THE
WRITERS
DIRECTORY
2006

THE WRITERS DIRECTORY 2006

TWENTY-FIRST EDITION

VOLUME 1: A-L

Editor
Michelle Kazensky

ST. JAMES PRESS

An imprint of Thomson Gale, a part of The Thomson Corporation

THOMSON
™
GALE

Detroit • New York • San Francisco • San Diego • New Haven, Conn. • Waterville, Maine • London • Munich

The Writers Directory 2006

Project Editor
Michelle Kazensky

Editorial
Katy Balcer, Sara Constantakis, Joshua Kondek, Lisa Kumar, Tracey Matthews, Julie Mellors, Joyce Nakamura, Mary Ruby, Lemma Shomali, Maikue Vang

Data Capture
Katrina Coach

Programmer/Analyst
Natasha Mikheyeva

Composition and Electronic Capture
Gary Leach

Manufacturing
Rhonda Dover

ISBN 1-55862-551-8 [Set]
ISBN 1-55862-552-6 (V. 1)
ISBN 1-55862-553-4 (V. 2)
ISSN 0084-2699

BRITISH LIBRARY CATALOGUING IN PUBLICATION DATA
A catalogue record for this book is available from the British Library

Printed in the United States of America
10 9 8 7 6 5 4 3 2 1

Contents

Preface

The Writers Directory 2006 is the newly revised and expanded twenty-first edition of this acclaimed reference work. It lists over 20,290 writers—writing under 21,728 names—from all countries of the world who have had at least one work published in English.

The main section of the Directory lists approximately 20,110 living writers of fiction and non-fiction who have published at least one full-length work in English. Listees run the gamut from the best-known, best selling authors of fiction and the most prominent non-fiction writers to those writers just embarking on their literary careers. Included in this section are nearly 750 writers whose listings have not appeared in a previous edition of The Writers Directory.

The **Obituaries** Section contains the entries for approximately 179 writers whose listings have appeared in previous editions of The Writers Directory and whose passing was made known to us in preparing this edition.

Compilation Methods

Selection of writers to appear in The Writers Directory is based primarily on reference value. Biographical and career information is researched for each writer, then a copy of the entry is sent to the writer for his or her approval and updates. By this process, the editors can assure comprehensive, current information. At the same time, entries in the previous edition were rigorously reviewed with an eye toward their current research value. As a result, some writers' entries have been retired to make way for those of new writers.

How to Read a Citation

Entries in The Writers Directory contain some or all of the following elements (please note that this is a sample entry for demonstration purposes only):

> ❚1❚ WILLIAMS, Mae. ❚2❚ (Allison May Williams) ❚3❚ Also writes as William Allison. ❚4❚ American (born Malta), ❚5❚ b. 1945. ❚6❚ **Genres:** Novels, Biography. ❚7❚ **Career:** Freelance writer. ❚8❚ **Publications:** Paris, L'amour, 1972; (ed.) Running through the Weeds, 1982; (as William Allison) Louis, My Love (biography), 1987; The Waves at My Back, 1997. ❚9❚ **Address:** 27500 Drake Rd., Farmington Hills, MI 48331 U.S.A. ❚10❚ **Online address:** maewil@aol.com ❚11❚ Died 1997.

❚1❚ Name of writer with fuller name information in parentheses

❚2❚ Full name of writer if different from writing name or pseudonyms but not used for writing

❚3❚ Pseudonym information

❚4❚ Nationality—if birthplace is different from nationality, it will follow the nationality in parentheses

❚5❚ Birth year

❚6❚ Genres—corresponds to **Index to Writing Categories**

❚7❚ Brief career information

❚8❚ Publications: title, year of publication, pseudonym if used, special awards

❚9❚ Address

❚10❚ Online address and/or web site

❚11❚ Death notation and year (in **Obituaries** Section only)

Cross references appear in the following form:

To main entry in main section: **ALLISON, William.** See **WILLIAMS, Mae.**

From main section to main entry in **Obituaries** section: **WILLIAMS, Mae.** See Obituaries.

From pseudonym in main section to main entry in **Obituaries** section: **ALLISON, William.** See **WILLIAMS, Mae** in the Obituaries.

Writers (and cross references) are listed alphabetically by surname which are sorted letter-by-letter. In cases where surnames are identical, writers are listed first by surname, then by given and middle names, and finally by suffixes such as Jr., Sr., II, or III. Surnames beginning with a prefix (such as Du, Mac, or Van), however spaced, are listed alphabetically under the first letter of the prefix and treated as if there were no space. Other compound surnames, hyphenated names, and names with apostrophes are alphabetized as if there were no space or punctuation. Surnames beginning with Saint or St. appear after names beginning with Sains and before names beginning with Sainu.

Entries in the **Obituaries** Section follow the same style as those in the main entries with the addition of the notation Died and the death year (if known) at the end of the entry.

Features

The Writers Directory contains many features to enhance its usefulness:

Boldface Rubrics allow quick and easy scanning for specifics on genre, career, publication, and mailing and on-line addresses.

The Obituaries Section lists the entries for those writers whose listing appeared in previous editions of *The Writers Directory* and whose passing was made known to us in preparing this edition. Cross references have been provided in the main body of the *Directory* to those deceased writers.

Indexing

The Writers Directory includes two indexes. In the **Index to Writing Categories**, one can locate writers by the type of works they write. New categories are added to *The Writers Directory* as needed to reflect new topics of interest and to define a writer's body of work more accurately. The **Country of Citizenship Index** lists writers by their country of citizenship as provided by the writer. Users are advised that one writer with multiple citizenship may appear under one country grouping (e.g., Canada-England) while another with the same citizenships may appear under a different grouping (e.g., England-Canada) depending on how the writer submitted the information.

The **Index to Writing Categories** and **Country of Citizenship Index** can be found at the end of the *Directory* following the **Obituaries** Section.

Also Available in Electronic Formats

Licensing. The Writer's Directory is available for licensing. The complete database is provided in a fielded format and is deliverable on such media as disk or CD-ROM. For more information, contact Gale's Business Development Group at 1-800-877-GALE, or visit us on our web site at www.gale.com/bizdev.

Online. The Writer's Directory is accessible as part of the Gale Biographies database (File GALBIO) through Lexis-Nexis. For more information, contact LexisNexis, P.O. Box 933, Dayton, OH 45401-0933; phone (937) 865-6800; toll-free: 800-227-4908.

Suggestions Welcome

Comments and suggestions from users of *The Writers Directory* on any aspect of the product as well as suggestions for writers to be included in a future edition are cordially invited. Please write:

The Editor
The Writers Directory
St. James Press
Thomson Gale
27500 Drake Rd.
Farmington Hills, Michigan 48331-3535.

Entry in *The Writers Directory* is at the discretion of the editor.

Abbreviations Used In The Writers Directory

A

AB	Alberta
ABC	American Broadcasting Company
ACT	Australian Capital Territory
AK	Alaska
AL	Alabama
Apt.	Apartment
AR	Arkansas
Assn.	Association
Assoc.	Associate
Asst.	Assistant
Ave.	Avenue
AZ	Arizona

B

b.	born
BBC	British Broadcasting Corporation
BC	British Columbia
Beds.	Bedfordshire
Berks.	Berkshire
Bldg.	Building
Blvd.	Boulevard
Brig.	Brigadier
Bros.	Brothers
Bucks.	Buckinghamshire

C

CA	California
Cambs.	Cambridgeshire
Can.	Canada
Capt.	Captain
CBC	Canadian Broadcasting Company
CBS	Columbia Broadcasting System (US)
CIA	Central Intelligence Agency (US)
CO; co.	Colorado; Company; County
Co-ed.	Co-editor
Co-trans.	Co-translator
Col.	Colonel
Contrib.	Contributor; Contributing
Corp.	Corporation
CPA	Certified Public Accountant
Cres.	Crescent
CT; Ct.	Connecticut; Court

D

DC	District of Columbia
DE	Delaware
Dept.	Department
Derbys.	Derbyshire
Dir.	Director
Div.	Division
Dr.	Doctor; Drive

E

E.	East
Ed.	Editor; Edition
Exec.	Executive

F

FBI	Federal Bureau of Investigation (US)
FL	Florida
Ft.	Fort

G

GA	Georgia
Gen.	General
Glam.	Glamorgan
Glos.	Glouchestershire
Gov.	Governor
Govt.	Government

H

Hants.	Hampshire
HE	His Eminence; His/Her Excellency
Herts.	Hertfordshire
HI	Hawaii
HM	His/Her Majesty
HMS	His/Her Majesty's Ship; His/Her Majesty's Service
Hon.	Honorable; Honorary

I

IA	Iowa
ID	Idaho
IL	Illinois
IN	Indiana
Inc.	Incorporated
Inst.	Institute
Intl.	International

J

Jr.	Junior

K

KS	Kansas
KY	Kentucky

L

LA	Louisiana
Lab.	Laboratory
Lancs.	Lancashire
Leics.	Leicestershire
LI	Long Island
Lincs.	Lincolnshire
Lt.	Lieutenant
Ltd.	Limited

M

MA	Massachusetts
Mag.	Magazine
Maj.	Major
MB	Manitoba
MD	Maryland
ME	Maine
Mgr.	Manager
MI	Michigan
Middx.	Middlesex
MN	Minnesota
MO	Missouri
MP	Member of Parliament
MT; Mt.	Montana; Mount, Mountain

N

N.	North
NASA	National Aeronautics and Space Administration
NATO	North Atlantic Treaty Organization
NB	New Brunswick
NBC	National Broadcasting System (US)
NC	North Carolina
NE	North East
NF	Newfoundland
NH	New Hampshire
NJ	New Jersey
NL	Newfoundland and Labrador
NM	New Mexico

No.	Number
Northants.	Northamptonshire
Notts.	Nottinghamshire
nr.	Near
NS	Nova Scotia
NSW	New South Wales
NT	Northern Territory (Australia); Northwest Territories (Canada)
NU	Nunavut
NV	Nevada
NW	North West
NWT	Northwest Territories
NY	New York
NYC	New York City

O

OH	Ohio
OK	Oklahoma
ON	Ontario
OR	Oregon
Orch.	Orchestra
Org.	Organization
Oxon.	Oxfordshire

P

PA	Pennsylvania
PE, PEI	Prince Edward Island
PEN	Poets, Playwrights, Essayists, Editors, Novelists
Pl.	Place
PO	Post Office
Pres.	President
Prof.	Professor
Prog.	Program
Publrs.	Publishers
Publs.	Publications

Q

QC	Quebec
QLD	Queensland

R

Rd.	Road
Rep.	Representative
Rev. ed.	Revised edition
RI	Rhode Island
RR	Rural Route
Rte.	Route

S

S.	South
SA	South Australia
Salop.	Shropshire
SC	South Carolina
Sch.	School
SD	South Dakota
SE	South East
Sec	Secretary
SK	Saskatchewan
Soc.	Society
Sq.	Square
Sr.	Senior
St.	Saint; Street
Staffs.	Staffordshire
Ste.	Suite
Supt.	Superintendent
SW	South West

T

Tas.	Tasmania
Terr.	Terrace
TN	Tennessee
Trans.	Translator; Translation
Treas.	Treasurer
TX	Texas

U

UK	United Kingdom
UN	United Nations
Unesco	United Nations Educational, Scientific and Cultural Organization

Unicef	United Nations Children's Emergency Fund
Univ.	University
US; USA	United States, United States of America
USS	United States Ship; United States Service
USSR	Union of Soviet Socialist Republics
UT	Utah

V

VA	Virginia
VIC	Victoria
Vol(s).	Volume(s)
VT	Vermont

W

W.	West
WA	Washington; Western Australia
Warks.	Warwicks; Warwickshire
WHO	World Health Organization
WI	Wisconsin
Wilts.	Wiltshire
Worcs.	Worcestershire
WV	West Virginia
WY	Wyoming

Y

YM-YWHA	Young Men's-Young Women's Hebrew Association
YMCA	Young Men's Christian Association
Yorks.	Yorkshire
YWCA	Young Women's Christian Association
YT	Yukon Territory

A

AAKER, Everett. British, b. 1954. **Genres:** Communications/Media. **Career:** Businessperson. London Academy of Music and Dramatic Art, associate, 1977. **Publications:** Television Western Players of the Fifties, 1997; Television Crimebusters of the Fifties, 2005. Contributor to magazines. **Address:** c/o McFarland and Co., Highway 88, Box 611, Jefferson, NC 28640, U.S.A.

AALTONEN, Sirkku. Finnish, b. 1952. **Genres:** Theatre, Translations. **Career:** University of Vaasa, Vaasa, Finland, lecturer in English, 1982-. **Publications:** Acculturation of the Other: Irish Milieux in Finnish Drama Translation (monograph), 1996; (ed.) Käännetyt illuusiot (monograph), 1998; Time-Sharing on Stage, 2000. Contributor to books and professional journals. **Address:** Faculty of English, University of Vaasa, PO Box 700, 65101 Vaasa, Finland. **Online address:** siaa@uwasa.fi

AAMODT, Donald. American. **Genres:** Science fiction/Fantasy. **Career:** Writer. **Publications:** A Name to Conjure With, 1989; Troubling Along the Border, 1991. **Address:** c/o Avon Books, 1350 Avenue of the Americas, New York, NY 10019, U.S.A.

AARON, Chester. American, b. 1923. **Genres:** Novels, Novellas/Short stories, Agriculture/Forestry, Children's fiction, Autobiography/Memoirs. **Career:** Chief X-Ray Technician, Alta Bates Hospital, Berkeley, CA, 1958-71; Technical Writer, MKI Engineering, San Francisco, 1971-72; Professor of English, St. Mary's College, Moraga, CA, 1972-94. **Publications:** About Us (novel), 1967; Better Than Laughter (children's fiction) 1972; An American Ghost, 1973; Hello to Bodega, 1975; Spill, 1977; Catch Calico!, 1979; Gideon, 1982; Duchess, 1982; Out of Sight, Out of Mind, 1984; Lackawanna, 1986; Alex, Who Won His War, 1991; Garlic Is Life (memoir), 1996; The Great Garlic Book, 1997; Garlic Kisses (memoir), 2002; Black and Blue Jew (novel), 2002; Home to the Sea (young adult novel), 2004; Whispers (novel), 2004. **Address:** PO Box 388, Occidental, CA 95465, U.S.A. **Online address:** chgarlic@comcast.net

AARON, James E. American, b. 1927. **Genres:** Education, Transportation. **Career:** Consultant, Office of Supt. of Public Instruction, 1960-; Consultant, Office of the Illinois Secretary of State; Member, Traffic Education and Training Committee, National Safety Council, 1972-, and Transportation Research Board, 1975-. Teacher of Driver Education, New York University, NYC, 1956-57; Administration and Teacher, Southern Illinois University, Carbondale, 1957-88; Member, National Highway Safety Advisory Committee, 1970-73; Safety and Health Hall of Fame, chairman, 1986-89. **Publications:** The Police Officer and Alcoholism, 1963; Driver and Traffic Safety Education: Content, Method, Organization, 1966, 1977; Driver Education: Learning to Drive Defensively, 1973; Driving Task Instruction: Dual Control, 1974; First Aid and Emergency Care, 1979; Fundamentals of Safety Education, 1981; (contrib.) Responsible Driving: AAA, 1993; How to Drive: AAA, 1993. **Address:** P.O. Box 1404, Sagamore Beach, MA 02562, U.S.A.

AARONS, Leroy. *See* Obituaries.

ABAS, Syed Jan. British (born India), b. 1936. **Genres:** Information science/Computers, Mathematics/Statistics. **Career:** University of Wales, Bangor, lecturer in maths and information technology, 1966-. Manchester University Computer Graphics Unit, research fellow; Journal of Speculations in Science and Technology, member of editorial board. **Publications:** Computers in Health and Fitness, 1988; (with J.R. Mondrayon) Pascal: An Interactive Text (textbook), 1990; Rapid Turbo Pascal Graphics Tutor (textbook), 1992; (with A.S. Salman) Symmetries of Islamic Geometrical Patterns, 1995, 2nd ed., 1998. **Address:** School of Informatics, University of Wales, Bangor, Gwynedd LL57 IUT, Wales. **Online address:** s.j.abas@bangor.ac.uk; www. bangor.ac.uk/~mas009

ABBAS. Iranian, b. 1934. **Genres:** Translations, Adult non-fiction. **Career:** Al Chaab (newspaper), Algiers, reporter and photographer, 1962-63; Olympic Games Committee, Mexico City, Mexico, photographer, 1968-69; Jeune Afrique (magazine), Africa, freelance photographer, 1970-71; Agences SIPA and Gamma, Paris, press photographer, 1974-80; Magnum Photos, Paris, photographer, 1981-. Has worked on photo assignments for periodicals. Photography represented in individual and group exhibitions. **Publications:** PHOTOGRAPHS, EXCEPT WHERE INDICATED: Le Zaire Aujourd'hui (title means: Zaire Today), 1974; Gamma: Le Secret des Grandes Photos (title means: Gamma: Behind Great Photos), 1978; Iran: La Revolution Confisquee (title means: Iran: The Revolution Stolen), 1980; (with others) Magnum Concert (exposition catalog), 1985; Retornos a Oapan, 1986; Return to Mexico: Journeys beyond the Mask, 1992; (author of text) Allah O Akbar: A Journey through Militant Islam, 1994. **Address:** c/o Magnum Photos, 19 Rue H Moreau, 75018 Paris, France.

ABBAS, Jailan. Egyptian, b. 1952. **Genres:** Mythology/Folklore, Children's fiction. **Career:** School of Tourism and Hotel Management, Helwan University, Cairo, professor of guiding methodology, 1979-93; Cairo American College, Cairo, Egypt, teacher of Egyptian culture, 1981-. Active in community volunteer activities. Guest lecturer on Egyptian history and culture in many cultural and educational institutions. **Publications:** FOR CHILDREN: The Festivals of Egypt, 1994; The Palm Tree in the Egyptian Culture, forthcoming. FOR ADULTS (in Arabic): Metals and Jewelry of Islamic Egypt, 1987; The Monuments of Ancient Egypt as Seen by Middle Ages Travelers, 1992; Athar Misr Al-Islameyyah Fi Kitabat Al-Rahalah, forthcoming. **Address:** Cairo American College, PO Box 39, Maadi, Cairo 11431, Egypt.

ABBOT, Sara. *See* ZOLOTOW, Charlotte.

ABBOTT, John Patrick. British, b. 1930. **Genres:** Air/Space topics, Genealogy/Heraldry. **Career:** Headmaster, St. Paul's V.C.J.M. School, Shepton Mallet, 1970-89. Formerly teacher in Birmingham, Wiltshire and Nottinghamshire. **Publications:** Family Patterns, 1971; Airship The Story of R.34, 1973, rev. ed., 1994; The British Airship at War, 1914-1918, 1989; Airships, 1991; British Airships in Pictures, 1998. **Address:** 30 Vibart Rd, Yardley, Birmingham, England.

ABBOTT, Pamela. British, b. 1947. **Genres:** Medicine/Health, Social sciences, Sociology, Women's studies and issues. **Career:** Borough of Enfield, London, ratings assistant, 1970-71, schoolteacher, 1972-74, head of social studies dept., 1974-75; Northwest Kent College of Technology, England, lecturer, 1975-80; Open University, Milton Keynes, England, research assistant and consultant, 1982-84; Brighton Polytechnic, England, lecturer in sociology, 1984-85; Plymouth Polytechnic (now part of University of Plymouth), England, lecturer, 1987-90, senior lecturer in sociology and social policy, 1992; Polytechnic South West Plymouth (now University of Plymouth), principal lecturer in sociology and social policy, 1990-92;

University of Plymouth, social policy subject head, 1993-96; University of Derby, professor of sociology, and assistant dean, School of Education and Social Science; University of Teesside, School of Social Sciences, professor and director, 1996-99; Glasgow Caledonian University, pro vice chancellor, 2000-03, director of Center for Equality and Diversity, 2003-. **Publications:** (with R. Sapsford) Community Care for Mentally Handicapped Children, 1987; (with Sapsford) Women and Social Class, 1987, 2nd ed., 1996; (with C. Wallace) An Introduction to Sociology: Feminist Perspectives, 1990; (with Wallace) The New Right and the Family, 1992; (with Sapsford) Research into Practice, 1992; (with Ackers) Social Policy for Nurses and the Caring Professionals, 1996. EDITOR: (with Wallace, and contrib.) The Sociology of the Caring Professions, 1990; (with G. Payne, and contrib.) Women and Mobility, 1990; (with Payne, and contrib.) New Directions in the Sociology of Health, 1990; (with Wallace) Gender, Power, and Sexuality, 1991; (with Sapsford, and contrib.) Research Methods for Nurses and the Caring Professionals, 1992. **Address:** Glasgow Caledonian University, Low Caddens Rd, Glasgow G6 0BA, Scotland. **Online address:** p.abbott@gcal.ac.uk

ABDEL-MAGID, Isam Mohammed. Sudanese, b. 1952. **Genres:** Environmental sciences/Ecology. **Career:** General Corporation for Irrigation and Drainage, Wad Medani, Sudan, civil engineer, 1977; University of Khartoum, Sudan, assistant professor, 1982-87, associate professor of civil engineering, 1987-88; University of the United Arab Emirates, Al-Ain, assistant professor of civil engineering, 1988-91; Sultan Qaboos University, Oman, assistant professor of engineering, 1991-96; Omdurman Islamic University, professor of water resources and environmental engineering, 1996-97; Juba University, professor of water resources and environmental engineering, 1998; Sudan University for Science and Technology, professor of water resources and environmental engineering, 1997-. Sudanese Engineering Council, consultant engineer. **Publications:** Selected Problems in Water Supply, 1986; Selected Problems in Wastewater Engineering, 1987; (with D.R. Rowe) Handbook of Wastewater Reclamation and Reuse, 1995; (with Rowe and A.M. Hago) Modeling Methods for Environmental Engineers, 1997. IN ARABIC: (with B.M. El-Hassan and M.E. Siddig) Guidelines for the Operation and Maintenance of Slow Sand Filters in Rural Sudan, 1983; Water Treatment and Sanitary Engineering, 1986; (with El-Hassan) Water Supply in the Sudan, 1986; (with El-Hassan) Industry and the Environment: The Treatment of Industrial Wastes, 1986; Environmental Engineering, 1995; Pollution: Hazards and Control, 1995; (with A.D. Mohammed) Water, 1999; Wastewater, 2000. **Address:** Industrial Research & Consultancy Centre, Ministry of Science & Technology, PO Box 268, Khartoum, Sudan. **Online address:** isam_abdelmagid@hotmail.com

ABEL, Elie. *See* Obituaries.

ABEL, Emily K. American, b. 1942. **Genres:** Education, Women's studies and issues, Medicine/Health. **Career:** Writer, historian, educator. Professor of Health Services at the University of California-Los Angeles. **Publications:** (ed., with E. Abel) The Signs Reader: Women, Gender, and Scholarship, 1983; Terminal Degrees: The Job Crisis in Higher Education, 1984; Love Is Not Enough: Family Care of the Frail Elderly, 1987; (ed. with M.L. Pearson) Across Cultures: The Spectrum of Women's Lives, 1989; (ed. with M.K. Nelson) Circles of Care: Work and Identity in Women's Lives, 1990; Who Cares for the Elderly? Public Policy and the Experience of Adult Daughters, 1991. **Address:** UCLA School of Public Health, 200 UCLA Neducal Plaza, Los Angeles, CA 90095, U.S.A.

ABERBACH, David. British, b. 1953. **Genres:** Literary criticism and history, Social sciences, Theology/Religion. **Career:** Tavistock Clinic, London, England, nurse in children's nursery, 1980-82; McGill University, Montreal, QC, assistant professor, 1986-87, associate professor of Jewish studies and comparative literature, 1987-; writer; teaching posts, Oxford University, 1982-83, Cambridge University, 1982-83, Leo Baeck College, 1984, and Cornell University, 1985; visiting professor, University College, London, 1992-; visiting academic, London School of Economics, 1992-. **Publications:** At the Handles of the Lord: Themes in the Fiction of S.J. Agnon, 1984; Bialik, 1988; Surviving Trauma: Loss, Literature, and Psychoanalysis, 1989; Realism, Caricature, and Bias: The Fiction of Mendele Mocher Sefarim, 1993; Imperialism and Biblical Prophecy, 750-500 BCE, 1993; Charisma in Politics, Religion and the Media, 1996; Revolutionary Hebrew, Empire and Crisis, 1998; (co-author) The Roman-Jewish Wars and Hebrew Cultural Nationalism, 2000; Major Turning Points in Jewish Intellectual History, 2003; (ed.) C.N. Bialik: Selected Poems, 2004. **Address:** Dept of Jewish Studies, McGill University, 3438 McTavish St Rm 300, Montreal, QC, Canada H3A 1A9.

ABISH, Walter. American (born Austria), b. 1931. **Genres:** Novels, Novellas/Short stories, Poetry, Essays. **Career:** Wheaton College, Norton, MA, writer-in-residence, 1977; State University of New York at Buffalo, Visiting Butler Professor of English, 1977; Ingram Merrill Fellowship, 1977; Columbia University, NYC, lecturer in English and comparative literature, 1979-88; National Endowment for the Arts Fellowship, 1979, 1985; Conjunctions Magazine, contributing editor, 1981-; Guggenheim Fellowship, 1981; PEN/Faulkner Award, 1981; visiting professor, Yale University, New Haven, CT, 1985, Brown University, Providence, RI, 1986, and Cooper Union for the Advancement of Science and Art, 1987, 1993-94; John D. MacArthur Fellow, 1987-92; DAAD-Deutscher Akademischer Austauschdienst, Berlin, 1987; American Academy & Institute of Arts & Letters, Merit Medal for the Novel, 1991; Lila Wallace-Reader's Digest Fellowship, 1992-95; American Academy of Arts and Sciences, fellow, 1998. **Publications:** Duel Site (poetry), 1970; Double Vision (self-portrait), 2004. NOVELS: Alphabetical Africa, 1974; How German Is It, 1980; Eclipse Fever, 1993. SHORT FICTION: Minds Meet, 1975; In the Future Perfect, 1977; 99: The New Meaning, 1990. **Address:** PO Box 485, Cooper Station, New York, NY 10276, U.S.A.

ABLEMAN, Michael. American, b. 1954. **Genres:** Agriculture/Forestry, Environmental sciences/Ecology. **Career:** Fairview Gardens, farm manager, founder and executive director of Center for Urban Agriculture, 1981-. Photographer, with solo exhibitions throughout the US. Lecturer at educational institutions in the US and abroad; public speaker. Creator of food gardens at Santa Barbara AIDS Hospice, Midland School, and Jordan Downs (housing project), Los Angeles, CA. **Publications:** From the Good Earth, 1993; On Good Land: The Autobiography of an Urban Farm, 1998. Contributor of articles and photographs to periodicals. **Address:** 598 N Fairview Ave, Goleta, CA 93117, U.S.A. **Online address:** michaelabl@aol.com

ABLOW, Keith Russell. American, b. 1961. **Genres:** Novels, Medicine/Health, Psychiatry. **Career:** Tri-City Mental Health Center, Lynn, MA, medical director and psychiatrist; Heritage Hospital, Somerville, MA, associate medical director and psychiatrist. **Publications:** Medical School: Getting in and Staying Human, 1989, rev. ed., 1990; (with R.J. DePaulo) How to Cope with Depression: A Complete Guide for You and Your Family, 1989; To Wrestle with Demons: A Psychiatrist Struggles to Understand His Patients and Himself, 1992; Anatomy of a Psychiatric Illness, 1993; The Strange Case of Dr. Kappler, 1994; Denial, 1997; Projection, 1999; Compulsion, 2002. **Address:** 12 49th St., Newbury, MA 01951-1412, U.S.A.

ABOUZEID, Leila. Also writes as Laylá Abu Zayd. Moroccan, b. 1950. **Genres:** Area studies, Women's studies and issues. **Career:** Television anchorman, 1972-73; press secretary for the Moroccan prime minister, minister of information, and minister of equipment, 1974; writer, 1983-; press secretary for the Moroccan president of the parliament, 1990-92. Author. Has also worked in radio production. **Publications:** Return to Childhood: The Memoir of a Modern Moroccan Woman, 1993, and trans. with A. and H.L. Taylor, 2000; The Last Chapter: A Novel, trans. by J. Liechety, 2000. AS LAYLÁ ABU ZAYD: Bid' Sunbulat Khudr, 1978; 'Am al-fil, 1983, trans. by B. Parmenter as Year of the Elephant: A Moroccan Woman's Journey toward Independence, and Other Stories, 1989; Amrika: al-wajh al-akhar, 1991; al-Fasl al-akhir, 2000; Al-Ghareeb, qassas mina emaghrib, 2003. **Address:** 1 rue Oumerrabia Apt. 12, Agdal, Rabat, Morocco. **Online address:** abouzeid@iam.net.ma

ABRAHAM, A(ntoine) J. American, b. 1942. **Genres:** Area studies. **Career:** New York Institute of Technology, NYC, associate professor, 1975-. John Jay College of Criminal Justice of the City University of New York, associate professor, 1992-. Also taught at Hunter College of the City University of New York; guest lecturer at U.S. colleges and universities. Consultant to government agencies and international organizations. **Publications:** Lebanon at Mid-Century: Maronite-Druze Relations in Lebanon, 1840-1860; A Prelude to Arab Nationalism, 1981; Khoumani and Islamic Fundamentalism, 1983; Lebanon: A State of Siege, 1975-1984, 1984; Islam and Christianity: Crossroads in Faith, 1987; (with G. Haddad) The Warriors of God: Jihad (Holy War) and the Fundamentalists of Islam, 1990; The Awakening of Persia: The Reign of Nasr al-Din Shah, 1848-1896, 1993; The Lebanon War, 1996. Contributor of articles and reviews to periodicals. **Address:** John Jay College of Criminal Justice, City University of New York, 445 W. 59th St., New York, NY 10019, U.S.A.

ABRAHAM, Henry J. American (born Germany), b. 1921. **Genres:** Civil liberties/Human rights, Law, Politics/Government. **Career:** University of Pennsylvania, Philadelphia, assistant professor, 1953-57, associate professor, 1957-62, professor of political science, 1962-72; University of Virginia, Charlottesville, James Hart Professor of Government and Foreign Affairs, 1972-97, Emeritus, 1997-. **Publications:** Compulsory Voting, 1955; Government as Entrepreneur and Social Servant, 1956; Courts and Judges: An Introduction to the Judicial Process, 1959; (with J.A. Corry) Elements of Democratic Government, 1958, 4th ed., 1964; The Judicial Process: An Introductory Analysis of the Courts of the United States, England, and France, 1962, 7th ed., 1998; The Judiciary: The Supreme Court in the Governmental Process, 1965, 10th ed., 1997; Freedom and the Court: Civil Rights and Liberties in the United States, 1967, 8th ed., 2003; (with J.C. Phillips) Essentials of American National Government, 1971; Justices and Presidents: A Political History of Appointments to the Supreme Court, 1974, 3rd ed., 1992; (with W.E. Keefe) American Democracy, 3rd ed., 1989; Justices, Presidents, and Senators, 1999. **Address:** 250 Pantops Mtn Rd Apt 5311, Charlottesville, VA 22911-8704, U.S.A.

ABRAHAMS, Lionel (Isaac). South African, b. 1928. **Genres:** Poetry. **Career:** Clerk in father's business, 1950-53; The Purple Renoster (magazine), writer/editor, 1957-72; Renoster Books, co-founder/publisher, 1970-74; Bateleur Press, co-founder/co-editor, 1974-81; Sesame (magazine), publisher, 1981-92; creative writing teacher, 1976-2002. **Publications:** (with others) Thresholds of Tolerance (poems), 1975; The Celibacy of Felix Greenspan (novel), 1976; Journal of a New Man (poems), 1984; The Writer in Sand (poems), 1988; Lionel Abrahams: A Reader (essays, stories, and poems), 1988; A Dead Tree Full of Live Birds (poems), 1994. EDITOR: (with N. Gordimer) South African Writing Today, 1966; 7 vols. by Herman Charles Bosman, 1957-90; Ruth Miller: Poems, Prose, Plays, 1991. Contributor of stories, poems, articles, and reviews to magazines and literary journals and anthologies. **Address:** PO Box 260, Rivonia 2128, Republic of South Africa. **Online address:** renoster@mweb.co.za

ABRAHAMS, Peter. Jamaican (born Republic of South Africa), b. 1919. **Genres:** Novels, Novellas/Short stories, Autobiography/Memoirs, Documentaries/Reportage. **Career:** Regular Contributor, The Observer, London, and The Herald Tribune, NYC and Paris, 1952-64; Ed., West Indian Economist, and Controller, West Indian News, Jamaica, 1955-64; Chairman, Radio Jamaica, 1977-80. **Publications:** Dark Testament (short stories), 1942; Song of the City, 1945; Mine Boy, 1946; The Path of Thunder, 1948; Wild Conquest, 1950; Return to Goli (reportage), 1953; Tell Freedom: Memories of Africa, 1954: A Wreath for Udomo, 1956; A Night of Their Own, 1965; This Island Now, 1966; The View from Coyaba, 1985; The Coyaba Chronicles, 2000, also as The Black Experience in the 20th Century, 2000. **Address:** Red Hills, St. Andrew, Jamaica.

ABRAHAMS, Peter. American, b. 1947. **Genres:** Mystery/Crime/Suspense, Young adult fiction. **Career:** Writer. Worked as a spear fisherman in the Bahamas, 1968-70; Canadian Broadcasting Co., Toronto, Canada, producer. **Publications:** NOVELS: The Fury of Rachel Monette, 1980; Tongues of Fire, 1982; Red Message, 1986; Hard Rain, 1988; Pressure Drop, 1989; Revolution #9, 1992; Lights Out, 1994; The Fan, 1995; A Perfect Crime, 1998; Crying Wolf, 2000; Last of the Dixie Heroes, 2001; The Tutor, 2002; Their Wildest Dreams, 2003; Oblivion, 2005; Down the Rabbit Hole, 2005. **Address:** c/o Aaron M. Priest Literary Agency, 708 3rd Ave 23rd Fl, New York, NY 10017, U.S.A. **Online address:** pa@cape.com; www.peterabrahams.com

ABRAMO, J(oe) L. American. **Genres:** Mystery/Crime/Suspense. **Career:** Author, actor, educator, and journalist; theater director, producer, and set designer. **Publications:** MYSTERIES: Catching Water in a Net, 2001; Clutching at Straws, 2003; A Second Helping of Murder, 2003; Counting to Infinity, 2004. **Address:** c/o Author Mail, St. Martin's Press/Minotaur Books, 175 Fifth Ave., New York, NY 10010, U.S.A. **Online address:** jakediamond@att.net

ABRAMS, Douglas Carl. American, b. 1950. **Genres:** History. **Career:** Bob Jones University, Greenville, SC, professor of history, 1974-, director of Africa Mission Team, 1991-, head of Department of Social Studies Education, 1992-. **Publications:** Conservative Constraints: North Carolina and the New Deal, 1992; Selling the Old-Time Religion: American Fundamentalists & Mass Culture, 1920-1940, 2001. Work represented in reference works. Contributor of articles and reviews to history journals. **Address:** Department of Social Studies Education, Bob Jones University, PO Box 34627, Greenville, SC 29614, U.S.A. **Online address:** cabrams@bju.edu

ABRAMS, Jeffrey. (born United States), b. 1966. **Genres:** Plays/Screenplays. **Career:** Producer, director, actor, and screenwriter. Worked on television series under the name J. J. Abrams. **Publications:** SCREENPLAYS: (With Jill Mazursky) Taking Care of Business (also known as Filofax), 1991; Regarding Henry, 1991; Forever Young, 1992; (with Jill Mazursky) Gone Fishin', 1997; (As J. J. Abrams; with others) Armageddon,

1998; (As J. J. Abrams; with Clay Tarver) Joy Ride (also known as Road Kill), 2001. TELEVISION SERIES: AS J. J. ABRAMS; WITH OTHERS: Felicity, 1998-2002; Alias, 2001-. OTHER: With Breen Frazier, wrote the Alias video game, 2003. **Address:** Endeavor, 9701 Wilshire Blvd., 10th Floor, Beverly Hills, CA 90212, U.S.A.

ABRAMS, Linsey. American, b. 1951. **Genres:** Novels. **Career:** Sarah Lawrence College, Bronxville, New York, director of fiction writing, 1980-; City College of New York, writer in residence, 1986-; Global City Review, editor, currently. **Publications:** Charting by the Stars, 1979; Double Vision, 1984; Our History in New York, 1998. **Address:** c/o Harvey Klinger, Inc, 301 W 53rd St Ste 13B, New York, NY 10019, U.S.A.

ABRAMS, M(eyer) H(oward). American, b. 1912. **Genres:** Literary criticism and history. **Career:** Class of 1916 Professor Emeritus, Cornell University, Ithaca, NY (Assistant Professor, 1945-47, Associate Professor, 1947-53, Professor, 1953-60, and Frederic J. Whiton Professor, 1960-63). Advisory Ed., W.W. Norton and Co. Inc., NYC, 1961-; Member, Council of Scholars, Library of Congress, 1980-. Instructor, 1938-42, and Research Associate, Psycho-Acoustic Laboratory, 1942-45, Harvard University; Fulbright Lecturer, Royal University of Malta and Cambridge University, 1953; Roache Lecturer, University of Indiana, Bloomington, 1963; Alexander Lecturer, University of Toronto, 1964; Ewing Lecturer, University of California at Los Angeles, 1974. **Publications:** The Milk of Paradise: The Effect of Opium Visions on the Works of DeQuincey, Crabbe, Francis Thompson and Coleridge, 1934, 1970; The Mirror and the Lamp: Romantic Theory and the Critical Tradition, 1953; A Glossary of Literary Terms, 1957, 1998; Natural Supernaturalism: Tradition and Revolution in Romantic Literature, 1971; The Correspondent Breeze: Essays in English Romanticism, 1984; Doing Things with Texts: Essays in Criticism and Critical Theory, 1989. EDITOR: Literature and belief, 1958; The Poetry of Pope, 1958; English Romantic Poets: Modern Essays in Criticism, 1960, 1975; The Norton Anthology of English Literature, 1962, 1999; Wordsworth: A Collection of Critical Essays, 1972; (with others) Wordsworth's Prelude 1799-1850, 1979. **Address:** 378 Savage Farm Dr, Ithaca, NY 14850, U.S.A. **Online address:** mha@cornell.edu

ABRAMS, Nita. American, b. 1953. **Genres:** Romance/Historical. **Career:** Writer; teacher. **Publications:** HISTORICAL ROMANCES: A Question of Honor, 2002; The Exiles, 2002; The Spy's Bride, 2003; The Spy's Kiss, 2005.

ABRAMS, Ovid (S. McL.). American (born Guyana), b. 1939. **Genres:** Area studies, Business/Trade/Industry. **Career:** CNS News (wire service), NYC, city editor, 1972-75; Fairchild Publications, NYC, news editor, 1976-78; Publishers Weekly, NYC, assistant news editor, 1978-80; E.F. Hutton, vice-president and research analyst, 1980-89; McGraw-Hill Book Co., NYC, senior editor, 1989-. Ordained minister. **Publications:** How to Find the Job of Your Dreams, 1993; Let God Answer Your Prayers, 1994; Metegee: The History and Culture of Guyana, 1998; (with others) The Columbia University Guide to Business Journalism; 760 Degrees of Love (poetry), 2002; The Mystery of Christ Jesus, 2004. **Address:** 113-27 210th St, Queens Village, NY 11429, U.S.A. **Online address:** ovidabrams@baruch.cuny.edu; ovidabra@aol.com; ovid_abrams@mcg

ABRAMSON, Edward A. American, b. 1944. **Genres:** Area studies, Literary criticism and history. **Career:** East Carolina University, Greenville, NC, instructor, 1966-69; College of William and Mary, Williamsburg, VA, visiting professor, 1986-87; University of Hull, Hull, England, senior lecturer, 1971-. **Publications:** The Immigrant Experience in American Literature (pamphlet), 1982; Chaim Potok (monograph), 1986; Bernard Malamud Revisited (monograph), 1993. **Address:** Department of American Studies, University of Hull, Hull HU6 7RX, England. **Online address:** E.A.Abramson@amstuds.hall.ac.uk

ABRAMSON, Leslie W. American. **Genres:** Law. **Publications:** (ed.) Basic Bankruptcy: Alternatives, Proceedings, and Discharges (edited transcript of seminar proceedings), 1971; Criminal Detainers, 1979; Judicial Disqualification under Canon 3C of the Code of Judicial Conduct, 1986, rev ed, 1991; Criminal Practice and Procedure, 1987; (with C.D. Edwards) Questions and Answers: Criminal Law, 1988; Substantive Criminal Law, 1990; (with J.R. Cox) Civil Procedure Forms, 1994. **Address:** Louis D. Brandeis School of Law, University of Louisville, 2301 S. 3rd St., Louisville, KY 40292, U.S.A.

ABRAMSON, Rudy. American, b. 1937. **Genres:** Biography, History. **Career:** Los Angeles Times, Washington, DC, correspondent, 1965-93. **Publications:** Spanning the Century: The Life of W. Averell Harriman, 1891-1986,

1992; Hallowed Ground: Preserving America's Heritage, 1996. Contributor of reviews and articles to periodicals. **Address:** c/o Goodman Associates, 500 West End Ave., New York, NY 10024, U.S.A.

ABRESCH, Peter E. American, b. 1931. **Genres:** Mystery/Crime/Suspense, Writing/Journalism. **Career:** Retired from federal service as a computer programmer. **Publications:** MYSTERIES: Bloody Bonsai, 1998; Killing Thyme, 1999; Tip a Canoe, 2001; Painted Lady, 2003; Sheep in Wolf's Clothing, 2003. NONFICTION: Easy Reading Writing, Easy Reading about Writing Easy Reading, 2001 Contributor to magazines. **Address:** PO Box 548, Prince Frederick, MD 20678, U.S.A. **Online address:** peter@elderhostelmysteries.com

ABSALOM, Roger Neil Lewis. British, b. 1929. **Genres:** International relations/Current affairs, Language/Linguistics, History. **Career:** Freelance educational consultant, 1989-. Teacher of English, English Institute of Naples, and British Council School, Milan, 1956-60; Sr. Lecturer, 1966-70, and Principal Lecturer in Italian, 1970-73, Cambridgeshire College of Arts and Technology; Sheffield Hallam University, Head of Department of Modern Languages, Dean of Faculty of Humanities, Reader in Italian Studies, 1973-89, Hon. Research Fellow in Italian History, 1989. Corresponding member, Accademia toscana di scienze e lettere "La Colombaria," 1990; Consultant, ERASMUS Bureau and Senior Consultant at EC TEMPUS Office, 1989-93; Reporting Assessor, Higher Education Funding Council for England (part-time consultant), 1994. **Publications:** Modern English, 1958; Italian Phrase Book, 1960; "A" Level French, 1965; "A" Level Italian, 1968; Mussolini and the Rise of Italian Fascism, 1969; Comprehension of Spoken Italian, 1978; Gli alleati e la ricostruzione in Toscana, Vol. I, 1988, Vol. II, 2000; A Strange Alliance: Aspects of Escape and Survival in Italy 1943-45, 1991; Italy: A Nation in the Balance?, 1995; Perugia Liberata, 2000. EDITOR: Passages for Translation from Italian, 1967; France, 1968; The May Events, 1970; (with S. Potesta) Advanced Italian, 1970. **Address:** 5 The Mill, Edale, Hope Valley, Derbyshire S33 7ZE, England. **Online address:** r.absalom@shu.ac.uk

ABSE, Dannie. Welsh, b. 1923. **Genres:** Novels, Plays/Screenplays, Poetry, Autobiography/Memoirs. **Career:** Specialist in charge of Chest Clinic, Central London Medical Establishment, 1954-82. President, Poetry Society, London, 1978-92; President, Welsh Academy of Letters, 1995. Visiting Writer-in-Residence, Princeton University, NJ, 1973-74. **Publications:** After Every Green Thing, 1948; Walking under Water, 1952; Ash on a Young Man's Sleeve (novel), 1954; Some Corner of an English Field (novel), 1956; Fire in Heaven (play), 1956; Tenants of the House, 1957; The Eccentric (play), 1961; Poems, Golders Green, 1962; Dannie Abse: A Selection, 1963; Is the House Shut? (play), 1964; Medicine on Trial, 1967; Three Questor Plays, 1967; A Small Desperation, 1968; The Dogs of Pavlov (play), 1969; Demo, 1969; O. Jones, O. Jones (novel), 1970; Selected Poems, 1970; Funland, 1973; A Poet in the Family (autobiography), 1974; (with D.J. Enright & M. Langley) Penguin Modern Poets No. 2, 1974; Poetry Dimension Annual 4, 1976; Pythagoras Smith (play), 1976; Poetry Dimension Annual 5, 1977; Collected Poems 1948-1976, 1977; Gone in January (play), 1978; Way Out in the Centre (poems), 1981; Miscellany One, 1981; A Strong Dose of Myself, 1983; Ask the Bloody Horse (poems), 1986; Journals from the Ant-Heap, 1986; White Coat, Purple Coat: Collected Poems 1948-88, 1989; Remembrance of Crimes Past (poetry), 1990; The View from Row G (plays), 1990; Selected Poems, 1994; Intermittent Journals, 1994; On the Evening Road (Poetry), 1994; Arcadia, One Mile, 1998; Be Seated, There (poems), 2000; Goodby 20th Century (autobiography), 2001; The Strange Case of Dr Simmonds and Dr Glas (novel), 2002. EDITOR: (with H. Sergeant) Mavericks, 1957; European Verse, 1964; Poetry Dimension 2, 1974; Poetry Dimension Annual 3, 1975; (with J. Abse) Voices in the Gallery, 1986; (with J. Abse) The Music Lover's Literary Companion, 1988; The Hutchinson Book of Post-War British Poetry, 1989; 20th Century Anglo-Welsh Poetry, 1997. **Address:** 85 Hodford Rd, London NW11, England.

ABSE, Leo. British, b. 1917. **Genres:** Politics/Government, Psychology. **Career:** Cardiff City Labour Party, Cardiff, Wales, chairman, 1951-53; Cardiff City Council, Cardiff, member, 1953-58; British Parliament, London, England, Labour member for Pontypool, 1958-83, and for Torfaen, 1983-87; Welsh Parliamentary Party, chair, 1976-87; Winnicott Clinic of Psychotherapy, chairman, 1988-. Senior partner of a law firm in Cardiff, Wales. Member of Home Office Advisory Committees on the Penal System, 1968, and on Adoption, 1972; member of Select Committee on Abortion, 1975-76; first chair, Select Committee on Welsh Affairs, 1980; secretary of British-Taiwan Parliamentary Group, 1983-87; chair of Parliamentary Friends of the Welsh National Opera, 1985-87. Vice-President, Institute for the Study and Treatment of Delinquency, 1964-. University of Wales, member of court, 1981-87;

University of California, regents lecturer, 1984. **Publications:** Private Member: A Psychoanalytically Orientated Study of Contemporary Politics, 1973; Margaret, Daughter of Beatrice: A Psychobiography of Margaret Thatcher, 1989; Wotan, My Enemy: Can Britain Live with the Germans?, 1994; The Man behind the Smile: The Politics of Perversion, 1996; Fellatio, Masochism, Politics & Love, 2000; Tony Blair: The Man Who Lost His Smile, 2003. **Address:** 54 Strand-on-the-Green, London W4 3PD, England.

ABSHIRE, David Manker. American, b. 1926. **Genres:** International relations/Current affairs, Politics/Government. **Career:** President 1982-83 and since 1988, Executive Director, 1962-70, and Chairman, 1973-82, Center for Strategic and International Studies, Washington, D.C.; Assistant Secretary of State for Congressional Relations, 1970-73; U.S. Permanent Representative to NATO, 1983-87. Member, Congressional Committee on the Organization of Government for the Conduct of Foreign Policy, 1973-75; Chairman, U.S. Board for International Broadcasting, 1974-77; Director, National Security Group, Transition Office of President-Elect Reagan, 1980-81; Special Counselor to the President, 1987. **Publications:** (with others) Detente, 1965; The South Rejects a Prophet: The Life of Senator D.M. Key, 1967; Research Resources for the Seventies, 1971; International Broadcasting: A New Dimension of Western Diplomacy, 1976; Egypt and Israel: Prospects for a New Era, 1979; Foreign Policy Makers: President vs. Congress, 1981; Preventing WWIII: A Realistic Grand Strategy, 1988. EDITOR: National Security, 1963; Portuguese Africa, 1969. Contributor to books. **Address:** Ctr. Strategic & Intl. Studies, Suite 400, 1800 K St., NW, Washington, DC 20006, U.S.A.

ABT, Jeffrey. American, b. 1949. **Genres:** Art/Art history. **Career:** Teacher of adult education classes at public schools in Des Moines, IA, 1973-77; Wichita Art Museum, Wichita, KS, curator of collections, 1977-78; Billy Hork Galleries Ltd., Chicago, IL, general manager, 1978-80; University of Chicago, exhibitions coordinator at university library, 1980-86, assistant director, 1986-87, then acting director of David and Alfred Smart Museum of Art, 1987-89; Wayne State University, Detroit, MI, associate professor of art and art history, 1989-. Artist, with paintings and drawings exhibited throughout the Midwest and represented in public collections; sculptor. **Publications:** A Museum on the Verge: The Detroit Institute of Arts, 1882-2002, 2001. Illustrator of books by A.R. Hayes. Author of exhibition catalogues. Contributor of articles and reviews to periodicals. **Address:** Department of Art and Art History, 150 Art Building, Wayne State University, Detroit, MI 48202, U.S.A. **Online address:** j_abt@wayne.edu

ABU-JABER, Diana. American, b. 1959. **Genres:** Novels. **Career:** Portland State University, English department, associate professor. **Publications:** Arabian Jazz, 1993. **Address:** Department of English, Portland State University, Portland, OR 97205, U.S.A. **Online address:** abujaber@aol.com

ABU-LUGHOD, Lila. American, b. 1952. **Genres:** Literary criticism and history, Women's studies and issues. **Career:** Williams College, Williamstown, MA, assistant professor of anthropology, 1983-87; University of Pennsylvania, Philadelphia, Mellon fellow, 1988-89; American Research Center in Egypt, Cairo, senior fellow, 1989-90; Princeton University, Princeton, NJ, assistant professor of religion, 1990-91; New York University, NYC, associate professor of anthropology, 1991-. Chair and member, Social Science Research Council Committee for the Comparative Study of Muslim Society, 1988-91. **Publications:** Veiled Sentiments: Honor and Poetry in a Bedouin Society, 1986; (ed. with C.A. Lutz) Language and the Politics of Emotion, 1990; Writing Women's Worlds: Bedouin Stories, 1993. Contributor of articles to professional journals. **Address:** Department of Anthropology, New York University, 25 Waverly Pl., New York, NY 10003, U.S.A.

ABU ZAYD, Laylá. *See* **ABOUZEID, Leila.**

ABZUG, Robert Henry. American, b. 1945. **Genres:** History, Humanities. **Career:** University of California, Berkeley, instructor in history, 1976-77; University of California at Los Angeles, lecturer in history, 1977-78; University of Texas at Austin, assistant professor, 1978-84, associate professor, 1984-89, professor of history, 1990-96, director of American studies, 1990-96, director, Liberal Arts Honors, 1996-, Oliver H. Radkey Regents Professor of History, 2002-. Carver Museum of Black History, trustee, 1981-83; University of Munich, Eric Voegelin Visiting Professor, 1990-91. **Publications:** Passionate Liberator: Theodore Dwight Weld and the Dilemma of Reform, 1980; Inside the Vicious Heart: Americans and the Liberation of the Nazi Concentration Camps, 1985; (ed. with S. Maizlish) New Perspectives on Race and Slavery in America, 1986; Cosmos Crumbling: American Reform and the Religious Imagination, 1994; America Views the Holocaust, 1933-1945, 1999. **Address:** American Studies, University of Texas, Austin, TX 78712, U.S.A.

ACCAD, Evelyne. American/Lebanese, b. 1943. **Genres:** Novels, Literary criticism and history, Third World, Women's studies and issues, Autobiography/Memoirs. **Career:** Anderson College, IN, instructor in French, 1967-68; International College, Beirut, Lebanon, teacher and girls' counselor, 1968-70; University of Illinois at Urbana-Champaign, assistant professor, 1974-79, associate professor, 1979-88, professor of French comparative literature and member of core faculty at African Center, Women's Studies Center, and Center for Asian Studies, all 1988-. Northwestern University, visiting professor, 1991; lecturer at colleges and universities worldwide; gives readings from her works. **Publications:** Veil of Shame: The Role of Women in the Modern Fiction of North Africa and the Arab World, 1978; (trans.) N. Aba, Montjoie Palestine!; or, Last Year in Jerusalem (poem), 1980; L'Excisee (novel), 1982, trans. as The Excised, 1989; (with R. Ghurayyeb) Contemporary Arab Women Writers and Poets (monograph), 1986; Coquelicot du massacre (novel), 1988; Sexuality and War, 1990; Des femmes, des hommes et la guerre, 1993; Blessures des Mots: Journal de Tunisie (novel), 1993, trans. as Wounding Words: A Woman's Journal in Tunisia, 1996; Les filles de Tahar Haddad (play; adaptation of Blessures des Mots), 1995; Voyages en Cancer, 2000, trans. as The Wounded Breast: Intimate Journeys through Cancer, 2001. Contributor to books and periodicals. **Address:** Dept of French, 2090 Foreign Languages Bldg, University of Illinois at Urbana-Champaign, Urbana, IL 61801, U.S.A. **Online address:** e_accad@uiuc.edu

ACCAWI, Anwar F. American (born Lebanon), b. 1943. **Genres:** Autobiography/Memoirs. **Career:** University of Tennessee, Knoxville, ESL professor, 1979-. Has also taught at National Evangelical Institute, Sidon High School, Sidon, Lebanon, and American University of Beirut, Beirut, Lebanon. **Publications:** The Boy from the Tower of the Moon, 1999. Contributor of essays to anthologies and periodicals. **Address:** University of Tennessee, English Language Institute, 907 Mountcastle, Knoxville, TN 37996, U.S.A. **Online address:** aaccawi@utk.edu

ACCINELLI, Robert. American, b. 1939. **Genres:** Education. **Career:** University of Toronto, Toronto, Ontario, professor of history and modern American foreign relations, 1966-. **Publications:** Crisis and Commitment: U.S. Policy toward Taiwan, 1950-1955, 1996. **Address:** Department of History, University of Toronto, Toronto, ON, Canada M5S 3G3. **Online address:** Accinell@chass.utoronto.ca

ACHEBE, Chinua. Nigerian, b. 1930. **Genres:** Novels, Novellas/Short stories, Children's fiction, Poetry, Essays. **Career:** Emeritus Professor, University of Nigeria, Nsukka, 1984- (Professor of English, 1976-81; Sr. Research Fellow, 1967-72). Director, Heinemann Educational Books (Nigeria) Ltd., and Nwamife & Co. (Publishers) Ltd., Enugu, 1970-; Ed., Okike, Nigerian Journal of New Writing, 1971-. Talks Producer, Lagos, 1954-57, Controller, Enugu, 1958-61, Director, Lagos, 1961-66, Nigerian Broadcasting Corp.; Professor of English, University of Massachusetts, Amherst, 1972-74; Professor of English, University of Connecticut, Storrs, 1975; Pro-Chancellor and Chairman of Council, Anambra State University of Technology, Enugu, 1986-88. **Publications:** Things Fall Apart, 1958; No Longer at Ease, 1960; The Sacrificial Egg and Other Stories, 1962; Arrow of God, 1964; A Man of the People, 1966; Chike and the River, 1966; Beware Soul-Brother and Other Poems, 1971; Girls at War, 1972; How the Leopard Got His Claws, 1972; Christmas in Biafra and Other Poems, 1973; Morning Yet on Creation Day (essays), 1975; The Flute, 1977; The Drum, 1977; (co-ed.) Don't Let Him Die, 1978; The Trouble with Nigeria, 1983; Anthills of the Savannah, 1987; Hopes and Impediments (essays), 1987; The University and the Leadership Factor in Nigerian Politics, 1988; The African Trilogy (fiction), 1988; (co-ed.) African Short Stories, 1985; The Heinemann Book of Contemporary African Short Stories, 1992; The Voter, 1994; Conversations with Chinua Achebe, 1997; Another Africa, 1998; Home and Exile, 2000. **Address:** c/o Bard College, Dept of Language and Literature, Annandale on Hudson, NY 12504, U.S.A.

ACHESON, David C(ampion). American, b. 1921. **Genres:** Autobiography/Memoirs. **Career:** Atomic Energy Commission, Washington, DC, attorney in Office of the General Counsel, 1948-49; Covington & Burling, Washington, DC, associate, partner, 1950-61; U.S. attorney for the District of Columbia, 1961-65; special assistant for enforcement to the U.S. Secretary of the Treasury, 1965-67; Communications Satellite Corp., general counsel, 1967-74; Jones, Day, Reavis & Pogue, Washington, DC, partner, 1974-78; Drinker Biddle & Reath, Washington, DC, partner, 1978-883; Atlantic Council of the United States, president, 1993-99. **Publications:** (ed.) This Vast External Realm, 1973; (with D. McLellan) Among Friends: The Personal Letters of Dean Acheson, 1980; Acheson Country: A Memoir, 1993. **Address:** 2700 Calvert St NW Apt 414, Washington, DC 20008, U.S.A. **Online address:** dcampach@aol.com

ACKELSBERG, Martha A. American, b. 1946. **Genres:** Politics/Government, Urban studies, Women's studies and issues. **Career:** Smith College, Northampton, MA, lecturer, 1972-76, assistant professor, 1976-80, associate professor, 1980-87, professor of government, 1987-, principal investigator, Project on Women and Social Change, 1978-85. University of Sussex, visiting lecturer, 1977; Radcliffe College, Bunting Institute, fellow, 1983-84; Harvard University, Center for European Studies, faculty associate, 1983-84; Columbia University, visiting scholar, 1987-88; University of Massachusetts, visiting professor, 1989; lecturer. **Publications:** (ed. with R. Bartlett and R. Buchele) Women, Welfare, and Higher Education: Toward Comprehensive Policies, 1988; Free Women of Spain: Anarchism and the Struggle for the Emancipation of Women, 1991; Mujeres Libres: El anarquismo y la lucha por la emancipacion de las mujeres, 1999. Work represented in anthologies. Contributor to periodicals. **Address:** Dept of Government, Smith College, 10 Prospect #104, Northampton, MA 01063, U.S.A. **Online address:** mackelsb@smith.edu

ACKER, Bertie (Wilcox Naylor). American, b. 1922. **Genres:** Translations. **Career:** Worked with the Army Signal Corps as a cryptographer, and read mail for the Bureau of Censorship during World War II; Sherman Public Schools, Spanish teacher, 1956-57; Austin Public Schools, Austin, TX, Spanish teacher, 1957-59; University of Texas at Austin, instructor, 1959-60; Universidad del Valle, Cali, Colombia, technical advisor for the Rockefeller Foundation, 1964-65; University of Texas at Arlington, assistant professor, 1965-72, associate professor, 1972-85, professor, 1985-89, professor emerita of Spanish, 1990-. **Publications:** El Cuento mexicano contemporaneo: Rulfo, Arreola y Fuentes (temas y cosmovision), 1984; (trans.) Teresa de la Parra, Iphigenia (The diary of a young lady who wrote because she was bored), 1993. Contributor of articles and translations to anthologies. Contributor of articles, translations, and reviews to periodicals. **Address:** 1705 Briardale Ct., Arlington, TX 76013, U.S.A.

ACKERMAN, Diane. American, b. 1953. **Genres:** Poetry, Adult non-fiction, Children's non-fiction. **Career:** Washington University, St. Louis, director, Writer's Program, 1984-86; Cornell University, Ithaca, NY, Society for the Humanities, professor, 1999-. Visiting writer, Columbia University, University of Pittsburgh, Cornell University, and others; University of Richmond, National Endowment for the Humanities Distinguished Professor of English, 2001. **Publications:** POETRY: The Planets: A Cosmic Pastoral, 1976; Wife of Light, 1978; Lady Faustus, 1983; Reverse Thunder, 1988; Jaguar of Sweet Laughter: New and Selected Poems, 1991; I Praise My Destroyer, 1999; Origami Bridges: Poems of Psychoanalysis and Fire, 2002; Animal Sense (for children), 2002. OTHER: Twilight of the Tenderfoot: A Western Memoir, 1980; On Extended Wings, 1985, 1987; A Natural History of the Senses, 1990; A Natural History of Love, 1994; The Moon by Whale Light, 1991; Monk Seal Hideaway (children's nonfiction), 1995; The Rarest of the Rare, 1995; A Slender Thread, 1996; Deep Play, 1999; Cultivating Delight, 2001. Contributor to journals. **Address:** PMB 207, 907 Hanshaw Rd, Ithaca, NY 14850, U.S.A. **Online address:** inkdream@hotmail.com

ACKERMAN, James D. American, b. 1950. **Genres:** Horticulture, Botany. **Career:** University of Puerto Rico, San Juan, professor, 1981-. **Publications:** The Orchids of Puerto Rico and the Virgin Islands, 1992; An Orchid Flora of Puerto Rico and the Virgin Islands, 1995. Contributor of more than 60 articles to scientific journals. **Address:** University of Puerto Rico, P.O. Box 23360, San Juan, PR 00931-3360, U.S.A. **Online address:** ACKER MAN@UPRACD.UPR.CLU.EDU

ACKERMAN, James S(loss). American, b. 1919. **Genres:** Architecture, Art/Art history. **Career:** Yale University, New Haven, CT, part-time instr., 1946-48; American Academy in Rome, research fellow, 1949-52; University of California, assistant professor to professor, 1952-60; Art Bulletin, ed.-in-chief, 1956-60; Harvard University, professor, 1960-90, chairman, 1963-68, 1982-84, Arthur Kingsley Porter Professor of Fine Arts, 1982-90, emeritus, 1990-; Kings College, Cambridge, Slade Professor of Fine Arts and Fellow, 1969-70; Columbia University, Meyer Shapiro Professor, 1989-90; New York University, adjunct professor, 1992. **Publications:** The Cortile del Belvedere, 1964; The Architecture of Michelangelo, 1961, 1986 (Alice D. Hitchcock Award, Charles R. Morey Award); (with Rhys Carpenter) Art and Archaeology, 1963; Palladio, 1967; Palladio's Villas, 1967; The Villa: Form and Ideology of Country Houses, 1990; Distance Points: Essays in Theory and Renaissance Art and Architecture, 1991; Origins, Imitation, Conventions, 2002. **Address:** Sackler Museum, Harvard University, Cambridge, MA 02138, U.S.A. **Online address:** jsackerm@fas.harvard.edu

ACKERMAN, Jennifer G. American, b. 1959. **Genres:** Natural history. **Career:** Writer, 1989-. Contributing writer and editor to the New York

Times, National Geographic, and other publications; lecturer at colleges and organizations. **Publications:** The Curious Naturalist, 1991; Notes from the Shore, 1995; Chance in the House of Fate: A Natural History of Heredity, 2001. Contributor to anthologies. **Address:** c/o Melanie Jackson Agency, 41 W 72nd St., Apt 3F, New York, NY 10023, U.S.A.

ACKERMAN, Lowell J. Canadian, b. 1956. **Genres:** Animals/Pets. **Career:** Veterinarian and writer. Dermvet, Inc., Scottsdale, AZ, president, 1985-; PHI, Inc., Scottsdale, 1990-; Mesa Veterinary Hospital Ltd., Mesa, AZ, director of department of clinical resources, 1998-. **Publications:** Practical Canine Dermatology, 1989; Practical Equine Dermatology, 1989; Practical Feline Dermatology, 1989; Healthy Dog, 1993; Guide to Skin and Haircoat Problems in Dogs, 1994; Dr. Ackerman's Book of Boxers, 1996; Dr. Ackerman's Book of Cocker Spaniels, 1996; Dr. Ackerman's Book of Collies, 1996; Dr. Ackerman's Book of Dachshunds, 1996; Dr. Ackerman's Book of Dalmatians, 1996; Dr. Ackerman's Book of Doberman Pinscher, 1996; Dr. Ackerman's Book of Great Danes, 1996; Dr. Ackerman's Book of Poodles, 1996; Dr. Ackerman's Book of Shar-Pei, 1996; Dr. Ackerman's Book of Shih Tzu, 1996; Dr. Ackerman's Book of the German Shepherd, 1996; Dr. Ackerman's Book of the Golden Retriever, 1996; Dr. Ackerman's Book of the Labrador Retriever, 1996; Dr. Ackerman's Book of the Rottweiler, 1996; Dr. Ackerman's Book of the Yorkshire Terrier, 1996; (with Gary M. Landsberge and Wayne Hunthausen) Handbook of Behavior Problems of the Dog and Cat, 1997; (with Gene H. Nesbitt) Canine and Feline Dermatology: Diagnosis and Treatment, 1998; (Medical advisor) Dogs: The Ultimate Care Guide: Good Health, Loving Care, Maximum Longevity, 1998; Canine Nutrition: What Every Owner, Breeder, and Trainer Should Know, 1999; (with Arden Moore) The Guilt-free Guide for on-the-Go Dog Lovers, 2002; (with Arden Moore) Happy Dog: How Busy People Care for Their Dogs: A Stress-free Guide for All Dog Owners, 2003. EDITOR AND COMPILER: Skin and Coat Care for Your Dog, 1995; (with Gary Landsberg and Wayne Hunthausen) Dog Behavior and Training: Veterinary Advice for Owners, 1996; Skin and Coat Care for Your Cat, 1996; (with Gary Landsberg and Wayne Hunthausen) Cat Behavior and Training: Veterinary Advice for Owners, 1996; The Biology, Husbandry, and Health Care of Reptiles, 1997. EDITOR: Owner's Guide to Cat Health, 1996; Cat Health Encyclopedia, 1998; Contributor of articles to professional journals. **Address:** Mesa Veterinary Hospital, 858 North Country Club Dr., Mesa, AZ 85201, U.S.A.

ACKERMAN, Susan Yoder. American, b. 1945. **Genres:** Children's fiction, Children's non-fiction, Inspirational/Motivational Literature, Local history/ Rural topics, Autobiography/Memoirs. **Career:** Elementary school teacher, Newport News, VA, 1966-67, 1972; teacher of English as a foreign language, Lubumbashi, Zaire, 1969-70, and Kongolo, Zaire, 1979-80; high school English teacher, Dunn, NC, 1970-72; middle and high school French teacher, Newport News, 1984-86, 1989-96; day care director, Newport News, 1989-90; elementary school principal, 2000-03. Island Institute, Sitka, AK, resident fellow, 2000. Speaker on African experiences and on writing; leader of workshops on writing juvenile fiction. **Publications:** Copper Moons, 1990; The Flying Pie and Other Stories, 1996; See This Wonderful Thing, 1998. Contributor to reading textbook anthologies and testing materials. Contributor of stories and articles to periodicals. **Address:** 524 Marlin Dr, Newport News, VA 23602, U.S.A.

ACKLAND, Len. American, b. 1944. **Genres:** History. **Career:** Worked as a teacher for International Voluntary Services, as a researcher for RAND Corporation, and as a freelance writer, all in Vietnam, 1967-69; Brookings Institute, research assistant, 1969-71; reporter and editor for Denver, CO, and Washington, DC, publications, 1971-73; Cervi's Journal, Denver, CO, reporter, 1973-75; Des Moines Register, Des Moines, IA, reporter, 1975-78; Chicago Tribune, Chicago, IL, reporter, 1978-84; Bulletin of the Atomic Scientists, Chicago, IL, editor, 1984-91; University of Colorado, Boulder, associate professor, School of Journalism and Mass Communication, 1991-, and director, Center for Environmental Journalism, 1992-. **Publications:** (ed.) Why Are We Still in Vietnam?, 1970. HISTORY: Credibility Gap: A Digest of the Pentagon Papers, 1972; (coed) Assessing the Nuclear Age, 1986; Making a Real Killing: Rocky Flats and the Nuclear West, 1999. **Address:** University of Colorado, SJMC, Campus Box 287, Boulder, CO 80309, U.S.A. **Online address:** ackland@spot.colorado.edu

ACKMANN, Martha (A.). (born United States), b. 1951. **Genres:** Air/ Space topics. **Career:** Educator, journalist, and author. Mount Holyoke College, South Hadley, MA, lecturer in women's studies, 1987-, director of Community-Based Learning Program, Weissman Center for Leadership. Founding editor, LEGACY: A Journal of American Women Writers, University of Nebraska Press. **Publications:** The Mercury Thirteen: The Untold Story of Thirteen American Women and the Dream of Space Flight,

2003; Contributor to periodicals. **Address:** Porter Hall, Mount Holyoke College, 50 College St., South Hadley, MA 01075, U.S.A. **Online address:** mackmann@mtholyoke.edu

ACKROYD, Peter. British, b. 1949. **Genres:** Novels, Poetry, Literary criticism and history. **Career:** Social Commentary. Chief Book Reviewer, The Times, London, since 1986. Literary Ed., The Spectator, London, 1973-77; television critic, The Times, London, 1977-81. **Publications:** London Lickpenny (poetry), 1973; Notes for a New Culture: An Essay on Modernism, 1976; Country Life (poetry), 1978; Dressing up: Transvestism and Drag: The History of an Obsession, 1979; Ezra Pound and His World, 1981; The Great Fire of London (novel), 1982; The Last Testament of Oscar Wilde (novel), 1983; T.S. Eliot, 1984; Hawksmoor (novel), 1985; Chatterton (novel), 1987; The Diversions of Purley (poetry), 1987; First Light (novel), 1989; Dickens (biography), 1990; English Music (novel), 1992; The House of Doctor Dee (novel), 1993; Dan Leno and the Limehouse Golem (novel), 1994; The Trial of Elizabeth Cree, 1995; Blake, 1996; The Life of Sir Thomas More, 1998; The Plato Papers, 2000. **Address:** c/o Anthony Sheil Assocs. Ltd, 43 Doughty St, London WC1N 2LF, England.

ACZEL, Amir D. American (born Israel), b. 1950. **Genres:** Mathematics/ Statistics. **Career:** University of Alaska, associate professor of mathematics, 1982-88; Bentley College, Waltham, MA, associate professor of mathematics, 1988-. **Publications:** Statistics, 1993; How to Beat the IRS, 1995; Complete Business Statistics, 3rd ed., 1996; Fermat's Last Theorem, 1996; Infinity, in press. **Address:** Department of Mathematics, Bentley College, Waltham, MA 02451, U.S.A. **Online address:** aaczel@bentley.edu

ADAIR, Aaron J. (born United States), b. 1980. **Genres:** Autobiography/ Memoirs. **Career:** Writer. **Publications:** You Don't Know Where I've Been (autobiography), 2003. **Address:** 1111 Oak Tree No. 215D, Norman, OK 73072, U.S.A. **Online address:** hito10bb@hotmail.com

ADAIR, Christy. British, b. 1949. **Genres:** Cultural/Ethnic topics, Dance/ Ballet, Women's studies and issues. **Career:** Northern School of Contemporary Dance, Leeds, England, dance critic, dance historian, and lecturer in dance studies, 1993-; University of Hull, Scarborough Campus, dance critic, dance historian, and lecturer in dance studies, 1999-. **Publications:** Women and Dance: Sylphs and Sirens, 1992. Contributor of articles and reviews to periodicals and radio.

ADAIR, James R(adford). American, b. 1923. **Genres:** Theology/Religion, Autobiography/Memoirs, Biography. **Career:** Ed., Pacific Garden Mission News, 1949-; Sr. Ed., Victor Books Division, Scripture Press Publications Inc., Wheaton, 1970-97 (Ed., Power for Living, Free Way, Teen Power and Counselor weekly churchpapers, 1949-77). **Publications:** Saints Alive, 1951; The Old Lighthouse, 1966; The Man from Steamtown, 1967, 1988; M.R. DeHaan: The Man and His Ministry, 1969; Surgeon on Safari, 1976, 1985; (with J.B. Jenkins) A Greater Strength (biography), 1990; A New Look at the Old Lighthouse, 1996; The Story of Scripture Press, 1998. COMPILER: (with H. Verploegh) 101 Days in the Gospels with Oswald Chambers, 1992; (with H. Verploegh) 101 Days in the Epistles with Oswald Chambers, 1994; (with H. Verploegh) A New Testament Walk with Oswald Chambers, 1999. EDITOR: God's Power Within, 1961; (with T. Miller) We Found Our Way, 1964; Teen with a Future, 1965; God's Power to Triumph, 1965; Tom Skinner, Top Man of the Lords and Other Stories, 1967; Hooked on Jesus, 1971; Unhooked, 1971; Brothers Black, 1973; (with T. Miller) Escape from Darkness, 1982; Through the Year with Warren W. Wiersbe, 1999; Be Quoted-From A to Z with Warren W. Wiersbe, 2000. **Address:** 703 Webster Ave, Wheaton, IL 60187, U.S.A. **Online address:** jradair@juno.com

ADAM, Christina. Japanese (born Japan). **Genres:** Novellas/Short stories. **Career:** Author, cattle rancher. Owner of the Lazy DW Cattle Ranch, Victor, ID. Taught courses in creative writing, English, American literature, and film studies in OH and CA. **Publications:** Sleeping With the Buffalo and Other Stories, 1996; Any Small Thing Can Save You: A Bestiary, 2001. Contributor to publications. **Address:** c/o Author Mail, Penguin Putnam, 375 Hudson Street, New York, NY 10014, U.S.A.

ADAM, David. British, b. 1936. **Genres:** Inspirational/Motivational Literature, Theology/Religion. **Career:** Anglican vicar. National Coal Board, Northumberland, England, coal miner, 1951-54; ordained Anglican priest, 1959, serving in Auckland, England, 1959-63, West Hartlepool, England, 1963-67, and Danby, England, 1967-90; Holy Island, Berwick-upon-Tweed, England, vicar, 1990-. Conductor of religious retreats; lecturer and broadcaster. National Coal Board, chaplain. **Publications:** The Edge of Glory: Prayers in the Celtic Tradition, 1985; The Cry of the Deer: Meditations on the Hymn of St. Patrick, 1987; Tides and Seasons: Modern Prayers in the Celtic Tradition, 1989; The Eye of the Eagle: Meditations on the Hymn "Be Thou My Vision," 1990; (with J. Douglas) Visions of Glory for Voices (music), 1990; Border Lands: The Best of David Adam's Celtic Vision, 1991; Power Lines: Celtic Prayers about Work, 1992; Fire of the North: The Illustrated Life of St. Cuthbert, 1993; The Open Gate: Celtic Prayers for Growing Spiritually, 1994; The Rhythm of Life: Celtic Christian Prayer, 1996, in US asThe Rhythm of Life: Celtic Daily Prayer, 1997; (comp. and author of introd.) The Wisdom of the Celts: A Compilation, 1996; A Celtic Daily Prayer Book: A Compilation, 1997, in US as A Celtic Book of Prayer, 1997; Flame in My Heart: St. Aidan for Today, 1997; Clouds and Glory: Prayers for the Church Year; Year A, 1998; On Eagles' Wings: The Life and Spirit of St. Chad, 1999; Traces of Glory: Prayers for the Church Year; Year B, 1999; Forward to Freedom: A Journey into God, 1999, in US as Forward to Freedom: From Exodus to Easter, 2001; A Desert in the Ocean: God's Call to Adventurous Living, in US as A Desert in the Ocean: The Spiritual Journey according to St. Brendan the Navigator, 2000; Glimpses of Glory: Prayers for the Church Year; Year C; Landscapes of Light: An Illustrated Anthology of Prayers, 2001; (comp) A Celtic Psaltery: Psalms from the Celtic Tradition, 2001; Island of Light: An Illustrated Collection of Prayers, 2002; Walking the Edges: Celtic Saints along the Roman Wall, 2003. **Address:** The Old Granary, Waren Mill, Belford NE70 7EE, England.

ADAM, Paul. British, b. 1951. **Genres:** Environmental sciences/Ecology. **Career:** Cambridge University, England, research fellow at Emmanuel College, 1975-78; University of New South Wales, Sydney, Australia, lecturer, 1978-83, senior lecturer, 1983-90, associate professor of biology, 1991-. **Publications:** Coastal Wetlands of New South Wales, 1985; New South Wales Rainforests, 1987; Saltmarsh Ecology, 1990; Australian Rainforests, 1992. **Address:** School of Biological Science, University of New South Wales, Sydney, NSW 2052, Australia. **Online address:** p.adam@unsw.edu.au

ADAMEC, Christine. American, b. 1949. **Genres:** Adult non-fiction. **Career:** Free-lance writer, Palm Bay, FL, 1982-. Military service: Served in the U.S. Air Force; received Air Force Commendation Medal, 1974. **Publications:** There Are Babies to Adopt, 1987, 2nd ed., 1996; (with W.L. Pierce) The Encyclopedia of Adoption, 1991, rev. ed., 2000; How to Live with a Mentally Ill Person, 1996; When Your Pet Dies, 1996; (with J.L. Thomas) Do You Have Attention Deficit Disorder?, 1996; Is Adoption for You?, 1998; Complete Idiot's Guide to Adoption, 1998; Adoption Option Complete Handbook, 2000-2001, 1999; Writing Freelance, 2000. **Address:** 1921 Ohio St. N.E., Palm Bay, FL 32907, U.S.A. **Online address:** Adamec@aol.com

ADAMEC, Ludwig W. American (born Austria), b. 1924. **Genres:** Geography, History, International relations/Current affairs. **Career:** Professor, University of Arizona, Tucson, 1967- (Director, Near Eastern Center, 1975-85). U.S. Ed., Afghanistan Journal, 1973-75; Chief, Afghanistan Branch, Voice of America, Washington, DC, 1986-87. **Publications:** Afghanistan 1900-1923: A Diplomatic History, 1967; Tarikh-e Ravabet-e Siya-si-ye Afghanistan az Zaman-e Amir Abdur Rahman ta Isteqlal, 1970; Who Is Who of Afghanistan, 1974; Afghanistan's Foreign Affairs in the 20th Century: Relations with the U.S.S.R., Germany, and Britain, 1974; Historical Gazetteer of Iran, 4 vols., 1976-88; Biographical Dictionary of Contemporary Afghanistan, 1987; Historical Dictionary of Afghanistan, 1991; Dictionary of Afghan Wars, Revolutions, and Insurgencies, 1996; Historical Dictionary of Afghanistan, 1997; Historical Dictionary of Islam, 2001; The A to Z of Islam, 2002; (with F.A. Clements) Conflict in Afghanistan: An Encyclopedia, 2020, 2004. EDITOR: Afghanistan: Some New Approaches, 1969; Political and Historical Gazetteer of Afghanistan (6 vols.), 1972-74. **Address:** 3931 E Whittier, Tucson, AZ 85711, U.S.A. **Online address:** adamec@u.arizona.edu

ADAMS, Abby. American, b. 1939. **Genres:** Horticulture. **Career:** Writer. **Publications:** An Uncommon Scold, 1989; A Gardener's Gripe Book, 1996. **Address:** c/o Knox Burger, Knox Burger Associates Ltd., 425 Madison Ave, 10th Floor, New York, NY 10017-1110, U.S.A.

ADAMS, Art(hur). (born United States), b. 1963. **Genres:** Graphic Novels. **Career:** Graphic artist and writer. Dark Horse Comics, Milwaukie, OR, cofounder of Legend imprint. **Publications:** (Penciler) Walt Simonson, Stan Lee Presents the New Fantastic Four: Monsters Unleashed, 1992; (Illustrator) Art Adams' Creature Features, 1996; (And illustrator) Monkeyman and O'Brien (graphic novel), 1997; (And illustrator, with others) Godzilla: Age of Monsters, 1998; Creator and illustration of comic-book series. **Address:** c/o Dark Horse Comics, 10956 Southeast Main St., Milwaukie, OR 97222, U.S.A.

ADAMS, Carol J. American, b. 1951. **Genres:** Animals/Pets, Environmental sciences/Ecology, Social commentary, Theology/Religion, Women's studies and issues. **Career:** Women's Theological Coalition of the Boston Theological Institute, Boston, MA, staff member, 1974-75; Goddard College, Plainfield, VT, field faculty in feminist studies program of Goddard-Cambridge Graduate Program in Social Change, 1975-76; Chautauqua County Rural Ministry, Inc., Dunkirk, NY, executive director, 1977-81, 1983-87; State University of New York College at Fredonia, part-time lecturer, 1980-84; Chautauqua Institution, summer lecturer, 1977-85; Perkins School of Theology, Southern Methodist University, visiting lecturer, 1989, 1991, 1993, 1999, 2001; writer, campus lecturer, and independent scholar. **Publications:** The Sexual Politics of Meat, 1990, rev. ed., 2000; Woman-Battering, 1994; Neither Man nor Beast, 1994; (ed. with J. Donovan) Animals and Women, 1995; The Inner Art of Vegetarianism, 2000; Meditations on the Inner Art of Vegetarianism, 2001; (with B. Buchanan and S. Allison) Journey to Gameland, 2001; Living among Meat Eaters, 2001; The Pornography of Meat, 2003; Help! My Child Stopped Eating Meat!, 2004; Prayers for Animals and Animal Lovers, 2004. EDITOR: Ecofeminism and the Sacred, 1993; (with M. Fortune) Violence against Women and Children, 1995; (with J. Donovan) Beyond Animal Rights, 1996. Author of articles and reviews.

ADAMS, Charles. Canadian (born United States), b. 1930. **Genres:** Economics, History, Law, Money/Finance. **Career:** Attorney in general practice in Ventura, CA, 1957-69, and Encino, CA, 1969-71; Cayman Islands International College, professor of history, 1971-75. Adjunct scholar, Cato Institute and Von Mises Institute, Auburn, University, both 1994. National Archives, lecturer. **Publications:** Fight, Flight, Fraud, 1983; For Good and Evil: The Impact of Taxes on the Course of Civilization, 1993, 2nd ed., 1999; Those Dirty Rotten Taxes, 1998; When in the Course of Human Events, 2000. Contributor to periodicals. **Address:** PO Box 62, Pickering, ON, Canada L1V 2R2. **Online address:** cadams000@sympatico.ca

ADAMS, Charles J., III. American, b. 1947. **Genres:** Mythology/Folklore, Travel/Exploration. **Career:** Berks County Record, Reading, PA, editor, 1968-76; WEEU-Radio, Reading, broadcaster, 1976-. Reading Eagle-Times, chief travel correspondent, 1985-, and author of the biweekly feature "Berks the Bizarre." Exeter House Books, founder, 1982. Performer with rock music groups Milestones and Sound Reaction; songwriter and composer of musical arrangements for commercial advertisements. **Publications:** Ghost Stories of Berks County, 1982, Book Two, 1984, (with G.S. Clothier) Book Three, 1988; (with D.J. Seibold) Legends of Long Beach Island, 1985; (with D.J. Seibold) Shipwrecks Off Ocean City, 1986; (with D.J. Seibold) Shipwrecks and Legends 'round Cape May, 1987; Cape May Ghost Stories, 1988, Book 2, 1997; (with D.J. Seibold) Shipwrecks, Sea Stories, and Legends of the Delaware Coast, 1989; (with D.J. Seibold) Ghost Stories of the Delaware Coast, 1990; (with D.J. Seibold) Pocono Ghosts, Legends, and Lore, 1991, Book Two, 1995; Great Train Wrecks of Eastern Pennsylvania, 1992; (with D.J. Seibold) Ghost Stories of the Lehigh Valley, 1993; Pennsylvania Dutch Country Ghosts, Legends, and Lore, 1994; (with B.E. Trapani) Ghost Stories of Pittsburgh and Allegheny County, 1994; (with D.J. Seibold) Shipwrecks near Barnegat Inlet, 2nd ed., 1995; Berks the Bizarre, 1995; A Day Away in Sovereign Country (travel book), 1995; Curtains (mystery), 1995; Mysterious Cape May, 1996; New York City Ghost Stories, 1996; Philadelphia Ghost Stories, 1998; Bucks County Ghost Stories, 1999; Montgomery County Ghost Stories, 2000; Ghost Stories of Chester County and the Brandywine Valley, 2001; Reading, Pa.: A Postcard History, 2001. Author and producer of safety education programs for Pennsylvania State Police. **Address:** Exeter House Books, PO Box 8134, Reading, PA 19603, U.S.A. **Online address:** gohaunting@aol.com

ADAMS, Chuck. See **TUBB, E(dwin) C(harles).**

ADAMS, Colin C. American, b. 1956. **Genres:** Novellas/Short stories, Adult non-fiction, Mathematics/Statistics. **Career:** Oregon State University, Corvallis, professor of mathematics, 1983-85; Williams College, Williamstown, MA, professor of mathematics, 1985-; University of California, Santa Barbara, professor, 1988-89; University of California, Davis, professor, 1991-92. **Publications:** The Knot Book, 1994; How to Ace Calculus: The Streetwise Guide, 1998; How to Ace the Rest of Calculus: The Streetwise Guide, 2001; Why Knot?, 2004. **Address:** Department of Mathematics, Bronfman Science Center, Williams College, Williamstown, MA 01267, U.S.A. **Online address:** Colin.Adams@Williams.edu

ADAMS, Deborah. American, b. 1956. **Genres:** Mystery/Crime/Suspense. **Career:** Writer; Nashville State Technical Institute, adjunct faculty member (teaches online writing courses). **Publications:** All the Great Pretenders, 1992; All the Crazy Winters, 1992; All the Dark Disguises, 1993; All the Hungry Mothers, 1994; All the Deadly Beloved, 1995; All the Blood Relations, 1997. **Address:** Route 4, Box 664, Waverly, TN 37185, U.S.A.

ADAMS, Edward E. American, b. 1921. **Genres:** Administration/ Management. **Career:** American Can Co., Jersey City, NJ, plant safety supervisor, 1947-50; General Chemical, NYC, corporate safety manager, 1950-55; Diamond Match Co., NYC, corporate safety manager, 1955-59; General Baking, NYC, safety manager, 1959-63; Pet Inc., St. Louis, MO, director of loss prevention, 1963-87. **Publications:** Total Quality Safety Management: An Introduction, 1995. Contributor to magazines. **Address:** 3890 Four Ridge Rd., House Springs, MO 63051, U.S.A.

ADAMS, Ernest Charles. British, b. 1926. **Genres:** Technology. **Career:** Materials Testing and Concrete Engineer, George Wimpey & Co. Ltd., London, 1953-59; Lecturer, Crawley College of Further Education, 1959-71; Lecturer, then Sr. Lecturer, Leeds Polytechnic, 1971-84. **Publications:** Science in Building (3 vols.), 1964; Fundamentals of Building Science, 1980. **Address:** 10 Kenworthy Vale, Holt Park, Adel, Leeds LS16 7QG, England.

ADAMS, Eve. See **COONTS, Stephen (Paul).**

ADAMS, Gerald R. American, b. 1946. **Genres:** Sociology, Psychology, Education. **Career:** Utah State University, Logan, professor of human development, 1975-80; University of Guelph, Guelph, Ontario, professor of family studies, 1990-. **Publications:** (with T.P. Gullotta) Adolescent Life Experiences, 1983, 3rd ed. (with Gullotta and C. Markstrom), 1994; (with Gullotta and S. Alexander) Today's Marriages and Families: A Wellness Approach, 1986; (with Montemayor and Gullotta) Psychosocial Development during Adolescence. EDITOR (with T.P. Gullotta and R. Montemayor) The Biology of Adolescent Behavior and Development, 1989; From Childhood to Adolescence, 1990; Developing Social Competency in Adolescence, 1990; Adolescent Identity Formation, 1992; Adolescent Sexuality, 1993; Adolescent Drug Misuse, 1994. **Address:** Department of Family Studies, University of Guelph, Guelph, ON, Canada N1G 2W1.

ADAMS, Glenda. Australian, b. 1939. **Genres:** Novels, Novellas/Short stories, Essays, Plays/Screenplays. **Career:** Teachers and Writers Collaborative, NYC, Associate Director, 1973-76; Sarah Lawrence College, Bronxville, NY, Writing Workshop Instructor, 1976-90; Columbia University, NYC, Writing Workshop Instructor, 1978, Adjunct Associate Professor, School of the Arts. **Publications:** STORIES: Lies and Stories, 1976; The Hottest Night of the Century, 1979. NOVELS: Games of the Strong, 1981; Dancing on Coral, 1987; Longleg, 1990; The Tempest of Clemenza, 1996. PLAYS & SCRIPTS: Pride, 1993; Wrath, 1993; The Monkey Trap, 1998. **Address:** Writing Program, 612 Lewisohn, Columbia University, New York, NY 10027, U.S.A. **Online address:** ga40@columbia.edu

ADAMS, Hazard. American, b. 1926. **Genres:** Novels, Poetry, Literary criticism and history. **Career:** Cornell University, Ithaca, NY, instructor, 1952-56; University of Texas, assistant professor, 1956-59; Michigan State University, East Lansing, associate professor, and professor, 1959-64; University of California, Irvine, professor, 1964-74, chairman of the Dept. of English, 1964-69, dean of the School of Humanities, 1970-72, vice-chancellor for academic affairs, 1972-74; University of Washington, Seattle, professor of English, Lockwood Professor of Humanities in Comparative Literature, 1977-97, emeritus, 1997-. **Publications:** Blake and Yeats, 1955; William Blake: A Reading, 1963; The Contexts of Poetry, 1963; The Horses of Instruction (novel), 1968; The Interests of Criticism, 1969; The Truth about Dragons (novel), 1971; Lady Gregory, 1973; The Academic Tribes, 1976; Philosophy of the Literary Symbolic, 1983; Joyce Cary's Trilogies, 1983; The Book of Yeats's Poems, 1990; Antithetical Essays, 1990; The Book of Yeats's Vision, 1995; Farm at Richwood and Other Poems, 1997; Many Pretty Toys: A Novel, 1999; Four Lectures on the History of Criticism in the West, 2000; Home: A Novel, 2001. EDITOR: Poems by R.S. Adams, 1952; Poetry: An Introductory Anthology, 1968; Fiction as Process, 1968; William Blake, 1970; Critical Theory since Plato, 1972, 3rd ed., 2004; Critical Theory since 1965, 1986; Critical Essays on William Blake, 1991. **Address:** 3930 NE 157th Pl, Lake Forest Park, WA 98155, U.S.A. **Online address:** HAdams3048@aol.com

ADAMS, Jad. British, b. 1954. **Genres:** Biography. **Career:** Reporter for local newspapers prior to 1978; reporter for national newspapers, London, England, 1978-82; television producer and writer, 1982-. Affiliated with television programs, including AIDS: The Unheard Voices; The Mouse's Tale; Food: Fad or Fact?; The Dynasty, The Nehru-Gandhi Story; Kitchener: The Empire's Flawed Hero; The Clintons; and The Real Eastenders. London Borough of Lewisham, member of borough council, 1978-86; Nightwatch (charity for the homeless), chairperson, 1992-. **Publications:** AIDS: The HIV Myth, 1989; Tony Benn: A Biography, 1992; Double Indemnity: Murder for Insurance, 1994; The Dynasty: The Nehru Gandhi Story, 1997; Madder

Music, Stranger Wine: The Life of Ernest Dowson, 2000; Pankhurst, 2003; Hideous Absinthe: A History of the Devil in a Bottle, 2004. Author of television scripts. **Address:** 2 Kings Garth, 29 London Rd, London SE23 3TT, England.

ADAMS, James (Macgregor David). British, b. 1951. **Genres:** Novels, Plays/Screenplays, Military/Defense/Arms control, Politics/Government. **Career:** Affiliated with the Evening Chronicle, Newcastle, England, 1972-75; freelance writer in the U.S. and Africa, 1975-78; Eight Days Magazine, worked as reporter, head reporter, and news editor, 1978-81; Sunday Times, London, England, foreign manager, 1981-82, special assistant to the editor, 1982-84, defense correspondent, 1984-91, managing editor, 1989-91, Washington Bureau Chief, 1991-. **Publications:** (with P. Frischer) The Artist in the Marketplace, 1980; The Unnatural Alliance, 1984; The Financing of Terror, 1986; Secret Armies, 1988; (with R. Morgan and T. Bambridge) Ambush: The War between the SAS and the IRA, 1988; Engines of War, 1990; The Final Terror, 1991; Bull's Eye, 1992; The New Spies, 1994; Sell Out, 1995; The Next World War, 1997. FICTION: The Final Terror, 1991; Taking the Tunnel, 1993; Hard Targert, 1995; Crucible, 1997. SCREENPLAYS: The Great Game, 1995; SSN, 1996. **Address:** Ashland Institute for Strategic Studies, 103 High St, Ashland, OR 97520, U.S.A.

ADAMS, James F(rederick). American (born Democratic People's Republic of Korea), b. 1927. **Genres:** Psychology. **Career:** Assistant Professor of Psychology, Whitworth College, Spokane, Wash., 1952-55; Research Associate, Experimental Study in Instructional Procedures, Miami University, Oxford, Ohio, 1957-59; Professor of Psychology, 1959-80, Chairman of Counseling Psychology, 1973-80, and Coordinator, Division of Educational Psychology, 1974-80, Temple University, Philadelphia; Professor of Psychology, and Dean of Graduate School, University of Nevada, Las Vegas, 1980-85; Sr. Vice President (Academic), Longwood College, Farmville, Virginia, 1985-86. **Publications:** Problems in Counseling, 1962. EDITOR: Counseling and Guidance: A Summary View, 1965; Understanding Adolescence, 1968, 4th ed. 1980; The Philosophy of Human Nature, by J. Buchanan, 1972; Human Behavior in a Changing Society, 1973; Songs That Had to Be Sung, by B.N. Adams, 1979. **Address:** 130 Palacio Rd, Corrales, NM 87048, U.S.A.

ADAMS, Jeanne Clare. American, b. 1921. **Genres:** Information science/ Computers. **Career:** U.S. Army Air Forces, systems service analyst; Harvard University, Cambridge, MA, research statistician; National Center for Atmospheric Research, worked as deputy head of Computing Division, assistant for planning, director of Program for Atmospheric Science Graduate Students, and manager of university liaison, between 1960 and 1982; Colorado State University, Fort Collins, coordinator of CYBER 205 Project at Institute for Computational Studies, 1982-84; National Center for Atmospheric Research, consultant to Computational Support Group, Scientific Computing Division, 1985-97, software engineer emeritus, 1997-. American National Standards Institute, chairperson of Fortran Standards Committee, 1977-92. **Publications:** (with W.S. Brainerd and C.H. Goldberg) Programmer's Guide to Fortran 90, 1990, 2nd ed, 1994; (with Brainerd, J. Martin, B. Smith, and J. Wagener) Fortran 90 Handbook, 1992; (with Brainerd, Martin, and Smith) Fortran TOP 90, 1994; (with Brainerd and Goldberg) Programmer's Guide to F, 1996; (with Brainerd, Martin, Smith, and Wagener) Fortran 95 Handbook, 1997. Contributor to periodicals.

ADAMS, Jerome R(obertson). American, b. 1938. **Genres:** Area studies, Biography, Politics/Government. **Career:** Writer. **Publications:** Liberators and Patriots of Latin America: Biographies of Twenty-three Leaders from Dona Marina (1505-1530) to Bishop Romero (1917-1980), 1991; Notable Latin American Women: Liberators, Rebels, Poets, Battlers and Spies, 1500-1900, 1995. **Address:** 20 Banner Ave., Winston-Salem, NC 27127, U.S.A.

ADAMS, Kathleen M(arie). American, b. 1957. **Genres:** Anthropology/ Ethnology. **Career:** Women's Community Development Project, San Francisco, CA, research assistant with Women's Jail Study Group, 1979-80; Thomas Burke Memorial Washington State Museum, Seattle, WA, assistant curator of ethnology, 1981-82; Hasanuddin University, Ujung, Pandang, Indonesia, visiting researcher at Pusat Latihan Penelitian Ilmu Ilmu Sosial, 1984-85; Beloit College, Beloit, WI, assistant professor of anthropology, 1988-93, Mouat Assistant Professor of International Studies, 1990-93, research associate in Asian ethnology at Logan Museum, 1988-93; Loyola University Chicago, Chicago, IL, assistant professor, 1993-98, associate professor of anthropology, 1998-, coordinator of undergraduate anthropology program, 1998-2000, faculty fellow at Center for Ethics, 1998. Field Museum of Natural History, adjunct curator, 1998-. Northern Illinois University, adjunct faculty for Program for Southeast Asian Studies, 1990-96, guest lecturer, 1997, 1999; University of Pittsburgh, assistant professor for

Semester at Sea, Pacific Program, 1996; Soka University of America, professor and coordinator of social and behavioral science concentration, 2000-01; lecturer at other institutions. Conducted field research in Java, Tana Toraja, and Alor, Indonesia, in Singapore, and in San Juan Capistrano, CA. **Publications:** (ed., with S. Dickey, and contrib.) Home and Hegemony: Domestic Service and Identity Politics in South and Southeast Asia, 2000. Contributor to books. Contributor of articles and reviews to periodicals. **Address:** Department of Anthropology, Loyola University of Chicago, 6525 North Sheridan Ave., Chicago, IL 60626, U.S.A. **Online address:** kadams@luc.edu

ADAMS, Marilyn Jager. American, b. 1948. **Genres:** Psychology, Education. **Career:** Planning Research Corp., Washington, DC, programmer and research assistant, 1967; General Electric Information Systems Division, Bethesda, MD, systems programmer and student intern, 1969-70; Bolt, Beranek & Newman, Inc., Cambridge, MA, cognitive and developmental psychologist, 1975-; writer. Brown University, senior research scientist, 1989-, visiting professor, 1994-95; National Assessment of Educational Progress, member of planning committee for reading, 1992; University of Illinois at Urbana-Champaign, Center for the Study of Reading, member of senior staff; guest on radio and television programs. **Publications:** (ed. and contrib.) Odyssey: A Curriculum for Thinking, Vol. I: Foundations of Reasoning, Vol. II: Understanding Language, Vol. III: Problem Solving, Vol. IV: Decision Making, Vol. V: Inventive Thinking, 1986; Beginning to Read: Thinking and Learning about Print, Press, 1990; (with Y.J. Tenney, R.W. Pew) Strategic Workload and the Cognitive Management of Advanced Multi-task Systems, 1991; (senior author) Collections for Young Scholars, K-2, 1994. **Address:** Bolt, Beranek & Newman, Inc, 10 Moulton St, Cambridge, MA 02138, U.S.A.

ADAMS, Michael Evelyn. See Obituaries.

ADAMS, Nicholas. See DOYLE, Debra.

ADAMS, Nicholas. See MACDONALD, James D.

ADAMS, Nicholas. See PINE, Nicholas.

ADAMS, Nicholas. See SMITH, Sherwood.

ADAMS, Patch. (Hunter Adams). American, b. 1945?. **Genres:** Medicine/Health. **Career:** Physician, 1971-; author; Gesundheit! Institute, Hillsboro, WV, founder and president, 1971-. **Publications:** (with M. Mylander) Gesundheit!: Bringing Good Health to You, the Medical System, and Society through Physician Service, Complementary Therapies, Humor, and Joy, 1992; House Calls: How We Can All Heal the World One Visit at a Time, 1998; (author of foreword) J. Graham-Pole, Illness and the Art of Creative Self-Expression: Stories and Exercises from the Arts for Those with Chronic Illness, 2000. Contributor to books. **Address:** Gesundheit! Institute, PO Box 268, Hillsboro, WV 24946, U.S.A.

ADAMS, Richard (George). British, b. 1920. **Genres:** Novels, Novellas/Short stories, Children's fiction, Poetry, Autobiography/Memoirs. **Career:** Freelance writer. Formerly a Higher Civil Servant with Dept. of the Environment. **Publications:** NOVELS: Watership Down, 1972; Shardik, 1974; The Plague Dogs, 1977; The Girl in a Swing, 1980; Maia, 1984; Traveller, 1988. POETRY: The Tyger Voyage (narrative), 1976; The Ship's Cat (narrative), 1977; (ed. and contrib.) Occasional Poets, 1986; The Legend of Te Tuna (narrative), 1986. OTHER: (with M. Hooper) Nature through the Seasons, 1975; (with M. Hooper) Nature Day and Night, 1978; The Watership Down Film Picture Book, 1978; The Iron Wolf and Other Stories, 1980; (with R. Lockley) Voyage through the Antarctic, 1982; The Bureaucats, 1985; A Nature Diary, 1985; The Day Gone By (autobiography), 1990; Tales from Watership Down, 1996; The Outlandish Knight, 2000. **Address:** 26 Church St, Whitchurch, Hants. RG28 7AR, England.

ADAMS, Robert Merrihew. American, b. 1937. **Genres:** Philosophy. **Career:** Ordained Presbyterian minister, 1962. Montauk Community Church, Montauk, NY, pastor, 1962-65; University of Michigan, Ann Arbor, lecturer, 1968, assistant professor of philosophy, 1969-72; University of California, Los Angeles, associate professor, 1972-76, professor of philosophy, 1976-93; Yale University, professor of philosophy, 1993-; writer. Yale Divinity School, visiting professor of philosophical theology, 1988. **Publications:** The Virtue of Faith and Other Essays in Philosophical Theology, 1987; Leibniz: Determinist, Theist, Idealist, 1994; A Finite and Infinite Goods: A Framework for Ethics, 1999. **Address:** Yale University, Department of Philosophy, PO Box 208306, New Haven, CT 06520-8306, U.S.A.

ADAMS, Roy J(oseph). American/Canadian, b. 1940. **Genres:** Administration/Management, Business/Trade/Industry, Civil liberties/Human rights, Economics, Ethics, Industrial relations, Organized labor. **Career:** Chase Manhattan Bank, NYC, industrial relations specialist, 1967-68; McMaster University, Hamilton, ON, assistant professor, 1973-78, head of Human Resources and Labour Relations Area, 1976-78, associate professor, 1978-83, professor of industrial relations, 1984-97, director, Theme School on International Justice and Human Rights, 1996-97, professor emeritus, 1997-; Hamilton Civic Coalition, executive director, 2005-. Visiting professor, visiting scholar, and guest lecturer at colleges and universities worldwide. Comparative Industrial Relations Newsletter, editor and publisher, 1990-99; Hamilton Spectator, columnist, 1997-2002; Sphere, columnist, 1998-. **Publications:** White Collar Union Growth in Britain and Sweden, 1975; Industrial Relations under Liberal Democracy, 1995; (with G. Betcherman and B. Bilson) Good Jobs, Bad Jobs, No Jobs: Tough Choices for Canadian Labour Law, 1995. EDITOR: Comparative Industrial Relations, 1991; (with N.M. Meltz, and contrib.) Industrial Relations Theory, 1993. Contributor to books. Contributor of articles and reviews to professional journals, popular magazines, and newspapers. **Address:** Michael G. DeGroote School of Business, DeGroote Bldg, McMaster University, 1280 Main St W, Hamilton, ON, Canada L8S 4M4. **Online address:** AdamsR@McMaster.ca

ADAMS, Scott. American, b. 1957. **Genres:** Cartoons. **Career:** Crocker National Bank, San Francisco, CA, worked as a bank teller, computer programmer, financial analyst, product manager, and commercial lender, 1979-86; Pacific Bell, San Ramon, CA, 1986-95; creator and author of Dilbert comic strip, 1989-. Speaker at meetings and conventions. **Publications:** HUMOR: The Dilbert Principle: A Cubicle-Eye View of Bosses, Meetings, Management Fads and Other Workplace Afflictions, 1996; Dogbert's Top Secret Management Handbook, 1996; The Dilbert Future: Thriving on Stupidity in the 21st Century, 1997; The Joy of Work, 1998. DILBERT COMIC STRIP COLLECTIONS: Dogbert's Clues for the Clueless: All-New Original Cartoons Featuring Dogbert from the Nationally Syndicated Dilbert Strip, 1993; Always Postpone Meetings with Time-Wasting Morons, 1994; Build a Better Life by Stealing Office Supplies, 1994; Shave the Whales, 1994; It's Obvious You Won't Survive by Your Wits Alone, 1995; Bring Me the Head of Willie the Mailboy, 1995; Conversations with Dogbert, 1996; You Don't Need Experience If You've Got Attitude, 1996; Access Denied: Dilbert's Quest for Love in the Nineties, 1996; Fugitive from the Cubicle Police, 1996; Still Pumped from Using the Mouse, 1996; Casual Day Has Gone Too Far, 1997; The Boss: Nameless, Blameless & Shameless, 1997; The Dilbert Bunch, 1997; Work Is a Contact Sport, 1997; Don't Feed the Egos, 1997; You'd Better Watch Out, 1997; Seven Years of Highly Defective People: The Origins and Evolutions of Dilbert, 1997; I'm Not Anti-Business, I'm Anti-Idiot, 1998. OTHER: (author of foreword) G. Kawasaki, How to Drive Your Competition Crazy: Creating Disruption for Fun and Profit, 1996; Telling It Like It Isn't: A Tiptoe Approach to Communications-A Dilbert Little Book, 1996; Dilbert Postcard Book, 1997. **Address:** c/o United Media, 200 Madison Ave., New York, NY 10016, U.S.A. **Online address:** ScottAdams@aol.com

ADAMS, Sheila Kay. American, b. 1953. **Genres:** Novels. **Career:** Madison County Board of Education, Marshall, NC, teacher, 1975-92. **Publications:** NOVELS: Come Go Home with Me, 1995; My Old True Love, 2004. Contributor to periodicals. **Address:** PO Box 1401, Mars Hill, NC 28754, U.S.A. **Online address:** sheila@jimandsheila.com; www.jimandsheila.com

ADAMS, Timothy Dow. American, b. 1943. **Genres:** Literary criticism and history, Autobiography/Memoirs. **Career:** Northern Virginia Community College, Annandale, lecturer in English, 1971-72; Old Dominion University, Norfolk, VA, instructor in English, 1972-75; Christian Brothers College, Memphis, TN, adjunct assistant professor of English, 1978-79; University of Arkansas, Fayetteville, temporary assistant professor of English, 1979-81; McMurry College, Abilene, TX, assistant professor of English, 1981-82; West Virginia University, Morgantown, assistant professor, 1982-86, associate professor of English, 1986-91, professor, 1991-, chair, 2000-. **Publications:** Telling Lies in Modern American Autobiography, 1990; Light Writing and Life Writing: Photography in Autobiography, 2000; (assoc. ed.) Autobiography Studies. **Address:** English Department, West Virginia University, Morgantown, WV 26506, U.S.A. **Online address:** tadams@wvu.edu

ADAMS, William James. American, b. 1947. **Genres:** History, Economics. **Career:** University of Michigan, Ann Arbor, professor of economics, 1974-. University of Aix-Marseille, Aix-en-Provence, France, visiting professor, 1980-81; University of Paris I, Paris, France, visiting professor, 1989. **Publications:** French Industrial Policy, 1986; Restructuring the French Economy, 1989; Singular Europe, 1992. **Address:** University of Michigan, Department of Economics, Ann Arbor, MI 48109, U.S.A.

ADAMS, Zack. *See* **BUNGERT, D. Edward.**

ADAMSON, Donald. British, b. 1939. **Genres:** Novellas/Short stories, History, Literary criticism and history, Philosophy, Biography, Translations. **Career:** Manchester Grammar School, assistant master, 1962-64; J. Walter Thompson Co., Ltd., London, executive, 1965-67; St. George's School, Gravesend, head of Modern Languages, 1968; Goldsmiths' College, London, lecturer, 1969-70, sr. lecturer, 1970-77, and principal lecturer in French, 1977-89; Wolfson College, Cambridge, visiting fellow, 1989-90. **Publications:** The Genesis of Le Cousin Pons, 1966; Dusty Heritage: A National Policy for Museums and Libraries, 1971; (with P. Dewar) The House of Nell Gwyn: The Fortunes of the Beauclerk Family, 1670-1974, 1974; A Rescue Policy for Museums, 1980; Balzac: Illusions Perdues, 1981; Les Romantiques francais devant la Peinture espagnole, 1989; Blaise Pascal: Mathematician, Physicist, and Thinker about God, 1995; The Curriers' Company: A Modern History, 2000; Balzac and the Tradition of the European Novel, 2001; Pascal's Views on Mathematics and the Divine, 2005. EDITOR: T.S. Eliot: A Memoir, 1971; Rides round Britain, the Travel Journals of John Byng, 5th Viscount Torrington, 1996. TRANSLATOR: Balzac, The Black Sheep, 1970; Balzac, Ursule Mirouet, 1976; Maupassant, Bed 29 and Other Stories, 1993. Author of articles on French literature and historical and political subjects; contributor to the Internet. **Address:** Dodmore House, The Street, Meopham, Kent, England. **Online address:** aimsworthy@aol.com; www.dodmore.co.uk

ADAMSON, M(ary) J(o). Also writes as Yvonne Adamson. American, b. 1935. **Genres:** Mystery/Crime/Suspense. **Career:** High school English teacher in Seneca, IL, 1956-57; Humboldt State College (now University), Arcata, CA, instructor in English, 1967-68; University of Denver, Denver, CO, internship director of department of mass communications and lecturer, 1979-83; writer. **Publications:** Not till a Hot January, 1987; A February Face, 1987; Remember March, 1987; April When They Woo, 1989; (as Mary Jo Adamson) May Newfangled Mirth, 1989; (as Yvonne Adamson) Bridey's Mountain; The Blazing Tree, 2000; The Elusive Voice, 2001.

ADAMSON, Yvonne. *See* **ADAMSON, M(ary) J(o).**

ADAMZ-BOGUS, SDiane. Also writes as SDiane Bogus. American, b. 1946. **Genres:** Poetry, Education, Gay and lesbian issues, Inspirational/Motivational Literature, Women's studies and issues. **Career:** Northwestern University, Evanston, IL, student teaching supervisor of M.A. teaching program, 1972; Los Angeles Southwest Community College, Los Angeles, CA, English instructor, 1976-81; Compton Unified School District, English department chair, 1979-80; Woman in the Moon Publications, founder/owner, 1979-99; City College, San Francisco, CA, English instructor, 1985-86; California State University, Stanislaus, visiting lecturer, 1987-89, faculty mentor, 1988-90, faculty adviser for "Umoja" (black student union), 1987-88; DeAnza College, Cupertino, CA, professor of composition and literature, 1990-. **Publications:** I'm off to See the Goddamn Wizard, Alright!, 1971; Woman in the Moon, 1979; Dykehands, 1984; The Chant of the Women of Magdelena, 1990; For the Love of Men, 1991; Spirit in the Dark (autobiography), 1994; The Studenthood New Age Reader, 1994; Buddhism in the Classroom, 1995; The New Age Reader, 1998; Education by Metaphor, 1998; Bearstories, 2000; Spirit in the Dark (essays), 2001; Greatest Hits Collection, 2001. **Address:** English Dept, DeAnza College, 21250 Stevens Creek Blvd, Cupertino, CA 95014, U.S.A. **Online address:** sdiane adamzbogus@yahoo.com

ADCOCK, Fleur. British (born New Zealand), b. 1934. **Genres:** Poetry. **Publications:** The Eye of the Hurricane, 1964; Tigers, 1967; High Tide in the Garden, 1971; The Scenic Route, 1974; The Inner Harbour, 1979; Below Loughrigg, 1979; Selected Poems, 1983; The Virgin and the Nightingale: Medieval Latin Poems, 1983; The Incident Book, 1986; Time Zones, 1991; Looking Back, 1997; Poems 1960-2000, 2000. EDITOR: The Oxford Book of Contemporary New Zealand Poetry, 1982; The Faber Book of 20th Century Women's Poetry, 1987. **Address:** 14 Lincoln Rd, London N2 9DL, England.

ADDAE, Akili. *See* **OBIKA, Akili Addae.**

ADDERSON, Caroline. Canadian, b. 1963. **Genres:** Novels, Novellas/Short stories, Plays/Screenplays. **Career:** Instructor; writer. Received residencies at Banff School of Fine Arts, 1987 and 1991, Tyrone Guthrie Centre for Artists (Canada-Ireland Artist Exchange Program), 1989 and 1992, and Leighton Artist Colony, 1993. **Publications:** Bad Imaginings (short stories), 1993; Tokyo Cowboy (screenplay), 1993. NOVELS: A History of Forgetting, 1999; Sitting Practice, 2003. Contributor to anthologies and periodicals; work has been broadcast on the radio.

ADDINALL, Peter. British, b. 1932. **Genres:** Theology/Religion. **Career:** Teacher of religious studies and history at grammar schools in Great Britain, 1954-58; Methodist Missionary Society, teacher in southwestern Nigeria, 1959-68; teacher at comprehensive schools in Great Britain, 1968-83. Guest on television special Did God Design the Big Bang?, 1992. **Publications:** Philosophy and Biblical Interpretation: A Study in Nineteenth-Century Conflict, 1991. Contributor to periodicals. **Address:** Myrtle Grove, Carperby, Leyburn, Yorkshire DL8 4DA, England.

ADDINGTON, Arthur Charles. British, b. 1939. **Genres:** Genealogy/Heraldry. **Publications:** Royal House of Stuart: The Descendants of King James VI of Scotland, James I of England, vol. I, 1969, vol. II, 1971, vol. III, 1975; (ed.) The Lineage and Ancestry of H.R.H. Prince Charles, Prince of Wales, by Gerald Paget, 2 vols., 1977; (with Z. Burke) Origine et Famille de Felix Nicolaievitch Elston, Comte Soumarokov-Elston, 1983. **Address:** 6 Fairfield Close, Harpenden, Herts., England.

ADDINGTON, Larry Holbrook. American, b. 1932. **Genres:** History, Military/Defense/Arms control. **Career:** San Jose State College, CA, assistant professor of history, 1962-64; The Citadel, Military College of South Carolina, Charleston, assistant professor of history, 1964-66, associate professor, 1966-70, professor, 1970, chair, history department, 1989-94, professor emeritus, 1994-; consultant to the Institute of Advanced Studies, U.S. Army War College, Carlisle, PA, 1968-69. **Publications:** From Moltke to Hitler: The Evolution of German Military Doctrine, 1865-1939, 1967; The Blitzkrieg Era and the German General Staff, 1865-1941, 1971; The Patterns of War since the 18th Century, 1984, 2nd ed., 1994; The Patterns of War through the 18th Century, 1990; America's War in Vietnam, 2000. **Address:** 1341 New Castle St, Charleston, SC 29407, U.S.A. **Online address:** larrya103@aol.com

ADDISON, Linda D. American, b. 1952. **Genres:** Science fiction/Fantasy. **Career:** Writer, poet, and systems analyst. Bristol Myers Squibb, senior system analyst, 1991-99; AXA Financial Solutions, senior system analyst, 1999-. **Publications:** SCIENCE FICTION: Animated Objects, 1997; Consumed, Reduced to Beautiful Grey Ashes, 2001. Contributor to anthologies and periodicals.

ADDISON, Paul S. Scottish, b. 1966. **Genres:** Mathematics/Statistics. **Career:** Napier University, Edinburgh, Scotland, lecturer in fluid mechanics, 1992-. **Publications:** Fractals and Chaos, 1997. **Address:** School of the Built Environment, Napier University, Edinburgh, Scotland. **Online address:** p.addison@napier.ac.uk

ADDLETON, Jonathan S. American (born Pakistan), b. 1957. **Genres:** Area studies. **Career:** U.S. Agency for International Development, program officer in Islamabad, Pakistan, 1985-89, Sanaa, Yemen, 1989-91, Pretoria, South Africa, 1991-93, Almaty, Kazakstan, 1993-96, and Amman, Jordan, 1997-2001; Mission director in Ulaanbaatar, Mongolia, 2001-2004; Mission director in Phnom Penh, Cambodia, 2004-; Also worked for World Bank and Carnegie Endowment for International Peace, both Washington, DC. **Publications:** Undermining the Center: The Gulf Migration and Pakistan, 1992; Some Far and Distant Place (memoir), 1997. Contributor to periodicals. **Address:** c/o U.S. Dept of State-Cambodia, #16-18 St. 228, APO/FPO, Unit 8166 Box P, APO, AP 96546, U.S.A. **Online address:** jaddleton@usaid.gov

ADDONIZIO, Kim (Theresa). American, b. 1954. **Genres:** Novels, Poetry, Literary criticism and history. **Career:** Writer, 1986-. **Publications:** POETRY: (with L. Duesing and D. Laux) Three West Coast Women, 1987; The Philosopher's Club, 1994; Jimmy & Rita (verse novel), 1997; Tell Me, 2000; What Is This Thing Called Love, 2004. NOVELS: Crimes of Passion, 1984; In the Box Called Pleasure, 1999. OTHER: (with D. Laux) The Poet's Companion: A Guide to the Pleasures of Writing Poetry, 1997. Contributor to anthologies and periodicals.

ADELBERG, Doris. *See* **ORGEL, Doris.**

ADELL, Sandra. American, b. 1946. **Genres:** Adult non-fiction. **Career:** University of Wisconsin-Madison, associate professor of Afro-American studies, 1989-. **Publications:** Double-Consciousness/Double Bind, 1994. **Address:** Department of Afro-American Studies, University of Wisconsin-Madison, 455 North Park No. 4217, Madison, WI 53706, U.S.A.

ADELMAN, Clifford. American, b. 1942. **Genres:** Politics/Government, Social commentary, Education. **Career:** Sr. Associate, Office of Research, U.S. Dept. of Education, 1979-. Instructor and Lecturer, City College of New

York, 1968-71; Visiting Fellow, Yale University, New Haven, CT, 1972, 1973; Associate Dean for Academic Development and Research, and Associate Professor of Communications, William Paterson (State) College of New Jersey, Wayne, 1974-79. **Publications:** Generations: A Collage on Youthcult, 1972; No Loaves, No Parables: American Politics and the English Language, 1974; The Standardized Test Scores of College Graduates, 1985; Starting with Students, 1985; Performance and Judgment, 1988; A College Course Map, 1990, 2nd ed. as The New College Course Map, 1999; Light and Shadow on College Athletes, 1990; Women at Thirtysomething: Paradoxes of Attainment, 1991; The Way We Are: The Community College as American Thermometer, 1992; Tourists in Our Own Land: Cultural Literacies and the College Cirriculum, 1992; Lessons of a Generation: Education and Work in the Lives of the High School Class of 1972, 1994; Leading, Concurrent, or Lagging: The Knowledge Content of Computer Science in Higher Education and the Labor Market, 1997; Women and Men of the Engineering Path, 1998; Answers in the Tool Box, 1999; A Parallel Postsecondary Universe, 2000. EDITOR: Assessment in American Higher Education, 1986; Signs and Tracers: Indicators of College Student Learning, 1989. **Address:** 3819 Archer Pl, Kensington, MD 20895, U.S.A.

ADELMAN, Deborah. American, b. 1958. **Genres:** Novellas/Short stories, Literary criticism and history, Essays, Translations. **Career:** New York University, instructor of English, 1986-90; Loyola University of Chicago, IL, instructor of English, 1991-92; Oakton Community College, Des Plaines, IL, instructor of English, 1991-92; College of Du Page, Glen Ellen, IL, professor of English, 1992-. **Publications:** (author and co-trans.) The Children of Perestroika, 1992; The Children of Perestroika Come of Age, 1992. Short stories and essays. **Address:** Dept of English, College of Du Page, 425 Fawell Blvd, Glen Ellyn, IL 60137-6599, U.S.A. **Online address:** adelman@cdnet.cod.edu

ADELSON, Alan. American, b. 1943. **Genres:** History. **Career:** Journalist and author. Feature writer for the Wall Street Journal; executive director of the Jewish Heritage Project, NYC; writer. **Publications:** SDS, 1972; (ed. with R. Lapides) Lodz Ghetto: Inside a Community under Siege, 1989; (and codirector with K. Taverna, and producer) Lodz Ghetto (documentary film screenplay), 1989. **Address:** The Jewish Heritage Project, 150 Franklin St. No. 1W, New York, NY 10013, U.S.A.

ADELSON, Roger. American, b. 1942. **Genres:** History, Biography, Essays. **Career:** Arizona State University, Tempe, assistant professor, 1974-77, associate professor, 1977-96, professor of history, 1996-; The Historian, editor, 1990-95, consulting editor, 1996-2001. **Publications:** Mark Sykes: Portrait of an Amateur (biography), 1975; London and the Invention of the Middle East: Money, Power, and War, 1902-1922 (history), 1995; Speaking of History: Conversations with Historians, 1990-1995 (interviews), 1996. **Address:** Dept of History, Box 4302, Arizona State University, Tempe, AZ 85287-4302, U.S.A. **Online address:** adelsonr@asu.edu

ADEPOJU, Aderanti. Nigerian, b. 1945. **Genres:** Area studies, Demography, Economics, Social sciences. **Career:** University of Ife, Ile-Ife, Nigeria, lecturer to professor, 1969-84; University of Lagos, Nigeria, professor and dean, 1984-90; IDEP, Dakar, Senegal, training coordinator for United Nations Fund for Population Activities (UNFPA), 1988-98. **Publications:** The African Family in the Development Process, 1996. EDITOR: The Impact of Structural Adjustment on the Population of Africa, 1993; (with C. Oppong) Gender, Work, and Population in Sub-Saharan Africa, 1994. **Address:** 298 Leigh Hunt Dr, Southgate, London N14 6BZ, England. **Online address:** aadepoju@infoweb.abs.net

ADES, Dawn. British, b. 1943. **Genres:** Art/Art history, Photography. **Career:** University of Essex, Colchester, Dept. of Art, university lecturer, 1968-, and professor, 1989-. **Publications:** Dada and Surrealism, 1974; Photomontage, 1976, 1986; Dada and Surrealism Reviewed, 1978; Salvador Dali, 1982; Art in Latin America, 1989; Siron Franco, 1995; Surrealist Art, 1997; Marcel Duchamp, 1999; Dali's Optical Illusions, 2000. **Address:** Department of Art, University of Essex, Wivenhoe Park, Colchester, Essex, England.

ADEY, William Ross. American (born Australia), b. 1922. **Genres:** Medicine/Health. **Career:** Director, Research and Development, Loma Linda VA Medical Center, 1977-. Reader in Anatomy, University of Adelaide, 1951-53; Sr. Lecturer in Anatomy, University of Melbourne, 1955-56; Professor of Anatomy and Physiology, University of California, Los Angeles, 1957-77. **Publications:** Stereotaxic Atlas of the Brain of the Chimpanzee, 1966; Problems of Molecular Coding, 1968; A Stereotaxic Brain Atlas for Macaca Nemestrina, 1970; Nonlinear Electrodynamics in Biomolecular Systems, 1984; Magnetic Resonance-Imaging of the Brain, Head, and Neck, 1985. **Address:** Rte 1 Box 615, 31866 3rd Ave, Redlands, CA 92374-8237, U.S.A. **Online address:** RAdey43450@aol.com

ADICKES, Sandra. American, b. 1933. **Genres:** Literary criticism and history, Novels. **Career:** Winona State University, Winona, MN, professor of English, 1988-. Also worked at City University of New York and as a high school English teacher in NYC. WBAI-FM Radio, producer of the weekly series Urban Education, 1971-73. Member of Human Rights Commission of Winona; civil rights activist, 1963-64; anti-Vietnam war activist, 1965-72; feminist activist, 1967-. **Publications:** The Social Quest: The Expanded Vision of Four Women Travellers in the Era of the French Revolution, 1991; Legends of Good Women (novel), 1992; To Be Young Was Very Heaven: Women in New York before World War I, 1997. Contributor to professional journals and other magazines. **Address:** Department of English, Winona State University, Winona, MN 55987, U.S.A.

ADJIBOLOSOO, Senyo B.-S. K. Guyanese, b. 1953. **Genres:** Business/Trade/Industry, Economics. **Career:** Trinity Western University, Langley, British Columbia, professor of business and economics, 1988-. International Institute for Human Factor Development, founder and executive director, 1992-. A Night from Africa, master of ceremonies and chief storyteller, 1994 and 1996; African Leadership Development Institute, Pietermaritzburg, South Africa, teacher, 1997; University of Zimbabwe, workshop presenter, 1998; conducted field research in Dar es Salaam, Tanzania. Wattlekainum Cooperative, member of board of directors, 1991-93; Smile Africa International, member of board of directors, 1993-; African Enterprises, member of board of directors, 1995-98. **Publications:** The Human Factor in Developing Africa, 1995; Global Development the Human Factor Way, 1998; Rethinking Development Theory and Policy: A Human Factor Critique, 1999. EDITOR & CONTRIBUTOR: (with F. EzealaHarrison) Perspectives on Economic Development in Africa, 1994; The Significance of the Human Factor in African Economic Development, 1995; Human Factor Engineering and the Political Economy of African Development, 1996; International Perspectives on the Human Factor and Economic Development, 1998; (with B. Ofori-Amoah) Addressing Misconceptions about Africa's Development: Seeing beyond the Veil, 1998. Contributor to books. Contributor of articles and reviews to professional journals. **Address:** Faculty of Business and Economics, Trinity Western University, 7600 Glover Rd., Langley, BC, Canada V2Y 1Y1. **Online address:** adjibolo@twu.ca

ADKIN, Mark. British, b. 1936. **Genres:** International relations/Current affairs, Military/Defense/Arms control, Politics/Government. **Career:** British Army, infantry officer, 1954-67, served in Germany, Malaya, Mauritius, and Aden; Overseas Civil Service, district officer and administrative officer in the Solomon Islands and the Gilbert and Ellice Islands (now Kiribati), 1968-81; Barbados Defence Force, contract army officer, 1982-87, became major; Deputy Honorary Colonel (TA) for Bedfordshire, 1997-99; military historian and writer, 1987-. **Publications:** Urgent Fury, 1989; The Last Eleven?, 1991; Goose Green, 1992; (with M. Yousaf) The Bear Trap: Afghanistan's Untold Story, 1992; The Quiet Operator, 1993; (with G. Wright-North) Prisoner of the Tunipheads, 1994; The Charge: The Real Reason Why the Light Brigade Was Lost, 1996; The Sharpe Companion, 1998; The Waterloo Companion, 2001; The Sharpe Companion: The Early Years, 2003. Contributor to periodicals.

ADKINS, Lesley. British, b. 1955. **Genres:** Archaeology/Antiquities. **Career:** Archaeologist and writer. Milton Keynes (Eng.) Development Corp., archaeological asst., 1976; Surrey Archaeological Society, London, field officer, 1977-83; Museum of London, sr. archaeologist, 1983-87; Devon, Eng., archaeological consultant, 1987. **Publications:** Empires of the Plain, 2003. WITH R.A. ADKINS: A Thesaurus of British Archaeology, 1982; The Handbook of British Archaeology, 1983; Under the Sludge, Beddington Roman Villa, 1986; Archaeological Illustration, 1989; An Introduction to Archaeology, 1989; Talking Archaeology, 1990; Abandoned Places, 1990; Introduction to the Romans, 1991; A Field Guide to Somerset Archaeology, 1992; Handbook to Life in Ancient Rome, 1994; Dictionary of Roman Religion, 1996; Handbook to Life in Ancient Greece, 1997; The Keys of Egypt, 2000; The Little Book of Egyptian Hieroglyphs, 2001.

ADKINS, Roy A(rthur). British, b. 1951. **Genres:** Archaeology/Antiquities. **Career:** Archaeologist and writer. Milton Keynes (Eng.) Development Corp., assist. archaeologist, 1974-78; Surrey Archaeological Society, London, field officer, 1978-83; Museum of London, sr. archaeologist, 1983-87, consultant, 1987. **Publications:** Neolithic Stone and Flint Axes from the River Thames, 1978. WITH L. ADKINS: A Thesaurus of British Archaeology, 1982; Under the Sludge-Beddington Roman Villa, 1986; Archaeological Illustration, 1989;

An Introduction to Archaeology, 1989; Abandoned Places, 1990; Talking Archaeology: A Handbook for Lecturers and Organisers, 1990; Introduction to the Romans, 1991; A Field Guide to Somerset Archaeology, 1992; Handbook to Life in Ancient Rome, 1994; Dictionary of Roman Religion, 1996; Handbook to Life in Ancient Greece, 1997; The Keys of Egypt, 2000; The Little Book of Egyptian Hieroglyphs, 2001. Contributor to professional journals.

ADLARD, Mark. British, b. 1932. **Genres:** Novels, Science fiction/Fantasy. **Career:** Executive in the steel industry, 1956-76; teacher of economics, 1985-92. **Publications:** Interface, 1971; Volteface, 1972; Multiface, 1975; The Greenlander, 1978. **Address:** 43 Enterpen, Hutton Rudby, Yarm, Cleveland, England.

ADLER, C(arole) S(chwerdtfeger). American, b. 1932. **Genres:** Children's fiction, Young adult fiction. **Career:** Advertising Assistant, Worthington Corp., Harrison, NJ, 1952-54; English teacher, Niskayuna Middle Schools, New York, 1967-77. **Publications:** JUVENILE: The Magic of the Glits, 1979; The Silver Coach, 1979; In Our House, Scott Is My Brother, 1980; Shelter on Blue Barns Road, 1981; The Cat Was Left Behind, 1981; Down by the River, 1981; Footsteps on the Stairs, 1982; The Evidence that Wasn't There, 1982; The Once in a While Hero, 1982; Some Other Summer, 1982; Get Lost Little Brother, 1983; Roadside Valentine, 1983; The Shell Lady's Daughter, 1983; Shadows on Little Reef Bay, 1984; Fly Tree, 1984; With Westie and the Tin Man, 1985; Binding Ties, 1985; Good-bye, Pink Pig, 1985; Split Sisters, 1986; Kiss the Clown, 1986; Carly's Buck, 1987; Always and Forever Friends, 1988; If You Need Me, 1988; Eddie's Blue Winged Dragon, 1988; One Sister Too Many, 1989; The Lump in the Middle, 1989; Ghost Brother, 1990; Help, Pink Pig, 1990; A Tribe for Lexi, 1991; Mismatched Summer, 1991; Tuna Fish Thanksgiving, 1992; Daddy's Climbing Tree, 1993; Willie, The Frog Prince, 1994; That Horse Whiskey, 1994; Youn Hee & Me, 1995; What's to Be Scared of, Suki, 1996; More than a Horse, 1997; Her Blue Straw Hat, 1997; Not Just a Summer Crush, 1998; Winning, 1999; One Unhappy Horse, 2001; The No Place Cat, 2002. **Address:** 7041 N Cathedral Rock Pl, Tucson, AZ 85718-1303, U.S.A. **Online address:** csawrite@mindspring.com

ADLER, David A. American, b. 1947. **Genres:** Children's fiction, Children's non-fiction, Biography, Humor/Satire, Picture/board books. **Career:** Math teacher in New York, NY, 1968-77; author of books for young readers, 1972-; senior editor of books for young readers, 1979-90. **Publications:** FOR YOUNGER READERS. PICTURE BOOKS: A Little at a Time, 1976; The House on the Roof, 1976; The Children of Chelm, 1979; You Think It's Fun to Be a Clown!, 1980; My Dog and the Key Mystery, 1982; Bunny Rabbit Rebus, 1983; My Dog and the Knock Knock Mystery, 1985; My Dog and the Green Sock Mystery, 1986; My Dog and the Birthday Mystery, 1987; I Know I'm a Witch, 1988; Happy Hanukkah Rebus, 1989; Malke's Secret Recipe: A Hanukkah Story, 1989; Happy Thanksgiving Rebus, 1991; One Yellow Daffodil, 1995; Chanukkah in Chelm, 1997; The Babe and I, 1999; Andy and Tamika, 1999; School Trouble for Andy Russell, 1999; Parachuting Hamsters and Andy Russell, 2000; Andy Russell, NOT Wanted by the Police, 2001; It's a Baby, Andy Russell, 2005. YOUNG CAM JANSEN... SERIES: Young Cam Jansen's Chocolate Chip Mystery, 1996; ...Dinosaur Count, 1996; ...Loose Tooth Mystery, 1997; ...Ice Skate Mystery, 1998; ...and the Baseball Mystery, 1999; ...and the Pizza Shop Mystery, 2000; ...and the Library Mystery, 2001; ... and the Double Beach Mystery, 2002; ...and the Zoo Note Mystery, 2003; ...and the New Girl Mystery, 2004; ...and the Substitute Mystery, 2005. BIOGRAPHIES: Our Golda: The Story of Golda Meir, 1984; Martin Luther King Jr.: Free at Last, 1986; Thomas Jefferson: Father of Our Democracy, 1987; George Washington: Father of Our Country, 1988; Jackie Robinson: He Was the First, 1989; Thomas Alva Edison: Great Inventor, 1990; Christopher Columbus: Great Explorer, 1991; Benjamin Franklin: Inventor, Statesman, Printer, 1992; Lou Gehrig: The Luckiest Man, 1997; George Washington Carver, 1999; Sacagawea, 2000; America's Champion Swimmer: Gertrude Ederle, 2000. A PICTURE BOOK OF ... SERIES: Martin Luther King, Jr., 1989; Abraham Lincoln, 1989; George Washington, 1989; Benjamin Franklin, 1990; Thomas Jefferson, 1990; Helen Keller, 1990; Christopher Columbus, 1991; John F. Kennedy, 1991; Eleanor Roosevelt, 1991; Simon Bolivar, 1992; Florence Nightingale, 1992; Jesse Owens, 1992; Harriet Tubman, 1992; Frederick Douglass, 1993; Anne Frank, 1993; Rosa Parks, 1993; Sitting Bull, 1993; Robert E. Lee, 1994; Jackie Robinson, 1994; Sojourner Truth, 1994; Patrick Henry, 1995; Paul Revere, 1995; Davy Crockett, 1996; Thomas Edison, 1996; Louis Braille, 1997; Thurgood Marshall, 1997; Amelia Earhart, 1998; George Washington Carver, 1999; Sacagawea, 2000; Dwight David Eisenhower, 2002; Lewis and Clark, 2003; (with M.S. Adler) Sam Adams, 2005; (with M.S. Adler) John Hancock, 2005. NONFICTION: 3D, 2D, 1D, 1975; Roman Numerals, 1977;

Redwoods Are the Tallest Trees in the World, 1978; 3-2-1 Number Fun, 1981; Calculator Fun Book, 1982; Hyperspace! Facts and Fun from All over the Universe, 1982; Our Amazing Ocean, 1983; All about the Moon, 1983; World of Weather, 1983; Wonders of Energy, 1983; Amazing Magnets, 1983; All Kinds of Money, 1984; Prices Go Up, Prices Go Down: The Laws of Supply and Demand, 1984; Inflation: When Prices Go Up, Up, Up, 1985; Banks: Where the Money Is, 1985; A Picture Book of Jewish Holidays, 1981; A Picture Book of Passover, 1982; A Picture Book of Hanukkah, 1982; We Remember the Holocaust, 1987; The Number on My Grandfather's Arm, 1987; The Children's Book of Jewish Holidays, 1987; Breathe In, Breathe Out: All about Your Lungs, 1991; Hilde and Eli: Children of the Holocaust, 1994; Fractions Fun, 1996; Child of the Warsaw Ghetto, 1995; Kids' Catalog of Jewish Holidays, 1996; Easy Number Puzzles, 1997; Hiding from the Nazis, 1997; Shape Up: All about Triangles and Other Polygons, 1998; B. Franklin, Printer, 2001; Heroes of the Revolution, 2003; Kid's Catalog of Hanukkah, 2004; Enemies of Slavery, 2004; George Washington: An Illustrated Biography, 2004. FOR OLDER READERS. Eaton Stanley and the Mind Control Experiment, 1985; Benny, Benny, Baseball Nut, 1987; Rabbit Trouble and the Green Magician, 1987; The Many Troubles of Andy Russell, 1998; Andy and Tamika, 1999. CAM JANSEN... SERIES: Mystery of the Stolen Diamonds, 1980; Mystery of the U.F.O., 1980; Mystery of the Dinosaur Bones, 1981; Mystery of the Television Dog, 1981; Mystery of the Gold Coins, 1982; Mystery of the Babe Ruth Baseball, 1982; Mystery of the Circus Clown, 1983; Mystery of the Monster Movie, 1984; Mystery of the Carnival Prize, 1984; Mystery at the Monkey House, 1985; Stolen Corn Popper, 1986; Flight 54, 1988; Mystery at the Haunted House, 1992; Chocolate Fudge Mystery, 1993; Triceratops Pops Mystery, 1995; Ghostly Mystery, 1996; Scary Snake Mystery, 1997; The Catnapping Mystery, 1998; The Barking Treasure Mystery, 1999; Birthday Mystery, 2000; The School Play Mystery, 2001; The First Day of School Mystery, 2002; Tennis Trophy Mystery, 2003; Snowy Day Mystery, 2004. FOURTH FLOOR TWINS ADVENTURE... SERIES: Fish Snitch Mystery, 1985; Fortune Cookie Chase, 1985; Disappearing Parrot Trick, 1986; Silver Ghost Express, 1986; Skyscraper Parade, 1987; Sand Castle Contest, 1988. JEFFREY'S GHOST ADVENTURE... SERIES: Leftover Baseball Team, 1984; Fifth Grade Dragon, 1985; Ziffel Fair Mystery, 1987. T.F. BENSON MYSTERY ... SERIES: Funny Money Mystery, 1992; Dinosaur Madness Mystery, 1992; Eye Spy, 1992; Detective Dog Mystery, 1992. HOUDINI CLUB MYSTERIES: Onion Sundaes, 1994; Wacky Jacks, 1994; Lucky Stars, 1996; Magic Money, 1997. RIDDLE BOOKS: The Car Sick Zebra and Other Animal Riddles, 1983; The Twisted Witch and Other Spooky Riddles, 1985; The Purple Turkey and Other Thanksgiving Riddles, 1986; Remember Betsy Floss and Other Colonial American Riddles, 1987; The Dinosaur Princess and other Prehistoric Riddles, 1988; Wild Pill Hickok and Other Old West Riddles, 1988; A Teacher on Roller Skates and Other School Riddles, 1989; Calculator Riddles, 1995. OTHER: Hanukkah Fun Book, 1976; Passover Fun Book, 1978; Hanukkah Game Book, 1978; Bible Fun Book, 1979; Finger-spelling Fun Book, 1981; A Children's Treasury of Chassidic Tales, 1983; Jewish Holiday Fun, 1987; Cam Jansen Activity Books, 1992.

ADLER, Elizabeth. British. **Genres:** Novels, Romance/Historical. **Career:** Romance novelist. **Publications:** Leonie, 1985; Private Desires, 1985; Peach, 1986; The Rich Shall Inherit, 1989; The Property of a Lady, 1991; Fortune Is a Woman, 1992; Legacy of Secrets, 1993; The Secret of the Villa Mimosa, 1995; Now or Never, 1997; Sooner or Later, 1998; All or Nothing, 1999; In a Heartbeat, 2000; Last Time I Saw Paris, 2001. **Address:** c/o Anne Sibbald, Janklow & Nesbit Associates, 445 Park Ave Fl 13, New York, NY 10022, U.S.A.

ADLER, Jeffrey S(cott). American, b. 1957. **Genres:** History. **Career:** Wellesley College, Wellesley, MA, assistant professor, 1986-87; University of Florida, Gainesville, assistant professor, 1987-92, associate professor, 1992-. **Publications:** Yankee Merchants and the Making of the Urban West: The Rise and Fall of Antebellum St. Louis, 1991; (co-ed.) African-American Mayors, 2001. **Address:** Department of History, 211 Keene-Flint, University of Florida, PO Box 117320, Gainesville, FL 32611-7320, U.S.A. **Online address:** jadler@history.ufl.edu

ADLERMAN, Daniel. Also writes as Kin Eagle. American, b. 1963. **Genres:** Children's fiction. **Career:** Writer; children's publishing consultant. **Publications:** Africa Calling, 1996. WITH K. ADLERMAN AS KIN EAGLE: It's Raining, It's Pouring, 1994; Hey, Diddle Diddle, 1997; Rub a Dub Dub, 1999; Humpty Dumpty, 1999. **Address:** Kids at Our House, 47 Stoneham Pl., Metuchen, NJ 08840, U.S.A. **Online address:** BookKids@aol.com

ADLERMAN, Kimberly M. Also writes as Kin Eagle. American, b. 1964. **Genres:** Children's fiction. **Career:** Graphic designer, art director, and illustrator. Owner, Kids at Our House. **Publications:** AS KIN EAGLE (with D. Adlerman): It's Raining, It's Pouring, 1994; Hey, Diddle Diddle, 1997; Rub a Dub Dub, 1998; Humpty Dumpty, 1999. Illustrator of books by D. Adlerman. **Address:** Kids at Our House, 47 Stoneham Pl, Metuchen, NJ 08840, U.S.A. **Online address:** KimArts@aol.com

ADNAN, Etel. American (born Lebanon), b. 1925. **Genres:** Novels, Novellas/Short stories, Plays/Screenplays, Poetry. **Career:** Writer and artist. Worked for the Bureau de la Presse, Beirut, Lebanon, 1941-45; Al-Ahliya School for Girls, Beirut, teacher of French literature, 1947-49; Dominican College, San Rafael, CA, professor of philosophy, 1958-72; literary editor, al-SAFA and L'Orient-Le Jour (French-language newspapers), Beirut, 1972-75. Paintings exhibited in museums. **Publications:** POETRY: Moonshots, 1966; Five Senses for One Death, 1971; Jebu/L'Express Beyrouth-Enfer, 1973; (and illustrator) L' Apocalypse Arabe, 1980; From A to Z, 1982; Pablo Neruda Is a Banana Tree, 1982; The Indian Never Had a Horse, and Other Poems, 1985; (and illustrator and trans.) The Arab Apocalypse, 1989; The Spring Flowers Own & The Manifestations of the Voyage, 1990; Kitab Al Bahr (title means The Book of the Sea), 1994; There (prose poem), 1996; In/somnia, 2003. OTHER: Sitt Marie Rose (novel), 1978, trans. by G. Kleege, 1982; (and illustrator) Journey to Mt. Tamalpais (essay), 1986; Paris, When It's Naked (essay), 1993; Of Cities and Women (Letters to Fawwaz), 1993. Contributor of poetry, short fiction, and essays to anthologies. **Address:** 35 Marie St, Sausalito, CA 94965, U.S.A.

ADOFF, Arnold. American, b. 1935. **Genres:** Poetry, Novellas/Short stories. **Career:** Literary Agent, Yellow Springs, Ohio, 1977-. Teacher in the New York public schools, 1957-69. **Publications:** VERSE FOR CHILDREN: Mandala, 1971; Black Is Brown Is Tan, 1973; Make a Circle, Keep Us In: Poems for a Good Day, 1975; My Sister Tells Me That I'm Black, 1976; Tornado!, 1977; Under the Early Morning Trees, 1978; Where Wild Willy, 1978; Eats, 1979; I Am the Running Girl, 1979; Friend Dog, 1980; Today We Are Brother and Sister, 1981; OUTside INside Poems, 1981; Birds, 1982; All the Colors of the Race, 1982; The Cabbages Are Chasing the Rabbits, 1985; Sports Pages, 1986; Greens, 1988; Flamboyant, 1988; Chocolate Dreams, 1989; Hard to Be Six, 1991; In for Winter, Out for Spring, 1991; The Return of Rex and Ethel, 1993; Street Music: City Poems, 1995; Slow Dance Heart Break Blues, Vol. 1, 1995; Touch the Poem, 1996; Touch Stone, 1997. OTHER: Malcolm X, 1970; Love Letters, 1997; Basket Counts, 2000; Daring Dog & Captain Cat, 2001. EDITOR: I Am the Darker Brother: An Anthology of Modern Poems by Negro Americans, 1968; Black on Black: Commentaries by Negro Americans, 1968, rev. ed., 1997; City in All Directions: An Anthology of Modern Poems, 1969; Black Out Loud: An Anthology of Modern Poems by Black Americans, 1970; Brothers and Sisters: Modern Stories by Black Americans, 1970; It Is the Poem Singing into Your Eyes: An Anthology of New Young Poets, 1971; The Poetry of Black America: An Anthology of the 20th Century, 1973; My Black Me: A Beginning Book of Black Poetry, 1974; Celebrations: A New Anthology of Black American Poetry, 1977; Slow Dance Heartbreak Blues, 1995. **Address:** Box 293, Yellow Springs, OH 45387, U.S.A. **Online address:** ArnoldAdoff@aol.com

ADRIAN, Frances. See POLLAND, Madeleine A(ngela).

ADSHEAD, S(amuel) A(drian) M(iles). New Zealander. **Genres:** History. **Publications:** Debate on China, 1969; The Modernization of the Chinese Salt Administration, 19001920, 1970; The End of the Chinese Empire, 1973; Province and Politics in Late Imperial China: Viceregal Government in Szechwan, 1898-1911, 1984; China in World History, 1988; Salt and Civilization, 1992; Central Asia in World History, 1993; Material Culture in Europe and China, 1400-1800: The Rise of Consumerism, 1997. **Address:** History Department, University of Canterbury, Private Bag 4800, Christchurch 8020, New Zealand.

AERYNOG. See JAMES, David Geraint.

AFFRON, Charles. American, b. 1935. **Genres:** Film, Literary criticism and history. **Career:** Professor of French, New York University, NYC, since 1968 (Assistant Professor, 1965-68). Former Instructor and Assistant Professor of Romance Languages, Brandeis University, Waltham, Massachusetts. **Publications:** Patterns of Failure in La Comedie Humaine, 1966; A Stage for Poets: Studies in the Theatre of Hugo and Musset, 1971; Star Acting: Gish, Garbo, Davis, 1977; Cinema and Sentiment, 1982; Divine Garbo, 1985; Fellini's 8-1/2, 1987; Sets In Motion: Art Direction and Film Narrative, 1995; Lillian Gish: Her Legend, Her Life, 2001. **Address:** 171 W. 71st St., New York, NY 10023, U.S.A. **Online address:** ca1e@2.nyu.edu

AFKHAMI, Mahnaz. Iranian, b. 1941. **Genres:** Area studies, Women's studies and issues. **Career:** Abstracts of English Studies, Boulder, CO, assistant editor, 1965-66; University of Colorado, Colorado Springs, lecturer, 1966-67; National University of Iran, Teheran, assistant professor of English, 1967-68, department head, 1968-70; Women's Organization of Iran, secretary general, 1970-79; consultant on women and development, 1979-81; Foundation for Iranian Studies, executive director and publisher of Iran Nameh, 1981-. Oral History of Iran Archives, founder, 1982, director, 1982-. Government of Iran, member of High Council for Welfare, 1974-79, and High Council for Family Planning, 1975-79, minister of state for women's affairs and prime minister's deputy for South Teheran Urban Development and Welfare Project, both 1976-78; Sixth National Development Plan of Iran, chairperson of Quality of Life Planning Committee, 1977;. **Publications:** (with C. Albright) Iran: A Pre-Collegiate Handbook, 1992; Women in Exile, 1994; (ed. with E. Friedl) In the Eye of the Storm: Women in Post-Revolutionary Iran, 1994; (ed. and author of intro) Women and the Law in Iran, 1967-1978 (in Persian), 1994; (ed with G. Emami) Readings in Feminist Theory: An Anthology (in Persian), 1995. Work represented in anthologies. Contributor to periodicals. **Address:** 4343 Montgomery Ave., Bethesda, MD 20814, U.S.A.

AFZAL, Omar. American (born India), b. 1939. **Genres:** Cultural/Ethnic topics. **Career:** Gauhati University, Dibrugarh, India, teacher of English literature, 1965-68; American Institute of Indian Studies, teacher of Urdu and Hindi, 1970-72; Delhi University, Delhi, India, teacher of English language and literature, 1972-73; Cornell University, Ithaca, NY, Southeast Asia assistant, 1973-, chairperson of Center for Research and Communication, and adviser to MECA. Committee for Crescent Observation International, committee chairperson; Forum, national coordinator, 1981-96. **Publications:** The Life of Muhammad (biography), 1971; Aap ki uljhane, 1972; Issues in the Lunar Calendar, 1988; Calculating Prayer Times, 1993; (ed., with N.H. Barazangi and M.R. Zaman) Islamic Identity and the Struggle for Justice, 1996. Author of poetry under pseudonym Athar. Contributor of stories to magazines. **Address:** 1069 Ellis Hollow Rd, Ithaca, NY 14850, U.S.A. **Online address:** omarafzal1@yahoo.com

AGARD, John. British, b. 1949. **Genres:** Children's fiction, Poetry, Novellas/Short stories. **Career:** Writer. Commonwealth Institute, London, England, touring lecturer; South Bank Centre, London, writer-in-residence, 1993; British Broadcasting Corp., writer-in-residence for Windrush project. Also worked as an actor and a performer with a jazz group. **Publications:** JUVENILE AND YOUNG ADULT POETRY: I Din Do Nuttin and Other Poems, 1983; Say It Again, Granny! Twenty Poems from Caribbean Proverbs, 1986; The Calypso Alphabet, 1989; Go Noah, Go!, 1990; Laughter Is an Egg, 1990; (with G. Nichols) No Hickory, No Dickory, No Dock: A Collection of Caribbean Nursery Rhymes, 1991, in US as No Hickory, No Dickory, No Dock: Caribbean Nursery Rhymes, 1994; Grandfather's Old Bruk-a-down Car, 1994; (with others) Another Day on Your Foot and I Would Have Died, 1996; We Animals Would Like a Word with You, 1996; Get Back, Pimple!, 1996; From the Devil's Pulpit, 1997; Hello New! New Poems for a New Century, 2000; Points of View with Professor Peekaboo, 2000; Come Back to Me, My Boomerang, 2001; Einstein, the Girl Who Hated Maths, 2002; (with others) Number Parade, 2002; Hello H2O, 2003. CHILDREN'S FICTION: Letters for Lettie and Other Stories, 1979; Dig away Two-Hole Tim, 1981; Lend Me Your Wings, 1987; The Emperor's Dan-Dan, 1992; Oriki and the Monster Who Hated Balloons, 1994; The Monster Who Loved Telephones, 1994; The Monster Who Loved Cameras, 1994; The Monster Who Loved Toothbrushes, 1994; (with K. Paul) Brer Rabbit, the Great Tug-o-War, 1998. POETRY FOR ADULTS: Shoot Me with Flowers (poetry), 1974; Man to Pan: A Cycle of Poems to Be Performed with Drums and Steelpans, 1982; Limbo Dancer in the Dark, 1983; Limbo Dancer in Dark Glasses, 1983; Livingroom, 1983; Mangoes and Bullets: Selected and New Poems, 1972-84, 1985; Lovelines for a Goat-born Lady, 1990; A Stone's Throw from Embankment: The South Bank Collection, 1993; Weblines, 2000. OTHER: (with others) Wake Up, Stir About: Songs for Assembly (traditional tunes), 1989; The Great Snakeskin (children's play), 1993. EDITOR: Life Doesn't Frighten Me at All, 1989; (with G. Nichols, and contrib) A Caribbean Dozen: Poems from Caribbean Poets, 1994, in US as A Caribbean Dozen: A Collection of Poems, 1995; Poems in My Earphone, 1995; Why Is the Sky?, 1996; (with G. Nichols) Under the Moon and over the Sea: A Collection of Caribbean Poems, 2002. Work represented in anthologies. Contributor of poetry to periodicals. **Address:** c/o Jubilee Books, Eltham Green School Complex, Middle Park Avenue, London SE9 5EQ, England.

AGEE, Chris. American, b. 1956. **Genres:** Poetry. **Career:** Poet. Belfast Institute of Further and Higher Education, Belfast, Ireland, lecturer in literacy, 1979; Queen's University, School of Education, Ireland, lecturer, 1985-1990;

Open University in Northern Ireland, tutor; University of East London, Belfast branch, adult education advisor. **Publications:** POETRY: In the New Hampshire Woods, 1992; Scar on the Stone, 1998; The Sierra de Zacatecas, 1998. **Address:** c/o The Daedalus Press, 24 The Heath, Cypress Downs, Dublin 6W, Ireland.

AGEE, Jonis. American, b. 1943. **Genres:** Novels, Novellas/Short stories, Poetry, Autobiography/Memoirs, Essays. **Career:** College of St. Catherine, St. Paul, MN, teacher in English, 1975-2000; University of Michigan, Ann Arbor, teacher in creative writing and English, 1995-98; University of Nebraska, Lincoln, teacher in creative writing and English, 2000-; writer and editor. Has given readings and been awarded residencies at universities, colleges, arts centers, and bookstores; served as judge and panelist for prizes and arts councils. **Publications:** POETRY: Houses, 1976; Mercury, 1981; Two Poems, 1982. STORIES: Bend This Heart, 1989; Pretend We've Never Met, 1989; A .38 Special and a Broken Heart, 1995; Taking the Wall (stories), 1999; Acts of Love on Indigo Road, 2003. NOVELS: Sweet Eyes, 1991; Strange Angels, 1993; South of Resurrection, 1997; The Weight of Dreams, 1999. EDITOR: Border Crossings, 1984; Stiller's Pond, 1988, rev. ed., 1991. Work represented in anthologies. Contributor of fiction and poetry to periodicals. **Address:** Department of English, 215 Andrews Hall, University of Nebraska-Lincoln, Lincoln, NE 68588-0333, U.S.A. **Online address:** jagee@peoplepc.com

AGELL, Charlotte. Swedish, b. 1959. **Genres:** Children's fiction. **Career:** Author and illustrator. Conducts workshops for youths and adults; Has worked previously as a teacher and education consultant;. **Publications:** SELF-ILLUSTRATED: The Sailor's Book, 1991; Mud Makes Me Dance in the Spring, 1994; I Wear Long Green Hair in the Summer, 1994; Wind Spins Me Around in the Fall, 1994; I Slide into the White of Winter, 1994; Dancing Feet, 1994; I Swam with a Seal, 1995; To the Island, 1998; Up the Mountain, 2000. **Address:** c/o Edite Kroll Literary Agency, 12 Grayhurst Park, Portland, ME 04101, U.S.A.

AGICH, George J. American, b. 1947. **Genres:** Ethics, Medicine/Health, Philosophy. **Career:** University of Texas Medical Branch at Galveston, research fellow, 1975-76; Southern Illinois University, Springfield, assistant professor, 1976-81, associate professor, 1981-88, professor of medical humanities and psychiatry, 1988-97, director of Ethics and Philosophy of Medicine Program, 1976-86, and Medical Ethics Program, 1990-97; Cleveland Clinic Foundation, F.J. O'Neill Chair in Clinical Bioethics, 1997-; chairman, department of bioethics, 1997-2004, Transplantation Center, staff, 1998-. Memorial Medical Center, member of allied health professional staff and director of Ethics Consultation Service, 1991-. Sangamon State University, adjunct professor of philosophy, 1978-; Cambridge University, visiting scholar in history and philosophy of science, 1982-83; Wayne State University, Paul E. Ruble Memorial Lecturer, 1987; University of Basel, Switzerland, Freiwillige Akademische Gesellschaft Visiting Professor, 200304; Anne Frank Foundation Lectureship, 2004; lecturer at colleges and universities in the United States and abroad. **Publications:** Autonomy and Long-Term Care, 1993. EDITOR & CONTRIBUTOR: Responsibility in Health Care, 1982; (with C.E. Begley) The Price of Health, 1986. Work represented in books. Contributor of articles and reviews to scholarly journals. **Address:** Dept of Bioethics, Cleveland Clinic Foundation, 9500 Euclid Ave, Cleveland, OH 44195, U.S.A. **Online address:** agichg@ccf.org

AGNEW, Eleanor. American, b. 1948. **Genres:** Adult non-fiction. **Career:** Worked as feature writer, columnist, and reporter for the newspapers Berkshire Sampler and Worcester Telegram and Gazette, Worcester, MA, between 1970 and 1975; Francis Marion University, Florence, SC, instructor, 1986-89; Georgia Southern University, Statesboro, associate professor of writing, 1989-. **Publications:** (with S. Robideaux) My Mama's Waltz, 1998. Contributor to books and periodicals. **Address:** PO Box 8026, Georgia Southern University, Statesboro, GA 30460, U.S.A. **Online address:** eagnew@gsvms2.cc.gasou.edu

AGONITO, Rosemary. American, b. 1937. **Genres:** Novels, Business/Trade/Industry, Self help, Women's studies and issues. **Career:** Gender equity consultant and owner of New Futures Enterprises, 1983-. Taught at Maria Regina College, Syracuse, 1966-68, Syracuse University, 1968-73, Colgate University, Hamilton, New York, 1973-75, and Eisenhower College, 1976-83. **Publications:** History of Ideas on Woman: A Source Book, 1977; Promoting Self Esteem in Young Women: A Teacher's Manual, 1988; No More Nice Girl: Power, Sexuality, and Success in the Workplace, 1993; Your Dream Made Easy: How to Start a Successful Business, 1999; Dirty Little Secrets: Sex in the Workplace, 2000; A Good Day to Die (novel), 2005. **Address:** 4502 Broad Rd, Syracuse, NY 13215, U.S.A. **Online address:** nfutures@aol.com

AGRAN, Edward G. American, b. 1949. **Genres:** History. **Career:** Centre College, Danville, KY, assistant professor of American history, 1985-91; Wilmington College, Wilmington, OH, associate professor of American history, 1993-. **Publications:** Too Good a Town: William Allen White, Community, and the Emerging Rhetoric of Middle America, 1998. Contributor to academic journals. **Address:** Department of History, Wilmington College, Wilmington, OH 45177, U.S.A. **Online address:** eagran@wilmington.edu

AGUILAR, Rosario. Nicaraguan, b. 1938. **Genres:** Novels, Novellas/Short stories. **Publications:** NOVELS: Primavera Sonambula (title means: Sleepwalking Spring), 1964; Quince Barrotes de Izquierda a Derecha, 1965; Rosa Sarmiento (biographical novel), 1968; Aquel Mar sin Fondo ni Playa (title means: That Sea without Bottom or Beach), 1970; Las Doce y Veintinueve (title means: TwelveTwenty-Nine), 1975; Primavera Sonambula, 1976; 7 Relatos Sobre el Amor y la Guerra, 1986; La Nina Blanca y los Pajaros sin Pies (historical novel), 1992, as The Lost Chronicles of Terra Firma, 1997. SHORT STORIES: Siete Relatos sobre el Amor y la Guerra (title means: Seven Tales about Love and War), 1986. BIOGRAPHY: Soledad: tu eres el enlace (title means: Soledad: You Are the Link), 1995. **Address:** PO Box 162, Leon, Nicaragua. **Online address:** agfia@ibw.com.ni

AGUILAR MELANTZON, Ricardo. American, b. 1947. **Genres:** Poetry. **Career:** University of Texas at El Paso, instructor in Spanish, 1974-75; University of Washington, Seattle, lecturer in Chicano studies, 1975-77; University of Texas at El Paso, director of Chicano studies and assistant to the vice-president for academic affairs, 1977-80, assistant professor, 1977-83, associate professor, 1983-90, professor of Spanish and creative writing, 1990; New Mexico State University, Las Cruces, regents professor of Spanish, 1990-. **Publications:** AS RICARDO AGUILAR, EXCEPT AS NOTED; Caravana enlutada (poetry), 1975; En Son de lluvia (poetry), 1980; (ed. with A. Armengol and O.U. Somoza) Palabra nueva: Cuentos chicanos, 1984; Efrain Huerta, 1984; (ed. with Armengol and S.D. Elizondo) Palabra nueva: Poesia chicana, 1985; (ed. with Armengol and Elizondo) Palabra nueva: Cuentos chicanos II, 1987; (as Ricardo Aguilar Melantzon) Madreselvas en flor (autobiographical narrative), 1987; Glosario del calo de Ciudad Juarez, 1989; Aurelia, 1990; Jose Fuentes Mares, 1990. TRANSLATOR: (with B. Pollack) R. Arias, The Road to Tamazunchale; (with B. Pollack) D. Chavez, Loving Pedro Infante. Contributor to periodicals. **Address:** Dept of Languages and Linguistics, New Mexico State University, PO Box 300001 MSC 3L, Las Cruces, NM 88003-8001, U.S.A.

AGUOLU, Christian Chukwunedu. Nigerian, b. 1940. **Genres:** Information science/Computers, Librarianship, Bibliography. **Career:** French and Latin teacher, high sch., Oraukwu, Nigeria, 1965-66; Reference Librarian and Bibliographer, University of California, Santa Barbara, 1968-72; University of Maiduguri, Nigeria, Sr. Lecturer, 1977-79, Dean of Education, 1979-82, 1984-86, Associate Professor/Reader, 1979-82, Professor of Library Science, 1982-; University of Maiduguri Press, chairman, 1996-. **Publications:** Ghana in the Humanities and Social Sciences, 1900-1971: A Bibliography, 1973; Nigerian Civil War, 1967-70: An Annotated Bibliography, 1973; Nigeria: A Comprehensive Bibliography in the Humanities and Social Sciences, 1900-1971, 1973; Library Development in Borno State, 1984; Selecting Materials for School Libraries in a Developing Society, 1982; Libraries, Knowledge and National Development, 1989; What's Wrong with Your English?, 1994, 2nd ed., 1999; Libraries and Information Management in Nigeria, 2002. **Address:** Dept. of Library Science, University of Maiduguri, Maiduguri, Borno, Nigeria. **Online address:** Aguoluci@unimaid.edu.ng

AGYEMAN, Opoku. Ghanaian, b. 1942. **Genres:** Politics/Government, Third World. **Career:** Montclair State University, Upper Montclair, NJ, professor of political science, 1982-. **Publications:** The Pan-Africanist Worldview, 1985; Requisite Values for Political and Economic Development in Africa, 1990; Pan-Africanist Federalism, 1991; Nkrumah's Ghana and East Africa, 1992; Panafricanism and Its Detractors: A Response to Harvard's Race-Effacing Univeralists, 1998; Africa's Persistent Vulnerable Link to Global Politics, 2001; The Failure of Grassroots Pan-Africanism: The Case of the All-African Trade Union Federation, 2003. **Address:** Department of Political Science, Montclair State University, Upper Montclair, NJ 07043, U.S.A. **Online address:** OpokuAgyeman@cs.com

AHARONI, Reuben. Israeli (born Palestine), b. 1943. **Genres:** Politics/Government, Area studies, History. **Career:** Ministry of Defense, Tel-Aviv, Israel, staff member, 1968-90; Institute for Israeli Arab Studies, Beit Berl, Israel, field research coordinator, 1992-94; Haifa University, Haifa, Israel, teaching fellow, 1993-. **Publications:** (with S. Mishal) Speaking Stones, 1989; (with Y. Reiter) The Political Life of Arabs in Israel, 1992, 2nd ed., 1993; Leaning Masts, 1997; Twofold Pass, 1998. **Address:** Eretz Israel Studies, Haifa University, Haifa, Israel.

AHEARN, (Edward) Allen. American, b. 1937. **Genres:** Librarianship, Bibliography. **Career:** US Department of the Navy, Washington, DC, contracting officer, 1960-73; Office of the US Secretary of Defense, Arlington, VA, advisor on major systems acquisitions, 1973-80; Quill and Brush (antiquarian book store), partner, 1976-; defense procurement consultant in Rockville, MD, 1980-84. **Publications:** The Book of First Books, 1975, 4th ed., 1986; (with P. Ahearn) Book Collecting: A Comprehensive Guide, 1989, new ed., 2000; (with P. Ahearn) Collected Books: The Guide to Value, 1991, rev. ed., 2002. Co-author of privately printed price guides to the works of individual authors. **Address:** Quill and Brush, 1137 Sugarloaf Mtn Rd, Dickerson, MD 20842, U.S.A. **Online address:** Allen@QBbooks.com

AHEARN, Patricia. American, b. 1937. **Genres:** Librarianship, Bibliography. **Career:** Quill and Brush (antiquarian book store and art gallery), Bethesda, MD, partner, 1976-86; Quill and Brush (book store), Rockville, MD, partner, 1986-. **Publications:** (with A. Ahearn) Book Collecting: A Comprehensive Guide, 1989, rev. ed., 2000; (with A. Ahearn) Collected Books: The Guide to Value, 1991, rev. ed., 2002. Co-author of privately printed bibliographic price guides to the works of individual authors. **Address:** Quill and Brush, 1137 Sugarloaf Mtn Rd, Dickerson, MD 20842, U.S.A. **Online address:** firsts@qbbooks.com

AHLGREN, Gillian T. W. American, b. 1964. **Genres:** Theology/Religion, History. **Career:** Xavier University, Cincinnati, OH, associate professor of theology, 1990-. **Publications:** Teresa of Avila and the Politics of Sanctity, 1996. Contributor of articles and reviews to periodicals and books. **Address:** Department of Theology, Xavier University, 3800 Victory Parkway, Cincinnati, OH 45207, U.S.A.

AHMED, Akbar S(alahudin). Pakistani, b. 1943. **Genres:** International relations/Current affairs, Sociology, Theology/Religion. **Career:** Civil Service of Pakistan, assistant commissioner in Frontier Province and Punjab, 1966-71, deputy secretary, 1971-76, political agent, 1976-80, additional secretary, 1977. National Centre for Rural Development, Islamabad, Pakistan, director-general. Centre of Social Sciences, director; visiting professor at colleges and universities; consultant, 1980. **Publications:** Mansehra: A Journey, 1973; A Strategy for Cooperation: A Study of the North-West Frontier Province, 1973; (trans.) Mataloona: Pukhto Proverbs, 1973, rev. ed., 1975; Millennium and Charisma among Pathans, 1976; Social and Economic Change in the Tribal Areas, 1972-1976, 1977; Pieces of Green: The Sociology of Change in Pakistan, 1964-1974, 1977; A Bibliography of the North-West Frontier Province, 1979; More Lines (poems), 1980; Pukhtun Economy and Society, 1980; Religion and Politics in Muslim Society, 1983, as Resistance and Control in Pakistan, 1991; Pakistan Society, 1986; Toward Islamic Anthropology, 1986; Discovering Islam, 1988; Postmodernism and Islam, 1992; Living Islam, 1993; Jinnah, Pakistan and Islamic Identity, 1997; Islam Today, 1999; Islam under Siege, 2003. EDITOR: (with D.M. Hart) Islam in Tribal Societies: From the Atlas to the Indus, 1984; Pakistan: The Social Sciences' Perspective, 1990; (with H. Donnan) Islam, Globalization and Postmodernity, 1994; (with C. Shore) The Future of Anthropology, 1995. Contributor to journals. **Address:** School of International Service, American University, 4400 Massachusetts Ave NW, Washington, DC 20016-8071, U.S.A. **Online address:** akbar@american.edu

AIDELLS, Bruce. American, b. 1944. **Genres:** Food and Wine. **Career:** Imperial Cancer Research Fund, London, England, research fellow, 1974-77; National Institute of Health, Bethesda, MD, research fellow, 1977-78; Poulet Deli, Berkeley, CA, founder and chef, 1979-83; Aidells Sausage Co., CA, owner and chef, 1983-. KCBS-Radio, host of radio program, restaurant consultant, and new business adviser. **Publications:** Great Meals in Minutes: Salads, 1985; (with Goodman, Harlow, Wise, and others) Regional American Classics, 1987; (with R. Clark) Barbecuing, Grilling, and Smoking, 1988; (with D. Kelly) Hot Links and Country Flavors, 1990; (with D. Kelly) Real Beer and Good Eats, 1992; (with D. Kelly) Flying Sausages, 1995; (with D. Kelly) The Complete Meat Cookbook, 1998; (with D. Kelly) Bruce Aidells' Complete Sausage Book, 2000. Contributor to periodicals and books. **Address:** 618 Coventry Rd, Kensington, CA 94707, U.S.A. **Online address:** bruce@aidells.com

AIKEN, Lewis R(oscoe), Jr. American, b. 1931. **Genres:** Education, Psychology. **Career:** Professor of Psychology, Pepperdine University, Malibu, California, 1979-93. School Psychologist, North Carolina Dept. of Public Instruction; Psychodiagnostician, North Carolina Dept of Human Resources; Research Psychologist Consultant, Veterans Administration Former Dana Professor, and Chairman, Psychology Dept., Guilford College, North Carolina, 1966-74, and Former Associate Professor of Psychology, and Director of Testing, University of North Carolina, Greensboro 1960-65.

Professor, Sacred Heart College, Belmont, North Carolina, 1974-76, and University Pacific, Stockton, California, 1977-79. **Publications:** General Psychology: A Survey, 1969; Psychological and Educational Testing, 1971; (ed.) Readings in Psychological and Educational Testing, 1973; Psychological Testing and Assessment, 1975, 10th ed. 2000; Later Life, 1978, 3rd ed., 1989; Dying, Death and Bereavement, 1985, 4th ed., 2000; Assessment of Intellectual Functioning, 1986, 2nd ed., 1996; Assessment of Personality, 1989, 3rd ed., 1999; Personality: Theories, Research, and Application, 1993; Aging: An Introduction to Gerontology, 1994; Rating Scales and Checklists, 1996; Assessment of Adult Personality, 1997; Questionnaires and Inventories, 1997; Human Differences, 1999. **Address:** 248 Marjori Ave, Thousand Oaks, CA 91320, U.S.A. **Online address:** laiken@prodigy.net

AINSWORTH, Patricia. (Patricia Nina Bigg). Australian, b. 1932. **Genres:** Romance/Historical. **Career:** Secretary, 1948-55; Full-time writer since 1967. **Publications:** The Flickering Candle, 1968; The Candle Rekindled, 1969; Steady Burns the Candle, 1970; The Devil's Hole, 1970; Portrait in Gold, 1971; A String of Silver Beads, 1972; The Bridal Lamp, 1975; The Enchanted Cup, 1980. **Address:** 3/2 Lorraine Ave, Mitcham, SA 5062, Australia.

AIRD, Catherine. Also writes as Kinn Hamilton McIntosh. British, b. 1930. **Genres:** Mystery/Crime/Suspense, Local history/Rural topics. **Career:** Chairman, Finance Committee, Girl Guides Association, London, 1975-80, 1983-87, and Crime Writers' Association, 1990-91. **Publications:** The Religious Body, 1966; A Most Contagious Game, 1967; Henrietta Who?, 1968; The Complete Steel, 1969 (in U.S. as The Stately Home Murder, 1970); A Late Phoenix, 1971; His Burial Too, 1973; Slight Mourning, 1976; Parting Breath, 1978; Some Die Eloquent, 1979; Passing Strange, 1980; Last Respects, 1982; Harm's Way, 1984; A Dead Liberty, 1986; The Body Politic, 1990; A Going Concern, 1993; Injury Time, 1994; After Effects, 1996; Stiff News, 1998; Little Knell, 2000; Amendment of Life, 2002; Chapter and Hearse, 2003. EDITOR AS KINN HAMILTON McINTOSH: Fordwich: The Lost Port, 1975; Chislet and Westberc: Villages of the Stour Lathe, 1979; Hoath and Herne: The Last of the Forest, 1984; In Good Faith, 1995. **Address:** Invergordon, 1 Sturry Hill, Sturry, Canterbury, Kent CT2 0NG, England. **Online address:** www.catherineaird.com

AIRLIE, Catherine. *See* MACLEOD, Jean S.

AITCHISON, Ian J(ohnston) R(hind). British, b. 1936. **Genres:** Physics. **Career:** Fellow, Worcester College, and Lecturer in Theoretical Physics, Oxford University, 1966-96; Professor of Physics, Oxford University, 1996-. Research Associate, Brookhaven Natl. Laboratory, NYC, 1961-63; Collaborateur Temporaire Etranger, CEN Saclay, France, 1963-64; Research Associate, Cavendish Laboratory, Cambridge, 1964-66. **Publications:** Relativistic Quantum Mechanics, 1972; (co-ed.) Rudolf Peierls and Theoretical Physics, 1977; (with A.J.G. Hey) Gauge Theories in Particle Physics, 1982, 3rd ed. (vol. 1), 2002; An Informal Introduction to Gauge Field Theories, 1982; (co-ed.) Plots, Quarks and Strange Particles, 1991. **Address:** Department of Physics, Oxford University, Theoretical Physics, 1 Keble Rd, Oxford OX1 3NP, England.

AITCHISON, James. Scottish, b. 1938. **Genres:** Poetry, Literary criticism and history, Writing/Journalism. **Career:** Free-lance writer, 1968-. Worked as publicity copywriter, journalist, information officer, and lecturer. Scottish Arts Council, member of book awards panel, 1979-83. **Publications:** POETRY: Sounds before Sleep, 1971; Spheres, 1975; Second Nature, 1990; Brain Scans, 1998; Bird-Score, 2002. OTHER: (ed. with A. Scott) New Writing Scotland, Vol 1, 1983, Vol 2, 1984, Vol 3, 1985; The Golden Harvester: The Vision of Edwin Muir, 1988; The Cassell Guide to Written English, 1994; Dictionary of English Grammar, 1996. Work represented in anthologies. **Address:** Rosehill Rise, Hillcourt Rd, Cheltenham GL52 3JL, England.

AITKEN, Robert (Baker). American, b. 1917. **Genres:** Poetry, Essays, Translations. **Career:** Executive secretary of community associations in Honolulu, HI, and Wahiawa, HI, 1948-53; bookseller in South Pasadena, CA, 1953-55; English teacher and assistant director of a school in Ojai, CA, 1955-58; bookseller in Honolulu, 1958-61; East-West Center, Honolulu, counselor and director of student activities, 1961-65; University of Hawaii at Manoa, Honolulu, assistant director of Hawaii Upward Bound, 1966-68; Kapiolani Community College, Honolulu, English teacher and editor, 1968-69; Diamond Sangha, Honolulu, cofounder, 1959, junior teacher, 1969-74, apprentice teacher, 1974-85, master, 1985-, retired, 1996. Associated with peace, social justice, and environmental organizations. **Publications:** Zen Training: A Personal Account, 1960; A Zen Wave: Basho's Haiku and Zen,

1978; Taking the Path of Zen, 1982; The Mind of Clover: Essays in Zen Buddhist Ethics, 1984; The Dragon Who Never Sleeps: Zen Buddhist Practice, 1990; The Gateless Barrier, the Wumen kuan (Mumonkan): Translated with a Commentary, 1992; Encouraging Words: Zen Buddhist Teachings for Western Students, 1993; (with D. Steindl-Rast) The Ground We Share: Everyday Practice, Buddhist and Christian, 1994; The Practice of Perfection: The Paramitas from a Zen Buddhist Perspective, 1994; Original Dwelling Place: Zen Buddhist Essays, 1996; Zen Master Raven: Sayings and Doings of a Wise Bird, 2002; The Morning Star: New and Selected Zen Writings, 2003.

AITKEN, Rosemary. (born England), b. 1942. **Genres:** Romance/Historical. **Career:** Secondary teacher, Taumarunui, New Zealand, 1964-67; teacher-trainer and lecturer in higher education, Cheltenham, England, 1967-72, senior lecturer, 1972-87, tutor in charge of ESOL program, 1978-87; Trinity College, London, England, examiner and moderator, 1990-. Also consultant in English as a foreign language for schools in the United Kingdom, Dubai, and Singapore. Tutor in charge for the Quillen Postal Writing Course, 1990-2000. **Publications:** NOVELS. CORNISH SAGA SERIES: The Girl from Penvarris, 1995; The Tinner's Daughter, 1996; Cornish Harvest, 1999; Stormy Waters, 2001; The Silent Shore, 2001; The Granite Cliffs, 2003; Against the Tide, 2004. MYSTERY NOVELS. LIBERTUS SERIES; AS ROSEMARY ROWE: The Germanicus Mosaic, 1999; Pattern of Blood, 2000; Murder in the Forum, 2001; The Chariots of Calyx, 2002; The Legatus Mystery, 2003. OTHER: Make Up Your Mind (teaching materials), 1979. Teaching Tenses (teaching materials), 1992; Writing a Novel: A Practical Guide, Crowood 2004; Contributor of numerous short stories and publications and author of plays. **Address:** Dorian Literary Agency, Church Road, St. Mary Church, Torquay, Devon TQU 5UD, England.

AIZLEY, Harlyn. (born United States). **Genres:** Sex. **Career:** Author. **Publications:** Buying Dad: One Woman's Search for the Perfect Sperm Donor, 2003; Contributor of fiction and poetry to numerous magazines and journals. Contributor of nonfiction articles and anthologies. **Address:** c/o Author Mail, 6922 Hollywood Blvd., Ste. 1000, Los Angeles, CA 90028, U.S.A. **Online address:** buyingAlyson Booksdad@aol.com

AJAMI, Fouad. American (born Lebanon). **Genres:** Cultural/Ethnic topics, Politics/Government. **Career:** Lehrhman Institute, NYC, former research fellow; Department of Politics and Center of International Studies, Princeton University, Princeton, NJ, faculty member, until c. 1980; Paul Nitze School of Advanced International Studies, Johns Hopkins University, Washington, DC, associate professor and director of Middle East studies, became Majid Khadduri Professor of Islamic Studies and director of Middle East Studies, 1980-. Contributing editor, U. S. News and World Report; consultant, CBS News. **Publications:** The Vanished Imam: Musa al Sadr and the Shia of Lebanon, 1986; Beirut: City of Regrets, 1988; The Arab Predicament: Arab Political Thought and Practice since 1967, 1981, rev ed., 1992; The Dream Palace of the Arabs: A Generation's Odyssey, 1998. **Address:** Johns Hopkins University, Nitze Bldg Rm 200, 1740 Massachusetts Ave NW, Washington, DC 20036, U.S.A.

AKARLI, Engin Deniz. American, b. 1945. **Genres:** History, Area studies. **Career:** Princeton University, NJ, lecturer in Near Eastern studies, 1975-76; Bosphorus University, Istanbul, Turkey, assistant professor to associate professor of history, 1976-83; Yarmouk University, Irbid, Jordan, associate professor of history, 1983-89; Washington University, St. Louis, MO, associate professor of history, 1989-. Institute of Advanced Studies, Berlin, Germany, fellow, 1985-86. Yurt Publications, member of board of editors, 1980-83. **Publications:** (ed. with G. Ben-Dor, and contrib.) Political Participation in Turkey, 1974; Political Testaments of Ali and Fuad (in Turkish), 1977; Documents on Jordan (monograph; bilingual in English and Arabic), 1989; The Long Peace: Ottoman Lebanon, 1861-1920, 1993. Contributor to periodicals. **Address:** Department of History, Washington University, Campus Box 1062, St. Louis, MO 63130, U.S.A.

AKERMAN, Susanna (Kristina). Swedish, b. 1959. **Genres:** Intellectual history. **Career:** Uppsala Universitet, Uppsala, Sweden, History of Ideas Department, research fellow, 1989-92; Stockholm University, research fellow, 1992-97. **Publications:** Queen Christina of Sweden and Her Circle: The Transformation of a Seventeenth-Century Philosophical Libertine, 1991; Rose Cross over the Baltic: The Spread of Rosicrucianism in Northern Europe, 1998. **Address:** Artillerig, 57 III, 114 45, Stockholm, Sweden. **Online address:** susanna.akerman@zeta.telenordia.se

AKERS, Alan Burt. See BULMER, (Henry) Kenneth.

AKINS, Ellen. American. **Genres:** Novels, Novellas/Short stories. **Career:** University of Notre Dame Press, Notre Dame, IN, advertising director, 1983-85; University of Chicago Press, Chicago, IL, promotions manager, 1985-88; writer. Also worked as an office assistant and script reader for director Sydney Pollack. **Publications:** NOVELS: Home Movie, 1988; Little Woman, 1990; Public Life, 1993; Hometown Brew, 1998. OTHER: World Like a Knife (stories and novellas), 1991. **Address:** Cornucopia, WI 54827, U.S.A.

AKINSHA, Konstantin. Russian, b. 1960. **Genres:** Art/Art history. **Career:** ArtNews, NYC, Moscow correspondent, 1990-93; Kunstverein Bremen, Bremen, Germany, research fellow, 1993-95; Germanisches National Museum, Nuremberg, Germany, research fellow, 1995-96. Soros Centers of Contemporary Art, member of international advisory board, 1996. **Publications:** (with G. Kozlov) Stolen Treasure, 1995; (with Kozlov and S. Hochfield) Beautiful Loot: Russia's Treasure Troves of Stolen Art from World War II, 1995; (with Kozlow and C. Toussaint) Operation Beutekunst, 1995. **Address:** c/o ArtNews, 48 West 38th St., New York, NY 10018, U.S.A.

AKMAKJIAN, Alan P(aul). American, b. 1948. **Genres:** Poetry. **Career:** California State University-San Francisco, instructor in English, 1982-83; St. John's University, Jamaica, NY, fellow in literature, 1993-94; University of Texas-Dallas, fellow in humanities, 1994-. Member of California Poets in the Schools program, 1984-92; member of boards of advisors and boards of governors. Translator. **Publications:** POETRY: Treading Pages of Water, 1992; California Picnic, 1993; Let the Sun Go, 1993; Grounded Angels, 1994; Breaking the Silence, 1995; California Picnic and Other Poems, 1997. Work represented in anthologies. Contributor of poetry, articles, short stories, and translations to periodicals. **Address:** 27908 Ryan Rd, Warren, MI 48092-5133, U.S.A.

AKST, Daniel. American, b. 1956. **Genres:** Novels, Bibliography. **Career:** Worked odd jobs during high school and college, including doorman, pleating factory employee, and mimeo supply company employee; Los Angeles Times, Los Angeles, CA, reporter, editor, and columnist, 1985-c.95; Wall Street Journal, NYC, reporter, 1987-88. Consultant for companies. **Publications:** Wonder Boy: Barry Minkow, The Kid Who Swindled Wall Street (nonfiction), 1990; Saint Burl's Obituary: A Novel, 1996. Contributor of short stories to periodicals. Contributor of articles and reviews to periodicals. **Address:** c/o Sloan Harris, ICM, 40 W. 57th St., New York, NY 10019, U.S.A. **Online address:** dan.akst@latimes.com

AKYEAMPONG, Emmanuel K(waku). Ghanaian, b. 1962. **Genres:** History. **Career:** University of Virginia, Charlottesville, instructor in history, 1992; Harvard University, Cambridge, MA, assistant professor, 1993-97, associate professor of history, 1997-. Speaker at educational institutions. **Publications:** Drink, Power, and Cultural Change: A Social History of Alcohol in Ghana, c. 1800 to Recent Times, 1996. Contributor to books. Contributor of articles and reviews to periodicals. **Address:** Department of History, Harvard University, Cambridge, MA 02138, U.S.A. **Online address:** akyeamp@fas.harvard.edu

ALAGOA, Ebiegberi Joe. Nigerian, b. 1933. **Genres:** Area studies, History. **Career:** National Archives of Nigeria, archivist, 1959-62; University of Lagos, Nigeria, lecturer, 1965-66, professor of history, director of Centre for Cultural Studies, 1972-77; University of Ibadan, Institute of African Studies, senior research fellow, 1966-72; University of Port Harcourt, School of Humanities, Port Harcourt, Nigeria, first dean, 1977-80, first deputy vice chancellor, 1980-81, acting vice chancellor, 1982, dean of School of Graduate Studies, 1982-83, 1985-87; Niger Delta Research Group, Faculty of Humanities, chairman, 1990-98; Niger Delta University, Wilberforce Island, Beyelsa State, Nigeria, pro-chancellor. Onyoma Research Publications, chairman. **Publications:** The Akassa Raid 1895, 1960; The Small Brave City-State, 1964; Kien abibi onde fa pugu, 1967; Jaja of Opobo (juvenile nonfiction), 1970; (with A. Fombo) A Chronicle of Grand Bonny, 1972; A History of the Niger Delta, 1972; King Boy of Brass (juvenile nonfiction), 1975; (with N. Nzewunwa) The History of Ogbakiri, 1980; Sagbe Obasi, 1986; People of the Fish and Eagle, 1995; The Ijaw Nation in the New Millennium, 1999; The Land and People of Rivers State: Eastern Niger Delta, 2002. EDITOR: (with T.N. Tamuno) Eminent Nigerians of the Rivers State, 1980; (with K. Williamson) Ancestral Voices, 1981; More Days, More Wisdom: Nembe Proverbs, 1983; Oral Historical Traditions in Africa, 1987; (with F. Anozie and N. Nzewunwa) The Early History of the Niger Delta, 1988; (with T. Tamuno) Land and People of Nigeria, 1989; Oral Tradition and Oral History in Africa and the Diaspora, 1990; Dike Remembered, 1998; A History of the University of Port Harcourt 1977-1998, 1999; The Land and People of Bayelsa State, 1999; Okpu, 2001. **Address:** 11 Orogbum Crescent, G.R.A II, PO Box 8611, Federal Secretariat Post Office, Port Harcourt, Rivers, Nigeria. **Online address:** kala_joe@yahoo.com

ALAI. Tibetan, b. 1959. **Genres:** Science fiction/Fantasy. **Career:** Writer. Science Fiction Journal, China, president and editor-in-chief. **Publications:** Chen ai lou ding, 1998, trans. H. Goldblatt and S. Li-chun Lin as Red Poppies, 2002; Yue guang li de yin jiang, (title means: The Silversmith in the Moonlight), 1999; Da di de jie ti (title means: The Ladder of the Land), 2001; Anthology of Alai, 2001; Jiu zhe yang ri yi feng ying, (title means: Being Opulent from Day to Day), 2002. **Address:** Science Fiction World, 11, Section 4, South People's Road, Chengdu, Sichuan 610041, People's Republic of China. **Online address:** alai@sfw-cd.com

ALAMA, Pauline J. American, b. 1964. **Genres:** Novels. **Career:** Writer. Helen Keller International, New York, NY, public relations assistant, 1986-88; New York Mission Society, New York, NY, information officer, 1988-89; New York University, New York, NY, employee development senior project analyst, 1989-91; University of Rochester and Rochester Institute of Technology, Rochester, NY, instructor in English, 1991-99; Teach for America, New York, NY, development associate, 1999-2000; New York Foundling, New York, NY, associate director of development, 2000-. **Publications:** The Eye of the Night, 2002. Contributor to periodicals and collections. **Address:** 71 Chestnut St., Rutherford, NJ 07070, U.S.A. **Online address:** PJAlma@excite.com

ALAMEDDINE, Rabih. American. **Genres:** Novels. **Career:** Painter (work exhibited at galleries) and novelist, 1998-. **Publications:** Koolaids: The Art of War (novel), 1998. **Address:** c/o St Martin's Press Inc., 175 Fifth Ave., New York, NY 10010, U.S.A.

ALARCÓN, Francisco X. American, b. 1954. **Genres:** Poetry, Language/Linguistics. **Career:** University of California, Santa Cruz, lecturer, 1985-92; University of California, Davis, lecturer, 1992-, director of Spanish for Native Speakers Program. **Publications:** POETRY: Tattoos, 1985; (with R. Reyes and J.P. Gutierrez) Ya vas, Carnal (title means: Right on, Brother), 1985; Quake Poems, 1989; Body in Flames/Cuerpo en llamas, 1990; Loma Prieta, 1990; Of Dark Love/De amor oscuro, 1991; Snake Poems: An Aztec Invocation, 1992; No Golden Gate for Us, 1993; Sonnets to Madness and Other Misfortunes, 2001; From the Other Side of Night/Del otro lado de la noche: New and Selected Poems, 2002. POETRY FOR CHILDREN: Laughing Tomatoes and Other Spring Poems, 1997; From the Bellybutton of the Moon and Other Summer Poems, 1998; Angels Ride Bikes and Other Fall Poems, 1999; Iguanas in the Snow and Other Winter Poems, 2001. Contributor of poetry to anthologies and periodicals. TEXTBOOKS: Mundo 21; Pasaporte al Mundo 21; Tu Mundo; Nuestro Mundo, 2000. **Address:** Dept of Spanish and Classics, 1 Shields Ave, University of California, Davis, Davis, CA 95616, U.S.A. **Online address:** fjalarcon@ucdavis.edu; francis coxalarcon.com

ALAYA, Flavia. American, b. 1935. **Genres:** Cultural/Ethnic topics, History, Literary criticism and history, Urban studies, Women's studies and issues, Autobiography/Memoirs, Biography. **Career:** University of North Carolina at Greensboro, instructor, 1959-60; Barnard College, NYC, lecturer and assistant in English, 1960-62; Hunter College of the City University of New York, lecturer, 1962-66; New York University, Bronx, instructor, 1966-67, assistant professor of English, 1967-71; Ramapo College of New Jersey, Mahwah, associate professor, and director, School of Intercultural Studies, 1971-73, professor of literature and cultural history, 1971-, now emerita. Northeast Victorian Studies Association, president, 1977-81; City of Paterson Historic Preservation Commission, New Jersey, commissioner, 1988-98, chair, 1990-98; National Trust for Historic Preservation, adviser, 1991-2000. **Publications:** William Sharp-Fiona Macleod 1855-1905, 1970; The Imagination Is a Square Wheel, 1977; Gaetano Federici: The Artist as Historian, 1980; Silk and Sandstone, 1984; Signifying Paterson, 1989; (co-author) Bridge Street to Freedom: Landmarking a Station on the Underground Railroad, 1998; Under the Rose: A Confession, 1999. Contributor to periodicals and essay collections. **Address:** 520 E 28th St, Paterson, NJ 07514, U.S.A. **Online address:** falaya@ramapo.edu

AL-AZM, Sadik J. Syrian, b. 1934. **Genres:** International relations/Current affairs, Philosophy. **Career:** Yale University, New Haven, CT, Dept of Philosophy, assistant in instruction, 1960-61; Hunter College, NYC, instructor in philosophy, 1961-62; University of Damascus, lecturer in philosophy, 1962-63, professor of philosophy, 1977-99, chairman, Dept of Philosophy and Sociology, 1998-; American University of Beirut, assistant professor of philosophy, 1963-68, assistant professor, Cultural Studies Program, 1967-68; Beirut University College, lecturer in philosophy, 1965-68; University of Jordan, assistant professor of philosophy, 1968-69. Arab Studies Review, editor, 1969-73. Visiting professor, scholar, and fellow at universities and institutions worldwide. **Publications:** Studies in Modern Western Philosophy,

1966; Kant's Theory of Time, 1967; Of Love and Arabic Courtly Love, 1968; Self-Criticism after the Defeat, 1968; Critique of Religious Thought, 1970; The Origins of Kant's Arguments in the Antinomies, 1972; A Critical Study of the Palestinian Resistance Movement, 1973; Materialism and History: A Defense, 1990; Salman Rushdie and the Truth of Literature, 1992, 2nd ed., 1994; Unbehagen in Der Moderne: Aufkarung im Islam, 1993; Reading the Satanic Verses: A Reply to Critics, 1997; L'illuminismo Islamico, 2nd ed., 2002; The Satanic Verses Post Festum, 2002. Contributor to periodicals. **Address:** PO Box 11574, Damascus University, Damascus, Syrian Arab Republic. **Online address:** s_j_azmzade@postmaster.co.uk

ALAZRAKI, Jaime. American (born Argentina), b. 1934. **Genres:** Literary criticism and history. **Career:** Professor of Latin American Literature, Columbia University, New York, since 1987. Member, Editorial Board, Hispanic Review, Latin American Literary Review, PMLA, Hispania, Hispanic Journal, Revista Iberoamericana, and Discurso Literario-revista de temas hispanicos. Instructor, Columbia University, NYC, 1964-67; Assistant Professor, 1967-68, Associate Professor, 1968-71, and Professor of Spanish Literature, 1972-77, University of California at San Diego. Member, Executive Council, International Institute of Ibero-American Literature, 1975-77. Professor of Latin American Literature, Harvard University, 1977-87. Co-ed., Revista Hispanica Moderna, 1987. **Publications:** Poetica y poesia de Pablo Neruda, 1965; La Prosa Narrativa de Jorge Luis Borges, 1968, rev. ed. 1974; Jorge Luis Borges, 1971; Versiones/inversiones/reversiones: el espejo como modelo estructural del relato en los cuentos de Borges, 1977; En busca del unicornio: les cuentos de Julio Cortazar, 1983; Critical Essays on Jorge Luis Borges, 1987; Borges and the Kabbalah and Other Essays, 1988; Hacia Cortázar: aproximaciones a su obra, 1994. EDITOR: (co-) Homenaje a Andres Iduarte, 1976; Jorge Luis Borges: el escritor y la critica, 1976; (co-) The Final Island: The Fiction of Julio Cortazar, 1978; Rayuela, 1980; Antologia de la novela hispanoamericana, 2 vols., 1982; J. Cortázar, Obra Crítica, 1994; J. Cotázar, Final del juego, 1995. **Address:** Dept of Spanish and Portuguese, Columbia University, Casa Hispanica, 612 W 116th St, New York, NY 10027, U.S.A.

ALBAHARI, David. Yugoslav, b. 1948. **Genres:** Novels, Novellas/Short stories, Literary criticism and history. **Career:** Writer. **Publications:** NOVELS: Sudija Dimitrijevic (title means: Judge Dimitrijevic), 1978; Cink, 1988, trans. as Tsing, 1997; Kratka knjiga (Short Book), 1993; Snezni covek (Man of Snow), 1995; Mamac, 1996, trans. as Bait, 2001; Mrak (Darkness), 1997; Gec i Majer, 1998, trans. as Gotz and Meyer, 2003; Svetski putnik (Globetrotter), 2001. SHORT STORIES: Porodicno vreme (Family Time), 1973; Obicne price (Ordinary Tales), 1978; Opis smrti (Description of Death), 1982; Fras u supi (Shock in the Shed), 1984; Jednostavnost (Simplicity), 1988; Pelerina (The Cloak), 1993; Izabrane price (Selected Stories), 1994; Neobicne price (Extraordinary Tales), 1999; Drugi jezik (Second Language), 2003; Words Are Something Else: Writings from an Unbound Europe, 1996. ESSAYS: Prepisivanje sveta (Copying the World), 1996. NONFICTION: (with others) Drugom stranom: Almanah novog talasa u SFRJ (rock music history and criticism), 1983; (author of preface) S.B. Finci, Seacanja (history), 1995. Contributor to periodicals. EDITOR: Savremena svetska prica (Contemporary World Short Stories), 1982; (with M. Pantic) Najbolje price 1989 (short stories), 1989; Savremena americka knjizevnost (Contemporary American Literature; fiction and poetry), 1989; Uhvati ritam: Rok i knjizevnost (Catch the Rhythm: Rock and Literature), 1990; Najkrace price na svetu (The Shortest Stories in the World), 1993; Antologija jevrejskih pripovedaca (Anthology of Jewish Storytellers), 1998. Translator of books into Serbian. **Address:** 15 Chatham Dr NW, Calgary, AB, Canada T2L 0Z4. **Online address:** albahard@telus.net

ALBANY, James. *See* **RAE, Hugh C(rawford).**

ALBARELLA, Joan K. American, b. 1944. **Genres:** Novels, Poetry. **Career:** Alpha Press Publishing, Gardenville, NY, founder, owner, and publisher, 1973-. Western New York Catholic, Buffalo, NY, writer and photographer, 1983-86; State University of New York-Buffalo, associate professor of writing at Educational Opportunity Center, 1986-. Director, performer, and playwright for children's theater productions; gives lectures and readings from her works. **Publications:** POETRY: Mirror Me, 1973; Poems for the Asking, 1975; Women, Flowers, Fantasy, 1987; Spirit and Joy, 1993. NOVELS: Agenda for Murder, 1999; Called to Kill, 2000; Close to You, 2003. Contributor of poetry, articles, and short stories to magazines and newspapers. **Address:** Alpha Press Promotions, 3574 Clinton St, Buffalo, NY 14224, U.S.A. **Online address:** alba@buffalo.edu

ALBARN, Keith. British, b. 1939. **Genres:** Art/Art history, Design. **Career:** Free-lance artist and designer, 1961-63; Keith Albarn and Partners Ltd.

(design consultants), London, England, managing director, 1963-71; visiting lecturer in art and design, 1971-81; North East London Polytechnic, London, principal lecturer in fine art, 1981-89; Colchester Institute, Colchester, England, head of School of Art and Design, 1989-97. Vice chairman, Colchester Borough Arts Forum, 1987-90; chairman of steering committee, Cuckoo Farm (artist studios project), 1989-91. **Publications:** (with J. Miall-Smith and S. Fraser-Steele) The Language of Pattern, 1974; (with J. Miall-Smith) Diagram: Instrument of Thought, 1977.

ALBEE, Edward (Franklin). American, b. 1928. **Genres:** Plays/Screenplays. **Career:** Producer, New Playwrights Unit Workshop, later Albarwild Theatre Arts, and Albar Productions, NYC. President, Edward F. Albee Foundation Inc. **Publications:** The Zoo Story, 1958; The Death of Bessie Smith, 1959; The Sandbox, 1959; Fam and Yam, 1959; The American Dream, 1960; Who's Afraid of Virginia Woolf?, 1961/2; (adapter) The Ballad of the Sad Cafe, 1963; Tiny Alice, 1964; (adapter) Malcolm, 1965; A Delicate Balance, 1966 (Pulitzer Prize); (adapter) Everything in the Garden, 1967; Box and Quotations from Chairman Mao Tse-Tung, 1968; All Over, 1971; Seascape, 1974 (Pulitzer Prize); Listening, 1975; Counting the Ways, 1976; The Lady from Dubuque, 1977/9; (adapter) Lolita, 1979; The Man Who Had Three Arms, 1981; Finding the Sun, 1982; Marriage Play, 1986/7; Three Tall Women, 1990/1 (Pulitzer Prize, 1994); The Lorca Play, 1992; Fragments, 1993; The Play about the Baby, 1996; (with S. Hunter) Tony Rosenthal, 2000; The Goat or Who Is Sylvia, 2002. **Address:** c/o Edward Albee Foundation, 91 Fairview Ave, Montauk, NY 11954, U.S.A.

ALBERT, Bill. American, b. 1942. **Genres:** Novels. **Career:** University of East Anglia, Norwich, England, reader in economic history, 1968-93. **Publications:** NOVELS: Et Rodriguez alors?, 1990; Desert Blues, 1994; Castle Garden, 1996. **Address:** 6 Mousehold House, Norwich NR1 4PH, England. **Online address:** w.albert@uea.ac.uk

ALBERT, Hans. German, b. 1921. **Genres:** Sociology, Philosophy. **Career:** University of Cologne, Cologne, Germany, assistant professor, 1952-58, dozent, 1958-63; University of Mannheim, Mannheim, Germany, professor and chair of philosophy of science and sociology, 1963-89; writer and editor. **Publications:** Oekonomische Ideologie und politischen Theorie: Das oekonomische Argument in der ordnungspolitischen Debatte, 1954; Marktsoziologie und Entscheidungslogik: Oekonomische Probleme in soziologischer Perspektive, 1967, 2nd ed., 1972; Traktat ueber kritische Vernunft, 1968, 5th ed., 1991, trans. M.V. Rorty as Treatise on Critical Reason, 1985; Plaedoyer fuer kritischen Rationalismus, 1971; Konstruktion und Kritik: Aufsaetze zur Philosophie des kritischen Rationalismus, 1972; Theologische Holzwege: Gerhard Ebeling und der rechte Gebrauch der Vernunft, 1973; Transzendentale Traumerien: Karl Otto Apels Sprachspiele und sein hermeutisches Gott, 1975; Rationaliteit in wetenschap en Samenleving, 1976; Aufklaerung und Steuerung: Aufsaetze zur Sozialphilosophie und zur Wissenschaftslehre der Sozialwissenschaft, 1976; Kritische Vernunft und menschliche Praxis, 1977; Traktat ueber rationale Praxis, 1978; Das Elend der Theologie: Kritische Auseinandersetzung mit Hans Kueng, 1979; Die Wissenschaft und die Fehlbarkeit der Vernunft, 1982; Freiheit und Ordnung: Zwei Abhandlungen zum Problem einer offenen Gesellschaft, 1986; Kritik der reinen Erkenntnislehre: Das Erkenntnisproblem in realistischer Perspektive, 1987; Kritik Der Reinen Hermeneutik: Der Antirealismus Und Das Problem Des Verstehens, 1994. EDITOR: (with F. Karrenberg) Sozialwissenschaft und Gesellschaftsgestaltung, 1963; Theorie und Realitaet: Ausgewaehlte Aufsaetze zur Wissenschaftslehre der Sozialwissenschaften, 1964; Sozialtheorie und soziale Praxis: Eduard Baumgarten zum siebzigsten Geburtstag, 1971; (with E. Topitsch) Werturteilsstreit, 1971, rev ed., 1979; Rechtstheorie als Grundlagenwissenschaft der Rechtswissenschaft, 1972; (with H. Keuth) Kritik der Kritischen Psychologie, 1973; (with K.H. Stapf) Theorie und Erfahrung, 1979; Oekonomisches Denken und soziale Ordnung: Festschrift fuer Erik Boettcher, 1984. **Address:** H Freiburger Strasse 62, D 69126, Heidelberg, Germany.

ALBERT, Michael. American, b. 1947. **Genres:** Administration/Management. **Career:** Writer and activist. Z Magazine, Woods Hole, MA, editorial writer and columnist. Formerly affiliated with South End Press (cofounder). **Publications:** What Is to Be Undone: A Modern Revolutionary Discussion of Classical Left Ideologies, 1974; (with Robin Hahnel) Unorthodox Marxism: An Essay on Capitalism, Socialism, and Revolution, 1978; (ed. and contributor, with David Dellinger) Beyond Survival: New Directions for the Disarmament Movement, 1983; (with others) Liberating Theory, 1986; (with Robin Hahnel) Quiet Revolution in Welfare Economics, 1990; (with Robin Hahnel) Looking Forward: Participatory Economics for the Twenty-first Century, 1991; (with Robin Hahnel) The Political Economy of Participatory Economics, 1991; Stop the Killing Train: Radical Visions for Radical Change, 1994; Moving Forward: Programme for a Participatory

Economy, 2000; The Trajectory of Change: Activist Strategies for Social Transformation, 2002; Parecon: Life after Capitalism, 2003. **Address:** 18 Millfield St., Woods Hole, MA 02543, U.S.A.

ALBERT, Neil. American, b. 1950. **Genres:** Mystery/Crime/Suspense. **Career:** Attorney, Lancaster, PA, 1976-. **Publications:** MYSTERIES: The January Corpse, 1991; The February Trouble, 1992; Burning March, 1993; Cruel April, 1994; Appointment in May, 1996; Tangled June, 1997. **Address:** 22 S. Duke St., Lancaster, PA 17602, U.S.A. **Online address:** nalbert@epix.net

ALBERT, Richard N(orman). American, b. 1930. **Genres:** Music. **Career:** High school English teacher and department head in Neenah, WI, 1957-63, and Normal, IL, 1965-78; Illinois State University, Normal, assistant professor to associate professor of English, 1978-93. **Publications:** (ed.) From Blues to Bop: A Collection of Jazz Fiction, 1990; (compiler) An Annotated Bibliography of Jazz Fiction and Jazz Fiction Criticism, 1996. Contributor to periodicals. **Address:** 1003 Dillon Dr., Normal, IL 61761, U.S.A. **Online address:** rnalber@mail.ilstu.edu

ALBERT, Steve. American, b. 1950. **Genres:** Documentaries/Reportage, Politics/Government. **Career:** Miami Review, Miami, FL, reporter, 1985-90; Recorder, San Francisco, CA, associate editor, 1990-95; freelance journalist, 1995-. **Publications:** The Case against the General: Manuel Noriega and the Politics of American Justice, 1993. Contributor of poetry to anthologies. **Address:** Jane Dystel Literary Management, 1 Union Sq. West, 9th floor, New York, NY 10003, U.S.A.

ALBERT, Susan Wittig. Also writes as Robin Paige. American, b. 1940. **Genres:** Mystery/Crime/Suspense, Young adult fiction, Literary criticism and history, Writing/Journalism. **Career:** University of San Francisco, CA, instructor, 196971; University of Texas, Austin, assistant professor, 1972-77, associate professor, 1977-79, associate dean of graduate school, 1977-79; Sophie Newcomb College, New Orleans, LA, dean, 1979-81; Southwest Texas State University, San Marcos, graduate dean, 1981-82, vice president for academic affairs, 1982-86, professor of English, 1981-87; full-time writer, 1987-. **Publications:** NONFICTION: (trans. with others, and ed.) The Poetics of Composition, 1973; Steps to Structure (textbook), 1975; (ed.) Structuralism, 1976; Stylistic and Narrative Structures in the Middle English Verse Romances, 1977; (with others) The Participating Reader (textbook), 1979; Work of Her Own: How Women Create Success and Fulfillment off the Traditional Career Track, 1992, as Work of Her Own: A Woman's Guide to Success off the Career Track, 1994; Writing from Life, 1997. CHINA BAYLES MYSTERY NOVELS: Thyme of Death, 1992; Witches' Bane, 1993; Hangman's Root, 1994; Rosemary Remembered, 1995; Rueful Death, 1996; Love Lies Bleeding, 1997; Chile Death, 1998; Lavender and Lies, 1999; Mistletoe Man, 2000; Bloodroot, 2001; Indigo Dying, 2003; A Dilly of a Death, 2004; The Tale of Hill Top Farm, 2004. AS ROBIN PAIGE. KATE AND CHARLES MYSTERY NOVELS (with Bill Albert): Death at Bishop's Keep, 1994; Death at Gallow's Green, 1995; Death at Daisy's Folly, 1997; Death at Devil's Bridge, 1998; Death at Rottingdean, 1999; Death at Whitechapel, 2000; Death at Epsom Downs, 2001; Death at Dartmoor, 2002; Death at Glamis Castle, 2003; Death in Hyde Park, 2004. Author/co-author of children's books, including several mysteries in the "Nancy Drew" and "Hardy Boys" series. **Address:** Box 1616, Bertram, TX 78605, U.S.A. **Online address:** china@tstar.net

ALBINSKI, Henry Stephen. American/Australian, b. 1931. **Genres:** International relations/Current affairs, Politics/Government. **Career:** Pennsylvania State University, Australia and New Zealand Studies Center, director, professor political science and Australian and New Zealand Studies, 1959-; Australian Natl University, visiting fellow, 1963-64, 1978-79, 1995; University of Western Ontario, visiting professor, 1969; Research Analysis Corp, consultant, 1969, Georgetown University Center for Strategic and International Studies, 1972-73; US Department of State, consultant, 1978, 1993, 1994; Australian Maritime Museum, 1987-88, Deakin University, 1993. Visiting appointments: University of Queensland, 1970; University of Sydney, 1974-75; Flinders University, 1974; University of Melbourne, 1985-86; Australiian Defence Force Academy, 1988-89, 1992; Curtin University 1995-96. **Publications:** Australia and the China Problem During the Korean War Period, 1964; Australian Policies and Attitudes Toward China, 1965; The Australian Labor Party and the Aid to Parochial Schools Controversy, 1966; (with L.K. Pettit) European Political Processes, 1968, rev. ed. 1974; Australia in Southeast Asia, 1970; Politics and Foreign Policy in Australia, 1970; Australian External Policy under Labor, 1977; The Australian-American Security Relationship, 1982; ANZUS: The United States and Pacific Security, 1987; The Australian-American Alliance: Prospects for the

1990s, 1990; The United States, Australia, and Regional Nation Defense Interactions in Asia-Pacific, 1993. EDITOR & CONTRIBUTOR: Asian Political Processes, 1971; Canadian and Australian Politics in Comparative Perspective, 1973; Australia and the United States, Strategic and Defence Cooperation Futures, 1993; Australia's Envolving American Relationship, 1994. **Address:** Australia-New Zealand Studies Center, Pennsylvania State University, University Park, PA 16802, U.S.A.

ALBOM, Mitch. American, b. 1958. **Genres:** Sports/Fitness, Biography. **Career:** Sports columnist, Detroit Free Press, 1985-. Formerly sportswriter for Ft. Lauderdale News and Sun-Sentinel, Florida. Panelist, ESPN's Sports Reporters. Feature reporter, ESPN-TV. Contributing Commentator, ESPN radio; WLLZ-FM (Detroit), sports director, 1985-; Sunday Sports Albom, co-host, 1988-; WDIV-TV (Detroit), broadcaster and commentator, 1987-. **Publications:** The Live Albom, 1988; (with B. Schembechler) Bo, 1989; The Live Albom II, 1990; The Live Albom III, 1992; Tuesdays with Morrie, 1997; Five People You Meet in Heaven, 2003. **Address:** c/o Detroit Free Press, 321 W Lafayette, Detroit, MI 48226, U.S.A.

ALBOROUGH, Jez. British, b. 1959. **Genres:** Children's fiction, Plays/Screenplays, Poetry, Illustrations. **Career:** Writer and illustrator. **Publications:** FOR CHILDREN Bare Bear, 1984; Running Bear, 1985; Willoughby Wallaby, 1986; The Grass Is Always Greener, 1987; Esther's Trunk, 1988; Hillary Hic-Cup, 1988; The Candle Story, The Clock Story, The Mirror Story, The Umbrella Story ("Featherby House Fables"), 1988; Cupboard Bear, 1989; Beaky, 1990; Archibald, 1991; Shake before Opening, 1992; Where's My Teddy, 1992; Cuddly Dudley, 1993; Washing Line, 1993; Hide and Seek, 1993; There's Something at the Letterbox, 1994; It's the Bear, 1994; Can You Jump Like a Kangaroo?, Can You Peck Like a Hen?, 1996; Watch Out! Big Bro's Coming, 1997; My Friend Bear, 1998; Balloon, 1998; Duck in the Truck, 1999. **Address:** Walker Books, 87 Vauxhall Walk, London SE11 5MJ, England.

ALBRECHT, Ernest (Jacob). American, b. 1937. **Genres:** Cultural/Ethnic topics, Recreation. **Career:** East Brunswick High School, East Brunswick, NJ, teacher, 1960-65; Middlesex Community College, Edison, NJ, assistant professor of English, 1967-. Spectacle: A Quarterly Journal of the Circus Arts, editor/publisher. **Publications:** A Ringling by Any Other Name, 1989; The New American Circus, 1995. **Address:** PO Box 1412, Edison, NJ 08818-1412, U.S.A. **Online address:** circusplus@aol.com

ALBRECHT, Gary L(ouis). American, b. 1937. **Genres:** Medicine/Health, Sociology. **Career:** Emory University, assistant professor of sociology and psychiatry, 1968-72; Northwestern University, associate professor of management and sociology, 1972-80; University of Illinois at Chicago, professor of public health, 1981-. American Sociological Association, Medical Sociology Section, chair, 1987-88; Society of the Study of Social Problems, Publications Committee, chair, 1992-93; Oxford University, visiting fellow, 1992-93, 1995-96. Has worked with the World Health Organization, Geneva, Switzerland, Global Programme on AIDS, and Project Hope, Washington, DC, on international AIDS studies. **Publications:** The Disability Business: Rehabilitation in America, 1992. EDITOR: (with P. Higgins) Health, Illness, and Medicine, 1979; Cross-National Rehabilitation Policies, 1981; (with J. Levy) Advances in Medical Sociology, Vol 2: Chronic Disease across the Life Course, 1992; (with R. Fitzpatrick and S. Scrimshaw) Handbook of Social Studies in Health and Medicine, 2000; (with K. Seelman and M. Bury) Handbook of Disability Studies, 2001. **Address:** School of Public Health, University of Illinois at Chicago, 1601 W Taylor St, Chicago, IL 60612, U.S.A.

ALBRECHT, Steve. American, b. 1963. **Genres:** Business/Trade/Industry, Law. **Career:** Police officer in San Diego, CA, 1984-85; Albrecht Training and Development, Alpine, CA, writer and seminar leader, 1985-. San Diego Police Reserve, officer. **Publications:** (with K. Albrecht) The Creative Corporation, 1987; (with J. Morrison) Contact and Cover, 1990; Streetwork, 1992; One-Strike Stopping Power, 1992; The Paralegal's Desk Reference, 1993; (with Albrecht) Added Value Negotiating, 1993; (with M. Mantell) Ticking Bombs, 1994; Service, Service, Service!, 1994; (with J. Clemens) Timeless Leaders, 1995; Corporate Self-Defense, 1995. FILM SCRIPTS: White Fire, Red Horse Down, and the television pilot Decoy Cops. **Address:** P.O. Box 1540, Alpine, CA 91903-1540, U.S.A.

ALCALDE, Miguel. See **REGINALD, Robert.**

ALCOSSER, Sandra (B.). American, b. 1944. **Genres:** Poetry. **Career:** Mademoiselle, NYC, associate editor, 1966-69; writer-in-residence and workshop director, 1973-85; Poets-in-the-Park, NYC, director, 1975-77;

Louisiana State University, instructor, 1982-85, assistant professor of English, 1985-87; San Diego State University, associate professor of English, 1986-89; professor, 1990-, director of creative writing program, 1988-91; University of Michigan, Ann Arbor, visiting professor of creative writing, 1994. Guest on National Public Radio and Public Television programs. **Publications:** POETRY: Each Bone a Prayer, 1982; A Fish to Feed All Hunger, 1986; Sleeping inside the Glacier, 1997; Except by Nature, 1998. Contributor to books and periodicals. Work represented in anthologies. **Address:** 5791 West County Line Rd., Florence, MT 59833, U.S.A. **Online address:** alcosser@mail.sdsu.edu

ALDCROFT, Derek Howard. British/Australian, b. 1936. **Genres:** Economics, History, Transportation, Bibliography. **Career:** University of Glasgow, teaching assistant, 1960-62, lecturer, 1964-67; University of Leicester, assistant lecturer, 1962-63, sr. lecturer, 1967-70, reader, 1970-73, professor of economic history, 1976-94, head of dept., 1976-94, fellow, 2002-; University of Sydney, Dept. of Economic History, professor and head, 1973-76; Manchester Metropolitan University, research professor in economic history, 1994-2001. Journal of Transport History, Editorial Committee, chairman, 1969-73; Business History Review, editorial adviser, 1971-73; Economic Review, Advisory Panel, 1982-; Independent Research Services, Oxford, Advisory Board, 1986-. **Publications:** British Railways in Transition, 1968; (with H.W. Richardson) Building in the British Economy between the Wars, 1968; (with H.W. Richardson) The British Economy, 1969; (with H.J. Dyos) British Transport, 1969; The Inter-War Economy, Britain 1919-1939, 1970; Studies in British Transport History 1879-1970, 1974; British Transport since 1914, 1975; From Versailles to Wall Street, 1977; The East Midlands Economy, 1979; The European Economy, 1914-80, 1980; Full Employment, 1984; The British Economy: Vol I, Years of Turmoil, 1920-1951, 1986; Education, Training and Economic Performance 1944-1990, 1992; The European Economy, 1914-1990, 1993; Bibliography of European Economic and Social History 1750-1939, 1993; Economic Change in Eastern Europe since 1918, 1995; Studies in the Interwar European Economy, 1997. EDITOR: The Development of British Industry and Foreign Competition 1875-1914, 1968; (with P. Fearon) Economic Growth in Twentieth Century Britain, 1969; (with P. Fearon) British Economic Fluctuations 1790-1939, 1972; (with M.J. Oliver) Trade Unions and the Economy: 1870-2000, 2000. **Address:** 10 Linden Dr, Evington, Leics. LE5 6AH, England.

ALDEN, Patricia. American. **Genres:** Literary criticism and history. **Career:** St. Lawrence University, Canton, NY, instructor, 1976-78, assistant professor, 1978-84, associate professor, 1985-92, professor of English, 1993-; writer. **Publications:** Social Mobility in the English Bildungsroman: Gissing, Hardy, Bennett, and Lawrence, 1986; (ed. with D.T. Lloyd and A.I. Samatar) African Studies and the Undergraduate Curriculum, 1994; (with L. Tremaine) Nuruddin Farah, 1999. Contributor to books and periodicals. **Address:** Department of English, St. Lawrence University, Canton, NY 13617, U.S.A. **Online address:** palden@stlawu.edu

ALDEN, Sue. See **FRANCIS, Dorothy Brenner.**

ALDER, Ken(neth L.). American. **Genres:** History, Novels. **Career:** Northwestern University, Evanston, IL, assistant professor, 1991, associate professor of history, 1997-. **Publications:** The White Bus (novel), 1987; Engineering the Revolution: Arms and Enlightenment in France, 1763-1815 (nonfiction), 1997. Contributor to periodicals. **Address:** Department of History, Northwestern University, Evanston, IL 60201, U.S.A. **Online address:** k-alder@nwu.edu

ALDERMAN, Ellen. American, b. 1957?. **Genres:** Law. **Career:** Attorney and author. **Publications:** (with C. Kennedy) In Our Defense: The Bill of Rights in Action (nonfiction), 1991; (with Kennedy) The Right to Privacy (nonfiction), 1995. Contributor to journals. **Address:** c/o Author Mail, Random House, 1745 Broadway #B1, New York, NY 10019-4305, U.S.A.

ALDERSEY-WILLIAMS, Hugh. American/British, b. 1959. **Genres:** Design, Architecture, Business/Trade/Industry, Sciences, Chemistry. **Career:** Free-lance writer, London, England, 1986-. **Publications:** New American Design, 1988; Hollington Industrial Design, 1990; King and Miranda: Poetry of the Machine, 1991; World Design: Nationalism and Globalism in Design, 1992; The Most Beautiful Molecule: The Discovery of the Buckyball, 1995. Contributor to magazines and newspapers in the United Kingdom and the United States. **Address:** 33 Hugo Rd., London N19 5EU, England.

ALDERSON, Sue Ann. American, b. 1940. **Genres:** Young adult fiction, Children's fiction. **Career:** Simon Fraser University, Vancouver, BC, instructor in English, 1967-71; Capilano College, Vancouver, instructor in English,

1972-80; University of British Columbia, Vancouver, assistant professor, 1980-84, associate professor, 1984-92, professor, Creative Writing Dept., 1992-. **Publications:** Bonnie McSmithers You're Driving Me Dithers, 1974; Hurry Up, Bonnie!, 1976; The Adventures of Prince Paul, 1977; The Finding Princess, 1977; Bonnie McSmithers Is at It Again!, 1979; Comet's Tale, 1983; The Not Impossible Summer, 1983; The Something in Thurlo Darby's House, 1984; Ida and the Wool Smugglers, 1987; Maybe You Had to Be There, by Duncan, 1989; Chapter One, 1990; Sure as Strawberries, 1992; A Ride for Martha, 1993; Ten Mondays for Lots of Boxes, 1995; Pond Seasons, 1997; Wherever Bears Be, 1999. **Address:** UBC Creative Writing Program, University of British Colombia, Buchanan E462-1866 Main Hall, Vancouver, BC, Canada V6T 1Z1.

ALDING, Peter. See **JEFFRIES, Roderic.**

ALDISS, Brian (Wilson). British, b. 1925. **Genres:** Novels, Novellas/Short stories, Science fiction/Fantasy, Poetry, Autobiography/Memoirs. **Career:** Oxford Mail, literary editor, 1958-69; Penguin Science Fiction, editor, 1961-64; World SF, president, 1982-84; Avernus Publishing, managing director, 1988-; West Buckland School, vice-president, 1990-; Royal Society of Literature, fellow, 1991-; Grand Master of Science Fiction, 2000. **Publications:** The Brightfount Diaries, 1955; Space Time and Nathaniel, 1957; Non-Stop (in US as Starship), 1958; No Time Like Tomorrow, 1959; Vanguard from Alpha, 1959; Canopy of Time, 1959; Male Response, 1959; Bow Down to Nul, 1960; Galaxies Like Grains of Sand, 1960; Equator, 1961; Primal Urge, 1961; The Interpreter, 1961; Hothouse (in US as Long Afternoon of Earth), 1962; Airs of Earth, 1963; The Dark Light Years, 1964; Introducing SF, 1964; Greybeard, 1964; Starswarm, 1964; Earthworks, 1965; Best SF Stories of Brian W. Aldiss (in US as Who Can Replace a Man?), 1965; The Saliva Tree and Other Strange Growths, 1966; Cities and Stones: A Traveller's Jugoslavia, 1966; An Age (in US as Cryptozoic!) 1967; Farewell Fantastic Venus (in US as All About Venus), 1968; Report on Probability A, 1968; A Brian Aldiss Omnibus, 1969; Intangibles Inc. and Other Stories, 1969; Barefoot in the Head, 1969; Neanderthal Planet, 1970; The Shape of Further Things, 1970; The Hand-Reared Boy, 1970; A Soldier Erect, 1971; Brian Aldiss Omnibus 2, 1971; The Moment of Eclipse, 1971; The Comic Inferno, 1972; Frankenstein Unbound, 1973; Billion Year Spree: The History of Science Fiction, 1973; The Eighty-Minute Hour, 1974; Space Opera, 1974; Science Fiction Art, 1975; The Malacia Tapestry, 1976; Last Orders, 1977; Brothers of the Head, 1977; A Rude Awakening, 1978; Enemies of the System, 1978; Distant Encounters (play), 1978; New Arrivals, Old Encounters, 1979; This World and Nearer Ones, 1979; Pile (verse), 1979; Life in the West, 1980; Foreign Bodies, 1981; Moreau's Other Island, 1980; Helliconia Spring, 1982; Helliconia Summer, 1983; Science Fiction Quiz, 1983; Seasons in Flight, 1984; Pale Shadow of Science, 1985; Helliconia Winter, 1985; ...And the Lurid Glare of the Comet, 1986; Trillion Year Spree, 1986; Cracken at Critical, 1987; Ruins, 1987; Forgotten Life, 1988; Best Short Stories of Brian Aldiss, 1988 (in US as Man in His Time, 1989); Science Fiction Blues, 1989; A Romance of the Equator: Best Fantasy Stories of Brian W. Aldiss, 1989; Bury My Heart at W. H. Smith's: A Writing Life, 1990; Dracula Unbound, 1991; Home Life with Cats, 1992; Remembrance Day, 1993; A Tupolev Too Far, 1993; Somewhere East of Life; The Detached Retina, 1995; At the Caligua Hotel, 1995; The Secret of This Book, 1995; Songs from the Steppes of Central Asia, 1996; Common Clay, 1996; The Twinkling of an Eye or My Life as an Englishman, 1999; When the Feast Is Finished, 1999; White Mars, 1999; Art after Apogee, 2000; Supertoys Last All Summer Long, 2001; Super-State, 2002; The Cretan Teat, 2002; Affairs at Hampden Ferrers, 2004; Jocasta, 2005. EDITOR: Penguin Science Fiction, 1961; More Penguin Science Fiction, 1962; Best Fantasy Stories, 1962; Yet More Penguin Science Fiction, 1964; (with H. Harrison) Nebula Award Stories II, 1967; (with H. Harrison) Best SF 1967 to 1975, 1968-76; (with H. Harrison) The Astounding-Analog Reader, vol. I, 1972, vol. II, 1973; Penguin Science Fiction Omnibus, 1973; Space Odysseys, 1975; (with H. Harrison) Hell's Cartographers, 1975; Evil Earths, 1975; (with C. Foss) Science Fiction Art, 1975; (with H. Harrison) Decade: The 1940's, 1950's, 1960's, 1975-77; Galactic Empires, 1976; Perilous Planets, 1978; Mini Sagas from the Daily Telegraph Competition, 1997. **Address:** Hambleden, 39 St. Andrews Rd, Old Headington, Oxford OX3 9DL, England. **Online address:** aldiss@dial.pipex.com

ALDRICH, Ann. See **MEAKER, Marijane (Agnes).**

ALDRIDGE, A. Owen. American, b. 1915. **Genres:** Literary criticism and history, Philosophy, Biography. **Career:** Professor Emeritus of Comparative Literature, University of Illinois, Urbana, 1967-86; Will and Ariel Durant Chair, St. Peter's College, Jersey City, 1986-87; Fulbright Professor, Korea, 1988; Distinguished Chair, National Chenchi University, Taiwan, 1990;

National Tsing Hua University, 1991; Ed., Comparative Literature Studies journal, since 1963. **Publications:** Shaftesbury and the Deist Manifesto, 1951; Benjamin Franklin and His French Contemporaries, 1957; Man of Reason: The Life of Thomas Paine, 1959; Essai sur les personnages des Liaisons Dangereuses en tant que types litteraires, 1960; Jonathan Edwards, 1964; Benjamin Franklin: Philosopher and Man, 1965; Benjamin Franklin and Nature's God, 1967; Voltaire and the Century of Light, 1975; Comparative Literature East-West, 1979; Thomas Paine's American Ideology, 1984; Fiction in Japan and the West, 1985; The Reemergence of World Literature: A Study of Asia and the West, 1986; The Dragon and the Eagle: The Presence of China in the American Enlightenment, 1993. EDITOR: Comparative Literature: Matter and Method, 1969; The Iberoamerican Enlightenment, 1970. **Address:** 101 East Chalmers St, Champaign, IL 61820, U.S.A.

ALDRIDGE, Delores P(atricia). American. **Genres:** Sociology, Cultural/Ethnic topics. **Career:** Tampa Urban League, Tampa, FL, associate director, 1966; Greater Lafayette Community Centers, director of community development, 1969-70, executive director, 1969-71; Emory University, Atlanta, GA, founding director of the department of Afro-American and African studies, 1971-90, assistant professor, 1971-75, associate professor, 1975-88, professor of sociology, 1988-, Grace Towns Hamilton Distinguished Professor of Sociology, 1990-. Shaw University, Raleigh, NC, and Spelman College, Atlanta, GA, adjunct associate professor of sociology, 1971-75; Clark Atlanta University, member of board of trustees, 1988-. Consultant and panelist for the National Science Foundation, the National Endowment of the Humanities, and the Department of Health, Education, and Welfare, 1971-; consultant for organizations, including Southern Regulatory Council, 1972-78, Southern Association of College and Schools, 1973-, and Center for the Study of Black Family Life, 1975-. **Publications:** A Statement on Racial Ethnic, 1987; (ed.) Black Male-Female Relationships: A Resource Book of Selected Materials, 1989; Focusing: Black Male-Female Relationships, 1991. **Address:** Department of Sociology, Emory University, 201 B Candler Library Bldg., Atlanta, GA 30322, U.S.A.

ALDRIDGE, (Harold Edward) James. Australian, b. 1918. **Genres:** Novels, Children's fiction, Plays/Screenplays, Travel/Exploration. **Career:** Writer, Melbourne Herald and Sun, 1937-38, and London Daily Sketch and Sunday Dispatch, 1939; European and Middle East War Correspondent, Australian Newspaper Service and North American Newspaper Alliance, 1939-44; Tehran correspondent, Time and Life, 1994. **Publications:** NOVELS: Signed with Their Honour, 1942; The Sea Eagle, 1944; Of Many Men, 1946; The Diplomat, 1950; The Hunter, 1951; Heroes of the Empty View, 1954; I Wish He Would Not Die, 1957; The Last Exile, 1961; A Captive in the Land, 1962; The Statesman's Game, 1966; My Brother Tom (in U.S. as My Brother Tom: A Love Story), 1966; A Sporting Proposition, 1973; Mockery in Arms, 1974; The Untouchable Juli, 1975; One Last Glimpse, 1977; Goodbye Un-America, 1979. SHORT STORIES: Gold and Sand, 1960. PLAYS: The 49th State, 1946; One Last Glimpse, 1981. FOR CHILDREN: The Flying 19, 1966; The Marvelous Mongolian, 1974; The Broken Saddle, 1983; The True Story of Lilli Stubeck, 1984; The True Story of Spit MacPhee, 1986; The True Story of Lola Mackellar, 1992. OTHER: Undersea Hunting for Inexperienced Englishmen, 1955; (with P. Stand) Living Egypt, 1969; Cairo: Biography of a City, 1969. **Address:** c/o Curtis Brown, 28/29 Haymarket, London SW1Y 4SP, England.

ALDRIDGE, John W(atson). American, b. 1922. **Genres:** Novels, Novellas/Short stories, Literary criticism and history. **Career:** Professor of English, University of Michigan, Ann Arbor, 1964-91, Professor Emeritus, 1991-. Member, National Book Critics Circle. Lecturer in Criticism, 1948-50, and Assistant Professor of English, 1950-55, University of Vermont, Burlington; Christian Gauss Lecturer in Criticism, Princeton University, New Jersey, 1953-54; Member of the Literature Faculty, Sarah Lawrence College, Bronxville, New York, and The New School for Social Research, NYC; Professor of English, Queens College, NYC, 1956-57; Berg Professor of English, New York University, 1957-58; Fulbright Lecturer, University of Munich, 1958-59, and the University of Copenhagen, 1962-63; Writer-in-Residence, Hollins College, Virginia, 1960-62; Book Critic, New York Herald Tribune Book Week, 1965-66, and Saturday Review, NYC, 1969-79; Special Adviser for American Studies, U.S. Embassy, Bonn, 1972-73; Book Commentator, MacNeil/Lehrer News Hour, 1983-84; Writers' America, film series WETA public television, special adviser. **Publications:** After the Lost Generation: A Critical Study of the Writers of Two Wars, 1951; The Party at Cranton (novel), 1960; Time to Murder and Create: The Contemporary Novel in Crisis, 1966; In the Country of the Young, 1970; The Devil in the Fire: Retrospective Essays on American Literature and Culture 1951-1972, 1972; The American Novel and the Way We Live Now, 1983; Talents and Technicians, 1992; Classics and Contemporaries, 1992. EDITOR: Critiques and Essays on Modern Fiction 1920-1951, 1952; Discovery 1, 1952; In Search of Heresy: American Literature in the Age of Conformity, 1956; Selected Stories, by P.G. Wodehouse, 1958. **Address:** 381 N Main St, Madison, GA 30650-1336, U.S.A.

ALESHIRE, Peter. American, b. 1952. **Genres:** History. **Career:** Arizona State University West, Phoenix, AZ, professor of American studies, 1992-2002; writer. Phoenix Magazine, associate editor. Freelance writer, Arizona Highways and others. Former journalist, for Arizona Republic, Oakland Tribune, Contra Costa Times, Indio Daily News, and Palm Springs Desert Sun. **Publications:** Reaping the Whirlwind: The Apache Wars, 1998; The Fox and the Whirlwind: General George Crook and Geronimo, 2000; Warrior Woman: The Story of Lozen, Apache Warrior and Shaman, 2001; Cochise: The Life and Times of the Great Apache Chief, 2001. Contributor to periodicals. **Address:** Department of American Studies, Arizona State University West, PO Box 37100, Phoenix, AZ 85069, U.S.A. **Online address:** peter.aleshire@asu.edu; westinfo@asu.edu

ALESSANDRA, Tony. American, b. 1947. **Genres:** Administration/Management, Business/Trade/Industry. **Career:** Georgia State University, Atlanta, instructor in marketing, 1973-76; University of San Diego, San Diego, CA, assistant professor of marketing, 1976-78; Alessandra and Associates Inc., La Jolla, CA, partner, professional speaker, and writer, 1979-. **Publications:** The Art of Managing People, 1980; The Business of Selling, 1984; NonManipulative Selling, 1987; Selling by Objectives, 1988; Be Your Own Sales Manager, 1990; Publish and Flourish, 1992; Collaborative Selling, 1993; Communicating at Work, 1993; People Smarts, 1994; The Sales Manager's Idea-a-Day Guide, 1996; The Sales Professional's Idea-a-Day Guide, 1996; The Platinum Rule, 1996; Charisma, 1998. **Address:** Alessandra and Associates Inc., PO Box 2767, La Jolla, CA 92038, U.S.A. **Online address:** tony@alessandra.com

ALEXANDER, Adele Logan. American, b. 1938. **Genres:** History, Race relations, Women's studies and issues. **Career:** Previously, instructor at University of Maryland, Howard University and Trinity College. Currently, associate professor of history, George Washington University, writer and lecturer. **Publications:** Ambiguous Lives: Free Women of Color in Rural Georgia, 1789-1879, 1991; Homelands and Waterways, 1999. Contributor of chapters to books and articles and reviews to periodicals and journals. **Address:** Dept of History, 335 Phillips Hall, George Washington University, Washington, DC 20052, U.S.A. **Online address:** alalex@gwu.edu

ALEXANDER, Caroline. British (born United States), b. 1956. **Genres:** Travel/Exploration. **Career:** University of Malawi, Zomba, Malawi, lecturer in classics, 1982-85; writer. **Publications:** One Dry Season: In the Footsteps of Mary Kingsley, 1990; The Way to Xanadu, 1993; Battle's End, 1995; The Bounty, 2003. **Address:** c/o Sheil Land Assoc., 43 Doughty St, London WC1N 2LF, England.

ALEXANDER, Doris (Muriel). American, b. 1922. **Genres:** Literary criticism and history, Biography, Psychology. **Career:** City University of New York, NYC, head of English department at Staten Island, 1956-63; University of Athens, Greece, Fulbright professor, 1966-67; Pennsylvania State University, University Park, visiting professor and fellow, Institute of Humanities and Arts, 1968. **Publications:** The Tempering of Eugene O'Neill, 1962; Creating Characters with Charles Dickens, 1991; Eugene O'Neill's Creative Struggle: The Decisive Years, 1924-1933, 1992; Creating Literature out of Life: The Making of Four Masterpieces, 1996. Contributor to language and literature journals. **Address:** San Trovaso 1116, Dorsoduro, 30123 Venice, Italy. **Online address:** dalex1@tin.it

ALEXANDER, Elizabeth. American, b. 1962. **Genres:** Poetry. **Career:** University of Chicago, Chicago, IL, assistant professor of English, 1991-; poet and writer. **Publications:** The Venus Hottentot (poems), 1990; Body of Life (poems), 1996. **Address:** Department of African American Studies, Yale University, PO Box 2033, New Haven, CT 06520, U.S.A.

ALEXANDER, Floyce. American, b. 1938. **Genres:** Poetry. **Career:** Freelance Ed., University of New Mexico Press, Albuquerque, 1983-. Editorial Assistant, Washington State University Press, Pullman, 1963-70; Teaching Assistant, Washington State University, Pullman, 1970-71, and University of Massachusetts, Amherst, 1972-74; Teaching Assistant, 1978-81, and Lecturer in Film, 1987-89, University of New Mexico, Albuquerque. **Publications:** Ravines, 1971; Machete, 1972; Bottom Falling out of the Dream, 1976; Red Deer, 1982; Memory of the Future, 1998; Succor, 2002; American Fires, 2003. **Address:** 1211 Beltrami NW, Bemidji, MN 56601, U.S.A. **Online address:** fmklalex@paulbunyan.net

ALEXANDER, Gary. American, b. 1941. **Genres:** Mystery/Crime/Suspense, Novels, Novellas/Short stories. **Career:** Writer. **Publications:** Pigeon Blood (novel), 1988; Unfunny Money (novel), 1989; Kiet and the Golden Peacock (novel), 1989; Kiet and the Opium War (novel), 1990; Deadly Drought (novel), 1991; Kiet Goes West, 1992; Blood Sacrifice, 1993; Dead Dinosaurs, 1994. Approximately 80 short stories, most to mystery magazines. **Address:** 4611 Devereaux Street, Philadelphia, PA 19135-3607, U.S.A.

ALEXANDER, Harriet Semmes. American, b. 1949. **Genres:** Literary criticism and history. **Career:** Oklahoma State University, Stillwater, OK, assistant reference librarian, 1974-77; University of Memphis, Memphis, TN, reference librarian, 1977-. Tennessee Librarian, editor, 1996-98. **Publications:** American and British Poetry: A Guide to the Criticism, 1925-1978, 1984; English Language Criticism on the Foreign Novel, 1989; American and British Poetry: A Guide to the Criticism, 1979-1990, 1997. **Address:** 1117 Robin Hood Lane, Memphis, TN 38111, U.S.A. **Online address:** halexndr@postmaster.memphis.edu

ALEXANDER, Jeffrey C(harles). American, b. 1947. **Genres:** Sociology, Anthropology/Ethnology. **Career:** Sociologist, educator, and writer. University of California-Berkeley, lecturer, 1974-76; University of California-Los Angeles, assistant professor, 1976-81, full professor, 1981-2001, chair, sociology department, 1989-92, professor emeritus, beginning 2001; Yale University, professor of sociology, 2001-. Visiting professor at European universities. **Publications:** Theoretical Logic in Sociology, 1982; Twenty Lectures: Sociological Theory since World War II, 1987; Action and Its Environments: Toward a New Synthesis, 1988; Structure and Meaning: Relinking Classical Sociology, 1989; Fin de Siecle Social Theory: Relativism, Reduction, and the Problem of Reason, 1995; The Meanings of a Social Life: A Cultural Sociology, 2003. EDITOR: Neofunctionalism, 1985; The Micro-Macro Link, 1987; Durkheimian Sociology: Cultural Studies, 1988; (with S. Seidman) Culture and Society: Contemporary Debates, 1990; (with P. Colomy) Differentiation Theory and Social Change: Comparative and Historical Perspectives, 1990; (with P. Sztompka) Rethinking Progress: Movements, Forces, and Ideas at the End of the 20th Century, 1990; (with R. Boudon and M. Cherkaoui) The Classical Tradition in Sociology: The American Tradition, 1997; Neofunctionalism and After, 1998; Real Civil Societies: Dilemmas of Institutionalization, 1998; (with N.J. Smelser) Diversity and Its Discontents: Cultural Conflict and Common Ground in Contemporary American Society, 1999; Mainstream and Critical Social Theory: Classical, Modern, and Contemporary, 2001; (with P. Smith) The Cambridge Companion to Durkheim, 2004. Contributor to books. **Address:** Department of Sociology, Yale University, PO Box 208265, New Haven, CT 06520, U.S.A. **Online address:** jeffrey.alexander@yale.edu

ALEXANDER, John Thorndike. American, b. 1940. **Genres:** History, Biography. **Career:** University of Kansas, assistant professor, 1966-70, associate professor, 1970-74, professor of history and Russian and East European studies, 1974-. **Publications:** Autocratic Politics in National Crisis: The Imperial Russian Government and Pugachev's Revolt 1773-1775, 1969; Emperor of the Cossacks: Pugachev and the Frontier Jacquerie of 1773-1775, 1973; Bubonic Plague in Early Modern Russia: Public Health and Urban Disaster, 1980; Catherine the Great: Life and Legend, 1989. TRANSLATOR: (and ed.) S.F. Platonov, The Time of Troubles, 1970; E.V. Anisimov, The Reforms of Peter the Great, 1993; E.V. Anisimov, Empress Elizabeth, 1995. Contributor to books. **Address:** Dept. of History, University of Kansas, Lawrence, KS 66045, U.S.A. **Online address:** jatalex@falcon.cc.ukans.edu

ALEXANDER, Joseph H(ammond). American, b. 1938. **Genres:** Military/Defense/Arms control, History, Plays/Screenplays, Documentaries/Reportage. **Career:** U.S. Marine Corps, career officer, 1960-88, including two combat tours in Vietnam, five years at sea, company commander in Vietnam, battalion commander in Okinawa, chief of staff for Third Marine Division, director of Marine Corps Research and Development Center, and service in the Caribbean, Mediterranean, and Northern Europe, retiring as colonel; independent military historian and writer, 1989-. Marine Corps Heritage Foundation, life member; consultant to Smithsonian magazine, 1993, National Geographic Television, 1995. **Publications:** MONOGRAPHS: Across the Reef: The Marine Assault on Tarawa, 1993; Closing In: Marines in the Seizure of Iwo Jima, 1995; Final Campaign: Marines in the Victory on Okinawa, 1996; 20th Century Marines: Three Touchstone Battles, 1997. NONFICTION: (with M.E. Bartlett) Sea Soldiers in the Cold War: Amphibious Warfare, 1945-91, 1994; Utmost Savagery: The Three Days of Tarawa, 1995; Storm Landings, 1997; (with D. Horan and N.C. Stahl) A Fellowship of Valor, 1998. TELEVISION DOCUMENTARIES: Death Tide at Tarawa,

1993; Admiral "Bull" Halsey, 1994; Iwo Jima: Hell's Volcano, 1995; Okinawa: The Final Battle, 1995; Imperial Sunset at Saipan, 1995; The Bloody Hills of Peleliu, 1995; V-J Day: The Day That Changed the World, 1995; Chesty Puller, the Marine's Marine, 1998; America's Five-Star Heroes, 1998; The Spanish American War, 1998; A Fellowship of Valor, 1997; Fire & Ice, 1999. Contributor to books. Contributor to history and military journals. **Address:** 18 Sunset Summit, Asheville, NC 28804, U.S.A.

ALEXANDER, Lloyd (Chudley). American, b. 1924. **Genres:** Novels, Novellas/Short stories, Children's fiction, Translations. **Career:** Director, Carpenter Lane Chamber Music Society, Philadelphia, 1970-; Member, Editorial Advisory Board, Cricket mag., Peru, IL, 1973-. Author-in-Residence, Temple University, Philadelphia, 1970-74. Recipient, Newbery Medal, 1968; National Book Award, 1970; American Book Award, 1981. **Publications:** And Let the Credit Go, 1955; My Five Tigers, 1956; Border Hawk: August Bondi, 1958; The Flagship Hope: Aaron Lopez, 1960; Janine Is French, 1960; My Love Affair with Music, 1960; (with L.J. Camuti) Park Avenue Vet, 1962; Time Cat: The Remarkable Journeys of Jason and Gareth, 1963; The Book of Three, 1964; Fifty Years in the Doghouse, 1964; The Black Cauldron, 1965; Coll and His White Pig, 1965; The Castle of Llyr, 1966; Taran Wanderer, 1967; The High King, 1968; The Marvelous Misadventures of Sebastian, 1970; The King's Fountain, 1971; The Four Donkeys, 1972; The Cat Who Wished to Be a Man, 1973; The Foundling and Other Tales of Prydain, 1973; The Wizard in the Tree, 1975; The Town Cats and Other Tales, 1977; The First Two Lives of Lukas-Kasha, 1978; Westmark, 1981; The Kestrel, 1982; The Beggar Queen, 1984; The Illyrian Adventure, 1986; The El Dorado Adventure, 1987; The Drackenberg Adventure, 1988; The Jedera Adventure, 1989; The Philadelphia Adventure, 1990; The Remarkable Journey of Prince Jen, 1991; Fortune Tellers, 1992; The House Gobbaleen, 1995; The Iron Ring, 1997; Gypsy Rizka, 1999; How the Cat Swallowed Thunder, 2000; The Gawgon and the Boy, 2001; The Rope Trick, 2002. TRANSLATOR: J.-P. Sartre, The Wall and Other Stories, 1948, as Intimacy and Other Stories, 1949; J.-P. Sartre, Nausea, 1949; P. Eluard, Selected Writings, 1951; P. Vialar, The Sea Rose, 1952. **Address:** 1005 Drexel Ave, Drexel Hill, PA 19026, U.S.A.

ALEXANDER, M(ichael) J(oseph). British, b. 1941. **Genres:** Poetry, Literary criticism and history, Translations. **Career:** Employed by William Collins, publishers, London, 1963-65; Princeton University Graduate School, NJ, Fellow, 1965-66; University of California at Santa Barbara, lecturer, 1966-67; Andre Deutsch, publishers, London, editor, 1967-68; University of East Anglia, Norwich, lecturer in English, 1968-69; University of Stirling, Scotland, lecturer, 1969-77, sr. lecturer, 1977-85, reader in English studies, 1985; University of St. Andrews, Scotland, Berry Professor of English Literature, 1985-. **Publications:** The Poetic Achievement of Ezra Pound, 1979, 2nd ed., 1998; Twelve Poems, 1980; The Prologue to the Canterbury Tales, 1980, 2nd ed., 1999; The Knight's Tale, 1981; A History of Old English Literature, 1983, 3rd ed., 2002; The Miller's Tale, 1986; A History of English Literature, 2000. TRANSLATOR: The Earliest English Poems, 1966, 3rd ed., 1991; Beowulf: A Verse Translation, 1973, rev. ed., 2001; Old English Riddles from the Exeter Book, 1980, 3rd ed., 1984; Beowulf and Grendel, 1995. EDITOR/CO-EDITOR: Macmillan Anthologies of English Literature, Vols. 1-5, 1989; Beowulf: A Glossed Text, 1995; Sons of Ezra, 1995; The Canterbury Tales: The First Fragment, 1996; The Canterbury Tales: Illustrated Prologue, 1996; The Merchant of Venice, 1998. Author of articles and essays on Hardy, T.S. Eliot, David Jones and more recent poets. **Address:** School of English, The University, St. Andrews KY16 9AL, Scotland. **Online address:** mja4@st-andrews.ac.uk

ALEXANDER, (Robert) McNeill. British, b. 1934. **Genres:** Zoology. **Career:** University College of North Wales, Bangor, assistant lecturer, 1958-61, lecturer, 1961-68, sr. lecturer, 1968-69; University of Leeds, professor of zoology, 1969-99. **Publications:** Functional Design in Fishes, 1967, 3rd ed., 1974; Animal Mechanics, 1968; Size and Shape, 1971; The Chordates, 1975; Biomechanics, 1975; (with G. Goldspink) Mechanics and Energetics of Animal Locomotion, 1977; The Invertebrates, 1979; Locomotion of Animals, 1981; Optima for Animals, 1982; Elastic Mechanisms in Animal Movement, 1988; Dynamics of Dinosaurs, 1989; Animals, 1990; Exploring Biomechanics, 1992; The Human Machine, 1992; Bones, 1994; Energy for Animal Life, 1999; Locomotion of Animals, 2003. **Address:** School of Biology, University of Leeds, Leeds LS2 9JT, England.

ALEXANDER, Meena. American (born India), b. 1951. **Genres:** Novels, Plays/Screenplays, Poetry, Literary criticism and history, Autobiography/Memoirs. **Career:** University of Khartoum, tutor in English, 1969; lecturer in English, University of Delhi, 1974, and Central Institute of English and Foreign Languages, Hyderabad, 1975-77; Jawaharlal Nehru University New

Delhi, CSIR fellow, 1975; University of Hyderabad, lecturer, 1977-79, reader, 1979 ; Sorbonne, Paris, visiting fellow, 1979; Fordham University, Bronx, NY, assistant professor of English, 1980-87; University of Minnesota, Minneapolis, visiting assistant professor, 1981; Hunter College and the Graduate Center, City University of New York, assistant professor, 1987-89, associate professor, 1989-91, professor of English, 1992-, professor of creative writing, 1993-, distinguished professor of English, 1999-. Visiting University Grants Commission Fellow, English Institute, University of Kerala, Trivandrum, 1987; Columbia University, NYC, writer-in-residence, Center for American Culture Studies, 1988, lecturer in poetry, 1991-; American College, Madurai, poet in residence, 1994; Arts Council of England, international writer in residence, 1995; Asian American Renaissance, Lila Wallace writer in residence, 1995. **Publications:** POETRY: The Bird's Bright Wing, 1976; I Root My Name, 1977; Without Place, 1978; Stone Roots, 1980; House of a Thousand Doors, 1988; The Storm, 1989; Night-Scene, The Garden, 1992; The Shock of Arrival (and essays), 1996; River and Bridge, 1996. OTHER: In the Middle Earth (play), 1977; The Poetic Self: Towards a Phenomenology of Romanticism, 1979; Women in Romanticism: Mary Wollstonecraft, Dorothy Wordsworth, and Mary Shelley, 1989; Nampally Road (novel), 1991; Fault Lines (memoir), 1993, rev. ed., 2003; Manhattan Music (novel), 1997; Illiterate Heart, 2002; Raw Silk, 2004; (ed.) Indian Love Poems, 2005. **Address:** Dept of English, Hunter College, City University of New York, 695 Park Ave, New York, NY 10021, U.S.A. **Online address:** malexander@gc.cuny.edu

ALEXANDER, Peter F. Australian (born Republic of South Africa), b. 1949. **Genres:** Literary criticism and history, Biography. **Career:** University of New South Wales, Kensington, lecturer, 1978-83, senior lecturer, 1983-88, associate professor of English, 1989-95, professor of English, 1996-; writer. Cambridge University, visiting fellowship at Clare Hall, 1990-91, distinguished visiting scholar at Christ's College, 2003-04; Duke University, visiting professor, 1996; Princeton University, visiting fellow, Summer 1996; Australian Academy of the Humanities, fellow. **Publications:** Roy Campbell: A Critical Biography, 1982; William Plomer (biography), 1989; Leonard and Virginia Woolf: A Literary Partnership, 1992; Alan Paton, 1994; Les Murray: A Life in Progress, 2000. EDITOR: The Selected Poems of Roy Campbell, 1982; (with M. Chapman and M. Leveson) The Collected Works of Roy Campbell, Vol. 1, 1986, Vol. 2, 1987, Vol. 3, 1988, Vol. 4, 1989. Author of articles in periodicals and professional journals. **Address:** English Dept., University of South Wales, Sydney 2052, Australia.

ALEXANDER, Robert J(ackson). American, b. 1918. **Genres:** Economics, History, International relations/Current affairs, Politics/Government, Biography. **Career:** Professor Emeritus of Economics and Political Science, Rutgers University, New Brunswick, NJ, 1989- (Instructor, 1947-50; Assistant Professor, 1950-56; Associate Professor, 1956-61; Professor, 1961-89). Assistant Economist, Board of Economic Warfare, 1942, Office of Inter-American Affairs, Washington, DC, 1945-46. **Publications:** The Peron Era, 1951; Communism in Latin America, 1957; The Bolivian National Revolution, 1958; (with C.O. Porter) The Struggle for Democracy in Latin America, 1961; A Primer of Economic Development, 1962; Prophets of the Revolution, 1962; Labor Relations in Argentina, Brazil and Chile, 1962; Today's Latin America, 1962; Latin America, 1964; The Venezuelan Democratic Revolution, 1964; Organized Labor in Latin America, 1965; Latin American Politics and Government, 1965; An Introduction to Argentina, 1969; The Communist Party of Venezuela, 1969; Trotskyism in Latin America, 1973; Latin American Political Parties, 1973; Aprismo: The Ideas and Doctrines of Victor Raul Haya de la Tore, 1973; Agrarian Reform in Latin America, 1974; Three Alexander Families of Wayne County, Ohio, 1975; A New Development Strategy, 1976; Arturo Alessandri: A Biography, 1977; The Tragedy of Chile, 1978; Juan Peron: A History, 1979; The Right Opposition, 1981; Romulo Betancourt and the Transformation of Venezuela, 1981; Bolivia: Past, Present and Future of Its Politics, 1982; Venezuela's Voice for Democracy, 1990; International Trotskyism, 1929-1985, 1991; Juscelino Kubitschek and the Development of Brazil, 1991; The ABC Presidents, 1992; The Bolivarian Presidents, 1994; Presidents of Central America, Mexico, Cuba and Hispaniola, 1995; Presidents, Prime Ministers and Governors of the English Speaking West Indies and Puerto Rico, 1997; The Anarchists in the Spanish Civil War, 1999; International Maoism in the Developing World, 1999. EDITOR: Political Parties of the Americas, 1982; Biographical Dictionary of Latin American and Caribbean Political Leaders, 1988. **Address:** 944 River Rd, Piscataway, NJ 08854, U.S.A.

ALEXANDER, Ruth M. American, b. 1954. **Genres:** Women's studies and issues, History. **Career:** Colorado State University, Fort Collins, assistant professor, 1988-93, associate professor of history, 1993-, acting director of American Studies Program, 1993-94; professor of history and department chair, 1999-. **Publications:** The "Girl Problem": Female Sexual Delinquency in New York, 1900-1930, 1995; (ed. with M.B. Norton) Major Problems in American Women's History, 2nd ed, 1996. Contributor to books. Contributor of articles and reviews to periodicals. **Address:** Department of History, Colorado State University, Fort Collins, CO 80523, U.S.A.

ALEXANDER, Sally Hobart. American, b. 1943. **Genres:** Children's fiction, Autobiography/Memoirs. **Career:** Elementary school teacher in Long Beach, CA, 1965-69; Guild for the Blind, Pittsburgh, PA, teacher, 1969-70; St. Francis Hospital, Pittsburgh, child therapist, 1973-76. Western Pennsylvania School for Blind Children, consultant, 1976-77. **Publications:** Mom Can't See Me, 1990; Sarah's Surprise, 1990; Mom's Best Friend, 1992; Maggie's Whopper, 1992; Taking Hold: My Journey into Blindness (nonfiction), 1994; On My Own, 1997. **Address:** 5648 Marlborough Rd., Pittsburgh, PA 15217, U.S.A.

ALEXANDER, Shana. American, b. 1925. **Genres:** Social commentary, Women's studies and issues, Biography, Adult non-fiction, Communications/Media, Writing/Journalism, Autobiography/Memoirs, Documentaries/Reportage. **Career:** Member, New York State Council on the Arts, 1978-81; With PM Newspaper, 1944-49, Harper's Bazaar, 1946-47, Flair mag., 1950; Life Magazine, reporter, 1951-54, correspondent, 1954-61, staff writer, 1961-64, columnist, The Feminine Eye, 1964-69; editor, McCall's mag., NYC, 1969-71; Vice President, Norton Simon Inc, 1971-72; radio and TV commentator, Spectrum, CBS News, 1971-74; Columnist, Newsweek mag., 1972-75; Commentator, Sixty Minutes, CBS-TV, 1974-79. **Publications:** The Feminine Eye, 1970; Shana Alexander's State-by-State Guide to Women's Rights, 1975; Talking Woman, 1976; Anyone's Daughter, 1979; Very Much a Lady, 1983; Nutcracker, 1985; The Pizza Connection, 1988; When She Was Bad, 1990; Happy Days: My Mother, My Father, My Sister & Me, 1995; The Astonishing Elephant, 2000. **Address:** c/o Robert F. Levine, Levine, Thall, Plotkin and Menin, 1740 Broadway, New York, NY 10019, U.S.A.

ALEXANDER, Victoria N. American, b. 1965. **Genres:** Novels. **Career:** Hunter College, NYC, adjunct instructor and tutor, 1988-94; Dactyl Foundation for the Arts and Humanities, director, NYC, 1996-; writer. Worked as a stripper, c. 1991-93. **Publications:** NOVELS: Smoking Hopes, 1996; Naked Singularity, 2003. Contributor of short fiction and literary criticism to periodicals. **Address:** Dactyl Foundation, 64 Grand St, New York, NY 10013, U.S.A.

ALEXIE, Sherman (Joseph), (Jr.). American, b. 1966. **Genres:** Novels, Novellas/Short stories. **Career:** Writer. **Publications:** POETRY: I Would Steal Horses, 1992; The Business of Fancydancing, 1992; First Indian on the Moon, 1992; Old Shirts & New Skins, 1993; Water Flowing Home, 1994; Seven Mourning Songs for the Cedar Flute I Have Yet to Learn to Play, 1994; The Summer of Black Widows, 1996; The Man Who Loves Salmon, 1998; One Stick Song, 1999. NOVELS: Reservation Blues, 1995; Indian Killer, 1996. SHORT STORIES: The Ranger and Tonto Fistfight in Heaven, 1993; The Toughest Indian in the World, 2000; Ten Little Indians, 2003. OTHER: Smoke Signals (screenplay), 1998. **Address:** c/o Christy Cox, Falls Apart Productions, Inc, PMB 2294, 10002 Aurora Ave N #36, Seattle, WA 98133-9334, U.S.A. **Online address:** www.fallsapart.com

ALEXIS, Andre. Canadian (born Trinidad and Tobago), b. 1957. **Genres:** Novels, Novellas/Short stories. **Career:** Playwright, radio writer, poet, and writer of fiction. **Publications:** Despair and Other Stories of Ottawa, 1994; Childhood (novel), 1998. Author of stage and radio plays. **Address:** c/o McClelland & Stewart Inc., 481 University Ave., Toronto, ON, Canada M5G 2E9.

ALFEYEVA, Valeria. Russian. **Genres:** Autobiography/Memoirs. **Career:** Journalist and writer. **Publications:** Pilgrimage to Dzhvari: A Woman's Journey of Spiritual Awakening, 1989, trans. by S. and J. Robertson, 1992. **Address:** c/o Bell Tower, Harmony Books, 201 East 50th St., New York, NY 10022, U.S.A.

ALFINO, Mark (R.). American, b. 1959. **Genres:** Philosophy. **Career:** University of Kentucky, Lexington, instructor in philosophy, 1984-86; University of Texas at Austin, instructor in philosophy, 1987-88; Blinn College, Brenham, TX, instructor in philosophy, 1988; St. Edward's University, Austin, instructor in philosophy, 1989; Gonzaga University, Spokane, WA, assistant professor, 1989-95, associate professor of philosophy, 1995-. Lecturer at colleges and universities. **Publications:** (with L. Pierce) Information Ethics for Librarians, 1997; (ed., with R. Wynyard and J. Caputo, and contrib) McDonaldization Revisited: Critical Essays in Consumer Culture,

1998. Contributor to periodicals. **Address:** Department of Philosophy, Gonzaga University, Spokane, WA 99258, U.S.A. **Online address:** alfino@gonzaga.edu; alfino.org

ALFORD, B(ernard) W(illiam) E(rnest). British, b. 1937. **Genres:** Economics, History. **Career:** professor of economic and social history, 1982-, and chairman, School of History, 1990-, University of Bristol (assistant lecturer, 1962-64, lecturer, 1964-73, sr. lecturer, 1973-76, and reader, 1976-82). Treasurer, Economic History Society, 1988-. Assistant lecturer in economic history, London School of Economics, 1961-62; member, Lord Chancellor's Advisory Committee on the Public Records, 1989-94; member, Research Grants Board, 1989-93. **Publications:** (with T.C. Barker) A History of the Carpenters' Company, 1968; Depression and Recovery? British Economic Growth 1918-1939, 1972; W.D. & H.O. Wills and the Development of the U.K. Tobacco Industry 1786-1965, 1973; British Economic Performance, 1945-75, 1988; (with R. Lowe and N. Rollings) Economic Planning in Britain, 1943-1951, 1992; Britain in the World Economy since 1880, 1995. **Address:** 13-15 Woodland Rd, Clifton, Bristol BS8 1TB, England. **Online address:** B.Alford@bristol.ac.uk

ALFORD, Edna. Canadian, b. 1947. **Genres:** Novellas/Short stories. **Career:** Writer. Has worked as a psychotherapist. Founder and co-editor of Dandelion (literary magazine), with Joan Clark, 1974-80. Writer-inresidence, Regina Public Library, 1985-86. **Publications:** A Sleep Full of Dreams (short stories), 1981; The Garden of Eloise Loon (short stories), 1986; (ed. with C. Harris) Kitchen Talk: Contemporary Women's Prose and Poetry, 1992. Contributor of stories to anthologies and journals. Alford's stories have been broadcast on CBC radio. **Address:** Box 179, Livelong, SK, Canada S0M 1J0.

ALFORD, Jeffrey. American. **Genres:** Food and Wine. **Career:** Writer. Cook and baker; partner with wife, Naomi Duguid, in Asia Access, a photography, journalism, and slide presentation business, Toronto, Ontario, Canada. **Publications:** WITH N. DUGUID: Flatbreads and Flavors: A Baker's Atlas, 1995; Seductions of Rice, 1998. Contributor of articles and/or photographs to periodicals. **Address:** Asia Access, 64 Henry St., Toronto, ON, Canada M5T 1X2. **Online address:** asiaaccess@sympatico.ca

ALFORD, Kenneth D. American, b. 1939. **Genres:** Military/Defense/Arms control. **Career:** Worked at the Signet Bank in Richmond, VA, 1958-94; author. **Publications:** The Spoils of World War II: The American Military's Role in Stealing Europe's Treasures, 1994; Great Treasure Stories of World War II, 2000. **Address:** 8711 Huguenot Rd, Richmond, VA 23235, U.S.A.

ALGEO, John. American, b. 1930. **Genres:** Language/Linguistics. **Career:** Professor Emeritus, University of Georgia, Athens, 1994- (member of faculty 1971-94; Head of the Dept., 1975-79; Alumni Foundation Distinguished Professor of English). Assistant Professor, Professor, and Assistant Dean of Graduate School, University of Florida, 1961-71. Editor, American Speech mag., 1971-81; National President, Theosophical Society in America, 1993-2002; International Vice President, Theosophical Society, 2002-; Editor, Quest mag. 1995-. **Publications:** Problems in the Origins and Development of the English Language, 1966, rev. ed., 2004; (with T. Pyles) English: An Introduction to Language, 1970; On Defining the Proper Name, 1973; Exercises in Contemporary English, 1974; (with T. Pyles) Origins and Development of the English Language, 1982, rev. ed., 2004; Reincarnation Explored, 1987; Fifty Years among the New Words, 1991; (with S.J. Nicholson) The Power of Thought, 2001; Unlocking the Door, 2001. EDITOR: T. Pyles: Selected Essays on English Usage, 1979; (assoc.) The Oxford Companion to the English Language, 1992; Cambridge History of the English Language, vol. 6: English in North America, 2001; The Letters of H.P. Blavatsky, vol. 1, 2003. **Address:** PO Box 80206, Athens, GA 30608-0206, U.S.A. **Online address:** JohnAlgeo@aol.com

ALI, Shahrazad. American, b. 1947. **Genres:** Human relations/Parenting, Self help. **Career:** Editor: Cincinnati Enquirer, OH, contributing editor, 1965-67; Cincinnati Call Newspaper, news and feature editor, 1966-67; Cincinnati Post, news and feature editor, 1966-67; Cincinnati Herald, editor, 1966-67; affiliated with Cincinnati Hi-Lites Magazine, 1967-75; medical transcriptionist, 1977-83; Clark College, Atlanta, GA, assistant to vice president, 1983-85; Civilized Publications, Atlanta, founder, 1985; Ali's Unlimited Accessories, executive assistant, 1986-89; Temple University, Philadelphia, PA, PASCEP Program for Independent Publishing, teacher, 1989. Nutritionist; free-lance writer. **Publications:** How Not to Eat Pork: Or Life without the Pig, 1985; The Blackman's Guide to Understanding the Blackwoman, 1990; The Blackwoman's Guide to Understanding the Blackman, 1992; Are You Still a Slave?, 1994; Things Your Parents Should Have Told You, 1998; Day by Day, 1996; Urban Survival for the Year 2000, 1999; How to Tell if Your Man Is Gay or Bisexual, 2003. VIDEO: Blackman's Guide on Tour, 1992. **Address:** Civilized Publications, 2026 S 7th St, Philadelphia, PA 19148-2439, U.S.A. **Online address:** civpub2003@yahoo.com

ALIBER, Robert Z(elwin). American, b. 1930. **Genres:** Money/Finance. **Career:** Professor of International Economics and Finance, and Director, Center for Studies in International Finance, Graduate School of Business, University of Chicago. Staff Economist, Commission on Money and Credit, 1959-61, and Committee for Economic Development, 1961-64; Sr. Economic Adviser, Agency for Intl. Development, U.S. Dept. of State, 1964-65. **Publications:** (ed and contrib.) National Monetary Policies and the International Financial System, 1974; International Money Game, 1979, 3rd ed., 2001; Exchange Risk and Corporate International Finance, 1979; (co-author) Money, Banking and Economic Activity, 1981, 3rd ed., 1990; Your Money and Your Life, 1982; Handbook of International Finance and Management, 1990; Readings in International Business, 1993; The Multinational Paradigm, 1993. **Address:** Graduate School of Business, University of Chicago, 5801 S Blis Ave, Chicago, IL 60637, U.S.A.

ALIKI. (Aliki Brandenberg). American, b. 1929. **Genres:** Children's fiction, Children's non-fiction, Illustrations. **Publications:** The Story of William Tell, 1961; The Wish Workers, 1962; My Five Senses, 1962; My Hands, 1962; The Story of Johnny Appleseed, 1963; The Story of William Penn, 1964; George and the Cherry Tree, 1964; A Weed Is a Flower, 1965; Keep Your Mouth Closed, Dear, 1966; Three Gold Pieces, 1967, New Year's Day, 1967; Hush Little Baby: A Folk Lullaby, 1968; Diogenes, 1969; The Eggs, 1969; My Visit to the Dinosaurs, 1969; Fossils Tell of Long Ago, 1972; June 7!, 1972; The Long Lost Coelacanth and Other Living Fossils, 1973; Go Tell Aunt Rhody, 1974; Green Grass and White Milk, 1974; At Mary Bloom's 1976; Corn Is Maize: The Gift of the Indians, 1976; The Many Lives of Benjamin Franklin, 1977; Wild and Wooly Mammoths, 1977; The Twelve Months, 1978; Mummies Made in Egypt, 1979; The Two of Them, 1979; Digging Up Dinosaurs, 1981; We Are Best Friends, 1982; Use Your Head, Dear, 1983; A Medieval Feast, 1983; Feelings, 1984; Dinosaurs Are Different, 1985; Jack and Jake, 1986; How a Book is Made, 1986; Overnight at Mary Bloom's, 1987; Welcome Little Baby, 1987; Dinosaur Bones, 1988; King's Day: Louis XIV of France, 1989; My Feet, 1990; Manners, 1990; Christmas Tree Memories, 1991; I'm Growing!, 1992; Milk: From Cow to Carton, 1992; Communication, 1993; My Visit to the Aquarium, 1993; Gods and Goddesses of Olympus, 1994; Tabby: A Story in Pictures, 1995; Best Friends Together Again, 1995; Hello!, Goodbye!, 1996; Those Summers, 1997; My Visit to the Zoo, 1997; Marianthe's Story: Painted Words, Spoken Memories, 1998; William Shakespeare and the Globe, 1999; All by Myself!, 2000; One Little Spoonful, 2000; Ah, Music!, 2003; A Play's the Thing, 2005. Illustrator of books by F. Brandenberg, H. Clare, M.K. Phelan, P. Showers, etc. **Address:** 17 Regent's Park Terrace, London NW1 7ED, England.

ALINDER, Mary Street. American, b. 1946. **Genres:** Photography, Biography. **Career:** The Weston Gallery, Carmel, CA, manager, 1978-79; executive editor and assistant to photographer Ansel Adams, Carmel, 1979-84; Ansel Adams Publishing Rights Trust, Carmel, executive editor and business manager, 1984-87; independent scholar specializing in photography, 1988-; Alinder Gallery, Gualala, CA, co-owner, 1990-; author. Lecturer on Ansel Adams's photography; contributor as food critic: Coast Magazine, 1993-98; bizTravel.com, 1997-98. **Publications:** Ansel Adams: The Eightieth Birthday Retrospective, 1982; (with Ansel Adams) Ansel Adams: An Autobiography, 1985; (ed. with Andrea Gray Stillman) Ansel Adams: Letters and Images, 1916-1984, 1988; Seeing Straight: The Group f/64 Revolution, 1992; Ansel Adams: A Biography, 1996. Contributor to books. **Address:** The Alinder Gallery, PO Box 1146, Gualala, CA 95445, U.S.A. **Online address:** alinders@mcn.org

ALKALI, Zaynab. Nigerian. **Genres:** Novels, Novellas/Short stories, Literary criticism and history. **Career:** Nasarawa State University, Keffi, associate prefessor. **Publications:** NOVELS: The Stillborn, 1984; The Virtuous Woman, 1987. OTHER: (ed with A. Imfeld) Vultures in the Air: Voices from Northern Nigeria (stories), 1995; Cobwebs & Other Stories, 1997. **Address:** Dept of English, Nasarawa State University, Keffi, PMB 1022, Keffi, Nasarawa State, Nigeria.

ALKIVIADES, Alkis. Also writes as Luke Sharp. British (born Cyprus), b. 1953. **Genres:** Science fiction/Fantasy, Information science/Computers. **Career:** Civil Service Commission, executive officer, 1977-79; Kilburn Skills College, lecturer, 1979-85; London Software Studio, London, England, graphic designer, 1985-87; freelance writer, 1987-91; MicroProse Software

Ltd., copywriter, 1991-92, communications manager, 1992-95, product information manager, 1995-99; The Write Stuff, managing director, 1999-. **Publications:** The Sports Game, 1985; Star Strider, 1986; Daggers of Darkness, 1988; Dotto and the Pharaoh's Mask: An Interactive Connect-the-Dots Adventure, 1997; Dotto and the Minotaur's Maze: An Interactive Connect-the-Dots Adventure, 1998. AS LUKE SHARP (with S. Jackson, I. Livingstone, and R. Nicholson) Steve Jackson and Ian Livingstone Present Chasms of Malice, 1987; Steve Jackson and Ian Livingstone Present Fangs of Fury, 1989. **Address:** Anchor Cottage, Brownshill, Stroud, Glos. GL6 8AG, England. **Online address:** aalkivia@aol.com

ALKON, Paul K. American. **Genres:** Literary criticism and history. **Career:** University of California, Berkeley, instructor to assistant professor of English, 1962-70; University of Maryland at College Park, associate professor of English, 1970-71; University of Minnesota-Twin Cities, Minneapolis, associate professor, 1971-73; professor of English, 1973-80; University of Southern California, Los Angeles, Leo S. Bing Professor of English, 1980-. Ben Gurion University of the Negev, visiting professor, 1977-78. **Publications:** Samuel Johnson and Moral Discipline, 1967; Defoe and Fictional Time, 1979; Origins of Futuristic Fiction, 1987; Science Fiction before 1900, 1994. Contributor to books. Contributor of articles and reviews to scholarly journals. **Address:** Department of English, University of Southern California, Los Angeles, CA 90089-0354, U.S.A. **Online address:** Alkon@usc.edu

ALLABY, (John) Michael. British, b. 1933. **Genres:** Environmental sciences/Ecology, Meteorology/Atmospheric sciences. **Career:** Freelance writer, 1973-. Drama Student, then Actor, 1954-64; Editorial Dept. of the Soil Association, 1964-72; Associate Ed., 1970-72, and Managing Ed., 1972-73, Ecologist mag. **Publications:** The Eco-Activists, 1971; Who Will Eat?, 1972; (with F. Allen) Robots behind the Plow, 1974; Ecology, 1975; (with others) The Survival Handbook, 1975; Inventing Tomorrow, 1975; (with C. Tudge) Home Farm, 1977; World Food Resources, Actual and Potential, 1977; Wildlife of North America, 1979; Animals That Hunt, 1979; Making and Managing a Smallholding, 1979; (with D. Baldock and C. Blythe) Food Policy and Self Sufficiency, 1979; (with P. Bunyard) The Politics of Self Sufficiency, 1980; A Year in the Life of a Field, 1980; (with P. Crawford) The Curious Cat, 1982; Animal Artisans, 1982; (with J. Lovelock) The Great Extinction, 1983; (with J. Lovelock) The Greening of Mars, 1984; The Food Chain, 1984; 2040, 1985; (with J. Burton) Nine Lives, 1985; The Woodland Trust Book of British Woodlands, 1986; Ecology Facts, 1986, 2nd ed. as Green Facts, 1989; (with J. Burton) Dog's Life, 1986; The Ordnance Survey Outdoor Handbook, 1987; (with J. Burton) A Pony's Tale, 1987; Conservation at Home, 1988; Guide to Gaia, 1989; Thinking Green, 1989; (with A. Allaby) The Concise Oxford Dictionary of Earth Sciences, 1990; Living in the Greenhouse, 1990; Into Harmony with the Planet, 1990; The Concise Oxford Dictionary of Zoology, 1991; Elements: Air, 1992, Water, 1992, Earth, 1993, Fire, 1993; The Concise Oxford Dictionary of Botany, 1992; The Concise Oxford Dictionary of Ecology, 1994; How the Weather Works, 1995; Facing the Future, 1995; (with N. Curtis) Planet Earth, 1995; How It Works: The Environment, 1996; (with M. Kent) Collins Pocket Reference Biology, 1996; Basics of Environmental Science, 1996; Dangerous Weather, 6 vols., 1997-98; Ecosystem: Temperate Forests, 1999, Deserts, 2001; Biomes of the World, 9 vols., 2000; DK Guide to Weather, 2000; Plants and Plant Life, 5 vols., 2000; Encyclopedia of Weather and Climate, 2 vols., 2001; How It Works: The World's Weather, 2002; Facts on File Weather and Climate Handbook, 2002. EDITOR: A Dictionary of the Environment, 1977; The Oxford Dictionary of Natural History, 1986. **Address:** Braehead Cottage, Tighnabruaich, Argyll PA21 2ED, Scotland. **Online address:** mike_allaby@compuserve.com

ALLAHAR, Anton L. Trinidadian, b. 1949. **Genres:** History, Local history/Rural topics. **Career:** University of Toronto, Ontario, assistant professor, 1981-84; University of Western Ontario, London, assistant professor of sociology, 1994-89, associate professor of sociology, 1989-95, professor of sociology, 1996-, member of Centre for Interdisciplinary Historical Studies and Political Economy Research Group. Has lectured and given conference papers at colleges and universities. **Publications:** The Sugar Planters of Colonial Cuba, 1982; Sociology and the Periphery: Theories and Issues, 1989, rev. ed., 1995; Class, Politics, and Sugar in Colonial Cuba, 1990; (with J.E. Cote) Generation on Hold: Coming of Age in Advanced Industrial Society, 1994; (with J.E. Cote) Richer and Poorer: The Structure of Inequality in Canada, 1998. EDITOR: (with R.G. Cecil) Is There Life after Debt?, 1993; Caribbean Charisma: Reelections on Leadership, Legitimacy and Populist Politics, 2001. Contributor to books. Contributor to scholarly journals. **Address:** Department of Sociology, Social Science Center, University of Western Ontario, London, ON, Canada N6A 5C2.

ALLAN, Adrian R. British. **Genres:** Librarianship. **Career:** University of Liverpool, Liverpool, England, university archivist. **Publications:** University

Bodies: A Survey of Inter- and Supra-University Bodies and Their Records, 1990; (ed. with A.L. Mackenzie) Redbrick University Revisited: The Autobiography of Bruce Truscot, 1996. Contributor to periodicals. **Address:** Sydney Jones Library, University of Liverpool, PO Box 123, Liverpool L69 3DA, England. **Online address:** ara@liv.ac.uk

ALLAN, David. British, b. 1964. **Genres:** History. **Career:** University of Lancaster, Bailrigg, England, administrator, 1990-95, lecturer in history and independent studies, 1995-, vice-principal of Pendle College, 1994-. **Publications:** Virtue, Learning, and the Scottish Enlightenment: Ideas of Scholarship in Early Modern History, 1993. **Address:** Department of History, University of Lancaster, Bailrigg LA1 4YG, England.

ALLAN, Keith. British/Australian, b. 1943. **Genres:** Language/Linguistics. **Career:** Monash University, Clayton, Australia, professor of linguistics, 1978-. **Publications:** Linguistic Meaning, 1986; (with K. Burridge) Euphemism and Dysphemism: Language Used as Shield and Weapon, 1991; Natural Language Semantics, 2001. Contributor to language and linguistic journals. **Address:** Linguistics Program, LCL, Menzies Bldg, Monash University, Clayton, VIC 3800, Australia. **Online address:** www.arts.monash. edu.au/ling/ka.html

ALLAN, Robin. British (born Malawi), b. 1934. **Genres:** Children's fiction, Film. **Career:** Artistic Director, InterTheatre, since 1987. Typographical Designer, Eyre and Spottiswoode Ltd., London, 1957-60; Lecturer in English, Kuwait, 1961-65, Television Officer in Malta, 1965-67, and Iran, 1967-70, Assistant Director, Educational Aids Dept., London, 1970-71, all for British Council; Lecturer in Drama, Basingstoke Technical College, 1972-73; Lecturer in Drama and Film, College of Adult Education, Manchester, 1973-87. President, International Theatre of Teheran, Iran, 1969-70; Chairman, Green Room Theatre, Manchester, 1975-77. **Publications:** Come Into My Castle, 1964; Beyond the Blue Mountains, 1979; Walt Disney and Europe, 1999. Contributor to books. **Address:** 10 Dale Rd, New Mills, High Peak, Derbyshire SK22 4NW, England. **Online address:** robinallan@intertheatre. ndo.co.uk

ALLASON, Rupert (William Simon). Also writes as Nigel West. British, b. 1951. **Genres:** Criminology/True Crime, History, International relations/Current affairs. **Career:** Special constable, 1975-82; British Broadcasting Corporation, London, England, journalist, 1978-82; Intelligence Quarterly, European editor, 1985-; Conservative member of Parliament representing Torbay, Devon, England, 1987-97. **Publications:** NONFICTION: The Branch: A History of the Metropolitan Police Special Branch, 1883-1983, 1983. FICTION: The Blue List, 1989; Cuban Bluff, 1991; Murder in the Commons, 1992; Murder in the Lords, 1994; Murder in the Cabinet, 1998. NONFICTION AS NIGEL WEST: (with R. Deacon) Spy!, 1980; MI5: British Security Service Operations 1909-1945, 1981; A Matter of Trust: MI5 1945-1972, 1982; MI6: British Secret Intelligence Service Operations 1909-1945, 1983; The Circus: MI5 Operations 1945-1972, 1983; Unreliable Witness, 1984; A Thread of Deceit, 1985; (with J. Pujol) Operation Garbo, 1985; GCHQ: The Secret Wireless War, 1900-1986, 1986; Molehunt, 1987; The Friends, 1988; The SIGINT Secrets: The Signals Intelligence War, 1900 to Today: Including the Persecution of Gordon Welchman, 1988; Games of Intelligence: The Classified Conflict of International Espionage, 1989; Seven Spies Who Changed the World, 1991; Secret War: The Story of SOE, 1992; The Illegals, 1993; The Secret War for the Falklands, 1997; Counterfeit Spies, 1998; (with O. Tsarev) The Crown Jewels: The British Secrets at the Heart of the KGB Archives, 1998; Venona, 1998; The Third Secret, 1999. EDITOR: The Faber Book of Espionage, 1993; The Faber Book of Treachery, 1995. Contributor to periodicals. **Address:** PO Box 2, Goring on Thames, Berks. RG8 9SB, England. **Online address:** nigel@westintel.co.uk

ALLCORN, Seth. American, b. 1946. **Genres:** Business/Trade/Industry, Medicine/Health. **Career:** University of Missouri-Columbia, internal auditor, 1972-75, administrative manager in Department of Medicine, 1975-87; University of Rochester, Rochester, NY, program administrator for Medicine Service and administrator of Department of Medicine, both 1987-90; Loyola University of Chicago, Chicago, IL, associate dean for fiscal affairs, Stritch School of Medicine, 1990-95; DYAD Mgt and Organizational Consulting Co., principal, 1995-. **Publications:** Internal Auditing for Hospitals, 1979; Workplace Superstars in Resistant Organizations, 1991; Codependency in the Workplace, 1992; (with T.S. Wirth) Creating New Hospital-Physician Collaboration, 1993; Anger in the Workplace, 1994; Working Together: Building Integrated Healthcare Organization through Improved Executive/Physician Collaboration, 1995; (with others) The Human Costs of a Management Failure: Organizational Downsizing at General Hospital, 1996; (with M. Diamond) Managing People during Stressful Times: The Psychologically

Defensive Workplace, 1997; Death of the Spirit in the American Workplace, 2002; The Dynamic Workplace: Present Structure and Future Redesign, 2003. Work represented in anthologies. **Address:** 39 Woodcrest Rd, Asheville, NC 28804, U.S.A. **Online address:** sethallcorn@msn.com

ALLEGRETTO, Michael. American, b. 1944. **Genres:** Mystery/Crime/Suspense. **Publications:** JACOB LOMAX MYSTERY NOVELS: Death on the Rocks, 1987; Blood Stone, 1988; The Dead of Winter, 1989; Blood Relative, 1992; Grave Doubt, 1995. OTHER THRILLER/MYSTERY NOVELS: Night of Reunion, 1990; The Watchmen, 1991; The Suitor, 1993; Shadow House, 1994. **Address:** c/o Dominick Abel Literary Agency, 146 W 82nd St Apt 1B, New York, NY 10024, U.S.A.

ALLEN, Alex B. See **HEIDE, Florence Parry.**

ALLEN, Barry. American/Canadian, b. 1957. **Genres:** Philosophy. **Career:** University of Chicago, IL, lecturer in philosophy, 1984-86; McMaster University, Hamilton, ON, Canada, professor of philosophy, 1986-. Common Knowledge, associate editor. **Publications:** Truth in Philosophy, 1993; Knowledge and Civilization, 2004. Work represented in books. Contributor to philosophy and interdisciplinary journals. **Address:** Department of Philosophy, McMaster University, Hamilton, ON, Canada L8S 4K1. **Online address:** bgallen@mcmaster.ca

ALLEN, Charlotte Vale. Also writes as Katharine Marlowe. Canadian, b. 1941. **Genres:** Novels. **Career:** Actress and singer, London, 1961-64, Toronto, 1964-66, and in the United States, 1966-70; full-time writer, 1974-. **Publications:** Hidden Meanings, 1976; Love Life, 1976; Sweeter Music, 1976; Another Kind of Magic, 1977; Becoming, 1977; Gentle Stranger, 1977; Mixed Emotions, 1977; Running Away, 1977; Gifts of Love, 1978; Julia's Sister, 1978; Meet Me in Time, 1978; Believing in Giants, 1978; Acts of Kindness, 1979; Moments of Meaning, 1979; Times of Triumph, 1979; Promises, 1980; Daddy's Girl (autobiography), 1980; The Marmalade Man (in paperback as Destinies), 1981; Intimate Friends, 1983; Pieces of Dreams, 1984; Matters of the Heart, 1985; Time/Steps, 1986; Illusions, 1987; Dream Train, 1988; Night Magic, 1989; Painted Lives, 1990; Leftover Dreams, 1992; Dreaming in Color, 1993; Somebody's Baby, 1995; Claudia's Shadow, 1996; Mood Indigo, 1998; Parting Gifts, 2001; Grace Notes, 2002; Fresh Air, 2003. AS KATHARINE MARLOWE: Hearts' Desires, 1991; Secrets, 1992; Nightfall, 1993. **Address:** 144 Rowayton Woods Dr, Norwalk, CT 06854, U.S.A. **Online address:** cvaleallen@earthlink.net; www.charlottevaleallen. com

ALLEN, Conrad. See **MILES, Keith.**

ALLEN, Craig M(itchell). American, b. 1954. **Genres:** Communications/Media. **Career:** Station KPTV, Portland, OR, reporter and anchor, 1976-78; KRDO-TV, Colorado Springs, CO, news director, 1981-82; KMGH-TV, Denver, CO, news manager, 1982-84; University of Alabama, Tuscaloosa, assistant professor of communications, 1989-91; Arizona State University, Tempe, associate professor of communications, 1991-. **Publications:** Eisenhower and the Mass Media, 1993; News Is People, 2001; The Global Media Revolution, 2001. Contributor to mass communications journals. **Address:** Walter Cronkite School of Journalism and Telecommunication, Arizona State University, Tempe, AZ 85287, U.S.A. **Online address:** craig.allen@asu.edu

ALLEN, Dean. American, b. 1950. **Genres:** Economics. **Career:** Interamerican Management Group, president and chief executive officer, 1974-99. **Publications:** Freedom 2000, 1999. **Address:** PO Box 1732, Forest City, NC 28043, U.S.A. **Online address:** dean@deanallen.com

ALLEN, Dick. American, b. 1939. **Genres:** Poetry, Literary criticism and history. **Career:** Full-time writer. Brown University, Providence, RI, Teaching Associate, 1962-64; Wright State University, Instructor in English and Creative Writing, 1964-68; University of Bridgeport, CT, Assistant Professor of Creative Writing and American Literature, 1968-72, Associate Professor, 1971-76, Director of Creative Writing, 1972-2001, Professor, 1976-2001, Dana Professor of English, 1979-2001, Charles A. Dana Professor Emeritus of English, 2001-. **Publications:** POETRY: Anon and Various Time Machine Poems, 1971; Regions with No Proper Names, 1975; Overnight in the Guest House of the Mystic, 1984; Flight and Pursuit, 1987; Ode to the Cold War: Poems New and Selected, 1997; The Day Before: New Poems, 2003. EDITOR/CO-EDITOR: Science Fiction: The Future, 1971, 1982; Detective Fiction: Crime and Compromise, 1974; Looking Ahead: The Vision of Science Fiction, 1975; Expansive Poetry: The New Formalism and the New Narrative, 1989. **Address:** 74 Fern Circle, Trumbull, CT 06611, U.S.A. **Online address:** rallen285@earthlink.net

ALLEN, Diogenes. American, b. 1932. **Genres:** Philosophy, Theology/Religion. **Career:** Clergyman. Windham Presbyterian Church, New Hampshire, Minister, 1958-61; York University, Toronto, Dept. of Philosophy, Assistant Professor, 1964-66, Associate Professor, 1966-67; Princeton Theological Seminary, NJ, Associate Professor, 1967-74, Professor, 1974-81, Stuart Professor of Philosophy, 1981-2002, Stuart Professor of Philosophy Emeritus, 2002-. **Publications:** (ed.) Leibniz' Theodicy, 1966; The Reasonableness of Faith, 1968; Finding Our Father, 1974, as The Path to Perfect Love, 1990; Between Two Worlds, 1977, new ed. as Temptation, 1986; Traces of God, 1981; Three Outsiders: Pascal, Kierkegaard, and Simone Weil, 1983; Mechanical Explanations and the Ultimate Origins of the Universe According to Leibniz, 1983; Philosophy for Understanding Theology, 1985; Love: Christian Romance, Marriage, Friendship, 1987; Christian Belief in a Postmodern World, 1989; Quest, 1990; The Path to Perfect Love, 1992; Primary Readings in Philosophy for Understanding Theology, 1992; (with E. Springsted) Spirit, Nature, and Community, 1994; Spiritual Theology, 1997; Steps along the Way, 2000. **Address:** 70 Lillie St, Princeton Jct, NJ 08550, U.S.A.

ALLEN, E. John B. American (born England), b. 1933. **Genres:** History, Sports/Fitness. **Career:** Plymouth State College, NH, assistant professor to professor of history, 1968-, now emeritus. **Publications:** Post and Courier Service in the Diplomacy of Early Modern Europe, 1972; Reflections of Berlin, 1984; Teaching and Technique: A History of Professional Ski Instruction, 1987, 2nd ed., 1987; From Skisport to Skiing: One Hundred Years of an American Sport, 1840-1940, 1993; New England Skiing 1870-1940, 1997; New Hampshire on Skis, 2002; (ed.) International Ski History Congress: Selected Papers, 2002; Le Ski en France 1840-1940, 2003. Work represented in books. Contributor of articles and reviews to periodicals. **Address:** PO Box 23, Rumney, NH 03266, U.S.A. **Online address:** jallen@mail.plymouth.edu

ALLEN, Edward (Hathaway). American, b. 1948. **Genres:** Novels. **Career:** Writer and educator. Worked in the 1970s and early 1980s as butcher, meat salesman, bartender, dishwasher, ranch hand, and truck driver; Mark Brothers Ltd., Goshen, NY, meat trimmer, 1974-76; Ottman and Co., NYC, butcher, 1976-78; Barry Packing Co., NYC, butcher and shipping clerk, 1978-79; Upstate Wholesale Meats, Congers, NY, butcher and truck driver, 1979-80; Suffern High School, substitute teacher, 1980-81; LHD Meats, Spring Valley, NY, butcher, 1982-84; Ohio University, Athens, OH, teaching assistant, 1984-89; Rhodes College, Memphis, TN, assistant professor, 1989-91; freelance writer, 1989-. **Publications:** NOVELS: Straight Through the Night, 1989; Mustang Sally, 1992. Contributor of short stories to periodicals. **Address:** 110 Forest Ave. Apt 303, Vermillion, SD 57069-3151, U.S.A.

ALLEN, Fergus. Irish (born England), b. 1921. **Genres:** Poetry. **Career:** Hydraulics Research Station, Wallingford, Oxfordshire, director, 1958-65; Cabinet Office, London, chief scientific officer, 1965-69; Civil Service Commission, London, civil service commissioner, 1969-74, first civil service commissioner, 1974-81. **Publications:** POETRY: The Brown Parrots of Providencia, 1993; Who Goes There?, 1996; Mrs Power Looks over the Bay, 1999. Author of poems, articles, and reviews published in literary magazines. **Address:** Dundrum, Wantage Rd, Streatley, Reading, Berks. RG8 9LB, England. **Online address:** fergusallen@btinternet.com

ALLEN, Jeffner. American, b. 1947. **Genres:** Gay and lesbian issues, Philosophy. **Career:** State University of New York at Binghamton, professor of philosophy and women's studies, 1987-. **Publications:** Lesbian Philosophy and Explorations, 1986; (co-editor) The Thinking Muse: Feminism and Recent French Thought, 1989; (ed.) Lesbian Philosophies and Cultures, 1991; reverberations across the shimmering CASCADAS, 1994; Sinuosities: Lesbian Poetic Politics, 1996. **Address:** Department of Philosophy, State University of New York at Binghamton, Binghamton, NY 13902, U.S.A.

ALLEN, John E(lliston). Also writes as Paul M. Danforth. British, b. 1921. **Genres:** Air/Space topics, Children's non-fiction, Design, Design, Education, Institutions/Organizations, Intellectual history, Local history/Rural topics, Military/Defense/Arms control, Technology, Transportation. **Career:** Scientific officer, Royal Aircraft Establishment, 1941-44; senior scientific officer, Marine Aircraft Experimental Establishment, 1944-50; principal scientific officer, Royal Aircraft Establishment, Farnborough, 1950-54; head of aerodynamics, Projects and Assessment Dept., A. V. Roe & Co., Ltd., Weapons Research Division, Manchester, 1954-63; deputy chief engineer, Advanced Projects Group, Hawker Siddeley Aviation, 1963-69; and chief future projects engineer, 1969-83, British Aerospace, Kingston upon Thames; visiting professor, Aerospace Design, College of Aeronautics Cranfield (UK); visiting professor, Kingston University (UK), 1999-. Consultant to Rolls-

Royce, Raychem, Ove Arup, BA Systems, 1997-, etc. Chairman, Working Party on Transport, Watt Committee on Energy Ltd. **Publications:** (as Paul M. Danforth) Transport Control, 1970; (co-ed.) The Future of Aeronautics, 1970; (co-author) Energy and Humanity; Aeronautics in a Finite World, 1974; (as Paul M. Danforth) The Channel Tunnel, 1974; Have Energy, Will Travel, 1977; Aerodynamics, 1982; Chambers Air and Space Dictionary, 1990; Chambers Bibliographic Dictionary, 1990; The Future of Aircraft Propulsion, 1992; The Motor Car in 2065 AD, 1993; (with E.M. Goodger) Transport Fuels Technology, 2000; Global Energy Issues Affecting Aeronautics Progress in Aerospace Sciences, 1999; Quest for a Novel Force: A Revolution in Aerospace, 2003. Contributor to professional journals. **Address:** The Gabriels, Angel Lane, Blythburgh, Suffolk IP19 9LU, England.

ALLEN, John Jay. American, b. 1932. **Genres:** Literary criticism and history. **Career:** Professor of Spanish, University of Kentucky, Lexington, since 1983. Assistant Professor, 1960-66, Associate Professor, 1966-72, and Professor of Spanish, 1972-83, University of Florida, Gainesville. **Publications:** Don Quixote: Hero or Fool?, 1969, part II, 1979; (ed.) Don Quijote de La Mancha, 1977; The Reconstruction of a Spanish Golden Age Playhouse: El Corral del Principe 1583-1744, 1983. **Address:** 1153 Stirling Dr, Danville, KY 40422, U.S.A.

ALLEN, Jonathan B(urgess). British, b. 1957. **Genres:** Children's fiction, Illustrations. **Career:** Children's book illustrator and writer. **Publications:** SELF-ILLUSTRATED FOR CHILDREN: Guthrie Comes Clean, 1984; My Cat, 1986; My Dog, 1987; Who's at the Door?, 1992; Keep Fit Canaries, 1993; Mucky Moose, 1990; Two by Two by Two, 1994; Sweetie, 1994; Chicken Licken, 1996; Fowl Play, 1996; Wake Up, Sleeping Beauty!, 1997; Wolf Academy, 1997; Jonathan Allen Picture Book, 1997; Flying Squad, 1998. WIZARD GRIMWEED SERIES: B.I.G. Trouble, 1993; Potion Commotion, 1993; The Funniest Man in the World, 1994; Nose Grows, 1994; The Witch Who Couldn't Spell, 1996; Dragon Dramatics, 1996. FRED CAT BOARD BOOKS SERIES: Dressing Up, 1997; My Noisy Toys, 1997; Weather and Me, 1997; What My Friends Say, 1997. JONATHAN ALLEN BOARD BOOKS SERIES: Purple Sock, Pink Sock, 1992; Big Owl, Little Towel, 1997; One with a Bun, 1997; Up the Steps, Down the Slide, 1997. POETRY: A Bad Case of Animal Nonsense, 1981; A Pocketful of Painful Puns and Poems, 1983. Illustrator of books by: D.H. Wilson, M. Mahy, F. O'Rourke, S. Wyllie, C. Mellor, R. Impey, B. Grossman. **Address:** Acorn Cottage, South Street, Lillington nr Royston, Herts. SG8 0QR, England.

ALLEN, Laura Jean. American. **Genres:** Children's fiction, Illustrations. **Career:** Writer and illustrator of books for children. Artist; fabric designer; creator of greeting cards. **Publications:** SELF-ILLUSTRATED FOR CHILDREN: A Fresh Look at Flowers, 1963; Mr. Jolly's Sidewalk Market: A Story Told in Pictures, 1963; Ottie and the Star, 1979; Rollo and Tweedy and the Case of the Missing Cheese, 1983. Where Is Freddy?, 1986; Rollo and Tweedy and the Ghost at Dougal Castle; The Witches Secret; The Secret Snow Country. Illustrator of books by J. Kofield, F. Allen.

ALLEN, Michael Patrick. American, b. 1945. **Genres:** Sociology. **Career:** Washington State University, Pullman, assistant professor, 1972-78, associate professor of sociology, 1978-. **Publications:** The Founding Fortunes: A New Anatomy of the Super-Rich Families in America, 1988; Understanding Regression Analysis, 1997. **Address:** Dept of Sociology, Wilson 204, Washington State University, Pullman, WA 99164-4020, U.S.A. **Online address:** allenm@wsu.edu

ALLEN, Myron B. American, b. 1954. **Genres:** Mathematics/Statistics. **Career:** University of Wyoming, Laramie, professor of mathematics, 1983-, associate vicepresident of university, 1999-. **Publications:** Numerical Analysis for Applied Science, 1997; three other books. Contributor to scientific journals. **Address:** Office of Academic Affairs, University of Wyoming, Laramie, WY 82071, U.S.A. **Online address:** allen@uwyo.edu

ALLEN, Nancy. American, b. 1938. **Genres:** Adult non-fiction. **Career:** North Kingstown School Department, RI, art teacher, 1964-69; Pine School, Stuart, FL, art teacher, 1971-73; boating journalist, 1973-78; real estate broker and salesperson, Stuart, FL, 1978-; nonfiction writer. **Publications:** Fair Seafarer: A Honeymoon Adventure with the Merchant Marine, 1997. Contributor to periodicals. **Address:** 1641 Binney Dr., Ft. Pierce, FL 34949, U.S.A. **Online address:** seafarer30@hotmail.com

ALLEN, Pamela (Kay). New Zealander, b. 1934. **Genres:** Children's fiction, Illustrations. **Career:** Art teacher, Pio Pio District High School, New Zealand, 1956, and Rangitoto College, Auckland, 1957-58, 1960-64; writer and illustrator, 1979-. **Publications:** SELF-ILLUSTRATED FOR CHIL-

DREN: Mr. Archimedes' Bath, 1980; Who Sank the Boat?, 1982; Bertie and the Bear, 1983; A Lion in the Night, 1985; Simon Said, 1985; Herbert and Harry, 1986, in US as Hidden Treasure, 1987; Mr. McGee, 1987; Fancy That!, 1988; Simon Did, 1988; Watch Me Now, 1988; I Wish I Had a Pirate Suit, 1989; My Cat Maisie, 1990; Black Dog, 1991; Belinda, 1992; Mr. McGee Goes to Sea, 1992; Alexander's Outing, 1993; Mr. McGee and the Blackberry Jam, 1993; Clippity Clop, 1994; Waddle Giggle Gargle!, 1996; The Bear's Lunch, 1997; Mr. McGee and the Biting Flea, 1998; The Pear in the Pear Tree, 1999; Mr McGee and the Perfect Nest, 2000; Inside Mary Elizabeth's House, 2000; Can You Keep a Secret?, 2001; Brown Bread and Honey, 2001; The Potato People, 2002; Daisy All-Sorts, 2002. Illustrator of books by J. Farr, T.E. Wilson, S. Fitzgerald, M. Vaughan, N. Antel. **Address:** c/o Curtis Brown Ltd., 27 Union St, Paddington, Sydney, NSW 2021, Australia.

ALLEN, Paula Gunn. American, b. 1939. **Genres:** Novellas/Short stories, Poetry, Children's non-fiction, Cultural/Ethnic topics, Intellectual history, Literary criticism and history, Mythology/Folklore, Third World, Women's studies and issues. **Career:** University of California, Los Angeles, Professor of English, now emeritus; University of California, Berkeley, formerly in Native American Studies. San Francisco State University, Native American Studies, Lecturer, and Dept. Chair; Lecturer, University of New Mexico, Albuquerque, and Fort Lewis College, Durango, CO. **Publications:** The Blind Lion (poetry), 1974; Coyote's Daylight Trip (poetry), 1978; A Cannon between My Knees (poetry), 1981; Shadow Country (poetry), 1982; The Woman Who Owned the Shadows (novel), 1983; Sacred Hoop: Recovering the Feminine in American Indian Traditions, 1986; Skins and Bones (poetry), 1988; Grandmother of the Light, Medicine Woman's Sourcebook 1990; (with P.C. Smith) As Long as the Rivers Flow, 1996; Off the Reservation, 1998. EDITOR: From the Center: A Folio of Native American Art and Poetry, 1981; Studies in American Indian Literature: Critical Essays and Course Designs, 1983; Spider Woman's Granddaughters: Traditional Tales and Contemporary Writing by Native American Women, 1990; The Voice of the Turtle: American Indian Literature 1900-1970, 1994; Song of the Turtle, 2001; Hozho: Walking in Beauty (short stories), 2001. **Address:** Department of English, Rolfe 222S, University of California, Los Angeles, Box 951530, Los Angeles, CA 90025-1530, U.S.A.

ALLEN, Philip M(ark). American, b. 1932. **Genres:** Travel/Exploration, Third World. **Career:** U.S. Department of State, Washington, DC, foreign service officer in Hamburg and Bonn, Germany, and Antananarivo, Madagascar, 1956-66; African-American Institute, NYC, regional representative for French-speaking Africa in Lagos, Nigeria, and Abidjan, Ivory Coast, and director of training and program development in NYC, 1966-70; University of Vermont, Burlington, associate professor of African studies, beginning in 1970; Johnson State College, Johnson, VT, associate professor of social science, until 1978, chairperson of Humanities Division, 1978-81, professor of humanities, 1986-87; Frostburg State University, Frostburg, MD, dean of arts and humanities, 1987-99, distinguished university professor, 1999-. Senior Fulbright lecturer, University of Dakar, 1981-82, University of Constantine, 1985-86, and University of Antananarivo, 1999-2000. Haiti Ministry of Agriculture, director of management training seminar, 1977-78. **Publications:** Self-Determination in the Western Indian Ocean, 1966; (with A. Segal) The Traveler's Africa, 1973; (ed. and author of introduction) Vermont and the Year 2000, 1972; (with J.M. Ostheimer) Africa and the Islands of the Western Indian Ocean, 1976; Security and Nationalism in the Indian Ocean: Lessons from the Latin Quarter Islands, 1987; Madagascar: Conflicts of Authority, 1995. Contributor to books. Contributor of articles, stories, and poems to periodicals. **Address:** Performing Arts Center 127, Frostburg State University, Frostburg, MD 21532, U.S.A. **Online address:** pallen@frostburg.edu

ALLEN, Roberta L. American, b. 1945. **Genres:** Novels, Novellas/Short stories, How-to books, Information science/Computers, Self help, Third World, Travel/Exploration, Women's studies and issues, Writing/Journalism, Autobiography/Memoirs. **Career:** Parsons School of Design, NYC, adjunct instructor in creative writing, 1986; Art Gallery of Western Australia, Perth, Australia, artist in residence, 1989; The Writer's Voice, adjunct instructor, 1992-97; New School for Social Research, adjunct instructor, 1993-; Department of Continuing Education, New York University, adjunct instructor, 1993-2000; Columbia University, School of the Arts, adjunct assistant professor, 1998-99; University of the South, Tennessee Williams Fellow, 1998. Works exhibited in solo shows at galleries and museums in cities worldwide. **Publications:** The Traveling Woman (short stories), 1986; The Daughter (novella in stories), 1992; Certain People (short stories), 1997; The Dreaming Girl (novel), 2000. NONFICTION: Amazon Dream (travel memoir), 1993; Fast Fiction, 1997; The Playful Way to Serious Writing, 2000; The Playful Way to Knowing Yourself, 2003. Work represented in anthologies. Contributor to periodicals. **Address:** c/o DeAnna Heindel, Gerorges Borchardt Inc Literary Agency, 136 E 57th St, New York, NY 10021, U.S.A. **Online address:** Roall@aol.com

ALLEN, Ronald J. American, b. 1948. **Genres:** Law. **Career:** University of Nebraska, visiting professor of law, 1973-74; State University of New York at Buffalo, assistant professor, 1974-77, associate professor of law, 1977-79; University of Iowa, Iowa City, visiting professor, 1978-79, professor of law, 1979-84; Northwestern University, School of Law, Chicago, IL, visiting professor, 1984, professor, 1984-, Stanford Clinton Jr. Research Professor, 1990-91, John Henry Wigmore Professor of Law, 1992-, fellow of Center for the Humanities, 1994-95. University of Michigan, visiting professor, 1982; Duke University, professor, 1983; Federal Judicial Center, lecturer, 1987; University of Adelaide, university distinguished visiting scholar, 1991; Marshall University, distinguished lecturer, 1991. **Publications:** Constitutional Criminal Procedure: An Examination of the Fourth, Fifth, and Sixth Amendments and Related Areas, 1985, 2nd ed. (with Kuhns), 1991, 3rd ed. (with Kuhns and Stuntz), 1995, teacher's manual, 1985, 2nd ed. (with Kuhns), 1991, 3rd ed. (with Kuhns and Stuntz), 1995; (with Kuhns) An Analytical Approach to Evidence: Text, Problems, and Cases, 1989, 2nd ed. (with Kuhns and Swift), 1997, teacher's manual, 1989, 2nd ed. (with Kuhns and Swift), 1996; (with Kuhns) Federal Rules of Evidence with Legislative History and Case Supplement, 1989, 2nd ed. (with Kuhns and Swift), 1996; (with Brander and Stulberg) Arthritis of the Hip and Knee: The Active Person's Guide to Taking Charge, 1998; The Nature of Juridical Proof, 1999; (with others) Criminal Procedure, 2001. Contributor to law books and to law journals. **Address:** School of Law, Northwestern University, 357 E Chicago Ave, Chicago, IL 60611, U.S.A. **Online address:** rjallen@northwestern.edu

ALLEN, Samuel W(ashington). Also writes as Paul Vesey. American, b. 1917. **Genres:** Poetry. **Career:** Professor Emeritus of English, Boston University, since 1981 (Professor of English and Afro-American Studies, 1971-81). Avalon Professor of Humanities, Tuskegee Institute, Alabama, 1968-70; Visiting Professor of English, Wesleyan University, Middletown, Conn., 1970-71. **Publications:** Ivory Tusks, 1956; Ivory Tusks and Other Poems, 1968; (co-ed.) Pan-Africanism Reconsidered, 1962 (ed.) Poems From Africa, 1973; Paul Vesey's Leger, 1975; Every Round, 1987. **Address:** 1155 N. Miranda St. Apt D7, Las Cruces, NM 88005-2065, U.S.A.

ALLEN, William Sheridan. American, b. 1932. **Genres:** History. **Career:** Professor of History, State University of New York, Buffalo, since 1970. Instructor, Bay City Jr. College, Michigan, 1957-58, and Massachusetts Institute of Technology, Cambridge, 1960-61; Assistant Professor University of Missouri, Columbia, 1961-67; Associate Professor, Wayne State University, Detroit, 1967-70. President, New York State Association of European Historians, 1983-84; State Univeristy of New York, History Dept, chair, 1987-90. **Publications:** The Nazi Seizure of Power, 1965, 1984; (ed. and trans.) The Infancy of Nazism, 1975. **Address:** 164 Woodward Ave, Buffalo, NY 14214, U.S.A.

ALLEN, Woody. American, b. 1935. **Genres:** Novels, Plays/Screenplays. **Career:** Comedian, actor, writer, and film director. Former staff writer for NBC. **Publications:** SCREENPLAYS: What's New, Pussycat, 1965; What's Up, Tigerlily, 1967; Take the Money and Run, 1969; Bananas, 1970; Everything You Always Wanted to Know about Sex but Were Afraid to Ask, 1972; Sleeper, 1974; Love and Death, 1975; Annie Hall, 1978; Interiors, 1978; Manhattan, 1979; Stardust Memories, 1980; A Midsummer Night's Sex Comedy, 1982; Zelig, 1983; Broadway Danny Rose, 1984; The Purple Rose of Cairo, 1985; Hannah and Her Sisters, 1986; Radio Days, 1987; September, 1988; Another Woman, 1988; Oedipus Wrecks, 1989; Crimes and Misdemeanors, 1989; Alice, 1990; Husbands and Wives, 1992; Shadow and Fog, 1992; Manhattan Murder Mystery, 1993; Bullets over Broadway, 1995; Mighty Aphrodite, 1995; Everyone Says I Love You, 1996; Deconstructing Harry, 1997; Small Time Crooks, 2000. PLAYS: Don't Drink the Water, 1967; Play It Again, Sam, 1969, screenplay, 1972; Getting Even, 1971; Death Defying Acts: 3 One-Act Comedies, 1995. OTHER: Without Feathers, 1975; Side Effects, 1980; The Floating Light Bulb, 1982; Woody Allen on Woody Allen, 1994. **Address:** c/o Jack Rollins, Rollins & Joffe, 1775 Broadway Ste 708, New York, NY 10019, U.S.A.

ALLENDE, Isabel. American (born Peru), b. 1942. **Genres:** Novels, Children's fiction. **Career:** United Nations Food and Agricultural Organization, Santiago, Chile, secretary, 1959-65; Paula magazine, Santiago, journalist, editor, and advice columnist, 1967-74; Mampato magazine, Santiago, journalist, 1969-74; television interviewer for Canal 13/Canal 7 (television station), 1970-75; worked on movie newsreels, 1973-75; El Nacional newspapers, Venezuela, journalist, 1975-84; Colegio Marroco, Caracas, Venezuela, administrator, 1981-2004; writer. Guest teacher at Montclair State College, NJ, spring, 1985, and University of Virginia, fall, 1988; Gildersleeve Lecturer, Barnard College, spring, 1988; teacher of creative writing, University of California, Berkeley, spring, 1989. **Publications:** Civilice a su troglodita: Los impertinentes de Isabel Allende (humor), 1974; La casa de los espiritus, 1982, trans by M. Bogin as The House of the Spirits, 1985; La gorda de porcelana (juvenile; title means: The Fat Porcelain Lady), 1984; De amor y de sombra, 1984, trans by M.S. Peden as Of Love and Shadows, 1987; Eva Luna, trans by Peden, 1988; Cuentos de Eva Luna, 1990, trans by Peden as The Stories of Eva Luna, 1991; El Plan infinito, trans by Peden as The Infinite Plan, 1993; Paula (autobiography), 1995; Afrodita: Recetas, cuentos y otros afrodisiacos, 1997, trans by Sayers Peden, as Aphrodite: A Memoir of the Senses, 1998; Daughter of Fortune, 1999; Portrait in Sepia, 2001; City of the Beasts, 2002; My Invented Country, 2003; Kingdom of the Golden Dragon, 2004. Author of several plays and stories for children. Contributor to books.

ALLEYNE, Mervyn C. Trinidadian, b. 1933. **Genres:** Anthropology/Ethnology, Language/Linguistics. **Career:** University of West Indies, Kingston, Jamaica, professor of sociolinguistics, 1960-2003; University of Puerto Rico, professor, 2003-. **Publications:** Les Noms des Vents en Gallo-Roman, 1962; Krio Language Training Manual, 1965; Comparative Afro-American: An Historical Comparative Study of English-Based Afro-American Dialects of the New World, 1980; Theoretical Issues in Caribbean Linguistics, 1984; Studies in Saramaccan Language Structure, 1987; The Roots of Jamaican Culture, 1988; Syntaxe Historique Creole, 1995; The Construction and Representation of Race and Ethnicity in the Caribbean and the World, 2002; The Folk Medicine of Jamaica, 2004. **Address:** Dept of English, College of Humanities, University of Puerto Rico, Rio Piedras, Puerto Rico 7. **Online address:** mcalleyne@lycos.com

ALLFREY, Anthony. British, b. 1930. **Genres:** History, Biography. **Career:** Historian and writer. **Publications:** Man of Arms: The Life and Legend of Sir Basil Zaharoff, Weidenfeld & Nicolson, 1989; Edward VII and His Jewish Court, Weidenfeld & Nicolson, 1991. **Address:** Santo Antonio, Casal Meirames, 2710 Varzea de Sintra, Portugal.

ALLGOOD, Myralyn F(rizzelle). American, b. 1939. **Genres:** Biography, Translations. **Career:** Samford University, Birmingham, AL, instructor, 1963-68, assistant professor, 1968-86, associate professor, 1986-89, professor of world languages and cultures, 1989-, chairperson of department, 1982-. Professor in residence with student study groups in Spain and Latin America. Alabama Commission on Higher Education Consortium for the Advancement of Foreign Languages, university representative, 1984-; oral proficiency tester (Spanish) for state, city, and regional organizations. **Publications:** (ed.) Another Way to Be: Selected Works of Rosario Castellanos in English Translation, University of Georgia Press, 1990; (ed.) Remembering Rosario, Scripta Humanistica, 1990. **Address:** Department of World Languages and Cultures, Samford University, 800 Lakeshore Dr., Birmingham, AL 35229-2298, U.S.A.

ALLIN, Lou. (born Canada), b. 1945. **Genres:** Mystery/Crime/Suspense. **Career:** Ohio State University, Columbus, lecturer in English, 1968-71; Cambrian College, Sudbury, Ontario, Canada, professor of English, 1977-. **Publications:** Northern Winters Are Murder, 2000; Blackflies Are Murder, 2002; Bush Poodles Are Murder, 2003. Additional works represented in anthologies. **Address:** 1903 West Bay Rd., Garson, ON, Canada P3L 1V3. **Online address:** murdereh@sympatico.ca

ALLINGTON, Maynard. American, b. 1931. **Genres:** Novels, Writing/Journalism. **Career:** U.S. Air Force, career officer, 1951-76, retiring as lieutenant colonel; novelist, 1976-. **Publications:** The Grey Wolf, 1986; The Fox in the Field, 1994; The Court of Blue Shadows, 1995. Contributor to periodicals and anthologies. **Address:** 336 Lake Victoria Cir., Melbourne, FL 32940, U.S.A.

ALLISON, Amy. American, b. 1956. **Genres:** Children's non-fiction. **Career:** Writer. Also works as copy editor, proofreader, and teacher. **Publications:** Machu Picchu, 1993; Shakespeare's Globe, 1999; Life in Ancient China, 2000; Roger Williams: Founder of Rhode Island, 2000; Antonio Banderas, 2001; John Leguizamo, 2001; Edwin Stanton: Secretary of War, 2001; Gargoyles on Guard, 2002; Luis Alvarez and the Bubble Chamber, 2002. Contributor of poetry to periodicals. **Address:** c/o Author Mail, Chelsea House Publishers, 1874 Sproul Rd. Suite 400, Broomall, PA 19008, U.S.A. **Online address:** tsotskelah@aol.com.

ALLISON, Henry E(dward). American, b. 1937. **Genres:** Philosophy. **Career:** State University of New York College at Potsdam, assistant professor of philosophy, 1964-65; Pennsylvania State University, State College, assistant professor of philosophy, 1965-68; University of Florida, Gainesville, associate professor, 1968-72, professor of philosophy, 1972-73; University of California, San Diego, La Jolla, professor of philosophy, 1973-, chairman of department, 1978-82. **Publications:** Lessing and the Enlightenment: His Philosophy of Religion and Its Relation to Eighteenth-Century Thought, 1966; (ed.) The Kant-Eberhard Controversy: An English Translation Together with Supplementary Materials, 1973; Benedict de Spinoza, 1975, rev. ed. as Benedict de Spinoza: An Introduction, 1987; Kant's Transcendental Idealism: An Interpretation and Defense, 1983; Kant's Theory of Freedom, 1990; Idealism and Freedom, 1996; Kant's Theory of Taste, 2001; (ed.) Kant, I: Theoretical Philosophy after 1781, 2002. **Address:** Department of Philosophy, Boston University, 745 Commonwealth Ave Rm 516, Boston, MA 02215, U.S.A.

ALLMAND, C. T. British. **Genres:** History. **Career:** Liverpool University, Liverpool, England, professor of medieval history. **Publications:** Henry V (pamphlet), 1968; Lancastrian Normandy, 1415-1450: The History of a Medieval Occupation, 1983; The Hundred Years War: England and France at War, c. 1300-c. 1450, 1988; Henry V, 1992. EDITOR: (and compiler) Society at War: The Experience of England and France during the Hundred Years War, 1973; War, Literature, and Politics in the Late Middle Ages: Essays in Honour of G.W. Coopland, 1976; (with C.A.J. Armstrong) English Suits before the "Parlement" of Paris 1420-1436, 1982. **Address:** University of Liverpool, Department of History, PO Box 147, Liverpool L69 3BX, England.

ALLRED, Alexandra Powe. Also writes as Alexandra Powe-Allred. German, b. 1965. **Genres:** Sports/Fitness, Recreation, Animals/Pets. **Career:** Writer. Member of the U.S. Women's Bobsled team, 1994-98; crew member for the U.S. Men's Olympic Bobsled team, 2002 Olympic Games. Board member; freelance writer for periodicals on parenting and fitness; has worked with science and sports summer camps for underprivileged children. **Publications:** (as Alexandra Powe-Allred) The Quiet Storm: A Celebration of Women in Sport, 1998, rev. ed., 'Atta Girl! A Celebration of Women in Sport, 2003; Entering the Mother Zone: Balancing Self, Health, and Family, 2000; Passion Rules! Inspiring Women in Business, 2001; Teaching Basic Obedience: Train the Owner, Train the Dog, 2001; Hummer, the Bee Who Couldn't Buzz, 2002; Your Outta Control Puppy, 2002; Atticus Weaver and His Triumphant Leap from Outcast to Hero and Back Again, 2002; The Code, 2002; Crossing the Line, 2003; Retold Middle Eastern Myths: Folktales for Children, 2003. Contributor to periodicals. **Address:** 4610 Whitehead Rd., Midlothian, TX 76065, U.S.A. **Online address:** alex@alexandrapoweallred.com

ALLSOBROOK, David Ian. Welsh, b. 1940. **Genres:** Education, Music. **Career:** High school teacher of history and music, 1963-70; Loughborough University, lecturer in education, 1970-72; Cardiff University, lecturer in history of education, 1972-. **Publications:** Schools for the Shires: The Reform of Middle-Class Education in Mid-Victorian England, 1986; Liszt: My Travelling Circus Life, 1991; Music for Wales: Walford Davies and the National Council of Music, 1918-41, 1992. **Address:** University of Wales, Cardiff, Wales.

ALLSOPP, (Stanley Reginald) Richard. Guyanese/Barbadian, b. 1923. **Genres:** Language/Linguistics. **Career:** Senior French teacher at secondary school in Georgetown, Guyana, 1949-60, became deputy headmaster, then headmaster, 1961-63; University of the West Indies, Cave Hill, Barbados, lecturer, 1963-70, senior lecturer, 1970-79, reader, 1979-90. Language consultant for new Book of Common Prayer, Anglican Church of the West Indies Province. **Publications:** Dictionary of Caribbean English Usage, 1996; Language and National Unity, 1998; A Book of Afric Caribbean Proverbs, 2001. **Address:** 1 Poinsettia Way, Cave Hill, St. Michael, Barbados. **Online address:** rallsopp@uwichill.edu.bb

ALLSTON, Aaron. American, b. 1960. **Genres:** Science fiction/Fantasy. **Career:** Science fiction and fantasy writer. Space Gamer magazine, circulation manager, assistant editor, and editor, 1980-83; freelance computer games scripter and designer of roleplaying game supplements, full-time since 1983. Worked briefly for the Austin American-Statesman, Austin, TX. **Publications:** Poor Wizard's Almanac & Book of Facts, 1992; Web of Danger, 1988; Galatea in 2-D, 1993; Double Jeopardy, 1994; Doc Sidhe, 1995; (with H. Lisle) Thunder of the Captains, 1996; (with H. Lisle) Wrath of the Princes, 1997; Wraith Squadron, 1998; Iron Fist, 1998. Writer for computer games; writer for game supplements. **Address:** PO Box 564, Round Rock, TX 78680, U.S.A.

ALLWARD, Maurice (Frank). British, b. 1923. **Genres:** Air/Space topics, Crafts, History. **Career:** Draughtsman, Hawker Aircraft, 1941-45; Chief Draughtsman, Palmer Tyre Co., London, 1946-56; Deputy Manager, Technical Publs., Civil Aircraft Division, British Aerospace, 1957-88. Regular Contributor, Putnam Aeronautical Review, Air Pictorial, and Jane's All the World Aircraft, 1961-2003. Pitcairn Island, modeller and historian. **Publications:** (with J. Taylor) Spitfire, 1946; (with J. Taylor) Wings for Tomorrow, 1951; (ed.) Encyclopaedia of Space; Milestones in Science, 1958; Objective-Outer Space, 1961; Daily Mirror Book of Space; Aircraft, 1965; Safety in the Air, 1967; Triumphs of Flight, 1968; Source Book of Aircraft, 1970; Story of Flight, 1970; Look It Up Book of Transport; Look It Up Book of Space; Marvels of Jet Aircraft, 1973; The Earth in Space; Hurricane Special, 1975; The Sabre Story; The Buccaneer, 1981; Gloster Javelin, 1983; (with J. Taylor) The de Havilland Aircraft Company, 1996; Pitcairn Island: Refuge of the Bounty Mutineers, 2000. **Address:** 14 Chantry Ln, Hatfield, Herts. AL10 9HP, England.

ALLYN, Doug. American, b. 1942. **Genres:** Mystery/Crime/Suspense. **Career:** Devil's Triangle (rock music group), musician, singer, and songwriter, 1975-. Edgar Award, 1996. **Publications:** The Cheerio Killings, 1989; Motown Underground, 1993; Icewater Mansions, 1995; Black Water, 1996; A Dance in Deep Water, 1997; All Creatures Dark and Dangerous, 1999; Welcome to Wolf Country, 2001; The Hard Luck Club, 2003. Contributor of stories to magazines and anthologies. **Address:** 325 E State, Montrose, MI 48457-9005, U.S.A.

AL-MARAYATI, Abid A(min). American (born Iraq), b. 1931. **Genres:** International relations/Current affairs, Politics/Government. **Career:** Professor Emeritus, Dept. of Political Science, University of Toledo, 1990- (Professor and Director, Center for International Studies, 1968-90). UN Intern, 1954; Secretary, Delegation of Iraq 1955, and Delegation of Yemen 1956-60, UN General Assembly; Instructor, Dept. of Government, University of Massachusetts, Amherst, 1960; Technical Assistance Officer, Division of Economic and Technical Assistance, International Atomic Energy Agency, Vienna, Austria, 1960-62; Associate Professor of Political Science, State University, College of New York, Plattsburg, 1962-64; Research Fellow, Harvard University, 1964-65; Associate Professor, Arizona State University, Tempe, 1965-68; Lecturer and International Education Consultant, American Institute for Foreign Trade, Glendale AZ, 1965-68; Hawaii Pacific University, National Endowment for the Humanities, Distinguished Scholar, 2001. **Publications:** A Diplomatic History of Modern Iraq, 1961; Middle Eastern Constitutions and Electoral Laws, 1968; (with others) The Middle East: Its Governments and Politics, 1972; (ed.) International Relations of the Middle East and North Africa, 1985. Contributor of articles and papers to professional journals. **Address:** University of Toledo, 2109 Terrace View W, Toledo, OH 43607, U.S.A. **Online address:** a_almarayati@yahoo.com

ALMOG, Ruth. Also writes as Almog Etinger. Israeli, b. 1936. **Genres:** Novels, Novellas/Short stories, Children's fiction. **Career:** Author and journalist. Ha'aretz newspaper, literary editor. **Publications:** Hasade ha-lailah shel Margaretah, 1969; Ahare tu bi-Shevat (stories), 1979; Nashim (stories; title means: Women), 1986; Rakefet, ahavati ha-rishonah (title means: Rakefet, My First Love), 1992; Tikun omanuti (stories; title means: Artistic Emendation), 1993. NOVELS: Be-erets gezerah (title means: Don't Hurry the Journey), 1971; Et ha-zar veha-oyev, 1980; Mavet ba-gashem, 1982, trans. by D. Bilu as Death in the Rain, 1993; Shorshe avir (title means: Dangling Roots), 1987; The Inner Lake, 2001. CO-WRITER, AS ALMOG ETINGER: A Perfect Lover; Eshtelina My Love. JUVENILE: Nafi, nesikh ha-karnapim, 1979; Tso'anim ba-pardes (title means: Gypsies in the Orchard), 1986; Gilgil, 1986; Kadur ha-kesef (title means: Silver Ball), 1986; My Journey with Alex, 2000. Contributor to newspapers. Novellas included in anthologies. **Address:** c/o David R. Godine Publisher, 9 Hamilton Place, Boston, MA 02108, U.S.A.

ALMON, Russell. *See* **DOWNING, David A(lmon).**

ALMOND, Brenda. Also writes as Brenda Cohen. British, b. 1937. **Genres:** Education, Ethics, Medicine/Health, Philosophy. **Career:** University of Surrey, Guildford, England, lecturer to reader in philosophy, 1974-86; University of Hull, England, reader in philosophy and education, 1986-92, professor of moral and social philosophy, 1992-. University of Connecticut, visiting lecturer, 1969-70; also taught at University of Brighton, University of Keele, University of Exeter, and University of Ghana. **Publications:** Educational Thought: An Introduction, 1969; Education and the Individual, 1981; Means and Ends in Education, 1982; Moral Concerns, 1987; The Philosophical Quest, 1990, 2nd ed. as Exploring Philosophy, 1995; Exploring Ethics: A Traveller's Tale, 1998. EDITOR & CONTRIBUTOR: (with B. Wilson)

Values: A Symposium, 1988; (with G. Enderle and A. Argandona) People in Corporations: Ethical Responsibilities and Corporate Effectiveness, 1990; AIDS, a Moral Issue: The Ethical, Legal, and Social Aspects, 1990, 2nd ed., 1996; (with D. Hill) Applied Philosophy: Morals and Metaphysics in Contemporary Debate, 1991; Introducing Applied Ethics, 1995; (with M. Parker) Ethical Issues in the New Genetics, 2002. Contributor to books. Contributor to philosophy and education journals. **Address:** Social Values Research Centre, Philosophy, Humanities, University of Hull, Hull, E. Sussex HU6 7RX, England.

ALOFF, Mindy. American, b. 1947. **Genres:** Poetry, Dance/Ballet, Humanities, Literary criticism and history, Writing/Journalism, Essays. **Career:** University of Portland, OR, instructor in English, 1973-75; free-lance writer and editor in Portland, 1975-80, NYC, 1988-; Dance, NYC, national staff correspondent, 1976-80, associate critic, 1979-80, senior critic, 1980-91; Vassar Quarterly, Poughkeepsie, NY, editor, 1980-88; Nation, dance critic, 1983-93; New Yorker, weekly writer for Goings on About Town and contrib to Talk of the Town, 1987-92; New Republic, dance critic, 1993-2001. Princeton University, visiting lecturer, 1996; Barnard College, adjunct associate professor, 1999-2000, assistant professor of professional practice, 2002-03; George Balanchine Foundation, consultant, 1999-; lecturer at workshops, consultant. **Publications:** Night Lights (poems), 1979.

ALOFSIN, Anthony. American, b. 1949. **Genres:** Novellas/Short stories, Architecture, Art/Art history, Biography. **Career:** University of Texas at Austin, associate professor of architecture, 1987-, adjunct professor of art and art history, 1988-, Sid W. Richardson Centennial fellow in architecture, 1987-98, Kermacy Professor, 1999-2000, Roland Roessner Centennial Professor, 2000-. Designer and exhibition curator. Lecturer at colleges and universities in the United States and abroad. **Publications:** (ed. and author of intro) Frank Lloyd Wright: An Index to the Taliesin Correspondence, 1988; Frank Lloyd Wright: The Lost Years, 1910-1922, 1993; (preface) Studies and Executed Buildings by Frank Lloyd Wright, 1998; Frank Lloyd Wright: Europe and Beyond (essays), 1999; The Struggle for Modernism: Architecture, Landscape Architecture and City Planning at Harvard, 2002. Work represented in books. Contributor of articles and reviews to art and architecture journals and exhibition catalogs. **Address:** School of Architecture, Goldsmith Hall, University of Texas at Austin, Austin, TX 78712, U.S.A. **Online address:** alofsin@mail.utexas.edu

ALPERT, Cathryn. American, b. 1952. **Genres:** Novels. **Career:** Centre College, Danville, KY, assistant professor of dramatic arts, 1980-84; free-lance writer, 1987-; San Francisco Chronicle, book reviewer. Bread Loaf Writers' Conference, fellow in fiction, 1997. **Publications:** Rocket City (novel), 1995. Work represented in anthologies. Contributor of stories, articles, poems, and reviews to magazines. **Address:** PO Box 624, Aptos, CA 95001, U.S.A.

ALPHIN, Elaine Marie. American, b. 1955. **Genres:** Children's fiction, Young adult fiction, Children's non-fiction, How-to books. **Career:** Rice Thresher, Houston, TX, writer and department editor, 1974-76; Houston (magazine), Houston, TX, feature editor and writer, 1978-79; freelance writer, 1978-; A-Square Company, Cornwall-on-Hudson, NY, Madison, IN, and Bedford, KY, advertising manager and technical service, 1982-93; Hieroglyphics Unlimited, Madison, IN, and Bedford, KY, owner and cross-stitch designer, 1986-; Institute of Children's Literature, West Redding, CT, instructor, 1992-. Speaker at conferences, workshop, and schools. **Publications:** The Ghost Cadet, 1991; The Proving Ground, 1992; 101 Bible Puzzles, 1993; Tournament of Time, 1994; Rainy Day/Sunny Day/Any Day Activities, 1994; A Bear for Miguel, 1996; Counterfeit Son, 2000; Creating Characters Kids Will Love, 2000; Ghost Soldier, 2001; Simon Says, 2002; Germ Hunter: A Story about Louis Pasteur, 2003; Davy Crockett, 2003; Dinosaur Hunter, 2003; Picture Perfect, 2003; I Have not Yet Begun to Fight: A Story about John Paul Jones, 2004; Dwight Eisenhower, 2004; The Perfect Shot, 2005. HOUSEHOLD HISTORY SERIES: Vacuum Cleaners, 1997; Irons, 1998; Toasters, 1998; Telephones, 2000. Contributor of stories and articles to anthologies; contributor of stories and articles to periodicals. **Address:** PO Box 10023, Bozeman, MT 59719-0023, U.S.A. **Online address:** Elaine MAlphin@aol.com

ALPHONSO-KARKALA, John B. *See* **KARKALA, John A.**

ALS, Hilton. American. **Genres:** Women's studies and issues, Art/Art history. **Career:** Journalist. Village Voice, staff writer; New Yorker, staff writer, 1994-; Vibe, editor-at-large; Grand Street, advisory editor. **Publications:** The Women (nonfiction), 1997. Contributor to periodicals; screenwriter for films; contributor to exhibition catalogs and books. **Address:** 49 Beach St. No. 5, New York, NY 10013, U.S.A.

ALSHAWI, Hiyan. American, b. 1957. **Genres:** Language/Linguistics, Technology. **Career:** Cambridge University, Cambridge, England, postdoctoral research fellow, 1984-85; SRI International, Cambridge, senior computer scientist, 1986-92; American Telephone & Telegraph, Bell Laboratories, Murray Hill, NJ, staff member, 1993-. **Publications:** Memory and Context for Language Interpretation, Cambridge University Press, 1987; (ed.) The Core Language Engine, MIT Press, 1992. Member of editorial board, Computational Linguistics. **Address:** American Telephone & Telegraph, Bell Laboratories 2D-435, 600 Mountain Ave., Murray Hill, NJ 07974, U.S.A.

ALSON, Peter (H.). American, b. 1955. **Genres:** Autobiography/Memoirs, Sports/Fitness. **Career:** Writer. Worked as a bookmaker in a betting parlor, NYC. **Publications:** Confessions of an Ivy League Bookie, 1996. Contributor of articles to periodicals and short stories to anthologies. **Address:** c/o Elizabeth Shinkman, Elaine Markson Literary Agency, 44 Greenwich Ave, New York, NY 10011, U.S.A. **Online address:** Peteralson@aol.com

ALT, Betty Sowers. American, b. 1931. **Genres:** History, Sociology. **Career:** University of Colorado, Colorado Springs, instructor in sociology, 1989-95; Colorado State University-Pueblo, instructor in sociology, 1991-; free-lance writer. Lecturer at Hawaii Pacific College, Christopher Newport College, University of Maryland extension on Okinawa, and Auburn University at Montgomery. **Publications:** (with B.D. Stone) Uncle Sam's Brides, 1990; (with Stone) Campfollowing: A History of the Military Wife, 1991; (with S. Folts) Weeping Violins: The Gypsy Tragedy in Europe, 1996; (with W.K. Patterson) Slaughter in Cell House 3, 1997; (with S. Wells) Wicked Women, 2000; (with W. Alt) Black Soldiers-White Wars, 2002; (with W.K. Patterson) Keeper of the Keys: A Warden's Notebook, 2003; (with S. Wells) Fleecing Grandma & Grandpa, 2004. **Address:** The Seymour Agency, 475 Miner St, Canton, NY 13617-9614, U.S.A. **Online address:** balt@aol.com

ALTEMEYER, Bob. American, b. 1940. **Genres:** Psychology. **Career:** University of Manitoba, Winnipeg, Canada, professor of psychology, 1968-. **Publications:** Right-Wing Authoritarianism, 1981; Enemies of Freedom: Understanding Right-Wing Authoritarianism, 1988; The Authoritarian Specter, 1996; (with B. Hunsberger) Amazing Conversions: Why Some Turn to Faith and Others Abandon Religion, 1997. **Address:** Department of Psychology, University of Manitoba, Winnipeg, MB, Canada R3T 2N2.

ALTEN, Steve. American, b. 1959. **Genres:** Horror. **Career:** Writer. Former self-employed water purification systems salesman and general manager of a wholesale meat plant. **Publications:** Meg: A Novel of Deep Terror (horror-thriller novel), 1997. **Address:** c/o Ken Atchity, Atchity Editorial/ Entertainment International, 400 S. Burnside Ave, Apt 11B, Los Angeles, CA 90036-5439, U.S.A.

ALTER, Judy. (Judith MacBain Alter). American, b. 1938. **Genres:** Novels, Children's fiction, Children's non-fiction, Local history/Rural topics, Biography. **Career:** Freelance writer, 1973-; Columnist, Roundup mag. and Ft. Worth Star Telegram, 1974-75; Instructor of English as a Second Language, 1975-76; Associate Director of News and Information, Texas College of Osteopathic Medicine, Ft. Worth, 1978-80 (Director of Publs., 1972); Director, Texas Christian University Press, Ft. Worth, 1987- (Ed., 1982-87). **Publications:** (with P. Russell) The Quack Doctor, 1974; After Pa Was Shot, 1978; (with S. Pearson) Single Again, 1978; The Texas ABC Book, 1981; (with J. Roach) Texas and Christmas, 1983; Luke and the Van Zandt County War, 1984; Thistle Hill: The History and the House, 1987; Mattie, 1988; Elmer Kelton, 1989; Maggie and a Horse Named Devildust, 1989; Maggie and the Search for Devildust, 1989; Women of the Old West, 1989; Growing Up in the Old West, 1989; Maggie and Devildust Ridin' High, 1990; Eli Whitney, 1990; American Osteopathic College of Radiology: A 50 Year History, 1990; Texas College of Osteopathic Medicine: The First 20 Years, 1990; Katie and the Recluse, 1991; A Ballad for Sallie, 1992; Libbie, 1993; Jessie, 1995; Cherokee Rose, 1996; Callie Shaw, Stableboy, 1996; Beauty Pageants: Tiaras, Roses and Runways, 1997; Wild West Shows: Rough Riders and Sure Shots, 1997; Meet Me at the Fair: County, State and World's Fairs and Expositions, 1997; Amusement Parks: Rollercoasters, Ferris Wheels and Cotton Candy, 1997; Cissie Palmer, 1998; Extraordinary Woman of the American West, 1999; Sam Houston, 1997; The Santa Fe Trail, 1998; Sundance, Butch, and Me, 2002; Sam Houston Is My Hero, 2003. **Address:** Box 298300, Fort Worth, TX 76129, U.S.A.

ALTER, Robert B. American, b. 1935. **Genres:** Literary criticism and history, Theology/Religion, Biography. **Career:** Class of 1937 Professor of Hebrew and Comparative Literature, University of California, Berkeley, 1989- (Professor, 1967-89). Instructor to Assistant Professor of English, Columbia University, NYC, 1962-66; Contributing Ed., Commentary, 1971-87. **Publications:** Rogue's Progress: Studies in the Picaresque Novel, 1965; Fielding and the Nature of the Novel, 1968; After the Tradition (critical essays), 1969; Partial Magic: The Novel as a Self-Conscious Genre, 1975; (ed.) Modern Hebrew Literature, 1975; Defenses of the Imagination (critical essays), 1978; A Lion for Love: A Critical Biography of Stendhal, 1979; The Art of Biblical Narrative, 1981; Motives for Fiction, 1984; The Art of Biblical Poetry, 1985; The Invention of Hebrew Prose, 1988; The Pleasures of Reading in an Ideological Age, 1989; Necessary Angels, 1991; The World of Biblical Literature, 1992; Hebrew and Modernity, 1994; Genesis: Translation and Commentary, 1996; The David Story: A Translation with Commentary of 1 and 2 Samuel, 1999; Canon and Creativity, 2000. **Address:** Dept of Comparative Literature, University of California, Berkeley, CA 94720-2510, U.S.A. **Online address:** altos@uclink4.berkeley.edu

ALTERMAN, Eric (Ross). American, b. 1960. **Genres:** Politics/ Government. **Career:** Business Executives for National Security, Washington, DC, associate for public policy, 1983-84; World Policy Institute, NYC, senior fellow, 1985-; Stanford University, Stanford, CA, peace studies fellow, 1992. Critic-at-large for the World Policy Journal, 1992-; Mother Jones (magazine), columnist, 1992-. **Publications:** Sound and Fury: The Washington Punditocracy and the Collapse of American Politics, 1992; It Ain't No Sin to Be Glad You're Alive, 1999; (with M. Green) The Book on Bush, 2004. Contributor to periodicals.

ALTERMAN, Glenn. (born United States), b. 1946. **Genres:** Self help. **Career:** Actor and writer. **Publications:** Street Talk: Character Monologues for Actors, 1991; Uptown: Original Monologues, 1992; Two Minutes and Under: Original Character Monologues for Actors, 1993; (ed.) What to Give Your Agent for Christmas: And 100 Other Suggestions for the Working Actor, 1995; Beginnings: Monologues of the Stars, 1996; Promoting Your Acting Career, 1998; Two-Minute Monologs: Original Audition Scenes for Professional Actors, 1998; Creating Your Own Monologue, 1999; An Actor's Guide: Making It in New York, 2002; More Two Minutes and Under: Character Monologues for Actors, 2002; The Perfect Audition Monologue, 2003; Additional works represented in anthologies, film scripts and plays. **Address:** 400 West 43rd St. No. 7G, New York, NY 10036, U.S.A. **Online address:** glennalt@rcn.com

ALTHER, Lisa. American, b. 1944. **Genres:** Novels, Novellas/Short stories, Writing/Journalism. **Career:** Atheneum Publishers, NYC, staff member, 1967. **Publications:** Kinflicks, 1976; Original Sins, 1981; Other Women, 1984; Bedrock, 1990; Birdman and the Dancer, 1993; Five Minutes in Heaven, 1995. **Address:** 24 Harbor Watch Rd, Burlington, VT 05401, U.S.A. **Online address:** lalther@aol.com

ALTICK, Richard Daniel. American, b. 1915. **Genres:** Cultural/Ethnic topics, Literary criticism and history. **Career:** Regents' Professor Emeritus of English, Ohio State University Columbus, since 1982 (joined faculty, 1945; Regents' Professor of English, 1968-82). **Publications:** Preface to Critical Reading, 1946, 6th rev. ed. 1984; The Cowden Clarkes, 1948; The Scholar Adventurers, 1950; The English Common Reader: A Social History of the Mass Reading Public, 1800-1900, 1957; The Art of Literary Research, 1963, 4th ed. 1993; Lives and Letters: A History of Literary Biography in England and America, 1965; (with J.F. Loucks) Browning's Roman Murder Story, 1968; To Be in England, 1969; Victorian Studies in Scarlet, 1970; Victorian People and Ideas: A Companion for the Modern Reader of Victorian Literature, 1973; The Shows of London, 1978; Paintings from Books: Art and Literature in Britain 1760-1900, 1985; Deadly Encounters: Two Victorian Sensations (in UK as Evil Encounters), 1986; Writers, Readers, and Occasions: Selected Essays on Victorian Literature and Life, 1988; The Presence of the Present: Topics of the Day in the Victorian Novel, 1991; Of a Place and a Time: Remembering Lancaster, 1991; Punch: The Lively Youth of a British Institution, 1841-1851, 1997. EDITOR: Carlyle: Past and Present, 1965; Browning: The Ring and the Book, 1971. **Address:** 276 W. Southington Ave., Worthington, OH 43085, U.S.A.

ALTMAN, Dennis. Australian, b. 1943. **Genres:** Sex, Social commentary, Gay and lesbian issues, Politics/Government. **Career:** University of Sydney, lecturer, 1969-75, Sr. Lecturer, 1975-80; Regents Lecturer, University of California, Santa Cruz, 1983; Policy Fellow, University of California, San Francisco, 1984-85; La Trobe University, Victoria, professor, reader and lecturer, 1986-94, professor, 1994-. **Publications:** Homosexual: Oppression and Liberation, 1972, rev. ed., 1992; Coming Out in the Seventies, 1979; Rehearsals for Change, 1980; The Homosexualization of America, 1982;

AIDS and the New Puritanism, 1986; AIDS in the Mind of America, 1986; The Comfort of Men, 1993; Power and Community, 1994; Defying Gravity, 1997; Global Sex, 2001. **Address:** Politics Department, La Trobe University, Bundoora, VIC 3083, Australia.

ALTMAN, Suzanne. *See* **ORGEL, Doris.**

ALTMANN, Simon L(eonardo). British (born Argentina), b. 1924. **Genres:** Poetry, Philosophy, Physics, Sciences. **Career:** University of Buenos Aires, Argentina, demonstrator, 1952, professor of chemical physics, 1957-58; Oxford University, research assistant at Mathematical Institute, 1953-57, lecturer in theory of metals, 1959-91, Brasenose College, fellow and lecturer in mathematical physics, 1964-91, vice-principal, 1990-91. University of Rome, lecturer, 1963, 1965, 1967, 1970, visiting professor, 1972, 1985; lecturer: Shell Research Laboratories (Amsterdam), 1963, UK Atomic Energy Authority (Harwell), 1966, University of Darmstadt, 1972, University of Perugia, 1982; visiting professor: University of Stockholm, 1972, Technische Hochschule (Vienna), 1975, Technion-Israel Institute of Technology, 1978, Johns Hopkins University, 1986, University of Vienna, 1992; Instituto Rocasolano (Madrid), British Council exchange visitor, 1976; University of Texas at Austin, distinguished lecturer, 1979; University of Zaragoza, visiting professor, 1979, visiting lecturer, 1991; Technical University of Vienna, guest professor, 1986; Catholic University of Louvain, Vlaamse Leergangen Professor, 1989-90. **Publications:** Band Theory of Metals: The Elements, 1970; Induced Representations in Crystals and Molecules: Point, Space, and Non-grid Molecule Groups, 1977; Rotations, Quaternions, and Double Groups, 1986; Band Theory of Solids, 1991; Icons and Symmetries, 1992; (with P. Herzig) Point-Group Theory Tables, 1994; Is Nature Supernatural?, 2002. Contributor to scientific journals and poetry publications. **Address:** Brasenose College, Oxford University, Oxford OX1 4AJ, England. **Online address:** simon.altmann@bnc.ox.ac.uk

ALTOFF, Gerard T(homas). American, b. 1949. **Genres:** History, Military/Defense/Arms control. **Career:** U.S. Forest Service, Ashley National Forest, Dutch John, UT, forest aide, 1972; National Park Service, Washington, DC, park technician at Zion National Park, Springdale, UT, 1972-75, district naturalist at Theodore Roosevelt National Park, Medora, ND, 1975-79, chief ranger and historian at Perry's Victory and IPM, Put-in-Bay, OH, 1979-. Speaker at schools. **Publications:** Deep Water Sailors-Shallow Water Soldiers: Manning the United States Fleet on Lake Erie, 1813, 1993; Amongst My Best Men: African-Americans and the War of 1812, 1996; (with DC Skaggs) A Signal Victory: The Lake Erie Campaign, 1812-1813, 1997; Oliver Hazard Perry and the Battle of Lake Erie, 1999. Contributor to books and periodicals. **Address:** National Park Service, 93 Delaware Ave, PO Box 549, Put in Bay, OH 43456, U.S.A. **Online address:** gerryaltoff@nps.gov

ALTSCHULER, Glenn C. American, b. 1950. **Genres:** Music. **Career:** Administrator, educator, and author. Cornell University, Ithaca, NY, 1981-, currently Thomas and Dorothy Litwin Professor of American Studies, School of Continuing Education and Summer Sessions, dean, 1991. **Publications:** Andrew D. White: Educator, Historian, Diplomat, 1979; Race, Ethnicity, and Class in American Social Thought, 1865-1919, 1982; (with Jan M. Saltzgaber) Revivalism, Social Conscience, and Community in the Burned-over District: The Trial of Rohad Bement, 1983; Better Than Second Best: Love and Work in the Life of Helen Magill, 1990; (with David I. Grossvogel) Changing Channels: America in TV Guide, 1992; (with Stuart M. Blumin) Rude Republic: Americans and Their Politics in the Nineteenth Century, 2000; All Shook Up: How Rock 'n Roll Changed America, 2003. (with Isaac Kramnick and R. Laurence Moore) The 100 Most Notable Cornellians, 2004. Contributor of articles to newspapers and academic journals. **Address:** B-20 Day Hall, Cornell University, Ithaca, NY 14853, U.S.A. **Online address:** gca1@cornellats.edu

ALUKO, T(imothy) M(ofolorunso). Nigerian, b. 1918. **Genres:** Novels. **Career:** Town Engineer, Lagos Town Council, 1956-60; Director and Permanent Secretary, Ministry of Works and Transport, Western Nigeria, 1960-66; Sr. Research Fellow in Municipal Engineering, University of Lagos, 1966-78; Associate Professor of Public Health Engineering, University of Lagos, 1978. Partner, Scott Wilson Kirkpatrick and Partners, Lagos, 1979-88. **Publications:** One Man, One Wife, 1959; One Man, One Matchet, 1964; Kinsman and Foreman, 1966; Chief the Honourable Minister, 1970; His Worshipful Majesty, 1973; Wrong Ones in the Dock, 1982; A State of Our Own, 1986; Conduct Unbecoming, 1993; My Years of Service, 1994; First Year at State College, 1999. **Address:** 53 Ladipo Oluwole Rd, Apapa, Lagos, Nigeria. **Online address:** toucaluko@hotmail.com

ALVARADO (GREEN), Manuel (Bernardo). British (born Guatemala), b. 1948. **Genres:** Communications/Media, Young adult non-fiction. **Career:**

Teacher of English at comprehensive schools in London, England, 1971-72; City College, London, lecturer in film and TV studies, 1972-74; Society for Education in Film and Television, London, education officer, 1975-78; University of London, lecturer, 1975-79; Institute of Education, London, lecturer in TV and film studies, 1978-83; Universite de Picardie, teacher of an annual course on British TV, 1978-; lecturer in Australia, 1980, 1982, 1984; British School of Motoring, head of education and instructor training, 1984; Ithaca College, lecturer, 1984-87; UNESCO and Broadcasting Research Unit, London, research fellow and director of Intl Video Flow Research Project, 1984-86; Boston University, London Centre, head of journalism and communications, 1986-88; Institute of Media Training, London, asst director of studies, 1987-88; John Libbey Media Publications, editorial director, 1988-; British Broadcasting Corp., senior assistant, 1989; British Film Institute, London, head of education in Research Division, 1989-93; Research on Media Associates, co-founder and co-director, 1991; Nottingham Trent University, England, reader in media studies, 1993-95; University of Luton, senior research fellow, 1995, professor of media arts, 1996-. **Publications:** (with C. Mottershead) Television and the Image, 1974; (with J. Caughie) Metz's Grande Syntagmatique and Godard's Tout Va Bien, 1974; Practical Television Work, 1976; (with E. Buscombe) Hazell: The Making of a TV Series, 1978; (with B. Ferguson) The Troubles, 1980; Audience/Education/Television, 1981; (with J. Tulloch) Doctor Who: The Unfolding Text, 1983; (with J. Stewart) Made for Television: Euston Films Limited, 1985; Media Imperialism, the New Information Order, and the International Flow of Television, 1985; (with R. Gutch and T. Wollen) Learning the Media, 1987; Television and Video (for teenagers), 1987; Mexican Food and Drink (for teenagers), 1988; (with others) East of Dallas, 1988; Countries of the World: Spain (for teenagers), 1989; The Place and Function of Media Education, 1990; Media Education in the 1990s, 1992. EDITOR: Video World-Wide, 1988; (with J.O. Thompson) The Media Reader, 1990; (with O. Boyd-Barrett, and contrib.) Media Education, 1992; (with Buscombe and R. Collins) The Screen Education Reader, 1993; (with J. King and A. Lopez) Mediating Two Worlds, 1993. Contributor to books and periodicals. **Address:** 49 Tremadoc Rd, Clapham, London SW4 7NA, England. **Online address:** manuel@alvarado.demon.co.uk

ALVAREZ, A(lfred). British, b. 1929. **Genres:** Novels, Poetry, Literary criticism and history. **Career:** The Observer, London, advisory poetry editor and poetry critic, 1956-66; Princeton University, NJ, Gauss lecturer, 1957-58; New Statesman, London, drama critic, 1958-60; Penguin Modern European Poets in Translation, advisory editor, 1965-75. **Publications:** NOVELS: Hers, 1974; Hunt, 1978; Day of Atonement, 1991. POETRY: (Poems), 1952; The End of It, 1958; Twelve Poems, 1968; Lost, 1968; (with R. Fuller and A. Thwaite) Penguin Modern Poets 18, 1970; Apparition, 1971; The Legacy, 1972; Autumn to Autumn and Selected Poems 1953-1976, 1978; New and Selected Poems, 2002. OTHER: The Shaping Spirit: Studies in Modern English and American Poets, in US as Stewards of Excellence: Studies in Modern English and American Poets, 1958; The School of Donne, 1961; Under Pressure: The Writer in Society: Eastern Europe and the USA, 1965; Beyond All This Fiddle: Essays, 1955-67, 1968; The Savage God: A Study of Suicide, 1971; Beckett, 1973; Life after Marriage: Scenes from Divorce, in US as Life after Marriage: Love in an Age of Divorce, 1982; The Biggest Game in Town, 1983; Offshore: A North Sea Journey, 1986; Feeding the Rat: Profile of a Climber, 1988; (with C. Blackman) Rainforest, 1988; Night: An Exploration of Night Life, Night Language, Sleep & Dreams, 1995; Where Did It All Go Right? (autobiography), 1999; Poker: Bets, Bluffs, and Bad Beats, 2001; The Writer's Voice, 2004. EDITOR: The New Poetry: An Anthology, 1962; The Faber Book of Modern European Poetry, 1992. **Address:** c/o Gillon Aitken Associates Ltd, 29 Fernshaw Rd, London SW10 0TG, England.

ALVAREZ, Julia. American, b. 1950. **Genres:** Novels, Young adult fiction, Poetry, Essays. **Career:** Poet-in-the-Schools in Kentucky, Delaware, and North Carolina, 1975-78; Phillips Andover Academy, Andover, MA, instructor in English, 1979-81; University of Vermont, Burlington, visiting assistant professor of creative writing, 1981-83; George Washington University, Washington, DC, Jenny McKean Moore Visiting Writer, 1984-85; University of Illinois, Urbana, assistant professor of English, 1985-88; Middlebury College, Middlebury, VT, associate professor of English, 1988-97, writer-in-residence, 1997-; writer. **Publications:** NOVELS: How the Garcia Girls Lost Their Accents, 1991; In the Time of Butterflies, 1994; "Yo!," 1997; In the Name of Salome, 2000. POETRY: (ed.) Old Age Ain't for Sissies, 1979; The Housekeeping Book, 1982; Homecoming, 1984, rev. ed., 1995; The Other Side/El Otro Lado, 1995; Seven Trees, 1999. OTHER: Something to Declare (nonfiction), 1999; The Secret Footprints (children's), 2000; How Tia Lola came to Stay (young adult), 2001; A Cafecito Story, 2001; Before We Were Free (young adult), 2002. Work represented in anthologies. Contributor to periodicals. **Address:** Susan Bergholz Literary Services, 17 W 10th St No 5, New York, NY 10011-8769, U.S.A. **Online address:** susan@susanbergholz. com

ALVI, Moniza. Pakistani, b. 1954. **Genres:** Poetry. **Career:** Scott Lidgett School, London, teacher, 1978-80; Aylwin School, London, teacher, 1980-, English department head, 1989-. **Publications:** POETRY: (with P. Daniels) Peacock Luggage, 1992; The Country at My Shoulder, 1993. **Address:** c/o Oxford University Press, Walton St., Oxford OX2 6DP, England.

AMABILE, George. Canadian (born United States), b. 1936. **Genres:** Novels, Novellas/Short stories, Mystery/Crime/Suspense, Plays/Screenplays, Poetry, Songs/Lyrics and libretti, Essays. **Career:** Professor of English, 1971-97, Senior Scholar, 1998-, University of Manitoba, Winnipeg. Ed., Northern Light mag. **Publications:** Blood Ties, 1972; Open Country, 1976; Flower and Song, 1978; Ideas of Shelter, 1981; The Presence of Fire, 1982; (ed. with K. Dales) No Feather, No Ink, 1985; Four of a Kind, 1994; Rumours of Paradise/Rumours of War, 1995; Tasting the Dark, 2001. **Address:** Dept. of English, University of Manitoba, Winnipeg, MB, Canada R3T 2N2. **Online address:** gamabile@shaw.com

AMADI, Elechi. Nigerian, b. 1934. **Genres:** Novels, Plays/Screenplays, Ethics, Autobiography/Memoirs. **Career:** Science teacher, 1960-63, and army officer, 1963-67; government divisional officer, and sr. assistant secretary, Ahoada and Port Harcourt, Nigeria, 1968-; permanent secretary, 1973; Rivers State College of Education, dean of arts, 1985-86, commissioner for education, 1988-89. Nigerian Academy of Education, fellow, 2003. **Publications:** The Concubine, 1966; The Great Ponds, 1969; Sunset in Biafra, 1974; The Slave, 1978; Ethics in Nigerian Culture, 1982; Estrangement (novel), 1986; Speaking and Singing (essays and poems), 2003. PLAYS: Peppersoup, and The Road to Ibadan, 1977; Isiburu, 1973; Dancer of Johannesburg, 1979; The Woman of Calabar, 2003. **Address:** c/o Heinemann Educational Books, Inc., Hanover St, Portsmouth, NH 03802-3959, U.S.A.

AMANN, Janet. American, b. 1951. **Genres:** Education, Children's fiction. **Career:** Art teacher in Bangor, WI, 1973-86; elementary librarian and art teacher in La Crosse, WI, 1986-91; North Woods Elementary School, La Crosse, library and media director, 1992-. Art salesperson. Girl Scout leader, 1982-86; Cub Scout leader, 1986-93. **Publications:** The T-206 Honus Wagner Caper, 1991; Theme Teaching with Great Visual Resources, 1993. Contributor to educational magazines. **Address:** North Woods Elementary School, 2541 Sablewood Dr, La Crosse, WI 54601, U.S.A. **Online address:** jaamann@mail.sdlax.ki2.wi.us

AMAR, Akhil Reed. American, b. 1958. **Genres:** Law. **Career:** Law professor, writer. Law clerk, Judge Stephen Breyer, U.S. Court of Appeals, 1st Circuit, 1984-85; Yale University Law School, assistant professor and associate professor of law, 1985-90, professor of law, 199093, Southmayd professor of law, 1993-. **Publications:** The Constitution and Criminal Procedure: First Principles, 1997; (with A. Hirsch) For the People: What the Constitution Really Says about Your Rights, 1998; The Bill of Rights: Creation and Reconstruction, 1998. **Address:** Yale Law School, PO Box 208215, New Haven, CT 06520, U.S.A. **Online address:** amar@mail.law.yale.edu

AMATO, Carol A. American, b. 1942. **Genres:** Children's fiction. **Career:** Language-learning specialist in the Boston, MA, area, 1965-. **Publications:** YOUNG READERS SERIES: The Truth about Sharks, 1995; Captain Jim and the Killer Whales, 1995; To Be a Wolf, 1995; Raising Ursa, 1996; Adios, Chi Chi: The Adventures of a Tarantula, 1996; The Bald Eagle: Free Again!, 1996; Penguins of the Galapagos, 1996; On the Trail of the Grizzly, 1997; Chessie, the Meandering Manatee, 1997; The Giant Panda, Hope for Tomorrow, 2000; Backyard Pets-Activities for Exploring Wildlife Close to Home, 2002. **Address:** c/o Barron's Educational Series, 250 Wireless Blvd, Hauppauge, NY 11788, U.S.A.

AMATO, Mary. American, b. 1961. **Genres:** Children's fiction. **Career:** Writer, puppeteer, choreographer, and teacher. Cofounder of Firefly Shadow Theater (puppet company.). **Publications:** The Word Eater, 2000; The Riot Brothers (short stories), in press. Contributor of articles, essays, and poems to periodicals for children and adults. **Address:** c/o Author Mail, Holiday House, 425 Madison Ave., New York, NY 10017, U.S.A. **Online address:** amato@erols.com

AMBERT, Anne-Marie. Canadian. **Genres:** Human relations/Parenting, Sociology. **Career:** University of Texas, Austin, research associate at Rehabilitation Research and Training Center in Mental Retardation, 1969-70, director of the center, 1970-71, assistant professor of social work, 1969-71;

York University, Toronto, ON, Canada, assistant professor, 1971-74, associate professor of sociology, 1974-; writer. **Publications:** The Effect of Children on Parents, 1992, 2nd ed., 2001; Parents, Children, and Adolescents, 1997; The Web of Poverty, 1998; Families in the New Millennium, 2001. Contributor to scholarly journals.

AMBLER, Scott W. Canadian, b. 1966. **Genres:** Information science/ Computers. **Career:** Writer, mentor, and development consultant specializing in object-oriented architectural modeling. Ambysoft Inc., founder. **Publications:** The Object Primer, 1995, 3rd ed., 2004; Building Object Applications That Work: Your Step-by-Step Handbook for Developing Robust Systems with Object Technology, 1997; Process Patterns: Building Large-Scale Systems Using Object Technology, 1998; More Process Patterns: Developing Large-Scale Systems Using Object Technology, 1998; The Unified Process Series, 2000-02; Agile Modeling, 2002; Agile Database Techniques, 2003; The Elements of UML 2.0 Style, 2005. Contributor to computer-related periodicals.

AMBROSE, Bonnie Holt. American, b. 1943. **Genres:** Fashion/Costume, Theatre. **Career:** Performing Arts Supply Co., Houston, TX, president, c. 1970-. Costume Workshop, Houston, owner; seminar lecturer on costume construction; presenter of the local public television series The Costume Workshop, 1997. **Publications:** The Little Hatmaking Book: A Workbook on Turn-of-the-Century Hats, Vol. 1, 1994; The Little Bodice Construction Book: A Workbook on Period Bodices, 1995; The Little Corset Construction Book: A Workbook on Period Underwear, 1997; Introduction to Costuming, 1997; The Costume Workshop; Costume Crew, 2004. **Address:** Costume Workshop, 417 Reinicke, Houston, TX 77007, U.S.A. **Online address:** bhambrose@netscape.net; info@performingartssupply.com

AMBROSINI, Richard. Italian, b. 1955. **Genres:** Literary criticism and history, Translations. **Career:** University of Rome, Rome, Italy, English language assistant, 1986-94, researcher, 1994- Military service: Italian Army, 1981-82; served in the Grenadier Corps. **Publications:** Conrad's Fiction as Critical Discourse, Cambridge University Press, 1991; Introduzione a Conrad, Laterza, 1991. Translator into Italian, Joseph Conrad's An Outcast of the Islands and The Secret Agent, Robert Louis Stevenson's Treasure Island, and several works on Contemporary history. Author of a column in Il Messaggero, 1993-94. Contributor to periodicals. **Address:** Department of English, University of Rome, Via Carlo Fea, 2-00161 Rome, Italy.

AMBURN, Ellis. Also writes as Edward Douglas. American, b. 1933. **Genres:** Biography. **Career:** Coward McCann, NYC, executive editor and secretary of board of directors, 1960-71; Delacorte Press, NYC, editor in chief, 1971-78; William Morrow & Co. Inc., NYC, senior editor, 1978-80; G.P. Putnam's Sons, NYC, editorial director, 1980-85; free-lance writer, 1985-. Volunteer worker with recovering alcoholics and addicts. **Publications:** (with T. Sanchez) Up and Down with the Rolling Stones, 1979; (with S. Winters) Shelley, Also Known as Shirley, 1980; (with P. Presley) Elvis and Me, 1985; (with M. Edwards) Priscilla, Elvis, and Me, 1988; (with S. Winters) Shelley II, 1989; Dark Star: The Tragic Story of Roy Orbison, 1990; Pearl: The Obsessions and Passions of Janis Joplin, 1992; Buddy Holly: The Real Story, 1995; Subterranean Kerouac: The Hidden Life of Jack Kerouac, 1998; The Most Beautiful Woman in the World: The Obsessions, Passions and Courage of Elizabeth Taylor, 2000; The Sexiest Man Alive: A Biography of Warren Beatty, 2002; (as Edward Douglas) Jack: The Great Seducer-The Live and Many Loves of Jack Nicolson, 2004. **Address:** c/o Elaine Markson, 44 Greenwich Ave, New York, NY 10011, U.S.A.

AMERY, Francis. See STABLEFORD, Brian M(ichael).

AMES, Christopher. American, b. 1956. **Genres:** Literary criticism and history. **Career:** Stanford University, Stanford, CA, teaching administrator, 1983-84, and lecturer in English; Thacher School, Ojai, CA, instructor in English and department head, 1984-86; Agnes Scott College, Decatur, GA, associate professor of English and department head, 1986-2001; Oglethorpe University, provost, 2001-. Georgia State University, guest lecturer, 1993; University of Southern California, guest lecturer, 1994. **Publications:** The Life of the Party: Festive Vision in Modern Fiction, 1991; Movies about the Movies: Hollywood Reflected, 1997. Contributor of articles and reviews to journals. **Address:** Provost, Oglethorpe University, 4484 Peachtree Rd, Atlanta, GA 30319, U.S.A. **Online address:** cames@oglethorpe.edu

AMES, Felicia. See BURDEN, Jean.

AMES, Jonathan. American, b. 1964. **Genres:** Novels. **Career:** Writer and performance artist. Worked briefly as a boxer. **Publications:** I Pass like

Night (novel), 1989; The Extra Man (novel), 1998; Oedipussy, (one-man show), 1999; What's Not to Love?: The Adventures of a Mildly Perverted Young Writer, 2000; My Less than Secret Life: A Diary, Fiction, Essays, 2002. **Address:** 181 Wyckoff St., Brooklyn, NY 11217, U.S.A. **Online address:** amesjon@aol.com

AMES, Kenneth L. American, b. 1942. **Genres:** Antiques/Furnishings, History, Bibliography. **Career:** Franklin and Marshall College, Lancaster, PA, assistant professor of art history, 1967-73, acting chair of department of art, 1971-72; Winterthur Museum, director of Winterthur Summer Institute, 1975-82, chair of Office of Advanced Studies, 1978-88, professor of Early American Culture, 1989-90; New York State Museum, Albany, chief of historical survey. University of Delaware, adjunct assistant professor, 1974-76, adjunct associate professor, 1976-88, adjunct professor, 1988-90; lecturer at colleges and universities; consultant. **Publications:** Beyond Necessity: Art in the Folk Tradition, 1977; Death in the Dining Room and Other Tales of Victorian Culture, 1992; On Bishop Street, 1996. EDITOR: (with G.W.R. Ward) Decorative Arts and Household Furnishings in America, 1650-1920: An Annotated Bibliography, 1989; (with B. Franco and T. Frye) Ideas and Images: Developing Interpretive History Exhibits, 1992; (with K. Martinez) The Material Culture of Gender, the Gender of Material Culture, 1997. Work represented in anthologies. Contributor of articles and reviews to art and history journals. **Address:** Bard Graduate Center, 18 W 86th St, New York, NY 10024, U.S.A.

AMIS, Martin (Louis). British, b. 1949. **Genres:** Novels, Novellas/Short stories. **Career:** Editorial Assistant, Times Literary Supplement, London, 1972-75; Assistant Literary Ed., 1975-77, and Literary Ed., 1977-79, New Statesman, London. Contributor, Times Literary Supplement, Observer newspaper, and the New Statesman mag., Sunday Times, New York Times, and Sunday Telegraph. **Publications:** The Rachel Papers, 1973; Dead Babies, 1975, as Dark Secrets, 1977; Success, 1978; Einstein's Monsters (short stories), 1987; Invasion of the Space Invaders, 1982; Other People: A Mystery Story, 1981; Money, 1984; The Moronic Inferno and Other Visits to America, 1986; Einstein's Monsters (short stories), 1987; London Fields, 1989; The Information, 1995; Night Train, 1997; Heavy Water and Other Stories, 1998; Experience, 2000. **Address:** c/o The Wylie Agency, 36 Parkside, 52 Knightsbridge, London SW1X 7JP, England.

AMMACHI. See AMRITANANDAMAYI, Mataji.

AMMER, Christine (Parker). American (born Austria), b. 1931. **Genres:** Business/Trade/Industry, Economics, Language/Linguistics, Medicine/Health, Music. **Publications:** Musician's Handbook of Foreign Terms, 1971; Harper's Dictionary of Music, 1972; (with D.S. Ammer) Dictionary of Business and Economics, 1977, 1984; Unsung: A History of Women in American Music, 1980, rev. ed., 2001; The A to Z of Women's Health: A Concise Encyclopaedia, 1982; (with N.T. Sidley) The Common Sense Guide to Mental Health Care 1982; The Harper Dictionary of Music, 1986; The A to Z of Investing, 1986; It's Raining Cats and Dogs...and Other Beastly Expressions, 1988; The New A to Z of Women's Health, 1989, 4th ed., 2000; Fighting Words...from War, Rebellion and Other Combative Capers, 1989, 2nd ed., 1999; The A to Z of Foreign Musical Terms, 1989; Getting Help: A Consumer's Guide to Therapy, 1991; HarperCollins Dictionary of Music, 1991, 3rd ed., 1995; Have a Nice Day-No Problem! A Dictionary of Cliches, 1992; Seeing Red or Tickled Pink: Color Terms in Everyday Language, 1992; Southpaws and Sunday Punches and Other Sporting Expressions, 1993; Fruitcakes and Couch Potatoes and Other Delicious Expressions, 1995; American Heritage Dictionary of Idioms, 1997; Cool Cats, Top Dogs and Other Beastly Expressions, 1999; Facts on File Dictionary of Cliches, 2001. **Address:** 6 Filer Ln, Lexington, MA 02420-1231, U.S.A.

AMMERMAN, Nancy T(atom). American, b. 1950. **Genres:** Theology/Religion. **Career:** Emory University, Atlanta, GA, teacher of university courses in religion, 1984-95, assistant professor at Candler School of Theology, 1984-90, associate professor of sociology of religion, 1990-95, director of Center for Religious Research, 1985-95, director of Baptist Studies program, 1991-95; Hartford Seminary, Hartford, CT, professor of sociology of religion, Center for Social and Religious Research, 1995-. Georgia State University, fellow in gerontology and theological education, 1986-87; Princeton University, visiting scholar at Center for the Study of American Religion, 1993-94. Lecturer and visiting faculty member at colleges and universities. **Publications:** Bible Believers: Fundamentalists in the Modern World, 1987; Baptist Battles: Social Change and Religious Conflict in the Southern Baptist Convention, 1990; (ed. and contrib.) Southern Baptists Observed: Multiple Perspectives on a Changing Denomination, 1993; (ed. with W.C. Roof) Work, Family, and Religion in Contemporary Society, 1995; Congregation

and Community, 1997; (ed. with J. Carroll, C.S. Dudley, and W. McKinney) Studying Congregations, 1998. **Address:** Center for Social and Religious Research, Hartford Seminary, 77 Sherman St., Hartford, CT 06105, U.S.A. **Online address:** nta@hartsem.edu

AMOIA, Alba della Fazia. American, b. 1928. **Genres:** Theatre, Literary criticism and history, Biography. **Career:** Barnard College, NYC, instructor in French, 1951-59; Hunter College of the City University of New York, NYC, associate professor of French, 1960-75, now emerita associate professor; writer. United Nations Language Training, teacher of French and English, 1949-64; Columbia University, lecturer, 1950-54. **Publications:** Jean Anouilh, 1969; The Italian Theatre Today (interviews), 1975; Edmond Rostand, 1978; Albert Camus, 1990; Women on the Italian Literary Scene: A Panorama, 1992; Feodor Dostoevsky, 1993; Twentieth-Century Italian Women Writers, 1996; (with E. Bruschini) Stendhal's Rome: Then and Now, 1997; No Mothers We!: Italian Women Writers and Their Revolt against Maternity, 2000. EDITOR: (with B.L. Knapp and N. Dormoy-Savage) An Anthology of Modern Belgian Theatre, 1982; Thomas Mann's Fiorenza, 1990; (with B.L. Knapp) Multicultural Authors from Antiquity to 1945, 2001. Contributor of articles and reviews to periodicals.

AMOS, James H., Jr. American, b. 1946. **Genres:** Novels, Business/Trade/Industry. **Career:** Brice Foods, Dallas, TX (positions include: director of franchising, director of marketing and sales, national director of consultant training, vice-president; CEO, 1988-96; Mail Boxes Etc., San Diego, CA, president & CEO, 1996-. Consultant. **Publications:** NOVELS: The Memorial, 1989; Focus or Failure: America at the Crossroads. **Address:** 3660 Bear Creek Rd., Thompsons Station, TN 37179-9739, U.S.A.

AMOS, William (David). British, b. 1933. **Genres:** Local history/Rural topics. **Career:** Liverpool Daily Post, daily columnist, 1963-70; Lancashire Life, editor, 1970-86; Whitethorn Press, director, 1974-85, editor in chief, 1982-86; Hotel Publishing International, editor in chief, 1986-89; Warwickshire & Worcestershire Life, editor, 1989-91; freelance editor, 1991-. **Publications:** Literary Liverpool, 1971; (ed.) Just Sithabod: Dialect Verse from "Lancashire Life," 1975; (ed.) Steam-up in Lancashire: Railwayana from "Lancashire Life," 1976; (ed.) Cheyp at T'Price: Dialect Verse from "Lancashire Life," 1978; The Originals: Who's Really Who in Fiction, 1985, (in U.S. as The Originals: An A-Z of Fiction's Real-Life Characters, 1986); Derbyshire, 1995; Tales of Old Cumbria, 1996. **Address:** Hacket Forge, Little Langdale, Ambleside, Cumbria LA22 9NU, England.

AMRITANANDAMAYI, Mataji. Also writes as Ammachi. Indian, b. 1953. **Genres:** Inspirational/Motivational Literature. **Career:** Operated as a trance medium until the late 1970s; Mata Amritanandamayi Center, Kerala, India, founder and Hindu spiritual teacher. Also affiliated with a center named after her in San Ramon, CA; conducted a world tour, 1987, including travel across the United States; United Nations Millennium Peace Summit, invited participant, 2000. Sometimes uses the name Ammachi. **Publications:** For My Children: Spiritual Teachings of Mata Amritanandamayi, 1986; Awaken, Children! Dialogues with Sri Sri Mata Amritanandamayi (originally Amritanandamayi sambhashanangal), 2 vols, trans. Swami Amritaswarupananda, 1990, rev. ed., 1998; Eternal Wisdom: Upadeshamritam, trans M.N. Namboodiri, 1999. **Address:** c/o Author Mail, Mata Amritanandamayi Center, PO Box 613, San Ramon, CA 94583, U.S.A. **Online address:** mam@amritapuri.org

AMSDEN, David. American, b. 1980. **Genres:** Adult non-fiction. **Career:** Author, journalist. **Publications:** Important Things That Don't Matter, 2003; Contributor to magazines. **Address:** c/o Author Mail, William Morrow/HarperCollins, 10 E. 53rd Street, 7th Floor, New York, NY 10022, U.S.A.

ANAND, Mulk Raj. See Obituaries.

ANANIA, Michael (Angelo). American, b. 1939. **Genres:** Novels, Poetry, Essays. **Career:** Professor of English, University of Illinois, Chicago, 1970- (Instructor, 1968-70); Literary Ed., Swallow Press, Chicago, 1968-74; member, Board of Dirs., 1971-76 (Chmn of the Board and President 1974-76); Executive Committee, 1972-; Coordinating Council of Literary Mags. Bibliographer, Lockwood Library, State University of New York, Buffalo, 1963-64; Ed., Audit, 1963-64; Co-Ed., Audit/Poetry, Buffalo, 1963-67; Instructor in English, State University of New York, Fredonia, 1964-65; Northwestern University, Evanston, Illinois, 1965-68. **Publications:** The Color of Dust, 1970; Set/Sorts, 1974; Riversongs, 1978; The Red Menace (novel), 1984; Constructions/Variations, 1985; The Sky at Ashland, 1986; Two Poems, 1986; In Plain Sight (essays), 1991; Selected Poems, 1994; In Natural Light (poetry), 1999. EDITOR: New Poetry Anthology I, 1969;

Gardening the Skies, 1988. **Address:** Dept. of English, University of Illinois at Chicago, Chicago, IL 60680, U.S.A.

ANASTAS, Benjamin. American, b. 1971. **Genres:** Essays. **Career:** Writer. Former fiction editor of Iowa Review. **Publications:** An Underachiever's Diary, 1998. Contributor of short stories and book reviews to periodicals. **Address:** c/o Dial Press, 1540 Broadway, New York, NY 10036, U.S.A.

ANATI, Emmanuel. Italian, b. 1930. **Genres:** Anthropology/Ethnology, Archaeology/Antiquities, Art/Art history. **Career:** University of Tel Aviv, professor of prehistory, 1968-78; University of Lecce, professor ordinarius of paleoethnology, 1980-99; Centro Camuno di Studi Preistorici, Capo Di Ponte, director and ed.-in-chief, 1964-. International Association for the Study of Prehistoric and Primitive Religions, general secretary, 1982-91; Institut des Arts Prehistoriques et Ethnographiques, Paris, president, 1992-; Intl Council on Monuments and Sites, ICOMOS-CAR, Intel Committee on Rock Art, chairman, 1980-90. **Publications:** La Grande Roche de Naquane, 1959; Camonica Valley, 1961; Palestine before the Hebrews, 1963; (with F. Roiter and C. Roy) Naquane: Decouverte d'un Pays et d'une Civilisation, 1966; Arte Preistorica in Valtellina, 1967; Origini della Civilta Camuna, 1968; Arte Rupestre nelle regioni Occidentali della Penisola Iberica, 1968; Rock Art in Central Arabia, 4 vols., 1972-75; Le Statue stele della'Italia Settrionale, 1972; (with M. Avnimelech, N. Haas and E. Meyerhof) Hazorea I, 1973; Evolution and Style in Camunian Rock Art, 1976; Methods of Recording and Analysing Rock Engravings, 1977; L'art rupestre: Negev et Sinai, 1979; Le Statue Stele delle Lunigiana, 1981; I Camuni alle Radici della Civilta Europea, 1982; Gli Elementi Fondamentali della Cultura, 1983; Har Karkom, Montagna sacra nel deserto dell'Esodo, 1984; La Prehistoire des Alpes, 1986; The Mountain of God, 1988; Origini dell'arte e della concettualita, 1988; Les Origines de l'Art, 1989; 10,000 Anni di Storia in Valcamonica, 1990; Felsbilder Wiege der Kunst und des Geistes, 1991; Radici della Cultura, 1992; Har Karkom in the Light of New Discoveries, 1993; World Rock Art, The Primordial Language, 1993; Valcamonica Rock Art, 1994; La religione delle origini, 1995; La racines de la culture, 1995; Brescia preistorica, 1995; Il museo immaginario della preistorica, 1995; I segni della storia, 1997; Esodo tra mito e storia, 1997; L'art rupestre dans le monde, 1997; Hohlenmalerei, 1997; La religion des origines, 1999; Har Karkom: 20 anni di ricerche archeologiche, 1999; Les mysteres du mont Sinai, 2000; (gen. ed.) 40,000 anni di arte contemporanea: Materiali per una esposizione sull'arte preistorica d' Europa, 2000; The Riddle of Mount Sinai, Archaeological Discoveries at Har Karkom, 2001; Gobustan, Azerbaijan, 2001; La struttura elementare dell'arte, 2002; Lo stile come fattore diagnostico nell'arte preistorica, 2002; Arte preistorica: Una rassegna regionale, 2002; Introduzione all'arte preistorica e tribale, 2003; Aux Origines de l'art, 2003. **Address:** Centro Camuno di Studi Prehistorici, 25044 Capo di Ponte, Italy. **Online address:** ccsp@tin.it

ANAYA, Rudolfo A(lfonso). American, b. 1937. **Genres:** Novels, Novellas/Short stories, Children's fiction, Poetry. **Career:** Teacher in the Albuquerque public schools, 1963-72; University of Albuquerque, director of counseling center, 1972-74; University of New Mexico, Albuquerque, professor of English, 1974-93, professor emeritus, 1993-. Coordinating Council of Literary Magazines, vice-president, 1974-80; American Book Review, NYC, associate editor, 1980-85. **Publications:** NOVELS: Bless Me, Ultima, 1972; Heart of Aztlan, 1976; Tortuga, 1979; The Legend of La Llorona, 1984; Lord of the Dawn, 1987; Alburquerque, 1992; Zia Sammer, 1995; Jalamanta, 1995; Rio Grande Fall, 1996; Shaman Winter, 1998; Jemez Spring, 2005. PLAYS: Who Killed Don Jose?; Matachines; Billy the Kid. FOR CHILDREN: The Farolitos of Christmas, 1987; Maya's Children, 1997; Farolito's for Abuelo, 1998; The Santero's Miracle, 2004. OTHER: The Silence of Llano (short stories), 1982; The Adventures of Juan Chicaspatas (poetry), 1985; Conversations with Rudolfo Anaya, 1998 with Rudolfo Anaya, 1998; Serafina's Stories (folk tales), 2004. EDITOR: (with A. Marquez) Cuentos Chicanos, 1980; (with J. Griego) Tales from the Hispanic Southwest (bilingual folk tales), 1980. **Address:** 5324 Canada Vista NW, Albuquerque, NM 87120, U.S.A.

ANCELET, Barry Jean. Also writes as Jean Arceneaux. American, b. 1951. **Genres:** Cultural/Ethnic topics, Poetry, Songs/Lyrics and libretti. **Career:** Worked as aide to Council for the Development of French in Louisiana, 1973-74; Indiana University-Bloomington, associate instructor in French, 1974-76; University of Louisiana, Lafayette, director of Center for Acadian and Creole Folklore, 1977-80; folklorist at Center for Louisiana Studies, 1980-83; director of Festival de Musique Acadienne, 1980-; professor of French, 1985-. Festival director of Tribute to Cajun Music, 1974, 1976-80; Louisiana Folklife Commission, chairman, 1984-90; Festival de Musique Acadienne/Cajun Music Festival, president and member of executive board,

1980-. Consultant to U.S. Department of State, National Geographic Society, National Park Service and Acadian Village Folklife Museum; television and film consultant. Producer of folk theater project and tour "Nous Autres," 1977-79; coproducer of a weekly radio program "Chez Nous Autres," 1979-80; producer and presenter of "Bonjour, Louisiane," daily radio program, 1980-82; host, "Rendez-vous des Cadiens," live weekly radio show, Eunice, LA, 1987-. **Publications:** The Makers of Cajun Music: Musiciens cadiens et creoles, 1984; (with M. Allain) History on the Table: An Annotated Cookbook of Cajun and Creole Cuisine, 1984; (with J. Edwards and G. Pitre) Cajun Country, 1991; Cajun Music: Origins and Development, 1989; Cajun and Creole Folktales, 1994. EDITOR: Jean l'Ours et la fille du roi (title means: John the Bear and the King's Daughter), 1979; Acadie Tropicale, 1983; (with K. James) Vivre pour manger: Cajun and Acadian Cooking, 1983. AS JEAN ARCENEAUX. POETRY: Je suis Cadien (I Am Cajun), 1994; Suite du Loup, 1999. EDITOR & CONTRIBUTOR: Cris sur le bayou: Naissance d'une poesie acadienne et creole en Louisiane (Cries on the Bayou: Birth of an Acadian and Creole Poetry in Louisiana), 1980; (with M. Allain) Anthologie de la litterature francaise de Louisiane (Anthology of Louisiana French Literature), 1981. **Address:** Dept of Modern Languages, University of Louisiana, Box 4-3331, Lafayette, LA 70504, U.S.A. **Online address:** ancelet@louisana.edu

ANCONA, George. American, b. 1929. **Genres:** Children's fiction, Children's non-fiction. **Career:** Photographer and author. Illustrator of books for children. **Publications:** Monsters on Wheels, 1974; (with R. Charlip and Mary Beth) Handtalk: An ABC of Finger Spelling and Sign Language, 1974; And What Do You Do?, 1975; I Feel: A Picture Book on Emotions, 1977; Growing Older, 1977; It's a Baby!, 1979; Dancing Is..., 1981; Monster Movers, 1984; Bananas, 1984; Teamwork, 1984; Freighter, 1985; Sheepdog, 1985; Helping Out, 1985; (with R. Charlip and Mary Beth) Handtalk Birthday, 1987; Turtle watch, 1987; (with Mary Beth) Handtalk Zoo, 1989; Riverkeeper, 1989; Aquarium, 1991; PowWow, 1992; My Camera, 1992; Pablo Remembers, 1993; The Pinata Maker, 1994; The Golden Lion Tamarin Comes Home, 1994; Mayeros, 1997; Fiesta Fireworks, 1997; Barrio, 1998; Charro, 1999; Carnaval, 1999; Cuban Kids, 2000; Harvest, 2001; Viva Mexico series: The Fiestas, The People, The Food, The Folk Arts, The Past, 2001; Murals, Walls That Sing, 2003. **Address:** 35 Calle Enrique, Santa Fe, NM 87507, U.S.A.

ANDELSON, Robert V. American, b. 1931. **Genres:** Economics, Ethics, Philosophy, Politics/Government, Social sciences, Sociology, Theology/Religion. **Career:** Ordained minister of Congregationalist Church, 1959; Arlington College, faculty member, CA, 1955-58; San Diego Extension, Henry George School of Social Science, CA, executive director, 1959-62; Northland College, WI, instructor in philosophy and religion, 1962-63; Northwestern State University, Natchitoches, LA, assistant professor of philosophy and government, 1963-65; Auburn University, Alabama, assistant professor, 1965-69, associate professor, 1969-73, professor, 1973-92, professor emeritus of philosophy, 1992-. Ludwig von Mises Institute, member, academic staff, 1983-; American Institute of Economic Research, distinguished research fellow, 1992-; International Union for Land-Value Taxation and Free Trade, president, 1997-; Robert Schalkenbach Foundation, vice president, 1998-. **Publications:** Imputed Rights: An Essay in Christian Social Theory, 1971; (with J.M. Dawsey) From Wasteland to Promised Land: Liberation Theology for a Post-Marxist Era, 1992. EDITOR: Critics of Henry George, 1979; Commons without Tragedy: Protecting the Environment from Overpopulation - A New Approach, 1991; Land-Value Taxation around the World, 2nd ed., 1997, 3rd ed., 2000. Contributor to scholarly journals. **Address:** 534 Cary Dr, Auburn, AL 36830, U.S.A. **Online address:** rvandelson@mindspring.com

ANDERS, Allison. American, b. 1954. **Genres:** Plays/Screenplays. **Career:** Screenwriter, film director, and producer. Director of films, 1987-; producer of films, 1997-. **Publications:** SCREENPLAYS: (co-author) Border Radio, 1982; Gas Food Lodging, 1992; Mi vida loca (title means: My Crazy Life), 1994; (co-author), Four Rooms, 1995; Grace of My Heart, 1996. **Address:** c/o UTA, 9560 Wilshire Blvd., Beverly Hills, CA 90210, U.S.A.

ANDERS, Isabel. American, b. 1946. **Genres:** Theology/Religion, Inspirational/Motivational Literature. **Career:** David C. Cook Publishing Co., Elgin, IL, religion editor, 1969-76; Tyndale House Publishers, Wheaton, IL, book editor, 1976-83; Synthesis Publications, Chattanooga, TN, managing editor, 1990-. **Publications:** Awaiting the Child: An Advent Journal, 1987; (with R.H. Calkin) Letters to Kristi (juvenile), 1990; The Faces of Friendship, 1992; The Lord's Prayer: Peace and Self-Acceptance for Those in Recovery, 1992; The Lord's Blessings: Hope and Peace for Those in Recovery, 1992; Walking with the Shepherd (devotional), 1994; Standing on

High Places: The Story of Hannah Hurnard and Hinds' Feet on High Places (biography), 1994; A Book of Blessings for Working Mothers, 1994; The Wisdom of Little Women, 1995; Sand and Shells, Carousels, Silver Bells: A Child's Seasons of Prayer, 1996; Simple Blessings for Sacred Moments, 1998; The Real Night before Christmas, 1999; Soul Moments, 2000; Easter ABCs, 2000; The Lord's Prayer for a New Millennium, 2001. **Address:** PO Box 277, Winchester, TN 37398, U.S.A. **Online address:** piander@earthlink. net; www.andersgroup.com; www.soulopenings.com

ANDERS, Leslie. American, b. 1922. **Genres:** History, Politics/Government. **Career:** Central Missouri State University, Warrensburg, assistant professor, 1955-58, associate professor, 1958-63, professor, 1963-87, professor emeritus of history, 1987-. Historian, Engineer Historical Division, Dept. of the Army, 1951-55. **Publications:** The Ledo Road: General Joseph W. Stilwell's Highway to China, 1965; The Eighteenth Missouri, 1968; Education for Service: Centennial History of Central Missouri State College, 1971; The Twenty-First Missouri: From Home Guard to Union Regiment, 1975; Gentle Knight: The Life and Times of Major General Edwin F. Harding, 1985; Confederate Roll of Honor: Missouri, 1990; The Test of Time, 1998. **Address:** Dept. of History, Central Missouri State University, Warrensburg, MO 64093, U.S.A.

ANDERSEN, Dennis Alan. American. **Genres:** Architecture. **Career:** Lutheran minister and author. Bethany Lutheran Church, Seattle, WA, pastor. Formerly curator at University of Washington Libraries, Special Collections Division. Also served on the Seattle Landmarks Preservation Board, the Board of Governors of the Book Club of Washington, the Pacific Northwest Lutheran Historical Society, Board of Trustees of the Friends of the Seattle Public Library, and as president of the Lutheran Ecumenical Representatives Network, 2000-. **Publications:** (with Jeffrey Karl Ochsner) Distant Corner: Seattle Architects and the Legacy of H. H. Richardson, 2003; Also contributor to Shaping Seattle Architecture: A Historical Guide to the Architects, 1994. **Address:** 410 W. Roy St., Seattle, WA 98119, U.S.A.

ANDERSEN, Kurt Byars. American, b. 1954. **Genres:** Novels, Plays/Screenplays. **Career:** NBC-TV, NYC, writer, 1976-80; Time Magazine, NYC, writer, 1981-84, architecture critic, 1984-93, columnist, 1993-94; Spy Magazine, NYC, co-founder, co-editor, 1986-93; New York Magazine, editor-in-chief, 1994-96; New Yorker, columnist, 1996-. **Publications:** The Real Thing, 1980; (with others) Tools of Power, 1980; How to be Fameous (for TV), 1990; The Hit List, 1992; Loose Lips (play), 1994; Turn of the Century, 1999. **Address:** c/o New Yorker, 4 Times Square, New York, NY 10036, U.S.A.

ANDERSON, Burton. American, b. 1938. **Genres:** Food and Wine. **Career:** Rome Daily American, Rome, Italy, reporter, 1962-63, news editor, 1965-67; Tehran Journal, Tehran, Iran, reporter, 1963; Minneapolis Tribune, Minneapolis, MN, reporter, 1964-65; Honolulu Advertiser, Honolulu, HA, reporter, 1965; International Herald Tribune, Paris, France, news editor, 1968-77. **Publications:** Vino: The Wines and Winemakers of Italy, 1980; Burton Anderson's Guide to the Wines of Italy, 1982, rev ed as The Simon & Schuster Guide to the Wines of Italy, 1992; The Wine Atlas of Italy, 1990; Treasures of the Italian Table, 1994, in UK as Pleasures of the Italian Table. **Address:** c/o Doe Coover Agency, PO Box 668, Winchester, MA 01890, U.S.A.

ANDERSON, David. American, b. 1952. **Genres:** Literary criticism and history, Business/Trade/Industry. **Career:** University of Rome, Italy, lecturer, 1979-80; University of Pennsylvania, Philadelphia, assistant professor, 1980-87; American Academy in Rome, Mellon fellow, 1988-89; Universitat Tubingen, wissenschaftlicher assistant, 1990-95; Empire Valuation Consultants, associate, 19972000. **Publications:** (ed. and author of intro.) Pound's Cavalcanti: An Edition of the Translations, Notes, and Essays, 1983; (ed. and author of intro.) Sixty Bokes Olde and Newe, 1986; Before the Knight's Tale: Imitation of Classical Epic in Boccaccio's "Teseida," 1988; Boccaccio's Glosses on Statius, 1994. **Address:** Dept. of English, University of Rochester, Rochester, NY 14627, U.S.A. **Online address:** andersonif@aol. com

ANDERSON, David Daniel. American, b. 1924. **Genres:** Novels, Literary criticism and history, Biography. **Career:** University Distinguished Professor, Dept. of American Thought and Language, Michigan State University, East Lansing, 1957-. Ed., Midwestern Miscellany Annual. Executive Secretary, Society for the Study of Midwestern Literature (President, 1971-73). **Publications:** Louis Bromfield, 1964; Critical Studies in American Literature, 1964; Sherwood Anderson, 1967; Sherwood Anderson's Winesburg, Ohio, 1967; Brand Whitlock, 1968; Abraham Lincoln, 1970; Robert Ingersoll, 1972;

Woodrow Wilson, 1978; Ignatius Donnelly, 1980; William Jennings Bryan, 1981; Critical Essays on Sherwood Anderson, 1981; Michigan: A State Anthology, 1982; Route Two, Titus, Ohio, 1993; The Path in the Shadow, 1998; Command Performances, 2003; Ohio in Myth, Memory, and Imagination, 2004. EDITOR: (in-chief) The Black Experience, 1969; The Literary Works of Abraham Lincoln, 1970; (with R. Wright) The Dark and Tangled Path, 1971; Sunshine and Smoke, 1971; Mid-America I-XXVII, 1974-2001; Sherwood Anderson: Dimensions of His Literary Art (essays), 1976; Sherwood Anderson: The Writer at His Craft, 1979; The Durability of Raintree County, 1998; Lieutenant William E. Sleight and the 102nd Regiment, U.S. Colored Infantry, in the Civil War, 2003. **Address:** Dept of American Thought and Language, Michigan State University, East Lansing, MI 48824, U.S.A.

ANDERSON, Donna K. American, b. 1935. **Genres:** Music, Bibliography, Biography. **Career:** MacPhail School of Music, Minneapolis, MN, piano teacher, 1956-59; Summit School, St. Paul, MN, piano teacher, 1959-61; Neighborhood Music School, Bronx, NY, piano teacher, 1965-66; New York Public Library for the Performing Arts, research assistant in Music Division, 1966-67; State University of New York College at Cortland, assistant professor, 1967-70, associate professor, 1970-78, professor of music, 1978-, head of department, 1985-92, professor of music emeritus, 1997, coordinator, first year program, 1997-98. Piano soloist and accompanist; guest on radio programs. City of Cortland, member of Zoning Board of Appeals, 1987-93, chairperson, 1990-93. **Publications:** Charles T. Griffes: An Annotated Bibliography-Discography, 1977; The Works of Charles T. Griffes: A Descriptive Catalogue, 1983; Charles T. Griffes: A Life in Music, 1993. EDITOR (all by C.T. Griffes): Three Preludes, 1967; Four Impressions, 1970; (and trans) Four German Songs, 1970; De Profundis, 1977; Song of the Dagger, 1983; Nachtlied, 1983; Seven English Songs, 1986; (and trans) Seven German Songs, 1986; Rhapsody in B Minor, 1992; The Pleasure Dome of Kubla-Khan, 1993; Charles T. Griffes: A Winter Landscape, 1997. Contributor of articles and reviews to music journals and newspapers. **Address:** Department of Performing Arts, State University of New York College at Cortland, PO Box 2000, Cortland, NY 13045, U.S.A. **Online address:** Andersond@ snycorva.cortland.edu

ANDERSON, Douglas A(llen). American, b. 1959. **Genres:** Literary criticism and history, Bibliography. **Career:** Worked as bookseller in Ithaca, NY, 1983-94; freelance writer, 1994-. **Publications:** (annotator) J.R.R. Tolkien, The Annotated Hobbit, 1988, rev. ed., 2002; (with W.G. Hammond) J.R.R. Tolkien: A Descriptive Bibliography, 1993; The 100 Best Writers of Fantasy and Horror, 2005. EDITOR: (with C. Tolkien and author of intro. note) J.R.R. Tolkien, The Lord of the Rings, 1987, rev. ed., 2002; K. Morris, The Chalchiuhite Dragon: A Tale of Toltec Times, 1992. EDITOR AND AUTHOR OF INTRO.: L. Cline, The Lady of Frozen Death, and Other Weird Tales, 1992; The Dragon Path: Collected Tales of Kenneth Morris, 1995; G.R. Wormser, The Scarecrow and Other Tales, 2001; J.R.R. Tolkien, The Hobbit, 2001; (with S.T. Joshi and D.E. Schultz) Eyes of the God: The Weird Fiction and Poetry of R.H. Barlow, 2002; Tales before Tolkien: The Roots of Modern Fantasy, 2003; Seekers of Dreams, 2005; V. Meik, Devil's Drums, 2005; Adrift on the Haunted Seas: The Best Stories of William Hope Hodgson, 2005; (with M.J. Burn) On Tolkien: Interviews, Reminiscences and Other Essays, 2005. Author of numerous introductions of books. **Address:** PO Box 493, Marcellus, MI 49067, U.S.A. **Online address:** nodens100@hotmail. com

ANDERSON, Duane. American, b. 1943. **Genres:** Anthropology/Ethnology. **Career:** Sanford Museum and Planetarium, Cherokee, IA, director, 1966-75; University of Iowa, Iowa City, state archaeologist, 1975-86, member of executive committee of Museum of Natural History, 1977-86; Dayton Museum of Natural History, Dayton, OH, executive director, 1986-92; School of American Research, Santa Fe, NM, vice president, 1992-, and director of Indian Arts Research Center. **Publications:** Western Iowa Prehistory, 1975; (ed. with H.A. Semken, Jr.) The Cherokee Excavations: Holocene Ecology and Human Adaptations in Northwestern Iowa, 1980; Eastern Iowa Prehistory, 1981; Mill Creek Ceramics: The Complex from the Brewster Site, 1981; All That Glitters: The Emergence of Native American Micaceous Art Pottery in Northern New Mexico, 1999; (ed.) Legacy: Southwest Indian Art at the School of American Research, 1999. **Address:** c/o School of American Research Press, PO Box 2188, Santa Fe, NM 87504, U.S.A.

ANDERSON, Elijah. American, b. 1943. **Genres:** Sociology. **Career:** Swarthmore College, Swarthmore, PA, assistant professor of sociology, 1973-75; University of Pennsylvania, Philadelphia, assistant professor, 1975-80, associate professor, 1981-88, professor of sociology, 1988-, Max and Heidi Berry Term Professor in the Social Sciences, 1988-90, Charles and William Day Professor of the Social Sciences, 1990-. **Publications:** A Place on the

Corner, 1978; Streetwise: Race, Class, and Change in an Urban Community, 1990; Code of the Street: Decency, Violence, and the Moral Life of the Inner City, 1999. **Address:** University of Pennsylvania, Department of Sociology, 3718 Locust Walk, Philadelphia, PA 19104, U.S.A.

ANDERSON, Elizabeth (S.). American, b. 1959. **Genres:** Ethics, Philosophy, Women's studies and issues. **Career:** Swarthmore College, Swarthmore, PA, visiting instructor in philosophy, 1985-86; University of Michigan, Ann Arbor, professor of philosophy and women's studies, 1987-, Arthur F. Thurnau Professor, 1994. **Publications:** Value in Ethics and Economics, 1993. Contributor to books. Contributor of articles and reviews to philosophy and law journals. **Address:** Department of Philosophy, 435 S State St, University of Michigan, Ann Arbor, MI 48109-1003, U.S.A. **Online address:** eandersn@umich.edu

ANDERSON, Gary L. American, b. 1948. **Genres:** Education. **Career:** Teacher of English and Spanish at junior and senior high schools in Swea City, IA, 1971-73; Inlingua Languages, Buenos Aires, Argentina, teacher trainer and instructor in English as a second language, 1973-74; Higher Education Development Fund-Harlem Center, NYC, teacher and director of bilingual programs, 1974-79; bilingual coordinator at an intermediate school in NYC, 1979-81; State University of New York, NYC, lecturer at Equal Opportunity Center, Harlem Center, 1981-82; American School of Puebla, Puebla, Mexico, high school principal, 1982-84; Ohio State University, Columbus, instructor and field supervisor, 1984-87; Western Maryland College, Westminster, adjunct faculty member, 1987-88; University of New Mexico, Albuquerque, assistant professor, 198894, associate professor of education, 1994-, director of Latin American Programs in Education, 1991-93, coordinator of Language, Literacy, and Socio-Cultural Studies Division, 1993-94. University of San Martin, Fulbright lecturer, 1996; University of California, Irvine, member of advisory board, Center for Collaborative Research in Education; speaker at educational institutions. **Publications:** (with K. Herr and A. Nihlen) Studying Your Own School: An Educator's Guide to Qualitative, Practitioner Research, 1994; (with J. Blase, J. Blase, and S. Dungan) Democratic Principals in Action: Eight Pioneers, 1995; (with Blase) The Micropolitics of Educational Leadership: From Control to Empowerment, 1995; (ed. and translator, with M. Montero-Sieburth) Educational Qualitative Research in Latin America: The Struggle for a New Paradigm, 1997. Contributor to books. **Address:** College of Education, 222 Hokona Hall, University of New Mexico, Albuquerque, NM 87131, U.S.A. **Online address:** Garyand@unm.edu.

ANDERSON, H(ugh) George. American, b. 1932. **Genres:** Theology/Religion. **Career:** Lutheran Theological Southern Seminary, Columbia, SC, faculty member until 1970, president, 1970-; Luther College, Decorah, IA, president, 1982-; Minnesota Public Radio, director, 1984-90; Evangelical Lutheran Church in America, presiding bishop, 1995-2001. **Publications:** Lutheranism in the Southeastern States, 1860-1886: A Social History, 1969; A Good Time to Be the Church: A Conversation with Bishop H. George Anderson, 1997. EDITOR: (with T.A. Murphy and J.A. Burgess) Justification by Faith, 1985; (with J.R. Crumley, Jr.) Promoting Unity: Themes in Lutheran-Catholic Dialogue, 1989; (with J.F. Stafford and J.A. Burgess) The One Mediator, the Saints, and Mary, 1992; Lutherans and Catholics in Dialogue (series). **Address:** c/o Augsburg Books, PO Box 1209, Minneapolis, MN 55440, U.S.A. **Online address:** hgeorgea@earthlink.net

ANDERSON, Henry L(ee Norman). Also writes as Norhm Lee. American, b. 1934. **Genres:** Education, Gay and lesbian issues, Human relations/Parenting, Medicine/Health, Race relations. **Career:** Academic administrator, free-lance writer, lecturer, radio and television host, and licensed marriage, family, and child counselor. Los Angeles County Schools, teacher, 1961-66; Los Angeles Unified Schools District, instructor, administrator, 1967-68; University of California, Los Angeles, Dept of Special Education Programs, associate director, 1968-69; Loyola University, Los Angeles, Graduate School of Education, and California State University, Los Angeles, supervisor of student teachers, 1972-73; Windsor University, Los Angeles, vice-president, 1973-75; City University, Los Angeles, chancellor, 1974-. Evaluations and Management International, Inc., director, 1971. Hosts weekly talk radio program and wellness TV series. Founder and chancellor of the Martin Luther King Memorial Urban Core Multi-Versity. Founder of the Organic Wellness Crusade and Imahe Wellness Village. Consultant and lecturer in wellness and other fields; real estate developer. **Publications:** You and Race...A Christian Reflects, 1960; No Use Cryin' (novel), 1961; Revolutionary Urban Teaching, 1973; Helping Hand: Eight-Day Diet Programs for People Who Care about Wellness, 1986; Ihre gesundheit liegt in ihrer hand, 1992; Organic Wellness Fasting Technique, 1992; African: Born in America, 1993; The Nature and Purpose of Disease: Definitive Guide for Peoples with

Melanin, 2001. Contributor to professional journals. **Address:** PO Box 45227, Los Angeles, CA 90045-5227, U.S.A. **Online address:** dranderson@cula.edu; truth@organicwellness.com

ANDERSON, James. British. **Genres:** Mystery/Crime/Suspense, Plays/Screenplays. **Publications:** Assassin, 1969; The Alpha List, 1972; The Abolition of Death, 1974; The Affair of the Blood-Stained Egg Cosy, 1975; Appearance of Evil, 1977; Angel of Death, 1978; Assault and Matrimony, 1980; The Affair of the Mutilated Mink, 1982; Auriol, 1982; The Murder of Sherlock Holmes, 1985; Hooray for Homicide, 1985; Lovers and Other Killers, 1986; Additional Evidence, 1988; The Animals' Christmas, a Nativity Play for Children, 1995; The Affair of the Thirty-Nine Cufflinks, 2003. **Address:** 4 Church Rd, Penarth, Glamorgan, Wales. **Online address:** james-anderson@tesco.net

ANDERSON, James G. American, b. 1936. **Genres:** Education, Information science/Computers, Medicine/Health, Sociology. **Career:** Purdue University, West Lafayette, IN, Professor of Sociology, Dept. of Sociology and Anthropology, 1970-, Director, Social Research Institute, 1995-, Professor of Communication, 2004-. Instructor in Mathematics, Mount St. Agnes College, 1962-64; Administrative Assistant to the Dean, 1964-65, and Director, Division of Engineering, 1965-66, Evening College, Johns Hopkins University, Baltimore, MD; Research Professor of Educational Administration, New Mexico State University, Las Cruces, 1966-70; Methodist Hospital of Indiana, Graduate Medical Education Program, adjunct professor of medical sociology, 1991-; Co-director of the Rural Center for AIDS/STD Prevention, Indiana University and Purdue University, 1994-. **Publications:** Bureaucracy in Education, 1968; (with J. Sullivan) Simulation in Health Care, 1991; Medical Sciences Simulation Conference, 1998; Simulation in the Health and Medical Sciences, 2001; (with C. Aydin) Evaluating the Organizational Impact of Health Care Information Systems, 2005. EDITOR: (with S.J. Jay) Use and Impact of Computers in Clinical Medicine, 1987; Simulation in Health Care and Social Services, 1992; (with M. Katzper) Simulation in the Health Sciences and Services, 1993; (with C. Aydin and S. Jay) Evaluating Health Care Information Systems, 1994; (with M. Katzper) Simulation in the Health Sciences, 1994; (with M. Katzper) Health Sciences, Physiological and Pharmacological Simulation Studies, 1995; (with M. Katzper) Simulation in the Medical Sciences, 1996; (with M. Katzper) Simulation in the Medical Sciences, 1997; (with M. Katzper) 1998; (with M. Katzper) Health Sciences Simulation, 1999, rev. ed., 2005; (with K.W. Goodman) Ethics and Information Technology: A Case-Based Approach to a Health Care System in Transition, 2002. **Address:** 4141 Black Forest Ln, West Lafayette, IN 47906, U.S.A. **Online address:** Andersonj@sri.soc.purdue.edu

ANDERSON, Janet A. See Obituaries.

ANDERSON, Joanne M. American, b. 1949. **Genres:** Food and Wine, Travel/Exploration. **Career:** Clay Corner Inn, Blacksburg, VA, owner and innkeeper, 1994-. Also worked as public relations director and technical writer. **Publications:** Small-Town Restaurants in Virginia, 1998; Solomon Says: Observations of an Innkeeper Dog, 2001. Contributor to magazines and newspapers. **Address:** 401 Clay St SW, Blacksburg, VA 24060, U.S.A. **Online address:** jmawriter@aol.com

ANDERSON, John B(ayard). American, b. 1922. **Genres:** Politics/Government. **Career:** Chairman, National Unity Party, Washington, D.C. Foreign Service Officer on staff of the U.S. High Commissioner to Germany, 1952-55; practiced law, Rockford, Illinois, 1955-60; State's Attorney, Winnebago County, Illinois, 1956-60; Member for the 16th district of Illinois (Republican), U.S. House of Representatives, 1969-79: Chairman, House Republican Conference, and Member, House Rules Committee, and Joint Committee on Atomic Energy. Independent Candidate for President of the U.S., 1980. **Publications:** Between Two Worlds: A Congressman's Choice, 1970; (ed.) Congress and Conscience, 1970; Vision and Betrayal in America, 1976; The American Economy We Need-And Won't Get from the Republicans or the Democrats, 1984; A Proper Institution, 1988. **Address:** 3917 Massachusetts Ave NW, Washington, DC 20016, U.S.A. **Online address:** bauco@aol.com

ANDERSON, Jon Lee. American, b. 1957. **Genres:** Military/Defense/Arms control. **Career:** Freelance journalist, writer, and documentary filmmaker. New Yorker magazine, staff writer, 1998-. **Publications:** (with S. Anderson) Inside the League: The Shocking Expose of How Terrorists, Nazis, and Latin American Death Squads Have Infiltrated the World Anti-Communist League, 1986; (with S. Anderson) War Zones: Voices from the World's Killing Zones, 1988; Guerrillas, 1992; Che Guevara: A Revolutionary Life, 1997; The

Lion's Grave: Dispatches from Afghanistan, 2002; The Fall of Baghdad, 2004. **Address:** c/o Grove/Atlantic Inc., 841 Broadway, New York, NY 10003, U.S.A.

ANDERSON, Judy. American, b. 1943. **Genres:** Human relations/Parenting, Business/Trade/Industry, Sports/Fitness. **Career:** Gateway Technical Institute, Kenosha, WI, assistant registrar and adjunct instructor, 1971-79; Long Island University, Greenvale, NY, associate registrar, 1979-85; American Express Financial Services, Mineola, NY, financial planner, 1985-86; Dime Savings Bank of New York, Uniondale, trainer and counselor, 1986-93; Business Golf Unlimited, Utica, MI, golf and business coach and professional speaker, 1991-. **Publications:** Teeing Off to the Green: Using Golf as a Business Tool, 1995. **Address:** 42253 Parkside Cir, Apt. 105, Sterling Heights, MI 48314-3398, U.S.A. **Online address:** judy@bizgolf.com

ANDERSON, Kay. Australian, b. 1958. **Genres:** Cultural/Ethnic topics, Geography, History. **Career:** Durham University, professor of geography; University of Western Sydney, professor of cultural research. **Publications:** Vancouver's Chinatown: Racial Discourse in Canada, 1875-1980, 1991. EDITOR: (with F. Gale) Cultural Geographies, 1999; (with M. Domosh, S. Pile, and N. Thrift) Handbook of Cultural Geography, 2002. Contributor of book chapters and articles to collective works and periodicals. **Address:** Centre for Cultural Research, University of Western Sydney, Parramatta Campus EBa, Locked Bag 1797, Penrith South DC, NSW 1797, Australia. **Online address:** k.anderson@uws.edu.au

ANDERSON, Kenneth Norman. American, b. 1921. **Genres:** Military/Defense/Arms control, Medicine/Health, Food and Wine. **Career:** Executive Ed., Publishers Editorial Services; President, Editorial Guild. News Editor, Radio Station KOIL, Omaha, NE, 1946-47; Intrnational News Service, Omaha and Kansas City, 1947-56; Assistant Editor, Better Homes and Gardens, 1956-57; Associate Editor, Popular Mechanics, 1957-59; Editor-in-Chief, Today's Health (AMA), 1959-65; Ed., Holt, Rinehart & Winston, Inc., New York, 1965-70; Executive Director, Coffee Information Institute, NYC, 1970-81; President, Pubs. Editorial Services, Katonah, NY, 1981-90. **Publications:** (co-author) Lawyer's Medical Cyclopedia, 1962; (with R. Addison) The Family Physician, 1963; (with W. Baver) Today's Health Guide, 1965; (with Robert Addison) Pictorial Medical Guide, 1967; Field and Stream Guide to Physical Fitness, 1969; (with P. Kuhn) Home Medical Encyclopedia, 1973; Sterno Guide to the Outdoors, 1977; Eagle Claw Fish Cookbook, 1977; The Newsweek Encyclopedia of Family Health and Fitness, 1980; (with W. Glanze) Bantam Medical Dictionary, 1980, 1982; How Long Will You Live, 1981; (with D. Tver) Dictionary of Dangerous Pollutants, Ecology, and Environment, 1981; The Pocket Guide to Coffees and Teas, 1982; (with L. Urdang) Mosby's Medical & Nursing Dictionary, 1982, 5th ed. 1998; Orphan Drugs, 1983, 1988; (with W. Glanze and R. Goldenson) Longman Dictionary of Psychology and Psychiatry, 1984; (with J. Murphy) History of the U.S. Marines, 1984; U.S. Military Operations: 1945-85, 1984; The Gourmet's Guide to Fish and Shellfish, 1984; (with L. Harmon Anderson) Prentice-Hall Dictionary of Nutrition and Health, 1985; (with L. Harmon Anderson and W. Glanze) Mosby's Medical Encyclopedia, 1985, rev. ed, 1992; (with D. Tver) Industrial Medicine Desk Reference, 1986; (with R. Goldenson) The Language of Sex from A to Z, 1986 (with R. Wagman and others) The Medical & Health Encyclopedia, Symptoms After Forty, 1987; (with E. Brace) The New Pediatric Guide to Drugs & Vitamins, 1987; (with I. Settle) Pictorial History of Television, 1987; (with R. Goldenson) Sex A to Z, 1989; (with L. Anderson) Mosby's Pocket Dictionary of Medicine, Nursing, and Allied Health, 1990, 3rd ed., 1998; History of U.S. Military Operations since World War II, 1992; (with L. Anderson) The International Dictionary of Food and Nutrition, 1993; (with L. Anderson) The International Menu Speller, 1993. **Address:** 1278 Kingswood Blvd., Mountain Home, AR 72653-8083, U.S.A.

ANDERSON, Kent. American, b. 1945. **Genres:** Adult non-fiction. **Career:** Writer. **Publications:** Television Fraud: The History and Implications of the Quiz Show Scandals, 1978; Sympathy for the Devil, 1987; Night Dogs, 1996. **Address:** c/o Bantam Books, 1540 Broadway, New York, NY 10036, U.S.A.

ANDERSON, Kevin J(ames). Also writes as Gabriel Mesta. American, b. 1962. **Genres:** Science fiction/Fantasy, Young adult fiction. **Career:** Lawrence Livermore National Laboratory, Livermore, CA, technical writer/editor, 1983-95; Materials Research Society, Pittsburgh, PA, columnist, 1988-94; International Society for Respiratory Protection, Salem, OR, copy editor, 1989-95. **Publications:** WITH D. BEASON: Lifeline, 1991; The Trinity Paradox, 1991; Assemblers of Infinity, 1993; Ill Wind, 1995; Virtual Destruction, 1996; Ignition, 1997; Fallout, 1997; Lethal Exposure, 1998. WITH K.K.

RUSCH: Afterimage, 1992; Aftershock, 1998. THE X-FILES SERIES: Ground Zero, 1995; Ruins, 1996; Antibodies, 1998. SCIENCE FICTION: Resurrection Inc., 1988; Climbing Olympus, 1994; Blindfold, 1995; (ed.) War of the Worlds: Global Dispatches (anthology), 1996; Dogged Persistence, 2002; (as K.J. Anderson) Captain Nemo, 2002; Hopscotch, 2002. DUNE SERIES (with B. Herbert): Dune: House Atreides, 1999; House Harkonnen, 2000; House Corrino, 2001; The Butlerian Jihad, 2002; The Machine Crusade, 2003; The Battle of Corrin, 2004. SAGA OF THE SEVEN SUNS SERIES: Hidden Empire, 2002; A Forest of Stars, 2003; Horizon Storms, 2004. GAMEARTH SERIES: Gamearth, 1989; Gameplay, 1989; Game's End, 1990. FOR YOUNG ADULTS: (with J.G. Betancourt) Born of Elven Blood, 1995; Darksaber, 1995. STAR WARS: JEDI ACADEMY TRILOGY: Jedi Search, 1994; Dark Apprentice, 1994; Champions of the Force, 1994. STAR WARS: YOUNG JEDI KNIGHTS SERIES (with R. Moesta): The Lost Ones, 1995; Shadow Academy, 1995; Heirs of the Force, 1995; Darkest Knight, 1996; Lightsabers, 1996; Jedi under Siege, 1996; Shards of Alderaan, 1997; Delusions of Grandeur, 1997; Diversity Alliance, 1997; The Emperor's Plague, 1997; Jedi Bounty, 1997; Return to Ord Mantell, 1998; Trouble on Cloud City, 1998; Crisis on Crystal Reef, 1998. EDITOR, STAR WARS ANTHOLOGIES SERIES: Star Wars: Tales from the Mos Eisley Cantina, 1995; Tales from Jabba's Palace, 1995; Tales of the Bounty Hunters, 1996. STAR WARS: TALES OF THE JEDI SERIES: Dark Lords of the Sith, 1996; Golden Age of the Sith, 1997. OTHER: The Illustrated Star Wars Universe, 1995; (with R. Moesta) Star Wars: The Mos Eisley Cantina Pop-Up Book, 1995. WITH R. MOESTA AS GABRIEL MESTA: Shadow of the Xel'Naga, 2001. Work represented in anthologies. Contributor of short stories, articles, and reviews to periodicals.

ANDERSON, Kirk. American, b. 1965. **Genres:** Translations. **Career:** Independent translator, 1990-. **Publications:** TRANSLATOR: P. Almodovar, Patty Diphusa and Other Writings, 1992; half of the essays in For Rushdie, 1994; works by F. Varela, F. Duran Ayanegui, J.M. Asensi, J.L. Sampedro, Su Tong, Zhong Ling, Zheng Da, and others. **Address:** 2455 Flamingo Dr No. 401, Miami Beach, FL 33140-4635, U.S.A. **Online address:** paellero@aol.com

ANDERSON, Lauri (Arvid). American, b. 1942. **Genres:** Novellas/Short stories. **Career:** U.S. Peace Corps, volunteer teacher at Bornu Teachers' College, Maiduguri, Nigeria, 1965-67; high school English teacher in Newport, VT, 1967-69; Mizpah Mission School, Moen, Truk, East Carolines, English teacher, department chair, and dean of boys, 197172; American Collegiate Institute, Izmir, Turkey, English teacher and department chair, 1972-76; Finlandia University, Hancock, MI, chair of English language and literature department, 1976-, also director of Humanities Program and rural studies coordinator. Indiana University-Bloomington, teacher of technical writing, 1983-84; Phillips Academy (private secondary school), teacher of English at summer camps, 1995 and 1997. FinnFest, guest writer and lecturer, 1996, 1997; presents workshops, including programs at elderhostels; gives readings from his works. **Publications:** Snow White and Others (poetry), 1971; Small Winter Wars (short fiction), 1983; Hunting Hemingway's Trout (short fiction), 1990; Heikki Heikkinen and Other Stories of Upper Peninsula Finns, 1995; Children of the Kalevala (short fiction), 1997; Misery Bay (short fiction), 2001. Work represented in anthologies. Author of a series of weekly fictional profiles in Mining Journal, 1992-94. Contributor of poetry, essays, and short stories to periodicals and professional journals. **Address:** Dept of English, Finlandia University, Hancock, MI 49930, U.S.A. **Online address:** lauri.anderson@finlandia.edu

ANDERSON, M. T(obin). American, b. 1968. **Genres:** Novels, Mystery/Crime/Suspense, Horror, Science fiction/Fantasy, Children's fiction, Young adult fiction, Music, Biography, Picture/board books. **Career:** Writer. Candlewick Press, Cambridge, MA, editorial assistant, 1993-96; Boston Review, intern; WCUW-Radio, disc jockey; Vermont College, MFA program in Writing for Children, faculty member, 2000-. Has also worked as sales clerk at a department store. **Publications:** Thirsty (horror novel), 1997; Burger Wuss, 1999; Handel, Who Knew What He Liked (picture book), 2001; Feed, 2002; Strange Mr. Satie, 2004; The Game of Sunken Places, 2004; The Serpent came to Gloucester, 2005; Whales on Stilts, 2005. **Address:** c/o Candlewick Press, 2067 Massachusetts Ave, Cambridge, MA 02140, U.S.A.

ANDERSON, Malcolm. British, b. 1934. **Genres:** History, Politics/Government, Translations. **Career:** Professor of Politics, University of Edinburgh, since 1979. Lecturer in Government, University of Manchester, 1960-64; Sr. Lecturer, 1965-73, and Professor of Politics, 1973-79, University of Warwick. **Publications:** (co-author) The Right in France, 1890-1919, 1962; (trans.) An Introduction to the Social Sciences: With Special Reference to Their Methods, by Maurice Duverger, 1964; Government in France, 1971;

Conservative Politics in France, 1974; Frontier Regions in Western Europe, 1983; Women, Equality and Europe, 1988; Policing the World: Interpol and the Politics of International Police Co-operation, 1989; (co-ed.) Policing across National Boundaries, 1993; (co-author) Policing the European Union, 1995; Frontiers: Territory and State Formation in the Modern World, 1996. **Address:** Dept. of Politics, University of Edinburgh, Edinburgh EH8 9JT, Scotland.

ANDERSON, Margaret Jean. American (born Scotland), b. 1931. **Genres:** Young adult fiction, Young adult non-fiction. **Career:** Statistician, East Malling Research Station, Kent, England, 1953-1955; entomologist, Canada Department of Agriculture, Summerland, BC, 1955-1956; statistician, Oregon State University, Corvallis, 1956-1957; writer, 1957-. **Publications:** FOR CHILDREN AND YOUNG ADULTS. FICTION: To Nowhere and Back, 1975; In the Keep of Time, 1977; Searching for Shona, 1978; In the Circle of Time, 1979; The Journey of the Shadow Bairns, 1980; The Brain on Quartz Mountain, 1982; Light in the Mountain, 1982; The Mists of Time, 1984; The Druid's Gift, 1989; The Ghost Inside the Monitor, 1990. NON-FICTION: Exploring the Insect World, 1974; Exploring City Trees, and the Need for Urban Forests, 1976; Food Chains: The Unending Cycle, 1991; Charles Darwin, Naturalist, 1994; (with N. Field and K. Stephenson) Ancient Forests: Discovering Nature, 1995; Bizarre Insects, 1996; Isaac Newton: The Greatest Scientist of All Time, 1996; Carl Linnaeus, Prince of Botany/Father of Classification, 1997; Children of Summer: Henri Fabre's Insects, 1997; (with N. Field and K. Stephenson) Leapfrogging through Wetlands, 1998; (with K. Stephenson) Scientists of the Ancient World, 1999; (with R.G. Vivian) Chaco Canyon, 2002. **Address:** 3325 NW 60th Street, Corvallis, OR 97330, U.S.A. **Online address:** mja@peak.org

ANDERSON, Marilyn D. American, b. 1943. **Genres:** Children's fiction. **Career:** Self-employed writer, 1983-. Former music teacher; instructor at Institute of Children's Literature. **Publications:** The Horse Lover's Handbook (nonfiction), 1983; All for a Horse, 1983, published as The Wild Arabian, 1987; The Horse That Came to Breakfast, 1983; No Home for Shannon, 1984; Hot Fudge Pickles, 1984; But Maggie Wanted a Pony, 1984, as Maggie's Wish, 1987; Barkley, Come Home, 1985, as Come Home, Barkley, 1996; A Horse Named Bandit, 1985; The Bridesmaid Wears Trackshoes, 1985; Hungry as a Lion (picture book), 1985; Marshmallow Pickles, 1986; I Don't Want a New Horse, 1986; We Have to Get Rid of These Puppies, 1986; The Bubble Gum Monster, 1987; Nobody Wants Barkley, 1987; The Bubble Gum Monster Strikes Again, 1989; The Revenge of the Bubble Gum Monster, 1992; Bring Back Barkley, 1998; (with J. Chaitin and S.S. Estabrook) The Fourth Wise Man (play), 1998; Chris Farley (biography), 2001; The Vice Presidency (nonfiction), 2001; Sarah Michelle Gellar (biography), 2002; Will Smith (biography), 2003. Stories and articles have been published popular and professional journals. **Address:** 10957 U.S. Hwy 50 W., Bedford, IN 47421, U.S.A. **Online address:** mandka@dmrtc.net

ANDERSON, Mark M. American, b. 1955. **Genres:** Literary criticism and history, Language/Linguistics. **Career:** Columbia University, NYC, assistant professor, 1985-90, associate professor of German and comparative literature, 1991-, director of Deutsches Haus, 1986-88 and 1989-90; chairman, department of Germanic languages, 1993-. **Publications:** Kafka's Clothes: Ornament and Aestheticism in the Habsburg Fin de Siecle, 1992; EDITOR: (And translator and author of introduction) Ingeborg Bachmann, In the Storm of Roses: Selected Poems by Ingeborg Bachmann, 1986; Reading Kafka: Prague, Politics, and the Fin de Siecle, 1989; (And author of introduction) Franz Kafka, The Sons, 1989; (And author of introduction) Bachmann, Three Paths to the Lake, 1989; (And author of afterword) Bachmann, Malina, 1990; Hitler's Exiles: Personal Stories of the Flight from Nazi Germany to America, 1998. **Address:** Department of Germanic Languages, Columbia University, New York, NY 10027, U.S.A.

ANDERSON, Matthew Smith. British, b. 1922. **Genres:** History. **Career:** London School of Economics, lecturer in political history, 1953-61, reader, 1961-72, professor of international history, 1972-85. **Publications:** Britain's Discovery of Russia, 1553-1815, 1958; Europe in the Eighteenth Century, 1713-1783, 1961, rev. ed., 2000; The Eastern Question, 1774-1923, 1966; Eighteenth Century Europe, 1713-1789, 1966; The Ascendancy of Europe, 1815-1914, 1972, 3rd ed., 2003; Peter the Great, 1978, rev. ed., 1995; Historians and Eighteenth Century Europe, 1979; War and Society in Europe of the Old Regime, 1618-1789, 1988; The Rise of Modern Diplomacy, 1450-1919, 1993; The War of the Austrian Succession, 1740-1748, 1995; The Origins of the Modern European State System, 1494-1618, 1998. EDITOR: The Great Powers and the Near East, 1774-1923, 1970; Studies in Diplomatic History: Essays in Memory of David Bayne Horn, 1970. **Address:** 45 Cholmeley Cres, London N6 5EX, England.

ANDERSON, Molly D(elCarmen). American, b. 1955. **Genres:** Agriculture/Forestry. **Career:** Tufts University, Medford, MA, assistant professor of nutrition, 1991-, director of degree program in agriculture, food, and the environment, 1994-. **Publications:** (with W. Lockertz) Agricultural Research Alternatives, 1993. **Address:** School of Nutrition, Tufts University, Medford, MA 02155-7028, U.S.A.

ANDERSON, Olive Ruth. British, b. 1926. **Genres:** History. **Career:** University of London, Westfield College, assistant lecturer, 1949-57, lecturer, 1958-69, reader, 1969-86, professor of history, 1986-89, Queen Mary and Westfield College, professor of history, 1989-91, emeritus, 1991-, fellow, 1994-. Royal Historical Society, vice-president, 2001-. **Publications:** A Liberal State at War: English Politics and Economics during the Crimean War, 1967; Suicide in Victorian and Edwardian England, 1987. **Address:** 45 Cholmeley Cres, Highgate, London N6 5EX, England.

ANDERSON, Patricia J. Canadian, b. 1950. **Genres:** Literary criticism and history, Social commentary. **Career:** High school teacher and freelance copyeditor/proofreader in Vancouver, British Columbia, Canada, 1973-89; independent scholar, London, England, 1989-91; freelance writer and historian, 1993-; literary consultant, 1999-. **Publications:** The Printed Image and the Transformation of Popular Culture, 1790-1860, 1991; When Passion Reigned: Sex and the Victorians, 1995; Passion Lost: Public Sex, Private Desire in the Twentieth Century, 2001. EDITOR (with J. Rose): Dictionary of Literary Biography, Vol. 106: British Literary Publishing Houses, 1820-1880, 1991, Vol. 112: British Literary Publishing Houses, 1881-1965, 1991. Contributor to periodicals. **Address:** c/o Lettie Lee, Ann Elmo Agency, 60 E 42nd St, New York, NY 10165, U.S.A. **Online address:** patriciaanderson@helpingyougetpublished.com

ANDERSON, Rachel. (Rachel Bradby). British, b. 1943. **Genres:** Novels, Children's fiction, Plays/Screenplays, Literary criticism and history. **Publications:** Pineapple, 1965; Tomorrow's Tomorrow (radio play), 1972; The Purple Heart Throbs, 1974; Moffatt's Road, 1978; Dream Lovers, 1978; Fairy Snow and the Disability Box (play for children), 1981; The Poacher's Son, 1982; Little Angel Comes to Stay, 1984; The War Orphan, 1986; French Lessons, 1988; Little Angel, Bonjour, 1988; Best Friends, 1989; The Bus People, 1989; The Boy Who Laughed, 1989; Jessy Runs Away, 1989; For the Love of Sang, 1990; Happy Christmas Little Angel, 1990; The Working Class, 1993; Jessy & the Long-Short Dress, 1993; Princess Jazz & the Angels, 1994; Black Water, 1994; The Dolls' House, 1995; Letters from Heaven, 1995; Julie and the Queen of Tonga, 1996; Carly's Luck, 1997; Ollie and the Trainers, 1997; The Scavenger's Tale, 1998; Big Ben, 1998; Grandmother's Footsteps, 1999; Bloom of Youth, 1999; Warlands, 2000; Joe's Story, 2001; Stronger Than Mountains, 2001. TRANSLATOR: The Cat's Tale, 1985; (with D. Bradby) Renard the Fox, 1986; Wild Goose Chase, 1986; Little Lost Fox, 1992. **Address:** c/o Oxford University Press, Walton St, Oxford OX4 6DP, England.

ANDERSON, Richard Lloyd. American, b. 1926. **Genres:** History, Theology/Religion. **Career:** Emeritus Professor of Ancient Scripture, Brigham Young University, Provo, Utah, 1996-, professor, 1962-96, faculty member from 1955. Lecturer in Classical and Medieval Rhetoric, University of California, 1960-61. **Publications:** Joseph Smith's New England Heritage, 1971; Investigating the Book of Mormon Witnesses, 1981; Understanding Paul, 1983. Author of articles. **Address:** 3736 No. Little Rock Drive, Provo, UT 84604, U.S.A.

ANDERSON, Robert (David). British (born India), b. 1927. **Genres:** Archaeology/Antiquities, Art/Art history, Music. **Career:** Record News, London, assistant editor, 1954-56; Gordonstoun School, assistant master and director of music, 1956-62; Moray Choral Union, conductor, 1958-62; Spoleto Festival, assistant conductor, 1962; St. Bartholomew's Hospital Choral Society, conductor, 1965-90; University of London, London, England, extramural lecturer on Egyptology, 1966-77; Musical Times, critic and associate editor, 1967-85; Egypt Exploration Society, excavations at Qasr Ibrim, administrative director, 1977-79. Contributor to British Broadcasting Corporation Music Weekly and other programs. **Publications:** Catalogue of Egyptian Antiquities in the British Museum, III, Musical Instruments, 1976; Wagner: A Biography, with a Survey of Books, Editions, and Recordings, 1980; (ed. with Ibrahim Fawzy) Egypt Revealed: Scenes from Napoleon's Description de l'Egypte, 1987; Elgar in Manuscript, 1990; Elgar, 1993; Elgar and Chivalry, 2002. **Address:** 54 Hornton St, London W8 4NT, England.

ANDERSON, Sarah. British, b. 1947. **Genres:** Travel/Exploration. **Career:** Travel Bookshop, London, England, founder and owner, 1979-2004. **Publications:** Anderson's Travel Companion, 1995; The Virago Book of Spirituality (in US as Heaven's Gate Thinly Veiled), 1996; Inside Notting Hill, 2001; Sarah Anderson's Travel Companion: Africa and Middle East, 2004. Contributor to periodicals. **Address:** Travel Bookshop, 13 Blenheim Cres., London W11 2EE, England. **Online address:** sarah@umbrellabooks.com

ANDERSON, Terry (A.). American, b. 1949. **Genres:** Autobiography/Memoirs. **Career:** Reporter for Associated Press, 1974-85, assigned to South Africa, 1981-83, chief Middle East correspondent and bureau chief in Beirut, Lebanon, 1983-85; held hostage by terrorists in Beirut, 1985-1991; writer and lecturer; founder of New York Renaissance (a grassroots, non-partisan organization concerned with political reform). **Publications:** Den of Lions: Memoirs of Seven Years, 1993. Contributor of articles to periodicals. **Address:** c/o Janklow & Nesbit, 445 Park Ave, Fl 13, New York, NY 10022, U.S.A.

ANDERSON, Trevor A(ndrew). Australian, b. 1959. **Genres:** Biology. **Career:** University of Newcastle, Australia, research assistant in medicine, 1981; New South Wales Institute of Technology, tutor in physiology, 1985; Nepean College, tutor in physiology, 1986-87; Department of Primary Industries and Energy, Canberra, Australia, scientist with Bureau of Rural Research, 1988; Deakin University, senior tutor, 1988-90, lecturer in aquaculture, 1990-93; James Cook University of North Queensland, Townsville, Australia, senior lecturer in aquaculture, 1994-. **Publications:** (with S.S. De Silva) Fish Nutrition in Aquaculture, 1995. Contributor of articles and reviews to scientific journals. **Address:** School of Marine Biology and Aquaculture, James Cook University of North Queensland, Townsville, QLD 4811, Australia.

ANDERSON, Virginia DeJohn. American, b. 1954. **Genres:** History. **Career:** University of Colorado, Boulder, assistant professor, 1985-92, associate professor of U.S. history, 1992-. **Publications:** New England's Generation: The Great Migration and the Formation of Society and Culture in the Seventeenth Century, 1991. Contributor of articles to New England Quarterly and William and Mary Quarterly. **Address:** Department of History, University of Colorado 234UCB, Boulder, CO 80309, U.S.A. **Online address:** virginia.anderson@colorado.edu

ANDERSON, Wilda (Christine). American, b. 1951. **Genres:** Chemistry, History, Literary criticism and history. **Career:** Johns Hopkins University, Baltimore, MD, assistant professor, 1978-84, associate professor, 1984-89, professor of French, 1989-. Emory University, visiting professor, autumn, 1989; Ecole Pratique des Hautes Etudes, Paris, visiting professor, 1994. **Publications:** Between the Library and the Laboratory: The Language of Chemistry in Eighteenth-Century France, Johns Hopkins University Press, 1984; Diderot's Dream, Johns Hopkins University Press, 1990; Contributor to books. **Address:** Department of French, Johns Hopkins University, Baltimore, MD 21218, U.S.A.

ANDERSON, William L(ouis). American, b. 1941. **Genres:** History, Anthropology/Ethnology. **Career:** Western Carolina University, Cullowhee, NC, assistant professor, 1969-76, associate professor, 1976-86, professor of history, 1986-; writer. Conducted archival research in Spain, Canada, England, and France. Museum of the Cherokee Indian, member of advisory board; Friends of Junaluska, member of board of directors, 1990-. Journal of Cherokee Studies, editor, 1995-. **Publications:** (with J. Lewis) Guide to Cherokee Documents in Foreign Archives, 1983; (with N. Anderson) Southern Treasures, 1987; (ed.) Cherokee Removal: Before and After, 1991; (with N. Anderson) Heritage of Healing: A Medical History of Haywood County, 1994. **Address:** Department of History, Western Carolina University, Cullowhee, NC 28723, U.S.A.

ANDERS-RICHARDS, Donald. British, b. 1928. **Genres:** Theology/Religion. **Career:** Primary and secondary sch. teacher. 1951-57; Sr. Curate, St. Francis, Bournemouth, 1962-64; Assistant Chaplain, Quainton Hall School, Harrow, Middx., 1964-68; Lecturer, 1968-71, and Sr. Lecturer, 1971-76, Totley-Thornbridge College of Education, Sheffield; Sr. Lecturer in Education, University of Hallam, 1976-88. **Publications:** The Drama of the Psalms, 1968. **Address:** Laburnum Cottage, Gwern-y-Brenin, near Oswestry, Salop SY10 8AS, England.

ANDES, Karen. American, b. 1956. **Genres:** Sports/Fitness, Women's studies and issues. **Career:** Andes Productions, San Rafael, CA, owner and producer of written, audio, and visual materials, 1988-; personal trainer, dance-movement teacher, and fitness consultant. **Publications:** A Woman's Book of Strength, 1995; A Woman's Book of Power, 1997; The Complete Book of Fitness, 1999; The Complete Book of Stretching, 2000; A Woman's Book of Balance, 2000. **Address:** 1 H St, Apt 306, San Rafael, CA 94901-1786, U.S.A. **Online address:** kandes@worlddancer.com; www.worlddancer.com

ANDRE, Judith. American, b. 1941. **Genres:** Philosophy, Ethics. **Career:** Elementary teacher for sixth, seventh, and eighth grades in Wisconsin, 1963-66; Mercy College of Detroit, adjunct professor of philosophy, 1973-76; Wayne County Community College, Detroit, adjunct professor of philosophy, 1973-76; Bowling Green State University, Ohio, adjunct instructor, 1976-77; Washburn University of Topeka, Kansas, visiting instructor, 1977-78; Loyola Marymount University, Los Angeles, CA, visiting instructor and adjunct instructor, 1978-80; Old Dominion University, Norfolk, VA, assistant professor, 1980-85, associate professor of philosophy, 1986-91, associate professor of women's studies, 1990-91, director of Institute of Applied Ethics, 1985-88; Michigan State University, East Lansing, associate professor of philosophy, 1991-95 professor, 1995-. Lecturer at colleges and universities. **Publications:** EDITOR: (with W. Brenner, and contrib.) Essays in Introduction to Philosophy, 1985; (with D. James) Rethinking College Athletics, 1991. Work represented in anthologies and academic journals. **Address:** Center for Ethics and Humanities in the Life Sciences, C-208 East Fee Hall, Michigan State University, East Lansing, MI 48824-1316, U.S.A. **Online address:** andre@msu.edu

ANDRE, Michael. Also writes as T. W. Fretter, Laura LeNail. Canadian, b. 1946. **Genres:** Poetry. **Career:** Unmuzzled Ox, NYC, editor, 1971-; Art News, NYC, editorial associate, 1972-76; City College of New York, lecturer in English, 1973. **Publications:** My Regrets, 1976; Studying the Ground for Holes, 1978; Letters Home, 1979; (ed.) The Poets' Encyclopedia, 1979; Like a Few Things, 1981; Jabbing the A Is High Comedy, 1984; It as It, 1991; Experiments in Banal Living, 1998. **Address:** Unmuzzled Ox, 105 Hudson St, New York, NY 10013, U.S.A. **Online address:** mandreox@aol.com

ANDRESKI, Stanislav Leonard. British/Polish, b. 1919. **Genres:** History, Military/Defense/Arms control, Politics/Government, Sociology. **Career:** Lecturer in sociology, Rhodes University, Grahamstown, South Africa, 1947-53; sr. Research fellow in anthropology, Manchester University, Lancs., 1954-56; lecturer in economics, Acton Technical College, London, 1956-57; lecturer in management studies, Brunel College of Technology, London, 1957-60; professor of sociology, School of Social Sciences, Santiago, Chile, 1960-61; sr. research fellow, Nigerian Institute of Social and Economic Research, Ibadan, 1962-64; visiting professor of sociology and anthropology, City College, City University of New York, 1968-69; professor emeritus of sociology, University of Reading, Berks., 1984- (professor and dept. head, 1964-84); professor (part-time): Polish University in London, 1978-98; DUXX Graduate School of Business, Monterey, Mexico, 1994-98; Faculty of Economics & Management, WSJOE University, Czestochawa, Poland, 1998-2002. **Publications:** Military Organization and Society, 1954, 2nd ed., 1968; (with J. Ostaszewski et al.) Class Structure and Social Development (in Polish), 1964; Elements of Comparative Sociology in US as The Uses of Comparative Sociology, 1964; Parasitism and Subversion: The Case of Latin America, 1966, 2nd ed., 1969; The African Predicament, 1968; Social Sciences as Sorcery, 1972; The Prospects of a Revolution in the USA, 1973; Max Weber's Insights and Errors, 1984; Syphilis Puritanism and Witchhunts, 1989; Wars, Revolutions, Dictatorships, 1992. EDITOR: H. Spencer, Structure, Function and Evolution, 1971; The Essential Comte, 1974; Reflections on Inequality, 1975; Max Weber on Capitalism, Bureaucracy and Religion, 1983. **Address:** Farriers, Village Green, Upper Basildon, West, Berks. RG8 8LS, England.

ANDREW, Edward. Canadian, b. 1941. **Genres:** Philosophy, Politics/Government. **Career:** University of Toronto, professor of political science. **Publications:** Closing the Iron Cage, 1981; Shylock's Rights: A Grammar of Lockean Claims, 1988; The Genealogy of Values: The Aesthetic Economy of Nietzsche and Proust, 1995; Conscience and Its Critics: Protestant Conscience, Enlightenment, Reason and Modern Subjectivity, 2003. **Address:** Dept of Political Science, Sidney Smith Hall, University of Toronto, 100 St. George St. Rm 3036, Toronto, ON, Canada M5S 3G3. **Online address:** eandrew@chass.utronto.ca

ANDREW, Joseph J(erald). American, b. 1960. **Genres:** Mystery/Crime/Suspense. **Career:** Attorney and author. Served as a law clerk for Judge Joel Flaum of the United States Court of Appeals, Seventh Circuit, 1985-86; affiliated with law firm Baker and Daniels, 1987-88; served on the campaign of the Democratic candidate for the Indiana Senate, 1988; appointed Deputy Secretary of State for the State of Indiana, 1989; Bingham, Summers, Welsh & Spilman (law firm), Indianapolis, IN, attorney, 1991, partner, 1992-95. Chairman of the Indiana Democratic Party, 1995-. Historic preservation and pro bono legal work. **Publications:** The Disciples (spy thriller), 1993. **Address:** One N. Capitol, Ste. 200, Indianapolis, IN 46204, U.S.A.

ANDREW, Sheila M. British/Canadian, b. 1938. **Genres:** History, Local history/Rural topics. **Career:** St. Thomas University, Fredericton, New Brunswick, professor of history, 1988-. Orienteering New Brunswick, past president. **Publications:** The Development of Elites in Acadian New Brunswick, 1861-1881, 1997. **Address:** Edmund Casey Hall Rm 328, St. Thomas University, 51 Dineen Dr, Fredericton, NB, Canada E3B 5G3. **Online address:** sandrew@stu.ca

ANDREWS, Andy. (born United States), b. 1959. **Genres:** Communications/Media. **Career:** Comedian, motivational speaker. **Publications:** Andy Andrews Live at Caesars, Tahoe (sound recording), 1988; Storms of Perfection, Volume 1: In Their Own Words, 1991, Volume 2: Letters from the Heart, 1994, Volume 3: A Pathway to Personal Achievement, 1996, Volume 4: Letters from the Past, 1997. Andy Andrews' Tales from Sawyerton Springs, 1995. The Traveler's Gift: Seven Decisions that Determine Personal Success, , 2002. The Lost Choice: A Legend of Personal Discovery, 2004. **Address:** c/o Author Mail, Thomas Nelson Inc., POB 141000, Nashville, TN 37214, U.S.A.

ANDREWS, Colin. British, b. 1946. **Genres:** Paranormal. **Career:** A.M.F. Legg, Andover, England, electrician, 1963-73; Brinklow Ltd., Andover, electrical technician, 1973-74; Test Valley Borough Council, Andover, supervisor, 1974-76, superintendent, 1976-78, coordinator, 1978-84, senior technical support services officer, 1984-. **Publications:** (With Pat Delgado) Circular Evidence, Bloomsbury Publishing, 1989. (With Delgado) Crop Circles: The Latest Evidence, Bloomsbury Publishing, 1990.

ANDREWS, Edgar Harold. British, b. 1932. **Genres:** Chemistry, Physics, Sciences, Theology/Religion. **Career:** Technical Officer, ICI Ltd., Welwyn Garden City, 1953-55; Sr. Physicist, Rubber Producers' Research Association, Welwyn Garden City, 1955-63; Professor of Materials, Queen Mary and Westfield College, University of London, 1968-98 (Reader in Materials Science, 1963-68). President, Biblical Creation Society, 1978-. **Publications:** (co-author) Chemistry and Physics of Rubberlike Substances, 1963; Fracture in Polymers (monograph), 1968; Is Evolution Scientific?, 1977; From Nothing to Nature (A Young People's Guide to Evolution and Creation), 1978; (ed. and co-author) Developments in Polymer Fracture, 1979; The Promise of the Spirit, 1982; Christ and the Cosmos, 1986; Free in Christ (commentary), 1996. **Address:** 25 Russellcroft Rd, Welwyn Garden City, Herts. AL8 6QX, England.

ANDREWS, Elmer. British, b. 1948. **Genres:** Plays/Screenplays, Literary criticism and history. **Career:** Mohammed V University, Rabat, Morocco, Senior Lecturer in English, 1976-79; University of Ulster, Coleraine, Northern Ireland, lecturer in English, 1980-. **Publications:** The Boundary (radio play; screenplay), 1982; The Rest Is Silence (screenplay), 1986; The Poetry of Seamus Heaney: All the Realms of Whisper, 1988; The Art of Brian Friel, 1995. EDITOR, INTRODUCTION, & CONTRIBUTOR: Contemporary Irish Poetry: A Collection of Critical Essays, 1990; Seamus Heaney: A Collection of Critical Essays, 1990. **Address:** Department of English, University of Ulster, Cromore Rd, Coleraine, Northern Ireland.

ANDREWS, George Reid. American, b. 1951. **Genres:** Area studies, Cultural/Ethnic topics, History, Race relations. **Career:** Social Science Research Council, NYC, staff associate, 1978-81; University of Pittsburgh, Pittsburgh, PA, assistant professor, 1981-83, associate professor, 1983-91, professor of history, 1991-. **Publications:** The Afro-Argentines of Buenos Aires, 1800-1900, 1980; Blacks and Whites in Sao Paulo, Brazil, 1888-1988, 1991; Afro-Latin America, 1800-2000, 2004. Work represented in anthologies. Contributor of articles and reviews to history and Latin American studies journals. **Address:** Dept of History, University of Pittsburgh, Pittsburgh, PA 15260, U.S.A. **Online address:** reid1@pitt.edu

ANDREWS, J(ames) S(ydney). Also writes as Jim Andrews. British, b. 1934. **Genres:** Medicine/Health, Children's fiction, Adult non-fiction. **Publications:** The Bell of Nendrum, 1969, in U.S. as The Green Hill of Nendrum, 1970; The Man from the Sea, 1970; Cargo for a King, 1972; Catamarans for Cruising, 1974. FOR ADULTS (AS JIM ANDREWS): Simple Sailing, 1975; (with J. Andrews) Food for Arthritics, Based on Dr. Dong's Diet, 1982; Twelve Ships A-Sailing: Thirty-Five Years of Home-Water Cruising, 1986. **Address:** Dove Wood, Storrs Park, Windermere, Cumbria LA23 3LB, England.

ANDREWS, Jim. See ANDREWS, J(ames) S(ydney).

ANDREWS, John. See MALCOLM, John.

ANDREWS, Lyman. American, b. 1938. **Genres:** Poetry. **Career:** Lecturer in American Literature, University of Leicester, 1965-88. Visiting Professor of English, Indiana University, Bloomington, 1978-79. Poetry Critic, The Sunday Times, London, 1968-79. **Publications:** Ash Flowers, 1958; Fugitive Visions, 1962; The Death of Mayakovsky and Other Poems, 1968; Kaleidoscope: New and Selected Poems, 1973; Denver Hometown Summer, 1994. **Address:** Flat 4-32, Victoria Centre, Nottingham NG1 3PA, England.

ANDREWS, Nin. American, b. 1958. **Genres:** Poetry. **Career:** Poet. **Publications:** POETRY: The Book of Orgasms, 1994; Spontaneous Breasts, 1998. Contributor of poems to anthologies and periodicals. **Address:** c/o Pearl Editions-Pearl Magazine, 3030 East Second St., Long Beach, CA 90803, U.S.A.

ANDREWS, Russell. See HANDLER, David.

ANDREWS, Sam S. American, b. 1942. **Genres:** Medicine/Health. **Career:** Private practice of endocrinology, New Orleans, LA. Mahorner Clinic, president, 1990; Mercy-Baptist Hospital, vice-president, 1995. **Publications:** Sugar Busters!, 1998. **Address:** 2820 Napoleon Ave. Suite 890, New Orleans, LA 70115, U.S.A. **Online address:** DrSSA@aol.com

ANDREWS, Sarah. American, b. 1949?. **Genres:** Novels. **Career:** Writer. U.S. Geological Survey, Wyoming, field geologist, c. 1976-80; Amoco Oil Company, Denver, CO, geologist, 1980-83; Angus Petroleum, Golden, CO, geologist, 1983-86; consultant geologist, c. 1990-; Sonoma State University, Rohnert Park, CA, instructor in geology. **Publications:** NOVELS: Tensleep, 1994; A Fall in Denver, 1995; Mother Nature, 1997. **Address:** Sonoma State University, Department of Geology, 1801 East Cotati Ave., Rohnert Park, CA 94928, U.S.A. **Online address:** canyonwren@aol.com

ANDREWS, Wendy. See SHARMAT, Marjorie Weinman.

ANDREWS, William L(eake). American, b. 1946. **Genres:** Literary criticism and history, Novellas/Short stories. **Career:** Texas Tech University, Lubbock, assistant professor of English, 1973-77; University of Wisconsin-Madison, assistant professor, 1977-78, associate professor, 1978-84, professor of English, 1984-88; University of Kansas, Lawrence, Joyce and Elizabeth Hall Professor of American Literature, 1989-96; University of North Carolina-Chapel Hill, E. Maynard Adams professor of English, 1997-. University of Geissen, visiting professor, 1984. **Publications:** EDITOR: Literary Romanticism in America, 1981; Critical Essays on W.E.B. duBois, 1985; Sisters of the Spirit: Three Black Women's Autobiographies of the Nineteenth Century, 1986; Frederick Douglass, My Bondage and My Freedom, 1987; Six Women's Slave Narratives, 1988; James Weldon Johnson, The Autobiography of an Ex-Colored Man, 1990; Three Classic African-American Novels, 1990; William Pickens, Bursting Bonds, 1991; Critical Essays on Frederick Douglass, 1991; Collected Stories of Charles W. Chesnutt, 1992; The African-American Novel in the Age of Reaction: Three Classics, 1992; The Oxford Frederick Douglass Reader, 1996. CO-EDITOR: Journeys in New Worlds: Early American Women's Narratives, 1990; African-American Literature, 1991; Norton Anthology of African American Literature, 1997; Oxford Companion to African American Literature, 1997; Frederick Douglass, Narrative, 1997. **Address:** 108 Cottonwood Ct., Chapel Hill, NC 27514, U.S.A.

ANDRUS, Hyrum Leslie. American, b. 1924. **Genres:** Theology/Religion, History, Social sciences. **Career:** Formerly, Professor of Church History and Doctrine, Brigham Young University, Provo, Utah. **Publications:** Helps for Missionaries, 1949; Doctrinal Themes of the Doctrine and Covenants, 1957; Joseph Smith and World Government, 1958; Joseph Smith the Man and Seer, 1960; The Glory of God and Man's Relation to Deity, 1965; Liberalism, Conservatism and Mormonism, 1965; Mormonism and the Rise of Western Civilization, 1966; Anticipation of the Civil War in Mormon Thought, 1966; Doctrinal Commentary on the Pearl of Great Price, 1967; God, Man and the Universe, 1968; Principles of Perfection, 1970; Doctrines of the Kingdom, 1973; (with Helen Mae Andrus) They Knew the Prophet, 1974. **Address:** 630 N. Patterson Lane, Alpine, UT 84004, U.S.A.

ANDRUS, Jeff. American, b. 1947. **Genres:** Novels. **Career:** Novelist; television writer 1972-; credits include television dramas; University of California at Los Angeles Extension Program, instructor of screenwriting, 1991-92; speaker and panelist, 1993-. **Publications:** NOVELS: Tracer Inc.,

1994; Neighborhood Watch, 1996. **Address:** The Writing Company, 13908 Fiji Way No. 162, Marina del Rey, CA 90292, U.S.A.

ANDRYSZEWSKI, Tricia. (Tricia Andryszewski Shapiro). American, b. 1956. **Genres:** Children's non-fiction, Young adult non-fiction, Adult non-fiction. **Career:** Girard College, Philadelphia, PA, taught high school social studies, 1978-79; GKSW: Human Service and Behavioral Science Consultants, Glenside, PA, 1979-80; Warner Books, NYC, 1980-81; Scholarly Resources, Wilmington, DE, project editor, 1988-89; assistant to Leonard Bernstein (composer/conductor), NYC, and Fairfield, CT, 1989-91; researcher/manager for Elizabeth Drew (writer), Washington, DC, 1992-93; freelance editor, writer, and researcher, full and part time, 1981-. Researched and wrote news analyses, brief biographies, and historical essays for CD-ROMs, 1994-99; copyedited bimonthly newsletters, 1994-98; copyedited full-length books for children and adults. **Publications:** The Dust Bowl: Disaster on the Plains, 1993; Marjory Stoneman Douglas: Friend of the Everglades, 1994; Immigration: Newcomers and Their Impact on the U.S., 1995; The Seminoles: People of the Southeast, 1995; The Environment and the Economy, 1995; What to Do about Nuclear Waste, 1995; The Amazing Life of Moe Berg, 1995; Abortion Rights, Options, and Choices, 1996; 1963: Gathering to Be Heard, the March on Washington, 1996; The Militia Movement in America, 1997; School Prayer, 1997; Communities of the Faithful, 1997; Step by Step along the Appalachian Trail, 1998; Step by Step along the Pacific Crest Trail, 1998; Kosovo: The Splintering of Yugoslavia, 1999; Bill Bradley, 1999; The Reform Party, 1999; Gay Rights, 1999; Terrorism in America, 2002. **Address:** 12 A River Rd, West Cornwall, CT 06796, U.S.A. **Online address:** andryszews@aol.com

ANEES, Munawar Ahmad. American, b. 1948. **Genres:** Cultural/Ethnic topics, Literary criticism and history, Medicine/Health, Sciences, Theology/Religion, Third World. **Career:** Zahra Publications, San Antonio, TX, President, 1984; Asas Inc., Houston, Director, 1984-85; East-West University, Chicago, Director of Research and Development, 1986-; Knowledge Management Systems, executive director, 1989-. **Publications:** Health Sciences in Early Islam, 1984; Guide to Sira and Hadith Literature, 1986; Islam and Biological Futures, 1989; The Kiss of Judas, 1989; Computers Don't Byte, 1990; Communication and Information: Ethical Perspectives, 1991; Periodica Islamica, 1991; Journals-Search-Journal of Arabic and Islamic Studies (Brattleboro, Vermont); International Journal of Islamic and Arabic Studies (Bloomington, IN); Journal of Islamic Science (Aligarh, India); Inquiry (London, England) Ultimate Reality and Meaning (Toronto, Canada) Christian-Muslim Relations: Yesterday, Today, Tomorrow, 1991. **Address:** 925 N 11th Ave, Tucson, AZ 85705-7627, U.S.A. **Online address:** dranees@att.net

ANGEL, Heather. British, b. 1941. **Genres:** Natural history, Photography. **Career:** Royal Photographic Society, president, 1984-86; writer, photographer, and lecturer on biology and natural history, currently. **Publications:** Your Book of Fishes, 1972; Nature Photography: Its Art and Techniques, 1972; The World of an Estuary, 1975; (with M. Angel) All Colour Book of Ocean Life, 1975; Photographing Nature: Trees, Seashore, Insects, Flowers, Fungi, 5 vols., 1975; Seashore Life on Rocky Shores, 1975; Seashore Life on Sandy Beaches, 1975; The World of a Stream, 1976; Sea Shells of the Seashore, 1976; Wild Animals in the Garden, 1976; Life on the Seashore, 1976; Life in the Oceans, 1976; Life in Our Rivers, 1977; Life in Our Estuaries, 1977; British Wild Orchids, 1977; The Countryside of the New Forest, 1977; Seaweeds of the Seashore, 1977; The Countryside of South Wales, 1977; Fungi, 1979; Lichens, 1980; Mosses and Ferns, 1980; The Country Side of Devon, 1980; The Guinness Book of Seashore Life, 1981; The Book of Nature Photography, 1982; The Book of Close-Up Photography, 1983; Heather Angel's Countryside, 1983; A Camera in the Garden, 1984; A View from the Window, 1988; Nature in Focus, 1988; Landscape Photography, 1989; Animal Photography, 1991; Kew: A World of Plants, in US as The World of Plants: Treasures from the Royal Botanic Gardens, Kew, 1993; Photographing the Natural World, 1994; Outdoor Photography 101 Tips & Hints, 1997; How to Photograph Flowers, 1998; Pandas, 1998; How to Photograph Water, 1999; Natural Visions, 2000. **Address:** Highways, 6 Vicarage Hill, Farnham, Surrey GU9 8HJ, England. **Online address:** hangel@naturalvisions.co.uk; www.naturalvisions.co.uk

ANGELA, Alberto. Italian, b. 1962. **Genres:** Zoology. **Career:** Worked at Institute of Marine Zoology, Naples, Italy, 1979; field researcher on the origins of man in Zaire, 1983-84, Tanzania, 1986-88, Oman, 1989, and Ethiopia, 1991; participated in research on the leopard in Serengeti National Park, Tanzania, 1990, which resulted in the documentary films One Day of Two Million Years Ago and In Search of the Leopard, 1990-91; Albatros (TV series), creator and presenter for Swiss television, 1991; writer and supervisor of a television program on animal behavior, for Swiss television, 1991; RAI-TV (Italian TV company), co-creator and co-presenter of a series on dinosaurs, 1993. **Publications:** Musei e mostre a misura d'Uomo, 1988; (with P. Angela) La straordinaria Storia dell'Uomo, 1989, trans. as The Extraordinary Story of Human Origins, 1993; (with P. Angela) La straordinaria Storia della vita sulla Terra, 1992, trans. as The Extraordinary Story of Life on Earth, 1996; (with P. Angela) Il pianeta dei Dinosauri, 1993; (with A. Angela and A.L. Recchi) Squali, trans. as Sharks!, 1997. Contributor to periodicals. **Address:** Via Pieve di Cadore, 30-00135 Rome, Italy.

ANGELL, Roger. American, b. 1920. **Genres:** Social commentary, Documentaries/Reportage, Essays, Humor/Satire. **Career:** Fiction Ed., The New Yorker, since 1956. Ed., Magazine X, 1946-47; Sr. Ed., Holiday, 1947-56. **Publications:** The Stone Arbor, 1961; A Day in the Life of Roger Angell, 1971; The Summer Game, 1972; Five Seasons, 1977; Late Innings, 1982; Season Ticket, 1988; Once More Around the Park, 1991; (ed) Nothing but You, Love Stories from the New Yorker, 1997; A Pitcher's Story: Innings with Davie Cone, 2001; Game Time, 2003. **Address:** 1261 Madison Ave, New York, NY 10028, U.S.A.

ANGELOU, Maya. (Marguerita Annie Johnson). American, b. 1928. **Genres:** Novels, Plays/Screenplays, Poetry. **Career:** First Reynolds Professor of American Studies, Wake Forest University, Winston-Salem, NC, 1981- (lifetime appointment). Former stage and screen actor and dancer; Associate Ed., Arab Observer, Cairo, Egypt, 1962-63; writer, Ghanaian Times, Accra, 1963-65, and Ghanaian broadcasting Corp., 1963-65; Assistant Administration, Institute of African Studies, School of Music and Drama, University of Ghana, Accra, 1963-65; Feature Ed., African Review, Accra, 1965-66; Lecturer, University of California, 1966. **Publications:** The Best of These, 1966; The Clawing Within, 1966; Adjoa Amissah, 1967; I Know Why the Caged Bird Sings, 1970, teleplay 1977; Just Give Me a Cool Drink of Water 'Fore I Die (poetry), 1971; Georgia, Georgia (screenplay), 1972; Gather Together in My Name, 1974; All Day Long (screenplay), 1974; Oh Pray My Wings Are Gonna Fit Me Well (poetry), 1975; Singin' and Swingin' and Gettin' Merry Like Christmas, 1976; And Still I Rise (poetry), 1978; Sisters (teleplay), 1978; The Heart of a Woman, 1981; Shaker, Why Don't You Sing? (poetry), 1983; All God's Children Need Traveling Shoes (autobiography), 1986; The Heart of a Woman, 1986; Now Sheba Sings the Song (poetry), 1987; Conversations with Maya Angelou, 1988; Moon on a Rainbow Shaw! (play), 1988; I Shall not Be Moved, 1990; Wouldn't Take Nothing for My Journey Now, 1993; On the Pulse of Morning, 1993; My Painted House, My Friendly Chicken and Me, 1994; The Complete Collected Poems of Maya Angelou, 1994; Kofi and His Magic, 1996; Even the Stars Look Lonesome, 1997; Phenomenal Woman, 2000; A Song Flung Up to Heaven, 2002. **Address:** c/o Dave La Camera, Lordly and Dame, Inc, 51 Church St, Boston, MA 02116, U.S.A.

ANGLE, Barbara. American, b. 1947. **Genres:** Novellas/Short stories, Novels. **Career:** Freelance writer and novelist. Bureau of National Affairs, Washington, DC, editor, 1968(?)-75; Laurel Run Mine, Mt. Storm, WV, coal miner, 1975-78; substitute teacher and writer in Keyser, WV, 1978-. **Publications:** Rinker (novella), 1979; Those That Mattered (novel), 1994. **Address:** Route 5, Box 66, Keyser, WV 26726, U.S.A.

ANGLESEY, Marquess of. (George Charles Henry Victor Paget). British, b. 1922. **Genres:** Military/Defense/Arms control, Biography, History. **Publications:** One-Leg: The Life and Letters of Henry William Paget, First Marquess of Anglesey, K.G., 1768-1854, 1961, reprint, 1996; A History of the British Cavalry 1816-1919, 8 vols., 1978-97. EDITOR: The Capel Letters 1814-1817, 1955; Sergeant Pearman's Memoirs, 1968; Little Hodge, 1971. **Address:** Plas Newydd, Llanfairpwll, Anglesey, Wales.

ANGLESEY, Zoe (Rita). American, b. 1941. **Genres:** Poetry. **Career:** Voice Literary Supplement, NYC, senior editor, 1994-. Baruch College, Manhattan, and Long Island University, Brooklyn, adjunct instructor of writing. Coordinator of poetry readings; participant in literary festivals. Painter. **Publications:** Something More Than Force: Poems for Guatemala, 1971-1982, 1983; (trans. with others) Forrest Gander, ed, Mouth to Mouth: Poems by Twelve Contemporary Mexican Women, 1993. EDITOR: Ixok Amargo: Central American Women's Poetry for Peace, 1987; North American Women's Poetry/Poesia de Mujeres de los Estados Unidos, 1989; Word Up!: Hope for Youth Poetry, 1992; (and comp) Stone on Stone/Piedra Sobre Piedra: Poetry by Women of Diverse Heritages, trans by Rodolfo Dada and Myena Nieves, 1994. Work represented in anthologies. Translations included in anthologies. Contributor of stories, poems, translations, and reviews to periodicals. **Address:** 113 South Oxford St., No. 2, Brooklyn, NY 11217-4207, U.S.A.

ANGLIM, Christopher Thomas. American/Irish, b. 1957. **Genres:** Librarianship, Bibliography, Law. **Career:** South Texas College of Law, Houston, government documents librarian and archivist, 1990-98; University of St. Thomas, Houston, TX, law librarian, 1998-2000; St. Mary's University, San Antonio, TX, consultant, 1998-2000, Sarita Kenedy East Law Library, professor and government documents librarian and archivist, 2000, Hispanic Governance Center, manager; Lee College, Baytown, TX, member of library staff, 1999-2000. Certified archivist; independent consultant and researcher. Worked in legal positions at Smith & Breecher, Scottsdale, AZ, Maricopa County Defender's Office, Arizona Attorney General's Office-Civil Division, Rice and Associates, Ostriecher & Vatz, and Pollock & More, all Phoenix, AZ, and Reynolds, Rhodes & Golston, Mesa, AZ; worked in library positions at Law Library of Winston & Strawn, Maricopa County Law Library, and City of Tempe Public Library. **Publications:** Special Collections Policies, Procedures, and Guidelines: A Model Plan for Special Collections, 1993; Special Collections at South Texas College of Law: An Annotated Catalog, 1994; Labor, Employment, and the Law: A Dictionary, 1997; Religion and the Law, 1999; Survey on Emergency Preparedness Planning, 2000; Joined in Common Enterprise, 2001. Contributor to periodicals. **Address:** Sarita Kenedy East Law Library, St. Mary's University, 1 Camino Santa Maria, San Antonio, TX 78228, U.S.A. **Online address:** anglimc@law.stmarytx.edu

ANGLIN, Douglas G(eorge). Canadian, b. 1923. **Genres:** International relations/Current affairs, Politics/Government. **Career:** Carleton University, Ottawa, professor, 1958-89, professor emeritus, 1993-. University of Zambia, vice-chancellor, 1965-69. **Publications:** Africa: The Political Pattern, 1961; The St. Pierre and Miquelon Affaire of 1941, 1966, reprinted as Free French Invasion, 1999; Conflict and Change in Southern Africa, 1978; Canada, Scandinavia and Southern Africa, 1978; Zambia's Foreign Policy: Studies in Diplomacy and Dependence, 1979; Zambian Crisis Behaviour: Confronting Rhodesia's Unilateral Declaration Of Independence, 1965-1966, 1994; Confronting Rwandan Genocide: The Military Options, 2002. **Address:** Dept. of Political Science, Carleton University, Ottawa, ON, Canada K1S 5B6.

ANGUS, Ian. *See* MACKAY, James Alexander.

ANGUS, Tom. *See* POWELL, Geoffrey (Stewart) in the Obituaries.

ANMAR, Frank. *See* NOLAN, William F(rancis).

ANNE, Princess. *See* PRINCESS ROYAL, The.

ANNERINO, John. American/Italian. **Genres:** Adult non-fiction, History, Natural history, Photography, Race relations, Social commentary, Travel/Exploration. **Career:** Wilderness guide and instructor, 1972-82. Gamma-Liaison Picture Agency, NYC, freelance photojournalist, 1983-96; Liaison International, NYC, contract photographer, 1996-2000; TimePix, NYC, contract photographer, 2001-03; Landov LLC Picture Agency, NYC, contract photographer, 2003-. **Publications:** Hiking the Grand Canyon, 1986, 3rd ed., 2006; Adventuring in Arizona, 1991, 3rd ed., 2003; Running Wild: Through the Grand Canyon, 1992; Running Wild: An Extraordinary Adventure of the Human Spirit, 1998; Canyoneering, 1999; Dead in Their Tracks: Crossing America's Desert Borderlands, 1999, rev. ed., 2003; Desert Survivor, 2001. PHOTO ESSAYS: High Risk Photography, 1991; Canyons of the Southwest, 1993; The Wild Country of Mexico/La Tierra Salvaje de Mexico, 1994; People of Legend, 1996; Apache: The Sacred Path to Womanhood, 1999; Roughstock: The Toughest Events in Rodeo, 2000; Grand Canyon Wild, 2004; The Photographer's Guide to the Grand Canyon, 2005; Canyon Country, 2005. **Address:** 2325 W Wagon Wheels Dr, Tucson, AZ 85745, U.S.A.

ANSA, Tina McElroy. American, b. 1949. **Genres:** Novels, History. **Career:** Copy editor, editor, feature writer, and news reporter for Atlanta Constitution and Charlotte Observer; Clark College, Atlanta, GA, instructor on mass media; Spelman College, Brunswick, GA, writing workshop supervisor. **Publications:** Not Soon Forgotten: Cotton Planters and Plantations of the Golden Isles of Georgia, c. 1987. NOVELS: Baby of the Family, 1989; Ugly Ways, 1993; The Hand I Fan With, 1996; You Know Better, 2002. Contributor to newspapers. **Address:** PO Box 20602, St. Simons Island, GA 31522, U.S.A. **Online address:** TinaMcElroyAnsa.com

ANSARY, Mir Tamim. Afghani, b. 1948. **Genres:** Children's non-fiction, Education, Children's fiction. **Career:** Portland Scribe, Portland, OR, staff writer, 1972-76; The Asia Foundation, San Francisco, CA, assistant editor of Asian Student, 1976-78, became editor of development publications, 1979;

Harcourt Brace Jovanovich, Orlando, FL, school department editor, 1980-89; freelance writer, educational consultant, and columnist, 1990-. **Publications:** Afghanistan: Fighting for Freedom, 1991; Matter: Solids, Liquids, and Gases, 1996; Score Booster Handbook: For Reading and Language Arts, 2000; West of Kabul, East of New York: An Afghan American Story (memoir), 2002. CAUGHT READING SERIES: Carmen's Card, 1995; The Sea House, 1995; Spiders from Outer Space, 1995; The Lost Boy, 1995. COOL COLLECTIONS SERIES: Model Cars, 1997; Stamps, 1997; Dolls, 1997; Natural Objects, 1997; Insects, 1997. SUPER READERS SERIES: Mysterious Places, 1997; Creepy Creatures, 1997; Unbelievable Beasts, 1998; Baffling Disappearances, 1998; Great Crime Busters, 1998. HOLIDAY HISTORIES SERIES: Veterans Day, 1999; Labor Day, 1999; Martin Luther King, Jr., Day, 1999; Memorial Day, 1999; Columbus Day, 1999; Presidents' Day, 1999; Earth Day, 2000; Thanksgiving Day, 2001; Election Day, 2002; Independence Day, 2002; Flag Day, 2002; Arbor Day, 2002. ADVENTURES PLUS SERIES (educational comic books): Alien Alert, 2000; Treasure Hunt, 2000; Lost in Time, 2000; Runaway Spaceship, 2000; That's Some Dog, 2000; Case of the Missing Millie, 2000. NATIVE AMERICANS SERIES: Plains Indians, 2000; California Indians, 2000; Eastern Woodlands Indians, 2000; Southwest Indians, 2000; Northwest Coast Indians, 2000; Great Basin Indians, 2000; Arctic Peoples, 2000; Plateau Indians, 2000; Southeast Indians, 2000; Subarctic Indians, 2002. STATE STUDIES. CALIFORNIA SERIES: California History, 2002; All around California: Regions and Resources, 2002; People of California, 2002; (with S. Feinstein) Uniquely California, 2003; (with S. Feinstein) California Plants and Animals, 2003; (with S. Feinstein) California Native Peoples, 2003. Contributor of chapters on Islamic history to books, and fiction and nonfiction selections to reading anthology. **Address:** c/o Julie Castiglia, 1155 Camino Del Mar, Ste. 510, Del Mar, CA 92014, U.S.A. **Online address:** JACLAgency@aol.com

ANSAY, A. Manette. American, b. 1964. **Genres:** Novels, Novellas/Short stories. **Career:** Cornell University, lecturer in English, 1991-92; Phillips Exeter Academy, George Bennett Fellow, 1992-93; Vanderbilt University, Nashville, TN, assistant professor of English, 1993-. Instructor with Sewanee Younger Writer's Conference and Northshore Younger Writer's Conference. Has performed readings as part of the Visiting Writers Series at schools. **Publications:** Vinegar Hill (novel), 1994; Read This and Tell Me What It Says (short stories), 1995; Sister (novel), in press; American Family Values (collection of poems); The Road Ends at the Orchard (novel); Midnight Champagne, 1999; Limbo, 2001. Contributor of stories to periodicals and anthologies. **Address:** Box 1654, Station B, Vanderbilt University, Nashville, TN 37235, U.S.A.

ANSBERRY, Clare. American, b. 1957. **Genres:** Local history/Rural topics. **Career:** Writer. Journal, Lorain, OH, reporter, 1979-84; Wall Street Journal, Pittsburgh bureau chief, 1984-. **Publications:** The Women of Troy Hill: The Back-Fence Virtues of Faith and Friendship, 2000. **Address:** One Mellon Center Suite 2750, Pittsburgh, PA 15219, U.S.A. **Online address:** Clare.ansberry@wsj.com

ANSCOMBE, Roderick. American (born England), b. 1947. **Genres:** Novels. **Career:** Beth Israel Hospital, Boston, MA, resident in psychiatry, became chief resident, 1976-80, associate in psychiatry, 1990-; Bridgewater State Hospital, Bridgewater, MA, staff psychiatrist, 1989-91; Harvard Medical School, Boston, MA, assistant clinical professor, 1992-; Tewksbury Hospital, Tewksbury, MA, staff psychiatrist, 1993-98; Bridgewater State Hospital, Bridgewater, MA, staff psychiatrist, 1998-; writer. **Publications:** The Secret Life of Laszlo, Count Dracula (novel), 1994; Shank (novel), 1996. Contributor to psychiatric journals; author of papers on schizophrenia, psychotherapy, and the unconscious. **Address:** 31 Eastern Point Rd., Gloucester, MA 01930, U.S.A.

ANSEL, Talvikki. American, b. 1962. **Genres:** Poetry. **Career:** Writer. Lynchburg College, Lynchburg, VA, Richard H. Thornton writer in residence, 1997. **Publications:** My Shining Archipelago (poems), 1997. **Address:** PO Box 4, Old Mystic, CT 06372, U.S.A.

ANSHAW, Carol. American, b. 1946. **Genres:** Novels. **Career:** Vermont College of Norwich University, Montpelier, faculty member, 1994-99; School of the Art Institute of Chicago, adjunct associate professor, 1996-. **Publications:** NOVELS: Aquamarine, 1992; Seven Moves, 1996; Lucky in the Corner, 2002. Work represented in anthologies.

ANTAL, Dan. Romanian, b. 1954. **Genres:** Novels, Novellas/Short stories, Autobiography/Memoirs. **Career:** English teacher in general school in Romania, 1978-83; West Heath College, Watford, England, French teacher, 1991-94; freelance language teacher, interpreter, lecturer and consultant on history, politics, and Romanian culture in London, England, 1992-. Former president of a company in Bacau, Romania. **Publications:** Out of Romania (autobiography), 1994; The Pinguin (novel); Maria (short stories). **Address:** 17 Mortimer Crescent, London NW6 5NP, England.

ANTHES, Richard A. American, b. 1944. **Genres:** Meteorology/Atmospheric sciences. **Career:** National Hurricane Research Laboratory, Miami, research meteorologist, 1968-71; Pennsylvania State University, professor of meteorology, 1971-81; consultant to the U.S. National Weather Service, 1972-81; National Center for Atmospheric Research, Boulder, director of the Atmospheric Analysis and Prediction Division, 1981-86, and director of the center, 1986-88; University Corporation for Atmospheric Research, Boulder, president, 1988-. **Publications:** Meteorology, 1967, 7th ed. 1997; (with others) The Atmosphere, 1975, 3rd ed., 1981; (with W. Cotton) Storm and Cloud Dynamics, 1989; Tropical Cyclones, 1982. **Address:** University Corporation for Atmospheric Research, PO Box 3000, Boulder, CO 80307, U.S.A.

ANTHONY, Evelyn. (Evelyn Bridget Patricia Ward-Thomas). British, b. 1928. **Genres:** Mystery/Crime/Suspense, Romance/Historical. **Career:** Author. **Publications:** Imperial Highness (in US as Rebel Princess), 1953; Curse Not the King (in US as Royal Intrigue), 1954; Far Flies the Eagle, 1955; Anne Boleyn, 1957; Victoria and Albert, 1958, as Victoria, 1959; Elizabeth (in US as All the Queen's Men), 1960; Charles the King, 1961; Clandara, 1963; The Heiress, 1964, in US as The French Bride, 1964; Valentina, 1966; The Rendezvous, 1967; Anne of Austria (in US as The Cardinal and the Queen), 1968; The Legend, 1969; The Assasin, 1970; The Tamarind Seed, 1971; The Poellenberg Inheritance, 1972; The Occupying Power (in US as Stranger at the Gates) 1973; The Malaspiga Exit (in US as Mission to Malaspiga), 1974; The Persian Ransom (in US as The Persian Price), 1975; The Silver Falcon, 1977; The Return, 1978; The Grave of Truth, 1979, in US as The Janus Imperative, 1980; The Defector, 1980; The Avenue of the Dead, 1981; Albatross, 1982; The Company of Saints, 1983; Voices on the Wind, 1985; No Enemy But Time, 1987, in US as A Place to Hide, 1987; The House of Vandekar, 1988; The Scarlet Thread, 1990; The Relic, 1991; The Doll's House, 1992; Exposure, 1993; Blood Stones, 1994; The Legacy, 1997. **Address:** Horham Hall, Thaxted, Essex, England.

ANTHONY, Joseph Patrick. American, b. 1964. **Genres:** Children's fiction, Young adult fiction. **Career:** Author and screenwriter. Also works as a carpenter. **Publications:** FOR CHILDREN: The Dandelion Seed, 1997; In a Nutshell, 1999. YOUNG ADULT FICTION: Innerworld, 2002. **Address:** Hwy 633, Buckingham, VA 23921, U.S.A. **Online address:** joseph@moonstar.com

ANTHONY, Michael. Trinidadian, b. 1932. **Genres:** Novels, Novellas/Short stories, History, Travel/Exploration. **Career:** Researcher, Ministry of Culture, 1972-88; Journalist, Reuters News Agency, London, 1964-68; Assistant Ed., Texaco Trinidad, 1970-72. **Publications:** The Games Were Coming (novel), 1963; The Year in San Fernando (novel), 1965; Green Days by the River (novel), 1967; Cricket in the Road (short stories), 1973; Sandra Street and Other Stories, 1973; Glimpses of Trinidad and Tobago, 1974; (ed. with A. Carr) David Frost Introduces Trinidad and Tobago, 1975; Profile Trinidad, 1975; Streets of Conflict (novel), 1976; Folk Tales and Fantasies (short stories), 1976; The Making of Port of Spain 1757-1939, 1978; All That Glitters (novel), 1982; Bright Road to El Dorado (novel), 1981; Port of Spain in a World at War, 1984; First in Trinidad, 1985; Heroes of the People of Trinidad and Tobago, 1986; A Better and Brighter Day, 1987; Towns and Villages of Trinidad and Tobago, 1988; Parade of the Carnivals of Trinidad, 1839-1989, 1989; The Golden Quest-The Four Voyages of Christopher Columbia (history), 1992; The Chieftain's Carnival (short stories), 1993; In the Heat of the Day, 1996; Historical Dictionary of Trinadad & Tobego, 1997; Green Days by the River, 2000. **Address:** 99 Long Circular Rd, St. James, Port of Spain, Trinidad and Tobago.

ANTHONY, Patricia. American, b. 1947. **Genres:** Novels, Novellas/Short stories, Science fiction/Fantasy, Plays/Screenplays. **Career:** Writer. University of Lisbon, Lisbon, Portugal, visiting professor of English literature; Universidade Federal de Santa Catarina, Florianopolis, Brazil, associate professor of English; Southern Methodist University, adjunct professor of creative writing. **Publications:** Cold Allies, 1993; Brother Termite, 1993; Conscience of the Beagle, 1993; Happy Policeman, 1994; Cradle of Splendor, 1996; God's Fires, 1997; Flanders, 1998; Eating Memories, 1997. Contributor of short stories to magazines. **Address:** 9712 Amberton Pkwy, Dallas, TX 75243, U.S.A. **Online address:** patanthony@mindspring.com

ANTHONY, Peter. *See* SHAFFER, Peter (Levin).

ANTHONY, Piers. (Piers Anthony Dillingham Jacob). American (born England), b. 1934. **Genres:** Novels, Romance/Historical, Science fiction/Fantasy, Westerns/Adventure, Young adult fiction, Autobiography/Memoirs. **Career:** Writer. **Publications:** Chthon, 1967; (with R.E. Margoff) The Ring, 1968; Macroscope, 1969; (with Margoff) The E.S.P. Worm, 1970; Prostho Plus, 1973; Race against Time, 1973; (with R. Fuentes) Kiai!, 1974; (with Fuentes) Mistress of Death, 1974; Triple Detente, 1974; (with Fuentes) Bamboo Blood Bath, 1974; Rings of Ice, 1974; Phthor, 1975; (with Fuentes) Ninja's Revenge, 1975; (with Fuentes) Amazon Slaughter, 1976; Steppe, 1976; (with R. Coulson) But What of Earth, 1976, 1989; Hasan, 1977; (with F.T. Hall) Pretender, 1979; Mute, 1981; Anthonology, 1985; Shade of the Tree, 1986; Ghost, 1986; (with Margoff) Dragon's Gold, 1987; Serpent's Silver, 1988; Chimaera's Copper, 1990; Orc's Opal, 1990; Mouvar's Magic, 1992; Bio of an Ogre (autobiography), 1988; (with R. Kornwise) Through the Ice, 1989; (with J.L. Nye) Visual Guide to Xanth, 1989; Total Recall, 1989; Pornucopia, 1989; (with Fuentes) Dead Morn, 1990; Firefly, 1990; Hard Sell, 1990; Balook, 1990; Tatham Mound, 1991; Mercycle, 1991; Alien Plot, 1992; (with P.J. Farmer) Caterpillar's Question, 1992; Killobyte, 1993; Letters to Jenny, 1993; (with M. Lackey) If I Pay Thee Not in Gold, 1993; (with A. Tella) The Willing Spirit, 1996; Volk, 1996; (with C.A. Pickover) Spider Legs, 1998; Quest for the Fallen Star, 1998; Realty Check, 1998; (with J. Brady) Dream a Little Dream, 1999; (with R. Leming) The Gutbucket Quest, 2000; (with J.A. Taeusch) The Secret of Spring, 2000; How Precious Was That While: An Autobiography, 2001; Up in a Heaval, 2002; Magic Fart, 2003; Key to Havoc, 2003; Key to Chroma, 2003; Cube Route, 2003. BATTLE CIRCLE TRILOGY: Sos the Rope, 1968; Var the Stick, 1973; Neq the Sword, 1975. OF MAN AND MANTA TRILOGY: Omnivore, 1968; Orn, 1971; Ox, 1976. CLUSTER SERIES: Cluster, 1977; Chaining the Lady, 1978; Kirlian Quest, 1978; Thousand Star, 1980; Viscous Circle, 1982. XANTH SERIES: A Spell for Chameleon, 1977; The Source of Magic, 1979; Castle Roogna, 1979; Centaur Aisle, 1982; Ogre, Ogre, 1982; Night Mare, 1983; Dragon on a Pedestal, 1983; Crewel Lye, 1985; Colem in the Gears, 1986; Vale of the Vole, 1987; Heaven Cent, 1988; Man from Mundania, 1989; Isle of the View, 1990; Question Quest, 1991; The Color of Her Panties, 1992; Dreams Don't Dream, 1993; Harpy Thyme, 1994; Geis of the Gargoyle, 1995; Yon Ill Wind, 1996; Faun & Games, 1997; Zombie Lover, 1998; Xone of Contention, 1999; The Dastard, 2000; Swell Foop, 2001. TAROT TRILOGY: God of Tarot, 1979; Vision of Tarot, 1980; Faith of Tarot, 1980. ADEPT SERIES: Split Infinity, 1980; Blue Adept, 1981; Juxtaposition, 1982; Out of Phaze, 1987; Robot Adept, 1988; Unicorn Point, 1989; Phaze Doubt, 1990. INCARNATIONS OF IMMORTALITY SERIES: On a Pale Horse, 1983; Bearing an Hourglass, 1984; With a Tangled Skein, 1985; Wielding a Red Sword, 1986; Being a Green Mother, 1987; For Love of Evil, 1988; And Eternity, 1990. BIO OF A SPACE TYRANT SERIES: Refugee, 1983; Mercenary, 1984; Politician, 1985; Executive, 1985; Statesman, 1986. MODE SERIES: Virtual Mode, 1991; Fractal Mode, 1992; Chaos Mode, 1993; DoOon Mode, 2001. GEODYSSEY SERIES (historical): Isle of Woman, 1993; Shame of Man, 1994; Hope of Earth, 1997; Muse of Art, 1999. EDITOR: (co-) Uncollected Stars, 1986; (with R. Gilliam) Tales from the Great Turtle (anthology), 1994. **Address:** c/o AMG/Renaissance, 9465 Wilshire Blvd, Beverly Hills, CA 90212, U.S.A. **Online address:** PiersAnthony@hipiers.com; www.hipiers.com

ANTIEAU, Kim. (born United States). **Genres:** Novellas/Short stories. **Career:** Librarian and researcher. Daughters of Nyx: A Magazine of Goddess Stories, Mythmaking, and Fairy Tales, editor, 1994-96. **Publications:** Blossoms, 1991; Trudging to Eden: A Collection of Short Stories, 1994; The Jigsaw Woman, 1996; The Gaia Websters, 1997; Coyote Cowgirl, 2003; Also author of numerous short stories and creative nonfiction. **Address:** c/o Author Mail, Forge, 175 Fifth Avenue, New York, NY 10010, U.S.A. **Online address:** Kim@Kimantieau.com

ANTIN, Steven (Howard). (born United States), b. 1961. **Genres:** Business/Trade/Industry. **Career:** Actor, producer, and screenwriter. **Publications:** FILM SCREENPLAYS, UNLESS OTHERWISE NOTED: Gloria (adapted from a 1980 screenplay by John Cassavetes), 1999; (with others) Young Americans (television series), 2000; (with Laura Angélica Simón) Chasing Papi, 2003; OTHER: (With John Boskovich) Inside Monkey Zetterland, 1992. **Address:** International Creative Management, 8942 Wilshire Blvd, Beverly Hills, CA 90211, U.S.A.

ANTOL, Marie Nadine. American, b. 1930. **Genres:** Biography, Medicine/Health, Ghost Writer. **Career:** Worked for an international company as vice president of marketing and sales, 1977-85; free-lance writer, 1985-. **Publications:** (with N. Johnson) A Dud at Seventy-A Stud at Eighty! An Autobiography, 1982; Healing Teas: A Practical Guide to the Medicinal Teas of the World, 1996. Ghostwriter. Contributor to periodicals. Some writings appear under the name Nikki Antol.

ANTON, Ted. American, b. 1957. **Genres:** Documentaries/Reportage. **Career:** DePaul University, Chicago, IL, associate professor of English, 1989-. **Publications:** (ed. with R. McCart) The New Science Journalists, 1995; Eros, Magic, and the Murder of Professor Culianu (nonfiction), 1996. Contributor to anthologies. Contributor to periodicals. **Address:** Department of English, DePaul University, 802 West Belden Ave., Chicago, IL 60614, U.S.A.

ANTONETTA, Susanne. American, b. 1956. **Genres:** Adult non-fiction. **Publications:** Body Toxic: An Environmental Memoir, 2001. POETRY: Bardo. **Address:** c/o Author Mail, Perseus Books Group, 10 E. 53rd Street, 23rd Floor, New York, NY 10022, U.S.A.

ANTONI, Brian. Bahamian, b. 1959. **Genres:** Novels. **Career:** Attorney at law in Miami, FL, 1995-. Real estate developer. **Publications:** Paradise Overdose (novel), 1994. Contributor to periodicals. **Address:** 451 Broome St. #9W, New York, NY 10013, U.S.A.

ANTONI, Robert (William). American/Trinidadian/Bahamian, b. 1958. **Genres:** Novels, Novellas/Short stories. **Career:** University of Miami, Coral Gables, FL, assistant professor of creative writing and literature, 1992-. **Publications:** NOVELS: Divina Trace, 1991; Blessed Is the Fruit, 1997; My Grandmother's Erotic Folk Tales, 2001; Carnival, 2005. Work represented in anthologies. Contributor to periodicals. **Address:** 110 W 25th Street, #7, New York, NY 10001, U.S.A. **Online address:** www.robertantoni.com

ANTONUCCI, Francesco. Italian, b. 1956. **Genres:** Food and Wine. **Career:** Worked as a chef for El Toula (restaurant chain), Italy; as a sous chef for Valentino Restaurant, Santa Monica, CA; has worked as a chef for DDL Foodshow; has worked as a chef for DDL Bistro, NYC; worked as an executive chef for Alo Alo Restaurant, NYC, until 1987; Remi Restaurant Inc., NYC, co-owner and chef, 1987-. Co-owner of Remi Restaurants in Santa Monica, 1990-, Mexico City, Mexico, 1993-, and Tel Aviv, Israel, 1994-. Delonghi, national spokesperson. **Publications:** (with F. Fabricant) Venetian Taste, 1994; Il Sapore della Memoria, trans. as The Art of Italian Regional Cooking, 1995. **Address:** Remi Restaurant Inc., 145 W 53rd St, New York, NY 10019, U.S.A. **Online address:** remirestaurant@earthlink.net

ANTRIM, Donald. American, b. 1959?. **Genres:** Novels. **Career:** Novelist. **Publications:** NOVELS: Elect Mr. Robinson for a Better World, 1993; The Hundred Brothers, 1997; The Verificationist, 2000. **Address:** c/o Melanie Jackson Agency, 41 W 72nd St., Apt 3F, New York, NY 10023, U.S.A.

ANUNOBI, Fredoline O. American, b. 1956. **Genres:** Economics, Politics/Government. **Career:** Alabama A & M University, Normal, instructor in economics, 1984-85; Morris Brown College, Atlanta, GA, teaching assistant in economics, 1987-88; Selma University, Selma, AL, assistant professor of political science, head of Division of Business Administration and Social Sciences, and director of Third World studies, 1988-92; Xavier University of Louisiana, New Orleans, assistant professor of political science, 1992-. **Publications:** The Implications of Conditionality: The International Monetary Fund and Africa, 1992; International Dimensions of African Political Economy: Trends, Challenges, and Realities, 1994. Work represented in anthologies. Contributor to political science and African studies journals and newspapers. **Address:** Department of Political Science, Xavier University of Louisiana, 7325 Palmetto St., New Orleans, LA 70125, U.S.A.

ANZALDÚA, Gloria. See Obituaries.

APHRONTIS, Hippoclides. See HUMEZ, Nicholas (David).

APONTE, Harry J. American, b. 1935. **Genres:** Psychiatry, Social work. **Career:** Catholic Charities Family Service, NYC, staff member, 1959-60; Menninger Clinic, Topeka, KS, staff member, 1961-68; Philadelphia Child Guidance Clinic, Philadelphia, PA, staff member, 1968-69, coordinator of clinical services, 1969-74, director of outpatient department, 1974-75, director of the clinic, 1975-79; private practice of family therapy in Philadelphia, 1979-. Family Therapy Training Program of Philadelphia, director, 1982-. Drexel University, clinical associate professor, 1983-. **Publications:** Bread and Spirit: Therapy with the New Poor, 1994. Contributor to books. Contributor of articles and reviews to professional journals in the United States and Latin America. **Address:** 1401 Walnut St Ste 1M, Philadelphia, PA 19102, U.S.A.

APOSTOLOU, Anna. See DOHERTY, P(aul) C.

APPACH, Anjana. Indian, b. 1956. **Genres:** Novellas/Short stories. **Career:** National Endowment for the Arts Creative Writing Fellowship; O. Henry Festival prize; 2 Hawthornden fellowships. **Publications:** Incantations & Other Stories, 1991; Listening Now (novel), 1998. **Address:** c/o Victoria Gould Pryor, Arcadia, 31 Lake Place N, Danbury, CT 06810, U.S.A.

APPELL, Scott D. American, b. 1954. **Genres:** Horticulture. **Career:** Brooklyn Botanic Garden, Brooklyn, NY, part-time assistant to orchidologist, 1969-71, assistant to taxonomist, 1974-77; WCMH-TV, Columbus, OH, host of The Garden Spot (weekly gardening program), 1989; York Wildlife Conservancy, Bronx Zoo, Bronx, NY, horticulturist and gardener, 1994, and Central Park Zoo, 1996; Ken Druse Studio, Brooklyn, NY, staff horticulturist, 1994-95; The Green Man Inc., New York, NY, horticultural consultant, 1994-; Smith & Hawken, New York, NY, senior horticulturist, 1994-96; New Hort-in-Site Ltd. (Internet Web site), New York, NY, coeditor and staff horticulturist, 1994-98; Horticultural Society of New York, director of education, 1996-. Ohio Nurserymen's Association, certified nurseryman, 1987; guest on television and radio programs. **Publications:** Pansies, 1999; Tulips, 1999; Lilies, 2000; Orchids, 2001. Contributor to books and periodicals. **Address:** c/o Horticultural Society of New York, 128 W 58th St, New York, NY 10019-2103, U.S.A.

APPELT, Kathi. American, b. 1954. **Genres:** Children's fiction, Young adult fiction, Children's non-fiction. **Career:** Texas A&M University, College Station, TX, instructor in continuing education, 1992, assistant lecturer, 2002-; Jacques' Toys and Books, Bryan, TX, children's books buyer, 1992-94, consultant, 1994-; Rice University, Houston, TX, instructor in continuing education, 1996-2000; Vermont college, faculty, 2003-. **Publications:** Elephants Aloft, 1993; Bayou Lullaby, 1995; Bat Jamboree, 1996; The Thunderherd, 1996; Watermelon Day, 1996; A Red Wagon Year, 1996; I See the Moon, 1997; Just People & Paper/Pen/Poem, 1997; Bats on Parade, 1999; Cowboy Dreams, 1999; Someone's Come to Our House, 1999; The Toddler Two-Step, 2000; Bats around the Clock, 2000; Hushabye, Baby Blue, 2000; Kissing Tennessee, and Other Stories from the Stardust Dance, 2000; Oh My Baby, Little One, 2000; Down Cut Shin Creek, 2001; Rain Dance, 2001; Bubbles, Bubbles, 2001; Bubba and Beau: Best Friends, 2002; The Alley Cat's Meow, 2002; Where, Where Is Swamp Bear, 2002; Poems from Home Room, 2002; Best Kind of Gift, 2003; Piggies in a Polka, 2003; Bubba and Beau Go Night-Night, 2003; Incredible Me, 2003. **Address:** 1907 Comal Circle, College Station, TX 77840, U.S.A. **Online address:** kappelt@tca.net; www.kathiappelt.com

APPIAH, (K.) Anthony. British, b. 1954. **Genres:** Philosophy, Cultural/Ethnic topics, Novels. **Career:** University of Ghana, Legon, teaching assistant, 1975-76; Yale University, New Haven, CT, visiting fellow, 1979, assistant professor, became associate professor of philosophy, 1981-86; Cornell University, Ithaca, NY, associate professor, 1986-89, professor of philosophy, 1989; Duke University, Durham, NC, professor of philosophy and literature, 1990-91; Harvard University, Cambridge, MA, professor of Afro-American studies and philosophy, 1991-. Cambridge University, visiting fellow of Clare College, 1983-84. **Publications:** Assertion and Conditionals, 1985; For Truth in Semantics, 1986; Necessary Questions: An Introduction to Philosophy, 1989; Avenging Angel, 1990; In My Father's House: Africa in the Philosophy of Culture, 1992; Nobody Likes Lehtia, 1993; Another Death in Venice, 1995; (with A. Gutmann) Color Conscious: The Political Morality of Race, 1996; (with H.L. Gates Jr.) A Dictionary of Global Culture, 1996. EDITOR: (and author of intro) Early African-American Classics, 1990; (with H.L. Gates Jr.) Identities, 1995. Contributor to periodicals. **Address:** Department of African-American Studies, Harvard University, 12 Quincy Street, Cambridge, MA 02138, U.S.A.

APPLE, Hope. American, b. 1942. **Genres:** Adult non-fiction. **Career:** Skokie Public Library, Skokie, IL, part-time reference librarian, 1971-, and past head of reference section. Jackson House, owner, 1993-. **Publications:** (with M. Jacob) To Be Continued, 1995. **Address:** 1614 Main St., Unit B, Evanston, IL 60202, U.S.A.

APPLE, Max (Isaac). American, b. 1941. **Genres:** Novels, Novellas/Short stories, Plays/Screenplays, Autobiography/Memoirs. **Career:** Professor of English, Rice University, Houston, since 1980 (Assistant Professor, 1972-76; Associate Professor, 1976-80). **Publications:** (with others) Studies in English, 1975; The Oranging of America and Other Stories, 1976; Zip: A Novel of the Left and the Right, 1978; (ed.) Southwest Fiction, 1980; Free Agents, 1984; The Propheteers, 1987; The Air Up There (screenplay), 1994; Roommates (memoir), 1994. **Address:** Kelly Writers House, University of Pennsylvania, 3805 Locust Walk, Philadelphia, PA 19104, U.S.A.

APPLE, Rima D. American, b. 1944. **Genres:** Medicine/Health, Women's studies and issues, Bibliography. **Career:** State University of New York at

Stony Brook, lecturer in community and preventive medicine and project coordinator at Center for Photographic Images of Medicine and Health Care, both 1981-83; University of Melbourne, Parkville, Australia, visiting research fellow in history and philosophy of science, 1983; University of Wisconsin-Madison, member of women's studies program, 1983-92, fellow in history of medicine, 1985-92, assistant professor, 1992, associate professor, 1992-94, professor of consumer science and women's studies, 1994-. University of Wisconsin-Milwaukee, lecturer, 1984, adjunct assistant professor, 1986-90; University of Auckland, visiting lecturer, 1990; University of Trondheim, visiting researcher, 1992-94. **Publications:** (comp.) Illustrated Catalogue of the Slide Archive of Historical Medical Photographs at Stony Brook, 1984; Mothers and Medicine: A Social History of Infant Feeding, 1890-1950, 1987; (asst. ed.) The History of Women and Science, Health and Technology: A Bibliographic Guide to the Professions and the Disciplines, 1988, 2nd ed. (assoc. ed.), 1993; (ed. and contrib.) Women, Health, and Medicine in America: A Historical Handbook, 1990; Vitamania: Vitamins in American Culture, 1996. Contributor to books. Contributor of articles and reviews to scientific and women's studies journals. **Address:** Department of Consumer Science, School of Human Ecology, University of Wisconsin - Madison, 1300 Linden Dr, Madison, WI 53706, U.S.A.

APPLEBAUM, Anne. American, b. 1964. **Genres:** International relations/ Current affairs. **Career:** Journalist, editor, author. The Independent, London, England, Warsaw correspondent, 1988-90; The Economist, London, England, writer/editor, 1988-92; The Spectator, London, England, foreign editor, 1993-, deputy editor, 1994-; The Daily Telegraph, London, England, weekly columnist, 1994-. **Publications:** Between East and West: Across the Borderlands of Europe, 1994; Gulag: A History, 2003 (Pulitzer Prize, 2004). Contributor of articles and reviews to newspapers and periodicals. **Address:** The Spectator, 56 Doughty St., London WC1N 2LL, England.

APPLEBAUM, Victor. *See* **MACDONALD, James D.**

APPLEBOME, Peter. American. **Genres:** Sociology. **Career:** Journalist. Texas Monthly, reporter; New York Times, Atlanta correspondent. **Publications:** Dixie Rising: How the South Is Shaping American Values, Politics, and Culture, 1996. **Address:** 376 Pinecrest Rd NE, Atlanta, GA 30342, U.S.A.

APPLEBY, Louis. British, b. 1955. **Genres:** Medicine/Health. **Career:** Victoria University of Manchester, Manchester, England, senior lecturer in psychiatry, 1991-. Physician and psychiatrist. **Publications:** A Medical Tour through the Whole Island of Great Britain, 1994. **Address:** 15 Danesmoor Rd., Didsbury, Manchester, England.

APPLEGATE, Katherine (Alice). American, b. 1956. **Genres:** Children's fiction, Young adult fiction, Children's non-fiction, Young adult non-fiction. **Career:** Freelance writer. **Publications:** FOR JUVENILES: The Story of Two American Generals: Benjamin O. Davis Jr., and Colin L. Powell (nonfiction), 1992; Zoey Fools Around (novel), 1994; Sharing Sam (novel), c. 1995; Escape (picture book), 1998. Author of many other juvenile novels, including installments in the "Sweet Valley Twin" series, some Disney books, and two Harlequin romances for adults. ANIMORPHS SERIES FOR JUVENILES (AS K.A. APPLEGATE): The Invasion, 1996; The Visitor, 1996; The Message, 1996; Capture, 1997; The Stranger, 1997; The Andalites Gift, 1997; The Alien, 1997; The Secret, 1997; Android, 1997; Forgotten, 1997; The Reaction, 1997; The Andalite Chronicles, 1997; The Change, 1997; The Unknown, 1998; Animorphs Warning, 1998; Animorphs Underground, 1998; Animorphs in the Time of the Dinosaurs, 1998. **Address:** c/o Scholastic Inc., 555 Broadway, New York, NY 10012, U.S.A. **Online address:** kaapplegate@scholastic.com

APPLEMAN, Philip (Dean). American, b. 1926. **Genres:** Novels, Poetry, Anthropology/Ethnology, Biology, Demography. **Career:** Indiana University, Bloomington, instructor, 1955-58, assistant professor, 1958-63, associate professor, 1963-67, professor of English, 1967-82, distinguished professor, 1982-86, distinguished professor emeritus, 1986-. **Publications:** POETRY: Kites on a Windy Day, 1967; Summer Love and Surf, 1968; Open Doorways, 1976; Darwin's Ark, 1984; Darwin's Bestiary, 1986; Let There Be Light, 1991; New and Selected Poems, 1956-1996, 1996. NOVELS: In the Twelfth Year of the War, 1970; Shame the Devil, 1981; Apes and Angels, 1989. OTHER: The Silent Explosion, 1965. EDITOR: (co-) 1859: Entering an Age of Crisis, 1959; Darwin, 1970, rev. ed., 2000; The Origin of Species, 1975, rev. ed., 2001; Malthus: An Essay on the Principle of Population, 1976, rev. ed., 2003. **Address:** PO Box 5058, East Hampton, NY 11937-6073, U.S.A. **Online address:** applemanmp@yahoo.com

APPLETON, Sheldon Lee. American, b. 1933. **Genres:** International relations/Current affairs, Politics/Government. **Career:** With Public Reports Office, U.S. AID, 1955-56; U.S. foreign service officer, 1956-57; Oakland University, Rochester, MI, assistant professor, 1960-64, associate professor, 1964-69, associate dean, 1979-87, associate provost, 1987-93, professor, 1969-2002, distinguished professor of political science, 2002-. University of Hawaii, visiting professor of political science, 1969-70. **Publications:** The Eternal Triangle?: Communist China, the United States, and the United Nations, 1961; United States Foreign Policy, 1968. **Address:** Department of Political Science, Oakland University, Rochester, MI 48309-4401, U.S.A. **Online address:** appleton@oakland.edu

APPLETON, Victor. *See* **DOYLE, Debra.**

APPLEWHITE, James. American, b. 1935. **Genres:** Poetry, Literary criticism and history. **Career:** Duke University, professor of English and former director of Institute of the Arts. **Publications:** POETRY: War Summer: Poems, 1972; Statues of the Grass, 1975; Following Gravity, 1980; Forseeing the Journey, 1983; Ode to the Chinaberry Tree and Other Poems, 1986; River Writing: An Eno Journal, 1988; Lessons in Soaring, 1989; A History of the River: Poems, 1993; Daytime and Starlight, 1997; Quartet for Three Voices, 2002. OTHER: Seas and Inland Journeys: Landscape and Consciousness from Wordsworth to Roethke, 1985. **Address:** 606 November Dr, Durham, NC 27712, U.S.A. **Online address:** jwa@duke.edu

APPLEYARD, Bryan (Edward). British, b. 1951. **Genres:** Biography, Philosophy. **Career:** Newspaper journalist in Surrey, England, and London, England, 1974-77; United Newspapers, London, journalist, 1977-78; Times, London, assistant financial editor, 1978-81, deputy arts editor, 1981-84; Sunday Times, London, contributor and columnist, 1984-91; Independent, London, contributor, 1989, special features writer, c. 1993-; Sunday Times Magazine, special features writer, 1994-. **Publications:** The Culture Club: Crisis in the Arts, 1984; Richard Rogers: A Biography, 1986; The Pleasures of Peace: Art and Imagination in Postwar Britain, 1986; Understanding the Present: Science and the Soul of Modern Man, 1992; Brave New Worlds: Genetics and Human Experience, 1998. Contributor to periodicals. Contributor to television shows.

APPY, Christian G. American. **Genres:** Cultural/Ethnic topics. **Career:** Writer. Harvard University, Cambridge, MA, taught undergraduate history and literature; Massachusetts Institute of Technology, Cambridge, MA, associate professor of history. **Publications:** (with Thomas V. DiBacco and Lorna C. Mason) History of the United States, 1991; Working-Class War: American Combat Soldiers and Vietnam, University of 1993. (ed. and contrib.) Cold War Constructions: The Political Culture of United States Imperialism, 2000; Patriots: The Vietnam War Remembered from All Sides, 2003. **Address:** 11 Walter Griffin Rd, Sharon, MA 02067, U.S.A. **Online address:** Chrisappy@aol.com

APTER, David Ernest. American, b. 1924. **Genres:** Politics/Government, Sociology. **Career:** Northwestern University, Evanston, IL, Assistant Professor, 1954-57; University of Chicago, Associate Professor, 1957-61; University of California, Berkeley, Professor, 1961-69, Director, Institute of International Studies, 1963-69; Yale University, New Haven, CT, Dept of Sociology, Henry J. Heinz Professor of Comparative Political and Social Development, 1969-2000, Henry J. Heinz Professor Emeritus, 2000-, Chairman, 1997-99, Senior Research Scientist, 2000-. **Publications:** Ghana in Transition, 1955, rev. ed., 1972; The Political Kingdom in Uganda, 1961, rev. ed., 1999; The Politics of Modernization, 1965; Some Conceptual Approaches in the Study of Modernization, 1968; Choice and Politics of Allocation, 1971 (Woodrow Wilson Award); Political Change, 1974; An Introduction to Political Analysis, 1977; (with N. Sawa) Against the State: Politics and Social Protest in Japan, 1984; (with C. Andrain) Political Protest and Social Change, 1986; Rethinking Development: Modernization, Dependency, and Post-Modern Politics, 1987; (with C.G. Rosberg) Political Development and the New Realism in Sub-Saharan Africa, 1993; (with T. Saich) Discourse and Power: The Revolutionary Process in Mao's Republic, 1994. AUTHOR AND EDITOR: Ideology and Discontent, 1963; (with J. Joll) Anarchism Today, 1972; (with L. Goodman) The Multinational Corporation and Development, 1976. EDITOR: (with H. Eckstein) Comparative Politics, 1963; (with C. Andrain) Contemporary Analytical Theory, 1972; The Legitimization of Violence, 1997. **Address:** Dept. of Political Science, Yale University, New Haven, CT 06520, U.S.A. **Online address:** david.apter@yale.edu

APTER, Emily (S.). American, b. 1954. **Genres:** Language/Linguistics, Literary criticism and history. **Career:** Williams College, Williamstown, MA, assistant professor, 1983-88, associate professor of Romance languages,

1988-90; University of California, Davis, associate professor of French and Italian, 1990-93; University of California, Los Angeles, Dept of Comparative Literature, professor of French and comparative literature, 1993-97, 2000-, chair, 2000-; University of Pennsylvania, visiting professor, 1993; Cornell University, professor of comparative literature, 1997-2000. **Publications:** Andre Gide and the Codes of Homotextuality, 1987; Feminizing the Fetish: Psychoanalysis and Obsession in Turn-of-the-Century France, 1991; Continental Drift: From National Characters to Virtual Subjects, 1999. Contributor of articles and reviews to literature and language journals. **Address:** Department of Comparative Literature, and French and Francophone Studies, 212 Royce Hall, University of California, Los Angeles, Los Angeles, CA 90095, U.S.A. **Online address:** apter@humnet.ucla.edu

APTER, Michael John. British, b. 1939. **Genres:** Information science/Computers, Psychiatry, Psychology. **Career:** Education and Scientific Developments Ltd., Bristol, Head of Research and Validation Dept., 1964-67; University College, Cardiff, Lecturer, 1967-73, Sr. Lecturer, 1973-84, Reader in Psychology, 1984-88; Apter International, Director, 1998-. **Publications:** Cybernetics and Development, 1966; An Introduction to Psychology, 1967; The New Technology of Education, 1968; The Computer Simulation of Behaviour, 1970; The Experience of Motivation: The Theory of Psychological Reversals, 1982; Reversal Theory: Motivation, Emotion and Personality, 1989; The Dangerous Edge: The Psychology of Excitement, 1992. CO-EDITOR: (with G. Westby) The Computer in Psychology, 1973; Reversal Theory: Applications and Development, 1985; Progress in Reversal Theory, 1988; Adult Play: A Reversal Theory Approach, 1990; Stress and Health: A Reversal Theory Perspective, 1997; Motivational Styles in Everyday Life, 2001. **Online address:** MJApter@aol.com

APTER, T(erri) E. American, b. 1949. **Genres:** Literary criticism and history, Psychology. **Career:** Cambridge University, England, English and American literature teacher, Betty Behvens Research Fellow, Clare Hall, fellow and tutor; writer. **Publications:** Silken Lines and Silver Hooks, 1976; Adonis Garden, 1977; Thomas Mann: The Devil's Disciple, 1978; Virginia Woolf: A Study of Her Novels, 1979; Fantasy Literature: An Approach to Reality, 1982; Why Women Don't Have Wives: Professional Success and Motherhood, 1985; Altered Loves: Mothers and Daughters during Adolescence, 1990; Working Women Don't Have Wives: Professional Success in the 1990s, 1994; Secret Paths: Women in the New Midlife, 1995; The Confident Child: Raising Children to Believe in Themselves, 1997; Best Friends: The Pleasures and Perils of Girls and Women's Friendships, 1998; You Don't Really Know Me!: Why Mothers and Teenage Daughters Argue, 2004. **Address:** 9 Huntingdon Rd, Cambridge CB3 0HH, England.

APTHEKER, Bettina. American, b. 1944. **Genres:** Education, Gay and lesbian issues, Race relations, Women's studies and issues, Autobiography/Memoirs, Bibliography. **Career:** University of California at Santa Cruz, Women's Studies, professor. **Publications:** (with R. Kaufman and M.B. Folsom) FSM (Free Speech Movement), 1965; Big Business and the American University, 1966; Higher Education and the Student Rebellion in the United States 1960-69 (bibliography), 1969, rev. ed., 1972; (with H. Aptheker) Racism and Reaction in the United States: Two Marxian Studies, 1971; (with A.Y. Davis) If They Come in the Morning: Voices of Resistance, 1971; The Academic Rebellion in the United States: A Marxist Appraisal, 1972; The Morning Breaks: The Trial of Angela Y. Davis, 2nd ed., 1999; Mary Church Terrell and Ida B. Wells: A Comparative Rhetoric/Historical Analysis, 1976; (ed.) The Unfolding Drama: Studies in U.S. History by Herbert Aptheker, 1978; Woman's Legacy: Essays on Race, Sex and Class in American History, 1982; Tapestries of Life: Women's Work, Women's Consciousness, and the Meaning of Daily Experience, 1989; Intimate Politics: Autobiography as Witness, 2006. Contributor to books. **Address:** Kresge College, University of California, 1156 High St, Santa Cruz, CA 95064, U.S.A. **Online address:** bettinaf@ucsc.edu

ARAI, Masami. Japanese, b. 1953. **Genres:** Romance/Historical, Area studies. **Career:** Osaka City University, Osaka, Japan, instructor, 1984-86, assistant professor, 1986-88, associate professor in Faculty of Letters, 1988-92; Tokai University, Tokyo, Japan, associate professor in Faculty of Letters, 1992-95; Tokyo University of Foreign Studies, Japan, professor of Turkish studies, 1995-. Osaka University, lecturer, 1991-92. **Publications:** Turkish Nationalism in the Young Turk Era, 1992; My Father Nobunaga (novel), 2003. **Address:** 9-9, Koyama 2-chome, Shinagawa-ku, Tokyo 142, Japan.

ARAKAWA, Yoichi. American. **Genres:** Music. **Publications:** Top Hits of the Country Superstars, 1993; Best of Count Basie, 1993; Best of Miles Davis, 1993; You Too Can Play Jazz Guitar, 1993; Jim Croce-The Greatest Hits, 1994; A Fingerstyle Christmas (guitar solo), 1995; Jazz Riffs for Guitar,

1995; Guitar Chords and Accompaniment, 1998; More Guitar Chords and Accompaniment, 1999; More Jazz Guitar Chords and Accompaniment, 2002; Country Guitar Chords and Accompaniment, 2003; Rock Guitar Chords and Accompaniment, 2003; Blues Guitar Chords and Accompaniment, 2003. **Address:** c/o Six Strings Music Publishing, PO Box 7718-157, Torrance, CA 90504, U.S.A. **Online address:** contact@sixstringsmusicpub.com

ARCENEAUX, Jean. *See* **ANCELET, Barry Jean.**

ARCHER, Chalmers, Jr. American, b. 1938. **Genres:** Cultural/Ethnic topics, History, Military/Defense/Arms control. **Career:** Saints Junior College, Lexington, MS, assistant to the president and registrar, 1968-70; Tuskegee Institute, Tuskegee Institute, AL, career and placement counselor and coordinator of cooperative program, 1972-74, assistant dean for admissions and records, 1974-76, assistant to the vice-president for administration, 1976-79, associate dean for admissions and records and assistant professor of educational administration and counseling, 1979-83; Northern Virginia Community College, coordinator of admissions and records at Annandale Campus, 1983-85, director of financial aid at Alexandria Campus, 1985; Consortium for the Recruitment of Black Students from Northern Cities, past chair and member of board of directors; Alabama State Steering Committee for Advanced Placement of High School Students, past chair. **Publications:** Growing up Black in Rural Mississippi: Memoirs of a Family, Heritage of a Place, 1992; An Invisible Hand at Work in the Community: Black Courage and Family Wisdom, 1995; My Twelve Years as a Green Beret: From Ike to LBJ: Green Berets in the Vanguard, 2001. Author of a weekly newspaper column and contributing editor, Jackson Advocate. Author of articles. **Address:** 785 Flager Circle, Manassas, VA 20109-7435, U.S.A. **Online address:** DrArcher97@aol.com

ARCHER, Gleason Leonard, Jr. American, b. 1916. **Genres:** Theology/Religion, Translations. **Career:** Fuller Theological Seminary, Pasadena, California, Professor of Biblical Languages, 1948-65, Acting Dean of Faculty, 1948-49, 1960-62; Trinity Evangelical Divinity School, Deerfield, Illinois, Emeritus Professor, 1987-, Professor of Old Testament, 1965-86, Emeritus 1987- Chairman, Dept. of Old Testament, 1965-75. **Publications:** The Epistle to the Hebrews: Study Manual, 1957; (trans.) Jerome's Commentary on Daniel, 1958; Epistle to the Romans: A Study Manual, 1959; Survey of Old Testament Introduction, 1964, 1974, 3rd ed. 1994; (assoc. ed.) The Zondervan Pictorial Encyclopedia of the Bible, 1975; (assoc. ed.) Theological Wordbook of the Old Testament; (assoc. ed.) Theological Wordbook of the Old Testament, 1980; Job: God's Answer to Undeserved Suffering, 1982; Encyclopedia of Bible Difficulties, 1982; (with G. C. Chirichigno) Old Testament Quotations in the New Testament: a Complete Survey, 1983; Secret History (trans. from Danish of J. Ahmanson), 1984; The Rapture: Pre-, Mid-, or Post-Tribulation?, 1984; (co-ed.) Disciple's Study Bible, 1988. **Address:** 812 Castlewood Lane, Deerfield, IL 60015, U.S.A.

ARCHER, Ian W. British, b. 1960. **Genres:** Economics, Sociology, History. **Career:** Cambridge University, Cambridge, England, research fellow at Girton College, 1988-89, research fellow and director of studies in history at Downing College, 1989-91; Oxford University, Oxford, England, fellow and tutor in modern history at Keble College and lecturer, 1991-; writer. Royal Historical Society, Bibliographies on British History, general editor. **Publications:** (ed. with C.M. Barron and V. Harding) Hugh Alley's Caveat: The London Markets in 1598, 1988; The Pursuit of Stability: Social Relations in Elizabethan London, 1991; The History of the Haberdashers Company, 1991. **Address:** Keble College, Oxford University, Oxford OX1 3PG, England.

ARCHER, Lord Jeffrey (Howard). British, b. 1940. **Genres:** Novels, Novellas/Short stories, Children's fiction, Plays/Screenplays. **Career:** Member of the Greater London Council for Havering, 1966-69; Conservative Member of Parliament for Louth, 1969-74; Deputy Chairman of the Conservative Party, 1985-86. Life Peer, 1992. **Publications:** Not a Penny More, Not a Penny Less, 1976; Shall We Tell the President?, 1977; Kane and Abel, 1979; The Prodigal Daughter, 1982; First among Equals, 1984; A Matter of Honour, 1986; As the Crow Files, 1991; Honour among Thieves, 1993; The Fourth Estate, 1996; The Eleventh Commandment, 1998; A Prison Diary, vols. 1-3, 2002-04; Sons of Fortune, 2002. SHORT STORIES: A Quiver Full of Arrows, 1980; A Twist in the Tale, 1989; Twelve Red Herrings, 1994; Collected Short Stories, 1997; To Cut a Long Story Short, 2000. PLAYS: Beyond Reasonable Doubt, 1987; Exclusive, 1989; The Accused, 2000. CHILDREN'S FICTION: The First Miracle, 1980; Willy and the Killer Kipper, 1981. **Address:** The Penthouse, 93 Albert Embankment, London SE1 7TY, England.

ARCHER, John Hall. Canadian, b. 1914. **Genres:** Children's non-fiction, History. **Career:** President Emeritus, University of Regina, since 1976

(President, 1974-76; Professor of History, 1976-80). Legislative Librarian, Saskatchewan, 1951-64; Assistant Clerk of Legislature, Saskatchewan, 1956-61; Provincial Archivist, 1957-62; Director of Libraries McGill University, Montreal, 1964-67; University Archivist and Associate Professor of History, Queen's University, Kingston; Principal, University of Saskatchewan, 1970-74. **Publications:** Historic Saskatoon, 1948; (co-author) The Story of a Province: A Junior History of Saskatchewan, 1955; (co-author) The Hudson's Bay Route, 1957; (co-author) Footprints in Time: Saskatchewan, 1967; Order of Canada, 1982; Honoured with the Burden: History of Regina Board of Education, 1987; (co-author) Bernard Amtman: A Personal Memoir, 1987. EDITOR: Search for Stability, 1958; West of Yesterday, 1967; Land of Promise, 1970; Saskatchewan History; Americana; A History of Saskatchewan, 1980. Contributor to reference books. **Address:** 1530 MacPherson Ave, Regina, SK, Canada S4S 4C9.

ARCHER, Jules. American, b. 1915. **Genres:** History, International relations/Current affairs, Law, Biography, Plays/Screenplays, Young adult non-fiction, Humor/Satire, Mystery/Crime/Suspense, Novellas/Short stories, Adult non-fiction, Children's non-fiction, Civil liberties/Human rights, Organized labor, Human relations/Parenting, Humanities, Military/Defense/Arms control, Politics/Government. **Publications:** (with A. Green) Show Biz, 1959; Front-Line General: Douglas MacArthur, 1963; Twentieth-Century Caesar: Benito Mussolini, 1964; Man of Steel: Joseph Stalin, 1965; Fighting Journalist: Horace Greeley, 1966; Laws That Changed America, 1967; The Dictators, 1967; World Citizen: Woodrow Wilson, 1967; Battlefield President: Dwight D. Eisenhower, 1967; Red Rebel: Tito of Yugoslavia, 1968; The Unpopular Ones, 1968; From Whales to Dinosaurs, 1968; African Firebrand: Kenyatta of Kenya, 1969; The Extremists: Gadflies of American Society, 1969; Angry Abolitionist: William Lloyd Garrison, 1969; Philippines' Fight for Freedom, 1970; Indian Foe, Indian Friend, 1970; Colossus of Europe: Metternich, 1970; Hawks, Doves, and the Eagle, 1970; Who's Running Your Life, 1971; 1968: Year of Crisis, 1971; Revolution in Our Time, 1971; Treason in America: Disloyalty versus Dissent, 1971; Ho Chi Minh: The Legend of Hanoi, 1971; Uneasy Friendship: France and the United States, 1972; Strikes, Bombs, and Bullets: Big Bill Haywood and the I.W.W., 1972; Cho En-lai, 1973; Mexico and the United States, 1973; The Plot to Seize the White House, 1973; Resistance, 1973; They Made a Revolution, 1776, 1973; Trotsky: World Revolutionary, 1973; Famous Young Rebels, 1973; Mao Tse-tung: A Biography, 1973; China in the Twentieth Century, 1974; Washington Versus Main Street, 1974; Riot: A History of Mob Action in the United States, 1974; The Russians and the Americans, 1975; Watergate: America in Crisis, 1975; Legacy of the Desert, 1976; The Chinese and the Americans, 1976; Police State, 1976; Epidemic!, 1977; Hunger on Planet Earth, 1977; Superspies, 1977; You and the Law, 1978; You Can't Do That to Me, 1980; Winners and Losers: How Elections Work in America, 1984; Jungle Fighters: A G.I. War Correspondent's Experiences in the New Guinea Campaign, 1985; The Incredible Sixties: The Stormy Years That Changed America, 1986; Breaking Barriers: The Feminist Revolution, 1991; Earthquake!, 1991; Tornado!, 1991; Hurricane!, 1991; They Had a Dream, 1992; Rage in the Streets: Violence in America, 1994; Midnight Jules (radio book), 1994; A House Divided: Lives of Ulysses S. Grant and Robert E. Lee, 1995; Special Interest, 1997; To Save the Earth, 1998. **Address:** 225 Mt. Hermon Rd, #59, Scotts Valley, CA 95066, U.S.A.

ARCHER, Keith (Allan). Canadian, b. 1955. **Genres:** Politics/Government. **Career:** Duke University, Durham, NC, R. Taylor Cole instructor, 1983-84; University of Calgary, Alberta, assistant professor, 1984-88, associate professor, 1988-95, professor of political science, 1995-, associate dean of social sciences, 1995-; writer; Pollstar Research, Inc, (opinion consultants), partner. **Publications:** Political Choices and Electoral Consequences, 1990; (ed. with R. Gibbins and S. Drabek) Canadian Political Life: An Alberta Perspective, 1990; (with R. Gibbins, R. Knopff, and L. Pal) Parameters of Power, 2nd ed., 1999; (with A. Whitehorn) Political Activists: The NDP in Convention, 1997; (with R. Gibbons and L. Youngman) Explorations: A Navagator's Guide to Quantitive Research in Canadian Political Science, 1998. **Address:** Department of Political Science, University of Calgary, 2500 University Dr. N.W, Calgary, AB, Canada T2N 1N4. **Online address:** kaarcher@ucalgary.ca

ARCHER OF SANDWELL, Lord. (Peter Kingsley Archer). British, b. 1926. **Genres:** Civil liberties/Human rights, Law, Politics/Government. **Career:** Labour M.P. (U.K.) for Warley West, 1974-92, and Member of Shadow Cabinet, 1981-87, (Member for Rowley Regis and Tipton, 1966-74; Parliamentary Private Secretary to the Attorney General, 1967-70; Solicitor General, 1974-79); Privy Councillor, 1978-. Chairman, Society of Labour Lawyers, and British Section of Amnesty International, 1971-74; Chairman, Council on Tribunals, 1992-98; Chairman, Enemy Property Compensation

Panel, 1998-. **Publications:** The Queen's Courts, 1956; (ed.) Social Welfare and the Citizen, 1957; Communism and the Law, 1963; (co-author) Freedom at Stake, 1966; Human Rights, 1969; (co-author) Purpose in Socialism, 1973; The Role of the Law Officers, 1978; (co-ed.) More Law Reform Now, 1984. **Address:** House of Lords, London SW1A 0PW, England.

ARCHERY, Helen. See ARGERS, Helen.

ARDEN, John. British, b. 1930. **Genres:** Novels, Plays/Screenplays, Literary criticism and history, Novellas/Short stories. **Career:** Freelance writer and director; Architectural Assistant, London, 1955-57; Fellow in Playwriting, University of Bristol, 1959-60. **Publications:** Serjeant Musgrave's Dance, 1960; (with M. D'Arcy) The Business of Good Government (play), 1963; The Workhouse Donkey, 1964; Three Plays: The Waters of Babylon, Live Like Pigs, The Happy Haven, 1964; Ironhand (adaptation), 1965; Armstrong's Last Goodnight, 1965; Left-Handed Liberty, 1965; (with M. D'Arcy) The Royal Pardon, 1967; Soldier, Soldier and Other Plays, 1967; (with M. D'Arcy) The Hero Rises Up, 1969; Two Autobiographical Plays: The True History of Squire Jonathan and His Unfortunate Treasure, and the Bagman, 1971; (with M. D'Arcy) The Island of the Mighty, 1974; (with M. D'Arcy) The Non-Stop Connolly Show, 5 vols., 1977-78; To Present the Pretence (essays), 1977; Pearl, 1979; (with M. D'Arcy) The Little Gray Home in the West, 1979; (with M. D'Arcy) Vandaleur's Folly, 1981; Silence among the Weapons (novel), 1982, in U.S. as Vox Pop, 1983; (with M. D'Arcy) Whose Is the Kingdom?, 1988; Books of Bale, 1988; (with M. D'Arcy) Awkward Corners, 1988; Cogs Tyrannic: Four Stories, 1991; Jack Juggler and the Emperor's Whore (novel), 1995. **Address:** c/o Casarotto Ramsay & Associates Ltd, National House, 60-66 Wardour St, London W1V 3HP, England.

ARDEN, Judith. See TURNER, Judith.

ARDEN, William. See LYNDS, Dennis.

ARELLANO, Juan Estevan. American, b. 1947. **Genres:** Documentaries/Reportage. **Career:** Writer. Worked as a reporter. Co-founder of Academia de la Nueva Raza, 1970. **Publications:** (ed.) Entre verde y seco, 1972; (And photographer) Palabras de la vista/Retratos de la pluma (poetry: title means: Sight Words/Pen Portraits), 1984; Inocencio: Ni siembra, ni escarda y siempre se come el mejor elote (novel: title means: Inocencio: Neither Plant nor Dig and You'll Always Eat the Best Corn), 1991. Work represented in anthologies. Contributor to periodicals. **Address:** c/o Taos News, 226 Albright St., PO Box U, Taos, NM 87571, U.S.A.

ARENA, Felice. (born Austria), b. 1968. **Genres:** Children's fiction. **Career:** Children's author. Formerly an actor. Presenter for children's television. **Publications:** Dolphin Boy Blue, 1996; Mission Buffalo, 1997; Wish, 1999; Bravo, Billy!, HarperCollins (Pymble, New South Wales, Australia), 2000; Breakaway John, 2001. SPECKY MAGEE SERIES; WITH GARRY LYON: Specky Magee, 2002; Specky Magee and the Great Footy Contest, 2003; Specky Magee and the Season of Champions, 2004. BOYZ RULE! SERIES; WITH PHIL KETTLE: Yabby Hunt, 2003, published as Crawfish Hunt, 2004; Golf Legends, 2004; Test Cricket, 2003; Bull Riding, 200;. Basketball Buddies, 2003; Bike Daredevils, 2003; Rock Star, 2003; Skateboard Dudes, 2003; Camping Out, 2003 Water Rats, 2003; Gone Fishing, 2003; Secret Agent Heroes, 2004; Park Soccer, 2003. Tree House, 2004. Tennis Ace, 2004. Wet World, 2004; Battle of the Games, 2004; Olympic Champions, 2004; On the Farm, 2004; Pirate Attack, 2004, published as Pirate Ship, 2004; Hit the Beach, 2004; Halloween Gotcha!, 2004; Race Car Dreamers, 2004; Rotten School Day, 2004. **Address:** c/o Booked Out Speakers Agency, POB 2321, Prahran, VIC 3181, Australia. **Online address:** felicearena@hotmail.com

ARENDS, Carolyn. Canadian, b. 1968. **Genres:** Philosophy, Human relations/Parenting, Inspirational/Motivational Literature. **Career:** Musician and writer. **Publications:** Living the Questions: Making Sense of the Mess and Mystery of Life, 2000; We've Been Waiting for You, 2002. **Address:** PO Box 74018, Surrey, BC, Canada V4N 5H9. **Online address:** carolyn@carolynarends.com; www.carolynarends.com

ARENS, Katherine (Marie). American, b. 1953. **Genres:** Intellectual history, Literary criticism and history. **Career:** University of Texas at Austin, assistant professor, 1980-86, associate professor, 1986-93, professor of Germanic languages and studies, 1993-. **Publications:** Functionalism and Fin de siecle, 1984; Structures of Knowing, 1989; (with J. Swaffar and H. Byrnes) Reading for Meaning, 1991; Austria and Other Margins, 1996; Empire in Decline, 2001. **Address:** Dept of Germanic Studies, E. P. Schoch 3.102, University of Texas at Austin, Austin, TX 78712-0304, U.S.A. **Online address:** k.arens@mail.utexas.edu

ARESTIS, Philip. British (born Cyprus), b. 1941. **Genres:** Economics. **Career:** University of Greenwich, London, England, lecturer, 1969-71, senior lecturer, 1971-77, principal lecturer in economics, 1977-88; Cambridge University, part-time lecturer, 1971-80; University of East London, Dagenham, England, head of economics department, 1988-97, research professor of economics, 1997-2000; South Bank University, London, professor, 2000-02; Levy Economics Institute of Bard College, director of research and professor of economics, 2002-. **Publications:** Introducing Macroeconomic Modelling, 1982; The Post-Keynesian Approach to Economics, 1992; Money, Pricing, Distribution, and Economic Integration, 1997. EDITOR/CO-EDITOR: Post-Keynesian Economic Theory, 1985; Post-Keynesian Monetary Economics, 1988; Contemporary Issues in Money and Banking: Essays in Honour of Stephen Frowen, 1988; Theory and Policy in Political Economy (essays), 1990; Recent Developments in Post-Keynesian Economics, 1992; A Biographical Dictionary of Dissenting Economists, 1992, 2nd ed., 2000; Money and Banking: Issues for the Twenty-first Century: Essays in Honour of Stephen F. Frowen, 1993; The Elgar Companion to Radical Political Economy, 1994; Finance, Development, and Structural Change, 1995; The Political Economy of Full Employment, 1995; Keynes, Money, and the Open Economy, 1996; Employment, Economic Growth, and the Tyranny of the Market, 1996; Capital Controversy, Post-Keynesian Economics and the History of Economic Thought, 1997; The Relevance of Keynesian Economic Policies Today, 1997; Markets, Unemployment, and Economic Policy, 1997; The Political Economy of Economic Policies, 1998; Money and Macroeconomic Policy, 1998; The Political Economy of Central Banking, 1998; Method, Theory, and Policy in Keynes: Essays in Honour of Paul Davidson, 1998; Money and Macroeconomic Policies: Essays in Macroeconomics in Honour of Bernard Corry and Maurice Peston, Vol. 1, 1999; The History and Practice of Economics: Essays in Honour of Bernard Corry and Maurice Peston, Vol. 2, 1999; Regulation, Strategies and Economic Policies: Essays in Honour of Bernard Corry and Maurice Peston, Vol. 3, 1999; What Global Economic Crisis?, 2001; Money, Finance and Capitalist Development, 2001; Economics of the Third Way, 2001; The Euro, 2001; Money, Macroeconomics and Keynes: Essays in Honour of Victoria Chick, Vol. 1, 2002; Methodology, Microeconomics and Keynes: Essays in Honour of Victoria Chick, Vol. 2, 2002; Monetary Union in South America, 2003; Globalization, Regionalism and Economic Policy, 2003. Contributor to economic journals. **Address:** Cambridge Center for Public Policy, University of Cambridge, 19 Silver St, Cambridge CB3 9EP, England. **Online address:** p.arestis@sbu.ac.uk

ARETXAGA, Begoña. American. **Genres:** Anthropology/Ethnology. **Career:** University of Texas, Austin, assistant professor. **Publications:** NONFICTION: Los funerales en el nacionalismo radical vasco: ensayo antropologico, 1988; Shattering Silence: Women, Nationalism, and Political Subjectivity in Northern Ireland, 1997. **Address:** Anthropology and Archeology, Campus Mail Code: C3200, University of Texas, Austin, TX 78712, U.S.A. **Online address:** aretxaga@mail.utexas.edu

ARGERS, Helen. Also writes as Helen Archery. American. **Genres:** Novels, Novellas/Short stories, Romance/Historical, Plays/Screenplays, Music, Race relations, Theatre, Writing/Journalism, Humor/Satire. **Career:** Lecturer, Metropolitan Writers Conference and Historical Society of New Jersey; Worrall Newspapers, music and play reviewer, and columnist, The Art of Laughter. **Publications:** NOVELS: A Lady of Independence, 1982; A Scandalous Lady, 1991; A Captain's Lady, 1991; An Unlikely Lady, 1992; Noblesse Oblige, 1994; The Gilded Lily, 1998. OTHER: The Home Visit (one-act play), 1986. NOVELS AS HELEN ARCHERY: The Age of Elegance, 1992; The Season of Loving, 1992; Lady Adventuress, 1994; Duel of Hearts, 1994.

ARGIRI, Laura. American, b. 1958. **Genres:** Novels. **Career:** Novelist, editor, and proofreader. **Publications:** The God in Flight, 1994. Contributor of chapter 14 to Pete and Shirley: The Great Tar Heel Novel, 1995. **Address:** c/o Endeavor Agency, 9601 Wilshire Blvd 10th Fl, Beverly Hills, CA 90212, U.S.A.

ARICO, Santo L. American, b. 1938. **Genres:** Literary criticism and history. **Career:** Teacher at the elementary, high school, college and university levels, 1960-. Held school principal and department chair positions. **Publications:** (ed.) Contemporary Women Writers in Italy: A Modern Renaissance, 1990; The Art of Persuasion in Rousseau's "La Nouvelle Heloise," 1994. **Address:** 200 Sivley St., Oxford, MS 38655, U.S.A.

ARIFF, Mohamed. Australian, b. 1942. **Genres:** Money/Finance. **Career:** Worked in industry in Singapore for ten years; worked at National University of Singapore for fourteen years; Monash University, Melbourne, Australia, staff member, c. 1997-. Also works as management accountant. **Publica-**

tions: Stock Pricing in Singapore, 1990; Stock Pricing in Malaysia, 1998; APEC Development Cooperation, 1998; Liberalization, Growth, and the Asian Financial Crisis, 2000; Taxation Compliance Costs in Asia Pacific. **Address:** 5/18 Mackay Ave., Glenhuntly, VIC 3163, Australia. **Online address:** mohamed.ariff@buseco.monash.edu.au

ARINZE, Cardinal Francis. Nigerian, b. 1932. **Genres:** Theology/Religion. **Career:** Ordained Roman Catholic priest, elevated to Cardinal; archbishop of Onitsha, Nigeria, 1967-85; Pontifical Council for Inter-religious Dialogue, Vatican City, Italy, president, 1984-; writer. **Publications:** Sacrifice in Ibo Religion, 1970; Answering God's Call, 1983; Living Our Faith, 1983; Alone with God, 1986; Progress in Christian-Muslim Relations Worldwide, 1988; Church in Dialogue, 1990; Meeting Other Believers, 1999; Brucken Bauen, 2000; The Holy Eucharist, 2001; Religions for Peace, 2002. **Address:** I-00120 Vatican City, Italy.

ARKIN, Marcus. South African, b. 1926. **Genres:** Economics, History, Theology/Religion, Reference. **Career:** Contributor and Consultant Ed., Dictionary of South African Biography. Professor of Economics and Head of Dept. of Economics and Economic History, Rhodes University, Grahamstown, 1967-73; former Director-General, South African Zionist Federation; Department of Economics, University of Durban-Westville (retired). Chairman, Editorial Board, Hashalom (monthly journal), Durban. **Publications:** John Company at the Cape, 1962 (Founders' Medal and prize, Economic Society of South Africa); Supplies for Napoleon's Gaolers, 1964; Agency and Island, 1965; South African Economic Development: An Outline Survey, 1966; Economists and Economic Historians, 1968; Introducing Economics: The Science of Scarcity, 1971; The Economist at the Breakfast Table, 1971; Storm in a Teacup: The Cape Colonists and the English East India Company, 1973; Aspects of Jewish Economic History, 1975; The Zionist Idea: A History and Evaluation, 1977; (ed.) South African Jewry, 1984; One People, One Destiny: Some Explorations in Jewish Affairs, 1989. **Address:** PO Box 22179, Glenashley, Kwazulu-Natal 4022, Republic of South Africa. **Online address:** arkin@iafrica.com

ARKOUN, Mohammed. French (born Algeria). **Genres:** History, Humanities, Philosophy. **Career:** Lycee d'Al-Harrach, Algeria, professor of Arabic, 1951-54; Universite de Sorbonne, Paris, France, professor of Islamic thought, 1962-. Visiting professor at universities worldwide. Arabica, journal of Arabic and Islamic Studies, director; Library of Congress, scientific counselor. **Publications:** Critique de la Raison Islamique, 1986; Essais sur la Pensee Islamique, 1986; Rethinking Islam Today, 1987; (ed.) Arab Thought, 1988; Ouvertures sur l'Islam, 1989, trans. as Rethinking Islam: Common Questions, Uncommon Answers, 1994; La Pensee arabe, 1996; L'Islam Approche Critique, 2002; The Unthought in Contemporary Islamic Thought, 2002; From Manhattan to Bagdad: Beyond Good and Evil, 2003; Humanism and Islam: Struggles and Proposals, 2005; Islam: To Reform or to Subvert, 2005. Contributor of articles on Islamic thought, history, and culture to Arabic French, German, and English language journals. **Address:** 44 Bld Magenta, 75010 Paris, France.

ARKUSH, Michael. American, b. 1958. **Genres:** Sports/Fitness, Biography. **Career:** Los Angeles Times, Los Angeles, CA, reporter, 1988-; writer. **Publications:** (with S. Springer) Sixty Years of USC-UCLA Football, 1991; Rush!: An Up-Close Look at Rush Limbaugh, 1993. Contributor to periodicals. **Address:** 20000 Pranie St., Chatsworth, CA 91311, U.S.A.

ARLINGTON, Taryn. See PALMER, Randy.

ARLUKE, Arnold. American, b. 1947. **Genres:** Animals/Pets, Sociology. **Career:** Northeastern University, Boston, MA, professor of sociology, 1978-. Tufts University, senior fellow of Center for Animals, 1990-; consultant to Massachusetts Society for the Prevention of Cruelty to Animals. **Publications:** The Making of Rehabilitation: A Political Economy of Medical Specialization, 1985; Gossip: The Inside Scoop, 1987; Sociology: Snapshots and Portraits of Society, 1996; Regarding Animals, 1996; Great Apes and Humans, 2001; Brute Force: Animal Police and the Challenge of Cruelty, 2004. **Address:** Department of Sociology, Northeastern University, Boston, MA 02115, U.S.A. **Online address:** profarluke@aol.com

ARMAH, Ayi Kwei. Ghanaian, b. 1939. **Genres:** Novels. **Career:** Former Trans., Revolution Africaine mag., Algiers. Scriptwriter for Ghana Television, and English Teacher, Navrongo School, Ghana, 1966; Ed., Jeune Afrique mag., Paris, 1967-68. **Publications:** The Beautiful Ones Are Not Yet Born, 1968; Fragments, 1970; Why Are We So Blest?, 1972; The Two Thousand Seasons, 1973; The Healers, 1978; Osiris Rising: A Novel of

Africa Past, Present and Future, 1995. Contributor of poetry to anthologies and short stories to magazines. **Address:** c/o Per Ankh Publishers, B.P.2, Popenguine, Senegal.

ARMANTROUT, (Mary) Rae. American, b. 1947. **Genres:** Poetry, Autobiography/Memoirs. **Career:** California State University, San Francisco, teaching assistant, 1972-74; California State University, San Diego, lecturer, 1980-82; University of California, San Diego, La Jolla, lecturer, 1980-. **Publications:** POETRY: Extremities, 1978; The Invention of Hunger, 1979; Precedence, 1985; Necromance, 1991; Made to Seem, 1995; Memoir: True, 1998; The Pretest, 2001; Veil: New and Selected Poems, 2001. **Address:** 4774 E Mountain View Dr, San Diego, CA 92116, U.S.A. **Online address:** raeal00900@aol.com

ARMISTEAD, John. American, b. 1941. **Genres:** Mystery/Crime/Suspense, Children's fiction. **Career:** Waimea Baptist Church, Waimea, HI, pastor, 1975-77; Kailua Baptist Church, Kailua, HI, pastor, 1977-79; Calvary Baptist Church, Tupelo, MS, pastor, 1979-94; Daily Journal, Tupelo, religion editor, 1995-. **Publications:** Cruel as the Grave, 1996; The $66 Summer, 2000; The Return of Gabriel, 2002. NOVELS: A Legacy of Vengeance, 1994; A Homecoming for Murder, 1995. **Address:** 5148 Woodlake Cove, Tupelo, MS 38801, U.S.A.

ARMITAGE, David. New Zealander, b. 1943. **Genres:** Children's fiction. **Career:** Author and illustrator. **Publications:** WITH R. ARMITAGE AND ILLUSTRATOR: The Lighthouse Keeper's Lunch, 1977; The Trouble with Mr. Harris, 1978; Don't Forget Matilda!, 1979; The Bossing of Josie, 1980, as The Birthday Spell, 1981; Ice Creams for Rosie, 1981; One Moonlit Night, 1983; Grandma Goes Shopping, 1984; The Lighthouse Keeper's Catastrophe, 1986; The Lighthouse Keeper's Rescue, 1989; Watch the Baby, Daisy, 1991; When Dad Did the Washing, 1992; Looking after Chocolates, 1992; A Quarrel of Koalas, 1992, published as Harry Hates Shopping!, 1992; The Lighthouse Keeper's Picnic, 1993; The Lighthouse Keeper's Cat, 1995. FOR CHILDREN (AND ILLUSTRATOR): Portland Bill's Treasure Trove (activity book), 1987; Giant Stories, 1988; Jasper Who Jumps, 1990. Illustrator of books by L. Hinds, J.P. Rutland, F. Linde, J.C. Siddons, M. Smith, P. Pearce, J. Corbalis, S. Berry, P. Visman. **Address:** Old Tiles Cottage, Church Lane, Hellingly, E. Sussex BN27 4HA, England.

ARMITAGE, Frank. *See* **NELSON, Ray.**

ARMITAGE, Ronda (Jacqueline). New Zealander, b. 1943. **Genres:** Children's fiction. **Career:** Infant Teacher, Duvauchelles, 1964-66, and Auckland, 1968-69; Supply Teacher, London, 1966; Adviser on Children's Books, Dorothy Butler Ltd., booksellers, Auckland, 1970-71; Assistant Librarian, Lewes Priory Comprehensive School, Sussex, 1976-77; Supply teacher, East Sussex County Council, from 1978. **Publications:** The Lighthouse Keeper's Lunch, 1977; The Trouble with Mr. Harris, 1978; Don't Forget Matilda, 1979; The Bossing of Josie, 1980, as The Birthday Spell, 1981; Ice Creams for Rosie, 1981; One Moonlight Night, 1983; Grandma Goes Shopping, 1985; The Lighthouse Keeper's Catastrophe, 1986; The Lighthouse Keeper's Rescue, 1987; When Dad Did the Washing, 1989; Watch the Baby, Daisy, 1990; Looking after Chocolates, 1991; A Quarrel of Koalas, 1992; The Lighthouse Keeper's Picnic, 1993; The Lighthouse Keeper's Cat, 1995; The Lighthouse Keeper's Favourite Stories, 1999; Queen of the Night, 1999. **Address:** Old Tiles Cottage, Church Lane, Hellingly, E. Sussex BN27 4HA, England.

ARMSTRONG, Alexandra. American, b. 1939. **Genres:** Money/Finance. **Career:** Ferris & Co., Washington, DC, executive secretary, 1961-66; New York Stock Exchange, registered representative, 1966-; Julia Walsh & Sons, Washington, DC, senior vice president, 1977-83; Alexandra Armstrong Advisors, Inc., Washington, DC, chairman, 1983-91; Armstrong, MacIntyre & Severns, Inc. (financial planning and investment firm), Washington, DC, chairman, 1991-. Guest on national television shows. **Publications:** (with M. Donahue) On Your Own: A Widow's Passage to Emotional and Financial Well-Being, 1993, 3rd ed., 2000. **Address:** Armstrong, MacIntyre & Severns, Inc., 1155 Connecticut Ave NW Ste 250, Washington, DC 20036-4306, U.S.A.

ARMSTRONG, David. (born England), b. 1946. **Genres:** Art/Art history. **Career:** Has taught adult education at a college in Shropshire, England. **Publications:** Night's Black Agents (novel), 1993; Less than Kind (novel), 1994; Until Dawn Tomorrow (novel), 1995; Thought for the Day (novel), 1997; Small Vices (novel), 2001; How NOT to Write a Novel (nonfiction), 2003. Also author of poems, short stories, and plays. Contributor to periodicals. **Address:** c/o Author Mail, Bon Marche Centre, 241 Ferndale Rd., London SW9 8BJ, England.

ARMSTRONG, David Malet. Australian, b. 1926. **Genres:** Philosophy. **Career:** Birkbeck College, University of London, Assistant Lecturer in Philosophy, 1954-55; Melbourne University, Lecturer and Sr. Lecturer in Philosophy, 1956-63; Sydney University, Challis Professor of Philosophy, 1964-91, Emeritus Professor of Philosophy, 1992-. **Publications:** Berkeley's Theory of Vision, 1960; Perception and the Physical World, 1961; Bodily Sensations, 1961; A Materialist Theory of the Mind, 1968; Belief, Truth and Knowledge, 1973; Universals and Scientific Realism, 1978; The Nature of Mind and Other Essays, 1980; What Is a Law of Nature?, 1983; (with N. Malcolm) Consciousness and Causality, 1984; A Combinatorial Theory of Possibility, 1989; Universals, 1989; (with C.B. Martin and U.T. Place) Dispositions; A Debate, 1996; A World of States of Affairs, 1997; The Mind-Body Problem, 1999. EDITOR: Berkeley's Philosophical Writings, 1965; (co-) Locke and Berkeley, 1968. **Address:** c/o Dept of Philosophy, Sydney University, Sydney, NSW 2006, Australia. **Online address:** david. armstrong@arts.usyd.edu.au

ARMSTRONG, Diane (Julie). Australian (born Poland), b. 1939. **Genres:** Novels, History. **Career:** Freelance writer. **Publications:** Mosaic: A Chronicle of Five Generations, 2001; The Voyage of Their Life: The Story of the SS Derna and Its Passengers, 2001; Winter Journey (novel), 2005. Contributor to periodicals. **Address:** 181 Military Rd, Dover Heights, Sydney, NSW 2030, Australia.

ARMSTRONG, Gillian (May). Australian, b. 1950. **Genres:** Plays/Screenplays. **Career:** Director, producer, art director, and screenwriter. Director of television commercials; also worked as production assistant, assistant designer, and assistant editor of industrial and educational films. Worked as a waitress. Associated with Women's Film Group, Sydney, Australia. **Publications:** SCREENPLAYS: Gretel, (short film), 1973; Smokes and Lollies (documentary), 1975; (with J. Pfeffer) The Singer and the Dancer, 1976; Fourteen's Good, Eighteen's Better (documentary), 1980; A Busy Kind of Bloke, 1980; Touch Wood (documentary), 1980; Not Just a Pretty Face, 1983; Not Fourteen Again (documentary; also known as Now They Are Fourteen and Not 14 Again!), 1996. Contributor to periodicals. **Address:** c/o Creative Artists Agency, 9830 Wilshire Blvd., Beverly Hills, CA 90212, U.S.A.

ARMSTRONG, Jeannette C. Canadian, b. 1948. **Genres:** Novels, Children's fiction, Mythology/Folklore. **Career:** En'owkin Cultural Center, Penticton, British Columbia, Canada, staff member, 1978-, director, 1985-; University of Victoria, Victoria, British Columbia, co-founder and director of En'owkin School of International Writing, 1989-. Penticton Band, member of council. **Publications:** Enwhisteetkwa: Walk on Water (juvenile fiction), 1982; Neekna and Chemai (juvenile fiction), 1984; Slash (novel), 1985, rev. ed., 1988; (ed.) Looking at the Words of Our People: An Anthology of First Nation Literary Criticism, 1993; The Native Creative Process: A Collaborative Discourse (non-fiction), 1991; Breathtracks (poetry), 1991; Whispering in Shadows (novel), 2000. Contributor of poems and short stories to periodicals and anthologies. **Address:** En'owkin School of International Writing, En'owkin Centre, RR#2, S-50, C-8, Penticton, BC, Canada V2A 6J7. **Online address:** theytusbooks@vip.net

ARMSTRONG, Jennifer. Also writes as Julia Winfield. American, b. 1961. **Genres:** Novels, Children's fiction, Young adult fiction, Children's non-fiction. **Career:** Cloverdale Press, NYC, assistant editor, 1983-85; freelance writer, 1985-; teacher. Leader of writing workshops. **Publications:** Steal Away (novel), 1992; Shipwreck at the Bottom of the World (non-fiction), 1998; (adapter) P. Jennings and T. Brewster, The Century for Young People, 1999. PICTURE BOOKS: Hugh Can Do, 1992; Chin Yu Min and the Ginger Cat, 1993; That Terrible Baby, 1994; Little Salt Lick and the Sun King, 1995; The Whittler's Tale, 1995; Pockets, 1998; Pierre's Dream, 1999; Spirit of Endurance, 1999; Audubon: Painter of Birds in the Wild Frontier, 2003; Magnus at the Fire, 2004. MIDDLE GRADE NOVELS: The Puppy Project, 1990; Too Many Pets, 1990; Hillary to the Rescue, 1990; That Champion Chimp, 1990; Theodore Roosevelt: Letters from a Young Coal Miner, 2000; Thomas Jefferson: Letters from a Philadelphia Bookworm, 2000. YOUNG ADULT FICTION. The Dreams of Mairhe Mehan, 1996; Mary Mehan Awake, 1997; The Kindling, 2002; The Keepers of the Flame, 2002; The Kiln, 2003. WILD ROSE INN SERIES: Bridie of the Wild Rose Inn, 1994; Ann of the Wild Rose Inn, 1994; Emily of the Wild Rose Inn, 1994; Laura of the Wild Rose Inn, 1994; Claire of the Wild Rose Inn, 1995; Grace of the Wild Rose Inn, 1995. JUVENILE NOVELS: Black-Eyed Susan, 1995; The Snowball, 1996; Sunshine, Moonshine, 1997. JUVENILE NON-FICTION: A Three-Minute Speech, 2003. CHAPTER BOOKS: Patrick Doyle Is Full of Blarney, 1996; Foolish Gretel, 1997; Lili the Brave, 1997. ANTHOLOGIES: Shattered, 2002; What a Song Can Do, 2004. YOUNG ADULT NON-

FICTION: In My Hands, 1999. YOUNG ADULT FICTION AS JULIA WINFIELD: Only Make-Believe, 1987; Private Eyes, 1989; Partners in Crime, 1989; Tug of Hearts, 1989; On Dangerous Ground, 1989. **Address:** PO Box 335, Saratoga Springs, NY 12866, U.S.A. **Online address:** www.jennifer-armstrong.com

ARMSTRONG, John. (born Scotland), b. 1966. **Genres:** Art/Art history. **Career:** Art dealer. University of London, London, England, director of aesthetics program; Monash University, Melbourne, Australia, director of Centre for Public Philosophy; University of Melbourne, senior research fellow in philosophy. **Publications:** Looking at Pictures: An Introduction to the Appreciation of Art, 1996; Move Closer: An Intimate Philosophy of Art, 2000; Conditions of Love: The Philosophy of Intimacy, 2003. **Address:** University of Melbourne, Department of Philosophy, Old Quad, Melbourne, VIC 3010, Australia.

ARMSTRONG, John Alexander. American, b. 1922. **Genres:** Administration/Management, History, International relations/Current affairs, Politics/Government. **Career:** Emeritus Professor of Political Science, University of Wisconsin, Madison, since 1986 (Assistant Professor, 1954-57; Associate Professor, 1958-60; Professor, 1960-78; Executive Secretary, Russian Area Studies Program, 1959-63 and 1964-65; Acting Chairman, Western European Area Program 1967; Philippe de Commynes Professor, 1978-86). President, American Association for the Advancement of Slavic Studies, 1965-67; Consultant, Bureau of Intelligence and Research, U.S. Dept of State, Washington, D.C., 1972-81 (member, Advisory Panel, Bureau of European Affairs, 1966-69). **Publications:** Ukrainian Nationalism, 1955, 1963, 1990; The Soviet Bureaucratic Elite, 1959, 1966; The Politics of Totalitarianism, 1961; Ideology, Politics and Government in the Soviet Union, 1962, 4th ed. 1979; (co-author and ed.) Soviet Partisans in World War II, 1964; The European Administrative Elite, 1973; Nations Before Nationalism, 1982. **Address:** 40 Water St, Saint Augustine, FL 32084, U.S.A.

ARMSTRONG, Judith (Mary). Australian. **Genres:** Novels, Literary criticism and history, Biography. **Career:** University of Melbourne, Russian Dept., member, 1974-96. **Publications:** The Novel of Adultery, 1976; (trans.) In the Land of Kangaroos and Goldmines, by Oscar Comettant, 1980; (ed. with R. Slonek) Essays to Honour Nina Christesen, 1980; The Unsaid Anna Karenina, 1988; The Christesen Romance, 1996; Anya, Countess of Adelaide, 1998; The Cook and the Maestro, 2001; The French Tutor, 2003. **Address:** 157 Newry St, N Carlton, VIC 3056, Australia. **Online address:** j.armstrong@unimelb.edu.au

ARMSTRONG, Karen (Anderson). British, b. 1944. **Genres:** Theology/Religion, Autobiography/Memoirs. **Career:** Writer and historian. Writer and presenter of The First Christian (6-part documentary TV series on the life of St. Paul), 1984. **Publications:** Through the Narrow Gate (autobiography), 1981; Beginning the World (autobiography), 1983; The Gospel According to Woman: Christianity's Creation of the Sex War in the West, 1986; Holy War: The Crusades and Their Impact on Today's World, 1988; Muhammad: A Biography of the Prophet, 1992; A History of God: The 4,000-Year Quest of Judaism, Christianity, and Islam, 1993; The Battle for God, 2000; Islam: A Short History, 2000; Jerusalem: One City, Three Faiths, 1996; Buddha, 2001; The Spiral Staircase, 2004. EDITOR: Tongues of Fire: An Anthology of Religious and Poetic Experience, 1985; (and trans.) The English Mystics of the Fourteenth Century, 1991. **Address:** c/o Curtis Brown Agency, 10 Astor Pl, New York, NY 10003, U.S.A.

ARMSTRONG, Kelley L. Canadian, b. 1968. **Genres:** Novels. **Career:** Writer and computer programmer. **Publications:** NOVELS: Bitten, 2001; Stolen, 2002. **Address:** RR #4, Aylmer, ON, Canada N5H 2R3. **Online address:** karmstg@hotmail.com

ARMSTRONG, Mary (Elizabeth) Willems. American, b. 1957. **Genres:** Film. **Career:** WNDU-TV, South Bend, IN, actress in Beyond Our Control, 1973-75; Friends of the Hardin County Public Libraries, Elizabethtown, KY, publicity coordinator, 1984-86; WQXE-FM Radio, Elizabethtown, film critic on Mary's Movie Minute, 1988-89; writer, 1989-; speech-language pathologist, 1993-. **Publications:** (with R.B. Armstrong) The Movie List Book: A Reference Guide to Film Themes, Settings, and Series, 1990, 2nd ed. 1994. **Address:** c/o Betterway Books, 4700 E Galbraith Rd, Cincinnati, OH 45236, U.S.A.

ARMSTRONG, Richard B(yron). American, b. 1956. **Genres:** Film. **Career:** WXII-TV, Winston-Salem, NC, intern in writing and production, 1977-78; U.S. Army Armor School, Fort Knox, KY, instructional developer, 1982-. **Publications:** (with M.W. Armstrong) The Movie List Book: A Reference

Guide to Film Themes, Settings, and Series, 1990, 2nd ed., 1994; Encyclopedia of Film Themes, Settings and Series, 2001. **Address:** c/o McFarland & Company, Inc., Publishers, Box 611, Jefferson, NC 28640, U.S.A.

ARMSTRONG, Robert Laurence. American, b. 1926. **Genres:** Philosophy. **Career:** Professor and Chairman, Dept. of Philosophy and Religious Studies, University of West Florida, Pensacola, since 1969 (Associate Professor, and Chairman, 1967-69). Assistant Professor of Philosophy, University of Nevada, Reno, 1962-67. **Publications:** Metaphysics and British Empiricism, 1970; (trans. with Daniel J. Herman) Investigations into the Origin of Language and Consciousness, by Tran Duc Thao, 1984. **Address:** Dept. of Philosophy and Religious Studies, University of West Florida, Pensacola, FL 32514, U.S.A.

ARNAUD, Claude. French, b. 1955. **Genres:** Novels, Plays/Screenplays, Biography. **Career:** Worked as a printer in Paris, France, 1973-74; Cinematographe (cinema review magazine), journalist, 1977-83; free-lance writer, 1984-. **Publications:** (with B. Minoret) Les Salons (play), 1985; Chamfort (biography), 1989, trans. by D. Dusinbere, 1992; Les Histoires d'Amour finissent mal en general (screenplay), 1993; Le Cameleon (novel; title means: The Chameleon), 1994; Le Jeu des Quatre Coins (novel; title means: Press in the Corner), 1998; Cocteau (biography), 2003. **Address:** 13 rue de Verneuil, 75007 Paris, France. **Online address:** cl_arns_@club-internet.fr

ARNETT, Peter (Gregg). American (born New Zealand), b. 1934. **Genres:** Autobiography/Memoirs. **Career:** Southland Times, Invercargill, New Zealand, reporter, 1951-54; Standard, Wellington, New Zealand, reporter, 1955-56; Sun, Sydney, Australia, reporter, 1957; Bangkok World, Bangkok, Thailand, associate editor, 195860; Vientiane World, Vientian, Laos, editor, 1960; Associated Press, correspondent in Jakarta, Indonesia, 1961-62, Vietnam, 1962-70, and NYC, 1970-81; Cable News Network (CNN-TV), international correspondent, 1981-; writer. **Publications:** Live from the Battlefield: From Vietnam to Baghdad: Thirty Five Years in the World's War Zones, 1994. **Address:** CNN Building, 820 First St. NE, Ninth Floor, Washington, DC 20002, U.S.A.

ARNETT, Ronald C. American, b. 1952. **Genres:** Communications/Media, Ethics, Philosophy. **Career:** St. Cloud State University, MN, assistant professor of speech communication, 1977-84; Marquette University, Milwaukee, WI, chair of communication and rhetorical studies, 1984-87; Manchester College, North Manchester, IN, professor of communications, dean/vice-president of the college, 1987-93; Duquesne University, Pittsburgh, PA, professor of communication and chair of Dept of Communication and Rhetorical Studies, 1993-. **Publications:** Dwell in Peace: Applying Nonviolence to Everyday Relationships, 1980; Communication and Community: Implications of Martin Buber's Dialogue, 1986; Dialogic Education: Conversations about Ideas and between Persons, 1992; Dialogic Civility in a Cynical Age: Community, Hope, and Interpersonal Relationships, 1999. CO-EDITOR: The Reach of Dialogue: Confirmation, Voice, and Community, 1994; Communication Ethics in an Age of Diversity, 1996. Contributor to scholarly journals. **Address:** Dept of Communication and Rhetorical Studies, Duquesne University, Pittsburgh, PA 15282, U.S.A. **Online address:** arnett@duq.edu

ARNEY, James. *See* RUSSELL, Martin (James).

ARNHEIM, Rudolf. American (born Germany), b. 1904. **Genres:** Art/Art history, Communications/Media, Film, Psychology. **Career:** Sarah Lawrence College, Bronxville, NY, Member of Psychology Faculty, 1943-68; Harvard University, Professor, 1968-74, Emeritus Professor, Psychology of Art, 1974-; Univ of Michigan, Ann Arbor, Visiting Professor, 1974-84. **Publications:** Art and Visual Perception, 1954, rev. ed. 1974; Film as Art, 1957; Genesis of a Painting, 1962; Toward a Psychology of Art, 1966; Entropy and Art, 1971; Radio: An Art of Sound, 1971; The Dynamics of Architectural Form, 1977; The Power of the Center, 1982, 1988; New Essays on the Psychology of Art, 1986; Parables of Sunlight, 1989; To the Rescue of Art, 1992; The Split and the Structure, 1996. **Address:** 1200 Earhart Rd #224N, Ann Arbor, MI 48105, U.S.A.

ARNOLD, A(lbert) James, Jr. American, b. 1939. **Genres:** Literary criticism and history. **Career:** Hamilton College, Clinton, NY, instructor in Romance languages, 1961-62; University of Virginia, Charlottesville, 1966-, assistant professor to professor of French, 1966-. Exchange professor of comparative literature at Sorbonne Nouvelle, Universite de Paris III, spring, 1981. **Publications:** Paul Valery and His Critics, 1970; (with J.-P. Piriou) Genese et critique d'une autobiographie: "Les Mots" de Jean-Paul Sartre, 1973; Modernism and Negritude: The Poetry and Poetics of Aime Cesaire,

1981. EDITOR: Albert Camus, Caligola: Testo inedito del 1941, 1983; Fourteen volumes in the CARAF BOOKS series, 1987-1994; New World Studies series, 1993-; A History of Literature in the Caribbean, 3 vols., 1994-. **Address:** Department of French, 302 Cabell Hall, University of Virginia, Charlottesville, VA 22903, U.S.A. **Online address:** aja@virginia.edu

ARNOLD, Arnold F. American, b. 1929. **Genres:** Ethics, Crafts, Education, Mathematics/Statistics. **Career:** Graphic, and industrial designer, 1946-; cyberneticist, writer and consultant in systems analysis and operational research, London, 1976-. Workshop School, New York, director, 1949-52; Arnold Arnold Design Inc, New York, president, 1960-66; Manuscript Press Inc, New York, president, 1963-66; Rutledge Books, New York, consultant ed, 1962-65; Collector and owner of the Arnold Arnold Collection of Culture of Childhood. Children's books, toys and games. **Publications:** Your Child's Play, 1955; The Arnold Arnold Book of Toy Soldiers, 1963; Tongue Twisters and Double Talk, 1964; Look and Do Books Series, 1964; Games, 4 vols., 1965; Violence and Your Child, 1969; Pictures and Stories from Forgotten Children's Books, 1969; Your Child and You, 1970; The Yes and No Book, 1970; Career Choices for the '70s, 1971; Teaching Your Child to Learn from Birth to School Age, 1971; The World Book of Children's Games, 1972; (ed.) Antique Paper Dolls, 1915-1920, 1975; The World Book of Arts and Crafts for Children, 1977; Winners and Other Losers in War and Peace, 1989; The Corrupted Sciences, 1992. **Address:** c/o Tina Betts, Andrew Mann Ltd, Literary Agents, 1 Old Compton St., London W1V 5PH, England.

ARNOLD, Edmund Clarence. American, b. 1913. **Genres:** Advertising/Public relations, Communications/Media, Design, History, Writing/Journalism. **Career:** State Journal, Lansing, Michigan, night editor, 1952-54; Linotype News, editor, 1954-60; Syracuse University, NY, School of Public Communications, Graphic Arts Dept., chairman, 1960-75; Virginia Commonwealth University, Richmond, professor, 1975-83; distinguished professor emeritus, 1983. American Press Institute, Print & Graphics, Publisher's Auxiliary, Editor's Workshop, contributing editor; Trailblazer Magazine, editor; National Newspaper Institute, faculty, 1960-. **Publications:** Functional Newspaper Design, 1956; Profitable Newspaper Advertising, 1960; Feature Photos That Sell, 1960; Ink on Paper: A Handbook of the Graphic Arts, 1963; The Student Journalist, 1963; Tipografia y Diagramados, 1965; The Yearbook, 1966; Copy Preparation, 1966; Graphic Arts Procedures, 1966; Layout for Advertising, 1966; Advertising Design, 1966; Type Handbook, 1966; Modern Newspaper Design, 1969; Ink on Paper 2, 1972; Editing the Yearbook, 1973; (with H. Kreigbaum) Handbook of Student Journalism, 1976; Arnold's Ancient Axioms, 1978; Designing the Total Newspaper, 1980; Editing the Organizational Publication, 1981; Fliers, Folders and Brochures, 1984; 34 Outstanding Organizational Publications, 1986; The Trailblazers: A History of the 70th Infantry Division, 1989; 40 Keys to Typography, 1995; A Number of Things: Recollections of a Depression Kid, 2004. **Address:** 3804 Brandon Ave SW Apt 415, Roanoke, VA 24018-7006, U.S.A. **Online address:** edvi@rev.net

ARNOLD, Eleanor. American, b. 1929. **Genres:** Local history/Rural topics, Women's studies and issues, History. **Career:** Farm homemaker, 1950-. Volunteer leader of oral history projects for Indiana Humanities Council, National Endowment for the Humanities, Indiana Extension Homemakers Association, and National Extension Homemakers Council; leader of oral history workshops; public speaker. Historic Landmarks Foundation of Indiana, member of board of directors; Indiana Rural Preservation Council, member; Rush County Heritage, vice-president. **Publications:** EDITOR: Rush County Sesquicentennial History, privately printed, 1973; Feeding Our Families, 1983; Party Lines, Pumps, and Privies, 1984; Buggies and Bad Times, 1985; Voices of American Homemakers, 1985; Girlhood Days, 1987; Going to Club, 1988; Living Rich Lives, 1989; (co-author) Rich Lives (play), 1986; (co-author) Hoosier Rich Lives (play), 1988. **Address:** 1744 N 450 E, Rushville, IN 46173, U.S.A.

ARNOLD, Guy. British, b. 1932. **Genres:** History, Industrial relations, International relations/Current affairs, Politics/Government, Third World, Travel/Exploration. **Career:** Freelance writer. Adviser on youth problems, Government of Northern Rhodesia, 1963-64; Researcher, Overseas Development Institute, London, 1965-66; Director, Africa Bureau, London, 1968-72. **Publications:** Longhouse and Jungle, 1959; Towards Peace and a Multiracial Commonwealth, 1964; Economic Co-operation in the Commonwealth, 1967; Kenyatta and the Politics of Kenya, 1974; The Last Bunker, 1976; Modern Nigeria, 1977; (with R. Weiss) Strategic Highways of Africa, 1977; Britain's Oil, 1978; Aid in Africa, 1979; Held Fast for England: G.A. Henty, Imperialist Boys' Writer, 1980; The Unions, 1981; Modern Kenya, 1981; Datelines of World History, 1983; Aid and the Third World, 1985; Third World

Handbook, 1989; Down the Danube, 1989; Britain since 1945, 1989; Journey round Turkey, 1990; Wars in the Third World since 1945, 1991; South Africa: Crossing the Rubicon, 1992; Brain Wash, 1992; The End of the Third World, 1993; Political and Economic Encyclopaedia of Africa, 1993; Historical Dictionary of Aid and Development Organizations, 1996; The Maverick State Gaddafi and The New World Order, 1996; World Government by Stealth, 1997; The Resources of the Third World, 1997; Historical Dictionary of Civil Wars in Africa, 1999; Mercenaries, 1999; World Strategic Highways, 2000; The New South Africa, 2000; A Guide to African Political & Economic Development, 2001; Historical Dictionary of the Crimean War, 2002. **Address:** 163 Seymour Pl, London W1H 4PL, England.

ARNOLD, H(arry) J(ohn) P(hilip) (Douglas). British, b. 1932. **Genres:** Astronomy, Information science/Computers, Photography, Biography. **Career:** Foreign News Ed., Financial Times newspaper, London, 1956-60; Assistant to Managing Director and Public Relations Adviser, Kodak Ltd., London, 1966-74; Managing Director, Space Frontiers Ltd., 1974-2000. **Publications:** Aid to Developing Countries, 1961; Aid for Development, 1966; Photographer of the World: Biography of H. G. Ponting, 1969; Another World, 1975; William Henry Fox Talbot: Photographic Pioneer and Man of Science, 1977; Images from Space, 1979; Night Sky Photography, 1988; (ed.) Man in Space, 1993; Astrophotography: An Introduction, 1995; The Photographic Atlas of the Stars, 1997; Eclipse '99, 1999; Astrophotography: An Introduction to Film and Digital Imaging, 2002. **Address:** 30 Fifth Ave, Denvilles, Havant, Hants. PO9 2PL, England. **Online address:** hjp.arnold@btconnect.com

ARNOLD, Kenneth L. American, b. 1957. **Genres:** Information science/Computers. **Career:** Tulsa Equipment Manufacturing, Tulsa, OK, co-owner and president, 1993-. **Publications:** The Manager's Guide to ISO 9000, 1994; Quality Assurance Methods and Technologies, 1994. **Address:** 4045 North Garnett Rd., Tulsa, OK 74116, U.S.A.

ARNOLD, Peter. American, b. 1943. **Genres:** Criminology/True Crime, How-to books, Medicine/Health, Travel/Exploration. **Publications:** (ed. with J. Lewis) The Total Filmmaker, 1971; Burgler-Proof Your Home and Car, 1971; Off the Beaten Track in Copenhagen, 1972; Lady Beware (crime prevention), 1974; Check List for Emergencies (health), 1974; Crime and Youth, 1976; How to Protect Your Child against Crime, 1977; Emergency Handbook, 1980; (with R. Germann) Bernard Haldane Associates' Job and Career Building, 1980; (with R. Germann and D. Blumenson) Working and Liking It, 1983; (with E.J. Wallach) The Job Search Companion, 1984; (with B.A. Percelay) Packaging Your House for Profit, 1985. **Address:** 1 Hollis St. #350, Wellesley, MA 02482-4631, U.S.A.

ARNOLD, Tedd. American, b. 1949. **Genres:** Children's fiction. **Career:** Tallahassee, FL, textbook illustrator, owner of a graphic design studio, 1973-84; New York City, book designer, 1984-86; Elmira, NY, freelance author and illustrator, 1986-. **Publications:** FOR CHILDREN: Sounds, 1985; Actions, 1985; Opposites, 1985; Colors, 1985; My First Drawing Book, 1986; No Jumping on the Bed, 1987; Ollie Forgot, 1988; Mother Goose's Words of Wit and Wisdom: A Book of Months, 1990; (and designer of samplers) Cross-Stitch Patterns for Mother Goose's Words of Wit and Wisdom Samplers to Stitch, 1990; The Signmaker's Assistant, 1992; The Simple People, 1992; Green Wilma, 1993; No More Water in the Tub, 1995; Five Ugly Monsters, 1995; Bialosky's Bedside Books, 1996; Parts, 1997; Huggly Gets Dressed, 1997; Huggly Takes a Bath, 1998; Huggly and the Toy Monster, 1998; Huggly's Pizza, 2000; Huggly Goes to School, 2000; More Parts, 2001; Huggly's Big Mess, 2001; Huggly's Christmas, 2001; Huggly's Snow Day, 2002; Huggly's Trip to the Beach, 2002; Huggly's Halloween, 2002; Huggly's Thanksgiving Parade, 2002; Huggly's Valentines, 2003; Huggly Goes Camping, 2003. ILLUSTRATOR OF BOOKS BY: R. Atlas, B. Bagert, A.S. Capucilli, R. Coyle, R. Failing, P. Glassman, A. Kostick, R. Pulver, D. Rosenbloom, J. Sardegna, D. Schiller, and H. Witty. **Address:** c/o Dial Books for Young Readers, 345 Hudson St, New York, NY 10014, U.S.A. **Online address:** www.teddarnold.com

ARNOTT, Peter. Scottish, b. 1962. **Genres:** Plays/Screenplays. **Career:** Playwright, songwriter, and writer for television, c. 1983-. Leader of writer's workshops; active in community theatre. **Publications:** PLAYS: The Boxer Benny Lynch, 1985; White Rose, 1985; The Death of Elias Sawney, 1985; Thomas Muir's Voyage to Australia, 1986; (adapter) C. Dickens, A Christmas Carol, 1986; Losing Alec, 1988; (with P. Mullan) Harmony Row, 1989; Century's End, 1990; Salvation, 1990; Hyde, 1996; (trans.) B. Brecht, Puntila and His Man Matti, 1998; The Wire Garden, 1998; A Little Rain, 2000; The Breathing House, 2003; (with P. Mullen) Miles Better (teleplay). Songwriter. **Address:** c/o Tron Theatre Company, 63 Trongate, Glasgow G1 5HB, Scotland.

ARNZEN, Michael A. American, b. 1967. **Genres:** Novels, Novellas/Short stories, Horror, Film, Poetry. **Career:** Freelance writer, 1987-. University of Idaho, Moscow, ID, instructional assistant, 1992-94; University of Oregon, Eugene, OR, graduate teaching fellow, 1994-99; Seton Hill University, Greensburg, PA, associate professor, 1999-. **Publications:** (ed.) Psychos: An Anthology of Psychological Horror in Verse, 1992; Grave Markings (novel), 1994. POETRY: Chew and Other Ruminations, 1991; Writhing in Darkness, vols. 1 and 2, 1997; Paratabloids, 1999; Dying, 2003; Freakcidents, 2004; Gorelets: Unpleasant Poems, 2003. SHORT STORIES: Needles and Sins, 1993; Fluid Mosaic, 2001; 100 Jolts, 2004. Contributor to anthologies. Contributor of essays to academic and popular journals. Contributor of poetry and short stories to periodicals. **Address:** Dept of English, Seton Hill University, Greensburg, PA 15601, U.S.A. **Online address:** arnzen@gorelets.com; www.gorelets.com

AROM, Simha. French/Israeli (born Germany), b. 1930. **Genres:** Anthropology/Ethnology, Cultural/Ethnic topics, Music. **Career:** Israel Broadcasting Corp., first horn in Symphonic Orchestra, 1958-63; National Museum Barthelemy Boganda, Bangui, Central African Republic, founder and director, 1963-67; Centre National de la Recherche Scientifique, Paris, France, ethnomusicologist and researcher, 1967-, director of research, 1978-. Israel Broadcasting Corp., head of Music Division, 1980-82. **Publications:** Conte et chantefables ngbaka-ma'bo: Republique Centrafricaine, 1970; (with J.M.C. Thomas) Les mimbo: genies du piegeage et le monde surnaturel des Ngbaka-Ma'bo: Republique Centrafricaine, 1975; Polyphonies et Polyrythmies instrumentales d'Afrique Centrale: Structure et methodologie, 2 vols., 1985, trans. as African Polyphony and Polyrhythm: Musical Structure and Methodology, 1991. **Address:** LMS, Centre National de la Recherche Scientifique, 7 rue Guy Moquet, 94801 Villejuif Cedex, France. **Online address:** arom@vjf.cnrs.fr

ARON, Michael. American, b. 1946. **Genres:** Politics/Government. **Career:** Harper's, NYC, associate editor, 1975-76; Rolling Stone, NYC, associate editor, 1977; New Jersey Monthly, Princeton, editor, 1978-82; New Jersey Network, Trenton, senior political correspondent, 1982-. **Publications:** Governor's Race: A TV Reporter's Chronicle of the 1993 Florio/Whitman Campaign, 1993. **Address:** NJN News, New Jersey Network, PO Box 777, Trenton, NJ 08625-0777, U.S.A.

ARONIE, Nancy S(lonim). American, b. 1941. **Genres:** Writing/Journalism. **Career:** Writer. Worked as a stage actress and stand-up comic. Founder of Chilmark Writing Workshop in 1986; contributor to National Public Radio. Writer-in-residence at Trinity College in Hartford, CT, for three years; artist-in-residence for Gardner Museum, Boston, MA. **Publications:** Writing from the Heart: Tapping the Power of Your Inner Voice, 1998. Contributor of essays to magazines. **Address:** 1 W Meadow, Chilmark, MA 02535, U.S.A.

ARONOFF, Craig E(llis). American, b. 1951. **Genres:** Business/Trade/Industry. **Career:** Georgia State University, Atlanta, assistant professor, 1975-79, associate professor of management, 1979-83; Kennesaw State University, Marietta, GA, professor of management and Dinos Distinguished Professor of Private Enterprise, both 1983-, department head, 1984-86, eminent scholar, 1999-, and founder and director of Cox Family Enterprise Center; Family Business Consulting Group, Inc., principal and co-founder, 1994-. Family Business Advisor, newsletter, executive editor, 1992-. Consultant to family-owned business firms and professional service providers. **Publications:** (with O. Baskin) Interpersonal Communication in Organizations, 1980; (with O. Baskin, H. Davis, and R. Hays) Getting Your Message Across: A Practical Guide to Business Communication, 1983; (with O. Baskin) Public Relations: The Profession and the Practice, 1983, (and with D. Lattimore) 4th ed., 1997; (with M. Cauley) A Century of Service: A History of Cobb and Its Bank, 1987; (with Ward and others) The Family Business Leadership Series, 15 vols., 1991-; (with J. Pearl) Winning: The NSI Story, 1997. EDITOR: Business and the Media, 1979; (with J. Ward) The Future of Private Enterprise, 3 vols, 1984-86; (with J. Ward) Initial Public Offerings Annual: 1989, 1990; (with J. Ward) Family Business Sourcebook, 1991, (and with J. Astrachon) 3rd ed., 2003; (with J. Ward) Contemporary Entrepreneurs, 1992. **Address:** 2061 E Side Dr, Marietta, GA 30062-6079, U.S.A. **Online address:** aronoff@efamilybusiness.com

ARONOWITZ, Stanley. American, b. 1933. **Genres:** Cultural/Ethnic topics, Education. **Career:** University of California, Irvine, professor of social science and comparative literature, 1977-82; Graduate Center of the City University of New York, New York, N.Y., professor of sociology, 1983-; CUNY Center for Cultural Studies, director, currently. **Publications:** Honor America: The Nature of Fascism, Historic Struggles Against It, and a Strategy for Today, 1971; False Promises: The Shaping of American Working Class Consciousness, 1973; Food, Shelter, and the American Dream, 1974; The Crisis in Historical Materialism: Class, Politics, and Culture in Marxist Theory, 1981; Working Class Hero: Evolution of the American Labor Movement, 1983; Science as Power, 1989; Post Modern Education, 1991; Politics of Identity, 1992; Roll over Beethoven, 1993; The Jobless Future, 1994; Death & Rebirth of American Radicalism, 1996; From the Ashes of the Old, 1998; The Knowledge Factory, 2000. EDITOR: The Sixties without Apology: An Anthology, 1984; (co-) PostWork: The Wages of Cybernation, 1998. **Address:** 1 Washington Sq Vlg, New York, NY 10012-1632, U.S.A. **Online address:** S.Aronowitz@igc.org

ARONSON, I(rwin) Michael. American, b. 1942. **Genres:** History, Area studies. **Career:** Kendall College, Evanston, IL, instructor, 1968; Roosevelt University, Chicago, IL, instructor, 1968-70; Lawrence University of Wisconsin, Appleton, instructor, 1970-71; Haifa University, Haifa, Israel, lecturer, 1972-80; State of Israel, Tel Aviv, researcher and translator for Ministry of Foreign Affairs, 1981-. Northwestern University, visiting assistant professor, summer, 1974; University of London, foreign guest lecturer, 1990. **Publications:** Troubled Waters: The Origins of the 1881 Anti-Jewish Pogroms in Russia, 1990. Work represented in anthologies. Contributor to history and Russian studies journals. **Address:** Rechov Borochov 23A, Raanana, Israel.

ARRIETY, Richmond. See NOONAN, Tom.

ARRINGTON, Stephen L(ee). American, b. 1948. **Genres:** Recreation. **Career:** U.S. Navy, frogman in Navy bomb disposal unit, including service in Vietnam, 1966-71, leaving the service as chief petty officer; Boron Prison Camp, inmate fireman, 1982-85; College of Oceaneering, air diving supervisor, 1985-87; Cousteau Society, expedition leader and chief diver, 1987-93; motivational and drug education speaker and writer, 1993-; special effects stuntperson for films, including Top Gun and Oceans of Fire; American Red Cross, instructor in cardiopulmonary resuscitation (CPR); Dream Machine Foundation, founder and president; also teacher of karate and scuba diving. **Publications:** Journey into Darkness: Nowhere to Land (memoir), 1992; Expedition and Diving Operations Handbook, 1993; High on Adventure: Stories of Good, Clean, Spine-Tingling Fun, 1995; (creator) Out of the Night (video), 1995; High on Adventure II: Dreams Becoming Reality, 1996; High on Adventure III: Building the Adventure Machine, 1997. **Address:** PO Box 3234, Paradise, CA 95967, U.S.A. **Online address:** steve@drugsbite.com; www.drugsbite.com

ARROW, Kenneth (Joseph). American, b. 1921. **Genres:** Economics, Mathematics/Statistics. **Career:** University of Chicago, asst. professor, 1948; Stanford University, assistant professor, 1949-50, associate professor, 1950-53, professor of economics, statistics, and operations research, 1953-68, Joan Kenney Professor of Economics and Professor of Operations Research, 1979-91, emeritus professor, 1991-; Harvard University, professor of economics, 1968-74, James Bryant Conant University Professor, 1974-79; Center for Advanced Study in the Behavioral Sciences, Palo Alto, CA, fellow, 1956-57; Council of Economic Advisors, U.S. Government, economist, 1962; Churchill College, Cambridge, fellow, 1963-64, 1970, 1973. Nobel Memorial Prize in Economics, Recipient, 1972. **Publications:** Social Choice and Individual Values, 1951; (with others) Studies in Linear and Non-Linear Programming, 1958; (with others) Studies in the Mathematical Theory of Inventory and Production, 1958; (with W.M. Capron) Dynamic Shortages and Price Rises, 1958; (with M. Hoffenberg) A Time Series Analysis of Interindustry Demands, 1959; (with A.C. Enthoven) Quasi-Concave Programming, 1959; Economic Welfare and the Allocation of Resources for Invention, 1960; The Economic Implications of Learning by Doing, 1962; (with M. Nerlove) Optimal Advertising Policy under Dynamic Conditions, 1962; Uncertainty and the Welfare Economics of Medical Care, 1963; Control in Large Organizations, 1963; Optimal Capital Policy with Irreversible Investment, 1968; (with D. Levhari) Uniqueness of the Internal Rate of Return with Variable Life of Investment, 1969; Essays in the Theory of Risk-Bearing, 1971; (with F.H. Hahn) General Competitive Analysis, 1971; Models of Job Discrimination, 1972; Gifts and Exchanges, 1972; Coinsurance Rates, 1973; The Limits of Organization, 1974; Two Notes on Inferring Long Run Behavior from Social Experiments, 1975; (with others) Energy, the Next 20 Years, 1979; (with J.P. Kalt) Petroleum Price Regulation: Should We Decontrol?, 1979; (with S. Chang) Optimal Pricing, Use, and Exploration of Uncertain Resource Stocks, 1980; Optimal and Voluntary Income Redistribution, 1981; (with others) On Partitioning a Sample with Binary-Type Questions in Lieu of Collecting Observations, 1981; Collected Papers, 6 vols., 1983-85; Innovation in Large and Small Firms, 1983; (with H. Raynaud) Social Choice and Multicriterion Decision-Making, 1986; The Demand for Information and the Distribution of Income, 1987; Informational Equivalence of Signals, 1992; Information and the Organization of Industry, 1994; Innovation and Increasing Returns to Scale, 1998; Discounting, Morality, and Gaming, 1999; Economic Transitions: Speed and Scope, 2000. EDITOR: (with L. Hurwicz) Studies in Resource Allocation Processes, 1977; (with others) Applied Research for Social Policy: The United States and the Federal Republic of Germany, 1979; (with M.D. Intriligator) Handbook of Mathematical Economics, 1981. **Address:** Dept. of Economics, Stanford University, Stanford, CA 94305-6072, U.S.A. **Online address:** arrow@leland.stanford.edu

ARTEAGA, Alfred. American, b. 1950. **Genres:** Poetry, Essays. **Career:** San Jose City College, San Jose, CA, instructor in MexicanAmerican studies, 1977-87; University of Houston, Houston, TX, assistant professor of English, 1987-90; University of California, Berkeley, assistant professor of English, 1990-98. **Publications:** Cantos (poems), 1991; (ed.) An Other Tongue: Nation and Ethnicity in the Linguistic Borderlands, 1994; First Words: Origins of the European Nation, 1994; House with the Blue Bed (essays), 1997; Chicano Poetics: Heterotexts and Hybridities, 1997; Love in the Time of Aftershocks (poems), 1998. Work represented in anthologies. Contributor of essays and poems to print electronic journals. **Address:** Dept of Ethnic Studies, University of California-Berkeley, 506 Barrows Hall 2570, Berkeley, CA 94720-2570, U.S.A. **Online address:** bluebed@hotmail.com; arteaga@socrates.berkeley.edu

ARTELL, Mike. American, b. 1948. **Genres:** Children's fiction, Children's non-fiction, How-to books, Trivia/Facts, Cartoons, Humor/Satire, Picture/board books. **Career:** Freelance author/illustrator, television cartoonist, and conference speaker, 1987-. **Publications:** Big Long Animal Song, 1992; How to Create Picture Books, 1993; The Earth and Me, 1994; Weather Whys, 1995; Writing Start-Ups, 1996; Write Fast-Write Funny, 1996; Parties Kids Love, 1996; Rainy Day Recess, 1996; Classroom Cartooning for the Artistically Challenged, 1996; Starry Skies, 1997; Awesome Alphabets, 1999; Little Giant Book of Tongue Twisters, 1999; Backyard Bloodsuckers, 2000; Petite Rouge: A Cajun Red Riding Hood, 2001; Cartooning for Kids, 2001; Oodles of Doodles, 2003. **Address:** Box 3997, Covington, LA 70434, U.S.A. **Online address:** mikeartell@aol.com; www.mikeartell.com

ARTER, David. American. **Genres:** Politics/Government. **Career:** University of Helsinki, Helsinki, Finland, professor of politics; University of Jyvaskyla, Jyvaskyla, Finland, lecturer; Leeds Metropolitan University, Leeds, England, professor of European Integration; University of Aberdeen, Aberdeen, Scotland, professor of Nordic politics. University of Stockholm, visiting research fellow, 1981; Social science research council scholar, Oslo, Norway, 1982. Finnish Institute in London, Vice-Chair of the Executive; Economics and Social Research Council, evaluator in Politics, 1994-. **Publications:** On the Emergence of a Strong Peasant Party in Finland: A Classification of Leaders and Conceptual Analysis of Support for the Nascent Agrarian Party, 1977; Bumpkin Against Bigwig: The Emergence of a Green Movement in Finnish Politics, 1978; (with N. Elder) The Consensual Democracies? The Government and Politics of the Scandinavian States, 1982, rev. ed, 1988; The Nordic Parliaments: A Comparative Analysis, 1984; Politics and Policy-Making in Finland, 1987; The Politics of European Integration in the Twentieth Century, 1993; Parties and Democracy in the Post-Soviet Republics: The Case of Estonia, 1996; Scandinavian Politics Today, 1999; (ed.) From Farmyard to City Square?: The Electoral Adaptation of the Nordic Agrarian Parties, 2001. **Address:** Edward Wright Building, University of Aberdeen, Dunbar St., Aberdeen AB24 3QY, Scotland. **Online address:** d.arter@abdn.ac.uk

ARTERBURN, Stephen. American, b. 1953. **Genres:** How-to books, Human relations/Parenting, Autobiography/Memoirs. **Career:** Comprehensive Care Corp., nurse's aide to vice president of operations, 1977-86; Westworld Community Healthcare, chair, 1986-88; Minirth Meier New Life Clinics, Laguna Beach, CA, cofounder, 1988, chair, 1988-; host of national call-in radio program for Christian counseling; guest on national television programs. **Publications:** Hooked on Life, 1985, rev. ed., 1989; Growing Up Addicted, 1987; How Will I Tell My Mother?, 1988, 3rd ed., 1990; (with D. Stoop) When Someone You Love Is Someone You Hate, 1988; (with J. Burns) Drug-Proof Your Kids, 1989; (with J. Felton) Toxic Faith, 1991, as Faith That Hurts, Faith That Heals, 1992; Addicted to "Love," 1991; (with C. Dreizler) Fifty-Two Simple Ways to Say I Love You, 1991; (executive ed. with Stoop) The Life Recovery Bible, 1992; (with Stoop) The Twelve-Step Life Recovery Devotional, 1992; (with M. Ehemann and V. Lamphear) Gentle Eating, 1993; Hand-Me-Down Genes and Second-Hand Emotions, 1993; (with Burns) When Love Is Not Enough, 1993; Winning at Work without Losing at Love, 1995; The Every Man series, 2000; Flashpoints, 2001. Contributor to periodicals. **Address:** New Life Ministries, 570 Glenneyre Ste 107, Laguna Beach, CA 92651, U.S.A.

ARTHUR, Chris. Irish, b. 1955. **Genres:** Theology/Religion. **Career:** Essayist, poet, and educator. Worked as a warden on a nature reserve in Lough Neagh in Northern Ireland, TV researcher, and schoolteacher; Department of Theology, Religious Studies & Islamic Studies, University of Wales, Lampeter, senior lecturer in religious studies. **Publications:** In the Hall of Mirrors: Some Problems of Commitment in a Religiously Plural World, 1986; Biting the Bullet-Some Personal Reflections on Religious Education, 1990; (ed.) Religion and the Media: An Introductory Reader, 1993; Globalization of Communications: Some Religious Implications, 1998; Irish Nocturnes, 1999; Irish Willow, 2000; Religious Pluralism: A Metaphorical Approach, 2000. Contributor of essays to books. Writings have appeared in literary publications. **Address:** Department of Theology Religious Studies and Islamic Studies, University of Wales, Lampeter, Ceredigion SA48 7ED, Wales. **Online address:** arthurc@lamp.ac.uk

ARURI, Naseer H. American (born Palestine), b. 1934. **Genres:** Area studies, International relations/Current affairs, Politics/Government. **Career:** Texas Technological (now Texas Tech) University, Lubbock, instructor in political science, 1962-63; Greenfield Community College, Greenfield, MA, instructor in political science, 1964-65; University of Massachusetts at Dartmouth, instructor, 1965-66, assistant professor, 1966-68, associate professor, 1968-73, professor, 1973-96, Chancellor Professor of Political Science, 1996-. University of Kuwait, visiting professor, 1973-74; lecturer at colleges and universities; guest on television and radio programs in the US and abroad. **Publications:** The Palestine Resistance to Israel's Occupation, 1970; (with E. Ghareeb) Enemy of the Sun: Poems of Palestinian Resistance, 1970; Jordan: A Study in Political Development, 1921-1965, 1972; (trans. into Arabic, with A. Tarabein) V. Brodine and M. Seldon, Open Secret: The Nixon-Kissinger Doctrine in Asia, 1974; (ed.) Middle East Crucible: The Arab-Israeli Confrontation of October, 1973, 1975; (co-ed. and contrib.) Lebanon: A Challenge to the Arab World, 1977; (with F. Moughrabi and J. Strok) Regan and the Middle East, 1983; Occupation: Israel over Palestine, 1983; The Obstruction of Peace: The U.S., Israel, and the Palestinians, 1995; Palestinian Refugees: The Right of Return, 2001. Contributor to books and scholarly journals. **Address:** Department of Political Science, University of Massachusetts at Dartmouth, North Dartmouth, MA 02747, U.S.A. **Online address:** naruri@aol.com; naruri@umassd.edu

ARVENSIS, Alauda. See FURDYNA, Anna M.

ARVEY, Michael. American, b. 1948. **Genres:** Poetry, Paranormal. **Career:** University of Colorado, Boulder, teacher of creative writing in correspondence study division, 1986-. Has taught classes in meditation. **Publications:** OPPOSING VIEWPOINTS SERIES: ESP, 1988; Reincarnation, 1989; UFOs, 1990; Miracles, 1991; End of the World, 1992. Contributor of poems to many publications. **Address:** PMB 220, 637 B South Broadway, Boulder, CO 80305, U.S.A. **Online address:** spiritmed@rocketmail.com

ASANTE, Molefi K. (Arthur L. Smith). American, b. 1942. **Genres:** Novels, Poetry, Cultural/Ethnic topics, Speech/Rhetoric. **Career:** Purdue University, Lafayette, Indiana, professor, 1968-69; University of California, Los Angeles, professor, 1969, director, Center for Afro-American Studies, 1970-73; Temple University, Philadelphia, African American Studies, professor. Journal of Black Studies, editor, 1970-; Imhotep, editor; Journal of Afrocentric American Studies, editor. **Publications:** Break of Dawn (poetry), 1964; Rhetoric of Black Revolution, 1969; Toward Transracial Communication, 1970; (with A. Rich) Rhetoric of Revolution, 1970; (with A. Allen and D. Hernandez) How to Talk with People of Other Races, 1971; Transracial Communication, 1973; Epic in Search of African Kings, 1978; Contemporary Black Thought, 1979; Mass Communication, 1979; Handbook of Intercultural Communication, 1979; Afrocentricity, 1980; The Afrocentric Idea, 1987; Kemet, Afrocentricity, and Knowledge, 1990; Historical and Cultural Atlas of African Americans, 1991; Classical Africa, 1993; Malcolm X as Cultural Hero, 1994; African American History: A Journey of Liberation, 1995; African American Atlas, 1998; Scream of Blood, 1999; The Painful Demise of Eurocentrism, 2000; The Egyptian Philosophers, 2000; (with J. Mitchell) Discovery Essays for Teachers, 2001; Scattered to the Wind (novel), 2002; 100 Greatest African Americans, 2002; Culture and Customs of Egypt, 2002; Erasing Racism: The Survival of the American Nation, 2003. EDITOR: (with S. Robb) The Voice of Black Rhetoric, 1971; Language, Communication and Rhetoric in Black America, 1972. **Address:** Dept of African American Studies, Temple University, Philadelphia, PA 19122, U.S.A. **Online address:** masante@Temple.edu

ASCHAN, Ulf. Swedish, b. 1937. **Genres:** Novels. **Career:** Assistant professional hunter in Kenya, 1954-57; worked in the travel trade business in Sweden and Kenya, 1960-70; Ulf Aschan Safaris (hunting and photographic),

Nairobi, Kenya, owner, 1970-. Africa Air Rescue Health Services, director. **Publications:** The Man Whom Women Loved, 1987. **Address:** Helen Brann Agency Inc., 157 West 57th St., New York, NY 10019, U.S.A. **Online address:** ULF.KIWAYU@SWIFTKENYA.COM

ASCHER, Barbara Lazear. American, b. 1946. **Genres:** Adult non-fiction. **Career:** Writer. Webster & Sheffield (law firm), New York City, attorney, 1979-81. National Public Radio, wrote and read essays for "Morning Edition," 1990; public speaker. **Publications:** Playing after Dark (essays), 1986; The Habit of Loving (essays), 1989; Landscape without Gravity: A Memoir of Grief, 1994. Contributor of essays to newspapers and periodicals. **Address:** Lantz Harris Agency, 156 Fifth Ave, Ste. 617, New York, NY 10010, U.S.A.

ASCHERSON, (Charles) Neal. Scottish, b. 1932. **Genres:** History, International relations/Current affairs. **Career:** East African Institute of Social Research, Kampala, researcher, 1955-56; Guardian, London, journalist, 1956-58; Scotsman, London, journalist, 1959-60, Edinburgh, journalist, 1975-79; The Observer, London, reporter, 1960-75, columnist, 1979-89, associate ed., 1985-89; The Independent on Sunday, assistant editor, 1989-98; Institute of Archaeology, London, lecturer, 1998-. **Publications:** The King Incorporated, 1963; The French Revolution, 1975; The Polish August, 1981; The Fourth Reich: Klaus Barbie and the Neo-Fascist Connection (in U.S. as The Nazi Legacy: Klaus Barbie and the International Fascist Connection), 1984; The Struggles for Poland, 1987; Games with Shadows, 1988; Black Sea, 1995; Stone Voices, 2002. **Address:** 27 Corsica St, London N5, England.

ASH, Constance (Lee). American, b. 1950. **Genres:** Science fiction/Fantasy. **Career:** Writer. **Publications:** FANTASY NOVELS: The Horsegirl, 1988; The Stalking Horse, 1990; The Stallion Queen, 1992. **Address:** c/o Publicity Director, Ace Publishing, 375 Hudson, New York, NY 10014, U.S.A.

ASH, Jennifer. (Jennifer Rudick). American, b. 1964. **Genres:** Documentaries/Reportage. **Career:** Women's Wear Daily, associate editor, 1986-87; Town and Country, contributing editor, 1992-. **Publications:** Private Palm Beach: Tropical Style, 1992; (with A. Brott) The Expectant Father: Facts, Tips, and Advice for Dads-to-Be, 1995. **Address:** 285 Birch Hill Rd, Locust Valley, NY 11560, U.S.A.

ASH, Stephen V. American, b. 1948. **Genres:** History. **Career:** Independent historian in Knoxville, TN, 1983-90; University of Tennessee, Knoxville, instructor, 1989-95, assistant professor of American history, 1995-98, associate professor, 1998-2003, professor, 2003-. University of Tennessee, Chattanooga, adjunct instructor, 1994. **Publications:** Meet Me at the Fair! A Pictorial History of the Tennessee Valley Agricultural and Industrial Fair, 1985; Tennessee's Iron Industry Revisited: The Stewart County Story, 1986; The Knoxville News-Sentinel: A Century of Front Pages, 1986; Beyond Their Dreams (video documentary), 1986; Middle Tennessee Society Transformed, 1860-1870: War and Peace in the Upper South, 1988; Messages of the Governors of Tennessee, Vol. IX: 1907-1921, Vol. X: 1921-1933, 1990; Past Times: A Daybook of Knoxville History, 1991; When the Yankees Came: Conflict and Chaos in the Occupied South, 1861-1865, 1995; Secessionists and Other Scoundrels: Selections from Parson Brownlow's Book, 1999; Tennesseans and Their History, 1999; A Year in the South: Four Lives in 1865, 2002. Contributor of articles and reviews of books. Contributor to periodicals. **Address:** Dept of History, 6th Floor, Dunford Hall, University of Tennessee, Knoxville, TN 37996, U.S.A. **Online address:** sash@utk.edu

ASH, William Franklin. British (born United States), b. 1917. **Genres:** Novels, History, Autobiography/Memoirs. **Career:** Sr. Script Ed., BBC Radio Drama Dept., until 1980 (joined BBC, 1948). Adapted novels to radio dramas. **Publications:** The Lotus in the Sky, 1961; Choice of Arms, 1962; The Longest Way Round, 1963; Marxism and Moral Concepts, 1964; Ride a Paper Tiger, 1968; Take Off, 1969; Pickaxe and Rifle: The Story of the Albanian People, 1974; Morals and Politics: The Ethics of Revolution, 1977; A Red Square (autobiography), 1978; Incorporated, 1979; Right Side Up, 1984; The Way to Write Radio Drama, 1985; Bold Riot, 1992; What's the Big Idea, 1993; But My Fist Is Free, 1997; Rise Like Lions, 1998; Marxist Morality (philosophy), 1998. **Address:** Flat 9, Chenies House, 43 Moscow Rd, London W2, England.

ASHABRANNER, Melissa. American, b. 1950. **Genres:** Children's non-fiction, How-to books. **Career:** Affiliated with the Association of American Medical Colleges, Washington, DC, 1972-77; Hill Rag, Inc. (publisher of community newspaper), owner and editor, 1980-88; Fagon Publishing Group (publisher of community newspapers), Washington, DC, co-owner, 1989-.

Publications: (with B. Ashabranner) Into a Strange Land: Unaccompanied Refugee Youth in America, 1987; (with B. Ashabranner) Counting America, 1989. **Address:** Fagon Publishing Group, 224 7th St. S.E, Washington, DC 20003, U.S.A.

ASHALL, Frank. British, b. 1957. **Genres:** Medicine/Health. **Career:** Eleanor Roosevelt Institute for Cancer Research, Denver, CO, postdoctoral researcher, 1982-85; University of London, London, England, postdoctoral researcher at London School of Hygiene and Tropical Medicine, 1985-89, senior research fellow at Imperial College of Science and Technology, 1989-92; Washington University, St. Louis, MO, assistant professor, 1992-94. **Publications:** Remarkable Discoveries!, 1994; (ed. with A.M. Goate) Plaques and Tangles in Alzheimer's Disease, 1995. Contributor to academic journals. **Address:** Washington University, Campus Box 8121, One Brookings Dr, St. Louis, MO 63130, U.S.A.

ASHBERY, John (Lawrence). American, b. 1927. **Genres:** Novels, Plays/Screenplays, Poetry, Translations. **Career:** Charles P. Stevenson Jr., Professor of Languages & Literature, Bard College, Annandale-on-Hudson, NY, 1990-. Publicity Dept, Oxford University Press, NYC, 1951-54; Copywriter, McGraw-Hill Book Co., NYC, 1954-55; Art Critic, European Ed. of New York Herald Tribune, Paris, 1960-65, and Art International, Lugano, Switzerland, 1961-63; Ed., Locus Solus mag., Lans-en-Vercors, France, 1960-62; Ed., Art and Literature, Paris, 1964-67; Executive Ed., 1965-72, Art News, NYC; Professor of English, and Co-Director of the MFA Program in Creative Writing, Brooklyn College, NY, 1974-90; Poetry Ed., Partisan Review, NYC, 1976-80; Art Critic, New York mag., 1978-80; Art Critic, Newsweek, NY, 1980-85; Charles Eliot Norton Professor of Poetry, Harvard University, 1989-90. Recipient, Pulitzer Prize, National Book Award, and National Book Critics Circle Award, 1976. **Publications:** POETRY: Turandot and Other Poems, 1953; Some Trees, 1956; The Poems, 1960; The Tennis Court Oath, 1962; Rivers and Mountains, 1966; Selected Poems, 1967; Sunrise in Suburbia, 1968; Three Madrigals, 1968; Fragment, 1969; The Double Dream of Spring, 1970; The New Spirit, 1970; Three Poems, 1972; The Vermont Notebook, 1975; Self-Portrait in a Convex Mirror, 1975; Houseboat Days, 1977; As We Know, 1979; Shadow Train, 1981; A Wave, 1984; Selected Poems, 1985; April Galleons, 1987; The Ice Storm, 1987; Flow Chart, 1991; Hotel Lautreamont, 1992; Three Books: Poems, 1993; And the Stars Were Shining, 1994; Can You Hear, Bird, 1995; The Mooring of Starting Out: The First Five Books of Poetry, 1997; Wakefulness, 1998; Girls on the Run, 1999; Your Name Here, 2000; As Umbrellas Follow Rain, 2001; Chinese Whispers, 2002. TRANSLATOR: J.-J. Mayoux, Melville, 1960; J. Dupin, Alberto Giacometti, 1963; Selected Poems by Germaine Bree, 1991; Hebdomeros and Other Writings by G. De Chirico, 1992. OTHER: The Philosopher (play), 1964; (with J. Schuyler) A Nest of Ninnies (novel), 1969; (with L. Harwood & T. Raworth) Penguin Modern Poets 19, 1971; Three Plays, 1978; Fairfield Porter (non-fiction), 1983; (with others) R.B. Kitaj (non-fiction), 1989; Reported Sightings (essays and criticism), 1989; Other Traditions (essays and criticism), 2000. EDITOR: (co-) American Literary Anthology 1, 1968; Penguin Modern Poets 24, 1973; Muck Arbour, by B. Marcus, 1974. **Address:** Dept of Languages and Literature, Bard College, PO Box 5000, Annandale On Hudson, NY 12504-5000, U.S.A.

ASHBY, Franklin C. (born United States), b. 1954. **Genres:** Adult non-fiction. **Career:** Dale Carnegie & Associates, Inc., Garden City, NY, vice president and chief educational officer, 1984-98; Manchester Training, Inc., Philadelphia, PA, president, 1998-2000; Manchester Partners International, Inc., Philadelphia, executive vice president, 1998-2000; Leadership Capital Group, LLC, Stony Brook, NY, chairman, 2000-. Member of board of directors of Performance Resources Organization, 1998-99, and Manchester Partners, 1998-2000. Radio talk show host and presenter of career clinics, 1986-87. **Publications:** Effective Leadership Programs, 1999; Revitalize Your Corporate Culture, 1999; The Complete Idiot's Guide to Team Building, 1999; (with Arthur R. Pell) Embracing Excellence, 2001; (Author of foreword) The Complete Idiot's Guide to Human Resource Management, 2002; (Author of foreword) The Complete Idiot's Guide to Managing People, 2003. Contributor to articles. **Address:** c/o Ellen Schneid Coleman, ESC Literary Services, 131 Ridge Dr., Montville, NJ 07045, U.S.A. **Online address:** ellen6@aol.com

ASHBY, Godfrey W. British, b. 1930. **Genres:** Inspirational/Motivational Literature, Theology/Religion. **Career:** Church of the Province of South Africa, priest to bishop, 1957-88; priest of the Church of England, 1988-95. Taught at Rhodes University, 1969-75, and University of the Witwatersrand, 1985-88. **Publications:** Sacrifice, 1988; Go Out and Meet God: Exodus, 1998. **Address:** Box 2685, Knysna 6570, Republic of South Africa. **Online address:** gashby@cyberperk.co.za

ASHBY, Gwynneth Margaret. British, b. 1922. **Genres:** Children's fiction, Children's non-fiction, Geography, Travel/Exploration. **Career:** Freelance writer, 1945-. **Publications:** Mystery of Coveside House, 1946; The Secret Ring, 1948; The Cruise of the Silver Spray, 1951; The Land and People of Sweden 1951; The Land and People of Belgium, 1955; Let's Look at Austria, 1966; Looking at Norway, 1967; Looking at Japan, 1969; Let's Go to Japan, 1980; Korean Village, 1986; A Family in South Korea, 1987; School by a Volcano, 1994; We Go to School in Japan, 2001. **Address:** 12D Blenheim Dr, De Havilland Way, Christchurch, Dorset BH23 4JH, England. **Online address:** gwyn@ashbybooks.co.uk

ASHE, Geoffrey Thomas. British, b. 1923. **Genres:** History, Mythology/Folklore, Paranormal, Writing/Journalism. **Career:** Lecturer at Polish, University College, London, 1948-50; Administrative Assistant, Ford Motor Co. of Canada, 1952-54; Lecturer in Mgmt. Studies Polytechnic, London, 1956-68; Secretary, Camelot Research Committee, London, 1965-. **Publications:** The Tale of the Tub, 1950; King Arthur's Avalon, 1957; From Caesar to Arthur, 1960; Land to the West, 1962; The Land and the Book, 1965; Gandhi, 1968; (ed.) The Quest for Arthur's Britain, 1968; All about King Arthur (in U.S. as King Arthur in Fact and Legend), 1969; Camelot and the Vision of Albion, 1971; The Art of Writing Made Simple, 1972; The Finger and the Moon, 1973; Do What You Will, 1974, as The Hell-Fire Clubs, 2000; The Virgin, 1976; The Ancient Wisdom, 1977; Miracles, 1978; A Guidebook to Arthurian Britain, 1980; Kings and Queens of Early Britain, 1982; Avalonian Quest, 1982; The Discovery of King Arthur, 1985, rev. ed., 2003; (assoc. ed.) The Arthurian Encyclopaedia, 1986; The Landscape of King Arthur, 1987; (with others) The Arthurian Handbook, 1988; Mythology of the British Isles, 1990; King Arthur, the Dream of a Golden Age, 1990; Dawn behind the Dawn, 1992; Atlantis, 1992; The Traveller's Guide to Arthurian Britain, 1997; The Book of Prophecy, 1999; Encyclopedia of Prophecy, 2001; Merlin, 2001. **Address:** Chalice Orchard, Well House Lane, Glastonbury, Somerset BA6 8BJ, England. **Online address:** AsheMail@tinyworld.co.uk

ASHER, Harry. See FREEMANTLE, Brian (Harry).

ASHER, Jane. British, b. 1946. **Genres:** Food and Wine, Novellas/Short stories, Children's fiction. **Career:** Actress, 1957-, writer and businesswoman. Screen credits include: Greengage Summer, Alfie, Deep End, Henry VIII and His Six Wives, Runners, Dream Child, Paris by Night. Radio and television actress. Member of Bristol Old Vic and National Theatre Company; Molecule Theatre, board of governors, 1985-92; BAFTA; RADA, associate member. **Publications:** Jane Asher's Party Cakes, 1982; Jane Asher's Fancy Dress, 1983; Silent Night for You and Your Baby, 1984; Jane Asher's Quick Party Cakes, 1985; The Moppy Stories, 1987; Easy Entertaining, 1987; Keep Your Baby Safe, 1998; Children's Parties, 1988; Calendar of Cakes, 1989; Eats for Treats, 1990; Jane Asher's Complete Book of Cake Decorating Ideas, 1993; Round the World Cookbook, 1994; Rhymes for All Seasons, 1995; Time to Play, 1995; 101 Things I Wish I'd Known Before…, 1996; The Longing, 1996; The Best of Good Living, 1998; Good Living at Christmas, 1998; The Question, 1998; Tricks of the Trade, 1999; Losing It, 2002. **Address:** c/o Blake Friedman, 122 Arlington Rd, London NW1 7HP, England.

ASHER, Miriam. See MUNDIS, Hester (Jane).

ASHER, R. E. British, b. 1926. **Genres:** History, Language/Linguistics, Literary criticism and history, Reference, Translations. **Career:** University of London, School of Oriental and African Studies, England, assistant lecturer, 1953-56, lecturer in linguistics, 1956-67, lecturer in Tamil, 1957-65; University of Edinburgh, Scotland, senior lecturer, 1965-70, reader, 1970-77, professor of linguistics, 1977-93, head of department, 1976-80, 1983-86, Faculty of Arts, associate dean, 1985-86, dean, 1986-89, associate director of Centre for Speech Technology Research, 1984-93, director, 1994, member of University Court, 1989-92, vice-principal, 1990-93, curator of patronage, 1991-93, professor emeritus, 1993-. Visiting professor at colleges and universities worldwide. **Publications:** (with R. Radhakrishnan) A Tamil Prose Reader, 1971; Some Landmarks in the History of Tamil Prose, 1973; Tamil, 1982; Malayala Bhasa-Sahitya Pathanangal (title means: Linguistic and Literary Studies on Malayalam), 1989; National Myths in Renaissance France, 1993; (with T.C. Kumari) Malayalam, 1997; Basheer: Malayattinre sarga vismayam (critical studies), 1999; (with E. Annamalai) Colloquial Tamil, 2002. TRANSLATOR FROM MALAYALAM: T.S. Pillai, Scavenger's Son (novel), 1986, rev. trans., 1993; (with A. Coilparampil) V.M. Basheer, "Me Grandad 'ad an Elephant!" Three Stories of Muslim Life in South India, 1980; (with N. Gopalakrishnan) What the Sufi Said, 2002. EDITOR: (with E.J.A. Henderson) Towards a History of Phonetics, 1981; (with C. Moseley) Atlas of the World's Languages, 1994; (in-chief) The Encyclopedia of Language and Linguistics, 10 vols., 1994; (with E.F.K. Koerner) Concise History of the Language Sciences, 1995; Basheer svatantrya samara kathakal (title means: Basheer-Stories of the Freedom Struggle), 1998; (with R. Harris) Linguisticoliterary-A Festschrift for Professor D.S. Dwivedi, 2000; (with V. Abdula) Wind Flowers: Contemporary Malayalam Short Fiction, 2004. **Address:** Theoretical and Applied Linguistics, University of Edinburgh, Adam Ferguson Bldg, George Sq, Edinburgh EH8 9LL, Scotland.

ASHER, Sandy. (Sandra Fenichel Asher). American, b. 1942. **Genres:** Children's fiction, Young adult fiction, Plays/Screenplays, Children's non-fiction, Writing/Journalism, Young adult non-fiction, Picture/board books. **Career:** Author and playwright. WFIU-Radio, Bloomington, IN, scriptwriter, 1963-64; Ball Associates (advertising agency), Philadelphia, PA, copywriter, 1964; Spectator, Bloomington, drama critic, 1966-67; Drury University, Springfield, MO, instructor in creative writing, 1978-85, writer in residence, 1985-2003; Institute of Children's Literature, instructor, 1986-96. Instructor in creative writing for children's summer programs, 1981-. Speaker at conferences, workshops, and schools. **Publications:** NOVELS: Summer Begins, 1980 in US as Summer Smith Begins, 1986; Daughters of the Law, 1980 in UK as Friends and Sisters, 1982; Just Like Jenny, 1982; Things Are Seldom What They Seem, 1983; Missing Pieces, 1984; Teddy Teabury's Fabulous Fact, 1985; Everything Is Not Enough, 1987, in Germany as Sunnyboy und Aschenputtel, 1990; Teddy Teabury's Peanutty Problems, 1987; Best Friends Get Better, 1989; Mary-in-the-Middle, 1990; Pat's Promise, 1990; Can David Do It?, 1991; Out of Here: A Senior Class Yearbook, 1993. PLAYS (as Sandra Fenichel Asher): The Ballad of Two Who Flew, 1976; Witling and the Stone Princess, 1979; Dover's Domain, 1980; The Insulting Princess, 1988; The Mermaid's Tale, 1988; A Song of Sixpence, 1988; Little Old Ladies in Tennis Shoes, 1989; A Woman Called Truth, 1989; The Wise Men of Chelm, 1991; All on a Saturday Morning, 1992; Blind Dating, 1992; Perfect, 1992; Sunday, Sunday, 1994; Dancing with Strangers, 1994; Once, in the Time of Trolls, 1995; Across the Plains: The Journey of the Palace Wagon Family, 1997; Emma, 1997; The Wolf and Its Shadows, 1999; I Will Sing Life, 1999; Little Women, 2001; Blackbirds and Dragons, Mermaids and Mice, 2003; Somebody Catch My Homework, 2004; Romeo and Juliet Together (and Alive!) at Last, 2004; In the Garden of the Selfish Giant, 2004. OTHER: The Great American Peanut Book, 1977; Where Do You Get Your Ideas? Helping Young Writers Begin, 1987; Wild Words! How to Train Them to Tell Stories, 1989; Princess Bee and the Royal Good-night Story (picture book), 1990; But That's Another Story, 1996; With All My Heart, with All My Mind, 1999; Stella's Dancing Days (picture book), 2001; Discovering Cultures: China, 2002; Discovering Cultures: Mexico, 2002; (with J. Robinette and K. Brown) 125 Original Audition Monologues, 2003; On Her Way, 2004; Why Rabbit's Nose Twitches, 2004; Too Many Frogs!, 2005. Contributor of stories, poetry, and plays to anthologies. Contributor of stories, poetry, and articles to books and magazines.

ASHFORD, Jeffrey. See JEFFRIES, Roderic.

ASHFORD, Nigel (John Gladwell). British, b. 1952. **Genres:** Politics/Government. **Career:** European Democrat Students, London, England, executive director, 1976-78; Paisley College, Paisley, Scotland, assistant professor, 1979-83; University of Strathclyde, Glasgow, Scotland, assistant professor, 1983-84; Staffordshire University, Stoke-on-Trent, England, associate professor, 1984-; Bowling Green University, Ohio, visiting scholar, 2000. Politics, member of editorial board. **Publications:** (ed. with Stephen Davies) A Dictionary of Conservative and Libertarian Thought, 1991; (ed. with G. Jordan) Public Policy and The Impact of The New Right, 1993; (with E. Ashbee) U.S. Politics Today, 1999. **Address:** Institute for Humane Studies, George Mason University, 3381 N Fairfax Dr Ste 440, Arlington, VA 22201, U.S.A. **Online address:** n.ashford@staffs.ac.uk

ASHLEY, Bernard. British, b. 1935. **Genres:** Novellas/Short stories, Children's fiction, Children's non-fiction. **Career:** Teacher, Kent Education Committee, Gravesend, 1957-65, Hertfordshire Education Committee, Hertford Heath, 1965-71, and Hartley Jr. School, Newham, London, 1971-76; Charlton Manor Jr. School, London, head-teacher, 1977-95; full-time writer, 1995-. **Publications:** The Men and the Boats: Britain's Life-Boat Service, 1968; Weather Men, 1970; The Trouble with Donovan Croft, 1974; Terry on the Fence, 1975; All My Men, 1977; A Kind of Wild Justice, 1978; Break in the Sun, 1980; I'm Trying to Tell You (short stories), 1981; Dinner Ladies Don't Count, 1981; Dodgem, 1981; Linda's Lie, 1982; High Pavement Blues, 1983; Your Guess Is as Good as Mine, 1983; A Bit of Give and Take, 1984; Janey, 1985; Running Scared, 1986; Down and Out, 1988; Bad Blood, 1988; The Royal Visit, 1988; The Clipper Street series, 1988-89; The Country Boy, 1989; The Secret of Theodore Brown (play), 1989; All I Ever Ask, 1989; The Dockside School Stories, 1990; Seeing Off Uncle Jack, 1991;

(with C. Ashley) Three Seven Eleven, 1993; Johnnie's Blitz, 1995; Justin and the Demon Drop Kick, 1997; Roller Madonnas, 1997; Flash, 1997; Framed, 1997; Mean Street, 1997; The Scam, 1997; Stitch-Up, 1997; Tiger without Teeth, 1998; King Rat, 1998; Justin and the Big Fight, 1999; Rapid, 1999; Little Soldier, 2001; Playing against the Odds, 2001; Justin Strikes Again, 2001; Revenge House, 2002; Freedom Flight, 2003. READERS: Don't Run Away, 1965; Wall of Death, 1966; Space Shot, 1967; The Big Escape, 1967. PICTURE BOOKS: Cleversticks, 1992; I Forgot Said Troy, 1996; A Present for Paul, 1996; Growing Good, 1999; Double the Love, 2002; The Bush, 2003. **Address:** 128 Heathwood Gardens, London SE7 8ER, England. **Online address:** bernardashley@talktalk.net

ASHLEY, Leonard R(aymond) N(elligan). American, b. 1928. **Genres:** Novels, Novellas/Short stories, Poetry, Gay and lesbian issues, Language/ Linguistics, Literary criticism and history, Military/Defense/Arms control, Paranormal, Social sciences. **Career:** University of Utah, 1953-56; RCAF, asst to the air historian, 1956-58; University of Rochester, 1958-61; Brooklyn College, CUNY, instructor, 1961-65, assistant professor, 1965-68, associate professor, 1968-71, professor of English, 1972-95, professor emeritus, 1995-. New School for Social Research, NYC, part-time faculty member, 1962-72. **Publications:** (with F.F. Liu) A Military History of Modern China, 1956; Colley Cibber, 1965; Nineteenth-Century British Drama, 1968; Authorship and Evidence, 1968; History of the Short Story, 1968; George Peele, 1970; Other People's Lives: 34 Stories, 1970; Ripley's Believe It or Not Book of the Military, 1977; The Wonderful World of Superstition, Prophecy and Luck, 1983; The Wonderful World of Magic and Witchcraft, 1986; The Amazing World of Superstition, Prophecy, Luck, Magic and Witchcraft, 1988; Elizabethan Popular Culture, 1988; What's in a Name?, 1989; The Complete Book of Superstition, 1995; The Complete Book of Magic and Witchcraft, 1995; The Complete Book of Devils and Demons, 1996; The Complete Book of the Devil's Disciples, 1996; The Complete Book of Spells, Curses and Magical Recipes, 1997; What I Know about You (novel), 1998; The Complete Book of Vampires, 1999; The Complete Book of Ghosts and Poltergeists, 2000; George Alfred Henty and the Victorian Mind, 1999; Language and Society, 2001; The Complete Book of Sex Magic, 2002; Names in Literature, 2002; The Complete Book of Numerology, 2002; Names in Popular Culture, 2002; Names of Places, 2002; Art Attack, 2002; Cornish Names, 2002. EDITOR/CO-EDITOR: (with S.L. Astor) British Short Stories, 1968; A Narrative of the Life of Mrs. Charlotte Clarke, 1969; Phantasms of the Living, 2 vols., 1970; Reliques of Irish Poetry: A Memoir of Miss Brooke, 1970; Shakespeare's Jest Book, 1970; Suhrab and Rustam, 1972; The Picture of Dorian Grey, 1972; Ballad Poetry of Ireland, 1973; Enriched Classics (11 vols. to date); Tales of Mystery and Melodrama, 1978; Geolinguistic Perspectives, 1987; Language in Contemporary Society, 1993; Language and Communication in the New Century, 1998; A Garland of Names, 2003; Languages across Borders, 2001; Language and Identity, 2004. Contributor of poetry to journals and anthologies. Contributor of articles to periodicals. **Address:** 1901 Ave H, Brooklyn, NY 11230-7402, U.S.A.

ASHLEY, Trisha. (born England). **Genres:** Humor/Satire. **Career:** Novelist. Has worked for a stained-glass maker and a plumber. **Publications:** NOVELS: Good Husband Material, 2000; The Urge to Jump, 2001; Every Woman for Herself, 2003; Singled Out, 2004; The Generous Gardener, 2005. **Address:** The Marsh Agency, 111 Dover St., London W1S 4LJ, England. **Online address:** Trisha.Ashley@tesco.net

ASHRAWI, Hanan (Mikhail). Also writes as Hanan Mikhail-Ashrawi. Palestinian, b. 1946. **Genres:** Literary criticism and history, History, Autobiography/Memoirs. **Career:** General Union of Palestinian Students (GUPS), Lebanese delegate at conference in Amman, Jordan, 1969; Bir Zeit University, West Bank, English professor, 1973-, English department founder, 1973, English department chair, 1973-78 and 1981-84, Legal Aid Committee/ Human Rights Documentation Project, founder, 1974, chair, 1974-95, dean of arts, 1986-90. Palestinian Liberation Organization (PLO), member of political committee, 1988-93, member of diplomatic committee, 1990-93, official spokesperson, 1991-93; Palestinian Legislative Council, Jerusalem District, member of council and head of political committee, 1996-; Palestinian National Authority, Ministry of Higher Education, Minister of Higher Education, 1996-; Bethlehem 2000, Secretary General of international committee and head of steering committee, 1996-. Lecturer at institutions and symposia. Appeared in print, radio, and television interviews. **Publications:** Contemporary Palestinian Literature under Occupation, 1976; (with S. Shahruri) Al-Qissah al-qasirah fi al-ard al-muhtallah (title means: The Short Story in the Occupied Territories), 1986; This Side of Peace: A Personal Account, 1995. Author of fiction and poetry and a contributor to periodicals. **Address:** c/o Bob Barnett, Simon & Schuster, 1230 Avenue of the Americas, New York, NY 10020, U.S.A.

ASHTON, Dianne. American, b. 1949. **Genres:** Theology/Religion, Literary criticism and history, History, Bibliography. **Career:** University of Pennsylvania, Philadelphia, teacher of general studies, 1987; La Salle University, Philadelphia, lecturer in religion, 1986-88; Rowan University, Glassboro, NJ, professor of religion, 1987-, and director of American studies, past chairperson of Department of Philosophy and Religion. Lecturer at colleges and universities. **Publications:** (ed. with E.M. Umansky, and coauthor of intros) Four Centuries of Jewish Women's Spirituality: A Sourcebook, 1991; The Philadelphia Group: A Guide to Archival and Bibliographic Collections, 1993; Jewish Life in Pennsylvania, 1998; Rebecca Gratz: Women and Judaism in Antebellum America, 1998. Contributor to books and periodicals. **Address:** Department of Philosophy and Religion, Bunce Hall, Rowan University, 201 Mullica Hill Rd., Glassboro, NJ 08028, U.S.A. **Online address:** ashton@jupiter.rowan.edu

ASHTON, Dore. American. **Genres:** Art/Art history, Cultural/Ethnic topics, History, Biography. **Career:** Arts mag. (formerly Art Digest), associate editor, 1951-54, contributing editor, 1965-; New York Times, NYC, art critic, 1955-60; Pratt Institute, art history instructor, 1962-64; Cooper Union, NYC, professor of art history; Yale University, senior lecturer, 2000-. **Publications:** Abstract Art before Columbus, 1957; Poets and the Past, 1959; Philip Guston, 1960; (co-author) Redon, Moreau, Bresdin, 1961; The Unknown Shore, 1962; Rauschenberg's Dante, 1964; Modern American Sculpture, 1968; A Reading of Modern Art, 1969; Richard Lindner, 1969; The Sculpture of Pol Bury, 1971; Picasso on Art, 1972; The New York School: A Cultural Reckoning, 1973; A Joseph Cornell Album, 1974; Yes, But...A Critical Biography of Philip Guston, 1976; A Fable of Modern Art, 1980; (with D.B. Hare) Rosa Bonheur: A Life and a Legend, 1981; American Art since 1945, 1982; About Rothko, 1983; Twentieth Century Artists on Art, 1985; Out of the Whirlwind, 1987; Fragonard in the Universe of Painting, 1988; Noguchi East and West, 1992; Terence LaNoue, 1992; The Delicate Thread: Teshigahara's Life in Art, 1996; The Walls of the Heart, 2000; The Black Rainbow; The Work of Fernando de Szyszlo, 2002. **Address:** 217 E 11th St, New York, NY 10003, U.S.A.

ASHTON, Robert. British, b. 1924. **Genres:** History. **Career:** Professor Emeritus of English History, University of East Anglia, Norwich, since 1989 (Professor, 1963-89; Dean, School of English Studies, 1964-67). Assistant Lecturer in Economic History, 1952-54, Lecturer, 1954-61, and Sr. lectr., 1961, University of Nottingham; Visiting Fellow, All Souls College, Oxford, 1973 and 1987; James Ford Special Lecturer in history, Oxford University, 1982. **Publications:** The Crown and the Money Market 1603-1640, 1960; James I by His Contemporaries, 1969; The English Civil War, 1978, 1989; The City and the Court 1603-1643, 1979; Reformation and Revolution 1558-1660, 1984; Counter Revolution: The Second Civil War and Its Origins, 1646-48, 1994. **Address:** The Manor Hse, Brundall, Norwich NR13 5JY, England.

ASHTON, Rosemary. Scottish, b. 1947. **Genres:** Literary criticism and history, Biography. **Career:** University College London, England, lecturer, 1974-86, reader, 1986-91, professor of English, 1991-2002, Quain Professor English Language and Literature, 2002-; writer. Examiner and lecturer. OBE, 1999. Royal Society of Literature, fellow, 1999; English Association, founding fellow, 1999; British Academy, fellow, 2000; Royal Society of Arts, fellow, 2002. **Publications:** The German Idea: Four English Writers and the Reception of German Thought, 1800-1860, 1980; George Eliot, 1983; Little Germany: Exile and Asylum in Victorian England, 1986; The Mill on the Floss: A Natural History, 1990; G.H. Lewes: A Life, 1991; The Life of Samuel Taylor Coleridge: A Critical Biography, 1995; George Eliot: A Life, 1996; Thomas and Jane Carlyle: Portrait of a Marriage, 2002. EDITOR: George Eliot: Selected Critical Writings, 1992; Versatile Victorian: Selected Writings of G.H. Lewes, 1992; G. Eliot, The Mill on the Floss, 1992; Eliot, Silas Marner, 1993; Eliot, Middlemarch, 1994. **Address:** University College London, Gower St, London WC1E 6BT, England. **Online address:** r.ashton@ucl.ac.uk

ASHWORTH, Andrea. British, b. 1969. **Genres:** Bibliography. **Career:** Writer. Jesus College, Oxford, junior research fellow in English literature, 1997-. **Publications:** Once in a House on Fire: A Memoir, 1998. **Address:** Jesus College, Oxford OX1 3DW, England. **Online address:** andrea.ashworth@ell.ox.ac.uk

ASHWORTH, (Lewis) William. American, b. 1942. **Genres:** Environmental sciences/Ecology, Natural history, Sciences, Travel/Exploration. **Career:** Ashland Public Library, Jackson County, OR, reference librarian, 1985-2002; writer. **Publications:** Hell's Canyon: The Deepest Gorge on Earth, 1977; The Wallowas: Coming of Age in the Wilderness, 1978; The Carson Factor,

1979; Under the Influence: Congress, Lobbies, and the American Pork-Barrel System, 1981; Nor Any Drop to Drink: The American Water Crisis, 1982; The Late, Great Lakes: An Environmental History, 1986; The Encyclopedia of Environmental Studies, 1991; Bears of North America, 1992; Penguins, Puffins, and Auks, 1991; The Economy of Nature: Rethinking the Connections between Ecology and Economics, 1995; The Left Hand of Eden: Meditations on Nature and Human Nature, 1999; Great Lakes Journey: A New Look at America's Freshwater Coast, 2000. **Address:** c/o Max Gartenberg Literary Agent, 12 Westminster Dr, Livingston, NJ 07039, U.S.A. **Online address:** william_ashworth@yahoo.com

ASIMOV, Janet Jeppson. American, b. 1926. **Genres:** Novels, Novellas/Short stories, Children's fiction, Writing/Journalism. **Career:** Physician, 1952-. Training and supervising analyst, W.A. White Psychoanalytic Institute, 1969- (director of training, 1974-82). Science columnist for the Los Angeles Times Syndicate, now Tribune Media Services, 1992-. Associate ed., Contemporary Psychoanalysis, 1970-94. **Publications:** The Second Experiment, 1974; The Last Immortal, 1980; (with I. Asimov) Norby, The Mixed-up Robot, 1983; (with I. Asimov) Norby's Other Secret, 1984; (with I. Asimov) Norby and the Lost Princess, 1985; The Mysterious Cure and Other Stories of Pshrinks Anonymous, 1985; (with I. Asimov) Norby and the Invaders, 1985; (with I. Asimov) Norby and the Queen's Necklace, 1986; (with I. Asimov) Norby Finds a Villain, 1987; (with I. Asimov) How to Enjoy Writing, 1987; Mind Transfer, 1988; The Package in Hyperspace, 1988; (with I. Asimov) Norby Down to Earth, 1988; (with I. Asimov) Norby and Yobo's Great Adventure, 1989; (with I. Asimov) Norby and the Oldest Dragon, 1990; (with I. Asimov) Norby and the Court Jester, 1991; (with I. Asimov) Frontiers II, 1993; Murder at the Galactic Writers' Society, 1995; Norby and the Terrified Taxi, 1997. EDITOR: (with I. Asimov) Laughing Space, 1982; I. Asimov, It's Been a Good Life. **Address:** 10 W 66th St, New York, NY 10023, U.S.A.

ASIMOW, Michael. American, b. 1939. **Genres:** Law. **Career:** Irell & Manella, Los Angeles, CA, associate, 1964-66; University of California, Los Angeles, professor of law, 1967-, associate dean of Law School, 1992-93. Visiting professor at universities worldwide. Loeb & Loeb, of counsel, 1986-91; Bet Tzedek Legal Services, volunteer attorney, 1993-; AME Church-Temple Isaiah, founder of Public Counsel Legal Service Program, 1993, supervising attorney, 1993-. **Publications:** Advice to the Public from Federal Administrative Agencies, 1973; (with A. Bonfield) State and Federal Administrative Law, 1989, supplements, 1993, 1997; (with P. Bergman) Reel Justice: The Courtroom Goes to the Movies, 1996. Contributor to books and law journals. **Address:** 1330 Longworth Dr., Los Angeles, CA 90049, U.S.A.

ASINOF, Eliot. American, b. 1919. **Genres:** Novels, Social commentary, Sports/Fitness. **Publications:** Man on Spikes, 1955; Eight Men Out, 1963; The Bedfellow, 1967; Seven Days to Sunday, 1968; The Name of the Game Is Murder, 1968; People vs Blutcher, 1968; Craig and Joan, 1971; (with W. Hinckle and W. Turner) The Ten Second Jailbreak, 1973; The Fox Is Crazy Too, 1976; Say It Ain't So, Gordon Littlefield, 1977; Bleeding between the Lines, 1979; Nineteen Hundred and Nineteen: America's Loss of Innocence, 1990; (with J. Bouton) Strike Zone, 1994; Off Season, 2000. **Address:** 416 Wood Ct, Ancramdale, NY 12503, U.S.A.

ASKEW, Thomas A(delbert), Jr. American, b. 1931. **Genres:** History. **Career:** Wheaton College, Wheaton, IL, instructor, 1960-62, assistant professor, 1962-68; National College of Education, Evanston, IL, professor of social science, 1968-72, associate dean of the college, 1971-72; Gordon College, Wenham, MA, professor of history, 1972-2000, assistant dean, 1975-76, chairman of department, 1976-, director of the Centennial, 1986-89, assistant dean, 1993-94, East West Institute of International Studies, executive director, 1996-2005. Member of visiting faculty at University of Illinois at Chicago Circle, 1970-72. Publisher of Christian Scholar's Review, 1979-86. Member of board of trustees of Essex Institute and Museum, Salem, MA, 1979-86; member of advisory planning committee of House of Seven Gables, Salem, 1987-. **Publications:** (with J.M. Askew) Beverly, Massachusetts, and the American Revolution: One Town's Experience, 1974; (with P.W. Spellman) The Churches and the American Experience: Ideals and Institutions, 1984; (ed. with R.A. Wells) Liberty and Law: Reflections on the Constitution in American Life and Thought, 1987; (with J.M. Askew) Gordon College: A Centennial History, 1988; (with R.V. Pierard) The American Church Experience: A Concise History, 2004. **Address:** Dept of History, East West Institute, Gordon College, Wenham, MA 01984, U.S.A. **Online address:** jethaskwe@aol.com

ASPER, Kathrin. Swiss, b. 1941. **Genres:** Psychology. **Career:** Private practice of psychoanalysis and psychotherapy, 1978-. C.G. Jung Institute,

member of Curatorium, 1982-99. Lecturer and seminar leader in Europe, Canada, the Philippines, and the United States; also worked as a teacher, including a year in Paris. **Publications:** Verlassenheit und Selbstentfremdung, 1987, trans. as The Abandoned Child Within: On Losing and Regaining Self-Worth, 1993; Von der Kindheit zum Kind in uns, 1988, trans. as The Inner Child in Dreams, 1992; Schritte im Labyrinth-Tagebuch Einer Psychotherapeutin, 1992; Fenster im Alltag-Psychologisches Skizzenbuch, 1995. Contributor to psychology journals. **Address:** Plattenstrasse 98, CH-8706 Meilen, Switzerland. **Online address:** kathrin.asper@bluewin.ch

ASPREY, Robert Brown. American, b. 1923. **Genres:** History, Military/Defense/Arms control, Biography. **Career:** US Marine Corps, captain, 1942-52; US Army, intelligence analyst, 1951-52; military correspondent, 1954-65; author, currently. **Publications:** The Panther's Feast, 1959; The First Battle of the Marne, 1962; (with A. A. Vandegrift) Once a Marine, 1964; At Belleau Wood, 1965, 2nd ed., 1996; Semper Fidelis, 1967; War in the Shadows: The Guerrilla in History, 2 vols., 1977, 2nd ed., 1 vol., 1994; Operation Prophet, 1975; Frederick the Great: The Magnificent Enigma, 1986; The German High Command at War: Hindenburg and Ludendorff Conduct World War One, 1991. Asprey's books appear on tape. **Address:** Apartado Nueva Andalucia, Malaga, Spain.

ASSMANN, Jan. German, b. 1938. **Genres:** Archaeology/Antiquities. **Career:** University of Heidelberg, Heidelberg, Germany, faculty member, 1972-, professor of Egyptology, 1976-. **Publications:** Das Kulturelle Gedaechtnis, 1992; Aegypten. Eine Sinngeschichte, 1996; Moses the Egyptian, 1997. **Address:** Institute of Egyptology, University of Heidelberg, Marstallhof 4, 69117 Heidelberg, Germany. **Online address:** ae3@ix.urz.uni-heidelberg.de

ASSOULINE, Pierre. Moroccan, b. 1953. **Genres:** History, Biography, Adult non-fiction. **Career:** Journalist, biographer, and writer. Lire (magazine), France, editor. **Publications:** BIOGRAPHIES: Monsieur Dassault, 1983; Gaston Gallimard: un demi-siecle d'edition francaise, 1984, trans. by H.J. Salemson as Gaston Gallimard: A Half-Century of French Publishing, 1988; Une eminence grise: Jean Jardin (1904-1976), 1986; L'homme de l'art: D.-H. Kahnweiler, 1884-1979, 1988, trans. by C. Ruas as An Artful Life: A Biography of D.H. Kahnweiler, 1884-1979, 1990; Albert Londres: vie et mort d'un grand reporter, 1884-1932, 1989; Simenon: biographie, 1992, trans. by J. Rothschild as Simenon: A Biography, 1997; Trois hommes d'influence, 1994; Herge: biographie, 1996. OTHER NONFICTION: (with P. Dampenon) De nos envoyes speciaux: les coulisses du reportage, 1977; Lourdes: histoires d'eau, 1980; Les nouveaux convertis: enquete sur les chretiens, des juifs et des musulmans pas comme les autres, 1982; L'epuration des intellectuels, 1944-1945 (history), 1985; Le fleuve Combelle, 1997. **Address:** 72 boulevard Flandrin, 75016 Paris, France.

ASTARITA, Tommaso. Italian, b. 1961. **Genres:** History. **Career:** Georgetown University, Washington, DC, associate professor of history, 1994-, assistant professor of history, 1989-94. Wright State University, visiting assistant professor, 1988-89. **Publications:** The Continuity of Feudal Power, Cambridge University Press, 1992. **Address:** History Department, Georgetown University, Washington, DC 20057, U.S.A.

ASTELL, Ann W. American. **Genres:** History. **Career:** Purdue University, West Lafayette, IN, currently professor of English. **Publications:** The Song of Songs in the Middle Ages, 1990; Job, Boethius, and Epic Truth, 1994; Divine Representations: Postmodernism and Spirituality, 1994; Chaucer and the Universe of Learning, Cornell University Press 1996; Political Allegory in Late Medieval England, 1999; (ed., with Bonnie Wheeler) Lay Sanctity, Medieval and Modern: A Search for Models, 2000; Joan of Arc and Spirituality, 2003; Joan of Arc and Sacrificial Authorship, 2003. **Address:** Purdue University, Department of English, 500 Oval Dr., West Lafayette, IN 47907, U.S.A. **Online address:** astell@purdue.edu

ASTIN, Patty Duke. See DUKE, Anna Marie.

ASTLEY, Neil. British, b. 1953. **Genres:** Novels, Poetry, Literary criticism and history. **Career:** Stand (magazine), Newcastle upon Tyne, England, production editor, 1975-78; Morden Tower (poetry readings organization), Newcastle upon Tyne, publications editor, 1976-78; Bloodaxe Books Ltd., Newcastle upon Tyne, founder, editor, and managing director, 1978-; poet and writer. Worked as a journalist. **Publications:** POETRY: The Speechless Act, 1984; Darwin Survivor, 1988; Biting My Tongue, 1995. EDITOR (anthologies unless noted): Ten North-East Poets, 1980; Poetry with an Edge, 1988, new ed., 1993; Tony Harrison (criticism), 1991; Wordworks, 1992; New Blood, 1999; Staying Alive: Reqal Poems for Unreal Times, 2003; Pleased to See Me: 69 Very Sexy Poems, 2002; Do not Go Gentle: Poems for Funerals, 2003; Bloodaxe Poems of the Year, 2003. OTHER: The End of My Tether (novel), 2002. **Address:** c/o Bloodaxe Books Ltd, Highgreen, Tarset, Northd. NE48 1RP, England. **Online address:** editor@bloodaxebooks. demon.co.uk

ASTLEY, Thea (Beatrice May). *See* Obituaries.

ASTOR, Gerald. American, b. 1926. **Genres:** Social commentary, Sports/ Fitness, Biography. **Publications:** The Charge Is Rape, 1974; Capitol Hell, 1974; A Question of Rape, 1974; (with A. Villano) Brick Agent, 1978; The Disease Detectives: Deadly Medical Mysteries and the People Who Solve Them, 1983; The "Last" Nazi: The Life and Times of Dr. Joseph Mengele, 1985; The Baseball Hall of Fame 50th Anniversary Book, 1988; A Blood-Dimmed Tide, 1991; Battling Buzzards, 1992; June 6, 1944, 1994; The Greatest War: Americans in Combat 1941-1945, 1999; The Bloody Forest, 2000; Terrible Terry Allen, 2003. **Address:** 50 Sprain Valley Rd, Scarsdale, NY 10583, U.S.A.

ATHAS, Daphne. American, b. 1923. **Genres:** Novels. **Career:** Lecturer in Creative Writing, University of North Carolina, Chapel Hill, since 1966. Fulbright Professor of American Literature, Tehran University, Iran, 1973-74. **Publications:** Weather of the Heart, 1947; The Fourth World, 1956; (with G. Campbell) Sit on the Earth (play), 1957; Greece by Prejudice, 1963; Entering Ephesus, 1971; Cora, 1978; Crumbs for the Bogeyman, 1991. **Address:** Box 224, Chapel Hill, NC 27514, U.S.A.

ATHERDEN, Margaret Ann. British, b. 1947. **Genres:** Natural history. **Career:** York St. John College, York, England, principal lecturer in geography, 1971-2003, director of research, 1998-2003, research development officer, 2003-; University of Bradford, visiting lecturer and honorary research fellow, 1978-; University of York, hon. research fellow, 2004-. **Publications:** Upland Britain: A Natural History, 1992. EDITOR/CO-EDITOR: (with R.A. Butlin) Woodland in the Landscape: Past and Future Perspectives, 1998; Wetlands in the Landscape: Archaeology, Conservation, Heritage, 2001; (and contrib.) Historical Atlas of North Yorkshire, Section 2: The Physical Landscape, 2003; Global Warming: A Yorkshire Perspective, 2003. Contributor to books. Author of articles on the vegetation history of North York Moors and environmental change in Greece. Contributor to academic journals. **Address:** York St. John College, Lord Mayor's Walk, York YO31 7EX, England. **Online address:** m.atherden@yorksj.ac.uk

ATKIN, Flora B. American, b. 1919. **Genres:** Children's fiction, Plays/ Screenplays, Theatre. **Career:** Lecturer, director, playwright, and consultant on children's theatre at universities and conferences, 1979-. Director, Recreational Arts Dept., 1940-44, and Founding Director, Creative Arts Day Camp, 1941-44, Jewish Community Center, Washington, DC; Instructor in Dance Education, Howard University, Washington, D.C., 1942-43; free-lance creative arts educator and children's theatre dir., 1953-80; Founding Director and Playwright, In-School Players, Adventure Theatre, Montgomery County, Maryland, 1969-79. **Publications:** PLAYS: Tarradiddle Tales, 1969; Tarradiddle Travels, 1970; Golliwhoppers!, 1972; Skupper-Duppers, 1974; Dig 'n Tel, 1977; Grampo/Scampo, 1981; Shoorik and Puffchik, 1983; Hold that Tiger, 1986; Tales from the Rebbe's Table, 1994; Twenty-Eight Steps Below, 1999. Contributor to professional periodicals. **Address:** 5507 Uppingham St, Chevy Chase, MD 20815, U.S.A. **Online address:** matkin1@compuserve. com

ATKINS, Russell. American, b. 1926. **Genres:** Plays/Screenplays, Poetry, Music. **Career:** Creative Writing Instructor, Karamu House and Theatre, since 1971. Ed., Free Lance Magazine, since 1950. Member, Ohio Arts Council, 1974-75. **Publications:** Psychovisual Perspective for Musical Composition, 1956-1958, 3rd ed. 1969; Phenomena (poetry and play), 1961; Objects (poetry), 1963; Heretofore (poetry and play), 1968; Here In The (poetry), 1976; Whichever, 1978; Juxtapositions (poetry, criticism), 1991. **Address:** 6005 Grand Ave, Cleveland, OH 44104, U.S.A.

ATKINS, Stephen E. American, b. 1941. **Genres:** International relations/ Current affairs, Librarianship, Military/Defense/Arms control, Politics/ Government. **Career:** University of Iowa, Iowa City, copy cataloger, 1973-83; University of Illinois, Urbana, political science subject specialist, 1983-89; Texas A&M University, College Station, head of collection development at Sterling C. Evans Library, 1989-97, AUL for Collection Management, 1997-2003, associate dean for collection management, 2003-. Also served on the board of directors of ACCESS: A Security Information Service, 1989-94. **Publications:** Arms Control and Disarmament, Defense and Military, International Security and Peace: An Annotated Guide to Sources, 1980-1987, 1989; The Academic Library in the American University, 1991; Terror-

ism: A Reference Handbook, 1992; Historical Encyclopedia of Atomic Energy, 2000; Encyclopedia of American Extremism, 2002. **Address:** 301B Library Annex, 5000 TAMUS, Texas A&M University Libraries, College Station, TX 77843-5000, U.S.A. **Online address:** s-atkins@tamu.edu

ATKINSON, Anthony Barnes. British, b. 1944. **Genres:** Economics, Social commentary. **Career:** University of Essex, professor of economics, 1970-76; University College, London, professor and head of Dept. of Political Economy, 1976-79; London School of Economics, professor of economics, 1980-92; University of Cambridge, professor of political economy, 1992-94; Nuffield College, Oxford, warden, 1994-. Journal of Public Economics, editor, 1972-97. **Publications:** Poverty in Britain and the Reform of Social Security, 1969; Unequal Shares, 1972; The Economics of Inequality, 1975; (with A.J. Harrison) Distribution of Personal Wealth in Britain, 1978; (with J.E. Stiglitz) Lectures on Public Economics, 1980; Social Justice and Public Policy, 1983; (with A. Maynard and C. Trinder) Parents and Children, 1985; (with J. Micklewright) Unemployment Benefits and Unemployment Duration, 1988; Poverty and Social Security, 1989; (with J. Micklewright) The Distribution of Income in Eastern Europe, 1992; Public Economics in Action, 1995; Incomes and the Welfare State, 1996; Poverty in Europe, 1998; Economic Consequences of Rolling Back the Welfare State, 1999; Social Indicators, 2002. **Address:** Nuffield College, Oxford OX1 1NF, England.

ATKINSON, James. British, b. 1914. **Genres:** Theology/Religion. **Career:** Director, Centre for Reformation Studies, University of Sheffield; Canon Theologian of Sheffield Cathedral, 1970-. Reader in Theology, University of Hull, 1956-67; Professor of Biblical Studies, University of Sheffield, 1967-79; Theological Adviser to Archbishop of Canterbury, 1955-79. **Publications:** Luther's Early Theological Works, 1962; Rome and Reformation, 1965; (ed.) Luther's Works, Vol. 44, 1967; Luther and the Birth of Protestantism, 1968, 1982; The Reformation, 1968; The Trial of Luther, 1971; Erasmus of Rotterdam (television script), 1974; Martin Luther, Prophet to the Church Catholic, 1983; The Darkness of Faith, 1987; Faith Lost: Faith Regained, 2005. **Address:** Leach House, Hathersage, Hope Valley S32 1BA, England.

ATKINSON, Kate. Scottish. **Genres:** Novels, Novellas/Short stories. **Publications:** Behind the Scenes at the Museum, 1996; Human Croquet, 1997. Also author of short stories. **Address:** c/o St. Martins Press, 175 Fifth Avenue, New York, NY 10010, U.S.A.

ATKINSON, Michael (J.). American. **Genres:** Literary criticism and history. **Career:** Classical scholar. **Publications:** (trans. and commentator) Plotinus, Ennead V. 1: On the Three Principal Hypostases, 1983. **Address:** c/o Oxford University Press, 198 Madison Ave., New York, NY 10016, U.S.A.

ATKINSON, Rick. American (born Germany), b. 1952. **Genres:** Military/ Defense/Arms control. **Career:** Pittsburg Morning Sun, Pittsburg, KS, reporter, 1976-77; Kansas City Times, Kansas City, MO, reporter, 1977-83; Washington Post, Washington, DC, investigative reporter, 1983-85, 1989-91, deputy national editor, 1985-87, Berlin bureau chief and Central Europe correspondent, 1993-96, assistant managing editor, 1996-. Guest on television programs. **Publications:** The Long Gray Line: The American Journey of West Point's Class of 1966, 1989; Crusade: The Untold Story of the Persian Gulf War, 1995; An Army at Dawn: The War in North Africa, 1942-1943, 2002 (Pulitzer Prize, History, 2003); In the Company of Soldiers, 2004. **Address:** c/o Raphael Sagalyn Agency, 7201 Wisconsin Ave Ste 675, Bethesda, MD 20814-7213, U.S.A.

ATLAS, James (Robert). American, b. 1949. **Genres:** Poetry, Novellas/ Short stories, Education. **Career:** Harvard Advocate, Cambridge, MA, editor, 1969-70; Time, NYC, book reviewer and staff writer, 1977-78; New York Times Book Review, NYC, assistant editor, 1979-81; Atlantic Monthly, NYC, associate editor, 1981-85; Vanity Fair, contributing editor, 1985-87; New York Times Magazine, assistant editor, 1988-; Lipper/Viking Penguin "Lives" series, general editor; Lipper Publications, president. **Publications:** Delmore Schwartz: The Life of an American Poet, 1977; The Great Pretender, 1986; The Book Wars: What It Takes to Be Educated in America, 1990, repr. as Battle of the Books: The Curriculum Debate in America, 1992; Bellow: A Biography, 2000. EDITOR: (with G. Goemoeri) Attila Jozsef: Selected Poems and Texts, trans. J. Batki, 1973; Ten American Poets: An Anthology of Poems by Alan Williamson, Jonathan Galassi, Paul Smyth, Peggy Rizza, James Martin, Richard Tillinghast, Robert B. Shaw, Jane Shore, Frank Bidart, and John Koethe, 1973; (and intro) D. Schwartz, In Dreams Begin Responsibilities, and Other Stories, 1978. Contributor of articles and poetry to periodicals. **Address:** c/o Lipper & Co., 101 Park Ave, Floor 6, New York, NY 10178-0002, U.S.A.

ATTANASIO, Paul. American, b. 1959. **Genres:** Plays/Screenplays. **Career:** Cravath, Swaine & Moore, 1984-; Washington Post, Washington, DC, journalist and film critic. **Publications:** SCREENPLAYS: Disclosure, 1994; Quiz Show, 1994; Donnie Brasco, 1995. TELEPLAYS: Homicide: Life on the Street (also known as H: LOTS and Homicide), 1993; Gideon's Crossing. Contributor to periodicals. **Address:** c/o David O'Connor, Creative Artists Agency Inc., 9830 Wilshire Blvd, Beverly Hills, CA 90212, U.S.A.

ATTEMA, Martha. Dutch, b. 1949. **Genres:** Children's fiction, Young adult fiction. **Career:** Kindergarten teacher in Giekerk, the Netherlands, 1969-73; teacher of kindergarten and grade one in North Bay, Ontario, 1987-. **Publications:** The Unhappy Pinetree (picture book), 1992. NOVELS FOR YOUNG ADULTS: A Time to Choose (historical), 1995; A Light in the Dunes, 1997; Daughter of Light (historical), 2001. Contributor to periodicals. **Address:** 376 Voyer Rd, Corbeil, ON, Canada P0H 1K0. **Online address:** martatte@Vianet.on.ca; www.marthaattema.com

ATTENBOROUGH, Richard (Samuel). British, b. 1923. **Genres:** Philosophy, Biography, Essays, Film, Social commentary. **Career:** Actor in stage productions and motion pictures; producer and director of motion pictures; writer. **Publications:** In Search of Gandhi, 1982; (compiler) The Words of Gandhi, 1982; (author of afterword and ed. of photographic selections) Richard Attenborough's Chorus Line, 1985; Richard Attenborough's Cry Freedom: A Pictorial Record, 1987. Author of introductions to publications.

ATTFIELD, Robin. British, b. 1941. **Genres:** Ethics, Intellectual history, Philosophy. **Career:** University of Wales, Cardiff, assistant lecturer, 1968-70, lecturer, 1971-77, senior lecturer, 1977-81, reader in philosophy, 1981-92, professor of philosophy, 1992-. University of Ife, visiting lecturer, 1972-73; University of Nairobi, Inter-University Council visiting lecturer, 1975. World Development Movement, chair of Cardiff branch, 1986-98; member of Cardiff Centre for Applied Ethics. **Publications:** God and the Secular, 1978, 2nd ed., 1993; The Ethics of Environmental Concern, 1983, 2nd ed., 1991; A Theory of Value and Obligation, 1987; (co-ed.) Values, Conflict, and the Environment, 1989, 2nd ed., 1996; (co-ed.) International Justice and the Third World, 1992; (coed.) Philosophy and the Natural Environment, 1994; Environmental Philosophy, 1994; Value, Obligation and Meta-Ethics, 1995; The Ethics of the Global Environment, 1999; Environmental Ethics, 2003. **Address:** Philosophy Section, Cardiff School of English, Communication and Philosophy, Cardiff University, Cardiff CF10 3XB, Wales.

ATWOOD, Margaret. Canadian, b. 1939. **Genres:** Novels, Novellas/Short stories, Children's fiction, Poetry, Literary criticism and history. **Career:** University of British Columbia, Vancouver, lecturer in English, 1964-65; instructor in English, Sir George Williams University, Montreal, 1967-68, and University of Alberta, Edmonton, 1969-70; York University, Toronto, assistant professor of English, 1971-72; writer-in-residence, University of Toronto, 1972-73, University of Alabama, Tuscaloosa, 1985, Macquarie University, N. Ryde, NSW, 1987, and Trinity University, San Antonio, TX, 1989; New York University, NYC, Berg Chair, 1986. President, Writers' Union of Canada, 1981-82, and International PEN, Canadian Centre (English Speaking), 1984-86. Recipient of numerous awards for poetry and fiction. **Publications:** POETRY: The Circle Game, 1964; Kaleidescopes Baroque, 1965; Talismans for Children, 1965; Speeches for Doctor Frankenstein, 1966; The Animals in that Country, 1969; The Journals of Susanna Moodie, 1970; Procedures for Underground, 1970; Power Politics, 1971; You Are Happy, 1974; Selected Poems, 1976; Marsh, Hawk, 1977; Two-Headed Poems, 1978; True Stories, 1981; Notes towards a Poem That Can Never Be Written, 1981; Snake Poems, 1983; Interlunar, 1984; Selected Poems II: 1976-1986, 1987; Selected Poems, 1966-1984, 1990; Margaret Atwood Poems, 1965-1975, 1991; Morning in the Burned House, 1995. FICTION: The Edible Woman, 1969; Surfacing, 1972; Lady Oracle, 1976; Dancing Girls (stories), 1977; Life before Man, 1979; Bodily Harm, 1981; Encounters with the Element Man, 1982; Murder in the Dark, 1983; Bluebeard's Egg and Other Stories, 1983; Unearthing Suite (stories), 1983; The Handmaid's Tale, 1985; Cat's Eye, 1988; Wilderness Tips, 1991; Good Bones, 1992; The Robber Bride, 1993; Alias Grace, 1996; The Blind Assassin, 2000 (Booker Prize); Oryx and Crake, 2003. CHILDREN'S BOOKS: Up in the Tree, 1978; Anna's Pet, 1980; For the Birds, 1990; Princess Prunella and the Purple Peanut, 1995; Rude Ramsay and the Roaring Radishes, 2003. NON-FICTION: Survival: A Thematic Guide to Canadian Literature, 1972; Days of the Rebels, 1815-1840, 1977; Second Words: Selected Critical Prose, 1982; Negotiating with the Dead, 2002. OTHER: New Oxford Book of Canadian Verse, 1982; (with R. Weaver) The Oxford Book of Short Stories, in English, 1986; (ed.) The Canlit Food Book, 1987; (ed. with S. Ravenel) The Best American Short Stories 1989, 1989; Strange Things: The

Malevolent North in Canadian Literature, 1995. **Address:** c/o McClelland & Stewart, 481 University Ave Ste 900, Toronto, ON, Canada M5G 2E9.

ATWOOD, William G(oodson). American, b. 1932. **Genres:** Biography. **Career:** University of Kansas Hospitals, Kansas City, MO, intern, 1950-59; Columbia-Presbyterian Medical Center, New York City, resident, 1961-64; physician (dermatologist) in private practice, 1964-. Columbia University College of Physicians and Surgeons, associate professor, beginning in 1987. **Publications:** The Lioness and the Little One: The Liaison of George Sand and Frederic Chopin, 1980; Fryderyk Chopin, Pianist from Warsaw, 1987; The Parisian Worlds of Frederic Chopin, 1999. Contributor of articles on dermatology to scientific journals. **Address:** 555 Park Ave., New York, NY 10021, U.S.A.

ATXAGA, Bernardo. (Joseba Irazu Garmendia). Spanish, b. 1951. **Genres:** Novels, Children's fiction. **Career:** Writer and translator. **Publications:** NOVELS: Ziutateaz, 1976; Bi anai, 1984; Obabakoak, 1988, trans., 1992; The Lone Man, trans., 1997. OTHER: Sugeak txoria'ri begiratzen dionean, 1983, 2nd ed., 1985. Author of children's books and poetry. **Address:** c/o Harvill, 2 Aztec Row, Berners Rd, London N1 0PW, England.

AUBERT, Alvin. American, b. 1930. **Genres:** Plays/Screenplays, Poetry, Education. **Career:** Southern University, Baton Rouge, LA, instructor, 1960-62, assistant professor, 1962-65, associate professor of English, 1965-70; State University of New York, Fredonia, associate professor, 1970-74, professor, 1974-79; Wayne State University, Detroit, professor, 1979-92, professor emeritus of English, 1992-. Founding Ed., Obsidian mag., Fredonia, NY. **Publications:** Against the Blues, 1972; Feeling Through, 1975; New and Selected Poems, 1985; Collected Poems, 1994; Harlem Wrestler, 1995; The Way I Do, 2004. **Address:** 1550 Cherboneau Pl Apt 117, Detroit, MI 48207-2861, U.S.A. **Online address:** ad8722@wayne.edu

AUBERT, Jacques. French, b. 1932. **Genres:** Literary criticism and history. **Career:** University of Lyon, Lyon, France, professor, 1971-, member of University Scientific Council and director of Centre d'Etudes et de Recherches Anglaises et Nord-Americaines. Visiting professor at universities worldwide. **Publications:** Introduction a l'esthetique de James Joyce, 1973; (trans. into French) James Joyce, Dubliners, 1974, rev. ed., 1992; (with M. Jolas) Joyce and Paris, 1979; (trans. into French) Joyce, Oeuvres, Vol. I, 1982, Vol. II, 1995; (with F. Senn) Cahier James Joyce, 1986; Joyce avec Lacan, 1987; The Aesthetics of James Joyce, 1992. **Address:** 16 rue de Tourvielle, 69005 Lyon, France.

AUCH, Mary Jane. American. **Genres:** Children's fiction, Young adult fiction. **Career:** Worked as an occupational therapist at a children's hospital, and as a designer, graphic artist, and illustrator for Pennywhistle Press. **Publications:** SELF-ILLUSTRATED PICTURE BOOKS: The Easter Egg Farm, 1992; Bird Dogs Can't Fly, 1993; Peeping Beauty, 1993; Monster Brother, 1994; Hen Lake, 1995; Eggs Mark the Spot, 1996; Bantam of the Opera, 1997; Noah's Aardvark, 1999; The Nutquacker, 1999; (with H. Auch) Poultrygeist, 2002; (with H. Auch) The Princess and the Pizza, 2002. NOVELS: The Witching of Ben Wagner, 1987; Cry Uncle!, 1987; Mom Is Dating Weird Wayne, 1988; Pick of the Litter, 1988; Glass Slippers Give You Blisters, 1989; Angel and Me and the Bayside Brothers, 1989; Kidnapping Kevin Kowalski, 1990; A Sudden Change of Family, 1990; Seven Long Years until College, 1991; Out of Step, 1992; The Latchkey Dog, 1994; Journey to Nowhere, 1997; I Was a Third-Grade Science Project, 1998; Frozen Summer, 1998; The Road Home, 2000; I Was a Third-Grade Spy, 2001; Ashes of Roses, 2002. Illustrator of books by S. Pennypacker, V. Vande Velde. **Address:** c/o Holiday House, 425 Madison Ave., New York, NY 10017, U.S.A. **Online address:** jmawebsite@aol.com; www.mjauch.com

AUCHINCLOSS, Louis (Stanton). American, b. 1917. **Genres:** Novels, Novellas/Short stories, Plays/Screenplays, Literary criticism and history, Autobiography/Memoirs, Essays. **Career:** Associate Lawyer, Sullivan & Cromwell, NYC, 1941-51; Associate, 1954-58, and Partner, 1958-86, Hawkins, Delafield & Wood, attorneys-at-law, NYC. President, Museum of the City of New York, 1967-90. **Publications:** (as Andrew Lee, later reprinted as Auchincloss) The Indifferent Children, 1947; The Injustice Collectors, 1950; Sybil, 1952; A Law for the Lion, 1952; The Romantic Egoists: A Reflection in 8 Minutes, 1954; The Great World and Timothy Colt, 1956; Venus in Sparta, 1958; Pursuit of the Prodigal, 1959; The House of Five Talents, 1960; Edith Wharton, 1961; Reflections of a Jacobite, 1961; Portrait in Brownstone, 1962; Powers of Attorney, 1963; The Rector of Justin, 1964; Ellen Glasgow, 1964; Pioneers and Caretakers: A Study of 9 American Women Novelists, 1965; The Embezzler, 1966; Tales of Manhattan, 1967; The Club Bedroom, (play), 1967; A World of Profit, 1968; Motiveless

Malignity, 1969; Second Chance, 1970; Henry Adams, 1971; Edith Wharton: A Woman in Her Time, 1971; I Come as a Thief, 1972; Richelieu, 1972; The Partners, 1974; Writer's Capital (autobiography), 1974; Reading Henry James, 1975; The Winthrop Covenant, 1976; The Dark Lady, 1977; The Country Cousin, 1978; Persons of Consequence, 1979; The House of the Prophet, 1980; Life, Law, and Letters, 1980; The Cat and the King, 1981; The Unseen Versailles, 1981; Watchfires, 1982; Narcissa and Other Fables, 1983; Exit Lady Masham, 1983; The Book Class, 1984; Honorable Men, 1985; Diary of a Yuppie, 1986; Skinny Island, 1987; The Golden Calves, 1988; Fellow Passengers, 1989; The Vanderbilt Era (essays), 1989; The Lady of Situations, 1990; J.P. Morgan: The Financier as Collector, 1990; Love without Wings: Some Friendships in Literature and Politics, 1991; False Gods, 1992; Three Lives, 1993; (text) Deborah Turbeville's Newport Remembered, 1994; The Style's the Man (essays), 1994; Tales of Yesteryear, 1994: The Collected Stories of Louis Auchincloss, 1994; The Education of Oscar Fairfax, 1995; The Man behind the Book, 1996; La Gloire, 1996; The Atonement, and Other Stories, 1997; (with others) Century of Arts & Letters, 1998; The Anniversary and Other Stories, 1999; Woodrow Wilson, 2000; Her Infinite Variety, 2000; Theodore Roosevelt, 2001; Manhattan Monologues, 2002; Scarlet Letters, 2003. EDITOR: An Edith Wharton Reader, 1965; Fables of Wit and Elegance, 1972; Hone & Strong Diaries of Old Manhattan, 1989. **Address:** 1111 Park Ave, New York, NY 10128-1234, U.S.A.

AUDEH, Azmi S. American (born Palestine), b. 1932. **Genres:** Adult nonfiction, Race relations, Autobiography/Memoirs. **Career:** 3M Co., Camarillo, CA, senior engineer, 1963-66; Ampex Corp., Culver City, CA, engineering manager, 1966-71; Burroughs Corp., Westlake Village, CA, vice-president for engineering, 1971-82; Storage Technology Corp., Louisville, CO, chief engineer, 1982-88, retiring in 1988. Worked as writer and as a consultant to control-system component suppliers. Holder of patents related to the design of control systems, such as computer digital tape instrumentation and computer peripherals. **Publications:** Carpenter from Nazareth: A Palestinian Portrait, 1998. Contributor to engineering journals. **Address:** 5546 Homestead Way, Boulder, CO 80301, U.S.A. **Online address:** asaudeh@worldnet.att.net

AUEL, Jean M(arie). American, b. 1936. **Genres:** Novels. **Publications:** The Clan of the Cave Bear, 1980; The Valley of Horses, 1982; The Mammoth Hunters, 1985; The Plains of Passage, 1990; The Shelters of Stone, 2002. **Address:** c/o Jean V. Naggar Literary Agency, 216 E 75th St, New York, NY 10021, U.S.A.

AUER, James M(atthew). American, b. 1928. **Genres:** Plays/Screenplays. **Career:** George Banta Co., Menasha, WI, accounting clerk, 1950-51; Twin City News-Record, Neenah, WI, reporter, 1953-56, assistant to the editor, 1957-60, news editor, 1960-61; Appleton Post Crescent, Appleton, WI, assistant Sunday editor, 1960-65; Milwaukee Journal, Milwaukee, WI, Sunday editor, 1965-72; Milwaukee Journal, Milwaukee, WI, art critic and feature writer, 1972-. Attic Theatre, Inc., presiding officer, 1959-62; Friends of Bergstrom Art Center, president, 1967-68; Ego Productions and Studio Door Artfilms, owner and president, 1983-; member of Neenah Municipal Museum Foundation, Inc. **Publications:** The Spirit Is Willing, 1960; The City of Light (play), 1961; Tell It to Angela (play), 1971; has also written screenplays. **Address:** 1849 N 72nd St, Milwaukee, WI 53213, U.S.A. **Online address:** jauer53406@aol.com

AUERBACH, Loyd. American, b. 1956. **Genres:** Paranormal. **Career:** Paranormal investigator, professor, media consultant, professional speaker, and author; The Office of Paranormal Investigations, founder and director, 1989-; John F. Kennedy University, Orinda, CA, adjunct professor, 1983-; Rosebridge Graduate School for Integrative Psychology in Concord, CA, Core Faculty member, 1996-98; FATE Magazine, consulting editor and Psychic Frontiers columnist, 1991-2004; American Society for Psychical Research, New York, public information and media consultant, 1982-83; Lexis-Nexis, consultant, 1984-. Also performing mentalist/psychic entertainer. **Publications:** ESP, Hauntings, and Poltergeists, 1986; Psychic Dreaming, 1991, rev. ed., 1999; Reincarnation, Channeling, and Possession: a Parapsychologist's Handbook, 1993; Mind over Matter, 1996; Ghost Hunting: How to Investigate the Paranormanl, 2004; Hauntings & Poltergeists: A Ghost Hunter's Guide, 2004. **Address:** Office of Paranormal Investigations, PO Box 875, Orinda, CA 94563, U.S.A. **Online address:** esper@california.com; www.mindreader.com

AUERBACH, Michael. American, b. 1949. **Genres:** Medicine/Health. **Career:** Cleveland Clinic, Cleveland, OH, in internal medicine, 1978; Columbia University, NYC, in hematology and oncology, 1981; Franklin Square Hospital Center, Baltimore, MD, chief of hematology and oncology and director of Comprehensive Cancer Center, 1986-. Georgetown University,

clinical professor. **Publications:** Conversations about Cancer, 1997. Contributor to medical journals. **Address:** 17 Jackson Manor Ct., Phoenix, MD 21131, U.S.A. **Online address:** michaela@helix.org

AUGENBRAUM, Harold. American, b. 1953. **Genres:** Cultural/Ethnic topics, Bibliography. **Career:** Teacher of English as a foreign language in Barcelona, Spain, 1976-79; United Way of NYC, account executive, 1980; Bruce Porter Co., NYC, staff consultant, 1981-84; Hunter College of the City University of New York, NYC, director of external affairs at Brookdale Center on Aging, 1984-87; Museum of the City of New York, NYC, deputy director for external affairs, 1987-89; Mercantile Library, NYC, director, 1990-2004; National Book Foundation, executive director, 2004-. Consultant to Ballad Theatre and Myerhoff Center. **Publications:** Latinos in English: A Selected Bibliography of Latino Fiction Writers of the United States, 1992; (ed. with I. Stavans) Marc Jaffe, Growing Up Latino: Memoirs and Stories, 1993; The Latino Reader, 1997: U.S. Latino Literature: A Critical Guide for Students and Teachers, 2000. Contributor to periodicals. **Address:** National Book Foundation, 95 Madison Ave Ste 709, New York, NY 10019, U.S.A. **Online address:** haugebraum@nationalbook.org

AUGER, C(harles) P(eter). British, b. 1931. **Genres:** Language/Linguistics. **Career:** Lucas Industries, Solihull, England, research manager, 1957-88; Peter Auger Research Services, Redditch, England, information consultant, 1988-. **Publications:** Engineering Eponyms, 1975; Use of Reports Literature, 1975; Information Sources in Grey Literature, 1989, 3rd ed, 1994; (ed.) Information Sources in Patents, 1992. **Address:** 82 Malvern Rd., Redditch, Worcestershire B97 5DP, England.

AUGUST, Bille. Danish, b. 1948. **Genres:** Plays/Screenplays. **Career:** Cinematographer, screenwriter, and film director; worked as cinematographer for television films and for motion pictures, 1973-79. Director of films and television dramas. Also director of Danish television series. **Publications:** SCREENPLAYS: Honning Maane (title means: Honeymoon), 1978; (with B. Reuter) Zappa, c. 1984; (with Reuter) Tro, hab og Karlighed, 1984, in US as Twist and Shout, c. 1986; (with P.O. Enquist and Reuter) Pelle Erovraren (also known as Pelle Erobreren), 1987, in US as Pelle the Conqueror, c. 1988; The House of the Spirits, 1993; Jerusalem, 1996; A Song for Martin, 2000. **Address:** c/o Fred Specktor, Creative Artists Agency, 9830 Wilshire Blvd, Beverly Hills, CA 90212-1825, U.S.A. **Online address:** fspecktor@caa.com

AUILER, Dan Rose. American. **Genres:** Film. **Career:** Critic and teacher of film and cinema; film historian. Founding participant of the Texas Film Festival. **Publications:** Vertigo: The Making of a Hitchcock Classic, 1998; Hitchcock's Notebooks: An Authorized and Illustrated Look inside the Creative Mind of Alfred Hitchcock, 1999; (ed., with A. Castle) Some Like It Hot, 2001. **Address:** c/o HarperCollins, 1350 Avenue of the Americas, New York, NY 10019, U.S.A.

AULICH, James. British, b. 1952. **Genres:** Art/Art history, History, Politics/Government. **Career:** Manchester Metropolitan University, Manchester, England, reader in visual culture, Manchester Institute for Innovation and Research, Art and Design. **Publications:** (with M. Sylvestrova) Political Posters in Central and Eastern Europe 1945-95: Signs of the Times, 2000. CONTRIBUTING EDITOR: (with J. Walsh) Vietnam Images: War and Representation, 1989; Nationhood, Identity, and Culture: The Falklands War, 1991; (with T. Wilcox) Europe without Walls: Art, Posters and Revolution 1989-93, 1993; (with J. Lynch) Critical Kitaj: Essays on the Work of R.B. Kitaj, 2000. **Address:** MIRIAD, Manchester Metropolitan University, Cavendish St, All Saints, Manchester M15 6BX, England.

AUNE, James Arnt. American, b. 1953. **Genres:** Economics. **Career:** University of Virginia, Charlottesville, assistant professor, 1981-86; St. Olaf College, Northfield, MN, assistant professor to associate professor, 1986-94; University of St. Thomas, St. Paul, MN, associate professor, 1994-96; Texas A&M University, College Station, TX, associate professor, 1996-. **Publications:** Rhetoric and Marxism, 1994; Selling the Free Market, 2001. **Address:** Rhetorical Theory, 4234 TAMU, 209A Bolton, Texas A&M University, College Station, TX 77843-4234, U.S.A. **Online address:** jamesarntaune@yahoo.com

AUSTER, Paul. American, b. 1947. **Genres:** Novels, Novellas/Short stories, Plays/Screenplays, Poetry, Literary criticism and history, Translations. **Career:** Princeton University, NJ, teacher of creative writing, 1986-90. Formerly, variously employed as a merchant seaman, census taker, tutor, telephone operator, translator, and writer. **Publications:** White Spaces (short prose), 1980; The Invention of Solitude, 1982; City of Glass, 1985; Ghosts,

1986; The Locked Room, 1986; In the Country of Last Things, 1987; Moon Palace, 1989; The Music of Chance, 1990; Leviathan, 1992; The Art of Hunger, 1992; Mr. Vertigo, 1994; Smoke and Blue in the Face: 2 Films (screenplay), 1995; Why Write? (literary criticism and history), 1996; Hand to Mouth (autobiography), 1997; Lulu on the Bridge (screenplay), 1998; Timbuktu (novel), 1999; The Book of Illusions, 2002; The Red Notebook (true stories), 2002; (with S. Messer)The Story of My Typewriter (essay), 2002; Oracle Night (novel), 2003; Collected Prose (nonfiction), 2003; Auggie Wren's Christmas Story, 2004. POETRY: Unearth, 1974; Wall Writing, 1976; Facing the Music, 1980; Disappearances, 1988; Collected Poems, 2003. EDITOR: The Random House Book of Twentieth-Century French Poetry, 1982; I Thought My Father Was God and Other True Tales from NPR's National Story Project, 2001. TRANSLATIONS: A Little Anthology of Surrealist Poems, 1972; Fits and Starts: Selected Poems of Jacques Dupin, 1974; (with L. Davis) S. Friedlander and M. Hussein, Arabs and Israelis: A Dialogue 1975; The Uninhabited: Selected Poems of Andre de Bouchet, 1976; (with L. Davis) J.P. Sartre, Life/Situations, 1978; (with L. Davis) J. Chesneaux, China: The People's Republic, 1979; (with L. Davis) J. Chesneaux and others, China from the 1911 Revolution to Liberation, 1979; (and ed.) The Notebooks of Joseph Joubert: A Selection, 1983; S. Mallarme, A Tomb for Anatole, 1983; M. Blanchot, Vicious Circles, 1985; P. Petit, On the High Wire, 1985; (with M. Rowell) J. Miro, Selected Writings, 1986; Translations, 1996; P. Clastres, Chronicle of the Guuyaki Indians, 1998. Address: c/o Carol Mann Agency, 55 Fifth Ave, New York, NY 10003, U.S.A.

AUSTERLITZ, Paul. American (born Finland), b. 1957. **Genres:** Music. **Career:** City University of New York, NYC, adjunct lecturer at Hunter College and City College, 1990; Wesleyan University, Middletown, CT, lecturer in music, 1992; University of Michigan, Ann Arbor, visiting assistant professor of music, 1993-94, visiting scholar, 1994-95; Autonomous University of Santo Domingo, Santo Domingo, Dominican Republic, Fulbright visiting professor of music, 1996; University of Miami, Coral Gables, FL, visiting professor of music, 1996-97; Brown University, Providence, RI, assistant professor of music, 1997-. Bowling Green State University, adjunct professor, 1995; Dominican Conservatory of Music, Fulbright visiting professor, 1996; lecturer at educational institutions. Saxophonist with a Latin jazz group and various Dominican music groups. **Publications:** Merengue: Dominican Music and Dominican Identity, 1997. Contributor to books. Contributor of articles and reviews to periodicals. **Address:** Department of Music, Brown University, Providence, RI 02912, U.S.A. **Online address:** paul_austerlitz@brown.edu

AUSTIN, Guy. British, b. 1966. **Genres:** Film. **Career:** University of Sheffield, England, lecturer in French, 1992-. **Publications:** Contemporary French Cinema: An Introduction, 1996; Claude Chabrol, 1999; Stars in Modern French Film, 2003. Contributor to French Cultural Studies. **Address:** Department of French, University of Sheffield, Sheffield S10 2TN, England.

AUSTIN, Jim. See REASONER, Livia Jane Washburn.

AUSTIN, M(ichel) M(ervyn). British (born Australia), b. 1943. **Genres:** History. **Career:** University of St. Andrews, Fife, Scotland, Lecturer, 1968-85, Sr. Lecturer in Ancient History, 1985-2000. **Publications:** Greece and Egypt in the Archaic Age, 1970; (with P. Vidal-Naquet) Economies et societes en Grece ancienne, 1972, 1973, as Economic and Social History of Ancient Greece: An Introduction, 1977; The Hellenistic World from Alexander to the Roman Conquest, 1981. **Address:** Dept. of Ancient History, University of St. Andrews, St. Andrews, Fife, Scotland.

AUSTIN, R. G. See LAMB, Nancy.

AVAKIAN, Arlene Voski. American, b. 1939. **Genres:** History, Women's studies and issues, Autobiography/Memoirs. **Career:** University of Massachusetts at Amherst, associate professor of women's studies, 1986-2001, director and professor of women's studies, 2001-; writer. Smith College, part-time member of social work faculty, 1990-93. **Publications:** Lion Woman's Legacy: An Armenian-American Memoir, 1992; (ed.) Through the Kitchen Window: Women Explore the Intimate Meaning of Food & Cooking, 1997; (co-ed.) African American Women and the Vote 1837-1965, 1997. **Address:** Women's Studies Program, 208 Bartlett, University of Massachusetts at Amherst, Amherst, MA 01003-0530, U.S.A. **Online address:** avakian@wost.umass.edu

AVELLA, Steven M. American, b. 1951. **Genres:** Theology/Religion. **Career:** Marquette University, Milwaukee, WI, associate professor of history, 1991-. **Publications:** (ed.) Milwaukee Catholicism, 1991; This Confident Church, 1992; (with E. Skerrett and E. Kantowicz) Catholicism, Chicago

Style, 1993; The History of the Society of the Divine Savior in the United States, Vol II: The Moment of Grace, 1994. **Address:** Department of History, Charles L. Coughlin Hall, Marquette University, Milwaukee, WI 53223, U.S.A.

AVERILL, Gage. American, b. 1954. **Genres:** Music. **Career:** Station WORT, Madison, WI, world music programmer, 1979-82, host of the talk show A Public Affair, 1980-82; Station KRAB, Seattle, WA, world music programmer, 1982-85; University of Washington, Seattle, instructor in music, 1986-89; Columbia University, NYC, visiting assistant professor of music, 1989-90; Wesleyan University, Middletown, CT, assistant professor, 1990-96, associate professor of music, 1996-97, director of graduate studies in music, 1993-, resident fellow at Center for the Humanities, 1992; New York University, Music Dept, associate professor, 1997-, head of Ethnomusicology Program, 1997-98, dept chair, 2000-. Speaker at colleges and universities; guest on TV and radio programs; coproducer of sound recordings; film consultant. **Publications:** (ed. with R. Ohmann, M. Curtin, and D. Shumway, and contrib.) Making and Selling Culture, 1996; A Day for the Hunter, a Day for the Prey: Popular Music and Power in Haiti, 1997; Four Parts, No Waiting: A Social History of American Barbershop Harmony. Contributor to books. Author of liner notes for sound recordings. Contributor of articles and reviews to periodicals. **Address:** Dept of Music, New York University, 24 Waverly Pl Rm 268, New York, NY 10003-6789, U.S.A. **Online address:** gage.averill@nyu.edu

AVERY, Evelyn. American, b. 1940. **Genres:** Literary criticism and history. **Career:** Towson University, Towson, MD, professor of English, 1975-, coordinator of Jewish studies, 1997-. Formerly taught at schools in New York, NY, and in Uganda. **Publications:** Rebels and Victims: The Fiction of Richard Wright and Bernard Malamud, 1979; Sex and the Modern Jewish Woman: An Annotated Bibliography, 1986; The Magic Worlds of Bernard Malamud, 2001. **Address:** Department of English, 218 Linthicum Hall, Towson University, 800 York Rd., Towson, MD 21252, U.S.A. **Online address:** eavery@towson.edu

AVERY, Fiona Kai. American. **Genres:** Agriculture/Forestry. **Career:** Writer, poet, archeologist, historian. **Publications:** No Honor: Set 1, Volumes 1-4, 2001; (with Billy Tan and Steve Firchow) Witchblade: Obakemono (graphic novel), 2002; Also author of The Lucky Strike (movie screenplay), 2000. Author of comic book series, writer for television and comic book series, interviewer for periodicals, and additional works represented in anthologies. **Address:** c/o Author Mail, Top Cow Productions Inc., 10390 Santa Monica Blvd., Los Angeles, CA 90025, U.S.A.

AVERY, Gillian (Elise). British, b. 1926. **Genres:** Novellas/Short stories, Children's fiction, Literary criticism and history. **Career:** Jr. Reporter, Surrey Mirror, Redhill, Surrey, 1944-47; Staff Member, Chambers Encyclopedia, London, 1947-50; Assistant Illustrations Ed., Clarendon Press, Oxford, 1950-54. **Publications:** The Warden's Niece, 1957; Trespassers at Charlcote, 1958; James without Thomas, 1959; The Elephant War, 1960; To Tame a Sister, 1961; The Greatest Gresham, 1962; The Peacock House, 1963; The Italian Spring, 1964; Mrs. Ewing, 1964; (with A. Bull) 19th Century Children: Heroes and Heroines in English Children's Stories 1780-1900, 1965; Call of the Valley, 1966; Victorian People in Life and Literature, 1970; A Likely Lad, 1971; Ellen's Birthday, 1971; Jemima and the Welsh Rabbit, 1972; The Echoing Green Memories of Victorian and Regency Youth, 1974; Ellen and the Queen, 1974; Book of Strange and Odd, 1975; Childhood's Pattern: A Study of the Heroes and Heroines of Children's Fiction 1770-1950, 1975; Freddie's Feet, 1976; Huck and Her Time Machine, 1977; Mouldy's Orphan, 1978; Sixpence, 1979; The Lost Railway, 1980; Onlookers, 1983; The Best Type of Girl: A History of Girls' Independent School, 1991; Behold the Child: American Children and Their Books, 1621-1922, 1994; The Everyman Anthology of Poetry for Children, 1994; Russian Fairy Tales, 1995; Cheltenham Ladies: A History of Cheltenham Ladies's College, 2003. EDITOR: J.H. Ewing, A Flat Iron for Farthing, 1959; J.H. Ewing, Jan of the Windmill, 1960; The Sapphire Treasury of Stories for Boys and Girls, 1960; In the Window Seat, 1960; A. Keary, Father Phim, 1962; Unforgettable Journeys, 1965; School Remembered, 1967; J.H. Ewing, A Great Emergency, and a Very Ill-Tempered Family, 1967; A. Lang, The Gold of Fairnilee and Other Stories, 1967; C. Yonge, Village Children, 1967; M. Roberts, Banning and Blessing, 1967; The Hole in the Wall and Other Stories, 1968; Brenda, Mrs. Gatty and F.H. Burnett, Victoria Bess and Others, 1968; G.E. Farrow, The Wallypug of Why, 1968; Brenda, Froggy's Little Brother, 1968; M.L. Molesworth, My New Home, 1968; anonymous, The Life and Adventures of Lady Anne, 1969; M. Roberts, Stephanie's Children, 1969; E.V. Lucas, Anne's Terrible Good Nature and Other Stories for Children, 1970; A. Keary, The Rival Kings, 1970; (with others) Authors' Choice 1, 1971; Red Letter Days,

1971; (with J. Briggs) Children & Their Books, 1989; (with K. Reynolds) Representations of Childhood Death, 1999. **Address:** 32 Charlbury Rd, Oxford OX2 6UU, England.

AVERY, Kevin J. American, b. 1950. **Genres:** Art/Art history. **Career:** Metropolitan Museum of Art, NYC, Chester fellow, 1983-84, Andrew Mellon fellow, 1984-85, associate curator of American paintings and sculpture, 1988-. Hunter College of the City University of New York, adjunct assistant professor, 1982-. **Publications:** (with P.L. Fodera) John Vanderlyn's Panoramic View of the Palace and Gardens of Versailles, 1988; Church's Great Picture; The Heart of the Andes, 1993. Author of exhibition catalogs. Contributor to art journals. **Address:** Department of American Paintings and Sculpture, Metropolitan Museum of Art, 1000 Fifth Ave., New York, NY 10028, U.S.A.

AVI. (Avi Wortis). American, b. 1937. **Genres:** Children's fiction, Young adult fiction. **Career:** Lincoln Center Library of the Performing Arts, staff member, 1962-70; Lambeth Public Library, staff member, 1968; Trenton State College, asst professor, humanities librarian, 1970-86; writer. **Publications:** Things That Sometimes Happen, 1970, rev. ed., 2002; Snail Tale, 1972; No More Magic, 1975; Captain Grey, 1977; Emily Upham's Revenge, 1978; Night Journeys, 1979; Encounter at Easton, 1980; The History of Helpless Harry, 1980; Man from the Sky, 1980; A Place Called Ugly, 1981; Who Stole the Wizard of Oz?, 1981; Sometimes I Think I Hear My Name, 1982; Shadrach's Crossing, 1983, as Smugglers Island, 1994; Devil's Race, 1984; The Fighting Ground, 1984; S.O.R. Losers, 1984; Bright Shadow, 1985; Wolf Rider, 1986; Romeo and Juliet, Together (and Alive!), at Last, 1987; Something Upstairs: A Tale of Ghosts, 1988; The Man Who Was Poe, 1989; The True Confession of Charlotte Doyle, 1990; Windcatcher, 1991; Nothing but the Truth, 1991; Blue Heron, 1992; Who Was That Masked Man, Anyway?, 1992; Punch with Judy, 1993; City of Light, City of Dark, 1993; The Barn, 1994; The Bird, The Frog, and the Light, 1994; Poppy, 1995; Tom, Babette and Simon, 1995; Beyond the Western Sea, vol. 1, 1996; The Escape from Home, vol. 2, 1996; Lord Kirkle's Money, 1996; Finding Providence, 1997; What Do Fish Have to Do with Anything?, 1997; Perloo the Bold, 1998; Poppy and Rye, 1998; Abigail Takes the Wheel, 1999; Ragweed, 1999; Midnight Magic, 1999; Keep Your Eye on Amanda, 1999; Amanda Joins the Circus, 1999; (with others) Second Sight, 1999; Ereth's Birthday, 2000; The Christmas Rat, 2000; The Secret School, 2001; Prairie School, 2001; Don't You Know There's a War On?, 2001; The Good Dog, 2001; Crispin, 2002 (Newbery Medal, 2003); Silent Movie, 2003; Mayor of Central Park, 2003; (with R. Vail) Never Mind!, 2004; End of the Beginning, 2004. **Address:** c/o Gale Hochman, Brandt & Hochman Literary Agents, 1501 Broadway Ste 2310, New York, NY 10036, U.S.A. **Online address:** awortis@uswest.net

AVISE, John C. American. **Genres:** Natural history, Sciences, Zoology. **Career:** University of Georgia, Athens, assistant professor of zoology, 1975-79, associate professor, 1979-84, professor of genetics, 1984-. **Publications:** Molecular Markers: Natural History and Evolution, 1994; (ed. with J.L. Hamrick) Conservation Genetics: Case Histories from Nature, 1996; The Genetic Gods: Evolution and Belief in Human Affairs, 1998; Phylogeography: The History and Formation of Species, 1999; Captivating Life: A Naturalist in the Age of Genetics, 2001; Genetics in the Wild, 2002; The Hope, Hype, and Reality of Genetic Engineering, 2003. Contributor to scientific journals. **Address:** Department of Genetics, University of Georgia, Athens, GA 30602, U.S.A.

AVNI, Haim. Israeli (born Austria), b. 1930. **Genres:** Cultural/Ethnic topics, History. **Career:** Hebrew University of Jerusalem, Israel, professor of contemporary Jewish history and head of Division for Latin America, Spain, and Portugal, both 1967-, and head of institute, 1981-83, 1991-93, all at Institute for Contemporary Jewry, senior lecturer, 1974-79, associate professor, 1979-85, professor, 1985-. Academic co-director for Judaic Studies Program, Universidad Iberoamericana, Mexico City, 1981-98; director of Latin American Project, International Center for University Teaching of Jewish Civilization, 1983-95; academic director of the Central Zionist Archives, Jerusalem, 2000-. **Publications:** Argentine Jewry: Its Socio-Political Status and Organizational Patterns (in Hebrew and English), 1972; Argentine, the Promised Land: Baron de Hirsch's Colonization Project in the Argentine Republic (in Hebrew), 1973; Spain, the Jews, and Franco, 1982; Argentina y la historia de la immigracion Judia, 1810-1950 (in Spanish and Hebrew), 1983; Emancipation and Jewish Education: A Century of Argentinian Jewry's Experience, 1884-1984 (in Hebrew), 1985; Argentina and the Jews: A History of Jewish Migration, 1991; Judios en America: Cinco Siglos de Historia, 1992. EDITOR: Estudios Judaicos en Universidades Latinoamericanas, 1985; (with G. Shimoni) Zionism and Its Jewish Opponents (in Hebrew),

1990; (with L. Senkman) Del campo al campo, colonos de Argentina en Israel, 1993; (with S. Steindling) D. Steindling, Hitting Back, an Austrian Jew in the French Resistance, 2000. **Address:** Division for Latin America, Spain, and Portugal, Institute of Contemporary Jewry, Hebrew University of Jerusalem, Mount Scopus, 91905 Jerusalem, Israel. **Online address:** heavni@h2.hum.huji.ac.il

AVRAMIDES, Anita. American, b. 1952. **Genres:** Philosophy. **Career:** Oxford University, Oxford, England, lecturer at Oriel College, 1980, Exeter College, 1981-82, Balliol College, 1982, Queen's College, 1983-90. Bedford College, visiting lecturer, 1980-82; St. Hilda's College, Oxford University, Southover Manor Trust fellow in philosophy, 1990-. **Publications:** Meaning and Mind: An Examination of a Gricean Account of Meaning, 1989; Women of Ideas, 1995; Other Minds, 2001. **Address:** Department of Philosophy, St. Hilda's College, Oxford University, Oxford OX1 4AW, England. **Online address:** anita.avramides@st-hildas.ox.ac.uk

AVZ. See **VON ZELEWSKY, Alexander.**

AWDRY, Christopher Vere. British, b. 1940. **Genres:** Novellas/Short stories, Children's fiction, Transportation. **Career:** Writer. **Publications:** Really Useful Engines, 1983; James and the Diesel Engines, 1984; Great Little Engines, 1985; More about Thomas the Tank Engine, 1986; Gordon, the High-speed Engine, 1987; Percy and the Postman: Sticker Book, 1988; Thomas and the Evil Diesel, 1988; Thomas and the Lost Cat: Sticker Book, 1988; Thomas and the Missing Christmas Tree, 1988; Toby, Trucks and Trouble, 1988; Henry Pulls the Express Train, 1989; James and the Rescue Train, 1989; Meet Thomas the Tank Engine and His Friends, 1989; Percy, the Seaside Train, 1989; Thomas and the Twins, 1989; Thomas's Book of Colours, 1989; Thomas's Big Book of Games and Puzzles, 1989; Thomas and the Goods Train, 1989; Thomas Gets Tricked and Other Stories, 1989; Thomas the Tank Engine and the Great Race, 1989; Thomas the Tank Engine's Noisy Trip, 1989; Trouble for Thomas and Other Stories, 1989; Up and Down with Percy, 1989; Thomas the Tank Engine's ABC's, 1990; Breakfast Time for Thomas, 1990; Jock the New Engine, 1990; Catch Me, Catch Me!, 1990; Happy Birthday, Thomas!, 1990; Henry and the Elephant, 1990; Encyclopedia of British Railway Companies, 1990; Thomas Visits a Farm, 1991; Thomas and the Great Railway Show, 1991; Thomas Comes Home, 1992; Brunel's Broad Gauge Railway, 1992; Tell the Time with Thomas, 1992; Henry and the Express, 1993; Over the Summitt, 1993; Wilbert the Forest Engine, 1994; The Fat Controller's Engines, 1995; Awdry's Steam Railways, 1995; Thomas the Tank Engine Easy to Read Treasury, 1995; New Little Engine, 1996; Railways Galore, 1996. **Address:** The Old Station House, Oundle, Peterborough PE8 5LA, England.

AWE, Susan C. American, b. 1948. **Genres:** Reference. **Career:** University of Wisconsin-Madison, information specialist, 1980-87; Northern Arizona University, Flagstaff, business reference librarian, 198790, senior reference librarian, 1988-90; Natrona County Public Library, Casper, WY, supervisor of Information Services Department, 1990-91; Jefferson County Library System, Arvada Library, Arvada, CO, library manager, 1991-. **Publications:** (ed.) The ARBA Guide to Subject Encyclopedias and Dictionaries, 2nd edition, 1997. Contributor of articles and reviews to library journals and other periodicals. **Address:** Arvada Library, Jefferson County Library System, 8555 West 57th Ave., Arvada, CO 80002, U.S.A. **Online address:** sawe@jefferson.lib.co.us

AWIAKTA, Marilou. American, b. 1936. **Genres:** Anthropology/Ethnology, History, Women's studies and issues. **Career:** Poet and author. Lecturer at institutions. Worked as civilian liaison officer and translator for US Air Force, Laon Air Force Base, France, 1964-67. Consultant for film The Good Mind (Native American Spirituality), 1982; consultant for Aaron Copland Festival. Has performed her works on television and radio programs. **Publications:** Abiding Appalachia: Where Mountain and Atom Meet, 1978, 8th ed., 1995; Rising Fawn and the Fire Mystery: A Story of Heritage, Family, and Courage, 1833 (children's book), 1983, rev. ed., 1992; Selu: Seeking the Corn-Mother's Wisdom, 1993. MONOGRAPHS: A Bridge Is a Gift to the People, 1994; Grandmothers, 1995; Southern Women, 1996; Southeastern Indian Women, 1996. Contributor to anthologies and periodicals. **Address:** c/o Fulcrum Publishing, 16100 Table Mtn Pky #300, Golden, CO 80403, U.S.A. **Online address:** fulcrum@fulcrum-books.com

AWOONOR, Kofi. Ghanaian, b. 1935. **Genres:** Novels, Plays/Screenplays, Poetry, Novellas/Short stories. **Career:** Research Fellow, Institute of African Studies, Legon, 1960-64; Director, Ghana Ministry of Information Film Corp., 1964-67; Research Fellow, University College, London, 1967-68; Assistant Professor, 1968-72, and Associate Professor, 1973-75, State University of New York at Stony Brook; Visiting Professor, University of Texas, Austin, 1972-73; Professor, University of Cape Coast, Ghana, 1977-82; Ambassador of Ghana to Brazil, 1983-88; Ghana's Ambassador to Cuba, 1988-90; Ghana's Ambassador to the United Nations, 1990-94. Former Ed., Okyeame, Accra, and Co-Ed., Black Orpheus, Ibadan. Recipient, Commonwealth Poetry Prize, 1989. **Publications:** Rediscovery and Other Poems, 1964; This Earth, My Brother: An Allegorical Tale of Africa, 1970; (ed. with G. Adali-Martty) Messages: Poems from Ghana, 1970; Night of My Blood (poetry), 1971; Ancestral Power (play), 1972; Lament (play), 1972; Ride Me, Memory (poetry), 1973; Guardians of the Sacred Word (poetry), 1974; The Breast of the Earth (essays), 1975; The House by the Sea (poetry), 1978; The Ghana Revolution (personal perspective), 1984; Fire in the Valley (folk stories), 1984; Until the Morning After: Collected Poems 1963-1985, 1987; Ghana: A Political History, 1990; Comes the Voyager at Last (fiction), 1992; Latin American and Caribbean Notebook (poetry), 1993; Africa: The Marginalized Continent, 1995. **Address:** PO Box C 536, Accra, Ghana.

AWRET, Irene. Israeli/American (born Germany), b. 1921. **Genres:** Children's fiction, Young adult fiction, Autobiography/Memoirs. **Career:** Painter and ceramist, with group and solo shows in Israel and the eastern United States; work represented at Jewish Museum of New York, in schools in Montgomery County, Md., and at synagogue in Skokie, Ill.; creator of peace posters presented by the government of Israel to Egyptian President Anwar Sadat. Past chairperson of Safed Artists' Colony. **Publications:** Days of Honey: The Tunisian Boyhood of Rafael Uzan (juvenile), 1985; But First You Have to Catch Me (memoir), 2003. **Address:** c/o Leona Schecter, 3748 Huntington NW, Washington, DC 20015, U.S.A. **Online address:** ireneawret@hotmail.com

AXELROD, Amy. American. **Genres:** Children's fiction. **Career:** Author. **Publications:** The News Hounds in the Great Balloon Race: A Geography Adventure, 2000; The News Hounds Catch a Wave: A Geography Adventure, 2001; My Last Chance Brother, 2002. PIGS WILL BE PIGS SERIES: Pigs Will Be Pigs, 1994; Pigs on a Blanket, 1996; Pigs Go to Market: Fun with Math and Shopping, 1997; Pigs in the Pantry: Fun with Math and Cooking, 1997; Pigs on the Ball: Fun with Math and Sports, 1998; Pigs on the Move: Fun with Math and Travel, 1999; Pigs at Odds: Fun with Math and Games, 2000; Pigs in the Corner: Fun with Math and Dance, 2001. **Address:** c/o Dutton's Childrens Books Publicity, 345 Hudson St., New York, NY 10014, U.S.A.

AXELROD, Mark (R.). American, b. 1946. **Genres:** Plays/Screenplays, Literary criticism and history, Novels. **Career:** University of Edinburgh, Edinburgh, Scotland, lecturer, 1989-90; Chapman University, Orange, CA, associate professor of comparative literature, 1990-; artist and writer. Art work exhibited at institutions and galleries. Writer in residence at Governor Dummer Academy and Metropolitan Arts Council of Indianapolis, both 1976. **Publications:** Neville Chamberlain's Chimera; or, Nine Metaphors of Vision, 1979; An Author's Mother (screenplay), 1990; The Politics of Style in the Fiction of Balzac, Beckett, and Cortazar, 1992; Bombay California; or, Hollywood, Somewhere West of Vine (novel), 1994; (ed., contrib., and author of intro.) Review of Contemporary Fiction, 1995; Ti amo Lucia Olivetti (2-act play); Cardboard Castles (novel), 1996; Cloud Castles (novel), 1998; Of Gold & Ashes (screenplay), 1998; Poetics of Novels (literary criticism), 1999; Capital Castles (novel), 2000; Aspects of the Screenplay (film), 2001. Author of teleplays. Work represented in anthologies and periodicals. **Address:** Department of English and Comparative Literature, Chapman University, Orange, CA 92866, U.S.A. **Online address:** axelrod@chapman.edu

AXLER, Leo. See LAZUTA, Gene.

AXTON, David. See KOONTZ, Dean R(ay).

AYALA, Francisco José. American (born Spain), b. 1934. **Genres:** Biology, Philosophy. **Career:** Rockefeller University, New York, Research Associate, 1964-65, Assistant Professor, 1967-71; Providence College, Rhode Island, Assistant Professor, 1965-67; University of California, Davis, Professor of Genetics (joined faculty 1971; Director, Institute of Ecology, 1977-81; Associate Dean of Environmental Studies, 1977-81); University of California, Irvine, Distinguished Professor of Biology, 1987-89, Donald Bren Professor of Biological Sciences, 1989-, University Professor, 2003-. **Publications:** Studies in the Philosophy of Biology, 1974; Molecular Evolution, 1976; Evolution, 1977; Evolving: The Theory and Processes of Organic Evolution, 1979; Population and Evolutionary Genetics, 1982; Modern Genetics, 2nd ed., 1984. **Address:** Dept of Ecology and Evolutionary Biology, University of California, Irvine, CA 92697-2525, U.S.A. **Online address:** fjayala@uci.edu

AYCKBOURN, Sir Alan. British, b. 1939. **Genres:** Plays/Screenplays, Theatre. **Career:** Playwright. BBC Radio Drama Producer, 1964-70; Artistic Director, Stephen Joseph Theatre, Scarborough, N. Yorks., 1971-; National Theatre Company Director, 1986-88. Knighted 1997. **Publications:** PLAYS: Mr Whatnot, 1963; Relatively Speaking, 1965; How the Other Half Loves, 1969; Ernie's Incredible Illucinations, 1971; Time and Time Again, 1971; Absurd Person Singular, 1972; The Norman Conquests Trilogy (Table Manners; Living Together; Round and Round the Garden), 1973; Absent Friends, 1974; Confusions, 1974; Bedroom Farce, 1975; Just between Ourselves, 1976; Ten Times Table, 1977; Joking Apart, 1978; Family Circles, 1978; Sisterly Feelings, 1979; Taking Steps, 1979; Suburban Strains, 1980; Season's Greetings, 1980; Way Upstream, 1981; Me, Myself & I, 1981; Intimate Exchanges, 1982; It Could Be Any One of Us, 1983; A Chorus of Disapproval, 1984; Woman in Mind, 1985; A Small Family Business, 1987; Henceforward..., 1987; Man of the Moment, 1988; Mr. A's Amazing Maze Plays, 1988; The Revengers' Comedies, 1989; Invisible Friends, 1989; Body Language, 1990; This Is Where We Came In, 1990; Callisto 5, 1990; Wildest Dreams 1991; My Very Own Story, 1991; Time of My Life, 1992; Dreams from a Summer House, 1992; Communicating Doors, 1994; A Word from Our Sponsor, 1995; The Champion of Paribanou, 1996; Things We Do for Love, 1997; Comic Potential, 1998; The Boy Who Fell into a Book, 1998; Gizmo, 1999; House & Garden, 1999; Whenever, 2000; Damsels in Distress Trilogy (GamePlan; FlatSpin; RolePlay), 2001; Snake in the Grass, 2002; The Jollies, 2002; Orvin-Champion of Champions, 2003; My Sister Sadie, 2003. NON-FICTION: (with I. Watson) Conversations with Ayckbourn, 1981; The Crafty Art of Playmaking, 2002. **Address:** c/o Casarotto Ramsay & Associates, National House, 60-66 Wardour St, London W1V 4ND, England.

AYCLIFFE, Jonathan. See MACEOIN, Denis.

AYERS, William. American, b. 1944. **Genres:** Education. **Career:** University of Illinois at Chicago, Chicago, IL, Distinguished Professor of Education. Taught at private schools in Ann Arbor, MI, and Cleveland, OH. **Publications:** The Good Preschool Teacher: Six Teachers Reflect on Their Lives, 1989; To Teach: The Journey of a Teacher, 1993; A Kind and Just Parent: The Children of Juvenile Court, 1997; Teaching for Social Justice: A Democracy and Reader, 1998; (as Bill Ayers) Fugitive Days: A Memoir, 2001. EDITOR: (with W.H. Schubert) Teacher Lore: Learning from Our Own Experience, 1992; To Become a Teacher: Making a Difference in Children's Lives, 1995; (with P. Ford) City Kids, City Teachers: Reports from the Front Row, 1996; (with J. Miller) A Light in Dark Times: Maxine Green and the Conversation, 1998; (with M. Klonsky and G. Lyon) A Simple Justice: The Challenge of Small Schools, 2000; (with R. Ayers and B. Dohrn) Zero Tolerance: Resisting the Drive for Punishment: A Handbook for Parents, Students, Educators, and Citizens, 2002. **Address:** College of Education, University of Illinois at Chicago, 1040 West Harrison 3145, Chicago, IL 60607, U.S.A. **Online address:** bayers@uic.edu

AYITTEY, George B. N. Ghanaian, b. 1945. **Genres:** Politics/Government, Area studies. **Career:** Economist, writer. American University, Washington, DC, visiting associate professor. **Publications:** Indigenous African Institutions, 1991; Africa Betrayed, 1992; Africa in Chaos, 1998. Contributor to works concerning African social and economic policy. **Address:** c/o St. Martin's Press, 175 Fifth Ave., Rm. 1715, New York, NY 10010, U.S.A. **Online address:** ayittey@american.edu

AYLEN, Leo. British (born Republic of South Africa). **Genres:** Plays/Screenplays, Poetry, Theatre. **Career:** Freelance writer and film dir. Poet-in-Residence, Fairleigh Dickinson University, New Jersey, 1972-74; Hooker Distinguished Visiting Professor, McMaster University, Ontario, 1982; former Producer for BBC TV. **Publications:** Greek Tragedy and the Modern World, 1964; Discontinued Design, 1969; I Odysseus, 1971; Greece for Everyone, 1976; Sunflower, 1976; Return to Zululand, 1980; The Apples of Youth, 1980; Red Alert: This Is a God Warning, 1981; Jumping-Shoes, 1983; The Greek Theater, 1985; Rhymoceros, 1989; Dancing the Impossible-New & Selected Poems, 1997; (co) Gods and Generals (screenplay), 2003. **Address:** The Coach House, Court St, Sherston, Malmesbury, Wilts. SN16 0LL, England. **Online address:** leo@leoaylen.demon.co.uk; www.leoaylen.com

AYLESWORTH, Jim. American, b. 1943. **Genres:** Children's fiction. **Career:** First grade teacher, Oak Park, IL, 1971-96; professor of children's literature; writer, 1980-. **Publications:** CHILDREN'S FICTION: Hush Up! 1980; Tonight's the Night, 1981; Mary's Mirror, 1982; Siren in the Night, 1983; The Bad Dream, 1985; Shenandoah, Noah, 1985; Two Terrible Frights, 1987; One Crow, 1988; Hanna's Hog, 1988; Mother Halverson's New Cat, 1989; Mr. McGill Goes to Town, 1989; The Completed Hickory Dickory

Doc, 1990; Country Crossing, 1991; The Folks in the Valley, 1991; Old Black Fly, 1992; The Cat & the Fiddle & More, 1992; The Good-Night Kiss, 1993; My Son John, 1994; McGraw's Emporium, 1995; Wake Up, Little Children, 1996; My Sister's Rusty Bike, 1996; Teddy Bear Tears, 1997; The Gingerbread Man, 1998; Through the Night, 1998; Jim Aylesworth's Book of Bedtime Stories, 1998; Aunt Pitty Patty's Piggy, 1999; The Full Belly Bowl, 1999; The Tale of Tricky Fox, 2001; The Burger and the Hot Dog, 2001; Naughty Little Monkeys, 2003; Goldilocks and the Three Bears, 2003. **Address:** 55 W Delaware Place #407, Chicago, IL 60610, U.S.A. **Online address:** oldfly@ayles.com; www.ayles.com

AYRES, E. C. (Gene Ayres). American, b. 1946. **Genres:** Mystery/Crime/Suspense, Plays/Screenplays, Literary criticism and history. **Career:** Producer, writer and director of educational films, 1969-72; Children's Television Workshop, NYC, producer, writer and director, 1973-74; producer, writer and director for television network documentaries and public television programs, 1975-80; Jack Arnold Productions, Universal City, CA, writer and associate producer, 1980-82; Roll Over Beethoven Productions, Los Angeles, CA, feature film development writer, 1983-89; WTSP-TV, St. Petersburg, FL, television film critic, 1990-91; 2020 Productions, Santa Fe, NM, writer and creative producer, 1992-94; freelance novelist, 1994-. Future Wave Inc., writer and creative producer, 1992-94. Eckerd College, guest lecturer for Elderhostel Program of Continuing Education. Supporter of environmental causes. **Publications:** MYSTERIES: Hour of the Manatee, 1994; Eye of the Gator, 1995; Night of the Panther, 1997; Lair of the Lizard, 1998. OTHER: Hunter (feature film), 1994. Author of television episodes for animation series. Contributor to periodicals. **Address:** 1620 Fairway Ave S, St. Petersburg, FL 33712, U.S.A. **Online address:** ECAyres@juno.com

AYRES, Mary Jo. American, b. 1953. **Genres:** Education. **Career:** Teacher in Leland, MS, 1975-93; speaker, trainer, consultant. **Publications:** Happy Teaching and Natural Learning, Vol. I, 1992, Vol. II, 1994; Natural Learning from A-Z, 1997, 2nd ed., 2002. SOUND RECORDINGS: Natural Learning Fun Songs, 1999; More Natural Songs from A-Z; Natural Learning Songs from A-Z. **Address:** Natural Learning, 103 Sycamore St, Leland, MS 38756, U.S.A. **Online address:** nlearn@naturallearning.com

AYRES, Pam. British, b. 1947. **Genres:** Children's fiction, Poetry, Humor/Satire. **Career:** Writer and performer in television, film, and radio, 1975-. Performs one-woman comedy show throughout Great Britain and internationally; hosted weekly BBC radio show, 1996-99. **Publications:** FOR CHILDREN: When Dad Cuts down the Chestnut Tree, 1988; When Dad Fills in the Garden Pond, 1988; Guess What?, 1988; Guess Who?, 1988; Piggo and the Nosebag, 1991; The Bear Who Was Left Behind, 1991; Piggo Has a Train Ride, 1992; Jack Crater, 1992; Guess Where?, 1994; Guess Why?, 1994; The Nubbler, 1997. OTHER: The Works: Selected Poems (light verse), 1992; With These Hands (poetry), 1997. **Address:** PO Box 64, Cirencester, Gloucestershire GL7 5YD, England. **Online address:** acornents@btconnect.com; www.pamayres.com

AYRES, Philip. Australian, b. 1944. **Genres:** Novels, Novellas/Short stories, History, Literary criticism and history. **Career:** Monash University, Clayton, Australia, lecturer, 1972-79, senior lecturer in English, 1980-94, associate professor, 1995-; Vassar College, visiting professor, 1993; Boston University, visiting fellow and professor, 2001. **Publications:** The Revenger's Tragedy, 1977; The English Roman Life, 1980; Malcolm Fraser: A Biography, 1987; Classical Culture and the Idea of Rome in Eighteenth-Century England, 1997; Douglas Mawson: A Biography, 1999; Owen Dixon, 2003. EDITOR: Ben Jonson, Sejanus His Fall, 1990; Shaftesbury, Characteristics, 1999. Contributor to scholarly journals. Contributor of short stories to periodicals. **Address:** Department of English, Monash University, Clayton, VIC 3168, Australia.

AYRES, Thomas (R.). American, b. 1936. **Genres:** History, Local history/Rural topics, Mythology/Folklore, Trivia/Facts. **Career:** Freelance writer. Dallas Times Herald, Dallas, TX, state features writer and investigative reporter; WFAA-TV, Dallas, TX, investigative reporter; also worked as radio commentator. **Publications:** That's Not in My American History Book, 2000; Dark and Bloody Ground, 2001; Dammit Sam and Me, 2002. Newspaper columnist. Contributor to magazines and newspapers. **Address:** 1383 Transport Rd, Jonesboro, LA 71251, U.S.A. **Online address:** tayres@pineynet.com

AZOULAY, Dan. Canadian, b. 1960. **Genres:** History. **Career:** Trent University, Peterborough, ON, sessional instructor, 1989-2002; McMaster University, Hamilton, OH, sessional instructor in history, 1992-; York University, North York, ON, sessional instructor in history, 1995-. **Publications:** Keeping the Dream Alive: The Survival of the Ontario CCF/NDP, 1950-1963, 1997; (ed.) Canadian Political Parties: Historical Readings, 1998; Only the Lonely: Finding Romance in the Personal Columns of the Western Home Monthly, 1905-1924. Contributor to books. Contributor of articles and reviews to periodicals.

B

B., Dick. *See* BURNS, Richard Gordon.

BAANTJER, Albert Cornelis. Dutch, b. 1923. **Genres:** Mystery/Crime/ Suspense. **Career:** Worked as a clerk, 1939-43; Amsterdam Police Force, Amsterdam, Holland, police officer, 1945-54, detective, 1955-83; writer. Author of column for Het Nieuws van de Dag. **Publications:** INSPECTOR De COCK DETECTIVE NOVELS: De Cock en het sombere naakt, 1964, trans. as DeKok and the Somber Nude, 1992; De Cock en de wurger op zondag, 1965, trans. as DeKok and the Sunday Strangler, 1993; De Cock en het lijk in de kerstnacht, 1965, trans. as DeKok and the Corpse on Christmas Eve, 1993; De Cock en de dode harlekijn, 1968, trans. as DeKok and the Dead Harlequin, 1993; De Cock en de treurende kater, 1969, trans. as De-Kok and the Sorrowing Tomcat, 1993; De Cock en de ontgoochelde dode, 1970, trans. as DeKok and the Disillusioned Corpse, 1993; De Cock en de zorgvuldige moordenaar, 1971, trans. as DeKok and the Careful Killer, 1993; De Cock en de romance in moord, 1972, trans. as DeKok and the Romantic Murder, 1993; De Cock en de stervende wandelaar, 1972, trans. as DeKok and the Dying Stroller, 1993; De Cock en het lijk aan de kerkmuur, 1973, trans. as DeKok and the Corpse on the Church Wall, 1993; De Cock en de dansende dood, 1974, trans. as DeKok and the Dancing Death, 1993; De Cock en de naakte juffer, 1978, trans. as DeKok and the Naked Lady, 1993; De Cock en de broeders van de zachte dood (title means: DeKok and the Brothers of the Easy Death), 1979; De Cock en het dodelijk akkoord (DeKok and the Deadly Accord), 1980; De Cock en moord in seance (DeKok and the Murder in Seance), 1981; De Cock en moord in extase (DeKok and the Murder in Ecstacy), 1982; De Cock en de smekende dood (DeKok and the Begging Death), 1982; De Cock en de ganzen van de dood (DeKok and the Geese of Death), 1983; De Cock en moord op melodie (DeKok and the Murder by Melody), 1983; De Cock en de dood van een clown (DeKok and the Death of a Clown), 1984; De Cock en een variant op moord (DeKok and the Variations on Murder), 1984; De Cock en moord op termijn (DeKok and the Murder by Installments), 1985; De Cock en moord op de Bloedberg (DeKok and the Murder on Blood Mountain), 1985; De Cock en de dode minnaars (DeKok and the Dead Lovers), 1986; De Cock en het masker van de dood (DeKok and the Mask of Death), 1987; De Cock en het lijk op re-tour (DeKok and the Corpse by Return), 1987; De Cock en moord in brons (DeKok and Murder in Bronze), 1988; De Cock en de dodelijke dreiging (DeKok and the Deadly Warning), 1988; De Cock en moord eerste klasse (DeKok and Murder First Class), 1989; De Cock en de bloedwraak (DeKok and the Vendetta), 1989; De Cock en moord a la carte, 1990, trans. as De-Kok and Murder on the Menu, 1992; De Cock en een moord in beeld (DeKok and Murder Depicted), 1990; De Cock en dans macabre (DeKok and Dance Macabre), 1991; De Cock en de onluisterende dood (DeKok and the Disfiguring Death), 1991; De Cock en een duivels complot (DeKok and the Devil's Conspiracy), 1992; De Cock en het duel in de nacht (Dekok and the Duel at Night), 1992; De Cock en kogels voor een bruid (DeKok and Bullets for the Bride), 1993; De Cock en de dood van een profeet (DeKok and the Death of a Prophet), 1993; Murder in Amsterdam (contains DeKok and the Sunday Strangler and DeKok and the Corpse on Christmas Eve), 1993; De Cock en Kogch voor een brunid, 1993; De Cock en de dode meesters (DeKok and the Dead Masters), 1994; De Cock en de sluimerende dood (DeKok and the Dozing Death), 1994; De Cock en 't wassend kwadd (DeKok and the Rising of Evil), 1995; De Cock en het roodsatijnen nachthemd (DeKok and the Red Satin Nightshirt), 1996; De Cock en moord bij maanlicht (DeKok and the Moonlit Murder), 1996; De Cock en de geur van rottend hout (DeKok and the Smell of Rotting Wood), 1996; De Cock en een dodelijk rendez-vou (DeKok and a Deadly Rendez-vous), 1997; De Cock en tranen aan de Leie (DeKok and Tears at the Leie), 1997; De Cock en het likj op drift (DeKok and a Body Adrift), 1998; De Cock en de onsterfelijke dood (DeKok and the Immortal Death), 1998; De Cock en de dood in antiek (DeKok and Death in Antiques), 1999; De Cock en een deal met de duivel (DeKok and a Deal with the Devil), 1999; De Cock en dood door hamerslag (DeKok and Death by a Stroke of a Hammer), 2000; De Cock en de dwaze maagden (DeKok and the Foolish Virgins), 2000; De Cock en de dode tempeliers (DeKok and the Dead Templars), 2001; De Cock en de blijde Bacchus (DeKok and the Happy Bacchus), 2001; De Cock en moord op bestelling (DeKok and Murder on Delivery), 2002; De Cock en de dood van de Helende Meesters (DeKok and the Death of the Great Healers), 2002; De Cock en de moord in reclame (DeKok and the Murder in Advertising), 2003; De Cock en geen excuus veer moord (DeKok and No Excuse for Murder), 2003; De Cock en de gebrand-merlite doden (DeKok and the Branded Dead), 2004; De Cock en een veld papavers (DeKok and a Field of Poppies), 2004. OTHER DETECTIVE NOVELS: Het mysterie van de doodshoofden (title means: The Mystery of the Skulls), 1963; De dertien katten (The 13 Cats), 1963; Een strop voor Bobbie (A Loss for Bobbie), 1964; Doden spreken niet (Dead Men Tell No Tales), 1966, rev. ed., 1981; De moord op Anna Bentveld (The Murder of Anna Bentveld), 1967; Het moraal van het cliche (The Moral of the Cliche), 1981; Moord en doodslag in het Warmoesstraat (Murder and Mayhem in Warmoes Street), 1982; De zotte Warmoesstraat (That Crazy Warmoes Street), 1984; De misdaadmachine van de Warmoesstraat (The Crime Machine of Warmoes Street), 1985; De magische zeven (The Magic 7), 1986; Het achtste wonder (The 8th Wonder), 1987. OTHER: Vijf maal acht grijpt in (stories; title means: 9-1-1 Responds), 1959; Leerboekje recherche (teaching manual; Plain Clothes Police Manual), 1977; Baantjer vertelt (collected columns; Baantjer Talks), vol. 1, 1978, vol. 2, 1979, vol. 3, 1980; Misdaad in het verleden (nonfiction; Crimes of the Past), 1982; Script voor Moord in extase (screenplay), 1984; Ik heb mijn man vermoord (story; I Killed My Husband), 1986; Negen heit de klok (collected columns; Nine O'Clock and All Is Well), 1988; Een tien met een griffel (collected columns; Whipped Cream and a Cherry on Top), 1988; Het malle elfje (collected columns; The Silly Little Elf), 1989; Een, twee, hopla (collected columns; One, Two, Skiddoo), 1991. **Address:** Poortweydt 4, 1671 RC Medemblik, Netherlands.

BAARS, Bernard J(oseph). American (born Netherlands), b. 1946. **Genres:** Psychology. **Career:** State University of New York at Stony Brook, assistant professor of psychology, 1977; University of California, San Diego, La Jolla, Sloan Cognitive Science Scholar at Center for Human Information Process-ing, 1979-80; University of California, San Francisco, visiting scientist in John D. and Catherine T. MacArthur Foundation Program on Conscious and Unconscious Mental Processes, at Langley Porter Neuropsychiatric Institute, 1985-86; Wright Institute, Berkeley, CA, associate professor, 1986-. University of Wisconsin-Milwaukee, university fellow, 1975; University of Minnesota-Twin Cities, traveling scholar, Center for Research in Human Learning, 1975. Appeared in the threepart television program Thinking Al-lowed, broadcast by Public Broadcasting Service in 1994. **Publications:** The Cognitive Revolution in Psychology, 1986; A Cognitive Theory of Conscious-ness, 1988; (ed.) The Experimental Psychology of Human Error: Implica-tions for the Architecture of Voluntary Control, 1992; In the Theater of Consciousness: The Workspace of the Mind, 1996. Contributor to books and scientific journals. **Address:** 3616 Chestnut St. No. 3, Lafayette, CA 94549, U.S.A. **Online address:** bbaars@wrightinst.edu

BABB, Sanora. American, b. 1907. **Genres:** Novels, Novellas/Short stories, Poetry. **Career:** Newspaper reporter; University of California Extension, Los Angeles, teacher of short story writing, 1958. **Publications:** The Lost Traveler, 1958; An Owl on Every Post, 1970; The Dark Earth (stories), 1987; Cry of the Tinamou (stories), 1998; Told in the Seed (poems), 1999. Contributor to periodicals and books. **Address:** 1562 Queens Rd, West Hollywood, CA 90069, U.S.A.

BABB, Valerie (Melissa). American, b. 1955. **Genres:** Biography, Local history/Rural topics, Cultural/Ethnic topics, Literary criticism and history. **Career:** Georgetown University, Washington, DC, asspciate professor of English, 1981-. **Publications:** Ernest Gaines, 1991; (with C.R. Gibbs and K.M. Lesko) Black Georgetown Remembered: A History of Its Black Community from the Founding of "The Town of George" in 1751 to the Present Day, 1991. Contributor to scholarly publications.

BABBITT, Natalie. American, b. 1932. **Genres:** Children's fiction, Young adult fiction. **Publications:** Dick Foote and the Shark, 1967; Phoebe's Revolt, 1968; The Search for the Delicious, 1969; Kneeknock Rise, 1970; The Something, 1970; Goody Hall, 1971; The Devil's Storybook, 1974; Tuck Everlasting, 1975; The Eyes of the Amaryllis, 1977; Herbert Rowbarge, 1982; The Devil's Other Storybook, 1984; Nellie: A Cat on Her Own, 1989; Bub-Or the Very Best Thing, 1994; (reteller) Ouch!: A Tale from Grimm, 1998; Elsie Times Eight, 2001. Illustrator of books by V. Worth. **Address:** 81 Benefit St, Providence, RI 02904, U.S.A.

BABBITT, Susan E. Canadian (born United States), b. 1953. **Genres:** Philosophy. **Career:** Queen's University, Kingston, Ontario, assistant professor of philosophy, 1990-. **Publications:** Impossible Dreams: Rationality, Integrity, and Moral Imagination, 1996. Contributor of articles and reviews to books and scholarly journals. **Address:** Department of Philosophy, Watson Hall, Queen's University, Kingston, ON, Canada K7L 3N6. **Online address:** babbitts@qucdn.queensu.ca

BABER, Carolyn Stonnell. American, b. 1936. **Genres:** Novels, Novellas/Short stories, Romance/Historical, Animals/Pets, Children's non-fiction, Autobiography/Memoirs, Biography, Illustrations. **Career:** Elementary schoolteacher at public schools in Cumberland County, VA, 1963-75, elementary supervisor, 1976-80; Huguenot Academy, Powhatan, VA, elementary teacher, 1985-89; Southside Livestock Markets Inc., Blackstone, VA, president, 1993-. Stonnell Timberlands, Powhatan, Amelia, and Cumberland, VA, manager, 1979-; Gibralter Wood Corp., Cumberland, president, 1981-85. Virginia Federation of Garden Clubs, nature conservancy chairperson for Piedmont District, 1993-96, state board, 1996-. **Publications:** Pony, 1991; Little Billy, 1994. Contributor to magazines. **Address:** Doubletree Farm, 246 Meador Rd, Cumberland, VA 23040, U.S.A.

BABICH, Babette E. American, b. 1956. **Genres:** Philosophy. **Career:** Denison University, Granville, OH, visiting assistant professor, 1987-88; Marquette University, Milwaukee, WI, assistant professor of philosophy, 1988-89; Fordham University, NYC, professor of philosophy, 1989-. Georgetown University, adjunct research professor, 1994-. **Publications:** Nietzsche's Philosophy of Science: Reflecting Science as the Ground of Art and Life, 1994. EDITOR: From Phenomenology to Thought: Essays in Honor of William J. Richardson, S.J., 1995; Nietzsche, Theories of Knowledge, Critical Theory, 1999; Nietzsche, Epistemology, and Philosophy of Science, 1999; Hermeneutic Philosophy of Science, Van Gogh's Eyes, and God: Essays in Honor of Patrick A. Heelan, SJ, 2001; Habermas, Nietzsche and Critical Theory, 2004. **Address:** Department of Philosophy, Fordham University, 113 W 60th St, New York, NY 10023, U.S.A. **Online address:** Babich@Fordham.edu

BABINGTON, Anthony Patrick. British (born Ireland), b. 1920. **Genres:** Criminology/True Crime, Law, Autobiography/Memoirs. **Career:** Circuit Judge, London, 1972-90. Metropolitan Stipendiary Magistrate, London, 1964-72. **Publications:** No Memorial, 1954; The Power to Silence, 1968; A House in Bow Street, 1969; The English Bastille, 1971; The Only Liberty, 1975, as The Rule of Law in Brtain; For the Sake of Example, 1983; Military Intervention in Britain, 1990; The Devil to Pay, 1991; Shell-Shock, 1997; An Uncertain Voyage, 2000. **Address:** Thydon Cottage, Chilham, Canterbury, Kent CT4 8BX, England.

BABUSHKA. *See* **MALAMUD-GOTI, Jaime.**

BACHE, Ellyn. Also writes as E. M. J. Benjamin. American. **Genres:** Novels, Novellas/Short stories, Children's fiction, Young adult fiction, Social commentary. **Career:** Novelist, editor, and journalist. **Publications:** Culture Clash, 1982; The Value of Kindness (short stories), 1993. NOVELS: Safe Passage, 1988; Festival Fire Season, 1992; The Activist's Daughter, 1997; (as E.M.J. Benjamin) Takedown, 1999; Holiday Miracles, 2001; Daddy and the Pink Flash, 2003; Riggs Park, 2005; Daughters of the Sea, 2005. **Address:** 2314 Waverly Dr, Wilmington, NC 28403, U.S.A. **Online address:** erbache@aol.com

BACHELDER, Thomas. Canadian, b. 1958. **Genres:** Food and Wine. **Career:** WINE TIDINGS (magazine), Montreal, Quebec, Canada, assistant editor, 1988-92, columnist, 1988-; Hour Magazine, wine columnist, 1993-; wine writer & winemaker. **Publications:** For the Love of Wine, 1990; You Made This?!: Making the Wine Nobody Knows Is Homemade, 1992; The Best B.Y.O.B. Restaurants of Montreal, 1994, 3rd ed., 2000. **Address:** c/o Lemelson Vindyards, 12020 NE Stag Hollow Rd, Carlton, OR 97111, U.S.A.

BACHER, John. (born Canada), b. 1954. **Genres:** Environmental sciences/Ecology. **Career:** Researcher, educator, and writer. Instructor in environmental topics at McMaster University and University of Toronto, Toronto, Ontario, Canada. Ontario Drainage Tribunal, hearing officer, 1991-97; Preservation of Agricultural Lands Society, researcher. Member, Niagara River Restoration Council; political candidate for federal office, 2000; lecturer, presenter at conferences and freelance writer. **Publications:** (with others) Niagara Conservation Strategy, 1988; Keeping to the Marketplace: The Evolution of Canadian Housing Policy, 1900-1990, 1993; (with Wayne Roberts and Brian Nelson) Get a Life, 1994; Petrotyranny, 2000. Contributor of articles and reviews to periodicals. **Address:** 134 Church St., St. Catharines, ON, Canada L2R 3E4. **Online address:** pals@becon.org

BACHMAN, Richard. *See* **KING, Stephen.**

BACHMAN, W(illiam) Bryant, Jr. American, b. 1941. **Genres:** Mythology/Folklore. **Career:** U.S. Army, career officer, 1965-75, leaving the service as captain; University of Southwestern Louisiana, Lafayette, professor of English, 1976-. **Publications:** Four Old Icelandic Sagas, 1985; (with G. Erlingsson) The Saga of Finnbogi the Strong, 1990; (with Erlingsson) The Sagas of King Half and King Hrolf, 1991; Forty Old Icelandic Tales, 1992; (with Erlingsson) Six Old Icelandic Sagas, 1993; (with Erlingsson) Svarfdale Sagas and Other Tales, 1994. **Address:** Department of English, University of Southwestern Louisiana, Lafayette, LA 70504, U.S.A.

BACHO, Peter. American, b. 1950. **Genres:** Novels, Novellas/Short stories. **Career:** Novelist and short-story writer. Has worked as an attorney and as a journalist; University of Washington, Seattle, professor of law and Philippine history; freelance writer, c. 1991-. **Publications:** Cebu (novel), 1991; Dark Blue Suit and Other Stories, 1997. Contributor of short stories to periodicals. **Address:** University of Washington Press, PO Box 50096, Seattle, WA 98145-5096, U.S.A.

BACKER, Sara. American, b. 1957. **Genres:** Novels. **Career:** Fiction and poetry writer. Shizuoka University, Japan, visiting professor of English. **Publications:** American Fuji: A Novel, 2001. Contributor of poetry to periodicals. **Address:** c/o Author Mail, G. P. Putnam's Sons, 375 Hudson St., New York, NY 10014, U.S.A. **Online address:** info@sarabacker.com

BACKES, David James. American, b. 1957. **Genres:** Travel/Exploration. **Publications:** Canoe Country: An Embattled Wilderness, 1991; (compiler and author of introduction) The Wilderness Companion, 1992; A Wilderness Within: The Life of Sigurd F. Olson, 1997. Contributor to periodicals. **Address:** University of Wisconsin, PO Box 413, Milwaukee, WI 53201-0413, U.S.A. **Online address:** backes@uwm.edu

BACKSCHEIDER, Paula R(ice). American, b. 1943. **Genres:** Literary criticism and history, Bibliography. **Career:** Rollins College, Winter Park, FL, assistant professor, 1973-75; University of Rochester, NY, assistant professor, 1975-78, associate professor, 1978-87, vice provost for academic concerns, 1981-82, professor of English, 1987-, Roswell Burrows Professor of English, 1991; Auburn University, Auburn, AL, Pepperell-Philpott Eminent Scholar, 1992-. Associated with University of Edinburgh's Institute for Advanced Studies, 1980-. **Publications:** NONFICTION: (with F. Nussbaum and P. Anderson) An Annotated Bibliography of 20th-Century Studies of Women and Literature, 1660-1800, 1977; A Being More Intense: The Prose Works of Bunyan, Swift, and Defoe, 1984; Daniel Defoe: Ambition and Innovation, 1986; Daniel Defoe: His Life, 1989; Moll Flanders: The Making of a Criminal Mind, 1990; Spectacular Politics, 1993; Reflections on Biography, 1999. EDITOR: Probability, Time, and Space in 18th-Century Literature, 1979; Eighteenth-Century Drama (69 vols.), 1979-83; The Plays of Charles Gildon, 1979; The Plays of Elizabeth Inchbald, 2 vols., 1980; (with D.

Howard) The Plays of Samuel Foote, 3 vols., 1983; Dictionary of Literary Biography, Vol. 80: Restoration and Eighteenth-Century Dramatists, 1st Series, 1989, Vol. 84: Restoration and 18nth-Century Dramatists, 2nd Series, 1989, Vol. 89: Restoration and 18th-Century Dramatists, 3rd Series, 1989; D. Defoe, A Journal of the Plague Year, 1992; (with T. Dystal) Intersections of the Public and Private Spheres in Early Modern England, 1996; (with J.J. Richetti) Popular Fiction by Women, 1660-1730, 1996; (with H.D. Cotton) Excursion, 1997; Selected Fiction and Drama of Eliza Haywood, 1999; Revising Women, 2000. **Address:** Department of English, 9030 Haley, Auburn University, Auburn, AL 36849, U.S.A. **Online address:** pkrb@eng.auburn.edu

BACKUS, George Edward. American, b. 1930. **Genres:** Earth sciences, Physics. **Career:** Professor of Geophysics, University of California San Diego, at La Jolla, since 1962 (Associate Professor, 1960-62). Royal Society Arts Fellow, London, 1970-90; Co-Chairman, Intl. Working Group on Magnetic Field Satellites, since 1983; member, visiting cttee., Institut de Physique du Globe de Paris, since 1987. Assistant Examiner, University of Chicago, 1949-50; Jr. Mathematician, Institute for Air Weapons Research, University of Chicago, 1951-54; Physicist, Project Matterhorn, Princeton University, New Jersey, 1957-58; Assistant Professor of Mathematics, Massachusetts Institute of Technology, Boston, 1959-60. Member, American Academy of Arts and Sciences, 1962, and National Academy of Sciences, 1969; Foreign Associate, Acadaemie des Sciences, Institut de France, 1989. **Publications:** Self-Sustaining Dissipative Kinematic Fluid Dynamo, 1958; Rotational Splitting of the Free Oscillations of the Earth, 1961; Propagation of Short Waves on a Slowly Rotating Earth, 1962; Magnetic Anomalies over Oceanic Ridges, 1964; Possible Forms of Seismic Anistropy, 1962, 3rd ed., 1970; Potentials for Tangent Tensor Fields in Spheroids, 1966; (with F. Gilbert) Inversion of Seismic Normal Mode Data, 1966; Geomagnetic Data and Core Motions, 1967; (with F. Gilbert) Inversion of Earth Normal Mode Data, 1968; Inference from Inaccurate and Inadequate Data, 1971, 1972; Mathematical Representation of Seismic Sources, 1976; Computing Extrema of Multidimensional Polynomials, 1980; Relative Importance of Tectonic Plate-Driving Forces, 1981; Construction of Geomagnetic Field Models, 1982; Mantle Conductivity, 1983; Core Motion, 1986; Statistical Inference, 1989; (with C. Constable and R.L. Parker) Foundations of Geomagnetism, 1996. **Address:** Institute of Geophysics and Planetary Physics, University of California, San Diego, La Jolla, CA 92093-0225, U.S.A.

BACON, Donald C(onrad). American, b. 1935. **Genres:** History, Politics/Government, Biography. **Career:** Wall Street Journal, NYC, staff writer, 1957-61; Washington Star, Washington, DC, staff writer, 1962-63; Newhouse News Service, Washington, DC, congressional correspondent to White House correspondent, senior correspondent, and columnist, 1962-75; U.S. News and World Report, Washington, DC, associate editor, 1975-79, senior editor, 1979-81, assistant managing editor, 1981-88; senior editor of Nation's Business, 1988-89; Encyclopedia of the U.S. Congress, Washington, DC, project director and co-editor, 1989-. **Publications:** The New Millionaires, 1961; Congress and You, 1969; (with D.B. Hardeman) Rayburn: A Biography, 1987; (co-ed) Encyclopedia of the US Congress, 1995. **Address:** 3809 East-West Highway, Chevy Chase, MD 20815-5918, U.S.A. **Online address:** donbacon@erols.com

BACON, George Edward. British, b. 1917. **Genres:** Chemistry, Physics. **Career:** Professor Emeritus of Physics, University of Sheffield, since 1981 (Professor, 1963-81). Deputy Chief Scientist, Atomic Energy Research Establishment, Harwell, 1946-63; Ed., Zeitschrift fur Kristallographie, 1963-90. **Publications:** Neutron Diffraction 1955, 3rd ed. 1975; Applications of Neutron Diffraction in Chemistry, 1963; X-ray and Neutron Diffraction, 1966; Neutron Physics, 1969; Neutron Scattering in Chemistry, 1977; The Architecture of Solids, 1981; (ed.) 50 Years of Neutron Diffraction, 1987. **Address:** Windrush Way, Guiting Power, Cheltenham GL54 5US, England.

BACON, Margaret. British. **Genres:** Novels, Children's fiction, Travel/Exploration. **Publications:** Journey to Guyana (travel), 1970; A Packetful of Trouble (children's fiction), 1974. NOVELS: The Episode, 1971; Kitty, 1972; The Unentitled, 1974; The Package, 1975; Snow in Winter, 1978; The Kingdom of the Rose, 1982; The Chain, 1984; The Serpent's Tooth, 1987; Other Women, 1994; Friends and Relations, 1996; The Ewe Lamb, 1999; Mother Nature, 2000; Northrop Hall, 2003; The Years Between, 2004; For Better for Worse, 2005. **Address:** Hill House, Highworth, Wilts. SN6 7BZ, England.

BACON, R(onald) L(eonard). New Zealander (born Australia), b. 1924. **Genres:** Novels, Children's fiction, Children's non-fiction. **Career:** Retired, formerly Principal, Favona Primary School, Auckland. Children's Literature

Society of New Zealand Inc, Award for Service to Children's Literature, 1994. **Publications:** In the Sticks, 1963; Along the Road, 1964; The Boy and the Taniwha, 1966; Rua and the Sea People, 1968; Auckland: Gateway to New Zealand, 1968; Again the Bugles Blow, 1973; Auckland: Town and Around, 1973; The House of the People, 1977; Hatupatu and the Bird Woman, 1979; Wind, 1984; The Bay, 1985; The Fish of Our Fathers, 1985; The Home of the Winds, 1985; Hemi Dances, 1985; A Legend of Kiwi, 1987; Hemi and the Whale, 1988; The Green Fish of Ngahui, 1989; The Clay Boy, 1990; A Mouse Singing in the Reeds, 1990; Three Surprises for Hemi, 1990; The Banjo Man, 1990; Hemi and the Skateboard and Sasquatch Harrison, 1992; Bone Tree, 1994; The Naming of the Land, 1997; The Great Jellification at the House of Ebenezer, 2003. **Address:** 3/5a McIntyre Rd, Mangere Bridge, Auckland 1701, New Zealand.

BADA, Constantina. Greek, b. 1950. **Genres:** Anthropology/Ethnology, Local history/Rural topics. **Career:** University of Ioannina, Greece, assistant professor, 1978-83, curator of university museum, 1978-83, lecturer, 1983-90, senior lecturer, 1990-97, reader, 1997-2004, professor in popular culture and anthropology, 2004-. **Publications:** (with P. Sant Cassia) The Making of the Modern Greek Family, 1992; Costume Codes of Childhood and Youth and Their Socio-Historical Equivalent (in Greek), 1993; The World of Work: The Fishermen of the Messologi Lagoon, 2004. **Address:** Dept of History and Archaeology, University of Ioannina, 45 110 Ioannina, Greece. **Online address:** kbada@cc.uoi.gr

BADAMI, Anita Rau. Canadian (born India), b. 1962. **Genres:** Novels. **Career:** Novelist. Worked as a copywriter at advertising agencies in Bombay, Bangalore, and Madras, India; former journalist. **Publications:** Tamarind Mem, 1996; The Hero's Walk, 2000. **Address:** c/o Random House of Canada Limited, 1 Toronto St., Unit 300, Toronto, ON, Canada M5C 2V6.

BADAWI, Mohamed Mustafa. British (born Egypt), b. 1925. **Genres:** Novels, Novellas/Short stories, Plays/Screenplays, Poetry, Literary criticism and history. **Career:** Lecturer, Oxford University and Brasenose College, 1964-92; Fellow, St. Antony's College, Oxford, since 1967. Co-ed., Journal of Arabic Literature, Leiden, 1970-96. Research Fellow, 1947-54, Lecturer, 1954-60, and Assistant Professor of English, 1960-64, Alexandria University, Egypt. Member, Cttees. of Ministry of Culture, Egypt, 1961; Unesco Expert on Modern Arabic Culture, 1974. Awarded King Faisal International Prize in Arabic Literature, 1992. **Publications:** Coleridge, Critic of Shakespeare, 1973; A Critical Introduction to Modern Arabic Poetry, 1975; Background to Shakespeare, 1981; Modern Arabic Literature and the West, 1985; Modern Arabic Drama in Egypt, 1987; Early Arabic Drama, 1988; A Short History of Modern Arabic Literature, 1993. TRANSLATOR: The Saint's Lamp and Other Stories, by Yahya Haqqi, 1973; Sara, by A.M. El Aqqad, 1978; The Thief and the Dogs, by N. Mahfouz, 1984. EDITOR: An Anthology of Modern Arabic Verse, 1970; Modern Arabic Literature, The Cambridge History of Arabic Literature, 1992. **Address:** St. Antony's College, Oxford, England.

BADCOCK, Christopher Robert. British, b. 1946. **Genres:** Psychology, Sociology. **Career:** Polytechnic of the South Bank, London, lecturer in sociology, 1969-73; London School of Economics, reader in sociology. **Publications:** Levi-Strauss: Structuralism and Sociological Theory, 1975; The Psychoanalysis of Culture, 1980; Madness and Modernity, 1984; The Problem of Altruism: Freudian-Darwinian Solutions, 1986; Essential Freud: An Introduction to Classical Psychoanalysis, 1988; Oedipus in Evolution, 1990; Evolution and Individual Behavior, 1991; PsychoDarwinism, 1994; Evolutionary Psychology: A Critical Introduction, 2000. **Address:** London School of Economics, Houghton St, London WC2A 2AE, England. **Online address:** c.badcock@lse.ac.uk

BADCOCK, Gary D. Canadian, b. 1961. **Genres:** Theology/Religion. **Career:** University of Aberdeen, Aberdeen, Scotland, teaching fellow, 199192; University of Edinburgh, Edinburgh, Scotland, lecturer, 1993-, associate dean of divinity faculty, 1997-. **Publications:** Light of Truth and Fire of Love, 1997; The Way of Life: A Theology of Christian Vocation, 1998. EDITOR: (with D.F. Wright) Disruption to Diversity: Edinburgh Divinity, 1846-1996, 1996; Theology after the Storm, 1996. **Address:** New College, University of Edinburgh, Mound Pl., Edinburgh, Scotland. **Online address:** g.badcock@ed.ac.uk

BADDOCK, James. British, b. 1950. **Genres:** Novels, Mystery/Crime/Suspense. **Career:** Assistant manager of a tailor's shop, 1968-71; Training College, teacher, 1971-74; Bedfordshire Education Authority, Bedford, England, teacher, 1974-. **Publications:** The Faust Conspiracy, 1985; The

Radar Job, 1986, as The Dutch Caper, 1990; (with R. Gordon) Gold Run, 1986; Emerald, 1987; The Alaska Project, 1989; Piccolo, 1992.

BADENI, June. Also writes as June Wilson. British, b. 1925. **Genres:** Novels, History, Biography. **Publications:** AS JUNE WILSON: The Bitter Journey, 1947; One Foolish Heart, 1948; Second Hearing, 1949; Green Shadows: A Life of John Clare, 1951. AS JUNE BADENI: Wiltshire Forefathers, 1960; The Slender Tree: A Life of Alice Meynell, 1981; Past People in Wiltshire and Gloucestershire, 1992. **Address:** Garden Cottage, Norton, Malmesbury, Wilts., England.

BADGLEY, John Herbert. American, b. 1930. **Genres:** Novels, Politics/Government. **Career:** Assistant Professor, Miami University, Ohio, 1962-66; Associate Professor, 1967-70, and Director of Asian Studies, 1970-73; Johns Hopkins University, Washington, DC; Institute of the Rockies, Missoula, 1973-94; Curator, Southeast Asia Collection, Cornell University, Ithaca, NY, 1986-. **Publications:** Politics among Burmans, 1970; Asian Development, 1971; A Clear Gathering of Miraculous Success in Peace & Security, Vol 7, #1, 1992; Intellectuals and the National Vision: The Burmese Case: In Literature and Society in Southeast Asia, 1981; The Foreign Policy of Burma in the Political Economy of Foreign Policy in Southeast Asia, 1990; Remodelling Myanmar in Myanmar Dilemmas and Options, 1990; Cornell in the Killing Fields, A Play in Three Acts, 1994; Red Peacocks, 1995; The Strategist, 1996. **Address:** 9911 220th St SW, Edmonds, WA 98020-4563, U.S.A.

BADIAN, Ernst. American (born Austria), b. 1925. **Genres:** History, Classics. **Career:** University of Leeds, professor of ancient history, 1964-69; State University of New York, Buffalo, professor of classics and history, 1969-71; Harvard University, professor of history, 1971-81, John Moors Cabot Professor of History, 1982-98, John Moors Cabot Professor of History Emeritus, 1998-. American Journal of Ancient History, editor, 1976-2001. **Publications:** Foreign Clientelae 264-70 B.C., 1958; Studies in Greek and Roman History, 1964; Roman Imperialism in the Late Republic, 1967; Publicans and Sinners, 1972; From Plataea to Potidaea, 1993; Zollner und Sunder, 1997. EDITOR: Polybius, 1966; (and contrib.) Ancient Society and Institutions, 1966; G. Susini, The Roman Stonecutter, 1973; R. Syme, Roman Papers, 2 vols., 1979. Contributor of articles to classical and historical journals. **Address:** Dept of History, Harvard University, Cambridge, MA 02138, U.S.A.

BADT, Karin L(uisa). American, b. 1963. **Genres:** Documentaries/Reportage, Children's fiction. **Career:** University of Chicago Continuing Education Program, Chicago, IL, basic program instructor, 1989-90, open program instructor, 1993-94; John Cabot University, lecturer, 1991-93; University of Rome, La Sapienza, Italy, lecturer, 1992; University of Chicago, lecturer, 1994-95; American University of Paris, Paris, France, assistant professor, 1995-; University of Paris, lecturer, 1995-; Science Po, Paris, lecturer, 1996-. Parsons School of Design (Paris), cinema instructor, summer, 1996. **Publications:** The Mississippi Flood of 1993, 1993; Charles Eastman: Sioux Physician and Author, 1994; The Underground Railroad (play), 1995; (with M. Bartok) The Southeast Indians, 1995; Ohiyesa (play), 1996; The Southwest Indians, 1996. A WORLD OF DIFFERENCE SERIES: Good Morning, Let's Eat, 1994; Greetings, 1994; Hair There and Everywhere, 1994; Let's Go!, 1994; On Your Feet!, 1994; Pass the Bread!, 1994. **Address:** American University of Paris, 31, avenue Bosquet, 75007 Paris, France.

BAEHR, Kingsley M. American (born People's Republic of China), b. 1937. **Genres:** Novels, Poetry, Ethics. **Career:** Adamsville School, Bridgewater, NJ, English teacher, 1959-71; Cedarcroft Bible Chapel, South Plainfield, NJ, teacher, preacher, youth worker, and elder, 1971-; Timothy Christian School, Piscataway, NJ, Bible teacher, 1973-2004, middle school principal, 1987-2002. **Publications:** Hope in a Scarlet Rope, 1994. **Address:** 1512 Kenyon Ave, South Plainfield, NJ 07080, U.S.A.

BAER, Greg. American. **Genres:** Self help. **Career:** Worked as ophthalmologist and eye surgeon; became full-time writer, teacher, and public speaker, including appearances at Unity churches. Guest on more than one hundred television and radio programs. **Publications:** The Wart King: The Truth about Love and Lies, 1997; The Truth about Relationships: A Simple and Powerfully Effective Way for Everyone to Find Real Love and Loving Relationships, published as Real Love: A Simple and Powerfully Effective Way for Everyone to Find Unconditional Love and Loving Relationships, 2003; The Wise Man: The Truth about Sharing Real Love, 2003. Author of other self-help books. **Address:** c/o Author Mail, Gotham Books, 375 Hudson St., New York, NY 10014, U.S.A.

BAERWALD, Hans H. American (born Japan), b. 1927. **Genres:** Politics/Government. **Career:** Professor Emeritus of Political Science, 1991-, and Professor of Political Science, University of California at Los Angeles, 1969-91 (Lecturer, 1962-65; Associate Professor, 1965-69). Assistant Professor, 1956-61, and Associate Professor of Government, 1961-62, Miami University, Oxford, Ohio. **Publications:** The Purge of Japanese Leaders Under the Occupation, 1959, 1977; (with P.H. Odegard) American Government: Structure, Problems, Policies, 1962; (with D.N. Jacobs) Chinese Communism: Selected Documents, 1963; (with Odegard) The American Republic, Its Government and Politics, 1964, rev. ed. with W. Havard, 1969; Japan's Parliament: An Introduction, 1974; Party Politics in Japan, 1986. **Address:** 2221 Barnett Road, St. Helena, CA 94574, U.S.A. **Online address:** hanbwald@napanet.net

BAGDIKIAN, Ben Haig. American (born Turkey), b. 1920. **Genres:** Communications/Media, Criminology/True Crime, Politics/Government, Race relations, Sociology, Writing/Journalism, Autobiography/Memoirs, Documentaries/Reportage. **Career:** Professor Emeritus, Graduate School of Journalism, University of California, Berkeley, 1990- (Professor, 1977-90; Dean, 1985-88). Chief Washington Correspondent, The Providence Journal, Rhode Island, 1947-61; Contributor Ed., Saturday Evening Post, 1963-67; Assistant Managing Ed., for National News, Washington Post, 1970-72. **Publications:** (ed.) Man's Contracting World in an Expanding Universe, 1960; In the Midst of Plenty: The Poor in America, 1964; The Information Machines, 1970; The Shame of the Prisons, 1972; The Effete Conspiracy and Other Crimes by the Press, 1972; Caged, 1976; Bagdikian on Political Reporting, Newspaper Economics, Law, and Ethics, 1977; The Media Monopoly, 1983, 7th ed. as The New Media Monopoly, 2004; Double Vision, 1995. **Address:** 25 Stonewall Rd, Berkeley, CA 94705, U.S.A. **Online address:** benmar@uclink4.berkeley.edu

BAGERT, Brod. American, b. 1947. **Genres:** Children's fiction, Poetry. **Career:** Writer; teacher and performer at schools around the country. **Publications:** FOR CHILDREN: Let Me Be the Boss: Poems for Kids to Perform, 1992; Chicken Socks: And Other Contagious Poems, 1994; Elephant Games and Other Playful Poems, 1995; The Gooch Machine, 1997; (ed.) Poetry for Young Readers: Edgar Allan Poe, 1995. FOR ADULTS: A Bullfrog at Cafe du Monde (poetry), 1986; Steel Cables (poetry), 1992; Throw Me Somethin Mistuh, 1995; Rainbows, Head Lice, and Pea Green Tile (poetry). **Address:** 6011 Chamberlain Dr, New Orleans, LA 70122, U.S.A. **Online address:** brodbagert@aol.com

BAGGE, Peter (Christian Paul). (born United States), b. 1957. **Genres:** Graphic Novels. **Career:** Graphic artist, writer, and creator of alternative comics. Creator of animated commercials and print ads for commercial clients. **Publications:** COLLECTIONS; SELF-ILLUSTRATED: The Bradleys, 1989; Studs Kirby: The Voice of America, 1989; The Adventures of Junior and Tragic Tales about Other Losers, 1990; Stupid Comics, 1991. HATE COLLECTIONS; SELF-ILLUSTRATED: Hey Buddy!, 1993; Buddy the Dreamer, 1994; Fun with Buddy and Lisa, 1995; Buddy Go Home, 1997; Buddy's Got Three Moms, 1999; Buddy Bites the Bullet!, 2001; Buddy's at the End of the Line, 2003. Author and/or illustrator of comic-books series and comic strips. Contributor of writing, illustrations, and strips to periodicals. Creator of short cartoons. **Address:** Author Mail, 7563 Lake City Way NE, Seattle, WA 98115, U.S.A. **Online address:** Booksagge@earthlink.net

BAGGOTT, Julianna. American, b. 1970?. **Genres:** Novels, Poetry. **Career:** Writer and poet. **Publications:** This Country of Mothers (poetry), 2001; Girl Talk, 2001; The Miss America Family, 2002; The Madam: A Novel, 2003. Contributor of short stories and poems to literary journals. **Address:** c/o Author Mail, Simon & Schuster, 1230 Avenue of the Americas, New York, NY 10020, U.S.A. **Online address:** email@juliannabaggott.com

BAGLEY, Mary (C.). American, b. 1958. **Genres:** Literary criticism and history, Adult non-fiction. **Career:** Missouri Baptists College, St. Louis, MO, professor, 1983-. America Alive! (cable program), St. Louis, MO, writer and broadcaster, 1983-85; Save the Ambassador Theatre, president; lecturer, editor, and broadcaster. **Publications:** The Front Row: Missouri's Grand Theatres, 1984; The Art of Writing Well, 1987; Handbook for Professional and Academic Writing, 1988; Professional Writing Types, 1989; Selected Readings in Nineteenth- and Twentieth-Century Literature, 1994; Poetics of Realism, 1994; Willa Cather's Myths, 1996; Business Communications; Art of Business Writing. Contributor of articles and short stories to journals and other periodicals. **Address:** Department of English, Missouri Baptist College, One College Park Dr., St. Louis, MO 63141, U.S.A. **Online address:** Robin@galaxy5.com

BAHAL, Aniruddha. (born India), b. 1967. **Genres:** Novellas/Short stories. **Career:** Investigative journalist and novelist. Worked for India Today and Outlook; cofounder and CEO of Tehelka.com; founder and editor and chief of Cobrapost.com. **Publications:** A Crack in the Mirror, 1991; Bunker Thirteen, 2003;. **Address:** Author Mail, Farrar, Straus & Giroux, 19 Union Square West, New York, NY 10003, U.S.A.

BAHN, Paul (Gerard). British, b. 1953. **Genres:** Archaeology/Antiquities, Translations. **Career:** University of Liverpool, England, postdoctoral research fellow in archaeology, 1979-82; University of London, England, V. Canada Blanch research fellow in archaeology, 1982-83; J. Paul Getty research fellow in the history of art and humanities, 1985-86; freelance writer, translator, and broadcaster, 1986-. **Publications:** Pyrenean Prehistory, 1984; (with J. Hawkes) The Shell Guide to British Archaeology, 1986; (with G. Daniel) Ancient Places, 1987; (with J. Vertut) Images of the Ice Age, 1988; The Bluffer's Guide to Archaeology, 1989, rev. ed., 1999; (with C. Renfrew) Archaeology, 1991, 4th ed., 2004; (with J. Flenley) Easter Island, Earth Island, 1992; (with A. Lister) Mammoths, 1994, rev. ed.; Archaeology, a Very Short Introduction, 1996; The Cambridge Illustrated History of Prehistoric Art, 1997; (with J. Vertut) Journey through the Ice Age, 1997; The Easter Island Enigma, 1997; Geoglyphs, 1997; (with B. Tidy) Disgraceful Archaeology, 1999; (with J. Flenley) The Enigmas of Easter Island, 2003. TRANSLATOR: P. Courbin, What Is Archaeology?, 1988; M. Rodna, The Bluffer's Guide to Modern Art, 1990; S. Gruzinski, The Aztecs, 1992; M. Krafft, Volcanoes, 1993; C. Bernand, The Incas, 1994; H. Thomas, The First Humans, 1995; C. and M. Orliac, The Silent Gods, Mysteries of Easter Island, 1995; J.-M. Chauvet and others, Dawn of Art, 1996; V. Berinstain, Mughal India, 1998; D. Vialou, Our Prehistoric Past, 1998; C. Debaine-Francfort, The Search for Ancient China, 1999, D. Lavallee, The First South Americans, 2000; P. Tort, Charles Darwin, 2001; J. Clottes, ed., Chauvet Cave, 2003. EDITOR & CONTRIBUTOR: The Collins Dictionary of Archaeology, 1992; 100 Great Archaeological Discoveries, 1995; The Cambridge Illustrated History of Archaeology, 1996; Tombs, Graves and Mummies, 1996; Lost Cities, 1997; Wonderful Things, 1999; Atlas of World Archaeology, 2000; Penguin Archaeology Guide, 2001; The Archaeology Detectives, 2001; The Definitive Guide: Archaeology, 2001; Written in Bones, 2003. **Address:** Watson Little Ltd., Capo Di Monte, London NW3 6RY, England.

BAHR, Alice Harrison. American, b. 1946. **Genres:** Librarianship, Bibliography. **Career:** Lehigh University, Bethlehem, PA, assistant reference librarian, 1970-74; Cedar Crest College, Allentown, PA, adjunct faculty member, 1978-82; Libraries at Cedar Crest and Muhlenberg Colleges, Allentown, project librarian, 1980-88; Spring Hill College, Mobile, AL, director of library, 1988-, adjunct member of English faculty, 1989, associate professor, 1993-99, professor, 1999-. Institute for Legal and Ethical Issues in the New Information Era, participant, 2000. **Publications:** Book Theft and Library Security Systems, 1978-79, 1978, 2nd ed. as Book Theft and Library Security Systems, 1981-82, 1981; Microforms: The Librarian's View, 1978-79, 1978; Automated Library Circulation Systems, 1979-80, 1979. EDITOR: Future Teaching Roles for Academic Librarians, 2000; InPrint: A Directory of Publishing Opportunities for College Librarians (Internet publication), 2001. Contributor to books. Contributor of articles, poems, and short fiction to library journals and other periodicals. **Address:** Library, Spring Hill College, 4000 Dauphin St., Mobile, AL 36608, U.S.A. **Online address:** bahr@shc.edu

BAHR, Ehrhard. German, b. 1932. **Genres:** Literary criticism and history, Biography, Translations. **Career:** University of California, Berkeley, teaching assistant, 1962-66; University of California, Los Angeles, acting assistant professor, 1966-68, assistant professor, 1968-70, associate professor, 1970-72, professor of German, 1972-, chairman, Dept. of Germanic Languages, 1981-84, 1993-98. **Publications:** (co-trans.) Nelly Sachs: Beryll Sees in the Night (play), 1969; Die Ironie in Goethes Spatwerk (criticism), 1972; (with R.G. Kunzer) Georg Lukacs (biography), 1972; Ernst Bloch (biography), 1974; Nelly Sachs (biography), 1980; The Novel as Archive, 1998. EDITOR: Kant: What Is Enlightenment?, 1974; (with others) Lessing Yearbook Supplement: Humanitat und Dialog, 1982; History of German Literature (3 vols.), 1987-88; (co-) The Internalized Revolution: German Reactions to the French Revolution, 1789-1989, 1992. **Address:** Dept of Germanic Languages, University of California, Box 951539, Los Angeles, CA 90095-1539, U.S.A. **Online address:** bahr@humnet.ucla.edu

BAHR, Mary. *See* **FRITTS, Mary Bahr.**

BAHR, Robert. Also writes as Dr. Harold Litten. American, b. 1940. **Genres:** Novellas/Short stories, Gay and lesbian issues, Medicine/Health, Psychology, Sex, Writing/Journalism, Biography. **Career:** Rodale Press, Emmaus, PA, managing editor of Health Bulletin, 1965-67, senior editor of Prevention magazine, 1967-69, managing editor of Fitness for Living, 1969-71, and director of Educational Services Division, 1971-72. **Publications:** Man with a Vision (biography), 1961; Natural Way to a Healthy Skin, 1972; Physical Fitness in Business and Industry, 1973; The Virility Factor, 1976; Least of All Saints, 1979; The Blizzard, 1980; Blizzard at the Zoo, 1982; (ghostwriter) Kreskin's Fun Way to Mind Expansion, 1984; Good Hands, 1984; (with P. Whybrow) The Hibernation Response, 1988; The Joy of Solo Sex, 1990; Indecent Exposures (short stories), 1993; More Joy of Solo Sex, 1996; Harold Litten's Best Erotic Fantasies, 1998; Dramatic Technique in Fiction, 1998. **Address:** 5204 Dove Point Ln, Salisbury, MD 21801, U.S.A. **Online address:** FactorPress@earthlink.net

BAICKER-MCKEE, Carol. (born United States), b. 1958. **Genres:** Human relations/Parenting. **Career:** Child psychologist; writer; lecturer on child-rearing subjects. **Publications:** Mapped Out!: The Search for Snookums, 1997; Fussbusters at Home: Around-the-Clock Strategies and Games for Smoothing the Rough Spots in Your Preschooler's Day, 2002; Fussbusters on the Go: Strategies and Games for Stress-Free Outings, Errands, and Vacations with Your Preschooler, 2002. **Address:** c/o Author Mail, Peachtree Publishers Ltd, 1700 Chattahoochee Ave., Atlanta, GA 30318, U.S.A.

BAIL, Murray. Australian, b. 1941. **Genres:** Novels, Novellas/Short stories. **Career:** Australian National Gallery, Canberra, Member of the Council, 1976-81. **Publications:** Contemporary Portraits and Other Stories, 1975, in U.K. as The Drover's Wife, 1986; Homesickness (novel), 1980; Ian Fairweather, 1981; Holden's Performance (novel), 1987; (ed.) The Faber Book of Contemporary Australian Short Stories, 1988; Longhand, 1989; Eucalyptus, 1998; Homesickness, 1999. **Address:** c/o Pat Kavanagh, PFD, Drury House, 34-43 Russell St, London WC2B 5HA, England.

BAILEY, Anthony. British, b. 1933. **Genres:** Novels, Human relations/Parenting, Travel/Exploration, Autobiography/Memoirs, Documentaries/Reportage, Biography. **Career:** Staff Writer, The New Yorker, 1956-92. Chairman, The Greenwich Society, London, 1979-81, and The Burney St. Garden Project, London, 1981-90. **Publications:** Making Progress (novel), 1959; The Mother Tongue (novel), 1961; The Inside Passage (travel), 1965; Through the Great City (reportage), 1967; The Thousand Dollar Yacht (autobiography: boating), 1968; The Light in Holland (reportage), 1970; In the Village (human relations), 1971; A Concise History of the Low Countries, 1972; Rembrandt's House (biography), 1978; Acts of Union: Reports on Ireland, 1980; America, Lost and Found (autobiography), 1981; Along the Edge of the Forest: An Iron Curtain Journey, 1983; England, First and Last (autobiography), 1985; Spring Jaunts: Some Walks, Excursions, and Personal Explorations of City, Country, and Seashore, 1986; Major Andre (novel), 1987; The Outer Banks (travel), 1989; A Walk through Wales, 1992; Responses to Rembrandt, 1994; The Coast of Summer (travel), 1994; Turner (biography), 1997. **Address:** c/o Candida Donadio and Associates, 121 W. 27th St, New York, NY 10001, U.S.A.

BAILEY, Charles Waldo, (II). American, b. 1929. **Genres:** Novels, History, Politics/Government. **Career:** Washington Ed., National Public Radio, 1984-87. Former Ed., Minneapolis Tribune. **Publications:** (with F. Knebel) No High Ground, 1960; Seven Days in May, 1962; Convention, 1964; Conflicts of Interest: A Matter of Journalistic Ethics, 1984; The Land Was Ours, 1991. Contributor to books. **Address:** 3001 Albemarle St. NW, Washington, DC 20008, U.S.A.

BAILEY, D(avid) R. Shackleton. American/British, b. 1917. **Genres:** Classics, History, Translations. **Career:** Emeritus Professor, Harvard University, Cambridge, MA, 1988- (Visiting Lecturer, 1963; Professor of Greek and Latin, 1975-82; Pope Professor of Latin Language and Literature, 198288). Caius College, Fellow, 1944-55, Fellow, Deputy Bursar, and Sr. Bursar, 1964-68; Lecturer in Tibetan, Cambridge University, 1948-68; Fellow, Jesus College, 1955-64; University of Michigan, Ann Arbor, Professor of Latin, 1968-74, Adjunct Professor, 1989; Visiting Andrew V.V. Raymond Professor of Classics, State University of New York, Buffalo, 1973-74; Visiting Fellow, Peterhouse, Cambridge, 1980-81. Ed., Harvard Studies in Classical Philology, 1980-85. **Publications:** Propertiana, 1951; Cicero, 1971; Two Studies in Roman Nomenclature, 1976; Towards a Text of Anthologia Latina, 1979; Profile of Horace, 1982; Lucanus, 1988; Onomasticon to Cicero's Speeches, 1988; Martialis, 1990; Martial, 3 vols., 1993; Homoeoteleuton in Latin Dactylic Verse, 1994; Onomasticon to Cicero's Letters, 1995; Onomasticon to Cicero's Treatises, 1996; Selected Classical Papers, 1997; Valerius Maximus, 2 vols., 2000. EDITOR: Ciceronis Epistulae ad Atticum IX-XVI, 1961; Cicero, Letters to His Friends, 1977; Cicero: Epistulae ad Q. Fratrem et M.

Brutum, 1981; Anthologia Latina I, 1982; Horatius, 1985; Ciceronis Epistulae, 4 vols., 1987-88; Quintilianus, Declamationes Minores, 1989. TRANSLATOR: Cicero's Letters to Atticus, 1978; Cicero's Letters to His Friends, 2 vols., 1978; Back from Exile, 1991; Cicero, Letters to Atticus, 4 vols., 1999. EDITOR & TRANSLATOR: The Satapancasatka of Matrceta, 1951; Cicero's Letters to Atticus, 7 vols., 1965-70; Cicero, Philippics, 1985; Cicero, Letters to Friends, 3 vols., 2001. **Address:** 303 N Division, Ann Arbor, MI 48104, U.S.A.

BAILEY, Donna. Also writes as Veronica Bonar. British, b. 1938. **Genres:** Children's non-fiction, Medicine/Health, History, Animals/Pets, Environmental sciences/Ecology, Natural history, Sports/Fitness. **Career:** University of Sussex, Sussex, England, library assistant, 1962-64; Essex Education Authority, Margaret Tabor School, Braintree, Essex, England, teacher of English, 1967; Essex University Library, Essex, senior library assistant and assistant Russian cataloger, 1967-69; N. V. Philips Language Teaching Centre, Eindhoven, Netherlands, teacher of English as a Foreign Language (EFL), 1970-71; National Central Library, London, England, filing assistant, 1972; Macmillan, Basingstoke, Hampshire, England, free-lance editor, 1972-73, overseas book editor, 1974, senior overseas book editor, 1975-77, managing editor, 1978-79, secondary publishing manager, 1980, senior editor of children's books, 1980, publishing manager, 1981-84; writer. Publishing consultant and developer of "Computer Club" children's information series and "Debates" teenage information series, originator and packager of "Children in Conflict" teenage information series, and consultant for "Starters (Places)" children's information series (includes audiocassettes), all for Macdonald and Co.; publishing consultant for British Broadcasting Corporation (BBC) audiovisual English Language Teaching (ELT) course "Muzzy Comes Back". Worked in editorial and consulting positions in Germany, Denmark, and Holland; producer of ELT video course, for Paideia; lecturer for Macmillan/Southern Books, 1989 and 1991, and Publisher's Association. **Publications:** HEALTH FACTS series: All about Birth and Growth, 1990; All about Digestion, 1990; All about Heart and Blood, 1990; All about Skin, Hair, and Teeth, 1990; All about Your Brain, 1990; All about Your Lungs, 1990; All about Your Senses, 1990; All about Your Skeleton, 1990. READ TOGETHER series: 36 titles. MY WORLD series: 72 titles: Animal World; Sports World; Where we Live; FIRST FACTS series: 24 titles. DAYS TO REMEMBER series: 6 titles. SMALL WORLD series: 6 titles. THE STORY OF… series: 6 titles. HISTORY INSIGHTS series: 4 titles. WHAT CAN WE DO ABOUT… series: 6 titles. THE SCIENCE OF COLOUR series, in US as INVESTIGATING COLOR series: 4 titles. AS VERONICA BONAR: RUBBISH series, in US as TRASH BUSTER series: 6 titles. TAKE A SQUARE OF … series, in US as ECO-JOURNEY series: 6 titles. **Address:** Reeds Cottage, Appleshaw, North Andover, Hampshire SP11 9AA, England.

BAILEY, F(rancis) Lee. American, b. 1933. **Genres:** Novels, Law, Young adult fiction. **Career:** Admitted to the Bar of Massachusetts, 1960; Bailey, Fishman and Leonard, Boston, MA, senior partner; founder of private detective agency; host of weekly prog., Good Company, 1967; Gallery mag., publisher, 1972-; Enstrom Helicopter Corp., president, 1972-. **Publications:** (with H.P. Rothblatt) Criminal Law Library, Vols. 1-11, 1969-82; (with H. Aronson) The Defense Never Rests: The Art of Cross-Examination, 1971; (with J Greenya) For the Defense, 1975; (with Greenya) Cleared for Approach: F. Lee Bailey in Defense of Flying, 1977; Secrets (novel), 1978; (with Rothblatt) Complete Manual of Criminal Forms: Federal and State, 2 vols., 1968, 1974, suppl. 1987; How to Protect Yourself Against Cops in California and Other Strange Places, 1982; How to Be a Trial Lawyer, 1982; (with K.J. Fishman) Supplements to the Bailey-Rothblatt Criminal Law Series, 1986-; (with Fishman) Handling Misdemenor Cases, 2nd ed, 1992; (with Fishman) Complete Manual of Criminal Forms, 3rd ed, 1993; (with Fishman) Criminal Trial Techniques, 1994. **Address:** Fishman, Anker & Horstmann LLP, 200 Berkeley St. Fl 16, Boston, MA 02116-5022, U.S.A.

BAILEY, Frederick George. British, b. 1924. **Genres:** Anthropology/Ethnology, Politics/Government, Social commentary, Third World. **Career:** Professor of Anthropology, University of California at San Diego, since 1971. Professor, University of Sussex, Brighton, 1964-71. **Publications:** Caste and the Economic Frontier, 1957; Tribe, Caste and Nation: A Study of Political Activity and Political Change in Highland Orissa, 1960; Politics and Social Change: Orissa in 1959, 1963; Stratagems and Spoils: A Social Anthropology of Politics, 1969; Morality and Expediency: The Folklore of Academic Politics, 1977; The Tactical Uses of Passion, 1983; Humbuggery and Manipulation: The Art of Leadership, 1988; The Prevalence of Deceit, 1991; The Kingdom of Individuals, 1993; The Witch-Hunt, 1994; The Civility of Indifference, 1996. EDITOR: Gifts and Poisons: The Politics of Reputation, 1971; Debate and Compromise: The Politics of Innovation, 1973. **Address:** Dept. of Anthropology, University of California at San Diego, La Jolla, CA 92093-0532, U.S.A.

BAILEY, Gordon (Keith). British, b. 1936. **Genres:** Poetry, Education, Theology/Religion, Humor/Satire. **Career:** Film editor, 1956-59; sales manager, 1959-62; Gordon Bailey series, ATV Network Ltd., Birmingham, 1973-75; Schools Outreach, executive director, 1986-. Voluntary youth worker, 1962-; freelance broadcaster, 1968-. **Publications:** Plastic World, 1971; Moth-balled Religion, 1972; Patchwork Quill, 1975; Can a Man Change?, 1979; 100 Contemporary Christian Poets, 1983; I Want to Tell You How I Feel, God, 1983; Stuff and Nonsense, 1989; Mix and Match, 1999. **Address:** The Coop, Inksmoor Ct, Tedstone Wafre, Herts. HR7 4PP, England. **Online address:** schoolsoutreach@aol.com

BAILEY, Hilary. American, b. 1936. **Genres:** Novels, Bibliography. **Career:** Worked as a publicist and an editor. **Publications:** NOVELS: Polly Put the Kettle On, 1975; Mrs. Mulvaney, 1978; All the Days of My Life, 1984; Hannie Richards, or, The Intrepid Adventures of a Restless Wife, 1985, in US as Hannie Richards; As Time Goes By, 1988; A Stranger to Herself, 1989; In Search of Love, Money and Revenge, 1990; The Cry from Street to Street, 1992; Cassandra: Princess of Troy, 1993; The Strange Adventures of Charlotte Holmes, 1994; Frankenstein's Bride, 1995. OTHER: Vera Brittain (biography), 1987. Contributor of stories, articles and fiction reviews to journals. **Address:** c/o Simon and Schuster Trade, 1230 Avenue of the Americas, New York, NY 10020, U.S.A.

BAILEY, Kathleen C. American, b. 1949. **Genres:** Military/Defense/Arms control. **Career:** U.S. Department of State, Washington, DC, deputy assistant secretary, 1985-87; Arms Control and Disarmament Agency, Washington, DC, assistant director, 1987-90; National Institute for Public Policy, Washington, DC, vice-president, 1990-92; Lawrence Livermore National Laboratory, Livermore, CA, fellow, 1992-. **Publications:** Doomsday Weapons in the Hands of Many: The Arms Control Challenge of the Nineties, 1991; Strengthening Nuclear Nonproliferation, 1993; (ed.) Weapons of Mass Destruction: Costs Versus Benefits, 1994; The UN Inspections in Iraq: Lessons for On-Site Verification, 1995; Death for Cause (novel), 1995. Some writings appear under the name K. C. Bailey. **Address:** National Institute for Public Policy, 3031 Javier Rd., Ste 300, Fairfax, VA 22031-4662, U.S.A.

BAILEY, Kathryn. American. **Genres:** Music. **Career:** Writer and editor, 1991-. **Publications:** NONFICTION: The Twelve-Note Music of Anton Webern: Old Forms in a New Language, 1991; (ed.) Webern Studies, 1996; The Life of Webern, 1998. Contributor to periodicals. **Address:** c/o Cambridge University Press, 40 West 20th St., New York, NY 10011, U.S.A.

BAILEY, Linda. Canadian, b. 1948. **Genres:** Children's fiction, Young adult fiction. **Career:** Writer. **Publications:** How Come the Best Clues Are Always in the Garbage?, 1992; How Can I Be a Detective If I Have to Babysit?, 1993; Who's Got Gertie? And How Can We Get Her Back?, 1994; How Can a Frozen Detective Stay Hot on the Trail?, 1996; What's a Daring Detective Like Me Doing in the Doghouse?, 1997; Gordon Loggins and the Three Bears, 1997; Petula, Who Wouldn't Take a Bath, 1998. **Address:** c/o Kids Can Press Ltd., 29 Birch Ave., Toronto, ON, Canada M4V 1E1.

BAILEY, Maria T. American. **Genres:** Business/Trade/Industry. **Career:** Bailey Innovative Marketing, past president; Broward Community College, past vice president of marketing and interim executive director of Broward Community College Foundation; AutoNation USA, vice president of loyalty marketing; BSM Media (marketing and media company), Pompano Beach, FL, founder, chief executive officer, and creator of Internet Web site BlueSuitMom.com, 2000-. Host of Mom Talk Radio, broadcast by WFLT-Radio, and Mom Talk TV, broadcast in South Florida; guest on other media programs, including ABC World News Tonight. Formerly held management positions with Miami Herald and McDonald's Restaurants. South Florida Parenting Conference, founder, 1990; Nova Southeastern University, member of advisory board of Family Center; Broward County Library Foundation, chair of Night of Literary Feasts; past president of Hospice Hundred and Museum of Art Contemporaries. **Publications:** The Women's Home-based Business Book of Answers: Seventy-five Important Questions Answered by Top Women Business Leaders, 2001; Marketing to Moms: Getting Your Share of the Trillion-Dollar, 2002. Contributor to periodicals. **Address:** BSM Media, 2335 East Atlantic Blvd. Suite 300, Pompano Beach, FL 33062, U.S.A.

BAILEY, Martha (J.). American, b. 1929. **Genres:** Librarianship, Administration/Management, Reference. **Career:** Purdue University, West Lafayette, IN, assistant professor, physics librarian, associate professor, physics and geosciences librarian, professor of library service, 1980-95, life sciences librarian, 1980-95, professor emeritus, 1995-. Union Carbide Corp., technical librarian; E. I. DuPont and de Nemours and Co., Wilmington, DE, library assistant; Eli Lilly and Co., Indianapolis, IN. **Publications:** The Special Librarian as a Supervisor or Middle Manager, 1977, 2nd ed., 1986; Supervisory and Middle Managers in Libraries, 1981; American Women in Science: Colonial Times to 1950, a Biographical Dictionary, 1994; American Women in Science: 1950 to the Present, a Biographical Dictionary, 1998. Contributor to books and magazines.

BAILEY, Norman (Alishan). American, b. 1931. **Genres:** Plays/ Screenplays, International relations/Current affairs, Economics, Politics/ Government. **Career:** International Economist, Mobil Oil, 1959-61; President, Overseas Equity Inc., 1961-68, and Bailey Tondu Warwick & Co. Inc., 1968-74; Assistant Professor, 1962-64, Associate Professor, 1964-68, and Professor, 1968-83, Queen's College, City University of New York. Special Assistant to the President for National Security Affairs and Senior Director for International Economic Affairs, the National Security Council, 1981-84. Consultant and president, Norman A. Bailey, Inc., 1984-. **Publications:** (with R. Linney and D. Cascio) Ten Plays for Radio, 1954; (with R. Linney and D. Cascio) Radio Classics, 1956; Latin America: Politics, Economics and Hemispheric Security, 1965; Latin America in World Politics, 1967; (with others) Portuguese Africa, 1969; (with S. Feder) Operational Conflict Analysis, 1973; (trans.) Pirandello, Sicilian Comedies, 1983; (with R. Cohen) The Mexican Time Bomb, 1987; The Strategic Plan that Won the Cold War, 1998. **Address:** Norman A. Bailey Inc., 1311 Dolley Madison Blvd Ste 2-A, Mc Lean, VA 22101-3925, U.S.A. **Online address:** norman abailey@aol.com

BAILEY, Peter J. American, b. 1946. **Genres:** Literary criticism and history. **Career:** St. Lawrence University, Canton, NY, professor of English, 1980-, and director of Jeffrey Campbell Graduate Fellows Program. **Publications:** Reading Stanley Elkin, 1985; The Reluctant Film Art of Woody Allen, 2000. Contributor to periodicals. **Address:** Department of English, St. Lawrence University, Canton, NY 13617, U.S.A. **Online address:** pbailey@stlawu.edu

BAILEY, Robin W(ayne). American, b. 1952. **Genres:** Science fiction/ Fantasy. **Career:** Writer. **Publications:** FANTASY NOVELS: Frost, 1983; Skull Gate (Frost series), 1985; Bloodsongs (Frost series), 1986; Enchanter, 1989; The Lake of Fire, 1989; Nightwatch, 1990; The Lost City of Zork, 1991; Brothers of the Dragon, 1992; Straight on Till Mourning, 1993, in the US as Flames of the Dragon, 1994; Triumph of the Dragon, 1994. **Address:** c/o Richard Curtis, 171 East 74th Street, New York, NY 10021, U.S.A.

BAILEY, Rosemary. (born England), b. 1953. **Genres:** Adult non-fiction. **Career:** Journalist, travel writer, and author. **Publications:** Scarlet Ribbons: A Priest with AIDS, 1997; The National Geographic Traveler: France, 1999; Life in a Postcard: Escape to the French Pyrenees, 2002; The Man Who Married a Mountain: A Journey through the Pyrenees, 2005. EDITOR AND CONTRIBUTOR, WITH OTHERS: Tuscany, 1990; Loire Valley, 1991; Burgundy, 1992, updated edition, 2000; Cote d'Azur, 1992; Eyewitness Travel Guide to France, 1998; The French Riviera, 2nd edition, 1999; Gascony and the Pyrenees, updated edition, 2001. **Address:** c/o Author Mail, Transworld Publishers, 61-63 Uxbridge Road, London W5 5SA, England.

BAILLIE, Allan. Australian (born Scotland), b. 1943. **Genres:** Novels, Children's fiction, Young adult fiction. **Career:** Sun News Pictorial, Melbourne, Australia, reporter/sub-editor, 1961-64; sub-editor, Middlesex Advertiser, London, 1966-67, Australian Associated Press, Sydney, 1968-69, Sunday Telegraph, Sydney, 1970-73, Daily Telegraph, Sydney, 1973-74, ABC, Sydney, 1974-78, Women's Weekly, Sydney, 1978-80, Sun, Sun-Herald, Sydney, 1980-87; Australian Broadcasting Commission, Sydney, 1973-77; freelance writer, 1969-2004. **Publications:** YOUNG ADULT FICTION: Adrift, 1983; Little Brother, 1985; Riverman, 1986; Eagle Island, 1987; Creature, 1987; Drac and the Gremlin, 1989; Mates, 1989; Megan's Star, 1990; (with C.-C. Yeh) Bawshou Rescues the Sun: A Han Folktale, 1991; Hero, 1991; Little Monster, 1991; The Boss, 1992; The China Coin, 1992; The Bad Guys, 1993; Magician, 1993; Rebel!, 1994; Songman, 1994; Dream Catcher; 1995; Old Magic, 1996; DragonQuest, 1996; Secrets of Walden Rising, 1996; Last Shot, 1997; The Excuse, 1997; Star Navigator, 1997; Wreck!, 1997; (with J. Bentley) Archie: The Good Bad Wolf, 1998; Legends, 1998; Abbie Returns, 2000; Heroes, 2000; Foggy, 2001; j!mp, 2002; Treasure Hunters, 2002; Villains, 2003; Riding with Thunderbolt, 2004. ADULT FICTION: Mask Maker, 1975. Work represented in anthologies. Contributor to magazines. **Address:** 197 Riverview Rd, Clareville, NSW 2107, Australia. **Online address:** baillie_allan@hotmail.com

BAILYN, Lotte. American (born Austria), b. 1930. **Genres:** Administration/ Management, Human relations/Parenting, Social sciences. **Career:** Harvard University, Cambridge, MA, postdoctoral research associate in education,

1956-57, research associate, 1958-64, lecturer in social relations, 1963-67; Massachusetts Institute of Technology, Cambridge, instructor in economics and social science, 1957-58, research associate, 1969-70, lecturer, 1970-71, senior lecturer, 1971-72, associate professor, 1972-80, professor, 1980-91, T Wilson Professor of Management, 1991-. University of London, Imperial College of Science and Technology, visiting scholar in social and economic studies, 1982, academic visitor at Management School, 1991, 1995, 2000; Rockefeller Foundation Study and Conference Center, Bellagio, Italy, scholar in residence, 1983; University of Auckland, visiting university fellow in management studies, 1984; Cambridge University, visiting scholar at New Hall, 1986-87. **Publications:** Mass Media and Children: A Study of Exposure Habits and Cognitive Effects (monograph), 1959; (with E.H. Schein) Living with Technology: Issues at Mid-Career, 1980; (with M.B. Arthur, D.J. Levinson, and H.A. Shepard) Working with Careers, 1984; Breaking the Mold: Women, Men, and Time in the New Corporate World, 1993; (with R. Rapoport, et al.) Relinking Life and Work: Toward a Better Future, 1996; (with R. Rapoport, J.K. Fletcher, and B.H. Pruitt) Beyond Work & Family Balance: Advancing Gender Equity and Workplace Performance, 2002. Work represented in books. Contributor to periodicals. **Address:** Sloan School of Management, E52-585, Massachusetts Institute of Technology, Cambridge, MA 02139, U.S.A. **Online address:** lbailyn@mit.edu

BAIN, David Haward. American, b. 1949. **Genres:** History, Social commentary, Writing/Journalism. **Career:** Alfred A. Knopf, Inc., NYC, editorial assistant, 1973-76; Stonehill Publishers, NYC, editor, 1976-77; Crown Publishers, NYC, editor, 1977-78; writer, 1978-; Bread Loaf Writers' Conference, faculty, 1981-88, 2003, admissions board, 1987-; Middlebury College, lecturer, 1987-. **Publications:** Aftershocks, 1980; Sitting in Darkness, 1984; Whose Woods These Are, 1994; The College on the Hill, 1999. Empire Express: Building the First Transcontinental Railroad, 1999; The Old Iron Road, 2004. Contributor to periodicals. **Address:** c/o Ellen Levine Trident Media Group, 41 Madison Ave, New York, NY 10010, U.S.A.

BAIN, Kenneth (Ross). New Zealander, b. 1923. **Genres:** History, Cultural/ Ethnic topics, Human relations/Parenting, International relations/Current affairs, Politics/Government, Public/Social administration, Race relations, Third World, Autobiography/Memoirs. **Career:** Chairman, Commonwealth Consultants (BVI) Ltd., British Virgin Islands, 1985-96. Contributor to The Independent (London) newspaper. British colonial administrator, 1946-74: Government of Palestine, 1946-48; Government of Fiji, 1949-52; Secretary to Government of Tonga, 1953-56; Fiji, 1957-74; Commissioner for Pitcairn, 1965-70; Commissioner British South Pacific Office, 1965-70; Deputy High Commissioner for Fiji in London, 1970-74. Director of Finance and Field Personnel Services, Commonwealth Fund for Technical Cooperation, Commonwealth Secretarial, London, 1974-79; Financial Secretary and Deputy Governor, Government of the British Virgin Islands, 1980-85. **Publications:** Royal Visit to Tonga, 1954; Low Income Housing in the West Indies, 1958; The Friendly Islanders: A Story of Queen Salote and Her People, 1967; (ed.) A Guide to Pitcairn Island, 2nd ed., 1970; Treason at Ten: Fiji at the Crossroads, 1989; The New Friendly Islanders, 1993; St. Helena: The Island, Her People and Their Ship, 1993. **Address:** South Rigg, 115 Kippington Rd., Sevenaks, Kent TN13 2LW, England.

BAIN, Trevor. American, b. 1931. **Genres:** Business/Trade/Industry. **Career:** University of Arizona, Tucson, assistant professor of economics, 1964-67; University of Michigan, Ann Arbor, visiting associate professor of economics and research associate at Institute of Industrial and Labor Relations, 1967-69; Queens College of the City University of New York, Flushing, NY, associate professor of economics, 1969-74; University of Alabama, Tuscaloosa, professor of labor economics and industrial relations, 1974-2000, John R. Miller Professor of Management, 1983-93, director of Human Resources Institute, 1974-2000, professor emeritus of management and industrial relations, 2000-. Labor arbitrator. **Publications:** Banking the Furnace: Restructuring of the Steel Industry in Eight Countries, 1992. Contributor to books. Contributor to economic journals. **Address:** Graduate School of Business, University of Alabama, P.O. Box 870225, Tuscaloosa, AL 35487, U.S.A. **Online address:** tbain@cba.ua.edu

BAINBRIDGE, Beryl (Margaret). British, b. 1934. **Genres:** Novels. **Career:** Actress in repertory theatres in UK, 1949-60; Gerald Duckworth & Co. Ltd., publrs., London, clerk, 1971-73; Evening Standard, columnist, 1987-93. **Publications:** A Weekend with Claude, 1967, rev. ed., 1981; Another Part of the Wood, 1968, rev. ed., 1979; Harriet Said, 1972; The Dressmaker (in US as The Secret Glass), 1973; The Bottle Factory Outing, 1974; Sweet William, 1975; A Quiet Life, 1976; Injury Time, 1976; Young Adolf, 1978; Winter Garden, 1980; English Journey; or, The Road to Milton Keynes, 1984; Watson's Apology, 1984; Mum and Mr. Armitage, 1985; Forever England, 1986;

Filthy Lucre, 1986; An Awfully Big Adventure, 1990; The Birthday Boys, 1991; Something Happened Yesterday (essays), 1993; Collected Stories, 1994; Every Man for Himself, 1996; Master Georgie, 1998; According to Queeney, 2001. PLAYS: Tiptoe through the Tulips, 1976; The Warrior's Return, 1977; It's a Lovely Day Tomorrow, 1977; Journal of Bridget Hitler, 1981; Somewhere More Central (for TV), 1981; Evensong (for TV), 1986. FILMS: Sweet William; The Dressmaker; An Awfully Big Adventure. **Address:** 42 Albert St, London NW1 7NU, England.

BAINS, William (Arthur). British, b. 1955. **Genres:** Technology. **Career:** Stanford University, Stanford, CA, postdoctoral research fellow, 1982-85; University of Bath, Avon, England, lecturer in biochemistry, 1985-88; PA Consulting Group, technology consultant, 1988-. **Publications:** Genetic Engineering for Almost Everybody, 1987; (with J. Raggett) Artificial Intelligence from A to Z, 1991; Biotechnology from A to Z, 1993. Contributor to scientific journals. **Address:** 101 Beechwood Ave., Melbourn, Royston, Hants. SG8 6DP, England.

BAIR, Deirdre. American, b. 1935. **Genres:** Writing/Journalism, Biography. **Career:** Writer. Freelance journalist, 1957-69; University of Pennsylvania, Philadelphia, assistant professor and associate professor of English, 1976-88; independent scholar and writer, 1988-. **Publications:** BIOGRAPHIES: Samuel Beckett, 1978 (National Book Award, 1981); Simone de Beauvoir, 1990; Anais Nin, 1995; Jung: A Biography, 2003. Contributor of articles and book reviews to journals. **Address:** c/o Elaine Markson Agency, 44 Greenwich Ave, New York, NY 10011, U.S.A.

BAIRD, Alison. Canadian, b. 1963. **Genres:** Children's fiction. **Career:** Writer. **Publications:** The Dragon's Egg, 1994; White as the Waves: A Novel of Moby Dick, 1999; The Hidden World, 1999; The Wolves of Woden, 2001; The Witches of Willowmere, 2002. Work represented in anthologies. Contributor of short stories to magazines. **Address:** c/o Sternig & Byrne Literary Agency, 3209 South 55th St., Milwaukee, WI 53219, U.S.A.

BAITZ, Jon Robin. American, b. 1961. **Genres:** Plays/Screenplays. **Career:** Playwright, 1986-. Worked as a shortorder cook, tractor driver, and assistant to film producers. **Publications:** The Film Society (play), 1987; Dutch Landscape, 1989; Substance of Fire, 1993; The End of the Day (play), 1993; Three Hotels (play), 1993; A Fair Country (play), 1996. **Address:** c/o Creative Artists Agency, 9830 Wilshire Blvd, Beverly Hills, CA 90212-1825, U.S.A.

BAKALIAN, Anny. American (born Lebanon), b. 1951. **Genres:** Sociology. **Career:** American University of Beirut, Lebanon, sociology instructor, 1978-81; College of Notre Dame of Maryland, Baltimore, associate professor of sociology, 1989-2001; Diocese of Armenian Church in America, NYC, consultant, 1991-93; St. Nersess Armenian Seminary, New Rochelle, NY, teacher, 1993. **Publications:** Armenian-Americans: From Being to Feeling Armenian, 1993. **Address:** MEMEAC Graduate Center, City University of New York, 365 5th Ave, New York, NY 10016-4309, U.S.A. **Online address:** Abakalian@gc.cuny.edu

BAKER, Alan. British, b. 1939. **Genres:** Mathematics/Statistics. **Career:** Trinity College, Cambridge, fellow, 1964-; Cambridge University, professor of pure mathematics, 1974-. **Publications:** Transcendental Number Theory, 1975, 1990; A Concise Introduction to the Theory of Numbers, 1984. EDITOR: (with D.W. Masser) Transcendence Theory: Advances and Applications, 1977; New Advances in Transcendence Theory, 1988; (with B. Bollobas and A. Hajnal) A Tribute to Paul Erdos, 1990. **Address:** Trinity College, Cambridge CB2 1TQ, England. **Online address:** a.baker@dpmms.cam.ac.uk

BAKER, Calvin. American, b. 1972. **Genres:** Novels. **Career:** Writer. People magazine, NYC, staff writer. **Publications:** Naming the New World (novel), 1997. Contributor of articles and book reviews to periodicals. **Address:** c/o People Weekly, Rockefeller Center, New Time & Life Bldg., New York, NY 10020, U.S.A.

BAKER, Christina Looper. American, b. 1939. **Genres:** Women's studies and issues, Bibliography. **Career:** English professor and feminist scholar. Durham High School, Durham, NC, English teacher, 1961-63; University of Maine, Bangor, ME, assistant professor of English, 1978-84, associate professor, 1985-92, professor, 1993-. Elected to Maine House of Representatives, 1996-98. **Publications:** (with C.B. Kline) The Conversation Begins: Mothers and Daughters Talk about Living Feminism, 1996; In a Generous Spirit: A First-person Biography of Myra Page, 1996. **Address:** 85 Texas Ave., University College, Bangor, ME 04401, U.S.A. **Online address:** cbaker@maine.maine.edu

BAKER, Christopher W. American, b. 1952. **Genres:** Information science/Computers. **Career:** Brandslinger Naming Group, Sebastopol, CA, chief executive officer, 1999-. **Publications:** Computer Illusion in Film and TV, 1994; Scientific Visualization: The New Eyes of Science, 1994; Let There Be Life!: Animating with the Computer, 1997; Virtual Reality: Experiencing Illusion, 2000; A New World of Simulators: Training with Technology, 2001; Robots among Us: The Challenges and Promises of Robotics, 2002. **Address:** 8770 Cider Springs Rd., Sebastopol, CA 95472, U.S.A. **Online address:** books@brandslinger.com

BAKER, Hugh D(avid) R(oberts). British, b. 1937. **Genres:** Anthropology/Ethnology, Cultural/Ethnic topics, Language/Linguistics. **Career:** University of London, School of Oriental and African Studies, lecturer in Chinese, 1967-80, reader in modern Chinese, 1980-90, professor of Chinese, 1990-2002, dean (interface), 2001-, professor emeritus, 2002-. Hong Kong Government, Chinese language training adviser, 1974-75. **Publications:** The Five Great Clans of the New Territories of Hong Kong, 1966; A Chinese Lineage Village: Sheung Shui, 1968; Ancestral Images: A Hong Kong Album, 1979; Chinese Family and Kinship, 1979; More Ancestral Images: A Second Hong Kong Album, 1980; Ancestral Images Again: A Third Hong Kong Album, 1981; (with P.Y.L. Ng) New Peace County: A Chinese Gazetteer of the Hong Kong Region, 1983; The Overseas Chinese, 1987; (with S. Feuchtwang) An Old State in New Settings, 1991; (with P.C. T'ung) Chinese in Three Months, 1993; (with P.K. Ho) Teach Yourself Cantonese, 1995. **Address:** School of Oriental and African Studies, University of London, London WC1H 0XG, England. **Online address:** hb3@soas.ac.uk

BAKER, James W. American, b. 1926. **Genres:** Children's non-fiction, Essays, How-to books. **Career:** Richmond News Leader, Richmond, VA, reporter and education writer, 1951-63; U.S. Information Agency, Washington, DC, foreign service officer, 1963-83; Virginia Gazette, Williamsburg, VA, columnist and writer, 1983-. **Publications:** Illusions Illustrated: A Professional Magic Show for Young Performers, 1984; Valentine Magic, 1988; Halloween Magic, 1988; Christmas Magic, 1988; Birthday Magic, 1988; New Year's Magic, 1989; Presidents' Day Magic, 1989; April Fools' Day Magic, 1989; Thanksgiving Magic, 1989; Columbus Day Magic, 1990; St. Patrick's Day Magic, 1990; Arbor Day Magic, 1990; Independence Day Magic, 1991; Americans Abroad, 1992. **Address:** 510 Spring Trace, Williamsburg, VA 23188, U.S.A. **Online address:** mrmystic@widomaker.com

BAKER, Jeannie. British/Australian, b. 1950. **Genres:** Children's fiction, Art/Art history, Environmental sciences/Ecology, Film, Travel/Exploration, Picture/board books. **Career:** Author, illustrator, artist, designer, filmmaker. One Women Exhibitions, London, 1975, New York, 1983; One-Woman Travelling Exhibition, Australia, 1988-89, 1991-92, 1995-97, 2000-02, 2004-06; Collections include: Queensland State Gallery, State Gallery of West Australia, Powerhouse Museum Sydney, Dromkeen, James Fairfax, Quantos, Private collections internationally. **Publications:** Grandfather, 1977; Grandmother, 1978; Millicent, 1980; One Hungry Spider, 1981; Home in the Sky, 1984; Where the Forest Meets the Sea, 1988; Window, 1991; The Story of Rosy Dock, 1995; The Hidden Forest, 2000; Belonging/Home, 2004. **Address:** c/o Walker Books Australia, Locked Bag 22 Newtown, Sydney, NSW 2042, Australia. **Online address:** jeanniebaker.com

BAKER, Kage. American, b. 1952. **Genres:** Science fiction/Fantasy. **Career:** Penncorp Financial, Santa Monica, CA, customer service representative, 1980-87; Pierce National Life, Los Angeles, CA, customer service representative, 1987-92; Living History Center, Novato, CA, general office worker, 1993-94; PhotoAd/EasyAd, San Luis Obispo, CA, customer service representative, 1995-. Teacher of weekend classes in "Elizabethan English as a second language" and "folklore in Elizabethan England," 1978-. **Publications:** In the Garden of Iden (science fiction novel), 1998. Contributor of stories to Isaac Asimov's magazine. **Address:** c/o Virginia Kidd Agency Inc., 538 East Harford St., PO Box 278, Milford, PA 18337, U.S.A. **Online address:** kage@best1.net

BAKER, Kevin (Breen). American, b. 1958. **Genres:** Novels. **Career:** Gloucester Daily Times, Gloucester, MA, staff writer, 1971-80; Foundation Center, NYC, compiler of entries for reference books, 1980-85; Public Securities Association, NYC, free-lance writer on municipal bonds papers, 1986-87; letter writer for mayor's office, NYC, 1987-88; free-lance writer, 1988-. **Publications:** NOVELS: Sometimes You See It Coming, 1993; Dreamland, 1999; Paradise Alley, 2002. Contributor to books and periodicals. OTHER: (chief historical researcher) The American Century, by H. Evans. **Address:** c/o Dunow Carlson Literary Agency, 27 W 20rd St Ste 1003, New York, NY 10011, U.S.A.

BAKER, Kyle. (born United States), b. 1965. **Genres:** Graphic Novels. **Career:** Writer and illustrator; director of animated films. Founder of Kyle Baker Publishing. **Publications:** GRAPHIC NOVELS; SELF-ILLUSTRATED: The Cowboy Wally Show, 1988, Sixteenth Commemorative Edition, 2003; Why I Hate Saturn, 1993; You Are Here, 1999; King David, 2002; Undercover Genie: The Irreverent Conjurings of an Illustrative Aladdin, 2003. OTHER: (Illustrator) Aaron McGruder and Reginald Hudlin, Birth of a Nation: A Comic Novel, 2004. **Address:** c/o Author Mail, DC Comics, 1700 Broadway, New York, NY 10019, U.S.A. **Online address:** kylebaker@kylebaker.com

BAKER, Larry. American. **Genres:** Novels. **Career:** Worked as a hotel clerk, house detective, pizza restaurant manager, sports writer, and drive-in movie theater manager; Iowa City, IA, city councilor, 1993-97, currently serving second term, former zoning commission member; part-time teacher of history and literature; Waldenbooks, part-time employee. Novelist. **Publications:** The Flamingo Rising (novel), 1997. **Address:** Iowa City City Council, Civic Center, 410 E. Washington Street, Iowa City, IA 52240, U.S.A. **Online address:** baker@blue.weeg.uiowa.edu

BAKER, Lori. American, b. 1962. **Genres:** Novels, Novellas/Short stories, Medicine/Health, Psychiatry, Psychology. **Career:** Freelance writer of both nonfiction and fiction; Massachusetts General Hospital, Boston, MA, science writer in psychiatry research, 1989-90; Brown University, Providence, RI, senior technical writer in psychiatry, 1990-91; adjunct lecturer in creative writing, 1993-; Wheaton College, Norton, MA, visiting assistant professor of English, 1992-95. Gives readings of her works. **Publications:** (ed. with R.P. Galea and B.F. Lewis) AIDS and IV Drug Abusers: Current Perspectives (nonfiction), 1988; Scraps (fiction), 1995; Crazy Water: Six Fictions (short stories), 1996. Contributor to books. Contributor of both fiction and nonfiction to magazines and journals. **Address:** 11 Slater Ave, Providence, RI 02906, U.S.A. **Online address:** Lori_Baker@brown.edu

BAKER, Margaret J(oyce). British, b. 1918. **Genres:** Children's fiction, Biography. **Publications:** The Fighting Cocks, 1949; Nonsense Said the Tortoise (in U.S. as Homer the Tortoise), 1949; Four Farthings and a Thimble, 1950; A Castle and Sixpence, 1951; Benbow and the Angels, 1952; The Family That Grew and Grew, 1952; Treasure Trove, 1952; Homer Sees the Queen, 1953; The Young Magicians, 1954; Lions in the Potting Shed (in U.S. as Lions in the Woodshed), 1954; The Wonderful Wellington Boots, 1955; Anna Sewell and Black Beauty, 1956; Acorns and Aerials, 1956; The Bright High Flyer, 1957; Tip and Run, 1958; Homer Goes to Stratford, 1958; The Magic Seashell, 1959; The Birds of Thimblepins, 1960; Homer in Orbit, 1961; Into the Castle, 1962; The Cats of Honeytown, 1962; Away Went Galloper, 1962; Castaway Christmas, 1963; Cut Off from Crumpets, 1964; The Shoe Shop Bears, 1964; Homer Goes West, 1965; Hannibal and the Bears, 1965; Bears Back in Business, 1967; Porterhouse Major, 1967; Hi-Jinks Joins the Bears, 1970; Snails' Place, 1970; The Last Straw, 1971; Boots and the Ginger Bears, 1972; The Sand Bird, 1973; Prickets Way, 1973; Lock Stock and Barrel, 1974; Home from the Hill, 1968; Sand in Our Shoes, 1976; The Gift Horse, 1982; Catch as Catch Can, 1983; Beware of the Gnomes, 1985; The Waiting Room Doll, 1986; Fresh Fields for Daisy, 1987. **Address:** Prickets, Old Cleeve, Near Minehead, Somerset TA24 6HW, England.

BAKER, Mark. American, b. 1950. **Genres:** Military/Defense/Arms control, Sex. **Career:** Free-lance writer, 1979-. **Publications:** Nam: The Vietnam War in the Words of the Men and Women Who Fought There, 1981; Cops: Their Lives in Their Own Words, 1985; Women: American Women in Their Own Words, 1990; What Men Really Think about Women, Love, Sex, and Themselves, 1991; Sex Lives: A Sexual Self-Portrait of America, 1994; Bad Guys, 1996; Insider's Book of Business School Lists, 1997; Insider's Book of Law School Lists, 1997; DA, 1999. Contributor to periodicals. **Address:** c/o Esther Newberg, International Creative Management, 40 West 57th St, New York, NY 10019, U.S.A.

BAKER, Maureen. Canadian/New Zealander, b. 1948. **Genres:** Sociology. **Career:** Acadia University, Wolfville, NS, assistant professor of sociology, 1974-76; University of Toronto, ON, assistant professor of sociology, 1978-83; Parliament of Canada, Ottawa, ON, senior researcher, 1984-90; McGill University, Montreal, QC, associate professor and professor of social work, 1990-97; University of Auckland, New Zealand, professor of sociology, 1998-, head of sociology, 1998-2004. **Publications:** Families: Changing Trends in Canada, 1984, 5th ed., 2005; What Will Tomorrow Bring? (monograph), 1985; Aging in Canadian Society, 1988; Families in Canadian Society, 1989, 2nd ed., 1993; Canada's Changing Families: Challenges to Public Policy, 1994; Canadian Family Policies, 1995; (with D. Tippin) Poverty, Social Assistance and the Employability of Mothers: Restructuring Welfare States, 1999; Families, Labour and Love, 2001; Families, Social Policy & Globalization, forthcoming. **Address:** Dept of Sociology, University of Auckland, Auckland, New Zealand. **Online address:** ma.baker@auckland.ac.nz

BAKER, Paul R(aymond). American, b. 1927. **Genres:** Architecture, Area studies, History. **Career:** New York University, Professor of History and former Director of American Civilization Program, 1965-. **Publications:** The Fortunate Pilgrims: Americans in Italy, 1800-1860, 1964; (with W. Hall) The American Experience, vol. I, The American People, 1976, vol. II, Growth of a Nation, 1976, vol. III, Organizing a Democracy, 1979, vol. IV, The American Economy, 1979, vol. V, The United States in World Affairs, 1979; Richard Morris Hunt, 1980, 1986; The Architecture of Richard Morris Hunt, 1986; Stanny: The Gilded Life of Stanford White, 1989; Greenwich Village: Culture and Counterculture, 1993. EDITOR: Views of Society and Manners in America, by F.W. D'Arusmont, 1963; The Atomic Bomb: The Great Decision, 1968. **Address:** c/o Dept. of History, New York University, 53 Washington Sq S, New York, NY 10012, U.S.A.

BAKER, Richard A(llan). American, b. 1940. **Genres:** Politics/Government, History, Biography. **Career:** Holy Apostles College, Cromwell, CT, assistant professor of history, 1965-67; Library of Congress, Washington, DC, specialist in American history for Legislative Reference Service, 1968-69; U.S. Senate, Washington, DC, acting curator, 1969-70; Government Research Corp., Washington, DC, director of research, 1970-75; U.S. Senate, director of Historical Office, 1975-. University of Maryland at College Park, adjunct instructor, 1983-84; University of Texas at Arlington, Walter Prescott Webb Lecturer, 1984; Cornell University, adjunct professor in Cornell in Washington Program, 1987-90, 1992. **Publications:** The United States Senate: A Historical Bibliography, 1977; Conservation Politics: The Senate Career of Clinton P. Anderson, 1985; The Senate of the United States: A Bicentennial History, 1988. EDITOR: Proceedings: Conference on Research Use and Disposition of Senators' Papers, 1979; (with B. Dole, and contrib) Historical Almanac of the United States Senate, 1989; (with R.H. Davidson) First among Equals: Senate Leaders of the Twentieth Century, 1991. Work represented in anthologies. **Address:** Historical Office, U.S. Senate, Washington, DC 20510, U.S.A. **Online address:** HISTORIAN@SEC.SENATE.GOV

BAKER, Richard E. American, b. 1950. **Genres:** Literary criticism and history. **Career:** Front Range Community College, Denver, CO, instructor in liberal arts, 1985-90; University of Colorado, Boulder, instructor, 1988-91; Metropolitan State College, Denver, adjunct faculty member, 1989-94; Adams State College, Alamosa, CO, visiting assistant professor of Spanish, 1994-95, associate professor of English, 1995-. **Publications:** The Dynamics of the Absurd in the Existentialist Novel, 1993. Contributor to periodicals. **Address:** Dept of Arts and Letters, Adams State College, Alamosa, CO 81102, U.S.A.

BAKER, Russell (Wayne). American, b. 1925. **Genres:** Autobiography/Memoirs, Humor/Satire. **Career:** New York Times, editorial columnist, 1962-, Washington Bureau, 1954-62, Observer columnist, 1962-89; Baltimore Sun, staff member, 1947-54; Pulitzer Prize, recipient, 1979, 1983. **Publications:** An American in Washington, 1961; No Cause for Panic, 1964; All Things Considered, 1965; Our Next President, 1968; Poor Russell's Almanac, 1972; The Upside Down Man, 1977; So This Is Depravity, 1980; (with others) Home Again, Home Again, 1979; Growing Up, 1982; The Rescue of Miss Yaskell and Other Pipe Dreams, 1983; (ed) The Norton Book of Light Verse, 1986; The Good Times, 1989; There's a Country in My Cellar: The Best of Russell Baker, 1991; (ed) Russell Baker's Book of American Humor, 1993; (with others) Inventing the Truth: The Art and Craft of Memoir, 2nd ed., 1995, rev. ed., 1998; Looking Back, 2002. **Address:** New York Times, 229 W 43rd St, New York, NY 10036, U.S.A.

BAKER, Sharlene. American, b. 1954. **Genres:** Novels, Plays/Screenplays. **Career:** Writer. **Publications:** Finding Signs (novel), 1990; (with J.P. Eberhard) Love Always (screenplay), 1996. **Address:** c/o Paper Journey Press, 1202 Watts St., Durham, NC 27701, U.S.A.

BAKER, Stephen. See Obituaries.

BAKER, Thomas Harrison. American, b. 1933. **Genres:** Communications/Media, History. **Career:** Mississippi State College for Women, Columbus, assistant professor, 1963-68; University of Arkansas at Little Rock, professor of history, 1969-95, professor emeritus, 1995-. **Publications:** The Memphis Commercial Appeal: History of a Southern Newspaper, 1971; (co) An

Arkansas History for Young People, 1991, 3rd ed., 2003. **Address:** 2 Arrow Brook Ct, Little Rock, AR 72227, U.S.A.

BAKER, William. American (born England), b. 1944. **Genres:** Literary criticism and history, Autobiography/Memoirs, Bibliography, Reference. **Career:** City Literary Institute, London, lecturer in English, 1967-71; Thurrock Technical College, lecturer, 1969-71; Ben-Gurion University of the Negev, Beersheva, Israel, lecturer, 1971-77; Hebrew University of Jerusalem, lecturer, 1973-75; University of Kent at Canterbury, UK, lecturer, 1977-78; West Midlands College of Higher Education, senior lecturer, 1978-85; Pitzer College, Claremont, CA, visiting professor, 1981-82; Clifton College, Bristol, UK, housemaster, 1986-89; Northern Illinois University, DeKalb, associate professor, 1989-94, professor of English and library studies, 1994-2003, presidential research professor, 2003-. NEH Senior Fellowship, 2002-03. English Association, fellow. **Publications:** (with others) Harold Pinter, 1973; Critics on George Eliot, 1973; George Eliot and Judaism, 1975; Some George Eliot Notebooks, 4 vols., 1976-85; The George Eliot-George Henry Lewes Library, 1977; The Libraries of George Eliot and G.H. Lewes, 1981; Shakespeare: The Merchant of Venice, 1985; Shakespeare: Antony and Cleopatra, 1985, rev. ed., 1991; (with J. Kimber and M.B. Kinch) F.R. Leavis and Q.D. Leavis: An Annotated Bibliography, 1989; The Early History of the London Library, 1992; (with K. Womack) Recent Work in Critical Theory, 1989-1995 (bibliography), 1996; 20th-Century Bibliography and Textual Criticism, 2000; Wilkie Collins's Library, 2002; (with J.C. Ross) George Eliot: A Bibliographical History, 2002. EDITOR: The Letters of George Henry Lewes, 3 vols., 1995, 1999; (with J.H. Alexander) Sir Walter Scott: Tales of a Grandfather; The History of France, 2nd series, 1996; (with J. Wolfreys) Literary Theories, 1996; (assoc.) New Dictionary of National Biography, 1996-; (with K. Womack) Dictionary of Literary Biography, Vol. 184: 19th-Century British Bibliographers & Book Collectors, 1997, Vol. 201: 20th-Century British Bibliographers & Book Collectors, 1999, Vol. 213: Pre19th Century British Bibliographers & Book Collectors, 1999; The Letters of Wilkie Collins, 1999; G. Eliot, Felix Holt, the Radical, 2000; (with K. Womack) A Companion to the Victorian Novel, 2002. Contributor of articles and reviews to periodicals. **Address:** Dept of English, University Libraries, Northern Illinois University, DeKalb, IL 60115-2868, U.S.A. **Online address:** wbaker@niu.edu

BAKEWELL, Kenneth (Graham Bartlett). British, b. 1931. **Genres:** Administration/Management, Librarianship. **Career:** British Inst of Mgmt., librarian, 1961-64; Liverpool City Libraries, technical documentation officer and librarian, 1964-66; Liverpool John Moores University, lecturer, 1966-68, senior lecturer, 1968-78, principal lecturer, 1978-87, reader, 1987-91, professor of information and library management, 1991-93, emeritus professor, 1993-. Society of Indexers, president, 1987-91. **Publications:** (comp.) Productivity in British Industry, 1963; (ed.) Library and Information Services Throughout the World, 1969; How to Find Out: Management and Productivity, 2nd ed., 1970; A Manual of Cataloguing Practice, 1972; Management Principles and Practice: A Guide to Information Sources, 1977; Classification and Indexing Practice, 1978; (with E.J. Hunter) Cataloguing, 1979; (with K.D.C. Vernon and others) The London Classification of Business Studies, 2nd ed., 1979; (with G.A. Dare) The Manager's Guide to Getting the Answers, 1980, 1983; How to Organise Information, 1984; Business Information and the Public Library, 1987; Managing User-Centered Libraries and Information Services, 1991, rev. ed., 1997; (with P.L. Williams) Indexing Children's Books, 2000. **Address:** 9 Greenacre Rd, Liverpool L25 0LD, England.

BAKKER, Robert T. American, b. 1946. **Genres:** Novels, Zoology. **Career:** University Museum, University of Colorado, Boulder, CO, adjunct curator; Johns Hopkins University, Baltimore, ME, associate professor, 1976-1984; Tate Museum, Casper, WY, dinosaur curator. Consultant for Dinamation International Society and Sega Genesis. **Publications:** The Dinosaur Heresies: New Theories Unlocking the Mystery of the Dinosaurs and Their Extinction, 1986; Raptor Red (novel), 1995. **Address:** Tate Museum, Casper College, 125 College Dr., Casper, WY 82601, U.S.A.

BAL, Mieke (Maria Gertrudis). Dutch, b. 1946. **Genres:** Literary criticism and history, Theology/Religion, Women's studies and issues. **Career:** Associated with universities in The Netherlands; University of Utrecht, co-founder of the Women's Studies Program, 1981, director, 1982-; University of Rochester, Rochester, NY, professor of comparative literature and art history, Susan B. Anthony professor of women's studies, 1987-91, co-founder and director of the program in Comparative Arts (now Visual and Cultural Studies); University of Amsterdam, chair of the Theory of Literature, 1991-, founder and codirector of Amsterdam School of Cultural Analysis (a research center). Visiting professor at universities; research associate and visiting

lecturer at Harvard University Divinity School, 1985-86. Has appeared in radio presentations. **Publications:** NONFICTION: Complexite d'un roman populaire, 1974; Narratologie: Essais sur la signification narrative dans quatre romans modernes, 1977; rev. and trans. as Narratology: Introduction to the Theory of Narrative, 1985; De Theorie van vertellen en verhalen, 1978, 3rd ed, 1985; (with J. van Luxemburg and W. Weststeijn) Inleiding in de literatuurwetenschap, 1981, rev. 5th ed., 1987; (with F. van Dijk and G. van Ginneken) En Sara in haar tent lachte: Patriarchaat en verzet in bijbelverhalen, 1984; Femmes imaginaires: L'Ancien Testament au risque d'une narratologie critique, 1986; selections trans., rev., and published in the US as Lethal Love: Feminist Literary Readings of Biblical Love Stories, 1987; (with Luxemburg and Weststeijn) Over literatuur, 1987; Het Rembrandt Effect: Visies op kijken, 1987; Death and Dissymmetry: The Politics of Coherence in the Book of Judges, c. 1988; Murder and Difference: Gender, Genre, and Scholarship on Sisera's Death, c. 1988; Verkrachting verbeeld: Seksueel geweld in cultuur gebracht, 1988; On Storytelling: Essays in Narratology, 1991; Reading "Rembrandt": Beyond the Word-Image Opposition: The Northrop Frye Lectures in Literary Theory, 1991; On Meaning-Making: Essays in Semiotics, c. 1994; Double Exposures: The Subject of Cultural Analysis, 1996. EDITOR: Mensen van papier: Over personages in de literatuur, 1980; Literaire genres en hun gebruik, 1981; Anti-Covenant: Counter-Reading Women's Lives in the Hebrew Bible, 1989; (with I.E. Boer) The Point of Theory: Practices of Cultural Analysis, 1994. Contributor to books and periodicals. **Address:** University of Amsterdam, ALW/Spuistraat 210, 1012 VT Amsterdam, Netherlands.

BALAGURU, P(erumalsamy) N(aidu). American (born India), b. 1947. **Genres:** Engineering, Technology. **Career:** Coimbatore Institute of Technology, University of Madras, India, associate lecturer, 1970-73; Indian Institute of Technology, Madras, India, senior research scholar, 1973-74; University of Illinois at Chicago Circle, teaching and research assistant, 1975-77; Rutgers University, Piscataway, NJ, assistant professor, 1977-82, associate professor, 1982-88, professor of civil engineering, 1988-2002, distinguished professor, 2002-. Northwestern University, visiting professor, 1990; National Science Foundation, program director, 2001-04. Consulting engineer for DuPont, Allied Signal, 3M Co., FMC Corp. and Diversified Technology Corporations. **Publications:** (with S.P. Shah) Fiber Reinforced Cement Composites, 1992. EDITOR: (with V. Ramakrishnan) Computer Use for Statistical Analysis of Concrete Test Data, 1987; Thin Reinforced Concrete Products and Systems, 1994. Contributor to books and periodicals. **Address:** Rutgers University, Dept of Civil and Environmental Engineering, 623 Bowser Rd, Piscataway, NJ 08854-8014, U.S.A. **Online address:** balaguru@rci.rutgers.edu

BALAKRISHNAN, N. Canadian (born India), b. 1956. **Genres:** Mathematics/Statistics. **Career:** University of Guelph, Guelph, Ontario, visiting faculty member, 1984-85; McMaster University, Hamilton, Ontario, research fellow, 1985-86, assistant professor, 1986-89, associate professor, 1989-95, professor of mathematics and statistics, 1995-. Statpro Consulting, sole proprietor. **Publications:** (with B.C. Arnold) Relations, Bounds, and Approximations for Order Statistics, 1989; (with A.C. Cohen) Order Statistics and Inference: Estimation Methods, 1991; (with B.C. Arnold and H.N. Nagaraja) A First Course in Order Statistics, 1992; (with N.L. Johnson and S. Kotz) Continuous Univariate Distributions, Vol 1, 1994, Vol. 2, 1995; (with H.L. Harter) The CRC Handbook of Tables for the Use of Order Statistics in Estimation, 1996; The CRC Tables for the Use of Order Statistics in Tests of Hypotheses, 1997; (with Harter) The CRC Handbook of Tables for the Use of Range, 1997; (with Johnson and Kotz) Discrete Multivariate Distributions, 1997; (with W.W.S. Chen) CRC Handbook of Tables for Order Statistics from Inverse Gaussian Distributions with Applications, 1997. EDITOR: Handbook of the Logistic Distribution, 1992; Recent Advances in Life-Testing and Reliability, 1995; CRC Handbook of Applied Industrial Statistics, 1996; The Exponential Distribution: Theory, Methods and Applications, 1996; (with N.L. Johnson) Advances in the Theory and Practice of Statistics, 1997; Advances in Combinatorial Methods and Applications to Probability and Statistics, 1997. **Address:** Department of Mathematics and Statistics, McMaster University, Hamilton, ON, Canada L8S 4K1. **Online address:** bala@mcmail.cis.mcmaster.ca

BALCH, James F. American, b. 1933. **Genres:** Medicine/Health. **Career:** Self-employed surgeon, IN, 1960-96; Health Counseling Inc., physician and author, 1997-. **Publications:** (with P.A. Balch) Prescription for Nutritional Healing: An A-to-Z Guide to Supplements, 1996; The Super Antioxidants: Why They Will Change the Face of Healthcare in the Twenty-first Century, 1998; (with M. Walker) Heartburn and What to Do about It: A Guide to Overcoming the Discomforts of Indigestion Using Drug-Free Remedies, 1998; (with P.A. Balch) Prescription for Dietary Wellness: Using Foods to Heal, 1998; Ten Natural Remedies That Can Save Your Life, 2000. **Address:** 99 Trophy Club Drive, Trophy Club, TX 76262, U.S.A. **Online address:** Balch33@aol.com

BALCHIN, William George Victor. British, b. 1916. **Genres:** Geography. **Career:** University of London, King's College, Lecturer in Geography, 1945-54; University College of Swansea, Professor of Geography, 1954-78, Vice-Principal, 1964-66, 1970-73, now Professor Emeritus. Kings College, London, Fellow, 1984; Balchin Family Society Journal, 1994-. **Publications:** Cornwall: The Making of the Landscape, 1954; Cornwall: The Landscape through Maps, 1967; Concern for Geography, 1981; The Cornish Landscape, 1983; The Geographical Association: The First Hundred Years, 1993; The Joint School Story, 1997. EDITOR: Geography and Man, 1947, rev. ed., 1955; (with A.W. Richards) Climate and Weather Exercises, 1949; (with A.W. Richards) Practical and Experimental Geography, 1952; Geography for the Intending Student, 1970; Swansea and Its Region, 1971; The Living History of Britain, 1981. **Address:** 10 Low Wood Rise, Ben Rhydding, Ilkley, W. Yorkshire, England.

BALDASSARRI, Mario. Italian, b. 1946. **Genres:** Economics. **Career:** Catholic University of Milan, Milan, Italy, associate professor of economics, 1974-79; University of Bologna, Bologna, Italy, professor of economics, 1980-89; University of Rome, Rome, Italy, professor of economics, 1989-. Television commentator. **Publications:** Saggi di programmazione economica, 1977; Spesa pubblica, inflazione, crescita, 1978; The Italian Economy: Heaven or Hell, 1990; World Savings, Inflation, and Growth, 1992; The Italian Economy: A New Miracle, 1993; (co-ed) Eastern Europe's Transition to a Market Economy. Contributor to magazines and newspapers. **Address:** Department of Economics, University of Rome, Via del Castro Laurenziano 9, Rome, Italy.

BALDASTY, Gerald J. American. **Genres:** Writing/Journalism. **Career:** University of Washington, Seattle, WA, professor of communications and adjunct professor of women's studies, 1974-. Also, serves as senior editor of Journalism History and holds co-chair of two lectureships (the Jesse and John Danz Lectureship and the Walker-Ames Lectureship) at the University of Washington. **Publications:** The Commercialization of News in the Nineteenth Century, 1992; E.W. Scripps and the Business of Newspapers, 1999. Contributor to journalism monographs. **Address:** University of Washington, School of Communications, 343 Communications Building, Seattle, WA 98195, U.S.A. **Online address:** baldasty@u.washington.edu

BALDEOSINGH, Kevin. Trinidadian, b. 1963. **Genres:** Novels, Romance/Historical, Humor/Satire. **Career:** Education Ministry, secondary school teacher, 1985-88; Trinidad Express Newspapers, editorial writer, 1989-92; Trinidad Guardian Newspapers, assistant features editor, 1992-96; freelance writer, 1996-; Trinidad Newsday, specialist writer, 2003-. **Publications:** HUMOR: The Autobiography of Paras P, 1996; Virgin's Triangle, 1997. NOVELS: The Ten Incarnations of Adam Avatar, 2004.

BALDEROSE, Nancy Ward. American, b. 1952. **Genres:** Science fiction/Fantasy, Children's fiction, Children's non-fiction, Illustrations, Picture/board books. **Career:** Writer and illustrator of children's books; illustrator for Story Friends magazine; art teacher for kindergarten through 12th grades. **Publications:** AND ILLUSTRATOR: Pittsburgh: Our City, 1991; Once upon a Pony: A Mountain Christmas, 1992. **Address:** 1414 Pennsylvania Ave, Pittsburgh, PA 15233, U.S.A. **Online address:** NWBalderose@hotmail.com

BALDERSTON, Daniel. American, b. 1952. **Genres:** Translations, Literary criticism and history, Bibliography. **Career:** California State University, Chico, instructor, 1980; Earlham College, Richmond, IN, assistant professor, 1980-82; Wittenberg University, Springfield, OH, assistant professor, 1982-83; Tulane University, New Orleans, LA, assistant professor, 1983-87, associate professor, 1987-92, professor of Spanish and Portuguese, 1992-. Leader of Earlham foreign study group in Mexico, 1982. Taught at institutions including Universidade de Sao Paulo, 1987, Universidade Estadual de Campinas, 1993, and Universidade de Buenos Aires, 1994. **Publications:** El precursor velado: R.L. Stevenson en la obra de Borges, trans. by E.P. Leston, 1985; (author of intro., selection, and bibliog.) The Historical Novel in Latin America: A Symposium, 1986; The Latin American Short Story: An Annotated Guide to Anthologies and Criticism, 1992; The Literary Universe of Jorge Luis Borge: An Index to References and Allusions to Persons, Titles and Places in His Writings, 1992; Out of Context: Historical Reference and the Representation of Reality in Borges, 1993. Contributor to periodicals and newspapers. TRANSLATOR: J. Bianco, Shadow Play and The Rats: Two Novellas, 1983; S. Oliver, Figari, intro. by Jorge Luis Borges, 1984; S. Ocampo, Leopoldina's Dream, 1988; (with S. Molloy) Molloy, Certificate of Absence, 1989; (and author of intro.) Juan Carlos Onetti, Goodbyes and Stories, 1990; (and author of intro. and notes) Ricardo Piglia, Artificial Respiration, 1994. Contributor of translations to periodicals. **Address:** Department of Spanish and Portuguese, Tulane University, New Orleans, LA 70118, U.S.A.

BALDWIN, Frank. American, b. 1963. **Genres:** Novels. **Career:** Novelist. Formerly worked as a copy editor for an oil company's newsletter, first in NYC, then in San Francisco, CA, until 1994. **Publications:** Balling the Jack (novel), 1997. **Address:** c/o Simon & Schuster, 1230 Avenue of the Americas, New York, NY 10020, U.S.A.

BALDWIN, William J. American, b. 1937. **Genres:** Human relations/Parenting. **Career:** Pastoral counselor, Past Lives therapist, hypnotherapist, and international lecturer, trainer, and seminar leader of regression therapy. Dentist, c. 1970-82; Center for Human Relations, Enterprise, FL, co-director and president. **Publications:** Spirit Releasement Therapy: A Technique Manual, 1991, 2nd ed, 1995; (with J. Baldwin) From My Heart to Yours: A Transformational Guide to Unlocking the Power of Love, 1996; CE-VI: Close Encounters of the Possession Kind, 1999; Past Life Therapy: A Technique Manual, 2003; Healing Lost Souls, 2003. **Address:** Center for Human Relations, PO Box 4061, Enterprise, FL 32725, U.S.A. **Online address:** Doctorbill@aol.com

BALE, Don. American, b. 1937. **Genres:** Money/Finance, Recreation. **Career:** Bale Books and Bale Publs, president. **Publications:** Complete Guide for Profitable Coin Investing and Collecting, 1969; How to Invest in Singles, 1970; Fabulous Investment Potential of Singles, 1970; Fabulous Investment Potential of Uncirculated Singles, 1970; Fabulous Investment Potential of Liberty Walking Halves, 1971; A Gold Mine in Your Pocket, 1971; A Gold Mine in Gold, 1972; How to Invest in Uncirculated Singles, 1972; Out of Little Coins, Big Fortunes Grow, 1973, 3rd. ed., 1982; (ed.) How to Find Valuable Old and Scarce Coins, 1984; The Fabulous Collecting and Investing Potential of U.S. Copper Cents, 2002. **Address:** 5121 St Charles Ave Ste 13, New Orleans, LA 70115, U.S.A.

BALE, G. F. See **COX, Patsi Bale.**

BALEN, Malcolm. American, b. 1956. **Genres:** Biography. **Career:** Journalist and author. British Broadcasting Corporation (BBC), London, England, news trainee, 1978, regional journalist, Manchester, 1980-82; Channel Four News/Independent Television News (ITN), London, senior programming editor, 1989-94; BBC Nine o'Clock News, editor, 1994-97, BBC-TV and Radio News Bulletin, executive editor, 1997-2000; Independent Television (ITV), London, head of news, 2000-; appointed as editorial consultant on Middle East news coverage for the BBC, 2003. Occasional lecturer for the Council of Europe, 2000-. **Publications:** Kenneth Clarke, 1994; A Very English Deceit: The Secret History of the South Sea Bubble and the First Great Financial Scandal, 2002, also published as The Secret History of the South Sea Bubble: The World's First Great Financial Scandal, 2003, and as The King, the Crook, and the Gambler: The True Story of the South Sea Bubble and the Greatest Financial Scandal in History, 2004. **Address:** London Television Centre, 1 Upper Ground, London SE1 9LT, England.

BALESTER, Valerie M. American, b. 1952. **Genres:** Education. **Career:** Texas A&M University, College Station, associate professor of English, 1988-, director of English Computer Classroom, 1990-91, director of Writing Programs, 1995-2000, executive director of University Writing Center, 2001-. **Publications:** Cultural Divide: Case Studies of African American College-Level Writers, 1993. EDITOR: (with B. Johnstone) A.C. Johnstone, Uses for Journal Keeping: An Ethnography of Writing in a University Science Class, 1994; (with M.H. Kells) Attending to the Margins: Writing, Researching, and Teaching on the Front Lines, 1999; (with M.H. Kells and V. Villanueva) Latino/a Discourses and Teaching Composition as a Social Action, 2004. Contributor to books and scholarly journals. **Address:** Dept of English, Texas A&M University, College Station, TX 77843, U.S.A. **Online address:** v-balester@tamu.edu

BALGASSI, Haemi. American (born Republic of Korea), b. 1967. **Genres:** Children's fiction, Young adult fiction. **Career:** Author. **Publications:** Peacebound Trains, 1996; Tae's Sonata, 1997. Contributor of poems, articles, and stories to magazines and literary journals.

BALIAN, Lorna. American, b. 1929. **Genres:** Children's fiction. **Career:** Commercial artist, until 1964; author and illustrator of books for children, 1964-. **Publications:** SELF-ILLUSTRATED FOR CHILDREN: Humbug Witch, 1965; I Love You, Mary Jane, 1967; The Animal, 1972; Where in the World Is Henry?, 1972; Sometimes It's Turkey-Sometimes It's Feathers, 1973; Humbug Rabbit, 1974; The Sweet Touch, 1976; Bah! Humbug?, 1977; A Sweetheart for Valentine, 1979; Leprechauns Never Lie, 1980; Mother's Mother's Day, 1982; Humbug Potion, 1984; A Garden for a Groundhog, 1985; Amelia's Nine Lives, 1986; The Socksnatchers, 1988; Wilbur's Space Machine, 1990. **Address:** 400 S. 10th St., Watertown, WI 53094, U.S.A.

BALIT, Christina. British, b. 1961. **Genres:** Children's non-fiction, Plays/ Screenplays, Illustrations. **Career:** Illustrator and playwright. City and Guilds School of Art, London, tutor. **Publications:** (and illustrator) My Arabian Home: Leila and Mustapha's Story, 1988. Illustrator of books by M. Morpurgo, C.J. Moore, J. Riordan, J. Mitton. PLAYS: Agony for Beginners, 1989; Woman with Upturned Skirt, 1992; The Sentence, 1996. **Address:** Pym Lodge, Soles Hill Rd., Shottenden, Kent CT4 8JU, England.

BALKEN, Debra Bricker. Canadian, b. 1954. **Genres:** Art/Art history. **Career:** Brown University, Providence, RI, visiting associate professor, 1996-. Independent curator, 1990-. **Publications:** Philip Guston's Poem Pictures, 1994; Arthur Dove, 1997. **Address:** 183 Central St., Somerville, MA 02145, U.S.A. **Online address:** dbbalken@aol.com

BALL, Angela. American, b. 1952. **Genres:** Poetry. **Career:** University of Southern Mississippi, Hattiesburg, instructor, 1979-80, assistant professor, 1980-85, associate professor, 1985-91, professor of English, 1991-. Poetry Intl Festival, 1989. **Publications:** Recombinant Lives (pamphlet), 1987; Kneeling between Parked Cars, 1990; Quartet, 1995; Possession, 1995; The Museum of the Revolution, 1999. **Address:** Department of English, University of Southern Mississippi, Box 5037, Hattiesburg, MS 39406, U.S.A. **Online address:** Angball1@aol.com

BALL, Ann. American, b. 1944. **Genres:** Theology/Religion. **Career:** Teacher in parochial and public elementary, middle, and high schools in Texas and California, 1964-78; Marian Christian High School, Houston, TX, teacher, 1980-85; Security Guard Services, Houston, private investigator, 1981; M. Herman and Associates, Houston, private investigator, 1981; All State Guard Service Inc., Houston, president and owner, 1981-. **Publications:** Modern Saints, Their Lives and Faces, 1983, Book II, 1990; A Litany of Mary, 1988; Heroes of God: A Coloring Book for Children, 1989; The Holy Names of Jesus, 1990; The Persecuted Church, 1990; Handbook of Catholic Sacramentals, 1991; A Litany of Saints, 1993; Catholic Traditions in Cooking, 1993; Catholic Book of the Dead, 1995; Catholic Traditions in Crafts, 1997; Catholic Traditions in the Garden, 1998; Faces of Holiness, 1998, vol. 2, 2001; A Saint for Your Name-Boys, 1999; A Saint for Your Name-Girls, 1999; The Saints Guide to Joy That Never Fades, 2001; Prayers for Prisoners, 2002; OSU Encyclopedia of Catholic Devotion, 2003; Child's Catholic Encyclopedia. Contributor to periodicals. **Address:** All State Guard Service Inc., PO Box 7449, Houston, TX 77248, U.S.A. **Online address:** Annalert@aol.com

BALL, Donna. Also writes as Donna Boyd, Donna Carlisle, Rebecca Flanders, Leigh Bristol, Taylor Brady. American. **Genres:** Romance/ Historical. **Career:** Writer. **Publications:** Summer Masquerade, 1982; The Darkest Hour, 1992; Exposure, 1996; Just Before Dawn, 1997; Dark Angel, 1998. AS DONNA BOYD: The Passion, 1998. AS DONNA CARLISLE: Under Cover, 1988; A Man Around the House, 1989; Interlude, 1989; Matchmaker, Matchmaker, 1990; For Keeps, 1991; The Stormriders, 1991; Cast Adrift, 1992; It's Only Make Believe, 1992; Stealing Savannah, 1994. AS REBECCA FLANDERS (with L. Dano): Prom Twice in a Lifetime, 1983; A Matter of Trust, 1983; Best of Friends, 1983; Morning Song, 1983; Falkone's Promise, 1984; Suddenly Love, 1984; Gilded Heart, 1984; Second Sight, 1984; Desert Fire, 1984; The Third Time, 1984; Daydreams, 1984; The Key, 1984; Silver Threads, 1984; A Modern Girl, 1984; The Growing Season, 1985; Easy Access, 1985; Prom Afterglow, 1985; Open Hands, 1985; Rainbows and Unicorns, 1985; Uncertain Images, 1985; The Last Frontier, 1985; The Straight Game, 1986; Minor Miracles, 1986; After the Storm, 1986; Satin Fires, 1986; Obsessions, 1986; Painted Sunsets, 1987; Search the Heavens, 1988; The Sensation, 1990; Earthbound, 1990; Under the Mistletoe, 1991; Yesterday Comes Tomorrow, 1992; Once upon a Time, 1992; The Last Real Man, 1993; Sunchasers, 1993; Forever Always, 1994; Kissed by the Sea, 1994; Quinn's Way, 1994. MEN MADE IN AMERICA SERIES: After the Storm, 1994; The Last Frontier, 1995. HEART OF THE WOLF SERIES: Secret of the Wolf, 1995; Wolf in Waiting, 1995; Shadow of the Wolf, 1995. AS LEIGH BRISTOL (with S. Harper): Hearts of Fire, 1989; Sunswept, 1990; Twice Blessed, 1991; Angel, 1992; Legacy, 1993. FIELDING TRILOGY: Scarlet Sunrise, 1987; Amber Skies, 1987; Silver Twilight, 1987. AS TAYLOR BRADY: THE KINCAIDS SERIES: Raging Rivers, 1992; Prairie Thunder, 1993; Mountain Fury, 1993; Westward Winds, 1993. **Address:** c/o Belle Books, PO Box 67, Smyrna, GA 30081, U.S.A.

BALL, Edward. American, b. 1959. **Genres:** Documentaries/Reportage. **Career:** Journalist. Appeared on television programs. **Publications:** Slaves in the Family (nonfiction), 1998; Peninsula of Lies, 2004. **Address:** c/o Farrar, Straus & Giroux Inc., 19 Union Square West, New York, NY 10036, U.S.A.

BALL, Gordon. American, b. 1944. **Genres:** Adult non-fiction. **Career:** Apprentice to filmmaker Jonas Mekas, mid-1960s; manager, Allen Ginsberg's farm, 1968-1971; Old Dominion University, literature professor, 1981-85; Wasedo, Sophia, and Rikkyo Universities, Fulbright specialist lecturer in American Literature, 1983-84; Tougaloo College, professor, 1985-89; Virginia Military Institute, professor, 1989-. Taught in Poznan, Poland, 1986, 1988; worked with poet Allen Ginsberg on variety of projects; Independent filmmaker and photographer. **Publications:** '66 Frames: A Memoir, 1999. EDITOR: Allen Verbatim: Lectures on Poetry, Politics, and Consciousness, 1974; (and contrib with J.H. Richards) An Introduction to Film Criticism: Prepared for English 42 and Christopher Brookhouse and Howard Harper, 3rd ed, 1977; Allen Ginsberg, Journals: Early Fifties, Early Sixties, 1977; Allen Ginsberg, Journals Mid-fifties, 1954-1958, 1995. Contributed photographs to books and magazines. **Address:** Department of English and Fine Arts, Virginia Military Institute, Lexington, VA 24450, U.S.A. **Online address:** BallGV@mail.vmi.edu

BALL, Nelson. Canadian, b. 1942. **Genres:** Poetry. **Career:** Weed Flower Press, Kitchener and Toronto, Ontario, founder, editor, and publisher, 1965-74; William Nelson Books, Toronto, founder and proprietor, 1972-85; Nelson Ball, Bookseller, Paris, Ontario, proprietor, 1985-; poet. Library technician, University of Toronto Library, 1967-71; cataloger, Village Book Store, Toronto, 1970-73; also worked as laborer, chauffeur, clerk, seasonal forest ranger, record store clerk, and janitor. Participated in poetry readings. **Publications:** POETRY: Room of Clocks, 1965; Beaufort's Scale, 1967; Sparrows, 1968; Force Movements, 1969; Water-Pipes and Moonlight, 1969; The Pre-Linguistic Heights, 1970; Points of Attention, 1971; Round Stone, 1971; Dry Spell, 1973; Our Arms Are Featherless Wings, 1973; The Shore, 1974; With Issa: Poems 1964-71, 1991; Sightings, 1992; (ed.) Frank Harrington's Kristmiss Book, 1993; Bird Tracks on Hard Snow, 1994; Fifteen Poems, 1994; The Concrete Air, 1996; Almost Spring, 1999. **Address:** 31 Willow St, Paris, ON, Canada N3L 2K7.

BALL, Stuart. British, b. 1956. **Genres:** History, Politics/Government. **Career:** University of Leicester, England, lecturer in modern history, 1979-. **Publications:** Baldwin and the Conservative Party: The Crisis of 1929-1931, 1988; The Conservative Party and British Politics 1902-1951, 1995. EDITOR: Parliament and Politics in the Age of Baldwin and MacDonald: The Headlam Diaries 1923-1935, 1992; Conservative Century: The Conservative Party since 1900, 1994; Conservative Party since 1945, 1998; (co) Heath Government, 1970-74, 1996; Parliament and Politics in the Age of Churchill and Attlee: The Headlam Diaries 1935-1951, 1999. **Address:** Department of History, University of Leicester, University Rd, Leicester LE1 7RH, England. **Online address:** bal@le.ac.uk

BALL, Terence. American, b. 1944. **Genres:** Mystery/Crime/Suspense, Politics/Government. **Career:** University of Minnesota-Twin Cities, Minneapolis, assistant professor, 1972-75, associate professor, 1975-82, professor of political science, 1982-; Arizona State University, Dept of Political Science. Visiting professor at Oxford University, 1978-79, 1993, 1995, 1998, and University of California, San Diego, 1984. Conference for the Study of Political Thought, member of executive committee. Commentator for local television stations. **Publications:** (with J. Farr) After Marx, 1984; Idioms of Inquiry, 1987; Transforming Political Discourse, 1988; (ed. with J.G.A. Pocock) Conceptual Change and the Constitution, 1988; (ed. with J. Farr and R.L. Hanson) Political Innovation and Conceptual Change, 1989; (with R. Dagger) Political Ideologies and the Democratic Ideal, 1991, 4th ed., 2002; (ed.) James Mill: Political Writings, 1992; Reappraising Political Theory, 1995; (ed. with J. Appleby) Thomas Jefferson: Political Writings, 1997; Rousseau's Ghost: A Novel, 1998; (ed. with R. Bellamy) The Cambridge History of Twentieth-Century Political Thought, 2002. Contributor to political science journals. **Address:** Department of Political Science, Arizona State University, Tempe, AZ 85287-2001, U.S.A. **Online address:** terence.ball@asu.edu

BALLARD, Holley. See RUBINSKY, Holley.

BALLARD, J(ames) G(raham). British (born China), b. 1930. **Genres:** Novellas/Short stories, Science fiction/Fantasy. **Publications:** The Wind from Nowhere, 1962; The Voices of Time and Other Stories, 1962; The Drowned World, 1962; Billenium and Other Stories, 1962; The 4-Dimensional Nightmare, 1963; Passport to Eternity and Other Stories, 1963; Terminal Beach, 1964; The Drought, 1965; The Crystal World, 1966; The Disaster Area, 1967; The Day of Forever, 1968; The Overloaded Man, 1968; The Atrocity Exhibition (in U.S. as Love and Napalm: Export USA), 1970; Vermilion Sands, 1971; Crash!, 1972; The Concrete Island, 1974; High-Rise, 1975; Low-Flying Aircraft (stories), 1976; The Best of J.G. Ballard, 1977;

The Best Short Stories, 1978; The Unlimited Dream Company, 1979; Hello America, 1981; Myths of the Near Future (stories), 1982; Empire of the Sun, 1984; The Venus Hunters, 1986; The Day of Forever, 1986; The Day of Creation, 1987; Memories of the Space Age, 1988; Running Wild, 1988; Kindness of Women, 1991; War Fever, 1991; Hometown Hospital, 1991; Rushing to Paradise, 1994; The Best Stories of J.G. Ballard, 1995; A User's Guide to the Millennium, 1996; Cocaine Nights, 1996; Super-Cannes, 2001. **Address:** 36 Old Charlton Rd, Shepperton, Middx TW17 8AT, England.

BALLARD, Michael B. American, b. 1946. **Genres:** History. **Career:** Mississippi State University, Starkville, MS, university archivist, 1983-. **Publications:** A Long Shadow, 1986; Landscapes of Battle, 1988; Pemberton: A Biography, 1991; (co-ed.) A Mississippi Rebel in the Army of Northern Virginia, 1996; Campaign for Vicksburg, 1996; The Battle of Tupelo, 1996; Civil War Mississippi: A Guide, 2000; (co-author) Sonny Montgomery: The Veteran's Champion, 2003. **Address:** PO Box 5408, Mississippi State University Library, Mississippi State, MS 39762, U.S.A.

BALLARD, Terry. American, b. 1946. **Genres:** Librarianship. **Career:** Phoenix Public Library, Phoenix, AZ, library assistant, 1966-90; Adelphi University, Garden City, NY, systems librarian, 1990-95; New York University, NYC, library automation coordinator for School of Law, 1995-97; Quinnipiac University, Hamden, CT, automation librarian, 1997-. Author of a bimonthly column on library systems, Information Today, 1996-2001. **Publications:** INNOPAC: A Reference Guide to the System, 1995. Contributor to library journals. **Address:** Quinnipiac University, 275 Mount Carmel, Hamden, CT 06518, U.S.A. **Online address:** terry.ballard@quinnipiac.edu

BALLENDORF, Dirk Anthony. American, b. 1939. **Genres:** Area studies. **Career:** U.S. Peace Corps, Washington, DC, volunteer in the Philippines, then associate director in Micronesia and member of headquarters staff in Washington; College of Micronesia, Pohnpei, Eastern Caroline Islands, president; University of Guam, Mangilao, director of Micronesian Area Research Center, professor of history and Micronesian studies, and editor of MARC Print Publications. Visiting professor in Germany; lecturer at universities worldwide. **Publications:** Historical Dictionary of Guam and Micronesia, 1995; (with others) Pete Ellis: Amphibious Warfare Prophet, 1880-1923, 1997; Guam History Perspectives, Vol I, 1998. Author of seven other books. Contributor of articles and reviews to professional journals. **Address:** Micronesian Area Research Center, University of Guam, Mangilao, GU 96923, U.S.A. **Online address:** ballendo@uog9.uog.edu

BALLENTINE, Lee (Kenney). American, b. 1954. **Genres:** Poetry. **Career:** Worked as a singer, disc jockey, dealer in rare books and music, and salesman; Adam Osborne & Associates, Berkeley, CA, software engineer, 1978-80; Ocean View Press, publisher, 1981-86; Ocean View Books, publisher, 1986-2001; Professional Book Center, Denver, CO, cofounder and president, 1987-2000; Documents of Colorado Art, Denver, editor, 1991-2001; Poeisis (Colorado poetry calendar), founder and publisher, 1992-97; Permanence Press, San Diego, CA, editor, 1992-2001; UR-VOX, Denver, editor, 2000-01. Lecturer and guest speaker. **Publications:** Directional Information, 1981; Basements in the Music-Box, 1986; (ed.) POLY: New Speculative Writing, 1989; Dream Protocols, 1992; (art ed.) High Fantastic, 1995; Phase Language, 1995; Renounce the Emerald Piety, 1998. Work represented in anthologies. Contributor to periodicals. **Address:** PO Box 9249, Denver, CO 80209, U.S.A. **Online address:** lee@probook.net

BALLIETT, Whitney. American, b. 1926. **Genres:** Music, Poetry, Biography, Literary criticism and history, Autobiography/Memoirs. **Career:** Member of staff, New Yorker mag., NYC, since 1951. Originator and Technical Adviser, The Sound of Jazz, CBS-TV, 1957. **Publications:** The Sound of Surprise, 1959, 1978; Dinosaurs in the Morning, 1962, 1978; Such Sweet Thunder, 1966; Super Drummer: A Profile of Buddy Rich, 1968; Ecstasy at the Onion, 1971; Alec Wilder and His Friends, 1974, 1983; New York Notes, 1976; Improvising, 1977; American Singers, 1979, 1988; Night Creature, 1981; Duke Ellington Remembered, 1981; Jelly Roll, Jabbo and Fats, 1982; American Musicians: 56 Portraits in Jazz, 1986; Barney, Bradley and Max, 1989; Goodbyes and Other Messages, 1991; American Musicians II: 72 Portraits in Jazz, 1996; Collected Works: A Journal of Jazz, 1954-1999, 2000. **Address:** 114 E 90th St, New York, NY 10128-1550, U.S.A.

BALLING, Robert C., Jr. American, b. 1952. **Genres:** Earth sciences, Environmental sciences/Ecology. **Career:** University of Nebraska, assistant professor of geography, 1979-84; Arizona State University, Tempe, member of faculty, 1985-, currently associate professor of geography and director of Office of Climatology. Lecturer on the greenhouse effect debate in Australia, New Zealand, England, Canada, Kuwait, and the United States. **Publica-

tions:** The Heated Debate: Greenhouse Predictions Versus Climate Reality, Pacific Research Institute for Public Policy, 1992. Contributor of articles to scientific journals. **Address:** Office of Climatology, Arizona State University, Box 871508, Tempe, AZ 85287-1508, U.S.A.

BALMAIN, Lydia. *See* **TURNER, Judith.**

BALMER, Randall (Herbert). American, b. 1954. **Genres:** Theology/ Religion. **Career:** Columbia University, assistant professor, 1985-90, Tremaine Associate Professor of religion, 1990; Barnard College, Columbia University, associate professor, 1991-94, professor, 1994-, Ann Whitney Olin Professor of American Religion, 1996-. **Publications:** A Perfect Babel of Confusion: Dutch Religion and English Culture in the Middle Colonies, 1989; Mine Eyes Have Seen the Glory: A Journey into the Evangelical Subculture in America, 1989, 3rd ed, 1999; (ed. with E.L. Blumhofer) Modern Christian Revivals, 1993; (with J.R. Fitzmier) The Presbyterians, 1993; Grant Us Courage: Travels along the Mainline of American Protestantism, 1996; Blessed Assurance: The History of Evangelicalism in America, 1999; Religion in Twentieth-Century America, 2001; Growing Pains: Learning to Love My Father's Faith, 2001; Encyclopedia of Evangelicalism, 2002. TV DOCUMENTARIES: Crusade: The Life of Billy Graham, 1993; In the Beginning: The Creationist Controversy, 1994. Contributor of articles and columns to newspapers and magazines. **Address:** 323 Fairfield Avenue, Ridgewood, NJ 07450, U.S.A. **Online address:** rb281@columbia.edu

BALOGH, Mary. Canadian (born Wales), b. 1944. **Genres:** Novellas/Short stories, Romance/Historical. **Career:** Writer. Kipling High School, Saskatchewan, English teacher, 1967-82; Windthorst High School, SK, principal and English teacher, 1982-88. **Publications:** NOVELS: A Masked Deception, 1985; The Double Wager, 1985; A Chance Encounter, 1986; Red Rose, 1985; The Trysting Place, 1986; The First Snowdrop, 1987; The Wood Nymph, 1987; The Constant Heart, 1987; Gentle Conquest, 1987; Secrets of the Heart, 1988; The Ungrateful Governess, 1988; An Unacceptable Offer, 1988; Daring Masquerade, 1989; A Gift of Daisies, 1989; The Obedient Bride, 1989; Lady with a Black Umbrella, 1989; The Gilded Web, 1989; A Promise of Spring, 1990; Web of Love, 1990; The Incurable Matchmaker, 1990; Devil's Web, 1990; An Unlikely Duchess, 1990; A Certain Magic, 1991; Snow Angel, 1991; The Secret Pearl, 1991; The Ideal Wife, 1991; Christmas Beau, 1991; The Counterfeit Betrothal, 1992; The Notorious Rake, 1992; A Christmas Promise, 1992; Beyond the Sunrise, 1992; A Precious Jewel, 1993; Deceived, 1993; Courting Julia, 1993; Dancing with Clara, 1994; Tangled, 1994; Tempting Harriet, 1994; Dark Angel, 1994; A Christmas Belle, 1994; Longing, 1994; Lord Carew's Bride, 1995; Heartless, 1995; The Famous Heroine, 1996; Truly, 1996; The Plumed Bonnet, 1996; Indiscreet, 1997; Temporary Wife, 1997; Silent Melody, 1997; A Christmas Bride, 1997; Unforgiven, 1998; Thief of Dreams, 1998; Irresistible, 1998; The Last Waltz, 1998; Slightly Married, 2003; Slightly Wicked, 2003; Slightly Scandalous, 2003; Slightly Tempted, 2004; Slightly Sinful, 2004; Slightly Dangerous, 2004. NOVELLAS: A Regency Christmas, 1989; A Regency Christmas II, 1990; A Regency Valentine, 1991; A Regency Christmas III, 1991; A Regency Valentine II, 1992; A Regency Summer, 1992; Full Moon Magic, 1992; A Regency Christmas IV, 1992; Tokens of Love, 1993; Rakes and Rogues, 1993; Moonlight Lovers, 1993; A Regency Christmas V, 1993; From the Heart, 1994; A Regency Christmas VI, 1994; Blossoms, 1995; Dashing and Dangerous, 1995; A Regency Christmas VII, 1995; An Angel Christmas, 1995; Love's Legacy, 1996; Timeswept Brides, 1996; A Regency Christmas Feast, 1996; A Regency Christmas Carol, 1997; The Gifts of Christmas, 1998; Under the Mistletoe, 2003. **Address:** Box 571, Kipling, SK, Canada S0G 2S0.

BALSWICK, Judith K. American, b. 1939. **Genres:** Human relations/ Parenting. **Career:** Marriage and family therapist in private practice. Fuller Theological Seminary, associate professor of marriage and family therapy. **Publications:** (with J.O. Balswick) The Family, 1989, rev. ed., 1998; Mothers & Daughters Making Peace, 1993; (with J.O. Balswick) Raging Hormones-What to Say to Your Sexually Active Teenager, 1994; (with B. Piper) Life Ties: Cultivating Relationships, 1995; (with J.O Balswick) Dual Earner Marriage, 1995; (with B. Piper) Then They Leave Home, 1997; (with J.O Balswick) Authentic Human Sexuality, 1999. **Address:** Fuller Theological Seminary, 135 North Oakland, Pasadena, CA 91101, U.S.A.

BALTIMORE, Mary. *See* **DOSS, Margot P(atterson).**

BALUTANSKY, Kathleen M(arie). American (born Haiti), b. 1954. **Genres:** Literary criticism and history. **Career:** University of Virginia, assistant dean, 1985-86; Washington International School, Washington, DC, vice principal, 1986-87; University of Virginia, Charlottesville, assistant professor of English, 1988-92; St. Michael's College, Colchester, VT, professor of English, 1992-2004, associate dean for academic affairs, 2004-. **Publications:** The Novels of Alex La Guma, 1990; Caribbean Creolization: Reflections on the Cultural Dynamics of Language, Culture, and Identity, 1998; Haiti: Writing under Siege, 2004. **Address:** Dept of English, St. Michael's College, 1 Winooski Park, Colchester, VT 05439, U.S.A.

BAMBACH, Carmen C. Also writes as Carmen Bambach Cappel. American (born Chile), b. 1959. **Genres:** Art/Art history, History, Humanities, Biography, Essays. **Career:** Connecticut Trust for Historic Preservation, New Haven, assistant to education coordinator, 1982-83, managing editor of Connecticut Preservation News, 1983; Philadelphia Museum of Art, Philadelphia, PA, NEA curatorial intern in Department of Prints, Drawings, and Photographs, 1988-89; Fordham University, Bronx, NY, assistant professor of art history, 1989-95; Metropolitan Museum of Art, NYC, associate curator of drawings and prints, 1995-. Lecturer at universities and museums. **Publications:** (with N. Orenstein) Genoa: Drawings and Prints, 1530-1800, 1996; The Drawings of Fillippino Lippi and His Circle, 1997; Drawing and Painting in the Italian Renaissance Workshop: Practice and Theory, 1300-1600, 1999. Contributor to books. Contributor of articles, essays, and reviews to art and history journals. **Address:** Department of Drawings and Prints, Metropolitan Museum of Art, 1000 Fifth Ave., New York, NY 10028, U.S.A. **Online address:** Carmen.Bambach@metmuseum.org

BAMBOLA, Sylvia. Also writes as Margaret Miller. American (born Romania), b. 1945. **Genres:** Novels. **Career:** Novelist. **Publications:** NOVELS: (as Margaret Miller) A Vessel of Honor, 1998; Refiner's Fire, 2000; Tears in a Bottle, 2001. **Address:** c/o Linda Glasford, Alive Communications Inc., Goddard Street Suite 200, Colorado Springs, CO 80920, U.S.A. **Online address:** SBambola@aol.com

BAMFORD, Brian Reginald. *See* Obituaries.

BAN, Thomas Arthur. Canadian (born Hungary), b. 1929. **Genres:** Psychiatry. **Career:** Douglas Hospital, Verdun, Sr. Research Psychiatrist, 1961-66, Associate Director of Research, 1966-70, Chief of Research Services, 1970-72. McGill University, Montreal, Demonstrator, 1960-63, Lecturer, 1964-65, Assistant Professor, 1965-70, Associate Professor, and Director, Division of Psychopharmacology, 1970-76, Associate Member of Psychiatry, 1977-. Vanderbilt University, Nashville, TN, Professor of Psychiatry, 1976-94, Emeritus, 1995-. **Publications:** Conditioning and Psychiatry, 1964; Psychopharmacology, 1969; (with H.E. Lehmann) Nicotinic Acid in the Treatment of Schizophrenias: Progress Report I, 1970; (with H.E. Lehmann) Pharmacotherapy of Tension and Anxiety, 1970; (with H.E. Lehmann) Experimental Approaches to Psychiatric Diagnosis, 1971; Nicotinic Acid in the treatment of Schizophrenias: Introduction, 1971; Nicotinic Acid in the Treatment of Schizophrenias: Complementary Report A, 1971; Schizophrenia: A Psychopharmacological Approach, 1972; Recent Advances in the Biology of Schizophrenia, 1973; Depression and the Tricyclic Antidepressants, 1974; Introduction to the Psychopharmacology Doxepin, 1977; Psychopharmacology of Thiothixene, 1978; Psychopharmacology of Depression, 1981; Psychopharmacology for the Aged, 1980; (with M. Hollender) Psychopharmacology for Everyday Practice, 1981; Composite Diagnostic Evaluation of Depressive Disorders, 1989; Declino Cognitivo Nell' Anziano, 1991; Sostituire il Neurolettico, 1992; (with R.V. Udabe) Clasificacion de las Psicosis, 1995; (with P. Gaszner) Composite Diagnostic Evaluation of Hyperthymic Disorders, 1998. **Address:** 1177 Yonge St. #607, Toronto, ON, Canada M4T 2Y6. **Online address:** fmcp@attcanada.ca

BANASH, Stan. (Stanley D. Banash). American, b. 1940. **Genres:** Literary criticism and history. **Career:** Daniel J. Edelman Inc., Chicago, IL, account executive, 1972-73; office of the Lieutenant Governor, Chicago, IL, administrative assistant for press relations, 1973-74; selfemployed consultant, 1974-; Society of American Registered Architects, executive director, 1988-1996. **Publications:** EDITOR: Best of Dee Brown's West: An Anthology, 1998; Dee Brown's Civil War Anthology, 1998. Reviewer of nonfiction books about the American West and contributor of articles to national magazines. **Address:** 5940 North Neva Ave., Chicago, IL 60631, U.S.A.

BANAZEK, Jeanne M. (Carpenter). American, b. 1943. **Genres:** Documentaries/Reportage. **Career:** Onondaga County Department of Drainage and Sanitation, Syracuse, NY, secretary, 1987-99; retired. **Publications:** Naked as We Stand, 1997.

BANBURY, Jen(nifer Marie). American, b. 1966. **Genres:** Novels, Plays/Screenplays. **Career:** Writer. B-movie casting assistant, waitress, actor, researcher. **Publications:** Like a Hole in the Head (novel), 1998; How Alex Looks When She's Hurt (play). **Address:** c/o The Paul Chung Literary Agency, 6 W. 18th St., 10th Floor, New York, NY 10011, U.S.A. **Online address:** bittermews@aol.com

BANCROFT, Anne. British, b. 1923. **Genres:** Theology/Religion. **Publications:** Religions of the East, 1974; Twentieth Century Mystics and Sages, 1976; Zen: Direct Pointing to Reality, 1980; The Luminous Vision: Six Medieval Mystics, 1982; Chinese New Year, 1984; Festivals of the Buddha, 1984; The Buddhist World, 1984; The New Religious World, 1985; Origins of the Sacred, 1987; Weavers of Wisdom, 1989; The Spiritual Journey, 1991; Women in Search of the Sacred, 1996; The Dhammapada, 1996. EDITOR: The Buddha Speaks, 2000; The Wisdom of Zen, 2001. **Address:** Cobberton, Denys Rd, Totnes, Devon TQ9 5TL, England.

BANDARAGE, Asoka. American, b. 1950. **Genres:** Politics/Government. **Career:** Writer. **Publications:** Colonialism in Sri Lanka: The Political Economy of the Kandyan Highland, 1833-86 (presented as Ph.D. dissertation), 1983; Woman, Population, and Global Crisis: A Political Economic Analysis, 1996. **Address:** Women's Studies, 106 Dickinson House, Mt. Holyoke College, South Hadley, MA 01075, U.S.A.

BANDELE, Biyi. American, b. 1967. **Genres:** Novels, Plays/Screenplays. **Career:** Playwright and novelist. Royal Court Theatre, London, associate writer, 1992-; Talawa Theatre Company, writer-in-residence, 1994-95; Royal National Theatre Studio, resident dramatist, 1996. **Publications:** The Man Who Came in from the Back of Beyond, 1991; The Sympathetic Undertaker and Other Dreams, 1991. PLAYS: Rain, 1991; Marching for Fausa, 1993; Two Horsemen, 1994; Resurrections, 1994; Death Catches the Hunter, 1995; Things Fall Apart, 1997; Thieves Like Us, 1998. SCREENPLAYS: Not Even God is Wise Enough, 1993; Bad Boy Blues, 1996. **Address:** c/o Leah Schmidt, The Agency, 24 Pottery Ln., Holland Park, London W11 4LZ, England.

BANDRAUK, Andre D. German, b. 1941. **Genres:** Physics. **Career:** Universite de Sherbrooke, Sherbrooke, Quebec, member of chemistry faculty. **Publications:** Atoms and Molecules in Laser Fields, 1988; Coherent Phenomena, 1992; (ed.) Molecules in Laser Fields, 1994; Molecular Physics in Intense Laser Fields, in press. **Address:** Faculty of Science, Universite de Sherbrooke, Sherbrooke, QC, Canada J1K 2R1.

BANDURA, Albert. American (born Canada), b. 1925. **Genres:** Psychology. **Career:** David Starr Jordan Professor of Social Science in Psychology, Stanford University, 1953-. Fellow, Center for Advanced Study in the Behavioural Sciences, 1969-70. President, American Psychological Association, 1974, and Western Psychological Assn, 1980; Honorary President, Canadian Psychological Association, 1999. **Publications:** (with W.H. Walters) Adolescent Aggression, 1959; (with W.H. Walters) Social Learning and Personality Development, 1963; Principles of Behavior Modification, 1969; Aggression: A Social Learning Analysis, 1973; Social Learning Theory, 1977; Social Foundations of Thought and Action, 1986; Self-Efficacy: The Exercise of Control, 1997. EDITOR: Psychological Modeling: Conflicting Theories, 1971; Self-Efficacy in Changing Societies, 1995. **Address:** Dept. of Psychology, Stanford University, Stanford, CA 94305-2130, U.S.A. **Online address:** bandura@psych.stanford.edu

BANERJEE, Asit. Indian, b. 1940. **Genres:** Physics. **Career:** Jadavpur University, Calcutta, India, lecturer, 1964-78, reader, 1978-86, professor of physics, 1986-, and coordinator of Relativity and Cosmology Research Centre. Institut Henri Poincare, postdoctoral fellow, 1971-72; Federal University of Rio de Janeiro, visiting professor, 1979-81; Inter-University Centre for Astronomy and Astrophysics, Pune, senior associate. **Publications:** (co-author) General Relativity, Astrophysics, and Cosmology, 1992; (co-author) The Special Theory of Relativity, 2002. Contributor to scientific journals. **Address:** Department of Physics, Jadavpur University, Calcutta 700032, India. **Online address:** asitb@cal3.vsnl.net.in

BANERJI, S(riranjan). Indian, b. 1938. **Genres:** Physics, Translations. **Career:** University of Burdwan, Burdwan, West Bengal, India, lecturer, 1961-74, reader, 1974-79, professor of physics, 1979-. Inter-University Centre for Astronomy and Astrophysics, senior associate, 1990-93 and 1993-96. **Publications:** (trans. from German to Bengali, with K. Mukherjee and R.S. Banerjee) Wolfgang Borchert, Duarer Bahirey (stories and a play; title means: Outside the Door), 1975; Apekshikata Tattva (in Bengali; title means: Theory of Relativity), 1982; Sudur Niharika (in Bengali; title means: Distant Nebulae), 1987; (with A. Banerjee and A.K. Raychaudhuri) General Relativity, Astrophysics, and Cosmology, 1992. Work represented in anthologies.

Contributor to scientific journals. **Address:** Department of Physics, University of Burdwan, Burdwan 713104, India.

BANFIELD, Stephen. British, b. 1951. **Genres:** Music. **Career:** University of Keele, England, lecturer, 1978-88, senior lecturer in music, 1988-92, department head, 1988-90; University of Birmingham, England, head of School of Performance Studies, 1992-95, Elgar Professor of Music, 1992-2003; University of Bristol, Stanley Hugh Badock Professor of Music, 2003-. Tallis Scholars Trust, member of board of trustees. **Publications:** Sensibility and English Song, 1985; Sondheim's Broadway Musicals, 1993; (ed. and contrib.) The Blackwell History of Music in Britain, Volume VI: The Twentieth Century, 1995; Gerald Finzi, 1997. **Address:** Dept of Music, University of Bristol, Victoria Rooms, Queens Rd, Bristol B58 1SA, England. **Online address:** s.d.banfield@bristol.ac.uk

BANG, Molly Garrett. American. **Genres:** Children's fiction, Illustrations. **Career:** Author, illustrator, and translator; English teacher, Doshisha University, Kyoto, Japan, 1965-67; interpreter of Japanese, Asahi Shimbun, New York, 1969; reporter, Baltimore Sunpapers, Baltimore, 1970. Illustrator and consultant for UNICEF, Johns Hopkins Center for Medical Research and Training, and Harvard Institute for International Development. **Publications:** SELF-ILLUSTRATED FOR CHILDREN: (comp.) The Goblins Giggle, and Other Stories (folktales), 1973; (trans. and compiler as Garrett Bang) Men from the Village Deep in the Mountains, and Other Japanese Folk Tales, 1973; The Grey Lady and the Strawberry Snatcher, 1980; (Adaptor and ed) Tye May and the Magic Brush (Chinese folktale), 1981; Ten, Nine, Eight, 1983; (Adaptor) Dawn (Japanese folktale), 1983; (Adaptor) The Paper Crane (Chinese folktale), 1985; Delphine, 1988; Yellow Ball, 1991; One Fall Day, 1994; Sunshine's Book, 1994; Goose, 1996; Chattanooga Sludge, 1996; Common Ground: The Water, Earth, and Air We Share, 1997; When I Get Angry, 1998. OTHER: Picture This: Perception and Composition, 1991. EDITOR: Wiley and the Hairy Man, 1975; The Buried Moon and Other Stories (folktales), 1977. Illustrator of works by: B. Bang, J.B. Richardson, S. Cassedy and S. Kunihirs. **Address:** 89 Water St., Woods Hole, MA 02543, U.S.A.

BANG-CAMPBELL, Monika. American. **Genres:** Children's fiction. **Career:** Sailor and writer. **Publications:** Little Rat Sets Sail, 2002; Little Rat Rides, in press. **Address:** c/o Author Mail, Harcourt Children's Books, 525 B Street Suite 1900, San Diego, CA 92101, U.S.A.

BANGS, Nina. American. **Genres:** Romance/Historical. **Career:** Author. Has worked as an elementary school teacher for over twenty years. **Publications:** ROMANCE FICTION: An Original Sin, 1999; (with Madeline Baker, Ann Lawrence, and Kathleen Nance) Paradise, 1999; (with Lisa Cach, Thea Devine, and Penelope Neri) Seduction by Chocolate, 2000; (with Claudia Dain and Shirl Henke) Unwrapped, 2000; The Pleasure Master, 2001; (with Jenelle Denison and Erin McCarthy) Men at Work, 2001; Night Games, 2002; From Boardwalk with Love, 2003; (with Cheryl Holt, Kimberly Raye, and Patricia Ryan) Burning Up: Four Novellas of Erotic Romance, 2003; Master of Ecstasy, 2004. **Address:** c/o Author Mail, St. Martin's Press, 175 Fifth Ave, New York, NY 10027, U.S.A.

BANISADR, Abol-Hassan. Iranian, b. 1933. **Genres:** Politics/Government, International relations/Current affairs. **Career:** Member of Iranian anti-Shah movement, 1953; wounded by police and served prison term for demonstrating against Shah's government, 1963; lived in exile, Paris, France, 1963-79; returned to Iran after revolution, 1978; Republic of Iran, acting minister of Foreign Affairs, 1979, Minister of Economy and Foreign Affairs, 1979-80, president, 1980-81. Central Bank of Iran, member of supervisory board, 1979; Constituent Assembly, member, beginning in 1979; Revolutionary Council, member of supervisory board, 1979-80, president, 1980-81. Founder of Mossadegh, Modaress, and 15 Khordad publishing houses. **Publications:** (with P. Vieille) Petrole et violence: Terreur blanche et resistance en Iran (title means: Oil and Violence: White Terror and Resistance in Iran), 1974; Quelle revolution pour l'Iran, 1980; (trans.) Mohammad R. Ghanoonparvar, The Fundamental Principles and Precepts of Islamic Government, c. 1981; L'esperance trahie, c. 1982; Bani Sadr racconta l'Iran, 1984; Le complot des ayatollahs, 1989, translation published as My Turn to Speak: Iran, the Revolution and Secret Deals with the United States, 1991; Usul-i hakem bar qazavat-i Islami: va Huquq-i bashar dar Islam, c. 1989; Le coran et le pouvoir, 1993. Author of articles and books about politics and Islamic law. Bani-Sadr's writings have been translated into Arabic, German, Serbian, and Italian. **Address:** 5 rue du General Pershing, 78000 Versailles, France. **Online address:** abanisadr@aol.com

BANKER, James R. American, b. 1938. **Genres:** History, Human relations/Parenting. **Career:** North Carolina State University, Raleigh, assistant profes-

sor, 1971-76, associate professor, 1976-85, professor of history, 1988-. **Publications:** Death in the Community, 1988. **Address:** Department of History, Box 8108, North Carolina State University, Raleigh, NC 27695-8108, U.S.A. **Online address:** james_banker@ncsu.edu

BANKER, Mark T(ollie). American, b. 1951. **Genres:** Local history/Rural topics. **Career:** Teacher and head of social studies department, Menaul School, Albuquerque, NM, 1976-81, dean of students, 1981-83; University of New Mexico, Valencia Campus, instructor in history, 1986; history teacher, Albuquerque Academy, 1986-87; Webb School of Knoxville, Knoxville, TN, history teacher, 1987-, department head, 1990-92. Menaul Historical Library of the Southwest, archival assistant, 1981-83. **Publications:** Presbyterian Missions and Cultural Interaction in the Far Southwest, 1850-1950, 1992; Toward Frontiers Yet Unknown: A Ninetieth Anniversary History of Warren Wilson College, 1985; Warren Wilson College: A Centennial Portrait, 1994. Work represented in anthologies. Contributor to history journals. **Address:** Webb School of Knoxville, 9800 Webb School Dr, Knoxville, TN 37923, U.S.A. **Online address:** mark_banker@webbschool.org

BANKIER, David. Israeli (born Germany), b. 1947. **Genres:** History. **Career:** Hebrew University of Jerusalem, Jerusalem, Israel, professor. **Publications:** The Germans and the Final Solution: Public Opinion Under Nazism, 1992. IN SPANISH: (ed.) La emancipacion judia, 1983; (ed.) El Holocausto, 1986; (ed.) El sionismo y la cuestion palestina, 1989. **Address:** Institute of Contemporary Jewry, Hebrew University of Jerusalem, Jerusalem, Israel. **Online address:** Bankier@surfree.net.il

BANKS, Geraldine. (Jeri). American, b. 1942. **Genres:** Animals/Pets, Education. **Career:** Teacher of language arts at a high school in Chicago, IL, 1963-67; substitute elementary schoolteacher in Chicago, 1967-70; teacher at a hearing impaired preschool in Chicago, 1970-80; John H. Kinzie Elementary School, Chicago, replication specialist in a program for the retrieval and acceleration of promising young handicapped and talented children, 1985-86, teacher, 1986-92, assistant principal, 1992-. St. Xavier University, instructor at Illinois Renewal Institute. **Publications:** All Animals, 1978; (as Jeri Banks) All of Us Together: The Story of Inclusion at the Kinzie School, 1994. Contributor to periodicals. **Address:** John H. Kinzie School, 5625 South Mobile, Chicago, IL 60638, U.S.A.

BANKS, Leslie. British, b. 1920. **Genres:** History, Air/Space topics, Travel/Exploration. **Career:** Clerk for a local government service in London, England, 1935-40; career military officer, serving as a wing commander for the British Army, Royal Air Force, and U.S. Air Force, 1940-63; International Business Machines (IBM) Ltd., worked in England as sales instructor, marketing representative, academic consultant, and in personnel, 1963-85; Jetbond Ltd. (conference management firm), chairperson, 1985-. **Publications:** Polar Air Navigation, 1947; Grid Navigation in All Latitudes, 1950; (with C.S. Stanley) Britain's Coastline: A History from the Air, 1986; (with C.S. Stanley) The Thames: A History from the Air, 1990. **Address:** 22 Minister Court, Hillcrest Rd, Ealing, London W5 1HH, England.

BANKS, Lynne Reid. British, b. 1929. **Genres:** Novels, Children's fiction, Young adult fiction, Plays/Screenplays, History, Writing/Journalism. **Career:** Actress in British repertory companies, 1949-53; interviewer, reporter and scriptwriter, Independent Television News, London, 1955-62; teacher of English, Israel, 1963-71. Writer, teacher, lecturer. **Publications:** The L-Shaped Room, 1960; An End to Running (in U.S. as House of Hope), 1962; Children at the Gate, 1968; The Backward Shadow, 1970; One More River, 1972; Two Is Lonely, 1974; The Adventures of King Midas, 1974; Sarah and After, 1975; Dark Quartet, 1976; The Farthest-Away Mountain, 1976; Path to the Silent Country, 1977; My Darling Villain, 1977; I, Houdini, 1978; The Indian in the Cupboard, 1980; Defy the Wilderness, 1981; The Writing on the Wall, 1981; Maura's Angel, 1984; The Warning Bell, 1984; The Fairy Rebel, 1985; Return of the Indian, 1986; Casualties, 1986; Melusine: A Mystery, 1988; The Secret of the Indian, 1989; The Magic Hare, 1992; Mystery of the Cupboard, 1993; Broken Bridge, 1994; Harry the Poisonous Centipede, 1996; Angela and Diabola, 1997; Key to the Indian, 1998; Moses in Egypt, 1998; Alice-by-Accident, 2000; Harry the Poisonous Centipede's Big Adventure, 2000; The Dungeon, 2002; Stealing Stacey, 2003; Tiger, Tiger, 2004; Harry the Poisonous Centipede Goes West, 2005. PLAYS: Miss Pringle Plays Portia; It Never Rains, 1954; The Killer Dies Twice, 1956; All in a Row, 1956; Already It's Tomorrow, 1962; The Travels of Yoshi and the Tea-Kettle, 1991. NON-FICTION: Letters to My Israeli Sons, 1979; Torn Country, 1981. **Address:** c/o Sheila Watson, Capo di Monte, Windmill Hill, Hampstead, London NW3 6RJ, England. **Online address:** www.lynnereidbanks.com

BANKS, Russell (Earl). American, b. 1940. **Genres:** Novels, Novellas/Short stories. **Career:** Plumber in New Hampshire, 1959-64; Publisher and

Ed., Lillabulero Press, and Co-Ed., Lillabulero mag., Chapel Hill, North Carolina, and Northwood Narrows, New Hampshire, 1966-75; taught at Emerson College, Boston, 1968-71, University of New Hampshire, Durham, 1968-75, New England College, Henniker, NH, 1975, 1977-82, and Princeton University, New Jersey, 1982. **Publications:** STORIES: Searching for Survivors, 1975; The New World, 1978; Trailerpark, 1981; Success Stories, 1986; Angel on the Roof, 2000. NOVELS: Family Life, 1975; Hamilton Stark, 1978; The Book of Jamaica, 1980; The Relation of My Imprisonment, 1983; Continental Drift, 1985; Affliction, 1989; The Sweet Hereafter, 1991; Rule of The Bone, 1995; Cloudsplitter, 1998. OTHER: Invisible Stranger, 1999. **Address:** Trident Media Group LLC, 41 Madison Ave Fl 36, New York, NY 10010, U.S.A.

BANN, Stephen. British, b. 1942. **Genres:** Cultural/Ethnic topics. **Career:** Writer and editor. University of Kent at Canterbury, England, professor of modern cultural studies, 1988-. **Publications:** (trans.) F. Popper, Origins and Development of Kinetic Art, 1968; Experimental Painting: Construction, Abstraction, Destruction, Reduction, 1970; The Clothing of Clio: A Study of the Representation of History in Nineteenth-Century Britain and France, 1984; The True Vine: On Visual Representation and Western Tradition, 1989; The Inventions of History, 1990; Under the Sign: John Bargrave as Traveler, Collector and Witness, 1994; Romanticism and the Rise of History, 1995; Paul Delaroche: History Painted, 1997. EDITOR: Concrete Poetry: An International Anthology, 1967; (with J. Bowlt) Russian Formalism: A Collection of Articles and Texts in Translation, 1973; The Tradition of Constructivism, 1974; Bernard Lassus, Les pins, 1983; (with W. Allen, and contrib.) Interpreting Contemporary Art, 1991; (with K. Kumar) Utopias and the Millennium, 1993; Frankenstein, Creation and Monstrosity, 1994. Contributor to periodicals. **Address:** Rutherford College, University of Kent at Canterbury, Canterbury, England.

BANNATYNE-CUGNET, (Elizabeth) Jo(-Anne). Canadian, b. 1951. **Genres:** Children's fiction, Picture/board books. **Career:** Writer, 1980-. Saskatchewan Ministry of Health, Weyburn, Saskatchewan area, rural public health nurse, 1974-1977; Souris Valley Regional Care Centre, Weyburn, part-time nursing supervisor, 1977-1994. Active in community and school-related activities. **Publications:** PICTURE BOOKS: A Prairie Alphabet, 1992; Estelle and the Self-Esteem Machine, 1993; A Prairie Year, 1994; From Far and Wide, 1998; Heartland: A Prairie Sampler, 2002. FICTION: Grampa's Alkali, 1993. **Address:** Box 1150, Weyburn, SK, Canada S4H 2L5.

BANNER-HALEY, Charles T. American, b. 1948. **Genres:** History, Race relations. **Career:** Colby College, Waterville, ME, assistant professor of history, 1977-79; State University of New York College at Oneonta, assistant professor of history, 1979-80; State University of New York College at Cortland, lecturer in history and black studies, 1980-85; University of Rochester, Rochester, NY, postdoctoral fellow at Frederick Douglass Institute, 1985-86; Martin Luther King, Jr. Papers Project, Atlanta, GA, assistant editor, 1988-89; Colgate University, Hamilton, NY, assistant professor, 1989-93, associate professor of history, 1994-. **Publications:** To Do Good and to Do Well, 1993; The Fruits of Integration, 1994. **Address:** Department of History, Colgate University, Hamilton, NY 13346, U.S.A.

BANNISTER, Sir Roger (Gilbert). British, b. 1929. **Genres:** Medicine/Health, Sports/Fitness. **Career:** Consultant neurologist, 1963-; The Sports/Council, London, chairman, 1971-74; Pembroke College, Oxford, Master, 1985-93. Athletic achievements include: world record for one mile (first four minute mile), 1954; European 1500 metres title and record, 1954. **Publications:** First Four Minutes, 1955; Four Minute Mile, 1989; Brain and Bannister's Clinical Neurology, 7th ed., 1992; (ed. with C.J. Mathias) Autonomic Failure: A Textbook of Clinical Disorders of the Autonomic Nervous System, 3rd ed., 1992, 4th ed., 1999. **Address:** Pembroke College, Oxford OX1 1DW, England.

BANNOCK, Graham. British, b. 1932. **Genres:** Business/Trade/Industry, Economics. **Career:** Market Research Manager, Rover Co., Solihull, 1958-60 and 1962-67; Sr. Administration, Economics Division, Organization for Economic Co-operation and Development, Paris, 1960-62; Manager, Advanced Planning, Ford of Europe Inc., Dunton, 1967-69; Director, Research Committee of Inquiry on Small Firms, Dept. of Trade, London, 1969-71; Managing Director, Economists Advisory Group Ltd., London, 1971-81, and Economist Intelligence Unit Ltd., 1981-84. **Publications:** (with A.J. Merrett) Business Economics and Statistics, 1962; The Juggernauts: The Age of the Giant Corporation, 1971, 1973; (with R.E. Baxter and R. Rees) Dictionary of Economics, 1972, 5th ed., 1998; How to Survive the Slump, 1975; The Smaller Business in Britain and Germany, 1976; The Economics of Small Firms, 1981; (with A. Doran) Going Public, 1987; (with A. Peacock)

Governments and Small Business, 1989; (with W.A.P. Manser) A Dictionary of International Finance, 1989; Taxation in the European Community, 1990; (with H. Albach) Small Business Policy in Europe, 1991; (with M. Daly) Small Business Statistics, 1994; International Dictionary of Finance, 1999. **Address:** Bannock Consulting, 47 Marylebone Ln, London WIU 2LD, England.

BANNON, David Race. (born United States), b. 1963. **Genres:** History. **Career:** Former Interpol agent and college science instructor. Worked as computer trainer for Information Architects; previously taught at Duke University, University of South Carolina, and Wake Technical College. Has appeared on cable television on the Discovery Channel, A&E, and the History Channel. **Publications:** Race against Evil: The Secret Missions of the Interpol Agent Who Tracked the World's Most Sinister Criminals, 2003. Published articles and books on the martial arts, Korean history, and computers. **Address:** c/o Author Mail, New Horizon Press Publishers, POB 669, Far Hills, NJ 07931, U.S.A.

BANSEMER, Roger. American, b. 1948. **Genres:** Area studies. **Career:** Artist and author. **Publications:** The Art of Hot-Air Ballooning, 1987; Southern Shores, 1989; Rachael's Splendifilous Adventure, 1991; At the Water's Edge, the Birds of Florida, 1991; Mountains in the Mist, 1992; Bansemer's Book of Florida Lighthouses, 1999. **Address:** 2352 Alligator Creek Rd., Clearwater, FL 33765, U.S.A. **Online address:** bansemer@bansemer.com

BANTA, Trudy W. American. **Genres:** Education. **Career:** University of Tennessee, Knoxville, special assistant to the chancellor, 1979-82, assistant professor to professor of education, 1979-92, research professor at Learning Research Center, 1986-89, director of National Assessment Resource Center, 1986-89, founding director of Center for Assessment Research and Development, 1989-92; Indiana University-Purdue University Indianapolis, professor of higher education and vice chancellor for planning and institutional improvement, 1992-. Bryn Mawr Summer Institute for Women in Higher Education Administration, guest faculty member; conference speaker and workshop presenter in the US and elsewhere. **Publications:** (with C. Palomba) Assessment Essentials, 1999. EDITOR & CONTRIBUTOR: Performance Funding in Higher Education: A Critical Analysis of Tennessee's Experience, 1986; Implementing Outcomes Assessment: Promise and Perils, 1988; Making a Difference: Outcomes of a Decade of Assessment in Higher Education, 1993; (with V.M.H. Borden) Using Performance Indicators to Guide Strategic Decision Making, 1994; Building a Scholarship of Assessment, 2002. Contributor to books and professional journals. **Address:** AO 140, Indiana University-Purdue University Indianapolis, 355 N Lansing St, Indianapolis, IN 46202-2896, U.S.A.

BANVILLE, John. Irish, b. 1945. **Genres:** Novels, Novellas/Short stories. **Career:** Irish Times, Dublin, chief literary critic and associate literary editor. **Publications:** Long Lankin (short stories), 1970. NOVELS: Nightspawn, 1971; Birchwood, 1973; Doctor Copernicus, 1976; Kepler, 1981; The Newton Letter, 1982; Mefisto, 1986; The Book of Evidence, 1989; Ghosts, 1993; Athena, 1995; The Untouchable, 1997; Eclipse, 2000; Shroud, 2003. **Address:** Gillon Aitken Associates, 29 Fernshaw Rd, London SW10 0TG, England.

BARABTARLO, Gennady. American (born Russia), b. 1949. **Genres:** Poetry, Literary criticism and history, Translations. **Career:** Pushkin Literary Museum, Moscow, U.S.S.R. (now the Russian Federation), senior research fellow, 1970-78; University of Missouri-Columbia, professor of Russian, 1984-. **Publications:** Phantom of Fact, 1989; Aerial View: Essays on Nabokov's Art and Metaphysics, 1993; (with C. Nicol) A Small Alpine Form, 1993; In Every Place (verse and adaptations), 1999; (ed.) Cold Fusion (essays), 2000; The Shimmering Wheel, 2003. TRANSLATOR: V. Nabokov, Pnin, 1983; Solzhenitsyn, What a Pity (short stories), 1999; Nabokov, Ebbing of Time (short stories), 2001. **Address:** 451 GCB, German and Russian Studies, University of Missouri, Columbia, MO 65211, U.S.A.

BARAKA, Imamu Amiri. Also writes as (Everett) LeRoi Jones. American, b. 1934. **Genres:** Novels, Plays/Screenplays, Poetry, Music, Race relations. **Career:** State University of New York at Stony Brook, assistant professor, 1980-83, associate professor, 1983-85, professor of African Studies, 1986-. Visiting professor, Rutgers University, New Brunswick, NJ, 1988-. Founder, Yugen mag. and Totem Press, NYC, 1958; co-ed., Floating Bar mag., NYC, 1961-63; member of faculty, New School for Social Research, NYC, 1961-64; founding director, Black Arts Repertory Theatre, Harlem, NYC, 1964-66, and Spirit House, Newark, NJ, 1966-72. **Publications:** Spring and Soforth, 1960; Preface to a 20 Volume Suicide Note, 1961; Blues People: Negro

Music in White America, 1963; The Dead Lecturer (poetry), 1964; Dutchman, and The Slave, 1964; The System of Dante's Hell (novel), 1965; Jello, 1965; Black Art (poetry), 1966; Home: Social Essays, 1966; Tales, 1967; Black Music, 1967; Arm Yourself and Harm Yourself, 1967; The Baptism, and The Toilet, 1967; Slave Ship, 1967; Black Magic: Poetry 1961-67, 1969; Four Black Revolutionary Plays, 1969; It's Nationtime (poetry), 1970; In Our Terribleness, 1970; A Black Value System, 1970; Poem for Black Hearts, 1970; Raise Race Rays Raze: Essays since 1965, 1971; Spirit Reach (poetry), 1972; African Revolution (poetry), 1973; The Creation of the New Ark, 1974; Hard Facts (poetry), 1976; The Motion of History and Other Plays, 1978; Selected Plays and Prose, 1979; Selected Poetry, 1979; AM/TRAK (poetry), 1979; Spring Song, 1979; Reggae or Not, 1981; The Autobiography of LeRoi Jones, 1984; (with Amina Baraka) The Music: Reflections on Jazz and Blues, 1987; The LeRoi Jones/Amiri Baraka Reader, 1991, 2nd ed., 2000; Thornton Dial, 1993; Jesse Jackson and Black People, 1994; Wise, Why's, Y's, 1994; Transbluency, 1995; Eulogies, 1996; The Fiction of Leroi Jones, 2000. EDITOR: Four Young Lady Poets, 1962; The Moderns: New Fiction in America, 1964; (with L. Neal) Black Fire: An Anthology of Afro-American Writing, 1968; African Congress: A Documentary of the First Modern Pan-African Congress, 1972. Work represented in anthologies. **Address:** c/o Joan Brandt, Sterling Lord Literistic Inc., 65 Bleecker St, New York, NY 10012-2420, U.S.A.

BARAM, Amatzia. Israeli, b. 1938. **Genres:** Area studies, History. **Career:** Science teacher at the high school in Kibbutz Kfar Menachem, Israel, 1968-73; Hebrew University of Jerusalem, Israel, tutor, 1976-80; University of Haifa, Israel, lecturer to professor in modern history of the Middle East, 1982-, Jewish-Arab Center and Gustav Heinemann Institute for Middle Eastern Studies, deputy director, 1992-93, director, 1999-2002. Hebrew University of Jerusalem, research fellow in advanced studies, 1986-87; Oxford University, senior associate member of St. Antony's College, 1988, 1990; Smithsonian Institution, fellow at Woodrow Wilson International Center for Scholars, 1989, 1993-94; US Inst of Peace, senior fellow, 1997-98. Member of the Israeli prime minister's advisory team on Middle Eastern affairs, 1984-88. Analyst for U.S. television and radio news programs; guest on television and radio programs in England, Europe, and Japan. **Publications:** Culture, History, and Ideology in the Formation of Ba'thist Iraq, 1968-1989, 1991; (ed., with B. Rubin) Iraq's Road to War, 1994; Building toward Crisis: Saddam Hussein's Strategy for Survival, 1998. Work represented in books. Contributor to Middle East studies journals. **Address:** Dept of Modern History of the Middle East, University of Haifa, 31905 Haifa, Israel. **Online address:** baram@research.haifa.ac.il

BARANCZAK, Stanislaw. American (born Poland), b. 1946. **Genres:** Poetry, Politics/Government, Literary criticism and history, Translations. **Career:** Adam Mickiewicz University, Poznan, Poland, Institute of Polish Philology, assistant professor, 1969-77, associate professor of literature, 1980-81; Harvard University, associate professor of Slavic language and literature, 1981-84, Alfred Jurzykowski professor of Polish language and literature, 1984-, member of cultural advisory committee for the Alfred Jurzykowski Foundation, 1989-. Cofounder and member of human rights group KOR, 1976-81. **Publications:** POETRY: Korekta twarzy (title means: Proofreading of a Face), 1968; Jednym tchem (title means: In One Breath), 1970; Dziennik poranny: Wiersze 1967-1971 (title means: A Morning Diary: Poems 1967-1971), 1972; Ja wiem, ze to niesluszne: Wiersze z lat 1975-1976 (title means: I Know It's Improper: Poems from 1975-1976), 1977; Sztuczne oddychanie (title means: Artificial Respiration), 1978; Tryptyk z betonu, zmeczenia i sniegu (title means: A Tryptych of Concrete, Weariness, and Snow), 1980; Under My Own Roof: Verses for a New Apartment, trans by F. Kujawinski, 1980; Wiersze prawie zebrane (title means: The Almost Collected Poems), 1981; Atlantyda i inne wiersze z lat 1981-1985 (title means: Atlantis and Other Verses from 1981-1985), 1986; Widokowka z tego swiata i inne rymy z lat 1986-1988 (title means: A Postcard from This World and Other Rhymes from 1986-1988), 1988; The Weight of the Body: Selected Poems, trans by M.J. Krynski, R. Lourie, R.A. Maguire, and S. Baranczak, 1989; 159 wierszy: 1968-1988 (title means: 159 Poems: 1968-1988), 1990; Poezje wybrane (title means: Selected Verse), 1990; Zwierzeca zajadlosc: Z zapiskow zniecheconego zoologa (title means: Brute Beasts: Notes of a Disenchanted Zoologist), 1991; Biografioly: Poczet 56 jednostek slawnych, slawetnych, i ostawionych (title means: Biographollies: A Galaxy of 56 Famous, Notorious, and Illreputed Individuals), 1991; Zupelne zezwierzecenie (title means: Absolute Animals), 1993; Podroz zimowa (Winter Journey), 1994; Bog, Traba i Ojczyzna: Slon a sprawa polska oczami poetow od Reja do Rymkiewicza (title means: Patriotic Tusks: The Elephant versus the Polish Cause As Seen by Poets from the Dark Ages to Our Time), 1995; Zegam cie Nosorozcze: Kompletne bestiarium zniecheconego zoologa (title means: See You Later, Rhinoceros: Complete Bestiary of the Disenchanted Zoologist), 1995. ESSAYS & CRITICISM, EXCEPT WHERE NOTED:

Nieufni i zadufani: Romantyzm i klascycyzm w mlodej poezji lat szescdziesiatych (title means: The Distrustful and the Overconfident: Romanticism and Classicism of Young Polish Poetry of the 1960s), 1971; Ironia i harmonia: Szkice o najnowszej literaturze polskiej (title means: Irony and Harmony: Essays on Modern Polish Literature), 1973; Jezyk poetycki Mirona Bialoszewskiego (title means: Miron Bialoszewski's Poetic Language), 1974; Etyka i poetyka: Szkice 1970-1978 (title means: Ethics and Poetics: Essays 1970-1978), 1979; Ksiazki najgorsze 1975-80 (title means: The Worst Books 1975-80), 1981, enlarged ed, 1990; Czytelnik ubezwlasnowolniony: Perswazja w masowej kulturze literackiej PRL (title means: The Incapacitated Reader: Persuasion in the Polish People's Republic's Mass Literary Culture), 1983; Uciekinier z Utopii: O poezji Zbigniewa Herberta, 1984, 2nd ed, 1994, trans as A Fugitive from Utopia: The Poetry of Zbigniew Herbert, 1987; Przed i po: Szkice o poezji krajowej przelo mu lat siedemdziesiatych i osiemdziesiatych (title means: Before and After: Essays on Polish Poetry of the Turn of the 1970s/1980s), 1988; Breathing under Water, and Other East European Essays, 1990; Tablica z Macondo: Osiem nascie prob wytlumaczenia, po co i dlaczego sie pisze (title means: The Macondo License Plate: Eighteen Ways of Trying to Explain the Reasons for Writing), 1990; Ocalone w tlumaczeniu (title means: Saved in Translation), 1992, 2nd ed, 1994; Zaufac nieufnosci: Osiem rozmow o sensie poezji 1990-1992 (interviews; title means: To Trust Distrustfulness), 1993; Pomyslane przepascie: Osien interpretacij (title means: The Thought of Precipices: Eight Interpretations), 1995. Contributor of articles and reviews to periodicals. EDITOR & TRANSLATOR: D. Thomas, Wiersze wybrane (title means: Selected Poems), 1974; O. Mandelshtam, Pozne wiersze (title means: The Late Poems), 1977; I. Brodskii, Wiersze i poematy (title means: Poems, Short and Long), 1979; G.M. Hopkins, Wybor poezji (title means: Selected Poems), 1981; Antologia angielskiej poezji metafizycznej XVII stulecia (title means: An Anthology of 17th-Century English Metaphysical Poetry), 1982, enlarged ed, 1991; J. Donne, Wiersze wybrane (title means: Selected Poems), 1984; (with R.A. Davies and J.M. Gogol) R. Krynicki, Citizen R.K. Does Not Live: Poems, 1985; T. Venclova, Rozmowa w zimie: Wybor wierszy (title means: The Winter Talk: Selected Poems), 1989; G. Herbert, Wiersze wybrane (title means: Selected Poems), 1990; J. Merrill, Wybor poezji (title means: Selected Poems), 1990; Zwierze slucha zwierzen: Male bestiarium z angielskiego (title means: The Animal Confessors: A Little English and American Bestiary), 1991; Z Toba wiec ze Wszystkim: 222 arcydziela angielskiej i amerykanskiej liryki religijnej (title means: With Thee, Therefore with All: 222 Masterpieces of English and American Religious Verse), 1992; (with C. Cavanagh) Polish Poetry of the Last Two Decades of Communist Rule: Spoiling Cannibals' Fun, 1991; C. Simic, Madonny z dorysowana szpicbrodka oraz inne wiersze, prozy poetyckie ie eseje (title means: Madonnas Touched up with a Goatee, and Other Poems, Prose Poems, and Essays), 1992; Milosc jest wszystkim, co istnieje: 300 najslawniejszych angielskich i amerykanskich wierszy milosnych (title means: That Love Is All There Is: 300 Most Famous English and American Love Poems), 1993; Fioletowa krowa: 333 najslawniejsze okazy angielskiej i amerykanskiej poezji niepowaznej od Williama Shakespeare'a do Johna Lennona (title means: The Purple Cow: 333 Most Famous Specimens of English and American Light Verse from William Shakespeare to John Lennon), 1993; Od Chaucera do Larkina: 400 niesmiertelnych wieszy 125 poetow anglojezycznych z 8 stuleci (title means: From Chaucer to Larkin: 400 Immortal Poems of 125 Poets of the English Language from 8 Centuries), 1993; (with Cavanagh) W. Szymborska, View with a Grain of Sand: Selected Poems, 1995; (with Cavanagh) 77 Translations, 1995. Translator of works into Polish by: A.A. Milne, e.e. cummings, U.K. Le Guin, Brodskii, W. Shakespeare, E. Dickinson, P. Larkin, R. Herrick, R. Frost, A. Marvel, T. Hardy, W.H. Auden, S. Heaney, T. Campion, T.S. Eliot, E. Bishop, J. Kochanowski. Editor of untranslated works by: W. Weintraub. **Address:** Harvard University, 313 Boylston Hall, Cambridge, MA 02138, U.S.A.

BARASCH, Frances K. American, b. 1928. **Genres:** Literary criticism and history. **Career:** Baruch College, City University of New York, Assistant Professor, 1965-72, Associate Professor, 1972-77, Professor of English, 1977-. Consultant, Choice, 1968-; Publr., Release: A Newsletter for Adult and Continuing Educators, 1979-. Assistant to Director and Instructor of English, New York University, 1959-61; Adjunct Associate Professor of English, Pace College, New York, 1961-69; Assistant Prof of English, Long Island University, 1964-65. **Publications:** Shakespeare's Second Part of Henry IV, 1964; (bib.) Modern British Authors, vol. III, 1966; The Grotesque: A Study of Meanings, 1971; Academic Women and Unions, 1974. EDITOR: Study Guide Series: Julius Caesar, Merchant of Venice, Othello, Romantic Poets, 1964-66; Wright's History of Caricature and the Grotesque, 1968; The Critical Temper, vol. II, 1969; PSC Clarion, 1972-73. Contributor of articles and reviews to periodicals. **Address:** 93-26 86th Ave, Woodhaven, NY 11421, U.S.A. **Online address:** Fbarasch@aol.com

BARASH, David P(hilip). American, b. 1946. **Genres:** Sociology, Psychology, Politics/Government, Military/Defense/Arms control, Zoology. **Career:** State University of New York, Oneonta, assistant professor of biology, 1970-73; University of Washington, Seattle, associate professor, 1973-80, professor of psychology and zoology, 1980-. **Publications:** Sociobiology and Behavior, 1977, rev. ed., 1982; The Whisperings Within, 1979; Stop Nuclear War!: A Handbook, 1982; Aging: An Exploration, 1983; The Caveman and the Bomb, 1985; The Hare and the Tortoise: Culture, Biology, and Human Nature, 1986; The Arms Race and Nuclear War, 1987; Marmots: Social Behavior and Ecology, 1989; The Great Outdoors, 1989; Introduction to Peace Studies, 1991; The L Word: An Unapologetic, Thoroughly Biased, Long-overdue Explication and Celebration of Liberalism, 1992; Beloved Enemies: Exploring Our Need for Opponents, 1994; Ideas of Human Nature, 1997; Approaches to Peace, 2000; Peace and Conflict Studies, 2001; Gender Gap, 2001; The Myth of Monogamy, 2002; The Survival Game, 2003. **Address:** Psychology Dept, Box 351525, University of Washington, Seattle, WA 98195, U.S.A.

BARASH, Samuel T. American, b. 1921. **Genres:** Money/Finance. **Career:** Author and self-employed real estate appraiser. **Publications:** Standard Real Estate Appraising Manual, 1979; How to Reduce Your Real Estate Taxes, 1979; How to Cash in on Little-Known Local Real Estate Investment Opportunities, 1980; Complete Guide to Condominium and Cooperative Appraising, 1981; Encyclopedia of Real Estate Appraisal Forms and Model Reports, 1983. **Address:** 466 Lakes Rd, Monroe, NY 10950, U.S.A. **Online address:** samba1@frontiernet.net

BARAT, Kahar. (born People's Republic of China), b. 1950. **Genres:** History. **Career:** Academia Sinica, Taipei, Taiwan, visiting fellow, 1996; Fokuang University, Chiayi, Taiwan, visiting associate professor, 1997-98; Harvard University, Cambridge, MA, research affiliate, 1998-99; Comverse, Inc., Cambridge, MA, linguistic engineer, 2000-01; Harvard University, Cambridge, MA, assistant cataloger, 2001, 2003-. **Publications:** The Uygur-Turkic Biography of the Seventh-Century Chinese Buddhist Pilgrim Xuanzang: Ninth and Tenth Chapters, 2000. Contributor to periodicals. **Address:** 295 Windsor St., No. 8, Cambridge, MA 02139, U.S.A. **Online address:** barat@post.harvard.edu

BARATTA, Joseph Preston. American, b. 1943. **Genres:** History, Politics/Government. **Career:** Worcester State College, professor, 1999-. Coalition for a Strong United Nations, founding member and chair of executive committee, 1994-99. **Publications:** The World Federalist Movement: A Collection of Mainstream Journals, 1989; Human Rights: Improving U.N. Mechanisms for Compliance, 1990; The United Nations System: Meeting the World Constitutional Crisis, 1995; What Happened to One World, 2003. **Address:** 32 Hilltop Circle, Worcester, MA 01609, U.S.A. **Online address:** jbaratta@worcester.edu

BARBA, Harry. Also writes as Baron Mikan, Ohan. American, b. 1922. **Genres:** Novels, Novellas/Short stories, Science fiction/Fantasy, Plays/Screenplays, Poetry, Songs/Lyrics and libretti, Education, Writing/Journalism. **Career:** Publisher and Conference Director, Harian Creative Books, 1967-; Ed., Harian Creative Awards series, 1981-. Instructor, Wilkes College, Wilkes-Barre, PA, 1947; Instructor, Univ of Connecticut, Hartford Campus, 1947-49; Teacher, Seward Park High School, NY, 1955-59; Instructor, University of Iowa, 1959-63; Fulbright Professor-American Specialist, University of Damascus, Syria, 1963-64; Reader and Lecturer, USIS Library, Damascus, 1963-64; Assistant Professor and Associate Professor, Skidmore College, Saratoga Springs, NY, 1964-68; Professor of English and Director of Writing, Marshall University, Huntington, WV, 1968-70; Director of Writing Arts in West Virginia, 1969-70; Distinguished Visiting Lecturer in Contemporary Literature and Consultant to the Writing Committee, SUNY, 1976-77. **Publications:** For the Grape Season, 1960; The Bulbul Bird, 1963, 3 by Harry Barba, 1967; How to Teach Writing. 1969; Teaching in Your Own Write, 1970; The Case for Socially Functional Education, 1973; Two Connecticut Yankees Teaching in Appalachia, 1974; One of a Kind: The Many Faces and Voices of America, 1976; The Day the World Went Sane, 1979; (with M. Barba) What's Cooking in Congress?, 2 vols., 1979-82; (as Baron Mikan) The Gospel According to Everyman, 1981; Round Trip to Byzantium, 1985; Mona Lisa Smiles, 1993; The Marriage of Heaven & Hell, 2004. **Address:** 47 Hyde Blvd, Ballston Spa, NY 12020, U.S.A.

BARBARESE, J. T. American. **Genres:** Novellas/Short stories, Poetry, Literary criticism and history. **Career:** Rutgers University, Camden Campus, adjunct professor, 1988-97, associate professor, 1999-2005. **Publications:** Under the Blue Moon, 1985; New Science, 1989; Euripides' Children of Herakles, 1999. POETRY: A Very Small World, 2004; The Black Beach, 2005. **Address:** 7128 Cresheim Rd, Philadelphia, PA 19119, U.S.A. **Online address:** jt.barbarese@verizon.net

BARBASH, Shepard. American, b. 1957. **Genres:** Art/Art history. **Career:** Patriot Ledger, Quincy, MA, correspondent for music and film reviews, 1981-82; Associated Press, NYC, statistical worker-newsperson, 1982-83; Hudson Dispatch, Union City, NJ, court and county politics reporter, 1983-84; Advocate, Stamford, CT, business reporter and real estate columnist; Houston Chronicle, Houston, TX, bureau chief for Mexico and Central America, 1987-88. Stringer, freelance writer for Barron's, AP-Dow Jones, Newsday, American Banker, Euromoney's Latin Finance magazine, 1986-89; stringer for the New York Times, covering real estate, 1992-. **Publications:** Oaxacan Woodcarving: The Magic in the Trees, 1993. **Address:** 1732 Meadowdale Ave., Atlanta, GA 30306, U.S.A.

BARBASH, Tom. American. **Genres:** Novellas/Short stories. **Career:** Author. Syracuse Post Standard, Oswego, NY, reporter; University of Iowa, lecturer; Stanford University, fellow and lecturer. **Publications:** The Last Good Chance, 2002; On Top of the World, 2003. Contributor of short stories to periodicals. **Address:** c/o Picador USA, 175 Fifth Avenue, New York, NY 10010, U.S.A.

BARBATO, Joseph. American, b. 1944. **Genres:** Adult non-fiction, Environmental sciences/Ecology, How-to books, Writing/Journalism. **Career:** New York University, NYC, news writer and editor, 1964-68, alumni communications director, 1969-74, senior development writer, 1976-78; Shell Oil Co., staff writer, 1968-69; City University of New York, NYC, public information director and manager of media relations office at LaGuardia Community College, 1974-76, adjunct lecturer in journalism; independent consultant to nonprofit institutions, 1978-90; Nature Conservancy, Arlington, VA, director of development communications and special editorial project leader for Book Publishing Group, 1990-99; Barbato Associates, president, 1999-. Publishers Weekly, contributing editor. **Publications:** (with A. Luks) You Are What You Drink: The Authoritative Report on What Alcohol Does to Your Body, Mind, and Longevity, 1989; (with F. Gurlich) Writing for a Good Cause, 2000. EDITOR/CO-EDITOR: How Your Mind Affects Your Health, 1990; Patchwork of Dreams: Voices from the Heart of the New America, 1994; Heart of the Land: Essays on the Last Great Places, 1995; Off the Beaten Path, 1998. Contributor to magazines and newspapers. **Address:** Barbato Associates, 5420 Gary Pl, Alexandria, VA 22311, U.S.A. **Online address:** jabarbato@aol.com

BARBEAU, Edward J(oseph). Canadian, b. 1938. **Genres:** Mathematics/Statistics. **Career:** University of Western Ontario, London, assistant professor of mathematics, 1964-66; Yale University, New Haven, CT, postdoctoral research fellow, 1966-67; University of Toronto, assistant professor, 1967-69, associate professor, 1969-88, professor of mathematics, 1988-, now emeritus. **Publications:** Polynomials, 1989; After Math: Puzzles and Brainteasers, 1995; (with M. Klamkin and M. Moser) Five Hundred Mathematical Challenges, 1995; Power Play, 1997; Fallacies, Flaws and Flimflam, 1999; Pell's Equation, 2003. **Address:** Department of Mathematics, University of Toronto, Toronto, ON, Canada M5S 3G3. **Online address:** barbeau@math.utoronto.ca

BARBER, Benjamin R(eynolds). American, b. 1939. **Genres:** Novels, Plays/Screenplays, Politics/Government, Education, Philosophy. **Career:** Walt Whitman Professor of Political Science, Rutgers University and Director, Whitman Center for the Culture and Politics of Democracy (member of faculty, 1969-). Lecturer in Ethics and Politics, Albert Schweitzer College, Churwalden, Switzerland, 1962-64; Assistant Professor of Political Science, University of Pennsylvania. Philadelphia, 1966-69. Ed-in-Chief, Political Theory, 1972-84; Bodies Electric, chairman. **Publications:** (with C.J. Friedrich and M. Curtis) Totalitarianism in Perspective: Three Views, 1969; Superman and Commen Men: Freedom, Anarchy and the Revolution, 1971; The Death of Communal Liberty: A History of Freedom in a Swiss Mountain Canton, 1974; Liberating Feminism, 1976; Marriage Voices: A Novel, 1981; The Artist and Political Vision, 1982; Strong Democracy, 1984; The Conquest of Politics, 1988; (with P. Watson) The Struggle for Democracy (TV series and companion book), 1989; Jihad versus McWorld, 1995; A Passion for Democracy (essays), 1999; My Affair with Clinton: An Intellectual Memoir, 2001; The Truth of Power, 2001. PLAYS: The People's Heart, 1969; Delly's Oracle, 1970; The Bust, 1971; (with M. Best) From Our Dissension, 1971; Doors, 1972; (with J. Duffy and R. Lamb) Fightsong (musical), 1975; (with G. Quincy) Home and the River (opera), 1982; Making Kaspar, 1984; An Aristocracy of Everyone, 1992. **Address:** Walt Whitman Center, Department of Political Science, Rutgers University, New Brunswick, NJ 08903, U.S.A.

BARBER, E(lizabeth) J. W(ayland). American, b. 1940. **Genres:** Archaeology/Antiquities, Language/Linguistics, Mythology/Folklore. **Career:** Chinese Linguistics Project, Princeton University, Princeton, NJ, research associate, 1968-69; Occidental College, Los Angeles, CA, 1970-, became professor of linguistics and archaeology. Consultant to Asia Foundation on Chinese machine translation project, 1974; lecturer for the Archaeological Institute of America, 1974-76, 1983-84, 1993-99, and 2002-03; lecturer for Phi Beta Kappa, 2001-02. **Publications:** Archaeological Decipherment, 1974; Prehistoric Textiles: The Development of Cloth in the Neolithic and Bronze Ages, 1991; Women's Work-The First 20,000 Years, 1994; The Mummies of Urumchi, 1999; When They Severed Earth from Sky: How the Human Mind Shapes Myth, 2005. Contributor to books and periodicals. **Address:** Language Dept, Occidental College, 1600 Campus Dr, Los Angeles, CA 90041, U.S.A.

BARBER, James David. *See* Obituaries.

BARBER, John (Douglass). British, b. 1944. **Genres:** History, Politics/Government. **Career:** University of Birmingham, Centre for Russian and East European Studies, hon. research fellow, 1980-; Cambridge University, fellow of King's College, and senior lecturer in politics. **Publications:** Soviet Historians in Crisis 1928-1932, 1981; (with M. Harrison) The Soviet Home Front, 1941-1945, 1991; (ed. with M. Harrison) The Soviet Defence-Industry Complex from Stalin to Khrushchev, 2000. **Address:** King's College, Cambridge CB2 1ST, England. **Online address:** jdb6@cam.ac.uk

BARBER, Karin. Swedish. **Genres:** Cultural/Ethnic topics, Language/Linguistics. **Career:** St. Mary's Teacher Training College, Bukedea, Mbale, Nigeria, teacher, 1967-68; University of Ife, Nigeria, assistant lecturer, 1977-79, lecturer in African languages and literatures, 1979-84; City Literary Institute, London, England, part-time instructor in Yoruba language, 1984-85; University of Birmingham, England, lecturer in West African studies, 1985-93, senior lecturer, 1993-. University of California, Los Angeles, principal instructor in Yoruba, summer, 1982. Institute for Advanced Study and Research in The African Humanities, Northwestern University, preceptor, 1993-94; consultant to Screenlife Ltd. **Publications:** Yoruba Dun un So: A Beginners' Course in Yoruba, Part I, 1984; I Could Speak until Tomorrow, 1991; (with J. Collins and A. Ricard) West African Popular Theatre, 1997; Generation of Plays, 2000. EDITOR: (with P.F. de Moraes Farias, and contrib.) Discourse and Its Disguises, 1989; (with P.F. de Moraes Farias, and contrib.) Self-Assertion and Brokerage, 1990; (and trans. with B. Ogundijo)Yoruba Popular Theatre, 1994; Readings in African Popular Culture, 1997. PLAYS IN YORUBA: Fenu monu (title means: Keep Your Mouth Shut); Ijapa ati Apata (title means: The Tortoise and the Rock); Ode Alaigboran (title means: The Disobedient Hunter); Okoo Bisi (title means: Bisi's Husband); Aropin ni teniyan (title means: Let Them Do Their Worst); Eni a fe la mo (title means: We Know Who We Love); Bischofswerda, 1992. Work represented in anthologies. Contributor of articles and reviews to African studies journals. **Address:** Centre of West African Studies, School of Historical Studies, University of Birmingham, Edgbaston, Birmingham B15 2TT, England. **Online address:** K.J.Barber@bham.ac.uk

BARBER, Lucy G(race). American, b. 1964. **Genres:** Civil liberties/Human rights. **Career:** Educator and historian. California State Archives, Sacramento, archivist. Teacher of U.S. history at universities and colleges, including Brown University, Rhode Island School of Design, and University of California-Davis. **Publications:** Marching on Washington: The Forging of an American Political Tradition, 2002. Contributor to periodicals. **Address:** California State Archives, 1020 O St., Sacramento, CA 95814, U.S.A. **Online address:** lgbarber@yahoo.com

BARBER, Paul (Thomas). American, b. 1941. **Genres:** Novels, Mythology/Folklore. **Career:** Princeton University, Princeton, NJ, instructor, 1967-68, assistant professor of Germanic languages and literatures, 1968-70; Pasadena City College, Pasadena, CA, part-time instructor in creative writing, 1972-76; Occidental College, Los Angeles, CA, instructor in literature, mythology, and folklore, 1974-78; owner of a piano repair and restoration business, 1978-. Part-time teacher at Glendale City College, 1972-76; research associate at Fowler Museum of Cultural History, University of California, Los Angeles; lecturer at Ludwigsburg Teachers College in Swabia, 1992. **Publications:** Vampires, Burial, and Death: Folklore and Reality, 1988. Contributor to periodicals and encyclopedias. **Address:** Fowler Museum of Cultural History, University of California, 405 Hilgard Ave, Los Angeles, CA 90024-1549, U.S.A. **Online address:** grendel33@hotmail.com

BARBER, Phyllis (Nelson). American, b. 1943. **Genres:** Novellas/Short stories, Children's fiction, Young adult fiction, Poetry, Literary criticism and history, Autobiography/Memoirs, Essays. **Career:** Professional pianist, Salt Lake City, UT, and Summit County, CO, 1964-; Vermont College, faculty member, M.F.A.-in-Writing-Program, 1990-; Colorado Mountain College,

Breckenridge, faculty member, 1992-94; University of Missouri, Columbia, visiting writer, 1994; Rochester, MN, Community Education, teacher, 1999; University of Utah, Park City, Lifelong Learning, teacher, 2000-01; writer. Pioneer Craft House, creative writing instructor. Has given readings and delivered lectures at colleges, schools, conferences, and bookstores. Served as judge for arts council awards and other writing competitions. **Publications:** Smiley Snake's Adventure (juvenile), 1980; (and ed.) Writers at Work (TV documentary), 1987; The School of Love (short stories), 1990; Legs: The Story of a Giraffe (juvenile), 1991; And the Desert Shall Blossom (novel), 1991; How I Got Cultured: A Nevada Memoir, 1992; Parting the Veil, 1999. Work represented in anthologies. Contributor of short stories, poems, essays, articles, and reviews to magazines and journals. **Address:** c/o MFA in Writing Program, Vermont College, 38 College St, Montpelier, VT 05602, U.S.A.

BARBER, Richard (William). British, b. 1941. **Genres:** Food and Wine, History, Literary criticism and history, Mythology/Folklore, Travel/Exploration. **Career:** Boydell and Brewer Ltd., managing director. **Publications:** Arthur of Albion, 1961, rev. ed. as King Arthur: Hero and Legend, 1986; Henry Plantagenet, 1963; (with F. Camps) The Investigation of Murder, 1965; The Knight and Chivalry, 1970, rev. ed., 1995; Samuel Pepys Esq., 1970; (with A. Riches) A Dictionary of Fabulous Beasts, 1971; The Figure of Arthur, 1972; Cooking and Recipes from Rome to the Renaissance, 1974; Aubrey's Brief Lives, 1975; A Strong Land and a Sturdy, 1976; Companion Guide to South West France, 1977, rev. ed. as Companion Guide to Gascony and the Dordogne, 1991; The Devil's Crown, 1978; Tournaments, 1978; Edward Prince of Wales and Aquitaine, 1978; The Arthurian Legends, 1979; A Companion to World Mythology, 1979; The Reign of Chivalry, 1980; Living Legends, 1981; The Pastons, 1981; Penguin Guide to Medieval Europe, 1984; The Worlds of John Aubrey, 1986; Fuller's Worthies, 1986; (with J. Barker) Tournaments, 1989; Pilgrimages, 1991; Bestiary, 1993; British Myths and Legends, 1998; Legends of King Arthur, 2000; The Holy Grail: Imagination and Belief, 2004. **Address:** Stangrove Hall, Alderton Near Woodbridge, Suffolk IP12 3BL, England.

BARBIER, Patrick. French, b. 1956. **Genres:** Music. **Career:** Universite Catholique de l'Ouest, Angers, France, professor of music history. **Publications:** Histoire de Castrats, 1989, trans. as The World of the Castrati, 1996; Graslin, Nantes et l'Opera, 1993; Farinelli, le castrat des Lumiers, 1994; Opera in Paris, 1800-1850, 1995; La Maison des Italiens (les castrats a Versailles), 1998. Author of theatrical monologues on Mozart, Beethoven, Bach, and Schubert, for young adults.

BARBIERI, Elaine. Also writes as Elaine Rome. American, b. 1936. **Genres:** Novels, Young adult fiction. **Career:** Novelist. **Publications:** Captive Ecstasy, 1980; Amber Fire (first novel in trilogy), 1981; Love's Fiery Jewel, 1982; Amber Treasure (second novel in trilogy), 1983; Sweet Torment, 1984; Amber Passion (third novel in trilogy), 1985; Race for Tomorrow, 1985; Passion's Dawn, 1985; Defiant Mistress, 1986; Ecstasy's Trail, 1987; Untamed Captive, 1987; Tarnished Angel, 1988; Wings of a Dove, 1990; Wishes on the Wind, 1991; (as Elaine Rome) Stark Lightning, 1991; Tattered Silk, 1991; More Precious than Gold, 1992; Dance of the Flame, 1995; Dangerous Virtues series: Honesty, 1996, Purity, 1997, Chastity, 1998; Eagle, 1999; Hawk, 1999; Night Raven, 2000; The Wild One, 2001; To Meet Again, 20001; Miranda and the Warrior (young adult), 2002; Renegade Moon, 2003; Texas Star, 2004; Texas Glory, 2004; Texas Triumph, 2005. **Address:** PO Box 536, West Milford, NJ 07480, U.S.A.

BARBOUR, Douglas. Canadian, b. 1940. **Genres:** Novellas/Short stories, Poetry, Literary criticism and history. **Career:** Professor, University of Alberta, Edmonton, 1982- (Assistant Professor, 1969-77; Associate Professor, 1977-81). Poetry Ed., Canadian Forum, 1978-80; Former Ed., Quarry mag., Kingston, Ont. **Publications:** Land Fall, 1971; A Poem as Long as the Highway, 1971; White, 1972; Songbook, 1973; He & She &, 1974; Visions of My Grandfather, 1977; Shore Lines, 1979; Vision/Sounding, 1980; (with S. Scobie) The Pirates of Pen's Chance, 1981; The Harbingers, 1984; Visible Visions: The Selected Poems of Douglas Barbour, 1984; Story for a Saskatchewan Night, 1990; John Newlove and His Works, 1992; Daphne Marlatt and Her Works, 1992; bpNichol and His Works, 1992; Michael Ondaatje, 1993; Fragmenting Body etc, 2000; Lyric/Anti-lyric: Essays on Contemporary Poetry, 2001; Breath Takes, 2001-02; A Flame on the Spanish Stairs, 2003. EDITOR/COEDITOR: The Maple Laugh Forever: An Anthology of Canadian Comic Poetry, 1981; Writing Right: Poetry by Canadian Women, 1982; Three Times Five: Short Stories by Harris, Sawai, Stenson, 1983; R. Sommer, Selected and New Poems, 1984; Tesseracts II, 1987; Beyond Tish: New Writing Interviews, Critical Writing, 1991. **Address:** 11655 72 Ave NW, Edmonton, AB, Canada T6G 0B9. **Online address:** doug.barbour@ualberta.ca

BARBOUR, John D. American, b. 1951. **Genres:** Literary criticism and history, Theology/Religion. **Career:** St. Olaf College, Northfield, MN, professor of religion, 1982-. **Publications:** Tragedy as a Critique of Virtue, 1984; The Conscience of the Autobiographer, 1992; Versions of Deconversion: Autobiography and the Loss of Faith, 1994; The Value of Solitude: The Ethics and Spirituality of Aloneness in Autobiography, 2004. **Address:** Dept of Religion, St. Olaf College, Northfield, MN 55057, U.S.A.

BARBOUR, Julian B. British (born Palestine), b. 1937. **Genres:** Physics. **Career:** Independent theoretical physicist and historian of science. **Publications:** Absolute or Relative Motion? Vol. 1: The Discovery of Dynamics, 1989, repr. as The Discovery of Dynamics, 2001, Vol.2: The Frame of the World, forthcoming; (ed. with H. Pfisher) Mach's Principle: From Newton's Bucket to Quantum Gravity, 1995; The End of Time: The Next Revolution in Physics, 1999. **Address:** College Farm, South Newington, Banbury, Oxon. OX15 4JG, England. **Online address:** julian@platonia.com

BARCLAY, Bill. *See* **MOORCOCK, Michael (John).**

BARCLAY, Donald A. American, b. 1958. **Genres:** Librarianship, Literary criticism and history. **Career:** Librarian, author, and editor. New Mexico State University, Las Cruces, coordinator of Library Institute, 1990-96; University of Houston, Houston, TX, coordinator of Electronic Publishing Center, 1996-97; Houston Academy of Medicine-Texas Medical Center Library, Houston, assistant director for systems and informatics, 1997-2002; University of California-Merced, assistant university librarian, 2002-. **Publications:** (with J.H. Maguire and P. Wild) Into the Wilderness Dream: Exploration Narratives of the American West, 1500-1805, 1994; (ed. and contrib.) Teaching Electronic Information Literacy, 1995; (with J.H. Maguire and P. Wild) A Rendezvous Reader: Tall, Tangled, and True Tales of the Mountain Men, 1997; Managing Public-Access Computers: A How-to-Do-It Manual for Librarians, 2000; (with D.D. Halsted) The Medical Library Association Consumer Health Reference Service Handbook, 2001; (with J.H. Maguire and P. Wild) Different Travellers, Different Eyes; Artists' Narratives of the American West, 1810-1920, 2001; Teaching and Marketing Electronic Information Literacy, 2003. Contributor to text and reference books. Contributor of articles and reviews to periodicals. **Address:** Library, Box 2039, University of California-Merced, Merced, CA 95344, U.S.A. **Online address:** dbarclay@ucmerced.edu

BARCLAY, Max. *See* **SHERWOOD, Ben.**

BARCLAY, Robert. British/Canadian, b. 1946. **Genres:** Anthropology/Ethnology, Cultural/Ethnic topics, Music. **Career:** Canadian Conservation Institute, Ottawa, ON, Canada, senior conservator of instruments, 1975-. Trumpet-maker and instructor in brass-instrument making; conservator of museum artifacts, specializing in musical instruments. Author of the quarterly column, Musae Museae. **Publications:** (ed. and contrib.) Anatomy of an Exhibition: The Look of Music, 1983; The Art of the Trumpet-Maker, 1992; The Preservation and Use of Historic Musical Instruments, 2004. Contributor to periodicals. **Address:** Canadian Conservation Institute, 1030 Innes Rd, Ottawa, ON, Canada K1A 0M5. **Online address:** bob_barclay@pch.gc.ca

BARD, Mitchell G. American, b. 1959. **Genres:** Politics/Government, History. **Career:** California Employment Development Department, Sacramento, analyst, 1980-81; American Enterprise Institute for Public Policy Research, Washington, DC, analyst, 1982; University of California, Irvine, postdoctoral fellow, 1986-87; George Bush for President Survey Research Group, Washington, DC, senior analyst, 1988; Near East Report, Washington, DC, editor, 1989-92; American Israel Public Affairs Committee, Washington, DC, associate director of research and information, 1992; American-Israeli Cooperative Enterprise, Washington, DC, executive director, 1993; writer, 1993-. **Publications:** The Water's Edge and Beyond: Defining the Limits to Domestic Influence on U.S. Middle East Policy, 1991; U.S.-Israel Relations: Looking to the Year 2000, 1991; (with J. Himelfarb) Myths and Facts: A Concise Record of the Arab-Israeli Conflict, 1992; Partners for Change: How U.S.-Israel Cooperation Can Benefit America, 1993; Forgotten Victims: The Abandonment of Americans in Hitler's Camps, 1994; The Complete Idiot's Guide to World War II, 1998; The Complete Idiot's Guide to the Middle East, 1999. Contributor to books. Contributor of articles and reviews to magazines and newspapers. **Address:** 2810 Blaine Dr., Chevy Chase, MD 20815, U.S.A.

BARDEN, Dan. American. **Genres:** Novels. **Career:** Freelance writer. **Publications:** John Wayne: A Novel, 1997. **Address:** c/o Doubleday, 1540 Broadway, New York, NY 10036, U.S.A.

BARDEN, Thomas E(arl). American, b. 1946. **Genres:** Mythology/Folklore. **Career:** University of Virginia, Charlottesville, acting assistant professor of English, 1975-76; University of Toledo, Toledo, OH, assistant professor, 1976-80, associate professor, 1980-90, professor of English, 1990-, director of program in American studies, 1991-96, director of graduate studies in English, 1996-99, associate dean for the Humanities College of Arts and Sciences, 1999-; University of Swansea, Wales, Senior Fulbright Lecturer, 1993-94. Ohio Foundation on the Arts, member of board of trustees, 1978-80; Ohio Arts Council, member of traditional and ethnic arts advisory panel, 1978-82; Arts Commission of Greater Toledo, member of general arts advisory panel, 1987-89. Executive producer of the record albums It's a Mighty Pretty Waltz: The Music of Bernard Johnson, Ocooch Mountain Records, 1983; and Two Aces and a Jack: Hot as You Got, Blue Suit Records, 1987. **Publications:** (coauthor) An Annotated Listing of the Virginia WPA Folklore, Norwood, 1979; (coauthor) Weevils in the Wheat: Interviews with Virginia Ex-Slaves, 1980; The Travels of Peter Woodhouse: Memoir of an American Pioneer, 1981; Virginia Folk Legends, 1991; (coauthor) Hungarian-American, 2000. **Address:** College of Arts and Sciences, University of Toledo, Toledo, OH 43606, U.S.A. **Online address:** tbarden@uoft02.utoledo.edu

BARDHAN, Pranab. Indian, b. 1939. **Genres:** Economics. **Career:** Massachusetts Institute of Technology, assistant professor to associate professor of economics, 1966-69; Indian Statistical Institute, New Delhi, professor, 1969-73; Delhi School of Economics, professor, 1973-76; University of California, Berkeley, professor of economics, 1976-. **Publications:** Economic Growth, Development, and Foreign Trade, 1970; Land, Labor, and Rural Poverty, 1984; The Political Economy of Development in India, 1984, 2nd ed., 1998; Endogenous Growth Theory in a Vintage Capital Model, 1996; Role of Governance in Economic Development, 1997; (with C. Udry) Development Microeconomics, 1999; Social Justice in a Global Economy, 2000. EDITOR: (with T.N. Srinivasan) Rural Poverty in South Asia, 1988; The Economic Theory of Agrarian Institutions, 1989; Conversations between Economists and Anthropologists, 1989; (with J. Roemer) Market Socialism, 1993. **Address:** 1266 Grizzly Peak Blvd, Berkeley, CA 94708, U.S.A.

BARDWICK, Judith M(arcia). American, b. 1933. **Genres:** Business/Trade/Industry, Institutions/Organizations, Psychology, Women's studies and issues. **Career:** University of California, San Diego, clinical professor of psychology, 1984-; Judith M. Bardwick, PhD, Inc., management consultants, La Jolla, CA, president. **Publications:** (with others) Feminine Personality and Conflict, 1970, 1981; Psychology of Women, 1971; (ed. and contrib.) Readings in the Psychology of Women, 1972; In Transition, 1979; Essays on the Psychology of Women, 1981; The Plateauing Trap, 1986; Danger in the Comfort Zone, 1991; In Praise of Good Business, 1998; Seeking the Calm in the Storm, 2002. **Address:** 1389 Caminito Halago, La Jolla, CA 92037-7165, U.S.A. **Online address:** wyck@pacbell.net

BAREHAM, Lindsey. American, b. 1948. **Genres:** Food and Wine, Travel/Exploration. **Career:** Food writer, author, and broadcaster. Sell Out (consumer section of Time Out magazine), editor, 1970-85; LBC-Radio, weekly broadcast on restaurants and cookbooks on First Edition, 1992-; Sunday Telegraph, restaurant critic and food columnist, food writer, 1990-93; Evening Standard, daily recipe, 1996-. **Publications:** The Time Out Guide to Shopping in London, 1983; In Praise of the Potato: Recipes from around the World, 1989; Pauper's London, 1990; A Celebration of Soup, 1993; (with S. Hopkinson) Roast Chicken and Other Stories, 1994; (with S. Hopkinson) The Prawn Cocktail Years, 1997; The Big Red Book of Tomatoes, 1999; Wolf in the Kitchen, 2000. **Address:** c/o Bruce Hunter, David Higham, 5-8 Lower John St, Golden Sq, London W1R 4HA, England.

BAREHAM, Terence. British, b. 1937. **Genres:** Literary criticism and history, Bibliography. **Career:** University of Rhodesia, Lecturer in English, 1963-67; University of York, Lecturer in English, 1967-68; The New University of Ulster, Coleraine, Sr. Lecturer in English, 1968-, Professor of English, 1990-2001, now retired. **Publications:** George Crabbe: A Critical Study, 1977; (co-author) A Bibliography of George Crabbe, 1978; Malcolm Lowry, 1987. EDITOR: Anthony Trollope, 1980; Robert Bolt, A Man for All Seasons, 1980; T.S. Eliot: Murder in the Cathedral, 1981; Shakespeare's Two Gentlemen of Verona, 1982; Anthony Trollope, Barsetshire Novels, 1982; Tom Stoppard: A Casebook, 1987; Charles Lever: New Evaluations, 1992. **Address:** Dept. of English, The New University, Coleraine, Northern Ireland.

BARER, Burl (Roger). American, b. 1947. **Genres:** Communications/Media. **Career:** Creative consultant, radio personality, writer. On-air personality, Seattle, WA, radio stations, 1967-. Mind Development Inc., Seattle, WA, teacher and consultant, 197374, vice president, 1978-; Barer/

McManus, Bellevue, WA, creative director and on-air personality, 1975-77; Merklingar Labs, Denver, CO, regional vice president, 1977-; Barer/Goldblatt & Associates, Bellevue, WA, president, 1978-; B. Barer & Sons Inc., director, 1980-; Barer Cable Advertising, president, 1982-. **Publications:** The Saint: A Complete History in Print, Radio, Film, and Television of Leslie Charteris' Robin Hood of Modern Crime, Simon Templar, 1928-1992, 1993; Maverick: The Making of the Movie and the Official Guide to the Television Series, 1994. **Address:** c/o Deadly Alibi Press, PO Box 5947, Vancouver, WA 98668-5947, U.S.A.

BARFIELD, Woodrow. American, b. 1950. **Genres:** Information science/Computers. **Career:** George Washington University, Washington, DC, assistant professor of engineering management, 1985-87; University of Washington, Seattle, assistant professor, 1987-91, associate professor of industrial engineering, 1991-96; Virginia Polytechnic Institute and State University, Blacksburg, professor of industrial and systems engineering, 1996-. University of London, visiting professor of computer science, 1996; University of Washington, Seattle, affiliate professor, 1997-98; speaker at colleges and universities worldwide. **Publications:** (with A. Majchrzak, T.C. Chang, and others) Human Aspects of Computer-Aided Design, 1987; (ed. with T. Furness, and contrib) Virtual Environments and Advanced Interface Design, 1995; (coed) Human Factors in the Design of Tactical Display Systems for the Individual Soldier, 1995; (ed. with T. Dingus, and contrib.) Human Factors in Intelligent Transportation Systems, 1998; (ed. with Dingus, and contrib.) Wearable Computers and Augmented Reality, in press. Contributor to books. Contributor of articles and reviews to technical and scientific journals. **Address:** Department of Industrial and Systems Engineering, Virginia Polytechnic Institute and State University, Blacksburg, VA 24061, U.S.A. **Online address:** barfield@vt.edu

BARHAM, Patte B. American. **Genres:** Autobiography/Memoirs. **Career:** Journalist, author, syndicated columnist; war correspondent in Korea, assigned by William Randolph Hearst; Herald-Examiner; acting secretary of state in California, appointed by March Fong, 1980-81. **Publications:** Pin up Poems; Operation Nightmare; Rasputin: The Man behind the Myth: A Personal Memoir with Maria Rasputin, 1977; Peasant to Palace, Rasputin's Cookbook with Maria Rasputin, 1990; Marilyn: The Last Take, 1992.

BARICCO, Alessandro. Italian, b. 1958. **Genres:** Novels. **Career:** Writer, musicologist. La Repubblica, Italy, music critic; La Stampa, cultural correspondent; Holden School of Writing, Turin, Italy, founder. Producer of L'amore X un dardo (title means "Love is a Dart") for public television channel RAI3, 1993, and Pickwick, del leggere e dello scrivere (title means "Pickwick: Of Reading and Writing"). **Publications:** IN ENGLISH TRANSLATION: Oceano Mare, 1993, trans as Ocean Sea, 1999; Seta, 1996, trans. by G. Waldman as Silk, 1997. UNTRANSLATED WORKS: Castelli di rabbia, 1991. OTHER: Novecento (stage monologue), 1994; essays. **Address:** c/o Alfred A. Knopf Inc., 201 East 50th St., New York, NY 10022, U.S.A.

BARICH, Bill. American, b. 1943. **Genres:** Novels, Novellas/Short stories, Travel/Exploration, Essays. **Career:** U.S. Peace Corps volunteer in Nigeria and Biafra, 1966-67; Somerset Hills School, Somerset, NJ, teacher, 1967-69; L.S. Distributors, San Francisco, CA, stockperson and book salesperson, 1969-71; Alfred A. Knopf, San Francisco and New York City, publicity assistant and editorial assistant, 1972-75; New Yorker, New York City, staff writer, 1981-94. Visiting professor of creative writing at University of California, Berkeley and Santa Cruz; and Jack Kerouac School of Disembodied Poetics at Naropa University, Boulder, CO. Faculty member of Squaw Valley Community of Writers. **Publications:** Laughing in the Hills (autobiography), 1980; Traveling Light (essays), 1984; Hard to Be Good (short stories), 1987; Hat Creek and the McCloud, 1988; Big Dreams: Into the Heart of California, 1994; Carson Valley (novel), 1997; Crazy for Rivers (essay), 1999; The Sporting Life, 1999; A Fine Place to Daydream: Racehorses, Romance, and the Irish, 2005. Contributor to periodicals. Work represented in anthologies. **Address:** c/o Amanda Urban, International Creative Management, 40 W 57th St, New York, NY 10019, U.S.A.

BARISH, Evelyn. Also writes as Evelyn Barish Greenberger. American. **Genres:** Literary criticism and history. **Career:** Cornell University, Ithaca, NY, instructor, 1964-66, assistant professor of English, 1966-69; assistant professor of English at Briarcliff College, 1970; City University of New York, New York City, associate professor at College of Staten Island, 1971-75; professor of English at College of Staten Island, 1976-, professor at Graduate Center, CUNY, 1988-, member of board of trustees of Research Foundation, CUNY, 1983-84. **Publications:** (as Evelyn Barish Greenberger) Arthur Hugh Clough: Growth of a Poet's Mind, 1970; Emerson in Italy,

1989; Emerson: The Roots of Prophecy, 1989. Contributor to books on Emerson and literature. **Address:** 244 W 74th St #6D, New York, NY 10023, U.S.A. **Online address:** Barish@i-2000.com

BAR-JOSEPH, Uri. Israeli, b. 1949. **Genres:** International relations/Current affairs, Politics/Government. **Career:** Writer. **Publications:** (with A. Perlmutter and M. Handel) Two Minutes over Baghdad, 1982; The Best of Enemies: Israel and Transjordan in the War of 1948, 1987; Intelligence Intervention in the Politics of Democratic States: The U.S.A., Britain, and Israel, 1995; The Watchman Fell Asleep: The Surprise of Yom Kippur and Its Sources (in Hebrew), 2001; (ed.) Israel's National Security towards the 21st Century, 2001. Contributor to periodicals. **Address:** Department of Political Science, Haifa University, 31905 Haifa, Israel. **Online address:** barjo@poli.haifa.ac.il

BARKAN, Joanne. Also writes as J. B. Wright. American. **Genres:** Children's fiction, Adult non-fiction. **Career:** Editor, Croft-NEI Publications, 1976-78; national news editor, Seven Days Magazine, 1978; book editor and staff writer for "The Muppets," Jim Henson Productions, 1985-87; editor and project coordinator, Brooke-House Publishing, 1988-92; executive editor, Dissent magazine; freelance writer and editor. **Publications:** Visions of Emancipation: The Italian Workers' Movement since 1945 (adult nonfiction), 1984. FOR CHILDREN: Baby Piggy and the Thunderstorm, 1987; The Christmas Toy, 1987; Kermit's Mixed-up Message, 1987; Baby Gonzo's Unfinished Dream, 1988; Baby Kermit's Old Blanket, 1988; Boober's Colorful Soup, 1988; Doozers Big and Little, 1988; My Cooking Pot, 1989; My Cooking Spoon, 1989; My Frying Pan, 1989; My Measuring Cup, 1989; My Rolling Pin, 1989; My Spatula, 1989; What's So Funny, 1989; The Girl Who Couldn't Remember, 1989; The Secret of the Sunken Treasure, 1989; Abraham Lincoln: A Biography, 1990; Air, Air, All Around, 1990; Fire, Fire, Burning Bright, 1990; Rocks, Rocks, Big and Small, 1990; Water, Water, Everywhere, 1990; My Pruning Shears, 1990; My Rake, 1990; My Trowel, 1990; My Watering Can, 1990; Whiskerville Bake Shop, 1990; Whiskerville Firehouse, 1990; Whiskerville Post Office, 1990; Whiskerville School, 1990; Anna Marie's Blanket, 1990; Glow in the Dark Spooky House, 1990; Creatures That Glow, 1991; My Birthday Adventure with TeddyO (a computer-personalized picture book), 1991; A Very Scary Haunted House, 1991; A Very Scary Jack O'Lantern, 1991; Easter Egg Fun, 1991; Easter Surprise, 1991; Where Do I Put My Toys?, 1991; Where Do I Put My Clothes?, 1991; Where Do I Put My Books?, 1991; Where Do I Put My Food?, 1991; Whiskerville Train Station, 1991; Whiskerville Theater, 1991; Whiskerville Grocery, 1991; Whiskerville Toy Shop, 1991; (as J.B. Wright) Dinosaurs, 1991; Boxcar, 1992; Caboose, 1992; Locomotive, 1992; Passenger Car, 1992; A Very Merry Santa Claus Story, 1992; A Very Merry Snowman Story, 1992; A Very Scary Ghost Story, 1992; A Very Scary Witch Story, 1992; That Fat Hat, 1992; Animal Car, 1993; Circus Locomotive, 1993; Clown Caboose, 1993; Performers' Car, 1993; The Magic Carpet's Secret, 1993; Elves for a Day, 1993; Numbers Add Up at Home, 1993; The Ballet Mystery, 1994; Home, Creepy Home, 1994; The Krystal Princess and the Grand Contest, 1994. Contributor to anthologies. Contributor (sometimes under undisclosed pseudonyms) of original stories for reading textbooks and author of social studies textbooks. Contributor to periodicals. **Address:** 711 West End Ave., New York, NY 10025, U.S.A.

BARKER, Clive. British, b. 1952. **Genres:** Mystery/Crime/Suspense, Plays/Screenplays, Novels, Novellas/Short stories, Horror. **Career:** Full-time writer, director, producer, illustrator, actor, playwright. **Publications:** Clive Barker's Books of Blood (six vols.) 1984-85 (vol. 4 in U.S. as The Inhuman Condition; vol. 5 in U.S. as In the Flesh); Underworld (screenplay), 1985; The Damnation Game, 1985; Rawhead Rex (screenplay), 1987; Hellraiser (screenplay), 1987; (author of intro.) Scared Stiff: Tales of Sex and Death, 1987; (author of intro.) Night Visions 4, 1987; Weaverworld (novel), 1987; The Hellbound Heart (stories), 1988; Cabal (novel), 1988; The Great and Secret Show (novel), 1989; Galilee, 1998; Coldheart Canyon, 2001; Abarat, 2002. Contributor to anthologies. **Address:** c/o Creative Artists Agency, 9830 Wilshire Blvd., Beverly Hills, CA 90212-1825, U.S.A.

BARKER, David J. P. British, b. 1938. **Genres:** Medicine/Health. **Career:** Professor of Clinical Epidemiology and Director of the Medical Research Council Environmental Epidemiology Unit, University of Southampton, and Hon. Consultant Physician, Royal South Hampshire Hospital Research Fellow, Dept. of Social Medicine, 1963-66, and Lecturer, Dept. of Medicine, 1966-69, University of Birmingham; Hon. Lecturer in Epidemiology, Makerere University, Uganda, 1969-72. **Publications:** Practical Epidemiology, 1973, 4th ed., 1991; (with G. Rose) Epidemiology in Medical Practice, 1976, 5th ed., 1998; (with G. Rose) Epidemiology for the Uninitiated, 1979, 3rd ed., 1993; (ed.) Fetal and Infant Origins of Adult Disease, 1992; Mothers,

Babies and Disease in Later Life, 1994, 2nd ed. as Mothers, Babies and Health in Later Life, 1998; (co-ed.) Fetal Programming, 1999; Fetal Origins of Cardiovascular and Lung Disease, 2001; The Best Start in Life, 2003. **Address:** Manor Farm, East Dean, nr Salisbury SP5 1HB, England. **Online address:** pjf@mrc.soton.ac.uk

BARKER, Dennis (Malcolm). British, b. 1929. **Genres:** Novels, Plays/Screenplays, Communications/Media, Crafts, Military/Defense/Arms control, Self help, Social commentary, Writing/Journalism, Documentaries/Reportage. **Career:** Suffolk Chronicle and Mercury, Ipswich, reporter, 1947-48; East Anglian Daily Times, Ipswich, reporter, feature writer, theatre and film critic, 1948-58; Express and Star, Wolverhampton, estates and property editor, feature writer, theatre critic and columnist, 1958-63. The Guardian, London, Midlands correspondent, Birmingham, 1963-67, reporter, feature writer, columnist, media correspondent, and obituarist, 1967-. **Publications:** Candidate of Promise, 1969; Candidate of Promise (screenplay); The Scandalisers, 1974; Soldiering On: An Unofficial Portrait of the British Army, 1981; One Man's Estate, 1983; Parian Ware, 1985; Ruling the Waves: An Unofficial Portrait of the Royal Navy, 1986; Winston Three Three Three, 1987; Guarding the Skies: An Unofficial Portrait of the Royal Air Force, 1989; Fresh Start, 1990; The Craft of the Media Interview, 1998; How to Deal with the Media, 2000. Contributor to books. **Address:** 67 Speldhurst Rd, London W4 1BY, England.

BARKER, Eileen (Vartan). British, b. 1938. **Genres:** Theology/Religion, Sociology. **Career:** Professor of sociology, London School of Economics, 1992-, lecturer, 1970-85; dean, Undergraduate Studies, 1982-86, senior lecturer, 1985-90, reader, 1990-92; director, INFORM (Information Network Focus on Religious Movements), London, 1988-93, 1999-; visiting part-time lecturer, Brunel University, 1974-75; vice dean, Faculty of Economics, University of London, 1986-88; visiting fellow, Dept of Religious Studies, University of California, Santa Barbara, 1987; visiting professor, Dept of Sociology, University of New England, Australia, 1988. **Publications:** The Making of a Moonie: Choice or Brainwashing?, 1984 (Distinguished Book Award, Society for the Scientific Study of Religion); Sects and New Religious Movements, 1988; New Religious Movements: A Practical Introduction, 1989. EDITOR: New Religious Movements: A Perspective for Understanding Society, 1982; Of Gods and Men: New Religious Movements in the West, 1984; Secularization, Rationalism and Sectarianism, 1993; LSE on Freedom, 1995; 20 Years On: Changes in New Religions, 1995. **Address:** Dept. of Sociology, London School of Economics and Political Science, Houghton St, London WC2A 2AE, England.

BARKER, Elspeth. Scottish, b. 1940. **Genres:** Novels. **Career:** Teacher at a boys' private school, 1961-63; teacher of classics at a girls' private school, 1982-93. **Publications:** : O Caledonia (novel), 1991; (ed.) Loss (anthology), 1998. Contributor of articles and reviews to periodicals and short stories to anthologies. **Address:** Bintry House, Itteringham, Aylsham, Norfolk NR11 7AT, England.

BARKER, Garry. American, b. 1943. **Genres:** Novels, Novellas/Short stories, Poetry, Crafts, Essays. **Career:** Southern Highland Handicraft Guild, Asheville, NC, assistant director, 1965-71; Kentucky Guild of Artists and Craftsmen, executive director, 1971-80; Morehead State University, Kentucky, communications coordinator, 1984-85; Berea College Student Crafts Program, assistant director, 1985-94, director, 1994-97; Kentucky Folk Art Center at Morehead State University, director, 1997-2002, university editor, 2003-. **Publications:** Fire on the Mountain, 1983; Copperhead Summer, 1985; Mountain Passage and Other Stories, 1986; All Night Dog, 1988; The Handcraft Revival in Southern Appalachia, 1930-1990, 1991; Mitchell Tolle: American Artist, 1992; Bitter Creek Breakdown (poetry), 1989; Notes From A Native Son (essays), 1995; Berea Hospital: The First Century, 1996. **Address:** 692 Orchard Rd, Bald Hill, KY 41041, U.S.A. **Online address:** garrybarker@netscape.net

BARKER, Jonathan. British, b. 1949. **Genres:** Literary criticism and history, Bibliography, Librarianship. **Career:** Royal Borough of Kensington and Chelsea, London, England, library assistant, 1970-72; Arts Council of Great Britain, London, poetry librarian, 1973-88; British Council, London, literature officer and deputy director of literature department, 1988-. **Publications:** A Bibliography of Poetry in Britain and Ireland since 1970, 1995. EDITOR: (and author of postscript) Arts Council Poetry Library Short-Title Catalogue, 6th ed., 1981; (and author of introduction, chronology, and bibliography) Selected Poems of W.H. Davies, 1985, rev. ed., 1992; (and author of introduction) Poetry Book Society Anthology, 1986/87, 1986; (and author of chronology and bibliography) The Art of Edward Thomas, 1987; (and author of introduction) Thirty Years of the Poetry Book Society, 1956-1986, 1988;

(with W. Hope, and author of introduction) Norman Cameron, Collected Poems and Selected Translations, 1990. Work represented in anthologies. Contributor of articles and reviews to periodicals. **Address:** Literature Department, British Council, 10 Spring Garden, London SW1A 2BN, England. **Online address:** jonathan.barker@britishcouncil.org

BARKER, Pat(ricia). British, b. 1943. **Genres:** Novels. **Career:** Booker Prize, 1995; Guardian Fiction Prize, 1993; Northern Electric Special Art's Award, 1993; Joint winner of Fawcett Prize, 1982. **Publications:** Union Street, 1982; Blow Your House Down, 1984; The Century's Daughter, 1986, as Liza's England, 1996; The Man Who Wasn't There, 1989; Regeneration, 1991; The Eye in the Door, 1993; The Ghost Road, 1995; Another World, 1999; Border Crossing, 2001; Double Vision, 2003. **Address:** c/o Gillon Aitken Associates Ltd, 29 Fernshaw Rd, London SW10 0TG, England. **Online address:** mail@aitkenassoc.demon.co.uk

BARKER, Paul. British, b. 1935. **Genres:** Sociology. **Career:** Worked as staff journalist for periodicals and newspapers in England, 1959-64; New Society, London, deputy editor, 1965-68, editor, 1968-86; independent writer and broadcaster, London, 1986-. Institute of Community Studies, London, senior research fellow, 2000-. **Publications:** A Sociological Portrait, 1972; One for Sorrow, Two for Joy, 1972; The Social Sciences Today, 1975; Arts in Society, 1977; The Other Britain, 1982; Founders of the Welfare State, 1985; Gulliver and Beyond, 1996; (ed.) Living as Equals, 1996. Contributor to books, magazines, newspapers, and BBC. **Address:** 15 Dartmouth Park Ave, London NW5 1JL, England.

BARKER, Philip. British/Canadian, b. 1929. **Genres:** Psychiatry. **Career:** Professor of Psychiatry and Paediatrics, University of Calgary, and Psychiatrist, Albert Children's Hospital, Calgary, since 1980, now emeritus. Consultant, Dundee Child Psychiatry Service, 1962-67; Lecturer University of St. Andrews, 1962-69; Consultant, Burns Clinic, Birmingham, and Lecturer, University of Birmingham, 1967-75; Director of Inpatient Services, 1975-79, and Director of Psychiatric Education, 1979-80, Thistletoun Regional Centre, Toronto; Professor of Psychiatry, Univ of Toronto, 1975-80. Ed., Journal of the Associate of Workers for Maladjusted Children, 1978-80. **Publications:** Basic Child Psychiatry, 1971, 6th ed., 1995; Care Can Prevent, 1973; (ed.) The Residential Psychiatric Treatment of Children, 1974; Basic Family Therapy, 1981, 4th ed., 1998; Using Metaphors in Psychotherapy, 1985; Clinical Interviews with Children and Adolescents, 1990; Psychotherapeutic Metaphors: A Guide to Theory and Practice, 1996. **Address:** 2217 23rd St SW, Calgary, AB, Canada T2T 5H6. **Online address:** jazz@canuck.com

BARKER, Raffaella. British, b. 1964. **Genres:** Novels. **Career:** Free-lance writer, 1988-. Worked as a features writer for Harpers and Queen. **Publications:** NOVELS: Come and Tell Me Some Lies, 1994; The Hook, 1996; Hens Dancing, 1999; Summertime, 2002. **Address:** c/o Alexandra Pringle, Toby Eady Associates, 9 Orme Ct., London W.2, England.

BARKER, Ralph Hammond. British, b. 1917. **Genres:** Military/Defense/Arms control. **Career:** RAF, flight lieutenant, retired; writer. **Publications:** Strike Hard, Strike Sure, 1963, rev. ed., 2003; The Hurricats, 1978; Down in the Drink; The Ship Busters; The Last Blue Mountain; The Thousand Plane Raid; Great Mysteries of the Air; Verdict on a Lost Flyer; The Schneider Trophy Races; The Blockade Busters; Not Here but in Another Place; The RAF at War; Good Night, Sorry for Sinking You; Children of the Benares; That Eternal Summer; The Royal Flying Corps in France; The Royal Flying Force in France, Vol. 2, 1995; A Brief History of the Royal Flying corps, 2002; Men of the Bombers, 2005. Contributor to periodicals. **Address:** Old Timbers, 16 Aldercrombe Ln, Caterham, Surrey CR3 6ED, England.

BARKEY, Karen. American (born Turkey), b. 1958. **Genres:** History. **Career:** University of Wisconsin-Madison, assistant professor of sociology, 1988-89; Columbia University, NYC, assistant professor, 1989-93, associate professor of sociology, 1993-. **Publications:** Bandits and Bureaucrats: The Ottoman Route to State Centralization, 1994; (ed. with M. von Hagen) After Empire: Multiethnic Societies and Nation-Building; The Soviet Union and the Russian, Habsburg, and Ottoman Empires, 1997. **Address:** Department of Sociology, Columbia University, 1180 Amsterdam Ave., New York, NY 10027, U.S.A.

BARKIN, Jill. See JOHNSON, Susan (M.).

BARKOW, Al. American, b. 1932. **Genres:** History, Sports/Fitness. **Career:** Ed.-in-chief, Golf Illustrated Magazine, 1985-91; chief writer, Shell's Wonderful World of Golf television series, 1962-68; ed.-in-chief, Golf

Magazine, 1969-71; editor/publisher, Al Barkow's Golf Report (newsletter). **Publications:** Golf's Golden Grind, 1974; (with B. Casper) The Good Sense of Golf, 1978 (with K. Venturi) The Venturi Analysis, 1981; The Venturi System, 1983; (with G. Low) The Master of Putting, 1983; (with P. Rodgers) Play Lower Handicap Golf, 1986; Gettin' to the Dance Floor: An Oral History of American Golf, 1986; The History of the PGA Tour, 1989; (with C. Lohren) Getting Set for Golf, 1995; (with D. Stockton) Putt to Win; The Golden Era of Golf: How America Rose to Dominate the Old Scotsgame, 2000; That's Golf: The Best of Al Barkow, 2001; Gene Darazen and Shell's Wonderful World of Golf, 2003. **Address:** 410 Evelyn Ave #303, Albany, CA 94706, U.S.A. **Online address:** abark@sbcglobal.net

BARKS, Coleman Bryan. American, b. 1937. **Genres:** Poetry, Translations. **Career:** University of Southern California, Los Angeles, instructor of English, 1965-67; University of Georgia, Athens, assistant professor, 1967-72, associate professor, 1972-78, professor emeritus of English, 1978-97. **Publications:** The Juice, 1972; New Words, 1976; We're Laughing at the Damage, 1977; Gourd Seed (poetry), 1993; Xenia (poetry), 1994; Tentmaking (poetry), 2001; Club (poetry), 2001. TRANSLATOR: (with R. Bly) Night and Sleep, Versions of Rumi, 1981; (with J. Moyne) Open Secret, by Rumi, 1984; (with J. Moyne) Unseen Rain, by Rumi, 1986; (with J. Moyne) We Are Three, by Rumi, 1987; (with J. Moyne) These Branching Moments, by Rumi, 1988; (with J. Moyne) This Longing, by Rumi, 1988; Delicious Laughter, by Rumi, 1990; Like This, by Rumi, 1990; One-Handed Basket Weaving, by Rumi, 1991; Naked Song, by Lalla, 1992; Stallion on a Frozen Lake, by Sixth Dalai Lama, 1992; Birdsong, by Rumi, 1993; The Hand of Poetry, selection from Rumi, Sanai, Attar, Saadi, and Hatiz, 1993; Say I Am You, by Rumi, 1994; The Essential Rumi, by Rumi, 1995; The Illuminated Rumi, by Rumi, 1997; The Glance, by Rumi, 1999; The Soul of Rumi, 2001; The Book of Love, by Rumi, 2002; The Drowned Book, by Tumi's father, Bahavddin, 2004. **Address:** 196 Westview Dr, Athens, GA 30606, U.S.A. **Online address:** colemanb196@home.net

BARLAY, Stephen. British (born Hungary), b. 1930. **Genres:** Novels, Plays/Screenplays, Documentaries/Reportage. **Publications:** (with P. Sasdy) Four Black Cars, 1958; Sex Slavery (in U.S. as Bondage), 1968; Aircrash Detective (in U.S. as The Search for Air Safety), 1969; Fire, 1972; Double Cross (in U.S. as The Secrets Business), 1973; (creator with J. Elliot) The Double Dealers (radio and TV series), 1972, 1974; Blockbuster (novel), 1976; That Thin Red Line (documentary), 1976; Point of No Return (radio play), 1977; Crash Course, (novel), 1979; Cuban Confetti (novel; in U.S. as In the Company of Spies), 1981; The Ruling Passion (novel), 1982; The Price of Silence (novel), 1983, radio serial 1983; Tsunami (novel), 1986; The Final Call: Air Disasters ... When Will They Ever Learn?, 1990 (in the U.S. as The Final Call: Why Airline Disasters Continue to Happen, 1991); Cleared For Take Off: Behind The Scenes of Air Travel, 1994. **Address:** c/o Curtis Brown, 4th Floor, Haymarket House, 28-29 Haymarket, London SW1Y 4SP, England.

BARLETT, Peggy F. American, b. 1947. **Genres:** Anthropology/Ethnology, Economics, Local history/Rural topics, Women's studies and issues. **Career:** Queens College of the City University of New York, Flushing, NY, lecturer in anthropology, 1972; Carleton College, Northfield, MN, assistant professor of anthropology, 1974-76; Emory University, Atlanta, GA, assistant professor, 1976-82, associate professor, 1982-89, professor of anthropology, 1989, department head, 1991-94. Society for Economic Anthropology, president, 1989-90. Conducted anthropological field work in Costa Rica, 1968, 1972-73, 1977, 1980, Ecuador, 1970, and U.S.A. (Georgia), 1982-83, 1987; consultant to Institute for the Study of Human Systems Arkleton Trust (Scotland); Faculty for Human Rights in El Salvador and Central America, member of delegation to Honduras, Guatemala, El Salvador, and Nicaragua, 1985. **Publications:** (ed. and author) Agricultural Decision Making: Anthropological Contributions to Rural Development, 1980; Agricultural Choice and Change: Decision Making in a Costa Rican Community, 1982; American Dreams, Rural Realities: Family Farms in Crisis, 1993; Sustainability on Campus: Stories and Strategies for Changes, 2004. Work represented in anthologies. Contributor to anthropology, rural sociology, and economics journals. **Address:** Dept of Anthropology, Emory University, Atlanta, GA 30322, U.S.A.

BARLEY, Janet Crane. American, b. 1934. **Genres:** Literary criticism and history. **Career:** Xenia Daily Gazette, Xenia, OH, women's editor, 1956-57; freelance writer, 1968-. Worked as writer, editor, and public relations specialist for organizations. **Publications:** Winter in July: Visits with Children's Authors Down Under, 1995. **Address:** 846 Sandalwood Rd W, Perrysburg, OH 43551, U.S.A.

BARLOW, Frank. British, b. 1911. **Genres:** History, Biography. **Career:** Professor Emeritus, University of Exeter, 1976- (Lecturer, 1946-49; Reader

1949-53; Professor of History, 1953-76; Deputy Vice-Chancellor, 1961-63; Public Orator, 1974-76; Hon. Fellow, 2001). Fereday Fellow, 1934-38, St. John's College, Oxford; Assistant Lecturer, University College, London, 1936-40. CBE; FBA. **Publications:** Durham Jurisdictional Peculiars, 1950; The Feudal Kingdom of England, 1955, 5th ed., 1999; The English Church 1000-1066, 1963; William I and the Norman Conquest, 1965; Edward the Confessor, 1970; (with M. Biddle, O. von Feilitzen and D.J. Keene) Winchester in the Early Middle Ages, 1976; The English Church 1066-1154, 1979; William Rufus, 1983; The Norman Conquest and Beyond, 1983; Thomas Becket, 1986; Introduction to the Devonshire Domesday, 1991; The Godwins, 2002. EDITOR: The Letters of Arnulf of Lisieux, 1939; Durham Annals and Documents of the Thirteenth Century, 1945; (and trans.) The Life of King Edward the Confessor, 1962, 2nd ed., 1992; English Episcopal Acta, XI (1046-1184), XII (1186-1257), 1996; (and trans.) The Carmen de Hastingae Proelio of Guy Bishop of Amiens, 1999. **Address:** Middle Court Hall, Kenton, Exeter EX6 8NA, England.

BARLOW, Maude. Canadian, b. 1947. **Genres:** Economics, Education, Politics/Government. **Career:** City of Ottawa, ON, director of equal opportunities, 1980-83; senior adviser to Prime Minister Pierre Trudeau, Ottawa, 1983-84; Council of Canadians, Ottawa, chairperson, 1988-. Visiting scholar, University of Ottawa, 1991. Member of council of advisers, Canadian Centre for Arms Control and Disarmament; consultant on equality and social justice issues. **Publications:** Women and Disarmament, 1988; Parcel of Rogues, 1990; (with B. Campbell) Take Back the Nation, 1991; (with H-J. Robertson) Class Warfare, 1994; (with B. Campbell) Straight through the Heart, 1995; (with J. Winter) The Big Black Book, 1997; (with T. Clarke) MAI: The Multilateral Agreement on Investment and the Threat to Canadian Sovereignty, 1997; (with T. Clarke) MAI: The Multilateral Agreement on Investment and the Threat to American Freedom, 1997; The Fight of My Life, 1998; (with T. Clarke) MAI: The Multilateral Agreement on Investment Round 2, 1998; (with E. May) Frederick Street, 2000; (with T. Clarke) Global Showdown, 2001; (with T. Clarke) Blue Gold, 2002; Profit Is not the Cure, 2002. Contributor to reference works, periodicals and journals. **Address:** 525 C Bay St, Ottawa, ON, Canada K1R 6B4.

BARLOW, Tani E. American, b. 1950. **Genres:** Cultural/Ethnic topics, Intellectual history, Women's studies and issues, Translations. **Career:** Shanghai Teachers University, Shanghai, China, lecturer in American culture, 1981-; University of Missouri-Columbia, assistant professor of history, 1985-92; Positions: East Asia Cultures Critique, founding editor, 1992-. **Publications:** (with D.M. Lowe) Chinese Reflections: Americans Teaching in the People's Republic, 1985, rev. ed. as Teaching China's Lost Generation: Foreign Experts in the People's Republic of China, 1987; The Question of Women in Chinese Feminism, 2004. **Address:** Box 354345, University of Washington, Seattle, WA 98195, U.S.A. **Online address:** position@u.washington.edu

BARLOW, William. American, b. 1943. **Genres:** Adult non-fiction, Communications/Media, Cultural/Ethnic topics, Music, Theatre. **Career:** Howard University, Washington, DC, professor of communications, 1980-92; writer. Smithsonian Institution, Blues Foundation, consultant; music programmer and producer for Pacifica Radio. **Publications:** An End to Silence, 1972; Looking Up at Down: The Emergence of Blues Culture, 1989; (ed. with J.L. Dates, and contrib.) Split Image: African Americans in the Mass Media, 1990; From Cakewalks to Concert Halls, 1991; (with C. Finley) From Swing to Soul, 1994; Voice Over, 1999. **Address:** Department of Radio/TV/Film, Howard University, 2400 6th St NW, Washington, DC 20059, U.S.A. **Online address:** wbarlow@howard.edu

BARLOWE, Raleigh (Bruce). American, b. 1914. **Genres:** Novels, Economics. **Career:** Michigan State University, East Lansing, Lecturer, 1948-50, Associate Professor, 1950-52, Professor, 1952-81, Chairman, Dept. of Resource Development, 1959-71, 1980-81, Adjunct Professor, 1981-84. Agricultural Economist, U.S. Dept. of Agriculture, 1943-57. **Publications:** (with V.W. Johnson) Land Problems and Policies, 1954; Land Resource Economics, 1958, 4th ed., 1986; Barlowe Ancestral Heritage, 1992; Fain Would I Climb, 1996; Saint's Second Season, 1999, 2nd ed. as The Blackening of Richard III, 2002. **Address:** 907 Southlawn, East Lansing, MI 48823, U.S.A.

BARLOWE, Wayne Douglas. American, b. 1958. **Genres:** Science fiction/Fantasy. **Career:** Parson's School of Design, New York City, teacher of science fiction courses, 1979-80; artist and writer, 1980-. Paintings exhibited at galleries. **Publications:** Barlowe's Guide to Extraterrestrials, 1979; Expedition, 1990; (with P. Dobson) A Dinosaur ABC, 1993; A Traveler's Guide to Hell, 1995; Barlowe's Guide to Fantasy, 1996; Barlowe's Inferno, 1998.

BARLTROP, Robert. British, b. 1922. **Genres:** History, Literary criticism and history, Writing/Journalism. **Career:** Socialist Standard, editor, 1972-77; Cockney Ancestor, editor, 1983-86; Recorder Newspapers, feature writer, 1985-. **Publications:** The Monument: Story of the Socialist Party of Great Britain, 1975; Jack London: The Man, the Writer, the Rebel, 1977; (ed.) Revolution: Stories and Essays, 1978; (with J. Wolveridge) The Muvver Tongue, 1981; My Mother's Calling Me, 1984; A Funny Age, 1985; Bright Summer Dark Autumn, 1986; A Cockney Dictionary, 1988. **Address:** 77 Idmiston Rd, Stratford, London E15 1RG, England.

BARMANN, Lawrence (Francis). American, b. 1932. **Genres:** History, Theology/Religion. **Career:** St. Louis University, assistant professor, 1970-73, associate professor, 1973-78, professor of history, 1978-2002, professor of American studies, 1981-2002, professor of theological studies, 1996-2002, professor emeritus, 2002-. Recipient of academic awards and grants. **Publications:** Baron Friedrich von Hugel and the Modernist Crisis in England, 1972; The Letters of Baron Friedrich von Hugel and Professor Norman Kemp Smith, 1981. EDITOR: Newman at St. Mary's 1962; Newman on God and Self, 1965; Sanctity and Secularity, 1999. Contributor to professional journals. **Address:** The Lindell Terrace (12-A), 4501 Lindell Blvd, St. Louis, MO 63108, U.S.A.

BARNABY, Charles Frank. British, b. 1927. **Genres:** International relations/Current affairs, Military/Defense/Arms control. **Career:** Scientist, U.K. Atomic Energy Authority, Aldermaston, 1951-57; Member of Scientific Staff, Medical Research Council, University College, London, 1957-69; Executive Secretary, Pugwash Conferences on Science and World Affairs, London, 1969-71; Defence Consultant, New Scientist Magazine, London, 1970-71; Director, Stockholm International Peace Research Institute, 1971-81. **Publications:** The Nuclear Future, 1969; Radionuclides in Medicine, 1970; Man and the Atom, 1971; (with R. Huiskens) Arms Uncontrolled, 1975; The Nuclear Age, 1976; Prospects for Peace, 1981; The Automated Battlefield, 1986; Star Wars Brought Down to Earth, 1986; The Invisible Bomb, 1989; The Role and Control of Arms in the 1990's, 1992; How Nuclear Weapons Spread, 1993; Instruments of Terror, 1996. EDITOR: (with A. Boserup) Anti-Ballistic Missile Systems, 1970; Preventing the Spread of Nuclear Weapons, 1971; (with C. Shaerf) Arms Control and Disarmament, 1972; Future Warfare, 1984; The Gaia Peace Atlas, 1988; How to Build a Nuclear Bomb, 2003. **Address:** Brandreth, Station Rd, Chilbolton, Stockbridge, Hants. SO20 6AW, England.

BARNACLE, Hugo. British, b. 1958. **Genres:** Novels. **Career:** Writer. **Publications:** NOVELS: Promise, 1988; Day One, 1998. **Address:** c/o Lisa Eveleigh, 11/12 Dover St, London W1S 4LJ, England.

BARNAO, Jack. See **WOOD, Edward John.**

BARNARD, Frederick Mechner. British/Canadian (born Czech Republic), b. 1921. **Genres:** Intellectual history, Philosophy, Politics/Government, Sociology. **Career:** Professor Emeritus of Political Science, University of Western Ontario, 1990- (Professor, 1970-90). Member, International Political Science Association. Head of Economics Dept., Wyggeston Grammar School, Leicester, 1948-59; Extra-Mural Lecturer, Leicester University and Leicester College of Technology, 1948-59; Sr. Lecturer and Director of Social Studies, Univ of Salford, 1959-64; Associate Professor, 1964-67, and Professor of Political Science, 1967-70, University of Saskatchewan. **Publications:** Between Enlightenment and Political Romanticism, 1964; J. G. Herder's Social and Political Thought, 1965; (ed.) Herder on Social and Political Culture, 1969; Socialism with a Human Face: Slogan and Substance, 1973; Self-Direction and Political Legitimacy, 1988; Pluralism, Socialism, and Politics, 1991; Democratic Legitimacy: Plural Values and Political Power, 2001; Herder on Nationality, Humanity, and History, 2003; Rational Purpose and Political Self-Enactment: Vignettes of Modernity, 2004. **Address:** RR1, Miller Lake, ON, Canada N0H 1Z0.

BARNARD, Judith. Also writes as Judith Michael. American, b. 1934. **Genres:** Novels, Romance/Historical, Education. **Career:** Writer. Worked as reporter and critic. **Publications:** ROMANCE NOVELS AS JUDITH MICHAEL (with M. Fain): Deceptions, 1982; Possessions, 1984; Private Affairs, 1986; Inheritance, 1988; A Ruling Passion, 1990; Sleeping Beauty, 1991; Pot of Gold, 1993; A Tangled Web, 1995: Acts of Love, 1997. OTHER: The Past and Present of Solomon Sorge (novel), 1967. Also author of textbooks and scripts for education films. Contributor to periodicals. **Address:** c/o Poseidon Press, Simon & Schuster Bldg, 1230 Avenue of the Americas, New York, NY 10020, U.S.A.

BARNARD, Nicholas. British, b. 1958. **Genres:** Crafts, Design, Homes/Gardens. **Career:** Writer. **Publications:** (with A. Hull) Living with Kilims, 1988; Living with Decorative Textiles, 1989; (with J. Gillow) Traditional Indian Textiles, 1991; Living with Folk Art, 1991; (with P. Adler) Asafo, 1992; African Majesty, 1992; Arts and Crafts of India, 1993; The Complete Home Decorating Book, 1994; New Decor, 1999; The Step-by-Step Home Decorating Book, 2000. **Address:** c/o DK Publishing, 375 Hudson St, New York, NY 10014, U.S.A.

BARNARD, Robert. Also writes as Bernard Bastable. British, b. 1936. **Genres:** Novellas/Short stories, Mystery/Crime/Suspense, Literary criticism and history. **Career:** Full-time writer, 1983-. Lecturer in English Literature, University of New England, New South Wales, 1961-66; Lecturer and Sr. Lecturer, Bergen University, Norway, 1966-76; Professor of English Literature, Tromso University, Norway, 1976-83. **Publications:** MYSTERIES: Death of an Old Goat, 1974; A Little Local Murder, 1976; Death on the High C's, 1977; Blood Brotherhood, 1977; Unruly Son, 1978; Posthumous Papers, 1979; Death in a Cold Climate, 1980; Mother's Boys, 1981; Sheer Torture, 1981; Death and the Princess, 1982; The Missing Bronte, 1983; Little Victims, 1983; A Corpse in Gilded Cage, 1984; Out of the Blackout, 1985; The Disposal of the Living, 1985; Political Suicide, 1986; Bodies, 1986; Death in Purple Prose, 1987; The Skeleton in the Grass, 1987; At Death's Door, 1988; Death of a Salesperson (short stories), 1989; Death and the Chaste Apprentice, 1989; A City of Strangers, 1990; A Scandal in Belgravia, 1991; A Fatal Attachment, 1992; A Hovering of Vultures, 1993; Masters of the House, 1994; The Bad Samaritan, 1995; The Habit of Widowhood (short stories), 1996; No Place of Safety, 1998; The Corpse at the Haworth Tandoori, 1999; A Murder in Mayfair, 2000; The Bones in the Attic, 2001; The Mistress of Alderley, 2002; Cry from the Dark, 2003. LITERARY CRITICISM: Imagery and Theme in the Novels of Dickens, 1974; A Talent to Deceive: An Appreciation of Agatha Christie, 1980; A Short History of English Literature, 1984; Emily Bronte, 2000. AS BERNARD BASTABLE: To Die Like a Gentleman, 1993; Dead, Mr. Mozart, 1995; Too Many Notes, Mr. Mozart, 1995; A Mansion and Its Murder, 1998. **Address:** Hazeldene, Houghley Lane, Leeds LS13 2DT, England.

BARNARD, Tom. See **GELDENHUYS, Deon.**

BARNES, Annie S. American, b. 1932. **Genres:** Sociology, Race relations. **Career:** High school teacher of American history and government, 1954-65; Hampton Institute, Hampton, VA, instructor in sociology, 1965-68; Norfolk State University, Norfolk, VA, associate professor, 1971-76, professor of anthropology and sociology, 1976-. Lecturer at colleges and universities, including Old Dominion University; workshop leader; guest on television and radio programs. **Publications:** The Black Middle Class Family: A Study of Black Subsociety, Neighborhood, and Home in Interaction, 1985; (ed.) Social Science Research Skills Handbook, 1985; Black Women: Interpersonal Relationships in Profile, 1986; Single Parents in Black America: A Study in Culture and Legitimacy, 1987; Retention of African-American Males in High School, with video cassette, 1992; Research Skills in the Social Sciences, 1993. Work represented in books. Contributor to sociology and anthropology journals. **Address:** Department of Sociology, Norfolk State University, 2401 Corprew Ave., Norfolk, VA 23504-3907, U.S.A.

BARNES, Burton V(erne). American, b. 1930. **Genres:** Environmental sciences/Ecology. **Career:** U.S. Forest Service, Washington, DC, forester, 1953-59, research forester at Intermountain Forest and Range Experiment Station, 1959-63; Baden-Wurttemberg Forest Research Station, Stuttgart, NSF Postdoc Fellowship, 1963-64; University of Michigan, Ann Arbor, 1964-, professor of forestry, 1970-88, Stephen H. Spurr Distinguished Professor of Forestry, 1989-; Matthaei Botanical Gardens, University of Michigan, forest botanist, 1967-. **Publications:** (with S.H. Spurr) Forest Ecology, 2nd ed., 1973, (with D.R. Zak, S.R. Denton, S.H. Spurr) 4th ed., 1998; (with W.H. Wagner Jr.) Michigan Trees: A Guide to the Trees of Michigan and the Great Lakes Region, 1981. **Address:** School of Natural Resources & Environment, University of Michigan, 430 E University Ave, Ann Arbor, MI 48109-1115, U.S.A.

BARNES, Christopher J(ohn). British, b. 1942. **Genres:** Literary criticism and history, Music, Biography, Translations. **Career:** University of St. Andrews, St. Andrews, Scotland, lecturer in Russian language and literature, 1967-89; University of Toronto, Toronto, Ontario, professor of Slavic languages and literatures and chairman of department, 1989-. Broadcaster; lecturer; pianist. **Publications:** Boris Pasternak: A Literary Biography, Vol. 1: 1890-1928, 1989, Vol. 2, 1998. EDITOR: Studies in Twentieth-Century Russian Literature, 1976; (and trans.) Boris Pasternak, Collected Short Prose, 1977; (and trans.) Pasternak, The Voice of Prose, Vol. 1, 1986, Vol. 2, 1990; Boris Pasternak and European Literature, 1990. **Address:** Department of Slavic Languages and Literatures, University of Toronto, Toronto, ON, Canada M5S 1A1.

BARNES, Douglas. British, b. 1927. **Genres:** Education. **Career:** English teacher in secondary schools, 1950-66; reader in education, University of Leeds, 1966-89. Chairman, National Association for the Teaching of English, 1967-69. **Publications:** (with J. Britton and H. Rosen) Language, The Learner and the School, 1969, 4th ed. (with J. Britton and M. Torbe), 1990; Language in the Classroom, 1973; From Communication to Curriculum, 1976, 2nd ed., 1992; (with F. Todd) Communication and Learning in Small Groups, 1977; Practical Curriculum Study, 1982; (with D. Barnes and S.R. Clarke) Versions of English, 1984; (with Y. Sheeran) School Writing: Discovering the Ground Rules, 1991; (with K.M. Pierce and C.J. Gilles) Cycles of Meaning, 1993; (with F. Todd) Communication and Learning Revisited, 1995; Becoming an English Teacher, 2000. EDITOR: (with R. Egford) Twentieth Century Short Stories, 1958; Short Stories of Our Time, 1963; (and contrib.) Drama in the English Classroom, 1968. **Address:** 16 Cholmeley Lodge, Cholmeley Park, London N6 5EN, England. **Online address:** dougbarnes@dougbarnes.f9.co.uk

BARNES, Edward F. *See* **MARQUIS, Max.**

BARNES, H. Lee. American, b. 1944. **Genres:** Novellas/Short stories. **Career:** Community College of Southern Nevada-Las Vegas, professor of English, 1992-; University of Las Vegas, Las Vegas, NV, adjunct instructor, 1993-96. **Publications:** SHORT STORIES: Gunning for Ho, 2000; Talk to Me, James Dean, 2003. OTHER: Dummy Up and Deal, 2002; The Lucky (novel), 2003. **Address:** Community College of Southern Nevada, 6375 W Charleston, Las Vegas, NV 89146, U.S.A. **Online address:** Lee_Barnes@ccsn.nevada.edu

BARNES, James J. American, b. 1931. **Genres:** History. **Career:** Amherst College, MA, instructor in history, 1959-62; Wabash College, Crawfordsville, IN, assistant professor, 1962-66, associate professor, 1966-76, professor of history, 1976-, Hadley Professor and chairman of the dept., 1979-. **Publications:** Free Trade in Books: A Study of the London Book Trade since 1800, 1964; Authors, Publishers and Politicians: The Quest for an Anglo-American Copyright Agreement, 1815-1854, 1974; (with P.P. Barnes) Hitler's Mein Kampf in Britain and America 1930-39, 1980; (with P.P. Barnes) James Vincent Murphy: Translator and Interpreter of Fascist Europe, 1880-1946, 1987; (with P.P. Barnes) Private and Confidential: Letters from British Ministers in Washington to Their Foreign Secretaries in London, 1844-67, 1993; (with P.P. Barnes) Nazi Refugee Turned Gestapo Spy: The Life of Hans Wesemann, 1895-1971; (with P.P. Barnes) The American Civil War through British Eyes: Diplomatic Dispatches from British Diplomat, Vol. I-Nov 1860-April 1862, 2003. **Address:** Dept of History, Wabash College, Crawfordsville, IN 47933, U.S.A. **Online address:** barnesj@wabash.edu

BARNES, Jay. American, b. 1958. **Genres:** Meteorology/Atmospheric sciences. **Career:** North Carolina Aquarium, Pine Knoll Shores, exhibits curator, 1980-89, director, 1989-. Carteret sports leadership mentor. **Publications:** North Carolina's Hurricane History, 1995, 3rd ed., 2000; Florida's Hurricane History, 1997; Faces from the Flood, 2004. **Address:** North Carolina Aquarium, Pine Knoll Shores, NC 28512, U.S.A.

BARNES, John (Allen). American, b. 1957. **Genres:** Science fiction/Fantasy, Westerns/Adventure, Young adult fiction, Theatre. **Career:** Middle South Services, New Orleans, LA, systems analyst, 1982-84; computer consultant, 1985-94; self-employed, 1988-90; writer. **Publications:** The Man Who Pulled down the Sky, 1986; Sin of Origin, 1987; Orbital Resonance, 1991; A Million Open Doors, 1992; Wartide, 1992; Battle Cry, 1992; Union Fires, 1992; Mother of Storms, 1994; Kaleidoscope Century, 1995; One for the Morning Glory, 1996; (with B. Aldrin) Encounter with Tibor, 1996; Earth Made of Glass, 1997; Patton's Spaceship, 1997; Washington's Dirigible, 1997; Caesar's Bicycle, 1997; Finity, 1998; Apostrophes and Apocalypses, 1998; Candle, 2000; (with B. Aldrin) The Return, 2000; The Merchants of Souls, 2001; The Sky So Big and Black, 2002; The Duke of Uranium, 2002; A Princess of the Aerie, 2003; In the Hall of the Martian King, 2003. **Address:** c/o Ashley Grayson, 1342 18th St, San Pedro, CA 90732, U.S.A. **Online address:** johnbarnes@sprintmail.com

BARNES, John Arundel. Australian/British, b. 1918. **Genres:** Anthropology/Ethnology, Sociology. **Career:** University of Sydney, Professor of Anthropology, 1956-58; Australian National University, Canberra, Professor of Anthropology, 1958-69; Churchill College, Cambridge, Fellow, 1969-; Cambridge University, Professor, 1969-82, Professor Emeritus of Sociology, 1982-. **Publications:** Marriage in a Changing Society, 1951; Politics in a Changing Society, 1954; Inquest on the Murngin, 1967; Sociology in Cambridge, 1970; Three Styles in the Study of Kinship, 1971; Social Networks, 1972; The Ethics of Inquiry in Social Science, 1977; Who Should

Know What?, 1979; Models and Interpretations, 1990; A Pack of Lies, 1994. **Address:** Churchill College, Cambridge CB3 0DS, England.

BARNES, Jonathan. British, b. 1942. **Genres:** Philosophy. **Career:** University of Chicago, lecturer in philosophy, 1967; Oriel College, fellow, 1968-78; visiting professor, University of Massachusetts at Amherst, 1973, and University of Texas, Austin, 1981; Oxford University, professor of ancient philosophy, and fellow and tutor, Balliol College, 1978-94; University of Geneva, professor of ancient philosophy, 1994-2002; University of Paris, 2002-. **Publications:** (trans.) G. Patzig, Aristotle's Theory of the Syllogism, 1969; The Ontological Argument, 1972; Aristotle's Posterior Analytics, 1976; The Presocratic Philosophers, 1979; Terms and Sentences: Theophrastus on Hypothetical Syllogisms, 1985; The Modes of Scepticism, 1985; Early Greek Philosophy, 1987; Philosophia Togata, 1989; The Toils of Scepticism, 1990; Sextus Empiricus: Outlines of Scepticism, 1993; Logic and the Imperial Stoa, 1999; The Cambridge History of Hellenistic Philosophy, 2000; Porphyry: Introduction, 2003. EDITOR: Articles on Aristotle, 1975; Doubt and Dogmatism, 1980. **Address:** Les Charmilles, L'Auvergne, 36200 Ceaulmont, France. **Online address:** Jonathan.Barnes@paris4.sorbonne.fr

BARNES, Joyce Annette. American, b. 1958. **Genres:** Novels, Plays/Screenplays. **Career:** Catonsville Community College, Catonsville, MD, assistant professor of English, 1986-; Agitprov Players, Catonsville, creative director, 1991-. **Publications:** The Baby Grand, the Moon in July, and Me (adapted from the play The Baby Grand), 1994. PLAYS: The Metamorphosis, 1984; The Baby Grand (television play), 1984; Whatcha Gonna Do?, 1991; Brute Absolute, 1993; Not Another World, 1994. **Address:** English Department, Catonsville Community College, Catonsville, MD 21228, U.S.A.

BARNES, Linda (Joyce Appelblatt). American, b. 1949. **Genres:** Mystery/Crime/Suspense, Plays/Screenplays. **Career:** Chelmsford High School, MA, teacher of theater, 1971-76; Lexington Public Schools, MA, drama director, 1977-78. **Publications:** MYSTERY NOVELS: Blood Will Have Blood, 1982; Bitter Finish, 1983; Dead Heat, 1984; Cities of the Dead, 1986; A Trouble of Fools, 1987; The Snake Tattoo, 1989; Coyote, 1990; Steel Guitar, 1991; Snapshot, 1993; Hardware, 1995; Cold Case, 1997; Flashpoint, 1999; The Big Dig, 2001; Deep Pockets, 2004. PLAYS: Wings, 1973; Prometheus, 1974. **Address:** 56 Seaver St, Brookline, MA 02445, U.S.A. **Online address:** linda@lindabarnes.com

BARNES, Lynard. American, b. 1948. **Genres:** Science fiction/Fantasy. **Career:** Department of Justice, Chicago, IL, program analyst for 7 years; Trices Co., Chicago, IL, publisher for 10 years. **Publications:** SCIENCE FICTION NOVELS: Phobos Lock, 1999; Rolun, 2000. **Address:** Trices Co, PO Box 12560, Chicago, IL 60612, U.S.A. **Online address:** lynard@lynard.net

BARNES, Michael (Anthony). British, b. 1947. **Genres:** Theology/Religion. **Career:** Gregorian University, Rome, Italy, lecturer in Buddhist studies, 1979-81; University of London, Heythrop College, London, England, lecturer in religious studies, 1982-, senior tutor, 1983-91. Diocesan Interfaith Agency, director of Westminster Interfaith, 1991-95. The Way, editor, 1996-. **Publications:** Christian Identity and Religious Pluralism, 1989, in UK as Religions in Conversation; God East and West, 1991. Contributor of articles and reviews to periodicals. **Address:** Heythrop College, Kensington Square, London W8 5HQ, England.

BARNES, Mike. (born United States), b. 1955. **Genres:** Poetry. **Career:** Private English tutor to high school and university students and to speakers of English as a second language, Toronto, Ontario, Canada, 1995-. Also worked as an elementary and high school English teacher at schools in Ontario. **Publications:** Calm Jazz Sea,1996; Aquarium, 1999; The Syllabus, 2002; Contrary Angel, 2004. Work represented in anthologies. Contributor of more than 125 poems and short stories to periodicals. **Address:** 43 Highview Crescent, Toronto, ON, Canada M6H 2Y3. **Online address:** mh.barnes@sympatico.ca

BARNES, Peter. *See* Obituaries.

BARNES, Samuel Henry. American, b. 1931. **Genres:** Politics/Government. **Career:** University of Michigan, Ann Arbor, instructor to professor of political science and program director, Center for Political Studies, 1957-91; Georgetown University, Graf Goltz Professor and Director, Center for German and European Studies, School of Foreign Service, now emeritus. **Publications:** Party Democracy: Politics in an Italian Socialist Federation, 1967; Representation in Italy, 1977; (with others) Political Action, 1979;

Politics and Culture, 1989; (co-author) Continuities in Political Action, 1990. **Address:** 1801 Hoban Rd NW, Washington, DC 20007, U.S.A. **Online address:** barness@georgetown.edu

BARNES, Simon. British, b. 1951. **Genres:** Sports/Fitness, Biography, Novels, Environmental sciences/Ecology, Children's non-fiction. **Career:** The Times, London, Sportswriter and Ecological Reporter, 1983-; The Spectator, Sportswriter, 1996-. **Publications:** Phil Edmonds: A Singular Man, 1986; (ed) There Was a Young Fellow Called Glover: Sporting Limericks, 1987; Horsesweat and Tears, 1989; A Sportswriter's Year, 1989; Sportswriter's Eye: An Anthology, 1989; Flying in the Face of Nature, 1991; Tiger!, 1994; Rogue Lion Safaris, 1997; Hong Kong Belongers, 1998; Miss Chance, 2000; Planet Zoo, 2000. **Address:** c/o The Times, 1 Pennington St, London, Herts. E1 9XN, England.

BARNET, Miguel. Cuban, b. 1940. **Genres:** Poetry, Mythology/Folklore. **Career:** Ethnologist, poet, and novelist. Escuela de Instruciones de Arte, Havana, Cuba, professor of folklore, 1961-66. Also worked at Editorial Nacional, a Cuban publishing house, during the 1960s. Researcher at the Institute of Ethnology and Folklore of the Academy of Science. **Publications:** La piedra fina y el pavorreal, 1963; Isla de guijes, 1964; Biografía de un cimarron, 1966; trans. by J. Innes as The Autobiography of a Runaway Slave, 1966; La sagrada familia (poems), 1967; Cancion de Rachel, 1969, trans. by W.N. Hall as Rachel's Song: A Novel, 1991; Akeke y la jutia, 1978; Orikis y otros poemas, 1980; Gallego, 1981; Carta de noche, 1982; La fuente viva, 1983; (ed.) F. Ortiz, Ensayos etnograficos, 1984; La vida real, 1986; Claves por Rita Montaner, 1987; Viendo mi vida pasar, 1987; Oficio de angel, 1989; (with E.P. Barnet and J.G. Espinosa) La bella del Alhambra (screenplay) 1990. Contributor of poetry to anthologies. Contributor to periodicals. **Address:** c/o Smithsonian Institution Press, 470 L'Enfant Plaza, Room 7100, Washington, DC 20560, U.S.A.

BARNETT, Anthony. British. **Genres:** Politics/Government. **Career:** Founder and former director of Charter 88, an organization devoted to achieving a written constitution for the United Kingdom; author, c. 1982-. **Publications:** NONFICTION: Iron Britannia, 1982; (with N. Bielski) Soviet Freedom, 1988; (ed. with C. Ellis and P. Hirst) Debating the Constitution: New Perspectives on Constitutional Reform, 1993; (ed. and author of intro) The Power and the Throne: The Monarchy Debate, 1994; This Time: Our Constitutional Revolution, 1997. Contributor to periodicals. **Address:** Charter 88, 16-24 Underwood St., London N1 7JQ, England. **Online address:** info@charter88.org.uk

BARNETT, Correlli (Douglas). British, b. 1927. **Genres:** Economics, Education, Engineering, History, Industrial relations, Military/Defense/Arms control, Politics/Government, Social sciences, Technology, Biography. **Career:** Keeper of the Churchill Archives Centre, 1977-95. Fellow, Churchill College, Cambridge, 1977-. Defence Lecturer, Cambridge University, 1980-83. **Publications:** The Hump Organisation (novel), 1957; (co-author) The Channel Tunnel, 1958; The Desert Generals, 1960; The Swordbearers, 1963; (co-author) The Great War (TV series), 1964; (co-author) The Lost Peace (TV series), 1966; Britain and Her Army, 1970; The Collapse of British Power, 1972; The Commanders (TV series), 1973; Marlborough, 1974; Strategy and Society, 1975; Bonaparte, 1978; The Great War, 1979; The Audit of War, 1986; Engage the Enemy More Closely: The Royal Navy in the Second World War, 1991; The Lost Victory: British Dreams, British Realities, 1945-1950, 1995; The Verdict of Peace: Britain between Her Yesterday and the Future, 1945-1950, 2001. **Address:** Catbridge House, East Carleton, Norwich NR14 8JX, England.

BARNETT, Matthew. American, b. 1974. **Genres:** Theology/Religion. **Career:** Evangelist. Los Angeles International Church, Los Angeles, CA, pastor, 1994-. **Publications:** The Church That Never Sleeps: The Amazing Story That Will Change Your View of Church Forever, 2000. **Address:** Los Angeles International Church, 2301 Bellevue Avenue, Los Angeles, CA 90026, U.S.A. **Online address:** mbpub@dreamcenter.org

BARNETT, Paul. Australian, b. 1935. **Genres:** Theology/Religion. **Career:** Rector of Anglican churches in Sydney and Adelaide, Australia; Robert Menzies College, master; Macquarie University, teacher; Anglican bishop of North Sydney. **Publications:** The Second Letter of Paul to the Corinthians, 1997; Jesus and the Logic of History, 1997; Jesus and the Rise of Early Christianity, 1999. **Address:** 59 Essex St, Epping, NSW 2121, Australia. **Online address:** pbarnett@laurel.ocs.mq.edu.au

BARNETT, Robert. See SHAGAN, Steve.

BARNETT, S(amuel) Anthony. Australian (born England), b. 1915. **Genres:** Anthropology/Ethnology, Biology, Environmental sciences/Ecology, Psychology, Public/Social administration, Zoology. **Career:** Professor Emeritus, Australian National University, Canberra, 1980(Professor and Head, Dept. of Zoology, 1971-80). Scientific Officer, 1943-46 and Principal Scientific Officer and Head of Research Unit on Mammalian Pests, 1946-51, Ministry of Food; Sr. Lecturer in Zoology, Glasgow University, 1951-71; Part-time Consultant, Ford Foundation, India, 1968-75. **Publications:** The Human Species, 1950, 1971; The Rat: A Study in Behavior, 1963, 1981; "Instinct" and "Intelligence," 1967, 1970; (with I. Prakash) Rodents of Economic Importance in India, 1975; Modern Ethology, 1981; Biology and Freedom, 1988; The Science of Life, 1998; Science, or Myth and Magic?, 2000. EDITOR: A Century of Darwin, 1958; Ethology and Development, 1973. **Address:** 3 Galali Place, Canberra, ACT 2614, Australia. **Online address:** tonybarnett@currawong.net

BARNETT, Victoria (Joan). American, b. 1950. **Genres:** History, Theology/Religion, Translations. **Career:** University of Hamburg, Germany, Missionsakademie, World Council of Churches fellow, 1979-80; Fortress Press, associate general editor of Dietrich Bonhoeffer Works series, English edition. Writes, teaches, and lectures on history of churches during the Holocaust. U.S. Holocaust Memorial Museum, Washington, DC, consultant to Church Relations Department, 1994-. **Publications:** For the Soul of the People: Protestant Protest against Hitler, 1992; Bystanders: Conscience and Complicity during the Holocaust, 1999. EDITOR & TRANSLATOR: W. Gerlach, And the Witnesses Were Silent: The Confessing Church and the Jews, 2000; E. Bethge, Dietrich Bonhoeffer: A Biography, 2000. Author of articles, book chapters, and book reviews. **Address:** c/o Publicity Director, Oxford University Press, 198 Madison Ave, New York, NY 10016, U.S.A. **Online address:** vjbarnett@worldnet.att.net

BARNETTE, Martha. American, b. 1957. **Genres:** Language/Linguistics, Medicine/Health. **Career:** Hebrew Union College, volunteer digger at Tel Dan excavation in Israel, 1977; Norton Psychiatric Clinic, Louisville, KY, psychiatric aide, 1977-78; Louisville Times, Louisville, feature and medical writer, 1981-85; Washington Post, national news intern, 1981, special correspondent; free-lance journalist; Allure magazine, writer; A Way with Words, KPBS-FM, San Diego, cohost. **Publications:** The Bill Schroeder Story: An Artificial Heart Patient's Historic Ordeal and the Amazing Family Effort that Supported Him, 1987; A Garden of Words, 1992; Ladyfingers and Nun's Tummies, 1997; Dog Days and Dandelions, 2003. **Address:** c/o Russell Galen, Scovil, Chichak, Galen, Literary Agency, Inc, 381 Park Ave S Ste 1020, New York, NY 10016, U.S.A. **Online address:** martha@funwords.com; www.funwords.com

BARNHARDT, Deanna. See KAWATSKI, Deanna.

BARNHILL, David Landis. (born United States), b. 1949. **Genres:** Literary criticism and history. **Career:** Guilford College, Greensboro, NC, Dana Professor of Religious Studies, 1986-2003; University of Wisconsin, Oshkosh, director of department of environmental studies, 2003-. **Publications:** At Home on the Earth: Becoming Native to Our Place: A Multicultural History, 1999; (With Roger S. Gottlieb) Deep Ecology and World Religions: New Essays on Sacred Grounds, 2001; Basho's Haiku: Selected Poetry of Matsuo Basho, 2004; Basho's Journey: The Literary Prose of Matsuo Basho, 2004. Contributor to journals. **Address:** University of Wisconsin, Department of Environmental Studies, Oshkosh, WI 54901, U.S.A. **Online address:** barnhill@uOshkoshwosh.edu

BARNIE, John. Welsh, b. 1941. **Genres:** Poetry, History, Literary criticism and history. **Career:** Copenhagen University, lecturer in English literature, 1969-82; Planet, editor. **Publications:** War in Medieval Society: Social Values and the Hundred Years War 1337-99, 1974; Borderland, 1984; Lightning Country, 1987; Clay, 1989; The King of Ashes, 1989; The Confirmation, 1992; Y Felan a Finnau, 1992; The City, 1993; Heroes, 1996; No Hiding Place, 1996; The Wine Bird, 1998; Ice, 2001; At the Salt Hotel, 2003. **Address:** Greenfields, Comins Coch, Aberystwyth, Ceredigion SY23 3BG, United Kingdom. **Online address:** planet.enquiries@planetmagazine.org.uk

BARNOUW, Dagmar. American (born Germany), b. 1936. **Genres:** Literary criticism and history, Area studies. **Career:** Stanford University, Stanford, CA, guest instructor in German, 1962-63; Yale University, New Haven, CT, lecturer in German literature, 1968-69; University of California at San Diego, La Jolla, lecturer in German and comparative literature, 1969-72; University of Heidelberg, Heidelberg, Germany, guest lecturer in German literature, 1974; Purdue University, West Lafayette, IN, associate professor of German, 1977-78; University of Pittsburgh, Pittsburgh, PA, associate professor of German, 1978-79; Brown University, Providence, RI, associate professor, 1979-81, professor of German and comparative literature, 1981-85; University of Texas at Austin, professor of German and English, 1985-88; University of Southern California, Los Angeles, professor of German and comparative literature, 1988-. University of Rostock, guest professor, 1982. **Publications:** Entzueckte Anschauung: Sprache und Realitaet in der Lyrik Eduard Moerikes, 1971; (with Hans R. Vaget) Thomas Mann: Studien zu Fragen der Rezeption, 1975; Elias Canetti, 1979; Die versuchte Realitaet: Utopischer Diskurs von Thomas Morus zur feministischen Science Fiction, 1985; Weimar Intellectuals and the Threat of Modernity, 1988; Visible Spaces: Hannah Arendt and the German-Jewish Experience, 1990; Critical Realism: History, Photography, and the Work of Siegfried Kracauer, 1994; Germany 1945: Views of War and Violence, 1996; Deutschland 1945: Krieg und gewalt in der Photographie, 1997. Work represented in anthologies. Contributor of articles and reviews to scholarly journals. **Address:** Department of German, 402 THH, University of Southern California, University Park, Los Angeles, CA 90089-0351, U.S.A.

BARNUM, Barbara (J.) Stevens. American, b. 1937. **Genres:** Medicine/Health. **Career:** Mound Park Hospital, St. Petersburg, FL, charge nurse in labor, delivery, and obstetrics, 1958-59; Augustana Hospital School of Nursing, Chicago, IL, instructor in medical-surgical nursing, 1959-62; Swedish Covenant Hospital, Chicago, staff and supervisory nurse, 1962-63; Augustana Hospital School of Nursing, instructor in medical-surgical nursing, 1963-68, associate director of nursing education, 1968-70, director of nursing services, 1970-71; University of Chicago, Chicago, director of nursing for staff education, Chicago Hospitals and Clinics, 1971-72, director of nursing for staff and community education, 1972-73; writer and consultant, 1973-74; University of Illinois at Chicago Circle, assistant professor, 1974-76, associate professor, 1976-78, professor of nursing service administration, 1978-79; Columbia University, Teachers College, NYC, professor of nursing and director, Division of Health Services, Sciences, and Education, 1979-87, chairperson, Department of Nursing, 1979-85; writer and consultant, 1987-88; Barnum Communications (medical advertising firm), NYC, chief executive officer, 1989-90, chairperson, 1989-92; Columbia-Presbyterian Medical Center, NYC, editor and consultant in Division of Nursing, 1992-95; Columbia University, professor of clinical nursing, 1995-98. Catholic Medical Center of Brooklyn and Queens, member of board of directors, 1984-90; consultant to Office of the Surgeon General, U.S. Air Force. **Publications:** (with K.M. Kerfoot) The Nurse as Executive, 1975, 4th ed, 1994; Nursing Theory: Analysis, Application, Evaluation, 1979, 5th ed, 1998; Writing and Getting Published: A Primer for Nurses, 1995; Spirituality in Nursing: From Traditional to New Age, 1996. Contributor to periodicals. **Address:** School of Nursing, Columbia University, 617 West 168th St., New York, NY 10016, U.S.A.

BARNWELL, William (Curtis). American, b. 1943. **Genres:** Science fiction/Fantasy, Writing/Journalism, Novels. **Career:** Writer-in-Residence, Columbia College, South Carolina, 1979. Assistant Professor of English, University of South Carolina, Columbia, 1970-77. **Publications:** The Blessing Papers, 1980; The Sigma Curve, 1981; Imram, 1981; Writing for a Reason (non-fiction), 1983; The Spearman Novel, 1984; The Book of Romes, 1994; Supreme Candy, 1996; Our Lady of the Stars, 1999. **Address:** c/o Curtis Brown Ltd., 10 Astor Pl, New York, NY 10003, U.S.A.

BAROLINI, Helen. American, b. 1925. **Genres:** Novels, Poetry, Food and Wine, Literary criticism and history. **Career:** Author, lecturer, translator, 1948-; Trinity College, Hartford, CT, teacher in a program in Rome, Italy, 1971-73, 1988; Kirkland College, Clinton, NY, instructor in Italian, 1974-75; teacher of oral history for adult education program in Dobbs Ferry, NY, 1976; librarian, Chappaqua, NY, 1984-90; Pace University, Pleasantville, NY, lecturer, 1990-. Adjunct faculty member, Westchester Community College, 1988; writer-in-residence, Quarry Farm Center, Elmira College, 1989; resident scholar, Bellagio Center of Rockefeller Foundation, Lake Como, Italy, 1991; visiting artist, American Academy in Rome, 2001. **Publications:** (with A. Barolini) Duet (poems in English and Italian), 1966; Umbertina (novel), 1979, repr., 1999; (ed. and author of intro.) The Dream Book: An Anthology of Writing by Italian American Women, 1985, rev. ed., 2000; Love in the Middle Ages (novel), 1986; Festa: Recipes and Recollections of Italian Holidays, 1988, rev. ed., 2002; Aldus and His Dream Book: An Illustrated Essay, 1991; Chiaroscuro: Essays of Identity, 1997, rev. ed., 1999; More Italian Hours, 2001. Contributor to anthologies. Translator of books from Italian. Contributor to periodicals. **Address:** 86 Maple Ave, Hastings On Hudson, NY 10706, U.S.A. **Online address:** helenbarolini@juno.com

BARON, Beth. American, b. 1958. **Genres:** Women's studies and issues, History, Area studies. **Career:** City University of New York, City College,

assistant professor of history, 1989-93, associate professor of history, 1994-, Graduate School and University Center, member of the doctoral faculty, 1995-. **Publications:** (ed. with Nikki R. Keddie, and contrib.) Women in Middle Eastern History: Shifting Boundaries in Sex and Gender, 1991; The Women's Awakening in Egypt: Culture, Society, and the Press, 1994. Work represented in anthologies. Contributor to Middle East and women's history journals. **Address:** Department of History, City College of the City University of New York, 138th at Convent Ave., New York, NY 10031, U.S.A.

BAR-ON, Dan. Israeli, b. 1938. **Genres:** Cultural/Ethnic topics, Education, History, Psychiatry, Psychology, Social commentary, Social sciences, Autobiography/Memoirs. **Career:** Farmer in a kibbutz, Revivim, Israel, 1960-79; secretary, 1973-75; Ben-Gurion University of the Negev, Beer Sheva, Israel, lecturer, 1981-87, senior lecturer, 1987-91, associate professor, 1991-. Visiting professor at University of Wuppertal, 1985, 1986, and University of Osnabrueck, 1989-; chair of Beer Sheva branch of Association for Civil Rights, 1990-91; visiting scholar at Massachusetts Institute of Technology and Harvard University, 1991-92; president of Reconciliation Trust Inc., 1992; consultant to organizations; Peace Research Institute in the Middle East, co-director. **Publications:** (ed. with F. Beiner and M. Brusten) Der Holocaust: Familiale und Geselltschafliche Folgen-Aufarbeitung in Wissenschaft und Erziehung? (title means: Family and Social Consequences of the Holocaust), 1988; (with A. Niv) The Size Dilemma of the Kibbutz from an Organizational Learning Perspective, 1988; Legacy of Silence: Encounters with Children of the Third Reich, 1989; Fear and Hope; Three Generations in a Family, 1995; Third Generation in Israel and Germany after the Holocaust, 1993; The Indescribable and the Undiscussible, 1999; Bridging the Gap, 2000; The Others in Us, 2001. Contributor of articles and chapters to books. Contributor to scientific journals. **Address:** Dept of Behavioral Sciences, Ben-Gurion University of the Negev, PO Box 653, 84105 Beer Sheva, Israel. **Online address:** danbaron@bgumail.bgu.ac.il

BARON, Denis Neville. British, b. 1924. **Genres:** Medicine/Health. **Career:** University of London, Royal Free Hospital School of Medicine, Professor, 1963-88, Prof Emeritus of Chemical Pathology, 1988-. **Publications:** (with K. Lee and J. T. Whicher) A New Short Textbook of Chemical Pathology, 5th ed., 1989; (ed.) Units, Symbol and Abbreviations, 5th ed., 1994. **Address:** 47 Holne Chase, London N2 0QG, England. **Online address:** d.baron@btinternet.com

BARON, Mike. American, b. 1949. **Genres:** Graphic Novels. **Career:** Writer, comic book creator. **Publications:** Badger, 1986; Robotech, the Graphic Novel: Genesis (based on a plot by Carl Macek), pencilled by Neil D.Vokes, edited by Diana Schutz, 1986; Original Nexus, 1986; The World of Ginger Fox, 1986; Hexbreaker: A Badger Graphic Novel, 1988; Stan Lee Presents the Punisher in Intruder, 1989; Dead Man: Book 1, 1990; Next Nexus, 1990; (with Jim Homan) The Complete Blankbook, 1992; (with others) The Punisher: G Force, 1992; Nexus: One, 1993; Nexus: Two, 1993; (with Kelley Jones and Les Dorscheid) Lost Souls, 1995; Deadmen: Lost Souls, 1995; Bruce Lee, 1995; Nexus: Alien Justice, 1996; (with Timothy Zahn) Star Wars: Heir to the Empire, 1996; (with Timothy Zahn) Star Wars: Dark Force Rising, 1998; Star Wars: The Last Command, 1999; (with Jack Herman and Carl Macek) The Macross Saga, Volume 1, 2003; Witchblade: Demons, 2003; (with Scott Lobdell) Kiss: Men and Monsters, 2003; Kiss: Unholy War, 2004. Writer for comic series. Author of stories, novels, and screenplays. **Address:** c/o Author Mail, Dark Horse Comics, 10956 Southeast Main St., Milwaukie, OR 97222, U.S.A. **Online address:** baron.m@attbi.com

BARON, Naomi S(usan). American, b. 1946. **Genres:** Language/Linguistics. **Career:** Brown University, Providence, RI, assistant professor, 1972-78, associate professor of linguistics, 1978-85, associate dean of the college, 1981-83; American University, Washington, DC, professor of language and foreign studies, 1987-, associate dean for undergraduate affairs, 1987-92, associate dean for curriculum and faculty development, 1992-94. Rhode Island School of Design, visiting faculty member, 1982-83; Emory University, visiting National Endowment for the Humanities chair, 1983-84; University of Texas at Austin, visiting scholar, 1984-85; Southwestern University, Brown Visiting Chair, 1985-87. **Publications:** Language Acquisition and Historical Change, 1977; Speech, Writing, and Sign, 1981; Computer Languages: A Guide for the Perplexed, 1986; Pigeon-Birds and Rhyming Words: The Role of Parents in Language Learning, 1990; Growing Up with Language: How Children Learn to Talk, 1992; Alphabet to Email: How Written English Evolved and Where It's Heading, 2000. Contributor to encyclopedias and periodicals. **Address:** Department of Language and Foreign Studies, American University, Washington, DC 20016-8045, U.S.A. **Online address:** nbaron@american.edu

BARON, Wendy. British, b. 1937. **Genres:** Art/Art history. **Career:** Director, Government Art Collection, Department of National Heritage, London, 1978-97. **Publications:** Sickert, 1973; Miss Ethel Sands and Her Circle, 1977; The Camden Town Group, 1979; (ed. with R. Shone) Sickert Paintings, 1992. **Address:** 139 Albert St, London NW1 7NB, England.

BARON-COHEN, Simon. British, b. 1958. **Genres:** Psychiatry. **Career:** Clinical psychologist. Institute of Psychiatry, London, England, staff psychologist, 1985-87, lecturer in developmental psychology, 1988-94; University College, London, and St. Mary's Hospital Medical School, London, lecturer in psychology, 1987-88; University of Cambridge, lecturer in psychopathology, 1994-2001, professor of developmental psychopathology, 2001-; writer. **Publications:** (ed. with H. Tager-Flusberg and D.J. Cohen) Understanding Other Minds: Perspectives from Autism, 1993; (with P. Bolton) Autism: The Facts, 1993; Mindblindness: An Essay on Autism and Theory of Mind, 1995; The Essential Difference: Men, Women, and the Extreme Male Brain, 2003. Contributor to professional periodicals. **Address:** Departments of Experimental Psychology and Psychiatry, University of Cambridge, Downing St, Cambridge CB2 3EB, England.

BARR, Alwyn. American, b. 1938. **Genres:** History, Race relations. **Career:** Southwestern Historical Quarterly, Austin, TX, editorial assistant, 1961-66; Purdue University, Lafayette, IN, assistant professor, 1966-69; Texas Tech University, associate professor, 1969-75, chmn. of the dept., 1978-85, professor of history, 1975-. **Publications:** Polignac's Texas Brigade, 1964, 2nd ed., 1998; Reconstruction to Reform: Texas Politics, 1876-1906, 1971, 2nd ed. 2000; Black Texans: A History of Negroes in Texas, 1528-1971, 1974, 2nd ed. as Black Texans: A History of African Americans in Texas, 1528-1995, 1996; Texans in Revolt: The Battle for San Antonio 1935, 1990. EDITOR: Charles Porter's Account of the Confederate Attempt to Seize Arizona and New Mexico, 1964; (with Calvert) Black Leaders: Texans for Their Times, 1981; N. Smithwick, The Evolution of a State or Recollections of Old Texas Days, 1995. **Address:** Dept. of History, Texas Tech University, Lubbock, TX 79409, U.S.A.

BARR, Andrew. British, b. 1961. **Genres:** Food and Wine, History. **Career:** Journalist, broadcaster, and writer on food and drink, 1983-. **Publications:** Wine Snobbery: An Insider's Guide to the Booze Business, 1988; Guide to Pinot Noir, 1992; Drink: An Informal Social History, 1995; Drink: A Social History of America, 1999. **Address:** c/o Andrew Lowmie Literary Agency, 17 Sutherland St, London SW1V 4JU, England.

BARR, James. British, b. 1924. **Genres:** Language/Linguistics, Theology/Religion. **Career:** Presbyterian College, Montreal, Professor of New Testament, 1953-55; University of Edinburgh, Professor of Old Testament, 1955-61; Princeton Theological Seminary, NJ, Professor of Old Testament, 1961-65; University of Manchester, Professor of Semitic Languages and Literatures, 1965-76; Oxford University, Oriel Professor of the Interpretation of Holy Scripture, 1976-78, Regius Professor of Hebrew, 1978-89; Vanderbilt University, Nashville, TN, Professor of Hebrew Bible, 1989-94, Distinguished Professor of Hebrew Bible, 1994-98, Emeritus, 1998-. **Publications:** The Semantics of Biblical Language, 1961; Biblical Words for Time, 1962; Old and New in Interpretation, 1965; Comparative Philology and the Text of the Old Testament, 1968; The Bible and the Modern World, 1973; Fundamentalism, 1977; Explorations in Theology 7, 1980; Holy Scripture: Canon, Authority, Criticism, 1983; Escaping from Fundamentalism, 1984; The Variable Spellings of the Hebrew Bible, 1989; The Garden of Eden and the Hope of Immortality, 1992; Biblical Faith and Natural Theology, 1993; The Concept of Biblical Theology, 1999; History and Ideology in the Old Testament, 2000. **Address:** 1432 Sitka Court, Claremont, CA 91711-2734, U.S.A. **Online address:** JmsBarr@aol.com

BARR, Nevada. American, b. 1952?. **Genres:** Mystery/Crime/Suspense, Novels. **Career:** Novelist and park ranger. Classic Stage Company, NYC, performer in shows Off-Broadway; performed in television commercials and corporate and industrial films, Minneapolis, MN; United States National Park Service, law enforcement ranger in National Parks, including Guadalupe Mountains, TX, Isle Royale, MI, Mesa Verde, CO, Natchez Trace Parkway, MS, and Horsefly Fire Camp, ID, 1989-. **Publications:** ANNA PIGEON MYSTERIES: Track of the Cat, 1993; A Superior Death, 1994; Ill Wind, 1995; Firestorm, 1996; Deep South, 2000; Blood Lure, 2001; Hunting Season, 2002; Flashback, 2003; High Country, 2004. OTHER NOVELS: Bittersweet, 1984; Spinsters/Aunt Lute (San Francisco), 1989. **Address:** c/o Putnam Publishing Group, 375 Hudson, New York, NY 10014, U.S.A.

BARR, Nicholas. British, b. 1943. **Genres:** Education, Money/Finance. **Career:** University of London, London School of Economics and Political Science, England, lecturer to senior lecturer in economics, 1971-. Consultant to World Bank. **Publications:** Self-Assessment for Income Tax, 1977; (with A.R. Prest) Public Finance in Theory and Practice, 1979, 7th ed., 1985; The Economics of the Welfare State, 1987, 3rd ed., 1998; (with A.J.L. Barnes) Strategies for Higher Education: The Alternative White Paper, 1988; Student Loans: The Next Steps, 1989; State of Welfare, 1990; Income Transfers and the Social Safety Net in Russia, 1992; Poland: Income Support and the Social Safety Net during the Transition, 1993; The Welfare State as Piggy Bank, 2001. EDITOR: (with D. Whynes) Current Issues in the Economics of Welfare, 1993; Labor Markets and Social Policy in Central and Eastern Europe, 1994; Economic Theory and the Welfare State, 2001. Contributor to economic journals. **Address:** London School of Economics and Political Science, University of London, Houghton St., London WC2A 2AE, England. **Online address:** n.barr@lse.ac.uk

BARR, Patricia (Miriam). British, b. 1934. **Genres:** Novels, History, Women's studies and issues, Biography. **Career:** Full-time writer, Norwich. **Publications:** NONFICTION: The Coming of the Barbarians, 1967; The Dear Cry Pavilion, 1968; The Elderly: Handbook on Care and Services, 1968; Foreign Devils: Westerners in the Far East, 1970; Curious Life for a Lady (biography), 1970; To China with Love, 1972; The Memsahibs: Women of Victorian India, 1976; Taming the Jungle, 1977; The Framing of the Female, 1978; (with R. Desmond) Simla: A Hill Station in British India, 1978; Japan (guidebook), 1980; The New Sourcebook for the Disabled, 1981; The Dust in The Balance: British Women in India 1905-1945, 1989. NOVELS: Chinese Alice, 1981; Jade, 1982; Kenjiro, 1985; Coromandel, 1988. **Address:** c/o Sara Menguc, 4 Hatch Place, Kingston-upon-Thanes, Surrey KT2 5NB, England.

BARR, Sheldon. American, b. 1938. **Genres:** Art/Art history. **Career:** Writer. **Publications:** Venetian Glass: Confections in Glass, 1855-1914, 1998. **Address:** Gardner & Barr Inc., 213 East 60th St., New York, NY 10022, U.S.A. **Online address:** gardbar@aol.com

BARRACLOUGH, June (Mary). See BENN, June.

BARRANGER, M(illy Hilliard) S(later). American, b. 1937. **Genres:** Literary criticism and history, Theatre, Biography. **Career:** Louisiana State University, New Orleans, special lecturer in English, 1964-69; Tulane University, New Orleans, Dept. of Theatre and Speech, associate professor and chairman, 1971-82; University of North Carolina, Chapel Hill, Dept. of Dramatic Art, professor and chairman, 1982-99, alumni distinguished professor, 1997-2003, alumni distinguished professor, 2003-. PlayMakers Repertory Co., producing director, 1982-99; president, American Theatre Association, 1978-79, and National Theatre Conference, 1988-90; College of Fellows of the American Theatre, 1984-. **Publications:** (co-ed.) Generations: An Introduction to Drama, 1971; Theatre: A Way of Seeing, 1980, 5th ed., 2002; Theatre: Past and Present, 1984, rev. ed., 2001; (co-ed.) Notable Women in the American Theatre, 1989; Understanding Plays, 1990, 3rd ed., 2003; Jessica Tandy, 1991; Margaret Webster, 1994; Margaret Webster: A Life in the Theater, 2004. **Address:** 10 Banbury Ln, Chapel Hill, NC 27517-2500, U.S.A. **Online address:** mbarrang@mindspring.com

BARRATT, Barnaby B. British, b. 1950. **Genres:** Psychology, Philosophy, Sex. **Career:** Wayne State University, Detroit, MI, professor of family medicine, psychiatry, and behavioral neurosciences, 1994-. Private practice of sexuality counseling and psychoanalysis, 1979-. **Publications:** Psychic Reality and Psychoanalytic Knowing, 1984; Psychoanalysis and the Postmodern Impulse, 1993.

BARRATT, Iris K. American, b. 1954. **Genres:** Paranormal, Self help. **Career:** Universal Life minister. Worked as transpersonal hypnotherapist, ten years, in "visionary palmistry," twenty years, and as private investigator, twenty years, all in Sun Valley, ID. **Publications:** Divination for Decision Makers, 1989; The Power of Forgiveness, 1989; Advanced Investigative Techniques, 1996; The Divination Workbook: An Expert's Guide to Awakening the Power and Wisdom of Your Soul, 1998; Surgery: Before and After, 1999. **Address:** PO Box 509, Horseshoe Bend, ID 83629, U.S.A. **Online address:** ourgoddessiris@juno.com

BARRATT BROWN, Michael. British, b. 1918. **Genres:** Economics, Environmental sciences/Ecology, History. **Career:** Director, Bertrand Russell Peace Foundation and Third World Information Network and Twin Trading Ltd. Special Assistant, to Chief of Balkan Mission, U. N. Relief and Rehabilitation Administration, 1944-47; Lecturer, 1961-66, and Sr. Lecturer, 1966-78, Dept. of Extra-Mural Studies, University of Sheffield; Principal, Northern College, 1978-83. **Publications:** After Imperialism, 1963, 2nd rev.

ed. 1970; What Economics is About, 1970; Essays on Imperialism, 1972; From Labourism to Socialism, 1972; The Economics of Imperialism, 1974; Resources and the Environment, 1976; Information at Work, 1978; Models in Political Economy, 1984, rev. ed., 1995; European Union: Fortress or Democracy, 1990; Short Changed: Africa in World Trade, 1992; Fair Trade: Reforming the International Trading System, 1993; Africa's Choices: After 30 Years of the World Bank, 1995; (with K. Coates) The Blair Revelation: Deliverance for Whom?, 1996; Defending the Welfare State, 1998; Young Person's Guide to the Global Crisis, 1999. **Address:** Robin Hood Farm, Baslow, Near Bakewell, Derbyshire, England. **Online address:** robinh@globalnet.co.uk

BARRAZ, David. *See* **FRIEDEBERG-SEELEY, Frank (J. B.).**

BARRE, Richard. American, b. 1943. **Genres:** Mystery/Crime/Suspense. **Career:** Barre Advertising, Santa Barbara, CA, owner, 1975-90. **Publications:** MYSTERY NOVELS: The Innocents, 1995; Bearing Secrets, 1996; The Ghosts of Morning, 1998; Blackheart Highway, 1999. **Address:** Santa Barbara, CA 93117, U.S.A. **Online address:** barres@aol.com

BARRECA, Regina. American, b. 1957. **Genres:** Women's studies and issues, Humor/Satire. **Career:** Queens College of the City University of New York, Flushing, graduate assistant and adjunct lecturer, 1981-87; University of Connecticut, Storrs, assistant professor, 1987-91, associate professor of English and feminist theory, 1991-. Writer, lecturer. **Publications:** They Used to Call Me Snow White...But I Drifted: Women's Strategic Uses of Humor, 1991; "Untamed and Unabashed": Essays on Women and Comedy, 1993; Perfect Husbands and Other Fairy Tales: Demystifying Marriage, Men, and Romance, 1993; Sweet Revenge, 1995; Too Much of a Good Thing Is Wonderful, 2000; A Sit-Down with the Sopranos: Watching Italian American Culture on TV's Most Talked about Series, 2002; The ABC of Vice: An Insatiable Women's Guide, 2003; I'm with Stupid: One Man, One Woman, and 10,000 Years of Misunderstanding between the Sexes Cleared Right Up, 2004. EDITOR & (OFTEN) CONTRIBUTOR: Last Laughs: Perspectives on Women and Comedy, 1988; Sex and Death in Victorian Literature, 1990; New Perspectives on Women and Comedy, 1992; Women of the Century: Thirty Modern Short Stories, 1993; Penguin Book of Women's Humor, 1994; Fay Weldon's Wicked Fiction, 1994; The Erotics of Instruction, 1997; The Signet Book of American Humor, 1999; Lit: Literature Interpretation Theory; Don't Tell Mama: The Penguin Book of Italian American Writing, 2002. Contributor to periodicals. **Address:** Box U-4025, Department of English, University of Connecticut, 215 Glenbrook Rd, Storrs Mansfield, CT 06269-4025, U.S.A.

BARRETO, Amílcar Antonio. Puerto Rican, b. 1965. **Genres:** Politics/Government. **Career:** Educator and author. Alfred State College, Alfred, NY, assistant professor of political science, 1993-95; Northeastern University, Boston, MA, assistant professor of political science, 1995-. **Publications:** Language, Elites, and the State: Nationalism in Puerto Rico and Quebec, 1998; The Politics of Language in Puerto Rico, 2001; Vieques, the Navy, and Puerto Rican Politics, 2002. Contributor to books and journals. **Address:** Northeastern University, 303 Meserve Hall, Boston, MA 02115, U.S.A. **Online address:** a.barreto@neu.edu

BARRETO, Mascarenhas. Portuguese, b. 1923. **Genres:** Poetry, History, Literary criticism and history, Popular Culture, Translations. **Career:** Services director for television studio, 1963-74; teacher of sociology, design, marketing, and publicity, now retired; freelance writer; Served as an editor for Livros do Brasil and for Aster during the 1970s; competed in the 1951 Olympic Games in Helsinki, Finland, as a fencer. **Publications:** Touros em Portugal, 1962; Origens liricas e motivacao poetica, trans. by as Lyrical Origins and Poetic Motivation, 1970; Historia da policia em Portugal, 1979; O Portugues Cristovao Colombo, agente secreto do Rei Dom Joao II, 1988, trans. as The Portuguese Columbus, Secret Agent of King John II, 1992; A Verdadeira Identidade de Criostovao Colombo (The True Identity of Christopher Columbus-Documental Proof). Translator of works into Portuguese. **Address:** Avenida da Liberdade 262 c/e, 1150-279 Lisbon, Portugal.

BARRETT, Andrea. American, b. 1954. **Genres:** Novels, Novellas/Short stories. **Career:** Writer. **Publications:** NOVELS: Lucid Stars, 1988; Secret Harmonies, 1989; The Middle Kingdom, 1991; The Forms of Water, 1993; The Voyage of the Narwhal, 1998. SHORT FICTION: Ship Fever and Other Stories, 1996. Work represented in anthologies. Contributor to periodicals. **Address:** c/o Wendy Weil Literary Agency, 232 Madison Ave Suite 1300, New York, NY 10016, U.S.A.

BARRETT, Anthony A(rthur). British/Canadian, b. 1941. **Genres:** Classics, History, Law. **Career:** Carleton University, Ottawa, ON, lecturer, 1965-66; University of British Columbia, Vancouver, professor, 1968-. **Publications:** (with M. Havers and P. Shankland) The Rattenbury Case, 1989; Caligula: The Corruption of Power, 1990; Agrippina: Sex, Power and Politics in the Early Empire, 1996; Livia: First Lady of Imperial Rome, 2002. **Address:** Department of Classical, Near Eastern and Religious Studies, University of British Columbia, Vancouver, BC, Canada V6T 1Z1. **Online address:** aab@interchange.ubc.ca

BARRETT, Buckley Barry. American, b. 1948. **Genres:** Bibliography, Reference. **Career:** South Dakota State Library, public library consultant & film librarian, 1973-75; California State Library, assistant librarian, Books for the Blind, 1975-78; Marymount Palos Verdes College, assistant director, director of library, 1978-82; California State University, San Bernardino, assistant head of materials services at Pfau Library, 1982-87, head of technical services, 1987-94, head of automation services, 1994-, library tenure committee, 1996-, faculty senate, 1994-, executive committee of faculty senate, 1999-2000, statewide academic senator, 2000-06. committee, 1996-, faculty senate, 1994-, executive committee of faculty senate, 1999-2000. **Publications:** The Barstow Printer: A Personal-Name and Subject Index..., 1985; (with M. Bloomberg) Stalin: An Annotated Guide to Books in English, 1993; (with Bloomberg) The Jewish Holocaust: An Annotated Guide to Books in English, 2nd ed., 1995; World War I: A Cataloging Reference Guide, 1995; World War II: A Cataloging Reference Guide, 1998; Winston S. Churchill: A Concise Bibliography, 2000. Contributor to periodicals. **Address:** Pfau Library, California State University, San Bernardino, CA 92407, U.S.A. **Online address:** bbarrett@csusb.edu

BARRETT, Charles Kingsley. British, b. 1917. **Genres:** Theology/Religion. **Career:** University of Durham, lecturer, 1945-54, sr. lecturer, 1954-58, professor of divinity, 1958-82, now retired. **Publications:** The Holy Spirit and the Gospel Tradition, 1947; The Gospel According to St. John, 1955, 1978; The Epistle to the Romans, 1957, 1991; Luke the Historian in Recent Study, 1961; From First Adam to Last, 1962; The Pastoral Epistles, 1963; Jesus and the Gospel Tradition, 1967; The First Epistle to the Corinthians, 1968; The Signs of an Apostle, 1970; Das Johannesevangelium und das Judentum, 1970; New Testament Essays, 1972; The Second Epistle to the Corinthians, 1973; The Gospel of John and Judaism, 1975; Essays on Paul, 1982; Essays on John, 1982; Freedom and Obligation, 1985; Church, Ministry, and Sacraments in the New Testament, 1985; Paul: An Introduction to His Thought, 1994; The Acts of the Apostles, Vol. 1, 1994, Vol. 2, 1998; Jesus and the Word and Other Essays, 1996; Acts: A Shorter Commentary, 2002; On Paul: Essays on His Life, Work and Influence in the Early Church, 2003. EDITOR: The New Testament Background: Selected Documents, 1956, 1987; Donum Gentilicium: New Testament Studies in Honour of David Daube, 1978. **Address:** 22 Rosemount, Durham DH1 5GA, England.

BARRETT, David M(arshall). American, b. 1951. **Genres:** History, Politics/Government. **Career:** WLOI-Radio, La Porte, IN, news director, 1974; WNIT Public Television, South Bend, IN, public affairs director, 1975-84; University of Wisconsin-Milwaukee, visiting assistant professor of political science, 1989-90; Villanova University, Villanova, PA, assistant professor of political science, 1990-. **Publications:** Uncertain Warriors: Lyndon Johnson and His Vietnam Advisers, 1993; Lyndon Johnson's Vietnam Papers: A Documentary Collection, 1997. Work represented in anthologies. Contributor articles and reviews to political science journals. **Address:** Department of Political Science, Villanova University, 262 St. Augustine Center, Villanova, PA 19085, U.S.A.

BARRETT, John G(ilchrist). American, b. 1921. **Genres:** History. **Career:** Virginia Military Institute, Lexington, professor emeritus of history. **Publications:** Sherman's March through the Carolinas, 1956; North Carolina as a Civil War Battleground, 1960; The Civil War in North Carolina, 1963. EDITOR: (with R.K. Turner) Letters of a New Market Cadet, 1961; Yankee Rebel: The Civil War Journal of Edmund Dewitt Patterson, 1966; (with W.B. Yearns) North Carolina Civil War Documentary, 1980; So Much Water, So Little Land: Life in World War II's Waterbug Navy, 2001. **Address:** 6 Junkin Pl, Lexington, VA 24450, U.S.A.

BARRETT, Joyce Durham. American, b. 1943. **Genres:** Novels, Children's fiction. **Career:** Teacher at public elementary schools in Georgia, beginning in 1966; Pickens Sentinel, Pickens, SC, reporter, 1980-83; Tri-County Technical College, Pendleton, SC, instructor in English, 1982; Easley Progress, Easley, SC, reporter, 1983; Clemson University, Clemson, SC, editor in department of news services, 1983-86; Lamar County Elementary School, Barnesville, GA, author-in-residence, 1989-92; Teacher of Creative Writing,

Gordon College, authors-in-schools program participant, 1993-. Heart of Georgia Resa, visiting author, 1990. Friends of the Arts of Pickens County, secretary, 1986. **Publications:** JUVENILE FICTION: Willie's Not the Hugging Kind, 1989; Gift of the White Dolphin, 1998; After the Flood, 1998. ADULT FICTION: Quiet-Crazy: A Novel, 1993; A Day in the Blue Ridge Mountains. Contributor to magazines. **Address:** 39 Ninety-two Place, Griffin, GA 30223, U.S.A. **Online address:** JBARR92371@aol.com

BARRETT, Julia. *See* **KESSLER, Julia Braun.**

BARRETT, Nancy Smith. American, b. 1942. **Genres:** Economics. **Career:** American University, Washington, DC, Dept. of Economics, assistant professor, 1966-74, and professor, 1974-88; Fairleigh Dickinson University, Samuel J. Silberman College of Business Administration, Teaneck, NJ, dean, 1989-91; Western Michigan University, provost, 1991-96; University of Alabama, provost, 1996-. **Publications:** The Theory of Macroeconomic Policy, 1972, 1975; (with G. Gerhardi and T. Hart) Prices and Wages in U.S. Manufacturing, 1973; The Theory of Microeconomic Policy, 1973. **Address:** Office for Academic Affairs, University of Alabama, PO Box 87011, Tuscaloosa, AL 35487, U.S.A. **Online address:** NBarrett@aalan.ua.edu

BARRETT, Tracy. American, b. 1955. **Genres:** Children's fiction, Young adult fiction, Children's non-fiction. **Career:** Vanderbilt University, Nashville, TN, senior lecturer in Italian, 1984-. **Publications:** NONFICTION FOR CHILDREN: Nat Turner and the Slave Revolt, 1993; Harpers Ferry: The Story of John Brown's Raid, 1994; Growing Up in Colonial America, 1995; Virginia, 1997, Tennessee, 1998; Kidding around Nashville, 1998, Kentucky, 1999; The Trail of Tears: An American Tragedy, 2000; The Ancient Greek World, 2004. OTHER: (trans. and author of intro.) Cecco, as I Am and Was: The Poems of Cecco Angiolieri, 1994; Anna of Byzantium (young adult fiction), 1999; Cold in Summer, 2003. Author of five children's stories for the educational series "Reading Works," 1975. **Address:** PO Box 120061, Nashville, TN 37212, U.S.A. **Online address:** scbwi.midsouth@juno.com

BARRIE, Alexander. British/German, b. 1923. **Genres:** Children's fiction, Children's non-fiction, History. **Career:** Principal, Alexander Barrie Assocs. (PR), London, 1986-89. Ed., Business Papers, MacLean Hunter, 1952-56; Managing Director, House Information Services Ltd., 1970-86. **Publications:** War Underground, 1961, 10th ed., 2000; Fly for Three Lives, 1974; Operation Midnight, 1974; Let Them All Starve, 1974; Jonathan Kane's Jungle Run, 1977; Jonathan Kane Climbs High, 1978; Ben Goes for Gold, 1991; Flight, Automobiles, Ships and Boats, 1993; Prehistoric World, 1995. **Address:** 33 Manor Way, London SE3 9XG, England.

BARRIE, Thomas (Matthew). American, b. 1955. **Genres:** Architecture, Urban studies. **Career:** Architectural Resources Cambridge Inc., Cambridge, MA, architect, 1980; Huygens & DiMella Inc., Boston, MA, architect, 1981-83; Payette Associates Inc., Boston, architect, 1983-87; Roger Williams University, Bristol, RI, adjunct professor of design, 1987-90; Boston Architectural Center, Boston, instructor in drawing, 1990; Manchester Metropolitan University, Manchester, England, visiting lecturer in design, history, and theory of architecture, 199091; Victoria University of Manchester, Manchester, visiting lecturer in design, history, and theory of architecture, 199192; Lawrence Technological University, Southfield, MI, associate professor of design, history, and theory of architecture, 1993-, head of faculty council, 1997-. Thomas Barrie Architects, architect, (in Boston), 1987-90, and (in Royal Oak, MI), 1993-; work represented in exhibitions; guest lecturer at universities. **Publications:** Spiritual Path, Sacred Place: Myth, Ritual, and Meaning in Architecture, 1996; Community Visions of Royal Oak: Rebuilding the American Small City, 1997. Contributor of articles and reviews to architecture journals and local periodicals. **Address:** College of Architecture and Design, Lawrence Technological University, 21000 West Ten-Mile Rd., Southfield, MI 48075, U.S.A. **Online address:** barrie@ltu.edu

BARRON, Judy. American, b. 1939. **Genres:** Medicine/Health. **Career:** Lyricist, 1978-. **Publications:** (with son, Sean Chapman Barron) There's a Boy in Here, 1992; I Want To Learn To Fly, 1994. **Address:** 529 W 42nd St, 7F, New York, NY 10036, U.S.A.

BARRON, Stephanie. American, b. 1950. **Genres:** Art/Art history. **Career:** Solomon R. Guggenheim Museum, NYC, intern and curatorial assistant, 1971-72; Toledo Museum of Art, Toledo, OH, National Education Association intern in education, 197374; Jewish Museum, NYC, exhibition coordinator, 1975-76; Los Angeles County Museum of Art, Los Angeles, associate curator of modern art, 1976-80, curator, 1980-94, coordinator of curatorial affairs, 1993-96, senior curator of twentieth-century art, 1995-, vice president of education and public programs, 1996-. Has lectured and served on panels

about art throughout the United States; has worked on films and television programs about art. **Publications:** The Museum as Site: Sixteen Projects, 1981; German Expressionist Sculpture, 1983; Gallery Guides to the Collection of Modern Art, 1987; German Expressionism 19151925: The Second Generation, 1988; Degenerate Art: The Fate of the Avant-Garde in Nazi Germany, 1991; Exiles and Emigres: The Flight of European Artists from Hitler, 1997. EDITOR: (with M. Tuchman) The Avant-Garde in Russia, 1910-1930: New Perspectives, 1980; (with W.D. Dube) German Expressionism: Art and Society, 1997. Contributor to periodicals, books, and exhibition catalogues. **Address:** Los Angeles County Museum of Art, 5905 Wilshire Blvd., Los Angeles, CA 90036, U.S.A. **Online address:** sbarron@lacma.org

BARRON, T. A. American, b. 1952. **Genres:** Novels, Children's fiction, Young adult fiction, Natural history, Politics/Government, Popular Culture, Self help, Young adult non-fiction, Picture/board books. **Career:** Writer. **Publications:** Heartlight, 1990; The Ancient One, 1992; To Walk in Wilderness, 1993; The Merlin Effect, 1994; Rocky Mountain National Park: A 100 Year Perspective, 1995; The Lost Years of Merlin, 1996; The Seven Songs of Merlin, 1997; The Fires of Merlin, 1998; The Mirror of Merlin, 1999; The Wings of Merlin, 2000; Where Is Grandpa, 2000; Tree Girl, 2001; The Hero's Trail, 2002; High as a Hawk, 2004; The Great Tree of Avalon, 2004.

BARRON-TIEGER, Barbara. American. **Genres:** Business/Trade/Industry, Film. **Career:** Author, consultant, trainer. **Publications:** WITH P.D. TIEGER: Do What You Are: Discover the Perfect Career for You through the Secrets of Personality Type, 1992; The Personality Type Tool Kit: The Career Professional's Guide to Do What You Are, 1995; Nurture by Nature: Understand Your Child's Personality Type-and Become a Better Parent, 1997; The Art of Speedreading People: Harness the Power of Personality Type and Create What You Want in Business and in Life, 1998, as The Art of Speedreading People: How to Size People Up and Speak Their Language, 1999; Just Your Type: Create the Relationship You've Always Wanted Using the Secrets of Personality Type, 2000. **Address:** PersonalityType.com, 20 Beverly Rd., West Hartford, CT 06119, U.S.A. **Online address:** info@personalitytype.com

BARROW, G(eoffrey) W(allis) S(teuart). Scottish (born England), b. 1924. **Genres:** History. **Career:** University College, London, lecturer in history, 1950-61; University of Newcastle upon Tyne, Kings College, professor of medieval history, 1961-74; University of St. Andrews, Scotland, professor of scottish history, 1974-79; University of Edinburgh, Sir William Fraser Professor of Scottish History and Paleography, 1979-92, professor emeritus, 1992-. **Publications:** Feudal Britain, 1956; Acts of Malcolm IV, King of Scots, 1960; Robert Bruce and the Community of the Realm of Scotland, 1965, 3rd ed., 1988; Acts of William I, King of Scots, 1971; The Kingdom of the Scots, 1973; (ed.) The Scottish Tradition: Essays in Honor of R.G. Cant, 1974; The Anglo-Norman Era in Scottish History, 1980; Kingship and Unity, 1981; Scotland and Its Neighbors in the Middle Ages, 1992; The Charters of King David I: The Written Acts of David I King of Scots 1124-53 and of His Son Henry Earl of Northumberland 1139-52, 1999; St Ninian and Pictomania, 2004. **Address:** Dept of Scottish History, University of Edinburgh, 17 Buccleuch Pl, Edinburgh EH8 9LN, Scotland.

BARROW, John D(avid). British, b. 1952. **Genres:** Astronomy. **Career:** University of Sussex, Brighton, professor of astronomy, director of the Astronomy Centre, 1981-99; University of Cambridge, professor of mathematical sciences and director of Millennium Mathematics Project, 1999-. **Publications:** (with J. Silk) The Left Hand of Creation: The Origin and Evolution of the Expanding Universe, 1983, 2nd ed., 1994; (with F. Tipler) L'Homme et le Cosmos, 1984; (with F. Tipler) The Anthropic Cosmological Principle, 1986; The World within the World, 1988; Theories of Everything, 1991; Pi in the Sky 1992; Perche il mondo e matematico?, 1992; The Origin of the Universe, 1994; The Artful Universe, 1995; Impossibility, 1998; Between Inner Space and Outer Space, 1999; The Universe that Discovered Itself, 2000; The Book of Nothing, 2000; Infinities, 2002; The Constants of Nature, 2002; The Infinite Book, 2005; The Artful Universe Expanded, 2005. **Address:** Dept of Applied Mathematics & Theoretical Physics, Centre for Mathematical Sciences, Cambridge University, Wilberforce Rd, Cambridge CB3 0WA, England. **Online address:** J.D.Barrow@damtp.cam.ac.uk

BARROW, Robin (St. Clair). British/Canadian, b. 1944. **Genres:** Classics, Education, History, Philosophy. **Career:** City of London School for Boys, asst master, 1968-72; University of Leicester, lecturer, 1972-80, reader in education, 1980-85; Simon Fraser University, Burnaby, BC, professor of education, 1982-, dean of education, 1990-2002. Royal Society of Canada, fellow, 1996. **Publications:** Athenian Democracy, 1973; Moral Philosophy for Education, 1975; (with R.G. Woods), Introduction to Philosophy of Education, 1975; Plato, Utilitarianism, and Education, 1975; Sparta, 1975; Common Sense and the Curriculum, 1976; Greek and Roman Education, 1976; Plato and Education, 1976; Plato: The Apology of Socrates, 1977; Radical Education, 1978; The Canadian Curriculum, 1979; Happiness, 1980; The Philosophy of Schooling, 1981; Injustice, Inequality, and Ethics, 1982; Language and Thought, 1982; Giving Teaching Back to Teachers, 1984; (with G. Milburn) Critical Dictionary of Educational Concepts, 1986; Understanding Skills, 1990; Utilitarianism: A Contemporary Statement, 1991; Language, Intelligence and Thought, 1993; (ed. with P. White) Beyond Liberal Education, 1993. **Address:** Faculty of Education, Simon Fraser University, Burnaby, BC, Canada V5A 1S6.

BARRY, Dave. American, b. 1947. **Genres:** Social commentary, Humor/Satire. **Career:** Columnist for the Miami Herald, 1983-. Syndicated newspaper columnist. Recipient of Pulitzer Prize for Commentary, 1988. **Publications:** Taming of the Screw: Several Million Homeowner's Problems Sidestepped, 1983; Babies and Other Hazards of Sex: How to Make a Tiny Person in Only Nine Months with Tools You Probably Have around the Home, 1984; Bad Habits: A One Hundred Percent Fact Free Book, 1985; Stay Fit and Healthy Until You're Dead, 1985; Claw Your Way to the Top, 1987; Dave Barry's Guide to Marriage and/or Sex, 1987; Dave Barry's Greatest Hits, 1988; Homes and Other Black Holes: The Happy Homeowner's Guide, 1988; Dave Barry Slept Here: A Sort of History of the United States, 1989; Dave Barry Turns 40, 1990; Dave Barry Talks Back, 1991; Dave Barry Does Japan, 1992; Dave Barry Is Not Making This Up, 1994; Dave Barry's Guide to Guys, 1995; Dave Barry in Cyberspace, 1996; (with others) Naked Came the Manatee, 1997; Dave Barry Turns 50, 1998; Big Trouble, 1999; Dave Barry Is Not Taking This Sitting Down, 2000; Dave Barry Hits Below the Beltway, 2001; Tricky Business, 2002; Boogers Are My Beat, 2003; (with R. Pearson) Peter and the Starcatchers, 2004. **Address:** c/o Miami Herald, 1 Herald Plaza, Miami, FL 33101, U.S.A.

BARRY, James P. American, b. 1918. **Genres:** Environmental sciences/Ecology, History, Marine sciences/Oceanography. **Career:** With U.S. Army Artillery, 1940 until retirement with rank of Col. in 1966; Administration, Capital University, Columbus, OH, 1967-71; freelance writer and ed., 1971-77. Director, Ohioana Library Association, and Ed., Ohioana Quarterly, 1977-88. **Publications:** Georgian Bay: The Sixth Great Lake, 1968, 3rd ed., 1995; The Battle of Lake Erie, 1970; Bloody Kansas, 1972; The Noble Experiment, 1972; (author and photographer) The Fate of the Lakes: A Portrait of the Great Lakes, 1972; The Louisiana Purchase, 1973; Henry Ford and Mass Production, 1973; Ships of the Great Lakes: 200 Years of Navigation, 1973, rev. ed. 1996; 1936 Olympics-Berlin, 1975; The Great Lakes, 1976; Lake Erie, 1980; Wrecks and Rescues of the Great Lakes, 1981; Georgian Bay: An Illustrated History, 1992; Old Forts of the Great Lakes: Sentinels in the Wilderness, 1994; Hackercraft, 2002; American Powerboats, 2003. **Address:** 353 Fairway Blvd, Columbus, OH 43213, U.S.A.

BARRY, John M. American, b. 1947. **Genres:** Documentaries/Reportage. **Career:** Football coach, journalist, and author of nonfiction. **Publications:** The Ambition and the Power: A True Story of Washington, 1989; (with S.A. Rosenberg) The Transformed Cell: Unlocking the Mysteries of Cancer, 1992; Rising Tide: The Great Mississippi Flood of 1927 and How It Changed America, 1997; Power Plays: Politics, Football, and Other Blood Sports, 2001; The Great Influenza: The Epic Story of the Deadliest Plague in History, 2004. Contributor of articles and book reviews to periodicals. **Address:** c/o Raphael Sagalyn Agency, 7201 Wisconsin Ave Ste 675, Bethesda, MD 20814-7213, U.S.A.

BARRY, P(atricia) S(teepee). Canadian (born United States), b. 1926. **Genres:** Poetry, Songs/Lyrics and libretti, Anthropology/Ethnology, Art/Art history, History, Literary criticism and history, Military/Defense/Arms control, Illustrations. **Career:** Rochester Democrat and Chronicle, Rochester, NY, journalist, 1943-53; Cornell University, Ithaca, NY, research assistant at School of Industrial and Labor Relations; performed biological field research in the western Canadian Arctic, 1959-69; University of Alberta, Edmonton, instructor in English, 1968-69, 1974-75; free-lance writer, editor, and researcher. Province of Alberta, registered historian, Historical Resources and Site Services. Public speaker on drama, art, and historical topics. Exhibition of art works in Alberta galleries. **Publications:** The King in Tudor Drama, 1977; The Canol Project: An Adventure of the U.S. War Department in Canada's Northwest, 1985, rev. ed., 1998; Snow Geese of the Western Arctic, 1958-1983, 1985; Mystical Themes in Milk River Rock Art, 1991. Contributor of articles, stories, poems, songs, and drawings to periodicals. **Address:** 14322 Ravine Dr, Edmonton, AB, Canada T5N 3M3.

BARRY, Robert Everett. American, b. 1931. **Genres:** Children's fiction, Education. **Career:** Pava Prints, San Juan, Puerto Rico, partner, 1957-63;

member of faculty, Averett College, Danville, VA, 1967-68, and Texas Woman's University, Denton, 1968-69; University of Massachusetts-Dartmouth, professor, 1969-96, professor emeritus, 1996-. **Publications:** Faint George, 1957; Just Pepper, 1957; Boo, 1957; Next Please, 1962; The Musical Palm Tree, 1964; Animals around the World, 1964; The Riddle of Castle Hill, 1964; Ramon and the Pirate Gull, 1966; Snowman's Secret, 1975; Mr. Willowby's Christmas Tree, 2000. **Address:** PO Box 817, Newport, RI 02840, U.S.A.

BARRY, Sheila Anne. See Obituaries.

BARRY, Tom. American, b. 1950. **Genres:** Economics, Geography, International relations/Current affairs, Military/Defense/Arms control, Politics/Government. **Career:** Seers Weekly, Albuquerque, NM, reporter and editor, 1971-77; Maricopa County Organizing Project, El Mirage, AZ, publicity coordinator, 1977; Navajo Times, Shiprock, NM, reporter, 1978; Interhemispheric Education Resource Center, Albuquerque, senior analyst and writer, 1978-. **Publications:** Dollars and Dictators, 1982; (with B. Wood and D. Preusch) The Other Side of Paradise, 1984; The Central America Fact Book, 1986; Roots of Rebellion, 1987; (with D. Preusch) The Soft War, 1988; Belize: A Country Guide, 1989; (with R. Garst) Feeding the Crisis, 1990; Guatemala: A Country Guide, 1990; Honduras: A Country Guide, 1990; Panama: A Country Guide, 1990; (with K. Norsworthy) Nicaragua: A Country Guide, 1990; Central America Inside Out, 1991; Costa Rica: A Country Guide, 1991; El Salvador: A Country Guide, 1991; (with D. Vernon) Inside Belize, 1992; Inside Guatemala, 1992; Mexico: A Country Guide, 1992; (with K. Norsworthy) Inside Honduras, 1993; (with B. Sims) On Foreign Soil, 1993; (co-author) Crossing the Line: U.S.-Mexico Relations in the 1990s, 1993; (co-author) The Challenge of Cross-Border Environmentalism, 1994; (co-author) Great Divide, 1994; (with B. Sims) For Richer, for Poorer, 1994; (with D. Vernon) Inside Panama, 1995; (with K. Murray) Inside El Salvador, 1995; Zapata's Revenge, 1995; (with S. Lara and P. Simonson) Inside Costa Rica, 1995; (with E. Leaver) Next 50 Years, 1996; (with M. Honey) Global Focus, 1997. **Address:** Interhemispheric Resource Center, PO Box 2178, Silver City, NM 88062, U.S.A.

BARSKY, Robert F. Canadian, b. 1961. **Genres:** History, Bibliography, Literary criticism and history. **Career:** Trans-Canada Social Policy Research Centre, Montreal, Quebec, Canada, content analysis researcher, 1985-91; Institut quebecois de recherche sur la culture, Montreal, ethnic studies and refugee studies researcher, 1991-93; Institut national de la recherche scientifique, Montreal, refugee studies researcher, 1993-95; University of Western Ontario, London, assistant professor of English, 1995-; Yale University, visiting fellow, 2000; Immigration and Refugee Board, expert witness. **Publications:** Constructing a Productive Other: Discourse Theory and the Convention Refugee Hearing (refugee study), 1994; (ed. with M. Holquist) Bakhtin and Otherness, 1991; Introduction a la theorie litteraire (literary theory), 1997; Noam Chomsky: A Life of Dissent (biography), 1997; Arguing and Justifying (refugee study), 2000. Contributor to periodicals. **Address:** Department of English, University of Western Ontario, London, ON, Canada N6A 3K7. **Online address:** rbarsky@uwo.ca

BARSTOW, Stan(ley). British, b. 1928. **Genres:** Novels, Plays/Screenplays, Autobiography/Memoirs. **Career:** Draftsman and sales exec. in the engineering industry, 1945-62. **Publications:** A Kind of Loving, 1960; The Desperadoes, 1961; Ask Me Tomorrow, 1962; Joby, 1964; The Watchers on the Shore, 1966; (with A. Bradley) Ask Me Tomorrow (play), 1966; A Raging Calm (in US as The Hidden Part), 1968; (ed.) Through the Green Woods: An Anthology of Contemporary Writing about Youth and Children, 1968; (with A. Bradley) A Kind of Loving (play), 1970; Listen for the Trains, Love (play), 1970; A Season with Eros, 1971; (with A. Bradley) Stringer's Last Stand (play), 1971; The Right True End, 1976; An Enemy of the People (play), 1977; A Brother's Tale, 1980; Joby (TV Play), 1977; A Kind of Loving: The Vic Brown Trilogy, 1982; The Glad Eye, 1984; Just You Wait and See, 1986; The Human Element (TV play), 1984; Albert's Part (TV play), 1984; "B-Movie," 1987; Give Us This Day, 1989; Next of Kin, 1991; In My Own Good Time, 2001. **Address:** c/o Lemon, Unna and Durbridge Ltd, 24 Pottery Lane, London W11 4LZ, England.

BARTEK, Edward J. American, b. 1921. **Genres:** Philosophy, Psychology. **Career:** Instructor of Philosophy and Psychology, Manchester, Middlesex, and Tunxis Community Colleges, Connecticut; lectr. at colls. Instructor in Philosophy, University of Connecticut Experimental College, Storrs, and Instructor in Labor Union Philosophy, University of Connecticut Extension Service. **Publications:** Treasury of Parables (philosophy), 1959; To Relax Tensions, 1965; Truth and Wisdom I, II, III, IV (philosophical-poetry), 1965; The Mind of Future Man 1965; The Ultimate Philosophy-Trinityism, 1968;

Unifying Principles of the Mind, 1969; Trinitarian Philosophical Psychology, vol. I, 1973, vol. II, 1978; The Philosophy of Trinityism, vol. I, 1973, vol. II, 1975; Ultimate Principles in Theology, 1983; G.U.T. Pending, 1984; Ultimate Principles, I, II, III, 1987; Truth and Wisdom Poems I, II, III, IV, 1988; Trinitarian Philosophy of History, 1988; Dream-Analysis for Self-Analysis, 1988; Universal Trinitarian Ethics, 1988; Trintityism Applied I, II, III, 1988; Trinitarian Philosophy, 1988. **Address:** 68 Walnut St, East Hartford, CT 06108, U.S.A. **Online address:** Trinitine@aol.com

BARTH, J(ohn) Robert. American, b. 1931. **Genres:** Literary criticism and history. **Career:** Entered Society of Jesus, 1948; ordained Roman Catholic Priest, 1961; Canisius College, Buffalo, NY, Assistant Professor of English, 1967-70; Harvard University, Cambridge, MA, Assistant Professor of English, 1970-74; University of Missouri at Columbia, Professor of English, 1974-88; Boston College, College of Arts and Sciences, Dean, 1988-99, James P. McIntyre Professor of English, 1999-. **Publications:** Coleridge and Christian Doctrine, 1969, rev. ed., 1987; The Symbolic Imagination: Coleridge and the Romantic Tradition, 1977, rev. ed., 2001; Coleridge and the Power of Love, 1988; Romanticism and Transcendence: Wordsworth, Coleridge, and the Religious Imagination, 2003. EDITOR/CO-EDITOR: Religious Perspectives in Faulkner's Fiction: Yoknapatawpha and Beyond, 1972; Coleridge, Keats and the Imagination: Romanticism and Adam's Dream, 1990; The Fountain Light: Studies in Romanticism and Religion-Essays in Honor of John L. Mahoney, 2002. **Address:** Boston College, 24 Quincy Rd, Chestnut Hill, MA 02467, U.S.A.

BARTH, John (Simmons). American, b. 1930. **Genres:** Novels, Novellas/Short stories, Essays. **Career:** Pennsylvania State University, instructor to associate professor, 1953-65; State University of New York, Buffalo, professor, 1965-73. Johns Hopkins University, junior instructor, 1951-53, Alumni Centennial Professor of English, 1973-90, professor emeritus, 1990-. **Publications:** The Floating Opera, 1956, 1967; The End of the Road, 1958, 1967; The Sot-Weed Factor, 1960, 1967; Giles Goat-Boy: or The Revised New Syllabus, 1966; Lost in the Funhouse: Fiction for Print, Tape, Live Voice, 1968; Chimera, 1972 (National Book Award); Letters, 1979; Sabbatical: A Romance, 1982; The Literature of Exhaustion, 1982; The Friday Book, 1984; Don't Count on It, 1984; The Tidewater Tales: A Novel, 1987; The Last Voyage of Somebody the Sailor, 1991; Once upon Time: A Floating Opera, 1994; Further Fridays, 1995; On with the Story, 1996; Coming Soon!!!, 2001; The Book of Ten Nights and a Night: Eleven Stories, 2004. **Address:** c/o Writing Seminars, Johns Hopkins University, Baltimore, MD 21218, U.S.A.

BARTH, Kelly L. American. **Genres:** Children's non-fiction. **Career:** Author and editor of books for children and young adults. **Publications:** Birds of Prey, 2000; Snakes, 2001; Native Americans of the Northwest Plateau, 2002. AT ISSUE IN HISTORY SERIES; EDITOR: The Delcaration of Independence, 2003; The Tianamen Square Massacre, 2003; The Rise and Fall of the Taliban, 2005. **Address:** c/o Author Mail, Lucent Books, 10911 Technology Place, San Diego, CA 92127, U.S.A.

BARTH, R(obert) L(awrence). American, b. 1947. **Genres:** Poetry. **Career:** Poet and editor. Proprietor of a small press, 1980-. **Publications:** POETRY: Forced-Marching to the Styx: Vietnam War Poems, 1983; Anniversaries, Hours, and Occasions, 1984; Looking for Peace, 1985; A Soldier's Time: Vietnam War Poems, 1987; (with T, Cassity and W. Hope) Mainstreaming: Poems of Military Life, 1988; Simonides in Vietnam, and Other Epigrams, 1990; Small Arms Fire, Epigrammatist Press (Davis, CA), 1998. OTHER: (with S. Barth) A Bibliography of the Published Works of Charles Gullans, 1946-1986, 1986; EDITOR: Y. Winters, The Selected Poems of Yvor Winters, 1999; J. Lewis, The Selected Poems of Janet Lewis, 2000; Y. Winters, The Selected Letters of Yvor Winters, 2000. Contribytor to anthologies. **Address:** 3122 Royal Windsor Drive, Edgewood, KY 41017, U.S.A.

BARTHELME, Frederick. American, b. 1943. **Genres:** Novels, Novellas/Short stories. **Career:** Professor of English, Director of the Center for Writers, and Ed. of Mississippi Review, University of Southern Mississippi, Hattiesburg, since 1977. **Publications:** Rangoon (short stories), 1970; War and War (novel), 1971; Moon Deluxe (short stories), 1983; Second Marriage (novel), 1984; Tracer (novel), 1985; Chroma and Other Stories, 1987; Two Against One (novel), 1988; Natural Selection (novel), 1990; The Brothers (novel), 1993; Painted Desert (novel), 1995; Bob the Gambler, 1997; (with S. Barthelme) Double Down: Reflections on Gambling and Loss, 1999; The Law of Averages: New and Selected Stories, 2000. **Address:** University of Southern Mississippi, Southern Station, Box 5144, Hattiesburg, MS 39406-5144, U.S.A.

BARTHELME, Steve(n). American, b. 1952. **Genres:** Novels, Novellas/Short stories, Essays, Humor/Satire. **Career:** Texas Observer, Austin, review editor, 1972-73; copywriter for advertising agencies in Austin and Houston, TX, 1973-83; Northeast Louisiana University, Monroe, instructor, 1984-86; University of Southern Mississippi, Hattiesburg, associate professor of English, 1986-; writer. **Publications:** And He Tells the Little Horse the Whole Story (stories), Johns Hopkins University Press, 1987. **Address:** Andrew Wylie, 250 West 57th St., Suite 2106, New York, NY 10107, U.S.A.

BARTHOLET, Elizabeth. American, b. 1940. **Genres:** Law, Social commentary. **Career:** NAACP Legal Defense and Educational Fund, Inc., NYC, staff attorney, 1968-72; Legal Action Center, NYC, founder, 1973, president and director, 1973-77; member of board of directors, 1977-; Harvard University, Cambridge, MA, assistant professor, 1977-83, professor of law, 1983-, now Morris Wasserstein Professor. **Publications:** Family Bonds: Adoption and the Politics of Parenting, 1993, rev. ed. as Family Bonds: Adoption, Infertility, and the New World of Child Protection, 1999; Nobody's Children: Abuse and Neglect, Foster Drift, and the Adoption Alternative, 1999. Work represented in anthologies. Contributor of articles and chapters to books. **Address:** Law School, Hauser 422, Harvard University, Cambridge, MA 02138, U.S.A.

BARTKY, Sandra Lee. American, b. 1935. **Genres:** Women's studies and issues. **Career:** Writer and educator. University of Illinois at Chicago, associate professor of philosophy, 1970-, and chairman of women's studies program. **Publications:** Philosophy and Feminism, 1977, as Philosophy and Women, 1979; Femininity and Domination: Studies in the Phenomenology of Oppression, 1990; (ed. with N. Fraser) Revaluing French Feminism: Critical Essays on Difference, Agency, and Culture, 1992. Contributor of essays to journals. **Address:** Department of Philosophy, University of Illinois at Chicago, 601 South Morgan St., Chicago, IL 60607, U.S.A.

BARTLETT, Christopher John. British, b. 1931. **Genres:** History, Biography. **Career:** University of the West Indies, Jamaica, lecturer in Modern History, 1959-62; University of Dundee, lecturer in Modern History, 1962-68, reader in International History, 1968-78, professor of Intl History, 1978-96, Emeritus Professor of International History, 1996-. **Publications:** Great Britain and Sea Power 1815-53, 1963; Castlereagh, 1966; (ed.) Britain Pre-Eminent: Studies in British World Influence in the Nineteenth Century, 1969; The Long Retreat: A Short History of British Defence Policy 1945-70, 1972; The Rise and Fall of the Pax Americana, 1974; A History of Postwar Britain 1945-1974, 1977; The Global Conflict 1880-1970, 1984; British Foreign Policy in the Twentieth Century, 1989; The Special Relationship: Anglo-American Relations since 1965, 1992; Defence and Diplomacy: Britain and the Great Powers 1815-1914, 1993; The Global Conflict, 1880-1990, 1994; Peace, War and the European Powers, 1814-1914, 1996. **Address:** Dept of History, University of Dundee, Dundee DD1 4HN, Scotland.

BARTLETT, Elizabeth. British, b. 1924. **Genres:** Poetry. **Career:** Clerk, Bells Ltd., 1940-41, Caffyns Ltd., 1941-42, and Barclays Bank, 1942-43, all Lewes, Sussex; Lecturer, Workers Education Association, Burgess Hill, Sussex, 1960-63; receptionist and secty., WS Health Authority, and home help, W. Sussex Co. Council, both Burgess Hill, 1966-86. **Publications:** A Lifetime of Dying, 1979; Strange Territory, 1983; The Czar Is Dead, 1986; Instead of A Mass, 1991; Look, No Face, 1992; Two Women Dancing: New & Selected Poems, 1994; Appetites of Love, 2000. **Address:** 17 St. John's Ave, Burgess Hill, W. Sussex RH15 8HJ, England.

BARTLETT, Eric George. British, b. 1920. **Genres:** Novels, Sports/Fitness. **Career:** Postal Officer (Retired 1984); Instructor, Yudachi School of Judo, Cardiff, since 1976; Instructor, Sakura Academy of Judo, New Tredegar, 1953-74. **Publications:** The Case of the Thirteenth Coach, 1958; The Complete Body Builder, 1961; Judo and Self Defence, 1962; Self Defence in the Home (in U.S. as New Ways of Self Defense), 1967; Basic Judo, 1974; Basic Fitness, 1976; Smoking Flax, 1977; Summer Day at Ajaccio, 1979; Basic Karate, 1980; Weight Training, 1984; Healing without Harm, 1985; (with M. Southall) Weight Training for Women, 1986; (with M. Southall) Weight Training for the Over-35's, 1987; World of Sport-Judo, 1988; Strangers in Eden, 1989; Mysterious Stranger, 1990; Jungle Nurse, 1990; Clouded Love, 1991; Beloved Hostage, 1991; Master of Kung Fu, 1992; Traditional Judo, 1996. **Address:** 5 Bryngwyn Rd, Cardiff CF23 6PQ, Wales.

BARTLETT, Jennifer Losch. American, b. 1941. **Genres:** Art/Art history, Novels. **Career:** University of Connecticut, Storrs, instructor in painting, 1968-72; Art Institute of Chicago, Chicago, IL, visiting artist, 1972; School of Visual Arts, New York City, instructor in painting, beginning in 1972; artist and writer. Member of board of directors, The Kitchen, New York City.

Work represented in collections at Museum of Modern Art, Metropolitan Museum of Art, and Whitney Museum of American Art, and in solo and group exhibitions. **Publications:** Cleopatra I-IV, Adventures in Poetry Press, 1971. In the Garden (drawing collection), Abrams, 1982. Rhapsody, introduction by Roberta Smith, Abrams, 1985. The History of the Universe (novel), Moyer-Bell, 1985. **Address:** 135 Charles St. #114, New York, NY 10014-2538, U.S.A.

BARTLETT, Sarah. American, b. 1955. **Genres:** Money/Finance. **Career:** Fortune, NYC, reporter, 1981-83; Business Week, NYC, editor, 1983-88; New York Times, NYC, reporter, 1988-92; Business Week, assistant managing editor, 1992-98; Oxygen Media, editor in chief, 1999-. **Publications:** The Money Machine: How KKR Manufactured Power and Profits (nonfiction), 1991. Contrib. to periodicals.

BARTOLETTI, Susan Campbell. American, b. 1958. **Genres:** Education, Children's non-fiction, Young adult non-fiction. **Career:** Textbook and children's book writer, teacher. North Pocono Middle School, Moscow, PA, English teacher, 1979-; educational consultant, 1983-; Keystone Junior College, adjunct faculty, 1984-86; International Correspondence School, commissioned author and editor, 1990-. North Pocono Middle School Faculty Advisory Committee, North Pocono Middle School literary magazine (past advisor), Student Assistance Program counselor. **Publications:** Easy Writer, Levels G and H (textbook), 1987; (with E. Lisandrelli) The Study Skills Workout (textbook), 1988; Silver at Night (picture book), 1994; Growing Up in Coal Country (nonfiction), 1996; Dancing with Dziadziu (picture book), in press. SCREENPLAYS: Wooden Angel, 1988; The Seed, 1989. Author of 15 textbooks, on composition, grammar, child abuse, medical assistance, and other topics. Stories have appeared children's magazines. Stories and educational articles have appeared in journals and anthologies. **Address:** 708 Pine St., Moscow, PA 18444, U.S.A.

BARTOLOMEO, Joseph F(rancis). American, b. 1958. **Genres:** Literary criticism and history. **Career:** University of Massachusetts, Amherst, MA, assistant professor, 1986-92, associate professor of English, 1992-. Twayne Publishers, NYC, eighteenth-century field editor, Twayne English Authors Series. **Publications:** A New Species of Criticism, 1994. Contributor to academic journals. **Address:** Department of English, Bartlett Hall, University of Massachusetts, Amherst, MA 01003, U.S.A.

BARTON, Anne. Also writes as Anne Righter. American, b. 1933. **Genres:** Literary criticism and history. **Career:** Ithaca College, NY, lecturer in the history of art, 1958-59; Cambridge University, England, Rosalind Carlisle fellow of Girton College, 1960-62, official fellow in English, 1962-72, assistant lecturer, 1962-64, lecturer, 1964-74; University of London, Bedford College, England, Hildred Carlile Professor of English and head of department, 1972-74; Oxford University, England, fellow of New College and tutor in English, 1974-84; Cambridge University, Grace 2 Professor of English, 1984-2000, fellow of Trinity College, 1986-. **Publications:** (as Anne Righter) Shakespeare and the Idea of the Play, 1962; Ben Jonson, Dramatist, 1984; The Names of Comedy, 1990; Byron, Don Juan, 1992; Essays, Mainly Shakespeare, 1994. Work represented in anthologies. Contributor to scholarly journals. **Address:** Trinity College, Cambridge University, Cambridge CB2 1TQ, England. **Online address:** ab10004@hermes.cam.ac.uk

BARTON, Erle. See FANTHORPE, R(obert) Lionel.

BARTON, James. See HARVEY, John B.

BARTON, John. British, b. 1948. **Genres:** Theology/Religion. **Career:** Oxford University, Oxford, England, lecturer, 1974-89, reader, 1989-91, professor, 1991-; writer. **Publications:** Amos's Oracles against the Nations, 1980; Reading the Old Testament: Method in Biblical Study, 1984; Oracles of God: Perceptions of Ancient Prophecy in Israel after the Exile, 1986; People of the Book: The Authority of the Bible in Christianity, 1988; Love Unknown: Meditations on the Death and Resurrection of Jesus, 1990; What Is the Bible?, 1991; Isaiah 1-39, 1996; The Spirit and the Letter, 1997; Making the Christian Bible, 1998; Ethics and the Old Testament, 1999; Understanding Old Testament Ethics, 2003. **Address:** Oriel College, Oriel Sq., Oxford OX1 4EW, England.

BARTON, Jon. See HARVEY, John B.

BARTON, Lee. See FANTHORPE, R(obert) Lionel.

BARTON, Tamsyn (S.). British, b. 1962. **Genres:** History. **Career:** Cambridge University, Cambridge, England, research fellow at Newnham

College, 1989-92; volunteer development worker for Action Aid and other non-government organizations in India, 1993-94; British Overseas Development Administration, New Delhi, India, social development advisor to Water and Sanitation Office, 1994-. Oxfam, fundraiser and coordinator, 1986-92. **Publications:** Power and Knowledge: Astrology, Physiognomics, and Medicine Under the Roman Empire, 1994; Ancient Astrology, 1994. Contributor of articles to academic journals. **Address:** B2 Anand Niketan, New Delhi 110 021, India.

BARTON, (Samuel) Wayne. American, b. 1944. **Genres:** Westerns/Adventure, Novels. **Career:** Arco Oil and Gas Co., Midland, TX, sr. engineer, 1967-94. Western Writers of America, membership chairman and member of Board of Dirs., 1985-87; Roundup mag., "Bookmarks for Westerns," columnist, 1985-88; Writer's Digest Schools, editorial associate, 1987-94. Recipient, Western Writers of America Spur Award, 1980. **Publications:** WESTERNS: Ride down the Wind, 1981; Return to Phantom Hill, 1983; High Country, 1993; Lockhart's Nightmare, 1998. WESTERNS WITH STAN WILLIAMS: Warhorse, 1988; Live by the Gun, 1989; Manhunt, 1992; High Country, 1993; Shadow of Doubt, 1994; Wildcat, 1995; Fairchild's Passage, 1997. OTHER: (ed.) What Do I Read Next? 1990-99. **Address:** 2509 Emerson, Midland, TX 79705, U.S.A.

BARTOSZEWSKI, Wladyslaw T(eofil). Polish, b. 1955. **Genres:** History. **Career:** Catholic University of Lublin, Lublin, Poland, assistant in Department of History and Culture, 1980; Max Weinreich Center for Advanced Jewish Studies, YIVO Institute for Jewish Research and Columbia University, NYC, research fellow, 1982-83; Hebrew University of Jerusalem, Jerusalem, Israel, visiting fellow in Department of Anthropology and Sociology, 1984-85; University of Cambridge, Cambridge, England, visiting lecturer in Department of Social Anthropology, 1985; St. Antony's College, Oxford, England, research fellow, 1985-89, senior associate member, 1989-90; Institute of Polish-Jewish Studies, Oxford, secretary, 1985-92, director, 1985-; Sarah Lawrence College Year Abroad Programme at Wadham College, Oxford, tutor in modern history and politics, 1986-90; London School of Economics and Political Science, London, England, research assistant in Department of International History, 1987-91; historical adviser in the War Crime Enquiry, Home Office, London, 1988-89; Oxford Year Abroad at Lady Margaret Hall, Oxford, tutor in modern history and politics, 1988-90; Institute of Russian, Soviet, and East European Studies, University of Oxford, Oxford, senior associate, 1988-90; University of London, London, tutor in Jewish history, 1989-90; University of Warwick, lecturer in Department of History, 1989-91; British and European Studies Group, London, lecturer in East European history, 1990; COBA-M.I.D., London, associate, 1990-91; Central Europe Trust, London, manager, 1991-93, senior manager, 1993-94, director, CIS, 1994-. Lecturer on Israel, Radio Free Europe/Radio Liberty, 1986. **Publications:** The Convent at Auschwitz, 1990. EDITOR: S. Willenberg, Surviving Treblinka, 1989; (with A. Polonsky) The Jews of Warsaw, 1991; S.W. Slowes, The Road to Katyn: A Soldier's Story, 1992. Contributor to books. Contributor of articles and reviews to scholarly publications. **Address:** Ministry of Foreign Affairs, Aleje 1 Szucha 23, 00-580 Warsaw, Poland.

BARTOV, Omer. Israeli/American (born Israel), b. 1954. **Genres:** Novels, History, Intellectual history, Military/Defense/Arms control. **Career:** Tel-Aviv University, Israel, senior lecturer in modern history, 1983-92; Harvard University, junior fellow at the Society of Fellows, 1989-92; Rutgers University, Visiting Raoul Wallenberg Professor for Human Rights, 1992-94, associate professor of modern European history, 1994-96, professor, 1996-2000; Brown University, John P. Birkelund Distinguished Professor of European History, 2000-, professor of history, 2000-; writer. **Publications:** The Eastern Front, 1941-1945: German Troops and the Barbarization of Warfare, 1985; Ptikhat tsir (novel; title means: Border Patrol), 1988; Karev Yom (novel; title means: Surrogate Killers), 1989; Hitler's Army: Soldiers, Nazis, and War in the Third Reich, 1991; Murder in Our Midst: The Holocaust, Industrial Killing, and Representation, 1996; Mirrors of Destruction: War, Genocide, and Modern Identity, 2000; Germany's War and the Holocaust: Disputed Histories (essays), 2003; The "Jew" in Cinema: From The Golem to Don't Touch My Holocaust, 2005. EDITOR/CO-EDITOR: The Holocaust: Origins, Implementation, Aftermath, 2000; In God's Name: Genocide and Religion in the Twentieth Century, 2000; Crimes of War: Guilt and Denial in the 20th Century, 2002. **Address:** Dept of History, Box N, Brown University, Providence, RI 02912, U.S.A. **Online address:** Omer_Bartov@brown.edu

BARTRUM, Giulia. American. **Genres:** Art/Art history. **Career:** British Museum, London, England, assistant keeper of prints and drawings, 1979-. **Publications:** (Coeditor, with John Rowlands) The Age of Dürer and Holbein: German Drawings, 1400-1550, 1988; German Renaissance Prints, 1490-1550, 1995; (ed.) Albrecht Dürer and His Legacy: The Graphic Work of a Renaissance Artist, 2002. **Address:** Department of Prints and Drawings, The British Museum, London WC1B 3DG, England.

BARTZ, Albert. American, b. 1933. **Genres:** Mathematics/Statistics, Psychology. **Career:** Concordia College, Moorhead, MN, Assistant Professor, Associate Professor, 1965-70, Chairman, Dept. of Psychology, 1972, Professor of Psychology, 1970-. **Publications:** Descriptive Statistics, 1979; Basic Statistical Concepts, 1988, rev. ed., 1999. **Address:** Dept. of Psychology, Concordia College, Moorhead, MN 56562, U.S.A.

BARUCH, Elaine Hoffman. American. **Genres:** Literary criticism and history, Women's studies and issues. **Career:** Queens College, Flushing, NY, lecturer, 1960-62, instructor, became assistant professor of English, 1967-77; York College, City University of New York, Jamaica, NY, associate professor of English, 1978-. **Publications:** NONFICTION: (with L.J. Serrano) Women Analyze Women: In France, England, and the United States, 1988; Women, Love, and Power: Literary and Psychoanalytic Perspectives, 1991; (with L.J. Serrano) She Speaks/He Listens: Women on the French Analysts' Couch, 1995. EDITOR: (and author of intro with R. Rohrlich) Women in Search of Utopia: Mavericks and Mythmakers, 1984; (with A.F. D'Adamo, Jr., and J. Seager) Embryos, Ethics, and Women's Rights: Exploring the New Reproductive Technologies, 1988. Contributor and editor (with others) to books and periodicals. **Address:** Department of English, York College, City University of New York, 150-14 Jamaica Ave., Jamaica, NY 11451, U.S.A.

BARUCHELLO, Gianfranco. Italian, b. 1924. **Genres:** Art/Art history. **Career:** Painter, writer, performance artist, and filmmaker. Has created and appeared in films and videos. **Publications:** Mi viene in mente, 1966; Multipurpose Object, 1966; La quindicesima riga, 1967; Avventure nell'armadio di plexigass, 1968; Una settantina di idee, 1968; Come ho dipinto certi miei quadri, 1976; (with G. Lascault) Alphabers d'Eros, 1976; (with H. Martin) Fragments of a Possible Apocalypse, 1978; Sentito vivere, 1978; La stazione del Conte Goluchowsky, 1978; L'Altra Casa, 1981; Marcel Duchamp in 20 Photos, 1981; Agricola Cornelia Soc. per Azioni, 1981; La scomparsa di Amanda Silvers, 1982; (with H. Martin) How to Imagine: A Narrative on Art and Agriculture, 1983; (with Martin) Why Duchamp: An Essay on Aesthetic Impact, 1985; Uomini di Pane, 1986; Mille Titoli, 1987; Bellissimo il Giardino, 1989; Se tanto mi da canto, 1990; Dall'archivio dei Cinque Cuori, 1991; Miss Omissis, 1991; Al Polo Nord, rotolando, 1992. **Address:** Via di Santa Cornelia, m. 695 (Prima Porta), Rome, Italy.

BARZUN, Jacques. American (born France), b. 1907. **Genres:** History, Intellectual history, Literary criticism and history, Music, Philosophy, Social commentary, Speech/Rhetoric, Biography, Reference, Translations, Language/Linguistics, Literary criticism and history. **Career:** Columbia University, University Professor of History, 1967-75, Emeritus, 1975- (faculty member, 1927-; Assistant Professor, 1938-42; Associate Professor, 1942-45; Professor, 1945-55; Dean of Graduate Faculties, 1955-58; Dean of Faculties and Provost, 1958-67; Seth Low Professor of History, 1960); Churchill College, Cambridge, Extraordinary Fellow, 1961-; Encyclopedia Britannica, Board of Editors, member, 1962-; Literary Consultant to Charles Scribner's Sons, publrs., 1975-93. **Publications:** The French Race: Theories of Its Origin, 1932; Race: A Study in Modern Superstition, 1937; Of Human Freedom, 1939; Darwin, Marx, Wagner, 1941; Teacher in America, 1945, 4th ed., 1981; Berlioz and the Romantic Century, 1950, 3rd ed., 1969; Pleasures of Music, 1951, 3rd ed., 1977; God's Country and Mine, 1954; The Energies of Art, 1956; Music in American Life, 1956; (with H. Graff) The Modern Researcher, 1957, 6th ed., 2003; The House of Intellect, 1959; Classic Romantic and Modern, 1961; Science: The Glorious Entertainment, 1964; The American University, 1968; (with W.H. Taylor) A Catalogue of Crime, 1971; On Writing, Editing and Publishing, 1971; Clio and the Doctors, 1974; The Use and Abuse of Art, 1974; Simple and Direct, 1975; Critical Questions, 1982; A Stroll with William James, 1983; A Word or Two before You Go, 1986; The Culture We Deserve, 1989; Begin Here, 1991; An Essay on French Verse for Readers of English Poetry, 1991; From Dawn to Decadence: 500 Years of Western Cultural Life, 2000; A Jacques Barzun Reader, 2001. TRANSLATOR: Diderot: Rameau's Nephew, 1952; Flaubert: Dictionary of Accepted Ideas, 1954, 3rd ed., 1968; (and ed.) New Letters of Berlioz, 1954; Courteline: A Rule Is a Rule, 1960; Beaumarchais: The Marriage of Figaro, 1961. EDITOR: Selected Letters of Lord Byron, 1953; Selected Writings of John Jay Chapman, 1957; (with others) Follett's Modern American Usage, 1966. **Address:** 18 Wolfeton Way, San Antonio, TX 78218-6045, U.S.A.

BASCH, Rachel. American, b. 1959. **Genres:** Novels. **Career:** Writer. **Publications:** Degrees of Love, 1998; The Passion of Reverend Nash, 2003.

Contributor of short stories to magazines. **Address:** c/o Alice Fried Martell, The Martell Agency, 545 Madison Ave 7th Fl, New York, NY 10022, U.S.A.

BASE, Graeme (Rowland). Australian (born England), b. 1958. **Genres:** Children's fiction. **Career:** Worked in advertising at design studios, including The Art Producers, Stannard Patten Samuelson, and Paul Pantelis & Partners, 1979-80; keyboard player in band Riki-Tiki-Tavi, with wife, 1980-85; author and illustrator of books for children. **Publications:** SELF-ILLUSTRATED BOOKS FOR CHILDREN: My Grandma Lived in Gooligulch, 1983; Animalia, 1986; The Eleventh Hour: A Curious Mystery, 1988; The Sign of the Seahorse, 1992; The Discovery of Dragons, 1996; The Worst Band in the Universe, 1999; The Waterhole, 2001. Illustrator of books by S. Burke, L. Carroll, M. Dann. **Address:** c/o Penguin Books Australia Ltd, 250 Camberwell Rd., Camberwell, VIC 3124, Australia.

BASH, Frank N(ess). American, b. 1937. **Genres:** Astronomy. **Career:** Edmonds Regents' Professor of Astronomy, since 1986, and Director, McDonald Observatory, since 1989, Univ of Texas, Austin (Associate Professor, 1975-81; Professor, 1982-86; Chairman, 1982-87). **Publications:** (with D. Schiller and Dilip Balamore) Astronomy, 1977. **Address:** McDonald Observatory, University of Texas, Mail Code C1402, Austin, TX 78712, U.S.A.

BASHE, Philip (Scott). American, b. 1954. **Genres:** History, Sports/Fitness, Biography, Medicine/Health. **Career:** Foxtrot (magazine), Buffalo, NY, publisher and editor in chief, 1975-77; WBUF-FM Radio, Buffalo, announcer, 1977-78; Buffalo Evening News, Buffalo, writer, 1978-79; Good Times (magazine), Long Island, NY, managing editor, 1979-80; Circus (magazine), New York City, senior editor, 1980-84; International Musician and Recording World (magazine), New York City, managing editor, 1984-86. Volunteer, Helen Keller Services for the Blind, Hempstead, NY. **Publications:** (with K. Barun, W. King, and M. Shore) Rolling Stone Rock Almanac, 1983; Heavy Metal Thunder: The Music, Its History, Its Heroes, 1985; (with D. Snider) Dee Snider's Teenage Survival Guide: How to Be a Legend in Your Own Lunch Time, 1987; (with M. Blanc) That's Not All, Folks!, 1988; (with K. Barun) How to Keep the Children You Love Off Drugs, 1988; Teenage Idol, Travelin' Man: The Complete Biography of Rick Nelson, 1992; (with G. and C. Gaes) You Don't Have to Die, 1992; Dog Days: The New York Yankees' Fall from Grace and Return to Glory, 1964 to 1976, 1994; (with S.J. Winawer and M. Shike) Cancer Free: The Comprehensive Prevention Program, 1995; (with physicians at Yale University School of Medicine) The Patient's Guide to Tests and Procedures, 1997; (with R. McFarlane) The Complete Bedside Companion: No-Nonsense Advice on Caring for the Seriously Ill, 1998; (with P. Teeley) Fight for Your Life: How to Get the Best Cancer Care Available, 1998; Caring for Your Teenager, 2000. **Address:** 974 Station Ave., Baldwin, NY 11510, U.S.A.

BASINGER, Jeanine (Deyling). American, b. 1936. **Genres:** Film. **Career:** Corwin-Fuller Professor of Film, Wesleyan University, Middletown, CT (Professor since 1984; joined faculty, 1971). Trustee, American Film Institute, National Center for Film and Video Preservation. **Publications:** Shirley Temple, 1975; Gene Kelly, 1976; Lana Turner, 1977; Anthony Mann: A Critical Analysis, 1979; World War II Combat Films: Anatomy of a Genre, 1985; A Woman's View, 1991; American Cinema: 100 Years of Filmmaking, 1994; Silent Stars, 1999. EDITOR: (with J. Frazer and J.W. Reed) Working with Kazan, 1973; The It's a Wonderful Life Book, 1986. **Address:** c/o Wesleyan Cinema Archives, 301 Washington Terrace, Wesleyan University, Middletown, CT 06457, U.S.A.

BASINSKI, Michael. American, b. 1950. **Genres:** Poetry. **Career:** Poet, 1975-. **Publications:** POETRY: B (text broadside), 1982; The Wicked Old Woman (broadside), 1983; The Women Are Called Girls, 1983; A-Part (broadside), 1991; (with B. Tedlock) Egyptian Gods 6 (broadside), 1991; Moon Bok, 1992; Red Rain Too, 1992; Her Roses (broadside), 1992; It Is an Open... (Christmas broadside), 1992; Cnyttan, 1993; Flight to the Moon, 1993; Vessels, 1993; Worms, 1993; So Up, 1994; SleVep, 1995; Duende, 1995; Catachresis Mum, 1995; Odalesque, 1995; The Sink, 1995; Coupid (broadside), 1996; Barstokai, 1996; Wen, 1996; Empty Mirror, 1996; Heebee-Jeebees, 1996; Idyll, 1996; Words, 1997; Nome, 1997; By, 1999; The Doors, 2000; Beseechers, 2000; Shards ov Shampoo, 2000; Mool3Ghosts, 2001; Strange Things Begin to Happen When a Meteor Crashes in the Arizona, 2001; The Lay of Fraya Wray, 2001; Mool, 2001; Heka, 2001; The Sound Pome Today Must Come to Bum Impoemvisational, 2001; A Poet Dreams about Poetry, 2001; Two Toons, 2002; Poemeserss, 2002; Abzu, 2003. **Address:** 30 Colonial Ave, Lancaster, NY 14086, U.S.A.

BASKIN, Judith R. American (born Canada), b. 1950. **Genres:** Theology/Religion, Women's studies and issues. **Career:** University of Massachusetts at Amherst, assistant professor of Judaic studies, 1976-81; Yale University, New Haven, CT, visiting assistant professor of religious studies, 1981-83; University of Massachusetts at Amherst, associate professor of Judaic and Near Eastern studies, 1984-88; State University of New York at Albany, associate professor of Judaic studies and chair of department, 1988-95, professor and chairman of department, 1995-. **Publications:** Pharaoh's Counsellors: Job, Jethro, and Balaam in Rabbinic and Patristic Tradition, 1983. EDITOR & CONTRIBUTOR: Jewish Women in Historical Perspective, 1991, 2nd ed., 1998; Women of the Word: Jewish Women and Jewish Writing, 1994; (with S. Tenenbaum) Gender and Jewish Studies: A Curriculum Guide, 1994. Work represented in anthologies. **Address:** Department of Judaic Studies, Humanities 284, State University of New York at Albany, Albany, NY 12222, U.S.A. **Online address:** baskin@cas.albany.edu

BASRA, Amarjit S(ingh). Indian, b. 1958. **Genres:** Agriculture/Forestry, Botany. **Career:** University of Western Sydney Hawkesbury, research fellow, 1983-85; Wageningen Agricultural University, senior research fellow, 1989; Punjab Agricultural University, Ludhiana, India, assistant professor, 1983-92, associate professor of botany, 1992-2000; University of California, Davis, 2000-02; Central Plains Crop Technology, Wichita, KS, 2002-. International Parliament for Safety and Peace, deputy member of assembly. Journal of Crop Improvement, founding editor-in-chief; Journal of New Seeds, founding editor-in-chief. **Publications:** EDITOR: Mechanisms of Plant Growth and Improved Productivity: 1994; (and contrib.) Stress-Induced Gene Expression in Plants, 1995; Seed Quality, 1995; (with R.K. Basra) Mechanisms of Environmental Stress Resistance in Plants, 1997; Crop Sciences, 1998; Cotton Fibers, 1999; Heterosis and Hybrid Seed Production in Agronomic Crops, 1999; Crop Responses and Adaptations to Temperature Stress, 2000; Hybrid Seed Production in Vegetables, 2000; Plant Growth Regulators in Agriculture and Horticulture, 2000; (with L.S. Randhawa) Quality Improvement in Field Crops, 2002. **Address:** 2011 N Frederic Ave, Wichita, KS 67206, U.S.A. **Online address:** asbasra@cox.net

BASS, Bernard M(orris). American, b. 1925. **Genres:** Administration/Management, Psychology. **Career:** Distinguished Professor of Management and Director, Center for Leadership Studies, 1977-93, Emeritus, 1993-, State University of New York at Binghamton. Professor, University of Rochester, NY 1968-77. Executive Ed., Leadership Quarterly, 1988-91. **Publications:** Objective Approach to Personality Assessment, 1959; Leadership, Psychology and Organizational Behavior, 1960; Conformity and Deviation, 1961; Leadership and Interpersonal Behavior, 1961; Organizational Psychology, 1965, 2nd ed. 1979; Psychology of Learning for Managers, 1965; Training in Industry, 1967; Man, Work and Organizations, 1972; Assessment of Managers, 1979; People, Work, and Organizations, 1981; Stogdill's Handbook of Leadership, 1981; Interpersonal Communications in Organizations, 1982; Organizational Decision-making, 1983; Leadership and Performance beyond Expectations, 1985; Advances in Organizational Psychology: An International Review, 1987; Bass and Stogdill's Handbook of Leadership, 1990; Improving Organizational Effectiveness through Transformational Leadership, 1994; A New Paradigm of Leadership, 1996; Transformational Leadership: Industrial, Military, and Educational Impact, 1998. **Address:** Center for Leadership Studies, Binghamton University, SUNY, Binghamton, NY 13902-6015, U.S.A. **Online address:** Bernard_M_Bass@Compuserve.com

BASS, Cynthia. American, b. 1949. **Genres:** Novels. **Career:** Novelist. **Publications:** NOVELS: Sherman's March, 1994; Maiden Voyage, 1996. Contributor of short stories and articles to periodicals. **Address:** 1926 Contra Costa Blvd. No. 217, Pleasant Hill, CA 94523, U.S.A.

BASS, Harold F. American, b. 1948. **Genres:** Politics/Government. **Career:** Ouachita Baptist University, Arkadelphia, AR, instructor to Moody Professor of Political Science, 1976-; member of boards of directors. **Publications:** Historical Dictionary of United States Political Parties, 2000. **Address:** Department of Political Science, Ouachita Baptist University, Box 3781, Arkadelphia, AR 71998, U.S.A. **Online address:** bassh@obu.edu

BASS, Howard. British, b. 1923. **Genres:** Sports/Fitness. **Career:** Winter Sports Correspondent, Telegraph, London, since 1960, Evening Standard, London, since 1973, and Mail, London, since 1987. Text Authority, Encyclopaedia Britannica, and Guinness Book of Records, since 1963. Ed., Winter Sports, 1948-68; Managing Director, Howard Bass Publs. Ltd., 1948-70. **Publications:** The Sense in Sport, 1943; This Skating Age, 1958; The Magic of Skiing, 1959; Winter Sports, 1966; Success in Ice Skating, 1970; International Encyclopaedia of Winter Sports, 1971; Let's Go Skating, 1970; Tackle Skating, 1978; Ice Skating for Pleasure, 1979; Ice Skating, 1980; The Love of Skating, 1980; Elegance on Ice, 1980; (with Robin Cousins) Skating for Gold, 1980; Glorious Wembley, 1982; Super Book of Ice Skating, 1988; Ski Sunday, 1988. **Address:** 256 Willow Rd, Enfield, Middx, England.

BASS, Jack. American, b. 1934. **Genres:** History, Politics/Government, Social commentary, Biography. **Career:** ; Harvard University, Nieman fellow, 1965-66; Charlotte Observer, Columbia, Bureau Chief, 1966-73; Duke University, Durham, NC, Inst of Policy Sciences and Public Affairs, Visiting Research Fellow, 1973-75; South Carolina State College, Orangeburg, Writer-in-Residence, 1975-78; University of South Carolina, Columbia, Research Fellow and Director of American South Special Projects, 1979-85; University of Mississippi, Oxford, Professor of Journalism, 1987-98; College of Charleston, Professor of Humanities and Social Sciences, 1999-. **Publications:** (with J. Nelson) The Orangeburg Massacre, 1970; Porgy Comes Home, 1972; (with W. DeVries) The Transformation of Southern Politics, 1976; Unlikely Heroes, 1981; (ed. with T.E. Terrill) The American South Comes of Age, 1985; Taming the Storm: The Life and Times of Judge Frank M. Johnson, Jr. and the South's Fight over Civil Rights, 1993; (with M. Thompson) Ol' Strom: An Unauthorized Biography of Strom Thurmond, 1998; (with M. Thompson) Strom: The Complicated Personal and Political Life of Strom Thurmond, 2005. **Address:** 100 Queen St, Charleston, SC 29401, U.S.A. **Online address:** bassj@cofc.edu

BASS, Ronald. American. **Genres:** Novels, Plays/Screenplays. **Career:** Lawyer, film producer, and screenwriter. **Publications:** SCREENPLAYS: Code Name: Emerald, 1985; (with L.Z. Dane) Heavenly Bodies, 1985; Target, 1985; Black Widow, 1986; (with B. Morrow) Gardens of Stone, 1987; (with Morrow) Rain Man, 1988; Sleeping with the Enemy, 1991; (with A. Tan) The Joy Luck Club, 1993; (with A. Franken) When a Man Loves a Woman, 1994; Reunion (television movie), 1994; The Enemy Within (television movie), 1994; (with T. McMillan) Waiting to Exhale, 1995; Dangerous Minds, 1995; My Best Friend's Wedding, 1997; Moloney (television). Sometimes credited as Ron Bass. NOVELS: Lime's Crisis, 1982; The Emerald Illusion, 1984; The Perfect Thief. **Address:** c/o Nancy Seltzer & Associates, 6220 Del Valle Dr, Los Angeles, CA 90048, U.S.A.

BASS, T. J. (Thomas J. Bassler). American, b. 1932. **Genres:** Science fiction/Fantasy, Medicine/Health. **Career:** In private practice as a pathologist, 1964-. Deputy Medical Examiner, Los Angeles, 1961-64. Ed. American Medical Joggers Newsletter. **Publications:** Half Past Human, 1971; The Godwhale, 1974. **Address:** 27558 Sunnyridge Rd, Palos Verdes Peninsula, CA 90274, U.S.A.

BASS, Thomas A. American, b. 1951. **Genres:** Business/Trade/Industry, Economics, Money/Finance, Sciences. **Career:** Writer. **Publications:** The Eudaemonic Pie, 1985 (in U.K. as The Newtonian Casino, 1990); Camping with the Prince and Other Tales of Science in Africa, 1990; Reinventing the Future, 1994; Vietnamerica, 1996; The Predictors, 1999. **Address:** c/o Michael Carlisle, Ink Well Management, 521 5th Ave, New York, NY 10175, U.S.A. **Online address:** tbass@albany.edu

BASSETT, Elizabeth. American, b. 1950. **Genres:** Travel/Exploration. **Career:** Intern teacher in Canton, MA, 1972-73; Beacon Hill Travel, Boston, MA, travel agent, 1973-75; Paul Browne Associates, San Francisco, CA, travel agent and assistant manager, 1975-77; Thomas Cook Inc., San Francisco, manager of travel agency, 197779; Cole Surveys Inc., Boston, project manager; Bank of New York, NYC, compensation manager and assistant vice-president, 1981-82; Kanoo Travel, Jeddah, Saudi Arabia, travel agent, 1983-85; freelance writer, 1985-. **Publications:** Nature Walks in Northern Vermont and the Champlain Valley, 1998. **Address:** 1989 Mt Philo Rd, Charlotte, VT 05445, U.S.A.

BASSIL, Andrea. Also writes as Anna Nilsen. British, b. 1948. **Genres:** Children's fiction, Art/Art history, Children's non-fiction, Illustrations, Picture/board books. **Career:** Mussleburgh Grammar School, assistant teacher of art, 1973-74; St. Margaret's School, Newington, assistant teacher of art, 1974-85; Bournemouth & Poole College of Art and Design, England, course director in natural history illustration, 1985-90; Anglia Polytechnic University, head of graphic arts and illustration, 1990-94; full-time artist, writer, and illustrator, 1995-. Lamp of Lothian Art Centre, evening class lecturer, 1973-74. Pixel Magic, art director, screen designer, and games consultant, 1995-96; educational games consultant to Multimedia Corp. Artwork exhibited in solo and group shows in England and Scotland. **Publications:** CHILDREN'S BOOKS AS ANNA NILSEN: Jungle, 1994; Farm, 1994; Friends, 1994; Wheels, 1994; Dinosaurs, 1994; Terrormazia, 1995; Flying High, 1996; Fairy Tales, 1996; Under the Sea, 1996; Drive Your Car, 1996; Drive Your Tractor, 1996; Where Are Percy's Friends?, 1996; Where Is Percy's Dinner?, 1996; Percy the Park Keeper Activity Book, 1996; Follow the Kite, 1997; Dig and Burrow, 1998; Hang and Dangle, 1998; Leap and Jump, 1998; Swim and Dive, 1998; I Can Spell Three Letter Words, 1998; I Can Count from 1-10, 1999; I Can Add, 1999; I Can Subtract,

2000; Art Fraud Detective, 2000; Mousemazia, 2000; I Can Multiply, 2001; Magnificent Mazes, 2001; Let's Learn ...Numbers, ...Words, ...Colours, ...Shapes, 2001; Let's Learn ...Actions, ...Noises, ...Sizes, ...Opposites, 2002; The Great Race, 2002; Pirates, 2003; Busy Digger, Zooming Plane, Racing Car, Sailing Boat, 2003. LEGO PUZZLE BOOKS: Spycatcher, Treasure Smuggler, Gold Robber, Jewel Thief, Insectoid Invasion, 1998-99. OTHER: Jaguar Expedition to Belize, 1989; Design in Partnership, 1989. Contributor of illustrations to journals. **Address:** 16 Emery St, Cambridge CB1 2AX, England. **Online address:** abassil@globalnet.co.uk

BASSIN, Donna. American, b. 1950. **Genres:** Psychology. **Career:** State University of New York Downstate Medical Center, Brooklyn, clinical instructor in psychiatry, 1977-80, director of art therapy, 1977-81; Pratt Institute, Brooklyn, assistant professor of psychology, 1980-85; Psychoanalytic Psychotherapy Study Center, NYC, faculty member and training supervisor, 1989-93; Institute for Psychoanalytic Training and Research, NYC, lecturer, 1993-, assistant director of Clinical Center and director of Women's Center, 1993. Lecturer at colleges and universities. Contemporary Center for Advanced Psychoanalytic Studies, training and supervising faculty member, 1993-94; Columbia University, Teachers College, adjunct assistant professor, 1994; Pratt Institute, associate professor, 1994-. Private practice of clinical psychology; Pratt Institute, clinical supervisor of Art Therapy Internship Program, 1977-81; State University of New York Downstate Medical Center, research assistant at infant-toddler laboratory, 1979-80, primary therapist in infant-toddler therapeutic nursery, 1980-82. **Publications:** EDITOR: (with M. Honey and M. Kaplan, and contrib.) Representations of Motherhood, 1994; Clinical Classics in Process: Women and Psychoanalysis, in press. FILMS: Buddy and the Monster: A Children's Orientation to Psychiatric Hospitalization, 1979. Contributor to books and psychology journals. **Address:** 31 West 11th St. No. 5C, New York, NY 10011, U.S.A.

BASSLER, Gerhard P. Canadian (born Germany), b. 1937. **Genres:** Area studies, Cultural/Ethnic topics, History. **Career:** University of Kansas-Lawrence, assistant instructor in western civilization, 1963-65; Memorial University of Newfoundland, St. John's, Newfoundland, Canada, professor of history, 1965-2002, professor emeritus, 2003-. German-Canadian Congress, member of national council, 1990-. **Publications:** (ed. and translator, with others) The German Canadians, 1750-1937: Immigration, Settlement, and Culture, 1986; The German Canadian Mosaic Today and Yesterday: Identities, Roots, and Heritage, 1991; Sanctuary Denied: Refugees from the Third Reich and Newfoundland Immigration Policy, 1906-1949, 1992; Alfred Valdmanis and the Politics of Survival, 2000. Contributor to books. **Address:** Department of History, Memorial University of Newfoundland, St. John's, NL, Canada A1C 5S7. **Online address:** gbassler@mun.ca

BASSO, Keith H(amilton). American, b. 1940. **Genres:** Language/Linguistics, Anthropology/Ethnology. **Career:** University of Arizona, Tucson, assistant professor, 1967-71, associate professor, 1972-76, professor of cultural anthropology, 1977-81; Yale University, New Haven, Conn., professor of cultural anthropology, 1982-87; University of New Mexico, Albuquerque, professor of cultural anthropology, 1987-. Member of Institute for Advanced Study, Princeton, N.J., 1975-76; Weatherhead fellow at School for American Research, Santa Fe, N.M., 1977-78; consultant to the White Mountain and San Carlos Apache tribes. **Publications:** Western Apache Witchcraft, 1969; The Cibecue Apache, 1970; Portraits of "The Whiteman": Linguistic Play and Cultural Symbols among the Western Apache, 1979; Western Apache Language and Culture: Essays in Linguistic Anthropology, 1990; Wisdom Sits in Places: Landscape and Language among the Western Apache, 1996. EDITOR: (with Morris Opler) Apachean Culture History and Ethnology, 1971; Western Apache Raiding and Warfare: From the Notes of Grenville Goodwin, 1971; (with Henry A. Selby) Meaning in Anthropology, 1976; (with S. Feld) Senses of Place, 1996. **Address:** Department of Anthropology, University of New Mexico, Albuquerque, NM 87131, U.S.A.

BASSOFF, Evelyn S(ilten). American, b. 1944. **Genres:** Human relations/Parenting, Psychology. **Publications:** Mothers and Daughters: Loving and Letting Go, 1988; Mothering Ourselves: Help and Healing for Adult Daughters, 1992; Between Mothers and Sons: The Making of Vital and Loving Men, 1994; Cherishing Our Daughters: How to Raise a Healthy, Confident Daughter, 1997. Contributor to professional journals. **Address:** 1634 Walnut St., no. 221, Boulder, CO 80302, U.S.A.

BASTA, Lofty L. Egyptian, b. 1933. **Genres:** Medicine/Health. **Career:** Ains Shams University, Cairo, Egypt, intern at university hospital, 1955-56, resident, 1956-58, instructor in clinical medicine, 1958-63, lecturer in cardiology, 1963-70, assistant professor, 1970-71; University of Iowa, Iowa City, senior fellow, 1971-72, research associate in cardiology, 197273, assistant

professor of medicine, 1973-74; University of Oklahoma Health Sciences Center, Oklahoma City, professor of medicine and head of Cardiovascular Section, 1974-76; St. John Medical Center, Tulsa, OK, director of cardiology, 1976-83; Hillcrest Medical Center, Tulsa, OK director of cardiology, 1976-92; Tampa General Hospital, Tampa, FL, chief of clinical cardiology, 1993-. Hammersmith Hospital, research fellow, 1960-61; Tulsa Heart Center, founder, 1976, consulting cardiologist, 197693. University of Oklahoma, Tulsa Medical Center, clinical professor, 1966-93; University of South Florida, professor, 1993-, director of Division of Cardiology, 1995-; visiting professor at educational institutions; public speaker on the history of medicine and on Egyptian history and medicine; guest on television programs. **Publications:** Essentials of Primary Care, 1983; A Graceful Exit: Life and Death on Your Own Terms, 1996. Contributor to medical books and medical journals. **Address:** Department of Internal Medicine, College of Medicine, University of South Florida, 12901 Bruce B. Downs, Tampa, FL 33612-4742, U.S.A.

BASTA, Samir Sanad. Egyptian/French, b. 1943. **Genres:** Novels, Novellas/Short stories, Humanities, Medicine/Health, Psychology, Writing/Journalism. **Career:** Writer. National Institute of Nutrition, Mexico, researcher, 1968-70; National Institute of Nutrition, Bogor, Indonesia, researcher and field team leader, 1971-73; World Bank, Washington, DC, nutrition expert, 1973-82; United Nations, UNICEF, representative in Khartoum, Sudan, 1982-86, director of evaluation department, New York, NY, 1986-90, director of Office for Europe, Geneva, Switzerland, 1990-95. Oxford University, visiting scholar in experimental psychology at Wolfson College, 1996; University of Geneva, member of Humanitarian Action Group at Institute of Legal Medicine; guest speaker at other institutions. **Publications:** Culture, Conflict, and Children, 2000. Contributor to books and professional and scholarly journals.

BASTABLE, Bernard. *See* BARNARD, Robert.

BASTIANICH, Lidia Matticchio. American (born Italy), b. 1947. **Genres:** Food and Wine. **Career:** Buonavia Restaurant, Forest Hills, NY, owner, 1972-81; Felidia Restaurant, NYC, owner, 1981-. Villa Secondo (Fresh Meadows, NY), owner, 1979-81; Becco Restaurant, coowner, 1992-; Frico Bar and Restaurant, co-owner, 1995-; Lidia's Restaurant (Kansas City, MO), co-owner, 1998-; Lidia's Flavors of Italy, partner. Esperienze Italian Travel, president, 1997-. Guest on television programs. **Publications:** (with J. Jacobson) La Cucina di Lidia, 1990; Lidia's Italian Table, 1998. **Address:** Felidia Restaurant, 243 East 58th St., New York, NY 10022, U.S.A. **Online address:** lidia@lidiasitaly.com

BASTIEN, Joseph William. American, b. 1935. **Genres:** Anthropology/Ethnology, Mythology/Folklore. **Career:** Roman Catholic mission priest of the Maryknoll Fathers, Maryknoll, NY, 1963-69; University of Texas at Arlington, professor of anthropology, 1977-. Tulane University, scholar in residence, 1978; consultant. **Publications:** (ed.) Health in the Andes, 1981; Mountain of the Condor: Metaphor and Ritual in an Andean Ayllu, 1985; Healers of the Andes: Kallawaya Herbalists and Their Medicinal Plants, 1987; Drum and Stethoscope: Integrating Ethnomedicine and Biomedicine in Bolivia, 1992; The Kiss of Death: Chaga's Disease in the Americas, 1998. **Address:** Department of Anthropology, University of Texas at Arlington, Box 19599, Arlington, TX 76012, U.S.A. **Online address:** bastien@uta.edu

BASTON, Lewis. American. **Genres:** Politics/Government. **Career:** Researcher and media consultant. Kingston University, research fellow. Historical consultant for BBC Television series; election commentator. **Publications:** (with A. Seldon) Major: A Political Life, 1997; Sleaze: The State of Britain, 2000; (with S. Henig) The Political Map of Britain, 2002; Reggie: The Life of Reginald Maulding, 2003; (with S. Henig) Politico's Guide to the General Election, 2003. Contributor to books. **Address:** Faculty of Human Science, Kingston University, Penrhyn Road, Kingston-upon-Thames, Surrey KT1 2EE, England.

BASWELL, Christopher. American, b. 1952. **Genres:** Literary criticism and history. **Career:** Universite de Geneve, Geneva, Switzerland, assistant, 1981-84; Barnard College, New York City, associate professor of English, 1984-, also cofounder and director of Barnard New Women Poets Prize. **Publications:** (co-ed) The Passing of Arthur, 1988; Virgil in Medieval England, 1995; (ed) Barnard Series of New Women Poets. **Address:** Department of English, Barnard College, 3009 Broadway, New York, NY 10027, U.S.A.

BATAILLE, Christophe. French, b. 1971. **Genres:** Novels. **Career:** Fiction writer. Ed. Grasset, Paris, France, editor. **Publications:** Annam, 1993, trans. by R. Howard, 1996; Absinthe, 1994; Le Maitre des Heures, 1997; Vive l'enfer, 1999; J'envie la felicite des betes, 2002. **Address:** 50 rue Lily, 92140 Clamart, France. **Online address:** cbatille@grasset.fr

BATALI, Mario. American, b. 1960. **Genres:** Food and Wine. **Career:** Chef, restaurant owner, and author. Po', New York, NY, chef/co-owner, 1993-; Babbo Ristorante Enoteca, New York, NY, chef/co-owner, 1998-; Lupa, New York, NY, chef/co-owner; Esca, New York, NY, chef/co-owner; Italian Wine Merchants, New York, NY, co-owner; The Food Network, New York, NY, television host of Molto Mario and Mario Eats Italy. **Publications:** Simple Italian Food: Recipes from My Villages, 1998; Holiday Food: Family Recipes for the Festive Time of the Year, 2000; The Babbo Cookbook, 2002. **Address:** Babbo Ristorante Enoteca, 110 Waverly Place, New York, NY 10011, U.S.A.

BAT-AMI, Miriam. American, b. 1950. **Genres:** Children's fiction. **Career:** University of Pittsburgh, PA, teaching fellow in English, 1980-84; Southwest Missouri State University, Springfield, instructor in English, 1984-89; Western Michigan University, Kalamazoo, assistant professor, 1989-94, associate professor, 1994-2000, professor of English, 2001-. **Publications:** Sea, Salt, and Air (picture book), 1993; When the Frost Is Gone, 1994; Dear Elijah (middle-grade novel), 1995; Two Suns in the Sky (young adult novel), 1999. Contributor of critical essays to journals. Contributor of short stories and poetry to periodicals. **Address:** Department of English, Western Michigan University, Kalamazoo, MI 49008, U.S.A. **Online address:** batami@wmich.edu

BATCHELOR, David. British, b. 1943. **Genres:** Novels, Novellas/Short stories. **Publications:** Brogan and Sons, 1976; A Dislocated Man, 1978; Children in the Dark, 1982; Why Tilbury?, 1985; Extracts from the Diary of Walter Nye (1874), 1999. **Address:** 52 Onslow Sq, London SW7, England.

BATCHELOR, John. British, b. 1942. **Genres:** Novels, Art/Art history, Literary criticism and history, Biography. **Career:** Birmingham University, lecturer in English, 1968-76; Oxford University, New College, fellow, 1976-90, senior tutor, 1985-87; University of Newcastle upon Tyne, Joseph Cowen Professor of English, 1990-, head of department, 1992-94; University of Lancaster, Ruskin Programme, honorary adjunct professor, 2002-. English Association, fellow, 1999-, chair of Higher Education Committee, 2001-. **Publications:** Breathless Hush, 1974; Mervyn Peake, 1974; The Edwardian Novelists, 1982; H.G. Wells, 1985; Lord Jim, 1988; Virginia Woolf: The Major Novels, 1991; Joseph Conrad: A Critical Biography, 1994; John Ruskin: No Wealth but Life (biography), 2000. EDITOR: Lord Jim, by Conrad, 1983; Victory, by Conrad, 1986; The Art of Literary Biography, 1995; Shakespearean Continuities, 1997. **Address:** Dept of English, University of Newcastle, Newcastle NE1 7RU, England.

BATCHELOR, R. E. British, b. 1934. **Genres:** Language/Linguistics, Literary criticism and history. **Career:** University of Besancon, France, teacher of English, 1957-59; English teacher in San Sebastian, Spain, 1959-60; University of Nottingham, England, teacher of French and Spanish, 1961-, now retired. Teacher and researcher at European universities. **Publications:** Unamuno, Novelist: A European Perspective, 1972; (with M. Offord) Using French: A Guide to Contemporary Usage, 1982, 3rd ed, 1999; (with C. Pountain) Using Spanish: A Guide to Contemporary Usage, 1992, 2nd ed., 2003; (with M. Offord) Using French Synonyms, 1993; Using Spanish Synonyms, 1994; (with M. Chebli Saadi) French for Marketing, 1997; (with M. Chebli Saadi) Usage Pratique et courant des synonymes anglais, 1998; L'Uso dei sinonimi (spagnolo), 2000; (with M.A. San Jose) Using Spanish Vocabulary, 2003; L'uso dei sinonimi inglese, 2003. Contributor to European studies journals. **Address:** 20 Moor Lane, Bramcote, Nottingham NG9 3FH, England. **Online address:** ronald@ronald48.fsnet.co.uk

BATE, Jonathan. British, b. 1958. **Genres:** Literary criticism and history, Novels. **Career:** Cambridge University, Cambridge, England, research fellow at St. Catharine's College, 1983-85, fellow of Trinity Hall and director of studies in English, 1985-90; University of Liverpool, Liverpool, England, King Alfred Professor of English Literature, 1991-. **Publications:** Shakespeare and the English Romantic Imagination, 1986; Shakespearean Constitutions: Politics, Theatre, Criticism, 1730-1830, 1989; Romantic Ecology: Wordsworth and the Environmental Tradition, 1991; Shakespeare and Ovid, 1993; The Genius of Shakespeare, 1997; The Cure for Love, 1998; The Song of the Earth, 2000. EDITOR: Charles Lamb: Essays of Elia, 1987; The Romantics on Shakespeare, 1992; The Arden Shakespeare: Titus Andronicus, 1995; Shakespeare: An Illustrated Stage History, 1996. **Address:** Department of English, University of Liverpool, Liverpool L69 3BX, England.

BATES, Craig D. American, b. 1952. **Genres:** Natural history, Anthropology/Ethnology. **Career:** National Park Service, Yosemite National Park, CA,

park technician in Division of Interpretation, 1973-76, Indian cultural specialist, 1976-80, assistant curator, 1980-82, curator of ethnography, 1982-. Merced Community College, instructor, 1974; California Department of Parks and Recreation, instructor, 1977-84; Point Reyes Field Seminars, instructor, 1978-88; Humboldt State University, instructor, 1980; Santa Barbara Museum of Natural History, research associate, 1983-; Miwok Archaeological Preserve of Marin, instructor at Coast Miwok/Pomo Dance Regalia Workshop, 1990, consultant to museums. **Publications:** (with F. La Pena) Legends of the Yosemite Miwok, 1981; The Indian Cultural Museum: A Guide to the Exhibits, 1985, rev. ed. (with M.J. Lee), 1987; (with M.J. Lee) Tradition and Innovation: A Basket History of the Indians of the Yosemite-Mono Lake Area, 1990; The Miwok in Yosemite: Southern Miwok Life, History and Language in the Yosemite Region, 1996; (with B.B. Kahn and B.L. Lanford) An Introduction to the Cheyenne-Arapaho Ledger Book from the Pamplin Collection, 1999. Work represented in anthologies. **Address:** Yosemite Museum, National Park Service, PO Box 577, Yosemite National Park, CA 95389, U.S.A. **Online address:** craig_bates@nps.gov

BATES, Karen Grigsby. American, b. 1951?. **Genres:** Novels. **Career:** Writer, and journalist. People, Los Angeles, CA, reporter for West Coast Bureau,; Los Angeles Times, Los Angeles, CA, contributing columnist; National Public Radio, commentator. **Publications:** (with K.E. Hudson) Basic Black: Home Training for Modern Times, 1996; Plain Brown Wrapper: An Alex Powell Novel, 2001. **Address:** c/o Carrie Feron, Avon Books/HarperCollins, 10 East 53rd St., New York, NY 10022, U.S.A.

BATESON, Mary Catherine. American, b. 1939. **Genres:** Anthropology/Ethnology, Autobiography/Memoirs. **Career:** Harvard University, instructor in Arabic, 1963-66, visiting scholar in anthropology, 1979-80; Ateneo de Manila University, Philippines, 1966-68, professor, then associate professor of anthropology; Brandeis University, Waltham, MA, senior research fellow in psychology and philosophy, 1968-69; Massachusetts Institute of Technology, research staff member, 1969-71; Northeastern University, Boston, MA, visiting professor of anthropology, 1969-71, 1974-75; organized Iranian National Character Study Group, Tehran, 1972-74; Damavand College, Tehran, professor of anthropology and dean of graduate studies, 1975-77; University of Northern Iran, Babolsar, professor of anthropology and dean of social science and humanities, 1977-79; Amherst College, MA, professor of anthropology, 1980-86, dean of faculty, 1980-83; George Mason University, Fairfax, VA, professor of anthropology and English, 1986-2002. President, Institute for Intercultural studies, NYC, 1979-. **Publications:** (ed. with T.A. Sebeok and A.S. Hayes) Approaches to Semiotics, 1964; Arab Language Handbook, 1967; Structural Continuity in Poetry: A Linguistic Study of Five Pre-Islamic Odes, 1970; Our Own Metaphor, 1972; With a Daughter's Eye: A Memoir of Margaret Mead and Gregory Bateson, 1984; (with G. Bateson) Angels Fear, 1987; Thinking AIDS, 1988; Composing a Life, 1990; Peripheral Visions: Learning along the Way, 1994; Full Circles, Overlapping Lives: Culture and Generation in Transition, 2000. Contributor to books. Contributor of articles on cultural anthropology, linguistics, and current affairs to professional journals. **Address:** 172 Lexington Ave, Cambridge, MA 02138, U.S.A. **Online address:** info@MaryCatherineBateson.com

BATT, Tanya Robyn. New Zealander, b. 1970. **Genres:** Mythology/Folklore. **Career:** Storyteller, author, and early childhood specialist. Imagined Worlds, Auckland, New Zealand, owner, 1995-. Facilitator at workshops for teachers and caregivers; teacher of creative dance and drama to children. **Publications:** Faery Favourites (audio recording), 2000; (Reteller) The Fabrics of Fairytale: Stories Spun from Far and Wide (with audio recording), 2000; Mermaid Tales (audio recording), 2001; The Terrible Queue, 2001; Imagined Worlds: A Journey through Expressive Arts in Early Childhood, 2001; A Child's Book of Fairies, 2002; The Fairy's Gift, 2002. Contributor of poetry to periodicals. **Address:** Imagined Worlds, PO Box 24566, Royal Oak, Auckland, New Zealand. **Online address:** faerybatt@hotmail.com

BATTERSBY, Christine. British, b. 1946. **Genres:** Art/Art history, Literary criticism and history, Philosophy, Women's studies and issues. **Career:** Greater London Council, London, England, administrative assistant, 1968-69; University of Warwick, Coventry, West Midlands, England, senior lecturer in philosophy, 1972-. **Publications:** Gender and Genius: Towards a Feminist Aesthetics, 1989; The Phenomenal Woman, 1998. Author of articles on feminism, philosophy, and aesthetics. **Address:** Department of Philosophy, University of Warwick, Coventry, W. Midlands CV4 7AL, England. **Online address:** c.battersby@warwick.ac.uk

BATTESTIN, Martin Carey. American, b. 1930. **Genres:** Literary criticism and history, Biography. **Career:** Wesleyan University, Middletown, CT, instructor, 1956-58, assistant professor, 1958-61; University of Virginia,

Charlottesville, assistant professor, 1961-63, associate professor, 1963-67, professor, 1967-75, Kenan Professor of English Literature, 1975-98, Emeritus, 1998-, Chairman of Dept., 1983-86. **Publications:** The Moral Basis of Fielding's Art, 1959; The Providence of Wit: Aspects of Form in Augustan Literature and the Arts, 1974; New Essays by Henry Fielding: His Contributions to the Craftsman (1734-1739) and Other Early Journalism, 1989; Henry Fielding: A Life, 1989; A Henry Fielding Companion, 2000. EDITOR/CO-EDITOR: Fielding's Joseph Andrews and Shamela, 1961; Fielding's Joseph Andrews, 1967; Twentieth-Century Interpretations of Tom Jones, 1968; Fielding's Tom Jones, 1975; Fielding's Amelia, 1983; British Novelists 1660-1800, 1985; The Correspondence of Henry and Sarah Fielding, 1993; (trans. by T. Smollett) The History and Adventures of the Renowned Don Quixote, 2003.

BATTIE, David. British, b. 1942. **Genres:** Antiques/Furnishings. **Career:** Reader's Digest, London, England, book designer, 1963-67; Sotheby's, London, expert and director, 1967-; writer. Regular broadcaster on radio and television; international lecturer. **Publications:** The Price Guide to Nineteenth- and Twentieth-Century British Porcelain, 1975, as Guide to Understanding Nineteenth- and Twentieth-Century British Porcelain, 1994; (with Turner) The Price Guide to Nineteenth- and Twentieth-Century British Pottery, 1979. EDITOR: Sotheby's Concise Encyclopedia of Porcelain, 1990; Sotheby's Concise Encyclopedia of Glass, 1991. **Address:** Sotheby's, 34/35 New Bond St, London W1A 2AA, England.

BATTISCOMBE, Georgina. British, b. 1905. **Genres:** Biography. **Publications:** Charlotte Mary Yonge, 1943; Two on Safari, 1946; English Picnics, 1949; Mrs. Gladstone, 1956; John Keble, 1963; Queen Alexandra, 1969; Lord Shaftesbury, 1974; Reluctant Pioneer: The Life of Elizabeth Wordsworth, 1978; Christina Rossetti, 1981; The Spencers of Althorp, 1985; Winter Song (anthology), 1992. **Address:** Thamesfield, Wargrave Rd, Henley on Thames, Oxon. RG9 2LX, England.

BATTLE, Richard V. (born United States), b. 1951. **Genres:** Business/Trade/Industry. **Career:** Burroughs Corp., Office Products Group, sales representative in Austin, TX, 1973-76, zone sales manager in Montgomery, AL, 1976-77; Bell & Howell Co., Microfilm Products Division, Austin, sales representative, 1977-86; Datatron Communication, Austin, sales representative, 1986-87; Bell & Howell Co., Austin, sales representative, 1987-88, western area sales manager, 1987-2001; KeyTrak, Austin, national sales manager, 2001-. Public speaker and trainer in leadership, personal development, volunteering, and sales techniques. Celebrity Golf Tournament, Inc., member of board of directors, 1981-86; John Ben Shepperd Public Leadership Forum, chair, 1986, member of board of directors, 1988-92, 1996-, board chair, 1990-91. **Publications:** The Volunteer Handbook: How to Organize and Manage a Successful Organization, 1988; Surviving Grief by God's Grace, 2002. **Address:** 124 Lido, Austin, TX 78734, U.S.A. **Online address:** rbat1@attglobal.net

BATTLES, Matthew. American. **Genres:** Air/Space topics. **Career:** Widener Library, selector of the HD Push Project; Houghton Library, librarian; Harvard Library Bulletin at Houghton Library, coordinating editor. **Publications:** Library: An Unquiet History, 2003. Contributor to publications. **Address:** Harvard University, Library, Cambridge, MA 02138, U.S.A. **Online address:** mbattles@fas.harvard.edu

BAUCOM, Donald R. American, b. 1940. **Genres:** Military/Defense/Arms control. **Career:** U.S. Air Force, career officer with aeronautical navigation rating, 1962-90, retired as lieutenant colonel; Strategic Defense Initiative Organization (now Ballistic Missile Defense Organization), Washington, DC, Air Force historian, 1987-90, civilian historian, 1990-. Served as communications and electronics officer in Spain and Thailand; U.S. Air Force Academy, teacher of military history; Air War College, faculty member; Airpower Research Institute, director of research. **Publications:** The Origins of SDI, 1944-1983, 1992. **Address:** 2418 Childs Lane, Alexandria, VA 22308-2124, U.S.A.

BAUDOT, Georges. French (born Spain), b. 1935. **Genres:** History. **Career:** Prytanee Militaire, paratrooper and professor, 1962-63; Ecole des Hautes Etudes Hispaniques, Madrid, Spain, member of Casa de Velazquez, 1963-66; Universite de Toulouse II-Le Mirail, France, associate professor, 1967-75, professor, 1976-, now emeritus, and director of Institut Pluridisciplinaire d'Etudes sur l'Amerique Latine. **Publications:** WORKS IN ENGLISH TRANSLATION: Utopie et Histoire au Mexique: Les premiers chroniqueurs de la civilisation mexicaine, 1520-1569, 1977, trans. as Utopia and History in Mexico: The First Chroniclers of Mexican Civilization, 1520-1569, 1995. OTHER: Les Lettres precolombiennes, 1976; Los sistemas politicos en His-

panoamerica, 1976; La vie quotidienne dans l'Amerique espagnole de Philippe II: XVIeme siecle, 1981; (with T. Todorov) Recits azteques de la conquete, 1983; La pugna franciscana por Mexico, 1990; (trans.) Poesie nahuatl d'amour et d'amitie, 1991; La Corona y la fundacion de los reinos americanos, 1992; (author of intro. and notes) Fray Andres de Olmos, Tratado sobre los siete pecados mortales, Instituto de 1996; Mexico y los albores del discurso colonial, 1996; (with M.A. Mendez) Armores prohibidos: La palabra condenada en el Mexico de los virreyes, 1997. EDITOR: Tratado de hechicerias y sortilegios de Fray Andres de Olmos, 1979; (and author of intro. and notes) Fray Toribio de Motolinia, Historia de los Indios de la Nueva Espana, 1985; (with J. de Durant-Forest and contrib.) Mille ans de civilisation mesoamericaine: Des Mayas aux Azteques, Vol I: Danse avec les Dieux, Vol II: La quete du Cinquieme Soleil, 1995; (with B.G. Cuaron) Historia de la Literatura Mexicana, Vol I: Las literaturas amerindias de Mexico y la literatura en espanol del siglo XVI, 1996. **Address:** Residence de l'Observatoire, 1 rue des Redoutes, 31500 Toulouse, France. **Online address:** baudot@univ-tlsed.fr

BAUER, Caroline Feller. American, b. 1935. **Genres:** Novellas/Short stories, Children's fiction, Children's non-fiction, Literary criticism and history. **Career:** Lecturer and educational consultant; Children's librarian, New York Public Library, NYC, 1958-59, 1961; Librarian, Colorado Rocky Mountain School, Carbondale, 1963-66; Associate Professor of Library Science, University of Oregon, Eugene, 1966-79; Producer, Caroline's Corner, KOAP-TV, 1973-74. **Publications:** Children's Literature: A Teletext, 1973; Getting It Together with Books, 1984; Storytelling, 1974; Caroline's Corner, 1974; Handbook for Storytellers, 1977; Children's Literature, 1978; My Mom Travels a Lot, 1981; This Way to Books, 1983; Too Many Books, 1974; Celebrations: Read-Aloud Holiday and Theme Book Program, 1985; Presenting Reader's Theater Plays and Poems to Read Aloud, 1987; Midnight Snowman, 1987; Halloween: Stories and Poems, 1988; Windy Day: Stories and Poems, 1988; Read For the Fun of It, 1992; Putting on a Play, 1993; New Handbook for Storytellers, 1994; Thanksgiving Day, 1994. LEADING KIDS TO BOOKS THROUGH... SERIES: Magic, 1996; Puppets, 1997; Crafts, 2000. EDITOR: Rainy Day: Stories and Poems, 1986; Snowy Day: Stories and Poems, 1986; Valentines Day, 1993; The Poetry Break, 1995. **Address:** 10150 Collins Ave, Miami, FL 33154-1654, U.S.A.

BAUER, Douglas. American, b. 1945. **Genres:** Local history/Rural topics. **Career:** Better Homes and Gardens, advertising copywriter; Playboy, associate editor; freelance journalist; Bennington College, member of core faculty for MFA program in writing and literature. **Publications:** Prairie City, Iowa: Three Seasons at Home, 1979; Dexterity, 1989; The Very Air, 1993; The Book of Famous Iowans, 1997. **Address:** 227 W Canton St, Boston, MA 02116-5860, U.S.A.

BAUER, Henry H. Also writes as Josef Martin. American (born Austria), b. 1931. **Genres:** Education, Sciences. **Career:** University of Sydney, Australia, lecturer and senior lecturer in agricultural chemistry, 1958-65; University of Michigan, Ann Arbor, visiting scientist, department of chemistry, 1965-66; University of Kentucky, associate professor, 1966-69, professor of chemistry, 1969-78; Virginia Polytechnic Institute and State University, Blacksburg, professor of chemistry and science studies, 1978-99, dean, College of Arts & Sciences, 1978-86. University of Southampton, visiting professor of chemistry, 1972-73; Rikagaku Kenkyusho, Tokyo, visiting professor, Japan Society for the Promotion of Science, 1974. Journal of Scientific Exploration, editor-in-chief, 2002-. **Publications:** (with B. Breyer) Alternating Current Polarography and Tensammetry, 1963; Electrodics-Modern Ideas Concerning Electrode Reactions, 1972; (ed. with G.D. Christian and J.E. O'Reilly) Instrumental Analysis, 1978; Beyond Velikovsky: The History of a Public Controversy, 1984; The Enigma of Loch Ness: Making Sense of a Mystery, 1986; (as Josef Martin) To Rise above Principle: The Memoirs of an Unreconstructed Dean, 1988; Scientific Literacy and the Myth of the Scientific Method, 1992; Science or Pseudoscience, 2001; Fatal Attractions: The Troubles with Science, 2001. Contributor to periodicals and academic journals. **Address:** 1306 Highland Circle, Blacksburg, VA 24060-5623, U.S.A. **Online address:** hhbauer@vt.edu; www.henryhbauer.homestead.com

BAUER, Marion Dane. American, b. 1938. **Genres:** Children's fiction, Young adult fiction, Young adult non-fiction, Picture/board books. **Career:** Writer. High school teacher, Waukesha, WI, 1962-64; Hennepin Technical Center, Minneapolis, MN, instructor in creative writing for adult education program, 1975-78; instructor, University of Minnesota Continuing Education for Women, 1978-85, Institute for Children's Literature, 1982-85, and The Loft, 1987-95; Vermont College, Faculty-MFA in Writing for Children and Young Adults, 1995-. **Publications:** FOR YOUNG ADULTS. FICTION: Shelter from the Wind, 1976; Foster Child, 1977; Tangled Butterfly, 1980;

Rain of Fire, 1983; Like Mother, Like Daughter, 1985; On My Honor, 1986; Touch the Moon, 1987; A Dream of Queens and Castles, 1990; Face to Face, 1991; Ghost Eye, 1992; A Taste of Smoke, 1993; A Question of Trust, 1994; (ed. and contrib.) Am I Blue? Coming out from the Silence, 1994; An Early Winter, 1999; Runt, 2002; Land of the Buffalo Bones, 2003. NONFICTION: What's Your Story?: A Young Person's Guide to Writing Fiction, 1992; A Writer's Story: From Life to Fiction, 1995; Our Stories: A Fiction Workshop for Young Authors, 1996. FOR CHILDREN. PICTURE BOOKS: When I Go Camping with Grandma, 1995; Alison's Wings, 1996; Alison's Fierce and Ugly Halloween, 1997; Alison's Puppy, 1997; Turtle Dreams, 1997; If You Were Born a Kitten, 1997; Bear's Hiccups, 1998; Christmas in the Forest, 1998; Sleep, Little One, Sleep, 1999; Jason's Bears, 2000; My Mother Is Mine, 2001; If You Had a Nose Like an Elephant's Trunk, 2001; Frog's Best Friend, 2002; Love Song for a Baby, 2002; The Kissing Monster, 2002; Uh-Oh, 2002; Toes, Ears and Nose, 2003; Snow, 2003; Clouds, 2003; Why Do Kittens Purr?, 2003; The Very Best Daddy, 2004; Rain, 2004; Wind, 2004. **Address:** 8861 Basswood Rd, Eden Prairie, MN 55344, U.S.A. **Online address:** mdanebauer@aol.com

BAUER, Susan Wise. (born United States), b. 1968. **Genres:** Education. **Career:** Writer. Peace Hill Press, editorial director. College of William and Mary, faculty member. **Publications:** The Revolt, 1996; Though the Darkness Hide Thee, 1998; (with Jessie Wise) The Well-trained Mind: A Guide to Classical Education at Home, 1999; The Story of the World: History for the Classical Child, Volume 1: Ancient Times, 2002, Volume 2: The Middle Ages, 2003; The Well-educated Adult, forthcoming. Contributing editor. **Address:** Richard Henshaw, Richard Henshaw Group, 127 West 24th St., 4th Floor, New York, NY 10011, U.S.A.

BAUER, Tricia. American. **Genres:** Novels, Novellas/Short stories. **Career:** Writer. Millbrook Press, Brookfield, CT, director of special markets and rights for children's books. **Publications:** Working Women and Other Stories (short stories), 1995. Boondocking (novel), 1997. Contributor of fiction and poetry to anthologies and periodicals. Contributor of travel features to the New York Times and the International Herald Tribune (Paris). **Address:** Millbrook Press, 2 Old New Milford Rd., Brookfield, CT 06804, U.S.A.

BAUER, Yehuda. Israeli (born Czech Republic), b. 1926. **Genres:** History. **Career:** Professor, and Head, Dept. of Holocaust Studies, 1968-95, and International Center for the Study of Antisemitism, 1983-95, Hebrew University, Jerusalem. Chair, International Institute for Holocaust Studies, Yad Vashem, Jerusalem, Editorial Board, Yad Vashem Studies, and Yalkut Moreshet. **Publications:** From Diplomacy to Resistance, 1970; Flight and Rescue, 1970; They Chose Life, 1973; My Brother's Keeper, 1974; The Holocaust in Historical Perspective, 1978; The Jewish Emergence from Powerlessness, 1978; American Jewry and the Holocaust, 1981; A History of the Holocaust, 1982; Out of the Ashes, 1989; Jews for Sale?, 1994; Rethinking the Holocaust, 2001. **Address:** 8, Hagana St., 97852 Jerusalem, Israel.

BAUERLEIN, Mark (Weightman). American, b. 1959. **Genres:** Literary criticism and history. **Career:** University of California, Los Angeles, lecturer in English, 1988-89; Emory University, Atlanta, GA, assistant professor of English, 1989-. **Publications:** Whitman and the American Idiom, 1991; (ed.) Purloined Letters; (ed.) Turning Word, 1996; Pragmatic Mind, 1997; Literary Criticism: An Autopsy, 1997; Negrophobia, 2001. **Address:** Department of English, Emory University, 302 N Callaway, Atlanta, GA 30322, U.S.A. **Online address:** engmb@emory.edu

BAUGHAN, Peter Edward. British, b. 1934. **Genres:** History, Area studies, Transportation. **Career:** Technical Assistant, Parliamentary Office, Chief Civil Engineer's Dept., British Railways, London, 1960-66; Technical Officer, Dept. of Transportation & Development, GLC, 1966-86. **Publications:** North of Leeds, 1966; The Railways of Wharfedale, 1969; The Chester & Holyhead Railway, vol. I, 1972; A Regional History of the Railways of Great Britain, vol. XI, North and Mid Wales, 1980; Midland Railway North of Leeds, 1987; The North Wales Coast Railway, 1988. **Address:** 55 Coulstock Rd, Burgess Hill, Sussex RH15 9XZ, England.

BAUGHMAN, Michael. American, b. 1937. **Genres:** Adult non-fiction, Philosophy. **Career:** Writer. **Publications:** NONFICTION: The Perfect Fishing Trip, 1985; Ocean Fishing, 1986; Mohawk Blood, 1995; A River Seen Right, 1995. Contributor to magazines. **Address:** 125 Reiten Dr, Ashland, OR 97520, U.S.A.

BAUGHMAN, T. H. American, b. 1947. **Genres:** History. **Career:** CBS Inc., in marketing and sales, 1976-84; John Wiley and Sons Inc., NYC, manager, 1984-85; Wesleyan College, Macon, GA, instructor, 1985-88; John Wiley and Sons Inc., manager, 1988-90; Benedictine College, Atchison, KS, associate professor and head of department, 1990-2000, dean, College of Liberal Arts, 2000-04, professor of history, 2004-. **Publications:** Before the Heroes Came: Antarctica in the 1890s, 1994; Ice: The Antarctic Diary of Charles Passel, 1995; Pilgrims on the Ice: Robert Falcon Scott's First Expedition, 1999; A Companion to Modern World History, 2003. Contributor to periodicals. **Address:** Dept of History, University of Central Oklahoma, Edmond, OK 73034-5209, U.S.A. **Online address:** tbaughman@ucok.edu

BAUM, Bernard H. American (born Germany), b. 1926. **Genres:** Administration/Management, Sociology. **Career:** University of Illinois at Chicago, professor of management and sociology, 1969-, professor of health policy and administration, 1973-. **Publications:** Decentralization of Authority in a Bureaucracy, 1961; (with R.W. French) Basics for Business, 1968. EDITOR: (with P.F. Sorensen Jr.) Perspectives on Organizational Behavior, 1973; (with others) Dimensions in Organization Behavior: Influence, Authority and Power, 1975; (with R. Babcock and P. Sorensen) Intervention: The Management Use of Organizational Research, 1975; As if People Mattered: Dignity in Organization, 2005. **Address:** School of Public Health, Health Policy and Administration (M/C923), University of Illinois at Chicago, 1601 W Taylor St, Chicago, IL 60612, U.S.A. **Online address:** bhbaum@uic.edu

BAUMAN, Christian. American, b. 1970. **Genres:** Novels. **Career:** Writer, musician, songwriter, cook, house painter, clerk, editor, and laborer. **Publications:** The Ice beneath You, 2002. **Address:** c/o Publicity Department, Simon & Schuster, 1230 Avenue of the Americas, New York, NY 10020, U.S.A. **Online address:** christianbauman@pobox.com

BAUMAN, Janina (G.). British (born Poland), b. 1926. **Genres:** Novellas/Short stories, Autobiography/Memoirs. **Career:** Film Polski, Warsaw, Poland, translator, researcher, and script editor, 1948-68; John Smeaton High School, Leeds, England, librarian, 1974-79; writer. **Publications:** Winter in the Morning: A Young Girl's Life in the Warsaw Ghetto and Beyond, 1939-1945, 1986; A Dream of Belonging: My Years in Postwar Poland, 1988. Three books and many short stories in Polish published in Poland, 1989-2000. **Address:** 1 Lawnswood Gardens, Leeds, W. Yorkshire LS16 6HF, England.

BAUMAN, Richard W. Canadian, b. 1951. **Genres:** Law. **Career:** Private practice of law in Edmonton, Alberta, 1982-83; Dalhousie University, Halifax, Nova Scotia, assistant professor, 1984-85; Alberta Law Reform Institute, Admonton, counsel, 1987-88; University of Alberta, Edmonton, professor of law, 1988-. Duke University, visiting scholar, 1994-95. **Publications:** (ed. with J. Hart) Explorations in Difference: Law, Culture, and Politics, 1996; Critical Legal Studies: A Guide to the Literature, 1996; Aristotle's Logic of Education, 1998. **Address:** 409 Law Centre, University of Alberta, Edmonton, AB, Canada. **Online address:** rbauman@law.ualberta.ca

BAUMAN, Zygmunt. British (born Poland), b. 1925. **Genres:** Sociology. **Career:** University of Leeds, Professor of Sociology, 1971-, now Emeritus. Sr. Lecturer, University of Warsaw, 1956-59; Dozent to Professor of Sociology, University of Tel Aviv, 1968-71. **Publications:** Between Class and Elite, 1972; Culture as Praxis, 1973; Towards a Critical Sociology, 1976; Socialism: The Active Utopia, 1976; Hermeneutics and Social Science, 1978; Memories of Class, 1982; Legislators and Interpreters: On Modernity, Postmodernity and Intellectuals, 1987; Freedom, 1988; Modernity and the Holocaust, 1989; Thinking Sociologically: An Introduction for Everyone, 1990; Modernity and the Ambivalence, 1991; Intonations of Postmodernity, 1992; Mortality, Immortality, and Other Life Strategies, 1992; Postmodern Ethics, 1994; Life in Fragments, 1995; Postmodernity and Its Discontents, 1997; Work, Consumerism and the New Poor, 1998; Globalization: The Human Consequences, 1998; Liquid Modernity, 1999; Individualized Society, 2000; Community: Seeking Safety in an Uncertain World, 2001. **Address:** Dept. of Sociology, University of Leeds, Leeds LS2 9JT, England.

BAUMANN, Carol Edler. American, b. 1932. **Genres:** International relations/Current affairs. **Career:** University of Wisconsin-Madison, Dept. of Political Science, instructor, 1957-61, National Security Studies Group, project associate, 1958-61; University of Wisconsin-Milwaukee, lecturer, 1961-62, assistant professor, 1962-67, director of Institute of World Affairs, 1964-97, associate professor, 1967-72, professor of political science, 1972-97, director of Office of Intl. Studies and Programs, 1982-88; Dept. of State, deputy assistant secretary for Assessments and Research, 1979-81. **Publications:** Political Cooperation in NATO, 1960; Western Europe: What Path to Integration?, 1967; (with K. Wahner) Great Decisions-1968, 1969; The Diplomatic Kidnappings, 1973; Europe in NATO, 1987. Contributor to books. **Address:** W6248 Lake Ellen Dr, Cascade, WI 53011, U.S.A. **Online address:** cbaumann@excel.net

BAUMBACH, Jonathan. American, b. 1933. **Genres:** Novels, Novellas/ Short stories, Literary criticism and history. **Career:** Stanford University, California, instructor, 1958-60; OH State University, Columbus, instructor, 1961-62, assistant professor, 1962-64; New York University, NYC, assistant professor, 1964-66; Brooklyn College, City University of New York, associate professor, 1966-70, 1971-72, professor of English, 1972-. Film Critic, Partisan Review, 1974-. **Publications:** NOVELS: A Man to Conjure With, 1965; What Comes Next, 1968; Reruns, 1974; Babble, 1976; Chez Charlotte and Emily, 1979; My Father More or Less, 1982; Separate Hours, 1990; Seven Wives: A Romance, 1994; D-tours: A Novel, 1998; B: A Novel, 2002. SHORT STORIES: The Return of Service, 1980; The Life and Times of Major Fiction, 1987; On the Way to My Father's Funeral: New and Selected Stories, 2005. CRITICISM: The Landscape of Nightmare: Studies in the Contemporary American Novel, 1965; Statements: New Fiction from the Fiction Collective, 1974. EDITOR: (with A. Edelstein) Moderns and Contemporaries (anthology), 1968; Writers as Teachers, Teachers as Writers, 1970; (with P. Spielberg) Statements 2: New Fiction, 1977. **Address:** Dept. of English, Brooklyn College, Brooklyn, NY 11210, U.S.A.

BAUMGARDNER, Jennifer. American, b. 1970. **Genres:** Women's studies and issues, Ghost Writer. **Career:** Writer; public speaker; Ms., New York, NY, former editor; Farrar, Straus & Giroux, Feminist Classics Series, editor, 2001. **Publications:** (with A. Richards) Manifesta: Young Women, Feminism, and the Future, 2000; (ghostwriter) G. Feldt, Abortion from a Global Perspective, 2002; Recipe-Tested, 2004; Look Both Ways, forthcoming. Contributor to books and magazines. **Address:** c/o Author Mail, Farrar, Straus & Giroux, 19 Union Sq W, New York, NY 10003, U.S.A. **Online address:** jennifer@manifesta.net

BAUMOL, William J. American, b. 1922. **Genres:** Economics. **Career:** Professor Emeritus of Economics and Senior Research Economist, Princeton University, NJ (joined faculty, 1949). Professor of Economics, New York University, NYC, 1971-. President, Association of Environmental and Resource Economists, and Eastern Economic Association, 1978-79, American Economic Association, 1981, and Atlantic Economic Society, 1985. **Publications:** Economic Dynamics, 1951; Welfare Economics and the Theory of the State, 1952, rev. ed., 2001; (with L.V. Chandler) Economic Processes and Policies, 1954; Business Behavior, Value and Growth, 1959, rev. ed., 1966; Economic Theory and Operations Analysis, 1961, 4th ed., 1976; The Stock Market and Economic Efficiency, 1965; (with W.G. Bowen) Performing Arts: The Economic Dilemma, 1966; Portfolio Theory, 1970; (with M. Marcus) Economics of Academic Libraries, 1973; (with W.E. Oates) The Theory of Environmental Policy, 1974; (with W.E. Oates and S.A. Batey Blackman) Economics, Environmental Policy, and the Quality of Life, 1978; (with A.S. Blinder) Economics: Principles and Policy, 1979, 6th ed., 1994; (with J.C. Panzar and R.D. Willig) Contestable Markets and the Theory of Industry Structure, 1982; Superfairness, 1986; Microtheory, 1986; (with L. Osberg and E.N. Wolff) The Information Economy and the Implications of Unbalanced Growth, 1989; (with S.A. Batey Blackman and E.N. Wolff) Productivity and American Leadership, 1989; (with S.M. Goldfeld et al.) Economics of Mutual Fund Markets, 1990; (with S.A. Batey Blackman) Perfect Markets and Easy Virtue, 1991; Entrepreneurship, Management & the Structure of Payoffs, 1993; (with G. Sidak) Toward Competition in Local Telephony, 1994; (with G. Sidak) Transmission Pricing and Stranded Costs in the Electric Power Industry, 1995. EDITOR: (with S.M. Goldfeld) Precursors in Mathematical Economics, 1968; Public and Private Enterprise in a Mixed Economy, 1980; (with H. Baumol) Inflation and the Performing Arts, 1984; (with K. McLennan) Productivity Growth and U.S. Competitiveness, 1985; (with R.R. Nelson & E.N. Wolff) Convergence of Productivity, 1994; (with W.E. Becker) Assessing Educational Practices, 1995; (with A.S. Bloinder) Microeconomics: Principles and Policy, 1996. **Address:** Dept. of Economics, New York University, 269 Mercer St, New York, NY 10003, U.S.A.

BAUMS, Roosevelt. American, b. 1946. **Genres:** Inspirational/Motivational Literature, Theology/Religion. **Career:** Preacher; motivational speaker, poet. Ordained Methodist elder, 1997. Worldwide Love and Brotherhood Ministry, Syracuse, NY, founder. **Publications:** A Minority View of How to Campaign for Political Office, 1982; In Search of the Dove That Brings Love (children's prayers), 1997; Welcome to Our Child's World (poems). Author of poems and songs. **Address:** Worldwide Love and Brotherhood Ministry, 436 W Ostrander Ave, Syracuse, NY 13205, U.S.A. **Online address:** r.baums@worldnet.att.net

BAUMSLAG, Naomi. American (born Republic of South Africa), b. 1936. **Genres:** Medicine/Health. **Career:** Baragwanath Hospital, Johannesburg, South Africa, 1959-62; Department of Health and Human Services, Rockville, MD, director of International Health Nutrition Division, 1979-84;

Women's International Public Health Network, Bethesda, Maryland, founder and president, 1987-; Georgetown University Medical School, Washington, DC, clinical professor of pediatrics, 1987-. **Publications:** (ed.) Family Care: A Guide, 1973; (with C.D. Williams and D.B. Jelliffe) Mother and Child Health: Delivering the Services, 1985; (with D.L. Michels) A Woman's Guide to Yeast Infections, 1992; (with D.L. Michels) Milk, Money, and Madness: The Culture and Politics of Breastfeeding, 1995. **Address:** Women's International Public Health Network, 7100 Oak Forest Ln, Bethesda, MD 20817, U.S.A. **Online address:** wiphn@erols.com

BAUSCH, Richard. American, b. 1945. **Genres:** Novels, Novellas/Short stories. **Career:** Writer. National Endowment for the Arts Creative Writing Fellow, 1982; Guggenheim Fellow in Fiction, 1984. **Publications:** NOVELS: Real Presence, 1980; Take Me Back, 1981; The Last Good Time, 1984; Mr. Field's Daughter, 1989; Violence, 1992; Rebel Powers, 1993; In the Night of the Season, 1998. STORIES: Spirits and Other Stories, 1987; Fireman's Wife and Other Stories, 1990; Rare and Endangered Species, 1994; Someone to Watch over Me, 1999. **Address:** English Dept, 4400 University Drive, George Mason University, Fairfax, VA 22030-4444, U.S.A.

BAVLY, Dan A(braham). Israeli, b. 1929. **Genres:** Economics, International relations/Current affairs. **Career:** Jerusalem Post, Jerusalem, Israel, economics journalist, 1955-57; Bavly Millner & Co. Tel-Aviv, Israel, executive partner, 1961-95. **Publications:** (with D. Kimche) The Sandstorm: The Arab-Israeli War of June 1967; Prelude and Aftermath, 1968; The Subterranean Economy, 1982; (with E. Salpeter) Fire in Beirut, 1983; Corporate Governance and Accountability, 1998. **Address:** Harashin, 24954 Galilee, Israel. **Online address:** dan_b@netvision.net.il

BAWCUTT, Priscilla (June). British, b. 1931. **Genres:** Literary criticism and history. **Career:** Independent scholar and writer. University of Liverpool, past member of literature faculty. **Publications:** Gavin Douglas: A Critical Study, 1974; Dunbar the Makar, 1992; The Poems of William Dunbar, 1998. EDITOR: The Shorter Poems of Gavin Douglas, 1967; (with F. Riddy) Longer Scottish Poems, 1987; (with F. Riddy) Selected Poems of Henryson and Dunbar, 1992.

BAWDEN, Nina (Mary). British, b. 1925. **Genres:** Novels, Mystery/Crime/ Suspense, Children's fiction. **Career:** Novelist, magistrate. **Publications:** Who Calls the Tune (in U.S. as Eyes of Green), 1953; The Odd Flamingo, 1954; Change Here for Babylon, 1955; The Solitary Child, 1956; Devil by the Sea, 1957; Just Like a Lady (in U.S. as Glass Slippers Always Pinch), 1960; In Honour Bound, 1961; Tortoise by Candlelight, 1963; The Secret Passage (in U.S. as The House of Secrets), 1963; On the Run (in U.S. as Three on the Run), 1964; Under the Skin, 1964; A Little Love, A Little Learning, 1966; The White Horse Gang, 1966; The Witch's Daughter, 1966; A Handful of Thieves, 1967; A Woman of My Age, 1967; The Grain of Truth, 1968; The Runaway Summer, 1969; The Birds on the Trees, 1970; Squib, 1971; Anna Apparent, 1972; Carrie's War; George beneath a Paper Moon, 1974; The Peppermint Pig, 1975; Afternoon of a Good Woman, 1976; Rebel on a Rock, 1978; Familiar Passions, 1979; Walking Naked, 1981; Kept in the Dark, 1982; The Ice House, 1983; The Finding, 1985; Circles of Deceit, 1987; Keeping Henry, 1988; The Outside Child, 1989; Family Money, 1991; Humbug, 1992; The Real Plato Jones, 1993; In My Own Time-Almost an Autobiography, 1994; Granny the Pag, 1994; A Nice Change, 1997; Off the Road, 1998; Ruffian on the Stair, 2001. **Address:** 22 Noel Rd, London N1 8HA, England.

BAX, Martin (Charles Owen). British, b. 1933. **Genres:** Children's fiction, Medicine/Health, Novels. **Career:** Research Community Paediatrician, Charing Cross/Westminster Medical School, London, since 1974. Ed., Ambit Magazine, since 1959. **Publications:** The Hospital Ship, 1959; (with J. Bernal) Your Child's First Five Years, 1974; (with H. Hart and S.M. Jenkins) Child Development and Child Health; Edmund Went Far Away (children's story book, illustrated by Michael Foreman). **Address:** 17 Priory Gardens, Highgate, London N6 5QY, England.

BAXTER, Brian. See Obituaries.

BAXTER, Craig. American, b. 1929. **Genres:** History, International relations/Current affairs, Politics/Government. **Career:** University of Pennsylvania, Philadelphia, instructor in history, 1955-56; U.S. Dept. of State, foreign service officer, 1956-80; Juniata College, Huntingdon, PA, professor of politics and history, 1981-99, professor emeritus, 1991-. American Institute of Bangladesh Studies, president, 1989-98; American Institute of Pakistan Studies, president, 1993-99. **Publications:** The Jana Sangh: A Biography of an Indian Political Party, 1969; District Voting Trends in India: A Research Tool, 1969; Bangladesh: A New Nation in an Old Setting, 1984; From Martial Law to Martial Law: Politics in the Punjab 1919-1958, 1985; Zia's Pakistan: Politics and Stability in a Frontline State, 1985; Government and Politics in South Asia, 1987, 5th ed., 2002; Historical Dictionary of Bangladesh, 1989, 3rd ed., 2003; Pakistan under the Military: Eleven Years of Zia ul-Haq, 1991; Pakistan: Authoritarianism in the 1980s, 1991; Bangladesh: From a Nation to a State, 1997; Pakistan 1997, 1997; Pakistan 2000, 2000; Pakistan at the Brink, 2004. **Address:** RR4 Box 103, Huntingdon, PA 16652, U.S.A. **Online address:** cbaxter@penn.com

BAXTER, John. Australian, b. 1939. **Genres:** Novels, Science fiction/Fantasy, Film, Biography. **Career:** Director of Publicity, Australian Commonwealth Film Unit., Sydney, 1968-70; Lecturer in Film and Theatre, Hollins Coll, 1974-78; freelance TV producer and screenwriter, 1978-87; Visiting Lecturer, Mitchell College, Australia, 1987; freelance journalist and broadcaster, Paris and Los Angeles, 1989-. **Publications:** The Off Worlders, 1966, in Australia as The God Killers, 1968; (adaptor) Adam's Woman, 1968; Hollywood in the Thirties, 1968; (ed.) The Pacific Book of Australian Science Fiction, 1970; The Australian Cinema, 1970; Science Fiction in the Cinema, 1970; The Gangster Film, 1970; The Cinema of Josef von Sternberg, 1971; The Cinema of John Ford, 1971; (ed.) The Second Pacific Book of Australian Science Fiction, 1971; Hollywood in the Sixties, 1972; Sixty Years of Hollywood, 1973; An Appalling Talent: Ken Russell, 1973; Stunt: The Story of the Great Movie Stunt Men, 1974; The Hollywood Exiles, 1976; (with T.R. Atkins) The Fire Came By, 1976; King Vidor, 1976; The Hermes Fall, 1978; The Bidders (in U.K. as Bidding), 1979; The Kid, 1981; (with B. Norris) The Video Handbook, 1982; The Black Yacht, 1982; Who Burned Australia? The Ash Wednesday Fires, 1984; Filmstruck, 1987; The Time Guardian (screenplay), 1988; Bondi Blues, 1992; Fellini, 1993; Bunuel, 1994; Steven Spielberg: The Unauthorized Biography, 1996; Woody Allen, 1998; George Lucas, 1999. **Address:** Curtis Brown, 28/29 Haymarket, London SW1Y 4SP, England.

BAXTER(-WRIGHT), Keith (Stanley). Welsh, b. 1935. **Genres:** Plays/Screenplays. **Career:** Actor, director, and writer. Made stage debut in Oxford and Worthing Repertories, 1956-57. Appeared in films; appeared in British Broadcasting Corporation (BBC-TV) specials. **Publications:** PLAYS: 56 Duncan Terrace, 1982; Cavell, England, 1982; Barnaby and the Old Boys, 1987. OTHER: My Sentiments Exactly, 1999. **Address:** c/o Chatto & Linnit, 123A Kings Rd, London SW3 4Pl, England.

BAXTER, Mary Lynn. American, b. 1943. **Genres:** Romance/Historical. **Career:** Houston Independent Schools, Houston, TX, librarian, 1965-72. **Publications:** ROMANCE NOVELS: Saddle Up, 1996; Hot Texas Nights, 1996; A Day in April, 1996; Southern Fires, 1996. **Address:** 807 W. Frank Ave., Lufkin, TX 75904, U.S.A.

BAXTER, Paula A. American, b. 1954. **Genres:** Art/Art history. **Career:** State University of New York College at Purchase, visual arts librarian, 1981-83; Museum of Modern Art, New York, NY, associate librarian in reference department, 1983-87; New York Public Library, New York, NY, curator of Art and Architecture Collection, 1987-. Workshop instructor; public speaker; library advisor to Republic of Singapore. **Publications:** Encyclopedia of Native American Jewelry, 2000; Southwest Silver Jewelry, 2001. Author of exhibition catalogs. Contributor of articles and reviews to periodicals. **Address:** New York Public Library, 476 5th Ave Rm 313, New York, NY 10018, U.S.A. **Online address:** pbaxter@nypl.org

BAXTER, Stephen. British, b. 1957. **Genres:** Science fiction/Fantasy, Novellas/Short stories, Information science/Computers. **Career:** Worked as a teacher of mathematics, physics, and information technology; full-time writer, 1995-. **Publications:** SCIENCE FICTION NOVELS: Anti-Ice, 1993; The Time Ships, 1995; Web 2027, 1999; (with A.C. Clarke) The Light of Other Days, 2000; Evolution, 2002. XEELEE SEQUENCE: Raft, 1991; Timelike Infinity, 1992; Flux, 1993; Ring, 1994; Vacuum Diagrams (stories), 1997. NASA TRILOGY: Voyage, 1996; Titan, 1997; Moonseed, 1998. MAMMOTH TRILOGY: Silverhair, 1999; Longtusk, 2001; Icebones, 2002. MANIFOLD SERIES: Manifold: Time, 1999; Manifold: Space, 2000; Manifold: Origin, 2001; Phase Space, 2002. NONFICTION: Angular Distribution Analysis in Acoustics, 1986; (with D. Lisburn) Reengineering Information Technology: Success through Empowerment, 1994; The Role of the IT/IS Manager, 1996; Deep Future, 2001; Omegatropic, 2001. OTHER: Irina (e-book), 1996; Gulliverzone (young adult novel), 1997; Webcrash (young adult novel), 1998; Traces (science fiction stories), 1998. Writer for television. Work represented in science fiction anthologies. Contributor of articles, short stories, and reviews to scientific and computing journals and science fiction magazines. **Address:** c/o PFD, Drury House, 34-43 Russell Street, London WC2B 5HA, England. **Online address:** sbaxter100@aol.com

BAY, Jeanette Graham. American, b. 1928. **Genres:** Novellas/Short stories. **Career:** Bay's Nursery School, Macedon, NY, founder and teacher, 1963-74; YMCA Preschool, Canandaigua, NY, director and teacher, 1974-85; Wee Wonders, Victor, NY, teacher, 1987-89; Child Time Children's Center, Fairport, NY, teacher, 1990-93. President of the woman's group of her church as well as a Sunday School teacher and member of the senior choir. **Publications:** Alleyside Book of Flannelboard Stories, 1991; A Treasury of Flannelboard Stories, 1995. **Address:** 770 Victor Rd., Macedon, NY 14502, U.S.A.

BAYBARS, Taner. Also writes as Timothy Bayliss. British (born Cyprus), b. 1936. **Genres:** Novels, Poetry, Autobiography/Memoirs, Translations. **Career:** Full-time writer, 1988-. Book Promotion Officer, British Council, London, 1983-88 (joined Council, 1956). **Publications:** To Catch a Falling Man, 1963; A Trap for the Burglar (novel), 1965; Plucked in a Far-Off Land, 1970; (ed. with O. Turkay) Modern Poetry in Translation: Turkey, 1971; Susila in the Autumn Woods, 1974; Narcissus in a Dry Pool, 1978; Pregnant Shadows, 1981; A Sad State of Freedom, 1990; Selected Poems, 1997; Fox and the Cradle Makers, 2001; Collected Poems, 2005. TRANSLATOR: Selected Poems of Nazim Hikmet, 1967; Moscow Symphony, 1970; Day before Tomorrow, 1972; E.J. Keats, The Snowy Day, 1980; E.J. Keats, Peter's Chair, 1980; M. Yashin, Don't Go Back to Kyrenia (poems), 2001. **Address:** 2 rue de l'Eveque, 34360 Saint-Chinian, France. **Online address:** tbaybars@wanadoo.fr

BAYER, William. Also writes as Leonie St. John, David Hunt. American, b. 1939. **Genres:** Novels, Mystery/Crime/Suspense, Plays/Screenplays, Film. **Career:** With U.S. Foreign Service, Washington, DC, 1963-68. **Publications:** NOVELS: In Search of a Hero, 1966; Stardust, 1974; Visions of Isabelle, 1976; Tangier, 1978; Punish Me with Kisses 1980; Peregrine, 1981 (Edgar Allan Poe Award); Switch, 1984; Pattern Crimes, 1987; Blind Side, 1989; Wallflower, 1991; Mirror Maze, 1994; The Dream of the Broken Horses, 2002. NOVELS AS DAVID HUNT: The Magician's Tale, 1996; Trick of Light, 1998. OTHER: (as Leonie St. John: with N. Harmon) Love with a Harvard Accent, 1962. NONFICTION: Breaking Through, Selling Out, Dropping Dead and Other Notes on Filmmaking, 1971; The Great Movies, 1973. **Address:** 1592 Union St #475, San Francisco, CA 94123, U.S.A. **Online address:** crimenovelist@aol.com

BAYLEN, Joseph O. American, b. 1920. **Genres:** History, International relations/Current affairs, Biography. **Career:** Emeritus Regents' Professor of History, Georgia State University, Atlanta, 1982- (Professor and Chairman, Dept. of History 1966-69; Regents' Professor 1969-82). Assistant Professor, to Associate Professor of History, New Mexico Highlands University, Las Vegas, 1950-54; Professor and Chairman, Division of Social Science, Delta State Teachers College, MS, 1954-57; Professor of History, Mississippi State University, State College, 1957-61; Professor of History, 1961-66, Chairman, Dept. of History, 1964-66, University of Mississippi, University; Part-time lecturer, University of Sussex and City University, London, 1985-; consultant, BBC-TV; British Library, Consultative Group on Newspapers, 1990-2000; Board of Editors, Southern Humanities Review, 1970-; Board of Editors, Encyclopedia of 1948 Revolutions, 1988-; Board of Advisers, Encyclopedia of the World Press, 1999-. **Publications:** Madame Juliette Adam, Gambetta, and the Idea of a Franco-Russian Alliance, 1960; Lord Kitchener and the Viceroyalty of India 1910, 1965; (with A. Conway) Soldier-Surgeon: The Crimean War Letters of Dr. Douglas A. Reid, 1855-1856, 1968; The Tsar's Lecturer-General: W. T. Stead and the Russian Revolution of 1905, 1969; (with others) Dictionary of Labour Biography, 1977; Biographical Dictionary of Internationalists, 1983; British Literary Magazines, 1984; Biographical Dictionary of Peace Leaders, 1985; Victorian Britain, 1988; Papers for the Millions, 1988; Biographical Dictionary of American Journalism, 1989; Encyclopedia of the British Press, 1992; 1890s, An Encyclopedia of British Literature, Art, and Culture, 1993; Twentieth Century Britain, 1995; Diplomacy and Publicity in the Twentieth Century, 1995; Shaping the Collective Memory, 1996; A Journalism Reader, 1997. EDITOR: (with O.S. Pidhainy) East European and Russian Studies in the American South, 1972; (with N.J. Gossman) Biographical Dictionary of Modern British Radicals, vol. I, 1770-1830, 1979, vol. II, 1830-1870, 1984, vol III, 1870-1914, 1988.

BAYLEY, Barrington John. British, b. 1937. **Genres:** Novels, Science fiction/Fantasy. **Career:** Former civil servant, and coal miner. **Publications:** The Star Virus, 1970; Annihilation Factor, 1972; Empire of Two Worlds, 1972; Collision Course, 1973; The Fall of Chronopolis, 1974; The Soul of the Robot, 1974; The Garments of Caean, 1976; The Grand Wheel, 1977; Star Winds, 1978; The Knights of the Limits (anthology), 1978; The Seed of Evil (anthology), 1979; The Pillars of Eternity, 1982; The Zen Gun, 1983; The Forest of Peldain, 1985; The Rod of Light, 1985; Eye of Terror, 1999;

The Great Hydration, 2002; The Sinners of Erspia, 2002. **Address:** 48 Turreff Ave, Donnington, Telford, Salop TF2 8HE, England.

BAYLEY, John (Oliver). British, b. 1925. **Genres:** Novels, Poetry, Literary criticism and history. **Career:** Warton Professor of English Literature, and Fellow, St. Catherine's College, Oxford University, 1974- (Lecturer and Fellow, New College, Oxford, 1955-74). Member, St. Anthony's and Magdalen Colls., Oxford, 1951-55. **Publications:** El Dorado: The Newdigate Prize Poem, 1950; In Another Country (novel), 1955; The Romantic Survival: A Study in Poetic Evolution, 1957; The Characters of Love: A Study in the Literature of Personality, 1960; Tolstoy and the Novel, 1966; Pushkin: A Comparative Commentary, 1971; The Uses of Division: Unity and Disharmony in Literature, 1976; An Essay on Hardy, 1978; Selected Essays, 1980; Shakespeare and Tragedy, 1981; The Line Order of Battle at Trafalgar, 1985; The Short Story: Henry James to Elizabeth Bowen, 1987; Housman's Poems, 1992; Alice (novel), 1994; The Queer Captain (novel), 1995; George's Lair (novel), 1996; The Red Hat (novel), 1997; Elegy for Iris, 1999; Iris & Her Friends, 2000; Widower's House, 2001; The Power of Delight (essays), 2005. **Address:** St. Catherine's College, Oxford, England.

BAYLEY, Peter (Charles). British, b. 1921. **Genres:** Literary criticism and history. **Career:** Oxford University, Fellow, University College, 1947-72, Praelector in English, 1949-72, University Lecturer, 1952-72; University of Durham, Collingwood College, Master, 1972-78; University of St. Andrews, Fife, Berry Professor and Head of English Dept., 1978-85, Berry Professor Emeritus, 1985-. University College, Oxford, Emeritus Fellow. **Publications:** Edmund Spenser, Prince of Poets, 1971; Poems of Milton, 1982; An ABC of Shakespeare, 1985; University College, Oxford: A Guide and Brief History, 1992. EDITOR: The Faerie Queene, by Spenser, Book II, 1965, Book I, 1966, 1970; Loves and Deaths, 1972; A Casebook on Spenser's Faerie Queene, 1977. **Address:** 63 Oxford St, Woodstock, Oxon. OX20 1TJ, England.

BAYLEY, Stephen. Welsh, b. 1951. **Genres:** Architecture, Art/Art history, Design. **Career:** Eye-Q Ltd., London, principal, 1990-. Lecturer in art history, Liverpool Polytechnic, 1972-74, Open University, 1974-76, and University of Kent, 1977-80; director of the Conran Foundation (which created Boilerhouse Project, and the Design Museum), then chief executive, the Design Museum, London, 1981-90; contributor to the Times, The Sunday Times, The Daily Mail, GQ, and others. **Publications:** In Good Shape: Style in Industrial Products 1900-1960, 1979; The Albert Memorial, 1981; Harley Earl and the Dream Machine, 1983; The Conran Directory of Design, 1985; Twentieth Century Style and Design, 1986; Sex, Drink and Fast Cars, 1986; Commerce and Culture, 1989; Taste, 1991; Labour Camp, 1998; Moving Objects, 1999; General Knowledge, 2000; Sex, 2001. **Address:** 176 Kennington Park Rd, London SE11 4BT, England.

BAYLIS, Janice H(inshaw). American, b. 1928. **Genres:** Psychology, Paranormal. **Career:** Schoolteacher in California, including Los Angeles, 1950-60; Santa Ana Unified Schools, Santa Ana, CA, reading specialist, 1964-86. Cypress Community College, instructor in dream study; presents dream study workshops at Santa Ana Community College and Golden West Community College. **Publications:** Sleep on It!: The Practical Side of Dreaming, 1977; Dream Dynamics and Decoding: An Interpretation Manual, 1977; (with A. Bartlow) Palmistry Dictionary, 1986; (with Bartlow) Dowsing Dictionary, 1986; Sex, Symbols, and Dreams, 1997. **Address:** 1180 Oakmont Rd. No. 51-J, Seal Beach, CA 90740, U.S.A. **Online address:** jbaylis@earthlink.net

BAYLIS, John. British, b. 1946. **Genres:** International relations/Current affairs, Military/Defense/Arms control. **Career:** University of Liverpool, Lecturer, 1969-71; University of Wales, Aberystwth, Dept. of International Politics, Lecturer, 1971-83, Sr. Lecturer, 1983-89, Reader, 1989-92, Professor and Dean of Social Sciences, 1989-. National Defence College, Latimer, Academic Adviser, 1975-82. **Publications:** (co-author) Contemporary Strategy: Theories and Policies, 1975; (ed.) British Defence Policy in Changing World, 1977; Anglo-American Defence Relations 1939-80, 1980, 1984; (ed.) Soviet Strategy, 1980; (co-author) Nuclear War, Nuclear Peace, 1983, 1988; (ed.) Alternative Approaches to British Defence Policy, 1984; (co-author) Contemporary Strategy: Theories and Concepts, vol. I, 1987; (co-author) Contemporary Strategy: The Nuclear Powers, vol. II, 1987; (with others) Britain, NATO and Nuclear Weapons, 1989; British Defence Policy: Striking the Right Balance, 1989; (co-ed.) Makers of Nuclear Stategy, 1990; Dilemmas of World Politics, 1992; (co-ed.) The Diplomacy of Pragmatism, 1993; Ambiguity and Deterrence: British Nuclear Strategy, 1945-63, 1995; (co-ed.) Alternative Nuclear Futures: The Role of Nuclear Weapons in the Post-Cold War Era, 2000. **Address:** Dept. of International Politics, University of Wales, Aberystwyth, Dyfed, Wales. **Online address:** jjb@aber.ac.uk

BAYLISS, Timothy. See **BAYBARS, Taner.**

BAYME, Steven. American, b. 1950. **Genres:** Cultural/Ethnic topics, Theology/Religion. **Career:** Yeshiva University, NYC, visiting lecturer, 1973-75, instructor, 1975-77, assistant professor of history, 1977-79; Hadassah, national Jewish education director, 1979-82; American Jewish Committee, NYC, assistant director of Jewish Communal Affairs Department, Institute of Human Relations, 1982-86, acting director, 1986-87, national director, 1987-, director of Institute on American Jewish Israel Relations, 1992-. Jewish Theological Seminary, lecturer, summers, 1973-74; Hebrew Union College, lecturer, 1976, 1981; Yeshiva University, adjunct assistant professor, 1979-87; adjunct professor at Wurzweiler School of Social Work, 1991-; Queens College of the City University of New York, adjunct assistant professor, 1986. **Publications:** Facing the Future: Essays on Contemporary Jewish Life, 1989; (ed. with D. Blankenhorn and J. Bethke Elshtain and contrib.) Rebuilding the Nest: A New Commitment to the American Jewish Family, 1990; (ed. with D. Ellenson and contrib.) Religious Pluralism: Implications for Israel Diaspora Relations, 1992; (ed. with G. Rosen) The Jewish Family and Jewish Continuity, 1994. Contributor to books. Contributor of articles and reviews to periodicals. **Address:** 3720 Independence Ave., Apt. 1E, Bronx, NY 10463, U.S.A.

BAYNE, Nicholas (Peter). British, b. 1937. **Genres:** Economics, International relations/Current affairs, Politics/Government. **Career:** British Foreign and Commonwealth Office, London, England, served in British embassy in Manila, Philippines, 1963-66, and in Bonn, West Germany, 1969-72, attached to Treasury in London, 1974-75, financial counselor at British embassy in Paris, France, 1975-79, head of economic relations department in London, 1979-82, attached to Royal Institute of International Affairs, London, 1982-83, British ambassador to Zaire (and non-resident ambassador to Congo, Rwanda, and Burundi), 1983-84, diplomatic service chairman of Civil Service Selection Board, London, 1985, representative to Organization for Economic Cooperation and Development, 1985-88, deputy under secretary for economic affairs in Foreign and Commonwealth Office, 1988-92; British High Commissioner to Canada, 1992-96. London School of Economics and Political Science, International Trade Policy Unit, fellow, 1998-. **Publications:** (with R.D. Putnam) Hanging Together: The Seven-Power Summits, 1984, rev. ed., 1987; Hanging in There: The 97 and 98 Summit in Maturity and Renewal, 2000; (with S. Woolcock) The New Economic Diplomacy: Decision-Making and Negotiation in International Economic Relations, 2002; Staying Together: The 98 Summit Confronts the 21st Century, 2005. **Address:** 2 Chetwynd House, Hampton Court Green, East Molesey, Surrey KT8 9BS, England.

BAYNES, Sir John (Christopher Malcolm). British, b. 1928. **Genres:** History, Military/Defense/Arms control. **Career:** Former Lt. Col., H.M. Forces. **Publications:** Morale: A Study of Men and Courage, 1968, 1987; The Jacobite Rising of 1715, 1970; The History of the Cameronians: The End of Empire 1948-1968, vol. IV, 1971; The Soldier in Modern Society, 1971; Soldiers of Scotland, 1988; The Forgotten Victor: The Life of General Sir Richard O'Connor, 1989; (with H. Maclean) A Tale of Two Captains, 1990; No Reward but Honour?, 1991; Lake Vyrnwy: The Story of a Sporting Hotel, 1992; Urquhart of Arnhem, 1993; (with A.J. Maxse) Far from a Donkey: The Life of General Sir Ivor Maxse, 1995; For Love of Justice, 1997. **Address:** Talwrn Bach, Llanfyllin, Powys, Wales.

BAYNES, Ken. British, b. 1934. **Genres:** Design, Art/Art history. **Career:** Designer, educator, editor, and author. Royal College of Art, research associate, 1974; Loughborough University, Department of Design and Technology, Loughborough, Leicestershire, England, visiting professor. **Publications:** Industrial Design and the Community, 1967; Attitudes in Design Education, 1969; (with B. Langslow and C.C. Wade) Evaluating New Hospital Buildings, 1969; War, 1970; Work, 1970; (ed.) Scoop, Scandal, and Strife: A Study of Photography in Newspapers, 1971; Worship, 1971; Sex, 1972; (with K. Baynes and A. Robinson) Art in Society, 1975; About Design, 1976; The Railway Cartoon Books, 1976; (with F. Pugh) The Art of the Engineer, 1978; (with K. Baynes) The Shoe Show: British Shoes since 1790, 1979; Gordon Russell, 1981; (with K. Brochocka and B. Saunders) Fashion and Design, 1990. **Address:** Department of Design and Technology, Loughborough University, Loughborough, Leicestershire LE11 3TU, England.

BAYNES, Kenneth R(ichard). American, b. 1954. **Genres:** Philosophy. **Career:** University of Massachusetts at Boston, instructor, 1982-85; Boston University, assistant professor of philosophy, 1986-87; State University of New York at Stony Brook, assistant professor, 1987-93, associate professor of philosophy, 1993-2002, director of undergraduate studies in philosophy, 1993-94, graduate director, 1998-2000; Syracuse University, professor, 2003-. Guest lecturer at institutions world wide. **Publications:** (ed. with J. Bohman and T. McCarthy) After Philosophy: End or Transformation?, 1987; (trans.) Axel Honneth, The Critique of Power, 1991; The Normative Grounds of Social Criticism: Kant, Rawls, and Habermas, 1992. Work represented in anthologies. Contributor of articles, translations, and reviews to professional journals. **Address:** Department of Philosophy, 541 Hall of Languages, Syracuse University, Syracuse, NY 13244, U.S.A. **Online address:** krbaynes @sry.edu

BAZZONI, Jana O'Keefe. American, b. 1941. **Genres:** Film, Theatre. **Career:** United Service Organizations, performer and choreographer for a tour of Seventeen, 1963; J. Walter Thompson, casting associate, 1964-65; Doyle, Dane, Bernbach, casting director, 1965-67; Guinness-Harp Corp., administrative assistant for advertising and public relations, 1969-72, office manager for Wine Division, 1972-73; Italian Theatre Festival, administrative manager, 1974; Images Unlimited (casting consultants), founding partner, 1975-77; lecturer at US universities, 1976-81; Elizabeth Seton College, Yonkers, NY, instructor in language and literature, 1975-86, academic adviser, 1981-87; Bernard M. Baruch College of the City University of New York, NYC, adjunct assistant professor, 1980-85, assistant professor, 1985-94, associate professor of speech, 1995-98, associate dean, 1998-. City University of New York Readers Theatre, founding member, producer, writer, and performer, 1979-90; producer and director of plays produced off-off-Broadway, 1974-86. **Publications:** (with N.D. Nichols) Pirandello and Film, 1995; (trans. and intro.) Edoardo Sangheti, Natural Stories #1, 1998. Contributor to books. Contributor of articles, translations, and reviews to periodicals. **Address:** Weissman School of Arts & Sciences, Bernard M. Baruch College/CUNY, 17 Lexington Ave, Box A1503, New York, NY 10010, U.S.A. **Online address:** jana_o'keefe_bazzoni@baruch.cuny.edu

BEACH, Hugh. American, b. 1949. **Genres:** Cultural/Ethnic topics. **Career:** Researcher for Swedish National Immigration Board and National Labor Market Board, 1981; Uppsala University, Sweden, research assistant in cultural anthropology, 1981-84, lecturer, 1984-90, associate professor of cultural anthropology, 1990-2001; professor, 2001-, departmental dean, 1985-86, founder and leader of Minority Interest Group, 1985-90. Umeaa University, researcher at Center for Arctic Cultural Research, 1987-90. Minority Rights Group, member of board of directors of Swedish branch, 1985-, chairperson, 1989-91. Conducted field studies at a Navajo Indian Reservation in Arizona, 1969; in Hong Kong, Bali, Sri Lanka, India, Kenya, and Tanzania, 1971-72, in Swedish Lapland, 1973-77, in Kotzebue, AK, 1982-83, in Sovkhoz Topolini, Yakutia, 1984, in Mogadishu, Somalia, 1986, to regions in Swedish Lapland affected by contamination from the Chernobyl disaster in Russia, 1987-, and among the Saami reindeer herders of the Kola Peninsula, Lovozero, 1991. **Publications:** Reindeer-Herd Management in Transition: The Case of Tuorpon Saameby in Northern Sweden, 1981; A New Wave on a Northern Shore: The Indochinese Refugees in Sweden, 1982; Gaest hos samerna, 1988; A Year in Lapland: Guest of the Reindeer Herders, 1993; The Saami of Lapland, 1994. Work represented in anthologies. Contributor to books and periodicals. **Address:** Department of Cultural Anthropology, Uppsala University, Traedgaardsgatan 18, 75309 Uppsala, Sweden. **Online address:** Hugh.Beach@antro.uu.se

BEACHAM, Richard C. American, b. 1946. **Genres:** Theatre. **Career:** Yale University, New Haven, CT, dramaturg at Yale Repertory Theatre, 1969-72, visiting lecturer in theater studies, 1970-72, resident fellow and visiting professor, 1979, 1982-83; Hiram College, Hiram, OH, assistant professor of theater studies and chairperson of department, 1972-74; University of Warwick, Coventry, England, began as lecturer, became reader in theater studies, 1976-, and acting chairperson of Joint School of Theatre Studies. University of California, Santa Barbara, visiting professor, 1989; American Institute for Foreign Study, lecturer. BBC World Service, German language broadcaster. **Publications:** Adolphe Appia, Theatre Artist, 1987; (ed.) A. Appia, Essays, Scenarios, and Designs, 1989; The Roman Theatre and Its Audience, 1991; Adolphe Appia: Texts on Theatre, 1993; Adolphe Appia: Artist and Visionary of the Modern Theatre, 1994; Spectacle of Entertainment in Eatly Imperial Rome, 1999. FILMS: Staging Greek Tragedy: Insights on Sites; Staging Roman Comedy: Pompeian Painting and Plautus; The Italian Renaissance Stage: The Idea and Image of Antiquity; Revolution and Rebirth: Modern Theatrical Reform and Its Debt to Antiquity; Gluck's Orpheus and Eurydice: A Production Inspired by Appia and Dalcroze's 1913 Staging at Hellerau. Work represented in anthologies. Contributor to scholarly journals and newspapers. **Address:** Joint School of Theatre Studies, University of Warwick, Office #088, Coventry CV4 7AL, England. **Online address:** tsrai@titanic.csv.warwick.ac.uk

BEAGLE, J. Robert. See REGALBUTO, Robert J.

BEAGLE, Peter S(oyer). American, b. 1939. **Genres:** Novels, Novellas/Short stories, Plays/Screenplays, Songs/Lyrics and libretti. **Publications:** A Fine and Private Place, 1960; I See by My Outfit, 1965; The Last Unicorn, 1968; The California Feeling, 1969; The Lady and Her Tiger, 1976; The Dove (screenplay), 1977; The Lord of the Rings (screenplay), 1978; The Fantasy Worlds of Peter S. Beagle, 1978; The Last Unicorn (screenplay), 1982; The Garden of Earthly Delights, 1982; The Folk of the Air (novel), 1987; The Innkeeper's Song (novel), 1993; The Midnight Angel (opera libretto), 1993; (with P. Derby & G. Molina) In the Presence of Elephants, 1995; (with J. Berliner) Peter S. Beagle's Immortal Unicorn (anthology), 1995; The Unicorn Sonata (novel), 1996; Giant Bones (stories), 1997. **Address:** c/o Sebastian Literary Agency, 172 6th St E, St. Paul, MN 55101, U.S.A.

BEAGLEY, Brenda E. (Marin Thomas). American, b. 1962. **Genres:** Romance/Historical. **Career:** Writer. **Publications:** ROMANCE FICTION: Chance of a Lifetime, 2001; The Cowboy and the Bride, 2004; Daddy by Choice, 2005; Homeward Bound, 2005. **Address:** c/o Paige Wheeler, Creative Media Agency, 240 W 35th St Ste 500, New York, NY 10001, U.S.A. **Online address:** marin@marinthomas.com; www.marinthomas.com

BEAL, Peter. British, b. 1944. **Genres:** Literary criticism and history, Bibliography. **Career:** Bowker Publishing and Mansell Publishing Ltd., research editor, 1974-79; Sotheby's, London, England, Department of Books and Manuscripts, English manuscripts expert 1980-, deputy director, 1990-96, director 1996-. University of Reading, English Department, visiting professor, 2000-02; University of London, Institute of English Studies, senior research fellow, 2002-. British Academy, fellow, 1993-. Has given lectures and presentations to colleges and universities internationally. Serves as adviser and consultant to presses and projects. **Publications:** Index of English Literary Manuscripts, Vol. 1 (parts 1 and 2: 1450-1625), 1980, Vol. 2 (part 1: 1625-1700, authors A-K), 1987, Vol. 2, (part 1: 1625-1700, authors L-Z), 1993; In Praise of Scribes: Manuscripts and their Makers in Seventeenth Century England, The Lyell Lectures, Oxford, 1995-96, 1998. EDITOR: (general) English Verse Miscellanies of the Seventeenth Century, 5 Vols., 1990; (co-) English Manuscript Studies, 1100-1700, 11 vols., 1989-2002. Author of academic articles and reviews. **Address:** Department of Books & Manuscripts, Sotheby's, 34-35 New Bond St, London WIA 2AA, England. **Online address:** peter.beal@sothebys.com

BEALES, D(erek) E(dward) D(awson). British, b. 1931. **Genres:** History. **Career:** Cambridge University, Assistant Lecturer, 1962-65, Lecturer, 1965-80, Chairman, Faculty Board of History, 1979-81, Member, General Board of Faculties, 1987-89, Professor, 1980-97, and Emeritus Professor of Modern History, 1997-, Sidney Sussex College, Research Fellow, 1955-58, Fellow, 1958-, Tutor, 1961-70, and Vice-Master, 1973-75. Reading University, Stenton Lecturer, 1992; Trinity College, Cambridge, Birkbeck Lecturer, 1993. Historical Journal, Editor, 1971-75, Chairman, Editorial Board, 1990-97. British Academy, Fellow, 1989-. Royal Historical Society, Member of the Council, 1984-88. **Publications:** England and Italy 1859-60, 1961; From Castlereagh to Gladstone, 1969; The Risorgimento and the Unification of Italy, 1971, rev. ed. (with E.F. Biagini), 2002; History and Biography, 1981; Joseph II: In the Shadow of Maria Theresa, 1741-1780, 1987; Mozart and the Habsburgs, 1993; Prosperity and Plunder: European Catholic Monasteries in the Age of Revolution, 16501815, 2002; Enlightenment and Reform in the Eighteenth Century, 2004. EDITOR: (with G.F.A. Best) History, Society and the Churches, 1985; (with H.B. Nisbet) Sidney Sussex College Quatercentenary Essays, 1996; Cassell's Companion to Eighteenth Century Britain, 2001; Cassell's Companion to Twentieth Century Britain, 2001. **Address:** Sidney Sussex College, Cambridge CB2 3HU, England.

BEALEY, Frank William. British, b. 1922. **Genres:** Industrial relations, Politics/Government. **Career:** Professor of Politics, University of Aberdeen, 1964-90, emeritus, 1990-. Lecturer in Political Institutions, University of Keele, 1952-64. **Publications:** (with H. Pelling) Labour and Politics, 1958; (with J. Blondel and W.P. McCann) Constituency Politics, 1965; The Social and Political Thought of the British Labour Party, 1970; The Post Office Engineering Union, 1976; (with J. Sewel) The Politics of Independence, 1981; Democracy in the Contemporary State, 1988; (with R.A. Chapman and M. Sheehan) Elements in Political Science, 1999; The Blackwell Dictionary of Political Science, 1999; Power in Business and the State, 2001. **Address:** 11 Viewforth Terrace, Edinburgh EH10 4LH, Scotland. **Online address:** fwsbealey@btopenworld.com

BEALL, Anne E. American, b. 1966. **Genres:** Psychology. **Career:** National Analysts, Philadelphia, PA, project manager, 1994-. **Publications:** (ed. with R.J. Sternberg) The Psychology of Gender, 1993. **Address:** National Analysts, 1835 Market St, Philadelphia, PA 19103-2981, U.S.A.

BEAMAN, Joyce Proctor. American, b. 1931. **Genres:** Young adult fiction, Education, Psychology, Self help. **Career:** Snow Hill High School, North

Carolina, English and French teacher, 1953-59; Saratoga Central High School, 1959-78; Elm City Middle School, North Carolina, librarian, 1978-82; Spaulding Elementary School, librarian, 1987-92; retired. **Publications:** Broken Acres, 1971; All for the Love of Cassie, 1973; Bloom Where You Are Planted, 1975; You Are Beautiful: You Really Are, 1981; Teaching: Pure and Simple, 1998. **Address:** PO Box 187, Saratoga, NC 27873, U.S.A.

BEAN, Gregory (K.). American, b. 1952. **Genres:** Mystery/Crime/Suspense. **Career:** Wyoming News, Cody, WY, reporter to associate editor, 1978-80; Howard Publications, Casper, WY, police reporter for Casper Star Tribune to assistant city editor, 1980-83, editor. Wyoming Horizons, 1983-85; Freeport Journal Standard, Freeport, IL, editor, 1985-86; Community Newspapers Co., Boston, MA, editor of North Shore Sunday, Danvers, MA, 1986-91, Region, Ipswich, MA, 1990-91, Merrimack Valley Sunday, 1991-92, Seacoast Sunday, 1991-92, editor for the parent company, 1992; Greater Media Newspapers, East Brunswick, NJ, executive editor, 1993-. University of Wyoming, instructor, 1979-85. **Publications:** MYSTERY NOVELS: No Comfort in Victory, 1995; Long Shadows in Victory, 1996; A Death in Victory, in press. **Address:** Greater Media Newspapers, 3499 US Highway 9 #10, Freehold, NJ 07728, U.S.A.

BEAN, Jonathan J. American, b. 1962. **Genres:** Business/Trade/Industry, History, Politics/Government, Race relations. **Career:** Southern Illinois University, Carbondale, assistant professor, 1995-99, associate professor , 1999-2003, professor of history, 2003-. **Publications:** Beyond the Broker State: Federal Policies toward Small Business, 1936-1961, 1996; Big Government and Affirmative Action: The Scandalous History of the Small Business Administration, 2001. Contributor to books. Contributor of articles and reviews to academic journals and newspapers. **Address:** Dept of History, Southern Illinois University at Carbondale, Carbondale, IL 62901, U.S.A. **Online address:** jonbean@siu.edu

BEAR, Greg(ory Dale). American, b. 1951. **Genres:** Science fiction/Fantasy. **Career:** Freelance writer since 1975. Lecturer, San Diego Aerospace Museum, 1969-72; writer and planetarium operator, Fleet Space Theatre, San Diego, 1973. **Publications:** SCIENCE FICTION: Hegira, 1979; Psychlone, 1979; Beyond Heaven's River, 1980; Strength of Stones, 1981; Corona, 1984; The Infinity Concerto, 1984; Blood Music, 1985; Eon, 1985; The Serpent Mage, 1986; The Forge of God, 1987; Eternity, 1988; Queen of Angels, 1990; Heads, 1990; Anvil of Stars, 1992; Songs of Earth and Power, 1992; Moving Mars, 1993; Legacy, 1995; (ed.) New Legends; 1995; Slant, 1997; Dinosaur Summer, 1998; Foundation and Chaos, 1998; Darwin's Radio, 1999. SHORT STORIES: The Wind from a Burning Woman, 1983; Sleepside Story, 1998; Early Harvest, 1988; Tangents, 1989; Sisters, 1992; The Venging, 1992; Bear's Fantasies: Six Stories in Old Paradigms, 1992. **Address:** 506 Lakeview Rd, Lynnwood, WA 98037, U.S.A. **Online address:** www.gregbear.com

BEARANGER, Marie. (Claire Messier). American, b. 1956. **Genres:** Zoology. **Career:** Gareth Stevens Inc., Milwaukee, WI, marketing associate, 1987-. Horizon Travel, travel consultant, 1988-. **Publications:** COLORS OF THE SEA SERIES (with E. Ethan): Coral Reef Builders, 1997; Coral Reef Feeders, 1997; Coral Reef Hunters, 1997; Coral Reef Partners, 1997; Coral Reef Survival, 1997. **Address:** c/o Gareth Stevens Publishing, 330 W Olive St Ste 100, Milwaukee, WI 53212, U.S.A. **Online address:** ClaireM@myexcel.com

BEARD, Darleen Bailey. American, b. 1961. **Genres:** Novels, Children's fiction. **Career:** Dental assistant in Oklahoma City and Norman, OK, 1979-83; freelance writer for McGraw-Hill, School Book Division, Oklahoma City, 1989-90; part-time receptionist, Oklahoma City, 1991-95. **Publications:** The Pumpkin Man from Piney Creek, 1995; The Flimflam Man, 1998; Twister (picture book), 1999. NOVELS: The Babbs Switch Story, 2002; Operation: Clean Sweep, 2004. Contributor to anthologies and children's magazines. **Address:** 1627 Briarcliff Ct, Norman, OK 73071-3811, U.S.A. **Online address:** dbbookgal@aol.com

BEARD, Geoffrey. British, b. 1929. **Genres:** Architecture, Art/Art history, Crafts. **Career:** Director's Assistant, Leeds City Art Gallery, 1957-61; Director, Cannon Hall Art Gallery, Barnsley, 1961-66; Sr. Lecturer, Manchester Polytechnic, 1966-72; Director, Visual Arts Centre, University of Lancaster, 1972-82. **Publications:** XIXth Century Cameo Glass, 1956; Collecting Antiques on a Small Income, 1957; Georgian Craftsmen and Their Work, 1966; Modern Glass, 1968; Modern Ceramics, 1969; Decorative Plasterwork in Great Britain, 1975; International Modern Glass, 1976; The Work of Robert Adam, 1978; The Greater House in Cumbria, 1978; (with G. Berry) The Lake District: A Century of Conservation, 1980; Robert Adam's Country

Houses, 1981; Craftsmen and Interior Decoration 1660-1820, 1981; The Work of Christopher Wren, 1981; Stucco and Decorative Plasterwork in Europe, 1982; The National Trust Book of English Furniture, 1985; The Work of John Vanbrugh, 1986; (ed. with C.G. Gilbert) Dictionary of English Furniture Makers 1660-1840, 1986; (with Lady Goodison) English Furniture 1500-1840, 1987; The Work of Grinling Gibbons, 1989; The National Trust Book of the English House Interior, 1990; The Compleat Gentleman, 1991; Upholsterers and Their Work in England, 1530-1840, 1997.

BEARD, Jo Ann. American, b. 1955. **Genres:** Novels. **Career:** Writer. Formerly worked as a secretary and editor of a journal. **Publications:** The Boys of My Youth, 1998. Contributor to periodicals. **Address:** c/o Little Brown and Co., 1271 Avenue of the Americas, New York, NY 10020, U.S.A.

BEARD, Patricia. American, b. 1947. **Genres:** Animals/Pets. **Career:** Author and editor. Elle, New York, NY, editor-at-large. **Publications:** The Voice of the Wild: An Anthology of Animal Stories, 1992; Growing up Republican: Christie Whitman, the Politics of Character, 1996; Good Daughters: Loving Our Mothers as They Age, 1999; Class Action, 2000; After the Ball: Gilded-Age Secrets, Boardroom Betrayals, and the Party That Ignited the Great Wall Street Scandal of 1905, 2003. Contributing writer to many national magazines. **Address:** Harper Collins, 10 East 53rd St., New York, NY 10022, U.S.A.

BEARD, Richard. British, b. 1967. **Genres:** Novels. **Career:** Writer. **Publications:** X20: A Novel of (Not) Smoking, 1997. **Address:** c/o Arcade Publishing, 141 Fifth Ave., New York, NY 10010, U.S.A.

BEARD, William R. (born Canada), b. 1946. **Genres:** Film. **Career:** University of Alberta, Edmonton, Alberta, Canada, professor of English and film, 1976-. **Publications:** Persistence of Double Vision: Essays on Clint Eastwood, 2000; The Artist as Monster: The Cinema of David Cronenberg, 2001; (With Jerry White) North of Everything: English Canadian Cinema since 1980, 2002. **Address:** Department of English and Film, Edmonton, Albertan, Canada T6G 2E6. **Online address:** william.beard@ualbeUniversity of Albertarta.ca

BEARDEN, Milton. American, b. 1940. **Genres:** Mystery/Crime/Suspense. **Career:** Writer. Worked as an agent for the Central Intelligence Agency. **Publications:** The Black Tulip, 1998. **Address:** c/o Random House Inc., 201 East 50th St., New York, NY 10022, U.S.A.

BEARDSELL, Peter R. British, b. 1940. **Genres:** Cultural/Ethnic topics, Literary criticism and history, Translations. **Career:** University of Manchester, England, lecturer in Spanish, 1965-66; University of Sheffield, England, lecturer/senior lecturer in Hispanic studies, 1966-93; University of Hull, England, chair of Hispanic studies, 1993-. Society for Latin American Studies, president, 1995-97. Manchester Hispanic Texts, general editor, 1990-2002. **Publications:** Critical Edition of Ricardo Guiraldes: Don Segundo Sombra, 1973; Winds of Exile: The Poetry of Jorge Carrera Andrade, 1977; Quiroga: Cuentos de amor de locura y de muerte, 1986; A Theatre for Cannibals: Rodolfo Usigli and the Mexican Stage, 1992; Critical Edition of Julio Cortazar: Siete cuentos, 1993; Gods and Demons, Self and Other, 1994; Europe and Latin America: Returning the Gaze, 2000. **Address:** Department of Hispanic Studies, University of Hull, Hull HU6 7RX, England. **Online address:** P.R.Beardsell@hull.ac.uk

BEARDSLEE, Karen E. American, b. 1965. **Genres:** Literary criticism and history. **Career:** Burlington County College, Pemberton, NJ, adjunct professor, 1991-99, lecturer in English, 1999-2002; independent scholar and folklorist, 2002-. Camden County College, adjunct professor, 1992; Rowan College of New Jersey, adjunct professor, 1995; teacher of history and English at a private secondary school in Philadelphia, PA, 1998-99. Moorestown Barnes and Noble Monthly Senior Memoirs Writing Group, co-facilitator, 2000. **Publications:** Literary Legacies, Folklore Foundations: Selfhood and Cultural Tradition in Nineteenth- and Twentieth-Century American Literature, 2001. Work represented in anthologies. Contributor of articles and poetry to periodicals. **Address:** 2777 Livingston Loop, Virginia Beach, VA 23456, U.S.A. **Online address:** Leejogger@aol.com

BEARDSLEY, Theodore S., Jr. American, b. 1930. **Genres:** Songs/Lyrics and libretti, Literary criticism and history, Music. **Career:** University of Wisconsin, Madison, member of faculty, 1962-65, 1995; The Hispanic Society of America, director, 1965-95, president, 1995-; New York University, NYC, adjunct professor, 1967-69, 1980. **Publications:** Hispano-Classical Translations, 1482-1699, 1970; Tomas Navarro Tomas: A Tentative Bibliography 1908-1970, 1971; (trans.) Maria Sabina (libretto), 1973; Ponce de Leon (libretto), 1973; The Hispanic Impact on the United States, 1990; also author of public radio (WBGO-FM) series, 1979-85. EDITOR: Enric Madriguera, 1994; (co-) Celestina, Early Texts, 1997; Carlos Molina, 2000. Contributor to professional journals. **Address:** 613 W 155th St, New York, NY 10032, U.S.A.

BEARY, Michael J. (born United States), b. 1956. **Genres:** Biography. **Career:** Writer and historian. **Publications:** Black Bishop: Edward T. Demby and the Struggle for Racial Equality in the Episcopal Church, 2001. **Address:** POB 4173, Batesville, AR 72503, U.S.A.

BEASLEY, Bruce. American, b. 1958. **Genres:** Poetry. **Career:** Poet. Western Washington University, Bellingham, WA, associate professor of English, 1992-. **Publications:** POETRY: Spirituals, 1988; The Creation, 1994; Summer Mystagogia, 1996. Contributor of poems to periodicals. **Address:** Department of English, Western Washington University, Bellingham, WA 98225, U.S.A.

BEASLEY, Faith E. American, b. 1958. **Genres:** History, Autobiography/ Memoirs, Essays. **Career:** Dartmouth College, Hanover, NH, associate professor of French, women's studies, and comparative literature, 1986-. **Publications:** Revising Memory: Women's Fiction and Memoirs in Seventeenth-Century France, 1990; (co-ed.) Approaches to Teaching Lafayette's the Princess of Cleves, 1998. **Address:** Dept of French and Italian, 315 Dartmouth Hall, Hinman Box 6087, Dartmouth College, Hanover, NH 03755, U.S.A. **Online address:** Faith.E.Beasley@dartmouth.edu

BEASLEY, William Gerald. British, b. 1919. **Genres:** History, International relations/Current affairs. **Career:** Professor Emeritus of the History of the Far East, School of Oriental and African Studies, University of London, since 1984 (Professor, 1954-83). **Publications:** Great Britain and the Opening of Japan 1833-1858, 1951; The Modern History of Japan, 1963, 3rd ed., 1981; The Meiji Restoration, 1972; Japanese Imperialism 1894-1945, 1987; The Rise of Modern Japan, 1990; Japan Encounters the Barbarian: Japanese Travellers in America and Europe, 1995; The Japanese Experience: A Short History of Japan, 1999. EDITOR: (and trans.) Select Documents on Japanese Foreign Policy 1853-1868, 1955; (with E.G. Pulleyblank) Historians of China and Japan, 1961; Modern Japan: Aspects of History, Literature and Society, 1975. **Address:** 172 Hampton Rd, Twickenham TW2 5NJ, England.

BEASON, Doug. American, b. 1953. **Genres:** Novels. **Career:** Writer. Kirkland Air Force Base, Deputy Director of Advanced Weapons and Survivability. **Publications:** NOVELS: Return to Honor, 1989; Assault on Alpha Base, 1990; Strike Eagle, 1991. NOVELS WITH K.J. ANDERSON: Lifeline, 1990; The Trinity Paradox, 1991; Assemblers of Infinity, 1993; Ill Wind, 1995; Virtual Destruction, 1996; Ignition, 1997; Fallout, 1997; Lethal Exposure, 1998. **Address:** c/o Tor Books, 175 Fifth Ave., 14th floor, New York, NY 10010, U.S.A.

BEATTIE, Ann. American, b. 1947. **Genres:** Novels, Novellas/Short stories, Art/Art history. **Career:** University of Virginia, Charlottesville, visiting lecturer, 1976-77, 1980, Edgar Allan Poe Professor of Creative Writing, 2001-; Harvard University, Cambridge, MA, Briggs Copeland Lecturer in English, 1977-78. **Publications:** NOVELS: Chilly Scenes of Winter, 1976; Falling in Place, 1980; Love Always, 1985; Picturing Will, 1989; Another You, 1995; My Life, Starring Dara Falcon, 1997; The Doctor's House, 2002. STORIES: Distortions, 1976; Secrets and Surprises, 1978; The Burning, 1982; Where You'll Find Me and Other Stories, 1986; What Was Mine, 1990; Perfect Recall, 2000. OTHER: Alex Katz (art criticism), 1987. **Address:** c/o Janklow & Nesbit, 445 Park Ave Fl 13, New York, NY 10022-1614, U.S.A.

BEATTIE, L(inda) Elisabeth. American, b. 1953. **Genres:** Women's studies and issues. **Career:** Director of a holiday home for the handicapped elderly in Chigwell, England, 1974; George Washington University, Washington, DC, administrative assistant in Oral History Program, 1978-79; Alston Wilkes Society, Columbia, SC, public information specialist, 1980-81; Bruccoli Clark Research, Columbia, editor and copy editor, 1981-82; Retired Senior Volunteer Program, Columbia, assistant director, 1982-84; Bellarmine College, Louisville, KY, adjunct instructor in English literature and composition, 1988-89; high school teacher of English and journalism in Shelbyville, KY, 1989-90; Elizabethtown Community College, Elizabethtown, KY, instructor, 1990-91, assistant professor, 1991-97, associate professor of English and journalism, 1997-99; Midway College, Midway, KY, associate professor of English, writer in residence, and shares Robert L. Botkin Chair, 1999-. Kentucky Writers' Oral History Project, director, 1990-; University of Kentucky, associate of Appalachian Center, 1996-99; Kentucky Humanities

Council, featured speaker, 1998-99. **Publications:** Conversations with Kentucky Writers, 1996; Savory Memories, 1998; Conversations with Kentucky Writers II, 1999; (with M.A. Shaughnessy) Sisters in Pain: Battered Women Fight Back, 2000. Work represented in anthologies. Contributor of articles and reviews to periodicals. **Address:** Midway College, 512 East Stephens St., Midway, KY 40347, U.S.A. **Online address:** lebeattie@ntr.net

BEATTIE, Melody (Lynn). American, b. 1948. **Genres:** Psychology, Social sciences. **Career:** Worked as an advertising secretary after high school; worked as a chemical dependency counselor in Minneapolis, MN, beginning in the mid-1970s; free-lance author of articles and books, 1979-. **Publications:** (with C. Owens) A Promise of Sanity, 1982; Denial, 1985; Codependent No More: How to Stop Controlling Others and Start Caring for Yourself, 1986; Crack: The Facts, 1987; Beyond Codependency: And Getting Better All the Time, 1989; The Language of Letting Go, 1990; Codependents' Guide to the Twelve Steps: How to Find the Right Program for You and Apply Each of the Twelve Steps to Your Own Issues, 1990; (ed.) A Reason to Live, 1991; Talk, Trust, and Feel: Keeping Codependency Out of Your Life, 1991; Lessons of Love, 1994; Journey into the Heart, 1995; Stop Being Mean to Yourself, 1997. Contributor to periodicals. **Address:** c/o Ballantine Books, 201 E. 50th St., New York, NY 10022, U.S.A.

BEATTY, Barbara (R.). American, b. 1946. **Genres:** Education, History. **Career:** Kindergarten teacher at public schools in Boston, MA, 1968-72; Lesley College, Cambridge, MA, assistant professor of education, 1973-81, administrative director of Lesley Ellis School, 1973-78; Wellesley College, Wellesley, MA, assistant professor, 1981-94, associate professor of education, 1994-, department head, 1988-89, 1995-96, head of Campus Task force on Minority Retention, 1988-92. Education Development Center (Newton, MA), coordinator of child care project, 1973; Boston Higher Education Compact, college coordinator, 1985-. **Publications:** Preschool Education in America: The Culture of Young Children From the Colonial Era to the Present, 1995. Contributor to books. Contributor of articles and reviews to education journals. **Address:** Department of Education, Wellesley College, Wellesley, MA 02481, U.S.A.

BEATTY, Jack. American, b. 1945. **Genres:** History, Biography. **Career:** Writer and magazine editor; has worked for Newsweek and New Republic; Atlantic Monthly, Boston, senior editor, 1983-. **Publications:** The Rascal King: The Life and Times of James Michael Curley (1874-1958): An Epic of Urban Politics and Irish America, 1992; The World According to Peter Drucker, 1998. **Address:** 7 Faraway Ln, Hanover, NH 03755, U.S.A.

BEATY, Betty (Smith). Also writes as Karen Campbell, Catherine Ross. British, b. 1919. **Genres:** Novels, Biography. **Career:** Former WAAF Officer, airline hostess and medical social worker, London. **Publications:** Maiden Flight, 1956; South to the Sun, 1956; Amber Five, 1958; The Butternut Tree, 1958; Top of the Climb, 1958; The Atlantic Sky, 1958; The Path of the Moonfish, 1964; Miss Miranda's Walk, 1967; The Swallows of San Fedora, 1973; Love and the Kentish Maid, 1973; Head of Chancery, 1974; Master at Arms, 1975; Fly Away, Love, 1976; Exchange of Hearts, 1977; (with D. Beaty) Wings of the Morning, 1982; The Missionary's Daughter, 1983; Matchmaker Nurse, 1983; Airport Nurse, 1986; Wings of Love, 1988; That Special Joy, 1992; Winged Life: A Biography of David Beaty. AS CATHERINE ROSS: From This Day Forward, 1959; The Colours of the Night, 1962; The Trysting Tower, 1964; Battle Dress, 1979; The Shadow of the Peak, 1984. AS KAREN CAMPBELL: Suddenly, in the Air, 1969; Thunder on Sunday, 1971; Wheel of Fortune, 1973; Death Descending, 1976; The Bells of St. Martin, 1979; Fatal Union, 1994. AS BETTY CAMPBELL BEATY: Winged Life: A Biography of David Beaty. **Address:** Manchester House, Church Hill, Slindon, near Arundel, W. Sussex, England.

BEAUCHAMP, Cari. American. **Genres:** Film. **Career:** Film reporter and writer. Reporter for National Public Radio. **Publications:** (with H. Behar) Hollywood on the Riviera: The Inside Story of the Cannes Film Festival, 1992; Without Lying Down: Frances Marion and the Powerful Women of Early Hollywood, 1997. **Address:** c/o Author Mail, University of California Press, 2120 Berkeley Way, Berkeley, CA 94704-1012, U.S.A.

BEAUCHAMP, Kenneth. American, b. 1939. **Genres:** Psychology. **Career:** California State Polytechnic University, Pomona, assistant professor, 1965-69; University of the Pacific, College of the Pacific, associate professor of psychology, 1969-78, professor of psychology, 1978-. **Publications:** (with D.W. Matheson and R.L. Bruce) Experimental Psychology, 1970, 3rd ed., 1978; (ed. with D.W. Matheson and R.L. Bruce) Contemporary Topics in

Experimental Psychology, 1970. **Address:** Psychology Dept, College of the Pacific, University of the Pacific, Stockton, CA 95211, U.S.A. **Online address:** kbeauchamp@pacific.edu

BEAUD, Michel. French, b. 1935. **Genres:** Economics, History, Essays. **Career:** University of Lille, France, assistant professor, 1965-66, associate professor of economics, 1966-69; University of Paris VIII, France, associate professor, 1969-70, professor of economics, 1970-91, and department head; University of Paris VII, professor of economics, 1991-98, and department head, emeritus, 1998-. **Publications:** Histoire du capitalisme, 1981, rev. ed. trans. as A History of Capitalism, 1500-2000, 2001; Le Socialisme a l'epreuve de l'histoire, 1982, trans. as Socialism in the Crucible of History, 1993; (with G. Dostaler) Le Pensee economique depuis Keynes, 1993, trans. as Economic Thought since Keynes, 1994, 2nd ed., 1997. UNTRANSLATED WORKS: (with P. Danjou and J. David) Une multinationale francaise, 1975; (with P. Allard, B. Bellon, and others) Dictionnaire des groupes industriels et financiers en France, 1978; (ed. with G. de Bernis and J. Masini), La France et le Tiers-Monde, 1979; La Politique economique de la gauche, Vol. 1: Le mirage de la croissance, 1983, Vol. 2: Le grand ecart, 1985; L'Art de la these, 1985; Le Systeme national/mondial hierarchise, 1987; L'Economie mondiale dans les annees 1980, 1989; (with R. Alvayay and G. Marin) El Socialismo en el umbral del Siglo XXI, 1990; (author of preface) L.R. Brown, C. Flavin and S. Postel, Le defi planetaire: Pour une economie, ecologique et durable, 1992; (ed. with L. Bouguerra and C. Beaud) L'Etat de l'environnement dans le monde, 1993; Le Basculement du monde, 1997; Le Journal du Basculement du monde: 2000, 2001; Naissance d'un siecle: 2001, 2004. Contributor to books and periodicals. **Address:** 14 Impasse Saint-Vincent, 85200 L'Orbrie, France. **Online address:** m.beaud@wanadoo.fr

BEAUDOIN, Tom. American. **Genres:** Theology/Religion. **Career:** Author; minister to GenXers at the Paulist Center Catholic Community in Boston. **Publications:** Virtual Faith: the Irreverent Spiritual Quest of Generation X, 1998. Contributor of articles to periodicals. **Address:** Carney Hall 420, Boston College, 140 Commonwealth Ave, Chestnut Hill, MA 02467, U.S.A. **Online address:** thomas.beaudoin.1@bc.edu

BEAUFOY, Simon. British, b. 1967. **Genres:** Plays/Screenplays. **Career:** Screenwriter; director. **Publications:** SCREENPLAYS: Cello, 1991; The Full Monty, 1997; Among Giants, 1998; The Tower Men, in development. DOCUMENTARY FILMS: The Frontier; Shattered Dream (documentary). PLAYS: Saddam's Arms. **Address:** c/o Creative Artists Agency, 9830 Wilshire Blvd., Beverly Hills, CA 90212, U.S.A.

BEAUMAN, Nicola. American, b. 1944. **Genres:** Literary criticism and history, Biography. **Career:** Writer. **Publications:** A Very Great Profession: The Woman's Novel, 1914-39, 1983; Cynthia Asquith (biography), 1987; Morgan: A Biography of the Novelist E.M. Forster, 1993. **Address:** c/o Amanda Urban, International Creative Management, 40 West 57th St., New York, NY 10019, U.S.A.

BEAUMAN, Sally. Also writes as Vanessa James. British, b. 1944. **Genres:** Novels. **Career:** Writer. Worked as a writer and editor for magazines and newspapers in the US and UK. **Publications:** (ed.) The Royal Shakespeare Company's Production of "Henry V" for the Centenary Season at the Royal Shakespeare Theatre, 1976; The Royal Shakespeare Company: A History of Ten Decades, 1982; Destiny (novel), 1987; Dark Angel (novel), 1990; Lovers and Liars (novel), 1994; Danger Zones, 1996; Sextet, 1997; Rebecca's Tale, 2001. AS VANESSA JAMES: Piers Clarendon, 1980; The Dark One, 1982; The Fire and the Ice, 1982; The Devil's Advocate, 1983; Ever After, 1983; Chance Meetings, 1984; The Object of the Game, 1985; Give Me This Night, 1986; Prisoner, 1986; Try to Remember, 1987. **Address:** c/o PFD, Drury House, 34-43 Russell St, London WC2B 5HA, England.

BEAUSEIGNEUR, James. (born United States), b. 1953. **Genres:** Science fiction/Fantasy. **Career:** Novelist and writing consultant. Has also worked as a political science instructor, technical writer, political campaign manager, lobbyist, and newspaper publisher. Served in U.S. Army, including assignment as an intelligence analyst for the National Security Agency, 1976-1981. **Publications:** In His Image, 1997; Birth of an Age, 1997; Acts of God, 2003. Contributor to many newspaper and magazine articles, and published manuals. Has written lyrics for published songs. **Address:** c/o Author Mail, Warner Books, 1271 Avenue of the Americas, New York, NY 10020, U.S.A.

BEAVAN, Colin. American. **Genres:** Criminology/True Crime. **Career:** Journalist. Liverpool Echo, Liverpool, England, former theater critic. **Publications:** Fingerprints: The Origins of Crime Detection and the Murder Case

That Launched Forensic Science, 2001. **Address:** c/o Hyperion Boks, 77 W 66th St 11th Fl, New York, NY 10023, U.S.A.

BEAVER, Bruce (Victor). Australian, b. 1928. **Genres:** Novels, Poetry. **Career:** Freelance journalist. Recipient, Patrick White Award for Literature, 1982. **Publications:** Under the Bridge: Poems, 1961; Seawall and Shoreline: Poems, 1964; The Hot Spring (novel), 1965; You Can't Come Back (novel), 1966; Open at Random: Poems, 1967; Letters to Live Poets: Poems, 1969 (Captain Cook Bi-Centenary Prize: Grace Leven Prize; Poetry Society of Australia Award); Lauds and Plaints: Poems (1968-1972), 1974; Odes and Days, 1975; Death's Directives, 1978; As It Was, 1979; Selected Poems, 1979; Headlands: Prose Sketches, 1986; Charmed Lives: Poems, 1988; New and Selected Poems (1960-1990), 1991; Anima and Other Poems, 1994. **Address:** 14 Malvern Ave, Manly, NSW 2095, Australia.

BEBBINGTON, D(avid) W(illiam). British, b. 1949. **Genres:** History, Theology/Religion. **Career:** University of Stirling, Scotland, lecturer, 1976-89, senior lecturer in history, 1989-92, reader in history, 1992-99, professor of history, 1999-. **Publications:** Patterns in History, Inter-Varsity Press, 1979; The Nonconformist Conscience: Chapel and Politics, 1870-1914, 1982; Victorian Nonconformity, 1992; William Ewart Gladstone: Faith and Politics in Victorian Britain, 1993; Holiness in Nineteenth-Century England, 2000. EDITOR/CO-EDITOR: The Baptists in Scotland: A History, 1988. Evangelicalism in Modern Britain: A History from the 1730s to the 1980s, 1989; Evangelicalism: Comparative Studies of Popular Protestantism in North America, the British Isles and Beyond, 1700-1990, 1994; Gladstone Centenary Essays, 2000. **Address:** Department of History, University of Stirling, Stirling FK9 4LA, Scotland.

BECHARD, Margaret. American, b. 1953. **Genres:** Young adult fiction. **Career:** Freelance writer. **Publications:** FOR YOUNG ADULTS: My Sister, My Science Report, 1990; Tory and Me and the Spirit of True Love, 1992; Really No Big Deal, 1994; Star Hatchling, 1995; My Mom Married the Principal, 1998; If It Doesn't Kill You, 1999; Hanging on to Max, 2002. **Address:** 12180 SW Ann Pl, Tigard, OR 97223, U.S.A.

BECHLER, Curt. American, b. 1958. **Genres:** Communications/Media. **Career:** Camp Friedenswald Inc., Cassopolis, MI, executive director, 1984-90; Denison University, Granville, OH, assistant professor of communication, 1990-. **Publications:** (with R.L. Weaver) Listen to Win: A Guide to Effective Listening, 1994. Contributor to books and professional journals. **Address:** Department of Communication, Denison University, Granville, OH 43023, U.S.A.

BECHTEL, Stefan D. American, b. 1951. **Genres:** Sex. **Career:** Triad, Greensboro, NC, executive editor, 1978-79; Burlington Daily Times-News, Burlington, NC, reporter, 1979-81; Rodale Press, Emmaus, PA, associate editor, 1981-82, senior editor, 1982-85, executive editor, 1985-87, managing editor of Newsletter Group, 1986-87; freelance writer, 1988-; Men's Health magazine, founding editor. Guest on television and radio programs. **Publications:** (with K. Castle) Katherine, It's Time, 1989; The Practical Encyclopedia of Sex and Health, 1993; (with L.R. Stains) Sex: A Man's Guide, 1996; (with L.R. Stains) The Good Luck Book, 1997; (with L.R. Stains) What Women Want, 2000; Growing a Fortune, 2002. Contributor to periodicals. **Address:** 302 Park St, Charlottesville, VA 22902, U.S.A. **Online address:** dhand302@aol.com

BECK, James. American, b. 1930. **Genres:** Art/Art history. **Career:** Professor of Art History, Columbia University, NYC, since 1972 (joined faculty, 1964). **Publications:** Michelangelo: A Lesson in Anatomy, 1975; Raphael, 1976; (co-author) Masaccio: The Documents, 1978; Leonardo's Rules of Painting, 1979; Italian Renaissance Painting, 1981; The Doors of the Florentine Baptistry, 1985; (ed.) Raphael Before Rome, 1986; The Sepulcral Monument for Ilaria del Carretto by Jacopo della Quercia, 1988; Jacopa della Quercia, 2 vols., 1991; The Tyranny of the Detail: Contemporary Art in an Urban Setting, 1992; The Restoration Establishment: The Culture, the Business and the Scandal, 1993 and 1996; Raphael: Camera della Segnatura, 1993. In progress: The Social World of the Young Michelangelo. **Address:** Dept. of Art History, Columbia University, 931 Schermerhorn Hall, New York, NY 10027, U.S.A.

BECK, John C. American. **Genres:** Economics. **Career:** Harvard University, Cambridge, MA, lecturer; University of Western Ontario, adjunct professor; Asian Business Information, president; Asian Century, editor; Monitor Company, Far-East advisor; United Nations, co-director of project on strategies of the world's largest fifty companies; Cambodian Prime Minister's office, senior strategic advisor; Accenture Institute for Strategic

Change, associate partner and director of international research; University of California, Los Angeles, visiting professor. **Publications:** (with T.H. Davenport) The Attention Economy: Understanding the New Currency of Business, 2001; (with M.E. Wade) DoCoMo: Japan's Wireless Tsunami, 2002. Author of articles and business reports on business in Asia, strategic management, globalization, leadership, and organizational behavior. **Address:** c/o AMACOM, 1601 Broadway, New York, NY 10019, U.S.A.

BECK, Mary L. (Giraudo). American, b. 1924. **Genres:** Mythology/Folklore, Sociology, Young adult non-fiction, History, Inspirational/Motivational Literature, Biography. **Career:** University of Alaska, Ketchikan, instructor, 1954-69, assistant professor, 1969-74, became associate professor of English, 1974, professor emeritus, 1983-; writer, 1983-. Member of library advisory board at University of Alaska, Ketchikan. **Publications:** Heroes and Heroines in Tlingit-Haida Legend, and Their Counterparts in Classical Mythology, 1989; Shamans and Kushtakas, 1991; Potlatch: Native Ceremony and Myth on the Northwest Coast, 1993; Kagunda: Alaskan Pioneer Teacher, Missionary, Leader, 1999. **Address:** c/o Rocky Point Publishing, 2855 Tongas Ave, Ketchikan, AK 99901, U.S.A.

BECK, Robert J. American, b. 1961. **Genres:** Military/Defense/Arms control, Law. **Career:** University of Virginia, Charlottesville, visiting assistant professor of government, 1989-90; University of Minnesota-Twin Cities, Minneapolis, visiting assistant professor of political science, 1990-91; University of Virginia, assistant professor of government, 1991-. **Publications:** The Grenada Invasion, 1993; (with A.C. Arend) International Law and the Use of Force, 1993; (Principal editor) International Rules, 1996. **Address:** Department of Government, University of Virginia, Charlottesville, VA 22901, U.S.A.

BECKER, Charles M(axwell). American, b. 1954. **Genres:** Economics, Urban studies, Demography. **Career:** Vanderbilt University, Nashville, TN, assistant professor of economics, 1981-86; Economics Institute, Boulder, CO, deputy director of academic program, 1987-89, president, 1990-. University of Colorado, Boulder, adjunct associate professor and research associate in population processes, Institute of Behavioral Science, both 1987-; University of Colorado at Denver, member of advisory council of Center for International Business Education and Research, 1993-. **Publications:** (with E.S. Mills) Studies in Indian Urban Development, 1986; (with T. Bell, H. Ali Khan, and P. Pollard) The Impact of Sanctions on South Africa, Part I: The Economy, 1990; (with E.S. Mills and J.G. Williamson) Indian Urbanization and Economic Development, 1992; (with A. Hamer and A. Morrison) Beyond Urban Bias: African Cities in an Age of Structural Adjustment, 1994. Contributor to economic and international studies journals. **Address:** Dept of Economics, 305 Social Science Bldg, Box 90097, Duke University, Durham, NC 27708-0097, U.S.A. **Online address:** cbecker@econ.duke.edu

BECKER, Elizabeth. American, b. 1947. **Genres:** Military/Defense/Arms control, History. **Career:** War correspondent in Cambodia for the Washington Post, Newsweek, and National Broadcasting Corporation (NBC) Radio, 1973-74; Washington Post, Washington, DC, reporter, 1975-78, editor of Maryland desk, 1978-80; Center for International Policy, Washington, DC, creator and director of the Indochina Project, 1978-80; freelance writer on international diplomacy, Paris, France, 1986-90; National Public Radio, senior foreign editor, 1993-95; New York Times, assistant Washington editor, 1996-98, Washington correspondent, 1999-; writer. Institute for Policy Studies, visiting scholar, 1981-83; member of Women's Refugee Commission study in Cambodia, 1991. **Publications:** When the War Was Over: The Voices of Cambodia's Revolution and Its People, 1986, rev. ed., 1998; America's Vietnam War: A Narrative History, 1992. Contributor to periodicals. **Address:** 4514 Connecticut Ave., Apt 203, Washington, DC 20008, U.S.A.

BECKER, Ethan. American, b. 1945. **Genres:** Food and Wine. **Career:** Operated a student travel agency in the 1960s; served as an assistant in the revision of The Joy of Cooking from the late 1960s to 1976. **Publications:** COOKBOOKS WITH I.S. ROMBAUER AND M.R. BECKER: Joy of Cooking: Christmas Cookies, 1996; The New Joy of Cooking, 1997; Quick Weeknight Meals, 1999; Joy of Cooking: Great Chicken Dishes, 1999; Joy of Cooking: All about ... series, 12 vols., 2000; Joy of Cooking Cookie Kit, 2001. **Address:** c/o Scribner, 1230 Avenue of the Americas, New York, NY 10020, U.S.A. **Online address:** joyofc@aol.com

BECKER, Gary S. American, b. 1930. **Genres:** Economics. **Career:** Columbia University, NYC, Assistant to Associate Professor of Economics, 1957-60, Professor, 1960-68, Arthur Lehman Professor of Economics, 1968-69. University of Chicago, Assistant Professor, 1954-57, Visiting Professor, 1969-70, Professor, 1970-83, University Professor, Dept. of Economics and Sociology, 1983-. Sr. Fellow, Hoover Institution, 1990-. Columnist, Business Week mag., 1985-. Research Associate, Economics Research Center, National Opinion Research Center, 1980-. John Bates Clark Medal, 1967; Nobel Prize for Economics, 1992; National Medal of Science, 2000. **Publications:** The Economics of Discrimination, 1957, rev. ed., 1971; Human Capital, 1964, rev. ed., 1993; Human Capital and the Personal Distribution of Income: An Analytical Approach, 1967; Economic Theory, 1971; (with G. Ghez) The Allocation of Time and Goods over the Life Cycle, 1975; The Economic Approach to Human Behaviour, 1976; A Treatise on the Family, 1981, rev. ed., 1991; Accounting for Tastes, 1996; (with G. Nashat) The Economics of Life, 1996; Familie, Gesellschaft und Politik, 1996; (with K.M. Murphy) Social Economics, 2000. EDITOR: (with W.M. Landes) Essays in the Economics of Crime and Punishment, 1974; Essays in Labor Economics in Honor of H. Gregg Lewis, 1976 Lewis, 1976. **Address:** Dept. of Economics, University of Chicago, 1126 E 59th St, Chicago, IL 60637, U.S.A.

BECKER, Jasper. British, b. 1956. **Genres:** Geography, History, Travel/Exploration. **Career:** Journalist in Brussels, Belgium, 1980-83; Associated Press, Geneva, Switzerland, journalist, 1983-85; Guardian, London, England, journalist in London and China, 1985-91; British Broadcasting Corp., London, journalist; South China Morning Post, Beijing bureau chief; The Independent, Beijing correspondent. **Publications:** The Lost Country: Mongolia Revealed, 1991; Hungry Ghosts: China's Secret Famine, 1996; The Chinese, 2000; Rogue State: The Continuing Threat of North Korea, 2005. Work represented in anthologies. **Address:** 3-31 Legend Garden, 89 Capital Airport Rd, Beijing 101300, People's Republic of China. **Online address:** jsprjas@aol.com

BECKER, Josh. American, b. 1958. **Genres:** Essays. **Career:** Director and screenwriter. Actor in films. **Publications:** SCREENPLAYS: (with Bruce Campbell, Sheldon Lettich, and Scott Spiegel) Stryker's War (also known as Thou Shalt Not Kill . . . Except), 1985; (And lyricist) Lunatics: A Love Story, 1991; (with Peter Choi) Running Time, 1997; If I Had a Hammer, 1999. Also author of short stories, essays, and magazine articles. **Address:** Panoramic Pictures, 3315 Little Applegate Rd., Jacksonville, OR 97530, U.S.A.

BECKER, Jürgen. German, b. 1932. **Genres:** Poetry, Novellas/Short stories. **Career:** Westdeutscher Rundfunk (radio), writer, 1959-64; Rowohlt Verlag, reader, 1964-65; writer, 1965-. Suhrkamp-Theaterverlag, director, 1974. Deutschlandfunk Koeln, head of drama department. Warwick University, writer in residence, 1988. **Publications:** (with W. Vostell) Phasen, 1960; Felder (short stories; title means: Fields), 1964; Raender (short stories), 1968, excerpted trans. by A.L. Wilson as Margins in Dimension, Vol 1, No 2, 1968; Umgebungen (short stories; title means: Surroundings), 1970; Erzaehlen bis Ostende (short stories; title means: Narration until Ostende), 1981; Die Tuere zum Meer (title means: The Door to the Sea), 1983; Frauen mit dem Ruecken zum Betrachter, 1989. POETRY: Schnee: Gedichte, 1971; Das Ende der Landschaftsmalerei: Gedichte, 1974; Erzaehl mir nichts vom Kreig: Gedichte, 1977; In der verbleibenden Zeit: Gedichte, 1979; Gedichte 1965-1980 (title means: Poems, 1965-1980), 1981; Fenster und Stimmen: Gedichte, 1982; Odenthals Kuenste, 1986; Das englische Fenster, 1990; Foxtrott im Erfurter Stadion: Gedichte, 1993. EDITOR: (with W. Vostell) Happenings; Fluxus; Pop Art; Nouveau Realisme: Eine Dokumentation, 1965; Elisabeth Borchers, Gedichte (poetry), 1976. OTHER: Bilder, Haeuser: Hausfreunde: Drei Hoerspiel (radio play), 1969; Eine Zeit ohne Woerter (photographs; title means: A Time without Words), 1971; Die Zeit nach Harrimann: 29 Szenen fuer Nora, Helen, Jenny und den stummen Diener Moltke, 1971; Die Abwesenden: Drei Hoerspiel (radio plays), 1983; (with R. Bohne) Frauen mit dem Rucken zum Betrachter, 1989. **Address:** Am Klausenberg 84, 51109 Koeln-Brueck, Germany.

BECKER, Palmer (Joseph). American, b. 1936. **Genres:** Theology/Religion. **Career:** Relief worker in Taiwan, 1958-63; First Mennonite Church, Clinton, OK, pastor, 1965-69; Commission on Home Ministries, Newton, KS, administrative executive, 1969-79; Peace Mennonite Church, Richmond, BC, founding pastor, 1979-88; Point Grey Fellowship, Vancouver, BC, founding pastor, 1988-91; Mennonite Simons Center, Vancouver, chaplain 1988-91; Bethel Mennonite Church, Mountain Lake, MN, senior pastor, 1991-94; Calvary Mennonite Church Aurora, OR, senior pastor, 1994-98; Hesston College, director of Pastoral Ministries, 1998-. **Publications:** Daily Thoughts, 4 vols., 1961; Congregational Goals Discovery Plan, 1976; You and Your Options, 1979; Creative Family Worship, 1984; Called to Care: A Training Manual for Small Group Leaders, 1993; Called to Equip: A Small Group Training and Resource Manual for Pastors, 1993; Called to Lead: A Training Video and Guide for Small Group Leaders, 1994; The

Ministry of Membership Preparation, 1995. **Address:** 221 Kingsway, Hesston, KS 67062, U.S.A. **Online address:** Palmerb@southwind.net

BECKERMAN, Paul. American, b. 1948. **Genres:** Economics, Area studies. **Career:** U.S. Peace Corps, Washington, DC, volunteer in Bolivia and Colombia, 1969-71; University of Illinois at Urbana-Champaign, Urbana, assistant professor of economics, beginning in 1977; Boston University, Boston, MA, assistant professor of economics; Fordham University, Bronx, NY, assistant professor of economics, until 1984; Marine Midland Bank, NYC, economist, 1984-85; Federal Reserve Bank of New York, NYC, economist, 1985-88; World Bank, Washington, DC, economist, 1988-. **Publications:** The Economics of High Inflation, 1991. Work represented in anthologies. Contributor to economic and Latin American studies journals. **Address:** World Bank, 1818 H St. N.W., Washington, DC 20433, U.S.A.

BECKERMAN, Wilfred. British, b. 1925. **Genres:** Economics. **Career:** Lecturer in Economics, University of Nottingham, 1950-52; with OEEC (later OECD), Paris, 1952-62; with NIESR, London, 1962-64; Governor, and Member of Executive Committee, National Institute, of Economic and Social Research, London, 1972-94 (Member of Staff, 1962-64); Fellow and Tutor in Economics, Balliol College, Oxford, 1964-69; Economic Adviser to President of Board of Trade (on leave from Oxford), 1967-69; Professor of Political Economy, University College London, 1969-75; Fellow, Balliol College, Oxford, 1975-92. Member, Royal Commission on Environmental Pollution, 1970-73; Royal Economic Society, council, 1990-93. **Publications:** (co-author) The British Economy, in 1975, 1965; International Comparisons of Real Income, 1966; An Introduction to National Income Analysis, 1968; In Defence of Economic Growth (in U.S. as Two Cheers for the Affluent Society), 1974; Measures of Equality, Leisure and Welfare, 1979; Poverty and the Impact of Income Maintenance Payments, 1979; (with S. Clark) Poverty and Social Security in Britain since 1961, 1982; Small Is Stupid, 1995; Growth, the Environment and the Distribution of Incomes, 1995; (with J. Pasek) Justice, Posterity, and the Environment, 2001. EDITOR: Labour Government's Economic Record, 1964-70, 1972; Slow Growth In Britain: Causes and Consequences, 1979; Wage Rigidity and Unemployment, 1986.

BECKET, Henry S. A. See **GOULDEN, Joseph C.**

BECKLEY, Harlan R. American, b. 1943. **Genres:** Ethics, Theology/Religion. **Career:** Minister of United Methodist churches in Kingston Springs, TN, 1971-74; Washington and Lee University, Lexington, VA, instructor to associate professor, 1974-89, professor of religion, 1989-, department head, 1989-, adjunct professor of business ethics, 1984-91. **Publications:** (ed. with C.M. Swezey and co-author of intro) James M. Gustafson's Theocentric Ethics: Interpretations and Assessments, 1988; Passion for Justice: Retrieving the Legacies of Walter Rauschenbusch, John A. Ryan, and Reinhold Niebuhr, 1992. Contributor of articles and reviews to journals of religious studies and law. **Address:** Department of Religion, Washington and Lee University, Lexington, VA 24450, U.S.A.

BECKMAN, Gail M(cKnight). American, b. 1938. **Genres:** Law. **Career:** Professor, Georgia State University, Atlanta, since 1976 (Associate Professor, 1971-76). Lawyer, Morgan Lewis & Bockius, Philadelphia, 1963-66; Research Associate, American Philosophical Association, 1966-70; Lecturer, Faculty of Law, University of Glasgow, 1967-71. **Publications:** Estate Planning Considerations for U.S. Citizens Abroad, 1974; (co-author) Law for Business and Management, 1974; (ed.) Statutes at Large of Pennsylvania 1680-1700, 1976. **Address:** Box 106, Georgia State University, University Plaza, Atlanta, GA 30303, U.S.A.

BECKWITH, Harry. American, b. 1949. **Genres:** Business/Trade/Industry. **Career:** Gearin, Cheney, Landis, Aebi & Kelly (law firm), Portland, OR, associate attorney, 197677; City of Portland, assistant city attorney, 1977-82; Carmichael-Lynch, Minneapolis, MN, writer, 1982-85, creative supervisor, 1985-88; Beckwith Advertising and Marketing, Minneapolis, principal, 1988-. Lecturer at University of St. Thomas and University of Minnesota-Twin Cities; guest on television programs. **Publications:** Selling the Invisible, 1997. **Address:** Beckwith Advertising and Marketing, 600 Lumber Exchange, 10 South Fifth, Minneapolis, MN 55402, U.S.A. **Online address:** invisible@bitstream.net

BECKWITH, Jonathan R(oger). (born United States), b. 1935. **Genres:** Medicine/Health. **Career:** Geneticist. Harvard University Medical School, Boston, MA, faculty member 1965-, professor of microbiology, 1969-, American Cancer Society Research Professor of Microbiology and Molecular Genetics, 1971-. University of California-Berkeley, visiting professor, 1985; member of advisory boards, including board of Ethical, Legal, and Social

Implications Research Program, Human Genome Project. **Publications:** (Editor with David Zipser) The Lactose Operon (conference papers), 1970; (Editor with Julian Davies and Jonathan A. Gallant) Gene Function in Prokaryotes (symposium papers), 1983; (Editor with Thomas J. Silhavy) The Power of Bacterial Genetics: A Literature-based Course, 1992; Making Genes, Making Waves: A Social Activist in Science (memoir), 2002; (As Jon Beckwith; editor, with others) The Double-edged Helix: Social Implications of Genetics in a Diverse Society, 2002. Contributor of articles and reviews to periodicals. **Address:** 8A Appleton Rd., Cambridge, MA 02138, U.S.A. **Online address:** jbeckwith@hms.harvard.edu

BECKWITH, Lillian. British, b. 1916. **Genres:** Novels, Children's fiction, Food and Wine, Autobiography/Memoirs, Novellas/Short stories. **Career:** Writer. **Publications:** The Hills Is Lonely, 1959; The Sea for Breakfast, 1961; The Loud Halo, 1964; Green Hand, 1967; A Rope in Case, 1968; About My Father's Business, 1971; Lightly Poached, 1973; The Spuddy, 1974; Beautiful Just!; The Lillian Beckwith Omnibus, 1976; The Lillian Beckwith Hebridean Cookbook, 1976; Bruach Blend, 1978; A Shine of Rainbows, 1984; A Proper Woman, 1986; A Hebridean Omnibus, 1987; The Bay of Strangers, 1988; The Small Party, 1989; A Proper Woman, 1991; An Island Apart, 1992.

BEDARD, Michael. Canadian, b. 1949. **Genres:** Children's fiction. **Career:** St. Michael's College Library, Toronto, ON, Canada, library assistant, 1971-78; pressman at a small press, 1978-81; full-time writer, 1982-. **Publications:** JUVENILE: Woodsedge and Other Tales (fairy tales), 1979; Pipe and Pearls: A Gathering of Tales (fairy tales), 1980; A Darker Magic (novel), 1987; The Lightning Bolt, 1989; Redwork (novel), 1990; The Tinderbox (retelling), 1990; The Nightingale (retelling), 1991; Painted Devil (novel), 1994; The Clayladies, 1999; The Wolf of Gubbio, 2000; Stained Glass (novel), 2001. BIOGRAPHY: Emily, 1992; The Divide, 1997; Glass Town, 1997. **Address:** c/o Linda McKnight, Westwood Creative Artists, 94 Harbord St, Toronto, ON, Canada M5S 1G6.

BEDARD, Michelle. See **FINNIGAN (MACKENZIE), Joan.**

BEDAU, Hugo Adam. American, b. 1926. **Genres:** Civil liberties/Human rights, Criminology/True Crime, Ethics, Humanities, Law, Philosophy, Politics/Government. **Career:** Dartmouth College, 1953-54; Princeton University, 1954-61; Reed College, Portland, OR, associate professor of philosophy, 1962-66; Tufts University, Medford, MA, professor of philosophy, 1966-99. **Publications:** The Courts, the Constitution, and Capital Punishment, 1977; Death Is Different, 1987; Making Mortal Choices, 1997; Thinking and Writing about Philosophy, 1997, 2nd ed., 2002. CO-AUTHOR: Nomos VI: Justice, 1963; Nomos IX: Equality, 1967; The Concept of Academic Freedom, 1972; Philosophy and Political Action, 1972; Philosophy, Morality, and International Affairs, 1974; Victimless Crimes: Two Views, 1974; Justice and Punishment, 1977; Human Rights and U.S. Foreign Policy, 1979; Making Decisions, 1979; The Imposition of Law, 1979; Matters of Life and Death, 1980; Ethical Issues in Government, 1981; And Justice for All, 1982; Social Justice, 1982; Group Decision Making, 1984; Human Rights, 1984; Nomos XXVII: Criminal Justice, 1985; Current Issues and Enduring Questions, 1987, 6th ed., 2001; In Spite of Innocence, 1992; Critical Thinking, Reading, and Writing, 1993, 4th ed., 2001. EDITOR: The Death Penalty in America, 1964, 3rd ed., 1997; Civil Disobedience: Theory and Practice, 1969; Justice and Equality, 1971; Civil Disobedience in Focus, 1991. **Address:** c/o Dept. of Philosophy, Tufts University, Medford, MA 02155, U.S.A.

BEDERMAN, Gail. American, b. 1952. **Genres:** History. **Career:** University of Notre Dame, Notre Dame, IN, assistant professor of history, 1992-. **Publications:** Manliness and Civilization: American Debates about Race and Gender, 1880-1917, 1995. Contributor to books and periodicals. **Address:** Department of History, 255 Decio Faculty Hall, Notre Dame, IN 46556, U.S.A.

BEDFORD, Deborah. American, b. 1958. **Genres:** Romance/Historical. **Career:** Author. Evergreen Today, Evergreen, CO, editor; advertising agency account executive and copywriter in Colorado, 1982-. **Publications:** Touch the Sky, 1985; Passages, 1988; To Weave Tomorrow, 1989; Chikadee, 1995; Timberline, 1996; A Child's Promise, 1997; (with R.L. Hatcher and A.E. Hunt) The Story Jar, 2001; A Rose by the Door, 2001; On Wings of Morning, 2002; Harvest Dance; Blessing. **Address:** PO Box 9175, Jackson Hole, WY 83001, U.S.A.

BEDFORD, Henry Frederick. American, b. 1931. **Genres:** History. **Career:** History teacher, Albuquerque Acad., New Mexico, 1988-90. At Phillips Exeter Academy, New Hampshire: Instructor in History, 1957-66; Chairman of the History Dept., 1966-69; Dean of the Faculty, 1969-73; Cowles Professor in the Humanities, 1973-82; Librarian, 1973-77; Vice-Principal, 1979-82. Dean of Admissions, Amherst College, Massachusetts, 1982-87. **Publications:** The Union Divides, 1963; Socialism and the Workers in Massachusetts, 1966; From Versailles to Nuremburg, 1969; (co-author) The Americans: A Brief History, 1972, 4th ed. 1985; Trouble Downtown, 1977; Seabrook Station, 1990; Their Lives and Numbers, 1995. **Address:** 20 Drake Ln, Scarborough, ME 04074-7414, U.S.A.

BEDFORD, Martyn. British, b. 1959. **Genres:** Novels. **Career:** South London Press, London, England, reporter and features writer, 1980-85; South Wales Echo, Cardiff, sports writer, 1985-87; Citizen, Gloucester, England, reporter, 1988; Oxford Mail and Times, Oxford, England, features writer and subeditor, 1988-93; Bradford Telegraph and Argus, Bradford, England, subeditor, 1994-95; free-lance writer, 1995-; University of Manchester, lecturer in creative writing, 2001-. **Publications:** (ed. and contrib.) Matrix, 1994. NOVELS: Acts of Revision, 1996; Exit, Orange and Red, 1997; The Houdini Girl, 1999; Black Cat, 2000. Work represented in anthologies. **Address:** c/o Jonny Geller, Curtis Brown, Haymarket House 4th Fl, 28-29 Haymarket, London SW1Y 4SP, England.

BEDFORD, Sybille. British (born Germany), b. 1911. **Genres:** Novels, Food and Wine, Law, Travel/Exploration, Biography. **Career:** Writer. Vice President, English P.E.N.; Fellow, Royal Society of Literature. OBE, C. Lit, 1982. **Publications:** A Sudden View: A Mexican Journey, 1953, as A Visit to Don Otavio, 1982; A Legacy (novel), 1956; The Best We Can Do: The Trial of Doctor Bodkin Adams (in U.S. as The Trial of Dr. Adams), 1958; The Faces of Justice, 1961; A Favourite of the Gods (novel), 1962; A Compass Error (novel), 1968; Aldous Huxley: A Biography, vol. I, 1894-1939, 1973, vol. II, 1939-63, 1974; Jigsaw: An Unsentimental Education (novel), 1989; As It Was: Pleasure, Landscapes (collected essays), 1990. **Address:** c/o Lutyens & Rubinstein, 231 Westbourne Park Rd, London W11 1EB, England.

BEDINI, Silvio A. American, b. 1917. **Genres:** History, Sciences, Biography. **Career:** Historian Emeritus, Smithsonian Institution, Washington, DC. **Publications:** Early American Scientific Instruments and Their Makers, 1964; (with W. Van Braun and F. Whipple) Moon: Man's Greatest Adventure, 1970; The Life of Benjamin Banneker, 1972, rev. ed., 1999; Thinkers and Tinkers: Early American Men of Science, 1975; The Spotted Stones, 1978; Declaration of Independence Desk; Relic of Revolution, 1981; Thomas Jefferson and His Copying Machines, 1984; Clockwork Cosmos, 1986; Thomas Jefferson: Statesman of Science, 1990; The Pulse of Time, 1990; The Trail of Time, 1993; Science and Instruments in Seventeenth Century Italy, 1994; Patrons, Artisans and Instruments of Science, 1999; The Pope's Elephant, 1997; The Jefferson Stone, 1999; With Compass and Chain: Early American Surveyors and Their Instruments, 2001. **Address:** 4303 47th St NW, Washington, DC 20016-2449, U.S.A. **Online address:** sbedini@att.net

BEE, Ronald J. American, b. 1955. **Genres:** Novels, History, International relations/Current affairs, Military/Defense/Arms control. **Career:** International Atomic Energy Agency, Vienna, Austria, public information assistant, 1981; Congressional Research Service, Washington, DC, foreign-affairs analyst, 1982; Palomar Corp., Washington, DC, special assistant for national security affairs, 1982-87; Robert Bosch Foundation Fellow and adviser in West Germany, 1987-88; National Security Archive, consultant, 1989; ACCESS, director of publications and research, 1990-92; Youth for Understanding Freedom Support Act, consultant, 1992-94; University of California, Institute on Global Conflict and Cooperation, senior analyst, 1994-2003, director of special projects, Middle East, 2003-; writer. **Publications:** (with C.B. Feldbaum) Looking the Tiger in the Eye: Confronting the Nuclear Threat, 1988; (with B. Seymore and S. Young) One Nation Becomes Many: The ACCESS Guide to the Former Soviet Union, 1992; Russia and the Central Asian Republics: After Independence, New Directions?, 1993; Nuclear Proliferation: The Post Cold War Challenge, 1995. Contributor to periodicals. **Address:** 7904 Caminito Dia No 1, San Diego, CA 92122, U.S.A. **Online address:** beehive@fastwave.net

BEEBE, Ralph K. American, b. 1932. **Genres:** History, Theology/Religion. **Career:** Professor Emeritus, George Fox College, Newberg, OR, 1997- (Professor, 1974-96; Dean of Men, and Director of Athletics, 1955-57). History Teacher, Willamette High School, Eugene, OR, 1957-66, and Churchill High School, Eugene, 1966-74. **Publications:** A Garden of the Lord: A History of Oregon Yearly Meeting of Friends Church, 1968; The Worker and Social Change: The Pullman Strike of 1894, 1970; Thomas Jefferson, the Embargo and the Decision for Peace, 1972; (with J. Lamoreau) Waging Peace: A Study in Biblical Pacifism, 1980; (with A.G. Rantisi) Blessed Are

the Peacemakers: A Palestinian Christian in the Occupied West Bank, 1990, new ed., 2003s; George Fox College, 1891-1991: A Heritage of Honor, a Future to Fulfill, 1991. **Address:** 1015 E Cherry St #4, Newberg, OR 97132, U.S.A. **Online address:** rbeebe@georgefox.edu

BEEBY, Dean. Canadian, b. 1954. **Genres:** Documentaries/Reportage. **Career:** Canadian Press, Ottawa, ON, deputy bureau chief, 1983-. **Publications:** NONFICTION: Moscow Despatches, 1987; In a Crystal Land, 1994; Cargo of Lies, 1996; Deadly Frontiers, 2001. **Address:** Canadian Press, PO Box 595, Station B, Ottawa, ON, Canada K1P 5P7. **Online address:** dbeeby@cp.org

BEECH, H. R(eginald). British, b. 1925. **Genres:** Psychology. **Career:** Consultant Psychologist, North West Regional Health Authority; Professor of Clinical Psychology, University of Manchester. Sr. Lecturer, Institute of Psychiatry, London, 1963-69; Consultant Psychologist, S. W. Metropolitan Region, 1969-72. Former Ed., British Journal of Social & Clinical Psychology. **Publications:** (with F. Fransella) Research and Experiment in Stuttering, 1968; Changing Man's Behaviour, 1969; (ed.) Obsessional States, 1974; (with M. Vaughan) Behavioural Treatment of Obsessional States, 1978; (with L. E. Burns and B. F. Sheffield) Behavioural Approaches to the Management of Stress; Staying Together, 1986.

BEECHER, Donald A(llen). Canadian (born United States), b. 1942. **Genres:** Humanities, Intellectual history, Literary criticism and history, Music, Theatre. **Career:** Carleton University, Ottawa, ON, lecturer, 1967-69, assistant professor, 1969-80, associate professor, 1980-87, professor of English, 1987-, director of Centre for Renaissance Studies, 1978-. Director, Dovehouse Editions; lecturer at universities. Visiting lecturer or fellow: Chiba University, Japan, 1999-2001; Jacksonville State University, AL, 2001; UCLA Center for Renaissance Studies, 2001; University of Victoria, BC. **Publications:** EDITOR: (and trans. and author of intro.) O. de Turnebe, Satisfaction All Around: Les contens, 1979; (with B. Gillingham) C. Simpson, Divisions for Treble, Bass Viol, and Keyboard, 1979; (and trans. with M. Ciavolella, and coauthor of intro.) A. Caro, The Scruffy Scoundrels: Gli straccioni, 1981; (and trans. with Ciavolella, and coauthor of intro.) G. Bernini, The Impresario, 1985; (with Ciavolella) Comparative Critical Approaches to Renaissance Comedy, 1986; (with Ciavolella and trans.) A Treatise on Love, Part I: Jacques Ferrand and the Tradition of Erotic Melancholy in Western Culture, Part II: Jacques Ferrand, Of Lovesickness or Erotic Melancholy, 1989; (with Ciavolella) Eros and Anteros, 1992; B. Riche, The Farewell to Military Profession, 1992; (and trans., with Ciavolella, and coauthor of intro.) L. de Sommi, The Three Sisters, 1993; (with U. Rappen) W. Young, 29 Movements in the French Style for Bass Viol Solo, 1993; Anon, The Dialogue between Solomon and Marcolphus, 1994; T. Lodge, Rosalind, 1996; Ariosto/Gascoigne, Supposes, 1998; G.B. della Porta, The Sister, 2000; T. Overbury, Characters, 2002; (and trans.) Calderon, The Phantom Lady, 2001; (with J. Butler and C. Di Biase) The Fables of Bidpai, 2002; (with H. Janzen) T. Lodge, A Margarite of America, 2005; O. Vecchi, The Veglie di Siena, 46 madrigals. **Address:** Dept of English, Carleton University, 1125 Colonel By Dr, Ottawa, ON, Canada K1S 5B6. **Online address:** donald_beecher@carleton.ca

BEECHER, Maureen Ursenbach. Also writes as Valerie March. Canadian, b. 1935. **Genres:** Theology/Religion, Autobiography/Memoirs, Biography. **Career:** Elementary and high school teacher in Alberta and Quebec; McGill University, Montreal, Quebec, lecturer, 1963-65, 1966-68; Western Humanities Review, managing editor, 1969-72; Church of Jesus Christ of Latter-day Saints, Salt Lake City, UT, editor and senior research associate, History Division, 1972-80; Brigham Young University, Provo, UT, associate professor, 1981-89, professor of English, 1990-, research historian, Joseph Fielding Smith Institute for Church History, 1981-. Charles Redd Center for Western Studies, member of advisory board, 1989-; Mormon History Association, president, 1984-85; Cornerstone: Mormon Architectural Heritage, president, 1972-73. **Publications:** (ed. with L.F. Anderson) Sisters in Spirit: Mormon Women in Historical and Cultural Perspective, 1987; (ed. with D. Bitton, and co-author of introduction) New Views of Mormon History: A Festschrift in Honor of Leonard J. Arrington, 1987; Eliza and Her Sisters, 1991. Work represented in anthologies. Contributor to periodicals. **Address:** 2161 Prince Wales Dr, Ottawa, ON, Canada K2B 7A4.

BEEMAN, Robin. American, b. 1940. **Genres:** Novellas/Short stories, Plays/Screenplays. **Career:** English teacher and part-time librarian. Sonoma State University, adjunct professor, 1990-95. **Publications:** A Parallel Life and Other Stories, 1992; A Minus Tide, 1995. FILMS: Brazil, 1989. Work represented in anthologies. Contributor of stories, articles and reviews to magazines. **Address:** PO Box 963, Occidental, CA 95465, U.S.A. **Online address:** robinbee@wclynx.com

BEER, Dame Gillian (Patricia Kempster). British, b. 1935. **Genres:** Literary criticism and history. **Career:** Bedford College, London, Assistant Lecturer, 1959-62; University of Liverpool, part-time Lecturer, 1962-64; University of Cambridge, Fellow of Girton College, 1965-94, Assistant Lecturer, 1966-71, Lecturer to Reader in Literature and Narrative, 1971-89, Professor of English, 1989-2002, President of Clare Hall College, 1994-2001, Professor Emeritus, 2002-. **Publications:** Meredith: A Change of Masks, 1970; The Romance, 1970; (ed. with J. Beer) Delights and Warnings: A New Anthology of Poems, 1979; Darwin's Plots, 1983, 2nd ed., 2000; George Eliot, 1986; Arguing with the Past, 1989; Forging the Missing Link: Interdisciplinary Stories, 1992; Open Fields: Science in Cultural Encounter, 1996; Virginia Woolf: The Common Ground, 1996. **Address:** Clare Hall, University of Cambridge, Cambridge CB3 9AL, England. **Online address:** gpblooo@cam.ac.uk

BEERE, Peter. British, b. 1951. **Genres:** Science fiction/Fantasy, Mystery/Crime/Suspense, Young adult fiction. **Career:** Writer, 1980-. Presents writing workshops; public speaker. Manager of a night shelter for the homeless in Lancaster, England, 1991-94; volunteer worker for an adult literacy project. Also worked as laboratory assistant, gardener, truck driver, construction laborer and office worker. **Publications:** SCIENCE FICTION NOVELS: Urban Prey, 1984; The Crucifixion Squad, 1984; Silent Slaughter, 1985. CRIME NOVELS: The Squad, 1987; The Fifth Man, 1987; The Sixth Day, 1988. JUVENILE SUSPENSE NOVELS: Crossfire, 1991; Underworld, 1992; Underworld II, 1992; Underworld III, 1992. JUVENILE CRIME NOVELS: School for Death, 1993, in the US as School for Terror; Kiss of Death, 1994. JUVENILE FANTASY NOVELS: Doom Sword, 1993; Star Warriors, 1995. OTHER: Riot (juvenile drama), 1995; Bod's Mum's Knickers (juvenile humor), 1995; Death House (young adult horror novel), in press. **Address:** 12 Sherman Dr., Rainhill, Merseyside L35 6PW, England.

BEERS, Burton Floyd. American, b. 1927. **Genres:** History, International relations/Current affairs, Young adult non-fiction. **Career:** North Carolina State University, Raleigh, Instructor, 1955-57, Assistant Professor, 1957-61, Associate Professor, 1961-66, Professor of History, 1966-96, Alumni Distinguished Professor, 1970-96, Professor Emeritus, 1997-. **Publications:** Vain Endeavour: Robert Lansing's Attempts to End the American-Japanese Rivalry, 1962; (with P.H. Clyde) The Far East: A History of Western Impacts and Eastern Responses, 6th ed. 1976; China in Old Photographs, 1978; (sr. writer) World History: Patterns of Civilization, 6th ed. 1993; (with M.S. Downs) North Carolina State: A Pictorial History, 1986; (ed. in-chief) Living in Our World, 4 vols., 1998. **Address:** 201 John Wesley Rd, Greenville, NC 27858, U.S.A.

BEERS, Mark H. American, b. 1954. **Genres:** Gerontology/Senior issues, Medicine/Health. **Career:** Massachusetts General Hospital, Boston, research assistant in developmental biology, 1975-77; New England Medical Center, Boston, intern, 1982-83, assistant in medicine, 1982-84; junior assistant resident, 1983-84; Mount Sinai Hospital, NYC, senior assistant resident and assistant in medicine, 1984-85; Beth Israel Hospital, Boston, clinical fellow, 1985-87; University of California, Los Angeles, assistant professor of medicine and medical director of Inpatient Geriatric Unit at university Medical Center, 1987-92, medical adviser to Dept of Coordinated Care and Discharge Planning, 1988-92; Merck and Co. Inc., West Point, PA, associate editor, 1992-. Harvard University, Medical School, clinical fellow in geriatric medicine and fellow of Program for the Analysis of Clinical Strategies, Division on Aging, 1985-87; Brigham and Women's Hospital, clinical fellow, 1985-87; Hebrew Rehabilitation Center for the Aged, Boston, clinical fellow, 1985-87; Jewish Memorial Hospital, Boston, attending physician, 1985- 86; RAND Corp., senior natural scientist, 1989-92; California Department of Health, member of Aging Program advisory board, 1989-. **Publications:** (with I.M. Rollingher) A Guide to Medications for Older Persons, 1991; (with S.K. Urice) Aging in Good Health, 1992. EDITOR: The Merck Manual of Diagnosis and Therapy, 17th ed., 1999; The Merck Manual of Geriatrics, 2000. Work represented in anthologies. Contributor of articles and reviews to medical journals. **Address:** Merck and Co Inc, BLA-22, PO Box 4, West Point, PA 19486, U.S.A.

BEETH, Howard. American, b. 1942. **Genres:** History. **Career:** Houston Public Library, Metropolitan Research Center, Houston, TX, head of Afro-American Collection, 1981-87; Texas Southern University, Houston, associate professor of history, 1988-. **Publications:** (ed. with C. Wintz) Black Dixie: Afro-Texan History and Culture in Houston, 1992. Contributor of articles and reviews to history journals. **Address:** Department of History, Texas Southern University, 3100 Cleburne Ave., Houston, TX 77004, U.S.A. **Online address:** howard.beeth@excite.com

BEGELMAN, Mitchell (Craig). American, b. 1953. **Genres:** Astronomy. **Career:** University of Colorado at Boulder, assistant professor, 1982-87, as- sociate professor, 1987-91, professor of astrophysical, planetary, and atmospheric sciences, 1991-, department head, 1995-98, member of Joint Institute for Laboratory Astrophysics, 1982-84, fellow, 1984-, member of Center for Astrophysics and Space Astronomy, 1986-. Cambridge University, fellow of Institute of Astronomy, 1978-79, 1981-82; University of California, Berkeley, postgraduate research astronomer, 1979-82; N. Copernicus Astronomical Center, Warsaw, Poland, visiting scientist, 1980. **Publications:** (with M. Rees) Gravity's Fatal Attraction: Black Holes in the Universe, 1996; Turn Right at Orion: Travels through the Cosmos, 2000. Contributor to books and scientific journals and popular magazines. **Address:** Joint Institute for Laboratory Astrophysics, University of Colorado at Boulder, Campus Box 440, Boulder, CO 80309, U.S.A. **Online address:** mitch@jila.colorado.edu

BEGLEY, Louis. American (born Poland), b. 1933. **Genres:** Novels. **Career:** Admitted to the Bar of New York State, 1961; Debevoise & Plimpton (law firm), NYC, associate, 1959-67, partner, 1968-; writer; lecturer. Senior visiting lecturer at University of Pennsylvania, 1985 and 1986. **Publications:** NOVELS: Wartime Lies, 1991; The Man Who Was Late, 1993; As Max Saw It, 1994; About Schmidt, 1996; Mistler's Exit, 1998; Schmidt Delivered, 2000; Shipwreck, 2003. Contributor to periodicals.

BEHAR, Ruth. American (born Cuba), b. 1956. **Genres:** Anthropology/Ethnology. **Career:** University of Michigan, Ann Arbor, assistant professor, 1986-89, associate professor, 1989-94, professor of anthropology, 1994-. **Publications:** Santa Maria del Monte: The Presence of the Past in a Spanish Village, 1986, repr. as The Presence of the Past in a Spanish Village: Santa Maria del Monte, 1991; Translated Woman: Crossing the Border With Esperanza's Story, 1993; Las Visiones de una Bruja Guachichil en 1599: Hacia una Perspectiva Indaigena Sobre la Conquista de San Luis Potosai, 1995 The Vulnerable Observer: Anthropology That Breaks Your Heart, 1996. EDITOR: Bridges to Cuba/Puentes a Cuba (anthology), 1995; (with D.A. Gordon) Women Writing Culture, 1995. Contributor of poetry to magazines; contributor to journals and anthologies. **Address:** Department of Anthropology, University of Michigan, 1020 LSA Bldg, Ann Arbor, MI 48109, U.S.A. **Online address:** rbehar@umich.edu

BEHLE, William Harroun. American, b. 1909. **Genres:** Zoology, Biography. **Career:** University of Utah, Salt Lake City, Professor, 1937-, now Professor Emeritus of Biology. **Publications:** Biography of Augustus C. Behle, M. D., 1948; The Bird Life of Great Salt Lake, 1958; (with M. L. Perry) Utah Birds: Check-List, Seasonal and Ecological Occurrence Charts and Guides to Bird Finding, 1975; The Birds of Northeastern Utah, 1981; (with E. D. Sorenson and C. M. White) Utah Birds: A Revised Checklist, 1985; Utah Birds: Geographic Distribution and Systematics, 1985; Utah Birds: Historical Perspectives and Bibliography, 1990; History of Biology at the University of Utah (1869-2000), 2002. **Address:** 1233 E 800 South St, Salt Lake City, UT 84102-3704, U.S.A.

BEHN, Robert Dietrich. American, b. 1941. **Genres:** Public/Social administration. **Career:** Massachusetts Institute of Technology, Lincoln Laboratory, Lexington, engineer, 1964-65; RAND Corp., Santa Monica, CA, consultant, 1966; Ripon Society, Cambridge, MA, research director, 1968-69, executive director, 1970-73; Commonwealth of Massachusetts, Boston, assistant for urban affairs to the governor, 1969-70; Duke University, Durham, NC, associate professor, 1973-88, professor of policy sciences and public affairs, 1988-, director of Institute of Policy Sciences and Public Affairs, 1982-85, director of Governors Center, 1984-. Harvard University, lecturer in business administration, 1972-73; State University of New York at Albany, chair of organization and workforce study for the New York State Department of Social Services, 1991-92. **Publications:** (ed.) The Lessons of Victory, 1969; (with J.W. Vaupel) Quick Analysis for Busy Decision Makers, 1982; (ed.) Governors on Governing, 1990; Leadership Counts: Lessons for Public Managers from the Massachusetts Welfare, Training, and Employment Program, 1991; (ed.) Innovation in American Government, 1997; Rethinking Democratic Accountability, 2001. Work represented in anthologies. Contributor to periodicals. **Address:** Kennedy School of Government, Harvard University, 79 John F Kennedy St, Cambridge, MA 02138, U.S.A.

BEHR, Edward. British, b. 1926. **Genres:** Novels, International relations/Current affairs, Politics/Government, Autobiography/Memoirs. **Career:** Contributing Ed., Newsweek International, since 1987 (Newsweek Bureau Chief, S.E. Asia, 1966-68, and Paris Bureau, 1968-73; European Ed., 1973-83; Cultural Ed., Paris, 1984-87). Reuters Correspondent, 1951-54; Correspondent, Time Magazine, 1957-63; Contributing Ed., Saturday Evening Post, 1963-65. **Publications:** The Algerian Problem, 1961; (with S. Liu) The Thirty Sixth Way, 1969; Bearings, 1978 (in U.K. as Anyone Here Been

Raped-and Speaks English?, 1981); Getting Even (novel), 1980; The Last Emperor, 1987; Hirohito: Behind the Myth, 1989; The Making of Les Miserables, 1989; Indonesia: A Voyage through the Archipelago, 1990; Kiss the Hand You Cannot Bite, 1991; (with M. Steyn) The Story of Miss Saigon, 1991; Thank Heaven for Little Girls (in U.S., The Good Frenchman: The Life and Times of Maurice Chevalier), 1993; The Rise and Fall of Ceausescu (for TV); Une Amerique Qui Fait Peur, 1995; Prohibition, the 13 Years That Changed America, 1997.

BEHREND, George (Henry Sandham). British, b. 1922. **Genres:** Poetry, Air/Space topics, Art/Art history, Geography, History, International relations/ Current affairs, Marine sciences/Oceanography, Transportation, Travel/ Exploration, Autobiography/Memoirs. **Career:** Br 8th Army, 1942-46; part-time personal assistant to Benjamin Britten, 1947-58; part-time farmer, Hampshire, England, 1947-56; freelance writer, 1962-. **Publications:** Grand European Expresses: The Story of Wagons-Lits, 1962; Pullman in Europe, 1962; Railway Holiday in France, 1963; Railway Holiday in Switzerland, 1965; Stanley Spencer at Burghclere, 1965; Jersey Airlines, 1968; Gone with Regret: Recollections of the Great Western Railway 1922-1947, 4th ed., 1992; (with V. Kelly) Yatakli-Vagon: Turkish Steam Travel, 1969; (with I. Scott-Hill) Channel Silver Wings, 1972; Steam over Switzerland, 1974; History of Trains de Luxe, 1982; Luxury Trains, 1982; (with G. Buchanan) Night Ferry: Britain's Only International Train, 1985; (trans.) The Orient Express: A Century of Railway Adventures, 1988; Don't Knock the Southern, 1993; Pullman and the Orient Expresses: 1872-2000, 2001, rev. ed., 2003; (with M. Kelharman) Shooting the Net, 2004; British Fishing 1923-2003, 2004. **Address:** 9 Station Rd, Findochty, Buckie, Morayshire AB56 4PN, Scotland. **Online address:** georgebehrend@aol.com; www.georgebehrend. co.uk

BEHRENS, Ellen. American, b. 1957. **Genres:** Novels, Novellas/Short stories, Education, Essays. **Career:** Adjunct instructor at colleges and universities, 1990-94; Delphi Automotive, Sandusky, OH, educational development counselor, 1994-99, Flint, MI, 1999-2000; Novations Learning Technologies, Lansing, MI, manager of instructional design, 2000-. Ohio Arts Council, artist in residence, 1991-2000; Firelands College, member of Technologies Advisory Board; BGSU Board of Directors, Creative Writing Alumni Association. **Publications:** None But the Dead and the Dying (novel), 1996. Work represented in anthologies. Contributor to periodicals. **Address:** Novations Learning Technologies, 3245 Technology Blvd, Lansing, MI 48910, U.S.A. **Online address:** ellenbehr@aol.com

BEHRENS, John C. (Jack). American, b. 1933. **Genres:** Business/Trade/ Industry, History, How-to books, Money/Finance, Music, Writing/Journalism. **Career:** Professor of Journalism, 1965-, Curator, Student Press Archives, 1967-, Director, PR/J Programs, 1986-92, Utica College of Syracuse University; Ed., Commerce Commentary, 1967-. Columnist, American Printer, 1978-99. Business Columnist, The Elks, 1976-. Journalist, Pacific Stars and Stripes, 1957-58; Newspaper ed. in Ohio, 1958-62; Chairman, Journalism Dept., Ohio Wesleyan University, Delaware, 1962-63; Assistant Professor of Journalism, Marshall University, Huntington, W. Virginia, 1963-65; Editor, Laubach's Literary Advance, 1984-86; Editor, Home Business Journal, 1995-2001. **Publications:** Magazine Writers' Workbook, 1968, 3rd ed., 1983; Reporting Worktext, 1974; Typewriter Guerrillas: Closeups of 20 Top Investigative Reporters, 1977, 2nd ed., 1979; Student Press Archives Directory, 1987; The Writing Business, 1991; Pioneering Generations: The Utica College Story, 1997; The Big Band Days: A Memoir and Source Book, 2003; Presidential Profiles: An Intimate Collection of Portraits and Documents, 2003. EDITOR: Wood and Stone: Landmarks of Mohawk Valley, 1972; Munson-Williams-Proctor Institute's Biennials, 1988-1998; The School of Art: The 1st 50 Years at M-W-P, 1991; Mohawk Valley Almanac (NY) 1994; CMA Student Press: A Bibliography of Cases, 1994; CMA Student Press Annotated Guide to Cases, 1994. **Address:** 57 Stebbins Dr, Clinton, NY 13323, U.S.A. **Online address:** writerjack@aol.com; writerjackweb.com

BEI DAO. (Zhao Zhenkai). Chinese, b. 1949. **Genres:** Novellas/Short stories, Poetry. **Career:** Writer. Today (Jintian), literary magazine, co-founder, 1978. **Publications:** The August Sleepwalker (poetry), 1990; Waves (short stories), 1990; Old Snow (poetry), 1991; Forms of Distance (poetry), 1994; Landscape over Zero (poetry), 1996; Unlock (poetry), 2000; Blue House (essay), 2000.

BEIDERWELL, Bruce. American, b. 1952. **Genres:** Literary criticism and history. **Career:** University of California, Los Angeles, lecturer in writing, 1985-. **Publications:** Power and Punishment in Scott's Novels, University of Georgia Press, 1992. Contributor of articles and reviews to literature journals. **Address:** Writing Programs, University of California, 405 Hilgard Ave., Los Angeles, CA 90024, U.S.A.

BEIDLER, Peter G. American, b. 1940. **Genres:** Education, Literary criticism and history, Race relations. **Career:** Lehigh University, Bethlehem, PA, assistant professor, 1968-72, associate professor, 1972-77, professor, 1977-78, Lucy G. Moses Distinguished Professor of English, 1978-, director of Freshman Writing Program, 1989-90. University of Kent at Canterbury, research professor, 1983-84; Sichuan University, Fulbright professor, 1987-88; Baylor University, Robert Foster Cherry Visiting Distinguished Teaching Professor, 1995-96. **Publications:** Fig Tree John: An Indian in Fact and Fiction, 1977; (with M.F. Egge) The American Indian in Short Fiction: An Annotated Bibliography, 1979; Distinguished Teachers on Effective Teaching, 1986; Ghosts, Demons, and Henry James, 1989; Writing Matters, 1990; Henry James, The Turn of the Screw: Text and Five Contemporary Critical Essays, 1995; Geoffrey Chaucer, The Wife of Bath: Complete, Authoritative Text with Biographical and Historical Contexts, Critical History, and Essays from Five Contemporary Critical Perspectives, 1996; (with E.M. Biebel) The Wife of Bath's Prologue and Tale: An Annotated Bibliography, 1998; (with G. Barton) A Reader's Guide to the Novels of Louise Erdrich, 1999; (with Egge) The Native American in the Saturday Evening Post, 1897-1969, 2000; (with Egge and H.J. Brown) The Native American in Short Fiction in the Saturday Evening Post, 2001; Why I Teach, 2002. EDITOR & CONTRIBUTOR: John Gower's Literary Transformations in the Confessio Amantis, 1982; Masculinities in Chaucer, 1998. Contributor to books. Contributor of articles and reviews to periodicals. **Address:** Dept of English, Lehigh University, 33 Sayre Dr, Bethlehem, PA 18015-3076, U.S.A. **Online address:** pgb1@lehigh.edu

BEIFUSS, John, (Jr.). American, b. 1959. **Genres:** Documentaries/ Reportage. **Career:** Newspaper reporter, Memphis, TN, 1981-. **Publications:** Armadillo Ray, 1995. **Address:** 495 Union, Memphis, TN 38103, U.S.A.

BEINHART, Larry. American, b. 1947. **Genres:** Novels. **Career:** Writer. **Publications:** No One Rides for Free, 1987; You Get What You Pay For, 1988; Foreign Exchange, 1991; American Hero, 1993; How to Write a Mystery, 1996. **Address:** c/o Joy Harris Agency, 156 5th Ave. No. 617, New York, NY 10010-7002, U.S.A.

BEISNER, Robert L. American, b. 1936. **Genres:** History. **Career:** University of Chicago, Instructor in the Social Science, 1962-63; Colgate University, Hamilton, NY, Instructor of History, 1963-65; American University, Washington, D.C., Assistant Professor, 1965-67, Associate Professor, 1967-71, Professor of History, 1971-97, Dept. Chair, 1981-90, Dir. of General Education, 1993-97, Emeritus Professor, 1997-. Society of Historians of American Foreign Relations, President, 2002-. **Publications:** Twelve against Empire: The Anti-Imperialists, 1898-1900, 1968, 1985; From the Old Diplomacy to the New, 1865-1900, 1975, 1986; (co-ed.) Arms at Rest: Peacemaking and Peacekeeping in American History, 1987. **Address:** 3851 Newark St NW, Washington, DC 20016-3026, U.S.A. **Online address:** huskerindc@rcn.com

BEISSEL, Henry (Eric). Canadian (born Germany), b. 1929. **Genres:** Plays/Screenplays, Poetry, Geography, Travel/Exploration, Essays, Translations. **Career:** Concordia University, Montreal, assistant professor, 1966-68, associate professor, 1968-76, professor, 1976-95, emeritus professor of English, 1995-, distinguished emeritus professor, 1999-. Visiting professor at universities worldwide. **Publications:** Introduction to Spain, 1955; Witness the Heart, 1963; The World Is a Rainbow, 1969; A Trumpet for Nap, 1973; The Salt I Taste, 1975; Kanada: Romantik und Wirklichkeit, 1981; Inuk, 2000. PLAYS: The Curve, 1963; Mister Skinflint: A Marionette Play, 1969; Inook and the Sun, 1973; For Crying Out Loud, 1977; (ed.) Cues and Entrances, 1977; Goya, 1978; Under Coyote's Eye, 1980; (adaptation) The Emigrants, 1981; The Noose and Improvisations for Mr. X, 1989. POETRY: New Wings for Icarus: A Poem in Four Parts, 1966; Face on the Dark, 1970; Cantos North (epic), 1980; Season of Blood, 1984; Poems New and Selected, 1987; Ammonite, 1987; Stones to Harvest, 1991; Dying I Was Born, 1992; The Dragon and the Pearl, 2002; Across the Sun's Warp, 2030. TRANSLATOR: W. Bauer, The Price of Morning: Selected Poems, 1969; A Different Sun, 1976; Three Plays by Tankred Dorst, 1976; T.A. Bringsvaerd, The Glass Mountain, 1989. **Address:** PO Box 339, Alexandria, ON, Canada K0C 1A0. **Online address:** beifran@glen-net.ca

BEISSINGER, Steven R. American, b. 1953. **Genres:** Environmental sciences/Ecology, Biology. **Career:** National Institute for Urban Wildlife, Columbia, MD, field biologist, 1978; Florida Game and Fresh Water Fish Commission, contract biologist, 1979; University of Michigan, Ann Arbor, lecturer in ecology and environmental science, 1984-85; University of Florida, Gainesville, adjunct assistant professor of wildlife science, 1986-88; Yale University, New Haven, CT, assistant professor, 1988-91, associate professor of ecology and conservation biology, 1991-. Lecturer at colleges and universities. **Publications:** (ed. with N.F.R. Snyder, and contrib.) New World Parrots in Crisis: Solutions from Conservation Biology, 1992. Contributor to books. Contributor of articles and reviews to scientific journals and popular magazines. **Address:** School of Forestry and Environmental Sciences, Yale University, 205 Prospect St., New Haven, CT 06511, U.S.A.

BEJA, Morris. American, b. 1935. **Genres:** Film, Literary criticism and history. **Career:** Ohio State University, instructor to professor of English, 1961-94, chairman of English, 1983-94, professor emeritus, 1995-. **Publications:** Epiphany in the Modern Novel, 1971; Film and Literature, 1979; Critical Essays on Virginia Woolf, 1985; James Joyce: A Literary Life, 1992; Joyce in the Hibernian Metropolis, 1996; Perspectives on Orson Welles, 1995; Virginia Woolf's Mrs. Dalloway, 1996. EDITOR: Virginia Woolf's To the Lighthouse: A Selection of Critical Essays, 1970; Psychological Fiction, 1971; James Joyce's Dubliners and A Portrait of the Artist as a Young Man: Selection of Critical Essays, 1973; (with S.E. Gontarski and P. Astier) Samuel Beckett: Humanistic Perspectives, 1982; (co) James Joyce: The Centennial Symposium, 1987; (co) Coping with Joyce, 1989. **Address:** Department of English, Ohio State University, 164 W 17th Ave, Columbus, OH 43210, U.S.A. **Online address:** beja.1@osu.edu

BELAND, Pierre. Canadian, b. 1947. **Genres:** Novels, Animals/Pets. **Career:** Glacialis Productions, Montreal, Quebec, screenplay writer. International Joint Commission, member, 1995-. **Publications:** Beluga: A Farewell to Whales, 1996; Trois Jours en Juin (Three days in June), 1998: Passagers Clandestines (Stowaways), 2005. **Address:** 5040 Rue de Mentana, Montreal, QC, Canada H2J 3C3. **Online address:** belandp@sympatico.ca

BELBIN, David. British, b. 1958. **Genres:** Children's fiction, Young adult fiction. **Career:** Teacher of English, drama, and media studies in Nottingham, England, 1985-94; writer, 1994-; Nottingham Trent University, senior lecturer in creative writing, 2002-. **Publications:** FOR YOUNG ADULTS: The Foggiest, 1990; Shoot the Teacher, 1993, in US as Deadly Secrets, 1994; Final Cut, 1994; Avenging Angel, 1994; Break Point, 1995; Deadly Inheritance, 1996; Dark Journey, 1997; The David Belbin Collection: Three Degrees of Murder, 1997; Haunting Time (stories), 1998; Love Lessons, 1998; Dying for You, 1999; Festival, 2000; The Last Virgin, 2002; Denial, 2004. FOR CHILDREN: Runaway Train, 1999; The Right Moment, 2000; Boy King, 2002. THE BEAT SERIES: Missing Person, 1995; Black and Blue, 1995; Smokescreen, 1996; Asking for It, 1996; Dead White Male, 1996; Losers, 1997; Sudden Death, 1997; Night Shift, 1998; Victims, 1998; Suspects, 1999; Fallen Angel, 2000. EDITOR FOR ADULTS: City of Crime (stories), 1997; (with J. Lucas) Stanley Middleton at Eighty, 1999. Work represented in anthologies. Contributor to periodicals. **Address:** 27 Devonshire Rd, Sherwood, Nottingham NG5 2EW, England. **Online address:** david.belbin@ntu.ac.uk

BELEN. *See* KAPLAN, Nelly.

BELIEU, Erin. American, b. 1965. **Genres:** Poetry. **Career:** Writer. **Publications:** Infanta (poetry), 1995. Contributor to periodicals. **Address:** c/o Copper Canyon Press, P. O. Box 271, Port Townsend, WA 98368, U.S.A.

BELIN, Esther G. American, b. 1968. **Genres:** Poetry. **Career:** Writer. **Publications:** From the Belly of My Beauty (poetry), 1999. **Address:** c/o Author Mail, University of Arizona Press, 355 South Euclid Suite 103, Tucson, AZ 85719, U.S.A. **Online address:** bitterwater@hotmail.com

BELKAOUI, Ahmed R. (Ahmed Riahi-Belkaoui). American (born Tunisia), b. 1943. **Genres:** Money/Finance, Novels, Administration/Management, Politics/Government. **Career:** University of Ottawa, ON, assistant professor to associate professor, 1973-79, associate professor, 1980-81; University of Illinois at Chicago, professor of accounting, 1981-. University of Chicago, visiting associate professor, 1979-80; lecturer at universities worldwide. **Publications:** The Conceptual Foundations of Management Accounting, 1980; Cost Accounting, 1983; Industrial Bond Ratings and the Rating Process, 1983; Socio-Economic Accounting, 1984; Theorie Comptable, 2nd ed., 1984; Public Policy and the Problems and Practices of Accounting, 1985; International Accounting, 1985; The Learning Curve, 1986; Handbook of Management Control Systems, 1986; Quantitative Models in Accounting, 1987; The New Environment in International Accounting, 1987; Inquiry and Accounting, 1987; The Coming Crisis in Accounting, 1989; Behavioral Accounting, 1989; Human Information Processing in Accounting, 1989; Judgment in International Accounting, 1990; (with E. Pavlik) Determinants of Executive Compensation, 1991; Multinational Management Accounting, 1991; Multinational Financial Accounting, 1991; Handbook of Cost Account-

ing, 1991; (with J. Monti-Belkaoui) Accounting for Economic Dualism, 1991; Accounting Theory, 3rd ed., 1992; Value Added Reporting, 1992; The New Foundations of Management Accounting, 1992; (with Pavlik) Accounting for Corporate Reputation, 1992; Morality in Accounting, 1992; Human Resource Valuation, 1995; (with J. Monti-Belkaoui); Fairness in Accounting, 1996; (with J. Monti-Belkaoui); Sherazade and Her Two Lovers, 1996. **Address:** College of Business Administration, University of Illinois at Chicago Circle M/C 006, 601 Morgan St, Chicago, IL 60607-7123, U.S.A. **Online address:** belkaoui@uic.edu

BELKIN, Lisa. American, b. 1960. **Genres:** Medicine/Health, Regional/Urban planning, Women's studies and issues, Autobiography/Memoirs. **Career:** New York Times, NYC, reporter, 1982-87, national correspondent 1987-91, health care reporter, 1991-93. **Publications:** First Do No Harm, 1993; Show Me a Hero, 1999; Life's Work: Confessions of an Unbalanced Mom, 2002. **Address:** c/o Karpfinger Agency, 357 W 20th St, New York, NY 10011, U.S.A.

BELKNAP, Robert L. American, b. 1929. **Genres:** Education, Literary criticism and history. **Career:** Columbia University, NYC, professor of Russian, 1970- (joined faculty as instructor, 1957). **Publications:** The Structure of The Brothers Karamazov, 1966; (with R. Kuhns) Tradition and Innovation, General Education and the Reintegration of the University, 1977; (ed.) Russianness, 1989; The Genesis of the Brothers Karamazov, 1990. **Address:** 305 Faculty House, Columbia University, New York, NY 10027, U.S.A. **Online address:** rb12@columbia.edu

BELL, Albert A., Jr. American, b. 1945. **Genres:** Mystery/Crime/Suspense, Children's fiction, History, Theology/Religion, Bibliography. **Career:** Hope College, Holland, MI, professor of history, 1978-. **Publications:** Daughter of Lazarus, 1988; (with J.B. Allis) Resources in Ancient Philosophy: An Annotated Bibliography of Scholarship in English, 1965-1989, 1991; A Guide to the New Testament World, 1994; Exploring the New Testament World, 1998; All Roads Lead to Murder, 2002; Kill Her Again, 2000; The Case of the Lonely Grave, 2000. Contributor of articles and stories to periodicals. **Address:** Department of History, Lubbers Hall, Hope College, PO Box 9000, Holland, MI 49422-9000, U.S.A. **Online address:** bell@hope.edu

BELL, Betty Louise. American, b. 1949. **Genres:** Novels. **Career:** Native American literary scholar and novelist; associated with the English department of the University of Michigan, Ann Arbor. **Publications:** Faces in the Moon, 1994. **Address:** Department of English, Haven Hall, University of Michigan, Ann Arbor, MI 48104, U.S.A.

BELL, Charles G(reenleaf). American, b. 1916. **Genres:** Sciences, Novels, History, Poetry, Philosophy. **Career:** Blackburn College, Carlinville, IL, instructor in English, 1939-40; Iowa State College, Ames, instructor and assistant professor of English, then of physics, 1940-45; Princeton University, NJ, research assistant in electronics, then assistant professor of English, 1945-49; University of Chicago, assistant professor of humanities, 1949-56; University of Puerto Rico, Mayaguez, guest professor and director of honors program, 1955-56; St. John's College, Annapolis, Maryland, tutor, 1956-67; Technische Hochschule, Munich, Fulbright professor of art and philosophy, 1958-59; St. John's College, Santa Fe, NM, tutor, 1967-. **Publications:** Songs for a New America, 1953, rev. ed., 1966; Delta Return, 1956, rev. ed. 1969; The Married Land (novel), 1962; The Half Gods (novel), 1968; Five Chambered Heart, 1985. **Address:** 1260 Canyon Rd, Santa Fe, NM 87501, U.S.A.

BELL, David Owen. American, b. 1949. **Genres:** Children's non-fiction, Environmental sciences/Ecology, Marine sciences/Oceanography, Picture/board books. **Career:** Writer and photographer, 1977-; Master Mariner, 1981-. President, Environmental Fund for Maryland, 1996-98. **Publications:** The Celestial Navigation Mystery: Solved, 1977; Dockmanship, 1992; Awesome Chesapeake: A Kid's Guide to the Bay, 1994; (ed.) Hands On! Feet Wet!, 1997; If Dads Can Eat, Dads Can Cook!, 1997; Chesapeake Bay Walk, 1998. **Address:** c/o Tidewater Publishers, Box 456, Centreville, MD 21617, U.S.A.

BELL, Hazel K(athleen). (born England), b. 1935. **Genres:** Animals/Pets. **Career:** Editor, indexer, and writer. National Housewives Register, editor of National Newsletter, 1976-80; Society of Indexers, editor of The Indexer, 1978-95; Association of Learned and Professional Publishers, editor of Learned Publishing, 1984-96; Malaysian Rubber Research and Development Association, editor of Rubber Developments, 1990; editor of Journal of the Angela Thirkell Society, 1997-98; Barbara Pym Society, editor of Green Leaves, 1999-. Compiler of more than 600 published indexes to books and journals. Has also worked as a teacher and as a member of educational examining boards. **Publications:** Situation Books for Under-Sixes, 1970; Indexing Biographies and Other Stories of Human Lives, foreword by A. S. Byatt, 1992; (editor) Indexers and Indexes in Fact and Fiction, 2001. Contributor of articles, reports, and reviews to periodicals. **Address:** 139 The Ryde, Hatfield, Hertfordshire AL9 5DP, England.

BELL, Ian Mackay. Scottish. **Genres:** Literary criticism and history, Area studies, Biography, Novels. **Career:** The Scotsman, Scotland, literary editor; journalist. **Publications:** The Dominican Republic, 1981; Dreams of Exile: Robert Louis Stevenson, a Biography, 1993; (ed. and author of intro.) R.L. Stevenson, The Complete Short Stories, 1994. **Address:** c/o Henry Holt & Co Inc, 115 W 18th St, New York, NY 10011, U.S.A. **Online address:** ibell@scotsman.com

BELL, James Edward. American, b. 1941. **Genres:** Psychology. **Career:** Professor of Psychology, Howard Community College, Columbia, Maryland, 1971-; instructor, University of Minnesota, Minneapolis, 1965-66; asst professor of psych, Hanover College, Indiana, 1966-68; asst professor of psych, Elmira College, New York, 1968-71. **Publications:** A Guide to Library Research in Psychology, 1971; (ed.) Ideas and Issues in Psychology, 7th ed., 1993; Evaluating Psychological Information: A Guide to Critical Thinking in Psychology, 3rd ed., 1999. **Address:** Howard Community College, Columbia, MD 21044, U.S.A. **Online address:** jbell@howardcc.edu

BELL, Madison Smartt. American, b. 1957. **Genres:** Novels, Novellas/ Short stories. **Career:** Johns Hopkins University, writing seminars, visiting associate professor, 1989-93; Goucher College, English Department, writer in residence, creative writing program, director, 1989-86, 1988-. **Publications:** The Washington Square Ensemble, 1983; Zero DB (short stories), 1987; Soldier's Joy, 1989; Barking Man and Other Stories, 1990; Doctor Sleep, 1991; Save Me, Joe Louis, 1993. NOVELS: Waiting for the End of the World, 1985; Straight Cut, 1986; The Year of Silence, 1987; All Souls Rising, 1994; Ten Indians, 1996; Master of the Crossroads, 2000; Anything Goes, 2002. **Address:** Kratz Center for Creative Writing, Goucher College, Towson, MD 21204, U.S.A.

BELL, Malcolm. See HOUGAN, Carolyn.

BELL, Marvin (Hartley). American, b. 1937. **Genres:** Poetry, Literary criticism and history, Autobiography/Memoirs, Essays. **Career:** Statements mag., visiting editor, 1959-64; North American Review, Mount Vernon, IA, poetry editor, 1964-69; University of Iowa, Iowa City, lecturer, 1965, assistant professor, 1966-69, associate professor, 1970-74, professor, 1975-85, Flannery O'Connor Professor of Letters, 1986-; Iowa Review, poetry editor, 1969-71; American Poetry Review, columnist, 1975-78, 1990-92; University of Redlands, Lila Wallace-Reader's Digest Writing Fellow, 199193; Pushcart Prize Volumes, series editor, poetry, 1997-. Iowa poet laureate, 2000-; Woodrow Wilson Visiting Fellow: St Mary's College of California, 1995; Nebraska-Wesleyan University, 1996; Pacific University, 1997; Hampden-Sydney College, 1999; West Virginia Wesleyan College, 2000; Birmingham Southern College, 2001; Illinois College, 2002; Bethany College, WV, 2003. **Publications:** (ed.) Iowa Workshop Poets 1963, 1963; Things We Dreamt We Died For, 1966; Poems for Nathan and Saul, 1966; A Probable Volume of Dreams: Poems, 1969; The Escape into You: A Sequence, 1971; Woo Havoc, 1971; Residue of Song, 1974; Stars Which See, Stars Which Do Not See, 1977, 2nd ed., 1992; These Green-Going-to-Yellow, 1981; William Stafford and Marvin Bell: Segues, 1983; Old Snow Just Melting: Essays and Interviews, 1983; Drawn by Stones, by Earth, by Things that Have Been in the Fire, 1984; New and Selected Poems, 1987; William Stafford and Marvin Bell: Annie-Over, 1988; Iris of Creation (poetry), 1990; The Book of the Dead Man (poetry), 1994; A Marvin Bell Reader: Selected Poetry and Prose, 1994; Ardor: The Book of the Dead Man, vol. 2, 1997; Wednesday, 1998; Poetry for a Midsummer's Night, 1998; Nightworks: Poems 1962-2000, 2000; Rampant, 2004. **Address:** Writers Workshop, University of Iowa, Iowa City, IA 52242, U.S.A.

BELL, Mary Reeves. American, b. 1946. **Genres:** Children's fiction. **Career:** Writer. Romanian Christian Enterprises (relief organization), executive director. **Publications:** The Secret of the Mezuzah, 1995; The Sagebrush Rebellion, 1999; Checkmate in the Carpathians, 2000. Contributor to periodicals. **Address:** 21058 Unison Rd, Middleburg, VA 20117, U.S.A. **Online address:** snarkhunt2@aol.com

BELL, Nancy. American, b. 1932. **Genres:** Mystery/Crime/Suspense. **Career:** Novelist. **Publications:** NOVELS: Biggie and the Poisoned Politician,

1996; Biggie and the Mangled Mortician, 1997; Biggie and the Fricasseed Fat Man, 1998. **Address:** c/o St. Martin's Press, 175 Fifth Ave., Rm. 1715, New York, NY 10010, U.S.A.

BELL, Richard H. American, b. 1938. **Genres:** Philosophy, Theology/ Religion. **Career:** Yale University, New Haven, CT, dean of Berkeley College, 1966-69, lecturer in religious studies, 1967-69; College of Wooster, Wooster, OH, assistant professor, 1969-75, associate professor, 1975-81, professor, 1981-84, Frank H. Ferris Professor of Philosophy, 1984-. **Publications:** (ed. with R.E. Hustwit and author of intro) Essays on Kierkegaard and Wittgenstein: On Understanding the Self, 1978; Sensing the Spirit, 1984; (gen. ed.) Spirituality and the Christian Life series, 1984; (ed. and author of intro) The Grammar of the Heart: New Essays in Moral Philosophy and Theology, 1988; (ed. and contrib.) Simone Weil's Philosophy of Culture: Readings towards a Divine Humanity, 1993; (with B.L. Battin) Seeds of the Spirit: Wisdom of the Twentieth-Century, 1995; Simone Weil: The Way of Justice as Compassion, 1998. Contributor to periodicals. **Address:** Department of Philosophy, College of Wooster, Scovel Hall, 944 College Mall, Wooster, OH 44691-2363, U.S.A. **Online address:** rbell@acs.wooster.edu

BELL, Robin. British, b. 1945. **Genres:** Plays/Screenplays, Poetry. **Career:** Secretary, Poetry Association of Scotland, since 1983. Worked in publishing and broadcasting, and as a univ. teacher, 1968-82. Recipient, Sony Award for Best Radio Documentary in Britain, 1985. **Publications:** POETRY: The Invisible Mirror, 1965; Culdee, Culdee, 1966; Sawing Logs, 1980; Strathinver: A Portrait Album 1943-1953, 1980; Radio Poems, 1989; Scanning the Forth Bridge, 1994. RADIO VERSE PLAYS: Strathinver, 1986; The Other Thief, 1986; Melville Bay, 1987. OTHER: Attic Archives (TV documentary), 1987. EDITOR: Collected Poems of James Graham, Marquis of Montrose, 1970; Guide book series to Scottish Ancient Monuments, 1978; Best of Scottish Poetry: An Anthology of Living Scottish Poets, 1989; Bittersweet within My Heart, the Collected Poems of Mary, Queen of Scots, 1992. **Address:** The Orchard, Mairton, Auchterardes, Perthshire PH3 1ND, Scotland.

BELL, Thornton. See FANTHORPE, R(obert) Lionel.

BELL, William. Canadian, b. 1945. **Genres:** Young adult fiction, Children's fiction. **Career:** High school teacher of writing and literature, Orillia and Barrie, Ontario, 1970-; English teacher, Harbin, China, 1982-83, and Beijing, China, 1985-86. **Publications:** FOR YOUNG ADULTS: Crabbe, 1986 in US as Crabbe's Journey, 1987; Metal Head, 1987; The Cripples' Club, 1988, as Absolutely Invincible, 1991; Death Wind, 1989; Five Days of the Ghost, 1989; Forbidden City, 1990; No Signature, 1992; Speak to the Earth, 1994; Zack, 1998. FOR CHILDREN: The Golden Disk, 1995; River My Friend, 1996. **Address:** c/o Doubleday Canada, 105 Bond St., Toronto, ON, Canada M5B 1Y3. **Online address:** willbell@barint.on.ca

BELLAMY, Christopher (David). British, b. 1955. **Genres:** History, Military/Defense/Arms control. **Career:** British Ministry of Defence, 1978-87; Independent, London, England, defense correspondent, 1990-. Institute of Linguists, associate, 1981. **Publications:** The Future of Land Warfare, 1986; Red God of War, 1987; The Times Atlas of the Second World War, 1989; The Evolution of Modern Land Warfare, 1990; Expert Witness, 1993; Knights in White Armour, 1996. **Address:** Independent, 1 Canada Sq., Canary Wharf, London E14 5DL, England. **Online address:** C.Bellamy@independent.co.uk

BELLAMY, David James. British, b. 1933. **Genres:** Botany, Natural history. **Career:** University of Durham, Hon. Professor of Adult and Continuing Education. TV and Radio writer and presenter: series include Life in Our Sea, 1970; Bellamy on Botany, 1973; Bellamy's Britain, 1975; Bellamy's Europe, 1977; Botanic Man, 1978; Up a Gum Tree, 1980; Backyard Safari, 1981; The Great Seasons, 1982; Bellamy's New World, 1983; Seaside Safari, 1986; Bellamy's Bugle, 1986-87; On Top of the World, 1988; Bird's Eye View, 1989; Moa's Ark, 1990. Founding Director, Conservation Foundation; President, WATCH, 1982-91; President, Youth Hostels Association, 1983; President, Population Concern, 1989-. O.B.E. 1994; Honorary Professor of Adult and Continuing Education, University of Durham. **Publications:** books connected with TV series; also: Peatlands, 1974; Life Giving Sea., 1977; Half of Paradise, 1979; The Great Seasons, 1981; Discovering the Countryside with David Bellamy, 4 vols., 1982-83; The Mouse Book, 1983; The Queen's Hidden Garden, 1984; Turning the Tide, 1986; The Vanishing Bogs of Ireland, 1986; Bellamy's Changing Countryside, 4 vols., 1988; Moa's Ark, 1990; Wilderness Britain, 1990; Britain's Last Wilderness Wetlands, 1990; How Green Are You?, 1991; Tomorrow's Earth, 1992; World Medicine, 1992; Blooming Bellamy, 1993; Trees of the World, 1994; Por You and the Potoroo's Loo, 1997. **Address:** Mill House, Bedburn, Bishop Auckland, Durham DL13 3NN, England.

BELLAMY, Richard (Paul). Scottish, b. 1957. **Genres:** History, Philosophy, Politics/Government. **Career:** University of Pisa, Italy, lecturer in English, 1981-82; Oxford University, postdoctoral research fellow at Nuffield College, 1983-86, lecturer in political studies at Christ Church, 1984-86; Cambridge University, England, fellow and lecturer in history at Jesus College and lector at Trinity College, 1986-88; University of Edinburgh, lecturer in politics and member of Centre for Criminology and the Social and Philosophical Study of Law, 1988-92; University of East Anglia, professor of politics, 1993-96; University of Reading, professor of politics, 1996-2002; University of Essex, professor of government, 2002-. Critical Review of International Social and Political Philosophy, co-editor, 2002-; European Consortium for Political Research, academic director, 2003-. **Publications:** Modern Italian Social Theory, 1987; Liberalism and Modern Society, 1992; (with D. Schecter) Gramsci and the Italian State, 1993; Liberalism and Pluralism, 1999; Rethinking Liberalism, 2000. EDITOR: A Gramsci, Pre-Prison Writings; C. Beccaria, On Crimes and Punishments and Other Writings, 1995. EDITOR & CONTRIBUTOR: Liberalism and Recent Legal and Social Philosophy, 1989; Victorian Liberalism, 1990; Theories and Concepts of Politics, 1993; (with D. Castiglione) Constitutionalism in Transformation, 1996; (with A. Warleigh) Citizenship and Governance in the European Union, 2001; (with A. Mason) Political Concepts, 2003; (with T. Ball) The Cambridge History of 20th Century Political Thought, 2003. Work represented in anthologies. Contributor of articles and reviews to history and political science journals. **Address:** Dept of Government, University of Essex, Colchester C04 3S0, England.

BELLE, Kathryn. See LYNN (RUIZ), Kathryn.

BELLER, Susan Provost. American, b. 1949. **Genres:** Genealogy/Heraldry, History. **Career:** Fairfax City Adult Education, Fairfax, VA, genealogy instructor, 1980-82; Christ The King School, Burlington, VT, librarian, 1982-86; Bristol Elementary School, Bristol, VT, librarian, 1986-93; writer, 1993-. Has also worked as an instructor at the University of Vermont; created and conducts a hands-on history program for schools. **Publications:** Roots for Kids: A Genealogy Guide for Young People, 1989; Cadets at War: The True Story of Teenage Heroism at the Battle of New Market, 1991; Woman of Independence: The Life of Abigail Adams, 1992; Medical Practices in the Civil War, 1992; Mosby and His Rangers: Adventures of the Gray Ghost, 1992; To Hold This Ground: A Desperate Battle at Gettysburg, 1995; Never Were Men So Brave: The Irish Brigade during the Civil War, 1998; Confederate Ladies, 1999; Billy Yank and Johnny Reb: Soldiering in the Civil War, 2000; Revolutionary War: Letters from the Home Front, 2001; American Voices from the Revolutionary War, 2002; American Voices from the Civil War, 2002; Yankee Doodle and the Redcoats! Soldiering in the Revolutionary War, 2003. **Address:** 187 Stone Wall Ln, Charlotte, VT 05445, U.S.A. **Online address:** kidsbks@msn.com

BELLER, Tom. American, b. 1965. **Genres:** Novellas/Short stories. **Career:** Open City (magazine), Manhattan, NY, co-founder and co-editor. Has worked in a bagel factory and as a bike messenger. **Publications:** Seduction Theory: Stories, 1995; Sleep-Over Artist, 2000. Contributor of short stories and articles to magazines. **Address:** c/o Mary Evans Inc., 242 East 5th St., New York, NY 10003, U.S.A.

BELLESILES, Michael A. American. **Genres:** History, Documentaries/Reportage. **Career:** Educator and historian. Emory University, Atlanta, GA, associate professor until December, 2002; teacher in Scotland, 2003-. **Publications:** Revolutionary Outlaws: Ethan Allan and the Struggle for Independence in the Early American Frontier, 1993; (ed.) Lethal Imagination: Violence and Brutality in History, 1999; Arming America: The Origins of a National Gun Culture, 2000, rev. ed, 2003. Contributor to books. **Address:** c/o Author Mail, Soft Skull Press, 71 Bond St., Brooklyn, NY 11217, U.S.A.

BELLI, Gioconda. Nicaraguan, b. 1949. **Genres:** Poetry, Novels. **Career:** Alfa Omega Advertising Co., Nicaragua, account executive, 1973-75; Garnier Advertising, San Jose, Cost Rica, creative director, 1976-78; Sandinista National Liberation Front, Nicaragua, diplomat, 1978-79; Ministry of Economic Planning, Nicaragua, director of communications and public relations, 1979-82; Sandinista National Liberation Front, international press liaison, 1982-83, executive secretary and spokesperson, 1983-84; Nicaragua Writer's Union, Nicaragua, foreign-affairs secretary, 1983-88; Sistema Nacional de Publicidad, Nicaragua, managing director, 1984-86; writer, 1986-. **Publications:** POETRY IN ENGLISH TRANSLATION: De las costilla de Eva, 1987, trans. by S.F. White as From Eve's Rib, 1989; Nicaragua under Fire, 1989. OTHER POETRY: Sobre la grama ("On the Grass"), 1974; Linea de fuego ("Line of Fire"), 1978; Truenos y arco iris ("Thunder and

Rainbows"), 1982; Amor insurrecto ("Insurrect Love"), 1984; El ojo de la mujer ("Through a Woman's Eye"), 1991; Sortilegio contra el frio, 1992. Work represented in anthologies. Contributor of poetry to periodicals. NOVELS IN ENGLISH TRANSLATION: La mujer habitada, 1988, trans. by K. March as The Inhabited Woman, 1994. OTHER NOVELS: Sofia de las presagios ("Sophie and the Omens"), 1990; Waslala, 1995. OTHER: Nicaragua in Reconstruction and at War, 1985; "The Workshop of the Butterflies" (for children), 1994. **Address:** 703 Twelfth St., Santa Monica, CA 90402, U.S.A.

BELLIOTTI, Raymond A(ngelo). American, b. 1948. **Genres:** Law, Philosophy. **Career:** Miami-Dade Community College South, adjunct instructor, 1976-78; Virginia Commonwealth University, Richmond, assistant professor of philosophy, 1978-79; Phillips, Nizer, Benjamin, Krim & Ballon, NYC, summer associate, 1981; Barrett, Smith, Schapiro, Simon & Armstrong, NYC, attorney, 1982-84; State University of New York College at Fredonia, assistant professor, 1984-86, associate professor, 1986-91, head of Faculty Council, 1989-90, professor of philosophy, 1991-99, distinguished teaching professor, 1999-. **Publications:** Justifying Law: The Debate over Foundations, Goals, and Methods, 1992; Good Sex: Perspectives on Sexual Ethics, 1993; Seeking Identity: Individualism versus Community in an Ethnic Context, 1995; Stalking Nietzsche, 1998; What Is the Meaning of Human Life?, 2001; Happiness Is Overrated, 2003. Work represented in anthologies. Contributor of articles and reviews to philosophy and law journals. **Address:** Department of Philosophy, State University of New York College at Fredonia, Fredonia, NY 14063, U.S.A. **Online address:** belliott@fredonia.edu

BELLM, Dan. American, b. 1952. **Genres:** Poetry, Education. **Career:** Writer, poet, and translator. **Publications:** Story in a Bottle (poetry), 1991; (and ed) Family Day Care Handbook, 1993; (trans.) A. Blanco, Angel's Kite/ Estrella de Angel, (children's fiction), 1994; (with M. Whitebook and P. Hnatiuk) The Early Childhood Mentoring Curriculum: A Handbook for Mentors, 1996; (with M. Whitebook) Taking on Turnover: An Action Guide for Child Care Center Teachers and Directors, 1998; (with M. Fisk and F. Hamer) Terrain (poetry), 1998; One Hand on the Wheel (poetry), 1999; Buried Treasure (poetry), 1999. Contributor of articles, book reviews, and poetry to publications. **Address:** 61 Ford St., San Francisco, CA 94114, U.S.A. **Online address:** danbellm@aol.com

BELLMAN, Samuel I. American, b. 1926. **Genres:** Education, Literary criticism and history. **Career:** Emeritus Professor of English, California State Polytechnic University, Pomona, 1996 (joined faculty, 1959). Taught at Fresno State College, California, 1955-57, California State Polytechnic College, San Luis Obispo, 1957-59; and Portsmouth Polytechnic, HM, England, 1975-76. **Publications:** Marjorie Kinnan Rawlings, 1974; Constance Mayfield Rourke, 1981. EDITOR: The College Experience (essays), 1962; Survey and Forecast (essays), 1966. Contributor of fiction, poetry, essays, and reviews to journals and a wide variety of literary publications. **Address:** Dept. of English and Foreign Languages, California State Polytechnic University, Pomona, CA 91768, U.S.A. **Online address:** sibellman@csupomona.edu

BELLOLI, Andrea P. A. American, b. 1947. **Genres:** Art/Art history. **Career:** Managing editor and editor in chief at museums, 1978-92; Macmillan Publishers, London, England, editor, 1992-93; Prestel-Verlag, New York and London, editorial director and consulting editor, 1993-. **Publications:** Oriental Ceramics from the Collection of Justice and Mrs. G. Mennan Williams, 1980; (with E. Savage-Smith) Islamicate Celestial Globes, 1986; Guide to the Museum and Its Gardens, J. Paul Getty Museum, 1990; Make Your Own Museum: An Activity Package for Children, 1994. **Address:** 5 Hosford House, 48 Devonshire Rd., London SE23 3SU, England.

BELLOS, David. British, b. 1945. **Genres:** Literary criticism and history, Translations. **Career:** University of Edinburgh, Scotland, lecturer in French, 1972-82; University of Southampton, England, professor of French, 1982-85; University of Manchester, Lancashire, England, professor of French, 1986-96; Princeton University, Princeton, NJ, professor of French and comparative literature, 1997-. **Publications:** TRANSLATOR: (and ed.) L. Spitzer, Essays on Seventeenth-Century French Literature, 1983; G. Perec, Winter Journey, 1985; Perec, Life: A User's Manual, 1987; Perec, W: Or the Memory of Childhood, 1988; Perec, Things: A Story of the Sixties, 1990; Perec, "53 Days," 1992; Kadare, The Pyramid, 1996; Kadare, The File on H, 1996; Kadare, Spring Flowers, Spring Frost, 2002. MONOGRAPHS: Honore de Balzac, La Cousine Bette, 1980; Balzac, Old Goriot, 1987. OTHER: Balzac Criticism in France, 1976; Georges Perec: A Life in Words (biography), 1993; Jacques Tati: His Life and Art (biography), 1999. **Address:** Department of French and Italian, 330 E Pyne, Princeton University, Princeton, NJ 08544-5264, U.S.A. **Online address:** dbellos@princeton.edu

BELLOTTI, Laura Golden. American, b. 1947. **Genres:** Human relations/Parenting. **Career:** Jeremy P. Tarcher, Inc. (book publisher), Los Angeles, CA, editor, 1980-85; free-lance writer and editor, 1985-. **Publications:** (ed.) Robin Norwood, Women Who Love Too Much: When You Keep Wishing and Hoping He'll Change, St. Martin's, 1985; (ed.) Norwood, Letters from Women Who Love Too Much: A Closer Look at Realtionship Addiction and Recovery, Pocket Books, 1988; (with Laurie Levin) You Can't Hurry Love: An Intimate Look at First Marriages after Forty, Dutton, 1992. **Address:** c/o Susan Schulman, Susan Schulman Literary Agency, 454 West 44th St., New York, NY 10036, U.S.A.

BELLOW, Adam. American, b. 1957. **Genres:** History. **Career:** Doubleday Press, New York, NY, editor-at-large, 1997-. Editorial director, Free Press. **Publications:** In Praise of Nepotism: A Natural History, 2003. **Address:** 64 Grand St., New York, NY 10013, U.S.A.

BELLOW, Saul. See Obituaries.

BELLOWS, Barbara L(awrence). American, b. 1950. **Genres:** History. **Career:** University of Tennessee, Knoxville, research assistant with "The Papers of Andrew Johnson," 1972-73; Spring Valley High School, Columbia, SC, teacher, 1973-77; University of South Carolina at Columbia, teaching assistant, 1977-80; Middlebury College, Middlebury, VT, assistant professor, 1983-90, associate professor of history, 1990-. **Publications:** (with T.L. Connelly) God and General Longstreet: Essays on the Lost Cause and the Southern Mind, 1982; Benevolence Among Slaveholders: Assisting the Poor in Charleston, 1670-1860, 1993. Work represented in anthologies. Contributor of articles and reviews to history journals. **Address:** 260 Stone Hill Rd, Pound Ridge, NY 10576-1421, U.S.A.

BELLOWS, Nathaniel. (born United States), b. 1972. **Genres:** Novels. **Career:** Writer of poetry and fiction; visual artist. **Publications:** On This Day (novel), 2003. Poetry published in periodicals and literary journals. **Address:** c/o Author Mail, HarperCollins, 10 E. 53rd St., 7th floor, New York, NY 10022, U.S.A.

BELLUSH, Bernard. American, b. 1917. **Genres:** International relations/Current affairs, Organized labor, Biography. **Career:** Hunter College (now of the City University of New York), New York City, tutor, 1946-49; City College of the City University of New York, New York City, assistant professor, 1951-61, associate professor and sub-chairman of department, 1961-68, professor, 1968-78, resident professor of history, 1978-81. Lecturer at Ballard School, 1950-53; Columbia University, lecturer at Teachers College, 1960, visiting associate professor, 1964-66; lecturer at Cooper Union, 1961; Fulbright professor at State University of Utrecht, The Netherlands, 1966-67 and 1970-71; member of faculty at Henry George School of Social Science, 1978-81; lecturer on union power and its future. American Civil Liberties Union, member, 1963-84, chairperson of Academic Freedom Committee, 1976-81; Americans for Democratic Action, member of national board of directors, 1971-, chairman of New York State chapter, 1971-73, president of Nassau County chapter 1976-; U.S. representative of World Veterans Federation non-governmental observer at the United Nations, 1980-; roving correspondent at The Forward, 1986-. **Publications:** Franklin D. Roosevelt as Governor of New York, 1955; He Walked Alone: A Biography of John Gilbert Winant, 1968; The Failure of the NRA, 1975; (with J. Bellush) Union Power and New York: Victor Gotbaum and District Council 37, 1984. **Address:** 55 Grasslands Rd Apt D252, Valhalla, NY 10595-1660, U.S.A.

BELMONTE, Kevin Charles. (born United States). **Genres:** Biography. **Career:** Author and lecturer. Gordon College, Wenham, MA, director of Wilberforce Project, 1998-2002; Wilberforce Forum, Washington, DC, fellow; film consultant. **Publications:** (editor) William Wilberforce, A Practical View of Christianity, introduction by Charles Colson, foreword by Garth M. Rosell, 1996; Hero for Humanity: A Biography of William Wilberforce, 2002. Contributor to periodicals. **Address:** Wilberforce Forum, POB 5484, Baltimore, MD 21285, U.S.A.

BELNAP, Nuel. American, b. 1930. **Genres:** Philosophy. **Career:** Yale University, instructor, 1958-60, assistant professor of philosophy, 1960-63; University of Pittsburgh, associate professor, 1963-66, professor of philosophy, sociology, and history and philosophy of science, 1966-, director of graduate studies in philosophy, 1964-67, 1970-72, senior research associate at Center for the Philosophy of Science, 1964-78, fellow of the center, 1979-, ex officio member of Humanities Council, 1974-75, Alan Ross Anderson Lecturer, 1983-84, Alan Ross Anderson Distinguished Professor, 1984-, professor in Intelligent Systems Program, 1988-. Oxford University, senior research fellow with Programming Research Group, 1970; University of California, Irvine, visiting professor, winter, 1973; Australian National University, visiting fellow, 1976; Indiana University Bloomington, Visiting Oscar R. Ewing Professor of Philosophy, autumns, 1977-79; U.S.S.R. Academy of Sciences, visiting scholar of Institute of Philosophy, 1991; University of Padua, visiting professor, 1991. University of Illinois Foundation, member, 1973-; consultant to Office of Naval Research, Westinghouse Research Laboratory, and System Development Corp. **Publications:** Entailment: The Logic of Relevance and Necessity, Vol. I (with A.R. Anderson), 1975, Vol. II (with Anderson and J.M. Dunn), 1992; (with T.B. Steel) The Logic of Questions and Answers, 1976; (with A. Gupta) The Revision Theory of Truth, 1993. Work represented in anthologies. Contributor of articles and reviews to scholarly journals. **Address:** Department of Philosophy, University of Pittsburgh, Pittsburgh, PA 15260, U.S.A.

BELOFF, John. British, b. 1920. **Genres:** Psychology. **Career:** University of Illinois, Champaign, research assistant, 1952; Queen's University, Belfast, Northern Ireland, lecturer in psychology, 1953-62; University of Edinburgh, Edinburgh, Scotland, senior lecturer in psychology, 1963-85, honorary fellow in department of psychology, 1985-95. Visiting professor at Cornell University, 1966. **Publications:** NONFICTION: Existence of Mind, 1962; Psychological Sciences: A Review of Modern Psychology, 1973; The Relentless Question: Reflections on the Paranormal, 1990; Parapsychology: A Concise History, 1993. EDITOR: New Directions in Parapsychology, 1974; (with J.R. Smythies) The Case for Dualism, 1989. Contributor to periodicals. **Address:** Blacket Place 6, Edinburgh EH9 1RL, Scotland. **Online address:** john.beloff@ed.ac.uk

BELOOF, Robert Lawrence. American, b. 1923. **Genres:** Poetry, Literary criticism and history, Psychology. **Career:** Prof of Rhetoric, University of California, Berkeley. **Publications:** The One-Eyed Gunner (poems), 1956; The Performing Voice in Literature, 1966; (co-author) The Oral Study of Literature, 1967; (co-author) The Craft of Writing, 1969; Good Poems, 1973; The Children of Venus and Mars, 1974. Book chapters. **Address:** Dept. of Rhetoric, University of California, Berkeley, CA 94720, U.S.A.

BELSEY, Catherine. British, b. 1940. **Genres:** Literary criticism and history. **Career:** New Hall, Cambridge, England, fellow in English, 1969-75; University College Cardiff, Wales, lecturer in English, 1975-89, professor of English, 1989-; writer. Centre for Critical and Cultural Theory, Chair. Visiting professor at McMaster University, 1986. **Publications:** Critical Practice, 1980; The Subject of Tragedy: Identity and Difference in Renaissance Drama, 1985; John Milton: Language, Gender, Power, 1988; (ed. with J. Moore) The Feminist Reader: Essays in Gender and the Politics of Literary Criticism, 1989, 1997; Desire: Love Stories in Western Culture, 1994. **Address:** Centre for Critical and Cultural Theory, University of Wales, Cardiff, P.O. Box 94, Cardiff CF1 3XB, England.

BELSHAW, Patrick (Edward Blakiston). British, b. 1936. **Genres:** Novels, Novellas/Short stories, Poetry, Biography. **Career:** Served as a teacher in secondary, primary, and special schools, 1958-66; advisory teacher, 1966-69; Darlington College of Education, senior lecturer, 1969-76; Local Education Authority adviser, 1976-80; served as Her Majesty's Inspector of Schools, 1980-91; retired, 1991. **Publications:** A Kind of Private Magic (group biography), 1994. **Address:** Hilltop Cottage, Whashton, Richmond, N. Yorkshire DL11 7JN, England.

BELTING, Hans. German, b. 1935. **Genres:** Art/Art history. **Career:** School for New Media, Karlsruhe, Germany, professor of art history and new media. **Publications:** Das Bild und sein Publikum im Mittelalter: Form und Funktion fruher Bildtafeln der Passion, 1981, trans. by M. Bartusis and R. Meyer as The Image and Its Public in the Middle Ages: Form and Function of Early Paintings of the Passion, 1990; (with D. Eichberger) Jan van Eyck als Erzahler: fruhe Tafelbilder im Umkreis der New Yorker Doppeltafel, 1983; Das Ende der Kunstgeschichte?, 1983, trans. by C. Wood as The End of the History of Art?, 1987; Max Beckmann: die Tradition als Problem in der Kunst der Moderne, 1984, trans. by P. Wortsman as Max Beckmann: Tradition as a Problem in Modern Art, 1989; (with others) Der Mensch und seine Gefuhle: Beitrage, 1985; Giovanni Bellini, Pieta: Ikone und Bilderzahlung in der venezianischen Malerei, 1985; (with D. Blume) Malerei und Stadtkultur in der Dantezeit: die Argumentation der Bilder, 1989; Bild und Kult: eine Geschichte des Bildes vor dem Zeitalter der Kunst, 1990, trans. by E. Jephcott as Likeness and Presence: A History of the Image before the Era of Art, 1994; Die Deutschen und ihre Kunst: ein schwieriges Erbe, 1992; Thomas Struth: Museum Photographs, 1993; The Invisible Masterpiece, 2001; Bild-Anthropologie, 2001; Art History after Modernism, 2004. **Address:** Sophienstrasse 105, 76135 Karlsruhe, Germany.

BELTMAN, Brian W. American, b. 1945. **Genres:** History. **Career:** Wisconsin State Historical Society, historical researcher, 1974-75; professor of American history successively at Hamilton College, Clinton, NY, Dartmouth College, Hanover, NH, Arizona State University, Tempe, University of Mid-America, Lincoln, NE, and University of South Carolina, Columbia, SC, 1975-80; South Carolina Electric and Gas Co., coordinator of regulatory affairs, 1980-. University of South Carolina at Columbia, adjunct professor, 1980-. **Publications:** Dutch Farmer in the Missouri Valley: The Life and Letters of Ulbe Eringa, 1866-1950, 1996. Contributor of articles, chapters, and reviews to periodicals. Contributor to books and anthologies. **Address:** 3950 Rockbridge Rd, Columbia, SC 29206, U.S.A.

BELTON, Sandra (Yvonne). American, b. 1939. **Genres:** Children's fiction, Adult non-fiction. **Career:** West Elementary School, DC Public Schools, Washington, DC, teacher, 1964-69; Scott, Foresman and Company, Glenview, IL, associate editor, 1969-72, executive editor/editorial manager, 1978-2001; Lyons & Carnahan, Chicago, IL, editor, 1972-74; Encyclopaedia Britannica Educational Corp., Chicago, senior editor; City Colleges of Chicago, reading teacher, 1976-78. **Publications:** CHILDREN'S FICTION: From Miss Ida's Porch, 1993; May'naise Sandwiches and Sunshine Tea, 1994; Ernestine & Amanda, 1996; Ernestine & Amanda: Summer Camp, Ready or Not, 1997; Ernestine & Amanda: Members of the C.L.U.B., 1997; Ernestine & Amanda: Mysteries on Monroe Street, 1998; McKendree, 2000.

BELUE, Ted Franklin. American, b. 1954. **Genres:** History. **Career:** Murray State University, Murray, KY, lecturer in history, 1991-. Muzzleloader, staff member; Kentucky Humanities Council, member of speakers' bureau; public lecturer and historical consultant. **Publications:** The Long Hunt: Death of the Buffalo East of the Mississippi, 1996; (ed.) P. Houston, A Sketch of the Life and Character of Daniel Boone, 1997; (ed.) L.C. Draper, The Life of Daniel Boone, 1998. Contributor to books and periodicals. **Address:** Department of History, Murray State University, PO Box 9, Murray, KY 42071, U.S.A.

BENARDE, Melvin Albert. American, b. 1924. **Genres:** Environmental sciences/Ecology, Medicine/Health, Travel/Exploration. **Career:** Professor and Director, Asbestos-Lead Center, Temple University, Philadelphia, 1987-. Member of faculty, Rutgers University, New Brunswick, NJ, 1962-67; Professor and Chairman, Dept. of Community Medicine and Environmental Health, Hahnemann University, Philadelphia, 1967-83. Associate Director, Environmental Studies Institute, Drexel University, Philadelphia, 1983-87. **Publications:** Race against Famine, 1968; Our Precious Habitat, 1970, rev. ed., 1989; The Chemicals We Eat, 1973, rev. ed., 1975; Beach Holidays: Portugal to Israel, 1974; The Food Additives Dictionary, 1981; Global Warning/Global Warming, 1992; You've Been Had!: How the Media and Environmentalists Turned America into a Nation of Hypochondriacs, 2002. EDITOR & CONTRIBUTOR: Disinfection, 1970; Asbestos: The Hazardous Fiber, 1990. **Address:** 6 Thorngate Ct, Princeton, NJ 08540, U.S.A. **Online address:** dickiedare1a@comcast.net

BENCE-JONES, Mark. Irish (born England), b. 1930. **Genres:** Novels, Architecture, History. **Career:** Consultant Ed., Burke's Irish Family Records, 1973-76. **Publications:** All a Nonsense: Paradise Escaped; Nothing in the City; The Remarkable Irish; Palaces of the Raj; Clive of India; The Cavaliers; Burke's Guide to Irish Country Houses; (with Hugh Montgomery-Massingberd) The British Aristocracy; The Viceroys of India, 1982; Ancestral Houses, 1984; Twilight of the Ascendancy, 1987; Guide to Irish Country Houses, 1989; The Catholic Families, 1992; Life in an Irish Country House, 1996.

BENCHLEY, Peter (Bradford). American, b. 1940. **Genres:** Plays/Screenplays, Novels, Children's fiction. **Career:** Reporter, Washington Post, 1963; Associate Ed., Newsweek, NYC., 1964-67; Staff Assistant to the President, White House, Washington, D.C., 1967-69; freelance television news corresp., 1969-72. **Publications:** NOVELS: Jaws, 1974, screenplay (with C. Gottlieb) 1975; The Deep, 1976, screenplay (with T.K. Wynn), 1977; The Island, 1979, screenplay, 1980; The Girl of the Sea of Cortez, 1982; Q Clearance, 1986; Rummies, 1989; Beast, 1991; White Shark, 1994. OTHER: Time and A Ticket, 1964; Jonathan Visits the White House (children's novel), 1964; Ocean Planet: Writings and Images of the Sea, 1995; Shark Trouble, 2002. **Address:** c/o Amanda Urban, International Creative Mgmt, 40 W. 57th St, New York, NY 10019-4001, U.S.A.

BENCHLEY, Rob. (Robert Benchley, III). American, b. 1950. **Genres:** Local history/Rural topics, Marine sciences/Oceanography, Documentaries/Reportage. **Career:** Freelance writer and photographer. **Publications:** (with J. Patrick) Scallop Season, a Nantucket Chronicle, 2002. Contributor of articles and photographs to periodicals. **Address:** Box 600, Siasconset, MA 02564, U.S.A. **Online address:** benchley@comcast.net

BENCKE, Matthew. *See* **VON BENCKE, Matthew Justin.**

BENDALL, Molly. American, b. 1961. **Genres:** Poetry. **Career:** Writer. **Publications:** After Estrangement (poetry), 1992. **Address:** English Department, University of Southern California, Los Angeles, CA 90089, U.S.A.

BENDELL, Frederick H. *See* **MCCARTY, Hanoch.**

BENDER, Sheila. American, b. 1948. **Genres:** Poetry, Writing/Journalism. **Career:** Poet, author, educator, editor, writing coach. Pima Community College, Tucson, AZ, instructor in writing and literature; Colorado Mountain Writer's Workshop, Steamboat Springs, guest instructor; guest writer or instructor. **Publications:** Love Along the Coastal Route (poems), 1983; Near the Light, 1983; (with C. Killien) Writing in a Convertible with the Top Down: A Unique Guide for Writers, 1992, rev. ed., 1997; Writing Personal Essays: How to Shape Your Life Experiences for the Page, 1995; (ed.) The Writer's Journal: 40 Contemporary Authors and Their Journals, 1997; Writing Personal Poetry: Creating Poems From Your Life Experiences, 1998; Sustenance: New and Selected Poems, 1999; A Year in the Life: Journaling for Self-Discovery, 2000; Keeping a Journal You Love, 2001. **Address:** c/o Wales Literary Agency, 1508 10th Ave. East, Seattle, WA 98102, U.S.A. **Online address:** SBender1@aol.com; www.writingitreal.com

BENDER, Thomas. American, b. 1944. **Genres:** History, Intellectual history, Urban studies. **Career:** University of Wisconsin at Green Bay, assistant professor of history and urban studies, 1971-74; New York University, assistant professor, 1974-76, associate professor, 1976-77, Samuel Rudin Professor of Humanities, 1977-82, professor of history, 1977-, university professor of humanities, 1982-. Intellectual History Group Newsletter, editor, 1978-85. **Publications:** Toward Urban Vision, 1975; Community and Social Change in America, 1978; (with E. Rozwenc) The Making of American Society, 1978; New York Intellect: A History of Intellectual Life in New York City from 1750 to the Beginnings of Our Own Time, 1987; Intellect and Public Life, 1993; The Unfinished City: New York and the Metropolitan Idea, 2002; (co) The Education of Historians for the Twenty-First Century, 2004. EDITOR/CO-EDITOR: Democracy in America, 1981; The University and the City: From Medieval Origins to the Present, 1989; The Anti-Slavery Debate, 1992; Budapest and New York: Studies in Metropolitan Transformation, 1870-1930, 1994; American Academic Culture in Transformation, 1998; City and Nation: Rethinking Place and Identity, 2001; Rethinking American History in a Global Age, 2002. **Address:** Dept of History, New York University, 53 Washington Sq S 7th Fl, New York, NY 10012, U.S.A. **Online address:** Thomas.Bender@nyu.edu

BENDERSKY, Margaret (Irene). American, b. 1949. **Genres:** Medicine/Health. **Career:** University of Medicine and Dentistry of New Jersey, New Brunswick, professor of pediatrics at Robert Wood Johnson Medical School, 1982-. **Publications:** (ed. with M. Lewis) Mothers, Babies and Cocaine: The Role of Toxins in Development, 1995. **Address:** Institute for the Study of Child Development, University of Medicine and Dentistry of New Jersey, Robert Wood Johnson Medical School, 97 Paterson St., New Brunswick, NJ 08903, U.S.A. **Online address:** bendersk@umdnj.edu

BENDIX, Deanna Marohn. American, b. 1938. **Genres:** Art/Art history. **Career:** Waseca Daily Journal, Waseca, MN, photojournalist and arts and education reporter, 1971-78; University of Minnesota, Waseca, instructor, 1977, 1980; art historian, researcher, lecturer, artist, and writer, 1989-96; Minneapolis Institute of Arts, Minneapolis, MN, instructor, 1997. **Publications:** Diabolical Designs: Paintings, Interiors, and Exhibitions of James McNeill Whistler, 1995. Contributor to periodicals. **Address:** 36078 Clear Lake Dr., Waseca, MN 56093, U.S.A.

BENDIXSON, Terence. British, b. 1934. **Genres:** Transportation, Urban studies. **Career:** Policy Analyst and Writer. Planning Correspondent, The Guardian, London, 1963-69; Member, Environment Bureau of The Observer, London, 1970-71. **Publications:** Instead of Cars, 1974; The Peterborough Effect, 1988; Milton Keynes: Image and Reality, 1991. **Address:** 39 Elm Pk Gardens, London SW10 9QF, England. **Online address:** t.bendixson@robox.com

BENDROTH, Margaret Lamberts. American, b. 1954. **Genres:** Human relations/Parenting, Theology/Religion. **Career:** Northern Virginia Community College, Alexandria, instructor in history, 1983-86; Northeastern University, Boston, MA, adjunct member of philosophy, religion, and history faculty, 1987-92; Divinitas Books, Cambridge, MA, assistant manager, 1992-93; Andover Newton Theological School, Newton Center, MA, adjunct lecturer in church history, 1993-. Center for Urban Ministerial Education,

Boston, adjunct faculty member, 1992-; Women and Twentieth-Century Protestantism, project codirector, 1995-98. Valparaiso Project on the Education and Formation of People in Faith, project member. **Publications:** Fundamentalism and Gender, 1875 to the Present, 1993; (ed. with P. Airhart) Families: Past, Present, and Future, 1996. Contributor to books and scholarly journals. **Address:** 510 Mulford Dr. SE, Grand Rapids, MI 49507-3518, U.S.A.

BENEDEK, Barbara. American. **Genres:** Plays/Screenplays. **Career:** Writer. **Publications:** SCREENPLAYS: (with L. Kasdan) The Big Chill, 1983; Immediate Family, 1989; (with P. Brickman) Men Don't Leave, 1990; (with D. Rayfiel) Sabrina, 1995. Author of scripts for television shows, including I'm a Big Girl Now, 1980-81; Making a Living, 1981; and Laverne and Shirley, 1982. **Address:** 9560 Wilshire Blvd., Fl. 5, Beverly Hills, CA 90212, U.S.A.

BENEDETTI, Jean (Norman). British, b. 1930. **Genres:** Translations. **Career:** Actor, director, and writer. Toured with the British Arts Council, 1959; performed in and directed regional theater, 1960-62; performed on and directed radio and television programs, 1962-64; appeared in and directed Beyond the Fringe, Mayfair Theatre, London, 1964-65; performed in and directed film and television productions, 1965-72; Rose Bruford College of Speech and Drama, principal, 1970-87, honorary fellow, 1991. **Publications:** TRANSLATIONS: G. Michel, A Sunday Walk, 1968; Edward II, A Respectable Wedding, 1970; F. Arrabal, The Architect and the Emperor of Assyria, The Grand Ceremonial, Plays, Vol. III, 1971; (and editor) The Moscow Art Theatre Letters, 1991; (and editor) Dear Writer, Dear Actress: The Love Letters of Olga Knipper and Anton Chekhov, 1997. NONFICTION: Gilles de Rais: The Authentic Bluebeard, 1971, in US as Gilles de Rais, 1972; Stanislavski: An Introduction, 1982, 2nd rev ed, 1989; Stanislavski: A Biography, 1989. Contributor to periodicals and books. OTHER: dramatist and/or translator of scripts: The Good Shoemaker and the Poor Fish Peddler, 1965; File on Harry Jordan, 1966; These Men Are Dangerous (trilogy), 1968; Lily, 1969; The Architect and the Emperor of Assyria, 1971; A Respectable Wedding, 1980; A Bolt From the Blue (dramatized documentary), 1987. **Address:** c/o Toby Eady, 18 Park Walk, London SW10 OA4, England.

BENEDICT, Barbara M. American, b. 1955. **Genres:** Literary criticism and history. **Career:** Trinity College, Hartford, CT, instructor, 1984-85, assistant professor, 1985-91, associate professor, 1991-96, professor of English, 1997-, Charles A. Dana Professor of English Literature, 2002-. **Publications:** Framing Feeling: Sentiment and Style in English Prose Fiction, 1745-1800, 1994; Making the Modern Reader: Cultural Mediation in Early Modern Literary Anthologies, 1996; Curiosity: A Cultural History of Early-Modern Inquiry, 2001. Contributor to books. Contributor of articles, poems, and reviews to academic journals. **Address:** Dept of English, Trinity College, 300 Summit St, Hartford, CT 06106-3100, U.S.A. **Online address:** barbara.benedict@trincoll.edu

BENEDICT, Elizabeth. American, b. 1954. **Genres:** Novels, Writing/Journalism. **Career:** Mexican American Legal Defense and Educational Fund, San Francisco, CA, and Washington, DC, legislative advocate and publicist, 1978-82; writer. Visiting writer at Swarthmore College, 1987-89, 1991, 1996, Haverford College, 1990, 1991; Davidson College, 1992, Writers' Workshop at University of Iowa, 1993, Princeton University, 1994-98, Harvard Extension School, 2002-03. Book reviewer and freelance journalist. Commentator for National Public Radio. **Publications:** NOVELS: Slow Dancing, 1985; The Beginner's Book of Dreams, 1988; Safe Conduct, 1993; Almost, 2001; The Practice of Deceit, 2005. OTHER: The Joy of Writing Sex: A Guide for Fiction Writers, 1996, rev. ed., 2002. **Address:** c/o Gail Hochman, Brandt & Hochman Literary Agents, 1501 Broadway Ste 2310, New York, NY 10036, U.S.A. **Online address:** info@elizabethbenedict.com

BENEDICT, Helen. American/British, b. 1952. **Genres:** Novels, Women's studies and issues, Writing/Journalism. **Career:** New Wings, Novato, CA, managing editor, 1979; Independent and Gazette, Richmond, CA, reporter and feature writer, 1980; Columbia University, NYC, professor of journalism, 1986-. University of California, Berkeley, visiting lecturer, 1991. **Publications:** NONFICTION: (with others) Women Making History: Conversations with Fifteen New Yorkers, 1985; Recovery: How to Survive Sexual Assault, 1985, 1994; Safe, Strong, and Streetwise (for young adults), 1987; Portraits in Print, 1991; Virgin or Vamp: How the Press Covers Sex Crimes, 1992. NOVELS: A World Like This, 1990; Bad Angel, 1996; The Sailor's Wife, 2001. Work represented in anthologies, contributor to periodicals. **Address:** Graduate School of Journalism, Columbia University, New York, NY 10027, U.S.A.

BENEDICT, Howard (S.). American, b. 1928. **Genres:** Air/Space topics. **Career:** Associated Press, staff member, 1953-90, correspondent in Salt Lake City, UT, NYC, and Tampa, FL, 1953-59, senior aerospace writer, 1959-90, correspondent from Cape Canaveral, FL, 1959-74, and Washington, DC, 1974-84, White House correspondent, 1975-77, correspondent from Cape Canaveral, 1984-90; Astronaut Scholarship Foundation, Titusville, FL, executive director, 1990-. **Publications:** NASA: A Quarter Century of Space Achievement, 1984; NASA: The Journey Continues, 1990; (with A. Shepard, D. Slayton, and J. Barbree) Moon Shot: The Inside Story of America's Race to the Moon, 1994; A Home in Space, 1995. Contributor to newspapers. **Address:** Astronaut Scholarship Foundation, 6225 Vectorspace Blvd, Titusville, FL 32780, U.S.A. **Online address:** mercurysun@aol.com

BENEDICT, Philip (Joseph). American, b. 1949. **Genres:** History. **Career:** Cornell University, Ithaca, NY, visiting assistant professor of history, 1975-76; University of Maryland, College Park, assistant professor of history, 1976-78; Brown University, Providence, RI, assistant professor, 1978-82, associate professor, 1982-92, professor of history, 1992-. Visiting professor or fellow: Institute for Advanced Study, 1983-84, EHESS (Paris), 1986, 2002, All Soul's College, Oxford, 2001-02, Universite de Lyon-II, 2003. **Publications:** Rouen during the Wars of Religion: 1981; The Huguenot Population of France, 1600-1685, 1991; The Faith and Fortynes of France's Huguenots, 1600-1685, 2001; Christ's Churches Purely Reformed: A Social History of Calvinism, 2002. EDITOR: Cities and Social Change in Early Modern France, 1989; Reformation, Revolt and Civil War in France and the Netherlands, 155-1585, 1999. **Address:** Dept of History, Brown University, Providence, RI 02912, U.S.A.

BENEDICT, Pinckney. American, b. 1964. **Genres:** Novellas/Short stories, Novels. **Career:** Writer, 1987-. Hope College, Holland, MI, associate professor (English); Pushcart Anthology Series, contributing editor. Has also taught creative writing at Ohio State University, Oberlin College, and Princeton University. **Publications:** Town Smokes (stories), 1987; The Wrecking Yard and Other Stories (stories), 1992; Dogs of God (novel), 1994. Contributor of stories and nonfiction to publications. Also writes one-act, full-length, and musical plays. **Address:** c/o Doubleday, 1540 Broadway, New York, NY 10036, U.S.A. **Online address:** benedict@hope.edu

BENERIA, Lourdes. Spanish, b. 1939. **Genres:** Women's studies and issues. **Career:** Rutgers University, New Brunswick, NJ, assistant professor, 1975-81, associate professor of economics, 1981-86, executive officer of Institute for Research on Women, 1982-83, and acting director, 1985-86; Cornell University, Ithaca, NY, professor of city and regional planning and women's studies, 1987-93, director of Program on International Development and Women, 1988-93, director of Latin American Studies Program, 1993-96; visiting faculty member and guest lecturer at colleges and universities in the United States and abroad; guest on radio and television programs in Mexico, Spain, Canada, and the United States. **Publications:** (trans.) Los Engranajes de la Economia Nacional, by J.M. Albertini, 1965; (with J. Grigoll and others) Planificacion y Desarrollo, 1965; Mujer, Economia, y Patriarcado Durante el Periodo Franquista, 1977; (with others) Mujeres: Ciencia y Practica Politica, 1987; (with M. Roldan) The Crossroads of Class and Gender: Homework, Subcontracting, and Household Dynamics in Mexico City, 1987. EDITOR: Women and Development: The Sexual Division of Labor in Rural Societies, 1982; (with C. Stimpson) Women, Households, and the Current Economy, 1987; (with S. Feldman, and contrib.) Unequal Burden: Economic Crises, Persistent Poverty, and Women's Work, 1992; (with S. Bisnath) Global Tensions, 2003; Gender, Development and Globalization, 2004. Work represented in anthologies. Contributor of articles and reviews to magazines and newspapers. **Address:** Dept of City and Regional Planning, West Sibley Hall, Cornell University, Ithaca, NY 14853, U.S.A.

BENEZRA, Neal. American, b. 1953. **Genres:** Art/Art history. **Career:** Des Moines Art Center, Des Moines, IA, curator, 1983-85; Art Institute of Chicago, Chicago, IL, curator, 1985-91; Hirshhorn Museum and Sculpture Garden, Washington, DC, chief curator, 1992-2002; San Francisco Museum of Modern Art, director, 2002-. **Publications:** Robert Arneson, 1986; Affinities and Intuitions: Gerald Elliott Collection of Contemporary Art, 1990; (with others) Ed Paschke, 1990; Martin Puryear, 1991; Bruce Nauman (exhibition catalog), 1994; Stephan Balkenhol, 1995; Distemper, 1996; Franz West, 1999; Regarding Beauty, 1999; Ed Ruscha, 2000; Juan Munoz, 2001. **Address:** San Francisco Museum of Modern Art, 151 3rd St, San Francisco, CA 94103-3159, U.S.A.

BENFORD, Gregory (Albert). Also writes as Sterling Blake. American, b. 1941. **Genres:** Mystery/Crime/Suspense, Science fiction/Fantasy. **Career:** Lawrence Radiation Laboratory, Livermore, CA, fellow, 1967-69, research physicist, 1969-72; University of California, Irvine, assistant professor, 1971-73, professor of physics, 1973-. **Publications:** Deeper Than the Darkness,

1970, as The Stars in Shroud, 1978; Jupiter Project, 1974; (with G. Eklund) If the Stars Are Gods, 1977; In the Ocean of Night, 1977; (with G. Eklund) Find the Changeling, 1980; Timescape, 1980; (with W. Rotsler) Shiva Descending, 1980; Against Infinity, 1983; Across the Sea of Suns, 1984; Of Space-Time and the River, 1985; Artifact, 1985, In Alien Flesh, 1985; (with D. Brin) Heart of the Comet, 1986; Great Sky River, 1987; Tides of Light, 1989; (with A.C. Clarke) Beyond the Fall of Night, 1990; (as Sterling Blake) Chiller, 1993; Furious Gulf, 1994; Matter's End, 1994; Sailing Bright Eternity, 1995; Foundation's Fear, 1997; Cosm, 1998; The Martian Race, 1999; Deep Time, 1999; Eater, 2000; Beyond Infinity, 2004.

BENGTSON, Vern L. American, b. 1941. **Genres:** Sociology. **Career:** University Professor of Gerantology AARP, since 1989, Professor of Sociology, since 1977, Chief, Laboratory of Social Organization and Behavior, Preceptor in Sociology, since 1971, and Principal Investigator, Socio-Cultural Contexts of Aging, since 1972, University of Southern California, Los Angeles (Assistant Professor, 1967-70; Associate Professor, 1970-71). Member of Executive Board, Sociology of Education, since 1967; Member of Ed. Board, Journal of Marriage and the Family, Los Angeles, since 1973. Fellow in Adult Development and Aging, 1963-67, and Research Coordinator of the Cross-National Study of Patterns of Aging, 1965-67, University of Chicago. Member, Finance Committee, Gerontological Society, Washington, 1973-75. **Publications:** The Social Psychology of Aging, 1973. EDITOR: (with J. Robertson) Grandparenthood, 1985; (with J.E. Birren) Emergent Theories of Aging, 1989; (with K.W. Schaie) The Course of Later Life: Research and Reflections, 1989. **Address:** University of Southern California, Andrus Gerontology Center, University Park, Los Angeles, CA 90089, U.S.A.

BENIG, Irving. American, b. 1944. **Genres:** Novels. **Career:** Schoolteacher in Brooklyn, NY, 1967-71; Avon Books, NYC, editor, 1971-72; advertising executive, NYC, 1972-84; business executive, NYC, 1984-. **Publications:** The Children: Poems and Prose of Bedford-Stuyvesant (children's anthology), 1971; The Messiah Stones (novel), 1995. **Address:** c/o Barbara Lowenstein, Lowenstein Associates Inc., 121 West 27th St. Suite 601, New York, NY 10001, U.S.A.

BENISON, C. C. See **WHITEWAY, Doug(las) Alfred.**

BENITEZ, Sandra (Ables). American, b. 1941. **Genres:** Novels. **Career:** Gaunt High School, Affton, MO, ninth grade Spanish and English teacher, 1963-68; Northeast Missouri State University, Kirksville, teaching assistant, 1974; Wilson Learning Corporation, Eden Prairie, MN, free-lance Spanish/English translator, 1975-76, marketing liaison in international division, 1977-80; University of San Diego, Knapp Chair in Humanities, 2000. Loft Inroads Program, Hispanic mentor, 1989-92. Fiction writer and creative writing teacher; member of the National Writers' Voice Project Reading Tour, 1994-95. Edelstein-Keller Writer of Distinction, 1997; American Book Award, 1998. **Publications:** A Place Where the Sea Remembers, 1993; Bitter Grounds, 1997; The Weight of All Things, 2001. Contributor of English and Spanish articles to periodicals. **Address:** c/o Ellen Levine, Trident Media Group, 41 Madison Ave, Fl 36, New York, NY 10010-2257, U.S.A.

BENJAMIN, Carol Lea. American. **Genres:** Animals/Pets, Mystery/Crime/Suspense. **Career:** Writer. Has worked as private investigator, teacher, and dog trainer. **Publications:** NONFICTION OFTEN ILLUSTRATOR: Dog Training for Kids, 1976; (with A.J. Haggerty) Dog Tricks: New Tricks for Old Dogs, Old Tricks for New Dogs, and Ageless Tricks That Give Wise Men Paws, 1978; Running Basics, 1979; Dog Problems: A Professional Trainer's Guide to Preventing and Correcting Aggression, 1981; Cartooning for Kids, 1982; Mother Knows Best: The Natural Way to Train Your Dog, 1985; Writing for Kids, 1985; Second-hand Dog: How to Turn Yours into a First-Rate Pet, 1988; The Chosen Puppy: How to Select and Raise a Great Puppy from an Animal Shelter, 1990; Surviving Your Dog's Adolescence: A Positive Training Program, 1993; Dog Training in Ten Minutes, 1997. FICTION: The Wicked Stepdog, 1982; Nobody's Baby Now, 1984. RACHEL ALEXANDER AND DASH MYSTERIES: This Dog for Hire, 1996; The Dog Who Knew Too Much, 1997; Dash P. I., 1997; A Hell of a Dog, 1998; Lady Vanishes, 1999; The Wrong Dog, 2000; The Long Good Boy, 2001; Fall Guy, 2004. **Address:** c/o Brandt & Brandt Literary Agents, 1501 Broadway Suite 2310, New York, NY 10036, U.S.A. **Online address:** cb@CarolLeaBenjamin.com

BENJAMIN, Denis R(ichard). American (born Republic of South Africa), b. 1945. **Genres:** Medicine/Health. **Career:** Johannesburg General Hospital, Johannesburg, South Africa, intern in surgery, 1969; Non-European Hospital, Johannesburg, intern in medicine, 1969; Transvaal Memorial Hospital for Children, intern in pediatrics, 1970; University of Washington, Seattle,

resident in anatomic pathology at University and Affiliated Hospitals, 1970-72, and clinical pathology, 1972-74, chief resident in laboratory medicine, 1973-74, assistant professor, 1975-80, associate professor, 1980-90, professor of laboratory medicine and pathology, and adjunct professor of pediatrics, 1990-. Children's Orthopedic Hospital and Medical Center, assistant pathologist, 1974, head of Division of Laboratory Medicine, 1975, director of School of Medical Technology, 1975, associate director of Department of Laboratories, 1977-84, director of the laboratory, 1984-; Children's Hospital and Medical Center, member of medical executive committee, 1984-, and hospital steering committee, 1994-. Children's Cancer Study Group, pathologist for acute myeloid leukemia, 1980-90; consultant to Project Hope and Harvard Medical International. **Publications:** Mushrooms: Poisons and Panaceas, 1995. Contributor to medical books, medical journals and popular magazines. **Address:** Children's Hospital and Medical Center, 4800 Sandpoint Way N.E., Seattle, WA 98105, U.S.A.

BENJAMIN, E. M. J. See **BACHE, Ellyn.**

BENJAMIN, Harold H. American, b. 1924. **Genres:** Medicine/Health. **Career:** Attorney in NYC and Beverly Hills, CA, 1950-81; Wellness Community, Santa Monica, CA, founder and president, c. 1982-. **Publications:** From Victim to Victor, 1988; The Wellness Community Guide to Fighting for Recovery From Cancer, 1994. **Address:** Wellness Community, 2716 Ocean Park Blvd. No. 1040, Santa Monica, CA 90405, U.S.A.

BENJAMIN, Joan. American, b. 1956. **Genres:** Homes/Gardens. **Career:** Flower and Garden Magazine, Kansas City, MO, editorial assistant, 1977; Shelter Insurance Company, Columbia, MO, gardener, 197880; Apple Valley Farm, Waverly, MO, farm manager, 1981-82; Columbia Parks and Recreation Department, Columbia, MO, landscape technician, 1982-88; Callaway Gardens, Pine Mountain, GA, interpretive horticulturist, 1990-92; Rodale Press Inc., Emmaus, PA, associate editor, 1992-. **Publications:** (with B.W. Ellis and D.L. Martin) Rodale's Low-Maintenance Gardening Techniques: Shortcuts and Time-Saving Hints for Your Greatest Garden Ever, 1995; (ed., with E. Hynes) Great Garden Shortcuts: Hundreds of All-New Tips and Techniques That Guarantee You'll Save Time, Save Money, Save Work, 1996; (ed., with B.W. Ellis) Rodale's No-Fail Flower Garden: How to Plan, Plant and Grow a Beautiful, Easy-Care Garden, 1997. **Address:** c/o Rodale Press Inc., 33 East Minor St., Emmaus, PA 18098-0099, U.S.A.

BENJAMIN, Saragail Katzman. American, b. 1953. **Genres:** Children's fiction, Plays/Screenplays, Songs/Lyrics and libretti. **Career:** New York metropolitan area entertainer, musician and singer, 1977-. Teaching artist, leading workshops in music, theater, and fiction; children's author, 1990-. Has a one-woman children's music show called A Joyful Noise. **Publications:** PLAYS: The Furnished Room (musical), 1984; The DYBBUK (musical), 1992. CHILDREN'S PLAYS: The Alexandria Municipal Reading Library (musical). CHILDREN'S SONGS: Goodnight, 1992; Take Good Care of the Earth, 1992. CHILDREN'S FICTION: My Dog Ate It, 1994. **Address:** 27 Kewanee Rd, New Rochelle, NY 10804, U.S.A.

BENN, June. Also writes as June (Mary) Barraclough. British, b. 1930. **Genres:** Novels, Romance/Historical, Women's studies and issues, Translations. **Career:** Teacher of modern languages, 1955-61, and part-time teacher, at independent and state grammar schools in London, England, 1967-71, 1978-85; London Colleges of Education, lecturer, 1974-78; University of London, "Extra Mural" lecturer, 1979-85; writer. **Publications:** (as June Barraclough, trans.) Marquis de Condorcet, Sketch for a Historical Picture of the Progress of the Human Mind, 1955; (ed.) The Woman's View (anthology), 1967; (ed.) Memorials (anthology), 1986; First Finds: A Yorkshire Childhood (fictionalized memoir), 1998; First Loves: A Yorkshire Adolescence (fictionalized memoir), 1999. NOVELS AS JUNE BARRACLOUGH: The Heart of the Rose, 1985; Rooks Nest, 1986; Kindred Spirits, 1988; A Time to Love, 1989; Generations, 1990; Time Will Tell, 1992; Familiar Acts, 1993; Ghosts at Cockcrow, 1994; Portrait of Maud, 1994; Swifter Wings than Time, 1994; Daughter of Haworth, 1995; Family Snapshots, 1996; No Time Like the Present, 1997; The Villa Violetta, 1997; Another Summer, 1998; Loving and Learning (historical), 1999; The Family Face, 200; Stephanie and Josephine, 2001; Emma Eliza, 2002; The Ways of Love, 2003; Family Circle, 2004. **Address:** St Andrews House, 113 Mycenae Rd, Blackheath, London SE3 7RX, England.

BENN, Tony. (Anthony Neil Wedgood Benn). British, b. 1925. **Genres:** Politics/Government. **Career:** Labour M.P. for Bristol South-East, 1950-60, 1963-83, and for Chesterfield, since 1984 (Chairman, Labour Party's Broadcasting Advisory Committee, 1957-64; Member, Select Committee on Procedure, 1958; Principal Labour Spokesman on Transport Policies, 1959;

Postmaster-General, 1964-66; Minister of Technology, 1966-70; Minister of Power, 1969-70; Chairman of the Labour Party, 1971-72; Secretary of State for Industry, 1974-75, for Energy, 1975-79; Chairman EEC Council of Energy Ministers, 1977; President of the Socialist Campaign Group of Labour MPs). Producer, BBC North American Service, 1949-50. Member, Executive Committee, British-American Parliamentary Group, 1953; Founder Member, Movement for Colonial Freedom, 1954; Member of the Executive, H-Bomb National Campaign, 1954; Chairman, Fabian Society, 1964-65; Candidate, Labour Party leadership, 1976, 1988. **Publications:** The Privy Council as a Second Chamber, 1957; The Regeneration of Britain, 1964; The New Politics, 1970; Speeches, 1974; Arguments for Socialism, 1979; Arguments for Democracy, 1981; Sizewell Syndrome, 1984; (ed.) Writings on the Wall, 1984; Out of the Wilderness: Diaries 1963-67, 1987; Office without Power: Diaries 1968-72, 1988; Fighting Back: Speaking Out for Socialism in the Eighties, 1988; Against the Tide: Diaries, 1973-1976, 1989; Conflicts of Interest: Diaries, 1977-80, 1990; The End of an Era: Diaries 1980-90, 1992; Common Sense, 1993; Speaking Up in Parliament, 1993; Benn Tapes, 1994; Year of Hope: Diaries 1940-1962, 1994; The Benn Diaries 1940-1990, 1995. **Address:** House of Commons, London SW1A 0AA, England.

BENNAHUM, David S. American/French, b. 1968. **Genres:** Music. **Career:** Writer. Established MEME (bi-weekly newsletter), beginning in 1995. **Publications:** In Their Own Words: The Beatles after the Breakup, 1991; k.d. lang, 1994; In Her Own Words: k.d. lang, 1995; Extra Life: Coming of Age in Cyberspace, 1998. Contributor to newspapers and periodicals. **Address:** 144 West 19th St., New York, NY 10011, U.S.A. **Online address:** davidsol@panix.com

BENNAHUM, Judith Chazin. American, b. 1937. **Genres:** Dance/Ballet, Fashion/Costume. **Career:** Professional ballet dancer, 1954-64; choreographer; University of New Mexico, Albuquerque, head of Dance Program, 1987-92, professor of theater and dance, 1988-. Santa Fe Opera, teacher of body movement; worked as a ballet dancer with Robert Joffrey, George Balanchine, and Antony Tudor at the Metropolitan Opera Ballet Company; danced on Broadway with Agnes de Mille. **Publications:** Dance in the Shadow of the Guillotine, 1988; The Ballets of Antony Tudor: Studies in Psyche and Satire, 1994; The Living Dance: An Anthology of Essays on Movement and Culture, 2003. Contributor of articles and reviews to scholarly journals. **Address:** Department of Theatre & Dance, University of New Mexico, Albuquerque, NM 87131, U.S.A. **Online address:** gigiben@unm.edu

BENNASSAR, Bartolomé. French, b. 1929. **Genres:** Novels, History. **Career:** University of Toulouse, France, professor, 1950-90. **Publications:** Le Dernier Saut (novel and screenplay), 1970; (with J. Jacquart) Le XVIe Siecle, c. 1972; L'Homme Espagnol: Attitudes et Mentalites du XVIe au XIXe Siecle, 1975, trans. as The Spanish Character: Attitudes and Mentalities from the 16th to the 19th Century, 1979; (with P. Chaunu) L'Ouverture du Monde: XIVe-XVIe Siecles, 1977; L'inquisition Espagnole: XVe-XIXe Siecle, 1979; Un Siecle d'or Espagnol: Vers 1525-Vers 1648, 1982; Histoire des Espagnols (series), 1985-92; La America Espagnola y la America Portuguesa, 1986; La Europa del Renacimiento, 1988; La Europa del siglo XVII, 1989; (with L. Bennassar) Les Chretiens D'Allah: L'histoire Extraordinaire des Renegats, XVIe et XVIIe Siecles, 1989; (with B. Bessiere) Le Defi Espagnol, 1991; (with L. Bennassar) 1492: Un monde noveau?, 1991; Histoire de la Tauromachie: Une Societe du Spectacle, 1993; Franco, 1995; Les Tribulations de Mustafa des Six-Fours (novel), 1995; (with B. Vincent) Le Temps de l'Espagne, 1999; (with R. Marin) Histoire du Brisil 1500-2000; Cortes, le conquezant de l'impossible, 2001; Toute les Colombies (novel), 2002. **Address:** 11 Allee du Val D'Aran, 31240 Saint Jean, France. **Online address:** bennassa@univ-tlse2.fr

BENNETT, Alan. British, b. 1934. **Genres:** Novellas/Short stories, Plays/Screenplays. **Publications:** (with P. Cook, J. Miller, and D. Moore) Beyond the Fringe (revue), 1963; Forty Years On, 1969; Getting On, 1972; Habeas Corpus, 1973; The Old Country, 1977; Enjoy, 1980; Office Suite (2 plays), 1981; Objects of Affection, 1983; A Private Function, 1984; The Writer in Disguise, 1985; The Complete beyond the Fringe, 1987; Prick Up Your Ears, 1987; Two Kafka Plays, 1987; Talking Heads, 1988; Single Spies, 1989; Poetry in Motion, 1990; Wind in the Willows (adapted), 1990; The Madness of George III, 1991, as The Madness of King George, 1995; Plays One, 1991; Writing Home, 1994; Plays Two, 1998; The Clothes They Stood Up In, 1998; Talking Heads 2, 1998; The Complete Talking Heads, 1998; The Lady in the Van, 1999; Father! Father! Burning Bright, 2000; Telling Tales, 2000; The Laying on of Hands, 2001; The History Boys, 2004. **Address:** c/o PFD, Drury House, 34-43 Russell St, London WC2B 5HA, England.

BENNETT, Carl D(ouglas). American, b. 1917. **Genres:** Humanities, Literary criticism and history. **Career:** West Georgia College, Carrollton, instruc-

tor in English, 1941-42; Wesleyan College, Macon, GA, assistant professor to associate professor of English, 1944-59; St. Andrews Presbyterian College, Laurinburg, NC, professor of English, 1959-82, distinguished professor, 1982-88, emeritus, 1989-, past department head and chair of Humanities and Fine Arts Division. Seinan Gakuin University, visiting professor, 1980-81; Mercer University, visiting professor; lecturer at Japanese colleges. Fulbright scholar, India, 1964. **Publications:** Joseph Conrad, 1991. Work represented in anthologies, contrib. of articles and reviews to scholarly journals. **Address:** Department of English, St. Andrews Presbyterian College, Laurinburg, NC 28352, U.S.A.

BENNETT, Charles A. American, b. 1947. **Genres:** Adult non-fiction. **Career:** Advertising and marketing specialist, motivational speaker, and writer. Volunteer Central (Internet clearing house for volunteering), founder. **Publications:** Volunteering: The Selfish Benefits, 2001. **Address:** PO Box 343, Oak View, CA 93022, U.S.A. **Online address:** bennettasc@aol.com

BENNETT, Cherie. American, b. 1960. **Genres:** Young adult fiction, Plays/Screenplays. **Career:** Author, playwright, and syndicated columnist. Performer in Broadway, Off-Broadway, and regional theater productions. Theatre director at regional and Off-Broadway productions. Has appeared on television and radio talk shows and as a lecturer in schools. Author of nationally syndicated advice column, "Hey Cherie!". **Publications:** YOUNG ADULT NOVELS: Good-Bye, Best Friend, 1993; Girls in Love, 1996; Bridesmaids, 1996; Searching for David's Heart, 1998; Life in the Fat Lane, 1998. SUNSET ISLAND SERIES: Sunset Island, 1991; Sunset Kiss, 1991; Sunset Dreams, 1991; Sunset Farewell, 1991; Sunset Reunion, 1991; Sunset Heat, 1992; Sunset Paradise, 1992; Sunset Promises, 1992; Sunset Scandal, 1992; Sunset Secrets, 1992; Sunset Whispers, 1992; Sunset after Dark, 1993; Sunset after Hours, 1993; Sunset after Midnight, 1993; Sunset Deceptions, 1993; Sunset Embrace, 1993; Sunset on the Road, 1993; Sunset Surf, 1993; Sunset Wishes, 1993; Sunset Touch, 1993; Sunset Wedding, 1993; Sunset Fantasy, 1994; Sunset Fire, 1994; Sunset Glitter, 1994; Sunset Heart, 1994; Sunset Illusions, 1994; Sunset Magic, 1994; Sunset Passion, 1994; Sunset Revenge, 1994; Sunset Sensation, 1994; Sunset Stranger, 1994; Sunset Fling, 1995; Sunset Love, 1995; Sunset Spirit, 1995; Sunset Tears, 1995; Sunset Forever, 1997. CLUB SUNSET ISLAND TRILOGY: Too Many Boys!, 1994; Dixie's First Kiss, 1994; Tori's Crush, 1994. SURVIVING SIXTEEN TRILOGY: Did You Hear about Amber?, 1993; The Fall of the Perfect Girl, 1993; Only Love Can Break Your Heart, 1994. WILD HEARTS SERIES: Hot Winter Nights, 1994; On the Edge, 1994; Passionate Kisses, 1994; Wild Hearts, 1994; Wild Hearts Forever, 1994; Wild Hearts on Fire, 1994. OTHER SERIES: (with J. Gottesfeld) Teen Angels series, 1996; Hope Hospital series, 1996-97; (with J. Gottesfeld) Trash series, 1997; (with J. Gottesfeld) Mirror Image series, 1999-2000; (with J. Gottesfeld) University Hospital series, 2000-2001. PLAYS: Honky Tonk Angels, 1988; John Lennon and Me (also known as Candy Store Window), 1993; Sex and Rage in a Soho Loft, 1994; Anne Frank and Me, 1995; Cyra and Rocky, 1996; Zink the So-Called Zebra, 1997; Searching for David's Heart, 1998, teleplay, 2002. SCREENPLAYS: Angel from Montgomery, 1993; Wild Hearts, 1995. OTHER: Samantha Tyler's Younger Sister (in German translation only); (with J. Gottesfeld) Anne Frank and Me, 2001. **Address:** PO Box 150326, Nashville, TN 37215, U.S.A.

BENNETT, Clinton. British, b. 1955. **Genres:** Education, Theology/Religion. **Career:** Ordained Baptist minister, 1978; Government of New South Wales, Sydney, Australia, clerical officer, 1972-74; Baptist Missionary Society, Bangladesh, missionary, 1979-83; Birmingham Ethnic Education and Advisory Service, Birmingham, England, tutor, 1983-86; British Council of Churches, London, England, executive secretary, 1987-92; Westminster College, Oxford, England, senior lecturer, 1992-98; Baylor University, TX, associate professor, 1998-2001; Birmingham University, honorary research fellow, 2001-. **Publications:** Victorian Images of Islam, 1992; In Search of the Sacred, 1996; (with C. Higgins and L. Foreman-Peck) Researching Teaching Methods in Colleges and Universities, 1996; In Search of Muhammad, 1998; In Search of Jesus, 2001; Muslims and Modernity, 2005. **Address:** 89 Oval Rd, Erdington, Birmingham B24 8PY, England. **Online address:** cb@clintonbennett.net

BENNETT, Colin J. British/Canadian, b. 1955. **Genres:** Politics/Government. **Career:** University of Victoria, BC, assistant professor, 1986-91, associate professor of political science, 1991-. **Publications:** (with P. Hennessy) A Consumers' Guide to Open Government: Techniques for Penetrating Whitehall, 1980; Regulating Privacy: Data Protection and Public Policy in Europe and the United States, 1992; (ed) Visions of Privacy, 1999. Contributor of articles and reviews to political science journals. **Address:** Department of Political Science, Cornett Bldg Rm A323, University of Victoria, Box 3050, Victoria, BC, Canada V8W 3P5. **Online address:** cjb@uvic.ca

BENNETT, Edward M. American, b. 1927. **Genres:** History, International relations/Current affairs. **Career:** Texas A&M University, College Station, instructor, 1960-61; Washington State University, Pullman, assistant professor, 1961-66, associate professor, 1966-71, professor, 1971-94. **Publications:** Recognition of Russia: An American Foreign Policy Dilemma, 1970; As the Storm Clouds Gathered: European Perceptions of American Foreign Policy in the Nineteen Thirties, 1979; Franklin D. Roosevelt and the Search for Security: American-Soviet Relations, 1933-1939, 1985; Franklin D. Roosevelt and the Search for Victory: American-Soviet Relations, 1939-1945, 1990; Separated by a Common Language: Franklin Delano Roosevelt and Anglo-American Relations, 1933-1939, 2002. EDITOR: Polycentrism: Growing Dissidence in the Communist Bloc?, 1967; (co) Diplomats in Crisis: U.S.-Sino-Japanese Relations, 1919-1941, 1974. **Address:** 1240 SE Harvest Dr, Pullman, WA 99163-2443, U.S.A.

BENNETT, Elizabeth. *See* **HARROD-EAGLES, Cynthia.**

BENNETT, Georgette. American (born Hungary), b. 1946. **Genres:** Civil liberties/Human rights, Criminology/True Crime, International relations/Current affairs. **Career:** City University of New York, assistant professor of sociology, 1970-77; NYC Office of Management and Budget, deputy assistant director for administration of justice, 1977-78; NBC News, NYC, network correspondent, 1978-80; Bennett Associates, NYC, owner and president, 1980-87, 1992-; First New York Bank for Business (formerly First Women's Bank), vice president and marketing director, 1987, first vp and chief marketing officer, 1987-88, senior vp and division executive of domestic and international and private banking, 1988-92; Tanenbaum Center for Interreligious Understanding, president, 1992-. Host of Walter Cronkite's PBS-TV program, Why in the World?; host, guest, and consultant on local and national TV and radio programs. **Publications:** (with A. Abramovitz, C. Milton, and E. Mintz) Women in Policing: A Manual, 1975; (with R. Waldron and others) Law Enforcement and Criminal Justice: An Introduction, 1979; Unlocking America, 2 vols., 1981; Protecting against Crime, 1982; A Safe Place to Live, 1982; Crimewarps: The Future of Crime in America, 1987. Contributor of articles to popular professional and scholarly publications. **Address:** Tanenbaum Center for Interreligious Understanding, 350 5th Ave Ste 3502, New York, NY 10118, U.S.A. **Online address:** gfbennett@msn.com

BENNETT, Hal Zina. American, b. 1936. **Genres:** Self help, Writing/Journalism, Medicine/Health, Adult non-fiction. **Career:** Writer; Teacher, Workshops & Seminars in Writing. **Publications:** Behind the Scenes, 1967; The Vanishing Pirate, 1967; Battle of Wits, 1968; Brave the Dragon, 1969; No More Public School, 1970; The Well Body Book, 1973; Be Well, 1974; Spirit Guides, 1975; Cold Comfort, 1979; Sewing for the Outdoors, 1980; The Doctor Within, 1981; (co-author) John Marino's Bicycling Book, 1981; The Complete Bicycle Commuter, 1982; (with C.A. Garfield) Peak Performance, 1984; Mind Jogger, 1986; Inner Guides, Visions, Dreams, 1986; The Lens of Perception, 1987; (with M. Larsen) How to Write with a Collaborator, 1988; (with S.J. Sparrow) Follow Your Bliss, 1990; Zuni Fetishes, 1994; Write from the Heart, 1995. EDITOR: The Tooth Trip, 1972; The New Dimensions Books Series, 1994-95; Emerging from Invisibility, 1997.

BENNETT, James Richard. American, b. 1932. **Genres:** Civil liberties/Human rights, Communications/Media, Humanities, Literary criticism and history, Military/Defense/Arms control, Politics/Government. **Career:** University of Montana, assistant professor, 1960-62; University of Western Washington, assistant professor, 1962-65; University of Arkansas, Fayetteville, assistant professor, 1965-66, associate professor, 1966-71, professor, 1971-98, professor emeritus, 1998-; Myers Center for the Study of Human Rights, founder and director, 1984-98; Whistleblowers Research Center, founder and director, 1998-2002; Peace Research Center, director, 1998-; Omni Center for Peace, Justice, and Ecology, founder and director. Style, founder and editor, 1966-82; Fulbright Lecturer, Yugoslavia 1968-69. **Publications:** Prose Style: A Historical Approach through Studies, 1972; Bibliographies: Stylistics and Related Criticism, 1986; Control of Information in the United States, 1987; Control of the Media in the United States, 1991; Political Prisoners and Trials, 1995; Peace Movement Directory, 2001. **Address:** 2582 Jimmie Ave, Fayetteville, AR 72703, U.S.A. **Online address:** JBennet@uark.edu

BENNETT, John M(ichael). American, b. 1942. **Genres:** Poetry. **Career:** Ohio State University, Columbus, assistant professor of Hispanic literature, 1969-76; Luna Bisonte Prods, Columbus, OH, publisher, 1974-; Ohio State University Libraries, Avant Writing Collection, curator, 1998-. **Publications:** Works, 1973; (with P. Virumbrales) La Revolucion, 1976; White Screen, 1976; Meat Dip, 1976; Do Not Cough, 1976; Meat Watch, 1977; Contents,

1978; Time Release, 1978; Nips Poems, 1980; (with C.M. Bennett) Pumped Gravel, 1980; Main Road, 1980; Motel Moods, 1980; (with R. Crozier) Meat Click, 1980; Puking Horse, 1980; Jerks, 1980; (with C.M. Bennett) Applied Appliances, 1981; (with C.M. Bennett) Some Blood, 1982; Blender, 1983; Burning Dog, 1983; Antpath, 1984; Nose Death, 1984; No Boy, 1985; 13 Splits, 1986; (with B. Smith) Ax Tongue, 1986; (with B. Smith) The Blur, 1987; The Poems, 1987; Cascade, 1987; Stones in the Lake, 1987; Twitch, 1988; Swelling, 1988; Regression, 1988; Lice, 1989; Live Chains, 1990; Milk, 1990; (with S.E. Murphy) Lens Rolled in a Heart, 1990; Span, 1990; Bell-Nail, 1991; Was Ah, 1991; Fenestration, 1991; (with J. Berry) The Lemurs, 1991; (with J. Brewton) Somation, 1992; Neuf Poemes, 1992; Bleached, 1992; (with D. Clark and C. Culhane) Bag Talk, 1992; (with T. Furgas, D. Clark, and W. Drake) Pod King/Uttered Thought Climatology, 1992; Leg, 1992; Wave, 1993; Blind on the Temple, 1993; Blanksmanship, 1994; (with M. Hovancsek) Autophagia, 1993; (with F. Straugulensis) Coruscation Drain, 1993; (with D. Metcalf) Bone-flag, 1994; Just Feet, 1994; Infused, 1994; Spinal Speech, 1995; Fish, Man, Control, Room, 1995; Eddy, 1995; Prime Sway: A Transduction of Primero Sueno by Sor Juana Ines de la Cruz, 1996; Ridged, Poeta, 1996; (with S.E. Murphy) Milky Floor, 1996; Door Door, 1997; Know Other, 1998; Sendero Luminoso in Context, 1998; Mailer Leaves Ham, 1999; Rolling Combers, 2001; (with I. Arguelles) Chac Prostibulario, 2001; (with R. Crozier) The Chapters, 2002; Historietas Alfabeticas, 2003; Public Cube, 2003; The Peel, 2004. **Address:** Luna Bisonte Prods, 137 Leland Ave, Columbus, OH 43214, U.S.A. **Online address:** bennett.23@osu.edu

BENNETT, Lerone, Jr. American, b. 1928. **Genres:** History. **Career:** Atlanta Daily World, reporter, 1949-1952, city editor, 1952-53; Jet magazine, Chicago, associate editor, 1953; Ebony magazine, Chicago, associate editor, 1954-57, senior editor, 1958-87, executive editor, 1987-; visiting professor of history, Northwestern University, 1968-69. **Publications:** NONFICTION: Before the Mayflower: A History of the Negro in America, 1619-1966, 1962, 5th ed, 1982; The Negro Mood, and Other Essays, cago, Johnson Publishing Co., 1964; What Manner of Man: A Biography of Martin Luther King, Jr., 1929-1968, 1964, 4th rev ed, 1976; Confrontation: Black and White, 1965; Black Power USA: The Human Side of Reconstruction, 1867-1877, 1967; Pioneers in Protest, 1968; The Challenge of Blackness, 1972; The Shaping of Black America, 1975; Wade in the Water: Great Moments in Black History, 1979; (with J.H. Johnson) Succeeding Against the Odds, 1989, repr. as Succeeding Against the Odds: The Inspiring Autobiography of One of America's Wealthiest Entrepreneurs, 1993; The Shaping of Black America, 1993; Forced into Glory: Abraham Lincoln's White Dream, 2000. Contributor to books. **Address:** c/o Ebony, 820 South Michigan Ave., Chicago, IL 60605, U.S.A.

BENNETT, Merit. American, b. 1947. **Genres:** Law. **Career:** Tinkler & Bennett (law firm), Santa Fe, NM, partner, 1975-. **Publications:** Law and the Heart: A New Paradigm for Lawyer-Client Relationships, 1994, as Law and the Heart: A Practical Guide for Successful Lawyer/Client Relationships, 1997. **Address:** Tinkler & Bennett, 309 Johnson St, Santa Fe, NM 87501-1828, U.S.A.

BENNETT, Neville. British, b. 1937. **Genres:** Education. **Career:** University of Lancaster, Former Professor of Educational Research; University of Exeter, Professor of Primary Education. **Publications:** Teaching Styles and Pupil Progress, 1976; Focus on Teaching, 1979; Open Plan Schools, 1980; The Quality of Pupil Learning Experiences, 1984; Recent Advances in Classroom Research, 1985; A Good Start: Four Year Olds in Infant Schools, 1989; Special to Ordinary: Case Studies in Integration, 1989; Learning and Instruction, vols. II and III, 1989; Talking and Learning in Groups, 1990; Managing Classroom Groups, 1992; Learning to Teach, 1993; Teaching through Play, 1996; Skills Development in Higher Education and Employment, 2000. **Address:** School of Education, University of Exeter, Exeter, England.

BENNETT, R(eginald) G(eorge) Stephen. Also writes as Elliot Long. British, b. 1928. **Genres:** Westerns/Adventure. **Career:** Has worked as a drift miner, apprentice butcher, lorry driver, bus driver, limestone quarryman, and cement plant operative; served in the British Royal Navy, retired, 1988-. **Publications:** AS ELLIOT LONG: The Brothers Gant, 1990; Savage Land, 1990; Incident at Ryker's Creek, 1990; Death on High Mesa, 1991; Wassala Valley Shootout, 1991; Marshal of Gunsight, 1991; A Killing at Tonto Springs, 1992; Lawless Range, 1992; Showdown at Crazy Man Creek, 1992; Trail to Nemesis, 1993; Stopover at Rever, 1993; Warpath, 1994; Mankiller, 1995; Death Trail, 1995; Sixgun Predator, 1996; The Hanging Man, 1996; Last Texas Gun, 1996; Meet at Ipona Basin, 1997; Return to Callyville, 1997; Bushwhack at Wolf Valley, 1997; Welcome to Hell, 1998; Scallon's Law, 1999; Retribution Day, 1999; Guntalk at Catalee, 1999; Wolf, 2000;

Hot Day at Noon, 2001; Hard-Dying Man, 2002. **Address:** 61 Heathfield Nook Rd, Harpur Hill, Buxton, Derbyshire SK17 9SA, England.

BENNETT, Ronan. Irish, b. 1956. **Genres:** Novels. **Career:** Institute of Historical Research, London, England, research fellow, 1986-87; writer. **Publications:** (with P. Hill) Stolen Years, 1990; Love Lies Bleeding (screenplay), 1990; The Second Prison, 1991; Overthrown by Strangers, 1992; Double Jeopardy, 1993; Catastrophist (novel), 1998; Face, 2000. **Address:** c/o Tessa Sayle Agency, 11 Jubilee Pl, London SW3 3TE, England.

BENNETT, Shelley M. American, b. 1947. **Genres:** Art/Art history, History, Bibliography. **Career:** University of Illinois at Chicago Circle, Chicago, assistant professor of art history, 1977-78; University of Iowa, Iowa City, assistant professor of art history, 1978-80; Henry E. Huntington Art Gallery, San Marino, Calif., assistant curator, 1980-83, associate curator of British and continental art, 1983-91, curator, 1991-. Visiting professor at University of California, Los Angeles, 1981-93, California Institute of Technology, 1987-, and University of Southern California, 1990-. **Publications:** (with P. Crown) English Book Illustration Circa 1800, 1979; Prints by the Blake Followers (exhibition catalog), 1981; British Narrative Drawings and Watercolors in the Huntington Collection, 1660-1880, 1986; Thomas Stothard: The Mechanisms of Art Patronage in England Circa 1800, 1988. Contributor to books, periodicals and reference works. **Address:** Henry E. Huntington Art Gallery, San Marino, CA 91108, U.S.A.

BENNETT-ENGLAND, Rodney (Charles). British, b. 1936. **Genres:** Antiques/Furnishings, Communications/Media, Fashion/Costume, Food and Wine, Homes/Gardens, Writing/Journalism. **Career:** Sunday Express, reporter and columnist, 1961-68; contributing editor, Penthouse, 1967-70, and Men Only, 1970-73; National Council in the Training of Journalists, chairman, 1968-69, 1977-79, 1984-85, 2001-04, director, 1994-; RBE Assocs Ltd., chairman and managing director, 1968-81; B&E International, London Ed., 1977-79; Connections (Press and PR) Ltd., chairman, 1982, managing director, 1985-87; Media Society, secretary, 1984-96; Chartered Institute of Journalists, president, 1985-86; Newsline UK, editor-in-chief, 1993-98; Journalism Training, editor, 1994-; The Journal, editor, 1996-2003. **Publications:** (ed.) Inside Journalism, 1967; Dress Optional-The Revolution in Menswear, 1967; As Young as You Look, 1970; The Dale Cottage Cookbook, 1980. Author of pamphlets; contributor to periodicals and books. **Address:** Church Cottage, East Rudham, Norfolk PE31 8QZ, England. **Online address:** r.b-e@virgin.net; rbe@ion.co.uk

BENNETT-GOLEMAN, Tara. American. **Genres:** Medicine/Health. **Career:** Omega Institute, Rhinebeck, NY, psychotherapist and workshop teacher. **Publications:** (with D. Goleman and American Health editors) The Relaxed Body Book: A High-Energy Anti-Tension Program, 1986; Emotional Alchemy: How the Mind Can Heal the Heart, 2001. **Address:** Omega Institute, 150 Lake Drive, Rhinebeck, NY 12572, U.S.A.

BENNING, Elizabeth. *See* **RICE, Bebe Faas.**

BENOIT, William L. American, b. 1953. **Genres:** Communications/Media. **Career:** Miami University of Ohio, Oxford, visiting assistant professor of communication, 1979-80; Bowling Green State University, OH, assistant professor, 1980-84; University of Missouri-Columbia, assistant professor to professor of communication, 1984-. **Publications:** (ed.) Readings in Argumentation, 1992; Accounts, Excuses, Apologies, 1995; Candidates in Conflict, 1996; Campaign '96, 1998. **Address:** Department of Communication, 115 Switzler Hall, University of Missouri-Columbia, Columbia, MO 65211, U.S.A. **Online address:** commwlb@showme.missouri.edu

BEN-RAFAEL, Eliezer. Israeli (born Belgium), b. 1938. **Genres:** Cultural/Ethnic topics, Language/Linguistics, Sociology. **Career:** Centre de Sociologie Rurale, Ecole des Hautes Etudes en Sciences Sociales, associate director of studies, 1984-85; Tel Aviv University, Israel, associate professor, 1987-91, professor of sociology and anthropology, 1991-, member of academic committee, Tami Shtinmatz Center for Peace Research, 1993-. Stanford University, visiting professor, 1984; Oxford University, Centre for Postgraduate Hebrew Studies, visiting scholar, 1989-90. Klal-Israel Project, cofounder and co-director, 2001-; International Institute of Sociology, president, 2001-. Consultant to International Peace Research Association and Commission on Peace Building in the Middle East. **Publications:** (with M. Lissak) Social Aspects of Guerilla and Anti-Guerilla Warfare, 1979; (with M. Konopnicki and P. Rambaud) Le Nouveau Kibboutz, 1979; The Emergence of Ethnicity, 1982; (with Konopnicki and Rambaud) Le Kibboutz, 1983; Israel-Palestine: A Guerrilla Conflict in International Politics, 1987; Status, Power, and Conflict in the Kibbutz, 1988; (with S. Sharot) Ethnicity, Religion, and Class

in Israeli Society, 1991; Language, Identity, and Social Division, 1994; (with H. Ayalon and A. Yogev) Community in Transition, 1994; Crisis and Transformation, 1997; (with Y. Sternberg) Identity, Culture, and Globalization, 2001; Jewish Identities, 2002. EDITOR: (with E. Olshtain) Language and Society in Israel, 2 vols., 1994; (with H. Herzog) Language and Communication in Israel, 2001. **Address:** Department of Sociology and Anthropology, Tel Aviv University, Rm 629 Naftali Bldg, 69 978 Tel Aviv, Israel. **Online address:** saba@post.tau.ac.il

BENSEL, Richard Franklin. American, b. 1949. **Genres:** History, Politics/Government. **Career:** Texas A & M University, College Station, assistant professor, 1977-82; University of Texas at Dallas, assistant professor, 1982-84; New School for Social Research, NYC, associate professor, 1984-90, professor, 1990-93; Cornell University, Ithaca, NY, professor, 1993-. **Publications:** Sectionalism and American Political Development, 1880-1980, 1984; Yankee Leviathan: The Origins of Central State Authority in America, 1859-1877, 1990; The Political Economy of American Industrialization, 1877-1900, 2000; The American Ballot Box in the Mid-Nineteenth Century, 2004. **Address:** Government Department, White Hall, Cornell University, Ithaca, NY 14853, U.S.A. **Online address:** rfb2@cornell.edu

BENSLEY, Connie. British, b. 1929. **Genres:** Poetry, Plays/Screenplays. **Career:** Office worker, including work for physicians and at House of Commons. **Publications:** Progress Report, 1981; Moving In, 1984; Central Reservations (poems), 1990; Choosing to Be a Swan (poems), 1994; The Back and the Front of It (poems), 2000. RADIO PLAYS: Loving Room, 1979; Changing Partners, 1980. **Address:** 49 Westfields Ave, Barnes, London SW13 0AT, England.

BENSMAN, David. American, b. 1949. **Genres:** History, Documentaries/Reportage. **Career:** Rutgers State University, director of graduate program in labor studies, 1985-89, associate professor, 1989-94. **Publications:** The Practice of Solidarity: American Hat Finishers in the Nineteenth Century, 1985; (with R. Lynch) Rusted Dreams: Hard Times in a Steel Community, 1987; Lives of the Graduates of the Central Park East School, 1994. Contributor to books and periodicals. **Address:** Department of Labor Studies & Employment Relations, Rutgers State University, School of Management & Labor Relations, 50 Labor Center Way, New Brunswick, NJ 08901, U.S.A. **Online address:** dbensman@rci.rutgers.edu

BENSON, Ann. American. **Genres:** Crafts, Mystery/Crime/Suspense. **Career:** Writer. **Publications:** Beadweaving: New Needle Techniques and Original Designs, 1993; Ann Benson's Beadwear: Making Beaded Accessories and Adornments, 1994; Beadwork Basics, 1994; Two-Hour Beaded Projects: More than Two Hundred Designs, 1996; The Plague Tales (thriller), 1997. **Address:** c/o Delacorte Press, 1540 Broadway, New York, NY 10036, U.S.A.

BENSON, Frank Atkinson. British, b. 1921. **Genres:** Technology. **Career:** Professor Emeritus of Electronic and Electrical Engineering, University of Sheffield, since 1987 (Lecturer, 1949-59; Sr. Lecturer, 1959-61; Reader in Electronics, 1961-67; Professor, 1967-87; Pro-Vice-chancellor, 1972-76). **Publications:** Electrical Engineering Problems with Solutions, 1954; Voltage Stabilized Supplies, 1957; Problems in Electronics with Solutions, 1958; (with D. Harrison) Electric Circuit Theory, 1959; Voltage Stabilization, 1965; Electric Circuit Problems with Solutions, 1967; (ed. and Contributor) Millimetre and Submillimetre Waves, 1969; (with T M Benson) Fields, Waves and Transmission Lines, 1991. **Address:** 64 Grove Rd, Sheffield S7 2GZ, England.

BENSON, Gerard. British, b. 1931. **Genres:** Poetry, Autobiography/Memoirs. **Career:** Central School of Speech and Drama, senior lecturer, 1965-85; Wordsworth Trust: Centre for British Romanticism, Grasmere, England, poet in residence, 1994; British Council Residencies: Cairo, 1997; Alexandria, 1997; Oslo, 1996; Stavanger Festival of Literature & Freedom of Speech, 1998; Kristiansand, 1998. Barrow Poets, leading performer. **Publications:** Name Game, 1971; Gorgon, 1984; The Magnificent Callisto, 1992; Evidence of Elephants, 1995; In Wordsworth's Chair, 1995; (with J. Cherniak and C. Herbert) London Poems on the Underground, 1996; (with J. Cherniak and C. Herbert) Comic Poems on the Underground, 1996; (with J. Cherniak and C. Herbert) Love Poems on the Underground, 1996; Bradford and Beyond: A Sonnet Journal, 1997; Help! 15 Poems, 2001; To Catch an Elephant (poetry for children), 2002, 2003. EDITOR: (with W.B. Wright and C. Herbert) Barrow Poems, 1976; This Poem Doesn't Rhyme (for young people), 1990; (with J. Cherniak and C. Herbert) 100 Poems on the Underground, 1991, as Poems on the Underground, 9th ed., 1999; Does W Trouble You?, 1994; (and comp.) Nemo's Almanac (annual), 1997, rev. ed.,

2000. **Address:** 46 Ashwell Rd, Manningham, Bradford, W. Yorkshire BD8 9DU, England. **Online address:** gerardjbenson@hotmail.com

BENSON, Jackson J. American, b. 1930. **Genres:** Novellas/Short stories, Literary criticism and history, Biography. **Career:** San Diego State University, California, professor of American literature, 1966-97. **Publications:** Hemingway: The Writer's Art of Self-Defense, 1969; The True Adventures of John Steinbeck, Writer, 1984; Looking for Steinbeck's Ghost, 1988; Wallace Stegner: His Life and Work, 1996; Wallace Stegner: A Study of the Short Fiction, 1998; Down by the Lemonade Springs: Essays on Wallace Stegner, 2001; The Ox-Bow Man: A Biography of Walter van Tilburg Clark, 2004. EDITOR: Hemingway in Our Time, 1974; The Short Stories of Ernest Hemingway: Critical Essays, 1974; The Fiction of Bernard Malamud, 1977; The Short Novels of John Steinbeck: Critical Essays, 1990; The Short Stories of Ernest Hemingway: New Critical Essays, 1991. **Address:** 9428 Haley Ln, La Mesa, CA 91941, U.S.A.

BENSON, John. British, b. 1945. **Genres:** Economics, History. **Career:** Sunderland Polytechnic, Sunderland, England, lecturer in history, 1973-74; Lady Mabel College of Education, Rotherham, England, lecturer in history, 1974-76; Wolverhampton Polytechnic, Wolverhampton University, England, lecturer, 1976-77, senior lecturer, 1977-86, professor of history, 1986-. **Publications:** British Coal Miners in the Nineteenth Century, 1980; The Penny Capitalists: A Study of Nineteenth-Century Working-Class Entrepreneurs, 1983; The Working Class in Britain: 1850-1939, 1989; Entrepreneurism in Canada, 1990; The Rise of Consumer Society in Britain 1880-1980, 1994; Prime Time: A History of the Middle Aged in Twentieth-Century Britain, 1997. EDITOR: (with R.G. Neville) Studies in the Yorkshire Coal Industry, 1976; (with R.G. Neville and C.H. Thompson) Bibliography of the British Coal Industry, 1981; The Working Class in England: 1875-1914, 1984; (with G. Shaw) The Evolution of Retail Systems, c. 1800-1914, 1992. Author of articles, chapters, reviews. **Address:** History Div., University of Wolverhampton, Wultruna St, Wolverhampton WV1 1SB, England.

BENSON, Judi. American, b. 1947. **Genres:** Poetry, Human relations/ Parenting. **Career:** Jacksonville Symphony Orchestra, Jacksonville, FL, public relations director, 1975-78; Antioch University International, London, England, assistant director, 1980-87; Foolscap magazine, editor, 1987; freelance artist and writer, 1987-92; Royal London Hospital, London, bereavement counselor, 1992-94; Dumfries & Galloway Royal Infirmary, writer in residence, 2004-. Participant in community theater in Pennsylvania, New Jersey, and Florida, 1970-78. Teacher of residential writing workshops in England. **Publications:** Somewhere Else, 1990; In the Pockets of Strangers, 1993; Call It Blue (Poetry), 2000. EDITOR/CO-EDITOR: Klaonica: Poems for Bosnia, 1993; What Poets Eat (poems and recipes), 1994; (with A. Falk) The Long Pale Corridor (bereavement poems), 1995; K. Smith, You AgainLast Poems and Other Words, 2004. Contributor of poems to periodicals. **Address:** 78 Friars Rd, East Ham, London E6 1LL, England. **Online address:** judi_benson2001@yahoo.com

BENSON, Peter. British, b. 1956. **Genres:** Novels, Novellas/Short stories. **Career:** Writer. **Publications:** The Levels (novel), 1987; A Lesser Dependency (novel), 1989; The Other Occupant (novel), 1990; Odo's Hanging (novel), 1993; Riptide (novel), 1994; Short stories represented in anthologies. ADAPTATIONS: The Levels and A Lesser Dependency, have both been adapted for television. **Address:** c/o Tessa Sayle, 11 Jubilee Place, London SW3 3TE, England.

BENSTOCK, Shari. American, b. 1944. **Genres:** Literary criticism and history, Biography. **Career:** University of Miami, professor of English and associate dean for Faculty Affairs of Arts & Sciences. **Publications:** Who's He When He's at Home, 1980; Women of the Left Bank: Paris 1900-1940, 1986; Feminist Issues in Literary Scholarship, 1987; The Private Self, 1988; No Gifts from Chance: A Biography of Edith Wharton, 1994; Textualizing the Feminine, 1991; On Fashion, 1994; Edith Wharton, House of Mirth, 1994; (ed. with S. Ferris) Footnotes: On Shoes, 2001; (with S. Ferris and S. Woods) A Handbook of Literary Feminism, 2002. **Address:** Department of English, University of Miami, Coral Gables, FL 33124, U.S.A. **Online address:** sbenstock@umiami.iv.miami.edu

BENT, Timothy (David). American. **Genres:** Translations. **Career:** Penguin USA (publisher), NYC, assistant to the chief executive officer, 1990-91; Arcade Publishing, NYC, senior editor, 1991-99; St. Martin's Press, senior editor, 1999-. **Publications:** TRANSLATOR: Henry Miller: The Paris Years, 1996; The Lost Museum, 1997; Memoir in Two Voices, 1999; The Character of Rain, 2002. **Address:** St. Martin's Press, 175 5th Ave 18th Fl, New York, NY 10010, U.S.A. **Online address:** Tim.Bent@stmartins.com

BENTLEY, James. *See* Obituaries.

BENTLEY, Joanne. American, b. 1928. **Genres:** Biography. **Career:** Psychologist in private practice in New York, N.Y., 1974-88; Asthmatic Children's Foundation, Ossining, N.Y., director in charge of psychological services, 1974-88; writer for World Authors, 1992-; Volunteer Counseling Service of Rockland County, supervisor, 1993-. **Publications:** Hallie Flanagan: A Life in the American Theatre, Knopf, 1988. **Address:** 2 Castle Heights Ave., Upper Nyack, NY 10960, U.S.A.

BENTLEY, Joyce. Also writes as Josie Collins. British, b. 1928. **Genres:** Novels, Romance/Historical, Biography. **Career:** Worked as a common law clerk in Manchester, England, 1944-49, and as a secretary, 1970-; Blackburn & Darwen, free-lance writer, 1958-; Blackburn Adult Centre, lecturer in creative writing, 1983-; Open University, lecturer in creative writing. Constable Trophy for Northern Writers (now absorbed by North West Arts Council), founder and secretary, 1975-83. **Publications:** NOVELS: Dangerous Refuge, 1974 (in US as Secret of Strangeways, 1976); Ring of Fate, 1979; (as Josie Collins) The Mad Major, 1980; Proud Riley's Daughter, 1988; Sing Me a New Song, 1990; Peterloo Shadows, 1995. OTHER: The Importance of Being Constance: A Biography of Oscar Wilde's Wife, 1983. **Address:** Silk Hall, Tockholes, Darwen, Lancs. BB3 0NQ, England.

BENTLEY, Michael (John). British, b. 1948. **Genres:** History, Politics/ Government. **Career:** University of Sheffield, England, professor of history, 1977-95; University of St. Andrews, professor of modern history, 1995-. **Publications:** The Liberal Mind, 1914-1929, 1977; (ed. with J. Stevenson) High and Low Politics in Modern Britain: Ten Studies, 1983; Politics without Democracy; Great Britain, 1815-1914: Perception and Preoccupation in British Government, 1984; The Climax of Liberal Politics: British Liberalism in Theory and Practice, 1868-1918, 1987; (ed.) Public and Private Doctrine: Essays in British History Presented to Maurice Cowling, 1993; Companion to Historiography, 1997; Modern Historiography, 1999; Lord Salisbury's World, 2001. **Address:** Department of Modern History, University of St. Andrews, St. Andrews KY16 9AL, Scotland.

BENTLEY, Nancy. American, b. 1946. **Genres:** Children's fiction, Plays/ Screenplays, Children's non-fiction, How-to books. **Career:** Dancer-Fitzgerald-Sample, San Francisco, CA, production department assistant, 1968-70; San Mateo Educational Resources Center, San Mateo, CA, educational research assistant, 1972-74; Colorado Springs School District, Colorado Springs, CO, media specialist, 1974-78, teacher, 1979-95, media specialist and coordinator of information & technology, 1995-2002. **Publications:** I've Got Your Nose!, 1991; (with D. Guthrie) The Young Author's Do-It-Yourself Book, 1994; (with D. Guthrie) The Young Producer's Video Book, 1995; (with D. Guthrie) Putting on a Play, 1996; (with D. Guthrie) The Young Journalist's Book, 1998; (with D. Guthrie) Writing Mysteries, Movies, Monsters, and More, 2001; The Case of the Sneaky Stinger, 2003; The Case of the Garden Monster, 2003; The Case of the Missing Bluebirds, 2003. BUSY BODY BOARD BOOK SERIES: Let's Go, Feet!, Do This, Hands!, Listen to This, Ears!, What's on Top, Head?, 1987. VIDEOTAPE SCRIPTS: The Making of a Storybook: Mary Calhoun, Storyteller, 1991; I've Got Your Nose!, 1992. **Address:** 1220 W High Point Ln, Colorado Springs, CO 80904, U.S.A.

BENTON, D(ebra) A. American, b. 1953. **Genres:** Administration/ Management. **Career:** Benton Management Resources, Fort Collins, CO, owner, public speaker, and consultant, 1976-. Rocky Mountain News, contributing editor, 1993. **Publications:** Lions Don't Need to Roar: Using the Leadership Power of Professional Presence to Stand Out, Fit In, and Move Ahead, 1992; How to Think Like a CEO, 1996; $100K Club, 1998; Secrets of a CEO Coach, 1999; How to Act Like a CEO, 2001. Contributor to management and finance journals and newspapers. **Address:** 2221 W Lake St, Fort Collins, CO 80521, U.S.A. **Online address:** www. TopSellingBooks.com

BENTON, Megan L. American, b. 1954. **Genres:** Literary criticism and history. **Career:** Institute of Early American History and Culture, Williamsburg, VA, editorial apprentice, 1978-79; freelance editor, 1979-86; Pacific Lutheran University, Tacoma, WA, adjunct professor, 1986-94, assistant professor, 1994-98, associate professor of English, 1998-, director of Publishing and Printing Arts Program, 1986-. Studio work in "fine printing" has been included in exhibitions on "book arts.". **Publications:** Beauty and the Book, 1999; (ed., with P. Gutjahr, and contrib) Illuminating Letters: Typography and Literary Interpretation, 2000. Contributor to books and periodicals. **Address:** Department of English, Pacific Lutheran University, Tacoma, WA 98447, U.S.A. **Online address:** bentonml@plu.edu

BENTSEN, Cheryl. American, b. 1950. **Genres:** Cultural/Ethnic topics, Public/Social administration, Sports/Fitness, Technology. **Career:** Change (magazine), New York City, assistant editor, 1971-72; Los Angeles Times, Los Angeles, CA, feature and sports writer, 1973-76; New York Post, NYC, feature writer, 1976-77; freelance writer, 1977-; CIO (magazine), senior editor, 2001; Darwin (magazine), senior editor, 2001. **Publications:** Maasai Days, 1989. **Address:** c/o Amanda Urban, ICM Agency, 40 W 57th St 17th Fl, New York, NY 10019, U.S.A. **Online address:** cherylbentsen@yahoo. com

BEN-YEHUDA, Nachman. Israeli, b. 1948. **Genres:** Sociology. **Career:** Hebrew University of Jerusalem, member of dept. of sociology, 1978-. Visiting professor at colleges and universities; consultant to U.S.-Israel Binational Science Foundation and Israeli Academy of Science. **Publications:** Deviance and Moral Boundaries: Witchcraft, the Occult, Deviant Sciences and Scientists, 1985; The Politics and Morality of Deviance: Moral Panics, Drug Abuse, Deviant Science, and Reversed Stigmatization, 1989; Political Assassinations by Jews: A Rhetorical Device for Justice, 1993; (with E. Goode) Moral Panics: The Social Construction of Deviance, 1994; The Masada Myth: Collective Memory and Mythmaking in Israel, 1995; Betrayals and Treason: Violations of Trust and Loyalty, 2001; Sacrificing Truth: Archaeology and the Myth of Masada, 2002. **Address:** Department of Sociology and Anthropology, Hebrew University of Jerusalem, 91905 Jerusalem, Israel. **Online address:** msnahman@pluto.mscc.huji.ac.il

BERBERIAN, Viken. American. **Genres:** Novels. **Career:** Writer. Former researcher of exchange-traded companies for investment firm in New York, NY. **Publications:** The Cyclist, 2002. **Address:** c/o Author's Mail, Simon & Schuster, 1230 Avenue of the Americas, New York, NY 10020, U.S.A.

BERBERICK, Nancy Varian. American, b. 1951. **Genres:** Science fiction/Fantasy, Novels, Novellas/Short stories, Children's fiction. **Career:** Writer. **Publications:** FANTASY NOVELS: Stormblade: Dragonlance Saga Heroes Vol. 2, 1988; The Jewels of Elvish, 1989; A Child of Elvish, 1992. "GARROC SERIES": Shadow of the Seventh Moon, 1991; The Panther's Hoard, 1994; (with L.P. Baker) Tears of the Night Sky, 1998; Dalamar the Dark, 2000; The Inheritance, 2001. **Address:** c/o Maria Carvainis Agency, 235 West End Ave, New York, NY 10024, U.S.A. **Online address:** Nancy_Berberick@yahoo.com

BERCK, Judith. American, b. 1960. **Genres:** Social commentary, Writing/Journalism, Young adult non-fiction. **Career:** Free-lance writer. Staff member or consultant to: Coalition for the Homeless, 1986, Citizen's Committee for Children, 1987-90, New York Civil Liberties Union, 1991. **Publications:** No Place to Be: Voices of Homeless Children, 1992. Contributor of articles to newspapers. **Address:** 2441 NE 41st Ave, Portland, OR 97212-5424, U.S.A.

BERCOVITCH, Jacob. New Zealander (born Romania). **Genres:** International relations/Current affairs. **Career:** University of Canterbury, Christchurch, New Zealand, professor of politics, 1981-. **Publications:** Social Conflict and Third Parties, 1984; (with R. Jackson) International Conflict, 1997. EDITOR: ANZUS in Crisis, 1986; (with M. Efrat) Superpowers and Client States in the Middle East, 1991; (with J.Z. Rubin) Mediation in International Relations: Multiple Approaches to Conflict Management, 1992; Resolving International Conflicts: The Theory & Practice of Mediation, 1996; Studies in International Mediation, 2002. **Address:** Department of Politics, University of Canterbury, Christchurch, New Zealand. **Online address:** J.bercovitch@pols.canterbury.ac.nz

BERDANIER, Carolyn D. American, b. 1936. **Genres:** Medicine/Health. **Career:** U.S. Department of Agriculture, Beltsville, MD, research nutritionist at Nutrition Institute, 1968-75; University of Nebraska-Lincoln, associate professor of biochemistry and medicine, 1975-77; University of Georgia, Athens, professor of nutrition, 1977-, head of Department of Foods and Nutrition, 1977-88, and member of executive council, College of Family and Consumer Sciences. University of Maryland at College Park, assistant professor, 1970-75; Hebrew University of Jerusalem, visiting scientist, 1970-72; Guy's Hospital Medical School (London, England), visiting professor, 1976; University of Vermont, visiting professor, 1994; Oregon State University, visiting professor, 1994; University of Washington, Seattle, visiting professor, 1994; National Yang-Ming Medical College (Taiwan), visiting professor, 1994; University of Pennsylvania, visiting professor, 1995. **Publications:** Advanced Nutrition: Macronutrients, 1995; Nutrition and Gene Expression: Clinical Aspects, 1996; Desk Reference for Nutrition, 1998; Advanced Nutrition: Micronutrients, 1998. EDITOR & CONTRIBUTOR: Carbohydrate Metabolism: Regulation and Physiological Role, 1976; (with J.L. Hargrove) Nutrition and Gene Expression, 1993. Contributor to books. Contributor of

articles and reviews to scientific journals. **Address:** Department of Foods and Nutrition, Dawson Hall, University of Georgia, Athens, GA 30602, U.S.A.

BEREBITSKY, Julie. American. **Genres:** History. **Career:** University of the South, Sewanee, TN, assistant professor of history and director of the Women's Studies Program. Hopewell-Furnace National Historic Site, consultant. **Publications:** Like Our Very Own: Adoption and the Changing Culture of Motherhood, 1851-1950, 2000. Contributor to journals and anthologies. **Address:** University of the South, Walsh Ellet 209, 735 University Ave., Sewanee, TN 37383, U.S.A. **Online address:** jberebit@sewanee.edu

BERENBAUM, Michael. American, b. 1945. **Genres:** History, Theology/Religion, Biography. **Career:** Colby-Sawyer College, New London, NH, instructor, 1969-71; Wesleyan University, Middletown, CT, university Jewish chaplain and adjunct assistant professor, 1973-80; Zachor, NYC, associate director, 1978; President's Commission on the Holocaust, Washington, DC, deputy director, 1979-80; Jewish Community Council of Greater Washington, DC, executive director, 1980-83; George Washington University, Washington, DC, associate professorial lecturer, 1981-83; U.S. Holocaust Memorial Museum, Washington, research fellow, 1987-88, project director, 1988-93, director of U.S. Holocaust Research Institute, 1993-97; University of Judaism, director of Sigi Ziering Institute, 2002-; Berenbaum Group, president. Adjunct professor, Georgetown University, 1983-97, American University, 1987; visiting professor, University of Maryland, 1983, Richard Stockton College, 1999-2000, Clark University, 2000; Claremont-McKenna College, 2003; Religious Action Center, senior scholar, 1986-88. **Publications:** The Vision of the Void, 1979, as Elie Wiesel: God, the Holocaust, and the Children of Israel, 1994; After Tragedy and Triumph: Modern Jewish Thought and the American Experience, 1990; The World Must Know: A History of the Holocaust, 1993; Witness to the Holocaust, 1997; A Promise to Remember, 2003. EDITOR: From Holocaust to New Life, 1985; (with J. Roth) Holocaust: Religious and Philosophical Implications, 1989; A Mosaic of Victims: Non-Jews Persecuted and Murdered by the Nazis, 1990; (with I. Gutman) Anatomy of the Auschwitz Death Camp, 1994; (with B.R. Rubenstein) What Kind of God?, 1994; (with A. Peck) The Holocaust and History, 1998; (with M. Neufeld) Bombing of Auschwitz, 2000. **Address:** 1024 S Orlando Ave, Los Angeles, CA 90035, U.S.A.

BERENDT, John. American, b. 1939. **Genres:** Local history/Rural topics. **Career:** Esquire, NYC, associate editor, 1961-69; Holiday, NYC, senior staff editor, 1969; associate producer for the David Frost Show, 1969-71, and for the Dick Cavett Show, 1973-75; New York Magazine, NYC, editor, 1977-79; writer. **Publications:** Midnight in the Garden of Good and Evil: A Savannah Story (nonfiction), 1994. Contributor to periodicals.

BERENZY, Alix. American, b. 1957. **Genres:** Children's fiction, Illustrations. **Career:** Glassman Advertising Agency, Fairfield, NJ, assistant art director, 1977-78; free-lance sign painter, 1977-79; Mark Color Studios (advertising agency), Fairfield, art director, 1978-79; free-lance illustrator, 1982-; writer. Part-time art instructor at schools in Philadelphia, PA. Works exhibited at galleries and shows worldwide. **Publications:** SELF-ILLUSTRATED RETELLINGS: A Frog Prince, 1989; Rapunzel, 1995; What's the Matter, Sammy?, 2005. Illustrator of books by B. Guiberson, A.P. Sayre, B.A. Schwartz. **Address:** 447 S Franklin St Apt C, Wilkes Barre, PA 18702, U.S.A.

BERESFORD, Anne. British, b. 1929. **Genres:** Plays/Screenplays, Poetry. **Career:** Drama teacher, Wimbledon Girls High School, London, 1969-73, and Arts Educational School, 1973-76. **Publications:** (with M. Hamburger) Struck by Appollo (radio play), 1965; Walking without Moving, 1967; The Lair, 1968; The Villa (radio play), 1968; Footsteps in the Snow, 1972; The Courtship, 1972; The Curving Shore, 1975; (with M. Hamburger) Words, 1977; Unholy Giving, 1977; Songs a Thracian Taught Me, 1980; The Songs of Almut from God's Country, 1980; Duet for Three Voices, 1983; The Sele of the Morning, 1988; Snapshots from an Album 1884-1895, 1992; Landscape with Figures, 1994; Selected Poems, 1997; No Place for Cowards, 1998; Hearing Things, 2002. **Address:** Marsh Acres, Middleton, Saxmundham, Suffolk IP17 3NH, England.

BERESFORD, Maurice (Warwick). British, b. 1920. **Genres:** Economics, History. **Career:** Member, Leeds Prison Parole Board, and Leeds Probation Committee. Lecturer, 1948-55, Reader, 1955-59, and Professor of Economic History, 1959-85, University of Leeds. Visiting Professor of History, University of Strathclyde, 1987-91. Member, Yorkshire Dales National Park Committee, 1964-72; Chairman, Yorkshire Citizens Advice Bureaux Committee, 1965-70; Member, Consumer Council, 1965-71, Hearing Aid Council, 1967-71, and Royal Commission on Historical Monuments, 1979-90. **Publications:** The Leeds Chambers of Commerce, 1951; The Lost Villages of England, 1954; History on the Ground, 1957, 1971; (with J.K. St. Joseph) Medieval England: An Aerial Survey, 1958, 1979; Time and Place, 1962; New Towns of the Middle Ages, 1967, 1988; (ed. with G. Jones) Leeds and Its Region, 1967; Deserted Medieval Villages, 1971; (with H.P.R. Finberg) English Medieval Boroughs, 1973; (with B.J. Barber) The West Riding County Council 1889-1974, 1979; Walks round Red Brick, 1980; Time and Place: Collected Papers, 1985; East End, West End, 1988; (with J.G. Hurst) Wharram Percy: Deserted Medieval Village, 1990. **Address:** 4 Claremont Ave., Leeds 3, Yorks, England.

BERG, A. Scott. American, b. 1949. **Genres:** Biography. **Career:** Full-time writer. **Publications:** Max Perkins: Editor of Genius, 1978; Goldwyn, 1989; Lindbergh, 1998 (Pulitzer Prize for Biography 1999); Kate Remembered, 2003. **Address:** c/o Janklow and Nesbit Assocs., 445 Park Ave., Fl 13, New York, NY 10022-1614, U.S.A.

BERG, Elizabeth. American, b. 1948. **Genres:** Novels, How-to books. **Career:** Writer. **Publications:** NOVELS: Durable Goods, 1993; Talk Before Sleep, 1993; What We Keep, 1998; Until the Real Thing Comes Along, 1999; Open House, 2000; Never Change, 2001. STORIES: Ordinary Life, 2002. OTHER: Family Traditions: Celebrations for Holidays and Everyday (nonfiction), 1992. Contributor to periodicals. **Address:** c/o Lisa Bankoff, International Creative Management, 40 West 57th St., New York, NY 10019, U.S.A.

BERG, John C. American, b. 1943. **Genres:** Politics/Government. **Career:** Suffolk University, Boston, MA, instructor, 1974-75, assistant professor, 1975-80, associate professor, 1980-85, professor of government, 1985-, director of graduate studies, 1993-. Boston Center for International Visitors, lecturer, 1993 and 1994. New Political Science, reviews editor, 1997-. **Publications:** Unequal Struggle: Class, Gender, Race, and Power in the U.S. Congress, 1994. Contributor to books. Contributor to political science and education journals. **Address:** Department of Government, Suffolk University, 41 Temple St., Boston, MA 02114, U.S.A. **Online address:** jberg@suffolk.edu

BERG, Leila. British, b. 1917. **Genres:** Novellas/Short stories, Children's fiction, Children's non-fiction, Civil liberties/Human rights, Education, Human relations/Parenting, Mythology/Folklore, Theology/Religion, Autobiography/Memoirs. **Publications:** FOR CHILDREN: The Adventures of Chunky, 1950; Little Pete Stories, 1952; Trust Chunky, 1954; The Story of the Little Car, 1955; Fire Engine by Mistake, 1955; The Hidden Road, 1958; A Box for Benny, 1958; My Dog Sunday, 1968; Folk Tales for Reading and Telling, 1966; The Nippers and Little Nippers series, 24 titles, 1968-76; Snaps series, 4 titles, 1977; Tales for Telling, 1983; Topsy Turvy Tales, 1984; Hanukka, 1985; Christmas, 1985; Time for One More, 1986; Dear Billy, 1992. SERIES: Chatterbooks, 4 titles, 1981; Small World, 8 titles, 1983-85; Steep Street Stories, 4 titles, 1987. FOR ADULTS: Risinghill: Death of a Comprehensive School, 1968; Children's Rights, 1971; (with P. Chapman) The Train Back: A Search for Parents, 1972; Look at Kids, 1972; Reading and Loving, 1977; Flickerbook, 1997; The God Stories, 1999. **Address:** Alice's Cottage, Brook St, Wivenhoe, Near Colchester, Essex C07 9DS, England.

BERG, Stephen. American, b. 1934. **Genres:** Poetry, Translations. **Career:** Assistant Professor, Philadelphia College of Art, Pa. Former Instructor in English, Temple University, Philadelphia, Pa.; Poetry Ed., Saturday Evening Post, Philadelphia, 1961-62; Founder and Co-Ed., The American Poetry Review, Philadelphia. **Publications:** Berg Goodman Mezey: Poems, 1957; Bearing Weapons: Poems, 1963; The Queen's Triangle: A Romance, 1970 (Frank O'Hara Prize); The Daughters: Poems, 1971; Grieve Like This, 1974; Grief: Poems and Versions of Poems, 1975; With Akhmatova at the Black Gates, 1981; Singular Voices: American Poetry Today, 1985; In It: Poems, 1986; Crow with No Mouth: Ikkyu Fifteenth Century Zen Master, 1989; First Song, Bankei, 1653, 1989; Homage to the Afterlife, 1991; New and Selected Poems, 1992; Oblivion: Poems, 1995; The Steel Cricket: Versions 1958-1997. TRANSLATOR: (co-) Cantico: Selections, by Jorge Guillen, 1965; Nothing in the Word, 1972; (co-) Clouded Sky, by Miklos Radnoti, 1973; (with D. Clay) Oedipus the King, by Sophocles, 1978. EDITOR: (with R. Mezey) Naked Poetry: Recent American Poetry in Open Forms, and Naked Poetry 2, 1969, 1974; (with S.J. Marks) Between People, 1972; (with S.J. Marks) Doing the Unknown, 1974; (with R. Mezey) The New Naked Poetry, 1976; In Praise of What Persists, 1983. **Address:** 2005 Mt. Vernon St., Philadelphia, PA 19130, U.S.A.

BERGÉ, Carol. American, b. 1928. **Genres:** Novels, Novellas/Short stories, Poetry, Antiques/Furnishings, Art/Art history, Social commentary, Biography, Essays. **Career:** 1947-56: Simon & Schuster, Forbes Magazine, Hart Publishing, Syndicate Publications, Green-Brodie Advertising, Pendray Industrial Public Relations: copywriting, copy editing, book reviews, advertising copy, account supervision. Merryle Rukeyser, Financial Columnist: Assistant. **Publications:** POETRY: (with others) Four Young Lady Poets, 1962; The Vulnerable Island, 1964; Lumina, 1965; Poems Made of Skin, 1968; The Chambers, 1969; Circles, as in the Eye, 1969; An American Romance, 1969; From a Soft Angle, 1971; The Unexpected, 1976; Rituals and Gargoyles, 1976; A Song, a Chant, 1978; Alba Genesis, 1979; Alba Nemesis (The China Poems), 1979. FICTION: The Unfolding, 1969; A Couple Called Moebius, 1972; Acts of Love: An American Novel, 1973; Timepieces, 1977; The Doppler Effect, 1979; Fierce Metronome, 1981; Secrets, Gossip and Slander, 1984; Zebras (collected fiction), 1991. OTHER: The Vancouver Report (reportage), 1965. **Address:** 2070 Calle Contento, Santa Fe, NM 87505, U.S.A. **Online address:** carolberge@earthlink.net

BERGEIJK, Peter A(drianus) G(errit) van. Dutch, b. 1959. **Genres:** Economics, International relations/Current affairs. **Career:** ABN Bank, Amsterdam, Netherlands, affiliated with Amsterdam Economist Country Risk Department, 1985-1987; Groningen University, Groningen, Netherlands, assistant professor of international economics, 1985-87; Ministry of Economic Affairs, The Hague Senior Economist, directorate general of international economic affairs, 1989-92, Economic Policy Directorate (research unit), 1992-. Consultant; professional trainer in government finance and economic policy. **Publications:** Handel en diplomatie (title means: Trade and Diplomacy), 1990; Handel, politiek, and handelspolitiek (title means: Trade, Politics, and Trade Policy), 1991; (with J. van Sinderen and E.W.M.T. Westerhout) Anticiperen en reageren op de Europese uitdaging (title means: The European Challenge: Strategies), 1992; (ed., with L.A. Geelhoed and van Sinderen) Met distantie: J.E. Andriessen en het economische bestuur (title means: Liber Amoricum for J.E. Andriessen, Former Minister of Economic Affairs), 1993; Economic Diplomacy, Trade, and Commercial Policy: Positive and Negative Sanctions in a New World Order, 1994; (with R.C.G. Haffner) Deregulation, Privatization, and the Macroeconomy: Measurement, Modelling, and Policy, 1996. Contributor to books. Contributor to periodicals and journals. **Address:** Ministry of Economic Affairs, P.O. Box 20101, 2500 EL The Hague, Netherlands.

BERGEN, Candice. American, b. 1946. **Genres:** Plays/Screenplays, Autobiography/Memoirs. **Career:** Actress and writer. Worked as model, during 1960s; freelance photographer and writer in late 1960s; commentator on Today Show, NBC-TV, 1975. Actress in motion pictures and television productions. **Publications:** Knock Wood (autobiography), 1984; The Freezer (play), 1968. Contributor to periodicals. **Address:** c/o Creative Artists Agency, 9830 Wilshire Blvd, Beverly Hills, CA 90212-1825, U.S.A.

BERGER, Arthur A(sa). American, b. 1933. **Genres:** Anthropology/Ethnology, Communications/Media, Film, Literary criticism and history, Humor/Satire. **Career:** University of Milan, Italy, Fulbright lecturer, 1963-64; San Francisco State University, Broadcast & Electronic Communication Arts Dept., professor, 1965-2003, emeritus professor, 2003-. University of Southern California, Los Angeles, Annenberg School of Communications, visiting professor, 1984-85. **Publications:** Li'l Abner: A Study in American Satire, 1970; The Evangelical Hamburger, 1970; (collaborator) Language in Thought and Action, 3rd ed., 1972, 4th ed., 1978; Pop Culture, 1973; The Comic-Stripped American, 1974; The TV-Guided American, 1976; Television as an Instrument of Terror, 1980; Media Analysis Techniques, 1982; Signs in Contemporary Culture, 1984; Seeing Is Believing, 1989; Agitpop, 1990; Scripts: Writing for Radio and Television, 1990; Media Research Techniques, 1991; Reading Matter, 1992; Popular Culture Genres, 1992; An Anatomy of Humor, 1993; Improving Writing Skills, 1993; Blind Men and Elephants, 1994; Cultural Criticism, 1994; Essentials of Mass Communication Theory, 1995; Manufacturing Desire, 1996; Narratives in Popular Culture, Media & Everyday Life, 1997; The Genius of the Jewish Joke, 1997; Bloom's Morning, 1997; The Art of Comedy Writing, 1997; Postmortem for a Postmodernist, 1997; The Postmodern Presence, 1997; Media & Communication Research Methods, 2000; Ads, Fads & Consumer Culture, 2000; Jewish Jesters, 2000; Video Games, 2002; The Agent in the Agency, 2001; The Mass Comm Murders, 2002; Media & Society, 2003. EDITOR: About Man, 1974; Film in Society, 1980; Television in Society, 1987; Humor, the Psyche and Society, 1987; Visual Sociology and Semiotics, 1987; Political Culture and Public Opinion, 1988. **Address:** 118 Peralta Ave, Mill Valley, CA 94941-3519, U.S.A. **Online address:** aberger@sfsu.edu

BERGER, Barbara Helen. American, b. 1945. **Genres:** Children's fiction, Autobiography/Memoirs, Essays, Illustrations, Picture/board books. **Career:**

Freelance artist, author, and book illustrator. Exhibited artwork at gallery shows in Seattle and the US. **Publications:** SELF-ILLUSTRATED: Animalia, 1982; Grandfather Twilight, 1984; The Donkey's Dream, 1985; When the Sun Rose, 1986; Gwinna, 1990; The Jewel Heart, 1994; A Lot of Otters, 1997; Angels on a Pin, 2000; All the Way to Lhasa: A Tale from Tibet, 2002. Contributor of essays to anthologies. **Address:** c/o Philomel Books, Penguin Putnam Books for Young Readers, 345 Hudson St, New York, NY 10014, U.S.A.

BERGER, Bruce. American, b. 1938. **Genres:** Poetry, Environmental sciences/Ecology, Natural history, Travel/Exploration. **Career:** Writer. Professional pianist, 1965-74; operator, Aspen Recycling Center, Colorado, 1976-78; American Way, contributing editor. **Publications:** There Was a River, 1979; Hanging On (non-fiction), 1980; Notes of a Half-Aspenite, 1987; A Dazzle of Hummingbirds (ornithology), 1989; The Telling Distance: Conversations with the American Desert, 1989; Almost an Island, 1998; Music in the Mountains, 2001. **Address:** Box 482, Aspen, CO 81612, U.S.A.

BERGER, Charles R. American. **Genres:** Language/Linguistics. **Career:** Illinois State University, Normal, assistant professor of psychology, 1968-71; Northwestern University, Evanston, IL, assistant professor, 1971-74, associate professor, 1974-78, professor of communication, 1978-87, Van Zelst Research Professor of Communication, 1987-88; University of California, Davis, visiting professor of communication, 1989; Northwestern University, professor of communication, 1989-90; University of California, Davis, professor of communication, 1991-, head of department, 1995-. Stanford University, visiting professor, 1983; lecturer at educational institutions worldwide. **Publications:** (with J.J. Bradac) Language and Social Knowledge: Uncertainty in Interpersonal Relations, 1982; (ed. with M.E. Roloff, and contrib.) Social Cognition and Communication, 1982; (ed. with S.H. Chaffee, and contrib.) Handbook of Communication Science, 1983; (ed. with M. Burgoon, and contrib.) Communication and Social Influence Processes, 1995; Planning Strategic Interaction: Attaining Goals through Communicative Action, 1997. **Address:** 5237 Cowell Blvd., Davis, CA 95616, U.S.A.

BERGER, Fredericka. American, b. 1932. **Genres:** Plays/Screenplays, Young adult non-fiction. **Career:** Haverford College, Haverford, Pa., librarian, 1954-55; English teacher at Friends' school in Jenkintown, Pa., 1955-56, junior high school in Wellesley, Mass., 1956-57, and high school in Newton, Mass., 1957-58; homemaker, 1958-79; Riverdale Presbyterian Church, University Park, Md., founder and director of Side Door Cafe, 1979-. Wesley Theological Seminary, Washington, D.C., team teacher in theology and the arts, 1983-, adjunct professor of drama, 1987-, religion and drama lecturer, 1995. Associate director of Episcopal Foundation for Drama; co-chairman of Interdenominational Drama Festivals for the Greater Washington Area. **Publications:** Nuisance (young adult novel), 1983. ONE-ACT PLAYS: What's New with Noah, 1975; The Light of the Gift, 1975; The Center of Time, 1976; Voices of Babel, 1977; Me and Myself, 1977; Storm, 1978; Robots: What They Are, What They Do, 1992; The Green Bottle and the Silver Kite, 1993. **Address:** 4209 Sheridan St, University Park, MD 20782, U.S.A.

BERGER, John (Peter). British, b. 1926. **Genres:** Novels, Novellas/Short stories, Art/Art history, Literary criticism and history, Sociology, Essays. **Career:** Full-time writer; began career as a painter and art teacher; art critic for Tribune and New Statesman, London. **Publications:** A Painter of Our Time, 1958; Permanent Red: Essays in Seeing (in U.S. as Towards Reality: Essays in Seeing), 1960; The Foot of Clive, 1962; Corker's Freedom, 1964; The Success and Failure of Picasso, 1965; A Fortunate Man: The Story of a Country Doctor, 1967; Art and Revolution: Ernst Niezvestny and the Role of the Artist in the U.S. S. R., 1969; The Moment of Cubism and Other Essays, 1969; The Look of Things (essays), 1971; G, 1972; Ways of Seeing, 1972; (with J. Mohr) A Seventh Man: Migrant Workers in Europe, 1975; Pig Earth, 1979; About Looking, 1980; (with J. Mohr) Another Way of Telling, 1982; And Our Faces, My Heart, Brief as Photos, 1984; (with N. Bielski) Question of Geography (play), 1984; The White Bird, 1985 (in U.S. as The Sense of Sight: Writings, 1986); Once in Europe (short stories), 1987; Lilac and Flag (novel), 1990; Into Their Labours (trilogy), 1991; Keeping A Rendezvous (essays), 1991; Pages of the Wound (poems), 1994; To the Wedding, 1995; Photocopies, 1995; (with K.B. Andreadakis) Titian: Nymph & Shepherd, 1996; King: A Street Story (novel), 1999; (with J. Christie) I Send You This Cadmium Red, 2000; The Shape of a Pocket (essays), 2001; John Berger: Selected Essays, 2001.

BERGER, Joseph. American (born Russia), b. 1945. **Genres:** Adult non-fiction. **Career:** English teacher in Bronx, NY, 1967-71; New York Post, New York, NY reporter, 1971-78; Newsday, New York, NY, reporter and

religion writer, 1978-84; New York Times, New York, NY, began in metro rewrite, became religion correspondent, 1985-87, national education correspondent, 1987-90, NYC education reporter, 1990-, Westchester, NY, bureau chief 1993-. **Publications:** The Young Scientists: America's Future and the Winning of the Westinghouse, 1994; Displaced Persons: Growing up American after the Holocaust, 2001. **Address:** Metropolitan Bureau, New York Times, 229 W 43rd St., New York, NY 10036, U.S.A.

BERGER, Samantha (Allison). American, b. 1969. **Genres:** Children's fiction, Children's non-fiction. **Career:** City and Country School, New York, NY, teacher, 1994; C.O.L.L.A.G.E. Comics, Philadelphia, PA, designer, editor, and writer, 1994-97; Scholastic, New York, NY, editor and writer, 1997-2000; Nickelodeon, New York, NY, head writer and editorial director of Nickelodeon, Nick Junior, and Nicktoons TV on-air creative group, 2000-. **Publications:** Baby Bird, 1999; Light, 1999; Honk! Toot! Beep!, 2000; Please Don't Tell about Mom's Bell, 2002; Spend a Day in Backwards Bay, 2002; Jan and Stan, 2002; Ride and Slide, 2002; Junior Goes to School, 2003. WITH P. CHANKO: Markets, 1998; Scientists, 1998; Big and Little, 1998; School, 1999; The Boat Book, 1999; Electricity, 1999; Festivals, 1999; It's Spring, 2000. WITH S. CANIZARES: Clay Art with Gloria Elliot, 1998; What Do Artists Use?, 1998; Building Shapes, 1998; Tedd and Huggly, 1998; Pelé, the King of Soccer, 1999; Canada, 1999; (with the Jim Henson Legacy) Meet Jim Henson, 1999; (with the Jim Henson Foundation) Puppets, 1999; The Voyage of Mae Jemison, 1999; Tools, 1999; Restaurant, 2000; At Home, 2000. WITH D. MORETON: Why Write?, 1998; Patterns, 1998; Then and Now, 1998; It's a Party, 1998; Celebrations, 1999; A Day in Japan, 1999; Games, 1999; (with L.E. Huberman) Junior in the City, 2002; (with L.E. Huberman) Junior on the Farm, 2002, WITH B. CHESSON: Hello, 1998; In the Air, 1999; Apples, 1999. OTHER: (with A. Kennedy) Fifi Ferret's Flute, 2001; (with M. Phillips) Worm's Wagon, 2001; (with M. Chambliss) Hide-and-Seek Hippo, 2001. **Address:** c/o Author Mail, Harry N. Abrams, 100 Fifth Ave., New York, NY 10011, U.S.A.

BERGER, Sidney. American, b. 1936. **Genres:** Plays/Screenplays, Songs/Lyrics and libretti, Theatre. **Career:** University of Kansas, Lawrence, assistant instructor, 1958-63; Michigan State University, East Lansing, assistant professor, 1964-66, associate professor, 1966-69; University of Houston, TX, professor to John and Rebecca Moores Professor of Theatre, 1969-, director of plays, 1969-. Houston Shakespeare Festival, producing director, 1975-; Children's Theatre Festival, producer, 1978-; Stages Repertory Theatre, artistic director, 1992-96, and director of plays; Alley Theatre, associate artist, 1989-, and member of advisory board. Director of films and television series, 1986-88; Public Broadcasting Service, producer and director of Centerstage, 1991-94; director of Houston Public Television presentations; narrator of Houston Public Television documentaries. Member of boards of directors. **Publications:** (ed. with J. Luere) The Playwright versus the Director, 1994; (with Luere) The Theatre Team, 1997. PLAYS: (and lyricist) The Mudlark, 1970; The Fall and Rise of Bertolt Brecht (adaptation), 1977; (and lyricist) The Little Match Girl, 1982; (and lyricist) The Last Temptation of Christ, 1984; Snow White, 1984; Bird Boy, 1985; (and lyricist) America! (musical), 1985; (librettist with R. Nelson) Tickets, Please (opera), 1985; (librettist) The Demon Lover (opera), 1987; Where Is the Sun? (oratorio), 1988; Rapunzel, 1990; Was It a Dream?, 1991; (librettist with Nelson) American Anthem (musical), 1991; End of the Line, 1992; Old Secrets. DOCUMENTARY FILMS: Upstream, U.S.A., 1985; House of the Jaguar, 1988. FILMS: The Search for Shakespeare, 1986; Good Buddies; Duets for Cannibals; Reina de la Selva. Contributor of articles and reviews to periodicals. **Address:** School of Theatre, University of Houston, Houston, TX 77204-4016, U.S.A. **Online address:** sberger@uh.edu

BERGER, Stefan. German, b. 1964. **Genres:** History, Organized labor, Politics/Government. **Career:** University of Plymouth, England, lecturer in British social history, 1990-91; University of Wales, Cardiff, senior lecturer in European studies, 1991-2000; University of Glamorgan, professor of history, 2000-. **Publications:** The British Labour Party and the German SPD, 1994; The Force of Labour, 1995; The Search for Normality, National Identity and Historical Consciousness in Germany since 1800, 1997; Labour, Nationalism and Ethnicity 1820-1939, 1999; Writing National Histories, 1999; Social Democracy and the Working Class in 19th & 20th Century Germany, 2000; Policy Concentration and Social Partnership in Western Europe: Lessons for the 21st Century, 2002; Labour and Social History in Great Britain, 2002; Historikerdialoge: Geschichte, Mythos und Gedachtnis im deutsch-britischen kulturellen Austausch 1750-2000, 2003; Writing History: Theory and Practice, 2003. Contributor to journals and newspapers. **Address:** Dept of History, University of Glamorgan, Pontypridd, Wales. **Online address:** sberger@glam.ac.uk

BERGER, Thomas (Louis). American, b. 1924. **Genres:** Novels, Westerns/Adventure, Plays/Screenplays. **Career:** Rand School of Social Science,

NYC, librarian, 1948-51; New York Times Index, staff member, 1951-52; Popular Science Monthly, NYC, associate ed., 1952-54; Southampton College,distinguished visiting professor, 1975-76; Yale University, New Haven, CT, visiting lecturer, 1981, 1982; University of California-Davis, regent's lecturer, 1982. **Publications:** NOVELS: Crazy in Berlin, 1958; Reinhart in Love, 1962; Little Big Man, 1964; Killing Time, 1967; Vital Parts, 1970; Regiment of Women, 1973; Sneaky People, 1975; Who Is Teddy Villanova?, 1977; Arthur Rex, 1978; Neighbors, 1980; Reinhart's Women, 1981; The Feud, 1983; Nowhere, 1985; Being Invisible, 1987; The Houseguest, 1988; Changing the Past, 1989; Orrie's Story, 1990; Meeting Evil, 1992; Robert Crews, 1994; Suspects, 1996; The Return of Little Big Man, 1999; Best Friends, 2003; Adventures of the Artificial Woman, 2004. OTHER: Other People (play), 1970. **Address:** c/o Don Congdon Associates, 156 5th Ave Ste 625, New York, NY 10010-7002, U.S.A.

BERGER, Thomas R(odney). Canadian, b. 1933. **Genres:** Law. **Career:** Practiced Law in Vancouver, BC, 1963-71; Served as member of Parliament (NDP) for Vancouver-Burrard, 1962-63, and Legislative Assembly (NDP) for Vancouver-Burrard, 1966-69; Judge, Supreme Court of BC, 1971-83; Royal Commission on Family and Children's Law, chair, 1973-75; Commissioner for Mackenzie Valley Pipeline Inquiry, 1974-77, Indian and Inuit Health Consultation, 1979-80, and Alaska Native Review Commission, 1983-85; Returned to practice of law in Vancouver, BC, 1986; Order of Canada, 1990; Freeman of City of Vancouver, 1992. **Publications:** Northern Frontier, Northern Homeland, 1977, rev. ed., 1989; Fragile Freedoms: Human Rights and Dissent in Canada, 1981; Village Journey: The Report of the Alaska Native Review Commission, 1985; A Long and Terrible Shadow, 1991; One Man's Justice, 2002. **Address:** 1440-355 Burrard St, Vancouver, BC, Canada V6C 2G8.

BERGER-KISS, Andres. American (born Hungary), b. 1927. **Genres:** Novels, Novellas/Short stories, Poetry, Autobiography/Memoirs, Humor/Satire. **Career:** State of Oregon, Portland, chief psychologist and director of mental health education, 1965-67; private practice of clinical psychology, 1968-90. **Publications:** Hijos de la Madrugada (novel), 1987, trans. as Children of the Dawn, 1999; Voices from the Earth (bilingual poetry collection), 1997. Contributor of short fiction to periodicals and anthologies.

BERGERON, Arthur W(illiam), Jr. American, b. 1946. **Genres:** History, Local history/Rural topics, Military/Defense/Arms control. **Career:** Louisiana State Archives, head of archives section, 1977-81; Louisiana Office of State Parks, Baton Rouge, curator of Port Hudson State Commemorative Area, 1981-86, historian, 1987-96. Pamplin Historical Park, Petersburg, VA, historian, 1996-; Louisiana State University, visiting assistant professor, summers, 1980 and 1987. Consultant to Louisiana Office of Historic Preservation for Historical Markers and National Register of Historic Places, both 1977-, and to Coastal Environments, Inc., 1989-; has conducted historical research for organizations; commentator and public speaker to genealogical and historical associations. **Publications:** Calendar of Documents of the Opelousas Post, 1764-1789, 1979; Reminiscences of Uncle Silas: A History of the Eighteenth Louisiana Infantry, 1981; (with L.L. Hewitt) Post Hospital Ledger, Port Hudson, Louisiana, 1862-1863, 1981; Civil War Records at the Louisiana State Archives, 1981; (with Hewitt) Miles' Louisiana Legion: A History and Roster, 1984; (with Hewitt) Boone's Louisiana Battery: A History and Roster, 1986; Guide to Louisiana Confederate Military Units, 18611865, 1989; Confederate Mobile, 1861-1865, 1991; The Civil War Reminiscences of Major Silas T. Grisamore, Confederate States Army, 1993; Tudor Hall: The Boisseau Family Farm, 1998. Contributor to book. Contributor of Contributor to historical journals; associate editor, Dictionary of Louisiana Biography, 1983-88.

BERGERUD, Eric M. American, b. 1948. **Genres:** Military/Defense/Arms control. **Career:** Lincoln University, San Francisco, CA, associate professor, 1983-. San Francisco PC Users Group, OS/2 SIG leader. **Publications:** The Dynamics of Defeat, 1991; Red Thunder, Tropic Lightning, 1993; Touched by Fire, 1996; Fire in the Sky, 2000. **Address:** 531 Kains, Albany, CA 94706, U.S.A. **Online address:** rickt@cris.com

BERGES, Emily Trafford. American, b. 1937. **Genres:** Novels, Sex, Self help. **Career:** New Jersey City University (formerly Jersey City State College), Jersey City, NJ, professor of English, 1969-. **Publications:** (with S. Neiderbach, B. Rubin, and others) Children and Sex: The Parents Speak, 1983; The Flying Circus (novel), 1984. **Address:** Department of English, New Jersey City University, 2039 Kennedy Blvd, Jersey City, NJ 07305, U.S.A. **Online address:** eberges@njcu.edu

BERGHAHN, Volker R. German, b. 1938. **Genres:** History, Politics/Government. **Career:** University of East Anglia, Norwich, Reader in

European History, 1971-75; University of Warwick, Coventry, Professor of History, 1975-88; Brown University, Providence, Rhode Island, Professor of History, 1988-98; Columbia University, Professor of History, 1998-. **Publications:** Der Stahlhelm, B.D.F. 1918-1935, 1966; Der Tirpitz-Plan, 1971; Rustung und Machtpolitik, 1973; Germany and the Approach of War in 1914, 1973; Militarism, 1981; Modern Germany, 1982; The Americanization of West German Industry, 1945-1973, 1986; Otto A. Friedrich. Ein Politischer Unternehmer, 1993; Imperial Germany, 1871-1914, 1994; America and the Intellectual Cold Wars in Europe, 2001. **Address:** Dept. of History, Columbia University, New York, NY 10027, U.S.A.

BERGIN, Thomas J. (Tim). American, b. 1940. **Genres:** History, Information science/Computers. **Career:** U.S. Veterans Administration, Washington, DC, systems manager, 1966-82; American University, Washington, DC, professor of computer science, 1982-, curator and director of Computing History Museum. Consultant to government agencies. IEEE Annals of the History of Computing, editor-in-chief, 1999-2003. **Publications:** Microcomputer Based Primer on Structural Behavior, 1986; Computer Aided Software Engineering, 1993; (co-ed.) History of Programming Languages, 1996; 50 Years of Army Computing, from ENIAC to MSRC, 2000. **Address:** Department of Computer Science, American University, 4400 Massachusetts Ave NW, Washington, DC 20016, U.S.A. **Online address:** tbergin@american.edu

BERGLAND, Martha. American, b. 1945. **Genres:** Novels, Poetry. **Career:** St. Matthew Grade School, Champaign, IL, teacher, 1967-68; Santiago College, Santiago, Chile, teacher, 1971-72; University of Wisconsin, Milwaukee, teaching assistant, 1974-77, lecturer in English, 1981; State University of New York at Albany, lecturer in freshman composition, 1979-80; Marquette University, Milwaukee, lecturer in English and journalism, 1981-82; Milwaukee Area Technical College, Oak Creek, WI, part-time lecturer, 1982-84; Milwaukee Center for Photography, lecturer in English, 1983-85; Milwaukee Area Technical College, instructor in English, 1984-2001. **Publications:** Fish (chapbook), 1975. NOVELS: A Farm under a Lake, 1989; Idle Curiosity, 1997. **Address:** 7460 N Longview Ave, Milwaukee, WI 53209-2152, U.S.A.

BERGMAN, Andrew. Also writes as Warren Bogle. American, b. 1945. **Genres:** Novels, Plays/Screenplays, Film. **Career:** Writer. Director of motion pictures, including So Fine, 1981, The Freshman, 1990, Honeymoon in Vegas, 1992, It Could Happen to You, 1994, Striptease, 1996, and Isn't She Great, 2001. Executive producer of motion picture Little Big League, 1994. Made cameo appearance in motion picture Big Trouble, 1986. **Publications:** We're in the Money: Depression America and Its Films (nonfiction), 1971; James Cagney (monograph), 1973; The Big Kiss-Off of 1944: A Jack LeVine Mystery (novel), 1974; Hollywood and LeVine (novel), 1975; Sleepless Nights (novel), 1994; Tender Is LeVine (novel), 2001. PLAYS: Social Security (two-act), 1986. SCREENPLAYS: (with M. Brooks, R. Pryor, A. Uger, and N. Steinberg) Blazing Saddles (based on Bergman's story), 1974; The In-Laws, 1979; So Fine, 1981; Oh God! You Devil, 1984; Fletch, 1985; (as Warren Bogle) Big Trouble, 1986; The Freshman, 1990; (with R. Harling) Soapdish, 1991; Honeymoon in Vegas, 1992; (with A. Brooks, M. Johnson, and L. Fonvielle) The Scout (based on a story by R. Angell), 1994; Striptease, 1996.

BERGMAN, Eugene. American (born Poland), b. 1930. **Genres:** Theatre, Biography, Novels. **Career:** Galludet University, Washington, DC, associate professor, 1971-92; writer. **Publications:** (with B. Bragg) Tales from a Club Room, 1980; (with T. Batson) Angels and Outcasts, 1982; (with Bragg) Lessons in Laughter, 1984; The Deaf and the Mute. **Address:** 5225 Pooks Hill Rd, Bethesda, MD 20814, U.S.A.

BERGMAN, Tamar. Israeli, b. 1939. **Genres:** Children's fiction, Children's non-fiction, Young adult fiction, Novels, Biography. **Career:** Israeli Broadcasting Authority, Jerusalem, radio play writer, 1970-82; writer. **Publications:** FOR CHILDREN: Hamassa Legan Hashoshanim (title means: The Journey to the Rose Garden), 1976; Danny Holeh Lemirpe'at Hashina'in (title means: Danny Goes to the Dentist), 1976; Al Shumklum ve-'al Shumakom (title means: About Nothing in Nowhere), 1976; Mi Rotze Lehitarev? (title means: Who Wants to Bet?), 1977; Beshabat Baboker (title means: On Saturday Morning), 1979; Shinayim tsohakot (title means: Laughing Teeth), 1980; Simlat Haksamim (title means: The Magic Dress), 1980; (with C. Gutman) Kol Ehad Ha'ya Pa'am Yeled (title means: We Were All Children Once), 1983; Ha Yeled mi-shamah, 1983, trans. as The Boy from Over There, 1988; Mehapsim Et Osnat (title means: Looking for Osnat), 1985; Gozal Shel Aba Ve'ima (title means: Mom and Dad's Chick), 1987; Leoreh Hamessila, 1987, trans. as Along the Tracks, 1991; Rav Hovel Shav Ela'ich (title means: The Captain Has Returned), 1990; Kunchiat Hassodot (title means: Conch of Secrets), 1996; Eifo?, trans. as Where Is?, 1998; Ina Afa im Hatziporim (title means: Ina Is Flying with the Birds), 1999; Mook, 2003. FOR ADULTS: Kemara Letusha (title means: As a Polished Mirror), 1996. **Address:** 6 Hanassi St., 92188 Jerusalem, Israel. **Online address:** zevtamar@netvision.net.il

BERGON, Frank. American, b. 1943. **Genres:** Literary criticism and history, Novels. **Career:** Vassar College, Poughkeepsie, NY, professor of English, 1972-. University of Washington, Seattle, visiting associate professor, 1980-81. **Publications:** Stephen Crane's Artistry, 1975. NOVELS: Shoshone Mike, 1987; The Temptations of St. Ed & Brother S, 1993; Wild Game, 1995. EDITOR: (with Z. Papanikolas) Looking Far West: The Search for the American West in History, Myth, and Literature, 1978; The Western Writings of Stephen Crane, 1979; The Wilderness Reader, 1980, rev. ed., 1994; A Sharp Lookout: Selected Nature Essays of John Burroughs, 1987; The Journals of Lewis and Clark, 1989. **Address:** Vassar College, Box 94, 124 Raymond Ave, Poughkeepsie, NY 12601-0094, U.S.A. **Online address:** bergou@vassar.edu

BERGONZI, Bernard. British, b. 1929. **Genres:** Novels, Poetry, Literary criticism and history. **Career:** Emeritus Professor of English, University of Warwick, Coventry, 1992- (Sr. Lecturer, 1966-71; Professor, 1971-92). **Publications:** The Early H.G. Wells, 1961; Heroes' Twilight, 1965, 1996; The Situation of the Novel, 1970, 1979; T.S. Eliot, 1972, 1978; The Turn of a Century, 1973; Gerard Manley Hopkins, 1977; Reading the Thirties, 1978; Years: Sixteen Poems, 1979; The Roman Persuasion (novel), 1981; The Myth of Modernism and Twentieth Century Literature, 1986; Exploding English, 1990; Wartime and Aftermath, 1993; David Lodge, 1995; War Poets and Other Subjects, 1999; A Victorian Wanderer, 2003. EDITOR: Innovations: Essays on Art and Ideas, 1968; T.S. Eliot: Four Quartets: A Casebook, 1969; H.G. Wells: Collection of Critical Essays, 1975; Poetry 1870-1914, 1980. **Address:** 19 St. Mary's Crescent, Leamington Spa CV31 1JL, England.

BERGQUIST, William Hastings. American, b. 1940. **Genres:** Psychology, Education. **Career:** University of Idaho, Moscow, assistant professor of psychology, 1969-72; Western Interstate Commission for Higher Education, Boulder, CO, director of special higher education programs, 1972-74; William Bergquist and Associates, director, 1974-; Professional School of Psychology, San Francisco, CA, president, 1986-. **Publications:** (with R.A. Gould and E.M. Greenberg) Designing Undergraduate Education, 1981; (with J.L. Armstrong) Planning Effectively for Quality, 1986; (with S. Phillips) Solutions: A Guide to Better Problem-Solving, 1987; The Four Cultures of the Academy, 1992; The Postmodern Organization: Managing the Art of Irreversible Change, 1993; (with G.A. Klaum and Greenberg) In Our Fifties: Voices of Men and Women Reinventing Their Lives, 1993; (with D. Meuel and J. Betwee) Building Strategic Relationships, 1994; (with B. Weiss) Freedom! The Social-Psychological Experiences of Liberation in Eastern Europe, 1994; (with R. McLean and B. Kobylin) Stroke Survivors, 1994; Quality and Access: An Essential Unity in Higher Education, in press. **Address:** Professional School of Psychology, Inc., 9912 Business Part Dr. Ste 170, Sacramento, CA 95827-1724, U.S.A.

BERGREEN, Laurence. American, b. 1950. **Genres:** Writing/Journalism, Biography, History. **Career:** Assistant to the President, Museum of Broadcasting, NYC, 1977-78; Member of the faculty, New School for Social Research, NYC, 1981-82. **Publications:** Look Now, Pay Later: The Rise of Network Broadcasting, 1980; James Agee: A Life, 1984; As Thousands Cheer: The Life of Irving Berlin, 1990; Capone: The Man and the Era, 1994; Louis Armstrong: An Extravagant Life, 1997. **Address:** c/o The Wylie Agency, 250 W. 57th St., Suite 2106, New York, NY 10107, U.S.A.

BERGSTROM, Elaine. Also writes as Marie Kiraly. American, b. 1946. **Genres:** Mystery/Crime/Suspense, Romance/Historical. **Career:** Novelist. WOS teacher. **Publications:** NOVELS: Shattered Glass, 1989; Blood Alone, 1990; Blood Rites, 1991; Daughter of the Night, 1992; Tapestry of Dark Souls, 1993; Baroness of Blood, 1995. NOVELS AS MARIE KIRALY: Mina, 1994; Leanna, 1996; Madeline, 1997; The Door through Washington Square, 1998; Blood to Blood, 1999; Nocturne, 2003. Work represented in anthologies. **Address:** 2918 S Wentworth Ave, Milwaukee, WI 53207, U.S.A. **Online address:** MKiraly@juno.com

BERGSTROM, Joan M(argosian). American, b. 1940. **Genres:** Human relations/Parenting, How-to books, Education. **Career:** University of Rhode Island, Kingston, instructor in child development and family relations, 1963-64; Cornell University, Ithaca, NY, instructor to assistant professor of child development and family relations, 1964-66, Project Head Start, regional training officer, 1966; Wheelock College, Boston, MA, Project Head Start

regional training officer, 1967-70, faculty member in department of professional studies in early childhood, 1972-, chair of department, 1975-, professor, 1978-, director of Center for International Education and Leadership, 1992-. Guest lecturer and visiting professor internationally. Served as consultant and resource for local, federal, and private agencies and corporations. **Publications:** School's Out-What Now?: Creative Choices for Your Child-Afternoons, Weekends, Vacations, 1984, 2nd ed, 1990; (with C. Bergstrom) All the Best Contests for Kids, 1988, 4th ed, 1994; It's Summer: School's Out!, 1992. Contributor to books and periodicals. **Address:** Director, Center for International Education & Leadership, Wheelock College, 200 Riverway, Boston, MA 02215, U.S.A. **Online address:** jbergstrom@wheelock.edu

BERKENSTADT, Jim. American, b. 1956. **Genres:** Music. **Career:** Pollina & Phelan, Chicago, IL, associate, 1982-85; Axley Brynelson, Madison, WI, associate, 1985-86; Wisconsin Cheeseman Inc., Madison, vice-president and corporate counsel, 1987-. Consultant to Apple Corps (Beatles), Dark Horse (Geo. Harriosn) and Garbage. **Publications:** (co-ed.) John, Paul, and Me: Before the Beatles, 1997. CO-AUTHOR: Black Market Beatles, 1995; Nevermind Nirvana, 1998; The Goldmine Beatles Digest, 2000. Contributor to periodicals. **Address:** c/o TWC, PO Box 1, Madison, WI 53701, U.S.A.

BERKEY, Jonathan P. American, b. 1959. **Genres:** History. **Career:** Princeton University, Princeton, NJ, lecturer in history, 1988-90; Mount Holyoke College, South Hadley, MA, assistant professor of religion, 1990-93; Davidson College, Davidson, NC, assistant professor of history, 1993-96; associate professor, 1996-. **Publications:** The Transmission of Knowledge in Medieval Cairo: A Social History of Islamic Education, 1992; Popular Preaching and Religious Authority in the Medieval Islamic Near East, 2001; The Formation of Islam: Religion and Society in the Near East, 600-1800, 2003. **Address:** Dept of History, Davidson College, PO Box 6911, Davidson, NC 28035-6911, U.S.A. **Online address:** joberkey@davidson.edu

BERKOFF, Steven. British, b. 1937. **Genres:** Novels, Novellas/Short stories, Plays/Screenplays, Travel/Exploration, Autobiography/Memoirs. **Career:** Writer, Director and Actor. Founding Director, London Theatre Group, 1973-. Formerly acted in repertory in Nottingham, Liverpool, Coventry, and at the Citizens' Theatre, Glasgow. **Publications:** Gross Intrusion and Other Stories, 1979; Decadence and Greek, 1980; The Trial and Metamorphosis, 1981; West, Lunch, and Harry's Christmas, 1985; Kvetch, and Acapulco, 1986; Sink the Belgrano!, 1987; Massage, 1987; Steve Berkoff's America, 1988; The Trial, Metamorphosis, In the Penal Colony: Three Theatre Adaptations from Franz Kafka, 1988; I Am Hamlet, 1989; A Prisoner in Rio (memoir), 1989; Decadence and Other Plays: East/West/Greek, 1989; (intro. to Faber text) Salome, 1989; (journal) Coriolanus in Deutschland, 1992; The Theatre of Steven Berkoff, 1992; Free Association (autobiography), 1996; Graft: Tales of an Actor, 1998; Shopping in the Santa Monica Mall (travel), 2000; The Secret Love Life of Ophelia (play), 2001; Tough Sets (journal), 2003. **Address:** c/o Rosica Colin Ltd, 1 Clareville Grove Mews, London SW7 5AH, England.

BERKOVITCH, Nitza. Israeli, b. 1955. **Genres:** Women's studies and issues. **Career:** Tel-Aviv University, Tel-Aviv, Israel, visiting lecturer in management and sociology, 1986-88, visiting lecturer in sociology, 1994-95; Stanford University, Stanford, CA, statistical consultant in libraries and information resources, 1991-93; adjunct lecturer in sociology, 1992-94; Ben-Gurion University, Beer Sheva, Israel, lecturer in behavioral sciences, 1995-, co-director of women's studies program, 1996-, head of sociology program, 1997-98. Western Washington University, adjunct lecturer, 1993. Adva Research Institute, member of editorial board of Lexicon on Inequality, 1998-; consultant to Israel Science Foundation, Ministry of Science, and Megamot. **Publications:** From Motherhood to Citizenship: Women's Rights and International Organizations, 1999. Contributor to books. Contributor of articles and reviews to periodicals in Israel and elsewhere. **Address:** Department of Behavioral Sciences, Ben-Gurion University, 84105 Beer Sheva, Israel. **Online address:** nberko@bgumail.bgu.ac.il

BERKOVITZ, Jay R. American, b. 1951. **Genres:** History, Cultural/Ethnic topics. **Career:** University of Massachusetts at Amherst, assistant professor, 1982-88, associate professor , 1988-2000, director of Center for Jewish Studies, 1989-, chairman of Department of Judaic and Near Eastern Studies, 1990-95, professor of Jewish history, 2000-; writer. **Publications:** The Shaping of Jewish Identity in Nineteenth-Century France, 1989; Rites and Passages: The Beginnings of Modern Jewish Culture in France, 1650-1860. **Address:** Dept of Judaic and Near Eastern Studies, Herter Hall, University of Massachusetts at Amherst, Amherst, MA 01003, U.S.A. **Online address:** jrb@judnea.umass.edu

BERKOWITZ, Dan. American. **Genres:** Plays/Screenplays. **Career:** Playwright. Alliance of Los Angeles Playwrights, chair. **Publications:** A . . .

My Name Is Still Alice (musical revue), 1992; Simply Divine (play), 1996; Miami Beach Monsters (musical), 1999; (with Shirley Hillard) There's No Place like Hollywood (musical), music and lyrics by Wayne Moore, produced in Hollywood, CA, 2001.Contributor to periodicals. **Address:** c/o Alliance of Los Angeles Playwrights, 7510 Sunset Blvd. Suite 1050, Los Angeles, CA 90046, U.S.A. **Online address:** ICIMEDIA@aol.com

BERKOWITZ, Peter. American, b. 1959. **Genres:** Ethics, Politics/Government. **Career:** Harvard University, Cambridge, MA, assistant professor, 1990-94, associate professor of government, 1994-. Lecturer at colleges and universities in U.S. and elsewhere. **Publications:** Nietzsche: The Ethics of an Immoralist, 1995. Contributor to books. Contributor of articles and reviews to periodicals. **Address:** Department of Government, Littauer Center, Harvard University, Cambridge, MA 02138, U.S.A.

BERKSON, Bill. American, b. 1939. **Genres:** Poetry, Art/Art history, Literary criticism and history. **Career:** Professor, San Francisco Art Institute, 1984- (Director, Letters & Science, 1994-98.) Editorial Board, Modern Painters, 2002-. Correspondent Ed., Art in America mag., 1988-. Editorial Associate, Portfolio and Art News Annual, NYC, 1960-63; Associate Producer, Art-New York series, WNDT-TV, NYC, 1964-65; taught at New School for Social Research, NYC, 1964-69; Guest Ed., Museum of Modern Art, NYC, 1965-69; Poet-teacher, Poets in the Schools, 1968-84; Ed., Best and Company mag., 1969; Teaching Fellow, Ezra Stiles College, Yale University, New Haven, CT, 1969-70; Adjunct Professor, Southampton College, 1979-80; Ed., Big Sky mag. and Big Sky Books, Bolinas, CA, 1971-78. **Publications:** Saturday Night: Poems 1960-61; Shining Leaves, 1969; (with L. Fagin) Two Serious Poems and One Other, 1972; Recent Visitors, 1973; Ants, 1974; (with F. O'Hara) Hymns of St. Bridget, 1974; Enigma Variations, 1975; Blue Is the Hero, 1976; Start Over, 1983; Red Devil, 1983; Lush Life, 1984; Ronald Bladen: Early and Late, 1991; A Copy of the Catalogue, 1999; (with A. Waldman) Young Manhattan, 2000; Serenade, 2000; Fugue State, 2001; (with F. O'Hara) Hymns of St. Bridget & Other Writings, 2001; The Sweet Singer of Modernism and Other Art Writings, 2004. EDITOR: In Memory of My Feelings, by Frank O'Hara, 1967; (with I. Sandler) Alex Katz, 1971; (with J. LeSueur) Homage to Frank O'Hara, 1978. **Address:** 800 Chestnut St, San Francisco, CA 94133, U.S.A. **Online address:** berkson@pacbell.net

BERLAN, Kathryn Hook. American, b. 1946. **Genres:** Children's fiction. **Career:** Hamilton Local Schools, Columbus, OH, third-grade teacher, 1969-70; Newark City Schools, Newark, OH, sixth-grade and elementary art teacher, 1971-77; Licking Valley Local Schools, Newark, second- and third-grade teacher, 1978-85. Freelance creator of workshops and teacher in-service projects, Cleveland, OH; Cleveland City Schools, creator and facilitator of classroom publishing project, 1991-. Owner and founder, ImagiBooks. Has given presentations for libraries and P.T.A. groups on writing with children. **Publications:** Andrew's Amazing Monsters, 1993. **Address:** 5034 Hartley Dr., Lyndhurst, OH 44124, U.S.A.

BERLFEIN, Judy Reiss. American, b. 1958. **Genres:** Young adult nonfiction. **Career:** KPBS Radio, San Diego, CA, science reporter, 1984-87; KUNC Radio, Greeley, CO, science reporter, 1985; Bernardo News, San Diego, CA, editorial assistant, 1986; Holt, Rinehart & Winston Inc., NYC, science editor and writer, 1987; freelance science writer and reporter, 1987-. **Publications:** Teen Pregnancy, 1992. Author of articles for magazines and newspapers.

BERLINER-GLUCKMAN, Janet. Also writes as Janet Gluckman. American (born Republic of South Africa), b. 1939. **Genres:** Novels, Novellas/Short stories, Mystery/Crime/Suspense, Horror, Science fiction/Fantasy, Biography. **Career:** Writer, editor, agent, and translator. Previously worked as a teacher; Professional Media Services (editorial consulting service), Las Vegas, NV, founder, 1978-. Founder, Berliner Productions (media production company), 1995. **Publications:** NOVELS AS JANET GLUCKMAN: (with W. Greer) The Execution Exchange, 1980; Rite of the Dragon, 1981, rev. ed. as Janet Berliner, 2001. MADAGASCAR MANI-FESTO SERIES (with G. Guthridge) (as Janet Gluckman): Child of the Light, 1992, rev. ed. as Janet Berliner, 1996; Child of the Journey, 1996; Children of the Dusk, 1997. EDITOR: (with P.S. Beagle) Peter S. Beagle's Immortal Unicorn, 1995; David Copperfield's Tales of the Impossible, 1995; (with M.H. Greenberg and U. Luserke) Desire Burn: Women's Stories from the Dark Side of Passion, 1995; (with D. Copperfield) David Copperfield's Beyond Imagination, 1996; (with M. Crichton) Michael Crichton Companion; (with J.C. Oates) Snapshots: 20th Century Mother-Daughter Fiction, 2000. Contributor of short fiction to periodicals and anthologies.

BERLINGER, Joe. American, b. 1961. **Genres:** Plays/Screenplays. **Career:** Director, producer, writer, and editor. Affiliated with McCann-Erickson, 1983-84, and Ogilvy & Mather, 1984-; Maysles Films, became executive producer; with Bruce Sinofsky, owner of production company Creative Thinking International. **Publications:** (with D. Beebe) Book of Shadows: Blair Witch 2 (screenplay), 2000. **Address:** c/o Innovative Artists, 3000 West Olympic Blvd., Building 4, Suite 1200, Santa Monica, CA 90404, U.S.A.

BERLO, Janet Catherine. American. **Genres:** Art/Art history. **Career:** Educator and historian. University of Missouri, St. Louis, member of art history faculty; University of Rochester, Rochester, NY, professor of art history, and Susan B. Anthony chair of gender and women's studies. **Publications:** Teotihuacan Art Abroad: A Study of Metropolitan Style and Provincial Transformation in Incensario Workshops, 1984; The Art of Pre-Hispanic Mesoamerica: An Annotated Bibliography, 1985; (with others) Native Paths: American Indian Art from the Collection of Charles and Valerie Diker, 1998; (with R.B. Phillips) Native North American Art, 1998; Spirit Beings and Sun Dancers: Black Hawk's Vision of the Lakota World, 2000; Quilting Lessons: Notes from the Scrap Bag of a Writer and Quilter, 2001. EDITOR: (with R.A. Diehl, and contrib) Mesoamerica after the Decline of Teotihuacan, A.D. 700-900, 1989; (with M.B. Schevil and E.B. Dwyer) Textile Traditions of Mesoamerica and the Andes: An Anthology, 1991; Art, Ideology, and the City of Teotihuacan: A Symposium at Dumbarton Oaks, 8th and 9th October 1988, 1992; The Early Years of Native American Art History: The Politics of Scholarship and Collecting, 1992; (with L.A. Wilson) Arts of Africa, Oceania, and the Americas, 1993; Plains Indian Drawings, 1865-1935: Pages from a Visual History, 1996. Contributor to books. **Address:** Department of Art and Art History, University of Rochester, 601 Elmwood Ave. Suite 656, 421 Morey, Rochester, NY 14642, U.S.A. **Online address:** brlo@mail. rochester.edu

BERLOW, Alan. American, b. 1950. **Genres:** Documentaries/Reportage. **Career:** Reporter, National Public Radio, 1979-89; freelance writer, 1989-. **Publications:** NONFICTION: Dead Season: A Story of Murder and Revenge on the Philippine Island of Negros, 1996. SOUND RECORDINGS FOR NATIONAL PUBLIC RADIO (NPR): Genetic Screening/Genetic Engineering, July 27, 1981; Watergate, Ten Years After, June 22, 1982; Vietnam Veterans in the Wake of War, November, 1982; Vietnam Veterans' Memorial Dedication, November 13, 1982; Reagan Administration Nuclear Weapons Policies, Parts I-V, March, 1983; The Hotel Intrigue: The United States and Human Rights in Honduras, April 22, 1984; Mexico City Earthquake, October 8, 1985; The Philippines, 1986; Davao City, Philippines: Laboratory for a Revolution, February 4, 1986; New Hope for Philippine Democracy, September 18, 1986; The New People's Army on Negros, February, 1987; Land Reform in the Philippines, April 14-15, 1987; Cambodia Ten Years after "Liberation", December 17, 1988; The War against Rangoon, 1989; and others. **Address:** 9 East Melrose St., Chevy Chase, MD 20815, U.S.A.

BERMAN, Claire. Also writes as Noelle Gallant. American, b. 1936. **Genres:** Gerontology/Senior issues, Human relations/Parenting, Psychology. **Career:** Secretary, American Society of Journalists and Authors. Sr. Ed., Cosmopolitan, 1958-63; Contributor Ed., New York mag., 1972-78; former Director of Public Education, Permanent Families for Children, Child Welfare League of America. **Publications:** A Great City for Kids: A Parent's Guide to a Child's New York, 1969; We Take This Child: A Candid Look at Modern Adoption, 1974; Making It as a Stepparent, 1980; What Am I Doing in a Stepfamily?, 1982; A Hole in My Heart: Adult Children of Divorce Speak Out, 1992; (with A. Elgart) Golden Cradle: How the Adoption Establishment Works and How to Make It Work for You, 1992; Caring for Yourself While Caring for Your Aging Parents, 1996, 2nd ed., 2001; The Day the Voices Stopped, 2001.

BERMAN, David. American, b. 1939. **Genres:** Politics/Government. **Career:** American University, Washington, DC, lecturer in political science, 1962-64; National League of Cities, Washington, DC, research associate, 1964-66; Arizona State University, Tempe, assistant professor, 1966-72, associate professor, 1973-80, professor of political science, 1981-, Institute of Public Administration, acting director, 1966-67, assistant director, 1966-69, senior fellow of Morrison Institute. Researcher, Democratic National Committee and American Law Division, Legislative Reference Service, Library of Congress, both 1962-64. Arizona Consumers Council, member of board of directors, 1970-79. KTSP-TV, political consultant, 1990, 1992; consultant to Salt River Pima-Maricopa Indian Community Council. **Publications:** State and Local Politics, 1975, 9th ed., 2001; American Government: Politics and Policy-Making, 1979, 3rd ed., 1988; Reformers, Corporations, and the Electorate: An Analysis of Arizona's Age of Reform, 1992; Arizona Government and Politics, 1998; Local Government and the States, 2003. EDITOR: Government Finances, 1967-70; (with J.C. Bollens, and contrib.) American Government: Ideas and Issues, 1981; (and contrib.) County Governments in an Era of Change, 1993; Contributor to books. Contributor of articles and reviews to political science and social science journals. **Address:** Department of Political Science, Arizona State University, Tempe, AZ 85287, U.S.A.

BERMAN, David. American, b. 1942. **Genres:** History, Philosophy, Psychology. **Career:** University of Dublin, Trinity College, Ireland, 1968-, lecturer, senior lecturer, associate professor, head of the Philosophy Dept, 1999-2000; writer and editor. **Publications:** A History of Atheism in Britain: From Hobbes to Russell, 1988; George Berkeley: Idealism and the Man, 1994; Berkeley: Experimental Philosophy, 1997. EDITOR: George Berkeley's Alciphron in Focus, 1993; Arthur Schopenhauer's World as Will and Idea, 1995. **Address:** Arts Building, University of Dublin Trinity College, Dublin 2, Ireland.

BERMAN, Jeffrey. American, b. 1945. **Genres:** Literary criticism and history, Writing/Journalism. **Career:** Cornell University, Ithaca, NY, lecturer in English, 1971-73; State University of New York at Albany, assistant professor, 1973-79, associate professor, 1979-88, professor of English, 1988-; writer. **Publications:** Joseph Conrad: Writing as Rescue, 1977; The Talking Cure: Literary Representations of Psychoanalysis, 1985; Narcissism and the Novel, 1990; Diaries to an English Professor, 1994; Surviving Literary Suicide, 1999; Risky Writing: Self-Disclosure and Self-Transformation in the Classroom, 2001. **Address:** Department of English, State University of New York at Albany, Albany, NY 12222, U.S.A. **Online address:** JBerman@albany.edu

BERMAN, Morris. American, b. 1944. **Genres:** Anthropology/Ethnology, History, Humanities, Intellectual history, Psychology, Social commentary. **Career:** Rutgers University, New Brunswick, NJ, assistant professor of history, 1970-75; Concordia University, Montreal, Quebec, assistant professor of history, 1980-82; University of Victoria, BC, Lansdowne professor of history, 1982-87; free-lance writer, lecturer, social critic, and cultural historian. Visiting professor: Seattle University, 1990, Evergreen State College, 1991, and University of Kassel, 1991-92, Simon Fraser University, 1997, Johns Hopkins University, 1999-2000, and Catholic University of America, 2003-; Incarnate Word College, San Antonio TX, Amy Freeman Lee Chair in the Humanities, 1993; University of New Mexico, Garrey Carruthers Chair in Honors, 1994-95; Weber State University, Ogden, UT, Eccles Chair in Honors, 1997. **Publications:** Social Change and Scientific Organization, 1978; The Reenchantment of the World, 1981; Coming to Our Senses: Body and Spirit in the Hidden History of the West, 1989; Wandering God: A Study in Nomadic Spirituality, 2000; The Twilight of American Culture, 2000; Colossus Adrift, 2005. **Address:** 3701 Connecticut Ave NW #618, Washington, DC 20008-4507, U.S.A. **Online address:** mberman@flash.net

BERMAN, Ruth. American, b. 1958. **Genres:** Animals/Pets, Children's non-fiction, Young adult non-fiction, Zoology. **Career:** Lerner Publications, Minneapolis, MN, children's book editor, became senior editor, 1987-95; Bowtie Press, Irvine, CA, editor-in-chief, 1995-2000. Freelance children's book writer and editor. **Publications:** American Bison, 1992; Sharks, 1995; Peacocks, 1996; Ants, 1996; Squeaking Bats, 1998; Fishing Bears, 1998; Buzzing Rattlesnakes, 1998; Spinning Spiders, 1998; Climbing Tree Frogs, 1998; Watchful Wolves, 1998. **Address:** 11517 Tulane Ave, Riverside, CA 92507, U.S.A. **Online address:** lineeditor@earthlink.net

BERMAN, Sanford. American, b. 1933. **Genres:** Communications/Media, Cultural/Ethnic topics, Librarianship, Sex, Bibliography. **Career:** Public Library, Washington, DC, Acquisitions Dept., assistant chief, 1957-62; U.S. Army Special Services Libraries, Germany, librarian, 1962-66; Schiller College, Kleiningersheim, Germany, librarian, 1966-67; University of California, Los Angeles, Research Library, periodicals librarian, 1967-68; University of Zambia, Lusaka, assistant librarian, 1968-70; Makerere Institute of Social Research, Kampala, Uganda, librarian, 1971-72; Hennepin County Library, Minnetonka, MN, head cataloguer, 1973-99. Contributing editor/editorial adviser to professional journals. **Publications:** Spanish Guinea: An Annotated Bibliography, 1961; Prejudices and Antipathies: A Tract on the LC Subject Heads Concerning People, 1971; Joy of Cataloging, 1981; Worth Noting: Editorials, Letters, Essays, an Interview and Bibliography, 1988. COMPILER: African Liberation Movements and Support Groups: A Directory, 1972; Subject Headings Employed at the Makerere Institute of Social Research Library, 1972. EDITOR/CO-EDITOR: Subject Cataloging: Critiques and Innovations, 1984; Alternative Library Literature, biennially, 1984-, Cataloging Special Materials: Critiques and Innovations, 1986. **Address:** 4400 Morningside Rd, Edina, MN 55416, U.S.A.

BERMANN, Sandra L. American, b. 1947. **Genres:** Literary criticism and history. **Career:** Princeton University, Princeton, NJ, professor of compara-

tive literature, 1976-. **Publications:** (trans.) Alessandro Manzoni, On the Historical Novel, 1984; The Sonnet over Time: A Study in the Sonnets of Petrarch, Shakespeare, and Baudelaire, 1988. **Address:** Department of Comparative Literature, Princeton University, 325 East Pyne, Princeton, NJ 08544, U.S.A.

BERMEO, Nancy G. American, b. 1951. **Genres:** Politics/Government. **Career:** Gladstone Associates, Washington, DC, research assistant, 1973-75; Dartmouth College, Hanover, NH, lecturer in politics, 1981-82; Princeton University, Princeton, NJ, assistant professor, 1983-89, associate professor of politics, 1989-. **Publications:** The Revolution within the Revolution, 1986. EDITOR: Liberalization and Democratization, 1992; Civil Society before Democracy, 2000; Unemployment in Southern Europe, 2000; Unemployment in the New Europe, 2001; (with U. Amoretti) Federalism and Territorial Cleavages, 2003. **Address:** Department of Politics, 230 Corwin Hall, Princeton University, Princeton, NJ 08540, U.S.A. **Online address:** bermeo@princeton.edu

BERNARD, Andre. American, b. 1956. **Genres:** Writing/Journalism. **Career:** Worked as bookstore clerk in the Berkshires; hand bookbinder in Boston, MA; Viking Penguin, New York City, member of editorial department; David R. Godine Publishers, Inc., Boston, executive editor; Simon & Schuster, Inc., New York City, senior editor of Touchstone Books. **Publications:** (ed.) Rotten Rejections: A Literary Companion, 1990. (ed. with Bill Henderson) The Complete Rot, 1991. **Address:** c/o Pushcart Press, P.O. Box 380, Wainscott, NY 11975, U.S.A.

BERNARD, Kenneth. Also writes as La Fanu Smerdnack. American, b. 1930. **Genres:** Novels, Novellas/Short stories, Plays/Screenplays, Poetry. **Career:** Member, English Dept., Long Island University, Brooklyn, NY, 1959-2003. Vice-President, New York Theatre Strategy, 1974-80; Assistant Ed., 1975-85, Advisory Ed., 1985-, Confrontation. **Publications:** The Maldive Chronicles (novel and short fiction), 1970; Night Club and Other Plays, 1971; Two Stories, 1973; How We Danced While We Burned and La Justice, or the Cock that Crew (plays), 1990; Curse of Fool (plays), 1992; From the District File (fiction), 1992; The Baboon in the Night Club (poetry), 1993; Clown at Wall: A Kenneth Bernard Reader (fiction, poetry, plays, collage), 1996; The Qui Parle Plays and Poems, 1999; Nullity (short fiction), 2000; The Man in the Stretcher (fiction), 2005. **Address:** 800 Riverside Dr #8H, New York, NY 10032, U.S.A. **Online address:** k.bernard@verizon.net

BERNARD, Oliver. British, b. 1925. **Genres:** Poetry, Autobiography/Memoirs, Translations. **Career:** English and Drama Teacher, West Suffolk, 1965-73; West Norfolk Area Drama Specialist, Norfolk Education Committee, 1974-81. Co-Chairman, Christian CND, 1986. **Publications:** Country Matters, 1960; Moons and Tides, 1978; Poems, 1983; Five Peace Poems, 1985; The Finger Points at the Moon, 1989; Getting Over It (autobiography), 1992; Verse &c., 2001. EDITOR & TRANSLATOR: Rimbaud: Collected Poems, 1961; Apollinaire: Selections, 1965; Formes et Paroles, by S. Espriu, 1990. **Address:** 1 E Church St, Kenninghall, Norwich NR16 2EP, England.

BERNARD, Patricia. Also writes as Judy Bernard Waite. Australian, b. 1942. **Genres:** Young adult fiction. **Career:** Writer and lecturer. **Publications:** FOR CHILDREN: We Are Tam, 1983; Aida's Ghost, 1988; Riddle of the Trumpalar, 1990; Challenge of the Trumpalar, 1990; Monkey Hill Gold, 1992; The Outer Space Spy, 1992; Dream Door of Shinar, 1992; Kangaroo Kids, 1992; Jacaranda Shadow, 1993; JB and the Worry Dolls, 1994; Outerspace Spy, 1994; Monster Builder, 1996; Duffy: Everyone's Dog Story (picture book), 1997; Spook Bus, 1997; The Outcast, 1997; The Punisher, 1997; The Rule Changer, 1998; No Sooks on the Starship, 1998; Wolf-Man, Pizza-Man, Jumping Dogs & Jellyfish, 1998; Into the Future, 2000; Techno Terror, 2000; Greening the Earth, 2001; Temple of Apis, 2001; Fords & Flying Machines, 2002; Duffy & the Invisible Crocodile, 2003; Stegosaurus Stone, 2003; The Mask, 2005; Basil Bigboots, 2005. FOR ADULTS: Sex Is a Deadly Exercise, 1987; Sex Is a Deadly Weapon, 1990; Deadly Sister Love, 1998; With the Kama Sutra under My Arm, 2004. **Address:** 54 Birrell St, Queens Park, Sydney, NSW 2022, Australia. **Online address:** patricia bernard@sdodo.com.au

BERNARDI, Daniel (Leonard). American, b. 1964. **Genres:** Film. **Career:** University of California, Los Angeles, assistant professor, 1996-98; University of Arizona, Tucson, assistant professor of new media, 1998-. **Publications:** Birth of Whiteness: Race and the Emergence of U.S. Cinema, 1996; Star Trek and History: Race-ing toward a White Future, 1998; Classic Hollywood, Classic Whiteness, 2002. **Address:** Department of Media Arts, University of Arizona, Tucson, AZ 85721, U.S.A. **Online address:** bernardi@email.arizona.edu

BERNARDINI, Joe. American, b. 1937. **Genres:** Novels. **Career:** Social worker in New York City, 1968-82; writer. **Publications:** Singapore: A Novel of the Bronx, 1983. **Address:** PO Box 669, Greenwood Lake, NY 10925, U.S.A. **Online address:** bernardi@optonline.net

BERNHARDT, William. American, b. 1960. **Genres:** Mystery/Crime/Suspense. **Career:** Hall, Estill, Hardwick, Gable, Golden & Nelson (law firm), Tulsa, OK, trial lawyer, 1986-95; Hawk Publishing Group, owner. **Publications:** NOVELS: Primary Justice, 1992; Blind Justice, 1992; The Code of Buddyhood, 1993; Deadly Justice, 1993; Perfect Justice, 1994; Double Jeopardy, 1995; Cruel Justice, 1996; Silent Justice, 2000; Murder One, 2001; Criminal Intent, 2002; Death Row, 2003; Hate Crime, 2004. Work represented in anthologies. Contributor of stories to magazines. **Address:** c/o Hawk Publishing Group, 7107 S Yale Ave #345, Tulsa, OK 74136-1619, U.S.A. **Online address:** wb@williambernhardt.com

BERNHEIM, Emmanuele. French, b. 1955. **Genres:** Novels. **Career:** Attended Cahiers du Cinema, Paris, France, 1979-83; reader of motion picture scripts for French television networks, 1983-93. **Publications:** Le Cran d'Arret, 1985; Un couple, 1988; Sa Femme; or, The Other Woman, 1993; Vendredi Soir (novel), 1998; Under the Sands (screenplay). Author of television scripts. **Address:** 56 rue de l'Universite, 75007 Paris, France.

BERNIKOW, Louise. American, b. 1940. **Genres:** Human relations/Parenting, Literary criticism and history, Women's studies and issues, Writing/Journalism. **Career:** Writer. Research fellow at Columbia University, 1962; U.S. Fulbright Fellowship to Spain, 1963-64; instructor in writing at The Juilliard School, New York City, 1965-70, Barnard College and Hunter College, 1973-75, and New York University, 1978-81. Curriculum consultant and founder of women's studies programs at Hunter College, 1970, and at Jersey City State College. Consultant to television news magazines. Guest on television programs. Frequent lecturer at conferences. **Publications:** Abel, 1970; (ed.) The World Split Open: Four Centuries of Women Poets in England and America, 1552-1950, 1974; Among Women, 1980; Let's Have Lunch: Games of Sex and Power, 1981; Alone in America: The Search for Companionship, 1986; The American Women's Almanac: An Irreverent History, 1997; Bark if You Love Me, 2001. Contributor to magazines. **Address:** 318 W 105 St #4A, New York, NY 10025, U.S.A.

BERNSTEIN, Burton. American, b. 1932. **Genres:** Novels, Biography, Documentaries/Reportage, Literary criticism and history, Air/Space topics, Autobiography/Memoirs, Humor/Satire. **Career:** Staff Writer, The New Yorker, NYC, 1957-92; Freelance Writer and Editor, 1992-. **Publications:** The Grove, 1961; The Lost Art, 1964; The Sticks, 1972; Thurber, 1975; Look Ma, I Am Kool! and Other Casuals, 1977; Sinai: The Great and Terrible Wilderness, 1979; Family Matters, 1982, rev. ed., 2000; Plane Crazy, 1986. **Address:** PO Box 238, Bridgewater, CT 06752, U.S.A.

BERNSTEIN, Charles. American, b. 1950. **Genres:** Poetry, Songs/Lyrics and libretti, Essays. **Career:** State University of New York, Buffalo, David Gray Professor of Poetry and Letters, 19892003; University of Pennsylvania, Regan Professor of English, 2003-. L=A=N=G=U=A=G=E, NYC, editor with Bruce Andrews, 1978-81. **Publications:** Parsing, 1976; Shade, 1978; Poetic Justice, 1979; Senses of Responsibility, 1979; (with others) Legend, 1980; Controlling Interests, 1980; Disfrutes, 1981; The Occurrence of Tune, 1981; Stigma, 1981; Islets/Irritations, 1983; Resistance, 1983; (ed. with B. Andrews) The L=A=N=G=U=A=G=E Book, 1984; Content's Dream: Essays 1975-1984, 1985; The Sophist, 1987; (ed.) The Politics of Poetic Form: Poetry and Public Policy, 1990; Rough Trades, 1991; The Absent Father in Dumbo, 1991; A Poetics, 1992; Dark City, 1994; Log Rhythms, 1998; My Way: Speeches & Poems, 1999; Republics of Reality: Poems 1975-1995, 2000; With Strings, 2001.

BERNSTEIN, David E(liot). (born United States), b. 1967. **Genres:** Civil liberties/Human rights. **Career:** Law clerk to U.S. Court of Appeals Judge David A. Nelson, 1991-92; Crowell & Moring (law firm), Washington, DC, associate, 1992-94; Columbia University, New York, NY, fellow in Julius Silver Program in Law, Science, and Technology, 1994-95; George Mason University, Fairfax, VA, assistant professor, 1995-98, associate professor of law, 1998-. Georgetown University, visiting professor, 2003; speaker at other institutions, including University of Michigan, Boston University, Vanderbilt University, Washburn University, and University of Chicago. **Publications:** (Coeditor and contribributor) Phantom Risk: Scientific Inference and the Law, 1993; Only One Place of Redress: African-Americans, Labor Regulations, and the Courts from Reconstruction to the New Deal, 2001; (with others) The New Wigmore: Volume on Expert and Demonstrative Evidence, 2002. Contributor to books. Contributor of articles and reviews to law journals and other periodicals. **Address:** 3301 North Fairfax Dr., George Mason University, Fairfax, VA 22030-4444, U.S.A.

BERNSTEIN, Ellen. American, b. 1953. **Genres:** Environmental sciences/Ecology, Theology/Religion. **Career:** Berkeley Community Health Project, Berkeley, CA, producer of educational and selfhelp materials, 1975-77; high school biology teacher, Berkeley, 1977-79; physical therapist in Philadelphia, PA, 1983-87; Shomrei Adamah: Keepers of the Earth (Jewish environmental organization), Philadelphia, founder and director, 1988-96; Jewish Federation of Greater Philadelphia, Philadelphia, director of Jewish Continuity Initiative, 1996-; consultant; public speaker. **Publications:** Let the Earth Teach You Torah, 1992; Ecology and the Jewish Spirit, 1998; An American Tu B'Sh'vat, 1999. Contributor to periodicals. **Address:** c/o Jewish Federation of Greater Philadelphia, 2100 Arch St, Philadelphia, PA 19103, U.S.A.

BERNSTEIN, Jared. American, b. 1955. **Genres:** Economics, Organized labor. **Career:** Economic Policy Institute, Washington, DC, labor economist, 1992-. **Publications:** (co-author) The State of Working America, 1993, rev. ed., 1999. **Address:** Economic Policy Institute, 1660 L St NW Suite 1200, Washington, DC 20036, U.S.A.

BERNSTEIN, Laurie. American. **Genres:** History. **Career:** Vassar College, Poughkeepsie, NY, assistant professor, 1987-89; Swarthmore College, Swarthmore, PA, visiting assistant professor, 1989-90; Drew University, Madison, NJ, assistant professor, 1991-92; Rutgers University, Camden, NJ, assistant professor, 1992-97, associate professor of history, 1997-, director of Women's Studies Program, 2001-. **Publications:** Sonia's Daughters: Prostitutes and Their Regulation in Imperial Russia, 1995; (ed., and author of intro with R. Weinberg) M.M. Leder, My Life in Stalinist Russia: An American Woman Looks Back, 2001. Contributor to books. Contributor of essays and reviews to journals. Contributor of translations to books. **Address:** Department of History, Rutgers University, Camden, NJ 08102, U.S.A. **Online address:** lbernste@camden.rutgers.edu

BERNSTEIN, Mark. American, b. 1950. **Genres:** Communications/Media. **Career:** Writer of history and biography. **Publications:** Paper with Presence: A Gilbert Century, 1987; Miami Valley Hospital: A Centennial History, 1990; Grand Eccentrics: Turning the Century: Dayton and the Inventing of America, 1996; New Bremen, 1999; New Bremen 2000, 2000; (with Alex Lubertozzi) World War II on the Air, 2003. Contributor to magazines. **Address:** 830 Xenia Ave., Yellow Springs, OH 45387, U.S.A.

BERNSTEIN, Richard. American, b. 1944. **Genres:** Documentaries/Reportage. **Career:** Journalist and author. Began as foreign correspondent for Washington Post in Taiwan, later for Time magazine in Hong Kong, becoming bureau chief in Beijing, China; New York Times, New York, NY, 1982-, first as Paris bureau chief, later United Nations bureau chief, national cultural correspondent, 1987-95, daily book critic, 1995-. **Publications:** From the Center of the Earth: The Search for the Truth about China, 1982; Fragile Glory: A Portrait of France and the French, 1990; Dictatorship of Virtue: Multiculturalism and the Battle for America's Future, 1994, 2nd ed. as Dictatorship of Virtue: How the Battle over Multiculturalism Is Reshaping Our Schools, Our Country, and Our Lives, 1995; (with R.H. Munro) The Coming Conflict with China, 1997; Ultimate Journey: Retracing the Path of an Ancient Buddhist Monk Who Crossed Asia in Search of Enlightenment, 2001; (with the staff of the New York Times) Out of the Blue: A Narrative of September 11, 2001, 2002. **Address:** New York Times, 229 West 43rd St., New York, NY 10036, U.S.A.

BERRIDGE, G. R. British, b. 1947. **Genres:** Politics/Government, International relations/Current affairs. **Career:** Metropolitan Police College, Ashford, England, assistant lecturer, 1969-71; teacher at a secondary school in Farnsborough, England, 1975-78; University of Leicester, Leicester, England, lecturer, 1978-89, reader, 1989-93, professor of politics, 1993-. **Publications:** Economic Power in Anglo-South African Diplomacy: Simontown, Sharpeville, and After, 1981; (ed. with A. Jennings, and contrib.) Diplomacy at the UN, 1985; The Politics of the South Africa Run: European Shipping and Pretoria, 1987; International Politics: States, Power, and Conflict since 1945, 1987, 2nd ed, 1992; Return to the UN: United Nations Diplomacy in Regional Conflicts, 1991; South Africa, the Colonial Powers, and "African Defence": The Rise and Fall of the White Entente, 1948-60, 1992; (with D. Heater) An Introduction to International Relations, 1993; Talking to the Enemy: How States without "Diplomatic Relations" Communicate, 1994. Work represented in anthologies. Contributor to political science and international studies journals. **Address:** Department of Politics, University of Leicester, Leicester LE1 7RH, England.

BERRIGAN, Daniel J. American, b. 1921. **Genres:** Plays/Screenplays, Poetry, Social commentary, Theology/Religion, Autobiography/Memoirs. **Career:** Writer, teacher, and political activist. Ordained Roman Catholic priest, 1952; member, Society of Jesus. Taught French and philosophy, Brooklyn Preparatory School, New York, 1954-57; Professor of New Testament Studies, LeMoyne College, Syracuse, NY, 1957-63; Director of United Christian Work, Cornell University, Ithaca, NY, 1967-68; jailed for antiwar activities, 1970-72; convicted of destroying unarmed nuclear warheads in PA, 1981, and sentenced to time served, 1990. **Publications:** Time without Number, 1957; The Bride: Essays in the Church, 1959; Encounters 1960; The Bow in the Clouds, 1961; The World for Wedding Ring: Poems, 1962; No One Walks Waters, 1966; False Gods, Real Men: New Poems, 1966; They Call Us Dead Men, 1966; Consequences: Truth and..., 1967; Go from Here: A Prison Diary, 1968; Love, Love at the End: Parables, Prayers and Meditations, 1968; Night Flight to Hanoi: War Diary with 11 Poems, 1968; Crime Trial, 1970; (with T. Lewis) Trial Poems, 1970; The Trial of the Catonsville Nine (play), 1970; No Bars to Manhood, 1970; The Dark Night of Resistance, 1971: The Geography of Faith: Conversations between Daniel Berrigan, When Underground, and Robert Coles, 1971; Absurd Convictions, Modest Hopes: Conversations after Prison with Lee Lockwood, 1972; American is Hard to Find, 1972; Jesus Christ, 1973; Selected and New Poems, 1973; Prison Poems, 1973; Prison Poems, 1974; Lights on in the House of the Dead: A Prison Diary, 1974; (with Thich Nhat Hanh) The Raft Is not the Shore: Conversations toward Buddhist/Christian Awareness, 1975; Uncommon Prayer, 1978, new ed. 1998; Beside the Sea of Glass, 1978; The Discipline of the Mountain, 1979; We Die before We Live, 1980; Ten Commandments for the Long Haul, 1981; Portraits: Of Those I Love, 1982; The Nightmare of God, 1983; Journey to Black Island, 1984; The Mission: A Film Journal, 1986; To Dwell in Peace: An Autobiography, 1987; (with M. Parker) Stations, 1988; Daniel Berrigan: Poetry, Drama, Prose, 1988; Sorrow Built a Bridge, 1989; Whereon to Stand, 1991; Jubilee: Poems, 1991; Tulips in the Prison Yard: Selected Poems, 1992; Minor Prophets, Major Themes, 1995; Isaiah: Spirit of Courage, Gift of Tears, 1996; Ezekiel: Vision in the Dust, 1997; And the Risen Bread: Selected Poems 1957-1997, 1998; Daniel; Under the Siege of the Divine, 1998; Jeremiah: The World, the Wound of God, 1999; Bride: Images of the Church, 2000; Job: Why Forsake Me?, 2001. **Address:** 220 W 98th St., #11-L, New York, NY 10025, U.S.A.

BERRINGTON, Hugh Bayard. British, b. 1928. **Genres:** Politics/Government. **Career:** University of Keele, Staffs., assistant lecturer, and subsequently lecturer, 1956-65; University of Newcastle upon Tyne, reader, 1965-70, professor of politics, 1970-94, emeritus, 1994-. **Publications:** (with S.E. Finer and D.J. Bartholomew) Backbench Opinion in the House of Commons, 1955-59, 1961; How Nations Are Governed (textbook), 1964; Backbench Opinion in the House of Commons, 1945-55, 1973. EDITOR: Change in British Politics, 1984; Britain in the '90s, 1998. **Address:** University of Newcastle, 40-42 Great North Rd, Newcastle upon Tyne, Tyne and Wear NE1 7RU, England. **Online address:** hugh.berrington@net1.co.uk

BERRINGTON, John. See BROWNJOHN, Alan (Charles).

BERRY, Adrian M. British, b. 1937. **Genres:** Science fiction/Fantasy, Astronomy, Sciences. **Career:** Fellow, Royal Astronomical Society, London, 1973-; Sr. Fellow, British Interplanetary Society, 1986-; Science Correspondent, Daily Telegraph, 1977-. Former member of science staff, Daily Telegraph, London; Correspondent, Time mag., NYC, 1965-67. **Publications:** The Next Ten Thousand Years: A Vision of Man's Future in the Univese, 1974; The Iron Sun: Crossing the Universe through Black Holes, 1977; From Apes to Astronauts, 1981; The Super Intelligent Machine, 1983; High Skies and Yellow Rain, 1983; Koyama's Diamond (fiction), 1984; Labyrinth of Lies (fiction), 1985; Ice with Your Evolution, 1986; Harrap's Book of Scientific Anecdotes, 1989; Eureka: The Book of Scientific Anecdotes, 1993; The Next 500 Years, 1996; Galileo and the Dolphins, 1997; The Giant Leap: Mankind Heads for the Stars. **Address:** 11 Cottesmore Gardens, Kensington, London W8, England. **Online address:** Adrian Berry@safe-mail.net

BERRY, Andrew. (born England). **Genres:** Animals/Pets. **Career:** Geneticist. Harvard University, Museum of Comparative Zoology, Cambridge, MA, research associate. Also worked as an instructor at Harvard University. **Publications:** (editor) Infinite Tropics: An Alfred Russel Wallace Anthology, 2002; (with James D. Watson) DNA: The Secret of Life, 2003. Also author of screenplays, and contributor to numerous scientific and popular journals. **Address:** Museum of Comparative Zoology, Harvard University, 26 Oxford St., Cambridge, MA 02138, U.S.A.

BERRY, Brian Joe Lobley. American/British (born United Kingdom), b. 1934. **Genres:** Novels, Economics, Geography, Regional/Urban planning,

Autobiography/Memoirs. **Career:** Lloyd Viel Berkner Regental Professor and Professor of Political Economy, University of Texas, Dallas, 1986-. Professor, Univ. of Chicago, 1958-76; Member of faculty, Brookings Institution, Washington, D.C., 1966-76; Professor, Harvard University, Cambridge, Massachusetts, 1976-81; Professor and Dean, School of Urban and Public Affairs, Carnegie Mellon University, Pittsburgh, 1981-86. **Publications:** Growth Centers in the American Urban System, 1960-1970, 1973; The Human Consequences of Urbanization: Divergent Paths in the Urban Experience of the Twentieth Century, 1973; (with others) Land Use, Urban Form, and Environmental Quality, 1974; (with Frank E. Horton) Urban Environmental Management: Planning for Pollution Control, 1974; The Open Housing Question: Race and Housing in Chicago 1966-76, 1979; Comparative Urbanization, 2nd ed., 1983; (with others) Economic Geography, 1987; (with others) Market Centers and Retail Location, 1988; Long-Wave Rhythms in Economic Development and Political Behavior, 1991; America's Utopian Experiments, 1992; (with others) The Global Economy, 1993; The Global Economy in Transition, 1997; (with others) The Rhythms of American Politics, 1998; Bali Burning, 2004; editor of books. **Address:** School of Social Science, University of Texas-Dallas, Richardson, TX 75083, U.S.A. **Online address:** bjlb@comcast.net

BERRY, Carmen Renee. American, b. 1953. **Genres:** Theatre. **Career:** Motivational lecturer, certified massage therapist, and author. **Publications:** (with Mark Lloyd Taylor) Loving Yourself As Your Neighbor: A Recovery Guide for Christians Escaping Burnout and Codependency, 1990; Are You Having Fun Yet? How to Bring the Art of Play into Your Recovery, 1992; (with poetry by Juanita Ryan) Coming Home to Your Body: 365 Simple Ways to Nourish Yourself Inside and Out, 1996; (with Mark W. Baker) Who's to Blame?: Escape the Victim Trap and Gain Personal Power in Your Relationship, 1996; Is Your Body Trying to Tell You Something? Why It Is Wise to Listen to Your Body and How Massage and Body Work Can Help, 1997; (with Lynn Barrington) Daddies and Daughters, 1998; When Helping You Is Hurting Me: Escaping the Messiah Trap, 1998, revised and updated edition, 2003; (with mother, Mary Ellen Berry) Reawakening to Life: Renewal after a Husband's Death, 2002; The Unauthorized Guide to Choosing a Church, 2003. WITH TAMARA TRAEDER: Girlfriends: Invisible Bonds, Enduring Ties, Wildcat 1995; The Girlfriends Keepsake Book: The Story of Our Friendship, 1996; Girlfriends Talk about Men: Sharing Secrets for a Great Relationship, 1997; Women's Rites: Girlfriends' Rituals, 1998; Girlfriends Are Forever, 1998; Girlfriends for Life: Friendships Worth Keeping Forever, 1998; A Friendship Meant to Be, 2000; A Girlfriend's Gift: Reflections on the Extraordinary Bonds of Friendship, 2000; (with Janet Hazen) Girlfriends Get Together: Food, Frolic, and Fun Times, 2001. **Address:** c/o Author Mail, HarperCollins Publishers, 10 East Fifty-third Street, Seventh Floor, New York, NY 10022, U.S.A.

BERRY, Carole. American. **Genres:** Mystery/Crime/Suspense. **Career:** Author of mystery novels; works as legal secretary in a New York law firm. Has also been a waitress, teacher, publisher's assistant, office manager, sales clerk, and typist. **Publications:** BONNIE INDERMILL MYSTERY NOVELS: The Letter of the Law, 1987; The Year of the Monkey, 1988; Goodnight, Sweet Prince, 1990; Island Girl, 1991; The Death of a Difficult Woman, 1994; The Death of a Dancing Fool, 1996; Death of a Dimpled Darling, 1997; Death of a Downsizer, 1999. SUSPENSE NOVEL: Nightmare Point, 1993. **Address:** c/o Berkley Publishing Group, Berkley Prime Crime, 375 Hudson St, New York, NY 10014, U.S.A.

BERRY, Chad. American, b. 1963. **Genres:** History. **Career:** Educator and author. Maryville College, Maryville, TN, assistant professor to associate professor of history, 1995-. **Publications:** Southern Migrants, Northern Exiles, 2000. **Address:** Division of Humanities, Maryville College, Anderson Hall 205C, Maryville, TN 37804, U.S.A. **Online address:** berry@maryvillecollege.edu

BERRY, Cicely. British, b. 1926. **Genres:** Speech/Rhetoric. **Career:** Central School of Speech and Drama, London, Teacher of Voice and Speech, 1948-65; Royal Shakespeare Company, Stratford-on-Avon, Voice Director, 1969-. **Publications:** Voice and the Actor, 1973; Your Voice and How to Use It, 1975; The Actor and the Text, 1987; Text in Action, 2001.

BERRY, Eliot. American, b. 1949. **Genres:** Literary criticism and history, Sports/Fitness. **Career:** Professional squash player in Boston, MA, 1975; teacher at a secondary school in Paris, France, 1976; Richmond College, London, England, lecturer in English and American literature, 1977; professional squash player in Munich, Germany, 1978; Fulbright lecturer in Kassel, Germany, 1979-80; realtor, 1981-85; independent real estate appraiser, 1986-. **Publications:** Four Quarters Make a Season, 1973; The Fiction of John

Hawkes: A Poetry of Force and Darkness, 1979; Tough Draw: The Path to Tennis Glory, 1992; Topspin, 1996. **Address:** 9 E 40th St 14 Fl, New York, NY 10016, U.S.A.

BERRY, Faith D. American, b. 1939. **Genres:** Literary criticism and history, Biography, Translations, Humanities, Essays, Cultural/Ethnic topics, Writing/Journalism, Race relations. **Career:** New Yorker, NYC, editorial assistant, 1962-64; free-lance writer, editor, and translator in Paris, France, and Washington, DC, 1964-70; National Gallery of Art, Washington, DC, assistant editor, 1972-75; Dispatch News Service International, senior editor, 1972; WETA-TV, Washington, DC, staff writer, 1975-78; President's Advisory Committee for Women, Washington, DC, media coordinator, 1979; U.S. Department of Labor, Washington, DC, speechwriter for Women's Bureau, 1980; Faith Berry and Associates, partner, 1980-82; Florida Atlantic University, Boca Raton, professor of American literature and comparative literature, 1988-93; University of California, Santa Barbara, professor of Afro-American literature, 1993-. Appointed to Task Force on Africa, National Association for the Advancement of Colored People, 1977. **Publications:** (ed. and author of intro.) Good Morning Revolution: Uncollected Social Protest Writings by Langston Hughes, 1973; Langston Hughes: Before and beyond Harlem; A Biography, 1983; (ed. and author of intro.) J. Saunders Redding, A Scholar's Conscience: Selected Writings, 1992. Contributor of articles and reviews to books, newspapers and magazines. **Address:** c/o Interdisciplinary Humanities Center, Univ. of California, Santa Barbara, 552 University Ave, Santa Barbara, CA 93106-0002, U.S.A. **Online address:** berryf@alishaw.ucsb.edu

BERRY, Francis. British (born Malaysia), b. 1915. **Genres:** Novels, Poetry, Literary criticism and history. **Career:** Professor Emeritus of English, Royal Holloway, University of London, since 1980 (Professor, 1970-80). Assistant Lecturer, subsequently Lecturer, Sr. Lecturer, Reader and Professor, University of Sheffield, 1947-70. **Publications:** Gospel of Fire, 1933; Snake in the Moon, 1936; The Iron Christ: A Poem, 1938; Fall of a Tower and Other Poems, 1943; Murdock and Other Poems, 1947; The Galloping Centaur: Poems 1933-1951, 1952; Herbert Read, 1953; Poets' Grammar: Person, Time and Mood in Poetry, 1958; Morant Bay and Other Poems, 1961; Poetry and the Physical Voice, 1962; The Shakespeare Inset: Word and Picture, 1965; Ghosts of Greenland, 1966; Thoughts on Poetic Time, 1972; I Tell of Greenland (novel), 1977; From the Red Fort (poetry), 1984; Collected Poems, 1994. EDITOR: An Anthology of Medieval Poems, 1954; Essays and Studies 1969. **Address:** 4 Eastgate St, Winchester SO23 8EB, England.

BERRY, J. Bill. American, b. 1945. **Genres:** Literary criticism and history, History. **Career:** University of Central Arkansas, Conway, associate professor of history, dean of faculty, and vice president for academic affairs, 1989-. **Publications:** Located Lives: Place and Idea in Southern Autobiography, 1989; Home Ground: Southern Autobiography, 1991. **Address:** Provost and Vice Chancellor for Academic Affairs, 615 McCallie Ave., 102 Founders Hall 5555, The University of Tennessee at Chattanooga, Chattanooga, TN 37403, U.S.A.

BERRY, J. W. Canadian, b. 1939. **Genres:** Psychology. **Career:** University of Sydney, Australia, lecturer in psychology, 1966-69; Queen's University, Kingston, Ontario, professor of psychology, 1969-99. Cross-Cultural/Multicultural Associates Inc., president. **Publications:** (co-ed.) Ethnicity and Culture in Canada, 1994; Handbook of Cross-Cultural Psychology, 3 vols., 1997;(with others) Cross-Cultural Psychology Research and Applications, 2002. **Address:** Dept of Psychology, Queen's University, Kingston, ON, Canada K7L 3N6. **Online address:** berryj@post.queensu.ca

BERRY, Jeffrey M. American, b. 1948. **Genres:** Politics/Government. **Career:** Tufts University, Medford, MA, assistant professor to professor of political science, 1974-, Graduate Program in Public Policy and Citizen Participation, co-founder and director, 1980-82, 1984-85; chairman, Department of Political Science, 1990-93. Guest scholar, lecturer, and visiting fellow at universities. **Publications:** (with R.L. Peabody, W.G. Frasure, and J. Goldman) To Enact a Law: Congress and Campaign Financing, 1972; Lobbying for the People: The Political Behavior of Public Interest Groups, 1977; The Interest Group Society, 1984, 3rd ed, 1997; Feeding Hungry People: Rulemaking in the Food Stamp Program, 1984; (with K. Janda and J. Goldman) The Challenge of Democracy: Government in America, 1987, 6th ed, 1999; (with K.E. Portney and K. Thomson) The Rebirth of Urban Democracy, 1993; (with K. Janda and J. Goldman) The Challenge of Democracy: The Essentials, 1999; The New Liberalism: The Rising Power of Citizen Groups, 1999. Contributor of articles to scholarly journals, newspapers, and newsmagazines. **Address:** Department of Political Science, Tufts University, Medford, MA 02155, U.S.A.

BERRY, John Stevens. American, b. 1938. **Genres:** Poetry, History. **Career:** Berry & Kelly (law firm), Lincoln, NE, senior partner, beginning in 1977. Admitted to state and federal courts in Nebraska, 1965, U.S. Court of Military Appeals, 1970, U.S. District Court for the District of South Dakota, 1973, U.S. State Court of Appeals for the 8th Circuit, 1974, U.S. Tax Court, 1975, and U.S. Supreme Court, 1979; U.S. Court of Veterans Appeals, 1996; Fellow American Board of Criminal Lawyers. **Publications:** Darkness of Snow (poems), 1973; Those Gallant Men on Trial in Vietnam, 1984. **Address:** Berry & Kelly, 2650 N 48th, Lincoln, NE 68504, U.S.A.

BERRY, Linda. American, b. 1940. **Genres:** Mystery/Crime/Suspense. **Career:** Writer, 1974-. Weekly columnist, Accent newspaper, 1991-93. **Publications:** Death and the Easter Bunny, 1998; Death and the Hubcap, 2000; Death and the Icebox, 2003. **Address:** 11558 E Wesley Ave, Aurora, CO 80014, U.S.A.

BERRY, Philippa. British, b. 1955. **Genres:** Literary criticism and history. **Career:** University of Fès, Fès, Morocco, research assistant, 1980-84; University of East Anglia, Norwich, England, lecturer, 1984-85; West London Institute of Higher Education, London, England, lecturer, 1985-88; Cambridge University, Cambridge, England, fellow and director of studies in English at King's College, 1988-. **Publications:** Of Chastity and Power: Elizabethan Literature and the Unmarried Queen, 1989; (ed., with A. Wernick) Shadow of Spirit: Postmodernism and Religion, 1993; Shakespeare's Feminine Endings, 1999. **Address:** King's College, Cambridge University, Cambridge CB2 1ST, England. **Online address:** 510300

BERRY, Thomas. American, b. 1914. **Genres:** Philosophy, Theology/Religion, History. **Career:** Director, Riverdale Center for Religious Research, Bronx, New York, 1970-93. Associate Professor of Asian History, Institute for Asian Studies, Seton Hall University, South Orange, New York, 1957-61; Associate Professor of Asian History, Center for Asian Studies, St. John's University, Jamaica, New York, 1961-65; Associate Professor, Dept. of History of Religions, Fordham University, Bronx, New York, 1966-79. **Publications:** Historical Theory of Giambattista Vico, 1949; Buddhism, 1966; Religions of India: Hinduism, Yoga, Buddhism, 1971; The Dream of the Earth, 1988; (with B. Swimme) The Universe Story, 1992; The Great Work, Our Way Into the Future, 1999.

BERRY, Wendell (Erdman). American, b. 1934. **Genres:** Novels, Poetry, Agriculture/Forestry, Environmental sciences/Ecology, Essays. **Career:** University of Kentucky, Lexington, mjember of English Dept., 1964-77, 1987-93. **Publications:** November Twenty-Six, Nineteen Hundred Sixty-Three, 1964; Findings, 1969; The Hidden Wound, 1970; Farming: A Hand Book, 1970; The Country of Marriage, 1973; Sayings and Doings, 1975; The Unsettling of America, 1977; The Gift of Good Land, 1981; Standing by Words, 1985; Home Economics, 1987; What Are People For?, 1990; Harlan Hubbard: Life and Work, 1990. NOVELS: Nathan Coulter, 1960; A Place on Earth, 1967; The Memory of Old Jack, 1974; Remembering, 1988; A World Lost, 1996; Jayber Crow, 2000. POETRY: The Broken Ground, 1964; Openings, 1969; An Eastward Look, 1974; To What Listens, 1975; Horses, 1975; The Kentucky River: Two Poems, 1976; Three Memorial Poems, 1977; Clearing, 1977; The Wheel, 1982; Collected Poems, 1985; Sabbaths, 1987; Entries, 1994; A Timbered Choir, 1999; Selected Poems, 1999. ESSAYS: The Long-Legged House 1969; The Unforeseen Wilderness: An Essay on Kentucky's Red River Gorge, 1971; A Continuous Harmony: Essays Cultural and Agricultural, 1972; Recollected Essays, 1981; Sex, Economy, Freedom and Community, 1993; The Art of the Commonplace, 2002; Citizenship Papers, 2003. STORIES: The Wild Birds, 1986; Fidelity, 1992; Watch with Me, 1994. **Address:** PO Box 1, Port Royal, KY 40058, U.S.A.

BERRYMAN, Jack W. American, b. 1947. **Genres:** History, Medicine/Health, Sports/Fitness. **Career:** University of Massachusetts at Amherst, instructor, 1971-72; University of Washington, Seattle, assistant professor, 1976-81, associate professor of medical history and ethics, 1981-95, professor, 1995-. Ball State University, Phi Alpha Theta Lecturer, 1981; American College of Sports Medicine, D. B. Dill Historical Lecturer, 1994, 2004; consultant on environmental history, and on sport history and the history of sports medicine. Contributor to Northwest fishing and travel magazines, 1977-. **Publications:** (ed. with R.J. Park) Sport and Exercise Science: Essays in the History of Sports Medicine, 1992; Out of Many, One: A History of the American College of Sports Medicine, 1995. **Address:** Dept of Medical History and Ethics, Box 357120, School of Medicine, University of Washington, Seattle, WA 98195, U.S.A. **Online address:** berryman@u.washington.edu

BERRYMAN, Phillip E. American, b. 1938. **Genres:** Area studies, Theology/Religion. **Career:** St. Philip Church, Pasadena, CA, administrator and counselor, 1963-65; Parroquia de Fatima, Chorrillo, Panama City, Panama, pastoral worker, 1965-73; Opportunities Industrialization Center, San Jose, CA, counselor, 1973-76; American Friends Service Committee, Guatemala, Central American program director, 1976-81, consultant, translator, and writer, 1981-; writer, 1981-. Has taught at Villanova University, 1987; Rosemont College, 1989; Stockton State College, 1990; and Temple University, 1993-95. Also has given lectures on tour in over forty states. **Publications:** What's Wrong in Central America and What To Do about It, 1983; The Religious Roots of Rebellion: Christians in Central American Revolutions, 1984; Inside Central America: The Essential Facts Past and Present on El Salvador, Nicaragua, Honduras, Guatemala, and Costa Rica, 1985; Liberation Theology: The Essential Facts about the Revolutionary Movement in Latin America and Beyond, 1987, also published as Liberation Theology: The Essential Facts about the Revolutionary Religious Movement in Latin America and Beyond, 1987; Our Unfinished Business: The Bishops' Letters on Peace and the Economy, 1989; Stubborn Hope: Religion, Politics, and Revolution in Central America, 1994; Religion in the Megacity: Catholic and Protestant Portraits from Latin America, 1996. TRANSLATOR: J. Sobrion, Juan Hernandez Pico, Theology of Christian Solidarity, 1985; T. Cabestrero (ed), Revolutionaries for the Gospel: Testimonies of Fifteen Christians in the Nicaraguan Government, 1986; F. Hinkelammert, The Ideological Weapons of Death: A Theological Critique of Capitalism, 1986; P. Casaldaliga, Prophets in Combat: The Nicaraguan Journal of Bishop Pedro Casaldaliga, 1987; P. Richard, Death of Christendoms, Birth of the Church, 1987; C. Boff, Feet-on-the-Ground Theology, 1987; E.F. Mignone, Witness to the Truth: The Complicity of Church and Dictatorship in Argentina, 1987; National Conference of Catholic Bishops, Justicia Economica para Todos: Carta Pastoral Sobre la Ensenanza Social Catolica y la Economia de los E.U.A., 1987; R.G. Treto, The Church and Socialism in Cuba, 1988; E. Cleary (ed), Path from Puebla: Significant Documents of the Latin American Bishops Since 1979, 1989; I. Gebara and M.C.L. Bingemer, Mary, Mother of God and Mother of the Poor, 1990; N. Jaen, Toward a Spirituality of Liberation, 1991; J. Hasset and H. Lacey (ed), Towards a Society that Serves Its People: The Intellectual Contribution of El Salvador's Murdered Jesuits, 1991; J.L. Segundo, The Liberation of Dogma: Faith, Revelation, and Dogmatic Teaching Authority, 1992; L. Boff, The Path to Hope: Fragments from a Theologian's Journey, 1993; Report of the Chilean National Commission on Truth and Reconciliation, 2 vols., 1993; Fourth General Conference of Latin American Bishops, Santo Domingo Conclusions, 1993. Contributor to periodicals in the U.S. Chile, Uruguay, Panama, and Guatemala. Contributor of columns to newspapers. Author of booklets and reports for the American Friends Service Committee and the Institute for Food and Development Policy. **Address:** 3818 Hamilton St., Philadelphia, PA 19104, U.S.A.

BERT, Norman A(llen). American, b. 1942. **Genres:** Theatre, Plays/Screenplays. **Career:** Choma Secondary School, Choma, Zambia, teacher and deputy headmaster, 1969-70; Messiah College, Grantham, PA, assistant professor of Drama, 1975-81; Eastern Montana College, Billings, assistant professor to professor, 1981-, member of the Graduate Faculty, for Communication Arts/Theatre Department, chair, Communication Arts Department, 1991-. Has also been an artistic consultant, director, and actor. **Publications:** (and ed) One-Act Plays for Acting Students, 1987; A History and Genealogy of Peter Bert, 1987; (and ed) The Scenebook for Actors: Great Monologs and Dialogs from Contemporary and Classical Theatre, 1990; (and ed) Theatre Alive!, 1991; (and editor) Scenes from Classic Plays, 1993; (with D. Bert) Play It Again: More One-Act Plays for Acting Students, 1993. PLAYS: The Planting of the Lord, 1972; And They Shall Be Mine, 1972; Dayspring, 1974; Phonecall from Sunkist, 1974,; The Bottsologuing of Miss Jones, 1975; Woolman, 1976; Jeremiah of Anathoth, 1978; Shake the Country, 1981; Post Office, 1982; Cat Games, 1982, new version titled Happy Hour at Velma's Place, 1989; Yellowstone, Hurrah!, 1982; The Dove, The Hawk, and the Phoenix, 1983; Mixed Doubles, 1986; A Visit From Harry, 1987; Pilgrimage, 1988; When the Bough Breaks, 1989; Breakfast, 1993; The Montana Times, 1989; Cowboy Serenade, or Duck Riders on the Sly, 1990; (with M. Martin) Uncross Junction, 1993; Dr. Dixie Duzzett's Delight, 1993. FILM SCRIPTS: And They Shall Be Mine, 1972; The Planting of the Lord, 1972. Contributor to journals. **Address:** Communication Arts/Theatre, Montana State University-Billings, 1500 North 30th St., Billings, MT 59101, U.S.A.

BERTAGNA, Julie. (born Scotland), b. 1962. **Genres:** Young adult fiction. **Career:** Freelance writer. Formerly worked as a magazine editor and a primary school teacher in Barmulloch, Glasgow, Scotland. **Publications:** The Spark Gap, 1996; The Ice-Cream Machine, 1998, 2004; Clumsy Clumps and the Baby Moon, 1999; Soundtrack, 1999; Dolphin Boy, 1999; Bungee Hero, 1999; Exodus, 2002; The Opposite of Chocolate, 2003. Author of newspaper columns. **Address:** Caroline Walsh, David Higham Associates Ltd., 5-8 Lower John St., Golden Square, London W1F 9HA, England. **Online address:** julie@juliebertagna.com

BERTEMATTI, Richard. American, b. 1971. **Genres:** Mystery/Crime/Suspense. **Publications:** MYSTERIES: Project Death, 1997; Puerto Rican Paradise, forthcoming. **Address:** PO Box 7727, North Bergen, NJ 07047, U.S.A. **Online address:** bertematti@mail.com

BERTLING, Tom. American, b. 1956. **Genres:** Language/Linguistics. **Career:** Kodiak Media Group, Wilsonville, OR, president, 1989-. **Publications:** A Child Sacrificed, 1994; No Dignity for Joshua, 1997. EDITOR: American Sign Language: Shattering the Myth, 1998; An Intellectual Look at American Sign Language, 2001; Communicating with Deaf Children, 2002. **Address:** Kodiak Media Group, PO Box 1029, Wilsonville, OR 97070, U.S.A.

BERTOLINO, James. American, b. 1942. **Genres:** Novellas/Short stories, Poetry, Writing/Journalism, Autobiography/Memoirs, Essays. **Career:** Editor, Abraxas mag. and Abraxas Press, Madison, WI, and Ithaca, NY, 1968-72; Washington State University, Pullman, teaching assistant; editor, Stone Marrow Press, Ithaca, and Cincinnati, OH, 1970-76; Epoch mag., Ithaca, assistant editor, 1971-73; Cornell University, Ithaca, teaching assistant, 1971-73, lecturer in creative writing, 1973-74; University of Cincinnati, assistant professor, 1974-77, associate professor of English, 1977-84; Cincinnati Poetry Review, co-editor, 1975-82; Eureka Review, Cincinnati, poetry editor, 1975-81; Skagit Valley College, instructor, 1984-89; Western Washington University, instructor, 1991-. **Publications:** Day of Change, 1968; Drool, 1968; Mr Nobody, 1969; Ceremony: A Poem, 1969; Maize: A Poem, 1969; Stone Marrow, 1969; Becoming Human: Poems, 1970; The Interim Handout, 1972; Employed, 1972; Edging Through, 1972; Soft Rock, 1973; Making Space for Our Living, 1975; Terminal Placebos, 1975; The Gestures, 1975; The Alleged Conception, 1976; New and Selected Poems, 1978; Are You Tough Enough for the Eighties?, 1979; Precinct Kali and the Gertrude Spicer Story, 1981; First Credo, 1986; Like a Planet, 1993; Snail River, 1995; Greatest Hits: 1965-2000, 2000; Pocket Animals, 2002. EDITOR: Quixote: Northwest Poets, 1968; The Abraxas/Five Anthology, 1972. **Address:** Dept of English, HU269, Western Washington University, Bellingham, WA 98225-9055, U.S.A. **Online address:** James.Bertolino@wwu.edu

BERTON, Pierre. See Obituaries.

BERTRAND, Diane Gonzales. American, b. 1956. **Genres:** Children's fiction, Young adult fiction, Essays. **Career:** at St. Mary's University, San Antonio, TX, writer in residence, creative writing and English composition. Presents workshops on creative writing for children, young adults, and adult audiences throughout Texas. **Publications:** Touchdown for Love, 1990; Close to the Heart, 1991; Carousel of Dreams, 1992; Sweet Fifteen, 1995; Alicia's Treasure, 1996; Sip, Slurp, Soup, Soup/Caldo, Caldo, Caldo (picture book), 1997; Lessons of the Game, 1998; Trino's Choice, 1999; Family, Familia (picture book), 1999; The Last Doll, 2000; Uncle Chente's Picnic, 2001; Trino's Time, 2001. Contributor to books and to magazines. **Address:** English Dept, St. Mary's University, 1 Camino Santa Maria, San Antonio, TX 78228, U.S.A.

BERTRAND, Lynne. American, b. 1963. **Genres:** Children's fiction. **Career:** Newspaper reporter and freelance journalist and writer, 1987-. **Publications:** One Day, Two Dragons, 1991; Good Night, Teddy Bear, 1992; Let's Go! Teddy Bear, 1992; Who Sleeps in the City?, 1994. Author of humorous columns for Working Mother. **Address:** Box 761, Williamsburg, MA 01096, U.S.A.

BERTRAND, Marsha. American, b. 1950. **Genres:** Money/Finance. **Career:** Coopers & Lybrand, Chicago, IL, personnel specialist and director of training and development, 1971-83; Allnet Communication Services Inc., Chicago, shareholder relations administrator, 1983-85; VMS Realty Partners, Chicago, assistant vice-president for investor relations, 1985-88; free-lance writer in Chicago and Orlando, FL, 1988-. **Publications:** Consumer Guide to the Stock Market, 1993; A Woman's Guide to Savvy Investing, 1997. Contributor to magazines. **Address:** 9107 Sloane St., Orlando, FL 32827, U.S.A. **Online address:** mbertrand@orlinter.com

BERUBE, Maurice R. American, b. 1933. **Genres:** Education. **Career:** Began as public schoolteacher; United Federation of Teachers, NYC, assistant editor, 1964-67; Queens College of the City University of New York, Flushing, NY, staff associate of Institute of Community Studies, 1968-73, assistant professor of urban studies, 1971-76; Old Dominion University, Norfolk, VA, professor of education, 1979-, eminent scholar. **Publications:**

(co-ed.) Confrontation at Ocean Hill Brownsville, 1969; (co-author) Local Control in Education, 1972; (co-author) School Boards and School Policy, 1973; The Urban University in America, 1978; Education and Poverty, 1984; Teacher Politics, 1988; American Presidents and Education, 1991; American School Reform, 1994; Eminent Educators, 2000; Beyond Modernism and Postmodernism, 2002; Radical Reformers, 2004. Contributor to periodicals. **Address:** Dept of Educational Leadership, Old Dominion University, Norfolk, VA 23508, U.S.A. **Online address:** mberube@odu.edu

BESNER, Hilda F. American (born Peru), b. 1950. **Genres:** Gay and lesbian issues, Human relations/Parenting, Psychology. **Career:** Washington University, St. Louis, MO, intern in clinical psychology at Malcolm Bliss Mental Health Center, 1975-76; clinical psychologist in private practice, St. Louis, 1976; Bessette, Farinacci and Associates, Fort Lauderdale, FL, clinical psychologist, 1977-81; Dade County Department of Youth and Family Development, clinical psychologist, 1977-78; Nova University, adjunct professor at Florida School of Professional Psychology, 1979-82; Southeast Biosocial Institute, director of clinical internship, 1980-81; clinical psychologist in private practice, Fort Lauderdale, 1981-. OptimaCare, vice-president, 1994-. **Publications:** (with S.J. Robinson) Understanding and Solving Your Police Marriage Problems, 1982; (with A. Besner and T.L. Perez) Rebuilding, 1992; (with A. Besner and Perez) After the Storm, 1992; (with C.I. Spungin) Gay and Lesbian Students: Understanding Their Needs, 1995; (with Spungin) Training Professionals to Work with Gays and Lesbians in Educational and Workplace Settings, 1997. Contributor to periodicals. **Address:** 915 Middle River Dr Ste 204, Fort Lauderdale, FL 33304, U.S.A.

BESNER, Neil K. Canadian, b. 1949. **Genres:** Literary criticism and history. **Career:** University of Regina, Saskatchewan, instructor in English, 1973-74, sessional lecturer in English, 1975-76; Epicenter Language Academy, Seville, Spain, instructor, 1975; Plains Community College, instructor, 1975-76; University of British Columbia, Vancouver, sessional lecturer, 1976-78, instructor at Centre for Continuing Education, 1978-80; Okanagan College, Penticton, BC, instructor in English, 1980-81; Kwantlen College, Vancouver, instructor in English, 1982-83; Mount Royal College, Calgary, AB, instructor in English, 1983-87, coordinator of composition, 1983-85, chairman of academic council, 1984-86; University of Winnipeg, MB, assistant professor, 1987-90, associate professor, 1990-95, chair of English department, 1993-2000, professor of English, 1995-, dean of humanities, 2002-. **Publications:** The Light of Imagination: Mavis Gallant's Fiction, 1988; Introducing Lives of Girls and Women, 1990; (ed. with D. Staines) The Short Story in English, 1991; (ed. with D. Schnitzer and A. Turner) Uncommon Wealth: An Anthology of Poetry in English, 1997; Rare and Commonplace Flowers: The Story of Elizabeth Bishop and Lota de Macedo Soares (trans. from Portuguese), 2001; Carol Shields: The Arts of a Writing Life, 2003. Work represented in anthologies. Contributor of articles and reviews to literature journals. **Address:** Dept of English, University of Winnipeg, 515 Portage Ave, Winnipeg, MB, Canada R3B 2E9. **Online address:** neilbesner@hotmail.com

BESSEL, Richard. British (born United States), b. 1948. **Genres:** History. **Career:** University of Southampton, England, Parkes fellow, 1977-79; Open University, Milton Keynes, England, lecturer in to reader in history, 1979-98; University of York, professor of twentieth-century history, 1998-. **Publications:** (ed. with E.J. Feuchtwanger) Social Change and Political Development in Weimar Germany, 1981; Political Violence and the Rise of Nazism, 1984; (ed.) Life in the Third Reich, 1987; Germany after the First World War, 1993; (ed.) Fascist Italy and Nazi Germany: Comparisons and Contrasts, 1996; (ed. with R. Jessen) Die Grenzen der Diktatur, 1996. **Address:** Department of History, University of York, Heilington, York YO10 5DD, England. **Online address:** rjb8@york.ac.uk

BESSETTE, Roland L. American. **Genres:** Bibliography. **Career:** Attorney specializing in labor and medical malpractice defense. **Publications:** Mario Lanza: Tenor in Exile, 1999. **Address:** 711 Balfour St., Grosse Pointe Park, MI 48230, U.S.A.

BES-SHAHAR, Eluki. Also writes as Rosemary Edghill. American, b. 1956. **Genres:** Romance/Historical. **Career:** Romance, science fiction, and occult novelist and short story writer;. **Publications:** NOVELS: Hellflower, 1991; Darktraders, 1992; Archangel Blues, 1993; Smoke and Mirrors, 1997; Time's Arrow Book III: The Future, 1998. Contributor of short stories to magazines and anthologies. NOVELS AS ROSEMARY EDGHILL: Turkish Delight, or, The Earl and the Houri, 1987; Two of a Kind: An English Trifle, 1988; The Ill-bred Bride, or, The Inconvenient Marriage, 1990; Fleeting Fancy, 1992; Speak Daggers To Her, 1994; The Sword of Maiden's Tears, 1994; The Cup of Morning Shadows, 1995; Book of Moons, 1995; The Bowl of Night, 1996; The Cloak of Night and Daggers, 1997; Met by

Moonlight, 1998; (with A. Norton) A Heart for Every Fate, 2000. **Address:** c/o St. Martin's Press, 175 Fifth Ave., New York, NY 10010, U.S.A. **Online address:** eluki@aol.com

BESSON, Luc. French, b. 1959. **Genres:** Plays/Screenplays. **Career:** Film director, producer, cinematographer, and screenwriter. Les Films du Loup, Paris, France, founder, 1982-. Director and producer of films; producer of films; and technical advisor. **Publications:** SCREENPLAYS: Le Dernier Combat, 1982, in the US as The Last Battle, 1984; Subway, 1984; (with R. Garland) Le Grand Bleu, 1988, in the US as The Big Blue, 1988; La Femme Nikita, 1990; Atlantis, 1991; The Professional, 1994; The Fifth Element, 1997; Taxi, 1998; The Messenger, 1999; Taxi 2, 2000; The Dancer, 2000; Yamakasi, 2001; Kiss of the Dragon, 2001. OTHER: (with C. Thivel) Atlantis, 1991. **Address:** Chez Les Films du Dauphin, 25 rue Yves-Toudic, 75010 Paris, France.

BEST, Don(ald M.). Also writes as John Lawless. American, b. 1949. **Genres:** How-to books, Architecture. **Career:** Oklahoma Daily, Norman, executive editor and sports editor, 1967-72; U.S. Peace Corps, Washington, DC, volunteer in Caazapa, Paraguay, 1972-74; Brazil Herald, Rio de Janeiro, managing editor and business editor, 1974-75; DataNews, Rio de Janeiro, founder, 1975, editor in chief, 1975-77; Corpus Christi Sun, Corpus Christi, TX, associate editor, 1977-78; freelance writer, 1978-80; Solar Age (now Custom Builder), Harrisville, NH, senior editor, 1981-86; freelance writer and editor, 1986-; editor, Energy Design Update, 1997-. **Publications:** (with R. Trethewey) This Old House: Heating, Ventilation, and Air Conditioning, 1994; (cont.) The Reader's Digest Complete Do-It-Yourself Manual; a how-to book on home emergencies, in press. Contributor to books. Author of regular columns. Contributor to magazines and newspapers. Some articles appear under the name D. Minor Best or the pseudonym John Lawless. **Address:** Paz CP 232, 68005-080 Santarem, Para, Brazil.

BEST, Geoffrey (Francis Andrew). British, b. 1928. **Genres:** History, Military/Defense/Arms control. **Career:** Cambridge University, England, fellow of Trinity Hall and assistant lecturer, 1955-61, Lees Knowles lecturer, 1970; Edinburgh University, Scotland, lecturer, 1961-66, Sir Richard Lodge Professor of History, 1966-74; Sussex University, professor of history, 1974-82, dean of School of European Studies, 1980-82. University of Chicago, visiting professor, 1964; All Souls College, Oxford, visiting fellow, 1969-70; Woodrow Wilson International Center for Scholars, fellow, 1978-79; University of Western Ontario, Joanne Goodman lecturer, 1981; University of London, visiting fellow, 1983-88; Australian National University, visiting fellow, 1984; St. Antony's College, Oxford, senior associate member, 1988-. Cambridge Review, editor, 1953-54; Victorian Studies, British editor, 1959-74; War and Society Newsletter, editor, 1972-82. British Academy, senior fellow, 2003. **Publications:** Shaftesbury, 1964, rev. ed., 1975; Temporal Pillars, 1964; Bishop Westcott and the Miners, 1967; Mid-Victorian Britain, 1851-1875, 1971, rev. ed., 1979; Humanity in Warfare: The Modern History of the International Law of Armed Conflicts, 1980; Honour among Men and Nations: Transformations of an Idea, 1981; War and Society in Revolutionary Europe, 1770-1870, 1982; Nuremberg and After: The Continuing History of War Crimes and Crimes against Humanity, 1984; War and Law since 1945, 1994; Churchill: A Study in Greatness, 2001. EDITOR: (and author of intro.) R.W. Church, Oxford Movement: Twelve Years, 1833-45, 1970; (with A. Wheatcroft) War, Economy, and the Military Mind, 1976; (with D. Beales) History, Society, and the Churches: Essays in Honour of Owen Chadwick, 1985; (and contrib.) The Permanent Revolution: The French Revolution and Its Legacy, 1789-1989, 1988. **Address:** 19 Buckingham St, Oxford OX1 4LH, England. **Online address:** geefab@fish.co.uk

BETANCOURT, Ingrid. Colombian, b. 1961. **Genres:** Area studies. **Career:** Activist, author, and politician. Elected to the Colombian congress, 1994, and senate, 1998; founder and presidential candidate of "Oxygen" (Green Party) in Colombia, 2002. Appeared on television and radio programs. **Publications:** Si Sabia, 1996; (with L. Duroy) La rage au coeur, 2001, trans. by S. Rendall as Until Death Do Us Part: My Struggle to Reclaim Colombia, 2002. **Address:** c/o Author Mail, Ecco Press, 18 West 30th St., New York, NY 10001, U.S.A.

BÉTEILLE, André. Indian, b. 1934. **Genres:** Sociology. **Career:** University of Delhi, Dept of Sociology, professor, 1972-. **Publications:** Caste, Class and Power: Changing Patterns of Stratification in a Tanjore Village, 1965; Castes: Old and New, 1969; Harmonic and Disharmonic Social Systems, 1971; Studies in Agrarian Social Structure, 1974; Six Essays in Comparative Sociology, 1974, rev. ed. as Essays in Comparative Sociology, 1987; (trans.) The Structure of Hindu Society, by Nirmal K. Bose, 1976; Inequality among Men, 1977; Ideologies and Intellectuals, 1980; The Backward Classes and the New Social Order, 1981; The Idea of Natural Inequality and Other Essays, 1983, rev ed, 1987; Society and Politics in India: Essays in a Comparative Perspective, 1991; The Backward Classes in Contemporary India, 1992; How Philosophy Makes the Stoic Sage Tranquil, 1997; Chronicles of Our Times, 2000; Antinomes of Society, 2000. EDITOR: Social Inequality: Selected Readings, 1969; (with T.N. Madan) Encounter and Experience: Personal Accounts of Fieldwork, 1975; Equality and Inequality: Theory and Practice, 1983. **Address:** Dept. of Sociology, University of Delhi, Delhi 110 007, India.

BETHELARD, Faith. American, b. 1953. **Genres:** Animals/Pets. **Career:** Licensed clinical psychologist in private practice. Has also worked in hospital outpatient clinics, at a community mental health center, at a college counseling center, and in a group private practice. Business consultant and executive coach; presenter of workshops for clinicians. **Publications:** (with Elisabeth Young-Bruehl) Cherishment: A Psychology of the Heart, 2000. Also author of professional articles published in psychoanalytic journals. **Address:** Free Press, Simon & Schuster, 1230 Avenue of the Americas, New York, NY 10020, U.S.A.

BETTEY, J(oseph) H(arold). British, b. 1932. **Genres:** History. **Career:** History teacher at boys' grammar school in Birmingham, England, 1957-60, head of history department, 1960-66; University of Bristol, England, lecturer, 1966-73, senior lecturer, 1973-89, reader in local history, 1989-. Society of Antiquaries, fellow; Royal Society of Arts, fellow; British Association for Local History, president. **Publications:** (ed.) English Historical Documents, 1906-1939, 1967; Dorset, 1975; Rural Life in Wessex, 1500-1900, 1977; The Landscape of Wessex, 1980; Church and Community, 1980; The Casebook of Sir Francis Ashley, J.P., 1982; The Calendar of the Correspondence of the Smyth Family of Ashton Court, 1548-1642, 1982; Bristol Observed, 1986; Wessex from A.D. 1000, 1986; Church and Parish: The English Parish Church and the Local Community, 1987; Suppression of the Monasteries in the West Country, 1989; Estates and the English Countryside, 1993; Man and the Land: Farming in Dorset 1846-1996, 1996; History of Farming in Dorset, 2000; Historic Churches & Church Life in Bristol, 2001. **Address:** Clayley Cottage, Compton Dando, Bristol BS39 4NX, England.

BETTINI, Maurizio. Italian, b. 1947. **Genres:** Anthropology/Ethnology, Archaeology/Antiquities, Classics. **Career:** University of Pisa, Italy, associate professor, 1975-81; University of Venice, Italy, professor, 1981-84; University of Siena, Italy, professor, 1984-85, dean of Faculty of Arts and Sciences, 1986-95. **Publications:** Anthropology and Roman Culture: Kinship, Time, Images of the Soul, trans., 1991; The Portrait of the Lover, trans., 1999; Classical Indiscretions, trans., 2001; To Be Born: History of Women, Weasels, Mothers, and Heroes, forthcoming. Author of many writings in German and Italian. Contributor to Italian periodicals. **Address:** Faculty of Arts and Sciences, University of Siena, Via Roma 47, 53100 Siena, Italy. **Online address:** bettini@unisi.it

BETTS, Clive. Welsh (born England), b. 1943. **Genres:** History, Language/Linguistics, Politics/Government, Regional/Urban planning, Transportation, Documentaries/Reportage. **Career:** Western Mail, Cardiff, Wales, national assembly editor and author of the weekly column, Clive Betts on Friday. **Publications:** Culture in Crisis, 1976; A Oedd Heddwch?, 1978; Cardiff and the Eisteddfod, 1978; The Political Conundrum, 1993. **Address:** Western Mail, National Assembly, Cardiff CF99 1NA, Wales. **Online address:** clive. g.betts@tinyonline.co.uk

BETTS, Doris. American, b. 1932. **Genres:** Novels, Novellas/Short stories. **Career:** Worked for Statesville Daily Record, 1946-50, and stringer for UPI and North Carolina newspapers, 1953-54, and later through 1957; taught typing for the North Carolina Highway Patrol, 1954; office manager and secretary-treasurer, Simplified Farm Record Book Company, Chapel Hill, 1955-57; full-time feature writer and daily columnist, Sanford Daily Herald, 1957-58; full-time editor, Sanford News Leader, 1960; University of North Carolina, Chapel Hill, lecturer, 1966-74, director of Freshman/Sophomore English, 1972-78, associate professor, 1974-78, professor, 1978-; visiting lecturer in creative writing, Duke University, 1971. **Publications:** NOVELS: Tall Houses in Winter, 1954; The Scarlet Thread, 1964; The River to Pickle Beach, 1972; Heading West, 1981; Souls Raised from the Dead, 1994; The Sharp Teeth of Love, 1997. STORY COLLECTIONS: The Gentle Insurrection, 1954; The Astronomer and Other Stories, 1966; Beasts of the Southern Wild & Other Stories, 1973. OTHER: Creative Writing: The Short Story, 1970. **Address:** English Department, CB# 3520, University of North Carolina, Chapel Hill, NC 27599, U.S.A. **Online address:** dbetts@ mindspring.com

BETTS, William Wilson, Jr. American, b. 1926. **Genres:** Literary criticism and history, Humor/Satire. **Career:** Professor of English, Indiana University of Pennsylvania, 1957-, now Emeritus (Associate Professor, 1955-57; Assistant Dean of Graduate School, 1968-71). Instructor, Ohio University, Athens, 1954-55. Outdoors Ed., Indiana Evening Gazette, 1973-80. **Publications:** (ed. with P.A. Shelley and A.O. Lewis) Anglo-German and American-German Crosscurrents, vol. I, 1957; Lincoln and the Poets, 1965; A Docketful of Wry (humor), 1970; Slips that Pass in the Night, the King's English Adrift on the Campus (humor), 2002. Contributor of essays and articles to nature magazines. **Address:** 71 Cedar Ln, Indiana, PA 15701-8490, U.S.A. **Online address:** wwjjbetts@earthlink.net

BEUMERS, Birgit. German, b. 1963. **Genres:** Theatre, Film. **Career:** University of Cambridge, England, lecturer, 1992-94; University of Bristol, England, lecturer, 1994-2001, senior lecturer in Russian, 2001-, teacher in continuing education, department of drama: theater, film, television. **Publications:** Yury Lyubimov at the Taganka Theatre, 1964-1994, 1997; (ed.) Russia on Reels: The Russian Idea in Post-Soviet Cinema, 1999; Burnt by the Sun, 2000; Nikita Mikhalkov, 2005. **Address:** Dept of Russian, University of Bristol, Bristol BS8 1TE, England. **Online address:** birgit.beumers@bris. ac.uk

BEVAN, James (Stuart). British, b. 1930. **Genres:** Medicine/Health. **Career:** Physician: partner in a medical general practice, London. Formerly, Automobile Association, Senior Medical Consultant; formerly, Foundation of Nursing Studies, Chairman; Charity Trustee Network, Trustee. **Publications:** State Final Questions and Answers for Nurses, 1962; Preliminary Questions and Answers for Nurses, 1963; Sex: The Plain Facts, 1966; A Pictorial Handbook of Anatomy and Physiology, 1979, rev. ed., 1998; The Pocket Medical and First Aid Guide, 1979; Your Family Doctor, 1980; The Family First Aid and Medical Guide, 1984; (ed.) Sex and Your Health, 1990.

BEVERLEY, Jo. British/Canadian, b. 1947. **Genres:** Romance/Historical. **Career:** Writer. Vocational guidance, 1971-76; member of Staffordshire and Nottinghamshire County Councils. **Publications:** Lord Wraybourne's Betrothed, 1988; The Stanforth Secrets, 1989; If Fancy Be the Food of Love, 1991; The Stolen Bride, 1990; Emily and the Dark Angel, 1991; The Fortune Hunter, 1991; Deirdre and Don Juan, 1993; An Arranged Marriage, 1991; The Christmas Angel, 1992; An Unwilling Bride, 1992; Forbidden, 1994, Black Satin, 1997; Dangerous Joy, 1995, Black Satin, 1997; Lord of My Heart, 1992; Dark Champion, 1993; The Shattered Rose, 1996; Lord of Midnight, 1998; My Lady Notorious, 1993; Tempting Fortune, 1995; Something Wicked, 1997; Forbidden Magic, 1998; Secrets of the Night, 1999; Devilish, 2000; The Devil's Heiress, 2001; The Dragon's Bride, 2001; Hazard, 2002; St. Raven, 2003; Winter Fire, 2003; Skylark, 2004. Contributor to anthologies. **Address:** c/o The Rotrosen Agency, 318 E 51st St, New York, NY 10022, U.S.A. **Online address:** jo@jobev.com; www.jobev.com

BEVIS, William W. American, b. 1941. **Genres:** Literary criticism and history, Environmental sciences/Ecology, Travel/Exploration, Novels. **Career:** Author. University of Montana, Missoula, associate professor of English, 1974-78, professor of English, 1978-. **Publications:** Mind of Winter: Wallace Stevens, Meditation, and Literature, 1988; Ten Tough Trips: Montana Writers and the West, 1990; Borneo Log: The Struggle for Sarawak's Forests, 1995; Shorty Harris, or, The Price of Gold, 1999. **Address:** University of Montana, Missoula, MT 59812, U.S.A.

BEW, Paul Anthony. Irish, b. 1950. **Genres:** Area studies, History. **Career:** Historian. Ulster College, Northern Ireland Polytechnic, Belfast, lecturer, 1975-79; Queen's University, Belfast, lecturer, 1979-86, reader, political science department, 1986; University of Pennsylvania, Philadelphia, visiting lecturer, 1982-83; radio and television commentator on Irish affairs. **Publications:** Land and the National Question in Ireland, 1858-82, 1979; (with P. Gibbon and H. Patterson) The State in Northern Ireland, 1921-72: Political Forces and Social Classes, 1979; C.S. Parnell (biography), 1980; (with H. Patterson) Sean Lemass and the Making of Modern Ireland, 1945-66, 1982; (with H. Patterson) The British State and the Ulster Crisis: From Wilson to Thatcher, 1985; Conflict and Conciliation in Ireland, 1890-1910: Parnellites and Radical Agrarians, 1987; (with E. Hazelkorn and H. Patterson) The Dynamics of Irish Politics, 1989; (with G. Gillespie) Northern Ireland: A Chronology of the Troubles, 1968-1993, 1993; (ed. with K. Darwin and G. Gillespie) Passion and Prejudice: Nationalist/Unionist Conflict in Ulster in the 1930s and the Origins of the Irish Association, Institute of Irish Studies, 1993; Ideology and the Irish Question: Ulster Unionism and Irish Nationalism, 1912-1916, 1994; (with P. Gibbon and H. Patterson) Northern Ireland, 1921-1994: Political Forces and Social Classes, 1995; (with H. Patterson and P. Teague) Between War and Peace: The Political Future of Northern Ireland, 1997. **Address:** Queens University, Department of Political Science, Belfast BT7, Ireland.

BEWES, Richard. British (born Kenya), b. 1934. **Genres:** Theology/ Religion. **Career:** Church of England Clergyman: Vicar, St. Peter's, Harold Wood, Essex, 1965-74, and Emmanuel Church, Northwood, Middx., 1974-83; Rector of All Souls, Langham Pl., London, 1983-2004. **Publications:** God in Ward 12, 1974; Advantage Mr. Christian, 1975; Talking about Prayer, 1979; John Wesley's England, 1981; The Church Reaches Out, 1981; The Pocket Handbook of Christian Truth, 1981; The Church Overcomes, 1984; On the Way, 1984; Quest for Truth, 1985; Quest for Life, 1985; The Church Marches On, 1986; When God Surprises, 1986; A New Beginning, 1989; The Resurrection, 1989; Does God Reign?, 1995; Speaking in Public Effectively, 1998; Great Quotations of the 20th Century, 1999; The Lamb Wins, 2000; Ten Steps in Prayer, 2001; The Stone That Became a Mountain, 2001; Words That Circled the World, 2002; The Top 100 Questions, 2002; Wesley Country, 2003; Beginning the Christian Life, 2004; 150 Pocket Thoughts, 2004. **Address:** Christian Focus, Geanies House, Fearn, Tain, Ross-shire, London 1V20 1TW, United Kingdom. **Online address:** richard. bewes@allsouls.org

BEYER, Werner W(illiam). American, b. 1911. **Genres:** Literary criticism and history, Novellas/Short stories. **Career:** Rebecca Clifton Reade Professor Emeritus of English and Head of English Dept., Butler University, Indianapolis (associate professor, 1948-51; professor, 1951-83). Jr. League Lecturer, 1963-96. Instructor in English, Drew University, Madison, NJ, 1943-45; assistant professor, Rutgers University, NJ, 1945-48; Columbia University, visiting assistant professor, 1948; Indiana University, visiting professor, comp. lit., 1966. **Publications:** The Prestige of C.M. Wieland in England, 1936; Keats and the Daemon King, 1947; The Enchanted Forest, 1963; (bibliographer) The World in Literature, 2 vols., 1967; Islands beneath the Moon (short stories), 1995; The Food of Love and Other Stories, 2002. **Address:** 5388 Thicket Hill Lane, Indianapolis, IN 46226-1457, U.S.A.

BEYFUS, Drusilla. British. **Genres:** Human relations/Parenting, Social commentary. **Career:** Editor, writer, broadcaster. Visiting tutor, Central St Martin's College of Art, 1989-; associate editor, Queen Magazine, 1959-63; home editor, The Observer, 1962-64; associate editor, Weekend Telegraph mag, 1963-71; editor, Brides and Setting Up Home mag, 1971-79; associate editor, Vogue mag, London, 1979-86; columnist, Sunday Telegraph, 1989-90, Telegraph mag, contributing editor, 1991-; You (The Mail on Sunday), columnist, 1994-2002. **Publications:** (with A. Edwards) Lady Behave, 1956, 1969; The English Marriage, 1968; The Brides Book, 1981; The Art of Giving, 1987; Modern Manners, 1992; Courtship Parties, 1992; Sex, Business, 1993.

BEYNON, Huw. British, b. 1942. **Genres:** Industrial relations, Sociology. **Career:** University of Bristol, lecturer in sociology; University of Durham, reader in sociology; University of Manchester, research fellow, 1973-74, professor in sociology; Cardiff University, School of Social Science, director. **Publications:** (with R.M. Blackburn) Perceptions of Work, 1972; Working for Ford, 1973; (with T. Nichols) Living with Capitalism, 1977; What Happened at Speke?, 1978; (with H. Wainwright) The Workers Report on Vickers Ltd., 1979; (with N. Hedges) Born to Work, 1982; (with R. Hudson and D. Sadler) A Tale of Two Industries: The Decline of Coal and Steel in the Northeast, 1991; A Place Called Teesside, 1994; (with T. Austrin) Masters and Servants: Class and Patronage in the Making of a Labour Organisation, 1994; (with A. Cox and R. Hudson) Digging up Trouble: Opencast Coal Mining, the Environment and Social Protest, 2000. EDITOR: Digging Deeper: Issues in the Miners Strike, 1985; (with P. Glavanis) Patterns of Social Inequality, 1999; (with S. Rowbotham) Looking at Class, 2001. **Address:** School of Social Sciences, Cardiff University, Glamorgan Bldg, King Edward VII Ave, Cardiff M13 9PL, England. **Online address:** BeynonH@ cardiff.ac.uk

BHALA, Raj K. Canadian (born Canada), b. 1962. **Genres:** Law, Money/ Finance. **Career:** Federal Reserve Bank of New York, NYC, attorney in Legal Department, 1989-93; College of William and Mary, Williamsburg, VA, associate professor of international law, 1993-. University of London, member of board of international scholars, Banking and Finance Unit, Centre for Commercial Law Studies, 1995-; Duke University, visiting professor, 1996; Bank of Japan, visiting scholar, 1997. **Publications:** Perspectives on Risk-Based Capital, 1989; (with E.T. Patrikis and T.C. Baxter, Jr.) Wire Transfers, 1993; Foreign Bank Regulation after BCCI, 1994; International Trade Law: Cases and Materials, 1996; Global Foreign Exchange Trading: Fundamentals, Market Practice, Law, and Policy, 1996; (with K. Kennedy) Contemporary International Trade Law, in press. Contributor to books. Contributor to law and banking journals. **Address:** School of Law, College of William and Mary, South Henry St., P.O. Box 8795, Williamsburg, VA 23187, U.S.A.

BHATT, Jagdish J(eyshanker). American (born India), b. 1939. **Genres:** Earth sciences, Marine sciences/Oceanography, Education. **Career:** Jackson Community College, Jackson, MI, instructor in physical science and chemistry, International Club, adviser, 1964-65; Panhandle State University, Goodwell, OK, instructor in physical science and geology, Geological Society, faculty advisor 1965-66; State University of New York, Buffalo, assistant professor, 1972-74; Community College of Rhode Island, Warwick, RI, professor of geology and oceanography, 1984-, Geological Club, adviser, 1974-, Applied Oceanography Student Workshop, project director, 1976-81. National Science Foundation, fellow, marine sciences training, University of San Diego & Scripps Institute of Oceanography, 1993; University of Rhode Island, School of Oceanography, visiting professor, 1995. **Publications:** Laboratory Manual on Physical Geology, 1966; Laboratory Manual on Physical Science, 1966; Environmentology, 1975; Geochemistry and Geology of South Wales Main Limestone, 1976; Geologic Exploration of Earth, 1976; Oceanography: Exploring the Planet Ocean, 1978; Applied Oceanography, 1979; Ocean Enterprise (textbook), 1984; Oceanography Year 2000 and Beyond, 1988; Oceanography-Concepts and Applications, 1994; Laboratory Studies in Historical Geology, 1995; Odyssey of the Damned (novel), 1995; Spinning Mind, Spinning Time, c'est la vie, 1999. FORTHCOMING: Laboratory Studies in Oceanography; Universe, Mind and Brahman.

BHATT, Sujata. Indian, b. 1956. **Genres:** Poetry. **Career:** Freelance writer and translator. University of Victoria, British Columbia, Lansdowne Visiting writer/professor, spring, 1992. **Publications:** POETRY: Brunizem, 1988; Monkey Shadows, 1991; Freak Waves (chapbook), 1992; The Stinking Rose, 1995. **Address:** Alexanderstrasse 38, 28203 Bremen, Germany.

BHATTACHARYA, Nalinaksha. Indian, b. 1949. **Genres:** Novels. **Career:** National Society for the Prevention of Blindness, New Delhi, India, proofreader of opthalmic journals, 1972-73; Directorate of Estates, Ministry of Works & Housing, New Delhi, assistant, 1973-81; Ministry of Agriculture, New Delhi, section officer, 1981-85; Ministry of Environment & Forests, New Delhi, section officer, 1985-94, under secretary, 1994-. **Publications:** NOVELS: Hem and Football, 1992; Hem and Maxine, 1995; A Fistful of Desire, 1997. Author of short stories. Contributor to books. **Address:** Sector 7/1204, R.K. Puramax, New Delhi 110022, India.

BHOTE, Keki R. Indian, b. 1925. **Genres:** Administration/Management, Business/Trade/Industry. **Career:** Motorola, Schaumburg, IL, director of quality and value assurance, 1970-80, director of quality for Quality and Productivity Improvement Group, 1980-85, senior corporate consultant, 1985-92; Keki R. Bhote Associates, Glencoe, IL, president, 1992-. Glencoe Board of Education, president, 1969-73; New Trier Township, president of board of trustees, 1977-85. **Publications:** (co-author) Value Analysis Methods, 1974; Supply Management, 1987; World Class Quality, 1988, 2nd ed., 1991; Strategic Supply Management, 1989; The Next Operation as Customer, 1991; Beyond Customer Satisfaction to Customer Loyalty, 1998; The Ultimate Six Sigma, 2000; The Power of Ultimate Six Sigma, 2003; World Class Reliability, 2004. **Address:** 493 Woodlawn, Glencoe, IL 60022, U.S.A. **Online address:** krbhote@msn.com

BIAL, Raymond. American, b. 1948. **Genres:** Children's non-fiction, Photography. **Career:** Parkland College Library, Champaign, IL, library director, 1988-. **Publications:** NONFICTION FOR CHILDREN; AND PHOTOGRAPHER: Corn Belt Harvest, 1991; County Fair, 1992; Amish Home, 1993; Frontier Home, 1993; Shaker Home, 1994; The Underground Rairoad, 1995; Portrait of a Farm Family, 1995. OTHER: Ivesdale: A Photographic Essay, 1982; In All My Years: Portraits of Older Blacks in Champaign-Urbana, 1983, rev. ed. 1985; Upon a Quiet Landscape: The Photographs of Frank Sadorus, 1983; There Is a Season, 1984; (with K. Kerr) First Frost, 1985; Common Ground: Photographs of Rural and Small Town Life, 1986; Stopping By: Portraits from Small Towns, 1988; (with L.L. Bial) The Carnegie Library in Illinois, 1988; From the Heart of the Country: Photographs of the Midwestern Sky, 1991; Looking Good: A Guide to Photographing Your Library, 1991; Champaign: A Pictorial History, 1993; Urbana: A Pictorial History, 1994; Visit to Amish Country, 1995; (photographer) Marcia Adams Heirloom Recipes; With Needle and Thread, 1996; Zoom Lens Photography, 1996; Mist Over the Mountains: Appalachia and Its People, 1997; The Strength of These Arms: Life in the Slave Quarters, 1997. **Address:** Parkland College Library, 2400 West Bradley Ave., Champaign, IL 61821, U.S.A.

BIALE, Rachel. Israeli, b. 1952. **Genres:** Children's fiction, Law. **Career:** Jewish Family and Children's Services of the East Bay, Berkeley, CA, clinical social worker and psychotherapy senior clinician, 1990-97. Jewish studies lecturer. **Publications:** LET'S MAKE A BOOK ABOUT IT SERIES (for children): (And illustrator) We Are Moving, 1996; (and illustrator) My Pet Died, 1997. OTHER: Women in Jewish Law, 1984. **Address:** c/o Jewish Family and Children's Services, 2484 Shattuck Ave, #210, Berkeley, CA 94704, U.S.A. **Online address:** biale@socrates.berkeley.edu

BIANCHI, Eugene Carl. American, b. 1930. **Genres:** Theology/Religion. **Career:** Professor of Religion, Emory University, Atlanta, Georgia, since 1968. Assistant Ed., American mag., NYC, 1963-66; Assistant Professor of Religion, 1966-68, and Director, Center for Study of Contemporary Values, 1967-68, University of Santa Clara, California; Distinguished Visiting Professor, California State University, Sacramento, 1974-75. **Publications:** John XXIII and American Protestants, 1968; Reconciliation: The Function of the Church, 1969; The Religious Experience of Revolutionaries, 1972; (with Rosemary R. Ruether) From Machismo to Mutuality, 1975; Aging As a Spiritual Journey, 1982; On Growing Older, 1985; (co-edited with Rosemary R. Ruether) A Democratic Catholic Church, 1992; Elder Wisdom: Crafting Your Own Elderhood, 1994. **Address:** Dept of Religion, Emory University, 1364 Clifton Rd NE, Atlanta, GA 30322-0001, U.S.A. **Online address:** releb@emory.edu

BIANCO, Anthony. American, b. 1953. **Genres:** Business/Trade/Industry, Biography. **Career:** Minneapolis Tribune, Minneapolis, MN, reporter, 1977; Willamette Week, Portland, OR, business writer, 1978-80; Business Week, New York City, San Francisco correspondent, 1980-82, staff editor, 1982, department editor in markets and investments, 1983-84, associate editor, 1984-85, senior writer, 1985-92, 1996-; writer. **Publications:** Rainmaker: The Saga of Jeff Beck, Wall Street's Mad Dog, 1991; The Reichmanns: Family, Faith, Fortune and the Empire of Olympia & York, 1997; Ghosts of 42nd Street: A History of America's Most Infamous Block, 2004. **Address:** 17 First St, Brooklyn, NY 11231, U.S.A. **Online address:** tony_bianco@businessweek.com

BIASIN, Gian-Paolo. Italian, b. 1933. **Genres:** Literary criticism and history, Anthropology/Ethnology. **Career:** Professor of Italian, University of California, Berkeley. Professor, University of Texas, Austin, 1973-81. Assistant Professor, 1964-67, and Associate Professor of Romance Studies, 1967-73, Cornell University, Ithaca, New York. **Publications:** The Smile of the Gods: A Thematic Analysis of C. Pavese's Works, 1968; Literary Diseases: Theme and Metaphor in the Italian Novel, 1975; Italian Literary Icons, 1985; Montale, Debussy and Modernism, 1989; The Flavors of Modernity: Food and the Novel, 1993. **Address:** Italian Studies Dept., University of California, Berkeley, CA 94720, U.S.A.

BICÂT, Tony. British, b. 1945. **Genres:** Plays/Screenplays, Education. **Career:** Co-founder and director of Portable Theatre, England, 1968-72; writer, director, and lyricist, 1972-. **Publications:** (co-author) All's Well That Ends, 1978; (with T. MacNabb) Creative Screenwriting. FILMS: Dinosaur, 1974. FILMS FOR TELEVISION: Electric in the City, 1981; A Cotswold Death, 1982; Facelift, 1982-83; A Christmas Present, 1986-87; Star Trap, 1988; The Children of Masha Cirkus (6-part series), 1989; The Laughter of God (in U.S. as Married to Murder), 1990; The Wordsworth Murders, 1991; An Exchange of Fire, 1992-93; The Scold's Bridle, 1998. STAGE PLAYS: A Buyer's Market, 2002; Robin of Wychwood, 2003. **Address:** c/o Berlin Associates, 14 Floral St, London WC2E 9DH, England.

BICCHIERI, Cristina. American (born Italy), b. 1950. **Genres:** Philosophy, Social sciences. **Career:** Carnegie-Mellon University, Pittsburgh, PA, professor of philosophy, 1989-. **Publications:** Ragioni per Credere..., 1989; Rationality and Coordination, 1993. EDITOR: (with M.L. Dalla Chiara) Knowledge, Belief, and Strategic Interaction, 1992; (with R. Jeffrey and B. Skyrms) The Dynamics of Norms, 1995; (with R. Jeffrey and B. Skyrms) The Logic of Strategy, 1999. **Address:** Department of Philosophy, Carnegie-Mellon University, Pittsburgh, PA 15213, U.S.A. **Online address:** cb36@andrew.cmu.edu

BICERANO, Jozef. American (born Turkey), b. 1952. **Genres:** Chemistry, Engineering. **Career:** University of California, Berkeley, postdoctoral researcher, 1981-82; Energy Conversion Devices Inc., Troy, MI, researcher, 1982-86; Dow Chemical Co., Midland, MI, researcher, 1986-. **Publications:** Prediction of Polymer Properties, 1993, 3rd ed., 2002. EDITOR: (with D. Adler) Proceedings of the International Conference on the Theory of the Structures of Non-Crystalline Solids, 1985; Computational Modeling of Polymers, 1992. Contributor to scientific journals. **Address:** Dow Chemical Co., 1702 Building, Midland, MI 48674, U.S.A. **Online address:** biceranoj@dow.com

BICKERSTAFF, Edwin Robert. British, b. 1920. **Genres:** Medicine/Health. **Career:** Sr. Consultant Neurologist, Midland Center for Neurosurgery and Neurology, Birmingham, 1954-83; Hon. Consultant Neurologist, United Birmingham Hosps.; Consultant Neurologist, Hereford Hosps., and Shrewsbury Hosps. **Publications:** Neurological Examination in Clinical Practice, 1963, 6th ed. (with J.A. Spillane) as Bickerstaff's Neurological Examination in Clinical Practice, 1996; Neurology for Nurses, 1965, 4th ed. 1987; Neurological Complication of the Oral Contraceptives, 1974. **Address:** St. Helens, The Close, Trevone, Padstow, Cornwall, England.

BICKERTON, David M. British, b. 1944. **Genres:** Librarianship. **Career:** University of Glasgow, Glasgow, Scotland, lecturer, 1969-86, senior lecturer in French, 1986-93, director of Language Centre, 1983-93; University of Plymouth, Plymouth, England, professor of modern languages, 1993-98, research professor, 1999-2001, director of modern languages, 1993-98; Institut National de Recherche Pédagogique, member of scientific council, 2001-. Centre for Modern Languages, member of national advisory board for Computers in Teaching Initiative, 1995-99; French Ministry of Education, member of Comité national de co-ordination de la recherche en éducation, 1996-99; University Council for Modern Languages, member of executive, 1998-2001; Subject Centre for Languages, Linguistics, and Area Studies, chair of Specialist Advisory Group, 2000-. Satellite Materials in Language Education, project director, 1989-93; University of Bergano, partner in Produzione di Materiali Didattici in Lingue inglese per orientatori nei Centri Informagiovani, 1992-94; Language Object Coding for Educational Purposes, project member, 1993-96; Rapid Authoring of Packages Using Innovative Development Tools, coordinator, 1997-98; Web Guide to Good Practice in Teaching and Learning Languages, Linguistics, and Area Studies, coordinating editor, 2001-02; consultant to University of Southampton. Producer of television documentaries. **Publications:** Marc-Auguste and Charles Pictet, the Bibliothèque britannique (1796-1815), and the Dissemination of British Literature and Science on the Continent, 1986, rev ed, The Bibliothèque britannique (1796-1815), 2002. EDITOR: (with J. Proud) The Transmission of Culture in Western Europe, 1750-1850: Papers Celebrating the Bicentenary of the Foundation of the Bibliothèque britannique (1796-1815) in Geneva, 1999; (with M. Gotti) Language Centres: Integration through Innovation, 1999; (with R. Sigrist) Marc-Auguste Pictet, Correspondance: Sciences et techniques, Vol 3: Les Correspondants britanniques, 2000. Contributor to books and periodicals. **Address:** 13 Albert Sq., London SW8 1BT, England. **Online address:** davidbick01@hotmail.com

BICKFORD-SMITH, Vivian. British, b. 1955. **Genres:** Area studies, Third World, History. **Career:** Rhodes University, Grahamstown, South Africa, assistant lecturer in history, 1980-81; University of Cape Town, Cape Town, South Africa, temporary lecturer, 1982-87, lecturer, 1987-95, senior lecturer in history, 1995-. **Publications:** (ed. with Elizabeth van Heyningen) The Waterfront, 1994; Ethnic Pride and Racial Prejudice in Victorian Cape Town, 1995; Cape Town, 1996. Contributor to books. **Address:** Department of History, University of Cape Town, Rondebosch 7700, Cape Town, Republic of South Africa.

BIDART, Frank. American, b. 1939. **Genres:** Poetry. **Career:** Wellesley College, faculty member, Dept. of English; poet. **Publications:** Poetry Collections: Golden State, 1973; The Book of the Body, 1977; The Sacrifice, 1983; In the Western Night: Collected Poems, 1965-90, 1990; Desire, 1997; Music Like Dirt, 2002. **Address:** English Dept, Wellesley College, 106 Central St, Wellesley, MA 02481-8268, U.S.A.

BIDDISS, Michael Denis. British, b. 1942. **Genres:** History, Intellectual history, International relations/Current affairs. **Career:** Downing College, Cambridge, Fellow, 1966-73, Director of Studies in History, 1970-73; University of Leicester, Lecturer, 1973-78, Reader in History, 1978-79; University of Reading, Professor of History, 1979-, Dean, Faculty of Letters and Social Sciences, 1982-85. Royal Historical Society, Vice President, 1995-99; Historical Association, President, 1991-94. **Publications:** Father of Racist Ideology: The Social and Political Thought of Count Gobineau, 1970; (with F.F. Cartwright) Disease and History, 1972, rev. ed., 2000; The Age of the Masses: Ideas and Society in Europe since 1870, 1977; The Nuremberg Trial and the Third Reich, 1992. EDITOR: Gobineau: Selected Political Writings, 1970; Images of Race, 1979; (with K. Minogue) Thatcherism: Politics and Personality, 1987; (with M. Wyke) The Uses and Abuses of Antiquity, 1999; (with S. Peters and I. Roe) The Humanities in the New Millennium, 2002. **Address:** School of History, University of Reading, Reading RG6 6AA, England. **Online address:** m.d.biddiss@reading.ac.uk

BIDDLE, Bruce Jesse. American, b. 1928. **Genres:** Education, Psychology, Sociology. **Career:** University of Kentucky, assistant professor of sociology, 1957-58; University of Kansas City, associate professor of education, 1958-60; University of Missouri, Columbia, associate professor, 1960-66, professor of psychology and sociology, 1966-2000, emeritus professor, 2000-. **Publications:** (with H.A. Rosencranz and E.F. Rankin) Studies in the Role of the Public School Teacher, 5 vols., 1961; The Present Status of Role Theory, 1961; (with R.S. Adams) Realities of Teaching: Explorations with Videotape, 1970; (with M.J. Dunkin) The Study of Teaching, 1974; (with T. Good and J. Brophy) Teachers Make a Difference, 1975; Role Theory: Expectations, Identities, and Behaviors, 1979; (with D.C. Berliner) The Manufactured Crisis: Myths, Freud, and the Attack on America's Public Schools, 1995; (with L.J. Saha) The Untested Accusation: Principals, Research Knowledge, and Policy Making in Schools, 2002. EDITOR: (with W.J. Ellena) Contemporary Research on Teacher Effectiveness, 1964; (with E.J. Thomas) Role Theory: Concepts and Research, 1966; (with P.H. Rossi) The New Media: Their Impact on Education and Society, 1966; (with D.S. Anderson) Knowledge for Policy: Improving Education through Research, 1991; (with T.L. Good and I.F. Goodson) International Handbook of Teachers and Teaching, 1997; Social Class, Poverty, and Education, 2001. **Address:** McAlester Hall Rm 210, University of Missouri, Columbia, MO 65211, U.S.A. **Online address:** biddleb@missouri.edu

BIDDLE, Martin. British, b. 1937. **Genres:** Archaeology/Antiquities. **Career:** British archeologist, writer, and educator. Ministry of Public Buildings and Works, assistant inspector of ancient monuments, 1961-63; University of Exeter, lecturer in medieval archeology, 1963-67; All Souls College, Oxford, visiting fellow, 1967-68; University of Pennsylvania, University Museum, director, and professor of anthropology and of history of art, 1977-81; Christ Church, Oxford, Lecturer of the House, 1983-86; University of Oxford, professor of archeology, 1997-. Director of several excavations and investigations including Nonsuch Palace, 1959-60, Repton (with wife), 1974-88, 1993, and many others; consultant for Canterbury Cathedral, St. Alban's Abbey, and Cathedral Church. Royal Commission on Historical Monuments of England, 1984-95. **Publications:** (with J. Dent) Nonsuch, 1960: The Banqueting House, 1960; (with D.M. Hudson and C.M. Heighway) The Future of London's Past, 1973; (ed.) Winchester in the Early Middle Ages, 1977; (with I.H. Goodall, D.A. Hinton, et al) Object and Economy in Medieval Winchester, Vols 1-2, 1990; The Tomb of Christ, 1999; The Church of the Holy Sepulchre, 2000; King Arthur's Round Table: An Archaeological Investigation, 2001. Contributor of papers on archeological, historical, and art-historical subjects to learned journals. **Address:** Oxford University, Hertford College, Catte Street, Oxford OX1 3BW, England. **Online address:** martin.biddle@hertford.ox.ac.uk

BIDDULPH, Steve. Australian. **Genres:** Human relations/Parenting. **Career:** Family therapist in Australia, c. 1981-; author, c. 1984-. **Publications:** NONFICTION: The Secret of Happy Children: A New Guide for Parents, 1984; (with S. Biddulph) The Making of Love, 1988, in US as The Secret of a Happy Family: Stay in Love as a Couple Through Thick and Thin-and Even with Kids, 1989; Raising Boys: Why Boys Are Different-And How to Help Them Become Happy and Well-Balanced Men, 1998; Manhood: An Action Plan for Changing Men's Lives, 1999; More Secrets of Happy Children, 1999. **Address:** c/o Manhood Online, PO Box 231, St. Leonards, NSW 2065, Australia.

BIDINI, Dave. Canadian, b. 1963?. **Genres:** Autobiography/Memoirs, Documentaries/Reportage. **Career:** Musician, and writer. **Publications:** On a Cold Road: Tales of Adventure in Canadian Rock, 1998; Tropic of Hockey: My Search for the Game in Unlikely Places, 2000. Contributor to periodicals. **Address:** c/o Author Mail, McClelland & Stewart Ltd., 481 University Ave Ste 900, Toronto, ON, Canada M5G 2E9.

BIDNEY, Martin. American, b. 1943. **Genres:** Literary criticism and history. **Career:** State University of New York at Binghamton, instructor, 1969-71, assistant professor, 1971-77, associate professor, 1977-89, professor, 1989-2004, emeritus professor of English and comparative literature, 2004-. **Publications:** Blake and Goethe: Psychology, Ontology, Imagination, 1988; Patterns of Epiphany: From Wordsworth to Tolstoy, Pater, and Barrett Browning, 1997. Contributor to books. Contributor of articles, translations, and reviews to academic journals. **Address:** 912 Taylor Dr, Vestal, NY 13850, U.S.A. **Online address:** mbidney@binghamton.edu

BIEBER, Konrad (F.). American (born Germany), b. 1916. **Genres:** Literary criticism and history, Biography, Translations. **Career:** Yale University, New Haven, CT, instructor in French, 1948-53; Connecticut College, New London, assistant professor, 1953-57, associate professor, 1957-60, professor of French, 1960-68, chair of department, 1960-64; State University of New York at Stony Brook, professor of French and comparative literature, 1968-86, professor emeritus, 1986-. Interallied Railroad Commission in Paris, military interpreter, 1944; Colonie Juliette (a Zionist-sponsored school for

war orphans), head counselor and teacher, 1946-47; instructor in German at New York University, Hunter College (now Lehmann College) and at City College of New York evening extension, 1948; Middlebury College, summer school instructor in French, 1949-51, 1956; University of Colorado, visiting lecturer in French and comparative literature, summer, 1952. Representative at the United Nations for the French movement against racism, 1969-88. **Publications:** L'Allemagne vue par les ecrivains de la Resistance francaise (title means: Germany Viewed by French Resistance Writers), 1954; Simone de Beauvoir, 1979; (trans.) L. Aubrac, Outwitting the Gestapo, 1993. **Address:** 1211 Foulkeways, Gwynedd, PA 19436, U.S.A.

BIEDER, Robert E. American, b. 1938. **Genres:** Anthropology/Ethnology. **Career:** Grinnell College, Grinnell, IA, assistant professor of history, 1972-73; Newberry Library, assistant director of Center for the History of the American Indian, 1973-74, associate director, 1974-75; University of Illinois at Chicago Circle, Chicago, assistant professor of Native American studies, 1977-80; University of Mainz, Mainz, Germany, senior Fulbright lecturer in ethnology and American studies, 1980-81; Indiana University-Bloomington, visiting assistant professor, summers, 1982-83, 1985, visiting associate professor of history, 1985-87, associate professor in Malaysian Program, 1987, associate professor of history, 1995-; Free University of Berlin, Berlin, Germany, senior Fulbright lecturer in history, 1988-89; L. Kossuth University, Debrecen, Hungary, Soros Foundation Professor of American Civilization, 1991, 1992, senior Fulbright lecturer in history, 1992-94. Expert witness for U.S. Departments of Justice and the Interior, Sault Ste. Marie Ojibwas, and Native American Rights Rund. **Publications:** (ed. and author of introduction) Johann G. Kohl, Kitchi-Gami: Life Among the Lake Superior Ojibway, 1985; Science Encounters the Indian: A Study of the Early Years of American Ethnology, 1820-1880, 1986; A Brief Historical Survey of the Expropriation of American Indian Remains, 1990; Contemplating Others: Cultural Contacts in Red and White America, 1990; Native American Communities in Wisconsin, 1600-1960: A Study of Tradition and Change, 1995. Contributor to books. Contributor of articles and reviews to journals. **Address:** Department of History, Ballantine Hall, Indiana University-Bloomington, Bloomington, IN 47405, U.S.A.

BIEK, David E. American, b. 1952. **Genres:** Horticulture. **Career:** Tacoma Public Library, Tacoma, WA, librarian and library manager, 1976-. **Publications:** Mushrooms of Northern California, 1984; Flora of Mount Rainier National Park, 2000. **Address:** Tacoma Public Library, 1102 Tacoma Ave. S., Tacoma, WA 98402, U.S.A. **Online address:** biek@popserv.wolfenet.com

BIEL, Steven. American, b. 1960. **Genres:** History. **Career:** Writer, historian, and teacher. Harvard University, Cambridge, MA, director of studies and lecturer in history and literature, 1990-93, 1998-, preceptor, expository writing, 1994-96; Brandeis University, Waltham, MA, lecturer, 1997-98. **Publications:** Independent Intellectuals in the United States, 1910-1945, 1992; Down with the Old Canoe: A Cultural History of the Titanic Disaster, 1996; Titanica: The Disaster of the Century in Poetry, Prose, and Song, 1998; American Disasters, 2001. Contributor to periodicals. **Address:** 23 Hancock St, Winchester, MA 01890, U.S.A. **Online address:** biel@fas.harvard.edu

BIELSKI, Alison (Joy Prosser). British, b. 1925. **Genres:** Poetry, Mythology/Folklore, Local history/Rural topics. **Career:** Self-employed writer and retired lectr. Formerly, Hon. Joint Secretary, Yr Academi Gymreig, English Language Section. **Publications:** Twentieth-Century Flood, 1964; Across the Burning Sand; The Story of the Welsh Dragon, 1969; Flower Legends of Wales, 1972; Chwedlau'r Cymry am Flodau, 1973; Eve, 1973; Shapes and Colours, 1973; Zodiac Poems, 1973; Mermaid Poems, 1974; Flower Legends of the Wye Valley, 1974; The Lovetree, 1974; Seth, 1980; Tales and Traditions of Tenby, 1981; Eagles, 1983; The Story of St. Mellons, 1985; That Crimson Flame: Selected Poems, 1996. **Address:** 92 Clifton Rd., Paignton, Devon TQ3 3LD, England.

BIEMAN, Elizabeth. Canadian, b. 1923. **Genres:** Poetry, Literary criticism and history, Writing/Journalism, Autobiography/Memoirs. **Career:** Ottawa Journal, Canada, reporter, 1944-46; University of Western Ontario, London, instructor to professor, 1966-88, professor emeritus, 1988-; writer. **Publications:** Plato Baptized: Towards the Interpretation of Spenser's Mimetic Fictions, 1988; William Shakespeare: The Romances, 1990. Contributor of articles and reviews to periodicals. **Address:** 250 Sydenham St Apt 205, London, ON, Canada N6A 5S1. **Online address:** ebieman@sympatico.ca

BIEN, Peter A. American, b. 1930. **Genres:** Language/Linguistics, Literary criticism and history, Translations. **Career:** Dartmouth College, Hanover, NH, professor of English, 1961-97, professor emeritus, 1997-. **Publications:**

L.P. Hartley, 1963; Constantine Cavafy, 1964; Kazantzakis and the Linguistic Revolution in Greek Literature, 1972; (ed. with E. Keeley) Modern Greek Writers, 1972; (with J. Rassias and C. Bien) Demotic Greek, 1972; Nikos Kazantzakis, 1972; (with N. Stangos) Yannis Ritsos: Selected Poems, 1974; (trans.) S. Myrivilis, Life in the Tomb, 1977, rev. ed., 2004; Antithesi kai synthesi sti poiisi tou Yanni Ritsou, 1980; (with J. Rassias, C. Bien and C. Alexiou) Demotic Greek II: O Iptamenos Thalamos, 1982; Three Generations of Greek Writers: Introductions to Cavafy, Kazantzakis, Ritsos, 1983; Tempted by Happiness: Kazantzakis' Post-Christian Christ, 1984; Kazantzakis: Politics of the Spirit, 1989; Nikos Kazantzakis, Novelist, 1989; Words, Wordlessness, and the Word, 1992; (with D.J.N. Middleton) God's Struggler: Religion in the Writings of Nikos Kazantzakis, 1996; (with C. Fager) In Stillness There Is Fullness, 2000; On Retiring to Kendal (and Beyond), 2003; (with P. Constantine, E. Keeley, and K. Van Dyck) A Century of Greek Poetry 1900-2000, 2004; (with D. Gondicas, J. Rassias, A. Karanika, and C. Yiannakou-Bien) Greek Today, 2004. TRANSLATOR (all by N. Kazantzakis): The Last Temptation of Christ, 1960; Saint Francis, 1962; Report to Greco, 1965. **Address:** 80 Lyme Rd #171, Hanover, NH 03755, U.S.A. **Online address:** peter.bien@dartmouth.edu

BIEN, Thomas (H.). (born United States), b. 1953. **Genres:** Psychology. **Career:** United Methodist minister, 1978-86; Veterans Administration Medical Center, Albuquerque, NM, clinical trainee, 1987; private practice of psychology, 1988-92; Health Psychology Associates, postdoctoral intern, 1992-93; Samaritan Counseling Center, psychotherapist, 1993-94; Health Psychology Associates, clinical psychologist, 1994-96; private practice of clinical psychology, Albuquerque, NM, 1996-. Veterans Administration Medical Center, therapist, 1993-94. Teacher of classes at University of New Mexico, 1988-90, 1993-94, and Albuquerque Technical-Vocational Institute, beginning 1992; presenter of seminars. **Publications:** (with Beverly Bien) Mindful Recovery: A Spiritual Path to Healing from Addiction, 2002; (with Beverly Bien) Finding the Center Within: The Healing Way of Mindfulness Meditation, 2003. Contributor to books. **Address:** 12517 Conejo N.E., N.E. Suite 205, Albuquerque, NM 87123, U.S.A.

BIENES, Nicholas Peter. Also writes as Judith Gould. American (born Austria), b. 1952. **Genres:** Novels, Documentaries/Reportage. **Publications:** NOVELS AS JUDITH GOULD (with W.R. Gallaher, Jr.): Sins, 1982; Love-Makers, 1986; Dazzle, 1989; Never Too Rich, 1990; Texas Born, 1992; Forever, 1992; Too Damn Rich, 1995; Second Love, 1998; Till the End of Time, 1998; Rapsody, 1999; Time to Say Good-Bye, 2000. **Address:** Judith Gould, c/o Dutton Publicity, 375 Hudson St., New York, NY 10014, U.S.A.

BIENVENU, Marcelle. American, b. 1945. **Genres:** Food and Wine. **Career:** Times-Picayune, New Orleans, LA, feature writer, 1967-71; Time-Life Books, NYC, researcher and consultant, beginning in 1971; Chez Marcelle, near Lafayette, LA, owner and operator, 1981-84; Times-Picayune, author of the weekly column "Cooking Creole," 1984-. Times of Acadiana, food writer 1986-. Emeril's Restaurant, cookbook writer, 1993-; catering director and public relations consultant for restaurants. Acadian Memorial Foundation, member, 1993-. **Publications:** (ed.) The Picayune's Creole Cook Book, 1987; Who's Your Mama, Are You Catholic, and Can You Make a Roux? (cookbook), 1991; Cajun Cooking for Beginners, 1994; (with E. Lagasse) Louisiana Real and Rustic, 1996. Contributor to books, magazines and newspapers. **Address:** 1056 Mimosa Lane, St. Martinville, LA 70582, U.S.A.

BIERDS, Linda. American, b. 1945. **Genres:** Poetry. **Career:** Credit Northwest Corporation, Seattle, WA, editor, 1971-80; University of Washington, Seattle, information specialist and part-time lecturer, 1981-91, full-time lecturer in English, 1991-95, associate professor of English, 1995-98, professor of English, 1998-; writer. **Publications:** POETRY: Snaring the Flightless Birds (chapbook), 1982; Flights of the Harvest-Mare, 1985; Off the Aleutian Chain (chapbook), 1985; The Stillness, the Dancing, 1988; Heart and Perimeter, 1991; Companions for the Slow Rowing, 1991; The Ghost Trio, 1994; The Profile Makers, 1997; The Seconds, 2002. Work represented in anthologies. Contributor to periodicals. **Address:** Department of English, Box 354330, University of Washington, Seattle, WA 98195, U.S.A. **Online address:** lbierds@u.washington.edu

BIERHORST, John. American, b. 1936. **Genres:** Cultural/Ethnic topics, Language/Linguistics, Mythology/Folklore, Natural history. **Publications:** The Fire Plume, 1969; The Ring in the Prairie, 1970; In the Trail of the Wind, 1971; Four Masterworks of American Indian Literature, 1974; Songs of the Chippewa, 1974; Black Rainbow, 1976; The Red Swan, 1976; The Girl Who Married a Ghost and Other Tales from the North American Indian, 1978; A Cry from the Earth, 1979; The Whistling Skeleton, 1982; The Sacred Path, 1983; The Hungry Woman, 1984; Spirit Child, 1984; The

Mythology of North America, 1985; Cantares Mexicanos, 1985; A Nahuatl-English Dictionary with a Concordance to the Cantares Mexicanos, 1985; The Monkey's Haircut and Other Stories Told by the Maya, 1986; Doctor Coyote, 1987; The Naked Bear, 1987; The Mythology of South America, 1988; The Mythology of Mexico and Central America, 1990; History and Mythology of the Aztecs, 1992; Codex Chimalpopoca, 1992; Lightning inside You and Other Native American Riddles, 1992; The Woman Who Fell from the Sky, 1993; On the Road of Stars, 1994; The Way of the Earth, 1994; The White Deer and Other Stories Told by the Lenape, 1995; Mythology of the Lenape, 1995; The Ashokan Catskills, 1995; The Dancing Fox, 1997; The Deetkatoo, 1998; The People with Five Fingers, 2000; (assoc. ed.) The Norton Anthology of World Literature, 2001; Is My Friend at Home?, 2001; Latin American Folktales, 2002. **Address:** PO Box 10, West Shokan, NY 12494, U.S.A.

BIERINGER, R(eimund). American, b. 1957. **Genres:** Theology/Religion. **Career:** Catholic University of Louvain, Louvain, Belgium, professor of theology, 1990-. **Publications:** (with J. Lambrecht) Studies on 2 Corinthians, 1994; (editor) The Corinthian Correspondence, 1996; (editor with D. Pollefeyt and F. Vanneuville) Anti-Judaism and the Fourth Gospel, 2001; (editor, with V. Koperski and B. Lataire) Resurrection in the New Testament: Festschrift J. Lambrecht, 2002; (with Mary Elsbernd) When Love Is Not Enough: A Theo-ethic of Justice, 2002. **Address:** Faculty of Theology, Catholic University of Louvaine, Sint Michielsstraat 6, 3000 Louvain, Belgium. **Online address:** reimund.bieringer@theo.kuleuven.ac.be

BIERMANN, Pieke. German, b. 1950. **Genres:** Novels, Mystery/Crime/Suspense, Novellas/Short stories, Documentaries/Reportage, Essays, Humor/Satire, Translations. **Career:** Professional translator from Italian and English into German. Radio writer, journalist and novelist. **Publications:** NOVELS: Potsdamer Ableben, 1987; Violetta, 1990, trans. by I. Rieder and J. Hannum, 1996; Herzrasen, 1993; Vier, Fuenf, Sechs, 1997. STORIES: Berlin, Kabbala, 1997; Herta & Doris, 2002. Work represented in anthologies. Contributor of stories and articles to magazines. **Address:** PF 151410, 10676 Berlin, Germany. **Online address:** pieke.biermann@t-online.de

BIESEL, David B. American, b. 1931. **Genres:** Sports/Fitness, Reference. **Career:** Worked as a sports writer in Washington, DC; American Institute of Physics, NYC, manager of editorial department, 1962-69; R.R. Bowker, NYC, managing editor to editor of reference books, 1969-73; Macmillan Publishing Co. Inc., NYC, senior editor in Professional and Reference Book Division, 1973-82; Elsevier Science Publishing Co., NYC, senior editor, 1982-84; R.R. Bowker, editor in chief of Book Division, 1984-86; M.E. Sharpe Inc., Armonk, NY, vice-president and editorial director, 1986-88; St. Johann Press, Haworth, NJ, president, 1988-. Scarecrow Press Inc., director of Association Publishing Program, 1991-98, Series Editor, American Sports History, 1992-. **Publications:** Can You Name That Team? A Guide to Professional Baseball, Football, Soccer, Hockey, and Basketball Teams and Leagues, 1991. **Address:** St. Johann Press, 315 Schraalenburgh Rd, Haworth, NJ 07641, U.S.A.

BIGELOW, Brian J(ohn). Canadian, b. 1947. **Genres:** Criminology/True Crime, Psychology. **Career:** Laurentian University, Sudbury, Ontario, member of psychology faculty. **Publications:** Learning the Rules, 1996. **Address:** Department of Psychology, Laurentian University, Ramsey Lake Rd, Sudbury, ON, Canada P3E 2C6. **Online address:** bbigelow@Nickel.laurentian.ca

BIGER, Gideon. Israeli, b. 1945. **Genres:** History, Area studies, Geography, Politics/Government. **Career:** Tel Aviv University, Tel Aviv, Israel, lecturer, 1979-83, senior lecturer, 1983-96, head of department, 1987-90, 1998-, associate professor, 1996-. **Publications:** Crown Colony or National Homeland?, 1983; (ed. with A.R. Baker) Ideology and Landscape in Historical Perspective: Essays on the Meanings of Some Places in the Past, 1992; An Empire in the Holy Land-Historical Geography of the British Administration in Palestine, 1994; The Encyclopedia of International Boundaries, 1995. **Address:** Department of Geography, Tel Aviv University, 61390 Tel Aviv, Israel. **Online address:** biger@post.tau.ac.il

BIGGS, Chester M(axwell), Jr. American, b. 1921. **Genres:** Military/Defense/Arms control, Autobiography/Memoirs. **Career:** U.S. Marine Corps, career marine, 1939-59, prisoner of war, 1941-45, served in Korea and China, retired as master sergeant; teacher at elementary schools in Oklahoma City, OK, 1963-64, and Wilmington, NC, 1964-69; Southeastern Community College, Whiteville, NC, director of audiovisual and printing services, 1969-86; retired, 1986. Public speaker; Marine Corps Historical Foundation, member. **Publications:** A Boot Marine (monograph), 1993; Behind the

Barbed Wire: Memoir of a World War II U.S. Marine, 1995; The U.S. Marines in North China, 1894-1942, 2002. Contributor to military magazines and local periodicals. **Address:** 8537 Independence Dr, Hope Mills, NC 28348, U.S.A.

BIGGS, John Burville. Australian, b. 1934. **Genres:** Education, Psychology. **Career:** Research Officer, National Foundation for Education Research, U.K., 1958-62; Lecturer in Psychology, University of New England, 1962-66; Education Research Officer, Monash University, 1966-69; Professor of Educational Psychology, University of Alberta, 1969-73; Professor of Education, University of Newcastle, 1973-87; Professor of Education, University of Hong Kong, 1987-95. **Publications:** Anxiety and Primary Mathematics, 1963; Mathematics and the Conditions of Learning, 1967; Information and Human Learning, 1972; (with K. Collis) Evaluating the Quality of Learning, 1982; Student Approaches to Learning and Studying, 1987; (with P. Moore) The Process of Learning, 1993; Teaching for Quality Learning at University, 1999. **Address:** 48 Ian St, Eleebana, NSW 2280, Australia.

BIGGS, Mary. American, b. 1944. **Genres:** Poetry, Education, Librarianship. **Career:** University of Evansville, Evansville, IN, humanities librarian, 1977-79; University of Chicago, Chicago, IL, assistant professor, 1982-87; Columbia University, New York City, assistant professor, 1987-89; Mercy College, Dobbs Ferry, NY, director of libraries, 1989-92; College of New Jersey, Trenton, dean of library and information services, 1992-. **Publications:** (ed.) Publishers and Librarians, 1984; (ed. with Morty Sklar) Editor's Choice: Fiction, Poetry, and Art from the U.S. Small Press, 1987; (ed. with Morty Sklar) Men and Women: Together and Alone (poems), 1988; A Gift That Cannot Be Refused: The Writing and Publishing of Contemporary American Poetry, 1990; Women's Words: The Columbia Book of Quotations by Women, 1996; (co-ed.) Columbia World of Quotations, 1996. Contributor to library and education journals. **Address:** Dept of English, College of New Jersey, 2000 Pennington Rd, PO Box 7718, Ewing, NJ 08628-0718, U.S.A.

BIGHAM, Darrel E. American, b. 1942. **Genres:** Local history/Rural topics. **Career:** University of Southern Indiana, Evansville, assistant professor, 1970-75, associate professor, 1975-81, professor of history, 1981-, director of Historic Southern Indiana, 1986-. Indiana State University, Evansville, codirector of regional archives, 1972-74. **Publications:** Reflections on a Heritage: The German Americans in Southwestern Indiana, 1980; We Ask Only a Fair Trial: A History of the Black Community of Evansville, Indiana, 1987; An Evansville Album: Perspectives on a River City, 1812-1988, 1988; Indiana Resource Book, 1997; Towns and Villages of the Lower Ohio, 1998; Evansville, 1998; Images of America: Evansville, 1999; Images of America: Southern Indiana, 2000. Contributor to books on Indiana and Midwestern history. Contributor of articles and reviews to journals. **Address:** Department of History, University of Southern Indiana, 8600 University Blvd, Evansville, IN 47712, U.S.A. **Online address:** dbigham@usi.edu

BIGNELL, Jonathan (Charles). (born England), b. 1963. **Genres:** Film. **Career:** University of Reading, Reading, England, lecturer in English, 1989-99; Royal Holloway College, London, London, England, senior lecturer in media arts, 1999-2002; University of Reading, reader in television and film studies, 2002-. Member of British Film Institute and National Film Theater, 1989-, and Institute for Learning and Teaching, 2001-. **Publications:** Media Semiotics: An Introduction, 1997, 2nd edition, 2002; (editor) Writing and Cinema, 1999; Postmodern Media Culture, 2000; (editor, with S. Lacey and M. Macmurraugh-Kavanagh) British Television Drama: Past, Present, and Future, 2000; An Introduction to Television Studies, 2003; (with Andrew O'Day) Terry Nation, 2004; Beckett on Screen: The Television Plays, forthcoming. Contributor to books. **Address:** Centre for Television Drama Studies, England University of Reading, Bulmershe Ct. and Woodlands Ave, Earley, Reading RG6 1HY, England. **Online address:** j.bignell@reading.ac.uk

BIGSBY, C(hristopher) W(illiam) E(dgar). British, b. 1941. **Genres:** Novels, Literary criticism and history, Theatre. **Career:** University of Wales, Aberystwyth, lecturer in English and American literature, 1966-69; University of East Anglia, Norwich, reader, 1969-84, professor of American studies, 1984-. **Publications:** Confrontation and Commitment: Study of Contemporary American Drama, 1967; Albee, 1969; Dada and Surrealism, 1972; Approaches to Popular Culture, 1976; Tom Stoppard, 1976; The Second Black Renaissance: Essays in Black Literature, 1980; Joe Orton, 1982; Critical Introduction to Twentieth Century American Drama, 3 vols., 1982-85; David Mamet, 1985; Miller and Company, 1990; Modern American Drama: 1945-1990, 1992, rev. ed., 1945-2000, 2000; Hester (novel), 1994; Pearl (novel), 1995; Still Lives (novel), 1996; Beautiful Dreamer (novel), 2002; The Black American Writer, 2 vols., 1969; Superculture: The Impact of American

Popular Culture on Europe, 1974; Edward Albee, 1975; Contemporary English Drama, 1981; The Radical Imagination and the Liberal Tradition, 1982; Cultural Change in the United States since World War II, 1986; Plays by Susan Glaspell, 1987; File on Miller, 1988; The Portable Arthur Miller, 1995; The Cambridge Companion to Arthur Miller, 1998; The Cambridge History of the American Theatre, 3 vols., 1998-2000; Contemporary American Playwrights, 1999. **Address:** 3 Church Farm, Colney, Norwich, England. **Online address:** c.bigsby@uea.ac.uk

BIHLER, Penny. See **HARTER, Penny.**

BILBY, Joanne Stroud. American, b. 1927. **Genres:** Literary criticism and history. **Career:** University of Dallas, Dallas, TX, member of literature department, 1972-84, and psychology department, 1977-82; Dallas Institute of Humanities and Culture, Dallas, founding fellow and lecturer, 1981-, director of publications, 1981-. **Publications:** (ed with G. Thomas) Images of the Untouched, 1982; The Bonding of Will and Desire, 1994; (ed and contrib) The Olympians, 1995, reprinted, 1996. Executive editor of a series of translations of the works of Gaston Bachelard. **Address:** Dallas Institute of Humanities and Culture, 2719 Routh St., Dallas, TX 75201, U.S.A.

BILGRAMI, Akeel. Indian, b. 1950. **Genres:** Philosophy, Politics/Government, History, Cultural/Ethnic topics. **Career:** Columbia University, NYC, Professor of philosophy, 1995-; chairman, Philosophy Dept. **Publications:** Belief and Meaning: The Unity and Locality of Mental Content, Basil Blackwell, 1992; Self-Knowledge and Intentionality, Harvard University Press, 1997; Secularism, Modernity & Cultural Identity, Harvard Unversity Press, 1997. ed., Journal of Philosophy. **Address:** 719 Philosophy Hall, Columbia University, New York, NY 10027, U.S.A.

BILLETDOUX, Raphaele. French, b. 1951. **Genres:** Novels, Plays/Screenplays, Autobiography/Memoirs, Essays. **Career:** Novelist and screenwriter. Director of the film La Femme-enfant, with Klaus Kinski, 1979. **Publications:** NOVELS: Jeune fille en silence (title means: Silent Girl), 1971; L'ouverture des bras de l'homme (title means: The Man's Embrace), 1973; Prends garde a la douceur des choses (title means: Beware the Sweetness of Things), 1976; Lettre d'excuse (title means: Letter of Apology) 1981; Mes nuits sont plus belles que vos jours, 1985, trans. as Night without Day, 1987; Entrez et fermez la porte (title means: Come in and Close the Door), 1991; Melanie dans un vent terrible (title means: Melanie in a Terrible Wind), 1994; Chere madame ma fille cadette, 1997; Je fremis en le racontant (essay), 2000. OTHER: La Femme-enfant (screenplay; title means: The Woman-child), 1979. **Address:** c/o Editions Grasset, 61 Rue des St. Peres, 75006 Paris, France.

BILLIAS, George Athan. American, b. 1919. **Genres:** History. **Career:** Prof. emeritus, 1989, Professor of American History, since 1962, and Jacob & Frances Hiatt Professor of History, since 1983, Clark University, Worcester, Massachusetts Professor of American History, University of Maine, Orono, 1954-61. **Publications:** Massachusetts Land Bankers of 1740, 1959; General John Glover and His Marblehead Mariners, 1960; Elbridge Gerry: Founding Father and Republican Statesman, 1976; The Republican Synthesis Revisited: Essay in Honor of George Athan Billian, 1992. EDITOR & CONTRIBUTOR: George Washington's Generals, 1964; The American Revolution: How Revolutionary Was It?, 1965, 3rd ed. 1980; George Washington's Opponents, 1969; American Constitutionalism Abroad, 1990; George Washington's General and Opponents: Their Exploits and Leadership, 1994. EDITOR: Law and Authority in Colonial America, 1965; (with G.N. Grob) Interpretations of American History, 1967; The Federalists: Realists or Idealogues?, 1970; (with G.N. Grob) American History: Retrospect and Prospect, 1971; (with A. Vaughan) Perspectives on Early American History, 1973;. **Address:** History Dept, Clark University, Worcester, MA 01610, U.S.A.

BILLINGSLEY, (Kenneth) Lloyd. American (born Canada), b. 1949. **Genres:** Theology/Religion, Film. **Career:** Writer. Editorial director, Pacific Research Institute for Public Policy, Sacramento, CA. **Publications:** The Generation that Knew Not Josef: A Critique of Marxism and the Religious Left, 1985; The Absence of Tyranny: Recovering Freedom in Our Time, 1986; A Year for Life, 1986; Religion's Rebel Son: Fanaticism in Our Time, 1986; The Seductive Image: A Christian Critique of the World of Film, 1989; From Mainline to Sideline: The Social Witness of the National Council of Churches, 1991; (ed.) Voices on Choice: The Education Reform Debate, 1994 Hollywood Party: The Untold Story of How Communism Seduced the American Film Industry in the 1930s and 1940s, 1998. Contributor to periodicals. **Address:** Pacific Research Institute for Public Policy, 1414 K. Street Suite 200, Sacramento, CA 95814, U.S.A. **Online address:** kenneth.billingsley@gte.net

BILLINGTON, David P(erkins). American, b. 1927. **Genres:** Art/Art history, Engineering, History. **Career:** Roberts & Schaefer Co., New York, structural engineer, 1952-60; Princeton University, Princeton, NJ, visiting lecturer, 1958-60, associate professor, 1960-64, professor of civil engineering, 1964-96, Gordon Y.S. Wu Professor of Engineering, 1996-; consultant; writer. Institute for Advanced Studies, Princeton, Visitor, 1974-75, 1977-78; Cornell University, A.D. White Professor-at-Large, 1987-93. **Publications:** Thin Shell Concrete Structures, 1965, rev. ed., 1982; Robert Maillart's Bridges: The Art of Engineering, 1979; The Tower and the Bridge: The New Art of Structural Engineering, 1983; Robert Maillart and the Art of Reinforced Concrete, 1990; The Innovators: The Engineering Pioneers Who Made America Modern, 1996; Robert Maillart: Builder, Designer, and Artist, 1997; The Art of Structural Design: A Swiss Legacy, 2003. **Address:** Dept of Civil and Environmental Engineering, Princeton University, Princeton, NJ 08544, U.S.A.

BILLINGTON, James H(adley). American, b. 1929. **Genres:** Cultural/Ethnic topics. **Career:** Harvard University, Cambridge, MA, instructor, 1957-58, assistant professor of history, 1958-61, fellow of Russian Research Center, 1958-59; Princeton University, NJ, associate professor, 1962-64, professor of history, 1964-73; Woodrow Wilson International Center for Scholars, Washington, DC, director, 1973-87; Library of Congress, Washington, DC, Librarian of Congress, 1987-. Writer. Guest professor at universities and research institutions in the USSR; visiting research professor and universities in Europe and Asia. Host of Humanities Film Forum (television series), 1973-74; Decorated Chevalier 1995 and Comdr., 1991, Order of Arts and Letters of France; Woodrow Wilson Award Princeton U., 1992; Knight comdr.'s Cross of Order of Merit, Fed. Republic of Germany, 1996. **Publications:** Mikhailovsky and Russian Populism, 1958; The Icon and the Axe: An Interpretive History of Russian Culture, 1966; (Author of intro) The Horizon Book of the Arts of Russia, 1970; Fire in the Minds of Men: Origins of the Revolutionary Faith, 1980; Russian Transformed: Breakthrough to Hope, Moscow, August 1991, 1992. Virtue, Public and Private, edited with a foreword by Richard John Neuhaus, 1986. **Address:** Office of the Librarian, The Library of Congress, 101 Independence Ave., S.E., Washington, DC 20540-1000, U.S.A.

BILLINGTON, Rachel. British, b. 1942. **Genres:** Novels, Children's fiction. **Publications:** All Things Nice, 1969; The Big Dipper, 1970; Lilacs out of the Dead Land, 1971; Cock Robin, 1973; Beautiful, 1974; A Painted Devil, 1975; A Woman's Age, 1979; Occasion of Sin, 1982;The Garish Day, 1985; Loving Attitudes, 1988; Theo and Matilda, 1990; The Family Year (non-fiction), 1992; Bodily Harm, 1992; The Great Umbilical (non-fiction), 1994; Magic and Fate, 1996; Perfect Happiness (sequel to Emma), 1996; The Life of Jesus, 1996; Tiger Sky, 1998; The Life of St. Francis, 1999; A Woman's Life, 2002; The Space Between, 2004. FOR CHILDREN: Rosanna and the Wizard-Robot, 1981; The First Christmas, 1983; Star-Time, 1984; The First Easter, 1987; The First Miracles, 1990; Far Out!, 2002. **Address:** c/o David Higham Associates Ltd., 5-8 Lower John St, Golden Sq, London W1R 4HA, England.

BILLINGTON, Ray(mond John). British, b. 1930. **Genres:** Philosophy, Theology/Religion. **Career:** Methodist minister, 1952-68. University of the West of England (formerly Bristol Polytechnic), principal lecturer in humanities, 1972-95; Open University, lecturer in philosophy, 1972-; Universities of Oxford and Cardiff, part-time lecturer, 1995-. **Publications:** The Basis of Pacifist Conviction, 1961; The Teaching of Worship, 1962; Concerning Worship, 1963, rev. ed. (with S. Hopkinson and J. Foster), 1967; (with T.M. Morrow) Worship and Preaching, 1967; The Liturgical Movement and Methodism, 1969; The Christian Outsider, 1971; A New Christian Reader, 1974; Living Philosophy, 1988, 3rd ed., 2003; East of Existentialism, 1990; Understanding Eastern Philosophy, 1997; Religion without God, 2001. **Address:** Springfield, Tintern, Chepstow NP16 6TH, England. **Online address:** philosophylive@aol.com

BILLSON, Anne. British, b. 1954. **Genres:** Novels, Film. **Career:** Time Out, Ltd., London, England, literary editor, 1985-86; Sunday Correspondent, London, film critic, 1989-90; New Statesman & Society, London, film critic, 1991-92; Sunday Telegraph, London, film critic, 1992-. **Publications:** Screen Lovers, 1988; Dream Demon, 1989; My Name Is Michael Caine: A Life in Film, 1991; Suckers (novel), 1993; Stiff Lips (novel), 1996; The Thing, 1997. **Address:** c/o Antony Harwood, Gillon Aitken Associates Ltd, 29 Fernshaw Rd, London SW10 0TG, England.

BILLSON, Janet Mancini. American (born Canada), b. 1941. **Genres:** Poetry, Sociology, Urban studies, Women's studies and issues. **Career:** Rhode Island College, Providence, professor of sociology and women's stud-

ies, 1973-91, acting associate dean of students and director of student life, 1984, assistant dean of faculty of arts and sciences, 198486; American Sociological Association, Washington, DC, assistant executive officer and director of the academic and professional affairs program, 1991-95; George Washington University, Washington, DC, adjunct professor of sociology and women's studies, 1993-95, professor of sociology, 1995-97 adjunct professor of sociology, 1998-. Director of Group Dimensions Research, Barrington, RI. **Publications:** Strategic Styles: Coping in the Inner City, 1980; (with R. Majors) Cool Pose: Dilemmas of Black Manhood in America, 1992; Keepers of the Culture: The Power of Tradition in Women's Lives, 1995; Pathways to Manhood: Young Black Males Struggle for Identity, 1996; The Power of Focus Groups for Social Policy and Research, 2000; (with K.M. Ries) Their Powerful Spirit: Inuit Women, a Century of Change, 2001. Work represented in anthologies. **Address:** 300 Narragansett Ave, Barrington, RI 02806-1338, U.S.A. **Online address:** jbillson@aol.com

BINA, Cyrus. American, b. 1946. **Genres:** Poetry, Economics, Philosophy. **Career:** Teacher of mathematics, social sciences, and English at a high school in Tehran, Iran, 1965-66; Iranian Treasury Department, Plan and Budget Organization, Tehran, foreign exchange analyst, 1966-68; Division of Social Security and Insurance, Tehran, chief auditor, 1969-71; Ball State University, Muncie, IN, instructor in economics, 1972-74; American University, Washington, DC, instructor in economics, 1977-79; Towson State University, Towson, MD, instructor in economics, 1979-80; EMAY Corp., McLean, VA, senior economist, 1980-81; Washington International College, Washington, DC, associate professor of economics and statistics, 1981-82; American University, Center for Technology and Administration, instructor, 1982; Olivet College, Olivet, MI, professor of economics and director of Economics Program, 1982-87; Providence College, Providence, RI, professor of economics, 1987-90; Harvard University, Cambridge, MA, faculty associate and visiting scholar at Center for Middle Eastern Studies, 1989-91, research associate, 1991-96; University of Redlands, Whitehead College, lead faculty for theses, honors, and research projects, and Director of the Center of Unified, Global, and Applied Research, 1996-98; California State University, Fullerton, School of Business and Economics, 1999-2000; University of Minnesota, professor of economics and management, 2000-. **Publications:** Accounting Handbook for Community Development, 1980; The Economics of the Oil Crisis, 1985; (ed. with H. Zangeneh and contrib.) Modern Capitalism and Islamic Ideology in Iran, 1992; (ed. with L. Clements and C. Davis) Beyond Survival: Wage Labor in the Late Twentieth Century, 1996; The Sun and the Earth (poetry), 1998. Contributor of articles and reviews to economic, political studies, and sociology journals. **Address:** Department of Economics, 206 Camden, University of Minnesota-Morris, 600 E 4th St, Morris, MN 56267, U.S.A. **Online address:** binac@mrs.umn.edu

BINCHY, Maeve. Irish, b. 1940. **Genres:** Novels, Novellas/Short stories. **Career:** Columnist, Irish Times, Dublin, 1968-. History and French teacher, Pembroke School, Dublin, 1961-68. **Publications:** End of Term (play), 1976; My First Book (journalism), 1976; The Central Line (short stories), 1978; The Half-Promised Land (play), 1979; Deeply Regretted By (screenplay), 1979; Maeve's Diary (journalism), 1979; Ireland of the Welcomes (screenplay), 1980; Victoria Line (short stories), 1980; Dublin Four (short stories), 1982; Light a Penny Candle, 1982; London Transports (short stories), 1983; The Lilac Bus (short stories), 1984; Echoes, 1985; Firefly Summer, 1987; Silver Wedding, 1989; Circle of Friends, 1990; The Copper Beech, 1992; The Glass Lake, 1994; This Year It Will Be Different, 1996; Evening Class, 1997; The Return Journey, 1998; Tara Road, 1999; Scarlet Feather, 2001; Quentins, 2002. **Address:** Dalkey, Dublin, Ireland.

BINDING, Paul. British, b. 1943. **Genres:** Novels, Literary criticism and history. **Career:** Has worked as university lecturer in Sweden, Italy and the United States. Oxford University Press, editor; New Statesman, deputy literary editor; freelance writer, 1990-. **Publications:** NONFICTION: Robert Louis Stevenson (juvenile biography), 1974; Separate Country: A Literary Journey Through the American South, 1979, 2nd ed, 1988; (ed.) Robert Louis Stevenson, Weir of Hermiston, and Other Stories, 1979; Lorca: The Gay Imagination, 1985; St. Martin's Ride (autobiography), 1990; The Still Moment: Eudora Welty: Portrait of a Writer, 1994; An Endless Quiet Valley: A Reappraisal of John Masefield, 1998. NOVELS: Harmonica's Bride Groom, 1984; Kingfisher Weather, 1990. OTHER: (with J. Horder) Dreams and Speculations (poetry). **Address:** 56 Mill St., Ludlow, Shropshire SY8 1BB, England.

BINDING, Tim. American. **Genres:** Novels. **Career:** Writer. Former editorial director of Penguin. **Publications:** NOVELS: In the Kingdom of Air, 1993; A Perfect Execution, 1996. **Address:** c/o Doubleday, 1540 Broadway, New York, NY 10036, U.S.A.

BINFORD, Lewis R(oberts). American, b. 1930. **Genres:** Archaeology/ Antiquities. **Career:** University of Michigan, Ann Arbor, research associate in archaeology, 1958-59, curator of Museum of Anthropology, 1960-61; University of Chicago, Chicago, Ill., assistant professor of anthropology, 1961-65; University of California, Santa Barbara, assistant professor of anthropology, 1965-66; University of California, Los Angeles, associate professor of anthropology, 1966-70; University of New Mexico, Albuquerque, associate professor of anthropology, beginning in 1970; Southern Methodist University, Dallas, associate professor of anthropology. Consultant to State of Michigan. **Publications:** Archaeology at Hatchery West, 1970; An Archaeological Perspective, 1972; Nunamiut Ethnoarchaeology, 1978; Bones: Ancient Men and Modern Myths, 1981; (with J.F. Cherry and R. Torrence) In Pursuit of the Past: Decoding the Archaeological Record, 1983; Faunal Remains From Klasies River Mouth (monograph), 1984; Debating Archaeology, 1989; Cultural Diversity Among Aboriginal Cultures of Coastal Virginia and North Carolina, 1991; Conversations with Lewis R. Binford, 1998; Constructing Frames of Reference, 2001. EDITOR: For Theory Building in Archaeology: Essays on Faunal Remains, Aquatic Resources, Spatial Analysis, and Systematic Modelling, 1977; Working at Archaeology, 1983. **Address:** Department of Anthropology, Univerity of New Mexico, Albuquerque, NM 87131, U.S.A.

BING, Leon. American, b. 1937. **Genres:** Adult non-fiction. **Career:** Fashion model; free-lance journalist; writer. **Publications:** Do or Die, 1991; Smoked, 1993; Wrongful Death, 1997. Contributor to periodicals.

BINGHAM, Charlotte. British, b. 1942. **Genres:** Novels, Plays/Screenplays, Autobiography/Memoirs, Biography. **Career:** Screen, play, and television writer. **Publications:** Coronet among the Weeds (autobiography), 1963; Coronet among the Grass (autobiography, vol. 2), 1972. WITH T. BRADY: Victoria (novel), 1972; Rose's Story (novel), 1972; Victoria and Company, 1974; No Honestly (biography), 1975. PLAY: I Wish, I Wish, 1987. TELEVISION, WITH T. BRADY: Upstairs, Downstairs; Nanny; Forever Green; Take Three Girls; No Honestly; Yes Honestly; Love with a Perfect Stranger; Magic Moments; Seventh Raven; Losing Connor; Oh Madeleine. NOVELS: Lucinda, 1965; Belgravia, 1984; Country Life, 1985; At Home, 1986; To Hear a Nightingale, 1988; The Business, 1989; In Sunshine or in Shadow, 1991; Stardust, 1993; Nanny, 1993; By Invitation Only, 1993; Change of Heart, 1994; Debutantes, 1995; The Nightingale Sings, 1996; Grand Affair, 1997; Love Song, 1998; The Kissing Garden, 1999. **Address:** c/o United Authors, Garden Studios 11/15, Betterton St, London WC2 9BP, England.

BINGHAM, June Rossbach. American, b. 1919. **Genres:** Plays/Screenplays, Medicine/Health, Biography. **Career:** Member of the Board, Member, Riverdale Mental Health Association; former trustee, Barnard College, NYC; founder of the T.L.C. (Trained Liaison Comforter) volunteer program at Columbia, Presbyterian Hospital in NYC. **Publications:** Do Cows Have Neuroses?, 1949; Do Babies Have Worries?, 1951; Do Teenagers Have Wisdom?, 1953; (with F. Redlich) The Inside Story: Psychiatry in Everyday Life, 1953; Courage to Change: An Introduction to the Life and Thought of Reinhold Niebuhr, 1961, 1992; U Thant: The Search for Peace, 1966; (with N. Tamarkin) The Pursuit of Health, 1985; Triangles (play), 1986; You and the I.C.U., 1991; Squanto and Love (musical), 1992; Young Roosevelts (musical), 1993; The Other Lincoln (musical), 1995; Eleanor and Alice (play), 1996. **Address:** 5000 Independence Ave, Bronx, NY 10471, U.S.A.

BINGHAM, Sallie. (Sarah (Montague) Bingham). American, b. 1937. **Genres:** Novels, Novellas/Short stories, Plays/Screenplays, Autobiography/ Memoirs. **Career:** Writer. Teacher of English and creative writing at University of Louisville and the College of Santa Fe. Founder, Kentucky Foundation for Women, The American Voice, and Santa Fe Stages. Founder, Sallie Bingham Archive for Women's Papers, Perkins Library, Duke University, Durham, NC, and Women's Project and Productions, New York, NY. Former director of the National Book Critics Circle. **Publications:** NOVELS: After Such Knowledge, 1960; Small Victories, 1992; Upstate, 1993; Matron of Honor, 1994; Straight Man, 1996. STORIES: The Touching Hand, and Six Short Stories, 1967; The Way It Is Now, 1972; Transgressions, 2002. PLAYS: Milk of Paradise, 1980; Paducah, 1985; In the Yurt; The Act; Couvade; No Time; Family; Country Boy. OTHER: Passion and Prejudice: A Family Memoir, 1989. Contributor to books and anthologies. Contributor of fiction to periodicals. **Address:** 369 Montezuma #316, Santa Fe, NM 87501, U.S.A. **Online address:** salliebingham@earthlink.net

BINION, Rudolph. American, b. 1927. **Genres:** History, Intellectual history, Literary criticism and history. **Career:** Leff Professor of History, Brandeis University, Waltham, MA, 1967-. Instructor in History, Rutgers University, NJ, 1955-56; Instructor in Humanities, Massachusetts Institute of Technol-

ogy, Cambridge, 1956-59; Assistant Professor of History 1959-63, and Associate Professor of History 1963-67, Columbia University, NYC. **Publications:** Defeated Leaders, 1960; Frau Lou, 1968; Hitler among the Germans, 1976; Soundings, 1981; Introduction à la psychohistoire, 1982; After Christianity, 1986; Love beyond Death, 1993; Freüd uber Aggression und Krieg, 1994; Sounding the Classics, 1997. **Address:** Brandeis University, Dept of History, PO Box 9110, Waltham, MA 02454, U.S.A. **Online address:** binion@brandeis.edu

BINNEMA, Theodore. Canadian, b. 1963. **Genres:** Area studies. **Career:** University of Northern British Columbia, Prince George, assistant professor, 2000-. **Publications:** (ed., with G. Eus and R.C. Macleod) From Rupert's Land to Canada, 2001; Common and Contested Ground: A Human and Environmental History of the Northwestern Plains, 2001. Contributor to periodicals. **Address:** University of Northern British Columbia, 3333 University Way, Prince George, BC, Canada V2N 4Z9. **Online address:** binnemat@unbc.ca

BINNS, Michael Ferrers Elliott. British, b. 1923. **Genres:** Theology/ Religion. **Career:** Charity Consultant, since 1983. Assistant Secretary to the Church Assembly 1949-63, Legal Secretary, 1963-70, and Assistant Secretary to the General Synod, 1970-76; Coordinator, Chiswick Family Rescue, 1978-80; Liaison Worker, Brixton Circle Projects, 1981-83. **Publications:** The Layman in Church Government, 1956; Guide to the Pastoral Measure, 1968; The Layman and His Church, 1970; North Downs Church, 1983; Realisation, 1993; Finding through War, 1995. **Address:** Quest Cottage, High St., N. Cadbury, Yeovil, Somerset BA22 7DH, England.

BINSKI, Paul. British, b. 1956. **Genres:** Art/Art history. **Career:** Yale University, New Haven, CT, assistant professor of art history, 1988-91; Victoria University of Manchester, Manchester, England, lecturer in art history, 1991-95; Cambridge University, lecturer in art history and fellow of Caius College, 1995-. **Publications:** The Painted Chamber at Westminster, 1986; Painters, 1991; Westminster Abbey and the Plantagenets, 1995; Medieval Death, Ritual, and Representation, 1996. Co-editor of an exhibition catalog. **Address:** Gonville and Caius College, Cambridge University, Cambridge CB2 1TA, England.

BINZEN, Peter (Husted). American, b. 1922. **Genres:** Writing/Journalism. **Career:** United Press International, New York City, reporter, 1947; Passaic Herald-News, Passaic, NJ, reporter, 1947-50; Philadelphia Bulletin, Philadelphia, PA, reporter and editor, 1951-82; Philadelphia Inquirer, Philadelphia, reporter, 1982-86, business columnist, 1986-. Military service: U.S. Army, 1943-45; received Bronze Star. **Publications:** Whitetown, U.S. A., Random House, 1970. (With Joseph R. Daughen) The Wreck of the Penn Central, Little, Brown, 1971. (With Daughen) The Cop Who Would Be King: The Honorable Frank Rizzo, Little, Brown, 1977. **Address:** Philadelphia Inquirer, 400 North Broad St, Philadelphia, PA 19101, U.S.A.

BIRCH, Anthony Harold. British/Canadian, b. 1924. **Genres:** Politics/ Government. **Career:** Lecturer, and Sr. Lecturer in Government, Manchester University, 1947-61; Professor of Political Studies, University of Hull, 1961-70; Professor of Political Science, University of Exeter, 1970-77. University of Victoria, BC, Professor, 1977-89, Professor Emeritus of Political Science, 1989-. **Publications:** Federalism. Finance and Social Legislation, 1955; Small-Town Politics, 1959; Representative and Responsible Government, 1964; The British System of Government, 1967, 10th ed., 1998; Representation, 1971; Political Integration and Disintegration in the British Isles, 1977; Nationalism and National Integration, 1989; The Concepts and Theories of Modern Democracy, 1993, 2nd ed., 2001. **Address:** 1901 Fairfield Rd, Victoria, BC, Canada V8S 1H2.

BIRCHMORE, Daniel A. American, b. 1951. **Genres:** Children's fiction. **Career:** Vanderbilt University Hospital, residency in internal medicine, 1976-79; University of Virginia Hospital, fellowship in rheumatology, 1979-81; private practice in rheumatology, Athens, GA, 1981-90; U.S. Veterans Hospital, Elsmere, DE, chief of division of rheumatology, 1990-97; U.S. Veterans Hospital, Nashville, TN, physician, 1997-. **Publications:** The Rock, 1996; Harry, the Happy Snake of Happy Hollow, 1996; The Reluctant Santa, or, Christmas Has Been Cancelled!, 1996; The White Curtain, 1996.

BIRD, Dennis Leslie. Also writes as John Noel. British, b. 1930. **Genres:** Public/Social administration, Sports/Fitness. **Career:** Course Director, Civil Service College, 1973-91; Contributor, Skating Magazine (USA), 1955-90, and Skating News, 1988-95. Historian, National Skating Association of Great Britain, 1977-. Monthly columnist as John Noel, Skating World, London, 1948-73; Joined R.A.F. 1949, retired as squadron leader in 1968; skating correspondent, The Observer, London, 1959-63, and The Times, London, 1959-78; Principal, Urban Program Division, Home Office, London, 1968-73; Contributor, Ice and Roller Skate monthly, London, 1973-86. **Publications:** (as John Noel) Figure Skating for Beginners, 1964; 1968 United States Olympic Book: Artistry on Ice, 1968; Our Skating Heritage, 1979; Know the Game: Ice Skating, 1985; Management in Government: A History of the Civil Service College, 1970-1995, 1995; (with T.M.A. Webb) Shoreham Airport Sussex, 1996, 2nd ed., 1999; More Tails of the Fifties: A Penguin in the Eyrie, 1998; (with R. Hopkins and R.J. Southway) The Schoolgirls' Own Library 1922-1963, 2001; Mixed Moss: Arthur Ransome the Yachtsman, 2001; The Independent: Arnold Gerschwiler, Inspired Ice-Skating Coach, 2003. **Address:** 37 The Avenue, Shoreham-by-Sea, Sussex BN43 5GJ, England.

BIRD, Richard. Canadian, b. 1938. **Genres:** Economics. **Career:** With Harvard University, Cambridge, MA, 1961-68; Professor of Economics Emeritus, and Director, International Tax Program, University of Toronto (Associate Professor, 1968-70; Director, Institute of Policy Analysis, 1980-85; Professor). Chief of tax policy div., International Monetary Fund, 1972-74. **Publications:** (co-author) Financing Urban Development in Mexico City, 1967; Taxation and Development: Lessons from Colombian Experience, 1970; The Growth of Government Spending in Canada, 1970; Taxing Agricultural Land in Developing Countries, 1974; Charging for Public Services, 1976; (with E. Slack) Residential Property Tax Relief in Ontario, 1978; Financing Canadian Government, 1979; (with M.W. Bucovetsky and D.K. Foot) The Growth of Public Employment in Canada, 1979; Taxing Corporations, 1980; Tax Incentives for Investment, 1980; (with others) Industrial Policy in Ontario, 1985; Federal Finance in Comparative Perspective, 1986; (with R.A. and P.B. Musgrave) Public Finance in Theory and Practice, 1987; (with S. Horton) Government Policy and the Poor in Developing Countries, 1989; (with S. Cnossen) The Personal Income Tax: Phoenix from the Ashes?, 1990; (with O. Oldman) Taxation in Developing Countries, 1990; More Taxing than Taxes?, 1991; Tax Policy and Economic Development, 1992; (with D. Brean and M. Krauss), Taxing International Portfolio Investment, 1992; (with E. Slack) Urban Public Finance in Canada, 1993; (with R. Ebel and C. Wallich) Decentralization of The Socialist State, 1995; (with F. Vaillancourt) Fiscal Decentralization in Developing Countries, 1998. **Address:** c/o Rotman School of Management, University of Toronto, Toronto, ON, Canada M5S 3E6.

BIRDSELL, Sandra. Canadian, b. 1942. **Genres:** Novels, Novellas/Short stories. **Career:** Writer. Writer in residence at University of Waterloo, 1987. Member: Association of Canadian Radio and Television Artists, Manitoba Writers Guild, Manitoba Association of Playwrights. **Publications:** Night Travellers (short stories), 1982; Ladies of the House (short stories), 1984; Agassiz Stories, 1987; The Missing Child (novel), 1989; The Chrome Suite (novel), 1992. **Address:** Milkweed Editions, 1011 Washington Ave. S. #300, Minneapolis, MN 55415, U.S.A.

BIRDSEYE, Tom. American, b. 1951. **Genres:** Children's fiction. **Career:** Elementary schoolteacher in Lincoln City, OR, and Sandpoint, ID, 1977-87; free-lance writer, 1984-. English teacher in Japan, 1983. **Publications:** FOR CHILDREN: I'm Going to Be Famous, 1986; Air Mail to the Moon, 1986; A Song of Stars, 1990; Tucker, 1990; Waiting for Baby, 1991; Soap! Soap! Don't Forget the Soap!, 1993; A Kids Guide to Building Forts, 1993; Just Call Me Stupid, 1993; A Regular Flood of Mishap, 1994; She'll Be Comin' round the Mountain, 1994; Tarantula Shoes, 1995; What I Believe: Kids Talk about Faith, 1996; Under Our Skin: Kids Talk about Race, 1997; The Eye of the Stone, 2000; Look Out Jack! The Giant Is Back!, 2001; Oh Yeah!, 2003; Attack of the Mutant Underwear, 2003. **Address:** 511 NW 12th St, Corvallis, OR 97330, U.S.A. **Online address:** www.tombirdseye.com

BIRELEY, Robert. American, b. 1933. **Genres:** History. **Career:** Entered Society of Jesus (Jesuits; S.J.), 1951, ordained Roman Catholic priest, 1964; teacher of European and American history, St. Ignatius High School, Cleveland, OH, 1958-61; Loyola University Chicago, IL, instructor, 1971-72, assistant professor, 1972-76, associate professor, 1976-82, professor of history, 1982-. Member of Institute for Advanced Study, Princeton, NJ, 1986-87; University of Chicago, member of executive committee, Renaissance Seminar, 1975-82; Newberry Library, member of executive committee, Center for Renaissance Studies, 1979-86; National Humanities Center, Fellow, 1998-99. **Publications:** Maximilian von Bayern, Adam Contzen, S.J., und die Gegenreformation in Deutschland, 1624-1635, 1975; Politics and Religion in the Age of the Counterreformation: Emperor Ferdinand II, William Lamormaini, S.J., and the Formation of Imperial Policy, 1981; The Counter-Reformation Prince: Antimachiavellianism or Catholic Statecraft in Early Modern Europe, 1990; The Refashioning of Catholicism, 1450-1700,

1999; The Jesuits and the Thirty Years War: Kings, Courts, and Confessors, 2003. Work represented in anthologies. Contributor to history journals. **Address:** Department of History, Loyola University Chicago, 6525 N Sheridan Rd, Chicago, IL 60626, U.S.A. **Online address:** rbirele@luc.edu

BIRENBAUM, Barbara. American. **Genres:** Children's fiction, Poetry, Songs/Lyrics and libretti, Children's non-fiction, Self help, Humor/Satire, Illustrations. **Career:** Educator, 1961-62, 1966-67, school psychologist, 1963-65, 1966, 1978; rehabilitation psychologist, 1965; teacher of creative writing workshops, 1976-78; Pinellas County, FL, poet-in-residence, 1980-82; author, illustrator, and composer, 1960-; Florida naturalist, 1987; Florida Department of State, Division of Cultural Affairs, literary representative, 1996-. **Publications:** Up Til Now, Yet..., 1964; (with G. Hoagland and N. Carter) Breaking through to Poetry, 1982; (with G. Hoagland and N. Carter) A Dance of Words, 1982; The Gooblins' Night, 1985; Light after Light, 1985; Lady Liberty's Light, 1986; The Hidden Shadow, 1986; The Lost Side of the Dreydl, 1987; Candle Talk, 1991; The Lighthouse Christmas, 1991; The Olympic Glow, 1994; Amazing Bald Eaglet, 1999; Groundhog Willie's Shadow, 2001; Quipnotes about Moms, 2003; Quipnotes about Dads, 2003; Groundhog Phil's Message, 2003; A Nation Stands United, 2005; Great Lives of the 21st Century, 2005; Top 100 Writers, 2005. ANTHOLOGIES: A Voyage to Remember, 1996; Best Poems of the 90s, 1996; Lyrical Heritage, 1997; Best Poems of 1997; Embedded Dreams, 1997; The Best Poems of 1998; Outstanding Poets of 1998; The Rustling Leaves, 1998; Captured Moments, 1999; Hearts of Glass, 1999; Poetic Voices of America, 2000; America in the Millennium, 2000; In-Between Days, 2001; America-Voices Coming Together, 2002; The Best Poems and Poets of 2002, 2003. **Address:** Peartree, PO Box 14533, Clearwater, FL 33766-2833, U.S.A.

BIRENBAUM, William M. American, b. 1923. **Genres:** Social commentary. **Career:** Director of Student Affairs, 1949-54, and Dean of Students, University College, 1955-57, University of Chicago; Assistant Vice President, Wayne State University, Detroit, 1957-61; Dean, New School for Social Research, NYC, 1961-64; Vice President and Provost, Brooklyn Center, Long Island University, 1964-67; President, Education Affiliate, Bedford-Stuyvesant Development Corp., Brooklyn, 1967-68; President, Staten Island College, City University of New York, 1968-76; Member of Faculty, New York University Graduate School of Education, 1969-70; President, Antioch College, Yellow Springs, Ohio, 1976-85. President, Association of Community Councils of Metropolitan Chicago, 1955-57. **Publications:** Overlive: Power, Poverty and the University, 1968; Something for Everybody Is Not Enough, 1972. **Address:** 108 Willow St, Brooklyn, NY 11201, U.S.A.

BIRKERTS, Sven. American, b. 1951. **Genres:** Literary criticism and history. **Career:** Literary critic. Bookstore clerk in Ann Arbor, MI, and Cambridge, 1973-83; Harvard University, Cambridge, MA, lecturer in expository writing, 1984-91; Boston Review, contributing editor, 1988-; Bennington Writing Seminars, member core faculty, 1995-; Mt. Holyoke College, lecturer, 1996-2004; Agni Review, editor, 2003-. Regular contributor to Boston Globe and New York Times Book Review. **Publications:** An Artificial Wilderness: Essays on Twentieth-Century Literature, 1987; The Electric Life: Essays on Modern Poetry, 1989; (with D. Hall) Writing Well, 7th ed., 1991; American Energies: Essays on Fiction, 1992; The Longwood Introduction to Fiction, 1992; Literature: The Evolving Canon, 1993; The Gutenberg Elegies: The Fate of Reading in an Electronic Age, 1994; (ed.) Tolstoy's Dictaphone: Technology and the Muse, 1996; Readings, 1999; My Sky Blue Trades, 2002. **Address:** 67 Dothan St, Arlington, MA 02474, U.S.A. **Online address:** CyberBirk@aol.com

BIRKLAND, Thomas A. American, b. 1961. **Genres:** Public/Social administration. **Career:** New Jersey Department of Transportation, Trenton, research analyst in Office of Policy Analysis, 1985-87; Office of the Governor, Trenton, aide in Independent Authorities Unit, 1987-88; New Jersey Department of Transportation, assistant manager of strategic planning, 1988-90; State University of New York at Albany, assistant professor of public affairs and political science and adjunct assistant professor of biological sciences, all 1995-, codirector of Biodiversity, Environment, and Conservation Program, 1995-, director of Public Policy Program, 1997-99. University of Washington, Seattle, worked as instructor. **Publications:** After Disaster: Agenda Setting, Public Policy, and Focusing Events, 1997. Contributor of articles and reviews to periodicals. **Address:** 217 Milne Hall, Nelson A. Rockefeller College of Public Affairs and Policy, State University of New York at Albany, 135 Western Ave., Albany, NY 12222, U.S.A. **Online address:** birkland@csc.albany.edu; www.albany.edu/~birkland.

BIRMINGHAM, Maisie. British (born India), b. 1914. **Genres:** Mystery/Crime/Suspense. **Career:** Personnel manager, 1936-41, 1943-45; H.M.

inspector of factories, 1941-43; University College of South Wales, lecturer in social science, 1945-49; Cwmbran New Town Development Corp., member, 1949-51; University of Ghana, lecturer in social studies, 1958-60. **Publications:** You Can Help Me, 1974; The Heat of the Sun, 1976; Sleep in a Ditch, 1978; The Mountain by Night, 1997. **Address:** Castle Hill House, Shaftesbury, Dorset SP7 8AX, England.

BIRMINGHAM, Walter (Barr). *See* Obituaries.

BIRN, Raymond Francis. American, b. 1935. **Genres:** History, Intellectual history. **Career:** University of Oregon, Eugene, instructor to assistant professor, 1961-66, associate professor, 1966-72, head, Dept. of History, 1971-78, professor, 1972-2001, professor emeritus of history, 2001-. Eighteenth-Century Studies, advisory editor, 1974-84, board of editors, 1999-2002; French Historical Studies, board of editors, 1977-80; College de France, visiting professor, 2001. **Publications:** Pierre Rousseau and the Philosophes of Bouillon, 1964; Crisis, Absolutism, Revolution: Europe 1648-1789/91, 1977, 2nd ed., 1992; (ed.) The Printed Word in the Eighteenth Century, 1984; Forging Rousseau: Print, Commerce, and Cultural Manipulation in the Late Enlightenment, 2001. **Address:** Dept of History, University of Oregon, Eugene, OR 97403, U.S.A. **Online address:** rbirn@oregon.uoregon.edu

BIRNBAUM, Jeffrey H. American. **Genres:** Documentaries/Reportage. **Career:** Author, journalist, and commentator. Miami Herald, Miami, FL, staff reporter, 1978; Wall Street Journal, on staff in New York, NY, 1979, and Washington, DC, 1982, White House correspondent, 1992; Time, Washington, DC, senior correspondent, 1995-. Commentator for All Things Considered, National Public Radio, 1994-. Lecturer; guest on television programs. **Publications:** (with A. Murray) Showdown at Gucci Gulch: Lawmakers, Lobbyists, and the Unlikely Triumph of Tax Reform, 1987; The Lobbyists: How Influence Peddlers Work Their Way in Washington, 1992; Madhouse: The Private Turmoil of Working for the President, 1996; The Money Men: The Real Story of Fund-raising's Influence on Political Power in America, 2000. **Address:** c/o Author Mail, Random House, 1745 Broadway, New York, NY 10019, U.S.A.

BIRNEY, Alice Lotvin. American, b. 1938. **Genres:** Literary criticism and history, Plays/Screenplays, Bibliography. **Career:** Literature specialist, Manuscript Division, Library of Congress, Washington, D.C., 1990(Literature and Theater Cataloguer, 1973-90). Associate Professor, Dept. of English, Mansfield State College, PA, 1968-69; Lecturer in Literature, University of California, San Diego, 1970-72. **Publications:** Satiric Catharsis in Shakespeare: A Theory of Dramatic Structure, 1973; The Literary Lives of Jesus: An International Bibliography, 1989; Poetry: 1959-1984. **Address:** 112 Fifth St NE, Washington, DC 20002, U.S.A. **Online address:** abir@loc.gov

BIRNEY, Betty G. American, b. 1947. **Genres:** Children's fiction. **Career:** Children's book author. Worked as an advertising copywriter for agencies in St. Louis, MO, and Chicago, IL; Disneyland, Anaheim, CA, advertising copywriter, 1977-79; Walt Disney Co., Burbank, CA, publicist, 1979-81; freelance television writer, 1982-. **Publications:** Disney Babies Bedtime Stories, 1990; Disney's Chip 'n Dale Rescue Rangers: The Rescue Rangers Save Little Red, 1991; Oh Bother, Somebody's Not Listening, 1991; Oh Bother, Somebody's Fibbing, 1991; (adaptor) Disney's The Little Mermaid, 1992; What's My Job?: A Riddle Flap Book, 1992; Who Am I?: A Riddle Flap Book, 1992; Oh Bother, Somebody's Grumpy, 1992; Walt Disney's Winnie the Pooh Half a Haycorn Pie, 1992; Walt Disney's Winnie the Pooh and the Missing Pots, 1992; Oh Bother, Somebody's Messy, 1992; Disney's Beauty and the Beast: The Tale of Chip the Teacup, 1992; Bambi's Snowy Day, 1992; Walt Disney's Winnie the Pooh and the Little Lost Bird, 1993; (adaptor) Disney's Beauty and the Beast, 1993; Oh Bother, Somebody Won't Share, 1993; Raja's Story, 1993; Walt Disney's Sleeping Beauty, 1993; Walt Disney's Winnie the Pooh: The Merry Christmas Mystery, 1993; Oh Bother, Somebody's Jealous, 1993; Oh Bother, Somebody's Afraid of the Dark, 1993; Walt Disney's I Am Winnie the Pooh, 1993; (adaptor) Black Beauty, 1994; Tyrannosaurus Tex, 1994; (adaptor) Disney's Toy Story, 1995; Meltdown at the Wax Museum, 1995; Pie's in the Oven, 1996; Let's Play Hide and Seek, 1997. SCRIPTS FOR LIVE-ACTION TELEVISION SERIES AND SPECIAL PROGRAMS: Mary Christmas; My Indian Summer; Fast Forward; Big Boys Don't Cry; But He Loves Me; Churchill Pictures; Talking with TJ; It Happened to Me; Zoobilee Zoo; Too Smart for Strangers; Welcome to Pooh Corner; Dumbo's Circus; Divorce Court; Secret Lives. SCRIPTS FOR ANIMATED TELEVISION PROGRAMS: Book of Virtues; The Good Samaritan; Little Mouse on the Prairie; Madeline; Where's Waldo; Camp Candy; Doug; Prince Valiant; Bobby's World; Maxie's World; Once upon a Forest; The Chipmunks; Fraggle Rock; The Moondreamers; The Snorks. INTERACTIVE SOFTWARE: The Crayon Factory; Berenstain Bears

on Their Own; Wacky Tales; Storypainting: The Wizard of Oz; Richard Scarry's Busiest Disc Ever; Richard Scarry's Busiest Neighborhood Ever; The Dark Fables of Aesop, I & II. **Address:** c/o Todd Koerner, Writers & Artists Agency Inc., 8383 Wilshire Blvd., Beverly Hills, CA 90211, U.S.A. **Online address:** bbirney@soca.com

BIRO, Val. (Balint Stephen Biro). British (born Hungary), b. 1921. **Genres:** Children's fiction, Education, Illustrations, Picture/board books. **Career:** Sylvan Press, studio manager, 1944-46; C and J Temple, production manager, 1946-48; John Lehmann Publishers, art director, 1948-51; Urban District Councillor, 1966-70; freelance author, illustrator, currently. **Publications:** WRITER-ILLUSTRATOR: Bumpy's Holiday, 1943; Gumdrop: The Adventures of a Vintage Car, series, 35+ vols., from 1966; The Honest Thief, 1972; A Dog and His Bone (reader), 1975; Hungarian Folk-Tales, 1981; The Magic Doctor, 1982; The Pied Piper, 1985; The Hobyahs, 1986; The Donkey That Sneezed, 1986; Tobias and the Dragon, 1989; Drango Dragon, 1989; Peter Cheater, 1989; Tales from Hans Andersen, 1989; Miranda's Umbrella, 1990; Look and Find ABC, 1990; Rub-a-Dub-Dub, 1991; The Monster Pack, 1993; My Oxford Picture Word Book, 1994; Lazy Jack, 1995; Jasper's Jungle Journey, 1995; Bears Can't Fly, 1996; Archie the Ugly Dinosaur, 1996; Hansel & Gretel, 1997; Goldilocks and The Three Bears, 1997; The Monster Birthday, 1997; The Dinosaurs' Dinner, 1997; Jennings Sounds the Alarm, 1999; Little Red Riding Hood, 2000; Aesop's Fables, 2001; The Joking Wolf, 2001. Illustrator of books by others. **Address:** Bridge Cottage, Brook Ave, Bosham, W. Sussex P018 8LQ, England.

BIRRELL, Anne (Margaret). British. **Genres:** Poetry, Anthropology/Ethnology, Area studies, Classics, Literary criticism and history, Mythology/Folklore, Theology/Religion, Women's studies and issues. **Career:** Writer; Sinologist. Member, Clare Hall, University of Cambridge, UK. Member: Royal Society of Literature. **Publications:** Chinese Love Poetry: New Songs from a Jade Terrace: A Medieval Anthology, 1982, rev. ed., 1995; Popular Songs and Ballads of Han China, 1988, rev. ed., 1993; Chinese Mythology: An Introduction, 1993; The Classic of Mountains and Seas, 1999; Chinese Myths: The Legendary Past, 2000; Games Poets Play: Readings in Medieval Chinese Poetry, 2004. **Address:** Clare Hall, University of Cambridge, Herschel Rd, Cambridge CB3 9AL, England.

BIRRELL, James Peter. Australian, b. 1928. **Genres:** Architecture, History, Autobiography/Memoirs, Biography. **Career:** Principal, James Birrell Architect and Town Planner, Maroochydore, Qld., since 1965. **Publications:** Walter Burley Griffin, 1964; (with Rory Barnes) Water from the Moon, 1989. **Address:** 104 Duporth Ave, Maroochydore, QLD, Australia.

BIRRINGER, Johannes (H.). German, b. 1953. **Genres:** Theatre, Literary criticism and history. **Career:** Yale University, New Haven, CT, lecturer, 1982-85; University of Texas at Dallas, Richardson, TX, visiting professor, 1985-87; Rice University, Houston, TX, visiting professor, 1989-90; Northwestern University, Evanston, IL, assistant professor, 1990-. Contemporary Art Museum, Houston, media and arts consultant; Southwest Alternate Media Project, Houston, media consultant. **Publications:** Marlowe's Dr. Faustus and Tamburlaine, 1984; Theatre, Theory, Postmodernism, 1991. Contributor to American, European, Mexican, and South African periodicals. **Address:** Department of Performance Studies, Northwestern University, 1979 Sheridan, Evanston, IL 60208, U.S.A.

BIRSTEIN, Ann. American, b. 1927. **Genres:** Novels, Novellas/Short stories, Writing/Journalism, Biography. **Publications:** Star of Glass, 1950; The Troublemaker, 1955; (ed. with A. Kazin) The Works of Anne Frank, 1959; The Sweet Birds of Gorham, 1967; Summer Situations, 1972; Dickie's List, 1973; American Children, 1980; The Rabbi on 47th Street, 1982; The Last of the True Believers, 1988; What I Saw at the Fair (biography), 2002. **Address:** 1623 Third Ave Apt 27 J W, New York, NY 10128, U.S.A. **Online address:** abirstein@aol.com

BIRYUKOV, Nikolai (Ivanovich). Russian, b. 1949. **Genres:** Politics/Government. **Career:** U.S.S.R. Trade Mission in Egypt, Cairo, interpreter, 1972-74; Moscow State Institute for International Relations, Moscow, Russia, research scientist, 1977-79, teacher (fellow), 1979-83, senior teacher (assistant professor), 1983-88, docent (associate professor) in philosophy, 1994-. All-Russia Knowledge Society, lecturer, 1984-88; Russian Academy of Sciences, senior research scientist at Center for the Analysis of Scientific and Industrial Policies, 1991-; State Duma, expert for Subcommittee on Science, Committee on Education, Science, and Culture, 1994-. **Publications:** (with V. Sergeyev) Russia's Road to Democracy: Parliament, Communism, and Traditional Culture, 1993; (with Sergeyev) Russian Politics in Transition, 1996. Contributor to books published in English, Russian, and German.

Contributor to scholarly journals. **Address:** Department of Philosophy, Laboratory for the Systematic Analysis of Int'l Relations, Moscow State Institute for International Relations, Vernadskogo 76 Prospekt, 117454 Moscow, Russia. **Online address:** nibiryukov@newmail.ru; http://nibiryukov.narod.ru

BISHOP, Courtney. *See* **RUEMMLER, John D(avid).**

BISHOP, Michael. Also writes as Philip Lawson. American, b. 1945. **Genres:** Novels, Novellas/Short stories, Mystery/Crime/Suspense, Science fiction/Fantasy, Plays/Screenplays, Poetry. **Career:** University of Georgia, Athens, instructor of English, 1972-74; freelance writer, 1974-. **Publications:** NOVELS: A Funeral for the Eyes of Fire, 1975, as Eyes of Fire, 1980; And Strange at Ecbatan the Trees, 1976, as Beneath the Shattered Moons, 1977; Stolen Faces, 1977; A Little Knowledge, 1977; Catacomb Years, 1979; Transfigurations, 1979; (with I. Watson) Under Heaven's Bridge, 1981; No Enemy but Time, 1982; Who Made Stevie Crye?, 1984; Ancient of Days, 1985; Philip K. Dick Is Dead, Alas, 1987; Unicorn Mountain, 1988; Count Geiger's Blues, 1992; Brittle Innings, 1994. NOVELS AS PHILIP LAWSON (with P. Di Filippo): Would It Kill You to Smile?, 1998; Muskrat Courage, 2000. POETRY: Windows & Mirrors, 1977; Time Pieces, 1998. STORIES: Blooded on Arachne 1980; One Winter in Eden, 1984; Close Encounters with the Deity, 1986; Emphatically Not SF, Almost, 1990; At the City Limits of Fate, 1996; Brighten to Incandescence, 2003. NOVELLAS: Apartheid, Superstrings, and Mordecai Thubana, 1989; Blue Kansas Sky, 2000. OTHER: Within the Walls of Tyre (screenplay), 1989. EDITOR: (with I. Watson) Changes (anthology), 1983; Light Years and Dark (anthology), 1984; Nebula Awards (anthologies), vols. 23-25, 1989-91. **Address:** Box 646, Pine Mountain, GA 31822, U.S.A. **Online address:** mlbishop@juno.com

BISHOP, Nic. New Zealander, b. 1955. **Genres:** Travel/Exploration, Natural history. **Career:** Masset University, Palmerston North, New Zealand, research fellow, 1977-80; University of Canterbury, Canterbury, New Zealand, tutor and researcher, 1980-86; writer and photographer, 1988-. Appeared in television documentaries; guest on radio programs in New Zealand. **Publications:** AUTHOR AND PHOTOGRAPHER: Untouched Horizons: Photographs from the South Island Wilderness, 1989; Natural History of New Zealand, 1992; From the Mountains to the Sea: The Secret Life of New Zealand's Rivers and Wetlands, 1994; New Zealand Wild: The Greenest Place on Earth, 1995. FOR CHILDREN: Leap Frog, 1994; Ready, Steady, Jump, 1995; The Secrets of Animal Flight, 1997; Strange Plants, 1997; The Green Snake, 1998; The Katydids, 1998; Gecko Flies, 1998; Mudskipper, 1998; Canoe Diary, 1998; Caught in a Flash, 1998; Digging for Bird Dinosaurs: An Expedition to Madagascar, 2000. Photographer for books by P. Quinn, O. Bishop, A. Bishop, J. Cowley, J. Buxton, D. Noonan, J. Eggleton, S. Montgomery, E.B. Jackson. Contributor to books. Photographs have appeared in calendars and magazines. **Address:** c/o Houghton Mifflin, 222 Berkeley St., Boston, MA 02116, U.S.A.

BISHOP, Wendy. American (born Japan), b. 1953. **Genres:** Education, Writing/Journalism. **Career:** Navajo Community College, Tsaile, AZ, chair of Communications, Humanities, and Fine Arts Division, 1984-85; University of Alaska, Fairbanks, visiting associate professor of English, 1985-89; Florida State University, Tallahassee, professor of English and former director of first-year writing, 1989-. **Publications:** Something Old, Something New: College Writing Teachers and Classroom Change, 1990; Released Into Language: Options for Teaching Creative Writing, 1990, 2nd ed, 1999; Working Words: The Process of Creative Writing, 1992; Teaching Lives: Essays and Stories, 1997; Ethnographic Writing Research: Writing It Down, Writing It Up, and Reading It, 1999; Thirteen Ways of Looking for a Poem: A Guide to Writing Poetry, 2000. EDITOR: The Subject Is Writing, 1993, 2nd ed, 1999; (with H. Ostrom) Colors of a Different Horse: Rethinking Creative Writing, 1994; (with H. Ostrom) Genres and Writing: Mapping the Territories of Discourse, 1997; (with D. Stavkey) In Praise of Pedagogy: Poems and Flash Fiction and Essays, 2000; The Subject Is Reading: Essays by Teachers and Students, 2000. Contributor to books and anthologies. **Address:** Department of English, Florida State University, Tallahassee, FL 32306-1036, U.S.A.

BISSELL, LeClair. American, b. 1928. **Genres:** Gay and lesbian issues, Sciences, Sociology. **Career:** New York Public Library, NYC, circulation librarian and branch librarian, 1952-59; Roosevelt Hospital, NYC, intern to resident in medicine, 1963-66; fellow in endocrinology and metabolism, 1966-68; coordinator and chief of Smithers Alcoholism Treatment and Training Center, 1968-79; Edgehill-Newport, Inc., Newport, RI, president and chief executive officer, 1979-81; researcher, writer, and consultant, 1981-. Member of permanent advisory commissions, task forces, advisory councils.

Guest on radio and television programs. **Publications:** (with R. Watherwax) The Cat Who Drank Too Much, 1982, 2nd ed., 1994; (with P.W. Haberman) Alcoholism in the Professions, 1984; (with J.E. Royce) Ethics for Addiction Professionals, 1987, 2nd ed., 1994; (with E.J. Sullivan and E. Williams) Chemical Dependency in Nursing: The Deadly Diversion, 1988; (with L. Crosby) To Care Enough: Intervention with Chemically Dependent Colleagues, 1989. **Address:** 1932 Woodring Rd, Sanibel, FL 33957-3433, U.S.A. **Online address:** LeClair@aol.com

BISSELL, Sallie. American. **Genres:** Novels. **Career:** Tennessee Writers Alliance, former director. Has worked as an advertising copywriter and art consultant. **Publications:** NOVELS: In the Forest of Harm, 2001; A Darker Justice, 2002. **Address:** 947 Gale Ln, Nashville, TN 37204, U.S.A. **Online address:** sallie@salliebissell.com

BISSETT, bill. Canadian, b. 1939. **Genres:** Poetry, Songs/Lyrics and libretti. **Career:** Ed. and Printer, Blewointmentpress, Vancouver, 1962-83. Artist and musician. **Publications:** Th jinx ship nd othr trips: pomes-drawings-collage, 1966; we sleep inside each other all, 1966; Fires in the Tempul, 1967; where is Miss Florence riddle, 1967; what poetiks, 1967; (th) Gossamer Bed Pan, 1967; Lebanon Voices, 1967; Of th Land/Divine Service Poems, 1968; Awake in the Red Desert!, 1968; Killer Whale, 1969; Sunday Work?, 1969; Liberating Skies, 1969; The Lost Angel Mining Co., 1969; S th Story I to, 1970; Th Outlaw, 1970; blew trewz, 1970; Nobody Owns th Earth, 1971; air 6, 1971; Tuff Shit Love Pomes, 1971; dragon fly, 1971; Rush what fukin thery, 1971; (with others) Four Parts Sand: Concrete Poems, 1972; th Ice bag, 1972; pomes for yoshi, 1972, 1977; drifting into war, 1972; air 10-11-12, 1972; Pass th Food, Release th Spirit Book, 1973; th first sufi line, 1973; Vancouver Mainland Ice & Cold Storage, 1973; Living with th vishyan, 1974; what, 1974; drawings, 1974; Medicine my mouths on fire, 1974; space travl, 1974; yu can eat it at th opening, 1974; th fifth sun, 1975; th wind up tongue, 1975; Stardust, 1975; an allusyun to macbeth, 1976; plutonium missing, 1976; sailor, 1978; Beyond Even Faithful Legends, 1979; th first snow, 1979; soul arrow, 1980; sa n th monkey, 1980; Selected Poems, 1980; northern birds in color, 1981; sa n his crystal ball, 1981; parlant, 1982; ready for framing, 1982; seagull on yonge street, 1983; canada gees mate for life, 1985; (ed.) last blewointment anghology, 1985; Animal Uproar, 1987; what we have, 1988; hard 2 beleev, 1989; (with others) Rezoning, 1989; inkorrect thots, 1992; th last photo uv th human soul, 1993; th influenza ur logih, 1995; loving without being vulnrabul, 1997; scars on the seehors, 1999; b leev abul char ak trs, 2000; th oranges uv orantangua, 2002; Peter among th towring boxes, text bites, 2002. **Address:** Box 272, Stn F, Toronto, ON, Canada M4Y 2L7.

BITTNER, Rosanne. American, b. 1945. **Genres:** Romance/Historical, Novellas/Short stories. **Career:** Worked as a secretary; full-time writer, 1984-. **Publications:** ROMANCE NOVELS: Savage Horizons, 1987; Frontier Fires, 1987; Destiny's Dawn, 1987; Tennessee Bride, 1988; Texas Bride, 1988; This Time Forever, 1988; Oregon Bride, 1990; Love Me Tomorrow, 1998; Texas Passions, 1999. HISTORICAL ROMANCES, SAVAGE DESTINY SERIES: Sweet Prairie Passion, 1983; Ride the Free Wind, 1984; River of Love, 1984; Embrace the Wild Land, 1984; Climb the Highest Mountain, 1985; Meet the New Dawn, 1986; Eagle's Song, 1996. OTHER HISTORICAL ROMANCES: Arizona Bride, 1985; Lawless Love, 1985; Rapture's Gold, 1986; Prairie Embrace, 1987; Heart's Surrender, 1988; Ecstasy's Chains, 1989; Arizona Ecstasy, 1989; Sweet Mountain Magic, 1990; Sioux Splendor, 1990; Comanche Sunset, 1991; Caress, 1992; Shameless, 1993; Unforgettable, 1994; Full Circle, 1994; Until Tomorrow, 1995; Texas Embrace, 1997; Mystic Dreamers, 1999. HISTORICAL SAGAS: Montana Woman, 1990; Embers of the Heart, 1990; In the Shadow of the Mountains, 1991; Song of the Wolf, 1992; Outlaw Hearts, 1993; Tender Betrayal, 1993; Wildest Dreams, 1994; Thunder on the Plains, 1992; The Forever Tree, 1995; Chase the Sun, 1995; Tame the Wild Wind, 1996. ANTHOLOGIES: Cherished Moments, 1994; Love by Chocolate, 1997; Cherished Love, 1997. **Address:** PO Box 1044, Coloma, MI 49038, U.S.A. **Online address:** bittner@parrett.net; www.parrett.net/~bittner

BITTON-JACKSON, Livia E(lvira). American/Israeli (born Czech Republic), b. 1931. **Genres:** Young adult non-fiction, Autobiography/Memoirs. **Career:** Hunter College of the City University of New York, New York, NY, lecturer in Hebrew literature, 1965-68; Academy of Jewish Religion, dean of students, 1972-75; Herbert H. Lehman College of the City University of New York, Bronx, NY, professor of Hebrew and Judaic studies, 1968-; Adjunct assistant professor of Hebrew language and literature at Brooklyn Center of Long Island University, 1965-68; assistant professor of Judaic studies at Brooklyn College of the City University of New York, 1972-76; professor of Jewish history at Tel Aviv University, 1979-82. **Publi-**

cations: AS LIVIA ELVIRA BITTON: A Decade of Zionism in Hungary, 1918-1928, 1971. AS LIVIA BITTON-JACKSON: Elli: Coming of Age in the Holocaust, 1980; Madonna or Courtesan: The Jewish Woman in Christian Literature, 1983; I Have Lived a Thousand Years, 1997; My Bridges of Hope, 1999. Contributor to books. **Address:** 12 Ussishkin St, 42273 Netanya, Israel. **Online address:** lbj@barak-online.net

BIZZARRO, Tina Waldeier. American. **Genres:** Architecture, Art/Art history. **Career:** Rosemont College, Rosemont, PA, associate professor of art history, 1977-, chair of Art History Dept, 1985-. Villanova University, part-time faculty member, 1983-. **Publications:** Romanesque Architectural Criticism: A Prehistory, 1992. Work represented in anthologies. Contributor to books and periodicals. **Address:** Arts Division, Rosemont College, Rosemont, PA 19010, U.S.A. **Online address:** rosieselavy@yahoo.com

BIZZELL, Patricia (Lynn). American, b. 1948. **Genres:** Education, Writing/Journalism, Bibliography. **Career:** Rutgers University, New Brunswick, NJ, assistant professor of English, 1975-78, director of remedial writing program, 1975-77, and teacher training program, 1977-78; College of the Holy Cross, Worcester, MA, assistant professor, 1978-81, associate professor, 1981-88, professor of English, 1988-, director of Writing across the Curriculum, 1981-94, director of Writing Workshop, 1982-87, 1992-94, director of Honors Program, 1994-98, chair, English dept., 2001-04; writer. Speaker at colleges and universities. **Publications:** (with B. Herzberg and R. Gorrell) The Bedford Bibliography for Teachers of Writing, 1983, (with B. Herzberg and N. Reynolds) 5th ed., 2000; (with B. Herzberg) The Rhetorical Tradition: Readings from Classical Times to the Present, 1990, 2nd ed., 2001; Academic Discourse and Critical Consciousness, 1992; (with B. Herzberg) Negotiating Difference: Cultural Case Studies for Composition, 1996. Work represented in anthologies. Contributor to language, literature, and education journals. **Address:** Department of English, College of the Holy Cross, 1 College St, Worcester, MA 01610, U.S.A. **Online address:** pbizzell@holycross.edu

BJARKMAN, Peter C(hristian). Also writes as Dr. Baseball. American, b. 1941. **Genres:** History, Sports/Fitness, Biography, Young adult fiction, Novellas/Short stories. **Career:** High school English teacher in Wethersfield, Conn., 1963-68; Colegio Panamericano, Bucaramanga, Colombia, instructor in English, 1968-69; Colegio Americano, Guayaquil, Ecuador, U.S. program director, 1971-72; English teacher at a private secondary school in Jacksonville, Fla., 1975-76; George Mason University, Fairfax, Va., assistant professor of English, 1976-79; Purdue University, West Lafayette, Ind., assistant professor of English, 1979-86, director of English-as-a-second-language programs, 1979-85; baseball and basketball historian and writer, 1986-. Adjunct associate professor at Butler University, autumn, 1986; visiting assistant professor at Ball State University, spring and fall, 1986, University of Colorado, spring, 1987, and Indiana University-Indianapolis, spring, 1988. Frequent guest on national television and radio talk shows, as Doctor Baseball. **Publications:** (ed. with V. Raskin, and contrib) The Real-World Linguist: Linguistic Applications in the 1980s, 1986; (ed. with R.M. Hammond, and contrib) American Spanish Pronunciation: Theoretical and Applied Perspectives, 1989; Baseball's Great Dynasties-The Dodgers, 1989; The Toronto Blue Jays, 1989; (ed. and contrib) Encyclopedia of Baseball Team Histories, Volume I: The American League, Volume II: The National League, 1990; (ed. and contrib) Baseball and the Game of Life: Stories for the Thinking Fan, 1991; Roberto Clemente (juvenile), 1991; The History of the NBA, 1992; Baseball's Great Dynasties-The Reds, 1991; The Brooklyn Dodgers, 1992; The Baseball Scrapbook, 1991; Baseball and the Game of Ideas: Essays for the Serious Fan, 1993; Encyclopedia of Major League Baseball Team Histories, Volume 1: American League, Volume II: National League, 1993; (ed. and contr.) The Inter-National Pastime: A Review of Baseball History, Volume 12, 1992; The Encyclopedia of Pro Basketball Team Histories, 1994; Duke Snider (juvenile), 1994; Baseball with a Latin Beat, 1994; Ernie Banks 1994; Warren Spahn (juvenile), 1994; Big Ten Basketball, 1994; Slam Dunk Superstars, 1994; Shaq: The Making of a Legend, 1994; Top 10 Baseball Base-Stealers (juvenile), 1995; Top 10 Basketball Slam-Dunkers, (juvenile), 1995; Hoopla: A Century of College Basketball, 1996; ACC-Atlantic Coast Conference Basketball, 1996; Sports Great Scottie Pipin (juvenile), 1996; Sports Great Dominique Wilkins (juvenile), 1996; The Biographical History of Basketball, 1997. **Address:** PO Box 2199, West Lafayette, IN 47906, U.S.A.

BJORGE, Gary J(ohn). American, b. 1940. **Genres:** History, Military/Defense/Arms control, Translations. **Career:** University of Wisconsin-Madison, library associate in Chinese, 1973-80; University of Kansas, Lawrence, East Asian librarian in Chinese, 1980-84; U.S. Army Command and General Staff College, Ft. Leavenworth, Kan., military historian and researcher, 1984-. **Publications:** (ed. and trans. with T.E. Barlow) I Myself

Am a Woman: Selected Works of Ding Ling, 1989; Merrill's Marauders: Combined Operations in Northern Burma in 1944, 1996; Moving the Enemy: Operational Art in the Chinese PLA's Huai Hai Campaign, 2004. **Address:** 1321 Jana Dr, Lawrence, KS 66049, U.S.A.

BJORK, Daniel W. American, b. 1940. **Genres:** Biography, History. **Career:** University of Alabama, Birmingham, assistant professor of history, 1974-81; Mercy College of Detroit, Detroit, MI, professor of history, 1983-91; St. Mary's University, San Antonio, TX, professor of history, 1991-. **Publications:** The Victorian Flight, University Press of America, 1978; The Compromised Scientist, Columbia University Press, 1983; William James: The Center of His Vision, Columbia University Press, 1988; B. F. Skinner: A Life, Basic Books, 1993. **Address:** Department of History, St. Mary's University, San Antonio, TX 78228, U.S.A.

BLACK, Arthur (Raymond). Canadian, b. 1943. **Genres:** Essays, Humor/Satire. **Career:** CBC-Radio, host of Radio Noon in Thunder Bay, ON, 1976-85, host of Basic Black in Toronto, ON, 1985-94, in Vancouver, BC, 1994-2001. Writer in residence, Kitchener Public Library, 1992; commentator, Global Television, 1992-94. Guest on television programs, including Journal and Midday; public speaker. Black and White, syndicated columnist, 1976-; Weird Homes, host, 1998-; Weird Wheels, 2000-. **Publications:** Old Fort William: A History; Basic Black, 1981; Back to Black, 1986; That Old Black Magic (essays), 1989; Arthur, Arthur!, 1991; Black by Popular Demand, 1993; Black in the Saddle Again, 1996; Black Tie and Tales, 1999; Flashback!, 2001. **Address:** 131 Lionel Crescent, Salt Spring Island, BC, Canada V8K 2E1.

BLACK, D(avid) M(acleod). British (born Republic of South Africa), b. 1941. **Genres:** Poetry. **Publications:** Theory of Diet, 1966; With Decorum, 1967; A Dozen Short Poems, 1968; (with D.M. Thomas and P. Redgrove) Penguin Modern Poets 11, 1968; The Educators, 1969; The Old Hag, 1972; The Happy Crow, 1974; Gravitations, 1979; A Place for Exploration, 1991; Collected Poems, 1964-87, 1991. **Address:** 30 Cholmley Gardens, London NW6 1AG, England.

BLACK, Donald. American, b. 1941. **Genres:** Law, Sociology. **Career:** Yale University, New Haven, CT, assistant professor of sociology and lecturer in law, 1970-74, associate professor of sociology, 1974-79; Harvard University, Cambridge, MA, research associate and lecturer in law, 1979-85; University of Virginia, Charlottesville, professor of sociology, 1985-88, University Professor of the Social Sciences, 1988-. **Publications:** The Behavior of Law, 1976; The Manners and Customs of the Police, 1980; Sociological Justice, 1989; The Social Structure of Right and Wrong, 1993, rev. ed., 1998. EDITOR: (with M. Mileski) The Social Organization of Law, 1973; Toward a General Theory of Social Control, 2 vols, 1984. **Address:** Dept of Sociology, Cabell Hall, University of Virginia, Charlottesville, VA 22904, U.S.A. **Online address:** Black@Virginia.edu

BLACK, Jeremy (Martin). British, b. 1955. **Genres:** History. **Career:** Oxford University, England, senior scholar of Merton College, 1979-80; University of Durham, England, lecturer in history, 1980-90, senior lecturer, 1990-91, reader, 1991-95, director of University Research Foundation and Society of Fellows, 1991-95, professor, 1994-95; University of Exeter, England, professor of history, 1995-. **Publications:** The British and the Grand Tour, 1985; British Foreign Policy in the Age of Walpole, 1985; The English Press in the 18th Century, 1986; Natural and Necessary Enemies, 1986; 18th Century Europe, 1700-1789, 1990; Culloden and the '45, 1990; The Rise of the European Powers, 1679-1793, 1990; Robert Walpole and the Nature of Politics in Early 18th-Century Britain, 1990; War for America, 1991; A Military Revolution?, 1991; A System of Ambition?, 1991; The Grand Tour, 1992; Pitt the Elder, 1992; The British Abroad, 1993; European Warfare 1660-1815, 1994; Divergence?, 1994; British Foreign Policy in an Age of Revolutions, 1783-1793, 1994; Warfare in the 18th Century, 1999; War and the World, 2000. Also author of other books. EDITOR: Britain in the Age of Walpole, 1984; (with K. Schweizer) Essays in European History in Honour of Ragnhild Hatton, 1985; The Causes of War in Early Modern Europe, 1987; (with E. Cruickshanks) The Jacobite Challenge, 1988; (with P. Woodfine) The British Navy and the Use of Naval Power in the 18th Century, 1988; Knights Errant and True Englishmen, 1989; (with Schweizer) Press and Politics in Hanoverian Britain, 1989; British Politics and Society from Walpole to Pitt, 1742-1789, 1990; (with J. Gregory) Culture, Politics and Society in Britain, 1660-1800, 1991. **Address:** SHiPSS, Amory Bldg, University of Exeter, Rennes Dr, Exeter, Devon EX4 4RJ, England.

BLACK, Noel (Anthony). American, b. 1937. **Genres:** Plays/Screenplays. **Career:** Director, producer, and writer. New York University, NYC, assistant professor at the Institute for Film and Television, Tisch School of the Arts, 1992-93. **Publications:** SCREENPLAYS: Skaterdater (short film), 1966; Pickup on 101, 1972; Mischief, 1985; (with others) Shakespeare's Child, 1996. TELEPLAYS; Trilogy: The American Boy, 1968. Contributor to periodicals.

BLACK, R(obert) D(enis) Collison. British (born Ireland), b. 1922. **Genres:** Economics, History, Intellectual history. **Career:** University of Dublin, Trinity College, Ireland, deputy for the professor of political economy, 1943-45; Queen's University, Belfast, Northern Ireland, assistant lecturer, 1945-46, lecturer, 1946-58, senior lecturer, 1958-61, reader, 1961-62, professor of economics and head of department, 1962-85, emeritus, 1985-, dean of faculty of economics and social sciences, 1967-70, pro-vice-chancellor of the university, 1971-75. Princeton University, Rockefeller fellow, 1950-51; Yale University, visiting professor, 1964-65. **Publications:** Centenary History of the Statistical Society of Ireland, 1947; Economic Thought and the Irish Question, 1817-1870, 1960; A Catalogue of Pamphlets on Economic Subjects Published Between 1750 and 1900, and Now Housed in Irish Libraries, 1969; Economic Theory and Policy in Context, 1995. EDITOR: Papers and Correspondence of William Stanley Jevons, Vol. I: Biography and Personal Journal, 1972, Vol. II: Correspondence, 1850-1862, 1973, Vol. III: Correspondence, 1863-1872, 1977, Vol. IV: Correspondence, 1873-1878, 1977, Vol. V: Correspondence, 1879-1882, 1977, Vol. VI: Lectures on Political Economy, 1875-1876, 1977, Vol. VII: Papers on Political Economy, 1981; Readings in the Development of Economic Analysis, 1776-1848, 1972; (with A.W. Coats and C.D. Goodwin) The Marginal Revolution in Economics, 1973; Ideas in Economics, 1986. **Address:** Dept of Economics, Queen's University, Belfast BT7 1NN, Northern Ireland.

BLACK, Robert. *See* **HOLDSTOCK, Robert.**

BLACK, Robert Perry. American, b. 1927. **Genres:** Economics, Money/Finance. **Career:** President, Federal Reserve Bank of Richmond, 1973-92 (Research Associate, 1954-55; Associate Economist, 1956-58; Economist, 1958-60; Assistant Vice President, 1960-62; Vice President, 1962-68; First Vice President. 1968-73). Assistant Professor of Finance, University of Tennessee, Knoxville, 1955-56. **Publications:** (with B.U. Ratchford) The Federal Reserve at Work, 1961, 5th ed. 1973; The Federal Reserve Today, 1964, 5th ed. 1971; (with D.E. Harless) Non-Bank Financial Institutions, 1965, 3rd ed. 1969. Contributor to professional journals. **Address:** 10 Dahlgren Rd., Richmond, VA 23233, U.S.A.

BLACK, Roger David. American, b. 1948. **Genres:** Administration/Management. **Career:** L.A. (weekly newspaper), Los Angeles, CA, art director, 1972; Rolling Stone, San Francisco and NYC, art director, 1976-78; New York and New West magazines, NYC and Los Angeles, design director, 1978-81; New York Times Magazine, NYC, art director, 1982-84; New York Times, NYC, director of editorial art, 1984-85; Newsweek, NYC, art director, 198587; Smart magazine, NYC, design director, 1988-90 and 1993-; also oversaw redesigns for Esquire, the San Francisco Examiner, and Advertising Age; launched Out, Fast Company, and Smart Money; Roger Black Inc. design consultants, NYC, president, 1981-; the Font Bureau, founder; Interactive Bureau, NYC, cofounder and president, 1994-. **Publications:** Getting Things Done, 1987; Roger Black's Desktop Design Power, 1991; (with S. Elder) Web Sites That Work, 1998. **Address:** 36 Gramercy Park E, New York, NY 10003-1741, U.S.A.

BLACK, Shane. American, b. 1962. **Genres:** Plays/Screenplays. **Career:** Screenwriter, actor, and executive producer. Worked as typist, data entry clerk, and movie theater usher. **Publications:** SCREENPLAYS: Lethal Weapon, 1987; (with F. Dekker) The Monster Squad, 1987; The Last Boy Scout, 1991; (with D. Arnott) Last Action Hero, 1993; The Long Kiss Goodbye, 1994; Shadow Company. **Address:** c/o OTML, 500 South Sepulveda Blvd., 5th Floor, Los Angeles, CA 90049, U.S.A.

BLACK, Veronica. *See* **PETERS, Maureen.**

BLACKBOURN, David. British, b. 1949. **Genres:** Area studies, History, Local history/Rural topics, Social sciences. **Career:** Cambridge University, England, research fellow in history at Jesus College, 1973-76; University of London, lecturer in history at Queen Mary College, 1976-79, Birkbeck College, lecturer, 1979-85, reader in history, 1985-89, professor, 1989-92; Harvard University, professor, 1992-. Stanford University, visiting professor, 1989-90; member of academic management committee of London's German Historical Institute, 1983-92, and of Institute for European History, Mainz, Germany, 1995-. Fellow of Royal Historical Society, 1986-. Research fellow, Alexander von Humboldt Foundation, 1984-85, Guggenheim Foundation,

1994-95. **Publications:** Class, Religion, and Local Politics in Wilhelmine Germany: The Centre Party in Wuerttemberg before 1914, 1980; (with G. Eley) Mythen deutscher Geschichtsschreibung: Die gescheiterte buergerliche Revolution von 1848 (title means: Myths of German Historiography), 1980; (with G. Eley) The Peculiarities of German History: Bourgeois Society and Politics in Nineteenth-Century Germany, 1984; Populists and Patricians: Essays in Modern German History, 1987; (ed. with R.J. Evans) The German Bourgeoisie, 1991; Marpingen: Apparitions of the Virgin Mary in Nineteenth-Century Germany, 1993; Germany in the Long Nineteenth Century, 1997. **Address:** Minda de Gunzburg Center for European Studies, Harvard University, 27 Kirkland St, Cambridge, MA 02138, U.S.A.

BLACKBURN, Fred M(onroe). American, b. 1950. **Genres:** Archaeology/Antiquities, History, Travel/Exploration. **Career:** Bureau of Land Management, Monticello, UT, ranger to chief ranger, 1974-79; Crow Canyon Archaeological Center, Cortez, CO, interpretive guide, 1979-81; self-employed interpreter, educator, guide, and researcher, 1981-. Cortez Historic Board, member, 1998; consultant to private and public schools. **Publications:** The Hiker's Guide to Utah, 1982; (with R. Williamson) An Approach to Vandalism of Archaeological Resources, 1990; (with V. Atkins) Handwriting on the Wall, 1993; (with Williamson) Cowboys and Cave Dwellers, 1997; Inscription History and Discover of Balcony House, 2000; Historical Inscriptions and the Expeditionary History of Balcony House, Cliff Palace, Hemenway House, Little Hemenway House, Honeymoon House, and Spruce Tree House, 2005. **Address:** 104 E Carpenter, Cortez, CO 81321, U.S.A. **Online address:** blackburn@msn.com

BLACKBURN, Julia. British, b. 1949?. **Genres:** Novels. **Career:** Writer. **Publications:** BIOGRAPHICAL FICTION: The White Men: The First Response of Aboriginal Peoples to the White Man, 1979; Charles Waterton, 1782-1865: Traveller and Conservationist, 1989; The Emperor's Last Island: A Journey to St. Helena, 1991; Daisy Bates in the Desert: One Woman's Life among the Aborigines, 1994. NOVELS: The Book of Colour, 1995; The Leper's Companion, 1999. **Address:** c/o Pantheon Publicity, 1540 Broadway, New York, NY 10036, U.S.A.

BLACKFORD, Mansel G(riffiths). American, b. 1944. **Genres:** Business/Trade/Industry, History. **Career:** Ohio State University, Columbus, OH, assistant professor, 1972-78, associate professor, 1979-84, professor, 1984-. Senior Fulbright lecturer to Japan, 1980-81 and 1985-86; member of Business History Conference. Boy Scouts of America, troop leader, 1987-90. **Publications:** Politics of Business in California, 1890-1920, 1977; Pioneering a Modern Small Business: Wakefield Seafoods and the Alaskan Frontier, 1979; A Portrait Cast in Steel: Buckeye International and Columbus, Ohio, 1881-1980, 1982; (with K.A. Kerr) Business Enterprise in American History, 1986, 3rd ed., 1994; The Rise of Modern Business in Great Britain, the United States, and Japan, 1988; (co-author) Local Businesses, 1990; A History of Small Business in America, 1991; The Lost Dream: Businessmen and City Planning on the Pacific Coast, 1890-1920, 1993; On Board the USS Mason: The World War II Diary of James A. Dunn, 1996; (with K.A. Kerr) BF Goodrich: Tradition and Transformation, 1870-1995, 1996; Fragile Paradise: The Impact of Tourism on Maui, 1959-2000, 2001. **Address:** Department of History, Ohio State University, 230 W 17th Ave, Columbus, OH 43210, U.S.A.

BLACKMAN, Malorie. British, b. 1962. **Genres:** Children's fiction, Young adult fiction, Children's non-fiction, Young adult non-fiction. **Career:** Reuters, London, England, computer programmer, 1983-85, database manager, 1986-90; Digital Equipment, London, software specialist, 1985-86; writer, 1990-. **Publications:** FOR YOUNG ADULTS: Not So Stupid!, 1990; Trust Me, 1992. FOR CHILDREN: That New Dress!, 1991, as A New Dress for Maya, 1992; Girl Wonder and the Terrific Twins, 1991; Elaine, You're a Brat!, 1991; Girl Wonder's Winter Adventures, 1992; Hacker, 1992; Betsey Biggalow Is Here!, 1992; Betsey Biggalow the Detective, 1992; Operation Gadgetman, 1993; Hurricane Betsey, 1993; Magic Betsey, 1994; Girl Wonder to the Rescue, 1994; Rachel vs. Bonecrusher the Mighty, 1994; Rachel and the Difference Thieves, 1994; My Friend's a Gris-Quok!, 1994; Thief!, 1995; Deadly Dare, 1995; Whizziwig, 1995; Jack Sweettooth, the 73rd, 1995; Mrs. Spoon's Family, 1995; Pig Heart Boy, 1996; Whizziwig, 1996; Dangerous Reality, 1999; Tell Me No Lies, 1999; Noughts and Crosses, 2000. Contributor of short stories and poems to anthologies. **Address:** c/o Hilary Delamere, The Agency, 24 Pottery Ln, Holland Park, London W11 4LZ, England.

BLACKMAN, Sue Anne Batey. American, b. 1948. **Genres:** Economics. **Career:** Princeton University, Princeton, NJ, research and administrative assistant in department of economics, 1972-78, research aide, 1979-84, research assistant, 1985-86, senior research assistant, 1987-. **Publications:** (with W.J.

Baumol and W.E. Oates) Economics, Environmental Policy, and the Quality of Life, 1979; (with W.J. Baumol and E.N. Wolff) Productivity and American Leadership: The Long View, 1989; (with W.J. Baumol) Perfect Markets and Easy Virtue: Business Ethics and the Invisible Hand, 1991.

BLACKMER, Donald L. M. American, b. 1929. **Genres:** International relations/Current affairs, Social sciences. **Career:** Massachusetts Institute of Technology, lecturer, 1960-61, assistant professor, 1961-67, Assistant Director, Center for International Studies, 1961-68, associate professor, 1967-73, Professor of Political Science, 1973-, Associate Dean, School of Humanities and Social Sciences, 1973-81, Director, Science, Technology, and Society Program, 1978-81, Head, Political Science Dept., 1981-88, now emeritus. **Publications:** (ed. with M.F. Millikan, and contrib.) The Emerging Nations: Their Growth and United States Policy, 1961; Unity in Diversity: Italian Communism and the Communist World, 1967; (ed. with S. Tarrow, and contrib.) Communism in Italy and France, 1974; (with A. Kriegel) The International Role of the Communist Parties of Italy and France, 1975. **Address:** Massachusetts Institute of Technology, E53-373, Cambridge, MA 02139, U.S.A.

BLACKMORE, Susan (Jane). British, b. 1951. **Genres:** Paranormal, Psychology, Autobiography/Memoirs. **Career:** University of Surrey, England, associate lecturer in parapsychology, 1975-80; University of Utrecht, Netherlands, temporary research fellow at Parapsychology Laboratory, 1980; University of Bristol, England, visiting research fellow at Brain and Perception Laboratory, 1980-88, lecturer in psychology, 1990-91; University of the West of England, Bristol, senior lecturer in psychology, 1992-99, reader in psychology, 1999-2000. North East London Polytechnic, lecturer, 1974-78; Thames Polytechnic, lecturer, 1977-78; University of Bath, lecturer, 1990-91; guest and presenter on radio and television programs. **Publications:** Beyond the Body: An Investigation of Out-of-the-Body Experiences, 1982, rev. ed., 1992; The Adventures of a Parapsychologist, 1986; Dying to Live: Near-Death Experiences, 1993; In Search of the light, 1996; The Meme Machine, 1999; Consciousness: An Introduction, 2003. Work represented in books. Contributor of articles and reviews to periodicals.

BLACKSTOCK, Terri. Also writes as Terri Herrington, Tracy Hughes. American, b. 1957. **Genres:** Novels, Mystery/Crime/Suspense, Romance/ Historical. **Career:** Writer. **Publications:** SUNCOAST CHRONICLES SERIES: Evidence of Mercy, 1995; Justifiable Means, 1996; Ulterior Motives, 1996; Presumption of Guilt, 1997. SECOND CHANCES SERIES: Never Again Goodbye, 1996; When Dreams Cross, 1996; Blind Trust, 1997; Broken Wings, 1998. NEWPOINTE 911 SERIES: Private Justice, 1998; Shadow of Doubt, 1998; Word of Honor, 1999; Trial by Fire, 2000. WITH B. LaHAYE: Seasons under Heaven, 1999; Showers in Season, 2000. AS TERRI HERRINGTON: Blue Fire, 1984; Head over Heels, 1986; Lovers' Reunion, 1986; Tender Betrayer, 1986; A Secret Stirring, 1986; Stolen Moments, 1987; Tangled Triumphs, 1987; Ticket to a Fantasy, 1987; Wife Wanted, 1988; Her Father's Daughter, 1991; Flashback, 1993; One Good Man, 1993; Silena, 1993; Winner Take All, 1995. AS TRACY HUGHES: Impressions, 1986; Quiet Lightning, 1986; Above the Clouds, 1988; Emerald Windows, 1989; Jo (Calloway Corner Series), 1989; White Lies & Alibis, 1990; Honorbound, 1991; Second Chances, 1991; Father Knows Best, 1992; Sand Man, 1992; Delta Dust, 1993; Catch a Falling Star, 1994; Heaven Knows, 1994; The Princess and the Pauper, 1994; To Heaven and Back, 1995; Daniel-Return to Calloway Corners, 1996. **Address:** c/o Author Mail, Zondervan, 5300 Patterson SE, Grand Rapids, MI 49530, U.S.A.

BLACKSTONE (OF STOKE NEWINGTON IN GREATER LONDON), Baroness. (Tessa Blackstone). British, b. 1942. **Genres:** Education, Politics/ Government, Social commentary. **Career:** London School of Economics, assistant lecturer, 1966-69, lecturer in social administration, 1969-75; Cabinet Office, Central Policy Review Staff, adviser, 1975-78; University of London, professor of educational administration, 1978-83; Inner London Education Authority, deputy education officer, 1983-86; Centre for Studies in Social Policy, London fellow, 1972-74; Policy Studies Institute, visiting fellow, 1987; University of London, Birkbeck College, master, 1987-97; Minister of State for Education and Employment, 1997-2001; Minister of State for the Arts, 2001-. **Publications:** (with K. Gales, R. Hadley and W. Lewis) Students in Conflict: L.S.E. in 1967, 1970; A Fair Start: The Provision of PreSchool Education, 1971; Education and Day Care for Young Children in Need: The American Experience, 1973; (with G. Williams and D. Metcalf) The Academic Labour Market: Economic and Social Aspects of a Profession, 1974; (with P. Lodge) Educational Policy and Education Inequality, 1982; (with J. Mortimore) Disadvantage and Education, 1982; (with G. Williams) Response to Adversity, 1983; (with others) Testing Children, 1983; (with W. Plowden) Inside the Think Tank: Advising the Cabinet 1971-83, 1988;

Prisons and Penal Reform, 1990; (ed. with B. Parekh and P. Saunders) Race Relations in Britain, 1997. **Address:** DCMS, 2-4 Cockspur St, London SW14 5DH, England.

BLACKSTONE, James. See BROSNAN, John.

BLACKWELL, Richard J. American, b. 1929. **Genres:** Sciences, Bibliography, Translations. **Career:** John Carroll University, Cleveland, OH, instructor, 1954-57, assistant professor, 1957-61; St. Louis University, Missouri, associate professor, 1961-66, professor of philosophy, 1966-, Danforth Chair in the Humanities, 1986-, now emeritus. The Modern Schoolman, associate ed., 1961-. **Publications:** (trans. with R. Spath and W. E. Thirlkel) Commentary on Aristotle's Physics, by St. Thomas Aquinas, 1963: (trans.) Preliminary Discourse on Philosophy in General, by Christian Wolff, 1963; Discovery in the Physical Sciences, 1969; Bibliography of the Philosophy of Science 1945-1981, 1983; (trans.) The Pendulum Clock, by C. Huygens, 1986; Galileo, Bellarmine, and the Bible, 1991; (trans. w/notes) Thomas Campanella, A Defense of Galileo, 1994. **Address:** Dept. of Philosophy, Saint Louis University, 3800 Lindell Blvd, PO Box 56907, St. Louis, MO 63156-0907, U.S.A.

BLACKWILL, Robert D. American, b. 1939. **Genres:** International relations/Current affairs, Politics/Government. **Career:** Career diplomat, 1967-. National Security Council, former director of West European Affairs; former Principal Deputy Assistant Secretary of State for Political-Military Affairs; served as United States Ambassador and Chief Negotiator at negotiations with Warsaw Pact on conventional forces in Europe. Served as Special Assistant to President George Bush for European and Soviet Affairs, 1989-90. Harvard University, John F. Kennedy School of Government, Executive Programs for United States and Russian General Officers and for members of the Russian State Duma, former associate dean, Executive Program for Senior Chinese Military Officers, and Initiative on United States-Chinese Relations, currently faculty chairman, currently Belfer Lecturer in International Security; Council on Foreign Relations, NYC, currently adjunct senior fellow. Former Peace Corps Volunteer in Malawi, Africa. **Publications:** (ed. with F.S. Larrabee) Conventional Arms Control and EastWest Security, 1989; (ed. with G.T. Allison and A. Carnesale) A Primer for the Nuclear Age, 1990; (with A. Carnesale) New Nuclear Nations, 1993; (ed. with S. Karaganov) Damage Limitation or Crisis? Russia and the Outside World, 1994; (with R. Braithwaite and A. Tanaka) Engaging Russia: A Report to the Trilateral Commission, 1995; (with M. Sturmer) Allies Divided: Transatlantic Policies for the Greater Middle East, 1997; The Future of Transatlantic Relations, 1999. Contributor of articles on European security and East-West relations to periodicals. **Address:** Harvard University, Kennedy School of Government, 79 JFK Street, Cambridge, MA 02138, U.S.A. **Online address:** Robert_Blackwill@harvard.edu

BLADES, Ann. Canadian, b. 1947. **Genres:** Children's fiction. **Career:** Children's book author and illustrator; Elementary sch. teacher, Peace River North School District, Mile 18, BC, 1967-68; Dept. of Indian Affairs and Northern Development, Tache, BC, 1969, and Surrey School District, BC, 1969-71; Clerk, London, ON, 1972; Registered Nurse, Vancouver General Hospital, 1974-75, and Mt. St. Joseph Hospital, Vancouver, part-time, 1975-80. **Publications:** Mary of Mile 18, 1971; A Boy of Tache, 1973; The Cottage at Crescent Beach, 1977; By the Sea: An Alphabet Book, 1985; The Seasons Boardbooks, 1990; Back to the Cabin, 1996; Wolf and the Seven Little Kids, 1999; Too Small, 2000. Illustrator of 11 books by others. **Address:** c/o Bella Pomer, 22 Shallmar Blvd. PH 2, Toronto, ON, Canada M5N 2Z8.

BLADES, John (D.). American, b. 1936. **Genres:** Novels, Plays/ Screenplays, Essays, Humor/Satire. **Career:** Illinois State Register, reporter, 1959; Miami Herald, Miami, FL, reporter, 1961-64; Chicago Sun-Times, Chicago, IL, Midwest magazine copy editor, 1964-65, managing editor, 1965-69; Chicago Tribune, Chicago, daily book editor, 1969-71; staff writer and articles editor for Sunday magazine, 1969-77, book editor, 1977-85, book critic, 1985-88, staff writer and book columnist for "Tempo" section, 1988-97. **Publications:** NOVELS: Small Game, 1992. PLAYS: The Last Million Miles; Someone's Been Riding My Rockinghorse. Contributor of short stories to periodicals. **Address:** 2111 Maple, Evanston, IL 60201, U.S.A. **Online address:** JDBlades@comcast.net

BLAGOJEVIC, Ljiljana. American, b. 1960. **Genres:** Architecture. **Career:** Architect and architectural historian. University of Belgrade, lecturer; School for History and Theory of Images, Belgrade, teacher. **Publications:** Modernism in Serbia: The Elusive Margins of Belgrade Architecture, 1919-1941, 2003. **Address:** c/o Author Mail, MIT Press, Five Cambridge Center, Cambridge, MA 02142, U.S.A.

BLAINE, Celia. See **MURPHEY, Cecil B(laine).**

BLAINEY, Geoffrey Norman. Australian, b. 1930. **Genres:** History, Biography. **Career:** University of Melbourne, Professor of Economic History, 1968-77, Ernest Scott Professor of History, 1977-88; Harvard University, Professor, 1982-83; University of Ballarat, Chancellor, 1994-98. Chairman: Commonwealth Literary Fund, 1971-73; Australia Council, 1977-81; Australia-China Council, 1979-84; National Council for the Centenary of Federation, 2001. **Publications:** The Peaks of Lyell, 1954; A Centenary History of the University of Melbourne, 1957; Gold and Paper, 1958; Mines in the Spinifex, 1960; The Rush That Never Ended, 1963; A History of Camberwell, 1964; (ed.) If I Remember Rightly: The Memoirs of W. S. Robinson, 1966; (co-author and ed.) Wesley College: The First Hundred Years, 1967; The Tyranny of Distance, 1966; Across a Red World, 1968; The Rise of Broken Hill, 1968; The Steel Master, 1971; The Causes of War, 1973; Triumph of the Nomads, 1975; Land Half Won, 1980; The Blainey View, 1982; Our Side of the Country, 1984; All for Australia, 1984; The Great Seesaw, 1988; A Game of Our Own: The Origins of Australian Football, 1990; Eye on Australia, 1991; Odd Fellows, 1992; The Golden Mile, 1993; Jumping over the Wheel, 1993; A Shorter History of Australia, 1994; White Gold, 1997; In Our Time, 1999; A Short History of the World, 2000; This Land Is All Horizons, 2001; Black Kettle and Full Moon, 2003; A Very Short History of the World, 2004. **Address:** PO Box 257, East Melbourne, VIC 3002, Australia.

BLAIR, Claude. British, b. 1922. **Genres:** Archaeology/Antiquities, Art/Art history. **Career:** Consultant, Christie's, London, since 1982. Assistant, Tower of London Armouries, 1951-56; Hon. Ed., Journal of Arms and Armour Society, 1953-77. Keeper of Metalwork, Victorian and Albert Museum, London, 1972-82 (Assistant Keeper of Metalwork, 1966-72; Deputy Keeper, 1966-72). **Publications:** European Armour, 1958; European and American Arms, 1962; Pistols of the World, 1968; Three Presentation Swords in the Victoria and Albert Museum, 1972; The James A. de Rothschild Collection at Waddesdon Manor: Arms, Armour and Base Metalwork, 1974. EDITOR: Pollard's History of Firearms, 1983; The History of Silver, 1987; Scottish Firearms, 1995; (and contrib.) The Crown Jewels, 1998. **Address:** 90 Links Rd, Ashtead, Surrey KT2I 2HW, England.

BLAIR, E(lizabeth) Anne. Australian, b. 1946. **Genres:** History, Politics/Government, Biography, Military/Defense/Arms control. **Career:** Monash University, Melbourne, research associate at National Center for Australia Studies. **Publications:** Lodge in Vietnam: A Patriot Abroad, 1995; There to the Bitter End: Ted Serong in Vietnam, 2001. **Address:** 41 Swallow St, Port Melbourne, VIC 3207, Australia. **Online address:** jablair@smartchat.net.au

BLAIR, Jessica. See **SPENCE, William John Duncan.**

BLAIR, L. E. See **CALHOUN, B. B.**

BLAIR, Sheila. American. **Genres:** Art/Art history. **Career:** Editor, Macmillan Dictionary of Art, Islamic section. **Publications:** (with O. Grabar) Epic Images and Contemporary History: The Illustrations of the Great Mongol Shahnama, 1980; The Ilkhanid Shrine Complex at Natanz, Iran, 1986; (ed. with J.M. Bloom) Images of Paradise in Islamic Art, 1991; The Monumental Inscriptions from Early Islamic Iran and Transoxiana, 1992; (with J.M. Bloom) The Art and Architecture of Islam, 1250-1800, 1994; Islamic Arts, 1997. **Address:** 85 2nd St. 6th Floor, San Francisco, CA 94105, U.S.A.

BLAIRMAN, Jacqueline. See **PINTO, Jacqueline.**

BLAIS, Andre. Canadian, b. 1947. **Genres:** Politics/Government. **Career:** University of Ottawa, ON, faculty member, 1972-74; Laval University, Quebec City, QC, faculty member, 1974-75; Universite de Montreal, Montreal, QC, teacher of political science, 1975-. **Publications:** The Budget Maximizing Bureaucrat, 1991; Letting the People Decide, 1992; The Challenge of Direct Democracy, 1996; A Question of Ethics, 1998; Governments, Parties, and Public Sector Employees, 1998; An Unsteady State: The 1997 Canadian Federal Election, 2000; To Vote or not to Vote? The Merits and Limits of Rational Choice, 2000. **Address:** Department of Political Science, Universite de Montreal, Montreal, QC, Canada H3C 3J7. **Online address:** blaisa@pol.umontreal.ca

BLAISDELL, Bob. (Robert). American, b. 1959. **Genres:** Children's fiction, Poetry, Education. **Career:** Kingsborough Community College of the City University of New York, Brooklyn, NY, associate professor. **Publica-**

tions: RETELLINGS; Robin Hood, 1994; Favorite Greek Myths, 1995; The Story of Hercules, 1997. ADAPTER, ABRIDGED EDITIONS: F.H. Burnett, The Secret Garden, 1994; L.F. Baum, The Wizard of Oz, 1995; C. Collodi, The Adventures of Pinocchio, 1995; L.M. Montgomery, Anne of Green Gables, 1995; K. Grahame, The Wind in the Willows, 1995; V. Hugo, The Hunchback of Notre Dame, 1995; D. Defoe, Robinson Crusoe, 1995; Burnett, A Little Princess, 1996; E.T.A. Hoffmann, The Story of the Nutcracker, 1996; R.L. Stevenson, Kidnapped, 1996; M. Twain, The Adventures of Tom Sawyer, 1996; Twain, The Prince and the Pauper, 1997; L.M. Alcott, Little Women, 1997; Alcott, Little Men, 1997; M.W. Shelley, Frankenstein, 1997; E.R. Burroughs, Tarzan, 1997; B. Stoker, Dracula, 1997; L. Carroll, Alice in Wonderland, 1998; J. Spyri, Heidi, 1998; Twain, The Adventures of Huckleberry Finn, 1998; W. Scott, Ivanhoe, 1999. EDITOR: T. Hardy, Hardy's Selected Poems, 1995; D.H. Lawrence, Snake and Other Poems, 1999; Tolstoy as Teacher: Leo Tolstoy's Writings on Education, 1999; Great Speeches by Native Americans, 2000; Classic Tales and Fables for Children by Leo Tolstoy, 2001; Irish Verse: An Anthology, 2002; Poems of Faith, 2003; The Civil War: A Book of Quotations, 2004; Elizabethan Poetry: An Anthology, 2005; Marcus Garvey: Selected Writings and Speeches, 2005. Contributor to periodicals. **Address:** 401 W 118th St No. 33, New York, NY 10027, U.S.A. **Online address:** rblaisdell@kbcc.cuny.edu

BLAISE, Clark. Canadian/American (born United States), b. 1940. **Genres:** Novels, Novellas/Short stories, Travel/Exploration. **Career:** University of Wisconsin, Milwaukee, instructor, 1964-65; Concordia University (previously Sir George Williams University), Montreal, lecturer, 1966-67, assistant professor, 1968-71, associate professor, 1971- 75, professor of English, 1976-78; York University, Toronto, professor of humanities, 1978-81; visiting professor: Skidmore College, 1981-84; Emory University, 1985-87; Columbia University, 1987-90; University of Iowa, 1990-98; University of California-Berkeley, 1998-99. **Publications:** A North American Education (short stories), 1973; Tribal Justice (short stories), 1974; (with B. Mukherjee) Days and Nights in Calcutta (travel memoir), 1977; Lunar Attractions (novel), 1979; Lusts, 1983; Resident Alien, 1986; Man and His World, 1992; I Had a Father, 1993; If I Were Me, 1997; Time Lord: Sir Sandford Fleming and the Creation of Standard Time, 2001; New and Selected Stories, 4 vols., 2000-05. **Address:** 130 Rivoli St, San Francisco, CA 94117, U.S.A. **Online address:** clarquito@aol.com

BLAKE, Andrea. See **WEALE, Anne.**

BLAKE, Jennifer. See **MAXWELL, Patricia Anne.**

BLAKE, Jon. British, b. 1954. **Genres:** Children's fiction, Plays/Screenplays, Novellas/Short stories. **Career:** Bretton Woods School, Peterborough, England, English and drama teacher, 1979-80; Chilwell Comprehensive, Nottingham, England, English teacher, 1980-81; Broxtowe College, Nottingham, lecturer in communications, 1982-84; International Community Centre, Nottingham, assistant warden, 1984-85; part-time community education worker in Cardiff, Wales, 1988-92; lecturer in creative writing, University of Glamorgan, 1994-; writer. **Publications:** YOUNG ADULT NOVELS: Yatesy's Rap, 1986; Geoffrey's First, 1988; Trick or Treat?, 1988; Holiday in Happy Street, 1989; Oddly, 1989; Roboskool, 1990; Roboskool: The Revenge, 1991; The King of Rock and Roll, 1991; The Likely Stories, 1991; The Melody of Oddly, 1992; How I Became a Star, 1995. CHILDREN'S BOOKS: Wriggly Pig, 1991; Binka and the Banana Boat, 1991; Impo, 1991; Daley B, 1991; Pilot Bird and Gums, 1991; The Ghost of Joseph Coney, 1994; Little Stupendo, 1995; FS3, 1995. OTHER: Direct Action (television play), 1986; Net (play), 1986; Showdown (stories), 1988; The Birdwoman of Normal Street (play), 1991; The Hell Hound of Hooley Street (stories), 1993; Life (tv play), 1995. **Address:** David Higham Associates, 5-8 Lower John St., Golden Square, London W1R 4HA, England.

BLAKE, Justin. See **BOWEN, John (Griffith).**

BLAKE, Ken. See **BULMER, (Henry) Kenneth.**

BLAKE, Laurel. See **PALENCIA, Elaine Fowler.**

BLAKE, Michael. American, b. 1943. **Genres:** Westerns/Adventure. **Career:** Writer. **Publications:** Stacy's Knights (screenplay), 1983; Dances with Wolves (novel), 1988, (screenplay), 1990; (with K. Costner and J. Wilson) Dances with Wolves: The Illustrated Story of the Epic Film, 1990; Airman Mortensen (novel), 1991; Marching to Valhalla, 1996; Holy Road, 2001.

BLAKE, Norman Francis. British (born Brazil), b. 1934. **Genres:** Language/Linguistics, Literary criticism and history, Biography, Translations.

Career: Professor of English Language, University of Sheffield, since 1973. Lecturer, to Sr. Lecturer, University of Liverpool, 1959-73. **Publications:** Caxton and His World, 1969; Caxton's Quattros Sermones, 1973; The English Language in Medieval Literature, 1977; Non-Standard Language in English Literature, 1981; Shakespeare's Language, 1983; Textual Tradition of the Canterbury Tales, 1985; Traditional English Grammar and Beyond, 1988; William Caxten and English Literary Culture, 1991; An Introduction to the Language of Literature, 1990; The Language of Literature, 1993; Essays on Shakespeare's Language, 1996; A History of the English Language, 1996. EDITOR: (and trans.) The Saga of the Jomsvikings, 1962; The Phoenix, 1964; William Caxton's Reynard the Fox, 1970; Middle English Religious Prose, 1972; Selections from William Caxton, 1973; Caxton's Own Prose, 1973; Caxton: England's First Publisher, 1976; William Caxton: A Bibliographical Guide, 1985; The Index of Printed Middle English Prose, 1985; Cambridge History of the English Language, vol. II, 1066-1476, 1992. **Address:** Dept. of English Language & Linguistics, Sheffield S10 2TN, England.

BLAKE, Patrick. See EGLETON, Clive.

BLAKE, Quentin. British, b. 1932. **Genres:** Children's fiction. **Career:** Illustrator for various British magazines, including Punch and Spectator, and for children's and educational books, 1948-. Visiting Tutor, 1986-, and Visiting Professor, 1989-, Royal Coll. of Art, London (Tutor, School of Graphic Design, 1965-78; Head of the Illustration Dept., 1978-86). **Publications:** SELF-ILLUSTRATED: Patrick, 1968; Jack and Nancy, 1969; A Band of Angels, 1969: Angelo, 1970; Snuff, 1973; Lester at the Seaside, 1975; Lester and the Unusual Pet, 1975; The Adventures of Lester, 1978; (ed.) Custard and Company: Poems by Ogden Nash, 1979; Mister Magnolia, 1980; Quentin Blake's Nursery Rhyme Book, 1983; The Story of the Dancing Frog, 1984; Mrs. Armitage on Wheels, 1987; Quentin Blake's ABC, 1989; All Join In, 1991; Cockatoos, 1992; Simpkin, 1993; Clown, 1995; The Quentin Blake Book of Nonsense Verse, 1995; The Quentin Blake Book of Nonsense Stories, 1996; Ten Frogs, 1997; The Green Ship, 1998; (with J. Yeoman) Up with Birds, 1998; Zagazoo, 1998; Fantastic Daisy Artichoke, 1999; Mrs. Armitage and the Big Wave, 1998; (with J. Cassidy) Drawing for the Artistically Undiscovered, 1999; Loveykins, 2002; Magic Pencil, 2002; Tell Me a Picture, 2003; Mrs. Armitage: Queen of the Road, 2003. Illustrator of books by R. Dahl; R. Hoban, M.-A. and E. Murail, B. Pitzorno, W. Steig. **Address:** c/o A.P. Watt Ltd., 20 John St, London WC1N 2DR, England. **Online address:** www.quentinblake.com

BLAKE, Raymond B. Canadian, b. 1958. **Genres:** History, Local history/Rural topics. **Career:** Teacher of social studies and history at a collegiate institute in St. Anthony, Newfoundland, 1979-86; Brock University, St. Catharines, ON, course director for Canadian social history, 1991; York University, Downsview, ON, course director for Canadian economic history, 1991-92; University of Alberta, Edmonton, visiting assistant professor of history, 1992-93; St. Thomas University, Fredericton, NB, assistant professor of history, 1993-94; Mount Allison University, Sackville, NB, professor of Canadian studies, 1994-, Winthrop Pickard Bell fellow at Centre for Canadian Studies, 1994-95, director of the center, 1995-; University of Regina, Saskatchewan Institute of Public Policy, director. Canadian Historical Review, bibliographer, 1988-91, proofreader, 1991. **Publications:** Canadians at Last: Canada Integrates Newfoundland as a Province, 1994; From Fishermen to Fish: Canada Integrates Newfoundland as a Province, 2000; The Trajectories of Rural Canada, 2003. CO-EDITOR: (with J. Keshen, and contrib.) A History of Social Welfare in Canada: Selected Readings, 1995; The Welfare State in Canada, 1997; Canada and World Order, 2000. Contributor to books. Contributor of articles and reviews to history and Canadian studies journals. **Address:** Saskatchewan Institute of Public Policy, University of Regina, Regina, SK, Canada S4S 0A2. **Online address:** Raymond.Blake@uregina.ca

BLAKE, Sally. See SAUNDERS, Jean.

BLAKE, Stephen P. American, b. 1942. **Genres:** Geography, Local history/Rural topics. **Career:** University of Minnesota, Minneapolis, visiting professor of history, 1974-84, and administrator; St. Olaf College, Northfield, MN, associate professor of history of India and the Middle East, 1986-. **Publications:** Shahjahanabad: The Sovereign City in Mughal India, Cambridge University Press, 1991. **Address:** Department of History, St. Olaf College, Northfield, MN 55057, U.S.A.

BLAKE, Sterling. See BENFORD, Gregory (Albert).

BLAKELY, Mary Kay. American, b. 1948. **Genres:** Novels, Autobiography/Memoirs, Essays. **Career:** Indiana University-Purdue University at Fort Wayne, instructor in women's studies, 1976-80; New School for Social Research, New York City, lecturer and instructor in writing, 1984-97; Missouri School of Journalism, associate professor, 1997-; free-lance writer for all major magazines. Contributing editor: Vogue, 1981-84; Lear's 1989-91; Ms. 1981-2001; Los Angeles Times Magazine, 1994-97. Organizer of and frequent lecturer at conferences. Cofounder of Cathryn Adamsky Women in Need Fund. **Publications:** (with G. Kaufman) Pulling Our Own Strings: A Collection of Feminist Humor and Satire, 1980; Wake Me When It's Over: A Journey to the Edge and Back, 1989; American Mom: Motherhood, Politics and Humble Pie, 1994; Red, White and Oh So Blue, 1996. **Address:** c/o Phyllis Wender, 38 E 29th St., 10th floor, New York, NY 10016, U.S.A.

BLAKEMORE, Colin (Brian). British, b. 1944. **Genres:** Biology, Medicine/Health, Psychology, Sciences. **Career:** Cambridge University, Physiological Laboratory, university demonstrator, 1968-72; fellow and director of Medical Studies, Downing Coll., and lecturer in physiology, Cambridge, 1977-79; Oxford University, Waynflete Professor of Physiology, 1979-, Magdalen Coll., professorial fellow, 1979-; Centre for Cognitive Neuroscience, Oxford, director, 1996-2003; European Dana Alliance for the Brain, vice-chairman, 1997-; Medical Research Council, chief executive, 2003-. Perspectives in Vision Research, Plenum, NY, series editor, 1981-; IBRO News, ed.-in-chief, 1986-2000; NeuroReport, associate ed., 1989-2003. British Assn for the Advancement of Science, president, 1997-98, chairman, 2001-03. President: British Neuroscience Association, 1997-2000, Physiological Society, 2001-03, Biosciences Federation, 2002-03, Association of British Science Writers, 2004-. Fellow, Royal Society, 1992-; Hon. Fellow, Institute of Biology, Chartered Biologist, 1996-. **Publications:** Mechanics of the Mind, 1977; The Mind Machine, 1988; (with S.D. Iversen) Sex & Society, 1999. EDITOR: Handbook of Psychobiology, 1975; Mindwaves, 1987; Images and Understanding, 1990; Vision: Coding and Efficiency, 1990; (section ed.) The Cognitive Neurosciences, 1995; (with S. Jennett) The Oxford Companion to the Body, 2001; (with A. Parker and A. Derrington) The Physiology of Cognitive Processes, 2003; (with C.A. Heywood and A.D. Milner) The Roots of Visual Awareness, 2003. **Address:** Medical Research Council, 20 Park Crescent, Oxford W1B 1AL, England. **Online address:** colin.blakemore@headoffice.mrc.ac.uk

BLAKESLEE, Sandra. American, b. 1943. **Genres:** Medicine/Health, Sciences. **Career:** New York Times, science writer, 1968-. **Publications:** (with L. Gillespie) You Don't Have to Live With Cystitis, 1987; (with J.S. Wallerstein) Second Chances: Men, Women, and Children a Decade After Divorce, 1989; (with J.S. Wallerstein) The Good Marriage: How & Why Love Lasts, 1995; (with W.S. Ramachardan) Phantoms in the Brain, 1998; (with J. Wallerstein and J. Lewis) The Unexpected Legacy of Divorce, 2000. **Address:** 16 Camino Delilah, Santa Fe, NM 87506-7937, U.S.A.

BLAKESLEY, Christopher L. American, b. 1945. **Genres:** Law. **Career:** U.S. Department of State (Office of the Legal Adviser), Washington, DC, attorney and adviser, 1973-75; Louisiana State University, Baton Rouge, assistant professor to associate professor of law, 1976-80; University of the Pacific, Sacramento, CA, professor of law, 1980-87; Louisiana State University, professor, 1987-, J.Y. Sanders Professor of Law, 1991-. Lecturer in Hungary, Austria, and France. **Publications:** (with Wardle and Parker) Treatise: Family Law in the United States, 4 vols, 1988; Terrorism, Drugs, International Law, and the Protection of Human Liberty, 1992; Louisiana Family Law, 1994; (with Oliver, Firmage, Scott, and Williams) The International Legal System, 4th ed, 1995. Work represented in anthologies. Contributor of articles and reviews to professional journals in the United States and abroad.

BLAKEY, Nancy. American, b. 1955. **Genres:** How-to books. **Career:** Author, journalist, columnist. Worked as able-bodied seaman on ferry boats in and around Seattle, WA, 1974-84. Professional model in Australia and in Seattle, 1978-80. Author of Mudpies, a column in Seattle's Child, also syndicated nationally, 1987-. **Publications:** The Mudpies Activity Book: Recipes for Invention, 1989; More Mudpies: 101 Alternatives to Television, 1994; Lotions, Potions, and Slime: Mudpies and More!, 1996; The Mudpies Book of Boredom Busters, 2000; Go Outside!, 2002. Contributor to magazines and anthologies. **Address:** 15890 Euclid Ave, Bainbridge Island, WA 98110, U.S.A.

BLAMIRES, Alcuin (Godfrey). British, b. 1946. **Genres:** Literary criticism and history, Women's studies and issues. **Career:** University of Wales, Lampeter, lecturer, 1970-99; Goldsmiths College, London, reader in English, 1999-. **Publications:** The Canterbury Tales (criticism), 1987; (ed. with K. Pratt and C.W. Marx) Woman Defamed and Woman Defended: An Anthology of Medieval Texts, 1992; The Case for Women in Medieval Culture,

1997. Contributor to medieval studies journals. **Address:** Department of English, Goldsmiths College, University of London, New Cross, London SE14 6NW, England.

BLAMIRES, Harry. British, b. 1916. **Genres:** Novels, Language/Linguistics, Literary criticism and history, Theology/Religion. **Career:** King Alfred's Coll., Winchester, head of English Dept., 1948-72, dean of Degrees, 1972-74, and dean of Arts, 1974-76. **Publications:** Repair the Ruins, 1950; English in Education, 1951; The Devil's Hunting Grounds, 1954; Cold War in Hell, 1955; Blessing Unbounded, 1955, as Highway to Heaven, 1984; The Faith and Modern Error, 1956, as The Secularist Heresy, 1980; The Will and the Way, 1957, as A God Who Acts, 1981; The Kirkbride Conversations, 1958; Kirkbride & Company, 1959; The Offering of Man, 1959; The Christian Mind, 1963; A Defence of Dogmatism (in US as The Tyranny of Time), 1965; The Bloomsday Book: Guide through Joyce's Ulysses, 1966; Word Unheard: A Guide through Eliot's Four Quartets, 1969; Milton's Creation: A Guide through Paradise Lost, 1971; A Short History of English Literature, 1974; Where Do We Stand?, 1980; Twentieth-Century English Literature, 1982; (ed.) Guide to Twentieth-Century Literature in English, 1983; On Christian Truth, 1983; Notes on "A Portrait of the Artist as a Young Man," 1984; Words Made Flesh, 1985, in UK as The Marks of the Maker, 1987; Studying James Joyce, 1987; Meat not Milk (in US as Recovering the Christian Mind), 1988; The Victorian Age of Literature, 1988; The Age of Romantic Literature, 1989; A History of Literary Criticism, 1991; Notes on John Betjeman: Selected Poems, 1992; The Queen's English, 1994; The Cassell Guide to Common Errors in English, 1997; The Post-Christian Mind, 1999; The Penguin Guide to Plain English, 2000; Compose Yourself-and Write Good English, 2003. **Address:** 3 Glebe Close, Keswick, Cumbria CA12 5QQ, England.

BLANCHARD, Olivier Jean. French, b. 1948. **Genres:** Economics. **Career:** Massachusetts Institute of Technology, Cambridge, instructor in economics, 1977; Harvard University, Cambridge, MA, assistant professor, 1977-81, associate professor, 1981-83; Massachusetts Institute of Technology, associate professor, 1983-85, professor of economics, 1985-. Visiting professor at Universite de Paris I, 1983, and Columbia University, 1987; London School of Economics and Political Science, academic visitor, 1986; National Bureau of Economic Research, research associate, 1979-; Center for Economic Performance, research associate and member of advisory board, 1992-. **Publications:** (with R. Dornbusch and R. Layard) Restoring Europe's Prosperity: Macroeconomic Papers From the Centre for European Policy Studies, 1986; (with S. Fischer) Lectures on Macroeconomics, 1989; World Imbalances, 1989; Reform in Eastern Europe, 1991; La desinflation competitive, le mark et les politiques budgetaires en Europe, 1991, trans. as Competitive Disinflation, the Mark, and Fiscal Policies in Europe, 1992; East-West Migration, 1992; (ed. with K. Froot and J. Sachs) The Transition in Eastern Europe, 1993. Work represented in anthologies. Contributor to economic and political studies journals. **Address:** Department of Economics, Massachusetts Institute of Technology, 50 Memorial Drive, Cambridge, MA 02142, U.S.A.

BLANCHARD, Stephen (Thomas). British, b. 1950. **Genres:** Novels. **Career:** Writer. Worked as carpenter, 1975-85, dealer in second-hand goods, 1985-90, and mail carrier, 1990-97, all in London, England. **Publications:** NOVELS: Gagarin and I, 1995; Wilson's Island, 1997. Contributor of stories and articles to magazines. **Address:** 74 Rectory Grove, London SW4 0ED, England.

BLANCO, Richard. American (born Spain), b. 1968. **Genres:** Poetry. **Career:** Poet. Butterfly Lightning (a poetry reading series), cofounder; consultant engineer. Central Connecticut State University, New Britain, CT, poet-in-residence, assistant professor of English and director of creative writing, 1999-; Hudson Valley Writers' Center, staff instructor. Has appeared on National Public Radio. **Publications:** City of a Hundred Fires, 1998. Contributor to periodicals and anthologies. **Address:** c/o Briarwood Writers Alliance, 61 Briarwood Circle, Needham Heights, MA 02494, U.S.A.

BLAND, Eleanor Taylor. American. **Genres:** Mystery/Crime/Suspense. **Career:** Author of mystery novels. Works as an auditor. **Publications:** Dead Time, 1992; Slow Burn, 1993; Gone Quiet, 1994; Done Wrong, 1995; Keep Still, 1996. **Address:** c/o St. Martin's Press, 175 Fifth Ave. Rm. 1715, New York, NY 10010, U.S.A.

BLAND, Peter. British/New Zealander, b. 1934. **Genres:** Plays/Screenplays, Poetry. **Career:** Free-lance writer and actor, London. Ed., Poetry prog., New Zealand Broadcasting Corp., 1960-64; Co-founder and Artistic Director, Downstage Theatre Co, Wellington, 1964-68; regular contributor, London Magazine, 1964-99. **Publications:** POETRY: (with J. Boyd and V. O'Leary)

Three Poets, 1958; My Side of the Story: Poems, 1960-1964, 1964; Domestic Interiors. 1964; The Man with the Carpet-Bag, 1972; Mr. Maui, 1976; Primitives, 1979; Stone Tents, 1981; The Crusoe Factor, 1985; Selected Poems, 1987, 1998; Paper Boats, 1990; Selected Poems, 1998. PLAYS: Father's Day, 1967; George the Mad Ad Man, 1967. **Address:** c/o Maureen Vincent, PFD, Drury House, 34-43 Russell St., London WC2B 5HA, England.

BLANK, G(regory) Kim. Canadian, b. 1952. **Genres:** Poetry, Literary criticism and history, Essays, Humor/Satire. **Career:** University of Victoria, BC, lecturer in English, 1978-80; University of Southampton, England, instructor in English, 1980-83; Open University, Milton Keynes, England, tutor, 1983-85; University of Namibia, lecturer in English, 1984-86; University of Victoria, assistant professor, 1986-90, associate professor, 1990-96, director of graduate studies, 1994-99, professor of English, 1996-, director of writing, 2002-05. **Publications:** Wordsworth's Influence on Shelley: A Study of Poetic Authority, 1987; (ed.) The New Shelley: Later Twentieth-Century Views, 1990; (co-ed.) Influence and Resistance in Nineteenth-Century English Poetry, 1993; Wordsworth and Feeling: The Poetry of an Adult Child, 1995; Sex, Life Itself, and the Original Nanaimo Bar Recipe, 1999; (co-author) The Writer's Block Calendar. Contributor to books. Contributor of articles, columns, chapters, and reviews to academic journals and newspapers. **Address:** Dept of English, MS 7236, University of Victoria, Box 3070, Victoria, BC, Canada V8W 3W1. **Online address:** gkblank@uvic.ca

BLANK, Harrod. American, b. 1963. **Genres:** Transportation. **Career:** Filmmaker, photographer, and author. Producer, director, and editor of the documentary films Wild Wheels, 1992, and Driving the Dream, 1997. **Publications:** Wild Wheels, 1993; Art Cars: The Cars, the Artists, the Obsession, the Craft, 2002; Automorphosis (film), 2005.

BLANK, Les. American, b. 1935. **Genres:** Plays/Screenplays. **Career:** Filmmaker. Flower Films, El Cerrito, Calif., founder and director, 1967-. Louis B. Mayer artist in residence at Dartmouth College, 1984; distinguished filmmaker in residence at San Diego State University, 1989-90. Lecturer abroad on behalf of U.S. Information Agency; Adjunct Asst. Professor, Film-University of California, Berkeley; Guggenheim Fellowship, 1977. **Publications:** "Till Death Should We Part" (one-act play), first produced in New Orleans, La., at Tulane University, 1959. "Quab" (threeact play), first produced in New Orleans at Tulane University, 1960. (Editor with James Bogan) Burden of Dreams: Screenplay, Journals, Reviews, Photographs, North Atlantic Books, 1985. **Address:** Flower Films, 10341 San Pablo Ave, El Cerrito, CA 94530, U.S.A.

BLANKENHORN, David (George), (III). American (born Germany), b. 1955. **Genres:** Sociology. **Career:** Writer and community organizer. Citizen Action, community organizer, 1978-84; Institute for American Values, NYC, founder, 1985, president, 1985-. **Publications:** Fatherless America: Confronting Our Most Urgent Social Problem, 1995. EDITOR: (with S. Bayme and J.B. Elshtain) Rebuilding the Nest: A New Commitment to the American Family, 1990; (with D. Mack) The Book of Marriage: The Wisest Answers to the Toughest Questions, 2001. **Address:** Institute for American Values, 1841 Broadway Ste 211, New York, NY 10023, U.S.A. **Online address:** info@americanvalues.org; www.americanvalues.org

BLASER, Robin (Francis). Canadian/American, b. 1925. **Genres:** Poetry, Essays, Translations. **Career:** Harvard Coll. Library, Cambridge, MA, Librarian, 1955-59; California Historical Society, Assistant Curator, 1960-61; San Francisco State Coll., Librarian, 1962-66; Simon Fraser University, BC, Lecturer in Poetry, 1966-72, Professor of English, 1972-86, Professor, Centre for the Arts, 1980-84, Professor Emeritus of English, 1986-. **Publications:** The Moth Poem, 1964; (trans.) Les Chimeres, by Nerval, 1965; Cups, 1968; The Holy Forest Section, 1970; Image-Nations 1-12, 1974; Image-Nations 13-14, 1975; Syntax, 1983; The Faerie Queen and The Park, 1987; Pell Mell, 1988; The Holy Forest, 1993; H. Birtwistle, The Last Supper (libretto), 2000; Wanders (poetry), 2002; Even on Sunday (poetry), 2002; The Irreparable (essays), 2003. EDITOR: The Collected Books of Jack Spicer, 1975; Particular Accidents by George Bowering, 1980; (co-) Art and Reality, 1986; L. Dudek, Infinite Worlds, 1988. **Address:** 1636 Trafalgar St, Vancouver, BC, Canada V6K 3R7.

BLASHFORD-SNELL, John Nicholas. British, b. 1936. **Genres:** Animals/Pets, Archaeology/Antiquities, Military/Defense/Arms control, Natural history, Travel/Exploration, Autobiography/Memoirs. **Career:** Regular Army Officer. Founder, Operations Drake and Raleigh, London, Chairman, Scientific Exploration Society. Trustee, Operation New World. Leader of: Great Abbai (Blue Nile) Expedition, 1968, Dahlak Quest Expedition, 1969-

70, British Trans-Americas Expedition, 1971-72, Zaire River Expedition, 1974-75, Operation Drake, 1978-80, Operation Raleigh, 1984-91, and many others. **Publications:** (with G.R. Snailham) The Expedition Organisers Guide, 1969; (with T. Wintringham) Weapons and Tactics, 1974; Where the Trails Run Out, 1974; In the Steps of Stanley, 1975; (with A. Ballantine) Expeditions: The Experts' Way, 1977; A Taste for Adventure, 1978; (with M. Cable) In the Wake of Drake, 1980; (with M. Cable) Operation Drake, 1981; Mysteries: Encounters with the Unexplained, 1984; Operation Raleigh: The Start of an Adventure, 1987; (with A. Tweedy) Operation Raleigh: Adventure Challenge, 1988; (with A. Tweedy) Operation Raleigh: Adventure Unlimited, 1990; Something Lost behind the Ranges, 1994; (with R. Lenska) Mammoth Hunt, 1996; (with G.R. Snailham) Kota Mama, 2000; (with G.R. Snailham) East to the Amazon, 2002. **Address:** c/o The Scientific Exploration Society, Expedition Base, Motocombe Nr Shaftesbury, Dorset SP7 9PB, England.

BLASI, Anthony J(oseph). American, b. 1946. **Genres:** Sociology, Theology/Religion. **Career:** University of Louisville, KY, assistant professor of sociology, 1976-78; Daemen College, Amherst, NY, associate professor of sociology and chairperson of department, 1978-80; University of Hawaii at Hilo, assistant professor of sociology, 1986-90; Muskingum College, New Concord, OH, associate professor of sociology, 1990-94; Tennessee State University, associate professor, 1994-99, professor of sociology, 2000-. **Publications:** A Phenomenological Transformation of the Social Scientific Study of Religion, 1985; Moral Conflict and Christian Religion, 1988; Early Christianity as a Social Movement, 1989; Making Charisma: The Social Construction of Paul's Public Image, 1991; A Sociology of Johannine Christianity, 1996; Organized Religion and Seniors' Mental Health, 1999; (ed.) Handbook of Early Christianity; Social Science Perspectives, 2003; A History of Sociological Teaching and Research at Catholic Notre Dame University, 2003. **Address:** Dept of Sociology, Tennessee State University, 3500 John A. Merritt Blvd, Nashville, TN 37209, U.S.A. **Online address:** blasi3610@cs.com

BLASING, Randy. American, b. 1943. **Genres:** Poetry, Translations. **Career:** Randolph-Macon College, Ashland, VA, instructor in English, 1966-67; College of William and Mary, Williamsburg, VA, instructor in English, 1967-69; Community College of Rhode Island, Lincoln, professor of English, 1969-; Pomona College, lecturer, 1977-79; Copper Beech Press, editor, 1983-. **Publications:** TRANSLATOR (with M. Konuk): Nazim Hikmet: Human Landscapes, 1982; Poems of Nazim Hikmet, 1994; Nazim Hikmet: Human Landscapes from My Country, 2002. POETRY: The Double House of Life, 1989; Graphic Scenes, 1994; Second Home, 2001. **Address:** Copper Beech Press, PO Box 2578, Providence, RI 02906, U.S.A.

BLATCHFORD, Claire H. American, b. 1944. **Genres:** Children's fiction, Children's non-fiction, Education, Inspirational/Motivational Literature. **Career:** Caritas Day Classes for Deaf Children, Rockville Center, NY, teacher of kindergarten and art, 1970-72; writer, 1972-; Clarke School for the Deaf, art teacher, 2000-. Arts and crafts teacher at elementary schools and public libraries, 1980-94; has also worked as a substitute teacher; co-founder of independent school, 1999-2001. **Publications:** Listening: Notes from a Kindergarten Journal, 1972; Yes, I Wear a Hearing Aid, 1976; All Alone (Except for My Dog Friday), 1983; Down the Path, 1992; A Surprise for Reggie, 1992; Shawna's Bit of Blue Sky, 1992; Nick's Mission, 1994; Turning, 1994, 2nd ed., 2001; Full Face, 1997; Many Ways of Hearing, 1997; Going with the Flow, 1997; Friend of My Heart (Meeting Christ in Everyday Life), 1999; Nick's Secret, 2000; Becoming, 2004. Work represented in anthologies. Contributor of stories and articles to magazines. **Address:** 286 Patten Rd, Shelburne Falls, MA 01370, U.S.A.

BLATNER, David. American, b. 1966. **Genres:** Information science/Computers. **Career:** Writer on computer topics and graphics consultant. Executive director, Afterlife (an organization which seeks to save archival internet material). **Publications:** The Desktop Publisher's Survival Kit, 1991; (with K. Stimely) The QuarkXpress Book, 1991; Real World Photoshop 3, 1992; (with E. Taub) QuarkXpress Tips & Tricks, 1992; (with S. Aukstakalnis) Silicon Mirage: The Art and Science of Virtual Reality, 1992; Real World Photoshop 4, 1997; Real World Quarkimmedia, 1997; The Joy of Pi, 1997; Real World Scanning and Halftones: The Definitive Guide to Scanning and Halftones from the Desktop World, 1998. **Address:** c/o Reid Boates Literary Agency, Box 328, 274 Crooks Crossroad, Pittstown, NJ 08867, U.S.A. **Online address:** david@moo.com

BLAU, Francine D. American, b. 1946. **Genres:** Economics, Women's studies and issues. **Career:** Frances Perkins Professor of Industrial and Labor Relations, Cornell University, 1994-; Professor of Economics and Labor and Industrial Relations, University of Illinois, Urbana, 1983-94

(Assistant Professor, 1975-78; Associate Professor, 1978-83). Research Associate, National Bureau of Economic Research, Cambridge, Massachusetts, since 1988. Trinity Coll, instructor, 1971-74; Research Associate, Centre for Human Resource Research, Ohio State University, Columbus, 1974-75. **Publications:** (with A. Simmons, A. Freedman, and M. Dunkle) Exploitation from 9 to 5: Report of the Twentieth Century Fund Task Force on Women and Employment, 1975; Equal Pay in the Office, 1977; (with M.A. Ferber) The Economics of Women, Men and Work, 1986, 3rd ed. (with M.A. Ferber and A.E. Winkler), 1998. **Address:** School of Industrial and Labor Relations, Cornell University, 265 Ives Hall, Ithaca, NY 14853-3901, U.S.A. **Online address:** fdb4@cornell.edu

BLAU, Joel. American, b. 1945. **Genres:** Social work. **Career:** New York City Human Resources Administration, New York City, policy analyst, 1983-86, project manager, 1986-87; Columbia University, adjunct lecturer, 1983-87; State University of New York at Stony Brook, assistant professor of social welfare, 1987-93, associate professor, 1993-2000, professor, 2000-; writer. **Publications:** The Visible Poor: Homelessness in the United States, 1992; Illusions of Prosperity: America's Working Families in an Age of Economic Insecurity, 1999; The Dynamics of Social Welfare Policy, 2003. Contributor to journals in the social sciences. **Address:** School of Social Welfare, State University of New York at Stony Brook, Stony Brook, NY 11794-8231, U.S.A.

BLAUNER, Bob. (Robert Blauner). American, b. 1929. **Genres:** Race relations, Sociology, Autobiography/Memoirs. **Career:** Professor of Sociology, University of California, Berkeley, since 1978 (Assistant Professor, 1963-67; Associate Professor, 1967-78). Assistant Professor of Sociology, San Francisco State University. 1961-62, and University of Chicago, 1962-63; field: men's studies. **Publications:** Alienation and Freedom: The Factory Worker and His Industry, 1964; Racial Oppression in America, 1972; Black Lives, White Lives: Three Decades of Race Relations in America, 1989; Our Mothers' Spirits: the Death of Mothers and the Grief of Men, 1998. Contributor to journals. **Address:** Dept. of Sociology, University of California, Berkeley, CA 94720, U.S.A.

BLAUNER, Peter. American, b. 1959. **Genres:** Novels, Mystery/Crime/Suspense. **Career:** Norwich Bulletin, Norwich, CT, general assignment reporter, 1980; Newark Star-Ledger, Newark, NJ, general assignment reporter, 1981; New York Magazine, New York City, contributing editor, 1982-92. **Publications:** NOVELS: Slow Motion Riot, 1991; Casino Moon, 1994; The Intruder, 1996; Man of the Hour, 1999; The Last Good Day, 2003. **Address:** c/o Richard Pine, 250 W 57th St, New York, NY 10019, U.S.A. **Online address:** slomoriot@aol.com

BLAUW, Wim. Dutch, b. 1942. **Genres:** Sociology. **Career:** High school teacher of commercial sciences, Rotterdam, Netherlands, 1965-66; Erasmus University, Rotterdam, assistant professor, 1971-77, associate professor of economic sociology, 1977-. Rotterdam School of Architecture, assistant professor, 1972-80. Housing Association of Schoonhoven, president, 1977-81. **Publications:** (with H. Van Dijke, T. Van Gils, and F. Van Wijnen) Luchtverontreiniging: laten de industriele leiders ons stikken? (title means: Air Pollution and the Societal Responsibility of Industrial Leaders), 1970; (with J.H. Elich) Emigreren (Emigration), 1983; Suburbanisatie en sociale contacten (Suburbanisation and Social Contacts), 1986; De ontsluiting van twee waarden (The Opening of Two Polders), 1989. EDITOR: (with C. Pastor) Soort by soort. Beschouwingen over ruimtelijke segregatie als maatschappelijk probleem (Essays on Spatial Segregation as a Social Problem), 1980; Ruimte voor Openbaarheid (Space for Public Life), 1989; (with E.D. Huttman and J. Saltman, and contrib.) Urban Housing Segregation of Minorities in Western Europe and the United States, 1991; (with W.A. Arts, C. Rijnvos, and G.A. van der Wal) Tempora Mutantur: Over maatschappelijke verandering en ontwikkelingen in het sociale denken (Tempora Mutantur: On Social Change and Developments of Social Thoughts), 1992. **Address:** Faculty of Economic Sciences, Erasmus University, PO Box 1738, 3000 DR Rotterdam, Netherlands.

BLAYNE, Diana. See KYLE, Susan S(paeth).

BLECHMAN, Elaine A(nn). American, b. 1943. **Genres:** Medicine/Health. **Career:** Brentwood Veterans Administration Hospital, Brentwood, CA, intern in clinical psychology, 1969-71; University of Maryland at College Park, assistant professor of psychology, 1971-73; Yale University, New Haven, CT, assistant professor of psychiatry, 1973-77; Wesleyan University, Middletown, CT, research associate professor, 1977-83, research professor, 1983-84; Yeshiva University, Albert Einstein College of Medicine, Bronx, NY, professor of psychiatry, 1984-89; NYC Department of Health, NYC, senior research scientist, 1990; University of Colorado at Boulder, professor of psychology, 1990-. State University of New York Health Sciences Center, Brooklyn, professor, 1990. National Institute of Mental Health, member of Family Research Consortium, 1982-90. **Publications:** Solving Child Behavior Problems: At Home and at School, 1985; Prosocial Family Therapy for Juvenile Offenders: A Practitioner's Guidebook, in press; Schools and Families Together: Cost-Effective Interventions for High-Risk Youth, in press. EDITOR & CONTRIBUTOR: Behavior Modification with Women, 1984; (with K.D. Brownell) Handbook of Behavioral Medicine for Women, 1988; Emotions and the Family: For Better or for Worse, 1990; (with E.M. Hetherington) Stress, Coping, and Resiliency in Children and Families, 1996; (with Brownell) Behavioral Medicine for Women: A Comprehensive Handbook, 1998. Contributor to books and professional journals. **Address:** Department of Psychology, Campus Box 345, Muenzinger Psychology Bldg., University of Colorado at Boulder, Boulder, CO 80309, U.S.A. **Online address:** eblechman@cu.campuscw.net

BLECKER, Robert A. American, b. 1956. **Genres:** Economics. **Career:** American University, Washington, DC, instructor, 1985-86, assistant professor, 1986-92, associate professor, 1992-98, professor of economics, 1998-. Economic Policy Institute, research associate, 1991-; public service work. **Publications:** Are Americans on a Consumption Binge? The Evidence Reconsidered, 1990; Beyond the Twin Deficits: A Trade Strategy for the 1990s, 1992; (with S.D. Cohen and J.R. Paul) Fundamentals of U.S. Foreign Trade Policy, 1994; (ed.) U.S. Trade Policy and Global Growth, 1994; Taming Global Finance, 1999. Work represented in books. Contributor of articles and reviews to economic journals. **Address:** Department of Economics, American University, Washington, DC 20016, U.S.A.

BLEDSOE, Glen L(eonard). American, b. 1951. **Genres:** Young adult fiction. **Career:** U.S. Steel Co., chemical technician, 1972-78; Rubino's Music Center, Portage, IN, luthier and seller of musical instruments, 1976-80; Keizer Elementary School, Keizer, OR, teacher, 1991-, team leader, 1995-, web page designer and webmaster of http://keizer.salkeiz.k12.or.us, 1995-. Lansing Art Gallery, Lansing, MI, interim director, 1981; also works as artist in residence. **Publications:** JUVENILES (WITH K. BLEDSOE): Classic Ghost Stories II, 1998; Classic Sea Stories, 1999; Creepy Classics III, 1999; Classic Mysteries II, in press; Classic Adventure Stories, in press. Contributor to periodicals. Contributor of art to Oregon Focus. Contributor of illustrations to the compact disc accompanying Real World Bryce II. **Address:** 4230 12th St SE, Salem, OR 97302, U.S.A. **Online address:** GlnBledsoe@aol.com; members.aol.com/SublimeArt/Studios

BLEDSOE, Jerry. American, b. 1941. **Genres:** Criminology/True Crime, Adult non-fiction, Documentaries/Reportage. **Career:** Reporter and columnist, Greensboro News & Record, 1966-77 and 1981-89; feature writer, Louisville Times, 1971; contributing editor, Esquire, 1972-76; columnist, Charlotte Observer, 1977-81; publisher and editor, Down Home Press, Asheboro, North Carolina, 1989-. **Publications:** TRUE CRIME BOOKS: Bitter Blood: A True Story of Southern Family Pride, Madness, and Multiple Murder, 1988; Blood Games, 1991; Before He Wakes: A True Story of Money, Marriage, Sex, and Murder, 1994; Death Sentence: The True Story of Velma Barfield's Life, Crimes and Execution, 1998. OTHER NONFICTION: The World's Number One, Flat-Out, All-Time Great, Stock Car Racing Book, 1975; You Can't Live on Radishes: Some Funny Things Happened on the Way Back to the Land, 1976; Just Folks: Visitin' with Carolina People, 1980; Carolina Curiosities: Jerry Bledsoe's Outlandish Guide to the Dadblamedest Things to See and Do in North Carolina, 1984; From Whalebone to Hot House: A Journey Along North Carolina's Longest Highway, U.S. 64, 1986; Country Cured: Reflections from the Heart, 1989; The Bare-Bottomed Skier and Other Unlikely Tales, 1990; Blue Horizons: Faces and Places from a Bicycle Journey Along the Blue Ridge Parkway, 1993; The Angel Doll: A Christmas Story, 1996. **Address:** Down Home Press, P.O. Box 4126, Asheboro, NC 27203, U.S.A.

BLEDSOE, Karen E(lizabeth). American, b. 1962. **Genres:** Young adult fiction. **Career:** Temporary and substitute teacher at public schools in Salem, OR, 1991-95; Western Oregon University, Monmouth, instructor in biology, 1995-. Oregon Academy of Science, science education cochairperson and web page designer, 1996-; Oregon Collaborative for Excellence in the Preparation of Teachers, faculty fellow, 1997-; Oregon Public Education Network, team coach for Master WEBster web page design contest, 1998-99. U.S. Forest Service, seasonal biological technician, 1985; City of Salem, seasonal recreational leader and environmental educator, 1989-94. **Publications:** JUVENILES (WITH G.L. BLEDSOE): Classic Ghost Stories II, 1998; Classic Sea Stories, 1999; Creepy Classics III, 1999; Classic Mysteries II, in press; Classic Adventure Stories, in press. OTHER JUVENILES: (with C.

Norvall) 365 Nature Crafts, 1997; Best Friends, 1997; School Memories Album, 1998; Millennium Album, 1998. **Address:** 4320 12th St SE, Salem, OR 97302-1870, U.S.A. **Online address:** KestrelB@aol.com; members/aol/com/SublimeArt/Studios

BLEDSOE, Timothy. American, b. 1953. **Genres:** Politics/Government. **Career:** University of South Carolina at Columbia, assistant professor of political science, 1984-89; Wayne State University, Detroit, MI, associate professor, 1989-96, professor of political science, 1996-. **Publications:** Urban Reform and Its Consequences, 1988; Careers in City Politics, 1993. **Address:** Department of Political Science, Wayne State University, Detroit, MI 48202, U.S.A.

BLEE, Kathleen M. American. **Genres:** Sociology, Women's studies and issues, History, Race relations. **Career:** University of Kentucky, Lexington, 1981-96, instructor to professor, director of women's studies program, 1987-89, associate dean of, College of Arts and Sciences, 1989-91, 1992, research professor, 1994-95; University of Pittsburgh, Pittsburgh, PA, professor of sociology and director of women's studies program, 1996-, affiliated appointment with department of history, 1997-. **Publications:** Women of the Klan: Racism and Gender in the 1920s, 1991; (with D.B. Billings) The Road to Poverty: The Making of Wealth and Hardship in Appalachia, 2000; Inside Organized Racism: Women in the Hate Movement, 2002. EDITOR: No Middle Ground: Women and Radical Protest, 1998; (with F.W. Twine) Feminism and Antiracism: International Struggles for Justice, 2001. **Address:** Department of Sociology, 2003 Forbes Quad, University of Pittsburgh, Pittsburgh, PA 15260, U.S.A. **Online address:** kblee@pitt.edu

BLEGEN, Daniel M. American, b. 1950. **Genres:** History, Plays/Screenplays, Young adult fiction. **Career:** Writer. Lutheran High School, Denver, CO, teacher, 1973-75; Vikan Junior High School, Brighton, CO, teacher and chair of language arts department, 1975-83, and Brighton High School, teacher, 1983-. **Publications:** (with M. Bacon) Bent's Fort: Crossroads of Cultures on the Santa Fe Trail, 1995. PLAYS: In My Time; Faith of Our Fathers. Contributor of poetry, articles, and theatre reviews to periodicals. **Address:** 1624 Adkinson Ave., Longmont, CO 80501, U.S.A. **Online address:** danblegen@aol.com

BLEI, Norbert. American, b. 1935. **Career:** City News Bureau, Chicago, IL, reporter, 1958-59; high school English teacher, 1960-68; writer, 1969-. Military service: Served in the U.S. Army Reserve. **Publications:** POETRY: The Watercolored Word, 1968; Door Steps (prose poems), 1983; Paint Me a Picture, Make Me a Poem, 1987. FICTION: The Second Novel (Becoming a Writer), 1978; The Hour of the Sunshine Now (short stories), 1978; Adventures in an American's Literature (novel), 1982; The Ghost of Sandburg's Phizzog and Other Stories (short stories), 1986. NONFICTION: Door Way, 1981; Door to Door, 1985; Neighborhood, 1987; Meditations on a Small Lake: (Requiem for a Diminishing Landscape) (essays), 1987; Chi Town, 1990; Chronicles of a Rural Journalist in America (essays), 1990; The Watercolor Way (essays), 1990. Work included in anthologies. Contributor to periodicals. **Address:** P.O. Box 33, Ellison Bay, WI 54210, U.S.A.

BLEILER, Everett F(ranklin). Also writes as Liberte E. LeVert. American, b. 1920. **Genres:** Bibliography. **Career:** Freelance writer, 1952-55; Dover Publications, NYC, advertising manager, 1955-60, managing director, 1960-65, executive vice president, 1965-77; Charles Scribner's Sons, NYC, editorial consultant, 1978-83. **Publications:** The Checklist of Fantastic Fiction: A Bibliography of Fantasy, Weird and Science Fiction Books Published in the English Language, 1948, rev ed The Checklist of Fantastic Fiction, 1978; (with W.C. Bennett) Northwest Argentine Archeology, 1948; (with G. Stern), Essential German Grammar, 1961; Essential Japanese Grammar, 1963; (as Liberte E. LeVert) Prophecies and Enigmas of Nostradamus, 1979; The Guide to Supernatural Fiction: A Full Description for 1,775 Books from 1750 to 1960 Including Ghost Stories, Weird Fiction, Stories of Supernatural Horror, Fantasy, Gothic Novels, Occult Fiction, and Similar Literature, 1983; Science-Fiction: The Early Years, 1990; Science-Fiction: The Gernsback Years, 1998. Contributor to periodicals Editor of fantastic fiction books, mystery stories, dime novels, childrens literature and others. **Address:** 4076 Interlaken Beach Rd., Interlaken, NY 14847, U.S.A.

BLENK, Katie. American, b. 1954. **Genres:** Education. **Career:** Kids Are People Preschool, director, 1980-; Kids Are People Elementary School, Boston, MA, administrator, 1992-. Massachusetts State Department of Education, consultant, 1993-94; Kenmore Business Association, member of board of directors; Kenmore Community and Economic Development Corp., vice-president. **Publications:** (with D.L. Fine) Making School Inclusion Work:

The Kids Are People School Experience, 1995. **Address:** Kids Are People Elementary School, 656 Beacon St, PO Box 15656, Boston, MA 02215, U.S.A.

BLENKINSOPP, Joseph. American (born England), b. 1927. **Genres:** Theology/Religion. **Career:** Chicago Theological Seminary, IL, Teacher of Biblical Studies, 1968-69; Hartford Seminary Foundation, CT, Associate Professor, 1969-70; University of Notre Dame, IN, professor, 1970-85, John A O'Brien Professor of the Hebrew Bible, 1985-. **Publications:** The Corinthian Mirror, 1964: The Promise to David, 1964; From Adam to Abraham, 1965; Jesus is Lord, 1967; Celibacy, Ministry, Church, 1969; Sexuality and the Christian Tradition, 1969; Gibeon and Israel, 1972; Prophecy and Canon: A Contribution to the Study of Jewish Origins, 1978; Wisdom and Law in the Old Testament, 1983; A History of Prophecy in Israel, 1984; Ezra-Nehemiah: A Commentary, 1988; Ezekiel, 1990; The Pentateuch: Introduction to the First Five Books of the Bible, 1992; Sage, Priest, Prophet: Religious and Intellectual Leadership in Ancient Israel, 1996.

BLESSINGTON, Francis C(harles). American, b. 1942. **Genres:** Novels, Novellas/Short stories, Poetry, Classics, Literary criticism and history, Translations. **Career:** Scituate Mass., high school teacher, 1963-64; Northeastern University, Boston, instructor, 1967-72, assistant professor, 1972-75, associate professor, 1975-84, professor of English, 1984-. **Publications:** Paradise Lost and the Classic Epic, 1979; (ed. with G.L. Rotella) The Motive for Metaphor: Essays on Modern Poetry in Honor of Samuel French Morse, 1983; Lantskip (poetry), 1987; Paradise Lost: Ideal and Tragic Epic, 1988; Lorenzo de' Medici (verse play), 1992; (trans.) Euripides: The Bacchae and Aristophanes: The Frogs, 1993; Wolf Howl (poetry), 2000; The Last Witch of Dogtown (novel), 2001. Author of poems, stories, essays, and reviews. **Address:** Department of English, Northeastern University, Boston, MA 02115, U.S.A.

BLETHEN, H(arold) Tyler. American, b. 1945. **Genres:** History. **Publications:** (with C.W. Wood) A Mountain Heritage, 1989; (with Wood) From Ulster to Carolina, 1998; Ulster and North America. **Address:** Department of History, Western Carolina University, Cullowhee, NC 28723, U.S.A. **Online address:** blethen@wcu.edu

BLEWETT, Daniel K(eith). American, b. 1957. **Genres:** History, Librarianship, Bibliography. **Career:** Louisiana State University, Baton Rouge, reference librarian at Troy H. Middleton Library, 1984-86; Johns Hopkins University, Baltimore, MD, reference librarian at Milton S. Eisenhower Library, 1986-90; Loyola University of Chicago, IL, reference librarian and bibliographer for history, political science, international studies, geography, and maps at Elizabeth M. Cudahy Memorial Library, 1990-2000, head of government documents, 1992-2000; College of DuPage Library, reference librarian, 2000-. **Publications:** American Military History: A Guide to Reference and Information Sources, 1995. Contributor to books. Contributor of articles and reviews to history and library journals. **Address:** College of DuPage Library, 425 Fawell Blvd, Glen Ellyn, IL 60137, U.S.A.

BLICKLE, Peter. German, b. 1938. **Genres:** History. **Career:** University of Saarbruecken, Germany, professor of modern history, 1972-80; University of Berne, Switzerland, professor of history, 1980-2004. **Publications:** Die Revolution von 1525, 1975, 4th ed., 2004, trans. by T.A. Brady Jr. and H.C. Erik Midelfort as The Revolution of 1525: The German Peasants War from a New Perspective, 1982; Gemeindereformation: Die Menschen des 16. Jahrhunderts auf dem Weg zum Heil, 1985, trans. by T. Dunlap as Communal Reformation, Humanities, 1992. IN GERMAN: Memmingen, 1967; Kempten, 1968; Landschaften im Alten Reich: Die staatliche Funktion des gemeinen Mannes in Oberdeutschland, 1973; (with R. Blickle) Dokumente zur Geschichte von Staat und Gesellschaft in Bayern, 1979; Deutsche Untertanen: Ein Widerspruch, 1981; Die Reformation im Reich: Uni-Taschenbuecher 1181, 1982, 3rd ed., 2000; Unruhen in der staendischen Gesellschaft, 1300-1800, 1988; Studien zur geschichtlichen Bedeutung des deutschen Bauernstandes, 1989; Kommunalismus, 2 vols., 2000; Von der Leibeigenschaft zu den Menschenrechten, 2003. **Address:** Institute for History, University of Berne, Laenggass-Strasse 49, CH 3000 Berne 9, Switzerland. **Online address:** peterblickle@hist.unibe.ch

BLIGHT, David W. American, b. 1949. **Genres:** History. **Career:** Affiliated with Northern High School, Flint, MI, 1971-78; North Central College, Naperville, IL, assistant professor, 1982-87; Harvard University, Cambridge, MA, assistant professor of history and Afro-American studies, 1987-89; Amherst College, Amherst, MA, assistant professor, beginning in 1987, became associate professor of history and Afro-American studies; writer. **Publications:** Frederick Douglass's Civil War: Keeping Faith in Jubilee, 1989; Race and Reunion: The Civil War in American Memory, 2001. EDITOR: C.H. Brewster, When This Cruel War Is Over: The Civil War Letters of Charles Harvey Brewster, 1992; F. Douglass, Narrative of the Life of Frederick Douglass, an American Slave, 1993. **Address:** Gilder Lehrman Center, Yale University, PO Box 208206, New Haven, CT 06520-8206, U.S.A. **Online address:** david.blight@yale.edu

BLIGHT, James G. American. **Genres:** International relations/Current affairs, Politics/Government. **Career:** Grand Valley State University, assistant professor of psychology and history of science, 1974-80; Harvard University, Andrew W. Mellon faculty fellow, National Endowment for the Humanities research fellow, lecturer at John F. Kennedy School of Government, 1984-90; Brown University, Watson Institute for International Studies, research fellow at Center for Foreign Policy Development, 1990-95, research professor of international relations, 1995-. Worked at Buick car factory; minorleague baseball pitcher; cofounder and director of Cuban Missile Crisis Project; director of Kennedy School of Government's Project on Avoiding Nuclear War, 1985-90; developer of "critical oral history" method for analyzing major post-World War II foreign policy crises and conflicts; consultant to U.S. and foreign broadcast organizations and to independent filmmakers on documentary films. **Publications:** Beyond Deterrence or beyond Utopian Ideology?: Thought Experiments for Antinuclear Movements in Crisis, 1986; (with D.A. Welch) On the Brink: Americans and Soviets Reexamine the Cuban Missile Crisis, 1989, 2nd ed., 1990; (with others) Superpowers and Regional Conflict in a Post-Cold War World: The Caribbean Basin and Southern Africa, 1990; The Shattered Crystal Ball: Fear and Learning in the Cuban Missile Crisis, 1990; (with B.J. Allyn and D.A. Welch) Cuba on the Brink: Castro, the Missile Crisis, and the Soviet Collapse, 1993, rev. ed, 2002; (with R.S. McNamara and R.K. Brigham) Argument without End: In Search of Answers to the Vietnam Tragedy, 1999; (with R.S. McNamara) Wilson's Ghost: Reducing the Risk of Conflict, Killing, and Catastrophe in the Twenty-first Century, 2001; (with P. Brenner) Sad and Luminous Days: Cuba's Struggle with the Superpowers after the Missile Crisis, 2002. EDITOR: (with T.G. Weiss) The Suffering Grass: Superpowers and Regional Conflict in Southern Africa and the Caribbean, 1992; (with B.J. Allyn and D.A. Welch) Back to the Brink: Proceedings of the Moscow Conference on the Cuban Missile Crisis, January 27-28, 1989, 1992; (with D.A. Welch) Intelligence and the Cuban Missile Crisis, 1998; (with P. Kornbluh) Politics of Illusion: The Bay of Pigs Invasion Reexamined, 1998. Contributor to journals. **Address:** Watson Institute, Brown University, Box 1970, Providence, RI 02912, U.S.A. **Online address:** James_Blight@brown.edu

BLINDER, Alan S(tuart). American, b. 1945. **Genres:** Economics. **Career:** Rider College, Trenton, NJ, instructor in finance, 1968-69; Boston State College, instructor in economics, 1969; Princeton University, NJ, assistant professor, 1971-76, associate professor, 1976-79, professor, 1979-82, Gordon S. Rentschler Memorial Professor of Economics, 1982-. Columnist for Boston Globe, 1981-85, and Business Week, 1985-92. Council of Economic Advisers, 1993-94; Board of Governors of the Federal Reserve System, vice chairman, 1994-96; The G7 Group, vice chairman, 1997-; Promontory Financial Group, partner, 2000-. **Publications:** (co-author) The Economics of Public Finance, 1974; Toward an Economic Theory of Income Distribution. 1974; (co-author) Economics: Principles and Policy, 1979, rev. ed., 1994; Economic Policy and the Great Stagflation, 1979: The Truce in the War on Poverty: Where Do We Go from Here?, 1982; Macroeconomics, Income Distribution and Poverty, 1986; Macroeconomics, 1986; Microeconomics, 1986; Hard Heads, Soft Hearts, 1987; Macroeconomics under Debate. 1989; Inventory Theory and Consumer Behavior, 1990; Central Banking in Theory and Practice, 1998; (co-author) Asking about Prices, 1998; (co-author) The Fabulous Decade: Macroeconomic Lessons from the 1990s, 2001; (co-author) How Do Central Banks Talk?, 2001; (co-author) Downsizing in America, 2003. EDITOR: (co) Natural Resources, Uncertainty and General Equilibrium Systems: Essays in Memory of Rafael Lusky, 1977; Paying for Productivity, 1990. **Address:** Department of Economics, Princeton University, 105 Fisher Hall, Princeton, NJ 08544-1021, U.S.A.

BLISS, Michael (J.). American, b. 1947. **Genres:** Film. **Career:** Instructor in English and film, 1979-91, including positions at University of Minnesota-Twin Cities, Metropolitan Community College, Hamline University, and Minneapolis public schools; Virginia Polytechnic Institute and State University, Blacksburg, instructor in English and film, 1991-. Minneapolis Film Festival, associate director and programmer, 1979-80; Cinemaland Theatres, copywriter, 1979-81. **Publications:** Brian De Palma, 1983; Martin Scorsese and Michael Cimino, 1985; Justified Lives: Morality and Narrative in the Films of Sam Peckinpah, 1993; (ed.) Doing It Right: The Best Criticism on Sam Peckinpah's "The Wild Bunch", 1994; The Word Made Flesh: Catholicism and Conflict in the Films of Martin Scorsese, 1995; (with C.

Banks) What Goes Around Comes Around: The Films of Jonathan Demme, 1995; (with D. Weddle) The Making of "The Wild Bunch", 1996. **Address:** Department of English, Virginia Polytechnic Institute and State University, Blacksburg, VA 24061, U.S.A. **Online address:** mbliss@vt.edu

BLITZER, Wolf. American (born Germany), b. 1948. **Genres:** International relations/Current affairs, Documentaries/Reportage. **Career:** Reuters News Agency, foreign correspondent at bureau in Tel Aviv, Israel, c. 1972; Jerusalem Post, Jerusalem, Israel, bureau chief and correspondent in Washington, DC, 1973-c. 1990; Cable News Network, Atlanta, GA, guest expert on Middle East, beginning c. 1980, Pentagon correspondent, beginning c. 1990, Sr. White House Correspondent, 1993. University of Maryland, instructor in political science, 1984. Served as consultant for television news programs 20/20, 1981, and 60 Minutes, 1987, and has made guest appearances on Meet the Press, Today, Nightline, Good Morning America, MacNeil-Lehrer Newshour, and Washington Week in Review. **Publications:** Between Washington and Jerusalem: A Reporter's Notebook, 1985; Territory of Lies: The Exclusive Story of Jonathan Jay Pollard, the American Who Spied on His Country for Israel and How He Was Betrayed, 1989. **Address:** CNN, 820 1st St. NE, Washington, DC 20002, U.S.A.

BLIX, Jacqueline. American, b. 1949. **Genres:** Documentaries/Reportage. **Career:** Mademoiselle (women's clothing store), San Francisco, CA, manager, 1975-79; Pacific Telephone, San Francisco, market administrator, 1979-80; American Telephone and Telegraph Co., market administrator for AT&T Long Lines, San Francisco, 1980-81, technical consultant to AT&T Communications, San Francisco, 1981-84, and Seattle, WA, 1984-88. Master gardener. **Publications:** (with D.A. Heitmiller) Getting a Life: Real Lives Transformed by Your Money or Your Life, 1997. Contributor to periodicals. **Address:** 1745 NW 59th St, Seattle, WA 98107, U.S.A. **Online address:** jacque@gettingalife.org

BLOCH, Douglas. American, b. 1949. **Genres:** Self help, How-to books, Psychology. **Career:** Writer. **Publications:** (with D. George) Asteroid Goddesses, 1986; Astrology for Yourself, 1987; Words That Heal, 1990; Listen to Your Inner Voice, 1991; I Am with You Always, 1992; Positive Self-Talk for Children, 1993; When Going through Hell, Don't Stop, 1999. **Address:** 4226 NE 23rd Ave., Portland, OR 97211, U.S.A. **Online address:** dbloch@teleport.com

BLOCK, Daniel I. Canadian, b. 1943. **Genres:** Theology/Religion. **Career:** Providend College and Theological Seminary, Otterburne, Manitoba, professor of Old Testament, 1973-83; Bethel Theological Seminary, St. Paul, MN, professor of Old Testament, 1983-95; Southern Baptist Theological Seminary, Louisville, KY, professor of Old Testament, 1995-. Also works as pastor, interim pastor, and lecturer. **Publications:** The Gods of the Nations, 1988; The Book of Ezekiel 1-24, 1997; The Book of Ezekiel 25-48, 1998; Judges and Ruth, 1999. **Address:** 7428 Falls Ridge Ct., Louisville, KY 40241, U.S.A. **Online address:** diblock@aol.com

BLOCK, Francesca (Lia). American, b. 1962. **Genres:** Science fiction/Fantasy, Novels, Novellas/Short stories, Young adult fiction, Plays/Screenplays, Poetry. **Career:** Writer. **Publications:** NOVELS: Weetzie Bat, 1989; Witch Baby, 1991; Cherokee Bat and the Goat Guys, 1991; Ecstasia, 1993; Missing Angel Juan, 1993; Primavera, 1994; The Hanged Man, 1994; Baby Be Bop, 1995; I Was a Teenage Fairy, 1998. OTHER: Girl Goddess (stories), 1996; (with H. Cartip) Zinescene (non-fiction), 1998; Dangerous Angels, 1998. **Address:** Lydia Willis, Artist's Agency, 230 W. 55th St., No. 29D, New York, NY 10019, U.S.A.

BLOCK, Geoffrey. American, b. 1948. **Genres:** Music, Theatre. **Career:** Director of music at a school in Ojai, CA, 1977-80; University of Puget Sound, Tacoma, WA, assistant professor to professor of music, 1980-. **Publications:** Charles Ives: A Bio-Bibliography, 1988; Ives: Concord Sonata, 1996; Enchanted Evenings: The Broadway Musical from Show Boat to Sondheim, 1997; Yale Broadway Masters: Richard Rodgers, 2003. EDITOR: (with J.P. Burkholder) Charles Ives and the Classical Tradition, 1996; The Richard Rodgers Reader, 2002. **Address:** Music Dept, University of Puget Sound, 1500 N Warner, Tacoma, WA 98416, U.S.A. **Online address:** Block@ups.edu

BLOCK, Joyce. American, b. 1951. **Genres:** Psychology, Women's studies and issues. **Career:** Private practice of psychology, 1985-. St. Mary's College and University of Notre Dame, adjunct professor. **Publications:** Motherhood as Metamorphosis: Change and Continuity in the Life of a New Mother, 1990; Family Myths: Living Our Roles, Betraying Ourselves, 1994. **Address:** 300 North Michigan St., South Bend, IN 46601, U.S.A.

BLOCK, Lawrence. Also writes as Chip Harrison, Paul Kavanagh. American, b. 1938. **Genres:** Novels, Novellas/Short stories, Mystery/Crime/Suspense, Recreation, Writing/Journalism. **Publications:** MYSTERY NOVELS: Death Pulls a Double Cross, 1961: Mona, 1961; The Case of the Pornographic Photos, 1961 (in UK as Marham: The Case of the Pornographic Photos, 1965); The Girl with the Long Green Heart, 1965; The Cancelled Czech, 1966; The Thief Who Couldn't Sleep, 1966; Deadly 1967; Tanner's Twelve Swingers, 1967; Two for Tanner, 1967; Here Comes a Hero, 1968; Tanner's Tiger, 1968; After the First Death, 1969; The Specialists, 1969; Me Tanner, You Jane, 1970; In the Midst of Death, 1976; Sin of the Fathers, 1977; Time to Murder and Create, 1977; Burglars Can't Be Choosers, 1977; The Burglar in the Closet, 1978; The Burglar Who Liked to Quote Kipling, 1979; Aniel, 1980; The Burglar Who Studied Spinoza, 1981; A Stab in the Dark, 1981; Eight Million Ways to Die, 1982; The Burglar Who Painted Like Mondrian, 1983; Like a Lamb to Slaughter (in UK as Five Little Rich Girls), 1984; When the Sacred Ginmill Closes, 1986; Into the Night (completion of C. Woolrich novel), 1987; Coward's Kiss, 1987; You Could Call It Murder, 1987; Random Walk, 1988; Spider Spin Me a Web, 1988; Out on the Cutting Edge, 1989; A Ticket to the Bone Yard, 1990; A Dance at the Slaughterhouse, 1991; A Walk among the Tombstones, 1992; The Devil Knows You're Dead, 1993; A Long Line of Dead Men, 1994; The Burglar Who Traded Ted Williams, 1994; The Burglar Who Thought He Was Bogart, 1995; Even the Wicked, 1997; The Burglar in the Library, 1997; Tanner on Ice, 1998; Everybody Dies, 1998; Hit Man, 1998; Hit List, 2000; Hope to Die, 2001; Small Town, 2003; The Burgler on the Prowl, 2004. NOVELS: Ronald Rabbit Is a Dirty Old Man, 1971; (with H. King) Code of Arms, 1981. OTHER: A Guide Book to Australian Coins, 1964; (with D.R. Krause) Swiss Shooting Talers and Medals, 1965; Writing the Novel, 1979; Telling Lies for Fun and Profit, 1981; (with C. Morrison) Real Food Places, 1981; Sometimes They Bite (short stories), 1984; Write for Your Life, 1985; Spider, Spin Me a Web, 1988; Some Days You Get the Bear (stories), 1993; After Hours, 1995. AS CHIP HARRISON: Make Out with Murder, 1974; The Topless Tulip Caper, 1975; No Score, 1970; Chip Harrison Scores Again, 1971; Introducing Chip Harrison (omnibus), 1984. NOVELS AS PAUL KAVANAGH: Such Men Are Dangerous, 1969; The Triumph of Evil, 1971; Not Comin' Home to You, 1974. **Address:** c/o HarperCollins Author Mail, 10 E 53rd St 7th Fl, New York, NY 10022, U.S.A. **Online address:** www.LawrenceBlock.com

BLOCK, Thomas H(arris). American, b. 1945. **Genres:** Novels. **Career:** US Airways, airline pilot (Captain). Flying Magazine, columnist, 1970-. **Publications:** Mayday, 1980; Orbit, 1982: Forced Landing, 1983; Airship Nine, 1984; Sky Fall, 1987; Open Skies, 1990.

BLOCKSMA, Mary. American, b. 1942. **Genres:** Children's fiction, Adult non-fiction, Children's non-fiction. **Career:** Junior high school English teacher in Baltimore, MD, 1964-65; U.S. Peace Corps, lecturer at University of Nigeria, Enugu, 1965-67; De Paul University, Chicago, IL, research librarian, 1968-69; Albany County Public Library, Laramie, WY, director, 1970-76; Addison-Wesley Publishing Co., Menlo Park, CA, staff writer, 1977-79; free-lance writer, 1980-. **Publications:** FOR CHILDREN: The Pup Went Up, 1983; Did You Hear That?, 1983; Apple Tree! Apple Tree!, 1983; Grandma Dragon's Birthday, 1983; (with D. Blocksma) Easy-to-Make Spaceships That Really Fly, 1983; Marvelous Music Machine: A Book about the Piano, 1984; The Best-Dressed Bear, 1984; Rub-a-Dub-Dub: What's in the Tub?, 1985; (with D. Blocksma) Easy-to-Make Water Toys, 1985; (with D. Blocksma) Space-Crafting, 1986; Amazing Mouths and Menus, 1986; Where's That Duck?, 1987; Why All My Toys Are on the Floor, 1987; (with D. Blocksma) Action Contraptions, 1988; Reading the Numbers, 1989; Yoo Hoo Moon!, 1992; Time Traveler's Catalog, Ticket to the Twenties, 1993; Naming Nature, 1992; The Fourth Coast, 1995; Lake Lover's Year, 2001; Necessary Numbers, 2002; Great Lakes Nature, 2003; What's on the Beach, 2003. **Address:** PO Box 40, Bay City, MI 48707-0040, U.S.A. **Online address:** mblocksma@yahoo.com; www.beaverislandarts.com

BLOCKSON, Charles L(eRoy). American, b. 1933. **Genres:** Cultural/Ethnic topics, History, Librarianship, Bibliography. **Career:** Pennsylvania Black History Committee, director, 1976-; Pennsylvania Afro-American Historical Board, director, 1976-; Governor's Heritage Affairs Commission, Afro-American commissioner, 1983-; Temple University, Philadelphia, PA, member of Centennial Committee, 1983-, curator of Charles L. Blockson Afro-American Collection, c. 1984-. Director of Pennsylvania State Historical and Record Advisory Board and Black History Advisory Board. Launched a project to erect 64 historical markers commemorating the contribution of African Americans to Philadelphia, 1989; served as moderator of Black Writer's Conference in Paris, France, 1992; lecturer; organizer of black study programs for schools and colleges; chair of the Valley Forge African-

American Revolutionary Soldier Monument; co-founder of the Afro-American Historical and Cultural Museum in Philadelphia. **Publications:** Pennsylvania's Black History, 1975; (with R. Fry) Black Genealogy, 1977; Handbook of Black Librarianship, 1977; The Underground Railroad in Pennsylvania, 1981; The Underground Railroad: First Person Narratives of Escapes to Freedom in the North, 1987; A Commented Bibliography of 101 Influential Books by and about People of African Descent, 1556-1982, 1989; The Journey of John W. Mosley: An African-American Pictorial, 1993; Philadelphia's Guide: African-American State Historical Markers, 1993; The Hippocrene Guide to the Underground Railroad, 1994; African-Americans in Pennsylvania: A History and Guide, 1994; Damn Rare: The Memoirs of an African American Bibliophile, 1998; Philadelphia: 1639-2000, 2000; African Americans in Pennsylvania, 2001. Contributor to books, magazines and scholarly journals. **Address:** Sullivan Hall, Temple University, Broad and Berks Streets, Philadelphia, PA 19122, U.S.A.

BLODGETT, (Anita) Jan. American (born Japan), b. 1954. **Genres:** Literary criticism and history. **Career:** West Texas A&M University, Canyon, assistant reference librarian, 198082; Texas Tech University, Lubbock, assistant archivist, 1982-89; Dickinson College, Carlisle, PA, college archivist, 1987-89; St. Mary's County Public Library, Leonardtown, NC, county archivist, 1989-94; Davidson College, Davidson, NC, college archivist, 1994-, adjunct member of humanities faculty, 1998, 1999. **Publications:** Land of Bright Promise: Advertising the Texas Panhandle and South Plains, 1870-1971, 1988; Protestant Evangelical Literary Culture and Contemporary Society, 1997. **Address:** E.H. Little Library, Davidson College, PO Box 7200, Davidson, NC 28035-7200, U.S.A. **Online address:** jablodgett@davidson.edu

BLODGETT, Peter J. American, b. 1954. **Genres:** History. **Career:** Yale University, New Haven, CT, teaching and research assistant in history, 1979-84; Huntington Library, San Marino, CA, curator of western manuscripts, 1985-. Loyola Marymount University, member of advisory board, Center for the Study of Los Angeles. **Publications:** Land of Golden Dreams: California in the Gold Rush Decade, 1848-1858, 1999. Contributor to books and periodicals. **Address:** Manuscripts Department, Huntington Library, 1151 Oxford Rd., San Marino, CA 91108, U.S.A.

BLOEMBERGEN, Nicolaas. American (born Netherlands), b. 1920. **Genres:** Physics. **Career:** Harvard University, junior fellow, 1949-51, associate professor, 1951-57, Gordon McKay Professor of Applied Physics, 1957-80, Gerhard Gade University Professor, 1980-90, professor emeritus, 1990-. **Publications:** Nuclear Magnetic Relaxation, 1961; Nonlinear Optics, 1965; Encounters in Magnetic Resonances, 1996; Encounters in Nonlinear Optics, 1996. EDITOR: (co) Proceedings of 3rd International Conference on Quantum Electronics, 1964; Nonlinear Spectroscopy, Course by Enrico Fermi, 1977. **Address:** Optical Sciences Center, University of Arizona, Tucson, AZ 85721, U.S.A. **Online address:** nbloembergen@optics.arizona.edu

BLOESCH, Donald George. American, b. 1928. **Genres:** Theology/Religion. **Career:** Professor of Theology, now Emeritus, Dubuque Theological Seminary, Iowa, 1957-. Past President, American Theological Society, Midwest Division. **Publications:** Centers of Christian Renewal, 1964; The Christian Life and Salvation, 1967; The Crisis of Piety, 1968; The Christian Witness in a Secular Age, 1968; (co-author) Christian Spirituality East and West, 1968; The Reform of the Church, 1970; (ed.) Servants of Christ, 1971; The Ground of Certainty, 1971; The Evangelical Renaissance, 1973; Wellsprings of Renewal, 1974; The Invaded Church, 1975; Jesus Is Victor!, 1976; Essentials of Evangelical Theology, 2 vols., 1978-79; The Struggle of Prayer, 1980; Faith and Its Counterfeits, 1981; Is the Bible Sexist?, 1982; The Future of Evangelical Christianity, 1983; Crumbling Foundations, 1984; Battle for the Trinity: The Debate Over Inclusive God-Language, 1985; Freedom for Obedience, 1987; A Theology of Word & Spirit, 1992; Holy Scripture, 1994; God the Almighty, 1995; Jesus Christ, 1997; The Holy Spirit, 2000; The Church, 2002; The Last Things, 2004. **Address:** Dubuque Theological Seminary, 2000 University Ave, Dubuque, IA 52001, U.S.A.

BLOM, Philipp. (Philipp Sievert). German, b. 1970. **Genres:** Novels. **Career:** Historian specializing in intellectual history and nationalism in Europe during the period between 1890 and 1914; high school teacher of German literature, philosophy, and violin. **Publications:** The Simmons Papers (novel), 1995. **Address:** 96a Banbury Rd., Oxford OX2 6JT, England.

BLONDEL, Jean (Fernand Pierre). French, b. 1929. **Genres:** Politics/Government. **Career:** University of Siena, Visiting Professor, 1996-. Swedish Royal Academy of Sciences, Member, 1990-. University of Keele, Staffs., Assistant Lecturer, Lecturer in Politics, 1958-63; Yale University, American

Council of Learned Societies Fellow, 1963-64; University of Essex, Colchester, Professor of Government, 1964-84; Carleton University, Ottawa, Visiting Professor of Political Science, 1969-70; Russel Sage Foundation, NY, Visiting Scholar, 1984-85; European University Institute, Florence, Professor of Political Science, 1985-94, External Professor, 1994. **Publications:** Voters, Parties and Leaders, 1963; (with F. Ridley) Public Administration in France, 1964; (with F. Bealey and P. McCann) Constituency Politics, 1965; An Introduction to Comparative Government, 1969; Comparing Political Systems, 1972; (with V. Herman) A Workbook for Comparative Government, 1972; Comparative Legislatures, 1973; The Government of France, 1974; Thinking Politically, 1976; Political Parties, 1979; World Leaders, 1980; The Discipline of Politics, 1981; The Organisation of Governments, 1982; Government Ministers in the Contemporary World, 1985; Political Leadership, 1987; Comparative Government, 1990; (with R. Sinnott and P. Svensson) People and Parliament in the European Union, 1998; (with F.M. Rommel) Cabinets in Eastern Europe, 2001. EDITOR: Comparative Government, 1971; (with F.M. Rommel) Cabinets in Western Europe, 1988; (with J.L. Thiebault) The Profession of Cabinet Minister in Western Europe, 1991; (with Rommel) Governing Together, 1993; (with M. Cotta) Party and Government, 1996; (with Cotta) The Nature of Party Government, 2000. **Address:** 15 Marloes Rd, London W8 6LQ, England.

BLOODSTEIN, Oliver. American, b. 1920. **Genres:** Medicine/Health. **Career:** Brooklyn College of the City University of New York, Brooklyn, NY, professor of speech pathology, 1948-, director of Speech and Hearing Center, 1985-. City University of New York, member of doctoral faculty. **Publications:** A Handbook on Stuttering, 1969, 5th ed, 1995; Speech Pathology: An Introduction, 1979, 2nd ed, 1984; Stuttering: The Search for a Cause and Cure, 1993. **Address:** Department of Speech, Brooklyn College of the City University of New York, 2900 Bedford Ave., Brooklyn, NY 11210, U.S.A.

BLOOM, Clive. British, b. 1953. **Genres:** Mystery/Crime/Suspense, Romance/Historical, Cultural/Ethnic topics, History, Literary criticism and history, Sex, Sociology. **Career:** Middlesex University, London, England, principal lecturer in English, 1980-. Chairman of the cooperative, Lumiere Press Ltd. Governor of Fullwood School. **Publications:** The "Occult" Experience and the New Criticism, 1986; Reading Poe, Reading Freud, 1988; Cult Fiction, 1996; Bestsellers, 2002; Literature, Politics, and Intellectual Crisis in Britain Today, 2001. EDITOR: (with G. Day, and contrib.) Perspectives on Pornography, 1988; (and contrib.) Jacobean Poetry and Prose, 1988; (with others, and contrib.) Nineteenth-Century Suspense, 1990; (and contrib.) Twentieth-Century Suspense, 1990; (and contrib.) Spy Thrillers, 1990; (with M. Roberts, and contrib.) Arcane Worlds, 1990; (with G.S. McCue) Dark Knights, 1990; (with D. Zadworna-Fjellerstad) Criticism towards 2000, 1990; (and contrib.) Voices from the Vault, 1991; Creepers, 1993; Literature and Culture in Modern Britain, 1993; American Drama, 1995; (with B. Docherty) American Poetry: The Modernist Ideal, 1995; Gothic Horror, 1998. Contributor to books and periodicals. **Address:** School of Arts, Faculty of Humanities, Middlesex University, White Hart Lane, London N17 8HR, England. **Online address:** cbloom4189@aol.com

BLOOM, Harold. American, b. 1930. **Genres:** Novels, Literary criticism and history. **Career:** Professor of Humanities, 1977-, and Sterling Professor of Humanities, 1983-, Yale University, New Haven, CT (joined Dept. of English, 1955; Professor of English, 1965-77; William Clyde De Vane Professor of Humanities, 1974-77). Berg Professor of English, New York University, 1987-. **Publications:** Shelley's Mythmaking, 1959; The Visionary Company, 1961; Blake's Apocalypse, 1963; Commentary to Blake's Poetry and Prose, 1965; Yeats, 1970; The Ringers in the Tower, 1971; The Anxiety of Influence, 1973; Kabbalah and Criticism, 1975; A Map of Misreading, 1975; Figures of Capable Imagination, 1976; Poetry and Repression, 1976; Wallace Stevens: The Poems of Our Climate, 1977; The Flight to Lucifer, 1978; (with A. Munich) Robert Browning, 1979; (coauthor) Deconstruction and Criticism, 1979; Agon: Towards a Theory of Revisionism, 1981; The Breaking of the Vessels, 1982; The Strong Light of the Canonical, 1987; Freud: Transference and Authority, 1988; Poetics of Influence: New and Selected Criticism, 1988; Ruin the Sacred Truths, 1988; The Book of J, 1990; The American Religion, 1992; The Western Canon, 1994; Omens of Millennium, 1996; Shakespeare: The Invention of the Human, 1998; How to Read and Why, 1999; Stories and Poems for Extremely Intelligent Children, 2001; Genius: A Mosaic of Exemplary Creative Minds, 2002. EDITOR: English Romantic Poetry (anthology), 1961; Romanticism and Consciousness, 1970; (with others) Oxford Anthology of English Literature, 2 vols., 1972; The Romantic Tradition in American Literature, 1972; (with L. Trilling) Romantic Prose and Poetry, 1973; Selected Poetry and Prose of Shelley, 1978; Selected Writings of Walter Pater, 1982.

BLOOM, James D. American, b. 1951. **Genres:** Literary criticism and history. **Career:** Muhlenberg College, Allentown, PA, Professor of English, 1982-. **Publications:** The Stock of Available Reality: R.P. Blackmur and John Berryman, 1984; Left Letters: The Culture Wars of Mike Gold and Joseph Freeman, 1992; The Literary Bent: In Search of High Art in Contemporary American Writing, 1997. **Address:** Department of English, Muhlenberg College, 24th and Chew St., Allentown, PA 18104, U.S.A.

BLOOM, Jonathan M(ax). American, b. 1950. **Genres:** Architecture, Art/ Art history, History. **Career:** University of California, Los Angeles, visiting assistant professor, 1980; Harvard University, Cambridge, MA, assistant professor of fine arts, 1981-87, research associate, 1987-88, faculty associate at Center for Middle Eastern Studies, 1988-93, affiliate in research, 1993-. Aga Khan Lecturer, Harvard University and Massachusetts Institute of Technology, 1980-81; University of Geneva, visiting professor, spring, 1985; Yale University, visiting lecturer, 1989; Trinity College, Hartford, CT, visiting associate professor, 1995; University of Bamberg, visiting professor, 1995-96; Boston College, Chestnut Hill, MA, Norma Jean Calderwood University Professor of Islamic and Asian Art, 2000-. Lecturer at colleges, universities, and art galleries around the world. **Publications:** Minaret: Symbol of Islam, 1989; (with S.S. Blair) The Art and Architecture of Islam, 1250-1800, 1994; (with S.S. Blair) Islamic Arts, 1996; (with S.S. Blair) Islam, a Thousand Years of Faint and Power, 2000; Paper before Print: The History and Impact of Paper in the Islamic Lands, 2001; Early Islamic Art and Architecture, 2002. Contributor to books. Contributor of articles and reviews to art, architecture, and Islamic studies journals. **Address:** Fine Arts Dept, Boston College, Chestnut Hill, MA 02467, U.S.A. **Online address:** jonathan.bloom@bc.edu

BLOOM, Lisa E. American, b. 1958. **Genres:** Art/Art history, Cultural/ Ethnic topics, Humanities, Photography, Travel/Exploration, Women's studies and issues. **Career:** University of California, Santa Cruz, lecturer in art history, 1989-91; University of California, Irvine, lecturer in art history, 1991-92; Brown University, Providence, RI, postdoctoral fellow at Pembroke Center, 1992-93; Rhode Island School of Design, Providence, lecturer in liberal arts, 1993; Stanford University, Stanford, CA, visiting assistant professor of art history and Mellon research fellow, 1993-94. **Publications:** Gender on Ice: American Ideologies of Polar Expeditions, 1993. Work represented in anthologies. Contributor of articles and reviews to professional journals. **Address:** Department of Human Services, Killian Bldg Rm 204, Western Carolina University, Cullowhee, NC 28723, U.S.A. **Online address:** Bloom@wcu.edu

BLOOM, Lynn (Marie Zimmerman). American, b. 1934. **Genres:** Literary criticism and history, Women's studies and issues, Writing/Journalism, Autobiography/Memoirs, Bibliography, Biography, Essays. **Career:** Western Reserve Univ., lectr. in English, 1962-63, instr., 1963-65, assoc., 1965-67; Butler Univ., asst. prof., 1970-73, assoc. prof., 1973-74; Univ. of New Mexico, Albuquerque, assoc. prof., 1975-78; College of William and Mary, assoc. prof. of English, 1978-82; Virginia Commonwealth University, Richmond, prof. of English, 1982-88; Univ. of Connecticut, Storrs, board of trustees distinguished professor, professor of English and holder, Aetna chair of writing, 1988-. Eastern VA Writing Project, co-dir., 1979-81. **Publications:** Dr. Spock: Biography of a Conservative Radical, 1972; (co) The New Assertive Woman, 1975, rev. ed., 2000; (co) American Autobiography: A Bibliography, 1945-1980, 1982; Strategic Writing, 1983; Fact and Artifact: Writing Non-Fiction, 1985, 2nd ed., 1994; Composition Studies as a Creative Art, 1998. EDITOR: Forbidden Diary, 1980, rev. ed., 2001; The Essay Connection, 1984, 7th ed., 2004; The Lexington Reader, 1987; Forbidden Family, 1989, rev. ed., 1998. CO-EDITOR: Bear, Man, and God: 7 Approaches to Faulkner's The Bear, 1964; Symposium, 1969; Symposium on Love, 1970; Bear, Man, and God: 8 Approaches to Faulkner's The Bear, 1971; Inquiry, 1993, rev. ed., 2004; Composition in the 21st Century, 1996; The St. Martin's Custom Reader, 2001; The Arlington Reader, 2003; Composition Studies in the New Millennium, 2004; The Arlington Shorter Reader, 2004. **Address:** English Dept, Box 4025, University of Connecticut, Storrs Mansfield, CT 06269-1025, U.S.A. **Online address:** Lynn.Bloom@uconn.edu

BLOOM, Miriam. American, b. 1934. **Genres:** Biology, Medicine/Health. **Career:** University of California, Los Angeles, visiting scholar in chemistry, 1972; University of Utah, Salt Lake City, assistant research professor of biology, 1973-74; University of South Florida, Tampa, biology research associate, 1974-75; Hillsborough Community College, Tampa, adjunct professor of biology, 1975-77; Georgetown University, Washington, DC, US Public Health service research fellow, 1977-79; US Consumer Product Safety Commission, Washington, DC, geneticist, 1979-88; SciWrite, Jackson, MS, president, 1989-. Hinds Community College, instructor, 1991; University Press of Mis-

sissippi, series editor, 1995-. **Publications:** Understanding Sickle Cell Disease, 1995. Contributor to books and magazines. **Address:** 4433 Wedgewood St, Jackson, MS 39211, U.S.A.

BLOOM, Murray Teigh. American, b. 1916. **Genres:** Plays/Screenplays, Law, Money/Finance. **Career:** American Society of Journalists and Authors, founder and former president; Llewellyn Miller Fund, trustee. **Publications:** Money of Their Own, 1957; The Man Who Stole Portugal, 1966; Leonora (play), 1966; The Trouble with Lawyers, 1969; Rogues to Riches, 1972; Lawyers, Clients, and Ethics, 1974; The Thirteenth Man, 1978; The Brotherhood of Money, 1984; The White Crow (play), 1984; Life Size, 1989. Contributor to magazines. **Address:** 40 Hemlock Dr, Kings Point, NY 11024, U.S.A.

BLOOM, Rebecca (S.). (born United States), b. 1975. **Genres:** Novels. **Career:** Speckles by Rebecca Bloom (jewelry and fashion design company), owner, 2001-. **Publications:** Girl Anatomy (novel), 2002; Tangled up in Daydreams (novel), forthcoming. Contributor to periodicals. **Address:** Jan Miller, Dupree/Miller, 100 Highland Park Village, Suite 350, Dallas, TX 75205, U.S.A. **Online address:** specklesb@aol.com

BLOOM, Samuel W. American, b. 1921. **Genres:** Medicine/Health, Sociology. **Career:** Professor of Sociology and Community Medicine, Mount Sinai School of Medicine, Director, Division of Behavioral Sciences, Dept. of Community Medicine. Research Associate, Bureau of Applied Social Research, Columbia University, NYC, 1953-56; Assistant Professor of Sociology, Baylor University Coll. of Medicine, Waco, TX, 1956-62; Associate Professor of Sociology in Administration, 1962-65, and Professor of Sociology in Psychiatry, 1965-68, State University of New York Coll. of Medicine, Downstate Medical Center; Professor Emeritus of Sociology, City University of New York Graduate Center, 1968-99. Visiting Professor at colleges and universities worldwide. **Publications:** The Doctor and His Patient: A Sociological Interpretation, 1963; Power and Dissent in the Medical School, 1973; The Word as Scalpel: A History of Medical Sociology, 2002. **Address:** Mount Sinai School of Medicine, Box 1043, New York, NY 10029, U.S.A. **Online address:** Samuel.Bloom@mssm.edu

BLOOM, Steven. American, b. 1942. **Genres:** Novels. **Career:** University of Heidelberg, Germany, part-time teacher, 1992-. Also worked as part-time teacher at New York University, Fordham University, and University of Maryland's European Division; lecturer on American topics in Germany, 1977-. **Publications:** No New Jokes (novel), 1997; Immer dieselben witze, 2000; Offene Ehe und anderer New York (short stories), 2004. Author of short stories. **Address:** Bogenstrasse 5, 69124 Heidelberg, Germany. **Online address:** gloomof@aol.com

BLOOMFIELD, Lincoln P(almer). American, b. 1920. **Genres:** International relations/Current affairs. **Career:** Senior Staff, Center for International Studies and Professor of Political Science Emeritus, Massachusetts Institute of Technology, Cambridge, 1963-. With U.S. Dept. of State, 1946-57, and Natl. Security Council, 1979-80. **Publications:** Evolution or Revolution?, 1957; The United Nations and U.S. Foreign Policy, 1960, rev. ed., 1967; (co-author and ed.) Outer Space: Prospects for Man and Society, 1962, rev. ed., 1968; International Military Forces, 1964, rev. ed. (with others) as The Power to Keep Peace, 1971; (with others) Khrushchev and the Arms Race, 1966; (with A.C. Leiss) Controlling Small Wars, 1967; In Search of American Foreign Policy, 1974; What Future for the U.N.?, 1977; The Foreign Policy Process, 1982; (ed. with H. Cleveland) Prospects for Peacemaking, 1987; (ed.) The Management of Global Disorder, 1987; Managing International Conflict, 1997; Accidental Encounters with History, 2005. **Address:** 37 Beach St, Cohasset, MA 02025, U.S.A. **Online address:** linc37@aol.com

BLOOMFIELD, Louis A(ub). American, b. 1956. **Genres:** Physics. **Career:** American Telephone & Telegraph Bell Laboratories, Murray Hill, NJ, member of technical staff, 1983-85; University of Virginia, Charlottesville, assistant professor, 1985-91, associate professor, 1991-96, professor of physics, 1996-. **Publications:** How Things Work: The Physics of Everyday Life, 1997, 2nd ed., 2001. **Address:** Department of Physics, University of Virginia, Box 400714, Charlottesville, VA 22904-4714, U.S.A. **Online address:** lab3e@virginia.edu

BLOOR, Edward (William). American, b. 1950. **Genres:** Young adult fiction. **Career:** Teacher in Florida public schools, 1983-86; Harcourt Brace School Publishers, Orlando, FL, executive editor, 1986-. **Publications:** Tangerine, 1997; Crusader, 1999; Story Time, 2003. **Address:** 12021 Windstone St, Winter Garden, FL 34787, U.S.A. **Online address:** ebloor@harcourtbrace.com

BLOS, Joan W. American, b. 1928. **Genres:** Children's fiction, Children's non-fiction. **Career:** Research assistant, Jewish Board of Guardians, New York, 1949-50; teaching asst., City Coll., New York, 1950-51; research asst., Child Study Center, Yale University, New Haven, CT, 1951-53; ed. and instructor, Bank St. Coll. of Education, New York, 1956-70; Medical Center research asst., 1970-72, and lecturer in education, 1972-80, University of Michigan, Ann Arbor; U.S. ed. Children's Literature in Education, 1976-81. **Publications:** "It's Spring," She Said, 1967; (with B. Miles) Just Think!, 1971; A Gathering of Days, 1979; Martin's Hats, 1984; Brothers of the Heart, 1985; Old Henry, 1987; Lottie's Circus, 1989; The Grandpa Days, 1989; One Very Best Valentine's Day, 1990; The Heroine of the Titanic, 1991; A Seed, a Flower, a Minute, an Hour, 1992; Brooklyn Doesn't Rhyme, 1994; The Days before Now, 1994; The Hungry Little Boy, 1995; Nellie Bly's Monkey, 1996; Bedtime, 1998; Hello, Shoes!, 1999. **Address:** c/o Curtis Brown Associates, 10 Astor Pl Fl 3, New York, NY 10003, U.S.A.

BLOSSFELD, Hans-Peter. German, b. 1954. **Genres:** Mathematics/ Statistics, Sociology. **Career:** University of Mannheim, Germany, research scientist, 1980-84; Max Planck Institute for Human Development and Education, Berlin, Germany, senior research scientist, 1984-89; European University Institute, Florence, Italy, professor of political and social sciences, 1989-92; external professor, 1992-95; University of Bremen, Germany, professor of sociology and social statistics, 1992-98; University of Bielefeld, Germany, professor of sociology, 1998-. **Publications:** Bildungsexpansion und Berufschancen, 1985; (with A. Hamerle and K.U. Mayer) Ereignisanalyse: Statistische Theorie und Anwendung in den Wirtschafts-und Sozialwissenschaften, 1986; Kohortendifferenzierung und Karriereprozess, 1989; (with Hamerle and Mayer) Event History Analysis, 1989; (ed. with Y. Shavit, and contrib.) Persistent Inequality: Changing Educational Attainment in 13 Countries, 1993; (ed. and contrib.) The New Role of Women: Family Formation in Modern Societies, 1995; (with G. Rohwer) Techniques of Event History Modeling, 1995; (ed. with C. Hakim, and contrib.) Between Equalization and Marginalization: Women's Part-Time Work in Europe and the United States of America, 1997; (ed. with G. Prein, and contrib.) Rational Choice Theory and Large-Scale Data Analysis, 1997; (with R. Stockmann) Globalization and Changes in Vocational Training Systems in Developing and Advanced Industrialized Societies, 1999; (with S. Drobnic) Careers of Couples in Modern Society, 2001. Contributor of articles and reviews to scholarly journals. **Address:** Lehrstuhl fuer Allgemeine Soziologie, Fakultaet fuer Soziologie, Universitaet Bielefeld, Postfach 100131, 33501 Bielefeld, Germany. **Online address:** hpb@uni-bielefeld.de

BLOUET, Olwyn M(ary). American (born England), b. 1948. **Genres:** International relations/Current affairs, History. **Career:** University of Nebraska, Lincoln, visiting assistant professor of history, 1979-80, 1981-83; Texas A & M University, visiting assistant professor of history, 1983-89; College of William & Mary, visiting assistant professor of history, 1990-91; Virginia State University, Petersburg, professor of history, 1992-. **Publications:** EDITOR: (with B.W. Blouet) Latin America: An Introductory Survey, 1982; (and contrib.) Latin America and the Caribbean: A Systematic and Regional Survey, 1993, rev. ed., 2002. Contributor of articles to periodicals; contributor of chapters to books. **Address:** Dept of History, Virginia State University, Petersburg, VA 23806, U.S.A.

BLOUIN, Lenora P. American, b. 1941. **Genres:** Librarianship, Literary criticism and history. **Career:** San Jose Public Library, San Jose, CA, reference librarian, 1976-86, senior librarian and head of reference department, 1986-96; writer and bibliographer, 1978-. **Publications:** May Sarton: A Bibliography, 1978, rev ed. as May Sarton: A Revised Bibliography, 2000. Contributor to books and periodicals.

BLOUNT, Roy, Jr. American, b. 1941. **Genres:** Novels, Poetry, Sports/ Fitness, Humor/Satire. **Career:** Atlanta Journal, Georgia, reporter and columnist, 1966-68; Sports Illustrated, NYC, staff writer and associate editor, 1968-75; The Atlantic, Boston, contributing editor, 1979; Men's Journal, New York, contributing editor, 1993. New York Public Library, Literary Lion, 1987. **Publications:** Larger than Life (screenplay), 1968; About Three Bricks Shy of a Load (sports), 1974; Crackers (humor), 1980; One Fell Soup (humor), 1982; What Men Don't Tell Women (humor), 1984; Not Exactly What I Had in Mind (humor), 1985; It Grows on You (semiotics), 1986; Soupsongs/Webster's Ark (poetry), 1987; Now Where Were We? (humor), 1989; About Three Bricks Shy and the Load Filled Up (sports), 1990; First Hubby (novel), 1990; Camels Are Easy, Comedy Is Hard (humor), 1991; Roy Blount's Book of Southern Humor, 1994; Be Sweet: A Conditional Love Story, 1998; If You Only Knew How Much I Smell You, 1998; I Am Puppy, Hear Me Yap, 2000; Am I Pig Enough for You Yet?: Voices of the Barnyard, 2001; Robert E. Lee, 2003; I Am the Cat, Don't Forget That,

2004; Feet on the Street: Rambles around New Orleans, 2005. **Address:** c/o Esther Newberg, International Creative Management, 40 W 57th St, New York, NY 10019, U.S.A.

BLOW, Michael. American, b. 1930. **Genres:** History, Sciences. **Career:** Editor with Collier's, Newsweek, American Heritage, Columbia Broadcasting System Inc, Earl Newsom and Co, Reader's Digest. **Publications:** Satellites, Ships and the Sea, 1960, 1966. Men of Science and Invention and The History of the Atomic Bomb, 1968; A Ship To Remember: The Maine and the Spanish-American War, 1992. **Address:** Editorial Services, 546 North St, Greenwich, CT 06830, U.S.A.

BLUEMEL, Kristin. American, b. 1964. **Genres:** Literary criticism and history. **Career:** Monmouth University, West Long Branch, NJ, associate professor of English, 1994-. **Publications:** Experimenting on the Borders of Modernism: Dorothy Richardson's Pilgrimage, 1997. **Address:** Dept of English, Monmouth University, West Long Branch, NJ 07764, U.S.A. **Online address:** kbluemel@mondec.monmouth.edu

BLUM, Bruce I(van). American, b. 1931. **Genres:** Information science/ Computers. **Career:** Fairleigh Dickinson University, Teaneck, NJ, instructor in history and social science, 1955-60; teacher at public schools in New Brunswick, NJ, 1960-62; Johns Hopkins University, Applied Physics Laboratory, Silver Spring, MD, senior staff mathematician, 1962-67; National Space Science Data Center, systems analyst and deputy project director, 1967-69, manager of information systems department and project director for Earth Resources Technology Satellite, 1969-70; Wolf Research and Development Corp., Riverdale, MD, vice-president and manager of information systems department, 1970-73; TRW Systems, McLean, VA, senior systems engineer and assistant manager of Fleet Command Support Center Program, 1973-74; Johns Hopkins University, School of Medicine, Baltimore, MD, assistant professor, 1975-83, associate professor of biomedical engineering, 1983-94, and assistant professor of oncology, also senior staff mathematician with Applied Physics Laboratory, Laurel, MD, 1974-79, principal professional staff member, 1979-94. Beijing Medical University, visiting professor, 1988; lecturer throughout the world. Photographer, with group and solo shows throughout the United States. **Publications:** Clinical Information Systems, 1986; TEDIUM and the Software Process, 1990; Software Engineering: A Holistic View, 1992; Beyond Programming To a New Era of Design, 1996. EDITOR: Proceedings: Sixth Annual Symposium on Computer Applications in Medical Care, 1982; Information Systems for Patient Care, 1984; (with R. Salamon and M. Jorgensen) MEDINFO-86, two vols, 1986; ACM Conference on the History of Medical Informatics, 1987; (with H.F. Orthner) Implementing Health Care Information Systems, 1989; (with J.P. Enterline and R.E. Lenhard) A Clinical Information System for Oncology, 1989; (with K. Duncan) A History of Medical Informatics, 1990; (with T. Timmers) Software Engineering in Medical Informatics, 1991; Computers in Medicine (series). Contributor to scientific journals. **Address:** 5605 Vantage Point Rd., Columbia, MD 21044, U.S.A. **Online address:** biblum@erols.com

BLUM, Deborah (Leigh). American, b. 1954. **Genres:** Adult non-fiction. **Career:** Journalist and nonfiction writer. Sacramento Bee, Sacramento, CA, science writer, 1984-. University of Wisconsin, Madison, WI, scientific writer in residence, 1994. **Publications:** The Monkey Wars, 1994. **Address:** Sacramento Bee, P.O. Box 15779, Sacramento, CA 95852, U.S.A.

BLUM, Howard. American, b. 1948. **Genres:** Novels, Adult non-fiction. **Career:** Former journalist for the New York Times and the Village Voice; author of fiction and nonfiction. **Publications:** Wanted! The Search for Nazis in America, 1977; Wishful Thinking (novel), 1985; I Pledge Allegiance-The True Story of the Walkers: An American Spy Family, 1987; Out There: The Government's Secret Quest for Extraterrestrials, 1990; Gangland: How the FBI Broke the Mob, 1993; The Gold of Exodus: The Discovery of the Real Mt. Sinai, 1998. **Address:** c/o Lynn Nesbit, Janklow & Nesbit Associates, 445 Park Ave., Fl 13, New York, NY 10022, U.S.A.

BLUM, Kristen Raub. American, b. 1967. **Genres:** Travel/Exploration. **Career:** Wanderlust Publishing, Seattle, WA, editor and publisher, 1997-; Rezworks, Seattle, editor, 1999-. Instructor in English at community colleges in Seattle. **Publications:** The Greater Evergreen Area Guide, 1999. **Address:** 4213 2nd Ave NE, Seattle, WA 98105-6509, U.S.A.

BLUM, Lenore (Carol). American, b. 1943. **Genres:** Mathematics/Statistics. **Career:** Air Force Office of Science and Research, fellow, 1968-69; University of California, Berkeley, lecturer in mathematics, 1969-71; adjunct professor of computer science, beginning in 1989, Mathematical Sciences Research Institute, deputy director, c. 1990-; Mills College, research associate in mathematics, 1971-77, mathematics and computer science department, founder, 1973, chair, 1973-86, associate professor of mathematics, 1977-, Letts-Villard chair of mathematics and computer science, 1978-, Letts-Villard professor, 1978-; International Computer Science Institute, Theory Group, research scientist, 1988-. Math/Science Network, Expanding Your Horizons Conferences, founder, co-director, 1975-81; member of Mathematics Panel, Project 2061. **Publications:** (with S. Smale and M. Shub) Complexity and Real Computation, 1997. Author of books and films for the Math/Science Network. Contributor to journals. **Address:** 700 Euclid Ave., Berkeley, CA 94708, U.S.A.

BLUM, Louise A(gnes). American, b. 1960. **Genres:** Gay and lesbian issues, Novels. **Career:** Worked as an inmate advocate in Georgia and as a community organizer in low-income neighborhoods in Columbus, OH, Pittsburgh, PA, and Atlanta, GA, 1982-85; University of Iowa, Iowa City, teaching assistant and instructor in creative writing, 1987-88; University of Nebraska, Lincoln, assistant professor of creative writing, 1988-89; Mansfield University, Mansfield, PA, associate professor of English, 1989-. Has worked as an assistant to the producer of radio documentary on storytelling; is active in community workshops on creative writing and on gay and lesbian issues. **Publications:** Good Girls, 1993; Amnesty (novel), 1995; You're Not from around Here, Are You?, A Lesbian in Smalltown America (memoir), 2001. Contributor of short stories to journals and anthologies. Contributor of poems to journals. **Address:** Mansfield University, Department of English, Mansfield, PA 16933, U.S.A.

BLUMBERG, Arnold. American, b. 1925. **Genres:** History, International relations/Current affairs. **Career:** Professor of History, Towson University, Baltimore (joined faculty, 1958, now emeritus). Abstractor, Historical Abstracts, and America, History and Life, publs.; Critic Reader, The American Historical Review and The Historian Journals; Book Reviewer for Choice mag., The Sunday Sun, Baltimore, etc. **Publications:** The Diplomacy of the Austro-Sardinian War of 1859, 1952; A History of Congregation Shearith Israel of Baltimore, 1970; A Manual for Under-graduate Term Papers, 1970; The Diplomacy of the Mexican Empire: 1863-1867, 1971, 1987; A View from Jerusalem 1849-1858: The Consular Diary of James and Elizabeth Ann Finn, 1980; Zion before Zionism 1838-1880, 1985; A Carefully Planned Accident: The Italian War of 1859, 1990; Great Leaders/Great Tyrants: Opposing Views of People Who Have Influenced History, 1995; The History of Israel, 1998. Author of scholarly journal articles and newspaper op/ed pieces. **Address:** 3415 Clark's Ln Apt A2, Baltimore, MD 21215, U.S.A.

BLUMBERG, Phillip Irvin. American, b. 1919. **Genres:** Law. **Career:** Professor Emeritus of Law and Business and Dean Emeritus, University of Connecticut School of Law, 1989- (Dean, 1974-84; Professor, 1984-89). Trustee emeritus, Connecticut Bar Foundation; professor of law, Boston University School of Law, 1966-74; formerly, Chairman, Finance Committee, Federated Development Co. (formerly Federated Mortgage Investors), NYC: Chairman, Executive Committee, Excess and Treaty Reinsurance Corp. **Publications:** Corporate Responsibility in a Changing Society, 1972; The Megacorporation in American Society: The Scope of Corporate Power, 1975; The Law of Corporate Groups: Procedure, 1983; The Law of Corporate Groups: Bankruptcy, 1985; The Law of Corporate Groups: Substantive Common Law, 1987; The Law of Corporate Groups: General Statutory Law, 1989; The Law of Corporate Groups: Specific Statutory Law, 1992; The Multinational Challenge to Corporation Law: The Search for a New Corporate Personality, 1993; The Law of Corporate Groups: State Statutory Law, 1995; The Law of Corporate Groups: Enterprise Liability, 1998. **Address:** University of Connecticut Law School, 65 Elizabeth St, Hartford, CT 06105-2290, U.S.A. **Online address:** pblumber@law.uconn.edu

BLUMBERG, Rhoda. American, b. 1917. **Genres:** Children's non-fiction. **Career:** Freelance writer. **Publications:** Firefighters, 1975; Sharks, 1975; First Ladies, 1977; Famine, 1978; Witches, 1979; Backyard Bestiary, 1979: UFO, 1979; The Truth about Dragons, 1980; First Travel Guide to the Moon, 1980; Freaky Facts, 1981; Southern Africa, 1982; Devils and Demons, 1982; (with L. Blumberg) Dictionary of Misinformation, 1982; First Travel Guide to the Bottom of the Sea, 1983: Monsters, 1983; Commodore Perry in the Land of the Shogun, 1985 (Golden Kite Award, Newbery Honor Book); (with L. Blumberg) Lovebirds, Lizards and Llamas, 1986; The Incredible Journey of Lewis and Clark, 1987; The Great American Gold Rush, 1989; The Remarkable Voyages of Captain Cook, 1991; Jumbo, 1992; Bloomers, 1993; Full Steam Ahead: The Race to Build a Transcontinental Rail Road, 1995; What's the Deal: Jefferson, Napoleon and the Louisiana Purchase, 1998; Shipwrecked: The True Adventures of a Japanese Boy, 2001. **Address:** 1305 Baptist Church Rd, Yorktown Heights, NY 10598, U.S.A.

BLUME, Harvey. American, b. 1946. **Genres:** Zoology. **Career:** Writer. **Publications:** (with Phillips V. Bradford) Ota Benga: The Pygmy in the Zoo, St. Martin's, 1992. **Address:** 1267 Cambridge St., Cambridge, MA 02139, U.S.A.

BLUME, Helmut. German, b. 1920. **Genres:** Geography, History, Genealogy/Heraldry. **Career:** Universitaet Marburg, Marburg, Germany, assistant lecturer, 1946-54; Universitaet Kiel, Germany, associate professor, 1954-63; Universitaet Tuebingen, Germany, professor, chair of physical geography, and director of the Department of Geography, 1963-85, professor emeritus, 1985-. **Publications:** The Caribbean Islands, 1974; Geography of Sugar Cane, 1985; The German Coast during the Colonial Era, 1722-1803, 1990; Color Atlas of the Surface Forms of the World, 1992. Also editor of Beihefte, Tuebinger Atlas des Vorderen Orients, Tuebinger Geographische Studien. **Address:** Geographisches Institut, Hoelderlinstr. 12, 72074 Tuebingen, Germany.

BLUME, Judy. American, b. 1938. **Genres:** Novels, Children's fiction, Young adult fiction. **Publications:** CHILDREN'S FICTION: Iggie's House, 1970; Are You There God? It's Me, Margaret, 1970; Freckle Juice, 1971; Then Again, Maybe I Won't, 1971; Tales of a Fourth Grade Nothing, 1972; It's Not the End of the World, 1972; Otherwise Known as Sheila the Great, 1972; Deenie, 1973; Blubber, 1974; Starring Sally J. Freedman as Herself, 1977; Superfudge, 1980; Judy Blume Diary, 1981; The One in the Middle Is the Green Kangaroo, 1981; The Pain and the Great One, 1984; Just as Long as We're Together, 1987; Fudge-a-mania, 1990; Here's to You, Rachel Robinson, 1993; Double Fudge, 2002. YOUNG ADULT FICTION: Forever, 1976; Tiger Eyes, 1981. ADULT FICTION: Wifey, 1978; Smart Women, 1984; Summer Sisters, 1998. OTHER: Letters to Judy: What Kids Wish They Could Tell You (nonfiction), 1986; (ed.) Places I Never Meant to Be: Original Stories by Censored Writers, 1999. **Address:** c/o William Morris Agency Inc, 1325 Avenue of the Americas, New York, NY 10019, U.S.A. **Online address:** www.judyblume.com

BLUMENKRANTZ, Jeff. American, b. 1965. **Genres:** Songs/Lyrics and libretti. **Career:** Actor, singer, songwriter, composer, arranger, orchestrator, musical director, and playwright. **Publications:** (with A. Kessler and L. Saines) Woman with Pocketbook (musical), 1998; (songs) Urban Cowboy (musical), 2002; (With L. Saines) Precious Little Jewel (musical). Author of songs and song cycles. **Address:** c/o Abrams Artists, 275 Seventh Ave., 26th Floor, New York, NY 10001, U.S.A.

BLUMENSON, Martin. American, b. 1918. **Genres:** Military/Defense/Arms control, Biography. **Career:** With US Army, 1942-46, 1950-57, retiring as Lt. Col.; Instructor in History, US Merchant Academy, Kings Point, NY, 1948-50; Sr. Historian, Office of Chief of Military History, Dept. of the Army, 1957-67; President, American Military Institute, 1967; Consultant in Domestic Matters, White House, 1967-69; Visiting Professor of Military and Strategic Studies, History or International Affairs at US universities. **Publications:** Breakout and Pursuit, 1961; The Duel for France, 1963; Anzio: The Gamble That Failed, 1963; Kasserine Pass (in U.K. as Rommel's Last Victory), 1967; Sicily: Whose Victory?, 1969; Salerno to Cassino, 1969; Bloody River: The Real Tragedy of the Rapido (in U.K. as Prelude to Mont Cassino), 1970; Eisenhower, 1972; The Patton Papers: vol. 1, 1885-1940, 1972, vol. 11, 1940-45, 1974; (co-author) Masters of the Art of Command, 1975; The Vilde Affair: Beginnings of the French Resistance, 1977; (co-author) Liberation, 1978; Mark Clark, 1984; Patton: The Man Behind the Legend, 1985; The Battle of the Generals, 1994; Heroes Never Die, 2001. **Address:** 3900 Watson Pl NW, Washington, DC 20016, U.S.A.

BLUMENTHAL, Gerda Renee. American (born Germany), b. 1923. **Genres:** Literary criticism and history. **Career:** Professor Emeritus of French and Comparative Literature, Catholic University of America. Washington, D.C. Professor of French, and Chairman, Dept. of Modern Languages, Washington Coll., 1955-68. **Publications:** Andre Malraux: The Conquest of Dread, 1960; The Poetic Imagination of Georges Bemanos, 1965; Thresholds: A Study of Proust, 1984. **Address:** 4530 Connecticut Ave. N. W, Washington, DC 20008, U.S.A.

BLUNDELL, Derek (John). British, b. 1933. **Genres:** Earth sciences. **Career:** University of Birmingham, England, lecturer, 1959-70; University of Lancaster, England, senior lecturer and reader, 1970-75; Chelsea College, London, England, professor, 1975-85; Royal Holloway and Bedford New College, London, professor, 1985-98, emeritus professor of geophysics, 1998-, Leverhulme Emeritus Fellow, 1998-2000. University of Ghana, visiting professor, 1974; British Institutions Reflection Profiling Syndicate advisory committee, chair 1981-93; EGT, Scientific Steering Committee,

1981-90; ESF, GEODE Steering Committee, 1998-. **Publications:** Tectonic Evolution of the North Sea Rifts, 1990; (co-ed.) A Continent Revealed, 1992; Lyell: The Past Is the Key to the Present, 1998; The Timing and Location of Major Ore Deposits in an Evolving Orogen, 2002. **Address:** Geology Department, Royal Holloway University of London, Egham, Surrey TW20 0EX, England. **Online address:** d.blundell@gl.rhul.ac.uk

BLUNDELL, Sue. British, b. 1947. **Genres:** History. **Career:** University of London, Birkbeck College, London, England, part-time lecturer in classical civilization, 1979-. Open University, part-time lecturer, 1979-; British Museum, lecturer. **Publications:** The Origins of Civilisation in Greek and Roman Thought, 1986; Women in Ancient Greece, 1995. The Sacred and the Feminine in Ancient Greece, 1998; Women in Classical Athens, 1998. Contributor to books. Adaptor of Homeric poems for public performance. **Address:** 59B Goodge St, London W1T 1TJ, England.

BLUNT, Giles. Canadian, b. 1952. **Genres:** Novels. **Career:** Novelist and scriptwriter. **Publications:** NOVELS: Cold Eye, 1989; Forty Words for Sorrow, 2000. Author of scripts for television series. **Address:** c/o Helen Heller, Helen Heller Agency, 32 Bayhampton Court, Toronto, ON, Canada M3H 5L6. **Online address:** gblunt99@yahoo.com

BLY, Robert (Elwood). American, b. 1926. **Genres:** Poetry, Adult nonfiction, Mythology/Folklore, Essays, Translations. **Career:** Founder and Ed., The Fifties mag (later the Sixties and the Seventies mags.), and the Fifties Press (later The Sixties Press and The Seventies Press), Madison, MI, 1958-. **Publications:** POETRY: (with J. Wright and W. Duffy) The Lion's Tail and Eyes, 1962; Silence in the Snowy Fields, 1962; The Light around the Body, 1967; Chrysanthemums, 1967; Ducks, 1968; The Morning Glory, 1969, rev. ed., 1973; The Teeth Mother Naked at Last, 1970; (with W.E. Stafford and W. Matthews) Poems for Tennessee, 1971; Christmas Eve Service at Midnight at St. Michael's, 1972; Water under the Earth, 1972; The Dead Seal near McClure's Beach, 1973; Leaping Poetry, 1973; Jumping Out of Bed, 1973; Sleepers Joining Hands, 1973; The Hockey Poem, 1974; Point Reyes Poems, 1974; Old Man Rubbing His Eyes, 1975; The Loon, 1977; This Body Is Made of Camphor and Gopherwood: Prose Poems, 1977; Visiting Emily Dickinson's Grave and Other Poems, 1979; This Tree Will Be Here for a Thousand Years, 1979, rev. ed., 1992; The Man in the Black Coat Turns, 1981; Finding an Old Ant Mansion, 1981; Four Rumages, 1983; The Whole Moisty Night, 1983; Out of the Rolling Ocean, 1984; Mirabai Versions, 1984; In the Month of May, 1985; Love of Minute Particulars 1985; Selected Poems, 1986; Loving a Woman in Two Worlds, 1987; The Moon on a Fence Post, 1988; The Apple Found in Plowing, 1989; Angels of Pompeii, 1991; What Have I Ever Lost by Dying (prose poems), 1992; Gratitude to Old Teachers, 1993; Meditations on the Insatiable Soul, 1994; Morning Poems, 1997; Holes the Crickets Have Eaten in Blankets, 1997; Saturday Nights in Marietta, 1999; Eating the Honey of Words, 1999; The Night Abraham Called to the Stars, 2001. TRANSLATIONS: H. Hvass, Reptiles and Amphibians of the World, 1960; (with J. Wright) Twenty Poems of Georg Trakl, 1961; S. Lagerlof, The Story of Gosta Berling, 1962; (with J. Wright and J. Knoepfle) Twenty Poems of Cesar Vallejo, 1962; (with E. Sellin and T. Buckman) Three Poems by Tomas Transtromer, 1966; K. Hamsun, Hunger, 1967; (with C. Paulston) G. Ekelof, I Do Best Alone at Night, 1967; (with C. Paulston) Late Arrival on Earth: Selected Poems of Gunnar Ekelof, 1967; (co) I. Goll, Selected Poems, 1968; (with J. Wright) Twenty Poems of Pablo Neruda, 1968; Forty Poems of Juan Ramon Jimenez, 1969; I. Kobayashi, Ten Poems, 1969; (with J. Wright and J. Knoepfle) Neruda and Vallejo: Selected Poems, 1971; Twenty Poems of Thomas Transtromer, 1971; The Fish in the Sea Is Not Thirsty, 1971; T. Transtromer, Night Vision, 1972; R.M. Rilke, The First Ten Sonnets of Orpheus, 1972; Lorca and Jimenez: Selected Poems, 1973; Martinson, Ekelof, Transtromer: Selected Poems, 1973; Basho, 1974; Selected Poems of Rainer Maria Rilke, 1981; Time Alone: Selected Poems of Antonio Machado, 1983; Tomas Transtromer: Selected Poems, 1954-86, 1987; (and ed.) Trusting Your Life to Water and Eternity: 20 Poems of Olav H. Hague, 1987; Ten Poems of Francis Ponge, 1990; (with S. Dutta) The Lightning Should Have Fallen on Ghalib: Selected Poems of Ghalib, 1999; The Half-Finished Heaven: The Best Poems of Tomas Transtromer, 2001; (with R. Hedin and R. Greenwald) The Roads Have Come to an End Now: Selected and Last Poems of Rolf Jacobsen, 2001. EDITOR: (with D. Ray) A Poetry Reading against the Vietnam War, 1966; The Sea and the Honeycomb (poems), 1966; Forty Poems Touching on Recent American History, 1970; Leaping Poetry, 1975; D. Ignatow, Selected Poems, 1975; News of the Universe (poems), 1979; 10 Love Poems, 1981; The Winged Life, 1986; (with others) The Rag and Bone Shop of the Heart, 1992; The Soul Is Here for Its Own Joy, 1995; The Darkness around Us Is Deep: Selected Poems of William Stafford, 1993; The Best American Poetry, 1999, 1999. OTHER: A Broadsheet against the New York Times Book

Review, 1961; Talking All Morning (interviews), 1980; A Little Book on the Human Shadow, 1986; The Pillow and the Key, 1987; American Poetry, 1990; Iron John: A Book about Men, 1990; Between Two Worlds (lyrics), 1991; The Sibling Society, 1996; (with M. Woodman) The Maiden King: The Reunion of Masculine and Feminine (prose), 1998. **Address:** 1904 Girard Ave S, Minneapolis, MN 55403, U.S.A.

BLYTH, Alan Geoffrey. British, b. 1929. **Genres:** Music, Biography. **Career:** Music critic, London; Board Member, Opera mag., London. Critic for Gramophone, Radio 3; Consulting Editor, Grove's Dictionary, 1996-. **Publications:** Enjoyment of Opera; Colin Davis; Janet Baker; Opera on Record; Remembering Britten; Wagner's Ring: An Introduction; Opera on Record 2, 1983; Opera on Record 3, 1984; Opera on CD, 1992; Opera on Video, 1995; Song on Record, vol. I, 1986, vol. II, 1988; Choral Music on Record, 1991. **Address:** 22 Shilling St, Lavenham, Suffolk C010 9RH, England. **Online address:** alan.blyth@tiscali.co.uk

BLYTH, Chay. (Charles). British, b. 1940. **Genres:** Travel/Exploration, Autobiography/Memoirs. **Career:** Sailing Ventures, Ltd., Hants, England, Co. Director and Managing Director, 1969-; The Challenge Business, Managing Director. Holds records for sailing. **Publications:** A Fighting Chance, 1967; Innocent Abroad, 1969; The Impossible Voyage, 1971; Theirs Is the Glory, 1974; The Challenge, 1993. **Address:** The Challenge Business, The Box Office, Box Lane, Minchinhampton, Glos. GL6 9HA, England.

BLYTH, John. See **HIBBS, John.**

BLYTHE, Martin. New Zealander, b. 1954. **Genres:** Film. **Career:** University of California, Los Angeles, programmer at Film and Television Archive, 1988-89; Buena Vista International, Los Angeles, became senior marketing manager, 1989-95; Buena Vista Home Video, Burbank, CA, director of public relations, 1995-. University of California, Los Angeles, extension lecturer. **Publications:** Naming the Other: Images of the Maori in New Zealand Film and Television, 1994. Contributor of articles and reviews to periodicals. **Address:** 8359 Rosewood Ave #5, Los Angeles, CA 90048, U.S.A.

BLYTHE, Ronald (George). British, b. 1922. **Genres:** Novels, Novellas/Short stories, History, Literary criticism and history, Local history/Rural topics. **Career:** Royal Society of Literature, fellow. John Clare Society, president. **Publications:** A Treasonable Growth (novel), 1960; Immediate Possession (short stories), 1961; The Age of Illusion 1963; Akenfield: Portrait of an English Village, 1969; The View in Winter, 1979; Places, 1981; From the Headlands, 1982; The Stories of Ronald Blythe, 1985; Divine Landscapes, 1986; Each Returning Day, 1989; Private Words: Letters and Diaries from the Second World War, 1991; England: The Four Seasons (essays), 1993; Word from Wormingford: A Parish Year, 1997; First Friends (biography), 1999; Out of the Valley (essays), 2000; The Circling Year: Perspectives from a Country Parish, 2001; Talking to the Neighbours, 2002; The Assassin, 2004. EDITOR: J. Austen, Emma, 1966; Components of the Scene: An Anthology of the Prose and Poetry of the Second World War, 1966; William Hazlitt: Selected Writings, 1970; Aldeburgh Anthology, 1972; T. Hardy, A Pair of Blue Eyes, 1976; L. Tolstoy, The Death of Ivan Ilyich, 1977; T. Hardy, Far from the Madding Crowd, 1978; H. James, The Awkward Age, 1987; George Herbert: The Country Person, 2003. **Address:** Bottengom's Farm, Wormingford, Colchester, Essex C06 3AP, England.

BOAG, Peter G. American, b. 1961. **Genres:** Environmental sciences/Ecology, History. **Career:** Oregon Historical Society, researcher, summer, 1982; University of Oregon, Eugene, adjunct assistant professor of history, 1989; Idaho State University, Pocatello, assistant professor, 1989-94, associate professor of history, 1994-, member of Mormon Migration Project, 1990. University of Oregon, visiting associate professor, 1994-95. **Publications:** Environment and Experience: Settlement Culture in Nineteenth-Century Oregon, 1992. Contributor of articles and reviews to history journals. **Address:** Department of History, Idaho State University, Pocatello, ID 83209-0009, U.S.A.

BOARDMAN, Sir John. British, b. 1927. **Genres:** Archaeology/Antiquities, Art/Art history, Classics. **Career:** Lincoln Professor of Classical Art and Archaeology, University of Oxford, 1978-94 (Assistant Keeper, Ashmolean Museum, 1955-59; Reader in Classical Archaeology, 1959-78). Fellow, British Academy, 1969-; Co-Ed., Oxford Monographs in Classical Archaeology. Assistant Director, British School at Athens, 1952-55; Ed., Journal of Hellenic Studies, 1958-65. **Publications:** (trans.) S. Marinatos and M. Hirmer: Crete and Mycenae, 1960; The Cretan Collection in Oxford, 1961; The Greeks Overseas, 1964, rev. ed., 1999; Island Gems, 1963; Greek Art, 1964, rev. ed., 1996; The Date of the Knossos Tablets, 1963; (with J. Hayes) Excavations at Tocra, 2 vols., 1966-73; (with J. Dorig, W. Fuchs, and M. Hirmer) Die Griechische Kunst, 1966; Greek Emporio, 1967; Pre-Classical Style and Civilisation, 1967; Engraved Gems, the Ionides Collection, 1968; Archaic Greek Gems, 1968; Greek Gems and Finger Rings, 1970; (with D.C. Kurtz) Greek Burial Customs, 1971; Athenian Black Figure Vases, 1974; Athenian Red Figure Vases: The Archaic Period, 1975; (with D. Scarisbrick) The Ralph Harari Collection of Finger Rings, 1978; (with E. la Rocca) Eros in Greece, 1978 Greek Sculpture, Archaic Period, 1978; (with M.L. Vollenweider) Catalogue of Gems and Finger Rings, vol. I, 1978; (with M. Robertson) Castle Ashby Corpus Vasorum, 1979; Greek Sculpture, Classical Period, 1985; The Parthenon and Its Sculptures, 1985; Athenian Red Figure Vases: Classical Period, 1989; The Diffusion of Classical Art in Antiquity, 1994; The Great God Pan, 1997; Early Greek Vase Painting, 1999; Persia and the West, 2000; The History of Greek Vases, 2001; The Archaeology of Nostalgia, 2002. EDITOR: (with M. Brown and T. Powell) The European Community in Prehistory, 1971; Oxford History of the Classical World, 1986; Oxford History of Classical Art, 1993. **Address:** 11 Park St, Woodstock, Oxon., England.

BOAS, Marie. See **HALL, Marie Boas.**

BOAST, Philip. British, b. 1952. **Genres:** Romance/Historical, History. **Career:** Writer. Worked in sales and as a sanitary inspector, asbestos molder, chicken farmer, and chauffeur. Norrice Green Farms Ltd., chief executive. **Publications:** The Assassinators, 1976; London's Child, 1987; The Millionaire, 1989; Watersmeet, 1990; Pride, 1991; London's Daughter, 1992; Gloria: Resurrection, 1996; City, 1996; The Foundling, 1997; Deus, 1998; Sion, 1999; Era, 2000. **Address:** c/o Dorian Literary Agency, 27 Church Rd, Torquay TQ1 4QY, England. **Online address:** philipboast@beeb.net

BOAZ, David. American, b. 1953. **Genres:** Politics/Government. **Career:** Cato Institute, Washington, DC, executive vice-president, 1981-. **Publications:** EDITOR: Left, Right, and Babyboom: America's New Politics, 1986; Assessing the Reagan Years, 1988; The Crisis in Drug Prohibition, 1990; Liberating Schools: Education in the Inner City, 1991; (co-ed.) Market Liberalism: A Paradigm for the 21st Century, 1993; The Libertarian Reader, 1997. AUTHOR: Libertarianism: A Primer, 1997. **Address:** Cato Institute, 1000 Massachusetts Ave. NW, Washington, DC 20001, U.S.A.

BOAZ, Noel T(homas). American, b. 1952. **Genres:** Anthropology/Ethnology, Sociology. **Career:** University of California, Los Angeles, lecturer in anthropology, 1977-78; New York University, NYC, assistant professor of anthropology, 1978-83; Virginia Museum of Natural History, Martinsville, director and curator, 1983-90; International Institute for Human Evolutionary Research, Bend, OR, research professor of anthropology and director of the institute, 1990-. Field work includes direction of International Sahabi Research Project in Libya, Senliki Research Expedition in Zaire, and Western Rift Research Expedition in Uganda. Virginia Museum of Natural History Foundation, president, 1984-89; International Foundation for Human Evolutionary Research, president, 1990-. **Publications:** Quarry: Closing in on the Missing Link, 1993. EDITOR: (with A.E. Arnanti, A. Gaziry, and others) Neogene Paleontology and the Geology of Sahabi, Libya, 1987; The Evolution of Environments and Hominidae in the African Western Rift Valley, 1990. **Address:** 4312 Two Woods Rd, Virginia Beach, VA 23455-4445, U.S.A.

BOBCAT. See **RESTALL ORR, Emma.**

BOBER, Natalie S. American, b. 1930. **Genres:** History, Young adult nonfiction, Biography. **Career:** Educator and consultant at junior high school and college level; author of biographies for young adults. Co-owner of children's bookstore, Once Upon a Time, 1985-93. Hunter College Alumnae Hall of Fame, 2001; International Center for Jefferson Studies, fellow, 2003; Jefferson Legacy Foundation, board of directors, 2003; consultant on Ken Burns's documentary film on Thomas Jefferson, 1997. **Publications:** William Wordsworth: The Wandering Poet, 1975; A Restless Spirit: The Story of Robert Frost, 1981, rev. ed., 1991; Breaking Tradition: The Story of Louise Nevelson, 1984; (comp.) Let's Pretend: Poems of Flight and Fancy, 1986; Thomas Jefferson: Man on a Mountain, 1988; Marc Chagall: Painter of Dreams, 1991; Abigail Adams: Witness to a Revolution, 1995; Countdown to Independence: A Revolution of Ideas in England and the American Colonies 1760-1776, 2001. Contributor to periodicals. **Address:** 7 Westfield Ln, White Plains, NY 10605, U.S.A. **Online address:** nsbober@optonline.net

BOBINSKI, George S. American, b. 1929. **Genres:** Librarianship. **Career:** State University Coll., Cortland, New York, Director of Libraries, 1960-67;

University of Kentucky, Lexington, Coll. of Library Science, Professor and Associate Dean, 1967-70; State University at Buffalo, School of Information Studies, Dean, 1970-99, Professor, 1970-99, Professor Emeritus, 2001-. **Publications:** Carnegie Libraries: Their History and Impact on American Public Library Development, 1969; Dictionary of American Library Biography, 1978; Current and Future Trends in Library and Information Science Education, 1986; Libraries in the Democratic Process, 1994; The School of Information and Library Studies of SUNY at Buffalo, 1919-1999, 2002. **Address:** 69 Little Robin Rd, Amherst, NY 14228-1125, U.S.A. **Online address:** bobinski@acsu.buffalo.edu

BOBRICK, Benson. American, b. 1947. **Genres:** History. **Career:** Historian and poet. **Publications:** Labyrinths of Iron: Subways in History, Myth, Art, Technology, and War, 1981; Parsons Brinckerhoff: The First Hundred Years, 1985; Fearful Majesty: The Life and Reign of Ivan the Terrible, 1987; East of the Sun: The Epic Conquest and Tragic History of Siberia, 1992; Knotted Tongues: Stuttering in History and the Quest for a Cure, 1995; Angel in the Whirlwind: The Triumph of the American Revolution, 1997; Wide as the Waters: The Story of the English Bible and the Revolution It Inspires, 2001. Testament: A Soldier's Story of the Civil War, 2003. **Address:** 345 8th Ave, New York, NY 10001, U.S.A.

BOCARDO, Claire. American, b. 1939. **Genres:** Novels, Novellas/Short stories. **Career:** Plano Morning Press, Plano, TX, writer and editor, 197677; Rockwell International, editor of technical documentation, 1978-83; freelance writer, 1984-89; real-estate editor and business writer for three suburban newspapers, 1990; full-time fiction writer. **Publications:** NOVELS: Maybe Later, Love, 1992; Sweet Nothings, 1993; Lovers and Friends, 1995. Contributor to anthologies. **Address:** 1498 Blanton Hill Rd, Whitewright, TX 75491, U.S.A.

BOCHIN, Hal W(illiam). American, b. 1942. **Genres:** History, Speech/Rhetoric, Bibliography. **Career:** California State University, Fresno, assistant professor, 1969-74, associate professor, 1974-78, professor of speech communication, 1978-, chair of speech communication program, 1980-83; writer. **Publications:** (with M. Weatherson) Hiram Johnson: A Bio-Bibliography, 1988; Richard Nixon: Rhetorical Strategist, 1990; (with M. Weatherson) Hiram Johnson: Political Revivalist, 1995. Author of debate handbooks. Work represented in anthologies. Contributor to periodicals. **Address:** Department of Speech Communication, California State University, Fresno, CA 93740, U.S.A. **Online address:** HALB@CSUFRESNO.EDU

BOCK, Gisela. German, b. 1942. **Genres:** History, Intellectual history, Women's studies and issues. **Career:** Free University of Berlin, Germany, assistant at John F. Kennedy Institute for North American Studies, 1971-76, assistant professor of history at Zentralinstitut fur Sozialwissenschaft, 1977-83, professor of Western European history, 1997-; European University Institute, Florence, Italy, professor of European history, 1985-89, director of European Culture Research Center, 1987-89; University of Bielefeld, Germany, professor of history, 1989-97. Harvard University Kennedy fellow at Center of European Studies, 1974-75; lecturer at University of Basel and University of Bern, 1985; fellow at Institute for Advanced Study, Berlin, 1995-96; Central European University at Budapest, guest professor, 2001-02. **Publications:** Thomas Campanella: Politische Intention and philosophische Spekulation, 1974; Die "andere" Arbeiterbewegung in den USA, 1905-1922, 1976; Zwangssterilisation im Nationalsozialismus, 1986; Storia, storia delle donne, storia di genere, 1988; Frauen in der europaischen Geschichte, 2000 as Woemn in European History, 2002. EDITOR: (and trans) E. Flexner, Hundert Jahre Kampf, 1978; (with G.N. Schiera) Il corpo delle donne, 1988; (with Q. Skinner and M. Viroli) Machiavelli and Republicanism, 1990; (with P. Thane) Maternity and Gender Policies, 1991; (with S. James) Beyond Equality and Difference, 1992; Lebenswege von Frauen im Ancien Regime, 1992; Rassenpolitik und Geschlechterpolitik im Nationalsozialismus, 1993; (with A. Cova) Writing Women's History in Southern Europe, 2003. Author of many articles. **Address:** Department of History, Free University of Berlin, Koserstr 20, D-14195 Berlin, Germany.

BOCK, Philip Karl. American, b. 1934. **Genres:** Anthropology/Ethnology, Plays/Screenplays, Songs/Lyrics and libretti. **Career:** University of New Mexico, Albuquerque, Professor, 1962-93, Emeritus Professor of Anthropology. Journal of Anthropological Research, Editor, 1982-94; Soc. for Psychological Anthropology, Past President. **Publications:** The Micmac Indians of Restigouche, 1966; Modern Cultural Anthropology, 1969, 3rd ed., 1978; Continuities in Psychological Anthropology, 1980; Shakespeare and Elizabethan Culture, 1984; The Formal Content of Ethnography, 1986; Rethinking Psychological Anthropology, 1988, 2nd ed., 1999. MUSICAL SATIRES: Not My Department; Cat on a Streetcar Named Iguana; Ms. Muffet, the Spider, and Dr. Rice. PLAYS: So Who Is This "Anne Frank"?; Peregrina. EDITOR: Peasants in the Modern World, 1969; Culture Shock, 1970; Handbook of Psychological Anthropology, 1994. Contributor to journals and books. **Address:** Dept. of Anthropology, University of New Mexico, Albuquerque, NM 87131, U.S.A. **Online address:** pbock@unm.edu

BODDY, Janice. Canadian, b. 1951. **Genres:** Anthropology/Ethnology, Biography, Women's studies and issues, History. **Career:** University of Toronto, lecturer in anthropology, 1978-79; University of Manitoba, Winnipeg, lecturer in anthropology, 1979-80; Lakehead University, Thunder Bay, ON, lecturer in anthropology, 1980-81; University of Toronto, 1981-82, assistant professor, 1982-90, associate professor, 1990-96, professor of anthropology, 1997-2004; University of British Columbia, professor of anthropology, 2004-. **Publications:** Wombs and Alien Spirits: Women, Men, and the Zar Cult in Northern Sudan, 1989; (co-author) Aman: The Story of a Somali Girl, 1994. **Address:** Dept of Anthropology and Sociology, University of British Columbia, Vancouver, BC, Canada V6T 1Z4.

BODEN, Margaret A(nn). British, b. 1936. **Genres:** Information science/Computers, Philosophy, Psychology. **Career:** University of Birmingham, lecturer in philosophy, 1959-65; University of Sussex, Brighton, lecturer and reader, 1965-80, professor of philosophy and psychology, 1980-2002, research professor of cognitive science, 2002-. **Publications:** Purposive Explanation in Psychology, 1972; Artificial Intelligence and Natural Man, 1977, 1987; Piaget, 1979, rev. ed., 1994; Minds and Mechanisms. 1981; Computer Models of Mind, 1988; Artificial Intelligence in Psychology, 1989; The Creative Mind, 1990, rev. ed., 2003. EDITOR: The Philosophy of Artificial Intelligence, 1990; Dimensions of Creativity, 1994; The Philosophy of Artificial Life, 1996; Artificial Intelligence, 1996. **Address:** School of Science and Technology, University of Sussex, Brighton, England.

BODENHAMER, David J(ackson). American, b. 1947. **Genres:** Law, Politics/Government, Social sciences. **Career:** University of Southern Mississippi, Hattiesburg, professor of history and assistant vice-president for academic affairs, 1976-88; Indiana University-Purdue University, Indianapolis, professor of history and director of Polis Center, 1989-. Member of boards of directors. **Publications:** The Pursuit of Justice: Crime and Law in Antebellum Indiana, 1986; Fair Trial: Rights of the Accused in American History, 1992; (with E.B. Monroe and L. Hulse) The Main Stem: The History and Architecture of North Meridian Street, 1992. EDITOR: (with J.W. Ely Jr.) Ambivalent Legacy: A Legal History of the South, 1984; (with J.W. Ely Jr.) The Bill of Rights in Modern America: After Two Hundred Years, 1993; The Encyclopedia of Indianapolis, 1994. Contributor to scholarly journals. **Address:** Polis Center, Indiana University-Purdue University at Indianapolis, 1200 Waterway Blvd Ste 100, Indianapolis, IN 46202, U.S.A.

BODETT, Tom. (Thomas Edward Bodett). American, b. 1955. **Genres:** Novels, Essays. **Career:** Writer and broadcaster: Commentator, "Alaska News Nightly," Alaska Public Radio, 1984-87; columnist, "We Alaskans," Anchorage Daily News, 1985-88. Logger and commercial fisherman, 1975-77; Owner, Bodett Construction Inc., Homer and Petersburg, AK, 1977-85; Commentator, "All Things Considered," National Public Radio, 1984-86; Bodett and Company, host. **Publications:** As Far as You Can Go without a Passport: The View from the End of the Road, 1985; Small Comforts, 1987; The End of the Road, 1989; The Big Garage on Clear Shot, 1990; The Free Fall of Webster Cummings, 1996; Williwaw, 1999. **Address:** PO Box 3249, Homer, AK 99603-3249, U.S.A. **Online address:** letters@bodett.com

BODMER, Sir Walter (Fred). British (born Germany), b. 1936. **Genres:** Biology, Medicine/Health. **Career:** Director General, Imperial Cancer Research Fund, 1991-, Research Director, 1979-91; President, European Association for Cancer Research, 1994-. Research Fellow, 1958-60, and Official Fellow, 1961, Clare Coll., Cambridge, and Demonstrator, Dept. of Genetics, Cambridge University, 1960-61; Fellow and Visiting Assistant Professor, 1961-62, Assistant Professor, 1962-66, Associate Professor, 1966-68, and Professor of Genetics, 1968-70, Stanford University School of Medicine, California; Professor of Genetics, Oxford University, 1970-79. Chairman of the Trustees, Natural History Museum, 1989-93; President, Organisation of European Cancer Institutes, 1990-93; President, International Federation of Associations for the Advancement of Science and Technology, 1992-94. **Publications:** (with L. Cavalli-Sforza) The Genetics of Human Population, 1971; (with A. Jones) Our Future Inheritance: Choice or Chance?, 1974; (with L. Cavalli-Sforza) Genetics, Evolution, and Man, 1976; (ed.) Inherited Susceptibility to Cancer in Man, 1982; (with R. McKie) The Book of Man, 1994. **Address:** Hertford College, Oxford OX1 3BW, England. **Online address:** walter.bodmer@hertford.ox.ac.uk

BOEGEHOLD, Alan L(indley). American, b. 1927. **Genres:** Classics. **Career:** University of Illinois at Urbana/Champaign, instructor, then as-

sistant professor of classics, 1957-60; Brown University, Providence, RI, assistant professor, then professor, 1960-2001, emeritus professor of classics, 2001-, department head, 1966-71, director of Ancient Studies Program, 1985-91, and director of summer sessions at American School of Classical Studies at Athens. Harvard University, visiting lecturer, 1967; American School of Classical Studies at Athens, visiting professor, 1968-69, research fellow, 1974-75, research fellow at Agora Excavations, 1980-81, senior associate member, 1983-84, 1990-91; Yale University, visiting professor, 1971; University of California, Berkeley, visiting professor, 1978; Amherst College, distinguished visiting professor of classics, 2001-; guest lecturer at colleges and universities. **Publications:** (revisor) C.A. Robinson Jr., Ancient History, 2nd ed., 1967; In Simple Clothes: Translations of 11 Poems, 1993; When a Gesture Was Expected: A Selection of Examples from Archaic and Classical Greek Literature, 1999. EDITOR & CONTRIBUTOR: Studies Presented to Sterling Dow, 1984; (with A.C. Scafuro) Athenian Identity and Civic Ideology, 1993; Lawcourts at Athens, 1995; Contributor to books. Contributor of articles, translations, and reviews to archaeology and classical studies journals. **Address:** Department of Classics, Brown University, Providence, RI 02912, U.S.A.

BOEHLING, Rebecca L. American, b. 1955. **Genres:** History. **Career:** Franklin and Marshall College, Lancaster, PA, visiting instructor in history, 1986-87; University of Dayton, Dayton, OH, assistant professor of history, 1987-89; University of Maryland, Baltimore County, Baltimore, instructor, 1989-90, assistant professor, 1990-96, associate professor of history, 1996-. **Publications:** A Question of Priorities: Democratic Reforms and Economic Recovery in Postwar Germany; Frankfurt am Main, Munich, and Stuttgart under U.S. Occupation, 1945-49, 1996. Contributor to books. Contributor of articles and reviews to periodicals. **Address:** Department of History, University of Maryland, Baltimore County, 1000 Hilltop Circle, Baltimore, MD 21250, U.S.A. **Online address:** boehling@umbc.edu

BOEHMER, Elleke. British (born Republic of South Africa), b. 1961. **Genres:** Novels, Humanities. **Career:** Literary critic specializing in postcolonial fiction, and novelist. **Publications:** NOVELS: Screens against the Sky, 1990; An Immaculate Figure, 1993; Bloodlines, 2000. NONFICTION: Colonial and Postcolonial Literature: Migrant Metaphors, 1995; Empire, the National and the Postcolonial (monograph), 2002. EDITOR: (with L. Chrisman and K. Parker) Altered State?: Writing and South Africa, 1994; Empire Writing: An Anthology, 1998; Scouting for Boys, 2004; C. Sorabji, India Calling, 2004. **Address:** c/o Oxford University Press, Walton St, Oxford OX2 6DP, England. **Online address:** elleke.boehmer@ntu.ac.uk

BOEHMER, Ulrike. (born Germany), b. 1959. **Genres:** Adult non-fiction. **Career:** Boston University, Boston, MA, instructor, 1997-2000, assistant professor at Center for Health Quality, Outcomes, and Economic Research, Bedford, MA, 2000-. **Publications:** (with Ilse Kokula) Die Welt gehört uns doch! Zusammenschluss lesbischer Frauen in der Schweiz der 30er Jahre, 1991; The Personal and the Political: Women's Activism in Response to the Breast Cancer and AIDS Epidemics, 2000. **Address:** 76 Garfield St., No. 4, Cambridge, MA 02138, U.S.A. **Online address:** boehmer@bu.edu

BOELTS, Maribeth. American, b. 1964. **Genres:** Children's non-fiction. **Career:** St. John/St. Nicholas School, Evansdale, IA, preschool teacher, 1988-91; substitute teacher, 1991-. **Publications:** With My Mom, with My Dad, 1992; Kids to the Rescue!: First Aid Techniques for Kids, 1992; Tornado, 1993; Dry Days, Wet Nights, 1994; Grace and Joe, 1994; The Lulla-Book, 1994; Summer's End, 1995; Little Bunny's Preschool Countdown, 1996; Little Bunny's Cool Tool Set, 1997; Little Bunny's Pacifier Plan, 1999; When Big Daddy Was Famous, 2000. **Address:** 3815 Clearview Dr., Cedar Falls, IA 50613-6107, U.S.A. **Online address:** mboelts@cfu-cybernet.net

BOERS, Arthur Paul. Canadian, b. 1957. **Genres:** Theology/Religion. **Career:** Church Community Services, Elkhart, IN, client counselor, 1981-82; Lombard Mennonite Peace Center, Lombard, IL, director, 1983; history teacher and business manager at an alternative high school for Latino youth in Chicago, IL, 1984-85; associate pastor of a United Methodist church in Chicago, 1985-87; pastor of a Mennonite fellowship in Windsor, Ontario, 1988-92; Bloomingdale Mennonite Church, Bloomingdale, Ontario, pastor, 1992-. **Publications:** On Earth as in Heaven: Justice Rooted in Spirituality, 1991; Justice That Heals: A Biblical Vision for Victims and Offenders, 1992; Lord, Teach Us to Pray: A New Look at the Lord's Prayer, 1992; Never Call Them Jerks: Healthy Responses to Difficult Behavior, 1999. Columnist, Christian Living and Christian Ministry. Contributor of articles and reviews to periodicals. Contributing editor, Other Side, 1988-; editorial adviser, Christian Ministry.

BOESSENECKER, John. American, b. 1953. **Genres:** History. **Career:** Attorney in private practice, San Francisco, CA, 1985-; writer. **Publications:** Badge and Buckshot: Lawlessness in Old California, 1988; (with M. Dugan) The Grey Fox: The True Story of Bill Miner, Last of the Old-Time Bandits, 1992; Lawman: The Life and Times of Harry Morse, 1998; Gold Dust and Gunsmoke: Tales of Gold Rush Outlaws, Gunfighters, Lawmen and Vigilantes, 1999; Against the Vigilantes: The Recollections of Dutch Charley Duane, 1999. **Address:** 220 Montgomery St, Suite 1500, San Francisco, CA 94104, U.S.A.

BOFF, Leonardo (Genezio Darci). Brazilian, b. 1938. **Genres:** Theology/Religion. **Career:** Ordained a priest of the Franciscan order in 1964. Roman Catholic priest, Petropolis, Brazil, 1964-92; Institute Teologico Franciscano, Petropolis, professor of systematic theology, Franciscan spirituality, and theology of liberation, 1971-92; University of Rio de Janeiro, Rio de Janeiro, Brazil, professor of theology, 1992-. Adviser to the Latin American Conference of religions, and to the National Conference of Brazilian Bishops, 1971-80. **Publications:** O Evangelho do Cristo cosmico: A Realidade de um mito e o mito de uma realidade, 1971; The Question of Faith in the Resurrection of Jesus, 1971; Vida Religiosa e secularizacao, 1971; (with others) A Oracao no mundo secular: Desafio e chance, 1971; Die Kirche als Sakrament im Horizont der Welterfahrung: Versuch einer Legitimation und einer struktur-funktionalistischen Grundlegung der Kirche im Anschluss an das II. Vatikanische Konzil, 1972; Jesus Cristo libertador: Ensaio de cristologia critica para o nosso tempo, 1972, trans by P. Hughes as Jesus Christ Liberator: A Critical Christology for Our Times, 1978; A Ressurreicao de Cristo e a nossa na morte: A Dimensao antropologica da esperanca crista, 1972; (with others) Credo para amamha, 1972; O Destino do homem e do mundo, 1973; A Atualidade da experiencia de Deus, 1973; Vida para alem da morte: O Futuro, a festa e a contestacao do presente, 1974; (with others) Experimentar Deus hoje, 1974; Minima Sacramentalia: Os Sacramentos da vida e a vida dos sacramentos, 1975; A Vida religiosa e a Igreja no processo de libertacao, 1975; Teologia desde el cautiverio, 1975; Pobreza, obediencia, realizacion personal en la vida religiosa, 1975; (with others) A Mulher na Igreja: Presenca e acao hoje, 1975; (with others) Nosso Irmao Francisco de Assis, 1975; (with others) Quem e Jesus Cristo no Brasil, 1975; Teologia da libertacao e do cativeiro, 1976; A Graca libertadora no mundo, 1976, trans by J. Drury as Liberating Grace, 1979; Paixao de Cristo-paixao do mundo: Os Fatos as interpretacoes e o significado ontem e hoje, 1976, trans by R.R. Barr as Passion of Christ, Passion of the World: The Facts, Their Interpretation, and Their Meaning Yesterday and Today, 1987; Encarnacao: A Humanidade e a jovialidade de nosso Deus, 1976; Testigos de Dios en el corazon del mundo, 1977; Eclesiogenese: As Comunidades eclesiais de base reinventam a Igreja, 1977, trans by Barr as Ecclesiogenesis: The Base Communities Reinvent the Church, 1986; Que es hacer teologia desde Amreica Latina, 1977; A Fe na periferia do mundo, 1978; Via-sacra da justica, 1978, trans by Drury as Way of the Cross-Way of Justice, 1980; (with others) Die lateinamerikanische Befreiungstheologie, 1978; (with others) Religiosita popolare e cammino di liberazione, 1978; (with others) Jesucristo: Fe y historia, 1978; (with others) Responsabilidades eclesiales y sociales de los religiosos, 1978; (with others) Renovacao carismatica catolica, 1978; O Rosto materno de Deus: Ensaio interdisciplinar sobre o feminino e suas formas religiosas, 1979, trans by Barr and J.W. Diercksmeier as The Maternal Face of God: The Feminine and Its Religious Expressions, 1987; O Pai-nosso: A Oracao de libertacao integral, 1979, trans by T. Morrow as The Lord's Prayer: The Prayer of Integral Liberation, 1983; Die Anliegen der Befreiungstheologie, 1979; (with others) Da libertacao: O Teologias das libertacoes socio-historicas, 1979; Pueblas Herausforderung an die Franziskaner (Berichte, Dokumente, Kommentare), 1979; (with others) Frontiers of Theology in Latin America, 1979; (with others) Roberto Burle Marx: Homenagem a natureza, 1979; Em Preparo: O Homem, o nao-homem, o homem novo: Ensaio de antropologia a partir do oprimido, 1980; Em Preparo: A Ave-Maria, o espirito santo e o feminino, 1980; O caminhar da Igreja com os oprimidos: Do Vale de lagrimas a terra prometida, 1980; Igreja, carisma e poder, 1981, trans by Diercksmeier as Church: Charism and Power: Liberation Theology and the Institutional Church, 1985; Vida segundo o espirito, 1982; Saint Francis: A Model for Human Liberation, 1982; (with C. Boff) Salvation and Liberation, 1984; (with Peter Eicher) Theologie der Befreiung im Gesprach, 1985; (with C. Boff) Bedrohte Befreiung, 1985; Francisco de Assis: Homem do paraiso, 1985; (with C. Boff) Teologia da libertacao no debate atual, 1985; Como pregar a cruz hoje numa sociedade de crucificados?, 1986; (ed. with V. Elizondo and M. Lefebure) The People of God Amidst the Poor, 1986; (ed. with Elizondo and Lefebure) Option for the Poor: Challenge to the Rich Countries, 1986; (with others) Teologos de la liberacion hablan sobre la mujer, 1986; A Trindade, a sociedade e a libertacao, 1986, trans by P. Burns as Trinity and Society, 1988; E a Igreja se fez povo: Eclesiogenese a Igreja que nasce de fe do povo, 1986; (with C. Boff) Como fazer teologia da libertacao, 1986, trans by Burns as Introducing Liberation Theology, 1987; (with C. Boff) Libera-

tion Theology: From Dialogue to Confrontation, trans by Barr, 1986; (with B. Kern and A. Muller) Werkbuch Theologie der Befreiung: Anliegen, Streitpunkte, Personen: Materialien und Texte, 1988; (ed. with Elizondo and J.A. Gardiner) Convergences and Differences, 1988; When Theology Listens to the Poor, trans by Barr, 1988; Faith on the Edge: Religion and Marginalized Existence, selections from Boff's works trans by Barr, 1989; (ed. with Elizondo) 1492-1992: The Voice of the Victims, 1990; Nova evangelizacao: Perspectiva dos oprimidos, 1990, trans by Barr as New Evangelization: Good News to the Poor, 1991; (with others) Direitos humanos, direitos dos pobres, 1991; (with others) Sobre la opcion por los pobres, 1991; America Latina: Da Conquista a nova evangelizacao, 1992; Ecologia, mundializacao, espiritualidade, a emergencia de um novo paradigma, 1993, trans as Ecology and Liberation: A New Paradigm, 1995; (ed. with Elizondo) Is There Room for Christ in Asia?, 1993; The Path to Hope: Fragments from a Theologian's Journey, trans by P. Berryman, 1993; (ed. with V. Elizando) Poverty and Ecology, 1995. Contributor to books and periodicals. **Address:** Pr. Martins Leao 12/204, Alto Vale Encantado, 20531-350 Rio de Janeiro, Brazil.

BOGACKI, Tomek. Polish, b. 1950. **Genres:** Children's fiction, Illustrations, Picture/board books. **Career:** Writer and illustrator of children's books. **Publications:** FOR CHILDREN, AND ILLUSTRATOR: Cat and Mouse, 1996; Cat and Mouse in the Rain, 1997; I Hate You! I Like You!, 1997; Cat and Mouse in the Night, 1998; The Story of a Blue Bird, 1998; Cat and Mouse in the Snow, 1999; My First Garden, 2000; Circus Girl, 2001; numerous others. Illustrator of books by K. Banks, E. Jenkins, W. Kreye. **Address:** c/o Farrar, Straus & Giroux Inc., 19 Union Sq W, New York, NY 10003, U.S.A.

BOGART, Eleanor A(nne). American, b. 1928. **Genres:** Writing/Journalism. **Career:** Free-lance writer. Worked as high school teacher and secretary for a magazine distributor. **Publications:** (with W.M. Smith) The Wars of Peggy Hull: The Life and Times of a War Correspondent, 1991. Contributor to magazines and newspapers. Some work appears under the name E.A. Bogart. **Address:** 2924 Walnut, Hays, KS 67601, U.S.A.

BOGART, Jo Ellen. American/Canadian, b. 1945. **Genres:** Children's fiction, Children's non-fiction, Songs/Lyrics and libretti. **Career:** Austin Independent School District, Austin, TX, substitute teacher, 1968; Margaret Roane Center, Ruston, LA, teacher of educable mentally retarded teenagers, 1973; Wellington County Board, ON, substitute teacher, grades K-6, 1983-92. Guelph Examiner, reporter, illustrator, photographer, editorial writer, 1980. St. George's-Laurine Public School, volunteer speech therapist, 1982-83; King George Senior Public School, volunteer library assistant, 1983-84. **Publications:** Dylan's Lullaby, 1988; Malcolm's Runaway Soap, 1988; 10 for Dinner, 1989; Daniel's Dog, 1990; Sarah Saw a Blue Macaw, 1991; Mama's Bed, 1993; Two Too Many, 1994; Gifts, 1994; Jeremiah Learns to Read, 1997; Money, Make It, Spend It, Save It, 2001; Capturing Joy: The Story of Maud Lewis, 2002; The Night the Stars Flew, 2001; Emily Carr: At the Edge of the World, 2003. **Address:** 172 Palmer St, Guelph, ON, Canada N1E 2R6.

BOGART, Stephen Humphrey. American, b. 1949. **Genres:** Mystery/Crime/Suspense, Autobiography/Memoirs. **Career:** Court TV, producer; author, 1995-. **Publications:** Play It Again (mystery), 1995; (with G. Provost) Bogart: In Search of My Father (biography/autobiography), 1995. **Address:** c/o Tor/Forge Books, 175 Fifth Ave., 14th Fl., New York, NY 10010, U.S.A.

BOGDAN, Radu J. American (born Romania). **Genres:** Philosophy. **Career:** Institute for Teachers Training, Bucharest, Romania, assistant professor, 1970-74; Stanford University, Stanford, CA, instructor, 1979-80; Tulane University, New Orleans, LA, assistant professor, 1980-86, associate professor, 1986-95, professor of philosophy, 1995-, director of Cognitive Studies Program, 1984-. Academy of Economic Sciences, Bucharest, lecturer, 1972-74; Stanford University, visiting assistant professor, 1981; University of Bucharest, guest professor, 1990-. **Publications:** (with A. Milcoveanu) Logic: An Introduction (in Romanian), 1974; Grounds for Cognition: How Goal-Guided Behavior Shapes the Mind, 1994; Interpreting Minds: The Evolution of a Practice, 1997; Minding Minds: Evolving a Reflexive Mind by Interpreting Others, in press. Contributor to journals. EDITOR: Logic, Methodology, and Philosophy of Science (in Romanian), 1971; (and contrib.) Jaakko Hintikka (in Romanian), 1972; (and contrib.) Mario Bunge (in Romanian), 1973; (with I. Niiniluoto) Logic, Language, and Probability, 1973; (and contrib.) Local Induction, 1976; Patrick Suppes, 1979; Keith Lehrer, 1981; Henry Kyburg and Isaac Levi, 1982; D.M. Armstrong, 1984; (and contrib.) Roderick Chisholm, 1986; (and contrib.) Belief, 1986; Jaakko Hintikka, 1987; (and contrib.) Mind and Common Sense, 1991. SERIES EDITOR: Profiluri si Sinteze, 1971-74; Profiles: An International Series on Contemporary Philosophers and Logicians,1977-90. **Address:** Department of Philosophy, Tulane University, New Orleans, LA 70118, U.S.A. **Online address:** bogdan@mailhost.tcs.tulane.edu

BOGDANOR, Vernon. British, b. 1943. **Genres:** Politics/Government. **Career:** Fellow and Tutor in Politics, Brasenose Coll., Oxford, 1966. Oxford University, Reader in Government, 1990-96, Professor of Government, 1996-. **Publications:** Devolution, 1979; The People and the Party System, 1981; Multi-Party Politics and the Constitution, 1983; What Is Proportional Representation?, 1984; (co-author) Comparing Constitutions, 1995; The Monarchy and the Constitution, 1995; Essays on Politics and the Constitution, 1996; Power and the People, 1997; Devolution in the United Kingdom, 1999. EDITOR: (co) The Age of Affluence 1951-1964, 1970; Lothair, by Disraeli, 1975; Liberal Party Politics, 1983; (co) Democracy and Elections, 1983; Coalition Government in Western Europe, 1983; Parties and Democracy in Britain and America, 1984; Science and Politics, 1984; Representatives of the People?, 1985; Blackwell's Encyclopaedia of Political Institutions, 1987; Constitutions in Democratic Politics, 1988; The British Constitution in the 20th Century. **Address:** Brasenose College, Oxford OX1 4AJ, England.

BOGEN, Hyman. American, b. 1924. **Genres:** Social work. **Career:** Assistant to press agent Bernard Simon, NYC, 1952; Human Resources Administration, NYC, staff member, 1954-73, director of Division of Family Homes for Adults, 1973-84; retired, 1984. **Publications:** The Luckiest Orphans: A History of the Hebrew Orphan Asylum of New York, University of Illinois Press, 1992. Work represented in collections, contrib. to periodicals. **Address:** 80 Knolls Cres., Bronx, NY 10463, U.S.A.

BOGIN, Magda. American, b. 1950. **Genres:** Novels, Translations. **Career:** Translator, editor, and novelist. City College, City University of New York, writing program faculty, 1984-; affiliated with School of the Arts, Columbia University, 1994-. **Publications:** (As Meg Bogin) The Women Troubadours, 1976; (As Meg Bogin) The Path to Pain Control, 1982; (trans.) Isabel Allende, The House of the Spirits (novel), 1985; (trans., and ed with C Vicuna) The Selected Poems of Rosario Castellanos, 1988; (trans. and ed.) Selected Poems of Salvador Espriu, 1989; (trans. and ed.) Miguel de Cervantes Saavedra, Don Quixote, 1991; Natalya, God's Messenger (novel), 1994. **Address:** 425 Riverside Dr., New York, NY 10025, U.S.A.

BOGLE, Donald. American. **Genres:** Film. **Career:** Historian, editor, and writer. Worked as a staff writer and assistant editor at Ebony magazine. Lectured at Lincoln University, University of Pennsylvania, and New York University's Tisch School of the Arts. **Publications:** Toms, Coons, Mulattoes, Mammies, and Bucks: An Interpretive History of Blacks in American Films, 1973, 4th ed, 2001; Brown Sugar: Eighty Years of America's Black Female Superstars, 1980; Blacks in American Films and Television: An Encyclopedia, 1988; (ed.) Black Arts Annual 1987/88, 1989; Dorothy Dandridge: A Biography, 1997; Primetime Blues: African Americans on Network Television, 2001. Contributor to books. **Address:** c/o Author Mail, Farrar Straus & Giroux, 19 Union Square W., New York, NY 10001, U.S.A.

BOGLE, Warren. See BERGMAN, Andrew.

BOGOSIAN, Eric. American, b. 1953. **Genres:** Plays/Screenplays, Novels. **Career:** Actor and writer. Cofounder of Woburn Drama Guild, Woburn, MA; director and founder of dance program at the Kitchen in New York City. Actor in stage productions, television series and productions, and in motion pictures. **Publications:** PLAYS: Careful Moment, 1977; Men Inside, 1982; Voices of America 1982; FunHouse, 1983; Drinking in America, 1986; Talk Radio, 1987, screenplay, 1988; Sex, Drugs, and Rock 'n' Roll, 1988; Men in Dark Times; Sheer Heaven; The Ricky Paul Show; The New World; Pounding Nails in the Floor with My Forehead, 1993; subUrbia, 1994, screenplay, 1997. OTHER: Eric Bogosian Takes a Look at Drinking in America (television production), 1986; Arena Brains (film), 1987; Notes from Underground (novel), 1993; Mall, 2000. Contributor to periodicals. **Address:** c/o George Lane, William Morris Agency, 1325 Avenue of the Americas, New York, NY 10019, U.S.A.

BOGUE, Lucile Maxfield. See Obituaries.

BOGUS, SDiane. See ADAMZ-BOGUS, SDiane.

BOHANNAN, Paul (James). American, b. 1920. **Genres:** Anthropology/Ethnology, Human relations/Parenting. **Career:** Oxford University, Lecturer in Social Anthropology, 1951-56; Princeton University, New Jersey, Associ-ate Professor of Anthropology, 1956-59; Northwestern University, Evanston, IL, Stanley G. Harris Professor of Social Sciences, 1959-75; University of California at Santa Barbara, Professor of Anthropology, 1976-82; University of Southern California, Los Angeles, Professor, and Dean of Social Sciences and Communications, 1982-87, Professor Emeritus, 1987-. **Publications:** (with L. Bohannan) The Tiv of Central Nigeria, 1953; Justice and Judgment among the Tiv, 1957; Social Anthropology, 1963; Africa and Africans (in U.K. as African Outline), 1964, 3rd ed., 1988; (with L. Bohannan) Tiv Economy, 1968; All the Happy Families, 1984; We, the Alien, 1991; Discovering the Alien, 1991; How Culture Works, 1995; Asking and Listening, 1998; Culture as Given, Culture as Choice, 1999. EDITOR: (and contrib.) African Homicide and Suicide, 1960; (with G. Dalton) Markets in Africa, 1962; (and contrib.) Divorce and After, 1970; (with M. Glazer) High Points in Anthropology, 1973. **Address:** 1610 N Tamarack St, Visalia, CA 93291, U.S.A.

BOHJALIAN, Chris. American, b. 1960. **Genres:** Novels, Adult non-fiction. **Career:** Burlington Free Press, Burlington, VT, columnist, 1987-; free-lance journalist and novelist. **Publications:** A Killing in the Real World, 1988; Hangman, 1991; Past the Bleachers, 1992; Water Witches, 1995; Midwives, 1997; The Law of Similars, 1999; Trans-Sister Radio, 2000; The Buffalo Soldier, 2002; Idyll Banter, 2003; Before You Know Kindness, 2004. **Address:** c/o Amanda Urban, c/o International Creative Management Inc, 40 W 57th St, New York, NY 10019, U.S.A.

BOHLMEIJER, Arno. Dutch, b. 1956. **Genres:** Novels, Adult non-fiction, Literary criticism and history. **Career:** University of Nymegen, Netherlands, teacher of English and French, 1978-92; freelance writer, 1993-. **Publications:** NOVELS: Something Very Sorry, 1996. Author of novels for adults and for children in various European languages. OTHER: The Intruder: A Jungian Study of Henry James, 1987; To an Angel Who's New, 2002. **Address:** 208 De Waarden, 7206 GN, Zutphen, Netherlands.

BOHMAN, James F. American. **Genres:** Philosophy. **Career:** St. Louis University, St. Louis, MO, Danforth professor of philosophy; with Thomas McCarthy, speaker at the symposium "Habermas's Political Theory" at the 1998 conference of the American Philosophical Association, Central Division; Washington University in St. Louis, MO, St. Louis, MO, member of the "Committee on Social Thought and Analysis.". **Publications:** NONFICTION: New Philosophy of Social Science: Problems of Indeterminacy, 1991; Public Deliberation: Pluralism, Complexity, and Democracy, 1996; EDITOR: (with K. Baynes and T. McCarthy) After Philosophy: End or Transformation?, 1987; (with D.R. Hiley and R. Shusterman) The Interpretive Turn: Philosophy, Science, Culture, 1991; (with W. Rehg) Deliberative Democracy: Essays on Reason and Politics, 1997; (with M. Lutz-Bachmann) Perpetual Peace: Essays on Kant's Cosmopolitan Ideal, 1997. Contributor to books and periodicals. **Address:** Dept. of Philosophy, St. Louis University, 3800 Lindell Blvd., POB 56907, St. Louis, MO 63156, U.S.A. **Online address:** bohmanjf@slu.edu

BOHNHOFF, Maya Kaathryn. American, b. 1954. **Genres:** Romance/Historical, Science fiction/Fantasy. **Career:** Writer and instructional software designer. Kelly Services, Nevada City, CA, manager of instructional design, 1994-95; formerly director of development, ComTrain Inc. (developers of training software). Singer, songwriter, with two self-produced albums. **Publications:** The Meri, 1992; Taminy, 1993; The Crystal Rose, 1995; The Spirit Gate, 1996. Contributor of short fiction to anthologies and periodicals. **Address:** 14708 Echo Ridge Dr, Nevada City, CA 95959-9631, U.S.A.

BOHNTINSKY, Dori. American, b. 1951. **Genres:** Speech/Rhetoric, Poetry. **Career:** Alameda County Medical Center, manager of department of speech pathology and audiology, 1980-2002; freelance writer and workshop presenter, 2002-. Also affiliated with Consultants for Enhanced Communication. **Publications:** Standard American English Pronunciation Training (workbook with audio tapes), 1994; Pragmatics for Effective Speaking (workbook), 1998; Once upon a Lunar Eclipse (poetry), 2000; The Healing Room: Discovering Joy through the Journal (nonfiction), 2002. **Address:** PO Box 20248, Castro Valley, CA 94546, U.S.A. **Online address:** inwordbound@aol.com

BOICE, James Montgomery. American, b. 1938. **Genres:** Theology/Religion. **Career:** Pastor, Tenth Presbyterian Church, Philadelphia, since 1968. Assistant Ed., Christianity Today, Washington, D.C., 1966-68. **Publications:** Witness and Revelation in the Gospel of John, 1970; Philippians: An Expositional Commentary, 1971; The Sermon on the Mount, 1972; How to Really Live It Up, 1973; The Last and Future World, 1974; How God Can Use Nobodies, 1974; The Gospel of John, 5 vols., 1975-79; Can You Run

Away from God?, 1977; God the Redeemer, 1978; The Sovereign God, 1978; Awakening to God, 1979; Making God's Word Plain, 1979; The Epistles of John, 1979; Does Inerrancy Matter?, 1979; God and History, 1980; Genesis, 3 vols., 1982-87; Parables of Jesus, 1983; Minor Prophets, 2 vols., 1983-86; The Christ of Christmas, 1983; Standing on the Rock, 1984; The Christ of the Empty Tomb, 1985; Foundations of the Christian Faith, 1986; Christ's Call to Discipleship, 1986; Daniel: An Expositional Commentary, 1989; Ephesians: An Expositional Commentary, 1989; Joshua: We Will Serve the Lord, 1989; Nehemiah: Learning to Read, 1990; Romans, 4 Volumes, 1992-95; The King Has Come, 1992; Amazing Grace, 1993; Mind Renewal in a Mindless Age, 1993; Psalms, 2 vols., 1994-96; Sure I Believe, So What!, 1994; Hearing God When You Hurt, 1995; Two Cities/Two Loves, 1996; Living by the Book, 1997; Acts: An Expositional Commentary, 1997; (with P.G. Ryken) The Heart of the Cross, 1999; The Foundations of the Church, 1999. EDITOR: Our Sovereign God, 1977; The Foundation of Biblical Authority, 1978; Our Savior God, 1980; Transforming Our World: A Call to Action, 1988; (with B.E. Sasse) Here We Stand: A Call from Confessing Evangelicals, 1996. **Address:** 1701 Delancey Pl., Philadelphia, PA 19103, U.S.A.

BOISSEAU, Michelle. American, b. 1955. **Genres:** Poetry, Literary criticism and history. **Career:** Educator and poet. Virginia Intermont College, Bristol, assistant professor of English and creative writing, 1985-87; Morehead State University, Morehead, KY, associate professor of English and creative writing, 1988-95; University of Missouri-Kansas City, associate professor of English and creative writing, 1995-. **Publications:** POETRY: No Private Life, 1990; Understory, 1996; Trembling Air: Poems, 2003; Some Will Tell You (chapbook). OTHER: (with R. Wallace) Writing Poems (textbook), 4th ed, 1995, 6th ed, 2004. Contributor of poems and short stories to periodicals. **Address:** University of Missouri-Kansas City, 5100 Rockhill Rd., Kansas City, MO 64110, U.S.A. **Online address:** boisseaum@umkc.edu

BOISVERT, Raymond D. American, b. 1947. **Genres:** Philosophy. **Career:** Clark College, Atlanta, GA, assistant professor of philosophy, 1978-84; Siena College, Loudonville, NY, professor of philosophy, 1984-; Senior Fulbright lecturer in Lyon, France. **Publications:** Dewey's Metaphysics, 1988; John Dewey: Rethinking Our Time, 1998. **Address:** Department of Philosophy, Siena College, Loudonville, NY 12211, U.S.A. **Online address:** Boisvert@siena.edu

BOITANI, Piero. Italian, b. 1947. **Genres:** Literary criticism and history, Translations. **Career:** Cambridge University, Cambridge, England, lector in Italian, 1971-74; University of Pescara, Italy, lecturer in English literature, 1974-79; University of Perugia, Italy, professor of English literature, 1979-85; University of Rome, Italy, chair of English literature, 1985-98, chair of comparative literature, 1998-. Cambridge University, visiting fellow, 1979-84; University of Connecticut, visiting professor, 1987-89; University of California, Berkeley, chair of Italian culture, 1990-. **Publications:** Prosatori negri Americani, 1973; Chaucer and Boccaccio, 1977; English Medieval Narrative, 1982; Chaucer and the Imaginary World of Fame, 1984; The Tragic and the Sublime, 1989; L'ombra di Ulisse, 1992, trans. as, The Shadow of Ulysses, 1994; Ri-Scritture, 1997, trans. as, Re-Scriptures: The Bible and Its Rewritings, 1999; Sulle orme di Ulisse, 1998; Il genio di migliorare un'invenzione, 1999. TRANSLATOR: Sir Gawain and the Green Knight; The Cloud of Unknowing, 1998. EDITOR: Chaucer and the Italian Trecento, 1983; (co-) The Cambridge Chaucer Companion, 1986; The European Tragedy of Troilus, 1989; (with A. Torti) Religion in the Poetry and Drama of the Late Middle Ages in England, 1991. **Address:** Department of English Literature, University of Rome, Via Carlo Fea 2, 00161 Rome, Italy.

BOK, Derek. American, b. 1930. **Genres:** Education, Law. **Career:** Harvard University, Cambridge, MA, assistant professor, 1958-61, professor of law, 1961, dean of the law school, 1968-71, president of the university, 1971-91. **Publications:** The First Three Years of the Schuman Plan, 1955; (ed. with A. Cox) Cases and Materials on Labor Law, 8th ed., 1977; (with J. Dunlop) Labor and the American Community, 1970; Beyond the Ivory Tower, 1982; Higher Learning, 1986; Universities and the Future of America, 1990; The Cost of Talent, 1993; (with W.G. Bowen) The Shape of the River, 1998; The Trouble with Government, 2000. **Address:** Kennedy School of Government, Harvard University, Cambridge, MA 02138, U.S.A.

BOK, Sissela. American (born Sweden), b. 1934. **Genres:** Ethics, Philosophy, Social commentary, Autobiography/Memoirs. **Career:** Distinguished Fellow, Harvard Center for Population and Development Studies, 1993-. Lecturer, Simmons Coll., Boston, 1971-72, Harvard-Massachusetts

Institute of Technology Division of Health Sciences and Technology, Cambridge, MA, 1975-82, and Harvard University, Cambridge, MA, 1982-84; Professor of Philosophy, Brandeis University, Waltham, MA, 1985-92. **Publications:** (ed. with J.A. Behnke) The Dilemma of Euthanasia, 1975; Lying: Moral Choice in Public and Private Life, 1978, 3rd ed., 1999; (ed. with D. Callahan) Ethics Teaching in Higher Education, 1980; Secrets: On the Ethics of Concealment and Revelation, 1983; A Strategy for Peace: Human Values and the Threat of War, 1989; Alva Myrdal: A Daughter's Memoir, 1991; Common Values, 1995, rev. ed., 2002; Mayhem: Violence as Public Entertainment, 1998; (with G. Dworkin and R. Frey) Euthanasia and Physician-Assisted Suicide, 1998. **Address:** Harvard Center for Population and Development Studies, 9 Bow St, Cambridge, MA 02138, U.S.A.

BOKINA, John. American, b. 1948. **Genres:** Politics/Government. **Career:** University of Illinois at Chicago, teaching assistant, 1971; University of Illinois at Urbana-Champaign, teaching assistant, 1972-74, 1975-76, instructor, 1973-76; University of Detroit, MI, visiting assistant professor, 1976-77, instructor, 1977-79, director of the honors program, 1977-80, assistant professor, 1979-81; University of Texas-Pan American, Edinburg, TX, assistant professor, 1982-85, associate professor, 1986-92, professor, 1992-. Conductor of workshops. **Publications:** (with J.P. Friedman and J. Miller) Contemporary Political Theory, 1977; (ed with T.J. Lukes) Marcuse: From the New Left to the Next Left, 1994; Opera and Politics: From Monteverdi to Henze, 1997. Contributor to anthologies and journals. **Address:** Department of Political Science, University of Texas-Pan American, Edinburg, TX 78539, U.S.A. **Online address:** jb83e8@panam.edu

BOLAM, Robyn. Also writes as Marion Lomax. British, b. 1953. **Genres:** Poetry, Songs/Lyrics and libretti, Literary criticism and history, Theatre, Women's studies and issues. **Career:** University of Reading Library, Berkshire, England, senior library assistant, 1975-77; King Alfred's College, Winchester, Hampshire, England, part-time lecturer in English, 1983-86; Open University, Bracknell and Newbury, Berkshire, part-time tutor and counsellor, 1983-88; University of Reading, Berkshire, part-time lecturer in English, 1983-87; St. Mary's College, Strawberry Hill, Twickenham, England, lecturer, 1987-89, senior lecturer in English, 1989-95, professor of literature 1995-; writer. Conducts writing workshops and gives poetry readings. **Publications:** ALL AS MARION LOMAX: Stage Images and Traditions: Shakespeare to Ford, 1987; The Peepshow Girl (poems), 1989; Beyond Men and Dreams (libretto), 1991; Raiding the Borders (poems), 1996. EDITOR: Time Present and Time Past: Poets at the University of Kent at Canterbury, 1965-1985, 1985; Tis Pity She's a Whore and Other Plays, J. Ford, 1995; The Rover, A.Behn, 1995; (with S. Hartman) Out of the Blue, 1998. **Address:** School of Communication, Culture & Creative Arts, St. Mary's College, Strawberry Hill, Twickenham TW1 4SX, England. **Online address:** bolamr@smuc.ac.uk

BOLAND, Eavan (Aisling). Irish, b. 1944. **Genres:** Poetry, Literary criticism and history. **Career:** Trinity College, Dublin, Ireland, junior lecturer, 1967-68; School of Irish Studies, Dublin, lecturer, 1968-88; visiting lecturer at universities worldwide, 1988-95; Stanford University, professor, 1995-; writer. Worked as a housekeeper at the Gresham Hotel, Dublin, c. 1962. **Publications:** POETRY: 23 Poems, 1962; Autumn Essay, 1963; Poetry, 1963; New Territory, 1967; The War Horse, 1975; In Her Own Image, 1980; Introducing Eavan Boland, 1981; Night Feed, 1982; The Journey, 1983; The Journey and Other Poems, 1987; Selected Poems, 1989; Outside History: Selected Poems, 1980-90, 1990; In a Time of Violence, 1994; An Origin Like Water: Collected Poems 1967-87, 1996; The Lost Land: Poems, 1998; Against Love Poetry, 2001. OTHER: (with M. MacLiammoir) W.B. Yeats and His World, 1971; A Kind of Scar: The Woman Poet in a National Tradition, 1989; Object Lessons, 1995. Work represented in anthologies. Contributor to newspapers and journals. **Address:** English Department, Building 460 Rm 219A, Stanford University, Stanford, CA 94305-2087, U.S.A. **Online address:** boland@stanford.edu

BOLAND, Janice. American. **Genres:** Children's fiction, Education. **Career:** Author, editor, and illustrator. Richard C. Owen Publishers, Katonah, NY, director of children's books, 1990-; graphic artist. Former school teacher and adjunct professor of writing and children's book illustration. **Publications:** Annabel, 1993; Annabel Again, 1994; A Dog Named Sam, 1996; The Fox, 1996; The Strongest Animal, 1996; El Zorro, 1996; (and photographer) The Pond, 1997; Zippers, 1997; Breakfast with John, 1997; Sunflowers, 1998; Mrs. Murphy's Crows, 1999; I Meowed, 2000; My Dog Fuzzy, 2001; Alley Cat, 2002; Strange Things, 2005. **Address:** Box 352, Cross River, NY 10518, U.S.A.

BOLDEN, Tonya. American, b. 1959. **Genres:** Young adult fiction, Cultural/Ethnic topics, Food and Wine, History, How-to books. **Career:** Charles Alan

Inc., NYC, salesperson, 1981-83; Raoulfilm Inc., NYC, office coordinator, 1985-87; research and editorial assistant to food and wine critic William E. Rice, 1987-88; Malcolm-King College, NYC, English instructor, 1988-89; College of New Rochelle, School of New Resources, NYC, English instructor, 1989-90, 1996-. Editorial consultant, MTA Arts for Transit Office, 1987-88, and Harlem River Press/Writers & Readers Publishing Inc., 1987, 1989-90. **Publications:** The Family Heirloom Cookbook, 1990; (with V. Higginsen) Mama, I Want to Sing (young adult novel), 1992; Starting a Business from Your Home, 1993; Mail-Order and Direct Response, 1994; Just Family (young adult novel), 1996; The Book of African-American Women: 150 Crusaders, Creators, and Uplifters, 1996; Through Loona's Door: A Tammy and Owen Adventure with Carter G. Woodson, 1997; And Not Afraid to Dare: The Stories of Ten African-American Women, 1998; Strong Men Keep Coming: The Book of African-American Men, 1999. EDITOR: Rites of Passage: Stories about Growing Up by Black Writers from around the World, 1994; 33 Things Every Girl Should Know: Stories, Songs, Poems, and Smart Talk by 33 Extraordinary Women, 1998. Contributor to reference works. Contributor of book reviews and articles to periodicals. **Address:** 3034 Tiemann Avenue, Bronx, NY 10469, U.S.A. **Online address:** tonbolden@aol.com; www.tonyabolden.com

BOLES, Philana Marie. (born United States). **Genres:** Novels. **Career:** Worked at 40 Acres & A Mule Filmworks and Glamour magazine; playwright. **Publications:** Blame It on Eve: A Novel, 2002. **Address:** c/o Author Mail, Random House, 1745 Broadway, New York, NY 10019, U.S.A.

BOLGER, Dermot. Irish, b. 1959. **Genres:** Novels, Poetry. **Career:** Editor, poet, and novelist. Raven Arts Press, Finglas, Dublin, Ireland, founder and editor, 1979-92; New Island Books, executive editor, 1992-. Member, Arts Council of Ireland, 1989-93, and Aosdana, 1991. **Publications:** NOVELS: Night Shift, 1985; The Woman's Daughter, 1987, rev. ed., 1991; The Journey Home, 1990; Emily's Shoes, 1992; A Second Life, 1994; Tinbars' Hotel, 1997; Father's Music, 1997; Temptation, 2000. POETRY: The Habit of Flesh, 1979; Finglas Lilies, 1980; No Waiting America, 1981; Internal Exiles, 1986; Leinster Street Ghosts, 1989; Taking My Letters Back: New and Selected Poems, 1998. EDITOR: (and author of intro.) Madeleine Stuart, Manna in the Morning: A Memoir 1940-1958, 1986; The Dolmen Book of Irish Christmas Stories, 1986; The Bright Wave: Poetry in Irish Now, 1986; 16 on 16: Irish Writers on the Easter Rising, 1988; Invisible Cities: The New Dubliners; A Journey through Unofficial Dublin, 1988; Invisible Dublin: A Journey through Dublin's Suburbs, 1991; Francis Ledwidge: Selected Poems, 1992; Wexford through Its Writers, 1992; The Picador Book of Contemporary Irish Fiction, 1993; (with A. Murphy) 12 Bar Blues, 1993; The New Irish Fiction, 2000. PLAYS: The Lament for Arthur Cleary (adapted from author's poem of same title), 1989; Blinded by the Light, 1990; In High Germany, 1990; The Holy Ground, 1990; One Last White Horse, 1991; A Dublin Quartet, 1992; The Dublin Bloom (adapted from Ulysses by J. Joyce), 1994; April Bright, 1995; The Passion of Jerome, 1999; Consenting Adults, 2000. OTHER: (with M. O'Loughlin) A New Primer for Irish Schools, 1985. Work represented in anthologies. **Address:** A. P. Watt, 20 John St., London WC1N 2DR, England. **Online address:** debolger@iol.ie

BOLGIANO, Chris(tina). American (born Germany), b. 1948. **Genres:** Agriculture/Forestry, Local history/Rural topics, Natural history, Zoology, Essays. **Career:** National Agricultural Library, Beltsville, MD, staff member, 1970-72; James Madison University, Harrisonburg, VA, member of library faculty until 1980, adjunct professor and curator of rare books and manuscripts, 1980-. Scriptwriter for the television series Virginia Outdoors, 1990-93. **Publications:** Mountain Lion: An Unnatural History of Pumas and People, 1995; The Appalachian Forest: A Search for Roots and Renewal, 1998; Living in the Appalachian Forest: True Tales of Sustainable Forestry, 2002. Contributor to magazines, newspapers, and anthologies. **Address:** Stackpole Books, 5067 Ritter Rd, Mechanicsburg, PA 17055, U.S.A. **Online address:** www.chrisbolgiano.com

BOLINO, August C. American, b. 1922. **Genres:** Economics. **Career:** Idaho State University, Pocatello, instructor, 1952-55; St. Louis University, Missouri, associate professor of economics, 1955-62; director, Economic Studies, Office of Manpower, Automation, and Training, 1962-64, and Evaluation of Manpower Branch, U.S. Office of Education, 1964-66; Catholic University of America, Washington, DC, professor of economics, 1966-90, professor emeritus, 1990-. **Publications:** The Development of the American Economy, 1961, 1966; Manpower and the City, 1969; Career Education: Contributions to Economic Growth, 1973; The Ellis Island Source Book, 1985, 1990; The Watchmakers of Massachusetts, 1987; A Century of Human Capital by Education and Training, 1989; From Depression to War: American Society in Transition-1939, 1998; Thomas Angel, American, 2001. **Address:** 8515 2nd Ave, Silver Spring, MD 20910-3465, U.S.A.

BOLLER, Paul F., Jr. American, b. 1916. **Genres:** History, Intellectual history. **Career:** Emeritus Professor of History, Texas Christian University, Fort Worth, since 1983 (Professor, 1976-83). Member of the faculty, Southern Methodist University, 1948-66, University of Massachusetts, 1966-76. **Publications:** (with J. Tilford) This Is Our Nation, 1961; George Washington and Religion, 1963; Quotemanship: The Use and Abuse of Quotations for Polemical and Other Purposes, 1967; American Thought in Transition 1865-1900, 1967; American Transcendentalism 1830-1860, 1974; Freedom and Fate in American Thought: From Edwards to Dewey, 1978; Presidential Anecdotes, 1981; Presidential Campaigns, 1984; (with R. Story) A More Perfect Union: Documents in American History, 1984; (with R. Davis) Hollywood Anecdotes, 1987; Presidential Wives, 1988; (with J. George) They Never Said It, 1989; Congressional Anecdotes, 1991; Memoirs of an Obscure Professor and Other Essays, 1992; Not So! Popular Myths from Columbus to Clinton, about the American Past, 1995; Presidential Inaugurations, 2001. **Address:** History Dept, Box 297260, Texas Christian University, Fort Worth, TX 76129, U.S.A.

BOLLES, Edmund Blair. American, b. 1942. **Genres:** Language/Linguistics, Natural history, Psychology. **Career:** Member, U.S. Peace Corps, Kidodi, Tanzania, 1966-68; Editor, FrameWords: A Newsletter about Political Rhetoric, 1991-92. **Publications:** (with P. Rosenthal) Readings in Psychology 1973/74 (college text), 1973; (with J. Sommer and J.F. Hoy) The Language Experience (essays), 1974; (with R. Fisher) Fodor's Old West (travel guide), 1976; (ed. with J. Fireman) Cat Catalog (essays), 1976; (with J. Fireman) TV book (essays), 1977; Animal Parks of Africa, 1978; The Beauty of America, 1979; So Much to Say! A Parent's Guide to Baby Talk from Birth to Five, 1982; The Penguin Adoption Handbook, 1984; Who Owns America?, 1984, rev. ed., 1993; (with D. Papalia) A Child's World (coll. text), 4th ed., 1987; Remembering and Forgetting, 1988; Learning to Live with Chronic Fatigue Syndrome, 1990; Relief from Chronic Backache, 1990; When Acting Out Isn't Acting, 1988; A Second Way of Knowing: The Riddle of Human Perception, 1991; (ed.) Galileo's Commandment: An Anthology of Great Science Writing, 1997; The Ice Finders: How a Poet, a Professor, and a Politician Discovered the Ice Age, 1999; Einstein Defiant: Genius versus Genius in the Quantum Revolution, 2004. **Address:** 414 Amsterdam Ave Apt 4N, New York, NY 10024, U.S.A. **Online address:** blair@ebbolles.com

BOLLES, Richard Nelson. American, b. 1927. **Genres:** How-to books. **Career:** Author, lecturer, and trainer, 1970-. Grace Cathedral, San Francisco, canon pastor, 1966-68; National Career Development Project, director, 1974-87; United Ministries in Higher Education, San Francisco, national staff member, 1978-87. **Publications:** What Color Is Your Parachute?: A Practical Manual for Job-Hunters and Career Changers, 1972- (revised annually); (with J. Crystal) Where Do I Go from Here with My Life?, 1974; The Three Boxes of Life and How to Get Out of Them, 1978; How to Find Your Mission in Life, 1991; Job-Hunting on the Internet, 1997; The What Color Is Your Parachute Workbook, 2000. **Address:** PO Box 379, Walnut Creek, CA 94597, U.S.A. **Online address:** RNB25@aol.com

BOLLINGER, Lee C. American, b. 1946. **Genres:** Law, Social commentary, Civil liberties/Human rights. **Career:** U.S. Court of Appeals for the Second Circuit, law clerk, 1971-72; U.S. Supreme Court, Washington, DC, law clerk to chief justice Warren E. Burger, 1972-73; University of Michigan, Ann Arbor, assistant professor, 1973-76, associate professor, 1976-78, professor of law, 1979-, dean of Law School, 1987-94, president, 1997; Dartmouth College, provost, 1994-96. Davis-Markert-Nickerson Lecturer, 1992. Cambridge University, visiting associate of Clare Hall, 1983. College of William and Mary, George Wythe Lecturer, 1984; Capital University, John E. Sullivan Lecturer, 1988; Columbia University, Rubin Lecturer, 1989; Southern Methodist University, Atwell Lecturer in Constitutional Law, 1992. **Publications:** (with J. Jackson) Contract Law in Modern Society, 2nd ed., 1980; The Tolerant Society: Freedom of Speech and Extremist Speech in America, 1986; Images of a Free Press, 1991. Work represented in anthologies. Contributor of articles and reviews to law journals. **Address:** President's Office, University of Michigan, Ann Arbor, MI 48109-1340, U.S.A. **Online address:** leecbol@umich.edu

BOLMAN, Lee G. American, b. 1941. **Genres:** Administration/Management. **Career:** Carnegie-Mellon University, Pittsburgh, PA, assistant professor of industrial administration and psychology, 1967-72; Harvard University, Cambridge, MA, lecturer in education, 1972-93, educational chairperson of Institute for Educational Management, 1983-88, and Management Development Program, 1986-88, director of National Center for Educational Leadership, 1988-94, principal investigator at Harvard School Leadership Academy, 1991-93; University of Missouri-Kansas City, Marion H. Bloch Missouri

Professor of Leadership and director of Center for Leadership Development, both 1993-. Cockpit Management Resources Inc., member of technical advisory board. **Publications:** (with T.E. Deal) Modern Approaches to Understanding and Managing Organizations, 1984; (with Deal) Reframing Organizations, 1991, rev. ed., 1996; (with Deal) The Path to School Leadership, 1993; (with Deal) On Becoming a Teacher-Leader, 1994; (with Deal and E.G. de Aldaz) Liderazgo, Arte y Devision (title means: Leadership, Art, and Decision), 1995; (with Deal and S.F. Rallis) Becoming a School Board Member, 1995; (with Deal) Leading with Soul, 1995, rev. ed., 2001; (with Deal) Escape from Cluelessness: A Guide for the Organizationally-Challenged, 2000. Contributor to books. Contributor of articles and reviews to professional journals. **Address:** Bloch School of Business and Public Administration, University of Missouri-Kansas City, 5100 Rockhill Rd., Kansas City, MO 64110, U.S.A. **Online address:** bolmanl@umkc.edu

BOLOTIN, Norman (Phillip). American, b. 1951. **Genres:** History. **Career:** Publishers Professional Services, Seattle, WA, editorial director, 1973-77; Alaska NW Publishing, Edmonds, WA, editor, 1978-84; KC Aly & Co. Communications, Bellevue, WA, partner and vice president, 1984; Laing Communications, Redmond, WA, president, 1985-99. University of Chicago, Business of Publishing Program, director, 1995-2000; History Bank, Woodinville, WA, managing partner, 2000-. **Publications:** Klondike Lost, 1980; A Klondike Scrapbook: Ordinary People, Extraordinary Times, 1987; The World's Columbian Exposition: The Chicago World's Fair of 1893, 1992, 2nd ed., 2002; For Home and Country: A Civil War Scrapbook, 1995; The Civil War, A-to-Z, 2001; A Season on the Coast, Day-by-Day with the 1961 Seattle Rainiers, 2003. **Address:** The History Bank, PO Box 1568, Woodinville, WA 98072, U.S.A. **Online address:** norm@thehistorybank.com

BOLSTER, Richard (H.). British. **Genres:** Literary criticism and history. **Career:** University of Kano, Kano, Nigeria, senior lecturer in French studies; University of Bristol, Bristol, England, senior lecturer in French. **Publications:** Stendhal, Balzac, et le féminisme romantique (nonfiction; title means: Stendhal, Balzac, and Romantic Feminism), 1970; (annotator) T. Gautier, La Vie de Balzac (biography; title means: The Life of Balzac), 1981; Stendhal: Le Rouge et le Noir, 1994; Balzac: Le Père Goriot, 2000; Marie d'Agoult: The Rebel Countess (biography), 2001. EDITOR: Documents littéraires de l'époque romantique (nonfiction), 1982; Baron de Trenck, La Vie extraordinaire du Baron de Trenck (autobiography), 1985; Histoire d'éléonore de Parme (fiction), 1997. **Address:** Department of French, University of Bristol, 17/19 Woodland Road, Bristol BS8 1TE, England. **Online address:** R.Bolster@bristol.ac.uk

BOLSTER, W(illiam) Jeffrey. American, b. 1954. **Genres:** History. **Career:** Southampton College, Southamptom, NY, instructor and ship's officer, 1977-83; Sea Education Association, Woods Hole, MA, captain of schoolship and instructor, 1978-85; Northeastern University, instructor and schoolship captain, 1982; University of New Hampshire, Durham, assistant professor, 1991-97, associate professor of history, 1997-. Consultant for film and television projects. **Publications:** Black Jacks: African American Seamen in the Age of Sail, 1997; (with H. Anderson) Soldiers, Sailors, Slaves and Ships: The Civil War Photographs of Henry P. Moore, 1999. Author of reviews in periodicals. **Address:** History Department, University of New Hampshire, Durham, NH 03824, U.S.A. **Online address:** jbolster@christa.unh.edu

BOLT, Bruce (Alan). American (born Australia), b. 1930. **Genres:** Earth sciences, Engineering, Mathematics/Statistics. **Career:** Lecturer, then Sr. Lecturer, Dept. of Applied Mathematics, University of Sydney, 1954-62; Professor of Seismology, and Director of the Seismographic Stations, University of California, Berkeley, 1963-89. Associate Ed., Journal of Computational Physics, 1973-79; Chairman, Geophysical Monograph Board, American Geophysical Union, 1976-78; Chairman, Panel on National Seismograph Networks, National Academy of Sciences, 1977-80; Berkeley Division, Academic Senate, University of California, Berkeley, chairman, 1993-94. **Publications:** (with others) Geological Hazards, 1975; Nuclear Explosions and Earthquakes: The Parted Veil, 1976; Earthquakes: A Primer, 1978, 5th ed., 2003; Inside the Earth, 1982; (with K.E. Bullen) Introduction to the Theory of Seismology, 4th ed., 1985; Earthquakes and Geological Discovery, 1993. EDITOR: (with B. Alder and S. Fernbach) Methods in Computational Physics, vol. XI: Seismology, Surface Waves and Earth Oscillations, 1972, vol. XII: Seismology, Body Waves and Sources, 1972, vol. XIII: Geophysics, 1973; Cumulative Index 1963-72, 1973; (with O. Anderson) Theory and Experiment Relevant to Geodynamic Processes: Tectonophysics, vol. XXXIV, 1976; (with D. Loewenthal) Journal of Computational Physics: Z. Alterman Memorial Vol. 29, 1978; Earthquakes and Volcanoes: Readings from "Scientific America," 1980; Seismic Strong Motion Synthetics, 1987. **Address:** Dept of Earth and Planetary Science, University of California, Berkeley, CA 94720, U.S.A. **Online address:** boltuc@socrates.berkeley.edu

BOLT, Jonathan. American, b. 1934. **Genres:** Plays/Screenplays. **Career:** Playwright. Started theatrical career as a scenic designer in summer stock; actor, Broadway debut, 1958; director, 1967-; Cleveland Playhouse, Cleveland, OH, associate director, 1971-73; Circle Repertory Company, NYC, company playwright, 1980-97; American Academy of Dramatic Arts, director, 1998-. Actor in stage plays; director of plays; actor for film and television. **Publications:** PLAYS: Threads, 1978; Eye and the Hands of God, 1980; (with composer T. Tierney and lyricist J. Forester) Teddy Roosevelt, 1980; (with Tierney and Forester) First Lady, 1984; Running Time; Plotline, 1985; The Whore and the H'Empress, 1987; Eleanor, an American Love Story, 1988; To Culebra, 1989; Oh, Dubrovnik, 1989; (with composer D. Cohen) Columbus!, 1990; Stephen Foster the Musical, 1997; Glimmerglass, 1998; and others. OTHER: Alamance Summer (screenplay); Unfinished Business (TV play). **Address:** 75 Laurel Ave., Bloomfield, NJ 07003, U.S.A.

BOLTON, Evelyn. See BUNTING, (Anne) Eve(lyn Bolton).

BOLTON, Ruthie. American, b. 1961. **Genres:** Biography. **Career:** Writer. Manager of a plant nursery. **Publications:** Gal: A True Life, 1994. **Address:** c/o Harriet Wasserman Literary Agency Inc., 137 East 36th St., New York, NY 10016, U.S.A.

BONADIO, Felice A(nthony). American. **Genres:** History. **Career:** University of California, Santa Barbara, professor of history. **Publications:** North of Reconstruction: Ohio Politics, 1865-1870, 1970; (ed.) Political Parties in American History: Vol 2, 1828-1890, 1974; A.P. Giannini: A Biography, 1994. Contributor to anthologies and periodicals. **Address:** Department of History, University of California, Santa Barbara, CA 93106, U.S.A.

BONADIO, William. American, b. 1955. **Genres:** Autobiography/Memoirs. **Career:** Cincinnati Children's Hospital, Cincinnati, OH, residency; Children's Hospital, St. Paul, MN, Assistant Clinical Professor of Pediatrics, attending Physician of Pediatric Medicine, 1984-. **Publications:** Julia's Mother: Life Lessons in the Pediatric ER, 2000. **Address:** Children's Hospital, 345 North Smith Avenue, St. Paul, MN 55102, U.S.A.

BONANSINGA, Jay R. American. **Genres:** Mystery/Crime/Suspense, Horror, Plays/Screenplays. **Career:** Suspense and horror novelist, screenwriter, and film director. **Publications:** The Black Mariah, 1994; Sick, 1995; The Killer's Game, 1997; Head Case, 1998. Author of short stories. Contributor to magazines. **Address:** c/o Simon & Schuster, 1230 Avenue of the Americas, New York, NY 10020, U.S.A.

BONAR, Veronica. See BAILEY, Donna.

BOND, C(hristopher Godfrey). British, b. 1945. **Genres:** Novels, Plays/Screenplays. **Career:** Artistic Director, Half Moon Theatre, London, Liverpool Playhouse, and Everyman Theatre, Liverpool, 1976-. Director of opera, musicals, and plays in the U.K. and Sweden. Actor, 1968-70, and Resident Dramatist, 1970-71, Victoria Theatre, Stoke on Trent. **Publications:** You Want Drink Something Cold (novel), 1969; Sweeney Todd: The Demon Barber of Fleet Street, 1974. **Address:** c/o Blanche Marvin Agency, 21a St. John's Wood High St, London NW8 7NG, England.

BOND, Edward. British, b. 1934. **Genres:** Plays/Screenplays, Poetry, Songs/Lyrics and libretti, Philosophy, Politics/Government, Social commentary, Theatre, Translations. **Publications:** PLAYS: The Pope's Wedding, 1962; Saved, 1965; Narrow Road to the Deep North, 1968; Early Morning, 1968; Passion, 1971; Black Mass, 1971; Lear, 1972; The Sea, 1973; Bingo: Scenes of Money and Death, 1974; The Fool, 1976; A-A-America (Grandma Faust, and The Swing), 1976; Stone, 1976; The Bundle, 1978; The Woman, 1978; The Worlds, 1980; Restoration, 1981; Summer, 1982; Derek, 1983; Human Cannon, 1984; War Plays (Red, Black and Ignorant; The Tin Can People; Great Peace), 1985; Jackets, 1989; In the Company of Men, 1990; September, 1990; Olly's Prison (for TV), 1993; Tuesday (for TV), 1993; Coffee: A Tragedy, 1995; At the Inland Sea: A Play for Young People, 1996; Eleven Vests, 1997; The Crime of the Twenty-First Century, 1999; The Children, 2000; Chair, 2000; Have I None, 2001; Existence, 2002; Born, 2003; The Balancing Act, 2003; Collected Plays 1977-2003, 7 vols., 2003. LIBRETTOS: We Come to the River, 1977; The English Cat, 1983. TRANSLATOR: Chekhov's Three Sisters, 1967; Wedekind's Spring Awakening, 1974; (with E. Bond-Pable) Wedekind's Lulu, 1992. OTHER: Theatre Poems and Songs, 1978; Collected Poems 1978-1985, 1987; Notes on Post-Modernism, 1990; Letters, 6 vols., 1994-2000; Selected Notebooks, vol. 1, 2000, vol. 2, 2001; The Hidden Plot: Notes on Theatre and the State, 2000. **Address:** c/o Casarotto Ramsay & Associates Ltd, National House, 60-66 Wardour St, London W1V 3HP, England.

BOND, George C(lement). American, b. 1936. **Genres:** Anthropology/Ethnology. **Career:** University of East Anglia, Norwich, England, lecturer, 1966-68; Columbia University, NYC, assistant professor, 1968-74, Teachers College, associate professor, 1974-82, professor of anthropology, 1982-, director of the university's Institute of African Studies, 1989-99, director of Center for African Education, 2004-. **Publications:** The Politics of Change in a Zambia Community, 1976. EDITOR/CO-EDITOR: African Christianity, 1978; Social Construction of the Past, 1994; AIDS in Africa and the Caribbean, 1995; Contested Terrain and Constructed Categories, 2001; Witchcraft Dialogues, 2002. **Address:** Program in Applied Anthropology, Box 10, Teachers College, Columbia University, New York, NY 10027, U.S.A. **Online address:** Bond@exchange.TC.Columbia.edu

BOND, Larry. American, b. 1951. **Genres:** Mystery/Crime/Suspense. **Career:** Writer and board game/computer game designer. Has worked as a computer programmer and as a naval analyst for defense consulting firms. **Publications:** (with T. Clancy) Red Storm Rising, 1986; Red Phoenix, 1989; Vortex, 1991; Cauldron, 1993; The Enemy Within, 1996; Day of Wrath, 1998. **Address:** c/o Author Mail, Warner Books, 1271 Avenue of the Americas, New York, NY 10020, U.S.A.

BOND, (Thomas) Michael. British, b. 1926. **Genres:** Novels, Children's fiction. **Career:** Cameraman, BBC Television, London, 1947-66. Director, Paddington and Company (Films) Ltd., London. **Publications:** FOR CHILDREN: FICTION: A Bear Called Paddington, 1958; More about Paddington, 1959; Paddington Helps Out, 1960; Paddington Abroad, 1961; Paddington at Large, 1962; Paddington Marches On, 1964; Here Comes Thursday, 1966; Paddington at Work, 1966; Paddington Goes to Town, 1968; Thursday Rides Again, 1968; Parsley's Good Deed, 1969; The Story of Parsley's Tail, 1969; Thursday Ahoy!, 1969; Paddington Takes the Air, 1970; Parsley's Last Stand, 1970; Parsley's Problem Present, 1970; Thursday in Paris, 1971; The Tales of Olga da Polga, 1971; Parsley the Lion, 1972; Parsley Parade, 1972; Paddington Bear, 1972; Paddington's Garden, 1972; The Day the Animals Went on Strike, 1972; Olga Meets Her Match, 1973; Paddington at the Circus, 1973; Paddington Goes Shopping, 1973 in US as Paddington's Lucky Day, 1974; Paddington on Top, 1974; Paddington's Blue Peter Story Book, 1974 in US as Paddington Takes to T.V.; Mr. Cram's Magic Bubbles, 1975; Windmill, 1975; Paddington at the Seaside, 1975; Paddington at the Tower, 1975; Olga Carries On, 1976; Paddington at the Station, 1976; Paddington Takes a Bath, 1976; Paddington Goes to the Sales, 1976; Paddington's New Room, 1976; Paddington Does It Himself, 1977; Paddington Hits Out, 1977; Paddington in the Kitchen, 1977; Paddington's Birthday Party, 1977; Paddington's Picture Book (collection), 1978; Paddington Takes the Test, 1979; J.D. Polson and the Liberty Head Dime, 1980; Paddington in Touch, 1980; Paddington and Aunt Lucy, 1980; Paddington Weighs In, 1980; Paddington at Home, 1980; Paddington Goes Out, 1980; J.D. Polson and the Dillogate Affair, 1981; Paddington On Screen: A Second Blue Peter Storybook, 1981; Paddington Has Fun, 1982; Paddington Works Hard, 1982; Olga Takes Charge, 1982; J.D. Polson and the Great Unveiling, 1982; The Caravan Puppets, 1983; Paddington's Storybook, 1983; Paddington on the River, 1983; Paddington and the Knickerbocker Rainbow, 1984; Paddington at the Zoo, 1984; Paddington at the Fair, 1985; Paddington's Painting Exhibition, 1985 in US as Paddington's Art Exhibition, 1986; Paddington at the Palace, 1986; Paddington Minds the House, 1986 in US as Paddington Cleans Up, 1986; Paddington Posts a Letter, 1986 in US as Paddington Mails a Letter, 1986; Paddington's Clock Book, 1986; Paddington at the Airport, 1986; On Four Wheels: Paddington's London, 1986 in US as Paddington's Wheel Book, 1986; Oliver the Greedy Elephant, 1986; Paddington and the Marmalade Maze, 1987; Paddington's Busy Day, 1987; A Mouse Called Thursday, 1988; Paddington's Magical Christmas, 1988; Paddington Meets the Queen, 1991; Paddington Rides On!, 1991; A Day by the Sea, 1992; Paddington at the Seashore, 1992; Paddington Breaks the Peace, 1992; Something Nasty in the Kitchen, 1992; Paddington's Picnic, 1993; Paddington Does the Decorating, 1993; Paddington's Disappearing Trick, 1993; Paddington's Things I Do, 1994; Paddington's Things I Feel, 1994; Bears & Forebears: A Life So Far, 1996; Paddington and the Christmas Surprise, 1997; Paddington at the Carnival, 1998; Paddington Bear All Day, 1998; Paddington Bear and the Busy Bee Carnival, 1998; Paddington Bear Goes to Market, 1998; Paddington Bear: My Scrapbook, 1999; Paddington Bear Goes to the Hospital, 2001; Olga Moves House, 2001; Olga Follows Her Nose, 2002; Paddington Bear in the Garden, 2002; Paddington and the Grand Tour, 2003. PLAYS: The Adventures of a Bear Called Paddington, 1974; Paddington on Stage, 1974; The Herbs (television series), 1970; The Adventures of Parsley (puppet series). OTHER: Herbs Annual, 1969-70; The Parsley Annual, 1971-72; How to Make Flying Things, 1975; Paddington's Loose-End Book: An ABC of Things to Do, 1976; Paddington's Party Book, 1976; The Great Big Paddington Book, 1976; Fun and Games with Paddington, 1977; Paddington's Pop-Up Book, 1977; Paddington's Colouring Books,

4 vols., 1977; Paddington Pastime series, 4 vols., 1977; Paddington's Suitcase, 1983; Paddington's First Puzzle Book, Paddington's Second Puzzle Book, 1987; Paddington's 123, 1990; Paddington's ABC, 1990; Paddington's Opposites, 1990; Paddington's Jar of Jokes, 1992; Paddington Book and Bear Box, 1993. FOR ADULTS: NOVELS: Monsieur Pamplemousse, 1984; Monsieur Pamplemousse and the Secret Mission, 1984; Monsieur Pamplemousse on the Spot, 1986; Monsieur Pamplemousse Takes the Cure, 1987; Monsieur Pamplemousse Aloft, 1989; Monsieur Pamplemousse Investigates, 1990; Monsieur Pamplemousse Rests His Case, 1991; Monsieur Pamplemousse on Location, 1992; Monsieur Pamplemousse Stands Firm, 1992; Monsieur Pamplemousse Takes the Train, 1993; Monsieur Pamplemousse Afloat, 1998; Monsieur Pamplemousse on Probation, 2000; Monsieur Pamplemousse on acation, 2002; Monsieur Pamplemousse Hits the Headlines, 2003. OTHER: The Pleasures of Paris, 1987; The Life and Times of Paddington Bear, 1988. **Address:** c/o The Agency, 24-31 Pottery Ln, London W11 4L7, England.

BOND, Nancy. American, b. 1945. **Genres:** Children's fiction. **Career:** Instructor in Children's Literature, Simmons Coll., Boston, 1979-. Head of Overseas Sales Publicity, Tutorial Books, Oxford University Press, London, 1967-68; Assistant Children's Librarian, Lincoln Public Library, Massachusetts, 1969-71; Head Librarian, Levi Heywood Memorial Library, Gardner, Massachusetts, 1973-75; Sr. Secretary, Massachusetts Audubon Society, Lincoln, 1976-77. **Publications:** A String in the Harp, 1976; The Best of Enemies, 1978; Country of Broken Stone, 1980; The Voyage Begun, 1981; A Place to Come Back To, 1984; Another Shore, 1988; Truth to Tell, 1994; The Love of Friends, 1997. **Address:** 109 The Valley Rd, Concord, MA 01742, U.S.A.

BOND, Ruskin. Indian, b. 1934. **Genres:** Novels, Novellas/Short stories, Children's fiction, Poetry, Children's non-fiction, Autobiography/Memoirs, Biography, Essays. **Career:** Author; freelance writer. **Publications:** The Room on the Roof, 1956; Grandfather's Private Zoo, 1967; The Last Tiger, 1971; Angry River, 1972; The Blue Umbrella, 1974; Once upon a Monsoon Time (memoirs), 1974; Man of Destiny: A Biography of Jawaharlal Nehru, 1976; Night of the Leopard, 1979; Big Business, 1979; The Cherry Tree, 1980; The Road to the Bazaar, 1980, 1991; A Flight of Pigeons, 1980; The Young Vagrants, 1981; Flames in the Forest, 1981; The Adventures of Rusty, 1981; Tales and Legends from India, 1982; A Garland of Memories (essays), 1982; To Live in Magic (verse), 1982; Tigers Forever, 1983; Earthquake, 1984; Getting Granny's Glasses, 1985; Cricket for the Crocodile, 1986; The Eyes of the Eagle, 1987; The Night Train at Deoli and Other Stories, 1988; Beautiful Garhwal (travelogue), 1988; Ghost Trouble, 1989; Time Stops at Shamli and Other Stories, 1989; Snake Trouble, 1990; Dust on the Mountain, 1990; Father's Moon and Other Stories, 1991; Our Trees Still Grow in Dehoa, 1992; Ganga Descends, 1992; Rain in the Mountains (memoirs), 1994; Tiger Roars, Eagle Soars, 1994; Quakes & Flames, 1994; Delhi Is not Far: The Best of Ruskin Bond, 1994; Binya's Blue Umbrella, 1995; The Ruskin Bond Children's Omnibus, 1995; When the Trees Walked & Other Stories, 1996; Strangers in the Nights, 1996; Scenes from a Writer's Life, 1997; The Lamp Is Lit, 1998; Seasons of Ghosts, 1999. **Address:** Ivy Cottage, Landour, Mussourie 248179, Uttar Pradesh, India.

BONDER, Nilton. Brazilian, b. 1957. **Genres:** Theology/Religion. **Career:** Rabbi and writer. **Publications:** A Tractade on Impunity, 1993; The Art of Saving Yourself, 1994; The Jewish Way of Problem Solving, 1995; Secret Portals (in Portuguese), 1996; The Kabbalah of Money, 1996; The Kabbalah of Envy, 1997; The Kabbalah of Food, 1998. **Address:** CJB, R. Prof. Milward, 226 Rio de Janeiro, Brazil. **Online address:** iibonder@ax.apc.org.br

BONE, J(esse) F(ranklin). American, b. 1916. **Genres:** Science fiction/Fantasy, Animals/Pets. **Career:** Officer, U.S. Army, 1937-46; Instructor of Veterinary Medicine, 1950-52, Assistant Professor, 1953-57, Associate Professor, 1958-65, and Professor, 1965-79, Oregon State University, Corvallis. **Publications:** Observations of the Ovaries of Infertile and Reportedly Infertile Dairy Cattle, 1954; Animal Anatomy, 1958, rev. ed. as Animal Anatomy and Physiology, 1975, 1982; (ed.) Canine Medicine. 1959, 1962; The Lani People, 1962; (co-ed.) Equine Medicine and Surgery, 1963, 1972; Legacy, 1976; The Meddlers, 1976; (with R. Myers) Gift of the Manti, 1977; Confederation Matador, 1978; Animal Anatomy and Physiology, 1979, 3rd ed., 1988. **Address:** 3017 E Braeburn St, Sierra Vista, AZ 85635, U.S.A.

BONELLO, Frank J. American, b. 1939. **Genres:** Economics. **Career:** University of Notre Dame, Notre Dame, IN, assistant professor, 1968-74, associate professor of economics, 1974-. Also worked for U.S. Agency for International Development, World Book Encyclopedia, and U.S. Chamber of Commerce. **Publications:** The Formulation of Expected Interest Rates, 1970;

Computer Assisted Instruction in Economic Education, 1974; Supply Side Economics, 1985; (with T. Swartz) Taking Sides: Clashing Views of Alternative Economic Issues, 1992, 107th ed., 1995; (ed.) Urban Finance Under Siege, 1993. **Address:** Department of Economics, 408 Decio, University of Notre Dame, Notre Dame, IN 46556, U.S.A.

BONGARD, David L(awrence). American, b. 1959. **Genres:** Military/Defense/Arms control. **Career:** National Archives and Records Administration, Washington, DC, archives aide, 1983-85; DMSI/HERO (research and consulting firm), Fairfax, VA, research associate, 1986-89, researcher, 1989-90; TNDA (research and consulting firm), McLean, VA, staff associate, 1990-92; Dupuy Institute, McLean, corporate secretary, researcher, and writer, 1992-. **Publications:** (with T.N. Dupuy, C. Johnson, and A.C. Dupuy) How to Defeat Saddam Hussein, 1991; (with T.N. Dupuy and C. Johnson) The Harper Encyclopedia of Military Biography, 1992; (ed. & contrib.) International Military and Defense Encyclopedia, Brassey's, 1993; (with T.N. Dupuy and R.C. Anderson) The Battle of the Bulge, 1994. **Address:** c/o Dupuy Institute, 3519 Beverly Dr, Annandale, VA 22003, U.S.A.

BONHAM-CARTER, Victor. British, b. 1913. **Genres:** Agriculture/Forestry, History, Biography. **Career:** Historian and Records Officer, Dartington Hall Estate, Devon, 1951-65; Secretary, Royal Literary Fund, 1966-82; Joint Secretary, Society of Authors, London. 1971-78; co-editor, The Exmoor Review, 1980-. **Publications:** The English Village, 1952; (with W. B. Curry) Dartington Hall, 1958; Exploring Parish Churches, 1959; Farming the Land, 1959; In a Liberal Tradition, 1960; Soldier True (in U.S. as The Strategy of Victory), 1965; (ed.) Surgeon in the Crimea 1968; The Survival of the English Countryside (in U.S. as Land and Environment), 1971; Authors by Profession, 2 vols., 1978-84; The Essence of Exmoor, 1991; What Countryman, Sir? (autobiography), 1996; A Filthy Barren Ground, 1998. **Address:** The Mount, Milverton, Taunton, Somerset TA4 1QZ, England.

BONIFACE, William. American, b. 1963. **Genres:** Children's fiction. **Career:** Publisher and children's author. **Publications:** Welcome to Dinsmore, the World's Greatest Store, 1995; Mystery in Bugtown, 1997; The Adventures of Max the Minnow, 1997; The Treasure Hunter, 1998. **Address:** c/o Jon Anderson, 313 West 22nd St., #2B, New York, NY 10011, U.S.A.

BONINGTON, Sir Chris(tian). British, b. 1934. **Genres:** Travel/Exploration, Autobiography/Memoirs. **Career:** Mountaineer, writer and photographer. Leader, successful British climb of Everest Southwest Face, 1975. **Publications:** I Chose to Climb, 1966; Annapurna South Face, 1971; Next Horizon, 1973; Everest Southwest Face: Ultimate Challenge, 1973; (with others) Changabang, 1975; Everest the Hard Way, 1976; Quest for Adventure, 1981; Kongur: China's Elusive Summit, 1982; (coauthor) Everest: The Unclimbed Ridge, 1983; The Everest Years, 1986; Mountaineer: 30 Years of Climbing, 1990; The Climbers, 1992; (with R. Knox-Johnston) Sea, Ice & Rock, 1992; (general ed.) Great Climbs, 1994; (coauthor) Tibet's Secret Mountain, 1999; Boundless Horizons, 2000; Quest for Adventure:1950-2000, 2000; Chris Bonington's Everest, 2002. **Address:** Badger Hill, Nether Row, Hesket Newmarket, Wigton, Cumbria CA7 8LA, England. **Online address:** chris@bonington.com; www.bonington.com

BONJOUR, Laurence Alan. American, b. 1943. **Genres:** Philosophy. **Career:** Philosopher and writer. **Publications:** The Structure of Empirical Knowledge, 1985; In Defense of Pure Reason: A Rationalist Account of A Priori Justification, 1998; Epistemology: Classic Problems and Contemporary Responses, 2002; (with E. Sosa) Epistemic Justification: Internalism vs. Externalism, Foundationalism vs. Virtues, 2003. **Address:** Department of Philosophy, Box 353350, University of Washington, Seattle, WA 98195, U.S.A. **Online address:** bonjour@u.washington.edu

BONNER, Arthur. American, b. 1922. **Genres:** Area studies, Biography, Documentaries/Reportage. **Career:** Journalist, Writer. Copy boy, New York Daily News, NYC, 1943-44; Newswriter, CBS Radio News, NYC, 1944-53; Freelance foreign corresp. in Asia, 1953-61; Documentary producer and foreign corresp. in New York, India, Africa. and S. America, CBS Radio and T.V. News, 1961-67; Documentary producer, NBC-TV News, NYC, 1968; Newswriter and producer, WNBC-TV News, NYC, 1968-84; Special corresp. in Afghanistan, New York Times, 1985-86; Freelance writer, 1986-. Recipient of Overseas Press Club Citations, 1955, 1988, and Emmy Award for Outstanding News Writer, 1976-77. **Publications:** Jerry McAuley and His Mission, 1967, 1990; Among the Afghans, 1987; Averting the Apocalypse, 1990; Democracy in India: A Hollow Shell, 1994; Alas! What Brought Thee Hither: The Chinese in New York 1800-1950, 1997; We Will not Be Stopped: Evangelical Persecution, Catholicism and Zapatistas in Chiapas, Mexico,

1999. **Address:** 40 W 106th St., Apt. 1, New York, NY 10025-3805, U.S.A. **Online address:** arthur_bonner@msn.com

BONNER, John Tyler. American, b. 1920. **Genres:** Biology. **Career:** George M. Moffett Professor Emeritus, 1990-, Princeton University, New Jersey, (joined faculty, 1947; George M. Moffett Professor, 1966-; Chairman, Dept. of Biology, 1965-77, 1983-84, and 1987-88). Oxford Surveys in Evolutionary Biology, editorial board, 1982-93. **Publications:** Morphogenesis: An Essay on Development. 1952; Cells and Societies, 1955; The Evolution of Development, 1958; The Cellular Slime Molds, 1959; (ed.) On Growth and Form, by D'Arcy Thompson, abridged ed., 1961; The Ideas of Biology, 1962; Size and Cycle, 1965; The Scale of Nature, 1969; On Development: The Biology of Form, 1974; The Evolution of Culture in Animals, 1980; (with T. A. McMahon) On Size and Life, 1983; The Evolution of Complexity, 1988; Researches on Cellular Slime Molds, 1991; Life Cycles, 1993; Sixty Years of Biology, 1996; First Signals, 2000; Lives of a Biologist, 2002. **Address:** Dept. of Ecology and Evolutionary Biology, Princeton University, Princeton, NJ 08544, U.S.A. **Online address:** jtbonner@princeton.edu

BONNER, Kieran (Martin). Irish/Canadian, b. 1951. **Genres:** Sociology. **Career:** Augustana University College, Camrose, AB, assistant professor, 1987-93, associate professor, 1993-99, professor of sociology, 1999, chairperson of Division of Interdisciplinary Studies and International Programs, 1997-99, founding member of Centre for Interdisciplinary Research in the Liberal Arts, 1990-97; University of Waterloo, ON, St. Jerome's University, professor of sociology, 1999-, vice-president and academic dean, 1999-. Teacher of extension courses for public schools in Toronto, ON, 1986; York University, visiting professor, 1987; Kings College, Edmonton, AB, visiting assistant professor, 1988; National University of Ireland, University College, Galway, visiting fellow in the humanities, 1994; University of Alberta, adjunct professor, 1999-2005; University of Queensland, associate doctoral supervisor, 1999; guest lecturer at educational institutions; public speaker at local churches, organizations, and libraries. **Publications:** A Great Place to Raise Kids: Interpretation, Science, and the Urban-Rural Debate, 1997; Power and Parenting: A Hermeneutic of the Human Condition, 1998. Contributor of articles and reviews to academic journals. **Address:** Dept of Sociology, St. Jerome's University, University of Waterloo, Waterloo, ON, Canada N2L 3G3. **Online address:** kmbonner@watarts.uwaterloo.ca

BONNER, Tracy Nelson. *See* YARBRO, Chelsea Quinn.

BONNOR, William Bowen. British, b. 1920. **Genres:** Astronomy, Mathematics/Statistics, Physics. **Career:** Visiting Professorial Research Fellow, Queen Mary Coll., University of London, 1987-. Lecturer, University of Liverpool, 1949-57; Reader, 1957-61, and Professor of Mathematics, 1962-84, Queen Elizabeth Coll., University of London; Sr. Research Officer, University of Cape Town, 1984-87. **Publications:** (with H. Bondi, R. A. Lyttleton and G. J. Whitrow) Rival Theories of Cosmology, 1960; The Mystery of the Expanding Universe. 1964; Status of General Relativity, 1969; (co-ed.) Classical General Relativity, 1983. Contributor to journals. **Address:** School of Mathematics, Queen Mary College, Mile End Rd, London E1 4NS, England. **Online address:** 100571.2247@compuserve.com

BONOMELLI, Charles J(ames). American, b. 1948. **Genres:** Novels. **Career:** Worked as a police officer in Pueblo, CO, for twenty-two years, retiring as sergeant. **Publications:** NOVELS: Of Life and Ecstasy, 1998; Mariana; Road to Insurrection. Work represented in anthologies. Contributor of poems to chapbooks and magazines. **Address:** 1610 Kings Royal Blvd., Pueblo, CO 81005, U.S.A.

BONONNO, Robert. American, b. 1949. **Genres:** Translations. **Career:** Free-lance photographer in NYC, 1972-85; free-lance translator, NYC, 1983; New York University, adjunct professor; Graduate Center of the City University of New York, lecturer. **Publications:** TRANSLATOR: Braque: Complete Graphic Work, 1983; A. Lorme, A Traitor's Daughter, 1993; M. Brun, Incident at Sakhalin: The True Mission of KAL 007, 1996; H. Guibert, Ghost Image, 1996; P. Levy, Collective Intelligence: Mankind's Emerging World in Cyberspace, 1997; P. Levy, Becoming Virtual; J. Douchet, French New Wave; P. Levy, Cyberculture; H. Lefebvre, The Urban Revolution; Baudrillard-Nouvel, Objects of Architecture; H. Raczymow, Swan's Way. Contributor of translations to periodicals. Contributor to magazines. **Address:** 109 E 2nd St Apt 6, New York, NY 10009, U.S.A. **Online address:** rb28@nyu.edu

BONSIGNORE, Joan. American, b. 1959. **Genres:** Children's non-fiction. **Career:** Teacher, beginning 1984. Center for Human Resources Development, Northhampton, MA, case manager for adults with developmental disabilities, 1994-99. **Publications:** Stick out Your Tongue!: Fantastic Facts, Features, and Functions of Animal and Human Tongues, 2001.

BONTA, Marcia Myers. American, b. 1940. **Genres:** Environmental sciences/Ecology, Natural history, Women's studies and issues. **Career:** Freelance nature writer, 1977-. **Publications:** Escape to the Mountain, 1980; Outbound Journeys in Pennsylvania, 1988; Appalachian Spring, 1991; Women in the Field: America's Pioneering Women Naturalists, 1991; Appalachian Autumn, 1994; (ed.) American Women Afield: Writings by Pioneering Women Naturalists, 1995; More Outbound Journeys in Pennsylvania, 1995; Appalachian Summer, 1999; Appalachian Winter, 2005. Contributor to state and national magazines. **Address:** PO Box 68, Tyrone, PA 16686, U.S.A. **Online address:** marciabonta@hotmail.com; www.marciabonta.com

BONTE, Pierre. French, b. 1942. **Genres:** Anthropology/Ethnology. **Career:** Affiliated with the Centre National de Recherche Scientifique, Paris, France, beginning in 1973, research director, second class, 1985-96, first class, 1996-. **Publications:** (with S. Bernus, L. Brock, and H. Claudot) Le Fils et le neveu: Jeux et enjeux de la parente touaregue, 1986; (with E. Conte, C. Hames, and Abd el Wedoud Ould Cheikh) Al-Ansab: La Quete des origines: Anthropologie historique de la societe tribale arabe, 1991. EDITOR: (with M. Izard) Dictionnaire de l'ethnologie et de l'anthropologie, 1991; (with J.G. Galaty) Herders, Warriors and Traders: Pastoralism in Africa, 1991; Epouser au plus proche. Inceste, prohibitions et strategies matrimoniales autour de la Mediterranee, 1994; (with A.-M. Brisebarre and A. Goualp) Sacrifices en Islam-Espaces et temps d'un ritual, 1999; (with E. Conte and P. Dresch) Emirs et Presidents: Figures de la parente et du politique dans le monde arabe, 2001; La montagne de fer. La SNIM (Mauritanie) une entreprise miniere Saharienne a l'heure de la mondialisation, 2001. **Address:** Laboratoire d'Anthropologie Sociale, 52 rue du Cardinal Lemoine, 75005 Paris, France. **Online address:** bonte@ehess.fr

BOOKER, Christopher (John Penrice). British, b. 1937. **Genres:** History, Documentaries/Reportage, Literary criticism and history, Humor/Satire, Mythology/Folklore, Psychology. **Career:** Free-lance journalist, 1960; Sunday Telegraph, jazz critic, 1961; Private Eye, London, England, founding editor, 1961-63; British Broadcasting Company (BBC-TV), resident scriptwriter for That Was the Week That Was (television satire), 1962-63; resident scriptwriter for Not So Much a Programme, 1963-64; contributor to television show Read All about It, 1975-77; Daily Telegraph, monthly columnist, 1973-90, author of "The Way of the World" column, 1987-90; Sunday Telegraph, columnist, 1990-; writer. **Publications:** (with W. Rushton and R. Ingrams) Private Eye on London, 1962; Private Eye's Romantic England, 1963; The Neophiliacs: A Study of the Revolution in English Life in the Fifties and Sixties, 1969, 1993; (with C.L. Green) Goodbye London: An Illustrated Guide to Threatened Buildings, 1973; The Booker Quiz, 1976; The Seventies: The Decade That Changed the Future, published in England as The Seventies: Portrait of a Decade, 1980; The Games War: A Moscow Journal, 1981; (with R. North) The Mad Officials, 1994; The Castle of Lies: Why Britain Must Get Out of Europe, 1996; A Looking Glass Tragedy: The Controversy over the Repatriations from Austria in 1945, 1997; The Seven Basic Plots of Literature: Why We Tell Stories, 2000. Coauthor of many private eye anthologies, 1966-99, including The Secret Diaries of John Major, 1991-96, and St. Albion's Parish News, 1998-99. **Address:** The Old Rectory, Litton, Bath BA3 4PW, England.

BOOKER, Sue. See **THANDEKA.**

BOOKMAN, Terry Allen. American, b. 1950. **Genres:** Theology/Religion. **Career:** Temple Sinai, Milwaukee, WI, rabbi/educator, 1984-95; Temple Beth Am, Miami, FL, senior rabbi, 1995-. **Publications:** The Busy Soul, 1999; God 101, 2001; A Soul's Journey, 2004. **Address:** Temple Beth Am, 5950 N Kendall Dr, Coral Gables, FL 33156, U.S.A. **Online address:** rebbeaid@aol.com

BOON, Debbie. British, b. 1960. **Genres:** Children's fiction. **Career:** Roy Walker Design Associates, Nottingham, England, illustrator-designer, 1980-83; Pencil Box Design, Nottingham, co-founder and co-managing director, 1983-97; Aspire Design, Leicestershire, England, co-founder and co-managing director, 1997-. **Publications:** SELF-ILLUSTRATED POETRY FOR CHILDREN: My Gran, 1997; Aunt Sal, 1998; Gio's Pizzas, 1998. **Address:** c/o Artist Partners Ltd, 14/18 Ham Yard, Great Windmill Street, London W1V 8DE, England.

BOONE, Daniel R. American, b. 1927. **Genres:** Medicine/Health, Speech/Rhetoric, Self help. **Career:** Case Western Reserve University, Cleveland,

OH, assistant professor, 1960-63; University of Kansas Medical School, Kansas City, associate professor, 1963-66; University of Denver, Colorado, professor, 1966-73; Consultant, BEH, U.S. Office of Education, 1968-; University of Arizona, Tucson, professor, Speech & Hearing Sciences, 1973-88, professor emeritus, 1988-. **Publications:** An Adult Has Aphasia, 1965; The Voice and Voice Therapy, 1971, 7th ed., 2005; Cerebral Palsy, 1973; Human Communication and Its Disorders, 1987, 2nd ed., 1993; Is Your Voice Telling on You?, 1991, 2nd ed., 1997. **Address:** 5715 N Genematas Dr, Tucson, AZ 85704, U.S.A. **Online address:** BOONVOZ@aol.com

BOORSTEIN, Sylvia. American. **Genres:** Inspirational/Motivational Literature. **Career:** Psychotherapist, teacher, retreat leader, and writer. Spirit Rock Meditation Center, Woodacre, CA, founder and teacher; Insight Meditation Society, Barre, MA, teacher. **Publications:** It's Easier than You Think: The Buddhist Way to Happiness, 1995; Don't Just Do Something, Sit There: A Mindfulness Retreat with Sylvia Boorstein, 1996; That's Funny, You Don't Look Buddhist: On Being a Faithful Jew and a Passionate Buddhist, 1997; Pay Attention, for Goodness' Sake: Practicing the Perfections of the Heart-the Buddhist Path of Kindness, 2002. Contributor to books; author and reader of sound recordings. **Address:** Spirit Rock Meditation Center, PO Box 169, Woodacre, CA 94973, U.S.A.

BOOSTROM, Robert E(dward). American, b. 1949. **Genres:** Education. **Career:** Laidlaw Brothers, River Forest, IL, editor, 1981-86; University of Southern Indiana, Evansville, assistant professor, 1993-. **Publications:** Developing Creative and Critical Thinking, 1992; (with Jackson and Hansen) The Moral Life of Schools, 1993. Contributor to periodicals. **Address:** University of Southern Indiana, 3600 University Blvd., Evansville, IN 47712, U.S.A.

BOOT, John C. G. Dutch (born Indonesia), b. 1936. **Genres:** Economics, Mathematics/Statistics. **Career:** Professor of Mgmt. Science, State University of New York, Buffalo, 1965-. **Publications:** Quadratic Programming, 1964; (co-author) Introduction to Operations Research and Management Science, 1964; Mathematical Reasoning in Economics and Management Science, 1967; (coauthor) Statistical Analysis for Managerial Decisions, 1970, 1974; Common Globe or Global Commons, 1974. **Address:** Jacobs Center, State University of New York, Buffalo, NY 14260-4000, U.S.A. **Online address:** jboot@buffalo.edu

BOOTH, Brian. American, b. 1936. **Genres:** History, Literary criticism and history, Local history/Rural topics, Biography. **Career:** Stoel Rives LLP, associate to partner, 1962-74; Tonkon Torp LLP, Portland, OR, partner and corporate attorney, 1974-. **Publications:** Wildmen, Wobblies, and Whistle Punks: Stewart Holbrook's Lowbrow Northwest, 1992. **Address:** Tonkon Torp LLP, 1600 Pioneer Tower, 888 SW Fifth Ave, Portland, OR 97204, U.S.A. **Online address:** brianb@tonkon.com

BOOTH, Edward. (Geoffrey Thornton Booth). British, b. 1928. **Genres:** History, Philosophy, Theology/Religion. **Career:** Entered English province of Order of Preachers (Dominicans), 1952, ordained Roman Catholic priest, 1958; engaged in parochial work and school teaching, 1960-71; lecturer at Pontifical Beda College, Rome, Italy, 1978-80, and at Pontifical University of St. Thomas (Angelicum), Rome, 1980-88; member of Commissio Leonina, 1981-88; priest, researcher, lecturer, and writer; contributor. **Publications:** Aristotelian Aporetic Ontology in Islamic and Christian Thinkers, 1983; Saint Augustine and the Western Tradition of Self-Knowing: The Saint Augustine Lecture 1986, 1989. Author of articles in collections, scholarly journals, and reference works. **Address:** Dominikanerinnen: Maria Viktoria, Vellarsweg 2, Wetten, D-47625 Kevelaer, Germany. **Online address:** booth@andris.de

BOOTH, Philip. American, b. 1925. **Genres:** Poetry. **Career:** Member of faculty, Wellesley Coll., Massachusetts, 1954-61; Associate Professor, 1961-65, and Professor of English and Poet-in-Residence, 1965-86, Syracuse University, New York. **Publications:** Letter from a Distant Land, 1957; (ed.) The Dark Island, 1960; The Islanders, 1961; (ed.) Syracuse Poems, 1965, 1970, 1973, 1978; Weathers and Edges, 1966; Margins, 1970; Available Light, 1976; Before Sleep, 1980; Relations: Selected Poems 1950-85, 1986; Selves, 1990; Pairs, 1994; Trying to Say It: Outlooks and Insights on How Poems Happen, 1996; Lifelines: Selected Poems 1950-1999, 1999. **Address:** Main St, Castine, ME 04421-0330, U.S.A.

BOOTH, Stanley. American, b. 1942. **Genres:** Mystery/Crime/Suspense, Plays/Screenplays, Songs/Lyrics and libretti, Art/Art history, Literary criticism and history, Music, Photography, Theology/Religion, Autobiography/Memoirs. **Career:** Writer. **Publications:** Dance with the Devil: The Rolling

Stones and Their Times, 1984; The True Adventures of the Rolling Stones, 1984; Rythm Oil, 1991; Keith: Till I Roll Over Dead (biography), 1994. **Address:** 104 Queens Ct, Brunswick, GA 31523-6282, U.S.A. **Online address:** sbooth@ktc.com

BOOTH, Wayne Clayson. American, b. 1921. **Genres:** Literary criticism and history, Speech/Rhetoric. **Career:** Professor emeritus, 1991-, George M. Pullman Distinguished Service Professor of English, University of Chicago, 1962-91 (Dean of Coll., 1964-69; Chairman, Committee on Ideas and Methods, 1972-75). Member, Editorial Board, Philosophy and Literature, Novel, Philosophy and Rhetoric, Critical Inquiry. Assistant Instructor of English, University of Chicago, 1947-50; Assistant Professor, Haverford Coll., Pa., 1950-53; Professor of English and Chairman of Dept., 1953-62, and Trustee, 1965-75, Earlham Coll., Richmond, Indiana; Co-Ed., Critical Inquiry, 1974-85. Member, Executive Council, 1971-75, and President, 1980-82, Modern Language Association. **Publications:** The Rhetoric of Fiction, 1961; (ed.) The Knowledge Most Worth Having, 1967; Now Don't Try to Reason with Me: Essays and Ironies for a Credulous Age, 1970; A Rhetoric of Irony, 1974; Modern Dogma and the Rhetoric of Assent, 1974; Critical Understanding: The Powers and Limits of Pluralism, 1979; (ed. with M. Gregory) The Harper and Row Reader, 1984; (with M. Gregory) The Harper and Row Rhetoric, 1987, 1991; The Company We Keep: An Ethics of Fiction, 1988; The Vocation of a Teacher: Rhetorical Occasions, 1967-88, 1989; The Art of Growing Older, 1992; (with Williams and Gregory) The Craft of Research, 1996; For the Love of It: Amateuring and Its Rivals, 1999.

BOPP, Mary S. (Mary R. Strow). American, b. 1946. **Genres:** Dance/Ballet. **Career:** Indiana University, Bloomington, IN, librarian, 1989-. **Publications:** Research in Dance: A Guide to Resources, 1994. **Address:** HPER Library, HPER Bldg 029, Indiana University, Bloomington, IN 47405, U.S.A. **Online address:** mstrow@indiana.edu

BORAINE, Alex(ander). American. **Genres:** International relations/Current affairs. **Career:** Ordained Methodist minister, 1956; Methodist Church of South Africa, elected president, 1970; Parliament of South Africa, member for Progressive Party, 1974-86; Institute for a Democratic Alternative in South Africa, co-founder, 1986; Truth and Reconciliation Commission, South Africa, vice chair, 1996-98; University of Cape Town, Cape Town, South Africa, visiting professor, 1998; New York University, New York, NY, professor of law (dignitary in permanent residence), 1999-; International Center for Transitional Justice, New York, NY, director, 2001-. Former chair, Progressive Party Federal Council. **Publications:** (with P.H. Baker and W. Krafchik) South Africa and the World Economy in the 1990s, 1993; A Country Unmasked: Inside South Africa's Truth and Reconciliation Commission, 2000. EDITOR: (with J. Levy and R. Scheffer) Dealing with the Past: Truth and Reconciliation in South Africa, 1994; (with J. Levy) The Healing of a Nation?, 1995. **Address:** International Center for Transitional Justice, 20 Exchange Place, New York, NY 10005, U.S.A. **Online address:** borainea@juris.law.nyu.edu

BORCHARDT, Frank L. American, b. 1938. **Genres:** Literary criticism and history. **Career:** Northwestern University, Evanston, IL, assistant professor of German, 1965-68; City University of New York, Queens Coll., Flushing, assistant professor of German and comparative literature, 1968-71; University of Wurzburg, W. Germany, Fulbright research fellow, 1971-72; Duke University, Durham, NC, associate professor, 1971-92, professor of German, 1992-. **Publications:** German Antiquity in Renaissance Myth, 1971; (ed. with M.C. Salinger) A Conversation Is the Life of Leland R. Phelps, 1987; Doomsday Speculation as a Strategy of Persuasion, 1990. **Address:** Duke University, Department of Germanic Language & Literature, Durham, NC 27708-0256, U.S.A. **Online address:** frankbo@duke.edu

BORCH-JACOBSEN, Mikkel. French/Danish/American, b. 1951. **Genres:** Psychology, Philosophy, History. **Career:** Writer. University of Washington, Seattle, professor of French and comparative literature. **Publications:** Le Sujet Freudien, 1982, trans. as The Freudian Subject, 1988; (with E. Michaud and J-L Nancy) Hypnoses, 1984; Le Lien Affectif, 1991, trans as The Emotional Tie: Psychoanalysis, Mimesis, and Affect, 1993; Lacan: The Absolute Master, trans. D. Brick, 1991; Souvenirs d'Anna O.: une mystification centenaire, 1995, trans. as Remembering Anna O.: A Century of Mystification, 1996. **Address:** Department of Comparative Literature, University of Washington, Box 354338, Seattle, WA 98195, U.S.A. **Online address:** mbj@u.washington.edu

BORCZ, Geri. (born United States). **Genres:** Novels. **Career:** Writer. **Publications:** HISTORICAL ROMANCE NOVELS: Devil's Knight, 1999; Loving Glory, 2000; Asking for Trouble, 2001; One Wild Rose, 2002. **Ad-**

dress: Stephanie Kip Rostan, Levine Greenberg Literary Agency, 307 Seventh Ave., Suite 1906, New York, NY 10001, U.S.A.

BORDO, Susan (Rebecca). American, b. 1947. **Genres:** Philosophy. **Career:** Duke University, visiting associate professor, graduate faculty, women's studies, 1989; Le Moyne College, Syracuse, NY, associate professor of philosophy, 1987-93, Joseph C. Georg professor, 1991-94; University of Kentucky, Otis A. Singletary Chair in the humanities, professor of philosophy, 1994-. **Publications:** The Flight to Objectivity: Essays on Cartesianism and Culture, 1987; Unbearable Weight: Feminism, Western Culture, and the Body, 1993; Twilight Zones: The Hidden Life of Cultural Images from Plato to O.J., 1997. EDITOR: (with A.M. Jaggar) Gender/Body/Knowledge: Feminist Reconstructions of Being and Knowing, 1989; Feminist Interpretation of Descartes, in press. **Address:** Department of Philosophy, University of Kentucky, Paterson Office Tower, Lexington, KY 40506, U.S.A.

BORDOWITZ, Hank. Also writes as C. Ben Issakson, Dr. Rock. American, b. 1955. **Genres:** Music. **Career:** Cannings Recording Studio, engineer, producer, and musician, 1978-81; Ben El Distributors/Crazy Eddie's Records, manager, 1981-84; Publishers Packaging Corp., managing editor of Concert Shots, Metal Mania, and Rock Scene, and senior editor of Rock Fever, Focalpoint, Heavy Metal Hall of Fame, Hot Metal, and Creem Specials, all 1985-90; Fama, writer and copy editor, 1992-94; Wizard: Guide to Comics, Congers, NY, managing editor, 1994; Interactive Quarterly, Montclair, NJ, editor, 1995-96; Sheet Music, Bedford, NY, editor, 1996-97; writer, educator, publicist, and music business consultant, 1997-. WEVD, engineer, 1978-79; Record World, writer, editor, and chart researcher, 1979; record producer. Bernard M. Baruch College of the City University of New York, instructor in the business of music. **Publications:** Bad Moon Rising: The Unauthorized History of Creedence Clearwater Revival, 1998. Scriptwriter for television and radio programs. Contributor of articles and reviews to periodicals. Some writings appear under the pseudonyms C. Ben Issakson and Dr. Rock;. **Address:** c/o Fran Liebowitz, Writers House, 21 West 26th St., New York, NY 10010, U.S.A. **Online address:** hankiam@aol.com

BORDWELL, David. American, b. 1947. **Genres:** Film. **Career:** University of Wisconsin-Madison, faculty member, 1973-, Jacques Ledoux Professor of Film Studies, 1990-, fellow of Institute for Research in the Humanities, 1987-88 and 1993-. Presenter of public lecture series. **Publications:** Filmguide to "La Passion de Jeanne d'Arc," 1973; (with K. Thompson) Film Art: An Introduction, 1979, 4th ed, 1992; French Impressionist Cinema: Film Culture, Film Theory, Film Style, 1980; The Films of Carl-Theodor Dreyer, 1981; (with Thompson and J. Staiger) The Classical Hollywood Cinema: Film Style and Mode of Production to 1960, 1985; Narration in the Fiction Film, 1985; Ozu and the Poetics of Cinema, 1988; Making Meaning: Inference and Rhetoric in the Interpretation of Cinema, 1989; The Cinema of Eisenstein, 1993; (with Thompson) Film History: An Introduction, 1994; (ed. with N. Carroll) Post-Theory: Reconstructing Film Studies, 1995. Contributor to film journals. **Address:** 6039 Vilas Communication Hall, Department of Communication Arts, University of Wisconsin-Madison, 821 University Ave., Madison, WI 53706, U.S.A.

BORENSTEIN, Emily Schwartz. American, b. 1923. **Genres:** Poetry. **Career:** Poet. Social Work Psychotherapist and Counselor, New York. **Publications:** Woman Chopping, 1978; Finding My Face, 1979; Cancer Queen, 1979: Night of the Broken Glass, 1981; From a Collector's Garden, 2001. **Address:** 189 Highland Ave, Middletown, NY 10940, U.S.A. **Online address:** eboren@warwick.net

BORG, Marcus J(oel). American, b. 1942. **Genres:** Philosophy, Theology/Religion. **Career:** Educator and writer. Concordia College, Moorhead, MN, instructor, 1966-69, then assistant professor, 1972-74; South Dakota State University, Brookings, assistant professor, 1975-76; Carleton College, Northfield, MN, assistant professor, 1976-79; Oregon State University, Corvallis, professor, 1979-, faculty council president, 1985-86, 1992-93, Hundere Professor of Religious Studies, 1993-. University of Puget Sound, Tacoma, WA, distinguished visiting professor, 1986-87; Pacific School of Religion, Berkeley, CA, visiting professor, 1989-91. Journal for the Study of the New Testament, member of editorial board, 1991-. **Publications:** Conflict and Social Change, 1971; Conflict, Holiness, and Politics in the Teachings of Jesus, 1984, rev. ed, 1998; Jesus, a New Vision: Spirit, Culture, and the Life of Discipleship, 1987; Jesus in Contemporary Scholarship, 1994; Meeting Jesus Again for the First Time: The Historical Jesus and the Heart of Contemporary Faith, 1994; (with J.D. Crossan and S. Patterson) The Search for Jesus: Modern Scholarship Looks at the Gospels, 1994; The God We Never Knew: Beyond Dogmatic Religion to Authentic Contemporary Faith, 1997; (with J. Kornfield and R. Riegert) Jesus and Buddha: The Parallel Sayings, 1997; (with N.T. Wright) The Meaning of Jesus: Two Visions, 1999; Reading the Bible Again for the First Time: Taking the Bible Seriously but Not Literally, 2001; The Heart of Christianity, 2003. EDITOR: (with M. Powelson and R. Riegert) The Lost Gospel Q: The Original Sayings of Jesus, 1996; Jesus at Two Thousand, 1997; (with R. Mackenzie) God at Two Thousand, 2000. **Address:** Department of Philosophy, Oregon State University, 208 Hovland Hall, Corvallis, OR 97331, U.S.A. **Online address:** mborg@orst.edu

BORGENICHT, David. American, b. 1968. **Genres:** Children's fiction, Children's non-fiction, Humor/Satire. **Career:** Nonfiction writer and editor; Quirk Productions (formerly Book Soup Publishing), Philadelphia, PA, president/publisher. **Publications:** FOR CHILDREN: (compiler) A Treasury of Children's Poetry, 1994; (reteller) Bible Stories: Four of the Greatest Stories Ever, 1994; (reteller) Brer Rabbit, 1995; (reteller) The Legend of King Arthur: A Young Reader's Edition of the Classic Story by Howard Pyle, 1996; Grimm's Fairy Tales: The Children's Classic Edition, 1997; Whose Nose Is This?, 2001; Whose Tail Is This?, 2001. WITH J. PIVEN: The Worst-Case Scenario Survival Handbook, 1999; (with J. Worick) The Worst-Case Scenario Survival Handbook: Dating and Sex, 2001; (with D. Concannon) The Worst-Case Scenario Survival Handbook: Travel, 2001. OTHER: Smile! Twenty-five Happy Reminders, 1995; Bytes of Wisdom: A User's Guide to the World, 1996; (compiler) Mom Always Said, Don't Play Ball in the House, 1996; The Little Book of Stupid Questions: 300 Hilarious, Embarrassing, Bold, Personal, and Basically Pointless Queries, 1999; Sesame Street Unpaved: Scripts, Stories, Secrets, Songs, 1998; The Jewish Mother Goose: Modified Rhymes for Meshugennah Times, 2000. EDITOR: The Best Little Book of One Liners, 1992; Golf: Great Thoughts on the Grand Game, 1995. **Address:** 215 Church Street, 1st Floor, Philadelphia, PA 19106, U.S.A. **Online address:** david@quirkproductions.com

BORITT, Gabor S(zappanos). American (born Hungary). **Genres:** History, Military/Defense/Arms control, Biography. **Career:** Held college teaching positions including Boston University, University of Maryland, Memphis State University, University of Michigan, Washington University, Harvard University, Darwin College of Cambridge University, University of London; Gettysburg College, associate professor, 1981-85, Robert C. Fluhrer Professor of Civil War Studies, 1986-. Civil War Institute, founder and director 1984-. Serves on boards of trustees and advisory boards. **Publications:** Lincoln and the Economics of the American Dream, 1978, reprint, 1994; (with H. Holzer and M.E. Neely, Jr.) The Lincoln Image: Abraham Lincoln and the Popular Print, 1984; Changing the Lincoln Image, 1985; Historian's Lincoln: Rebuttals, 1988. EDITOR: (with N.O. Forness) The Historian's Lincoln: Pseudohistory, Psychohistory, and History, 1988; Lincoln: The War President, 1992; Why the Confederacy Lost, 1992; Lincoln's Generals, 1994; War Comes Again: Comparative Vistas on the Civil War and World War II, 1995; Of the People, by the People, for the People, 1996; Why the Civil War Came, 1996; The Gettysburg Nobody Knows, 1997; Jefferson Davis's Generals, 1999; The Lincoln Enigma, 2000. Contributor to professional journals and the popular press. **Address:** Civil War Institute, Gettysburg College, Gettysburg, PA 17325, U.S.A. **Online address:** gboritt@gettysburg.edu

BORJAS, George J(esus). American (born Cuba), b. 1950. **Genres:** Economics, Money/Finance. **Career:** National Bureau of Economic Research, senior research analyst, 1972-78; Queens College, City University of New York, assistant professor of economics, 1975-77; University of Chicago, Chicago, IL, post-doctoral fellow, 1977-78; University of California at Santa Barbara, assistant professor of economics, 1978-80, associate professor, 1980-82, professor, 1982-90; National Bureau of Economic Research, Cambridge, MA, research associate, 1983-; Harvard University, visiting scholar, 1988-89; University of California at San Diego, professor of economics, 1990-95; Harvard University, professor of public policy, 1995-97, Pforzheimer Professor of Public Policy, 1998-. **Publications:** Union Control of Pension Funds: Will the North Rise Again?, 1979; Wage Policy in the Federal Bureaucracy, 1980; The Sensitivity of Labor Demand Functions to Choice of Dependent Variable, 1985; (with M. Tienda) The Economic Consequences of Immigration, 1986; International Differences in the Labor Market Performance of Immigrants, W. 1988; Friends or Strangers: The Impact of Immigrants on the U.S. Economy, 1990; Heaven's Door: Immigration Policy and the American Economy, 1999; Economic Research on the Determinants of Immigration: Lessons for the European Union, 1999. EDITOR: (with M. Tienda) Hispanics in the U.S. Economy, 1985; (with R.B. Freeman) Immigration and the Work Force: Economic Consequences for the United States and Source Areas, 1992; Labor Economics, 1996; Issues in the Economics of Immigration, 2000. Contributor to books, professional publications and journals. **Address:** Kennedy School of Government, Harvard University, 79 John F. Kennedy St., Cambridge, MA 02138, U.S.A. **Online address:** gborjas@harvard.edu

BORK, Robert H(eron). American, b. 1927. **Genres:** Law, Politics/Government. **Career:** Admitted to the Bar of Illinois, 1953, and the Bar of the District of Columbia, 1977; University of Chicago, IL, research associate, 1953-54; Kirkland, Ellis, Hodson, Chaffetz & Masters (corporate law firm), Chicago, and NYC, 1955-62, became partner; Yale University Law School, New Haven, CT, associate professor of law, 1962-65, professor of law, 1965-75, Chancellor Kent professor of law, 1977-79, Alexander M. Bickel professor of public law, 1979-81; Department of Justice, Washington, DC, acting attorney general of the U.S., 1973-74, solicitor general of the U.S., 1973-77; American Enterprise Institute for Public Policy Research, Washington, DC, resident scholar, 1977, adjunct scholar, 1977-82; Kirkland & Ellis (corporate law firm), Washington, DC, partner, 1981-82; U.S. Court of Appeals for the District of Columbia Circuit, Washington, DC, circuit judge, 1982-88; John M. Olin Scholar in Legal Studies at American Enterprise Institute, 1988-99, senior fellow, 2000-; writer. **Publications:** Government Regulation of Business: Cases from the National Reporter System, 1963; Political Activities of Colleges and Universities, 1970; The Antitrust Paradox, 1978; Tempting America, 1989; Slouching towards Gomorrah: Modern Liberalism and American Decline, 1996. **Address:** American Enterprise Institute for Public Policy Research, 1150 17th St NW, Washington, DC 20036, U.S.A. **Online address:** rbork@aei.org

BORKO, Harold. American, b. 1922. **Genres:** Information science/Computers, Librarianship. **Career:** University of California, Los Angeles, professor of library and information science, now emeritus. **Publications:** Computer Applications in the Behavioral Sciences, 1962; Automated Language Processing, 1967; (with H. Sackman) Computers and the Problems of Society, 1972; Targets for Research in Library Education, 1973: (with C.L. Bernier) Abstracting Concepts and Methods, 1975; (with C.L. Bernier) Indexing Concepts and Methods, 1978. **Address:** University of California, Graduate School of Education and Information Science, 405 Hilgard Ave, Los Angeles, CA 90024, U.S.A. **Online address:** hborko@ucla.edu

BORNEMAN, John W. American, b. 1952. **Genres:** Anthropology/Ethnology, Politics/Government. **Career:** Harvard University, Cambridge, MA, lecturer in social studies, 1989-90; University of California at San Diego, La Jolla, assistant professor of anthropology and political science, 1990-91; Cornell University, Ithaca, NY, assistant professor of anthropology, 1991-. Guest lecturer at universities in the US and Germany. Conducted field research in East and West Berlin, France, Lebanon, and Syria. **Publications:** After the Wall: East Meets West in the New Berlin, 1991; (ed. and author of intro.) Gay Voices from East Germany, 1991; Belonging in the Two Berlins: Kin, State, Nation, 1991; Sojourners, 1995; Retribution and Judgment, 1997; Settling Accounts, 1997; Subversions of International Order, 1998; Death of the Father, 2003. Contributor to books and periodicals. **Address:** Dept of Anthropology, Aaron Burr Hall, Princeton University, Princeton, NJ 08543, U.S.A.

BORNHOLDT, Jenny. (Jennifer Mary). New Zealander, b. 1960. **Genres:** Poetry. **Career:** Unity Books, Wellington, bookseller, 1989-92. Haines Recruitment Advertising, Wellington, copywriter, 1992-96; City Gallery, Wellington, part-time organiser of public Programmes, 1996-98. **Publications:** POETRY: This Big Face, 1988; Moving House, 1989; Waiting Shelter, 1991; How We Met, 1995; Miss New Zealand, 1998. EDITOR: (with G. O'Brien) My Heart Goes Swimming: New Zealand Love Poems, 1996; (with G. O'Brien and M. Williams) An Anthology of New Zealand Poetry in English, 1997. **Address:** c/o Victoria University Press, PO Box 600, Wellington, New Zealand.

BORNSTEIN, George. American, b. 1941. **Genres:** Literary criticism and history. **Career:** Massachusetts Institute of Technology, Cambridge, assistant professor of humanities, 1966-69; Rutgers University, New Brunswick, NJ, assistant professor of English, 1969-70; University of Michigan, Ann Arbor, associate professor, 1970-75, professor of English, 1975-95, C.A. Patrides Professor of Literature, 1996-. **Publications:** Yeats and Shelley, 1970; (with D. Fader) British Periodicals of the 18th and 19th Centuries, 1972; (with D. Fader) Two Centuries of British Periodicals, 1974; Transformations of Romanticism in Yeats, Eliot, and Stevens, 1976; The Post-Romantic Consciousness of Ezra Pound, 1977; Poetic Remaking: The Art of Browning, Yeats, and Pound, 1988; Representing Modernist Texts: Editing as Interpretation, 1991; Contemporary German Editorial Theory, 1995; The Iconic Page in Manuscript, Print, and Digital Culture, 1998; Material Modernism: The Politics of the Page, 2001. EDITOR: Romantic and Modern; Revaluations of Literary Tradition, 1977; Ezra Pound among the Poets, 1985; W.B. Yeats: The Early Poetry, vol. 1, 1987, vol. 2, 1994; W.B. Yeats: Letters to the New Island, 1990; Palimpsest: Editorial Theory in the Humanities, 1993. **Address:** Dept of English, University of Michigan, Ann Arbor, MI 48109-1003, U.S.A. **Online address:** georgeb@umich.edu

BORNTRAGER, Mary Christner. American, b. 1921. **Genres:** Children's fiction. **Career:** Full-time poet and writer; worked as youth social worker, 1966-78. Public speaker. **Publications:** Ellie, 1988; Rebecca, 1989; Rachel, 1990; Daniel, 1991; Reuben, 1992; Andy, 1993; Polly, 1994; Sarah, 1995; Mandy, 1996; Annie, 1997. **Address:** Herald Press, 616 Walnut Ave., Scottdale, PA 15683, U.S.A.

BOROVIK, Genrikh (Aviezerovich). Russian, b. 1929. **Genres:** Plays/Screenplays, Novels, International relations/Current affairs. **Career:** Journalist, novelist, playwright, and television personality. Chief Moscow correspondent for Literary Gazette and Novosti Press Agency, 1966-72; Writers Union of the U.S.S.R., secretary, 1976-89; served as president of the International Federation for Peace and Conciliation and vice president of the World Peace Council, 1987-93; served as People's Deputy of the Soviet Union and Deputy Chair of the Foreign Relations Committee of the Supreme Soviet, 1989-91; Vashe-TV, Moscow, president. **Publications:** Povest o Zelenov Yascheritse (title means:, A Story about a Green Lizard), 1961; Reportaj s fashistskih granits (title means:, Reportage from Fascist Borders), 1974; Mai v Lissabone (title means:, May in Lisboa), 1975; Kontora na Ulitse Montera (title means:, Office on Montera Street), 1978; Interviyu v Buenos Airese (selected plays; title means:, Interview in Buenos Aires), 1980; Istoria odnogo ubiystva (biography of Martin Luther King, Jr.; title means:, The Story of One Killing), 1980; Moment Istini (title means:, Moment of Truth), 1981; Prolog (novel-essay; title means:, Prologue), 1984; Agent 00 (play), 1986; Izbrannoe (selected works), 2 vols, 1987; The Philby Files: The Secret Life of Master Spy Kim Philby, 1994. Author of additional books, plays, and screenplays. Contributor to periodicals around the world. **Address:** c/o Vashe TV, 12 ul Koroleva, Moscow, Russia.

BOROWITZ, Andy (Seth). (born United States), b. 1958. **Genres:** Adult non-fiction. **Career:** Writer, humorist, film and television producer. Regularly appears on CNN's American Morning and National Public Radio's Weekend Edition. Executive producer and creator of The Fresh Prince of Bel Air, National Broadcasting Company (NBC), 1990-96. Producer of motion pictures. **Publications:** (with Henry Beard and John Boswell) Rationalizations to Live By, 2000; The Trillionaire Next Door: The Greedy Investor's Guide to Day Trading, 2000; Who Moved My Soap?: The CEO's Guide to Surviving in Prison, 2003; Governor Arnold: A Photodiary of His First 100 Days in Office, 2004; The Borowitz Report: The Big Book of Shockers, 2004. Contributor to periodicals and writer for television shows. **Address:** Bruce Vinokour, Creative Artists Agency, 9830 Wilshire Blvd., Beverly Hills, CA 90212, U.S.A. **Online address:** andy@borowitzreport.com

BORTNIK, Aida (Beatriz). Argentine, b. 1938. **Genres:** Plays/Screenplays. **Career:** Playwright, short-story writer, art critic, and journalist. **Publications:** SCREENPLAYS: La Tregua (title means: The Truce), 1974; Una Mujer, 1975; Crecer de Golpe, 1976; La Isla, 1979; Volver, 1983; No habra mas penas ni olvido (title means: Funny Dirty Little War), c. 1984; (with L. Puenzo) La Historia oficial, 1985; Pobre mariposa (title means: Poor Butterfly), 1986; Old Gringo, 1989; (with M. Pineyro) Tango feroz: la leyenda de Tanguito (title means: Wild Tango), 1993; Caballos salvajes (title means: Wild Horses), 1995. STAGE PLAYS: Doldados y Soldaditos, 1972; Tres por Chejov, 1974; Dale Nomas, 1975; Papa Querido, 1981; Domesticados, 1981. Author of television plays. OTHER: Guiones cinematograficos, 1981; Primaveras, 1985. Author of art criticism and short stories for magazines. **Address:** 595 Salta St., 1074 Buenos Aires, Argentina.

BORTON, D. B. See CARPENTER, Lynette.

BORTON, Della. See CARPENTER, Lynette.

BORTON, Lady. American, b. 1942. **Genres:** Autobiography/Memoirs, Children's fiction. **Career:** Westtown School, Westtown, PA, teacher of mathematics, 1964-67; Friends School, Philadelphia, PA, teacher of history, 1967-68; Overseas Refugee Program of American Friends Service Committee (AFSC), Philadelphia, PA, assistant director, 1968-69; Quaker Service (physical rehabilitation center), Quang Ngai, Vietnam, assistant director, 1969-71; freelance writer and photographer, 1972-; Careline Inc., Athens, OH, executive director, 1975-77; Pulau Bidong Refugee Camp, West Malaysia, health administrator for the Red Cross, 1980. Beacon School for Children with Mental Retardation and Developmental Disabilities, Athens, OH, bus driver, 1972-; works in home restoration, 1972-; B. Dalton Bookstore, Athens, OH, clerk, 1985-88; Quaker Service-Vietnam, Hanoi, Vietnam, interim director, 1990-91, field director, 1993-. Independent radio producer, 1987-; columnist for Akron Beacon Journal, Akron, OH, 1989-; commentator for Sunday Weekend Ed, National Public Radio, 1990-; affiliated with Faculty Writers' Workshop at the Joiner Center for the Study of War and Social Consequences, University of Massachusetts, Boston, summers, 1993 and 1994. **Publications:** Sensing the Enemy: An American Woman among the Boat People of Vietnam (nonfiction), 1984; Voyage of the Mekong Dragon, 1986; Fat Chance!, (juvenile fiction), 1993; Junk Pile (juvenile fiction), 1995; After Sorrow: An American among the Vietnamese (nonfiction), in press; Boat Boy (juvenile fiction). Contributor to books. Contributor of articles to periodicals. **Address:** Beacon School for Children with Mental Retardation, and Developmental Disabilities, 801 West Union St., Athens, OH 45701, U.S.A.

BORTZ, Fred. (Alfred B). American, b. 1944. **Genres:** Children's nonfiction, Sciences, Technology. **Career:** Bowling Green State University, OH, assistant professor of physics, 1970-73; Yeshiva University, NYC, research associate, 1973-74; Westinghouse Electric, Madison, PA, senior engineer, 1974-77; Essex Group, Inc., Pittsburgh, PA, staff scientist, 1977-79; Carnegie Mellon University, Pittsburgh, scientist, 1979-83, assistant director, Data Storage Systems Center, 1983-90, director of Special Projects for Engineering Education, 1990-92, senior fellow, Sci/Tech Education, 1992-94; Duquesne University, Pittsburgh, School of Education, sr. research fellow, 1994-96; freelance writer and book reviewer, 1996-. Consultant to publishers of children's science books; Chatham College, lecturer, 2000-. **Publications:** Superstuff! Materials That Have Changed Our Lives, 1990; Mind Tools: The Science of Artificial Intelligence, 1992; Catastrophe! Great Engineering Failure-and Success, 1995; Martian Fossils on Earth?: The Story of Meteorite ALH84001, 1997; To the Young Scientist: Reflections on Doing and Living Science, 1997; Dr. Fred's Weather Watch, 2000; Collision Course!: Cosmic Impacts and Life on Earth, 2001; Techno-Matter: The Materials behind the Marvels, 2001; The Library of Subatomic Particles, 6 vols., 2004. Contributor to books. Contributor of articles on theoretical and applied physics to periodicals. **Address:** 1312 Foxboro Dr, Monroeville, PA 15146, U.S.A. **Online address:** DrFredB@worldnet.att.net

BORYSENKO, Joan. American, b. 1945. **Genres:** Medicine/Health, Inspirational/Motivational Literature. **Career:** Psychologist, biologist, organizational official, health-care consultant, writer, and yoga instructor. Mind/Body Health Sciences, president; Claritas Institute for Interspiritual Inquiry and the Interspiritual Mentor Training Program, co-founder. Prevention magazine, columnist. **Publications:** (with L. Rothstein) Minding the Body, Mending the Mind, c. 1987; Guilt Is the Teacher, Love Is the Lesson, c.1990; (with J. Drescher) On Wings of Light, 1992; Fire in the Soul, 1993; Pocketful of Miracles, 1994; (with M. Borysenko) The Power of the Mind to Heal, 1994; A Woman's Book of Life, 1996; The Ways of the Mystic, 1997; A Woman's Journey to God, 1999; Inner Peace for Busy People, 2001; Inner Peace for Busy Women, 2003. Contributor to newsletters and a variety of lectures, workshops, and audiotapes. **Address:** Mind/Body Health Sciences Inc., 393 Dixon Rd, Boulder, CO 80302, U.S.A. **Online address:** www.Joanborysenko.com

BOSCO, Dominick. American, b. 1948. **Genres:** Medicine/Health, Ghost Writer. **Career:** Full-time writer. Editor of Prevention magazine. **Publications:** (ghostwriter) Robert S. Mendelsohn, Confessions of a Medical Heretic, 1979; The People's Guide to Vitamins and Minerals: From A to Zinc, 1980, rev ed, 1989; (with M.E. Rosenbaum) Super Fitness Beyond Vitamins: The Bible of Super Supplements, 1987; (with R.A. Markman) Alone with the Devil: Famous Cases of a Courtroom Psychiatrist, 1989; Bedlam: A Year in the Life of a Mental Hospital, 1992. Contributor to magazines. **Address:** c/o Russell Galen, Scovil Chichak Galen Literary Agency, Inc., 381 Park Ave. South, Ste1020, New York, NY 10016, U.S.A.

BOSCO, Joseph (Augustus). American, b. 1948. **Genres:** Adult non-fiction. **Career:** Worked as a painter, cab driver, restaurant manager, and actor; television writer, director, and producer, until 1984; full-time writer, 1984-. **Publications:** The Boys Who Would Be Cubs: A Year in the Heart of Baseball's Minor Leagues (nonfiction), 1990; Blood Will Tell: A True Story of Deadly Lust in New Orleans (nonfiction), 1993. **Address:** 3731 Rue Nicole, New Orleans, LA 70131-5461, U.S.A.

BOSCO, Monique. Canadian (born Austria), b. 1927. **Genres:** Novels. **Career:** Writer and professor. Freelance journalist, 1949-59; writer for National Film Board and Radio Canada; Universite de Montreal, Quebec, Canada, professor of literature, beginning in the early 1960s. **Publications:** Un Amour maladroit, 1961; Les Infusoires, 1965; La Femme de Loth, 1970 trans. by J. Glassco as Lot's Wife, 1975; Jericho, 1971; New Medea, 1974; Charles Levy, m.d., c. 1978; Schabbat 70-77, 1978; Portrait de Zeus peint par Minerve, 1982; Sara Sage, 1986; Boomerang, 1987; Cliches, 1988; BabelOpera, 1989; Miserere, 1991; Rememoration, L'Arbre, 1991; Ephemeres, c. 1993; Ephemerides, 1993; Le jeu des sept familles, 1995; Lamento, 1997;

Confiteor, 1998; Bis, 1999; Mea Culpa, 2001. Contributor to periodicals. **Address:** 4105 Cote des Neiges app. 15, Montreal, QC, Canada H3H 1W9.

BOSKIN, Joseph. American, b. 1929. **Genres:** History, Race relations, Social commentary, Humor/Satire. **Career:** Faculty member, State University of Iowa, 1959-60, and University of Southern California, Los Angeles, 1960-69; Professor of History and Afro-American Studies, and Director of Urban Studies and Public Policy Program, Boston University, MA, 1969-, now Emeritus. Member of advisory councils and task forces. **Publications:** (with F. Krinsky) The Oppenheimer Affair: A Political Play in Three Acts, 1968; Urban Racial Violence in the 20th Century, 1969; (with R.R. Rosenstone) Seasons of Rebellion: Protest and Radicalism in Recent America, 1971; Into Slavery: Racial Decisions in the Virginia Colony, 1976; Issues in American Society, 1978; Humor and Social Change in 20th Century America, 1979; Sambo: The Rise & Demise of an American Jester, 1986; Rebellious Laughter: People's Humor in American Culture, 1997. EDITOR: Opposition Politics: The Anti-New Deal Tradition, 1968; The Humor Prism in 20th Century America. **Address:** Dept of History, Boston University, 226 Bay State Rd, Boston, MA 02215, U.S.A. **Online address:** jboskin@bu.edu

BOSKOFF, Alvin. American, b. 1924. **Genres:** Politics/Government, Sociology, Urban studies, Regional/Urban planning. **Career:** Professor of Sociology, Emory University, Atlanta, since 1958. **Publications:** (with H. Becker) Modern Sociological Theory, l957: The Sociology of Urban Regions, 1962, rev. ed. 1970; (with W. Cahnman) Sociology and History, 1964; Theory in American Sociology, 1969; The Mosaic of Sociological Theory, 1972; (with J. Doby and W. Pendleton) Sociology: The Study of Man in Adaptation. 1973. **Address:** Dept. of Sociology, Emory University, Atlanta, GA 30322, U.S.A.

BOSMAJIAN, Haig. American, b. 1928. **Genres:** Civil liberties/Human rights, Language/Linguistics, Speech/Rhetoric. **Career:** University of Connecticut, Storrs, Assistant Professor, 1960-64; University of Washington, Seattle, Dept. of Speech, Professor, since 1964, now Emeritus. **Publications:** The Language of Oppression, 1974; Metaphor and Reason in Judicial Opinions, 1992; The Freedom Not to Speak, 1999. EDITOR: Readings in Speech, 1965; The Rhetoric of the Speaker, 1967; Readings in Parliamentary Procedure, 1968; (with H. Bosmajian) The Rhetoric of the Civil Rights Movement. 1969; The Principles and Practice of Freedom of Speech, 1971; The Rhetoric of Nonverbal Communication, 1971; Dissent: Symbolic Behavior and Rhetorical Strategies, 1972; (with H. Bosmajian) This Great Argument: The Rights of Women, 1972; Obscenity and Freedom of Expression, 1975; Justice Douglas and Freedom of Speech, 1980; Censorship, Libraries, and the law, 1982. FIRST AMMENDMENT IN THE CLASSROOM SERIES: vol. I, The Freedom to Read, 1987, vol. II, Freedom of Religion, 1987, vol. III, Freedom of Expression, 1988, vol. IV, Academic Freedom, 1988, vol. V, Freedom to Publish, 1989.

BOSS, Pauline. American, b. 1934. **Genres:** Human relations/Parenting. **Career:** University of Wisconsin-Madison, lecturer, 1973-75, assistant professor, 1975-80, associate professor of child and family studies, 1980-81; University of Minnesota-St. Paul, St. Paul, MN, associate professor, 1981-84, professor of family social science, 1984-, director of marital and family therapy program, 1984-87, director of graduate studies, 1987-91, chair of human subjects committee for behavioral Research, 1982-86, member of Children, Youth, and Family Consortium, 1990-. Workshop presenter, lecturer, visiting professor at educational institutions; conference speaker in the United States and abroad. Family therapist in private practice, 1976-; presenter of seminars and workshops; guest on media programs in the United States and elsewhere. **Publications:** (with others) The Father's Role in Family Systems: An Annotated Bibliography, 1979; Family Stress Management, 1988, rev ed, 2001; Ambiguous Loss: Learning to Live with Unresolved Grief, 1999; Losing a Way of Life: Ambiguous Loss in Farm Families, 2001; (with C. Mulligan) Classic and Contemporary Readings about Family Stress, 2002. EDITOR:(and contrib) Sourcebook of Family Theories and Methods: A Contextual Approach, 1993; Family Structures and Child Health in the Twenty-first Century, Maternal and Child Health Leadership Conference, 1993. Author of training films and videotapes. Contributor to books. Contributor of articles and reviews to periodicals. **Address:** Department of Family Social Science, 290 McNeal Hall, University of Minnesota-St. Paul, 1985 Buford Ave., St. Paul, MN 55108, U.S.A. **Online address:** pboss@che.umn.edu

BOSSELAAR, Laure-Anne. Belgian, b. 1943. **Genres:** Poetry. **Career:** Worked for radio and television stations in Belgium and Luxembourg; editor of poetry anthologies; poetry translator. **Publications:** POETRY: Artemis (in French), 1982; The Hour between Dog and Wolf, 1997; Small Gods of Grief,

2001. EDITOR: (with K. Brown) Night Out: Poems about Hotels, Motels, Restaurants, and Bars, 1997; Outsiders: Poems about Rebels, Exiles & Renegades (anthology); Urban Nature: Poems about Wildlife in the Cities (anthology). **Address:** c/o Boa Editions, 260 East Ave, Rochester, NY 14604, U.S.A.

BOSSONE, Richard M. American, b. 1924. **Genres:** Education, Language/Linguistics. **Career:** Professor Emeritus, 1993-, City University of New York, (Associate Professor of English Education, Richmond Coll., 1967-71: Professor of English. Baruch Coll., 1970-74; University Dean for Instructional Research and Professor of English, Graduate School, 1974-93). Associate Professor of English Education, University of California, Riverside, 1961-67. **Publications:** (ed.) Talks to Secondary English Teachers, 1963; Remedial English Instruction in California Public Junior Colleges: An Analysis and Evaluation of Current Practices, 1966; The Writing Problems of Remedial English Students in Community Colleges of the City University of New York, 1969; Reading Problems of Community College Students, 1970; (co-author) Basic English: ComputerAssisted Instruction, 1970; Teaching Basic English Courses: Readings and Comments, 1971; (coauthor) Handbook of Basic English Skills, 1971; (co-author) Three Modes of Teaching Remedial English: A Comparative Analysis, 1973; English Proficiency, 1979; The Writing Proficiency Program, 1982; (co-author) Writing: Process and Skills, 1986; (ed.) University/Urban Schools National Task Force Conference Proceedings, 1980-94.

BOSTDORFF, Denise M. American, b. 1959. **Genres:** Politics/Government, Speech/Rhetoric. **Career:** Purdue University, Lafayette, IN, visiting assistant professor, 1987-88, assistant professor, 1988-93, associate professor of communication, 1994; College of Wooster, OH, assistant professor, 1994-97, associate professor of communication, 1997-, chair, 1998-2002. **Publications:** The Presidency and the Rhetoric of Foreign Crisis, 1994. Work represented in anthologies. Contributor to communication journals and other scholarly periodicals. **Address:** 103 Wishart Hall, College of Wooster, Wooster, OH 44691, U.S.A. **Online address:** dbostdorff@wooster.edu

BOSTICCO, (Isabel Lucy) Mary. British. **Genres:** Administration/Management, Business/Trade/Industry, Novellas/Short stories, Novels. **Career:** Writer and Ed., Cement and Concrete Association, 1968-71; Associate Ed., International Mgmt., 1973-74; Press Officer, Bracknell Development Corp., 1974-82. **Publications:** Modern Personnel Management, 1964; Personal Letters for Businessmen, 1965, 3rd ed., 1986; Etiquette for the Businessman, at Home and Abroad, 1967; Instant Business Letters, 1968, 2nd ed., 1985; Top Secretary, 1970; (trans.) Modern Filing Methods and Equipment, 1970; Creative Techniques for Management, 1971; The Businessman's Wife, 1972; Teach Yourself Secretarial Practice, 1984; Uncle Ginger: Tales of Italy and Other Places, 1990; Autumn Leaves, 1996. **Address:** The Oasis, 7A Telston Close, Bourne End, Bucks. SL8 5TY, England.

BOSTOCK, David. British, b. 1936. **Genres:** Philosophy. **Career:** Fellow and Tutor in Philosophy, Merton Coll., Oxford, and Lecturer in Philosophy, Oxford University, since 1968. Temporary Lecturer in Philosophy, University of Leicester, 1963; Lecturer in Philosophy, Aust. Natl. University, Canberra, 1964-67; Loeb Research Fellow, Harvard University, Cambridge, Massachusetts, 1967-68. **Publications:** Logic and Arithmetic, 2 vols., 1974-79; Plato's Phaedo, 1986; Plato's Theaetetus, 1988; Aristotle: Metaphysics, books Z and H, 1994; (intro. and notes) Aristotle: Physics, trans. by R. Waterfield, 1996; Intermediate Logic, 1997; Aristotle's Ethics, 2000. **Address:** Merton College, Oxford, England.

BOSTOCK, Donald Ivan. British, b. 1924. **Genres:** Music. **Career:** Assistant Conductor, The Echelforde Singers, 1950-53, and Ashford and District Choral Society, 1954-58; Musical Director, Ashford Methodist Church, Middx., 1947-87. **Publications:** Choirmastery, 1966. **Address:** Kerridge, Gorse Hill Lane, Virginia Water, Surrey, England.

BOSTON, Jonathan. New Zealander (born England), b. 1957. **Genres:** Politics/Government. **Career:** New Zealand Treasury, Wellington, investigating officer, 1984; University of Canterbury, Christchurch, New Zealand, lecturer, 1985-87; Victoria University of Wellington, senior lecturer, 1987-93, associate professor, 1994-97, professor 1997-. Institute of Policy Studies (Wellington), research fellow, 1984, then member of executive. **Publications:** Incomes Policy in New Zealand, 1984; The Future of New Zealand Universities, 1988; (co-author) Public Management: The New Zealand Model, 1996; (co-author) New Zealand under MMP, 1996; Governing under Proportional Representation, 1998. EDITOR/COEDITOR: The Fourth Labour Government, 1987; Reshaping the State, 1991; The Decent Society?, 1992; Voices for Justice, 1994; The State under Contract, 1995; From

Campaign to Coalition, 1998; Redesigning the Welfare State in New Zealand, 1999; Electoral and Constitutional Change in New Zealand: An MMP Sourcebook, 1999; Left Turn: The New Zealand General Election of 1999. **Address:** School of Government, Victoria University of Wellington, PO Box 600, Wellington, New Zealand. **Online address:** jonathan.boston@vuw.ac.nz

BOSWELL, Robert. American, b. 1953. **Genres:** Novels, Novellas/Short stories, Plays/Screenplays. **Career:** University of Arizona, Tucson, teaching assistant, 1982-86; Northwestern University, Evanston, IL; assistant professor of creative writing, 1986-89; New Mexico State University, professor, 1989-; writer. **Publications:** SHORT STORIES: Dancing in the Movies, 1986; Living to Be 100, 1994. NOVELS: Crooked Hearts, 1987; The Geography of Desire, 1989; Mystery Ride, 1993; American Owned Love, 1997; Century's Son, 2002. **Address:** Dept of English, Box 3E, New Mexico State University, Las Cruces, NM 88005, U.S.A. **Online address:** RBoswell@NMSU.edu

BOSWORTH, R(ichard) J(ames) B(oon). Australian, b. 1943. **Genres:** History, International relations/Current affairs. **Career:** University of Sydney, lecturer, 1969-73, sr. lecturer, 1974-80, associate professor, 1981-86; University of Western Australia, Nedlands, professor of history, 1987-. May Foundation for Italian Studies, Deputy Director, 1981-. **Publications:** Benito Mussolini and the Fascist Destruction of Liberal Italy, 1973; (ed. with G. Cresciani) Altro Polo: A Volume of Italian Studies, 1979; Italy, The Least of the Great Powers: Italian Foreign Policy Before the First World War, 1979; Italy and the Approach of the First World War, 1983; (ed. with G. Rizzo) Altro Polo: Study of Ideas and Intellectuals in Contemporary Italy, 1983; (with J. Wilton) Old Worlds and New Australia: A History of Non-British Migration to Australia since the Second World War, 1984; La Politica estera dell'Italia giolittiana, 1985; (ed. with M. Melia) Aspects of Ethnicity in Western Australia, 1991; (ed. with S. Romano) Il Problema della politica estera italiana, 1991; (with M. Bosworth) Fremantle's Italy, 1993; (ed. with R. Ugolini) War, Internment and Mass Migration: the Italo-Australian Experience, 1940-1990, 1992; Explaining Auschwitz and Hiroshima: History Writing and the Second World War 1945-1990, 1993; Italy and the Wider World 1860-1960, 1996; The Italian Dictatorship, 1998; (ed. with P. Dogliani) Italian Fascism: History, Memory and Representation, 1999; Mussolini, 2002. **Address:** History Dept, University of Western Australia, Nedlands, WA 6009, Australia.

BOTEACH, Shmuley. (Shmuel). American. **Genres:** Theology/Religion. **Career:** Rabbi, writer, and public speaker. Founder, L'Chaim Society; cofounder, with Michael Jackson, Heal the Kids Foundation; Loveprophet. com (dating Web site), founder. Has appeared on television and radio shows. **Publications:** The Wolf Shall Lie with the Lamb: The Messiah in Hasidic Thought, 1993; Wrestling with the Divine: A Jewish Response to Suffering, 1995; Wisdom, Understanding, and Knowledge: Basic Concepts of Hasidic Thought, 1996; Kosher Sex: A Recipe for Passion and Intimacy, 1999; Dating Secrets of the Ten Commandments, 2000; Why Can't I Fall in Love: A Twelve-Step Program, 2001; (with U. Geller and D. Chopra) The Psychic and the Rabbi: A Remarkable Correspondence, 2001; An Intelligent Person's Guide to Judaism and Jewish Guide to Adultery. Contributor to periodicals. **Address:** c/o Random House, 1745 Broadway, New York, NY 10019, U.S.A.

BOTHWELL, Robert (Selkirk). Canadian, b. 1944. **Genres:** History, Biography. **Career:** University of Toronto, ON, Canada, lecturer, 1970-72, assistant professor, 1972-75, associate professor, 1975-81, professor of history, 1981-, member of executive committee of Trinity College, 1988-90; CJRT-FM, Toronto, academic broadcaster, 1989-99. **Publications:** (with B. Alexandrin) A Bibliography of the Material Culture of New France, 1970; (with Hillmer) Canada's Foreign Policy, 1919-1939, 1978; Pearson: His Life and World (biography), 1978; (with W. Kilbourn) C.D. Howe: A Biography, 1979; (with I. Drummond and J. English) Canada since 1945: Power, Politics, and Provincialism, 1981, rev. ed., 1989; Eldorado: Canada's National Uranium Company, 1984; (with D.J. Bercuson and J.L. Granatstein) The Great Brain Robbery: The Decline of Canada's Universities, 1984; A Short History of Ontario, 1986; (with Drummond and English) Canada, 1900-1945, 1987; Years of Victory, 1987; Loring Christie: The Failure of Bureaucratic Imperialism, 1988; Nucleus: This History of Atomic Energy of Canada Limited, 1988; (with Granatstein) Pirouette: Pierre Trudeau and Canadian Foreign Policy, 1990; Laying the Foundations, 1991; Canada and the United States: The Politics of Partnership, 1992; Canada and Quebec, 1995, rev. ed, 1998; The Big Chill: Canada and the Cold War, 1998; Traveller's History of Canada, 2001. EDITOR: (with M. Cross) Policy by Other Means, 1972; (with N. Hillmer) The In-Between Time, 1975. **Address:** International Relations Program, Trinity College, University of Toronto, Toronto, ON, Canada M5S 1H8. **Online address:** bothwell@chass.utoronto.ca

BOTKIN, Daniel B. American, b. 1937. **Genres:** Agriculture/Forestry, Environmental sciences/Ecology. **Career:** U.S. Peace Corps, Washington,

DC, volunteer, 1962-63; Worldwide Medical News Service, NYC, science writer, 1964; Yale University, New Haven, CT, professor of forestry, 1968-75; Ecosystems Center, Woods Hole, MA, research scientist, 1975-78; University of California, Santa Barbara, professor of biology and environmental studies, 1978-94, research professor, 1999-; Center for the Study of the Environment, President, 1992-; George Mason University, Professor of Biology and Director of Program on Global Change, 1994-99. **Publications:** (with E.A. Keller) Environmental Studies, 1982, 2nd ed., 1987; Discordant Harmonies: A New Ecology for the 21st Century, 1990; Forest Dynamics: An Ecological Model, 1993; Environmental Sciences, 1995, 3rd ed., 1999; Our Natural History: Lessons from Lewis & Clark, 1996; Passage of Discovery: The American Rivers Guide to the Missouri River of Lewis and Clark, 1999; No Man's Garden: Thoreau and a New Vision for Civilization and Nature, 2003; Strange Encounters: Adventures of a Renegade Naturalist, 2003. EDITOR: (with West and Shugart) Forest Succession, 1981; (with Caswell, Estes, and Orio) Changing the Global Environment, 1989. **Address:** 245 8th Ave #270, New York, NY 10011, U.S.A. **Online address:** danielbotkin@rcn.com

BOTTING, Douglas. British, b. 1934. **Genres:** History, Natural history, Travel/Exploration, Biography. **Career:** Freelance writer, photographer, and television film-maker, since 1958. Fellow, Royal Geographical Society, Royal Institute of International Affairs, and Society of Authors, London. **Publications:** Island of the Dragon's Blood (exploration), 1958; The Knights of Bornu (travel), 1961; One Chilly Siberian Morning (travel), 1965; Humboldt and the Cosmos (biography), 1973; Wilderness Europe, 1977; Rio de Janeiro (reportage), 1977; The Pirates (history), 1978; The Second Front (war), 1978; The U-Boats (war), 1979; The Great Airships (history), 1980; Aftermath Europe, 1982; Nazi Gold, 1984; In the Ruins of the Reich, 1985; Wild Britain, 1988; Hitler's Last General, 1989; America's Secret Army, 1989; Gavin Maxwell: A Life (biography), 1993; Sex Appeal: The Art and Science of Sexual Attraction, 1995; Gerald Durrell: The Authorized Biography, 1999. **Address:** c/o John Johnson Literary Agency, 45-47 Clerkenwell Green, London EC1R 0HT, England.

BOTTOMS, David. American, b. 1949. **Genres:** Poetry, Novels. **Career:** High school teacher of English, Douglasville, Georgia, 1974-78; Georgia State University, assistant professor of English, 1982-87, associate professor, 1987-; poet-in-residence, University of Montana, 1986. **Publications:** POETRY: Jamming with the Band at the VFW, 1978; Shooting Rats at the Bibb County Dump, 1980; In a U-Haul North of Damascus, 1983; Under the Vulture-Tree, 1987; Armored Hearts: Selected and New Poems, 1995. NOVELS: Any Cold Jordan, 1987; Easter Weekend, 1990. OTHER: (ed. with D. Smith) The Morrow Anthology of Younger American Poets, 1985. **Address:** Department of English, Georgia State University, Atlanta, GA 30303, U.S.A.

BOUCHER, Bruce (Ambler). American, b. 1948. **Genres:** Art/Art history. **Career:** University of London, London, England, lecturer, 1976-92, reader in art history, 1992-98; professor, 1998-. **Publications:** The Sculpture of Jacopo Sansavino, 1991; (ed.) Piero di Cosimo de'Medici: Art in the Service of the Medici, 1993; Andrea Palladio: The Architect in His Time, 1994; Italian Baroque Sculpture, 1998. **Address:** Department of the History of Art, University College, University of London, London WC1E 6BT, England. **Online address:** b.boucher@ucl.ac.uk

BOUCHER, Philip P. American, b. 1944. **Genres:** History. **Career:** Instructor in Charlotte, NC, 1973-74; University of Alabama, Huntsville, assistant professor, 1974-80, associate professor, 1980-89, professor, 1989-, distinguished professor, 1996-. **Publications:** Shaping of the French Colonial Empire, 1985; Les Nouvelles Frances, 1989; Cannibal Encounters, 1992. **Address:** History Department, RH 409, University of Alabama in Huntsville, Huntsville, AL 35899, U.S.A. **Online address:** boucherp@uah.edu

BOUDREAU, R(obert) L(ouis). Canadian, b. 1951. **Genres:** Young adult non-fiction. **Career:** Worked as a sea captain for thirty years; writer. Chief executive officer of Newport Yachts International, Sailing Holidays Ltd., and Yachting Holidays Ltd. **Publications:** The Man Who Loved Schooners (biography), 2000. **Address:** 1852 Crescent Rd., Victoria, BC, Canada V8S 2G8.

BOUGHTON, Doug(las Gordon). Australian, b. 1944. **Genres:** Education. **Career:** Elementary schoolteacher in Bankstown, Australia, 1963-64; high school art teacher in NSW, Australia, 1965-67; Riverina Area Office of Education, NSW, art adviser, 1968-70; elementary schoolteacher in Calgary, Alberta, 1971; junior high school art teacher in Calgary, 1971-72; art teacher and department head at a high school in Calgary, 1973-74; University of

Lethbridge, Lethbridge, Alberta, assistant professor of education, 1976-78; University of British Columbia, Vancouver, assistant professor of art education, 1978-79; Salisbury College of Advanced Education, Salisbury, Australia, senior lecturer, 1979-81, principal lecturer in art and art education, 1981-82; South Australian College of Advanced Education, principal lecturer in art and design education, 1982-90, head of School of Art and Design Education, 1985-90; University of South Australia, Underdale, associate professor, 1991-92, professor of art and design education, 1993-, head of School of Art and Design Education, 1993. Speaker at colleges and universities. Painter, with work exhibited in Alberta. **Publications:** Evaluation and Assessment of Visual Arts Education (monograph), 1994. EDITOR: (with J. Cunningham and DC Wilson) Curriculum Policies and the Expressive Arts (monograph), 1979; (with E.W. Eisner and J. Ligtvoet, and contrib.) Evaluating and Assessing the Visual Arts in Education: International Perspectives, 1996; (with K. Congdon, and contrib.) Evaluating Art Education Programs in Community Centers: International Perspectives of Conception and Practice, 1998. Contributor to books. Contributor of articles and reviews to academic journals. **Address:** School of Education, University of South Australia, Holbrooks Rd., Underdale, SA 5032, Australia. **Online address:** doug. boughton@unisa.edu.au

BOULEZ, Pierre. French, b. 1925. **Genres:** Music. **Career:** Composer. Compagnie Renaud/Barrault, Paris, France, theater music director, 1946-56; British Broadcasting Corporation (BBC-TV) Symphony Orchestra, London, chief conductor, 1971-77; New York Philharmonic Orchestra, NYC, music director, 1971-77; College de France, Paris, professor, 1976-95; Institut de recherche et coordination-acoustique/musique, Paris, director, 1976-92; Ensemble Intercontemporain, Paris, president, 1977-98. **Publications:** Penser la Musique Aujourd'hui (title means: Thinking about Music Today), 1963, trans by S. Bradshaw and R.R. Bennett as Boulez on Music Today, 1971; Releves d'apprenti (texts collected and presented by P. Thevenin), 1966, trans by H. Weinstock as Notes of an Apprenticeship, 1968, trans by S. Walsh as Stocktakings from an Apprenticeship, 1991; Par Volonte et Par Hasard: Entretiens avec Celestin Deliege (title means: Conversations with Deliege), 1975, trans by B. Hopkins as Conversations with Deliege, 1977; Points de Repere, ed. by J-J Nattiez, 1985, trans by M. Cooper as Orientations: Collected Writings, 1986; Jalons (Pour une Decennie), 1990. Contributor to books. **Address:** Institut de recherche et coordination acoustique/musique, 1, Place Igor Stravinsky, 75004 Paris, France.

BOULLATA, Issa J. American (born Palestine), b. 1929. **Genres:** Novels, Novellas/Short stories, Humanities, Intellectual history, Language/Linguistics, Literary criticism and history, Theology/Religion, Translations. **Career:** De La Salle College, Jerusalem, senior teacher of Arabic literature, 1949-52; Ahliyyah College, Ramallah, senior teacher of Arabic literature, 1952-53; St. George's School, Jerusalem, senior teacher of Arabic literature and deputy headmaster, 1953-68; Hartford Seminary, Hartford, CT, professor of Arabic literature and language, 1968-75; McGill University, Montreal, Quebec, professor of Arabic literature and language, 1975-1999; retired, 2000-. **Publications:** Outlines of Romanticism in Modern Arabic Poetry (in Arabic), 1960; Badr Shakir alSayyab: His Life and Poetry (in Arabic), 1971; Trends and Issues in Contemporary Arab Thought, 1990; 'A'id ila al-Quds (novel; title means: Return to Jerusalem), 1998. EDITOR: (and trans.) Modern Arab Poets, 1950-1975, 1976; Critical Perspectives on Modern Arabic Literature, 1980; (with T. DeYoung) Tradition and Modernity in Arabic Literature, 1997; Literary Structures of Religious Meaning in the Qur'an, 2000. Contributor to encyclopedias. Contributor of articles and reviews to scholarly journals. TRANSLATOR: A. Amin, My Life, 1978; E. Nasrallah, Flight against Time, 1987; J.I. Jabra, The First Well: A Bethlehem Boyhood, 1995; M. Berrada, The Game of Forgetting, 1996; G. Samman, The Square Moon, 1998; M. Berrada, Fugitive Light, 2002; J.I. Jabra, Princesses' Street, 2005. Translator from English into Arabic.

BOULTON, James T(hompson). British, b. 1924. **Genres:** Literary criticism and history. **Career:** Director, Institute for Advanced Research in Arts and Social Sciences, University of Birmingham, 1987- (Professor of English Studies, and Head of Dept., 1975-88). Professor of English Literature, University of Nottingham, 1964-75. **Publications:** The Language of Politics in the Age of Wilkes and Burke, 1963; Selected Letters of D.H. Lawrence, 1997. EDITOR: Edmund Burke: Philosophical Enquiry into...Sublime and Beautiful, 1958, 1987; C.F.G. Masterman's The Condition of England, 1960; Dryden's Essay of Dramatick Poesie, etc., 1964; Defoe: Prose and Verse, 1965; English Satiric Poetry: Dryden to Byron, 1966; Lawrence in Love: Letters from D.H. Lawrence to Louie Burrows, 1968; (with S.T. Bindoff) Research in Progress in English and Historical Studies, 2 vols., 1971-75; Samuel Johnson: The Critical Heritage, 1971; Defoe's Memoirs of a Cavalier, 1972, 1991; The Letters of D.H. Lawrence, vol. I, 1979, vol. 2, 1982, vol. 3,

1984, vol. 4, 1987, vol. 5, 1989, vol. 6, 1991, vol. 7, 1993, vol. 8, 2000; D.H. Lawrence, Last Essays and Articles, 2004; James Boswell, An Account of Corsica, 2005.

BOUNDS, Sydney J(ames). Also writes as Adam Clark, Sam Foster, Jack Greener, Wes Saunders, Will Sutton. British, b. 1920. **Genres:** Novellas/Short stories, Mystery/Crime/Suspense, Horror, Science fiction/Fantasy, Westerns/Adventure, Children's fiction, Writing/Journalism. **Career:** Freelance writer, 1951-. Worked for London Transport until 1951. **Publications:** Dimension of Horror, 1953; (as Wes Saunders) Vengeance Valley, 1953; The Moon Raiders, 1955; The World Wrecker, 1956; The Robot Brains, 1957; The Yaqui Trail, 1964; Gun Brothers, 1966; Lynching at Noon City, 1967; The Predators, 1977; Star Trail, 1978; The Cleopatra Syndicate, 1990; A Man Called Savage, 2000; (as Will Sutton) Ghost Town, 2000; (as Sam Foster) Nemesis Rides the Trail, 2001; (as Adam Clark) Shadow of the Noose, 2001; (as Jack Greener) The Long Chase, 2001; Savage's Feud, 2002; The Savage River, 2003; Border Savage, 2004; Savage-Manhunter, 2004. **Address:** 27 Borough Rd, Kingston-upon-Thames, Surrey KT2 6BD, England.

BOUQUET, Mary (Rose). British, b. 1955. **Genres:** Anthropology/Ethnology. **Career:** University of Lisbon, Lisbon, Portugal, lecturer, 1983-87; National Museum of Ethnology, Lisbon, exhibition developer, 1986-88; University of Amsterdam, Amsterdam, Netherlands, lecturer, 1989; National Museum of Natural History, Leiden, Netherlands, exhibition developer, 1992-93. **Publications:** Reclaiming English Kinship, 1993. Author of exhibition catalogues. **Address:** c/o Andrew B. Durnell, 43 High St., Tunbridge Wells, Kent TN1 1XL, England.

BOURDEAUX, Michael Alan. British, b. 1934. **Genres:** History, Theology/Religion. **Career:** London School of Economics, Centre for International Studies, Research Fellow, 1968-71; Keston Institute, Oxford (formerly Keston College, Kent), Director, 1970-99, Director Emeritus, 1999-2002, President, 2003-; Royal Institute of International Affairs, Research Staff Member, 1971-73. **Publications:** Opium of the People, 1965: Religious Ferment in Russia, 1968: Patriarch and Prophets, 1969; Faith on Trial in Russia, 1971; Land of Crosses: The Struggle for Religious Freedom in Lithuania, 1979; Risen Indeed: Lessons in Faith from the USSR, 1983; (with L. Bourdeaux) Ten Growing Soviet Churches, 1987; Gorbachev, Glasnost and the Gospel, 1990 (in US as The Gospel's Triumph over Communism, 1991); (with J. Witte Jr.) Proselytism and Orthodoxy in Russia, 1999. EDITOR: (with X.H. Johnston) Aida of Leningrad, 1972; The Politics of Religion in Russia and the New States of Eurasia, 1995. **Address:** 101 Church Way, Iffley, Oxford OX4 4EG, England. **Online address:** mbourdeaux@freenet.co.uk

BOURGEOIS, Paulette. Canadian, b. 1951. **Genres:** Children's fiction. **Career:** Royal Ottawa Hospital, Ottawa, ON, staff occupational therapist, 1975-76; Canadian Broadcasting Corp., reporter, 1977-78, 1980-81; freelance writer, 1981-. **Publications:** JUVENILE: Franklin in the Dark, 1986; Big Sarah's Little Boots, 1987; On Your Mark, Get Set: All about the Olympic Games, Then and Now, 1987; The Amazing Apple Book, 1987; The Amazing Paper Book, 1989; Hurry Up, Franklin, 1989; Grandma's Secret, 1989; The Amazing Dirt Book, 1990; Too Many Chickens, 1990; Amazing Potato Book, 1991 Franklin Is Lost, 1992; Franklin Is Bossy, 1993; Franklin Is Messy, 1994; (with M. Wolfish) Changes in You and Me: A Book about Puberty, Mostly for Boys (Girls), 2 vols, 1994; Many Hats of Mr. Minches, 1994; Franklin Goes to School, 1995; Franklin Plays the Game, 1995; Franklin Wants a Pet, 1995; Franklin's Blanket, 1995; Franklin and the Tooth Fairy, 1996; Franklin Has a Sleepover, 1996; Franklin's Halloween, 1996; Franklin's School Play, 1996; Franklin Rides a Bike, 1997; Franklin's Bad Day, 1997; Franklin's New Friend, 1997; Finders Keepers for Franklin, 1998; Franklin and the Thunderstorm, 1998; Franklin's Secret Club, 1998; Franklin's Class Trip, 1999; Franklin and the Baby, 1999; Franklin Goes to the Hospital, 2000; Franklin's Pet Problem, 2000; Franklin Says Sorry, 2000; Franklin's First Day at School, 2000; Franklin's Baby Sister, 2000; Franklin in the Dark, 2000; Franklin's Bicycle Helmet, 2000; Franklin's Special Blanket, 2000; Franklin and Harriet, 2001; Oma's Quilt, 2001; Franklin Says I Love You, 2002. **Address:** c/o Kids Can Press, 29 Birch Ave, Toronto, ON, Canada M4V 1E1.

BOURKE, Angela. Irish, b. 1952. **Genres:** Literary criticism and history. **Career:** Writer and scholar; senior lecturer in Irish, University College Dublin, Ireland. Visiting professor at Harvard University, 1992-93 and at University of Minnesota; has held academic posts in North America and in Italy. **Publications:** Caoineadh na dTri Muire: Teama na Paise I bhFiliocht Bheil na Gaeilge, 1983; Inion Ri na Cathrach Deirge, 1989; Inion Ri an Oileain Dhorcha, 1991; Caoineadh na Marbh: Siceoilfhiliocht, 1992; By Salt

Water, 1996; The Burning of Bridget Cleary, 2000; (ed.) Field Day Anthology: Irish Women's Writings and Tradition, 2002. **Address:** University College Dublin, Belfield, Dublin 4, Ireland.

BOURNE, Joyce. British, b. 1933. **Genres:** Music. **Career:** Medical assistant and anesthetist in Manchester, England, 1962-87; senior partner of a general medical practice in Salford, England, 1965-90. **Publications:** Who's Who in Opera, 1998. ASSOCIATE EDITOR: M. Kennedy, The Oxford Dictionary of Music, 1994; The Concise Oxford Dictionary of Music. **Address:** The Bungalow, Edilom Rd, Manchester M8 4HZ, England.

BOURNE, Larry Stuart. Canadian, b. 1939. **Genres:** Geography, Regional/Urban planning, Social sciences, Urban studies. **Career:** University of Toronto, assistant professor, 1966-69, associate professor 1969-73, director, Centre for Urban and Community Studies, 1972-84, professor of geography and planning, 1973-. Fellow, Royal Society of Canada, 1986. Recipient: Massey Medal, Royal Geographical Society, 2004. **Publications:** The Urban and Regional Economy of Yellowknife, N.W.T., 1964; Private Redevelopment of the Central City, 1967; Urban Systems: Strategies for Regulation, 1976; Progress in Settlement Systems Geography, 1986. EDITOR: (and contrib.) Internal Structure of the City: Readings on Space and Environment, 1971, 1982; (with R. Mackinnon, and contrib.) Urban Systems in Central Canada: Selected Papers, 1972; (with R. Mackinnon and J. Simmons) The Form of Cities in Central Canada: Selected Papers, 1973; (with R. Mackinnon, J. Simmons and J. Siegel) Urban Futures for Central Canada: Perspectives on Forecasting Growth and Form, 1974; (with J. Simmons) Systems of Cities: Readings on Structure, Growth and Policy, 1978; (with J. Hitchcock) Urban Housing Markets: Recent Directions in Research and Policy, 1980; The Geography of Housing, 1981; (with R. Sinclair, and contrib.) Urbanization and Settlement Systems. 1984; Urban Systems in Transition, 1986; The Changing Geography of Urban Systems, 1989; Urbanization and Urban Development, 1991; (with D. Ley) The Changing Social Geography of Canadian Cities, 1993; Portrait of a Region, 2000.

BOURNE, Russell. American, b. 1928. **Genres:** History. **Career:** Life, New York City, reporter, 1950-53; worked as assistant to Henry R. Luce; affiliated with Architectural Forum; American Heritage Publishing Co., NYC, editor of Junior Library and Horizon Caravel Books, 1960-69; National Geographic Society, Washington, DC, associate chief of Book Service, 1969-71; U.S. News and World Report Books, Washington, DC, consulting editor, 1975-76; Smithsonian Books, Washington, DC, senior editor of Exposition Books, 1977-79; Hearst Books, NYC, publisher of general books, 1980-81; American Heritage Publishing Co., publisher and editor, 1981-84. Bourne-Thompson & Associates, Washington, DC, partner, 1975-77; consultant. **Publications:** The View from Front Street: Travels through Historic New England Fishing Communities, 1989; The Red King's Rebellion: Racial Politics in New England, 1675-1678, 1990; Columbus and the Early Explorers, 1991; Floating West and Other American Canals, 1992; Americans on the Move, 1993; Invention in America, 1995; The Best of the Best Sparkman and Stephens Designs, 1996; Rivers of America, 1998; Gods of War, Gods of Peace, 2002. **Address:** Curtis Brown Ltd, 10 Astor Place, New York, NY 10003, U.S.A. **Online address:** RBourne@compuserve.com

BOURQUE, Antoine. See BRASSEAUX, Carl A(nthony).

BOUSON, J. Brooks. American. **Genres:** Literary criticism and history. **Career:** Mundelein College, Chicago, IL, assistant professor, 1980-86, associate professor of English, 1986-91; Loyola University, Chicago, IL, associate professor, 1991-2000, professor of English, 2000-. **Publications:** The Empathic Reader: A Study of the Narcissistic Character and the Drama of the Self, 1989; Brutal Choreographies: Oppositional Strategies and Narrative Design in the Novels of Margaret Atwood, 1993; Quiet as It's Kept: Shame, Trauma, and Race in the Novels of Toni Morrison, 2000. Contributor to books and periodicals. **Address:** Department of English, Crown Center, Loyola University of Chicago-Lake Shore Campus, 6525 N Sheridan Rd, Chicago, IL 60626, U.S.A.

BOUTILIER, Robert. Canadian, b. 1950. **Genres:** Marketing. **Career:** Freelance research consultant, Vancouver, British Columbia, 1981-85; Criterion Research Corp., Toronto, Ontario, vice president and partner, 1985-87; Boutilier and Associates (independent marketing research consultants), Burnaby, British Columbia, partner, 1987-. University of British Columbia, part-time teacher of psychology. **Publications:** Targeting Families: Marketing to and through the New Family, 1993. **Address:** 3968 Southwood St., Burnaby, BC, Canada V5J 2E6.

BOUTON, Gary David. American, b. 1953. **Genres:** How-to books, Information science/Computers. **Career:** Writer. **Publications:** CorelDRAW! for Non-Nerds, 1993; (with B.M. Bouton) Inside Adobe Photoshop for Windows, 1994; CorelDRAW! 5 for Beginners, 1994; Adobe Photoshop Now!, 1994; (with G. Kubicek) Adobe Photoshop 3 Filters and Effects, 1995; (with B.M. Bouton) Inside Adobe Photoshop 3, 1995; CorelDRAW! 6, 1996; Official Multimedia Publishing for Netscape: Make Your Web Pages Come Alive!, 1996; (with B.M. Bouton and G. Kubicek) Inside Adobe Photoshop 4, 1997; Inside Extreme 3D 2, 1997; Extreme 3D Fundamentals, 1997; Inside Adobe Photoshop 5.0, 1998. **Address:** c/o Macmillan Computer Publishing, 201 West 103rd St., Indianapolis, IN 46290, U.S.A.

BOUTROS-GHALI, Boutros. Egyptian, b. 1922. **Genres:** International relations/Current affairs. **Career:** University of Cairo, professor of international law and international relations, 1949-77; Al-Ahram Al-Iktisadi, editor, 1960-75; Al-Siyasa Al-Dawlyya (a foreign affairs journal), editor; Egyptian diplomat; acting Egyptian Minister of State for Foreign Affairs under Anwar Sadat, 1977-91; Foreign Minister of State of Egypt; Vice President of the Socialist International; Secretary General of the United Nations, 1992-96; author. **Publications:** An Agenda For Peace 1995, 1995; An Agenda for Development 1995, 1995; An Agenda for Democratization, 1996; Egypt's Road to Jerusalem: A Diplomat's Story of the Struggle for Peace in the Middle East, 1997. **Address:** 2 Avenue El-Nil Giza, Cairo, Egypt.

BOUVARD, Marguerite Guzman. American (born Italy), b. 1937. **Genres:** Poetry, Organized labor, Politics/Government, Psychology, Women's studies and issues. **Career:** Regis College, Weston, MA, professor of political science and poetry, 1966-90, and department head; Wellesley Center for Research on Women, MA, scholar, 1991-92; Brandeis University, Waltham, MA, resident scholar in women's studies, 1991-. University of Maryland at College Park, past writer in residence. Exhibitions: The Body's Burning Fields, poetry and drawings about illness, University of Massachusetts Medical School Gallery, 1995, and Butler Art Museum; (with K. Klein) She Who Has Gone Before: A Book on the Wall, poetry and drawings about mothers, Dreitzer Gallery, Brandeis University, 1994; (with sculptor K. Klein) The Intimate Life of Trees, poetry, Brandeis University and Natick Public Library, 2002-03. **Publications:** The Labor Movements in the Common Market Countries, 1972; The Search for Community: Building a New Moral World, 1975; Journeys over Water, 1982; Voices from an Island, 1985; Landscape and Exile, 1985; The Path through Grief, 1988, rev. ed., 1997; Of Light and Silence, 1990; With the Mothers of the Plaza de Mayo, 1993; Revolutionizing Motherhood: The Mothers of the Plaza de Mayo, 1994; Women Reshaping Human Rights, 1996; The Body's Burning Fields, 1997; Grandmothers: Granddaughters Remember, 1998; Wind, Frost and Fire, 2001; Prayers for Comfort in Difficult Time, 2004. Work represented in anthologies. Contributor of articles and poems to periodicals. **Address:** 6 Brookfield Circle, Wellesley, MA 02481, U.S.A. **Online address:** marguerite.bouvard@worldnet.att.net

BOVA, Ben(jamin William). American, b. 1932. **Genres:** Novels, Novellas/Short stories, Science fiction/Fantasy, Sciences, Social commentary. **Career:** Former editor, Upper Darby News, PA, former technical ed. Project Vanguard, Martin Co., Baltimore, MD; Script writer, Physical Science Study Committee, Cambridge; Marketing Manager. Avco Everett Research Laboratory, MA, 1960-71; Ed, Analog science fiction mag., 1971-78; Ed, Director, Omni, 1978-82. **Publications:** The Star Conquerors, 1959; The Milky Way Galaxy, 1961; Giants of the Animal World, 1962; Reptiles since the World Began, 1964; Star Watchman, 1964; The Uses of Space, 1965; The Weathermakers, 1967; Out of the Sun, 1968; The Dueling Machine, 1969; In Quest of Quasars, 1970; Planets, Life and LGM, 1970; Escape!, 1970; The Fourth State of Matter, 1971; Exiled from Earth, 1971; (with G. Lucas) THX 1138, 1971; The Amazing Laser, 1972; The New Astronomies, 1972; Flight of Exiles, 1972; As on a Darkling Plain, 1972; When the Sky Burned, 1972; Starflight and Other Improbabilities, 1973; Forward in Time, 1973; The Weather Changes Man, 1974; (with B. Berson) Survival Guide for the Suddenly Single, 1974; Workshops in Space, 1974; (with G.R. Dickson) Gremlins, Go Home!, 1974; End of Exile, 1975; Notes to a Science Fiction Writer, 1975; Through Eyes of Wonder, 1975; Science: Who Needs It?, 1975; The Starcrossed, 1975; Millennium, 1976; Multiple Man, 1976; City of Darkness, 1976; The Seeds of Tomorrow, 1977; (with T.E. Bell) Closeup: New Worlds, 1977; Viewpoint, 1977; Colony, 1978; Maxwell's Demons, 1978; Kinsman, 1979, 1981; The Exiles Trilogy, 1981; Voyagers, 1981; The High Road, 1981; Test of Fire, 1982; Vision of the Future, 1982; The Winds of Altair, 1983; Escape Plus (collection), 1984; Orion, 1984; Assured Survival, 1984; The Astral Mirror (collection), 1985; Privateers, 1985; Prometheans (collection), 1986; Voyagers II: The Alien Within, 1986; The Kinsman Saga, 1987; Welcome to Moonbase, 1987; Battle Station (collection), 1987; Vengeance of Orion, 1988; The Beauty of Light, 1988; (with Sheldon Glashow) Interactions, 1988; Peacekeepers, 1988; Cyber-books, 1989; Voyagers III: Star Brothers, 1990; Orion in the Dying Time, 1990; Future Crime, 1990; (with B. Pogue) The Trikon Deception, 1992; Mars, 1992; (with A.J. Austin) To Save the Sun, 1992; Triumph, 1993; Empire Builders, 1993; Challenges (collection), 1993; Sam Gunn, Unlimited, 1993; The Craft of Writing Science Fiction, 1994; Death Dream, 1994; (with A.J. Austin) To Fear the Light, 1994; Orion the Conqueror, 1994; The Watchmen, 1994; Orion among the Stars, 1995; Brothers, 1996; Moonrise, 1996; Twice Seven (collection), 1998; Moonwar, 1998; Immortality, 1998; Sam Gunn Forever, 1998; Return to Mars, 1999; Venus, 2000; Jupiter, 2001; The Precipice, 2001; The Story of Light, 2001; The Rock Rats, 2002; Saturn, 2003; Tales of the Grand Tour (collection), 2004; The Silent War, 2004; Faint Echoes, Distant Stars, 2004; Powersat, 2005; Mercury, 2005. EDITOR: The Many Worlds of SF, 1971; Analog 9, 1973; SFWA Hall of Fame, vol. 2, 1973; The Analog Science Fact Reader, 1974; Analog Annual, 1976; Analog Yearbook, 1978; Best of Analog, 1978; (with D. Myrus) Best of Omni Science Fiction, 1980-82; Best of the Nebulas, 1989; (with B. Preiss) First Contact, 1990; Aliens and Alien Societies, 1996; World Building, 1996; Space Travel, 1997; Time Travel, 1997.

BOVAIRD, Anne E(lizabeth). American, b. 1960. **Genres:** Language/Linguistics. **Career:** Grassroots Research, San Francisco, CA, journalist, 1989-; Universites de Paris X and XIII, Paris, France, teacher, 1991-. Journalist-on-staff for Transatlantic, a magazine for Americans living in Europe; freelance writer in the fields of education, translation, and journalism for a number of clients both in France and the United States. **Publications:** GOODBYE U.S.A. SERIES: Goodbye U.S.A.-Bonjour la France: A Language Learning Adventure, 1993, Vol. II, 1994. OTHER: (with L. Potier) Dictionnaire anglais-francais, 1990. **Address:** 521 Walnut St., Winnetka, IL 60093, U.S.A.

BOVON, François. Swiss, b. 1938. **Genres:** Theology/Religion. **Career:** Harvard University, Divinity School, Cambridge, MA, Frothingham Professor of the History of Religion. **Publications:** De vocatione gentium, 1967; Das Evangelium nach Lukas, 1989; Lukas in neuer Sicht, 1985; L'oeuvre de Luc, 1987; Luke the Theologian, 1987; Revelations et Ecritares, 1993; (ed. with A.G. Brock and C.R. Matthews) The Apocryphal Acts of the Apostles, 1999; (with B. Bouvier and F. Amsler) Acta Philippi, 1999; Luke (Hermenia), 2001. **Address:** Harvard University, The Divinity School, 45 Francis Ave, Cambridge, MA 02138, U.S.A. **Online address:** francois_bovon@harvard.edu

BOWDEN, Charles. American, b. 1945. **Genres:** Environmental sciences/Ecology, Literary criticism and history. **Career:** Writer. Tucson Citizen, Tucson, AZ, reporter; City Magazine, Tucson, editor; contributing editor, Esquire, Harper's. **Publications:** The Impact of Energy Development on Water Resources in Arid Lands: Literature Review and Annotated Bibliography, 1975; Killing the Hidden Waters, 1977; (with L. Kreinberg) Street Signs Chicago: Neighborhood and Other Illusions of Big City Life, 1981; Blue Desert (essays), 1986; Frog Mountain Blues, 1987; Mezcal (autobiography), 1988; Red Line, 1989; Desierto: Memories of the Future, 1991; The Sonoran Desert: Arizona, California, and Mexico, 1992; The Secret Forest, 1993; (with M. Binstein) Trust Me: Charles Keating and the Missing Billions, 1993; Seasons of the Coyote: The Legend and Lore of an American Icon (essays), 1994; Blood Orchid: An Unnatural History of America, 1995; Stone Canyons of the Colorado Plateau, 1996; Juarez: Laboratory of Our Future, 1998. **Address:** 1928 E 9th St., Tucson, AZ 85719, U.S.A.

BOWDEN, Jim. See SPENCE, William John Duncan.

BOWDEN, Mark. American, b. 1951. **Genres:** Documentaries/Reportage. **Career:** Baltimore News American, Baltimore, MD, staff writer, 1973-79; Philadelphia Inquirer, Philadelphia, PA, staff writer, 1979-. **Publications:** NONFICTION: Doctor Dealer, 1987; Bringing the Heat: A Pro Football Team's Quest for Glory, Fame, Immortality, and a Bigger Piece of the Action, 1994; Black Hawk Down: A Story of Modern War, 1999; Killing Pablo, 2001; Finders Keepers, 2002. **Address:** Philadelphia Inquirer, 400 N. Broad St., Philadelphia, PA 19101, U.S.A.

BOWDRING, Paul (Edward). Canadian, b. 1946. **Genres:** Novels, Poetry. **Career:** College of the North Atlantic, St. John's, Newfoundland, instructor in English, 1975-99; TickleAce literary magazine, editor and copublisher, 1979-87; The Fiddlehead literary magazine, associate editor; Editors & Co., editor; writer. **Publications:** NOVELS: The Roncesvalles Pass, 1989; The Night Season, 1997. OTHER: Home for Christmas (anthology), 1999; Voices from the Rock (anthology), 2001. **Address:** c/o Writers' Alliance of New-

foundland & Labrador, PO Box 2681, St. John's, NL, Canada A1C 5M5. **Online address:** pbowdring@thezone.net

BOWEN, Barbara C(herry). British, b. 1937. **Genres:** Intellectual history, Literary criticism and history. **Career:** University of Illinois, Urbana, instructor to professor, 1962-87; Vanderbilt University, Nashville, professor of French and comparative literature, 1987-2002. **Publications:** Les Caracteristiques essentielles de la farce francaise, et leur survivance dans les annees 1550-1620, 1964; The Age of Bluff: Paradox and Ambiguity in Rabelais and Montaigne, 1972; Words and the Man in French Renaissance Literature. 1983; Enter Rabelais, Laughing, 1998. EDITOR: Four Farces, 1967; The French Renaissance Mind, 1976; One Hundred Renaissance Jokes, 1988; Lapidary Inscriptions: Renaissance Studies for Donald A. Stone, Jr., 1991. **Address:** 1818 Cedar Ln, Nashville, TN 37212, U.S.A.

BOWEN, Gail. Canadian, b. 1942. **Genres:** Mystery/Crime/Suspense, Novellas/Short stories. **Career:** University of Saskatchewan, Saskatoon, instructor, 1976-79; Gabriel Dumont Institute, Regina, Saskatchewan, instructor, 1979-85; University of Regina, Dept of English, lecturer, 1979-85, assistant professor, 1986-97, associate professor of English, 1997-, department head, 1997-; writer. Canadian Broadcasting Corporation (CBC)-Radio, arts columnist. **Publications:** NOVELS: Deadly Appearances, 1990; Murder at the Mendel, 1991, as Love and Murder, 1993; The Wandering Soul Murders, 1992; A Colder Kind of Death, 1994; A Killing Spring, 1996; Verdict in Blood, 1998. OTHER: (with R. Marken) 1919: The Love Letters of George and Adelaide (novella), 1987. **Address:** SIFC/English, Room 210 College West, University of Regina, Regina, SK, Canada S4S 0A2.

BOWEN, John (Griffith). Also writes as Justin Blake. British (born India), b. 1924. **Genres:** Novels, Children's fiction, Plays/Screenplays. **Publications:** The Truth Will Not Help Us; Embroidery on an Historical Theme, 1956; Pegasus, 1957; The Mermaid and the Boy, 1958; After the Rain, 1958; The Centre of the Green, 1959; Storyboard. 1960; (with J. Bullmore, as Justin Blake) Garry Halliday series 5 vols., 1960-64; The Birdcage, 1962; The Essay Prize, with A Holiday Abroad and The Candidate: Plays for Television, 1962; I Love You, Mrs. Patterson, 1964; A World Elsewhere, 1964; After the Rain, 1967; The Fall and Redemption of Man, 1968; Little Boxes, 1968; The Disorderly Women, 1969; The Waiting Room, 1970; The Corsican Brothers, 1970; Heil Caesar!, 1974; Florence Nightingale, 1976; Squeak, 1983; The McGuffin, 1984; The Girls, 1986; Fighting Back, 1989; The Precious Gift, 1992; No Retreat, 1994; Cold Salmon, 1998; Plays One, 1999.

BOWEN, Michael. American, b. 1951. **Genres:** Mystery/Crime/Suspense, Law. **Career:** Foley & Lardner (law firm), Milwaukee, WI, partner, 1976-. **Publications:** MYSTERIES: Badger Game, 1989; Washington Deceased, 1990; Fielder's Choice, 1991; Faithfully Executed, 1992; Act of Faith, 1993; Corruptly Procured, 1994; Worst Case Scenario, 1996; Collateral Damage, 1999; Fourth Glorious Mystery, 2000; Screenscam, 2001. OTHER: (with G. Marshall and K. Freeman) Passing By: The United States and Genocide in Burundi, 1973; Can't Miss, 1987; (with B.E. Butler) The Wisconsin Fair Dealership Law, 1988. **Address:** Foley & Lardner, 777 East Wisconsin Ave., Suite 3900, Milwaukee, WI 53202, U.S.A.

BOWEN, Roger W. American, b. 1947. **Genres:** History, Biography. **Career:** Colby College, Waterville, ME, assistant professor, 1978-82, associate professor, 1982-87; Hollins College, Roanoke, VA, vice president for academic affairs, 1992-. St. Mary's University, Halifax, Nova Scotia, Canada, visiting professor, 1978; Japan Institute of Harvard University, associate in research, 1980-. **Publications:** Rebellion and Democracy in Meiji Japan: A Study of Commoners in the Popular Rights Movement, 1980; (ed.) E.H. Norman: His Life and Scholarship, 1984; Innocence Is Not Enough: The Life and Death of Herbert Norman, 1986. **Address:** Vice President for Academic Affairs, Hollins College, P.O. Box 9706, Roanoke, VA 24020, U.S.A.

BOWEN, William (Gordon). American, b. 1933. **Genres:** Economics, Education. **Career:** President, The Andrew W. Mellon Foundation, since 1988. Professor of Economics, 1958-88, and President, 1972-88, Princeton University, New Jersey. **Publications:** The Wage-Price Issue: A Theoretical Analysis, 1960; Wage Behaviour in the Postwar Period: An Empirical Analysis, 1960; Economic Aspects of Education: Three Essays, 1964; (with W.J. Baumol) Performing Arts: The Economic Dilemma, 1966; (with T.A. Finegan) The Economics of Labor Force Participation, 1969; Ever the Teacher, 1987; (with J.A. Sosa) Prospects for Faculty in the Arts and Sciences, 1989; (with N.L. Rudenstine) In Pursuit of the PhD, 1992; (with T.I. Nygren, S.E. Turner, and E.A. Duffy) The Charitable Nonprofits: An Analysis of Institutional Dynamics and Characteristics, 1994; Inside the Boardroom,

1994; (with D. Bok) The Shape of the River, 1998. **Address:** Andrew W. Mellon Foundation, 140 E. 62nd St, New York, NY 10021, U.S.A.

BOWEN, Zack. American, b. 1934. **Genres:** Literary criticism and history, Biography. **Career:** State University Coll., Fredonia, NY, assistant professor of English, 1960-64; State University of New York at Binghamton, assistant professor, to distinguished professor, and chairman of the English Dept., 1964-76; University of Delaware, Newark, professor and chmn of the English Dept., 1976-86; University of Miami, chairman of the English Dept., 1986-96, professor, 1986-. Irish Renaissance Annual, general ed., 1980-84; Essays in British Literature series, G. K. Hall/Twayne, general ed., 1984-; Florida University Press, James Joyce Series, general ed., 1994-; International James Joyce Foundation, president, 1996-2000. **Publications:** Padraic Colum: A Biographical-Critical Introduction, 1970; Musical Allusions in the Works of James Joyce, 1974; Mary Lavin, 1975; A Companion to Joyce Studies, 1984; Ulysses as a Comic Novel, 1989; A Reader's Guide to John Barth, 1993; Bloom's Old Sweet Song, 1994; (with D. Wilson) Science and Literature, 2001. **Address:** Dept. of English, University of Miami, Coral Gables, FL 33124, U.S.A. **Online address:** zbowen@miami.edu

BOWER, John Morton. British, b. 1942. **Genres:** Animals/Pets, Medicine/Health. **Career:** Associate veterinary surgeon in London, England, 1965-68, and Maidenhead, Berkshire, England, 1968-69; Veterinary Hospital, Plymouth, Devonshire, England, principal veterinarian, then senior partner, 1969-; writer. Pet Plan Insurance Co., consultant-adviser, 1991-; Veterinary Drug Co., director, 1993-98; genusxpress plc, consultant, 1998-. British Veterinary Association, president, 1989-90. **Publications:** (with D. Youngs) The Health of Your Dog, 1989; (with J. Gripper and D. Gunn) Veterinary Practice Management, 1989, rev. ed., 2000; The Dog Owners Veterinary Handbook, 1994; (with C. Bower) The Dog Owner's Problem Solver, 1998; (with C. Bower) The Cat Owner's Problem Solver, 1998. Contributor to periodicals. **Address:** Veterinary Hospital, Colwill Rd, Plymouth, Devon PL6 8RP, England. **Online address:** johnbower@plymouthvets.co.uk

BOWER, Tom. British, b. 1946. **Genres:** Writing/Journalism, Documentaries/Reportage. **Career:** British Broadcasting Company, London, England, producer and correspondent; writer. **Publications:** Blind Eye to Murder: Britain, America and the Purging of Nazi Germany-A Pledge Betrayed, 1981, in US as The Pledge Betrayed: America and Britain and the Denazification of Postwar Germany, 1982; Klaus Barbie: The Butcher of Lyons, 1984; The Paperclip Conspiracy: The Hunt for the Nazi Scientists, 1987, in UK as The Paperclip Conspiracy: The Battle for the Spoils and Secrets of Nazi Germany, 1987; The Red Web, 1990; Maxwell: The Outsider, 1988; Tiny Rowland: A Rebel Tycoon, 1993; Nazi Gold, 1997; Branson, 2000. **Address:** 10 Thurrow Rd, London NW3 5PL, England.

BOWERING, George. Canadian, b. 1938. **Genres:** Novels, Novellas/Short stories, Young adult fiction, Plays/Screenplays, Poetry, Essays. **Career:** University of Calgary, AB, professor, 1963-66; Sir George Williams University, Montreal, writer-in-residence, 1967-68, assistant professor of English, 1968-72; Simon Fraser University, Burnaby, BC, professor of English, 1972-. Imago mag., Vancouver, editor. **Publications:** A Home for Heroes (play), 1962; Baseball, 1967; Rocky Mountain Foot, 1969; The Gangs of Kosmos, 1969; Al Purdy, 1970; George, Vancouver, 1970; Sitting in Mexico, 1970; Geneve, 1971; Autobiology, 1971; The Sensible, 1972; Layers 1-13, 1973; Curious, 1973; In the Flesh, 1974; At War with the U.S., 1974; Allophanes, 1976; The Catch, 1976; The Concrete Island, 1977; A Short Sad Book, 1977; Concentric Circles, 1977; Protective Footwear, 1978; Another Mouth, 1979; Burning Water, 1980; West Window, 1982; Smoking Mirror, 1982; Errata (literary theory), 1987; George Bowering Selected, 1993; The Moustache (memoir), 1993; Bowering's B.C. (history), 1996; Egotists and Autocrats (history), 1999; Cars (memoir), 2002; A Magpie Life (memoir), 2001. NOVELS: Mirror on the Floor, 1967, screenplay, 1971; Caprice, 1987; Harry's Fragments, 1990; Shoot!, 1994; Parents from Space (young adult), 1994; Diamondback Dog (young adult), 1998; Piccolo Mondo, 1998. POETRY: Sticks and Stones, 1963; Points on the Grid, 1964; The Man in Yellow Boots, 1965; The Silver Wire, 1966; Two Police Poems, 1968; Selected Poems, 1971; Touch: Selected Poems 1960-1970, 1971; Poem and Other Baseballs, 1976; Particular Accidents: Selected Poems, 1981; Kerrisdale Elegies, 1984; Poems for People, 1985; Delayed Mercy, 1986; His Life, a Poem, 2000. STORIES: Flycatcher, 1974; A Place to Die, 1984; The Rain Barrel, 1994. ESSAYS: A Way with Words, 1982; The Mask in Place, 1983; Craft Slices, 1985-71; Imaginary Hand, 1988. EDITOR: Vibrations, 1970; The Story So Far, 1971; Likely Stories, 1992.

BOWERING, Marilyn (Ruthe). Canadian, b. 1949. **Genres:** Novels, Plays/Screenplays, Poetry. **Career:** Gregson Graham Marketing, Victoria, BC, edi-

tor and writer, 1978-82; University of Victoria, sessional lecturer, 1982-86, 1989, visiting lecturer, 1993-98. **Publications:** POETRY: The Liberation of Newfoundland, 1973; One Who Became Lost, 1976; The Killing Room, 1977; Third Child: Zian, 1978: The Book of Glass, 1978; Sleeping with Lambs, 1980; Giving Back Diamonds, 1982; The Sunday before Winter, 1984; Anyone Can See I Love You, 1987; Grandfather Was a Soldier, 1987; Calling All the World, 1989; Love as It Is, 1993; Autobiography, 1996; Human Bodies, New & Selected Poems 1987-1999; The Alchemy of Happiness, 2003. NOVELS: The Visitors Have All Returned, 1979; To All Appearances a Lady, 1989; Visible Worlds, 1997; Cat's Pilgrimage, 2004. EDITOR: (with D.A. Day) Many Voices: An Anthology of Contemporary Canadian Indian Poetry, 1977. **Address:** c/o The Writers' Union of Canada, 40 Wellington St. E, 3rd Floor, Toronto, ON, Canada M5E 1C7. **Online address:** bowerinm@mala.bc.ca

BOWERS, Jane Palatini. American, b. 1945. **Genres:** Literary criticism and history. **Career:** University of California, Davis, lecturer in English, 1981-87; John Jay College of Criminal Justice of the City University of New York, NYC, faculty member, 1987-93, professor of English, 1993-. University of Florence, visiting professor, 1986. **Publications:** "They Watch Me as They Watch This": Gertrude Stein's Metadrama, 1991; Women Writers: Gertrude Stein, 1993. Work represented in anthologies. Contributor to academic journals. **Address:** Department of English, John Jay College of Criminal Justice, 445 West 59th St., New York, NY 10019-1104, U.S.A.

BOWERS, Janice Emily. American, b. 1950. **Genres:** Botany, Horticulture, Essays. **Career:** University of Arizona, Tucson, research assistant and coordinator, 1976-82; U.S. Geological Survey, Tucson, hydrological assistant and botanist, 1982-. **Publications:** Seasons of the Wind: A Naturalist's Look at the Plant Life of Southwestern Sand Dunes, 1986; One Hundred Roadside Wildflowers of Southwest Woodlands, 1987; A Sense of Place: The Life and Work of Forrest Shreve, 1988; Chiricahua National Monument, 1988; One Hundred Desert Wildflowers of the Southwest, 1989; The Mountains Next Door, 1991; Shrubs and Trees of the Southwest Deserts, 1993; A Full Life in a Small Place and Other Essays from a Desert Garden, 1993; Fear Falls Away and Other Essays from Hard and Rocky Places, 1997; The Desert, 2000. **Address:** PO Box 86205, Tucson, AZ 85754, U.S.A.

BOWERS, John. American, b. 1928. **Genres:** Novels, Autobiography/Memoirs, Biography, Local history/Rural topics. **Career:** Columbia University, Faculty. **Publications:** The Colony (autobiography), 1971; The Golden Bowers, 1971; No More Reunions (novel), 1973; Helene, 1979; In the Land of Nyx, 1984; Stonewall Jackson: Portrait of a Soldier, 1989; Chic Kamauga and Chattanooga: The Battles that Doomed the Confedercy, 1994. **Address:** c/o Georges Borchardt Inc, 136 E. 57th St, New York, NY 10022, U.S.A.

BOWERS, Terrell L. American, b. 1945. **Genres:** Westerns/Adventure. **Career:** City Market Stores, Delta, CO, clerk, 1966-70; Safeway Stores, Inc., Glenwood Springs, CO, grocery dept. manager, 1970-74; Bold Petroleum, Grand Junction, CO, store/station manager, 1975-81; Desert Gateway, Mack, CO, store owner, 1981-85; Questar, dispatcher 1985-98; Mountain Fuel Supply, Salt Lake City, UT, meter setter, 1985-; Post Office, 1999-2000. **Publications:** Noose at Big Iron, 1979; A Man Called Banker, 1980; Rio Grande Death Ride, 1980; Crossfire at Twin Forks, 1980; Gunfire at Flintlock, 1981; Frozen Trail, 1981; Last Stand at Rio Blanco, 1981; Banyon's War, 1982; Chase into Mexico, 1982; Avery's Vengeance, 1982; Maverick Raid, 1982; The Fighting Peacemaker, 1983; Death at Devil's Gap, 1983; The Fighting McBride, 1983; Gold Trail, 1983; Dakota Bullets, 1984; Job for a Gunman, 1984; Sinclair's Double War, 1984; Culhane's Code, 1984; Deadly Bounty, 1985; Blood Vengeance, 1985; Banshee Raiders, 1985; The Masked Cowpoke, 1985; Skull Mountain Bandit, 1985; Vendetta, 1985; The Fighting Lucanes, 1986; Cheyenne Brothers, 1986; Trail to Justice, 1986; Petticoat War, 1986; Armageddon at Gold Butte, 1986; Delryan's Draw, 1986; Destiny's Trail, 1987; Lassito's Last War, 1987; The Railroad War, 1988; Black Cloud over Gunstock, 1988; Iron Claw's Revenge, 1988; The Shadow Killer, 1989; Justice at Black Water, 1990; Doctor Totes a Six-Gun, 1990; Tanner's Last Chance, 1990; Winter Vendetta, 1991; Secret of Snake Canyon, 1993; Ride against the Wind, 1996; Noose at Sundown, 1997; Trap at Broken Spoke, 1998; Gun Law at Broken Spoke, 1998; Crossfire at Broken Spoke, 1998; Destiny at Broken Spoke, 1998; Yancy's Luck, 2002; Battle at Lost Mesa, 2002; Mystery at Gold Vista, 2002; A Man Called Sundown, 2003; The Shadow Killers, 2003; Spenser's Law, 2003; The Guns at Three Forks, 2004; The Last Revenge, 2004. **Address:** PO Box 651, West Jordan, UT 84084, U.S.A.

BOWIE, Andrew (S.). British, b. 1952. **Genres:** Philosophy, Music, Literary criticism and history. **Career:** Free University of Berlin, Berlin, Germany, visiting scholar, 1976-80, instructor in aesthetics, 1980-81; Anglia Polytechnic University, Cambridge, England, professor, philosophy, 1981-99; University of London, Royal Holloway, professor of German, 1999-; writer; professional jazz musician. **Publications:** Aesthetics and Subjectivity: From Kant to Nietzsche, 1990; (trans. and author of intro.) F.W.J. Schelling, Lectures on the History of Modern Philosophy, 1993; Schelling and Modern European Philosophy: An Introduction, 1993; From Romanticism to Critical Theory. The Philosophy of German Literary Theory, 1997. EDITOR: (and author of intro.) Manfred Frank, The Subject & the Text, 1998; (and trans.) F.D.E. Schleiermacher, Hermeutics and Criticism and Other Texts, 1998. **Address:** Department of German, Royal Holloway, University of London, London, Egham, Surrey, England. **Online address:** a.bowie@rhul.ac.uk

BOWKER, Gordon. British, b. 1934. **Genres:** Literary criticism and history. **Career:** Biographer, literary critic, freelance journalist. Goldsmiths' College, University of London, teacher, 1966-91. Author of scripts for educational television and radio, 1966-75. **Publications:** The Lighthouse Invites the Storm (radio tribute), 1984; Pursued by Furies: A Life of Malcolm Lowry, 1993; Through the Dark Labyrinth: A Biography of Lawrence Durrell, 1996; (author of intro.) M. Lowry, Hear Us O Lord from Heaven Thy Dwelling Place, 2000; George Orwell, 2003. EDITOR: Under Twenty (anthology), 1966; Freedom: Reason or Revolution (anthology), 1970; Malcolm Lowry Remembered, 1985; M. Lowry, Malcolm Lowry: Under the Volcano, 1988; (with P. Tiessen) Apparently Incongruous Parts: The Worlds of Malcolm Lowry, 1990. **Address:** c/o Anthony Goff, David Higham Associates, 5-8 Lower John St, London W12 4HA, England.

BOWKETT, Stephen. Also writes as Ben Leech. Welsh, b. 1953. **Genres:** Novels, Plays/Screenplays, Novellas/Short stories, Horror, Poetry, Science fiction/Fantasy, Children's fiction, Education. **Career:** Lutterworth High School, Leicestershire, England, teacher, 1976-94; writer. Conductor of creative thinking workshops for children. **Publications:** Spellbinder, 1985; The Copy Cat Plan (two plays), 1986; Gameplayers, 1986; Dualists, 1987; Catch and Other Stories, 1988; Frontiersville High, 1990; The Community, 1993; The Bidden, 1994. **Address:** c/o Sheila Watson, Watson, Little Ltd, Capo Dimonte, Windmill Hill, London NW3 6RJ, England. **Online address:** steve@sbowkett.freeserve.co.uk

BOWLBY, Rachel. British, b. 1957. **Genres:** Literary criticism and history, Women's studies and issues. **Career:** Sussex University, Brighton, East Sussex, England, lecturer in English, 1984-93, professor of English, 1994-97; Oxford University, professor of English, 1997-99; York University, professor of English and French, 1999-. **Publications:** Just Looking, 1985; Virginia Woolf: Feminist Destinations, 1988; Still Crazy After All These Years, 1992; Shopping with Freud, 1993; Feminist Destinations and Further Essays on Virginia Woolf, 1997; Carried Away: The Invention of Modern Shopping, 2000. **Address:** Dept of English, York University, York YO10 5DD, England. **Online address:** rachel.bowlby@york.ac.uk

BOWLER, Tim. British, b. 1953. **Genres:** Science fiction/Fantasy. **Career:** Worked in the forestry and timber trade; seven years as a teacher of foreign languages and of English as a second language, ending as head of modern languages at a school in Newton Abbot, Devon, England; full-time freelancer, translator, and writer, 1990-. **Publications:** Midget, 1994; Dragon's Rock, 1995; River Boy, 1997; Shadows, 1999; Storm Catchers, 2001. Contributor to books. **Address:** c/o Caroline Walsh, David Hingham Associates Ltd., 5-8 Lower John Street, Golden Square, London W1R 4HA, England.

BOWLES, Samuel. American, b. 1939. **Genres:** Education, Economics. **Career:** Economist and writer. Harvard University, Cambridge, MA, assistant professor of economics, 1965-71, associate professor 1971-74; University of Massachusetts at Amherst, professor of economics, 1974-, chair of Department of Economics, 2000, then professor emeritus; Santa Fe Institute, Santa Fe, NM, research associate, 2000-; Research Network on Effects of Inequality on Economic Performance, founder and co-director, 1993-. Visiting professor, University of Siena, 1982-. Has worked as a musician, a high school teacher in Nigeria, and a participant in the civil rights movement. **Publications:** Planning Educational Systems for Economic Growth, 1969; (with others) Notes and Problems in Microeconomic Theory, 1970; (with H. Gintis) Schooling in Capitalist America: Educational Reform and the Contradictions of Economic Life, 1976; (with D.M. Gordon and T.E. Weisskopf) Beyond the Waste Land: A Democratic Alternative to Economic Decline, 1983; (with R. Edwards) Understanding Capitalism: Competition, Command, and Change in the U.S. Economy, 1985; (with H. Gintis) Democracy and Capitalism: Property, Community, and the Contradictions of Modern Social Thought, 1986; (with H. Gintis) Recasting Egalitarianism: New Rules for Communities, States, and Markets, 1989; (with D.M. Gordon

and T.E. Weisskopf) After the Waste Land: A Democratic Economics for the Year 2000, 1990; Microeconomics: Behavior, Institutions, and Evolution, 2003. EDITOR: (with H.B. Chenery) Studies in Development Planning, 1971; (with R. Edwards and W.G. Shepherd) Unconventional Wisdom: Essays on Economics in Honor of John Kenneth Galbraith, 1989; (with R.Edwards) Radical Political Economy, 1990; (with H. Gintis and B. Gustafsson) Markets and Democracy: Participation, Accountability, and Efficiency, 1993; (with T.E. Weisskopf) D.M. Gordon, Economics and Social Justice: Essays on Power, Labor, and Institutional Change, 1998; (with M. Franzini and U. Pagano), The Politics and Economics of Power, 1999; (with K. Arrow and S. Durlauf) Meritocracy and Economic Inequality, 2000. Contributor to periodicals and journals. **Address:** Santa Fe Institute, 1399 Hyde Park Rd., Santa Fe, NM 87501, U.S.A. **Online address:** bowles@santafe.edu

BOWLEY, Rex Lyon. British, b. 1925. **Genres:** Education, History, Local history/Rural topics, Theology/Religion, Travel/Exploration. **Career:** Boarding Housemaster, Reading School, 1960-70; Sr. History Master and Housemaster, Bancroft's School, Essex, 1970-85. **Publications:** Tresco: The Standard Guidebook to the Isle of Tresco, 1970; Teaching without Tears: A Guide to Teaching Technique, 4th ed., 1973; Scillonian Quiz-Book, 1974; Readings for Assembly, 1976; The Fortunate Islands: The Story of the Isles of Scilly, 8th ed., 1996, 9th ed., 2004; The Study: The Story of a Wimbledon Girls' School, 1996; The Isles of Scilly Standard Guidebook, 52nd ed., 1998, 55th ed., 2004; Scilly at War, 2002. **Address:** 15 Penlee Manor Dr, Penzance, Cornwall TR18 4HW, England.

BOWLING, Lewis. (born United States), b. 1959. **Genres:** History. **Career:** North Carolina Central University, Durham, NC, teacher of physical education, 1996-. Aerobics and Fitness Association of America, personal trainer certification examiner, 1999-. **Publications:** (with others) Lifetime Physical Fitness, 1999; Granville County: Images of America, 2002; Resistance Training: The Total Approach, 2003; Granville County Revisited, 2003. Fitness columnist. **Address:** 1735 Bowling Rd., Stem, NC 27581, U.S.A. **Online address:** lewis_bowling@yahoo.com

BOWLT, John E(llis). British, b. 1943. **Genres:** Art/Art history, Translations. **Career:** University of St. Andrews, Scotland, lecturer in Russian, 1968-69; University of Kansas, Lawrence, assistant professor of Russian, 1970-71; University of Texas at Austin, associate professor, 1971-81, professor of Russian, 1981-, director of Institute of Modern Russian Culture, 1979-; affiliated with University of Southern California, Los Angeles. Research fellow at National Humanities Institute, Yale University, 1977-78; consultant to Metropolitan Museum of Art, M. H. de Young Museum, and Thames & Hudson Ltd. **Publications:** (ed. with S. Bann) Russian Formalism, 1973; Russian Art, 1785-1975: A Collection of Essays, 1976; (ed. and trans.) Russian Art of the Avant Garde: Theory and Criticism, 1902-1934, 1976, 2nd ed., 1988; Stage Designs and the Russian Avant Garde, 1911-1929, 1976; (ed.) Benedikt Livshits, 1977; (ed. and trans.) B. Livshits, The One-and-a-Half-Eyed Archer, 1977; (with D.V. Sarabianov) Russian and Soviet Painting, 1977; Russian Theater and Costume Design from the Fine Arts Museums of San Francisco, 1979; (trans.) V. Krasovskaya, Nijinsky, 1979; (trans.) E.S. Sizov, Treasures from the Kremlin, 1979; Journey into Non-Objectivity, 1980; The Silver Age: Russian Art of the Early Twentieth Century and the "World of Art" Group, 1980, 2nd ed., 1982. (ed. with R.C. Washton Long and trans.) The Life of Vasilii Kandinsky in Russian Art, 1982, 2nd ed., 1984; Russian Stage Design: Scenic Innovation, 1900-1930, 1982; (ed. with N. Misler) Pavel Filonov: A Hero and His Fate, Collected Writings on Art and Revolution, 1910-40, 1983; (with A.E. Senn and D. Straskevicius) Mikalojus Konstantinas Ciurlionis: Music of the Spheres, 1986, (ed. and author of intro.) A. Lavrentiev, Varvara Stepanova: The Complete Work, 1988; (ed. with V. Misiano) Ten Plus Ten: Contemporary Soviet and American Painters, 1989; (with O. Matich) Laboratory of Dreams: The Russian Avant-Garde and Cultural Experiment, 1990; (with N. Misler): Russian and East European Painting in the Thyssen-Bornemisza Collection, 1993; Artists of the Russian Theater, Vol. 2, 1994; The Salon Album of Vera Sudeikin-Stravinsky, 1995; The Uncommon Vision of Sergei Konenkov, 2001. **Address:** University of Southern California, Department of Slavic Languages, University Park, Box 4353, Los Angeles, CA 90089-4353, U.S.A.

BOWMAN, Lady Christian. Also writes as Christian Miller. British, b. 1920. **Genres:** Novels, Travel/Exploration, Autobiography/Memoirs. **Career:** Technical Adviser to Ministry of Production, 1939-45; Racehorse breeder, 1952-92. **Publications:** AS CHRISTIAN MILLER: The Champagne Sandwich, 1969; Daisy, Daisy, 1980; A Childhood in Scotland, 1981. **Address:** The Walled Garden, Chamberlain Street, Wells, Somerset BA5 2PE, England.

BOWMAN, Crystal. American, b. 1951. **Genres:** Children's fiction, Songs/Lyrics and libretti. **Career:** Early childhood educator in Ann Arbor, MI, and (also director) Grand Rapids, MI; mathematics tutor for public schools in Holland, MI; FJH Music Co., children's lyricist, 1990-. Conducts poetry workshops. **Publications:** JUVENILES: Cracks in the Sidewalk (poems), 1993, rev. ed., 2001; Ivan and the Dynamos, 1997; If Peas Could Taste like Candy (poems), 1998; Windmills and Wooden Shoes, 1999; The M.O.P.S. series, 1999-2002; My ABC Bible/My ABC Prayers, 2001; Dinosaur Stomp, 2003. Author of lyrics for children's songs. ADULT NON-FICTION: Meditations for Moms, 2001. **Address:** 45 Lakeside Dr SE, Grand Rapids, MI 49506, U.S.A. **Online address:** bowmanmi@netscape.net

BOWMAN, David. American (born Greece), b. 1957. **Genres:** Novels, Novellas/Short stories, Mystery/Crime/Suspense, Children's fiction, Plays/Screenplays, Adult non-fiction, Film, History, Information science/Computers, Institutions/Organizations, Music, Literary criticism and history, Social commentary, Writing/Journalism, Young adult non-fiction. **Career:** Strand Bookstore, NYC, staff member, 1976-78; Scholastic Inc, NYC, editor, 1979-83; Holt, Rinehart & Winston, project editor, 1987-89; Sony Wonder, NYC, designer, 1993-94. **Publications:** NOVELS: Let the Dog Drive, 1993; Bunny Modern, 1998. **Address:** 60 East Fourth St. #15, New York, NY 10003, U.S.A.

BOWMAN, J. Wilson. American. **Genres:** Cultural/Ethnic topics, Education, Gerontology/Senior issues, How-to books. **Career:** Merritt College, Oakland, CA, professor and department head; Diablo Valley College, Pleasant Hill, CA, dean; Compton College, Compton, CA, dean and assistant superintendent; Mars Hill College, Mars Hill, NC, professor; R.J. Enterprises (consultant and publisher), president; national public speaker. Black Women Leadership Institute, co-founder. **Publications:** America's Black Colleges, 1992; America's Black and Tribal Colleges, 1996. **Address:** PO Box 1034, Skyland, NC 28776, U.S.A. **Online address:** rjeanc@earthlink.net

BOWN, Deni. British, b. 1944. **Genres:** Homes/Gardens, Horticulture, Natural history, Botany. **Career:** Laurence Urdang Associates, Aylesbury, England, etymologist, 1972-77; Newbury College, Newbury, England, lecturer, 1982-84; The Herb Society, chairman, 1997-; Norfolk, England, writer and photographer; Photo library, consultant editor. **Publications:** AUTHOR AND PHOTOGRAPHER: Aroids: Plants of the Arum Family, 1988, rev. ed., 2000; Fine Herbs, 1988, as Ornamental Herbs for Your Garden, 1993; Alba: The Book of White Flowers, 1989; Through the Seasons (juvenile), 6 vols including Pond, Stream, Wood, Park, Garden, and Field and Hedgerow, 1989; Westonbirt Arboretum, 1990; Orchids, 1991; Four Gardens in One: The Royal Botanic Garden, Edinburgh, 1992; The Encyclopedia of Herbs and Their Uses, 1995; Growing Herbs, 1995; Garden Herbs, 1998. Contributor to books. **Address:** Yaxham Park, Yaxham NF, England. **Online address:** DeniBown@aol.com

BOWNESS, Alan. British, b. 1928. **Genres:** Art/Art history. **Career:** University of London, Courtauld Institute of Art, London, England, lecturer, 1957-, reader, 1967-, professor of art history, 1978-79; Tate Gallery, London, director, 1980-88; Henry Moore Foundation, Hertfordshire, England, director. **Publications:** Henry Moore: Complete Sculpture, six volumes, 1965-88; Modern Sculpture, 1967; Barbara Hepworth: Complete Sculpture, 1960-69, 1971; Modern European Art, 1972; Ivon Hitchens, 1973; The Condition of Success, 1989. **Address:** 91 Castelnau, London SWI3 9EL, England.

BOWSER, Benjamin P(aul). American, b. 1946. **Genres:** Race relations, Sociology. **Career:** Cornell University, Ithaca, NY, assistant dean of Graduate School, 1975-82; Western Interstate Commission for Higher Education, director of Minority Education Office, 1982-83; University of Santa Clara, CA, director of Office of Black Student Affairs, 1983-85; Stanford University, CA, assistant to the director of information technology services, 1985-87; California State University, Hayward, associate professor, 1987-94, professor of sociology and social services, 1994-. Indiana University of Pennsylvania, visiting research scholar, 1984; University of California, San Francisco, associate research scientist, Treatment Research Unit, Substance Abuse Services, 1990-91; Bayview Hunter's Point Community Foundation, director of multicultural inquiry and research on AIDS, 1990-91. **Publications:** (with G. Auletta and T. Jones) Dealing with Diversity in the University, 1993. EDITOR: (with E. Mann and M. Oling) Census Data with Maps for Small Areas of NYC, 1910-1960, 1981; (with R. Hunt) Impacts of Racism on White Americans, 1981, 2nd ed., 1995; Black Male Adolescents: Parenting and Education in Community Context, 1991; (with T. Jones and G. Auletta) Toward the Multicultural University, 1995; Racism and Anti-Racism in World Perspective, 1995; (with L. Kushnick) Against the Odds: Scholars Who Challenged Racism in the 20th Century, 2002. Contributor to books

and academic journals. **Address:** Department of Sociology and Social Services, California State University, 25800 Carlos Bee Blvd, Hayward, CA 94542, U.S.A. **Online address:** bbowser@csuhayward.edu

BOWYER, Mathew Justice. American, b. 1926. **Genres:** Novels, Novellas/Short stories, Romance/Historical, Westerns/Adventure, Children's fiction, Antiques/Furnishings, Business/Trade/Industry, Children's non-fiction, Food and Wine, History, Information science/Computers, Local history/Rural topics, Bibliography, Essays, Humor/Satire, Ghost Writer. **Career:** Realtor, ghostwriter. **Publications:** They Carried the Mail: A Survey of Postal History and Hobbies, 1972; Collecting Americana, 1977; Encyclopedia of Mystical Terminology, 1979; Real Estate Investor's Desk Encyclopedia, 1982; Gen. Geo. Washington's Great Secret, 1998; Return to Memory, 1999; St. Elmo's Fire, 1999; The Post Office Delivers: Humor, 1999; Love on the Bridge, 2000; George Washington's Boy, 2001; A Generation Apart, 2003. **Address:** 3504 Pinnacle Dr, Roanoke, VA 24012, U.S.A. **Online address:** MatBowyer@matbowyerbooks.com

BOX, Edgar. See VIDAL, Gore.

BOXER, Arabella. British, b. 1934. **Genres:** Food and Wine, Travel/Exploration. **Career:** Contributor, Sunday Times Magazine, London. Food Correspondent, Vogue mag., London, 1965-67, and 1975-91. **Publications:** First Slice Your Cookbook, 1964; A Second Slice, 1966; Garden Cookbook, 1974; The Vogue Summer and Winter Cookbook, 1980; Mediterranean Cookbook, 1981; Wind in the Willows Country Cookbook, 1983; Sunday Times Complete Cookbook, 1983; Book of English Food, 1991; (with T. Traeger) A Visual Feast, 1991; The Hamlyn Herb Book, 1996; The Hamlyn Spice Book, 1997; The New First Slice Your Cookbook, 1998. **Address:** 44 Elm Park Rd, London SW3 6AX, England.

BOYD, Blanche McCrary. American, b. 1945. **Genres:** Novels, Essays. **Career:** Educator and writer. Connecticut College, New London, teacher of creative writing. **Publications:** NOVELS: Nerves, 1973; Mourning the Death of Magic, 1977; The Revolution of Little Girls, 1991. NONFICTION: The Redneck Way of Knowledge: Down-Home Tales (essays), 1981. Contributor to periodicals. **Address:** Connecticut College, PO Box 5421, 270 Mohegan Ave., New London, CT 06320, U.S.A.

BOYD, Brian (David). New Zealander (born Northern Ireland), b. 1952. **Genres:** Literary criticism and history, Biography. **Career:** Victoria University, Wellington, New Zealand, junior lecturer, 1974; University of Auckland, New Zealand, postdoctoral fellow, 1979-80, lecturer, 1980-85, senior lecturer, 1986-91, associate professor, 1992-98, professor, 1998-2001, University Distinguished Professor, 2001-. Universite de Nice-Sophia Antipolis, visiting professor, 1994-95; Nabokov Museum, visiting professor, 2002. **Publications:** Nabokov's Ada: The Place of Consciousness (criticism), 1985, 2nd ed., 2001; Vladimir Nabokov: The Russian Years (biography), 1990; Vladimir Nabokov: The American Years (biography), 1991; (ed.) Nabokov: Novels and Memoirs, 1941-1951, 1996; Nabokov: Novels 1955-1962, 1996; Nabokov: Novels 1969-1974, 1996; The Presents of the Past: Literature in English before 1900 (anthology/textbook), 1998; Nabokov's Pale Fire: The Magic of Artistic Discovery, 1999; (ed. with R.M. Pyle) Nabokov's Butterflies, 2000. Contributor to periodicals. **Address:** Department of English, University of Auckland, Private Bag 92019, Auckland 1, New Zealand.

BOYD, Candy Dawson. American, b. 1946. **Genres:** Children's fiction. **Career:** Overton Elementary School, Chicago, IL, teacher, 1968-71; Longfellow School, Berkeley, CA, teacher, 1971-73; University of California, Berkeley, extension instructor in the language arts, 1972-79; Berkeley Unified School District, Berkeley, district teacher trainer in reading and communication skills, 1973-76; St. Mary's College of California, Morgana, extension instructor in language arts, 1972-79, lecturer, 1975, assistant professor and director of reading leadership and teacher effectiveness programs, 1976-87, director of elementary education, 1983-88, tenured associate professor, 1983-91, professor of education, 1991-; writer. **Publications:** Circle of Gold, Scholastic, 1984; Breadsticks and Blessing Places, Macmillan, 1985, published as Forever Friends, Viking, 1986; Charlie Pippin, Macmillan, 1987; Chevrolet Saturday, Macmillan, 1992; Fall Secrets, Puffin, 1994; Daddy, Daddy Be There, Philomel, 1995. Also contributor of articles and essays to professional journals. Reviewer of children's literature for the Los Angeles Times and San Francisco Chronicle. **Address:** St. Mary's College of California, School of Education, Box 4350, Moraga, CA 94575, U.S.A. **Online address:** cboyd@stmarys-ca.edu

BOYD, Carl. American, b. 1936. **Genres:** History, International relations/Current affairs, Military/Defense/Arms control. **Career:** Ohio State

University, Columbus, instructor to assistant professor of history, 1969-75; Old Dominion University, Norfolk, VA, assistant professor to associate professor, 1975-85, professor of history, 1985-2001, university eminent scholar, director of graduate program in history, 1991-94, Louis I. Jaffe Professor, 1995-2001, eminent scholar emeritus and Louis I. Jaffe Emeritus Professor, 2001-. Visiting scholar at universities and institutions worldwide. Fulbright scholar, Poland, 1999-2000. **Publications:** The Extraordinary Envoy: General Hiroshi Oshima and Diplomacy in the Third Reich, 1934-1939, 1980; Hitler's Japanese Confidant: General Oshima Hiroshi and MAGIC Intelligence From Berlin, 1941-1945, 1993; The Japanese Submarine Force and World War II, 1995; American Command of the Sea through Carriers, Codes, and the Silent Service: World War II and Beyond, 1995. Work represented in anthologies. Contributor of articles and reviews to history and military studies journals. **Address:** 1229 Rockbridge Ave, Norfolk, VA 23520, U.S.A. **Online address:** CBoyd31480@aol.com

BOYD, Claude E. American, b. 1939. **Genres:** Environmental sciences/ Ecology. **Career:** University of Georgia, Athens, faculty member, 1969-71; Auburn University, Auburn, AL, professor, 1971-. **Publications:** Water Quality Management in Pond Aquaculture, 1982, rev. ed., 1998; Hydrology and Water Supply for Pond Aquaculture, 1994; Bottom Soils, Sediment and Pond Aquaculture, 1995; Water Quality, 2000. **Address:** Dept of Fisheries and Allied Aquacultures, Auburn University, Auburn, AL 36849, U.S.A. **Online address:** ceboyd@acesag.auburn.edu

BOYD, Donna. *See* **BALL, Donna.**

BOYD, Malcolm. American, b. 1923. **Genres:** Novellas/Short stories, Civil liberties/Human rights, Gay and lesbian issues, Race relations, Sex, Theology/ Religion, Autobiography/Memoirs. **Career:** Episcopal priest, 1955-. Yale University, Calhoun College, New Haven, CT, associate fellow, 1971-; St. Augustine-by-the-Sea Episcopal Church, Santa Monica, CA, writer priest-in-residence, 1980-96; Modern Maturity mag., columnist, 1990-2000; Episcopal Cathedral Center of Los Angeles, poet-in-residence, 1996-; Honorary Canon of Cathedral, 2002. PEN Center USA West, president, 1984-87. **Publications:** Crisis in Communication, 1957; Christ and Celebrity Gods, 1958; Focus, 1960; If I Go Down to Hell, 1962; The Hunger, The Thirst, 1964; Are You Running with Me Jesus?, 1965, rev. ed., 1990; Free to Live, Free to Die, 1967; Malcolm Boyd's Book of Days, 1968; The Fantasy Worlds of Peter Stone, 1969; As I Live and Breathe, 1969; My Fellow Americans, 1970; Human Like Me, Jesus, 1971; The Lover, 1972; (with P. Conrad) When in the Course of Human Events, 1973; The Runner, 1974; The Alleluia Affair, 1975; Christian: Its Meaning in an Age of Future Shock, 1975; Am I Running with You, God?, 1977; Take Off the Masks, 1978, rev. ed., 1993; Look Back in Joy, 1981, rev. ed., 1990; Half Laughing, Half Crying, 1986; Gay Priest, 1986; Edges, Boundaries, and Connections, 1992; Rich with Years, 1993; Go Gentle into That Good Night, 1998; Running with Jesus, 2000; Simple Grace, 2001; Prayers for the Later Years, 2002. EDITOR: On the Battle Lines, 1964; The Underground Church, 1968; (with N. Wilson) Amazing Grace: Stories of Lesbian and Gay Faith, 1991; (with C. Talton) Race and Prayer, 2003; (with J.J. Bruno) In Times Like These, 2005. **Address:** PO Box 512164, Los Angeles, CA 90051-2145, U.S.A.

BOYD, Nan Alamilla. American. **Genres:** History. **Career:** Writer. University of Colorado, Boulder, assistant professor of women's studies, 1999-2003; Sonoma State University, assistant professor, 2003-. **Publications:** Wide-Open Town: A History of Queer San Francisco to 1965, 2003. **Address:** 1801 E. Colati Ave., 51 Rachel Carson Hall, Rohnert Park, CA 94928, U.S.A. **Online address:** nan.alamilla.boyd@sonoma.edu

BOYD, Steven R(ay). American, b. 1946. **Genres:** History. **Career:** St. Olaf College, Northfield, MN, instructor, 1974-75; University of Texas at San Antonio, assistant professor, 1975-81, associate professor, 1981-94, professor of history, 1994-. **Publications:** The Politics of Opposition: Antifederalists and the Acceptance of the Constitution, 1979; (ed.) The Whiskey Rebellion: Past and Present Perspectives, 1985; The Constitution in State Politics: From the Calling of the Constitutional Convention to the Calling of the First Federal Elections, 1990; (ed.) Alternative Constitutions for the United States: A Documentary History, 1992. Contributor to books and periodicals. **Address:** Dept of History, University of Texas at San Antonio, San Antonio, TX 78249, U.S.A.

BOYER, Jay. American, b. 1947. **Genres:** Novels, Biography. **Career:** Arizona State University, Tempe, faculty member, 1976-, currently professor of English and chairperson of Film Studies Program. **Publications:** Richard Brautigan, 1987; As Far Away as China (novel), 1989; Ishmael Reed, 1993; Sidney Lumet, 1993; Bob Rafelson, 1996; Three Plays and a Bed, 2001;

Heartbeats, 2001; Making Out, 2001; Take It and Leave, 2001; The Third Planet from the Sun, 2001; Five Jewish Biker Chics, Out of Control, 2001; Wollicott's Traveling Rabbit's Foot Minstrels, 2002; Time Went By, But Slowly, 2002; Three New Plays, 2002; Urban/Rural, 2002; Six Tony Women, Shopping for Shoes, 2002; The Euripideads, 2002; Poaching Deer in Northern Arizona, 2002; Dancing My Mother to Sleep, 2002; Awkward Pauses, 2003. Contributor to periodicals. **Address:** Department of English, Language and Literature Bldg Rm B-504, Arizona State University, Tempe, AZ 85287-0302, U.S.A. **Online address:** j.boyer@asu.edu

BOYER, Rick. (Richard Lewis Boyer). American, b. 1943. **Genres:** Mystery/Crime/Suspense, Anthropology/Ethnology, Travel/Exploration. **Career:** New Trier Township High School, English teacher, 1968-70; Little Brown and Co., Boston, text book representative, 1971-73, acquisitions editor, 1973-78; Places Rated Partnership, Asheville, NC, founding partner, 1978-; Western Carolina University, Cullowhee, NC, writer-in-residence, 1988-. Recipient: Edgar Allan Poe Award, Mystery Writers of America, 1982. **Publications:** NOVELS: The Giant Rat of Sumatra, 1976; Billingsate Shoal, 1982; The Penny Ferry, 1984; The Daisy Ducks, 1986; Moscow Metal, 1987; The Whale's Footprints, 1988; Gone to Earth, 1990; Yellow Bird, 1991; Pirate Trade, 1995; The Man Who Whispered, 1998; A Sherlockian Quartet, 1998; Buck Gentry, forthcoming. NONFICTION: (with D. Savageau) Places Rated Almanac, 1981; Mzengu Mfinga (memoir), 2004. **Address:** Dept. of English, Western Carolina University, Cullowhee, NC 28723, U.S.A. **Online address:** boyer@wcu.edu

BOYERS, Robert. American, b. 1942. **Genres:** Literary criticism and history, Novellas/Short stories. **Career:** Tisch Professor of Arts & Letters, Professor of English, and Ed. of Salmagundi mag., Skidmore Coll., Saratoga Springs, New York, since 1969 (founded Salmagundi, Flushing, New York, 1965). Taught at the New School for Social Research, NYC, Fall 1967, Baruch School of the City University of New York, 1967-68, and Sullivan County Community Coll., 1968-69; Bennington Review, editor, 1977-83. **Publications:** (ed. with M. London) Robert Lowell: A Portrait of the Artist in His Time, 1970; (ed. with Robert Orrill) R. D. Laing and Anti-Psychiatry, 1971; (ed.) The Legacy of the German Refugee Intellectuals, 1972; (ed. with Robert Orrill) Psychological Man: Approaches to an Emergent Social Type, 1975; (ed.) Contemporary Poetry in America, 1975; Excursions: Selected Literary Essays of Robert Boyers, 1976; Lionel Trilling: Negative Capability and the Wisdom of Avoidance, 1977; F. R. Leavis: Judgment and The Discipline of Thought, 1978; R. P. Blackmur: Poet-Critic, 1980; (ed. with P. Boyers) The Salmagundi Reader, 1983, as The New Salmagundi Reader, 1996; Atrocity and Amnesia: The Political Novel since 1945, 1985; After the Avant-Garde: Essays on Art and Culture, 1987. **Address:** English Dept, Skidmore Coll, Saratoga Springs, NY 12866, U.S.A.

BOYES, Vivien (Elizabeth). British, b. 1952. **Genres:** Children's fiction, Poetry. **Career:** British Broadcasting Corp., London, England, radio studio manager, 1974-79, technical instructor, 1979-82; freelance writer, broadcast training instructor, and sound operator, 1982-. St. John's Primary School, governor, 1989-98. **Publications:** The Druid's Head, 1997; Science Scope (episode script). Contributor to periodicals. Poems have been broadcast on radio programs.

BOYETT, Jimmie T. American, b. 1948. **Genres:** Administration/ Management. **Career:** Management and systems analyst for federal agencies in Washington, DC, 1976-80; Tarkenton Software, Atlanta, GA, account executive, 1982-85; Bank South N.A., Atlanta, assistant vice president, 1985-90; consultant and writer. **Publications:** (with J.H. Boyett) Beyond Workplace 2000, 1995; (with J.H. Boyett) The Guru Guide, 1998. **Address:** 125 Stepping Stone Ln., Alpharetta, GA 30004, U.S.A. **Online address:** jimmie@jboyett.com; www.jboyett.com

BOYETT, Joseph H. American, b. 1945. **Genres:** Administration/ Management, Business/Trade/Industry. **Career:** Tarkenton, Conn & Co., Atlanta, GA, vice president and chief administrative officer, 1981-90; A. T. Kearney, Inc., Atlanta, principal, 1990-92, and cofounder of Executive Issues Center of Excellence; Boyett and Associates, Atlanta, cofounder and president, 1992-. **Publications:** Maximum Performance Management, 1988; Workplace 2000, 1991; The Competitive Edge, 1991; The Quality Journey, 1993; (with J.T. Boyett) Beyond Workplace 2000, 1995; (with J.T. Boyett) The Guru Guide, 1998; (with J.T. Boyett) Guru Guide to Entrepreneurship, 2001; (with J.T. Boyett) Guru Guide to the Knowledge Economy, 2001. Author of articles and case studies. **Address:** 125 Stepping Stone Ln, Alpharetta, GA 30004, U.S.A. **Online address:** joe@jboyett.com

BOYKIN, J. Robert III. (born United States), b. 1944. **Genres:** History. **Career:** Boykin Antiques and Appraisals, Inc., Wilson, NC, owner, 1980-.

International Society of Appraisers, certified appraiser of personal property, 1984. Indiana University, instructor in appraisal, 1986-92; public speaker. Wilson-Greene Mental Health Center, vice chair of board of trustees, 1973-2001; Arts Council of Wilson, president, 1973-75; Wilson City Council, council member, 1976-78, 1978-80; Friends of Wilson County Public Library, president, 1979-81; Wilson Historic Properties Commission, chair, 1984-86; Wilson County Chamber of Commerce, member of board of directors, 1997-99, vice president, 1999; Wilson Education Partnership, member of board of directors, 1999-2001. Historic Preservation Foundation of North Carolina, member of board of advisors, 1984-; member of Claims Prevention and Procedures Council, Inc., North Carolina Museum of History, North Carolina Museum of Art, and National Trust for Historic Preservation. **Publications:** 1880 Census of Wilson County, North Carolina, 1984; Marriages of Wilson County, North Carolina, 1855-1899, 1988; Wills of Wilson County, North Carolina, 1855-1899, 1992; Historic Wilson in Vintage Postcards, 2003. Contributor to professional journals. **Address:** 2112 Canal Dr., Appraisals Inc., POB 7440, Wilson, NC 27896, U.S.A. **Online address:** boykinappraisals@coastalnet.com

BOYKIN, Keith. American, b. 1965. **Genres:** Civil liberties/Human rights, Gay and lesbian issues, Race relations. **Career:** Author. Governor Michael Dukakis' presidential campaign, campaign worker, 1988; DeKalb County (GA) Public Schools, high school teacher, 1989; Bryan Cave (law firm), St. Louis, MO, legal intern, 1990; McCutchen, Doyle, Brown, and Enersen (law firm), San Francisco, CA, legal intern, 1991; Patton, Boggs, and Blow (law firm), Washington, DC, legal intern, 1991; Governor Bill Clinton's presidential campaign, campaign worker, 1992; special assistant to the president, 1993-95; National Black Gay and Lesbian Leadership Forum, executive director, 1995-. **Publications:** One More River to Cross, 1996; Respecting the Soul, 1999. Contributor to books. **Address:** PO Box 1229, New York, NY 10037, U.S.A.

BOYLAN, Clare. Irish, b. 1948. **Genres:** Novels, Literary criticism and history, Novellas/Short stories. **Career:** Radio Telefis Eireann, presenter; Dublin Evening Press, reporter, 1968-69, feature writer, 1973-78; Young Woman mag., Dublin, editor, 1969-71; Image mag., Dublin, editor, 1980-84; literary essays and criticism for Sunday Times, Los Angeles Times, Washington Post, Guardian, Independent, Irish Times. **Publications:** NOVELS: Holy Pictures, 1983; Last Resorts, 1984; Black Baby, 1988; Eleven Edward Street, 1992, in U.K. as Home Rule; Room for a Single Lady, 1997; Beloved Stranger, 1999; Emma Brown, 2004. STORIES: A Nail on the Head, 1983; Concerning Virgins, 1989; That Bad Woman, 1995. OTHER: (ed) The Agony and the Ego, 1993; The Literary Companion to CATS (anthology), 1994. **Address:** Rogers, Coleridge and White, 20 Powis Mews, London W11 1JN, England.

BOYLE, David (Courtney). British, b. 1958. **Genres:** Business/Trade/Industry, Economics, Politics/Government, Regional/Urban planning. **Career:** Oxford Star, Oxford, England, arts editor, 1983-85; Town and Country Planning, London, England, editor, 1985-88; Rapide Productions, London, manager, 1988-92; New Economics, editor, 1987-99; Liberal Democrat News, editor, 1992-98; New Economics Foundation, senior associate, 1998-; writer. **Publications:** Building Futures: A Layman's Guide to the Inner City Debate, 1989; (ed.) The New Economics of Information, 1989; What Is New Economics?, 1993; World War II in Photographs, 1998; Funny Money, 1999; Virtual Currencies, 1999; Why London Needs Its Own Currency, 2000; The Tyranny of Numbers, 2001; The Sum of Our Discontent, 2001; Authenticity, 2003. **Address:** 23 Camden Hill Rd, London SE19 1NX, England. **Online address:** davidboyle1958@cs.com

BOYLE, Gerry. American, b. 1956. **Genres:** Novels. **Career:** Rumford Falls Times, Rumford, ME, reporter and editor, 1979; Central Maine Morning Sentinel, Waterville, reporter and editor, 1981-87, columnist, 1987-99. **Publications:** NOVELS: Dead Line, 1993; Bloodline, 1995; Lifeline, 1996; Potshot, 1997; Borderline, 1998; Cover Story, 2000; Pretty Dead, 2003; Home Body, 2004. **Address:** c/o Helen Brann Agency, 94 Curtis St, Bridgewater, CT 06752, U.S.A.

BOYLE, Josephine. British, b. 1935. **Genres:** Mystery/Crime/Suspense, Local history/Rural topics. **Career:** Worked for Augener's Music Publisher and British Broadcasting Corp. Music Library, 1956-59; homemaker, 1960-82; writer, 1984-. **Publications:** NOVELS: A Spectre in the Hall, 1984; Summer Music, 1986; Maiden's End, 1988; Knock, Knock, Who's There?, 1989; Holy Terror, 1993; The Spirit of the Family, 2000. NON-FICTION: Builders of Repute: The Story of Reader Bros., 2002. **Address:** c/o Anne Dewe, Andrew Mann Ltd., 1 Old Compton St, London W1V 5PH, England.

BOYLE, Nicholas. British, b. 1946. **Genres:** Literary criticism and history. **Career:** Cambridge University, England, fellow at Magdalene College,

1968-, reader, 1993-2000, professor of German literary and intellectual history, 2000-; writer. **Publications:** (ed. with M. Swales) Realism in European Literature: Essays in Honor of J. P. Stern, 1986; Goethe, Faust, Part One, 1987; Goethe, the Poet and the Age, Vol. 1: The Poetry of Desire (1749-1790), 1991, Vol. 2: Revolution and Renunciation (1790-1803), 1999; Who Are We Now? Christian Humanism and the Global Market from Hegel to Heaney, 1998. **Address:** Magdalene College, Cambridge University, Cambridge CB3 0AG, England.

BOYLE, Thomas A. American, b. 1922. **Genres:** Information science/Computers, Sciences, Education. **Career:** Fenn College (now Cleveland State University), Cleveland, OH, laboratory instructor in physics, 1942-43; U.S. Naval Academy, Annapolis, MD, instructor in marine engineering, 1945; Lafayette College, Easton, PA, instructor in mechanical engineering, 1947-49; University of Michigan, Ann Arbor, instructor to assistant professor of mechanical engineering, 1949-56; Duke University, Durham, NC, associate professor of mechanical engineering, 1956-67; Purdue University, West Lafayette, IN, associate professor to professor of engineering, 1967-88; retired, 1988. Also taught at Indiana University-Bloomington, South Georgia College, Francis Marion College, Horry-Georgetown Technical College, and Coastal Carolina College, 1989-95. J.G. Hoad and Associates, Ypsilanti, MI, staff engineer, 1966-67. **Publications:** Enough Fortran, 1974, 3rd ed., 1980; Fortran 77 PDQ, 1985, 2nd ed., 1989; Precursory Physical Science, 1997. **Address:** 226 Lander Dr., Conway, SC 29526, U.S.A. **Online address:** tboyle@sccoast.net

BOYM, Svetlana. Russian, b. 1959. **Genres:** Novellas/Short stories, Plays/Screenplays. **Career:** Harvard University, instructor in Slavic and comparative literature, 1984-88, assistant professor of comparative literature and of history and literature (Russian studies), 1988-93, John L. Loeb Associate Professor of Humanities, 1993-; independent filmmaker and writer. Moscow Institute of Contemporary Art, member of advisory board. **Publications:** Flirting with Liberty (screenplay), 1989; The Woman Who Shot Lenin (play), 1990; Death in Quotation Marks: The Cultural Myths of the Modern Poet, 1991; Common Places: Mythologies of Everyday Life in Russia, 1994; The Future of Nostalgia, 2001. Contributor to anthologies and scholarly journals. **Address:** Dept of Slavic Languages & Literatures, Barker Center 311, Harvard University, 12 Quincy St, Cambridge, MA 02138, U.S.A. **Online address:** boym@fas.harvard.edu

BOYNE, Daniel J. American, b. 1959. **Genres:** Recreation. **Career:** Harvard University, Cambridge, MA, instructor, 1986-. Also worked as adult literacy instructor. **Publications:** Essential Sculling, 2000; The Red Rose Crew, 2000. Contributor to periodicals. **Address:** c/o Lane Zachary, Zachary Shuster Agency, 729 Boylston St., Boston, MA 02116, U.S.A. **Online address:** boyne@fas.harvard.edu

BOYNE, Walter J(ames). American, b. 1929. **Genres:** Novels, Air/Space topics, Cultural/Ethnic topics, Military/Defense/Arms control. **Career:** U.S. Air Force Colonel, Command Pilot, 1951-74; National Air and Space Museum, Washington, D.C., director, 1974-86; Flying Network, chairman of the board, 1986-; author, consultant. **Publications:** (ed. with D.S. Lopez) The Jet Age, 1979; Flying: An Introduction to Flight, 1980; Messerschmitt Me 262: An Arrow to the Future, 1980, 1994; Boeing B-52: A Documentary History, 1981, 1994; Aircraft Treasures of Silver Hill, 1982; DeHavilland DH-4: From Flaming Coffin to Living Legend, 1982; Phantom in Combat, 1985, 1994; The Leading Edge, 1986; (with S.L. Thompson) The Wild Blue (novel), 1986; The Smithsonian Book of Flight, 1987; The Smithsonian Book of Flight for Children, 1988; Power behind the Wheel: Creativity and the Evolution of the Automobile, 1988; Trophy for Eagles (novel), 1989; Flight, 1990; Weapons of Desert Storm, 1991; Gulf War, 1991; Eagles at War (novel), 1991; Air Force Eagles (novel), 1992; Classic Aircraft, 1992; Art in Flight, 1992; Silver Wings, the History of the USAF, 1993; Clash of Wings, World War II in the Air, 1994; Clash of Titans, World War II at Sea, 1995; Fly Past, Fly Present, 1995; Beyond the Wild Blue: A History of the USAF 1947-1997, 1997; Beyond the Horizons: The Lockheed Story, 1998; (with P. Handleman) Brassell's Air Combat Reader, 1999; Aces in Combat, 2001; The Best of Wings, 2001; Classic Aircraft, 2001; Aviation 100, Vol. I, Vol II. **Address:** 21028 Starflower Way, Ashburn, VA 20147-4700, U.S.A. **Online address:** WBoyne@cqi

BRABAZON, James. (Leslie James Seth-Smith). British (born Uganda), b. 1923. **Genres:** Plays/Screenplays, Biography. **Career:** Freelance film and TV writer and producer. Actor, 1946-54; advertising copywriter, 1954-58; Story Ed., 1963-68, and Drama Director, 1969, BBC TV; Drama Producer, Granada TV Ltd., 1970-74, 1978-82, and London TV Week-end Ltd., 1976-77. **Publications:** People of Nowhere (play), 1959; Albert Schweitzer, 1975, 2nd ed., 2000; Dorothy L. Sayers, 1981.

BRACE, Paul (R.). American, b. 1954. **Genres:** Politics/Government. **Career:** New York University, NYC, assistant professor of political science, 1986-90; University of Illinois at Chicago Circle, Chicago, associate professor of political science, 1990-93; Florida State University, Tallahassee, professor of political science, 1993-. **Publications:** The Presidency in American Politics, 1989; (co-author) Follow the Leader, 1992; State Government and Economic Performance, 1993. **Address:** Department of Political Science, Florida State University, Tallahassee, FL 32306, U.S.A.

BRACEGIRDLE, Brian. British, b. 1933. **Genres:** Archaeology/Antiquities, Biology, Photography, Sciences. **Career:** Research Consultant in Microscopy and Fellow, Science Museum, London, since 1990 (Assistant Director and Head of Collections Management, 1987-89). Technician in industry, 1950-57; Biology Master, Erith Grammar School. 1958-61; Sr. Lecturer in Biology, St. Katharine's Coll., London, 1961-64; Head, Depts. of Natural Science and Learning Resources, Coll. of All Saints, London, 1964-77; Keeper, Wellcome Museum of the History of Medicine, London, 1977-87. Secretary, then Chairman, Institute of Medicine and Biological Illustration, 1971- 75. Former Chairman, Fellowship and Associateship Panel, Royal Photographic Society. **Publications:** (with W.H. Freeman) An Atlas of Embryology, 1963, 1967, 1978; (with W.H. Freeman) An Atlas of Histology, 1966; Photography for Books and Reports, 1970; (with W.H. Freeman) An Atlas of Invertebrate Structure, 1971; (with P.H. Miles) An Atlas of Plant Structure, vol. I, 1971, vol. II, 1973; The Archaeology of the Industrial Revolution, 1973; (with P.H. Miles) Thomas Telford, 1973; (with P.H. Miles) The Darbys and the Ironbridge Gorge, 1974; (with W.H. Freeman) An Advanced Atlas of Histology, 1976; (with P.H. Miles) An Atlas of Chordate Structure, 1977; The Evolution of Microtechnique, 1978, 1986; (ed.) Beads of Glass: Leeuwenhoek and the Early Microscope, 1983; (ed.) Microscopal Papers from the Quekett, 1989; (with J.B. McCormick) The Microscopic Photographs of J.B. Dancer, 1993; (ed.) Cumulative Index to the Quekett Journals, 1994; Scientific PhotoMAC-ROgraphy, 1995; (with S. Bradbury) Modern PhotoMICROgraphy, 1995; Notes on Modern Microscope Manufacturers, 1996; Microscopical Mounts and Mounters, 1998; (with S. Bradbury) An Introduction to the Light Microscope, 1998. **Address:** Cold Aston Lodge, Cold Aston. Cheltenham, Glos. GL54 3BN, England.

BRACEWELL-MILNES, (John) Barry. British, b. 1931. **Genres:** Economics. **Career:** Freelance writer and economic consultant. Economic Adviser, Institute of Directors, London, 1973-96. Sr. Research Fellow, Institute of Economic Affairs, London, 1989-92. Economist, Iron and Steel Board, London, 1960-63, and Federation of British Industries, London, 1964-65; Assistant Economic Director, 1965-67, Deputy Economic Director, 1967-68, and Economic Director, 1968-73, Confedn. of British Industry, London. **Publications:** The Measurement of Fiscal Policy, 1971; Saving and Switching, 1971; Pay and Price Control Guide, 1973; Is Capital Taxation Fair?, 1974; Economic Integration in East and West, 1976; The Camel's Back, 1976; (with J.C.L. Huiskamp) Investment Incentives, 1977; (with others) International Tax Avoidance, vols. A and B 1978-79; Tax Avoidance and Evasion, 1979; The Economics of International Tax Avoidance, 1980; The Taxation of Industry, 1981; Land and Heritage, 1982; A Market in Corporation Tax Losses, 1983; Smoking and Personal Choice, 1985; The Public Sector Borrowing Requirement, 1985; Are Equity Markets Short-Sighted?, 1987; Caring for the Countryside, 1987; Taxes on Spending, 1988; (with B. Sutherland) A Capital Offence, 1989; Capital Gains Tax, 1989: A Tax on Trade, 1989; The Wealth of Giving, 1989; An ACT against Trade, 1992; False Economy, 1993; (with R. Carnaghan) Testing the Market, 1993; A Disorderly House, 1993; Will to Succeed, 1994; A House Divided, 1994; Captive Capital, 1995; A Pool of Resources, 1996; Capital Punishment, 1998; Is a Mast a Must?, 2001; Euthanasia for Death Duties, 2002. **Address:** 26 Lancaster Ct, Banstead, Surrey SM7 1RR, England.

BRACH, Tara. American. **Genres:** Animals/Pets. **Career:** Clinical psychologist, educator, and lecturer. Meditation teacher, 1975-, psychotherapist, 1980-, clinical psychologist, 1994-. Founder of the Insight Meditation Community of Washington. **Publications:** Radical Acceptance: Embracing Your Life with the Heart of a Buddha, 2003. **Address:** 8129 Hamilton Spring Road, Bethesda, MD 20817, U.S.A.

BRACKEN, James K. American, b. 1952. **Genres:** Librarianship. **Career:** Knox College, Galesburg, IL, reader services librarian, 1979-85; Purdue University, West Lafayette, IN, humanities bibliographer and assistant professor of library science, 1985-88; Ohio State University, Columbus, head of Second Floor Main Library Information Services and professor, university libraries, 1988-. **Publications:** Reference Works in British and American Literature, Vol. I: English and American Literature, 1990, Vol. II: English and American Writers, 1991, 2nd ed., 1998; (with E.S. Block) Communica-

tion and the Mass Media: A Guide to the Reference Literature, 1991; (with C.H. Sterling) Telecommunications Research Resources: An Annotated Guide, 1995; (with C.H. Sterling and S.M. Hill) Mass Communications Research Resources: An Annotated Guide, 1998. EDITOR (with J. Silver): The British Literary Book Trade, 1700-1820 (Dictionary of Literary Biography, vol. 154), 1995; The British Literary Book Trade, 1475-1700 (Dictionary of Literary Biography, vol. 170), 1996. Work represented in anthologies. Contributor of articles and reviews to professional journals. **Address:** University Libraries, Ohio State University, 1858 Neil Avenue Mall, Columbus, OH 43210-1286, U.S.A. **Online address:** bracken.1@osu.edu

BRACKEN, Len. American, b. 1961. **Genres:** Novels, History, Politics/Government, Biography. **Career:** Translator and editor. **Publications:** Freeplay, 1990; The East Is Black, 1992; Guy Debord: Revolutionary, 1997; The Arch Conspirator, 1999; Shadow Government: 9-11 and State Terror, 2002. **Address:** PO Box 5585, Arlington, VA 22205, U.S.A.

BRACKENBURY, Alison. British, b. 1953. **Genres:** Poetry. **Career:** Gloucestershire Col. of Arts and Technology, Cheltenham, librarian, 1976-83; Polytechnics Central Admissions System, Cheltenham, clerical asst., 1985-90; electro-plater, family business, 1990-. **Publications:** Journey to a Cornish Wedding, 1977; Two Poems, 1979; Dreams of Power and Other Poems, 1981; Breaking Ground and Other Poems, 1984; The Country of Afternoon (radio play), 1985; Christmas Roses and Other Poems, 1988; Selected Poems, 1991; 1829 and Other Poems, 1995; After Beethoven and Other Poems, 2000; Bricks and Ballads, 2004. **Address:** c/o Carcanet Press, 4th Floor, Conavon Court, 12-16 Blackfriars St, Manchester M3 5BQ, England. **Online address:** www.alisonbrackenbury.co.uk

BRACKETT, Peter. *See* **COLLINS, Max Allan.**

BRACKMAN, Barbara. American, b. 1945. **Genres:** Antiques/Furnishings, Crafts. **Career:** Educator in special education, University of Kansas and University of Illinois, 1970-85; freelance writer, 1976-. Also freelance consultant and museum curator for facilities such as the Spencer Museum of Art, Kansas Museum of History, and the Knoxville Museum of Art. **Publications:** Clues in the Calico: A Guide to Identifying and Dating Antique Quilts, 1989; Encyclopedia of Applique, 1993; Encyclopedia of Pieced Quilts, 1993; (ed.) Kansas Quilts and Quilters, 1993; (with M. Waldvogel) Patchwork Souvenirs, 1993. **Address:** 3115 West 6th, No. C-237, Lawrence, KS 66049, U.S.A.

BRADBURY, Edward P. *See* **MOORCOCK, Michael (John).**

BRADBURY, Jim. British, b. 1937. **Genres:** History, Literary criticism and history. **Career:** Shoreditch Comprehensive School, London, England, schoolteacher, 1959-61; Manhood Secondary School, schoolteacher, 1961-69; Borough Road College & West London Institute of Education, history lecturer, 1969-89, part-time lecturer, 1989-93; writer. **Publications:** Shakespeare and His Theatre (for children), 1975; The Medieval Archer, 1985; Introduction to Buckinghamshire Domesday, 1986; The Medieval Siege, 1992; Stephen and Matilda, the Civil War 1139-45, 1996; Philip Augustus, King of France, 1997; The Battle of Hastings, 1998. Contributor to books and journals. **Address:** 27 East St, Selsey, W. Sussex PO20 0BN, England. **Online address:** jim@bradbury21.fsnet.co.uk

BRADBURY, Ray (Douglas). American, b. 1920. **Genres:** Novels, Science fiction/Fantasy, Children's fiction, Plays/Screenplays, Poetry, Novellas/Short stories. **Publications:** Dark Carnival, 1947; The Meadow (play), 1948; The Martian Chronicles, 1950; The Illustrated Man, 1951; It Came from Outer Space (screenplay), 1952; Fahrenheit 451, 1953; The Golden Apples of the Sun, 1953; Moby Dick (screenplay), 1954; The October Country, 1955; Switch on the Night, 1955; Dandelion Wine, 1957; A Medicine for Melancholy (in U.K. as The Day It Rained Forever), 1959, The Day It Rained Forever (play), 1966; Icarus Montgolfier Wright (screenplay), 1961; R is for Rocket, 1962; Something Wicked This Way Comes, 1962; The Anthem Sprinters and Other Antics (play), 1963; The World of Ray Bradbury (play), 1964; The Machineries of Joy: Short Stories, 1964; The Vintage Bradbury, 1965; The Wonderful Ice-Cream Suit (play), 1965; The Autumn People, 1965; Tomorrow Midnight, 1966; The Pedestrian (play), 1966; S is for Space, 1966; The Picasso Summer (screenplay), 1968; I Sing the Body Electric!, 1969; Christus Apollo (cantata), 1969; Old Ahab's Friend, and Friend to Nosh, Speaks His Piece: A Celebration, 1971; The Halloween Tree, 1972; The Wonderful Ice Cream Suit and Other Plays: For Today, Tomorrow, and Beyond Tomorrow, 1972; When Elephants Last in the Dooryard Bloomed (poetry), 1972; The Small Assassin, 1973; Zen and the Art of Writing, 1973; Mars and the Mind of Man, 1973; That Son of Richard III, 1974; Long after

Midnight (stories), 1976; Pillar of Fire and Other Plays, 1976; Where Robot Mice and Robot Men Run Round in Robot Towns: New Poems Both Light and Dark, 1977; The Stories of Ray Bradbury, 1980; The Ghosts of Forever, 1981; The Haunted Computer and the Android Pope, 1981; The Last Circus, 1981; The Complete Poems of Ray Bradbury, 1982; The Love Affair, 1983; Dinosaur Tales, 1983; A Memory of Murder, 1984; Forever and the Earth, 1984; Death Is a Lonely Business, 1986; The Toynbee Convector, 1988; A Graveyard for Lunatics (novel), 1990; Folon's Folons, 1990; Yestermorrow: Obvious Answers to Impossible Futures, 1991; The Smile, 1991; Green Shadows, White Whale, 1992; Quicker than the Eye, 1996; With Cat for Comforter, 1997; Dogs Think that Every Day Is Christmas, 1997; Driving Blind, 1997; Ahmed and the Oblivion Machines: A Fable, 1998; Christus Apollo: Cantata Celebrating the Eighth Day of Creation and the Promise of the Ninth, 1998; (with others) You Are Here: The Jerde Partnership International, 1999; From the Dust Returned: A Family Remembrance, 2001; Ray Bradbury Collected Short Stories, 2001; Let's All Kill Constance, 2002; One More for the Road, 2002; The Cat's Pajamas: Stories, 2004. EDITOR: Timeless Stories for Today and Tomorrow, 1952; The Circus of Dr. Lao, 1956; A Day in the Life of Hollywood, 1992. **Address:** c/o Don Congdon, Harold Matson Co., 276 Fifth Ave, Room 903, New York, NY 10010, U.S.A.

BRADEN, Donna R. American, b. 1953. **Genres:** Social commentary, History, Art/Art history. **Career:** Henry Francis du Pont Winterthur Museum, Winterthur, DE, tour guide, 1975-76; Mercer Museum of the Bucks County Historical Society, Doylestown, PA, intern, 1976; Henry Ford Museum and Greenfield Village, Dearborn, MI, curator in historical resources unit, 1977-. Lecturer on domestic technology, kitchen evolution, and leisure and entertainment. **Publications:** Leisure and Entertainment in America, 1988; Eagle Tavern Cookbook, 1988; (co-author) Americans on Vacation, 1990. Contributor of chapters to books. **Address:** Henry Ford Museum and Greenfield Village, 20900 Oakwood Blvd., Dearborn, MI 48121, U.S.A.

BRADFIELD, Scott (Michael). American, b. 1955. **Genres:** Novellas/Short stories, Novels. **Career:** University of Connecticut, Storrs, professor of English, 1989-96; writer. **Publications:** The Secret Life of Houses (stories), 1988, expanded ed published in US as Dream of the Wolf: Stories, 1990; The History of Luminous Motion (novel), 1989; Greetings from Earth: New and Collected Stories, 1993; Dreaming Revolution: Transgression in the Development of American Romance (criticism), 1993; What's Wrong with America (novel), 1994. **Address:** c/o Picador U.S.A., St. Martin's Press, 175 5th Ave., New York, NY 10010, U.S.A.

BRADFORD, Barbara Taylor. American (born England), b. 1933. **Genres:** Novels. **Career:** Reporter, 1949-51, and Women's Ed., 1951-53, Yorkshire Evening Post, Leeds; Fashion Ed., Woman's Own, London, 1953-54; Columnist, Evening News, London, 1955-57; Ed., The London American; Features Ed.,Woman, London, 1962-64; Ed., National Design Center, NYC, 1964-68; syndicated columnist, Newsday, Long Island, NY, 1966. **Publications:** NOVELS: A Woman of Substance, 1979; Voice of the Heart, 1983; Hold the Dream, 1985; Act of Will, 1986; To Be the Best, 1988; The Women in His Life, 1990; Remember, 1991; Angel, 1993; Everything to Gain, 1994; Dangerous to Know, 1995; Love in Another Town, 1995; Her Own Rules, 1996; A Secret Affair, 1996; Power of a Woman, 1997; A Sudden Change of Heart, 1999; Where You Belong, 2000; The Triumph of Katie Bryne, 2001; Three Weeks in Paris, 2002. OTHER: Easy Steps to Successful Decorating, 1971; How to Solve Your Decorating Problems, 1976; Decorating Ideas for Casual Living, 1977; Making Space Grow, 1979; Luxury Designs for Apartment Living, 1981. **Address:** Bradford Enterprises, 450 Park Ave Ste 1903, New York, NY 10022, U.S.A. **Online address:** www.brabarataylorbradford.com

BRADFORD, Karleen. Canadian, b. 1936. **Genres:** Children's fiction, Young adult fiction. **Career:** West Toronto YWCA, social worker, 1959-62; writer, 1963-. **Publications:** FICTION FOR YOUNG ADULTS: The Nine Days Queen, 1986; Windward Island, 1989; There Will Be Wolves, 1992; Thirteenth Child, 1994; Shadows on a Sword, 1996; Dragonfire, 1997; Lionheart's Scribe, 1999; Whisperings of Magic, 2001; Angeline, 2004. FOR CHILDREN: A Year for Growing, 1977, as Wrong Again, Robbie, 1983; The Other Elizabeth, 1982; I Wish There Were Unicorns, 1983; The Stone in the Meadow, 1984; The Haunting at Cliff House, 1985; Write Now!, 1988, rev. ed., 1996; Animal Heroes, 1995, rev. ed., 2000; More Animal Heroes, 1996; A Different Kind of Champion, 1998; With Nothing but Our Courage, 2002; You Can't Rush a Cat, 2003. **Address:** RR #2, Owen Sound, ON, Canada N4K 5N4. **Online address:** karleen.bradford@sympatico.ca

BRADFORD, Sarah (Mary Malet). (Viscountess Bangor). British, b. 1938. **Genres:** Food and Wine, History, Biography. **Career:** Christie's, manuscript expert, 1974-80; Sotheby's, manuscript consultant, 1980-82; Times Literary Supplement, book and manuscript consultant, 1982-85; writer. **Publications:** HISTORY: The Englishman's Wine, 1969 as The Story of Port, 1978; Portugal & Madeira, 1969; Portugal, 1972. BIOGRAPHIES: Cesare Borgia, 1976; Disraeli, 1982; Princess Grace, 1984; King George VI, 1989, in US as The Reluctant King, 1990; Splendours and Miseries, 1993; (with others) The Sitwells and the Arts of the 1920s and 1930s, 1994; Elizabeth: A Biography of Britain's Queen, 1996; America's Queen: The Life of Jacqueline Kennedy Onassis, 2000. **Address:** c/o Gillon Aitken Associates, 29 Fernshaw Rd, London SW10 0TG, England.

BRADING, D. A. British, b. 1936. **Genres:** Area studies, Cultural/Ethnic topics, History, Theology/Religion. **Career:** University of California, Berkeley, assistant professor, 1965-71; Yale University, New Haven, CT, associate professor, 1971-73; Cambridge University, England, lecturer in history, 1973-91, director of Centre of Latin American Studies, 1975-90; reader in Latin American History, 1991-98, professor of Mexican history, 1999-2003; writer. **Publications:** Miners and Merchants in Bourbon Mexico, 1971; Haciendas and Ranchos in Mexican Bajio, 1979; Myth and Prophecy in Mexican History, 1984; The Origins of Mexican Nationalism, 1985; The First America, 1492-1867, 1991; Church and State in Bourbon Mexico 1749-1810, 1994; Mexican Phoenix: Our Lady of Guadalupe, 2001. **Address:** Clare Hall, Herschel Rd, Cambridge CB3 9AL, England.

BRADLEE, Benjamin (Crowninshield). American, b. 1921. **Genres:** International relations/Current affairs. **Career:** Vice President at-Large, 1991-, Washington Post, (Managing Ed., 1965-68; Executive Ed., 1968-91). Reporter, New Hampshire Sunday News, Manchester, 1946-48, and Washington Post, 1958-51; Press Attache American Embassy, Paris, 1951-53; European Correspondent, 1953-57, Reporter, Washington Bureau, 1957-61, and Sr. Ed. and Chief of Bureau, 1961-65, Newsweek mag. **Publications:** That Special Grace, 1964; Conversations with Kennedy, 1976; A Good Life-Newspapering and Other Adventures, 1995. **Address:** c/o Washington Post, 1150 15th St NW, Washington, DC 20071-0001, U.S.A.

BRADLEY, Blythe. See WAGNER, Sharon Blythe.

BRADLEY, David (Henry), (Jr.). American, b. 1950. **Genres:** Novels, Novellas/Short stories, Plays/Screenplays, Adult non-fiction, History, Intellectual history, Autobiography/Memoirs, Essays. **Career:** Lippincott, publishers, Philadelphia, reader and assistant ed., 1974-76; Temple University, Philadelphia, assistant professor, 1977-82, associate professor 1982-89, professor of English, 1989-96. University of Pennsylvania, Philadelphia, visiting lecturer, 1975; editorial consultant, Lippincott, 1977-78, and Ace Science Fiction, NYC, 1979; visiting professor, Colgate University, 1988, Massachusetts Institute of Technology, 1989, University of Oregon, 2000, University of Texas, 2000, Austin Peay University, 2001. Member, Executive Board, PEN American Center, 1982-84. Member, Author's Guild Council, 1988-. **Publications:** South Street, 1975; The Chaneysville Incident, 1981. **Address:** c/o Wendy Weil Agency, 232 Madison Ave, New York, NY 10016, U.S.A. **Online address:** YGTBK@aol.com

BRADLEY, John Ed(mund), (Jr.). American, b. 1958. **Genres:** Novels, Novellas/Short stories. **Career:** Washington Post, Washington, DC, staff writer, 1983-87; writer. **Publications:** NOVELS: Tupelo Nights, 1988; The Best There Ever Was, 1990; Love & Obits, 1992; Smoke, 1994; My Juliet, 2000. Also author of short stories. **Address:** 2035 Delmas St, Opelousas, LA 70570-4715, U.S.A.

BRADLEY, John Lewis. British, b. 1917. **Genres:** Literary criticism and history. **Career:** Instructor, Wellesley Coll., Massachusetts, 1948-51, and University of Maryland, College Park, 1952-53; Assistant Professor, Clark University, Worcester, Massachusetts, 1953-55; Assistant Professor, 1955-58, and Associate Professor, 1958-64, Mount Holyoke Coll., South Hadley, Massachusetts; Professor, Ohio State University, Columbus, 1964-66, Graduate Division, University of South Carolina, Columbia, 1966-69, University of Durham, England, 1969-78, and University of Maryland, College Park, 1978-82. **Publications:** An Introduction to Ruskin, 1971; Lady Curzon's India, 1985; A Shelley Chronology, 1993; A Ruskin Chronology, 1997. EDITOR: Ruskin's Letters from Venice 1851-1852, 1955; Ruskin's Letters to Lord and Lady Mount-Temple, 1964; Selections From Mayhew's London Labour and the London Poor, 1966; (with M. Stevens) Masterworks of English Prose, 1968; Ruskin: The Critical Heritage, 1984; (co-) The Correspondence of John Ruskin and Charles Eliot Norton, 1987. Contributor to encyclopedias. **Address:** Church Cottage, Hinton St. George, Somerset TA17 8SA, England.

BRADLEY, Patricia. American (born England). **Genres:** History. **Career:** KMJ-TV, Fresno, CA, anchor and reporter; freelance writer; Temple University, professor and chair of the Department of Journalism, School of Communications and Theater, director of College of Arts and Sciences American Studies Program, 1994-98. Previously at University of Georgia and Southern Methodist University. **Publications:** Slavery, Propaganda, and the American Revolution, 1998; Mass Media and the Shaping of U.S. Feminism, 2003. **Address:** Temple University School of Communications and Theater, 2020 N 13th St, Philadelphia, PA 19122, U.S.A.

BRADLEY, Shelley. American, b. 1968. **Genres:** Romance/Historical. **Career:** Novelist. **Publications:** HISTORICAL ROMANCES: The Lady and the Dragon, 1999; Sweet Enemy, 1999; One Wicked Night, 2000; His Stolen Bride, 2000; His Lady Bride, 2000; His Rebel Bride, 2001; A Christmas Promise, 2001; Strictly Seduction, 2002; Strictly Forbidden, 2002; Strictly Wanton, 2003. **Address:** PO Box 270126, Flower Mound, TX 75027, U.S.A. **Online address:** shelley@shelleybradley.com

BRADLEY, Will. See STRICKLAND, (William) Brad(ley).

BRADMAN, Tony. British, b. 1954. **Genres:** Children's fiction. **Career:** Parents magazine, UK edition, deputy editor, 1979-87; writer. Has worked as a reviewer of specialist children's books, magazines, and national press; founded Best Books for Babies, a children's book award, and has served as a judge for other awards; regularly visits schools to read from his own works. **Publications:** FOR CHILDREN: A Kiss on the Nose (poetry), 1984; The Bad Babies' Counting Book, 1985; John Lennon, 1985; One Nil, 1985; Let's Pretend, 1985; The Bad Babies' Book of Colors, 1986; See You Later, Alligator, 1986; At the Park, 1986; Hide and Seek, 1986; Play Time, 1986; Through My Window, 1986; The Lonely Little Mole (based on a story by Paule Alen), 1986; Night-Time, 1986; Will You Read Me a Story?, 1986; Baby's Best Book, 1987; The Baby's Bumper Book, 1987; The Bad Babies' Book of Months, 1987; Smile, Please!, 1987; I Need a Book!, 1987; The Little Cakemaker and the Greedy Magician (based on a story by Alen), 1987; Look Out, He's Behind You!, 1988; Wait and See, 1988; Not Like That, Like This!, 1988; Bedtime, 1988; The Cuddle, 1988; Our Cat, 1988; All Together Now! (poetry), 1989; Who's Afraid of the Big Bad Wolf?, 1989; Bub, 1989; Gary and the Magic Cat, 1989, published as The Magic Cat, 1992; Tracey's Wish, 1989; The Sandal: A Story, 1989; This Little Baby, 1990; Michael, 1990; Let's Go, Ben, 1990; Gerbil Crazy, 1990; Miranda the Magnificent, 1990; In a Minute, 1990; Five Minutes More!, 1991; Morning, 1991; That's Not a Fish!, 1991; Tommy Niner and the Planet of Danger, 1991; Billy and the Baby, 1992; It Came from Outer Space, 1992; Has Anyone Seen Jack?, 1992; Frankie Makes a Friend, 1992; My Family, 1992; My Little Baby Brother, 1992; That's Not My Cat!, 1992; Wally's New Face, 1992; Winnie's New Broom, 1992; A Bad Week for the Three Bears, 1993; The Invaders, 1993; Tommy Niner and the Mystery Spaceship, 1994; Night Night, Ben!, 1994; Two Minute Puppy Tales, 1994. RETELLER: The Ugly Duckling, 1990; The Gingerbread Man, 1991; Goldilocks and the Three Bears, 1991; The Little Red Hen, 1991. DILLY THE DINOSAUR SERIES: Dilly the Dinosaur, 1985; Dilly Visits the Dentist (in US as Dilly Goes to the Dentist), 1986; Dilly Tells the Truth, 1986; Dilly and the Horror Film (in US as Dilly and the Horror Movie), 1987; Dilly's Muddy Day, 1987; Dilly and the Tiger, 1988; Dilly, 1988; Dilly and the Ghost, 1989; Dilly Dinosaur, Superstar, 1989; Dilly Speaks Up, 1990; Dilly Goes on Holiday, 1990; Dilly the Angel, 1990; Dilly and His Swamp Lizard, 1991; Dilly and the Big Kids, 1991; Dilly's Birthday Party, 1991; Dilly Goes to School, 1992; Dilly and the Pirates, 1993; Dilly-The Worst Day Ever, 1993; Dilly Goes Swamp Wallowing, 1994; Dilly, Dinosaur Detective, 1994. DAISY TALES: Daisy and the Babysitter, 1986; Daisy and the Crying Baby, 1986; Daisy and the Washing Machine, 1986; Daisy Goes Swimming, 1986; Daisy Feels Ill, 1988; Daisy Goes to Playgroup, 1988. THE BLUEBEARDS SERIES: Adventure on Skull Island, 1988; Mystery at Musket Bay, 1989; Contest at Cutlass Cove, 1990; Search for the Saucy Sally, 1990; Peril at the Pirate School, 1990; Revenge at Ryan's Reef, 1991. SAM, THE GIRL DETECTIVE SERIES: Sam, the Girl Detective, 1989; The Cash Box Caper, 1990; The Case of the Missing Mummy, 1990; The Secret of the Seventh Candle, 1992; The Great Rock 'n' Roll Ransom, 1994. SELECTOR: The Magic Kiss, 1987; Animals Like Us, 1987; The Mad Family, 1987; The Best of Friends, 1988; What a Wonderful Day, 1988; Things That Go, 1989; You're Late, Dad, 1989; That Spells Magic, 1989; The Parents' Book of Bedtime Stories, 1990; Love Them, Hate Them, 1991; Our Side of the Playground, 1991; Hissing Steam and Whistles Blowing, 1991; Good Sports!, 1992; A Stack of Story Poems, 1992; Amazing Adventure Stories, 1994; Fantastic Space Stories, 1994. OTHER: The Essential Father, 1985; So You Want to Have a Baby?, 1985; Reading for Enjoyment, 0-6, 6th ed, 1989. Contributor of reviews to periodicals. ADAPTATIONS: Many of the Dilly books are available on cassette. **Address:** 175 Mackenzie Rd., Beckenham, Kent B43 4SE, England.

BRADSHAW, Michael. British, b. 1935. **Genres:** Geography, Earth sciences, Regional/Urban planning. **Career:** Teacher of geography and geology at a secondary school near Godalming, England, 1959-68; College of St. Mark and St. John, Plymouth, England, teacher of geography and geology and department head, 1968-93; retired, 1993. **Publications:** A New Geology, 1968, 2nd ed., 1973; (with E.A. Jarman) Reading Geological Maps, 1969; Geological Map Exercises, 1969; Earth, The Living Planet, 1977; (with J. Abbott and A. Gelsthorpe) Earth's Changing Surface, 1978; Earth: Past, Present, and Future, 1981; (with P. Guinness) North America: A Human Geography, 1984; Regions and Regionalism in the United States, 1988; Industrial Change: New England and Appalachia, 1988; The Appalachian Regional Commission, 1992; (with R. Weaver) Physical Geography, 1993; (with R. Weaver) Foundations of Physical Geography, 1995; The New Global Order, a World Regional Geography, 1997. **Address:** 57 Frensham Ave., Glenholt, Plymouth PL6 7JN, England.

BRADSHAW, Timothy. British, b. 1950. **Genres:** Theology/Religion. **Career:** Curate of the Church of England, 1976-79; Trinity College, Bristol, England, lecturer, 1979-90; Oxford University, Regents Park College, Oxford, England, senior tutor, 1990-. Ecumenical representative of the Church of England with the Orthodox Church; minister of a local church. **Publications:** Purity and Orthodoxy, 1984; The Olive Branch, 1992; (ed.) The Way Forward?, 1997; Grace and Truth in the Secular Age, 1998; Praying and Believing, 1998. **Address:** Regents Park College, Oxford University, Oxford OX1 2LB, England. **Online address:** timothy.bradshaw@regents.ox.ac.uk

BRADY, James B. American, b. 1939. **Genres:** Law. **Career:** State University of New York at Buffalo, Amherst, lecturer, 1967-70, assistant professor, 1970-73, associate professor of philosophy, 1973-, associate chair and director of undergraduate studies in department of philosophy, 1970-72, assistant provost, faculty of social sciences, 1972-73, associate provost, 1973-75, co-director of Baldy Center for Law and Social Policy, 1978-81. Oxford University, visiting senior member of Linacre College, 1975. **Publications:** (ed. with N. Garver) Justice, Law, and Violence, 1991. Contributor of articles and reviews to journals. **Address:** Department of Philosophy, 616 Baldy Hall, State University of New York at Buffalo, Buffalo, NY 14214, U.S.A.

BRADY, Joan. American/British, b. 1939. **Genres:** Novels. **Career:** Writer. Dancer with San Francisco Ballet, 1955-58, and NYC Ballet, 1960. National Endowment of the Arts, 1986; Whitbread Novel of the Year, 1992; Whitbread Book of the Year, 1993; Prix de Meilleur Livre Etranger, 1995. **Publications:** The Imposter, 1979; The Unmaking of a Dancer, 1982 (in U.K., rev., as Prologue, 1994); Theory of War, 1992; Death Comes for Peter Pan, 1995; The Emigre, 1999; Bleedout, 2005.

BRADY, John (Mary). Irish, b. 1955. **Genres:** Novels, Mystery/Crime/Suspense. **Career:** Bank of Ireland, Dublin, bank official, 1972-75; Royal Canadian Mounted Police, Yellowknife, Northwest Territories, police officer, 1975-76; schoolteacher in Terrace, British Columbia, 1981-84; St. Patrick's School, Schomberg, Ontario, teacher, 1988-. **Publications:** A Stone of the Heart (mystery novel), 1988; Unholy Ground (mystery novel), 1989; Kaddish in Dublin, 1990; All Souls, 1992; The Good Life, 1994; A Carra King, 2001.

BRADY, Kimberley S(mith). American, b. 1953. **Genres:** Adult non-fiction. **Career:** Tempe Unified School District, Tempe, AZ, elementary schoolteacher, 1977-81; Clovis Unified School District, Fresno, CA, substitute teacher, 1996-. **Publications:** Keeper for the Sea, 1997. **Address:** 55 Antrim Rd., Hancock, NH 03449, U.S.A. **Online address:** ksbrady@aol.com

BRADY, Patricia. Also writes as Patricia Brady Schmit. American, b. 1943. **Genres:** Anthropology/Ethnology, Cultural/Ethnic topics, Biography. **Career:** Dillard University, New Orleans, LA, instructor, 1969-73, assistant professor of history, 1973-80; Historic New Orleans Collection, New Orleans, editor of The Butler Papers, 1980-82, director of publications, 1982-2001; DivaBooks Publication Consulting, president, 2001-; writer. **Publications:** George Washington's Beautiful Nelly: The Letters of Eleanor Parke Custis Lewis to Elizabeth Bordley Gibson, 1794-1851, 1991. EDITOR (as Patricia Brady Schmit): Nelly Custis Lewis's Housekeeping Book, 1982; Encyclopaedia of New Orleans Artists, 1718-1918, 1987. **Address:** 170 Walnut St 8A, New Orleans, LA 70118, U.S.A. **Online address:** epcustis@msn.com

BRADY, Taylor. See BALL, Donna.

BRADY, William S. See HARVEY, John B.

BRADY, William S. *See* **WELLS, Angus.**

BRAGA, Newton C. Brazilian, b. 1946. **Genres:** Information science/Computers. **Career:** Educator, editor, and author. Editoria Saber Ltda., São Paulo, Brazil, technical director. Instituto Monitor, consultant, 1969-; Colegio Mater Amabilis, instructor in mechatronics, 1999-. Consultant. **Publications:** Fun Projects for the Experimenter, 1998; CMOS Projects and Experiments: Fun with the 4093 Integrated Circuit, 1999; Sourcebook for Electronics Calculations, Formulas, and Tables, 1999; Electronics for the Electrician, 2000; Electronics Projects from the Next Dimension: Paranormal Experiments for Hobbyists, 2001; CMOS Sourcebook, 2001; Pirate Radio and Video: Experimental Transmitter Projects, 2001; Robotics, Mechatronics, and Artificial Intelligence: Experimental Circuit Blocks for Designers, 2002; Mechatronics Sourcebook, 2003. UNTRANSLATED WORKS, includes: Eletronica Para Eletricistas, 2001; Instalacoes Eletricas Domiciliares, 2003; Curso de Eletronica Digital, 2003. Contributor to periodicals. **Address:** Rua Vera 247, Guarulhos, 07096, 020 Sao Paulo, Brazil. **Online address:** newtoncbraga@sili.com.br

BRAGDON, Kathleen J. American. **Genres:** Anthropology/Ethnology. **Career:** College of William and Mary, Williamsburg, VA, teacher of anthropology. **Publications:** (with I. Goddard) Native Writings in Massachusetts, 1988; Native People of Southern New England, 1500-1650, 1996. Contributor to academic journals. **Address:** Department of Anthropology, College of William and Mary, Williamsburg, VA 23185, U.S.A. **Online address:** bkbrag@farstaff.wm.edu

BRAGG, Melvyn. British, b. 1939. **Genres:** Novels, Plays/Screenplays, Biography. **Career:** Controller of Arts, and Ed. and Presenter, lTV Arts Program, London Weekend T.V., The South Bank Show, 1978-. Presenter and Producer, BBC Television, 1961-67 and 1974-77. Chairman, Arts Council Literature panel, 1977-78. **Publications:** For Want of a Nail, 1965; The Second Inheritance, 1966; Without a City Wall, 1968; A Place in England, 1970; The Nerve, 1971; The Hunt, 1972; Josh Lawton, 1972; The Silken Net, 1974; Speak for England, 1976; A Christmas Child, 1977; Autumn Manouvers, 1978; Kingdom Come, 1980: Love and Glory, 1983; Land of the Lakes, 1983: Laurence Olivier, 1984; (ed.) Cumbria in Verse, 1984; Rich: The Life of Richard Burton, 1988; The Seventh Seal: Ingmar Bergman; Credo, 1996; On Giants' Shoulders (nonfiction), 1998; The Adventure of English (nonfiction), 2003. NOVELS: The Hired Man, 1969; The Maid of Buttermere, 1987; A Time to Dance, 1990; Crystal Rooms, 1992; The Sword and the Miracle, 1997; The Soldier's Return, 1999; A Son of War, 2001; Crossing the Lines, 2003. SCREENPLAYS: Play Dirty, 1969; Isadora, 1969; The Music Lovers, 1971. **Address:** 12 Hampstead Hill Gardens, London NW3, England.

BRAGG, Steven M. American, b. 1960. **Genres:** Business/Trade/Industry, Administration/Management. **Career:** Certified public accountant; Teague Equipment Co., controller; Isolation Technologies, chief operating officer; Ernst & Young, consulting manager. **Publications:** Controllership, 1995; The Controller's Function, 1995; Justin-Time Accounting, 1996; Advanced Accounting Systems, 1997. **Address:** 6727 East Fremont Pl., Englewood, CO 80112, U.S.A. **Online address:** Brasto@aol.com

BRAGINSKY, Vladimir B. Russian, b. 1931. **Genres:** Physics. **Career:** Moscow State University, Moscow, Russia, senior lecturer, 1955-56, assistant professor, 1956-64, senior research scientist, 1964-68, professor of physics, 1968-, chair of department, 1986-. California Institute of Technology, research associate, 1993-96. **Publications:** Physical Experiments with Test Bodies, 1970; (with A. Manukin) Measurements of Weak Forces in Physics Experiments, 1977; (with V. Mitrofanov and V. Panov) Systems with Small Dissipation, 1985; (with F. Khalili) Quantum Measurement, 1992. **Address:** Department of Physics, Moscow State University, 119899 Moscow, Russia.

BRAHAM, (E.) Jeanne. American, b. 1940. **Genres:** Literary criticism and history, Poetry. **Career:** Allegheny College, Meadville, PA, professor, 1970-90; Clark University, Worcester, MA, visiting faculty member. Chautauqua Writers Center, creative writing teacher; visiting professor at Smith College, Hampshire College, University of New Hampshire, and College of the Holy Cross. Heatherstone Press, founding editor and chief. **Publications:** One Means of Telling Time (poems), 1982; Primary Sources (poems), 1983; A Sort of Columbus: The Fiction of Saul Bellow, 1985; Crucial Conversations, 1995; Starry, Starry Night, 1998. **Address:** Department of English, Clark University, Worcester, MA 01610, U.S.A.

BRAHMANANDA, Palahally Ramaiya. Indian, b. 1926. **Genres:** Economics. **Career:** Bombay University, research assistant, 1950-54, lecturer in economics, 1954-56, reader in monetary economics, 1956-63, professor, 1963-89, director Department of Economics, 1976-86; national fellow ICSSR, 1977-79; RBI Nat. Professor, 1990;Delhi University, visiting professor, 1985. **Publications:** (with C.N. Vakil) Planning for a Shortage Economy, 1952; (with C.N. Vakil) Economics of Electricity Planning, 1992; (with C.N. Vakil) Planning for an Expanding Economy, 1956; Studies in Welfare Maximization, 1959; The New Classical vs. the Neo-Classical Economics, 1967; The Gold-Money Rift: A Classical Theory of International Liquidity, 1969; Explorations in the New Classical Theory of Political Economy and a Connected Critique of Economic Theory, 1974; Determinants of Real National Income and of Price Level, 1976; The Falling Economy and How to Revive It, 1977; Planning for a Futureless Stockless Money, 1980; The I.M.F. Loan and India's Economic Future, 1982; Productivity in the Indian Economy: Rising Inputs for Falling Outputs, 1982; Employment Policy in a Developing Country, 1983; (ed) Development Process in the Indian Economy, 1986; Planning for a Wage-Goods Economy, 1994; Indian Economy: Crisis-Adjustment-Crisis, 1995; Money, Interest & Exchange Rates, 1997. Author of articles on different aspects of economic theory and the Indian economy. **Address:** The Indian Economic Journal, Srishaila Nilaya, No. 12, Kalappa Block, Basavanagudi, Bangalore 560 016, India.

BRAINARD, Cecilia Manguerra. American (born Philippines), b. 1947. **Genres:** Novellas/Short stories, Women's studies and issues. **Career:** Communications specialist, ranging from documentary scriptwriting to public relations work, 1969-81; freelance writer, 1981-. University of California Extension, Los Angeles, instructor in writing program, 1989-; Philippine American Literary House, partner, 1994-; workshop presenter; public speaker. **Publications:** Woman with Horns and Other Stories, 1988; The Philippine Woman in America, 1991; Song of Yvonne, 1991, as When the Rainbow Goddess Wept, 1994; Magdalena (novel), 2002; Cecilia's Diary 1962-1969, 2003. EDITOR: Seven Stories from Seven Sisters: A Collection of Philippine Folktales, 1992; Fiction by Filipinos in America, 1993; Contemporary Fiction by Filipinos in America, 1997; (co) Journey of 100 Years: Reflections on the Centennial of Philippine Independence, 1999; Growing up Filipino: Stories for Young Adults, 2003. Work represented in anthologies. Contributor of articles and stories to periodicals. **Address:** PO Box 5099, Santa Monica, CA 90409, U.S.A. **Online address:** CBrainard@aol.com; www.ceciliabrainard.com

BRAINE, David. British, b. 1940. **Genres:** Medicine/Health, Ethics. **Career:** University of Aberdeen, Aberdeen, Scotland, lecturer, 1965-89. University of Aberdeen, honorary lecturer, 1989-. **Publications:** Medical Ethics and Human Life, 1982; The Reality of Time and the Existence of God, 1988; (ed. and contributor with H. Lesser) Ethics, Technology and Medicine, 1988; The Human Person: Animal and Spirit, 1992. **Address:** 104/106 High St., Old Aberdeen AB2 3HE, Scotland.

BRAKE, Laurel. American, b. 1941. **Genres:** Literary criticism and history. **Career:** University of London, Birkbeck College, London, England, research assistant in English, 1970-73, reader in literature, 1988-; University of Wales, University College of Wales, Aberystwyth, lecturer in English, 1973-88; writer. Co-editor, Pater Newsletter, 1978-98. **Publications:** Subjugated Knowledges, 1994; Walter Pater, 1994; Print in Transition, 2001. EDITOR: The Year's Work in English Studies, Volumes 62-69, 1984-91; (with A. Jones and L. Madden) Investigating Victorian Journalism, 1990; (with I. Small) Pater in the 1990s, 1991; (with B. Bell and D. Finkelstein) Nineteenth-Century Media and the Construction of Identity, 2000. **Address:** FCE, Birkbeck College, University of London, 26 Russell Sq, London WC1B 5DQ, England.

BRAME, Charles L. American, b. 1926. **Genres:** Biography. **Career:** Teacher in Missouri and California, 1961-84. Producer of the radio show Inland Youth Forum. Professional Abraham Lincoln impersonator, 1985-, has appeared in solo stage shows and television series, as well as appearances in commercials, print advertisements, and CD-ROMs. Creator of The Living Lincoln (dramatic monologue); A Trip to Gettysburg (monologue); and We Must Think, Anew (motivational dialogue). **Publications:** Honestly Abe: A Cartoon Biography of Abraham Lincoln, 1998. Contributor to educational journals. **Address:** 6019 Falling Tree Ln, Alta Loma, CA 91737, U.S.A. **Online address:** abepress@eee.org

BRAMLY, Serge. French (born Tunisia), b. 1949. **Genres:** Biography, Novels. **Career:** Worked as a journalist, publisher, and art critic. **Publications:** Terre Wakan: Univers sacre des Indiens d'Amerique du Nord, 1974; (ed. and compiler) Macumba: Forces noires du Bresil: Les Enseignements de Maria-Jose, mere des dieux, 1975, trans. by M. Bogin as Macumba: The Teachings of Maria-Jose, Mother of the Gods, 1977, rev. ed. as Macumba: Forces noires du Bresil, 1981; Rudolf Steiner, prophete de l'homme nouveau, 1976; (with E. de Smedt and V. Bardet) La Pratique des arts divina-toires: Astrologie, tarots, chiromancie, geomancie, Yi-king, 1976; L'Itineraire du fou (novel), 1978; Un Piege a lumiere (novel), 1979; Man Ray, 1980; (with J-P.I. Amunategui) Le Livre des dates, 1981; La Danse du loup, 1982; Un Poisson muet, surgi de la mer, 1985; Leonard de Vinci, 1988, trans. by S. Reynolds as Leonardo: Discovering the Life of Leonardo da Vinci, 1991; L. de Vinci: Manuscrit sur le vol des oiseaux, 1989; Le grand cheval de Leonard: Le Projet monumental de Leonard de Vinci, 1990; Madame Satan (novel), 1992; Chambre Close, 1992, trans. by P. Goud; La Terreur dans le boudoir (novel), 1994; Mona Lisa, 1994; Le Reseau Melchior, 1996. **Address:** c/o Publicity Director, Jean Claude Lattes, 17 rue Jacob, F-75006 Paris, France.

BRAMPTON, Sally (Jane). British, b. 1955. **Genres:** Novels. **Career:** Freelance journalist. Vogue, fashion writer, 1978; Observer, fashion editor, 1981; Elle (United Kingdom), editor, 1985-1989; Mirabella, associate editor, 1990-1991. **Publications:** Good Grief, 1992; Concerning Lily, 1998. **Address:** 10a Wedderburn Road, London NW3, England.

BRAMSON, Leon. American, b. 1930. **Genres:** Sociology, Humanities, Social sciences. **Career:** Senior Program Officer, Division of Research, National Endowment for the Humanities, Washington, D.C., 1982-. Professor of Sociology, Swarthmore Coll., Pa., 1970-78 (Associate Professor, 1965-70). Instructor, 1959-61, and Assistant Professor, 1961-65, Dept. of Social Relations, Harvard University, Cambridge, Massachusetts; Program Officer, Exxon Education Foundation, NYC, 1978-80; Coordinator for Social Analysis, Corporate Planning Dept., Exxon Corp., 1980-82. **Publications:** The Political Context of Sociology, 1961; (ed.) Examining in Harvard College: A Collection of Essays by Members of the Harvard Faculty, 1963; (ed. with G.W. Goethals) War: Studies from Psychology, Sociology, Anthropology, 1964; (ed.) Robert MacIver: On Community, Society and Power, 1970. **Address:** National Endowment for the Humanities, 1100 Pennsylvania Ave NW, Washington, DC 20506, U.S.A.

BRANAGH, Kenneth (Charles). Irish, b. 1960. **Genres:** Plays/Screenplays, Film, Theatre. **Career:** Actor, director, producer, playwright, and screenwriter. Member of Royal Shakespeare Theater, 1983-85; Renaissance Theater Company, London, founder, producer, and director, with David Parfitt, 1987-; Renaissance Films PLC, c. 1987. **Publications:** Tell Me Honestly (play), 1985; Public Enemy (play), 1987; (Adapter) Henry V (film), 1989; Beginning (autobiography), 1989; (Adapter) Much Ado about Nothing (film), 1993; A Midwinter's Tale (film), 1995; Hamlet: The Making of the Movie Including the Screenplay, 1996. **Address:** 83 Berwick Street, London W1V 3PJ, England.

BRANCH, Alan E(dward). British, b. 1933. **Genres:** Business/Trade/Industry, Economics, Marketing, Transportation. **Career:** Sr. Lecturer, Basingstoke Coll. of Technology, retired. Visiting Professor of Shipping Economics, European Institute of Maritime Studies; Lecturer, University of Leicester; Lecturer, University of Reading; marketing, shipping, and export consultant. **Publications:** Elements of Shipping, 1964, 7th ed., 1996; Economics of Shipping Practice and Management, 1982; Dictionary of Shipping International Business Trade Terms and Abbreviations, 1983, 4th ed., 1995; Elements of Export Marketing and Management, 1984; Dictionary of Commercial Terms and Abbreviations, 1984; Elements of Port Operation and Management, 1986; Dictionary of English-Arabic Commercial, International Trade and Shipping Terms, 1988; Export-Import Shipping Documentation, 1989; Elements of Import Practice, 1990; Multilingual Dictionary of Commercial International Trade and Shipping Terms: English, French, Spanish, German, 1990; Export Practice and Management, 3rd ed., 1993, 4th ed., 2000; Maritime Economics Management Marketing, 3rd ed., 1997; Shipping and Air Freight Documentation for Exporters and Importers, 2nd ed., 2000; International Purchasing and Management, 2001. **Address:** 19 The Ridings, Emmer Green, Reading, Berks. RG4 8XL, England.

BRANCH, Edgar Marquess. American, b. 1913. **Genres:** Literary criticism and history, Biography, Bibliography. **Career:** Research Professor of English Emeritus and Research Associate in American Literature, Miami University, Oxford, Ohio, 1978- (Professor of English, 1941-64; Chairman of Dept., 1959-64; Research Professor of English, 1964-78). Sr. Fellow, National Endowment for the Humanities, 1971-72 and 1976-77; Guggenheim Fellow, 1979. **Publications:** The Literary Apprenticeship of Mark Twain, 1950; A Bibliography of the Writings of James T. Farrell, 1921-1957, 1959; Clemens of the "Call," 1969; James T. Farrell, 1971; (with F. Anderson) The Great Landslide Case, 1972; (ed. with R.H. Hirst) Mark Twain's Early Tales and Sketches, vol. I, 1851-64, 1979, vol. II, 1864-65, 1981; Men Call Me Lucky: Mark Twain and the Pennsylvania, 1985; (with R.H. Hirst) The Grangerford-

Shepherson Feud: Life and Death at Compromise, 1985; (ed. with M.B. Frank and K.M. Sanderson) Mark Twain's Letters, vol. I, 1853-66, 1988; Mark Twain and The Starchy Boys, 1992; (ed. with H. Smith) Roughing It, by Mark Twain, 1993; Studs Lonigan's Neighborhood and the Making of James T. Farrell, 1996; A Paris Year: Dorothy and James T. Farrell in Paris, 1931-1932, 1998. **Address:** 4810 Bonham Rd, Oxford, OH 45056-1423, U.S.A. **Online address:** ebranch@lib.muohio.edu

BRANCH, Muriel Miller. American, b. 1943. **Genres:** Children's fiction, Children's non-fiction, Education, History. **Career:** Richmond Public Schools, Richmond, VA, library media specialist, 1967-98. Maggie L. Walker Historical Foundation, secretary, vice president, and president. **Publications:** (with D. Rice) Miss Maggie: The Story of Maggie Lena Walker, 1984; (comp. with E.G. Evans) Hidden Skeletons and Other Funny Stories, 1995; (with E.G. Evans) A Step Beyond: Multimedia Activities for Learning American History, 1995; The Water Brought Us: The Story of the Gullah Speaking People, 1995; Juneteenth: Freedom Day, 1998; (with D. Rice) Pennies to Dollars: The Story of Maggie Lena Walker, 1997; (with E. Evans) 3-D Displays for Libraries, Schools and Media Centers, 2000; (with M.E. Lyons) Dear Ellen Bee: A Civil War Scrapbook of Two Union Spies, 2000; Fine Arts and Crafts, 2001. Contributor to professional journals. **Address:** 9315 Radborne Rd, Richmond, VA 23236, U.S.A. **Online address:** mbranch@mindspring.com

BRANCH, Taylor. American, b. 1947. **Genres:** Novels, Autobiography/Memoirs. **Career:** Washington Monthly, Washington, DC, staff member, 1970-73; Harper's, NYC, staff member, 1973-75; Esquire, NYC, staff member, 1975-76; writer. **Publications:** (ed. with C. Peters, and contrib.) Blowing the Whistle: Dissent in the Public Interest, 1972; (with B. Russell) Second Wind: The Memoirs of an Opinionated Man, 1979; The Empire Blues (novel), 1981; (with E.M. Propper) Labyrinth, 1982; Parting the Waters: America in the King Years, 1954-1963, 1988; Pillar of Fire: America in the King Years 1963-1965, 1998. **Address:** c/o George Diskant, 1033 Gayley Ave Ste 202, Los Angeles, CA 90024, U.S.A.

BRAND, Alice Glarden. American, b. 1938. **Genres:** Poetry, Psychology, Writing/Journalism, Essays. **Career:** Taught English and creative writing in New York and New Jersey Public Schools, 1960-78; writing instructor at Rutgers University, Middlesex County College, Somerset County College, and Rider College, 1978-80; University of Missouri-St. Louis, assistant professor, associate professor of English, 1987, 1980-87, director of communications programs and program director of the Gateway Writing Project, 1980-87; Clarion University of Pennsylvania, associate professor of English and director of writing, 1987-89; State University of New York at Brockport, associate professor, 1989-91, director of composition, 1989-92, professor of English, 1992-99, professor emerita, 2000-. Visiting scholar, University of California, Berkeley, 1982-83. Director of creative writing programs in New Jersey, State Teen Arts Festival. **Publications:** Therapy in Writing: A Psycho-Educational Enterprise, 1980; as it happens (poetry), 1983; Studies on Zone (poetry), 1989; The Psychology of Writing: The Affective Experience, 1989; (ed. with R.L. Graves) Presence of Mind: Writing and the Domain beyond the Cognitive, 1994; Court of Common Pleas (poetry), 1996. Contributor of poems, articles, and short stories to anthologies and periodicals. **Address:** State University of New York at Brockport, Brockport, NY 14420, U.S.A. **Online address:** abrand@brockport.edu

BRAND, Dionne. Canadian (born Trinidad and Tobago), b. 1953. **Genres:** Poetry, Race relations. **Career:** Poet, writer, and journalist. Associated with Black Education Project, Toronto, Ontario, Canada; Immigrant Women's Centre, Toronto, Caribbean women's health counselor; Agency for Rural Transformation, Grenada, information and communications officer, 1983. **Publications:** POETRY: 'Fore Day Morning, 1978; Earth Magic, 1980; Primitive Offensive, 1982; Winter Epigrams and Epigrams to Ernesto Cardenal in Defense of Claudia, 1983; Chronicles of the Hostile Sun, 1984; No Language Is Neutral, 1990; In Another Place, not Here, 1996; Land to Light On, 1997; Thirsty, 2002. OTHER: (with K.S. Bhaggiyadatta) Rivers Have Sources, Trees Have Roots: Speaking of Racism, 1986; Sans Souci, and Other Stories, 1989; (with L. De Shield) No Burden to Carry: Narratives of Black Working Women in Ontario, 1920s-1950s, 1991; Bread out of Stone, 1994; At the Full and Change of the Moon (novel), 1999. Contributor to periodicals. **Address:** c/o McClelland and Stewart Ltd, 481 University Ave Ste 900, Toronto, ON, Canada M5G 2E9.

BRAND, Oscar. American (born Canada), b. 1920. **Genres:** Children's fiction, Plays/Screenplays, Songs/Lyrics and libretti, Adult non-fiction, Communications/Media, Music, Documentaries/Reportage. **Career:** Freelance writer, composer and folk-singer. President, Harlequin Productions, and Gypsy Hill Music; Lecturer on Dramatic Writing, Hofstra University, Hempstead, NY; Coordinator of Folk Music, WNYC; host of television folksong progs.; Curator, Songwriters Hall of Fame, NYC. **Publications:** Courting Songs, 1952: Folksongs for Fun, 1957; The Ballad Mongers (autobiography), 1957; Bawdy Songs, 1958; (ed) Words about Music, 1969-; Songs of '76 (music history), 1972; When I First Came to This Land (children), 1974; Party Songs, 1985; Bunyan & the Termites, 1996; The High Road, 1998; The Gender Gap, 1999. AUTHOR & COMPOSER: The Gold Rush (ballet), 1961; In White American (play), 1962; A Joyful Noise (musical play), 1966; The Education of Hyman Kaplan (musical play), 1967; Celebrate (religious songs), 1968; How to Steal an Election (musical play), 1969, rev. ed., 2000; Thunder Rock (musical play), 1974. **Address:** Gypsy Hill Music, Box 1362, Manhasset, NY 11030, U.S.A. **Online address:** OscarBrand@ oscarbrand.com; www.oscarbrand.com

BRAND, Rebecca. *See* CHARNAS, Suzy McKee.

BRANDEN, Nathaniel. American (born Canada), b. 1930. **Genres:** Literary criticism and history, Psychology. **Career:** Psychotherapist in private practice and author, 1956-. Owner and Director, The Biocentric Institute (now the Branden Institute for Self-Esteem), Los Angeles, 1968-. Contributor, Cofounder and Co-editor with Ayn Rand, the Objectivist Newsletter, 1962-65, and under new title The Objectivist, 1966-68. **Publications:** Who Is Ayn Rand?: An Analysis of the Novels of Ayn Rand, 1962; The Psychology of Self-Esteem, 1969; Breaking Free, 1970; The Disowned Self, 1971; The Psychology of Romantic Love, 1980; The Romantic Love Question and Answer Book, 1982, rev. ed. (with E.D. Branden) as What Loves Asks of Us, 1987; If You Could Hear What I Cannot Say, 1983; Honoring the Self, 1984; To See What I See and Know What I Know, 1986; How to Raise Your Self-Esteem, 1987; Judgment Day: My Years with Ayn Rand, 1989; The Power of Self-Esteem, 1992; The Six Pillars of Self-Esteem, 1993; Taking Responsibility: Self-Reliance and the Accountable Life, 1996; The Art of Living Consciously, 1997; Self-Esteem Everyday, 1998; Self-Esteem at Work: How Confident People Make Powerful Companies, 1998; Woman's Self-Esteem: Struggles and Triumphs in the Search for Identity, 1998; My Years with Ayn Rand, 1999.

BRANDENBERG, Franz. Swiss, b. 1932. **Genres:** Children's fiction. **Publications:** I Once Knew a Man, 1970; Fresh Cider and Pie, 1973; A Secret for Grandmother's Birthday, 1975: No School Today, 1975: A Robber! A Robber!, 1976; 1 Wish I Was Sick Too!, 1976; Nice New Neighbors, 1977; What Can You Make of It?, 1977: A Picnic, Hurrah!, 1978: Six New Students, 1978; Everyone Ready? 1979: It's Not My Fault, 1980; Leo and Emily series, 4 vols., 1981-88; Aunt Nina series, 3 vols. 1983-88; Otto Is Different, 1985: The Hit of the Party, 1985; Cock-a-Doodle-Doo, 1986; What's Wrong with a Van?, 1987; A Fun Weekend, 1991. **Address:** 17 Regent's Park Terrace, London NW1 7ED, England.

BRANDENBURG, Jim. American, b. 1945. **Genres:** Zoology, Environmental sciences/Ecology, Photography. **Career:** Worked as a picture editor, Daily Globe, Worthington, MN, during the 1970s; National Geographic, Washington, DC, contract photographer, 1978-92. Commissioned by US Postal Service to photograph and design 10 stamps, released May 1981. Coproducer, director and cinematographer of documentary film, White Wolf, 1988. Has had exhibits in North America and Europe. **Publications:** (and photographer) White Wolf: Living with an Arctic Legend, 1988; (and photographer) Brother Wolf: A Forgotten Promise, 1993; (and photographer) To the Top of the World: Adventures with Arctic Wolves (for children), 1993; (and photographer) Sand and Fog: Adventures in Southern Africa (for children), 1994; (and photographer) An American Safari: Adventures on the North American Prairie, 1995; Scruffy: A Wolf Finds His Place in the Pack, 1996; Chased by the Light, 1998. Contributor of photographs to books and periodicals. **Address:** 14568 Moose Lake Rd, Ely, MN 55731, U.S.A. **Online address:** brthrwolf@aol.com; www.jimbrandenburg.com

BRANDES, Joseph. American (born Poland), b. 1928. **Genres:** History. **Career:** Professor of History, William Paterson University, Wayne, New Jersey, since 1958, now emeritus. Visiting Associate Professor of History, New York University, summers 1963-66; Research Associate, American Jewish History Center, since 1965. Member, Academic Council and Publication Committee, American Jewish Historical Society, since 1971. Consulting Economist, U.S. Dept. of Commerce, Washington, D.C., 1958-60; Public Member, District Ethics Comm, Supreme Court of New Jersey. **Publications:** (Contributing ed.) Pictorial History of the World, 1956; Herbert Hoover and Economic Diplomacy, 1962; Immigrants to Freedom, 1971; contributor to: Encyclopedia Judaica, Jewish-American History and Culture, various journals; review essays in various journals. **Address:** 16-36 Raymond St, Fair Lawn, NJ 07410, U.S.A.

BRANDES, Stuart D. American, b. 1940. **Genres:** History. **Career:** University of Wisconsin, Rock County, Janesville, professor of history, 1967-. **Publications:** American Welfare Capitalism: 1880-1940 (historical monograph), 1976; Warhogs: A History of War Profits in America (historical monograph), 1997. **Address:** University of Wisconsin Rock County, 2909 Kellogg Ave., Janesville, WI 53546, U.S.A. **Online address:** sbrandes@uwc. edu

BRANDEWYNE, Rebecca. American, b. 1955. **Genres:** Novels, Novellas/ Short stories, Mystery/Crime/Suspense, Horror, Romance/Historical, Science fiction/Fantasy, Westerns/Adventure. **Career:** Full-time writer. **Publications:** No Gentle Love, 1980; Forever My Love, 1982; Love, Cherish Me, 1983; Rose of Rapture, 1984; And Gold Was Ours, 1984; The Outlaw Hearts, 1986; Desire in Disguise, 1987; Passion Moon Rising, 1988; Upon a Moon-Dark Moor, 1988; Across a Starlit Sea, 1989; Heartland, 1990; Beyond the Starlit Frost, 1991; Rainbow's End, 1991; Devil's Keep (novella), 1992; Desperado, 1992; Moonstruck (novella), 1993; Swan Road, 1994; The Bounty (novella), 1995; The Jacaranda Tree, 1995; Wildcat, 1995; The Ice Dancers (novella), 1996; Dust Devil, 1996; Hasten Down the Wind (novella), 1996; Hired Husband, 1996; Glory Seekers, 1997; High Stakes, 1999; The Lioness Tamer, 1998.

BRANDI, John. American, b. 1943. **Genres:** Novellas/Short stories, Poetry. **Career:** Artist and poet. Peace Corps, member, South America, 1965-68; poet-in-the-schools, Arts Division, State of New Mexico, 1973-86, and State Council of the Arts, Nevada, Montana, Arkansas, New York, and Alaska, 1980s-1990s; poet-in-the-parks, Carlsbad Caverns and Guadalupe Mountains, NM, 1979; NEA Fellowship for Poetry, 1980; Just Buffalo/Literary Center, NY, writer-in-residence, 1989; Dejerassi Foundation, literature/visual arts residency, 1990; Navajo Nation, poetry, language arts residencies, 1986-. **Publications:** POETRY: Tehachapi Fantasy, 1964; A Nothing Book, 1964; Poem Afternoon in a Square of Guadalajara, 1970; Emptylots: Poems of Venice and L.A., 1971; Field Notes from Alaska, 1971; Three Poems for Spring, 1973; August Poems, 1973; San Francisco Lastday Homebound Hangover Highway Blues, 1973; A Partial Exploration of Palo Flechado Canyon, 1973; Smudgepots: For Jack Kerouac, 1973; Firebook, 1974; The Phoenix Gas Slam, 1974; Turning Thirty Poems, 1974; In a December Storm, 1975; Looking for Minerals, 1975; In a September Rain, 1976; The Guadalupes: A Closer Look, 1978; Poems from Four Corners, 1978; Andean Town circa 1980, 1979; As It Is These Days, 1979; Poems for the People of Coyote, 1980; Sky House/Pink Cottonwood, 1980; At the World's Edge, 1983; Zvleika's Book, 1983; Rite for the Beautification of All Beings, 1983; That Crow That Visited Was Flying Backwards, 1984; That Back Road In, 1985; Poems at the Edge of Day, 1984; (with S. Sanfield) Circling, 1988; Hymn for a Night Feast: Poems 1979-1987, 1989; Shadow Play: Poems 1987-1991, 1992; Turning 50 Poem, 1993; Weeding the Cosmos: Selected Haiku, 1994; Heartbeat Geography, 1995; (with S. Sanfield) No Reason at All, 1995; No Other Business Here, 1999; Stone Garland A Haiku Journey, Northern Vietnam, 2000; Visits to the City of Light, 2000; In What Disappears, 2003. SHORT STORIES: The Cowboy from Phantom Banks, 1983; In the Desert We Do not Count the Days, 1990; A Question of Journey, 1995; Reflections in the Lizard's Eye, 2000; One Cup and Another, 2004; Empty Moon, Belly Full, 2004. OTHER: Desde Alla, 1971; One Week of Mornings at Dry Creek, 1971; Towards a Happy Solstice, 1971; Y Aun Hay Mas, Dreams and Exploration: New and Old Mexico, 1972; Narrowgauge to Riobamba, 1973; Memorandum from a Caribbean Isle, 1977; Diary from Baja, California, 1978; Diary from a Journey to the Middle of the World, 1979. EDITOR: Chimborazo: Life on the Haciendas of Highland Ecuador, 1976; The Noose, 1980; Dog Day Blues, 1985. **Address:** PO Box 275, El Rito, NM 87530, U.S.A.

BRANDS, H. W. American, b. 1953. **Genres:** History. **Career:** Affiliated with Texas A&M University, College Station, beginning in 1987, became professor of history. **Publications:** Cold Warriors, 1988; The Specter of Nationalism, 1989; India and the United States, 1990; Inside the Cold War, 1991; Bound to Empire, 1992; The Devil We Knew, 1993; The Wages of Globalism, 1994; Into the Labyrinth, 1994; The United States in the World, 1994; The Reckless Decade, 1995, 2nd ed, 2002; Since Vietnam, 1996; TR: The Last Romantic, 1997; What America Owes the World, 1998; Masters of Enterprise, 1999; The First American, 2000; The Strange Death of American Liberalism, 2001; The Age of Gold, 2002; Woodrow Wilson, 2003; Lone Star Nation, 2004. EDITOR: The Foreign Policies of Lyndon Johnson, 1999; The Use of Force After the Cold War, 2000; Critical Reflections on the Cold War, 2000; Selected Letters of Theodore Roosevelt, 2001. **Address:** Department of History, Texas A&M University, College Station, TX 77843, U.S.A.

BRANDSTETTER, Alois. Austrian, b. 1938. **Genres:** Novels, Novellas/ Short stories. **Career:** University of Saarland, professor, 1972-74; University of Klagenfurt, professor, 1974. **Publications:** (with R. Rath) Zur Syntax des Wetterberichtes und des Telegrammes, 1968; Über Untermieter (limited edition), 1970; Stille Grösse (limited edition), 1971; Überwindung der Blitzangst, 1971, as Von den Halbschuhen der Flachländer und Der Majestät der Alpen, 1980; Prosaauflösung; Studien zur Rezeption der höfischen Epik im frühnenhochdeutschen Prosaroman, 1971; Ausfälle: Natur-und Kunstgeschichten, 1972, as Von den Halbschuhen der Flachländer und Der Majestät der Alpen, 1980; Zu Lasten der Briefträger: Roman (novel), 1974; Start: Erzählungen (short stories), 1976; Der Leumund des Löwen: Geschichten von grossen Tieren und Menschen (short stories), 1976; Die Abtei: Roman (novel), 1977, trans. by P. and E. Firchow as The Abbey, 1998; Vom Schnee der vergangenen Jahre (short stories), 1979; Von den Halbschuhen der Flachländer und der majestät der alpen: frühe prosa (selected prose works), 1980; Die Mühle: Roman (novel), 1981; Über den grünen Klee der Kindheit (short stories), 1982; Altenehrung: Roman (novel), 1983; Die Burg: Roman (novel), 1986; Landessäure: starke Stücke und schöne Geschichten, 1986; Kleine Menschenkunde, 1987; So wahr ich Feuerbach heise: Roman (novel), 1988; Romulus und WörtherSEE: ein poetisches Wörterbuch, 1989; Vom Manne aus Eicha: Roman (novel), 1991; Vom HörenSagen: eine poetische Akustik, 1992; Almträume: eine Erzählung, 1993; Herbert Wochinz: vom Endspiel zum Theater der Freude, 1994; Hier kocht der Wirt: Roman (novel), 1995; Schonschreiben, 1997; Die Rampe: porträt, 1998; Gros in Fahrt: Roman (novel), 1998; Meine besten Geschichten (selected short stories), 1999. EDITOR: (with R. Malter) Saarbrüker Beiträge zur ästhetik, 1966; Daheim ist daheim. Neue Heimatgeschichten (short stories), 1973; Katzenmusik: Prosa, 1974; Gegenwartsliteratur als Bildungswert, 1982; Österreichische Erzählungen des 20. Jahrhunderts, 1984; (with György Sebestyén) Der Ort, an dem wir uns befinden: ungarische Erzähler der Gegenwart, 1985; Österreichische Erzählungen des 19. Jahrhunderts, 1986. Contributor to books. **Address:** University of Klagenfurt, Universitasstrasse 65-67, A-9020 Klagenfurt, Austria. **Online address:** Alois.Brandstetter@uni.klu.ac.at

BRANDT, Allan M(orris). American, b. 1953. **Genres:** Medicine/Health. **Career:** Smith College, Northampton, MA, lecturer in American history, 1982; Harvard University, Cambridge, MA, assistant professor of history of medicine and science, 1983-87, associate professor, 1987-90; University of North Carolina, Chapel Hill, NC, department of social medicine and history, associate professor, 1990-92; Harvard University, Cambridge, Kass professor of history of medicine and professor of history of science, 1992-. **Publications:** No Magic Bullet: A Social History of Venereal Disease in the United States Since 1880, Oxford University Press, 1985. **Address:** Department of Social Medicine, Harvard Medical School, 641 Huntington Ave., Boston, MA 02115, U.S.A.

BRANDT, Clare. American, b. 1934. **Genres:** Biography. **Career:** Writer. **Publications:** An American Aristocracy: The Livingstons, 1986; The Man in the Mirror: A Life of Benedict Arnold, 1994. **Address:** c/o JCA Literary Agency Inc., 27 West 20th St. No. 1103, New York, NY 10011, U.S.A.

BRANDT, Deborah. American, b. 1951. **Genres:** Writing/Journalism, Documentaries/Reportage. **Career:** Vineland Times-Journal, Vineland, NJ, reporter, 1974-76; University of Wisconsin-Madison, assistant professor, 1983-89, associate professor of English, 1990-. **Publications:** Literacy as Involvement: The Acts of Readers, Writers, and Texts, 1990; Literacy in American Lives, 2001. Contributor to language and communication journals. **Address:** Department of English, 6187E Helen White Hall, University of Wisconsin-Madison, 600 N Park St, Madison, WI 53706, U.S.A. **Online address:** dlbrandt@facstaff.wisc.edu

BRANDT, Richard M. American, b. 1922. **Genres:** Education, Psychology. **Career:** Prof. Emeritus of Education, Univ. of Virginia, Charlottesville, since 1990 (Assoc. Prof., 1965-68; Prof. and Chmn., Dept. of Foundns. of Education, 1968-74; Dean, Sch. of Education, 1974-84; Curry Prof., 1975-90). Instr., 1953-54, Asst. Prof., 1954-57, and Assoc. Prof., 1957-65, Univ. of Maryland, College Park. **Publications:** Studying Behavior in Natural Settings, 1972, 1981; (ed.) Observational Methods in the Classroom, 1973; Public Education under Scrutiny, 1981; Incentive Pay and Career Ladders for Today's Teachers: A Study of Current Programs and Practices, 1990. **Address:** 6403 Rivendell Lane, Crozet, VA 22932, U.S.A.

BRANNEN, Julia (M.). British, b. 1944. **Genres:** Human relations/Parenting, Sociology, Social sciences, Women's studies and issues. **Career:** Central Middlesex Hospital, London, England, research officer and sociologist, 1978-80; University of London, London, England, research worker and sociologist at Bedford College, 1980-82, senior research officer, 1982-, and reader in sociology, 1994-, at Thomas Coram Research Unit, Institute of Education, Member: British Sociological Association, Association of

University Teachers. **Publications:** (with J. Collard) Marriages in Trouble: The Process of Seeking Help, 1982; (with P. Moss) New Mothers at Work: Employment and Childcare, 1988; (with P. Moss) Managing Mothers: Dual Earner Households after Maternity Leave, 1991; (with K. Dodd, A. Oakley, and P. Storey) Young People, Health and Family Life, 1994. EDITOR: (with G. Wilson) Give and Take in Families: Studies in Resource Distribution, 1987; Mixing Methods: Qualitative and Quantitative Research, 1992; (with M. O'Brien) Parenthood and Childhood, 1995; (with M. O'Brien) Children in Families: Research and Policy, 1996; (with B. Bernstein) Children, Research and Policy, 1996. **Address:** Thomas Coram Research Unit, Institute of Education, University of London, 27/28 Woburn Sq., London WC1H 0AA, England.

BRANNIGAN, Gary G(eorge). American, b. 1947. **Genres:** Education, Psychology. **Career:** State University of New York College at Plattsburgh, assistant professor, 1973-76, associate professor, 1976-82, professor of psychology, 1982-, director of Psychological Services Clinic, 1975-80. Clinical psychologist at public schools of Dover, DE, 1970-71, Veterans Administration Hospital (Perry Point, MD), 1971-72, at a school in Newark, DE, 1972, and at Devereux Foundation, 1972-73; Sibley Educational Research and Demonstration Center, school psychologist, 1978-80; consultant to Northern New York Center for the Emotionally Disturbed, Psychological Corp. (San Antonio, TX), Early Education Program, and Infant Intervention Project. **Publications:** (with A. Tolor) Research and Clinical Applications of the Bender-Gestalt Test, 1980; (with N. Brunner) The Modified Version of the Bender-Gestalt Test for Preschool and Primary School Children, 1989, rev. ed., 1996; The Social Psychologists: Research Adventures, 1995; The Developmental Psychologists: Research Adventures across the Life Span; (with M. Merrens) Experiences in Personality, 1998; The Sport Scientists, 1999; Experiencing Psychology: Active Learning Adventures, 2000; Guide to the Qualitative Scoring System for the Modified Version of the Bender-Gestalt Test, 2002; Experiences in Social Psychology: Active Learning Adventures, 2002. EDITOR: Psychoeducational Perspectives: Readings in Educational Psychology, 1982; (with M. Merrens) The Undaunted Psychologist: Adventures in Research, 1992; The Enlightened Educator: Research Adventures in the Schools, 1996; (with E. Allgeier and R. Allgeier) The Sex Scientists, 1998; (with S. Decker) Bender Visual Motor Gestalt Test, 2nd ed., 2003. Work represented in anthologies. **Address:** Department of Psychology, State University of New York College at Plattsburgh, 92 Broad St, Plattsburgh, NY 12901, U.S.A. **Online address:** gary.brannigan@plattsburgh.edu

BRANOVER, Herman. Israeli (born Latvia), b. 1931. **Genres:** Engineering, Physics, Theology/Religion. **Career:** Technical School, Latvia, lecturer in fluid mechanics, 1953-59; Academy of Sciences, Riga, senior scientific worker, 1959-70; Institute of Technology, Riga, professor of fluid mechanics, 1970-71; Ben-Gurion University of the Negev, Beer-Sheva, Israel, professor and head of Center for Magnetohydrodynamics, 1973-. Adjunct professor of applied science at New York University, 1987-. Scientific director of Solmecs Corp. and of Shamir Advanced Technologies Engineering Center Ltd. **Publications:** Textbook of Elementary Hydraulics and Pump Theory, 1960; (with O. Lielausis) Foundations of Hydraulics, 1963; Turbulent Magnetohydrodynamic Flows in Pipes, 1963; Elementary Hydrodynamics, 1967; (with A. Cinober) Magnetohydrodynamics of Incompressible Media, 1970; Magnetohydrodynamic Flow in Ducts, 1978; Return: A Philosophical Autobiography, 1983; (with Eidelman, Golbraikh, and Moisev) Turbulence and Structures, 1999; (with J. Ginsburg) How Great Are Thy Works God, 2000; (with A. Naveh) The Vision of the Heart, 2002. EDITOR: MHD-Flows and Turbulence, 1976, Vol. II (with A. Yakhot), 1979; (with P.S. Lykoudis and Yakhot) Liquid-Metal Flows and Magnetohydrodynamics, 1983; (with Lykoudis and M. Mond) Single- and Multi-Phase Flows in an Electromagnetic Field, 1985; (with Mond and Y. Unger) Liquid Metal Flows, 1988; (with Mond and Yakhot) Current Trends in Turbulent Research, 1988; (with A. Gottfryd and S. Lipskar) Fusion: Absolute Standards in a World of Relativity, 1989; (with Y. Unger) Metallurgical Technologies, Energy and Conversion, and Magnetohydrodynamic Flows, 1993; (Y. Unger) Advances in Turbulence Studies, 1993; (with I. Coven-Attia) Science in the Light of Torah, 1994; (with Y. Unger) Progress in Turbulence Research, 1995. **Address:** Center for MHD Studies, Dept. of Mechanical Engineering, Ben-Gurion University of the Negev, PO Box 653, 84 105 Beer-Sheva, Israel. **Online address:** branover@solmecs.co.il

BRANT, Marley. American, b. 1950. **Genres:** Biography. **Career:** Chrysalis Records, Beverly Hills, CA, executive in artist development, 1976-78; Paramount Television, Hollywood, CA, publicist, 1980-81; ICPR Public Relations, Los Angeles, CA, account executive, 1981-83; Sierra Records, Pasadena, CA, producer, 1983-91; free-lance writer, 1986-. **Publications:** The Outlaw Youngers: A Confederate Brotherhood, 1992; Outlaws: The Illustrated History of the James-Younger Gang, 1997; Jesse James: The Man and the Myth, 1998; Southern Rockers: The Roots and Legacy of Southern Rock, 1999; Freebirds: The Lynyrd Skynyrd Story, 2002; Tales from the Rock and Roll Highway, 2004; Lightning in a Bottle: Paramount Television's Golden Sitcoms, 1973-1983, 2005. Contributor to periodicals, history and music magazines; writer of entertainment and historical biography, and television documentaries. **Address:** PO Box 5175, Marietta, GA 30061, U.S.A. **Online address:** marleybrant.com

BRANTENBERG, Gerd. Norwegian, b. 1941. **Genres:** Novels, Literary criticism and history, Plays/Screenplays. **Career:** Norwegian novelist and feminist activist. High school teacher in Copenhagen, Denmark, 1971-74, and in Oslo, Norway, 1974-82; writer, 1982-. Cofounder of refugee center for women, the Women's High School, Denmark, and Literary Women's Forum, Norway. **Publications:** NOVELS: Opp alle jordens homofile (title means: Arise All Gays of the Earth), 1973, German trans., 1983, English trans. as What Comes Naturally, 1986; Egalia's dotre, 1977, trans. by L. Mackay as The Daughters of Egalia, 1985, another English trans. as Egalia's Daughters, 1985; Ja, vi slutter (title means: Stop Smoking), 1978; Sangem om St. Croix (title means: The Song of St. Croix) 1979, German trans., 1982; Favntak (title means: Embraces), 1983; Ved fergestedet (title means: At the Ferry Crossing) 1985; For alle vinder, 1989, English trans., 1996, title also rendered as Scattered by the Winds. MUSICALS: Egalia, 1982. LITERARY HISTORY AND CRITICISM: (with others) Pea sporet av den tapte lyst: Kjurlighet mellom kvinner som litterurt motiv, 1986; Eremitt og entertainer: Forfatteren moter sitt publikum, 1991. **Address:** c/o Aschehougs Forlag, Schestedsgt. 3, Oslo, Norway.

BRANTLINGER, Patrick (Morgan). American, b. 1941. **Genres:** Literary criticism and history. **Career:** Indiana University, Bloomington, assistant professor, 1968-72, associate professor, 1972-78, professor of English, 1978-, chair of department, 1990-94, director of Victorian Studies Program, 1978-90. **Publications:** The Spirit of Reform: British Literature and Politics, 1832-1867, 1977; Bread and Circuses: Theories of Mass Culture as Social Decay, 1984; Rule of Darkness: British Literature and Imperialism, 1830-1914, 1988; Energy and Entropy: Science and Culture in Victorian Britain; Essays from Victorian Studies, 1989; Crusoe's Footprints: Cultural Studies in Britain and America, 1990; (ed. with J. Naremore) Modernity and Mass Culture (essays), 1991; Fictions of State: Culture and Credit in Britain, 1694-1994, 1996; The Reading Lesson: The Threat of Mass Literacy in Nineteenth-Century British Fiction, 1998; Who Killed Shakespeare?: What's Happened to English since the Radical Sixties, 2001; (ed. with W. Thesing) The Blackwell Companion to the Victorian Novel, 2002; Dark Vanishings: Discourse on the Extinction of Primitive Races, 18001930, 2003. **Address:** Department of English, Indiana University, Bloomington, IN 47405, U.S.A.

BRASCHI, Giannina. American (born Puerto Rico), b. 1953. **Genres:** Poetry, Humor/Satire, Novellas/Short stories, Cultural/Ethnic topics, Women's studies and issues. **Career:** Writer. Gives bilingual readings from her works. **Publications:** Asalto al Tiempo (poems), 1981; La Poesia de Becquer (criticism), 1982; La Comedia Profana (poems), 1985; El Imperio de los Suenos (poems and a novella), 1988, rev. ed., 2000, trans. as Empire of Dreams, 1994; Yo-Yo Boing! (bilingual novel), 1998. **Address:** c/o Publicity Department, Yale University Press, PO Box 209040, New Haven, CT 06520-9040, U.S.A.

BRASHEAR, Jean. (born United States), b. 1949. **Genres:** Romance/Historical. **Career:** Novelist. **Publications:** ROMANCE NOVELS: Millionaire in Disguise, 2001; What the Heart Wants, 2002; The Healer, 2002; The Good Daughter, 2003; Real Hero, 2004; Author of other romance novels. OTHER: Contributor to magazines. **Address:** c/o Author Mail, Harlequin Enterprises, POB 5190, Buffalo, NY 14240, U.S.A. **Online address:** jean@jeanbrashear.com

BRASHER, Norman Henry. *See* Obituaries.

BRASSEAUX, Carl A(nthony). Also writes as Antoine Bourque. American, b. 1951. **Genres:** History, Bibliography, Reference, Translations. **Career:** University of Louisiana at Lafayette, Center for Cultural and Eco-Tourism, assistant director, 1975-2001, director, 2001-, curator of colonial records collection, 1980-, adjunct assistant professor, 1987-90, assistant professor, 1990-98, professor of history, 1998-, Center for Louisiana Studies, director, 2003-; writer. Louisiana History, managing editor, 2003-. Consultant to businesses, organizations, and institutions. **Publications:** HISTORY: (with G.R. Conrad and R.W. Robison) The Courthouses of Louisiana, 1977, 2nd ed., 1998; (comp. with Conrad) Gone but Not Forgotten, vol. 1: St. Peter's Cemetery, New Iberia, LA, 1983; Denis-Nicolas Foucault and the New Orleans Rebel-

lion of 1768, 1987; The Founding of New Acadia, 1987; (trans. with E. Garcia and J.K. Voorhies, annotator with Voorhies, and ed.) Quest for the Promised Land, 1989; In Search of Evangeline, 1989; Lafayette, Where Yesterday Meets Tomorrow, 1990; The Foreign French: French Immigration into the Mississippi Valley, 1820-1900, vol. 1: 1820-1839, 1990, vol. 2: 1840-1848, 1992, vol. 3: 1820-1900, 1993; Scattered to the Wind, 1991; Acadian to Cajun, 1992; Crevasse: The 1927 Flood in Acadiana, 1994; (with C. Oubre and K.P. Fontenot) Creoles of Color in the Bayou Country, 1995; A Refuge for All Ages, 1996; France's Forgotten Legion, 2000; Steamboats on Louisiana's Bayous, 2004; French, Cajun, Creole, Houma, forthcoming; (wit M. Bienvenu and R.A. Brasseaux) A History of Cajun Cuisine, forthcoming. REFERENCE WORKS: (with Conrad) A Selected Bibliography of Scholarly Literature on Colonial Louisiana and New France, 1982; (with Conrad) Louisiana History: The Journal of the Louisiana Historical Association: Index to Vols. 1-25, 1985, Index to Vol. 26-30, 1990; (with M.J. Foret) A Bibliography of Acadian History, Literature, and Genealogy, 1955-1985, 1986; (with Conrad) A Bibliography of Scholarly Literature on Colonial Louisiana and New France, 1992. OTHER: (as Antoine Bourque) Trois Saisons: Nouvelles, contes, et fables, 1988. EDITOR: (trans. and annotator) A Comparative View of French Louisiana: The Journals of Pierre Le Moyne d'Iberville and Jean-Jacques-Blaise d'Abbadie, 1979, 2nd ed., 1980; (with M. Allain) A Franco-American Overview: Louisiana, vol. 5, 1981, vol. 6, 1981, vol. 7: The Postbellum Period, 1982, vol. 8: French Louisiana in the 20th Century, 1982; (with Conrad, and annotator) M.deV. du Terrage, The Last Years of French Louisiana, 1982; (assoc.) Dictionary of Louisiana Biography, 1988, (with J.D. Wilson Jr.) Ten-Year Supplement, 1988-1998, 1998; (and annotator, with Conrad) The Road to Louisiana: The Saint-Domingue Refugees, 1792-1809, 1992. Work represented in anthologies. Contributor to periodicals. **Address:** Center for Cultural and Eco-Tourism, University of Louisiana at Lafayette, PO Box 40831, Lafayette, LA 70504, U.S.A. **Online address:** brasseaux@louisiana.edu

BRATT, James D. American, b. 1949. **Genres:** History, Theology/Religion. **Career:** University of Pittsburgh, PA, assistant professor to associate professor of religious studies, 1978-87; Calvin College, Grand Rapids, MI, professor of history, 1987-; Calvin Center for Christian Scholarship, director, 1998. **Publications:** Dutch Calvinism in Modern America, 1984; (ed.) Viewpoints: Exploring the Reformed Tradition, 1991; (with C. Meehan) Gathered at the River: Grand Rapids, Michigan, and Its People of Faith, 1993; (ed.) Abraham Kuyper: A Centennial Anthology, 1997. **Address:** Department of History, Calvin College, 1845 Knollcrest Circle SE, Grand Rapids, MI 49546-4402, U.S.A. **Online address:** jbratt@calvin.edu

BRAUDY, Leo. American, b. 1941. **Genres:** Film, History, Literary criticism and history, Social commentary. **Career:** Taught at Yale University, New Haven, CT, 1966-68, Columbia University, NYC, 1968-76, and Johns Hopkins, Baltimore, 1976-83; University of Southern California, Los Angeles, Leo S. Bing Professor of English, 1983-, University Professor, 1997-. **Publications:** Narrative Form in History and Fiction: Hume, Fielding, and Gibbon, 1970; Jean Renoir: The World of His Film, 1972; The World in a Frame: What We See in Films, 1977, 3rd ed., 2002; The Frenzy of Renown: Fame and Its History, 1986, 2nd ed., 1997; Native Informant: Essays on Film, Fiction and Popular Culture, 1992; From Chivalry to Terrorism: War and the Changing Nature of Masculinity, 2003; On the Waterfront, 2005. EDITOR: Norman Mailer: A Collection of Critical Essays, 1972; Focus on Shoot the Piano Player (film), 1972; (with M. Dickstein) Great Film Directors, 1978; (with M. Cohen and G. Mast) Film Theory and Criticism, 4th ed., 1992, 6th ed. (with M. Cohen), 2004. **Address:** Dept of English, University of Southern California, Los Angeles, CA 90089-0354, U.S.A. **Online address:** braudy@usc.edu

BRAULT, Jacques. Canadian, b. 1933. **Genres:** Poetry, Plays/Screenplays, Literary criticism and history. **Career:** Writer and educator. University of Montreal, Montreal, Quebec, professor. **Publications:** POETRY: (with R. Perusse and C. Mathieu) Trinome, (Montreal), 1957; (with M. Van Schendel and others) La Poesie et nous, 1958; Memoire, 1965, rev. and enlarged, 1968; Miron le magnifique, 1966; Suite fraternelle, 1969; L'en dessous, l'admirable, 1972, trans. by G. Sanderson as Within the Mystery, 1986; La Poesie ce matin, 1971; Trois Partitions, 1972; Poemes des quatre cotes, 1975; Chemin faisant, 1975; Droits des salaries et autogestion: propositions concretes pour les entreprises francaises, 1975; Les Hommes de paille, 1978; Migration, 1979; Vingt-quatre murmures en novembre, 1980; (with M. Beaulieu) P.V. Beaulieu, 1981; Trois fois passera precede de Jour et nuit, Noroit, 1981; Moments Fragiles, 1981, bilingual ed, with trans. by B. Callaghan, 1985; La Naissance des nuages, 1984; Ductus, 1985; Poemes I, 1986; La Poussiere du chemin, 1989; Il n'y a plus de chemin, 1990, trans. by D. Sobelman as On the Road No More, 1993; (with R. Melancon) Au petit matin, 1993. Poems have appeared in periodicals. PROSE: (with A. Brochu and A. Major) Nouvelles, 1963; Agonie, 1984, trans. by D. Lobdell as Deathwatch, 1987. TELEPLAYS: La Morte-Saison, 1968; Quand nous serons heureux, 1969. OTHER: Alain Grandbois, 1958, rev, 1967; (ed., with B. Lacroix) Saint-Denys Garneau: Oeuvres, 1971. Contributor of nonfiction to periodicals. **Address:** 231, Chemin Saint-Armand, Saint-Armand ouest, QC, Canada J0J 1T0.

BRAUN, Marta (A.). Canadian, b. 1946. **Genres:** Film, Photography. **Career:** Ryerson Polytechnic University, Toronto, ON, professor of film and photography, 1975-. Visiting professor at Ontario College of Art, 1978-79, and University of Waterloo, 1981-82; curator of exhibitions at Milan's Galleria Ciovasso, 1974, and Eastman House, 1982; Toronto Arts Awards, member of board of directors, 1989-; consultant on the early cinema and E.J. Marey and E.J. Muybridge; Opera Atelier, member of board of directors, 1988-91. **Publications:** Picturing Time: The Work of Etienne-Jules Marey, 1992. Contributor to periodicals. **Address:** Ryerson Polytechnic University, 350 Victoria St., Toronto, ON, Canada M5B 1K3. **Online address:** mbraun@acs.ryerson.ca

BRAUN, Matt(hew). American, b. 1932. **Genres:** Westerns/Adventure. **Career:** Journalist, 1956-69, then freelance writer. Member, Board of Dirs., Western Writers of America. Recipient: Golden Spur Award, Best Western Historical Novel, 1976; Stirrup Award, 1987, 1988; Cowboy Spirit Award, 1999; Eagle Feather Award, 1999; Doc Holliday Award, 1999; inducted into Cowboy Hall of Fame, 1999. **Publications:** Mattie Silks, 1972; Black Fox, 1972; The Savage Land, 1973; El Paso, 1973; Noble Outlaw, 1975; Bloody Hand, 1975; Cimarron Jordan, 1975; Kinch, 1975; Buck Colter, 1975; The Kincaids, 1976; The Second Coming of Lucas Brokaw, 1977; The Save-Your-Life Defense Handbook (nonfiction), 1977; Hangman's Creek, 1979; Lords of the Land, 1979; the Stuart Women, 1980; Jury of Six, 1980; Tombstone, 1981; The Spoilers, 1981; Manhunter, 1981; Deadwood, 1981; Deadwood, No. 6, 1981; The Judas Tree, No. 7, 1982; The Killing Touch, 1983; This Loving Promise, 1984; Santa Fe, 1985; Rio Hondo, 1987; Windward West, 1987; A Distant Land, 1988; Matt Braun's Western Cooking, 1988; How to Write Western Novels, 1988; A Time of Innocence, 1985; Tenbow, 1990; Westward of the Law, 1991; The Brannocks, 1986; Wyatt Earp, 1994; Outlaw Kingdom, 1995; Texas Empire, 1996; One Last Town, 1997; Doc Holliday, 1997; The Last Stand, 1998; Gentleman Rogue, 1998; Bloodsport, 1999; Deathwalk, 2000; Hickok & Cody, 2001; The Wild Ones, 2002; The Overlords, 2003; The Warlords, 2003. **Address:** c/o Richard Curtis Associate, Inc, 171 E 74th St Ste 2, New York, NY 10021, U.S.A. **Online address:** www.mattbraun.com

BRAUN, Richard Emil. American, b. 1934. **Genres:** Poetry, Translations. **Career:** University of Alberta, Edmonton, Dept. of Classics, Professor Emeritus, 1996- (Lecturer, 1962-64; Assistant Professor, 1964-69, Associate Professor, 1969-76, Professor, 1976-96). Poetry Editor, Modern Poetry Studies, 1970-77. **Publications:** Children Passing, 1962; Bad Land, 1971; The Foreclosure, 1972; (trans.) Sophocles: Antigone, 1973; (trans.) Euripides: Rhesos, 1978; (trans. and commentary) Persius: Satires, 1984; Last Man In, 1990; The Snow Man Is No One, 2001. **Address:** c/o Joan Daves, 21 W 26th St, New York, NY 10010-1003, U.S.A. **Online address:** krbraun@bcsupernet.com

BRAUN, Stephen R. American, b. 1957. **Genres:** Adult non-fiction. **Career:** Writer. New England Research Institutes, Boston, MA, executive producer, 1994-. **Publications:** Buzz: The Science and Lore of Alcohol and Caffeine, 1996. **Address:** New England Research Institutes, 9 Galen St., Watertown, MA 02472, U.S.A. **Online address:** stephenb@neri.org

BRAUND, Kathryn E. Holland. American, b. 1955. **Genres:** History. **Career:** Writer. **Publications:** Deerskins and Duffels: Creek Indian Trade with Anglo-America, 1685-1815, 1993. **Address:** c/o University of Nebraska Press, 901 North 17th St., Lincoln, NE 68588, U.S.A.

BRAUNMULLER, A(lbert) R(ichard). American, b. 1945. **Genres:** Literary criticism and history. **Career:** University of California, Los Angeles, assistant professor, 1971-76, associate professor, 1976-81, professor of English, 1982-. **Publications:** George Peele, 1983; Natural Fictions: George Chapman's Major Tragedies, 1992. EDITOR: (and author of intro) Bertolt Brecht, The Rise and Fall of the City of Mahagonny, 1976; The Captive Lady, 1982; A Seventeenth-Century Letter Book: A Facsimile Edition of Folger MS Va321, 1983; (with J. Bulman) Comedy from Shakespeare to Sheridan: Change and Continuity in the English and European Tradition, 1986; W. Shakespeare, King John, 1989; (with M. Hattway) Cambridge Companion to

English Renaissance Drama, 1990; W. Shakespeare, Macbeth, 1997. **Address:** Department of English, University of California, PO Box 90095, Los Angeles, CA 90095, U.S.A.

BRAUNTHAL, Gerard. American (born Germany), b. 1923. **Genres:** International relations/Current affairs, Politics/Government. **Career:** University of Massachusetts, Amherst, instructor, 1954-57, assistant professor, 1957-62, associate professor, 1962-67, professor, 1967-88, professor emeritus of political science, 1988-. **Publications:** The Federation of German Industry in Politics, 1965; The West German Legislative Process: A Case Study of Two Transportation Bills, 1972; Socialist Labor and Politics in Weimar Germany: The General Federation of German Trade Unions, 1978; The West German Social Democrats 1969-82: Profile of a Party in Power, 1983; 2nd ed. as The German Social Democrats since 1969: A Party in Power and Opposition, 1993; Political Loyalty and Public Service in West Germany: The 1972 Decree against Radicals and Its Consequences, 1990; Parties and Politics in Modern Germany, 1996. **Address:** 161 Red Gate Lane, Amherst, MA 01002, U.S.A. **Online address:** gbraunth@polsci.umass.edu

BRAVEBOY-WAGNER, Jacqueline Anne. American (born Trinidad and Tobago), b. 1948. **Genres:** International relations/Current affairs, Politics/Government. **Career:** Bowling Green State University, OH, assistant professor of political science, 1979-81; Friends World College (now part of Long Island University), coordinator of Latin American program, 1983-84; City College of the City University of New York, NYC, associate professor, 1984-91, professor of political science, 1999-2002; Graduate School and University Center of the City University of New York, associate professor, 1984-91, professor, 1991-. Tokyo Metropolitan University, visiting professor, 1988. United Nations, fellow of UN Institute for Training and Research, 1990-91; consultant to Caribbean Community and to local and regional organizations in Latin America and the Caribbean, 1986-. **Publications:** The Venezuela-Guyana Boundary Dispute: A Study in Conflict Resolution, 1984; Interpreting the Third World: Politics, Social and Economic Issues, 1986; The Caribbean in World Affairs: Foreign Policies of the English-Speaking Caribbean, 1989, 2nd ed., in press; (with W.M. Will, D.J. Gayle, and I. Griffith) The Caribbean in the Pacific Century, 1993; Caribbean Diplomacy, 1996; (ed. with Gayle) Caribbean Public Policy: Regional, Cultural, and Socioeconomic Issues for the Twenty-First Century, 1997; The Foreign Policies of the Global South: Re-Thinking Conceptual Frameworks, 2003. Contributor to professional journals. **Address:** Department of Political Science, City College of the City University of New York, 138th St and Convent Ave, New York, NY 10031, U.S.A. **Online address:** wiscc@cuny.edu

BRAVERMAN, Melanie. American, b. 1960. **Genres:** Novels, Poetry. **Career:** Writer. **Publications:** East Justice (novel), 1996. **Address:** 633 Commercial, Provincetown, MA 02657, U.S.A. **Online address:** melaniebraverman@earthlink.net

BRAVERMAN, Terry. American, b. 1953. **Genres:** Self help, Humor/Satire, Psychology. **Career:** Owner of laser art businesses in San Diego and Los Angeles, CA, 1982-93; professional speaker and humorist, 1992-. Professional standup comic, 1988-91; musician. **Publications:** When the Going Gets Tough, the Tough Lighten Up!, 1997. Contributor to magazines. **Address:** PO Box 11571, Marina Del Rey, CA 90295, U.S.A. **Online address:** mirthpro@netzero.net

BRAWLEY, Ernest. American, b. 1937. **Genres:** Novels. **Career:** Railroad brakeman, 1956-59; prison guard, 1962; English teacher, 1963-64, and 1969-70; barman, 1965; janitor, 1967-68; City University of New York, adjunct lecturer, 1985-97. **Publications:** The Rap, 1974; Selena, 1979; The Alamo Tree, 1984. **Address:** c/o John Hawkins and Assocs, 71 W. 23rd St., No. 1600, New York, NY 10010, U.S.A.

BRAWLEY, Robert L. American, b. 1939. **Genres:** Theology/Religion. **Career:** Memphis Theological Seminary, Memphis, TN, professor of the New Testament, 1979-92; McCormick Theological Seminary, Chicago, IL, Albert G. McGraw professor of the New Testament, 1992-. **Publications:** Luke-Acts and the Jews, 1987; Centering on God, 1990; Text to Text Pours Forth Speech, 1995; (ed. and contrib.) Biblical Ethics and Homosexuality, 1995. **Address:** McCormick Theological Seminary, 5460 S University Ave, Chicago, IL 60615, U.S.A.

BRAXTON, Joanne M(argaret). (Jodi). American, b. 1950. **Genres:** Literary criticism and history. **Career:** University of Michigan, Ann Arbor, Michigan Society of Fellows, 1976-79; College of William and Mary, Williamsburg, VA, assistant professor, 1980-86, associate professor, 1986-89,

Frances L. and Edwin L. Cummings Professor of American Studies and English, and professor of English, 1989-. **Publications:** (as Jodi Braxton) Sometimes I Think of Maryland, 1977; Black Women Writing Autobiography: A Tradition within a Tradition, 1989; (ed. with A.N. McLaughlin) Wild Women in the Whirlwind: Afra-American Culture and the Contemporary Literary Renaissance (anthology), 1990; (ed.) The Collected Poetry of Paul Laurence Dunbar, 1993; My Magic Pours Secret Libations, 1996. Contributor of essays to books and poetry to anthologies. **Address:** Department of English, College of William and Mary, Tucker Hall, Williamsburg, VA 23187, U.S.A. **Online address:** jmbrax@wm.edu; www.wm.edu/mid-pass

BRAYBON, (Charmian) Gail. British, b. 1952. **Genres:** History, Women's studies and issues. **Career:** University of Brighton, computer officer, 1985-; historian. **Publications:** Women Workers in the First World War, 1981; (with P. Summerfield) Out of the Cage, 1987; Evidence, History and the Great War: Histomans and the Impact of 1914-18, 2003. Contributor of essays and reviews to books and journals. **Address:** St. Peter's House Library, University of Brighton, Grand Parade, Brighton, E. Sussex BN2 2JY, England.

BRAYFIELD, Celia. British, b. 1945. **Genres:** Novels. **Career:** Writer. Nova, London, trainee journalist, 1968; Observer, London, fashion writer, 1969; Daily Mail, London, features writer, 1969-71; free-lance writer, 1971-74; Evening Standard, London, TV columnist, 1974-82; The Times, London, TV critic, 1982-88; feature writer, 1998-; Sunday Telegraph, columnist, 1989. **Publications:** NON-FICTION: Glitter: The Truth about Fame, 1985; Bestseller, 1996; Deep France, 2004. NOVELS: Pearls, 1987; The Prince, 1989; White Ice, 1993; Harvest, 1995; Getting Home, 1998; Sunset, 1999; Heartswap, 2000; Mister Fabulous and Friends, 2003; Wild Weekend, 2004.

BRAZAITIS, Mark. American, b. 1966. **Genres:** Novellas/Short stories. **Career:** Peace Corps volunteer, Santa Cruz Verapaz, Guatemala, 1990-93; Bowling Green Junior High School, Bowling Green, OH, creative writing instructor, 1993-94; Bowling Green State University, Bowling Green, OH, English instructor, 1993-95; Farmer-to-Farmer program, U.S. AID, Matehuala, San Luis Potosi, Mexico, technical consultant, 1995; World Learning Center, Santa Lucia Milpas Altas, Guatemala, technical trainer, 1995-96; Helene Fuld College of Nursing, NYC, adjunct English professor, 1996-; Fordham University, Bronx, NY, adjunct English professor, 1998-. **Publications:** The River of Lost Voices: Stories from Guatemala, 1998. Contributor of short stories to publications. Contributor of poems to periodicals. Contributor of articles to newspapers and publications. **Address:** 5483 30th St. NW, Washington, DC 20015, U.S.A.

BREAKWELL, Glynis M(arie). British, b. 1952. **Genres:** Psychology, Social sciences, Sociology. **Career:** University of Bradford, lecturer in social psychology, 1976-78; University of Oxford, Nuffield College, Prize Fellow, 1978-81; University of Surrey, Guildford, lecturer in social psychology, 1981-87, Manor Hall, warden, 1981-83, senior lecturer in psychology, 1987-88, reader, 1988-91, head of department of psychology, 1990-95, professor of psychology, 19912001, pro-vice-chancellor, 1994-2001, head of School of Human Sciences, 1997-2001; University of Bath, vice-chancellor, 2001-. **Publications:** (with C. Rowett) Social Work, 1982; The Quiet Rebel: Women at Work in a Man's World, 1985; Coping with Threatened Identities, 1986; Facing Physical Violence, 1990; (with C. Rowett) Interviewing, 1990; Managing Violence at Work, 1992; (with others) Careers and Identities, 1992; (with L. Millward) Basic Evaluation Methods, 1995; Coping with Aggressive Behaviour, 1997. EDITOR: (with H. Foot and R. Gilmour) Social Psychology, 1982; Threatened Identities, 1983; (with H. Foot and R. Gilmour) Doing Social Psychology, 1987; (and co-author) Social Psychology of Political and Economic Cognition, 1991; (and co-author) Social Psychology of Identity and the Self Concept, 1992; (and author with Canter) Empirical Approaches to Social Representations, 1993; (with S. Hammond and C. Fife-Schaw) Research Methods in Psychology, 1994, 2nd ed., 2000; (with E. Lyons) Changing European Identities, 1996; Doing Social Psychology Research, 2004. **Address:** Vice-Chancellor, University of Bath, Bath BA2 7AY, England. **Online address:** g.breakwell@bath.ac.uk

BREARS, Peter C. D. British, b. 1944. **Genres:** Crafts, Food and Wine, History. **Career:** Writer and Museums Consultant; Director, Leeds City Museums, 1979-94. Curator, Curtis Museum, Alton, Hants, 1967-69; Keeper, Shibden Hall, Halifax, 1969-72; Curator, Clarke Hall, Wakefield, 1972-75; Curator, The Castle Museum, York, 1975-79. **Publications:** The English Country Pottery: Its History and Techniques, 1971; The Collector's Book of English Country Pottery, 1971; Yorkshire Probate Inventories 1542-1685, 1972; St. Mary's Heritage Centre, York, 1976; York Castle Museum, 1978; Yorkshire Farmhouse Fare, 1978; The Castle Museum, York, Guidebook, 1978; The Kitchen Catalogue, 1979; The Dairy Catalogue, 1979; Horse

Brasses, 1981; The Gentlewoman's Kitchen, 1984; Food and Cooking in Britain, 1985; Traditional Food in Yorkshire, 1987; North Country Folk Art, 1989; Of Curiosities and Rare Things, 1989; Treasures for the People, 1989; Images of Leeds, 1992; Leeds Describ'd, 1993; Leeds Waterfront, 1994; The Country House Kitchen, 1996; The Old Devon Farmhouse, 1998; Ryedale Recipes, 1998; A Taste of Leeds, 1998; All the King's Cooks, 1999; The Compleat Housekeeper, 2000; The Boke of Kervynge, 2003. **Address:** 4, Woodbine Terrace, Headingley, Leeds LS6 4AF, England.

BREBNER, Philip. British, b. 1955. **Genres:** Adult non-fiction. **Career:** King Abdulaziz University, Jeddah, Saudi Arabia, assistant professor of architecture and planning, 1982-84; Universidade do Porto, Porto, Portugal, assistant professor of architecture and planning, 1985-90; writer. **Publications:** A Country of Vanished Dreams, 1992; The Fabulous Road, 1997; Contributor to periodicals. **Address:** c/o PFD, Drury House, 34-43 Russell Street, London WC2B 5HA, England.

BRECHER, Michael. Canadian, b. 1925. **Genres:** International relations/Current affairs, Politics/Government, Social sciences. **Career:** McGill University, Montreal, lecturer, 1952-54, assistant professor, 1954-58, associate professor, 1958-63, professor, 1963-93, R.B. Angus Professor of Political Science, 1993-. Visiting professor: Chicago, 1963, Hebrew University of Jerusalem, 1970-75, Berkeley, 1979, Stanford, 1980. **Publications:** The Struggle for Kashmir, 1953; Nehru: A Political Biography, 1959, abridged ed., 1961; The New States of Asia, 1963; Succession in India: A Study in Decision-Making, 1966; India and World Politics: Krishna Menon's View of the World, 1968; Political Leadership in India: An Analysis of Elite Attitudes, 1969; The Foreign Policy System of Israel: Setting, Images, Process, 1972; Israel, the Korean War and China, 1974; Decisions in Israel's Foreign Policy, 1974; Studies in Crisis Behavior, 1979; Decisions in Crisis: Israel 1967 and 1973, 1980; Crisis and Change in World Politics, 1986; Crises in the Twentieth Century, 2 vols., 1988; Crisis, Conflict, and Instability, 1989; Crises in World Politics, 1993; A Study of Crisis, 1997; Millennial Reflections on International Studies, 5 vols., 2002. **Address:** Dept of Political Science, McGill University, 855 Sherbrooke St W, Montreal, QC, Canada H3A 2T7. **Online address:** michael.brecher@mcgill.ca

BREDERO, Adriaan H(endrik). Dutch, b. 1921. **Genres:** History. **Career:** Bonifatiuscollege, Utrecht, Netherlands, professor of history, 1948-66; Theological Faculty, Tilburg, Netherlands, professor of church history, 1967-75; Free University, Amsterdam, Netherlands, professor of medieval history, 1976-86. **Publications:** Etudes sur la "Vita Prima" de Saint Bernard, 1960; Cluny et Citeaux au douzieme siecle, 1975; (ed.) Christendom and Christianity in the Middle Ages, 1994 (originally in Dutch, 1986); Bernard of Clairvaux, 1996 (originally in Dutch, 1993); The Dechristianization of the Middle Ages (in Dutch), 2000. Author of other publications. **Address:** Hoge Ham 55 zwart, 5104 JB Dongen, Netherlands.

BREEDEN, Joann Elizabeth. American, b. 1934. **Genres:** Human relations/Parenting. **Career:** Serenity Lane, Eugene, OR, lecturer, 1977-, supervisor of Family Program, 1977-87, director of Family Education Services, 1987-. Gives workshops and public lectures. **Publications:** Chemical Family, 1984; Love, Hope, and Recovery: Healing the Pain of Addiction, 1994. **Address:** Serenity Lane, 616 East 16th, Eugene, OR 97401, U.S.A.

BREHONY, Kathleen A. American. **Genres:** Self help. **Career:** Psychotherapist; clinical psychologist; personal coach; public speaker; author. **Publications:** Awakening at Midlife: Realizing Your Potential for Growth and Change, 1996; Ordinary Grace: An Examination of the Roots of Compassion, Altruism, and Empathy, and the Ordinary Individuals Who Help Others in Extraordinary Ways, 1999; (with R. Gass) Chanting: Discovering Spirit in Sound, 1999; After the Darkest Hour: How Suffering Begins the Journey to Wisdom, 2000. EDITOR: (with L.W. Frederiksen and L. Solomon) Marketing Health Behavior: Principles, Techniques, and Applications, 1984; (with E.D. Rothblum) Boston Marriages: Romantic but Asexual Relationships among Contemporary Lesbians, 1993. **Address:** c/o Henry Holt & Co., 115 West 18th St., New York, NY 10011, U.S.A. **Online address:** kathleen@jonesbrehony.com

BREIVIK, Patricia Senn. American, b. 1939. **Genres:** Librarianship, Education. **Career:** Fund raiser for church-related activities, NYC, 1962-67; school librarian, NYC, 1969-70; Brooklyn College of the City University of New York, Brooklyn, NY, humanities reference librarian, 1970; Pratt Institute, Brooklyn, lecturer, 1971-72, assistant professor and assistant dean of Graduate School of Library and Information Science, 1972-76; Sangamon State University, Springfield, IL, dean of library services and associate professor, 1976-79; University of Colorado at Denver, director of Auraria Library and professor, 1979-90, special assistant to the president, 1984-90; Towson State University, Towson, MD, associate vice-president for information resources, 1990-95; Wayne State University, Detroit, MI, dean of university libraries, 1995-. **Publications:** Open Admissions and the Academic Library, 1977; Planning the Library Instruction Program, 1982; (with E.G. Gee) Information Literacy: Revolution in the Library, 1989; (with J.A. Senn) Information Literacy: Educating Children for the Twenty-First Century, 1994, 2nd ed., 1998; Student Learning in the Information Age, 1997. EDITOR & CONTRIBUTOR: (with E.B. Gibson) Funding Alternatives for Libraries, 1979; Managing Programs for Learning outside the Classroom, 1986; (with R. Wedgeworth) Libraries and the Search for Academic Excellence, 1988. Contributor to library journals. **Address:** University Libraries, Wayne State University, 5155 Anthony Wayne Dr., Detroit, MI 48202, U.S.A. **Online address:** p.breivik@wayne.edu

BRENDON, Piers. British, b. 1940. **Genres:** Biography. **Career:** Freelance writer. Cambridgeshire College of Arts and Technology, Lecturer, 1971-76, Head of the History Dept., 1977-80; Cambridge University, Keeper of the Churchill Archives and Fellow of Churchill College, 1995-2001. **Publications:** Hurrell Froude and the Oxford Movement, 1974; Hawker of Morwenstow: Portrait of a Victorian Eccentric, 1975; Eminent Edwardians, 1979; The Life and Death of the Press Barons, 1982; Winston Churchill, 1984; Our Own Dear Queen, 1986; Ike: The Life and Times of Dwight D. Eisenhower, 1987; Thomas Cook: 150 Years of Popular Tourism, 1991; (with P. Whitehead) The Windsors: A Dynasty Revealed, 1994; The Motoring Century: The Story of the Royal Automobile Club, 1997; The Dark Valley: A Panorama of the 1930s, 2000. EDITOR (all with W. Shaw): Reading They've Liked, 1967; Reading Matters, 1969; By What Authority?, 1972. **Address:** 4b Millington Rd, Cambridge, England. **Online address:** pb204@cam.ac.uk

BRENER, Milton E(rnest). American, b. 1930. **Genres:** Anthropology/Ethnology, Art/Art history, Psychology, Documentaries/Reportage. **Career:** Orleans Parish, LA, assistant district attorney, 1956-58, part-time, 1962-63; Garon, Brener and Mc Neely, trial lawyer, 1958-91. Pilot, flight instructor, opera critic. **Publications:** The Garrison Case: a Study of the Abuse of Power, 1969; The Other Side of the Airport: The Private Pilot's World, 1982; Opera Offstage: Passion and Politics behind the Great Operas, 1996; Faces: The Changing Look of Humankind, 2000; Vanishing Points: Three Dimensional Perspectives in Art and History, 2004. **Address:** 1704 Audubon Trace, Jefferson, LA 70121, U.S.A. **Online address:** mebrener@aol.com

BRENNA, Duff. American. **Genres:** Novels. **Career:** California State University in San Marcos, teacher of creative writing. Former dairy farm worker. **Publications:** The Book of Mamie (novel), 1989; The Holy Book of the Beard, 1996; Too Cool, 1998; The Altar of the Body, 2001. **Address:** Department of English, California State University, 333 S. Twin Oaks Valley Rd., San Marcos, CA 92096, U.S.A. **Online address:** dbrenna@mailhost1.csusm.edu

BRENNAN, Herbie. See **BRENNAN, J(ames) H(erbert).**

BRENNAN, J(ames) H(erbert). Also writes as Herbie Brennan, Cornelius Rumstuckle, Maria Palmer, Jan Brennan. Irish, b. 1940. **Genres:** Children's fiction, Children's non-fiction, Science fiction/Fantasy, Paranormal. **Career:** Writer and lecturer. Full-time author, 1973-. Worked as a journalist, newspaper and magazine editor, hypnotherapist, counselor, marketer, and director of an advertising firm. Facilitator of seminars. Creator of computer software. Developer of boxed games. **Publications:** FOR CHILDREN. Marcus Mustard, 1994; The Mystery Machine, 1995; Blood Brothers, 1996; (as Cornelius Rumstuckle) The Book of Wizardry: The Apprentice's Guide to the Secrets of the Wizard's Guild, 2003. BARMY JEFFERS SERIES: Barmy Jeffers and the Quasimodo Walk, 1988; Return of Barmy Jeffers and the Quasimodo Walk, 1988; Barmy Jeffers and the Shrinking Potion, 1989. ICE AGE SERIES: Shiva: An Adventure of the Ice Age, 1989; The Crone: An Adventure of the Ice Age, 1990, in US as Shiva Accused: An Adventure of the Ice Age, 1991; Ordeal by Poison, 1992, in US as Shiva's Challenge: An Adventure of the Ice Age, 1992. HORRORSCOPE SERIES: (as Maria Palmer) Capricorn's Children, 1995; Cancer: The Black Death, 1995; The Gravediggers, 1996. FANTASY GAME BOOKS. SAGAS OF THE DEMONSPAWN SERIES: Demonspawn, 1984; Fire Wolf, 1984; The Crypts of Terror, 1984; Demonstration, 1984; Ancient Evil, 1985; Demondoom, 1985. GRAILQUEST SERIES; The Castle of Darkness, 1984; The Den of Dragons, 1984; The Gateway of Doom, 1984; Voyage of Terror, 1985; Kingdom of Horror, 1985; Realm of Chaos, 1986; Tomb of Nightmares, 1986; Legion of the Dead, 1987. OTHER FANTASY GAME BOOKS: The Curse of Frankenstein, 1986; Dracula's Castle, 1986; Monster Horrorshow, 1987. NONFICTION: Mindpower 1: Succeed at School, 1990; Mindpower 2:

Make Yourself a Success, 1990; The Young Ghost Hunter's Guide, 1990. FOR ADULTS. PARAPSYCHOLOGY: Discover Astral Projection: How to Achieve Out-of-Body Experiences, 1970, as The Astral Projection Workbook, 1989; Mindreach, 1985; Discover Reincarnation, 1992, in US as Discover Your Past Lives: A Practical Course, 1994. ESOTERIC WRITINGS: Astral Doorways, 1971, rev. ed., 1991; Five Keys to Past Lives, 1971, as Reincarnation: Five Keys to Past Lives, 1981; Experimental Magic, 1972; Beyond the Fourth Dimension, 1975; The Reincarnation Workbook: A Complete Course in Recalling Past Lives, 1989; (with E. Campbell) Aquarian Guide to the New Age, 1990, rev. ed. as Dictionary of Mind, Body, and Spirit: Ideas, People, and Places, 1994; Nostradamus: Visions of the Future, 1992; Ancient Spirit, 1993; Magick for Beginners: The Power to Change Your World, 1998; The Magical I Ching, 2000; (with D. Ashcroft-Nowicki) Magical Use of Thought Forms: A Proven System of Mental and Spiritual Empowerment, 2001; Occult Tibet: Secret Practices of Himalayan Magic, 2002. NONFICTION: The Occult Reich, 1974; An Occult History of the World, Vol. 1, 1976; Power Play, 1977; Getting What You Want: Power Play Techniques for Achieving Success, 1977, in UK as How to Get Where You Want to Go, 1991; The Good Con Guide (humor), 1978; Getting Rich: A Beginner's Manual, 1988; A Guide to Megalithic Ireland, 1994; Time Travel: A New Perspective, 1997. FICTION: The Greythorn Woman 1979; Dark Moon, 1980; (as Jan Brennan) Dream of Destiny, 1980. AS HERBIE BRENNAN. FOR CHILDREN. FANTASY GAME BOOKS: Aztec Quest, 1997; Egyptian Quest, 1997. NONFICTION FOR CHILDREN: Memory, 1997; Seriously Weird True Stories, 1997; Seriously Weird True Stories 2, 1998; Alien Contact, 1998; The Internet, 1998; Techno-Future, 2000; Space Quest: 111 Peculiar Questions Answered, 2003; A Spy's Handbook, 2003. INFORMATIONAL BOOKS FOR SCHOOLS: The Death of the Dinosaurs, 2001; Dr. Jenner and the Cow Pox, 2001; How to Remember Absolutely Everything, 2001; Leonardo da Vinci: The Greatest Genius Who Ever Lived?, 2001; Why Do Cats Purr?, 2001. FICTION: Emily and the Werewolf, 1993; Bad Manners Day, 1996; Dorothy's Ghost, 1996; Little House, 1996; The Thing from Knucker Hole, 1996; Mario Scumbini and the Big Pig Swipe, 1996; Kookabura Dreaming, 1997; Letters from a Mouse, 1997; Jennet's Tale: A Story about the Great Plague, 2000; Final Victory, 2000; Zartog's Remote, 2000; Fairy Nuff: A Tale of Bluebell Wood, 2001; Nuff Said: The New Bluebell Wood Adventure, in US as Nuff Said: Another Tale of Bluebell Wood, 2002; Frankenstella and the Video Shop Monster, in US as Frankenstella and the Video Store Monster, 2002; Faerie Wars, 2003. EDDIE THE DUCK SERIES: Eddie the Duck, 1998; Eddie and the Bad Egg, 1998; Eddie and the Dirty Dogs, 2001. FOR ADULTS. ESOTERIC: The Little Book of Nostradamus: Prophecies for the Twenty-First Century, 1999. NONFICTION: Martian Genesis: The Extraterrestrial Origins of the Human Race, 1998; The Atlantis Enigma, 1999; The Secret History of Ancient Egypt: Electricity, Sonics, and the Disappearance of an Advanced Civilization, 2000; Death: The Great Mystery of Life, 2002. Contributor of short stories to collections of science fiction. Contributor of science-fiction stories to periodicals. Contributor of humorous short fiction and romances to periodicals. **Address:** c/o Sophie Hicks, Ed Victor Ltd., 6 Bayley St., Bedford Square, London WC1B 3HB, England. **Online address:** herbie@eircom.net

BRENNAN, J. N. H. Also writes as John Welcome. Irish, b. 1914. **Genres:** Novels, Mystery/Crime/Suspense, Sports/Fitness, Novellas/Short stories. **Publications:** AS JOHN WELCOME: NOVELS: Grand National, 1976; Bellary Bay, 1979; A Call To Arms, 1985; Royal Stakes, 1993. MYSTERY NOVELS: Run for Cover, 1958; Stop at Nothing, 1959; Beware of Midnight, 1961; Hard to Handle, 1964; Wanted for Killing, 1965; Hell Is Where You Find It, 1968; On the Stretch, 1969; Go for Broke, 1972; A Painted Devil, 1988; Reasons of Hate, 1990. OTHER: The Cheltenham Gold Cup: The Story of a Great Steeplechase, 1957, 1973, 1984; Cheating at Cards: The Cases in Court, 1963 (in U.S. as Great Scandals of Cheating at Cards: Famous Court Cases, 1964); Fred Archer: His Life and Times, 1967; Neck or Nothing: The Extraordinary Life and Times of Bob Sievier, 1970; The Sporting Empress: The Story of Elizabeth of Austria and Bay Middleton, 1975; Infamous Occasions, 1980; The Sporting World of R. S. Surtees, 1982; (with R. Collens) Snaffles: The Life and Work of Charlie Johnson Payne, 1987; Snaffles on Racing and Point to Pointing, 1988; Snaffles on Hunting, 1989; Classic Lines More Great Racing Stories, 1991. EDITOR: (with V.R. Orchard) Best Hunting Stories, 1954; Best Motoring Stories, 1959; Best Secret Service Stories, 2 vols., 1960-65; Best Gambling Stories, 1961; Best Legal Stories, 2 vols., 1962-70; Best Crime Stories, 3 vols., 1964-68; (with D. Francis) Best Racing and Chasing Stories, 2 vols., 1966-69; Best Smuggling Stories, 1967; Best Spy Stories, 1967; (with D. Francis) The Racing Man's Bedside Book, 1969; Ten of the Best: Selected Short Stories, 1969; The Welcome Collection: Fourteen Racing Stories, 1972; (with D. Francis) Great Racing Stories, 1989; Winning Colours: Edgar Wallace's Racing Writing, 1991; Kipling on Horses, 1992.

BRENNAN, Jan. *See* **BRENNAN, J(ames) H(erbert).**

BRENNAN, Mary C. American, b. 1959. **Genres:** History. **Career:** Xavier University, Cincinnati, OH, instructor in history, 1983, 1984; Ohio State University, Columbus, instructor in history, 1988-90; Texas State University-San Marcos, assistant professor of history, 1990-. **Publications:** Turning Right in the Sixties: The Conservative Capture of the GOP, 1995. Contributor to academic journals. **Address:** Dept of History, Texas State University-San Marcos, San Marcos, TX 78666, U.S.A.

BRENNAN, Matthew C. American, b. 1955. **Genres:** Literary criticism and history, Poetry. **Career:** University of Minnesota, visiting assistant professor of English, 1984-85. Indiana State University, assistant professor of English, 1985-88, associate professor of English, 1988-92, professor of English, 1992-, director of graduate studies, 1994-96, 1998-99. **Publications:** LITERARY CRITICISM: Wordsworth, Turner, and Romantic Landscape: A Study of the Traditions of the Picturesque and the Sublime, 1987; The Gothic Psyche: Disintegration and Growth in Nineteenth-Century English Literature, 1997. POETRY: Seeing in the Dark: Poems, 1993; The Music of Exile, 1994; American Scenes: Poems on WPA Artworks, 2001. Contributor of poems, articles, and reviews to periodicals. **Address:** Dept of English, Indiana State University, Terre Haute, IN 47809, U.S.A. **Online address:** Mbrennan@indstate.edu

BRENNAN, Neil F. American, b. 1923. **Genres:** Literary criticism and history, Bibliography. **Career:** Professor of English Literature, Villanova University, PA (joined faculty, 1960), now retired. **Publications:** Anthony Powell, 1974, rev. ed. 1995; (with A.R. Redway) A Bibliography of Graham Greene, 2001. **Address:** 122 Buckingham Dr, Bryn Mawr, PA 19010-1010, U.S.A. **Online address:** nbren@earthlink.net

BRENNER, Joël Glenn. American, b. 1966. **Genres:** Documentaries/Reportage. **Career:** Des Moines Register, summer intern reporter, 1988; Washington Post, business reporter, 1989-95; freelance journalist and author, 1995-. **Publications:** The Emperors of Chocolate: Inside the Secret World of Hershey and Mars, 1999. Contributor to periodicals. **Address:** 425 New York Ave Ste 209, Huntington, NY 11743, U.S.A. **Online address:** JGBrennr@aol.com

BRENNER, Mayer Alan. Also writes as Rick North. American, b. 1956. **Genres:** Novels, Science fiction/Fantasy. **Career:** Designer of computer software and systems for health care; writer. **Publications:** FANTASY NOVELS: DANCE OF THE GODS SERIES: Catastrophes Spell, 1989; Spell of Intrigue, 1990; Spell of Fate, 1992; Spell of Apocalypse, 1994. OTHER: (as Rick North) Space Pioneers (novel), 1991. **Address:** 1815 Westholme Avenue #4, Los Angeles, CA 90025, U.S.A.

BRENNER, Michael. German, b. 1964. **Genres:** History. **Career:** Indiana University, Bloomington, IN, visiting assistant professor of Jewish history, 1993-94; Brandeis University, Waltham, MA, assistant professor of modern Jewish history, 1994-97; Tauber Institute for the Study of European Jewry, assistant director, 1995-97; University of Munich, Munich, Germany, professor of Jewish history and culture, 1997-. **Publications:** Am Beispiel Weiden: Jüdischer Alltag im Nationalsozialismus, 1983; Nach dem Holocaust: Juden in Deutschland, 1945-1950, 1995, trans. as After the Holocaust: Rebuilding Jewish Lives in Postwar Germany, 1997; The Renaissance of Jewish Culture in Weimar Germany, 1996; (with others) German-Jewish History in Modern Times, Vol. 2: 1780-1871, 1996; Zionism: A Brief History, trans. S. Frisch, 2002. EDITOR: (with D. Penslar) Circles of Community: Collective Jewish Identities in Germany and Austria, 1918-1932, 1998; (with D. Penslar) In Search of Jewish Community: Jewish Identities in Germany and Austria, 1918-1933, 1998; (with R. Liedtke and D. Rechter) Two Nations: British and German Jews in Comparative Perspective, 1999; (with Y. Weiss) Zionistische Utopie, israelische Realität: Religion und Nation in Israel, 1999; (with S. Rohrbacher) Wissenschaft vom Judentum: Annäherungen nach dem Holocaust, 2000. **Address:** Abteilung für Jedische Geschichte und Kultur, Historisches Seminar, Universitat Munchen, Geschwister-Scholl-Platz 1, 80539 Munich, Germany.

BRENNER, Philip (Joseph). (born United States), b. 1946. **Genres:** Economics. **Career:** Trinity College, instructor in political science, 1973-75; University of Maryland, Baltimore County, assistant professor of political science, 1975; American University, professor of international relations, chair of Inter-Disciplinary Council on the Americas. Institute for Policy Studies, associate fellow, 1972-; National Security Archive, researcher and member of advisory board, 1985-, United States Congress, staff member; consultant to John F. Kennedy Library, member of editorial boards of several journals.

Publications: The Limits and Possibilities of Congress, 1983; From Confrontation to Negotiation: U.S. Relations with Cuba, 1988; (with James G. Blight) Sad and Luminous Days: Cuba's Struggle with the Superpowers after the Missile Crisis, 2002; (editor with Robert Borosage and Bethany Weidner) Exploring Contradictions: Political Economy in the Corporate State, 1974; (with William M. LeoGrande, Donna Rich, and Daniel Siegel) The Cuba Reader: The Making of a Revolutionary Society, 1989. **Address:** School of International Service, American University, 4400 Massachusetts Ave. NW, Washington, DC 20016, U.S.A. **Online address:** pbrenne@american.edu

BRENNER, Reuven. Canadian/Israeli (born Romania), b. 1947. **Genres:** History, Law, Money/Finance, Politics/Government, Social sciences. **Career:** Bank of Israel, Jerusalem, economist, 1974-75; University of Chicago, IL, post-doctoral fellow and lecturer in department of economics, 1977-79; New York University, NYC, instructor in economics, 1979-80; McGill University, Montreal, QC, Canada, assistant professor of economics, 1980-82, Repap Chair of Economics in the School of Management, 1991-; Universite de Montreal, assistant professor, 1982-84, associate professor, 1984-89, professor of economics, 1989-91. Consultant; public speaker at conferences. **Publications:** History-The Human Gamble, 1983; Betting on Ideas: Wars, Invention, Inflation, 1985; Rivalry: In Business, Science, among Nations, 1987; (with G.A. Brenner) Gambling and Speculation: A Theory, a History, and a Future of Some Human Decisions, 1990, 1993; (ed. with D. Colander) Educating Economists, 1992; Labyrinths of Prosperity, 1993; The Financial Century, 2001; Forces of Finance, 2002.

BRENNER, Robert. American, b. 1945. **Genres:** Antiques/Furnishings, History. **Career:** Princeton High School, Princeton, WI, English teacher, 1968-. Lecturer at museums, art institutes, and public gatherings; consultant to Galloway Village, Smithsonian Institution, and Sheboygan Historical Society. **Publications:** Christmas Revisited, 1986, rev. ed., 1999; Christmas through the Decades, 1993, rev. ed., 2000; Christmas Past, 1996, rev. ed., 1998; Valentine Treasury, 1996; Celluloid Collectibles, 1999; Depression Glass, 1998; Christmas: 1940-1959, 2002; Christmas 1960-Present, 2003. Contributor to periodicals. **Address:** 316 W Main St, Princeton, WI 54968, U.S.A. **Online address:** rbrenner@dotnet.com

BRENNER, Wendy. American, b. 1966. **Genres:** Novellas/Short stories. **Career:** University of Florida, Gainesville, writer and creative writing teacher, 1993-96; State University of New York, Brockport, writer and creative writing teacher, 1996-97; University of North Carolina, Wilmington, writer and creative writing teacher, 1997-. **Publications:** STORIES: Large Animals in Everyday Life, 1996; Phone Calls from the Dead, 2001. Contributor of short stories to periodicals. **Address:** Department of English, University of North Carolina, Wilmington, NC 28403, U.S.A.

BRENNER, Yehojachin Simon. Dutch (born Germany), b. 1926. **Genres:** Economics, Novels. **Career:** University of Cape Coast, Ghana, Head of Economics Dept., 1962-67; Institute of Social Studies, The Hague, Deputy Chairman of Economic Planning Courses, 1967-69; Middle East Technical University, Ankara, Professor of Economics, 1969-72; University of Utrecht, Professor of Economics, 1972-96, Emeritus Professor, 1996-. Journal of Income Distribution, Editor, 1991-2002. **Publications:** Theories of Economic Development and Growth, 1966, 1969; A Short History of Economic Progress, 1969; Agriculture and the Economic Development of Low Income Countries, 1971; Introduction to Economics, 1972; A Short History of Economic Progress, 1973; Looking into the Seeds of Time, 1979; (co-author) Bezuinigen is geen Werk, 1981; Capitalism, Competition, and Economic Crisis, 1984; (co-author) Visies op Verdelng, 1986; The Theory of Income and Wealth Distribution, 1988; (co-author) Maatschappelijk Klimaat en Economisch Elan, 1990; The Rise and Fall of Capitalism, 1991; Income Distribution in Historical Perspective, 1991; A Theory of Full Employment, 1996; Ghana: A World Apart, 2003. NOVELS: Verboden Land, 1992; Dissidents, 1996. **Address:** Mozartlaan 23, 3723 JL Bilthoven, Netherlands. **Online address:** j.brenner@fss.uu.nl

BRENT, Madeleine. *See* **O'DONNELL, Peter.**

BRENTLINGER, John. American, b. 1934. **Genres:** Philosophy. **Career:** University of Massachusetts at Amherst, currently professor of philosophy. **Publications:** Plato's Symposium, 1972; The Best of What We Are: Reflections on the Nicaraguan Revolution, 1995; Villa sin miedo. **Address:** 64 Liberty St., Florence, MA 01062-2714, U.S.A.

BRENTON, Howard. British, b. 1942. **Genres:** Novels, Plays/Screenplays, Poetry, Songs/Lyrics and libretti. **Career:** Royal Court Theatre, London, resident dramatist, 1972-73; University of Warwick, resident writer, 1978-79. BBC TV, Spooks episodes, 2002-03. **Publications:** Notes from a Psychotic Journal and Other Poems, 1969; Revenge, 1970; Christie in Love and Other Plays, 1970; (co-author) Lay By, 1972; Plays for Public Places, 1972; (with D. Hare) Brassneck, 1973; Magnificence, 1973; Weapons of Happiness, 1976; Epsom Downs, 1977; Sore Throats, with Sonnets of Love and Opposition, 1979; (adapter) The Life of Galileo, 1980; The Romans of Britain, 1980; Plays for the Poor Theatre, 1980; Thirteenth Night and A Short Sharp Shock, 1981; (adapter) Danton's Death, 1982; (adapter) Bertolt Brecht: Conversations in Exile, 1982; The Genius, 1983; (with T. Ikoli) Sleeping Policemen, 1984; Bloody Poetry, 1985; (with D. Hare) Pravda, 1985; Dead Head (TV series), 1987; Greenland, 1988; (with T. Ali) Iranian Nights, 1989; Diving for Pearls (novel), 1989; H.I.D (Hess Is Dead), 1989; (with T. Ali) Moscow Gold, 1990; Berlin Bertie, 1992; Playing Away (opera), 1994; Hot Irons (essays and diaries), 1995; Goethe, Faust, 1995; In Extremis, 1997; (with T. Ali) Ugly Rumours, 1998; Nasser's Eden (radio play), 1998; (with T. Ali and A. de la Tour) Collateral Damage, 1999; (with T. Ali and A. de la Tour) Snogging Ken, 2000; Kit's Play, 2000; Democratic Demons, 2001. **Address:** c/o Casarotto Ramsay Ltd, National House, 60-66 Wadour St, London W1V 3HP, England.

BRESLIN, Jimmy. American, b. 1930. **Genres:** Novels, Documentaries/ Reportage. **Career:** Former reporter, WNBC-TV, and syndicated columnist, New York Herald Tribune, Paris Tribune, etc. **Publications:** Can't Anybody Here Play this Game?, 1963; The Gang that Couldn't Shoot Straight, 1969; How the Good Guys Finally Won: Notes from an Impeachment Summer, 1975; The World of Jimmy Breslin. 1976; World without End, Amen, 1976; (with D. Schaap) Forty-Four Caliber, 1978; Forsaking All Others, 1983; Queens: People and Places, 1984; The World According to Breslin, 1984; Table Money, 1986; He Got Hungry and Forgot His Manners, 1987; The Queen of the Leaky-Roof Circuit (play), 1988; Damon Runyon: A Life, 1991; I Want to Thank My Brain for Remembering Me, 1996; I Don't Want to Go to Jail: A Good Novel, 2001; The Short Sweet Dream of Edwardo Gutierrez, 2002. **Address:** c/o New York Newsday, 2 Park Ave, New York, NY 10016-5603, U.S.A.

BRESLIN, Rosemary. American, b. 1957. **Genres:** Adult non-fiction. **Career:** Writer and journalist. **Publications:** (with J. Hammer) Gerry!: A Woman Making History, 1984; Not Exactly What I Had in Mind, 1997. Contributor to periodicals. **Address:** c/o Flip Brophy, Sterling Lord Literistic, 65 Bleecker St. 12th floor, New York, NY 10012, U.S.A.

BRESLOW, Susan. American, b. 1951. **Genres:** Travel/Exploration. **Career:** American Society for the Prevention of Cruelty to Animals, New York City, head of publications, 1981-83; New York (magazine), NYC, marketing director, 1983-91; Honeymoons/Romantic Getaways from About.com, 1997-. **Publications:** (with S. Blakemore) I Really Want a Dog, 1990. **Address:** PO Box 32, Phoenicia, NY 12464, U.S.A.

BRESSOUD, David M(arius). American, b. 1950. **Genres:** Mathematics/ Statistics. **Career:** U.S. Peace Corps, Washington, DC, volunteer teacher of science and mathematics at Clare Hall School in Antigua, 1971-73; Pennsylvania State University, University Park, assistant professor, 1977-82, associate professor, 1982-86, professor of mathematics, 1986-94; Macalester College, professor of mathematics, 1994-. Visiting professor at University of Wisconsin-Madison, 1980-81, 1982, University of Minnesota-Twin Cities, 1983, 1998, and University of Strasbourg, 1985-86. Institute of Advanced Study, member, 1979-80. **Publications:** Analytic and Combinatorial Generalizations of the Rogers-Ramanujan Identities, 1980; Factorization and Primality Testing, 1989; Second Year Calculus from Celestial Mechanics to Special Relativity, 1991; A Radical Approach to Real Analysis, 1994; Proofs and Confirmations, 1999; A Course in Computational Number Theory, 2000. Contributor to mathematics journals. **Address:** Department of Mathematics and Computer Science, Macalester College, 1600 Grand Ave, St. Paul, MN 55105, U.S.A. **Online address:** bressoud@macalester.edu

BRETON, Albert. Canadian, b. 1929. **Genres:** Economics. **Career:** Professor of Economics, University of Toronto, 1970-. Member, Canadian Economic Policy Committee of the C.D. Howe Research Institute, 1974-88. Guest, Massachusetts Institute of Technology, 1959-60; Dir of Research, The Social Research Group, 1956-65; Assistant Professor of Economics, University of Montreal, 1957-65; Visiting Associate Professor, Carleton University, 1964-65; Lecturer, 1966-67, and Reader in Economics, 1967-69; London School of Economics; Visiting Professor, Catholic University, of Louvain, 1968-69; Visiting Professor of Canadian Studies, Harvard University, 1969-70; Visiting Professor, University of Paris, 1990, 1993. **Publications:** Discriminatory Government Policies in Federal Countries,

1967; A Conceptual Basis for an Industrial Strategy, 1974; The Economic Theory of Representative Government, 1974; (with A.D. Scott) The Economic Constitution of Federal States, 1978; (with R. Wintrobe) The Logic of Bureaucratic Conduct, 1982; Competitive Governments, 1996. Contributor to books on economics. **Address:** Dept. of Economics, University of Toronto, 150 St. George St, Toronto, ON, Canada M5S 3G7. **Online address:** albertbreton@sympatico.ca

BRETON, William. *See* **GURR, David.**

BRETT, Brian. Canadian, b. 1950. **Genres:** Novellas/Short stories, Poetry, Autobiography/Memoirs. **Career:** Writer and instructor. Vancouver International Writer's Festival, producer of poetry events, 1991. Worked as an editor, reviewer, and poetry critic. **Publications:** POETRY: Fossil Ground at Phantom Creek, 1976; Savage People Dressed in Skins, 1978; Monster, 1981; Smoke without Exit, 1984; Evolution in Every Direction, 1987; Poems: New and Selected, 1993; Allegories of Love and Disaster, 1993; The Colour of Bones in a Stream, 1998; Uproar's Your Only Music. NOVELS: The Fungus Garden, 1988; Coyote, 2004. OTHER: Tanganyika (short stories), 1991. Work represented in anthologies. **Address:** 191 Meyer Rd, Salt Spring Island, BC, Canada V8K 1X4. **Online address:** brett@saltspring.com

BRETT, Catherine. *See* **HUMPHREYS, Helen (Caroline).**

BRETT, Donna W(hitson). American, b. 1947. **Genres:** International relations/Current affairs, Writing/Journalism, Documentaries/Reportage, Essays. **Career:** Louisiana Training Institute, Bridge City, purchasing agent, 1976-79; Computer School of Sante Fe, Santa Fe, NM, administrative assistant, 1981-84; Santa Fe Research Corp., administrative assistant, 1981-84; University of Pittsburgh, academic adviser, 1988-. **Publications:** (with E.T. Brett) Murdered in Central America: The Stories of Eleven U.S. Missionaries, 1988. **Address:** University of Pittsburgh, 252 Thackeray Hall, Pittsburgh, PA 15260, U.S.A. **Online address:** dbrett@fcas.pitt.edu

BRETT, Edward T(racy). American, b. 1944. **Genres:** Novellas/Short stories, History, Theology/Religion, Third World, Writing/Journalism, Biography. **Career:** College of Santa Fe, Santa Fe, NM, assistant professor of history, 1980-83; Santa Fe Community College, instructor in history, 1983-84; La Roche College, Pittsburgh, PA, History Dept, associate professor, 1984-90; professor and chair, 1990-; writer. National Endowment for the Humanities visiting tutor, St. John's College, Santa Fe, 1984; Duquesne University, Pittsburgh, visiting professor, 1987-89. **Publications:** Humbert of Romans: His Life and Views of Thirteenth-Century Society, 1984; (with D.W. Brett) Murdered in Central America: The Stories of Eleven U.S. Missionaries, 1988; The US Catholic Press on Central America: From Cold War Anticommunism to Social Justice, 2003. Contributor to books and periodicals. **Address:** La Roche College, 9000 Babcock Blvd, Pittsburgh, PA 15237, U.S.A. **Online address:** brette1@laroche.edu

BRETT, Jan (Churchill). American, b. 1949. **Genres:** Children's fiction. **Career:** Painter; author and illustrator of children's books. Has exibited in galleries in New York and Massachusetts. **Publications:** SELF-ILLUSTRATED FOR CHILDREN: Fritz and the Beautiful Horses, 1981; Annie and the Wild Animals, 1985; Goldilocks and the Three Bears, 1987; The First Dog, 1988; Beauty and the Beast, 1989; The Mitten, 1989; The Wild Christmas Reindeer, 1990; Berlioz the Bear, 1991; Trouble With Trolls, 1992; Christmas Trolls, 1993; Town Mouse, Country Mouse, 1994; Armadillo Rodeo, 1995; Comet's Nine Lives, 1996; The Hat, 1997; On Noah's Ark, 2003. Illustrator of books by S. Krensky, M.L. Cuneo, S. Simon, E. Bunting, M. Taylor, B. Boegehold, D. Harding, R. Krauss, J.L. Groth, D.H. Cross, J. Perryman, A. Dellinger, D. Van Woerkom, P. Jane, J. Porazinska. **Address:** 132 Pleasant Street, Norwell, MA 02061, U.S.A. **Online address:** http://www.janbrett.com

BRETT, Leo. *See* **FANTHORPE, R(obert) Lionel.**

BRETT, Lionel (Gordon Baliol). *See* **Obituaries.**

BRETT, Michael. *See* **TRIPP, Miles (Barton)** in the Obituaries.

BRETT, Simon (Anthony Lee). British, b. 1945. **Genres:** Mystery/Crime/ Suspense, Plays/Screenplays. **Career:** Producer, BBC Radio, London, 1967-77, and London Weekend Television, 1977-79. **Publications:** PLAYS: Mrs. Gladys Moxon, 1970; Did You Sleep Well, and A Good Day at the Office, 1971; Third Person, 1972; Drake's Dream, 1977. NOVELS: Cast, In Order of Disappearance, 1975; So Much Blood, 1976; Star Trap, 1977; An Amateur

Corpse, 1978; A Comedian Dies, 1979; The Dead Side of the Mike, 1980; Murder Unprompted, 1982; Molesworth Rites Again, 1983; Murder in the Title, 1983; Not Dead, Only Resting, 1984; A Shock to the System, 1984; Dead Romantic, 1985; A Nice Class of Corpse, 1986; The Three Detectives and the Missing Superstar, 1986; Dead Giveaway, 1986; What Bloody Man Is That?, 1987; The Three Detectives and the Knight-in-Armour, 1987; Mrs. Pargeter, Presumed Dead, 1988; A Series of Murders, 1989; Mrs. Pargeter's Package, 1991; Corporate Bodies, 1992; Mrs. Pargeter's Pound of Flesh, 1993; A Reconstructed Corpse, 1994; Sicken and So Die, 1995; Singled Out, 1995; Mrs. Pargeter's Plot. STORIES: A Box of Tricks, 1985. OTHER: Frank Muir on Children, 1980; The Childowner's Handbook, 1983; Bad Form, 1984. EDITOR: The Faber Book of Useful Verse, 1981; The Faber Book of Parodies, 1984; The Faber Book of Diaries, 1987. **Address:** C/O Michael Motley, The Old Vicrage, Trendington, Gloucestershire GL20 7BP, England.

BRETTON, Barbara. American, b. 1950. **Genres:** Novels, Romance/ Historical, Autobiography/Memoirs. **Career:** Writer, 1983-. Cross Country, computer programmer, Syosset, NY, 1974-82. **Publications:** ROMANCE NOVELS: Love Changes, 1983; The Sweetest of Debts, 1984; No Safe Place, 1985; Starfire, 1985; The Edge of Forever, 1986; Promises in the Night, 1986; Shooting Star, 1986; Somewhere in Time, 1992; Tomorrow and Always, 1994; One and Only, 1994; The Invisible Groom, 1994; Destiny's Child, 1995; Maybe This Time, 1995; Guilty Pleasures, 1996; Operation: Baby, 1997; Sleeping Alone, 1997; Always, 1998; Operation: Family, 1998; Second Harmony; Nobody's Baby (as Men: Made in America); Mother Knows Best; Mrs. Scrooge (as By Request); Bundle of Joy (as Here Come the Grooms); Daddy's Girl; Renegade Lover; Sentimental Journey; Stranger in Paradise; Playing for Time; Honeymoon Hotel; A Fine Madness; All We Know of Heaven; The Bride Came C.O.D.; Operation: Husband; Once Around, 1998; The Day We Met, 1999; At Last, 2000; A Soft Place to Fall, 2001; Because You Loved Me, 2003. HISTORICAL NOVELS: The Perfect Wife, 1997; The Reluctant Bride; Fire's Lady; Midnight Lover. Contributor of novellas to anthologies. Contributor of short stories and articles to periodicals.

BREWARD, Christopher. British, b. 1965. **Genres:** Fashion/Costume. **Career:** Manchester Metropolitan University, England, lecturer in the history of art and design, 1992-94; Royal College of Art, London, England, tutor in the history of design, 1994-98; London College of Fashion, professor in historical and cultural studies, 1999-. **Publications:** The Culture of Fashion, 1995; Masculinity and Consumption in Gender and Material Culture, 1996; Material Memories, 1999; The Hidden Consumer, 1999; The Englishness of English Dress, 2001; Fashion, 2003. **Address:** Historical & Cultural Studies, London College of Fashion, 20 John Princes Street, London W1M 0BJ, England. **Online address:** c.breward@lcf.linst.ac.uk

BREWARD, Ian. New Zealander, b. 1934. **Genres:** History, Theology/ Religion. **Career:** Knox College, Dunedin, professor of church history, 1965-82; Ormond College, Parkville, professor of church history, 1982-2000. Presbyterian Church of N.Z., moderator, 1975; Radio N.Z., deputy chairman, 1976-77. **Publications:** Godless Schools?, 1967; Authority and Freedom, 1969;Grace and Truth, 1975; The Future of Our Heritage, 1984; Australia: The Most Godless Place under Heaven?, 1988; A History of Australian Churches, 1993; A History of the Churches in Australasia, 2001. EDITOR: The Work of William Perkins, 1970; John Bunyan, 1988; Thomas Cranmer, 1991; A Man of Grace, 2002; Reforming the Reformation, 2004. **Address:** 337 Howe Parade, Garden City, VIC 3207, Australia.

BREWER, Garry D(wight). American, b. 1941. **Genres:** Politics/ Government, Sociology, Environmental sciences/Ecology, Business/Trade/ Industry. **Career:** RAND Corp., Santa Monica California, member, Sr. Staff, 1970-74; Center for Advanced Studies in the Behavioral Sciences, Stanford, California, 1974-75; Yale University, New Haven, associate professor, 1975-78, professor, 1978-84, Frederick K. Weyerhaeuser Professor, 1984-90, Edwin W. Davis Professor, 1990-91; University of Michigan, Ann Arbor, professor and Dean of School of Natural Resources and Environment, 1991-95; Frederick A. Erb Environmental Management Institute, director, 1996-. **Publications:** (with Ronald D. Brunner) Organized Complexity: Empirical Theories of Political Development, 1971; Politicians, Bureaucrats and the Consultant: A Critique of Urban Problem-Solving, 1973; (ed. with Brunner and Contributor) Political Development and Change: A Policy Approach, 1974; (with J. Kakalik) Mental Health and Mental Retardation Services, 1976; (with M. Shubik) The War Game: A Critique of Military Problem Solving, 1979 (with J. Kakalik) Handicapped Children: Strategies for Improving Services, 1979; (with P. de Leon) The Foundations of Policy Analysis, 1983; (with M. Greenberger and others) Caught Unawares: The Energy

Decade in Retrospect, 1983. **Address:** University of Michigan, Dana Building, 430 E. University, Ann Arbor, MI 48109-1115, U.S.A.

BREWER, Jeannie A. American, b. 1960. **Genres:** Novels. **Career:** Teaching assistant, University of Chicago Medical School, 1983-86; resident and instructor, University of Pennsylvania Medical School, 1989; General Internal Medicine instructor, University of California, 1991-92; instructor, Introduction to Clinical Medicine, University of Southern California Medical School, 1993-. **Publications:** A Crack in Forever (novel), 1996. **Address:** 24067 Chestnut Way, Calabasas, CA 91302, U.S.A.

BREWER, William D(ean). American, b. 1955. **Genres:** Literary criticism and history. **Career:** Appalachian State University, Boone, NC, professor of English, 1987-. **Publications:** The Shelley-Byron Conversation, 1994; (coed.) Mapping Male Sexuality: NineteenthCentury England, 2000; The Mental Anatomies of William Godwin and Mary Shelley, 2001. Contributor to books and periodicals. **Address:** Department of English, Appalachian State University, Boone, NC 28608, U.S.A. **Online address:** brewerwd@appstate.edu

BREWERTON, Derrick (Arthur). British, b. 1924. **Genres:** Medicine/ Health. **Career:** Consultant rheumatologist in London, England, 1957-89. University of London, professor, 1982-89. Consultant physician at Royal National Orthopaedic Hospital, 1957-73, and Westminster Hospital, 1958-89. **Publications:** (ed.) Immunogenetics in Rheumatic Diseases, 1977; All About Arthritis: Past, Present, Future, 1992. Contributor to scientific and medical journals. **Address:** 173 Ashley Gardens, London SW1P 1PD, England. **Online address:** derrick.brewerton@btinternet.com

BREWSTER, David (C.). American, b. 1939. **Genres:** Communications/ Media, Cultural/Ethnic topics, Intellectual history, Politics/Government. **Career:** University of Washington, Seattle, acting assistant professor of English, 1965-68; Seattle Times, Seattle, copy editor and writer, 1968, columnist, 1997-2000; Seattle Magazine, associate editor, 1968-70; KING-TV News, assignment editor, 1971; Argus, managing editor, 1972-76; Sasquatch Publishing Co. Inc., Seattle, founder, president, publisher, 1976-94; Seattle Weekly, editorial director, editor/publisher, 1976-97; Town Hall Seattle (cultural center), executive director, 1998-. **Publications:** (co-ed.) The Seattle Book, 1982; (co-ed.) Washingtonians, 1989; (ed.) Northwest Best Places, 1975-83. **Address:** 1415 35th St, Seattle, WA 98122-3406, U.S.A. **Online address:** davidb@townhallseattle.org

BREWSTER, Elizabeth (Winifred). Canadian, b. 1922. **Genres:** Novels, Novellas/Short stories, Poetry, Autobiography/Memoirs. **Career:** Professor Emeritus of English, University of Saskatchewan, Saskatoon, 1990- (Assistant Professor, 1972-75; Associate Professor, 1975-80; Professor, 1980-90). Cataloguer, Carleton University Library, Ottawa, 1953-57, and Indiana University Library, Bloomington, 1957-58; Member of English Dept., Victoria University, BC, 1960-61; Reference Librarian, Mount Allison University Library, Sackville, NB, 1961-65; Cataloguer, New Brunswick Legislative Library, Fredericton, 1965-68, and University of Alberta Library, Edmonton, 1968-70. **Publications:** East Coast, 1951; Lillooet, 1954; Roads and Other Poems, 1957; Passage of Summer: Selected Poems, 1969; Sunrise North, 1972; In Search of Eros, 1974; The Sisters (novel), 1974; Sometimes I Think of Moving, 1977; It's Easy to Fall on the Ice (stories), 1977; The Way Home, 1982; Digging In, 1982; Junction (novel), 1982; A House Full of Women (short stories), 1983; Selected Poems 1944-1984, 2 vols., 1985; Visitations (short stories), 1987; Entertaining Angels (poetry), 1988; Spring Again (poetry), 1990; Invention of Truth (essays and stories), 1991; Wheel of Change (poems), 1993; Away from Home (essays and stories), 1995; Footnotes to the Book of Job (poems), 1995; Garden of Sculpture, 1998; Burning Bush (poems), 2000; Jacob's Dream (poems), 2002; Collected Poems, Vol. 1, 2003, Vol. 2, 2004. **Address:** #206, 910 - 9th St E, Saskatoon, SK, Canada S7H 0N1.

BREWSTER, Eva. British/Canadian (born Germany), b. 1922. **Genres:** Autobiography/Memoirs, Documentaries/Reportage. **Career:** 7th U.S. Army in Germany, interpreter, 1945; British Control Commission, 1945-47; short story writer in Western Africa, 1953-62; Newspaper columnist, 1971-96; Lethbridge Community College, guest lecturer. Newspaper columnist, 1971-96. **Publications:** Vanished in Darkness: An Auschwitz Memoir (autobiography), 1984; Progeny of Light/Vanished in Darkness (expanded autobiography), 1994; The Last of Nine Lives/Grandma Teach Me to Fly, 2001. **Address:** PO Box 238, Coutts, AB, Canada T0K 0N0.

BREWSTER, Hugh. Canadian (born England), b. 1950. **Genres:** Children's non-fiction. **Career:** Writer. Scholastic Canada, Toronto, Ontario, Canada, editor, 1972-81; Scholastic, NYC, editor, 1981-84; Madison Press Books, Toronto, editorial director, 1984-. Banff Publishing Workshop, instructor, 1993-95. **Publications:** The Complete Hoser's Handbook, 1983; Anastasia's Album, 1996; Inside the Titanic, 1997; 882 1/2 Answers to All Your Questions about the Titanic, 1998. **Address:** Madison Press Books, 1000 Yonge St Ste 200, Toronto, ON, Canada M4W 2K2. **Online address:** hbrewster@madisonpressbooks.com

BREYMAN, Steve. American, b. 1960. **Genres:** Engineering. **Career:** Marquette University, Milwaukee, WI, visiting assistant professor, 1991-93; Rensselaer Polytechnic Institute, Troy, NY, assistant professor, 1993-. **Publications:** Movement Genesis, 1997; Why Movements Matter, 1999. **Address:** Department of STS, Rensselaer Polytechnic Institute, Troy, NY 12180, U.S.A. **Online address:** breyms@rpi.edu

BREZIANU, Andrei. American (born Romania), b. 1934. **Genres:** Novels, Literary criticism and history, Area studies. **Career:** Voice of America, Washington, DC, international radio broadcaster, Romanian service chief, chief editor, 1986-. Also serves as English editor for "Secolul 20," and the World Literature Journal of the Romanian Writers Union. Taught at the University of Bucharest, 1970-79; Catholic University of America, 1990-91; University of Cluj-Napoca, Romania, 1998, and Free International University of Moldova, 1998, 1999, and 2000. **Publications:** Iesirea La Tarmuri (novel), 1978; Castelul Romanului (novel), 1981; Odiseu in Atlantic (studies in world literature), 1977; Translatii (essays in cross-cultural communication), 1982; (with others) Romania-A Case in Dynastic Communism, 1989; The Historical Dictionary of the Republic of Moldova, 2000. Romanian translator of plays and books. Author of articles. **Address:** c/o Scarecrow Press, 4720A Boston Way, Lanham, MD 20706, U.S.A.

BREZNITZ, Shlomo. Israeli (born Czech Republic), b. 1936. **Genres:** Psychology. **Career:** University of Haifa, Haifa, Israel, professor of psychology, 1974-, rector, 1975-77, director of R.D. Wolfe Center for the Study of Psychological Stress, 1979-. New School for Social Research, professor, 1985-. **Publications:** (ed. with L. Goldberger) Handbook of Stress, 1982, 2nd ed, 1993; Stress in Israel, 1982; Denial of Stress, 1983; Cry Wolf: The Psychology of False Alarms, 1984; Memory Fields, 1993. **Address:** 19 Hakhsharat Hayishuv, 34985 Haifa, Israel.

BRIAN, Cynthia. American, b. 1951. **Genres:** Inspirational/Motivational Literature. **Career:** Entrepreneur, television and radio host, producer, actress, and author. Formerly worked as a journalist; actress and model. Be the Star You Are! (nonprofit media library), founder and president; host and producer of weekly radio program; cohost of Animal Cuts for television and radio. Motivational speaker. **Publications:** Miracle Moments, 1997; (ed. with J. Canfield and M.V. Hansen) Chicken Soup for the Gardener's Soul: 101 Stories to Sow Seeds of Love, Hope, and Laughter, 2001; Be the Star You Are!: Ninety-nine Gifts for Living, Loving, Laughing, and Learning to Make a Difference, 2001; The Businesss of Show Business: A Comprehensive Career Guide for Actors and Models, 2002. Contributor to syndicated column. Author of scripts for television shows. **Address:** Starstyle Productions LLC, PO Box 422, Moraga, CA 94556, U.S.A. **Online address:** cynthia@starstyle.com

BRIDE, Nadja. See **NOBISSO, Josephine.**

BRIDGERS, Sue Ellen (Hunsucker). American, b. 1942. **Genres:** Novels, Young adult fiction. **Publications:** CHILDREN'S FICTION: Home Before Dark, 1976; All Together Now, 1979; Notes for Another Life, 1981; Permanent Connections, 1987; Keeping Christina, 1993. ADULT FICTION: Sara Will, 1985; All We Know of Heaven, 1996. **Address:** PO Box 248, Sylva, NC 28779, U.S.A.

BRIDGES, Ben. See **WHITEHEAD, David (Henry).**

BRIDGES, Laurie. (Lorraine Bruck). American, b. 1921. **Genres:** Science fiction/Fantasy, Young adult fiction. **Career:** New Haven Regional Center for the Retarded, New Haven, CT, public relations, 1965-66; Bruck Industries Inc., Westport, CT, marketing and public relations, 1968-77; Southbury Press Inc., Southbury, CT, projects coordinator/writer, 1980-82, vice president, 1982-86; The Bruck Corporation, Lake Havasu City, AZ, vice president, 1982-86; TWN Communications Inc., Dallas, TX, president, 1984-. Texas delegate for White House Conference on Small Business, 1986. **Publications:** DARK FORCES SERIES FOR JUVENILES: (with P. Alexander) Devil Wind, 1983; (with Alexander) Magic Show, 1983; (with Alexander) Swamp Witch, 1983; The Ashton Horror, 1984. Contributor to periodicals. **Address:** 4500 Claire Chennault, Dallas, TX 75248, U.S.A.

BRIDGLAND, Fred. British, b. 1941. **Genres:** Area studies, Earth sciences, Natural history, Travel/Exploration, Ghost Writer. **Career:** Reuters News Agency, London, England, foreign correspondent, 1969-78; Scotsman, Edinburgh, Scotland, diplomatic editor, 1978-88, assistant editor, 1995-97, Africa correspondent, 2001-; Sunday Telegraph, London, southern Africa correspondent, 1988-95; Melbourne Age, Africa correspondent, 2001-. **Publications:** Jonas Savimbi: A Key to Africa, 1987; The War for Africa: Twelve Months That Transformed a Continent, 1991; Katiza's Journey: The True Story of Winnie Mandela, 1997. **Address:** Flat 2/1, 59 Broughton St, Edinburgh EH1 3RJ, Scotland. **Online address:** fredk.bridgland@wol.co.za

BRIDWELL, Norman Ray. American, b. 1928. **Genres:** Children's fiction, Illustrations. **Career:** Freelance artist, 1950-62; author, illustrator, 1963-. **Publications:** Clifford the Big Red Dog, 1962; Zany Zoo, 1963; Bird in the Hat, 1964; Clifford Gets a Job, 1965; The Witch Next Door, 1965; Clifford Takes a Trip, 1966; Clifford's Halloween, 1966; A Tiny Family, 1968; The Country Cat, 1969; What Do They Do When It Rains?, 1969; Clifford's Tricks, 1969; How to Care for Your Monster, 1970; The Witch's Christmas, 1970; Monster Jokes and Riddles, 1972; Clifford the Small Red Puppy, 1972; The Witch's Vacation, 1973; Merton, the Monkey Mouse, 1973; The Dog Frog Book, 1973; Clifford's Riddles, 1974; Monster Holidays, 1974; Clifford's Good Deeds, 1974; Ghost Charlie, 1974; Boy on the Ceiling, 1976; The Witch's Catalog, 1976; The Big Water Fight, 1977; Clifford at the Circus, 1977; Kangaroo Stew, 1978; The Witch Grows Up, 1979; Clifford Goes to Hollywood, 1980; Clifford's ABC's, 1983; Clifford's Story Hour, 1983; Clifford's Family, 1984; Clifford's Kitten, 1984; Clifford's Christmas, 1984; Clifford's Grouchy Neighbors, 1985; Clifford's Pals, 1985; Count on Clifford, 1985; Clifford's Manners, 1987; Clifford's Birthday Party, 1988; Clifford's Puppy Days, 1989; Where Is Clifford?, 1990; Clifford, We Love You!, 1991; The Witch Goes to School, 1992; Clifford's Thanksgiving Visit, 1993; Clifford Follows His Nose, 1992; Clifford's Peeka Boo, 1992; Clifford's Bathtime, 1992; Clifford's Bedtime, 1992; Clifford Counts Bubbles, 1992; Clifford's Noisy Day, 1992; Clifford's Animal Noises, 1992; Clifford's Happy Easter, 1994; Clifford the Firehouse Dog, 1994; Clifford's First Christmas, 1994; Clifford and The Big Storm, 1995; Clifford's First Halloween, 1996; Clifford's Sports Day, 1996; Clifford's Happy Christmas Lacing Book, 1996; Clifford's Furry Friends, 1996; Clifford's First Valentine's Day, 1997; Clifford's Spring Clean-Up, 1997; Clifford's First Autumn, 1997; Clifford Makes a Friend, 1998; Clifford's First Snow Day, 1998; The Story of Clifford, 1998; Clifford's First School Day, 1999; Clifford Grows Up, 1999; Clifford's Big Book of Things to Know, 1999; Cooking with Clifford, 1999; Clifford and the Halloween Parade, 1999; Oops, Clifford!, 1999; Tiny Family, 1999; Clifford to the Rescue, 2000; Cat and the Bird in the Hat, 2000; Clifford Barks!, 2000; Clifford's Opposites, 2000; Clifford Visits the Hospital, 2000; Clifford's Best Friend, 2000; Clifford's Schoolhouse, 2000; Clifford's Happy Mother's Day, 2001; Clifford's Valentines, 2001; Clifford's Puppy Fun, 2001; Glow-in-the-Dark Christmas, 2001; Cleo Cooperates, 2002; T-Bone Tells the Truth, 2002; Clifford's Busy Week, 2002; Clifford Goes to Dog School, 2002; Clifford's Class Trip, 2003; Clifford's Day with Dad, 2003; Clifford's First Sleepover, 2004;. **Address:** Box 869, Edgartown, MA 02539, U.S.A.

BRIEN, Alan. British, b. 1925. **Genres:** Essays, Novels. **Career:** Film critic for Truth, 1954-55; Observer, London, England, television critic, 1955-56; Evening Standard, London, film critic, 1955-57; Spectator, London, drama critic, 1958-61; Telegraph, London, drama critic, 1961-68; Times, London, columnist, 1968-76, film critic, 1976-84; writer. **Publications:** Domes of Fortune (essays), 1979; Lenin (novel), 1987; And When Rome Falls (novel), 1993. Contributor to periodicals. **Address:** 15 Marlborough Yard, Holloway Rd., London N19 4ND, England.

BRIERLEY, Barry. American, b. 1937. **Genres:** Romance/Historical. **Career:** Joston's, Owatonna, MN, staff artist, 1970-79; Wincraft, Winona, MN, manager of special graphics, 1983-87; writer, 1993-. **Publications:** HISTORICAL NOVELS: Wasichu, 1993; Timeless Interlude at Wounded Knee, 1995; White Horse, Red Rider, 1996; Wasichu's Return, 1996. OTHER: Chesty's Traveling Road Show (screenplay). **Address:** 1720 Stonehouse Ln., Cincinnati, OH 45255, U.S.A.

BRIGGS, Asa. (Baron Briggs of Lewes). British, b. 1921. **Genres:** Economics, History. **Career:** Provost, Worcester College, Oxford, 1976-91 (Fellow, 1945-55); Chancellor, Open University, 1978-94. Reader in Recent Social and Economic History, Oxford University, 1950-55; Professor of Modern History, Leeds University, 1955-61; Dean of Social Studies, 1961-65, ProVice-Chancellor, 1961-97, Professor of History, 1961-76, and Vice-Chancellor, 1967-76, University of Sussex. **Publications:** (with D. Thomson and E. Meyer) Patterns of Peacemaking, 1945; History of Birmingham,

1952; Victorian People, 1954; Friends of the People, 1956; The Age of Improvement, 1959, rev. ed., 2000; A Study of the Work of Seebohm Rowntree, 1961; History of Broadcasting in the United Kingdom, 5 vols., 1961-95; From Ironbridge to the Crystal Palace, 1979; The Power of Steam, 1982; A Social History of England, 1984, rev. ed., 1999; Victorian Things, 1988; Haut-Brion, 1994; Michael Young, Social Entrepreneur, 2001. EDITOR: Chartist Studies, 1959; (with J. Saville) Essays in Labour History, 2 vols., 1960, 1971; They Saw It Happen 1897-1940, 1961; The Nineteenth Century, 1970; (with S. Briggs) Cap and Bell: Punch's Chronicle of English History in the Making, 1972; (gen. ed.) Essays in the History of Publishing, 1974; (co) Fins de siecle, 1996. **Address:** c/o Veronica Humphrey, 26 Oakmede Way, Ringmer, E. Sussex BN8 5JL, England.

BRIGGS, John. American, b. 1945. **Genres:** Novellas/Short stories, Literary criticism and history, Writing/Journalism. **Career:** Hartford Courant, Hartford, CT, reporter, 1965-68, copy editor, 1978-79; New York Quarterly, NYC, managing editor, 1972-77; Western Connecticut State University, Danbury, CSU distinguished professor, professor of English, 1987-. Member of adjunct faculty, New School for Social Research, 1973-87, and Mercy College, Dobbs Ferry, NY, 1974-87. Connecticut Review, senior editor. **Publications:** (with R. Monaco) The Logic of Poetry, 1974; (with F.D. Peat) Looking Glass Universe, 1984; Fire in the Crucible, 1988; (with Peat) Turbulent Mirror, 1989; (with Monaco) Metaphor: The Logic of Poetry, 1990; Fractals: The Patterns of Chaos, 1992; (with Peat) The Seven Life Lessons of Chaos, 1999; Trickster Tales, 2004. Contributor of fiction to periodicals. **Address:** Dept of English Language, Western Connecticut State University, 181 White St, Danbury, CT 06810-6639, U.S.A. **Online address:** briggsjp@wcsu.ctstateu.edu

BRIGGS, Julia. British, b. 1943. **Genres:** Literary criticism and history. **Career:** Associated with Hertford College, Oxford, England; writer. **Publications:** Night Visitors: The Rise and Fall of the English Ghost Story, 1977; This Stage-Play World: English Literature and Its Background, 1580-1625, 1983; (ed.) Don Crompton, A View from the Spire, 1984; A Woman of Passion: The Life of E. Nesbit, 1858-1924, 1987; (ed. with G. Avery) Children and Their Books: A Collection of Essays to Celebrate the Work of Iona and Peter Opie, 1989. Contributor to periodicals. **Address:** Hertford College, University of Oxford, Oxford OX1 3BW, England.

BRIGGS, Raymond (Redvers). British, b. 1934. **Genres:** Children's fiction, Illustrations. **Career:** Brighton Polytechnic, Faculty of Art, part-time lecturer in illustration, 1961-87. **Publications:** The Strange House, 1961; Midnight Adventure, 1961; Ring-a-Ring O'Roses (poems), 1962; Sledges to the Rescue, 1963; Jim and the Beanstalk, 1970; Father Christmas, 1973; Father Christmas Goes on Holiday, 1975; Fungus the Bogeyman, 1977; The Snowman, 1978; Gentleman Jim, 1980; When the Wind Blows, 1982; The Tin-Pot Foreign General and the Old Iron Woman, 1984; Party, 1985; Dressing Up, 1985; Building the Snowman, 1985; (with others) All in a Day, 1986; Unlucky Wally, 1987; Unlucky Wally Twenty Years On, 1989; The Snowman Storybook, 1990; The Snowman Flap Book, 1991; The Snowman Tell-the-Time Book, 1991; The Man, 1992; Father Christmas Having a Wonderful Time, 1993; The Bear, 1994; Snowman: Things to Touch and Feel, See and Sniff, 1994; Man, 1995; Ethel & Ernest, 1998; Ug, 2002; Blooming Books, 2003. Illustrator of books by: A. Ahlberg, A. Duggan, R. Manning-Sanders, E. Vipont, B.K. Wilson, and others. **Address:** Weston, Underhill Lane, Westmeston nr Hassocks, Sussex BN6 8XG, England.

BRIGGS, Ward W(right), Jr. American, b. 1945. **Genres:** Classics, Language/Linguistics, Literary criticism and history. **Career:** University of South Carolina at Columbia, instructor, 1973-, Carolina Distinguished Professor of Classics, 1996-, Louise Fry Scudder Professor of Humanities, 1996-, interim associate provost, 1996-97; writer. Visiting professor at US colleges. **Publications:** Narrative and Simile from Virgil's Georgics in the Aeneid, 1979; Basil Lanneau Gildersleeve: An American Classicist, 1986; Soldier and Scholar: The Southern Papers of Basil Lanneau Gildersleeve, 1998; Roman Authors, 1999. EDITOR: The Letters of Basil Lanneau Gildersleeve, 1987; (with W.M. Calder III) Classical Scholarship: A Biographical Encyclopedia, 1990; Selected Classical Papers of Basil L. Gildersleeve, 1991; Biographical Dictionary of North American Classicists, 1994; Greek Authors, 1997; Vergilius, 1986-95. **Address:** Department of French and Classics, University of South Carolina at Columbia, Columbia, SC 29208, U.S.A. **Online address:** wardbriggs@sc.edu

BRIGHT, Freda. American, b. 1929. **Genres:** Novels, Advertising/Public relations. **Career:** RCA Victor, New York City, literary editor, 1957-60; Batton, Barton, Durstine & Osborn, New York City, advertising copywriter, 1960-63; West, Weir & Bartel, New York City, advertising copywriter, 1963-

65; McCann Erikson, New York City, advertising copywriter, 1965-67; freelance advertising writer in New York City and London, England, 1967-. **Publications:** Options, Pocket Books, 1981. Futures, Pocket Books, 1983. Decisions, St. Martin's, 1985. Infidelities, Atheneum, 1987. Singular Women, Bantam, 1989. Parting Shots, Little Brown, 1993. **Address:** Carole Abel, 160 West 87th St, New York, NY 10024, U.S.A.

BRIGHT, Myron H. American, b. 1919. **Genres:** Law. **Career:** Wattam, Vogel, Bright & Peterson, Fargo, ND, lawyer, 1947-68; U.S. Court of Appeals, Fargo, judge, 1968-85, senior judge 1985-. St. Louis University, distinguished professor of law, 1985-89, emeritus professor of law, 1989-95. Member of Federal Advisory Committee on Appellate Rules 1989-90. **Publications:** (with others) Objections at Trial, 1990, 4th ed., 2001. **Address:** U.S. Court of Appeals, 8th Circuit, 655 1st Ave N Ste 340, Fargo, ND 58102-4952, U.S.A.

BRIGHTMAN, Carol. American, b. 1939. **Genres:** International relations/Current affairs, Social commentary, Biography, Documentaries/Reportage. **Career:** Journalist and educator. Founder and editor of Viet-Report: An Emergency News Bulletin on Southeast Asia Affairs, 1965-68; co-editor of Leviathan, 1969-70; associate editor of GEO magazine, 1982-85; freelance writer, 1976-. Central YMCA College, Chicago, IL, adjunct instructor, 1962-63; New York University, graduate assistant, 1964-65; New School College, New York, instructor, 1965-67; Southeastern Massachusetts University, instructor, 1969; Brooklyn College, full-time instructor, 1973-76; University of Maine, adjunct instructor, 1989-92. **Publications:** NONFICTION: (with L. Rivers) Drawings and Digressions, 1979; Writing Dangerously: Mary McCarthy and Her World, 1992; Sweet Chaos: The Grateful Dead's American Adventures, 1998; Total Insecurity: The Myth of American Omnipotence, 2004. EDITOR: (with S. Levinson) Venceremos Brigade: Young Americans Sharing the Life and Work of Revolutionary Cuba: Diaries, Letters, Interviews, Tapes, Essays, Poetry by the Venceremos Brigade, 1971; (and author of intro.) Between Friends: The Correspondence of Hannah Arendt and Mary McCarthy, 1949-1975, 1995. Contributor of articles and reviews to periodicals. **Address:** 44 Carl Bailey Rd, Walpole, ME 04573, U.S.A.

BRILL, Marlene Targ. American, b. 1945. **Genres:** Children's fiction, Adult non-fiction, Children's non-fiction. **Career:** Worked as a curriculum specialist, media coordinator and special education classroom teacher, 1967-80; Marlene Targ Brill Communications, Wilmette, IL, children's book author, speaker about writing, and writer/editor for businesses and textbook publishers, 1980-. Consultant and advocate for special education. **Publications:** JUVENILE: (with K. Checker) Unique Listening/Mainstreaming Stories, 1980; John Adams, 1986; I Can Be a Lawyer, 1987; Libya, 1987; James Buchanan, 1988; Hide-and-Seek Safety, 1988; Rainy Days and Rainbows, 1989; Algeria, 1990; Why Do We Have To?, 1990; Mongolia, 1992; Daniel in the Lion's Den, 1992; David and Goliath, 1992; Jonah and the Whale, 1992; Joseph's Coat of Many Colors, 1992; Noah's Ark, 1992; Allen Jay and the Underground Railroad, 1993; (with H. Targ) Guatemala, 1993; (with H. Targ) Guyana, 1994; Trail of Tears, 1994; Illinois, 1996; Small Paul and the Big Bully, 1996; Building the Capital City, 1996; Let Women Vote!, 1996; Extraordinary Young People, 1996; Journey for Peace: The Story of Rigoberta Menchu, 1996; Women for Peace, 1997; Indiana, 1997; Tooth Tales from around the World, 1998; Diary of a Drummer Boy, 1998; Shoes through the Ages, 1999; Winning Women in Soccer, 1999; Winning Women in Ice Hockey, 1999; Winning Women in Baseball/Softball, 2000; Winning Women in Basketball, 2000; Margaret Knight: Girl Inventor, 2001; Tourette Syndrome, 2002; Michigan, 2002; Minnesota, 2003; Broncho Charlie and the Pony Express, 2004; Garbage Trucks, 2004; Doctors, 2004; Veteran's Day, 2004. ADULT: Infertility and You, 1984; Keys to Parenting a Child with Down Syndrome, 1993; Keys to Parenting a Child with Autism, 1994, rev. ed., 2001; The AMA Book of Asthma, 1998; Raising Smart Kids for Dummies, 2003. **Address:** Marlene Targ Brill Communications, Wilmette, IL 60091, U.S.A. **Online address:** mtbrill@att.net

BRILLIANT, Richard. American, b. 1929. **Genres:** Archaeology/Antiquities, Art/Art history. **Career:** Assistant Professor, 1962-64, Associate Professor, 1964-69, and Professor, 1969-70, University of Pennsylvania, Philadelphia; Anna S. Garbedian Professor in the Humanities, Professor of Art History and Archaeology, Columbia University, NYC, 1970-. **Publications:** Gesture and Rank in Roman Art, 1963; The Arch of Septimus Severus in the Roman Forum, 1967; Arts of the Ancient Greeks, 1973; Roman Art, 1974; Pompeii AD 79, 1979; Visual Narratives, 1984; Portraiture, 1991; Commentaries on Roman Art, 1994; Facing the New World, 1997; My Laocoon, 2000; Un Americano A Roma, 2000. **Address:** Dept of Art History and Archaeology, Columbia University, New York, NY 10027, U.S.A.

BRIN, David. American, b. 1950. **Genres:** Science fiction/Fantasy, Sciences, Technology. **Career:** Hughes Research Laboratory, 1973-77; taught at

University of California and San Diego State University, 1980-83, Secretary, Science Fiction Writers of America. **Publications:** Sundiver, 1980; Startide Rising, 1983; The Practice Effect, 1984; The Postman, 1985; (with G. Benord) Heart of the Comet, 1986; The River of Time, 1986; The Uplift War 1987; Dr. Pak's Pre-School, 1988; (with T. Kuiper) Extraterrestrial Civilization (non-fiction/science), 1989; Earth, 1990; Glory Season, 1992; Otherness, 1994; Brightness Reef, 1995; Infinity's Shore, 1996; Heaven's Reach, 1997. **Address:** c/o SFWA Inc, PO Box 877, Chestertown, MD 21620, U.S.A.

BRINGHURST, Robert. Canadian (born United States), b. 1946. **Genres:** Poetry, Art/Art history, Design, Literary criticism and history, Translations. **Career:** University of British Columbia, Vancouver, visiting lecturer in creative writing, 1975-77, lecturer in English, 1979-80; Simon Fraser University, Burnaby, BC, lecturer in typographical history, 1983-84; poet-in-residence, Banff Centre School of Fine Arts, Alberta, 1983, University of Winnipeg, 1986, University of Edinburgh, 1989-90, and University of Western Ontario, 1998-99; Trent University, ON, Ashley lecturer, 1994. **Publications:** POETRY: The Shipwright's Log, 1972; Cadastre, 1973; Deuteronomy, 1974; Pythagoras, 1974; Eight Objects, 1975; Bergschrund, 1975; Jacob Singing, 1977; The Stonecutter's Horses, 1979; Tzuhalem's Mountain, 1982; The Beauty of the Weapons: Selected Poems 1972-82, 1982; Tending the Fire, 1985; The Blue Roofs of Japan, 1986; Pieces of Map, Pieces of Music, 1986; Conversations with Toad, 1987; The Calling: Selected Poems, 1970-1995, 1995; Elements, 1995; The Book of Silences, 2001; Ursa Major, 2003. TRANSLATOR: Nine Visits to the Mythworld, 2000; Being in Being: The Collected Works of Skaay, 2001; The Fragments of Parmenides, 2003. EDITOR: (with others) Visions: Contemporary Art in Canada, 1983; Solitary Raven: Selected Writings of Bill Reid. OTHER: (with B. Reid) The Raven Steals the Light: Stories, 1984; Ocean/Paper/Stone, 1984; Shovels, Shoes and the Slow Rotation of Letters, 1986; (with C. McClellan) Part of the Land, Part of the Water: A History of the Yukon Indians, 1987; The Black Canoe, 1991; The Elements of Typographic Style, 1992, rev. ed., 1996; A Story as Sharp as a Knife, 1999; (with W. Chappell) A Short History of the Printed Word, 1999. **Address:** Box 51, Heriot Bay, BC, Canada V0P 1H0.

BRINK, André. South African, b. 1935. **Genres:** Novels. **Career:** Rhodes University, Grahamstown, S. Africa, professor of Afrikaans and Dutch literature, 1961-90; University of Cape Town, professor of English, 1991-. **Publications:** Looking on Darkness, 1974; An Instant in the Wind, 1976; Rumours of Rain, 1978; A Dry White Season, 1979; A Chain of Voices, 1981; Mapmakers, 1983; The Wall of the Plague, 1984; The Ambassador, 1985; (ed. with J.M. Coetzee) A Land Apart: A South African Reader, 1986; States of Emergency, 1988; An Act of Terror, 1991; The First Life of Adamastor, 1993; On the Contrary, 1993; Imaginings of Sand, 1996; Reinventing a Continent, 1996; Destabilising Shakespeare, 1996; Die Jogger: 'n Drama in Twee Bedrywe, 1997; The Novel: Language and Narrative from Cervantes to Calvino, 1998; Devil's Valley, 1998; Reinventing a Continent: Writing and Politics in South Africa, 1998; Jan Vermeirian, 2000; The Rights of Desire, 2000; The Other Side of Silence, 2003; Praying Mantis, 2005. **Address:** Dept. of English Language and Literature, University of Cape Town, Private Bag, Rodebosch 7701, Republic of South Africa.

BRINK, Jean R. American, b. 1942. **Genres:** Education, History. **Career:** San Jose State University, San Jose, CA, visiting assistant professor, 1971-72 and 1973-74; Arizona State University, Tempe, assistant professor, 1974-79, associate professor, 1979-84, professor of English, 1984-, director of Arizona Center for Medieval and Renaissance Studies, 1981-94; Arizona Humanities Council, member of speakers' bureau; gives workshops for high school teachers. **Publications:** Michael Drayton Revisited, 1990; National Traditions: England and the European Renaissance, 1992. EDITOR: (and contrib.) Female Scholars: A Tradition of Learned Women, 1980; (and contrib.) The Computer and the Brain: Perspectives on Human and Artificial Intelligence, 1989; (with P.R. Baldini) Italian Renaissance Studies in Arizona, 1989; (with A. Coudert and M. Horowitz) The Politics of Gender in Early Modern Europe, 1989; Playing with Gender: A Renaissance Pursuit, 1991; Privileging Gender in Early Modern England, 1992; (with C.R. Haden) Innovative Models for University Research, 1992. **Address:** English Dept, Arizona State University, Tempe, AZ 85287-2301, U.S.A.

BRINKLEY, Alan. American, b. 1949. **Genres:** History. **Career:** Massachusetts Institute of Technology, Cambridge, assistant professor of history, 1978-82; Harvard University, Cambridge, MA, Dunwalke Associate Professor of American History, 1982-88; City University of New York Graduate School, NYC, professor of history, 1988-91; Columbia University, NYC, professor of history, 1991-98, Allan Nevins Professor of History, 1998-, provost, 2003-; Oxford University, Harmsworth Professor of American History, 1998-99. **Publications:** Voices of Protest: Huey Long, Father Coughlin,

and the Great Depression, 1982; American History: A Survey, 1994; The Unfinished Nation: A Concise History of the United States, 1993; The End of Reform: New Deal Liberalism in Recession and War, 1995; Liberalism and Its Discontents, 1998. **Address:** Office of the Provost, Columbia University, 205 Low Library, New York, NY 10027, U.S.A.

BRINKLEY, Douglas. American, b. 1960. **Genres:** History, Documentaries/Reportage. **Career:** Historian and educator. Hofstra University, New College, Hempstead, NY, associate professor of history and teaching fellow, 1989-94; University of Louisiana, associate professor; University of New Orleans, professor of history, 1994-, director of Eisenhower Center for American Studies, 1994-. Contributor to National Public Radio; consultant to television documentary projects. **Publications:** NONFICTION: Dean Acheson: The Cold War Years, 1953-1971, 1992; (with T. Hoopes) Driven Patriot: The Life and Times of James Forrestal, 1992; The Majic Bus: An American Odyssey, 1993; (with T. Hoopes) FDR and the Creation of the United Nations, 1997; (with S.E. Ambrose) Rise to Globalism, 8th ed., 1997; The Unfinished Presidency: Jimmy Carter's Journey beyond the White House, 1998; American Heritage History of the United States, 1998; Rosa Parks, 2000; (with S.E. Ambrose) The Mississippi and the Making of a Nation, 2002; Wheels of the World, 2003. EDITOR: (with C. Hackett) Jean Monnet: The Path to European Unity, 1991; Dean Acheson and the Making of U.S. Foreign Policy, 1993; (with N.A. Naylor and J.A. Gable) Theodore Roosevelt: Many-Sided American, 1993; (with D.R. Facey-Crowther) The Atlantic Charter, 1994; (with R. Griffiths) John F. Kennedy and Europe, 1999; (with S.E. Ambrose, A. Nevins, and H.S. Commager) Witness to America, 1999; (with P. Limerick) The Bernard DeVoto Reader, 2001; (advisory) The Penguin Encyclopedia of American History, 2003; (gen. ed.) The New York Times Living History, World War II: The Axis Assault, 1939-1942, 2003. Author of introductions to books by: J. Carter, T. Dreiser, C.T. Rowan. Contributor to periodicals. **Address:** Eisenhower Center for American Studies, 923 Magazine St, New Orleans, LA 70130, U.S.A.

BRISCO, P. A. *See* **MATTHEWS, Patricia.**

BRISCO, Patty. *See* **MATTHEWS, Patricia.**

BRISCOE, Connie. American, b. 1952. **Genres:** Novels. **Career:** Analytic Services Inc., Arlington, VA, research analyst, 197680; Joint Center for Political and Economic Studies, Washington, DC, associate editor, 1981-90; American Annals of the Deaf, Gallaudet University, Washington DC, managing editor, 1990-94; novelist, 1994-. **Publications:** NOVELS: Sisters and Lovers, 1994; Big Girls Don't Cry, 1996; A Long Way From Home, 1999. **Address:** c/o HarperCollins, 10 East 53rd St, Author Mail, 7th Floor, New York, NY 10022, U.S.A.

BRISKIN, Jacqueline. American (born England), b. 1927. **Genres:** Novels. **Career:** Published in Turkey, Greece, Poland, Russia, France, Germany, Italy, Israel, Japan, Spain, Portugal, Argentina, Brazil, Bulgaria, Canada, Sweden, Norway, Finland, Denmark, Netherlands, Slovenia, Czech Republic, UK, USA, Taiwan, Yugoslavia. LMV Peer Award, 1985. **Publications:** California Generation, 1970; Afterlove, 1974; Rich Friends, 1976; Paloverde, 1978; The Onyx, 1982; Everything and More, 1983; Too Much Too Soon, 1985; Dreams Are Not Enough, 1987; The Naked Heart, 1987; The Other Side of Love, 1991; Crimson Palace, 1995.

BRISKIN, Mae. American, b. 1924. **Genres:** Novels, Novellas/Short stories, History. **Career:** Brooklyn College (now of the City University of New York), Brooklyn, NY, instructor in economics, 1944-45; New York State Department of Labor, New York City, investigator, 1945-47; New York City Housing Authority, member of tenant selection and management staffs of housing projects, 1947-50; writer, 1973-. **Publications:** A Boy Like Astrid's Mother (stories), 1988; The Tree Still Stands (novel), 1991; A Hole in the Water (novel), 2002. **Address:** 3604 Arbutus Dr, Palo Alto, CA 94303, U.S.A.

BRISSENDEN, Alan (Theo). Australian, b. 1932. **Genres:** Dance/Ballet, Literary criticism and history, Theatre. **Career:** University of Adelaide, Dept. of English, Lecturer, 1963-68, Sr. Lecturer, 1968-82, Reader, 1982-94, Chairman of the Dept., 1985-86, Honorary Visiting Research Fellow, 1994-. Studies in Tudor and Stuart Literature, Joint General Ed., with F.H. Mares, 1973; Dance Magazine, Dance Critic, 1979-84; Dance Australia, Dance Critic, 1980-; Adelaide Festival of Arts, Governor, 1981-94, Hon. Life Member (Friends), 1998; Bibliographical Society of Australia and New Zealand, President, 1983-85; The Australian, Dance Critic, 1990-; Australian and New Zealand Shakespeare Association, President, 1992-94, Hon. Life Member, 1998; Friends of State Library of South Australia, President, 1994-2000.

Order of Australia, Member. **Publications:** Rolf Boldrewood, 1972; Shakespeare and the Dance, 1981. EDITOR: (with C. Higham) They Came to Australia (prose anthology), 1961; T. Middleton, A Chaste Maid in Cheapside, 1968, rev. ed., 2002; Lawson's Australia (prose/verse anthology), 1973; The Drover's Wife and Other Stories by Henry Lawson (prose anthology), 1974; (contributing ed.) Shakespeare and Some Others, 1976; Rolf Boldrewood (prose anthology), 1979; Aspects of Australian Fiction, 1990; As You Like It, 1993; What Makes a Masterpiece?, 2002. **Address:** Dept. of English, University of Adelaide, Adelaide, SA 5005, Australia.

BRISSON, Pat. American, b. 1951. **Genres:** Children's fiction. **Career:** St. Anthony of Padua School, Camden, NJ, elementary school teacher, 1973-75; Phillipsburg Free Public Library, Phillipsburg, NJ, library clerk, 1978-81, reference librarian, 1990-2000; Easton Area Public Library, Easton, PA, library clerk, 1981-88; writer. **Publications:** Your Best Friend, Kate, 1989; Kate Heads West, 1990; The Magic Carpet, 1991; Kate on the Coast, 1992; Benny's Pennies, 1993; Wanda's Roses, 1994; Hot Fudge Hero, 1997; The Summer My Father Was Ten, 1998; Little Sister, Big Sister, 1999; Sky Memories, 1999; Bertie's Picture Day, 2000; Hobbledy-Clop, 2003; Star Blanket, 2003; Beach Is to Fun, 2004; Mama Loves Me from Away, 2004. **Address:** 94 Bullman St, Phillipsburg, NJ 08865, U.S.A. **Online address:** brisson@enter.net; www.enter.net/~brisson

BRISTOL, Leigh. *See* **BALL, Donna.**

BRISTOW, Robert O'Neil. American, b. 1926. **Genres:** Novels. **Career:** Professor Emeritus of English and Communications, Winthrop College, Rock Hill, South Carolina, since 1988 (Assistant Professor, 1961-65; Associate Professor, 1966-74; Professor, 1974-88). **Publications:** Time for Glory, 1968; Night Season, 1970; A Faraway Drummer, 1973; Laughter in Darkness, 1974. **Address:** 613 1/2 Charlotte Ave, Rock Hill, SC 29730-3648, U.S.A. **Online address:** rbristow@cetlink.net

BRITAIN, Ian (Michael). Australian (born India), b. 1948. **Genres:** Art/Art history, Cultural/Ethnic topics, Education, History, Intellectual history, Biography. **Career:** Monash University, Clayton, Australia, research fellow, 1980-82, lecturer in cinema studies, 1994, Dept of History, senior research fellow, 1997-2002; University of Melbourne, Parkville, Australia, lecturer in modern British history, 1982-91, research associate, 1992; National Library of Australia, Harold White Research Fellow, 1992; Meanjin literary magazine, editor, 2001-. **Publications:** Fabianism and Culture: A Study in British Socialism and the Arts, 1884-1918, 1982; Once an Australian: Journeys with Barry Humphries, Clive James, Germaine Greer and Robert Hughes, 1997; (ed. with B. Niall) The Oxford Book of Australian Schooldays, 1997. **Address:** c/o Meanjin, 131 Barry St, Carlton, VIC 3052, Australia. **Online address:** i.britain@unimelb.edu.au

BRITE, Poppy Z. American, b. 1967. **Genres:** Novels, Novellas/Short stories, Horror, Food and Wine, Gay and lesbian issues. **Career:** Writer. Worked as candy maker, short-order cook, mouse caretaker, artists' model, and exotic dancer, 1985-91. **Publications:** NOVELS: Lost Souls, 1992; Drawing Blood, 1993; Exquisite Corpse, 1996; The Lazarus Heart, 1998; The Value of X, 2002; Liquor, 2004; (with C. Faust) Triads, 2004; Prime, 2005. STORIES: Swamp Foetus, 1993; Are You Loathsome Tonight?, 1998; The Devil You Know, 2003. OTHER: (ed.) Love in Vein (anthology), 1994; Love in Vein 2 (anthology), 1996; Courtney Love: The Real Story (biography), 1997. Work appears in anthologies. **Address:** c/o Donadio & Olson, 121 W 27th St, New York, NY 10001, U.S.A. **Online address:** AskPZB@aol.com

BRITNELL, R(ichard) H. British, b. 1944. **Genres:** History. **Career:** University of Durham, Durham, England, lecturer, 1966-86, senior lecturer in history, 1986-94, reader, 1994-97, professor, 1997-. Treasurer of Durham Medieval Drama Group and Durham Shakespeare Group. **Publications:** Growth and Decline in Colchester, 1300-1529, 1986; The Commercialisation of English Society, 1000-1500, 1993, 2nd ed., 1996; The Closing of the Middle Ages?, 1997. **Address:** Department of History, University of Durham, 43-46 North Bailey, Durham DH1 3EX, England. **Online address:** R.H. Britnell@durham.ac.uk

BRITT, Brian (Michael). American, b. 1964. **Genres:** History, Theology/Religion. **Career:** Virginia Polytechnic Institute and State University, Blacksburg, associate professor. **Publications:** Walter Benjamin and the Bible, 1996; Rewriting Moses: The Narrative Eclipse of the Text, 2003. Contributor of articles and reviews to periodicals. **Address:** 207 Major Williams (0135), Virginia Polytechnic Institute and State University, Blacksburg, VA 24061, U.S.A.

BRITTAIN, C. Dale. American, b. 1948. **Genres:** Science fiction/Fantasy. **Career:** Professor of medieval history and writer. **Publications:** FANTASY NOVELS: A Bad Spell in Yurt, 1991; The Wood Nymph and the Cranky Saint, 1993; Mage Quest, 1993; Voima, 1995; The Witch and the Cathedral, 1995; Daughter of Magic, 1996; (with R.A. Bouchard) Count Scar, 1997; Is This Apocalypse Necessary?, 2000. **Address:** 2006 Blair Blvd, Wooster, OH 44691, U.S.A. **Online address:** Bouchard@bright.net

BRITTAIN, William. American, b. 1930. **Genres:** Children's fiction, Children's non-fiction. **Career:** Union Free School District 15, teacher, 1954-86. **Publications:** Survival Outdoors, 1977; Sherlock Holmes, Master Detective (text), 1982; Children's novels: All the Money in the World, 1979; Devil's Donkey, 1981; The Wish Giver, 1983; Who Knew There'd Be Ghosts, 1985; Dr. Dredd's Wagon of Wonders, 1987; The Fantastic Freshman, 1988; My Buddy, The King, 1989; Professor Popkin's Prodigious Polish, 1990; Wings, 1991; The Ghost From Beneath the Sea, 1992; Shape-Changer, 1994; The Wizards and the Monster, 1994; The Mystery of the Several Sevens, 1994. **Address:** 308 Kyfields, Weaverville, NC 28787, U.S.A.

BRITTAN, Sir Samuel. British, b. 1933. **Genres:** Economics, Politics/Government. **Career:** Economics writer, 1966-, and Assistant Ed., 1978-, Financial Times, London (Member, Editorial staff, 1955-61). Economics Ed., Observer, London, 1961-64; Economic Adviser, Dept. of Economic Affairs, London, 1965. Research and Visiting Fellow, Nuffield College, Oxford, 1973-82; Visiting Professor, University of Chicago Law School, 1978. Member, Peacock Committee on Finance of the BBC, 1985-86. **Publications:** The Treasury Under the Tories, 1964, as Steering the Economy: The Role of the Treasury, 1969, 1971; Left or Right: The Bogus Dilemma, 1968; The Price of Economic Freedom: A Guide to Flexible Rates, 1970; Capitalism and the Permissive Society, 1973, new ed as A Restatement of Economic Liberalism, 1988; Is There An Economic Consensus? An Attitude Survey, 1973; Second Thoughts on Full Employment Policy, 1975; (with P. Lilley) The Delusion of Incomes Policy, 1977; The Economic Consequences of Democracy, 1977; How to End the "Monetarist" Controversy, 1981; The Role and Limit of Government, 1983; Capitalism with a Human Face, 1994; Essays, Moral, Political and Economic, 1998; Against the Flow, 2005. **Address:** c/o Financial Times, No 1 Southwark Bridge, London SE1 9HL, England.

BRITTON, Bruce K. American, b. 1944. **Genres:** Education, Psychology, Language/Linguistics. **Career:** University of Georgia, Athens, professor of psychology, 1976-. Winter Text Conference, organizer, 1988-. **Publications:** (with J. Black) Understanding Expository Text, 1985; (with S.M. Glynn) Executive Control Processes in Reading, 1987; (with Glynn) Computer Writing Environments: Theory, Research, and Design, 1989; (with A.D. Pellegrini) Narrative Thought and Narrative Language, 1990; (ed. with A. Woodward and M. Binkley) Learning From Textbooks: Theory and Practice, 1993; (with Glynn and R.H. Yaney) The Psychology of Learning Science; (with A.C. Graesser) Models of Text Comprehension, 1995. **Address:** Department of Psychology, University of Georgia, Athens, GA 30602, U.S.A. **Online address:** bbritton@arches.uga.edu

BRITTON, Celia (Margaret). British, b. 1946. **Genres:** Literary criticism and history. **Career:** King's College, London, London, England, lecturer in French, 1972-74; University of Reading, Reading, England, lecturer in French, 1974-91; University of Aberdeen, Aberdeen, Scotland, professor of French, 1991-. **Publications:** Claude Simon: Writing the Visible, 1987; The Nouveau Roman: Fiction, Theory, and Politics, 1992; (ed.) Claude Simon, 1993; Edouard Glissant and Postcolonial Theory: Strategies of Language and Resistance, 1999; Race and the Unconscious: Freudianism in French-Caribbean Thought, 2002. Contributor to books. **Address:** Dept of French, University College London, London WC1E 6BT, England. **Online address:** celiabritton@talk21.com

BRITTON, Denis (King). British, b. 1920. **Genres:** Agriculture/Forestry. **Career:** Lecturer, Agricultural Economics Research Institute, Oxford University, 1947-52; Economist, U.N. Food and Agriculture Organization, Geneva, 1952-59; General Manager, Marketing and Economic Research, Massey-Ferguson (U.K.) Ltd., Coventry, 1959-61; Professor of Agricultural Economics, Nottingham University, 1961-70, and Wye College, University of London, 1970-82. Honourary Fellow, Wye College, 1982. **Publications:** Cereals in the United Kingdom, 1969; (with B. Hill) Size and Efficiency in Farming, 1975; (with J.C. Dunning and R.M. Harley) Report on Research on the Integration of Farming and Forestry in Lowland Britain, 1984; (co-ed.) A Hundred Years of British Food and Farming: A Statistical Survey, 1988; (ed.) Agriculture in Britain: Changing Pressures and Policies, 1990. **Address:** 29 Chequers Park, Wye, Ashford, Kent TN25 5BB, England.

BRKIC, Courtney Angela. American, b. 1972. **Genres:** Mystery/Crime/ Suspense. **Career:** Writer. Worked as a freelance translator for the United Nations War Crimes Tribunal in The Hague, Netherlands, a sociological researcher and contract translator in Croatia, a forensic archeologist in Bosnia-Herzegovina after the Balkan wars, and a volunteer for Physicians for Human Rights, all 1990s. **Publications:** Stillness and Other Stories, 2003; The Stone Fields: An Epitaph for the Living (memoir), 2004. Contributor to literary journals. **Address:** Sandra Dijkstra Agency, 1155 Camino del Mar Suite 515, Del Mar, CA 92014, U.S.A.

BROAD, Kendal L. American, b. 1966. **Genres:** Sociology. **Career:** University of Florida, Gainesville, assistant professor of sociology, 1998-. **Publications:** (with V. Jenness) Hate Crimes: New Social Movements and the Politics of Violence, 1997. **Address:** Department of Sociology, University of Florida, PO Box 117330, Gainesville, FL 32611, U.S.A. **Online address:** kendal@soc.ufl.edu

BROAD, Robin. American, b. 1954. **Genres:** Economics. **Career:** Xavier University, Mindanao, Philippines, Henry Luce Foundation Fellow of economic development and environmental studies and research associate, 1977-78; Chulalonghorn University, Bangkok, Thailand, economic researcher, 1979; University of the Philippines, visiting research associate, 1980-81, 1988-89; U.S. Treasury Department, Office of Multilateral Development Banks, Washington, DC, international economist, 1983-84, Inter-American Development Bank desk officer, 1984-85; senior staff economist for U.S. Congressman Charles E. Schumer, Washington, DC, 1985-87; Carnegie Endowment for International Peace, resident associate, 1987-88; American University, Washington, DC, assistant professor of environment and development, 1990-96, associate professor, 1996-. **Publications:** Unequal Alliance: The World Bank, the International Monetary Fund, and the Philippines, 1988; (with J. Cavanagh) The Philippine Challenge: Sustainable and Equitable Development in the 1990s (monograph), 1991; (with J. Cavanagh) Plundering Paradise: The Struggle for the Environment in the Philippines, 1993; (ed.) Global Backlash, 2002. Work represented in anthologies. Contributor to professional journals and newspapers. **Address:** International Development Program, School of International Service, American University, 4400 Massachusetts Ave NW, Washington, DC 20016-8071, U.S.A.

BROADHURST, Kent. American, b. 1940. **Genres:** Plays/Screenplays. **Career:** Playwright and screenwriter, 1980-. Actors Theatre of Louisville (ATL), playwright in residence, 1981; director of plays; actor in motion pictures, Television, Broadway, Regional; Portrait painter, photographer, and inventor. **Publications:** PLAYS: They're Coming to Make It Brighter, 1980; The Eye of the Beholder (one-act), 1981; The Habitual Acceptance of the Near Enough (one-act), 1982; Lemons, 1982; Bound; Gala; Black Iris; Wild Iris (screenplay), 2001. **Address:** 24 Cornelia St No 20, New York, NY 10014, U.S.A.

BROADWIN, John. American, b. 1944. **Genres:** Translations. **Career:** University of Arizona, Tucson, catalog librarian, 1971-72; California State University Library, Sacramento, CA, assistant catalog librarian, 1972-74; Felix Dietrich Verlag, Osnabruck, FRG, indexer/translator, 1974-75; National Library of Medicine, Bethesda, MD, selector of medical literature, 1975-79; Letterman Army Institute of Research Library, San Francisco, CA, administrative librarian, 1979-83; Stanford University, CA, Engineering Library, head of reference and bibliographic instruction, 1983-88; Health Services Library, V.A. Medical Center, Palo Alto, CA, medical librarian, 1988-90; Foothill College, Los Altos Hills, CA, Hubert H. Semans Library, collection development librarian, 1990-. **Publications:** TRANSLATOR, NONFICTION: B. and K. Bock, Soviet Bloc Merchant Ships, 1981; J. Rohwer, Axis Submarine Successes, 1939-1945, 1983; T.W. Mason, Social Policy in the Third Reich, 1993; (with V.R. Berghahn) H. Hoffmann, The Triumph of Propaganda, 1996; R. Liepman, Maybe Luck Isn't Just Chance, 1997; H. Schipperges, Hildegard of Bingen, 1997; I. Hecht, To Remember Is to Heal, 1999; (with S.L. Frisch) P.O. Scholz, Eunuchs and Castrati, 2001; A. Konigseder and J. Wetzel, Waiting for Hope, 2001; H. Frankenthal, The Unwelcome One, 2002. **Address:** Foothill College Library, 12345 El Monte Road, Los Altos Hills, CA 94022, U.S.A. **Online address:** broadwinjohn@fhda.edu

BROBECK, Stephen. American, b. 1944. **Genres:** Business/Trade/Industry. **Career:** Case Western Reserve University, Cleveland, OH, assistant professor of American studies, 1970-79; Consumer Federation of America, Washington, DC, executive director, 1980-. Cornell University, visiting associate professor, 1989; University of Maryland at College Park, adjunct associate professor, 1990-92. Richmond Federal Reserve Bank, member of board of directors, 1990-96. **Publications:** The Product Safety Book, 1983;

The Bank Book, 1986; The Modern Consumer Movement: References and Resources, 1990; Encyclopedia of the Consumer Movement, 1997. **Address:** 4700 Connecticut Ave. N.W., Washington, DC 20008, U.S.A.

BROCH, Harald Beyer. Norwegian, b. 1944. **Genres:** Anthropology/ Ethnology. **Career:** University of Oslo, Norway, professor of anthropology, 1975-89; Ethnographic Museum, Oslo, anthropologist, 1990-; writer. Adviser to Royal Norwegian Ministry of Development Cooperation, 1987. **Publications:** Woodland Trappers: Hare Indians of Northwestern Canada, 1986; Growing up Agreeably: Bonerate Childhood Observed, 1990; Jangan Lupa, 2002. Contributor of anthropological articles to periodicals. **Address:** Dept of Social Anthropology, University of Oslo, PO Box 1091 Blindern, N-0317 Oslo, Norway. **Online address:** h.b.broch@sai.uio.no

BROCHU, André. Canadian, b. 1942. **Genres:** Novels, Poetry, Literary criticism and history, Essays. **Career:** Educator and writer. University of Montreal, Canada, professor of literature, 1963-97; fulltime writer, 1997-. **Publications:** POETRY: (with J.-A. Constant and Y. Dube) Etranges domaines, 1957; Privileges de l'ombre, 1961; Delit contre delit, 1965; Les matins nus, le vent, 1989; Dans les chances de l'air, 1990; Particulierement la vie change, 1990; Dela, 1994; L'inconcevable, 1998; Je t'aime, je t'ecris, 2001. NOVELS: Adeodat I, 1973; La vie aux trousses, 1993; Les epervieres, 1996; Le maitre reveur, 1997; Matamore premier, 2000. NOVELLAS: La Croix du nord, 1991; L'Esprit ailleurs, 1992; Fievres blanches, 1994; Adele intime, 1996. ESSAYS: (ed.) La Litterature par elle-meme, 1962; Hugo: Amour/Crime/Revolution: Essai sur Les Miserables, 1974; (with L. Mailhot and A. Le Grand) Le Reel, le realisme et la litterature quebecoise, 1974; (with G. Marcotte) La Litterature et le reste: Livre de lettres, 1980; L'Evasion Tragique-essai sur les romans d'Andre Langevin, 1985; La Visee critique: Essais autobiographiques et litteraires, 1988; Le Singulier pluriel, 1992; La Grande Langue: Eloge de l'anglais, 1993; Roman et enumeration De Flaubert a Perec, 1996; Une etude de Bonheur d'occasion de Gabrielle Roy, 1998; Anne Hebert, 2000; Rever la lune, 2002. OTHER: (with J. Brault and A. Major) Nouvelles (short stories), 1963; L'Instance critique: 1961-1973 (collected articles), 1974; Tableau du poeme, 1994; Saint-Denys Garneau, 1999. Contributor to periodicals. **Address:** 53 Avenue Wicksteed, Mont-Royal, QC, Canada H3P 1P9.

BROCK, Delia. See EPHRON, Delia.

BROCK, James. American, b. 1958. **Genres:** Poetry. **Career:** Indiana University-Bloomington, associate instructor, 1982-88; Belmont University, Nashville, TN, assistant professor, 1988-93; Idaho State University, Pocatello, visiting assistant professor, 1993-96; East Stroudsburg University, East Stroudsburg, PA, instructor, 1996-97. **Publications:** The Sunshine Mine Disaster (poems), 1995. Work represented in anthologies. Contributor of poems to magazines. **Address:** College of Arts & Sciences, Florida Gulf Coast University, 10501 Florida Gulf Coast University Blvd. S., Ft. Myers, FL 33965-6565, U.S.A. **Online address:** jbrock@fgcu.edu

BROCK, Michael (George). British, b. 1920. **Genres:** History. **Career:** Warden, St. George's House, Windsor Castle, 1988-93; Fellow and Tutor in Modern History and Politics, Corpus Christi College, Oxford, 1950-66; Vice President and Bursar, Wolfson College, Oxford, 1967-76; Professor of Education and Director of School of Education, Exeter University, 1977-78; Warden, Nuffield College, Oxford, 1978-88. **Publications:** The Great Reform Act, 1973. CO-EDITOR: H.H. Asquith: Letters to Venetia Stanley, 1982; Nineteenth-Century Oxford (History of Oxford University, vols. 6-7), Part 1, 1997, Part 2, 2000. **Address:** Flat 1, Ritchie Court, 380 Banbury Rd, Oxford OX2 7PW, England.

BROCK, Peter de Beauvoir. Canadian (born England), b. 1920. **Genres:** History. **Career:** University of Toronto, ON, lecturer, 1957-58, professor, 1966-85, professor emeritus of history, 1985-; University of Alberta, Edmonton, assistant professor of history, 1958-61; Columbia University, NYC, associate professor, 1961-65. **Publications:** The Political and Social Doctrines of the Unity of Czech Brethren in the 15th and Early 16th Centuries, 1957; Pacifism in the United States, 1968; Twentieth-Century Pacifism, 1970; Pacifism in Europe to 1914, 1972; Nationalism and Populism in Partitioned Poland, 1973; The Slovak National Awakening, 1976; Polish Revolutionary Populism, 1977; The Roots of War Resistance, 1981; The Mahatma and Mother India (essays), 1983; The Quaker Peace Testimony, 1660 to 1914, 1990; Freedom from Violence, 1991; Freedom from War, 1991; Studies in Peace History, 1991; Folk Cultures and Little Peoples, 1992; Bart de Ligt (1883-1938), 1994; Mahatma Gandhi as a Linguistic Nationalist, 1995; Varieties of Pacifism, 1998; Soviet Conscientious Objectors, 1917-1939, 1999; (with N. Young) Pacifism in the Twentieth Century, 1999; The Riddle of St. Maximilian of Tebessa, 2000; The Black Flower, 2001. EDITOR: (with H.G. Skilling) The Czech Renascence of the 19th Century, 1970; Records of Conscience, 1993; Testimonies of Conscience Sent from the Soviet Union to the War Resisters' International 1923-1929, 1997; (with T.P. Socknat) Challenge to Mars: Essays on Pacifism from 1918 to 1945, 1999; Pacifism since 1914, 2000; (with J.L.H. Keep) Life in a Penal Battalion of the Imperial Russian Army, 2001; Liberty and Conscience, 2002; Life in an Austro-Hungarian Military Prison, 2002; "These Strange Criminals": An Anthology of Prison Memoirs by Conscientious Objectors from the Great War to the Cold War, 2004. **Address:** Dept of History, University of Toronto, Toronto, ON, Canada M5S 3G3.

BROCK, William Hodson. British, b. 1936. **Genres:** History, Sciences. **Career:** University of Leicester, Lecturer, 1960-74, Director of the Victorian Studies Centre, 1974-90, Reader, 1974-93, Professor, 1993-98, Professor Emeritus of the History of Science, 1998-. Royal Institution Centre for History of Science and Technology, Chairman, Steering Committee, 1984-90. AMBIX, Ed., 1968-83; Royal Society British National Cttee for History of Science, Member, 1970-75, 1978-84; British Society for History of Science, President, 1978-80. **Publications:** (with R.M. MacLeod) Natural Knowledge in Social Context: The Journals of Thomas Archer Hirst, 1980; (with A.J. Meadows) The Lamp of Learning, 1984; From Protyle to Proton, 1985; Fontana History of Chemistry, 1992; Science for All, 1996; Justus von Liebig, 1997. EDITOR: The Atomic Debates, 1967; Science Case Histories, 1972; H.E. Armstrong and the Teaching of Science 1880-1930, 1973; (with N.D. McMillan and R.C. Mollan) John Tyndall: Essays on a Natural Philosopher, 1981; Liebig und Hofmann in ihren Briefen, 1984. **Address:** 56 Fitzgerald Ave, Seaford BN25 1AZ, England. **Online address:** william.brock@btinternet.com

BROCK, William Ranulf. British, b. 1916. **Genres:** History, Politics/Government. **Career:** Life Fellow, Selwyn College, Cambridge, 1967- (Fellow, from 1947). Fellow, British Academy, 1990-. Lecturer in History, Cambridge University, 1949-67; Professor of History, University of Glasgow, 1967-81. **Publications:** Lord Liverpool and Liberal Toryism, 1941; Britain and the Dominions, 1950; The Character of American History, 1960; An American Crisis, 1963; The Evolution of American Democracy, 1970; Conflict and Transformation in the U.S., 1844-1877, 1973; The United States, 1789-1890: Sources of History, 1975; Politics and Political Conscience, 1979; Scotus Americanus, 1981; Investigation and Responsibility, 1984; Welfare Democracy, and the New Deal, 1988; Selwyn College: A History, 1994. **Address:** 49 Barton Rd, Cambridge CB3 9LG, England. **Online address:** brock.wr@ntlworld.com

BROCK-BROIDO, Lucie. American, b. 1956. **Genres:** Poetry. **Career:** Harvard University, Cambridge, MA, Briggs-Copeland Assistant Professor in Poetry, 1988-93, and director, creative writing program, 1992-93; Bennington Writing Seminars, associate professor in poetry, 1993-; Columbia University, NY, professor and director of poetry, 1993-. **Publications:** POETRY: A Hunger, 1988; The Master Letters, 1995; Trouble in Mind, 2004. **Address:** c/o Dodge Hall, Writing Division, School of the Arts, Columbia University, New York, NY 10027, U.S.A. **Online address:** LB89@columbia.edu

BROCKETT, Oscar Gross. American, b. 1923. **Genres:** Theatre, Bibliography. **Career:** Instructor in English, University of Kentucky, Lexington, 1949-50; Assistant Professor of Drama, Stetson University, DeLand, FL, 1952-56; Assistant Professor, then Associate Professor of Drama, University of Iowa, Iowa City, 1956-63; Professor of Theatre, Indiana University, Bloomington, 1963-78; Z.T. Scott Family Chair in Drama, University of Texas at Austin, 1981-99 (Dean, College of Fine Arts, 1978-80); DeMille Professor of Drama, University of Southern California, Los Angeles, 1980-81. **Publications:** The Theatre: An Introduction, 1964, 4th ed., 1979; History of the Theatre, 1968, 9th ed., 2003; Perspectives on Contemporary Theatre, 1971; (with R. Findlay) Century of Innovation: A History of European and American Theatre and Drama since 1870, 1973, 2nd ed., 1991; The Essential Theatre, 1976, 8th ed., 2004; (with M. Pape) World Drama, 1984. EDITOR: (with S. Becker and D. Bryant) A Bibliographical Guide to Research in Speech and Dramatic Art, 1963; (with L. Brockett) Plays for the Theatre, 1967, 8th ed., 2004; Studies in Theatre and Drama, 1972. **Address:** Dept of Theatre & Dance, University of Texas, Austin, TX 78712, U.S.A. **Online address:** obrockett@mail.utexas.edu

BROCKINGTON, J(ohn) L(eonard). British, b. 1940. **Genres:** Theology/Religion, Language/Linguistics. **Career:** University of Edinburgh, Scotland, assistant lecturer, 1965-67, lecturer, 1967-82, director of studies, 1969-75, department head, 1975-99, senior lecturer, 1982-89, reader in Sanskrit, 1989-

98, professor of Sanskrit, 1998-. Guest lecturer, Cambridge University, 1979, Utkal University, 1981, 1994, Sri Jagannatha Sanskrit University, 1981, 1994, University of Calcutta, 1981, University of Zagreb, 1987, School of Oriental and African Studies, London, 1993, 2000, and Jadavpur University, 1993. **Publications:** The Sacred Thread: Hinduism in Its Continuity and Diversity, 1981; Righteous Rama: The Evolution of an Epic, 1985; Hinduism and Christianity, 1992; (comp. with P. Flamm, H. von Stietencron, and others) Epic and Puranic Bibliography: Up to 1985, 1992; The Sanskrit Epics, 1998; Epic Threads: John Brockington on the Sanskrit Epics, 2000. Contributor to books. Contributor to learned journals. **Address:** Sanskrit, School of Asian Studies, University of Edinburgh, 7 Buccleuch Pl., Edinburgh EH8 9LW, Scotland. **Online address:** J.L.Brockington@ed.ac.uk

BROCKWAY, Connie. American, b. 1954. **Genres:** Romance/Historical. **Career:** University of Minnesota-Duluth, graphic artist for School of Medicine, 1976-78; employed at Bachman's Nurser, Minneapolis, MN, 1978-80. University of Minnesota, Extension Office, master gardener. **Publications:** HISTORICAL ROMANCE NOVELS: Promise Me Heaven, 1994; Anything for Love, 1994; A Dangerous Man, 1996; As You Desire, 1997; All through the Night, 1997; My Dearest Enemy, in press. **Address:** PO Box 828, Hopkins, MN 55343, U.S.A. **Online address:** conbroc@aol.com

BROD, Harry. American (born Germany), b. 1951. **Genres:** Philosophy, Women's studies and issues. **Career:** University of Southern California, Los Angeles, lecturer, 1982-84, associate professor of philosophy, 1984-87; University of Delaware, assistant professor, 1994-2003; University of Northern Iowa, 2003-; writer. Lecturer and visiting instructor at US institutions. Men's Studies Review (now masculinities), founding editor, 1983-85, consulting editor, 1985-86, associate editor, 1992-. Guest editor of periodicals. **Publications:** Hegel's Philosophy of Politics: Idealism, Identity, and Modernity, 1992; (co-author) White Men Challenging Racism. EDITOR: The Making of Masculinities: The New Men's Studies, 1987; A Mensch among Men: Explorations in Jewish Masculinity, 1992; (with M. Kaufman) Theorizing Masculinity, 1994. Work represented in anthologies. Contributor to books and periodicals. **Address:** Dept of Philosophy & Religion, University of Northern Iowa, Cedar Falls, IA 50614-0501, U.S.A.

BRODE, Patrick. Canadian, b. 1950. **Genres:** Criminology/True Crime, History. **Career:** City Solicitor's Office, Windsor, Ontario, attorney, 1980-. **Publications:** Sir John Beverley Robinson: Bone and Sinew of the Compact, 1984; The Odyssey of John Anderson, 1989; The Charter of Wrongs, 1990; Casual Slaughters and Accidental Judgements: Canadian War Crimes Prosecutions, 1944-1948, 1997; Courted and Abandoned: Seduction in Canadian Law, 2002; Death in the Queen City: Clara Ford on Trial, 1895, 2005. **Address:** 243 Buckingham Dr, Windsor, ON, Canada.

BRODERICK, Damien. Australian, b. 1944. **Genres:** Science fiction/Fantasy, Novellas/Short stories, Plays/Screenplays, Paranormal, Sciences, Young adult fiction. **Publications:** A Man Returned (short stories), 1965; Sorcerer's World, 1970; The Dreaming Dragons, 1980; The Judas Mandala, 1982; (with R. Barnes) Valencies, 1983; Transmitters, 1984; The Black Grail, 1986; Striped Holes, 1988; The Dark Between the Stars (short stories), 1991; The Lotto Effect (parapsychology), 1992; Time Zones (radio play), 1992; The Sea's Furthest End, 1993; The Architecture of Babel (discourse of literature and science), 1994; Reading By Starlight: Post Modern Science Fiction, 1995; Schrodinger's Dog (radio play), 1995; Theory and Its Discontents, 1997; The White Abacus, 1997; The Spike (pop. science), 1997; The Last Mortal Generation (pop. science), 1999; (with R. Barnes) Stuck in Fast Forward, 1999; (with R. Barnes) The Book of Revelation, 1999. EDITOR: The Zeitgeist Machine, 1977; Strange Attractors, 1985; Matilda at the Speed of Light, 1988; Not the Only Planet, 1998; (with D.G. Hartwell) Centaurus, 1999.

BRODEUR, Paul (Adrian), (Jr.). American, b. 1931. **Genres:** Novels, Environmental sciences/Ecology, Novellas/Short stories. **Career:** Staff Writer, The New Yorker mag. 1958-96. **Publications:** The Sick Fox, 1963; The Stunt Man, 1970; Downstream (short stories), 1972; Expendable Americans, 1974; The Zapping of America, 1977; Restitution: The Land Claims of the Mashpee, Passamaguoddy, and Penobscot Indians of New England, 1985; Outrageous Misconduct: The Asbestos Industry on Trial, 1985; Currents of Death: Power Lines, Computer Terminals, and the Attempt to Cover Up Their Threat to Your Health, 1989; The Great Power Line Cover-Up: How the Utilities and the Government Are Trying to Hide the Cancer Hazards Posed by Electromagnetic Fields, 1993; Secrets: A Writer in the Cold War. **Address:** c/o The New Yorker, 4 Times Square, New York, NY 10036, U.S.A.

BRODY, Jane E(llen). American, b. 1941. **Genres:** Food and Wine, How-to books, Medicine/Health. **Career:** Minneapolis Tribune, lecturer reporter,

1962-65; New York Times, science writer, 1965-76, personal health column, writer, 1976-. **Publications:** (with R. Engquist) Secrets of Good Health, 1970; (with A.I. Holleb) You Can Fight Cancer and Win, 1977; Jane Brody's Nutrition Book, 1981; Jane Brody's The New York Times Guide to Personal Health, 1982; Jane Brody's Good Food Book: Living the High Carbohydrate Way, 1985; Jane Brody's Good Food Gourmet, 1990; Jane Brody's Good Seafood Book, 1994; Jane Brody's Cold & Flu Fighter, 1995; Jane Brody's Allergy Fighter, 1997; The New York Times Book of Women's Health, 2000; The New York Times Guide to Alternative Health, 2001. **Address:** c/o New York Times, 229 W 43rd St, New York, NY 10036, U.S.A.

BRODY, Jean. American. **Genres:** Science fiction/Fantasy. **Publications:** Gideon's House, 1984; A Coven of Women, 1987; Cleo, 1995; Elephants, 1995; The Tropical Rainforest, 1995. **Address:** Cambria Book Co., 784-C Main St., Cambria, CA 93428, U.S.A.

BRODY, Miriam. American, b. 1940. **Genres:** Writing/Journalism. **Career:** Ithaca College, Ithaca, NY, professor of writing. **Publications:** Manly Writing: Gender, Rhetoric, and the Rise of Composition, 1993. **Address:** Writing Program, Ithaca College, Ithaca, NY 14850, U.S.A.

BRODY, Stuart. American, b. 1959. **Genres:** Medicine/Health. **Career:** Veterans Administration Hospital, Montrose, NY, staff psychologist, 1984-88; psychologist in private practice, NYC, 1988-90; New York Family Court, NYC, senior psychologist, 1990-92; University of Tuebingen, Tuebingen, Germany, research associate professor, 1992-97, adjunct research associate professor, 1997-. Consultant and expert witness in behavioral research, including risk analysis and self-report, 1997-. **Publications:** Sex at Risk: Lifetime Number of Partners, Frequency of Intercourse, and the Low AIDS Risk of Vaginal Intercourse, 1997. Contributor to medical, psychological, public health, and physiological journals. **Address:** Gartenstrasse 29, 72074 Tuebingen, Germany.

BROER, Lawrence R(ichard). American, b. 1938. **Genres:** Literary criticism and history. **Career:** University of South Florida, Tampa, College of Arts and Sciences, instructor, 1965-68, assistant professor, 1968-73, associate professor, 1973-79, professor of English, 1979-2003. **Publications:** Hemingway's Spanish Tragedy, 1973; Counter Currents, 1973; (with Herb K. and C. Weingartner) The First Time, 1974; Sanity Plea: Schizophrenia in the Novels of Kurt Vonnegut, 1989, rev. ed., 1994; (with J. Walther) Dancing Fools and Weary Blues: The Great Escape of the Twenties, 1990; Rabbit Tales: Poetry and Politics in the Novels of John Updike, 1997; (with G. Holland) Hemingway and Women: Female Critics and the Female Voice, 2002. **Address:** Dept of English, University of South Florida, Tampa, FL 33620, U.S.A. **Online address:** LBruer@chumal.cas.usf.edu

BROEZE, Frank. Dutch, b. 1945. **Genres:** Business/Trade/Industry, History, Urban studies. **Career:** Writer. University of Western Australia, Nedlands, professor of history; Western Australian Maritime Museum, deputy chairperson; International Commission of Maritime History, president, 1990-95. **Publications:** De Stad Schiedam, 1978; A Merchant's Perspective, 1988; Private Enterprise, Government, and Society, 1992; Mr. Brooks and the Australian Trade: Imperial Business in the Nineteenth Century, 1993; Maritime History at the Crossroads, 1995; Island Nation: A History of Australians and the Sea, 1998. EDITOR: Brides of the Sea, 1989; (and contrib.) Gateways of Asia, 1998. Contributor to history and maritime journals. **Address:** Department of History, University of Western Australia, Nedlands, WA 6907, Australia. **Online address:** fjab@arts.uwa.edu.au

BROGAN, Elise. See URCH, Elizabeth.

BROGAN, Hugh. British, b. 1936. **Genres:** History. **Career:** Writer and historian. The Economist, staff member, 1959-63; St. John's College, Cambridge, fellow, 1963-74; University of Essex, Colchester, England, lecturer in history, 1974-92, R.A. Butler Professor of History, 1992-98. **Publications:** Tocqueville, 1973; The American Civil War: Extracts from "The Times," 1860-65, 1975; The Life of Arthur Ransome, 1984; The Longman History of the United States of America, 1985; Mowgli's Sons: Kipling and Baden-Powell's Scouts, 1987; (with C. Mosley) American Presidential Families, 1994; (with A.P. Kerr) Conversations et Correspondance d'Alexis de Tocqueville et Nassau William Senior, 1991; Kennedy, 1996. EDITOR: A. Ransome, Coots in the North and Other Stories, 1988; Signalling From Mars: The Letters of Arthur Ransome, 1997. Contributor of reviews to periodicals. **Address:** Department of History, University of Essex, Wivenhoe Park, Colchester CO4 3SQ, England.

BROIDO, Ethel. American/Israeli, b. 1917. **Genres:** Translations, Art/Art history, History. **Career:** Am Oved Publishing Co., art director, 1950-55;

Graphic designer and editor of publications for Histadruth, Israel's federation of labor; U.S. Information Service, worked in publication department, 1956-57; El Al Israel Airlines, advertising manager, 1958-62; ZIM Shipping Lines, advertising manager, 1962-65; Gordon Gallery, Tel Aviv, Israel, cofounder, 1965, director, 1965-69; American-Israel Culture Foundation, NYC, director of Gallery of Israeli Art, 1969-72; Bloomingdale's, NYC, worked in interior design department, 1973-74; NBC News, Israel Office, administrator and translator in Tel Aviv and Herzlia, 1975-87; free-lance writer and translator, 1987-. **Publications:** TRANSLATOR: M. Gil, A History of Palestine, 634-1099, 1992; I. Gutman: Resistance-The Warsaw Ghetto Uprising, 1994; City of Hope, Jerusalem from Biblical to Modern Times; Heroism and Bravery in Lithuania: Fustat on the Nile 1941-1945. EDITOR: Painting Palestine in the Nineteenth Century. Translator of scripts for documentary and action film and of texts of catalogs for art exhibits and art albums. Contributor of articles, translations, and reviews to periodicals. **Address:** 8 Bezalel St., 64683 Tel Aviv, Israel.

BROMBERG, Nicolette A. American. **Genres:** Local history/Rural topics. **Career:** Lower Columbia College, Longview, WA, director of media center and photography instructor, 1979-83; University of Kansas, Lawrence, photo archivist, 1983-93; Wisconsin Historical Society, Madison, curator of visual arts archive, 1993-2000; University of Washington, Seattle, curator of photographs and graphics, 2000-. **Publications:** Wisconsin Revisited: A Rephotographic Essay, 1998; Wisconsin Then and Now: The Wisconsin Sesquicentennial Rephotography Project, 2002. Contributor to journals. **Address:** University of Washington, Allen Library-Box 352900, Seattle, WA 98195, U.S.A. **Online address:** nxb@u.washington.edu

BROMBERT, Victor (Henri). American, b. 1923. **Genres:** Literary criticism and history. **Career:** Henry Putnam University Professor of Romance and Comparative Literature, Princeton University, NJ, 1975-. Formerly, Professor and Chairman, Dept of Romance Literatures, Yale University, New Haven, CT. **Publications:** The Criticism of T.S. Eliot, 1949; Stendhal et la Voie oblique, 1954; The Intellectual Hero, 1961; (ed.) Stendhal: A Collection of Critical Essays, 1962; The Novels of Flaubert, 1966; Stendhal: Fiction and the Themes of Freedom, 1968; (ed.) The Hero in Literature, 1969; Flaubert par lui-meme, 1971; The Romantic Prison, 1978; Victor Hugo and the Visionary Novel, 1984; The Hidden Reader, 1988; In Praise of Antiheroes: Figures and Themes in Modern European Literature, 1830-1980, 1999.

BROME, Vincent. See Obituaries.

BROMIGE, David (Mansfield). Canadian (born England), b. 1933. **Genres:** Novels, Poetry, Literary criticism and history, Plays/Screenplays, Novellas/Short stories. **Career:** Professor Emeritus of English, Sonoma State University, California (began as Assistant Professor, 1970). Contributor Ed., Avec, Penngrove, California, since 1987, and Kaimana, Honolulu, since 1989. Dairy farm worker, 1950-53; Mental hosp. attendant, 1954-55; Elementary School Teacher, England, 1957-58, and B.C., 1959-62; Freelance Reviewer, CBC, 1960-62; Ed., Raven mag., 1960-62; Poetry Ed., Northwest Review, Eugene, Oregon, 1963-64; Teaching Assistant, 1966-69, and Instructor in English, 1969-70, University of California, Berkeley; Lecturer, California College of Arts and Crafts, 1970. Editor of journals. **Publications:** Palace of Laments (play), 1957; The Medals (play), 1959; The Cobalt Poet (play), 1960; Save What You Can (play), 1961; The Gathering, 1965; Please Like Me, 1968; The Ends of the Earth, 1968; The Quivering Roadway, 1969; In His Image, 1970; Threads, 1971; The Fact So of Itself, 1971; They Are Eyes, 1972; Birds of the West, 1973; Three Stories, 1973; Tight Corners and What's Around Them, 1974; Ten Years in the Making, 1974; Spells and Blessings, 1974; Out of My Hands, (prose), 1974; Credences of Winter, 1976; Living in Advance (songs) 1976; Six of One, Half a Dozen of the Other, 1977; My Poetry, 1980; P-E-A-C-E, 1981; In the Uneven Steps of Hung-Chow (stories) 1982; It's the Same Only Different; 1984; You See, I & II, 1986; Red Hats, vol. 1, 1986; Broadside, 1987; Desire, 1988 (Western States Poetry Prize); Men, Women, and Vehicles (stories), 1990; American Testament, 1991; Tiny Courts, 1991; They Ate (novella), 1992; The Harbormaster of Hong Kong, 1993; A Cast of Tens, 1994; The Mad Career, 1995; From the First Century, 1995; The Art of Capitalism, 1996. **Address:** Dept. of English, Sonoma State University, Rohnert Park, CA 94928, U.S.A.

BROMILEY, Geoffrey William. British, b. 1915. **Genres:** Theology/Religion, Translations. **Career:** Professor Emeritus of Church History and Historical Theology, Fuller Theological Seminary, Pasadena, California, 1986- (Professor, 1958-86). Vice Principal, Trinity Theological College, Bristol, England, 1946-51; Rector, St. Thomas's Church, Edinburgh, 1951-58. **Publications:** Reasonable Service, 1949; Baptism and the Anglican Reformers, 1953; Thomas Cranmer, Theologian, 1956; Sacramental Teaching, 1957;

Unity and Disunity, 1958; Christian Ministry, 1959; Ellul's Ethics of Freedom, 1974; Thomas Cranmer, 1977; Historical Theology, 1978; Theology of Karl Barth, 1979; Children of Promise, 1979; God and Marriage, 1980. EDITOR: Standard Bible Encyclopedia, 1979-88. TRANSLATOR: Kasemann's Romans, 1980; Karl Barth's Letters, Ethics, Christian Life, 1981; Karl Barth's Theology of Schleiermacher, 1982; Helmut Thielicke's Being Human-Becoming Human, 1984; J. Ellul's Technological Bluff, 1990; Helmut Thielicke's Modern Faith and Thought, 1990; Gottingen Dogmatics I, by K. Barth, 1991; Systematic Theology I-3, by W. Pannenberg, 1991-98; The Theology of Calvin, by K. Barth, 1996. EDITOR & TRANSLATOR: Zwingli and Bullinger Classics, 1953; (co) Karl Barth's Church Dogmatics, vols. I-IV, 1956-74; DeSenarclens' Heirs of the Reformation, 1963; Theological Dictionary of the New Testament, vols. I-IX, 1964-74; Helmut Thielicke's Evangelical Faith, 3 vols., 1974-82; The Encyclopedia of Christianity, 3 vols., 1999-2003. **Address:** 2661 Tallant Rd #627, Santa Barbara, CA 93105, U.S.A.

BROMKE, Adam. Canadian/Polish (born Poland), b. 1928. **Genres:** International relations/Current affairs, Politics/Government. **Career:** Lecturer, Dept. of Economics and Political Science, McGill University, Montreal, 1957-60; Research Fellow, Russian Research Centre, Harvard University, Cambridge, Massachusetts, 1960-62; Professor Dept. of Political Science, Carleton University, Ottawa, 1962-73; Professor of Political Science, McMaster University, Hamilton, Ont., 1973-89, professor emeritus, 1989; Polish Academy of Sciences, professor of humanities, 1990. Grand Cross of Poland, 1998. **Publications:** Poland's Politics, Idealism vs. Realism, 1967; Poland: The Last Decade; Poland: The Protracted Crisis, 1983; Eastern Europe in the Aftermath of Solidarity, 1985; The Meanings and Uses of Polish History, 1987; Polak w swiecie (memoirs in Polish), 1996. EDITOR: The Communist States at the Crossroads, 1965; (with P.E. Uren) The Communist States and the West, 1967; (with T.H. Rakowski-Harmstone) The Communist States in Disarray, 1965-1973; (with J.W. Strong) Gierek's Poland, 1973; (with D. Novak) The Communist States in the Era of Daetente: 1971-77, 1978. **Address:** Bernardynska 22/26, 02-904, Warsaw, Poland.

BROMLEY, Simon. British, b. 1961. **Genres:** Politics/Government. **Career:** University of Leeds, Leeds, England, lecturer in international political economy. **Publications:** (with B. Jessop, K. Bonnett, and T. Ling) Thatcherism, 1988; American Hegemony and World Oil, 1991; Rethinking Middle East Politics, 1994. **Address:** Faculty of Social Sciences, Open University, Walton Hall, Milton Keynes MK7 6AA, England.

BRONER, E(sther) M(asserman). American, b. 1930. **Genres:** Novels, Novellas/Short stories, Plays/Screenplays, Literary criticism and history, Theology/Religion, Autobiography/Memoirs. **Career:** Wayne State University, Detroit, MI, professor of English and writer-in-residence, 1964-, now emerita. **Publications:** Summer Is a Foreign Land (verse-drama), 1966; Journal/Nocturnal and Seven Stories, 1968; (with M. Zieve) Colonel Higginson (musical drama), 1968; Her Mothers (novel) 1975; A Weave of Women (novel), 1978; The Body Parts of Margaret Fuller (play), 1978; (with C.N. Davidson) The Last Tradition: Mothers and Daughters in Literature, 1980; The Telling, 1993; Mornings and Mournings (autobiography), 1994; Ghost Stories (short stories), 1995; Bringing Home the Light: A Jewish Woman's Handbook of Rituals, 1999. **Address:** c/o Kane, 350 Central Park W 15F, New York, NY 10025, U.S.A. **Online address:** embroner@aol.com

BRONNER, Edwin Blaine. American, b. 1920. **Genres:** History, Theology/Religion, Biography. **Career:** Professor Emeritus of History, Haverford College, Pa., since 1990 (Professor and Curator of Quaker Collection, 1962-90; Librarian, 1969-86). Book Review Ed., Quaker History, 1974-90. President, Friends Historical Association, 1970-72 and 1974-77; President, Friends Historical Society (London), 1970. **Publications:** Thomas Earle as Reformer, 1948; William Penn's Holy Experiment, 1962; (ed.) American Quakers Today, 1966; (ed.) Walter Robson's Journal, 1970; The Other Branch, 1974; William Penn, 1975; (co-author) The Papers of William Penn, V, Bibliography, 1986; (ed.) The Quakers, by W. W. Comfort, 1986; (ed.) Everyman's William Penn, The Peace of Europe, The Fruits of Solitude, and other Writings, 1990. **Address:** 171 Crosslands, Kennett Square, PA 19348, U.S.A.

BRONNER, Leila Leah. American (born Czech Republic). **Genres:** Theology/Religion, Biography, History. **Career:** Witwatersrand University, tenured associate professor, 1960-84; Hebrew Teachers' College, senior lecturer, 1966-78; Harvard University, visiting fellow, 1984; Yeshiva University, visiting professor, 1985-87; University of Southern California, visiting scholar, 1986-87; University of Judaism, adjunct associate professor, 1987-90; Institute of Bible and Jewish Studies, professor, 1991-. Professionally affiliated throughout her career with Witwatersrand University Continu-

ing Adult Education, the Jewish Board of Deputies, and the Zionist Federation. **Publications:** Sects and Separatism During the Second Jewish Commonwealth, 1967; The Stories of Elijah and Elisha, 1968; Biblical Personalities and Archeology, 1974; From Eve to Esther: The Rabbinic Reconstruction of Biblical Women, 1994. Contributor to books and periodicals. **Address:** 180 North Las Palmas Avenue, Los Angeles, CA 90004, U.S.A. **Online address:** LeilaLeah@aol.com

BRONSON, Po. American, b. 1964. **Genres:** Novels. **Career:** First Boston Corporation, San Francisco, CA, bond salesman, 1986-88; Citi Respect ("San Francisco Politics"), 1988-89; Mercury House (non-profit publishing company), San Francisco, CA, associate publisher, 1989-95. Cofounder of the Writer's Grotto, San Francisco. **Publications:** NOVELS: Bombardiers, 1995; The First $20 Million is Always the Hardest, 1997; The Nudist on the Late Shift, 1999; What Should I Do With My Life, 2003. Contributor to magazines. **Address:** c/o Peter Ginsberg, Curtis Brown Ltd., 10 Astor Place, New York, NY 10003, U.S.A.

BRONZINO, Joseph D. American, b. 1937. **Genres:** Engineering, Ethics, Medicine/Health, Technology. **Career:** US Naval Postgraduate School, Monterey, CA, instructor, 1959-61; New York Telephone Co., NYC, transmission engineer, 1960-61, central office engineer, 1963-64; University of New Hampshire, Durham, instructor, 1964-66, assistant professor of electrical engineering, 1966-67; University of New Hampshire, Engineering Design and Analysis Laboratory, assistant director, 1964-67; Trinity College, Hartford, CT, associate professor, 1968-75, professor of engineering, 1975-, Vernon Roosa Professor of Applied Science, 1977-, chair of department, 1982-90; Hartford Graduate Center, Hartford, CT, director and chair of biomedical engineering program, 1969-97; Worcester Foundation for Experimental Biology, cooperating staff, 1968-97; University of Connecticut Health Center, clinical associate, 1971-77, project manager, 1980, administrative assistant, 1981, management and computer consultant, 1981-97; Boston University Medical School, adjunct faculty, 1989-98; Biomedical Engineering Alliance for Connecticut, director, 1997-2000; Beacon, president, 2000-. Aetna Institute, educational consultant, 1985-88; conference organizer; Connecticut Science Museum, scientific adviser, 1985-; reviewer for professional journals. **Publications:** Technology for Patient Care, 1977; Computer Applications for Patient Care, 1982; Biomedical Engineering and Instrumentation: Basic Concepts and Applications, 1986; (with V. Smith and M. Wade) Medical Technology and Society, 1990; Expert Systems: Basic Concepts and Applications, 1990; Management of Medical Technology, 1992; The BME Handbook, 1995, 2nd ed., 2000; Introduction to BME, 1999. **Address:** Dept of Engineering, Trinity College, Hartford, CT 06106, U.S.A. **Online address:** joseph.bronzino@trincoll.edu

BROOK, David. American, b. 1932. **Genres:** International relations/Current affairs. **Career:** Professor Emeritus, New Jersey City University, 2000- (Assistant Professor 1967-69; Associate Professor, 1969-70; Professor of Political Science, 1972-2000). Representative of International Studies Associate to the UN, 1981-91; Main Representative of Intl Public Policy Institute to the UN, 1993-. Chairman, UN Non-Governmental Organization Committee on the Youth, 1988-. Consultant, Dodd Mead & Co., publrs. Instructor, St. John University, NYC, 1961-63; Assistant Professor, City University of New York, 1964-67; Lecturer in Political Science, Rutgers University, New Brunswick, New Jersey, 1964-67. **Publications:** The United Nations and the China Dilemma, 1956; Preface to Peace: The United Nations and the Arab-Israel Armistice System, 1964; (ed.) Search for Peace: Readings in International Relations, 1970. **Address:** 135 Hawthorne St, Apt. 6-H, Brooklyn, NY 11225, U.S.A.

BROOK, Elaine (Isabel). British, b. 1949. **Genres:** Anthropology/Ethnology, Cultural/Ethnic topics, Environmental sciences/Ecology, Mythology/Folklore, Natural history, Philosophy, Travel/Exploration. **Career:** Primary school teacher in London, England, 1974-77; commercial artist in Calgary, Canada, 1977-80; mountain guide and freelance photojournalist in the United Kingdom and Nepal, 1980-85; freelance writer, 1985-; Himalayan Travel (a trekking agency), Buxton, England, 1987-94. Also worked as a mountain guide for Fantasy Ridge Alpinism in Colorado. Sponsored trek to Mt. Everest base camp with Julie Donnelly to support Guide Dogs for the Blind Association. Appeared in television film with Donnelly about communication between the sighted and the blind. **Publications:** The Wind Horse, 1986; Land of the Snow Lion, 1987; In Search of Shambhala, 1996. Contributor to periodicals. **Address:** c/o Jonathan Cape, 20 Vauxhall Bridge Rd, London SW1V 3EL, England. **Online address:** elaine@gaiacooperative.org

BROOK, Stephen. British, b. 1947. **Genres:** Food and Wine, Travel/Exploration. **Career:** Atlantic Monthly, Boston, MA, staff editor, 1970-73;

David R. Godine Inc. (publisher), Boston, editorial director, 1973-75; Routledge & Kegan Paul Ltd. (publisher), London, England, editor, 1976-80; writer, 1982-. **Publications:** New York Days, New York Nights, 1984; Honkytonk Gelato: Travels in Texas, 1984; The Dordogne, 1985; Maple Leaf Rag: Travels across Canada, 1987; Liquid Gold: Dessert Wines of the World, 1987; The Double Eagle: Vienna, Budapest, Prague, 1988; The Club: The Jews of Modern Britain, 1989; Winner Takes All: A Season in Israel, 1990; The Veneto, 1991; Prague, 1992; L.A. Lore, 1992; Sauvignon Blanc and Semillon, 1992; Claws of the Crab: Georgia and Armenia in Crisis, 1992; Vienna, 1994; Sauternes, 1995; Class, 1997; Pauillac, 1998; The Wines of California, 1999; Pocket Guide to Sweet and Fortified Wines, 2000; Bordeaux: People, Power and Politics, 2001. EDITOR: The Oxford Book of Dreams, 1983; The Penguin Book of Infidelities, 1994; The Penguin Book of Opera, 1995. Contributor of articles and reviews to periodicals. **Address:** 34 Carlton Mansions, Randolph Ave, London W9 1NP, England.

BROOK, Timothy (James). Canadian, b. 1951. **Genres:** Civil liberties/Human rights, History, Third World. **Career:** Needham Research Institute, research associate, 1978-79; University of Alberta, Edmonton, Canada, MacTaggart fellow, 1984-86; University of Toronto, ON, professor of history, 1986-2004; Stanford University, professor of history, 1997-99; University pf British Columbia, principal St. John's College, 2004-. **Publications:** Geographical Sources of Ming-Qing History, 1988; Quelling the People: The Military Suppression of the Beijing Democracy Movement, 1992; Praying for Power: Buddhism and the Formation of Gentry Society in Late-Ming China, 1993; The Confusions of Pleasure: Commerce and Culture in Ming China, 1998. EDITOR: The Asiatic Mode of Production in China, 1989; (with P.A. Kuhn) Min Tu-ki, National Polity and Local Power: The Transformation of Late Imperial China, 1989; (with Hy Van Luong) Culture and Economy: The Shaping of Capitalism in Eastern Asia, 1997; (with B.M. Frolic) Civil Society in China, 1997; (with G. Blue) China and Historical Capitalism: Genealogies of Sinological Knowledge, 1999; Documents on the Rape of Nanking, 1999; (with A. Schmid) Nation Work: Asian Elites and National Identities, 2000; (with B.T. Wakabayashi) Opium Regimes: China, Britain, and Japan, 1839-1952, 2001. Work represented in books. Contributor of articles and reviews to periodicals. **Address:** St. John's College, University of British Columbia, 2329 West Mall, Vancouver, BC, Canada V6T 1Z4.

BROOKE, Christopher N. L. British, b. 1927. **Genres:** History. **Career:** Fellow, Gonville and Caius College, Cambridge, 1949-56, 1977- (Lecturer in History, 1954-56). General Ed., Oxford (formerly Nelson's) Medieval Texts, 1959-87; Professor of Mediaeval History, University of Liverpool, 1956-67; Professor of History, Westfield College, University of London, 1967-77; Dixie Professor of Ecclesiastical History, University of Cambridge, 1977-94. **Publications:** (with W.J. Millor and H.E. Butler) The Letters of John of Salisbury, 2 vols., 1955-79; (with M. Postan) Carte Nativorum: A Peterborough Abbey Cartulary of the 14th Century, 1960; From Alfred to Henry III, 871-1272, 1961; The Saxon and Norman Kings, 1963, rev. ed., 2001; Europe in the Central Middle Ages, 1964, rev. ed., 2000; (with A. Morey) Gilbert Foliot and His Letters, 1965; (with A. Morey) The Letters and Charters of Gilbert Foliot, 1969; The Structure of Medieval Society, 1971; (with D. Knowles and V.C.M. London) The Heads of Religious Houses, England and Wales, 940-1216, 1972, rev. ed., 2001; (with W. Swaan) The Monastic World, 1000-1300, 1974; (with G. Keir) London, 800-1216: The Shaping of a City, 1975; (with D. Whitelock and M. Brett) Councils and Synods, I, 871-1204, 1981; (with R.B. Brooke) Popular Religion in the Middle Ages, 1984; A History of Gonville and Caius College, 1985; (with D.N. Dumville) The Church and the Welsh Border in the Central Middle Ages, 1986; (with R. Highfield and W. Swaan) Oxford and Cambridge, 1988; The Medieval Idea of Marriage, 1989; (with M. Brett and M. Winterbottom) Hugh the Chanter: History of the Church of York, 1990; A History of the University of Cambridge, IV: 1870-1990, 1993; (co-author) II: 1546-1750, 2004; Jane Austen: Illusion and Reality, 1999; (with S. Bendall and P. Collinson) A History of Emmanuel College Cambridge, 1999; Churches and Churchmen in Medieval Europe, 1999. **Address:** Gonville and Caius College, Trinity St, Cambridge CB2 1TA, England.

BROOKE, Jill. American, b. 1959. **Genres:** Adult non-fiction. **Career:** Journalist. Worked as a reporter for ABC's Nightline, columnist for the New York Post, and correspondent for CNN; Daily News, New York, NY, columnist; Avenue (magazine), New York, NY, editor-in-chief. **Publications:** Don't Let Death Ruin Your Life: A Practical Guide to Reclaiming Happiness After the Death of a Loved One, 2001. Contributor to publications. **Address:** c/o Show Circuit Magazine, 2341 Farringdon Ave, Pomona, CA 91768-1037, U.S.A.

BROOKE, Rosalind B(eckford). British, b. 1925. **Genres:** History, Politics/Government, Theology/Religion. **Career:** Mitcham County Grammar School

for Girls, temporary senior history mistress, 1949-50; Cambridge University, Cambridge, England, history supervisor for undergraduates, 1951-56; Birkenhead High School, Birkenhead, England, history mistress, 1958-59; Liverpool University, Liverpool, England, lecturer in palaeography, 1963; University of Liverpool, Liverpool, tutor, 1964-66; University College, London, England, part-time lecturer in medieval history, 1968-73, honorary research fellow, 1973-77; Cambridge University, history supervisor for undergraduates and lecturer in history, 1977-92; writer. **Publications:** Early Franciscan Government: Elias to Bonaventure, 1959; (ed. and trans.) Scripta Leonis, Rufini et Angeli sociorum S. Francisci, 1970, rev. ed., 1990; The Coming of the Friars: Historical Problems, Studies, and Documents, 1975; (with C. Brooke) Popular Religion in the Middle Ages: Western Europe, 1000-1300, 1984. Contributor to periodicals, including conference proceedings. **Address:** c/o Professor C.N.L. Brooke, Gonville and Caius College, Cambridge CB2 ITA, England.

BROOKE, William J. American, b. 1946. **Genres:** Children's fiction, Young adult fiction. **Career:** Employed by Metropolitan Opera, New York City, 1973-87; worked as word processor, 1987-90; actor; writer. **Publications:** FOR CHILDREN: Operantics, 1986; A Telling of the Tales, 1990; Untold Tales, 1992; A Brush with Magic, 1993; Teller of Tales, 1994; A Is for Aargh!, 1999. **Address:** 215 W 78th St No. 5C, New York, NY 10024, U.S.A. **Online address:** billbrooke@nyc.rr.com

BROOKE-LITTLE, John (Philip Brooke). British, b. 1927. **Genres:** Genealogy/Heraldry, History, Local history/Rural topics, Theology/Religion. **Career:** Ed., Dod's Peerage, and Dod's Parliamentary Companion, 1955-58; Clavenceux King of Arms, 1995-97 (Bluemantle Pursuivant of Arms, 1956-67; Richmond Herald of Arms, 1967-80; Norroy and Ulster King of Arms 1980-95). Officer of Arms, Royal Household, 1956-97. Hon. Ed., The Coat of Arms, 1950-2004. Fellow, Society of Antiquaries, and Heraldry Society. **Publications:** Royal London, 1953; Pictorial History of Oxford, 1954; (ed. with C. W. Scott-Giles) Boutell's Heraldry, 1963, (sole ed.) 9th ed., 1983; Knights of the Middle Ages, 1966; (ed.) Complete Guide to Heraldry, 1969; The Prince of Wales, 1969; (with A. Taute and D. Pottinger) The Kings and Queens of Great Britain, 1970; An Heraldic Alphabet, 3rd ed. 1985, 4th rev. ed. 1996; (with M. Angel) Beasts in Heraldry, 1974; Royal Arms, Beasts and Badges, 1977; The British Monarchy in Colour, 1977; Royal Ceremonies of State, 1980. **Address:** Heyford House, Lower Heyford, Bicester, Oxon. OX25 5NZ, England.

BROOKER, Jewel Spears. American, b. 1940. **Genres:** Poetry, Humanities, Intellectual history, Literary criticism and history. **Career:** University of Tampa and University of South Florida, adjunct appointments, 1977-80; Yale University, New Haven, CT, postdoctoral research fellow in English, 1980-81; Eckerd College, St. Petersburg, FL, associate professor to professor, 1981-; Colorado School of Mines, Hennebach Professor of Humanities, 2003-04; writer. St. Edmund's College, Cambridge, visiting scholar, 1987; visiting professor, Columbia University, 1988, and Doshisha University, Kyoto, Japan, 1992-94; Harvard University, Fellow in Literary Manuscripts, 1999; University of London, John Adams Fellow, 2000; South Atlantic Modern Language Assn, president, 2000-01 National Endowment for the Humanities, National Humanities Council, 2003-08. NEH Fellowship for Independent Study, 1980-81; NEH Fellowship for College Teachers, 1987-88; Pew Charitable Trust Fellowship, 1999-2000. **Publications:** (with J. Bentley) Reading "The Waste Land": Modernism and the Limits of Interpretation, 1990; Mastery and Escape: T.S. Eliot and the Dialectic of Modernism, 1994. EDITOR: (and contrib.) Approaches to Teaching T.S. Eliot's Poetry and Plays, 1988; (and contrib.) The Placing of T.S. Eliot, 1991; Conversations with Denise Levertov, 1998; T.S. Eliot and Our Turning World, 2000; (ed.) T.S. Eliot, The Contemporary Reviews, 2003. Contributor to books and journals. **Address:** Eckerd College, 4200 54th Ave S, St. Petersburg, FL 33733, U.S.A. **Online address:** jsbrooker@aol.com

BROOKE-ROSE, Christine. British (born Switzerland), b. 1923. **Genres:** Literary criticism and history, Novels, Novellas/Short stories, Autobiography/Memoirs. **Career:** Freelance journalist, London, 1956-68; Lecturer, 1969-75, and Professor, 1975-88, Dept. of English and American Literature, University of Paris. **Publications:** NOVELS: The Languages of Love, 1957; The Sycamore Tree, 1958; The Dear Deceit, 1960; The Middlemen: A Satire, 1961; Out, 1964; Such, 1966; Between, 1968; Thru, 1975; Amalgamemnon, 1984; Xorandor, 1986; The Christine Brooke-Rose Omnibus, 1986; Verbivore, 1989; Textermination, 1991; Next, 1998; Subscript, 1999. LITERARY CRITICISM: A Grammar of Metaphor, 1958; A ZBC of Ezra Pound, 1971; A Rhetoric of the Unreal, 1981; Stories, Theories and Things, 1991; Invisible Author, 2002. OTHER: Go When You See the Green Man Walking (short stories), 1969; Remake (autobiography), 1996.

BROOKES, John A. British, b. 1933. **Genres:** Homes/Gardens. **Career:** Nottingham Corp., parks department, Nottingham, England, apprentice; Architectural Design, assistant; John Brookes Design (landscape designers), principal, 1964-. Inchbald School of Landscape Design, past director; Inchbald School of Interior Design, founder, Teheran, Iran, 1978; Clock House School of Garden Design, founder, 1980; Royal Botanic Garden Kew, England, principal lecturer at School of Garden Design; lecturer at Institute of Park Administration and Regent Street Polytechnic. **Publications:** Room Outside, 1969; Gardens for Small Spaces, 1970; Garden Design and Layout, 1970; Living in the Garden, 1971; The Financial Times Book of Garden Design, 1975; Improve Your Lot, 1977; The Small Garden, 1977; The Garden Book, 1984; A Place in the Country, 1984; The Indoor Garden Book, 1986; Gardens of Paradise, 1987; The Country Garden, 1987; The New Small Garden Book, 1989; The Book of Garden Design, in UK as John Brookes' Garden Design Book, 1991; (with E. Price) Home & Garden Style, 1996; Natural Landscapes, 1998; John Brookes' Garden Masterclass, 2002. **Address:** Clock House, Denmans, Fontwell, near Arundel, W. Sussex BN18 0SU, England. **Online address:** jbrookes@denmans-garden.co.uk; www.denmans-garden.co.uk

BROOKES, Tim. British, b. 1953. **Genres:** Medicine/Health, Travel/Exploration. **Career:** University of Vermont, Burlington, instructor in English, 1974-99; writer. Regular commentator for Sunday Weekend Edition, National Public Radio, 1989-; worked as a soccer coach, singer/guitarist, and as a journalist for an alternative weekly in Vermont, a local daily, a rock station, an entertainment newsletter, and editor of the public radio program guide-cum-magazine. **Publications:** Catching My Breath: An Asthmatic Explores His Illness, 1994; (with others) The Blair Handbook: Instructor's Ed, 1994; Signs of Life: a memoir of dying and discovery, 1997; A Hell of a Place to Lose a Cow, 2000. Contributor to periodicals. **Address:** Department of English, 431 Old Mill, University of Vermont, Burlington, VT 05405, U.S.A. **Online address:** tbrookes@zoo.uvm.edu

BROOKHISER, Richard. American, b. 1955. **Genres:** History, Politics/Government, Social commentary. **Career:** National Review, NYC, senior editor, 1979-85, and 1988-, managing editor, 1986-87; writer. Speech writer for Vice President George Bush, 1982. **Publications:** The Outside Story: How Democrats and Republicans Re-elected Reagan, 1986; (ed.) William F. Buckley, Jr., Right Reason, 1986; The Way of the WASP: How It Made America and How It Can Save It, So to Speak, 1991; Founding Father: Rediscovering George Washington, 1996; Rules of Civility, 1997; Alexander Hamilton, American, 1999. Contributor of articles and reviews to periodicals. **Address:** National Review, 215 Lexington Ave 4th Fl, New York, NY 10016, U.S.A.

BROOKNER, Anita. British, b. 1928. **Genres:** Novels, Novellas/Short stories, Art/Art history. **Career:** University of Reading, lecturer, 1959-64; Cambridge University, Slade Professor, 1967-68; Courtauld Institute of Art, London, lecturer, 1964-77, reader, 1977-87. **Publications:** ART HISTORY & CRITICISM: J.A. Dominique Ingres, 1965; Watteau, 1968; The Genius of the Future, 1971; Greuze, 1972; Jacques-Louis David: A Personal Interpretation, 1974, rev. ed., 1987; Jacques-Louis David, 1980, rev. ed., 1987; Soundings, 1997; Romanticism and Its Discontents, 2000. NOVELS: A Start in Life (in US as The Debut), 1981; Providence, 1982; Look at Me, 1983; Hotel du Lac, 1984 (Booker Prize); Family and Friends, 1985; A Misalliance, 1986, in US as The Misalliance, 1987; A Friend from England, 1987; Latecomers, 1988; Lewis Percy, 1989; Brief Lives, 1990; A Closed Eye, 1991; Fraud, 1992; A Family Romance (in US as Dolly), 1993; A Private View, 1994; Incidents in the Rue Laugier, 1996; Altered States, 1997; Visitors, 1998; Falling Slowly, 1998; Undue Influence, 2000; The Bay of Angels, 2001; The Next Big Thing, 2002 (Booker Prize); Making Things Better, 2003. OTHER: An Iconography of Cecil Rhodes, 1956. AUTHOR OF INTRODUCTIONS: Troy Chimneys, 1985; The Island of Desire, 1985; Summer in the Country, 1985; Living on Yesterday, 1986; The House of Mirth, 1987; (and ed.) The Stories of Edith Wharton, vol. 2, 1988; The Collected Stories of Edith Wharton, 1998. TRANSLATOR: W. George, Utrillo, 1960; J.-P. Crespelle, The Fauves, 1962; M. Gauthier, Gauguin, 1963. Contributor to periodicals.

BROOKS, Andree (Nicole) Aelion. American (born England), b. 1937. **Genres:** Psychology, Writing/Journalism, History, Politics/Government. **Career:** Hampstead News, London, England, reporter, 1954-58; Photoplay, New York City, story editor, 1958-60; Australian Broadcasting Co., New York City, correspondent, 1961-68; Ladies' Home Journal, New York City, member of editorial staff, 1957-58; free-lance journalist, 1960-. Hertsmere Council, Conservative representative from Elstree, 1973-74; Fairfield University, adjunct professor of journalism, 1983-87; parent educator, 1987-;

Yale University, associate fellow, 1989-; columnist, regular contributor, New York Times, 1977-95; Guest on radio and television programs. Founder and first president, Women's Campaign School at Yale, 1994. Lecturer in Jewish history. **Publications:** NON-FICTION: Children of Fast-Track Parents, 1989; The Woman Who Defied Kings, 2002. Contributor to periodicals.

BROOKS, Betty. American, b. 1936. **Genres:** Romance/Historical. **Career:** Writer. **Publications:** HISTORICAL NOVELS: Savage Flame, 1987; Passion's Angel, 1987; Passion's Siren, 1988; Apache Sunset, 1988; Warrior's Embrace, 1989; Wild Texas Magnolia, 1990; Apache Captive, 1990; Comanche Embrace, 1991; Heart of the Mountains, 1991; Comanche Passion, 1992; Love's Endless Flame, 1992; Beloved Viking, 1994; Viking Mistress, 1994; Warrior's Destiny, 1995; Jade, 1997; Comanche Sunset, 1998; Sweet Words of Love, 1998; A Place in My Heart, 1999; Mail Order Love, 1999; The Wayward Heart, 1999; Texas Treasure, 2000. **Address:** 2201 SE 9th St, Mineral Wells, TX 76067, U.S.A. **Online address:** BettyBrooks1@yahoo.com

BROOKS, Bruce. American, b. 1950. **Genres:** Novels, Natural history. **Career:** Writer; worked as a letterpress printer, newspaper and magazine reporter, and teacher. **Publications:** FICTION: The Moves Make the Man, 1984; Midnight Hour Encores, 1986; No Kidding, 1989; Everywhere, 1990; What Hearts, 1992; Boys will Be, 1993; Asylum for Nightface, 1996; Cody, 1997; Woodsie, 1997; Zip, 1997; Billy, 1998; Boot, 1998; Dooby, 1998; Each a Piece, 1998; Prince, 1998; Reed, 1998; Barry, 1999; Subtle, 1999; Vanishing, 1999; Woodsie, Again, 1999; Throwing Smoke, 2000; All That Remains, 2001; Dolores, 2002. NONFICTION: On the Wing: The Life of Birds from Feathers to Flight, 1989; Predator!, 1991; Nature by Design, 1991; Making Sense, 1993; Those Who Love the Game, 1993; NBA by the Numbers, 1997; (ed.) The Red Wasteland, 1998; Shark, 1998. **Address:** c/o HarperCollins Children's Books, 1350 Avenue of the Americas, New York, NY 10019, U.S.A.

BROOKS, David (Gordon). Australian, b. 1953. **Genres:** Novels, Novellas/Short stories, Poetry, Literary criticism and history, Essays. **Career:** University of Toronto, Canada, 1976-80; University of New South Wales, Canberra, ACT, 1981; University of Western Australia, Perth, 1982-85; Australian National University, Canberra, 1986-91; University of Sydney, NSW, Australia, senior lecturer in Australian literature, 1991-. Open Door Press, founder, editor, and printer, 1974-77; Southerly, editor, 1999-. **Publications:** POETRY: Five Poems, 1981; The Cold Front, 1983; Walking to Point Clear, 2005. STORIES: The Book of Sei and Other Stories, 1986, rev. 1988; Sheep and the Diva, 1990; Black Sea, 1997. OTHER: The Necessary Jungle: Literature and Excess (essays), 1990; The House of Balthus (novel), 1995; De/Scription (art criticism), 2001. EDITOR: New South: Australian Poetry of the Late 1970s, 1980; (with B. Walker) Poetry and Gender: Statements and Essays on Australian Women Poets, 1989; Selected Poems of A.D. Hope, 1991; Suddenly Evening: Selected Poems of R.F. Brissenden, 1991; The Double Looking Glass: Essays on the Poetry of A.D. Hope, 2003. Works represented in anthologies. Contrib. of essays and reviews to periodicals. **Address:** University of Sydney, Sydney, NSW 2006, Australia.

BROOKS, Edwin. Australian (born Wales), b. 1929. **Genres:** Geography. **Career:** Lecturer, 1954-66, 1970-72, Sr. Lecturer in Geography 1972-77, and Dean of College Studies, 1975-77, University of Liverpool; Dean of Commerce, 1977-88, and Deputy Principal, 1988-89, Charles Sturt University-Riverina (formerly Riverina-Murray Institute of Higher Education), Wagga Wagga, N. S. W. Councillor, Birkenhead, Cheshire, 1958-67; Labour M.P. for Bebington, 1966-70. **Publications:** This Crowded Kingdom, 1973; (ed.) Tribes of the Amazon Basin in Brazil, 1973. **Address:** Inchnadamph, Gregadoo Rd, Wagga Wagga, NSW 2650, Australia.

BROOKS, Erik. (born United States), b. 1972. **Genres:** Children's fiction. **Career:** Author and illustrator of children's books. Carleton College, Northfield, MN, cross-country and track coach. **Publications:** The Practically Perfect Pajamas, 2000; Octavius Bloom and the House of Doom, 2003. ILLUSTRATOR: Shirley Climo, Monkey Business, 2004; Emme Aronson, What Are You Hungry For?, forthcoming. **Address:** 315 Cherry St., Northfield, MN 55057, U.S.A. **Online address:** brooks@rconnect.com

BROOKS, Fairleigh. (born United States), b. 1953. **Genres:** Novels. **Career:** Writer. **Publications:** Notes of a Would-Be Astronaut, 2002. Author of a monthly column. **Address:** 1104 Fenley Ave, Louisville, KY 40222, U.S.A. **Online address:** fairbrooks@att.net

BROOKS, George E., Jr. American, b. 1933. **Genres:** History. **Career:** Professor of History, Indiana University, Bloomington, 1975- (Asst Professor, 1962-68; Associate Professor, 1968-75); International Journal of African Historical Studies, Editorial Advisory Board, 1968-97; Liberian Studies Journal, 1968-77. **Publications:** (ed. with N.R. Bennett) New England Merchants in Africa: A History through Documents, 1802-1865, 1965; Yankee Traders, Old Coasters and Africa Middlemen: A History of American Legitimate Trade with West Africa in the Nineteenth Century, 1970; The Kru Mariner in the Nineteenth Century: An Historical Compendium, 1972; Themes in African and World History, 1973, 1983; Western Africa to c. 1860 A.D.: A Provisional Historical Schema Based on Climate Periods, 1985; Landlords and Strangers: Ecology, Society, and Trade in Western Africa, 1000-1630, 1993; Eurafricans in Western Africa: Commerce Social Status, Gender, and Religious Observance from the Sixteenth to the Eighteenth Century, 2003. **Address:** Dept. of History, Indiana University, Ballantine Hall 742, 1020 E Kirkwood Ave, Bloomington, IN 47405-7103, U.S.A. **Online address:** brooksg@indiana.edu

BROOKS, H(arold) Allen. American, b. 1925. **Genres:** Architecture. **Career:** University of Toronto, Dept. of Fine Art, joined faculty, 1958, professor emeritus. Society of Architectural Historians (USA), director, 1961-64, 1967-70, 1971-74, president, 1964-66. **Publications:** The Prairie School: Frank Lloyd Wright and His Midwest Contemporaries, 1972; Frank Lloyd Wright and the Prairie School, 1984; Le Corbusier's Formative Years: Charles-Edouard Jeanneret at La Chaux-de Fonds, 1997. Contributor to periodicals. EDITOR: Prairie School Architecture: Studies from the "Western Architect," 1975; (and contrib.) Writings on Wright: Selected Comment on Frank Lloyd Wright, 1981; (gen. and contrib.) The Le Corbusier Archive: The Drawings, 32 vols., 1982-85; (and contrib.) Le Corbusier, 1987. **Address:** 80 Lyme Rd Apt 373, Hanover, NH 03755, U.S.A.

BROOKS, Jeanne. See **BROOKS-GUNN, Jeanne.**

BROOKS, Kevin M. (born England), b. 1959. **Genres:** Young adult fiction. **Career:** Worked various jobs in England, including musician, gasoline station attendant, crematorium handyman, civil service clerk, hot dog vendor at the London Zoo, post office clerk, and railway ticket office clerk. Writer. **Publications:** Martyn Pig, 2002; Lucas, 2003; Kissing the Rain, 2004. **Address:** c/o Author Mail, Scholastic Inc, 524 Broadway, New York, NY 10012, U.S.A. **Online address:** fairbrooks@att.net

BROOKS, Martha. Canadian. **Genres:** Children's fiction, Novellas/Short stories. **Career:** Writer, 1972-; creative writing teacher in junior and senior high schools, through the Artist in the Schools program of the Manitoba Arts Council, beginning in early 1980s. **Publications:** A Hill for Looking, 1982; Paradise Cafe and Other Stories (young adults), 1988, 1990; Two Moons in August (young adult novel), 1991; Traveling on into the Light (young adult short stories), 1994. **Address:** 58-361 Westwood Dr, Winnipeg, MB, Canada R3K 1G4.

BROOKS, Peter Newman. British, b. 1931. **Genres:** History, Theology/Religion, Biography, Essays. **Career:** Cambridge University, England, professor of Reformation studies, 1970-98, fellow of Downing College, 1970-83, proctor of the university, 1977-78, fellow of Robinson College, 1983-98, fellow emeritus, 1998-; Cranmer Theological House, Shreveport, LA, emeritus professor of Reformation studies, 1999-2002, director of Graduate Studies, 1999-2002. Lecturer in the United States. South Cambridgeshire District Councillor, 1984-88; chairman of the Landbeach Society (a conservation and amenity body). **Publications:** Thomas Cranmer's Doctrine of the Eucharist: An Essay in Historical Development, 1965, 2nd ed., 1992; Cranmer in Context, 1989; Hymns as Homilies, 1997. EDITOR & CONTRIBUTOR: Christian Spirituality: Essays Presented to Gordon Rupp, 1975; Reformation Principle and Practice: Essays Presented to A.G. Dickens, 1980; Seven-Headed Luther: Essays in Commemoration of a Quincentenary, 1483-1983, 1983. Contributor to books. **Address:** Robinson College, Cambridge CB3 9AN, England.

BROOKS, Rodney (A.). Australian, b. 1954. **Genres:** Information science/Computers. **Career:** Massachusetts Institute of Technology, Cambridge, MA, professor of computer science, 1984-, artificial intelligence laboratory, director. **Publications:** Model-based Computer Vision, 1984; Programming in Common LISP, 1985; Cambrian Intelligence: The Early History of the New AI, 1999; Flesh and Machines: How Robots Will Change Us, 2002; Robot: The Future of Flesh and Machines, 2002. EDITOR: (with P. Maes) Artificial Life IV: Proceedings of the Fourth International Workshop on the Synthesis and Simulation of Living Systems, 1994; (with L. Steels) The Artificial Life Route to Artificial Intelligence Building Embodied, Situated Agents, 1995. Contributor to periodicals; author of papers in model-based computing, uncertainty analysis, path planning, artificial life, planetary exploration, autonomous robots, active vision, robot assembly, and compiler design. **Address:** MIT Artificial Intelligence Laboratory, 200 Technology Square, Cambridge, MA 02139, U.S.A. **Online address:** brooks@ai.mit.edu

BROOKS, Roy L(avon). American, b. 1950. **Genres:** Law, Politics/Government, Race relations. **Career:** University of San Diego, CA, Warren Distinguished Professor of Law, 1979-. **Publications:** Rethinking the American Race Problem, 1990; Civil Rights Litigation, 1995; Integration or Separation? 1996; Critical Procedure, forthcoming. **Address:** School of Law, University of San Diego, San Diego, CA 92110, U.S.A. **Online address:** rbrooks@sandiego.edu

BROOKS-GUNN, Jeanne. Also writes as Jeanne Brooks, Brooke Gunn. American, b. 1946. **Genres:** Education, Psychology, Sociology. **Career:** University of Pennsylvania, adjunct faculty, 1973-80, adjunct associate professor, 1985-; Educational Testing Service, Princeton, NJ, associate research scientist, 1974-77, research scientist, 1978-83, associate director of Institute for the Study of Exceptional Children, 1977-82, director of Adolescent Study Program, 1982-, senior research scientist for Division of Education Policy Research, 1983-92; St. Luke's-Roosevelt Hospital Center Pediatric Service, research scientist, 1978-95; Columbia University, assistant professor, 1978-86, Teachers College, Virginia & Leonard Marx Professor, 1991-, director of National Center for Children and Families, co-director of Institute of Child and Family Policy, 1998-, College of Physicians & Surgeons, professor, 2000-; visiting associate professor, Princeton University, 1981-84, Barnard College, 1982-83; Russell Sage Foundation, visiting scholar, 1988-89; writer. **Publications:** (with Matthews) He and She: How Children Develop Their Sex-Role Identity, 1979; (with Lewis) Social Cognition and the Acquisition of Self, 1979; (with Furstenberg Jr. and Morgan) Adolescent Mothers in Later Life, 1987; (with Graber and Petersen) Transitions through Adolescence, 1996; (with Cox) Conflict and Cohesion in Families, 1999. EDITOR/CO-EDITOR: (and contrib.) Girls at Puberty, 1983; (and contrib.) Women in Midlife, 1984; Time of Maturation and Psychosocial Functioning in Adolescence, 2 vols., 1985; (and contrib.) The Encyclopedia of Adolescence, 1990; The Emergence of Depression and Depressive Symptoms during Adolescence, 1991; Escape from Poverty, 1993; Consequences of Growing up Poor, 1997 Neighborhood Poverty, 2 vols., 1997; Early Childhood Development in the 21st Century, 2003; (series ed.) Adolescent Lives. **Address:** Teachers College, Columbia University, 525 W 120th St, New York, NY 10027, U.S.A.

BROOM, Neil D. New Zealander. **Genres:** Sciences. **Career:** Health Research Council of New Zealand, Auckland, research fellow, 1975-; University of Auckland, New Zealand, associate professor, 1989-. **Publications:** How Blind Is the Watchmaker?: Theism or Atheism: Should Science Decide?, 1998, in US as How Blind Is the Watchmaker?: Nature's Design and the Limits of Naturalistic Science, 2001. Contributor to journals. **Address:** Dept of Chemical and Materials Engineering, University of Auckland, Private Bag 92019, Auckland, New Zealand. **Online address:** nd.broom@auckland.ac.nz

BROOMALL, Robert W(alter). Also writes as Hank Edwards, Dale Colter. American, b. 1946. **Genres:** Westerns/Adventure, Mystery/Crime/Suspense, Romance/Historical. **Career:** Freelance writer since 1975. Copy Ed., Williams and Wilkins, publrs., Baltimore, 1968; civilian budget analyst, U.S. Army, Corps of Engineers, Baltimore, 1972-74; property administrator, U.S. Defense Contracts Supply Agency, Baltimore, 1974-75. **Publications:** The Bank Robber, 1985; Dead Man's Canyon, 1986; Dead Man's Crossing, 1987; Dead Man's Town, 1988; Texas Kingdoms, 1989; California Kingdoms, 1992; K Company, 1992; The Lawmen, 1993; Conroy's First Command, 1994; as Hank Edwards-Texas Feud, 1991; War Clouds, 1991; as Dale Colter-the Scalphunters, 1992; Pardise Mountain, 1992; Desert Pursuit, 1992; Montana Showdown, 1993;. **Address:** 8196 Gray Haven Rd, Baltimore, MD 21222, U.S.A.

BROOME, Errol. Australian, b. 1937. **Genres:** Children's fiction, Children's non-fiction. **Career:** The West Australian, Perth, Western Australia, journalist, 1958-60; Herald-Sun Television, Melbourne, Victoria, Australia, journalist, 1961; writer, 1978-. **Publications:** Wrinkles, 1978; Bird Boy, 1986; Town and Country Ducks, 1986; The Smallest Koala, 1987; A Year of Pink Pieces, 1988; Have a Go!, 1988; Dear Mr. Sprouts, 1991; Garry Keeble's Kitchen: How One Boy Left Home and Survived with 28 Recipes That Anyone Can Cook and Everyone Will Eat, 1992; Tangles, 1993; Rockhopper, 1995; Nightwatch, 1995; Splashback: A Great Greasy Journey, 1996; Fly with Me, 1996; Pets (series of eight), 1997; What a Goat!, 1997; Quicksilver, 1997; Tough Luck, 1998; Magnus Maybe, 1998; Missing Mem, 2000; Away with the Birds, 2000; Cry of the Karri, 2001; Gracie and the

Emperor, 2003; The Judas Donkey, 2003. **Address:** 33 Seymour Grove, Brighton Beach, VIC 3186, Australia. **Online address:** errolbroome@ bigpond.com

BROSNAHAN, L(eonard) F(rancis). New Zealander, b. 1922. **Genres:** Language/Linguistics. **Career:** Vice Chancellor (retired), University of South Pacific, Suva, Fiji, since 1983 (Professor, 1969-82; Deputy Vice-Chancellor, 1972-79; Vice-Chancellor, 1982-83). Former Lecturer, and Sr. Lecturer, University of Ibadan, Nigeria, and Professor, Victoria University of Wellington, New Zealand. **Publications:** Some Old English Sound Changes, 1953; Genes and Phonemes, 1957; The Sounds of Language, 1961-82; The English Language in the World, 1963; (with B. Malmberg) Introduction to Phonetics, 1970, 1975; Grammar Usage and the Teacher, 1971. **Address:** Lake Okareka, Rural Delivery 5, Rotorua 3221, New Zealand.

BROSNAN, John. Also writes as Harry Adam Knight, Simon Ian Childer, James Blackstone, John Raymond. Australian, b. 1947. **Genres:** Science fiction/Fantasy. **Career:** Science fiction writer and author of books on film and science fiction. Inland Revenue, Kensington, England, clerk; Foundation Press, Holborn, England, publicity manager; freelance writer, 1974-; science fiction and fantasy editorial consultant, Granada Paperbacks, 1977-82. Film columnist for Science Fiction Monthly and Starburst (periodicals); former lead book reviewer for The Dark Side (horror magazine). **Publications:** NOVELS: Skyship, 1981; The Midas Deep, 1983; The Opoponax Invasion, 1993; Damned and Fancy, 1995. SKYLORDS TRILOGY: The Skylords, 1988; War of the Skylords, 1989; The Fall of the Skylords, 1991. AS HARRY ADAM KNIGHT: (with L. Kettle) Slimer, 1983; Carnosaur, 1984; (with Kettle) The Fungus, 1985, in US as Death Spore, 1989. AS SIMON IAN CHILDER: (with Kettle) Tendrils, 1986; Worm, 1987. AS JAMES BLACK-STONE: (with J. Baxter) Torched, 1985. NOVELIZATIONS AS JOHN RAYMOND: Blind Eye, 1985; Lucky Streak, 1985; The Bogeyman, 1986; Dirty Weekend, 1986; The Jericho Scam, 1986; Partners in Brine, 1986; Bulman: Thin Ice, 1987. NONFICTION AS JOHN BROSNAN: James Bond in the Cinema, 1972, rev 2nd ed, 1981; Movie Magic: The Story of Special Effects in the Cinema, 1974, rev. ed., 1976; The Horror People, 1976; Future Tense: The Cinema of Science Fiction, 1978 as The Primal Screen, 1991; (with L. Mitchell) The Dirty Movie Book, 1988. Author of short stories. **Address:** c/o Victor Gollancz Ltd., 5 Upper St. Martins Lane, London WC2, England.

BROSS, Donald G. American, b. 1932. **Genres:** Novels, Adult non-fiction, Essays. **Career:** Southwestern Bell, Oklahoma City, OK, line worker, telephone installer, and supervisor, 1951-84. **Publications:** Surrogate Son (novel), 1992; Farewell, Ma Bell (humor), 1996; (coauthor) Mountain Madness (nonfiction), 1996. **Address:** 5350 W Camp Rd, Guthrie, OK 73044, U.S.A. **Online address:** dixidon@yahoo.com

BROSS, Irwin D. J. *See* Obituaries.

BROSTOFF, Anita. American, b. 1931. **Genres:** Writing/Journalism. **Career:** Carnegie-Mellon University, Pittsburgh, PA, assistant professor of English, 1972-75, assistant professor at Communication Skills Center, 1975-81; Brostoff Associates (communications consultants), Pittsburgh, PA, principal, 1981-94; writer, 1994-. University of Pittsburgh, lecturer and consultant to Graduate School of Business, 1983-86; Carnegie-Mellon University, instructor at Academy for Lifelong Learning, 1999-. Carnegie Museum of Art, docent, 1995-. **Publications:** Thinking through Writing, 1981. EDITOR: I Could Be Mute: The Life and Work of Gladys Schmitt, 1978; (with S. Chamovitz) Flares of Memory: Stories of Childhood during the Holocaust, 2001. **Address:** 1215 Murray Hill Ave., Pittsburgh, PA 15217, U.S.A. **Online address:** abrostoff@worldnet.att.net

BROTHERS, Joyce (Diane). American. **Genres:** Psychology. **Career:** Columnist, Good Houskeeping mag., and King Features Syndicate. Independent psychologist, writer since 1952. TV programs: Dr. Joyce Brothers, 1958-63; Consult Dr. Brothers, 1960-66; Ask Dr. Brothers, 1965-75; Living Easy with Dr. Joyce Brothers, 1972-75. **Publications:** Ten Days to a Successful Memory, 1959; Woman, 1961; The Brothers System for Liberated Love and Marriage, 1973; Better Than Ever, 1976; How to Get What You Want Out of Life, 1978; What Every Woman Should Know about Men, 1982; What Every Woman Ought to Know about Love and Marriage, 1984; Dr. Joyce Brothers' The Successful Woman: How You Can Have a Career, a Husband, a Family - And Not Feel Guilty about It, 1988; Widowed, 1990; Positive Plus - The Practical Plan for Liking Yourself Better, 1997. **Address:** c/o King Features Syndicate, 1530 Palisade Ave., Fort Lee, NJ 07024, U.S.A.

BROTHERSTON, Gordon. British, b. 1939. **Genres:** Literary criticism and history, Translations, Anthropology/Ethnology. **Career:** University of Essex,

Dept. of Literature, Lecturer, 1965-68, Sr. Lecturer, 1968-73, Reader, 1973-78, Professor, 1978-. Latin American Series, Pergamon Press, Oxford, Ed., 1965-. **Publications:** Manuel Machado: A Revaluation, 1968; Spanish American Modernista Poets: A Critical Anthology, 1968; Origins and Presence of Latin American Poetry, 1976; The Emergence of the Latin American Novel, 1977; Image of the New World, 1979; A Key to the Mesoamerican Reckoning of Time, 1982; Voices of the First America, 1985; Aesop in Mexico, 1987; Book of the Fourth World, 1992; Painted Books of Mexico, 1995 Mexico, 1995. EDITOR: Jose Enrique Rodo: Ariel, 1967; (with M. Vargas Llosa) Seven Stories from Spanish America, 1968, 1973; (and trans. with E. Dorn) Our Word, 1968; (and co-trans. with E. Dorn) Cesar Vallejo: Selected Poems, 1976; (with P. Hulme) Borges: Ficciones, 1976.

BROTTMAN, Mikita. British, b. 1966. **Genres:** Film, Intellectual history, Literary criticism and history. **Career:** Eastern Mediterranean University, Cyprus, assistant professor of English, 1992-94; University of East London, London, England, assistant professor of communication studies, 1994-98; Indiana University-Bloomington, visiting assistant professor of comparative literature, 1998-2000; Maryland Institute College of Art, professor of language and literature, 2001-. **Publications:** Offensive Films, 1997; Meat Is Murder!, 1998; Hollywood Hex, 1999. EDITOR: Jack Nicholson, Movie Top Ten, 2000; Car Crash Culture, 2002. Contributor to periodicals. **Address:** Department of Liberal Arts, Maryland Institute College of Art, 1300 Mt Royal, Baltimore, MD 21217, U.S.A. **Online address:** mbrottma@mica.edu

BROUGHTON, R(obert) Peter. Canadian, b. 1940. **Genres:** History, Astronomy. **Career:** Toronto Board of Education, Toronto, Ontario, Canada, teacher, 1964-97. **Publications:** Looking Up: A History of the RASC, 1994. Contributor to periodicals, encyclopedias, and biographical dictionaries. **Address:** 31 Killdeer Cres, Toronto, ON, Canada M4G 2W7.

BROUGHTON, T. Alan. American, b. 1936. **Genres:** Novels, Novellas/Short stories, Poetry. **Career:** Chair, Corse Professor of English and Director of Writers' Workshop Program, University of Vermont, 1966-2001. Has held teaching positions at University of Washington, 1962-64, Sweet Briar College, 1964-66. **Publications:** In the Face of Descent, 1975; Adam's Dream, 1975; The Man on the Moon, 1979; Far from Home, 1979; The Others We Are, 1979; Dreams before Sleep, 1982; Preparing to Be Happy, 1988; In the Country of Elegies, 1995; The Origin of Green, 2001. NOVELS: A Family Gathering, 1977; Winter Journey, 1980; The Horsemaster, 1981; Hob's Daughter, 1984. SHORT STORIES: The Jesse Tree, 1988; Suicidal Tendencies, 2003. **Address:** 124 Spruce St, Burlington, VT 05401, U.S.A. **Online address:** alan.broughton@verizon.net

BROUMAS, Olga. Greek, b. 1949. **Genres:** Poetry, Translations, Women's studies and issues, Gay and lesbian issues. **Career:** Poet-in Residence, Goddard College, Plainfield, VT, 1979-81; Founder and Associate Faculty Member, Freehand community of women writers and photographers, Provincetown, MA, 1982-87. Visiting Associate Professor, Boston University, 1988-90; Poet-in-Residence and director, creative writing, Brandeis University, Waltham, MA, 1990. **Publications:** POETRY: Restlessness, 1967; Caritas, 1976; Beginning with O, 1977; From Caritas: Poem 3, 1978; Soie Sauvage, 1979; Pastoral Jazz, 1983; Black Holes, Black Stockings, 1985; Perpetua, 1989; Sappho's Gymnasium, 1994; Helen Groves, 1994; Ithaca: Little Summer in Winter, 1996; Rave: Poems, 1975-1999, 1999. TRANSLATIONS: What I Love: Selected Translations of Odysseas Elytis, 1986; The Little Mariner, by Odysseas Elytis, 1988; Open Papers: Selected Essays of Odysseas Elytis, 1995; Eros, Eros, Eros: Odysseas Elytis: Poems, Selected and Last, 1998. **Address:** 162 Mill Pond Dr, Brewster, MA 02631, U.S.A.

BROUWER, Sigmund. Canadian, b. 1959. **Genres:** Children's fiction, Young adult fiction, Children's non-fiction, Young adult non-fiction. **Career:** Freelance writer. National Racquetball Magazine, editor; co-founder, lecturer, The Young Writer's Institute, 1993-. **Publications:** NOVELS: Morning Star, 1994; Moon Basket, 1994; Double Helix, 1995; Magnus, 1995; Sun Dance, 1995; Thunder Voice, 1995; Blood Ties, 1996; Blazer Drive, 1996; Chief Honor, 1997; Knights Honor, 1997; Pharaoh's Tomb, 1997; Pirate's Cross, 1997; Outlaw's Gold, 1997; Soldier's Aim, 1997; Galilee Man, 1997; Dance of Darkness, 1997. JUVENILE CHRISTIAN NOVELS. ACCIDENTAL DETECTIVE SERIES: Indians in the Deep Woods: A Ricky and Joel Adventure, 1988; The Mystery Tribe of Camp Blackeagle, 1990; Phantom Outlaw at Wolf Creek, 1990; The Disappearing Jewel of Madagascar, 1990; Lost beneath Manhattan, 1990; Race for the Park Street Treasure, 1991; Creature of the Mists, 1991; The Missing Map of Pirate's Haven, 1991; The Downtown Desperadoes, 1991; Madness at Moonshiner's Bay, 1992; Sunrise at the Mayan Temple, 1992; Short Cuts, 1993; Terror on Kamikaze Run,

1994. LIGHTNING ON ICE SERIES: Rebel Glory, 1995; All-Star Pride, 1995; Thunderbird Spirit, 1996; Winter Hawk Star, 1996. WINDS OF LIGHT SERIES: Wings of an Angel, 1992; Barbarians from the Isle, 1992; Legend of Burning Water, 1992; The Forsaken Crusade, 1992; A City of Dreams, 1993; Merlin's Destiny, 1993; The Jester's Quest, 1994. DR. DRABBLE SERIES (with W. Davidson): Dr. Drabble's Astounding Musical Mesmerizer, 1991; Dr. Drabble's Incredible Identical Robot Innovation, 1991; Dr. Drabble's Phenomenal Antigravity Dust Machine, 1991; Dr. Drabble's Remarkable Underwater Breathing Pills, 1991; Dr. Drabble's Spectacular Shrinker-Enlarger, 1994; Dr. Drabble and the Dynamic Duplicator, 1994. NONFICTION: Snowboarding-To the Extreme-Rippin', 1996; Mountain Biking-To the Extreme-Cliff Dive, 1996; Scuba Diving-To the Extreme-Off the Wall, 1996; Sky Diving-To the Extreme-'Chute Roll, 1997. **Address:** 15 Howarth St., Red Deer, AB, Canada T4N 6J6. **Online address:** www. sigmundbrouwer.com

BROWER, Kenneth. American, b. 1944. **Genres:** Environmental sciences/Ecology, Natural history. **Career:** Free-lance writer, 1971-. Ed., Sierra Club, San Francisco, 1964-69, and Friends of the Earth, San Francisco, 1969-71. **Publications:** Earth and the Great Weather: The Brooks Range, 1971; With Their Islands Around Them, 1974; Micronesia: Island Wilderness, 1975; The Starship and the Canoe, 1978; Wake of the Whale, 1979; Micronesia: The Land, the People and the Sea, 1980; A Song for Satawal, 1983; Yosemite, 1990; One Earth, 1990; Realms of the Sea, 1991; American Legacy: Our National Forests, 1997; The Winemaker's Marsh, 2001. CO-AUTHOR AND EDITOR: Galapagos: The Flow of Wildness, 1967; Maui: The Last Hawaiian Place, 1970; Cry Crisis, 1974. EDITOR: Navajo Wildlands, 1967; Kauai and the Park Country of Hawaii, 1967; Baja California and the Geography of Hope, 1967; Guale: The Golden Coast of Georgia, 1974; Primal Alliance: Earth and Ocean, 1974. **Address:** 2379 Humboldt Ave, Oakland, CA 94601, U.S.A.

BROWN, Alan. American. **Genres:** Literary criticism and history, Mythology/Folklore. **Career:** High school teacher of English and German, Flora, IL, 1974-76; high school English teacher and Writing Center director, Springfield, IL, 1976-86; University of West Alabama, Livingston, professor of composition and director of Writing Center, 1986-, trustee professor, 1996. Folklorist. **Publications:** Gabr'l Blow Sof': Ex-Slave Narratives, 1997; A Literary Tour Guide of New Orleans, 1998. EDITOR: Dim Roads and Dark Nights: The Collected Folklore of Ruby Pickens Tartt, 1993; (with K. Friday) Mama 'n' 'em: An Oral History of Thomaston, Alabama, 1994; The Face in the Window and Other Alabama Ghostlore, 1996; Shadows and Cypress, 2000; Haunted Places in the American South, 2002; Stories form the Haunted South, 2004. Contributor to books. Contributor of articles and reviews to academic journals. **Address:** 1516 57th Ct, Meridian, MS 39305-1425, U.S.A. **Online address:** anb@uwa.edu; anbrown@mississippi.net

BROWN, Archibald Haworth. British, b. 1938. **Genres:** Politics/Government. **Career:** Fellow, St. Antony's College, Oxford, 1971- (Sub-Warden, 1995-97). Professor of Politics, University of Oxford, 1989- (Lecturer 1971-89). British Council Exchange Scholar, Moscow University, 1967-68; Lecturer in Politics, Glasgow University, 1964-71; Visiting Professor, Yale University, New Haven, CT, 1980, Columbia University, NYC, 1985, and University of Texas, Austin, 1990-91; Distinguished Visiting Fellow, University of Notre Dame, 1998. Fellow, British Academy, 1991. Foreign Honorary Member, American Academy of Arts and Sciences, 2003. **Publications:** Soviet Politics and Political Science, 1974; The Gorbachev Factor, 1996. EDITOR/COEDITOR: (with M. Kaser) The Soviet Union since the Fall of Khrushchev, 1975, 2nd ed., 1978; (with J. Gray) Political Culture and Political Change in Communist States, 1977, 2nd ed., 1979; (with T.H. Rigby and P. Reddaway) Authority, Power and Policy in the USSR, 1980; The Cambridge Encyclopedia of Russia and the Soviet Union, 1982, 2nd ed., 1994; (with M. Kaser) Soviet Policy for the 1980s, 1982; Political Culture and Communist Studies, 1984; Political Leadership in the Soviet Union, 1989; The Soviet Union: A Biographical Dictionary, 1990; New Thinking in Soviet Politics, 1992; The British Study of Politics in the Twentieth Century, 1999; Contemporary Russian Politics: A Reader, 2001; Gorbachev, Yeltsin, and Putin: Political Leadership in Russia's Transition, 2001; The Demise of Marxism-Leninism in Russia, 2004. **Address:** St. Antony's College, Oxford OX2 6JF, England.

BROWN, Brian A. Canadian, b. 1942. **Genres:** International relations/Current affairs. **Career:** Minister of United Churches of Canada in British Columbia, Alberta, Saskatchewan, and Ontario, 1966-, including Lansing United Church, Toronto, Ontario. Presenter of radio editorials on moral, political, and social issues, 1976-85. Head of a royal commission on the postsecondary educational needs of northern British Columbia, 1973-75.

Publications: The Burning Bush, 1976; (with R. Levesque) Separatism, 1976; The New Confederation, 1977; Your Neighbor as Yourself: Race, Religion, and Region; North America into the Twenty-First Century, 1997; The Canadian Challenge. **Address:** Lansing United Church, 49 Bogert Ave., Toronto, ON, Canada M2N 1K4.

BROWN, Brooks. American, b. 1981. **Genres:** Young adult fiction. **Career:** Writer. Consultant on the film Bowling for Columbine, 2002. **Publications:** (with Rob Merritt) No Easy Answers: The Truth behind Death at Columbine, 2002. **Address:** c/o Lantern Books, 1 Union Square W. Suite 201, New York, NY 10003, U.S.A.

BROWN, Bryan T(urner). American, b. 1952. **Genres:** Natural history, Environmental sciences/Ecology. **Career:** Grand Canyon National Park, biological technician, 1976-80; University of Arizona, Tucson, research ecologist with Cooperative Park Studies Unit, 1983-87; self-employed research biologist in Tucson, 1986-90; Northern Arizona University, Flagstaff, research associate with Cooperative Park Studies Unit, 1990-91; self-employed research biologist in Tucson, specializing in applied avian ecology research on endangered or riparian birds in the Southwest, 1991-93; SWCA Environmental Consultants, Inc., Avian Ecologist, 1993-. **Publications:** (with S.W. Carothers and R.R. Johnson) Grand Canyon Birds: Historical Notes, Natural History, and Ecology, 1987; (with S.W. Carothers) The Colorado River through Grand Canyon: Natural History and Human Change, 1991. Contributor to periodicals. **Address:** 1015 South 1400 East, Salt Lake City, UT 84105-1616, U.S.A. **Online address:** bbrown@swca.com

BROWN, Clair. American, b. 1946. **Genres:** Economics. **Career:** University of California, Berkeley, professor of economics, 1973-. **Publications:** Women in the Labor Force, 1989; American Standards of Living, 1996; Work and Pay in the United States and Japan, 1997. **Address:** Department of Economics, University of California, Berkeley, CA 94720, U.S.A. **Online address:** cbrown@uclink.berkeley.edu

BROWN, Dale W. American, b. 1926. **Genres:** Theology/Religion. **Career:** Professor of Christian Theology, Bethany Theological Seminary, Oak Brook, Illinois, 1963-94. Director of Religious Life, and Assistant Professor of Philosophy and Religion, McPherson College, 1958-62. **Publications:** In Christ Jesus: The Significance of Jesus as the Christ, 1965; Four Words for the World, 1968; So Send I You, 1969; Brethren and Pacifism, 1970; The Christian Revolutionary, 1971; Flamed by the Spirit, 1978; Understanding Pietism, 1978; What About the Russians?, 1984; Biblical Pacifism, 1986. **Address:** Bethany Theological Seminary, Butterfield and Meyers Road, Oak Brook, IL 60521, U.S.A.

BROWN, Dan. American, b. 1964. **Genres:** Novels. **Career:** Author. Formerly an English teacher at Phillips Exeter Academy, Exeter, NH. **Publications:** Digital Fortress, 1998; Angels and Demons, 2000; Deception Point, 2001; The Da Vinci Code, 2003. **Address:** c/o Author Mail, Random House, 1745 Broadway, New York, NY 10019, U.S.A. **Online address:** www.danbrown.com

BROWN, Dona. American, b. 1956. **Genres:** History. **Career:** University of New Hampshire, Durham, assistant professor of history, 1990-93; University of Vermont, Burlington, assistant professor of history, 1994-96. **Publications:** Inventing New England, 1995. Contributor to books. **Address:** Department of History, Wheeler House, University of Vermont, Burlington, VT 05405, U.S.A.

BROWN, H. Jackson, Jr. American, b. 1940. **Genres:** Children's nonfiction. **Career:** END Inc. (advertising and marketing firm), Nashville, TN, president and creative director, 1974-92; writer. **Publications:** A Father's Box of Wisdom, 1989; Life's Little Instruction Book, 1991; Life's Little Treasure Book, 1994; Little Book of Christmas Joys, 1994; Life's Little Treasure Book of Christmas Traditions, 1996; Life's Little Treasure Book on Friendship, 1996; Life's Little Treasure Book on Hope, 1996; Complete Life's Little Instruction Book, 1997; Life's Little Treasure Book on Things that Really Matter, 1999; Life's Instructions on Wisdom, Success and Happiness, 2000; Life's Little Instruction Book for Incurable Romatics, 2000; Mothers to Daughters, 2000; Life's Little Instructions from the Bible, 2000; Book of Love For My Daughter, 2001; Highlighted in Yellow, 2001. COMPILER: Father's Book of Wisdom, 1988; P.S. I Love You, 1990; Live and Learn and Pass It On, 1991; When You Lick a Slug, Your Tongue Goes Numb, 1994; Wit and Wisdom from the Peanut Butter Gang, 1994; Life's Little Treasure Book on Love, 1995; Hero in Every Heart, 1996; Kids' Little Treasure Book on Happy Families, 1997; Life's Little Treasure Book of Christmas Memories, 1998; The Complete Live, Learn and Pass It On, 1998;

Book of Love for My Son, 2001. **Address:** END Inc., 2219 Elliston Pl., Nashville, TN 37203, U.S.A. **Online address:** www.instructionbook.com

BROWN, Harriet N(ancy). American. **Genres:** Documentaries/Reportage. **Career:** Wisconsin Trail magazine, editor. **Publications:** The Good-bye Window: A Year in the Life of a Day-Care Center, 1998; The Babysitter's Handbook, 1998; Welcome to Kit's World, 1999; Kit's Railway Adventure, 2002; Madison Walks, 2003; The Promised Land, 2004. **Address:** 2515 Chamberlain Ave, Madison, WI 53705, U.S.A. **Online address:** hnbrown@tds.net

BROWN, Harry Clifford. American, b. 1953. **Genres:** Novels, Essays. **Career:** Writer and environmental editor/consultant. **Publications:** Sundays in August, 1997. **Address:** 430 1/2 Prospectors Point, Grand Junction, CO 81503, U.S.A.

BROWN, Helen Gurley. American, b. 1922. **Genres:** Human relations/Parenting, Sex, Women's studies and issues. **Career:** Ed.-in-Chief, 1965-, and Editorial Director of foreign eds., 1972-, Cosmopolitan mag., NYC. Executive Secretary, Music Corp. of America, 1942-45, and William Morris Agency, 1956-47; Copywriter, Foote Cone and Belding Advertising Agency, Los Angeles, California, 1948-58; Advertising Writer and Account Executive, Kenyon and Eckhardt Advertising Agency, Hollywood, California, 1958-62. **Publications:** Sex and the Single Girl, 1962; Sex and the Office, 1965; The Outrageous Opinions of Helen Gurley Brown, 1967; Helen Gurley Brown's Single Girl's Cookbook, 1969; Sex and the New Single Girl, 1970; Having It All, 1982; The Late Show, 1993; The Writer's Rules, The Power of Positive Prose-How to Write It and Get It Published, 1998; I'm Wild Again, Snippets from My Life and a Few Brazen Thoughts, 2000. **Address:** Cosmopolitan, The Hearst Corp, 959 8th Ave, New York, NY 10019, U.S.A.

BROWN, Herbert C. See Obituaries.

BROWN, Irene Quenzler. (born Germany), b. 1938. **Genres:** Education. **Career:** Historian and educator. University of Hartford, Hartford, CT, lecturer, 1976-77, assistant professor of history, 1978; University of Connecticut, Storrs, director of women's studies program, 1979-85, assistant professor, 1985-86, associate professor of human development and family relations with joint appointment with department of history, 1987-2003, associate director of honors program, 1992-2002. Member, American Council of Learned Societies, 1983-84; Connecticut Coordinating Committee for the Promotion of History, 1983-; and Connecticut Campus Compact steering committee, 1998-2002. **Publications:** (with Richard D. Brown) The Hanging of Ephraim Wheeler: A Story of Rape, Incest, and Justice in Early America, 2003. Contributor of articles and reviews. Contributor to books. Author of academic papers and conference presentations. **Address:** 20 Utley Rd., Hampton, CT 06247, U.S.A. **Online address:** irene.q.brown@uconn.edu

BROWN, Isobel. See GRANT-ADAMSON, Lesley (Heycock).

BROWN, J(oseph) P(aul) S(ummers). American, b. 1930. **Genres:** Westerns/Adventure. **Career:** Boxer, motion picture stuntman and actor, and cattleman. Reporter, El Paso Herald Post, Texas, 1953-54. **Publications:** Jim Kane, 1970; in U.K. as Pocket Money, 1972; The Outfit: A Cowboy's Primer, 1971; The Forests of the Night, 1974; Steeldust, 1986; Steeldust II: The Flight, 1987; Blooded Stock, 1990; Outfit, 1990; The Horseman, 1991; Jim Kane, 1991; Ladino, 1991; Native Born, 1992; Keep the Devil Waiting, 1992; The Forests of the Night, 1992; The Cinnamon Colt, 1992. **Address:** PO Box 972, Patagonia, AZ 85624-0972, U.S.A. **Online address:** horsemn1020@cs.com

BROWN, James. American, b. 1957. **Genres:** Novels, Novellas/Short stories, Plays/Screenplays, Autobiography/Memoirs. **Career:** Santa Clara University, Santa Clara, CA, lecturer in composition and fiction writing, 1986-87; California State University, Hayward, lecturer in fiction writing, 1987-89; California State University, San Bernardino, associate professor of literature and fiction writing, 1989-. **Publications:** Second Chances (teleplay), 1991; 21 Jump Street (teleplay), 1991; The Second Story Theatre and Two Encores (short stories), 1994; The Los Angeles Diaries (memoir), 2003. NOVELS: Hot Wire, 1985; Final Performance, 1988; Lucky Town, 1994. **Address:** Dept of English, California State University, 5500 University Parkway, San Bernardino, CA 92407, U.S.A. **Online address:** jbrown@csusb.edu

BROWN, Jared. American, b. 1936. **Genres:** Plays/Screenplays, History, Theatre, Biography. **Career:** Western Illinois University, Macomb, assistant professor of speech and dramatic art, 1965-72, associate professor, 1972-78, acting chair of department of theater, 1977-78, professor of theater, 1978-89; Illinois Wesleyan University, Bloomington, professor of theater and director of School of Theatre Arts, 1989-2002. Illinois Sesquicentennial One-Act Play Competition, regional administrator and judge, 1968; Western Illinois University, academic director of Study Abroad in London program, 1979-80. **Publications:** BIOGRAPHIES: The Fabulous Lunts: A Biography of Alfred Lunt and Lynn Fontanne, foreword by Helen Hayes, 1986; Zero Mostel: A Biography, 1989; The Theatre in America during the Revolution, 1995; Alan J. Pakula: His Films and His Life, 2005. PLAYS: On Our Way (musical revue), 1954; Oh Say Can You See, 1959; The Social Event of the Season (musical), 1960; The Adventures of Peter Macaroon (children's play), 1975; The Peddler, 1980; The Preacher, 1981; Kathy on the Spot, 2004; I, Alpheus Pike, 2004; Russian Dressing, 2005. Contributor of articles on the history of theater to periodicals. **Address:** School of Theatre Arts, Illinois Wesleyan University, Bloomington, IL 61702, U.S.A. **Online address:** jbrown@titan.iwu.edu

BROWN, Jennifer S. H. American. **Genres:** Anthropology/Ethnology, Cultural/Ethnic topics, History. **Career:** Colby College, Waterville, ME, instructor in sociology, 1966-69; Northern Illinois University, DeKalb, assistant professor of anthropology and sociology, 1969-81; University of Winnipeg, MB, associate professor, 1983-88, professor of history, 1988-, director, Centre for Rupert's Land Studies, 1995-. Tulane University, Middle American Research Institute, publications editor, 1976-82; Indiana University-Bloomington, visiting assistant professor of anthropology, 1978-79; American Society for Ethnohistory, president, 1989-90. **Publications:** Strangers in Blood: Fur Trade Company Families in Indian Country, 1980; (ed. with J. Peterson, and contrib.) The New Peoples: Being and Becoming Metis in North America, 1985; (with R. Brightman) The Orders of the Dreamed: George Nelson on Cree and Northern Ojibwa Religion and Myth, 1823, 1988; (with E. Vibert) Reading beyond Words: Contexts for Native History, 1996, rev. ed., 2003. Contributor to books and periodicals. **Address:** Dept of History, University of Winnipeg, 515 Portage Ave, Winnipeg, MB, Canada R3B 2E9.

BROWN, John Gregory. American, b. 1960. **Genres:** Novels. **Career:** North Carolina State University, Raleigh, lecturer in English, 1984-87; Johns Hopkins University, Baltimore, MD, instructor in writing, 1988-89; Johns Hopkins University, instructor in writing, 1993-94; Sweet Briar College, Sweet Briar, VA, Julia Jackson Nichols Professor of English, and director of creative writing, 1994-. Gives readings from his works. **Publications:** NOVELS: Decorations in a Ruined Cemetery, 1994; The Wrecked, Blessed Body of Shelton Lafleur, 1996; Audubon's Watch, 2001. TELEPLAY: The Road Home (episode), 1994. Contributor of stories, articles, and reviews to periodicals. **Address:** Department of English, Sweet Briar College, Sweet Briar, VA 24595, U.S.A. **Online address:** brown@sbc.edu

BROWN, Jonathan (Mayer). American, b. 1939. **Genres:** Art/Art history. **Career:** Carroll and Milton Petrie Professor, Institute of Fine Arts, New York University, NYC, since 1984 (joined faculty, 1973). Taught at Princeton University, New Jersey, 1965-73; Slade Professor of Fine Art, Oxford University, 1981-82. **Publications:** (with R. Enggass) Italy and Spain, 1600-1750, 1970; Prints and Drawings by Jusepe de Ribera, 1973; Francisco de Zurburan, 1973; Murillo and His Drawings, 1976; Images and Ideas in Seventeenth-Century Spanish Painting, 1978; (with J.H. Elliott) A Palace for a King: The Buen Retiro and the Court of Philip IV, 1980; Velazquez, Painter and Courtier, 1986; (with R.G. Mann) Spanish Painting of the Fifteenth through Nineteenth Centuries: The Collections of the National Gallery of Art, 1990; The Golden Age of Painting in Spain, 1991; Kings and Connoisseurs: Collecting Art in Seventeenth-Century Europe, 1995; (ed. and contrib.) Picasso and the Spanish Tradition, 1996. **Address:** 1 E. 78th St, New York, NY 10021, U.S.A.

BROWN, Kevin. American, b. 1960. **Genres:** Art/Art history, Cultural/Ethnic topics, Film, Food and Wine, Humanities, Intellectual history, Language/Linguistics, Literary criticism and history, Music, Travel/Exploration, Autobiography/Memoirs, Biography, Essays, Reference. **Career:** Book reviewer, contributing editor, literary journalist, essayist, biographer, 1978-. **Publications:** Romare Bearden (biography), 1994; Malcolm X: His Life and Legacy, 1995; (contributing ed.) New York Public Library African-American Desk Reference, 1999. Contributor to magazines and newspapers. **Address:** 65-60 Booth St Apt 2E, Rego Park, NY 11374, U.S.A. **Online address:** wwwkevinbrown@aol.com

BROWN, (William) Larry. See Obituaries.

BROWN, Lee Ann. (born Japan), b. 1964. **Genres:** Film. **Career:** Educator, poet, and filmmaker. St. John's University, New York, NY, assistant professor of English; Naropa Institute, Boulder, CO, member of writing and poetics program; founder and editor of Tender Buttons Press. **Publications:** Polyverse (poems), 1999; The Sleep That Changed Everything (poems), 2003. **Address:** St. John's University, 101 Murray St., New York, NY 10007, U.S.A.

BROWN, Lester R(ussell). American, b. 1934. **Genres:** Agriculture/Forestry, Demography, Economics, Environmental sciences/Ecology. **Career:** US Dept of Agriculture, Washington, DC, international agricultural economist with the Economic Research Service, 1959-64, policy advisory secretary of agriculture, 1964-66; International Agricultural Development Service, administrator 1966-69; Overseas Development Council, senior fellow, 1969-74; Worldwatch Institute, Washington, DC, president, 1974-2000, founder and senior researcher, 1974-2001, chairman of the board, 2000-01; Earth Policy Institute, president and founder, 2001-; writer. Salzburg Seminar in American Studies, faculty member, 1971; guest scholar at Aspen Institute, 1972-74; participant in conferences. **Publications:** Man, Land, and Food, 1963; Increasing World Food Output, 1965; Seeds of Change, 1970; World without Borders, 1972; (with G.W. Finsterbusch) Man and His Environment, 1972; In the Human Interest, 1974; (with E.P. Eckholm) By Bread Alone, 1974; The Twenty-ninth Day, 1978; (with C. Flavin and C. Norman) Running on Empty, 1979; Building a Sustainable Society, 1981; (with others) State of the World, annual vol., 1984-2001; (with others) Saving the Planet, 1991; (ed.) The Worldwatch Reader, 1991, rev. ed. (with E. Ayres), 1998; (with others) Vital Signs, annual vol., 1992-2002; (with H. Kane) Full House, 1994; Who Will Feed China?, 1995; Tough Choices, 1996; Beyond Malthus, 1999; Eco-Economy: Building an Economy for the Earth, 2001; (with J. Larsen and B. Fischlowitz-Roberts) The Earth Policy Reader, 2002; Plan B: Rescuing a Planet under Stress & a Civilization in Trouble, 2030; Outgrowing the Earth, 2005. Contributor to journals. **Address:** c/o Earth Policy Institute, 1350 Connecticut Ave NW Ste 403, Washington, DC 20036, U.S.A. **Online address:** lesterbrown@earth-policy.org

BROWN, Lyn Mikel. American. **Genres:** Psychiatry, Psychology, Women's studies and issues. **Career:** CETA Program, Calais, ME, preschool teacher and coordinator, 1979-81; Connection Inc., Middletown, CT, substance abuse counselor, 1981-83; Harvard University, Cambridge, MA, director of Laurel-Harvard Project, 1986-89, lecturer in education, 1989-90, research associate in human development psychology, 1989-. Colby College, assistant professor and co-chair of education and human development program, 1991-. **Publications:** (with C. Gilligan) Meeting at the Crossroads: The Psychology of Women and the Development of Girls, 1992; Raising Their Voices, 1998; Girl Fighting, 2003. Work represented in anthologies. Contributor to periodicals. **Address:** Program in Education and Human Development, Colby College, 4422 Mayflower Hill, Waterville, ME 04901-8840, U.S.A. **Online address:** lmbrown@colby.edu

BROWN, Lynne P. American, b. 1952. **Genres:** Education, Politics/Government. **Career:** U.S. House of Representatives, Office of the Majority Whip, Washington, DC, legislative aide, 1978-82; New York University, NYC, vice president of university relations and adjunct professor of politics, 1982-. American University, adjunct professor, 1980-81. Manhattan College, member of the Board of Trustees. **Publications:** (with J. Brademas) The Politics of Education: Conflict and Consensus on Capitol Hill, 1987. **Address:** New York University, 70 Washington Sq S Rm 1214, New York, NY 10012, U.S.A.

BROWN, Margaret Lynn. American, b. 1958. **Genres:** Local history/Rural topics. **Career:** Educator and historian. Brevard College, Brevard, NC, associate professor of history, 1996-. Center for the Study of War and Society, University of Tennessee, Knoxville, organizer of oral history project of Korean war veterans. Lecturer. **Publications:** The Wild East: A Biography of the Great Smoky Mountains, 2000. Contributor to books and periodicals. **Address:** PO Box 21, Brevard, NC 28712, U.S.A. **Online address:** mbrown@brevard.edu

BROWN, Mary Ward. American, b. 1917. **Genres:** Novellas/Short stories. **Career:** Judson College, Marion, AL, publicity director, 1938-39; writer. Worked as a secretary for a short time during the 1970s; affiliated with Office of Guidance and Counseling, Marion Military Institute. PEN/Hemingway Award, 1987. **Publications:** Tongues of Flame (short story collection), 1986; It Wasn't All Dancing, 2002. Contributor of short stories to periodicals. **Address:** c/o Amanda Urban, 40 W 57th St, New York, NY 10019, U.S.A.

BROWN, Michael F(obes). American, b. 1950. **Genres:** Anthropology/Ethnology, Theology/Religion. **Career:** Williams College, Williamstown, MA, professor of anthropology, early 1980s-. **Publications:** Tsewa's Gift:

Magic and Meaning in an Amazonian Society, 1986; (with Eduardo Fernandez) War of Shadows: The Struggle for Utopia in the Peruvian Amazon, 1991; The Channeling Zone: American Spiritually in an Anxious Age, 1997. **Address:** Department of Anthropology and Sociology, Williams College, Williamstown, MA 01267-2606, U.S.A.

BROWN, Michael P. American, b. 1966. **Genres:** Genealogy/Heraldry, Geography, Politics/Government. **Career:** University of Canterbury, Christchurch, New Zealand, lecturer in geography, 1995-97; University of Washington, Seattle, acting assistant professor, 1998, assistant professor, 1998-2001, associate professor of geography, 2001-. LaTrobe University, visiting scholar at National Centre for Social Research in HIV/AIDS, 1997; University of Auckland, visiting scholar in geography, 1998; lecturer at colleges and universities. **Publications:** RePlacing Citizenship: AIDS Activism and Radical Democracy, 1997; Closet Space: Geographies of Metaphor from the Body to the Globe. Contributor to books. Contributor of articles and reviews to periodicals. **Address:** Department of Geography, Box 353550, University of Washington, Seattle, WA 98195, U.S.A. **Online address:** michaelb@u.washington.edu

BROWN, Michelle P(atricia). British, b. 1959. **Genres:** Archaeology/Antiquities, Art/Art history, History, Librarianship. **Career:** University of London, England, Courtauld Institute, information officer at galleries of art, 1982-83, and fellow, Birkbeck College and King's College, part-time lecturer in history and paleography, 1983-86, extramural lecturer, 1983-95, Inst of English Studies, visiting senior research fellow; British Library, London, curator of manuscripts, 1986-. Society of Antiquaries, fellow; Courtauld Institute, fellow. **Publications:** A Guide to Western Historical Scripts from Antiquity to 1600, 1990, rev. ed., 1999; Anglo-Saxon Manuscripts, 1991; (with J. Bately and J. Roberts) A Palaeographer's View: The Selected Papers of Julian Brown, 1993; Understanding Illuminated Manuscripts: A Glossary of Technical Terms, 1994; The Book of Cerne: Prayer, Patronage and Power in 9th Century England, 1996; (with L. Webster) The Transformation of the Roman World, 1997; The British Library Guide to Writing & Scripts, 1998; (with S. McKendrick) Illuminating the Book: Makers & Interpreters, 1998; (with P. Lovett) The British Library Source Book for Scribes, 1999; (with C. Farr) Mercia: An Anglo-Saxon Kingdom in Europe, 2001; Painted Labyrinth: The World of the Lindisfarne Gospels, 2003; The Lindisfarne Gospels: Society, Spirituality and the Scribe, 2003. Contributor of articles and reviews to academic journals. **Address:** Department of Manuscripts, British Library, 96 Euston Rd, London NW1 2DB, England.

BROWN, Montague. American, b. 1952. **Genres:** Ethics, Intellectual history, Philosophy. **Career:** Saint Anselm College, Manchester, NH, professor of philosophy, 1986-. **Publications:** The Romance of Reason: An Adventure in the Thought of Thomas Aquinas, 1993; The Quest for Moral Foundations: An Introduction to Ethics, 1996; The One-Minute Philosopher, 2001; Half-Truths, 2003. **Address:** Saint Anselm College, 100 St. Anselm Dr, Manchester, NH 03102, U.S.A.

BROWN, Murray. American, b. 1929. **Genres:** Economics. **Career:** Wharton School, University of Pennsylvania, Philadelphia, Dept. of Economics, Assistant Professor, 1956-62; George Washington University, Patent & Trademark Foundation, Consultant, 1958-60; Office of Business Economics, U.S. Dept. of Commerce, Washington, DC, 1962-65; Center of Economic Studies and Plans, Rome, NY, Research Associate, 1966-; State University of New York at Buffalo, Professor of Economics, 1967-96, Professor Emeritus, 1996-. **Publications:** On the Theory and Measurement of Technological Change, 1966; Tripartite Income Employment Contracts, Rand Journal of Economics, 1989; Uniqueness of Equilibrium, Games and Economic Behavior, 1991; Unsystematic Risk and Coalition Formation, 2002; Coalitions in Oligopolies, 2003. EDITOR: The Theory and Empirical Analysis of Production, 1967; (co) Regional National Econometric Modeling, 1978.

BROWN, Patricia Fortini. American, b. 1936. **Genres:** Art/Art history. **Career:** State of California, Department of Employment, employment and claims specialist in San Francisco and San Rafael, 1960-65; painter and graphic designer in San Rafael, 1963-76; Mills College, Oakland, Calif., lecturer in Italian Renaissance art, spring, 1983; Princeton University, Princeton, N.J., assistant professor, 1983-89, associate professor of art and archaeology, 1989-, professor of art and archaeology, 1997-, chair, Dept. of Art and Archaeology, 1999-. Fellow at American Academy in Rome, 1989-90; Guggenheim Fellow, 1992-93; Andrew W. Mellon associate professor in art and archaeology, 1991-95. **Publications:** La pittura nell' eta di Carpaccio: i grandi cicli narrativi, 1992; Venetian Narrative Painting in the Age of Carpaccio, 1988; Venice & Antiquity: The Venetian Sense of the Past, 1997; Art and Life in Renaissance Venice, 1997. Contributor to publications and journals. **Address:** Department of Art and Archaeology, Princeton University, Princeton, NJ 08544-1018, U.S.A. **Online address:** pbrown@princeton.edu

BROWN, Peter A. American, b. 1949. **Genres:** Politics/Government. **Career:** United Press International, political reporter, 1974-81; Scripps Howard News Service, Washington, DC, chief political writer, 1982-96; Orlando Sentinel, 1996-. **Publications:** Minority Party: Why Democrats Face Defeat in 1992 and Beyond, Regnery Gateway, 1991. **Address:** c/o Orlando Sentinel, 633 N. Orange, Orlando, FL 32801-1300, U.S.A.

BROWN, Peter G. American, b. 1940. **Genres:** Politics/Government. **Career:** McGill School of Environment, professor. Urban Institute, assistant vice president for research operations; Battelle Seattle Research Center, visiting fellow; consultant to Aspen Institute for Humanistic Studies, Academy for Contemporary Problems and National Academy of Public Administration. Has taught at Princeton University, University of Washington, St. John's College, and University of Maryland at College Park. **Publications:** Restoring the Public Trust: A Fresh Vision for Progressive Government in America, 1994; Ethics, Economics, and International Relations: Transparent Sovereignty in the Commonwealth of Life (in Canada as The Commonwealth of Life), 2000. EDITOR: (with H. Shue) Food Policy: The Responsibility of the United States in the Life and Death Choices, 1977; Human Rights and U.S. Foreign Policy: Principles and Applications, 1979; (with Shue) Boundaries: National Autonomy and Its Limits, 1981; (with others) Income Support, 1981; (with Shue) The Border That Joins: Mexican Migrants and U.S. Responsibility, 1983; Markets and Morals; Food Policy; Human Rights and U.S. Foreign Policy; Boundaries; The Border That Joins; Energy and the Future. Contributor to books and periodicals. **Address:** McGill School of Environment, 3534 University St, Montreal, QC, Canada H3A 2A7. **Online address:** peter.g.brown@mcgill.ca

BROWN, Rajeswary Ampalavanar. (born Malaysia). **Genres:** Business/Trade/Industry. **Career:** Writer. **Publications:** Chinese Big Business and the Wealth of Asian Nations, 2000. **Address:** c/o Author Mail, Palgrave, 175 Fifth Ave., New York, NY 10010, U.S.A. **Online address:** r.brown@rhul.ac.uk

BROWN, Richard E. American, b. 1946. **Genres:** Novels, Novellas/Short stories, Plays/Screenplays. **Career:** University of Nevada, Reno, assistant professor, 1972-77, associate professor, 1977-89, professor of English, 1989-, chairman of Faculty Senate, 1990-91. Taught in Nevada London Program, spring, 1984, 1993. **Publications:** Cubes in Arms: A Play in One Act, published in Capilano Review, Number 38, 1986. Chester's Last Stand, 1988; Fishing for Ghosts: 12 Short Stories, 1994. **Address:** Department of English, MS 098, University of Nevada, Reno, NV 89557, U.S.A. **Online address:** rebrown@unr.nevada.edu

BROWN, Richard E(arl). Canadian, b. 1948. **Genres:** Psychology, Zoology. **Career:** Dalhousie University, Halifax, Nova Scotia, professor of psychology and physiology, 1978-; writer. **Publications:** (ed. with D.W. Macdonald) Social Odors in Mammals (2 vols), 1985; An Introduction to Neuroendocrinology, 1994; Hormones and Behavior, in press. Contributor to periodicals. **Address:** Psychology Department, Dalhousie University, Halifax, NS, Canada B3H 4J1.

BROWN, Rita Mae. American, b. 1944. **Genres:** Novels, Plays/Screenplays, Poetry, Gay and lesbian issues, Translations. **Career:** American Artists Inc., Charlottesville, VA, president, 1981-; Sterling Publishing Co, NY, photo editor, 1969-70; Radicalesbians, NY, co-founder; Federal City College, Washington, DC, lecturer in sociology, 1970-71; Institute for Policy Studies, Washington, DC, research fellow, 1971-73; exec. officer with National Organization for Women (NOW), resigned 1970; a founder of Redstockings radical feminist group, NY; involved with lesbian separatist movement, early 1970s; active with National Gay Task Force, and National Women's Political Caucus, from mid-1970s; reviewer for magazines and newspapers. **Publications:** NOVELS: Rubyfruit Jungle, 1973; In Her Day, 1976; Six of One, 1978; Southern Discomfort, 1982; Sudden Death, 1983; High Hearts, 1986; Bingo, 1988; Venus Envy, 1993; Rest in Pieces, 1992; Wish You Were Here, 1990; Murder at Monticello, 1994; Dolley, 1994; Pay Dirt, 1995; Riding Shotgun, 1996; Murder, She Meowed, 1996; Murder on the Prowl, 1998; Loose Lips, 1999; Cat on the Scent, 1999; Outfoxed, 2000; Pawing through the Past, 2000; Claws and Effect, 2001; Alma Mater, 2001; Catch as Cat Can, 2002; Hotspur, 2002; Full Cry, 2003; Tail of the Tip-Off, 2003; Whisker of Evil, 2004. POETRY: The Hand That Cradles the Rock, 1971; Songs to a Handsome Woman, 1973. SCREENPLAYS: I Love Liberty, 1981; The Long Hot Summer, 1983; My Two Loves, 1985; Table Dancing, 1986; Girls of Summer, 1989; Rich Men, Single Women, 1989; Sweet Surrender, 1989;

Mary Pickford (documentary), 1997. OTHER: (trans.) Hrotsvitha: Six Medieval Latin Plays, 1971; A Plain Brown Rapper (essays), 1976; Starting from Scratch (writer's manual), 1988; Rita Will (memoir), 1997; Sneaky Pie's Cookbook for Mystery Lovers, 1999. **Address:** American Artists, Inc, PO Box 4671, Charlottesville, VA 22905-4671, U.S.A. **Online address:** www.ritamaebrown.org

BROWN, Robert G(oodell). American, b. 1923. **Genres:** Administration/Management, Information science/Computers, History, Theology/Religion. **Career:** President, Materials Mgmt. Systems Inc., Thetford Center, Vermont, since 1970. Visiting Professor, Northeastern University, Boston, 1960, Dartmouth College, Hanover, New Hampshire, 1963, Boston University, 1967, and Lehigh University, Bethlehem, Pa., 1971. **Publications:** Statistical Forecasting for Inventory Control, 1959; Smoothing, Forecasting and Prediction of Discrete Time Series, 1963; Decision Rules for Inventory Management, 1967; Management Decisions for Production Operations, 1971; (compiler) Source Book in Production Management, 1971; APL-Plus 747 Forecasting Users Guide, 1973; Materials Management Systems, 1977; Advanced Service Parts Inventory Control, 1982; Shirley He Hath Born, 1984; LOGOL Systems Manual, 1985, rev. ed., 1994; Twigs Systems Manual, 1988; Consultantmanship, 1993; The Tall Boy Scout Playing Tennis, 1994; The People of the Old Testament, 1994; My Psalter, 1994. **Address:** P. O. Box 239, Thetford Center, VT 05075, U.S.A.

BROWN, Robert L. American, b. 1921. **Genres:** History. **Career:** Teacher, Denver Public Schools, and University of Colorado. Staff member, University of Denver, 1948-51; Staff member, Regis College, Denver, 1956-66. **Publications:** Jeep Trails to Colorado Ghost Towns, 1963; An Empire of Silver, 1965, 1984; Holy Cross: The Mountain and the City, 1968; Ghost Towns of the Colorado Rockies, 1968; Colorado Ghost Towns: Past and Present, 1972; Uphill Both Ways: Hiking Colorado's High Country, 1976; Saloons of the American West: An Illustrated Chronicle, 1978; The Great Pike's Peak Gold Rush, 1985; Colorado on Foot, 1992; Cripple Creek: Then and Now, 1991; Central City and Gilpin County: Then and Now, 1994.

BROWN, Roberta Simpson. American, b. 1939. **Genres:** Novellas/Short stories, Horror, Writing/Journalism. **Career:** Jefferson County Board of Education, KY, teacher of language arts, 1963-, now retired; freelance writer, 1991-. Storyteller on radio and television programs. **Publications:** JUVENILE HORROR: The Walking Trees and Other Scary Stories, 1991; Queen of the Cold-Blooded Tales, 1993; Scared in School, 1997. **Address:** 11906 Lilac Way, Louisville, KY 40243-1409, U.S.A. **Online address:** robertasbrown@aol.com; robertasimpsonbrown.com

BROWN, Rosellen. American, b. 1939. **Genres:** Novels, Novellas/Short stories, Plays/Screenplays, Poetry. **Career:** Tougaloo College, MS, instructor in American and English literature, 1965-67; Goddard College, Plainfield, VT, instructor in creative writing; Boston University, visiting professor of creative writing, 1977-78; University of Houston, Texas, professor of creative writing, 1982-85, 1989-95; School of the Art Institute of Chicago, MFA in Writing, professor, 1996-. National Endowment for the Arts Fellow, 1973, 1982; Bunting Institute Fellow, 1973-75; Guggenheim Fellow, 1976; Ms. Magazine Woman of the Year, 1984. Recipient of American Academy and Institute of Arts and Letters Literature Award, 1987, and Ingram Merrill Grant, 1989-90. **Publications:** POETRY: Some Deaths in Delta and Other Poems, 1970; Cora Fry, 1977; Cora Fry's Pillow Book, 1994. NOVELS: The Autobiography of My Mother, 1976; Tender Mercies, 1978; Civil Wars, 1984; Before and After, 1992; Half a Heart, 2000. OTHER: Street Games (short stories), 1974, rev. ed., 2001; (adaptor with L. MacGregor) F.H. Burnett, The Secret Garden (musical play), 1983; A Rosellen Brown Reader, 1992. EDITOR: The Whole World Catalog, 1972; Ploughshares: Men Portray Women, Women Portray Men, 1978. **Address:** 5421 S Cornell Ave, Chicago, IL 60615, U.S.A. **Online address:** hoff@usi.uchicago.edu

BROWN, Ruth. British, b. 1941. **Genres:** Children's fiction. **Career:** Author and illustrator, 1979-. **Publications:** FOR CHILDREN SELF-ILLUSTRATED: Crazy Charlie, 1979; A Dark, Dark Tale, 1981; If at First You Do Not See, 1982; The Grizzly Revenge, 1983; The Big Sneeze, 1985; Our Cat Flossie, 1986; Our Puppy's Holiday, 1987, in the US as Our Puppy's Vacation; Ladybird, Ladybird, 1988, in the US as Ladybug, Ladybug; I Don't Like It!, 1989; The World That Jack Built, 1990; The Four-Tongued Alphabet: An Alphabet Book in Four Languages, 1991, in the US as Alphabet Times Four: An International ABC; The Picnic, 1992; One Stormy Night, 1992; Copycat, 1994; (Reteller) Greyfriars Bobby, 1995, in the US as The Ghost of Greyfriar's Bobby, 1996; The Tale of the Monstrous Toad, 1996, in the US as Toad, 1997; Baba, 1997, in the US as Cry Baby; Ruth Brown's Mad Summer Night's Dream, 1998; The Shy Little Angel, 1998. Illustrator of books by J. Miles, B. Parker, M. Harris, F. Zeissl, J. Herriot, J. Willis, F. Thomas, T. Forward, H. Oram. **Address:** Andersen Press Ltd, Random House, 20 Vauxhall Bridge Road, London SW1V 2SA, England.

BROWN, Sandra. Also writes as Laura Jordan, Rachel Ryan, Erin St. Claire. American, b. 1948. **Genres:** Novels, Mystery/Crime/Suspense, Romance/Historical. **Career:** Merle Norman Cosmetics Studios, Tyler, TX, manager, 1971-73; KLTV-TV, Tyler, weather reporter, 1972-75; WFAA-TV, Dallas, TX, weather reporter, 1976-79; Dallas Apparel Mart, model, 1976-87; writer. **Publications:** ROMANCE/SUSPENSE NOVELS: Breakfast in Bed, 1983; Heaven's Price, 1983; Relentless Desire, 1983; Tempest in Eden, 1983; Temptation's Kiss, 1983; Tomorrow's Promise, 1983; In a Class by Itself, 1984; Send No Flowers, 1984; Bittersweet Rain, 1984; Sunset Embrace, 1984; Words of Silk, 1984; Riley in the Morning, 1985; Thursday's Child, 1985; Another Dawn, 1985; 22 Indigo Place, 1986; The Rana Look, 1986; Demon Rumm, 1987; Fanta C, 1987; Sunny Chandler's Return, 1987; Adam's Fall, 1988; Hawk's O'Toole's Hostage, 1988; Slow Heat in Heaven, 1988; Tidings of Great Joy, 1988; Long Time Coming, 1989; Temperatures Rising, 1989; Best Kept Secrets, 1989; A Whole New Light, 1989; Another Dawn, 1991; Breath of Scandal, 1991; Mirror Image, 1991; French Silk, 1992; The Silken Web, 1992; Honor Bound, 1992; A Secret Splendor, 1992; Shadows of Yesterday (also as Relentless Desire), 1992; Where There's Smoke, 1993; Charade, 1994; The Witness, 1995; Exclusive, 1996; Fat Tuesday, 1997; Unspeakable, 1998; The Alibi, 1999; Standoff, 2000; The Switch, 2000; Envy, 2001; Not Even for Love, 2003; Hello Darkness, 2003. TEXAS! SERIES: Texas! Lucky, 1990; Texas! Sage, 1991; Texas! Chase, 1991. ROMANCE NOVELS AS LAURA JORDAN: Hidden Fires, 1982; The Silken Web, 1982. NOVELS AS RACHEL RYAN: Love beyond Reason, 1981; Love's Encore, 1981; Eloquent Silence, 1982; A Treasure Worth Seeking, 1982; Prime Time, 1983. NOVELS AS ERIN ST. CLAIRE: Not Even for Love, 1982; A Kiss Remembered, 1983; A Secret Splendor, 1983; Seduction by Design, 1983; Led Astray, 1985; A Sweet Anger, 1985; Tiger Prince, 1985; Above and Beyond, 1986; Honor Bound, 1986; The Devil's Own, 1987; Two Alone, 1987; Thrill of Victory, 1989.

BROWN, Steve. American, b. 1944. **Genres:** Mystery/Crime/Suspense. **Career:** Writer. Also sold life insurance and radio advertising space. **Publications:** Of Love and War, 1999; Color Her Dead, 1999; Dead Kids Tell No Tales, 2000; Stripped to Kill, 2000; Black Fire, 2000; Radio Secrets, 2000; America Strikes Back, 2001; Woman against Herself, 2001; Fallen Stars, 2001; When Dead Is Not Enough, 2001; Hurricane Party, 2002; Sanctuary of Evil, 2003. **Address:** c/o Author Mail, Chick Springs, PO Box 1130, Taylors, SC 29687, U.S.A.

BROWN, Stewart. British, b. 1951. **Genres:** Novellas/Short stories, Poetry, Literary criticism and history. **Career:** High school teacher in Jamaica, 1972-74; Bayero University, Kano, Nigeria, lecturer in English, 1980-83; University of Birmingham, England, lecturer in African and Caribbean literature, 1988-; writer and editor. **Publications:** Writers from Africa: A Readers' Guide, 1989; Kiss to Quarrel: Yoruba/English, Strategies of Mediation, 2000. POETRY: Mekin Foolishness, 1981; Zinder, 1986; Lugard's Bridge, 1989; Elsewhere: New & Selected Poems, 1999. EDITOR: Caribbean Poetry Now, 1984, 2nd ed., 1992; (with M. Morris and G. Rohler) Voiceprint: An Anthology of Oral and Related Poetry from the Caribbean, 1989; New Wave: The Contemporary Caribbean Short Story, 1990; The Art of Derek Walcott: A Collection of Critical Essays, 1991; (with I. McDonald) The Heinemann Book of Caribbean Poetry, 1992; The Art of Kamau Brathwaite: A Collection of Critical Essays, 1995; The Pressures of the Text: Orality, Texts and the Telling of Tales, 1995; Caribbean New Voices, 1995; African New Voices, 1997; (with J. Wickham) The Oxford Book of Caribbean Short Stories, 1999; All Are Involved: The Art of Martin Carter, 2000. **Address:** Centre of West African Studies, University of Birmingham, Edgbaston, Birmingham B15 2TT, England. **Online address:** s.brown@bham.ac.uk

BROWN, Theodore M. American, b. 1925. **Genres:** Architecture, Photography. **Career:** Professor Emeritus of History of Art, Cornell University, Ithaca, New York, since 1988 (Associate Professor, 1967-71; Professor, 1971-88). Assistant and Associate Professor of History of Art, University of Louisville, Kentucky, 1958-67. **Publications:** The Work of G. Rietveld, Architect, 1958; Introduction to Louisville Architecture, 1960; (with M. M. Bridwell) Old Louisville, 1961; Margaret Bourke-White, Photojournalist, 1972. **Address:** 92 Ithaca Rd, Ithaca, NY 14850, U.S.A.

BROWN, Thomas J. American, b. 1960. **Genres:** History. **Career:** University of South Carolina, Columbia, SC, currently assistant professor of history and assistant director of the Institute of Southern Studies. **Publica-**

tions: Dorothea Dix: New England Reformer, 1998. EDITOR: American Eras: Civil War and Reconstruction, 1850-1877, 1997; (with M.H. Blatt and D. Yacovone) Hope and Glory: Essays on the 54th Massachusetts Regiment, 2001. **Address:** Institute of Southern Studies, Gambrell Hall 107, University of South Carolina, Columbia, SC 29208, U.S.A. **Online address:** browntj@gwm.sc.edu

BROWN, Tony. (William Anthony Brown). American, b. 1933. **Genres:** Plays/Screenplays, Adult non-fiction. **Career:** Television journalist and writer. Worked briefly as a social worker, c. 1961; Detroit Courier, Detroit, MI, drama critic to city editor; WTVS-TV, Detroit, writer, producer, and/or host of programs; host of Black Journal, WNET-TV, 1970-77, Tony Brown's Journal, 1977 to c. 1980, 1982-, and Tony Brown at Daybreak, c. 1980-82. Founding dean of Howard University's School of Communications, 1971-74. Commentator for All Things Considered, National Public Radio. President of Tony Brown Productions, 1977-. **Publications:** The White Girl (screenplay), 1988; Black Lies, White Lies: The Truth According to Tony Brown (nonfiction), 1995. **Address:** Tony Brown Productions, 2350 5th Ave Ste 124, New York, NY 10037, U.S.A.

BROWN, V(ictor) I(vy). American, b. 1949. **Genres:** Law. **Career:** Writer. **Publications:** Veteran Preference Employment Statutes: A State-by-State and Federal Government Handbook, 2000. **Address:** c/o McFarland, PO Box 611, Jefferson, NC 28640, U.S.A. **Online address:** vbrown1845@aol.com

BROWNE, Anthony (Edward Tudor). British, b. 1946. **Genres:** Children's fiction. **Career:** University of Manchester, Royal Infirmary, medical artist, 1968-70; Gordon Fraser Greeting Cards, London, designer, 1971-87. **Publications:** Through the Magic Mirror, 1976; A Walk in the Park, 1977; Bear Hunt, 1979; Look What I've Got!, 1980; Hansel and Gretel (retelling), 1981; Bear Goes to Town, 1982; Gorilla, 1983; Willy the Wimp, 1984; Willy the Champ, 1985; Piggybook, 1986; The Little Bear Book, 1988; I Like Books, 1989; A Bear-y Tale, 1989; The Tunnel, 1989; Changes, 1990; Willy and Hugh, 1991; Through the Magic Mirror, 1992; Zoo, 1992; The Big Baby: A Little Joke, 1994; King Kong, 1994; The Topiary Garden, 1995; Willy the Wizard, 1996; Things I Like, 1997; Willy the Dreamer, 1997; Voices in the Park, 1998; My Dad, 2000; Willy's Pictures, 2000; Animal Fair, 2002; The Shape Game, 2003. **Address:** c/o Walker Books Ltd, 87 Vauxhall Walk, London SE11 5HJ, England.

BROWNE, Gerald A(ustin). American, b. 1928. **Genres:** Novels. **Career:** Grey Advertising, vice president; freelance writer. **Publications:** It's All Zoo, 1968; 11 Harrowhouse, 1972; Hazard, 1973; Slide, 1976; Green Ice, 1978; Nineteen Purchase Street, 1982; Stone 588, 1986; Hot Siberian, 1989; Eighteen Millimeter Blues, 1993; West Forty Seventh, 1996; Rush 929, 1998. **Address:** c/o Warner Books Inc., Time & Life Bldg., 1271 Avenue of the Americas 9th Fl., New York, NY 10020, U.S.A.

BROWNE, Michael Dennis. American (born England), b. 1940. **Genres:** Poetry, Songs/Lyrics and libretti. **Career:** University of Iowa, Iowa City, visiting lecturer in creative writing, 1967-68; Columbia University, NYC, adjunct assistant professor, 1968-69; Bennington College, VT, member of English Dept., 1969-71; University of Minnesota, Minneapolis, assistant professor, 1971-74, associate professor, 1975-83, professor of English, 1983-, director, program in creative writing, 1989-92. **Publications:** (with D. Lord) How the Stars Were Made, 1968; The Wife of Winter, 1970; (with D. Lord) Sea Journey, 1970; (with D. Lord) Non Songs, 1974; Sun Exercises, 1976; (with S. Paulus) Canticles, 1977; (with S. Paulus) Fountain of My Friends, 1977; (with S. Paulus) Mad Book, 1977; (with S. Paulus) North Shore, 1978; The Sun Fetcher, 1978; (with S. Paulus) A Village Singer, 1979; (with S. Paulus) All My Pretty Ones, 1981; Smoke from the Fires, 1985; (with J. Foley) As a River of Light, 1987; (with J. Foley) Able to Fall, 1988; (with S. Paulus) Harmoonia, 1991; You Won't Remember This, 1992; Selected Poems 1965-1995, 1997; (with S. Paulus) The Three Hermits, 1997; Sing Her the River (poetry for children), 2004; Things I Can't Tell You, 2005. **Address:** Dept of English, 207 Lind Hall, University of Minnesota, Minneapolis, MN 55455, U.S.A. **Online address:** mdb@umn.edu

BROWNELL, Charles E(dward), (III). American, b. 1943. **Genres:** Art/Art history, Architecture. **Career:** University of Virginia, Charlottesville, associate professor of architectural history; Virginia Commonwealth University, Richmond, professor of art history. **Publications:** (ed. with E.C. Carter and J.C. Van Horne) Benjamin H. Latrobe, Latrobe's View of America, 1795-1820: Selections from the Watercolors and Sketches, 1985; (with C. Loth, W.M. Rasmussen, and R. Wilson) The Making of Virginia Architecture, 1992; (with J.A. Cohen) The Architectural Drawings of Benjamin Henry Latrobe, 1994. **Address:** Department of Art History, Virginia Commonwealth University, 922 West Franklin St., Richmond, VA 23284-3046, U.S.A.

BROWNELL, Susan. American, b. 1960. **Genres:** Anthropology/Ethnology, Sports/Fitness, Women's studies and issues. **Career:** University of Missouri-St. Louis, associate professor of anthropology, 1994-. **Publications:** Training the Body for China: Sports in the Moral Order of the People's Republic, 1995; (ed. with J.N. Wasserstrom) Chinese Femininities/Chinese Masculinities: A Reader, 2002. **Address:** Department of Anthropology, University of Missouri-St. Louis, St. Louis, MO 63121, U.S.A. **Online address:** sbrownell@umsl.edu

BROWNE-MILLER, Angela. Also writes as Angela de Angelis. American, b. 1952. **Genres:** Novels, Plays/Screenplays, Self help, Social commentary, Social sciences, Theology/Religion, Writing/Journalism, Autobiography/Memoirs. **Career:** Cokenders Alcohol and Drug Program, Emeryville, CA, research and education director, 1983-89; University of California, Berkeley, lecturer in Schools of Social Welfare, Business and Public Policy, 1983-92; psychotherapist in private practice in Tiburon, CA, 1985-; Parkside Medical Services Corp., executive consultant, 1990-91; editor, illustrator, and painter. Involved in political campaigns. **Publications:** The Day Care Dilemma, 1990; Working Dazed: Why Drugs Pervade the Workplace and What Can Be Done about It, 1991; Transcending Addiction, 1993; Gestalting Addiction, 1993; Learning to Learn, 1994; Shameful Admissions, 1995; Intelligence Policy, 1995; Omega Point, 1996; Adventures in Death, 1996; Embracing Death, 1996; How to Die and Survive, 1997; How to Die and Survive Addictions, Crises, and Transitions, 1999; Rushing Water, 2003. **Address:** Metaterra, Inc, 98 Main St No 315, Tiburon, CA 94920, U.S.A. **Online address:** DoctorAngela1@aol.com

BROWNING, Christopher R(obert). American, b. 1944. **Genres:** History. **Career:** Allegheny College, Meadville, PA, instructor in history, 1969-71; Pacific Lutheran University, Tacoma, WA, assistant professor, 1974-79, associate professor, 1979-84, professor of history, 1984-99; University of North Carolina at Chapel Hill, Frank Porter Graham Professor of History, 1999-. **Publications:** The Final Solution and the German Foreign Office, 1978; Fateful Months: Essays on the Emergence of the Final Solution, 1941-42, 1984; Ordinary Men: Reserve Police Battalion 101 and the Final Solution in Poland, 1992; The Path to Genocide: Essays on Launching the Final Solution, 1992; Nazi Policy, Jewish Workers, German Killers, 2000; Collected Memories: Holocaust History and Postwar Testimony, 2003; The Origins of the Final Solution: The Evolution of Nazi Jewish Policy, 2004. **Address:** Dept of History, University of North Carolina, Chapel Hill, Chapel Hill, NC 27599, U.S.A. **Online address:** cbrownin@email.unc.edu

BROWNING, Dixie Burrus. Also writes as Zoe Dozier, Bronwyn Williams. American, b. 1930. **Genres:** Romance/Historical. **Career:** President and Co-Owner, Browning Artworks, Frisco, NC, since 1984. Founder and Co-Director, Art Gallery Originals, Winston-Salem, NC, 1968-73; Co-Director, Art V Galley, Clemmons, NC, 1974-75. **Publications:** Warm Side of the Island, 1977; Tumbled Wall, 1980; Unreasonable Summer, 1980; Chance Tomorrow, 1981; East of Today, 1981; Winter Blossom, 1981; Wren of Paradise 1981; Finders Keepers, 1982; Island on the Hill, 1982; Logic of the Heart, 1982; The Loving Rescue, 1982; Renegade Player, 1982; Practical Dreamer, 1983; Reach Out to Cherish, 1983; A Secret Valentine, 1983; Shadow of Yesterday, 1983; First Things Last, 1984; The Hawk and the Honey, 1984; Image of Love, 1984; Journey to Quiet Waters, 1984; Just Desserts, 1984; Late Rising Moon, 1984; The Love Thing, 1984; Stormwatch, 1984; Time and Tide, 1984; Visible Heart, 1984; A Bird in Hand, 1985; By Any Other Name, 1985; Matchmaker's Moon, 1985; Something for Herself, 1985; The Tender Barbarian, 1985; Reluctant Dreamer, 1986; The Security Man, 1986; In the Palm of Her Hand, 1986; A Winter Woman, 1986; Belonging, 1987; Henry the Ninth, 1987; A Matter of Timing, 1987; There Once Was a Lover, 1987; Along Came Jones, 1988; Fate Takes a Holiday, 1988; Thin Ice, 1989; Beginner's Luck, 1989; Ships in the Night, 1990; Twice in a Blue Moon, 1990; The Homing Instinct, 1990; Just Say Yes, 1991; Not A Marrying Man, 1991; Gus And The Night Lady, 1992; Best Man For The Job, 1992; Hazards Of The Heart, 1993; Kane's Way, 1993; Keegan's Hunt, 1993; Grace and the Law, 1994; Lucy and the Stone, 1994; Two Hearts, Shlightly Used, 1994; Alex and the Angel, 1995; Single Female (reluctantly) Seeks, 1995; The Beast, the Beauty and the Baby, 1996; The Baby Notion, 1996; Stryker's Wife, 1996; Sunshine, 1997. AS ZOE DOZIER: Home Again My Love, 1977. AS BRONWYN WILLIAMS (with M. Williams): White Witch, 1988; Dandelion, 1989; Stormwalker, 1990; Gideon's Fall, 1991; Mariner's Bride, 1991; A Promise Kept, 1992; The Warfield Bride, 1994; Bedeviled, 1995; Slow Surrender, 1995; Halfway Home, 1996; Seaspell, 1997. **Address:** 5316 Robinhood Rd, Winston-Salem, NC 27106, U.S.A.

BROWNING, Don. American, b. 1934. **Genres:** Ethics, Psychiatry, Psychology, Theology/Religion. **Career:** Alexander Campbell Professor of Ethics and the Social Sciences, Divinity School, University of Chicago, 1980-(Instructor, 1965-66; Assistant Professor, 1967-68; Associate Professor, 1968-77; Professor of Religion and Psychological Studies, 1977-80; Dean, Disciples Divinity House, 1977-83). Consultant, Center for Religion and Psychotherapy, 1970-. Counselor, William Healy School, 1962-63; Assistant Professor of Theology and Pastoral Care, Graduate Seminary, Phillips University, Enid, OK, 1963-65. **Publications:** Atonement and Psychotherapy, 1966; Generative Man: Society and Good Man in Philip Reff, Norman Brown, Erich Fromm, and Erik Erikson, 1973; The Moral Context of Pastoral Care, 1976; Pluralism and Personality: William James and Some Contemporary Cultures of Psychology, 1980; (ed.) Practical Theology, 1983; Religious Ethics and Pastoral Care, 1983; Religious Thought and the Modern Psychologies, 1986; A Fundamental Practical Theology, 1991; From Culture Wars to Common Ground, 1997; Reweaving the Social Tapestry: Toward a Public Philosophy and Policy for Families, 2002; Marriage and Modernization: How Globalization Threatens Marriage and What to Do about It, 2003. **Address:** Divinity School, University of Chicago, 1025 E 58th St, Chicago, IL 60637, U.S.A.

BROWNING, Wilfrid (Robert Francis). British, b. 1918. **Genres:** Theology/Religion. **Career:** Canon of Christ Church Cathedral, Oxford, 1965-88, and Lecturer in New Testament Studies, Oxford University. **Publications:** (co-trans.) Vocabulary of the Bible, 1958; (ed.) The Anglican Synthesis, 1964; Meet the New Testament, 1964; Saint Luke's Gospel, 6th ed., 1981; Handbook of the Ministry, 1985; Dictionary of the Bible, 1996, rev. ed., 2004. **Address:** Christ Church Cathedral, Oxford OX1 1DP, England.

BROWNJOHN, Alan (Charles). Also writes as John Berrington. British, b. 1931. **Genres:** Novels, Poetry, Literary criticism and history, Translations. **Career:** Wandsworth Borough Councillor, London, 1962-65; Sr. Lecturer in English, Battersea College of Education, now University of the South Bank, London, 1965-79; Member, Arts Council Literature Panel, 1968-72; Poetry Critic, New Statesman, London, 1968-76, Encounter, 1978-80, and Sunday Times, 1990-; Chairman, Literature Panel, Greater London Arts Association, 1973-77; Deputy President, Poetry Society, London, 1988-92 (Chairman, 1982-88). **Publications:** POETRY: Travellers Alone, 1954; The Railings, 1961; The Lions' Mouths, 1967; Oswin's Word (libretto for children), 1967; Sandgrains on a Tray, 1969; (with M. Hamburger and C. Tomlinson) Penguin Modern Poets 14, 1969; Brownjohn's Beasts, 1970; Warrior's Career, 1972; A Song of Good Life, 1975; A Night in the Gazebo, 1980; Collected Poems 1952-1983, 1983; The Old Flea-Pit, 1987; Collected Poems 1952-88, 1988; The Observation Car, 1990; In The Cruel Arcade, 1994; The Cat without E-mail, 2001; The Men around Her Bed, 2004. NOVELS: (as John Berrington) To Clear the River, 1964; The Way You Tell Them, 1990; The Long Shadows, 1997; A Funny Old Year, 2001. OTHER: The Little Red Bus Book, 1972; Philip Larkin, 1975. TRANSLATIONS: Torquato Tasso, by Goethe, 1985; Horace, by Corneille, 1996. EDITOR: First I Say This (poems), 1969; (with S. Heaney and J. Stallworthy) New Poems 1970-71, 1971; (with M. Duffy) New Poetry 3, 1977; New Year Poetry Supplement, 1982; (with S. Brownjohn) Meet and Write, I, II and III, 1985-87; (with K.W. Gransden) The Gregory Anthology, 1990. **Address:** 2 Belsize Park, London NW3 4ET, England.

BROWNLEE, David B(ruce). American, b. 1951. **Genres:** Architecture. **Career:** University of Pennsylvania, Philadelphia, assistant professor, 1980-85, associate professor of art history, 1985-93, professor, 1993-, member of Graduate Groups in History of Art, Architecture, and Historic Preservation. **Publications:** The Law Courts: The Architecture of George Edmund Street, MIT Press, 1984. Friedrich Weinbrenner, Architect of Karlsruhe, University of Pennsylvania Press, 1986. Building the City Beautiful: The Benjamin Franklin Parkway and the Philadelphia Museum of Art, Philadelphia Museum of Art, 1989. (With David G. De Long) The Architecture of Louis I. Kahn, Rizzoli, 1991. **Address:** Department of the History of Art, Jaffe Building, University of Pennsylvania, Philadelphia, PA 19104-6208, U.S.A.

BROWNMILLER, Susan. American, b. 1935. **Genres:** Human relations/Parenting, Women's studies and issues. **Career:** Freelance writer. Formerly: Reporter, NBC-TV, Philadelphia, 1965; network newswriter, ABC-TV, NYC, 1965-67; researcher, Newsweek mag., NYC, and staff writer, Village Voice newspaper, NYC. **Publications:** Shirley Chisholm, 1970; Against Our Will: Men, Women and Rape, 1975; Femininity, 1984; Waverly Place, 1989; Seeing Vietnam: Encounters of the Road and Heart, 1994; In Our Time: Memoir of a Revolution, 1999. **Address:** c/o Frances Goldin Literary Agency, Inc., 57 E 11th St, New York, NY 10003, U.S.A.

BROWNRIDGE, William R(oy). Canadian, b. 1932. **Genres:** Children's fiction. **Career:** KB Graphic Design, Calgary, Alberta, partner for fourteen years; Francis, Williams & Johnson (advertising and public relations firm), Calgary, associate creative director for twenty years. Artist. Artwork has been represented in a national touring exhibition and exhibits throughout Canada; artwork included in Calgary's print and film presentation for the 1988 Olympic Winter Games; designer of uniforms for the Calgary Flames hockey club, 1993. **Publications:** The Moccasin Goalie (self-illustrated), 1995. **Address:** 705 145 Point Dr. N.W., Calgary, AB, Canada T3B 4W1.

BROWNSTEIN, Gabriel. American, b. 1966. **Genres:** Novellas/Short stories. **Career:** Educator and author of short stories. State University of New York at Stony Brook, lecturer in English. **Publications:** The Curious Case of Benjamin Button, Apt. 3W, 2002. Contributor of short stories to periodicals. **Address:** c/o Paul Cirone, Aaron Priest Literary Agency, 708 3rd Ave. 23rd Floor, New York, NY 10017, U.S.A. **Online address:** gbrownstein @ms.cc.sunysb.edu

BROX, Jane (Martha). American, b. 1956. **Genres:** Poetry, Adult non-fiction. **Career:** Has worked as a baker, a cook, and a bookstore clerk; has worked on her family farm; Harvard Extension School, Cambridge, MA, instructor and tutor in writing, workshop leader, 1994-; freelance writer and poet, 1985-. Has also taught classes and workshops for the Brockport Writers' Forum, Harvard Summer School, Provincetown Fine Arts Work Center, and Centrum Writers Conference; The Loft, Minneapolis, MN, nonfiction writer-in-residence, 1996; Vermont Studio Center, writer-in-residence; Harvard University, Cambridge, visiting lecturer in creative writing, 2002-04. Has written commentary for National Public Radio's Living on Earth program. NEA grant, 1994. **Publications:** EDITOR: (with K. Aponick and P. Marion, and contrib.) Merrimack: A Poetry Anthology, 1992. NONFICTION: Here and Nowhere Else: Late Seasons of a Farm and Its Family, 1995; Five Thousand Days Like This One: An American Family History, 1999; Clearing Land: Legacies of the American Farm, 2004. Contributor to books. Contributor of poetry, reviews, prose, and essays to periodicals. **Address:** 1334 Broadway, Dracut, MA 01826, U.S.A.

BROYLES, Michael. American, b. 1939. **Genres:** Music. **Career:** University of Maryland, Baltimore County, Catonsville, assistant professor, 1967-71, associate professor, 1971-87, professor of music, 1987-93, presidential research professor, 1993-94, director of honors program in music, 1980-94; Pennsylvania State University, State College, distinguished professor of music and professor of American history, 1994-. Johns Hopkins University, lecturer, 1990-; John F. Kennedy Center for the Performing Arts, lecturer, 1994; American Antiquarian Society, research associate, 1990. **Publications:** The Emergence and Evolution of Beethoven's Heroic Style, 1987; A Yankee Musician in Europe: The 1837 Journals of Lowell Mason, 1990; Music of the Highest Class: Elitism and Populism in Antebellum Boston, 1992. Work represented in anthologies. Contributor of articles and reviews to music journals. **Address:** School of Music, Pennsylvania State University, State College, PA 16802, U.S.A.

BROZ, J. Lawrence. American, b. 1956. **Genres:** Politics/Government. **Career:** University of California, Los Angeles, instructor in political science, 1992; Harvard University, Cambridge, MA, assistant professor, 1992-95, associate professor of government, 1995-, faculty associate of Weatherhead Center for International Affairs, 1992-. **Publications:** The International Origins of the Federal Reserve System, 1997. **Address:** Weatherhead Center for International Affairs, Harvard University, 1737 Cambridge St., Cambridge, MA 02138, U.S.A. **Online address:** lbroz@cfia.harvard.edu

BRUCCOLI, Matthew J. American, b. 1931. **Genres:** Literary criticism and history, Bibliography, Biography. **Career:** Bruccoli Clark Layman Publishers, Columbia, SC, president, 1972-; University of South Carolina, Columbia, Jefferies Professor of English, 1976-, professor of English and director of the Center for Editions of American Authors, 1969-76. Editor: Fitzgerald Newsletter, 1958-68; Fitzgerald/Hemingway Annual, 1969-79; New Black Mask, 1985-87; Matter of Crime, 1988-89. **Publications:** Notes on the Cabell Collection at the University of Virginia, 1957; The Composition of Tender Is the Night, 1963; Raymond Chandler: A Checklist, 1968; Profile of F. Scott Fitzgerald, 1971; Kenneth Millar/Ross Macdonald: A Checklist, 1971; John O'Hara: A Checklist, 1972; The O'Hara Concern, 1975; (with R. Layman) Ring Lardner: A Descriptive Bibliography, 1976; The Last of the Novelists, 1977; Scott and Ernest, 1978; John O'Hara: A Descriptive Bibliography, 1978; Raymond Chandler: A Descriptive Bibliography, 1979; Some Sort of Epic Grandeur, 1981; Ross Macdonald: A Descriptive Bibliography, 1983; James Gould Cozzens, 1983; Ross Macdonald, 1984; The Fortunes of Mitchell Kennerley, Bookman, 1986; (with J. Baughman) James Dickey: A Descriptive Bibliography, 1990; Fitzgerald and Hemingway, 1994; (with J. Baughman) Reader's Companion to F. Scott

Fitzgerald's Tender Is the Night, 1996; 150 Years of the American Short Story, 1998; Classes on F. Scott Fitzgerald, 2001; Classes on Ernest Hemingway, 2002; Joseph Heller: A Descriptive Bibliography, 2002. EDITOR: The Profession of Authorship in America 1800-1970: The Papers of William Charvat, 1968; (with J.R. Bryer) F. Scott Fitzgerald in His Own Time, 1971; (with J.M. Atkinson) As Ever, Scott Fitz, 1972; F. Scott Fitzgerald: A Descriptive Bibliography, 1972, 1987; (with C.F. Clark Jr.) Hemingway at Auction, 1972; (with S.F. Smith and J. Kerr) The Romantic Egoists, 1974; An Artist Is His Own Fault, 1976; (with R. Layman) Some Champions, 1976; The Notebooks of F. Scott Fitzgerald, 1978; Selected Letters of John O'Hara, 1978; (with M. Duggan) Correspondence of F. Scott Fitzgerald, 1980; The Short Stories of F. Scott Fitzgerald, 1989; (with D. Nabokov) Vladimir Nabokov: Selected Letters, 1940-1977, 1989; F. Scott Fitzgerald Manuscripts, 18 vols., 1990; The Cambridge University Press Edition of the Works of F. Scott Fitzgerald, 1991; (with J. Baughman) Bibliography of American Fiction, 1992; Ring around the Bases, 1992; John O'Hara, Gibbsville, PA, 1992; (with J. Baughman) Essential Bibliography of American Fiction, 3 vols., 1993; F. Scott Fitzgerald: A Life in Letters, 1994; F.S. Fitzgerald, Tender Is the Night 1996; (with R. Trogdon) The Only Thing That Counts: The Ernest Hemingway/Maxwell Perkins Correspondence, 1996; (with J. Baughman) F. Scott Fitzgerald on Authorship, 1996; F.S. Fitzgerald, Fie! Fie! Fi-Fi! 1996; F. Scott Fitzgerald Centenary Exhibition: The Matthew J. and Arlyn Bruccoli Collection, 1996; American Expatriate Writers, 1997; J.G. Cozzens, By Love Possessed, 1998; C. Schnee, The Bad and the Beautiful, 1998; F.S. Fitzgerald, The Rich Boy and Other Stories, 1998; Crux: The Letters of James Dickey, 1999; F.S. Fitzgerald, The Great Gatsby: A Documentary Volume, 2000; F.S. Fitzgerald, Trimalchio, 2000; T. Wolfe, O Lost, 2000; "To Loot My Life Clean": The Thomas Wolfe/Maxwell Perkins Correspondence, 2000; James Gould Cozzens: An Exhibition, 2000; F. Scott Fitzgerald before Gatsby, 2001; Hemingway and the Thirties, 2001; The Last Romantic, 2002; Catch as Catch Can, 2003; F.S. Fitzgerald, Tender Is the Night, 2003; Conversations with F. Scott Fitzgerald, 2003; The Sons of maxwell Perkins, 2004; The Easiest Thing in the World, 2004; Conversations with John le Carre, 2004. **Address:** Dept of English, University of South Carolina, Columbia, SC 29208, U.S.A.

BRUCE, Colin John. Scottish, b. 1960. **Genres:** Military/Defense/Arms control, History. **Career:** Elmwood College, Cupar, Scotland, librarian, 1984-85; Imperial War Museum, London, England, map curator, 1985-. National Trust for Scotland, guest lecturer in modern history. **Publications:** (with Edward Smithies) War at Sea, 1992; War on the Ground, 1995; Invaders, 1999. Creator of the board game Knights of Justice: The Siege of Malta, 1565. **Address:** Imperial War Museum, Lambeth Rd., London SE1 6HZ, England.

BRUCE, Dickson Davies, Jr. American, b. 1946. **Genres:** History. **Career:** Professor, University of California, Irvine, 1971-. Visiting Professor, Attila Jozsef University, Szeged, Hungary, 1987-88. **Publications:** And They All Sang Hallelujah: Plain-Folk Camp-Meeting Religion, 1800-1845, 1974; Violence and Culture in the Antebellum South, 1979; The Rhetoric of Conservatism: The Virginia Convention of 1829-30 and the Conservative Tradition in the South, 1982; Black American Writing from the Nadir: The Evolution of a Literary Tradition 1877-1915, 1989; Archibald Grimke: Portrait of a Black Independent, 1993; The Origins of African American Literature, 1680-1865, 2001. **Address:** Dept of History, University of California, Irvine, CA 92697, U.S.A.

BRUCE, (William) Harry. Canadian, b. 1934. **Genres:** Area studies, Young adult non-fiction, Young adult non-fiction. **Career:** Ottawa Journal, reporter, 1955-59; Globe and Mail, reporter, 1959-61; Maclean's, assistant editor, 1961-64; Saturday Night, managing editor, 1964-65; Canadian Magazine, managing editor, 1965-66; Star Weekly, associate editor and featured columnist, 1967-68; Toronto Daily Star, columnist, 1968-69; Maclean's, columnist and reports and reviews editor, 1970-71; Nova Scotia Light and Power Co. Ltd., executive editor, 1971; Atlantic Insight, editor, 1979-80, executive editor, 1981; Atlantic Salmon Journal, editor, 1991-. Freelance writer, 1973-79. Gazette East Coast Editorial Ltd., Canadian Broadcasting Corporation (CBC), Halifax, TV talk-show host, 1972. **Publications:** NONFICTION FOR ADULTS: The Short Happy Walks of Max MacPherson, 1968; Nova Scotia, 1975; Lifeline, 1977; R.A.: The Story of R.A. Jodrey, Entrepreneur, 1979; A Basket of Apples: Recollections of Historic Nova Scotia, 1982; The Gulf of St. Lawrence, 1984; Each Moment as It Flies, 1984; Movin' East: The Further Writings of Harry Bruce, 1985; The Man and the Empire: Frank Sobey, 1985; Down Home: Notes of a Maritime Son, 1988. NONFICTION FOR YOUNG ADULTS: Maud: The Life of L.M. Montgomery, 1992. Contributor of essays, reviews, and articles to commentaries, anthologies, and periodicals. **Address:** c/o Writers' Federation of Nova Scotia, 1113 Marginal Rd, Halifax, NS, Canada B3H 4P9.

BRUCE, Robert S. (born England), b. 1955. **Genres:** Paranormal. **Career:** Writer and workshop presenter. **Publications:** Astral Dynamics: A New Approach to Out-of-Body Experience, 1999; Practical Psychic Self-Defense: Understanding and Surviving Unseen Influences, 2002; (with C. E. Lindgren) Capturing the Aura, 2002. Author of short stories and poetry. **Address:** c/o Author Mail, Hampton Roads Publishing Co., 1125 Stoney Ridge Rd., Charlottesville, VA 22902, U.S.A. **Online address:** robert@astralpulse.com

BRUCE, Victoria. American. **Genres:** Documentaries/Reportage. **Career:** NASA, Washington, DC, former science writer; Portland Oregonian, Portland, OR, former science reporter; freelance writer and documentary film producer. **Publications:** No Apparent Danger: The True Story of Volcanic Disaster at Galeras and Nevado del Ruiz, 2001. **Address:** PO Box 551, Riva, MD 21140, U.S.A. **Online address:** vbruce@victoriabruce.com

BRUCE LOCKHART, Robin. British, b. 1920. **Genres:** Biography, Theology/Religion, History. **Career:** Member, Stock Exchange, London, since 1960. Foreign Manager, Financial Times, London, 1946-52; with Beaverbrook Newspapers Ltd., London, 1953-59. **Publications:** Ace of Spies: Biography of Sidney Reilly, 1967; Halfway to Heaven: The Hidden Life of the Sublime Carthusians, 1985; Reilly: The First Man, 1987; Listening to Silence, 1997; O Bonitos, Hushed to Silence, 2000. **Address:** 37 Adelaide Crescent, Hove, Sussex BN3 2JL, England.

BRUCHAC, Joseph. American, b. 1942. **Genres:** Novellas/Short stories, Children's fiction, Young adult fiction, Plays/Screenplays, Children's nonfiction, History, Literary criticism and history, Mythology/Folklore. **Career:** Teachers for West Africa, Ghana, English teacher and liaison officer, 1966-69; Skidmore College, English instructor, 1969-73; Great Meadow Correctional Facility, instructor and coordinator for the writing program, 1974-81; Hamilton College, faculty member, 1983, 1985, 1987; SUNY/Albany, faculty adjunct, 1987-88; Greenfield Review Literary Center, director, and Greenfield Review Press, Greenfield Center, NY, founder and co-editor, 1969-. **Publications:** FOR YOUNG ADULTS. FICTION: Turtle Meat and Other Stories, 1992; Dawn Land, 1993; Long River, 1995; Dog People, 1995; Children of the Longhouse, 1996; Eagle Song, 1997; The Arrow over the Door, 1998; The Waters Between, 1998; The Heart of a Chief, 1999; Sacajawea, 2000; Skeleton Man, 2001; The Journal of Jesse Smoke, 2001; Pocahontas, 2003; Hidden Roots, 2004. FOLK STORIES: Turkey Brother and Other Tales, 1975; Stone Giants & Flying Heads, 1978; Iroquois Stories, 1985; The Wind Eagle, 1985; The Faithful Hunter, 1988; The Return of the Sun, 1990; Hoop Snakes, Hide-Behinds and Sidehill Winders, 1991; Native American Stories, 1991; Native American Animal Stories, 1992; Flying with the Eagle, Racing the Great Bear, 1993; (with G. Ross) The Girl Who Married the Moon, 1994; Four Ancestors (songs & poems) 1994; The Boy Who Lived with the Bears, 1995; Native American Plant Stories, 1995; When the Chenoo Howls, 1998. NONFICTION: (with M.J. Caduto) Keepers of the Earth, 1988; (with M.J. Caduto) Keepers of the Animals, 1990; The Native American Sweat Lodge, History and Legends, 1993; (with M.J. Caduto) Keepers of Life, 1994; (with M.J. Caduto) Keepers of the Night, 1994; (ed.) Native Wisdom, 1995; Roots of Survival, 1996; Tell Me a Tale, 1997; Lasting Echoes, 1997; Bowman's Store (autobiography), 1998. FOR CHILDREN. FOLK STORIES: The First Strawberries, 1993; The Great Ball Game, 1994; Gluskabe and the Four Wishes, 1995; (with G. Ross) The Story of the Milky Way, 1995; Between Earth and Sky, 1996; The Maple Thanksgiving, 1996; (with M.J. Fawcett) Makiawisug, 1997. PICTURE BOOKS: (with J. London) Thirteen Moons on Turtle's Back (poetry), 1992; Fox Song, 1993; The Earth under Sky Bear's Feet, 1995; The Circle of Thanks (songs and poetry), 1996; Many Nations, 1997; Crazy Horse' s Vision, 2000; Squanto's Journey, 2001; (with James Bruchac) How Chipmunk Got His Stripes, 2001; (with James Bruchac) Turtle's Race with Beaver, 2003. NONFICTION: A Boy Called Slow, 1995; Trail of Tears, 2000; Navajo Long Walk, 2002. PLAYS: Pushing up the Sky, 2000. FOR ADULTS. POETRY: Indian Mountain and Other Poems, 1971; The Buffalo in the Syracuse Zoo, 1972; Great Meadow Poems, 1973; The Manabozho Poems, 1973; Flow, 1975; This Earth Is a Drum, 1976; Entering Onondaga, 1978; There Are No Trees inside the Prison, 1978; Mu'undu Wi Go, 1978; The Good Message of Handsome Lake, 1979; Translator's Son, 1980; Ancestry, 1981; Remembering the Dawn, 1983; Tracking, 1985; Walking with My Sons, 1985; Near the Mountains, 1986; Langes Gedachtnis/Long Memory, 1988; No Borders, 1999; Ndakinna/Our Land, 2003; Above the Line, 2003. NONFICTION: Survival This Way, 1990; Roots of Survival, 1996; (with M.J. Caduto) Native American Gardening, 1996; Trails of Tears, Paths of Beauty, 2001; Our Stories Remember, 2003. STORIES: Foot of the Mountain & Other Stories, 2004. EDITOR: Songs from This Earth on Turtle's Back, 1983; Breaking Silence, 1984; The Light from Another Country, 1984; North Country, 1986; New Voices from the Longhouse, 1988; Raven Tells Stories, 1991; Singing of Earth, 1993;

Returning the Gift, 1994; Aniyunwiya/Real Human Beings, 1995; Smoke Rising, 1995. **Address:** PO Box 308, Greenfield Center, NY 12833, U.S.A. **Online address:** www.greenfieldreview.org

BRUCK, Connie. American, b. 1946. **Genres:** Documentaries/Reportage, Business/Trade/Industry. **Career:** Free-lance journalist, 1970-79; American Lawyer (magazine), staff reporter, 1979-1989; New Yorker, staff writer, 1989-. **Publications:** The Predators' Ball: The Junk Bond Raiders and the Man Who Staked Them, 1988; Master of the Game, 1994; When Hollywood Really had a King, 2003. Contributor to periodicals. **Address:** c/o The New Yorker, 4 Times Square, New York, NY 10036, U.S.A.

BRUCKNER, Pascal. French, b. 1948. **Genres:** Novels, Adult non-fiction. **Career:** Writer. Visiting professor at universities worldwide. **Publications:** NOVELS: Monsieur Tac, 1976; Allez jouer ailleurs, 1977; Lunes de fiel, 1981, trans. as Evil Angels, 1987; Parias, 1985; Le divin enfant, 1992, trans. as The Divine Child: A Novel of Prenatal Rebellion, 1994; Les voleurs de beaute, 1997. NONFICTION: Fourier, 1975; Le nouveau desordre amoureux, 1977; Au Coin de la rue, 1979; Le sanglot de l'homme blanc: Tiers-monde culpabilite, 1983, trans. as The Tears of the White Man: Compassion as Contempt, 1986; La melancolie democratique, 1990; La tentation de l'innocence, 1995, trans. as The Temptation of Innocence Living in the Age of Entitlement, 2000; L'euphorie perpetuelle, 2000. OTHER: Le palais des claques (children's fiction), 1986. **Address:** 8 rue Marie-Stuart, 75002 Paris, France. **Online address:** bruchuer@wanadoo.fr

BRUEMMER, Fred. Canadian (born Latvia), b. 1929. **Genres:** Anthropology/Ethnology, Natural history. **Career:** Freelance photographer; writer. Recipient of Order of Canada award, 1983. **Publications:** The Long Hunt, 1969; Seasons of the Eskimo, 1971; Encounters with Arctic Animals, 1972; The Arctic, 1974; The Life of the Harp Seal, 1977; Children of the North, 1979; Summer at Bear River, 1980; The Arctic World, 1985; Arctic Animals, 1986; Seasons of the Seal, 1988; World of the Polar Bear, 1989; Seals (with Eric S. Grace), 1991; The Narwhal, 1993; Arctic Memories: Living with the Inuit, 1993; (with A. Delaunois) Nanook and Nauja: The Polar Bear Cubs, 1995; (with A. Delaunois) Kotik: The Baby Seal, 1995; (with T. Mangelsen) Polar Dance: Born of the North Wind, 1997; Seals in the Wild, 1998; Glimpses of Paradise: The Marvel of Massed Animals, 2002. **Address:** 2 Strathearn S, Montreal, QC, Canada H4X 1X4.

BRUER, John T. American, b. 1949. **Genres:** Education. **Career:** Educator and administrator. Rockefeller Foundation, Health Science Division, visiting research fellow and associate director, 1978-81; Josiah Macy, Jr. Foundation, program administrator, 1981-86; James S. McDonnell Foundation, St. Louis, MO, president, 1986; Washington University, adjunct professor of philosophy; serves on the boards of several universities. **Publications:** (ed. with W. Goffman and K.S. Warren) Research on Selective Information Systems: A Bellagio Conference, October 23-27, 1979, 1980; (ed. with H. Zuckerman and J.R. Cole) The Outer Circle: Women in the Scientific Community, 1991; Schools for Thought: A Science of Learning in the Classroom, 1993; The Myth of the First Three Years: A New Understanding of Early Brain Development and Lifelong Learning, 1999; (with S.M. Fitzpatrick) Carving Our Destiny: Scientific Research Faces a New Millennium, 2001. Contributor to books. **Address:** c/o Author Mail, The Free Press/Simon & Schuster, 1230 Avenue of the Americas, New York, NY 10020, U.S.A.

BRUGIONI, Dino A. American, b. 1921. **Genres:** Air/Space topics, Earth sciences, History, Military/Defense/Arms control, Photography, Politics/Government, Technology, Writing/Journalism, Illustrations. **Career:** US Army Air Corps, 1942-45; Tennessee Valley Authority, Washington, DC, part-time liaison officer, 1945-48; National Photographic Interpretation Center, Central Intelligence Agency, Washington, DC, senior officer and expert on aerial reconnaissance and photographic interpretation, 1948-82; free-lance writer, lecturer, and consultant, 1982-. Member of National Intelligence Study Center; U.S. Holocaust Museum and Smithsonian Air and Space Museum, adviser. Visiting scholar and lecturer at colleges and universities in the U.S.; has helped with and appeared on television programs. Testified before U.S. Senate and House of Representatives. **Publications:** The Holocaust Revisited: A Retrospective Analysis of the Auschwitz-Birkenau Extermination Complex, 1979; The Civil War in Missouri as Seen from the Capital City, 1987; Eyeball to Eyeball: The Inside Story of the Cuban Missile Crisis, 1991; From Balloons to Blackbirds, 1993; Photo Fakery: The History and Techniques of Photographic Deception and Manipulation, 1999. Contributor to journals, magazines, and newspapers. **Address:** 301 Storck Rd, Fredericksburg, VA 22406-4731, U.S.A.

BRUGMAN, Alyssa (F.). (born Australia), b. 1974. **Genres:** Children's fiction. **Career:** Writer. Worked variously as an after-school tutor for

Aboriginal children, a business college instructor, an operations manager, and in public relations. **Publications:** Finding Grace (young adult novel), 2001; Walking Naked (young adult novel), 2002. **Address:** c/o Author Mail, St. Leonards, Allen & Unwin, POB 8500, St. Leonards, New South Wales 1590, Australia. **Online address:** alyssabrugman@yahoo.com.au

BRUHNS, Karen Olsen. American, b. 1941. **Genres:** Anthropology/ Ethnology. **Career:** University of California, Los Angeles, acting assistant professor of anthropology, 1967-68; University of Calgary, Calgary, Alberta, assistant professor of anthropology, 1968-70; San Jose State University, San Jose, CA, assistant professor of anthropology, 1970-72; San Francisco State University, San Francisco, CA, faculty member, 1972-80, professor of anthropology, 1980-. California Academy of Sciences, research associate in anthropology, 1984-; Museo del Banco Central de Ecuador, research associate in archaeology, 1986-94. Crew member for projects in northern California, 1959-63, and Mexico, 1964; field class instructor at sites in Santa Cruz County, CA, 1971, 1972; director of field projects in Colombia, Ecuador, and Peru, 1969-70, at Zapatera Island, Nicaragua, 1974, Cihuatan Settlement, El Salvador, 1975-79, 1994-95, Cuello Project, Belize, 1980, Merced County, CA, 1987-88, and Paute Valley, Ecuador, 1980-. **Publications:** (with T.W. Weller) A Coloring Album of Ancient Mexico and Peru, 1971, rev. bilingual ed., 1974; Ancient South America, 1994; (with K.E. Stothert) Women in Ancient America, 1996. Contributor to books. Contributor of articles and reviews to periodicals. **Address:** Department of Anthropology, San Francisco State University, 1600 Holloway, San Francisco, CA 94132, U.S.A.

BRUIN, John. See **BRUTUS, Dennis (Vincent).**

BRULOTTE, Gaetan. American (born Canada), b. 1945. **Genres:** Novels, Novellas/Short stories, Plays/Screenplays, Humanities, Literary criticism and history, Sex, Essays. **Career:** Trois-Rivieres College, QC, Canada, assistant professor, 1970-72, associate professor of French, 1972-83; University of South Florida, Tampa, visiting professor, 1984-88, professor of French, 1988-, director of graduate studies in French, 1985-90; writer. Visiting professor of French at universities. Consultant to libraries; translator. **Publications:** FICTION IN ENGLISH TRANSLATION: L'Emprise (novel; The Ascendancy), 1979, rev. ed., 1988, trans. as Double Exposure, 1988; Le Surveillant (short stories), 1982, rev. ed., 1995, trans. as The Secret Voice, 1990. OTHER FICTION: Ce qui nous tient (short stories; What Holds Us), 1988; Epreuves (short stories), 1999; Le Client (play), 2001; La vie de Biais (short stories), 2002. ESSAYS: L'Imaginaire et l'ecriture: Ghelderode (Writing and the Configuration of Imagination: Ghelderode), 1972; Aspects du texte erotique (Aspects of the Erotic Text), 1978; L'univers de Jean Paul Lemieux, 1996; Oeuvres de chair of figures du discours erotique, 1998; Les cahiers de Limentinus: Lectures fin de siecle, 1998; La Chambre des Lucidites, 2003. RADIO PRODUCTIONS: Seuils (Thresholds), 1979; Les Ecrivains (The Writers), 1980-81; Le Client (The Customer), 1983. Author of 10 stories adapted and produced by Radio-Canada, 1979-87. OTHER: (with J. Sarrazin) L'Emprise (teleplay), 1980; (with M. Poulette) L'Emprise (screenplay), 1981; Dicionnaire bio-bibliographique, critique et anthologique/ Ecrivains de la Mauricie (Bio-bibliographical Dictionary of the Writers of the Mauricie Region), 1981. Contributor to anthologies and periodicals. **Address:** World Language Education, University of South Florida, Tampa, FL 33620, U.S.A. **Online address:** brulotte@chuma1.cas.usf.edu

BRUMFIELD, William Craft. American, b. 1944. **Genres:** Architecture, Literary criticism and history, Photography, Urban studies. **Career:** Harvard University, Cambridge, MA, assistant professor of Russian literature, 1974-79, fellow at Russian Research Center, 1980-81; Tulane University, New Orleans, LA, assistant professor, 1981-83, associate professor, 1984-91, professor of Russian studies, 1992-. University of Wisconsin, visiting lecturer in Russian literature, 1973-74; American Council of Teachers of Russian, Pushkin Institute, resident director, 1979-80; University of Virginia, visiting associate professor, 1985-86; NEH Summer Institute, Moscow, co-director, 1994. **Publications:** (and photographs) Gold in Azure: 1,000 Years of Russian Architecture, 1983; (with B. Ruble and A. Kopp) Architecture and the New Urban Environment, 1988; The Origins of Modernism in Russian Architecture, 1991; A History of Russian Architecture, 1993; An Architectural Survey of St. Petersburg, 1840-1916: Building Inventory, 1994; Lost Russia: Photographing the Ruins of Russian Architecture, 1995; Landmarks of Russian Architecture: A Photographic Survey, 1997. EDITOR: Reshaping Russian Architecture, 1990; (with M. Velimirovich) Christianity and the Arts in Russia, 1991; (with B. Ruble) Russian Housing in the Modern Age, 1993; (with B. Ruble) Zhilishche v Rossii: vek XX, 2001; (with B. Ananich and Y. Petrov) Commerce in Russian Urban Culture, 2001; (with B. Ananich and Y. Petrov) Predprinimatelstvo i gorodskaia kultura v Rossii, 2002. **Address:**

Dept of Germanic and Slavic Studies, Tulane University, New Orleans, LA 70118, U.S.A. **Online address:** brumfiel@tulane.edu

BRUNDAGE, James A. American, b. 1929. **Genres:** History. **Career:** Ahmanson-Murphy Distinguished Professor of History and Courtesy Professor of Law, University of Kansas, Lawrence, 1989-. Associate Ed., Journal of Medieval History, 1974-. Instructor, Fordham University, NYC, 1953-57; Assistant Professor, 1957-60, Associate Professor, 1960-64, Professor of History, 1964-88, and Chairman of Dept., 1972-76, University of Wisconsin, Milwaukee. President, American Catholic Historical Association, 1980. **Publications:** The Chronicle of Henry of Livonia, 1961; The Crusades: A Documentary History, 1962; (ed.) The Crusades: Motives and Achievements, 1964; (with J. Donnelly) Old World Heritage, 1965; Medieval Canon Law and the Crusader, 1969; Richard Lion-Heart: A Biography, 1974; (with V.L. Bullough) Sexual Practices and the Medieval Church, 1982; Law, Sex, and Christian Society in Medieval Europe, 1988; Sex, Law and Marriage in the Middle Ages, 1993; Medieval Canon Law, 1995; (with V.L. Bullough) Handbook of Medieval Sexuality, 1996; The Profession and Practice of Medieval Canon Law, 2004. **Address:** Dept of History, University of Kansas, Lawrence, KS 66045-2130, U.S.A. **Online address:** jabrun@ku.edu

BRUNDIGE, Donald G. American, b. 1940. **Genres:** Travel/Exploration, Recreation. **Career:** Rockwell International Corp., Seal Beach, CA, member of technical staff, 1962-79; Aerospace Corp., El Segundo, CA, senior project engineer, 1979-96; writer. 1996-. Aerospace Corp., consultant, 1996-. **Publications:** (all with S.L. Brundige): Bicycle Rides: Los Angeles and Orange Counties, 1986; Bicycle Rides: San Fernando Valley and Ventura County, 1987; Bicycle Rides: Orange County, 1988; Bicycle Rides: Los Angeles County, 1989; Bicycle Rides: Inland Empire, 1990; Bicycle Rides: San Diego and Imperial Counties, 1991; Bicycle Rides: Santa Barbara and Ventura Counties, 1992; Mountain Biking L.A. County (Southern Section), 1996; Outdoor Recreation Checklists, Outdoor Recreation Equipment, 1998. **Address:** 122 Mirabeau Ave., San Pedro, CA 90732, U.S.A. **Online address:** bnyduk@aol.com

BRUNDIGE, Sharron L(ea). American, b. 1943. **Genres:** Travel/ Exploration, Recreation. **Career:** Rockwell International Corp., El Segundo, CA, member of technical staff, 1965-89; writer, 1989-. **Publications:** (all with D.G. Brundige): Bicycle Rides: Los Angeles and Orange Counties, 1986; Bicycle Rides: San Fernando Valley and Ventura County, 1987; Bicycle Rides: Orange County, 1988, rev. ed., 2001; Bicycle Rides: Los Angeles County, 1989, rev. ed., 2000; Bicycle Rides: Inland Empire, 1990; Bicycle Rides: San Diego and Imperial Counties, 1991; Bicycle Rides: Santa Barbara and Ventura Counties, 1992; Mountain Biking L.A. County (Southern Section), 1996; Outdoor Recreation Checklists, Outdoor Recreation Equipment, 1998. **Address:** 122 Mirabeau Ave, San Pedro, CA 90732, U.S.A. **Online address:** bnyduk@aol.com

BRUNELLI, Jean. American, b. 1934. **Genres:** Medicine/Health, Young adult non-fiction. **Career:** ABC Unified School District, Cerritos, CA, school nurse and program director, 1975-. Southeast Council Serving Young Children with Special Needs and Their Families, chair; member of California Perinatal Substance Abuse Commission and California Alliance Concerned with School Aged Parents. **Publications:** (with Jeanne Warren Lindsay) Teens Parenting: Your Pregnancy and Newborn Journey, Morning Glory, 1991. **Address:** 5782 Shasta Circle, La Palma, CA 90623, U.S.A.

BRUNER, Jerome S(eymour). American, b. 1915. **Genres:** Education, Psychology, Law. **Career:** University Professor, Research Professor of Psychology, Senior Research Fellow in Law, New York University, NYC, 1984-. Associate Director, Office of Public Opinion Research, Princeton, New Jersey, 1942-44; Lecturer, 1945-48, Associate Professor, 1948-52, Professor of Psychology, 1957-72, and Director of the Center for Cognitive Studies, 1961-72, Harvard University, Cambridge, Massachusetts; Watts Professor of Psychology, Oxford University, 1972-80; G. H. Mead University Professor, New School for Social Research, NYC, 1981-88. President, American Psychological Association, 1964-65. **Publications:** Mandate from the People, 1944; (with J.J. Goodnow and G.A. Austin) A Study of Thinking, 1956; (with others) Opinions and Personality, 1956; (with others) Contemporary Approaches to Cognition, 1957; Logique et perception, 1958; On Knowing: Essays for the Left Hand, 1962; Man: A Course of Study, 1965; (with others) Studies in Cognitive Growth, 1966; Processes of Cognitive Growth: Infancy, 1968; The Relevance of Education, 1971; Beyond the Information Given: Studies in the Psychology of Knowing, 1973; Patterns of Growth, 1974; Under Five in Britain, 1980; In Search of Mind: Essays in Autobiography, 1983; Child's Talk, 1983; Actual Minds, Possible Worlds, 1986; Acts of Meaning, 1990; The Culture of Education, 1996; Minding the

Law, 2000. EDITOR: Perception and Personality: A Symposium, 1950; The Growth of Competence, 1974; Play: Its Role in Development and Evolution, 1976; (with A. Garton) Human Growth and Development, 1978. **Address:** 200 Mercer St, New York, NY 10012, U.S.A. **Online address:** jerome. bruner@nyu.edu

BRUNO, Richard L(ouis). American, b. 1954. **Genres:** Medicine/Health. **Career:** Psychophysiologist. New York State Psychiatric Institute, New York, NY, clinical research scientist, 1978-81; Columbia University, New York, fellow, 1981-84; College of Physicians and Surgeons, clinical research coordinator, faculty of medicine, 1984-88; Kessler Institute for Rehabilitation, East Orange, NJ, director of post-polio rehabilitation and research service; Harvest Center, Hackensack, NJ, president; New Jersey Medical School, assistant professor. International Post-Polio Task Force, chair, 1984-; Mount Sinai School of Medicine, New York, NY, associate professor; Englewood Hospital and Medical Center, Englewood, NJ, director of Post-Polio Institute and International Center for Post-Polio Education and Research. Consultant and adviser to US government and international groups. **Publications:** The Polio Paradox: Uncovering the Hidden History of Polio to Understand and Treat Post-Polio Syndrome and Chronic Fatigue, 2002; Post-Polio Sequelae Monograph Series, 1996-2002. Contributor to medical journals. **Address:** c/o Post Polio Institute, Englewood Hospital and Medical Center, 350 Engle St., Englewood, NJ 07631, U.S.A. **Online address:** postpolioinfo@aol.com

BRUNS, Don. American, b. 1947. **Genres:** Mystery/Crime/Suspense. **Career:** Musician, songwriter, advertising executive, and author. Produced music CD Last Flight Out, Whitesand Records, 2002. **Publications:** Jamaica Blue, 2002; Barbados Heat, 2003. **Address:** 768 North Mail, Lima, OH 45801, U.S.A. **Online address:** Don@holditsystems.com

BRUNS, Roger A. American, b. 1941. **Genres:** History, Young adult nonfiction, Biography, Humor/Satire. **Career:** National Historical Publications and Records Commission, National Archives, Washington, DC, archivist, 1967-69, supervisory archivist, 1969-77, director of publications program, 1977-88, acting executive director, 1988, deputy executive director, 1989-. Consultant. **Publications:** (ed. with A. Schlesinger Jr.) Congress Investigates: A Documented History, 5 vols, 1975; (ed.) Am I Not a Man and a Brother: The Antislavery Crusade of Revolutionary America, 1688-1787, 1977; Knights of the Road: A Hobo History, 1980; (with G. Vogt) Your Government Inaction: Or in God We'd Better Trust (humor), 1980; The Damndest Radical: The Life and World of Dr. Ben Reitman (biography), 1986; Thomas Jefferson (young adult biography), 1986; Abraham Lincoln (young adult biography), 1986; (with H. Richardson) Bermuda, 1986; George Washington (young adult biography), 1987; Julius Caesar (young adult biography), 1987; Preacher: Billy Sunday and Big-Time American Evangelism (biography), 1992; The Bandit Kings: From Jesse to Pretty Boy, 1995; John Wesley Powell, 1997; Jesse James, 1998; Almost History, 2000; Billy the Kid, 2000; Desert Honkytonk, 2000. Contributor of articles to periodicals. **Address:** National Archives, 700 Penn Ave NW, Washington, DC 20408-0001, U.S.A.

BRUNS, William John, Jr. American, b. 1935. **Genres:** Administration/Management, Economics. **Career:** Yale University, New Haven, CT, assistant professor of economics and industrial administration, 1962-66; University of Washington, Seattle, professor of accounting, 1966-72; Harvard University, Boston, MA, visiting associate professor, 1969-70, professor, 1972-93, Henry R. Byers Professor of Business Administration, 1993-; Northeastern University, visiting professor, 2001-. Addison-Wesley Publishing Co., advisory ed. **Publications:** Accounting for Decisions: Business Game, 1966; (ed. with D.T. DeCoster) Accounting and Its Behavioral Implications, 1969; Introduction to Accounting: Economic Measurement for Decisions, 1971; (with R. Vancil) A Primer on Replacement Cost Accounting, 1976; (with M.E. Barrett) Case Problems in Management Accounting, 1982, 2nd ed., 1985; (ed. with R.S. Kaplan) Accounting and Management: Field Study Perspectives, 1987; (with S.M. McKinnon) The Information Mosaic, 1992; Performance Measurement, Evaluation, and Incentives, 1992; Accounting for Managers: Text and Cases, 1994, 3rd ed., 2005. **Address:** Harvard Business School, Soldiers Field, Boston, MA 02163, U.S.A. **Online address:** wbruns@hbs.edu

BRUNSKILL, Ronald William. British, b. 1929. **Genres:** Architecture. **Career:** University of Manchester, lecturer, 1960-73, sr. lecturer, 1973-83, reader, 1984-89, hon. Fellow in architecture, 1989-95; De Montfort University, visiting professor, lecturer, 1994-2001. Historic Bldgs. Council for England, member, 1978-83; Cathedrals Advisory Commission for England, member, 1981-91; Royal Commission on Ancient and Historical Monuments of Wales, member, 1983-97; Historic Bldgs. and Monuments

Commission (English Heritage), commissioner, 1989-95, president of Vernacular Architecture Group, 1974-77; Ancient Monuments Society, chairman, 1990-2000. **Publications:** Illustrated Handbook of Vernacular Architecture, 1970, 4th ed. as Vernacular Architecture: An Illustrated Handbook, 2000; Vernacular Architecture of the Lake Counties, 1974; (with A. Clifton-Taylor) English Brickwork, 1978; Traditional Buildings of Britain, 1981, 3rd ed., 1999; Houses, 1982; Traditional Farm Buildings of Britain, 1982, 3rd ed. as Traditional Farm Buildings of Britain and Their Conservation, 1999; Timber Buildings of Britain, 1985, 2nd ed., 1993; Brick Buildings of Britain, 1990; Houses and Cottages of Britain, 1997; Traditional Buildings of Cumbria, 2002. **Address:** Three Trees, 8 Overhill Rd, Wilmslow, Cheshire SK9 2BE, England.

BRUSH, Kathleen (E.). American, b. 1956. **Genres:** Administration/Management. **Career:** Siemens, Boca Raton, FL, computer analyst, 1979-85; Boole & Babbage, Sunnyvale, CA, marketing management, 1985-91; Intek Management, Cape Canaveral, FL, consultant, 1992-. **Publications:** (with W. Davies) High Tech Industry Marketing: The Elements of a Sophisticated Global Strategy, 1997; (with W. Davies) Managing Product Development in the High-Tech Industry, 1997; (with W. Davies and S. Dill) Managing Unsatisfactory Employee Performance, 1997; Export Management, 1999; High-Tech Strategies in the Internet Era, 2000. **Address:** c/o Rogue Wave Software, 5500 Flatiron Pky, Boulder, CO 80301, U.S.A. **Online address:** intek_management@msn.com

BRUSSAT, Frederic. American. **Genres:** Inspirational/Motivational Literature. **Career:** Inspirational writer. United Church of Christ, clergyman. Cultural Information Service, co-founder and co-director with his wife, Mary Ann Brussat; Values & Visions Circles, co-director. **Publications:** EDITOR WITH M.A. BRUSSAT: 100 Ways to Keep Your Soul Alive: Living Deeply and Fully Every Day, 1994; Spiritual Literacy: Reading the Sacred in Everyday Life, 1996; 100 More Ways to Keep Your Soul Alive, 1997. Has also produced a series of viewer's guides for television and film, and co-wrote Values & Visions, a magazine offering resources for making spiritual journeys. **Address:** Values & Visions Circles, 15 W 24th St Fl 10, Madison Square Station, New York, NY 10010-3214, U.S.A.

BRUSSAT, Mary Ann. American. **Genres:** Inspirational/Motivational Literature. **Publications:** EDITOR (with F. Brussat): 100 Ways to Keep Your Soul Alive: Living Deeply and Fully Every Day, 1994; Spiritual Literacy: Reading the Sacred in Everyday Life, 1996; 100 More Ways to Keep Your Soul Alive, 1997; Values and Visions: A Resource Companion for Spiritual Journeys (bimonthly magazine); Values and Visions Circles Newsletter. **Address:** Values & Visions Circles, 15 W 24th St Fl 10, New York, NY 10010-3214, U.S.A.

BRUSTEIN, Robert. American, b. 1927. **Genres:** Theatre. **Career:** American Repertory Theatre, artistic leader, founder. Drama critic, New Republic, Washington, DC, 1959-67, 1979-. Host and writer, Opposition Theatre, network TV, 1966-; contributor, New York Times, 1967-. Founder and publisher, Yale/Theatre, 1967-. Advisory ed., Theatre Quarterly, 1967-. Lecturer to professor, Columbia University, New York, 1957-66; professor of English, dean of Drama School, and artistic director, Yale Repertory Theatre, Yale University, New Haven, CT, 1966-79; professor of English, Harvard University, Cambridge, MA, 1979-2003. **Publications:** The Theatre of Revolt, 1963; Introduction to the Plays of Chekhov, 1964; (ed.) The Plays of Strindberg, 1964; Season of Discontent, 1965; The Third Theatre, 1969; Revolution as Theatre, 1971; The Culture Watch, 1975; Making Scenes, 1981; Who Needs Theatre, 1987; Reimagining American Theatre, 1991; Dumbocracy in America: Studies in the Theatre of Guilt, 1994; Cultural Calisthenics: Writings on Race, Politics, and Theatre, 1998; Siege of the Arts, 2001; Letters to a Young Actor, 2005. Adapter of plays; Demons; Shlemiel the First; Nobody Dies on Friday; Spring Forward, Fall Back. **Address:** Loeb Drama Centre, 64 Brattle St, Cambridge, MA 02138, U.S.A. **Online address:** brustein@fas.harvard.edu

BRUSTEIN, William I. American, b. 1947. **Genres:** History, Sociology, Politics/Government. **Career:** University of Washington, Seattle, instructor, 1979-81, Stewart Carter Dodd Instructor in Sociology, 1979-80; University of Utah, Salt Lake City, assistant professor, 1981-87, associate professor of sociology, 1987-88; University of Minnesota-Twin Cities, Minneapolis, assistant professor, 1988-89, associate professor, 1989-94, director of Center for European Studies, 1992-95, professor of sociology and adjunct professor of political science, both 1994-2000, Morse Alumni Distinguished Teaching Professor of Sociology, 1994-2000, department head, 1995-98, McKnight Distinguished University Professor, 2000; University of Pittsburgh, professor of sociology, political science, and history, 2001-, University Center for

International Studies, director 2001-, professor, 2001-. Lecturer at universities worldwide. **Publications:** The Social Origins of Political Regionalism: France, 1849 to 1981, 1988; The Logic of Evil: The Social Origins of the Nazi Party, 1925-1933, 1996; Roots of Hate: Anti-Semitism in Europe before the Holocaust, 2003. Contributor to books. Contributor of articles and reviews to periodicals. **Address:** University Center for International Studies, 4G40 Wesley W. Posvar Hall, University of Pittsburgh, Pittsburgh, PA 15260, U.S.A. **Online address:** Brustein@ucis.pitt.edu

BRUTUS, Dennis (Vincent). Also writes as John Bruin. South African (born Zimbabwe), b. 1924. **Genres:** Poetry, Literary criticism and history, Politics/Government, Third World. **Career:** Northwestern University, Evanston, IL, professor of English, 1971-85; Swarthmore College, PA, Cornell Professor of English Literature, 1985-86; University of Pittsburgh, Dept. of Africana Studies, professor of African literature and writing, 1986-99, chairman & professor, 1994-99, professor emeritus, 1999-. South African Sports Association, secretary, 1959-; South African Non-Racial Olympic Committee, president, 1963-; director, Campaign for Release of South African Political Prisoners, London, and staff member, International Defence and Aid Fund, London, 1966-71; International Campaign Against Racism in Sport, chairman, 1972-; Africa Today, Denver, member of the Editorial Board, 1976-; Africa Network, chairman, 1984-; Program of African Writing in Africa and the Diaspora, program director, 1989-. Served 18 months in Robben Island Prison, South Africa, for opposition to apartheid, 1964-65; visiting professor at colleges worldwide. Chicago State University, Gwendolen Brooks Center, inducted into Intl Hall of Fame of Writers of African Descent, 2004. **Publications:** Sirens, Knuckles, Boots: Poems, 1963; Letters to Martha and Other Poems from a South African Prison, 1968; The Denver Poems, 1969; Poems from Algiers, 1970; (as John Bruin) Thoughts Abroad, 1971; A Simple Lust: Collected Poems of South African Jail and Exile, 1973; China Poems, 1975; Strains, 1975; Stubborn Hope (poems), 1978; Salutes and Censures, 1982; Airs and Tributes, 1988; Still the Sirens, 1993; Remembering, 2004; Leafdrift, 2005. **Address:** Dept of Africana Studies, 3T01 Forbes Quadrangle, University of Pittsburgh, Pittsburgh, PA 15260-0001, U.S.A. **Online address:** dennisbrutus2002@yahoo.com

BRYAN, Ford R. American, b. 1912. **Genres:** History, Biography. **Career:** Lawrence Institute of Technology, Southfield, MI, instructor, 1935-36; high school principal in Port Hope, MI, 1937-41; Ford Motor Co., Dearborn, MI, research engineer, 1941-51, scientific laboratory supervisor, 1951-74; Edison Institute, Dearborn, volunteer researcher, 1980-. Secretary, Dearborn Historical Commission, 1989-; member of chancellor's cabinet, University of Michigan-Dearborn. **Publications:** The Fords of Dearborn: An Illustrated History, 1987; Beyond the Model T: The Other Ventures of Henry Ford, 1990; Henry's Lieutenants, 1993; Henry's Attic, 1995. **Address:** 15091 Ford Rd Apt 610, Dearborn, MI 48126, U.S.A.

BRYAN, Lynne. British, b. 1961. **Genres:** Novels, Novellas/Short stories. **Career:** Theatre Royal, Glasgow, Scotland, deputy box office manager, 1989-90; Women's Support Project, Glasgow, information worker, 1990-94; Archway Housing Project (hostel), Norwich, England, relief worker, 1994-95. Harpies and Quines (feminist magazine), founding director, 1992-93. Also worked as a teller, clerk, retail assistant, and factory worker. **Publications:** Envy at the Cheese Handout (stories), 1995; Gorgeous (novel), 1999; Like Rabbits (novel), 2002. Work represented in anthologies. Contributor to periodicals. **Address:** c/o Judith Murray, Greene & Heaton, 37 Goldhawk Rd, London W12 8QQ, England.

BRYANT, Christopher G. A. British, b. 1944. **Genres:** Politics/Government, Sociology. **Career:** British sociologist; University of Salford, Greater Manchester, England, professor of sociology and formerly dean of Faculty of Arts, Media and Social Sciences. **Publications:** NONFICTION; Sociology in Action: A Critique of Selected Conceptions of the Social Role of a Sociologist, 1976; Positivism in Social Theory and Research, 1985; Practical Sociology: Post-Empiricism and the Reconstruction of Theory and Application, 1995. Editor of books. **Address:** European Studies Research Institute, University of Salford, Salford, Greater Manchester M5 4WT, England. **Online address:** c.g.a.bryant@salford.ac.uk

BRYANT, Dorothy (Calvetti). American, b. 1930. **Genres:** Novels, Plays/Screenplays, Literary criticism and history, Speech/Rhetoric. **Career:** Publisher, Ata Books, 1978-. English Teacher, San Francisco Public Schools, 1953-56, and Lick-Wilmerding High School, 1956-61; Instructor in English, San Francisco State University, 1962, and Golden Gate College, San Francisco, 1963; Instructor in English and Creative Writing, Contra Costa College, San Pablo, California, 1964-76. **Publications:** The Comforter, 1971, retitled The Kin of Ata Are Waiting for You, 1976; Ella Price's Journal,

1972; Miss Giardino, 1978; Writing a Novel (nonfiction), 1979; The Garden of Eros, 1979; Prisoners, 1980; Killing Wonder, 1981; A Day in San Francisco, 1983; Myths to Lie By, 1984; Confessions of Madame Psyche, 1986; The Test, 1991; Anita, Anita (novel), 1993; Literary Lynching, 2005. PLAYS: Dear Master, 1990; Tea with Mrs. Hardy, 1991; The Panel, 1993; Posing for Gauguin, 1998; The Trial of Cornelia Connelly, 2004; The Berkeley Pit, 2005. **Address:** 1928 Stuart St, Berkeley, CA 94703, U.S.A.

BRYANT, Edward (Arnot). Canadian, b. 1948. **Genres:** Geography, Earth sciences. **Career:** Macquarie University, North Ryde, Australia, computer operator, 1976-77; Technical and Field Surveys, Sydney, Australia, minerals researcher, 1978-79; Wollongong University, Australia, associate professor of geography, 1979-, head of department, 1990-92, head of School of Geosciences, 1999-. Macquarie University, member of the company of Dunmore Lang College. **Publications:** Natural Hazards, 1991; (ed. with G.D. Calvert, C.E. Ewan, and J.A. Garrick, and contrib.) Health in the Greenhouse: The Medical and Environmental Health Effects of Global Climate Change, 1993; Climate and Process Change, 1997. Work represented in anthologies. Contributor to geology and geography journals. **Address:** School of Geosciences, University of Wollongong, Northfields Ave, Wollongong, NSW 2522, Australia. **Online address:** ted_bryant@uow.edu.qu

BRYANT, Howard. American, b. 1968. **Genres:** Sports/Fitness. **Career:** Journalist. San Jose Mercury News, San Jose, CA, sportswriter, 1995-2001; Bergen Record, sportswriter, 2001-. Oakland Tribune, Oakland, CA, journalist. **Publications:** Shut Out: A Story of Race and Baseball in Boston, 2002. Contributor to books. **Address:** Record, 1 Garret Mountain Plaza, PO Box 471, West Paterson, NJ 07424, U.S.A. **Online address:** sports@northjersey.com

BRYANT, Jennifer F(isher). American, b. 1960. **Genres:** Science fiction/Fantasy, Children's fiction, Poetry, Children's non-fiction, Biography. **Career:** Writer, 1989-. High school teacher of foreign languages; writing and poetry instructor for public schools; Pennsylvania Council on the Arts, artist in residence; West Chester University, Writing/English Dept, professor. **Publications:** WORKING MOMS SERIES: Anne Abrams, Engineering Drafter, 1991; Ubel Velez, Lawyer, 1991; Sharon Oehler, Pediatrician, 1991; Zoe McCully, Park Ranger, 1991; Jane Sayler, Veterinarian, 1991; Carol Thomas-Weaver, Music Teacher, 1991. EARTH KEEPERS SERIES: Marjory Stoneman Douglas: Voice of the Everglades, 1992; Margaret Murie: A Wilderness Life, 1993. PHYSICALLY CHALLENGED SERIES: Louis Braille: Inventor, 1994; Henri de Toulouse-Lautrec: The Artist Who Was Crippled, 1995. GREAT ACHIEVERS SERIES: Lucretia Mott: A Guiding Light, 1996; Thomas Merton: Poet, Prophet, Priest, 1997. NOVELS: The Trial, 2004. PICTURE BOOKS: Into Enchanted Woods, 2001; Georgia's Bones, 2005; Music for the End of Time, 2005. OTHER: Birds of a Feather (adult nature anthology), 1993; Hand-Crafted (poetry chapbook), 2001; The Whole Measure (poetry chapbook), 2005. Contributor to literary magazines. **Address:** PO Box 816, Uwchland, PA 19480, U.S.A.

BRYANT, Jonathan M. American, b. 1957. **Genres:** History. **Career:** Emory University, Atlanta, GA, Mellon fellow in southern studies, 1992-93; University of Baltimore, Baltimore, MD, director of Jurisprudence Program, 1993-96; Georgia Southern University, Statesboro, assistant professor of history, 1996-, and director of special collections at Henderson Library. **Publications:** How Curious a Land: Conflict and Change in Greene County, Georgia, 1850-1885, 1996. **Address:** Department of History, Box 8054, Georgia Southern University, Statesboro, GA 30460, U.S.A. **Online address:** jbryant@gasou.edu

BRYANT, Lynwood. American, b. 1908. **Genres:** History, Engineering. **Career:** Massachusetts Institute of Technology, Cambridge, professor of history, 1937-75; writer. **Publications:** (with L.C. Hunter) A History of Industrial Power in the United States, 1780-1930, Vol. III: The Transmission of Power, 1991. Contributor to scholarly journals. **Address:** 46 Heard Rd, Center Sandwich, NH 03227, U.S.A.

BRYANT, Robert Harry. American, b. 1925. **Genres:** Theology/Religion. **Career:** Professor Emeritus of Constructive Theology, United Theological Seminary of the Twin Cities, New Brighton, Minnesota, 1991- (Professor of Systematic Theology, 1961-71; Professor of Constructive Theology, 1971-91). Visiting Assistant Professor of Theology, School of Religion, Vanderbilt University, Nashville, TN, 1953-54; Assistant Professor of Religion, Mt. Holyoke College, South Hadley, Massachusetts, 1956-58; Associate Professor of Philosophy and Religion, Centre College of Kentucky, Danville, 1958-61; Visiting Professor, St. John's University, Collegeville, Minnesota, 1971-72; and Adams United College, Federal Theological Seminary, S. Africa, 1973-

74; Official Visitor; East West Center, Honolulu, HI, 1993. **Publications:** The Bible's Authority Today, 1968; various chapters in books and journal articles. **Address:** 700 John Ringling Blvd Apt N308, Sarasota, FL 34236-1501, U.S.A.

BRYCE ECHENIQUE, Alfredo. Peruvian, b. 1939. **Genres:** Novels. **Career:** Writer and novelist, 1965-. **Publications:** Huerto cerrado, 1968; Un Mundo para Julius, 1970, trans. by D. Gerdes as A World for Julius, 1992; Muerte de Sevilla en Madrid; Antes de la cita con los Linares, 1972; La felicidad, ja, ja, 1974; La Pasion segun San Pedro Balbuena que fue tantas veces Pedro y que nunca pudo negar a nadie, 1977; Avuelo de buen cubero y otras cronicas, 1977; Todos los cuentos, 1979; Cuentos completos, 1981; La vida exagerada de Martin Romana, 1981; El hombre que hablaba de Octavia de Cadiz, 1985; Magdalena peruana y otros cuentos, 1986; Goig, 1987; La ultima mudanza de Felipe Carrilo, 1988; Dos senoras conversan; Un sapo el desierto; Los grandes hombres son asi, y tambien asa, 1990. **Address:** c/o Editorial Palenta SA, Edifici Palenta, Diagonal, 662-664, 08034 Barcelona, Spain.

BRYDEN, John (Herbert). Canadian, b. 1943. **Genres:** History, Military/Defense/Arms control. **Career:** Hamilton Spectator, Hamilton, Ontario, reporter, feature writer, and city editor, 1969-77; Globe and Mail, Toronto, Ontario, copy editor and science editor, 1977-79; Toronto Star, feature editor, senior news editor, business editor, and magazine editor, 1979-89; writer; Member of Parliament for Hamilton-Wentworth, 1993-. **Publications:** Deadly Allies: Canada's Secret War, 1937-1947, 1989; Best Kept Secret: Canadian Secret Intelligence in the Second World War, 1993; Special Interest Group Funding, 1994; A Prescription for Unity, 1995; Canada's Charities: A Need for Reform, 1996. **Address:** 83 Lynden Rd, Lynden, ON, Canada L0R 1T0.

BRYNER, Gary C. American, b. 1951. **Genres:** Politics/Government. **Career:** Brigham Young University, Provo, UT, assistant professor, 1982-88, associate professor of political science, 1989-. **Publications:** Bureaucratic Discretion: Law and Policy in Federal Regulatory Agencies, 1987; (with R. Vetterli) In Search of the Republic, 1987; (with N.B. Reynolds) Constitutionalism and Rights, 1987; Blue Skies, Green Politics: The Clean Air Act of 1990, 1992. EDITOR: (with D.L. Thompson) The Constitution and the Regulation of Society, 1988; Global Warming and the Challenge of International Cooperation: An Interdisciplinary Assessment, 1992; Science, Technology, and Politics: Policy Analysis in Congress, 1992. **Address:** Natural Resources Law Center, University of Colorado School of Law, Campus Box 401, Boulder, CO 80309-0401, U.S.A.

BRYSK, Alison. American, b. 1960. **Genres:** International relations/Current affairs, Politics/Government. **Career:** University of New Mexico, Albuquerque, assistant professor, 1990-92; Pomona College, Claremont, CA, assistant professor, 1992-95; University of California, Irvine, professor of political science and international studies, 1997-. Consultant and member of boards and committees. **Publications:** The Politics of Human Rights in Argentina: Protest, Change, and Democratization, 1994; From Tribal Village to Global Village, 2000. EDITOR: Globalization and Human Rights, 2002; People out of Place: Globalization and the Citizenship Gap, 2003. Contributor to edited collections and series; contributor to scholarly periodicals. **Address:** Department of Politics, 3151 Social Science Plaza, University of California-Irvine, Irvine, CA 92697, U.S.A. **Online address:** abrysk@uci.edu

BRYSON, John. American, b. 1923. **Genres:** Biography. **Career:** Life, New York City, correspondent, bureau chief, and picture editor, 1947-55; free-lance photojournalist, 1955-87; contributing editor, New York; contributor to magazines around the world. **Publications:** (and photographer) The World of Armand Hammer, introduction by Walter Cronkite, 1985; The Private World of Katharine Hepburn, 1990.

BRYSON, Norman. Scottish, b. 1949. **Genres:** Art/Art history. **Career:** King's College, Cambridge, England, fellow in English Studies, 1976-; University of Rochester, Rochester, NY, professor of comparative arts, 1988-90; Harvard University, Cambridge, MA, professor of art history, 1990-99; University College, London, Slade School of Art, professor of art history and theory, 1999-; writer. **Publications:** Word and Image: French Painting of the Ancien Regime, 1982; Vision and Painting: The Logic of the Gaze, 1983; Tradition and Desire: From David to Delacroix, 1984; Looking at the Overlooked: Four Essays on Still Life Painting, 1990; (with B. Barryte) In Medusa's Gaze: Still Life Paintings from Upstate New York Museums (essay; catalogue by B. Barryte), 1991; (with R. Krauss) Cindy Sherman, 1979-1993, (essay; other text by Krauss), 1993. EDITOR: Teaching the Text, 1983; Calligram: Essays in New Art History from France, 1987; (with M.A.

Holly and K. Moxey) Visual Theory, 1991; (with M.A. Holly and K. Moxey) Visual Culture: Images and Interpretations, 1993; Cambridge New Art History series. Contributor to periodicals.

BRZEZINSKI, Zbigniew. American (born Poland), b. 1928. **Genres:** International relations/Current affairs, Politics/Government. **Career:** Counselor, Center for Strategic and International Studies, Washington, D.C., 1981-. Robert E. Osgood Professor of American Foreign Policy, Paul Nitze School of Advanced International Studies, Johns Hopkins University, Washington, DC, 1989-. Trustee, Trilateral Commission, NYC. Teacher and Researcher, Harvard University, Cambridge, MA, 1953-60; Member, Policy Planning Council, of Dept. of State, Washington, DC, 1966-68; White House National Security Adviser, 1977-81; Herbert Lehman Professor of Government, and Director, Research Institute on International Change (formerly, Research Institute on Communist Affairs), Columbia University, NYC, 1960-89. **Publications:** Political Controls in the Soviet Army, 1954; The Permanent Purge: Politics in Soviet Totalitarianism, 1956; (co-author) Totalitarian Dictatorship and Autocracy, 1957; The Soviet Bloc: Unity and Conflict, 1960; Ideology and Power in Soviet Politics, 1962; (ed. and contrib.) Africa and the Communist World, 1963; (co-author) Political Power: USA/USSR, 1964; Alternative to Partition: For A Broader Conception of America's Role in Europe, 1965; Dilemmi Internazionali in Un'Epoca Tecnetronica, 1969; (ed. and contrib.) Dilemmas of Change in Soviet Politics, 1969; Between Two Ages: America's Role in the Technetronic Era, 1970; The Fragile Blossom: Crisis and Change in Japan, 1972; Power and Principle: Memoirs of the National Security Adviser 1977-1981, 1983; Game Plan: How to Conduct the U.S.-Soviet Contest, 1986; Promise or Peril: The Strategic Defense Initiative, 1986; The Grand Failure: The Birth and Death of Communism in the 20th Century, 1989; Out of Control: Global Turmoil on the Eve of the Twenty-First Century, 1993; The Grand Chessboard: American Primacy and Its Geostrategic Imperatives, 1997. **Address:** Center for Strategic and International Studies, 1800 K St., N. W, Washington, DC 20006, U.S.A.

BUBE, Richard H. American, b. 1927. **Genres:** Engineering, Physics, Theology/Religion, Autobiography/Memoirs. **Career:** Senior Scientist, RCA Laboratories, Princeton, NJ, 1948-62; Stanford University, California, Professor, 1962-92, Chairman of Materials Science and Engineering, 1975-86, Associate Chairman, 1980-81, Professor Emeritus, 1992-. Ed., Journal of the American Scientific Affiliation, 1969-83; Associate Ed., Annual Review of Materials Science, 1969-83; Member, Ed. Board, Solid-State Electronics, since 1975; Associate Ed., Materials Letters, 1981-89. Sr. Research Staff, RCA Labs., Princeton, New Jersey, 1948-62. **Publications:** A Textbook of Christian Doctrine, 1955; Photoconductivity of Solids, 1960; The Encounter Between Christianity and Science, 1968; The Human Quest: A New Look at Science and Christian Faith, 1971; Electronic Properties of Crystalline Solids, 1974; Electrons in Solids, 1981; Fundamentals of Solar Cells, 1983; Science and the Whole Person, 1985; Photoelectronic Properties of Semiconductors, 1992; Putting It All Together: Seven Patterns for Relating Science and Christian Faith, 1994; One Whole Life: Personal Memoirs, 1994; Photo-Induced Defects in Semiconductors, 1995; Photovoltaic Materials, 1998. **Address:** Dept of Materials Science and Engineering, Stanford University, Stanford, CA 94305-2205, U.S.A.

BUCCINI, Stefania. American, b. 1959. **Genres:** Literary criticism and history. **Career:** University of Wisconsin-Madison, professor of Italian, c. 1988-. **Publications:** Il Dilemma della Grande Atlantide: Le Americhe nella Letteratura Italiana del Sette Ottocento, 1990, trans. as The Americas in Italian Literature and Culture, 1700-1825, 1997. **Address:** Dept of French and Italian, 618 Van Hise Hall, University of Wisconsin-Madison, Madison, WI 53706, U.S.A. **Online address:** stefania@gmacc.wisc.edu

BUCHANAN, Anne L. American, b. 1960. **Genres:** Bibliography. **Career:** University of North Carolina at Wilmington, reference librarian at Randall Library, 1984-88; Purdue University, West Lafayette, IN, assistant management and economics librarian at Krannert Management and Economics Library and assistant professor of library science, 1990-96; King's College, Wilkes-Barre, PA, reference librarian at D. Leonard Corgan Library, 1996-. **Publications:** (compiler with J-P V.M. Herubel) The Doctor of Philosophy Degree: A Selective, Annotated Bibliography, 1995. Contributor to books. Contributor of articles and reviews to scholarly journals. **Address:** D. Leonard Corgan Library, King's College, Wilkes Barre, PA 18711, U.S.A. **Online address:** albuchan@kings.edu

BUCHANAN, Colin (Ogilvie). British, b. 1934. **Genres:** Theology/Religion. **Career:** Assistant curate, Cheadle Parish Church, Cheshire, 1961-64; librarian, 1964-69, registrar, 1969-74, director of studies, 1974-75, vice principal, 1975-78, and principal, 1979-85, St. John's College, Bramcote, Notts; Bishop

Suffragan of Aston, 1985-89; Diocese of Rochester, hon. Asst. Bishop, 1989-96; vicar, St. Marks, Gillingham, 1991-96; Bishop of Woolwich, 1996-2004. **Publications:** New Communion Service-Reasons for Dissent, 1966; A Guide to the New Communion Service, 1966; A Guide to 2nd Series Communion Service, 1968; (with P.S. Dawes) Proportional Representation in Church Elections, 1969, as Election by Preference, 1970; Evangelical Structures for the Seventies, 1969; (co-author) Growing into Union, 1970; (co-author) Growing into Union and Six Methodist Leaders, 1970; The Clarified Scheme Examined, 1971; Baptismal Discipline, 1972; The Job Prospects of the Anglican Clergy, 1972; Patterns of Sunday Worship, 1972; Recent Liturgical Revision in the Church of England, 1973, Supplement for 1976-78, 1978; A Case for Infant Baptism, 1973; (with J.D. Pawson) Infant Baptism under Cross-Examination, 1974; Liturgy for Infant Baptism: Series 3, 1975; What Did Cranmer Think He Was Doing?, 1976; Inflation, Deployment and the Job Prospects of the Clergy, 1976; Encountering Charismatic Worship, 1977; The End of the Offertory, 1978; One Baptism Once, 1978; Liturgy for Initia-tion: The Series 3 Services, 1979; Liturgy for Communion: The Revised Series 3 Service, 1979; (comp.) The Development of the New Eucharistic Prayers of the Church of England, 1979; The Role and Calling of an Evangelical Theological College in the 1980's, 1980; Leading Worship, 1981; The Kiss of Peace, 1982; (with D. Wheaton) Liturgy for the Sick, 1983; ACIC and Lima on Baptism and Eucharist, 1983; The Christian Conscience and Justice in Representation, 1983; Latest Liturgical Revision in the Church of England 1978-1984, 1984; Evangelical Anglicans and Liturgy, 1984; Adult Baptisms, 1985; Anglican Eucharistic Liturgy 1975-1985, 1985; Anglican Confirmation, 1986; Policies for Infant Baptism, 1987; Anglicans and Worship in Local Ecumenical Projects, 1987; Lambeth and Liturgy 1988, 1989; Revising the ASB, 1989; Children in Communion, 1990; Open to Others, 1992; Infant Baptism in Church of England, 1992; The Heart of Sunday Worship, 1992; The Renewal of Baptismal Vows, 1993; Infant Baptism and the Gospel, 1993; Cut the Connection, 1994; The Lord's Prayer in the Church of England, 1995; (co) Six Eucharistic Prayers as Proposed in 1996, 1996; (co) The New Initiation Rites, 1998; Eucharistic Consecration, 1998; Is the Church of England Biblical?, 1998; (co) The Eucharistic Prayer of Order One, 2000; Services of Wholeness and Healing, 2000; Infant Baptism in Common Worship, 2001; Mission in South East London, 2002. EDITOR: Prospects for Reconciliation, 1967; Modern Anglican Liturgies 1958-68, 1968; Evangelical Essays on Church and Sacraments, 1972; Unity on the Ground, 1972; Further Anglican Liturgies 1968-1975, 1975; (jt.) Anglican Worship Today, 1980; Anglo-Catholic Worship, 1983; Eucharistic Liturgies of Edward VI, 1983; Background Documents to Liturgical Revision 1547-1549, 1983; Essays on Eucharistic Sacrifice in the Early Church, 1984; Latest Anglican Liturgies 1976-1984, 1985; Liturgies of the Spanish and Portuguese Reformed Episcopal Churches, 1985; Nurturing Children in Communion: Essays from the Boston Consultation, 1985; Bishop Hugh-With Affection, 1987; Modern Anglican Ordination Rites, 1987; The Bishop in Liturgy, 1988; Michael Vasey-Liturgist and Friend, 1999; (jt. consulting) Common Worship Today, 2001; The Savoy Conference Revisited, 2002. **Address:** 21 The Drive, Alwoodley, Leeds LS17 7QB, England. **Online address:** cobtalk@onetel.com

BUCHANAN, Edna. American, b. 1949. **Genres:** Novels, Novellas/Short stories, Mystery/Crime/Suspense, Criminology/True Crime, Autobiography/Memoirs, Writing/Journalism. **Career:** Western Electric Co., Paterson, NJ, switchboard wirer; affiliated with Miami Beach Daily Sun, 1965-70; Miami Herald, Miami, general assignment and criminal court reporter, 1970-73, police beat reporter, 1973-88. Pulitzer Prize for general reporting, 1986. **Publications:** NONFICTION: Carr: Five Years of Rape and Murder, 1979; The Corpse Had a Familiar Face: Covering Miami, America's Hottest Beat, 1987; Never Let Them See You Cry, 1991. NOVELS: Nobody Lives Forever, 1990; Contents under Pressure, 1992; Miami, It's Murder, 1994; Suitable for Framing, 1995; Act of Betrayal, 1996; Margin of Error, 1997; Pulse, 1998; Garden of Evil, 1999; You Only Die Twice, 2001; The Ice Maiden, 2002. **Address:** c/o Michael Congdon, Don Congdon Associates, 156 Fifth Ave, Suite 625, New York, NY 10010, U.S.A.

BUCHANAN, James J. American, b. 1925. **Genres:** Classics. **Career:** Professor Emeritus of Classical Languages, Tulane University, New Orleans, Louisiana, since 1987 (Professor, 1964-87). Assistant Professor of Classics, Princeton University, New Jersey, 1953-60; Dean of Arts and Sciences College, and Chairman, Dept. of Classics, Southern Methodist University, Dal-las, Texas, 1960-64. **Publications:** (ed. and trans.) Boethius: The Consolation of Philosophy, 1957; Theorika: A Study of Monetary Distributions to the Athenian Citizenry during the Fifth and Fourth Centuries B. C., 1962; (trans. with Harold T. Davis) Zosimus: Historia Nova, 1967. **Address:** Canterbury Pl #501, 310 Fisk St, Pittsburgh, PA 15201, U.S.A.

BUCHANAN, Marie. See CURZON, Clare.

BUCHANAN, Paul G. American, b. 1954. **Genres:** Social sciences. **Career:** Naval Postgraduate School, Monterey, CA, assistant professor, 1985-87; University of Arizona, Tucson, assistant professor, 1987-95; New College, Sarasota, FL, assistant professor of social sciences, 1995-. U.S. Department of Defense, regional policy analyst, 1993-94. **Publications:** State, Labor, Capital: Democratizing Class Relations in the Southern Cone, 1995. Contributor of articles and reviews to periodicals. **Address:** Department of Political Studies, University of Auckland, Private Bag 92019, Auckland, New Zealand. **Online address:** pa.buchanan@auckland.ac.nz

BUCHANAN, Robert Angus. British, b. 1930. **Genres:** Archaeology/Antiquities, History. **Career:** University of Bath, professor of the history of technology, and director, Centre for the History of Technology, Science and Society, 1960-95, emeritus professor, 1995-. Annual Journal of the Bristol Industrial Archaeological Society, editor, 1968-74; Technology and Society, editor, 1971-74. OBE, 1993; Society for the History of Technology, Le-onardo da Vinci Medal, 1989. **Publications:** Technology and Social Progress, 1965; (with N. Cossons) Industrial Archaeology of the Bristol Region, 1969; (with N. Cossons) Industrial History in Pictures: Bristol, 1969; The Industrial Archaeology of Bath, 1969; Industrial Archaeology in Britain, 1972; (with G. Watkins) Industrial Archaeology of the Stationary Steam Engine, 1976; History and Industrial Civilisation, 1979; (with C.A. Buchanan) Industrial Archaeology of Central Southern England, 1980; (with M. Williams) Brunel's Bristol, 1982; The Engineers: A History of the Engineering Profession in Britain 1750-1914, 1989; The Power of the Machine, 1992; Brunel: The Life and Times of Isambard Kingdom Brunel, 2002. **Address:** Centre for the His-tory of Technology, Science & Society, University of Bath, Claverton Down, Bath BA2 7AY, England. **Online address:** hssraab@bath.ac.uk

BUCHEISTER, Patt. Also writes as Patt Parrish. American, b. 1942. **Genres:** Novels, Novellas/Short stories, Romance/Historical. **Career:** Clear Lake, Iowa, Chamber of Commerce, 1959-60. Former editor of the newslet-ter Brushstrokes. Artist. Romance Writer. **Publications:** AS PATT PARRISH: Make the Angel Weep, 1979 (in U.S. as His Fierce Angel, 1983); Summer of Silence, 1980 (in U.S. as A Gift to Cherish, 1985); Feather in the Wind, 1981; The Sheltered Haven, 1981; The Amberley Affair, 1983; Lifetime Af-fair, 1985; Escape the Past, 1985. AS PATT BUCHEISTER: Night and Day, 1986; The Dragon Slayer, 1987; Touch the Stars, 1987; Two Roads, 1988; The Luck o' the Irish, 1988; Flynn's Fate, 1988; Time Out, 1988; Near the Edge, 1989; Fire and Ice, 1989; Elusive Gypsy, 1989; Once Burned, Twice as Hot, 1990; The Rogue, 1990; Relentless, 1990; Tropical Heat, 1990; Tropical Storm, 1991; Hot Pursuit, 1991; Island Lover, 1992; Mischief and Magic, 1992; Struck by Lightning, 1992; Tilt at Windmills, 1992; Stroke by Stroke, 1993; Tame a Wildcat, 1993; Strange Bedfellows, 1994; Unpredict-able, 1994; Hot Southern Nights, 1995; Instant Family, 1995; Wild in the Night, 1995; Gypsy Dance, 1997; Below the Salt: A Gentlewoman's Com-monplace Book, 1999. Contributor of articles and stories to magazines. **Ad-dress:** PSC 817 Box 31, FPO, AE 09622-0031, U.S.A. **Online address:** raypatt@mindspring.com

BUCHHOLZ, Todd G. American, b. 1961. **Genres:** Business/Trade/Industry, Economics. **Career:** Harvard University, Department of Econom-ics, teaching fellow, 1984-87; Breed, Abbott, and Morgan, NYC, attorney, 1987-89; White House, Washington, DC, director of economic policy, 1989-93; G7 Group Inc., Washington, DC, president, 1993-96; Tiger Management, LLC, managing director, 1996-98; Victoria Capital, LLC, chairman, 1998-. Public Broadcasting Service, commentator on the television program Nightly Business Report; commentator for television network and cable programs; Worth magazine, columnist; Wall Street Journal, columnist. **Publications:** New Ideas from Dead Economists, 1989; From Here to Economy, 1995; Market Shock, 1999. Contributor to economic and law journals. **Address:** 214 Gibson Pt, Solana Beach, CA 92075-4200, U.S.A.

BUCHIGNANI, Walter. Canadian, b. 1965. **Genres:** Young adult non-fiction. **Career:** Journalist. The Gazette, Montreal, Canada, feature writer and copy editor, 1987-. **Publications:** Tell No One Who You Are: The Hid-den Childhood of Regine Miller (juvenile nonfiction), 1994. Contributor to periodicals. **Address:** The Gazette, 250 St. Antoine West, Montreal, QC, Canada H2Y 3R7. **Online address:** walterb@thegazette.southam.ca

BUCHMANN, Stephen L. American. **Genres:** Zoology. **Career:** Entomologist. Carl Hayden Bee Research Center, 1979-; University of Arizona, Tuscon, AZ, research associate in the Department of Ecology and Evolutionary Biology, then adjunct associate professor in the Department of Entomology; ArizonaSonora Desert Museum, research associate; American Museum of Natural History, research associate. **Publications:** (ed. with A. Matheson, with C. O'Toole) The Conservation of Bees, 1996; (with G.P.

Nabhan) The Forgotten Pollinators, 1996; Buzz Pollination in Angiosperms, The Ecology of Oil Flowers and Their Bees; (with J.H. Cane) Bees Assess Pollen Returns while Sonicating Solanum Flowers; (with J.G. Rozen) Nesting Biology and Immature Stages of the Bees Centris caesalpiniae and the Cleptoparasite ericrocis lata; (with J.O. Schmidt) Other Products of the Hive. **Address:** Carl Hayden Bee Research Center, 2000 East Allen Rd., Tucson, AZ 85719, U.S.A. **Online address:** buchmann@tuscon.ars.ag.gov

BUCHOLZ, Arden. American, b. 1936. **Genres:** History, Military/Defense/Arms control. **Career:** Amerikan Orta Okulu, Talas-Kayseri, Turkey, teacher of English, 1958-60; Latin School of Chicago, Chicago, IL, teacher of history, 1965-70; State University of New York College at Brockport, distinguished SUNY board of trustees teaching professor, 1970-, codirector of program at Brunel University, Uxbridge, England, 1987-88. **Publications:** Hans Delbruck and the German Military Establishment, 1985; Moltke, Schlieffen, and Prussian War Planning, 1991; Delbruck's Modern Military History, 1997; Moltke and the German Wars, 1864-1871, 2001. **Address:** Department of History, State University of New York College at Brockport, Brockport, NY 14420, U.S.A. **Online address:** abucholz@brockport.edu

BUCHWALD, Art. American, b. 1925. **Genres:** Humor/Satire. **Career:** Journalist: syndicated columnist, 1962-. Paris columnist, New York Herald Tribune, 1949-62. **Publications:** Paris after Dark, 1950; Art Buchwald's Paris, 1954; The Brave Coward, 1957; I Chose Caviar, 1957; More Caviar, 1958; A Gift from the Boys, 1958; Don't Forget to Write, 1960; Art Buchwald's Secret List to Paris, 1961; How Much Is That in Dollars, 1961; Is It Safe to Drink the Water, 1962; I Chose Capitol Punishment, 1963; And Then I Told the President, 1965; Son of the Great Society, 1966; Have I Ever Lied to You, 1968; The Establishment Is Alive and Well in Washington, 1969; Sheep on the Runway (play), 1970; Getting High in Government Circles, 1971; I Never Danced at the White House, 1973; Irving's Delight, 1975; Washington Is Leaking, 1976; Down the Seine and Up the Potomac: 25 Years of Art Buchwald's Best Humor, 1977; The Buchwald Stops Here, 1978; (with Ann Buchwald) Seems Like Yesterday, 1980; While Reagan Slept, 1983; You Can Fool All of the People All the Time, 1985; I Think I Don't Remember, 1987; Whose Rose Garden Is It Anyway?, 1989; Lighten Up, George, 1991; Leaving Home: A Memoir, 1993; I'll Always Have Paris, 1996; Stella in Heaven: Almost a Novel, 2000; We'll Laugh Again, 2002. **Address:** c/o The Washington Post, 1150 15th St NW, Washington, DC 20071, U.S.A.

BUCHWALTER, Andrew. American, b. 1949. **Genres:** Philosophy. **Career:** University of Massachusetts at Boston, lecturer in management and professional studies, 1980-81; Bentley College, Waltham, MA, adjunct professor of philosophy, 1985-86; University of North Florida, Jacksonville, assistant professor, 1987-94, associate professor, 1994-, director of Center for the Humanities, 1990-92, chairperson of Humanities Council, 1993-, chairperson of Department of Philosophy, 1999-. Yale University, visiting assistant professor, 1992; University of Bochum, Fulbright guest professor, 1992-93. **Publications:** (trans. and author of intro) J. Habermas, ed, Observations on "The Spiritual Situation of the Age": Contemporary German Perspectives, 1984; (ed. and author of intro) Culture and Democracy: Social and Ethical Issues in Public Support for the Arts and Humanities, 1992. Work represented in anthologies. Contributor of articles and reviews to philosophy and political studies journals. **Address:** Department of Philosophy, University of North Florida, 4567 St Johns Bluff Rd S, Jacksonville, FL 32224, U.S.A. **Online address:** abuchwal@unf.edu

BUCK, Craig. American, b. 1952. **Genres:** Self help, Adult non-fiction. **Career:** Writer. **Publications:** WITH S. FORWARD: Betrayal of Innocence: Incest and Its Devastation, 1979; Toxic Parents: Overcoming Their Hurtful Legacy and Reclaiming Your Life, 1989; Obsessive Love: When Passion Holds You Prisoner, 1991; Money Demons: Keep Them from Sabotaging Your Relationships and Your Life, 1994. Author of pieces for television and film.

BUCK, Detlev. German, b. 1962. **Genres:** Plays/Screenplays. **Career:** Film director, actor, producer, cinematographer and writer. **Publications:** SCREENPLAYS: Eist die Arbeit und Dann?, 1984; Hopnick, 1990; Karnigels, 1991; Kleine Haie, 1992; Wir Koennen Auch Anders, 1993; (As D.W. Buck) Maennerpension, 1996; Liebe Deine Daechste!, 1998; Sonnenalle, 1999. **Address:** c/o Sabine Lutter, Above the Line GmbH, Oranienburger Strasse 5, 10178 Berlin, Germany.

BUCK, Harry M. American, b. 1921. **Genres:** Theology/Religion. **Career:** Professor of Religion Studies, Wilson College, Chambersburg, Pa., since 1959. Ed., ANIMA: An Experiential Journal. Assistant Professor of Biblical History, Literature and Interpretation, Wellesley College, Massachusetts, 1951-59; Executive Director, American Academy of Religion, 1958-72; Managing Ed., Journal of the American Academy of Religion, 1961-73. **Publications:** Johannine Lessons in the Greek Gospel Lectionary, 1958; People of the Lord: The History, Scripture and Faith of Ancient Israel, 1966; Spiritual Discipline in Hinduism, Buddhism, and the West, 1981. EDITOR: (with G. Yocum) Structural Approaches to South India Studies, 1974; (with L. Hammann) Religious Traditions and the Limits of Tolerance, 1988. **Address:** 1053 Wilson Ave, Chambersburg, PA 17201, U.S.A.

BUCK, Rinker. American, b. 1950. **Genres:** Air/Space topics, Autobiography/Memoirs. **Career:** Berkshire Eagle, MA, reporter; worked for New York, Life, and Adweek. **Publications:** Flight of Passage, 1997; If We Had Wings, 2001; First Job, 2002. Contributor to magazines and newspapers.

BUCK, Susan J. American, b. 1947. **Genres:** Law, Politics/Government, Public/Social administration. **Career:** Virginia Institute of Marine Science, Gloucester, laboratory specialist, 1976-79; Northern Arizona University, Flagstaff, assistant professor, 1984-88; University of North Carolina at Greensboro, assistant professor, 1988-93, associate professor of political science, 1993-. **Publications:** Understanding Environmental Administration and Law, 1990, 2nd ed., 1996; Public Administration: Concepts in Practice, 1993; Global Commons, 1998. **Address:** Department of Political Science, University of North Carolina at Greensboro, Greensboro, NC 27402, U.S.A.

BUCKELEW, Albert R., Jr. American, b. 1942. **Genres:** Zoology. **Career:** Bethany College, Bethany, WV, professor of biology and department head, c. 1969-. West Virginia Nongame Wildlife Advisory Council, member. **Publications:** Endangered and Threatened Species in West Virginia, 1990; The West Virginia Breeding Bird Atlas, 1994. **Address:** Department of Biology, Bethany College, Bethany, WV 26032, U.S.A.

BUCKLEY, Cornelius M(ichael). American, b. 1925. **Genres:** History, Theology/Religion, Translations. **Career:** Entered Jesuits, and 1950, in California; ordained Roman Catholic priest, 1962, in France; St. Ignatius College Preparatory, San Francisco, CA, rector and president, 1970-73; University of San Francisco, San Francisco, trustee, 1970-83, professor of history, 1973-. Trustee of Santa Clara University, 1971-78, St. Patrick's College, 1972-74, and Fellowship of Catholic Scholars, 1992-. Chaplain at Thomas More Society, Hastings College of Law, University of California, San Francisco, and San Francisco City Jail. **Publications:** A Frenchman, a Chaplain, a Rebel, 1980; Your Word, O Lord, 1987; Nicolas Point, S.J.: His Life and Northwest Indian Chronicles, 1989; When Jesuits Were Giants, 1999. TRANSLATOR: S. Decloux, The Ignatian Way, 1991; A. Ravier, A Do-It-at-Home Retreat, 1991; C. de Dalmases, Francis Borgia, 1991; (ed. and author of preface) J. Ignacio Tellechea Idigoras, Ignatius of Loyola: The Pilgrim Saint, 1993; A. Ravier, Like a Child, 1997. **Address:** Thomas Aquinas College, 10000 N Ojai Rd, Santa Paula, CA 93060, U.S.A.

BUCKLEY, Francis Joseph. American, b. 1928. **Genres:** Theology/Religion, Psychology, Sociology. **Career:** Professor of Dogmatic and Pastoral Theology, 1972-, University of San Francisco, California (Instructor, 1960-63; Assistant Professor, 1963-68; Chairman, Dept. of Theology, 1971-73, 1978-79; 1988-92; Director, Dept. of Religious Education and Pastoral Ministries, 1974-75, 1979-82, 1986-87, 1992-96). President, College Theology Society of the U.S. and Canada, 1972-74. **Publications:** Christ and the Church According to Gregory of Elvira, 1964; (with M. de la Cruz Aymes) On Our Way (series), 1966-70; (with M. de la Cruz Aymes) New Life (series), 1971-74; (with J. Hofinger) The Good News and Its Proclamation, 1968; (ed. with C. Miller) Faith and Life (series), 1971-72; Children and God: Communion, Confession, Confirmation, 1970, rev. ed., 1973; "I Confess"-The Sacrament of Penance Today, 1972; (with M. de la Cruz Aymes) Jesus Forgives, 1974; (with M. de la Cruz Aymes) Lord of Life (series), 1978-80; Reconciling, 1981; (with M. de la Cruz Aymes) We Share Forgiveness, 1981; (with M. de la Cruz Aymes) We Share Reconciliation, 1981; (with M. de la Cruz Aymes and T.H. Groome) God with Us (series), 1982-85; (with M. de la Cruz Aymes) Fe y Cultura, 1985; Come Worship with Us, 1987; (with D.B. Sharp) Deepening Christian Life: Integrating Faith and Maturity, 1987; (with M. de la Cruz Aymes) Familia de Dios (series), 1990-96; Team Teaching: What, Why, How, 1999; Growing in the Church: From Birth to Death, 2000; The Church in Dialogue: Culture and Tradition, 2000. **Address:** University of San Francisco, San Francisco, CA 94117, U.S.A. **Online address:** buckleyf@usfca.edu

BUCKLEY, Gail Lumet. American, b. 1937. **Genres:** Autobiography/Memoirs. **Career:** Marie-Claire, Paris, France, journalist, 1959-63; Life, New York City, journalist, 1959-62, reporter, 1962-63; National Scholarship

Service and Fund for Negro Students, NYC, student counselor, 1961-62; writer. Democratic National Convention, delegate-at-large for Edward M. Kennedy, 1980. Volunteer for president John F. Kennedy, 1960. **Publications:** The Hornes: An American Family, 1986; American Patriots, 2001. Contributor to periodicals. **Address:** c/o Lynn Nesbit, Janklow & Nesbit Associates, 445 Park Ave Fl 13, New York, NY 10022, U.S.A.

BUCKLEY, John (F.). American, b. 1961. **Genres:** Law. **Career:** National Legal Research Group, Charlottesville, VA, senior attorney, 1987-. **Publications:** (with M. Lindsay) Defense of Equal Employment Claims, 1995; State by State Guide to Human Resources Law, 1995. Author of several jurisprudence articles. **Address:** 2421 Ivy Rd., Charlottesville, VA 22901, U.S.A.

BUCKLEY, Mary (Elizabeth Anne). (born England), b. 1951. **Genres:** Adult non-fiction. **Career:** Social scientist and author. Edinburgh University, Edinburgh, Scotland, lecturer, 1983-91, senior lecturer, 1991-94, reader in politics, 1994-2000; University of London, London, England, professor of politics, 2000-02. Visiting fellow at the Centre for Research in the Arts, Social Sciences, and Humanities, Cambridge University, 2004. **Publications:** (editor) Soviet Social Scientists Talking: An Official Debate about Women, 1986; (editor, with Malcom Anderson) Women, Equality, and Europe, 1988; Women and Ideology in the Soviet Union, 1989; (editor) Perestroika and Soviet Women, 1992; Redefining Russian Society and Polity, 1993; (editor) Post-Soviet Women: From the Baltic to Central Asia, 1997; (Coeditor, with Sally N. Cummings) Kosovo: Perceptions of War and Its Aftermath, 2001; (editor, with Rick Fawn) Global Responses to Terrorism: 9/11, the War in Afghanistan, and Beyond, 2003. Also contributor to numerous academic journals. **Address:** c/o Author Mail, Routledge Press, 11 New Fetter Lane, London EC4P 4EE, England.

BUCKLEY, Thomas. American, b. 1932. **Genres:** History, Biography. **Career:** University of Tulsa, Oklahoma, Jay P. Walker Research Professor of American History, 1981- (Associate Dean of the Graduate School, 1995-2000; Chairman, Dept. of History, 1971-81). Member of faculty, University of South Dakota, Vermillion, 1960-69, and Indiana University, Bloomington, 1969-71. **Publications:** The United States and the Washington Conference, 1921-1922, 1970; Challenge Was My Master, 1979; Walter H. Helmerich, Independent Oilman, 1980; (with E. Strong) American Foreign and National Security Policies 1914-1945, 1987. **Address:** Dept. of History, University of Tulsa, 600 S College Ave, Tulsa, OK 74104, U.S.A.

BUCKLEY, William F(rank), Jr. American, b. 1925. **Genres:** Mystery/Crime/Suspense, Politics/Government, Essays. **Career:** National Review, NYC, Founder, Ed., 1955-90, Editor-at-Large, 1991-. Syndicated Columnist, On the Right, 1962-. Host, weekly TV show, Firing Line, 1966-99. Member, USIA Advisory Commission, 1969-72; Public Member, U.S. Delegation to 28th UN General Assembly, 1973. **Publications:** God and Man at Yale, 1951; (co-author) McCarthy and His Enemies, 1954; Up from Liberalism, 1959; Rumbles Left and Right, 1963; The Unmaking of a Mayor, 1966; The Jeweler's Eye, 1968; The Governor Listeth, 1970; Cruising Speed, 1971; Inveighing We Will Go, 1972; Four Reforms, 1973; United Nations Journal, 1974; Execution Eve, 1975; Airborne, 1976; A Hymnal, 1978; Atlantic High, 1982; Overdrive, 1983; Right Reason, 1985; Racing through Paradise, 1987; On the Firing Line: The Public Life of Our Public Figures, 1989; Stained Glass, 1978, (play), 1989; Gratitude: Reflections on What We Owe Our Country, 1990; Windfall, 1992; In Search of Anti-Semitism, 1992; Happy Days Were Here Again: Reflections of a Libertarian Journalist, 1993; Buckley: The Right Word, 1996; Nearer My God, 1997; The Lexicon, 1998; Let Us Talk of Many Things: The Collected Speeches, 2000; The Fall of the Berlin Wall, 2004; Miles Gone By: A Literary Autobiography, 2004. NOVELS: Saving the Queen, 1976; Who's On First, 1980; Marco Polo, If You Can, 1982; The Story of Henri Tod, 1984; See You Later, Alligator, 1985; The Temptation of Wilfred Malachey, 1985; High Jinx, 1986; Mongoose, R.I.P., 1988; Tucker's Last Stand, 1991; A Very Private Plot, 1994; The Blackford Oakes Reader, 1995; Brothers No More, 1995; The Redhunter, 1999; Spytime: The Undoing of James Jesus Angleton, 2000; Elvis in the Morning, 2001; Nuremberg: the Reckoning, 2002; Getting It Right, 2002. EDITOR: The Committee and Its Critics, 1962; Odyssey of a Friend, 1970; Did You Ever See a Dream Walking?: American Conservative Thought in the 20th Century, 1970. **Address:** c/o National Review, 215 Lexington 4th Fl, New York, NY 10016, U.S.A.

BUCKNALL, Barbara Jane. Canadian (born England), b. 1933. **Genres:** Children's fiction, Poetry, Literary criticism and history. **Career:** Instructor, 1962-66, and Assistant Professor, 1966-69, Dept. of French, University of Illinois, Champaign-Urbana; Associate Professor, Dept. of French, Italian and Spanish, Brock University, 1971-94 (Assistant Professor, 1969-71). **Publications:** The Religion of Art in Proust, 1969; Ursula K. Le Guin, 1981; (ed.) Critical Essays on Marcel Proust, 1987; Marcel Proust Revisited, 1992; The Witch Poems, 1995; Barbara Bucknall's Fairy Tales for the Young at Heart, 2000, vol. 2, 2000, vol. 3, 2002. **Address:** 160 Highland Ave, St. Catharines, ON, Canada L2R 4J6.

BUCKNER, Rheuben. *See* **MCCOY, Max.**

BUCKSER, Andrew (S.). American, b. 1964. **Genres:** Anthropology/Ethnology. **Career:** Research and Planning Inc., Cambridge, MA, researcher, 1986; teacher of English, physics, and American history at a high school in Whitinsville, MA, 1987; Hartwick College, Oneonta, NY, assistant professor of anthropology, 1993-95; Purdue University, West Lafayette, IN, assistant professor of anthropology, 1995-. Conducted anthropological field work in St. Pierre and Miquelon, 1988, and in Denmark, 1989-97. **Publications:** Communities of Faith: Sectarianism, Identity, and Social Change on a Danish Island, 1996. Contributor to periodicals. **Address:** Department of Sociology and Anthropology, Purdue University, West Lafayette, IN 47907, U.S.A. **Online address:** bucksera@sri.soc.purdue.edu

BUCUVALAS, Tina. American, b. 1951. **Genres:** Mythology/Folklore, Local history/Rural topics. **Career:** Historical Museum of Southern Florida, Miami, curator, 1986-91; freelance folklorist in Maine, Florida, and Washington, DC, 1991-. **Publications:** (with S. Poyser) Introduction to Arkansas Folklore: A Teacher-Student Guide, 1986; Native American Foodways and Recipes: Hopi, Navajo, Hualapai, Laguna, 1986; South Florida Folk Arts: A Teacher Guide, 1988; (with P. Bulger and S. Kennedy) South Florida Folklife, 1994. Author of booklets. Contributor to periodicals. **Address:** Historical Resources Div., 500 S. Bronough St., Tallahassee, FL 32399-6504, U.S.A.

BUDBILL, David. American, b. 1940. **Genres:** Novels, Novellas/Short stories, Children's fiction, Plays/Screenplays, Poetry, Music. **Career:** Full-time writer. **Publications:** PLAYS: Mannequins Demise, 1964; Thingy World!, 1990; Judevine, 1992; Little Acts of Kindness, 1993; Fleeting Animal (opera libretto), 2001. SHORT STORIES: Snowshoe Trek to Otter River, 1976; (ed.) Rowland Robinson, Danvis Tales, 1995. POETRY: Barking Dog, 1968; The Chain Saw Dance, 1977; Pulp Cutter's Nativity, 1981; From Down to the Village, 1981; Why I Came to Judevine, 1987; Judevine, 1991; Moment to Moment, 1999; While We Still Have Feet, 2005. OTHER: Christmas Tree Farm (for children), 1974; The Bones on Black Spruce Mountain (novel), 1978. **Address:** 4592 E Hill Rd, Wolcott, VT 05680, U.S.A. **Online address:** budbill@sover.net

BUDD, Holly. *See* **JUDD, Alan.**

BUDDE, Michael L(eo). American, b. 1958. **Genres:** Theology/Religion. **Career:** Auburn University, Auburn, AL, assistant professor of political science, 1990-93; DePaul University, Chicago, IL, associate professor of political science, 1993-. **Publications:** The Two Churches: Catholicism and Capitalism in the World System, 1992; The (Magic) Kingdom of God: Christianity and Global Culture Industries, 1997; (ed. with R.W. Brimlow) Paths That Lead to Life: The Church as Counterculture, in press. Contributor to journals. **Address:** Department of Political Science, DePaul University, 2320 North Kenmore, Chicago, IL 60614, U.S.A.

BUDDEN, Julian (Medforth). British, b. 1924. **Genres:** Music. **Career:** Writer. Music library clerk, 1951-55, music information assistant, 1955-56, music producer, 1956-71, chief producer of opera, 1971-76, and external services music organizer, 1976-83, all for the British Broadcasting Corporation (BBC), England. Member: Royal Musical Association, Critics' Circle. **Publications:** The Operas of Verdi, Vol. 1: From Oberto to Rigoletto, 1973, Vol. 2: From Il Trovatore to Il Forza del Destino, 1979, Vol. 3: From Don Carlos to Falstaff, 1981; Verdi, 1985; Puccini, 2002. **Address:** Via Fratelli Bandiera, 9, 50137 Florence, Italy.

BUDDENSIEG, Tilmann. German, b. 1928. **Genres:** Architecture, Art/Art history, Business/Trade/Industry, International relations/Current affairs. **Career:** Art History Institute, Freie University, Berlin, Germany, assistant, 1962-65, professor, beginning in 1968; affiliated with Freie University, 1965-78; Rheinische FriedrichWilhelms-University, Bonn, Germany, professor, beginning in 1978. Visiting professor at Harvard University, 1967, Warburg Institute, 1969, Stanford University, 1971, University of California at Berkeley, 1971, Hebrew University of Jerusalem, 1984, and Columbia University, 1985; Slade Professor of Fine Arts, Cambridge, 1974; Humboldt University, Berlin, honorary professor, 1995-. Chair of advisory board of art of KPM, Berlin; member of board "Villa Stuck" in Munich; Adviser Senator for city development in Berlin; Einstein Forum, Potsdam, board member. **Publications:** (with H. Rogge and others) Industriekultur: Peter Behrens und die AEG, 1979, in English as Industriekultur: Peter Behrens and the AEG, 1907-14, 1984; Die Nuetzlichen Kuenste: Gestaltende Technik und Bildende Kunst seit der Industriellen Revolution, 1981; Keramik in der Weimarer Republik, 1919-1933 (catalog), 1985; (with others) Berlin, 1900-1933: Architecture and Design (catalog), 1987; Ein Mann vieler Eigenschaften: Walther Rathenau und die Kultur der Moderne, 1990; Berliner Labyrinth, Berlin, 1993, rev. ed., 1999. **Address:** Kunstgeschichtliches Seminar, Humboldt Universitaet Berlin, Unter den Linden 6, 10099 Berlin, Germany.

BUDERI, Robert. American, b. 1954. **Genres:** Technology. **Career:** Daily Republic, Fairfield, CA, reporter of police news, 1977-79; contributor to magazines, 1982-90; Business Week, NYC, technology editor, 1990-92; Upside, San Mateo, CA, columnist, 1998-2000; Technology Review, editor at large, 2000-02, editor in chief, 2002-. Consultant: Science at War, a documentary television series, British Broadcasting Corp.; History Channel. **Publications:** The Invention That Changed the World, 1996; Engines of Tomorrow, 2000. **Address:** Technology Review, 1 Main St 7th Fl, Cambridge, MA 02142, U.S.A. **Online address:** Bob.Buderi@technologyreview.com

BUDGE, Ian. British, b. 1936. **Genres:** Philosophy, Politics/Government, Social sciences, Speech/Rhetoric. **Career:** Professor, University of Essex, Colchester, 1976- (on faculty, 1966-). Assistant Lecturer, University of Edinburgh, 1962-64; Assistant Lecturer, 1963-64, and Lecturer, 1964-66, University of Strathclyde, Glasgow. **Publications:** (with D.W. Urwin) Scottish Political Behaviour, 1966; Agreement and the Stability of Democracy, 1970; (with C. O'Leary) Belfast: Approach to Crisis: A Study of Belfast Politics 1613-1970, 1973; (with D. Farlie) Party Identification and Beyond, 1976; Voting and Party Competition, 1977; Explaining and Predicting Elections, 1983; Ideology, Strategy and Party Movement: Election Programmes in 19 Democracies, 1987; (with H.E. Keman) Parties and Democracy: Coalition Formation and Government Functioning in 20 Countries, 1990; The New Challenge of Direct Democracy, 1996. WITH OTHERS: Political Stratification and the Functioning of Democracy, 1972; The New British Political System, 1983, rev. ed., 1993; Party Policy and Government Coalitions, 1992; Developing Democracy, 1994; Parties, Policies and Democracy, 1994; The Politics of the New Europe: Atlantic to Urals, 1997; The New British Politics, 1998; Party Government in 48 Democracies 1945-1998, 2000; Mapping Policy Preferences: Estimates for Parties, Electors, and Governments, 1945-1998, 2000.

BUDIANSKY, Stephen (Philip). American, b. 1957. **Genres:** Environmental sciences/Ecology, Animals/Pets, History. **Career:** American Chemical Society, Washington, DC, writer, 1979-82; Nature, Washington, DC, Washington editor, 1982-85; U.S. Congress, Office of Technology Assessment, Washington, DC, Congressional fellow, 1985-86; U.S. News & World Report, Washington, DC, senior writer, 1986-. **Publications:** The Covenant of the Wild, 1992; Nature's Keepers, 1995; The Nature of Horses, 1997; If a Lion Could Talk, 1998; The World According to Horses, 2000; Battle of Wits, 2000; The Truth About Dogs, 2000; The Character of Cats, 2002.

BUDNITZ, Judy. American, b. 1973. **Genres:** Novellas/Short stories. **Career:** Village Voice, NYC, cartoonist, 1996-; freelance writer. Residency, Fine Arts Work Center, Provincetown, NJ. **Publications:** Flying Leap (short stories), 1998. Contributor of short stories to literary magazines. **Address:** 58 West Eight St., Apt. 4F, New York, NY 10011, U.S.A.

BUDRYS, Algis. American (born Lithuania), b. 1931. **Genres:** Science fiction/Fantasy. **Career:** Assistant Ed., Gnome Press, NYC, 1952, and Galaxy mag., NYC, 1953; on staff, Royal Publs., NYC, 1958-61; Ed.-in-Chief, Regency Books, Evanston, Illinois, 1961-63; Editorial Director, Playboy Press, Chicago, 1963-65; magazine manager, Woodall Publishers, 1973-74; President, Unifont Co., Evanston, since 1974. **Publications:** False Night, 1953, as Some Will Not Die, 1961; Man of Earth, 1955; Who?, 1958; The Falling Torch, 1959, 1990; The Unexpected Dimension, 1960; Rogue Moon, 1960; The Furious Future, 1964; The Iron Thorn, 1968; Michaelmas, 1977; Blood and Burning, 1978; Benchmarks: Galaxy Bookshelf, 1985; (ed.) L. Ron Hubbard Presents Writers of the Future, 19 vols., 1986-2002; Hard Landing, 1993. **Address:** 824 Seward St, Evanston, IL 60202, U.S.A.

BUECHNER, (Carl) Frederick. American, b. 1926. **Genres:** Novels, Theology/Religion, Autobiography/Memoirs. **Career:** Clergyman, English Master, Lawrenceville School, NJ, 1948-53; Head of Employment Clinic, East Harlem Protestant Parish, NYC, 1954-58; Chairman of Religion Dept.,

1958-67, and School Minister, Phillips Exeter Academy, Exeter, NH. **Publications:** A Long Day's Dying, 1950; The Season's Difference, 1952; The Return of Ansel Gibbs, 1958; The Final Beast, 1965; The Magnificent Defeat (meditations), 1966; The Hungering Dark (meditations), 1969; The Entrance to Porlock, 1970; The Alphabet of Grace (autobiography), 1970; Lion Country, 1971; Open Heart, 1972; Wishful Thinking: A Theological ABC, 1973; Love Feast, 1974; The Faces of Jesus, 1974; Telling the Truth, 1977; Treasure Hunt, 1977; Peculiar Treasures: A Biblical Who's Who, 1979; The Book of Bebb, 1979; Godric, 1980; The Sacred Journey (autobiography), 1982; Now and Then (autobiography), 1983; A Room Called Remember (essays and sermons), 1984; Brendan, 1987; Whistling in the Dark, 1988; The Wizard's Tide, 1990; Telling Secrets (autobiography), 1991; The Clown in the Belfry: Writings on Faith and Fiction, 1992; The Son of Laughter, 1993; Listening to Your Life, 1996; The Longing for Home: Recollections and Reflections, 1996; On the Road with the Archangel (novel), 1997; The Storm (novel), 1998; The Eyes of the Heart (memoir), 1999; Speak What We Feel, 2001; Beyond Words, 2004. **Address:** 3572 State Rte 315, Pawlet, VT 05761, U.S.A.

BUEHLER, Evelyn Judy. American, b. 1953. **Genres:** Novellas/Short stories, Poetry, Photography. **Career:** Poet, writer, and photographer. **Publications:** Tales of Summer (poems), 1998. Contributor of poetry, short stories, and phonographs to anthologies. **Address:** 5658 S Normal Blvd, Chicago, IL 60621-2966, U.S.A. **Online address:** Evelyn_Judy_Buehler@yahoo.com

BUEHNER, Caralyn M. American, b. 1963. **Genres:** Picture/board books. **Career:** Writer. **Publications:** PICTURE BOOKS: The Escape of Marvin the Ape, 1992; A Job for Wittilda, 1993; It's a Spoon, Not a Shovel, 1995; Fanny's Dream, 1996; I Did It, I'm Sorry, 1998; I Want to Say I Love You, 2002; Snowmen at Night, 2002; Superdog, the Heart of a Hero, 2004. **Address:** 2646 Alden St, Salt Lake City, UT 84106, U.S.A. **Online address:** m.buehner@comcast.net

BUELER, William Merwin. Also writes as William Merwin. American, b. 1934. **Genres:** Novels, History, International relations/Current affairs, Politics/Government, Travel/Exploration. **Career:** Defense Language Institute, Monterey, California, retired professor of Chinese. **Publications:** Mountains of the World: A Handbook for Climbers and Hikers, 1970; U.S. China Policy and the Problem of Taiwan, 1971; (comp.-trans.) Chinese Sayings, 1972; Roof of the Rockies: A History of Colorado Mountaineering, 1974, 3rd ed., 2000; The Teton Controversy: Who Climbed the Grand?, 1980; (as William Merwin) The Restructuring of America, 1991; An Agenda for Sustainability, 1997; Tablet of the Gods (novel), 2000.

BUELL, Frederick (Henderson). American, b. 1942. **Genres:** Poetry, Literary criticism and history. **Career:** Professor of English, Queens College, Flushing, New York, since 1980 (Instructor, 1971-72; Assistant Professor, 1972-74; Associate Professor, 1974-79). **Publications:** Theseus and Other Poems, 1971; W. H. Auden as a Social Poet, 1973; Full Summer, 1979; National Culture and the New Global System, 1994. **Address:** Dept. of English, Queens College, Flushing, NY 11367, U.S.A.

BUELL, Victor P. American, b. 1914. **Genres:** Administration/Management, Advertising/Public relations, Marketing. **Career:** Professor Emeritus of Marketing, School of Management, University of Massachusetts, Amherst, since 1983 (Professor, 1970-83). Marketing Consultant, McKinsey & Co., 1951-55; Manager, Marketing Division, Hoover Co., 1955-59; Vice-President, and Director of Marketing, Archer Daniels Midland Co., 1959-64; Corporate Vice-President, Marketing, American Standard Inc., 1964-70. **Publications:** Marketing Management in Action, 1966; (co-ed.) Handbook of Modern Marketing, 1970, 2nd ed, 1986; Changing Patterns in Advertising Decision-making and Control, 1973; British Approach to Improving Advertising Standards and Practices, 1977; Organizing for Marketing/Advertising Success in a Changing Business Environment, 1982; Marketing Management: A Strategic Planning Approach, 1984; (with others) Marketing Definitions: A Glossary of Marketing Terms, 1989, rev. ed., 1995. **Address:** 1Fleet Landing Blvd #611-612, Atlantic Beach, FL 32233-4599, U.S.A.

BUETTNER, Dan. American, b. 1960. **Genres:** Travel/Exploration. **Career:** Explorer, journalist, and photographer. AfricaTrek (bicycle tour), leader, 1992-93; MayaQuest (series of interactive expeditions), leader, 1995, 1996, 1997; participant in other record-setting bicycle expeditions, including Americastrek, 1986-87, and Sovietrek, 1990; guest on radio and television programs; holder of 3 Guinness World Records in cycling. **Publications:** (and photographer) Sovietrek: A Journey by Bicycle across Russia, 1994; MayaQuest: The Interactive Expedition, 1996; AfricaTrek, 1996; Inside

Grand Bahama; AfricaQuest, 1998; AsiaQuest, 1999. **Address:** Classroom Connect, 8000 Marina 4th Blvd., Brisbane, CA 94005, U.S.A. **Online address:** dan@classroom.com

BUFFETT, Jimmy. American, b. 1946. **Genres:** Young adult fiction, Songs/ Lyrics and libretti, Autobiography/Memoirs. **Career:** Songwriter and performer, 1960s-; Billboard Publications, Nashville, TN, writer, 1971-73; writer. **Publications:** (with S.J. Buffett) The Jolly Mon (juvenile), 1988; Tales from Margaritaville: Fictional Facts and Factual Fictions (short story and autobiographical sketch collection), 1989; (with S.J. Buffett) Trouble Dolls (juvenile), 1991; Where Is Joe Merchant? A Novel Tale (novel), 1992; A Pirate Looks at Fifty (autobiography), 1998. Contributor to oeriodicals. RECORD ALBUMS, LYRICS AND MUSIC: Down to Earth, 1972; A White Sport Coat and a Pink Crustacean, 1973; Living and Dying in 3/4 Time, 1974; A-1-A, 1974; Rancho Deluxe (soundtrack), 1975; High Cumberland Jamboree, Barnaby, 1976; Havana Daydreamin', 1976; Changes in Latitudes, Changes in Attitudes, 1977; Son of a Son of a Sailor, 1978, Jimmy Buffett Live, You Had to Be There, 1978; Volcano, 1979; Somewhere over China, 1981; Coconut Telegraph, 1981; One Particular Harbor, 1983; Riddles in the Sand, 1984; Last Mango in Paris, 1985; Songs You Know by Heart: Jimmy Buffett's Greatest Hits, 1986; Floridays, 1986; Hot Water, 1988; Off to See the Lizard, 1989; Boats, Beaches, Bars, and Ballads, 1992; Before the Beach (reissue of Down to Earth and High Cumberland Jamboree), 1993. **Address:** c/o Cindy Thompson, Margaritaville Inc, 424-A Fleming St, Key West, FL 33040, U.S.A.

BUFFIE, Margaret. Canadian, b. 1945. **Genres:** Children's fiction, Young adult fiction. **Career:** Illustrator, Hudson's Bay Co., Winnipeg, Manitoba, 1968-70; painting instructor, Winnipeg Art Gallery, 1974-75; high school art teacher, River East School Division, Winnipeg, 1976-77; freelance illustrator and painter, 1977-84. Writer, 1984-. **Publications:** CHILDREN'S FICTION: Who Is Frances Rain?, 1987, in US as The Haunting of Frances Rain, 1989; The Guardian Circle, 1989, in US as The Warnings, 1991; My Mother's Ghost, 1992, in US as Someone Else's Ghost, 1994; The Dark Garden, 1995; Angels Turn Their Backs, 1998; The Watcher, 2000; The Seeker, 2002; The Finder, 2004.

BUFORD, Bill. American, b. 1954. **Genres:** Travel/Exploration, Literary criticism and history, Biography, Social commentary. **Career:** Granta magazine, editor, 1979-95; chair of Granta Publications; New Yorker, Literary and fiction editor, 1995-. **Publications:** NONFICTION: Among the Thugs: 1991; (ed.) Granta Book of Travel, 1992; Granta Book of Reportage, 1993; Granta Book of the Family, 1995. EDITOR OF GRANTA MAGAZINE ISSUES: The End of the English Novel, 1981; Best of Young British Novelists, 1983; Dirty Realism, 1983; Greetings from Prague, 1984; Travel Writing, 1984; Richard Ford-The Womanizer, 1992; Biography, 1993; Krauts!, 1993; The Best of Young British Novelists II, 1993. **Address:** c/o The New Yorker, 4 Times Square, New York, NY 10036-7440, U.S.A.

BUGAJSKI, Janusz. American (born United Kingdom), b. 1954. **Genres:** International relations/Current affairs. **Career:** BBC-TV, London, England, consultant, 1981-83; Radio Free Europe, Munich, Germany, senior research analyst, 1984-85; Center for Strategic and International Studies, Washington, DC, director of East European studies, 1986-. American University, adjunct lecturer, 1991; lecturer at Smithsonian Institution, Foreign Service Institute, Woodrow Wilson Center, and U.S. universities; consultant to International Republican Institute, International Research and Exchanges Board, Institute for Democracy in Eastern Europe, and U.S. Department of Defense. **Publications:** Czechoslovakia: Charter 77's Decade of Dissent, 1987; (with M. Pollack) East European Fault Lines, 1989; Sandinista Communism and Rural Nicaragua, 1990; Fourth World Conflicts: Communism and Rural Societies, 1991; Nations in Turmoil: Conflict and Cooperation in Eastern Europe, 1993, rev. ed., 1995; Ethnic Politics in Eastern Europe, 1994; Political Parties of Eastern Europe: A Guide to Politics in the Post-Communist Era, 2002; (ed.) Toward an Understanding of Russia, 2002; Cold Peace: Russia's New Imperialism, 2004. Contributor to periodicals and encyclopedias. **Address:** Center for Strategic and International Studies, 1800 K St NW, Washington, DC 20006, U.S.A. **Online address:** jbugajsk@csis.org

BUGEJA, Michael J. American. **Genres:** Poetry, Education, Literary criticism and history. **Career:** United Press International, Sioux Falls, SD, state editor, 1975-79; Oklahoma State University, Stillwater, associate professor of journalism, 1979-86; Ohio University, Athens, professor of journalism, 1986-. **Publications:** What We Do for Music (poetry chapbook), 1990; The Visionary, 1990; Platonic Love, 1991; Culture's Sleeping Beauty: Essays on Poetry, Prejudice, and Belief, 1992; After Oz, 1993; Flight from Valhalla, 1993; The Art & Craft of Poetry, 1994; Academic Socialism: Merit and

Morale in Higher Education, 1994; Living Ethics, 1995; Poet's Guide, 1995; Little Dragons, 1995; Visionary, 1995; Talk, 1997; Family Values, 1997; Guide to Writing Magazine Nonfiction, 1998; Millennium's End, 1999; Living without Fear: Understanding Cancer and the New Therapies, 2001; Crown and Garland, 2001. **Address:** Hamilton Hall, Iowa State University, Ames, IA 50011, U.S.A. **Online address:** bugeja@oak.cats.ohiou.edu

BUGENTAL, James F(rederick) T(homas). American, b. 1915. **Genres:** Psychology, Adult non-fiction, Reference. **Career:** Self-employed psychotherapist, since 1950. Member, Adjunct Faculty, Saybrook Institute, San Francisco; Lecturer, Stanford Medical School, California (Consultant, Stanford Research Institute, 1968-71). Assistant Professor of Psychology, University of California, Los Angeles, 1948-54; Partner, Psychological Service Assocs., Los Angeles, 1953-68. **Publications:** Psychological Interviewing, 1951, 3rd ed 1966; The Search for Authenticity: An Existential-Analytic Approach to Psychotherapy, 1965, 1988; (ed) Challenges of Humanistic Psychology, 1967; The Human Possibility, 1971; The Search for Existential Identity: Patient-Therapist Dialogues in Existential-Humanistic Psychotherapy, 1976; Psychotherapy and Process: The Fundamentals of an Existential-Humanistic Approach, 1978; Talking: The Fundamentals of Humanistic Professional Communication, 1981; The Art of the Psychotherapist, 1987; Intimate Journeys, 1990; Pyschotherapy Isn't What You Think, 1999; Handbook of Humanistic Psychology, forthcoming.

BUGOS, Glenn E. American, b. 1961. **Genres:** Air/Space topics. **Career:** California Institute of Technology, Pasadena, faculty member, 1988-90; University of California, Berkeley, faculty member, 1990-91; Wissenschaftszentrum, Berlin, Germany, faculty member, 1991-93; Prologue Group, Redwood City, CA, historian, 1993-. **Publications:** Engineering the F-4 Phantom II: Parts into Systems, 1996; Atmosphere of Freedom: Sixty Years at NASA Ames Research Center, 2000. Contributor to journals devoted to the history of science, technology, and business. **Address:** Prologue Group, 188 King St, Redwood City, CA 94062, U.S.A. **Online address:** glenn@ prologuegroup.com; www.prologuegroup.com

BUGUL, Ken. *See* **MBAYE, Marietou (Bileoma).**

BUHNER, Stephen Harrod. American, b. 1952. **Genres:** Poetry, Cultural/ Ethnic topics, Environmental sciences/Ecology, Medicine/Health, Self help. **Career:** Wilderness survival training in Colorado, 1972-75; builder of custom furniture and solar homes, 1975-84; workshop leader, lecturer, teacher, 1980-; psychotherapist in private practice, 1981-95; proprietor of rare book and manuscript business, 1985-92; clinical herbalist, 1988-95; Healer's Review, editor, 1990-95; writer, 1995-. Ordained practitioner of Church of Gaia, 1990. **Publications:** Sacred Plant Medicine: Explorations in the Practice of Indigenous Herbalism, 1996; One Spirit, Many Peoples: A Manifesto for Earth Spirituality, 1997; Sacred and Herbal Healing Beers: The Secrets of Ancient Fermentation, 1998; Herbal Antibiotics: Natural Alternatives for Drug-Resistant Bacteria, 1999; Herbs for Hepatitis C and the Liver, 2000; The Lost Language of Plants: The Ecological Importance of Plant Medicines to Life on Earth, 2002; The Taste of Wild Water: Poems and Stories Found While Walking in Woods, 2002; Vital Man, 2003; The Fasting Path, 2003; The Secret Teachings of Plants, 2004. **Address:** 505 Flint Rd, Randolph, VT 05060-8769, U.S.A.

BUITENHUIS, Peter M. Canadian, b. 1925. **Genres:** Literary criticism and history. **Career:** Yale University, New Haven, CT, Member of faculty, 1955-59, University of Toronto, Member of faculty, 1959-66; Professor of English, McGill University, Montreal, 1967-75; Professor, Dept. of English, Simon Fraser University, Burnaby, BC, 1975-, Chairman, 1975-81, now emeritus. **Publications:** Five American Moderns, 1965; Hugh MacLennan, 1969; The Grasping Imagination: The American Writings of Henry James, 1970; The Restless Analyst: Essays by Henry James, 1980; The Great War of Words: British, American and Canadian Fiction and Propaganda 1914-1933, 1987; The House of Seven Gables: Severing Family and Colonial Ties, 1991. EDITOR: French Writers and American Women: Essays by Henry James, 1960; Selected Poems by E. J. Pratt, 1968; Twentieth Century Interpretations of The Portrait of a Lady, 1968; George Orwell: A Reassessment, 1988. **Address:** 7019 Marine Dr W, Vancouver, BC, Canada V5A 1S6. **Online address:** buitenhu@sfu.ca

BUJOLD, Lois McMaster. American, b. 1949. **Genres:** Science fiction/ Fantasy. **Career:** Ohio State University Hospitals, pharmacy technician, 1972-78; homemaker, 1979-; writer, 1982-. Writing workshop instructor at Thurber House, spring, 1988, and Ohio State University, summers, 1990-92. **Publications:** SCIENCE FICTION: Shards of Honor, 1986; Ethan of Athos, 1986; The Warrior's Apprentice, 1986; Falling Free, 1988; Brothers in Arms,

1989; Borders of Infinity, 1989; The Vor Game, 1990; Mirror Dance, 1994; Cetaganda, 1996; Memory, 1996; Komarr, 1998; A Civil Campaign, 1999; OTHER: The Spirit Ring (fantasy), 1992; The Mountains of Mourning (novella). Contributor to periodicals. **Address:** c/o Spectrum Literary Agency, 320 Central Park West Ste 1-D, New York, NY 10025, U.S.A. **Online address:** lmbujold@mu.uswest.net

BUKEY, Evan Burr. American, b. 1940. **Genres:** History. **Career:** University of Arkansas, Fayetteville, assistant professor, 1969-75, associate professor, 1975-86, professor of history, 1986-. Visiting instructor at U.S. Military Academy, West Point, N.Y., 1982; University of Cambridge, visiting fellow, Wolfson College, 1993-94. **Publications:** Hitler's Hometown: Linz, Austria, 1908-1945, 1986; Hitler's Austria: Popular Sentiment in the Nazi Era, 1938-1945, 2000. **Address:** Department of History, University of Arkansas, Fayetteville, AR 72701, U.S.A. **Online address:** ebukey@comp.uark.edu

BUKIET, Melvin Jules. American. **Genres:** Novellas/Short stories. **Career:** Mt. Vernon Public Library, writing teacher, 1983; The Writer's Voice, writing teacher, 1988-1993; Tikkun, NYC, fiction editor, 1992-; Sarah Lawrence College, Bronxville, NY, visiting professor, 1993-; Columbia University, NYC, visiting professor, 1996. **Publications:** Sandman's Dust, 1986; Signs and Wonders, 1999. STORIES: Stories of an Imaginary Childhood, 1992; While the Messiah Tarries, 1995; After, 1996. Contributor of short stories, essays, reviews, and editorials to periodicals. **Address:** 529 W. 113th St., New York, NY 10025, U.S.A.

BULBECK, Chilla. Australian, b. 1951. **Genres:** Women's studies and issues. **Career:** Officer of Australian Public Service, 1972-75; Murdoch University, Australia, tutor, 1980, senior tutor in social and political theory, 1981-83; Griffith University, Nathan, Australia, lecturer, 1983-87, senior lecturer, 1988-93, associate professor of humanities, 1993-96; University of Adelaide, professor of women's studies, 1998-. Visiting scholar, University of Beijing, 1991-92, 1993, and Australian Studies Centre, 1993. **Publications:** (with C. Heath) Shadow of the Hill, 1985; One World Women's Movement, 1988; Social Sciences in Australia, 1992, rev. ed., 1998; Australian Women in Papua New Guinea: Colonial Passages, 1920-1960, 1992; Living Feminism: The Import of the Women's Movement on Three Generations of Australian Women, 1997; Reorienting Western Feminism: Women's Diversity in a Postcolonial World, 1998; Facing the Wild, 2004. Contributor to periodicals. **Address:** Social Inquiry, University of Adelaide, Adelaide, SA 5005, Australia. **Online address:** chilla.bulbeck@adelaide.edu.au

BULGER, Peggy A. American, b. 1949. **Genres:** Music, Mythology/Folklore. **Career:** Bureau of Cultural Affairs, Albany, NY, oral historian, 1975; Appalachian Museum, Berea, KY, research and participants coordinator for Traditional Folklife Project, 1975-76; Florida Department of State, state folk arts coordinator for Florida Folk Arts Program, 1976-79, folklife programs administrator for Bureau of Florida Folklife Programs, 1979-89; Southern Arts Federation, Atlanta, GA, coordinator of Regional Folk Arts Program, 1989-92, director of the program, 1992-. Producer of documentary videotapes and films, for educational television and radio networks, and sound recordings; consultant to organizations, including Marine Resources Council of Florida, National Folk Festival, and National Black Arts Festival. **Publications:** (ed.) Musical Roots of the South, 1992; (with T. Bucuvalas and S. Kennedy) South Florida Folklife, 1994. Contributor to books. Contributor to history and folklore journals. **Address:** 4849 Pine Hill Ct W, Stone Mountain, GA 30088, U.S.A. **Online address:** PBulger@southarts.org

BULKELEY, Kelly. American, b. 1962. **Genres:** Psychology. **Career:** Graduate Theological Union, Berkeley, CA, visiting scholar, 1993-. University of Santa Clara, lecturer, 1996-. **Publications:** The Wilderness of Dreams, 1994; Spiritual Dreaming, 1995; (ed.) Among All These Dreamers, 1996; An Introduction to the Psychology of Dreaming, 1997; (with A. Siegel) Dreamcatching, 1998; Visions of the Night, 1999. **Address:** 226 Amherst Ave., Kensington, CA 94708, U.S.A. **Online address:** 76633.1555@compuserve.com

BULKOWSKI, Thomas N. (born United States), b. 1957. **Genres:** Business/Trade/Industry. **Career:** Raytheon, Missile Systems Division, Bedford, MA, hardware design engineer, 1979-81; Tracor Westronics, Fort Worth, TX, software manager for process monitoring systems, 1981-82; Tandy Corp., Fort Worth, senior software engineer, 1982-93; IMI Systems (consulting service), Dallas, TX, consultant, 1993; freelance writer, 1993-. Vice chair of a local recycle task force committee, 1992; Keller Parks and Recreation Board, chair, 1990-95; Keep Keller Beautiful, president, 1990-92; Friends of

the Keller Library, vice president, 1990; Keller Chamber of Commerce, vice president for membership, 1994, treasurer, 1995. **Publications:** Encyclopedia of Chart Patterns, 2000; Trading Classic Chart Patterns, 2002. Contributor to periodicals. **Address:** c/o Author Mail, Wiley Publishing Group, 605 Third Ave., New York, NY 10158, U.S.A. **Online address:** tbul@hotmail.com

BULL, Angela (Mary). British, b. 1936. **Genres:** Children's fiction, Literary criticism and history, Novellas/Short stories, Children's non-fiction. **Career:** Teacher, Casterton School, Kirkby Lonsdale, Westmorland, 1961-62; Assistant, Medieval Manuscript Room, Bodleian Library, Oxford, 1962-63. **Publications:** The Friend with a Secret, 1965; (with G. Avery) Nineteenth Century Children: Heroes and Heroines in English Children's Stories, 1780-1900, 1965; Wayland's Keep, 1966; Child of Ebenezer, 1974; Treasure in the Fog, 1976; Griselda, 1977; The Doll in the Wall, 1978; The Machine Breakers, 1980; The Bicycle Parcel, 1980; The Accidental Twins, 1982; Noel Streatfeild, 1984; Anne Frank, 1984; Florence Nightingale, 1985; Marie Curie, 1986; The Visitors, 1986; A Hat for Emily, 1986; Elizabeth Fry, 1987; A Wish at the Baby's Grave, 1988; Up the Attic Stairs, 1989; The Jiggery-Pokery Cup, 1990; Pink Socks, 1990; The Shadows of Owlsnap, 1992; The Winter Phantoms, 1993; The Kitchen Maid, 1994; Yellow Wellies, 1994; Blue Shoes, 1996; Purple Buttons, 1996; A Patchwork of Ghosts, 1996; The Terrible Birthday Present, 1998; Ghost Hunting, 1998; Flying Ace, 2000; Joan of Arc, 2000; Free at Last, 2000; Time Traveller, 2000; Robin Hood, 2000. **Address:** The Vicarage, Gargrave, Skipton, North Yorkshire BD23 3NQ, England.

BULL, Barry L. American, b. 1947. **Genres:** Education, Philosophy. **Career:** Wellesley College, Wellesley, MA, assistant professor of education, 1979-84; University of Hawaii at Manoa, Honolulu, assistant professor to associate professor of education, 1986-89; University of Minnesota-Twin Cities, Minneapolis, associate professor of education, 1989-90; Indiana University-Bloomington, professor of education, 1990-. **Publications:** (with R. Fruehling and V. Chatterby) The Ethics of Multicultural and Bilingual Education, 1992; Education in Indiana: An Overview, 1994. **Address:** Education Bldg, Indiana University-Bloomington, Bloomington, IN 47405, U.S.A. **Online address:** bbull@indiana.edu

BULL, Bartle. British/American, b. 1939. **Genres:** Novels, Travel/Exploration. **Career:** Attorney, publisher, and novelist. Cadwalader, Wickersham & Taft (law firm), associate, 1964-69; Village Voice, president and publisher, 1970-76; director of New York Magazine, Village Voice, and New West. Political positions include campaign coordinator for Robert Kennedy, NYC, 1968; chairman, New Yorkers for Giuliani for Senate, 2000; executive director, Citizens for McGovern/Shriver Campaign, 1972; executive director, Citizens for Hugh Carey for Governor, 1974; New York State campaign coordinator for Jimmy Carter campaign, 1976; alternate delegate, Democratic National Convention, 1976. **Publications:** TRAVEL: Safari: A Chronicle of Adventure, 1988; Around the Sacred Sea: Mongolia and Lake Baikal on Horseback, 1999. NOVELS: The White Rhino Hotel, 1992; A Cafe on the Nile, 1998; The Devil's Oasis, 2001. **Address:** 439 E 51st St., New York, NY 10022, U.S.A.

BULL, Christopher Neil. American (born England), b. 1940. **Genres:** Gerontology/Senior issues. **Career:** University of Oregon, Eugene, OR, instructor, 1969-71; University of Missouri-Kansas City, Kansas City, MO, assistant professor, 1971-75, associate professor, 1976-92, professor and lecturer in medicine, 1992-, chair of department of sociology, 1976-81, associate dean of College of Arts and Sciences, 1993-97. Institute for Community Studies, Kansas City, MO, research associate, 1971-81; Center on Rural Elderly, codirector, 1987-90; The National Resource Center for Rural Elderly, principal investigator, 1988-92; University of New South Wales, Sydney, Australia, School of Sociology, visiting fellow, 1989. **Publications:** (with D. Howard) Evaluating Rural Elderly Transportation Systems (monograph), 1990; (with Howard) Challenges and Solutions to the Provision of Programs and Services to Rural Elders (monograph), 1991; (with S.D. Bane) The Future of Aging in America: Proceedings of a National Symposium 1991, 1991; (ed.) Aging in Rural America, 1993; (with N. Levine) The Older Volunteer: An Annotated Bibliography, 1993; (ed. with R. Coward, J. Galliher, and G. Kakulka) Health Services for Rural Elders, 1993. Contributor to books. **Address:** Center on Aging, University of Missouri-Kansas City, 5215 Rockhill Rd, Kansas City, MO 64110, U.S.A.

BULL, Schuyler M. American, b. 1974. **Genres:** Travel/Exploration. **Career:** Soundprints (publisher), Norwalk, CT, editorial assistant, 1996-97; Grosset & Dunlap (publisher), New York, NY, editorial assistant, 1997-98; Office of Paul Hastings (law practice), Stamford, CT, associate attorney, 2001-. **Publications:** Through Tsavo: A Story of an East African Savanna,

1998; (adaptor) The Nutcracker, 1999; Along the Luangwa: A Story of an African Floodplain, 1999. **Address:** c/o Hastings Janofsky & Walker, 1055 Washington Blvd., 10th Floor, Stamford, CT 06902, U.S.A. **Online address:** sky@minckler.org

BULLA, Clyde Robert. American, b. 1914. **Genres:** Novels, Children's fiction, Translations, Novellas/Short stories. **Career:** Farmer until 1943; Linotype Operator and Columnist, Tri-County News, King City, Missouri, 1943-49. **Publications:** These Bright Young Dreams, 1941; The Donkey Cart, 1946; Riding the Pony Express, 1948; The Secret Valley, 1949; Surprise for a Cowboy, 1950; A Ranch for Danny, 1951; Johnny Hong of Chinatown, 1952; Song of St. Francis, 1952; Star of Wild Horse Canyon, 1953; Eagle Feather, 1953; Squanto, Friend of the White Men, 1954, as Squanto, Friend of the Pilgrims, 1969; Down the Mississippi, 1954; White Sails to China, 1955; A Dog Named Penny (reader), 1955; John Billington, Friend of Squanto, 1956; The Sword in the Tree, 1956; Old Charlie, 1957; Ghost Town Treasure, 1957; Pirate's Promise, 1958; The Valentine Cat, 1959; Stories of Favorite Operas, 1959; A Tree Is a Plant, 1960; Three-Dollar Mule, 1960; The Sugar Pear Tree, 1961; Benito, 1961; What Makes a Shadow?, 1962; The Ring and the Fire: Stories from Wagner's Niebelung Operas, 1962; Viking Adventure, 1963; Indian Hill, 1963; St. Valentine's Day, 1965; More Stories of Favorite Operas, 1965; Lincoln's Birthday, 1966; White Bird, 1966; Washington's Birthday, 1967; Flowerpot Gardens, 1967; Stories of Gilbert and Sullivan Operas, 1968; The Ghost of Windy Hill, 1968; Mika's Apple Tree; A Story of Finland, 1968; The Moon Singer, 1969; New Boy in Dublin: A Story of Ireland, 1969; Jonah and the Great Fish, 1970; Joseph the Dreamer, 1971; Pocahontas and the Strangers, 1971; (trans.) M. Bollinger, Noah and the Rainbow, 1972; Open the Door and See All the People, 1972; Dexter, 1973; The Wish at the Top, 1974; Shoeshine Girl, 1975; Marco Moonlight, 1976; The Beast of Lor, 1977; (with M. Syson) Conquista!, 1978; Last Look, 1979; The Stubborn Old Woman, 1980; My Friend the Monster, 1980; Daniel's Duck, 1980; A Lion to Guard Us, 1981; Almost a Hero, 1981; Dandelion Hill, 1982; Poor Boy, Rich Boy, 1982; Charlie's House, 1983; The Cardboard Crown, 1984; A Grain of Wheat, 1985; The Chalk Box Kid, 1987; Singing Sam, 1989; The Christmas Coat, 1990; A Place for Angels, 1995; The Paint Brush Kid, 1999.

BULLARD, Beth. American, b. 1939. **Genres:** Music. **Career:** Dickinson College, Carlisle, PA, instructor in music, 1968-79, 1983-87, 1993-94, member of artist faculty in music, 1987-92; Temple University, Philadelphia, PA, visiting assistant professor of music, 1994-95. University of Rochester, member of visiting faculty at Eastman School of Music, 1994. Flutist. **Publications:** EDITOR: (with A. Krantz) Harold Zabrak, Three Pieces for Flute and Guitar, 1984; (and trans.) Musica getutscht: A Treatise on Musical Instruments (1511) by S. Virdung, 1993. Contributor to music journals. **Address:** 364 W. South St., Carlisle, PA 17013, U.S.A.

BULLINS, Ed. American, b. 1935. **Genres:** Novels, Novellas/Short stories, Plays/Screenplays. **Career:** Black Arts/West, San Francisco, cofounder, 1965, producer, 1965-67; Black Arts Alliance, cofounder and cultural director until 1966; New Lafayette Theatre, Harlem, NYC, resident playwright and associate director, 1968-73; New York Shakespeare Festival, 1975-82; Peoples School of Dramatic Arts, San Francisco, CA, teacher, 1983; City College of San Francisco, instructor, drama department, 1984-88; Sonoma State University, lecturer in American multicultural studies dept., 1987-89; Contra Costa College, San Pablo, CA, instructor in African American Humanities/Theatre, 1989-93; San Francisco State University, lecturer in black studies, 1993; Northeastern University, professor of theatre, 1995, distinguished artist in residence, 2000. Playwright in residence, instructor, and director at colleges and universities and for theater groups. **Publications:** How Do You Do? A Nonsense Drama (one-act), 1967; Five Plays by Ed Bullins, 1969, in UK as The Electronic Nigger and Other Plays, 1970; The Duplex, 1971; The Hungered One (short stories), 1971; Four Dynamite Plays, 1972; The Theme Is Blackness: The Corner and Other Plays, 1972; Four Dynamite Plays, 1972; The Reluctant Rapist (novel), 1973; New/Lost Plays, 1995. Author of unpublished plays. EDITOR & CONTRIBUTOR: New Plays from the Black Theatre, 1969; The New Lafayette Theatre Presents, 1974.

BULLITT, Dorothy. American, b. 1955. **Genres:** Adult non-fiction. **Career:** Lawyer and writer. Office of the Washington State Attorneys General, Assistant Attorney General, 1980-85; Harbor Properties Inc., Seattle, chief operating officer, 1985-92; management consultant and arbitrator, 1993-. **Publications:** Filling the Void: Six Steps from Loss to Fulfillment, 1996; (with J. Wickwire) Addicted to Danger: A Memoir about Affirming Life in the Face of Death, 1998. Contributor to periodicals. **Address:** 821 Second Ave. Suite 2000, Seattle, WA 98104, U.S.A. **Online address:** dbullitt@bigplanet.com

BULLOCK, Michael (Hale). Also writes as Michael Hale. British/Canadian (born United Kingdom), b. 1918. **Genres:** Novels, Novellas/Short stories, Plays/Screenplays, Poetry, Translations. **Career:** University of British Columbia, Vancouver, professor, 1969-83, professor emeritus of creative writing, 1983-. Translators Association, London, chairman, 1964-67. **Publications:** Transmutations, 1938; World without Beginning, Amen!, 1963; Zwei Stimmen in Meinem Mund, 1967; A Savage Darkness, 1969; 16 Stories as They Happened, 1960; Green Beginning Black Ending (short stories), 1971; Not to Hong Kong (play), 1972; Randolph Cranstone and the Pursuing River (short stories), 1975; The Man with Flowers through His Hands (fables), 1985; The Double Ego: An Autocollage (novella), 1985; The Burning Chapel (novella), 1991; The Invulnerable Ovoid Aura and Other Stories, 1993, 2nd ed., 1995; Sokotra (play), 1997; Selected Works 1936-1996 (poetry & fiction), 1997. POETRY: Sunday Is a Day of Incest, 1961; Black Wings White Dead, 1978; Lines in the Dark Wood, 1981; Quadriga for Judy, 1982; Prisoner of the Rain, 1983; Poems on Green Paper, 1988; Vancouver Moods, 1989; The Walled Garden, 1992; The Secret Garden, 1990; Labyrinths, 1992; Brambled Heart, 1985; Dark Water, 1987; Avatars of the Moon, 1990; Stone and Shadow, 1993; The Sorcerer with Deadly Nightshade Eyes, 1993; The Inflowing River, 1994; Moons and Mirrors, 1994; Dark Roses, 1994; Sonnet in Black and Other Poems, 1998; Erupting in Flowers, 1999; Nocturnes: Poems of Night, 2000; Wings of the Black Swan, 2001; Colours, 2003. NOVELS: Randolph Cranstone and the Glass Thimble, 1977; Randolph Cranstone and the Veil of Maya, 1986; The Story of Noire, 1987; Randolph Cranstone Takes the Inward Path, 1989; Voices of the River, 1993. TRANSLATOR: (with J. Ch'en) Poems of Solitude, 1961; The Tales of Hoffmann, 1962; The Stage and Creative Arts, 1969; K. Krolow, Foreign Bodies, 1969; K. Krolow, Invisible Hands, 1969; M. Tremblay, Stories for Late Night Drinkers, 1978; T. Pavel, The Persian Mirror, 1988; C. Charbonneau-Tissot, Compulsion, 1989; O. Volta, Eric Satie Seen through His Letters, 1989; A. Carpentier, The Bread of Birds (short stories), 1993; M. Tremblay, The City in the Egg, 1999; M. Frisch, Three Plays, 2002. **Address:** 103-3626 W 28th Ave, Vancouver, BC, Canada V6S 1S4. **Online address:** michaelhbullock@hotmail.com

BULLOUGH, Robert V., Jr. American, b. 1949. **Genres:** Education. **Career:** University of Utah, Salt Lake City, professor of teacher educational studies, 1976-99, emeritus professor of educational studies, 1999-; Brigham Young University, professor of teacher education, 1999-; writer. Park fellow, 1980; consultant to secondary schools and teachers' professional associations. **Publications:** Democracy in Education: Boyd H. Bode, 1981; (with S. Goldstein and L. Holt) Human Interests in the Curriculum: Teaching and Learning in a Technological Society, 1984; The Forgotten Dream of American Public Education, 1988; First Year Teacher: A Case Study, 1989; (with J.G. Knowles and N.A. Crow) Emerging as a Teacher, 1991; (with A. Gitlin) Becoming a Student of Teaching: Methodologics for Exploring Self and School Context, 1995; (co-ed.) Teachers and Mentors: Profiles of Distinguished Twentieth-Century Professors of Education, 1996; (with K. Baughman) First Year Teacher-After Eight Years: An Inquiry into Teacher Development, 1997; Uncertain Lives: Children of Promise, Teachers of Hope, 2001; (with A. Gitlin) Becoming a Student of Teaching: Linking Knowledge Production and Practice, 2001. **Address:** 413 4th Ave, Salt Lake City, UT 84103, U.S.A. **Online address:** Bob_Bullough@byu.edu

BULLOUGH, Vern L. American, b. 1928. **Genres:** History, Medicine/Health, Paranormal, Sex, Sociology, Women's studies and issues, Bibliography, Biography. **Career:** California State University, Northridge, professor of history, 1959-79, outstanding professor emeritus, 1993-; Youngstown University, Youngstown, OH, professor, 1954-59; State University of New York, Buffalo, dean of the faculty of natural and social sciences, 1980-90, distinguished professor, 1987-93, distinguished professor emeritus, 1993-; University of Southern California, visiting professor, 1993-. **Publications:** (with B. Bullough) Emergence of Modern Nursing, 1964; History of Prostitution, 1964; Development of Medicine as a Profession, 1966; Man in Western Civilization, 1970; (with B. Bullough) Poverty, Ethnic Identity and Health Care, 1972; The Subordinate Sex, 1973; (with R. and F. Naroll) Military Deference in History, 1974; Sex, Society, and History, 1976; Sexual Variance in Society and History, 1976; (with others) An Annotated Bibliography of Homosexuality, 1976; (with B. Bullough and B. Elcano) A Bibliography of Prostitution, 1977; (with B. Bullough) Sin, Sickness, and Sanity, 1977; (with B. Bullough) Prostitution, 1977; (with B. Bullough) Expanding Horizons in Nursing, 1977; (with B. Bullough) The Care of the Sick, 1978; Homosexuality: A History, 1979; (with B. Elcano and B. Bullough) A Bibliography of the History of Nursing, 1980; (with J. Brundage) Sexual Practices and the Medieval Catholic Church, 1982; (with B. Bullough) Health Care for the Other Americans, 1982; (with B. Bullough and M.C. Soukup) Nursing Issues and Strategies for the Eighties, 1983; (with B. Bullough) History, Trends and Politics of Nursing, 1984; (with B. Bullough, J. Garvey and K. Allen) Issues in Nursing, 1985; (with B. Bullough) Women and Prostitution, 1987; American Nursing: A Biographical Dictionary, (with O. Church and A. Stein) vol. 1, 1988, (with L. Sentz and A. Stein) vol. 2, 1992, (with L. Sentz) vol. 3, 2000; (with B. Shelton and S. Slavin) The Subordinated Sex, 1988; (with B. Bullough) Nursing in the Community, 1990; (with B. Bullough and M.A. Stanton) Nightingale and Her Era, 1990; (with B. Bullough), Contraception Today, 1990, 2nd ed., 1997; (with L. Sentz) Prostitution: A Guide to Sources, 1992; (with B. Bullough), Cross Dressing, Sex and Gender, 1993; (with S. Freeman) A Guide to Fertility and Alternatives, 1993; (with B. Bullough) Nursing Issues and Strategies for the Nineties, 1993; (with B. Bullough) Encyclopedia of Human Sexual Behavior, 1993; (with T. Madigan) Toward a New Enlightenment: The Philosophy of Paul Kurtz, 1993; Science in the Bedroom, 1994; (with B. Bullough) Sexual Attitudes, 1995; (with J. Brundage) A Handbook of Medieval Sexuality, 1996; (with B. Bullough and others) How I Got into Sex, 1996; (with B. Bullough and J. Elias) Gender Blenders, 1997; (with J. Elias) Prostitutes, Pimps & Whores, 1998; (with J. and V. Elias) Porn 101, 1999; Encyclopedia of Birth Control, 2001; Before Stonewall, 2002; Universities, Medicine and Science in the Medieval West, 2003. EDITOR: (with B. Bullough) Issues in Nursing, 1966; The Scientific Revolution, 1971; (with B. Bullough) New Directions in Nursing, 1971; The Frontiers of Sex Research, 1979. Contributor of chapters to books and articles to popular and professional journals. **Address:** 3304 W Sierra Dr, Westlake Village, CA 91362-3542, U.S.A. **Online address:** vbullough@csun.edu; vbullough@adelphia.net

BULMER, (Henry) Kenneth. Also writes as Alan Burt Akers, Ken Blake, Ernest Corley, Arthur Frazier, Adam Hardy, Bruno Krauss, Neil Langholm, Charles R. Pike, Dray Prescot, Andrew Quiller, Richard Silver. British, b. 1921. **Genres:** Novels, Science fiction/Fantasy, Romance/Historical. **Career:** Ed., New Writing in Science Fiction, London, since 1972. Former Ed., Sword and Sorcery mag., Newcastle. **Publications:** AS HENRY KENNETH BULMER: (with A.V. Clarke) Space Treason, 1952; (with A.V. Clarke) Cybernetic Controller, 1952; Encounter in Space, 1952; Space Salvage, 1953; The Stars Are Ours, 1952; Galactic Intrigue, 1953; Empire of Chaos, 1953; World Aflame, 1954; Challenge, 1954; City under the Sea, 1957; The Secret of ZI (in U.K. as The Patient Dark), 1958; The Changeling Worlds, 1959; (with J. Newman) The True Book about Space Travel, 1960; The Earth Gods Are Coming (in U.K. as Of Earth Foretold), 1960; No Man's World (in U.K. as Earth's Long Shadow), 1961; Beyond the Silver Sky, 1961; New Writings in SF No. 26, (29), 1975; The Diamond Contessa, 1983. AS ALAN BURT AKERS: The Dray Prescot Saga 1972-83; New Writings in SF No. 30, 1978; Allies of Antares, 1981; Mazes of Scorpio, 1982; Delia of Vallia, 1982; Fires of Scorpio, 1983; Talons of Scorpio, 1983; Masks of Scorpio, 1984; Seg the Bowman, 1984; Werewolves of Kregen, 1985; Witch of Kregen, 1985. AS KEN BLAKE: Where the Jungle Ends, 1978; Long Shot, 1978; Stake-Out, 1978; Hunter Hunted, 1978; Blind Run, 1979; Fall Girl, 1979; Dead Reckoning, 1980; No Stone, 1981; Spy Probe, 1981; Foxhole, 1981. AS ERNEST CORLEY: White-Out, 1960, 1969; The Fatal Fire, 1962; Wind of Liberty, 1962; Defiance, 1963; The Wizard of Starship, 1963; The Million Year Hunt, 1964; Demon's World (in U.K. as The Demons), 1964; Land Beyond the Map, 1965; Behold the Stars, 1965; Worlds for the Taking, 1966; To Outrun Doomsday, 1967; The Key to Irunium, 1967; The Key to Venudine, 1968; The Doomsday Men, 1968; Cycle of Nemesis, 1968; The Star Venturers, 1969; The Wizards of Senchuria, 1969; Kandar, 1969; The Ships of Durostorum, 1970; Blazon (in U.K. as Quench the Burning Stars), 1970; The Ulcer Culture, 1970; Star Trove, 1970; Swords of the Barbarians, 1970; The Hunters of Jundagai, 1971; The Chariots of Ra, 1971; On the Symb Socket Circuit, 1972; Pretenders, 1972; Roller Coaster World, 1972. AS ARTHUR FRAZIER: Wolfshead series, 6 vols., 1973-75; (ed.) New Writings in SF No. 22, (24, 25) 3 vols., 1973-74. AS ADAM HARDY: Fox series, 14 vols., 1972-77; New Writings in SF No. 28, 1976; Strike Force Falklands, 6 vols., 1984-85. AS BRUNO KRAUSS: Shark series, 8 vols., 1978-82. AS NEIL LANGHOLM: The Dark Return, 1975; Trail of Blood, 1976. AS ANDREW QUILLER: The Land of Mist, 1976; Sea of Swords, 1977; New Writings in SF No. 29, 1976. AS RICHARD SILVER: Captain Shark: By Pirate's Blood, 1975; Captain Shark: Jaws of Death, 1976. AS CHARLES R. PIKE: Brand of Vengeance, 1978. AS DRAY PRESCOT: Warlord of Antares, 1988; Dray Prescot, Vols 38 to 50, 1991-1995.

BULOT, Blaise. See HORNE, R(alph) A(lbert).

BUMILLER, Elisabeth. Danish, b. 1956. **Genres:** Biography, Documentaries/Reportage. **Career:** Washington Post, Washington, DC, reporter for "Style" section, 1979-87, reporter from Washington, New Delhi, Tokyo, and NYC, 1990-91, 1995; New York Times, NYC, reporter on metropolitan staff, 1995-. **Publications:** May You Be the Mother of a Hundred Sons: A Journey Among the Women of India, 1990; The Secrets of

Mariko: A Year in the Life of a Japanese Woman and Her Family, 1995. **Address:** New York Times, 229 West 43rd St., New York, NY 10036, U.S.A.

BUMSTED, J(ohn) M(ichael). Canadian (born United States), b. 1938. **Genres:** History. **Career:** Tufts University, Medford, MA, Instructor, 1965-67; McMaster University, Hamilton, ON, Assistant Professor, 1967-69; Simon Fraser University, Burnaby, BC, Associate Professor, 1969-75, Professor of History, 1975-80; University of Manitoba, Winnipeg, Fellow of St. John's College, 1980-, Professor of History, 1980-. **Publications:** (ed.) Documentary Problems in Canadian History, 2 vols., 1969; (ed.) The Great Awakening in Colonial America: The Beginnings of Evangelical Pietism, 1970; Henry Alline 1748-1784, 1971; (ed.) Canada before Confederation: Readings and Interpretations, 1972, 1979; (with J. Van de Wetering) "What Must I Do to be Saved?": The Great Awakening in Colonial America, 1976; The People's Clearance, 1982; (ed. with R. Fisher) The Journal of Alexander Walker, 1982; (ed.) The Collected Writings of Lord Selkirk 1799-1809, 1984; (ed.) Interpreting Canada's Past, 2 vols., 1986; Understanding the Loyalists, 1986; Land, Settlement and Politics in 18th Century Prince Edward Island, 1987; The Collected Writings of Lord Selkirk 1810-1820, 1988; The Peoples of Canada: A Pre-Confederation History; The Peoples of Canada: A Post-Confederation History, 1992; The Red River Rebellion, 1996; The Fur Trade Wars: The Origins of Western Canada, 1999; The Dictionary of Manitoba Biography, 1999. **Address:** Dept. of History, University of Manitoba, Winnipeg, MB, Canada R3T 2N2.

BUNCK, Julie Marie. American, b. 1960. **Genres:** Politics/Government. **Career:** University of Louisville, Louisville, KY, assistant professor of political science, 1994-. **Publications:** Fidel Castro and the Quest for a Revolutionary Culture in Cuba, 1994; (with M.R. Fowler) Law, Power, and the Sovereign State: The Evolution and Application of the Concept of Sovereignty, 1995. **Address:** Department of Political Science, Louisville, KY 40292, U.S.A.

BUNDLES, A'Lelia Perry. American, b. 1952. **Genres:** Biography. **Career:** Producer for NBC News in Washington, DC, Atlanta, GA, Houston, TX, and NYC, 1976-89; ABC News, Washington, DC, producer for World News Tonight, 1989-96, deputy bureau chief, 1996-99, director of talent development, 2000-. **Publications:** Madam C.J. Walker: Entrepreneur, 1991; On Her Own Ground: The Life and Times of Madam C.J. Walker, 2001. Contributor to books and periodicals. **Address:** ABC News, 1717 DeSales St NW, Washington, DC 20036, U.S.A.

BUNGERT, D. Edward. Also writes as Zack Adams, Edward Hess. American, b. 1957. **Genres:** Novels. **Career:** World-Wide Business Centres, NYC, 1977-, began working in the mailroom, became vice-president, 1988-. **Publications:** Deep Cover, 1993; Stranglehold, 1994; Pursuit, 1996. **Address:** World-Wide Business Centres, 575 Madison Ave., New York, NY 10022, U.S.A.

BUNGEY, John Henry. British, b. 1944. **Genres:** Engineering. **Career:** Scott, Wilson, Kirkpatrick and Partners, London, Assistant (under agreement), 1966-68; North West Rd. Construction Unit, Cheshire Sub-Unit, Assistant Engineer, 1969-71; University of Liverpool, Lecturer, 1971-81, Senior Lecturer, 1981-93, Reader, 1993-94, Professor in Civil Engineering, 1994-. **Publications:** (with W.H. Mosley) Reinforced Concrete Design, 1976, 4th ed., 1990; The Testing of Concrete in Structures, 1982. **Address:** Dept. of Civil Engineering, University of Liverpool, Brownlow St, Liverpool L69 3GQ, England. **Online address:** bungey@liv.ac.uk

BUNIM, Amos. American, b. 1929. **Genres:** Biography. **Career:** Garden Fabrics Corp., New York City, president, 1973-. Torah Academy for Girls, chairman of board of directors, 1963-82; Kennedy Foundation in Israel, president, 1965-85; Sh'or Yoshuv Institute, national chairman, 1972-; Beth Medrash Govoha, chairman of board of governors, 1985-; Torah Schools for Israel, national co-chairman, 1987-. **Publications:** A Fire in His Soul (biography), 1989. **Address:** Garden Fabrics Corp, 450 7th Ave, New York, NY 10123, U.S.A.

BUNKERS, Suzanne L. American, b. 1950. **Genres:** Children's non-fiction, Education, History, Humanities, Literary criticism and history, Women's studies and issues, Young adult non-fiction, Autobiography/Memoirs, Humor/Satire. **Career:** Minnesota State University, Mankato, MN, assistant professor, 1980-84, associate professor, 1984-89, professor of English, 1989-, director of university honors program, 1999-2002. Host of "The Weekly Reader" program on KMSU-Radio, 1990-2003; consultant for Capstone Press' "Diaries, Memoirs" series, 1996-2001. **Publications:** (with F.W. Klein) Good Earth, Black Soil, 1981; In Search of Susanna: An Auto/

biography, 1996; A Midwestern Farm Girl's Diary, 2000. EDITOR: The Diary of Caroline Seabury, 1991; "All Will Yet Be Well": The Diary of Sarah Gillespie Huftalen, 1993; (with C. Huff) Inscribing the Daily: Critical Essays on Women's Diaries, 1996; Diaries of Girls and Women: A Midwestern American Sampler, 2001. **Address:** Dept of English, 230 Armstrong Hall, Minnesota State University, Mankato, MN 56001, U.S.A. **Online address:** suzanne.bunkers@mnsu.edu; www.intech.mnsu.edu/bunkers

BUNT, Gary R. British. **Genres:** Theology/Religion. **Career:** University of Wales-Lampeter, lecturer in Islamic studies, 1996-. **Publications:** Virtually Islamic: Computer-Mediated Communication and Cyber Islamic Environments 2000; The Good Web Guide to World Religions, 2001; Islam in the Digital Age, 2003. Contributor to websites, periodicals and academic journals. **Address:** Dept. of Theology and Religious Studies, University of Wales, Lampeter SA48 7ED, Wales. **Online address:** bunt@virtuallyislamic.com

BUNTING, A. E. See **BUNTING, (Anne) Eve(lyn Bolton).**

BUNTING, (Anne) Eve(lyn Bolton). Also writes as Evelyn Bolton, A. E. Bunting. American/Irish, b. 1928. **Genres:** Children's fiction, Young adult fiction. **Career:** Freelance writer. **Publications:** FICTION: A Gift for Lonny, 1973; Box, Fox, Ox, and the Peacock, 1974; The Wild One, 1974; We Need a Bigger Zoo, 1974; The Once-a-Year Day, 1974; Barney the Beard, 1975; The Dinosaur Machines, 4 vols., 1975; No Such Things...?, 4 vols., 1976; Josefina Finds the Prince, 1976; Blacksmith at Blueridge, 1976; Skateboard Saturday, 1976; One More Flight, 1976; Skateboard Four, 1976; Winter's Coming, 1977; The Big Cheese, 1977; Cop Camp, 1977; Ghost of Summer, 1977; Creative Science Fiction, 8 vols., 1978; Creative Romance, 10 vols., 1978; The Big Find, 1978; Magic and the Night River, 1978; Going against Cool Calvin, 1978; The Haunting of Kildoran Abbey, 1978; The Big Red Barn, 1979; The Cloverdale Switch, 1979, as Strange Things Happen in the Woods, 1984; Yesterday's Island, 1979; Mr. Pride's Umbrella, 1980; The Robot Birthday, 1980; Demetrius and the Golden Goblet, 1980; Terrible Things, 1980; St. Patrick's Day in the Morning, 1980; Blackbird Singing, 1980; The Empty Window, 1980; The Skate Patrol, The Skate Patrol Rides Again, and the Skate Patrol and the Mystery Writer, 3 vols., 1980-82; Goose Dinner, 1981; Jane Martin and the Case of the Ice Cream Dog, 1981; Rosie and Mr. William Star, 1981; The Waiting Game, 1981; The Spook Birds, 1981; The Happy Funeral, 1982; The Ghosts of Departure Point, 1982; The Travelling Men of Ballycoo, 1983; The Valentine Bears, 1983; Karen Kepplewhite Is the World's Best Kisser, 1983; Clancy's Coat, 1984; The Ghost behind Me, 1984; If I Asked, Would You Stay, 1994; The Man Who Could Call Down Owls, 1984; Monkey in the Middle, 1984; Someone Is Hiding on Alcatraz Island, 1984; Mohammed's Monkey, 1984; Jane Martin, Dog Detective, 1984; Surrogate Sister, 1985, in US as Mother, How Could You!, 1987; Face at the Edge of the World, 1985; Janet Hamm Needs a Date for the Dance, 1985; The Mother's Day Mice, 1986; Sixth Grade Sleepover, 1986; Ghost's Hour, Spook's Hour, 1987; Will You Be My POSSLQ?, 1987; Happy Birthday, Dear Duck, 1988; How Many Days to America, 1988; Is Anybody There, 1988; A Sudden Silence, 1988; The Wednesday Surprise, 1989; The Ghost Children, 1989; No Nap, 1989; In the Haunted House, 1990; The Wall, 1990; Such Nice Kids, 1990; Our Sixth Grade Sugar Babies, 1990; Fly Away Home, 1991; A Perfect Father's Day, 1991; The Hideout, 1991; Jumping the Nail, 1991; Night Tree, 1991; Sharing Susan, 1991; A Turkey for Thanksgiving, 1991; The Bicycle Man, 1992; Day before Christmas, 1992; Our Teacher's Having a Baby, 1992; Summer Wheels, 1992; Coffin on a Case, 1992; For Always, 1992; Just Like Everyone Else, 1992; Nobody Knows but Me, 1992; Eve Bunting Signature Library, 1992; Survival Camp, 1992; Red Fox Running, 1993; Someday a Tree, 1993; Flower Garden, 1994; Smoky Night, 1994 (1995 Caldecott Medal); Spying on Miss Muller, 1995; Market Day, 1996; Sunflower House, 1996; Going Home, 1996; Secret Place, 1996; I Am the Mummy Herb-Nefert, 1997; Ducky, 1997; My Backpack, 1997; On Call Back Mountain, 1997; The Christmas House, 1997; Your Move, 1997; Twinnies, 1997; Some Frog, 1997; The Pumpkin Fair, 1997; The Day the Whale Came, 1998; So Far from the Sea, 1998; Your Move, 1998; Blackwater, 1999; Butterfly House, 1999; Can You Do This, Old Badger?, 1999; Dreaming of America: An Ellis Island Story, 1999; I Have an Olive Tree, 1999; Rudi's Pond, 1999; Dear Wish Fairy, 2000; Doll Baby, 2000; I Like the Way You Are, 2000; Wanna Buy an Alien?, 2000; Swan in Love, 2000; Peepers, 2000; The Days of Summer, 2001; Too Many Monsters, 2001; Riding the Tiger, 2001; The Summer of Riley, 2001; Jin Woo, 2001; Gleam and Glow, 2001; Little Badger, Terror of the Seven Seas, 2001; (with L. Gore) Who Was Born this Special Day?, 2001; We Were There: A Nativity Story, 2001; Little Badger's Just-about Birthday, 2002; Sing a Song of Piglets, 2002; Little Bear's Little Boat, 2002; One Candle, 2002; The Bones of Fred Mcfee, 2002; Christmas Cricket, 2002; Girls: A-Z, 2002; Whales Passing, 2003. OTHER: The Two Giants (Irish folktale), 1972;

Say It Fast (tongue twisters), 1974; Skateboards, 1977; The Sea World Book of Sharks, 1979; The Sea World Book of Whales, 1980; The Giant Squid, 1981; The Great White Shark, 1982; Scary, Scary, Halloween (poetry), 1986; Once upon a Time, 1995; The Blue and the Grey, 1996; SOS Titanic, 1996; Moonstick, 1997. FICTION AS EVELYN BOLTON: Stable of Fear, 1974; Lady's Girl, 1974; Goodbye, Charlie, 1974; Ride When You're Ready, 1974; The Wild Horses, 1974; Dream Dancer, 1974. FICTION AS A.E. BUNTING: Pitcher to Center Field, 1974; Surfing Country, 1974; High Tide for Labrador, 1975; Springboard to Summer, 1975.

BURACK, Elmer H(oward). American, b. 1927. **Genres:** Administration/Management, Civil liberties/Human rights. **Career:** Director of Doctoral Studies, Dept. of Management, University of Illinois, Chicago, 1990-96, (Professor and Head of Dept., 1977-82). Co-Founder and Director, Midwest Human Resources Group, 1981-95. Consultant, Booz, Allen and Hamilton, 1959-60; Lecturer, 1960-64, Associate Professor, 1964-66, and Professor of Management, 1966-77, Illinois Institute of Technology, Chicago. Chairman, Personnel and Human Resource Division, 1975, and Health Care Division, 1977, National Academy of Mgmt.; Board Director and "Pioneer", Personnel Accreditation Institute, Society for Human Resource Management, 1975-87; Illinois Management Training Institute, president, co-founder, 1977-78; Associate Chairman, Illinois Gov ernor's Advisory Council on Employment/Training, 1978-80; Board Director and co-founder, Midwest Human Resource Planner's Group, 1986-95. **Publications:** Strategies for Manpower Planning and Programming, 1972; (co-author) Human Resource Planning: Technology, Policy, Change, 1973; Organization Design, 1973; Organizational Analysis, 1975; Personnel Management, 1977; The Manager's Guide to Change, 1979; Human Resource Planning, 1980, rev. ed., 2001; Career Management in Organizations, 1980; Growing: Women's Career Guide, 1980; Personnel Management, 1982; Introduction to Management, 1983; Creative Human Resource Planning, 1988; Corporate Resurgence and the New Employment Relationships, 1993; Retiring Retirement, 2002. **Address:** College of Business Administration (M/C 240), University of Illinois, Chicago, c/o 1 Ct of Harborside, 305, Northbrook, IL 60062, U.S.A.

BURAK, Carl S. American, b. 1942. **Genres:** Medicine/Health. **Career:** Physician specializing in family medicine and psychiatry. Diplomate of National Board of Medical Examiners, American Board of Family Practice, and American Board of Psychiatry and Neurology; fellow of American College of Legal Medicine; author. **Publications:** (with M.G. Remington) The Cradle Will Fall, 1994. **Address:** 482 Jacksonville Dr, Jacksonville Beach, FL 32250, U.S.A.

BURAYIDI, Michael A. Ghanaian, b. 1958. **Genres:** Reference. **Career:** University of Science and Technology, Kumasi, Ghana, instructor for two years; University of Louisville, Louisville, KY, instructor for two years; University of Wisconsin-Oshkosh, professor, 1994-. **Publications:** EDITOR: Multiculturalism in a Cross-National Perspective, 1997; (with A.T. Kisubi) Race and Ethnic Relations in the First Person, 1998; Urban Planning in a Multicultural Society, 1999; Downtowns: Revitalizing the Centers of Small Urban Communities, 2001. **Address:** University of Wisconsin-Oshkosh, Department of Geography, 800 Algoma Boulevard, Oshkosh, WI 54901, U.S.A. **Online address:** Burayidi@uwosh.edu

BURCH, Geoff. British, b. 1951. **Genres:** Administration/Management, Business/Trade/Industry. **Career:** Has worked in advertising and in sales; founder of Sales Coach, a business consulting firm. Has worked in a consultant capacity with the staffs of many corporations and companies throughout the world. **Publications:** Resistance Is Useless, 1994, in U.S. as The Art and Science of Business Persuasion: Mastering the Power of Getting What You Want, 1996; Go It Alone: Streetwise Secrets of SelfEmployment; Writing on the Wall: A Campaign for Commonsense Business, 2002; The Way of the Dog, 2005. **Address:** 94A Leckhampton Rd, Cheltenham GL53 0BN, England. **Online address:** geoff@geoffburch.com

BURCH, Joann J(ohansen). American. **Genres:** Children's non-fiction, Travel/Exploration, Biography. **Career:** American Airlines, Dallas, TX, flight attendant; teacher of social studies, English, and Spanish in California and Germany; teacher of English as a second language in Los Angeles, CA. Editor of newsletters for several organizations; volunteer for charity groups and civic organizations. **Publications:** Fine Print: A Story of Johann Gutenberg, 1991; Isabella of Castile: Queen on Horseback, 1991; Kenya, 1992, rev. ed., 1999; A Fairy Tale Life: A Story about Hans Christian Andersen, 1994; Marion Wright Edelman: Children's Champion, 1994; Chico Mendes: Defender of the Rainforest, 1994; Jefferson Davis: President of the Confederacy, 1998. Contributor of travel articles and photographs to newspapers and articles to magazines.

BURCH, Robert. American, b. 1925. **Genres:** Children's fiction. **Publications:** The Traveling Bird, 1959; (trans.) A Jungle in the Wheat Field, 1960; A Funny Place to Live, 1962; Tyler, Wilkin and Skee, 1963; Skinny, 1964; D. J.'s Worst Enemy, 1965; Queenie Peavy, 1966; Renfroe's Christmas, 1968; Joey's Cat, 1969; Simon and the Game of Chance, 1970; Doodle and the Go-Cart, 1972; The Hunting Trip, 1971; Hut School and the War-time Home-Front Heroes, 1974; The Jolly Witch, 1975; Two that Were Tough, 1976; The Whitman Kick, 1977; Wilkin's Ghost, 1978; Ida Early Comes over the Mountain, 1980; Christmas with Ida Early, 1983; King Kong and Other Poets, 1986. **Address:** 2021 Forest Dr, Fayetteville, GA 30214, U.S.A.

BURCHELL, R(obert) A(rthur). British, b. 1941. **Genres:** History. **Career:** Sr. Lecturer in American History and Institutions, 1980-91; Professor of American Studies, 1991-96, and Head of Dept., 1989-93, University of Manchester (Assistant Lecturer, 1965-68; Lecturer, 1968-80). Chairman, British Association for American Studies, 1989-92; Director, The Eccles Centre for American Studies, British Library, 1991-. **Publications:** Westward Expansion, 1974; The San Francisco Irish 1848-80, 1980; The End of Anglo-America, 1991; Harriet Martineau and America, 1995. **Address:** Eccles Centre for American Studies, The British Library, 96 Euston Rd, London NW1 2DB, England.

BURCHFIELD, Robert William. *See* Obituaries.

BURCHILL, Julie. British, b. 1959. **Genres:** Novels, Plays/Screenplays. **Career:** Writer. **Publications:** (with T. Parsons) The Boy Looked at Johnny: The Obituary of Rock and Roll, 1978; Love It or Shove It, 1985; Damaged Gods: Cults and Heroes Reappraised, 1986; Girls on Film, 1986; Ambition (novel), 1989; Prince (screenplay), 1991; Sex & Sensibility, 1992; No Exit (novel) 1993; Diana, 1998; I Knew I Was Right, 1998; Married Alive (novel), 1999; The Guardian Columns, 2001; Beckham, 2002. **Address:** Capel & Land, 29 Wardour St, London W1, England.

BURDEN, Jean. Also writes as Felicia Ames. American, b. 1914. **Genres:** Poetry, Animals/Pets, Essays. **Career:** Poetry Ed., Yankee mag., since 1955. Contributor author to Atlantic, Family Weekly, Ladies Home Journal, Good Housekeeping, Mademoiselle, Poetry, Georgia Review, American Scholar and others. Pet Ed., Woman's Day, 1973-82. Public Relations Officer, Meals for Millions Foundation, 1956-65; owner, public relations agency, 1966-72. **Publications:** Naked as the Glass, 1963; Journey Toward Poetry, 1966; (ed.) A Celebration of Cats, 1974; The Classic Cats, 1975; The Woman's Day Book of Hints for Cat Owners, 1980, 1984; Taking Light from Each Other, 1992. AS FELICIA AMES: The Cat You Care For, 1968; The Dog You Care For, 1968; The Bird You Care For, 1970; The Fish You Care For, 1971. **Address:** 1129 Beverly Way, Altadena, CA 91001, U.S.A.

BURDETT, John. British, b. 1951. **Genres:** Novels. **Career:** Barrister at law in London, England; Government of Hong Kong, barrister in Attorney General's Department; Johnson, Stokes & Master, Hong Kong, partner; currently full-time writer. **Publications:** NOVELS: A Personal History of Thirst, 1996; The Last Six Million Seconds, 1997; Bangkok 8, 2003; Bangkok Tattoo, 2005. **Address:** 2 Old Brompton Rd Ste 241, London SW7 3DQ, England.

BURDICK, Carol (Ruth). American, b. 1928. **Genres:** Women's studies and issues, Writing/Journalism. **Career:** Homemaker, 1949-60; elementary school teacher in Hamburg, NY, and Portland, ME, 1960-68; high school teacher in Yarmouth, ME, 1968-73; Alfred University, Alfred, NY, associate director of development, 1973-78, assistant professor in English, 1986-99, assistant professor in English emerita, 1999-; State University College at Oswego, master teacher at Oswego Campus School, 1978-79; Ossabaw Island Project (for writers and artists), co-director 1979-82. Member of Wee Playhouse, A.S.L.E. **Publications:** Destination Unknown, 1967; Stop Calling Me Mr. Darling!, 1988; Woman Alone: A Farmhouse Journal, 1989. FORTHCOMING: Killing Mother. **Address:** Pondhouse, Alfred Station, NY 14803, U.S.A. **Online address:** burdickc@alfred.edu

BURFIELD, Eva. *See* EBBETT, Eve.

BURG, Steven L. American, b. 1950. **Genres:** Politics/Government. **Career:** Brandeis University, Waltham, MA, lecturer, 1979-80, assistant professor, 1980-86, associate professor of political science, beginning in 1986, now professor of politics, dean of College of Arts and Sciences, 1990-92. **Publications:** Conflict and Cohesion in Socialist Yugoslavia: Political Decision-making since 1966, 1978; The Political Integration of Yugoslavia's Muslims: Determinants of Success and Failure, 1983; (with R.C. Macridis) Introduction to Comparative Politics: Regimes and Change, 1991; War or Peace?:

Nationalism, Democracy, and American Foreign Policy in Post-Communist Europe, 1996; (with P.S. Shoup) The War in Bosnia-Herzegovina: Ethnic Conflict and International Intervention, 1999. Contributor to political science journals. **Address:** Department of Politics, Brandeis University, 415 South St., Olin-Sang 204 Mail Stop 058, Waltham, MA 02454, U.S.A. **Online address:** burg@binah.cc.brandeis.edu

BURGER, Joanna. American, b. 1941. **Genres:** Biology, Environmental sciences/Ecology, Marine sciences/Oceanography, Natural history, Zoology. **Career:** State University of New York College at Buffalo, instructor in biology, ecology, and comparative anatomy, 1964-68; Rutgers University, Newark Campus, postdoctoral research fellow at Institute of Animal Behavior, 1972-73; Rutgers University, Piscataway, NJ, assistant professor, 1973-76, associate professor, 1976-81, professor of biological sciences, 1981-, director of Ecology Graduate Program, 1978-92; Cornell University, Shoals Marine Laboratory, associate professor, 1979. **Publications:** Pattern, Mechanism, and Adaptive Significance of Territoriality in Herring Gulls (Larus argentatus) (monograph), 1984; (with M. Gochfeld) The Black Skimmer: Social Dynamics of a Colonial Species, 1990; (with M. Gochfeld) The Common Tern: Its Breeding Biology and Behavior, 1991; (with D.N. Nettleship and M. Gochfeld) Seabirds on Islands: Threats, Case Studies, and Action Plans, 1992; A Naturalist along the Jersey Shore, 1996; Oil Spills, 1997; (with M. Gochfeld) Butterflies of New Jersey, 1997; The Parrot Who Owns Me, 2001; Biology of Marine Birds, 2001. EDITOR & CONTRIBUTOR: (with B. Olla) Behavior of Marine Animals: Perspectives in Research, Vol. IV (and H. Winn): Marine Birds, 1980, Vol. V: Breeding Behavior and Populations, 1984, Vol. VI: Migration and Foraging Behavior, 1984; Seabirds and Other Marine Vertebrates: Competition, Predation, and Other Interactions, 1988; Anatomy of an Oil Spill: The Arthur Kill, 1990. **Address:** Nelson Biology Lab, Rutgers University, 604 Allison Rd, Piscataway, NJ 08855-1059, U.S.A.

BÜRGER, Peter. German, b. 1936. **Genres:** Literary criticism and history. **Career:** University of Lyon, Lyon, France, lecturer in German language and literature, 1961-63; University of Bonn, Bonn, Germany, assistant in French literature, 1964-70; University of Erlangen, Erlangen, Germany, assistant professor, 1970-71; University of Bremen, Bremen, Germany, professor of French and comparative literature, 1971-. **Publications:** Der französische Surrealismus, 1971, 2nd ed., 1995; Theorie der Avantgarde, 1974, 9th ed, 1993, trans. as Theory of the Avant-Garde, 1984; The Decline of Modernism, 1992; (with C. Bürger) The Institutions of Art, 1992. IN GERMAN: Zur Kritik der idealistischen Aesthetik, 1983; (with C. Bürger) Postmoderne: Alltag, Allegorie, und Avantgarde, 1987; (with C. Bürger) Prosa der Moderne, 1988, 2nd ed, 1992; Das Denken des Herrn: Bataille zwischen Hegel und dem Surrealismus (title means: The Thinking of the Master), 1992; Die Traenen des Odysseus (title means: The Tears of Ulysses), 1993. **Address:** Fachbereich 10, University of Bremen, Postbox 333440, D-28334 Bremen, Germany.

BURGES, Dennis. American. **Genres:** Geography. **Career:** Educator and writer. Longwood University, Farmville, VA, English professor. Worked as a teacher in AZ, carpenter, musician, and guitar builder. **Publications:** Graves Gate, 2003. **Address:** Longwood University, Department of English and Modern Languages, Farmville, VA 23909, U.S.A. **Online address:** burges7@earthlink.net

BURGESS, Charles. American, b. 1932. **Genres:** History, Biography. **Career:** Chairman, Educational Policy Studies, and Professor of History of Education, University of Washington, Seattle, since 1970 (Assistant Professor, 1964-66; Associate Professor, 1966-70). National Post-Doctoral Fellow, Harvard University, Cambridge, Massachusetts, 1967-68; President, History of Education Society, 1971-72, and Division F, American Educational Research Association, 1977-79. Foreign Expert, People's Republic of China, 1984-85. **Publications:** Nettie Fowler McCormick: Profile of an American Philanthropist, 1962; (ed. with C. Strickland) Health, Growth, and Heredity: G. Stanley Hall on Natural Education, 1965; (with M. L. Borrowman) What Doctrines to Embrace: Studies in the History of American Education, 1969; Western Ideas and the Shaping of America, 1985. **Address:** 2111 SW 174th St., Seattle, WA 98166-3529, U.S.A.

BURGESS, Granville Wyche. American, b. 1947. **Genres:** Plays/Screenplays, Songs/Lyrics and libretti, Children's fiction. **Career:** Central State University, Edward, OK, artist in residence, 1985-87; Walnut Street Theatre, Philadelphia, PA, director of theatre school, 1988-95; playwright. Columbia Broadcasting System, staff writer for television soap opera Capitol; member of Circle Repertory Company. **Publications:** The Freak (three-act play), 1983; Dusky Sally (play), 1987; Play It as It Lies (play), 1991; Conrack (musical), 1992; A Country Carol (musical), 1998; the Death of Dracula, 1997. TELEVISION: episode "The Deal" for series Tales from the Darkside;

The Turtle Stone; Hell Hath No Fury..., Paul Revere Rides Again. **Address:** c/o The Wilma Theater, Broad & Spruce Streets, Philadelphia, PA 19107, U.S.A. **Online address:** gbprodinc@aol.com

BURGESS, M. R. *See* REGINALD, Robert.

BURGESS, Melvin. British, b. 1954. **Genres:** Novels. **Career:** Writer. **Publications:** The Cry of the Wolf, 1990; Burning Issy, 1992; An Angel for May, 1992; The Baby and Fly Pie, 1993; Loving April, 1995; Earth Giant, 1995; Junk, 1996; Tiger, Tiger, 1996; Kite, 1997. **Address:** 4 Hartley St., Garby, Lancashire BB8 GNL, England.

BURGESS, Michael. *See* REGINALD, Robert.

BURGESS, Patricia. Also writes as Patricia Burgess Stach. American, b. 1947. **Genres:** Regional/Urban planning. **Career:** Journal of the American Planning Association, managing editor, 1978-83; Illinois State University, Normal, assistant professor of history, 1988-89; University of Texas at Arlington, assistant professor of urban and public affairs, 1989-91; Iowa State University, Ames, assistant professor, 1991-94, associate professor of community and regional planning, 1994-95; consulting historian and urban planner, Shaker Heights, OH, 1995-. **Publications:** Planning for the Private Interest: Land Use Controls and Residential Patterns in Columbus, Ohio, 1900-1970, 1994. Contributor to books. Contributor of articles and reviews to professional journals. Prior to 1991, some articles appeared under the name Patricia Burgess Stach. **Address:** 3283 Norwood Rd, Shaker Heights, OH 44122, U.S.A. **Online address:** paburge@attglobal.net

BURGESS, Robert J(ohn). American, b. 1961. **Genres:** Business/Trade/ Industry. **Career:** United Bank of Colorado, Denver, analyst, 1984-85; Coors Brewing, Golden, CO, senior analyst, 1985-88; U.S. West Telecommunications, Englewood, CO, in marketing, 1988-91; Marketing Advocates Inc., Englewood, founder, 1990, president, 1991-. Adjunct faculty member, University of Denver and University of Colorado at Denver, both 1991-. South Metropolitan Denver Chamber of Commerce, small business counselor, 1992-; Denver Entrepreneurship Academy, member of board of directors, small business counselor, 1992-. **Publications:** Silver Bullets: A Soldier's Story of How Coors Bombed the Beer Wars, St. Martin's, 1993. Author of "Quick Consult," a monthly column, Denver Business Journal, 1993. **Address:** 7273 S. Allison Way, Littleton, CO 80128-4355, U.S.A.

BURGESS, Stephen F(ranklin). American, b. 1952. **Genres:** International relations/Current affairs. **Career:** University of Zambia, Lusaka, lecturer in development studies, 1980-82; Vanderbilt University, Nashville, TN, instructor in political science, 1991-92; Hofstra University, Hempstead, NY, assistant professor of political science, 1992-99; U.S. Air War College, Maxwell Air Force Base, AL, assistant professor of international security studies, 1999-, currently professor of strategy and international security and chair of department; associate of U.S. Air Force Counter-Proliferation Center. **Publications:** Smallholders and Political Voice in Zimbabwe, 1997; The United Nations under Boutros Boutros-Ghali, 1992-1997, 2001; (with H. Purkitt) The Rollback of the South African Chemical and Biological Warfare Program, 2001; (with H. Purkitt) South Africa's Weapons of Mass Destruction, in press. **Address:** U.S. Air War College, 325 Chennault Cir., Maxwell AFB, AL 36112, U.S.A. **Online address:** StvBurgess@aol.com

BURGOYNE, Bruce E. American, b. 1924. **Genres:** History, Translations. **Career:** U.S. Navy, 1942-46; U.S. Army 1948-54; U.S. Air Force, 1954-64, retiring as master sergeant; civilian in military intelligence, 1965-71. **Publications:** TRANSLATIONS: J.C. Doehla, A Hessian Diary of the American Revolution, 1990; H. Kuemmell and V. Asteroth, Diaries of a Hessian Chaplain and the Chaplain's Assistant, 1991; (compiler) Waldeck Soldiers of the American Revolutionary War: A Hessian Diary of the American Revolution, 1993; Eighteenth Century America, 1995; Georg Pausch's Journal and Reports of the Campaign in America, 1996; (and compiler) Enemy Views: The American Revolutionary War as Recorded by the Hessian Participants, 1997. **Address:** 1131 S. Bay Rd., Lot 185, Dover, DE 19901, U.S.A.

BURIAN, Jarka M. American, b. 1927. **Genres:** Theatre. **Career:** State University of New York, Albany, Dept. of Theatre, assistant professor, 1955-59, associate professor, 1959-63, professor, 1963-93, emeritus, 1993, chairman, 1971-74, 1977-78. **Publications:** Americke Drama a Divadelnictvi, 1966; The Scenography of Josef Svoboda, 1971 (Special Award, U.S. Institute of Theatre Technology, 1973); Josef Svoboda's Scenography for Richard Wagner's Operas, 1983; (trans. and ed.) Josef Svoboda's The Secret of Theatrical Space, Applause Books, 1993; Modern Czech Theatre: Reflector

and Conscience of a Nation, 2002; Leading Creators of Twentieth Century Czech Theatre, 2002. **Address:** 71 Berkshire Blvd, Albany, NY 12203-2319, U.S.A.

BURK, Frank. American, b. 1942. **Genres:** Mathematics/Statistics. **Career:** California State University, Chico, member of mathematics faculty. **Publications:** Lebesgue Measure and Integration, 1997. **Address:** 2280 Oak Park Ave., Chico, CA 95928, U.S.A. **Online address:** fburk@csuchico.edu

BURK, Kathleen. American, b. 1946. **Genres:** History, International relations/Current affairs, Money/Finance, Politics/Government, Biography. **Career:** University of Dundee, Scotland, tutorial assistant in modern history, 1976-77; University of London, England, lecturer in history and politics at Imperial College of Science and Technology, 1980-90; University College London, lecturer in history, 1990-93, reader in modern and contemporary history, 1993-95; professor of modern and contemporary history, 1995-. **Publications:** Britain, America, and the Sinews of War, 1914-1918, 1985; The First Privatisation: The Politicians, the City and the Denationalisation of Steel, 1988; Morgan Grenfell 1838-1988: The Biography of a Merchant Bank, 1989; (with A. Cairncross) Goodbye, Great Britain: The 1976 IMF Crisis, 1992; (with M. Pohl) Deutsche Bank in London 1873-1998, 1998; Troublemaker: The Life and History of A.J.P. Taylor, 2000. EDITOR: (and contrib.) War and the State: The Transformation of British Government, 1914-1919, 1982; (with M. Stokes) The United States and the Western Alliance since 1945, 1999. **Address:** Dept. of History, University College London, Gower St, London WC1E 6BT, England.

BURK, Robert F(rederick). American, b. 1955. **Genres:** Politics/ Government, Sports/Fitness, Biography. **Career:** University of Wisconsin-Madison, lecturer in history, 1983; University of Cincinnati, OH, visiting assistant professor of history, 1983-84; Muskingum College, New Concord, OH, assistant professor, 1984-89, associate professor of history, 1989-, college archivist, 1988-. **Publications:** The Eisenhower Administration and Black Civil Rights, 1984; Dwight D. Eisenhower: Hero and Politician, 1986; The Corporate State and the Broker State: The du Ponts and American National Politics, 1925-40, 1990; Never Just a Game: Players, Owners, and American Baseball to 1920, 1994; Much More Than a Game: Players, Owners, and American Baseball since 1921, 2001. **Address:** Department of History, Muskingum College, New Concord, OH 43762, U.S.A. **Online address:** burk@muskingum.edu

BURKE, Carolyn. Australian. **Genres:** Literary criticism and history. **Career:** Art critic, translator, and writer. University of California, Santa Cruz, research associate in humanities, c. 1998-. **Publications:** (trans. with G.C. Gill) L. Irigaray, An Ethics of Sexual Difference (philosophy), 1993; (ed. with N. Schor and M. Whitford) Engaging with Irigaray: Feminist Philosophy and Modern European Thought (philosophy), 1994; Becoming Modern: The Life of Mina Loy (biography), 1996. Contributor to art journals. **Address:** c/o The University of California Press, 2120 Berkeley Way, Berkeley, CA 94720, U.S.A.

BURKE, James. British, b. 1936. **Genres:** History, Sciences. **Career:** Producer, writer and host of TV documentaries and news series, 1965-. Director, English School, Bologna, 1961-63, and Rome, 1963-65. **Publications:** (with R. Baxter) Tomorrow's World, vol. I, 1970, vol. II, 1972; Connections, 1978; The Day the Universe Changed, 1985; Chances, 1991; (with R. Ornstein) The Axemaker's Gift, 1994; Connections, 1995; The Pinball Effect, 1996; The Knowledge Web, 1998; Circles, 2000; Twin Tracks, 2003. **Address:** c/o Royce Carlton Inc, 866 UN Plaza, New York, NY 10017-1881, U.S.A.

BURKE, Martyn. Canadian, b. 1947. **Genres:** Novels, Plays/Screenplays, Documentaries/Reportage. **Career:** Journalist, screenwriter, and novelist. Freelance correspondent, covered the Vietnam War and Afghan War; director of documentary films for the Canadian Broadcasting Corporation (CBC-TV). **Publications:** Laughing War, 1980; The Commissar's Report, 1984; Ivory Joe, 1991. NOVELS: Tiara, 1995; The Shelling of Beverly Hills, 2000; When the Glass Comes Out of the Ground, 2005. SCREENPLAYS: Connections; State of Shock; The Last Chase; Power Play; Sugartime; Pentagon Wars, 1998; Pirates of Silicon Valley, 1999.

BURKE, Richard E. American, b. 1953. **Genres:** Politics/Government. **Career:** Administrative assistant/chief of staff for U.S. Senator Edward Kennedy, Washington, DC, 1971-81. American Electro Products (electronics), senior vice president for marketing and director of human resources; Congress Video Group, chair and CEO; National Entertainment Group (producer and distributor of video cassettes), president; affiliated with The

European Gourmet: Guide to Best Restaurants in Europe. On board of trustees, Martha Graham Dance Company. **Publications:** (with William Hoffer and Marilyn Hoffer) The Senator: My Ten Years with Ted Kennedy, St. Martin's, 1992. **Address:** John Hawkins & Associates Inc., 71 W. 23rd St., Ste. 1600, New York, NY 10010, U.S.A.

BURKE, Sean. Welsh, b. 1961. **Genres:** Plays/Screenplays, Literary criticism and history. **Career:** Freelance journalist, 1989-92; University of Durham, Durham, England, lecturer in English, 1992-. **Publications:** The Revolutionist (play), 1987; The Death and Return of the Author (literary theory), 1992, 2nd ed., 1998; Authorship: From Plato to the Postmodern (literary theory), 1995; Deadwater (novel), 2002. Contributor to anthologies and academic journals. **Address:** Department of English Studies, University of Durham, Durham DH1 3JT, England. **Online address:** j.m.burke@durham.ac.uk

BURKEY, Stan. Norwegian (born United States), b. 1938. **Genres:** Third World. **Career:** Redd Barna, Oslo, Norway, program coordinator, 1977-81, Sri Lanka representative, 1981-84; ACORD, Uganda representative, 1986-90; Quaker Service Norway, Uganda representative, 1990-97; Uganda Change Agent Association, executive secretary, 1997-. **Publications:** People First: A Guide to Self-Reliant Participatory Rural Development, 1993; Bookkeeping for Development Groups, Quaker Service of Norway, 1993. **Address:** PO Box 2922, Kampala, Uganda. **Online address:** ucaa@infocom.co.ug

BURKITT, Ian. British, b. 1956. **Genres:** Psychology. **Career:** Leeds Area Health Authority, Leeds, England, office clerk, 1975-78; Denison Brothers Printers, Yorkshire, England, fork lift driver, 1978-79; Bradford Social Services, Bradford, England, social worker, 1983-85; University of Bradford, lecturer in social psychology, 1992-. **Publications:** Social Selves: Theories of the Social Formation of Personality, 1991; Bodies of Thought, 1999. Contributor to philosophy and history journals. **Address:** Dept of Applied Social Sciences, University of Bradford, Bradford BD7 1DP, England. **Online address:** i.burkitt@bradford.ac.uk

BURKS, Brian. American, b. 1955. **Genres:** Westerns/Adventure. **Career:** Writer. Owner and operator of horse rental stables. Worked as a rancher, lumber yardman, surveyor, engineering technician, heavy equipment operator, ambulance and truck driver, and musician. **Publications:** Runs with Horses, 1995; Soldier Boy, 1997; Walks Alone, 1998; Wrango, 2000. MURPHY SERIES (with G. Paulsen): Murphy's Stand, 1993; Murphy's Ambush, 1995; Murphy's Trail, 1996. **Address:** 18 Burks Rd, Tularosa, NM 88352, U.S.A.

BURKS, Jean M. American, b. 1949. **Genres:** Antiques/Furnishings. **Career:** Cooper-Hewitt Museum, NYC, research assistant to curator of decorative arts, 1983-84, adjunct professor at the Parsons School of Design, 1986-87, 2003, and 2005; Philadelphia Museum of Art, Philadelphia, PA, assistant curator of American decorative arts, 1984-86; Henry Francis du Pont Winterthur Museum, Winterthur, DE, research assistant, 1987; Shaker Village Inc., Canterbury, NH, curator of collections, 1987-90; Strong Museum, Rochester, NY, curator of recreational artifacts, 1991-93; Bard Graduate Center for Studies in the Decorative Arts, NYC, adjunct professor, 1993-95; Shelburne Museum, curator of decorative arts, Shelburne, VT, 1995-. Lecturer on furniture and base metals consultant. **Publications:** Birmingham Brass Candlesticks, 1987; (with T. Rieman) The Complete Book of Shaker Furniture, 1993; The Encyclopeida of Shaker Furniture, 2003; The Shaker Furniture Handbook, 2005. Documented Furniture (booklet). Contributor to periodicals. **Address:** Shelburne Museum, U.S. Route 7, PO Box 10, Shelburne, VT 05482-7007, U.S.A.

BURLEW, A(nn) Kathleen. American. **Genres:** Psychology. **Career:** University of Cincinnati, Cincinnati, OH, professor of psychology, 1993-. **Publications:** (with W.P. Smith, M. Mosely, and W.M. Whitney) Minority Issues in Mental Health, 1978; (with Smith, Mosely, and Whitney) Reflections on Black Psychology, 1979; (with W.C. Banks, H.M. McAdoo, and D. Azibo) African American Psychology: Theory, Research, and Practice, 1992. **Address:** Department of Psychology, 334 Dyer, ML No. 0376, University of Cincinnati, Cincinnati, OH 45221, U.S.A.

BURLEY, W(illiam) J(ohn). British, b. 1914. **Genres:** Novels, Mystery/Crime/Suspense. **Career:** Full-time writer since 1974. Engineer and Manager for South Western Gas and Water Co. Ltd. in southwest England, 1936-50; Head of the Biology Dept., Richmond Grammar School, Surrey, 1953-55; Head of Biology, 1955-59, and Tutor, 1959-74, Newquay School, Cornwall. **Publications:** A Taste of Power, 1966; Three-Toed Pussy, 1968; Death in Willow Pattern, 1969; To Kill a Cat, 1970; Guilt Edged, 1971; Death in a

Salubrious Place, 1973; Death in Stanley Street, 1974; Wycliffe and the Pea-Green Boat, 1975; Wycliffe and the Schoolgirls, 1976; The Schoolmaster, 1977; Centenary History of the City of Truro, 1977; The Sixth Day (non-mystery novel), 1978; Wycliffe and the Scapegoat, 1978; Charles and Elizabeth, 1979; Wycliffe in Paul's Court, 1979; The House of Care, 1981; Wycliffe's Wild Goose Chase, 1982; Wycliffe and the Beales, 1983; Wycliffe and the Four Jacks, 1985; Wycliffe and the Quiet Virgin, 1986; Wycliffe and the Windsor Blue, 1987; Wycliffe and the Tangled Web, 1988; Wycliffe and the Cycle of Death, 1990; Wycliffe and the Dead Flautist, 1991; Wycliffe and the Last Rites, 1992; Wycliffe and the Dunes Mystery, 1993; Wycliffe and the House of Fear, 1995; Wycliffe and the Redhead, 1997; Wycliffe and the Guild of Nine, 2000. **Address:** St. Patricks, Holywell, Newquay, Cornwall TR8 5PT, England.

BURLING, William J. American, b. 1949. **Genres:** Literary criticism and history, Reference. **Career:** Auburn University, Auburn, AL, assistant professor of English, 1985-89; Southwest Missouri State University, Springfield, associate professor, 1989-94, professor of English, 1994-. Producer, codirector, audio engineer, and musical director of the documentary videotape The Spirit of Pioneer Women, 1993. **Publications:** A Checklist of New Plays and Entertainments on the London Stage, 1700-1737, 1992; Summer Theatre in London, 1661-1820 and the Rise of the Haymarket Theatre, 2000; (ed. with T.J. Viator) The Plays of Colley Cibber, 2000; (with O. Johnson) The Colonial American Stage, 1665-1774: A Documentary Calendar, 2001. Contributor to scholarly journals. **Address:** Department of English, Southwest Missouri State University, 901 South National, Springfield, MO 65804, U.S.A. **Online address:** wjb692f@mail.smsu.edu

BURLINGAME, Michael. American, b. 1941. **Genres:** History. **Career:** Connecticut College, New London, professor of history, 1968-. Abraham Lincoln Institute of the Mid-Atlantic, member of board of directors; Abraham Lincoln Studies Center, member of board of advisers. **Publications:** The Inner World of Abraham Lincoln, 1994; An Oral History of Lincoln, 1996; Inside Lincoln's White House, 1997; Lincoln Observed, 1998. **Address:** Department of History, Connecticut College, New London, CT 06320, U.S.A. **Online address:** mabur@conncoll.edu

BURMAN, Edward. British, b. 1947. **Genres:** Novels, History. **Career:** University of Rome, Rome, Italy, lecturer, 1972-74; Government of Iran, Tehran, editor, 1974-79; University of L'Aquila, L'Aquila, Italy, lecturer, 1979-84; full-time writer, 1988-. **Publications:** Silvestro Aquilano, 1981; The Inquisition: The Hammer of Heresy, 1984; The Templars: Knights of God, 1986; The Assassins: Holy Killers of Islam, 1987; Italian Dynasties: The Great Families of Italy from the Renaissance to the Present Day, 1989; The World before Columbus: 1100-1492, 1989; (ed.) Logan Pearsall Smith: An Anthology, 1989; The Image of Our Lord (fiction), 1990; Emperor to Emperor: Italy before the Renaissance, 1991; Supremely Abominable Crimes: The Trial of the Knights Templar, 1994. **Address:** A. M. Heath & Co. Ltd, 79 St. Martin's Lane, London WC2N 4RE, England.

BURNET, Jean R. Canadian, b. 1920. **Genres:** Cultural/Ethnic topics, History. **Career:** Editor, Ontario History, 1990-95. Instructor, 1945-49, Assistant Professor, 1954-64, and Associate Professor of Sociology, 1964-67, University of Toronto; Professor of Sociology, York University, Toronto, 1967-85; Chair of Board of Dirs. and Chief Executive Officer, Multicultural History Society of Ontario, Toronto, 1985-90. **Publications:** Next Year Country: A Study of Rural Social Organization in Alberta, 1951, reprinted, 1978; Ethnic Groups in Upper Canada, 1972; (with H. Palmer) Coming Canadians: An Introduction to a History of Canada's Peoples, 1988; Multiculturalism in Canada, 1988. EDITOR: Looking into My Sister's Eyes, 1986; Migration and the Transformation of Cultures, 1992. **Address:** 494 St Clements Ave, Toronto, ON, Canada M5N 1M4.

BURNETT, Alan. New Zealander, b. 1932. **Genres:** Economics. **Career:** Worked for New Zealand Foreign Service, 1956-69; Australian National University, Canberra, senior research fellow, 1970-92; author. **Publications:** The Western Pacific: The Challenge of Sustainable Growth, Edward Elgar, 1992. **Address:** 13 Coles Place, Torrens, Canberra, ACT 2607, Australia.

BURNETT, Alfred David. British, b. 1937. **Genres:** Poetry, Intellectual history, Librarianship, Literary criticism and history, Translations. **Career:** Glasgow University Library, library assistant, 1959-64; Durham University Library, assistant librarian, 1964-90, part time, 1990-96. **Publications:** Mandala, 1967; Diversities, 1968; A Ballad upon a Wedding, 1969; Columbaria, 1971; Shimabara, 1972; 30 Snow Poems, 1973; Fescennines, 1973; (with S. Simsova and R.K. Gupta) Studies in Comparative Librarianship, 1973; The True Vine, 1974; The Abbott Collection of Literary Manuscripts, 1975; Hero and Leander, 1975; He and She, 1976; The Heart's Undesign, 1977; Figures and Spaces, 1978; (with E. Havard-Williams) International Library and Information Programmes, 1978; Jackdaw, 1980; (with H.A. Whatley) Language and Literacy, 1981; Thais, 1981; Romans, 1983; Vines, 1984; Arabic Resources, 1986; Autolycus, 1987; Technology for Information in Development, 1988; Kantharos, 1989; Pharos, 1989; Lesbos, 1990; Root and Flower, 1990; The Presence of Japan, 1991; Crystal and Flint, 1991; (with J. Cayley) Mirror and Pool, 1992; 9 Poets, 1993; Temenos, privately printed, 1993; The Olive of Odysseus, 1993; The Island: A Poem, 1994, 2nd. ed., 1996; 12 Poems, 1994; Something of Myself, 1994; 6 Poems, 1995; Transfusions: Poems from the French, 1995; Transfusions: An Introduction, 1995; Hokusai, 1996; Marina Tsvetaeva, 1996; Moschatel and Morning Star, 1997; Chesil Beach: A Poem, 1997; Akhmatova, 1998; The Engraved Title-Page of Bacon's Instauratio Magna, 1998; A Thinker for All Seasons, 2000; Butterflies, 2000; Cinara, 2001; Evergreens, 2002; Sister Margaret Tournour, 2003; Quoins for the Chase, 2003. **Address:** 33 Hastings Ave, Merry Oaks, Durham DH1 3QG, England.

BURNETT, Charles. American, b. 1944. **Genres:** Plays/Screenplays. **Career:** Director, producer, cinematographer, editor, and writer. **Publications:** SCREENPLAYS: Killer of Sheep, 1978; My Brother's Wedding, 1983; Bless Their Little Hearts, 1984; To Sleep with Anger, 1990; The Glass Shield, 1995; The Horse. **Address:** c/o Broder Kurland Webb Offner, 9242 Beverly Blvd. Suite 200, Beverly Hills, CA 90210, U.S.A.

BURNETT, Gail Lemley. American, b. 1953. **Genres:** Medicine/Health. **Career:** Reporter for two small daily newspapers in California, 1977-81; Journal Tribune, Biddeford, ME, news reporter, 1981-82, wire editor and copy editor, 1982-89, feature writer and author of the column "Home Front," 1989-94, editor of editorial page, 1994-. **Publications:** Muscular Dystrophy, 1995. **Address:** Journal Tribune, PO Box 627, Biddeford, ME 04005, U.S.A. **Online address:** burnett@gwi.net

BURNETT, John. British, b. 1925. **Genres:** Economics, Food and Wine, History, Autobiography/Memoirs, Bibliography. **Career:** Professor of Social History, Brunel University, 1972- (now emeritus), head, Dept of General Studies, 1962-66, reader, social and economic history, 1966-72; lecturer, social history, London University, 1952-72; head, Division of Liberal Studies, Borough Polytechnic (now University of the South Bank), 1959-62; chair, Social History Society of the UK, 1985-90. **Publications:** Plenty and Want: A Social History of Diet in England from 1815 to the Present Day, 1966, 1989; A History of Cost of Living, 1969, 1993; The Challenge of the 19th Century, 1970; Housing: A Social History 1815-1985, 1987; Destiny Obscure: Autobiographies of Childhood, 1982, 1994; Idle Hands, The Experience of Unemployment, 1790-1990, 1994; Liquid Pleasures: A Social History of Drinks in Modern Britain, 1999; England Eats Out: A Social History 1830Present, 2004. EDITOR: Useful Toil: Autobiographies of Working People from the 1820s to the 1920s, 1974, 1994; (co-) The Autobiography of the Working Class: A Critical Annotated Bibliography, vol. 1, 1984, vol. 2, 1987, vol. 3, 1989. **Address:** Castle Dene, 11 Burgess Wood Rd, Beaconsfield, Bucks. HP9 1EQ, England.

BURNETT, Ron. Canadian (born England), b. 1947. **Genres:** Communications/Media, Cultural/Ethnic topics, Film, Popular Culture. **Career:** McGill University, Instructional Communications Centre, Montreal, QC, television cameraman, 1968-69, professor of communications, 1970-82; Vanier College, Montreal, founder and chair of media, fine arts, photography and theatre department, 1972-75, 1977-80; LaTrobe University, Melbourne, Australia, professor of film studies, 1983-88; McGill University, Montreal, associate professor of cultural studies, 1988-96, director of Graduate Program in Communications, 1990-96; Emily Carr Institute of Art and Design, Vancouver, BC, president, 1996-. Director of documentary videotapes. **Publications:** (ed. and author of intro.) Explorations in Film Theory, 1991; Cultures of Vision: Images, Media and the Imaginary, 1995; How Images Think, 2004. Contributor to books on film and video both in English and French. Contributor to periodicals. **Address:** Emily Carr Institute of Art and Design, 1399 Johnston St, Vancouver, BC, Canada V6H 3R9. **Online address:** RBurnett@eciad.bc.ca

BURNHAM, Terence (Charles). American. **Genres:** Psychology. **Career:** Writer; former employee of Goldman, Sachs & Co., New York, NY; Harvard University, Cambridge, MA, assistant professor of economics, Kennedy School of Government, 1997-, became visiting scholar, Harvard Business School. Co-founder, Progenics Pharmaceuticals Inc. **Publications:** (with J. Phelan) Mean Genes: From Sex to Money to Food, Taming Our Primal Instincts, 2000. Contributor to journals and periodicals. **Address:** Harvard Business School, Soldiers Field, Boston, MA 02163, U.S.A.

BURNINGHAM, John (Mackintosh). British, b. 1936. **Genres:** Children's fiction, Cultural/Ethnic topics. **Career:** Author, designer, illustrator. **Publications:** Borka: The Adventures of a Goose with No Feathers, 1963; Trubloff: The Mouse Who Wanted to Play the Balalaika, 1964; ABC, 1964; Humbert, Mister Firkin and the Lord Mayor of London, 1965; Cannonball Simp, 1966; Birdland: Wall Frieze, 1966; Lionland: Wall Frieze, 1966; Storyland: Wall Frieze, 1966; Harquin: The Fox Who Went Down to the Valley, 1967; Jungleland: Wall Frieze, 1968; Wonderland: Wall Frieze, 1968; Seasons, 1969; Mr. Gumpy's Outing, 1970; Around the World: Two Wall Friezes, 1972; Around the World in Eighty Days, 1972; The Baby (reader), 1974; The Rabbit (reader), 1974; The School (reader), 1974; The Snow (reader), 1974; Mr. Gumpy's Motor Car, 1974; The Blanket, 1975; The Cupboard (reader), 1975; The Dog (reader), 1975; The Friend (reader), 1975; Come Away from the Water, Shirley, 1977; Time to Get Out of the Bath, Shirley, 1978; Would You Rather, 1978; The Shopping Basket, 1980; Avocado Baby, 1982; Granpa, 1984; Opposites, Colours, 1985; John Patrick Norman McHennessy-The Boy Who Is Always Late, 1987; Hey! Get off Our Train, 1990; Aldo, 1992; England, 1992; Harvey Slumfenberger's Christmas Present, 1993; Courtney, 1994; Cloudland, 1996; France, 1998; Whadyamean, 1999; Hushabye, 2001; The Time of Your Life, 2002; The Magic Bed, 2003. Illustrator of books by I. Fleming, K. Grahame, L. Schantz. **Address:** c/o Jonathan Cape Ltd, 20 Vauxhall Bridge Rd, London SW1V 2FA, England.

BURNS, Ailsa (Milligan). Australian, b. 1930. **Genres:** Human relations/Parenting, Psychology, Self help, Women's studies and issues. **Career:** Macquarie University, North Ryde, Australia, lecturer to associate professor of psychology. **Publications:** Breaking Up: Separation and Divorce in Australia, 1980; (with J.J. Goodnow) Children and Families in Australia: Contemporary Issues and Problems, 2nd ed., 1985; (with Goodnow) Home and School, 1985; (with R. Dunlop) Don't Feel the World Is Caving In, 1988; (with C. Scott) Mother-Headed Families and Why They Have Increased, 1994. Contributor to books and professional journals. EDITOR: (with G. Bottomley and R. Jools) The Family in the Modern World, 1983; (with N. Grieve) Australian Women: New Feminist Perspectives, 1986; (with Grieve) Australian Women: Contemporary Feminist Thought, 1994. **Address:** Dept of Psychology, Macquarie University, North Ryde, NSW 2109, Australia. **Online address:** aburns@psy.mq.edu.au

BURNS, Alan. British, b. 1929. **Genres:** Novels, Plays/Screenplays. **Career:** Barrister-at-Law. Professor, University of Minnesota, Minneapolis, 1977-90; Lancaster University, 1990-96. **Publications:** Buster, 1961; Europe after the Rain, 1965; Celebrations, 1967; Babel, 1969; Palach (play), 1970; Dreamerika!, 1972; The Angry Brigade, 1974; The Day Daddy Died, 1981; (with C. Sugnet) The Imagination on Trial (non-fiction), 1981; Revolutions of the Night, 1986; (with W. Harris) The Review of Contemporary Fiction, 1997. **Address:** Flat 2, 6 Upper Park Rd, London NW3 2UP, England.

BURNS, Anna. Irish, b. 1962. **Genres:** Novels. **Career:** Writer. **Publications:** No Bones, 2001. Contributor of short fiction to periodicals. **Address:** c/o Author Mail, W. W. Norton Co., 500 Fifth Ave., New York, NY 10110, U.S.A.

BURNS, Carol. British, b. 1934. **Genres:** Novels, Art/Art history. **Career:** City Literary Institute, London, Lecturer in Art History, 1972, Lecturer in Creative Writing, 1973-2001. City Literary Institute Magazine, Ed., Matrix. Artist. **Publications:** Infatuation, 1968; The Narcissist, 1968; Stumato (novel), forthcoming. **Address:** Flat 2, 6 Upper Park Rd, Belsize Park, London NW3 2UP, England. **Online address:** caburns90@hotmail.com

BURNS, Diane L. American, b. 1950. **Genres:** Children's fiction, Children's non-fiction, Humor/Satire. **Career:** Elementary schoolteacher, Rhinelander, WI, 1972-74; U.S. Forest Service, Bitterroot National Forest, MT, relief fire tower lookout, 1980; Institute of Children's Literature, Redding, CT, instructor by correspondence, 1989-2003; writer. Founder and director of Story Cottage (writing workshops for children) and a local writers' support group; Festival of Performing Arts, Rhinelander Area Children's Arts Program, chairman, 1979; Cooperative Children's Book Center, member; Rhinelander District Library Foundation, vice president, 2000-01. **Publications:** FOR YOUNG PEOPLE: Elephants Never Forget! A Book of Elephant Jokes, 1987; Snakes Alive! Jokes about Snakes, 1987; Hail to the Chief! Jokes about Presidents, 1988; Here's to Ewe: Jokes about Sheep, 1989; Arbor Day, 1989; Sugaring Season: Making Maple Syrup, 1990; Rocky Mountain Seasons, 1993; Cranberries: Fruit of the Bogs, 1994; Home on the Range!, 1994; Trees, Leaves and Bark, 1995; Snakes, Salamanders and Lizards, 1995; Berries, Nuts & Seeds, 1996; Frogs, Toads & Turtles, 1997; Wildflowers, 1997; (with J.A. Burns) Plant a Garden in Your Sneaker, 1998. **Address:** 4099 N Shore Dr, Rhinelander, WI 54501, U.S.A.

BURNS, Edward. American, b. 1946. **Genres:** Documentaries/Reportage. **Career:** Public school teacher. Has also served with the Baltimore Police Dept., Baltimore, MD, as a patrol officer and as a detective. **Publications:** (with D. Simon) The Corner: A Year in the Life of an Inner-City Neighborhood (nonfiction), 1997. **Address:** c/o Broadway Books, 1540 Broadway, New York, NY 10036, U.S.A.

BURNS, Edward. British, b. 1955. **Genres:** Theatre. **Career:** University of Liverpool, Liverpool, England, lecturer in English. **Publications:** Restoration Comedy: Crises of Desire and Identity, 1987; Character: Acting and Being on the Pre-Modern Stage, 1990. **Address:** English Dept., University of Liverpool, PO Box 147, Liverpool L693BX, England.

BURNS, Grant (Francis). American, b. 1947. **Genres:** Adult non-fiction. **Career:** University of Michigan-Flint, MI, reference librarian, 1977-92, head librarian of public services, 1992-. **Publications:** The Atomic Papers, 1984; The Sports Pages, 1987; Affordable Housing, 1989; The Nuclear Present, 1992; Librarians in Fiction, 1998. Contributor to professional journals. **Address:** Thompson Library, University of Michigan-Flint, Flint, MI 48502, U.S.A. **Online address:** gfburns@flint.umich.edu

BURNS, James MacGregor. American, b. 1918. **Genres:** Administration/Management, History, Politics/Government, Biography. **Career:** Williams College, Williamstown, MA, assistant professor, 1947-50, associate professor, 1950-53, professor, 1953-88, professor emeritus of political science, 1988-; University of Maryland, Academy of Leadership, senior scholar; University of Richmond, Jepson School of Leadership Studies, senior scholar, 2001-04. Project 87, interdisciplinary study of constitution during bicentennial era, co-chairman, 1976-87. **Publications:** Congress on Trial, 1949; (with J.W. Peltason) Government by the People: The Dynamics of American National Government, 1952; (with Peltason) Government by the People: The Dynamics of American State & Local Government, 1952; (with Peltason) Government by the People: The Dynamics of American National State & Local Government (rev. of 2 previous books), 1954, (with Peltason, Cronin and D.B. Magleby) 16th ed., 1994; Roosevelt: The Lion and the Fox, 1956; (ed. with Peltason) Functions and Policies of American Government, 1958, 3rd ed., 1967; John Kennedy: A Political Profile, 1960; The Deadlock of Democracy: 4-Party Politics in America, 1963; (with others) Dialogues in Americanism, 1964; Presidential Government, 1966; (with others) Our American Government Today, 1966; (ed.) Lyndon Baines Johnson: To Heal and to Build, 1968; Roosevelt: The Soldier of Freedom, 1970 (Pulitzer Prize, National Book Award); Uncommon Sense, 1973; Leadership, 1978; The Vineyard of Liberty, 1982; The Power to Lead, 1984; The Workshop of Democracy, 1985; The Crosswinds of Freedom, 1989; (with S. Burns) A People's Charter, 1991; (with G.J. Sorenson) Dead Center, 1999; (with S. Dunn) The Three Roosevelts, 2001; Transforming Leadership, 2003; (with S. Dunn) George Washington, 2004. **Address:** Dept. of Political Science, Williams College, Williamstown, MA 01267, U.S.A.

BURNS, Jim. British, b. 1936. **Genres:** Novellas/Short stories, Poetry, Literary criticism and history. **Career:** Regular Contributor, Tribune, London, and Ambit, London, 1964-. Ed., Move mag., Preston, 1964-68, and Palantir, Preston, 1976-83; Beat Scene, jazz editor, 1990-. **Publications:** Some Poems, 1965; Some More Poems, 1966; My Sad Story and Other Poems, 1967; Cells: Prose Pieces, 1967; Saloon Bar: 3 Jim Burns Stories, 1967; The Store of Things, 1969; Types: Prose Pieces and Poems, 1970; A Single Flower, 1972; Leben in Preston, 1973; Easter in Stockport, 1976; Fred Engels in Woolworths, 1975; Playing It Cool, 1976; The Goldfish Speaks from Beyond the Grave, 1976; Catullus in Preston, 1979; Aristotle's Grill, 1979; Notes from a Greasy Spoon, 1980; Internal Memorandum, 1982; The Real World, 1986; Out of the Past: Selected Poems 1961-1986, 1987; Poems for Tribune, 1988; The Gift, 1989; Confessions of an Old Believer, 1996; As Good a Reason as Any, 1999; Beats, Bohemians, Intellectuals: Selected Essays, 2000; Take It Easy, 2003. **Address:** 11 Gatley Green, Gatley, Cheadle, Cheshire, England.

BURNS, Ken(neth Lauren). American, b. 1953. **Genres:** History, Military/Defense/Arms control, Sports/Fitness, Documentaries/Reportage. **Career:** Producer, director, cinematographer, and writer. Maker of motion picture and television documentaries. Television appearances include Public Television: Public Debate with Charlie Rose, PBS, 1992. Member of board of trustees, New Hampshire Humanities Council; member of board of directors, MacDowell Colony; trustee, Hampshire College; member of professional council, The New School of Design. **Publications:** FILM AND TELEVISION SCRIPTS: The Brooklyn Bridge, 1981; The Shakers: Hands to Work, Hearts to God, 1984; (with G.C. Ward) Huey Long, 1985; Thomas Hart Benton, 1988; The Congress, 1988; (with Ward and R. Burns) The Civil War, 1990;

Lindbergh, 1990; Empire of the Air: The Men Who Made Radio, 1991; The Songs of the Civil War, 1992; (with Ward) Baseball, 1994; The West, 1996; Thomas Jefferson, 1997. BOOKS: (with A.S. Burns) The Shakers: Hands to Work, Hearts to God: The History and Visions of the United Society of Believers in Christ's Second Appearing from 1774 to the Present (companion to documentary), 1987; (with G.C. Ward and R. Burns) The Civil War: An Illustrated History (companion to television series), 1990; (with G.C. Ward) Baseball (companion to televison series), 1994; (with Ward and D. Duncan) Mark Twain: An Illustrated Biography, 2001. Contributor to books. Retrospectives of Burns's work have been featured at the Smithsonian Institution, 1991, and the Walker Arts Center, Minneapolis, MN, 1991. **Address:** P.O. Box 613, Walpole, NH 03608, U.S.A.

BURNS, Khephra. American, b. 1950. **Genres:** Plays/Screenplays, Biography. **Career:** Freelance writer, NYC, 1978-. Writer and associate producer, WNET-13, 1978-80. **Publications:** (with W. Miles) Black Stars in Orbit: NASA's African American Astronauts, 1994; (with S.L. Taylor) Confirmation: The Spiritual Wisdom That Has Shaped Our Lives, 1997; Mamsa Musa, the Lion of Mali, 2001. TELEVISION PROGRAMS: Black Champions, 1986; Images & Realities, I: African American Men, 1992, II: The African American Family, 1993, III: The African American Woman, 1993, IV: African American Children, 1994; Triple Threat, 1992; The Power of One, 1997; (co-author and co-producer) The Essence Awards, 1992-2003; NAACP/UNCF Gospel Music Festival, 1998. SCREENPLAY: Marie Laveau. MUSICAL: Stackalee. Contributor to books and periodicals. Author of liner notes for recordings of jazz artists. **Address:** Taylor Burns Inc., 220 Riverside Blvd PH3A, New York, NY 10069, U.S.A.

BURNS, Marilyn. American, b. 1941. **Genres:** Children's fiction, Children's non-fiction, Education. **Career:** Writer and educator. **Publications:** FOR CHILDREN. NONFICTION: The Hanukkah Book, 1981; The Hink Pink Book: Or, What Do You Call a Magician's Extra Bunny?, 1981; The $1.00 Word Riddle Book, 1990; How Many Feet? How Many Tails? A Book of Math Riddles, 1996. Designer of math activities for "Hello Math Reader" series, 1997-. BROWN PAPER SCHOOL SERIES: The I Hate Mathematics! Book, 1975; The Book of Think: Or, How to Solve a Problem Twice Your Size, 1976; I Am Not a Short Adult! Getting Good at Being a Kid, 1977; Good for Me! All about Food in 32 Bites, 1978; This Book Is about Time, 1978; Math for Smarty Pants: Or, Who Says Mathematicians Have Little Pig Eyes, 1982. FICTION: The Greedy Triangle, 1994; Spaghetti and Meatballs, 1997. FOR ADULTS. NONFICTION: A Collection of Math Lessons: Grades 3-6, 1987; (with B. Tank) A Collection of Math Lessons: Grades 1-3, 1988; (with C. Humphreys) A Collection of Math Lessons: Grades 6-8, 1990; Math by All Means: Multiplication, Grade 3, 1991; About Teaching Mathematics: A K-8 Resource, 1992; Math and Literature: K-3, 1992; Writing in Math Class: A Resource for Grades 2-8, 1995; Fifty Problem-solving Lessons, 1995. **Address:** PO Box 820, Sausalito, CA 94966-0820, U.S.A.

BURNS, Ralph. American, b. 1949. **Genres:** Poetry. **Career:** University of Arkansas at Little Rock, professor, 1985-. **Publications:** POETRY: Us, 1983; Any Given Day, 1985; Mozart's Starling, 1991; Swamp Candles, 1996. **Address:** University of Arkansas at Little Rock, 23rd and University Ave., Little Rock, AR 72204, U.S.A. **Online address:** rmburns@ualr.edu

BURNS, Ric. American, b. 1955. **Genres:** History. **Career:** Film director and producer. Co-producer of the television documentary The Civil War, 1990; producer and director of television specials. **Publications:** TELEVISION SCRIPTS: (with K. Burns and G.C. Ward; also coproducer) The Civil War, 1990; (also producer and director) The Donner Party, 1992; (with L. Ades; also producer) The Way West, 1995; (with L. Ades) New York, 1998. BOOKS: (with Burns and Ward) The Civil War: An Illustrated History (companion volume to the television documentary), 1990; (with J. Sanders and L. Ades) New York: An Illustrated History, 1999. **Address:** c/o Steeplechase Films, 2095 Broadway Ste 503, New York, NY 10023, U.S.A.

BURNS, Richard Gordon. Also writes as Dick B. American, b. 1925. **Genres:** History, Inspirational/Motivational Literature, Medicine/Health, Psychology, Self help, Theology/Religion, Biography, Bibliography, Reference. **Career:** Admitted to the Bar of California State, 1951; attorney in San Francisco, CA, 1951-61, and Corte Madera, CA, 1961-86; public-records analyst, 1987-90; writer, 1990-. Almonte District Sanitary Board, director, 1952-60; Wyoming Pacific Oil Company, consultant 1955-. President, Almonte District Improvement Club, 1956, Corte Madera Chamber of Commerce, Corte Madera Center Merchant Council, Mill Valley Community Church, and Community Church Retirement Center. **Publications:** NONFICTION AS DICK B: Dr. Bob and His Library, 1992, 3rd ed., 1998; The Oxford Group & Alcoholics Anonymous, 1992, 2nd ed., 1998; The

Akron Genesis of Alcoholics Anonymous, 1992, 2nd ed., 1998; The Books Early AAs Read for Spiritual Growth, 1993, 7th ed., 1998; Anne Smith's Journal, 1994, 3rd ed., 1998; New Light on Alcoholism, 1994, 2nd ed., 1999; (with Bill P.) Courage to Change, 1994; The Good Book and the Big Book, 1995; Good Morning!, 1996; That Amazing Grace, 1996; Turning Point, 1997; Utilizing Early AAs Spiritual Roots for Recovery Today, 1998; Hope!, 1998; The Golden Text of AA, 1999; By the Power of God, 1999; Why Early AA Succeeded, 2001; Making Known the Biblical Roots of AA, 2000; God and Alcoholism, 2001; Cured, 2002; When Early AAs Were Cured, and Why, 2003; Twelve Steps for You, 2003. **Address:** PO Box 837, Kihei, HI 96753-0837, U.S.A. **Online address:** dickb@dickb.com; www.dickb.com/index.shtml

BURR, David (Dwight). American, b. 1934. **Genres:** History. **Career:** Educator, historian, and author. Virginia Polytechnic Institute and State University, Blacksburg, 1966-, assistant professor to professor of history, 1977-2001, professor emeritus, 2001-. **Publications:** The Persecution of Peter Olivi, 1976; Eucharistic Presence and Conversion in Late Thirteenth-Century Franciscan Thought, 1984; Olivi and Franciscan Poverty: The Origins of the Usus Pauper Controversy, 1989; Petrus Ioannis Olivi's Quaestio de Usu Paupere and Tractatus de Usu Paupere, 1992; Olivi's Peaceable Kingdom: A Reading of the Apocalypse Commentary, 1993; Pierre de Jean Olieu: Franciscain Persécuté, 1997; The Spiritual Franciscans: From Protest to Persecution in the Century after Saint Francis, 2001. Contributor to books and journals. **Address:** Dept. of History, Virginia Polytechnic Institute, Blacksburg, VA 24061, U.S.A. **Online address:** olivi@vt.edu

BURRESON, Jay. American. **Genres:** Chemistry. **Career:** Worked as an industrial chemist; Mega Tech of Oregon, Corvallis, OR, currently general manager. **Publications:** (with Penny Cameron Le Couteur) Napoleon's Buttons: How Seventeen Molecules Changed History, 2003. **Address:** Mega Tech of Oregon, 33866 Southeast Eastgate Cir., Corvallis, OR 97333, U.S.A.

BURRIDGE, Trevor David. British (born Wales), b. 1932. **Genres:** History. **Career:** Schoolteacher in England, France, and Canada, 1954-65; McGill University, Montreal, Quebec, assistant professor of history and philosophy of education, 1966-70; Universite de Montreal, Montreal, associate professor, 1974-86, professor of British history, 1986-. Radio and television commentator on British politics. **Publications:** What Happened in Education, Allyn & Bacon, 1970; British Labour and Hitler's War, Deutsch, 1976; Clement Attlee: A Political Biography, J. Cape, 1986. Contributor of articles and reviews to history journals and newspapers. **Address:** Department of History, Universite de Montreal, C.P. 6128A, Montreal, QC, Canada H3C 3J7.

BURROUGH, Bryan. American, b. 1961. **Genres:** Documentaries/Reportage, Business/Trade/Industry. **Career:** Journalist and author. Wall Street Journal, NYC, worked in Dallas, TX, bureau while in college, reporter assigned to Houston, TX, bureau, 1983-85, assigned to Pittsburgh, PA, bureau, 1986-87, reporter on mergers and acquisitions, 1987-. Has also worked as a reporter for Columbia Missourian and Waco Tribune-Herald. **Publications:** (with J. Helyar) Barbarians at the Gate: The Fall of RJR Nabisco, 1990; Vendetta: American Express and the Smearing of Edmond Safra, 1992; Dragon Fly, 1998. Contributor to periodicals. **Address:** Wall Street Journal, 200 Liberty St., New York, NY 10281, U.S.A.

BURROUGHS, William James. British, b. 1942. **Genres:** Environmental sciences/Ecology, Geography, Marine sciences/Oceanography, Meteorology/Atmospheric sciences, Technology. **Career:** National Physical Laboratory, Teddington, Middlesex, England, researcher, 1964-71; British Embassy, Washington, DC, scientific attache, 1971-74; Department of Energy, London, policy official, 1974-87; Department of Health, London, policy official, 1987-91, director of research management, 1991-93, head of international relations, 1993-95; Author of columns in London Times, 1987-90; writer. **Publications:** Lasers, 1976; Understanding Lasers, 1982; Lasers, 1984; Watching the World's Weather, 1991; Weather Cycles: Real or Imaginary?, 1992; Mountain Weather: A Guide for Skiers and Hillwalkers, 1995; (co-author) The Nature Company Guide to the Weather, 1996; Does the Weather Really Matter?, 1997; The Climate Revealed, 1999; (co-author) Maritime Weather and Climate, 1999; Climate Change: A Multidisciplinary Approach, 2001; (ed.) Climate: Into the 21st Century, 2003. Contributor to periodicals. **Address:** Squirrels Oak, Clandon Rd, West Clandon, Surrey GU4 7UW, England. **Online address:** BillSqoak@aol.com

BURROW, J(ohn) A(nthony). British, b. 1932. **Genres:** Literary criticism and history. **Career:** Oxford University, Jesus College, fellow, 1961-75; University of Bristol, Winterstoke professor of English, 1976-98, emeritus professor, 1998-. Early English Text Society, hon. director, 1983-. **Publica-**

tions: A Reading of Sir Gawain and the Green Knight, 1965; Ricardian Poetry: Chaucer, Gower, Langland, and the Gawain Poet, 1971; Medieval Writers and Their Work, 1982; Essays on Medieval Literature, 1984; The Ages of Man, 1986; (with T. Turville-Petre) A Book of Middle English, 1992; Langland's Fictions, 1993; Thomas Hoccleve, 1994; The Gawain-Poet, 2001; Gestures and Looks in Medieval Narrative, 2002. EDITOR: Geoffrey Chaucer: A Critical Anthology, 1969; Sir Gawain and the Green Knight, 1972; English Verse 1300-1500, 1977; Hoccleve's Complaint and Dialogue, 1999; (with A.I. Doyle) Thomas: Hoccleve: A Facsimile of the Autograph Manuscripts, 2002. **Address:** 9 The Polygon, Clifton, Bristol, England.

BURROWAY, Janet (Gay). American, b. 1936. **Genres:** Novels, Children's fiction, Plays/Screenplays, Poetry, Autobiography/Memoirs, Essays. **Career:** University of Sussex, Brighton, lecturer in English literature, 1965-70; reviewer, New Statesman, London, 1970-75, New York Times Book Review, 1989-; Florida State University, Tallahassee, member of faculty, 1972-2002, Robert O. Lawton Distinguished Professor Emerita of Literature and Writing, 2002-. **Publications:** Descend Again, 1960; But to the Season (poetry), 1961; The Dancer from the Dance, 1965; Eyes, 1966; The Buzzards, 1970; The Truck on the Track, 1971; (with J. V. Lord), The Giant Jam Sandwich, 1972; Raw Silk, 1977; Material Goods (poetry), 1981; Writing Fiction, 1982, 6th ed., 2002; Opening Nights (novel), 1985; Cutting Stone (novel), 1992; Medea with Child (play), 1997; Sweepstakes (play), 1999; Embalming Mom (essays), 2002; Imaginative Writing, 2002; Parts of Speech (play), 2003; (ed.) From Where You Dream (lectures), 2004. **Address:** 240 De Soto St, Tallahassee, FL 32303, U.S.A. **Online address:** jburroway@english.fsu.edu

BURROWS, Edwin G(wynne). American, b. 1943. **Genres:** History. **Career:** Marymount College, Tarrytown, NY, instructor in history, 1970-71; Lehman College, City University of New York, NYC, adjunct lecturer in history, 1971-72; Brooklyn College, CUNY, instructor and assistant professor, 1972-79, associate professor, 1980-86, professor, 1986-, Claire and Leonard Tow Professor of History, 1999-, distinguished professor of history, 2003-. Dyckman House Museum, member of board of directors; New York Historical Society, member of academic advisory panel; Society of American Historians, fellow, 2000. Consultant to organizations. Recipient: Pulitzer Prize in History, 1999. **Publications:** Albert Gallatin and the Political Economy of Republicanism, 1761-1800, 1986; (with M. Wallace) Gotham: A History of NYC to 1898, 1999; (intro.) T.A. Janvier, In Old New York, 2000; New York in the Revolution, forthcoming. Contributor to books. Contributor of articles and reviews to periodicals. **Address:** 14 Clipper Dr, Northport, NY 11768, U.S.A. **Online address:** eburrows@brooklyn.cuny.edu

BURRS, Mick. (Steven Michael Berzensky). Canadian (born United States), b. 1940. **Genres:** Poetry, Plays/Screenplays. **Career:** Poet, playwright, and songwriter. CKUA-Radio, Edmonton, Alberta, Canada, host of radio programs; Waking Image Press, Regina, Saskatchewan, Canada, founder, 1971. Warm Poets for Cold Nights (reading series), founder, 1975, organizer, 1975-77; Parkland Writers Alliance, cofounder, 1985; presenter of workshops and readings; guest on Canadian radio programs. **Publications:** CHAPBOOKS; In the Dark the Journeyman Landed, 1971; Adventures of the Midnight Janitor, 1972; Game Farm: Poems for Interreflection, 1975; Sockpan, 1976; Walls, 1977; (And illustrator) The Hillside Poems: A Poem Sequence, 1981; (ed.) Sonnet's End and Other Lyrical Catastrophes: An Anthology of Poems, 1981; Pages Torn from Trees: Some Poems Recently Rediscovered, Written Originally in Vancouver, Edmonton, and Regina between 1969 and 1976, 1981; Word Crumbs: Poems, 1981; Listening to the Crows: Poems and Collages, 1983; (And illustrator) From My Box of Dreams: Poems, 1986; Lit like Gold: Poems, 1988. POETRY: Moving in from Paradise, 1976; Children on the Edge of Space, 1977; Seeds of Light, 1978; Aurora: Poems, 1980; The Blue Pools of Paradise, 1983; Ghostwriters and Bookworms, 1984; Junkyard of Dreams: Poetry, 1992; Dark Halo, 1993; The Silence of Horizons, 1996; Variations on the Birth of Jacob, 1997; Rainbows in the Dark, 1998. PLAYS: Gettin' Cuckoo, 1979; Emily Meets the Emperor of Rock & Roll, 1986. EDITOR: Going to War: Found Poems of the Metis People, 1975; The Waking Image Bedside Companion, 1982; (with others) Video Verses: Yorkton TV's Poem of the Month Contest Winners, 1986. Work represented in anthologies. Contributor to periodicals. **Address:** PO Box 639, Yorkton, SK, Canada S3N 2W7.

BURSTEIN, Andrew. American. **Genres:** History. **Career:** University of Northern Iowa, Cedar Falls, assistant professor of history. **Publications:** The Inner Jefferson: Portrait of a Grieving Optimist, 1995; Sentimental Democracy: The Evolution of America's Romantic Self-Image, 1999; America's Jubilee: How in 1826 a Generation Remembered Fifty Years of Independence, 2001. Contributor to periodicals. **Address:** University of Tulsa, 600 South College, Tulsa, OK 74104, U.S.A. **Online address:** andrewburstein@utulsa.edu

BURSTEIN, Fred. American, b. 1950. **Genres:** Children's fiction. **Career:** Writer. Played the role of Laslo Novotny on the television daytime drama Ryan's Hope, ABC-TV, 1984-86; Rondout Valley Middle School, Accord, NY, reading specialist, 1993-. **Publications:** Rebecca's Nap, 1988; Anna's Rain, 1990; Whispering in the Park, 1992; The Dancer, 1993. **Address:** 674 Samsonville Rd, Kerhonkson, NY 12446, U.S.A.

BURSTON, Daniel. Israeli, b. 1954. **Genres:** Psychology. **Career:** Duquesne University, Pittsburgh, PA, professor of psychology. **Publications:** The Legacy of Erich Fromm, 1991; The Wing of Madness: The Life and Work of R.D. Laing, 1996. **Address:** Psychology Dept., Duquesne University, Pittsburgh, PA 15282, U.S.A. **Online address:** burston@duq3.ec.duq.edu

BURSTOW, Bonnie. Canadian, b. 1945. **Genres:** Psychiatry. **Career:** Memorial University of Newfoundland, St. John's, lecturer in English, 1968-69; Brock University, St. Catharines, Ontario, lecturer in English, 1968-69, and drama, 1973-76; guest lecturer at Canadian universities, 1979-87; University of Manitoba, Winnipeg, assistant professor of social work, 1987-88; Carleton University, Ottawa, Ontario, assistant professor, 1988-89, faculty liaison for social work placement students in Toronto, 1989-. Private practice of feminist therapy, 1978-87 and 1988-, and social service training, 1980-; guest on television programs. **Publications:** (ed. with D. Weitz) Shrink Resistant: The Struggle against Psychiatry in Canada, 1988; Radical Feminist Therapy: Working in the Context of Violence, 1992. Contributor to books, periodicals, and professional journals. **Address:** 441 Clinton St., Toronto, ON, Canada M6G 2Z1.

BURT, Nathaniel. American, b. 1913. **Genres:** Novels, Poetry, Social commentary. **Publications:** Rooms in a House, 1947; Question on a Kite, 1950; Scotland's Burning, 1954; Make My Bed, 1957; Leopards in the Garden, 1968; The Perennial Philadelphians, 1963; War Cry of the West, 1964; First Families, 1970; Palaces for the People, 1977; Jackson Hole Journal, 1983; Wyoming Guide, 1991. **Address:** 2117 Windrow Dr, Princeton, NJ 08540, U.S.A.

BURTCH, Brian. Canadian, b. 1949. **Genres:** Law. **Career:** Researcher for the attorney general of British Columbia, Canada, 1977-80; Simon Fraser University, Burnaby, BC, instructor, 1985-87, assistant professor, 1987-92, associate professor, 1992-, professor of criminology, 1998-. Writers' Union of Canada, BC/Yukon regional representative. **Publications:** The Sociology of Law: Critical Approaches to Social Control, 1992; Trials of Labour: The Re-Emergence of Midwifery, 1994; (ed. with N. Larsen) Law in Society: Canadian Perspectives, 1999. **Address:** School of Criminology, Simon Fraser University, Burnaby, BC, Canada V5A 1S6. **Online address:** burtch@sfu.ca

BURTCHAELL, James Tunstead. American, b. 1934. **Genres:** Education, Ethics, Theology/Religion. **Career:** University of Notre Dame, IN, Professor of Theology, 1966-92, Dept. of Theology, Chairman, 1968-70, Provost, 1970-77. **Publications:** Catholic Theories of Biblical Inspiration since 1810: A Review and Critique, 1969; Philemon's Problem: The Daily Dilemma of the Christian, 1973; Bread and Salt, 1978; Rachel Weeping, and Other Essays on Abortion, 1982; For Better for Worse: Sober Thoughts on Passionate Promises, 1985; There Is No More Just War: The Teaching and Trial of Don Lorenzo Milani, 1988; The Giving and Taking of Life: Essays Ethical, 1989; From Synagogue to Church, 1992; The Dying of the Light: The Disengagement of Colleges and Universities from Their Christian Churches, 1998; Philemon's Problem: A Theology of Grace, 1998. EDITOR: Marriage among Christians: A Curious Tradition, 1977; Abortion Parley, 1980. **Address:** Casa Santa Cruz, 7126 N 7th Ave, Phoenix, AZ 85021-8608, U.S.A. **Online address:** jtbcsc@aol.com

BURTLESS, Gary. American, b. 1950. **Genres:** Economics. **Career:** US Department of Health, Education, and Welfare, Washington, DC, economist, 1977-79; US Department of Labor, Washington, DC, economist, 1979-81; Brookings Institution, Washington, DC, senior fellow, 1981-; Journal of Human Resources, co-editor, 1988-96; consultant. **Publications:** (with H. Aaron and B. Bosworth) Can America Afford to Grow Old?, 1989; A Future of Lousy Jobs?, 1990; (with M. Baily and R. Litan) Growth with Equity, 1993; (with R. Lawrence and R. Litan) Globalphobia: Confronting Fears about Open Trade, 1998; (with D. Friedlander) Five Years After: The Long-Term Effects of Welfare to Work Programs, 1994. **Address:** Brookings Institution, 1775 Massachusetts Ave NW, Washington, DC 20036, U.S.A. **Online address:** Brookinfo@Brookings.edu

BURTON, Anthony. British, b. 1934. **Genres:** Novels, History, Transportation, Travel/Exploration, Biography. **Career:** Self-employed writer, 1968-. Ed., Weidenfeld and Nicolson, London, 1963-67; Publicity Manager, Penguin Books, London, 1967-68. **Publications:** Programmed Guide to Office Warfare (humour), 1969; The Jones Report (humour), 1970; The Canal Builders, 1972, 1981, 1993; The Reluctant Musketeer (novel), 1973; Canals in Colour, 1974; Remains of a Revolution, 1974; The Master Idol (novel), 1975; The Navigators (novel), 1976; (with D. Pratt) Canal, 1976; Josiah Wedgwood, 1976; The Miners, 1976; A Place to Stand (novel), 1977; Back Door Britain, 1977; Industrial Archaeological Sites of Britain, 1977; (with P. Burton) The Green Bag Travellers, 1978; The Past at Work, 1980; The Rainhill Story, 1980; The Changing River, 1982; The Past Afloat, 1982; The Shell Book of Curious Britain, 1982; The National Trust Guide to Our Industrial Past, 1983; The Waterways of Britain, 1983; The Rise and Fall of King Cotton, 1984; (co-ed.) Canals: A New Look, 1984; Walking the Line, 1985; Wilderness Britain, 1985; (with J. Morgan) Britain's Light Railways, 1985; The Shell Book of Undiscovered Britain & Ireland, 1986; (with J. May) Landscape Detective, 1986; Britain Revisited, 1986; Opening Time, 1987; Steaming Through Britain, 1987; Walk the South Downs, 1988; Walking through History, 1988; The Yorkshire Dales and York, 1989; The Great Days of the Canals, 1989; Cityscapes, 1990; Astonishing Britain, 1990; Slow Roads, 1991; The Railway Builders, 1992; Canal Mania, 1993; (with N. Curtis) The Grand Union Canal Walk, 1993; The Railway Empire, 1994; The Rise and Fall of British Shipbuilding, 1994; The Coswold Way, 1995; The Dales Way, 1995; The West Highland Way, 1996; The Southern Upland Way, 1997; The Wye Valley Walk, 1997; William Cobbett Englishman, 1997; The Caledonian Canal, 1998; Best Foot Forward, 1998; The Cumbria Way, 1999; The Wessex Ridgeway, 1999; Thomas Telford, 1999; Weekend Walks: Dartmoor & Exmoor, 2000, The Yorkshire Dales, 2000, The Peak District, 2001; Traction Engines, 2000; Richard Trevithick: Giant of Steam, 2000; The Orient Express, 2001; The Anatomy of Canals: The Early Years, 2001, The Nania Years, 2002, Decline & Renewal, 2003; The Daily Telegraph Guide to Britain's Working Past, 2001; Hadrian's Wall Path, 2003; The Daily Telegraph Guide to Britain's Maritime Past, 2003; On the Rails, 2004; The Ridgeway, 2005. **Address:** c/o Sara Menguc, 4 Hatch Pl, Kingston upon Thames, Surrey KT2 5NB, England.

BURTON, Humphrey (McGuire). British, b. 1931. **Genres:** Music. **Career:** British Broadcasting Corp., London, England, BBC-Radio, sound studio manager, 1955-58, BBC-Television, director, then editor of Monitor (program), 1958-62, executive producer of music programs, 1963-64, head of music and arts programing, 1965-67, 1975-81, program host, 1975-89; London Weekend TV, London, head of drama, arts, and music, 1967-69, editor and presenter of Aquarius (program), 1970-75; Hollywood Bowl summer festival, guest director, 1983; Barbican Centre, artistic director of Tender Is the North, 1989-92. Director and producer of television documentaries and over 160 musical performances. Conductor of orchestral performances. **Publications:** Leonard Bernstein, 1994; Yehudi Menuhi: A Life, 2000; Sir William Walton: The Romantic Loner, 2002. **Address:** 17 Wendell Rd., London W12 9RS, England.

BURTON, Ivor (Flower). British, b. 1923. **Genres:** History, Politics/Government. **Career:** Professor Emeritus of Social Policy, Royal Holloway and Bedford New College, University of London, since 1988 (joined faculty, 1950; Professor, 1983-88). **Publications:** The Captain General: The Career of John Churchill, 1st Duke of Marlborough, 1702-11, 1968; (with Gavin Drewry) Legislation and Public Policy: Public Bills in the 1970-4 Parliament, 1980. **Address:** 21 Downs View Lodge, Surbiton, Surrey KT6 6EG, England.

BURTON, John Andrew. British, b. 1944. **Genres:** Animals/Pets, Natural history, Zoology, Travel/Exploration. **Career:** Natural History Museum, London, exhibition secretary, 1963-69; Birds of the World, assistant editor, 1969-71; Friends of the Earth, London, natural history consultant, 1971-75; New Scientist, regular contributor, 1974-85; Fauna and Flora Preservation Society, executive secretary, 1975-88; Birds International, editor, 1974-76; Fauna and Flora Preservation Society U.S.A., director, 1982-89; Wildlife Works Ltd., director, 1990-; IUCN, Species Survival Commission, member emeritus, 1990-; World Land Trust, chief executive, 1991-; Authors & Artists for Conservation, founder, 1995; Wyld Court Rainforest Ltd., director, 1996-; regular broadcaster on BBC radio and TV. **Publications:** Extinct Animals, 1972; Birds of the Tropics, 1973; Fossils, 1974; The Naturalist in London, 1974; (with D.H.S. Risdon) Love of Birds, 1975; Nature in the City, 1976; (with E.N. Arnold) A Field Guide to the Reptiles and Amphibians of Europe, 1978; Rare Animals, 1978; Gem Guide to Wild Animals, 1980; The Guinness Book of Mammals, 1982; Gem Guide to Zoo Animals, 1984; Collins' Guide to Rare Mammals of the World, 1987; Close to Extinction, 1988; Mammals of America, 1990; The Book of Snakes, 1991; The Atlas of Endangered Species, 1992; Collins' Wild Guide to Wild Animals, 1998; Eye Witness 3D Reptile, 1998; The Pocket Guide to Mammals of North

American, 1999. EDITOR: Owls of the World, 1974, 3rd ed., 1992; National Trust Book of Wild Animals, 1984. **Address:** c/o Kingfisher Publications, New Penderel House, 283-288 High Holborn, London WC1V 7HZ, England. **Online address:** john.a.burton@lineone.net

BURTON, L(awrence) DeVere. American, b. 1943. **Genres:** Agriculture/ Forestry, Environmental sciences/Ecology. **Career:** Church of Jesus Christ of Latter-day Saints, missionary in Texas, 1962-64; agriculture teacher at county schools in Brigham City, UT, 1967-68, Morgan, UT, 1968-70, Rupert ID, 1972-79, and Burley, ID, 1979-84; Iowa State University, Ames, instructor in agricultural engineering, 1984-87; Idaho State Division of Vocational Education, Pocatello, area coordinator for vocational education, 1987-88; State of Idaho, state supervisor of agricultural education, 1989-. Affiliate assistant professor at Idaho State University, 1987-88, and University of Idaho, 1987-97. **Publications:** Agriscience and Technology, 1991; Ecology of Fish and Wildlife, 1995; Forestry Science, 1997. Contributor to professional journals and popular periodicals. **Address:** College of Southern Idaho, 315 Falls Ave, PO Box 1238, Twin Falls, ID 83303-1238, U.S.A. **Online address:** dburton@csi.edu

BURTON, Rebecca B(rown). Also writes as Rebecca Winters. American, b. 1940. **Genres:** Romance/Historical. **Career:** Novelist. Granite School District, Salt Lake, UT, French teacher, 1987-99. **Publications:** By Love Divided, 1979; The Loving Season, 1979; To Love Again, 1987. AS REBECCA WINTERS: Blind to Love, 1989; Fully Involved, 1990; The Story Princess, 1991; Rites of Love, 1991; Rescued Heart, 1991; Blackie's Woman, 1991; The Marriage Bracelet, 1992; Meant for Each Other, 1992; Both of Them, 1992; Hero on the Loose, 1993; Bride of My Heart, 1994; The Mermaid Wife, 1994; The Rancher and the Redhead, 1994; The Nutcracker Prince, 1994; A Man for All Time, 1995; The Baby Business, 1995; The Wrong Twin, 1995; Return to Sender, 1995; For Better, for Worse, 1996; Kit and the Cowboy, 1996; The Badlands Bride, 1996; Not without My Child, 1996; Strangers When We Meet, 1997; No Wife Required, 1997; Second-best Wife, 1997; Laura's Baby, 1997; Three Little Miracles, 1997; Deborah's Son, 1998; Until There Was You, 1998; Baby in a Million, 1998; Bride by Day, 1998; A Daddy for Christmas, 1998; Undercover Husband, 1999; Undercover Baby, 1999; Undercover Bachelor, 1999; Undercover Fiancee, 1999; If He Could See Me Now, 1999; The Family Way, 1999; Husband Potential, 2000; The Faithful Bride, 2000; The Unknown Sister, 2000; Sarah's First Christmas (anthology), 2000; The Billionaire and the Baby, 2000; His Very Own Baby, 2001; The Baby Discovery, 2001; Accidentally Yours, 2001; The Toddler's Tale, 2001; My Private Detective, 2001; Husband for a Year, 2001; Claiming His Baby, 2001; Beneath a Texas Sky, 2002; The Bridegroom's Vow, 2002; The Prince's Choice, 2002; She's My Mom, 2002; The Baby Dilemma: Philippe's Story 2002; The Tycoon's Proposition, 2002; Another Man's Wife, 2003; Bride Fit for a Prince, 2003; Rush to the Altar, 2003; Manhattan Merger, 2003; Home to Copper Mountain, 2003. **Address:** c/o Author Mail, Harlequin Enterprises Ltd., 225 Duncan Mill Rd, Don Mills, ON, Canada M3B 3K9. **Online address:** becky485@earthlink.net

BURTON, Thomas G(len). American, b. 1935. **Genres:** Mythology/ Folklore, Theology/Religion. **Career:** High school teacher in Nashville, TN, 1957; East Tennessee State University, Johnson City, faculty member, 1958-95, professor of English, 1967-95, professor emeritus, 1996-. **Publications:** Some Ballad Folks, 1981; Serpent-Handling Believers, 1993; The Serpent and the Spirit, 2004. EDITOR: (with A.N. Manning) A Collection of Folklore by Undergraduate Students of East Tennessee State University, 1966; (with Manning) The East Tennessee State University Collection of Folklore: Folksongs, 1967; (with Manning) The East Tennessee State University Collection of Folklore: Folksongs II, 1969; Essays in Memory of Christine Burleson, 1969; Tom Ashley, Sam McGee, Bukka White: Tennessee Traditional Singers, 1981. **Address:** East Tennessee State University, PO Box 23117, Johnson City, TN 37614, U.S.A. **Online address:** i22burt@mail.etsu.edu

BURTSCHI, Mary Pauline. American, b. 1911. **Genres:** History, Biography, Novellas/Short stories, Architecture. **Career:** Research Historian, since 1966, and Vice-President, since 1972, Vandalia Historical Society, Illinois Director, James Hall Library, since 1966. Site Interpreter and Writer, Little Brick House, since 1961. Director and Poetry Consultant, Fayette County Cultural and Arts Association, since 1974. Teacher of English and French, Carlyle High School, Illinois, 1936-39, and Effingham High School, Illinois, 1939-70. Director, 1965-68, and Vice-President, 1969-77, Illinois State Historical Society. **Publications:** Biographical Sketch of Joseph Charles Burtschi, 1962; Vandalia: Wilderness Capital of Lincoln's Land, 1963; A Portfolio for James Hall, 1968; A Guide Book of Historical Vandalia, 1974; James Hall of Lincoln's Frontier World 1978; General George Washington,

1980; European Journey, 1983; A Descriptive Sketch of the Little Brick House in Historic Vandalia, Illinois, 1987; The Virgin Forest of Vandalia, Illinois, 1994; Old Buildings in Vandalia, vol. I & vol. II. EDITOR: Seven Stories by James Hall, 1975; Sesquicentennial Celebration of the Antiquarian and Historical Society of Illinois 1827-1977, 1981. **Address:** 307 N. Sixth St, Vandalia, IL 62471, U.S.A.

BURWELL, Jennifer. Canadian, b. 1962. **Genres:** Sociology. **Career:** Northwestern University, Evanston, IL, instructor in English and writing, 1989-93; Ryerson Polytechnic University, Toronto, Ontario, instructor in continuing education program, 1994-95; Wesleyan University, Middletown, CT, visiting assistant professor of English, 1996-97; Ryerson Polytechnic University, assistant professor of English, 1997-. Literacy instructor at Council Fire Native Centre and Women's Native Resource Centre, both Toronto, 1994-95; speaker at universities. **Publications:** Notes on Nowhere: Utopian Logic, Feminism, and Social Transformation, 1997. Contributor to periodicals. **Address:** Jorgenson Hall, Ryerson Polytechnic University, 350 Victoria St., Toronto, ON, Canada. **Online address:** atenx001@tc.umn.edu.

BUSBEE, Shirlee. American, b. 1941. **Genres:** Romance/Historical. **Publications:** Gypsy Lady, 1977; Lady Vixen, 1980; While Passion Sleeps, 1983; Deceive Not My Heart, 1984; The Tiger Lily, 1985; Spanish Rose, 1986; Midnight Masquerade, 1988; Whisper to Me of Love, 1991; Each Time We Love, 1993; Love a Dark Rider, 1994; Lovers Forever, 1996; A Heart for the Taking, 1997; Love Be Mine, 1998; For Love Alone, 2000; At Long Last, 2000; Swear by the Moon, 2001. **Address:** Warner Books, Time-Life Bldg., 1271 Ave. of the Americas, New York, NY 10020, U.S.A.

BUSBY, F(rancis) M(arion). American, b. 1921. **Genres:** Novels, Novellas/ Short stories, Science fiction/Fantasy. **Career:** Freelance writer, 1970-. Project Supvr., Alaska Communication System, Seattle, 1947-53; telegraph engineer, 1953-70. Vice-President, Science Fiction Writers of America, 1974-76. **Publications:** Cage a Man, 1973; The Proud Enemy, 1975; Rissa Kerguelen, (and) The Long View, 1976, combined as Rissa Kerguelen, 1977, reissued in 3 parts, Young Rissa, Rissa and Tregare, The Long View, 1984; All These Earths, 1978, 1985; Zelde M'tana, 1980, 1986; The Demu Trilogy, 1980; Star Rebel, 1984; The Alien Debt, 1984; Rebel's Quest, 1985, reissued (together with Star Rebel) as The Rebel Dynasty, vol. I, 1987; Rebels' Seed, 1986, reissued (together with The Alien Debt) as The Rebel Dynasty, vol. II, 1988; Getting Home (short stories), 1987; The Breeds of Man, 1988; Slow Freight, 1991; The Singularity Project, 1993; The Islands of Tomorrow, 1994; Arrow from Earth, 1995; The Triad Worlds, 1996. Over 20 uncollected shorter works. **Address:** 2852 14th Ave W, Seattle, WA 98119, U.S.A. **Online address:** fmbusby001@aol.com

BUSBY, Mark. American, b. 1945. **Genres:** Novels, Literary criticism and history. **Career:** Indiana-Purdue University, Indianapolis, associate faculty instructor, 1970-72; University of Colorado, Boulder, instructor in English and black education, 1972-76; Texas A&M University, College Station, assistant professor, 1977-83, associate professor, 1983-91; Texas State University, San Marcos, associate professor, 1991-93, professor of English and director of Center for the Study of the Southwest, 1993-. Co-editor, Southwestern American Literature, 1992-, and Texas Books in Review, 1996-. **Publications:** Preston Jones, 1983; Lanford Wilson, 1987; Ralph Ellison, 1991; Fort Benning Blues (novel), 2001. EDITOR & CONTRIBUTOR: The Frontier Experience and the American Dream: Essays on American Literature, 1989; New Growth/2: Contemporary Short Stories by Texas Writers, 1993; Larry McMurtry and the West: An Ambivalent Relationship, 1995; From Texas to the World and Back: The Journeys of Katherine Anne Porter, 2001; The Greenwood Encyclopedia of American Regional Cultures: The Southwest, 2004. Contributor to books. Contributor of articles and reviews to periodicals. **Address:** Center for the Study of the Southwest, Texas State University, San Marcos, San Marcos, TX 78666, U.S.A. **Online address:** MB13@swt.edu

BUSCALL, Jon. British, b. 1970. **Genres:** Novels. **Career:** Educator and novelist. Stockholm University, Stockholm, Sweden, instructor in creative writing. **Publications:** College.com, 1999. Editor of literary Web site www. seriously.com. **Address:** Department of English, Universitetsvaagen 10F, 106 91 Stockholm, Sweden. **Online address:** jonbuscall@english.su.se

BUSCH, Briton Cooper. American, b. 1936. **Genres:** History, International relations/Current affairs. **Career:** William R. Kenan Jr. Professor of History, Colgate University, Hamilton, New York, since 1978 (Instructor, 1962-63; Assistant Professor, 1963-65; Associate Professor, 1965-73; Professor, 1973-78; Chairman, 1980-85; Director, International Relations, 1984-85; Director, Social Sciences Division, 1985-91). **Publications:** Britain and the Persian

Gulf 1894-1914, 1967; Britain, India and the Arabs 1914-1921, 1971; Mudros to Lausanne: Britain's Frontier in West Asia 1918-1923, 1976; Hardinge of Penshurst: A Study in the Old Diplomacy, 1980; Master of Desolation: The Memoirs of Capt. Joseph Fuller, 1980; Alta California 1840-1842: The Journal and Observations of William Dane Phelps, Master of the Ship Alert, 1983; The War against Seals: A History of the North American Seal Fishery, 1985; Fremont's Private Navy: The 1846 Journal of Captain William Dane Phelps, 1987; Whaling Will Never Do for Me: The American Whaleman in the Nineteenth Century, 1993; (with B.M. Gough) Fur Traders from New England: The Boston Men, 1787-1800, 1996. **Address:** Dept. of History, Colgate University, Hamilton, NY 13346, U.S.A.

BUSCH, Charles. American, b. 1954. **Genres:** Novels, Plays/Screenplays. **Career:** Playwright; actor in stage plays. Worked as portrait artist, encyclopedia salesperson, memorabilia shop manager, ice cream scooper, sports handicapper, and artist's model, 1976-84. **Publications:** STAGE PLAYS: Hollywood Confidential (1-person show), 1978; Alone with a Cast of Thousands (1-person show), 1980; Theodora, She-Bitch of Byzantium, 1984; Vampire Lesbians of Sodom, 1985; Times Square Angel, 1985; Pardon My Inquisition, or Kiss the Blood off My Castanets, 1986; Psycho Beach Party, 1987, screenplay, 2000; The Lady in Question (2-act), 1989; Four Plays by Charles Busch (contains Vampire Lesbians of Sodom, Sleeping Beauty or Coma, Psycho Beach Party, The Lady in Question), 1990; Red Scare on Sunset, 1991; Three Plays by Charles Busch (contains Theodora, She-Bitch of Byzantium, Times Square Angel, Pardon My Inquisition, or Kiss the Blood off My Castanets), 1992; Charles Busch Revue, 1993; You Should Be So Lucky, 1995; (with L.T. Bond and W. Repicci) Swingtime Canteen, 1996; Flipping My Wig (1-person show), 1997; The Green Heart (libretto), 1997; Queen Amarantha, 1998; Shanghai Moon, 1999; Die, Mommy, Die!, 1999, screenplay, 2002; The Tale of the Allergist's Wife and Other Plays (contains title play, Vampire Lesbians of Sodom, Psycho Beach Party, The Lady in Question, Red Scare on Sunset), 2001; Shanghai Moon, 2002. OTHER: Whores of Lost Atlantis (novel), 1993. Contributor to magazines. **Address:** c/o Marc Glick, Glick and Weintraub, 1501 Broadway Ste 2401, New York, NY 10036, U.S.A.

BUSCH, Frederick. American, b. 1941. **Genres:** Novels, Novellas/Short stories, Literary criticism and history. **Career:** Colgate University, Hamilton, NY, staff member, 1966-, professor of English, 1976-87, Fairchild Professor of Literature, 1987-2003. **Publications:** I Wanted a Year without Fall, 1971; Hawkes: A Guide to His Fictions, 1973; Manual Labor, 1974; When People Publish (essays), 1987; A Dangerous Profession (essays), 1998; (ed.) Letters to a Fiction Writer, 1999. NOVELS: The Mutual Friend, 1978; Rounds, 1980; Take This Man, 1981; Invisible Mending, 1984; Sometimes I Live in the Country, 1986; Harry and Catherine, 1990; Closing Arguments, 1991; Long Way from Home, 1993; Girls, 1997; The Night Inspector, 1999; A Memory of War, 2003. STORIES: Breathing Trouble, 1974; Domestic Particulars, 1976; Hardwater Country, 1979; Too Late American Boyhood Blues, 1984; Absent Friends, 1989; The Children in the Woods: New & Selected Stories, 1994; Don't Tell Anyone, 2000. **Address:** c/o Elaine Markson Literary Agency, 44 Greenwich Ave, New York, NY 10011, U.S.A.

BUSCH, Lawrence (Michael). American, b. 1945. **Genres:** Sociology, Ethics. **Career:** U.S. Peace Corps, Washington, DC, volunteer in Labe, Guinea, 1965-66, and Lome, Togo, 1967-68; Volunteers in Service to America (VISTA), Washington, DC, supervisor of Community Action Council, Rose Hill, NC, 1968-70; University of Kentucky, Lexington, assistant professor, 1974-79, associate professor, 1979-84, professor of sociology, 1984-89; Michigan State University, East Lansing, professor of sociology, 1990-96, University Distinguished Professor, 1997-. University of Trondheim, visiting professor, 1994, 1995, 1996, 1999, 2004. Guest on television and radio programs in the United States and Canada. **Publications:** (with W.B. Lacy) Science, Agriculture, and the Politics of Research, 1983; (with W.B. Lacy, L.R. Lacy, and J. Burkhardt) Plants, Power, and Profit, 1991; (with Lacy, Burkhardt, and others) Making Nature, Shaping Culture: Plant Biodiversity in Global Context, 1995; The Eclipse of Morality, 2000. EDITOR: (and contrib.) Science and Agricultural Development, 1981; (with W.B. Lacy, and contrib.) Food Security in the United States, 1984; (with Lacy) The Agricultural Scientific Enterprise: A System in Transition, 1986; (with W.H. Friedland, F.H. Buttel, and A. Rudy) Toward a New Political Economy of Agriculture, 1991; (with Friedland, A. Bonanno, and others) From Columbus to Conagra: The Globalization of Agriculture, 1994. Contributor to books and academic journals. Author of professional papers. **Address:** Department of Sociology, 316 Berkey Hall, Michigan State University, East Lansing, MI 48824, U.S.A. **Online address:** LBusch@msu.edu; www.msu.edu~busch

BUSE, D(ieter) K(urt). Canadian (born Germany), b. 1941. **Genres:** History, Politics/Government, Bibliography. **Career:** University of Saskatchewan, Regina, member of faculty, 1966-67; Laurentian University, Sudbury, Ontario, lecturer, 1969-71, assistant professor, 1971-75, associate professor, 1975-85, professor of history, 1985-. University of Adelaide, visiting lecturer, 1983-84. Kommission fuer die Geschichte des Parlamentarismus und der politischen Parteien, researcher, 1975-76. Ontario Council of Universities, member of History Discipline Group, 1978-81; Ministry of Colleges and Education, member of Universities Validation Committee, 1984-85. **Publications:** (trans. with J.L. Black, and contrib.) G.F. Mueller and Siberia, 1733-43, 1988. EDITOR: Parteiagitation und Wahlkreisvertretung: Eine Dokumentation ueber Friedrich Ebert und seinen Wahlkreis Elberfeld-Barmen, 1910-1918, 1975; (with J. Doerr, and contrib.) German Nationalisms: A Bibliographical Approach, 1985; (with J. Doerr) Modern Germany: An Encyclopedia of History, People and Culture, 2 vols., 1998. Work represented in anthologies. Contributor of articles, translations, and reviews to periodicals. **Address:** Department of History, Laurentian University, Ramsey Lake Rd., Sudbury, ON, Canada P3E 2C6.

BUSER, Pierre. French, b. 1921. **Genres:** Psychology, Sciences. **Career:** University of Paris, Paris, France, assistant professor, 1944-50, associate professor, 1950-55, professor of neurosciences, 1955-91, professor emeritus, 1991-. **Publications:** Neurophysiologie, 1975; Psychophysiologie, 1982; (with M. Imbert) Audition, 1987, trans. by R.H. Kay, 1992; (with M. Imbert) Vision, 1987, trans. by R.H. Kay, 1992; Neurobiologie, 1993; Regulations neurovegetatives, 1994; Cerveau de soi, cerveau de l'autre, 1998. **Address:** University of Paris, 9 Quai St. Bernard, 75005 Paris, France. **Online address:** pierre.buser@snv.jussieu.fr

BUSH, Anne Kelleher. American, b. 1959. **Genres:** Science fiction/Fantasy, Romance/Historical. **Career:** Writer. **Publications:** SCIENCE FICTION/FANTASY NOVELS: Daughter of Prophecy, 1995; Children of Enchantment, 1996; The Misbegotten King, 1996; A Once & Future Love, 1998; The Knight, the Harp and the Maiden, 1999; The Ghost & Katie Coyle, 1999; Love's Labyrinth, 2000. **Address:** c/o Donald Maass, Donald Maass Literary Agency, 160 W. 95th St., Ste 1B, New York, NY 10025, U.S.A.

BUSH, Barney (Furman). American. **Genres:** Novels, Poetry, Songs/Lyrics and libretti. **Career:** University of Wisconsin, Milwaukee, Native American specialist, 1973-74; National Indian Youth Council, Albuquerque, NM, and Institute of the Southern Plains, Hammond, OK, educational specialist, 1974-75; Milwaukee Area Technical College, Milwaukee, WI, instructor in American Indian literature and history, 1976-78; poet-in-residence in OK and IL, 1980-88; Council of Redwinds College, spokesman, 1996-. **Publications:** My Horse and a Jukebox, 1979; Petroglyphs, 1982; Inherit the Blood: Poetry and Fiction, 1985. Work represented in anthologies. Contributor to periodicals. **Address:** Box 22779, Santa Fe, NM 87502, U.S.A.

BUSH, Barry (Michael). British, b. 1938. **Genres:** Animals/Pets, Medicine/Health. **Career:** Veterinary surgeon since 1961. Sr. Veterinary Adviser, Hill's Pet Nutrition, Hatfield, Herts., since 1990. Lecturer and Course Adviser, Hounslow Borough College, 1962-90; Lecturer, 1964-80, and Sr. Lecturer, 1980-90, Royal Veterinary College, University of London. Lecturer, College for the Distributive Trades, London, 1967-88. Member of Council, 1968-69, Hon. Secretary, 1969-70, Jr. Vice President, 1970-73, President, 1973-74 and Sr. Vice President, 1974-75, Central Veterinary Society; Member, Small Animal Committee, 1969-72, and Member of Council, 1969-72 and 1973-74, British Veterinary Association. **Publications:** Veterinary Laboratory Manual, 1975; First Aid for Pet Animals, 1980, rev. ed. as First Aid for Pets, 1984; The Cat Care Question and Answer Book, 1981; The Dog Care Question and Answer Book, 1982; Interpretation of Laboratory Results for Small Animal Clinicians, 1991. **Address:** Hill's Pet Nutrition Ltd, 1 The Beacons, Beaconsfield Road, Hatfield, Herts. AL10 8EQ, England.

BUSH, Catherine. Canadian, b. 1961. **Genres:** Novels, Young adult non-fiction. **Career:** Novelist, journalist, 1983-. **Publications:** FOR CHILDREN: Elizabeth I, 1985; Gandhi, 1985. NOVELS: Minus Time, 1993; Rules of Engagement, 2000; Claire's Head, 2004. Contributor to books. **Address:** c/o Bukowski Agency, 14 Prince Arthur Ave, Ste 202, Toronto, ON, Canada M5R 1A9. **Online address:** catebush@aol.com

BUSH, Duncan. British, b. 1946. **Genres:** Novels, Plays/Screenplays, Poetry. **Career:** Writer. **Publications:** POETRY: Aquarium, 1983; Salt, 1985; Black Faces, Red Mouths, 1986; Masks, 1994; Midway, 1998; The Hook, 1998. PLAYS: Cocktails for Three, 1979; Ends, 1980; Sailing to America, 1982, for television, 1992. RADIO PLAYS: In the Pine Forest, 1991; Are There Still Wolves in Pennsylvania?, 1991. NOVELS: The Genre of Silence, 1988; Glass Shot, 1991. **Address:** Godre Waun Oleu, Brecon Rd, Ynyswen, Penycae, Powys SA9 1YY, Wales.

BUSH, M(ichael) L(accohee). British, b. 1938. **Genres:** History, Social commentary, Social sciences, Local history/Rural topics, Philosophy. **Career:** Victoria University of Manchester, Manchester, England, lecturer in history, 1962-76, sr. lecturer, 1976-88, reader, 1988-94; Manchester Metropolitan University, research professor in history, 1999-. **Publications:** Renaissance, Reformation, and the Outer World, 1450-1660, 1966, 2nd ed., 1971; The Government Policy of Protector Somerset, 1976; The European Nobility, Vol I: Noble Privilege, 1983, Vol II: Rich Noble, Poor Noble, 1988; The English Aristocracy: A Comparative Synthesis, 1984; (ed.) Social Orders and Social Classes in Europe since 1500, 1992; The Pilgrimage of Grace, 1996; (ed.) Serfdom and Slavery, 1996; What Is Love? Richard Carlile's Philosophy of Love, 1998; The Defeat of the Pilgrimage of Grace, 1999; Durham and the Pilgrimage of Grace, 2000; Servitude in Modern Times, 2000. Contributor to periodicals. **Address:** 7 Hesketh Ave, Didsbury, Manchester M20 2QN, England.

BUSH, Ronald. American, b. 1946. **Genres:** Literary criticism and history. **Career:** Harvard University, Cambridge, MA, assistant professor, 1974-79, associate professor of English, 1979-82; California Institute of Technology, Pasadena, associate professor, 1982-85, professor of literature, 1985-; Oxford University, Drue Heinz Professor of American Literature; writer. **Publications:** The Genesis of Ezra Pound's Cantos, 1976; T.S. Eliot: A Study in Character and Style, 1984; (ed.) T.S. Eliot: The Modernist in History, 1991; (ed. with E. Barkan) Prehistories of the Future: The Primitivist Project and the Culture of Modernism, 1995. **Address:** St. John's College, Oxford OX1 3PJ, England. **Online address:** ron.bush@english.ox.ac.uk

BUSHELL, Agnes. American, b. 1949. **Genres:** Novels, Mystery/Crime/Suspense. **Career:** Portland School of Art, instructor in liberal arts, 1983-92; instructor in liberal arts, San Francisco Art Institute, 1993; Maine College of Art, associate professor, 1996-, editor and writer. Cofounder, Maine Writers and Publishers Alliance, 1975. **Publications:** NOVELS: Shadowdance, 1989; Local Deities, 1990; Death by Crystal, 1993; Days of the Dead, 1995; The Enumerator, 1997; Asian Vespers, 2000. EDITOR: Balancing Act, 1975. **Address:** 18 Exeter St, Portland, ME 04102, U.S.A. **Online address:** ABushell@meca.edu

BUSHEY, Jeanne. American, b. 1944. **Genres:** Children's fiction, Crafts. **Career:** Beal Business College, Bangor, ME, English teacher, 1967-70; teacher at an elementary school in Iqaluit, Northwest Territories, 1974-78; teacher at an American community school in Uxbridge, England, 1978-80; N. J. Macpherson School, Yellowknife, Northwest Territories, elementary teacher, 1980-. **Publications:** A Sled Dog for Moshi (fiction), 1994; Holiday Hangups: Crafts for Every Season, 1995. Contributor to magazines. **Address:** #304-8380 Jones Rd., Richmond, BC, Canada V6Y 1L6. **Online address:** jbushey@intergate.ca

BUSHMAN, Richard Lyman. American, b. 1931. **Genres:** History. **Career:** Assistant Professor, 1960-66, and Assoc Professor, 1966-68, Brigham Young University, Provo, Utah; Professor of History, Boston University, 1968-77; Professor of History, University of Delaware, 1977-89; Professor, 1989-2001, Emeritus Professor of History, 2001-, Columbia University, NYC. **Publications:** (ed.) Religion at Harvard, 1957; From Puritan to Yankee: Character and the Social Order in Connecticut 1690-1765, 1967; (ed.) The Great Awakening, 1970; (co-ed.) Uprooted Americans, 1979; Joseph Smith and the Beginnings of Mormonism, 1984; King and People in Provincial Massachusetts, 1985; The Refinement of America: Persons, Houses, Cities, 1992. **Address:** Dept. of History, Columbia University, New York, NY 10027, U.S.A.

BUSHNELL, Candace. American, b. 1959?. **Career:** Writer and journalist. New York Observer, New York, NY, columnist, 1994-c. 1998; Sex, Lives, and Video Clips (talk show on VH-1), host, 1997. **Publications:** Sex and the City, 1996; Four Blondes, 2000; Trading Up, 2003. **Address:** c/o Author Mail, Atlantic Monthly Press, 841 Broadway, New York, NY 10003, U.S.A.

BUSHNELL, Jack. American, b. 1952. **Genres:** Children's fiction, Literary criticism and history. **Career:** Rutgers University, New Brunswick, NJ, assistant professor and lecturer, 1974-84; DMB&B Advertising, NYC, senior account planner, 1984-88; Geer, DuBois Advertising, NYC, vice president, 1988-92; Nabisco Foods, New Jersey, associate manager of business information, 1992-93; University of Wisconsin, Eau Claire, adjunct assistant professor, 1994-95; full-time writer, 1993-. **Publications:** FOR CHILDREN: Circus of the Wolves, 1994; Sky Dancer, 1996. OTHER: Midnight Run; Bayou Song; Great Grandfather's Farm; White Deer; The World According to Jumping Spiders; Exploring the Aurora Borealis. LITERARY ESSAYS: Where is the Lamb for a Burnt Offering? in The Wordsworth Circle, 1981;

Maggie Tulliver's Stored Up Force in Studies in the Novel, 1984; The Daughter's Dilemma (a scholarly book review) in Configuration, 1994. **Address:** University of Wisconsin - Eau Claire, Hibbard 431, 105 Garfield Ave, Box 4004, Eau Claire, WI 54702-4004, U.S.A.

BUSHONG, Carolyn Nordin. American, b. 1947. **Genres:** Human relations/Parenting, Psychology, Self help. **Career:** Worked as kindergarten teacher, 1969-73, and school counselor, 1973-75; Aspen Counseling and Tutoring, Aspen, CO, founder and operator, 1977-84; Carolyn Bushong Psychotherapy Associates Inc., Denver, CO, private practice of psychotherapy, 1984-; radio talk show host, 1996-. Guest on national television programs. **Publications:** Loving Him without Losing You, 1991; The Seven Dumbest Relationship Mistakes Smart People Make, 1997; Bring Back the Man You Fell in Love With, 2003. **Address:** Carolyn Bushong Psychotherapy Associates Inc., 210 St Paul St Ste 205, Denver, CO 80206, U.S.A. **Online address:** www.CarolynSays.com

BUSIA, Akosua. Ghanaian. **Genres:** Novels. **Career:** Actress on stage, television, and in films, writer and artist; artwork on display in the National Museum of Art in London. **Publications:** The Seasons of Beento Blackbird: A Novel, 1996. Illustrator of books by others. **Address:** c/o Little Brown & Co., Time & Life Building, 1271 Avenue of the Americas, New York, NY 10020, U.S.A.

BUSKIN, Richard. British, b. 1959. **Genres:** Biography. **Career:** Writer. **Publications:** John Lennon: His Life and Legend, 1991; The Films of Marilyn Monroe, 1992; Princess Diana: Her Life Story, 1997; The Complete Idiot's Guide to British Royalty, 1997; The Complete Idiot's Guide to the Beatles, 1998; Inside Tracks: A First-Hand History of Popular Music from the World's Greatest Record Producers and Engineers, 1999; Blonde Heat: The Sizzling Screen Career of Marilyn Monroe, 2001; Sheryl Crow: No Fool to This Game, 2002; (with P. Diller) Like a Lampshade in a Whorehouse: My Life in Comedy, 2005. Contributor to newspapers and magazines.

BUSLIK, Gary. Also writes as Rex Harlan. American, b. 1946. **Genres:** Novels. **Career:** Lloyds Security, Chicago, IL, president, 1969-97. Licensed private detective, 1970-; freelance travel writer, 1990-. University of Illinois at Chicago Circle, founder of Gary and Janice Buslik Caribbean Studies Program. **Publications:** NOVELS: (as Rex Harlan) Black Blood, 1989; The Missionary's Position, 1999. Contributor to magazines. **Address:** c/o Marcia Amsterdam, Amsterdam Literary Agency, 41 West 82nd St., New York, NY 10024, U.S.A.

BUSS, David M. American, b. 1953. **Genres:** Psychology. **Career:** Harvard University, Cambridge, MA, assistant professor of psychology, 1981-85; University of Michigan, Ann Arbor, associate professor, 1985-91, professor of psychology, 1991-2000; University of Texas, professor, 2000-. **Publications:** (with N. Cantor) Personality Psychology, 1989; The Evolution of Desire, 1994; Sex, Power, Conflict, 1996; Evolutionary Psychology: The New Science of the Mind, 1999; The Dangerous Passion: Why Jealousy Is as Necessary as Love and Sex, 2000. Contributor to scientific journals. **Address:** University of Texas, Department of Psychology, Austin, TX 78712, U.S.A.

BUSS, Helen M. *See* **CLARKE, Margaret.**

BUSS, Robin (Caron). British, b. 1939. **Genres:** Poetry, Film, Translations. **Career:** British Foreign Office, London, England, research assistant, 1967-74; Woolwich College, London, lecturer in French, 1978-92; Independent on Sunday, critic, 1990-2001; freelance writer and translator, 1992-. **Publications:** The One-Way Glass (poems), 1971; Vigny: Chatterton, 1984; Cocteau: Les Enfants terribles, 1986; The French through Their Films, 1988; Italian Films, 1989; (ed. and author of intro. and notes) Stendhal, Lucien Leuwen, 1991; French Film Noir, 1994. TRANSLATOR: Marquis de Custine, Letters from Russia, 1991; Madame de Lafayette, The Princesse de Cleves, 1992; J. Cocteau, The Art of Cinema, 1992; H. de Balzac, Cesar Birotteau, 1994; A. Dumas, The Count of Monte-Cristo, 1996; J. Green, Stars of the South, 1996; J.-N. Liaut, Cover Girls and Supermodels, 1996; R. Bober, What News of the War?, 1998; E. Zola L'Assommoir, 2000; E. Zola, Au Bonheur des Dames, 2001; A. Camus, The Plague, 2001; A. Dumas, The Black Tulip, 2003; E. Zola, Therese Raquin, 2004. Contributor to books and periodicals. **Address:** 6, Park Place House, Park Vista, London SE10 9ND, England.

BUSVINE, James Ronald. *See* Obituaries.

BUTALA, Sharon (Annette). Canadian, b. 1940. **Genres:** Novels, Novellas/Short stories, Environmental sciences/Ecology. **Career:** Educator, artist, and author. Teacher of English, then special education, in Saskatchewan, Nova Scotia, and British Columbia, 1963-83; full-time writer, 1983-. **Publications:** NOVELS: Country of the Heart, 1984; The Gates of the Sun, 1986; Luna, 1988; Upstream, 1991; The Fourth Archangel, 1992; The Garden of Eden, 1998. SHORT STORY COLLECTIONS: Queen of the Headaches, 1985; Fever, 1990; Real Life, 2002. OTHER: Harvest, 1992; The Perfection of the Morning: An Apprenticeship in Nature, 1994; Coyote's Morning Cry: Meditations and Dreams from a Life in Nature, 1995; Wild Stone Heart, 2000; Old Man on His Back, 2002. Author of plays. Contributor to Canadian literary magazines and periodicals. **Address:** Box 428, Eastend, SK, Canada S0N 0T0. **Online address:** sharon.noble@sk.sympatico.ca

BUTCHER, Kristin. Canadian, b. 1951. **Genres:** Children's non-fiction, Young adult fiction. **Career:** Teacher in Manitoba and British Columbia, Canada, 1972-96; Education International, Victoria, Canada, technical writer, 1996-97, author, 1997-. Worked as a real estate sales administer, property manager assistant, office manager, item records clerk, tour package organizer, and cashier. **Publications:** The Runaways, 1998; The Tomorrow Tunnel, 1999; The Gramma War, 2001; Cairo Kelly and the Mann, 2002; Summer of Suspense, 2002; The Hemingway Tradition, 2002; The Trouble with Liberty, 2003; Zee's Way, in press. Contributor of book reviews to periodicals. **Address:** 4451 Wilkerson Rd., Victoria, BC, Canada V8Z 5C2. **Online address:** kristinbutcher@shaw.ca

BUTLER, Daniel Allen. American, b. 1957. **Genres:** History. **Career:** Writer. 42nd Royal Highland Regiment (Black Watch) Re-enactment Group, regimental sergeant major. Active in Scottish-American community in south and central Florida. **Publications:** "Unsinkable": The Full Story of RMS Titanic, 1998. **Address:** c/o Stackpole Books, 5067 Ritter Rd., Mechanicsburg, PA 17055, U.S.A. **Online address:** Butler1918@aol.com

BUTLER, David (Edgeworth). British, b. 1924. **Genres:** Politics/Government. **Career:** Fellow, Nuffield College, Oxford, 1951-; Personal Assistant to the British Ambassador, Washington, D.C., 1955-56. Companion of the Order of the British Empire. **Publications:** The British General Election of 1951, 1952; The Electoral System in Britain since 1918, 1953, 1962; The British General Election of 1955, 1955; The Study of Political Behaviour, 1958; (ed.) Elections Abroad, 1958; (with R. Rose) The British General Election of 1959, 1960; British Political Facts, 1963, 8th ed., 2001; (with A.S. King) The British General Election of 1964, 1965; (with A.S. King) The British General Election of 1966, 1966; (with M. Pinto-Duschinsky) The British General Election of 1970, 1971; (with D. Stokes) Political Change in Britain, 1969, 1973; The Canberra Model, 1973; (with D. Kavanagh) The British General Election of February 1974, 1974; (with D. Kavanagh) The British General Election of October 1974, 1975; (with U.W. Kitzinger) The 1975 Referendum, 1976; (with A.H. Halsey) Policy and Politics, 1978; (with A. Ranney) Referendums, 1978; (with D. Kavanagh) The British General Election of 1979, 1980; (with D. Marquand) European Elections and British Politics, 1981; (with A. Ranney) Democracy at the Polls, 1981; (with V. Bogdanor) Democracy and Elections, 1983; Governing without a Majority, 1983; (with D. Kavanagh) The British General Election of 1983, 1984; A Compendium of Indian Elections, 1984; (with P. Jowett) Party Strategies in Britain, 1985; (with G. Butler) British Political Facts 1900-94, 1994; (with D. Kavanagh) The British General Election of 1987, 1988; British Elections since 1945, 1989; (with A. Low) Sovereigns and Surrogates, 1991; (with P. Roy) India Decides, 1952-91, 1996; (with B. Cain) Congressional Redistricting, 1991; (with A. Ranney) Electioneering, 1992; (with D. Kavanagh) The British General Election of 1992, 1992; (with A. Adonis and T. Travers) Failure in British Government: The Politics of the Poll Tax, 1994; (with M. Westlake) British Politics and European Elections, 1994, 1995; (with I. Maclean) Fixing the Boundaries, 1996; (with D. Kavanagh) The British General Election of 1997, 1997. **Address:** Nuffield College, Oxford OX1 3DP, England.

BUTLER, Dorothy. New Zealander, b. 1925. **Genres:** Children's fiction, Novellas/Short stories, Children's non-fiction, Education, Literary criticism and history. **Career:** High school English teacher; worked as play center supervisor, university lecturer in children's literature, and teacher of night classes for Auckland Technical Institute, 1946-65; Dorothy Butler Children's Bookshop Ltd., Auckland, NZ, owner and managing director, 1965-90; Dorothy Butler Reading Centre, owner, 1978-84; Reed Methuen, children's editor, 1984. OBE, 1993. **Publications:** Cushla and Her Books, 1979; (with M. Clay) Reading Begins at Home, 1979; Babies Need Books, 1980, 3rd ed., 1995; The Dorothy Butler Pre-Reading Kit, 1980; Five to Eight, 1985; Come Back, Ginger, 1987; A Bundle of Birds, 1987; My Brown Bear Barney, 1988; Bears, Bears, Bears, 1989; Lulu, 1989; A Happy Tale, 1990; Higgledy Piggledy Hobbledy Hoy, 1991; Another Happy Tale, 1991; Good Morning,

Mrs. Martin, 1992; The Little, Little Man, 1992; Farmyard Fiasco, 1992; By Jingo!, 1992; Where's Isabella?, 1992; My Brown Bear, Barney in Trouble, 1993; Birthday Rain, 1993; The Breakdown Day, 1993; My Brown Bear Barney at School, 1994; Farm Boy, City Girl, 1994; What Peculiar People, 1994; My Monkey Martha, 1995; Behave Yourself, Martha, 1995; Just a Dog, 1995; Hector: An Old Bear, 1995; Children, Books & Families, 1995; What a Birthday!, 1996; There Was a Time (autobiography), 1999; My Brown Bear, Barney at the Party, 2000; O'Reilly and the Real Bears, 2002. EDITOR: The Magpies Said: Stories and Poems from New Zealand, 1980; For Me, Me, Me, 1983; I Will Build You a House, 1984. **Address:** The Old House, Kare Kare, Auckland W, New Zealand.

BUTLER, Geoff. Canadian, b. 1945. **Genres:** Children's fiction, Art/Art history, Military/Defense/Arms control, Humor/Satire, Illustrations. **Career:** Artist and writer, Granville Ferry, NS, 1980-. Soccer coach, Annapolis Royal, NS, 1994-. **Publications:** Art of War: Painting It out of the Picture, 1990. SELF-ILLUSTRATED: The Killick: A Newfoundland Story (children's), 1995; The Hangashore (children's), 1998; Ode to Newfoundland, 2003. Illustrator of books by A. Walsh, P. Wyman. Creator of book cover illustrations. **Address:** PO Box 29, Granville Ferry, NS, Canada B0S 1K0. **Online address:** gbutler@auracom.com; www.auracom.com/~gbutler

BUTLER, Gregory S. American, b. 1961. **Genres:** Politics/Government. **Career:** Catholic University of America, Washington, DC, assistant professor of political science, 1989-90; New Mexico State University, Las Cruces, associate professor of government, 1990-, trainer for Central American Peace Scholarship Program, Center for Latin American Studies, 1993. Intercollegiate Studies Institute, faculty associate; Washington Center for Internships and Academic Seminars, internship coordinator, 1991-. **Publications:** In Search of the American Spirit: The Political Thought of Orestes Brownson, 1992; (with J.D. Slack) U.S. Educational Groups: Institutional Profiles, 1994. Work represented in books. Contributor to periodicals. **Address:** Department of Government, New Mexico State University, Box 3BN, Las Cruces, NM 88003, U.S.A.

BUTLER, Gwendoline (Williams). Also writes as Jennie Melville. British. **Genres:** Mystery/Crime/Suspense, Romance/Historical, Literary criticism and history. **Career:** Historian, lecturer, author. Royal Society of Arts, fellow; Crime Time magazine, historical crime fiction critic, 1998-. **Publications:** Receipt for Murder, 1956; Dead in a Row, 1957; The Dull Dead, 1958; The Murdering Kind, 1958; The Interloper, 1959; Death Lives Next Door (in U.S. as Dine and Be Dead), 1960; Make Me a Murderer, 1961; Coffin in Oxford, 1962; Coffin for Baby, 1963; Coffin Waiting, 1963; Coffin in Malta, 1964; A Nameless Coffin, 1966; Coffin Following, 1968; Coffin's Dark Number, 1969; A Coffin from the Past, 1970; A Coffin for Pandora, 1973, in U.S. as Olivia, 1974; A Coffin for the Canary (in U.S. as Sarsen Place), 1974; The Vesey Inheritance, 1975; Brides of Friedberg (in U.S. as Meadowsweet), 1977; The Red Staircase, 1979; Albion Walk, 1982, as Cavalcade, 1984; Coffin in the Water, 1986; Coffin in Fashion, 1987; Coffin Underground, 1988; Coffin in the Black Museum, 1989; Coffin and the Paper Man, 1990; Coffin on Murder Street, 1991; Cracking Open a Coffin, 1992; A Coffin for Charley, 1993; The Coffin Tree, 1994; A Dark Coffin, 1995; A Double Coffin, 1996; Butterfly, 1996. AS JENNIE MELVILLE: Come Home and Be Killed, 1962; Burning Is a Substitute for Loving, 1963; Murderers' Houses, 1964; There Lies Your Love, 1965; Nell Alone, 1966; A Different Kind of Summer, 1967; The Hunter in the Shadows, 1969; A New Kind of Killer, an Old Kind of Death, 1970, in U.S. as A New Kind of Killer, 1971; Ironwood, 1972; Nun's Castle, 1973; Raven's Forge, 1975; Dragon's Eye, 1976; Axwater (in U.S. as Tarot's Tower), 1978; Murder Has a Pretty Face, 1981; The Painted Castle, 1982; The Hand of Glass, 1983; Listen to the Children, 1986; Death in the Garden, 1987; Windsor Red, 1988; A Cure for Dying (in U.S. as Making Good Blood), 1989; Witching Murder, 1990; Footsteps in the Blood, 1990; Dead Set, 1992; Whoever Has the Heart, 1993; Baby Drop (in U.S. as A Death in the Family), 1994; The Morbid Kitchen, 1995; The Woman Who Was Not There, 1996; Revengeful Death, 1997; Stone Dead, 1998; Dead Again, 1999.

BUTLER, Jack. American, b. 1944. **Genres:** Novels, Poetry, Novellas/Short stories, Food and Wine. **Career:** Actuarial Analyst, Blue Cross, Little Rock, Arkansas, 1981-84; Supervisor for Capital Recovery, Arkansas Public Service Commission, Little Rock, 1985-88; Hendrix College, Conway, AR, assistant dean, 1988-93; The College of Santa Fe, Santa Fe, NM, professor of creative writing, 1993-. **Publications:** West of Hollywood: Poems from a Hermitage, 1980; Hawk Gumbo and Other Stories, 1982; The Kid Who Wanted to Be a Spaceman and Other Poems, 1984; Jujitsu for Christ (novel), 1986; Nightshade (novel), 1989; Living in Little Rock with Miss Little Rock (novel), 1993; Dreamer (novel,), 1998; Jack's Skillet (food), 1997.

BUTLER, Jon. American, b. 1940. **Genres:** History, Theology/Religion. **Career:** California State College, Bakersfield, assistant professor of history, 1971-75; University of Illinois at Chicago, 1975-85, assistant professor, professor of history; Yale University, New Haven, CT, William Robertson Coe Professor of American History and professor of religious studies and American studies, 1985-. **Publications:** Religion and Witch Craft in Early American Society, 1974; The Origins of American Denominational Order: The English Churches in the Delaware Valley, 1680-1730, 1978; The Huguenots in America: A Refugee People in New World Society, 1983; Awash in a Sea of Faith: Christianizing the American People, 1990; Religion in American History: A Reader, 1997; Becoming America: The Revolution before 1776, 2000; Religion in Colonial America, 2000. **Address:** Dept of History, Yale University, PO Box 208324, New Haven, CT 06520-8324, U.S.A.

BUTLER, Joseph T(homas). American, b. 1932. **Genres:** Antiques/ Furnishings, Architecture. **Career:** Historic Hudson Valley, Tarrytown, NY, Museum Operations, senior director, 1957-94, curator emeritus, 1994-; Columbia University, NYC, adjunct associate professor of architecture, 1970-80; Fashion Institute of Technology, NYC, professor, 1987-97. The Connoisseur, American editor, 1967-77. Art and Antiques, editorial board member, 1978-83; Julia Dyckman Andrus Memorial Foundation, board member, 1993-. **Publications:** Washington Irving's Sunnyside, 1962, 1974; American Antiques 1800-1900: A Collector's History and Guide, 1965; (with others) World Furniture, 1965; Candleholders in America 1650-1900, 1967; The Family Collections at Van Cortlandt Manor, 1967; (with others) The Arts in America: The 19th Century, 1969; American Furniture, 1973; (with others) The Collectors' Encyclopedia of Antiques, 1973; The Story of Boscobel and Its Builder: States Morris Dyckman, 1974; Van Cortlandt Manor, 1978; Sleepy Hollow Restorations. A Cross Section of the Collection, 1983; A Field Guide to American Antique Furniture, 1985. **Address:** 222 Martling Ave, Tarrytown, NY 10591, U.S.A.

BUTLER, Judith P. American. **Genres:** Philosophy. **Career:** Educator and writer. University of California, Berkeley, professor of rhetoric and comparative literature. **Publications:** Subjects of Desire: Hegelian Reflections in Twentieth-Century France, 1987; Gender Trouble: Feminism and the Subversion of Identity, 1990; (ed. with J.W. Scott) Feminists Theorize the Political, 1992; Bodies That Matter: On the Discursive Limits of "Sex", 1993; (ed. with L. Singer and M. MacGrogan) Erotic Welfare: Sexual Theory and Politics in the Age of Epidemic, 1993; Excitable Speech: A Politics of the Performative, 1997; The Psychic Life of Power: Theories in Subjection, 1997; Antigone's Claim: Kinship between Life and Death, 2000. **Address:** Department of Rhetoric, University of California Berkeley, 7408 Dwinelle Hall MC 2670, Berkeley, CA 94720, U.S.A.

BUTLER, Lance St. John. British, b. 1947. **Genres:** Literary criticism and history. **Career:** University of Stirling, Scotland, lecturer to senior lecturer in English studies, 1972-. **Publications:** (ed. and contrib.) Thomas Hardy after Fifty Years, 1977; Thomas Hardy, 1978; D.H. Lawrence's Sons and Lovers, 1980; Henry Fielding's Tom Jones, 1981; Daniel Defoe's Moll Flanders, 1982; Samuel Beckett and the Meaning of Being: A Study in Ontological Parable, 1984; Studying Thomas Hardy, 1986; (ed. with R. Davis) Make Sense Who May: Samuel Beckett's Later Plays, 1988; (ed. and contrib.) Alternative Hardy, 1989; (ed. with P.J. Wordie, and contrib.) The Royal Game, 1989; Victorian Doubt: Literary and Cultural Discourses, 1990; (ed. with R. Davis) Rethinking Beckett, 1990; (ed.) Critical Essays on Samuel Beckett, 1993; Registering the Difference, 1999. Work represented in anthologies. **Address:** Dept of English Studies, University of Stirling, Stirling FK9 4L0, Scotland. **Online address:** l.s.j.butler@stir.ac.uk

BUTLER, Marilyn (Speers). British, b. 1937. **Genres:** Literary criticism and history. **Career:** Current Affairs Producer, BBC, 1960-63; Research Fellow, St. Hilda's College, Oxford, 1970-73; Fellow and Tutor, St. Hugh's College, and Lecturer in English Literature, Oxford University, 1976-86; King Edward VII Professor of English Literature, Cambridge University, 1986-93; Rector, Exeter College, Oxford, 1994-. **Publications:** Maria Edgeworth: A Literary Biography, 1972; Jane Austen and the War of Ideas, 1975; Peacock Displayed: A Satirist in His Context, 1979; Romantics, Rebels, and Reactionaries: English Literature and Its Background 1760-1830, 1981. EDITOR: Burke, Paine, Godwin and the Revolution Controversy, 1984; (with J. Todd) The Works of Mary Wollstonecraft, 1989; Edgeworth's Castle Rackrent and Ennui, 1992; Mary Shelley's Frankenstein, 1993; Austen's Northanger Abbey, 1995; Works of Maria Edgeworth, 1999-2000. **Address:** Exeter College, Oxford, England. **Online address:** rector@exeter.ox.ac.uk

BUTLER, Octavia E. American, b. 1947. **Genres:** Science fiction/Fantasy. **Career:** Writer. **Publications:** Pattermaster, 1976; Mind of My Mind, 1977;

Survivor, 1978; Kindred, 1979; Wild Seed, 1980; Clay's Ark, 1984; Dawn, 1987; Adulthood Rites, 1988; Imago, 1989; The Evening and the Morning and the Night, 1991; Parable of the Sower, 1993; Bloodchild and Other Stories, 1995; Parable of the Talents, 1998; Lilith's Brood, 2000. **Address:** c/o Warner Books, 1271 Avenue of the Americas, New York, NY 10020, U.S.A.

BUTLER, Patrick. *See* **DUNBOYNE, Lord** in the Obituaries.

BUTLER, Pierce A. Irish, b. 1952. **Genres:** Novels, Literary criticism and history. **Career:** National University of Ireland, Cork, assistant lecturer in engineering design, 1976-79; Harvard University, Cambridge, MA, instructor in creative writing, 1983; University of Massachusetts, Boston, lecturer in English, 1982-83; Bentley College, Waltham, MA, adjunct assistant professor of communication, 1983-84; Babson College, Wellesley, MA, preceptor in English, 1984-88; Bentley College, writer in residence, 1988-. Gives readings from his works. **Publications:** A Malady (novel), 1982; Sean O'Faolain: A Study of the Short Fiction, 1993; Riddle of Stars, 2000. Work represented in anthologies. Contributor to periodicals. **Address:** 24 Harris St., Waltham, MA 02454, U.S.A. **Online address:** pierce.butler@pop.rcn.com

BUTLER, Robert Olen. American, b. 1945. **Genres:** Novels, Novellas/ Short stories. **Career:** High school teacher in Granite City, IL, 1973-74; Electronic News, NYC, editor/reporter, 1972-73; reporter, Chicago, 1974-75; Energy User News, editor-in-chief, 1975-85; member of faculty at writers' conferences, 1988-; McNeese State University, Lake Charles, LA, assistant professor, 1985-93, professor of fiction writing, 1993-. **Publications:** NOVELS: The Alleys of Eden, 1981; Sun Dogs, 1982; Countrymen of Bones, 1983; On Distant Ground, 1985; Wabash: A Novel, 1987; The Deuce, 1989; They Whisper, 1994; Fragments, 1997; The Deep Green Sea, 1998; Mr. Spaceman, 2000; Fair Warning, 2001. SHORT STORY COLLECTIONS: The Deuce, 1989; A Good Scent from a Strange Mountain: Stories, 1992; Tabloid Dreams, 1996. **Address:** Department of English, McNeese State University, 4100 Ryan Street, Lake Charles, LA 70609, U.S.A.

BUTLER, Ruth (Ann). American, b. 1931. **Genres:** Art/Art history. **Career:** University of Maryland, assistant professor of art history, 1969-72; University of Massachusetts, Boston, associate professor, 1973-76, chairperson of art department, 1976-80, professor emerita of art history, 1976-. **Publications:** (ed. with J. Van Nimmen) Nineteenth-Century French Sculpture: Monuments for the Middle Class, 1971; Western Sculpture: Definitions of Man, 1975; (ed.) Rodin in Perspective, 1980; Rodin: The Shape of Genius, 1993. Contributor to books. **Address:** 41 Holden St., Cambridge, MA 02138, U.S.A.

BUTLIN, Martin (Richard Fletcher). British, b. 1929. **Genres:** Art/Art history. **Career:** Keeper of the Historic British Collection, Tate Gallery, London, 1967-89 (Assistant Keeper, 1955-67); Consultant to Christie's, 1989-. **Publications:** Catalogue of the Works of William Blake in the Tate Gallery, 1957, 3rd ed., 1990; Samuel Palmer's Sketch Book of 1824, 1962; Turner Watercolours, 1962; (with J. Rothenstein) Turner, 1965; (co-author) Tate Gallery Catalogues: Modern British Paintings, Drawings and Sculpture, 1964; The Later Works of J.M.W. Turner, 1965; William Blake, 1966; The Blake-Varley Sketchbook of 1819, 1969; (with A. Wilton and J. Gage) Turner 1775-1851 (exhibition catalog), 1974; (with E. Joll) The Paintings of J.M.W. Turner, 1977, 2nd ed., 1984; William Blake (exhibition catalog) 1978; The Paintings and Drawings of William Blake, 1981; Aspects of British Painting 1550-1800, 1988; (with M. Luther and I. Warrell) Turner and Petworth, 1989; (with T. Gott) William Blake in the Collection of the National Gallery of Victoria, 1989; (with G. Schiff) William Blake (exhibition catalog), 1990; (ed. with E. Joll and L. Herrmann) The Oxford Companion to J.M.W. Turner, 2001. Author of articles and reviews. **Address:** 74C Eccleston Square, London SW1V 1PJ, England.

BUTLIN, Ron. Scottish, b. 1949. **Genres:** Novels, Novellas/Short stories, Plays/Screenplays, Poetry, Songs/Lyrics and libretti. **Career:** Has worked as a footman, model, computer operator, security guard, laborer, and city messenger. Writer-in-residence, University of Edinburgh, 1982, 1985, and for Midlothian Region, 1989-90, and Craigmillar Literacy Trust, 1997-98; University of New Brunswick, Fredericton, Scottish/Canadian Exchange Writing Fellow, 1984-85; Stirling University, writing fellow, 1993; University of St Andrews, novelist in residence, 1998-99. **Publications:** POETRY: Stretto, 1976; Creatures Tamed by Cruelty, 1979; Ragtime in Unfamiliar Bars, 1985; Histories of Desire, 1995. OPERA LIBRETTOS: Markheim, 1990; Dark Country, 1992; Faraway Pictures, 2001. STORIES: Tilting Room, 1983; No More Angels, 2004; Vivaldi and the Number 3, 2004. NOVELS: The Sound of My Voice, 1987; Night Visits, 1997. EDITOR: Mauritian

Voices, 1997; When We Jump We Jump High!, 1998. OTHER: (trans. with K. Chevalier) The Exquisite Instrument: Imitations from the Chinese, 1982; (adaptor) Blending In (play), 1989. **Address:** 7 West Newington Place, Edinburgh EH9 1QT, Scotland.

BUTMAN, John. American, b. 1951. **Genres:** Business/Trade/Industry, Social commentary, Biography, Humor/Satire. **Career:** Friends of the Performing Arts, Concord, MA, manager, 1972-76; Silver and Light Productions, Concord, director, 1976-80; Envision Corporation, Boston, MA, creative director, 1980-86; Spectrum Communications Ltd., London, England, creative director, 1986-88; Butman Company, Boston, principal, 1989-. **Publications:** Car Wars, 1991; Flying Fox: A Business Adventure in Teams & Teamwork, 1993; Introduction to Managerial Breakthrough, 1994; The Book That's Sweeping America! or Why I Love Business!, 1997; J.M. Juran, A Lifetime of Influence, 1997; Townie, 2002; (co-author) Sparkly Perfect, 2005. COLLABORATOR: Real Boys, 1998; Real Boys' Voices, 2000; The Change Monster, 2001; Trading Up, 2003; Hardball, 2004. Contributor to books. **Address:** 37 Main St Ste 4, Concord, MA 01742, U.S.A. **Online address:** john@butman.us

BUTOW, Robert J. C. American, b. 1924. **Genres:** Area studies, International relations/Current affairs, History. **Career:** Professor Emeritus, Jackson School of International Studies, University of Washington, Seattle, since 1990 (Associate Professor, 1960-66; Professor, 1966-90). Instructor in History, 1954-59, and Assistant Professor, 1959-60, Princeton University, New Jersey. **Publications:** Japan's Decision to Surrender, 1954; Tojo and the Coming of the War, 1961; The John Doe Associates: Backdoor Diplomacy for Peace 1941, 1974. **Address:** Jackson School of International Studies, University of Washington, Box 353650, Seattle, WA 98195-3650, U.S.A.

BUTSCH, Richard (J.). American, b. 1943. **Genres:** Communications/Media, History, Popular Culture. **Career:** Esso Research and Engineering, research engineer, 1967-69; Rider University, Lawrenceville, NJ, 1976-, professor of sociology and American Studies. Center for Contemporary Cultural Studies, University of Birmingham, visiting scholar, 1987. **Publications:** (ed. and contrib.) For Fun and Profit: The Transformation of Leisure into Consumption, 1990; The Making of American Audiences, 2000. **Address:** Department of Sociology, Rider University, Lawrenceville, NJ 08648-3099, U.S.A.

BUTTERWORTH, Nick. British, b. 1946. **Genres:** Children's fiction. **Career:** Author and illustrator of children's books. Graphic designer; TV AM (UK), presenter for Rub-a-Dub-Tub. **Publications:** AUTHOR AND ILLUSTRATOR: B.B. Blacksheep and Company: A Collection of Favourite Nursery Rhymes, 1981; My Mom Is Excellent, 1989; My Dad Is Awesome, 1989; (ed.) Nick Butterworth's Book of Nursery Rhymes, 1990; My Grandma Is Wonderful, 1991; My Grandpa Is Amazing, 1991; Amanda's Butterfly, 1991; Jack the Carpenter and His Friends, 1991; Jill the Farmer and Her Friends, 1991; Busy People, 1992; Making Faces, 1993; When It's Time for Bed, 1994; When There's Work to Do, 1994; When We Go Shopping, 1994; When We Play Together, 1994; All Together Now!, 1994; Thud!, 1997; 1-2-3-London, 1998; A-B-C-London, 1998; Jingle Bells, 1998; QPootle5, 2000; Albert LeBlanc, 2002, in US as Albert the Bear; QPootle5 in Space, 2003. UPNEY JUNCTION SERIES: Treasure Trove at Upney Junction, 1983; A Windy Day at Upney Junction, 1983; Invasion at Upney Junction, 1983; A Monster at Upney Junction, 1983. PERCY THE PARK KEEPER SERIES: One Snowy Night, 1989; After the Storm, 1992, in US as One Blowy Night; The Rescue Party, 1993; The Secret Path, 1993; A Year in Percy's Park, 1995; The Cross Rabbit, 1995; Percy the Park Keeper Press-Out Book, 1995; The Fox's Hiccups, 1995; The Treasure Hunt, 1996; The Hedgehog's Balloon, 1996; The Badger's Bath, 1996; Tales from Percy's Park, 1996; Percy the Park Keeper Activity Book, 1996; Percy Helps Out: Sticker Book, 1996; The Owl's Flying Lesson, 1997; One Warm Fox, 1997; Four Feathers in Percy's Park, 1998; Percy the Park Keeper A-B-C, 1998; Percy in the Park 1-2-3; Percy in the Park Games Book; Percy in the Park Coloring Book; Percy in the Park Sticker and Story Book; A Year with Percy Coloring Book. WITH M. INKPEN: The Nativity Play, 1985; The House on the Rock, 1986; The Precious Pearl, 1986; The Lost Sheep, 1986; The Two Sons, 1986; Nice and Nasty: A Book of Opposites, 1987, in US as Nice or Nasty: A Book of Opposites; I Wonder at the Zoo, 1987; I Wonder in the Garden, 1987; I Wonder in the Country, 1987; I Wonder at the Farm, 1987, in US as I Wonder on the Farm, 1987; Who Made...In the Country, 1987; Who Made...On the Farm, 1987; Who Made...At the Zoo, 1987; Who Made...In the Garden, 1987; Sports Day, 1988; The Magpie's Story: Jesus and Zacchaeus, 1988; The Mouse's Story: Jesus and the Storm, 1988; The Cat's Tale: Jesus at the Wedding, 1988; The Fox's Tale: Jesus Is Born, 1988; The Good Stranger, 1989; Just Like Jasper!, 1989; The Little Gate, 1989; The Rich Farmer, 1989; The

Ten Silver Coins, 1989; The School Trip, 1990; Wonderful Earth!, 1990; Field Day, 1991; Jasper's Beanstalk, 1992; Stories Jesus Told, 1994; Opposites, 1997. Illustrator of books by E. Lawrence, A. Butterworth, M. and M. Doney. Contributed illustrations to a series of Christian books for children. **Address:** c/o HarperCollins Publishers, 77-85 Fulham Palace Rd., Hammersmith, London W6 8JB, England.

BUTTITTA, Tony. American, b. 1907. **Genres:** Children's fiction, Plays/Screenplays, Theatre, Autobiography/Memoirs. **Career:** Former theatrical press agent in New York and California; also United Press Correspondent for various U.S. newspapers. Ed., Contempo, 1931-34. **Publications:** Singing Piedmont (play), 1937; After the Good Gay Times: A Season with F. Scott Fitzgerald, 1974; Uncle Sam Presents: A Memoir of the Federal Theatre, 1935-39, 1982; The Lost Summer: A Memoir of F. Scott Fitzgerald, 1987; The Singing Tree (children's fiction), 1990; Never a Stranger (memoir), forthcoming.

BUTTON, Kenneth J(ohn). British, b. 1948. **Genres:** Economics, Transportation. **Career:** Loughborough University, Leicestershire, lecturer, sr. lecturer, and reader, 1973-89; professor of applied economics and transport, 1989-; University of British Columbia, Vancouver, visiting professor, 1982; University of California, Berkeley, visiting fellow, 1982; Tinbergen Institute, Amsterdam, VSB visiting professor of transport and the environment, 1991-; OECD, Paris, counsellor, 1994; George Mason University, professor of public policy, 1996-. **Publications:** (with P.J. Barker) Case Studies in Cost Benefit Analysis, 1975; Urban Economics, 1976; (with D. Gillingwater) Case Studies in Regional Economics, 1976; The Economics of Urban Transport, 1977; (with A.D. Pearman) The Economics of Urban Freight Transport, 1981; (with A.D. Pearman and A.S. Fowkes) Car Ownership Modelling and Forecasting, 1982; Transport Economics, 1982, 2nd ed., 1993; (with A.D. Pearman) The Practice of Transport Investment Appraisal, 1983; Transport Policy, Economics and the Environment, 1983; Road Haulage Licensing and EC Transport Policy, 1984; (with A.D. Pearman) Applied Transport Economics, 1985; (with D. Gillingwater) Future Transport Policy, 1986; (with A.J. Westaway) The Economic Impact of Aid Policy on Donor Country's Economies, 1989; Market and Intervention Failures in Transport Policy, 1992; (with others) Academic Links and Communications, 1993; Transport, the Environment an d Economic Policy, 1993; (with others) Transport Policy, 1994; (with others) Missing Transport Networks in Europe, 1994; (with others) The Future of International Air Transport Policy, 1997; (with others) Meta-analysis in Environmental Economics, 1997; (with K. Haynes and R. Stough) Flying into the Future, 1998; (with E. Pentecost) Economic convergence in Europe, 1999. EDITOR WITH OTHERS: Transport Location and Spatial Policy, 1983; International Railway Economics, 1985; The Collected Essays of Harvey Leibenstein, 2 vols., 1989; The Age of Regulatory Reform, 1989; Transport Policy and the Environment, 1990; Airline Deregulation: An International Perspective, 1990; Transport in a Free Market Economy, 1991; Transport, the Environment and Sustainable Development, 1992; Location Theory, 2 vols., 1996; Regional Dynamics, 2 vols., 1996; Analytical Urban Economics, 1996; Regional Labour and Housing Markets, 1996; Regional Policy and Regional Integration, 1996; Transport and Land Use, 1996; Transport Networks in Europe, 1993; Road Pricing, Traffic Congestion and th Environment, 1998; Transport Policy, 1998; Environment and Transport, 1999; Global Aspects of the Environment, 2 vols., 1999; Ecosystems and Nature, 1999; Environment, Land Use and Urban Policy, 1999; Environment Economics and Development, 1999; Environmental Instruments and Institutions, 1999; Environmental Evaluation, 2 vols., 1999; Air Transport Networks, 2000; Handbook of Transport Modelling, 2000; Handbook of Logistics and Supply-Chain Management, 2001; Handbook of Transport Systems and Traffic Control, 2001; Maritime Transport, 2002; Air Transport, 2002; Railways, 2002; Transport Infrastructure, 2002. **Address:** School of Public Policy, 116D Finley Bldg 3C6, George Mason University, 4400 University Dr, Fairfax, VA 22030-4444, U.S.A. **Online address:** kbutton@gmu.edu

BUTTS, Anthony. American, b. 1969. **Genres:** Adult non-fiction. **Career:** Writer. KOPN-FM Radio, cohost of the interview show Different Voices;. **Publications:** Fifth Season, 1997; Evolution, 1998. **Address:** 107 Tate Hall, University of Missouri at Columbia, Columbia, MO 65211, U.S.A.

BUTTS, Dennis. British, b. 1932. **Genres:** Literary criticism and history, Bibliography. **Career:** University of Reading, Reading, England, part-time lecturer. **Publications:** Robert Louis Stevenson, 1966; (ed.) Stories and Society, 1992; Mistress of Our Tears: A Literary and Bibliographical Study of Barbara Hofland, 1992. **Address:** 219 Church Rd., Earley, Reading RS6 1HW, England.

BUZO, Alexander. Australian, b. 1944. **Genres:** Novels, Plays/Screenplays, Adult non-fiction. **Career:** David Jones Ltd., Sydney, salesman, 1960; E.L.

Davis & Co., Sydney, messenger, 1961; McGraw-Hill Book Co., Sydney, storeman-packer, 1967; N.S.W. Public Service, Sydney, clerk, 1967-68; Melbourne Theatre Co., resident playwright, 1972-73; University of Central Queensland, writer in residence, 1991. **Publications:** Macquarie, 1971; Norm and Ahmed, Rooted, and The Roy Murphy Show: Three Plays, 1973; Coralie Lansdowne Says No, 1974; Tom, 1975; Martello Towers, 1976; Makassar Reef, 1978; Meet the New Class, 1981; Big River, The Marginal Farm, 1985; Pacific Union (play), 1995. NOVELS The Search for Harry Allway, 1985; Prue Flies North, 1991. NON-FICTION: Tautology, 1981; Glancing Blows, 1987; The Young Person's Guide to the Theatre, 1988; The Longest Game, 1990; Kiwese, 1994; A Dictionary of the Almost Obvious, 1998. **Address:** 14 Rawson Ave, Bondi Junction, Sydney, NSW 2022, Australia. **Online address:** ajbu@ozemail.com.au

BUZZEO, Toni. American, b. 1951. **Genres:** Children's fiction, Education, Librarianship, Bibliography. **Career:** Author, library media specialist, and book reviewer. Baxter Memorial Library, Gorham, ME, children's librarian, 1988-; Margaret Chase Smith School, Sanford, ME, library media specialist, 1990-; Longfellow Elementary School, Portland, ME, library media specialist, 1993-. Visiting author at schools; conducts workshops and training sessions at conferences and in school districts. **Publications:** (with J. Kurtz) Terrific Connections with Authors, Illustrators, and Storytellers: Real Space and Virtual Links, 1999; (with J. Kurtz) 35 Best Books for Teaching U.S. Regions: Using Fiction to Help Students Explore the Geography, History, and Cultures of the Seven U.S. Regions, 1999; Collaborating to Meet Standards, Teacher/Librarian Partnerships for K-6, 2002; Collaborating to Meet Standards, Teacher/Librarian Partnerships for 7-12, 2002. JUVENILE: The Sea Chest, 2002; Dawdle Duckling, 2003; Little Loon and Papa, 2004. Contributor of book reviews to professional journals.

BYALICK, Marcia. American, b. 1947. **Genres:** Children's fiction, Young adult fiction, Self help, Essays, Humor/Satire. **Career:** Writer. Hofstra University, writing teacher, 1993-; Long Island University and C.W. Post Campus, 1995-. **Publications:** (co-author) The Three Career Couple (humorous self-help), 1993; (co-author) How Come I Feel So Disconnected...If This Is Such a User Friendly World?, 1995; (co-author) The Craving Brain: The Biobalance Approach to Controlling Addiction, 1997; Quit It (for children), 2003. YOUNG ADULT NOVELS You Don't Have to Be Perfect to Be Excellent, 1993; It's a Matter of Trust, 1995. Contributor to magazines and newspapers. **Address:** 22 Lydia Ct, Albertson, NY 11507, U.S.A.

BYARS, Betsy (Cromer). American, b. 1928. **Genres:** Children's fiction, Novellas/Short stories. **Publications:** Clementine, 1962; The Dancing Camel, 1965; Rama, the Gypsy Cat, 1966; The Groober, 1967; The Midnight Fox, 1968; Trouble River, 1969; The Summer of the Swans, 1970; Go and Hush the Baby, 1971; The House of Wings, 1972; The 18th Emergency, 1973; The Winged Colt of Casa Mia, 1973; After the Goat Man, 1974; The Lace Snail, 1975; The T.V. Kid, 1976; The Pinballs, 1977; The Cartoonist, 1978; Goodbye, Chicken Little, 1979; Night Swimmers, 1980; The Animal, The Vegetable, and John D. Jones, 1981; The Two Thousand Pound Goldfish, 1981; The Cybil War, 1982; The Glory Girl, 1983; The Computer Nut, 1984; Cracker Jackson, 1985; The Blossoms Meet the Vulture Lady, 1986; The Golly Sisters Go West, 1986; The Not-Just-Anybody Family, 1986; A Blossom Promise, 1987; The Blossoms and the Green Phantom, 1987; Sugar and Other Stories, 1987; The Burning Questions of Bingo Brown, 1988; Beans on the Roof, 1988; Bingo Brown and the Language of Love, 1989; Hooray for the Golly Sisters!, 1990; Bingo Brown, Gypsy Lover, 1990; Seven Treasure Hunts, 1991; Wanted--Mud Blossom, 1991; Bingo Brown's Guide to Romance, 1992; Coast to Coast, 1992; The Moon & I, 1992; McMummy, 1993; The Dark Stairs: A Herculeah Jones Mystery, 1994; The Golly Sisters Ride Again, 1994; Tarot Says Beware, 1996; The Joy Boys, 1996; My Brother Ant, 1996; Tornado, 1996; Dead Letter, 1996; Death's Door, 1997; Ant Plays Bear, 1997; Disappearing Acts, 1998; My Dog, My Hero, 2000; Me Tarzan, 2000; Little Horse, 2001; Keeper of the Doves, 2002; Little Horse on His Own, 2004; (with others) The SOS File, 2004. **Address:** 401 Rudder Ridge, Seneca, SC 29678, U.S.A.

BYATT, A(ntonia) S(usan). British, b. 1936. **Genres:** Novels, Novellas/Short stories, Literary criticism and history. **Career:** London University, extra-mural lecturer, 1965-72; University College, London, lecturer, 1972-81, sr. lecturer, 1981-83. **Publications:** The Shadow of the Sun, 1964; Degrees of Freedom: The Novels of Iris Murdoch, 1965; The Game, 1967; Wordsworth and Coleridge in Their Time, 1970; Iris Murdoch, 1976; The Virgin in the Garden, 1978; Still Life, 1985; Sugar and Other Stories, 1987; Possession: A Romance, 1990 (Booker Prize); Still Life: A Novel, 1991; Passions of the Mind, 1992; Angels and Insects (novellas), 1992; The Matisse Stories, 1993; The Djinn in the Nightingale's Eye, 1995; Imagining Characters,

1995; Babel Tower, 1996; Elementals: Stories of Fire and Ice, 1999; The Biographer's Tale, 2001; On Histories and Stories: Selected Essays, 2001; Portraits in Fiction, 2001; (with V. Schrager) Bird Hand Book, 2001; A Whistling Woman, 2002; Little Black Book of Stories, 2003. EDITOR: G. Eliot, The Mill on the Floss, 1979; G. Eliot, Selected Essays, Poems & Other Writings, 1991; The Oxford Book of English Short Stories, 1998. **Address:** 37 Rusholme Rd, London SW15 3LF, England.

BYE, Beryl (Joyce Rayment). British, b. 1926. **Genres:** Children's fiction, Children's non-fiction, Theology/Religion. **Publications:** Three's Company, 1961; Wharf Street, 1962; Prayers at Breakfast, 1964; Teaching Our Children the Christian Faith, 1965; Please God, 1966; About God, 1967; Nobody's Pony, 1967; Looking into Life, 1967; Jesus Said, 1968; Pony for Sale, 1969; Learning from Life, 1969, Jesus at Work, 1969; Start the Day Well, 1970; Prayers for All Seasons, 1971; People Like Us, 1971; More People Like Us, 1972; To be Continued, 1972; Belles Bridle, 1973; Following Jesus, 1974; What about Lifestyle?, 1977; Time for Jesus, 1980; Hear a Minute, 1990; Hello God! It's Me!, 1992. **Address:** Cotswold, Priory Lane, Bishops Cleeve, Glos., England.

BYER, Kathryn Stripling. American, b. 1944. **Genres:** Poetry. **Career:** Western Carolina University, Cullowhee, NC, instructor in English, 1968-. **Publications:** POETRY: Search Party, 1979; Alma, 1983; The Girl in the Midst of the Harvest, 1986; Wildwood Flower, 1992; Black Shawl, 1998; Catching Light, 2002. **Address:** Department of English, Western Carolina University, Cullowhee, NC 28723, U.S.A.

BYERS, John A. American, b. 1948. **Genres:** Animals/Pets, Sciences, Zoology. **Career:** Brookfield Zoo, Chicago, IL, research associate in animal behavior, 1977; University of Idaho, Moscow, faculty member, 1980-, professor of zoology, 1993-. Lecturer at colleges and universities; consultant. **Publications:** American Pronghorn: Social Adaptations and the Ghosts of Predators Past, 1997; (ed. with M. Bekoff, and contrib.) Animal Play: Evolutionary, Comparative, and Ecological Perspectives, 1998; Built for Speed: A Year in the Life of Pronghorn, 2003. Contributor to books. Contributor of articles and reviews to scientific journals. **Address:** Dept of Biological Sciences, 345 Life Science South, University of Idaho, Moscow, ID 83844, U.S.A. **Online address:** jbyers@uidaho.edu

BYNUM, Victoria E. American, b. 1947. **Genres:** History. **Career:** Texas State University at San Marcos, professor of history, 1986-. **Publications:** Unruly Women: The Politics of Social and Sexual Control in the Old South, 1992; The Free State of Jones: Mississippi's Longest Civil War, 2001. **Address:** Department of History, Texas State University at San Marcos, San Marcos, TX 78666, U.S.A. **Online address:** vb03@txstate.edu

BYRD, Max. American, b. 1942. **Genres:** Mystery/Crime/Suspense, Literary criticism and history, Romance/Historical. **Career:** Professor, University of California, Davis, since 1981 (Associate Professor, 1976-81). Assistant Professor of English, 1970-75, and Associate Professor, 1975-76, Yale University, New Haven, Conn. Recipient, Private Eye Writers of America Shamus Award, 1982. **Publications:** MYSTERY NOVELS: California Thriller, 1981; Fly Away, Jill, 1981; Finders Weepers, 1983; Target of Opportunity, 1988; Fuse Time, 1991. HISTORICAL NOVELS: Jefferson, 1993; Jackson, 1997; Grant, 2000. OTHER: Visits to Bedlam: Madness and Literature in the Eighteenth Century, 1974; (ed.) Daniel Defoe: A Collection of Critical Essays, 1976; London Transformed: Images of the City in the 18th Century, 1978; Tristram Shandy, 1985.

BYRNE, Donn. American, b. 1931. **Genres:** Psychology. **Career:** California State University, San Francisco, instructor, 1957-59; University of Texas, assistant professor to professor, 1959-69; Purdue University, West Lafayette, IN, professor of psychological sciences, 1969-79; State University of New York, Albany, professor of psychology, 1979-91, chairman of dept., 1984-89, distinguished professor of psychology, 1991-2001, distinguished professor emeritus, 2001-. **Publications:** The Attraction Paradigm, 1971; (with H. and G. Lindgren) Current Research in Personality, 1971; (with R. Baron) Social Psychology, 1974, 10th ed., 2003; An Introduction to Personality, 3rd ed., 1981; (with H. Lindgren) Psychology, 4th ed., 1975; (with R. Baron and B. Kantowitz) Psychology, 1977; (with W.A. Fisher) Adolescents, Sex, and Contraception, 1983; (with K. Kelley) Alternative Approaches to the Study of Sexual Behavior, 1986; (with R. Baron and J. Suls) Exploring Social Psychology, 1989, 4th ed. (with R. Baron and B. Johnson), 1998; (with K. Kelley) Exploring Human Sexuality, 1992. EDITOR: (with P. Worchel) Personality Change, 1964; (with M. Hamilton) Personality Research, 1966; (with L. Byrne) Exploring Human Sexuality, 1977. **Address:** 15 Indian Hill Rd, Feura Bush, NY 12067-2602, U.S.A. **Online address:** vyaduckdb@aol.com

BYRNE, Robert. American, b. 1930. **Genres:** Novels, Language/Linguistics, Recreation, Writing/Journalism. **Career:** Former trade journal editor. **Publications:** Writing Rackets, 1969; McGoorty, 1972; (ed.) Mrs. Byrne's Dictionary of Unusual Words, 1974; Byrne's Standard Book of Pool and Billiards, 1978; Byrne's Treasury of Trick Shots in Pool and Billiards, 1982; The 637 Best Things Anybody Ever Said, 1982; Cat Scan, 1983, in England as The Quotable Cat, 1985; The Other 637 Best Things Anybody Ever Said, 1984; The Third 637 Best Things Anybody Ever Said, 1986; Every Day Is Father's Day, 1989; The Fourth 637 Best Things Anybody Ever Said, 1990; Byrne's Advanced Technique in Pool and Billiards, 1990; The Fifth 637 Best Things Anybody Ever Said, 1993; Byrne's Wonderful World of Pool and Billiards, 1996; Byrne's New Standard Book of Pool and Billiards, 1998; The 2,548 Best Things Anybody Ever Said, 2003; Byrne's Complete Book of Pool Shots, 2003. NOVELS: Memories of a Non-Jewish Childhood, 1971; The Tunnel, 1977; The Dam, 1981; Always Catholic, 1981; Skyscraper, 1984; Mannequin (in England as Death Train), 1988; Thrill, 1995. **Address:** 198 Main St, Dubuque, IA 52001-3114, U.S.A. **Online address:** bob@byrne.org

BYRT, Edwin Andrew. Australian, b. 1932. **Genres:** Mathematics/Statistics. **Career:** Teacher, Education Dept. of Vic., 1954-66, and Suva Grammar School, Fiji, 1967-68; Lecturer, University of the South Pacific, Fiji, 1969; Sr. Lecturer, Victoria College, Rusden, 1970-88; Research Assistant, Royal Children's Hospital, Vic., 1989-98. **Publications:** Contemporary Mathematics, 4 vols., 1969-72. **Address:** 60 Rolling Hills Rd, Chirnside Park, VIC 3116, Australia.

C

CABOT, Meg(gin Patricia). Also writes as Patricia Cabot, Jenny Carroll. American, b. 1967. **Genres:** Novels, Romance/Historical, Young adult fiction. **Career:** Novelist. **Publications:** FOR ADULTS: She Went All the Way, 2002. FOR YOUNG ADULTS: PRINCESS DIARY SERIES: The Princess Diaries, 2000; Princess in the Spotlight, 2001; Princess in Love, 2002; Princess in Waiting, 2003; Princess in Pink, 2004. ALL AMERICAN GIRL SERIES: All American Girl, 2002; Boy Next Door, 2002; Boy Meets Girl, 2004. NICOLA & THE VISCOUNT (historical romance): Victoria and the Rogue, 2002; Haunted, 2003. AS PATRICIA CABOT (adult historical romance): Where Roses Grow Wild, 1998; Improper Proposal, 1999; Portrait of My Heart, 1999; Little Scandal, 2000; Educating Caroline, 2001; Lady of Skye, 2001. FOR YOUNG ADULTS AS JENNY CARROLL. THE MEDIATOR SERIES: Shadow Land, 2000; Ninth Key, 2001; Reunion, 2001; Darkest Hour, 2001. 1-800-WHERE-R-YOU SERIES: When Lightning Strikes, 2001; Codename Cassandra, 2001; Safe House, 2002; Sanctuary, 2002.

CABOT, Patricia. *See* **CABOT, Meg(gin Patricia).**

CABRERA, Jane. British, b. 1968. **Genres:** Children's fiction. **Career:** Apollo Arts and Antiques (magazine), art director, 1989-91; freelance graphic designer for clients including the British Broadcasting Corporation (BBC) Children's Books, Reed Children's Books, Dorling Kindersley, HarperCollins, Tiger Print (design group), and HIT Entertainment PLC, 1991-98; illustrator, 1997-. Speaker on children's book design and illustration at schools in England. **Publications:** SELF-ILLUSTRATED FICTION FOR CHILDREN: Cat's Colours, 1997, in the US as Cat's Colors; Dog's Day, 1998; Panda Big and Panda Small, 1998. Illustrator of books by J. Dunbar. Contributor of illustrations to travel magazine. **Address:** 7 Saint Marks Mansions, Balderton Street, London W1Y 1TG, England.

CACHIA, Pierre (Jacques Elie). British (born Egypt), b. 1921. **Genres:** Language/Linguistics, Literary criticism and history. **Career:** Professor Emeritus, Columbia University, NYC, 1991- (Professor of Arabic Language and Literature, 1975-91; Chairman, Dept. of Middle Eastern Languages and Cultures, 1980-83). Joint Ed., Journal of Arabic Literature, Leiden, 1970-96. Assistant Lecturer, 1949-50, Lecturer, 1950-65, Sr. Lecturer, 1965-69, and Reader in Arabic, 1969-76, Edinburgh University. **Publications:** Taha Husayn: His Place in the Egyptian Literary Renaissance, 1956; (with W. Watt) A History of Islamic Spain, 1965; (comp.) The Monitor: A Dictionary of Arabic Grammatical Terms, Arabic/English. English/Arabic, 1973; Popular Narrative Ballads of Modern Egypt, 1989; An Overview of Modern Arabic Literature, 1990; The Arch Rhetorician or the Schemer's Skimmer: A Handbook of Late Arabic Badi, 1998; (with A. Cachia) Landlocked Islands: Two Alien Lives in Egypt, 1999; Arabic Literature: An Overview, 2002. EDITOR: The Book of the Demonstration by Eutychius of Alexandria, vol. l, 1960, vol. 2, 1961; (joint) Islam: Past Influence and Present Challenge, 1979. TRANSLATOR: The Prison of Life by Tawfiq al-Hakim, 1992; Blood and Mud by Y. Haqqi, 1999. **Address:** 456 Riverside Dr Apt 8A, New York, NY 10027-6811, U.S.A. **Online address:** pjc1@columbia.edu

CADDEN, Tom Scott. (Thomas Scott). American, b. 1923. **Genres:** Film, Music. **Career:** KSTL-Radio, St. Louis, MO, continuity director and publicity director, 1948-51; WIL-Radio, St. Louis, continuity director and publicity director, 1950-51; Smith, Taylor & Jenkins, Pittsburgh, PA, television and radio writer and producer, 1951-53; Krupnick and Associates, St. Louis, director of television and radio, 1954-55; Geoffrey Wade, Chicago, television and radio writer, 1955-56; Tatham-Laird & Kudner, Chicago, vice-president, member of board of directors, and director of commercial production for television and radio, 1956-70; free-lance writer, producer, and musician, 1971-; writer of words and music for TV commercial jingles, including the Mr. Clean jingle. **Publications:** What a Bunch of Characters! An Entertaining Guide to Who Played What in the Movies, 1984. **Address:** 707 Arbor Ln, Glenview, IL 60025, U.S.A.

CADDY, Caroline. Australian, b. 1944. **Genres:** Poetry. **Career:** Self-employed in farming, 1965-; olive grower, olive oil producer. **Publications:** POETRY: Singing at Night, 1981; Letters from the North, 1984; Beach Plastic, 1990; Conquistadors, 1991; Antarctica, 1996; Working Temple, 1997; Editing the Moon, 1998; New & Selected, 2006.

CADDY, (Michael) Douglas. American, b. 1938. **Genres:** Business/Trade/Industry, Politics/Government. **Career:** McGraw-Edison Co., New York City, executive director of committee on public affairs, 1960-61; assistant to the lieutenant governor of the state of New York, 1962-65; NAM, New York City, assistant to the executive vice president, 1966-67; General Foods Corp., Washington liaison, 1968-70; Gall, Lane, Powell & Kilcullen (law firm), associate, 1970-74; National Association of Realtors, legislative counsel, 1975-76; office of the Texas secretary of state, attorney, 1980-81; attorney-at-law in Houston, TX, 1982-. **Publications:** The One-Hundred-Million-Dollar Pay-Off, 1975; How They Rig Our Elections, 1976; Understanding Texas Insurance, 1984; Legislative Trends in Insurance Regulation, 1986; Exploring America's Future, 1987. **Address:** 166 Stoney Creek Dr, Houston, TX 77024-6220, U.S.A. **Online address:** DouglasCaddy@justice.com

CADLE, Farris W(illiam). American, b. 1952. **Genres:** Geography, History, Law. **Career:** Delta Engineers and Surveyors, Smyrna, GA, land surveyor's assistant, 1976-78; Donaldson Surveys, Metter, GA, land surveyor's assistant, 1979-82; Helmly and Associates, Savannah, GA, land surveyor, 1982-84, 1986-89; Belford Land Title Co., Savannah, title abstractor, 1989-91, 1996-2002; Farris Cadle, Inc., president, 2002-. Registered land surveyor, Georgia, 1986-. **Publications:** Georgia Land Surveying History and Law, 1991. **Address:** 21 Colonial Trail #10, Garden City, GA 31408, U.S.A. **Online address:** fcadle@bellsouth.net

CADNUM, Michael. American, b. 1949. **Genres:** Novels, Novellas/Short stories, Mystery/Crime/Suspense, Horror, Romance/Historical, Children's fiction, Young adult fiction, Plays/Screenplays, Poetry. **Career:** Writer. **Publications:** NOVELS: Nightlight, 1990; Sleepwalker, 1991; Saint Peter's Wolf, 1991; Calling Home, 1991; Breaking the Fall, 1992; Ghostwright, 1993; The Horses of the Night, 1993; Skyscape, 1994; Taking It, 1995; The Judas Glass, 1996; Zero at the Bone, 1996; Edge, 1997; In a Dark Wood, 1998; Heat, 1998; Rundown, 1999; The Book of the Lion, 2000; Redhanded, 2000; Raven of the Waves, 2001; The Leopard Sword, 2002; Daughter of the Wind, 2003; Ship of Fine, 2003; Blood Gold, 2004; Star Fall, 2004. POETRY: The Morning of the Massacre (chapbook), 1981; Invisible Mirror (chapbook), 1984; Foreign Springs (chapbook), 1985; Long Afternoon (chapbook), 1986; By Evening, 1992; The Cities We Will Never See, 1993; The Woman Who Discovered Math, 2001; Illicit, 2001. FOR CHILDREN: The Lost and Found House, 1997. Contributor to anthologies and periodicals. **Address:** c/o Laura Langlie Literary Agent, 275 President St No 3, Brooklyn, NY 11231, U.S.A.

CADUTO, Michael J. American, b. 1955. **Genres:** Children's fiction, Songs/Lyrics and libretti, Adult non-fiction, Cultural/Ethnic topics, Education,

Environmental sciences/Ecology, Mythology/Folklore, Natural history. **Career:** Audubon Society of Rhode Island, land management planner, 1975-78, teacher, 1976-78; W. Alton Jones Environmental Education Center, Greenwich, RI, teacher and naturalist, 1979; Pocono Lake Preserve, curator of exhibits and program director, 1979; VINS, worked in land management, 1982-85, and environmental education, 1982-83; Programs for Environmental Awareness and Cultural Exchange, Norwich, VT, founder, 1984, director, 1984-. Vermont Council on the Arts, touring artist; New Hampshire Council on the Arts, artist-in-residence; teacher at colleges; presents workshops on ecological education, native cultures, and storytelling. Vermont Council on the Humanities, speaker/performer, also senior instructor at Living Rivers Environmental Education Program, 1980. **Publications:** Ann Arbor Alive, 1981; A Guide on Environmental Values Education, 1985; Pond and Brook, 1990; (with J. Bruchac) Keepers of the Earth, 1988; (with J. Bruchac) Keepers of the Animals, 1991; (with J. Bruchac) Keepers of the Night, 1994; (with J. Bruchac) Keepers of the Life, 1994; All One Earth: Songs for the Generations, 1994; (with J. Bruchac) Native American Gardening: Stories, Projects, and Recipes for Families, 1996; The Crimson Elf: Italian Tales of Wisdom, 1997; Earth Tales from around the World, 1997; Remains Unknown: The Final Journey of a Human Spirit, 1999; A Time before New Hampshire: The Story of a Land and Native Peoples, 2003. Contributor to books. Contributor of articles and poems to magazines. **Address:** P.E.A.C.E., PO Box 1052, Norwich, VT 05055, U.S.A.

CAFFREY, Margaret M. American, b. 1947. **Genres:** Women's studies and issues, History. **Career:** University of Memphis, Memphis TN, assistant professor, 1988-93, associate professor of American history and women's history, 1993-; writer. **Publications:** Ruth Benedict: Stranger in This Land, 1989; The Family in America, 2001. Contributor to books and professional periodicals. **Address:** Department of History, University of Memphis, Memphis, TN 38152, U.S.A.

CAFRUNY, Alan W(eston). American, b. 1951. **Genres:** Economics, Politics/Government. **Career:** Colgate University, Hamilton, NY, visiting instructor, 1981; Cornell University, Ithaca, NY, instructor, 1982; University of Virginia, Charlottesville, assistant professor of government and foreign affairs, 1982-88; Hamilton College, Clinton, NY, assistant professor, 1988-91, associate professor of government, 1991-96, Henry Platt Bristol (Endowed) chair, 1991-, professor of government, 1996-, chair of the department, 1996-. Brookings Institution, guest scholar, 1986; George Mason University, visiting scholar at European Community Studies Center, 1990; European University Institute, visiting professor, 1993-94, external professor, 1994-; lecturer at colleges and universities. **Publications:** Ruling the Waves: The Political Economy of International Shipping, 1987. EDITOR & CONTRIBUTOR: (with G. Rosenthal) The State of the European Community, Vol II: The Maastricht Debates and Beyond, 1993; (with C. Lankowski) Europe's Ambiguous Unity: Conflict and Cooperation in the Post-Maastricht Era, 1995. Contributor to books. **Address:** Department of Government, Hamilton College, 198 College Hill Rd., Clinton, NY 13323, U.S.A. **Online address:** ACafruny@hamilton.edu

CAHALAN, James Michael. American, b. 1953. **Genres:** Literary criticism and history. **Career:** University of Massachusetts at Boston, instructor in English, 1979-81, lecturer in English and director of the Irish Studies Program, 1982-84; Northeastern University, Boston, instructor in English, 1981-82; Indiana University of Pennsylvania, Indiana, assistant professor, 1984-88, associate professor, 1988-92, professor of English, 1992-, director of graduate studies in literature, 1987-91. **Publications:** Great Hatred, Little Room: The Irish Historical Novel, 1983; The Irish Novel: A Critical History, 1988; Liam O'Flaherty: A Study of the Short Fiction, 1991; (ed. with D. Downing, and contrib.) Practicing Theory in Introductory College Literature Courses, 1991; Modern Irish Literature and Culture: A Chronology, 1993; Double Visions: Women and Men in Modern and Contemporary Irish Fiction, 1999; Edward Abbey: A Life, 2001. Contributor to books and scholarly journals. **Address:** Department of English, 110-B Leonard Hall, Indiana University of Pennsylvania, Indiana, PA 15705-1094, U.S.A. **Online address:** jcahalan@iup.edu

CAHILL, Jack. (John Denis). Canadian (born Australia), b. 1926. **Genres:** Biography, History. **Career:** Apprentice reporter for Australian newspapers, 1946-50; Daily Telegraph, Sydney, Australia, chief crime reporter, 1951-56; Sun, Vancouver, British Columbia, chief crime reporter, 1959, chief of British Columbia Legislature Bureau, 1959-63, chief of Ottawa Bureau, 1963-65; Star, Toronto, Ontario, chief of Legislative Bureau, 1966-69, national editor, 1969-70, chief of Ottawa Bureau, 1970-73, chief of Asian Bureau, Hong Kong, 1973-78, senior feature writer, 1978-91. **Publications:** If You Don't Like the War, Switch the Damn Thing Off!, 1979; Hot Box: The Mississauga

Disaster, 1980; John Turner: The Long Run (biography), 1984; Words of War, 1987; Forgotten Patriots, 1998. **Address:** Beverley Slopen, 131 Bloor St. W., Suite 711, Toronto, ON, Canada M5S 1S3.

CAHILL, Nicholas D. American. **Genres:** Air/Space topics. **Career:** University of Wisconsin, Madison, associate professor, 1993-. **Publications:** Household and City Organization at Olynthus, 2002. **Address:** Department of Art History, University of Wisconsin, Room 220, Elvehjem, 716 Langdon St., Madison, WI 53706, U.S.A. **Online address:** ndcahill@wisc.edu

CAHILL, Tim. American, b. 1943. **Genres:** Travel/Exploration, Essays. **Career:** Journalist and writer. Worked as a lifeguard, longshoreman, and warehouse worker; Rolling Stone, San Francisco, then NYC, associate editor and staff writer, 1971-; Outside, founding editor, 1976-77; freelance writer. **Publications:** Buried Dreams: Inside the Mind of a Serial Killer, 1987; Road Fever: A High-Speed Travelogue, 1991; (ed. and contrib.) Wild Places: Twenty Journeys into the North American Outdoors, 1996. ESSAYS: Jaguars Ripped My Flesh: Adventure Is a Risky Business, 1987; A Wolverine Is Eating My Leg, 1989; Pecked to Death by Ducks (essays), 1993; Pass the Butterworms: Remote Journeys Oddly Rendered, 1997; Hold the Enlightenment, 2003. FILMS: The Living Sea; Everest; Dolphins. Contributor to books and periodicals.

CAIL, Carol. Also writes as Kara Galloway. American, b. 1937. **Genres:** Mystery/Crime/Suspense, Romance/Historical. **Career:** Teacher of American history at a junior high school in Fayetteville, AR, 1961-63; Daily Office Supply, Longmont, CO, co-owner and operator, 1978-89; full-time writer, 1989-. Adult education teacher in Boulder, CO, 1991-98; Writer's Digest correspondence courses (fiction), teacher, 1994-. **Publications:** ROMANTIC SUSPENSE: (as Kara Galloway) Sleight of Heart, 1990; (as Kara Galloway) Love at Second Sight, 1991; Ivory Lies, 1992; Cupid's Ghost, 2003. MYSTERY NOVELS: Private Lies, 1993; Unsafe Keeping, 1995; If Two of Them Are Dead, 1996; Who Was Sylvia?, 2000; The Seeds of Time, 2001; Death Kindly Stopped, 2002; His Horror the Mayor, 2003.

CAIN, Christopher. See FLEMING, Thomas.

CAINE, Barbara. Australian (born Republic of South Africa), b. 1948. **Genres:** Women's studies and issues, History. **Career:** University of Sydney, Sydney, New South Wales, Australia, assistant professor of history and director of women's studies department, 1989-95; Monash University, professor of history, 1995-. **Publications:** Destined to Be Wives: The Sisters of Beatrice Webb, 1986; (ed. with E.A. Grosz and M. de Lepervanche) Crossing Boundaries: Feminisms and the Critique of Knowledges, 1988; Victorian Feminists, 1992; (ed. with R. Pringle) Transitions: A New Australian Feminism, 1995; English Feminism, 1780-1980, 1996; (gen. ed.) A Companion to Australian Feminism, 1998; (with G. Sluga) Gendering European History, 2000. **Address:** Department of History, Monash University, Clayton, VIC 2006, Australia. **Online address:** Barbara.Caine@arts.monash.edu.au

CAINE, Michael. British, b. 1933. **Genres:** Film, Trivia/Facts, Autobiography/Memoirs. **Career:** Screen, television, and stage actor. Westminster Repertory, Horsham, Sussex, England, assistant stage manager, 1953; Lowestoft Repertory, actor, 1953-55; Theatre Workshop, London, actor, 1955. Appeared in British television dramas, motion pictures and television miniseries. **Publications:** Not Many People Know That!: Michael Caine's Almanac of Amazing Information, 1984, in US as Michael Caine's Almanac of Amazing Information, 1986; Not Many People Know It's 1988!, 1987; Michael Caine's Moving Picture Show (film trivia), 1988; Acting in Film: An Actor's Take on Moviemaking, 1990; What's It All About? (autobiography), 1992. **Address:** c/o Pam RR Inc, 4401 Wilshire Blvd, Los Angeles, CA 90010-3728, U.S.A.

CAINE, Rebecca. See HILTON, Margery.

CAIRNS, Scott. American, b. 1954. **Genres:** Theology/Religion. **Career:** Kansas State University, Manhattan, instructor, 1981-84; University of Utah, Salt Lake City, teaching fellow, 1984-87; Westminster College, Salt Lake City, assistant professor, 1987-90; University of North Texas, Denton, assistant professor, 1990-94; Old Dominion University, Norfolk, VA, associate professor, 1994-. Director of creative writing, University of North Texas, 1990-94, and Old Dominion University, 1994-. **Publications:** The Theology of Doubt, 1985; The Translation of Babel, 1990; Figures for the Ghost, 1994. **Address:** English Department, Old Dominion University, Norfolk, VA 23529, U.S.A.

CALABRO, Marian. American. **Genres:** Business/Trade/Industry, Communications/Media, Institutions/Organizations, Writing/Journalism, Young adult non-fiction. **Career:** Publishing writer and manager, 1980s; freelance writer, Hasbrouck Heights, NJ, 1984-; Media and Methods, contributing editor; CorporateHistory.net LLC, president, 2004-; creative writing teacher, 2004-. **Publications:** Operation Grizzly Bear, 1989; ZAP!: A Brief History of Television, 1992; Great Courtroom Lawyers, 1996; The Perilous Journey of the Donner Party, 1999; A Wealth of History, 2001; Making Things Work: PSEG'S First Century, 2003; various children's books for Pearson, 2003-05; The Pep Boys Corporate History, 2005.

CALASSO, Roberto. Italian, b. 1941. **Genres:** Novels, Autobiography/Memoirs. **Career:** Adelphi Edizioni (publishing house), Milan, Italy, editorial director, 1968-. **Publications:** L'Impuro Folle, 1974; La rovina di Kasch, 1983, trans. as The Ruin of Kasch, 1988; (ed.) F.W. Nietzsche, Ecce homo: Come si diventa cio che si e (autobiography), 1985; Le Nozze di Cadmo e Armonia, 1988, trans. as The Marriage of Cadmus and Harmony, 1993; Ka, 1996; Literature and the Gods, 2001. Contributor of articles to professional journals. **Address:** Adelphi Edizioni SpA, Via S. Giovanni sul Muro 14, I-20121 Milan, Italy.

CALBERT, Cathleen. American, b. 1955. **Genres:** Poetry. **Career:** Poet. Rhode Island College, Providence, RI, assistant professor, 1990-95; associate professor, 1995-. **Publications:** My Summer As a Bride: Poems, 1995; Lessons in Space (poetry), 1997; Bad Judgment: Poems, 1999. Has contributed poems to publications. **Address:** Rhode Island College, 600 Mt. Pleasant, Providence, RI 02908, U.S.A. **Online address:** ccalbert@brainiac.com

CALDER, Angus. Scottish, b. 1942. **Genres:** Poetry, History, Literary criticism and history. **Career:** University of Nairobi, Lecturer in Literature, 1968-71; Open University in Scotland, Reader in Literature and Cultural Studies and Staff Tutor, 1979-93. **Publications:** (with J. Calder) Scott, 1969; The People's War: Britain 1939-1945, 1969; Russia Discovered: Nineteenth Century Fiction from Pushkin to Chekhov, 1976; Revolutionary Empire, 1981; T.S. Eliot, 1987; Byron, 1987; The Myth of the Blitz, 1991; Revolving Culture: Notes from the Scottish Republic, 1994; Waking in Waikato (poems), 1997; Horace in Tolleross (poems), 2000; Scotlands of the Mind, 2002; Colours of Grief (poems), 2002; Dipa's Bowl (poems), 2003. EDITOR: Dickens: Great Expectations, 1965; (with A. Gurr) Writers in East Africa, 1974; Scott: Old Mortality, 1975; (co) Speak for Yourself, 1984; (co) Burns: Selected Poems, 1992; (co) H. MacDiarmid, The Rauchle Tongue, Hitherto Uncollected Prose, 3 vols., 1996-98; (co) Time to Kill: The Soldier's Experience of War in the West 1939-45, 1997; R.L. Stevenson, Selected poems, 1998; Waugh: Sword of Honour, 1999; Wars (anthology), 1999. **Address:** 15 Spittal St, Edinburgh EH3 9DY, Scotland.

CALDER, John (Mackenzie). British (born Canada), b. 1927. **Genres:** Literary criticism and history. **Career:** Former director of Calders Ltd. (timber company); John Calder Publishers Ltd., London, England, founder, 1950, managing director, beginning in 1950. Managing director, Calder & Boyars Ltd., beginning in 1961. Organizer of literary conferences; founder, Ledlanet Nights (music and opera festival), 1963; chair, Federation of Scottish Theatres, 1972-74; director of Operabout Ltd., Riverrun Press, Inc. (US), and Canadian International Library Ltd. Candidate for Parliament for Kinross and West Perthshire, 1970, and Hamilton, 1974; candidate for European Parliament for Mid Scotland and Fife, 1979; lecturer in history, University of Nanterre; professor of English literature, Ecole Active Bilingue, 1994-95. Literary and political journalist and columnist. **Publications:** The Garden of Eros, The Philosophy of Samuel Beckett, 1996; What's Right, What's Wrong, 1999; Pursuit, 2001. EDITOR: A Samuel Beckett Reader, 1984; (with M. Esslin, B. Whitelaw, and D. Warrilow) As No Other Dare Fail: Festschrift for Samuel Beckett's Eightieth Birthday, 1986. **Address:** Calder Publications Ltd, 51 The Cut, London SE1 8LF, England. **Online address:** info@calderpublications.com

CALDER, Marie D(onais). Canadian, b. 1948. **Genres:** Children's fiction, International relations/Current affairs. **Career:** Teacher at elementary and junior high schools in Prince Albert, Saskatchewan, Canada, 1971-74; kindergarten teacher at schools in Thompson, Manitoba, Canada, 1976-78, and Estevan, Saskatchewan, 1978-80; Estevan Rural Schools, teacher of kindergarten and French, 1980-. Workshop leader. **Publications:** Humpty Dumpty Is a Friend of Mine, 1997. Also author of a parent/caregiver's resource package and a teacher's resource package for Humpty Dumpty Is a Friend of Mine. **Address:** 413 Maple Bay, Estevan, SK, Canada S4A 2E6.

CALDER, Nigel (David Ritchie). British, b. 1931. **Genres:** Sciences. **Career:** Physicist, Mullard Research Labs., 1954-56; Member, Editorial Staff, New Scientist, London, 1956-66; Science Ed., 1960-62, and Ed., 1962-66; Science Correspondent, New Statesman, London, 1959-62, 1966-71; Independent author and TV scriptwriter, 1966-. **Publications:** Electricity Grows Up, 1957; Robots, 1957; Radio Astronomy, 1958; The Environment Game (in U.S. as Eden Was No Garden); Violent Universe: An Eyewitness Account of the New Astronomy, 1969; Technopolis, 1969; The Mind of Man, 1970; Living Tomorrow, 1970; Restless Earth: A Report on the New Geology, 1972; The Life Game: Evolution and the New Biology, 1973; The Weather Machine, 1974; The Human Conspiracy, 1975; The Key to the Universe, 1977; Spaceships of the Mind, 1978; Einstein's Universe, 1979; Nuclear Nightmares, 1979; The Comet Is Coming!: The Feverish Legacy of Mr. Halley, 1980; 1984 and After, 1983; Timescale, 1983; The English Channel, 1986; The Green Machines, 1986; Spaceship Earth, 1991; Giotto to the Comets, 1992; Beyond this World, 1995; The Manic Sun, 1997; Magic Universe: The Oxford Guide to Modern Science, 2003. EDITOR: The World in 1984, 1965; Unless Peace Comes, 1968; Nature in the Round, 1973; Future Earth, 1988; Scientific Europe, 1990. Author of television series. **Address:** 26 Boundary Rd, Northgate, Crawley, W. Sussex RH10 8BT, England. **Online address:** nc@windstream.demon.co.uk

CALDERWOOD, James Lee. American, b. 1930. **Genres:** Literary criticism and history. **Career:** Emeritus Professor of English, 1994-, Associate Dean of Humanities. since 1974, University of California, Irvine (Assistant Professor, Los Angeles. 1963-66; Professor of English, 1966-94). Instructor, Michigan State University, East Lansing, 1961-63. **Publications:** (co-ed.) Forms of Poetry, 1968; (co-ed.) Perspectives on Poetry, 1968: (co-ed.) Perspectives on Fiction. 1968; (co-ed.) Perspectives on Drama, 1968; (co-ed.) Forms of Drama. 1969; (co-ed.) Essays in Shakespearean Criticism, 1969: Love's Labour's Lost, by Shakespeare, 1970; Shakespearean Metadrama, 1971; (co-ed.) Forms of Prose Fiction, 1972: (co-ed.) Forms of Tragedy, 1972; Metadrama in Shakespeare's Henriad, 1979; To Be and Not to Be, 1983: If It Were Done: Tragic Action in Macbeth, 1986; Shakespeare and the Denial of Death. 1987; The Properties of Othello, 1989; A Midsummer Night's Dream, 1992. **Address:** 1323 Terrace Way, Laguna Beach, CA 92651, U.S.A.

CALDWELL, David H(epburn). Scottish, b. 1951. **Genres:** Art/Art history. **Career:** Affiliated with National Museums, Edinburgh, Scotland; writer. **Publications:** The Scottish Armoury, 1979; Scotland's Wars & Warriors, 1998; Islay, Jura and Colonsay: A Historical Guide, 2001. EDITOR: (and contrib.) Scottish Weapons and Fortifications, 1100-1800, 1981; Angels, Nobles, and Unicorns: Art and Patronage in Medieval Scotland, 1982. **Address:** National Museums of Scotland, Chambers St, Edinburgh EH1 1JF, Scotland. **Online address:** d.caldwell@nms.ac.uk

CALDWELL, Grant. Australian, b. 1947. **Genres:** Poetry, Novellas/Short stories. **Career:** Secondary school teacher, 1971-73; worked in London, Morocco, and Spain, 1974-77; imprisoned for drug smuggling in Morocco, 1975-76; SCOPP (literary magazine), Sydney, Australia, editorial reader, 1977-79; freelance writer, c. 1979-; MEUSE (art and literature magazine), editor and publisher, 1980-82; Angus and Robertson Publishers, editorial reader, 1982-84; Darlinghurst Non-School of Writing, teacher and director, 1984-87; Going Down Swinging (literary magazine), guest editorial reader, 1992; Victoria College of the Arts, writer and teacher, 1995-97. Performed and read work at schools, theatres, universities, pubs, clubs, and festivals. **Publications:** POETRY: The Screaming Frog That Ralph Ate, 1979; The Bells of Mr. Whippy, 1982; The Nun Wore Sunglasses, 1984; The Life of a Pet Dog, 1993; You Know What I Mean, 1996. OTHER: The Revolt of the Coats (short stories), 1988; Malabata (autobiography), 1991. Contributor of stories to periodicals. Poetry, prose, and stories published in magazines, anthologies, and newspapers, and broadcast on television and radio worldwide. **Address:** c/o Hale & Iremonger, 19 Eve St., Erskineville, NSW 2043, Australia.

CALDWELL, Stratton F(ranklin). Also writes as Kerry Franklin. American, b. 1926. **Genres:** Poetry, Sports/Fitness. **Career:** University of California, Los Angeles, teaching assistant in physical education, 1953-54; Regina Young Men's Christian Association, Saskatchewan, director of physical education, 1954-56; athletic director and teacher of physical education, biology, social studies, and health education at a high school in Calgary, Alberta, 1956-57; University of California, Los Angeles, associate in physical education, 1957-65; California State University, Northridge, assistant professor, 1965-68, associate professor, 1968-71, professor of physical education and kinesiology, 1971-92, professor of kinesiology, 1992-93, emeritus professor, department of kinesiology, 1992-. Visiting professor at: University of California, Los Angeles, 1967, University of Washington, Seattle, 1968, University of California, Santa Barbara, 1969. American Biographical

Institute, member of national board of advisers, 1982-84, member of national research board of advisers, 1984-; International Biographical Centre, member of advisory council, 1990-. **Publications:** (with C. Hollingsworth and J. Martin) Golf, 1959; (with R. Cassidy) Humanizing Physical Education: Methods for the Secondary School Movement Program, 1974. Prose and poetry appears in over 500 publications. **Address:** 80 N Kanan Rd, Oak Park, CA 91377, U.S.A.

CALHOUN, B. B. Also writes as L. E. Blair. American, b. 1961. **Genres:** Young adult fiction, Young adult non-fiction. **Career:** Writer. Taught pre-school, elementary, and junior high school for twelve years. **Publications:** GIRL TALK SERIES: The New You, 1990; (as L.E. Blair) The Ghost of Eagle Mountain, 1990; Odd Couple, 1990; Baby Talk, 1991; Beauty Queens, 1991; (as L. E. Blair) The Bookshop Mystery, 1992; (as L. E. Blair) Allison, Shape Up!, 1992; (as L. E. Blair) Allison to the Rescue!, 1992; (as L. E. Blair) Allison's Babysitting Adventure, 1992. PINK PARROTS SERIES: All That Jazz, 1990; Fielder's Choice, 1991. DINOSAUR DETECTIVE SERIES: On the Right Track, 1994; Fair Play, 1994; Bite Makes Right, 1994; Out of Place, 1994; Scrambled Eggs, 1995; Night of the Carnotaurus, 1995; The Competition, 1995; The Raptor's Claw, 1995. FORD SUPERMODELS OF THE WORLD SERIES: The New Me, 1994; Party Girl, 1994; Having It All, 1994; Making Waves, 1994; Stepping Out, 1995; High Style, 1995; Model Sister, 1995; Cover Girl, 1995. SILVER BLADES SERIES: Center Ice, 1995; The Big Audition, 1995; Nutcracker on Ice, 1995; A New Move, 1996; Wedding Secrets, 1996; Rival Roommates, 1997. HIS & HERS SERIES: New in Town, 1997; Summer Dreams, 1998. **Address:** c/o Fran Lebowitz, Writers House, 21 West 26th Street, New York, NY 10010, U.S.A. **Online address:** bbcalhoun@earthlink.net

CALHOUN, Craig (Jackson). American, b. 1952. **Genres:** Anthropology/ Ethnology, History, Sociology. **Career:** Columbia University, NYC, research assistant at Bureau of Applied Social Research, 1974-75; University of North Carolina at Chapel Hill, instructor, 1977-79, assistant professor, 1979-85, associate professor, 1985-89, professor of sociology and history, 1989-96, director, Office of International Programs, 1990-93, director, program in social theory and cross-cultural studies, 1989-96, director, University Center for International Studies, 1993-96; New York University, professor, 1996-, director, Center for Applied Social Science Research, 1996-; Social Science Research Council, president, 1999-. Visiting research associate at Development Studies and Research Centre, University of Khartoum, 1983; Center for Psychosocial Studies, Chicago, Ill., research fellow, 1983, visiting fellow, 1985-, co-director of social theory program, 1988-91, member of council, 1993-; visiting professor at Center for Comparative Cultural Studies, Beijing Foreign Studies University, 1989. **Publications:** The Question of Class Struggle, 1982; (with D. Light and S. Keller) Sociology, 5th ed., 1989, 7th ed., 1997; Neither Gods nor Emperors, 1994; Critical Social Theory, 1995; Nationalism, 1997. EDITOR: (with F.A.J. Ianni) The Anthropological Study of Education, 1976; (with W.R. Scott and M. Meyer) Structures of Power and Constraint: Essays in Honor of Peter M. Blau, 1990; Habermas and the Public Sphere, 1992; (with E. LiPuma and M. Postone) Bourdieu: Critical Perspectives, 1993; Social Theory and the Politics of Identity, 1994; (with J. McGowan) Hannah Arendt and the Meaning of Politics, 1997; The Oxford Dictionary of the Social Sciences, 2002; (with others) The Classical Social Theory Reader, 2002; (with others) The Contemporary Social Theory Reader, 2002; (with P. Price and A. Timmer) Understanding September 11, 2002. Contributor to books and periodicals. **Address:** Dept. of Sociology, New York University, 269 Mercer, New York, NY 10003-6687, U.S.A.

CALHOUN, Richard J(ames). American, b. 1926. **Genres:** History, Literary criticism and history. **Career:** Clemson University, South Carolina, Assistant Professor, 1961-63, Associate Professor, 1963-67, Alumni Distinguished Professor, 1969-94, Emeritus, 1994-. Ed. Modern American Poetry Cassette Series, 1972-; Ed., South Carolina Review, 1973-. Fellow, Cooperative Program in Humanities, 1964-65; Fulbright Senior Lecturer, Yugoslavia, 1969-70, Denmark, 1975-76, Vienna, Austria, 1996. **Publications:** James Dickey, 1983: Witness to Sorrow: The Antebellum Autobiography of William J. Grayson, 1990; Galway Kinnell, 1992. EDITOR: James Dickey: The Expansive Imagination, 1973: (co-) A Tricentennial Anthology of South Carolina Literature, 1973; (co-) Two Decades of Change: The South since Desegregation, 1975. **Address:** 6 Clover Dr, Chapel Hill, NC 27517-2507, U.S.A. **Online address:** rcalhoun@mindspring.com

CALHOUN, Wes. See SADLER, Geoffrey Willis.

CALIAN, Carnegie Samuel. American, b. 1933. **Genres:** Theology/ Religion. **Career:** President and Professor of Theology, Pittsburgh Theological Seminary, 1981-. Assistant Pastor, Calvary Presbyterian Church, Haw-

thorne, California, 1958-60; Visiting Professor of Theology, 1963-67, Associate Professor, 1967-72, and Professor, 1972-81, University of Dubuque Theological Seminary, Iowa. **Publications:** The Significance of Eschatology in the Thoughts of Nicolas Berdyaev, 1965, rev. ed. as Berdyaev's Philosophy of Hope: A Contribution to Marxist-Christian Dialogue, 1968; Icon and Pulpit: The Protestant-Orthodox Encounter, 1968; Grace, Guts and Goods: How to Stay Christian in an Affluent Society, 1971; The Gospel According to The Wall Street Journal, 1975; Today's Pastor In Tomorrow's World, 1977, rev. ed., 1982; For All Your Seasons, 1979; Where's the Passion for Excellence in the Church?, 1989; Theology without Boundaries: Encounters of Eastern Orthodoxy and Western Tradition, 1992; Survival or Revival: Ten Keys to Church Vitality, 1999; The Ideal Seminary: Pursuing Excellence in Theological Education, 2001. **Address:** Pittsburgh Theological Seminary, 616 N. Highland Ave, Pittsburgh, PA 15206-2525, U.S.A.

CALIMANI, Riccardo. Italian, b. 1946. **Genres:** Intellectual history, Sciences. **Career:** Radiotelevisione Italiana (RAI), Venice, Italy, manager, 1977-2000; writer. **Publications:** Una di Maggio (novel; title means: One of May), 1974; Energia: Piu dubbi meno certezze (title means: Energy: More Doubts, Less Certainties), 1981; Storia del ghetto di Venezia, 1985, trans. by K.S. Wolfthal as The Ghetto of Venice, 1987; Energia e informazione (title means: Energy and Information), 1987; Di ebrei, di cose ebraiche e del resto (title means: About Jews, about Jewish Things and about the Rest), 1984; Storia dell'ebreo errante (title means: History of the Wandering Jew), 1987; Gesu ebreo (title means: Jesus as a Jew or Jesus the Jew), 1990; (with A. Lepschy) Feedback, 1990; Storie di marrani a Venezia (title means: Stories of Marranos in Venice), 1991; Stella gialla, Ebrei e pregiudizio (title means: Yellow Star: Jews and Prejudice), 1993; I Destini e le avventure dell'intellettuale ebreo (1650-1933) (title means: Destinies and Adventurzes of the Jewish Intellectual 1650-1933), 1996; Capitali europee dell'ebraismo (title means: Capital Cities of Judaism in Europe), 1998; Paolo, l'ebreo che fondo il Cristianesimo (title means: Paul, the Jew Who Founded Christianity), 1999; Ebrei e pregiudizio (title means: Jews and Prejudice), 2002; L'Inquisizione a Venezia (title means: The Inquisition in Venice), 2003; L'Europa degli ebrei (title means: Jews' Europe), 2003; Non e facile essere ebreo (title menas: It's not Easy to Be a Jew), 2004.

CALINESCU, Matei (Alexe). American (born Romania), b. 1934. **Genres:** Literary criticism and history. **Career:** University of Bucharest, Bucharest, Romania, 1963-72, assistant professor to associate professor of comparative literature; Indiana University-Bloomington, visiting associate professor, 1973-75, associate professor, 1976-78, professor of comparative literature, 1978-. **Publications:** Faces of Modernity: Avant-Garde, Decadence, Kitsch, 1977, enlarged ed., 1987; Rereading, 1993. EDITOR: (with D.W. Fokkema) Exploring Postmodernism, 1988; M. Eliade, Youth without Youth and Other Novellas, 1989. **Address:** Dept of Comparative Literature, Indiana University, Bloomington, IN 47405, U.S.A. **Online address:** calinesc@ indiana.edu

CALISHER, Hortense. Also writes as Jack Fenno. American, b. 1911. **Genres:** Novels, Novellas/Short stories, Autobiography/Memoirs. **Career:** Barnard Coll., adjunct professor of English, 1956-57; State University of Iowa, writer-in-residence, 1959-60; Sarah Lawrence Coll., faculty, 1962; Brandeis University, visiting professor of literature, 1963-64; University of Pennsylvania, writer-in-residence, 1965, visiting lectr., 1968; Columbia University, adjunct professor of English, 1968-70; University of California, regents professor, 1975; Brown University, distinguished professor, 1986. President, American P.E.N., 1986; President, American Academy/Inst. of Arts and Letters. 1987-90; winner of Lifetime Achievement Award, National Endowment for the Arts, 1989. **Publications:** NOVELS: False Entry, 1961; Tale for the Mirror, 1962; Textures of Life, 1963; Journal from Ellipsia, 1965; The New Yorkers, 1969; Queenie, 1971; Standard Dreaming, 1972; Eagle Eye, 1974; On Keeping Women, 1977; Mysteries of Motion, 1983; The Bobby-Soxer, 1986; Age, 1987; (as Jack Fenno) The Small Bang, 1992; In the Palace of the Movie-King, 1993; In the Slammer with Carol Smith, 1997; Sunday Jews, 2002. STORIES: In the Absence of Angels, 1951; Extreme Magic: A Novella and Other Stories, 1964; The Railway Police and The Last Trolley Ride (novellas), 1966; Collected Stories, 1975; Saratoga, Hot, 1985; The Novellas of Hortense Calisher, 1997. OTHER: Herself (autobiography), 1972; Kissing Cousins (memoir), 1988. **Address:** 205 W 57th St, New York, NY 10019, U.S.A.

CALKINS, Robert G. American, b. 1932. **Genres:** Art/Art history. **Career:** Cornell University, Ithaca, N.Y., associate professor, 1966-80, professor of medieval art and architecture, 1980-, chairman of department of history of art, 1976-81. International Center of Medieval Art, vice-president and member of board of directors, 1980-81, president, 1981-84. Member: College Art Association of America, Medieval Academy of America. **Publications:** Monuments of Medieval Art, 1985; Illuminated Books of the Middle Ages, 1983; Programs of Medieval Illumination, 1984; Medieval Architecture in Western Europe, 1998. **Address:** Department of History of Art, Goldwin Smith Hall, Cornell University, Ithaca, NY 14850, U.S.A. **Online address:** rgc1@cornell.edu

CALLAGHAN, Barry. Canadian, b. 1937. **Genres:** Novels, Novellas/Short stories, Poetry, Translations. **Career:** Artist. Teaching Fellow, University of Toronto, 1960-64; Professor, York University, Toronto, 1965-2003. Literary critic, "Umbrella" prog., 1964-66; Co-host, "The Public Eye," 1966-68, sr. producer of current affairs, 1967-71, and war corresp. in Lebanon and Jordan, 1969-71, Rhodesia and South Africa, 1975-77, all CBC TV; Literary Ed., Toronto Telegram. 1966-71; Co-owner, Villon Films, 1972-76; Critic of contemporary affairs, CTV Network, 1976-82; Host of dramatized novel series, OECA-T 1977. Founder and Publr., Exile mag., Toronto, 1972-. Publr., Exile Editions, Toronto, 1976-. Contributor Ed., Toronto Life mag., 1978-85. **Publications:** The Hogg Poems and Drawings, 1978; The Black Queen Stories, 1982; The Way the Angel Spreads Her Wings (novel), 1989; When Things Get Worst (novel), 1993; A Kiss Is Still A Kiss (stories), 1995; Barrelhouse Kings (memoir), 1998. POETRY: As Close as We Came, 1982; Stone Blind Love, 1988; Hogg: The Poems & Drawings, 1999; Hogg: The Seven Last Words, 2001. TRANSLATOR: Atlante by R. Marteau, 1979; Treatise on White and Tincture, by R. Marteau, 1979; Interlude, 1982; Singing at the Whirlpool and Other Poems, by M. Pavlovic, 1983; A Voice Locked in Stone by M. Pavlovic, 1985: Fragile Moments, by J. Brault, 1986; Flowers of Ice: Selected Poems by I. Ziedonis, 1987; Eidolon, by R. Marteau, 1991. EDITOR: Lord of Winter and of Love: A Book of Canadian Love Poems in English and French, 1983; Canadian Travellers in Italy, 1989; Fifteen Years in Exile, 2 vols., 1992; Exile's Exiles, 1992. **Address:** 20 Dale Ave, Toronto, ON, Canada M4W 1K4. **Online address:** exile@eol.ca

CALLAHAN, Bob. American, b. 1942. **Career:** Turtle Island Foundation, executive director, 1969-91; Bob Callahan Studios, San Francisco, CA, proprietor, 1991-. **Publications:** The Big Book of American Irish Culture, 1988; The New Comics Anthology, 1991; Who Shot JFK: A Guide to the Major Conspiracy Theories, 1993; Fireside, 1993; (ed. with Art Spiegelman) The Neon Lit Series, Avon, in progress. **Address:** Agent Norman Kurz, Lowenstein and Associates, 121 W 27th St., New York, NY 10001, U.S.A.

CALLAHAN, Daniel (J.). American, b. 1930. **Genres:** Education, Ethics, Humanities, Law, Medicine/Health, Politics/Government, Theology/Religion. **Career:** Teaching Fellow in Roman Catholic Studies, Harvard Divinity School, Cambridge, MA, 1961-68: Staff member, 1961-67, and Exec Ed., 1967-68, Commonweal, NYC; Hastings Center, Briarcliff Manor, NY, president, 1969-96, senior research associate, 1996-. Recipient, National Catholic Book Award, 1964, Thomas More Medal, 1970. **Publications:** The Mind of the Catholic Layman, 1963; Honesty in the Church, 1965; The New Church, 1966; (co) The Role of Theology in the University, 1967; Abortion: Law, Choice and Morality, 1970; Ethics and Population Limitation, 1971; The American Population Debate, 1972; The Tyranny of Survival and Other Pathologies of Civilized Life, 1973; Setting Limits; Medical Goals in an Aging Society, 1987; What Kind of Life? The Limits of Medical Progress, 1990; The Troubled Dream of Life, 1993; False Hopes, 1998. EDITOR: (co) Christianity Divided, 1961; Federal Aid and Catholic Schools, 1964; Generation of the Third Eye, 1965; The Secular City Debate, 1967; The Catholic Case for Contraception, 1969; God, Jesus and Spirit, 1969; (with H.T. Engelhardt Jr.) Science, Ethics and Medicine, 1976; (with Engelhardt) Knowledge, Value and Belief, 1977; (with Engelhardt) Morals, Science and Sociality, 1978; (with Engelhardt) Knowing and Valuing; The Search for Coinmon Roots, 1980; (with S. Bok) Ethics Teaching in Higher Education, 1980; (with P.G. Clark) Ethical Issues of Population Aid, 1981; (with A.L. Caplan) Ethics in Hard Times, 1981; (with Engelhardt) The Roots of Ethics; Science, Religion and Values, 1981; (with S. Callahan) Abortion: Understanding Differences, 1984; (co-ed.) Applying the Humanities, 1985; (with B. Jennings) Representation and Responsibility; Exploring Legislative Ethics, 1985. **Address:** Hastings Center, Rt. 9D, Garrison, NY 10524-5555, U.S.A.

CALLAHAN, Nelson J. American, b. 1927. **Genres:** Theology/Religion. **Career:** Pastor, St. Raphael Parish, Bay Village, Ohio, 1974-; Prosynodal Judge, Diocesan Matrimonial Tribunal, Cleveland; Assistant Pastor of St. Patrick, and St. Agatha; St. Peter High School, director of guidance, 1953-67; Assistant Professor of Theology, and Chaplain, St. John Col., Cleveland, 1967-74; Diocese of Cleveland, archivist, 1967-78. **Publications:** A Case for Due Process in the Church, 1971; The Role of an Ethnic Pastor in a Cleveland Parish, 1972; (ed.) A Catholic Journey Through Ohio, 1976; (co-author) The Irish and Their Communities of Cleveland, 1977; The Diary of

Richard Burtsell Priest of New York: The First Three Years (1865-1868), 1978; St. Ignatius High School 1886-1986, 1986; Years in Passing. **Address:** 525 Dover Rd, Bay Village, OH 44140, U.S.A.

CALLAHAN, North. American, b. 1908. **Genres:** History, Biography. **Career:** Professor Emeritus of History, New York University, NYC (Associate Professor, 1957-62; Professor 1962-73). Writer, syndicated column, So This Is New York, 1943-68; Public relations consultant, NYC, 1945-55; Professor of American History, Finch Coll., NYC. 1956-57. **Publications:** Armed Forces as a Career, 1947; Smoky Mountain Country, 1952; Henry Knox: General Washington's General, 1958; Daniel Morgan: Ranger of the Revolution, 1962; Tories of the American Revolution, 2 vols., 1963, 1967; Carl Sandburg: Lincoln of Our Literature, 1970; George Washington: Soldier and Man, 1972; TVA: Bridge over Troubled Waters, 1980; Peggy (novel), 1982; Daybreak (novel), 1985; Carl Sandburg: His Life and Work, 1987; Thanks Mr. President: The Trail-Blazing Second Term of George Washington, 1991. **Address:** 600 Pine St., Chattanooga, TN 37402, U.S.A.

CALLANAN, Frank. Irish, b. 1956. **Genres:** Politics/Government, Biography. **Career:** Barrister practicing in Dublin, Ireland, 1980-. **Publications:** (ed.) Edward Byrne, Parnell: A Memoir, 1991; The Parnell Split, 1890-91, 1992; 1993; T.M. Healy, 1996. **Address:** 9 Upper Mountpleasant Ave., Ranelagh 6, Dublin, Ireland. **Online address:** fcallanan@lawlibrary.ie

CALLANDER, Don. American, b. 1930. **Genres:** Science fiction/Fantasy. **Career:** George Washington University, Washington, DC, member of public relations staff; Washington Post, Washington, DC, copy boy to reporter; American Automobile Association, staff writer, editor, photographer, and graphic designer in Falls Church, VA, and Heathrow, FL, 1961-91; freelance writer, 1991-. **Publications:** NOVELS: Pyromancer, 1991; Aquamancer, 1992; Geomancer, 1993; Aeromancer, 1994; Dragon Rescue, 1995; Dragon Tempest, 1997; Marbleheart, 1998; Dragon Companion, 1998; Warlock's Bar & Grill, 2000. **Address:** 9B Azalea Dr, Orange City, FL 32763-6113, U.S.A. **Online address:** marbleheart@mpinet.net

CALLARD, D(avid) A(rthur). Welsh, b. 1950. **Genres:** Biography, Novellas/Short stories. **Career:** Writer. Teacher of English as a second language, 1972-88. **Publications:** BIOGRAPHIES: "Pretty Good for a Woman": The Enigmas of Evelyn Scott, J. Cape (London), 1985, Norton (New York), 1986; The Case of Anna Kavan: A Biography, Peter Owen (London), 1992; Rhys Davies: A Life in Writing, Redcliffe (Bristol, England), in press; OTHER: (with Geraint Jarman) Zutique (poetry), Second Aeon, 1968; (ed. and author of introduction) The Selected Rhys Davies, Redcliffe, 1995; Reading the Signals (story). Work represented in anthologies. Contributor to periodicals. **Address:** 136 Johnston Rd., Llanishen, Cardiff CF4 5HJ, Wales.

CALLAWAY, C. Wayne. American, b. 1941. **Genres:** Medicine/Health. **Career:** Northwestern University Medical School, rotating intern at Chicago Wesley Memorial Hospital, 1967-68, resident in internal medicine, 1968-69; Mayo Graduate School of Medicine, resident in internal medicine, 1971-73, advanced clinical resident in endocrinology and metabolism, 1973-75, instructor in medicine at the graduate school and Mayo Medical School, 1974-78, assistant professor of medicine and instructor in the history of medicine at the medical school, 1978-86, director of Nutrition Clinic and Nutrition Consulting Services, 1980-86, director of Lipid Clinic, 1982-86; George Washington University, Washington, DC, associate professor of medicine and director of Center for Clinical Nutrition at University Medical Center, 1986-88, associate clinical professor, 1988-; private practice of internal medicine, endocrinology and metabolism, and clinical nutrition in Washington, DC, 1988-. **Publications:** (with C. Whitney) The Callaway Diet: Successful Permanent Weight Control for Starvers, Stuffers, and Skippers, 1990; (with C. Whitney) Surviving with AIDS: A Comprehensive Program of Nutritional Co-therapy, 1991; (with M. B. Albert) Clinical Nutrition for the Housestaff Officer, 1991; (with others) American Medical Association Family Health Cookbook, 1997. **Address:** 2311 M St NW Ste 301, Washington, DC 20037, U.S.A.

CALLENBACH, Ernest. American, b. 1929. **Genres:** Science fiction/Fantasy, Environmental sciences/Ecology, Film, Human relations/Parenting, Social commentary. **Career:** Ed., Film Quarterly, and Film Book Ed., University of California Press, Berkeley, 1958-91. Founder, Banyan Tree Books, 1975. **Publications:** FICTION: Ecotopia, 1975; Ecotopia Emerging, 1981. OTHER: Our Modern Art: The Movies, 1955; Living Poor with Style, 1971; (with C. Leefeldt) The Art of Friendship, 1979; The Ecotopian Encyclopedia for the 80's, 1981; (with C. Leefeldt) Humphrey the Wayward Whale, 1985; (with M. Phillips) A Citizen Legislature, 1985; Publisher's Lunch,

1989; (with F. Capra, L. Goldman, R. Lutz, and S. Marburg) EcoManagement: The Elmwood Guide to Ecological Auditing and Sustainable Business, 1993; Bring Back the Buffalo! A Sustainable Future for America's Great Plains, 1996; Ecology: A Pocket Guide, 1998. **Address:** c/o Banyan Tree Books, 1963 El Dorado Ave, Berkeley, CA 94707, U.S.A. **Online address:** www.ernestcallenbach.com

CALLICOTT, J(ohn) Baird. American, b. 1941. **Genres:** Philosophy, Literary criticism and history. **Career:** Syracuse University, Ithaca, NY, lecturer in philosophy, 1965-66; Memphis State University, TN, instructor in philosophy, 1966-69; University of Wisconsin-Stevens Point, assistant professor, 1969-74, associate professor, 1974-82, professor of philosophy, 1982-95, director of environmental studies program, 1980-86, professor of natural resources, 1984-95; University of North Texas, professor of philosophy and religion studies, 1995-. Visiting professor, University of Florida, 1983, University of California, Santa Barbara, 1988, and University of Hawaii at Manoa, 1988. Institute for Comparative Philosophy, University of Hawaii at Manoa, fellow, 1984; University of California, Berkeley, research associate, 1987-90, visiting scholar, 1990-91. **Publications:** (with T.W. Overholt) Clothed-in-Fur and Other Tales, 1982; In Defense of the Land Ethic (essays), 1989; Earth's Insights: A Multicultural Survey of Ecological Ethics, 1994; Beyond the Land Ethic, 1999. EDITOR: (and contrib.) Companion to A Sand County Almanac (essays), 1987; (with R.T. Ames, and contrib.) Nature in Asian Traditions of Thought (essays), 1989; (with S.L. Flader, and author of intro.) A. Leopold, The River of the Mother of God and Other Essays, 1991; (with others) Environmental Philosophy, 1993; (with F. duRocha) Earth Summit Ethics, 1996; (with M.P. Nelson) The Great New Wilderness Debate, 1998; (with E.T. Freyfogle) For the Health of the Land. **Address:** Department of Philosophy and Religion Studies, University of North Texas, Denton, TX 76203, U.S.A.

CALLOW, Simon. British, b. 1949. **Genres:** Autobiography/Memoirs, Biography. **Career:** Actor, director, and writer. Worked as a theater box office attendant in London; member of National Theatre Co., London, 1979-. Actor in stage productions, motion pictures, and television productions. Director of stage productions and film documentary. **Publications:** Being an Actor (memoir), 1984; Charles Laughton: A Difficult Actor (biography), 1988; (with D. Makavejev) Shooting the Actor; or, The Choreography of Confusion (nonfiction), 1990; Acting in Restoration Comedy (nonfiction), 1992; Orson Welles, the Road to Xanadu, 1995; Snowdon on Stage, 1997; The National, 1997; Love Is Where It Falls, 1999; Oscar Wilde and His Circle, 2000; Shakespeare on Love, 2000; Night of the Hunter, 2001; Henry IV, Pt. 1, 2002, Pt. 2, 2003; Dickens' Christmas, 2003. **Address:** c/o BAT, 180 Wardour St, London W1V 3AA, England.

CALLOWAY, Colin G(ordon). British, b. 1953. **Genres:** History, Writing/Journalism, Bibliography. **Career:** College of Ripon and York, St. John, England, lecturer in history and American studies, 1979-82; high school teacher in Springfield, VT, 1983-85; Newberry Library, Chicago, IL, assistant director and editor of D'Arcy McNickle Center for the History of the American Indian, 1985-87; University of Wyoming, Laramie, assistant professor, 1987-91, associate professor of history, 1991-95; Dartmouth College, visiting assistant professor, 1990, 1991, visiting associate professor, 1993, professor of history and Native American studies, 1995-, chair, Native American studies, 1997. Native Americans of the Northeast series, co-editor. **Publications:** Crown and Calumet: British-Indian Relations, 1783-1815, 1987; The Abenaki (young adult), 1989; The Western Abenakis of Vermont, 1600-1800: War, Migration, and the Survival of an Indian People, 1990; The Indians of the Northeast (young adult), 1991; The American Revolution in Indian Country, 1995; New Worlds for All: Indians, Europeans, and the Remaking of Early America, 1997; First Peoples: A Documentary Survey of American Indian History, 1999, 2nd ed., 2004; One Vast Winter Court: The Native American West before Lewis and Clark, 2003. EDITOR: New Directions in Indian History: A Bibliography of Recent Writings in American Indian History, 1988; Dawnland Encounters: Indians and Europeans in Northern New England, 1991; North Country Captives: Selected Narratives of Indian Captivity from Vermont and New Hampshire, 1992.

CALLWOOD, June. Canadian, b. 1924. **Genres:** Social commentary, Women's studies and issues. **Career:** Brantford Expositor, reporter, 1941; Toronto Globe and Mail, reporter, 1942, columnist, 1975-78, 1983-89; TV host, CBC, 1975-78, VISION 1991-95. Writers' Union of Canada, founding member, 1973, chair, 1979, life member, 1994; Canadian Centre PEN, founding member, 1984, president, 1989; Toronto Arts Council, director, 1985-89. Yorkville Digger House, founder, 1966; Nellie's Hostel for Women, co-founder, 1974, president, 1974-78; Canadian Civil Liberties Assn, founding member, 1964, vice-president, 1964-88, life member, 1988; Law Society of Upper Canada, bencher 1987-91; Jessie's Centre for Teenagers, founder 1982, president, 1983-93; Casey House Hospice, founder, 1988, president 1988-89; honorary director, 1989; Casey House Foundation, president, 1992, honorary director, 1993; Justice for Children, founding member, 1978, president, 1979-80; Maggie's, Toronto Prostitutes Project, founding member, 1986, president, 1988-93; Feminists against Censorship, founding member, 1984; Electronic Rights Licensing Agency, founder, board of directors, 1998-; Women's Television Network Foundation, director, 1994-98. **Publications:** (with M. Hillard) A Woman Doctor Looks at Life and Love, 1957; Love, Hate, Fear, and Anger, 1964; (with M. Zuker) Canadian Women and the Law, 1971; (with B. Walters) How to Talk to Practically Anybody about Practically Anything, 1973; (with M. Zuker) The Law Is Not for Women, 1973; (with J. Densen-Gerber) We Mainline Dreams, 1974; Naughty Nineties: Canada's Illustrated Heritage, 1978: Portrait of Canada, 1981; (with H. Gahagan Douglas) A Full Life, 1981; Portrait of Canada, 1981; Emma, 1984; Emotions, 1986: Twelve Weeks in Spring, 1986, rev. ed., 2002; Jim: A Life with AIDS, 1988; The Sleepwalker, 1990; June Callwood's National Treasures, 1994; Trial without End, 1995; The Man Who Lost Himself, 2000. **Address:** 21 Hillcroft Dr, Toronto, ON, Canada M9B 4X4.

CALNE, Donald B. Canadian (born England), b. 1936. **Genres:** Psychology. **Career:** University of British Columbia, Vancouver, BC, Canada, professor of neurology, 1981-; Vancouver Hospital, Vancouver, BC, Canada, Director of Neurodegenerative Disorders Centre, 1990-2001. **Publications:** Within Reason: Rationality and Human Behavior, 1999. Author of three books and editor of eight books on neurology for physicians; contributor of papers and chapters on neurological subjects to journals and volumes. **Address:** Room M31, Purdy Pavilion, University of British Columbia Hospital, 2221 Westbrook Mall, Vancouver, BC, Canada V6T 2B5.

CALVERT, Patricia. American, b. 1931. **Genres:** Young adult fiction, History, Biography. **Career:** St. Mary's Hospital, Laboratory clerk, 1948-49; General Motors Acceptance Corp., clerk typist, 1950-51; Mayo Clinic, cardiac laboratory technician, 1961-64, enzyme laboratory technician, 1964-70. Senior editorial assistant in publications, 1970-92; Institute of Children's Literature, instructor, 1987-. **Publications:** FICTION FOR YOUNG ADULTS: The Snowbird, 1980; The Money Creek Mare, 1981; The Stone Pony, 1982; The Hour of the Wolf, 1983; Hadder MacColl, 1985; Yesterday's Daughter, 1986; Stranger, You and I, 1987; When Morning Comes, 1989; Picking Up the Pieces, 1993; Bigger, 1994; Glennis, Before and After, 1996; Great Lives: The American West, 1997; Sooner, 1998; Michael, Wait for Me, 2000; Stand Off at Standing Rock, 2000; Betrayed!, 2002; Daniel Boone: Beyond the Mountains, 2002; Robert E. Peary: To the Top of the World, 2002; Ernest Shackleton: By Endurance We Conquer, 2003; Hernando Cortes: Fortune Favored the Bold, 2003; Vasco Da Gama: So Strong a Spirit, 2004; Zebulon Pike: Lost in the Rockies, 2004; The Ancient Inca, 2004; The Ancient Celts, 2005. **Address:** 3548-3rd Pl NW, Rochester, MN 55901, U.S.A.

CALVERT, Peter (Anthony Richard). British, b. 1936. **Genres:** History, International relations/Current affairs, Politics/Government. **Career:** University of Michigan, Ann Arbor, teaching fellow, 1960-61; University of Southampton, professor of comparative and international politics, 1984-2002 (lecturer, 1964-71; sr. lecturer, 1971-74; reader, 1974-83). **Publications:** The Mexican Revolution 1910-1914, 1968; Latin America: Internal Conflict and International Peace, 1969: Revolution, 1970; A Study of Revolution, 1970; Mexico, 1973; The Mexicans: How They Live and Work, 1975; Emiliano Zapata, 1979; The Concept of Class, 1982; The Falklands Crisis, 1982; Politics, Power, and Revolution, 1983; Boundary Disputes in Latin America, 1983; Revolution and International Politics, 1984, rev. ed., 1996; Guatemalan Insurgency and American Security, 1984; Guatemala, a Nation in Turmoil, 1985; Britain's Place in the World, 1986; The Foreign Policy of New States, 1986; (with S. Calvert) Argentina: Political Culture and Instability, 1989; Revolution and Counterrevolution, 1990; (with S. Calvert) Latin America in the 20th Century, 1990, rev. ed., 1993; (with S. Calvert) Sociology Today, 1992; An Introduction to Comparative Politics, 1993; The International Politics of Latin America, 1994; (with S. Calvert) Politics and Society in the Third World, 1995, rev. ed., 2001; The Democratic Transition in Central America, 1998; (with S. Calvert) The South, the North and the Environment, 1999; Comparative Politics, 2002. EDITOR: The Process of Political Succession, 1987; The Central American Security System, 1988; Political and Economic Encyclopedia of South America and the Caribbean, 1991; (with P. Burnell) The Resilience of Democracy, 1999; (with P. Burnell) Civil Society in Democratization, 2004; Border and Territorial Disputes, 2004. **Address:** School of Social Sciences/Politics, University of Southampton, Highfield, Southampton S017 1BJ, England. **Online address:** pcpol@sosci.soton.ac.uk

CALVIN, William H(oward). American, b. 1939. **Genres:** Medicine/Health, Sciences, Essays. **Career:** Affiliate Associate Professor of Psychiatry,

University of Washington, Seattle, since 1992 (Instructor, 1967-69; Assistant Professor, 1969-73; Associate Professor of Neurological Surgery, 1974-86). Visiting Professor of Neurobiology, Hebrew University of Jerusalem, 1978-79. **Publications:** Inside the Brain (with George A. Ojemann), 1980; The Throwing Madonna: From Nervous Cells to Hominid Brains, 1983; The River That Flows Uphill: A Journey from the Big Bang to the Big Brain, 1986; The Cerebral Symphony: Seashore Reflections on the Structure of Consciousness, 1989; The Ascent of Mind: Ice Age Climates and the Evolution of Intelligence, 1990; How the Shaman Stole the Moon, 1991; Conversations with Neil Brain, 1994; How Brains Think, 1996; The Cerebral Code, 1996; (with D. Bickerton) Lingua Ex Machina: Reconsiling Darwin and Chomsky with the Human Brain, 2000. **Address:** 1543 17th Ave. E, Seattle, WA 98112, U.S.A.

CALVOCORESSI, Peter (John Ambrose). British (born Pakistan), b. 1912. **Genres:** History, International relations/Current affairs. **Career:** Called to the Bar, 1934; Wing Comdr., trial of major war criminals, Nuremberg, 1945-46; Member of Staff, 1949-54, and of Council, 1955-72, Royal Institute of International Affairs; Director, Chatto and Windus Ltd. and The Hogarth Press Ltd., publishers, London 1954-65; Reader, part-time, in International Relations, University of Sussex, Brighton, 196571; Editorial Director, 1972-73, and Publisher and Chief Executive, 1973-76, Penguin Books Ltd., London; Chairman, Open University Educational Enterprises, 1979-88. Member of the Council, Institute for Strategic Studies, 1961-71; Chmn, The Africa Bureau, 1963-71; Chmn, London Library, 1970-73. **Publications:** Nuremberg: The Facts, the Law and the Consequences, 1947; Survey of International Affairs, 5 vols., 1947- 54; (with G. Wint) Middle East Crisis, 1957; South Africa and World Opinion, 1961; World Order and New States, 1962; (with G. Wint) Total War, 1972, 1989; The British Experience 1945-1975, 1978; Top Secret Ultra, 1980; Independent Africa and the World, 1985; A Time for Peace, 1988; Who's Who in the Bible, 1988; Resilient Europe, 1991; Threading My Way, 1994; Fall Out: World War II and the Shaping of Postwar Europe, 1997; World Politics, 1945-2000, 2001. **Address:** 1 Queen's Parade, Bath BA1 2NJ, England.

CAMBIE, R(ichard) C(onrad). New Zealander, b. 1931. **Genres:** Chemistry. **Career:** University of Auckland, Auckland, New Zealand, junior lecturer, 1957, lecturer, 1958-60, senior lecturer, 1961-63, associate professor, 1964-69, professor of organic chemistry, 1970-97, head of department, 1984-91, professor emeritus, 1997-. Visiting professor at universities worldwide. **Publications:** (with S.G. Brooker and R.C. Cooper) New Zealand Medicinal Plants, 1981, 3rd ed., 1991; (with Brooker and Cooper) Economic Native Plants of New Zealand, 1988; (with Cooper) New Zealand's Economic Native Plants, 1991; Fijian Medicinal Plants, 1994; (with A.A. Brewis) Antifertility Plants of the Pacific, 1997. Contributor to periodicals. **Address:** 21D Southern Cross Rd., Kohimaramara, Auckland, New Zealand.

CAMERON, Alexander. (Alexander Cameron Gibson). Scottish, b. 1926. **Genres:** Novels. **Career:** Ordained minister of Church of Scotland; veterinary surgeon in Ayrshire, Scotland, and Devonshire, England, 1950-59; minister of Church of Scotland in Fenwick, 1962-68, Nairn Old, 1968-80, and in Eskdalemuir, Hutton, Corrie, and Tundergarth, 1980-90; writer. Founding member, Lochgoin and Fenwick Covenanters Trust; chairman of Nairn Health Council in the 1970s. **Publications:** Vet in the Vestry (novel), 1987; Poultry in the Pulpit (novel), 1988; Dog Collar Diary (memoirs), 1995. **Address:** Langleigh, 10 Rowan Place, Nairn IV12 4TL, Scotland.

CAMERON, Ann. See RIEFE, Alan.

CAMERON, Catherine M(ary). American (born Canada), b. 1946. **Genres:** Sociology. **Career:** Cedar Crest College, Allentown, PA, professor of anthropology, 1983-. Camwood Research Associates, partner. **Publications:** Dialectics in the Arts, 1996. Contributor to scholarly journals. **Address:** Dept of Social Sciences, Cedar Crest College, 100 College Dr, Allentown, PA 18104, U.S.A. **Online address:** ccameron@cedarcrest.edu

CAMERON, Charla. See SKINNER, Gloria Dale.

CAMERON, Ian. See PAYNE, Donald Gordon.

CAMERON, Julia. American. **Genres:** Inspirational/Motivational Literature. **Career:** Poet, playwright, songwriter, novelist, educator, and author of nonfiction. Director of film God's Will. Journalist; former special correspondent for Chicago Tribune. Teacher of creativity and writing workshops. **Publications:** ADULT NONFICTION: (with M. Bryan) The Money Drunk: Ninety Days to Financial Sobriety, 1992; (with M. Bryan) The Artist's Way: A Spiritual Path to Higher Creativity, 1992, 10th anniversary ed, 2002; (with M. Bryan) The Artist's Way Morning Pages Journal: A Companion Volume to "The Artist's Way," 1995; The Vein of Gold: A Journey to Your Creative Heart, 1996; Heart Steps: Prayers and Exercises for a Creative Life, 1997; (with M. Toms) The Well of Creativity, 1997; (with M. Bryan and C. Allen) The Artist's Way at Work: Riding the Dragon, 1998; Blessings: Prayers and Declarations for a Heartful Life, 1998; The Right to Write: An Invitation and Initiation into the Writing Life, 1998; The Artist's Date Book: A Companion Volume to "The Artist's Way," 1999; Transitions: Prayers and Declarations for a Changing Life, 1999; God Is No Laughing Matter: Observations and Objections on the Spiritual Path, 2000; God Is Dog Spelled Backwards, 2000; Supplies: A Pilot's Guide to Creative Flight, 2000, as Supplies: A Troubleshooting Guide for Creative Difficulties, 2003; Inspirations: Meditations from "The Artist's Way," 2001; Walking in This World: The Practical Art of Creativity, 2002; Prayers from a Nonbeliever: A Story of Faith, 2003; The Sound of Paper: Starting from Scratch, 2004. FOR CHILDREN: Prayers for the Little Ones, 1999; Prayers to the Nature Spirits, 1999. FICTION: The Dark Room (crime), 1998; Popcorn: Hollywood Stories, 2000. PLAYS: Avalon (musical); Four Roses; Public Lives; The Animal in the Trees. POEMS: This Earth; The Quiet Animal. Contributor to screenplays, anthologies, and periodicals. **Address:** c/o Author Mail, Penguin Putnam, 375 Hudson St., New York, NY 10014, U.S.A.

CAMERON, Lorna. See FRASER, Anthea.

CAMERON, M(alcolm) L(aurence). Canadian, b. 1918. **Genres:** Medicine/Health. **Career:** University of New Brunswick, Fredericton, Canada, research associate, 1953-55; University of Saskatchewan, Saskatoon, Canada, assistant professor to associate professor of biology, 1955-65; Dalhousie University, Halifax, Nova Scotia, Canada, assistant professor to professor, 1965-79, Campbell Professor of Biology, 1979-84. **Publications:** Anglo-Saxon Medicine, 1993. Contributor to scholarly journals. **Address:** 6306 Jubilee Rd., Halifax, NS, Canada B3H 2G7.

CAMERON, Maxwell A. American, b. 1961. **Genres:** Economics, Politics/Government. **Career:** Carleton University, Ottawa, Ontario, associate professor of international affairs, 1989-96; University of British Columbia, associate professor, 1996-2002, professor of political science, 2002-. **Publications:** Democracy and Authoritarianism in Peru, 1994; The Peruvian Labyrinth, 1997; The Making of NAFTA, 2000. EDITOR: (with R. Grinspun) The Political Economy of North American Free Trade, 1993; Democracy and Foreign Policy. **Address:** Dept of Political Science, University of British Columbia, Vancouver, BC, Canada V6T 1Z1. **Online address:** maxcamer@interchange.ubc.ca

CAMERON, Rondo. American, b. 1925. **Genres:** Economics, History. **Career:** William Rand Kenan Jr. Univ. Prof., Emory Univ., Altanta, Ga., since 1969. Member, Exec. Cttee., Intnl. Assn. of Economic History, 1973-86 (Vice-Pres., 1986-90). Ed., Journal of Economic History, 1975-81. **Publications:** (co-ed.) Europe in Review, 1957, 1964; France and the Economic Development of Europe 1800-1914, 1961, 1966; (with J. Blum and T. Barnes) The European World: A History, 1966, 1970; (co-author) Banking in the Early Stages of of Industrialization, 1967; (ed.) Essays in French Economic History, 1970; (ed.) Civilization Since Waterloo, 1971; (ed.) Banking and Economic Development: Some Lessons of History, 1972; (co-author) Civilizatins, Western and World, 1975; A Concise Economic History of the World from Paleolithic Times to the Present, 1989, 4th ed. 2001. Editor of books. **Address:** 885 Barton Woods Rd. NE, Atlanta, GA 30307-1305, U.S.A. **Online address:** kenanrc@Emory.edu

CAMERON, Stella. American. **Genres:** Novels. **Career:** Novelist. **Publications:** Fascination, 1993; His Magic Touch, 1993; Pure Delights, 1994; Charmed, 1995; Bride, 1995; True Bliss, 1996; Beloved, 1996; Guilty Pleasures 1997; Dear Stranger, 1997; Wait for Me, 1997; The Best Revenge, 1998; French Quarter, 1998; More and More, 1999; Key West, 1999; Glass Houses, 2000; All Smiles, 2000; Finding Ian, 2001; Tell Me Why, 2001; 7B, 2001; The Wish Club, 2001; The Orphan, 2002; Cold Day in July, 2002; About Adam, 2003. Contributor to books. **Address:** c/o Steven Axelrod Agency, 49 Main St Box 357, Chatham, NY 12037, U.S.A.

CAMERON, Sue. American, b. 1944. **Genres:** Romance/Historical, Food and Wine. **Career:** The Hollywood Reporter, daily columnist; former executive for the American Broadcasting Corporation; Beverly Hills 213, columnist. Appeared in episodes of television series; also appeared in programs on E! Entertainment Television. **Publications:** NOVELS: Honey Dust, 1993; Love, Sex, and Murder, 1996. NONFICTION: The Bible Cookbook: Nourishment for the Body and Soul, 1996. **Address:** c/o Warner Books, 1271 Avenue of the Americas, New York, NY 10020, U.S.A.

CAMINALS-HEATH, Roser. American (born Spain), b. 1956. **Genres:** Cartoons, Novels, Translations. **Career:** Private tutor in Barcelona, Spain, 1978-79; substitute teacher in Barcelona, 1979-81; Mount St. Mary's College, instructor, 1981; Hood College, Frederick, MD, instructor, 1981-86, assistant professor, 1986-92, associate professor of Spanish language and literature, 1992-97, professor of Spanish language and literature, 1997-. **Publications:** (trans. and author of intro.) Emilia Pardo Bazán, The House of Ulloa, 1992; Once Remembered, Twice Lived (novel), 1993; Les Herbes Secretes (novel), 1998; (co-trans. and author of intro.) Carme Riera: A Matter of Self-Esteem and Other Stories, 2001. Contributor to periodicals. **Address:** Department of Foreign Languages and Literatures, Hood College, 401 Rosemont Ave, Frederick, MD 21701, U.S.A. **Online address:** rheath@ hood.edu

CAMMERMEYER, Margarethe. American (born Norway), b. 1942. **Genres:** Gay and lesbian issues, Medicine/Health, Military/Defense/Arms control, Women's studies and issues. **Career:** Washington National Guard colonel and registered nurse. U.S. Army, private, 1961-62, lieutenant to captain, 1965-68, served in Vietnam, 1967-68, resigned, 1968, reenlisted in Army Reserve, 1972; Veteran's Hospital, Seattle, WA, staff nurse, 1970-73, clinical nurse specialist in neurology and epilepsy, 1976-81; Veteran's Medical Center, San Francisco, CA, clinical nurse specialist in neuro-oncology, 1981-86; Veteran's Medical Center, Tacoma, WA, clinical nurse specialist in neuroscience and nurse researcher, 1986-96; promoted to colonel, 1986; Army Reserve Hospital, Oakland, CA, assistant chief nurse and supervisor, 1985-88; Washington Army National Guard and National Guard Hospital, Tacoma, chief nurse, 1988-96, retired, 1997; gaybc.com, radio Internet talk show host, 1999-2001. Lecturer and author. **Publications:** (co-author) Neurological Assessment for Nursing Practice, 1984; (co-ed and contrib) to Core Curriculum for Neuroscience Nursing, 1990; (with C. Fisher) Serving in Silence (memoir), 1994. Contributor to professional periodicals. **Address:** 4632 S Tompkins Rd, Langley, WA 98260, U.S.A. **Online address:** grethe@ cammermeyer.com; www.cammermeyer.com

CAMNITZER, Luis. German, b. 1937. **Genres:** Art/Art history. **Career:** Escuela de bellas artes, Montevideo, Uruguay, instructor, 1961-64; Fairleigh Dickinson University, Madison, NJ, instructor in art, 1968-69; State University of New York College at Old Westbury, professor of art, 1969-. Studio Camnitzer, Valdottavo, Lucca, Italy, director. **Publications:** New Art of Cuba, 1993. Contributor to books and journals. **Address:** State University of New York College at Old Westbury, Old Westbury, NY 11568, U.S.A.

CAMP, Helen C(ollier). American, b. 1939. **Genres:** History, Politics/Government. **Career:** Manhattan College, Riverdale, NY, adjunct professor, 1973-78; State University of New York, Empire State College, NYC, adjunct professor, 1984-85; Pace University, NYC, adjunct professor of American history, 1985-86, 1987-98, instructor, 1998-2000. Teacher at Brooklyn College and Bernard M. Baruch College, both of the City University of New York, 1981, Herbert H. Lehman College of the City University of New York, 1982-83, 1985, and New York University, 1987. **Publications:** (ed. with B. Blumberg and K. Centola) From World War to Cold War: Readings in Foreign and Domestic Policy, 1988; Iron in Her Soul: Elizabeth Gurley Flynn and the American Left, 1995. Contributor to books and periodicals. **Address:** 8818 Dolphin Lane, Gulf Shores, AL 36547, U.S.A. **Online address:** fhcamp@gulftel.com

CAMP, Robert C. American, b. 1935. **Genres:** Administration/Management. **Career:** Xerox Corp., began as manager for planning in logistics and distribution, worked as manager of supplies inventory control, transportation, and quality, as program manager in customer service, and as manager of business analysis for Xerox Business Services, became manager of benchmarking competency in Quality Office, U.S. Customer Operations; Best Practice Institute, Rochester, NY, principal. Also worked for Mobil Oil Co. and DuPont. Rochester Institute of Technology, adjunct professor, 1972-85. **Publications:** Benchmarking: The Search for Industry Best Practices That Lead to Superior Performance, 1989; Business Process Benchmarking: Finding and Implementing Best Practices, 1994; Global Cases in Benchmarking: Best Practices from Organizations around the World, 1998. **Address:** Best Practice Institute, 218 Fall Creek Dr, Ithaca, NY 14850-2418, U.S.A. **Online address:** rcampbpi@att.net

CAMPAGNA, Palmiro. (born Canada), b. 1954. **Genres:** Military/Defense/Arms control. **Career:** Department of National Defence, Ottawa, Ontario, Canada, engineer and internal auditor, 1981-. CFRB-Radio, contributor to the weekly program Strange Days Indeed. **Publications:** Storms of Controversy: The Secret Avro Arrow Files Revealed, 1992, 3rd edition, 1998; The UFO Files: The Canadian Connection Exposed, 1997; Requiem for a Giant: A. V. Roe Canada and the Avro Arrow, 2003. Contributor to periodicals. **Address:** Department of National Defence, Colonel By Dr., Ottawa, ON, Canada K1A 0K2. **Online address:** maxcam@storm.ca

CAMPBELL, Alexandra. British, b. 1954. **Genres:** Novels, Homes/Gardens. **Career:** Journalist on the staff of periodicals; Good Housekeeping, managing editor; Women & Home, beauty and well-being editor; freelance contributor to newspapers and magazines; novelist. **Publications:** NOVELS: The Office Party, 1998; The Ex-Girlfriend, 2000; The Daisy Chain, 2001; That Dangerous Age, 2002. INTERIOR DESIGN GUIDES: East Meets West: Global Design for Contemporary Interiors, 1997; (with L. Bauwens) Spaces for Living: How to Create Multifunctional Rooms for Today's Homes, 1999; (with L. Bauwens) Country Chic: Country Style for Modern Living, 2001. **Address:** c/o Author Mail, Penguin Books Ltd., 80 Strand, London WC2 0RL, England. **Online address:** Niniacampb@aol.com

CAMPBELL, Alistair Te Ariki. New Zealander (born Cook Islands), b. 1925. **Genres:** Novels, Children's fiction, Plays/Screenplays, Poetry, Mythology/Folklore. **Career:** Taught at Newtown Primary School, 1944; Ed., Dept. of Education School Publications Branch, Wellington, 1955-72; Sr. Ed., New Zealand Council for Educational Research, Wellington, 1972-87. President, P.E.N., New Zealand, 1976-79; full-time writer. **Publications:** Mine Eyes Dazzle: Poems 1947-49, 1951; The Happy Summer (children's story), 1961; Sanctuary of Spirits (poem), 1963; Wild Honey (poems), 1964; Blue Rain (poems), 1967; Maori Legends, 1969; When the Bough Breaks (play), 1970; Kapiti: Selected Poems, 1947-71, 1972; Dreams, Yellow Lions (poems), 1975; The Dark Lord of Savaiki (poem) 1980; Collected Poems, 1981; Island to Island (memoirs), 1984; Soul Traps: Lyric Sequence, 1985; Triology: The Frigate Bird (novel), 1989; Sidewinder (novel), 1991; Tia (novel), 1993; Stone Rain: The Polynesian Strain (poems), 1992; Death and the Tagua (poems), 1995; Pocket Collected Poems, 1996; Fantasy with Witches (novel), 1998; Gallipoli and Other Poems, 1999; Maori Battalion (poem), 2001; Poets in Our Youth (poems), 2002. TV DOCUMENTARIES: Island of Spirits, 1973; Like You I'm Trapped, 1975. RADIO PLAYS: Sanctuary of Spirits, 1963; The Homecoming, 1964; The Proprietor, 1964; The Suicide, 1965; The Wairau Incident, 1967. **Address:** 4B Rawhiti Rd, Pukerua Bay, Wellington, New Zealand.

CAMPBELL, Beatrix. British, b. 1947. **Genres:** Civil liberties/Human rights, Criminology/True Crime, Psychology, Sociology, Women's studies and issues. **Career:** Journalist for Morning Star, 1967-77; Time Out, London, England, 1979-81; and City Limits, London, beginning in 1981. Guest on television and radio programs. Newcastle University, women's studies, visiting professor. **Publications:** (with A. Coote) Sweet Freedom: The Struggle for Women's Liberation, 1981; Wigan Pier Revisited: Poverty and Politics in the Eighties, 1984; The Iron Ladies: Why Do Women Vote Tory?, 1987; Unofficial Secrets: Child Sexual Abuse, 1988; Goliath, Britain's Dangerous Places, 1993; Diana, Princess of Wales: How Sexual Politics Shook the Monarchy, 1998. **Address:** 5 Heaton Grove, Newcastle upon Tyne NE6 5NN, England. **Online address:** beejaysway@dial.pipex.com

CAMPBELL, Bebe Moore. American, b. 1950. **Genres:** Novellas/Short stories, Women's studies and issues, Autobiography/Memoirs, Essays. **Career:** Novelist. NPR commentator. **Publications:** Successful Women, Angry Men: Backlash in the Two-Career Marriage, 1986, 2nd ed., 2000; Sweet Summer: Growing Up with and without My Dad, 1989; Your Blues Ain't Like Mine, 1992; Brothers and Sisters, 1994; Singing in the Comeback Choir, 1998; What You Owe Me, 2001; Sometimes My Mommy Gets Angry, 2002. **Address:** c/o Beth Swofford, William Morris Agency, 1 William Morris Place, Beverly Hills, CA 90212, U.S.A. **Online address:** www. bebemoorecampbell.com

CAMPBELL, Colin. (Georgia Arianna Ziadie). British/Jamaican, b. 1949. **Genres:** Biography. **Career:** Writer. **Publications:** Guide to Being a Modern Lady, 1986; Diana in Private: The Princess Nobody Knows, 1992; The Royal Marriages, 1993; A Life Worth Living, 1997; The Real Diana, 1998. **Address:** 45 Bourne St, London SW1W 8JA, England.

CAMPBELL, Donald E. Canadian, b. 1943. **Genres:** Economics. **Career:** University of Toronto, Toronto, Ontario, professor, 1970-92; College of William and Mary, Williamsburg, VA, CSX Professor of Economics and Public Policy, 1990-. **Publications:** Resource Allocation Mechanisms, 1987; Equity, Efficiency, and Social Choice, 1992; Incentives, 1995. **Address:** Department of Economics, College of William and Mary, Williamsburg, VA 23187, U.S.A. **Online address:** decamp@wm.edu

CAMPBELL, Drusilla. American. **Genres:** Business/Trade/Industry. **Career:** Writer, workshop instructor. Teacher, including in London, England,

and Changuinola, Panama; worked in Washington, DC, as a secretary, receptionist, and as an on-air personality for NPR affiliate WAMU-FM. **Publications:** The Frost and the Flame, 1980; A Dream of Fire, 1982; Silent Dreams, 1982; Stolen Passions, 1982; Tomorrow's Journey, 1982; Autumntide,1984; Men Like Gods, 1984; Reunion, 1985; (with Marilyn Graham) Drugs and Alcohol in the Workplace: A Guide for Managers, 1988; Wildwood, 2003; The Edge of the Sky, 2004. Also author of two other novels, published in the 1980s. **Address:** c/o Author Mail, Kensington Publishing Corp., 850 Third Ave., New York, NY 10022, U.S.A. **Online address:** drusilla.campbell@yahoo.com

CAMPBELL, Eddie. (born Scotland), b. 1955. **Genres:** Graphic Novels. **Career:** Illustrator and author of comic-book series and graphic novels, 1981-. Escape magazine, publisher; cofounder, Harrier New Wave Comics and Eddie Campbell Comics. **Publications:** (with Ed Hillyer and Todd Gesicht) Deadface: Immortality Isn't Forever, 1990; The Complete Alec, 1990; (Illustrator) Alan Moore, From Hell: Being a Melodrama in Sixteen Parts (graphic novel), 1999; Alec: How to Be an Artist, 2001; After the Snooter, 2002. Author and/or illustrator of comic-book series, and contributor to anthologies. **Address:** c/o Eddie Campbell Comics, POB 230, Paddington, Queensland 4064, Australia.

CAMPBELL, G(aylon) S(anford). American, b. 1940. **Genres:** Environmental sciences/Ecology. **Career:** Professor, Dept. of Crop and Soil Sciences, Washington State University, Pullman, since 1971. **Publications:** An Introduction to Environmental Biophysics, 1977; Soil Physics with BASIC, 1985; Biophysical Measurements and Instrumentation, 1990. **Address:** Dept. of Crop and Soil Sciences, Washington State University, Pullman, WA 99164, U.S.A.

CAMPBELL, Ian Barclay. New Zealander, b. 1916. **Genres:** Law. **Career:** Teaching Fellow, Massey University; Safety Director, Accident Compensation Commission; Secretary, Workers' Compensation Board. **Publications:** Hand Book to Workers' Compensation Act 1956, 1958; (with D.P. Neazor) Workers' Compensation Law in New Zealand, 1964; Safety Legislation and the Work Place, 1982; Legislating for Workplace Hazards in New Zealand, 1987; Compensation for Personal Injury in New Zealand: Its Rise and Fall, 1996; Health and Safety in Employment Act: An Overview, 1998. **Address:** 30 Field Way, Waikanae, New Zealand. **Online address:** iancampbell1@compuserve.com

CAMPBELL, James B. American, b. 1944. **Genres:** Geography. **Career:** Kansas Geological Survey, Lawrence, research assistant in Geologic Research Section, 1972-76; Virginia Polytechnic Institute and State University, Blacksburg, assistant professor, 1976-81, associate professor, 1981-88, professor of geography, 1988-, department head, 1993-. **Publications:** Mapping the Land: Aerial Imagery for Land Use Information, 1983; (with F.D. Hole) Soil Landscape Analysis, 1985; Introduction to Remote Sensing, 1987, 3rd ed., 2001. Contributor to professional journals. **Address:** Department of Geography, Virginia Tech, 0115, Blacksburg, VA 24061, U.S.A. **Online address:** jayhawk@vt.edu

CAMPBELL, Jo Ann (L.). American, b. 1958. **Genres:** Literary criticism and history. **Career:** Indiana University, Bloomington, English department, assistant professor, 1989-96, Center on Philanthropy, community service associate, Indianapolis, 1996-. **Publications:** (ed.) Towards a Feminist Rhetoric: The Writing of Gertrude Buck, 1996. **Address:** Center on Philanthropy, Indiana University, 550 West North St. Suite 301, Indianapolis, IN 46202, U.S.A. **Online address:** jocampbe@indiana.edu

CAMPBELL, John. Scottish, b. 1956. **Genres:** Philosophy, Adult nonfiction. **Career:** Oxford University. **Publications:** Past, Space, and Self, 1994. **Address:** New College, Oxford University, Oxford OX1 3BN, England.

CAMPBELL, Judith. (Marion Staplyton Pares). Also writes as Anthony Grant. British, b. 1914. **Genres:** Animals/Pets, Biography. **Career:** Journalist, and broadcaster. **Publications:** Family Pony, 1962; The Queen Rides, 1965; Horses in the Sun, 1966; Police Horse, 1967; Pony Events, 1969; World of Horses, 1969: Horses and Ponies, 1970; World of Ponies, 1970; Anne, Portrait of a Princess, 1970; (with N. Toyne) Family on Horseback, 1972; Princess Anne and Her Horses, 1972; Elizabeth and Philip, 1972; The Champions, 1973; Royalty on Horseback, 1974; The World of the Horse, 1975; Eventing, 1976; Anne and Mark, 1976; Your own Pony Club, 1979; Queen Elizabeth II, 1979; (as Anthony Grant) The Mutant, 1980; Charles, A Prince of His Time, 1980; The Royal Partners, 1982; Royal Horses, 1983;

Ponies, People and Palaces, forthcoming. **Address:** c/o A. M. Heath Ltd, 79 St. Martin's Lane, London WC2N 4AA, England.

CAMPBELL, Karen. See BEATY, Betty (Smith).

CAMPBELL, Mary B(aine). American, b. 1954. **Genres:** Literary criticism and history, Poetry. **Career:** Columbia University, New York City, research fellow, 1985-87; Harvard University, Cambridge, MA, lecturer in literature, 1987-88; Brandeis University, Waltham, MA, assistant professor of English, 1988-94, associate professor of English, 1994-, chair of creative writing committee, 1990-. Gives readings from her works; workshop leader. **Publications:** The Witness and the Other World: Exotic European Travel Writing, 400-1600, 1988; (ed. with M. Rollins) Begetting Images: Studies in the Art and Science of Symbol Production, 1989; The World, the Flesh, and Angels (poems), 1989. **Address:** Department of English, Brandeis University, PO Box 9110, Waltham, MA 02454, U.S.A.

CAMPBELL, Mavis C. American (born Jamaica). **Genres:** History. **Career:** Hunter College of the City University of New York, NYC, faculty member, 1971-77; Amherst College, Amherst, MA, professor of history, 1977-. University of Sierra Leone, visiting research scholar at Fourah Bay College, 1973; University of Guyana, visiting professor and director of Caribbean studies, 1979-80; University of Edinburgh, visiting fellow, 1985-86. **Publications:** The Dynamics of Change in a Slave Society, 1976; The Maroons of Jamaica, 1655-1796: A History of Resistance, Collaboration, and Betrayal, 1988; Nova Scotia and the Fighting Maroons: A Documentary History, 1988; Back to Africa: George Ross and the Maroons from Nova Scotia to Sierra Leone, 1993; Black Women of Amherst College, 1999. Contributor to chapters in books. Contributor of articles and reviews to history and Caribbean studies journals. **Address:** Department of History, Amherst College, Amherst, MA 01002, U.S.A.

CAMPBELL, Peter (Walter). British, b. 1926. **Genres:** Politics/Government. **Career:** Professor Emeritus of Politics, University of Reading, since 1991 (Professor of Political Economy, 1960-64: Professor of Politics, 1964-91; Dean, Faculty of Letters, 1966-69; Chairman, Graduate School of Contemporary European Studies, 1971- 73). Lecturer in Government, University of Manchester, 1949-60. **Publications:** (with W. Theimer) Encyclopaedia of World Politics, 1950; French Electoral Systems and Elections 1789-1957, 1958; (with B. Chapman) The Constitution of the Fifth Republic, 1958; French Electoral Systems and Elections since 1789, 1965, 1989. **Address:** 6 Treyarnon Ct, 37 Eastern Ave, Reading RG1 5RX, England.

CAMPBELL, Peter A. American, b. 1948. **Genres:** Picture/board books. **Career:** Artist. Has also worked as an art director and creative director for several Rhode Island advertising agencies. **Publications:** (and illustrator) Launch Day, 1995. **Address:** Stauch-Vetromile & Mitchell, 55 South Brow St., East Providence, RI 02914, U.S.A. **Online address:** svmpcampbl@aol.com

CAMPBELL, R(obert) Wayne. Canadian, b. 1941. **Genres:** Animals/Pets, Environmental sciences/Ecology, Natural history, Bibliography. **Career:** British Columbia Ministry of Recreation and Conservation, Victoria, park naturalist, 1964-68; University of British Columbia, Vancouver, curator of vertebrates at Cowan Vertebrate Museum, 1969-72; Royal British Columbia Museum, Victoria, curator of ornithology, 1973-92; British Columbia Ministry of Environment, Lands, and Parks, Victoria, senior research scientist, 1993-2000; Wild Bird Trust of British Columbia, WBT Wildlife Data Centre, director, 2000-. **Publications:** The Birds of British Columbia, 4 vols, 1997; The Reptiles and Amphibians of British Columbia. Author of additional titles. **Address:** WBT Wildlife Data Centre, Wild Bird Trust of BC, PO Box 6218 Station C, Victoria, BC, Canada V8P 5L5. **Online address:** rwcampbell@shaw.ca

CAMPBELL, Ramsey. British, b. 1946. **Genres:** Novels, Novellas/Short stories, Mystery/Crime/Suspense, Horror. **Career:** BBC, Liverpool, film critic. British Fantasy Society, president, 1976-. Tax officer, Liverpool, 1962-66; Liverpool Public Libraries, library assistant, 1966-73. **Publications:** The Inhabitant of the Lake and Less Welcome Tenants, 1964; Demons by Daylight, 1973; The Height of the Scream, 1976; The Doll Who Ate His Mother, 1976; The Face That Must Die, 1979; To Wake the Dead (in U.S. as the Parasite), 1980; The Nameless, 1981; Dark Companions, 1982; Night of the Claw, 1983; Incarnate, 1983; Obsession, 1985; Cold Print, 1985; The Hungry Moon, 1986; (with L. Tuttle and C. Barker) Night Visions 111, 1986; Scared Stiff, 1986; The Influence, 1987; Dark Feasts, 1987; Ancient Images, 1989; Midnight Sun, 1990; Needing Ghosts, 1990; The Count of Eleven, 1991; Waking Nightmares, 1991; Alone with the Horrors, 1993; Two Obscure

Tales, 1993; Strange Things and Stranger Places, 1993; The Long Lost, 1993; The One Safe Place, 1995; Far Away and Never, 1996; The House on Nazareth Hill (in U.S. as Nazareth Hill), 1996; The Last Voice They Hear, 1998; Ghosts and Grisly Things, 1998; Silent Children, 2000; The Darkest Part of the Woods, 2002; Ramsey Campbell, Probably, 2002; Told by the Dead, 2003; The Overnight, 2004. EDITOR/CO-EDITOR: Superhorror, 1976; New Terrors, 2 vols., 1980; New Tales of the Cthulhu Mythos, 1980; The Gruesome Book, 1983; Stories That Scared Me, 1987; Best New Horror, 1990. **Address:** 31 Penkett Rd, Wallasey, Merseyside CH45 7QF, England. **Online address:** ramsey@ramseycampbell.com

CAMPBELL, Rhonda. Also writes as Denise Turney. American, b. 1962. **Genres:** Novels. **Career:** U.S. Navy, staff writer, 1984-88; currently freelance writer; Merrill Lynch, Princeton, NJ, administrative assistant. **Publications:** Portia (novel), 1997; Love Has Many Faces (novel), 2000; Spiral (novel), 2003. **Address:** 2500 Knights Rd. No. 19-01, Bensalem, PA 19020, U.S.A. **Online address:** www.chistell.com

CAMPBELL, Robin. See STRACHAN, Ian.

CAMPBELL, Rod. Scottish, b. 1945. **Genres:** Children's fiction. **Career:** Worked as painter, 1972-81; free-lance artist, 1981-; illustrator and writer. **Publications:** CHILDREN'S BOOKS (and illustrator): An ABC, 1980; Dressing Up, 1980; A Grand Parade Counting Book, 1980; Great, Greater, Greatest, 1980; Eddie Enginedriver, 1981; Freddie Fireman, 1981; Charlie Clown, 1981; Nigel Knight, 1981; Gertie Gardener, 1981; Nancy Nurse, 1981; Dear Zoo, 1982; Rod Campbell's Book of Board Games, 1982; Wheels!, 1982; Look Inside! All Kinds of Places, 1983; Look Inside! Land, Sea, Air, 1983; Oh, Dear!, 1983; My Farm, 1983; My Zoo, 1983; My Pets, 1983; My Garden, 1983; Rod Campbell's Noisy Book, 1983; Rod Campbell's Magic Circus, 1983; Rod Campbell's Magic Fairground, 1983; Henry's Busy Day, 1984; Take the Wheel, 1984; Look Up at the Sky, 1984; How Many Hats?, 1984; What Color Is That?, 1984; Lots of Animals, 1984; Buster's Morning, 1984; Buster's Afternoon, 1984; From Gran, 1984; Toy Soldiers, 1984; Baby Animals, 1984; Pet Shop, 1984; Circus Monkeys, 1984; Buster's Bedtime, 1985; Playwheels with Moving Parts!, 1985; Funwheels with Moving Parts!, 1985; Big and Strong, 1985; Cars and Trucks, 1985; Road Builders, 1985; Speed!, 1985; Misty's Mischief, 1986; I'm a Mechanic, 1986; I'm a Nurse, 1986; My Bath, 1986; My Favorite Things, 1986; My Teatime, 1986; My Toys, 1986; My Day, 1986; It's Mine, 1987; Lift-the-Flap ABC, 1987; Lift-the-Flap 123, 1987; Make a Word, 1987; Numbers, 1988; Shapes, 1988; Alphabet, 1988; Buster Gets Dressed, 1988; Buster Keeps Warm, 1988; My Presents, 1989; The Pop-Up Pet Shop, 1990; We Have a Pet, 1990; We Have a Rabbit, 1990; We Have a Dog, 1990; We Have a Guinea Pig, 1990; Look, Touch, and Feel with Buster, 1991; My Stand Up Baby Animals, 1991; My Stand Up Farm Animals, 1991; My Stand Up Wild Animals, 1991; Naughty Henry, 1991; Henry in the Park, 1991; Noisy Farm, 1991; A Simple Rhyming ABC, 1991; Rod Campbell's Lift-the-Flap Animal Book, 1991; Misty, 1993; My Lift-the-Flap Nursery Book, 1993; I Won't Bite, 1993; My Pop-Up Garden Friends, 1993. Books also published in multititle editions. **Address:** 19 Hazeldon Rd., London SE4, England.

CAMPBELL, Scott. American, b. 1945. **Genres:** Novels, Human relations/Parenting. **Career:** Freelance writer, 1974-. Massachusetts Institute of Technology, writer and editor, 1979-, lecturer in writing, 1984-85; Emerson College, lecturer in fiction, 2001-. **Publications:** (with P. Silverman) Widower: When Men Are Left Alone (oral histories), 1987; Touched (novel), 1996. Work represented in anthologies. Contributor of stories, articles, and photographs to periodicals. **Address:** Richard Parks Agency, 138 E 16th St, New York, NY 10003, U.S.A.

CAMPBELL, Siobhan. Irish, b. 1962. **Genres:** Poetry. **Career:** Wolfhound Press, Dublin, Ireland, director. Ireland Literature Exchange (translators), member of founding board of directors. International Writers Festival, Ottawa, Ontario, guest reader, 1998; gives readings in Ireland, England, Canada, and the United States; work also broadcast on BBC-TV and RTE-Radio. **Publications:** The Permanent Wave (poems), 1996; That Other Walking Stick, 1999. Work represented in anthologies. Contributor of poems to magazines and newspapers. **Address:** 1240 Diamond St., San Francisco, CA 94131, U.S.A. **Online address:** Siobhan.Campbell@gte.net

CAMPBELL, Tom. American, b. 1938. **Genres:** Westerns/Adventure. **Career:** U.S. Marine Corps, career officer in Infantry, 1961-88; instructor in landing force operations at Marine Corps Command and Staff College, Quantico, VA, 1974-77, and instructor in naval operations at Naval War College, Newport, RI, 1983; Davis & Davis (law firm), Austin, TX, legal administrator, 1988-90; University of Texas at Austin, lecturer in manage-

ment, 1990-. Campbell Management Services, president; Southwest Art Export Co., president. **Publications:** The Old Man's Trail (action novel), 1995. Contributor to periodicals. **Address:** Department of Management, Red McCombs School of Business, 1 University Station Stop 86300, University of Texas at Austin, Austin, TX 78712, U.S.A. **Online address:** thomcamp@mail.utexas.edu

CAMPBELL, Tracy (A.). American, b. 1962. **Genres:** History. **Career:** Union College, Barbourville, KY, assistant professor of history and director of Appalachian Semester Program, 1989-91; Mars Hill College, Mars Hill, NC, assistant professor of history, 1991-. **Publications:** The Politics of Despair: Power and Resistance in the Tobacco Wars, 1993. Contributor to history journals. **Address:** Department of History, Mars Hill College, Mars Hill, NC 28754, U.S.A.

CAMPBELL-CULVER, Maggie. British. **Genres:** Horticulture. **Career:** Ballet Rambert, dancer; lecturer on garden history. **Publications:** The Origin of Plants, 2001. **Address:** c/o Author Mail, Hodder Headline, 338 Euston Road, London NW1 3BH, England.

CAMPBELL-KELLY, Martin. British, b. 1945. **Genres:** Information science/Computers. **Career:** Educator and author. Leicester Polytechnic, Leicester, England, reader in computer science, 1963-73; Sunderland Polytechnic, Sunderland, England, senior lecturer, 1973-80; University of Warwick, Warwick, England, lecturer, 1980-89, senior lecturer, 1989-94, reader in computer science, 1994-. Consultant to IBM UK, Oracle, SCO, ICL-Fujitsu, NPL, University College-Chester, and Manchester Business School. **Publications:** An Introduction to Macros, 1973; The Computer Age, 1978; ICL: A Business and Technical History, 1989;(with W. Aspray) Computer: A History of the Information Machine, 1996; From Airline Reservations to Sonic the Hedgehog: A History of the Software Industry, 2003. EDITOR: (with M.R. Williams) The Moore School Lectures: Theory and Techniques for Design of Electronic Digital Computers, 1985; (and author of intro. with M.R. Williams) The Early British Computer Conferences, 1989; The Works of Charles Babbage, 1989; (and author of intro.) Charles Babbage, Passages from the Life of a Philosopher, 1994. Contributor to books and periodicals. **Address:** University of Warwick, Department of Computer Science, Coventry CV4 7AL, England. **Online address:** mck@dcs.warwick.ac.uk

CAMPER, Carol. Canadian, b. 1954. **Genres:** Novellas/Short stories, Poetry. **Career:** Hassle Free Clinic, Toronto, Ontario, counselor, 1990-. Black Coalition for AIDS Prevention, past member of board of directors. **Publications:** (ed.) Miscegenation Blues, 1994. Work represented in anthologies. Contributor of stories, poems, and reviews to periodicals. **Address:** 253 Strathmore Blvd., Toronto, ON, Canada M4J 1P7.

CAMPION, Dan(iel Ray). American, b. 1949. **Genres:** Poetry, Literary criticism and history. **Career:** Encyclopaedia Britannica Inc., Chicago, IL, production editor, 1972-74; Follett Publishing Company, Chicago, children's book editor, 1977-78; University of Iowa, Iowa City, teaching and research assistant, 1978-84; visiting assistant professor of English, 1990-95; ACT Inc., Iowa City, test specialist and senior test editor, 1984-. **Publications:** (ed. with J. Perlman and E. Folsom) Walt Whitman: The Measure of His Song (criticism), 1981, 2nd ed., 1998; Calypso (poetry), 1981; Peter De Vries and Surrealism (criticism), 1995. Contributor of poetry and articles to periodicals. **Address:** ACT, 500 ACT Dr, PO Box 168, Iowa City, IA 52243-0168, U.S.A.

CAMPION, Jane. New Zealander, b. 1954. **Genres:** Plays/Screenplays. **Career:** Filmmaker and writer. Director of television productions, short films, and feature films. **Publications:** SCREENPLAYS. SHORT FILMS: Peel, 1982; Mishaps of Seduction and Conquest, 1984; (with G. Lee) Passionless Moments, 1984; A Girl's Own Story, 1984; After Hours, 1984. FEATURE FILMS: (with G. Lee) Sweetie, 1988; The Piano, 1992; (with A. Campion) Holy Smoke, 1999; (with S. Moore) In the Cut, 2003. **Address:** c/o HLA Management Pty Ltd, PO Box 1536, Strawberry Hills, NSW 2012, Australia. **Online address:** hla@hlamgt.com.au

CAMPION, Nicholas. British, b. 1953. **Genres:** Astronomy. **Career:** Writer. **Publications:** The Great Year, 1994; The New Astrology, 1999. **Address:** PO Box 1071, Bristol BS8 4TF, England. **Online address:** ncampion@caol.demon.co.uk

CAMPLING, Christopher Russell. British, b. 1925. **Genres:** Music, Theology/Religion. **Career:** Assistant Curate, Basingstoke, 1951-55; Chaplain, King's School, Ely, 1955-60, and Lancing Coll., Sussex, 1961-67; Vicar and Rural Dean of Pershore, and Canon of Worcester Cathedral, 1968-

76: Archdeacon of Dudley, 1976-84, Dean of Ripon, 1984-95, Dean Emeritus of Ripon, 1995-. Chairman of the Council for the Care of Churches, 1988-93. **Publications:** (co-author) Guide to Divinity Teaching, 1960: The Way, the Truth and the Life (series), 1965; (co-ed.) Words for Worship, 1970; (ed.) The Fourth Lesson, Book 1; 1973, Book 2, 1974; Music for Rite A Eucharist, 1988; The Food of Love: Reflections on Music and Faith, 1997. **Address:** Pebble Ridge, Aglaia Rd, Worthing, W. Sussex BN11 5SW, England.

CAMPO, Rafael. American, b. 1964. **Genres:** Poetry. **Career:** Poet and practicing physician; Beth Israel Hospital, Boston, MA, physician; Harvard Medical School, physician. **Publications:** The Other Man Was Me: A Voyage to the New World, 1994; What the Body Told, 1996; The Poetry of Healing: A Doctor's Education in Empathy, Identity, and Desire (essays), 1997; Diva, 1999. Contributor to collections. Contributor of poetry, essays, and reviews to periodicals. **Address:** Beth Israel Deaconess Medical Center, 330 Brookline Ave., General Medicine, Ly-314, Boston, MA 02215, U.S.A.

CAMPOS, Paul F. American, b. 1959. **Genres:** Law. **Career:** Sports Periodical Index, editor, 1985-86; Latham & Watkins, attorney, 1989-90; University of Minnesota, visiting professor of law, 1992; University of Colorado, professor of law, 1990-. **Publications:** Against the Law, 1996; Jurismania: The Madness of American Law, 1998. **Address:** Law School, University of Colorado, Kitteridge Dr., Campus Box 401, Boulder, CO 80309, U.S.A.

CAMPTON, David. British, b. 1924. **Genres:** Children's fiction, Plays/Screenplays. **Career:** Clerk, City of Leicester Education Dept., 1941-49, and East Midlands Gas Board, Leicester, 1949-56; actor, director, 1959-. **Publications:** Going Home, 1951: Honeymoon Express, 1951; Change Partners, 1951; Sunshine on thc Righteous, 1952; The Laboratory, 1955; The Cactus Garden, 1955: Doctor Alexander, 1956: Cuckoo Song, 1956; The Lunatic View: A Comedy of Mcnace, 1960; Roses Round the Door, 1958; Frankenstein: The Gift of Fire, 1959; Little Brother, Little Sister, 1960; Four Minute Warning, 1960; Funeral Dance, 1960: Passport to Florence, 1961; Silence on the Battlefield, 1961; Usher, 1962; Incident, 1962; On Stage: Containing Seventeen Sketches and One Monologue, 1964; Resting Place, 1964; The Manipulator, 1964; Split Down the Middle, 1965; Little Brother, Little Sister and Out of the Flying Pan, 1966; Two Leaves and a Stalk, 1967; Angel Unwilling, 1967; More Sketches, 1967; Ladies Night: Four Plays for Women. 1967; The Right Place, 1969; Laughter and Fear: 9 One-Act Plays, 1969; On Stage Again: Containing Fourteen Sketches and Two Monologues, 1969; The Life and Death of Almost Everybody, 1970; Now and Then, 1970; Timesneeze, 1970; Gulliver in Lilliput (reader), 1970; Gulliver in the Land of the Giants (reader), 1970: The Wooden Horse of Troy (reader), 1970; Jonah, 1971; The Cagebirds, 1971; Us and Them, 1972; Carmilla, 1972; Come Back Tomorrow, 1972; In Committee, 1972; Three Gothic Plays, 1973; Modern Aesop (reader), 1976; One Possessed, 1977; The Do-It-Yourself Frankenstein Outfit, 1978; What Are You Doing Here?, 1978; Zodiac, 1978; After Midnight: Before Dawn, 1978; Parcel, 1979; Everybody's Friend, 1979; Pieces of Campton, 1979; Who Calls?, 1980; Attitudes, 1980; Freedom Log, 1980; Dark Wings, 1981; Look- Sea, 1981; Great Whales, 1981; Who's a Hero?, 1981; But Not Here, 1984; Dead and Alive, 1983; Mrs. Meadowsweet, 1986; Singing in the Wilderness, 1986; Our Branch in Brussels, 1986; Cards, Cups and Crystal Ball, 1986; The Vampyre (children's book), 1986; Can You Hear the Music?, 1989; The Winter of 1917, 1989; Smile, 1990; Becoming a Playwright, 1992; Who's Been Sitting in My Chair?, 1992; Eskimos & Provisioning, 1993; The Evergreens, 1994; Permission to Cry, 1996. **Address:** 35 Liberty Rd, Glenfield, Leicester LE3 8JF, England.

CANADA, Geoffrey. American, b. 1952. **Genres:** Psychology. **Career:** Camp Freedom, Cambridge, MA, supervisor of camp at Center Ossipe, NH, 1974-75; Robert White School (alternative high school), Boston, MA, teacher and counselor, 1975-76, associate director, 1976-77, director, 1977-81; Health Care Inc., Lawrence, MA, executive director, 1981-83; Rheedlen Centers for Children and Families, NYC, director of Truancy Prevention Program and Center 54, 1983-90, president and chief executive officer, 1990-. Member of boards of trustees. **Publications:** Fist Stick Knife Gun, 1995; Reaching Up for Manhood, 1998. Contributor to magazines and newspapers. **Address:** Rheedlen Centers for Children and Families, 1916 Park Ave., New York, NY 10037-3736, U.S.A. **Online address:** Rheelen@rheelen.org

CANAVAGGIO, Jean (Francois). French, b. 1936. **Genres:** Literary criticism and history, Theatre. **Career:** Sorbonne University, assistant, 1966-69; University of Caen, France, assistant lecturer, 1969-75, professor, 1975-91; University of Virginia, Charlottesville, visiting professor, 1983; University of Paris X Nanterre, professor, 1991-; Casa de Velazquez, Madrid, director,

19962001. **Publications:** L'Espagne au temps de Philippe II, 1965; Cervantes dramaturge: un theatre a naitre, 1977; Theatre espagnol du XVIe siecle, 1983; Cervantes, Mazarine, 1986, trans., 1990; Theatre espagnol du XVIIe siecle, 1992-99; (ed.) Miguel de Cervantes Saavedra, Los Banos de Argel; Pedro de Urdemalas, 1992; Histoire de la litterature espagnole, 1993-94; Un mundo abreviado, 2000; Cervantes entre vida y creacion, 2000; (ed.) Cervantes, Oeuvres completes, 2001. **Address:** Universite de Paris X Nanterre, 200 av Republique, 32001 Nantere Cedex, France. **Online address:** jean.f.canavaggio@wanadoo.fr

CANDILIS, Wray O. American (born England), b. 1927. **Genres:** Economics. **Career:** Director, Information Industries Division, Office of Service Industries, International Trade Administration, U.S. Dept. of Commerce, Washington, DC, 1971-(former Special Assistant, for Financial Affairs, Office of Business Research and Analysis). Assistant Director, Dept. of Research, National Association of Real Estate Bds., Washington, DC, 1960-64; Sr. Economics Associate, Division of Statistics and Research, Institute of Life Insurance, NYC, 1964-66; Research Project Director, Dept. of Research and Planning, American Bankers Association, Washington, DC, 1966-71. **Publications:** The Economy of Greece 1944-66, 1968; Long-Range Planning in Banking, 1968; Financing America's States and Cities, 1970; Variable Rate Mortgage Plans, 1971; Consumer Credit-Factors Influencing Its Availability and Costs, 1976. EDITOR: (and co-author) The Future of Commercial Banking, 1975; Changing Minority Markets, 1978; (and co-author) Franchising in the Economy 1976-1978, 1978; Market Center Shifts, 1978; The Motor Vehicle Leasing and Rental Industry: Trends and Prospects, 1979; Measuring Markets: Guide to the Use of Federal and State Statistical Data, 1979; United States Service Industries Handbook, 1988; The Flowergarden (translated from Greek), 2001.

CANDISKY, Catherine A. American, b. 1961. **Genres:** Mystery/Crime/Suspense. **Career:** Columbus Dispatch, Columbus, OH, reporter, 1984-. **Publications:** (with Robin Yocum) Insured for Murder, Prometheus Books (Buffalo), 1993. **Address:** c/o Columbus Dispatch, 34 S. 3rd St., Columbus, OH 43215, U.S.A.

CANDLAND, Douglas Keith. American, b. 1934. **Genres:** Psychology. **Career:** Bucknell University, Lewisburg, PA, assistant professor, 1960-64, associate professor, 1964-67, professor, 1967-73, presidential professor of animal behavior, 1973-. Consulting editor for professional journals. **Publications:** (with J. Campbell) Exploring Behavior, 1960; (ed.) Emotion: Bodily Change, 1962; Psychology: The Experimental Approach, 1968, 2nd ed. (with R. Moyer), 1978; (with others) Emotion, 1977; Feral Children and Clever Animals, 1993; Fossils of the Mind, forthcoming. **Address:** 125 Stein Ln, Lewisburg, PA 17837, U.S.A. **Online address:** dcandlan@bucknell.edu

CANFIELD, Jack. American, b. 1944. **Genres:** Education, How-to books, Inspirational/Motivational Literature, Philosophy, Self help, Cartoons. **Career:** High school social studies teacher, Chicago, 1967-68; Clinton Job Corps Center, Clinton, IA, director of teacher program, 1968-69; W. Clement and Jessie V. Stone Foundation, Chicago, associate director of education, 1969-70; New England Center for Personal and Organizational Development, Amherst, MA, founder and director, 1971-77; Institute for Wholistic Education, Amherst, founder and director, 1975-80; Insight Training Seminars, Santa Monica, CA, director of educational services, 1981-83; Self-Esteem Seminars, Santa Barbara, CA, president, 1983-. Foundation for Self-Esteem, chairperson of board of directors, 1986-; Chicken Soup for the Soul Enterprises, CEO, 1998-. Maui Writers School, faculty member. Chicken Soup for the Soul, weekly column, 1995. **Publications:** (with H.C. Wells) About Me, 1971; (with Wells) 100 Ways to Enhance Self-Concept in the Classroom, 1976, rev. ed., 1993; Personalized Learning, 1976, as Loving to Learn, 1997; (with M. Reese, R. Rowland, S. Limina, and others) Self-Esteem in the Classroom, 1986; Self-Esteem and Peak Performance, 1991; (with F. Siccone) 101 Ways to Develop Student Self-Esteem and Responsibility in the Classroom, Vol. 1: The Teacher as Coach, 1992, Vol. 2: The Power to Succeed in School and Beyond, 1992, in 1 vol, 1994; Los Angeles Dodgers Team Esteem Program, 1992; (with M.V. Hansen) Dare to Win, 1994; (with K. Goldberg) Follow Your Dreams, 1994; (with Hansen) The Aladdin Factor, 1995; (with J. Miller) Heart at Work, 1996;(with Hansen and L. Hewitt) The Power of Focus, 2000. COMPILER (with M.V. Hansen and others) CHICKEN SOUP FOR THE SOUL SERIES: Chicken Soup for the Soul: 101 Stories to Open the Heart and Rekindle the Spirit, 1993; A Second Helping of ..., 1995; ... Cookbook, 1995; A Third Serving of ..., 1996; A Cup of ..., 1996; ... for the Surviving Soul, 1996; Condensed ..., 1996; ... for the Woman's Soul, 1996; ... at Work, 1996; A Fourth Course of ..., 1997; ... for the Teenage Soul, 1997, II, 1998, Journal, 1998, III, 2000, The Tough Stuff, 2001; ... for the Christian Soul, 1997; ... for the Mother's Soul, 1997; A Little

Sip of ..., 1997; Another Sip of ..., 1997; A Fifth Portion of ..., 1998; ... for the Pet Lover's Soul, 1998; ... for the Country Soul, 1998; ... for the Kid's Soul, 1998; A 2nd Helping ... for the Woman's Soul, 1998; ... for the Couple's Soul, 1999; A Sixth Bowl of ..., 1999; ... for the Golfer's Soul, 1999, A Second Round, 2002; A Little Spoonful of ..., 1999; A Little Spoonful ... for the Mother's Soul, 1999; A Little Spoonful ... for the Friend's Soul, 1999; A Little Spoonful ... for the Teenage Soul, 1999; ... for the College Soul, 1999; ... for the Unsinkable Soul, 1999; ... for the Single Soul, 1999; ... for the Cat & Dog Lover's Soul, 1999; ... for the Dental Soul, 1999; ... for the Golden Soul, 2000; ... for the Christian Family Soul, 2000; ... for the Writer's Soul, 2000; ... for the Expectant Mother's Soul, 2000; ... for the Prisoner's Soul, 2000; ... for the Parent's Soul, 2000; ... for the Pre-Teen Soul, 2000; ... for the Sport Fan's Soul, 2000; ... for the Father's Soul, 2001; ... for the Veteran's Soul, 2001; ... for the Nurse's Soul, 2001; ... for the Jewish Soul, 2001; ... for the Baseball Fan's Soul, 2001; ... Teenage Collection, 2001, Teenage Trilogy, 2001; ... Christmas Treasury, 2001; ... for the Traveler's Soul, 2002; ... of America, 2002; ... for the Grandparent's Soul, 2002; ... for the Teacher's Soul, 2002; ... for the Volunteer's Soul, 2002; ... for the Canadian Soul, 2002; ... for the Christian Woman's Soul, 2002; ... for the Sister's Soul, 2002; ... for the Teenage Soul on Love and Friendship, 2002; ... Christmas Treasury for Kids, 2002; ... for the Romantic Soul, 2003; ... for the Grieving Soul, 2003; ... for the Mother & Daughter 's Soul, 2003; ... Cartoon Collection for Moms, 2003; ... of NASCAR, 2003; ... of Hawaii, 2003; ... for the Chiropractic Soul, 2003; ... Celebrates Teachers, 2003; ... for the Healthy Soul, 2003; ... for the Christian Teenage Soul, 2003; ... for the Working Woman's Soul, 2003; ... for the Horse Lover's Soul, 2003; ... Living Your Dreams, 2003; ... Cartoon Collection for Dads, 2003; ... for the Ocean Lover's Soul, 2003. **Address:** PO Box 30880, Santa Barbara, CA 93130, U.S.A. **Online address:** webmaster@ chickensoupforthesoul.com.

CANHAM, Marsha. British. **Genres:** Romance/Historical. **Career:** Writer. **Publications:** ROMANCE NOVELS: China Rose, 1984; Bound by the Heart, 1984; The Wind and the Sea, 1986; Under the Desert Moon, 1992; Dark and Dangerous, 1992; Straight for the Heart, 1995; Across a Moonlit Sea, 1996; Pale Moon Rider, 1998; Swept Away, 1999. SCOTLAND TRILOGY: The Pride of Lions, 1988; The Blood of Roses, 1989; Midnight Honor, 2001. MEDIEVAL TRILOGY: Through a Dark Mist, 1991; In the Shadow of Midnight, 1994; The Last Arrow, 1997. **Address:** c/o Author Mail, Dell Publishing Co., 1540 Broadway, New York, NY 10036, U.S.A. **Online address:** marsha.canham@sympatico.ca

CANIN, Ethan. American, b. 1960. **Genres:** Novels, Novellas/Short stories, Medicine/Health, Travel/Exploration. **Publications:** Emperor of the Air (short stories), 1988; Blue River (novel), 1991; The Palace Thief (novellas), 1994; For Kings and Planets, 1998; Carry Me across the Water, 2001. **Address:** Maxine Groffsky Literary Agency, 2 Fifth Ave, New York, NY 10001, U.S.A.

CANN, Kate. British, b. 1954. **Genres:** Young adult fiction. **Career:** Time Life Books, London, England, copyeditor, 1979-83. Freelance editor; writer. **Publications:** FOR YOUNG ADULTS. FICTION: Diving In, 1996; In the Deep End, 1997; Sink or Swim, 1998; Footloose, 1999; Breaking Up, 2000; Hard Cash, 2000; Shacked Up, 2001; Fiesta, 2001; Speeding, 2002; Escape, 2003. **Address:** 34 Denton Rd., Twickenham, Middlesex TWI 2HQ, England. **Online address:** katescann@aol.com

CANNELL, Dorothy. American (born England). **Genres:** Mystery/Crime/Suspense. **Career:** Mystery writer. **Publications:** MYSTERY NOVELS: The Thin Woman: An Epicurean Mystery, 1984; Down the Garden Path: A Pastoral Mystery, 1985; The Widows Club, 1988; Mum's the Word, 1990; Femmes Fatal, 1992; How to Murder Your Mother-in-Law, 1994; How to Murder the Man of Your Dreams, 1995; God Save the Queen, 1996; The Spring Cleaning Murders, 1998. Author of short stories. **Address:** c/o Bantam Books, 1540 Broadway, New York, NY 10036, U.S.A.

CANNEY, Donald L. American, b. 1947. **Genres:** Military/Defense/Arms control. **Career:** Maranatha Christian High School, Columbus, OH, teacher, 1974-84; Blue and Grey, Columbus, member of editorial staff, 1984-87; U.S. Coast Guard, Washington, DC, registrar for Museum System, 1991-. **Publications:** The Old Steam Navy, Vol. 1: Frigates, Sloops, and Gunboats, 1989, Vol. 2: The Ironclads, 1842-1885, 1993; U.S. Coast Guard and Revenue Cutters, 1790-1935, 1995; Lincoln's Navy, 1998; Sailing Warships of the U.S. Navy, 2001. Author of booklets for U.S. Coast Guard. **Address:** 12618 Kornett Ln, Bowie, MD 20715, U.S.A.

CANNING, Peter. American, b. 1937. **Genres:** Biography. **Career:** Reader's Digest (magazine), Pleasantville, NY, 1965-88, managing editor, 1980-88.

Publications: American Dreamers: The Wallaces and Reader's Digest: An Insider's Story, 1996. **Address:** 1103 Horseneck Rd, Westport, MA 02790-1324, U.S.A.

CANNISTRARO, Philip V(incent). American, b. 1942. **Genres:** History. **Career:** Florida State University, Tallahassee, professor of history, 1971-82; Drexel University, Philadelphia, PA, professor of history, 1982-. **Publications:** La Fabbrica del consenso (monograph), 1975; (co-author) Civilizations of the World, 1990; (with B.R. Sullivan) Il Duce's Other Woman, 1993; Journey to Power: The Life and Times of Generoso Pope, in press; Western Perspective, 1998; Blackshirts in Little Italy, 1999. EDITOR: Italian Fascist Activities in the United States, 1977; (with R.N. Juliani) Italian Americans: The Search for a Usable Past, 1989. Contributor to history journals. **Address:** PhD Queens College, CUNY, 365 5th Ave Ste 5114, New York, NY 10016, U.S.A. **Online address:** philip-cannistraro@gc.edu; pvcnyc@aol.com

CANNON, Devereaux D(unlap), Jr. American, b. 1954. **Genres:** History. **Career:** Old Republic Title Co. of Tennessee, Nashville, vice-president and staff attorney, 1991-. Old Republic National Title Insurance Co., assistant vice-president and Tennessee state counsel. Flag Institute, member; consultant to National Archives. **Publications:** The Flags of the Confederacy: An Illustrated History, 1988; Flags of Tennessee, 1990; The Flags of the Union: An Illustrated History, 1994; The Wit and Wisdom of Robert E. Lee, 1997. Contributor to books on real estate and title law. Contributor to law journals and regional magazines. **Address:** 159 Womack Rd, Portland, TN 37148, U.S.A. **Online address:** dcannon.tenn@worldnet.att.net

CANNON, Dolores Eilene. American, b. 1931. **Genres:** Paranormal. **Career:** Regressive hypnotist, writer, and publisher. Ozark Mountain Publishing, Inc., owner and publisher. International speaker. **Publications:** Conversations with Nostradamus, Volume 1, 1989, Volume 2, 1990, Volume 3, 1992; Jesus and the Essenes: Fresh Insights into Christ's Ministry and the Dead Sea Scrolls, 1992; Conversations with a Spirit: Between Death and Life, 1993; A Soul Remembers Hiroshima, 1993; Keepers of the Garden, 1993; The Legend of StarCrash, 1994; Legacy from the Stars, 1996; They Walked with Jesus, 1994; The Custodians, 1999; The Convoluted Universe, 2001. Contributor to professional journals and periodicals. **Address:** c/o Ozark Mountain Publishing, PO Box 754, Huntsville, AR 72740, U.S.A. **Online address:** decannon@msn.com; www.ozarkmt.com

CANNON, Eileen E(mily). American, b. 1948. **Genres:** Mystery/Crime/Suspense, Plays/Screenplays. **Career:** Writer. **Publications:** SCREENPLAYS: Doubletalk, 1975. NOVELS: Convictions: A Novel of the Sixties, 1985; Mississippi Treasure Hunt (young adult), 1996. MYSTERY NOVELS: A Pocketful of Karma, 1993; Tangled Roots, 1995; Class Reunions Are Murder, 1996; Guns and Roses, 2000; The Tumbleweed Murders, 2001; Open Season on Lawyers, 2002; Murder Will Travel, 2002. **Address:** PO Box 2520, Carlsbad, CA 92018, U.S.A. **Online address:** tcannon@nctimes. net

CANNON, Frank. *See* **MAYHAR, Ardath (Hurst).**

CANNON, Garland. American, b. 1924. **Genres:** Language/Linguistics, Bibliography, Biography. **Career:** Columbia University, NYC, Teachers Coll., assistant professor, 1959-62; City University of New York, associate professor, 1963-66; Texas A&M University, College Station, professor of English and linguistics, 1966-, now emeritus, with visiting professorships at universities worldwide. **Publications:** Sir William Jones: Orientalist, 1952; Oriental Jones, 1964; A History of the English Language, 1972; An Integrated Transformational Grammar of English, 1978; Sir William Jones: A Secondary and Primary Bibliography, 1979; Historical Change and English Word-Formation, 1987; The Life and Mind of Oriental Jones, 1990; (with J.A. Pfeffer) German Loanwords in English, 1994; Arabic Loanwords in English, 1994; Japanese Loanwords in English, 1996; (with A. Kaye) Persian Loanwords in English, 2001. EDITOR: The Letters of Sir William Jones, 2 vols., 1970; The Collected Works of Sir William Jones, 13 vols., 1993; (with K. Brine) Objects of Enquiry: The Life and Mind of Sir William Jones, 1995. **Address:** Dept. of English, Texas A&M University, College Station, TX 77843, U.S.A.

CANNON, Michael. Australian, b. 1929. **Genres:** Area studies. **Career:** Journalist and historian in Melbourne and Sydney Australia and London, England; Historical Records of Victoria, Australia, chief editor, 1981-91. **Publications:** The Land Boomers, 1966, 2nd ed. as Land Boom and Bust, 1972; Who's Master? Who's Man? (vol. 1), 1971, Life in the Country (vol. 2), 1973, Life in the Cities (vol. 3), 1975; Lola Montes, 1973; An Australian

Camera, 1851-1914, Newton Abbott, 1973; That Damned Democrat: John Norton, an Australian Populist, 1858-1916, 1981; The Long Last Summer: Australia's Upper Class before the Great War, 1985; The Exploration of Australia, 1987; Who Killed the Koories?, 1990; Melbourne after the Gold Rush, 1993; The Woman as Murderer: Five Who Paid with Their Lives, 1994; Perilous Voyages to the New Land, 1995; The Human Face of the Great Depression, 1996; That Disreputable Firm: The Inside Story of Slater & Gordon, 1998. EDITOR: (and intro) The Vagabond Papers, 1969; (and intro.) Our Beautiful Homes, NSW, c. 1977; (and intro.) the Vagabond (John Stanley James, Julian Thomas), Vagabond Country: Australian Bush and Town Life in the Victorian Age, 1981; (and intro.) S.T. Gill, The Victorian Gold Fields, 1852-53: An Original Album, 1982; (with I. MacFarlane) The Early Development of Melbourne, 1984; (and intro.) J. Chandler, Forty Years in the Wilderness, 1990; (with I. MacFarlane) The Crown, the Land, and the Squatter, 1835-1840, 1991; (and intro) Hold Page One: Memoirs of Monty Grover, Editor, 1993; (with P. Jones) Beginnings of Permanent Government; The Aborigines of Port Phillip, 1835-1839; Aborigines and Protectors, 1838-1839; (with I. MacFarlane) Communications, Trade, and Transport. **Address:** PO Box 149, Foster, VIC 3960, Australia.

CANO, Daniel. American, b. 1947. **Genres:** Novels. **Career:** Santa Monica College, Santa Monica, CA, professor of English. Has held administrative positions at University of California Los Angeles, Los Angeles, California State University Dominguez Hills, University of California, Davis. **Publications:** Pepe Rios, 1991; Shifting Loyal Ties, 1995. **Address:** Department of English, Santa Monica College, 1900 Pico Blvd., Santa Monica, CA 90405, U.S.A. **Online address:** dcano@smc.edu

CANOVAN, Margaret Evelyn Leslie. British, b. 1939. **Genres:** Politics/Government, Philosophy. **Career:** University of Lancaster, lecturer in politics, 1965-71; Keele University, Staffs, lecturer to professor of political thought, 1974-. **Publications:** The Political Thought of Hannah Arendt, 1974; G.K. Chesterton: Radical Populist, 1977; Populism, 1981; Hannah Arendt: A Reinterpretation of Her Political Thought, 1992; Nationhood and Political Theory, 1996. **Address:** Dept. of Politics, Keele University, Keele, Staffs, England.

CANTER, Mark. American, b. 1952. **Genres:** Novels. **Career:** Feature writer for newspapers in South Florida; Men's Health, past editor. Blue Heron Zen Center, Tallahassee, FL, founder; Cloud Forest Zen Center, Monteverde, Costa Rica, founder. **Publications:** Ember From the Sun (novel), 1996. Contributor to periodicals. **Address:** 5012 Crestwood Ct., Tallahassee, FL 32311, U.S.A.

CANTON, Katia. Brazilian, b. 1962. **Genres:** Literary criticism and history. **Career:** University of Sao Paulo, Brazil, professor of contemporary art history and performance. Museum of Contemporary Art, Brazil, curator. **Publications:** The Fairy Tale Revisited: A Survey of the Evolution of the Tales, from Classical Literary Interpretations to Innovative Contemporary Dance Theatre Productions, 1994. **Address:** Universidade de Sao Paulo, Musem de Arte Contemporanian, Cidade Universitaria, Rua da Reitoria 160, 05508-900 Sao Paulo, SP, Brazil. **Online address:** katiacanton@uol.com.br

CANTOR, George (Nathan). American, b. 1941. **Genres:** Travel/Exploration, Geography, History, Civil liberties/Human rights. **Career:** Detroit Free Press, Detroit, MI, reporter and editor, 1963-77; Detroit News, Detroit, columnist, 1977-. Commentator for WWJRadio, 1981-, and WXYZ-TV, 1982-. Greater Detroit Area Hospital Council, member of board of directors, 1983. **Publications:** The Great Lakes Guidebook, Vol I: Lakes Ontario and Erie, 1978, 2nd ed, 1984, Vol II: Lake Huron and Eastern Lake Michigan, 1979, 2nd ed, 1985, Volume III: Lake Superior and Western Lake Michigan, 1980; Where the Old Roads Go: Driving the First Federal Highways of the Northeast, 1990; Civil War to Civil Rights: A Traveler's Guide to Black American Landmarks, 1991; Historic Black Landmarks: A Traveler's Guide, 1991; (ed.) Historic Landmarks of Black America, 1991; Incantations, 1991; Old Roads of the Midwest, 1997; Courtney's Legacy: A Father's Journal, 2002. **Address:** Detroit News, 615 Lafayette Blvd., Detroit, MI 48231, U.S.A. **Online address:** gcantor@detnews.com

CANTRELL, Lisa W. American, b. 1945. **Genres:** Horror, Mystery/Crime/Suspense. **Career:** Novelist in the horror and crime genres. **Publications:** The Manse, 1987; The Ridge, 1989; Torments, 1990; Boneman, 1992. Contributor to anthologies. **Address:** c/o Tor Books, 175 Fifth Ave., 14th Fl., New York, NY 10010, U.S.A.

CANTU, Norma Elia. (Elia). American (born Mexico), b. 1947. **Genres:** Novels, Poetry, Women's studies and issues, Documentaries/Reportage,

Education, Autobiography/Memoirs. **Career:** Texas A&M International University, Laredo, TX, professor of English, 1980-2000. University of Texas, San Antonio, professor of Latino Studies, 2000-; Visiting professor at Georgetown University School for Continuing Education, 1994-95; has read poetry, given lectures, and presented papers in locations throughout the United States, Mexico, and Paris, France. Has served as an editor or consultant for the University of New Mexico Press, Texas A&M University Press, and Chicana/Latina Studies Journal; produced and moderated "Fiesta Latina," a weekly public service radio program on KRNU; past director of Teatro Chicano/a at the University of Nebraska; past translator at the Development Center for Hispanic Affairs in Lincoln, NE; has served on several other community projects. **Publications:** Canícula: Snapshots of a Girlhood en la frontera, 1995; Telling the Line: Latina Feminist Testimonies, 2001; Chicana Traditions: Continuity and Change, 2002. Contributor of articles, stories, poems, and reviews to periodicals. Contributor to books. **Address:** Dept of English, Classics and Philosophy, University of Texas-San Antonia, 6900 N Loop 1604 W, San Antonio, TX 78249, U.S.A. **Online address:** necantu@omni.ucsb.edu

CAN XUE. See **DENG XIAOHUA.**

CAO, Lan. American, b. 1961. **Genres:** Novels, Reference. **Career:** Admitted to the Bar of New York State, 1989; Judge Constance Motley, U.S. District Court (Southern District), NYC, law clerk, 1988-89; Paul, Weiss, Rifking, Wharton and Garrison (law firm), New York City, associate, litigation department, 1987-88, 1990-91, associate, corporate law department, 1992-93; Brooklyn Law School, Brooklyn, NY, assistant professor, 1993-. **Publications:** (with H. Novas) Everything You Need to Know about Asian American History, 1996; Monkey Bridge (novel), 1997. Contributor to journals.

CAPE, Judith. See **PAGE, P(atricia) K(athleen).**

CAPEK, Michael. Also writes as Kari Christopher. American, b. 1947. **Genres:** Young adult fiction, Plays/Screenplays, Art/Art history, Children's non-fiction, History. **Career:** Walton-Verona High School, Walton, KY, teacher of English, 1969-96. **Publications:** Artistic Trickery: The Trompe L'Oeil Tradition, 1995; Murals: Cave, Cathedral, to Street, 1996; A Ticket to Jamaica, 1999; Globetrotter's Club: Jamaica, 1999; A Personal Tour of a Shaker Village, 2001. Contributor to textbooks. Contributor of stories and articles to periodicals. **Address:** 5965 Tip Dr, Taylor Mill, KY 41015, U.S.A. **Online address:** mcapek@goodnews.net

CAPIE, Forrest H(unter). Scottish, b. 1940. **Genres:** Money/Finance, Economics. **Career:** University of Warwick, Coventry, England, lecturer in economics, 1972-74; University of Leeds, England, lecturer in economic studies, 1974-79; City University, London, England, visiting lecturer, 1978-79, lecturer, 1979-82, senior lecturer, 1982-83, reader, 1983-86, professor of economic history, 1986-, head of Department of Banking and Finance, 1988-. University of Aix-Marseille, visiting professor, 1978-79; University of London, London School of Economics and Political Science, visiting professor, 1991-92; lecturer at universities around the world. **Publications:** (with M. Collins) The British Economy between the Wars, 1983; Depression and Protectionism: Britain between the Wars, 1983; (with A. Webber) A Monetary History of the United Kingdom, 1870-1982: Data Sources and Methods, 1985; (with M. Collins) Did the Banks Fail British Industry?, 1992; Commercial Policy in the Modern World Economy, 1994. EDITOR: (with G.E. Wood, and contrib.) Financial Crises and the World Banking System, 1986; (with G.E. Wood) Monetary Economics in the 1980s: Some Themes from Henry Thornton, 1989; A Directory of Economic Institutions, 1990; (with G.E. Wood, and co-author of intro) Unregulated Banking: Chaos or Order, 1991; (and contrib.) Major Inflations in History, 1991; (and contrib.) Protectionism in the World Economy, 1992; (with M. Bordo, and contrib.) Monetary Regimes in Transition, 1993; (and contrib.) A History of Banking, 10 vols., 1993. Co-editor of a series on monetary and financial history, 1988-; editor of a series on macroeconomic and financial history, 1989-94. Work represented in books. Contributor of articles and reviews to economic and finance journals. **Address:** Faculty of Finance, Cass Business School, 106 Bunhill Row, London EC1Y 8TZ, England. **Online address:** F.H. Capie@city.ac.uk

CAPITAN, William H(arry). American, b. 1933. **Genres:** Art/Art history, Philosophy, Theology/Religion, Ethics. **Career:** Instructor in Philosophy, University of Minnesota, Minneapolis. 1959-60; Instructor, University of Maryland, College Park, 1960-62; Assistant Professor, 1962-65, Associate Professor, 1965-70, and Chairman, Dept. of Philosophy, 196870, Oberlin Coll., Ohio: Dean, 1970-72, Vice-President, 1972-74, and Acting President,

1974-79, Saginaw Valley Coll., Michigan; President, Georgia Southwestern State University, Americus, 1979-96; University of Georgia, Athens, GA, President Emeritus, Adjunct Professor of Philosophy. **Publications:** Introduction to The Philosophy of Religion (textbook), 1972; Speak for Yourself, 1989; The Ethical Navigator, 2000. EDITOR: (with D.D. Merrill) Metaphysics and Explanation, 1966; (with Merrill) Art, Religion and Mind, 1967. **Address:** Georgia Southwestern State University, Americus, GA 31709, U.S.A.

CAPLAN, Arthur L(eonard). American, b. 1950. **Genres:** Humanities, Medicine/Health. **Career:** Columbia University, NYC, associate for social medicine, 1978-81 (instructor, School of Public Health, 1977-78; associate director, associate for the humanities, Hastings Center, 1977-87); University of Pittsburgh, visiting associate professor, 1986; University of Minnesota professor of philosophy, professor of surgery, and director, Center for Biomedical Ethics, 1987-94; University of Pennsylvania, trustee professor of bioethics, and director, Center for Bioethics, Medical Center, Division of Bioethics, chief, 1994-. **Publications:** Beyond Baby M, 1990; Everyday Ethics: Resolving Dilemmas in Nursing Home Life, 1990; When Medicine Went Mad, 1992; If I Were a Rich Man Could I Buy a Pancreas and Other Essays on Medical Ethics, 1992; Prescribing Our Future, 1993; Moral Matters, 1995; Due Consideration: Controversy in an Age of Medical Miracles, 1997; Am I My Brother's Keeper?, 1998; The Ethics of Organ Transplants: The Current Debate, 1999; Finding Common Ground, 2001; Who Owns Life?, 2002. EDITOR: The Sociobiology Debate, 1978; (with H.T. Engelhardt Jr.) Concepts of Health and Disease: Interdisciplinary Perspectives, 1980; (with D. Callahan) Ethics in Hard Times, 1981; In Search of Equity, 1983; (with B. Jennings) Darwin, Marx and Freud: Their Influence on Moral Theory, 1983; Scientific Controversies, 1985; (with T.H. Murray) Which Babies Shall Live?, 1985; (with R.A. Kane) Resolving Dilemmas in Nursing Home Life, 1989. Contributor to professional journals. **Address:** Center for Bioethics, University of Pennsylvania Medical Center, 3401 Market St Ste 320, Philadelphia, PA 19104-3308, U.S.A. **Online address:** caplan@mail.med.upenn.edu; caplan@fast.net

CAPLAN, Lincoln. American, b. 1950. **Genres:** Law. **Career:** New Republic, Washington, DC, staff writer, 1975-76; Connecticut Supreme Court, Hartford, law clerk, 1976-77; Boston Consulting Group, Boston, MA, management consultant, 1977-79; White House fellow, 1979-80; New Yorker, NYC, regular contributor, 1980-88, staff writer, 1988-92; Newsweek, contributing editor, Washington, DC, 1993-95; U.S. News & World Report, editor, special projects, 1996-; Yale Law School, Knight senior journalist, 1998-; Legal Affairs, editor and president, 2000-. **Publications:** NONFICTION: The Insanity Defense and the Trial of John W. Hinckley, Jr., 1984; The Tenth Justice: The Solicitor General and the Rule of Law, 1987; An Open Adoption, 1990; Skadden: Power, Money, and the Rise of a Legal Empire, 1993; Up against the Law: Affirmative Action and the Supreme Court, 1997. Contributor to books. **Address:** Knight Senior Journalist, Yale Law School, Box 208215, New Haven, CT 06520-8215, U.S.A.

CAPLAN, Mariana. American, b. 1969. **Genres:** Human relations/Parenting, Self help. **Career:** Writer, family counselor, and professor in Berkeley, CA. **Publications:** When Sons and Daughters Choose Alternative Lifestyles, 1996; When Holidays Are Hell...! A Guide to Surviving Family Gatherings, 1997; Untouched: The Need for Genuine Affection in an Impersonal World, 1998; Half Way up the Mountain: Presuming Enlightenment before Its Time, 1999; To Touch Is to Live, 2nd ed., 2002; Do You Need a Guru?: Understanding the Student-Teacher Relationship in an Era of False Prophets, 2002. **Address:** 2305 Prince St, Berkeley, CA 94705, U.S.A. **Online address:** mariana@realspirituality.com

CAPLAN, Suzanne H. American, b. 1943. **Genres:** Business/Trade/Industry. **Career:** PGM Group, Pittsburgh, PA, principal, 1998-2001; Crossroads Associates, Pittsburgh, partner, 2001. **Publications:** Saving Your Business: How to Survive Chapter 11 Bankruptcy and Successfully Reorganize Your Company, 1992; A Piece of the Action: How Women and Minorities Can Launch Their Own Successful Business, 1992; Turn Your Business Around, 1992; Small Business Insiders Guide to Bankers, 1997; Streetwise Finance and Accounting, 2000; Streetwise Small Business Success Kit, 2001. **Address:** c/o Laurie Harper, Sebastian Literary Agency, 172 E 6th St, St. Paul, MN 55101, U.S.A. **Online address:** suzcaplan@aol.com

CAPOBIANCO, Michael Victor. American, b. 1950. **Genres:** Mathematics/Statistics, Science fiction/Fantasy. **Career:** Writer. Developer of computer simulations and game software. **Publications:** (ed. with J.B. Frechen and M. Krolik) Recent Trends in Graph Theory: Proceedings of the First NYC Graph Theory Conference Held on June 11, 12 and 13, 1970, 1971; (with J.C. Molluzzo) Examples and Counterexamples in Graph Theory, 1978; (ed.)

Graph Theory and Its Applications, East and West: Proceedings of the First China-USA International Graph Theory Conference, 1989. SCIENCE FICTION: Burster, 1990; (with W. Barton) Iris, 1990; (with Barton) Fellow Traveler: Sputnik Mira, 1991; (with Barton) Alpha Centauri, 1997; (with Barton) White Light, 1998. Co-author with William Barton of articles in periodicals covering planetology and space exploration. **Address:** Science Fiction and Fantasy Writers of America Inc., 532 La Guardia Place No. 632, New York, NY 10012, U.S.A. **Online address:** michaelc@thebee.net

CAPON, Robert Farrar. American, b. 1925. **Genres:** Novels, Human relations/Parenting, Theology/Religion. **Career:** Ordained Episcopal priest, 1949. All Soul's Church, Stony Brook, NY, vicar, 1949-58; Christ Church, Port Jefferson, NY, vicar, 1949-77; writer. George Mercer Jr., Memorial School of Theology, dean, professor of dogmatic theology, and instructor in Greek, 1957-77. **Publications:** Bed and Board: Plain Talk about Marriage, 1965; An Offering of Uncles: The Priesthood of Adam and the Shape of the World, 1967; The Supper of the Lamb: A Culinary Reflection, 1969, 2nd ed., 1989, in UK as Angels Must Eat: A Culinary Entertainment, 1969; The Third Peacock: The Goodness of God and the Badness of the World, 1971; Hunting the Divine Fox: Images and Mystery in Christian Faith, 1974; Exit 36: A Fictional Chronicle, 1975; Food for Thought: Resurrecting the Art of Eating, 1978; Party Spirit: Some Entertaining Principles, 1979; A Second Day: Reflections on Remarriage, 1980; Between Noon and Three: A Parable of Romance, Law, and the Outrage of Grace (novel), 1982; Capon on Cooking, 1983; The Youngest Day: Shelter Island's Seasons in the Light of Grace, 1983; The Parables of the Kingdom, 1985; The Parables of Grace, 1988; The Parables of Judgment, 1989; Health, Money, and Love-and Why We Don't Enjoy Them, 1990; The Man Who Met God in a Bar: The Gospel According to Marvin (novel), 1990; The Mystery of Christ, 1993; The Romance of the Word, 1995; The Astonished Heart, 1996; The Foolishness of Preaching, 1998; The Fingerprints of God, 2000; Genesis, the Movie, 2003. **Address:** c/o Publicity Dept, Eerdmans Publishing, 255 Jefferson SE, Grand Rapids, MI 49503, U.S.A.

CAPONIGRO, Jeffrey R. American, b. 1957. **Genres:** Administration/Management. **Career:** Casey Communications Management Inc., Southfield, MI, worked as president and chief executive officer, prior to 1995; Caponigro Public Relations Inc., Southfield, president and chief executive officer, 1995-. **Publications:** The Crisis Counselor: The Executive's Guide to Avoiding, Managing, and Thriving on Crises That Occur in All Businesses, 1998. Work represented in anthologies. **Address:** Caponigro Public Relations Inc., 4000 Town Center, Southfield, MI 48075, U.S.A. **Online address:** jcap@caponigro.com

CAPP, Bernard (Stuart). British, b. 1943. **Genres:** History, Literary criticism and history, Women's studies and issues, Biography. **Career:** University of Warwick, Coventry, assistant lecturer, 1968-70, lecturer, 1970-80, senior lecturer in history, 1980-90, reader in history, 1990-94, professor of history, 1994-, chairman of history department, 1992-95. Royal Historical Society, fellow. **Publications:** The Fifth Monarchy Men: A Study in Seventeenth-Century English Millenarianism, 1972; English Almanacs: 1500-1800: Astrology and the Popular Press, 1979; Cromwell's Navy: The Fleet and the English Revolution, 1648-1660, 1989; The World of John Taylor the Water Poet, 1578-1653, 1994; When Gossips Meet: Women, Family and Neighbourhood in Early Modern England, 2003. **Address:** Dept of History, University of Warwick, Coventry CV4 7AL, England. **Online address:** b.s.capp@warwick.ac.uk

CAPPEL, Carmen Bambach. *See* **BAMBACH, Carmen C.**

CAPPELLI, Peter. American, b. 1956. **Genres:** Business/Trade/Industry. **Career:** University of Pennsylvania, Philadelphia, professor of management, 1985-. **Publications:** Change at Work, 1997; The New Deal at Work, 1999. **Address:** Wharton School, University of Pennsylvania, Philadelphia, PA 19104, U.S.A. **Online address:** cappelli@wharton.upenn.edu

CAPUTI, Anthony. American, b. 1924. **Genres:** Literary criticism and history, Theatre, Novels. **Career:** Professor of English, Cornell University, Ithaca, New York, since 1969 (Assistant Professor, 1960-63; Associate Professor, 1964-69). **Publications:** John Marston: Satirist, 1961; Loving Evie (novel), 1974; Buffo: The Genius of Vulgar Comedy, 1978; Storms and Son (novel), 1985; Pirandello and the Crisis of Modern Consciousness, 1988. EDITOR: Norton Anthology of Modern Drama, 1966; Masterworks of World Drama, 6 vols., 1968; Eight Modern Plays, 1991. **Address:** Dept. of English Literature, Cornell University, Ithaca, NY 14853, U.S.A.

CAPUTO, Philip. American, b. 1941. **Genres:** Novels, Novellas/Short stories. **Career:** Promotional writer and member of staff of a house paper,

3-M Corp., Chicago, Illinois, 1968-69; local correspondent, Chicago Tribune, Chicago, 1969-72; correspondent in Rome, Beirut, Saigon, and Moscow, 1972-77; writer and lecturer. **Publications:** A Rumor of War, 1977, repr. with a 20th anniversary postscript by the author, 1996; Horn of Africa, 1980; Del-Corso's Gallery, 1983; Indian Country, 1987; Means of Escape, 1991; Equation for Evil, 1996; Exiles: Three Short Novels, 1997; The Voyage, 1999; Ghosts of Tsavo, 2002. **Address:** c/o Aaron Priest Literary Agency, 708 3rd Ave., New York, NY 10017, U.S.A.

CARABELLI, Giancarlo. Italian, b. 1939. **Genres:** Philosophy. **Career:** University of Ferrara, Ferrara, Italy, lecturer, 1973-82, professor of the history of philosophy, 1983-. **Publications:** Hume e la retorica dell'ideologia: Uno studio dei "Dialoghi sulla religione naturale," 1972; Tolandiana: Materiali bibliografici per lo studio dell'opera e della fortuna di John Toland, 1670-1722, 1975; Intorno a Hume, 1992, trans. by K. Hall as On Hume and Eighteenth-Century Aesthetics: The Philosopher on a Swing, 1995; In the Image of Priapus, 1996. **Address:** Istituto di discipline filosofiche, Via Savonarola 38, I-44100 Ferrara, Italy.

CARAHER, Kim(berley Elizabeth). Australian (born Northern Ireland), b. 1961. **Genres:** Children's fiction, Young adult fiction, Picture/board books. **Career:** Writer. Northern Territory Department of Education, Darwin, Australia, teacher, 1985-. Northern Territory University, lecturer in gifted education, 1993-2001. **Publications:** There's a Bat on the Balcony, 1993; My Teacher Turns into a Tyrannosaurus, 1996; Up a Gum Tree, 1997; The Cockroach Cup, 1998; Yucky Poo, 1998; Goanna Anna, 1999; Zip Zap, 2001; Kakadu Nightmare, 2001; Clinging to the Edge, 2003; Mark of the Beast, 2004. **Address:** c/o Debbie Golvan, Golvan Arts Management, PO Box 766, Kew, VIC 3101, Australia. **Online address:** caraher@bigpond.net.au

CARAVANTES, Peggy. American, b. 1935. **Genres:** Biography. **Career:** Worked as an English teacher in several Texas school districts, 1956-82; East Central Independent School District, San Antonio, TX, worked as an assistant principal, principal, curriculum director, and deputy superintendent for instruction and personnel, 1982-99. Educational consultant and workshop presenter. **Publications:** Petticoat Spies: Six Women Spies of the Civil War, 2002; Marcus Garvey: Black Visionary, 2003; O. Henry: William Sidney Porter: Texas Cowboy Writer, 2003; Sam Houston: No Ordinary Man, 2004. Contributor to series. **Address:** 2518 Silver Ridge, San Antonio, TX 78232, U.S.A. **Online address:** pcaravantes@satx.rr.com

CARBO, Nick. Filipino, b. 1964. **Genres:** Poetry. **Career:** Poet and teacher. Member of Asian American Writer's Workshop. **Publications:** El Grupo McDonald's (poems), 1995; (ed.) Returning A Borrowed Tongue: An Anthology of Contemporary Filipino and Filipino-American Poetry, 1996. Contributor to periodicals. **Address:** c/o Coffee House Press, 27 North 4th St. Suite 400, Minneapolis, MN 55401, U.S.A. **Online address:** bulaklak61@aol.com

CARBONE, Elisa Lynn. American. **Genres:** Children's fiction, Young adult fiction, Education. **Career:** Full-time writer; visiting author at public and private schools, libraries, and conferences, 1993-. **Publications:** My Dad's Definitely not a Drunk, 1992; Corey's Story: Her Family's Secret, 1997; Teaching Large Classes: Tools and Strategies, 1998; Starting School with an Enemy, 1998; Stealing Freedom, 1998; Sarah and the Naked Truth, 2000; Storm Warriors, 2001; The Pack, 2003. **Address:** c/o Crown & Knopf Books for Young Readers, 1745 Broadway 9th Fl, New York, NY 10019, U.S.A. **Online address:** elcarbone@earthlink.net

CARCATERRA, Lorenzo. American, b. 1954. **Genres:** Novels, Plays/Screenplays, Adult non-fiction, Documentaries/Reportage. **Career:** Cop Talk (syndicated), creative consultant, 1988; Top Cops (CBS), NYC, managing editor, 1990-94; Law & Order (NBC), producer/writer, 2003-. **Publications:** NONFICTION: A Safe Place, 1993; Sleepers, 1995. NOVELS: Apaches, 1997; Gangster, 2001; Street Boys, 2001, screenplay, 2002. SCREENPLAYS: Italian Dressing, 1994; Dreamer, 1996; Doubt, 1997. TELEPLAYS: The Hall (pilot), 1996; Ringers (pilot), 1998; The Force (pilot), 1999; Law & Order, 2002; Couples, 2002.

CARD, Orson Scott. American, b. 1951. **Genres:** Novels, Science fiction/Fantasy, Plays/Screenplays, Novellas/Short stories. **Career:** Volunteer Mormon missionary in Brazil, 1971-73; operated repertory theatre, Provo, Utah, 1974-75; Proofreader, 1974, and Ed., 1974-76, Brigham Young University Press, Provo, Utah; Ed., Ensign Magazine, Salt Lake City, 1976-78, and Compute Books, Greensboro NC, 1983. **Publications:** Listen, Mom and Dad, 1978; Capitol (short stories), 1978; Unaccompanied Sonata and Other Stories, 1981; Saintspeak, 1981; (ed) Dragons of Darkness, 1981;

Ainge, 1982; (ed) Dragons of Light, 1983; Saints (A Woman of Destiny) (novel), 1984; Seventh Son (novel), 1987; Red Prophet (novel), 1988; Character and Viewpoint, 1988; Prentice Alvin (novel), 1989; Maps in a Mirror (stories), 1990; Earthfall, 1994; Earthborn, 1995; Alvin Journeyman, 1995; Pastwatch, 1996; Children of the Mind, 1996; Treasure Box, 1996; Stone Tables, 1997; Homebody, 1998; Heart Fire, 1998; Enchantment, 1999; Ender's Shadow, 1999. SCIENCE FICTION: Hot Sleep, 1978; A Planet Called Treason, 1979; Songmaster, 1980; Hart's Hope, 1983; The Worthing Chronicle, 1983; Ender's Game, 1985; Speaker for the Dead, 1986; Wyrms, 1987; Folk of the Fringe, 1989; The Abyss, 1989; Worthing Saga, 1990. **Address:** c/o Barbara Bova Literary Agency, 3951 Gulf Shore Blvd N PH 1B, Naples, FL 34103-3639, U.S.A.

CARDINAL, Roger. British, b. 1940. **Genres:** Art/Art history, Literary criticism and history. **Career:** University of Manitoba, Winnipeg, lecturer in French, 1965-67; University of Warwick, Coventry, lecturer in French, 1967-68; University of Kent, Canterbury, lecturer in French, 1968-81, reader in comparative literature, 1981-87, professor of literary and visual studies, 1987-. **Publications:** (with R. Short) Surrealism: Permanent Revelation, 1970; Outsider Art, 1972; German Romantics, 1975; (ed.) Sensibility and Creation: Studies in Twentieth Century French Poetry, 1977; Primitive Painters, 1978; Figures of Reality: A Perspective on the Poetic Imagination, 1981; Expressionism, 1985; Andre Breton: Nadja, 1986; The Landscape Vision of Paul Nash, 1989; (ed. with J. Elsner) The Cultures of Collecting, 1994; (with J.F. Hernandez and J. Beardsley) A.G. Rizzoli: Architect of Magnificent Visions, 1997; (with J. Beardsley) Private Worlds, 1998; (ed. with M. Lusardy) Messages d'Outre-Monde, 1999; Henry Moore: In the Light of Greece, 2000; (with A. van Berkum, J. ten Berge, and C. Rhodes) Marginalia, 2001. **Address:** Rutherford College, University of Kent, Canterbury, Kent CT2 7NX, England. **Online address:** r.cardinal@ukc.ac.uk

CARDONA, Manuel. Spanish/American, b. 1934. **Genres:** Sciences, Physics. **Career:** Physicist. RCA Laboratories, Switzerland and New Jersey, 1959-64; Brown University, associate professor of physics, 1964-66, full professor, 196671; Max Planck Institute of Solid State Research, Stuttgart, Germany, director, 1971-. Editor of technical journals. Solid State Communications, editor-in-chief. **Publications:** Modulation Spectroscopy, 1965; (with P.Y. Yu) The Physics of Semiconductors, 1994; (with P.Y. Yu) Fundamentals of Semiconductors: Physics and Materials Properties, 1996, 3rd ed., 2001. EDITOR: Light Scattering in Solids, Vols 1-8, 1975-99; (and contrib., with L. Ley) Photoemission in Solids, I, II, 1978-79; (with G.R. Castro) Lectures on Surface Science, 1987; (with others) International Conference on Modulation Spectroscopy, 1990; (with F.A. Ponce) Surface Science: Lectures on Basic Concepts and Applications, 1991. Contributor to journals and periodicals. **Address:** Max Planck Institute of Solid State Research, 70569 Stuttgart, Germany. **Online address:** cardona@kmr.mpi-stuttgart.mpg.de

CAREW, Jan (Rynveld). Canadian (born Guyana), b. 1920. **Genres:** Novels, Novellas/Short stories, Children's fiction, Plays/Screenplays, Poetry, History. **Career:** Professor Emeritus, Dept. of African-American Studies, Northwestern University, Evanston, IL, 1987- (Professor, 1972-87). Co-Chairman, Third World Energy Institute, 1978-. Lecturer in Race Relations, University of London Extra-Mural Dept., 1953-57; Writer and Ed., BBC Overseas Service, London, 1954-65; Ed., African Review, Ghana, 1965-66; CBC Broadcaster, Toronto, 1966-69; Sr. Fellow, Council of Humanities, and Lecturer, Dept. of AfroAmerican Studies, Princeton University, 1969-72; visiting professor in Latin American and Caribbean Literature, Hampshire College, Amherst, MA, 1987-88; Visiting Clarence J. Robinson Professor, George Mason University, Fairfax, VA, 1989-91; Visiting Distinguished Professor and Director, Center for the Humanities, Lincoln University, PA, 1993-95; Liberal Studies Visiting Scholar in Pan African Studies, University of Louisville, 2000. **Publications:** Streets of Eternity (poetry), 1952; Black Midas (in U.S. as A Touch of Midas), 1958; The Wild Coast. 1958; The Last Barbarian, 1961; Green Winter, 1964: University of Hunger (play), 1966; The Third Gift (children's fiction), 1976; The Origins of Racism and Resistance in the Americas, 1978; Children of the Sun (children's fiction), 1980; Sea Drums in My Blood (poetry), 1983; Grenada: The Hour Will Strike Again (history), 1985; Fulcrums of Change (essays), 1987, Rape of Paradise, 1994; Ghosts in Our Blood, 1994. **Address:** 115 Brownlea Dr. Apt 20, Greenville, NC 27858-1625, U.S.A.

CAREW, Sir Rivers (Verain). British, b. 1935. **Genres:** Poetry. **Career:** Assistant Ed., Ireland of the Welcomes mag, Dublin, 1964-67; Joint Ed., The Dublin Magazine, 1964- 69; Sub-Ed., 1967-77, Deputy Chief Sub-Ed., 1977-82, and Chief Sub-Ed., 1982-87, Radio Telefis Eireann, Dublin; Chief Sub-Ed., BBC World Service, 1987-93. **Publications:** (with T. Brownlow) Figures out of Mist, 1966. **Address:** Cherry Bounds, Hicks Lane, Girton, Cambs. CB3 0JS, England.

CAREY, Ernestine Gilbreth. American, b. 1908. **Genres:** Novels, Children's fiction, Autobiography/Memoirs, Biography. **Career:** R.H. Macy & Co., NYC, buyer, 1930-44; James Mccreery, NYC, buyer, 1947-49; lecturer, book reviewer, 1949-. **Publications:** (with F.B. Gilbreth) Cheaper by the Dozen, 1949; (with F.B. Gilbreth) Belles on Their Toes, 1951; Jumping Jupiter, 1952; Rings around Us, 1956; Giddy Moment, 1958. **Address:** 703 W Herbert Ave, Reedley, CA 93654-3941, U.S.A. **Online address:** erngilcarey@onemain.com

CAREY, George Wescott. American, b. 1933. **Genres:** Politics/Government. **Career:** Georgetown University, Washington, DC, professor of government. Political Science Reviewer, editor, 1973-. **Publications:** (with W. Kendall) The Basic Symbols of the American Political Tradition, 1970, 2nd ed., 1995; In Defense of the Constitution, 1989, rev. ed., 1995; The Federalist: Design for a Constitutional Republic, 1989. EDITOR: (with G.J. Graham Jr.) The Post-Behavioral Era: Perspectives on Political Science, 1972; (with J.V. Schall) Essays on Christianity and Political Philosophy, 1984; Freedom and Virtue: The Conservative/Libertarian Debate, 1984, rev. ed., 1998; Order, Freedom, and the Polity: Critical Essays on the Open Society, 1986; (with J. McClellan) The Federalist, 1990, Gideon ed., 2001; (with B. Frohnen) Community and Tradition: Conservative Perspectives on the American Experience, 1998; The Political Writings of John Adams, 2000. OTHER: (selector with C.S. Hyneman) A Second Federalist: Congress Creates a Government (selections from the Annals of Congress), 1967. Contributor to books. **Address:** Government Department, Georgetown University, Washington, DC 20057, U.S.A. **Online address:** careygw@georgetown.edu

CAREY, Jacqueline. American, b. 1954. **Genres:** Novels, Novellas/Short stories. **Career:** Freelance writer. **Publications:** Good Gossip (stories), 1992; The Other Family (novel), 1996; Wedding Pictures, 1997; The Crossley Baby (novel), 2003. **Address:** 318 Grove St, Montclair, NJ 07042-4209, U.S.A.

CAREY, Jacqueline. American, b. 1964. **Genres:** Science fiction/Fantasy. **Career:** Writer. **Publications:** Angels: Celestial Spirits in Art and Legend, 1997. NOVELS: Kushiel's Dart, 2001; Kushiel's Chosen, 2002; Kushiel's Avatar, 2003. Contributor of short stories, essays, articles and reviews to periodicals. **Address:** c/o Jane Dystel Literary Management, One Union Square West, Suite 904, New York, NY 10003, U.S.A. **Online address:** Contact@jacquelinecarey.com

CAREY, John. British, b. 1934. **Genres:** Literary criticism and history. **Career:** Oxford University, Lecturer, Christ Church, 1958-59, Tutorial Fellow, Keble Coll., 1960-64, and St. John's Coll., 1964-75, Merton Professor of English Literature, 1976-2001. **Publications:** Milton, 1969; The Violent Effigy: A Study of Dickens' Imagination, 1971, 2nd ed., 1991; Thackeray: Prodigal Genius, 1977; John Donne: Life, Mind, and Art, 1981 2nd ed., 1990; Original Copy: Selected Reviews and Journalism, 1987; The Intellectuals and the Masses, 1992; Pure Pleasure, 2000. EDITOR: (with A. Fowler) Poems of John Milton, 1968, 2nd ed., 1997; The Private Memoirs and Confessions of a Justified Sinner, by J. Hogg, 1969; William Golding: The Man and His Books, 1987; The Faber Book of Reportage, 1987; The Faber Book of Science, 1995; The Faber Book of Utopias, 1999. **Address:** 57 Stapleton Rd, Headington, Oxford, England. **Online address:** jcarey00@supanet.com

CAREY, Lisa. American. **Genres:** Novels. **Career:** Brookline Booksmith, Brookline, MA, sales clerk. **Publications:** The Mermaids Singing, 1998. **Address:** c/o Avon Books, 1350 Avenue of the Americas, New York, NY 10019, U.S.A.

CAREY, Patrick W. American, b. 1940. **Genres:** Theology/Religion, History. **Career:** St. Peter's College, Jersey City, NJ, assistant professor of theology, 1975-76; Elizabeth Seton College, assistant professor, 1976; Carleton College, Northfield, MN, assistant professor of theology, 1976-77; Gustavus Adolphus College, St. Peter, MN, assistant professor of theology, 1977-78; Marquette University, Milwaukee, WI, assistant professor, 1978-83, associate professor of religious studies, 1984-, department head, 1991-. **Publications:** Altogether: A Parish Family, 1974; An Immigrant Bishop: John England's Adaptation of Irish Catholicism to American Republicanism, 1982; People, Priests, and Prelates: Ecclesiastical Democracy and the Tensions of Trusteeism, 1987; (ed.) American Catholic Religious Thought, 1987; (ed.) Orestes A. Brownson: Selected Writings, 1991; The Roman Catholics, 1993, republished as The Roman Catholics in America, 1994. Work represented in anthologies. Contributor to history and religious studies journals. **Address:** Department of Theology, 100 Coughlin Hall, Marquette University, Milwaukee, WI 53233, U.S.A.

CAREY, Peter. Australian, b. 1943. **Genres:** Novels, Novellas/Short stories. **Career:** New York University and Princeton University, writing instructor; worked part time in advertising in Australia, 1962-88; full-time writer, currently. **Publications:** STORIES: The Fat Man in History, 1974, in U.K. as Exotic Pleasures, 1981; War Crimes, 1979. NOVELS: Bliss, 1981, as film, 1985; Illywhacker, 1985; Oscar and Lucinda (Booker Prize), 1988; The Tax Inspector, 1991; The Unusual Life of Tristan Smith, 1995; Jack Maggs, 1998; True History of the Kelly Gang, 2000 (Booker Prize, 2001); My Life as a Fake, 2003. OTHER: 30 Days in Sydney, 2001; Wrong about Japan, 2005. **Address:** c/o Amanda Urban, International Creative Management, 40 W 57th St, New York, NY 10019, U.S.A.

CAREY OF CLIFTON, Lord. (George (Leonard) Carey). British, b. 1935. **Genres:** Inspirational/Motivational Literature, Theology/Religion. **Career:** Worked for the London Electricity Board, c. 1950s; ordained as a deacon, 1962; St. Mary's Islington, London, assistant curate, 1962-66; Oak Hill Theological College, Southgate, England, lecturer, 1966-70; St. John's Theological College, Nottingham, England, lecturer and chaplain, 1970-75; St. Nicholas' Church, Durham, England, vicar, 1975-82; Trinity College, Bristol, England, principal, 1982-87; Bishop of Bath and Wells, 1987-91; archbishop of Canterbury, 1991-2002; life peer, 2002. **Publications:** NONFICTION: I Believe in Man, 1975; God Incarnate, 1976; (with others) The Great Acquittal, 1980; The Church in the Marketplace, 1984; The Meeting of the Waters, 1985; The Gate of Glory, 1986; The Message of the Bible, 1986, in US as The Bible for Everyday Life, 1996; The Great God Robbery, 1989; I Believe, 1991; The Charter for the Church: Sharing a Vision for the Twenty-first Century, 1993, in UK as Sharing a Vision, 1993; Spiritual Journey, 1994; My Journey, Your Journey, 1996; Canterbury Letters to the Future, 1998. Contributor of articles and essays to periodicals. **Address:** House of Lords, Westminster, London SW1A, England.

CARIN, Michael. Canadian, b. 1951. **Genres:** Novels. **Career:** Montreal Business Magazine, editor, 1994-. **Publications:** NOVELS: Five Hundred Keys, 1980; The Neutron Picasso, 1989. **Address:** 3475 St. Urbain No. 1402, Montreal, QC, Canada H2X 2N4. **Online address:** MHCarin@aol.com

CARKEET, David. American, b. 1946. **Genres:** Novels. **Career:** University of Missouri, St. Louis, Dept. of English, professor, 1973-. **Publications:** Double Negative, 1980; The Greatest Slump of All Time, 1984; I Been There Before, 1985; The Silent Treatment, 1988; The Full Catastrophe, 1990; Quiver River, 1991; The Error of Our Ways, 1997. **Address:** 418 Macey Rd., North Middlesex, VT 05682, U.S.A. **Online address:** carkeet@umsl.edu

CARL, JoAnna. See SANDSTROM, Eve K.

CARLE, Eric. American, b. 1929. **Genres:** Children's fiction, Children's non-fiction, Autobiography/Memoirs, Essays, Illustrations. **Career:** Freelance writer, illustrator and designer, 1963-. U.S. Information Ctr., Stuttgart, poster designer, 1950-52; New York Times, graphic designer, 1954-56; L. W. Frohlick and Co., NYC, art director, 1956-63; Pratt Institute, Brooklyn, guest instructor, 1964. **Publications:** Gravity at Work and Play, 1963; If You Can Count to 10, 1964; Red-Flannel Hash and Shoo-Fly Pie: American Regional Foods and Festivals, 1965; The Indoor & Outdoor Grow-It Book, 1966; The Say-with-Me ABC Book, 1967; In Search of Meaning, 1968; 1,2,3, to the Zoo, 1969; The Very Hungry Caterpillar, 1969; Pancakes, Pancakes!, 1970; The Boastful Fisherman, 1970; Tales of the Nimipoo from the Land of the Nez Perce Indians, 1970; The Tiny Seed, 1970, in U.K. as The Tiny Seed and the Giant Flower, 1970; Feathered Ones and Furry, 1971; The Scarecrow Clock, 1971; Do You Want to Be My Friend?, 1971; The Rooster Who Set Out to See the World, 1972, in U.K. as Rooster's Off to See the World, 1988; The Secret Birthday Message, 1972; The Very Long Tail, 1972; The Very Long Train, 1972; Walter the Baker, 1972; Have You Seen My Cat?, 1973, 1987; I See a Song, 1973; Do Bears Have Mothers, Too?, 1973; The Hole in the Dike, 1974; Why Noah Chose the Dove, 1974; All about Arthur (An Absolutely Absurd Ape), 1975; My Very First Library, includes, My Very First Book of Colors (Numbers, Shapes, Words, Food, Growth, Heads and Tails, Homes, Motion, Sounds, Tools, Touch), 12 vols., 1974, reprinted as My Very First Book of Colors (Numbers, Shapes, Words), 1986; The Mixed-Up Chameleon, 1975, 1985; Storybook: 7 Tales by the Brothers Grimm, 1976; The Grouchy Ladybug, 1977, in U.K. as The Bad-Tempered Ladybird, 1978; Watch Out! A Giant!, 1978; Seven Stories by Hans Christian Andersen, 1978; 12Tales from Aesop, 1980; The Honeybee and the Robber, 1981; Otter Nonsense, 1982; Catch the Ball!, 1982; Let's Paint a Rainbow, 1982; What's for Lunch?, 1982; The Very Busy Spider, 1984; The Foolish Tortoise, 1985; The Mountain That Loved a Bird, 1985; All around Us, 1986; Papa, Please Get the Moon for Me, 1986; A House for Hermit Crab,

1987; The Greedy Python & the Foolish Tortoise, 1987; Eric Carle's Fairy Tales and Fables, 1988; The Lamb and the Butterfly, 1988; (ed.) Treasury of Classic Stories for Children, 1988; Chip Has Many Brothers, 1989; Animals, Animals, 1989; The Very Quiet Cricket, 1990; Dragons, Dragons & Other Creatures That Never Were, 1991; (with B. Martin Jr.) Polar Bear, Polar Bear, 1991; (with B. Martin Jr.) Brown Bear, Brown Bear, What Do You See?, 1992; Draw Me a Star, 1992; Today Is Monday, 1993; My Apron, 1994; The Very Lonely Firefly, 1995; Little Cloud, 1996; The Art of Eric Carle (autobiography/essays), 1996; The Magical Papers of Eric Carle, 1997; From Head to Toe, 1997; Flora and Tiger, 1997; Hello, Red Fox, 1998; You Can Make a Collage, 1998; The Very Clumsy Click Beetle, 1999; Does a Kangaroo Have a Mother Too, 2000; Dream Snow, 2000; Oz: The 100th Anniversary Celebration, 2000; Slowly, Slowly, Slowly Said the Sloth, 2002; (with K. Iwamura) Where Are You Going? To See My Friend, 2003; (with B. Martin Jr.) Panda Bear, Panda Bear, What Do You See?, 2003; Mister Seahorse, 2004; 10 Little Rubber Ducks, 2005. Illustrator of books by N. Juster, B. Martin Jr., I.B. Singer. **Address:** PO Box 485, Northampton, MA 01060, U.S.A. **Online address:** www.eric-carle.com

CARLEBACH, Michael L(loyd). American, b. 1945. **Genres:** Photography. **Career:** Miami Herald, Miami, FL, staff photographer, 1969; Village Post, staff photographer, 1969-72; University of Miami, Coral Gables, FL, instructor, 1973-78, assistant professor, 1980-83, 1985-87, associate professor of photography, 1987-93, professor, 1993-, coordinator of Photography Sequence. U.S. Environmental Protection Agency, photographer for Project Documerica, 1973; U.S. State Department, documentary photographer for Cuban-Haitian Task Force, 1980; free-lance photographer, with group and solo exhibitions in the United States and abroad. Miami Dade Community College, guest curator at Wolfson Campus, 1986. **Publications:** (photographer) Arlene Brett and Eugene F. Provenzo Jr., The Complete Block Book, 1983; The Origins of Photojournalism in America, 1992; (with E. Provenzo) Farm Security Administration Photographs of Florida, 1993; (photographer) Arlene Brett, Robin Moore, and Eugene F. Provenzo Jr., The Complete Playground Book, 1993; American Photojournalism Comes of Age, 1997; This Way to the Crypt, 1998; Working Stiffs: Occupational Portraits in the Age of the Tintype, 2002. Contributor of articles and photographs to periodicals. **Address:** PO Box 248106, Dept of Art and Art History, University of Miami, Coral Gables, FL 33124, U.S.A. **Online address:** mcarleba@miami.edu

CARLEON, A. See O'GRADY, Rohan.

CARLESS, Jennifer. American, b. 1960. **Genres:** Environmental sciences/ Ecology. **Career:** Manager of research support for a consulting firm that specialized in strategic political and defense analyses, Monterey, CA, 1983-85; manager of European agents for a U.S. online information service, London, England, 1986-87; freelance technical writer of software users manuals, London, 1987-88; office manager and attorney's assistant for a law firm specializing in business litigation, contract law, and creditor bankruptcy work, Santa Cruz, CA, 1992-. **Publications:** Taking out the Trash: A No-Nonsense Guide to Recycling, 1992; Renewable Energy: A Concise Guide to Green Alternatives, 1993. **Address:** P.O. Box 7616, Santa Cruz, CA 95061-7616, U.S.A.

CARLEY, Lionel (Kenneth). British, b. 1936. **Genres:** Poetry, Music, Biography. **Career:** Teacher, lecturer, broadcaster, and translator in Stockholm, Sweden, 1962-63; government service, London, England, 1964-92. Freelance writer and lecturer, 1993-; Delius Trust, honorary archivist, 1965-, adviser, 1991-. **Publications:** Delius: The Paris Years, 1975; Night Watch (poems), 1976; (with R. Threlfall) Delius: A Life in Pictures, 1977; Delius: A Life in Letters, 1862-1908, 1983; Delius: A Life in Letters, 1909-1934, 1988; Grieg and Delius: Their Friendship and Their Correspondence, 1993; Frederick Delius: Music, Art and Literature, 1998; Edvard Grieg in England, 2005. Contributor to books.

CARLIN, Martha. American. **Genres:** Food and Wine, History, Technology, Reference. **Career:** Historian and writer. University of Wisconsin at Milwaukee, assistant professor, 1990-95, associate professor of history, 1995-, director of graduate studies, 1996-. **Publications:** Medieval Southwark (monograph), 1996; London and Southwark Inventories, 1316-1650: A Handlist of Extents for Debts (reference), 1997; (ed. with J.T. Rosenthal) Food and Eating in Medieval Europe, 1998. **Address:** Department of History, University of Wisconsin at Milwaukee, PO Box 413, Milwaukee, WI 53201, U.S.A.

CARLIN, Vivian F. American, b. 1919. **Genres:** Gerontology/Senior issues. **Career:** Clinical psychologist, 1940-45; vocational counselor, 1945-52; New Jersey State Division on Aging, Trenton, supervisor, 1969-84; self-employed consultant in gerontology, 1984-; writer. Past member of board of directors of Princeton Community Housing, Inc. New Jersey staff coordinator for 1981 White House Conference on Aging. **Publications:** (with R. Mansberg) If I Live to Be 100: Congregate Housing for Later Life, 1984, 2nd ed, 1989; (with Mansberg) Where Can Mom Live? A Family Guide to Living Arrangements for Older Parents, 1987; Can Mom Live Alone? A Family Guide to Helping Older People Stay in Their Own Homes, 1991; (with V. Greenberg) Should Mom Live with Us? And is Happiness Possible if She Does?, 1992. **Address:** 290 E. Winchester Ave. #409, Langhorne, PA 19047, U.S.A.

CARLING, Alan H(ugh). British, b. 1949. **Genres:** Social sciences. **Career:** University of Bradford, Bradford, England, senior lecturer, 1976-, association of university teachers, local president, 1992-94, 1995-97. **Publications:** Social Division, 1991. Contributor to periodicals. **Address:** Department of Interdisciplinary Human Studies, University of Bradford, Bradford, W. Yorkshire BD7 1DP, England.

CARLING, Paul J. American, b. 1945. **Genres:** Medicine/Health, Psychology, Public/Social administration, Self help, Theology/Religion. **Career:** American Friends Service Committee, NYC, projects director, 1966-68; Fellowship House Farm, Pottstown, PA, farm manager, 1968-69; Carling & Keitt, Philadelphia, PA, partner, contractor and carpenter, 1970-72; St. Joseph's College, Philadelphia, psychology intern at Counseling Center, 1973-74; Horizon House, Philadelphia, director of program development, director of residential services and intern, 1974-78; New Jersey Division of Mental Health and Hospitals, Trenton, chief of Bureau of Housing Policy and Development and acting chief of Bureau of Transitional Services, 1978-79; National Institute of Mental Health, Rockville, MD, special assistant to the director for mental health services, 1979-81; Vermont Department of Mental Health, Waterbury, deputy commissioner, 1981-83; University of Vermont, Burlington, research and clinical associate professor of psychology, 1982- and consultant to Behavior Therapy and Psychotherapy Center. University of Pennsylvania, lecturer, 1972-75; Boston University, research associate professor and director of community residential rehabilitation project at Center for Psychiatric Rehabilitation, 1984-87; Center for Community Change through Housing and Support, executive director, 1987-99; Trinity College of Vermont, professor and director of Graduate Program in Community Mental Health, 1993-99; consultant to federal, state and local mental health organizations, 1984-. Guest on television programs; testified before the U.S. Senate and several state legislatures. **Publications:** (ed. with J.W. Jacobson and S.N. Burchard) Community Living for People with Developmental and Psychiatric Disabilities, 1992; Return to Community: Building Support Systems for People with Psychiatric Disabilities, 1995. Contributor to books and professional journals. **Address:** 31 Vermont Ave, Brattleboro, VT 05301-6014, U.S.A. **Online address:** paul.carling@att.net

CARLISLE, Carris. See PEMBERTON, Margaret.

CARLISLE, Donna. See BALL, Donna.

CARLS, Stephen D(ouglas). American, b. 1944. **Genres:** History. **Career:** University of Minnesota, Minneapolis, MN, teaching assistant, 1970-71; Sterling College, Sterling, KS, assistant professor, 1971-81, associate professor, 1981-83; Union University, Jackson, TN, associate professor, 1983-90, professor, 1990-2000, chair of Department of History and Political Science, 1990-, university professor, 2000-. **Publications:** Louis Loucheur and the Shaping of Modern France, 1916-1931, 1993; Louis Loucheur: Ingenieur, homme d'etat, modernisateur de la France, 1872-1931, 2000. Contributor of book reviews. **Address:** Dept of History, Union University, 1050 Union University Dr, Jackson, TN 38305-3697, U.S.A. **Online address:** scarls@uu.edu

CARLSEN, Chris. See HOLDSTOCK, Robert.

CARLSON, Andrew R. American, b. 1934. **Genres:** Novels, History. **Career:** Archivist, Kalamazoo, Michigan, since 1976. Adjunct Professor of History, Western Michigan University, Kalamazoo, since 1990. Member of faculty, Michigan State University, East Lansing, 1964-65, Professor of Social Science, Eastern Kentucky University, Richmond, 1967-70, Ferris State Coll., Michigan, 1970-73, and Western Michigan University, 1974-75. **Publications:** German Foreign Policy 1890-1914, and Colonial Policy to 1914, 1970; Anarchism in Germany: The Early Years, 1972; Bulow, Holstein, Wilhelm II and the Daily Telegraph Affair, 1974; Can Life Begin Again (novel), 1982. Many reviews, chapters, and articles. **Address:** 968 124th St, Shelbyville, MI 49344, U.S.A. **Online address:** andrew.carlson@wmich.edu

CARLSON, Bernice Wells. American, b. 1910. **Genres:** Children's fiction, Children's non-fiction. **Publications:** Junior Party Book, 1939, rev. ed. 1948; Make It Yourself, 1950; Do It Yourself, 1952; Fun for One or Two, 1954; Act It Out, 1956; Make It and Use It, 1958; The Right Play for You, 1960; (with K. Hunt) Masks and Mask Makers, 1962; (with D. Ginglend) Play Activities for the Retarded Child, 1963; The Party Book for Boys and Girls, 1963; Listen and Help Tell the Story, 1965; (with C. W. Carlson) Water Fit to Use, 1966, 1972; You Know What? I Like Animals, 1967; (with D. Ginglend) Recreation for Retarded Teenagers and Young Adults, 1968; Play a Part, 1970; (with R. Wigg) We Want Sunshine in Our Houses, 1973; Let's Pretend it Happened to You, 1973; Funny-Bone Dramatics, 1974; Picture That!, 1978; (with D. Ginglend) Ready to Work?, 1978; Quick Wits and Nimble Fingers, 1979; Let's Find the Big Idea, 1982; My Very Own Pet, 1990; The Witch On A Windy Night, 1994. **Address:** 334 Skillmans Lane, Somerset, NJ 08873, U.S.A.

CARLSON, Joan. *See* **CHAPMAN, J. Dudley.**

CARLSON, Keith Thor. Canadian, b. 1966. **Genres:** Cultural/Ethnic topics, History. **Career:** Sto:lo Nation, Chilliwack, BC, Canada, historian, 1992-2001; University of Saskatchewan, Saskatoon, professor of history, 2001-. **Publications:** Twisted Road to Freedom, 1995; You Are Asked to Witness, 1997; I Am Sto:lo (juvenile nonfiction), 1998; A Sto:lo-Coast Salish Historical Atlas, 2001. **Address:** Dept of History, University of Saskatchewan, 9 Campus Dr, Saskatoon, SK, Canada S7N 5A5. **Online address:** keith. carlson@usask.ca

CARLSON, Laurie. American, b. 1952. **Genres:** Children's non-fiction, History. **Career:** High school home economics teacher in Deary, ID, 1976-77; artist and sculptor, with art work and sculptured dolls exhibited in galleries, 1977-86; elementary schoolteacher in Mesa, AZ, 1988-92. **Publications:** Home Study Opportunities: A Complete Guide to Going to School by Mail, 1989; Kids Create! (juvenile), 1990; Eco Art! Earth-Friendly Art and Craft Experiences for Three-to-Nine-Year-Olds, 1993; More Than Moccasins, 1994; Huzzah! Means Hooray!, 1994; Green Thumbs, 1995; (with J. Dammel) Kids Camp!, 1995; Westward Ho!, 1996; Colonial Kids!, 1997; Boss of the Plains: The Story of the Cowboy Hat, 1998; Classical Kids: An Activity Guide to Ancient Greece & Rome, 1989; On Sidesaddles to Heaven: The Women of the Rocky Mountain Mission, 1998; Fits & Fevers: Salem's Witches and the Forgotten Epidemic, 1999; Cattle: An Informal Social History, 2001; Seduced by the West: Jefferson's America and the Lure of the Spanish West, 2003; Queen of Inventions: How the Sewing Machine Changed the World, 2003. Contributor to periodicals. **Address:** 16502 W Stoughton Rd, Cheney, WA 99004-9616, U.S.A. **Online address:** lwcarls@tincan. tincan.org

CARLSON, Lori Marie. American, b. 1957. **Genres:** Picture/board books, Novels. **Career:** Writer. **Publications:** PICTURE BOOKS: Sol a Sol, 1998; Hurray for Three Kings Day!, 1999. NOVELS: The Sunday Tertulia, 2000; The Flamboyant, 2002. EDITOR: (with others) Where Angels Glide at Dawn: New Stories from Latin America (young adult), 1990; (with others) Return Trip Tango and Other Stories from Abroad, 1992; Cool Salsa: Bilingual Poems on Growing up Latino in the U.S. (young adult), 1994; American Eyes: New Asian American Short Stories for Young Adults, 1994; (and author of intro.) Barrio Streets, Carnival Dreams: Three Generations of Latino Artistry (young adult), 1996; You're On!: Seven Bilingual Plays (juvenile), 1999; Red Hot Salsa, 2005; Moccasin Thunder: American Indian Stories for Today, 2005. **Address:** c/o Jennifer Lyons, Writers House Inc., 21 W 26th St, New York, NY 10010, U.S.A.

CARLSON, Richard A. American, b. 1956. **Genres:** Psychology. **Career:** University of Illinois at Urbana-Champaign, research assistant, 1981-82, 1983-84, instructor in cognitive psychology, 1982, 1983, associate director of Human Attention Research Laboratory, 1984-85; Pennsylvania State University, University Park, assistant professor, 1985-91, associate professor, 1991-97, professor of psychology, 1997-, director of undergraduate studies in psychology, 1995-. **Publications:** Experienced Cognition, 1997. Contributor of articles and reviews to scholarly journals. **Address:** Department of Psychology, 613 Moore Bldg., Pennsylvania State University, University Park, PA 16802, U.S.A. **Online address:** racarlson@psu.edu

CARLSON, Richard C. American, b. 1942. **Genres:** Politics/Government, Social commentary. **Career:** U.S. Office of Management and the Budget, Washington, DC, budget analyst, 1965-69; Illinois Bureau of the Budget, assistant director, 1971-73; SRI International, Menlo Park, CA, senior regional economist, 1976-84; QED Research Inc., Palo Alto, CA, vice president and principal, 1984-88; Spectrum Economics Inc., Palo Alto, president, 1988-92,

chairperson, 1992-. **Publications:** Energy Future: Human Values and Lifestyles (future studies), 1982; 2020 Visions (future studies), 1991; I'll Surely Pay You Tuesday: Issues and Candidates in the 1992 Election (politics), 1992; (Coauthor) Fast Forward (future studies), 1994. **Address:** Spectrum Economics Inc., 201 San Antonio Cir Ste 105, Mountain View, CA 94040-1252, U.S.A. **Online address:** rccarl@sjm.inti.net

CARLSON, Ron. American, b. 1934. **Genres:** Criminology/True Crime, Law. **Career:** Fuller E. Callaway Professor of Law, University of Georgia, Athens, 1984-. Professor of Law, University of Iowa, Iowa City, 1965-73; Professor of Law, Washington University, St. Louis, Missouri, 1973-84. **Publications:** Criminal Justice Procedure, 1970, 6th ed., 1999; Criminal Law Advocacy, 1982; Successful Techniques for Civil Trials, 2nd ed., 1992; Adjudication of Criminal Justice, 1986; Materials for the Study of Evidence, 1986; Dynamics of Trial Practice, 1989, rev. ed., 2002; (with M. Bright) Objections at Trial: A Concise Guide, 1990, rev. ed., 2002; Evidence in the Nineties, 1991; Trial Handbook for Georgia Lawyers, 1993; (with E. Imwinkelried, E. Kionka, and K. Strachan) Evidence: Teaching Materials for an Age of Science and Statutes, 2002. **Address:** University of Georgia, School of Law, Athens, GA 30602, U.S.A. **Online address:** mlfield@arches.uga.edu

CARLSON, Ron. American, b. 1947. **Genres:** Novels, Novellas/Short stories. **Career:** Arizona State University, Tempe, asst. professor, 1986-88, assoc. professor, 1988-92, professor, 1992. Participant, Artist in the Schools for Utah, Idaho, and Alaska arts councils. English teacher, Hotchkiss School, Lakeville, CT, 1971-81. **Publications:** NOVELS: Betrayed by F. Scott Fitzgerald, 1977; Truants, 1981; The Speed of Light, 2003. STORIES: The News of the World, 1987; Plan B for the Middle Class, 1992; The Hotel Eden, 1997; At the Jim Bridger, 2002; A Kind of Flying, 2003. **Address:** c/o English Dept, Arizona State University, Tempe, AZ 85287, U.S.A. **Online address:** ron.carlson@asu.edu

CARLTON, David. British, b. 1938. **Genres:** History, International relations/Current affairs, Military/Defense/Arms control. **Career:** London Metropolitan University, formerly sr. lecturer in diplomatic history; University of Warwick, senior lecturer in international studies. **Publications:** MacDonald versus Henderson: The Foreign Policy of the Second Labour Government, 1970; Anthony Eden: A Biography, 1981; Britain and the Suez Crisis, 1988; Churchill and the Soviet Union, 2000. CO-EDITOR: The Dynamics of the Arms Race, 1975; International Terrorism and World Security, 1975; Arms Control and Technological Innovation, 1977; Terrorism: Theory and Practice, 1979; Contemporary Terror, 1981; The Hazards of the International Energy Crisis, 1982; The Arms Race in the 1980s, 1982; SouthEastern Europe after Tito, 1983; Reassessing Arms Control, 1984; The Nuclear Arms Race Debated, 1986; The Cold War Debated, 1988; The Arms Race in the Era of Star Wars, 1988; New Technologies and the Arms Race, 1989; Perspectives on the Arms Race, 1989; The Arms Race in an Era of Negotiations, 1991; Reducing Nuclear Arsenals, 1991; Space and Nuclear Weaponry, 1992; Controlling the International Transfer of Weaponry and Related Technology, 1995; Rising Tension in Eastern Europe and the Former Soviet Union, 1996; The Search for Stability in Russia and the Former Soviet Bloc, 1997. **Address:** University of Warwick, Coventry CV4 7AL, England. **Online address:** d.carlton@btconnect.com

CARLTON, Jim. American, b. 1955. **Genres:** Documentaries/Reportage. **Career:** West Coast technology reporter for the Wall Street Journal. **Publications:** Apple: The Intrigue, Egomania, and Business Blunders that Toppled an American Icon, 1997. **Address:** c/o Random House, 1745 Broadway 18th Fl, New York, NY 10019, U.S.A.

CARMICHAEL, Clair. *See* **MCNAB, Claire.**

CARMICHAEL, Joel. American, b. 1915. **Genres:** History, Biography, Translations. **Career:** Ed., Weizmann Letters and Papers, 1968-71, and Midstream mag., NYC, 1975-97. **Publications:** (ed. and trans.) The Russian Revolution 1917: A Personal Record by N. Sukhanov, 1955; (trans.) Anna Karenina by Tolstoy, 1962; The Death of Jesus, 1962; An Illustrated History of Russia, 1963; Karl Marx: The Passionate Logician, 1964; A Short History of the Russian Revolution, 1965; A Cultural History of Russia, 1966; The Shaping of the Arabs, 1967; Trotsky, 1975; Stalin's Masterpiece, 1976; Stehe auf und Rufe Deinen Herrn, 1982; The Birth of Christianity: Reality and Myth, 1989; A History of Russia, 1990; The Satanizing of the Jews, 1992; The Unriddling of Christian Origins, A Secular Account, 1995. **Address:** 302 W. 86th St, New York, NY 10024, U.S.A.

CARNALL, Geoffrey Douglas. British, b. 1927. **Genres:** Literary criticism and history, Biography. **Career:** Honorary Fellow, 1994-, University of Edinburgh (Lecturer, 1960-65; Sr. Lecturer, 1965-69; Reader in English Literature 1969-94). Lecturer in English, Queen's University, Belfast, 1952-60. **Publications:** Robert Southey and His Age: The Development of a Conservative Mind, 1960; Robert Southey, 1964, rev. ed., 1971; To Keep the Peace: The United Nations Peace Force, 1965; (with J. Butt) The Mid-Eighteenth Century, 1979 (as The Age of Johnson, 1990). EDITOR: J. Butt Pope, Dickens, and Others: Essays and Addresses, 1969; (with C. Nicholson) The Impeachment of Warren Hastings, 1989; M. Sykes, An Indian Tapestry: Quaker Threads in the History of India, Pakistan and Bangladesh, 1997. **Address:** School of Literatures, Languages & Cultures, David Hume Tower, George Sq, Edinburgh EH8 9JX, Scotland.

CARNEY, Judith A(nn). American. **Genres:** Anthropology/Ethnology. **Career:** University of California, Los Angeles, CA, professor of geography. **Publications:** Triticale Production in the Central Mexican Highlands: Smallholders' Experiences and Lessons for Research, 1990; Black Rice: The African Origins of Rice Cultivation in the Americas, 2001. **Address:** Department of Geography, University of California Los Angeles, 405 Hilgard Avenue, Los Angeles, CA 90024, U.S.A. **Online address:** carney@geog.ucla.edu

CARNEY, Pat. Canadian (born China), b. 1935. **Genres:** Autobiography/Memoirs. **Career:** Journalist and economic consultant in British Columbia, Canada; Elected to the Canadian House of Commons, February, 1980, from Vancouver's Centre district; served as Opposition Critic in House of Commons for Energy, Mines, Resources cabinet, Finance cabinet, and Secretary of State, 1980-84; appointed Minister of Energy, Mines, and Resources by Prime Minister Brian Mulroney, 1984, Minister of International Trade, and President of Treasury Board, until 1988; appointed to Senate of Canada, 1990. Also member of Cabinet Committee on Priorities and Planning; minister for Asia Pacific Initiative; University of British Columbia, School of Community and Regional Planning, adjunct professor, 1990-99; author. **Publications:** Trade Secrets: A Memoir, 2000. Contributor to Canadian newspapers and magazines. **Address:** Box 101, Saturna Island, BC, Canada V0N 2Y0. **Online address:** pcarney@gulfislands.com

CARNEY, Raymond. American, b. 1947. **Genres:** Film. **Career:** Stanford University, asst. professor; Boston University, professor; Middlebury College, Middlebury, VT, assistant professor of literature and film, beginning in 1978. Harvard Schools and Scholarship Committee, chairman, 1980-; consultant to Whitney Museum of American Art and The Museum of Modern Art. **Publications:** (ed. and author of introduction) Henry James, The Spoils of Poynton and What Maisie Knew, 1985; (ed. and author of introduction) Rudyard Kipling, Kim, 1985; American Vision: The Films of Frank Capra and the Transcendental Impulse, 1986; (ed., illustrator, and author of introduction) Henry Adams, Mont Saint Michel and Chartres, 1986; Speaking the Language of Desire, 1989; General editor, The Cambridge Film Classics, 25 volumes, 1989-93; The Films of John Cassavetes. Work represented in anthologies. Contributor to periodicals. **Address:** Boston University, Film and American Studies, College of Communication, 640 Commonwealth Ave, Boston, MA 02215, U.S.A.

CARNLEY, Peter Frederick. Australian, b. 1937. **Genres:** Theology/Religion. **Career:** Anglican Archbishop of Perth and Metropolitan of the Province of Western Australia, 1981-; Primate of the Anglican Church of Australia, 2000-. Deacon, 1962, and Priest, 1964, Diocese of Bath; Assistant Curate of Parkes, 1966; Diocese of Ely, England, 1966-69; Chaplain, Mitchell Coll. of Advanced Education, Bath, 1970- 72; St. John's Coll., Cambridge, Research Fellow, 1971-72, Fellow, 2000-; Warden, St. John's Coll., St. Lucia, Queensland, 1978-81; Residentiary Canon, St. John's Cathedral, Brisbane, 1975-81; Examining Chaplain to Archbishop of Brisbane, 1975-81; Fellow, Trinity College, University of Melbourne, 2000-. **Publications:** The Structure of Resurrection Belief, 1987; Faithfulness in Fellowship: Reflections on Homosexuality and the Church, 2001; The Yellow Wallpaper and Other Sermons, 2001. **Address:** GPO Box W2067, Perth, WA 6846, Australia. **Online address:** abcsuite@perth.anglican.org

CARNOCHAN, W. B. American, b. 1930. **Genres:** Literary criticism and history, Autobiography/Memoirs. **Career:** Stanford University, California, instructor, 1960-62, assistant professor, 1962-68, associate professor, 1968-73, professor, 1973-92, dean of grad studies, 1975-80, vice-provost, 1976-80, director of Stanford Humanities Center, 1985-91, Richard W. Lyman Professor of the Humanities, 1993-94, emeritus, 1994-. **Publications:** (ed.) The Man of Mode, by George Etherege, 1966; Lemuel Gulliver's Mirror for Man, 1968; Confinement and Flight: An Essay on English Literature of the Eighteenth Century, 1977; Gibbon's Solitude: The Inward World of the Historian, 1987; The Battleground of the Curriculum: Liberal Education and

American Experience, 1993; Momentary Bliss: An American Memoir, 1999. **Address:** English Dept, Stanford University, Stanford, CA 94305, U.S.A. **Online address:** carnochan@stanford.edu

CARO, Robert A. American. **Genres:** Biography, History. **Career:** Former staff member, Newsday newspaper, Long Island, New York, Author, Nieman Fellow Harvard; Pulitzer Prize for Biography, 1975. Francis Parkman Prize of Society of American Historians, 1975; Award in Literature from American Academy of Arts & Letters, 1982; H.L. Mencken Award, 1983; Carr Collins Award of Texas Institute of Letters, 1983. President, Authors Guild, 1977-78; Vice President, PEN American Center. **Publications:** The Power Broker: Robert Moses and the Fall of New York, 1974; The Years of Lyndon Johnson: vol. I, The Path to Power, 1982, vol. 2, Means of Ascent, 1990, Vol. 3, Master of the Senate, 2002 (Pulitzer Prize, Biography, 2003). **Address:** 91 Central Park West, New York, NY 10023, U.S.A.

CAROLE, Bovoso. See IONE, Carole.

CAROTHERS, Thomas. American, b. 1956. **Genres:** Politics/Government. **Career:** International lawyer and specialist in democracy promotion. U.S. Department of State, Washington, DC, attorney-adviser, 1980s; Arnold & Porter (law firm), Washington, DC, attorney, 1990-93; Carnegie Endowment for International Peace, director of research vice president for studies, 1997-2002; Central European University, Budapest, recurrent visiting professor, 2002-04. Democracy and Rule of Law Project, Carnegie Endowment for International Peace, founder and director; consultant and adviser to many organizations involved in promoting democracy worldwide. **Publications:** In the Name of Democracy: U.S. Policy toward Latin America in the Reagan Years, 1991; Assessing Democracy Assistance: The Case of Romania., 1996; Aiding Democracy Abroad: The Learning Curve, 1999; Critical Mission: Essays on Democracy Promotion, 2004. Contributor to books. Contributor to periodicals, journals, and books. **Address:** Carnegie Endowment for International Peace, 1779 Massachusetts Ave NW, Washington, DC 20036, U.S.A. **Online address:** tcarothers@ceip.org

CARPENTER, Bogdana. American (born Poland), b. 1941. **Genres:** Literary criticism and history, Translations. **Career:** University of Washington, Seattle, assistant professor of Polish, 1974-83; University of Michigan, Ann Arbor, associate professor, 1983-91, professor of Polish and comparative literature, 1991-; Wilson Center, member of advisory council for East European program, 1985-90; Cross Currents, associate editor, 1986-. **Publications:** The Poetic Avant-Garde in Poland, 1918-1939; Monumenta Polonica: The First Four Centuries of Polish Poetry, 1989; (author of intro. and ed. with M.G. Levine) C. Milos, To Begin Where I Am: Selected Essays, 2001. TRANSLATOR WITH J. CARPENTER, ALL BY Z. HERBERT: Selected Poems of Zbigniew Herbert, 1977; Report from the Besieged City and Other Poems, 1985; Still Life with a Bridle, 1991; Mr. Cogito, 1993; The King of the Ants, 1999; Elegy for the Departure and Other Poems, 1999. **Address:** Department of Slavic Languages and Literature, 3040 MLB, University of Michigan, Ann Arbor, MI 48104, U.S.A. **Online address:** bogdana@umich.edu

CARPENTER, Kenneth E(dward). American, b. 1936. **Genres:** Librarianship. **Career:** Harvard University, Cambridge, MA, assistant in reading room at Houghton Library, 1959-61, assistant to the librarian, 1961-62; Bowdoin College, Brunswick, ME, reference librarian, 1962-63; Harvard University, assistant to the editor of Bibliography of American Literature at Houghton Library, 1963-67, associate of Kress Library, 1967-68, curator, 1968-80, research and publications librarian, 1980-84, assistant director for research resources, 1984-. **Publications:** (with P. Barucci and others) Italian Economic Literature in the Kress Library, 1985; The First 350 Years of the Harvard University Library, 1986. EDITOR: British Labour Struggles: Contemporary Pamphlets, 1727-1850, 32 vols, 1975; Books and Society in History: Papers of the Association of College and Research Libraries Rare Books and Manuscripts Preconference, 24-28 June, 1980, Boston, Massachusetts, 1983. **Address:** Library, Wadsworth House, Harvard University, Cambridge, MA 02138, U.S.A.

CARPENTER, Lynette. Also writes as D. B. Borton, Della Borton. American, b. 1951. **Genres:** Mystery/Crime/Suspense, Literary criticism and history, Bibliography. **Career:** University of Cincinnati, OH, assistant professor of English, associate director, acting director of women's studies, 1980-89; Ohio Wesleyan University, Delaware, assistant professor, 1989-96, associate professor, 1996-2001, professor of English, 2001-. **Publications:** (ed. with W.K. Kolmar) Haunting the House of Fiction: Feminist Perspectives on Ghost Stories by American Women, 1991; Ghost Stories by Women: A Selected Annotated Bibliography. AS D.B. BORTON: One for the Money;

Two Points for Murder, 1993; Three Is a Crowd; Four Elements of Murder; Five Alarm Fire; Six Feet Under. AS DELLA BORTON: Fade to Black, 1999; Freeze Frame, 2000; Slow Dissolve, 2001; Seventh Deadly Sin, 2004. **Address:** Dept of English, Ohio Wesleyan University, Delaware, OH 43015, U.S.A. **Online address:** dbborton@delnet.net

CARPI, Daniel (V.). Israeli (born Italy), b. 1926. **Genres:** History, Theology/Religion. **Career:** Institute for Youth Leaders from Abroad, Jerusalem, Israel, teacher, 1951-58; Tel Aviv University, Israel, instructor, 1962-66, lecturer, 1966-68, senior lecturer, 1968-71, head of Institute for Zionist Research, 1968-73, 1983-84, 1992-94, associate professor, 1971-77, dean of Faculty of Humanities, 1972-75, Schapelsky Professor of Holocaust Studies, 1975-94, professor of Jewish history, 1977-94, head of School of Jewish Studies, 1984-85, department head, 1988-91, member of council of Diaspora Research Institute, 1992-, professor emeritus, 1994-. Visiting professor: Jewish Theological Seminary, NYC, 1976, Yeshiva University, 1976, Pontificia Universita Gregoriana, 1986; Oxford University, fellow in Sephardic studies at Centre for Postgraduate Hebrew Studies and senior associate member of St. Antony's College, both 1977, 1992; Hebrew University of Jerusalem, head of Research Group in Sephardic Studies at Institute for Advanced Studies, 1987; Sorbonne, University of Paris, associate director of studies in Ecole Pratique des Hautes Etudes, 1989. **Publications:** Between Mussolini and Hitler, 1994; L'individuo e la collettivita, 2001. BOOKS IN HEBREW: The Minute-Book of the Jewish Community of Padua, 1577-1603, 1974, 1604-1630, 1979; The Activity of the "Italian Synagogue" of Venice on Behalf of the Jewish Communities of Eretz-Israel during the Years 1576-1733, 1978; R. Itzhak Min-Halleviyyim's "Medabber Tahpuchoth", 1985; R. Yehuda Aryeh Mi-Modena's "Chayye' Yehuda," 1985; Between Renaissance and Ghetto, 1989; Zeev Jabotinsky's Letters, Vol I: 1898-1914, 1992, Vol II: 1914-1918, 1995, Vol III: 1918-1922, 1997, Vol IV: 1922-1925, 1998, Vol V: 1926-1927, 2000, Vol VI: 1928-1929, 2002; Ben Shevet le-Hesed, The Italian Authorities and the Jews of France and Tunisia during the Second World War, 1993; The Minutes Book of the "Italian" Jewish Community of Venice, 2003. Editor of books in Hebrew and English. Contributor to books and scholarly journals. **Address:** 2 Geiger St, 69341 Tel Aviv, Israel.

CARR, Caleb. American, b. 1955. **Genres:** Novels, Biography. **Career:** Writer and historian, 1980-. **Publications:** Casing the Promised Land (novel), 1980; (with J. Chace) America Invulnerable: The Quest for Absolute Security, from 1812 to Star Wars (nonfiction), 1988; Bad Attitudes (television movie), 1991; The Devil Soldier: The Story of Frederick Townsend Ward (biography), 1991; The Alienist (novel), 1994; The Angel of Darkness, 1997; Killing Time, 2000. Author of short stories and articles on military history. Contributor to periodicals. **Address:** c/o International Creative Management, 40 West 57th St., New York, NY 10019, U.S.A.

CARR, Duane. American, b. 1934. **Genres:** Novels, Poetry, Literary criticism and history. **Career:** University of Texas at El Paso, instructor, 1974 and 1979; University of Arkansas at Little Rock, instructor, 1983 and 1986-87; University of New Orleans, New Orleans, LA, instructor, 1987-88; Western Kentucky University, Bowling Green, instructor, 1988-95. Denver & Rio Grande Western Railroad, worked as agent and telegrapher throughout the southwest. **Publications:** The Bough of Summer, 1976; A Question of Class, 1996. Work represented in anthologies. **Address:** 10695 Venice Rd, Elkins, AR 72727, U.S.A.

CARR, Jonathan. British. **Genres:** Biography. **Career:** British foreign correspondent; writer for Economist. **Publications:** BIOGRAPHIES: Helmut Schmidt: Helmsman of Germany, 1985; Mahler, 1997. **Address:** c/o Caroline Dawnay, PFD, Drury House, 34-43 Russell St, London WC2B 5HA, England.

CARR, Margaret. Also writes as Martin Carroll, Belle Jackson, Carole Kerr. British, b. 1935. **Genres:** Novels, Mystery/Crime/Suspense, Romance/Historical. **Career:** Formerly a local government secretary. **Publications:** NOVELS: Spring into Love, 1967. MYSTERY NOVELS: Tread Warily at Midnight, 1971; Sitting Duck, 1972; Who's The Target, 1974; Wait for the Wake, 1974; Too Close for Comfort, 1974; Blood Will Out, 1975; Blindman's Bluff, 1976; Dare the Devil, 1976; Sharendel, 1976; Out of the Past, 1976; Twin Tragedy, 1977; The Witch of Wykham, 1978; Daggers Drawn, 1980; Deadly Pursuit, 1991; Dark Intruder, 1991. MYSTERY NOVELS AS MARTIN CARROLL: Begotten Murder, 1967; Blood Vengeance, 1968; Dead Trouble, 1968; Goodbye Is Forever, 1968; Too Beautiful to Die, 1969; Bait, 1970; Miranda Said Murder, 1970; Hear No Evil, 1971. AS BELLE JACKSON: In the Dark of the Day, 1988; Valdez's Lady, 1989. NOVELS AS CAROLE KERR: Not for Sale, 1975; Shadow of the Hunter, 1975; A Time to Surrender, 1975; Love All Start, 1977; Lamb to the Slaughter, 1978; An Innocent Abroad, 1979; When Dreams Come True, 1980; Stolen Heart, 1981. **Address:** Waverley, Wavering Lane, Gillingham, Dorset SP8 4NR, England.

CARR, Marvin N. American, b. 1927. **Genres:** Novels, Mystery/Crime/Suspense. **Career:** Writer. Active in EDC. **Publications:** Positively Negative (novel), 1994; Men Are Cruel, but Women Are Dangerous; The Deliquescent Lights. **Address:** 2311 W 16th Ave Spot #61, Spokane, WA 99224, U.S.A. **Online address:** TromPublishing@webtv.net

CARR, Roger Vaughan. Australian, b. 1937. **Genres:** Children's fiction. **Career:** Writer. Journalist, television writer, and screenwriter. Founder and owner of eKIDna Interactive, producer of educational CD-ROM programs. **Publications:** CHILDREN'S NOVELS: Surfie, 1966; Dead Man's Float, 1973; Old Cranky Jack, 1973; Surfboard, 1975; Noose over the Valley, 1977; Rollin' Through, 1979; The Split Creek Kids, 1988; Firestorm!, 1985; The Nearly-Always-Come-Home-Again Hat, 1989; The Clinker, 1989; Piano Bay, 1991; Nipper and the Gold Turkey, 1991; The Imprint, 1994; The Butterfly, 1996. Author of other children's novels. Author of short stories. **Address:** 69 Outer Crescent, Brighton, VIC 3186, Australia. **Online address:** eKIDna@onaustralia.com.au

CARRADICE, Ian A. British, b. 1953. **Genres:** Archaeology/Antiquities. **Career:** British Museum, London, England, curator in Department of Coins and Medals, 1977-89; University of St. Andrews, St. Andrews, Scotland, professor of art history and course director in museum and gallery studies, 1989-, keeper of university collections and museums, 1990-. **Publications:** Coinage and Finances in the Reign of Domitian, 1983; (ed.) Coinage and Administration in the Athenian and Persian Empires, 1987; Coinage in the Greek World, 1988; Greek Coins, 1995; Roman Provincial Coinage, Vol. II, 1999. **Address:** School of Art History, University of St. Andrews, St Andrews, Fife KY16 9AR, Scotland. **Online address:** iac@st-and.ac.uk

CARRAHER, Charles E., Jr. American, b. 1941. **Genres:** Chemistry. **Career:** University of South Dakota, Vermillion, instructor, 1967-68, asst professor, 1968-70, assoc professor, 1970-73, professor of chemistry, 1973-76, chairman of science division, 1971-74; Wright State University, Dayton, OH, professor of chemistry, 1976-85, chairman of dept, 1976-84; Florida Atlantic University, Boca Raton, professor of chemistry and dean of College of Science, 1985-95, associate professor, Florida Center for Environmental Studies, 1995-; writer. Artist, with exhibitions of pen and ink drawings and oil and water color paintings; professional musician. **Publications:** Chemistry Applied, 1970; Chemistry in Everyday Life, 1972, rev. ed., 1976; Chemistry in Our World, 1974; (ed.) Interfacial Synthesis, Vol. I (with F. Millich): Fundamentals, 1977, Vol. II (with Millich): Polymer Applications and Technology, 1977, Vol. III (with J. Preston): Recent Advances, 1982; (with J. Sheats and C. Pittman) Organometallic Polymers, 1978; (with M. Tsuda) Modification of Polymers, 1979, rev. ed., 1980; (with R. Seymour) Polymer Chemistry, 1981, 4th ed., 1996; (with Sheats and Pittman) Metallo-Organic Polymers, 1981; (with Sheats and Pittman) Advances in Organometallic Polymer Science, 1982; (with C. Gebelein) Polymeric Drugs, 1982; (with L. Sperling) Polymer Applications of Renewable-Resource Materials, 1983; (with J. Moore) Chemical Modification of Polymers, 1983; (with L. Mathias) Crown Ethers and Phase Transfer Agents for Polymer Applications, 1984; (with Sheats and Pittman) Metal-Containing Polymeric Systems, 1985; (with Gebelein) Bioactive Polymeric Systems, 1985; (with Gebelein) Polymeric Materials in Medication, 1985; (with Sperling) Renewable Resource Materials, 1986; (with Gebelein and V. Foster) Applied Bioactive Polymeric Systems, 1989; (with Seymour) Giant Molecules, 1990; (with others) Inorganic and Metal-Containing Polymeric Materials, 1990; (with Gebelein) Biotechnology, 1994; (with Gebelein) Industrial Biotechnological Polymers, 1995; (with others) Metal-Containing Polymers Materials, 1996; (with Swift and Bowman) Polymer Modification, 1997; (with Craver) Applied Polymer Science, 2000; Polymer Chemistry, 2000; (with others) Bonding, 2001; (with Swift) Functional Condensation Polymers, 2002. **Address:** Florida Atlantic University, Florida Center for Environmental Studies, Boca Raton, FL 33431, U.S.A.

CARREL, Annette Felder. American, b. 1929. **Genres:** Young adult fiction, Law. **Career:** Taught kindergarten and first grade in Marin County, CA, for ten years; former director of education at Sunny Hills, a residential treatment center for children with emotional problems. Docent for the Santa Barbara Historical Society, Trust for Historic Preservation, Symphony League, local court house, and the Santa Barbara Mission and Archive Library; public speaker; former commissioner of the Juvenile Justice/Delinquency Prevention Commission. **Publications:** It's the Law: A Young Person's Guide to Our Legal System, 1994. **Address:** 2010 Garden St., Santa Barbara, CA 93105, U.S.A.

CARRETTA, Vincent (Albert). American, b. 1945. **Genres:** Literary criticism and history. **Career:** Mount Mercy College, Cedar Rapids, Iowa, instructor in English, 1977; University of Maryland at College Park, assistant professor, 1978-83, associate professor, 1983-90, professor of English, 1990-. Visiting lecturer at University of Iowa, 1977; visiting fellow at Institute for Research in the Humanities, University of Wisconsin-Madison, 1978-79. **Publications:** "The Snarling Muse": Verbal and Visual Political Satire from Pope to Churchill, 1983; George III and the Satirists from Hogarth to Byron, 1990. EDITOR, AUTHOR OF INTRO. & NOTES: The Satires of Mr. (Paul) Whitehead, 1984; Olaudah Equiano's The Interesting Narrative and Other Writings, 1995; Unchained Voices: An Anthology of Black Authors in the English-Speaking World of the Eighteenth Century. **Address:** Department of English-ARHU, University of Maryland at College Park, 4117 Susquehanna Hall, College Park, MD 20742, U.S.A. **Online address:** vac@umd.edu

CARR-HILL, Roy A. British, b. 1943. **Genres:** Criminology/True Crime, Education, Mathematics/Statistics, Medicine/Health, Public/Social administration, Social sciences. **Career:** University of Sussex, Brighton, England, lecturer, 1971-74; Organization for Economic Cooperation and Development, Paris, France, administrator, 1974-77; Universdade Eduardo Mondlane, Maputo, Mozambique, professor, 1978-81; Medical Research Council, Aberdeen, Scotland, research fellow, 1981-83; University of York, Centre for Health Economics, Heslington, England, senior research fellow, 1984-96, professor in health and social statistics, 1996-; University of Hull, England, School of Social and Political Sciences, research coordinator, 1991-93; University of London, Institute of Education, England, professor, 1992-. **Publications:** (with O. Magnusson) Indicators of Performance of Educational Systems, 1973; (with N.H. Stern) Crime Police and Criminal Statistics, 1979; (with C. Pritchard) The Development and Exploitation of Empirical Birthweight Standards, 1985; (with others) The Functioning and Effects of the Tanzanian Literacy Programme, 1991; Social Conditions in Sub-Saharan Africa, 1991; (with others) Skill Mix and the Effectiveness of Nursing Care, 1992; (with C. Pritchard) Women's Social Standing, 1992; (with others) Les inegalities de sante en France et en Grande Borlagne, 1991; (with G. Carron) Non-formal Education, 1992; (with O'Ketch, Katahoise, and Ndiddie) Adult Literacy Programmes in Uganda, 1999; (co) The Fourth Way, 2000. **Address:** c/o Centre for Health Economics, University of York, Heslington, York YO10 5DD, England. **Online address:** irss23@york.ac.uk

CARRICK, Malcolm. British, b. 1945. **Genres:** Children's fiction, Novellas/Short stories. **Career:** Owner, Malcolm Carrick Productions, advertising agency, 1985-. Freelance writer, illustrator, and songwriter; author of scripts for children's television and radio light entertainment progs. **Publications:** Allsorts of Every Thing, 1973; The Wise Men of Gotham, 1973; The Extraordinary Hat-Maker, 1974; Mr. Pedagouge's Sneeze, 1974; Once There Was a Boy and Other Stories, 1974; The Little Pilgrim, 1975; Tramp, 1977; Today Is Shrew's Day, 1978; I Can Squash Elephants!, 1978; Happy Jack, 1979; Making Devil and Demon Masks, 1979; Mr. Tod's Trap, 1980; I'll Get You, 1981; Butterfingers!, 1985; Skem, 1994; "Oddjob" Is the Sandman, 1999; Oddjob's Lunch Box, 2002. **Address:** Flat 4 Vicarage Ct, 215 Church Rd, London SE19 2QQ, England. **Online address:** mickcarrick_2@hotmail.com

CARRIER, James G(olden). American, b. 1947. **Genres:** Anthropology/Ethnology. **Career:** University of Papua New Guinea, Port Moresby, lecturer, 1980-84, senior lecturer in anthropology and sociology, 1985-86, department head, 1984-86; University of Virginia, Charlottesville, lecturer in sociology, 1987-94; University of Durham, Durham, England, lecturer in anthropology, 1994-99; University of Edinburgh, reader in anthropology, 1999-2000l Oxford Brookes University, research asspciate in anthropology, 2002-. Conducted field work in Papua New Guinea, 1978-79. **Publications:** Learning Disability: Social Class and the Construction of Inequality in American Education, 1986; (with A. Carrier) Wage, Trade, and Exchange in Melanesia: A Manus Society in the Modern State, 1989; (with A. Carrier) Structure and Process in a Melanesian Society: Ponam's Progress in the Twentieth Century, 1991; Gifts and Commodities: Exchange and Western Capitalism Since 1700, 1994. EDITOR & CONTRIBUTOR: History and Tradition in Melanesian Anthropology, 1992; Occidentalism: Images of the West, 1995; (with J. Friedman) Melanesian Modernities, 1996; Meaning of the Market, 1997; (with D. Miller) Virtualism, 1998; Confronting Environments, 2004. Contributor to books. Contributor of articles and reviews to scholarly journals. **Address:** Headington Campus, Oxford Brookes University, Gipsy Ln, Oxford OX3 0BP, England. **Online address:** JGC@jgcarrier.demon.co.uk

CARRIER, Roch. Canadian, b. 1937. **Genres:** Novels, Children's fiction, Poetry, Young adult fiction, Novellas/Short stories. **Career:** Novelist, short story writer, poet, dramatist, and screenwriter. Held teaching positions at College Militaire Royal de Saint-Jean, Quebec, and at L'Universite de Mon-

treal, Montreal, Quebec; secretary-general at Theatre du Nouveau Monde, Quebec, 1971-. Chairman of Salon du Livre, Montreal. **Publications:** TRANSLATED WORKS: La Guerre, Yes Sir! (novel), 1968, trans. by S. Fischman, 1970; Floralie, ou es-tu? (novel), 1969, trans. by Fischman as Floralie, Where Are You?, 1971; Il est par la, le soleil (novel), 1970, trans. by Fischman as Is It the Sun, Philibert?, 1972; Le Deux-millieme etage (novel), 1973, trans. by Fischman as They Won't Demolish Me!, 1973; Le Jardin des delices (novel), 1975, trans. by Fischman as The Garden of Delights, 1978; Il n'y a pas de pays sans grand-pere (novel), 1977, trans. by Fischman as No Country Without Grandfathers, 1981; Les Enfants du bonhomme dans la lune (stories), 1979, trans. by Fischman published as The Hockey Sweater and Other Stories, 1979; La Dame qui avait des chaines aux chevilles (novel), 1981, trans. by Fischman as Lady With Chains, 1984; De l'amour dans la ferraille (novel), 1984, trans. by Fischman as Heartbreaks Along the Road, 1987; Canada: La Belle aventure, 1986, English and Japanese translations; Prieres d'un enfant tres tres sage, 1988, trans as Prayers of a Very Wise Child, 1991; Une Bonne et Heureuse Annee, 1991 trans. as A Happy New Year's Day; L'Homme dans le placard (novel), 1991, trans. as The Man in the Closet, 1992; Fin (novel), 1992, trans. as The End, 1994; Le plus long circuit, 1993, trans as The Longest Home Run; Basketball Player, 1996. UNTRANSLATED WORKS: Les Jeux incompris (poems), 1956; Cherche tes mots, cherche tes pas, 1958; Jolis Deuils: Petites Tragedies pour adultes (stories), 1964; L'Aube d'acier (poem), 1971; Les Fleurs vivent-elles ailleurs que sur la terre?, 1980; Les Voyageurs de l'arc-en-ciel, 1980; Le Cirque noir, 1982; Ne faites pas mal a l'avenir (juvenile), 1984; La Fleur et Autres Personnages (short stories), 1984; L'Ours et le kangourou, 1986; Un chameau en Jordanie, 1988; Enfants de la planete (short stories), 1989; L'Eau de Polguk SA (short stories), 1989; Le Canot dans les nuages, 1991; Un Champion, 1991; Le Martien de Noel, 1991; Petit homme tornade (novel), 1996. **Address:** Tundra Books of Northern New York, PO Box 1030, Plattsburgh, NY 12901, U.S.A.

CARRIER, Thomas J. (born United States), b. 1956. **Genres:** Travel/Exploration. **Career:** Writer. Arlington County Visitors Commission, member, 1990-92. U.S. Army, 82nd Airborne Division, 1976-79; received parachute wings. **Publications:** The Small Meetings Handbook, 1993; The Historic Walking Tour of Alexandria 1749, L. B. Prince Co., 1996. Washington, DC: A Historical Walking Tour, 1999. Historic Georgetown: A Walking Tour, 1999. The White House, the Capitol, and the Supreme Court: Historic Self-guided Tours, 2000. Complete Small Meetings Planner, 2003. Contributor to periodicals. **Address:** c/o Author Mail, Arcadia Press, 2 Cumberland St., Charleston, SC 29401, U.S.A. **Online address:** tcines@aol.com

CARRIER, Warren. American, b. 1918. **Genres:** Novels, Poetry, Translations. **Career:** Chancellor Emeritus, University of Wisconsin, Platteville, 1982(Chancellor, 1975-82). Associate Dean, Rutgers University, New Brunswick, New Jersey, 1968-69; Dean, California State University, San Diego, 1969-72; Vice-President, University of Bridgeport, Conn., 1972-75. Founder, and former Ed., Quarterly Review of Literature. **Publications:** NOVELS: The Hunt, 1952; Bay of the Damned, 1957; Death of a Chancellor, 1986; An Honorable Spy, 1992; Murder at the Strawberry Festival, 1993; Death of a Poet, 1999; Justice at Christmas, 1999; Coming to Terms, 2004. POETRY: The Cost of Love, 1953; Toward Montebello, 1966; Leave Your Sugar for the Cold Morning, 1978; The Diver, 1986; An Ordinary Man, 1997; Risking the Wind, 2000. TRANSLATOR: City Stopped in Time, 1949. EDITOR: (with P. Engle) Reading Modern Poetry, 1955, rev. ed., 1968; Guide to World Literature, 1980; (with B. Neumann) Literature from the World, 1981. **Address:** 69 Colony Park Circle, Galveston, TX 77551, U.S.A.

CARRIKER, S. David. American, b. 1951. **Genres:** History, Local history/Rural topics, Transportation. **Career:** Third Creek Presbyterian Church, Cleveland, NC, minister, 1998-; Heritage Publishing Co., publisher. **Publications:** The Carriker Family, 1977; The Geology of Richmond County, North Carolina, 1982; The Eighteenth-Century Churches of Richmond County, North Carolina, 1984; Railroading in the Carolina Sandhills, Vol I: The Nineteenth Century (1825-1900), 1985, Vol II: The Twentieth Century (1900-1985), 1987, Vol III, 1992; The Piedmont & Northern (Electric) Railway (videotape), 1986; North Carolina Railroads: The Common Carrier Railroads of North Carolina, 1988; The Aberdeen & Rockfish Railroad (videotape), 1989; The Laurinburg & Southern Railroad (videotape), 1989; N&W RY Number 1218: Through the Loops to Asheville, 1989; Sandhill Shorties!, 1991. EDITOR: The North Carolina Railroad Map, 1990; Railroading in the Carolina Sandhills, Vol. IV, 1991, Vol. V, 1996. **Address:** Heritage Publishing Co., 207 Kimrod Lane, Charlotte, NC 28270, U.S.A. **Online address:** Heritage@carolina.rr.com

CARRINGTON, Paul Dewitt. American, b. 1931. **Genres:** Law. **Career:** University of Wyoming, assistant professor, 1958-60; Indiana University,

Bloomington, assistant professor, 1960-62; Ohio State University, Columbus, associate professor, 1962-64, professor, 1964-65; University of Michigan Law School, Ann Arbor, professor of law, 1965-78; Duke University School of Law, Durham, NC, professor, 1978-, dean, 1978-88; Guggenheim Fellow, 1985-89. **Publications:** Accommodating the Workload of the United States Courts of Appeal, 1968; (ed.) Civil Procedure: Cases with Comment on the Process of Adjudication, 1969, 3rd ed., 1983; (with Meador and Rosenberg) Justice on Appeal, 1976; (with Meador and Rosenberg) Appellate Courts, 1995; (with Meador and Rosenberg) Stewards of Democracy, 1999; Spreading America's Word, 2004. **Address:** Duke University School of Law, Durham, NC 27708-0362, U.S.A. **Online address:** pdc@law.duke.edu

CARRINGTON, Ruth. See **HARTLAND, Michael.**

CARROLL, Brendan G. British, b. 1952. **Genres:** Biography. **Career:** Independent marketing consultant, music critic, and journalist. **Publications:** The Last Prodigy, 1997. **Address:** 2 South Bank Rd., Liverpool L19 9AR, England. **Online address:** brandan_carroll@compuserve.com

CARROLL, Cathryn. American. **Genres:** Adult non-fiction. **Career:** Gallaudet University, Washington, DC, managing editor at National Deaf Education Network and Clearinghouse, Laurent Clerc National Deaf Education Center. **Publications:** (with Susan M. Mather) Movers and Shakers: Deaf People Who Changed the World; Twenty-six Tales of Genius, Struggle, Perseverance, and Heroism, 1997. (with Catherine Hoffpauir Fisher) Orchid of the Bayou: A Deaf Woman Faces Blindness, 2001. **Address:** Gallaudet University, 800 Florida Ave. N.E., Washington, DC 20002, U.S.A. **Online address:** cathryn.carroll@gallaudet.edu

CARROLL, Colleen. American, b. 1974. **Genres:** Documentaries/ Reportage. **Career:** Freelance writer and public speaker, 1992-; Marquette Journal magazine, Milwaukee, WI, editor-in-chief, columnist, and staff writer, 1992-95; Washington Magazine, editorial intern, 1995; Milwaukee Journal Sentinel, Milwaukee, freelance writer, 1995-96; Memphis Commercial Appeal, news reporter, 1996-97; St. Louis Post-Dispatch, editorial writer and news reporter, 1997-2002; speechwriter to President George W. Bush, 2003. Media commentator for Public Broadcast System, CBS Radio, EWTN, Harvest Television Network, American Family Radio, Breakpoint Radio, Moody Broadcasting, and USA Radio Network. **Publications:** The New Faithful: Why Young Adults Are Embracing Christian Orthodoxy, 2002. Contributor to periodicals. **Address:** c/o Author Mail, Loyola Press, 3441 North Ashland Ave., Chicago, IL 60657, U.S.A. **Online address:** maryrose29@mindspring.com

CARROLL, Francis M(artin). (born United States), b. 1938. **Genres:** History. **Career:** South Dakota State University, faculty member, 1962-64; Kalamazoo College, Kalamazoo, MI, faculty member, 1967-68; University of Manitoba, Winnipeg, Manitoba, Canada, member of history faculty, 1969-98, senior scholar, 1999-, professor emeritus, 2002-. Dean of studies at St. John's College, 1976-78, acting warden, 1985-86, chair of assembly, 1989-90. Columbia University, visiting scholar in international law, 1980; National University of Ireland, University College, Dublin, Ireland, Mary Ball Washington Professor of American History, 1984-85; South Dakota State University, F. O. Butler Lecturer, 1988; University of Nottingham, guest lecturer, 1994; University of London, John Adams fellow at Institute of United States Studies, 1994-95; University of St. Thomas, visiting Irish historian, 2000. **Publications:** American Opinion and the Irish Question, 1910-23, 1978; (editor) The American Commission on Irish Independence, 1919: The Diary, Correspondence, and Report, 1985; Crossroads in Time: A History of Carlton County, Minnesota, 1988; (with Franklin R. Raiter) The Fires of Autumn: The Cloquet-Moose Lake Disaster of 1918, 1990; (with Marlene Wisuri) Reflections of Our Past: A Pictorial History of Carlton County, 1997; A Good and Wise Measure: The Search for the Canadian-American Boundary, 1783-1842, 2001; Money for Ireland: Finance, Diplomacy, Politics, and the First Dáil Éireann Loans, 1919-1936, 2002. Contributor to books, articles and reviews to academic journals. **Address:** 601 Wardlaw Ave., Winnipeg, Manitoba, Canada R3L 0M3. **Online address:** fcarrol@cc.umanitoba.ca

CARROLL, Jenny. See **CABOT, Meg(gin Patricia).**

CARROLL, Martin. See **CARR, Margaret.**

CARROLL, Matthew S. American, b. 1955. **Genres:** Environmental sciences/Ecology. **Career:** Black Hills National Forest, Rapid City, SD, seasonal forestry aide, 1975; U.S. Forest Service, Northeast Forest Experiment Station, Hamden, CT, research technician at Forest Insect and Disease Laboratory, 1976-77; University of Washington, Seattle, instructor in forest resources, 1982, Resources for the Future fellow in forest economics and policy, 1982-83, research analyst in Cooperative Park Studies Unit, College of Forest Resources, 1983-85; Pennsylvania State University, University Park, postdoctoral research associate, 1985-87; Washington State University, Pullman, assistant/associate professor of natural resource sciences and assistant/associate resource sociologist, 1987-. Consultant to President Clinton's Forest Ecosystem Management Assessment Team and Upper Columbia Basin Ecosystem Assessment Team. **Publications:** Community and the Northwestern Logger: Continuities and Change in the Era of the Spotted Owl, 1995. Contributor to books. Contributor of articles and reviews to periodicals. **Address:** Department of Natural Resource Sciences, 123 Johnson Hall, Washington State University, Pullman, WA 99164, U.S.A. **Online address:** carroll@mail.wsu.edu

CARROLL, Rebecca. American, b. 1969. **Genres:** Cultural/Ethnic topics. **Career:** Blackside Inc., Boston, MA, research assistant for the documentary film project Malcolm X: Make It Plain, 1992-93; Harvard University, Cambridge, MA, editorial and administrative assistant in department of Afro-American studies, 1993-94; Elle, NYC, assistant editor, 1994-. **Publications:** I Know What the Red Clay Looks Like, 1994; Swing Low, 1995; Sugar in the Raw: A Nonfiction Profile of Young Black Girls in America, in press. **Address:** 206 7th St., Brooklyn, NY 11215, U.S.A.

CARROLL, Richard J. American, b. 1957. **Genres:** Economics. **Career:** World Bank, Washington, DC, researcher, 1981-86; independent economic and financial consultant, 1988-. **Publications:** (with G. Meier) Industrial Adjustment in Sub-Saharan Africa, 1989; An Economic Record of Presidential Performance from Truman to Bush, 1995; Desk Reference on the Economy: More Than 600 Answers to Questions That Will Help You Understand News, Trends and Issues; NewsGuides Series on Controversial Issues, 2004. **Address:** PO Box 363, Glen Echo, MD 20812, U.S.A. **Online address:** richjcarroll@comcast.net

CARRUTH, Hayden. American, b. 1921. **Genres:** Poetry. **Career:** Syracuse University, New York, Professor of English, 1979-91. Member of Editorial Board, Hudson Review, NYC. Ed., Poetry, Chicago, 1949-50; Associate Ed., University of Chicago Press, 1950-51, and Intercultural Publs. Inc., NYC, 1952-53; Poetry Ed., Harpers Magazine, NYC, 1979-84. **Publications:** The Crow and the Heart, 1946-1959, 1959; Journey to a Known Place, 1961; The Norfolk Poems: 1 June to 1 September 1961, 1962; Appendix A, 1963, 1963; North Winter, 1964; (ed. with J. Laughlin) A New Directions Reader, 1964; Nothing for Tigers: Poems 1959-1964, 1965; After "The Stranger": Imaginary Dialogues with Camus, 1965; Contra Mortem, 1967; For You: Poems, 1970; The Clay Hill Anthology, 1970; (ed.) The Voice That Is Great Within Us: American Poetry of the Twentieth Century, 1970; (ed.) The Bird/Poem Book: Poems on the Wild Birds of North America, 1970; From Snow and Rock, From Chaos, 1973; Dark World, 1974; The Bloomingdale Papers, 1974; Loneliness, 1976; Aura, 1977; Brothers, I Loved You All, 1978; Working Papers, 1981; Sleeping Beauty, 1982; If You Call This Cry a Song, 1983; The Mythology of Dark and Light, 1983; Effluences From the Sacred Caves, 1984; Asphalt Georgies, 1985; The Oldest Killed Lake in North America, 1985; Mother, 1985; Lighter than Air Craft, 1985; The Selected Poetry of Hayden Carruth, 1986; Sitting In: Selected Writings on Jazz, Blues and Related Topics, 1986; Tell Me Again, 1989; Sonnets, 1989; Collected Shorter Poems, 1946-91, 1992; Suicides and Jazzers, 1992; Collected Longer Poems, 1994; Collected Essays and Reviews, 1996; Scrambled Eggs & Whiskey, 1996; Reluctantly, 1998; Beside the Shadblow Tree, 1999; Doctor Jazz, 2001. **Address:** RD1, Box 128, Munnsville, NY 13409, U.S.A.

CARSON, Anne (Regina). American, b. 1950. **Genres:** Literary criticism and history, Women's studies and issues, Novellas/Short stories, Theology/ Religion, Bibliography. **Career:** University of Pittsburgh, Pittsburgh, PA, library assistant, 1976-80; Brown University, Providence, RI, rare book cataloger, 1980-82; Cornell University, Ithaca, NY, reference librarian and selector for philosophy and religion, 1983-95, 1997-. Freelance researcher and editor, 1993-. **Publications:** Feminist Spirituality and the Feminine Divine: An Annotated Bibliography, 1986; (ed.) Spiritual Parenting in the New Age, 1989, as Caretaking a New Soul, 1999; Goddesses and Wise Women: The Literature of Feminist Spirituality, 1980-1992: An Annotated Bibliography, 1992. **Address:** 811 Mitchell St, Ithaca, NY 14850, U.S.A.

CARSON, Anne. Canadian, b. 1950. **Genres:** Poetry, Essays. **Career:** Poet and essayist. Princeton University, Princeton, NJ, former instructor; Emory University, Atlanta, GA, former instructor; McGill University, Montreal, Quebec, Canada, John MacNaughton Professor of Classics, 2000-. **Publications:** Eros the Bittersweet: An Essay, 1986; Short Talks, 1992; Plainwater:

Essays and Poetry, 1995; Glass, Irony, and God, 1995; Autobiography of Red: A Novel in Verse, 1998; Economy of the Unlost: Reading Simonides of Keos with Paul Celan, 1999; Men in the Off Hours, 2000; The Beauty of the Husband: A Fictional Essay in 29 Tangoes (poetry), 2001. Contributor to anthologies. Contributor of poetry to periodicals. **Address:** Department of History, Leacock Building Room 823, McGill University, 855 Sherbrooke Street West, Montreal, QC, Canada H3A 2T7. **Online address:** decreation@ hotmail.com

CARSON, Barbara Harrell. American, b. 1943. **Genres:** Literary criticism and history. **Career:** Towson State College, Baltimore, MD, assistant professor of English, 1968-71; University of Massachusetts, Amherst, assistant professor of English, 1971-72; Florida Technological University, Orlando, FL, adjunct instructor, 1973-79; Valencia Community College, Orlando, adjunct instructor, 1973-79; Rollins College, Winter Park, FL, adjunct instructor, 1973-79, assistant professor, 1979-81, associate professor, 1981-88, professor of English, 1988-94, Theodore Bruce and Barbara Lawrence Alford Professor of English, 1994-. **Publications:** Eudora Welty: Two Pictures at Once in Her Frame, 1992. Contributor to periodicals. **Address:** Box 2619, Rollins College, Winter Park, FL 32789, U.S.A.

CARSON, Benjamin S(olomon). American, b. 1951. **Genres:** Medicine/ Health, Autobiography/Memoirs. **Career:** Neurosurgeon. Johns Hopkins University, Baltimore, MD, chief resident neurosurgery, 1982-83, assistant professor of neurosurgery, 1984-, assistant professor of oncology, 1984-, assistant professor of pediatrics, 1987-, associate professor, 1991-, director of pediatric neurosurgery, 1985-91; Queen Elizabeth II Medical Center, Perth, Australia, senior registrar of neurosurgery, 1983-84. Has appeared on television programs. Gives presentations, especially to adolescents, about fulfilling personal potential. **Publications:** (with C. Murphey) Gifted Hands, The Ben Carson Story, 1990; Think Big: Unleashing Your Potential for Excellence, 1992; (ed. with C.R. Dufresne and S.J. Zinreich) Complex Craniofacial Problems: A Guide to Analysis and Treatment, 1992. Contributor to periodicals. **Address:** Johns Hopkins Medical Institutions, Meyer 5-109, 600 N Wolfe, Baltimore, MD 21205, U.S.A.

CARSON, Ciaran. Irish, b. 1948. **Genres:** Poetry, Music. **Career:** Traditional Arts Officer, Northern Ireland Arts Council, Belfast, 1975, Literature Officer, 1992-98. School Teacher, Belfast, 1974-75. **Publications:** The New Estate, 1976; The Lost Explorer, 1979; Pocket Guide to Irish Traditional Music, 1986; The Irish for No (poetry), 1987; Belfast Confetti (poetry), 1989; First Language (poetry), 1993; Opera Et Cetera (poetry), 1996; Last Night's Fun (prose), 1996; The Twelfth of Never (poetry), 1998; Fishing for Amber (prose), 1999; The Ballad of HMS Belfast (poetry), 1999; Shamrock Tea (prose), 2001. **Address:** 12 Glandore Ave, Belfast BT15 3FB, Northern Ireland.

CARSON, D(onald) A(rthur). Canadian, b. 1946. **Genres:** Theology/ Religion. **Career:** Ordained Baptist minister, 1972; Central Baptist Seminary, Toronto, lecturer in French, 1967-70; Northwest Baptist Theological College, Vancouver, lecturer, 1971-72, associate professor of New Testament, 1975-76, academic dean of Seminary, 1976-78; Trinity Evangelical Divinity School, Deerfield, IL, associate professor, 1978-82, professor, 1982-91, research professor of New Testament, 1991-. Lecturer at: Richmond College, 1969-70, Moore College, 1985, Ontario Bible College, 1991; Wycliffe Hall, Oxford, 1993; guest lecturer at colleges, universities, and theological schools in the United States and Canada. Pastor of Baptist church in Richmond, British Columbia, 1970-72; Gramcord Institute, founding chairperson, currently vice-chairperson; World Evangelical Fellowship, member of Theological Commission, 1981-82, member of executive committee of Theological Commission, 1986-90; Tyndale House, acting warden, 1986-87. Worked in radio and television as writer, executive producer, and on-screen interviewer; also worked as shipping clerk and salesperson for a tire company, statistics clerk for the Canadian government, and research assistant in air pollution laboratories. **Publications:** (author of revision) A.C. Thiselton, New Testament Commentary Survey, 1977, 4th ed., 1993; The Sermon on the Mount: An Exposition of Matthew 5-7, 1978; The King James Version Debate: A Plea for Realism, 1979; The Farewell Discourse and Final Prayer of Jesus: An Exposition of John 14-17, 1980, in UK as Jesus and His Friends: His Farewell-Message and Prayer in John 14 to 17, 1986; Divine Sovereignty and Human Responsibility: Biblical Themes in Tension, 1981; (ed. and author of introduction) From Sabbath to Lord's Day: A Biblical, Historical, and Theological Investigation, 1982; (ed. with J.D. Woodbridge, and contrib.) Scripture and Truth, 1983; Matthew, 1984; Exegetical Fallacies, 1984; From Triumphalism to Maturity: An Exposition of 2 Corinthians 10-13, 1984; (ed. and contrib.) Biblical Interpretation and the Church: Text and Context, Paternoster, 1984, published as Biblical Interpretation and the Church: The

Problem of Contextualization, 1985; God with Us: Themes from Matthew, 1985, 1995; Greek Accents: A Student's Manual, 1985; Redaction Criticism: The Nature of an Interpretative Tool, 1985; (ed. with J.D. Woodbridge, and contrib.) Hermeneutics, Authority, and Canon, 1986; Showing the Spirit: A Theological Exposition of 1 Corinthians 12-14, 1987; (ed. and contrib.) The Church in the Bible and the World: An International Study, 1987; When Jesus Confronts the World: An Exposition of Matthew 8-10, 1987; (ed. with H.G.M. Williamson, and contrib.) It Is Written: Scripture Citing Scripture; Essays in Honour of Barnabas Lindars, S.S.F., 1988; How Long, O Lord? Reflections on Suffering and Evil, 1990; (ed. and contrib.) Teach Us to Pray: Prayer in the Bible and the World, 1990; The Gospel According to John, 1991; (with L. Morris and D.J. Moo) An Introduction to the New Testament, 1991; A Call to Spiritual Reformation: Priorities From Paul and His Prayers, 1992; (co-author) An Evangelical Response to "Baptism, Eucharist, and Ministry," 1992; (ed.) Right With God: Justification in the Bible and the World, 1992; The Cross and Christian Ministry, 1993; (ed.) Worship: Adoration and Action, 1993; (ed. with J.D. Woodbridge, and contrib.) God and Culture: Essays in Honor of Carl F.H. Henry, 1993; (ed. with S.E. Porter) Biblical Greek Language and Linguistics: Open Quest, Current Research, 1993; (with J.D. Woodbridge) Letters Along the Way, 1993; Holy Sonnets of the Twentieth Century, 1994; (co-ed.) New Bible Commentary Revised, 1994; (ed. with S.E. Porter) On Discourse and Other Topics, 1995; The Gagging of God: Christianity Confronts Pluralism, 1996; Basics for Believers: An Exposition of Philippians, 1996. Work represented in anthologies. Contributor of articles and reviews to periodicals. **Address:** Trinity Evangelical Divinity School, 2065 Half Day Rd., Deerfield, IL 60015, U.S.A.

CARSON, Donald W. American, b. 1933. **Genres:** Biography. **Career:** Journalist and educator. Arizona Daily Star, Tucson, AZ, reporter and writer, 1957-61, associate editor, 1967-68; Associated Press, 1961-66, newsman in Washington, DC to assistant bureau chief in Phoenix, AZ; University of Arizona, Tucson, AZ, 1966-, assistant professor to professor of journalism, head of department, 1978-84. Editor, Goals for Tucson tabloid, 1982; Fulbright lecturer, Ecuador, 1988, 1989; semester-abroad professor, London, 1990; Fulbright senior scholar, Ecuador, 1993; visiting lecturer in Europe and South America. **Publications:** (with J.W. Johnson) Mo: The Life and Times of Morris K. Udall, 2001. Contributor to newspapers. **Address:** Department of Journalism, Franklin Bldg., Room 112F, University of Arizona, Tucson, AZ 85721, U.S.A. **Online address:** dcarson@u.arizona.edu

CARSON, Herbert L. American, b. 1929. **Genres:** Literary criticism and history, Philosophy. **Career:** Ferris State University, Big Rapids, MI, professor of humanities and philosophy, 1960-84, professor, 1984-94, professor emeritus, 1994-. Grand Rapids Press, Michigan, book reviewer, 1973-94. Formerly, Originator and Director, Workshop on Film, Ford Foundation and National Endowment for the Humanities, and Chataugua Tonight, Michigan Council for the Humanities. **Publications:** Steps in Successful Speaking, 1967; (ed. with A. Carson) The Impact of Fiction, 1970; (with A. Carson) Royall Tyler, 1979; (with A. Carson) Domestic Tragedy in England, 1982; (with A. Carson) The Image of the West, 1989.

CARSON, Mary Kay. (born United States), b. 1964. **Genres:** Children's non-fiction. **Career:** Freelance writer of books, articles and teaching materials for Newbridge, Science World, Scholastic, Inc., National Audubon Society, KidsBooks, Chicago Review Press, and other educational companies, 1994-. SuperScience, New York, NY, associate editor and writer, 1991-94; Don Bosco Center, Kansas City, MO, and Delta School, Astillero, Spain, teacher of English as a second language, 1993-96. Served as a U.S. Peace Corps volunteer in La Peñita Arriba, Dominican Republic, 1987-89; worked as a National Marine Fisheries Service observer in Seattle, Washington, 1990. **Publications:** Epilepsy, 1998; The Creepiest, Scariest, Weirdest Creatures Ever!, 2002; The Wright Brothers for Kids: How They Invented the Airplane, 2003; Mars, 2003; In the Deep, 2003; The Underground Railroad for Kids, 2004. LEVELED READERS: Cool Science Jobs, 2003; Gross Body Facts, 2003; Driving on Mars, 2004; The Bald Eagle Is Back, 2004; The Greatest Electrician in the World, 2004; The Return of Wild Whoopers, 2004. PROFESSIONAL TITLES FOR TEACHERS: Space: Hands-On Activities, the Latest Information &, a Colorful Learning Poster, 1996; Colonial America: A Complete Theme Unit Developed in Cooperation with the Colonial Williamsburg Foundation, 1999 The Wow's and Why's of Weather, 2000; Great Weather Activities: All the Background Info and How To's you Need for Teaching about the Wonders of Weather, 2000 Space: Quick & Easy Internet Activities for the One-Computer Classroom, 2001 Weather: Quick & Easy Activities for the One-Computer Classroom, 2002; Easy Science Activity Journals, 2003. Author of educational titles. **Address:** 3916 Tappan Ave., Cincinnati, OH 45223, U.S.A. **Online address:** mkcarson@nasw.org

CARSTENS, Catherine Mansell. *See* **MAYO, C(atherine) M(ansell).**

CARTER, Alden R(ichardson). American, b. 1947. **Genres:** Novels, Young adult fiction, Children's non-fiction, History, Young adult non-fiction. **Career:** Writer. Taught high school English and journalism for four years in Marshfield, WI. Speaker at workshops. **Publications:** YOUNG ADULT NONFICTION: (with W.J. LeBlanc) Supercomputers, 1985; Modern China, 1986; (with LeBlanc) Modern Electronics, 1986; Radio: From Marconi to the Space Age, 1987; Illinois, 1987; The Shoshoni, 1989; Last Stand at the Alamo, 1990; Battle of Gettysburg, 1990; The Colonial Wars: Clashes in the Wilderness, 1992; The American Revolution: War for Independence, 1992; The War of 1812: Second Fight for Independence, 1992; The Mexican War: Manifest Destiny, 1992; The Civil War: American Tragedy, 1992; The Spanish-American War: Imperial Ambitions, 1992; Battle of the Ironclads: The Monitor and the Merrimack, 1993; China Past, China Future, 1994. THE AMERICAN REVOLUTION SERIES: Colonies in Revolt, 1988; Darkest Hours, 1988; At the Forge of Liberty, 1988; Birth of the Republic, 1988. YOUNG ADULT FICTION: Growing Season, 1984; Wart, Son of Toad, 1985; Sheila's Dying, 1987; Up Country, 1989; RoboDad, 1990, as Dancing on Dark Water, 1994; Dogwolf, 1994; Between a Rock and a Hard Place, 1995; Bull Catcher, 1997; Crescent Moon, 1999; Brother's Keeper, 2003. CHILDREN'S NONFICTION: (with S.M. Carter) I'm Tougher Than Asthma, 1996; Big Brother Dustin, 1997; Seeing Things My Way, 1998; Dustin's Big School Day, 1999; Stretching Ourselves: Kids with Cerebral Palsy, 2000; I'm Tougher Than Diabetes, 2001. FOR ADULTS. FICTION: Bright Starry Banner: A Novel of the Civil War, 2004. NONFICTION: (ed.) Auschwitz Veterinarian, 2003. **Address:** 1113 W Onstad Dr, Marshfield, WI 54449, U.S.A. **Online address:** acarterwriter@tznet.com; www.aldencarter.com

CARTER, Ashton B. American, b. 1954. **Genres:** Military/Defense/Arms control. **Career:** Affiliated with the Congressional Office of Technology Assessment, U.S. Department of Defense, Washington, DC, 1981-82; Massachusetts Institute of Technology, Cambridge, research fellow, 1982-84; Harvard University, Cambridge, assistant professor, 1984-86, associate professor of public policy, 1986-88; Harvard University Center for Science and International Affairs, associate director and professor, 1988-90, director and professor of science and international affairs, 1990-. **Publications:** (ed. with D.N. Schwartz, and contrib.) Ballistic Missile Defense, 1984; Directed Energy Missile Defense in Space, 1984; (ed. with J. Steinbruner and C.A. Zraket, and contrib.) Managing Nuclear Operations, 1987; Ashton B. Carter on Arms Control, 1990; (with K. Campbell and others) Soviet Nuclear Fission, 1991; (with J. Alic and others) Beyond Spinoff: Military and Commercial Technologies in a Changing World, 1992; New Thinking and American Defense Technology, 1993; Preventive Defense, 1999; Keeping the Edge, 2001. Contributor to anthologies and scholarly journals. **Address:** Belfer Center for Science and International Affairs, John F. Kennedy School of Government, Littauer 374, 79 John F. Kennedy St, Cambridge, MA 02138, U.S.A. **Online address:** ashton_carter@harvard.edu

CARTER, Betty. American, b. 1944. **Genres:** Bibliography. **Career:** Librarian, educator. **Publications:** (with R.F. Abrahamson and the Committee on the Senior High School Booklist of the National Council of Teachers of English) Books For You: A Booklist for Senior High Students, 1988; (with R.F. Abrahamson) Nonfiction for Young Adults: From Delight to Wisdom, 1990; Best Books for Young Adults: The Selections, the History, the Romance, 1994. **Address:** c/o American Library Association, 50 East Huron St., Chicago, IL 60611, U.S.A.

CARTER, Betty Smartt. Also writes as Mary Carter. American, b. 1965. **Genres:** Children's fiction, Novels, Autobiography/Memoirs. **Career:** Novelist. **Publications:** I Read It in the Wordless Book, 1996; The Tower, the Mask & the Grave, 1997; Home is Always the Place you Just Left, 2001. Contributor of articles and reviews to periodicals. **Address:** c/o Paraclete Press, PO Box 1568, Orleans, MA 02653, U.S.A. **Online address:** bettycart@juno.com

CARTER, Charlotte. American. **Genres:** Mystery/Crime/Suspense. **Career:** Freelance editor, proofreader, and writer. **Publications:** Rhode Island Red, 1997; Coq au Vin, 1999. Contributor to periodicals. **Address:** c/o Mysterious Press, Warner Books, 1271 Avenue of the Americas, New York, NY 10020, U.S.A.

CARTER, Emily. American, b. 1960. **Genres:** Poetry. **Career:** Pulse (newspaper), Minneapolis, MN, columnist; Loft Literary Center, Minneapolis, MN, teacher; author. **Publications:** Glory Goes and Gets Some, 2000. Contributor to anthologies. **Address:** c/o Coffee House Press, 27 North Fourth St. Suite 400, Minneapolis, MN 55401, U.S.A.

CARTER, Frances Monet. American, b. 1923. **Genres:** Medicine/Health. **Career:** Professor Emerita of Psychiatric Nursing, University of San Francisco, since 1988 (Instructor to Associate Professor, 1957-70; Professor, 1970-88). Member, San Francisco Mental Health Advisory Board, 1969-78 (President, 1976). Fellow, American Academy of Nursing, 1990. World Health Organization Fellow 1961-62, 1970; Distinguished Teaching Award, Univ. of San Francisco, 1972; First Alumni Fellow Award, Univ. of Louisville, 1990. **Publications:** The Role of the Nurse in Community Mental Health, 1968; Psychosocial Nursing: Theory and Practice in Hospital and Community Mental Health, 1971, 3rd ed. 1981. **Address:** 55 Conrad St, San Francisco, CA 94131, U.S.A.

CARTER, Harold. British, b. 1925. **Genres:** Geography, Urban studies, Language/Linguistics. **Career:** University College of Wales, Aberystwyth, Lecturer, 1952-68, Gregynog Professor of Human Geography, 1968-86, Professor Emeritus, 1986-. **Publications:** Towns of Wales: A Study in Urban Geography, 1965; (ed.) Urban Essays: Studies in the Geography of Wales, 1970; The Study of Urban Geography, 1972, 4th ed. 1995; An Introduction to Urban Historical Geography, 1983; The Welsh Language 1961-1981: An Interpretive Atlas, 1988; An Urban Geography of England and Wales in the Nineteenth Century, 1990; A Geography of the Welsh Language, 1961-1991, 1994; Language, Economy and Society, 2000. **Address:** Tyle Bach Maes y Garn, Bow Street, Aberystwyth, Ceregigion SY24 5DS, Wales. **Online address:** 101571.3476@compuserve.com

CARTER, Jared. American, b. 1939. **Genres:** Poetry. **Publications:** POETRY: Early Warning, 1979; Work, for the Night Is Coming, 1981; Fugue State, 1984; Pincushion's Strawberry (poems and photographs), 1984; Millennial Harbinger, 1986; The Shriving, 1990; Situation Normal, 1991; Blues Project, 1991; After the Rain, 1993; Les Barricades Mysterieuses, 1999. Work represented in anthologies. Contributor to periodicals. **Address:** 1220 N State Ave, Indianapolis, IN 46201-1162, U.S.A. **Online address:** www.jaredcarter.com

CARTER, Jean Wilmont. *See* **WILMOT, Jeanne.**

CARTER, Jimmy. (James Earl Carter, Jr). American, b. 1924. **Genres:** Politics/Government, Autobiography/Memoirs, Inspirational/Motivational Literature. **Career:** Distinguished Professor, Emory University, Atlanta, 1982-. Chairman, Board of Trustees, Carter Center, Atlanta, Carter-Menil Human Rights Foundation, and Global 200, Inc., all 1986-. U.S. Navy, Lt., 1946-53; Businessman/Farmer (Carter Peanut Farms), 1953-77; Georgia State Senator, 1962-66; Governor of Georgia, 1971-74; President of the United States, 1977-81. Recipient: Nobel Prize for Peace, 2002. **Publications:** Why Not the Best?, 1975; A Government as Good as Its People, 1977; Letters to the Hon. William Prescott, 1977; Keeping Faith: Memoirs of a President, 1982; Negotiation: The Alternative to Hostility, 1984; The Blood of Abraham: Insights into the Middle East, 1985, new ed., 1993; (with R. Carter) Everything to Gain: Making the Most of the Rest of Your Life, 1987; An Outdoor Journal, 1988; Turning Point: A Candidate and a State Come of Age, 1992; Talking Peace: A Vision for the Next Generation, 1993; Always a Reckoning, and Other Poems, 1995; Living Faith, 1996; Lessons for Life, 1996; (with Amy Carter) The Little Baby Snoogle-Fleejer, 1996; Sources of Strength: Meditations on Scripture for Daily Living, 1997; The Virtues of Aging, 1998; Atlanta: The Right Kind of Courage, 2000; An Hour before Daylight: Memories of a Rural Boyhood, 2000; Christmas in Plains: Memories, 2001; As Time Goes By: Memories of the Past, A Legacy for the Future, 2001; The Hornet's Nest (novel), 2003. **Address:** The Carter Center, One Copenhill, 453 Freedom Parkway, Atlanta, GA 30307-1498, U.S.A.

CARTER, John T(homas). American, b. 1921. **Genres:** Children's fiction, Children's non-fiction. **Career:** Samford University, Birmingham, AL, professor, 1956-77, dean of education emeritus, 1987-. **Publications:** Mike and His Four-Star Coal, 1960; East Is West, 1964; Witness in Israel, 1966; (with F. Carter) Sharing Times Seven, 1970. **Address:** 2561 Rocky Ridge Rd, Birmingham, AL 35243, U.S.A. **Online address:** j-fcarter@juno.com

CARTER, Joseph H(enry), (Sr.). American, b. 1932. **Genres:** Biography. **Career:** United Press International (UPI), correspondent in Dallas, TX, 1959-64; Honolulu Advertiser, reporter, 1964-65; Oklahoma Journal, associate editor, 1964-68; White House staff assistant, Washington, DC, 1968 and 1980; served as executive assistant to governor of Oklahoma, 1971-74; Democratic National Committee, director of communications, 1972; White House Council on Wage and Price Stability, deputy assistant director, 1979-80; H/CA Inc., Washington, DC, president, 1980-85; Cameron University, Lawton, OK, vice president, 1985-89; Will Rogers Memorial Museums, Claremore, OK, director, 1989-99; writer. **Publications:** Never Met a Man I

Didn't Like: The Life and Writings of Will Rogers, 1991. **Address:** PO Box 2334, Claremore, OK 74018, U.S.A. **Online address:** joecarter@willrogers. com

CARTER, Martin R(oger). Canadian (born England), b. 1946. **Genres:** Agriculture/Forestry, Environmental sciences/Ecology. **Career:** Farm manager, prior to 1972; Agriculture Canada, assistant head of investigation section at PFRA Tree Nursery, Indian Head, Saskatchewan, 1977-80, officer in charge of Soils and Crops Substation, Vegreville, Alberta, 1981-83; Agriculture and Agri-Food Canada, Charlottetown, Prince Edward Island, research scientist, 1983-. Rutherglen Research Institute, Australia, visiting scientist, 1990-91; Nova Scotia Agricultural College, adjunct professor, 1993-98; Ballarat University, Australia, visiting fellow, 1995-96. **Publications:** (ed.) Soil Sampling and Methods of Analysis, 1993; (ed.) Conservation Tillage in Temperate Agroecosystems, 1994; (ed. with B.A. Stewart) Soil Structure and Organic Matter Storage in Agricultural Soils, 1996; (ed. with E.G. Gregorich) Soil Quality for Crop Production, 1997. **Address:** Research Centre, Research Branch, Agriculture and Agri-Food Canada, PO Box 1210, Charlottetown, PE, Canada C1A 7M8. **Online address:** carterm@ em.agr.ca

CARTER, Mary. See **CARTER, Betty Smartt.**

CARTER, Mike. British, b. 1936. **Genres:** Novels, Young adult fiction. **Career:** Secondary school teacher, 1961-89; writer, 1989-. **Publications:** Biggest Pool of All, 1995; Space Games, 2001. YOUNG ADULT NOVELS: Jessie, 2003; Access to the Universe, 2004. Contributor of short stories and articles to periodicals. **Address:** Te Kohanga Rd, Onewhero, R.D. 2 Tuakau, Auckland, New Zealand. **Online address:** diannacarter@clear.net.nz

CARTER, Nick. See **CRIDER, (Allen) Bill(y).**

CARTER, Nick. See **LYNDS, Dennis.**

CARTER, Nick. See **SMITH, Martin Cruz.**

CARTER, Raphael. American. **Genres:** Science fiction/Fantasy. **Publications:** The Fortunate Fall, 1996. **Address:** c/o Tor Books, 175 Fifth Ave., 14th Floor, New York, NY 10010, U.S.A. **Online address:** www. chaparraltree.com

CARTER, Rosalynn (Smith). American, b. 1927. **Genres:** Self help, Autobiography/Memoirs. **Career:** Wife of former U.S. President Jimmy Carter. First Lady of Georgia, 1971-75. Vice-chair, Board of Directors, The Carter Center; chair, Carter Center Mental Health Task Force; co-founder, Every Child by Two Campaign for Early Immunization; President, Rosalynn Carter Institute for Caregiving of Georgia Southwestern State University; member of Board of Advisers, Habitat for Humanity; member, Georgia Governor's Commission to Improve Services for the Mentally and Emotionally Handicapped, 1971; Hon. Chairman, Georgia Special Olympics, 1971-75; Honorary Chair, President's Commission on Mental Health, 1977-78; Honorary Chair, John F. Kennedy Center for the Performing Arts Board of Trustees, 1977-80. Board member emerita, National Association for Mental Health; recipient of humanitarian and public service awards. **Publications:** First Lady from Plains, 1984; (with J. Carter) Everything to Gain: Making the Most of the Rest of Your Life, 1987; Helping Yourself Help Others: A Book for Caregivers, 1994; Helping Someone with Mental Illness: A Compassionate Guide for Family, Friends, and Caregivers, 1998. **Address:** The Carter Center, 1 Copenhill, Atlanta, GA 30307, U.S.A.

CARTER, Stephen L(isle). American, b. 1954. **Genres:** Law. **Career:** Educator and writer. Admitted to the Bar of Washington, DC, 1981. U.S. Court of Appeals, District of Columbia Circuit, law clerk, 1979-80; U.S. Supreme Court, Washington, DC, law clerk for Justice Thurgood Marshall, 1980-81; Shea & Gardner (law firm), Washington, DC, associate, 1981-82; Yale University Law School, New Haven, CT, assistant professor, 1982-84, associate professor, 1984-85, professor, 1985-, William Nelson Cromwell Professor of Law. **Publications:** Reflections of an Affirmative Action Baby, 1991; The Culture of Disbelief: How American Law and Politics Trivialize Religious Devotion, 1993; Confirmation Mess, 1994; Integrity, 1996; Dissent of the Governed, 1998; Civility, 1998; God's Name in Vain, 2000; The Emperor of Ocean Park (novel), 2002. **Address:** Yale University Law School, P.O. Box 208215, New Haven, CT 06520, U.S.A. **Online address:** stephen. carter@yale.edu

CARTER, Steven. American, b. 1956. **Genres:** Psychology, Self help, Sex. **Career:** Writer. **Publications:** What Every Man Should Know about the

New Woman: A Survival Guide, 1984; (with J. Levine) How to Make Love to a Computer, 1984; (with H. Levinson) Phobia-Free: A Medical Breakthrough Linking Ninety Percent of All Phobia and Panic Attacks to a Hidden Physical Problem, 1985; (with J. Sokol) Men Who Can't Love: When a Man's Fear Makes Him Run from Commitment (and What a Smart Woman Can Do about It), 1986; (with Sokol) What Really Happens in Bed: A Demystification of Sex, 1988; (with Sokol) What Smart Women Know, 1990; Lives without Balance: When You're Giving Everything You've Got and Still Not Getting What You Hoped For, 1992; He's Scared, She's Scared, 1993; Men Like Women Who Like Themselves, 1996; Getting to Commitment, 1998; This Is How Love Work, 2001. **Address:** c/o M. Evans & Co., 216 E 49th St, New York, NY 10017, U.S.A. **Online address:** caspublic@ aol.com

CARTER, Steven R(ay). American, b. 1942. **Genres:** Mystery/Crime/Suspense, Literary criticism and history, Theatre. **Career:** Youngstown State University, Youngstown, OH, instructor in English, 1968-70, 1972, and 1973; University of Akron, part-time instructor, 1975-76; University of Sassari, Italy, lecturer, 1976-77; University of North Carolina, Wilmington, assistant professor of English, 1977-82; University of Puerto Rico, Rio Piedras, assistant professor of English, 1982-87, associate professor, 1988-96; Trenton State College, visiting professor, 1991-92; Salem State College, associate professor, 1996-98, professor, 1998-, chairperson of English Dept, 2004-. **Publications:** (ed. with M. Curran) Questioning: A Thematic and Rhetorical Reader, 1971; Hansberry's Drama: Commitment amid Complexity, 1991; James Jones: An American Literary Orientatlist Master, 1998. Contributor to anthologies. Contributor to periodicals. **Address:** Dept of English, Salem State College, Salem, MA 01970, U.S.A.

CARTER, (Elizabeth) Susanne. American, b. 1950. **Genres:** Education, Women's studies and issues, Literary criticism and history, Bibliography. **Career:** Springfield Daily News, Springfield, MO, news reporter, 1973-74; Missouri State Auditor's Office and Missouri Department of Natural Resources, Jefferson, staff writer, 1974-77; junior high school English teacher at public schools in Stockton, MO, 1977-80; Southwest Missouri State University, Springfield, microforms supervisor, 1980-92; University of Oregon, Eugene, information specialist at Western Regional Resource Center, 1992-95; University of Missouri, library coordinator, Center for Innovations in Special Education, 1995-99, grant writer, College of Education, 1999-. **Publications:** War and Peace through Women's Eyes: An Annotated Bibliography of American Women's Interpretations of War and Peace through Fiction, 1992; Mothers and Daughters in American Short Fiction: An Annotated Bibliography of Women's Writing, 1993. Contributor of articles and book reviews to magazines and local newspapers. **Address:** University of Missouri, 109 Hill Hall, Columbia, MO 65211, U.S.A. **Online address:** cartere@missouri.edu

CARTER, Tom. (Thomas Earl Carter). American, b. 1947. **Genres:** Biography. **Career:** Tulsa World, Tulsa, OK, columnist and general assignment writer, 1971-75, director of suburban news bureau, 1975-78, entertainment reporter and columnist, 1978-82, human interest columnist, 1982-88; writer. Presented music and talk shows for local radio and television networks, 1974-79. **Publications:** (with R. Milsap) Almost Like a Song, 1990; Memories: The Autobiography of Ralph Emery, 1991; (with R. Emery) More Memories, 1993; (with B. Killen) By the Seat of My Pants, 1993; (with G. Campbell) Rhinestone Cowboy, 1994; (with R. McEntire) Reba: My Story, 1994; (with G. Jones) I Lived to Tell It All, 1996; (with L,. Rhimes) Holiday in Your Heart, 1997; (with N. Jones) Nashville Wives, 1998; (with M. Haggard) Merle Haggard's My House of Memories, 1999; (with J. Daly) Tammy Wynette, 2000; First Lady of Tennis: Hazel Hotchkiss Wightman, 2001. **Address:** c/o Mel Berger, William Morris Agency, 1325 Avenue of the Americas, New York, NY 10019, U.S.A.

CARTER, Walter. American, b. 1950. **Genres:** Music. **Career:** Tennessean, Nashville, music reporter, 1978-82; Gruhn Guitars, Nashville, TN, writer and researcher, 1988-92; Gibson Guitar Corp., Nashville, historian, 1993-98; songwriter. **Publications:** (with E. Widner) The Oak Ridge Boys: Our Story, 1986; The Songwriter's Guide to Collaboration, 1988; (with G. Gruhn) Gruhn's Guide to Vintage Guitars, 1990; (with G. Gruhn) Acoustic Guitars and Other Fretted Instruments: A Photographic History, 1992; (with G. Gruhn) Electric Guitars and Basses: A Photographic History, 1993; (ed. and contrib.) Gibson Guitars: One Hundred Years of an American Icon, 1994; The Martin Guitar Book, 1995; Epiphone: The Complete History, 1995; The Ovation Story, 1995.

CARTER, Warren. (born New Zealand), b. 1955. **Genres:** Theology/Religion. **Career:** Saint Paul School of Theology, Kansas City, MO, instructor, 1990-91, assistant professor, 1991-95, associate professor, 1995-2000, Lindsey P. Pherigo Professor of New Testament, 2000-. **Publications:** What Are They Saying about Matthew's Sermon on the Mount?, 1994; Disciple-ship and Households: A Study of Matthew 19-20, 1994; Matthew: Storyteller, Interpreter, Evangelist, 1996; (with J. P. Heil) Matthew's Parables: Audience-Oriented Perspectives, 1998; Matthew and the Margins: A Religious and Socio-Political Reading, 2000; Matthew and Empire: Initial Explorations, 2001; (with D. Jacobson, C. J. Dempsey, and J. P. Heil) New Proclamation: Year A, 2001-2002, 2002; Pontius Pilate: Portraits of a Roman Governor, 2003 Got Life? John: Storyteller, Interpreter, Evangelist, forthcoming. Contributor to scholarly journals and religious magazines. **Address:** Saint Paul School of Theology, 5123 Truman Rd., Kansas City, MO 64127, U.S.A. **Online address:** wcarter@st.edu

CARTER, William E. American, b. 1939. **Genres:** Astronomy, Earth sciences. **Career:** Research geodesist, civil engineer. U.S. Air Force, 1961-72, Orlando, Fl, geodetic officer, 1961-63, Cheyenne, WY, geodetic officer, 1965-67, Great Falls, MT, missile launch officer; 1967-69, Tucson, AZ, research geodesist, 1969-72; University of Hawaii, Maui, research geodesist, 1972-76; National Oceanic and Atmospheric Administration, Silver Springs, MD, 1976-96, chief of geodetic research and development laboratory, 1992-96; University of Florida, Gainesville, adjunct professor of engineering, 1996-. **Publications:** (with M.S. Carter) Latitude: How American Astrono-mers Solved the Mystery of Variation, 2002. Author of scientific papers and articles; contributor to journals and periodicals. **Address:** 5154 Medoras Ave, St. Augustine, FL 32080, U.S.A. **Online address:** bcarter@ufl.edu

CARTMILL, Matt. American, b. 1943. **Genres:** Anthropology/Ethnology. **Career:** Duke University, Durham, NC, professor of biological anthropology and anatomy, 1969-. **Publications:** Human Structure, 1987; A View to a Death in the Morning: Hunting and Nature through History, 1993. **Address:** Department of Biological Anthropology, Medical Center, Duke University, Durham, NC 27710, U.S.A.

CARTON, Bernice. American, b. 1922. **Genres:** Novels, Travel/Exploration. **Career:** Travel writer and photographer, 1971-. Also worked as a nursery school teacher; volunteer for New York Philharmonic Orchestra. **Publica-tions:** Beyond the Brooklyn Bridge, 1998. Contributor to magazines and newspapers in the United States and Canada. **Address:** 880 5th Ave Apt 7G, New York, NY 10021-4951, U.S.A.

CARTWRIGHT, Justin. British (born Republic of South Africa), b. 1945. **Genres:** Novels. **Career:** Author and film director. **Publications:** The Revenge, 1978; The Horse of Darius, 1980; Freedom for the Wolves, 1983; Interior, 1988; Look at It This Way, 1990; Masai Dreaming, 1993; In Every Face I meet, 1995. NON-FICTION: Not Yet Home: A South African Journey, 1996. **Address:** c/o PFD, Drury House, 34-43 Russell Street, London WC2B 5HA, England.

CARUSONE, Al. American, b. 1949. **Genres:** Paranormal. **Career:** Accu-Weather, State College, PA, educational sales representative, 1989-. Worked as junior high school science teacher, ice cream maker, glass worker, and nuclear reactor operator. **Publications:** Don't Open the Door after the Sun Goes Down: Tales of the Real and Unreal, 1994; Behind the Sending Door, 1997; The Boy with Dinosaur Hands, 1998.

CARVER, Martin. Scottish, b. 1941. **Genres:** Archaeology/Antiquities, History, Urban studies. **Career:** H.M. Forces (British Army), Royal Tank Regiment, army officer, 1959-72; freelance archaeologist, 1972-76; Birmingham University Field Archaeology Unit, director, 1977-86; University of York, England, professor of archaeology, 1986-, director, Centre for Medieval Studies, 2001-02. Antiquity, editor, 2003-. **Publications:** Underneath English Towns, 1986; Arguments in Stone, 1993; Sutton Hoo Burial Ground of Kings?, 1998; Surviving in Symbols: A Visit to the Pictish Nation, 1999; Archaeological Value and Evaluation, 2003. EDITOR: Medieval Worcester, 1980; The Age of Sutton Hoo, 1992; In Search of Cult, 1993; The Cross Goes North, 2003. **Address:** Ella House, Ellerton, York YO42 4PB, England. **Online address:** martincarver@yahoo.co.uk

CARVER, Norman Francis, Jr. American, b. 1928. **Genres:** Architecture. **Career:** Lectures, Visiting Architect: Ill. Inst. of Tech., MIT, Yale, Carnegie Tech, King Faisel Univ., Saudi Arabia; architect, private practice in Kalama-zoo, MI, 1955-. **Publications:** Form and Space of Japanese Architecture, 1955; Form and Space of Japanese Architecture, 2nd ed., 1993; Silent Cities: Mexico and the Maya, 1965, 1986; Italian Hilltowns, 1979, 2nd ed., 1995; Iberian Villages, 1980; Japanese Folkhouses, 1984; North African Villages, 1989; Greek Island Villages, 2001.

CARVER, Terrell. American, b. 1946. **Genres:** History, Politics/Government, Biography. **Career:** University of Liverpool, Liverpool, England, lecturer in politics, 1974-79; University of Bristol, Bristol, England, lecturer, 1980-89, reader in politics, 1990-94, professor of politics, 1995-. **Publications:** Karl Marx: Texts on Method, 1975; Engels, 1981; Marx's Social Theory, 1982; Marx and Engels: The Intellectual Relationship, 1983; A Marx Dictionary, 1987; Friedrich Engels: His Life and Thought, 1990; Marx, 1991; Marx: Later Writings, 1996; Gender Is Not a Synonym for Women, 1996; The Postmodern Marx, 1998. EDITOR: (and trans.) J. Zeleny, The Logic of Marx, 1980; (and trans.) G. Bekerman, Marx and Engels: A Conceptual Concordance, 1983; (and trans.) H. Uchida, Marx's Grundrisse and Hegel's Logic, 1988; (with P. Thomas) Rational Choice Marxism, 1995. **Address:** Department of Politics, University of Bristol, Bristol BS8 1TU, England. **Online address:** t.carver@bristol.ac.uk

CARVILLE, (Chester) James, (Jr.). American, b. 1944. **Genres:** Politics/Government. **Career:** Taught middle school science, 1969-70; admitted to the Bar of Louisiana, 1973; McKernnan, Beychok, Screen and Pierson, Baton Rouge, LA, attorney, 1973-79; Gus Weill and Raymond Strother (political consulting firm), Baton Rouge, became a director of campaigns, 1979-80; administrative assistant to Mayor Pat Screen, Baton Rouge, 1980-81; campaign manager for Virginia's Lt. Governor Richard J. Davis's bid for the U.S. Senate, 1982; worked briefly as an organizer of the South for Democratic presidential candidate Gary Hart, 1983; campaign manager for Texas state senator Lloyd Doggett's bid for the U.S. Senate, 1983-84; direc-tor of Robert P. Casey's campaign for governor of Pennsylvania, 1986; director of Wallace Wilkinson's campaign for governor of Kentucky, 1987; manager of New Jersey Senator Frank R. Lautenberg's reelection campaign, 1988; manager of Fred Hofheinz's bid for mayor of Houston, TX, 1989; Car-ville & Begala (a consulting firm), Washington, DC, founding partner, 1989-; campaign manager for the reelection of Casey as governor of Pennsylvania, manager of Lieutenant Governor Zell Miller's campaign for governor of Georgia, and advisor to Texas state attorney general Jim Mattox's campaign for governor of Texas, all 1990; manager of Martha Wilkinson's campaign for governor of Kentucky and Pennsylvanian Harris Wofford's campaign for the U.S. Senate, 1991; chief strategist for Bill Clinton's presidential campaign, 1991-92; advisor to James J. Florio's reelection campaign as governor of New Jersey and Richard Katz's bid for mayor of Los Angeles, 1993. **Publications:** (with M. Matalin and P. Knobler) All's Fair: Love, War, and Running for President, 1994; And the Horse He Rode in on, 1998; Stickin': The Case for Loyalty, 2000. **Address:** c/o Washington Speakers Bureau, 1663 Prince St., Alexandria, VA 22314, U.S.A.

CARWARDINE, Richard J(ohn). British, b. 1947. **Genres:** History, Theology/Religion. **Career:** University of Sheffield, England, lecturer, 1971-90, senior lecturer, 1990-94, professor of history, 1994-2002; University of Oxford, England, Rhodes Professor of American History, 2002; University of North Carolina at Chapel Hill, research fellow, 1989. **Publications:** Transatlantic Revivalism: Popular Evangelicalism in Britain and America, 1790-1865, 1978; Evangelicals and Politics in Antebellum America, 1993; Lincoln, 2003.

CARWELL, L'Ann. See **MCKISSACK, Patricia C(arwell).**

CARY, Jud. See **TUBB, E(dwin) C(harles).**

CARY, Lorene. American, b. 1956. **Genres:** Novels, Autobiography/Memoirs. **Career:** Writer. Art Sanctuary, director. **Publications:** Black Ice (memoir), 1991; The Price of a Child, 1995; Pride, 1998. **Address:** Depart-ment of English, University of Pennsylvania, Bennett Hall, 34th and Walnut Sts, Philadelphia, PA 19104, U.S.A.

CARY, Margaret. American. **Genres:** Medicine/Health. **Career:** Completed medical internship and residency at University of California-San Francisco, and Community Hospital of Sonoma County, Santa Rosa, CA, 1978-81; private practice of medicine in Santa Rosa and Mammoth Lakes, CA, 1981-83; Rose Medical Center, medical director, 1983-86; private practice of medicine in Denver, CO, 1986-93; U.S. Department of Health and Human Services, regional director, 1994-2000, member of Managed Care Forum, 1996-98, and Partnership for Rural Opportunities, 1996-99; Vox Medica (health care communications group), Philadelphia, PA, chief medical officer and senior vice president, 2001-. University of Colorado-Denver, assistant clinical professor of family medicine, 1991-; member of advisory boards; guest on media programs; public speaker. **Publications:** (with A.W. Darkins) Telemedicine and Telehealth: Principles, Policies, Performance, and Pitfalls, 2000. Contributor to books and periodicals. **Address:** Vox Medica, 210 West Washington Sq., Philadelphia, PA 19106, U.S.A. **Online address:** mcary@voxmedica.com; maggicary@aol.com

CASANOVA, Mary. American, b. 1957. **Genres:** Children's fiction, Young adult fiction. **Career:** Author, lecturer, speaker, and writing instructor. **Publications:** MIDDLE GRADE NOVELS: Moose Tracks, 1995; Riot, 1996; Wolf Shadows, 1997; Stealing Thunder, 1998; Curse of a Winter Moon, 2000; When Eagles Fall, 2002; Cecile: Gates of Gold, 2002. PICTURE BOOKS: The Hunter, 2000; One Dog Canoe, 2003. OTHER: The Golden Retriever (nonfiction), 1990. **Address:** PO Box 141, Ranier, MN 56668-0141, U.S.A. **Online address:** www.marycasanova.com

CASATI, Roberto. Italian, b. 1961. **Genres:** Translations, Philosophy. **Career:** University of Neuchatel, Neuchatel, Switzerland, assistant professor, 1988-93; University of Aix-Marseille, Aix-en-Provence, France, researcher in Research Group on Epistemology, at Centre National de la Recherche Scientifique, 1994-. Swiss National Foundation for Scientific Research, researcher, 1988-92; Ecole Polytechnique, Paris, France, research associate at Centre de Recherche en Epistemologie Appliquee, 1993-. **Publications:** L'immagine (title means: Pictures), 1991; (with A. Varzi) Holes and Other Superficialities, 1994; (with J. Dokic) La philosophie du son (title means: The Philosophy of Sound), 1994; (with Varzi) Events: An Annotated Bibliography, 1994. TRANSLATOR: G. Frege, Logische Untersuchungen/Ricerche Logiche, 1989; A.J. Ayer, Russell, 1992. EDITOR: (with G. White) Philosophy and the Cognitive Sciences, 1993; (with White and B. Smith) Philosophy and the Cognitive Sciences, 1994; (with Varzi) Events, 1995. Contributor to books. Contributor of articles, translations, and reviews to philosophy journals and other scholarly periodicals. **Address:** Department of Philosophy, Centre National de la Recherche Scientifique, University of Aix-Marseille, 29 Av. Robert Schuman, 13621 Aix-en-Provence, France.

CASCONE, A. G. See CASCONE, Annette.

CASCONE, Annette. Also writes as A. G. Cascone. American, b. 1960. **Genres:** Children's fiction, Young adult fiction, Plays/Screenplays. **Career:** Writer. **Publications:** ALL WITH G. CASCONE AS A.G. CASCONE. FOR CHILDREN. The Attack of the Aqua Apes, 1995; Eye of the Fortuneteller, 1996. DEADTIME STORIES SERIES: Terror in Tiny Town, 1996; Invasion of the Appleheads, 1996; Along Came a Spider, 1996; Ghost Knight, 1996; Revenge of the Goblins, 1996; Little Magic Shop of Horrors, 1997; It Came from the Deep, 1997; Grave Secrets, 1997; Mirror, Mirror, 1997; Grandpa's Monster Movies, 1997; Nightmare on Planet X, 1997; Welcome to the TerrorGo-Round, 1997; The Beast of Baskerville, 1997; Trapped in Tiny Town, 1997; Cyber Scare, 1997; Night of the Pet Zombies, 1997; Faerie Tale, 1997. FOR YOUNG ADULTS: In a Crooked Little House, 1994; If He Hollers, 1995; There's No Place Like Home, 1997. SCREENPLAYS: Mirror, Mirror, Orphan Eyes, 1991. **Address:** 1 Arlington Ave, Spotswood, NJ 08884-1014, U.S.A. **Online address:** agcascone@bookwire.com

CASE, Bill. (Theodore Willard Case). American, b. 1920. **Genres:** Essays, Plays/Screenplays, Poetry, Gerontology/Senior issues, Children's fiction. **Career:** Bridgeport Post, Bridgeport, CT, reporter, 1947-49; U.S. Rubber Co., New York City, advertising writer, 1949-51; Research Institute of America, New York City, directing editor, 1954-76; free-lance writer, 1977-. **Publications:** Horses, 1985; Life Begins at Sixty, 1986. 51 TV plays, 1950-66. **Address:** 1 Crescent Ave., Apt. 15, Warwick, NY 10990, U.S.A.

CASE, George (Andrew Thomas). Canadian, b. 1967. **Genres:** Novels, Communications/Media, Social commentary, Essays. **Career:** Writer. **Publications:** Silence Descends: The End of the Information Age, 2000-2500 (fiction), 1997. Contributor to literary magazines and newspapers. **Address:** c/o Arsenal Pulp Press, 103-1014 Homer St, Vancouver, BC, Canada V6B 2W9. **Online address:** georgcas@vpl.ca

CASE, John. See HOUGAN, Carolyn.

CASEY, Barbara (Louise). (born United States), b. 1944. **Genres:** Education. **Career:** Writer, editor, and literary agent. North Carolina Wesleyan College, director of alumni and public relations, 1975-77; North Carolina State University, department of athletics, 1977-79; full-time writer, 1989-. Guest author and panelist at BookFest of the Palm Beaches, 1993-2000; judge for the Pathfinder Literary Awards, 1994-; founded own editorial consulting business and literary agency; editorial consultant, Jamaican Writers Circle. Publisher of Publishers Update, a directory of children's publishers and literary agents. **Publications:** Leilani Zan, 1992; Grandma Jock and Christabelle, 1994; Shyla's Initiative, 2002; The Coach's Wife, 2003; The Airs of Tillie, 2004; Slightest in the House, 2004; The House of Kane, 2004; Just Like a Family, 2004. Contributor to periodicals. **Address:** 11924 West Forest Hill Blvd., Ste. 22, Box 346, Wellington, FL 33414, U.S.A. **Online address:** barcafer@aol.com

CASEY, John (Dudley). American, b. 1939. **Genres:** Novels, Novellas/Short stories, Literary criticism and history, Essays, Translations. **Career:** University of Virginia, Charlottesville, professor of English, 1972-. **Publications:** NOVELS: An American Romance, 1977; Spartina, 1989; Supper at the Black Pearl, 1995; The Half-Life of Happiness, 1998. TRANSLATIONS: A. Boffa, You're an Animal, Viskovitz; L. Ferri, Enchantments. OTHER: Testimony and Demeanor (short stories), 1989. **Address:** Dept of English, Bryan Hall, University of Virginia, Charlottesville, VA 22903-3289, U.S.A.

CASEY, Maud. American. **Genres:** Novellas/Short stories, Novels. **Career:** Short-story writer and novelist. Worked in temporary positions; writing instructor at Illinois Wesleyan University, and H.E.L.P. Haven shelter; Lee Strasberg Theatre Institute, New York, NY, former staff member. **Publications:** The Shape of Things to Come (novel), 2001; Drastic (short stories), in press; The Art of Reading Barbara Comyns: Gather Your Hats While You May. Contributor of short stories and book reviews newspapers and periodicals. **Address:** c/o Alice Tasman, Jean V. Naggar Literary Agency, 216 East 75th St. Suite 1E, New York, NY 10021, U.S.A.

CASH, Anthony. British, b. 1933. **Genres:** Communications/Media, History. **Career:** Director, Lilyville Productions, independent TV production co., 1984-. Producer and Director, Granada TV's "Man and Music," since 1984. Assistant Master for Russian, Tottenham Grammar School, London, 1960-63; Program Assistant, Russian Section, External Service, 1963-68, and Producer and Director, 1968-77, BBC Television, London; Producer and Director, London Weekend Television, 1977-84. **Publications:** Great Neighbors: U.S.S.R., 1965; (co-trans.) Years of My Life, 1966; The Russian Revolution, 1967; Lenin, 1972. **Address:** 7 Lilyville Rd, London SW6 5DP, England. **Online address:** tony.cash@btclick.com

CASH, Jean W(ampler). American, b. 1938. **Genres:** Biography. **Career:** Taught at secondary schools in Virginia and Delaware, 1959-80; University of Mississippi, University, instructor, 1976-77; James Madison University, Harrisonburg, VA, 1980-, associate professor, 1986-96, professor of English, 1996-. **Publications:** Flannery O'Connor: A Life, 2002. **Address:** English Dept., Keezell 212, James Madison University, 800 South Main St., Harrisonburg, VA 22807, U.S.A. **Online address:** cashjw@jmu.edu

CASHDAN, Linda. American, b. 1942. **Genres:** Novels, Ghost Writer. **Career:** Voice of America, Washington, DC, broadcaster, reporter, and feature writer, 1967-83, economics correspondent, 1983-. Ghostwriter. **Publications:** Special Interests (novel), St. Martin's, 1990, It's Only Love (Novel), 1992. **Address:** Elaine Markson, Elaine Markson Literary Agency, Inc, 44 Greenwich Ave, New York, NY 10011, U.S.A.

CASIL, Amy Sterling. (born United States), b. 1962. **Genres:** Science fiction/Fantasy. **Career:** Family Service Association, Redlands, CA, executive director, 1988-97; Chapman University, Orange, CA, instructor in English, 1997-2000; Saddleback College, Mission Viejo, CA, instructor in English, 2000-. Pierce College, faculty member. Wildside Press, worked in marketing and publicity. Associates of Redlands Bowl, member, 1990-95. Founding member and officer for Volunteer Center of Inland Empire and San Bernardino County Homeless Coalition, 1992-95. **Publications:** Without Absolution (short stories and poetry), 2000; Imago (science fiction novel), 2002; Choosing a Career in Aircraft Maintenance (textbook), 2002; B-1 Lancer (nonfiction), 2003; Coping with Terrorism (young adult nonfiction), 2003; Trinity (science fiction novel), 2004. Author of other nonfiction titles. Contributor of short stories to periodicals. **Address:** Saddleback College, 20800 Marguerite Parkway, Mission Viejo, CA 92692, U.S.A. **Online address:** ASterling@aol.com

CASPER, Claudia. Canadian, b. 1957?. **Genres:** Novels. **Career:** Freelance typesetter and writer. Appeared on the radio show Morningside, CBC Radio, 1996. **Publications:** NOVELS: The Reconstruction, 1996; The Continuation of Love by Other Means, 2003. Author of short stories. **Address:** c/o Penguin Books Canada Ltd., 10 Alcorn Ave Ste 300, Toronto, ON, Canada M4V 3B2.

CASPER, Leonard (Ralph). American, b. 1923. **Genres:** Novels, Novellas/Short stories, Literary criticism and history. **Career:** Professor of English, Boston College, Chestnut Hill, MA, 1956-99. Visiting Professor, University of the Philippines, Quezon City, 1953-56; Fulbright lecturer, University of the Philippines, 1962-63; Fulbright lecturer, Ateneo University, Quezon City, 1973. Contributing Ed., Panorama, Manila, 1954-61, Drama Critique, 1959-62, Solidarity, Manila, 1966-68, Literature East and West, 1969-77, and Pilipinas, 1987-2002. **Publications:** Robert Penn Warren: The Dark and Bloody Ground, 1960; Wayward Horizon: Essays on Modern Philippine Literature, 1961; The Wounded Diamond: Studies in Modern Philippine Literature,

1964; New Writing from the Philippines: A Critique and Anthology, 1966; A Lion Unannounced: 12 Stories and a Fable, 1971; Firewalkers, 1987; In Burning Ambush, 1991; The Opposing Thumb, 1995; Sunsurfers Seen from Afar: Critical Essays 1991-96, 1996; The Blood-Marriage of Earth & Sky, 1997; The Circular Firing Squad, 1999; Green Circuits of the Sun, 2002. EDITOR: Six Filipino Poets, 1955; (with T.A. Gullason) The World of Short Fiction: An International Collection, 1962; Modern Philippine Short Stories, 1962. **Address:** 54 Simpson Dr, Saxonville, MA 01701, U.S.A.

CASPER, Monica J. American, b. 1966. **Genres:** Medicine/Health. **Career:** University of California, San Francisco, instructor in social and behavioral sciences, 1993-95, research associate, 1995; Stanford University, Stanford, CA, fellow in genomics, ethics, and society at Center for Biomedical ethics, 1995-96; University of California, Davis, lecturer in sociology, 1996; University of California, Santa Cruz, assistant professor of sociology. San Francisco State University, lecturer, 1994; guest speaker at universities; guest on television programs. **Publications:** (with C.L. Estes, J.H. Swan, and others) The Long Term Care Crisis: Elders Trapped in the No-Care Zone, 1992; The Making of the Unborn Patient: A Social Anatomy of Fetal Surgery, 1998. Contributor to books. Contributor of articles and reviews to periodicals. **Address:** 324 College No. 8, Santa Cruz, CA 95064, U.S.A. **Online address:** mjcasper@cats.ucsc.edu

CASPER, Scott E. American, b. 1964. **Genres:** History. **Career:** University of Nevada, Reno, assistant professor, 1992-97, associate professor of history, 1997-, member of Forum for the Future, 1995-96, chair of Dept of History, 2003-. **Publications:** Constructing American Lives: Biography and Culture in Nineteenth-Century America, 1999. EDITOR: (with R.O. Davies) Five Hundred Years: Exploring American Traditions, 1995, 3rd ed, 2000; (with Davies) Of Sagebrush and Slot Machines: This Curious Place Called Nevada, 1997; (with J.D. Groves and J.D. Chaison) Perspectives on American Book History: Artifacts and Commentary, 2001. Contributor to books. Contributor of articles and reviews to periodicals. **Address:** Dept of History, University of Nevada, Reno, NV 89557, U.S.A. **Online address:** casper@unr.nevada.edu

CASSADY, Marsh. American, b. 1936. **Genres:** Theatre, Novels, How-to books, Plays/Screenplays. **Career:** Kent State University, Kent, OH, teacher of theater; Montclair State College, Upper Montclair, NJ, teacher of theater; part-time teacher at San Diego State University, Long Island University, and University of California, San Diego, 1985-92; Long Ridge Writers Group, instructor, 1991-93; presents writing workshops. Daily Reporter, Dover, OH, staff reporter, 1960-63; appeared on the syndicated radio program On Location, Cleveland, OH, 1975-77; Los Hombres Press, editor and publisher, 1987-97. **Publications:** An Introduction to Theatre and Drama, 1975; Theatre: A View of Life, 1982; Characters in Action: A Guide to Playwriting, 1984; Playwriting Step-by-Step, 1985, 2nd edition, 1992; The Book of Scenes for Acting Practice, 1985; Melinda: A Survivor (biography), 1987; Acting Step-by-Step, 1988; The Book of Cuttings for Acting and Directing, 1989; Love Theme with Variations (novel), 1989; Storytelling Step-by-Step, 1990; (with J. Sturkie) Acting It Out: 74 Short Dramas for Conversations with Teenagers, 1990; Alternate Casts (science fiction mystery novel), 1990; (with R.L. Stone and Stephen Richard Smith) Triple Fiction (stories), 1990; Modern One-Act Plays, 1991; Creating Stories for Storytelling, 1991; Perverted Proverbs (humorous stories), 1992; Mind Swap (science fiction novel), 1992; The Theatre and You: A Beginning, 1992; (with Sturkie) Acting It Out Junior, 1992; The Music of Tree Limbs (poems), 1993; Short Plays for Small Casts, 1993; Acting Games, Improvisations, and Exercises, 1993; The Book of Scenes for Aspiring Actors, 1994; The Book of Monologues for Aspiring Actors, 1994; The Art of Storytelling, 1994; Light (novel), 1994; The Times of the Double Star (science fiction mystery novel), 1994; Perverted Proverbs/Sudden Drama (stories and plays), 1994; Playwriting the Easy Way, 1995; Great Scenes from Women Playwrights, 1995; To Ride a Wild Pony (novel), 1996; Tongues of Men and Angels (novella and stories), 1996; Theatre: An Introduction, 1997; Great Scenes from Minority Playwrights, 1997; Funny Business (one-act plays and comedy sketches), 1997; Vampire Wedding (play), Meriwether Publishing, 1998; (with J. Anderson) Newhall, 1998; Ice Cold Moon (vampire novel with audio book), in press. **Address:** c/o Helen McGrath, 1406 Idaho Ct., Concord, CA 94521, U.S.A. **Online address:** marsh@tis.cetys.mx

CASSEDY, James H(iggins). American, b. 1919. **Genres:** Demography, History, Medicine/Health. **Career:** Historian, National Library of Medicine, Bethesda, Maryland, and Ed., Bibliography of the History of Medicine, since 1968. Personnel Officer, U.S. Veterans Administration, 1946-48; Director, Binational Centers, Haiti, Burma and Pakistan, for U.S. Information Service, 1951-55 and 1960-62; Science Administration, National Insts. of Health,

1962-68. **Publications:** Charles V. Chapin and the Public Health Movement, 1962; Demography in Early America: Beginnings of the Statistical Mind 1600-1800, 1969; American Medicine and Statistical Thinking 1800-1860, 1984; Medicine and American Growth 1800-1860, 1986; Medicine in America: A Short History, 1991.

CASSELL, Eric J. American, b. 1928. **Genres:** Medicine/Health, Philosophy. **Career:** Bellevue Hospital, intern, 1954-55, asst resident, 1955-56, 1958-59, asst visiting physician, 1965-66; Cornell University Medical College, NYC, U.S. Public Health Service trainee, 1959-63, clinical instructor, 1961-65, clinical asst professor, 1964-65, clinical professor of public health, 1971-, director of program for study of ethics & values in medicine, 1981-86; New York University, NYC, lecturer and associate professor, 1965-66; Mount Sinai School of Medicine, associate clinical professor, 1966, 1968, associate professor, 1967-71, lecturer, 1971-73. French Hospital, asst attending physician, 1961-63, associate attending physician, 1963-65, attending physician, 1965-74; New York Hospital, physician to outpatients, 1961-65, asst attending physician to inpatients, 1971-77, associate attending physician, 1977-84, attending physician, 1984-; New York University Hospital, associate attending physician, 1965-66; Mt Sinai Hospital, associate attending physician and asst attending physician, both 1966-71, associate director of ambulatory care, 1966-68; New York Hospital/Cornell Medical Center, attending physician to inpatients, 1984-. Lecturer, distinguished medical scholar, visiting scholar and/or professor at colleges and universities throughout the world. **Publications:** The Healer's Art: A New Perspective on the Doctor-Patient Relationship, 1976, rev. ed., 1985; The Place of the Humanities in Medicine, 1984; Talking with Patients, Vol. 1: The Theory of Doctor-Patient Communication, Vol. 2: Clinical Technique, 1985; (ed. with M. Siegler, and contrib) Changing Values in Medicine, 1985; The Nature of Suffering, 1991, 2nd ed., 2004; Doctoring: Nature of Primary Care Medicine, 1997. Work represented in anthologies. **Address:** 28 Old Fulton St, Brooklyn, NY 11201, U.S.A. **Online address:** eric@ericcassell.com

CASSELL, Joan. American, b. 1929. **Genres:** Women's studies and issues, Anthropology/Ethnology. **Career:** Institute for Scientific Analysis, San Francisco, CA, research associate, 1975-77; Center for Policy Research, New York City, senior research associate, 1977-83; Institute for the Study of Human Issues, Philadelphia, PA, senior research associate, 1983-86; Washington University, St. Louis, MO, research associate in anthropology 1987-. Conducted field research in Jamaica, 1969, and in and around New York City, 1971-73; visiting fellow in anthropology, Princeton University, 1976-78; research fellow, Research Institute for the Study of Man, 1986-87. Visiting member, Hastings Center Research Group on Death, Suffering, and Well-Being, 1971-82. Also worked as advertising copywriter for Macy's, Daniel & Charles Agency, and Media Promotion Agency. **Publications:** A Group Called Women: Sisterhood and Symbolism in the Feminist Movement, 1977; A Fieldwork Manual for Studying Desegregated Schools, 1978; (ed. with M. L. Wax, and contrib.) Federal Regulations: Ethical Issues and Social Research, 1979; (ed. with S. Jacobs) Handbook of Ethical Issues in Anthropology, 1987; Children in the Field: Anthropological Experiences, 1987; Expected Miracles: Surgeons at Work, 1991; The Woman in the Surgeon's Body, 1998. **Address:** Department of Anthropology, Box 1114, Washington University, St. Louis, MO 63130, U.S.A.

CASSELS, Alan. British/Canadian, b. 1929. **Genres:** History, International relations/Current affairs. **Career:** Trinity College, Hartford, Conn., Instructor in History, 1959-62; University of Pennsylvania, Philadelphia, Assistant Professor of History, 1962-67; McMaster University, Hamilton, Ont., Associate Professor of History, 1967-71, Professor of History, 1971-94, Emeritus Professor of History, 1994-. Vice-President, 1978-80, and President, 1980-82, Society for Italian Historical Studies; Fellow, Royal Historical Society, 1983. **Publications:** Fascist Italy, 1968, 1985; Mussolini's Early Diplomacy, 1970; Fascism, 1975; Italian Foreign Policy 1918-1945; A Guide to Research and Research Materials, 1981, 1991; Ideology and International Relations in the Modern World, 1996. **Address:** Dept. of History, McMaster University, Hamilton, ON, Canada L8S 4L9. **Online address:** cassels@mcmaster.ca

CASSELS, J(ohn) W(illiam) S(cott). British, b. 1922. **Genres:** Mathematics/Statistics. **Career:** Manchester University, Manchester, England, lecturer, 1949-50; Cambridge University, Cambridge, England, fellow at Trinity College, 1949-, lecturer, 1950-63, reader in arithmetic, 1963-67, Sadleirian Professor of Pure Mathematics, 1967-84, head of department of pure mathematics and mathematical statistics, 1969-84, emeritus professor, 1984-. International Mathematical Union, vice president, 1974-78, member of executive board, 1978-82. **Publications:** An Introduction to Diophantine Approximation, 1957; An Introduction to the Geometry of Numbers, 1959, rev. ed, 1971; (ed. with A. Frohlich) Algebraic Number Theory: Proceedings of an Instructional Conference, 1967; Rational Quadratic Forms, 1978; Economics for Mathematicians, 1981, rev. ed., 1985; Local Fields, 1986; Lectures on Elliptic Curves, 1991, rev. ed., 1993; (with E.V. Flynn) Prolegomena to a Middlebrow Arithmetic of Curves of Genus 2, 1996. **Address:** Department of Pure Mathematics and Mathematical Statistics, Cambridge University, CMS, Wilberforce Rd, Cambridge CB3 0WB, England.

CASSIDY, David C(harles). American, b. 1945. **Genres:** Sciences. **Career:** University of California, Berkeley, postdoctoral research fellow, 1976-77; University of Stuttgart, Stuttgart, Germany, Alexander von Humboldt fellow, 1977-80; University of Regensburg, Regensburg, Germany, assistant professor, 1980-83; Princeton University Press, Boston, MA, associate editor of "Albert Einstein Papers," 1983-90; Hofstra University, Hempstead, NY, professor of the history of science, 1990-. **Publications:** (assoc. ed.) The Collected Papers of Albert Einstein, Vol. I, 1987, Vol. II, 1989; Uncertainty: The Life and Science of Werner Heisenberg, 1992; Einstein and Our World, 1995. Contributor to German- and English-language history of science journals. **Address:** Natural Science Program, New Science Bldg, Hofstra University, Hempstead, NY 11549, U.S.A.

CASSIDY, Michael. South African, b. 1936. **Genres:** Human relations/Parenting, Theology/Religion. **Career:** Founder and International Team Leader, African Enterprise, Pietermaritzburg, South Africa, 1962-. Religious Columnist, The Natal Witness, 1968-. Religious Columnist, Johannesburg Star, 1968-73; Chairman, National Initiative for Reconciliation, 1985-88. **Publications:** Decade of Decisions (in U.S. as Where Are You Taking the World Anyway?), 1970; Prisoners of Hope, 1974; Together in One Place, 1978; Christianity for the Open Minded, 1978; Bursting the Wineskins, 1983; Chasing the Wind, 1985; The Passing Summer, 1989; The Politics of Love, 1991; A Witness Forever, 1995; Michael Cassidy's Window on the Word, 1997. EDITOR: (with A. Blane and C. le Feuvre) The Relationship Tangle, 1974; I Will Heal Their Land, 1974; (co-) Facing the New Challenges, 1978. **Address:** c/o African Enterprise, PO Box 13140, Cascades 3202, Republic of South Africa. **Online address:** aesa@ae.org.za

CASSITY, (Allen) Turner. American, b. 1929. **Genres:** Poetry. **Career:** Assistant University Librarian, Emory University Library, Atlanta, 1962-. Assistant Librarian, Jackson Municipal Library, South Africa, 1959-61. **Publications:** Watchboy, What of the Night?, 1966; Steeplejacks in Babel, 1973; Yellow for Peril, Black for Beautiful, 1975; The Defense of the Sugar Islands, 1979; Keys to Mayerling, 1983; The Book of Alma: A Narrative of the Mormon Wars, 1985; Hurricane Lamp, 1986; Between the Chains, 1991; The Destructive Element, 1998; No Second Eden, 2002. **Address:** 510-J East Ponce de Leon Ave, Decatur, GA 30030, U.S.A.

CASSON, Mark (Christopher). British, b. 1945. **Genres:** Economics, Business/Trade/Industry. **Career:** University of Reading, England, lecturer, 1969-76, reader, 1976-81, professor of economics, 1981-, head of department, 1987-94. Royal Society of Arts, fellow. **Publications:** Introduction to Mathematical Economics, 1973; (with P.J. Buckley) The Future of the Multinational Enterprise, 1976; Alternatives to the Multinational Enterprise, 1979; Youth Unemployment, 1979; Unemployment: A Disequilibrium Approach, 1981; The Entrepreneur, 1982; Economics of Unemployment, 1983; Unemployment Theory before Keynes, 1983; (with P.J. Buckley) The Economic Theory of the Multinational Enterprise, 1985; (co-author) Multinationals and World Trade, 1986; The Firm and the Market, 1987; Enterprise and Competitiveness, 1990; The Economics of Business Culture, 1991; Entrepreneurship and Business Culture, 1995; Organization of International Business, 1995; Information and Organization, 1997; Economics of International Business, 2000; Enterprise and Leadership, 2000. EDITOR: The Growth of International Business, 1983; Entrepreneurship, 1990; Multinational Corporations, 1990; Global Research Strategy and International Competitiveness, 1991; International Business and Global Integration, 1992; (with P.J. Buckley) Multinational Enterprises in the World Economy: Essays in Honour of John Dunning, 1992; (with J. Creedy) Industrial Concentration and Economic Inequality: Essays in Honour of Peter Hart, 1993; (with A.C. Godley) Cultural Factors in Economic Growth, 2000. Contributor to journals in economics, business history, transport studies, political science, and social psychology. **Address:** Dept of Economics, Box 218, University of Reading, Reading RG6 2AA, England. **Online address:** m.c.casson@reading.ac.uk

CASSTEVENS, Thomas William. American, b. 1937. **Genres:** Politics/Government. **Career:** University of California at Berkeley, Institute of Governmental Studies, assistant research political scientist, 1963-66; Oakland University, Rochester, MI, assistant professor, 1966-69, associate prof, 1969-72, professor, 1972-2000, emeritus professor of political science, 2000-. **Publications:** Politics, Housing and Race Relations: The Defeat of Berkeley's Fair Housing Ordinance, 1965; Politics, Housing and Race Relations: The Rumford Act and Proposition 14, 1967; (co-ed.) The Politics of Fair Housing Legislation, 1968; (co-ed.) American Government and Politics, 1980. **Address:** 5805 S Campbell Rd, Greenacres, WA 99016-9768, U.S.A. **Online address:** cass@oakland.edu

CASSUTT, Michael (Joseph). American, b. 1954. **Genres:** Science fiction/Fantasy, Plays/Screenplays, Air/Space topics, Biography, Reference. **Career:** KHYT Radio, Tucson, AZ, disc jockey and operations manager, 1975-78; CBS Television, Los Angeles, CA, positions included children's programming executive, 1979-85; freelance writer and television producer, 1985-. Scifi.com, columnist, 2000-. **Publications:** TELEPLAYS: Love, Sidney, 1982; Gloria, 1982; It's Not Easy, 1983; Alice, 1983-84; Dungeons and Dragons, 1985; Rocky Road (syndicated), 1985; Misfits of Science, 1985; The Twilight Zone, 1985-87; CBS Storybreak, 1985; Centurions, (syndicated), 1986; Simon and Simon, 1986; The Wizard, 1987; Max Headroom, 1987-88; Beauty and the Beast, 1988; TV 101, 1988-89; WIOU, 1990; Eerie, Indiana, 1992; Sirens, 1993; Sea Quest, 1993; Strange Luck, 1995-96; Beverly Hills, 90210, 1997-98; Seven Days, 1999; Farscape, 2000; Stargate SG-1, 2000; Gene Roddenberry's Andromeda, 2002; The Dead Zone, 2003-04. OTHER: The Star Country (science fiction), 1986; Who's Who in Space (reference), 1987, 3rd ed., 1999; (author of intro) Valentin Lebedev, Diary of a Cosmonaut: 211 Days in Space, 1988; Dragon Season (fantasy), 1991; (ed. with A. Greeley and M.H. Greenberg) Sacred Visions (science fiction anthology), 1991; (with D.K. Slayton) Deke! U.S. Manned Space: Mercury to the Shuttle, 1994; Missing Man (novel), 1998; Red Moon (novel), 2001; (with T.P. Stafford) We Have Capture, 2001; Tango Midnight (novel), 2003. Contributor of short stories to periodicals and anthologies; contributor of nonfiction articles to periodicals and online sites. **Address:** 12241 Hillslope St, Studio City, CA 91604-3604, U.S.A.

CASTALDO, Nancy Fusco. American, b. 1962. **Genres:** Children's fiction, Children's non-fiction. **Career:** Writer. Worked as an environmental educator for New York State Department of Environmental Conservation and National Audubon Society; conducts children's workshops and adult ecology programs. **Publications:** FOR CHILDREN: Sunny Days and Starry Nights, 1996; Rainy Day Play!, 1996; The Little Hands Nature Book, 1996; Winter Day Play!, 2001. Contributor to magazines.

CASTANEDA, Christopher James. American, b. 1959. **Genres:** History. **Career:** Houston Community College, TX, lecturer in history, 1989-90; University of Houston, TX, adjunct professor, 1991-92; California State University, Sacramento, assistant professor, 1994-2003, professor of history, 2003-. Business History Group, partner. **Publications:** Regulated Enterprise: Natural Gas Pipelines and Northeastern Markets, 1938-1954, 1993; (with J. Pratt) From Texas to the East: A Strategic History of Texas Eastern Corporation, 1993; Invisible Fuel: Manufactured and Natural Gas in America, 1800-2000, 2000. Contributor of articles and reviews to history journals. **Address:** Department of History, California State University, 6000 J St, Sacramento, CA 95819-6059, U.S.A. **Online address:** cjc@csus.edu

CASTANEDA, Jorge G. Mexican, b. 1953. **Genres:** Politics/Government, International relations/Current affairs. **Career:** National Autonomous University of Mexico, Mexico City, professor of economics and international affairs, 1978-82, professor of political science, 1982-; writer. Visiting professor at University of California, Berkeley, 1990-92, and Princeton University, 1990-94. Advisor to Mexican government, 1980-82. **Publications:** (with E. Hett) El economismo dependentista, 1978; Nicaragua: Contradicciones en la revolucion, 1980; (with E. Semo and P. Lopez) La Renovacion del PCM, 1981; Los ultimos capitalismos, 1981; Mexico: El futuro en juego, 1987; (with R.A. Pastor) Limits to Friendship: The United States and Mexico, 1988; La casa por la ventana, 1993; Utopia Unarmed: The Latin American Left after the Cold War, 1993; La Vida Te Da Sorpresas, 1994; Perpetuating Power: How Mexican Presidents Were Chosen, 2000. Contributor to books and periodicals. **Address:** Department of Political Science, National Autonomous University of Mexico, Mexico City, Mexico.

CASTELL, Megan. See WILLIAMS, Jeanne.

CASTELLANI, Catherine. (born United States), b. 1965. **Genres:** Plays/Screenplays. **Career:** Playwright. **Publications:** Romance (play), 1984; Girl Friday (radio play), 1992; Marlboro Angel (radio play), 1995; Ashira 69: Superheroines Collide! (play), 1997; Profit (play), 1999; Rain (radio play), 2001. Contributor of feature articles. **Address:** c/o Mitchell Waters, Curtis Brown, 10 Astor Pl., New York, NY 10003, U.S.A. **Online address:** catherinecastellani@hotmail.com

CASTER, Andrew I. American, b. 1954. **Genres:** Medicine/Health. **Career:** Caster Eye Center, Beverly Hills, CA, medical director, 1984-. **Publications:** The Eye Laser Miracle: The Complete Guide to Better Vision, 1997. **Address:** Caster Eye Center, 9100 Wilshire Blvd Ste 265E, Beverly Hills, CA 90212, U.S.A. **Online address:** info@castervision.com

CASTILE, Rand. American, b. 1938. **Genres:** Art/Art history. **Career:** Free-lance writer and critic, 1963-67; Japan Society, New York City, education director, 1967-70, founding director of Japan House Gallery (now Japan Society Gallery), 1970-85; Asian Art Museum of San Francisco, CA, director, 1985-94, director emeritus, 1995-; lecturer on Japanese arts at U.S., Australian, and Japanese universities and museums. **Publications:** The Way of Tea, 1971, 2nd ed., 1979; Ikeda and Ida: Two New Japanese Printmakers, 1974; Japanese Art Now: Tadaaki Kuwayama and Rikuro Okamoto, 1980. Author of exhibition catalogs. Contributor to journals, newspapers, and magazines. **Address:** 9 Key St, Eastport, ME 04631, U.S.A. **Online address:** rcastile3@aol.com

CASTILLO, Debra A(nn Garsow). American, b. 1953. **Genres:** Literary criticism and history. **Career:** University of Maryland at College Park, instructor in English composition, 1981-82; University of Tulsa, Tulsa, OK, visiting assistant professor of English composition and Spanish, 1984-85; Cornell University, Ithaca, NY, Stephen H. Weiss Presidential Fellow and professor of romance studies and comparative literature, 1985-. **Publications:** The Translated Word: A Postmodern Tour of Libraries in Literature, 1984; Talking Back: Strategies for a Latin American Feminist Literary Criticism, 1992; Easy Women: Sex and Gender in Modern Mexican Fiction, 1998. **Address:** Department of Romance Studies, Morrill Hall, Cornell University, Ithaca, NY 14853, U.S.A. **Online address:** dac9@cornell.edu

CASTLE, Alfred L. American, b. 1948. **Genres:** History, Literary criticism and history, Philosophy, Social commentary, Theology/Religion, Essays. **Career:** New Mexico Military Institute, Roswell, professor of history, 1976-83, vice president for development, 1983-87; Hawaii Pacific University, Honolulu, vice president, 1987-95; California State University, San Marcos, vice president, 1995-98; Samuel N. and Mary Castle Foundation, executive director and treasurer, 1998-; Henry and Dorothy Castle Fund, trustee; Hawaii Council for the Humanities, trustee. **Publications:** A Century of Philanthropy, 1992, 2nd ed., 2004; Diplomatic Realism, 1998. Work represented in anthologies. Contributor to books, history journals, newspapers, and religious magazines. **Address:** c/o Castle Foundation, 733 Bishop St Ste 1275, Honolulu, HI 96813, U.S.A. **Online address:** acastle@aloha.net

CASTLE, Kathryn. American. **Genres:** History. **Career:** University of North London, London, England, principal lecturer in history, 1982-. **Publications:** Britannia's Children, 1996. Contributor to books. **Address:** Department of History, London Metropolitan University, 166-220 Holloway Rd, London N7 8DB, England. **Online address:** kcastle@unl.ac.uk

CASTLE, Linda. (Linda Lea Castle). American, b. 1952. **Genres:** Mystery/Crime/Suspense, Romance/Historical, Westerns/Adventure, Language/Linguistics, Paranormal. **Career:** Writer. **Publications:** ROMANCE NOVELS: Fearless Hearts, 1995; Abbie's Child, 1996; Lightening Lexicon, 1998; Territorial Bride, 1998; Gideon's Angel, 1999; Heart of the Lawman, 1999; By Kings Command, 2000; Addie & the Laird, 2000; Mattie & the Blacksmith, 2001; Lottie & the Rustler, 2001. OTHER NOVELS: The Return of Chase Cordell (historical), 1996; Temple's Prize (western), 1997; Promise the Moon, 2002; Surrender the Stars, 2002; Embrace the Sun, 2002.

CASTLEDEN, Rodney. British, b. 1945. **Genres:** Songs/Lyrics and libretti, Archaeology/Antiquities, Area studies, Earth sciences, Geography, History, Music, Mythology/Folklore, Theatre, Reference. **Career:** Geography master at grammar and high schools in Wellingborough, England, 1968-75, Overstone, England, 1975-76, and London, England, 1976-79; Roedean School, Brighton, England, head of geography department, 1979-90, head of humanities faculty, 1990-2001, head of social science faculty, 2001-04. **Publications:** Classic Landforms of the Sussex Coast, 1982, rev. ed., 1996; The Wilmington Giant, 1983; (co-ed.) Classic Landform Guides series, 1983-98; The Stonehenge People, 1987; The Knossos Labyrinth, 1989; Minoans, 1990; The Book of British Dates, 1991; Neolithic Britain, 1992; The Making of Stonehenge, 1993; World History: A Chronological Dictionary of Dates, 1994, rev. ed., 2003; The Cerne Giant, 1996; Knossos, Temple of the Goddess, 1997; Out in the Cold: Ideas on Glaciation, 1998; Atlantis Destroyed, 1998; The English Lake District, 1998; The Search for King Arthur, 1999; The Little Book of Kings and Queens of Britain, 1999; Ancient British Hill Figures, 2000; Winfrith: A Music Drama, 2000, rev. ed., 2001; The History

of World Events, 2003; Britain 3000 BC, 2003; Infamous Murderers, 2004; Serial Killers, 2004. Contributor to geography and prehistory journals. **Address:** 15 Knepp Close, Bevendean, Brighton, E. Sussex BN2 4LD, England. **Online address:** rodney@castleden.fsnet.co.uk; www.rodneycastleden.co.uk

CASTRO, Brian (Albert). Australian (born Hong Kong), b. 1950. **Genres:** Novels, Essays. **Career:** Australian novelist, short story writer, and educator. Mt. Druitt High School, New South Wales, Australia, teacher, 1972-76; Lycee Technique, Paris, France, assistant in languages, 1976-77; St. Joseph's College, Hunter's Hill, NSW, French master, 1978-79; Asiaweek magazine, Hong Kong, literary journalist, 1983-87; Mitchell College, NSW, writer-in-residence, 1985; Nepean College, Kingswood, NSW, visiting fellow, 1988; All-Asia Review of Books, Hong Kong, literary journalist, 1989-; University of Western Sydney, tutor in literary studies, 1989-90; writer-in-residence: University of Hong Kong, 1994, Cite des Arts, Paris, 2000. Australia Council for the Arts, Literature Fund, senior fellowship, 1997-98; University of Melbourne, Macgeorge Fellowship, 2005. **Publications:** NOVELS: Birds of Passage, 1982; Pomeroy, 1991; Double-Wolf, 1991; After China, 1992; Drift, 1994; Stepper, 1997; Shanghai Dancing, 2003; You Can Find Me in the Garden, 2005. OTHER: Looking for Estrellita (essays), 1999. **Address:** c/o Giramondo Publishing Group, PO Box 752, Artarmon, NSW 1570, Australia. **Online address:** bcastro@ozemail.com.au

CASTRO, Michael. American, b. 1945. **Genres:** Poetry, Literary criticism and history. **Career:** Writer. River Styx, founder; poet member of the jazz performance groups Human Arts Ensemble, 1971-75, and Harmony 1989-93; Lindenwood University, professor, 1980-; Poetry Beat (radio program), host, 1989-; Fred Tompkins Poetry & Music Ensemble, 1996-. Fulbright scholar, India, 1991. **Publications:** The Kokopilau Cycle (poem), 1975; Ghost Hiways and Other Homes (poems), 1976; Cracks, 1977; Interpreting the Indian: Twentieth-Century Poets and the Native American, 1983; The Man Who Looked into Coltrane's Horn, 1997; Human Rites, 2002; Swimming in the Ground: Contemporary Hungarian Poetry, 2001.

CASWELL, Brian. Australian (born Wales), b. 1954. **Genres:** Children's fiction, Young adult fiction. **Career:** New South Wales Department of Education, high school teacher of English and history, 1976-91. University of Western Sydney, writer in residence. **Publications:** FOR YOUNG ADULTS: Merryll of the Stones, 1989; A Dream of Stars, 1991; A Cage of Butterflies, 1992; Dreamslip, 1994; Deucalion, 1995; Asturias, 1996; (with D. Phu An Chiem) Only the Heart, 1997; The View from Ararat, 1999. FOR CHILDREN. Relax Max!, 1997. BOUNDARY PARK TRILOGY: Mike, 1993; Lisdalia, 1994; Maddie, 1995. ALIEN ZONES SERIES: TeeDee and the Collectors, 1998; Messengers of the Great Orff, 1998; Gladiators in the Holo-colosseum, 1998; Gargantua, 1998; What Were the Gremnholzs' Dimensions Again?, 1998; Whispers from the Shibboleth, 1998. Contributor to periodicals. **Address:** 17 Wagstaff St, Edensor Park, NSW 2176, Australia. **Online address:** brian@alienzones.com

CATALANO, Nick. American, b. 1940?. **Genres:** Biography, Music. **Career:** Musician, educator, and producer. Pace University, New York, NY, professor of music and literature, 1976-, became director of performing arts. Jazz saxophonist. producer of recordings and concerts; television producer. **Publications:** Clifford Brown: The Life and Art of the Legendary Jazz Trumpeter, 2000. Contributor of music reviews to Associated Press. **Address:** Department of Performing Arts, Dyson College of Arts and Sciences, Pace University, 78 North Broadway, Pleasantville, NY 10570, U.S.A. **Online address:** Ncatalano@pace.edu

CATALANOTTO, Peter. American, b. 1959. **Genres:** Children's fiction. **Career:** Free-lance illustrator, New York City, 1982-87; free-lance writer and illustrator of children's books, New York City, 1987-. Catalanotto's work is displayed with the Mazza Collection in Findlay, OH, and has been with the permanent collection at Elizabeth Stone Gallery in Birmingham, MI, 1991-. **Publications:** SELF-ILLUSTRATED: Dylan's Day Out, 1989; Mr. Mumble, 1990; Christmas Always..., 1991; The Painter, 1995; Dad and Me, 1999; Emily's Art, 2001; Matthew A.B.C., 2002; Daisy 1,2,3, 2003; Kitten Red, Yellow, Blue, 2005. Illustrator of books by: S. Fowler, A. Johnson, G.E. Lyon, M. McDonald, S. Patron, J. Ryder, C. Rylant. **Address:** PO Box 253, Holicong, PA 18928, U.S.A.

CATEURA, Linda Brandi. American. **Genres:** Art/Art history, Cultural/Ethnic topics, Theology/Religion. **Career:** Harper's Bazaar, New York City, associate literary editor, 7 years; Woman's Day, New York City, associate editor, 2 years; Family Circle, New York City, associate editor, 2 years; aide to New York State Senator William Giordano, 5 years; associate press officer to New York Secretary of State Mario Cuomo, 2 years; public information officer for New York Department of State, 3 years; writer, 1982-; Secretariat News (UN), columnist, 1998-. Member of board of governors, Brooklyn Heights Association, 3 years; member of local Planning Board, 4 years. **Publications:** Oil Painting Secrets from a Master, 1984; Growing Up Italian, 1986; Catholics USA, 1989; Protestant Portraits, 2002. **Address:** 136 Willow St, Brooklyn, NY 11201, U.S.A. **Online address:** cateura@earthlink.net

CATHCART, Jim. American, b. 1946. **Genres:** Business/Trade/Industry. **Career:** Co-founder, Professional Speaking Institute, North Carolina; corporate executive, training director, entrepreneur, psychological researcher, meeting planner, association executive, and personal development speaker, c. 1977-. **Publications:** Communication Dynamics, 1976; Executive Stress: How to Avoid Falling Face down on the Bottom Line, 1983; (co-author) The Business of Selling, 1984; Relationship Strategies (sound recording), 1982, print ed, 1985; Winning with People through Service and Customer Relationships, 1986; (with A.J. Alessandra and P. Wexler) Selling by Objectives, 1988; (with Alessandra and J. Monoky) Be Your Own Sales Manager, 1990; Relationship Selling: The Key to Getting and Keeping Customers, 1990; (with Alessandra and Baron) The Sales Professional's Idea-a-Day Guide: Two Hundred Fifty Ways to Increase Your Top and Bottom Lines-Every Selling Day of the Year, 1997; The Acorn Principle (Know Yourself-Grow Yourself): Discover, Explore, and Grow the Seeds of Your Greatest Potential, 1998; (with Alessandra) The Business of Selling: How to Be Your Own Sales Manager, 1998. **Address:** Cathcart Institute Inc., 6120 Paseo Del Norte Ste M-2, Carlsbad, CA 92009, U.S.A.

CATHERWOOD, Sir (Henry) Frederick (Ross). British, b. 1925. **Genres:** Social commentary, Theology/Religion. **Career:** Chief Executive, Richard Costain Ltd., 1955-60; Assistant Managing Director, 1960-62, and Managing Director, 1962-64, British Aluminium Co. Ltd; Chief Industrial Adviser, Dept. of Economic Affairs, 1964-66; Director General, National Economic Development Council, 1966-71; Managing Director, John Laing & Son Ltd., 1971-74; Director, Goodyear Great Britain Ltd., 1975-86; Chairman, British Overseas Trade Board, 1975-79; European II Parliament, member 1979-94; Chair Foreign Trade Committee, 1979-84, VP 1989-92; VP Foreign Affairs Committee, 1992-94; Evangelical Alliance, president, 1992-. **Publications:** The Christian in Industrial Society, 1964, 1980, in U.S. as Nine to Five, 1983; Britain with the Brakes Off, 1966; The Christian Citizen, 1969; A Better Way, 1976; First Things First, 1979; God's Time, God's Money, 1987; Pro Europe?, 1991; David: Poet, Warrior, King, 1993; At the Cutting Edge, 1995; Jobs & Justice, 1997; It Can Be Done, 2000; The Creation of Wealth, 2002. **Address:** Sutton Hall, Balsham, Cambridgeshire CB1 6DX, England.

CATO, Heather. New Zealander. **Genres:** Young adult fiction. **Career:** Writer. Operator of a horseback riding school. **Publications:** Dark Horses (novel), 1997. **Address:** 5 Arney Cres., Remuera, Auckland 5, New Zealand.

CATROW, David J. III. (born United States). **Genres:** Children's fiction. **Career:** Cartoonist, painter, and commercial illustrator. Springfield News-Sun, Springfield, OH, editorial cartoonist, 1984-; Copley News Service, syndicated cartoonist, 1988-. Worked as a paramedic for ten years. Freelance illustrator for Cleveland Plain Dealer and Akron Beacon-Journal; illustrator of Wild Things (weekly pet column). **Publications:** (Self-illustrated) We the Kids: The Preamble to the Constitution of the United States, 2002. ILLUSTRATOR; AS DAVID CATROW: Ethel Pochocki, Attic Mice, 1990; Charles Ghigna, Good Dogs, Bad Dogs, 1992; Charles Ghigna, Good Cats, Bad Cats, 1992; Robert Southey, The Cataract of Lodore, 1992; Harriet Berg Schwartz, Backstage with Clawdio, 1993; John Walker, Ridiculous Rhymes from A to Z, 1994; Kathryn Lasky, She's Wearing a Dead Bird on Her Head!, 1995; William Kotzwinkle, The Million-Dollar Bear, 1995; Lydia Maria Child, Over the River and through the Wood, 1996; Elizabeth Spurr, The Long, Long Letter, 1996; Robert Burleigh, Who Said That?: Famous Americans Speak, 1997; Sharon Arms Doucet, Why Lapin's Ears Are Long and Other Tales from the Louisiana Bayou, 1997; Candace Fleming, Westward Ho, Carlotta!, 1998; Howard W. Reeves, There Was an Old Witch, 1998; Laura Simms, Rotten Teeth, 1998; Stephen Phillip Policoff, Cesar's Amazing Journey, 1999; Kathryn Lasky, The Emperor's Old Clothes, 1999; Arthur Dorros, The Fungus That Ate My School, 2000; Mike Reiss, How Murray Saved Christmas, 2000; Robert D. San Souci, Cinderella Skeleton: A Fractured Fairy Tale in Rhyme, 2000; Patty Lovell, Stand Tall, Molly Lou Melon, 2001; Alan Katz, Take Me Out of the Bathtub, and Other Silly Dilly Songs, 2001; Margery Cuyler, That's Good! That's Bad!, 2001; Mike Reiss, Santa Claustrophobia, 2002; Jerdine Nolen, Plantzilla, 2002; Margery Cuyler, That's Good! That's Bad! in the Grand Canyon, 2002; Alan Katz, I'm Still Here in the Bathtub: Brand New Silly Dilly Songs, 2003; Robert D. San Souci, Little Pierre: A Cajun Story from Louisiana, 2003; Karin Ireland, Don't Take Your Snake for a Stroll, 2003; Mike Reiss, The Boy Who Looked

Like Lincoln, 2003; Alan Katz, Where Did They Hide My Presents?: Silly Dilly Christmas Songs, 2004; James Carville and Patricia C. McKissack, Lu and the Swamp Ghost, 2004; Karen Beaumont, I Like Myself!, 2004; Karen Kaufman Orloff, I Wanna Iguana, 2004. ILLUSTRATOR; CORNERSTONES OF FREEDOM SERIES: R. Conrad Stein, The Story of the Little Bighorn, 1983; R. Conrad Stein, The Story of Wounded Knee, 1983; R. Conrad Stein, The Story of the Johnstown Flood, 1984; R. Conrad Stein, The Story of the Oregon Trail, 1984; R. Conrad Stein, The Story of Apollo 11, 1985; R. Conrad Stein, The Story of the Trail of Tears, 1985; Zachary Kent, The Story of the Battle of Bull Run, 1986. **Address:** Springfield News-Sun, 202 North Limestone St., Springfield, OH 45503, U.S.A. **Online address:** dcatrow@coxohio.com

CATTERALL, Lee. American, b. 1944. **Genres:** Art/Art history. **Career:** Omaha World-Herald, Omaha, NE, general assignment reporter, 1969-70; Montgomery County Sentinel, Rockville, MD, general assignment reporter, 1971; Service Employees International Union, Washington, DC, writer, 1971-72; Mountain States News Service, Washington, owner and writer, 1973-77; Associated Press, Cheyenne, WY, news writer, 1977-80; Honolulu Star-Bulletin, Honolulu, HI, legal affairs reporter, 1980-. Stringer for KTWO Radio (Casper), KTWO-TV, and other affiliates of Harriscope Broadcasting Corp.; worked summers as a reporter in Wyoming for Riverton Ranger and Sheridan Press, and in England for Bradford Telegraph and Argus. **Publications:** The Great Dali Art Fraud and Other Deceptions, 1992. Contributor to periodicals. **Address:** 92-510 Akaula St, Kapolei, HI 96707, U.S.A. **Online address:** hicatt@pixi.com

CATTERALL, Peter. British, b. 1961. **Genres:** History, Bibliography. **Career:** Queen Mary and Westfield College, London, England, visiting lecturer in modern British history, 1987-; Institute of Contemporary British History, London, research fellow, 1988-89, director, 1989-; writer. Consultant at the London School of Economics for the British Political Archives project. Member of London's South East Valuation Tribunal. **Publications:** British History, 1945-1987: An Annotated Bibliography, 1990; (ed) Contemporary Britain: An Annual Review 1990, 1991, 1992, 1993, 1994, 1995; (ed. with C.J. Morris) Britain and the Threat to Stability in Europe 1918-1945, 1993; History of Electrex 1950-1993, 1993; (ed. with J. Obeluevicre) Understanding Post-War British Society, 1994; (ed. with S. McDougall) The Northern Ireland Question in British Politics, 1996. **Address:** Institute of Contemporary British History, Room 357, Senate House, Market St., London WC1E 7HU, England.

CAUDILL, (Charles) Edward. American, b. 1953. **Genres:** Writing/Journalism. **Career:** Columbus Citizen-Journal, Columbus, OH, copy editor, 1977-83; University of Tennessee, Knoxville, professor of journalism, 1985-. **Publications:** Darwin in the Press: The Evolution of an Idea, 1989; Darwinian Myths: The Legends and Misuses of a Theory, 1997. Contributor to books and periodicals. **Address:** 330 Communications Bldg., University of Tennessee, Knoxville, TN 37996, U.S.A.

CAUFIELD, Catherine. American. **Genres:** Environmental sciences/Ecology. **Career:** Writer. Freelance journalist, London, England, and California. **Publications:** NONFICTION: The Emperor of the United States of America and Other Magnificent British Eccentrics, c. 1981; Tropical Moist Forests: The Resource, the People, the Threat (monograph), c. 1982; In the Rainforest, 1985; Multiple Exposures: Chronicles of the Radiation Age, c. 1989; Masters of Illusion: The World Bank and the Poverty of Nations, 1997. Contributor to periodicals. **Address:** c/o Henry Holt & Co. Inc., 115 West 18th St., New York, NY 10011, U.S.A.

CAULDWELL, Frank. See KING, Francis (Henry).

CAULFIELD, Carlota. American (born Cuba), b. 1953. **Genres:** Poetry. **Career:** Cuban Ministry of Culture, Havana, educator and researcher, 1975-80; Spanish tutor, 1981; San Francisco State University, lecturer, 1983-85; Ediciones el gato tuerto, editor and publisher, 1984; El gato tuerto (literary journal), San Francisco, founding editor, 1984-90; Mills College, associate professor of Spanish and Spanish American Studies. Author of columns Resenas, in Tiempo Latino, 1992-95, and Entrevistas (interviews), in Tiempo Latino and El Bohemio News, 1992-96. Contributor of book reviews to Lateral (Barcelona), 1995-99. **Publications:** POETRY: Palabra Solar, plaquette No. 6, 1982; (and trans. with C. Allen) Fanaim (in English & Spanish), 1984; Oscuridad divina, 1985; (and trans. with C. Allen) Sometimes I Call Myself Childhood (in English & Spanish), 1985; El tiempo es una mujer que espera, 1986; 34th Street and Other Poems, 1987; Oscuridad divina, 1987; Angel Dust (in Spanish, English, and Italian), 1990; Visual Games for Words and Sounds (hyperpoems), 1993; Libro de los XXXIX escalones (in Spanish and Italian), 39 vols, 1995; Estrofas de papel, barro y tinta (plaquette), 1995; Book of the XXXIX Steps (hyperbook), 1995; A las puertas del papel con amoroso fuego, 1996, trans. as At the Gates of the Paper with Burning Desire, 2001; Autorretrato en ojo ajeno, 2001; The Book of Giulio Camillo (in English, Spanish, & Italian), 2003; Movimientos metalicos para juguettes abandonados, 2003; Quincunce/Quincunx, 2004; Ticket to Ride (essays and poems), 2005. EDITOR: Rosa Luxemburgo, 1977; Los socialistas anteriores a Marx, 3 vols, 1978; Pablo Lafargue, 1979; (with M. Zapata) Literary and Cultural Journeys: Selected Letters to Arturo Torres-Rioseco, 1995; Web of Memories: Interviews with 5 Cuban Poets, 1997; Voces viajeras, 2002; From the Forbidden Garden: Letters from Alejandra Pizarnik to Antonio Beneyto, 2004; (with J. Parra) The Other Poetry of Barcelona: Spanish and Spanish-American Women Poets, 2004. Contributor to anthologies. Contributor of poetry, essays, and book reviews to periodicals. **Address:** Mill College, 5000 MacArthur Blvd, Oakland, CA 94613, U.S.A. **Online address:** amach@mills.edu; www.intelinet.org/Caufield

CAUTE, (John) David. Also writes as John Salisbury. British (born Egypt), b. 1936. **Genres:** Novels, Plays/Screenplays, History, Politics/Government. **Career:** Fellow, All Souls College, Oxford, 1959-65; Visiting Professor, New York University and Columbia University, NYC, 1966-67; Reader in Social and Political Theory, Brunel University, Uxbridge, Middx., 1967-70; Regents Lecturer, University of California, 1974; Literary and Arts Ed., New Statesman, London, 1979-80; Visiting Professor, University of Bristol, 1985. Co-Chairman, Writers Guild of Great Britain, 1981-82. **Publications:** Communism and the French Intellectuals 1914-1960, 1964; The Left in Europe since 1789, 1966; (ed.) Essential Writings of Karl Marx, 1967; The Demonstration (play), 1969; Fanon, 1970; The Illusion, 1971; The Fellow-Travellers, 1973; Collisions: Essays and Review, 1974; Cuba, Yes?, 1974; The Great Fear: The Anti-Communist Campaign under Truman and Eisenhower, 1978; Under the Skin: The Death of White Rhodesia, 1983; The Espionage of the Saints, 1986; Sixty-Eight: The Year of the Barricades, 1988; Joseph Losey: A Revenge on Life, 1994; The Dancer Defects: The Struggle for Cultural Supremacy during the Cold War, 2003. NOVELS: At Fever Pitch (novel), 1959 (Author's Club Award, John Llewelyn Rhys Prize); Comrade Jacob, 1961; The Decline of the West, 1966; The Occupation, 1971; The K-Factor, 1983; News from Nowhere, 1986; Veronica or the Two Nations, 1989; The Woman's Hour, 1991; Dr. Orwell and Mr. Blair, 1994; Fatima's Scarf, 1998. AS JOHN SALISBURY: The Baby Sitters, 1978; Moscow Gold, 1980. **Address:** 41 Westcroft Sq, London W6 0TA, England.

CAUTHEN, (W.) Kenneth. American, b. 1930. **Genres:** Theology/Religion. **Career:** Mercer University, Georgia, assistant professor, 1957-60; associate professor of Christian ethics, 1960-61; Crozer Theological Seminary, Chester, PA, associate professor, 1961-63, professor of theology, 1963-70; Colgate-Rochester/Crozer Theological Seminary, professor of theology, 1970-92. **Publications:** The Impact of American Religious Liberalism, 1962; The Triumph of Suffering Love, 1966; Science, Secularization and God, 1969; (ed. and contrib.) Shailer Mathews: Jesus on Social Institutions, 1971; Christian Biopolitics, 1971; The Ethics of Enjoyment, 1975; Process Ethics, 1984; Systematic Theology, 1986; The Passion for Equality, 1987; Theological Biology, 1992; Toward a New Modernism, 1997; The Many Faces of Evil, 1997; Evil Has Many Faces, 1997; The Ethics of Assisted Death, 1999; The Ethics of Belief, 2002; Rejoicing in Life's "Melissa Moments," 2003; "I Don't Care What the Bible Says," 2003; Born into the Wrong World, 2004. **Address:** 46 Azalea Rd, Rochester, NY 14620, U.S.A. **Online address:** kenc@frontiernet.net

CAVAZOS-GAITHER, Alma E(lisa). American, b. 1955. **Genres:** Sciences, Reference. **Career:** Texas Employment Commission, McAllen, receptionist and clerk, 1978-79; Tri-City Steel Construction Co., Pharr, TX, bookkeeper, receptionist, and payroll clerk, 1980-82; TRW Seatbelt Division, McAllen, material control clerk, 1983-85; Birch Hill Ski Lodge and Chena Bend Golf Course, Fort Wainwright, AK, recreational aide to operations assistant, 1989-93; MARC Group Inc., Killeen, TX, bilingual telephone surveyor, 1994; test data collector at Fort Hunter Leggitt, CA, 1995; CARMA, Killeen, president. Free-lance writer, 1995-. **Publications:** WITH C.C. GAITHER: Statistically Speaking: A Dictionary of Quotations, 1996; Physically Speaking: A Dictionary of Quotations, 1997; Mathematically Speaking: A Dictionary of Quotations, 1998; Practically Speaking: A Dictionary of Quotations, 1998; Medically Speaking: A Dictionary of Quotations, 1998; Scientifically Speaking: A Dictionary of Quotations, 2000; Naturally Speaking: A Dictionary of Quotations, 2001; Chemically Speaking: A Dictionary of Quotations, 2002; Astronomically Speaking: A Dictionary of Quotations, 2003. **Address:** 502 Weiss, Killeen, TX 76542, U.S.A. **Online address:** cgaither6281@earthlink.net

CAVE, Emma. (Caroline Lassalle). British. **Genres:** Novels. **Career:** Picador Books, London, editor, 1972-77. Lives in Cyprus. **Publications:**

Little Angie, 1977; The Blood Bond, 1979; Cousin Henrietta, 1981; (as Caroline Lassalle) Breaking the Rules, 1986; Going Too Far, 1989; The Inferno Corridor, 1991; Bluebeard's Room, 1995; The Lair, 1997. **Address:** c/o Barrie and Jenkins, Random Century House, 20 Vayxhall Bridge Rd, London SW1V 2SA, England.

CAVE, Eric M. American (born Sweden), b. 1965. **Genres:** Philosophy. **Career:** Union College, Schenectady, NY, visiting assistant professor of humanities, 1994-95; Arkansas State University, State University, assistant professor, 1995-2000, associate professor of philosophy, 2001-. **Publications:** Preferring Justice: Rationality, Self-Transformation, and the Sense of Justice, 1998. Contributor to periodicals. **Address:** Department of English and Philosophy, Arkansas State University, PO Box 1890, State University, AR 72467, U.S.A. **Online address:** ecave@astate.edu

CAVE, Kathryn. British, b. 1948. **Genres:** Young adult fiction. **Career:** Penguin Publishing, London, England, editor, 1970-71; Blackwell (publishers), Oxford, England, editor, 1971-72; Metier (publishers), Hayes, England, technical editor, 1987-88; Frances Lincoln Ltd., London, England, editorial director for children's nonfiction, 1990-92; writer. **Publications:** Dragonrise, 1984; Many Happy Returns, 1986; Just in Time, 1988; Poor Little Mary, 1988; Henry Hobbs, Alien, 1990; Jumble, 1990; William and the Wolves, 1991; Out for the Count, 1991; Running Battles, 1992; Something Else, 1994; Best Friends for Ever, 1994; Andrew Takes the Plunge, 1994; My Journey Through Art, 1994; Something Else, 1998; W is For World, 1998; The Boy Who Became an Eagle, 2000; Henry's Song, 2000.

CAVELL, Benjamin. American. **Genres:** Communications/Media. **Career:** Short-story writer and novelist. **Publications:** Rumble, Young Man, Rumble (short stories), 2003. **Address:** c/o Author Mail, Alfred A. Knopf, 1745 Broadway, New York, NY 10019, U.S.A.

CAVELL, Marcia. American, b. 1931. **Genres:** Psychology. **Career:** State University of New York at Purchase, associate professor of philosophy, 1972-84; University of California-Berkeley, visiting associate professor of philosophy, 1986-89; New York University, NYC, visiting associate professor of philosophy, 1994. **Publications:** The Psychoanalytic Mind: From Freud to Philosophy, 1994. Contributor to philosophy and psychoanalytical journals. **Address:** 1570 Olympus Ave., Berkeley, CA 94708, U.S.A. **Online address:** CAVELL@UCLIN4.BERKELEY.EDU

CAVENEY, Graham. British. **Genres:** Literary criticism and history. **Career:** Writer. University of East Anglia, Norwich, Norfolk, England, lecturer in American literature. **Publications:** NONFICTION: (with E. Young) Shopping in Space: Essays on America's Blank Generation Fiction, 1992; The Priest, They Called Him: The Life and Legacy of William S. Burroughs, 1997, in US as Gentleman Junkie: The Life and Legacy of William S. Burroughs, 1998. **Address:** Department of American Literature, University of East Anglia, Earlham Rd., Norwich, Norfolk NR4 7TJ, England.

CAVES, Richard Earl. American, b. 1931. **Genres:** Economics. **Career:** University of California, Berkeley, assistant professor and associate professor, 1957-62; Harvard University, Cambridge, MA, professor of economics, 1962-. **Publications:** (with R.H. Holton) The Canadian Economy, 1959; Trade and Economic Structure, 1960; Air Transport and Its Regulators, 1962; American Industry, 1964; (with J.S. Bain and J. Margolis) Northern California's Water Industry, 1966; (with G.L. Reuber) Canadian Economic Policy and the Impact of International Capital Flows, 1969; (with G.L. Reuber) Capital Transfers and Economic Policy, 1971; (with R.W. Jones) World Trade and Payments, 1973; Diversification, Foreign Investment, and Scale in North American Manufacturing Industries, 1975; (with M. Uekusa) Industrial Organization in Japan, 1976; (with others) Studies in Canadian Industrial Organization, 1977; (with M.E. Porter and A.M. Spence) Competition in the Open Economy, 1980; Multinational Enterprise and Economic Analysis, 1982; (with S.W. Davies) Britain's Productivity Gap, 1987; (with D.R. Barton) Efficiency in U.S. Manufacturing Industries, 1990; Adjustment to International Competition, 1990; Creative Industries: Contracts between Art and Commerce, 2000. EDITOR & CONTRIBUTOR: (with H.G. Johnson and P.B. Kenen) Trade, Growth and the Balance of Payments, 1965; (with H.G. Johnson) Readings in International Economics, 1967; Britain's Economic Prospects, 1968; (with M.J. Roberts) Regulating the Product, 1975; (with L.B. Krause) Britain's Economic Performance, 1980; (with L.B. Krause) The Australian Economy, 1984; Industrial Efficiency in Six Nations, 1992; Creative Industries, 2000; Switching Channels, 2005. **Address:** Dept of Economics, Harvard University, Cambridge, MA 02138, U.S.A.

CAWS, Mary Ann. American/British, b. 1933. **Genres:** Art/Art history, Literary criticism and history, Essays, Translations. **Career:** Distinguished professor of English, French and comparative literature, Graduate Center, City University of New York, 1986- (assistant professor, 1966-70; associate professor, 1970-72; professor, 1972-86). Co-director, Henri Peyre Institute for the Humanities, 1981-2002; co-ed., Dada/Surrealism, University of Iowa; director, Le Siecle eclate, Paris; vice-president, 1982-83, and president, 1983-84, Modern Language Association. Faculty member, Barnard College, Columbia University, NYC, 1962-63, and Sarah Lawrence College, Bronxville, NY, 1963; visiting professor, Princeton University, NJ, 1974, Paris VII, 1993-94, School of Visual Arts, 1994. **Publications:** Surrealism and the Literary Imagination, 1966; The Poetry of Dada and Surrealism, 1970; Andre Breton, 1971; The Inner Theatre of Recent French Poetry, 1972; The Presence of Rene Char, 1976; The Surrealist Voice of Robert Desnos, 1977; Rene Char, 1977; La Main de Pierre Reverdy, 1979; A Metapoetics of the Passage, 1981; The Eye in the Text, 1982; L'Oeuvre Filante de Rene Char, 1983; (trans.) A. Breton, Mad Love, 1988; The Art of Interference, 1989; Women of Bloomsbury, 1990; (co-trans.) A. Breton, Communicating Vessels, 1990; (with S.B. Wright) Bloomsbury and France, 2000; Picasso's Weeping Woman, 2000; Virginia Woolf: Illustrated Lives, 2001. EDITOR: (and trans.) Approximate Man and Other Writings of Tristan Tzara, 1974; About French Poetry from Dada to Tel Quel, 1975; (and trans.) Selected Poems of Rene Char, 1976; (and co-trans.) Roof Slates and Other Poems of Pierre Reverdy, 1981; Stephane Mallarme: Selected Poetry and Prose, 1981; St. John Perse, Selected Poems, 1982; Writing in a Modern Temper, 1984; Reading Frames in Modern Fiction, 1985; Textual Analysis: Some Readers Reading, 1986; Perception in Philosophy, Art and Literature, 1989; Reading Proust Now, 1989; Selected Poems of Rene Char, 1991; City Images, 1991; Joseph Cornell, Theater of the Mind; Selected Diaries, Letters and Files, 1992; (chief ed.) HarperCollins World Reader, 1994; Manifesto, 2001; Surrealist Painters and Poets, 2001; Vita Sackville-West: Selected Writings, 2002; Robert Motherwell with Pen and Brush, 2002; Surrealist Love Poems, 2002; Mallarme in Prose, 2002; Surrealism, 2004. **Address:** 140 E 81st St Apt 11D, New York, NY 10028, U.S.A. **Online address:** cawsma@aol.com

CAWS, Peter (James). American (born England), b. 1931. **Genres:** Education, Philosophy, Sciences, Translations, Humanities. **Career:** University Professor of Philosophy, George Washington University, Washington, D.C., since 1982. Executive Associate, Carnegie Corp., NYC, 1962-65; Professor of Philosophy, Hunter College, NYC, 1965-82. **Publications:** The Philosophy of Science: A Systematic Account, 1965; (trans.) The Methods of Contemporary Thought, by J. M. Bochenski, 1965; Science and the Theory of Value, 1967; (with S.D. Ripley) The Bankruptcy of Academic Policy, 1972; Sartre, 1979; (ed.) Two Centuries of Philosophy in America, 1980; Structuralism: The Art of the Intelligible, 1988; (ed.) The Causes of Quarrel: Essays on Peace, War, and Thomas Hobbes, 1989; Yorick's World: Science and the Knowing Subject, 1993; The Capital Connection: Business, Science, and Government, 1993; Ethics from Experience, 1996. **Address:** 237 Cheltenham Rd., Newark, DE 19711-3617, U.S.A. **Online address:** pcaws@gwu.edu

CAWTHORNE, Nigel. British, b. 1951. **Genres:** Novels, Science fiction/Fantasy, Children's fiction, Young adult fiction, Architecture, Art/Art history, Astronomy, Criminology/True Crime, Ghost Writer, Fashion/Costume, Film, History, Human relations/Parenting, Intellectual history, Military/Defense/Arms control, Music, Physics, Sciences. **Career:** IPC Business Press (now Reed International Publishing), cub reporter for Electrical and Electronic Trader, 1975-76; Club International, NYC, writer, 1976-77; Hi-Fi Weekly, writer, 1977; Haymarket Publishing, writer for What Hi-Fi? and Popular Hi-Fi, 1977; New York Trib, NYC, reviewer and features writer, 1977-78; Davis Publications, member of editorial staff, 1978; Financial Times, writer and producer of World Business Weekly, 1978-79; free-lance writer, 1979-. Guest on television and radio programs in US and abroad. **Publications:** The Loving Touch, 1987; How to Assess Mortgages and Loans, 1988; How to Build an Airliner (juvenile), as Airliners, 1988; The Sixties Source Book, 1989; The Bamboo Cage, 1991; Great Record Labels, 1992; The Iron Cage, 1993; Spree Killers, 1993; Sex Killers, 1994; Killers, 1994; The Winning System, 1994; The Universe Explained, 1994; Sex Lives of the Kings and Queens of England, 1994; Satanic Murder, 1995; Sex Lives of the Popes, 1996; The New Look, 1996; The Art of Japanese Prints, 1996; Sex Lives of the U.S. Presidents, 1996; The Art of India, 1997; The Art of Native North America, 1997; A Century of Shoes, 1997; Sex Lives of the Hollywood Idols, 1997; The Secrets of Love, 1997; Sex Lives of the Hollywood Goddesses, 1997, vol. 2, 2004; Sex Lives of the Great Artists, 1998; Sex Lives of the Great Composers, 1998; Key Moments in Fashion, 1998; The Art of the Aztecs, 1999; 911 Exposed, 1999; Steps, 1999; Another Level, 1999; Five Take Five, 1999; BAssistantWitched, 1999; Images of the Cat, 1999; The Confessions of Ike Turner, 1999; The World's Greatest Alien Abductions, 1999; The World's Greatest Serial Killers, 1999; The World's Greatest Serial Cults, 1999; The World's Greatest Serial Royal Scandals, 1999; The World's Great-

est Political Scandals, 1999; The World's Worst Atrocities, 1999; The Art of Icons, 2000; The Art of Frescoes, 2000; The Vulva, 2000; Magical Mythery Tour, 2000; The History of the SS Cricket Team, 2000; The Alien Who Thought He Was Elvis, 2000; The World's Greatest UFO and Alien Encounters, 2000; The World's Greatest Alien Encounters, 2002; The World's Greatest UFO Sightings, 2002; The World's Greatest Alien Conspiracy Theories, 2002; A Life as History, 2002; Million Dollar Trivia, 2002; Turning the Tide, 2002; Fighting Them on the Beaches, 2002; Steel Fist, 2003; A History of Pirates, 2003; Witche Hunt, 2003; The Empress of South America, 2003; Vietnam: A War Lost and Won, 2003; Victory 100 Great Military Commanders, 2003; 100 Great Disasters, 2004; Alexander the Great, 2004; 100 Tyrants and Despots, 2004. **Address:** Flat D Bevan House, Boswell St, London WC1N 3BT, England. **Online address:** nigelcawthorne@compuserve.com; www.nigelcawthorne.com

CAYER, D. M. *See* **DUFFY, Maureen (Patricia).**

CAYLEFF, Susan E. American, b. 1954. **Genres:** Women's studies and issues. **Career:** University of Texas Medical Branch, Galveston, assistant professor of medical humanities, 1983-87, clinical adjunct in nursing, 1986-87, humanities faculty founder of Women's History Seminar Series, 1984-87; San Diego State University, San Diego, CA, associate professor, 1987-92, professor of women's studies, 1993-, department chair, 1997-, member of executive committee, Lipinsky Institute for Judaic Studies, 1990-. Loma Linda University, William Frederick Norwood Lecturer, 1988; University of Texas Medical Branch, Galveston, adjunct faculty at Institute for the Medical Humanities, 1987-; guest on radio and television programs; public speaker. **Publications:** Wash and Be Healed: The Water-Cure Movement and Women's Health, 1987; (ed. with Bair) "Wings of Gauze": Women of Color and the Experience of Health and Illness, 1993; Babe: The Life and Legend of "Babe" Didrikson Zaharias, 1995. Work represented in anthologies. Contributor of articles, poems, and reviews to academic journals.

CAZDEN, Courtney B(orden). American, b. 1925. **Genres:** Education. **Career:** Elementary school teacher in public schools, 1947-49, 1954-61, and 1974-75; Harvard University, Cambridge, MA, assistant professor, 1965-68, associate professor, 1968-71, professor, 1971-. Visiting professor at US and Australian colleges and universities. **Publications:** Environmental Assistance to the Child's Acquisition of Grammar, 1965; Child Language and Education, 1972; (ed. with V.P. John and D. Hymes) Functions of Language in the Classroom, 1972; (ed.) Language in Early Childhood Education, 1972; Classroom Discourse: The Language of Teaching and Learning, 1988; (coauthor) Whole Language Plus, 1992. Contributor to periodicals. **Address:** Harvard Graduate School of Education, Longfellow Hall 205, Cambridge, MA 02138, U.S.A.

CAZET, Denys. American, b. 1938. **Genres:** Children's fiction. **Career:** Teacher, Corcoran and St. Helena, California, 1960-75; Founder, Parhelion and Co., 1972-73; Elementary sch. librarian and media specialist, St. Helena, 1975-85; Faculty member and teacher of extension classes, University of California at Davis, 1976-78; Director, St. Helena School District Media Centers, 1979-81; Instructor, California College of Arts and Crafts, Oakland, 1985-86. **Publications:** SELF-ILLUSTRATED FOR CHILDREN: Requiem for a Frog, 1971; The Non-Coloring Book: A Drawing Book for Mind Stretching and Fantasy Building, 1973; The Duck with Squeaky Feet, 1980; Mud Baths for Everyone, 1981; You Make the Angels Cry, 1983; Lucky Me, 1983; Big Shoe, Little Shoe, 1984; Christmas Moon, 1984; Saturday, 1985; December Twenty-Fourth, 1986; Frosted Glass, 1987; A Fish in His Pocket, 1987; Sunday, 1988; Great-Uncle Felix, 1988; Mother Night, 1988; Good Morning Maxine!, 1989; Never Spit on Your Shoes, 1990; Daydreams, 1990; I'm Not Sleepy, 1992; Are There Any Questions?, 1992; Born in the Gravy, 1993; Nothing at All, 1994; Dancing, 1995; Night Lights: 24 Poems to Sleep On, 1997; Minnie and Moo Go to the Moon, 1998; Minnie and Moo Go Dancing, 1998; Minnie and Moo Save the Earth, 1999; Minnie and Moo Go to Paris, 1999; Minnie and Moo and the Musk of Zorro, 2000; Never Poke a Squid, 2000; Minnie and Moo and the Thanksgiving Tree, 2000; Minnie and Moo Meet Frankenswine, 2001. Illustrator of books by D. Maurer, L. Komaiko. **Address:** 1300 Ink Grade Rd, Pope Valley, CA 94567-9434, U.S.A.

CEBULASH, Mel. Also writes as Ben Farrell, Glen Harlan, Jared Jansen, Jeanette Mara. American, b. 1937. **Genres:** Novels, Novellas/Short stories, Children's fiction, Young adult fiction, Children's non-fiction, Sports/Fitness, Young adult non-fiction, Autobiography/Memoirs, Humor/Satire. **Career:** Cebulash Assocs., Phoenix, AZ, director, 1986-. Teacher, New Jersey Public Schools, 1962-65; Language Arts, associate ed., 1966-68, ed., 1969-72; Scholastic Magazine Inc, NYC, editorial director, reading skills, 1972-74, associate ed.-in-chief, 1974-76; Bowmar/Noble Publ. Inc., Los Angeles, ed.-in-chief, 1976-80; Fearon Books, San Francisco, vice president and publr., 1982-85. **Publications:** Through Basic Training with Walter Young, 1968; Man in the Green Beret, 1969; Benny's Nose, 1972; The See-Saw, 1972; Willie's Pet, 1972; The Ball That Wouldn't Bounce, 1972; Dictionary Skilz, 1972; Baseball Players Do Amazing Things, 1974; Football Players Do Amazing Things, 1974; Basketball Players Do Amazing Things, 1976; The Grossest Book of World Records, 1977, vol. II, 1978; The Champion's Jacket, 1978; The 1,000 Point Football Quiz Book, 1979; The 1,000 Point Baseball Quiz Book, 1979; Blackouts, 1979; A Horse to Remember, 1979; The Spring Street Boys Team Up, 1981; The Spring Street Boys Settle a Score, 1981; The Spring Street Boys Hit the Road, 1982; I'm an Expert, 1982; Ruth Marini of the Dodgers, 1982; Ruth Marini, Dodger Ace, 1983; The Kid with the Left Hook, 1984; The Face That Stopped Time, 1984; Ruth Marini, World Series Star, 1985; Hot Like the Sun, 1986; Carly & Company, 1989; Campground Caper, 1990; Part-time Shadow, 1990; Catnapper, 1993; Rattler, 1993; Snooperman, 1993; Batboy, 1993; Flipper's Boy, 1993; Muscle Bound, 1993; Willie's Wonderful Pet, 1993; Bases Loaded, 1993; Third and Goal, 1993; Lights Out, 1993; Fast Break, 1993; Dirty Money, 1993; Pet to Explode, 1993; A Sucker for Readheads, 1993; Knockout Punch, 1993; Scared Silly, 1995; Betting on Baseball in the 1950s, 2002. MOVIE NOVELIZATIONS: Monkeys, Go Home, 1967; The Love Bug, 1969; The Boatniks, 1970; Herbie Rides Again, 1974; The Strongest Man in the World, 1976; Ghostdad, 1990. AS GLEN HARLAN: Petey the Pup, 1972; Play Ball!, 1996. AS BEN FARRELL: Nancy and Jeff, 1972; Mad Dog 1984; Dad Saves the Day 1991; Let's Visit the Moon, 1996; What a Shower!, 1996; One More Time, 1996; My Family Band, 1996. AS JARED JANSEN: Penny the Poodle, 1972; Showtime! 1991. AS JEANETTE MARA: What Time Is It?, 1996. **Address:** 11820 N 112th St, Scottsdale, AR 85259, U.S.A. **Online address:** cebulash@att.net

CELENZA, Anna Harwell. American. **Genres:** Music. **Career:** Michigan State University, East Lansing, MI, assistant professor of musicology. **Publications:** The Farewell Symphony (juvenile, with CD), 2000; The Early Works of Niels W. Gade: In Search of the Poetic, 2001; (ed.) N.W. Gade, St. Hans' Evening Play Overture, 2001; Pictures at an Exhibition, 2003. Contributor of scholarly articles to collections. **Address:** 446 Kensington Rd., East Lansing, MI 48823, U.S.A. **Online address:** celenzaa@msu.edu

CELIZIC, Mike. American, b. 1948. **Genres:** Biography, Sports/Fitness, Self help. **Career:** Telegraph, Painesville, OH, reporter and photographer, 1970-72; Home News, New Brunswick, NJ, reporter for State House Bureau, 1972-76; Ruder & Finn, NYC, writer in New York and San Juan, PR, 1976-77; free-lance photographer and public relations consultant in El Salvador, 1977-78; The Record, Hackensack, NJ, sports columnist, 1979-. **Publications:** (with M. Wills) On the Run: The Never Dull and Often Shocking Life of Maury Wills, 1990; Courage, 1991; The Fall of '66 (nonfiction), 1992; (with R. Traum) A Victory for Humanity, 1993; (with R. Ruettiger) Rudy's Rules, 1994; The Biggest Game of Them All (nonfiction). **Address:** The Record, 150 River St., Hackensack, NJ 07602, U.S.A.

CELL, Edward Charles. American, b. 1928. **Genres:** Theology/Religion. **Career:** U.S. International University, San Diego, CA, professor of philosophy and chairman of Division of Comparative World Studies, 1972-74; Sangamon State University, Springfield, IL, professor of philosophy, 1974-. **Publications:** (ed.) Religion and Contemporary Western Culture, 1967; Language, Existence and God, 1971; Learning to Learn from Experience, 1984; Daily Readings from Quaker Spirituality, 1987; Organizational Life, 1998. **Address:** Dept of Philosophy, University of Illinois at Springfield, 1 University Plaza, Springfield, IL 62703, U.S.A. **Online address:** ecell1@uis.edu

CENDRARS, Blaise. *See* **HARSCH, Rich.**

CERAMI, Charles A. American. **Genres:** Adult non-fiction. **Career:** Economist. Kiplinger Washington Publications, Washington, DC, former editor. **Publications:** Successful Leadership in Business, 1955; How to Solve Management Problems, 1957; Stop Hiding from Success, 1958; Crisis, the Loss of Europe, 1975; More Profit, Less Risk: Your New Financial Strategy, 1982; (editor) A Marshall Plan for the 1990s: An International Roundtable on World Economic Development, 1989; Real Estate for Profit: New Trends & Strategies for the '90s, 1990; Benjamin Banneker: Surveyor, Astronomer, Publisher, Patriot, 2002; Jefferson's Great Gamble: The Remarkable Story of Jefferson, Napoleon, and the Men Behind the Louisiana Purchase, 2003. Contributor of articles to periodicals. **Address:** 4201 Massachusetts Ave. NW, Washington, DC 20016, U.S.A.

CERCIGNANI, Carlo. Italian, b. 1939. **Genres:** Mathematics/Statistics. **Career:** Politecnico di Milano, Milano, Italy, associate professor of aerodynamics, 1968-75, professor of theoretical mechanics, 1975-. Massachusetts Institute of Technology, visiting associate professor, 1966-67. **Publications:** Mathematical Methods in Kinetic Theory, 1969, 2nd ed, 1990; The Boltzmann Equation and Its Applications, 1988; (with R. Illner and M. Pulvirenti) The Mathematical Theory of Dilute Gases, 1994; (with V.I. Gerasimenko and D. Ya. Petrina), Many-Particle Dynamics and Kinetic Equations, 1997; Ludwig Boltzmann. The Man Who Trusted Atoms, 1998; Rarefied Gas Dynamics. From Basic Concepts to Actual Calculations, 2000. Author of papers published in scientific journals and proceedings of scientific meetings. **Address:** Via Tito Speri 1, 20154 Milano, Italy. **Online address:** carcer@mate.polimi.it

CERNADA, George P. American. **Genres:** Demography, Medicine/Health, Social sciences. **Career:** Population Council, resident representative in Taiwan, 1965-75, senior associate and director of Asian operations research, 1990-93, representative, Pakistan, 1993-95; University of Massachusetts at Amherst, professor of community health, 1976-90, 1995-2002, professor emeritus, 2003-. Consultant. **Publications:** Taiwan Family Planning Reader, 1970, 2nd ed., 1973; Knowledge into Action: Taiwan's Research Utilization, 1980; Spacing as an Alternative Strategy: India, 1996; Progress in Preventing AIDS?, 1998; Sexual and Reproductive Health Promotion in Latino Populations, 2003. Contributor to periodicals. **Address:** University of Massachusetts, PO Box 3585, Amherst, MA 01004-3585, U.S.A.

CERNY, Frank J. American, b. 1946. **Genres:** Medicine/Health, Sports/Fitness. **Career:** Educator and author. University of Windsor, Windsor, Ontario, Canada, instructor, 1974-76; Children's Hospital of Buffalo Children's Lung Center, cofounder and associate director, 1976-85; State University of New York at Buffalo, associate professor, 1985-, chair of Department of Exercise and Nutrition Sciences. Eden United Methodist Church, assistant pastor. **Publications:** (with H. Burton) Exercise Physiology for Health Professionals, 2001. Contributor to professional journals. **Address:** Department of Exercise and Nutrition Sciences, State University at Buffalo, 405 Kimball Tower, Buffalo, NY 14260, U.S.A. **Online address:** cerny@acsu.buffalo.edu

CERULLO, Mary M. American, b. 1949. **Genres:** Zoology. **Career:** RISE (Resources in Science Education), owner and consultant to schools and environmental organizations, 1988-. Friends of Casco Bay, Associate Director. **Publications:** Sharks: Challengers of the Deep, 1993; Lobsters: Gangsters of the Sea, 1994; Coral Reef: A City That Never Sleeps, 1996. **Address:** 101 Loveitt's Field Road, South Portland, ME 04106, U.S.A.

CERUZZI, Paul Edward. American, b. 1949. **Genres:** Information science/Computers. **Career:** Writer. Clemson University, SC, assistant professor of history of technology, 1981-; Smithsonian National Air and Space Museum, curator of aerospace engineering and computing. **Publications:** Reckoners: The Prehistory of the Digital Computer from Relays to the Stored Program Concept, 1935-1945, 1983; Beyond the Limits: Flight Enters the Computer Age, 1989; (with P.A. Kidwell) Landmarks in Digital Computing: A Smithsonian Pictorial History, 1994; A History of Modern Computing, 1945-1995, 1998. Contributor to books. **Address:** Space History Dept. (MRC 311), National Air & Space Museum, Smithsonian Institution, Washington, DC 20560, U.S.A. **Online address:** nasem001@sivm.si.edu

CERVENKA, Jarda. (Jaroslav). American/Czech, b. 1933. **Genres:** Novels, Novellas/Short stories, Children's fiction. **Career:** University of Minnesota, Minneapolis, professor of medical genetics, c. 1965-2000. **Publications:** Mal d'Afrique and Stories from Other Places (short stories), 1995; Revenge of Underwater Man (short stories), 2000. Contributor of stories to anthologies and periodicals. Translator of poems by Jaroslav Seifert. **Address:** 4205 Beverly Ave, Golden Valley, MN 55422, U.S.A. **Online address:** jardace@aol.com

CESPEDES, Frank V. American, b. 1950. **Genres:** Administration/Management, Business/Trade/Industry, Marketing. **Career:** Harvard University, Harvard Business School, Boston, MA, professor of business administration and leader of Strategic Marketing Management Program, 1978-95; Center for Executive Development, Cambridge, MA, managing partner. Consultant to companies in North and South America, Europe, and Asia. **Publications:** (with L. Micheli, D. Byker, and T. Raymond) Managerial Communications, 1984; (with E.R. Corey and V.K. Rangan) Case Studies in Industrial Distribution, 1989; (with Corey and Rangan) Going to Market: Distribution Systems for Industrial Products, 1989; Organizing and Implementing the Marketing Effort: Text and Cases, 1991; Concurrent Marketing: Integrating Product, Sales, and Service, 1995; Managing Marketing Linkages, 1996; Sales Management, 1998. Contributor to periodicals. **Address:** Center for Executive Development, 420 Boylston St Ste 408, Boston, MA 02116-4002, U.S.A.

CESSAC, Catherine. French, b. 1952. **Genres:** Music. **Career:** Musicologist. Centre de Musique Baroque, Versailles, France, CNRS, researcher. **Publications:** Marc-Antoine Charpentier, 1988, trans. 1995; Elisabeth Jacquet de la Guerre: Une femme compositeur sous le regne de Louis XIV, 1995; Nicolas Clerambault, 1998. **Address:** Centre de Musique Baroque, 22 Avenue de Paris, F-78000 Versailles, France. **Online address:** cc@cmbv.com

CEVASCO, G(eorge) A(nthony). Also writes as Serge O. Cogcave. American, b. 1924. **Genres:** Art/Art history, Environmental sciences/Ecology, Language/Linguistics, Literary criticism and history. **Career:** Fordham University, New York, lecturer, 1954-63; St. John's University, NY, professor of English, 1955-. **Publications:** J. K. Huysmans in England and America, 1962; (with J. Fee) Wordcraft, 1962; Grammar Self-Taught, 1963; (co-author) Functional English, 1963; Salvador Dali: Master of Surrealism and Modern Art, 1971; Oscar Wilde, 1972; The Population Problem, 1973; New Words for You, 1977; J. K. Huysmans: A Reference Guide, 1980; John Gray, 1982; The Sitwells: Edith, Osbert, Sacheverell, 1987; Three Decadent Poets: Ernest Dowson, John Gray and Lionel Johnson, 1989; The 1890s: An Encyclopedia of British Literature, Art and Culture, 1993; (co-author) Biographical Dictionary of American and Canadian Naturalists and Environmentalists, 1997; The Breviary of the Decadence: J.K. Huysmans's A Rebours and English Literature, 2001. **Address:** Dept. of English, St. John's University, Jamaica, NY 11439, U.S.A.

CHADWICK, Alex. See ZOSS, Joel.

CHADWICK, Cydney. American, b. 1959. **Genres:** Novels, Novellas/Short stories. **Career:** Chadwick Marketing, Penngrove, CA, regional sales manager, 1984-92; Syntax Projects for the Arts, executive director. Free-lance typesetter, designer, editor, and manuscript consultant. **Publications:** STORIES: Enemy Clothing, 1993; The Gift Horse's Mouth, 1994; Persistent Disturbances, 1995; Oeuvres, 1995; Interims, 1997. FICTION: Inside the Hours, 1998; Dracontic Nodes, 1999; Benched (novella), 2000; Flesh & Bone, 2001. **Address:** PO Box 1059, Penngrove, CA 94951, U.S.A. **Online address:** aveclivres@yahoo.com

CHADWICK, Elizabeth. See HERNDON, Nancy.

CHADWICK, Henry. British, b. 1920. **Genres:** Theology/Religion. **Career:** Master of Peterhouse, Cambridge, 1987-93, Regius Professor Emeritus of Divinity, Cambridge University, 1983- (Fellow, Queens College, 1946-58, and Magdalene College, 1979-87; Regius Professor, 1979-83). Regius Professor of Divinity, 1959-69, Canon of Christ Church, 1959-69, Dean of Christ Church, 1969-79, and Pro-Vice Chancellor, 1974-75, Oxford University. Editor, Journal of Theological Studies, 1954-85; Anglican-Roman Catholic International Commission, 1969-81, 1983-87. **Publications:** Origen: Contra Celsum, 1953; (with J.E.L. Oulton) Alexandrian Christianity, 1954; Lessing's Theological Writings, 1956; The Sentences of Sextus, 1959; Early Christian Thought and the Classical Tradition, 1966; The Early Church, 1967; (ed.) The Treatise on the Apostolic Tradition of St. Hippolytus of Rome, ed. by G. Dix, 1968; Priscillian of Avila, 1976; Boethius, 1981; History and Thought of the Early Church, 1982; Augustine, 1986; Heresy and Orthodoxy in the Early Church, 1991; Augustine's Confessions, 1991; Tradition and Exploration, 1994; The Church in Ancient Society, 2001; East and West, the Making of a Rift in the Church, 2002. **Address:** 46 St John St, Oxford OX1 2LH, England.

CHADWICK, (Sir) Owen. British, b. 1916. **Genres:** History, Intellectual history, Theology/Religion. **Career:** Cambridge University, Professor of Ecclesiastical History, 1958-68, Regius Professor of Modern History, 1968-83, and Vice-Chancellor, 1969-71. **Publications:** John Cassian, 1950, 1968; From Bossuet to Newman, 1957; (trans. and ed.) Western Asceticism, 1958; Mackenzie's Grave, 1959; Victorian Miniature, 1960; The Reformation, 1964, 15th ed., 1984; The Victorian Church, vol. 1, 1966, 3rd ed., 1972, vol. 2, 1970, 3rd ed., 1979; The Secularization of the European Mind, 1976; Catholicism and History, 1978; The Popes and European Revolution, 1981; Newman, 1983; Hensley Henson, 1983; Britain and the Vatican in the Second World War, 1986; Michael Ramsey, 1990; The Spirit of the Oxford Movement, 1990; The Christian Church in the Cold War, 1992; The History of Christianity, 1995; A History of the Popes, 1830-1914, 1998; Acton and History, 1998; The Early Reformation on the Continent, 2001. **Address:** Selwyn College, Cambridge CB3 9DQ, England. **Online address:** OC207@cam.ac.uk

CHADWICK, Whitney. American, b. 1943. **Genres:** Novels, Art/Art history. **Career:** Massachusetts Institute of Technology, Cambridge, lecturer to associate professor of art history, 1972-78; San Francisco State University, San Francisco, CA, professor of art, 1978-. University of California, Berkeley, visiting professor of art history, 1977. Member of boards of directors and advisory committees; Fellow, Mary Ingraham Bunting Institute, Radcliffe College, 1992-93. **Publications:** Myth in Surrealist Painting, 1929-1939, 1980; Women Artists and the Surrealist Movement, 1985; Women, Art, and Society, 1990; (ed. with I. de Courtivron) Significant Others: Creativity and Intimate Partnership, 1993; Leonora Carrington: La Realidad de Imaginacion, 1994; Framed (novel), 1998; Amazons in the Drawing Room: The Art of Romaine Brooks, 2000. **Address:** Art Department, San Francisco State University, 1600 Holloway Ave, San Francisco, CA 94132, U.S.A.

CHAFE, Wallace L. American, b. 1927. **Genres:** Novellas/Short stories, Anthropology/Ethnology, Language/Linguistics, Psychology. **Career:** Professor of linguistics, University of California, Berkeley, 1962-, and University of California at Santa Barbara, 1986-. **Publications:** Seneca Thanksgiving Rituals, 1961; Seneca Morphology and Dictionary, 1967; Meaning and the Structure of Language, 1970; The Caddoan, Iroquoian and Siouan Languages, 1976; The Pear Stories, 1980; Evidentiality, 1986; Discourse, Consciousness, and Time, 1994. **Address:** Dept. of Linguistics, College of Letters & Sciences, University of California, Santa Barbara, CA 93106, U.S.A. **Online address:** chafe@linguistics.ucsb.edu

CHAFEL, Judith A. American, b. 1945. **Genres:** Education. **Career:** Boston Redevelopment Authority, Roxbury, MA, relocation worker, 1968; John F. Kennedy Family Service Center, Charlestown, MA, assistant director of youth services, 1968-69; substitute teacher at elementary schools in Rochester, NY, 1971-72; elementary schoolteacher in Lakewood, NJ, 1972-74, and Sodus, NY, 1974-76; University of Texas at Austin, visiting assistant professor of curriculum and instruction, 1979-80; Indiana University-Bloomington, assistant professor, 1980-86, associate professor, 1986-2001, professor of curriculum and instruction, 2001-, adjunct associate professor of philanthropic studies, Center on Philanthropy, 1991-2001, coordinator of Early Childhood Program, 1988, 1992-93, co-coordinator, 1993-. U.S. House of Representatives, professional staff member, Committee on Ways and Means, 1989-90. **Publications:** (ed. and contrib.) Child Poverty and Public Policy, 1993; (with S. Reifel) Advances in Early Education and Day Care, 1997. Contributor to books. Contributor of articles and reviews to education and child study journals. **Address:** 3214 Education Bldg, School of Education, Indiana University-Bloomington, Bloomington, IN 47405, U.S.A.

CHAI, Arlene J. Australian (born Philippines), b. 1955. **Genres:** Novels. **Career:** Advertising copywriter in Manila, Philippines, and Sydney, Australia, 1976-. **Publications:** NOVELS: The Last Time I Saw Mother, 1995: Eating Fire and Drinking Water, 1996; On the Goddess Rock, 1998; Black Hearts, 2000. Work represented in anthologies. **Address:** c/o Sally Wofford Girand, Elaine Markson Literary Agency Inc., 44 Greenwich Ave., New York, NY 10011, U.S.A.

CHAI, May-Lee. American. **Genres:** Area studies. **Career:** Worked as teacher in Nanjing, China; Associated Press, reporter; University of California, Berkeley, research associate; writer. **Publications:** (ed. with W. Chai) Chinese-Mainland and Taiwan: A Study of Historical, Cultural, Economic and Political Relations with Documents, 1996; My Lucky Face (novel), 1997; (with W. Chai) The Girl from Purple Mountain: Love, Honor, War, and One Family's Journey from China to America (biography), 2001. Contributor to periodicals. **Address:** c/o Author Mail, Thomas Dunne Books, 175 Fifth Ave., New York, NY 10010, U.S.A.

CHAKRAVARTY, Sumita S(inha). Indian, b. 1951. **Genres:** Film. **Career:** Lucknow University, Lucknow, India, research fellow, 1971-74, lecturer in English, 1974-77; The New School for Social Research, NYC, faculty member, 1988-90, core faculty in communication and media studies, 1990-. **Publications:** National Identity in Indian Popular Cinema, 1947-1987, 1993. **Address:** Department of Communications, 2 West 13th St., 12th Floor, The New School for Social Research, New York, NY 10011, U.S.A.

CHALEFF, Ira. American, b. 1945. **Genres:** Poetry, Politics/Government. **Career:** Congressional Management Foundation, Washington, DC, executive director, 1982-89; Institute for Business Technology U.S. Inc., Washington, DC, president, 1989-97; Executive Coaching & Consulting Associates, president, 1998-. **Publications:** Setting Course: A Congressional Management Guide, 1986; Cutback Management for Congressional Offices, 1989; Secret Winds: Poems of a Spiritual Journey, 1990; The Courageous Follower: Standing Up to and for Our Leaders, 1995, 2nd ed., 2003. **Address:** Institute for Business Technology U.S. Inc., 513 Capitol Ct NE Ste 300, Washington, DC 20003, U.S.A. **Online address:** ira.chaleff@exe-coach.com

CHALFANT, William Y. American, b. 1928. **Genres:** History. **Career:** Partner of law firms in Hutchinson, KS, including Branine, Chalfant & Hill, 1956-. National Conference of Bar Examiners, member of Constitutional Law Drafting Committee for the Multi-State Bar Exam, 1974-85; Kansas Board of Law Examiners, 1966-92, chairman, 198692. **Publications:** Cheyennes and Horse Soldiers: The 1857 Expedition and the Battle of Solomon's Fork, 1989; Without Quarter, 1991; Dangerous Passage, 1994; Cheyennes at Dark Water Creek, 1996. **Address:** 1007 W 95th Ave, Hutchinson, KS 67502-8325, U.S.A.

CHALFONT, Lord. (Alun Arthur Gwynne Jones). British, b. 1919. **Genres:** History, Military/Defense/Arms control, Biography. **Career:** President, All Party Defence Group, House of Lords. Served as regular officer in the British Army, 1939-61; Defence Correspondent, The Times, London, 1961-64; Minister of State, Foreign and Commonwealth Office, 1964-70; Representative to the Council of the Western European Union, 1969-70; Foreign Affairs Correspondent, New Statesman, London, 1970-71; Chairman, U.N. Association, 1972-73; Director, Shandwick PLC, 1979-94; Director, IBM UK Ltd. 1983-90, and Lazard Bros. Ltd. 1982-90; Chairman, VSEL Consortium, 1987-95; Chairman, Radio Authority, 1990-94; Chairman, Marlborough Stirling Plc, 1994-99; Director, Television Corporation Plc, 1996-2002. **Publications:** The Sword and the Spirit, 1963; The Great Commanders, 1973; Montgomery of Alamein, 1976; (ed.) Waterloo, 1979; Star Wars: Suicide or Survival, 1985; Defence of the Realm, 1987; By God's Will: A Portrait of the Sultan of Brunei, 1989; The Shadow of My Hand, 2000.

CHALKER, Sylvia. British. **Genres:** Travel/Exploration, Language/Linguistics, Reference. **Career:** Worked as a journalist, public relations representative, and teacher of English as a foreign language. **Publications:** Going It Alone, 1978; Let's See Great Britain, 1979; Advanced English Course: Study Programmes, 1979; Police!, 1981; Fire!, 1981; Current English Grammar, 1984; Intermediate Grammar Workbooks, Volume I-III, 1987; Fast Forward 3 Resource Book, 1988, abridged ed (with M. Geddes), 1990; English Grammar Word by Word, 1991; A Student's English Grammar Workbook, 1992; (with E. Weiner) The Oxford Dictionary of English Grammar, 1994; The Little Oxford Dictionary of English Grammar, in press. Contributor to books. Contributor of articles and reviews to periodicals. **Address:** c/o Oxford University Press, 198 Madison Ave., New York, NY 10016-4308, U.S.A.

CHALLIS, Sarah. (born England). **Genres:** Dance/Ballet. **Career:** Writer, teacher. **Publications:** Killing Helen, 2000; Turning for Home, 2001; Blackthorn Winter, 2003; On Dancing Hill, 2004. **Address:** c/o Author Mail, St. Martin's Press, 175 Fifth Avenue, New York, NY 10010, U.S.A.

CHALLIS, Simon. See CHAMBERS, Peter.

CHALMERS, Alan D(ouglas). British, b. 1957. **Genres:** Literary criticism and history. **Career:** University of Southern California, Los Angeles, assistant lecturer, 198190; University of Oregon, Eugene, visiting assistant professor of English, 1990-91; University of South Carolina at Spartanburg, assistant professor, 1991-96, associate professor of English, 1996-. **Publications:** Jonathan Swift and the Burden of the Future, 1995. **Address:** University of South Carolina at Spartanburg, 800 University Way, Spartanburg, SC 29303, U.S.A. **Online address:** achalmers@gw.uscs.edu

CHALMERS, Penny. See KEMP, Penn.

CHALON, Jon. See CHALONER, John (Seymour).

CHALONER, John (Seymour). Also writes as Jon Chalon. British, b. 1924. **Genres:** Children's fiction. **Publications:** Three for the Road, 1954; Eager Beaver, 1965; Family Hold Back, 1975; To the Manner Born, 1978; Bottom Line, 1984; Occupational Hazard, 1991. AS JON CHALON: The Flying Steamroller, 1967; The House Next Door, 1967; Sir Lance-a-little and the Knights of the Kitchen Table, 1971; The Voyage of the Floating Bedstead, 1972; The Green Bus, 1973; The Dustmen's Holiday, 1976; The Great Balloon Adventure, 1984; Will o' the Wheels and Speedy Sue, 1990; Among the Missing, 2001. **Address:** 4 Warwick Sq, London SW1V 1NZ, England.

CHAMBERLAIN, Lesley. British, b. 1951. **Genres:** Food and Wine, Travel/Exploration, Autobiography/Memoirs, Literary criticism and history, Novellas/Short stories, Psychology, Philosophy. **Career:** Portsmouth Polytechnic, Portsmouth, England, lecturer in Russian and German, 1976-77; Reuters Agency, journalist, 1977-86; free-lance writer, critic, and teacher, 1986-. Reviewer on Russian literature for the LA Times, the Times Literary Supplement and national newspapers; occasional broadcaster and lecturer. **Publications:** The Food and Cooking of Russia, 1982; The Food and Cooking of Eastern Europe, 1989; (ed. and author of intro.) Marinetti La Cucina Futurista, 1989; In the Communist Mirror: Journeys in Eastern Europe, 1990; Volga Volga: A Journey down Russia's Great River, 1995; Nietzsche in Turin: The End of the Future, 1996; In a Place Like That (fiction), 1998; The Secret Artist: A Close Reading of Sigmund Freud, 2000. Contributor to periodicals. **Address:** David Higham Associates Ltd, 5-8 Lower John St, Golden Sq, London W1R 4HA, England. **Online address:** lesleychamb@aol.com

CHAMBERLAIN, Lorna M(arie). Canadian, b. 1945. **Genres:** Animals/Pets. **Career:** Whitby Psychiatric Hospital, Whitby, Ontario, Canada, psychometrist, 1971; Addiction Research Foundation, Sarnia, Ontario, community consultant, 1972-80; Sarnia General Hospital, Sarnia, associate director, 1980-92, director of addiction services, 1992-. **Publications:** (with R. Preece) Animal Welfare and Human Values, 1993. **Address:** Sarnia General Hospital, 220 North Mitton St., Sarnia, ON, Canada N7T 6H6.

CHAMBERLAIN, Mary (Christina). British, b. 1947. **Genres:** Area studies, History, Women's studies and issues. **Career:** Arms Control and Disarmament Research Unit, Foreign and Commonwealth Office, London, research officer, 1970-71; Richardson Institute for Peace and Conflict Research, London, research officer, 1972; Social Science Research Council, London, administrative officer, 1972; lecturer in liberal studies: Norfolk College of Art and Technology, King's Lynn, 1973-74, London College of Fashion, 1974-75, and Ipswich Civic College, 1977-87; London College of Printing, sr. lecturer in cultural studies, 1977-87; University of the West Indies, Cave Hill Campus, Barbados, part-time lecturer, 1988-91; University of Essex, fellow, 1991-93; National Life Story Collection of the British Library National Sound Archive, trustee, 1991-; International Yearbook of Oral History and Life Stories, associate reviews editor, 1992-; Oxford Brookes University, School of Humanities, senior lecturer, 1993, professor of modern history, 1995-; Routledge Studies in Memory and Narrative, founder and principal editor, 1997-; Barbados National Oral History Project, consultant, 1999-. Royal Historical Society, Fellow, 2002-. **Publications:** Fenwomen, 1975; Old Wives' Tales, 1981; Writing Lives, 1988; Growing Up in Lambeth, 1989; Narratives of Exile and Return, 1997; New Perspectives on Caribbean Families, forthcoming. EDITOR: Caribbean Migration: Globalised Identities, 1998; (with P. Thompson) Narrative and Genre, 1998; (with H. Goulbourne) Caribbean Families in Britain and the Trans-Atlantic World, 2001. **Address:** School of Humanities, Oxford Brookes University, Gipsy Lane, Oxford OX3 0BP, England. **Online address:** mcchamberlain@brookes.ac.uk

CHAMBERLIN, Ann. American, b. 1954. **Genres:** Novels, Plays/Screenplays. **Career:** Writer. **Publications:** NOVELS: The Virgin and the Tower, 1979; Tamar, 1994; Sofia, 1996; The Sultan's Daughter, 1997; The Reign of the Favored Women, 1998; Leaving Eden, 1999; The Merlin of St. Gilles' Well, 1999; The Merlin of the Oakwood, 2001. PLAYS: To Life, 1976; A Faerie Tale, 1978; Ex Cathedra, 1978; The Desert and the Sown, 1980; The Lorlei, 1981; Someone Like No Other, 1991; Simoom, 1991; The Giantkiller, 1992; The Sow's Bladder, 1993; Pas De Deux, 1993; A Christmas Wish, 1994; Fire Exit, 1996; Jihad, 1996; The Lamentable Tragedy of Sir Thomas More, 1999. UNPRODUCED PLAYS: Shadow Play; Acting Heads of State; The Piper Must Be Paid; Every Woman Blues. **Address:** PO Box 71114, Salt Lake City, UT 84171-1114, U.S.A. **Online address:** setzers@msn.com

CHAMBERLIN, Kate. American, b. 1945. **Genres:** Children's fiction. **Career:** Elementary schoolteacher in Newburgh, NY, 1967-69; Rochester Institute of Technology, Rochester, NY, departmental secretary for National Technical Institute for the Deaf, 1971-73; Wayne Central School District, Walworth, NY, substitute teacher and tutor, 1973-97. Rochester Museum and Science Center, instructor in youth program, 1976-82; Teddy Bear Trail Nursery School, teacher, 1984-86; Community Partners: The Homework Place, director, 1993-95. **Publications:** The Night Search, 1997. Work represented in anthologies. Contributor to magazines and newspapers. **Address:** 3901 Orchard St., Walworth, NY 14568, U.S.A. **Online address:** kathryngc@juno.com

CHAMBERS, Aidan. British, b. 1934. **Genres:** Literary criticism and history, Children's fiction, Plays/Screenplays, Children's non-fiction. **Career:** Freelance writer and ed. Ed., Topliners, Club 75, and Rockets series, Macmillan; Proprietor, Thimble Press, 1970-. Co-founder, Turton and Chambers (publrs.), 1989. **Publications:** PLAYS: Everyman's Everybody (for adults), 1957; Johnny Salter, 1966; The Car, 1967; The Chicken Run, 1968; The

Dream Cage (for adults), 1982; Only Once: A Play for Young Actors, 1998. OTHER: Cycle Smash, 1967; Marle, 1968; The Reluctant Reader (for adults), 1969; Haunted Houses, 1971; Mac and Lugs, 1971; Don't Forget Charlie, and The Vase, 1971; Ghosts 2, 1972; More Haunted Houses, 1973; Introducing Books to Children, 1973; Great British Ghosts, 1974; Great Ghosts of the World, 1974; (ed.) The Tenth (and Eleventh) Ghost Book, 1974-75; Snake River, 1975; Funny Folk, 1976; Ghost Carnival, 1977; Breaktime, 1978; Fox Tricks, 1980; Seal Secret, 1980; Dance on My Grave, 1982; The Present Takers, 1983; Booktalk, 1985; Now I Know, 1987; The Reading Environment, 1991; The Toll Bridge, 1992; Tell Me: Children, Reading and Talk, 1993; Postcards from No Man's Land (novel), 1999. Editor of books for children. **Address:** Lockwood, Station Rd, S. Woodchester, Stroud, Glos. GL5 5EQ, England.

CHAMBERS, John Whiteclay, II. American, b. 1936. **Genres:** History. **Career:** Independent, Star-News, Pasadena, CA, news reporter, 1958-60; Independent-Journal, San Rafael, CA, news reporter, 1960-61; KRON-TV, San Francisco, CA, newswriter and producer, 1961-65; Barnard College, Columbia University, New York City, assistant professor of history, 1972-82; Rutgers University, New Brunswick, NJ, History Dept, assistant professor, 1982-87, associate professor, 1987-93, professor, 1993-2000, dept chair, 1997-98, distinguished professor, 2002-. WNET-TV, director of research for "In Pursuit of Liberty" series, 1974-76; Rutgers Center for Historical Analysis, project director, 1993-95. **Publications:** The Tyranny of Change: America in the Progressive Era, 1890-1920, 1980, 3rd ed., 2001; To Raise an Army: The Draft Comes to Modern America, 1987. EDITOR: The Eagle and the Dove: The American Peace Movement and U.S. Foreign Policy, 1900-1922, 1976, 2nd ed., 1991; (with Charles C. Moskos) The New Conscientious Objection: From Sacred to Secular Resistance, 1993; (with D. Culbert) World War II, Film, and History, 1996; (in -chief) The Oxford Companion to American Military History, 1999. **Address:** Department of History, Rutgers University, 16 Seminary Pl, New Brunswick, NJ 08901-1108, U.S.A. **Online address:** chamber@rci.rutgers.edu

CHAMBERS, Leland H. American, b. 1928. **Genres:** Translations. **Career:** Central Michigan University, Mount Pleasant, instructor to assistant professor of English, 1958-63; University of Denver, CO, assistant professor to professor, 1963-92, emeritus professor of English and Comparative literature, 1992-. **Publications:** TRANSLATOR: E.Martinez Estrada, Holy Saturday and Other Stories, 1988; J. Campos, She Has Reddish Hair and Her Name Is Sabina (novel), 1993; J. Campos, The Fear of Losing Eurydice (novel), 1993; (ed. with E. Jaramillo Levi, and coordinator of trans.) Contemporary Short Stories from Central America, 1994; E. Jaramillo Levi, Duplications and Other Stories, 1994; J. Campos, Celina, or the Cats (novel), 1995; C. Boullosa, They're Cows, We're Pigs (novel), 1997; J. Stamadianos, Beer Cans in the Rio de la Plata (novel), 1998; Juan Tovar, Creature of a Day (novel), 2002. **Address:** 2884 S Raleigh, Denver, CO 80236, U.S.A.

CHAMBERS, Peter. Also writes as Simon Challis, Peter Chester, Philip Daniels, Dennis Phillips. British, b. 1924. **Genres:** Mystery/Crime/Suspense. **Career:** Director, since 1983, and Hon. Treasurer, since 1990, Author's Licencing and Collecting Society, London. Former professional jazz musician; has worked as a sr. manager in nationalized industry. Executive Councillor, Writers Guild of Great Britain, London, 1982-87; Chairman, Crime Writers Association, London, 1984-85. **Publications:** Murder Is for Keeps, 1961; Wreath for a Redhead, 1962; The Big Goodbye, 1962; Dames Can Be Deadly, 1963; Down-Beat Kill, 1963; Lady, This Is Murder, 1963; This'll Kill You, 1964; Nobody Lives Forever, 1964; You're Better Off Dead, 1965; Always Take the Big Ones, 1965; No Gold When You Go, 1966; Don't Bother to Knock, 1966; The Bad Die Young, 1967; The Blonde Wore Black, 1968; No Peace for the Wicked, 1968; Speak Ill of the Dead, 1968; (as Simon Challis) Death on a Quiet Beach, 1968; (as Dennis Phillips) Revenge Incorporated, 1970; They Call It Murder, 1973; Somebody Has to Lose, 1975; The Deader They Fall, 1979; Lady, You're Killing Me, 1979; The Day of the Big Dollar, 1979; The Beautiful Golden Frame, 1980; Nothing Personal, 1980; The Deep Blue Cradle, 1980; A Long Time Dead, 1981; The Lady who Never Was, 1981; Female-Handle with Care, 1981; Murder Is Its Own Reward, 1982; The Highly Explosive Case, 1982; A Miniature Murder Mystery, 1982; Jail Bait, 1983; Dragons Can Be Dangerous, 1983; Bomb-Scare Flight 147; The Moving Picture Writes, 1984; The Vanishing Holes Murders, 1985; The Day the Thames Caught Fire, 1989; The Hot Money Caper, 1992; No Place for a Lady, 1993. AS PETER CHESTER: Killing Comes Easy, 1958; Murder Forestalled, 1960; The Pay-Grab Murders, 1962; Blueprint for Larceny, 1963; The Traitors, 1964. AS PHILIP DANIELS: Goldmine, London W1, 1979; The Scarred Man, 1980; The Nice Quiet Girl, 1980; Alibi of Guilt, 1980; Foolproof, 190; Suspicious, 1981; The Inconvenient Corpse, 1982; A Genteel Little Murder, 1982; Nice Knight for Murder, 1982; The Dracula

Murders, 1983; Cinderella Spy, 1984; Enquiries Are Proceeding, 1986; The Hunting of Mr. Gloves, 1986. **Address:** Hillcrest House, 94 Highfield Lane, Maidenhead, Berks. SL6 3PF, England.

CHAMBERS, Veronica. American, b. 1970?. **Genres:** Film, Novels. **Career:** Memoirist, journalist, editor, novelist, and photographer; Glamour magazine, contributing editor. Worked as editor at Premiere, and New York Times Magazine; has also worked at Sassy, Seventeen, Essence, Life, and MTV. Photographs exhibited in a group show in Los Angeles, spring, 1990. **Publications:** (with J. Singleton; includes screenplay by Singleton and poems by M. Angelou) Poetic Justice: Filmmaking South Central Style, foreword by Spike Lee, 1993; Mama's Girl, 1996. **Address:** c/o Putnam Berkley Group Inc., 375 Husdon, New York, NY 10014, U.S.A.

CHAMOISEAU, Patrick. Martiniquian, b. 1953. **Genres:** Novels, Literary criticism and history, Autobiography/Memoirs. **Career:** Writer. **Publications:** Manman Dlo contre la fee Carabosse: theatre contae, 1982; Chronique des sept miseres (novel), 1986, trans as Chronicle of the Seven Sorrows, 2000; Solibo Magnifique (novel), 1988, trans. by R-M. Rejouis and V. Vinokurov as Solibo Magnificent, 1998; Martinique, 1988; (with J. Bernabe and R. Confiant) Eloge de la creolite (literary criticism), 1989; (with Confiant) Lettres creoles: Tracees antillaises et continentales de la litterature-Haiti, Guadeloupe, Martinique, Guyane 1635-1975 (literary criticism), 1991; Texaco (novel), 1992, trans. by Rejouis and Vinokurov, 1997; Antan d'enfance (memoir), 1993; Au temps de l'antan (folktales), trans. by L. Coverdale as Creole Folktales, 1994; Guyane: Traces-memoires du bagne, 1994; Chemin-d'ecole (memoir), 1994, trans. by Coverdale as School Days, 1997. **Address:** 31 Favorite, 97232 Larentin, Martinique.

CHAMPAGNE, Duane (Willard). American, b. 1951. **Genres:** Sociology. **Career:** Cultural Survival Inc., intern, 1982-83; University of Wisconsin-Milwaukee, assistant professor, 1983-84; University of California, Los Angeles, assistant professor, 1984-91, associate professor, 1991-97, professor of sociology, 1997-, director of American Indian Studies Center, 1991-2002. Member of many boards of advisers for Indian Affairs. **Publications:** Social Order and Political Change: Constitutional Governments among the Cherokee, the Choctaw, the Chickasaw, and the Creek, 1992. EDITOR: Native America: Portrait of the Peoples, 1994; (and contrib.) Native North American Almanac, 2 vols., 1994; (and author of intro.) Chronology of Native North American History, 1994; Reference Library of Native North America, Vols. 1-4, 1996; (with T. Johnson and J. Nagel, and contrib.) American Indian Activism: Alcatraz to the Longest Walk, 1997; (and contrib.) Contemporary Native American Cultural Issues, 1999; Native American Studies in Higher Education, 2002. Contributor to books. Contributor of articles and reviews to professional journals. **Address:** Department of Sociology, 264 Haines Hall, Box 951551, University of California, Los Angeles, CA 90095-1551, U.S.A. **Online address:** champagn@ucla.edu

CHAMPION, J(ustin) A. I. British, b. 1960. **Genres:** History, Intellectual history. **Career:** Royal Holloway College, University of London, Egham, England, senior lecturer in early modern history, 1992-. **Publications:** Pillars of Priestcraft Shaken: The Church of England and Its Enemies, 1660-1730, 1992; London's Dreaded Visitation: The Social Geography of the Great Plague, 1665, 1995. EDITOR: Early Modern History, 1991-92; Epidemic Disease in London, 1993; J. Toland, Nazareenus, 1999. **Address:** Department of History, Royal Holloway College, University of London, Egham TW20 0EX, England. **Online address:** J.Champion@rhul.ac.uk

CHAMPION, Larry S. American, b. 1932. **Genres:** Novellas/Short stories, Literary criticism and history, Bibliography. **Career:** Davidson College, North Carolina, Instructor in English, 1955-56; with U.S. Army, Panama, 1956-58; University of North Carolina, Chapel Hill, Dept. of English, Teaching Fellow, 1958-60; North Carolina State University, Raleigh, joined Dept. as Instructor, 1960, Associate Head, 1967-71, Head of Dept., 1971-84, Professor, 1971-94, Emeritus Professor of English, 1994-. **Publications:** Ben Jonson's Dotages, 1967; The Evolution of Shakespeare's Comedy, 1970; Shakespeare's Tragic Perspective, 1976; Tragic Patterns in Jacobean and Caroline Drama, 1977; Perspective in Shakespeare's English Histories, 1980; Thomas Dekker and the Traditions of English Drama, 1985; The Essential Shakespeare: An Annotated Bibliography of Major Modern Studies, 1986, 2nd ed., 1993; The Noise of Threatening Drum: Dramatic Strategy and Political Ideology in Shakespeare and the English Chronicle Plays, 1990. EDITOR: Quick Springs of Sense: Studies in the 18th Century, 1974; The Garland Shakespeare Bibliographies: King Lear, 2 vols., 1980. **Address:** 5320 Sendero Dr, Raleigh, NC 27612-1810, U.S.A. **Online address:** larrychampion@webtv.net

CHAMPLIN, Peggy. (Margaret Derby). American, b. 1925. **Genres:** History, Biography. **Career:** Sterling-Winthrop Research Institute, Rensselaer,

NY, assistant librarian, 1947-49; Chicago Public Library, Chicago, IL, librarian, 1949-50; California State University, Los Angeles, science reference librarian and coordinator of computerized reference services, 1972-86; Autry Museum of Western Heritage, library assistant, 1990-91. **Publications:** Raphael Pumpelly: Gentleman Geologist of the Gilded Age, 1994. Contributor to biographical dictionaries and encyclopedias.

CHAMPLIN, Tim. (John Michael Champlin). American, b. 1937. **Genres:** Westerns/Adventure. **Career:** Supervisor of Veterans Benefits Counselors, U.S. Dept. of Veterans' Affairs, Nashville, Tennessee, 1977-94 (employed by Dept. since 1970). Youth Director, Catholic Youth Organization, Nashville, 1965-67; Recreation resource specialist, Bureau of Outdoor Recreation, U.S. Dept. of the Interior, Ann Arbor, Michigan, 1967-68; Youth Director, Stewart Air Force Base, Smyrna, Tennessee, 1968-70. **Publications:** Summer of the Sioux, 1982; Dakota Gold, 1982; Staghorn, 1984; Shadow Catcher, 1985; Great Timber Race, 1986; Iron Trail, 1987; Colt Lightning, 1989; King of the Highbinders, 1989; Flying Eagle, 1990; The Last Campaign, 1996; The Survivor, 1996; Deadly Season, 1997; Swift Thunder, 1998; The Tombstone Conspiracy, 1999; Lincoln's Ransom, 1999; Treasure of the Templars, 2000; Wayfaring Strangers, 2000; A Trail to Wounded Knee, 2001; By Flare of Northern Lights, 2001; Raiders of the Western & Alantic, 2002. Short stories appear in anthologies. **Address:** c/o Dorchester Publishing Co Inc, PO Box 6640, Wayne, PA 19087, U.S.A.

CHAN, Gerald. New Zealander. **Genres:** Politics/Government. **Career:** Victoria University of Wellington, New Zealand, senior lecturer; Peking University, China, exchange scholar, 1995; National University of Singapore, East Asian Institute, visiting fellow, 1998. Member, advisory/editorial board, New Zealand Journal of East Asian Studies; coeditor, Political Science Journal. **Publications:** China and International Organizations: Participation in Non-Governmental Organizations since 1971, 1989; International Studies in China: An Annotated Bibliography, 1998; Chinese Perspectives on International Relations: A Framework for Analysis, 1999. **Address:** Room 104, 84 Fairlie Tce, Victoria University of Wellington, Wellington, New Zealand. **Online address:** Gerald.Chan@vuw.ac.nz

CHAN, Gillian. British/Canadian, b. 1954. **Genres:** Novellas/Short stories, Young adult fiction. **Career:** Writer, 1994-. Teacher-librarian, 1980-90. **Publications:** Golden Girl and Other Stories, 1994; Glory Days and Other Stories, 1996; The Carved Box, 2001; A Foreign Field, 2002. **Address:** 41 Thornton Trail, Dundas, ON, Canada L9H 6Y2. **Online address:** gillian.chan@sympatico.ca

CHANCE, Megan. American, b. 1959. **Genres:** Romance/Historical. **Career:** Romance novelist. Television news photographer, Seattle, WA, 198386; special events coordinator, Seattle, WA, 1987-89; commercial studio manager, 1988-95; full-time fiction writer, 1995-. **Publications:** A Candle in the Dark, 1993; After the Frost, 1994; The Portrait, 1995; A Heart Divided, 1996; Fall from Grace, 1997; The Way Home, 1997; The Gentleman Caller, forthcoming. **Address:** c/o Meg Ruley, Jane Rotrosen Agency, 318 East 51st St., New York, NY 10022, U.S.A.

CHANCE, Stephen. See TURNER, Philip (William).

CHANCER, Lynn S. American, b. 1955. **Genres:** Sociology. **Career:** Columbia University, Barnard College, NYC, assistant professor, 1989-. **Publications:** Sadomasochism in Everyday Life, 1992; Provoking Assaults: Gender, Class, and Race in High Profile Crimes; Reconcilable Differences, 1998. **Address:** Dept of Sociology & Anthropology, Fordham University, Rose Hill Campus, 441 E Fordham Rd, Bronx, NY 10458, U.S.A. **Online address:** chancer@fordham.edu

CHANCY, Myriam J(osephe) A(imee). Canadian (born Haiti), b. 1970. **Genres:** Literary criticism and history. **Career:** Vanderbilt University, Nashville, TN, assistant professor of English, 1994-97; Arizona State University, Tempe, AZ, associate professor of English, 1997-. **Publications:** Searching for Safe Spaces: Afro-Caribbean Women Writers in Exile, 1997; Framing Silence: Revolutionary Novels by Haitian Women, 1997. Contributor of essays and reviews to journals and anthologies, and fiction and poetry to journals. **Address:** Department of English, Arizona State University, Tempe, AZ 85287, U.S.A. **Online address:** mchancy@imap3.asu.edu

CHANDLER, Alfred D(upont), Jr. American, b. 1918. **Genres:** Business/Trade/Industry, Economics, History, Biography. **Career:** Massachusetts Institute of Technology, research associate to full professor, 1950-63; Johns Hopkins University, professor of history, 1963-71, dept. chairman, 1966-70, director, Center for the Study of Recent American History, 1964-71; Harvard

University, Graduate School of Business Administration, Straus Professor of Business History, 1971-89, professor emeritus, 1989-. **Publications:** The Origins of Progressive Leadership, 1954; Henry Varnum Poor, 1956; The Beginnings of Big Business in American Industry, 1959; Strategy and Structure, 1962; The Role of Business in the United States, 1968; The Changing Economic Order, 1968; (co-author) Pierre S. Dupont and the Making of the Modern Corporation, 1971, rev. ed., 2001; The Rise of Managerial Capitalism and Its Impact on Investment Strategy in the Western World and Japan, 1974; The Visible Hand, 1977 (Pulitzer Prize for History, 1978); Administrative Coordination, Allocation and Monitoring, 1977; Precursors of Modern Management, 1979; (co-author) Managerial Hierarchies, 1980; (with R. Tedlow) The Coming of Managerial Capitalism, 1985; The Evolution of Modern Global Competition, 1984; The Essential Alfred Chandler, 1988; Scale and Scope, 1990; The Enduring Logic of Industrial Success, 1990; Creating Competitive Capability, 1991; Organizational Capabilities and the Economic History of the Industrial Enterprise, 1992; Corporate Strategy, Structure, and Control Methods in the U.S. during the 20th Century, 1992; Organizational Capabilities and Industrial Restructuring, 1993; The Function of the HQ Unit in the Multibusiness Firm, 1993; Managerial Enterprise and the Entrepreneurial Function, 1994; The Competitive Performance of U.S. Industrial Enterprises since the Second World War, 1994; Entrepreneurial Achievements, 1996; (with T.K. McCraw and R.S. Tedlow) Management: Past and Present, 1996; Inventing the Electronic Century, 2002. EDITOR: (asst.) The Letters of Theodore Roosevelt, 4 vols., 1950-53; (gen.) Forces in Economic Growth Series, 1963-; The Railroads, 1965; Giant Enterprise, 1966; Papers of Dwight D. Eisenhower, 5 vols., 1970; The New American State Papers, 2 vols., 1972; Pioneers in Modern Factory Management, 1979; The Application of Modern Systematic Management, 1979; History of Management Thought and Practice, 1980; (with F. Amatori and T. Hikino) Big Business and the Wealth of Nations, 1997; (with P. Hagstrom and O. Sovell) The Dynamic Firm, 1998; (with J.W. Cortada) A Nation Transformed by Information, 2000. **Address:** Cumnock 300, Harvard Business School, Soldiers Field, Boston, MA 02163, U.S.A.

CHANDLER, Daniel Ross. American, b. 1937. **Genres:** Theology/Religion. **Career:** Augustana College, Rock Island, IL, instructor and associate debate coach, 1965-66; Central Michigan University, Mount Pleasant, assistant professor of communication, 1969-70; State University of New York College at New Paltz, assistant professor of communication, 1970-71; City University of New York, NYC, assistant professor of communication, 1971-75; Rutgers University, New Brunswick, NJ, assistant professor of communication, 1976-83; City University of New York, adjunct assistant professor to adjunct associate professor, 1983-90; Loyola University of Chicago, IL, lecturer, 1991-93; Northwestern University, Evanston, IL, visiting scholar, 1996-2000. Adjunct professor, visiting professor, and visiting scholar at US universities, 1974-. Minister of United Methodist Church. Union Theological Seminary, NYC, Masland Fellowship, 1975-76; Fulbright scholar, India, 1986. **Publications:** The Reverend Dr. Preston Bradley, 1971; The Rhetorical Tradition, 1978; The History of Rhetoric, 1990; The 1993 Parliament of the World's Religions, 1995; Toward Universal Religion: Voices of American and Indian Spirituality, 1996. Contributor of articles and reviews to books and periodicals.

CHANDLER, David (Geoffrey). See Obituaries.

CHANDLER, Frank. See GILMAN, George G.

CHANDLER, James K. American. **Genres:** Literary criticism and history. **Career:** University of Chicago, Chicago, IL, professor of English, 1978-, Director of the Franke Institute for the Humanities, 2001-. **Publications:** Wordsworth's Second Nature: A Study of the Poetry and Politics, 1984; (ed. with A.I. Davidson and H. Harootunian) Questions of Evidence: Proof, Practice, and Persuasion Across the Disciplines, 1994; England in 1819: The Politics of Literary Culture and the Case of Romantic Historicism, 1998. **Address:** University of Chicago, Department of English, Gates-Blake 324, 1050 E. 59th St., Chicago, IL 60637, U.S.A. **Online address:** docj@midway.uchicago.edu

CHANDLER, Laurel. See HOLDER, Nancy L.

CHANDLER, Marilyn R(uth). See MCENTYRE, Marilyn Chandler.

CHANDRA, Vikram. Indian, b. 1961. **Genres:** Novels, Novellas/Short stories. **Career:** University of Houston, Houston, TX, adjunct professor, 1987-93; George Washington University, Washington, DC, visiting writer, 1994-95. Letters and Light (computer programming and consulting firm), owner, 1987-94. Has also taught courses in writing and literature at Rice

University, Inprint Foundation, and Johns Hopkins University. **Publications:** Red Earth and Pouring Rain (novel), 1995; Tales of Love and Longing (stories), Faber, 1996; City of Gold (television series), 1996. Contributor of stories to periodicals. **Address:** 2020 Pennsylvania Ave. N.W. Suite 227, Washington, DC 20006, U.S.A. **Online address:** vchandra@mindspring.com; www.vikramchandra.com

CHANEY, Edward (Paul de Gruyter). British, b. 1951. **Genres:** History, Area studies, Travel/Exploration, Art/Art history, Humanities. **Career:** University of Pisa, Pisa, Italy, lecturer in English, 1979-85; Oxford University, Lincoln College, Oxford, England, research fellow in architectural history, 1985-90. Adjunct assistant professor at Charles A. Strong Center, Georgetown University Florence Program, Villa le Balze, Italy, 1982-83; part-time lecturer art history, Oxford Brookes University, 1991-96; historian, London Region of English Heritage, 1991-93. **Publications:** (ed. with N. Ritchie, and contrib.) Oxford, China, and Italy: Writings in Honour of Sir Harold Acton on His Eightieth Birthday, 1984; The Grand Tour and the Great Rebellion: Richard Lassels and the Voyage of Italy in the Seventeenth Century, 1985; (ed. with H. Acton) Florence: A Travellers' Companion, 1986; "Blue Guides" Series (author of introduction) P. Blanchard, ed., Southern Italy, 1982; (author of introduction) A. Macadam, ed., Sicily, 1988, rev. ed., 1990; (ed. with P. Mack) England and the Continental Renaissance, 1990; (ed. with P. Vassallo) Journal of Anglo-Italian Studies, vol. I, 1991, vol II, 1992; (ed. and contrib. with J. Bold) English Architecture: Public and Private, 1993; The Evolution of the Grand Tour, 1997. Contributor to booke. Contributor of articles to periodicals. **Address:** 40 Southfield Rd, Oxford OX4 1NZ, England.

CHANEY, Jill. (Jill Leeming). British, b. 1932. **Genres:** Children's fiction. **Publications:** On Primrose Hill, 1961; Half a Candle, 1968; A Penny for the Guy, 1970; Mottram Park, 1971; Christopher's Dig, 1972; Taking the Woffle to Pebblecombe on Sea, 1974; Return to Mottram Park, 1974; Woffle, R. A., 1976; Christopher's Find, 1976; The Buttercup Field, 1976; Canary Yellow, 1977; Angel Face, 1978; Vectis Diary, 1979; Leaving Mottram Park, 1989; Three Weeks in August, 1995. **Address:** Glen Rosa, Colleyland, Chorleywood, Herts., England.

CHANG, Iris. *See* Obituaries.

CHANG, Joan Chiung-huei. Taiwanese, b. 1962. **Genres:** Literary criticism and history. **Career:** Soochow University, Taipei, Taiwan, associate professor of English, 1997-. **Publications:** Transforming Chinese American Literature: A Study of History, Sexuality, and Ethnicity, 2000. **Address:** Department of English, Soochow University, Taipei, Taiwan. **Online address:** eugene@mail.scu.edu.tw

CHANG, Kang-i Sun. American (born China), b. 1944. **Genres:** Literary criticism and history. **Career:** Princeton University, Princeton, NJ, curator of Gest Oriental Library and East Asian Collections, 1980-81; Yale University, New Haven, CT, assistant professor, 1982-86, associate professor, 1987-90, professor of Chinese, 1990-. **Publications:** The Evolution of Chinese Tz'u Poetry, 1980; Six Dynasties Poetry, 1986; The Late-Ming Poet Ch'en Tzu-lung, 1991; Writing Women in Late Imperial China, 1997; Women Writers of Traditional China, 1999. **Address:** Department of East Asian Languages and Literatures, PO Box 208236, Yale University, New Haven, CT 06520, U.S.A. **Online address:** kang-i.chang@yale.edu

CHANG, Kevin O'Brien. Jamaican, b. 1958. **Genres:** Music. **Career:** Fontana Pharmacy, Montego Bay, Jamaica, managing director, 1989-. **Publications:** Reggae Routes: The Story of Jamaican Music, 1998. Contributor to newspapers. **Address:** Fontana Pharmacy, Mobay Shopping Centre, Montego Bay, Jamaica. **Online address:** superv@cwjamaica.com

CHANG, Leonard. American, b. 1968. **Genres:** Novels. **Career:** Antioch University, Los Angeles, CA, MFA faculty, 1998-2001; Mills College, distinguished visiting writer, 2001-03. **Publications:** NOVELS: The Fruit 'n Food, 1996; Dispatches from the Cold, 1998; Over the Shoulder, 2001; Underkill, 2003; Fade to Clear, 2004. Contributor of short stories to magazines.

CHANG, Maria Hsia. American (born Hong Kong), b. 1950. **Genres:** Area studies, International relations/Current affairs, Politics/Government, Theology/Religion. **Career:** Washington State University, Pullman, visiting assistant professor of political science, 1980-82; University of Puget Sound, Tacoma, WA, assistant professor of political science, 1983-89; University of Nevada, Reno, professor of political science, 1989-. U.S. Marine Corps War College, lecturer on China, 2003-; consultant on Chinese immigration and political asylum cases in the United States and Canada. **Publications:** (with others) The Taiwan Relations Act and the Defense of the Republic of China, 1980; (with others) Ideology and Development: Sun Yat-sen and the Economic History of Taiwan, 1981; (with others) The Republic of China and U.S. Policy, 1983; (with others) The Iron Triangle: A U.S. Security Policy for Northeast Asia, 1984; The Chinese Blue Shirt Society, 1985; (with Y. Wu and others) Human Rights in the People's Republic of China, 1985; (ed. with B. Lin and others) The Aftermath of the 1989 Tiananmen Crisis in Mainland China, 1992; The Labors of Sisyphus: The Economic Development of Communist China, 1998; Return of the Dragon: China's Wounded Nationalism, 2001; Falun Gong: The End of Days, 2004. Contributor to periodicals. **Address:** Dept of Political Science, University of Nevada, Reno, NV 89557, U.S.A. **Online address:** mariac@unr.nevada.edu

CHANOFF, David. American, b. 1943. **Genres:** Biography, International relations/Current affairs, History. **Career:** Sudbury Valley School, Framingham, MA, founding teacher and administrator, 1968-; writer. English instructor at Tufts University, 1977-80, and Harvard University, 1977-83. **Publications:** (with Truong Nhu Tang and Doan Van Toai) A Vietcong Memoir, 1985; (with Toai) The Vietnamese Gulag, 1986; (with Toai) Portrait of the Enemy, 1986; (with Bui Diem) In the Jaws of History, 1987; (with A. Sharon) Warrior: The Autobiography of Ariel Sharon, 1989; (with O. DeForest) Slow Burn: The Rise and Bitter Fall of American Intelligence in Vietnam, 1990; (with K. Good) Into the Heart: One Man's Pursuit of Love and Knowledge among the Yanomama, 1991, in UK as Into the Heart: An Amazonian Love Story; (with W. Crowe Jr.) The Line of Fire, 1993; (with F. Zandman) Never the Last Journey, 1995; (with J. Elders) Joycelyn Elders, M.D., 1996; (with W. Ungar) Destined to Live, 2000; (with E. Nuwere) Hacker Cracker. Contributor to periodicals. **Address:** c/o Owen Laster, William Morris Agency, 1325 Avenue of the Americas, 15th Fl, New York, NY 10019, U.S.A.

CHAO, Patricia. American, b. 1955. **Genres:** Novels, Children's fiction. **Career:** Writer. Sarah Lawrence College, Bronxville, NY, undergraduate writing workshop teacher. **Publications:** Monkey King (novel), 1997. CHILDREN'S STORIES: On the Silk Road; Mimi and the Tea Ceremony; The Lost and Found Twins. Contributor to anthologies. Contributor of short fiction and essays to periodicals. **Address:** 55 West 14th St. No. 11M, New York, NY 10011, U.S.A.

CHAPIN, F. Stuart, Jr. American, b. 1916. **Genres:** Regional/Urban planning. **Career:** Alumni Distinguished Professor Emeritus of Planning, Dept. of City and Regional Planning, University of North Carolina, Chapel Hill, since 1978 (Associate Professor, 1949-54; Professor, 1954-78). With Tennessee Valley Authority, 1940-42 and 1945-47; Director of Planning, City of Greensboro, North Carolina, 1947-49; Member, Committee on Urban Economics, Resources for the Future Inc., 1964-69; Member, President Johnson's Task Force on Cities, 1966-67; Member, Dept. of Urban Transportation, Highway Research Board, National Academy of Sciences, 1964-67; Guggenheim Fellow, 1973; Member, State of Washington Columbia River Gorge Commission, 1985-87; Member, Bistate Columbia River Gorge Commission, 1987-93. **Publications:** Communities for Living, 1941; Urban Land Use Planning, 1957, 4th ed. (co-author), 1995; (co-ed. and contrib.) Urban Growth Dynamics, 1962; (co-author) Across the City Line, 1974; Human Activity Patterns in the City, 1974.

CHAPIN, Miles. American, b. 1954. **Genres:** Autobiography/Memoirs, Art/Art history. **Career:** Professional actor, 1964-. Works in feature films, on stage, and in television series and radio commercials. **Publications:** (ed. with D. Katz) Tales from the Jungle, 1995; 88 Keys: The Making of a Steinway Piano, in press. **Address:** c/o Kristine Dahl, International Creative Management, 40 W 57th St, New York, NY 10019, U.S.A. **Online address:** blueelver@aol.com

CHAPIN, Sarah. American, b. 1931. **Genres:** History. **Career:** Independent Broadcast Associates, research adviser for National Public Radio (NPR) series Passages to India, 1986; Concord Free Public Library Special Collections, Concord, research scholar, 1989-. **Publications:** The Tin Box Collection: Letters of Roger Sessions, His Family and Friends, 1992; (ed.) Edward Jarvis, Traditions and Reminiscences of Concord, Massachusetts, 1779-1878, 1993; A Wreath of Joy, 1996; Images of Concord, 1997; Then and Now, Concord, MA, 2001; History of Concord, forthcoming. EDITOR OF TRANSCRIPTIONS: Journal of Alfred W. Hosmer (1888-1903); Thoreau-Salt's Biography (1896), grangerized by Alfred W. Hosmer; William Ellery Channing's Botanical Jottings (from Channing's copy of Gray's Manual, 1848); Concord Flora 1834-1836: Observed by Edward Jarvis. **Address:** 261 Sudbury Rd, Concord, MA 01742, U.S.A.

CHAPLIN, Elizabeth. *See* MCGOWN, Jill.

CHAPMAN, Herb. American, b. 1951. **Genres:** Novels, Mystery/Crime/ Suspense. **Career:** South Carolina Department of Mental Health, Columbia, SC, psychologist, 1976-80; Midlands Technical College, Columbia, SC, adjunct faculty, 1980-86; South Carolina Department of Juvenile Justice, Columbia, SC, psychologist, 1986-87; Baptist Medical Center, Columbia, SC, coordinator and manager of Center for Pain Management, 1987-98; writer, 1998-. **Publications:** The Book of Cain (thriller), 2001. **Address:** 5850 Wescott Hills Way, Alexandria, VA 22315, U.S.A.

CHAPMAN, J. Dudley. Also writes as Joan Carlson. American, b. 1928. **Genres:** Psychology, Sex. **Career:** Gynecologist, sex researcher, and writer. Ed.-in-Chief, Osteopathic Physician, since 1968; Clinical Professor, Ohio University College of Osteopathic Medicine; Faculty and member of Academic Board, The Institute for the Advanced Study of Human Sexuality, San Francisco, since 1979; Member of Executive Council, The Academy of Psychosomatic Medicine, since 1983; Editorial Consultant, Penthouse FORUM, The J. Am. Osteopathic Association and others. Associate Professor of Obstetrics and Gynecology, College of Osteopathic Medicine and Surgery, Des Moines, Iowa, 1955-58; President, American College of Osteopathic Obstetricians and Gynecologists, 1966-67; Former member, Editorial Consulting Board, Institute of Comprehensive Medicine, and Chronic Disease Mgmt. and Modern Medicine. **Publications:** The Feminine Mind and Body, 1967; The Sexual Equation, 1977. **Address:** P. O. Box 340, North Madison, OH 44057, U.S.A.

CHAPMAN, Lynne F(erguson). American, b. 1963. **Genres:** Biography. **Career:** Mayfield Publishing, Mountain View, CA, editorial assistant, 1985-87; Windsor Publications, Northridge, CA, photography editor, 1987-88; Dushkin Publishing, Guilford, CT, annual editions editor, 1988-89; freelance editor and writer, 1989-. **Publications:** Sylvia Plath, 1994; Leo Tolstoy, 1997. **Address:** c/o Creative Education, Inc., 123 S. Broad St., Mankato, MN 56001, U.S.A.

CHAPMAN, Paul K. American, b. 1931. **Genres:** Business/Trade/Industry. **Career:** Packard Manse, Stoughton, MA, director, 1957-75; Center for Seafarers' Rights, NYC, director, 1981-90; North American Maritime Ministry Association, NYC, executive secretary, 1991-; director, Employment Project, 1993-. **Publications:** Trouble on Board: The Plight of International Seafarers, 1992. **Address:** 237 Thompson St, New York, NY 10012, U.S.A.

CHAPMAN, Richard A(rnold). British, b. 1937. **Genres:** Administration/ Management, Politics/Government, Public/Social administration, Social sciences. **Career:** Air Ministry, London, clerk, 1953-55; Ministry of Pensions and National Insurance, London, executive officer, 1955-62; Inland Revenue, London, inspector of taxes, 1962; University of Leicester, assistant lecturer in politics, 1962-63; University of Liverpool, Leverhulme Lecturer in Public Administration, 1963-68, sub-dean of arts faculty, 1966-68; University of Birmingham, senior lecturer, 1968-71; University of Durham, reader, 1971-85, professor of politics, 1985-96, chair of board of studies in politics, 1973-75, 1988-91, deputy dean of faculty of social sciences, 1975-76, dean, 1976-78, honorary treasurer of St. Chad's College, 1976-79. **Publications:** Decision Making, 1957; The Higher Civil Service in Britain, 1970; Teaching Public Administration, 1973; (with J.R. Greenaway) The Dynamics of Administrative Reform, 1980; Leadership in the British Civil Service, 1984; Ethics in the British Civil Service, 1988; The Art of Darkness, 1988; (with P.K. Saxena) Public Sector Management: India and Britain, 1990; The Treasury in Public Policy-Making, 1997; (with F. Bealey and M. Sheehan) Elements in Political Science, 1999; The Civil Service Commission 1855-1991: A Bureau Biography, 2004. EDITOR: (with A. Dunsire) Style in Administration, 1971; The Role of Commissions in Policy Making, 1973; Public Policy Studies: The North East of England, 1985; (with M. Hunt) Open Government, 1987; Ethics in Public Service, 1993; Ethics in Public Service for the New Millennium, 2000. **Address:** Durham University Business School, Mill Hill Ln, Durham DH1 3LB, England.

CHAPMAN, Samuel Greeley. American, b. 1929. **Genres:** Criminology/ True Crime. **Career:** Professor of Political Science, University of Oklahoma, Norman, 1967-91. Member, Norman City Council, 1972-76; and since 1977 (Vice-Mayor, 1976, 1978, 1982-84). Patrolman, Dept. of Police, Berkeley, California, 1951-56; Police Consultant, Public Administration Service, Chicago, 1956-59; Assistant Professor, School of Police Administration Michigan State University, East Lansing, 1959-63; Police Chief, Multnomah County Sheriff's Police Dept., Portland Oregon, 1963-65; Assistant Director, President's Commission on Law Enforcement and Administration of Justice, Washington, D.C., 1965-67. **Publications:** Dogs in Police Work, 1960; (with E. St. Johnston) The Police Heritage in England and America, 1962; Police

Patrol Readings, 1964, rev. ed., 1970; (with D. Clark) Educational Backgrounds for Police, 1966; Perspectives on Police Assaults in the South Central United States, 1974; (with G. Eastman) Short of Merger: County-wide Police Resource Pooling, 1976; Police Murders and Effective Countermeasures, 1976; Police Dogs in America, 1979; Cops, Killers, and Staying Alive, 1986; Police Dogs in North America, 1990; Murdered on Duty: The Killing of Police Officers in America, 1999. **Address:** 680 Kane Ct, Reno, NV 89512-1354, U.S.A. **Online address:** sgchapman@renonevada. net

CHAPMAN, Walker. See SILVERBERG, Robert.

CHAPPELL, Audrey. British, b. 1954. **Genres:** Children's fiction. **Career:** Islington school, London, preschool teacher, 1976-83; Haringey school, London, preschool teacher, 1984-91. **Publications:** A Surprise for Oliver, 1989; An Outing for Oliver, 1990. **Address:** "The Old Forge", Berghapton, Mill Rd., Norwich NR15 1BQ, England. **Online address:** aud-chap@dircon. co.uk

CHAPPELL, Fred(erick Davis). American, b. 1936. **Genres:** Novels, Novellas/Short stories, Poetry, Literary criticism and history. **Career:** University of North Carolina, Greensboro, professor of English, 1964-2004; North Carolina's poet laureate, 1997-2002. **Publications:** NOVELS: It Is Time, Lord, 1963; The Inkling, 1965; Dagon, 1968; The Gaudy Place, 1972; I Am One of You Forever, 1985; Brighten the Corner Where You Are, 1989; More Shapes Than One, 1991; Farewell, I'm Bound to Leave You, 1996; Look Back All the Green Valley, 1999. POETRY: The World between the Eyes, 1971; River, 1975; The Man Twice Married to Fire, 1977; Bloodfire, 1978; Awakening to Music, 1979; Wind Mountain, 1979; Earthsleep, 1980; Driftlake: A Lieder Cycle, 1981; Midquest, 1981; Castle Tzingal, 1985; Source, 1985; First and Last Words, 1988; C, 1993; Spring Garden: New and Selected Poems, 1995; Family Gathering, 2000; Backsass, 2003. STORIES: Moments of Light, 1980. OTHER: The Fred Chappell Reader, 1987; Plow Naked: Selected Writings on Poetry, 1993; A Way of Happening: Observations of Contemporary Poetry, 1998. **Address:** 305 Kensington Rd, Greensboro, NC 27403, U.S.A.

CHAPPELL, Ruth Paterson. (Booie Chappell). American. **Genres:** Children's non-fiction. **Career:** Drayton Hall Plantation, Charleston, SC, member of education staff. Also worked as an elementary schoolteacher. **Publications:** AS BOOIE CHAPPELL: (with B.P. Shipe) The Mysterious Tail of a Charleston Cat (juvenile), 1995; All 'bout Charleston (juvenile), 1998; Counting the Ways to Love Charleston (juvenile), 2001. **Address:** Drayton Hall Plantation, 3380 Ashley River Rd, Charleston, SC 29414, U.S.A.

CHAPPLE, John Alfred Victor. British, b. 1928. **Genres:** History, Literary criticism and history, Women's studies and issues. **Career:** Professor Emeritus of English, Hull University, 1992- (Professor, 1971-92; Pro-Vice-Chancellor, 1985-88). President, Gaskell Society, 1999-. Assistant University College, London, 1953-55; Research Assistant, Yale University, New Haven, CT, 1955-58; Assistant, Aberdeen University, 1958-59; Assistant Lecturer, 1959-61, Lecturer, 1961-67, and Sr. Lecturer, 1967-71, Manchester University. **Publications:** (ed. with A. Pollard) The Letters of Mrs. Gaskell, 1966; Documentary and Imaginative Literature 1880-1920, 1970; Dryden's Earl of Shaftesbury, 1973; (with J.G. Sharps) Elizabeth Gaskell: A Portrait in Letters, 1980; Science and Literature in the Nineteenth Century, 1986; (with A. Wilson) Private Voices: The Diaries of Elizabeth Gaskell and Sophia Holland, 1996; Elizabeth Gaskell: The Early Life, 1997; (with K. Shelston) Further Letters of Mrs Gaskell, 2000. **Address:** 8 Lomax Close, Lichfield WS13 7EY, England.

CHAQUERI, Cosroe. See SHAKERI, Khosrow.

CHARBONNEAU, Eileen. American, b. 1951. **Genres:** Mystery/Crime/ Suspense, Romance/Historical, Young adult fiction, Plays/Screenplays. **Career:** Freelance writer, 1974-. Has worked as a teacher, waitress, and department store receiver. Community theater director and actress. Historical Novelists Society, reviewer. Washington Romance Writers of America, Lifetime Achievement Award, 2004. **Publications:** The Ghosts of Stony Clove, 1988; In the Time of the Wolves, 1994; Honor to the Hills, 1996; Manituwak (play), 1999. Z-FAVE YOU-SOLVE-IT MYSTERY SERIES: The Mound Builders' Secret, 1994; Disappearance at Harmony Festival, 1994; Waltzing in Ragtime, 1996; The Randolph Legacy, 1997; Rachel LeMoyne, 1998; The Conner Emerald, 2000. Contributor to periodicals. **Address:** c/o Susan Yuen, Susan Herner Rights Agency, PO Box 20, Cold Spring, NY 10516, U.S.A. **Online address:** EileenCharbonneau@hotmail.com

CHARBONNET, Gabrielle. American, b. 1961. **Genres:** Children's fiction. **Career:** Random House, NYC, production assistant, 1987-88; Daniel Weiss Associates Inc., NYC, associate editor, 1988-89, managing editor, 1989-93; writer. **Publications:** Snakes Are Nothing to Sneeze At, 1990; (adaptor) P. Lindenbaum, Else-Marie and Her Seven Little Daddies, 1991; (reteller) Lindenbaum, Boodil, My Dog, 1992; Tutu Much Ballet, 1994. Also the author of mass-market series books under a pseudonym. **Address:** c/o Henry Holt & Co., 115 West 18th St., 6th Floor, New York, NY 10011, U.S.A.

CHARD, Judy (Gordon). Also writes as Lyndon Chase. British, b. 1916. **Genres:** Novellas/Short stories, Mystery/Crime/Suspense, Romance/Historical, Travel/Exploration. **Career:** Devon Life, Exeter, editor, 1979-82; Writers News Home Study, Nairn, Scotland, director of studies, 1989-. **Publications:** NOVELS: Through the Green Woods, 1974; The Weeping and the Laughter, 1975; Encounter in Berlin, 1976; The Uncertain Heart, 1976; The Other Side of Sorrow, 1977; In the Heart of Love, 1978; Out of the Shadows, 1978; All Passion Spent, 1979; Seven Lonely Years, 1980; The Darkening Skies, 1981; When the Journey's Over, 1981; Haunted by the Past, 1982; Sweet Love Remembered, 1982; Where the Dream Begins, 1982; Rendezvous with Love, 1983; Hold Me in Your Heart, 1983; (as Lyndon Chase) Tormentil, 1984; To Live with Fear, 1985; Wings of the Morning, 1985; A Time to Love, 1987; Wild Justice, 1987; For Love's Sake Only, 1988; Person Unknown, 1988; To Be So Loved, 1988; Enchantment, 1989; Encounter in Spain. OTHER: Along the Dart, 1979; About Widecombe, 1979; Devon Mysteries, 1979; The South Hams, 1980; Along the Teign, 1981; Tales of the Unexplained in Devon, 1986; Haunted Happenings, Burgh Island, Traditional Cookery, Devon Companion, 1993; The Mysterious Lady of the Moor-The Story of Beatrice Chase; Murder and Mystery in Devon; A Guide to the South Hams; Devon Tales of Mystery and Murder. **Address:** Flat 57 Gilberd's House, Old Exeter Rd, Newton Abbot, Devon TQ12 2NH, England. **Online address:** d.chard1@btopenworld.com

CHARLEBOIS, Lucile C. American, b. 1950. **Genres:** Literary criticism and history. **Career:** Department of Public Welfare, Springfield, MA, social worker, 1968-69; College of Our Lady of the Elms, Chicopee, MA, instructor in Spanish, 1970-76, head of modern language department, 1975-76; Volunteers for Educational and Social Services, Austin, TX, teacher of Spanish in Uvalde, TX, 1976-77; College of Our Lady of the Elms, instructor in Spanish, 1977-78; Residencia Buendia, Cuenca, Spain, instructor in English, 1981; University of Nebraska-Lincoln, visiting assistant professor, 1982-83, assistant professor of Spanish, 1983-88, coordinator, basic language, 1983-88, graduate fellow, 1984-88; University of South Carolina at Columbia, assistant professor, 1988-94, associate professor of Spanish, 1994-, director of Spanish Tutorial Center, 1988-92, graduate director, 1995-98. Broadcaster, programmer, and scriptwriter for the Spanish-language radio program Encrucijada, West Springfield, MA, 1975-76. **Publications:** Understanding Camilo Jose Cela, 1998. Contributor to books. Contributor of articles and reviews to periodicals. **Address:** Department of Spanish Italian and Portuguese, 713 Welsh Humanities, University of South Carolina-Columbia, Columbia, SC 29208, U.S.A. **Online address:** charlelc@gwm.sc.edu

CHARLES, Hampton. *See* MARTIN, (Roy) Peter.

CHARLES, Henry. *See* HARRIS, Marion (Rose).

CHARLES, John. Canadian, b. 1965. **Genres:** Film. **Career:** Video Watchdog, Cincinnati, OH, associate editor and reviewer, 1992-; Hong Kong Digital Web site, host and reviewer, 2000-. **Publications:** The Hong Kong Filmography 1977-1997: A Complete Reference to 1,100 Films Produced by British Hong Kong Studios, 2000. **Address:** PO Box 30053, Park Mall Postal Outlet, 2 Quebec St, Guelph, ON, Canada N1H 8J5. **Online address:** dosun892@hotmail.com

CHARLES, Kate. American/British, b. 1950. **Genres:** Mystery/Crime/Suspense. **Career:** WGUC Radio, Cincinnati, OH, promotion assistant and record librarian, 1981-85; St. Paul's Church, Bedford, England, parish administrator, 1988-91; full-time writer, 1991-. **Publications:** A Drink of Deadly Wine, 1991; The Snares of Death, 1992; Appointed to Die, 1993; A Dead Man Out of Mind, 1994; Evil Angels among Them, 1995; Unruly Passions, 1998; Strange Children, 1999; Cruel Habitations, 2000. **Address:** The Chapter House, 4 St. George's Rd., Bedford MK40 2LS, England. **Online address:** KateCharles@mac.com

CHARLES, Lance. *See* WUBBELS, Lance.

CHARLES, Nicholas. *See* KUSKIN, Karla.

CHARLES, Sara C(onnor). American, b. 1934. **Genres:** Medicine/Health. **Career:** St. Vincent's Hospital and Medical Center, New York City, intern, 1964-65; Seton Institute, Baltimore, MD, resident in psychiatry, 1965-68; University of Notre Dame, Notre Dame, IN, psychiatrist, 1968-72; University of Illinois at the Medical Center, Chicago, assistant professor, 1972-79, associate professor, 1979-88, professor of clinical psychiatry, 1988-. **Publications:** WITH E. KENNEDY: Defendant: A Psychiatrist Stands Trial for Medical Malpractice; An Episode in America's Hidden Health Care Crisis, 1985; On Becoming a Counselor: A Basic Guide for Non-Professional Counselors, 1990, 2nd ed., 2001; Authority, 1997. **Address:** 1300 N Lake Shore Dr, Chicago, IL 60610-2167, U.S.A.

CHARLESWORTH, James H(amilton). American, b. 1940. **Genres:** Theology/Religion. **Career:** Ordained United Methodist minister, deacon, 1963, elder, 1972; Duke University, Durham, NC, assistant professor, 1969-74, associate professor of religion, 1974-84, director of International Center on Christian Origins, 1975-84; Princeton Theological Seminary, Princeton, NJ, George L. Collord Professor of New Testament Language and Literature, 1984-. American Schools of Oriental Research, Jerusalem, Thayer fellow, 1968-69; University of Tuebingen, Alexander von Humboldt fellow, 1983-84; Hebrew University of Jerusalem, Lady Davis Visiting Professor, 1988; Albright Institute, Jerusalem, annual professor, 1998-99. **Publications:** Tools for the Study of the Apocrypha, Pseudepigrapha, and Cognate Works, 1970; The Pseudepigrapha and Modern Research, 1976, rev. ed., 1981; Papyri and Leather Manuscripts of the Odes of Solomon, 1981; (with G.T. Zervos) The New Discoveries in St. Catharine's Monastery, 1981; The History of the Rechabites, vol. 1: The Greek Recension, 1982; The Old Testament Pseudepigrapha and the New Testament, 1985; The Discovery of a Dead Sea Scroll (4Q Therapeia), 1985; The New Testament Apocrypha and Pseudepigrapha, 1987; Jesus within Judaism, 1988; The Beloved Disciple 1995; Authentic Apocrypha, 1998; The Odes of Solomon, 1998; How Barisat Bellowed, 1998; The Millennium Guide for Pilgrims to the Holy Land, 2000. EDITOR: (and contrib.) John and Qumran, 1972; (and trans.) The Odes of Solomon, 1973, rev. ed., 1978; (and contrib.) The Old Testament Pseudepigrapha, vol. 1: Apocalyptic Literature and Testaments, 1983, vol. 2: Expansions of the "Old Testament" and Legends, 1985; Jews and Christians, 1990; (with J.M. O'Connor) Paul and the Dead Sea Scrolls, 1990; Graphic Concordance to the Dead Sea Scrolls, 1991; (with J.J. Collins) Mysteries and Revelations, 1991; Jesus's Jewishness, 1991; The Messiah, 1992; Jesus and the Dead Sea Scrolls, 1992; Overcoming Fear between Jews and Christians, 1992; (with W. P. Weaver) What Has Archaeology to Do with Faith?, 1992; (with K. Stendahl) The Scrolls and the New Testament, 1992; The Rule of the Community and Related Documents, 1993; (with W.P. Weaver) The Old and New Testaments, 1993; (with C.A. Evans) The Pseudepigrapha and Early Biblical Interpretation, 1993; (with W.P. Weaver) Images of Jesus Today, 1994; (with M. Harding and M. Kiley) The Lord's Prayer and Other Prayer Texts form the Greco-Roman Era, 1994; (with W.P. Weaver) Earthing Christologies, 1995; Damascus Document, War Scroll and Related Documents, 1995; Quran Questions, 1995; The Dead Sea Scrolls, 1996; Pseudepigrapha and Non-Masoretic Psalms, Daily Prayers, and Related Documents, 1997; (with L. Johns) Hillel and Jesus, 1997; (with W.P. Weaver) The Dead Sea Scrolls and Christian Faith, 1998; Caves of Enlightenment, 1998; Angelic Liturgy, 1999; (with W.P. Weaver) Jesus Two Thousand Years Later, 2000; (with others) Miscellaneous Texts from the Judaean Desert, 2000; The Hebrew Bible and Qumran, 2000. **Address:** Biblical Department, Box 821, Princeton Theological Seminary, Princeton, NJ 08542, U.S.A.

CHARLIER, Roger Henri. Also writes as Henri Rochard. American (born Belgium), b. 1921. **Genres:** Novels, Poetry, Earth sciences, Engineering, Environmental sciences/Ecology, Marine sciences/Oceanography. **Career:** Professor Emeritus of Geology, Geography and Oceanography, Northeastern Illinois University, Chicago (Director, Bureau of Educational Travel, 1961-64; Co-ordinator, Earth Science Area, 1961-65; Research Scholar in Oceanography, 1962-64; Director, Oceanography Program, 1966-71; Vice-Chairman, Dept. of Geography, 1962-70). Professor Emeritus, University of Brussels, Belgium; Hon. Prof, University of Bordeaux I, France; Collab, Royal Institute Natural Sciences, Belgium; Visiting Professor, University of Maryland (European Division), 1976-90. Scientific Adviser to Pres./CEO HAECON Inc. Drongen, Belgium, 1984-99; Vice Pres, Europe, Environmental Planning Group, Inc, Elk Grove Village, IL, 1992-95. **Publications:** Analyse-mathematique, 1941; The Gifted: A National Resource, 1960; Introductory Earth Science, 1961; The Physical Environment, 1966; Harnessing the Energies of the Ocean, 1970; The World around Us, 1971; The Study of Rocks, 1971; The Study of Oceans, 1971; Ocean Resources, 1976, 1978; Marine Science and Technology, 1980; Our Physical Environment, 1980; Marine Geology, 1980; Tidal Energy, 1982; Economic Oceanography, 1987; Ocean Energies, 1993; Coastal Erosion, 1998; Using Today's Knowledge for Black Sea Area's Tomorrow, 2000; 2nd Leadership Conference of Intl Ocean

Inst (Constantza), The Proceedings, 2003; Oceans bridging the Millenium, 2004. AS HENRI ROCHARD: I Was a Male War Bride (novel), 1950; For the Love of Kate (novel), 1963; Pensees (poetry), 1964. **Address:** 4055 N Keystone Ave, Chicago, IL 60641-2414, U.S.A. **Online address:** roger. charlier@pophost.eunet.be

CHARLIP, Remy. American, b. 1929. **Genres:** Reference, Plays/Screenplays, Poetry. **Career:** Director, International All-Star Dance Co., New York, 1977-. Choreographer, London Contemporary Dance Theatre, 1972-76; Choreographer, Scottish Theatre Ballet, 1973, and Welsh Dance Theatre, 1974. **Publications:** 31 picture books, including: Fortunately, 1964; (with B. Supree) Mother Mother I Feel Sick Send for the Doctor Quick Quick Quick, 1966; Arm in Arm, 1980; I Love You, 1981; Sleepytime Rhyme, 1999; Baby Hearts and Baby Flowers, 2002; Little Old Big Beard & Big Young Little Beard: A Short & Tall Tale, 2002. Illustrator of books by M.W. Brown. **Address:** 521 Precita Ave, San Francisco, CA 94110-4719, U.S.A. **Online address:** www.remycharlip.com

CHARLOT, Anita M. American, b. 1965. **Genres:** Gay and lesbian issues. **Career:** BSE, Chicago, IL, operations manager, 1999-. Also works as life coach for lesbian and bisexual women, as mentor for a lesbian and bisexual women youth group, and as a project manager consultant. **Publications:** Poetic Growing Pains, 2000; The Reality of Loving a Lesbian/Bisexual Mother, 2001; At Least My Mom's Not Gay, in press. **Address:** c/o Author Mail, Purrfect Harmony Unlimited, 1507 E 53rd St Ste 462, Chicago, IL 60615, U.S.A. **Online address:** purrfectharmonyunlimited@onebox.com

CHARLWOOD, D(onald) E(rnest Cameron). Australian, b. 1915. **Genres:** Novels, Novellas/Short stories, History, Autobiography/Memoirs. **Career:** Sr. Supervisior, Air Traffic Control, Dept. of Aviation, 1945-75; now retired. Appointed Member Order of Australia, 1992. **Publications:** No Moon Tonight (memoirs), 1956; All the Green Year (novel), 1965; An Afternoon of Time (short stories), 1966; Take-Off to Touchdown, 1967; The Wreck of the Loch Ard, 1971; Wrecks and Reputations, 1978; Settlers under Sail, 1978; Flight and Time (short stories), 1979; The Long Farewell, 1981; Marching as to War, (autobiography), 1990; Journeys into Night (autobiography), 1991. **Address:** Yarra Gardens, 7/2 Everard Dr, Warrandyte, VIC 3113, Australia.

CHARMÉ, Stuart Zane. American, b. 1951. **Genres:** Philosophy, Theology/Religion. **Career:** Rutgers University, Camden Campus, Camden, NJ, assistant professor, 1978-86, associate professor, 1986-98, professor, 1998-; writer. **Publications:** Meaning and Myth in the Study of Lives: A Sartrean Approach, 1983; Vulgarity and Authenticity: Dimensions of Otherness in the World of Jean-Paul Sartre, 1991. **Address:** Dept of Philosophy and Religion, Rutgers University, Camden, NJ 08102, U.S.A. **Online address:** scharme@crab.rutgers.edu

CHARMLEY, John. British, b. 1955. **Genres:** Politics/Government, History, Biography. **Career:** University of East Anglia, Norwich, England, lecturer, 1979-c. 1993; Westminster College, Fulton, MO, Churchill Memorial professor, c. 1993-; writer. **Publications:** Duff Cooper: The Authorized Biography, 1986; (ed.) Evelyn Shuckburgh, Descent to Suez: Foreign Office Diaries, 1951-56, 1987; Lord Lloyd and the Decline of the British Empire (biography), 1988; (ed. with E. Homberger) The Troubled Face of Biography, 1988; Chamberlain and the Lost Peace (biography), 1989; Churchill, The End of Glory: A Political Biography, 1992; Churchill's Grand Alliance, 1995; A History of Conservative Politics 1900-1996, 1996. **Address:** School of History, University of East Anglia, Norwich NR4 7TJ, England.

CHARNAS, Suzy McKee. Also writes as Rebecca Brand. American, b. 1939. **Genres:** Novellas/Short stories, Horror, Science fiction/Fantasy, Young adult fiction, Songs/Lyrics and libretti, Essays. **Career:** Freelance writer, 1969-. Formerly English and history teacher for the Peace Corps in Nigeria; teacher, New Lincoln School, NYC; and worker for Community Mental Health Organization, NYC. **Publications:** Walk to the End of the World, 1974; Motherlines, 1979; The Vampire Tapestry, 1980; The Bronze King, 1985; Dorothea Dreams, 1986; The Silver Glove, 1988; Listening to Brahms (novella), 1988; The Golden Thread (juvenile), 1989; Vampire Dreams (play), 1990; The Kingdom of Kevin Malone, 1993; The Furies, 1994; Beauty and the Opera, or the Phantom Beast (novella), 1996; (as Rebecca Brand) The Ruby Tear (science fiction), 1997; Bernard J. Taylor, Nosferatu (rev. lyrics), 1997; The Conqueror's Child (science fiction), 1999; My Father's Ghost (memoir), 2002. **Address:** 212 High St NE, Albuquerque, NM 87102, U.S.A. **Online address:** suzych@Highfiber.com

CHARNEY, Mark J. American, b. 1956. **Genres:** Literary criticism and history, Plays/Screenplays. **Career:** Clemson University, Clemson, SC,

instructor, 1980-82, assistant professor, 1987-91, associate professor of English, 1991-. Servo Productions (video production company), director. Lecturer on film. Director of community and university theater; member of local play selection committee and arts commission. **Publications:** Barry Hannah, Twayne, 1992. **Address:** Department of English, Strode Tower, Clemson University, Clemson, SC 29634-1503, U.S.A.

CHARNON-DEUTSCH, Lou. American, b. 1946. **Genres:** Language/Linguistics, Literary criticism and history. **Career:** State University of New York at Stony Brook, assistant professor, 1980-88, associate professor, 1988-95, professor of Hispanic languages and literature and women's studies, 1995-, chairperson of Hispanic studies, 1989-91, acting director, Humanities Institute, 1997. **Publications:** The Nineteenth-Century Spanish Short Story: Study of a Genre in Evolution, 1985; Gender and Representation: Women in Nineteenth-Century Spanish Realist Fiction (monograph), 1990; Narratives of Desire: Nineteenth-Century Spanish Fiction by Women, 1994; Fictions of the Feminine in the Nineteenth-Century Spanish Press, 2000. EDITOR: Estudios sobre escritoras hispanicas en honor de G. Sabat-Rivers, 1992; An Annotated Bibliography of Hispanic Feminist Criticism, 1994; (with J. Labanyi, and contrib.) Culture and Gender in Nineteenth-Century Spain, 1996. Contributor to academic journals. **Address:** Department of Hispanic Languages and Literature, State University of New York at Stony Brook, Stony Brook, NY 11794, U.S.A. **Online address:** ldeutsch@notes.sunysb.edu

CHARNY, Israel. American/Israeli, b. 1931. **Genres:** Human relations/Parenting, International relations/Current affairs, Psychology. **Career:** Tel Aviv University, Bob Shapell School of Social Work, associate professor, 1973-93; Hebrew University of Jerusalem, Martin Buber Center and Department of Psychology, professor of Psychology and Family Therapy, (founder and director, 1993-1997) advanced studies in integrative psychotherapy, 1993-. Executive Director, Institute on the Holocaust and Genocide, Jerusalem, 1979-. Director, Guidance Consultants Psychological Group Practice, Paoli, Pa. 1962-73. **Publications:** Individual and Family Developmental Review, 1964; Marital Love and Hate, 1972; Strategies Against Violence, 1978; How Can We Commit the Unthinkable?, 1982; Toward the Understanding and Prevention of Genocide, 1984; Genocide: A Critical Bibliographical Review, 1988; Genocide: A Critical Bibliographic Review, Volume 2, 1991; Holding on to Humanity: The Message of Holocaust Survivors, 1992; Existential/Dialectual Marital Therapy: Breaking the Secret Code of Marriage, 1992; (series ed.) R. Krell and M.I. Sherman, eds., Genocide: A Critical Bibliographic Review, vol. 3: The Widening Circle of Genocide, 1993, vol. 4: Medical and Psychological Effects of Concentration Camps on Holocaust Survivors, 1997; (with S. Totten and W. Parsons) Genocide in the Twentieth Century, 1995, as Century of Genocide, 1997; (ed.-inchief) Encyclopedia of Genocide, 1999; Facsicm and Democracy in the Human Mind, in progress. **Address:** PO Box 10311, 91102 Jerusalem, Israel. **Online address:** encygeno@mail.com

CHARPAK, Georges. French (born Poland), b. 1924. **Genres:** Physics. **Career:** Physicist. Centre Nation de la Recherche Scientifique, 1948-59; Centre Europeen pour la Recherche Nucleaire, Geneva, Switzerland, 1959-. Nobel Prize in physics, 1992. **Publications:** La Vie a Fil Tendu, 1993; Research on Particle Imaging Detectors, 1995; (with R.L. Garwin) Feux Follets et Champignous nucleaires, 1997; Enfants, Chercheurs et citoyens, 1998; (with R.L. Garwin) Megawatts and Megatones, 2001. **Address:** CERN Lab for Particle Physics, CH 1211 Geneva-23, Switzerland.

CHARRETTE, Robert N. American, b. 1953. **Genres:** Novels, Science fiction/Fantasy. **Career:** Freelance graphic artist, 1975-81; Fantasy Games Unlimited, New York, art director, 1981-82; freelance sculptor, 1982-84 and 1986-; Ral Partha Enterprises, Cincinnati, OH, staff sculptor, 1984-86; freelance writer, 1975-. **Publications:** NOVELS: Never Trust An Elf, 1992; Just Compensation, 1996; A Prince Among Men, 1994; The King Beneath the Mountain, 1995; A Knight Among Knaves, 1995. BATTLETECH SERIES: Wolves on the Border, 1989; Heir to the Dragon, 2000; Wolfpack, 1992. SECRETS OF POWER TRILOGY: Shadowrun: Never Deal with a Dragon, 1990; Shadowrun: Choose Your Enemies Carefully, 1991; Shadowrun: Find Your Own Truth, 1991. CHRONICLES OF AELWYN SERIES: Timespell, 1996; Eye of the Serpent, 1996; Wizard of Bones, 1996. ROLE-PLAYING GAMES: (with P. Hume) Bushido, 1975; (with P. Hume) Aftermath!, 1981; (with P. Hume) Daredevils, 1982; Land of Ninja, 1986; (with P. Hume and T. Dowd) Shadowrun, 1989. **Address:** c/o Donald Maass, Donald Maass Literary Agency, 160 W. 95th St., Ste 1B, New York, NY 10025, U.S.A.

CHARTERS, Ann. American, b. 1936. **Genres:** Literary criticism and history, Biography. **Career:** University of Connecticut, Storrs, professor of

English. **Publications:** A Bibliography of Jack Kerouac, 1968; Olson/Melville: A Study of Affinity, 1968; Scenes along the Road: Photographs of the Desolation Angels, 1970; Nobody: The Story of Bert Williams, 1970; Kerouac: A Biography, 1973, rev. ed., 1995; (with S. Charters) I Love, 1979; Beats and Company: Portrait of a Literary Generation, 1986; (with S. Charters) Literature and Its Writers, 1997, 3rd ed., 2003. EDITOR: The Special View of History: Charles Olson at Black Mountain College, 1970; The Dictionary of Literary Biography: Vol. 16: Beat Writers, 1983; The Story and Its Writer, 1983, 6th ed., 2002; G. Stein, Three Lives and Q.E.D., 1990; Major Writers of Short Fiction, 1992; Portable Beat Reader, 1992; Portable Kerouac Reader, 1995; Selected Letters of Jack Kerouac, Vol. I, 1995, Vol. II, 1999; The American Short Story and Its Writer, 2000; Beat Down to Your Soul, 2001; The Portable Sixties Reader, 2003. **Address:** Dept of English, University of Connecticut, Storrs Mansfield, CT 06269, U.S.A.

CHARTERS, Samuel. American, b. 1929. **Genres:** Novels, Poetry, Music. **Career:** Producer, Vanguard Recording Society, NYC, 1965-70; Producer, Sonet Grammofon AB, Stockholm, 1970-84; Owner Gazell Productions/Records, 1984-. **Publications:** Jazz: New Orleans, 1958; The Country Blues, 1959; (with L. Kunstadt) Jazz: The New York Scene, 1962; Heroes of the Prize Ring (poetry), 1963; The Poetry of the Blues, 1963; The Bluesmen, 1967; Days (poetry), 1967; To This Place (poetry), 1969; Some Poems/Poets (literary criticism), 1971; Sweet as the Showers of Rain (poetry), 1972; From a London Notebook (poetry), 1973; From a Swedish Notebook, 1973; Robert Johnson, 1973; (trans.) Baltics, by Tomas Transtruomer, 1975; The Legacy of the Blues, 1975; In Lagos (poetry), 1976; (trans.) We Women, by Edith Suodergran, 1977; Spelmannen, 1979; Of Those Who Died (poetry), 1980; (with A. Charters) I Love (poetry), 1980; The Roots of the Blues, 1981; (trans.) The Courtyard, by Bo Carpelan, 1982; Mr. Jabi and Mr. Smythe (novel), 1983; Jelly Roll Morton's Last Night at the Jungle Inn (novel), 1984; Louisiana Black (novel), 1986; A Country Year (memoir), 1992; Elvis Presley Calls His Mother after the Ed Sullivan Show (novel), 1992; The Day Is So Long and the Wages So Small (music/travel), 1998; (with A. Charters) Blue Faces (music/photo), 2000; Mambo Time, the Story of Bebo Valdes, 2001. **Address:** c/o Marion Boyars Publishers, 24 Lacy Rd, London SW15 1NL, England.

CHARYN, Jerome. American, b. 1937. **Genres:** Novels, Novellas/Short stories, Plays/Screenplays. **Career:** Dutton Review, NYC, Founding Ed., 1970. High School of Music and Art, and School of Performing Arts, NYC, English teacher, 1962-64; Stanford University, California, Assistant Professor of English, 1965-68; City University of New York, Herbert Lehman College, Professor of English, 1968-80; Princeton University, New Jersey, Lecturer in Creative Writing, 1980-86; City College of New York, Visiting Distinguished Professor of English, 1988-89; American University of Paris, Professor of Film Studies, 1995-. **Publications:** Once upon a Droshky, 1964; On the Darkening Green, 1965; The Man Who Grew Younger and Other Stories, 1967; Going to Jerusalem, 1967; American Scrapbook, 1969; Eisenhower, My Eisenhower, 1971; The Tar Baby, 1973; Blue Eyes, 1975; The Education of Patrick Silver, 1976; Marilyn the Wild, 1976; The Franklin Scare, 1977; Secret Isaac, 1978; The Seventh Babe, 1979; The Catfish Man, 1980; Darlin' Bill, 1980; Panna Maria, 1982; Pinocchio's Nose, 1983; The Isaac Quartet, 1984; War Cries over Avenue C, 1985; Metropolis: New York as Myth, Marketplace and Magical Land, 1986; Paradise Man, 1987; The Magician's Wife, 1987; Movieland, 1989; The Good Policeman, 1990; Elsinore, 1991; Maria's Girls, 1992; Margot in Badtown, 1992; Back to Bataan, 1993; Montezuma's Man, 1993; Little Angel Street, 1994; El Bronx, 1997; The Dark Lady from Belorusse, 1997; Death of a Tango King, 1998; Citizen Sidel, 1998; Captain Kidd, 1999; The Black Swan, 2000; Sizzling Chops and Devilish Spins, 2001; Hurricane Lady, 2001; Bronx Boy, 2002; Gangsters and Gold Diggers, 2003. EDITOR: The Single Voice: An Anthology of Contemporary Fiction, 1969; The Troubled Vision, 1970; The New Mystery, 1993. **Address:** Bosquet, American University of Paris, 31 Av Bosquet, 75007 Paris, France. **Online address:** jeromecharyn@aol.com

CHASE, Alyssa. American, b. 1965. **Genres:** Children's fiction. **Career:** Dial Books for Young Readers, NYC, assistant editor, 1989-90; Holiday House, NYC, associate editor, 1990-92; freelance copy writer, proofreader, copy editor, and researcher, 1990-; Buffalo Spree (magazine), Buffalo, NY, associate editor, 1992-95; Riverfront Times (newspaper) and St. Louis Magazine, St. Louis, MO, copy editor/writer, 1995-. Arts in Education Institute of Western New York, Cheektowaga, teaching artist, docent coordinator, and tour guide, 1995. **Publications:** Jomo and Mata, 1993; Tessa on Her Own, 1994. **Address:** 306 N Ridgeview Dr, Indianapolis, IN 46219, U.S.A.

CHASE, Elaine Raco. American, b. 1949. **Genres:** Mystery/Crime/Suspense, Romance/Historical, Criminology/True Crime. **Career:** Full-time writer. Narcotic Addiction Control Commission, Albany, NY, secretary, 1967-68; WGY-WRGB-TV, Schenectady, NY, audio-visual librarian, 1968-70; Beckman Advertising, Albany, copywriter, 1970-71. **Publications:** Rules of the Game, 1980; Tender Yearnings, 1981; A Dream Come True, 1982; Double Occupancy, 1982; Designing Woman, 1982; Calculated Risk, 1983; No Easy Way Out, 1983; Video Vixen, 1983; Best Laid Plans, 1984; Lady Be Bad, 1984; Special Delivery, 1984; Dare the Devil, 1987; Dangerous Places, 1987; Dark Corners, 1988; The Best of Elaine Raco Chase, vol. 1, 1990, vol. 2, 1991, Vol. 3, 1992, Vol. 4, 1992; Partners in Crime, 1994; Amateur Detectives, 1996. **Address:** 13134 Madonna Ln, Fairfax, VA 22033-3706, U.S.A. **Online address:** elainerc@juno.com

CHASE, Emily. See GARWOOD, Julie.

CHASE, Emily. See SACHS, Judith.

CHASE, Joan. American. **Genres:** Novels, Novellas/Short stories. **Career:** Ragdale Foundation, Lake Forest, IL, assistant director, 198084; writer. Taught at Iowa Writers Workshop, 1988, an Princeton University, 1990. **Publications:** During the Reign of the Queen of Persia (novel), 1983; The Evening Wolves (novel), 1989; Bonneville Blue (short stories), 1991. **Address:** c/o Ellen Levine, Trident, 41 Madison Ave, Fl 36, New York, NY 10010-2257, U.S.A.

CHASE, John Leighton. American, b. 1953. **Genres:** Design. **Career:** Walt Disney Imagineering, designer, 1986-87; John Chase Design, Los Angeles, principal, 1987-93; Chase & Burnett Inc. (design firm), Los Angeles and Marina Del Rey, CA, principal, 1993-96; City of West Hollywood, urban designer, 1996-. **Publications:** Exterior Decoration, 1982; (with F. Anderton) Las Vegas, The Success of Excess, 1997; (ed., with others) Everyday Urbanism, 1999; Glitter, Stucco, and Dumpster Diving, 2000. **Address:** c/o Planning Division, West Hollywood City Government, 8300 Santa Monica Blvd, West Hollywood, CA 90069, U.S.A. **Online address:** jchase@weho.org

CHASE, Karen. American, b. 1943. **Genres:** Poetry. **Career:** New York Hospital-Cornell Medical Center, New York, NY, writer-in-residence; Robert Frost Place, Franconia, NH, member of faculty; writer and teacher in western Massachusetts. Camel River Writing Center, Lenox, MA, founder. **Publications:** Kazimierz Square (poetry), 2000. Contributor of poetry to anthologies; contributor of poetry and stories to periodicals. **Address:** PO Box 634, Lenox, MA 01240, U.S.A. **Online address:** kchase@vgernet.net

CHASE, Karen Susan. American, b. 1952. **Genres:** Literary criticism and history. **Career:** University of Virginia, Charlottesville, assistant professor, 1979-85, associate professor, 1985-91, professor of English, 1992-. **Publications:** Eros and Psyche: the Representation of Personality in Charlotte Bronte, Charles Dickens, and George Eliot, 1984; George Eliot's Middlemarch, 1990; (with M. Levenson) The Spectacle of Intimacy: A Public Life for the Victorian Family, 2000. **Address:** University of Virginia, Department of English, 2219 Bryan Hall, Charlottesville, VA 22903, U.S.A. **Online address:** ksc3j@virginia.edu

CHASE, Loretta Lynda. American, b. 1949. **Genres:** Romance/Historical. **Career:** Writer. Worked in various fields, including retail, administration, and clerical. **Publications:** HISTORICAL ROMANCE NOVELS: Isabella, 1987; The English Witch, 1988; Viscount Vagabond, 1988; The Devil's Delilah, 1989; Knaves' Wager, 1990; The Sandalwood Princess, 1990; Falling Star: A Christmas Collection, 1992; The Lion's Daughter, 1992; Captives of the Night, 1994; Falling Star: A Christmas Present, 1994; Lord of Scoundrels, 1995; The Mad Earl's Bride: Three Weddings and a Kiss (short stories), 1995; The Last Hellion, 1998. **Address:** c/o Author Mail, Avon Books, HarperCollins Publishers, 10 E 53rd St, New York, NY 10022, U.S.A. **Online address:** lorettachase@yahoo.com

CHASE, Lyndon. See CHARD, Judy (Gordon).

CHASE, Nicholas. See HYDE, Anthony.

CHASE, Nicholas. See HYDE, Christopher.

CHAST, Roz. American, b. 1954. **Genres:** Cartoons. **Career:** New Yorker, NYC, cartoonist, 1979-; freelance illustrator for advertisements and children's books. **Publications:** CARTOONS: Unscientific Americans, 1982; Parallel Universes: An Assortment of Cartoons, 1984; Mondo Boxo: Cartoon Stories, 1987; The Four Elements, 1988; Proof of Life on Earth, 1991. Illustrator of books by A. Zobel, J.R. Martin and P. Marx, A-B. Olsen and M. Efron. Contributor of cartoons to periodicals. **Address:** 29 New St., Ridgefield, CT 06877, U.S.A.

CHATAWAY, Carol. Australian, b. 1955. **Genres:** Children's fiction. **Career:** Author. Worked as a school assistant in Salisbury, South Australia, 1975-83, and a school treasurer in Birdwood, South Australia, 1983-88. **Publications:** The Perfect Pet, 2001. **Address:** 9 Cave Ave., Bridgewater, SA 5155, Australia. **Online address:** carol.chataway@bigpond.com

CHATELLIER, Louis. French, b. 1935. **Genres:** Theology/Religion. **Career:** High school teacher in Strasbourg, France, 1963-66; Centre Nationale Recherche Scientifique, Strasbourg, research assistant, 1966-70; Universite de Strasbourg, assistant principal, 1970-80; Universite Lyon, professor, 1980-81; Universite Nancy II, professor, 1981-2003, professor emeritus, 2003-; Institut Universitaire de France, professor, 1996-2003; Ecole pratiques des Hautes Etudes, section des sciences religieuses, 1998-2003. **Publications:** Tradition christienne et remouveau catholique dans l'ancien diocese de Strasbourg (title means: Christian Tradition and Catholic Renewal in the Old Diocese of Strasbourg), 1981; L'Europe de devots, 1987, trans by J. Birrell as The Europe of the Devout: The Catholic Reformation and the Formation of a New Society, 1989; The Religion of the Poor: Rural Missions in Europe and the Formation of Modern Catholicism, c. 1500-1800, 1993, trans. 1997; (ed.) Religions en transition dans la seconde moitie du XVIII siecle, 2000; Les espaces infinis et le silence de Dieu, 2003. **Address:** Universite Nancy II, 23 Boulevard Albert I, 54000 Nancy, France. **Online address:** schonann@pt.lu

CHATFIELD, Cheryl A. American. **Genres:** How-to books, Money/Finance. **Career:** Worked as stockbroker; Chatfield, Dean and Co. Inc., founder, partner, and chief executive officer; Women Securities International Inc., founder and owner; worked as high school English teacher in Bristol, CT; district coordinator of language arts for public schools in New Britain, CT; Campfire (afterschool child care provider), supervisor and curriculum specialist; Center for Entrepreneurship and Economic Development, instructor; adjunct professor: University of Arizona and University of New Mexico; State Penitentiary of New Mexico, executive director of Alice King Family Center; National Association of Securities Dealers, registered representative, 1980, financial principal, 1984; registered investment adviser, 1981; Nottingham Institute (nonprofit educational organization), president; Central Connecticut State University, assistant professor; business and educational consultant. **Publications:** Low-Priced Riches: Investing in the OTC Market, 1985; Selling Low-Priced Riches: Being a Successful OTC Stock Broker, 1986; The Trust Factor: The Art of Doing Business in the 21st Century, 1997; Don't Fall off the Bicycle: Balancing Chaos & Order in Our Lives, 2002. **Address:** c/o Sunstone Press, PO Box 2321, Santa Fe, NM 87504-2424, U.S.A. **Online address:** NottInst@aol.com

CHATFIELD, E. Charles. American, b. 1934. **Genres:** History, Institutions/Organizations, Intellectual history, International relations/Current affairs, Biography. **Career:** Wittenberg University, Springfield, OH, instructor, 1961-65, assistant professor, 1965-69, associate professor, 1969-74, professor of history, 1974-99, H. Orth Hirt Professor of History Emeritus, 1999. Peace and Change, co-ed., 1980-83. University of Chicago Divinity School, Illinois, Danforth Theological Year, 1965-66. **Publications:** For Peace and Justice: Pacifism in America, 1914-1941, 1971; The Radical "No": The Correspondence and Writings of Evan Thomas on War, 1974; International War Resistance through 1945, 1975; The Life and Writings of Devere Allen, 1976; The Americanization of Gandhi: Images of the Mahatma, 1977; (with C. De Benedetti) Kirby Page and the Social Gospel, 1977; (with C. DeBenedetti), An American Ordeal: The Antiwar Movement of the Vietnam Era, 1990; The American Peace Movement: Ideals and Activism, 1992. EDITOR/CO-EDITOR: Peace Movements in America, 1973; (and contrib.) The Garland Library of War and Peace, 1974-78; Peace Movements and Political Cultures, 1988; (Russian American project) Peace/Mir: An Anthology of Historic Alternatives to War, 1994; Transnational Social Movements and Global Politics, 1997.

CHATMAN, Seymour. American, b. 1928. **Genres:** Literary criticism and history, Film, Speech/Rhetoric. **Career:** University of Pennsylvania, Philadelphia, Assistant Professor of English, 1956-60; University of California, Berkeley, Professor of Rhetoric, 1961-1993, Professor Emeritus and Professor in the Graduate School, 1993-. **Publications:** A Theory of Meter, 1965; Later Style of Henry James, 1972; Story and Discourse: Narrative Structure in Fiction and Film, 1978; Antonioni, or the Surface of the World, 1985; Coming to Terms: The Rhetoric of Narrative in Film and Fiction, 1990; Reading Narrative Fiction, 1992. EDITOR: (with S.R. Levin) Essays on the Language of Literature, 1967; (and trans.) Literary Style: A Symposium, 1971; Approaches to Poetics: English Institute Essays, 1973; (with U. Eco) A Semiotic Landscape, 1979; Benjamin Graham: Memoirs of the Dean of Wall Street, 1996. **Address:** Dept. of Rhetoric, University of California, Berkeley, CA 94720, U.S.A. **Online address:** Chatman@socrates.berkeley.edu

CHATTERJEE, Debjani. Indian, b. 1952. **Genres:** Children's fiction, Mythology/Folklore, Local history/Rural topics. **Career:** Sheffield Racial Equality Council, Sheffield, England, director, 1984-94; Oxfordshire Racial Equality Council, Oxford, England, director, 1994-; writer, storyteller, and poet. Worked in the steel industry, in education, and in community relations. Does occasional broadcasts for the BBC. **Publications:** FOR CHILDREN: The Elephant-Headed God and Other Hindu Tales, 1989; The Monkey God and Other Hindu Tales, 1993; (trans.) Rabindranath Tagore, The Parrot's Training, 1993; Nyamia and the Bag of Gold, 1994; Sufi Stories from around the World, 1994; The Most Beautiful Child, 1996. OTHER: The Role of Religion in a Passage to India, 1984; (ed. with Chris Searle) Peaces: Poems for Peace, 1987; (ed. and contrib.) I Was That Woman (poetry collection), 1989; (ed. with Rashida Islam) Barbed Lines (bilingual anthology), 1990; (ed. with William Scammell) Northern Poetry: Vol II, 1991; (ed. with John Lyons, Cheryl Martin, and Lemn Sissay, and contrib.) The Sun Rises in the North, 1992; (ed. with Rehana Choudhury, Karabi Ghosh, and Rashida Islam) Sweet and Sour (bilingual anthology), 1993; Author of an oral history account of the Bangladeshi community in Sheffield, Sheffield City Libraries, 1994. Contributor to periodicals. **Address:** Oxfordshire Racial Equality Council, Macclesfield House, Tidmarsh Lane, Oxford OX1 1NA, England.

CHATTERJEE, Upamanyu. Indian, b. 1959. **Genres:** Novellas/Short stories. **Career:** Indian Administrative Service, various regions of India, officer, became chief officer of Bombay Slum Improvement Board, c. 1983-; freelance writer, c. 1986-. **Publications:** FICTION: English, August: An Indian Story, 1988; The Last Burden, 1993. Contributor of short stories to periodicals. **Address:** c/o Faber and Faber Ltd., 3 Queen Sq., London WC1N 3AU, England.

CHATTERJI, Joya. Indian, b. 1964. **Genres:** History. **Career:** Cambridge University, Cambridge, England, fellow of Trinity College, 1989-94, senior research fellow at Centre for South Asian Studies, 1995-. **Publications:** Bengal Divided: Hindu Communalism and Partition, 1932-1947, 1994. **Address:** E/4 Hauz Khas Village, New Delhi 110016, India.

CHATTO, James. British, b. 1955. **Genres:** Novellas/Short stories, Food and Wine. **Career:** Journalist and freelance writer. Formerly worked as an actor and musician, London, England. **Publications:** SHORT STORIES: The Atheist, 1985; Tricky Customers, 1986. NONFICTION: The Seducer's Cookbook, 1981; (with W.L. Martin) A Kitchen in Corfu, 1987; The Man Who Ate Toronto: Memoirs of a Restaurant Lover, 1998. Contributor to cookbooks; contributor of columns and articles to periodicals. **Address:** Toronto Life Magazine, 59 Front St. E., Toronto, ON, Canada M5E 1B3.

CHAUDHURI, Amit. Indian, b. 1962. **Genres:** Novels. **Career:** Writer. Wolfson College, Oxford, creative arts fellow, 1992-95. **Publications:** A Strange and Sublime Address, 1991; Afternoon Raag, 1993; Freedom Song: Three Novels, 1999; A New World, 2000; (ed.) Picador Book of Modern Indian Literature, 2001; Real Time: Stories and a Reminiscence, 2002. Contributor to periodicals and anthologies. **Address:** 6 Sunny Park, Flat 10, 8th Fl, Calcutta 700019, India.

CHAUNCEY, George. American. **Genres:** Gay and lesbian issues. **Career:** University of Chicago, IL, began as assistant professor, currently professor of history. **Publications:** (ed. with M.B. Duberman and M. Vicinus) Hidden from History: Reclaiming the Gay and Lesbian Past, 1989; Gay New York: Gender, Urban Culture, and the Making of the Gay Male World, 1890-1940, 1994. **Address:** Department of History, University of Chicago, 1126 E 59th St, Chicago, IL 60637, U.S.A.

CHAURETTE, Normand. Canadian, b. 1954. **Genres:** Plays/Screenplays. **Career:** Playwright. **Publications:** Reve d'une nuit d'hopital, 1980; Provincetown Playhouse, juillet 1919, j'avais 19 ans, 1981; Fetes d'Automne, 1982; La Societe de Metis, 1983; Fragments d'une lettre d'adieu lus par des geologues, 1986; Scenes d'enfants, 1989; Les Reines, 1986, trans by L. Gaboriau as The Queens, 1992; Je vous ecris du Caire, 1996; Le Passage de l'Indiana, 1996. **Address:** c/o Union des ecrivains quebecois, 1030 rue Cherrier bur. 510, Montreal, QC, Canada H2L 1H9.

CHAVE, Anna C. American. **Genres:** Art/Art history. **Career:** Hunter College, instructor; Harvard University, Cambridge, MA, professor of fine arts.

Publications: ART CRITICISM: Mark Rothko: Subjects in Abstraction, 1989; Constantin Brancusi: Shifting the Bases of Art, 1993. Contributor to books. **Address:** PhD Program in Art History, The Graduate Center, City University of New York, 365 5th Ave., New York, NY 10016-4309, U.S.A.

CHECKLAND, Olive. *See* Obituaries.

CHECKOWAY, Julie. American, b. 1963. **Genres:** Autobiography/ Memoirs. **Career:** University of Iowa, Iowa City, instructor at Iowa Writer's Workshop, 1987; Johns Hopkins University, Baltimore, MD, instructor for Writing Seminars, 1988-95; University of Georgia, Athens, assistant professor of English, 1995-, director of Creative Writing Program, 1996-. Hebei Teachers University, Shijiazhuang, China, visiting professor; Gilman School, Baltimore, MA, director of Writing Center, 1989-95. **Publications:** Little Sister: Searching for the Shadow World of Chinese Women (memoir), 1996. Work represented in anthologies. Contributor of stories to magazines. **Address:** Creative Writing Program, 329A Park Hall, University of Georgia, Athens, GA 30602, U.S.A. **Online address:** jcheckow@uga.cc.uga.edu

CHEDID, Andree. French (born Egypt), b. 1920. **Genres:** Literary criticism and history, Poetry, Novels. **Career:** Writer, 1949-. Member of poetry juries. **Publications:** POETRY: Textes pour une figure, 1949; Textes pour un poeme, 1950; Textes pour le vivant, 1953; Textes pour la terre aimee, 1955; Terre et poesie, 1956; Terre regardee, 1957; Seul, le visage, 1960; Lubies, 1962; Double-pays, 1965; Contre-Chant, 1969; Visage premier, 1972; Fetes et lubies, 1973; Prendre corps, 1973; Fraternite de la parole, 1975; Ceremonial de la violence, 1976; Le Coeur et le temps, 1977; Cavernes et soleils, 1979; 7 Textes pour un chant, 1986; Ancienne Egypte, 1990. NOVELS: Le Sommeil delivre, 1952, trans. as From Sleep Unbound, 1983; Jonathan, 1955; Le Sixieme jour, 1960, trans. as The Sixth Day, 1988; Le Survivant, 1963; L'Autre, 1969; La Cite fertile, 1972; Nefertiti et le reve d'Akhnaton, 1974; Les Marches de sable, 1981; La Maison sans racines, 1985, trans. as The Return to Beirut, 1989; L'Enfant multiple, 1989; Le Message, 2000. STORY COLLECTIONS: Le Corps et le temps suivi de l'Etroite Peau, 1979; Mondes Miroirs Magies, 1988; A la mort, a la vie: Nouvelles, 1992. PLAYS: Theatre, 1981, Le Montreur, trans. as The Show-Man, 1984; Echec a la Reine, 1984. NONFICTION: Le Liban, 1974; Guy Levis-Mano, 1974. JUVENILE: Grandes Oreilles, toutes oreilles, 1976; Le Coeur et le temps, 1976; Lubies, 1976; Le Coeur suspendu, 1981; L'Etrange Mariee, 1983; Grammaire en fete, 1984. OTHER: The Prose and Poetry of Andree Chedid: Selected Poems, Short Stories, and Essays, 1990; Selected Poems, 1995; Fugitive Suns, 1999. **Address:** c/o Flammarion, 26 rue Racine, 75006 Paris, France.

CHEETHAM, Ann. *See* **PILLING, Ann.**

CHEEVER, Susan. American, b. 1943. **Genres:** Novels, Biography. **Career:** Colorado Rocky Mountain School, Carbondale, CO, teacher, 1965-67; Scarborough School, Scarborough, NY, teacher, 1968-69; Tarrytown Daily News, Tarrytown, NY, reporter, 1970-72; Westchester Rockland Newspapers, White Plains, NY, reporter, 1972; Newsweek mag., NYC, general editor and writer, 1974-79; Newsday, columnist; Bennington College, teacher, MFA Program, Yale College, New Haven, CT. **Publications:** Looking for Work (novel), 1980; A Handsome Man (novel), 1981; The Cage (novel), 1982; Home before Dark: A Biographical Memoir of John Cheever, 1984; Doctors and Women (novel), 1987; Elizabeth Cole (novel), 1989; Treetops: A Family Memoir, 1991; A Woman's Life: The Story of an Ordinary American and Her Extraordinary Generation, 1994; Note Found in a Bottle (memoir), 1998; As Good as I Could Be, 2001. **Address:** c/o Witherspoon Assoc., 235 E 31st St, New York, NY 10016, U.S.A.

CHEHAK, Susan Taylor. American, b. 1951. **Genres:** Novels. **Career:** Writer. **Publications:** NOVELS: The Story of Annie D. 1989; Harmony 1990; Dancing on Glass 1993; Smithereens 1995; Rampage, 1998. SHORT STORIES: End of the World Dreams, 1989; Coulda Been You, 1992. NONFICTION: Don Quixote Meets the Mob: The Craft of Fictions the Art of Life, 2001. **Address:** c/o Betsy Lerner, The Gernert Company, 136 E 57th St, New York, NY 10022, U.S.A.

CHELF, Carl P. American, b. 1937. **Genres:** Politics/Government. **Career:** Professor of Government, Western Kentucky University, Bowling Green, since 1968, (Assistant Professor of Government, 1964-68; Staff Assistant to Vice President, 1968-69; Assistant Dean of Faculties, 1970-71; Assistant Dean of Instruction, 1971-72; Associate Dean of Instruction, 1972-73; formerly, Dean of Public Service and Continuity Education, from 1974). Congressional Fellow, American Political Science Association, 1962-63; Legislative Service Fellow, American Political Science Association, 1971-73;

Academic Administration Intern and Fellow, American Council on Education, 1969-70. **Publications:** (co-author) 100 Questions about a Constitutional Convention, 1960; (co-author) Planning and Zoning Law in Kentucky, 1961; A Manual for Members of the Kentucky General Assembly, 1973; (co-author) Political Parties in the United States: A Systems Analysis, 1974; Congress in the American System, 1977; Public Policymaking in America: Difficult Choices, Limited Solutions, 1981; American Government: Kentucky Edition, 1991; Controversial Issues in Social Welfare Policy, 1991. **Address:** Dept. of Government, Western Kentucky University, Bowling Green, KY 42101, U.S.A.

CHEN, Joseph T. American (born People's Republic of China), b. 1925. **Genres:** History. **Career:** University of California, Berkeley, Center for Chinese Studies, Head Librarian, 1963-64; University of California, Santa Barbara, Guest Lecturer, 1970-73; California State University, Northridge, Professor of History, 1971-2001 (Assistant Professor, 1964-68; Associate Professor, 1968-71). **Publications:** The May Fourth Movement in Shanghai, 1971; trans. into Chinese, 1981. **Address:** Dept of History, California State University, Northridge, CA 91330, U.S.A.

CHEN, Patrizia. (born Italy), b. 1948. **Genres:** Autobiography/Memoirs. **Career:** Writer. Worked variously as an insurance broker, model, public relations executive, salesperson, and food writer. Founded a school in Rome, Italy, 1980s. **Publications:** Rosemary and Bitter Oranges: Growing up in a Tuscan Kitchen (memoir), 2003. **Address:** c/o Author Mail, Simon & Schuster, 1230 Avenue of the Americas, New York, NY 10020, U.S.A.

CHÉNETIER, Marc. French, b. 1946. **Genres:** Translations, Literary criticism and history. **Career:** Scholar and translator. Centre Pedagogique Regional de Tours, teacher of English in training, 1969-70; Stanford University, CA, lecturer in French, 1970-72, visiting professor, 1981; University of Paris III, Sorbonne Nouvelle, assistant professor, 1972-79; University of East Anglia, Norwich, England, visiting professor, 1979-80; University of Orleans, France, professor, 1980-91; visiting professor, University of Virginia, Charlottesville, 1983-84, Princeton University, 1987; Ecole Normale Superieure, Fontenay-aux-Roses, France, professor of American literature, 1990-97; Institut Universitaire de France, Professor Universite Paris VII, 1997-. **Publications:** TRANSLATOR: (with O. Chenetier) G.W. Parkyn, Vers un modele conceptuel d'education permanente, 1973; R. Brautigan, Dreaming of Babylon, 1981; J. Baumbach, Ce soir, on joue mes reves (Reruns), 1983; R. Brautigan, So the Wind Won't Blow It All Away, 1983; W. Byron, Cervantes, 1984; E. Swados, Lea and Lazar, 1984; W. Cather, Death Comes for the Archbishop, 1986; Cather, My Mortal Enemy, 1986; J. Charyn, Frog, 1988; Charyn, Pinocchio's Nose, 1990; Charyn, Un Bon Flic, 1990; Charyn, Elseneur, 1991; Charyn, Les Filles de Maria, 1994; W. Gass, Au coeur du coeur de ce pays; R. Coover, Demandez le programme; D. Johnson, Fiskadoro; R. Banks, Continents a la Derive; Pionniers, Une Dame Perdue, and Un des notres, all by Cather; Cather, La Maison du Professeur, 1993; R. Brautigan, Romans, 1994; G. Capenegro, Star Cafe, 1994; A. Theroux, Three Frogs. EDITOR: Selected Letters of Vachel Lindsay, 1979; (with R. Kroes) Impressions of a Gilded Age, 1983. OTHER: (with J. Barson) Textuellement, 1974; By Signs Obsessed, 1981, as L'Obsession des signes, 1984; Richard Brautigan, 1983; Critical Angles, 1985; Au-Dela du soupcon (Beyond Suspicion), 1989; La Fiction Americaine de 1960 a 1985 (American Fiction from 1960 to 1985), 1985; Brautigan Sauve du Vent, 1992; Sgraffites, Encres et Sanguines, 1994; De la Caverne a la Pyramide, 2000; La Perte de l'Amerique archeologie d'un amour, 2000; Steven Millhauser: la precision du l'impossible, 2003. Contributor to anthologies and periodicals. Editor or co-editor of special issues of scholarly journals. **Address:** 10 rue Charles V, 75004 Paris, France. **Online address:** marche@paris7.jussieu.fr

CHENEY, Martha. Also writes as Martha Palmer. American, b. 1953. **Genres:** Education. **Career:** Preschool teacher in Woodland Hills, CA, 1986-88; Los Angeles Unified School District, Los Angeles, CA, teacher, 1988-94; writer, 1995-. **Publications:** How to Develop Your Child's Gifts and Talents in Reading, 1996; How to Develop Your Child's Gifts and Talents in Vocabulary, 1997; How to Develop Your Child's Gifts and Talents in Writing, 1997. Author or coauthor of workbooks and activity books for Gifted and Talented Series; author or coauthor of curriculum supplements for Educational Publishers. AUDIO RECORDINGS: Witches' Brew, 1976; Tickly Toddle, 1981; Babysong, 1984. VIDEOTAPES: Babysongs, 1986; More Babysongs, 1987; Rock Me: A Family Celebration, 1991. Works published prior to 1986 appeared under the name Martha Palmer. **Address:** 32150 Ranch Lane, Huson, MT 59846, U.S.A.

CHENG, Christopher. Australian, b. 1959. **Genres:** Children's non-fiction. **Career:** Taronga Zoo, Sydney, Australia, public relations assistant, 1981- 84;

relief/substitute teacher, 1981-84; infants/primary teacher at Bourke Public School, Bourke, Australia, 1984-86, North Sydney Demonstration School, Sydney, 1987, and Dulwich Hill Public School, Sydney, 1994; education officer, Taronga Zoo Education Centre, Sydney, 1987-93; Dymocks Booksellers, Sydney, national children's development manager, 1994-98. Purdue University, author-education consultant, 1998-. Has served as author-in-residence at several public schools. **Publications:** (with L. Hathorn) Stuntumble Monday, 1990; The Eyespy Book of Night Creatures, 1990; The Eyespy Book of Endangered Animals, 1991; Bancks' Ginger Meggs and Friends Pet Care Book, 1992; The Eyespy Book of Rainforest Animals, 1994; The Eyespy Book of Party Animals, 1995; One Child, 1997; Rainforests, 1998; Alpine Regions, 1998. Author of several educational series books; contributor of articles and reviews to journals. **Address:** PO Box 279, Newtown, NSW 2042, Australia. **Online address:** chengc@ozemail.com.au

CHENG, J(ames) Chester. American, b. 1926. **Genres:** History, Politics/Government. **Career:** Professor of History, San Francisco State University, 1960-, now Emeritus. Consultant, Asia Foundation, 1983-. Research Associate, Hoover Institution, Stanford, California, 1964-. Lecturer in History, University of Hong Kong, 1952-59; Visiting Associate Professor of University of Oregon, Eugene, 1959-60; Consultant, U.S. Office of Education, 1960-61. **Publications:** Basic Principles Underlying Chinese Communist Approach to Education, 1961; Chinese Sources for the Taiping Rebellion in China 1850-1864, 1963; (ed.) The Politics of the Chinese Red Army, 1966; Documents of Dissent: Chinese Political Culture since Mao, 1980.

CHER, Ming. Chinese (born Singapore), b. 1947. **Genres:** Novels. **Career:** Worker as construction supervisor, seaman, and importer. **Publications:** Spider Boys (novel), 1995. **Address:** c/o Michael Gifkins and Associates, PO Box 6496, Auckland 1, New Zealand.

CHERCHI-USAI, Paolo. American (born Italy), b. 1957. **Genres:** Film. **Career:** Film curator and historian. University of Rochester, Rochester, NY, adjunct professor of English. Lavoro, Genoa, Italy, editor of arts section, 1982-88; George Eastman House, Rochester, assistant curator, 1989-92, senior curator of film, 1994-; Royal Film Archive, Brussels, Belgium, head of preservation projects, 1993-94; Cineteca del Friuli, Gemona, Italy, deputy curator, 1986-88; Selznick School of Film Preservation, Rochester, director, 1996-; teacher at University of Liege and International School for Film Preservation, Bologna, Italy. **Publications:** The Vitagraph Company of America (1897-1916), 1987; Burning Passions: An Introduction to the Study of Silent Cinema, 1995; Silent Cinema: An Introduction, 2000; The Death of Cinema: History, Cultural Memory, and the Digital Dark Age, 2001. EDITOR: Silent Witnesses: Russian Films, 1908-1917, 1989; (with C. Rowell) The Griffith Project, Volume 1: Films Produced 1907-1908, 2000, Volume 2: Films Produced in January-June 1909, 2000, Volume 3: Films Produced in July-December 1909, 2000, Volume 4: Films Produced in 1910, 2001, Volume 5: Films Produced in 1911, 2002. Contributor to journals. **Address:** George Eastman House, 900 East Avenue, Rochester, NY 14607, U.S.A. **Online address:** usai@mail.rochester.edu

CHERIPKO, Jan. American, b. 1951. **Genres:** Travel/Exploration, Politics/Government. **Career:** Sullivan County Democrat, Callicoon, NY, reporter and editor, 1979-1986; The Family School, Hancock, NY, English teacher, 1986-. Times Herald-Record, Middletown, NY, correspondent, 1989-1992; Boyds Mills Press, Honesdale, PA, institutional promotion specialist, 1990-. **Publications:** Voices of the River: Adventures on the Delaware, 1994; Imitate the Tiger, 1996; Get Ready to Play Tee Ball, 1998. **Address:** Boyds Mills Press, 815 Church St., Honesdale, PA 18431, U.S.A.

CHERNAIK, Warren L(ewis). American, b. 1931. **Genres:** Literary criticism and history. **Career:** University of London, England, Queen Mary and Westfield College, started as lecturer, became senior lecturer, reader, and professor, now professor emeritus; program director of Center for English Studies at University of London; University of Southampton, visiting professor; King's College, London, visiting professor. Held teaching positions at Yale University, Ohio State University, City College of New York, Boston University, University of Massachusetts (Boston) and University College of North Wales. **Publications:** The Poetry of Limitation: A Study of Edmund Waller, 1968; The Poet's Time: Politics and Religion in the Work of Andrew Marvell, 1983; (with C. Davis and M. Deegan), The Politics of the Electronic Text, 1993; Sexual Freedom in Restoration Literature, 1995; (with M. Deegan and A. Gibson) Beyond the Book: Theory, Culture and the Politics of Cyberspace, 1996; (with I. Willison and K. Gould) Modernist Writers and the Marketplace, 1996; (with P. Parrinder) Textual Monopolies: Literary Copyright and the Public Domain, 1997; (with M. Dzelzainis) Marvell and Liberty, 1999; (with M. Swales and R. Vilain) The Art of Detective Fiction, 2000; The Merchant of Venice, 2004. **Address:** 124 Mansfield Rd, London NW3 2JB, England.

CHERNOFF, Maxine. American, b. 1952. **Genres:** Novels, Novellas/Short stories, Poetry. **Career:** University of Illinois at Chicago Circle, lecturer in English, 1977-80; Columbia College, Chicago, instructor, 1978-85; Truman College, Chicago, associate professor of English, 1980-94; School of the Art Institute of Chicago, visiting lecturer, 1988-94; San Francisco State University, professor of creative writing, 1994-; Poetry Center, president and member of board of directors, 1982-87; Bard College, fellow of Simon's Rock. Illinois Arts Council, member of literature panel, 1981-83. **Publications:** POETRY: A Vegetable Emergency, 1977; Utopia TV Store, 1979; New Faces of 1952, 1985; Japan, 1988; Leap Year Day: New and Selected Poems, 1990; Next Song (poetry), 1998; World, 2001; Evolution of the Bridge, 2004; Among the Names, 2005. STORIES: Bop, 1987; Signs of Devotion, 1993; Some of Her Friends That Year, 2002. NOVELS: Plain Grief, 1991; American Heaven, 1996; A Boy in Winter, 1999. **Address:** 369 Molino, Mill Valley, CA 94941, U.S.A. **Online address:** maxpaul@sfsu.edu

CHERNOFSKY, Barbara J. American, b. 1949. **Genres:** Education, Human relations/Parenting. **Career:** Joyful Noise Family Daycare, director, 1983-89; Grossmont College, El Cajon, CA, instructor, 1989-. Barbara Chernofsky and Co., owner, 1986-; Advocates for Better Childcare Inc., executive director, 1986-; San Diego County Commission on Children, Youth, and Families, education chairperson; California Resource and Referral Network, member of advisory board of Partners in Prevention Project; member of San Diego County Child Care Planning Council, San Diego County Child Abuse Coordinating Council, and East County Child Care Task Force; parenting consultant. **Publications:** A Practical Approach to Family Daycare, 1986; A Family Daycare Primer, 1989; Who's in Charge Here?, 1991; An In-Home Study Course in Child Abuse Prevention for the Family Daycare, 1992; (with D. Gage) Change Your Child's Behavior by Changing Yours: Thirteen New Tricks to Teach Yourself to Get Kids to Cooperate, 1996. **Address:** P.O. Box 2291, La Mesa, CA 91943, U.S.A.

CHERNOW, Barbara A. American, b. 1948. **Genres:** Communications/Media, Biography, Reference. **Career:** Macmillan Publishing, NYC, associate editor of reference books, 1977-82; Chernow Editorial Services Inc., NYC, president, 1982-. New York University, Center for Publishing, lecturer, 2000-; lecturer at seminars and conferences. **Publications:** Robert Morris: Land Speculator, 1790-1801, 1979; Guide to the Research Collections of the Columbia University Libraries, 1984; (with S. Lindner) Retail Profitability, 2004. EDITOR: (managing ed.) International Encyclopedia of the Social Sciences Biographical Supplement, edited by D.L. Sills, 1979; (senior project ed.) Macmillan Encyclopedia of Architects, edited by A.K. Placzek, 1982; (series ed. with G.A. Vallasi) The Reader's Adviser, 6 vols., 1986-88; (with Vallasi) The Concise Columbia Encyclopedia, 2nd ed., 1989; (with Vallasi) The Columbia Encyclopedia, 5th ed., 1993; (assoc ed.) The Papers of Alexander Hamilton, edited by H.C. Syrett, Vols. 17-26, 1971-79. **Address:** Chernow Editorial Services Inc., 1133 Broadway, New York, NY 10010, U.S.A.

CHERNY, Andrei. American, b. 1975. **Genres:** Adult non-fiction. **Career:** U.S. Government, speechwriter for President Clinton, senior speechwriter for Vice President Gore; Democratic Party, platform director; California State Assembly, policy adviser to the Speaker of the State Assembly; New Democrat, contributing editor. **Publications:** The Next Deal: The Future of Public Life in the Information Age, 2000. **Address:** c/o Author Mail, Basic Books, 10 East 53rd Street 23rd floor, New York, NY 10022, U.S.A.

CHERNY, Robert W(allace). American, b. 1943. **Genres:** History, Biography. **Career:** San Francisco State University, CA, instructor, 1971-72, assistant professor, 1972-77, associate professor, 1977-81, professor of American history, 1981-, acting dean of School of Behavioral and Social Sciences, 1984-85; chair of history department, 1987-92; University of Nebraska, Lincoln, visiting associate professor, 1980, visiting professor, 1982; Moscow State University, Distinguished Fulbright Lecturer, 1996; University of Melbourne, visiting research scholar, 1997. **Publications:** Populism, Progressivism, and the Transformation of Nebraska Politics, 1885-1915, 1981; (with W. Issel) San Francisco: Presidio, Port, and Pacific Metropolis, 1981; A Righteous Cause: The Life of William Jennings Bryan, 1985; (with W. Issel) San Francisco, 1865-1932: Power, Politics, and Urban Development, 1986; (with C. Berkin, A. Brinkley, et al.) American Voices: A History of the United States, 1992; (with C. Berkin, C. Miller, J. Gormley) Making America: A History of the United States, 1995, 3rd ed., 2003; American Politics in the Gilded Age: 1868-1900, 1997; (ed. with W. Issel and K. Taylor) American Labor and the Cold War, 2004. **Address:** Department of History, San Francisco State University, 1600 Holloway Ave, San Francisco, CA 94132-4155, U.S.A. **Online address:** cherny@sfsu.edu

CHERNYKH, E(vgenij) N(ikolaevich). Russian, b. 1935. **Genres:** Archaeology/Antiquities, Engineering. **Career:** Russian Academy of Sciences, Moscow, scientist at Institute of Archaeology, 1958-72, professor of archaeology and head of the laboratory nature sciences in archaeology, 1972-. **Publications:** History of Ancient Metallurgy in Eastern Europe (in Russian), 1966; Ancient Mining and Metallurgy in Bulgaria (in Russian), 1978; Ancient Metallurgy in the USSR, 1992. Author of books in Russian on ancient metallurgy and mining in Eurasia. Contributor to scientific journals and popular magazines. **Address:** Institute of Archaeology, Russian Academy of Sciences, D. Ulyanova St. 19, 117036 Moscow, Russia. **Online address:** chernykh.e@g23.relcom.ru

CHERRILL, Jack. See PAXTON, John.

CHERRY, Bridget (Katherine). British, b. 1941. **Genres:** Architecture. **Career:** Architectural historian. Courtauld Institute, assistant librarian, 1964-68; Penguin, London, research assistant for "Buildings of England" series, 1968-83, editor 1983-. Member, English Heritage London advisory committee, 1985-, Historic Buildings advisory committee, 1986-, Royal Commission on Historical Monuments of England, 1987-94; commissioner, English Heritage, 1991-; trustee, Sir John Soane's Museum, 1995-. **Publications:** The Buildings of England, Ireland, Scotland, and Wales: A Short History and Bibliography (pamphlet), 1998. EDITOR BUILDINGS OF ENGLAND SERIES (by N. Pevsner): Surrey, 2nd ed, 1971; London 1: The Cities of London and Westminster, 1973; Wiltshire, 2nd ed, 1975; Hertfordshire, 2nd ed., 1977; London 2: South, 1983; London (contains London 1 and London 2), 1983; (with J. Newman) The Best Buildings of England, 1983; Devon, 1989; London 3: North West, rev ed, 1991; Northamptonshire, rev. ed, 1999; London 4: North, rev. ed, 1999. Editor, Buildings of Scotland, Ireland, and Wales series. Contributor of articles and reviews to architectural journals. **Address:** c/o Penguin Publicity, 80 Strand, London WC2R 0RL, England.

CHERRY, Charles Conrad. American, b. 1937. **Genres:** Theology/Religion. **Career:** Pennsylvania State University, University Park, professor of religious studies, 1964-81; Scholars Press, Atlanta, director, 1981-88; Indiana University, Indianapolis, distinguished professor of religious studies, 1988-2001, emeritus professor, 2001-. **Publications:** Theology of Jonathan Edwards, 1966; Nature and Religious Imagination, 1980; Religion on Campus, 2001. EDITOR: God's New Israel, 1970; Horace Bushnell, 1985; Religion, the Independent Sector, and American Culture; Hurrying toward Zion, 1995;.

CHERRY, Kelly. American. **Genres:** Novels, Novellas/Short stories, Poetry, Philosophy, Autobiography/Memoirs, Essays, Translations. **Career:** University of Wisconsin, Madison, professor of English and writer-in-residence, 1977-99, Evjue-Bascom Professor in the Humanities, 1993-99, Eudora Welty Professor of English, 1997-99, Eudora Welty Professor Emerita of English and Evjue-Bascom Professor Emerita in the Humanities, 1999-; University of Alabama in Huntsville, Humanities Center, Eminent Scholar, 1999-. Western Washington University, Bellingham, Visiting Professor, and Distinguished Visiting Writer, 1981; Rhodes College, Memphis, TN, Distinguished Visiting Professor, 1985; Hollins University, Wyndham Thompson Visiting Writer, 2000. **Publications:** (assoc. ed. and co-author) Lessons from Our Living Past, 1972, Teacher's Guide, 1972; Sick and Full of Burning, 1974; Lovers and Agnostics, 1975, rev. ed., 1995; Relativity, 1977, rev. ed., 2000; Augusta Played, 1979; Conversion, 1979; Songs for a Soviet Composer, 1980; In the Wink of an Eye, 1983; The Lost Traveller's Dream, 1984; Natural Theology, 1988; My Life and Dr. Joyce Brothers, 1990; The Exiled Heart, 1991; Benjamin John, 1993; God's Loud Hand, 1993; Time Out of Mind, 1994; Writing the World, 1995; Death and Transfiguration, 1997; The Society of Friends, 1999; The Poem, 1999; An Other Woman, 2000; Rising Venus, 2002; We Can Still Be Friends, 2003; Welsh Table Talk, 2004; History, Passion, Freedom, Death, and Hope: Prose about Poetry, 2005. Contributor to books.

CHERRYH, C. J. (Carolyn Janice Cherry). American, b. 1942. **Genres:** Science fiction/Fantasy. **Career:** Teacher of Latin and ancient history, Oklahoma City public schs., 1965-76. **Publications:** Brothers of Earth, 1976; Hunter of Worlds, 1977; The Faded Sun: Kesrith, 1977; The Faded Sun: Shon'Jir, 1978; Hestia, 1979; The Book of Morgaine, 1979 (trilogy: first published as Gates of Ivrel, 1976; Well of Shiuan, 1978; and Fires of Azeroth, 1979); The Faded Sun: Kutath, 1979; Serpent's Reach, 1980; Wave without a Shore, 1981; Ealdwood, 1981; Downbelow Station, 1981; Sunfall, 1981; Merchanter's Luck, 1982; The Port Eternity, 1982; The Pride of Chanur, 1982; The Tree of Swords and Jewels, 1983; The Dreamstone, 1983; Voyager in Night, 1984; Forty Thousand in Gehenna, 1984; Chanur's Venture, 1984; Cuckoo's Egg, 1985; The Kif Strikes Back, 1985; Angel with a Sword, 1985; Chanur's Homecoming, 1986; (with J. Morris) The Gates of Hell, 1986; (with J. Morris and L. Abbey) Soul of the City, 1986; (with J.

Morris) Kings in Hell, 1986; (ed.) Fever Season, 1987; (ed.) Festival Moon, 1987; The Faded Sun Trilogy, 1987; Glass and Amber, 1987; Legions of Hell, 1987; The Paladin, 1988; Exile's Gate, 1988; Cyteen, 1988; (ed.) Troubled Waters, 1988; (ed.) Smuggler's Gold, 1988; Rimrunners, 1989; Rusalka, 1989; (ed.) Divine Right, 1989; (ed.) O Flood Tide, 1990; Chernevog, 1990; Heavy Time, 1991; Endgame, 1991; Yvgenie, 1991; Hellburner, 1992; Chanur's Legacy, 1992; Goblin Mirror, 1993; Faery in Shadow, 1993; Foreigner, 1994; Tripoint, 1994; Rider at the Gate, 1995; Fortress in the Eye of Time, 1995; Invader, 1995; Cloud's Rider, 1996; Inheritor, 1996; Lois & Clark, 1996; Finity's End, 1997. **Address:** c/o Daw Books, 375 Hudson St., 3rd Fl., New York, NY 10014-3658, U.S.A.

CHERTOW, Marian R. American, b. 1955. **Genres:** Environmental sciences/Ecology. **Career:** Resource Recovery Systems, Inc., director of marketing and development, 1978-89; Town of Windsor, CT, assistant to the assistant town manager, 1983-86; Connecticut Resources Recovery Authority (bonding authority), Hartford, president, 1986-88; U.S. Conference of Mayors, Washington, DC, senior fellow, 1988-89; Yale University, New Haven, CT, director of industrial environmental management at School of Forestry and Environmental Studies, 1991-. **Publications:** Garbage Solutions: A Public Official's Guide to Recycling and Alternative Solid Waste Management Technologies, 1989; (ed. with D. Esty) Thinking Ecologically: The Next Generation of Environmental Policy, 1997. **Address:** School of Forestry and Environmental Studies, Yale University, 205 Prospect St, New Haven, CT 06511, U.S.A.

CHESEBROUGH, David B. See Obituaries.

CHESLER, Ellen. American, b. 1947. **Genres:** Women's studies and issues. **Career:** Open Society Institute, NY, senior fellow, currently; writer. **Publications:** Woman of Valor: Margaret Sanger and the Birth Control Movement in America, 1992. Contributor to periodicals. **Address:** Open Society Institute, 400 W 59th St, New York, NY 10019, U.S.A.

CHESMAN, Andrea. American, b. 1952. **Genres:** Food and Wine. **Career:** Free-lance writer and editor. **Publications:** (with P. Joan) Guide to Women's Publishing, 1978; Pickles and Relishes: One-Hundred-Fifty Recipes from Apples to Zucchini, 1983; Summer in a Jar: Making Pickles, Jams, and More, 1985; Salsas!, 1985; (with K. Scott) Sauces for Pasta!, 1990; Sun-Dried Tomatoes!, 1990; (with F. Raboff) The Great American Dessert Cookbook, 1990; Simply Healthful Pasta Salads, 1993; Simply Healthful Skillet Suppers, 1994; Salad Suppers, 1997; 366 Delicious Ways to Cook Rice, Beans, and Grains, 1998; Vegetarian Grill, 1998; The Roasted Vegetable, 2002; (with N.C. Ralston and M. Jordan) The Classic Zucchini Cookbook, 2002; (with F. Raboff) Mom's Best Desserts, 2002. **Address:** Box 185, Ripton, VT 05766, U.S.A. **Online address:** folkfood@sover.net

CHESNEY, Ann. See DUMMETT, (Agnes Margaret) Ann.

CHESNEY, Elizabeth Anne. See ZEGURA, Elizabeth Chesney.

CHESS, Richard. American, b. 1953. **Genres:** Poetry. **Career:** University of North Carolina, Charlotte, NC, lecturer, 1988-89; University of North Carolina, Asheville, NC, assistant professor of literature and language, 1989-; director of Creative Writing Program, 1989-; director of Center for Jewish Studies, 1989-. **Publications:** Tekiah: Poems by Richard Chess, 1994. Contributor of articles and essays to periodicals. **Address:** Department of Literature and Language, University of North Carolina at Asheville, Asheville, NC 28804, U.S.A. **Online address:** chess@bulldog.unca.edu

CHESTER, Mark (S.). American, b. 1945. **Genres:** Photography, Writing/Journalism. **Career:** American Society of Composers, Authors, and Publishers, New York, NY, director of photography and assistant director of public relations, 1970-72; freelance photographer and writer, 1972-. Work exhibited in galleries, institutions, and museums. **Publications:** (and photographer) No in America, 1986; (and photographer) Shanghai: In Black and White (exhibition catalog), 1987; Twosomes(photographs), 2004. Work featured in portfolios. Contributor of articles and photographs to books and periodicals. **Address:** Mark Chester Photography, PO Box 545, Woods Hole, MA 02543, U.S.A. **Online address:** info@markchesterphotography.com

CHESTER, Peter. See CHAMBERS, Peter.

CHESTER, Tessa Rose. Also writes as Rosi Re Beech. British, b. 1950. **Genres:** Poetry, Art/Art history, Bibliography, Illustrations. **Career:** Healer, poet, artist, and musician. Cambridge Central Library, Cambridge, England, assistant to divisional children's librarian, 1975-77; Bethnal Green Museum of Childhood, London, England, part-time employee, 1982-84, curator of Children's Book Collections, 1984-2001. Exhibitions of drawings and watercolors held under the pseudonym Donetta, in Cambridge, England, in the 1970s. **Publications:** (with J.I. Whalley) A History of Children's Book Illustration, 1988; Children's Books Research: A Practical Guide to Techniques and Sources, 1989; Sources of Information about Children's Books, 1989; Provisions of Light (poetry), 1996.

CHESTERS, Graham. British, b. 1944. **Genres:** Literary criticism and history, Education. **Career:** University College, Swansea, Tutor in French, 1969-70; Queen's University, Belfast, Lecturer in French, 1970-72; University of Hull, Lecturer, 1972-80, Senior Lecturer, 1980-88, Professor of French, 1988-, Computers in Teaching Initiative Centre for Modern Languages, Director, 1989-2000, Institute for Learning, Director, 1997-. **Publications:** Some Functions of Sound Repetition in Les Fleurs du Mal, 1975; (with P. Broome) The Appreciation of Modern French Poetry 1850-1950, 1976; Baudelaire and the Poetics of Craft, 1988; Baudelaire: Les Fleurs du Mal, 1995. EDITOR: (with P. Broome) An Anthology of Modern French Poetry 1850-1950, 1976; (with N. Gardner) The Use of Computers in the Teaching of Language and Languages, 1987; (with J. Thompson) Emancipation through Learning Technology, 1994. **Address:** Institute for Learning, University of Hull, Hull HU6 7RX, England.

CHETKOVICH, Carol A. American, b. 1948. **Genres:** Public/Social administration, Race relations, Sociology, Women's studies and issues. **Career:** Family Planning Alternatives, Sunnyvale, CA, vice-president and program director, 1972-85; Berkeley Planning Associates, Berkeley, CA, senior analyst and project director, 1987-89; University of California, Berkeley, instructor in public policy and in education, 1994-96, affiliated scholar with Beatrice M. Bain Research Group, 1994-95; Mills College, Oakland, CA, visiting assistant professor of government, 1996-97; Harvard University, Cambridge, MA, assistant/associate professor of public policy, 1997-. **Publications:** Real Heat: Gender and Race in the Urban Fire Service, 1997. Contributor to periodicals. **Address:** John F. Kennedy School of Government, Harvard University, 79 John F. Kennedy St, Cambridge, MA 02138, U.S.A. **Online address:** carol_chetkovich@harvard.edu

CHETWIN, Grace. American (born England). **Genres:** Mystery/Crime/Suspense, Horror, Science fiction/Fantasy, Children's fiction. **Career:** Full-time writer, 1983-. High sch. English and French teacher, Auckland New Zealand, 1958-62; High sch. English teacher and dept. head, Devon, England, 1962-63; Director, Modern Dance Group 1972-76, Auckland, 1972-76. **Publications:** On All Hallow's Eve, 1984; Out of the Dark World, 1985; The Atheling, 1988; Mr. Meredith and the Truly Remarkable Stone, 1989; Collidescope, 1990; Box and Cox, 1990; Child of the Air, 1991; Friends in Time, 1992; The Chimes of Alyafaleyn, 1993; Jason's Seven Magical Night Rides, 1994; Rufus, 1996; Briony's ABC of Abominable Children, 1997; Everychild and the Twelve Days of Christmas, 1997; Beauty and the Beast: A Retelling, 1998; Deathwindow, 1999; The Burning Tower, 2000; The Orborgon, 2000. TALES OF GOM IN THE LEGENDS OF ULM TETRALOGY: Gom on Windy Mountain, 1986; The Riddle and the Rune, 1987; The Crystal Stair, 1988; The Starstone, 1989. TALES OF ULM FROM HESTER'S HEARTH SERIES: Gerrad's Quest, 1998; THE LORDS OF AELYTH-KINTALYN: The Fall of Aelyth-Kintalyn 2002; The Foundling of Snawbyr Crygg 2003; Wycan 2004. **Address:** c/o Feral Press, Inc., 304 Strawberry Field Rd, Flat Rock, NC 28731, U.S.A. **Online address:** gchet@feralpressinc.com

CHEUSE, Alan. American, b. 1940. **Genres:** Novels, Literary criticism and history, Autobiography/Memoirs, Biography, Novellas/Short stories. **Career:** New Jersey Turnpike Authority, toll taker, 1961; Fairchild Publs., reporter, 1962-63; Kirkus Review Service, staff member, 1963-64; teacher of history and English, Guadalajara, Mexico, 1965-66; NYC Dept. of Welfare, caseworker, 1966-67; Bennington College, VT, member of Division of Literature and Languages, 1970-78, director of writing workshops, 1986-87; writer-in-residence, University of the South, Sewanee, TN, 1984, and University of Michigan, 1984-86; National Public Radio, book commentator, 1982-; George Mason University, Fairfax, VA, member of writing faculty, 1987-; The Sound of Writing, producer & host, 1991-97. **Publications:** (co-ed.) The Rarer Action: Essays in Honor of Francis Fergusson, 1971; Memories of the Future: A Critical Biography of Alejo Carpentier, 1974; Candace and Other Stories, 1980; The Bohemians: John Reed and His Friends Who Shook the World (novel), 1982; The Grandmother's Club (novel), 1986; Fall Out of Heaven: An Autobiographical Journey, 1987; The Light Possessed (novel), 1990; The Tennessee Waltz (stories), 1990; (co-ed.) The Sound of Writing, 1991; Listening to Ourselves, 1994; (ed. with N. Delbanco)

Talking Horse: Bernard Malamud on Life and Work, 1996; Lost and Old Rivers (stories), 1999; Listening to the Page (essays), 2001. **Address:** Dept. of English, George Mason University, 4400 University Dr, Fairfax, VA 22030, U.S.A.

CHEVALIER, Tracy. American, b. 1962. **Genres:** Novels. **Career:** Writer. **Publications:** NOVELS: The Virgin Blue, 1997; Girl with a Pearl Earring, 1999; Falling Angels, 2001; The Lady and the Unicorn, 2004. EDITOR: Twentieth-Century Children's Writers, 1989; Contemporary Poets, 5th ed., 1991; Contemporary World Writers, 1993; Encyclopedia of the Essay, 1997. **Address:** c/o Jonny Geller, Curtis Brown, Haymarket House, 28/29 Haymarket, London SWIY 4SP, England. **Online address:** tracy@tchevalier.com

CHEW, Allen F. American, b. 1924. **Genres:** History. **Career:** USAF intelligence officer, 1950-64; U.S. Air Force Academy, Colorado, associate professor of history, 1964-69; University of Wisconsin, Oshkosh, Dept. of History, professor and chairman, 1971-74; U.S. Army Command and General Staff College, Ft. Leavenworth, Kansas, research fellow and visiting associate professor, 1979-81. **Publications:** An Atlas of Russian History, 1967; The White Death: The Epic of the Soviet-Finnish Winter War, 1971; Fighting the Russians in Winter: Three Case Studies, 1981; Interregnum: Smoldering Embers from Russia's Troubled Past, 2002. **Address:** 18290 Spruce Rd, Monument, CO 80132-8210, U.S.A.

CHEYETTE, Bryan (Henry). British, b. 1959. **Genres:** Race relations, Literary criticism and history. **Career:** Spiro Institute, London, England, adult education lecturer, 1983-85; Hebrew University of Jerusalem, Jerusalem, Israel, research fellow, 1985-86; University of Leeds, Leeds, England, Montague Burton research fellow, 1986-89, British Academy fellow, 1989-92; University of London, Queen Mary and Westfield College, London, lecturer in English, 1992-, executive member of Centre for European Studies. Guest on television and radio programs. **Publications:** Constructions of "The Jew" in English Literature and Society Racial Representations, 1875-1945, 1993; (ed.) Between "Race" and Culture: Representations of "The Jew" in English and American Literature, 1995. Contributor to books. Contributor of articles and reviews to literature journals and newspapers. **Address:** School of English, Queen Mary and Westfield College, University of London, Mile End Rd., London E1 4NS, England.

CHIARELLA, Tom. American, b. 1961. **Genres:** Novellas/Short stories, Writing/Journalism. **Career:** DePauw University, Greencastle, IN, professor of English and head of department, 1988-. **Publications:** Foley's Luck (stories), 1992; Writing Dialogue (nonfiction), 1998. **Address:** Department of English, Asbury Hall, DePauw University, Greencastle, IN 46135, U.S.A. **Online address:** tchiarel@depauw.edu

CHIARELLO, Michael. American, b. 1962. **Genres:** Food and Wine. **Career:** Tra Vigne, St. Helena, CA, executive chef, 1986-2001. Napa Valley Kitchens, chairperson and culinary director, 1992-2001; Caffe Museo (San Francisco, CA), owner, 1994-; Ajax Tavern, owner, 1995-2001. **Publications:** (with P. Wisner) Flavored Oils, 1995; (with P. Wisner) Flavored Vinegars, 1996; (with P. Wisner)The Tra Vigne Cookbook, 1999; (with J. Fletcher) Napa Stories, 2001; Recipes from Michael Chiarello's Napa, 2001. **Address:** 801 Main St #B, St. Helena, CA 94574-2008, U.S.A. **Online address:** chefmc@napa.net

CHIBNALL, Marjorie McCallum. Also writes as Marjorie Morgan. British, b. 1915. **Genres:** History, Theology/Religion. **Career:** Fellow, Clare Hall, Cambridge, 1975- (Research Fellow, 1969-75). Assistant Lecturer, 1943-45, and Lecturer in History, 1945-47, University of Aberdeen; Lecturer in History and Fellow, Girton College, Cambridge, 1947-65; Fellow, British Academy, 1978. **Publications:** The English Lands of the Abbey of Bec, 1946, 1968; (with A.T. Gaydon) Victoria County History of Shropshire, vol. II, 1973; The World of Orderic Vitalis, 1984; Anglo-Norman England 1066-1166, 1986; The Empress Matilda, 1991; The Debate on the Norman Conquest, 1999; The Normans, 2000; Piety, Power and History in Medieval England and Normandy, 2000. EDITOR: Select Documents of the English Lands of the Abbey of Bec, 1951; (and trans.) The Historia Pontificalis of John Salisbury, 1956; (and trans.) The Ecclesiastical History of Orderic Vitalis, 6 vols., 1969-80; Anglo-Norman Studies, vols. 13-17, 1990-94; (and trans. with L. Watkiss) The Waltham Chronicle, 1994; (and trans. with R.H.C. Davis) The Gesta Guillelmi of William of Poitiers, 1998. **Address:** 7 Croftgate, Fulbrooke Rd, Cambridge CB3 9EG, England.

CHICHESTER CLARK, Emma. British, b. 1955. **Genres:** Children's fiction, Illustrations. **Career:** Illustrator and author of children's books, 1983-. Visiting lecturer at Middlesex Polytechnic and City and Guilds School of

Art, 1984-86. **Publications:** SELF-ILLUSTRATED FOR CHILDREN: Catch That Hat!, 1988; The Story of Horrible Hilda and Henry, 1988; Myrtle, Tertle, and Gertle, 1989; The Bouncing Dinosaur, 1990; I Never Saw a Purple Cow and Other Nonsense Rhymes, 1990; Tea with Aunt Augusta, 1991, in US as Lunch with Aunt Augusta, 1992; Across the Blue Mountains, 1993; Miss Bilberry's New House, 1994; Little Miss Muffet's Count-Along Surprise, 1997; I Love You, Blue Kangaroo!, 1999; More!, 1999; No More Kissing!, 2002; Follow the Leader!, 2003. Illustrator of books by others including: R. Dahl, P. Dickinson, D.J. Enright, J. Falloon, B. Frankel, G. Pollinger, M. Price, J. Reeves. **Address:** 3 Inglethorpe St, London SW6 6NS, England.

CHICK, Jean M. *See* **SNOOK, Jean M(cGregor).**

CHIFFOLO, Anthony F. American, b. 1959. **Genres:** Inspirational/Motivational Literature. **Career:** Praeger Publishers, Westport, CT, managing editor and acquisitions editor. **Publications:** Be Mindful of Us: Prayers to the Saints, 2000; One Hundred Names of Mary: Stories and Prayers, 2002; Advent and Christmas with the Saints, 2003; We Thank You, God for These, 2003. COMPILER & EDITOR: At Prayer with the Saints, 1997; In My Own Words: Pope John Paul II, 1998; In My Own Words: Pope John XXIII, 1999; Padre Pio: In My Own Words, 2000; (with T.J. Borchard) An Hour with . **Address:** c/o Author Mail, St. Anthony Messenger Press, 28 W Liberty St, Cincinnati, OH 45210, U.S.A.

CHILCOTE, Ronald H. American, b. 1935. **Genres:** Economics, Politics/Government. **Career:** University of California at Riverside, joined faculty, 1963, professor of political science, 1975-90, professor of political science and economics, 1990-. **Publications:** The Brasilian Communist Party: Conflict and Integration, 1922-1972, 1973; (with J. Edelstein) Latin America: The Struggle with Dependency and Beyond, 1974; Theories of Comparative Politics: The Search for a Paradigm, 1981, 2nd ed., 1994; Theories of Development and Underdevelopment, 1984; (with J. Edelstein) Latin America: Capitalist and Socialist Perspectives of Development and Underdevelopment, 1986; Power and the Ruling Classes in Northeast Brazil, 1990; Theories of Comparative Political Economy, 2000; The Political Economy of Imperialism, 2000. **Address:** Dept. of Economics, University of California at Riverside, Riverside, CA 92521, U.S.A.

CHILD, Julia. *See* Obituaries.

CHILD, Lincoln B. American, b. 1957. **Genres:** Novels. **Career:** St. Martin's Press, NYC, editor, 1979-88; Metropolitan Life Insurance Co., analyst, 1988-95; freelance writer, 1995-. **Publications:** NOVELS (with Douglas Preston): Relic, 1995; Mount Dragon, 1996; Reliquary, 1997; Riptide, 1998; Thunderhead, 1999; Ice Limit, 2000; Still Life with Crows, 2003. EDITOR: Dark Company: The Ten Greatest Ghost Stories, 1983; Dark Banquet: A Feast of Twelve Great Ghost Stories, 1985; Tales of the Dark, 1987; Tales of the Dark Two, 1987; Tales of the Dark Three, 1988. **Address:** PO Box 162, Convent Station, NJ 07961, U.S.A. **Online address:** lchild@ prestonchild.com

CHILDER, Simon Ian. *See* **BROSNAN, John.**

CHILDRESS, Mark. American, b. 1957. **Genres:** Novels, Children's fiction. **Career:** Full-time novelist since 1985. Staff writer, The Birmingham News, Alabama, 1977-80; Features Ed., Southern Living mag., Birmingham, Alabama, 1980-84; Regional Ed., The Atlanta Journal and Constitution, Georgia, 1984-85. **Publications:** A World Made of Fire, 1984; V for Victor, 1988; Tender, 1990; Crazy in Alabama, 1993; Joshua's Big Tooth, 1992; Joshua & the Big Bad Blue Crabs, 1995; Henry Bobbity Is Missing and It Is All Billy Bobbity's Fault, 1996. **Address:** c/o Wendy Weil Agency, 232 Madison Ave., New York, NY 10016, U.S.A.

CHILDS, Christopher. American, b. 1949. **Genres:** Environmental sciences/Ecology, Inspirational/Motivational Literature. **Career:** Writer, lecturer, and activist. Middlesex School, Concord, MA, English teacher and coach of skiing, soccer, and crew, 1970-73; actor, director, and designer for television, film, and stage productions, 1972-; Massachusetts Council on the Arts and Humanities, Theatre Advisory Panel, member, 1977-80, chair, 1981; American Premiere Stage, Boston, MA, member of the board of directors, 1980-82; Environmental Testing Service, Waltham, MA, technician, 1987; Greenpeace, Washington, DC, canvasser and campaigner for Boston, MA office, 1987-88, national speaker from Boston, MA office, 1988-92, national speaker from Los Angeles, CA office 1992-96; affiliated with the New Eden Foundation, Topanga, CA, 1996-98. **Publications:** (ed.) Clear Sky, Pure Light: Encounters with Henry David Thoreau, 1979; The Spirit's Terrain:

Creativity, Activism, and Transformation, 1998. Contributor of essays, theater reviews, and photographs to periodicals and the Internet. **Address:** 384 Hall Ave, St. Paul, MN 55107, U.S.A. **Online address:** worldgarden@igc.org; home.igc.org/~worldgarden

CHILDS, Craig. American, b. 1967. **Genres:** Literary criticism and history. **Career:** River guide, 1986-. Worked as editor, writer, photographer, and mechanic for Colorado newspapers, including Ouray County Plaindealer and Ridgeway Sun, 1990-92. **Publications:** Stone Desert: A Naturalist's Exploration of Canyonlands National Park, 1995; Crossing Paths: Uncommon Encounters with Animals in the Wild, 1997. **Address:** PO Box 112, Crawford, CO 81415, U.S.A.

CHILDS, David (Haslam). British, b. 1933. **Genres:** Area studies, History, International relations/Current affairs, Politics/Government, Reference. **Career:** University of Nottingham, lecturer, 1966-71, senior lecturer, 1971-76, reader, 1976-89, director of Institute of German, Austrian, and Swiss Affairs, 1986-92, professor of German politics, 1989-. **Publications:** From Schumacher to Brandt, 1966; East Germany, 1969; Germany since 1918, 2nd ed., 1980; Marx and the Marxists, 1973; Britain since 1945, 1979, 5th ed., 2001; (with J. Johnson) West Germany: Politics and Society, 1981; The GDR: Moscow's German Ally, 1983, rev. ed., 1988; East Germany to the 1990s, 1987; Germany on the Road to Unity, 1990; Germany in the 20th Century, 1991; Britain since 1939: Progress and Decline, 1995, 2nd ed., 2002; (with R. Popplewell) The Stasi: The East German Intelligence and Security System, 1996, 2nd ed., 2000; The Two Red Flags: European Social Democracy and Soviet Communism, 2000; The Fall of the GDR: Germany's Road to Unity, 2001. EDITOR/CO-EDITOR: The Changing Face of Western Communism, 1980; Honecker's Germany, 1985; East Germany in Comparative Perspective, 1989; Children in War, 1990. Contributor to books. **Address:** 1 Grange Park, West Bridgford, Nottingham NG2 6HW, England. **Online address:** david@jcit.co.uk

CHILDS, Elizabeth C(atharine). American, b. 1954. **Genres:** Art/Art history. **Career:** State University of New York College at Purchase, lecturer, 1987-89, assistant professor of art history, 1989-92; Princeton University, Princeton, NJ, Gould fellow in art and archaeology, 1992-93; Washington University, St. Louis, MO, assistant professor, 1992-98, associate professor of art history, 1998-. Metropolitan Museum of Art, lecturer and program assistant in museum education, 1976-81; National Gallery of Scotland, educational consultant, 1977-78; Museum of Modern Art, museum lecturer, 1979; National Gallery of Art, summer intern, 1980; Solomon R. Guggenheim Museum, curatorial consultant, 1984-85, research associate, 1987-91. Guest lecturer at colleges and universities. **Publications:** (with L. Flint) The Handbook of the Peggy Guggenheim Collection, Solomon R. Guggenheim Foundation, 1986; Daumier and Exoticism: Satirizing the French and the Foreign, 2004. EDITOR: (and author of intro.) Louis Provost, Honoré Daumier: A Thematic Index to the Oeuvre, 1989; Suspended License: Censorship and the Visual Arts, 1997. Contributor to art and art history journals. **Address:** Dept of Art History and Archaeology, Campus Box 1189, Washington University, 1 Brookings Dr, St. Louis, MO 63130, U.S.A.

CHILDS, Michael J. Canadian, b. 1956. **Genres:** History. **Career:** University of Lethbridge, Lethbridge, Alberta, Canada, assistant professor of history, 1987-88; Bishop's University, Lennoxville, Quebec, Canada, assistant professor, 1988-92, associate professor of history, 1992-. **Publications:** Labour's Apprentices, 1992. **Address:** Department of History, Bishop's University, Lennoxville, QC, Canada J1M 1Z7.

CHILSON, Peter. (born United States), b. 1961. **Genres:** Education. **Career:** Essayist, journalist, and educator. Peace Corps volunteer, Niger, Africa, 1985-87; Associated Press, freelance reporter, West Africa; High Country News, Paonia, CO, associate editor, 1997-98; Washington State University, Pullman, assistant professor of English, 1998-. **Publications:** Riding the Demon (nonfiction), 1999. Also author of short fiction, essays, and reports for several magazines and newspapers. **Address:** Department of English, Washington State University, Pullman, WA 99164, U.S.A. **Online address:** pchilson@mail.wsu.edu

CHILSON, Robert. American, b. 1945. **Genres:** Science fiction/Fantasy. **Career:** Freelance writer, since 1967. **Publications:** As the Curtain Falls, 1974; The Star-Crowned Kings, 1975; The Shores of Kansas, 1976; Refuge, 1988; Men Like Rats, 1989; Rounded with Sleep, 1990; Black as Blood, 1998. **Address:** PO Box 12583, Kansas City, KS 66112-0583, U.S.A.

CHILTON, Bruce. American, b. 1949. **Genres:** Theology/Religion. **Career:** Sheffield University, England, lecturer in biblical studies, 1976-85; Yale

University, New Haven, CT, Lillian Claus Professor of the New Testament, 1985-87; Bard College, Annandale, NY, Bernard Iddings Professor of Religion, 1987-. Church of St. John the Evangelist, rector, 1987-; Institute of Advanced Theology, executive director, 2000-. **Publications:** The Glory of Israel, 1983; A Galilean Rabbi and His Bible, 1984; Targumic Approaches to the Gospels (essays), 1986; (trans. & author of intro. & notes) The Isaiah Targum, 1987; Beginning New Testament Study, 1986; (with J.I.H. McDonald) Jesus and the Ethics of the Kingdom, 1988; Profiles of a Rabbi, 1989; The Temple of Jesus, 1992; A Feast of Meanings, 1994; Judaic Approaches to the Gospel, 1994; (with J. Neusner) Judaism in the New Testament, 1995; (with Neusner) Revelation: The Torah and the Bible, 1995; Pure Kingdom: Jesus' Vision of God, 1996; (with Neusner) The Body of Faith: Israel and the Church, 1996; (with Neusner) Trading Places: The Intersecting Histories of Judaism and Christianity, 1996; (with Neusner) The Intellectual Foundations of Christian and Jewish Discourse, 1997; Jesus' Prayer and Jesus' Eucharist, 1997; Rabbi Jesus: An Intimate Biography, 2000; Redeeming Time, 2002; (with Neusner and W. Graham) Three Faiths, One God, 2003; Rabbi Paul: An Intellectual Biography, 2004. EDITOR: (and author of intro.) The Kingdom of God in the Teaching of Jesus, 1984; (with C.A. Evans) Studying the Historical Jesus, 1994; (with Neusner) Trading Places Sourcebook, 1997. **Address:** Bard College, Annandale, NY 12504, U.S.A. **Online address:** Chilton@Bard.edu.

CHIN, Justin. Malaysian, b. 1969. **Genres:** Poetry. **Career:** Poet, writer, and performance artist. **Publications:** Bite Hard, 1997; Mongrel: Essays, Diatribe, and Pranks, 1999; Harmless Medicine (poetry), 2001; Burden of Ashes, 2002. Contributor of poetry, prose, and journalism to journals. **Address:** c/o Author Mail, Manic D Press, Box 410804, San Francisco, CA 94141, U.S.A.

CHINEN, Nate. (born United States). **Genres:** Autobiography/Memoirs. **Career:** Writer, editor, poet, music critic, musician. Music reporter for City Paper, Philadelphia, PA, and Billboard Online. Cofounder, Virgin House Band. **Publications:** (with George Wein) Myself among Others: A Life in Music, 2003. Contributor to magazines. **Address:** c/o Author Mail, Da Capo Press, 387 Park Avenue, 12th Floor, New York, NY 10016, U.S.A.

CHINERY, Michael. British, b. 1938. **Genres:** Biology, Natural history, Zoology. **Career:** Freelance writer, 1964-. **Publications:** Pictorial Dictionary of the Animal World, 1966; (with M. Gabb) Human Kind, 1966; (with M. Gabb) The World of Plants, 1966; (with D. Larkin) Patterns of Living, 1966; (with M. Gabb) The Life of Animals with Backbones, 1966; (with M. Gabb) The Life of Animals without Backbones, 1966; Breeding and Growing, 1966; Pictorial Dictionary of the Plant World, 1967; Visual Biology, 1968; Purnell's Concise Encyclopedia of Nature, 1971; Animal Communities, 1972; Animals in the Zoo, 1973; Field Guide to the Insects of Britain and Northern Europe, 1973; Life in the Zoo, 1976; The Natural History of the Garden, 1977; The Family Naturalist, 1977; Nature All Around, 1978; Discovering Animals, 1978; Killers of the Wild, 1979; (with M. Pledger) Garden Birds, 1979; Collins Gem Guide to Butterflies and Moths, 1981; The Natural History of Britain and Europe, 1982; Collins Guide to the Insects of Britain and Western Europe, 1986; Garden Creepy Crawlies, 1986; The Living Garden, 1986; Collins Gem Guide to Insects, 1986; Exploring the Countryside, 1987; New Generation Guide to the Butterflies and Day-Flying Moths of Britain and Europe, 1989; Countryside Handbook, 1990; Spiders, 1993; How Bees Make Honey, 1996; Secrets of the Rain Forest series: Plants and Plant Eaters, Predators and Prey, Poisoners and Pretenders, Partners and Parents; Resources and Conservation, People and Places. **Address:** Mousehole, Mill Road, Hundon, Suffolk CO10 8EG, England.

CHIN-LEE, Cynthia D. American, b. 1958. **Genres:** Business/Trade/Industry, Children's non-fiction, How-to books. **Career:** Freelance writer and consultant in technical writing, 1983-. De Anza College, instructor, 1984-89; Santa Clara University, adjunct lecturer, 1988-92; professional speaker, 1991-. **Publications:** FOR CHILDREN: Almond Cookies and Dragon Well Tea, 1993; A Is for Asia, 1997; (with T. de la Pena) A Is for the Americas, 1999; Amelia to Zora, forthcoming. FOR ADULTS: It's Who You Know: Career Strategies for Making Effective Personal Contacts, 1991; It's Who You Know: The Magic of Networking, in Person and on the Internet, 1998. **Address:** 666 Wildwood Ln, Palo Alto, CA 94303-3116, U.S.A. **Online address:** cynthia_chin-lee@post.harvard.edu

CHINN, Carl. British, b. 1956. **Genres:** History, Local history/Rural topics. **Career:** Bookmaker (bet taker) in Birmingham, England, 1980-84; University of Birmingham, Birmingham, lecturer in modern history and community historian, 1991-. Presenter of a weekly radio show broadcast by BBC-West Midland. **Publications:** They Worked All Their Lives: Women of the Urban Poor in England, 1880-1939, 1988; Better Betting with a Decent Feller: Bookmakers, Betting, and the British Working Class, 1750-1900, 1991; Homes for People: One Hundred Years of Council Housing in Birmingham, 1991; Birmingham: The Great Working City, 1994; Poverty Amidst Prosperity: The Urban Poor in England, 1834-1914, 1995; The Cadbury Story: A Short History of Cadbury, 1998. Columnist for a local Birmingham newspaper. Contributor to books and periodicals. **Address:** Department of Modern History, University of Birmingham, Birmingham B15 2TT, England.

CHINODYA, Shimmer. Also writes as B. S. Chiraska. Zimbabwean, b. 1957. **Genres:** Novels, Novellas/Short stories, Children's fiction, Plays/Screenplays, Poetry. **Career:** Curriculum Development Unit, Harare, Zimbabwe, editor in chief, 1983-. Zimbabwe Book Development Council, member of board of directors. **Publications:** Dew in the Morning, 1982; Farai's Girls, 1984; (ed.) Classroom Plays for Primary Schools, 1986; Harvest of Thorns, 1989; Traditional Tales of Zimbabwe, Books 1-6, 1989; (ed.) Poems for Primary Schools, 1990; Can We Talk and Other Stories, 1998. Author of educational and children's books, some under the name B. S. Chiraska. **Address:** 29 Lorraine Dr, Bluff Hill, Harare, Zimbabwe.

CHIOCCA, Olindo Romeo. Canadian, b. 1959. **Genres:** Food and Wine. **Career:** Writer. **Publications:** Dinner wit da Dons (cookbook), 1999; Mobsters and Thugs (nonfiction), 2000. **Address:** 4323 Stanley St., Nelson, BC, Canada V1L 1P9. **Online address:** mata_hari@uniserve.com

CHIPMAN, Bruce Lewis. American, b. 1946. **Genres:** Film, Social commentary. **Career:** Tufts University, Medford, MA, instructor of English, 1969-73; Tatnall School, Wilmington, DE, head of English Dept. and teacher of literature and writing, 1973-; University of Delaware, lecturer in English, 1977-. Fulbright Lectureship, University of Khartoum, Sudan, Africa, 1983. **Publications:** Hardening Rock, 1972; Hollywood: America's Dream-Dump, 1981; Into America's DreamDump, 1999. **Address:** 39 Tenby Chase Dr, Newark, DE 19711, U.S.A.

CHIPMAN, Donald. American, b. 1928. **Genres:** History. **Career:** University of North Texas, Denton, Associate Professor, 1964-67, Professor of History, 1967-. Handbook of Latin American Studies, contributing editor of History General Section; Locus: Regional and Local History of the Americas, co-editor, currently. **Publications:** Nuno de Guzman and the Province of Panuco in New Spain 1518-1533, 1967; (co-author) Dallas Cowboys and the NFL, 1970; Spanish Texas, 1519-1821, 1992; Texas en la Epoca Colonial, 1992; (co-author) Notable Men and Women of Spanish Texas, 1999; (co-author) Explorers and Settlers of Spanish Texas, 2001. **Address:** Dept. of History, University of North Texas, Denton, TX 76203, U.S.A. **Online address:** dchipman@unt.edu

CHIRA, Susan. American. **Genres:** Women's studies and issues. **Career:** New York Times, deputy foreign editor. **Publications:** A Mother's Place: Taking the Debate About Working Mothers Beyond Guilt and Shame, 1998. **Address:** c/o HarperCollins, Authors Mail 7th floor, 10 E. 53rd St., New York, NY 10022, U.S.A.

CHIRAS, Daniel D. American, b. 1950. **Genres:** Environmental sciences/Ecology. **Career:** Free-lance writer, 1980-. Adjunct professor, University of Denver and University of Colorado. Colorado Environmental Coalition, member of board of directors, 1987-90, head of Environmental Health Committee, 1988-93, president, 1990-92; Speakers for a Sustainable Future, co-founder, 1989, member of advisory board, 1989-; Colorado's Ocean Journey, member of scientific advisory board, 1991; Center for Environmental Solutions, member of board of directors, 1993-; Sustainable Futures Society, co-founder, 1993, president and director of sustainable development and policy analysis, 1993-. **Publications:** Environmental Science: Action for a Sustainable Future, 1985, 6th ed., 2001; Environmental Science: A Framework for Decision Making, 1989; (with O.S. Owen) Natural Resource Conservation, 5th ed., 1990, 8th ed., 2002; Beyond the Fray, 1990; Human Biology, 1991, 4th ed., 2002; Lessons from Nature, 1992; Biology: The Web of Life, 1993; Study Skills for Science Students, 1994; (ed.) Regional Issues: Supplement to Environmental Science, 1994; Voices for the Earth, 1995; The Natural House, 2000. Contributor to scientific journals and newspapers. **Address:** 9124 S. Armadillo Trl, Evergreen, CO 80439-6210, U.S.A. **Online address:** danchiras@uswest.net

CHIRASKA, B. S. See **CHINODYA, Shimmer.**

CHIROT, Daniel. American (born France), b. 1942. **Genres:** History, Politics/Government, Sociology. **Career:** University of Washington, Seattle, professor of international studies, 1975-. **Publications:** Social Change in a

Peripheral Society, 1976; Social Change in the Twentieth Century, 1977; Social Change in the Modern Era, 1986; Modern Tyrants, 1994; How Societies Change, 1994. EDITOR: The Origins of Backwardness in Eastern Europe, 1989; The Crisis of Leninism and the Decline of the Left, 1991; (co) Essential Outsiders, 1997; (co) Ethnopolitical Warfare, 2001. **Address:** Jackson School, Box 353650, University of Washington, Seattle, WA 98195, U.S.A.

CHISHOLM, Clive Scott. (born Canada), b. 1936. **Genres:** Autobiography/ Memoirs. **Career:** Writer. Utah State University, former associate professor and head of department of communication. **Publications:** Following the Wrong God Home: Footloose in an American Dream, 2003. Contributor to literary journals. **Address:** c/o Author Mail, University of Oklahoma Press, 1005 Asp Avenue, Norman, OK 73019, U.S.A.

CHISHOLM, Michael. British, b. 1931. **Genres:** Economics, Geography, Politics/Government. **Career:** Oxford University, Departmental Demonstrator in Agricultural Economics, 1954-59; University of London, Bedford College, Assistant Lecturer and Lecturer in Geography, 1960-64; University of Bristol, Lecturer to Reader, 1965-72, and Professor of Economic and Social Geography, 1972-76; University of Cambridge, Professor of Geography, 1976-96, Emeritus Professor, 1996-. Member, Social Science Research Council, 1967-72, Local Government Boundary Commission for England, 1971-78, and Rural Development Commission, 1981-90; Member, Local Government Commission for England, 1992-95. **Publications:** Rural Settlement and Land Use: An Essay in Location, 1962, 3rd ed., 1979; Geography and Economics, 1966, rev. ed. 1970; Research in Human Geography, 1971; (with P. O'Sullivan) Freight Flows and Spatial Aspects of the British Economy, 1973; (with J. Oeppen) The Changing Pattern of Employment: Regional Specialisation and Industrial Localisation in Britain, 1973; Human Geography: Evolution or Revolution?, 1975; Modern World Development: A Geographical Perspective, 1982; Regions in Recession and Resurgence, 1990; Britain on the Edge of Europe, 1995; Structural Reform of British Local Government: Rhetoric and Reality, 2000. EDITOR: (with A.E. Frey and P. Haggett) Regional Forecasting, 1971; Resources for Britain's Future, 1972; (with B. Rodgers) Studies in Human Geography, 1973; (co) Processes in Physical and Human Geography, 1975; (with D. Smith) Shared Space, Divided Space, 1990. **Address:** Dept. of Geography, Downing Place, Cambridge CB2 3EN, England.

CHISSELL, Joan Olive. British, b. 1919. **Genres:** Music. **Career:** Regular Broadcaster for BBC, and Reviewer for the Gramophone. Jury member at many international piano competitions. Lecturer, Extra-Mural Depts. of Oxford and London Univs., 1943-48; Piano Teacher, Jr. Special Talent Dept., Royal College of Music, London, 1943-53; Assistant Music Critic, The Times, London, 1948-84; City of Zwickau, Robert Schumann Prize, 1991. **Publications:** Schumann, 1948; (co-author) The Music of Britten, 1952; Chopin, 1965; Schumann's Piano Music, 1972; Brahms, 1977; Clara Schumann, A Dedicated Spirit, 1983; (co-author) A Companion to the Concerto, 1988. **Address:** 7 Abbey Rd, Flat D, St Johns Wood, London NW8 9AA, England.

CHITHAM, Edward. British, b. 1932. **Genres:** Children's fiction, History, Literary criticism and history, Biography, Education. **Career:** Education Consultant, National Association for Gifted Children, 1988-. Sr. Lecturer, Faculty of Education, The Polytechnic, Wolverhampton, 1977-88. Part-time Tutor, The Open University, 1970-, and Assistant Staff Tutor, 1991-. Master in charge of Latin, 1956-61, and Head of Library Dept., 1961-67, Rowley Regis Grammar School; Sr. Lecturer in English, Dudley College of Education, 1973-77. **Publications:** The Black Country, 1972; Ghost in the Water, 1973; The Poems of Anne Brontë, 1979; Brontë Facts and Brontë Problems, 1984; (with T. Winnifrith) The Brontës' Irish Background, 1985; A Life of Emily Brontë, 1987; (with T. Winnifrith) Literary Lives: Charlotte and Emily Brontë, 1989; A Life of Anne Brontë, 1990; A Bright Start, 1995; (with D. Roper) The Poems of Emily Brontë, 1996. **Address:** 11 Victoria Rd., Harborne, Birmingham B17 0AG, England.

CHITWOOD, Michael. American, b. 1958. **Genres:** Poetry, Documentaries/ Reportage. **Career:** Writer, poet, and journalist. Independent Weekly, Chapel Hill, NC, columnist, 1995-98; WUNC radio, Chapel Hill, NC, commentator, 1995-. Worked in maintenance at a fabric mill. **Publications:** Salt Works: Poems, 1992; Whet: Poems, 1995; The Weave Room, 1997; Hitting Below the Bible Belt: Blood Kin, Baptist Voodoo, Grandma's Teeth and Other Stories from the South, 1998. Contributor of poems, essays, and stories to national publications. **Address:** c/o Down Home Press, PO Box 4126, Asheboro, NC 27204, U.S.A.

CHIU, Hungdah. Chinese/Taiwanese, b. 1936. **Genres:** History, International relations/Current affairs, Law. **Career:** Professor of Law, University of Maryland School of Law, Baltimore, since 1977 (Associate Professor, 1974-77). Ed.-in-chief, Chinese Yearbook of International Law and Affairs, vols. 1-13, 1981-96. Associate Professor of International Law, National Taiwan University, 1965-66; Research Associate in Law, Harvard Law School, Cambridge, Massachusetts, 1966-70, and 1972-74; Professor of Law, National Chengchi University, Taipei, Taiwan, 1970-72. **Publications:** The Capacity of International Organization to Conclude Treaties, 1966; A Calendar, 1968; The People's Republic of China and the Law of Treaties, 1972; (with J.A. Cohen) People's China and International Law: A Documentary Study, 2 vols., 1974; Agreements of the People's Republic of China: A Calendar of Events, 1966-80, 1981; (with S. Leng) Criminal Justice in Post-Mao China, 1985; Hsien-tai Kur-chi-fa (Modern International Law) (in Chinese), 1995; (with G. Knight) International Law of the Sea: Cases, Documents and Readings, 1991; Hsien-tai-Kuo-Chi-fa Tsan-k'ao Wen-chien (Reference Documents of Modern International Law), 1996. EDITOR: (with D.M. Johnston) Agreements of the People's Republic of China, 1949-1967; (and contrib. with S. Leng) Law in Chinese Foreign Policy, 1972; (and contrib.) China and the Question of Taiwan: Documents and Analysis, 1973; (with D. Simon) Legal Aspects of U.S.-Republic of China Trade and Investment, 1977; Normalizing Relations with the People's Republic of China: Problems, Analysis and Documents, 1978; (and contrib.) China and the Taiwan Issue, 1979; (with K. Murphy) The Chinese Connection and Normalization, 1980; (with R. Downen) Multi-System Nations and International Law, 1981; (and contrib. with S. Leng) China, 70 Years After the 1911 Hsin-hai Revolution, 1984; (co-) The Future of Hong Kong: Toward 1997 and Beyond, 1987; (and contrib.) The Draft Basic Law of Hong Kong: Analysis and Documents, 1988. **Address:** University of Maryland School of Law, 500 West Baltimore St, Baltimore, MD 21201, U.S.A.

CHIVIAN, Eric. American, b. 1942. **Genres:** Medicine/Health. **Career:** Massachusetts Institute of Technology, Cambridge, staff psychiatrist, 1980-2000; Harvard Medical School, assistant clinical professor, 1988-, director, Center for Health and the Global Environment, 1996-. **Publications:** Last Aid: The Medical Dimensions of Nuclear War, 1982; (ed.) Critical Condition: Human Health and the Environment, 1993. **Address:** Center for Health and the Global Environment, Harvard Medical School, 260 Longwood Ave, Boston, MA 02115, U.S.A. **Online address:** eric_chivian@hms.harvard.edu

CHIZMAR, Richard T(homas). American, b. 1965. **Genres:** Adult nonfiction. **Career:** Cemetery Dance Publications, Forest Hill, MD, founder, editor-in-chief, and publisher, 1988-. **Publications:** Midnight Promises (short stories), 1996; Also author of over fifty published short stories. EDITOR: Cold Blood, 1991; The Earth Strikes Back: New Tales of Ecological Horror, 1994; Thrillers, 1994; Screamplays, 1997; Monsters and Other Stories, 1998; (with William Schafer) Subterranean Gallery, 1999; (with Robert Morrish) October Dreams: A Celebration of Halloween, 2000; The Best of Cemetery Dance, 2001; Night Visions 10, 2001; Trick or Treat: A Collection of Halloween Novellas, 2001; Shivers, 2002; Shivers II, 2003; (with Matt Schwartz) Shocklines: Fresh Voices in Terror, 2004; Cemetery Dance-A Fifteen Year Celebration, 2004. **Address:** c/o Author Mail, Cemetery Dance Publications, 132-B Industry Lane, Unit 7, Forest Hill, MD 21050, U.S.A. **Online address:** info@cemeterydance.com

CHMIELEWSKI, Wendy E. British, b. 1955. **Genres:** Women's studies and issues, History. **Career:** Swarthmore College, Swarthmore, PA, project editor for Peace Collection, 1986-87, archivist, 1987-88, George R. Cooley Curator, 1988-, lecturer in peace studies, 1991-. **Publications:** EDITOR: Guide to Sources on Women in the Swarthmore College Peace Collection, 1988; (with M.K. Hartzel and L. Kern, and contrib.) Women in Spiritual and Communitarian Societies in the United States, 1992. Work represented in anthologies. Contributor to academic journals. **Address:** Swarthmore College Peace Collection, 500 College Ave., Swarthmore, PA 19081-1399, U.S.A. **Online address:** wchmiel1@swarthmore.edu

CHOATE, Jean (Marie). American, b. 1935. **Genres:** History. **Career:** Northern Michigan University, Marquette, assistant professor, 1992-99; Coastal Georgia Community College, Brunswick, professor of history, 1999-. **Publications:** Disputed Ground: Farm Groups That Opposed the New Deal Agricultural Program, 2002; Eliza Johnson, Unknown First Lady, 2004. **Address:** Dept of General Studies, Coastal Georgia Community College, Brunswick, GA 31520, U.S.A. **Online address:** jchoate@cgcc.edu

CHOCIOLKO, Christina. Canadian, b. 1958. **Genres:** Ethics. **Career:** Transport Canada, Western Region, Edmonton, Alberta, radio operator in Calgary, Alberta, and Hay River, Northwest Territories, 1977-78; Arctic Exploration Services Ltd., Tuktoyaktuk, Northwest Territories, senior radio operator, 1979-83; MacDonald Dettwiler and Associates Ltd., Richmond,

British Columbia, hardware technologist for electro-optical products, 1984-85; British Columbia Institute of Technology, Burnaby, assistant instructor in microelectronics, 1985-86; University of British Columbia, Vancouver, research assistant in international relations, 1989; Simon Fraser University at Harbour Centre, Vancouver, research director at Centre for Policy Research on Science and Technology, 1990-94; Queen's University, Kingston, Ontario, research associate in environmental policies, 1994-, instructor in policy studies, 1995. **Publications:** (with W. Leiss) Risk and Responsibility, 1994. Contributor to periodicals. **Address:** 2910 Quebec St., Apt. 246, Vancouver, BC, Canada V5T 4P7.

CHOCOLATE, Debbi. (Deborah M. Newton Chocolate). American, b. 1954. **Genres:** Children's fiction, Children's non-fiction. **Career:** Writer. Riverside Publishing Co., Chicago, IL, editor, 1978-90; Triton College, River Grove, IL, English instructor, 1990-92. Oak Park Public Schools, writing workshop leader at Youth Author's Conference, 1985-95; AYA African Arts Festival, storyteller, 1990, 1991. Affiliated with Illinois Young Author's Conference hosted by the Illinois State Board of Education, 1992, 1995, 1997. **Publications:** NEATE to the Rescue!, 1992; Elizabeth's Wish, 1994; On the Day I Was Born, 1995; A Very Special Kwanzaa, 1996; Kente Colors, 1996; The Piano Man, 1998; Pigs Can Fly!: The Adventures of Harriet and Friends, 2003; El Barrio!, 2004. AS DEBORAH M. NEWTON CHOCO-LATE: Kwanzaa, 1990; My First Kwanzaa Book, 1992; Spider and the Sky God: An Akan Legend, 1993; Talk, Talk: An Ashanti Legend, 1993; Imani in the Belly, 1994. **Address:** c/o Jane Jordan Browne, 410 S Michigan Ave Ste 724, Chicago, IL 60605, U.S.A. **Online address:** dar60187@aol.com

CHODOROW, Nancy J. American, b. 1944. **Genres:** Women's studies and issues, Psychology. **Career:** Professor of Sociology, University of California, Berkeley. Psychoanalyst, Instructor in Women's Studies, Wellesley College, 1973-74; Lecturer, Assistant, Associate Professor of Sociology, University of California, Santa Cruz, 1974-86. **Publications:** The Reproduction of Mothering: Psychoanalysis and the Sociology of Gender, 1978; Feminism and Psychoanalytic Theory, 1989; Femininities, Masculinities, Sexualities: Freud and Beyond, 1994; The Power of Feelings: Personal Meaning in Psychoanalysis, Gender, and Culture, 1999. **Address:** Dept. of Sociology, University of California, Berkeley, Berkeley, CA 94720, U.S.A.

CHODOS, Robert. Canadian, b. 1947. **Genres:** Social commentary, Theology/Religion, Translations. **Career:** Last Post, Montreal, QC, and Toronto, ON, parliamentary correspondent, news editor, and member of editorial board, 1969-80; This Magazine, Toronto, briefings editor, 1986-94; Compass: A Jesuit Journal, Toronto, editor, 1987-97; Canadian Forum, Toronto, editor, 1998-2000; Voices across Boundaries, Montreal, managing editor, 2002-; Inroads, Montreal, managing editor, 2002-; freelance book editor and translator. Temple Shalom Religious School, principal, 1986-96. **Publications:** Right-of-Way, 1971; The CPR, 1973; (with P. Brown and R. Murphy) Winners, Losers: The 1976 Tory Convention, 1976; The Caribbean Connection, 1977; (with P. MacFadden and R. Murphy) Your Place or Mine? (novel), 1978; (with R. Murphy and N. Auf der Maur) Brian Mulroney, 1984; (with A. Leis) Write All about It, 1986; (with R. Murphy and E. Hamovitch) Selling Out, 1988; (with R. Murphy and E. Hamovitch) The Unmaking of Canada, 1991; (with E. Hamovitch) Quebec and the American Dream, 1991; (with R. Murphy and E. Hamovitch) Canada and the Global Economy, 1993; (with R. Murphy and E. Hamovitch) Lost in Cyberspace, 1997; (with R. Murphy and E. Hamovitch) Paul Martin, 1998; (with J. Swift) Faith and Freedom, 2002. EDITOR: (with N. Auf der Maur) Quebec: A Chronicle, 1968-1972, 1972; (with R. Murphy) Let Us Prey, 1974; Compass Points, 1999. Contributor to periodicals. Translator from French of books by: B. Bellon, M. Cornellier, R. Dupuis, R. Durocher, G. Gougeon, P.-A. Linteau, J.-F. Lisee, J. Niosi, R. Prevost, M. Raboy, F. Ricard, J.-C. Robert, N. St-Amand, M. Venne. **Address:** 28 Huron St, New Hamburg, ON, Canada N3A 1J5. **Online address:** leischod@rogers.com

CHODRON, Pema. American, b. 1936. **Genres:** Self help. **Career:** Buddhist nun, 1974-. Also worked as an elementary school teacher. **Publications:** The Wisdom of No Escape, 1991; Start Where You Are, 1994; When Things Fall Apart, 1997. **Address:** Gampo Abbey, Pleasant Bay, NS, Canada B0E 2P0.

CHOI, Frederick D. S. American, b. 1942. **Genres:** Business/Trade/Industry, Economics. **Career:** Bank of Hawaii, management trainee, 1965, 1966; Federal Deposit Insurance Corp., assistant bank examiner, 1967; University of Hawaii at Manoa, Honolulu, assistant professor, 1972-76, associate professor, 1976-79, professor of accounting, 1979, head of department, 1980-81; New York University, NYC, professor of accounting and international business, 1981-87, research professor, 1988-95, head of Dept of

Accounting, Taxation, and Business Law, 1983-86, and International Business Dept, 1994-95, director of Japan-American Business and Cultural Studies Program, 1981-83, director of Ross Institute of Accounting Research, 1983-85, chairperson of international business area, 1994-, dean of Undergraduate Business College at Stern School of Business, 1995-. Visiting professor/lecturer at universities worldwide. Financial consultant to industry, government, and educational institutions. **Publications:** (with G. Mueller) An Introduction to Multinational Accounting, 1978; (with others) Analyzing the Financial Ratios of the World's 1,000 Leading Industrial Companies, 1981; Accounting and Control, 1982; (with J. Czechowicz) Assessing Foreign Subsidiary Performance, 1982; (with Mueller) International Accounting, 1984, 4th ed. (with G. Meek and C.A. Frost), 2002; (with R. Levich) The Capital Market Effects of International Accounting Diversity, 1990; Handbook of International Accounting, 1991, 1993 Supplement, 1992, 2nd ed. as International Accounting and Finance Handbook, 1997; (with Mueller) Globalization of Financial Accounting and Reporting, 1994; (with Levich) International Capital Markets in a World of Accounting Differences, 1994; (with others) Barriers to Business in the Single European Equity Market, 1996. EDITOR: (with Mueller) Essentials of Multinational Accounting, 1979; Multinational Accounting, 1981; (with Mueller) Frontiers of International Accounting, 1985; (with R. Hawkins and T. Pugel, and contrib.) Essays on the American Economy, Business, and Finance for Japanese Executives, 1987; (with K. Hiramatsu) Accounting and Financial Reporting in Japan, 1987. **Address:** Stern School of Business, New York University, 40 West 4th St., New York, NY 10012, U.S.A. **Online address:** fchoi@stern.nyu.edu

CHOI, Hyaeweol. Korean, b. 1962. **Genres:** Adult non-fiction, Bibliography. **Career:** Research Institute of Korean History, Seoul, research fellow, 1987-89; State University of New York at Buffalo, visiting scholar at Center for Asian Studies and Comparative Education Center, 1993-94, assistant director of Korean Language and Culture Program at World Languages Institute, 1994; University of Kansas, Lawrence, visiting assistant professor of East Asian languages and cultures, 1994-. Yonsei University, instructor at Korean Language Institute, 1988; Sangmyung Women's University, lecturer, 1988-89. **Publications:** (with P.G. Altbach) Publishing and Book Development in the Third World, 1980-1993: Bibliography and Analysis, 1993; An International Scientific Community: Asian Professors in the United States, 1995. Contributor of articles and reviews to academic journals. **Address:** Department of East Asian Languages and Cultures, 2118 Wescoe Hall, University of Kansas, Lawrence, KS 66045, U.S.A.

CHOLDENKO, Gennifer. American, b. 1957. **Genres:** Humor/Satire. **Career:** Author. **Publications:** Moonstruck: The True Story of the Cow Who Jumped over the Moon, 1997; Notes from a Liar and Her Dog, 2001; Al Capone Does My Shirts, 2004. **Address:** c/o Author Mail, Putnam, 345 Hudson St, New York, NY 10014, U.S.A. **Online address:** choldenko@earthlink.net

CHOMSKY, Aviva. American, b. 1957. **Genres:** Economics, History. **Career:** Bates College, Lewiston, ME, assistant professor of history, 1990-97; Harvard University, visiting scholar, 1994; Institute for Health and Social Justice, faculty research associate, 1995-96; Salem State College, Salem, MA, associate professor, 1997-2002, professor of history, 2002-; speaker at colleges and universities. **Publications:** West Indian Workers and the United Fruit Company in Costa Rica, 1870-1940, 1996; (ed. with A. Lauria-Santiago, and contrib.) Identity and Struggle at the Margins of the Nation-State: The Laboring Peoples of Central America and the Hispanic Caribbean, 1998. **Address:** Department of History, Salem State College, Salem, MA 01970, U.S.A. **Online address:** achomsky@salemstate.edu

CHOMSKY, (Avram) Noam. American, b. 1928. **Genres:** International relations/Current affairs, Language/Linguistics, Philosophy, Politics/Government. **Career:** Massachusetts Institute of Technology, Cambridge, Dept. of Linguistics and Philosophy, assistant professor, 1955-58, associate professor, 1958-61, professor, 1961-66, Ferrari P. Ward professor, 1966-76, institute professor, 1976-, now retired. **Publications:** Syntactic Structures, 1957; Current Issues in Linguistic Theory, 1964; Aspects of the Theory of Syntax, 1965; Cartesian Linguistics, 1966; Topics in the Theory of Generative Grammar, 1966; (with M. Halle) Sound Pattern of English, 1968; Language and Mind, 1968; American Power and the New Mandarins, 1969; At War with Asia, 1970; Problems of Knowledge and Freedom, 1971; Studies on Semantics in Generative Grammar, 1972; (with E.S. Herman) Counterrevolutionary Violence, 1973; For Reasons of State, 1973; Peace in the Middle East?, 1974; The Logical Structure of Linguistic Theory, 1975; Reflections on Language, 1975; Essays on Form and Interpretation, 1977; Human Rights and American Foreign Policy, 1978; (with E.S. Herman) Political Economy of Human Rights, 2 vols., 1979; Rules and Representations, 1980; Lectures on Government and Binding, 1981, 7th ed., 1993; Radical Priorities, 1981; Towards a New Cold War, 1982; Some Concepts and Consequences of the Theory of Government and Binding, 1982; Fateful Triangle: The U.S., Israel and the Palestinians, 1983, rev. ed., 1999; Turning the Tide, 1985; Knowledge of Language, 1986; Barriers, 1986; Pirates and Emperors, 1986; On Power and Ideology, 1987; Language in a Psychological Setting, 1987; Language and Problems of Knowledge, 1987; The Chomsky Reader, 1987; The Culture of Terrorism, 1988; Language and Politics, 1988; Necessary Illusions, 1989; Deterring Democracy, 1991; Chronicles of Dissent, 1992; Year 501, 1993; Rethinking Camelot, 1993; Letters from Lexington, 1993; Language and Thought, 1994; World Orders, Old and New, 1994, rev. ed., 1996; The Minimalist Program, 1995; Powers and Prospects, 1996; Profit over People, 1998; The New Military Humanism, 1999; New Horizons in the Study of Language & Mind, 2000; A New Generation Draws the Line, 2000; Rogue States, 2000; Understanding Power, 2001; Language and Nature, 2002; Hegemony or Survival, 2003. **Address:** Massachusetts Institute of Technology, 77 Massachusetts Ave, Cambridge, MA 02139, U.S.A.

CHOPEY, Nicholas P. American. **Genres:** Engineering. **Career:** Esso Standard Oil Co., Linden and Bayonne, NJ, process engineer, 1955-59; McGraw-Hill Inc., NYC, member of editorial staff, 1960-. **Publications:** EDITOR: Handbook of Chemical Engineering Calculations, 1984, 2nd ed, 1994; Environmental Engineering in the Process Plant, 1992; Fluid Movers, 2nd ed, 1994. **Address:** Chemical Week Associates, 110 William St, New York, NY 10038, U.S.A.

CHOPRA, Deepak (K.). American (born India), b. 1946. **Genres:** How-to books, Medicine/Health, Self help, Sports/Fitness. **Career:** Physician, lecturer, and writer. Muhlenbert Hospital, Plainfield, NJ, intern, c. 1970-71; established private endocrinology practice in Boston, MA, 1971; affiliated with Tufts University, Medford, MA, Harvard University, Cambridge, MA, and Boston University, Boston, MA, 1971-c. 1985; New England Memorial Hospital (now Boston Regional Medical Center), Stoneham, MA, chief of staff, 1981-1985; Maharishi Ayur-Veda Products International, Inc., cofounder, 1985, sole stockholder, 1985-87, president, treasurer and clerk, 1985-88; Maharishi Ayur-Veda Health Center for Behavioral Medicine and Stress Management, Lancaster, MA, director, 1985-93; Sharp Institute for Human Potential and Mind/Body Medicine, La Jolla, CA, executive director, 1993-; Center for Mind/Body Medicine at L'Auberge, Del Mar, CA, director, 1993-95; associated with The Chopra Center for Well Being, La Jolla. Member of alternative medicine board of National Institute of Health. Coproducer of video Growing Younger, 1994. **Publications:** Creating Health: The Psychophysiological Connection, 1985, as Creating Health: Beyond Prevention, 1987, new ed. with new intro. as Creating Health: How to Wake Up the Body's Intelligence, 1991; Return of the Rishi: A Doctor's Search for the Ultimate Healer (autobiography), 1988, new ed. with new intro. as Return of the Rishi: A Doctor's Story of Spiritual Transformation and Ayurvedic Healing, 1991; Quantum Healing: Exploring the Frontiers of Mind/Body Medicine, 1989; (with R. Averbach and S. Rothenberg) Perfect Health: Maharishi Ayurveda, the Mind/Body Program for Total Well-Being, 1990; Perfect Health: The Complete Mind/Body Guide, 1991; Unconditional Life: Mastering the Forces That Shape Personal Reality, 1991, as Unconditional Life: Discovering the Power to Fulfill Your Dreams, 1992; Creating Affluence: Wealth Consciousness in the Field of All Possibilities, 1993; Ageless Body, Timeless Mind: The Quantum Alternative to Growing Old, 1993; Restful Sleep: The Complete Mind/Body Program for Overcoming Insomnia, 1994; The Seven Spiritual Laws of Success: A Practical Guide to the Fulfillment of Your Dreams, 1994; Perfect Weight: The Complete Mind/Body Program for Achieving and Maintaining Your Ideal Weight, 1994; Journey into Healing: Awakening the Wisdom within You, 1994, as Journey into Healing: A Step-by-Step Personal Guide Compiled from the Timeless Wisdom of Deepak Chopra, M.D., 1994; Perfect Digestion: The Key to Balanced Living, 1995; The Return of Merlin (novel), 1995; Living without Limits, 1995; Boundless Energy: The Complete Mind/Body Program for Overcoming Chronic Fatigue, 1995; The Way of the Wizard: Twenty Spiritual Lessons for Creating the Life You Want, 1996; How to Know God, 2000. Contributor to periodicals. **Address:** The Chopra Center at La Costa, 2013 Costa del Mar Rd, Carlsbad, CA 92009, U.S.A.

CHORAFAS, Dimitris N. Greek, b. 1926. **Genres:** Administration/Management, Business/Trade/Industry, Communications/Media, Engineering, Information science/Computers, Money/Finance. **Career:** Consultant in private practice; teacher, author. **Publications:** Operations Research for Industrial Management, 1958; Statistical Processes and Reliability Engineering, 1960; The Functions of Research in the Enterprise, 1960; Computer Theory, 1960; Computer Applications in Industry and Commerce, 1961;

Programming Systems for Electronic Computers, 1962; Industrial Strategy, 1962; New Methods of Economic Analysis, 1963; The Influence of the Computer on the Organization, 1964; Systems and Simulation, 1965; Control Systems Functions and Programming Approaches, 2 vols., 1966; La Direction des Produits Nouveaux, 1967; An Introduction to Product Planning, 1967; Sales Engineering, 1967; Managing Industrial Research for Profits, 1967; Selecting the Computer System, 1967; Developing the International Executive, 1967; The Knowledge Revolution, 1968; How to Manage Computers for Results, 1969; The Communication Barrier in International Management, 1970; Management Development, 1971; Information Systems Design, 1972; Computers in Medicine, 1972; Warehousing, 1973; Management Planning, 1973; Die Kranke Geselschaft, 1974; Microform and Computer Output to Microfilm, 1976; Computer Networks for Distributed Information Systems, 1980; Data Communication, 1980; Interactive Videotex, 1981; Office Automation, 1982; Money: The Banks of the 1980's, 1982; Information Systems in Financial Institutions, 1983; Microprocessors for Management, 1983; DBMS for Distributed Computers and Networks, 1983; Local Area Networks, 1984; Telephony, Today and Tomorrow, 1984; Software Handbook, 1985; Interactive Message Services, 1985; Handbook of Data Communications, 1986; Fourth and Fifth Generation Languages, 2 vols., 1986; Personal Workstations for Greater Productivity, 1986; Interactive Workstations, 1986; Engineering Productivity through CAD/CAM, 1987; The New Communications Disciplines, 1987; Applying Expert Systems in Business, 1987; Engineering Databases, 1988; Electronic Funds Transfer, 1988; (with H. Steinmann) High Technology at UBS, 1988; Implementing Networks for Banks and Financial Institutions, 1988; Handbook of Relational Databases and DBMS, 1989; Bank Profitability, 1989; Local Area Networks, 1989; System Architecture and System Design, 1989; New Technologies, 1989; Knowledge Engineering, 1989; Intelligent Networks, 1990; Supercomputers, 1990; The Handbook of Management, 1990; Risk Management in Financial Institutions, 1990; Expert Systems in Banking, 1991; Expert Systems in Manufacturing, 1992; Using High Technology in Foreign Exchange and the Treasury Business, 1992; Treasury Operations and the Foreign Exchange Challenge, 1992; Simulation, Optimization and Expert Systems in Securities Trading, 1992; The Globalization of Money and Securities, 1992; The New Information Technologies, 1992; (with E.M. Binder) Technoculture and Change, 1992; (with H. Steinmann) Object-Oriented Databases, 1993; Measuring Return on Technology Investments, 1993; Financial Models and Simulation, 1995; Derivative Financial Instruments, 1995; (with H. Steinmann) An Introduction to Communications Networks and the Information Superhighway, 1996; How to Understand and Use Mathematics for Derivatives, Vol., 1, 1995, Vol. 2, 1996; Rocket Scientists in Banking, 1996; Managing Derivatives Risk, 1996; The Money Magnet, 1996; Protocols, Servers and Projects, 1997; High Performance Networks, Mobile Computing and Personal Communications, 1997; Visual Programming Technology, 1997; Network Computers versus High Performance Computers, 1997; Internet Financial Services, 1998; Transaction Management, 1998; Agent Technology Handbook, 1998; Cost-Effective IT Solutions for Financial Services, 1998; The Market Risk Amendment, 1998; Understanding Volatility and Liquidity in Financial Markets, 1998; Commercial Banking Handbook, 1999; Setting Limits for Market Risk, 1999; Credit Derivatives and the Management of Risk, 2000; Managing Credit Risk, 2 vols., 2000; New Regulation of the Financial Industry, 2000; Reliable Financial Reporting and Internal Control, 2000; Managing Risk in the New Economy, 2001; Implementing and Auditing the Internal Control System, 2001; Managing Operational Risk, 2001; Internet Supply Chain, 2001; Integrating ERP, CRM, Supply Chain Management and Smart Materials, 2001; Enterprise Architecture and New Generation Information Systems, 2002; Liabilities, Liquidity, and Cash Management, 2002; The Management of Philanthropy in the 21st Century, 2002; Modelling the Survival of Financial and Industrial Enterprises, 2002; Outsourcing, Insourcing and IT for Enterprise Management, 2003; Stress Testing, 2003; Alternative Investments and the Mismanagement of Risk, 2003; Corporate Accountability, 2004; Management Risk, 2004; Operational Risk Control with Basle II, 2004; Economic Capital Allocation with Basle II, 2004; Rating Management Effectiveness, 2004; The Real-Time Enterprise, 2005; The Management of Bond Investments, 2005; The Management of Equity Investments, 2005. **Address:** Villa Romantic, 6354 Vitznau, Switzerland.

CHORBAJIAN, Levon. American, b. 1942. **Genres:** History, Organized labor, Sociology, Sports/Fitness. **Career:** U.S. Peace Corps, volunteer, 1966-68; University of Massachusetts, Lowell, professor of sociology, 1970-. Senior Fulbright lecturer in the USSR, 1986-87, and in the Republic of Armenia, 1996. Zoryan Institute for Contemporary Armenian Research and Documentation, chairperson of board of directors. Managing editor, Journal of Sport and Social Issues and ARENA Review, both 1982-86. **Publications:** The Caucasian Knot: The History and Geopolitics of Nagorno-Karabagh, 1994; (trans.) P. Verluise, Armenia in Crisis: The 1988 Earthquake, 1995;

Conflict and Struggle, 2004. EDITOR: Readings in Critical Sociology, 1989; The Hand in Your Pocket May Not Be Your Own, 1991; Studies in Comparative Genocide, 1999; The Making of Nagorno-Karabagh, 2001. **Address:** Department of Sociology, University of Massachusetts, Lowell, MA 01854, U.S.A. **Online address:** Lchor@comcast.net

CHORLTON, David. British (born Austria), b. 1948. **Genres:** Poetry, Essays, Translations. **Career:** Freelance writer and artist. Arizona Composers Forum, member of board of directors, 1987-89; Arizona Center to Reverse the Arms Race, member of board of directors, 1990-92. **Publications:** (trans.) H. Raimund, Viennese Ventriloquies, 1998; Assimilation, 2000; Common Sightings, 2001; A Normal Day Amazes Us, 2003; Return to Waking Life, 2004. **Address:** 118 W Palm Ln, Phoenix, AZ 85003, U.S.A. **Online address:** rdchorlton@netzero.com

CHOTZINOFF, Robin. American, b. 1958. **Genres:** Homes/Gardens. **Career:** Journalist and author. Westword, Denver, CO, staff writer, 1985-. Sold jewelry as a street vendor in Berkeley, CA, 1976-80; drilled oil wells in the western United States, 1980-84; shined shoes, Denver, CO, 1984-85. **Publications:** People with Dirty Hands: The Passion for Gardening, 1996; People Who Sweat: Ordinary People, Extraordinary Pursuits, 1999. Writes column for Garden Design. **Address:** PO Box 415, Indian Hills, CO 80454, U.S.A. **Online address:** twodogsinternationalerfold.com

CHOU, Tsu-Wei. American (born China), b. 1940. **Genres:** Engineering. **Career:** University of Delaware, Newark, Pierre S. du Pont Chair of Engineering, 1969-. **Publications:** Composite Materials and Their Use in Structures, 1975; Textile Structural Composites, 1988; Use of Composite Materials in Transportation Systems, 1991; Microstructural Design of Fiber Composites, 1992; Structure and Properties of Composite, 1993; Innovative Processing and Characterization of Composite Materials, 1995; Comprehensive Composite Materials, Vol. 1, 2000. **Address:** University of Delaware, Department of Mechanical Engineering, Newark, DE 19716, U.S.A.

CHOUDHURY, Ashok. American (born India), b. 1957. **Genres:** Engineering. **Career:** Oak Ridge National Laboratory, Oak Ridge, TN, member of development staff in Metals and Ceramics Division, 1989-92; UT-Battelle, LLC, Oak Ridge, commercialization manager, 1992-. **Publications:** (with C.R. Brooks) Metallurgical Failure Analysis, 1993; Failure Analysis of Engineering Materials, 2002. **Address:** Oak Ridge National Laboratory, 111 B Union Valley Rd, Oak Ridge, TN 37831, U.S.A.

CHOUDHURY, Masudul Alam. Also writes as Masud. Canadian (born India), b. 1948. **Genres:** Area studies, Economics, Third World. **Career:** Saskatchewan Department of Labour, Regina, SK, Canada, research economist, 1977-79; King Abdulaziz University, Jeddah, Saudi Arabia, assistant professor of economics, 1979-83; Islamic Development Bank, Jeddah, senior economist, 1983-85; University College of Cape Breton, Sydney, NS, Canada, professor of economics, 1985-, and director of Centre of Humanomics. National University of Malaysia, visiting professor; Ontario Institute for Studies in Education, University of Toronto, visiting professor; lecturer at colleges and universities. King Fahd University of Petroleum & Minerals, Dhahran, Saudi Arabia, Professor of Finance & Economics. **Publications:** (with U.A. Malik) The Foundations of Islamic Political Economy, 1992; The Unicity Precept and the Socio-Scientific Order, 1993; The Principles of Islamic Political Economy, 1993; Comparative Development Studies, 1993; Theory and Practice of Islamic Development Cooperation, 1993; Epistemological Foundations of the Islamic Economic, Social, and Scientific Order, six volumes and a booklet, 1995; Money in Islam, 1997; Studies in Islamic Social Sciences, 1998; Studies in Islamic Science & Polity, 1998; Reforming the Muslim World, 1998; Comparative Economic Theory, 1999; The Islamic World View, 2000. Contributor to scholarly journals. **Address:** University College of Cape Breton, Sydney, NS, Canada B1P 6L2.

CHOW, Claire S. American, b. 1952. **Genres:** Psychology. **Career:** Private practice of psychotherapy in San Ramon, CA, 1994-. John F. Kennedy University, adjunct faculty member, 1994-; Pleasanton Counseling and Training, clinical supervisor of interns, 1997-; Grief Healing and Resource Center, founding member. **Publications:** Leaving Deep Water, 1998; The Lives of Asian American Women. Contributor to periodicals. **Address:** 2551 San Ramon Valley Blvd. Suite 210, San Ramon, CA 94583, U.S.A. **Online address:** ClaireChow@aol.com

CHOWDHURY, Bernie. American (born England). b. 1959. **Genres:** Documentaries/Reportage. **Career:** Columbia University, NYC, data communications technician, 1982-87, senior data communications technician,

1987-89; Goldman, Sachs and Co., NYC, telecommunications analyst, 1989-94, senior staff analyst, 1994-95; Immersed (magazine), NYC, co-publisher and executive editor, 1995-. **Publications:** The Last Dive (nonfiction), 2000; Icelandic Cave Diving Expedition Special (television documentary), 2001. **Address:** PO Box 638, Chester, NY 10918, U.S.A. **Online address:** bernie@immersed.com

CHOWDHURY, Subir. Bangladeshi, b. 1967. **Genres:** Administration/Management, Engineering. **Career:** Ciproco Computers Ltd., Dhaka, Bangladesh, software and systems manager, 1989-91; Silocon magazine, founding editor, 1990; General Motors Corporation, Saginaw, MI, quality management consultant, 1993-97; American Supplier Institute, Livonia, MI, executive vice president, 1997-; Automotive Excellence, editor-in-chief, 1997-99; author, 1996-. **Publications:** QS-9000 Pioneers: Registered Companies Share Their Strategies for Success, 1996; (with G. Taguchi and S. Taguchi) Robust Engineering, 1999; Management 21C: Someday We'll All Manage This Way, 2000; The Power of Six Sigma: An Inspiring Tale of How Six Sigma Is Transforming the Way We Work, 2001; (with Genichi Taguchi and Yuin Wu) The Mahalanobis-Taguchi System, 2000; The Talent Era: Achieving a High Return on Talent, 2002; Design for Six Sigma, 2002; Organization 21C: Someday All Organizations Will Lead This Way, forthcoming; The Power of Design for Six Sigma, forthcoming. **Address:** American Supplier Institute, 38705 Seven Mile Road, Ste. 345, Livonia, MI 48152, U.S.A. **Online address:** subir.chowdhury@asiusa.com

CHOYCE, Lesley. Canadian (born United States), b. 1951. **Genres:** Novels, Novellas/Short stories, Mystery/Crime/Suspense, Science fiction/Fantasy, Young adult fiction, Literary criticism and history, Local history/Rural topics, Natural history, Travel/Exploration, Autobiography/Memoirs, Essays, Humor/Satire. **Career:** Referrals Workshop, Denville, NJ, rehabilitation counselor, 1973-74; Bloomfield College, NJ, coordinator, 1974; Montclair State College, Upper Montclair, NJ, instructor, 1974-78; Alternate Energy Consultants, Halifax, NS, writer and consultant, 1979-80; Dalhousie University, Halifax, instructor in English, 1981-. Founder of Pottersfield Press. Creative writing instructor for City of Halifax continuing education program, 1978-83; instructor: St. Mary's University, 1978-82, Nova Scotia College of Art and Design, 1981, and Mount St. Vincent University, 1982. Freelance broadcaster, 1972-; host of TV talk show "Choyce Words," 1985-. **Publications:** NON-FICTION: Edible Wild Plants of the Maritimes, 1977; An Avalanche of Ocean (autobiography), 1987; December Six/The Halifax Solution, 1988; Transcendental Anarchy (autobiography), 1993; Nova Scotia: Shaped by the Sea, 1996; The Coasts of Canada, 2002. EDITOR: Alternating Currents, 1977; (with P. Thompson) Atlantic Canada Community Energy Strategy Sourcebook, 1979; The Cape Breton Collection, 1984; Ark of Ice, 1992; (with R. Joe) The Mi'kmaq Anthology, 1997; Pottersfield Nation, 2004. POETRY: (ed.) Chezzetcook (and stories), 1977; Re-Inventing the Wheel, 1980; Fast Living, 1982; The End of Ice, 1985; The Top of the Heart, 1986; The Man Who Borrowed the Bay of Fundy, 1988; The Coastline of Forgetting, 1995; Beautiful Sadness, 1998; Caution to the Wind, 2000; Typographical Eras, 2003; Revenge of the Optimist, 2004. FICTION: Eastern Sure, 1981; Downwind, 1984; Billy Botzweiler's Last Dance, 1984; Conventional Emotions, 1985; Coming Up for Air, 1988; The Second Season of Jonas MacPherson, 1989; Magnificent Obsessions, 1991; Ecstasy Conspiracy, 1992; Margin of Error, 1992; The Republic of Nothing, 1994; Dance the Rocks Ashore, 1997; World Enough, 1998; The Summer of Apartment X, 1999; Cold Clear Morning, 2001; Shoulder the Sky, 2002; Sea of Tranquility, 2003. SCIENCE FICTION: (ed. with J. Bell) Visions from the Edge (anthology), 1981; The Dream Auditor (stories), 1986; Trap Door to Heaven, 1996. YOUNG ADULT FICTION: Skateboard Shakedown, 1989; Hungry Lizards, 1990; Wavewatch, 1990; Some Kind of Hero, 1991; Wrong Time, Wrong Place, 1991; Clearcut Danger, 1993; Full Tilt, 1993; Good Idea Gone Bad, 1993; Dark End of Dream Street, 1994; Big Burn, 1995; Falling through the Cracks, 1996; Couleurs Troubles, 1997; Roid Rage, 1999; Far Enough Island, 2000; Refuge Cove, 2002; Thunderbowl, 2004. CHILDREN'S: Go for It Carrie, 1997; Carrie's Crowd, 1998; Carrie's Camping Adventure, 2001. **Address:** East Lawrencetown, NS, Canada B2Z 1P8.

CHRAIBI, Driss. French (born Morocco), b. 1926. **Genres:** Novels, Plays/Screenplays. **Career:** Writer. University of Laval, professor, 1969-70. **Publications:** NOVELS IN ENGLISH: Le passe simple, 1954, trans by H.A. Harter as The Simple Past, 1990; Les boucs, 1955, trans by H.A. Harter as The Butts, 1983; Succession ouverte, 1962, trans by L. Ortzen as Heirs to the Past, 1972; La civilisation, ma mere!, 1972, trans by H.A. Harter as Mother Comes of Age, 1985; Une enquete au pays, 1981, trans by R. Roosevelt as Flutes of Death, 1985; La mere du printemps, 1982, trans by H. Harter as Mother Spring, 1989; Naissance a l'aube, 1986, trans. by Ann Woollcombe as Birth at Dawn, 1990; L'Inspecteur Ali, 1991, trans. by L. McGlashan as

Inspector Ali, 1994. OTHER FICTION: L'Ane (title means: The Ass), 1956; De tous les horizons, 1958; La foule (title means: The Crowd), 1961; Un ami viendra vous voir (title means: A Friend Will Come to See You), 1966; Mort au Canada, 1974; L'Homme du livre, 1992. OTHER: Contes pour enfants, 1992. Author of radio plays. **Address:** 15 Rue Paul Pons, 26400 Crest, France.

CHRISMAN, Miriam Usher. American, b. 1920. **Genres:** Cultural/Ethnic topics, History, Theology/Religion, Bibliography. **Career:** National Resources Planning Board, Washington, D.C., research assistant, 1941-43; National Planning Association, Washington, D.C., research assistant, 1943-46; teacher in private girls' schools in Wellesley, Mass., 1946-47, Baltimore, Md., 1947-49, and Northampton, Mass., 1949-57; Smith College, Northampton, instructor in history, 1955-57; University of Massachusetts at Amherst, instructor, 1962-63, assistant professor, 1963-68, associate professor, 1968-71, professor of early modern social history, 1972-86, professor emeritus, 1986-. **Publications:** Strasbourg and the Reform: A Study in the Process of Change, 1967; Bibliography of Strasbourg Imprints, 1480-1599, 1982; Lay Culture, Learned Culture: Books and Social Change in Strasbourg, 1480-1599, 1982; Conflicting Visions of Reform: German Lay Propaganda Pamphlets 1519-1530, 1996. EDITOR: (with K. Mellon, Jr.) Like It Was, Like It Is: People and Issues in the Western World: A Reader, Vol II, 1972; (with O. Grundler) Social Groups and Religious Ideas in the Sixteenth Century, 1978. **Address:** 32 Concord Ct, Bedford, MA 01730-2906, U.S.A.

CHRIST, Carol P(atrice). American/Greek (born United States), b. 1945. **Genres:** Theology/Religion, Women's studies and issues. **Career:** Columbia University, assistant professor of religion, 1972-77; San Jose State University, CA, professor of religious studies and women's studies, 1977-88; Harvard Divinity School, Boston, MA, visiting lecturer and research associate, 1986-87; Pomona College, Stauffacher Distinguished Visiting Professor of Religion, 1988; California Institute of Integral Studies, Rockefeller Distinguished Professor, 1994; Ariadne Institute for the Study of Myth and Ritual, director, 1995-. Journal of Feminist Studies in Religion, contributing editor. **Publications:** Diving Deep and Surfacing: Women Writers on Spiritual Quest, 1980; Laughter of Aphrodite: Reflections on a Journey to the Goddess, 1987; Odyssey with the Goddess: A Spiritual Quest in Crete, 1995; Rebirth of the Goddess: Finding Meaning in Feminist Spirituality, 1997; She Who Changes: Re-imagining the Divine in the World, 2003. EDITOR (with J. Plaskow): (and contrib.) Womanspirit Rising: A Feminist Reader in Religion, 1979; Weaving the Visions: New Patterns in Feminist Spirituality, 1989. **Address:** Molivos, 81108 Lesvos, Greece. **Online address:** www.goddessariadne.org

CHRIST, Henry I. American, b. 1915. **Genres:** Language/Linguistics, Literary criticism and history, Sports/Fitness, Biography. **Career:** Teacher, 1936-46; Andrew Jackson High School, St. Albans, NY, chairman of English, 1947-70. **Publications:** Winning Words, 1948, 3rd ed., 1967; (adaptor) Odyssey of Homer, 1948; Myths and Folklore, 1952; Modern English in Action 7-12, 1965; Modern Short Biographies, 1970; Language and Literature, 1972; Short World Biographies, 1973; The World of Sports, 2 vols., 1975, 1977; The Challenge of Sports, 1978; Going Places, 1980; Globe American Biographies, 1987; Globe World Biographies, 1987; English for the College Boards, 1987; Myths and Folklore, 1989; Greek Tragedies, 1992; English for the College Boards, 1994-95; Heroes and Villains, 1995; Themes in American and World Literature, 1997; Shakespeare for the Modern Reader, 2001; Lexicon for Lovers of Language, 2004. **Address:** PO Box 361062, Melbourne, FL 32936-1062, U.S.A.

CHRIST, Ronald. American, b. 1936. **Genres:** Architecture, Literary criticism and history, Translations. **Career:** Manhattan College, Riverdale, NY, assistant professor, 1961-63; Rutgers University, New Brunswick, NJ, professor of English, 1969-96, professor emeritus, 1996-. Review, editor, 1970-78; Sites, managing editor, 1979-95; Lumen Books, co-publisher, 1983-. Center for Inter-American Relations, director, Literature Program, 1973-78; American PEN, executive board, 1978-83; PEN New Mexico, president, 2002-. **Publications:** The Narrow Act: Borges' Art of Allusion, 1969; (with D. Dollens) Nomadic Design: New York; (ed.) The Brotherhood, by W. Vasulka, 1998. TRANSLATOR: (with G. Kolovakos) Capt. Pantoja and the Special Service, by M. Vargas Llosa, 1978; (with G. Kolovakos) The Cubs and Other Stories, 1979; Under a Mantle of Stars, by M. Puig, 1985; Augusto Torres, by G. Castillo, 1986; (with G. Waldman) Borges in/and/on Film, by E. Cozarinsky, 1988; The Architecture of Jujol, by J.M. Jujol, 1997; E. Luminata, by D. Eltit, 1997. **Address:** 40 Camino Cielo, Santa Fe, NM 87501, U.S.A. **Online address:** lumenbooks@earthlink.net

CHRISTE, Ian. American. **Genres:** Adult non-fiction. **Career:** Musician and writer. **Publications:** Sound of the Beast: The Complete Headbanging History of Heavy Metal, 2003. Composer of heavy-metal music, sometimes under the name Dark Noerd; contributor of articles and other entertainment/technology magazines. **Address:** 105 North Eighth Street, Brooklyn, NY 11211, U.S.A. **Online address:** ian@soundofthebeast.com

CHRISTENSEN, Allan Conrad. Italian (born United States), b. 1940. **Genres:** Literary criticism and history. **Career:** University of California, Los Angeles, assistant professor of English, 1967-73; New School, Rome, Italy, lecturer, 1973-81; John Cabot University, Rome, professor of English, 1981-. **Publications:** Edward Bulwer-Lytton: The Fiction of New Regions, 1976; A European Version of Victorian Fiction: The Novels of Giovanni Ruffini, 1996; (coed.) The Challenge of Keats: Bicentenary Essays, 2001. Contributor to scholarly journals. **Address:** John Cabot University, Via Lungara 233, 00165 Rome, Italy. **Online address:** allan.christensen@tin.it

CHRISTENSEN, Father Damascene. American, b. 1961. **Genres:** Theology/Religion. **Career:** Writer, editor, monk, and priest. **Publications:** Not of This World: The Life and Teaching of Fr. Seraphim Rose: Pathfinder to the Heart of Ancient Christianity, 1993; Christ the Eternal Tao, 1999. **Address:** St. Herman Monastery, PO Box 70, Platina, CA 96076, U.S.A.

CHRISTENSEN, Kate. American, b. 1962. **Genres:** Novels. **Career:** Novelist. Worked as an editorial assistant, waitress, secretary, and adult education teacher. **Publications:** In the Drink, 1999; Jeremy Thrane, 2001; The Epicure's Lament, 2004. **Address:** c/o Author Mail, Random House, 1745 Broadway, New York, NY 10019, U.S.A.

CHRISTENSEN, Kit Richard. American, b. 1953. **Genres:** Philosophy. **Career:** Indiana University-Purdue University at Indianapolis, teacher of philosophy, 1980; Moorhead State University, Moorhead, MN, teacher of philosophy, 1980-81; Bemidji State University, Bemidji, MN, professor of philosophy, 1981-. **Publications:** The Politics of Character Development: A Marxist Reappraisal of the Moral Life, 1994; (ed.) Philosophy and Choice: Selected Readings from Around the World, 1999, 2nd ed., 2002. Contributor to books and periodicals. **Address:** Department of Philosophy, Bemidji State University, Bemidji, MN 56601, U.S.A. **Online address:** kchristensen@bemidjistate.edu

CHRISTENSEN, Paul. American, b. 1943. **Genres:** Poetry, Literary criticism and history. **Career:** Eastern Publishing Co., Alexandria, VA, associate ed., 1967-68; Texas A&M University, College Station, Dept. of English, professor, 1974-; Quartet mag., College Station, TX, poetry ed., 1975-77; Poetry Southwest, KAMU-FM, TX, host, 1976-86; Cedarshouse Press, Bryan, TX, ed. publisher, 1979-. **Publications:** Charles Olson: Call Him Ishmael (criticism), 1979; Signs of the Whelming, 1982; Gulfsongs, 1982; The Complete Correspondence of Charles Olson and Edward Dahlberg, 1990; Minding the Underworld: Clayton Eshleman and Late Postmodernism, 1991; West of the American Dream, 2001; The Mottled Air, 2003. POETRY: Old and Lost Rivers, 1977; The Vectory, 1983; Weights and Measures, 1985; Blue Alleys: Prose Poems, 2001. **Address:** Dept of English, Texas A&M University, 201C Blocker Bldg MS 4227, College Station, TX 77843-4227, U.S.A. **Online address:** p-christensen@neo.tamu.edu

CHRISTENSON, James A. American, b. 1944. **Genres:** Adult non-fiction. **Career:** North Carolina State University, Raleigh, assistant professor, 1972-75, associate professor, 1975-76, and extension community development specialist, 1972-76; University of Kentucky, Lexington, associate professor, 1976, founder and director of Survey Research Center, 1979-82, professor of sociology, 1981-89, head of department, 1982-89; University of Arizona, Tucson, associate dean and director of Cooperative Extension, 1989-. International Research Group in Extension, cofounder, 1988. **Publications:** (ed. with J.W. Robinson, Jr.) Community Development in America, 1980; (with P.D. Warner) The Cooperative Extension Service: A National Assessment, 1984; (ed. with Robinson) Community Development in Perspective, 1989; (with C.B. Flora) Rural Policies for the 1990s, 1991; Rural Data, People, and Policy, 1994. Work represented in anthologies. Contributor to periodicals. **Address:** Cooperative Extension Forbes 301, College of Agriculture, University of Arizona, Tucson, AZ 85721, U.S.A.

CHRISTESEN, C(lement) B(yrne). Australian, b. 1911. **Genres:** Poetry, Literary criticism and history, Novellas/Short stories. **Career:** Founder and Ed., Meanjin Quarterly, Melbourne, 1940-75. **Publications:** (ed.) Australian Heritage, 1949; Coast to Coast, 1953, 1954; On Native Grounds, 1968; The Hand of Memory (stories and poems), 1970; The Gallery on Eastern Hill, 1971; Having Loved (poems), 1979; The Troubled Eyes of Women (stories), 1990.

CHRISTIAN, Carol Cathay. American/British, b. 1923. **Genres:** Novels, Children's fiction, Human relations/Parenting, Biography. **Publications:** Into Strange Country, 1958; (with G. Plummer) God and One Redhead: Mary Slessor of Calabar, 1970; Tales of the Cross River, 1972; Great People of Our Time, 1973; Proverbs and Rhymes, 1974; Johnny Ring, 1975; More People of Our Time, 1978; (with D. Christian) Famous Women of the 20th Century, 1982; (ed.) In the Spirit of Truth: A Reader in the Work of Frank Lake, 1991; Macmillan U.K. Bible Stories (18 titles), 1996-97. **Address:** 20 Pitfold Ave, Shottermill, Haslemere, Surrey GU27 1PN, England. **Online address:** ccarol@fish.co.uk

CHRISTIAN, Garna L. American, b. 1935. **Genres:** Architecture, History, Music. **Career:** South Texas Junior College, Houston, instructor, 1962-74; University of HoustonDowntown, professor of history, 1974-. **Publications:** Stay a Little Longer: The First Generation of Houston Country Music, 1983; Black Soldiers in Jim Crow Texas, 1899-1917, 1995; 40,000 Window Panes: The Story of the Merchants and Manufacturers Building, 1986. **Address:** Dept of Social Sciences, University of Houston-Downtown, 1 Main St, Houston, TX 77002, U.S.A. **Online address:** christiang@uhd.edu

CHRISTIAN, Jeffrey E. American, b. 1956. **Genres:** Business/Trade/Industry. **Career:** Christian & Timbers, Cleveland, OH, founder, chairman, and chief executive officer, 1980-. Commentator on employment issues for CNBC-TV and periodicals. **Publications:** Headhunter Confidential: How to Get the Best Jobs and the Best People-Exclusive Tips from One of the Top Headhunters in the Business, 2002. **Address:** Christian & Timbers Exchange, 25825 Science Park Drive, Suite 400, Cleveland, OH 44122, U.S.A.

CHRISTIAN, Roy Cloberry. British, b. 1914. **Genres:** History, Local history/Rural topics, Travel/Exploration. **Career:** Lecturer-in-Charge of Mature Students, Derby College of Further Education, 1966-76 (joined faculty, 1955). **Publications:** Ships and the Sea, 1962; Old English Customs, 1966; Ghosts and Legends, 1972; (ed.) Nature-Lover's Companion, 1972; Nottinghamshire, 1974; Factories, Forges, and Foundries, 1974; Peak District, 1976; Vanishing Britain, 1977; Derbyshire, 1978; (with J. E. Heath) Derby, 1985; Derbyshire, 1989; Butterley Brick, 1990. **Address:** 53 Littleover Lane, Littleover, Derby DE23 6JH, England.

CHRISTIAN, William. Canadian, b. 1945. **Genres:** Philosophy, Politics/Government, Biography. **Career:** Mount Allison University, Sackville, NB, assistant professor of political science, beginning in 1970, associate professor of political studies, ending in 1978; University of Guelph, ON, professor of political science, 1978-. Visiting professor at University of Toronto, 1987-90, and McMaster University, 1990. London School of Economics, academic visitor, 1976-77, 1984-85, 1989; University of Edinburgh, International Social Sciences Institute, visiting associate, 1996. **Publications:** (with C. Campbell) Political Parties and Ideologies in Canada, 1974, 3rd ed., 1990; George Grant: A Biography, 1993; (with C. Campbell) Parties, Leaders, and Ideologies in Canada, 1996. EDITOR: Idea File of Harold Adams Innis, 1980; Innis on Russia, 1981; G. Grant, Time as History, 1995; G. Grant, Philosophy in the Mass Age, 1996; Selected Letters of George Grant, 1996; The George Grant Reader, 1998. **Address:** Dept of Political Science, University of Guelph, Guelph, ON, Canada N1G 2W1. **Online address:** wchristie@uoguelph.ca

CHRISTIANSEN, Rupert. British, b. 1954. **Genres:** History, Music, Writing/Journalism. **Career:** Associated with Oxford University Press, 1979-82; freelance writer and editor, 1982-. Opera critic: Spectator, 1990-96; Daily Telegraph, 1996-. **Publications:** Prima Donna: A History, 1984; Romantic Affinities: Portraits from an Age, 1780-1830, 1988; (ed.) The Grand Obsession: A Collins Anthology of Opera, 1988; Tales of the New Babylon, 1869-1875, 1994; Cambridge Arts Theatre: A Collaboration, 1997; The Victorian Visitors, 2000; The Voice of Victorian Sex: Arthur Hugh Clough, 2001; A Pocket Guide to Opera, 2002. **Address:** c/o PFD, Drury House, 34-43 Russell St, London WC2B 5HA, England. **Online address:** rupec@dircon.co.uk

CHRISTIANSON, Paul. American, b. 1937. **Genres:** History. **Career:** Queen's University, Kingston, Ontario, professor of history, 1964-. **Publications:** Discourse on History, Law, and Governance in the Public Career of John Selden, c. 16101635, 1996; Reformers and Babylon: English Apocalyptic Visions from the Reformation to the Eve of the Civil War, 1998. **Address:** Department of History, Queen's University, Kingston, ON, Canada K7L 3N6. **Online address:** christia@post.queensu.ca

CHRISTIANSON, Sven-Åke. Swedish, b. 1954. **Genres:** Psychology. **Career:** University of Umea, assistant professor, 1984-87; associate professor of psychology, 1987-90; University of Stockholm, associate professor, 1990-99, professor of psychology, 1999-. Consultant at Department of Neurosurgery, Umea University Hospital, 1982-96; consultant at the Swedish National Police College, 1993-; Montreal Neurological Institute/Hospital, research fellow, 1984; University of Washington and University Hospital, visiting scientist and Fulbright scholar, 1988-89. **Publications:** The Handbook of Emotion and Memory: Research and Theory, 1992; Traumatic Memories, 1994; Crime and Memory, 1996; Forensic Psychology, 1996; Advanced Interrogation and Interviewing Technique, 1998. **Address:** Department of Psychology, Stockholm University, S-106 91 Stockholm, Sweden. **Online address:** scn@psychology.su.se

CHRISTIE, Ian. British, b. 1956. **Genres:** Business/Trade/Industry. **Career:** Policy Studies Institute, London, England, senior research fellow in industry, the environment, and employment, 1986-. Computer programmer and technical writer for the software industry; adult education lecturer; consultant. **Publications:** (with J. Northcott and A. Walling) The Employment Effects of New Technology, 1990; (with M. Fogarty) Companies and Communities, 1991; (with M. Carley and Fogarty) Profitable Partnerships: Business Investment in the Community, 1991; (ed. with N. Ritchie) Energy Efficiency: The Policy Agenda for the 1990s, 1992; (with Carley) Managing Sustainable Development, 1992. Contributor to periodicals. **Address:** AHRB Centre for British Film and Television Studies, Birkbeck, 43 Gordon Sq Rm 102, London WC1H 0PD, England.

CHRISTIE-MURRAY, David (Hugh Arthur). British, b. 1913. **Genres:** Genealogy/Heraldry, Paranormal, Theology/Religion. **Career:** Diocese of Rochester, youth organizer, 1942-46; Harrow School, Harrow-on-the-Hill, assistant master, 1946-73. **Publications:** Heraldry in the Churches of Beckenham, 1954; Armorial Bearings of British Schools, 1967 (originally published as School Heraldry); The Hamlyn Bible for Children, 1974; A History of Heresy, 1976; Voices From the Gods, 1978; Reincarnation, 1981; My First Prayer-Book, 1981; The Practical Astrologer, 1990; The Children's Bible, 1993.

CHRISTMAN, Al(bert B.). American, b. 1923. **Genres:** Military/Defense/Arms control. **Career:** Naval Weapons Center, China Lake, CA, technical writer and presentation specialist, 1951-62, historian and publications manager, 1962-79; Navy Material Command, San Diego, CA, historian of naval laboratories, 1979-82; freelance writer and historian, San Marcos, CA, 1982-. Red Rock Canyon State Park, founding member of advisory committee, 1969-74; Maturango Museum, member of board of directors, 1973-76; Naval Historical Foundation, member. **Publications:** (coauthor) Sailors, Scientists, and Rockets, 1971; (with J.D. Gerrard-Gough) Grand Experiment at Inyokerm, 1978; Naval Innovators, 1776-1900, 1989; (coauthor) Target Hiroshima: Deak Parsons and the Creation of the Atomic Bomb, 1998. **Address:** 1711 Birchwood Dr, San Marcos, CA 92069, U.S.A. **Online address:** janal@adnc.com

CHRISTMAS, Joyce. Also writes as Christmas Peterson. American, b. 1939. **Genres:** Mystery/Crime/Suspense. **Career:** Public Relations and Advertising Writer and Copy Ed., Writer mag., Boston, (Editorial Assistant, 1963-68; Associate Ed., 1973-76); Hotel computer consultant and Managing Ed., CKC Report: Hotel Technology Newsletter, NYC, 1981-. **Publications:** Blood Child, 1982; Dark Tide, 1983; Suddenly, in Her Sorbet, 1988; Simply to Die For, 1989; A Fete Worse than Death, 1990; A Stunning Way to Die, 1991; Friend or Faux, 1991; It's Her Funeral, 1992; This Business Is Murder, 1993; A Perfect Day for Dying, 1994; Death at Face Value, 1995; Mourning Gloria, 1996; Going Out in Style, 1998; Downsized to Death, 1999; Mood to Murder, 1999; Dying Well, 2000; A Better Class of Murder, 2000. **Address:** c/o Evan Marshall, 6 Tristam Pl., Pine Brook, NJ 07058, U.S.A. **Online address:** christmasj@aol.com

CHRISTMAS, Linda (Irene). British, b. 1943. **Genres:** Travel/Exploration. **Career:** Swindon Evening Advertiser, Swindon, England, journalist, 1966-68; Times Educational Supplement, London, England, journalist, 1969-70; Guardian, London, journalist, 1971-82; freelance writer, 1982-; City University, London, senior lecturer in journalism, 1989-. **Publications:** The Ribbon and the Ragged Square: An Australian Journey (nonfiction), 1986; Chopping Down the Cherry Trees: A Portrait of Britain in the Eighties, 1990. Author of radio documentaries. Parliamentary sketch writer for London Times, 1985. Contributor to periodicals, including London Times. **Address:** 47 Thornhill Sq., London N1 1BE, England.

CHRISTODOULOU, Demetrios. Cypriot, b. 1919. **Genres:** Agriculture/Forestry, Economics, Politics/Government, Sociology. **Career:** Government of Cyprus, Nicosia, teacher, 1940-45, lecturer in geography and teaching methods at Teachers' Training College in Morphou, 1949-53, inspector of secondary schools, 1955-56, land consolidation officer, 1956-60, agricultural development officer, 1958-60; Food and Agriculture Organization of the UN, Rome, Italy, senior officer and policy advisor involved with land tenure and settlement, 1960-81, secondment to serve in other international agencies on missions, 1960-1981, vice chair of conference, 1983; Government of Cyprus, Nicosia, minister of agriculture and natural resources, 1982-85; writer. **Publications:** Physical Geography, 1954; The Evolution of the Rural Land Use Pattern in Cyprus, 1959; The Unpromised Land: Agrarian Reform and Conflict Worldwide, 1990; Inside the Cyprus Miracle: The Labors of an Embattled Mini-Economy, 1992; Where the Cyprus Miracle Fell Short (in Greek), 1995. **Address:** Flat 201, Anemomylos Bldg, 6 Michael Karaolis St, Nicosia 1095, Cyprus.

CHRISTOPH, Florence A(nna). American, b. 1937. **Genres:** Genealogy/Heraldry, History. **Career:** High school mathematics teacher in Norwich, NY, 1959-60, and in Van Hornesville, NY, 1960-61; genealogist, 1973-83, certified genealogist, 1983-; historical editor, 1982-. **Publications:** Vital Records of Jerusalem Reformed Church, Feura Bush, Albany County, N.Y., 1987; Upstate New York in the 1760s, 1992; The Van Voorhees Family in America: The First Six Generations, 2000; The Van Voorhees Family in America: The Seventh and Eighth Generations, 2 vols., 2003. EDITOR (WITH P.R. CHRISTOPH): Books of General Entries of the Colony of New York, 1664-1688, 2 vols, 1982; Records of the People of the Town of Bethlehem, 1690-1880, 1982; Records of the Court of Assizes for the Colony of New York, 1665-1682, 1983; (sole ed.) Sources Pertaining to the Schuyler Families in America prior to 1800, 1987; The Andros Papers: Files of the Provincial Secretary of New York during the Administration of Governor Sir Edmund Andros, 1674-1680, 3 vols., 1989-91. **Address:** 181 Maple Ave, Selkirk, NY 12158, U.S.A.

CHRISTOPH, James B. American, b. 1928. **Genres:** Politics/Government. **Career:** Professor Emeritus of Political Science and West European Studies, Indiana University, Bloomington, since 1967 (Chairman of Dept., 1967-71; Director, West European Studies, 1973-74). Instructor, then Professor, Ohio State University, Columbus, 1955-66; Fulbright-Hays Professor of Political Science, Bologna Center of Johns Hopkins University, Baltimore, Maryland, 1966-67; Visiting fellow, Nuffield College, Oxford Univerisity, 1991. Member, Executive Council, American Political Science Association, 1975-77; President, British Politics Group, 1978-80. **Publications:** Capital Punishment and British Politics, 1962; Britain at the Crossroads, 1969; (ed. and author with B. Brown) Cases in Comparative Politics: Europe, 3rd ed. 1976. **Address:** 4875 Heritage Woods Rd, Bloomington, IN 47401, U.S.A.

CHRISTOPH, Peter R(ichard). American, b. 1938. **Genres:** Genealogy/Heraldry, History. **Career:** New York State Library, Albany, assistant cataloging librarian, 1965-68, senior librarian for manuscripts and history, 1968-72, associate librarian for manuscripts and special collections, 1972-88, editor of New York Historical Manuscripts, 1974-86, senior editor, 1986-, director of Project to Translate and Edit the Archives of New Netherland, 1974-87, associate librarian for New Netherland Project, 1988-91. **Publications:** Albert Andriessen Bradt: A Norwegian Settler in Rensselaerswyck, 1987; The Dongan Papers, 1683-1688, 2 vols., 1993-96; The Leisler Papers, 1689-1691, 2002. EDITOR: (with K. Scott and K. Stryker-Rodda) The Kingston Papers, 1661-1675, 2 vols., 1976; Administrative Papers of Governors Richard Nicolls and Francis Lovelace, 1664-1673, 1980; (with F.A. Christoph) Books of General Entries of the Colony of New York, 1664-1688, 2 vols., 1982; (with F. Christoph) Records of the People of the Town of Bethlehem, 1690-1880, 1982; (with F. Christoph) Records of the Court of Assizes for the Colony of New York, 1665-1682, 1983; (with F. Christoph) The Andros Papers: Files of the Provincial Secretary of New York during the Administration of Governor Sir Edmund Andros, 1674-1680, 3 vols., 1989-91. Work represented in anthologies. Contributor to genealogy and history journals and books. Author of introductions and prefaces to books.

CHRISTOPHER, John. See YOUD, Sam.

CHRISTOPHER, Kari. See CAPEK, Michael.

CHRISTOPHER, Renny (Teresa). American, b. 1957. **Genres:** Poetry, Literary criticism and history. **Career:** Horse Lovers' National, Burlingame, CA, features editor, 1976-79; Literature of Liberty, Menlo Park, CA, production editor, 1982; Gilroy Dispatch, graphic arts editor, 1983-84; San Jose State University, San Jose, CA, lecturer in English, 1986-87; Cabrillo Community College, Aptos, CA, instructor in English, 1988-95; California State University, Stanislaus, Turlock, assistant professor of English, 1995-. San Jose State University, lecturer, 1993-94; University of California, Santa Cruz, lecturer, 1992-95; University of Virginia, associate fellow of Institute for

Advanced Technology and the Humanities. Gives readings from her works. **Publications:** The Viet Nam War/The American War: Images and Representations in EuroAmerican and Vietnamese Exile Narratives, 1995; My Name Is Medea (poems), 1996; Viet Nam and California (poems), 1998; Longing Fervently for Revolution (poems), 1998. Contributor to books. Poetry represented in anthologies. Contributor of articles, stories, poems, and reviews to periodicals. **Address:** Department of English, California State University Stanislaus, 801 W Monte Vista, Turlock, CA 95382, U.S.A. **Online address:** rchristo@athena.csustan.edu

CHRYSSAVGIS, John. (born Australia), b. 1958. **Genres:** Education. **Career:** St. Andrew's Theleological College, Sydney, Australia, subdean, 1985-95; Sydney University, Sydney, Australia, lecturer, 1986-95; Holy Cross School of Theology, Boston, MA, professor, beginning 1995, acting dean, 1997-98; Hellenic College, Boston, director of religious studies, beginning 1995. Greek Orthodox Church in Australia, protodeacon, 1984-95; Greek Orthodox Archdiocese of America, deacon, beginning 1995. Member of standing committee of Liturgical Translations, member, 1997; Faith and Science Exchange, Boston, member, 1996. Member of Institute for Theology and the Arts, advisor 1990-95. **Publications:** Persons and Events: Historical Moments in the Development of Orthodox Christianity, 1985; Fire and Light: The Theology of the Human Person, 1989; Ascent to Heaven: The Theology of the Human Person according to Saint John of the Ladder, 1989 (with wife, Sophie Chryssavgis) The World My Church, 1990; The Desert Is Alive: Dimensions of Australian Spirituality, 1990; Repentance and Confession in the Orthodox Church, 1990; Love, Sexuality, and the Sacrament of Marriage, 1996; The Way of the Fathers: Exploring the Patristic Mind, 1998; Beyond the Shattered Image, 1999; Soul Mending: The Art of Spiritual Direction, 2000; In the Footsteps of Christ: The Ascetic Teaching of Abba Isaiah of Scetis, 2001; (trans. and author of introduction, with Pachomios Penkett) Abba Isaiah of Scetis Ascetic Discourses, 2002; In the Heart of the Desert: The Spirituality of the Desert Fathers and Mothers, 2003; (trans. and author of introduction) Letters from the Desert: A Selection of Questions and Responses, 2003; (editor) Cosmic Grace and Humble Prayer: The Ecological Vision of the Green Patriarch Bartholomew I, 2003; John Climacus: From the Egyptian Desert to the Sinaite Mountain, 2004; Light through Darkness: The Orthodox Tradition, 2004. Contributor of papers and chapters to numerous books. **Address:** 50 Goddard Ave, Brookline, MA 02445, U.S.A. **Online address:** JChryisavg@aol.com

CHU, Petra ten-Doesschate. Dutch, b. 1942. **Genres:** Art/Art history. **Career:** Seton Hall University, South Orange, NJ, assistant professor, 1972-77, associate professor, 1977-80, professor of art, 1980, chairperson of department of art and music, 1980-2001, academic director, MA Program Museum Professions, 2002-. Princeton University, visiting professor, 1990-92. Nineteenth-Century Art Worldwide (www.19thc-artworldwide.org), managing editor. **Publications:** French Realism and the Dutch Masters, 1974; Courbet in Perspective, 1977; Dominique Vivant Denon, part 1, 1985, part 2, 1988; Im Lichte Hollands: Hollandische Malerei: des 17. Jahrhunderts aus den Sammlungen des Fursten von Liechtenstein und aus Schweizer Besitz, 1987; Nineteenth-Century European Art, 2002. EDITOR & CONTRIBUTOR: Letters of Gustave Courbet, 1992; (with G. Weisberg) The Popularization of Images: Visual Culture under the July Monarchy, 1994; (with J. Zutter) Courbet: Artiste et promoter de son oeuvre, 1998. Work represented in anthologies. Contributor to art journals and exhibition catalogs. Contributor of articles to dictionaries. **Address:** Department of Art and Music, Seton Hall University, 400 S Orange Ave, South Orange, NJ 07079-2697, U.S.A. **Online address:** chupetra@shu.edu

CHUPACK, Cindy. (born United States), b. 1973. **Genres:** Advertising/Public relations. **Career:** Writer. Coach, television series producer, 1989; A Whole New Ballgame, television series scriptwriter, 1995; Everybody Loves Raymond, Columbia Broadcasting System, Inc. (CBS), television series scriptwriter, 1996-98; Sex and the City, Home Box Office (HBO), scriptwriter and executive producer, 1998-2004; Madigan Men, television series executive producer, 2000. **Publications:** The Between Boyfriends Book: A Collection of Cautiously Hopeful Essays, 2003. Contributor to periodicals, and scriptwriter. **Address:** c/o Home Box Office, 1100 Avenue of the Americas, New York, New York, NY 10036, U.S.A.

CHURCH, (Frank) Forrest(er), (IV). American, b. 1948. **Genres:** Literary criticism and history, Theology/Religion, Biography, Essays. **Career:** All Souls Unitarian Church, New York City, pastor, 1978-. **Publications:** Father and Son: A Personal Biography of Senator Frank Church of Idaho, 1985; The Devil and Dr. Church: A Guide to Hell for Atheists and True Believers, 1986; Entertaining Angels: A Guide to Heaven for Atheists and True Believers, 1987; Everyday Miracles (essays), 1988; The Seven Deadly Virtues: A

Guide to Purgatory for Atheists and True Believers, 1988; (with J.A. Buehrens) Our Chosen Faith: An Introduction to Unitarian Universalism, 1989; God and Other Famous Liberals, 1991; Lifelines: Holding on and Letting Go, 1996; Lifecraft: The Art of Meaning in the Everyday, 2000; Bringing God Home: A Traveler's Guide, 2002; The American Creed: A Spiritual & Patriotic Primer, 2003. EDITOR: (and author of preface) The Essential Tillich (anthology), 1987; (with T.J. Mulry) The Macmillan Book of Earliest Christian Hymns, 1988; (with T.J. Mulry) The Macmillan Book of Earliest Christian Prayers, 1988; (with T.J. Mulry) The Macmillan Book of Earliest Christian Meditations, 1989; (with T.J. Mulry) One Prayer at a Time, 1989; A.P. Davies, Without Apology: Meditations on Liberal Religion, 1998; Restoring Faith: America's Religious Leaders Answer Terror with Hope, 2001. **Address:** All Souls Unitarian Church, 1157 Lexington, New York, NY 10021, U.S.A.

CHURCHETT, Stephen. British, b. 1947. **Genres:** Plays/Screenplays. **Career:** Actor in films and television and playwright. **Publications:** PLAYS: Tom and Clem, 1997; Heritage, 1997. **Address:** c/o The Agency, 24 Pottery Lane, London W11 4LZ, England.

CHURCHILL, Caryl. British, b. 1938. **Genres:** Plays/Screenplays. **Career:** Royal Court Theatre, London, resident writer, 1974. **Publications:** Owners, 1973; Vinegar Tom, 1978; Light Shining in Buckinghamshire, 1976; Traps, 1978; Cloud Nine, 1979; Top Girls, 1982, 1989; Fen, 1983; Softcops, 1984; Collected Plays, vol. 1, 1985, vol. 2, 1988; (with D. Lan) A Mouthful of Birds, 1987; Serious Money, 1987; Ice Cream, 1989; Hot Fudge, 1990; Mad Forest, 1990; (with I. Spink and O. Gough) Lives of the Great Poisoners, 1991; Churchill Shorts: Short Plays, 1990; Top Girls, 1991; The Skriker, 1994; (trans.) Thyestes, 1994; Hotel, 1997; Blue Heart, 1997; This Is a Chair, 1998; Churchill: Plays Three, 1998; Far Away, 2000; A Number, 2002. **Address:** c/o Casarotto Ramsay & Associates Ltd, National House, 60-66 Wardour St, London WIV 4ND, England.

CHURCHILL, E. Richard. Also writes as Cora Verlag. American, b. 1937. **Genres:** Novellas/Short stories, Education, History, Recreation. **Career:** Freelance writer. Park-Washington Elementary School, School District No. 6, teacher, 1959-80. **Publications:** Colorado Quiz Bag, 1973; Doc Holliday, Bat Masterson and Wyatt Earp: Their Colorado Careers, 1974; Hidden Word Puzzles, 1975; Shaggy Dog Stories, 1975; Six-Million Dollar Cucumber, 1976; Hidden Word Puzzles 2, 1977; Holiday Hullabaloo!, 1977; Bionic Banana, 1979; New Puzzles, 1980; Classroom Activity Program, 1980; I Bet I Can!, 1981; Sneaky Tricks to Fool Your Friends, 1986; Instant Paper Toys, 1986; Quick and Easy Paper Toys, 1988; Instant Paper Airplanes, 1988; Paper Toys that Fly, Soar, Zoom, and Whistle, 1989; Optical Illusion Tricks and Toys, 1989; Fast and Funny Paper Toys You Can Make, 1989; Building with Paper, 1990; Science Paper Toys, 1990; Dartmoor Danger, 1990; Visions of Terror, 1990; Terrific Paper Toys, 1991; Amazing Science Experiments with Everyday Materials, 1991; Fabulous Paper Airplanes, 1991; Paper Tricks and Toys, 1992; Who I Am and Who I Want to Be, 1992; Holiday Paper Projects, 1992; Fantastic Paper Flying Machines, 1993; Paper Action Toys, 1993; No Fair Standing Still, 1994; Where Is It?, 1995; 45 Profiles in Modern Music, 1996; A Haunted Mine Is a Terrible Thing to Waste (juvenile novel), 1998; You and the Law, 1998; Understanding Our Economy, 1998; Short Lessons in U.S. History, 1999; American History Jeopardy, 2002. CO-AUTHOR: Games and Puzzles for Family Leisure, 1965; Fun with American History, 1966; Fun with American Literature, 1968; Short Lessons in World History, 1971; How Our Nation Became Great, 1971; Puzzle It Out, 1971; Everybody Came to Leadville, 1971; The McCartys, 1972; Community Civic Case Book, 1973; Enriched Social Studies Teaching, 1973; Puzzles and Quizzes, 1974; American History Activity Reader, 1974; World History Activity Reader, 1974. YOUNG ADULT NOVELS: Secret Fear, 1992; Fear the Fog, 1992; Images of Evil, 1993; Destination Horror, 1993; Fearful Shadows, 1998; Devil's Deep, 1998. **Address:** 25890 Weld County Rd 53, Kersey, CO 80644, U.S.A.

CHURCHILL, Winston S(pencer). British, b. 1940. **Genres:** History. **Career:** War correspondent in Yemen, the Congo, and Angola, 1963; British Broadcasting Corp. (BBC-Radio), London, England, presenter of "This Time of Day," 1964-65; correspondent in Borneo and Vietnam, 1966, the Middle East, 1967, and Chicago, IL, and Czechoslovakia, 1968; The Times, (London), correspondent in Nigeria, Biafra, and the Middle East, 1969-70; British Parliament, House of Commons, London, Conservative member of Parliament for Stretford, Lancashire, 1970-83, and Davyhulme, Manchester, 1983-. Parliamentary private secretary to minister of housing and construction, 1970-72, and to minister of state at Foreign and Commonwealth Office, 1972-73; secretary of Conservative Foreign and Commonwealth Affairs Committee, 1973-76; Conservative front-bench spokesman on defence, 1976-

78; Conservative Backbench 1922 Committee, executive, 1979-86, treasurer, 1987-88; vice-chairman of Conservative Defence Committee, 1979-83; Conservative party coordinator for defence and multilateral disarmament, 1982-84; member of Select Committee on Defence, 1984-. President of Trafford Park Industrial Council, 1971-; member of board of trustees of Winston Churchill Memorial Trust, 1968-, and National Benevolent Fund for the Aged, 1974-; member of board of governors of English Speaking Union, 1975-80. Special correspondent in China, 1972, and Portugal, 1975. **Publications:** First Journey, 1964; (with father, Randolph Spencer Churchill) The Six Day War, 1967; Defending the West, 1981; Memories and Adventures, 1989; His Father's Son, 1996. **Address:** Curtis Brown, 28/29 Haymarket, Haymarket House, 4th Fl, London SW1Y 4SP, England.

CHURCHLAND, Paul M. American (born Canada), b. 1942. **Genres:** Philosophy. **Career:** University of California, San Diego, professor of philosophy. **Publications:** Scientific Realism and the Plasticity of the Mind, 1979; Matter and Consciousness: A Contemporary Introduction to the Philosophy of the Mind, 1984; (ed. with C.A. Hooker) Images of Science: Essays on Realism and Empiricism, 1985; A Neurocomputational Perspective: The Nature of the Mind and the Structure of Science, 1990; The Engine of Reason, the Seat of the Soul, 1995; On the Contrary (essays), 1998. **Address:** Dept. of Philosophy, H&SS 8016, University of California, San Diego, 9500 Gilman Dr, La Jolla, CA 92093-0119, U.S.A. **Online address:** pchurchland@ucsd.edu

CHVIDKOVSKI, Dmitri. *See* **SHVIDKOVSKY, Dimitri.**

CHWAST, Seymour. American, b. 1931. **Genres:** Children's fiction, Illustrations, Adult non-fiction. **Career:** Graphic artist, designer, and illustrator, 1956-; New York Times, junior designer; worked for Esquire, House and Garden, and Glamour magazines; Push Pin Studios, NYC, founding partner, originator and director of studio publication, Push Pin Graphic, 1956-80, studio director, 1975-82; Pushpin, Lubalin, Peckolick Inc., NYC, partner, 1982-86; Pushpin Group, president and director, 1982-. Cooper Union Art School, NYC, instructor of design and illustration, 1975-81; Parsons School of Design, visiting lecturer; has had exhibitions and one-man shows worldwide. **Publications:** SELF-ILLUSTRATED FOR CHILDREN: (with M.S. Moskof) Still Another Alphabet Book, 1969; (with Moskof) Still Another Number Book, 1971; Still Another Children's Book, 1972; (with Moskof), Flip-Flap Limerickricks, 1972; Flip Flap Mother Gooooose, 1972; Bushy Bride: Norwegian Fairy Tale, 1983; Tall City, Wide Country: A Book to Read Forward and Backward, 1983; The Alphabet Parade, 1991; Paper Pets: Make Your Own Three Dogs, Two Cats, One Parrot, One Rabbit, One Monkey, 1993; The Twelve Circus Rings, 1993; Mr. Merlin and the Turtle, Books, 1996. OTHER: The Book of Battles, 1957; (with D.J.R. Bruckner and S. Heller) Art against War: 400 Years of Protest in Art, 1984; (self-illustrated) The Left-Handed Designer, 1985; (self-illustrated) Happy Birthday Bach, 1985; (with D. Barthelme) Sam's Bar, 1987; (with S. Heller) Graphic Style: From Victorian to Post-Modern, 1988; (with B. Cohen and S. Heller) Trylon and Perisphere: The 1939 New York World's Fair, 1989; (with V.G. Levi and S. Heller) You Must Have Been a Beautiful Baby: Baby Pictures of the Stars, 1992; (self-illustrated) Bra Fashions by Stephanie, 1994; (with S. Heller) Jackets Required: An Illustrated History of the American Book Jacket 1920-1950, 1995; (with J. Fraser and S. Heller) Japanese Modern: Graphic Design between the Wars, 1996. DESIGNER: Connoisseur Book of the Cigar, 1967; The Illustrated Cat, 1976; The Illustrated Flower, 1977. EDITOR: (with J-C Suares) The Literary Cat, 1977; (and comp. with S. Heller) The Art of New York, 1983; (and comp. with B. Cohen and S. Heller) New York Observed: Artists and Writers Look at the City, 1650 to the Present, 1987; (with S. Heller) Sourcebook of Visual Ideas, 1989. Illustrator of children's books by J. Gill, E. Merriam, P. La Farge, O. deKay Jr., S. Kroll, D. Weaver, H. Ziefert, B.D. Goldin, D. Johnston. Illustrator of adult books by E. Heller and V. Levites, S. Heller, V. Perrone, D.K. Holland. Creator of illustrations, posters, typographic designs and animated commercials for print and television advertising, book jackets, record albums, packages, brochures and magazines, and art for theatrical productions. **Address:** c/o Pushpin Group Inc., 55 E 9th St #1G, New York, NY 10003, U.S.A.

CIARAVINO, Helene. American, b. 1972. **Genres:** Adult non-fiction. **Career:** Editor, poet, and freelance writer; Our Lady of Mercy Academy, Syosset, NY, teacher of American literature and college writing. **Publications:** How to Pray: Tapping into the Power of Divine Communication, 2001; How to Publish Your Poetry: A Complete Guide to Finding the Right Publishers for Your Work, 2001. **Address:** c/o Author Mail, Square One Publishers, 6 Birch Hill Rd, Ballston Lake, NY 12019, U.S.A.

CICELLIS, Kay. Greek (born France), b. 1926. **Genres:** Novels, Translations, Novellas/Short stories. **Publications:** The Easy Way, 1950; No Name in the Street (novel), 1952; Death of a Town, 1954; Ten Seconds from Now (novel), 1957; The Way to Colonos: A Greek Triptych, 1960; (trans.) Their Most Serene Majesties, by Angel Vlachos, 1963; (trans.) Drifting Cities, by Stratis Tsirkas, 1974; (trans.) The Lost Center, by Zissimos Lorentzatos, 1980; (trans.) Koula, by Menis Koumandareas, 1991; (trans.) What Does Mrs. Freeman Want?, by Petros Abatzoglou, 1991; (trans.) The Life of Ismail Ferik Pasha, by Rhea Galanaki, 1996. **Address:** 13 Hatzikostas St, Mavili Sq, 11521 Athens, Greece.

CIMBALA, Stephen J. American, b. 1943. **Genres:** Military/Defense/Arms control, Politics/Government. **Career:** State University of New York at Stony Brook, assistant professor of political science, 1969-73; Pennsylvania State University, Delaware County Campus, Media, associate professor, 1973-86, professor of political science, 1986-, chief academic officer, 1973-81, distinguished professor, 2000-. Ohio State University, visiting associate professor, 1976; speaker at colleges and universities. **Publications:** Extended Deterrence: The U.S. and NATO Europe, 1987; Nuclear War and Nuclear Strategy, 1987; Rethinking Nuclear Strategy, 1988; Nuclear Strategizing: Deterrence and Reality, 1988; Nuclear Endings, 1989; NATO Strategy and Nuclear Escalation, 1990; Uncertainty and Control: Future Superpower Strategy, 1990; First Strike Stability, 1990; Conflict Termination in Europe, 1990; Strategy after Deterrence, 1991; Clausewitz and Escalation, 1991; Force and Diplomacy in the Future, 1992; U.S. Nuclear Strategy in the New World Order, 1993; U.S. Military Strategy and the Cold War Endgame, 1995; The Politics of Warfare, 1997; The Past and Future of Nuclear Deterrence, 1998; Nuclear Strategy in the 21st Century, 2000. EDITOR & CONTRIBUTOR: National Security Strategy, 1984; Strategic War Termination, 1986; The Reagan Defense Program, 1986; Soviet Command, Control, and Communications, 1987; Challenges to Deterrence, 1987; Intelligence and Intelligence Policy in a Democratic Society, 1987; The Technology, Strategy, and Politics of SDI, 1987; (with K. Dunn) Conflict Termination and Military Strategy, 1987; Artificial Intelligence and National Security, 1987; (with J. Douglass Jr.) Ending a Nuclear War, 1988; The Soviet Challenge in the 1990s, 1989; Strategic Arms Control after SALT, 1989; Strategic Air Defense, 1989; (with S.R. Waldman) Controlling and Ending Conflict, 1992; Clinton and Post-Cold War Defense, 1996; Coercive Military Strategy, 1998. Work represented in anthologies. Contributor of articles and reviews to professional journals. **Address:** Department of Political Science, 118 Vairo Library, Pennsylvania State University Delaware County Campus, Media, PA 19063, U.S.A. **Online address:** sjc2@psu.edu

CIMENT, James D. Canadian, b. 1958. **Genres:** Children's non-fiction. **Career:** City College of New York, New York, NY, lecturer, 1985-94; freelance writer and editor, 1992-2000; ABC-CLIO, Santa Barbara, CA, acquisitions editor, 2000-01; East River Books, Santa Barbara, CA, president, 2002-. **Publications:** Law and Order, 1995; Scholastic Encyclopedia of the North American Indian, 1996; The Kurds: State and Minority in Turkey, Iraq, and Iran, 1996; Algeria: The Fundamentalist Challenge, 1997; Angola and Mozambique: Postcolonial Wars in Southern Africa, 1997; Palestine/Israel: The Long Conflict, 1997; The Young People's History of the United States, 1998; Atlas of African-American History, 2001. EDITOR: (with I. Ness) Encyclopedia of Global Population and Demographics, 1999; Encyclopedia of Conflicts since World War II, 1999; (with I. Ness) Encyclopedia of Third Parties in America, 2000; Encyclopedia of the Great Depression and New Deal, 2001; Encyclopedia of American Immigration, 2001. **Address:** 2020 De La Vina, Apt. B, Santa Barbara, CA 93105, U.S.A. **Online address:** james.ciment@verizon.net

CIMENT, Jill. Canadian, b. 1953. **Genres:** Novels, Novellas/Short stories, Autobiography/Memoirs. **Career:** Author, 1986-. **Publications:** Small Claims (short stories and novella), 1986; The Law of Falling Bodies (novel), 1993; Half a Life (autobiography), 1996. Contributor to periodicals. **Address:** c/o Mary Evans, 242 E. Fifth Ave., New York, NY 10003, U.S.A.

CIMINO, Richard P. American. **Genres:** Theology/Religion. **Career:** Writer. **Publications:** Against the Stream: The Adoption of Traditional Christian Faiths by Young Adults, 1997; (with D. Lattin) Shopping for Faith: American Religion in the New Millennium, 1998; Trusting the Spirit: Renewal and Reform in American Religion, 2001. Author of articles magazines. **Address:** c/o Author Mail, Jossey-Bass, 989 Market St., San Francisco, CA 94103, U.S.A.

CIOCHON, Russell L. American, b. 1948. **Genres:** Anthropology/Ethnology, Archaeology/Antiquities, Earth sciences. **Career:** University of North Carolina at Charlotte, lecturer in anthropology, 1978-81; University of California, Berkeley, research specialist in paleontology, 1982-83, research associate at Institute of Human Origins, 1983-85; State University of New

York at Stony Brook, research associate in anatomical sciences, 1985-86; University of Arizona, Tucson, visiting lecturer in anthropology, 1987; University of Iowa, Iowa City, assistant professor, 1987-90, associate professor of anthropology and pediatric dentistry, 1990-95; professor of anthropology and pediatric dentistry, 1996-; chair, department of anthropology, 1998-. Writer and subject of television documentaries; guest on radio talk shows. **Publications:** (with J.G. Fleagle) Primate Evolution and Human Origins, 1985, rev. ed., 1987; (with J.W. Olsen and J. James) Other Origins: The Search for the Giant Ape in Human Prehistory, 1990; (with Fleagle) The Human Evolution Source Book, 1993. EDITOR: (with A.B. Chiarelli, and contrib.) Evolutionary Biology of the New World Monkeys and Continental Drift, 1980; (with R.S. Corruccini, and contrib.) New Interpretations of Ape and Human Ancestry, 1983; Advances in Human Evolution Series, 1991-; (with Corruccini, and contrib.) Integrative Paths to the Past: Paleoanthropological Advances in Honor of F. Clark Howell, 1994; (with R. Nisbett) The Primate Anthology, 1998; (with B. Wood) Human Evolution (series), 1998-. (with N. Boaz) Dragon Bone Hill: An Ice Age Saga of Homo erectus, 2004 Contributor to books. Television scriptwriter. Contributor of articles and reviews to scientific journals and popular magazines. **Address:** Department of Anthropology, MH114, University of Iowa, Iowa City, IA 52242, U.S.A. **Online address:** russell-ciochon@uiowa.edu

CIRESI, Rita. American, b. 1960. **Genres:** Novels, Novellas/Short stories. **Career:** Pennsylvania State University, University Park, science writer and editor for department of agriculture, 1989-92; Hollins College, Roanoke, VA, assistant professor of English, 1992-95; University of South Florida, associate professor of English, 1995-. **Publications:** STORIES: Mother Rocket, 1993; Sometimes I Dream in Italian, 2000. NOVELS: Blue Italian, 1996; Pink Slip, 1999; Remind Me Again Why I Married You, 2002. **Address:** Dept of English, University of South Florida, Tampa, FL 33620, U.S.A. **Online address:** rciresi@cas.usf.edu

CITRO, Joseph A. American. **Genres:** Science fiction/Fantasy. **Career:** Writer, lecturer, and teacher. **Publications:** FICTION: Shadow Child, 1987; Guardian Angels, 1988; The Unseen, 1990; Dark Twilight, 1991; Green Mountain Ghosts, Ghouls & Unsolved Mysteries, 1994; Deus-X, 1994; Passing Strange: True Tales of New England Hauntings and Horrors, 1996; Green Mountains, Dark Tales, 1999. OTHER: Monsters: Three Tales by Joseph A. Citro (sound recording), 1992. Contributor to books. **Address:** 217 St. Paul St., Burlington, VT 05401, U.S.A.

CIVIL-BROWN, Sue. *See* LEE, Rachel.

CLAGUE, Christopher K. American, b. 1938. **Genres:** Economics. **Career:** Harvard University, Cambridge, MA, instructor in economics, 1965-67; President's Council of Economic Advisers, Washington, DC, senior staff economist, 1967-68; University of Maryland at College Park, assistant professor, 1968-71, associate professor, 1971-79, professor of economics, 1979-, department head, 1980-82, director of research for Project on Institutional Reform and the Informal Sector, 1990-. Visiting professor at Boston University's Center for Latin American Development Studies, 1974-75, University of California, Berkeley, 1983, University of Hawaii at Manoa, 1990, and University of Nottingham, 1990. National Bureau of Economic Research, member of executive committee, Conference on Research in Income and Wealth, 1983-89; conducted field work in Peru, 1966, 1969, and 1971, and Haiti, 1968 and 1969; consultant to World Bank and Organization for Economic Cooperation and Development. **Publications:** (with R. Rotberg) Haiti: The Politics of Squalor, 1971; (with R. Betancourt) Capital Utilization: Theoretical and Empirical Analysis, 1981; (ed. with G. C. Rausser and contrib.) The Emergence of Market Economies in Eastern Europe, 1992. Work represented in anthologies. Contributor to economic journals. **Address:** Department of Economics, University of Maryland at College Park, College Park, MD 20742, U.S.A.

CLAIRE, Cherie. (Chere (Dastugue) Coen). American, b. 1960. **Genres:** Novels. **Career:** Novelist. **Publications:** A Cajun Dream, 1999; (with P. Conn and V. Dark) Snow Angels (anthology), 1999; Emilie, 2000; Rose, 2000; Gabrielle, 2001; Delphine, 2002. **Address:** c/o Author Mail, Kensington Publications Corp., 850 Third Ave., New York, NY 10022, U.S.A. **Online address:** ccoen@thevine.net

CLANCY, Flora Simmons. American. **Genres:** Architecture. **Career:** Colgate University, Hamilton, NY, lecturer, 1973-78; University of New Mexico, Albuquerque, 1979-, currently professor of art history. Contributor to symposia on Mayan art and architecture. **Publications:** Maya: Treasures of an Ancient Civilization, photographs by Stuart Rome, 1985; (editor, with Peter D. Harrison) Vision and Revision in Maya Studies, 1990; Pyramids,

1994; Sculpture in the Ancient Maya Plaza: The Early Classic Period, 1999. Contributor of scholarly articles to periodicals. **Address:** Department of Art and Art History, University of New Mexico, Albuquerque, NM 87131, U.S.A. **Online address:** flora@unm.edu

CLANCY, Tom. (Thomas L. Clancy, Jr). American, b. 1947. **Genres:** Novels, Novellas/Short stories, Military/Defense/Arms control, Biography. **Career:** Insurance agent in Baltimore, Md. and Hartford, Conn., until 1973; O.F. Bowen Agency (insurance company), Owings, Md., agent, 1973-, owner, 1980-; writer. **Publications:** FICTION: The Hunt for Red October, 1984; Red Storm Rising, 1986; Patriot Games, 1987; The Cardinal of the Kremlin, 1988; Clear and Present Danger, 1989; Sum of All Fears, 1991; Without Remorse, 1993; Debt of Honor, 1994; Executive Orders, 1996; SSN: Strategies of Submarine Warfare, 1996; Rainbow Six, 1998; Every Man a Tiger, 1999; The Bear and the Dragon, 2000; Red Rabbit, 2002; The Teeth of the Tiger, 2003. TOM CLANCY'S OP-CENTER SERIES WITH S. PIEC-ZENIK: Mirror Image, 1995; Game of State, 1997; Acts of War, 1997; Sea of Fire, 2003. OTHER: Submarine: A Guided Tour inside a Nuclear Warship, 1993; Armored Cav: A Guided Tour of an Armored Cavalry Regiment, 1994; Fighter Wing: A Guided Tour of an Air Force Combat Wing, 1995; Reality Check: What's Going On out There?, 1995; Marine: A Guided Tour of a Marine Expeditionary Unit, 1995; (with F. Franks Jr.) Into the Storm: A Study in Command, 1997; Airborne: A Guided Tour of an Airborne Task Force, 1997; (with Chuck Horner) Every Man A Tiger, 1999; Carrier: A Guided Tour of an Aircraft Carrier, 1999; (with Martin Greenberg) SSN: Strategies of Submarine Warfare, 2000; (with John Gresham) Special Forces: a Guided Tour of US Army Special Forces, 2001; (with C. Stiner and T. Koltz) Shadow Warriors: Inside the Special Forces, 2002; (with John Gresham) Submarine: A Guided Tour inside a Nuclear Warship, 2003; (with Tony Zinni and Tom Kolz) Battle Ready, 2004. **Address:** Red Storm Entertainment, 2000 Aerial Center Parkway Ste 110, Morrisville, NC 27560-9294, U.S.A.

CLAPHAM, Christopher. British, b. 1941. **Genres:** International relations/ Current affairs. **Career:** Lancaster University, sr. lecturer in politics, 1974-89, professor of politics and international relations, 1989-2002; Cambridge University, Centre of African Studies, professor, 2002-. **Publications:** Haile-Selassie's Government, 1969; Liberia and Sierra Leone: An Essay in Comparative Politics, 1976; Foreign Policy Making in Developing States, 1977; Private Patronage and Public Power, 1982; (ed.) Political Dilemmas of Military Regimes, 1984; Third World Politics, 1985; Transformation and Continuity in Revolutionary Ethiopia, 1988; Africa and the International System, 1996; African Guerrillas, 1998. **Address:** Centre of African Studies, Cambridge University, Free School Ln, Cambridge CB2 3RQ, England. **Online address:** csc34@cam.ac.uk

CLAPP, Nicholas. American, b. 1936. **Genres:** Documentaries/Reportage. **Career:** Documentary filmmaker and writer. **Publications:** The Road to Ubar: Finding the Atlantis of the Sands, 1998. **Address:** 1551 South Robertson Blvd., Los Angeles, CA 90035, U.S.A.

CLAPP, Rodney. American. **Genres:** Theology/Religion. **Career:** Writer, editor, and theologian. InterVarsity Press, Downers Grove, IL, senior editor for general and academic books. **Publications:** (with R.E. Webber) People of the Truth: the Power of the Worshiping Community in the Modern World, 1988; Families at the Crossroads: Beyond Traditional and Modern Options, 1993; A Peculiar People: The Church as Culture in a Post-Christian Society, 1996; (ed.) The Consuming Passion: Christianity and the Culture of Consumption, 1997. **Address:** c/o Author Relations, InterVarsity Press, PO Box 1400, Downers Grove, IL 60515, U.S.A.

CLAPPER, Gregory S(cott). American, b. 1951. **Genres:** Inspirational/ Motivational Literature, Theology/Religion. **Career:** Westmar College (now Teikyo Westmar University), LeMars, IA, assistant professor, 1985-89, associate professor of religion and philosophy, 1989-91; senior minister of United Methodist church in Waverly, IA, 1991-94; Huntingdon College, Montgomery, AL, associate professor in Chapman-Benson Chair of Christian Faith and Philosophy, 1994-98; University of Indianapolis, professor of religion and philosophy, 1998-. Metodistkirkens Studiesenter, Bergen, Norway, visiting professor, 1988; leader of workshops and retreats. **Publications:** John Wesley on Religious Affections, 1989; As if the Heart Mattered: A Wesleyan Spirituality, 1997; When the World Breaks Your Heart: Spiritual Ways to Live with Tragedy, 1999; Living Your Heart's Desire, 2005. Contributor of articles and reviews to periodicals. **Address:** 243 Hawthorne Ln, Greenwood, IN 46142, U.S.A. **Online address:** gclapper@uindy.edu.

CLARE, Ellen. See SINCLAIR, Olga (Ellen).

CLARE, George (Peter). British (born Austria), b. 1920. **Genres:** Autobiography/Memoirs, Documentaries/Reportage. **Career:** British Control Commission, Germany, 1946-54; Axel Springer Publishing Group, Hamburg, 1954-63, London, Managing Director, 1963-83. **Publications:** Last Waltz in Vienna, 1981 (W.H. Smith Literary Award, 1982); Berlin Days 1946-1947, 1989. **Address:** 62 Northways, College Crescent, London NW3 5DP, England. **Online address:** george@vincla.demon.co.uk

CLARE, Helen. See CLARKE, Pauline.

CLARK, A(ndrea) Kim. Canadian, b. 1964. **Genres:** History. **Career:** University of Western Ontario, London, assistant professor, 1995-99, associate professor of anthropology, 1999-. Universidad Andina Simon Bolivar, visiting professor, 1998; York University, associate fellow of Centre for Research on Latin America and the Caribbean; Taller de Estudios Historicos, associate fellow. **Publications:** The Redemptive Work: Railway and Nation in Ecuador, 1895-1930, 1998. Contributor to books published in Spanish and English. Contributor of articles and reviews to professional journals. **Address:** Department of Anthropology, University of Western Ontario, London, ON, Canada N6A 5C2. **Online address:** akc@uwo.ca

CLARK, A(ilsa) M. British, b. 1926. **Genres:** Zoology, Natural history, Marine sciences/Oceanography. **Career:** British Museum-National History (now Natural History Museum), London, England, curator of echinoderms, 1948-86. **Publications:** Starfishes and Related Echinoderms, 1962, 3rd ed. 1977; (with F.W.E. Rowe) Indo-Pacific Echinoderms, 1971; (with J. Courtman-Stock) Echinoderms of Southern Africa, 1976; (with M.E. Downey) Starfishes of the Atlantic, 1992; (with Y. Liao) Echinoderms of Southern China. **Address:** Gyllyngdune South Rd., Wivelsfield Green, Haywards Heath, Sussex RH17 7QS, England.

CLARK, Adam. See BOUNDS, Sydney J(ames).

CLARK, Andrew F. American. **Genres:** Area studies. **Career:** University of North Carolina at Wilmington, professor of African and global history, 1990-. **Publications:** From Frontier to Backwater: Economy and Society in the Upper Senegal Valley, 18501920, 1999; (with L.C. Phillips) Historical Dictionary of Senegal, 2nd ed., 1994; Lost and Found in West Africa: An American in Senegal, forthcoming. **Address:** Department of History, University of North Carolina at Wilmington, Wilmington, NC 28403, U.S.A. **Online address:** clarkaf@aol.com

CLARK, Andy. British, b. 1957. **Genres:** Medicine/Health, Psychology. **Career:** University of Glasgow, Scotland, temporary lecturer in philosophy, 1984-85; University of Sussex, Brighton, England, lecturer, 1985-92, senior lecturer to reader in philosophy and cognitive sciences, 1992-93; Washington University, St. Louis, MO, professor of philosophy and director of Philosophy/Neuroscience/Psychology Program, 1993-. Visiting fellow, professor and lecturer at universities worldwide. **Publications:** Microcognition: Philosophy, Cognitive Science, and Parallel Distributed Processing, 1989; Associative Engines: Connectionism, Concepts, and Representational Change, 1993; Being There: Putting Brain, Body, and World Together Again, 1997. EDITOR: (with R. Lutz) Connectionism in Context, 1992; (with L. May and M. Friedman, and contrib.) Mind and Morals: Essays on Ethics and Cognitive Science, 1996; (with P. Millican) Essays in Honour of Alan Turing, Vol I: The Theory of Computation, Vol II: Connectionism, Concepts, and Folk Psychology, 1996; (with J. Ezquerro and J. Larrazabal, and contrib.) Philosophy and Cognitive Science: Categories, Consciousness, and Reasoning, 1996. Contributor to books. Contributor of articles and reviews to periodicals. **Address:** Department of Philosophy, Sycamore 117, Indiana University, Bloomington, IN 47405-7005, U.S.A. **Online address:** andy@indiana.edu

CLARK, (Carter) Blue. American, b. 1946. **Genres:** Law. **Career:** University of Utah, Salt Lake City, program director, 1976-77; Morningside College, Sioux City, IA, assistant professor, 1977-79; California State University, Long Beach, associate professor to professor, 1979-92; Oklahoma City University, OK, executive vice-president, 1991-. **Publications:** Lone Wolf v. Hitchcock (ethnohistory/law), 1994. Contributor to books and periodicals. Some writings appear under the name C.B. Clark. **Address:** Law School Office 209, Bldg SC, Oklahoma City University, 2501 North Blackwelder, Oklahoma City, OK 73106, U.S.A. **Online address:** bclark@okcu.edu

CLARK, Carol Higgins. American, b. 1956. **Genres:** Mystery/Crime/Suspense. **Career:** Actress and novelist. Appeared off-Broadway, and in television films and miniseries. **Publications:** MYSTERY NOVELS: Decked,

1992; Snagged, 1993; Iced, 1995; Twanged, 1998; (with M.H. Clark) Deck the Halls, 2000; Popped, 2003. **Address:** c/o Scribner, 1230 Avenue of the Americas, New York, NY 10020, U.S.A.

CLARK, Charles E. American, b. 1929. **Genres:** History. **Career:** Reporter, Providence Journal, and Evening Bulletin, Rhode Island, 1956-61; Assistant Professor of History, Southeastern Massachusetts Technological Institute, North Dartmouth, 1965-67; University of New Hampshire, Durham, Assistant Professor, 1967-70, Associate Professor, 1970-75, Professor of History, 1975-97; Chairman of the Dept., 1977-80; James H. Hayes and Claire Short Hayes Professor of the Humanities, 1993-97; Professor Emeritus of History, 1998-. **Publications:** The Eastern Frontier: The Settlement of Northern New England, 1610-1763, 1970, 1983; Maine: A Bicentennial History, 1977, 1990; Printers, The People and Politics: The New Hampshire Press and Ratification, 1989; The Public Prints: The Newspaper in Anglo-American Culture, 1665-1740, 1994; The Meetinghouse Tragedy: An Episode in the Life of a New England Town, 1998. EDITOR: (with J.S. Leamon and K. Bowden) Maine in the Early Republic: From Revolution to Statehood, 1988; (with E.C. Nordbeck) Granite and Grace: Essays Celebrating the 200th Anniversary of the New Hampshire Conference United Church of Christ, 2001. **Address:** 2 Thompson Ln, Durham, NH 03824, U.S.A. **Online address:** charles.clark@unh.edu

CLARK, Charles Michael Andres. American, b. 1960. **Genres:** Economics. **Career:** St. John's University, Jamaica, NY, instructor, 1984-90, assistant professor, 1990-91, associate professor of economics, 1991-96, professor of economics, 1996-. Economic consultant. **Publications:** Economic Theory and Natural Philosophy, 1992; (ed.) History and Historians of Political Economy, 1994; Institutional Economics and the Theory of Social Value, 1995. (with J. Healy) Pathways to a Basic Income, 1997; (ed. with C. Kavanagh) Unemployment in Ireland, 1998; (with S. Lerner and R. Needham) Basic Income: Economic Security for All Canadians, 1999; (with J. Rosicka) Economic Transition in Historical Perspective, 2001; Basic Income Guarantee, 2002. **Address:** Department of Economics, St. John's University, Jamaica, NY 11439, U.S.A. **Online address:** Cleiroch@aol.com

CLARK, Curt. See WESTLAKE, Donald E.

CLARK, David. See HARDCASTLE, Michael.

CLARK, David Lindsey. British, b. 1926. **Genres:** Music, Reference. **Career:** Central Music Library, London, England, assistant to the music librarian, 1952-59; Blackwell's Music Shop, Oxford, England, assistant to the manager, 1959-62; Oxford University, Oxford, assistant to the music librarian at Bodleian Library, 1962-65; Exeter City Library, Exeter, England, music librarian, 1965-72; Oxford County Library, Oxford, music librarian, 1972-91. Presenter of concerts in libraries. **Publications:** Music for Wind Instruments: A Survey of Anthologies in Print, 1970; (with Stoneham and Gillespie) Wind Ensemble Sourcebook and Biographical Guide, 1997; (with Stoneham and Gillespie) The Wind Ensemble Catalog, 1998; Appraisals of Original Wind Music: A Survey and Guide, 1999; Settings for Shakespeare Plays in Music of His Time: A Bibliographical Survey and Discography, forthcoming. **Address:** 19 Lower King's Ave, Exeter, Devon EX4 6JT, England.

CLARK, David Ridgley. American, b. 1920. **Genres:** Theatre, Poetry, Literary criticism and history. **Career:** University of Massachusetts, Amherst, instructor, 1951-58, assistant professor, 1958, associate professor, 1958-65, professor, 1965-85, chairman, Dept. of English, 1975-76, emeritus professor of English, 1985-. **Publications:** (with G.S. Koehler, L.O. Barron, and R.G. Tucker) A Curious Quire (poetry), 1962; W.B. Yeats and the Theatre of Desolate Reality, 1965, rev. ed. (with R. Clark), 1993; Dry Tree (poetry), 1966; (with F.B. Millett and A.W. Hoffman) Reading Poetry, 1968; Lyric Resonance: Glosses on Some Poems of Yeats, Frost, Crane, Cummings and Others (essays), 1972; That Black Day: The Manuscripts of Crazy Jane on the Day of Judgment, 1980; Yeats at Songs and Choruses, 1983; The Winding Stair (1929), Manuscript Materials, 1995; Words for Music Perhaps and Other Poems (1932), Manuscript Materials, 1999; Parnell's Funeral and Other Poems, Manuscript Materials, 2003. EDITOR: (with R. Skelton) Irish Renaissance, 1965; Riders to the Sea, 1970; Studies in The Bridge, 1970; (with G.P. Mayhew) A Tower of Polished Black Stones: Early Versions of The Shadowy Waters, 1971; (with M.J. Sidnell and G.P. Mayhew) Druid Craft: The Writing of The Shadowy Waters, 1971; Twentieth Century Interpretations of Murder in the Cathedral, 1971; Critical Essays on Hart Crane, 1982; (with J. McGuire) W.B. Yeats: The Writing of Sophocles' King Oedipus, 1989; (with R.E. Clark) The Plays, vol. 2 of The Collected Works of W.B. Yeats, 2001. **Address:** 481 Holgerson Rd, Sequim, WA 98382-9536, U.S.A.

CLARK, Dick. (Richard Wagstaff Clark). American, b. 1929. **Genres:** History, Music. **Career:** Announcer at radio and television stations in Syracuse, NY, and Utica, NY, 1950-51; Philadelphia, PA, radio announcer, 1952-56; host of television program Bandstand (later American Bandstand), 1956-89; dick clark productions, Burbank, Calif., chairman and chief executive officer, 1956-; co-founder and principal owner of United Stations Radio Network; host of television programs; producer of: television series, specials, annual award programs, movies, syndicated radio programs; actor in and producer of feature films. **Publications:** Your Happiest Years, 1959; To Goof or Not to Goof, 1963; (with Richard Robinson) Rock, Roll, and Remember (autobiography), 1976; Dick Clark's Program for Success in Your Business and Personal Life, 1980; (with Bill Libby) Looking Great, Staying Young, 1980; (with Michael Shore) The History of American Bandstand, 1985; Dick Clark's Easygoing Guide to Good Grooming, 1986; Dick Clark's American Bandstand, 1997. **Address:** dick clark productions, 3003 West Olive Ave., Burbank, CA 91505, U.S.A.

CLARK, Emma Chichester. British, b. 1955. **Genres:** Children's fiction, Illustrations. **Career:** Illustrator and author of children's books, 1983-. Visiting lecturer at Middlesex Polytechnic and City and Guilds School of Art, 1984-86. **Publications:** SELF-ILLUSTRATED FOR CHILDREN: Catch That Hat!, 1988; Myrtle, Tertle, and Gertle, 1989; The Story of Horrible Hilda and Henry, 1988; The Bouncing Dinosaur, 1990; I Never Saw a Purple Cow and Other Nonsense Rhymes, 1990; Tea with Aunt Augusta, 1991, in US as Lunch with Aunt Augusta, 1992; Miss Bilberry's New House, 1993, in US as Across the Blue Mountains; (with others) Tom's Pirate Ship and Other Stories, 1996; Little Miss Muffet Counts to Ten, 1997, in US as Little Miss Muffet's Count-Along Surprise; (with others) Mostly Animal Poetry, 1997; More!, 1998; I Love You, Blue Kangaroo!, 1998; Follow My Leader!, 1998; Where Are You, Blue Kangaroo?, 1999; It Was You, Blue Kangaroo!, 2000; No More Kissing!, 2000; What Shall We Do, Blue Kangaroo?, 2001; I'll Show You Blue Kangaroo!, 2003; Up in Heaven, 2003. Illustrator of books by A. Ahlberg, E. Allcock, C. Ashton, H. Branford, L. Cecil, R. Dahl, P. Dickinson, D.J. Enright, J. Falloon, A. Fine, B. Frankel, D.W. Jones, P. Lockwood, M. Mahy, L. Mare, G. McCaughrean, K. McMullan, J. Nimmo, J. Reeves, J. Romer, R. Sutcliff, P. Thomson, A. Turnbull, J. Yeoman. **Address:** c/o Laura Cecil, 17 Alwyne Villas, London N 1, England.

CLARK, Eric. British, b. 1937. **Genres:** Novels, International relations/Current affairs. **Career:** Reporter, Daily Mail, London, 1962-64; Writer, The Guardian, London, 1964-66, and The Observer, London, 1966-72. **Publications:** (co-author) Len Deighton's London Dossier, 1967; Everybody's Guide to Survival, 1969; Corps Diplomatique (in U.S. as Diplomat: The World of International Diplomacy), 1973; Black Gambit, 1978; The Sleeper, 1979; Send in the Lions, 1981; Chinese Burn (in U.S. as China Run), 1984; The Want Makers: Lifting the Lid off the World Advertising Industry, 1988; Hide and Seek, 1997; The Secret Enemy, 2002. **Address:** c/o A.M. Heath, 79 St Martin's Lane, London WC2N 4AA, England.

CLARK, Geoffrey (D.). American, b. 1940. **Genres:** Novellas/Short stories. **Career:** Roger Williams University, Bristol, RI, teacher of creative writing, 1971-99. Also taught at University of Wisconsin-Superior. Ampersand Press, co-founder, 1980. **Publications:** STORIES: What the Moon Said, 1983; Ruffian on the Stair, 1988; Schooling the Spirit, 1993; All the Way Home; Rabbit Fever, 2000. NOVELS: Jackdog Summer, 1996; Wedding in October, 2002. EDITOR: The Best I Can Wish You (anthology); How the Weather Was (anthology). Work represented in anthologies. **Address:** PO Box 43, Bristol, RI 02809, U.S.A. **Online address:** waypamgeof@aol.com

CLARK, George. Canadian (born United States), b. 1932. **Genres:** Literary criticism and history. **Career:** University of Wisconsin-Madison, instructor in English, 1961-63; University of Texas at Austin, assistant professor of English, 1963-65; Queen's University, Kingston, Ontario, assistant professor, 1965-68, associate professor, 1968-74, professor of English, 1974-; writer. University of Helsinki, lecturer, 1966-67. **Publications:** Beowulf, 1990; (ed.) J.R.R. Tolkein and His Literary Resonances, 2000. **Address:** Department of English, Queen's University, Kingston, ON, Canada K7L 3N6. **Online address:** clarkg@post.QueensU.ca

CLARK, Gordon L. Australian, b. 1950. **Genres:** Law, Business/Trade/Industry, Economics. **Career:** Harvard University, Cambridge, MA, assistant professor, 1978-83; University of Chicago, Chicago, IL, associate professor, 1983-85; Carnegie-Mellon University, Pittsburgh, PA, professor, 1985-91; Monash University, Clayton, Australia, professor, 1989-. **Publications:** Inter-Regional Migration, National Policy, and Social Justice, 1983; State Apparatus, 1984; Judges and the Cities, 1985; Regional Dynamics, 1986; Unions and Communities Under Siege, 1989; Pensions and Corporate Restructuring in American Industry, 1993; Multiculturalism, Difference, Postmodernism, 1994; Asian NIEs in the Global Economy, 1995. **Address:** 13 Glenowan Rd., Mt Waverley, VIC 3149, Australia.

CLARK, J(onathan) C(harles) D(ouglas). British, b. 1951. **Genres:** History, Intellectual history, Theology/Religion. **Career:** Peterhouse, Cambridge, research fellow, 1977-81; All Souls College, Oxford, fellow, 1986-95; University of Chicago, Committee on Social Thought, Lurcy Visiting Professor, 1993; University of Kansas, Hall Distinguished Professor of British History, 1995-; University of Northumbria, visiting professor, 2001-. **Publications:** The Dynamics of Change: The Crisis of the 1750s and English Party Systems, 1982; English Society 1688-1832: Ideology, Social Structure and Political Practice during the Ancien Regime, 1985, 2nd ed. as English Society 1660-1832: Religion, Ideology and Politics during the Ancien Regime, 2000; Revolution and Rebellion: State and Society in England in the Seventeenth and Eighteenth Centuries, 1986; The Language of Liberty 1660-1832: Political Discourse and Social Dynamics in The Anglo-American World, 1993; Samuel Johnson: Literature, Religion and English Cultural Politics from the Restoration to Romanticism, 1994; Our Shadowed Present: Modernism, Postmodernism and History, 2003. EDITOR: The Memoirs and Speeches of James, 2nd Earl Waldegrave, 1742-1763, 1988; Ideas and Politics in Modern Britain, 1990; Edmund Burke, Reflections on the Revolution in France, 2000; (jt.) Samuel Johnson in Historical Context, 2002. **Address:** Dept of History, University of Kansas, 1445 Jayhawk Blvd, Lawrence, KS 66045-7590, U.S.A. **Online address:** jcdclark@ku.edu

CLARK, Jerome. American, b. 1946. **Genres:** Songs/Lyrics and libretti, Biology, History, Paranormal, Sciences, Theology/Religion. **Career:** Fate, Highland Park, IL, associate editor, 1976-87, senior editor, 1987-89, then in St Paul, MN, consulting editor, 1989-93; writer, 1989-. Songwriter, with Robin and Linda Williams, 1978-; J. Allen Hynek Center for UFO Studies, officer, 1987-. **Publications:** (with L. Coleman) The Unidentified: Notes toward Solving the UFO Mystery, 1975; (with L. Coleman) Creatures of the Outer Edge, 1978; (with D.S. Rogo) Earth's Secret Inhabitants, 1979; (with J.G. Melton and A.A. Kelly) New Age Encyclopedia, 1990, as New Age Almanac, 1991; The UFO Encyclopedia, Vol. I: UFOs in the 1980s, 1990, Vol. II: The Emergence of a Phenomenon: UFOs from the Beginning through 1959, 1992, Vol. III: High Strangeness: UFOs from 1960 through 1979, 1996; UFO Encounters: Sightings, Visitations, and Investigations, 1992; Encyclopedia of Strange and Unexplained Physical Phenomena, 1993, as Unexplained! 347 Strange Sightings, Incredible Occurrences, and Puzzling Physical Phenomena, 1993, 2nd ed., 1999; (with N. Pear) Strange and Unexplained Happenings: When Nature Breaks the Rules of Science, 3 vols. 1995; The UFO Encyclopedia, 2 vols., 1998; The UFO Book, 1998; (with L. Coleman) Cryptozoology A-Z, 1999; Extraordinary Encounters, 2000. Contributor to periodicals. **Address:** c/o L. T. Mead, 379 Burning Tree Ct, Half Moon Bay, CA 94019, U.S.A. **Online address:** jkclark@frontiernet.net

CLARK, Kelly James. American, b. 1956. **Genres:** Philosophy. **Career:** Young Life, South Bend, IN, area director, 1981-84; Gordon College, Wenham, MA, assistant professor, 1985-89; Calvin College, Grand Rapids, MI, former assistant professor, currently associate professor, 1989-. **Publications:** Return to Reason: A Critique of Enlightenment Evidentialism and a Defense of Reason and Belief in God, 1990; Our Knowledge of God: Essays on Natural and Philosophical Theology, 1992; (ed.) Philosophers Who Believe: The Spiritual Journey of 11 Leading Thinkers, 1994; When Faith Is Not Enough, 1997. **Address:** Department of Philosophy, Calvin College, Grand Rapids, MI 49546, U.S.A. **Online address:** kclark@calvin.edu

CLARK, LaVerne Harrell. American, b. 1929. **Genres:** Novels, Novellas/Short stories, Cultural/Ethnic topics, Literary criticism and history, Mythology/Folklore, Photography, Biography. **Career:** Lecturer, freelance writer and photographer. University of Arizona Poetry Center, Tucson, director, 1962-66. **Publications:** They Sang for Horses: The Impact of the Horse on the Folklore of the Navajo and Apache Indians, 1966, rev. ed., 2001; (ed. and photographer) The Face of Poetry: 101 Poets in Two Significant Decades: The Sixties and the Seventies, 1976, 2nd ed., 1979; Re-visiting the Plains Indian Country of Mari Sandoz, 1977; Focus 101, 1979; The Deadly Swarm and Other Stories, 1985, 2nd ed., 1987; Keepers of the Earth, 1997, 2nd ed., 2002; Mari Sandoz's Native Nebraska: The Plains Indian Country, 2000. **Address:** 604 Main St, Smithville, TX 78957, U.S.A. **Online address:** lhldclark@aol.com

CLARK, Martin Fillmore, Jr. American, b. 1959. **Genres:** Novels. **Career:** Twenty-first Judicial Circuit, Stuart, VA, district court judge, 1992-95; circuit court judge, 1995-. **Publications:** NOVELS: The Many Aspects of Mobile Home Living, 2000; Plain Heathen Mischief, 2004. **Address:** PO Box 762, Stuart, VA 24171, U.S.A.

CLARK, Mary Higgins. American, b. 1929. **Genres:** Mystery/Crime/Suspense. **Career:** Radio scriptwriter and producer for Robert G. Jennings, 1965-70; Aerial Communications, partner and vice-president, 1970-80; D.J. Clark Enterprises, creative director and chairman of the board, NYC, 1980-. Mystery Writers of America, president, 1987. **Publications:** NOVELS: Where Are the Children?, 1975; A Stranger Is Watching, 1978; The Cradle Will Fall, 1980; A Cry in the Night, 1982; Stillwatch, 1984; Aspire to the Heavens, 1986; Weep No More, My Lady, 1987; While My Pretty One Sleeps, 1989; Mary Higgins Clark, 3 vols., 1990; Loves Music, Loves to Dance, 1991; All around the Town, 1993; I'll Be Seeing You, 1993; Remember Me, 1994; Let Me Call You Sweetheart, 1995; Silent Night, 1995; Moonlight Becomes You, 1996; Pretend You Don't See Her, 1997; You Belong to Me, 1998; All through the Night, 1998; We'll Meet Again, 1999; Before I Say Goodbye, 2000; (with C. H. Clark) Deck the Halls, 2000; On the Street Where You Live, 2001; (with C. H. Clark) He Sees You When You're Sleeping, 2001; Daddy's Little Girl, 2002; Kitchen Privileges, 2002; Mount Vernon Love Story, 2002; The Second Time Around, 2003; Nighttime Is My Time, 2004. STORIES: The Anastasia Syndrome and Other Stories, 1989; The Lottery Winner: Alvirah and Willy Stories, 1994; My Gal Sunday, 1996. OTHER: Aspire to the Heavens: A Biography of George Washington, 1969. EDITOR: Murder on the Aisle: 1987 Mystery Writers of America Anthology, 1987; (and author of intro.) The International Association of Crime Writers Presents Bad Behavior, 1995. **Address:** c/o Eugene H. Winick, McIntosh and Otis Inc, 535 Lexington Ave, New York, NY 10016, U.S.A.

CLARK, Mary Jane Behrends. American. **Genres:** Cultural/Ethnic topics. **Career:** Writer. Columbia Broadcasting System, Inc., New York, NY, news writer and producer. **Publications:** The Commonwealth of Independent States, 1992; Do You Want to Know a Secret?, 1998; Do You Promise Not to Tell?, 1999; Let Me Whisper in Your Ear, 2000; Close to You, 2001; Nobody Knows, 2002; Nowhere to Run, 2003. **Address:** Laura Dail Literary Agency, 80 Fifth Avenue, Suite 1503, New York, NY 10011, U.S.A. **Online address:** maryjaneclark@maryjaneclark.com

CLARK, Mary T. American. **Genres:** Philosophy, Theology/Religion. **Career:** Manhattanville College, Purchase, NY, professor of philosophy, 1951-. Visiting professor, University of San Francisco, summers, 1967-71, Villanova University, 1980, Fordham University, 1981, 1991, 1993, St. John Neuman Seminary, 1982-, University of Santa Clara, 1983, State University of New York at Purchase, 1989-91, New York University, 1991, Fairfield University, 1992, and Marquette University, 1993. American Catholic Philosophical Association, executive council, 1961-64, 1971-74, vice-president, 1975-76, president, 1976-77; American Philosophical Association, executive committee, 1988-91; Metaphysical Society of America, president, 1992; Society in Medieval & Renaissance Philosophy, president, 1993-94, executive committee, 1994-; Personalist Forum, editorial board. **Publications:** Augustine, Philosopher of Freedom, 1959; (with Casey) Logic, a Practical Approach, 1963; Discrimination Today, 1966; Augustinian Personalism, 1970; (ed.) An Aquinas Reader, 1973, rev. ed., 2000; (ed.) Problem of Freedom, 1973; (trans.) Theological Treatises of Marius Victorinus, 1981; Augustine of Hippo, 1984; Augustine, an Introduction, 1994. Contributor to books and journals. **Address:** Manhattanville College, Purchase, NY 10577, U.S.A.

CLARK, Merle. See GESSNER, Lynne.

CLARK, Paul F. American, b. 1954. **Genres:** Politics/Government, Industrial relations, Organized labor. **Career:** United Mine Workers of America, Washington, DC, research assistant, 1975; Cornell University, Ithaca, NY, labor extension associate, 1979; Pennsylvania State University, University Park, instructor, 1979-87, associate professor of labor studies and industrial relations, 1987-; writer. **Publications:** The Miners' Fight for Democracy, 1981; A Union Member's Guide to the New Right, 1983; Industrial Relations: A Correspondence Study Course, 1985, 3rd ed., 1992; (ed. with P. Gottlieb and D. Kennedy) Forging a Union of Steel, 1987; Changing Labor's Image: A Union Member's Guide, 1989. Contributor to labor and industrial relations periodicals. **Address:** Department of Labor and Industrial Relations, Old Botany Building, Pennsylvania State University, University Park, PA 16802, U.S.A.

CLARK, Sally. Canadian, b. 1953. **Genres:** Plays/Screenplays. **Career:** Playwright and filmmaker, c. 1983-. Playwright-in-residence at Canadian theatres. Director of plays and films. **Publications:** PLAYS: Ten Ways to Abuse an Old Woman, 1983; Lost Souls and Missing Persons, 1984; The Trial of Judith K., 1985; Moo, 1988; Jehanne of the Witches, 1989; Life without Instruction, 1991; (with J. Mighton, R. Fulford, and D. MacIvor) Sleeproom, 1993; Saint Frances of Hollywood, 1994; Wasps, 1996; The

Widow Judith, 1998. SCREENPLAYS: Ten Ways to Abuse an Old Woman, 1992; The Art of Conversation, 1994. **Address:** c/o Shain Jaffe, Great Northern Artists, 350 Dupont St, Toronto, ON, Canada M5R 1V9.

CLARK, Suzanne. American. **Genres:** Literary criticism and history. **Career:** Writer and educator. University of Oregon, Eugene, OR, professor of English. **Publications:** Sentimental Modernism: Women Writers and the Revolution of the Word, 1991; Cold Warriors: Manliness on Trial in the Rhetoric of the West, 2000. **Address:** Department of English, 1286 University of Oregon, Eugene, OR 97403, U.S.A. **Online address:** sclark@oregon.uoregon.edu

CLARK, T(imothy) J(ames). British, b. 1943. **Genres:** Art/Art history. **Career:** Art historian. Essex University, Essex, England, lecturer, 1967-69; Camberwell School of Art, London, England, senior lecturer, 1970-74; University of California, Los Angeles, CA, associate professor, 1975-76; Leeds University, Leeds, England, chair of fine art, 1976-80; Harvard University, Cambridge, MA, professor, 1980-88; University of California, Berkeley, CA, professor, 1987-. University of California, Los Angeles, visiting professor, 1974-75. **Publications:** The Absolute Bourgeois: Artists and Politics in France, 1848-1851, 1973; Image of the People: Gustave Courbet and the Second French Republic, 1848-1851, 1973; The Painting of Modern Life: Paris in the Art of Manet and His Followers, 1985; Farewell to an Idea: Episodes from a History of Modernism, 1999. **Address:** History of Art Dept, 416 Doe Library #6020, University of California, Berkeley, CA 94720, U.S.A.

CLARK, Terry N(ichols). American, b. 1940. **Genres:** Sociology. **Career:** University of Chicago, assistant professor, 1966-71, associate professor, 1971-85, professor of sociology, 1985-, National Opinion Research Center, research associate, 1974-. Member, editorial bds.: American Journal of Sociology, 1966-, Comparative Urban Research, 1972-, Policy and Politics, 1973-. Comparative Study of Community Decision-Making, University of Chicago, director, 1967-; International Sociological Association, Research Committee on Community Research, president, 1970-. **Publications:** Prophets and Patrons, 1973; Community Power and Policy Outputs, 1973; (with I. Leif) Community Power and Decision-Making, 1974; Leadership in American Cities, 1974; (with J. Ben-David) Culture and Its Creators: Essays in Honor of Edward Shils, 1977; (with Schumaker and Getter) Policy Responsiveness and the Fiscal Strain in 51 American Communities, 1979; Urban Policy Analysis, 1981; (co-author) City Money, 1983; (with others) Financial Handbook for Mayors and City Managers, 1985; Monitoring Local Governments, 1990; Urban Innovation, 1994; New Political Culture, 1998; Breakdown of Class Politics, 2001. EDITOR: (and co-author) Community Structure and Decision-Making, 1968; Gabriel Tarde on Communication and Social Influence, 1969; (and author with C.M. Bonjean and R.L. Lineberry) Community Politics: A Behavioral Approach, 1971; (co, and co-author) Comparative Community Politics, 1974; (and co-author) Citizen Preferences and Urban Public Policy, 1976; Research in Urban Policy (annual), 1985-; (co) Citizen Responsive Government, 2000. **Address:** Dept. of Sociology, Soc Sci 322, University of Chicago, 1126 E. 59th St, Chicago, IL 60637, U.S.A. **Online address:** t-clark@uchicago.edu

CLARK, Tom. American, b. 1941. **Genres:** Novels, Plays/Screenplays, Poetry, Literary criticism and history. **Career:** Paris Review, NYC and Paris, poetry editor, 1963-73; University of Essex, Wivenhoe, instructor in American poetry, 1966-67; New College of California, member of core faculty, 1987-. **Publications:** Airplanes, 1966; The Sand Burg: Poems, 1966; The Emperor of the Animals (play), 1967; (with R. Padgett) Bun, 1968; Stones, 1969; Air, 1970; Green, 1971; John's Heart, 1972; (with T. Berrigan and R. Padgett) Back in Boston Again, 1972; Smack, 1972; Blue, 1974; Suite, 1974; Chicago, 1974; At Malibu, 1975; Baseball, 1976; Champagne and Baloney, 1976; Fan Poems, 1976; 35, 1977; (with M. Fidrych) No Big Deal, 1977; How I Broke in Six Modern Masters, 1978; The World of Damon Runyon, 1978; When Things Get Tough on Easy Street: Selected Poems, 1978; One Last Round for the Shuffler, 1979; Who Is Sylvia? (novel), 1979; The Master (novel), 1979; The Great Naropa Poetry Wars, 1980; The Last Gas Station and Other Stories, 1980; The End of the Line, 1980; A Short Guide to the High Plains, 1981; Nine Songs, 1981; Heartbreak Hotel, 1981; Under the Fortune Palms, 1982; Jack Kerouac, 1984; The Exile of Celine, 1987; Easter Sunday, 1987; Kerouac's Last Word: Jack Kerouac in Escapade, 1978; Disordered Ideas, 1987; Fractured Karma, 1990; Charles Olson: The Allegory of a Poet's Life, 1991; Sleepwalker's Fate: New and Selected Poems 1965-1991, 1992; Robert Creeley and the Genius of the American Common Place, 1993; Junkets on a Sad Planet: Scenes from the Life of John Keats, 1994; Like Real People, 1995; White Thought, 1997; Empire of Skin, 1997; The Spell: A Romance, 2000; Cold Spring: A Diary, 2000; Edward Dorn: A World of Difference, 2002. **Address:** 1740 Marin Ave, Berkeley, CA 94707, U.S.A.

CLARK, Wesley K. American, b. 1944. **Genres:** Military/Defense/Arms control. **Career:** U.S. Army, 1st Battalion, 77th Armor, 4th Infantry Division, Fort Carson, CO, Commander, 1980-82; Office of the Deputy Chief of Staff for Operations and Plans, Washington, DC, Plans Integration Division Chief, 1983; Office of the Chief of Staff of the Army, Washington, DC, Chief of the Army's Study Group, 1983-84; National Training Center, Fort Irwin, CA, Commander Operations Group, 1984-86; Cold War, 4th Infantry Division, 3rd Brigade, Commander, 1986-88; National Training Center, Fort Irwin, CA, Commander, 1989-91; Training and Doctrine Command, Fort Monroe, VA, Deputy Chief of Staff for Concepts, Doctrine and Developments, 1991-92; 1st Cavalry Division, Fort Hood, TX, Commander, 1992-94; Joint Staff, Director of Strategic Plans and Policy, 1994-96; U.S. Southern Commander, Panama, Commander-in-Chief, 1996-97; Supreme Allied Commander, Europe, 1997-2000; Commander-in-Chief, U.S. European Command, 1997-2000, retired General of U.S. Army; Center for Strategic and International Studies, distinguished senior adviser. **Publications:** Waging Modern War: Bosnia, Kosovo, and the Future of Combat, 2001. **Address:** c/o Author Mail, Public Affairs Ltd, 250 W 57th St Ste 1321, New York, NY 10107, U.S.A.

CLARK, Will. American, b. 1939. **Genres:** Administration/Management. **Career:** U.S. Air Force, career officer as logistics manager, 1957-78, retiring as major; real estate broker in Tracy, CA, 1978-80; ADT Security Systems, Memphis, TN, distribution manager, 1980-90; management and motivation consultant, 1990-. **Publications:** The Leadership Handbook, 1991; The Power of Positive Education, 1993; Who's Blaming Who? 1993; School Bells and Broken Tales: Exploring with Jack and Jill, 1998; Behold Leviathan, 1999; Simply Success. **Address:** 467 Gordon Rd., Union, MS 39365-8468, U.S.A. **Online address:** will01@aol.com

CLARK, William R. American, b. 1938. **Genres:** Medicine/Health. **Career:** Weizmann Institute of Science, Rehovot, Israel, trainee in cellular immunology, 1968-70; MCDB/UCLA, Los Angeles, CA, assistant professor of cell biology, 1970-74, associate professor, 1974-78, professor of immunology, 1978-. Head of Parvin Cancer Research Laboratories, 1975-; Stanford University, visiting scholar, 1977-78. **Publications:** The Experimental Foundations of Modern Immunology (textbook), 1980, 4th ed, 1991; (ed. with P. Golstein) Mechanisms of Cell-Mediated Cytotoxicity, 1982; At War Within: The Double-Edged Sword of the Immune System, 1995; Sex and the Origins of Death, 1996. **Address:** MCDB, UCLA - Medical School, 10833 Le Conte Ave. #12-138, Los Angeles, CA 90095-3075, U.S.A.

CLARKE, Alison (Jane). American. **Genres:** Adult non-fiction. **Career:** Winchester School of Art, University of Southampton, former senior lecturer; University of Brighton, former senior lecturer; Royal College of Art, senior tutor. Visiting professor in design history and theory, University of Applied Arts, Vienna, Austria. **Publications:** Tupperware: The Promise of Plastic in 1950s America, 1999. **Address:** c/o Author Mail, Smithsonian Institution Press, 750 Ninth St. NW Suite 4300, Washington, DC 20560, U.S.A. **Online address:** Alison.Clarke@rca.ac.uk

CLARKE, Anna. See Obituaries.

CLARKE, Arthur C(harles). British, b. 1917. **Genres:** Science fiction/Fantasy, Air/Space topics, Astronomy, Marine sciences/Oceanography, Travel/Exploration, Novellas/Short stories. **Career:** Engaged in underwater exploration and photography of the Great Barrier Reef of Australia and the coast of Ceylon, 1954-. Assistant Auditor, Exchequer and Audit Dept., London, 1936-41; Assistant Ed., Physics Abstracts, London, 1949-50; Chancellor, Univ of Moratuwa, Sri Lanka, 1979-2002; has made numerous radio and TV appearances, and has lectured widely in Britain and the U.S.; Commentator, for CBS-TV, on lunar landing flights of Apollo 11, 12, and 15. **Publications:** FICTION: Prelude to Space: The Sands of Mars, 1951; Islands in the Sky, 1952; Against the Fall of Night, 1953; Childhood's End, 1953; Earthlight, 1955; The City and the Stars, 1956; The Deep Range, 1957; Across the Sea of Stars, 1962; Dolphin Island, 1963; Glide Path, 1963; Prelude to Mars, 1965; An Arthur C. Clarke Omnibus, 1965; 2001: A Space Odyssey (novel and screenplay), 1968; An Arthur C. Clarke Second Omnibus, 1968; The Lion of Comarre, 1970; Rendezvous with Rama, 1972; Imperial Earth, 1975; The Fountains of Paradise, 1979; 2010: Odyssey Two, 1982; The Songs of Distant Earth, 1986; A Fall of Moondust, 1987; 2061: Odyssey Three, 1988; (with G. Lee) Cradle, 1988; (with G. Lee) Rama II, 1989; The Ghost from the Grand Banks, 1990; (with G. Lee) The Garden of Rama, 1991; The Hammer of God, 1993; (with G. Lee) Rama Revealed, 1994; (with M. McQuay) Richter 10, 1996; 3001: The Final Odyssey, 1997; The Trigger, 1999; (with Stephen Baxter) The Light of Other Days, 2000. SHORT STORIES: Expedition to Earth, 1953; Reach for Tomorrow, 1956; Tales of

White Hart, 1957; The Other Side of the Sky, 1958; Tales of Ten Worlds, 1962; The Nine Billion Names of God: The Best Short Stories of Arthur C. Clarke, 1967; The Wind from the Sun, 1972; Of Time and Stars, 1972; The Best of Arthur C. Clarke 1937-1971, 1973; The Sentinel, 1983; Tales from Planet Earth, 1989; More Than One Universe, 1990; Collected Stories, 2001. NON-FICTION: Interplanetary Flight: An Introduction to Astronautics, 1950; The Exploration of Space, 1951; The Young Traveler in Space (in U.S. as Going into Space), 1954, rev. ed. (with R. Silverberg) as Into Space: A Young Person's Guide to Space, 1971; (with R.A. Smith) The Exploration of the Moon, 1954; The Coast of Coral, 1956; The Making of a Moon: The Story of the Earth Satellite Program, 1957; The Reefs of Taprobane: Underwater Adventures around Ceylon, 1957; Voice across the Sea, 1958; (with M. Wilson) Boy beneath the Sea, 1958; The Challenge of the Spaceship, 1959; (with M. Wilson) The First Five Fathoms, 1960; The Challenge of the Sea, 1960; (with M. Wilson) Indian Ocean Adventure, 1961; Profiles of the Future, 1962; The Treasure of the Great Reef, 1964; (with M. Wilson) Indian Ocean Treasure, 1964; (with eds. of Life) Man and Space, 1964; Voices from the Sky, 1965; The Promise of Space, 1968; (co-author) First on the Moon, 1970; Report on Planet Three and Other Speculations, 1972; The Lost Worlds of 2001, 1972; (with C. Bonestell) Beyond Jupiter, 1972; (co-author) Technology and the Frontiers of Knowledge (lectures), 1975; The Best of Arthur C. Clarke, 2 vols., 1977; The View from Serendip, 1978; 1984: Spring: A Choice of Futures, 1984; Ascent to Orbit: A Scientific Autobiography: The Technical Writings of Arthur C. Clarke, 1984; (with P. Hyams) The Odyssey File, 1985; July 20, 2019: Life in the 21st Century, 1986; How the World Was One, 1992; By Space Possessed, 1993; The Snows of Olympus: A Garden on Mars; Greetings, Carbon-Based Bipeds!, 1999. EDITOR: Time Probe, 1966; The Coming of the Space Age, 1967. **Address:** 25 Barnes Place, Colombo 7, Sri Lanka.

CLARKE, Boden. *See* **REGINALD, Robert.**

CLARKE, Brenda. Also writes as Brenda Honeyman, Kate Sedley. British, b. 1926. **Genres:** Romance/Historical. **Career:** Full-time writer. Clerical officer in the Civil Service, Bristol, 1943-55. **Publications:** The Glass Island, 1978; The Lofty Banners, 1979; The Far Morning, 1982; All through the Day, 1983; A Rose in May, 1984; Three Women, 1985; Winter Landscape, 1986; Under Heaven, 1988; An Equal Chance, 1989; Sisters and Lovers, 1990; Beyond the World, 1991; A Durable Fire, 1993; Sweet Auburn, 1995. AS BRENDA HONEYMAN: Richard by Grace of God, 1968; The Kingmaker, 1969; Richmond and Elizabeth, 1970; Harry the King, 1971, in U.S. as The Warrior King, 1972; Brother Bedford, 1972; Good Duke Humphrey, 1973; The King's Minions, 1974; The Queen and Mortimer, 1974; Edward the Warrior, 1975; All the King's Sons, 1976; The Golden Griffin, 1976; At the King's Court, 1977; The King's Tale, 1977; Macbeth, King of Scots, 1977; Emma the Queen, 1978; Harold of the English, 1979. AS KATE SEDLEY: Death and the Chapman, 1991; The Plymouth Cloak, 1992; The Hanged Man, 1993; The Holy Innocents, 1994; The Eve of Saint Hyacinth, 1995; The Wicked Winter, 1996; The Brothers of Glastonbury, 1994; The Weaver's Inheritance, 1998; The St. John's Fern, 1999; The Goldsmith's Daughter, 2001; The Lammas Feast, 2002; Nine Men Dancing, 2003; The Midsummer Rose, 2004. **Address:** 25 Torridge Rd, Keynsham, Bristol BS31 1QQ, England.

CLARKE, Gillian. Welsh, b. 1937. **Genres:** Children's fiction, Plays/Screenplays, Poetry. **Career:** Freelance writer, 1985-. President for life, Taliesin Trust. Lecturer in Art History, Gwent College of Art and Design, Newport, 1975-84; Ed., Anglo-Welsh Review, Cardiff, 1976-84; Writing Fellow, St. David's University College, Lampeter, Dyfed, 1984-85; Chair, Welsh Academy, 1988-93. **Publications:** POETRY: Snow on the Mountain, 1971; The Sundial, 1978; Letter from a Far Country, 1982; Selected Poems, 1985; (ed.) Poetry Book Society Anthology, 1987-88, 1987; Letting in the Rumour, 1989; The King of Britain's Daughter, 1993; (ed.) The Whispering Room (for children), 1996; (ed.) I Can Move the Sea (for children), 1996; Collected Poems, 1997; Five Fields, 1998; The Animal Wall (for children), 1999; Nine Green Gardens, 2000; Making the Beds for the Dead, 2004. PLAYS: The Time of the Wolf, 1996; Talking to Wordsworth (radio play), 1996; The Blue Man (radio play), 1998; Honey (radio play), 2001; Letter from a Far Country, 2005; Shopping for Happiness, 2005. OTHER: One Moonlit Night (trans. from the Welsh of T.L. Jones, traditional Welsh stories for children). **Address:** Blaen Cwrt, Talgarreg Landysul, Ceredigion SA44 4EU, Wales. **Online address:** enquirer@gillianclarke.co.uk; www.gillianclarke.co.uk

CLARKE, Gus. British, b. 1948. **Genres:** Children's fiction, Illustrations. **Career:** Held jobs designing for print and packaging exhibitions, television and video productions for five years before forming partnership to do much the same sort of work. **Publications:** SELF-ILLUSTRATED FOR CHIL-

DREN: Eddie and Teddy, 1990; Along Came Eric, 1991; How Many Days to My Birthday?, 1992; E-I-E-I-O, 1992; Betty's Not Well Today, 1993; Ten Green Monsters, 1993; Helping Hector, 1994; Pat, the Dog, 1994; Too Many Teddies, 1995; Cheeky Monkey, 1995; Michael's Monsters, 1996; Scratch 'n' Sniff, 1996; Nothing But Trouble, 1997; Lucy's Bedtime Book, 1998, in US as Goodnight Lucy; Sammy's Waggy Tail, 1998; Can We Keep It Dad?, 1999; What Would We Do without Missus Mac?, 1999; The Sun Robbers, 2000; Let's Go Driving!, 2001; Nervous Norris, 2002; Max and the Rainbow Rainhat, 2002; Lucky, 2005. Illustrator of books by L. Sloss, K. May, C. d'Lacey. **Address:** c/o Anderson Press Ltd, 20 Vauxhall Bridge Rd, London SW1V 2SA, England.

CLARKE, John R. American, b. 1945. **Genres:** Art/Art history. **Career:** Vassar College, Poughkeepsie, NY, instructor in history of art, 1972-73; University of Michigan, Ann Arbor, visiting assistant professor, 1973-74; University of California, San Diego, assistant professor, 1974-75; Yale University, New Haven, CT, assistant professor, 1975-80; University of Texas at Austin, assistant professor, 1980-82, associate professor, 1982-87, professor of history of art, 1987-, E.W. Doty Professor, 1989-90, Annie Laurie Howard Regents Professor of Fine Arts, 1991-. Conducted archaeological field work in Italy and Greece; public speaker at universities and symposia; College Art Association, president, 1998-2000. 1998-2000. **Publications:** Roman Black-and-White Figural Mosaics, 1979; The Houses of Roman Italy, 100 BC-AD 250: Ritual, Space, and Decoration, 1991; Looking at Lovemaking: Constructions of Sexuality in Roman Art, 100 BC-AD 250, 1998; Art in the Lives of Ordinary Romans: Visual Representation and Non-Elite Viewers in Italy, 100 BC-AD 315, 2003; Roman Sex, 100 BC-AD 250, 2003. Contributor to books and periodicals. **Address:** Department of Art and Art History, University of Texas, 1 University Station D1300, Austin, TX 78712-0337, U.S.A. **Online address:** j.clarke@mail.utexas.edu

CLARKE, Judith. Australian, b. 1943. **Genres:** Novels, Novellas/Short stories. **Career:** Writer. **Publications:** The Boy on the Lake (stories), 1989, rev. ed. as The Torment of Mr. Gully: Stories of the Supernatural, 1990; Teddy B. Zoot, 1990; Luna Park at Night, 1991; Riffraff, 1992; Friend of My Heart, 1994; Big Night Out, 1995; Panic Stations, 1995; Lost Day, 1999; Night Train, 1998; Wolf on the Fold, 2001. AL CAPSELLA SERIES: The Heroic Life of Al Capsella, 1988; Al Capsella and the Watchdogs, 1990; Al Capsella on Holidays, 1992, in US as Al Capsella Takes a Vacation, 1993. **Address:** 31 Alice St, Mt. Waverley, Melbourne 3149, Australia.

CLARKE, Kenneth. American, b. 1957. **Genres:** Mystery/Crime/Suspense. **Career:** Sprint Corp., Dallas, TX, departmental assistant, 1987-2001. **Publications:** The Case of the Magnolia Murders, 1998; And Then You Die, 2003.

CLARKE, (Victor) Lindsay. British, b. 1939. **Genres:** Novels, Mythology/Folklore. **Career:** Sr. master in high school in Ghana, 1962-65; College of Further Education, Great Yarmouth, lecturer in English, 1965-67; Norwich City College, coordinator of liberal studies, 1967-70; Friends World College European Center, Norwich, co-dir., 1970-78; free-lance teacher, counselor, and writer, 1978-; University of Wales, Cardiff, writer-in-residence, 1996, associate lecturer in creative writing, 1997-. **Publications:** Sunday Whiteman, 1987; The Chymical Wedding, 1989 (Whitbread Fiction Prize); Alice's Masque, 1993; Cathal of the Woods, 1994; A Stone from Heaven, 1995; Essential Celtic Mythology, 1997; Parzival and the Stone from Heaven, 2001; The War at Troy, 2004. **Address:** c/o PFD, Drury House, 34-43 Russell St, London WC2B 5HA, England.

CLARKE, Margaret. Also writes as Helen M. Buss. Canadian, b. 1941. **Genres:** Novels, Literary criticism and history, Women's studies and issues, Autobiography/Memoirs. **Career:** High school English teacher in Dryden, Ontario, 1966-72, and in Winnipeg, Manitoba, 1972-83; University of Calgary, Alberta, professor of English, 1988-. **Publications:** The Cutting Season (novel), 1984; Gertrude and Ophelia (two-act play), 1993; Healing Song (novel), 1988; (as Helen M. Buss) Mapping Our Selves: Canadian Women's Autobiography, 1993; Memoirs from Away: A New Found Land Girlhood, 1999; Repossessing the World: Reading Memoirs by Contemporary Women, 2002. **Address:** Department of English, University of Calgary, Calgary, AB, Canada T2N 1N4. **Online address:** hbuss@ucalgary.ca

CLARKE, Mary. British, b. 1923. **Genres:** Dance/Ballet. **Career:** Assistant Ed., Ballet Annual, 1952-63; Ed., Dancing Times, London, 1963(Assistant Ed., 1954-63); London Ed., Dance News of New York, 1955-70; Dance Critic, The Guardian, 197794. **Publications:** The Sadler's Wells Ballet, 1955; Six Great Dancers, 1957; Dancers of Mercury: The Story of Ballet Rambert, 1962; (with C. Crisp) Ballet: An Illustrated History, 2nd ed., 1973; (with C. Crisp) Making a Ballet, 1974; (ed. with D. Vaughan) An

Encyclopedia of Dance and Ballet, 1977; (with C. Crisp) Design for Ballet, 1978; (with C. Crisp) The History of Dance, 1980; (with C. Crisp) Men in Dance, 1985; Ballerina, 1987. **Address:** 54 Ripplevale Grove, London N1 1HT, England. **Online address:** maryat@dancing-times.co.uk

CLARKE, Patricia. Australian, b. 1926. **Genres:** History, Women's studies and issues, Biography. **Career:** Australian News and Information Bureau, in Melbourne and Canberra, journalist; Australian Broadcasting Co., Canberra, journalist; M. Newton Publications, editor and journalist; National Capital Development Commission, editor and journalist. Editor, Canberra Historical Journal, 1987-2000. **Publications:** The Governesses: Letters from the Colonies, 1862-1882, 1985; A Colonial Woman: The Life and Times of Mary Braidwood Mowle, 1827-1857, 1986; Pen Portraits: Women Writers and Journalists in Nineteenth Century Australia, 1988; Pioneer Writer: The Life of Louisa Atkinson, Novelist, Journalist, Naturalist, 1990; Tasma: The Life of Jessie Couvreur, 1994; Rosa! Rosa! A Life of Rosa Praed, Novelist and Spiritualist, 1999. EDITOR: (with D. Spender) LifeLines: Australian Women's Letters and Diaries, 1788-1840, 1992; Tasma's Diaries, 1995; Steps to Federation, 2001. **Address:** 14 Chermside St, Deakin, Canberra, ACT 2600, Australia. **Online address:** clarke.patricia@netspeed.com.au

CLARKE, Pauline. (Pauline Hunter Blair). Also writes as Helen Clare. British, b. 1921. **Genres:** Novels, Novellas/Short stories, Children's fiction, Young adult fiction. **Career:** Full-time author, 1948-. **Publications:** The Pekinese Princess, 1948; The Great Can, 1952; The White Elephant, 1952; Smith's Hoard (in U.S. as Hidden Gold), 1955, retitled in U.K. as The Golden Collar, 1967; Sandy the Sailor, 1956; The Boy with the Erpingham Hood, 1956; James the Policeman series, 4 vols., 1957-63; Torolv the Fatherless, 1959; The Lord of the Castle, 1960; The Robin Hooders, 1960; Keep the Pot Boiling, 1961; The Twelve and the Genii (in U.S. as The Return of the Twelves), 1962; Silver Bells and Cockle Shells (verse), 1962; Crowds of Creatures, 1964; The Bonfire Party, 1966; The Two Faces of Silenus, 1972. AS HELEN CLARE: Five Dolls series, 5 vols., 1953-63; Merlin's Magic, 1953; Bel the Giant and Other Stories (in U.S. as The Cat and the Fiddle, and Other Stories), 1956; Seven White Pebbles, 1960. AS PAULINE HUNTER BLAIR: The Nelson Boy, 2000; A Thorough Seaman, 2000; Warscape, 2001; Jacob's Ladder, 2003. **Address:** Church Farm House, Bottisham, Cambridge CB5 9BA, England.

CLARKE, Peter Frederick. British, b. 1942. **Genres:** Economics, Politics/Government. **Career:** Cambridge University, professor of modern British history, 1991-, master of Trinity Hall, 2000- (lecturer and reader, 1980-91). University College, London, lecturer and reader, 1966-80. Review ed. of history, 1967-73; St. John's College, Cambridge, fellow, 1980-2000. **Publications:** Lancashire and the New Liberalism, 1971; (ed.) Democracy and Reaction by L. T. Hobhouse, 1972; (ed.) The Crisis of Liberalism by J. A. Hobson, 1974; Liberals and Social Democrats, 1978; The Keynesian Revolution in the Making, 1924-36, 1988; A Question of Leadership: From Gladstone to Thatcher, 1991; Hope and Glory: Britain, 1900-1990, 1996, 2nd ed., 1900-2000, 2004; The Keynesian Revolution and Its Economic Consequences, 1998; The Cripps Version: The Life of Sir Stafford Cripps, 2002. **Address:** The Master's Lodge, Trinity Hall, Cambridge CB2 1TJ, England. **Online address:** pfc1000@cam.ac.uk

CLARKE-RICH, Elizabeth L. American, b. 1934. **Genres:** Children's fiction, Poetry. **Career:** Writer. Elementary school teacher at public schools in Charlotte County, VA, 1950-52; social studies teacher and librarian at public schools in Charlotte County, 1953-55; elementary school principal in Mecklenburg County, VA, 1956-59; Prince George's County Public Schools, Prince George's County, VA, librarian, 1960-66, resource teacher, 1967-69, high school librarian, 1970-89. Worked as a university librarian in Maryland. **Publications:** We Ain't Arrived Yet (poems), 1991; The Big Mistake, 1995; And the Winner Is… 1998. **Address:** 11611 Tyre St., Upper Marlboro, MD 20772, U.S.A.

CLARKSON, Ewan. British, b. 1929. **Genres:** Novels, Children's fiction, Children's non-fiction. **Publications:** Break for Freedom (in U.S. as Syla the Mink), 1967; Halic, The Story of a Grey Seal, 1970; The Running of the Deer, 1972; In the Shadow of the Falcon, 1973; Wolf Country, a Wilderness Pilgrimage, 1975; The Badgers of Summercombe, 1977; The Many Forked Branch, 1980; Wolves, 1980; Reindeer, 1981; Eagles, 1981; Beavers, 1981; In the Wake of the Storm (novel), 1984; Ice Trek, 1986; King of the Wind, 1990; The Flight of the Osprey, 1996. **Address:** Moss Rose Cottage, Preston, Kingsteignton, Newton Abbot, Devon, England.

CLARKSON, J. F. See TUBB, E(dwin) C(harles).

CLARKSON, Wensley. British, b. 1956. **Genres:** Plays/Screenplays, Documentaries/Reportage, Biography. **Career:** Wimbledon News, London, England, reporter, 1977-79; Sunday Mirror, London, England, reporter, 1979-81; Mail on Sunday, London, England, reporter, 1981-82; Sunday Mirror, London, England, reporter, 1982-87. Has also produced commercials. **Publications:** Dog Eat Dog: Confessions of a Tabloid Journalist (autobiography), 1990; Hell Hath No Fury (true crime), 1990; Like a Woman Scorned (true crime), 1991; Love You to Death, Darling (true crime), 1991; Doctors of Death (true crime), 1992; Year in La La Land (autobiography), 1992; Mel: The Inside Story (biography), 1993; Tom Cruise Unauthorized (biography), 1994; Whatever Mother Says: An Incredible True Story of Death and Destruction Inside One Ordinary Family (true crime), 1994; Deadly Seduction (true crime), 1995; Quentin Tarantino: Shooting from the Hip (biography), 1995; John Travolta: Back in Character (biography), 1996; Sting (biography), 1996; Slave Girls (true crime), 1996; True Patriot (military/espionage), 1996; Caged Heat (true crime), 1997. Contributor to periodicals. SCREENPLAYS: The Thin Blue Line (documentary), 1989; Dog Eat Dog, 1991. Wrote television episodes for England's The Bill; co-author, with G. Cerello, of the cable television movie Tainted Blood, 1993. **Address:** c/o Blake Publishing Ltd., 3 Bramber Ct., 2 Bramber Rd., London W14 9PB, England.

CLARVOE, Jennifer. American. **Genres:** Poetry. **Career:** Kenyon College, Gambier, OH, associate professor of English; poet. **Publications:** Invisible Tender (poetry), 2000. **Address:** Department of English, Kenyon College, 102 College Dr., Gambier, OH 43022, U.S.A. **Online address:** clarvoe@kenyon.edu

CLARY, Killarney. American, b. 1953. **Genres:** Poetry. **Career:** Writer. **Publications:** By Me, by Any, Can or Can't Be Done, 1980; Who Whispered Near Me, 1989; By Common Salt, 1996. **Address:** 6224 Rockcliff Dr, Los Angeles, CA 90068-1652, U.S.A.

CLAUDE, Richard Pierre. American, b. 1934. **Genres:** Civil liberties/Human rights, Law. **Career:** Professor Emeritus, Dept. of Government and Politics, University of Maryland, College Park, 1993- (Associate Professor, 1965-78; Professor, 1978-93). Founding Ed., Human Rights Quarterly; Member, National Advisory Council, Amnesty International US, 1978-. Instructor in Political Science, Vassar College, Poughkeepsie, NY, 1962-64; Visiting Professor, College of William and Mary, Williamsburg, VA, 1964-65, University of the Philippines, 1991, Princeton University, 1996. Rockefeller Residency Fellow, Bellagio, Italy, 1985; Board of Dirs., Physicians for Human Rights, 1988; Vice-President, Survival International, US, 1988; Advisory Board of Pennsylvania Studies in Human Rights, 1989; Scientific Freedom and Responsibility Committee, American Association for the Advancement of Science, 1989; Fulbright Senior Research Professor, 1990-91, 1995; Board of Editors, Human Rights Journal (Sao Paulo), SUR. **Publications:** The Supreme Court and the Electoral Process, 1970; (co-author) Health Professionals and Human Rights in the Philippines, 1986; Human Rights Education in the Philippines, 1992; Educating for Human Rights, 1996; Bells of Freedom, 1994; Popular Education for Human Rights, 2000; Science in Service of Human Rights, 2002. EDITOR: Comparative Human Rights, 1976; Human Rights in the World Community, 1989, 3rd ed., 2005; Human Rights and Statistics, 1992; Human Rights Education for the 21st Century, 1997.

CLAUDE-PIERRE, Peggy. Canadian. **Genres:** Psychology. **Career:** Writer and therapist. Outpatient and residential therapist specializing in eating disorders, 1988-; Montreux Counselling Centre, Victoria, BC, Canada, founder, 1996-. **Publications:** The Secret Language of Eating Disorders, 1997. **Address:** Montreux Counselling Centre, Box 5460, Victoria, BC, Canada V8R 6S4. **Online address:** info@montreux.org

CLAUSEN, Andy. (born Belgium), b. 1943. **Genres:** Poetry. **Career:** Poet and educator. Naropa Institute, Boulder, CO, faculty member, 1980. Presently works as a stonemason, troubadour, and freelance teacher of creative writing for the NYC school system. Renegade, publisher. **Publications:** Extreme Unction, 1974; Austin, Texas, 1981; Without Doubt, 1991; Trek to the Top of the World, 1996; Fortieth Century Man: Selected Verse, 1996-1966, 1997; (editor, with Allen Ginsberg and Eliot Katz) Poems for the Nation: A Collection of Contemporary Political Poems, 1999. **Address:** c/o Author Mail, Seven Stories Press, 140 Watts St., New York, NY 10013, U.S.A.

CLAUSEN, Christopher (John). American, b. 1942. **Genres:** Literary criticism and history, Intellectual history, Politics/Government, Social commentary, Essays. **Career:** University of Hawaii at Manoa, Honolulu, instructor in English, 1965-66; Concord College, Athens, W.Va., assistant professor of English, 1966-68; Virginia Polytechnic Institute and State University, Blacksburg, visiting assistant professor, 1972, assistant professor, 1973-79, associate professor, 1979-84, professor of English, 1984-85; Pennsylvania State University, University Park, professor of English, 1985-. **Publications:** The Place of Poetry: Two Centuries of an Art in Crisis, 1981; The Moral Imagination: Essays on Literature and Ethics, 1986; My Life with President Kennedy, 1994; Faded Mosaic: The Emergence of Post-Cultural America, 2000. Contributor to periodicals. **Address:** Department of English, Pennsylvania State University, University Park, PA 16802, U.S.A. **Online address:** cqc1@psu.edu

CLAUSEN, Lowen. American. **Genres:** Mystery/Crime/Suspense. **Career:** Writer and business owner. Police officer for thirteen years in the Seattle, WA, police department. **Publications:** First Avenue: A Novel, 1999; Second Watch, 2003. **Address:** 2208 Northwest Market St., Ste. 505, Seattle, WA 98107, U.S.A. **Online address:** totheauthor@lowenclausen.com

CLAUSEN, Meredith L(eslie). American, b. 1942. **Genres:** Architecture, Art/Art history. **Career:** University of Santa Clara, Santa Clara, CA, teacher, 1976; Colorado College, Colorado Springs, teacher, 1976-77; Stanford University, Stanford, CA, acting assistant professor, 1977-78; University of Washington, Seattle, assistant professor, 1979-85, associate professor, 1985-93, professor of architectural history, 1993-. University of California, Berkeley, teacher, 1977; Stanford University, visiting assistant professor, 1984, 1985-86, visiting associate professor, 1987. **Publications:** Frantz Jourdain, Art Nouveau Theory and Criticism and the Samaritaine, 1987; Spiritual Space: The Religious Architecture of Pietro Belluschi, 1992; Pietro Belluschi, Modern American Architect, 1994. Contributor to books. Contributor of articles and reviews to professional journals. **Address:** Departments of Architecture and Art History, University of Washington, Seattle, WA 98195, U.S.A. **Online address:** mlc@u.washington.edu

CLAVEL, Pierre. American, b. 1935. **Genres:** Regional/Urban planning. **Career:** Blair Associates, Providence, RI, city planner, 1960-62; University of Puerto Rico, Rio Piedras, assistant professor of planning, 1965-67; Cornell University, Ithaca, NY, assistant professor to professor of city and regional planning, 1967-. **Publications:** Opposition Planning in Wales and Appalachia, 1983; The Progressive City: Planning and Participation, 1986; (with N. Krumholz) Reinventing Cities: Equity Planners Tell Their Stories, 1994. EDITOR: (with W.W. Goldsmith) Urban and Regional Planning in an Age of Austerity, 1980; (with W. Wiewel) Harold Washington and the Neighborhoods: Progressive City Government in Chicago, 1991. **Address:** Dept of City and Regional Planning, 201 West Sibley Hall, Cornell University, Ithaca, NY 14853, U.S.A. **Online address:** pc29@cornell.edu

CLAWSON, Calvin C. American, b. 1941. **Genres:** Mathematics/Statistics, Novels. **Career:** Seattle Police Department, Seattle, WA, systems analyst and planner, c. 1969-83; freelance writer, 1983-. South Seattle Community College, instructor in mathematics, 1994-. **Publications:** Conquering Math Phobia, 1992; The Mathematical Traveler, 1994; Mathematical Mysteries, 1996; Mathematical Sorcery, in press. Contributor of short stories and articles to periodicals. **Address:** 27106 Southeast 146th St., Issaquah, WA 98027, U.S.A.

CLAWSON, James G. American, b. 1947. **Genres:** Business/Trade/Industry, Administration/Management. **Career:** Mormon missionary in Hong Kong and Japan, 1967-69; Wells Fargo Bank, San Francisco, CA, international credit officer, 1973-75; Harvard University, Business School, Boston, MA, assistant professor, 1979-81; University of Virginia, Charlottesville, associate professor, 1981-. International University of Japan, visiting faculty member, 1991. **Publications:** Self-Assessment and Career Development, 1986, now in 3rd ed; An MBA's Guide to Self-Assessment and Career Development, 1987. **Address:** Darden School, University of Virginia Northgrounds, Box 6550, Charlottesville, VA 22906, U.S.A.

CLAY, G. A. See TROTTER, Michael H(amilton).

CLAY, Rita. See ESTRADA, Rita Clay.

CLAY, Rosamund. See OAKLEY, Ann.

CLAYSON, Alan. British, b. 1951. **Genres:** Music. **Career:** Performed as a vocalist and musician in avant-rock groups during the early 1970s; played viola in the Portsmouth Sinfonia, 1974-75; collaborated with such musical groups and performers as Dave Berry, Jim McCarty, Twinkle and Screaming

Lord Sutch; writer; organizer and coordinator of courses and lectures on popular music in Britain and the US. **Publications:** Call Up the Groups! The Golden Age of British Beat, 1962-67, 1985; Back in the High Life: A Biography of Steve Winwood, 1988; Only the Lonely: The Life and Artistic Legacy of Roy Orbison, 1989; The Quiet One: A Life of George Harrison, 1990; Ringo Starr: Straight Man or Joker?, 1991; Death Discs, 1992; (with P. Sutcliffe) Backbeat: Stuart Sutcliffe, the Lost Beatle (movie tie-in), 1994. Contributor of articles on popular music to publications. **Address:** c/o Carol Boyer, 894 Monterey Dr., Shoreview, MN 55126, U.S.A.

CLAYSON, (S.) Hollis. American. **Genres:** Art/Art history. **Career:** Pierce College, Athens, Greece, adviser on student affairs, 1968-69; California Institute of the Arts, Valencia, instructor in complementary studies, 1974-76; Schiller College, Strasbourg, France, instructor in English and art history, 1977-78; Wichita State University, KS, assistant professor of art history, 1978-82; Northwestern University, Evanston, IL, visiting assistant professor of art history, 1982-84, assistant professor, 1985-91, associate professor, 1991-2001, Charles Deering McCormick Professor of Teaching Excellence, 1993-96, associate dean of the graduate school, 1995-98, department chair, 2000-, professor of art history, 2001-, Martin J. and Patricia Koldyke Outstanding Teaching Professor, 2004-06; University of Illinois at Chicago Circle, assistant professor of the history of architecture and art, 1984-85. **Publications:** Painted Love: Prostitution in French Art of the Impressionist Era, 1991; Understanding Paintings: Themes in Art Explored and Explained, 2000; Paris in Despair: Art and Everyday Life under Siege (1870-71), 2002. Contributor of articles and reviews to art journals. **Address:** Dept of Art History, 3-400 Kresge Hall, Northwestern University, 1880 Campus Dr, Evanston, IL 60208, U.S.A. **Online address:** shc@northwestern.edu

CLAYTON, Elaine. American, b. 1961. **Genres:** Children's fiction, Illustrations. **Career:** Illustrator and author. Cesar Chavez Migrant Camp, Mobile, AL, head start teacher, 1980; High Museum of Art, Atlanta, GA, gallery instructor, 198085; St. Anthony's Summer Camp, Atlanta, art instructor, 1983; Woodruff Memorial Arts Center Gallery, Atlanta, gallery manager, 1984; Paideia School, Atlanta, assistant teacher and artist in residence, 1985-89; Mary Lin Elementary School, Atlanta, artist-in-residence, 1985; Atrium School, Watertown, MA, elementary teacher, 1990-94. Volunteer with Glen Mary Missionary. Has presented artwork at exhibitions throughout the US. **Publications:** SELF-ILLUSTRATED FOR CHILDREN: Pup in School, 1993; Ella's Trip to the Museum, 1996; Gregory Maguire, Six Haunted Hairdos, 1997; (ed.) Puzzle Gallery Books, 1997; The Yeoman's Daring Daughter and the Princes in the Tower. Illustrator of books by: A. Curasone, S. Greene, E. Woodruff, A.H. Wayland. Contributor of reviews and illustrations to magazines and newspapers.

CLAYTON, Lawrence (Otto), (Jr.). American, b. 1945. **Genres:** Psychology, Self help. **Career:** Diversa Inc., Newport, AR, mobile home sales representative, 1969-72; United Methodist Church, Central Texas Conference, Fort Worth, TX, pastor, 1973-81; Johnson County Mental Health Clinic, Cleburne, TX, director, 1981-83; United Methodist Counseling Services, Oklahoma City, administrator, 1983-88; Clayton Clinic, Oklahoma City, owner and president, 1988-90; Oklahoma Family Institute, Oklahoma City, executive director, 1990-95; Gospel Celebration Fellowship, Oklahoma City, assoc. pastor, 1996-98; retired; pastoral counselor; drug and alcohol counselor; presenter of professional workshops. Newspaper columnist, editor, and publisher. **Publications:** Assessment and Management of the Suicidal Adolescent, 1990; (with S. Carter) Coping with Depression, 1990; Coping with a Drug Abusing Parent, 1991; (with Carter) Coping with Being Gifted, 1992; (with J. Morrison) Coping with a Learning Disability, 1992; Careers in Psychology, 1992; (with B. Smith) Coping with Sports Injuries, 1992; (with R. Van Norstrand) The Professional Drug and Alcohol Counselor Supervisor's Handbook, 1993; Designer Drugs, 1994; Barbiturates and Other Depressants, 1994; Amphetamines and Other Stimulants, 1994; All You Need to Know about Sports Injuries, 1994; Steroids, 1995; Working Together against Drug Addiction, 1996; Drugs & Drug Testing, 1997; Tranquilizers, 1997; Alcohol, 1999; Diet Pills, 1999; Drug Testing, 2000; Delayed Gratification, 2001; Careers in Behavioral Science, 2002; Managing Suicidal Individuals and Their Families, 2002; Introduction to Alcohol and Drug abuse counseling, 29002; Behavioral Science Research, 2002; Personality Development, 2002; Stress Management, 2002; Lifespan Human Development, 2002; Small Groups, 2002; Biblical Concepts of Mental Health, 2002; Abnormal Psychology, 2002; Marriage and Family Development, 2002. Contributor to books and periodicals.

CLAYTON, Martin. British, b. 1967. **Genres:** Art/Art history. **Career:** Royal Library, Windsor Castle, England, assistant curator of Print Room, 1990-. **Publications:** (with R. Philo) Leonardo da Vinci: The Anatomy of

Man, 1992; Seven Florentine Heads, 1993; Poussin: Works on Paper, 1995; Leonardo da Vinci: A Curious Vision, 1996. **Address:** Royal Library, Windsor Castle, London SL4 1NY, England.

CLAYTON, Mary. See **LIDE, Mary.**

CLAYTON, Mary. Irish, b. 1954. **Genres:** Theology/Religion, Literary criticism and history. **Career:** National University of Ireland, University College, Dublin, lecturer, 1982-, professor, 1998-. **Publications:** The Cult of the Virgin Mary in Anglo-Saxon England, 1990; (ed. with H. Magennis) The Old English Lives of St. Margaret, 1994; The Apocryphal Gospels of Mary in Anglo-Saxon England, 1998. **Address:** University College, National University of Ireland, Belfield 4, Dublin, Ireland.

CLAYTON, Michael. British, b. 1934. **Genres:** Sports/Fitness. **Career:** Evening Standard, London, England, deputy news editor, 1961-64; Southern Television, news editor, 1964-65; British Broadcasting Corp., news and current affairs staff correspondent, 1965-73; Horse and Hound, London, editor, 1973-95; Press Complaints Commission, member 1991-93. IPC Magazines, director, 1994-97; editor-in-chief: Horse & Hound, Country Life, The Field, and The Shooting Times, 1994-97. **Publications:** A-Hunting We Will Go, 1967; Hickstead: The First Twelve Years, 1972; Cross Country Riding, 1977; The Hunter, 1980; The Golden Thread, 1984; Prince Charles: Horseman, 1987; The Chase, 1987; Fox Hunting in Paradise, 1993. **Address:** King's Reach Tower, Stamford St., London SE1 9LS, England.

CLAYTON, Peter A(rthur). British, b. 1937. **Genres:** Archaeology/Antiquities, Classics. **Career:** Islington Public Libraries, Islington, England, chartered librarian, 1954-58; St. Marylebone Public Libraries, chartered librarian, 1958-63; Thames & Hudson Ltd., London, England, archaeology editor, 1963-74; Longman Group Ltd., Harlow, England, humanities publisher, 1974; British Museum Publications, London, managing editor, 1974-79; B.A. Seaby Ltd., London, publications director, 1980-. University of Leiden, visiting lecturer, 1970; University of Padua, visiting professor, 1978. Minerva: The International Review of Ancient Art and Archaeology, consultant editor and book reviews editor, 1990-. **Publications:** Archaeological Sites of Britain, 1976, 2nd ed., 1985; (ed.) Manfred Lurker, The Gods and Symbols of Ancient Egypt: An Illustrated Dictionary, rev. ed., 1980; Companion to Roman Britain, 1980; The Rediscovery of Ancient Egypt: Artists and Travellers in the Nineteenth Century, 1983; David Roberts' Egypt, 1985; David Roberts' Holy Land, 1986; The Treasures of Ancient Rome, 1986; (ed. with M.J. Price) The Seven Wonders of the Ancient World, 1988; Great Figures of Mythology, 1990; Chronicle of the Pharaohs: The Reign-by-Reign Record of the Rulers and Dynasties of Ancient Egypt, 1994; Family Life in Ancient Egypt, 1995; The Valley of the Kings, 1995; Egyptian Mythology, forthcoming. **Address:** 41 Cardy Rd, Boxmoor, Hemel Hempstead HP1 1RL, England.

CLEALL, Charles. British, b. 1927. **Genres:** Literary criticism and history, Music, Theology/Religion. **Career:** Writer. Command Music Adviser to the Royal Navy, Plymouth Command, 1946-48; Professor of Solo Singing and Choral Repertoire, Trinity College of Music, London, 1949-52; Choral Scholar, Westminster Abbey, London, 1949-52; Conductor, Morley College Orchestra, 1950-52; Organist, Wesley's Chapel, City Rd, London, 1950-52; Conductor, Glasgow Choral Union, 1952-54; BBC Music Assistant, Midland Region, 1954-55; Music Master, Glyn County School, Ewell, 1955-66; Conductor, The Aldeburgh Festival Choir, 1957-60; Organist, St. Paul's, Portman Square London, 1957-61, and Holy Trinity, Guildford, 1961-65; Lecturer in Music, The Froebel Institute, Roehampton, 1967-68; Music Adviser, London Borough of Harrow, 1968-72; Music Specialist of the Northern Division of Her Majesty's Inspectorate of Schools in Scotland, Scottish Education Dept., 1972-87; Ed., Journal of The Ernest George White Society, 1983-88. **Publications:** Voice Production in Choral Technique, 1955, 1970; The Selection and Training of Mixed Choirs in Churches, 1960; (ed.) Sixty Songs from Sankey, 1960, 1966; (ed.) John Merbecke's Music for the Congregation at Holy Communion, 1963; Music and Holiness, 1964; Authentic Chanting, 1969; (ed.) Plainsong for Pleasure, 1969; A Guide to Vanity Fair, 1982; Walking Round the Church of St. James the Great Stonehaven, 1993; A Jewel of a Church, 2000. Scores of articles in the musical and educational press. **Address:** 14 Heathfields Way, Shaftesbury, Dorset SP7 9JZ, United Kingdom.

CLEARE, John S. British, b. 1936. **Genres:** Photography, Travel/Exploration. **Career:** Proprietor, Mountain Camera Photo Library and consultancy, 1976. Photographer, Queen Magazine, 1960-61; Director, Gamma Group, Photography and Design, Sargent/Gamma Ltd., 1961-69. **Publications:** (with T. Smythe) Rock-Climbers in Action in Snowdonia, 1966; (with

R. Collomb) Sea-Cliff Climbing in Britain, 1973; Mountains, 1974; World Guide to Mountains and Mountaineering, 1979; Mountaineering in Colour, 1980; (ed. and illustrator) Whymper's Scrambles amongst the Alps, 7th ed., 1986; (with Ordnance Survey) John Cleare's Fifty Best 100 Hill Walks in Britain, 1988; Trekking: Great Walks of the World, 1988; (with R. Smith) Walking the Great Views, 1991; (with M. Andrew) Discovering the English Lowlands, 1991; (with K. Sngden) Walking the Pilgrim Ways, 1991; (with R. Smith) On Foot in the Pennines, 1993; (with R. Smith) On Foot in the Yorkshire Dales, 1996; Mountains of the World, 1997; Distant Mountains, 1999; (with P. Ziegler and Francis Frith Archive) Britain Then and Now, 1999; (with R. Sale) On Top of the World, 2000; (with A. Alderson) Pembrokeshire: National Park, 2001; (with R.A. Dale) Tao Te Ching-A New Translation, 2002; Moods of Pembrokshire, 2004; Portrait of Bath, 2004; (with S. Banoobhai) Book of Songs, 2004; The Tao, 2005. **Address:** Mountain Camera, Fonthill Gifford, Salisbury, Wilts. SP3 6QW, England. **Online address:** cleare@btinternet.com; www.mountaincamera.com

CLEARY, Beverly. American, b. 1916. **Genres:** Children's fiction. **Career:** Children's librarian, Yakima, WA, 1939-40; U.S. Army Hospital, Oakland, CA, post librarian, 1942-45. **Publications:** Henry Huggins series, 5 vols., 1950-62; Ellen Tebbits, 1951; Otis Spofford, 1953; Ramona series, 7 vols., 1955-84; Fifteen, 1956; The Luckiest Girl, 1958; Jean and Johnny, 1959; The Hullabaloo ABC, 1960; The Real Hole, 1960; Two Dog Biscuits, 1961; Emily's Runaway Imagination, 1961; Sister of the Bride, 1963; Ribsy, 1964; The Mouse and the Motorcycle, 1964; Mitch and Amy, 1967; Runaway Ralph, 1970; Socks, 1973; Ralph S. Mouse, 1982; Dear Mr. Henshaw, 1983; Lucky Chuck, 1984; Janet's Thingamajigs, 1987; The Growing-Up Feet, 1987; A Girl from Yamhill: A Memoir, 1988; Here Come the Twins, 1989; The Twins Again, 1989; Muggie Maggie, 1990; Strider, 1991; Petey's Bedtime Story, 1993; My Own Two Feet: A Memoir, 1995; Ramona's World, 1999. **Address:** c/o HarperCollins Children's Books, 1350 Ave of the Americas, New York, NY 10019, U.S.A. **Online address:** www.beverlycleary.com

CLEARY, Brian P. American, b. 1959. **Genres:** Children's fiction, Children's non-fiction, Humor/Satire. **Career:** Humor writer, freelance copywriter. **Publications:** Jamaica Sandwich?, 1996; It Looks a Lot Like Reindeer, 1996; Give Me Bach My Schubert, 1996; You Never Sausage Love, 1996; A Mink, a Fink, a Skating Rink: What Is a Noun?, 1999; Hairy, Scary, Ordinary: What Is an Adjective?, 2000; To Root, to Toot, to Parachute: What Is a Verb?, 2000; Under, Over, by the Clover: What Is a Preposition?, 2001; Dearly, Nearly, Insincerely: What Is an Adverb?, 2003; I and You and Don't Forget Who: What Is a Pronoun?, 2004; Rainbow Soup: Adventures in Poetry, 2004. Contributor of humor articles, essays, features, and cartoons to local and national magazines.

CLEARY, Edward L. American, b. 1929. **Genres:** Area studies, Theology/Religion. **Career:** University of Pittsburgh, Pittsburgh, PA, assistant director of Latin American studies; Aquinas Institute, St. Louis, MO, academic dean and vice-president; Pontifical College Josephinum, Columbus, OH, professor and director of Hispanic studies, 1985-93; Providence College, Providence, RI, professor of Political Science, 1993-. Visiting professor at University of Pittsburgh, New York University, and Florida International University. **Publications:** (Ed.) Shaping a New World: An Orientation to Latin America, 1971; Crisis and Change: The Church in Latin America Today, 1985; (ed.) Path from Puebla: Significant Documents of the Latin American Bishops since 1979, 1989; (ed.) Born of the Poor: The Latin American Church since Medellin, 1990; (coed. and contrib.) Conflict and Competition: The Latin American Church in a Changing Environment, 1992; (coed. and contrib.) Power, Politics, and Pentecostals in Latin America, 1996. **Address:** Latin American Studies, Providence College, Providence, RI 02918, U.S.A.

CLEARY, Melissa. American. **Genres:** Mystery/Crime/Suspense. **Career:** Novelist. **Publications:** MYSTERY NOVELS. JACKIE WALSH AND JAKE SERIES: A Tail of Two Murders, 1992; Hounded to Death, 1993; Dead and Buried, 1994; First Pedigree Murder, 1994; Skull and Dog Bones, 1994; Dog Collar Crime, 1995; The Maltese Puppy, 1995; Murder Most Beastly, 1996; Old Dogs, 1997; And Your Little Dog, Too, 1998. **Address:** c/o Berkley Publishing Group, 375 Hudson St., New York, NY 10014, U.S.A.

CLEEK, Richard K. American, b. 1945. **Genres:** Architecture. **Career:** University of Wisconsin Colleges, Madison, chief information officer, 1970-. **Publications:** (with A.G. Noble) The Old Barn Book: A Field Guide to North American Barns and Other Farm Structures, 1995. **Address:** University of Wisconsin Colleges, 780 Regent St, Madison, WI 53708, U.S.A.

CLEESE, John (Marwood). British, b. 1939. **Genres:** Self help, Humor/Satire. **Career:** Actor, comedian, and writer. **Publications:** (With J. Hobbs and J. McGrath) The Strange Case of the End of Civilisation As We Know It, 1977; (with R. Skynner) Families and How to Survive Them, 1983; The Golden Skits of Wing Commander Muriel Volestrangler FRHS and Bar, 1984; (with C. Booth) The Complete Fawlty Towers, 1988; A Fish Called Wanda (screenplay), 1988; (with R. Skynner) Life and How to Survive It, 1993; (with B. Bates) The Human Face (nonfiction), 2001. **Address:** c/o David Wilkinson, 115 Hazlebury Rd, London SW6 2LX, England.

CLEGG, Holly Berkowitz. American, b. 1955. **Genres:** Food and Wine. **Career:** Cookbook author and media spokesperson. Guest on television programs; Cooking Light Magazine, contributing editor, 1997-99; Healthy Cooking magazine, bimonthly columnist; iVillage.com/food, cooking coach. **Publications:** A Trim and Terrific Louisiana Kitchen, 1993; Trim and Terrific American Favorites: Over 250 Fast and Easy Low-Fat Recipes, 1996; Trim and Terrific One-Dish Favorites, 1997; The Devils Food: A Dessert Cookbook, 1998; Meals on the Move: Rush Hour Recipes, 1999; Eating Well through Cancer: Easy Recipes & Recommendations During & After Treatment, 2001; The Holly Clegg Trim & Terrific Cookbook: More Than 500 Fast, Easy, and Healthy Recipes, 2002; Holly Clegg Trim & Terrific Home Entertaining the Easy Way, 2003. **Address:** 13431 Woodmont Ct, Baton Rouge, LA 70810-5334, U.S.A. **Online address:** info@hollyclegg.com; www.hollyclegg.com

CLEM, Alan L(eland). American, b. 1929. **Genres:** Politics/Government. **Career:** Professor of Political Science, University of South Dakota, Vermillion, 1964- (Assistant Professor, 1960-62; Associate Professor, 1962-64). Copywriter, Ayres Advertising Agency, Lincoln, Nebraska, 1950-52; Press Secretary, U.S. House of Reps., Washington, D.C., 1953-59; Information Specialist, Foreign Agricultural Service, Washington, DC, 1959-60. **Publications:** The Nomination of Joe Bottum, 1963; South Dakota Political Almanac, 2nd ed., 1969; Prairie State Politics, 1967; (sr. author) The Making of Congressmen: Seven Campaigns of 1974, 1976; American Electoral Politics: Strategies for Renewal, 1981; (with J. Rumbolz) Law Enforcement: The South Dakota Experience, 1982; The Government We Deserve, 1985, 5th ed., 1995; Congress: Powers, Processes, and Politics, 1989; Government by the People?: South Dakota Politics in the Last Third of the Twentieth Century, 2002. **Address:** 608 Colonial Court, Vermillion, SD 57069, U.S.A.

CLEM, Margaret H(ollingsworth). American, b. 1923. **Genres:** Children's fiction. **Career:** Writer. MEIS Department Store, Terre Haute, IN, assistant to the buyer/manager of the Boulevard Room (customer relations, community relations, ad writing, displays), weekly column writer for the Women's Department, 1962-86. **Publications:** (and illustrator) Elbert Ein Swine, Genius Pig, 1994; (and illustrator) Elbert Ein Swine Learns Line Dancing, 1995; Little Candles: A Collection of Poems and Stories, 1995.

CLEMENS, Brian (Horace). Also writes as Tony O'Grady. British, b. 1931. **Genres:** Plays/Screenplays. **Career:** Writer and producer of films and televisions shows and series. **Publications:** SCREENPLAYS: (As Tony O'Grady) At the Stroke of Nine, 1957; The Depraved, 1957; A Woman of Mystery, 1957; Operation Murder, 1957; Three Sundays to Live, 1957; Three Crooked Men, 1958; A Woman Possessed, 1958; On the Run, 1958; (as Tony O'Grady) The Secret Man, 1958; Moment of Indiscretion, 1958; Links of Justice, 1958; The Betrayal, 1958; A Woman's Temptation, 1959; Web of Suspicion, 1959; Top Floor Girl, 1959; Innocent Meeting, 1959; An Honourable Murder, 1959; High Jump, 1959; The Great Van Robbery, 1959; Crash Drive, 1959; The Child and the Killer, 1959; Two Wives at One Wedding, 1960; Identity Unknown, 1960; Highway to Battle, 1960; Transatlantic, 1961; Tarnished Heroes, 1961; Return of a Stranger, 1961; The Pursuers, 1961; The Middle Course, 1961; The Court Martial of Major Keller, 1961; The Tell-Tale Heart, 1962; The Spanish Sword, 1962; The Silent Invasion, 1962; Fate Takes a Hand, 1962; Station Six-Sahara, 1963; (as Tony O'Grady) Curse of the Voodoo, 1965; The Corrupt Ones, 1967; Buff: Original Story and Screenplay, 1970; And Soon the Darkness, 1970; See No Evil, 1971; Dr. Jekyll and Sister Hyde, 1972; The Golden Voyage of Sinbad, 1973; Captain Kronos: Vampire Hunter, 1974; The Watcher in the Woods, 1980; Highlander II: The Quickening (story), 1991. TELEPLAYS: Scene of the Crime, 1962; One Deadly Owner, 1974; Timestalkers, 1987; Perry Mason: The Case of the Glass Coffin, 1991; Perry Mason: The Case of the Reckless Romeo, 1992; Perry Mason: The Case of the Heartbroken Bride, 1992. PLAYS: The Edge of Darkness: A Play, 1978; Shock!: A Thriller, 1979; (with D. Spooner) A Sting in the Tail: A Thrilling Comedy in Two Acts, 1988; The Return of Brother Bernard, And, Who Was That Man, 1989; Rabbit Pie, 1990; (with D. Spooner) Anybody for Murder?: A Play, 1990; (with D. Spooner) Will You Still Love Me in the Morning?: A Farce, 1992; Inside Job: A Thriller, 1993. **Address:** c/o Samuel French, 45 N. 25th St., New York, NY 10010, U.S.A.

CLEMENS, Walter C., Jr. American, b. 1933. **Genres:** International relations/Current affairs. **Career:** Professor of Political Science, Boston University, 1966.- Adjunct Research Fellow, Harvard Center for Science and International Affairs, 1986-. Chairman, Language Dept., Iolani School, Honolulu, HI, 1960-61; Assistant Professor, Dept. of Political Science, University of California, Santa Barbara, 1961-63, and Massachusetts Institute of Technology, Cambridge, 1963-66; Associate, Russian Research Center, Harvard University, Cambridge, MA, 1963-. **Publications:** (comp.) Soviet Disarmament Policy, 1917-1963, 1965; (ed.) World Perspectives on International Politics, 1965; (ed.) Toward a Strategy of Peace, 1965; (with L. Bloomfield and F. Griffiths) Khrushchev and the Arms Race, 1966; Outer Space and Arms Control, 1966; The Arms Race and Sino-Soviet Relations, 1968; Die Tschechoslowakei unter Husak, 1970; (with others) The Soviet Union and Arms Control: A Superpower Dilemma, 1970; The Superpowers and Arms Control, 1973; The USSR and Global Interdependence, 1978; National Security and U.S.-Soviet Relations, 1981; Can Russia Change?, 1990; Baltic Independence and Russian Empire, 1991; Dynamics of International Relations: Conflict and Mutual Gain in an Era of Global Interdependence, 1998, 2nd ed., 2004; America and the World, 1898-2025: Achievements, Failures, Alternative Futures, 2000; The Baltic Transformed: Complexity Theory and European Security, 2001. **Address:** Dept of Political Science, Boston University, 232 Bay State Rd, Boston, MA 02215, U.S.A. **Online address:** wclemens@bu.edu

CLEMENT, Mary H. American, b. 1943. **Genres:** Law. **Career:** Attorney and educator. Virginia Commonwealth University, former professor of criminal justice and coordinator of dual-degree M.A. program in criminal justice and divinity. **Publications:** The Juvenile Justice System: Law and Process, 1997, 2nd ed, 2001; (with D. Humphry) Freedom to Die: People, Politics, and the Right-to-Die Movement, 1998; How to Die without a Lawyer: A Practical Guide to Creating an Estate Plan without Paying Legal Fees, 2000. Author of two other books. Contributor of articles to periodicals. **Address:** c/o Author Mail, St. Martin's Press, 175 Fifth Ave., New York, NY 10010, U.S.A.

CLEMENTS, Alan. American. **Genres:** Area studies. **Career:** Lecturer and spokesperson for Burma, c. 1983-; ordained a Buddhist monk; head of a human rights organization for Burma. **Publications:** Burma: The Next Killing Fields?, 1992; (with L. Kean) Burma's Revolution of the Spirit: The Struggle for Democratic Freedom and Dignity, 1995; (with Aung San Suu Kyi) The Voice of Hope: Conversations with Alan Clements, 1997. **Address:** c/o Seven Stories Press, 140 Watts St., New York, NY 10013, U.S.A.

CLEMENTS, Alan. British, b. 1948. **Genres:** Information science/Computers. **Career:** Loughborough University, Dept of Electronic Engineering, research fellow, 1974-76, lecturer, 1976-87, reader in computer science, 1987-92, School of Computing and Mathematics, Motorola Professor, 1992-; Technical Institute of Crete, Greece, visiting professor, 1989-90; Microprocessors and Microsystems, associate editor, 1986-; Manchester Metropolitan University, Manchester, England, external examiner for computer science degree, 1990-94; South Bank University, London, England, external examiner, 1991-95; International Institute for Computer Studies, Colombo, Sri Lanka, external examiner, 1992-94; University of Massachusetts, Boston, MA, adjunct professor, 1996-97. National Teaching Fellowship (UK), 2002. **Publications:** Microcomputer Design and Construction: Building Your Own System with the Motorola 6800, 1982; The Principles of Computer Hardware, 1985, rev. ed., 1993; Microprocessor Systems Design: 68000 Software, Hardware, and Interfacing, 1987, 3rd ed., 1997; Microprocessor Interfacing and the 68000: Peripherals and Systems, 1989; 68000 Family Assemblage Language, 1994. EDITOR: 68000 Sourcebook, 1990; Microprocessor Support Chip Sourcebook, 1991; Analog Interface and the DSP Sourcebook, 1993. VIDEO SERIES: Microprocessor Design, 1990. **Address:** University of Teesside, Borough Rd, Middlesbrough TS1 3BA, England. **Online address:** a.clements@tees.ac.uk

CLEMENTS, Andrew. Also writes as Andrew Elborn. American, b. 1949. **Genres:** Children's fiction, Young adult fiction. **Career:** Writer, editor, and educator. Sunset Ridge School, Northfield, IL, fourth grade teacher, 1972-74; Wilmette Junior High School, Wilmette, IL, eighth grade teacher, 1974-77; New Trier High School, Winnetka, IL, English teacher, 1977-79. Allen D. Bragdon Publishers, New York, NY, editor, 1980-82; Alphabet Press, Natick, MA, sales and marketing manager, editor, 1982-85; Keller Graduate School of Management, Chicago, IL, director, 1985-87; Picture Book Studio Ltd., Saxonville, MA, vice-president and editorial director, 1987-93; Christian Science Publishing Society, Boston, MA, editor, 1997-98; frequent speaker in schools and at writing and education conferences. **Publications:** FOR CHILDREN: Bird Adalbert, 1985; Big Al, 1987; Santa's Secret Helper, 1990; (as Andrew Elborn) Noah and the Ark and the Animals, 1991; Temple Cat, 1991; Mother Earth's Counting Book, 1992; Billy and the Bad Teacher,

1992; Who Owns the Cow?, 1995; Bright Christmas: An Angel Remembers, 1996; Frindle, 1996; (adaptor) Philipp's Birthday Book, 1996; Riff's BeBop Book, 1996; Real Monsters Go for the Mold!, 1997; Things That Go EEK on Halloween, 1997; Real Monsters Stage Fright, 1997; Music Time, Any Time!, 1997; Double Trouble in Walla Walla, 1997; Gromble's Haunted Halloween, 1998; The Landry News, 1998; Workshop, 1999; Hey Dad, Could I Borrow Your Hammer?, 1999; The Christmas Kitten, 2000; The Mouse Family, 2000; The Janitor's Boy, 2000; Circus Family, 2000; The School Story, 2001; Brave Norman, 2001; Dolores and the Big Fire, 2001; Ringo Save the Day, 2001; The Jacket, 2002; Things not Seen, 2002; Big Al and Shrimpy, 2002; A Week in the Woods, 2002; The Report Card, 2004; The Last Holiday, 2004. JAKE DRAKE SERIES: Bully Buster, Know-It-All, Teacher's Pet, 2001; Class Clown, 2002. READING PROGRAM BOOKS FOR SCHOOLS: Karen's Island, 1995; Three Wishes for Buster, 1995; Bill Picket, 1996; Hurricane Andrew, 1998; Ham and Eggs for Jack, 1998; Life in the Desert, 1998; Desert Treasure, 1998; Inventors: Making Things Better, 1998; Milo's Great Invention, 1998; The Big Gust, 2001; RoboCat, 2001; Once upon a Box, 2001; Ruthie's Perfect Poem, 2001; The Mummy Moved, 2001. TRANSLATOR/ADAPTOR: Where Is Mr. Mole?; The Christmas Teddy Bear; Brave as a Tiger; The Beast and the Boy; Little Pig; Bigger Trouble; A Dog's Best Friend; Where the Moon Lives.

CLEMENTS, Arthur L. American, b. 1932. **Genres:** Poetry, Literary criticism and history, Autobiography/Memoirs, Biography. **Career:** Syracuse University, NY, lecturer, 1962-64; State University of New York at Binghamton, Assistant Professor, 1964-69, Associate Professor, 1969-88, Professor of English Literature, 1988-. **Publications:** (ed.) John Donne's Poetry, 1966, 1992; The Mystical Poetry of Thomas Traherne, 1969; Common Blessings, 1987; Benedizioni Comuni, 1989; Poetry of Contemplation, 1990; Dream of Flying, 1994; The Book of Madness and Love, 2000; 500 Years of Italian-American Accomplishments, 2003. **Address:** Dept. of English, State University of New York at Binghamton, PO Box 6000, Binghamton, NY 13902-6000, U.S.A.

CLEMENTS, Bruce. American, b. 1931. **Genres:** Children's fiction. **Career:** Member of the Dept. of English, Eastern Connecticut State University, Willimantic, since 1967. Pastor in Schenectady, New York, 1957-64; Instructor, Union College, Schenectady, 1964-67. **Publications:** FICTION: Two Against the Tide, 1967; The Face of Abraham Candle, 1969; I Tell a Lie Every So Often, 1974; Prison Window, Jerusalem Blue, 1977; Anywhere Else But Here, 1980; Coming About, 1984; The Treasure of Plunderell Manor, 1986; Tom Loves Anna Loves Tom, 1989. OTHER: From Ice Set Free: The Story of Otto Kiep, 1972; Coming Home to a Place You've Never Been Before, 1975. **Address:** Eastern Connecticut State University, Willimantic, CT 06226, U.S.A.

CLEMENTS, Jonathan. American (born England), b. 1963. **Genres:** Money/Finance. **Career:** Euromoney, London, England, writer and researcher, 1985-86; Forbes, NYC, staff writer, 1986-90; Wall Street Journal, NYC, columnist, 1990-. **Publications:** Funding Your Future, 1993; Twenty-Five Myths You've Got to Avoid-If You Want to Manage Your Money Right, 1998; You've Lost It, Now What?, 2003. **Address:** c/o Wall Street Journal, 200 Liberty St., New York, NY 10281, U.S.A. **Online address:** jonathan. clements@wsj.com

CLEMMER, Richard O. American, b. 1945. **Genres:** Anthropology/ Ethnology. **Career:** University of California, Santa Barbara, reader, 1967; University of Illinois, Urbana, teaching assistant, 1969-70; State University of New York, Dept of Anthropology, Binghampton, visiting assistant professor, 1972-73; Brooklyn College, City University of New York, Brooklyn, Dept of Anthropology, assistant professor; University of British Columbia, Vancouver, Dept of Anthropology and Sociology, visiting member of extrasessional faculty, 1976-78 (summers); College of New Rochelle, School of New Resources, NY, adjunct faculty, 1976; California State University, Northridge, visiting lecturer, 1977-78, associate professor of anthropology and American Indian studies, 1978-79, adjunct associate professor, 1979-81; Human Environment Research Corporation, Santa Barbara, CA, consultant, 1981; Social and Economic Development Strategy Project, Southern Ute Indian Tribe, Ignacio, CO, head, 1983; Pinon Canyon Archaeological Project, University of Denver, Pinon Canyon, CO, seasonal staff member, 1984; University of Denver, CO, Dept of Anthropology, senior lecturer, 1983-86, associate professor, 1986-; Sacred Lands Film Project, La Honda, CA, adviser to director, 1985-; organizer of symposia, 1978-; consultant for anthropological films and organizations. **Publications:** Roads in the Sky: The Hopi Indians in a Century of Change, 1995; (ed.) Julian Steward and the Great Basin: The Making of an Anthropologist, 1999. Contributor to anthropology books. Author of articles and reviews published in periodicals; author of

papers and non-refereed publications and reports. **Address:** Department of Anthropology, University of Denver, Denver, CO 80208, U.S.A.

CLENDENIN, Daniel B. American. **Genres:** Theology/Religion. **Career:** Protestant theologian. Moscow State University, Moscow, Russia, visiting professor, 1991-95; InterVarsity Christian Fellowship of Stanford University, Palo Alto, CA, graduate staff member. **Publications:** Theological Method in Jacques Ellul, 1987; (author of intro.) J. Ellul, The Presence of the Kingdom, 1989; From the Coup to the Commonwealth: An Inside Look at Life in Contemporary Russia, 1992; Eastern Orthodox Christianity: A Western Perspective, 1994; Many Gods, Many Lords: Christianity Encounters World Religions, 1995. EDITOR: (with W.D. Buschart) Scholarship, Sacraments, and Service: Historical Studies in Protestant Tradition: Essays in Honor of Bard Thompson, 1990; Eastern Orthodox Theology: A Contemporary Reader, 1995. Contributor to periodicals. **Address:** c/o Baker Books, PO Box 6287, Grand Rapids, MI 49516, U.S.A.

CLENDINNEN, Inga. Australian, b. 1934. **Genres:** Novellas/Short stories, History, Anthropology/Ethnology. **Career:** University of Melbourne, Parkville, Australia, tutor, 1956-57, senior tutor in history, 1958-65 and 1968; La Trobe University, Bundoora, Australia, lecturer, 1969-82, senior lecturer, 1982-89, reader in history, 1989-91, emeritus scholar, 1992-. Princeton University, fellow at Shelby Cullom Davis Center for Historical Research, 1983-84; Institute for Advanced Study (Princeton, NJ), fellow at School for Historical Studies, 1987; University of Michigan, Arthur H. Aiton Memorial Lecturer, 1987; Fellow, Australian Academy of the Humanities, 1992. **Publications:** Ambivalent Conquests: Maya and Spaniard in Yucatan, 1517-1571, 1987; Aztecs: An Interpretation, 1991; Reading the Holocaust, 1999; True Stories: Boyer Lectures, 1999; Tiger's Eye, 2000; Dancing with Strangers, 2003. Work represented in anthologies. Contributor to history and anthropology journals. Contributor of short fiction to Australian journals. **Address:** Department of History, La Trobe University, Bundoora, VIC 3083, Australia.

CLEVELAND, Ceil. American, b. 1940. **Genres:** Mystery/Crime/Suspense, Literary criticism and history, Autobiography/Memoirs, Reference. **Career:** Scriptwriter for educational television, Spokane, WA, 1966-69, and Dallas, TX, 1970-72; Cincinnati Arts and Humanities Consortium, OH, director of curriculum, 1972-74; University Press, University of Cincinnati, associate editor, 1974-76; Columbia-The Magazine of Columbia University, NYC, founder and editor-in-chief, 1976-86; Cleveland Communications Inc. (marketing & editorial projects organization), founder and president, 1986-; Queens College of the City University of New York, NYC, vice president for university relations, 1991-95; State University of New York at Stony Brook, vice president for university affairs and associate professor of English and women's studies, 1995-98; New York University, adjunct professor of English, 1998-. Syzygy: A Journal of Short Fiction, co-founder, 1976; founder, Cincinnati Women's Press, and The Brook (magazine), c. 1996. Lecturer at colleges. **Publications:** The Bluebook Solution (mystery), 2002. NONFICTION: Iron, Gold, and Bronze Women, and a Few Made of Steel: Three Generations of Women and Their Relationship to Work, 1994; Whatever Happened to Jacy Farrow? (memoir), 1997; In the World of Literature; Better Punctuation, 2003. EDITOR: A. Briggs, Lord Briggs, English Musical Culture, 1776-1976, 1977; M. Mulder, Managing with Power, 1979. Contributor to periodicals, journals, and newspapers. **Address:** 11 Prospect Rd, Centerport, NY 11721, U.S.A. **Online address:** ceilc@ optonline.net

CLEVELAND, Harlan. American, b. 1918. **Genres:** Education, International relations/Current affairs, Politics/Government, Essays. **Career:** President, World Academy of Art and Science, 1991-. Executive Ed. and Publisher, The Reporter mag., 1953-56; Dean, Maxwell Graduate School of Citizenship and Public Affairs, Syracuse University, NY, 1956-61; Assistant Secretary of State for International Organization Affairs, Washington, DC, 1961-65; U.S. Ambassador, NATO, Paris, and Brussels, 1965-69; President, University of Hawaii, Honolulu, 1969-74; Director, Program in International Affairs, Aspen Institute, Princeton, NJ, 1974-80; Professor of Public Affairs and Dean, Hubert H. Humphrey Institute of Public Affairs, University of Minnesota, Minneapolis, 1980-88. **Publications:** (with others) The Overseas Americans, 1960; The Obligations of Power, 1966; NATO: The Transatlantic Bargain, 1970; The Future Executive, 1972; Seven Everyday Collisions in American Higher Education, 1974; China Diary, 1976; The Third Try at World Order, 1977; Humangrowth: An Essay on Growth, Values and the Quality of Life, 1978; (with others) National Perceptions and Cultural Identities, 1978; Triple Collision of Modernization, 1979; Toward a Strategy for the Management of Peace, 1983; The Knowledge Executive, 1985; (co-author) Rethinking International Cooperation, 1988; The Global Commons:

Policy for the Planet, 1990; Birth of a New World, 1993; Leadership and the Information Revolution, 1997; Nobody in Charge, 2002. EDITOR/CO-EDITOR: The Promise of World Tensions, 1961; Ethics and Bigness, 1962; The Ethics of Power, 1962; Bioresources for Development, 1980; Energy Futures of Developing Countries, 1980; The Management of Sustainable Growth, 1981; Prospects for Peacemaking, 1987. **Address:** 46891 Grissom St, Sterling, VA 20165, U.S.A. **Online address:** harlancleve@cs.com

CLEVELAND, Leslie. New Zealander (born Australia), b. 1921. **Genres:** Poetry, Communications/Media, Film, Mythology/Folklore, Photography. **Career:** Reader, Victoria University of Wellington, 1966-87. Ed., Political Science journal, 1969-75; Sr. Fellow, Smithsonian Institution, Washington, D.C., 1988-89; Research Associate, University of Wellington, 1992. **Publications:** The Songs We Sang, 1959; The Silent Land, 1966; The Anatomy of Influence, 1972; (with A. D. Robinson) Readings in New Zealand Government, 1972; The Iron Hand, 1979; The Politics of Utopia, 1979; The Great New Zealand Songbook, 1991; Dark Laughter, 1994; Six Decades, 1998. **Address:** 38 Havelock St, Wellington, New Zealand. **Online address:** lesandmary@hotmail.com

CLEVELAND, Ray L. American, b. 1929. **Genres:** History. **Career:** Professor Emeritus, 1994-, Professor of History, 1974-94, University of Regina, Sask., Canada; Research Fellow, American Foundation for the Study of Man, 1964-66; Associate Professor, 1966-72, Professor, 1972-74, University of Saskatchewan, Regina. **Publications:** An Ancient South Arabian Necropolis, 1965; The Middle East and South Asia, 1967, rev. annually 1967-88; Readings on the History of the Holy Land, 1979; (with K.B. Leyton-Brown) Alexander the Great: An Exercise in the Study of History, 1992. Author of articles and book reviews. **Address:** Dept. of History, University of Regina, Regina, SK, Canada S4S 0A2. **Online address:** ray.cleveland@uregina.ca

CLEVELAND-PECK, Patricia. British. **Genres:** Children's fiction, Plays/Screenplays, Homes/Gardens, Travel/Exploration, Writing/Journalism. **Career:** Freelance writer and journalist. **Publications:** (ed.) The Cello and the Nightingale: The Autobiography of Beatrice Harrison, 1985. PLAYS: Evasion Tango (radio), 1991; The Cello and the Nightingale (radio), 1992; Evasion Tango (stage). JUVENILE: The String Family, 1979; William the Wizard, 1980; The Birthday Cake, 1981; The String Family in Summer, 1983; Community Magic, 1984; The String Family Move House, 1986; Bus from Beyond, 1990; Shepherd Boy, 1990; The Wandering Wizard, 1990; Ark Angel, 1991; Much Too Much, 1991; City Cat, Country Cat, 1992, in UK as Freckle and Clyde. Contributor of articles on plants, gardens, travel, and gastronomy to periodicals. **Address:** Harelands, Ashurst Woods, East Grinstead, Sussex RH19 3SL, England.

CLEWELL, David. American, b. 1955. **Genres:** Poetry. **Career:** Webster University, Webster Groves, MO, professor of English, 1985-. **Publications:** Room to Breathe, 1977; The Blood Knows to Keep Moving, 1980; As Far as the Eye Can See, 1988; Blessings in Disguise, 1991; Lost in the Fire, 1993; Now We're Getting Somewhere, 1994; The Conspiracy Quartet, 1997; Jack Ruby's America, 2000; The Low End of Higher Things, 2003. Contributor to magazines. **Address:** Department of English, Webster University, 470 E Lockwood, Webster Groves, MO 63119, U.S.A.

CLIFFORD, Christine. American, b. 1954. **Genres:** Inspirational/Motivational Literature, Self help. **Career:** Humorist, public speaker, and businesswoman. The Cancer Club (firm marketing humorous and helpful products to cancer-affected individuals), Edina, MN, president and chief executive officer; formerly senior vice president, SPAR Marketing Services (information and merchandising services firm), Minneapolis, MN. Director and producer, One Move at a Time, an exercise video for cancer patients. Inspirational speaker throughout the U.S. and on radio and television programs. **Publications:** Not Now ... I'm Having a No Hair Day, 1996; Our Family Has Cancer, Too! (children's nonfiction), 1997; Inspiring Breakthrough Secrets to Live Your Dreams, 2001; Cancer Has Its Privileges: Stories of Hope & Laughter, 2002. AUDIOCASSETTES: (with A.M. Ronning) Ask a Woman; Laughter: A New Twist to the Old Illness of Cancer!. **Address:** c/o The Cancer Club, 6533 Limerick Dr, Edina, MN 55439-1224, U.S.A. **Online address:** Christine@cancerclub.com

CLIFFORD, Deborah Pickman. American, b. 1933. **Genres:** Biography, History. **Career:** Writer and historian, 1975-. Vermont Historical Society and Sheldon Museum, president, 1981-85; Middlebury College, visiting lecturer, 1981-82; University of Vermont, visiting lecturer, 1983, 1984. **Publications:** Mine Eyes Have Seen the Glory: A Biography of Julia Ward Howe, 1979; Crusader for Freedom: A Life of Lydia Maria Child, 1992; The Passion of

Abby Hemenway: Memory, Spirit, and the Making of History, 2001. **Address:** 125 Sherman Lane, New Haven, VT 05472-3085, U.S.A.

CLIFFORD, Mary Louise. American, b. 1926. **Genres:** Children's fiction, Children's non-fiction, History, Technology. **Career:** With U.S. Foreign Service, Beirut, Lebanon, 1949-51; Staff Associate, National Center for State Courts, 1977-87. **Publications:** The Land and People of Afghanistan, 1962, 3rd ed. 1989; The Land and People of Malaysia, 1968; The Land and People of Liberia, 1971; (co-author) The Noble and Noble African Studies Program, 1971; Bisha of Burundi (children's fiction), 1973; The Land and People of Sierra Leone, 1974; Salah of Sierra Leone (children's fiction), 1975; The Land and People of the Arabian Peninsula, 1976; State Court Model Statistical Dictionary, 1980, Supplement, 1984, 1989; Computer-Aided Transcription in the Courts, 1981; Court Case Management Information Systems Manual, 1983; State Trial Court Jurisdiction Guide for Statistical Reporting, 1985; When the Great Canoes Came, (children's fiction), 1993; Women Who Kept the Lights: An Illustrated History of Female Lighthouse Keepers, 1994; From Slavery to Freetown: Black Loyalists after the American Revolution, 1999; (co-author) Nineteenth Century Lights: Historic Images of American Lighthouses, 2000. **Address:** 109 Shellbank Dr, Williamsburg, VA 23185, U.S.A.

CLIFTON, Chas S. American, b. 1951. **Genres:** Paranormal, Theology/Religion. **Career:** Mountain States Collector, Colorado Springs, CO, publisher and editor, 1977-79; Colorado Springs Sun, Colorado Springs, reporter, 1979-82; Colorado College, Colorado Springs, staff writer, 1983-84; Johnson Books, Boulder, CO, marketing director, 1984-85; Colorado Outdoor Journal, Canon City, managing editor, 1986-87; Canon City Daily Record, Canon City, reporter and photographer, 1987-90; Pueblo Community College, adjunct instructor, 1988-92; University of Southern Colorado, Pueblo, lecturer in English, 1992-. **Publications:** Ghost Tales of Cripple Creek, 1982; Encyclopedia of Heresies and Heretics, 1992. EDITOR: The Modern Craft Movement, 1992; Modern Rites of Passage, 1993; Witchcraft and Shamanism, 1994. **Address:** Dept of English, Colorado State University-Pueblo, 2200 Bonforte Blvd, Pueblo, CO 81001-4901, U.S.A. **Online address:** chas.clifton@colostate-pueblo.edu; www.chasclifton.com

CLIFTON, Lucille. American, b. 1936. **Genres:** Novels, Children's fiction, Poetry. **Career:** Coppin State College, Baltimore, visiting writer, 1971-74; St. Mary's College of Maryland, distinguished professor of humanities, 1989-; Blackburn Professor of Creative Writing, Duke University, Spring 1998, 1999. **Publications:** POETRY: Good Times, 1969; Everett Anderson series, 7 vols., 1970-83; Good News About the Earth, 1972; An Ordinary Woman, 1974; Two-Headed Woman, 1980, 1984; Good Woman, 1987; Next, 1987; Ten Oxherding Pictures, 1988; Quilting: Poems 1987-1990, 1991; The Book of Light, 1993; Terrible Stories: Poems, 1998; Blessing the Boats: New and Selected Poems 1988-2000, 2000 (National Book Award); Mercy, 2004. FOR CHILDREN: The Black BC's, 1970; Some of the Days of Everett Anderson, 1970; Everett Anderson's Christmas Coming, 1971; All Us Come 'cross the Water, 1973; Good, Says Jerome, 1973; The Boy Who Didn't Believe in Spring, 1973; Don't You Remember?, 1973; Everett Anderson's Year, 1974; The Times They Used to Be, 1974; My Brother Fine with Me, 1975; Everett Anderson's Friend, 1976; Three Wishes, 1976; Amifica, 1977; Averett Anderson's 1 2 3, 1977; Everett Anderson's Nine Month Long, 1978; The Lucky Stone, 1979; My Friend Jacob, 1980; Sonora Beautiful, 1981; Everett Anderson's Goodbye, 1983; Dear Creator: A Week of Poems for Young People and Their Teachers, 1997; One of the Problems of Everett Anderson, 2001. OTHER: Generations: A Memoir, 1976. **Address:** Division of Arts & Letters, Montgomery Hall, 126, St. Mary's College of Maryland, Saint Marys City, MD 20686, U.S.A. **Online address:** lclifton@smcm.edu

CLIMO, Shirley. American, b. 1928. **Genres:** Children's fiction, Children's non-fiction, Mythology/Folklore. **Career:** Scriptwriter for weekly juvenile series "Fairytale Theatre," Cleveland, 1949-53; free-lance writer, 1976-. **Publications:** CHILDREN'S FICTION: The Cobweb Christmas, 1982; Gopher, Tanker, and the Admiral, 1984; Someone Saw a Spider, 1985; A Month of Seven Days, 1987; King of the Birds, 1988; T.J.'s Ghost, 1989; The Egyptian Cinderella, 1989; The Korean Cinderella, 1993; The Little Red Ant and the Great Big Crumb: A Mexican Fable, 1995; The Irish Cinderlad, 1996. OTHER FOR CHILDREN: Piskies, Spriggans, and Other Magical Beings: Tales from the Droll-Teller, 1981; City! New York, 1990; City! San Francisco, 1990; City! Washington, DC, 1991; The Match between the Winds, 1991; Stolen Thunder: A Norse Myth, 1994; Atalanta's Race: A Greek Myth, 1995; (comp. and reteller) A Treasury of Princesses: Princess Tales from around the World, 1996; (comp. and reteller) A Treasury of Mermaids: Mermaid Tales from around the World, 1997; (comp. and reteller) Magic and Mischief: Tales from Cornwall, 1999; The Persian Cinderella, 1999; Monkey

Business, 2004. Contributor to anthologies. **Address:** 24821 Prospect Ave, Los Altos, CA 94022, U.S.A. **Online address:** sbclimo@aol.com

CLINE, Foster W. American, b. 1940. **Genres:** Human relations/Parenting. **Career:** Evergreen Consultants, Evergreen, CO, child psychiatrist, 1970-. Cline-Fay Institute, co-founder. Colorado State University, off-campus instructor. **Publications:** (with J. Fay) Parenting with Love and Logic: Teaching Children Responsibility, 1991; (with Fay) Parenting Teens with Love and Logic: Preparing Adolescents for Responsible Adulthood, 1992; (with Fay) Grandparenting with Love and Logic: Practical Solutions to Today's Grandparenting Challenges, 1994; Conscienceless Acts, Societal Mayhem: Uncontrollable, Unreachable Youth in Today's Desensitized World, 1994; Hope for High Risk and Rage-Filled Children. **Address:** Love and Logic Institute, 2207 Jackson St Ste 102, Golden, CO 80401-2300, U.S.A. **Online address:** drfcline@netw.com

CLINE, Lynn Hunter. American (born Sweden), b. 1961. **Genres:** Travel/Exploration. **Career:** Writer, 1993-. Santa Fe Community College, teacher of writing courses; Santa Fe Writers' Conference, teacher. **Publications:** Romantic Days and Nights in Santa Fe (travel book), 1998. **Address:** 29 Ellis Ranch Loop, Santa Fe, NM 87505, U.S.A. **Online address:** lyncli@aol.com

CLINE, Wayne. American, b. 1945. **Genres:** Transportation. **Career:** Teacher, 1968-77; investment broker, 1978-82; license inspector, 1982-83; United States Department of Defense, Anniston, AL, quality assurance specialist, 1983-; author, 1997-. **Publications:** Alabama Railroads, 1997. **Address:** c/o University of Alabama Press, Box 870380, Tuscaloosa, AL 35487, U.S.A.

CLINE, William R. American, b. 1941. **Genres:** Economics, Money/Finance. **Career:** Princeton University, NJ, lecturer to assistant professor of economics, 1967-70; Ford Foundation, visiting professor in Rio de Janeiro and Sao Paulo, Brazil, 1970-71; U.S. Treasury, Washington, DC, deputy director of trade, development, and research, 1971-73; Brookings Institution, Washington, DC, senior fellow, 1973-81; Institute for International Economics, Washington, DC, senior fellow, 1982-. **Publications:** The Economic Consequences of a Land Reform in Brazil, 1970; International Monetary Reform and the Developing Countries, 1976; (with others) Trade Negotiations in the Tokyo Round: A Quantitative Assessment, 1978; (ed. with E. Delgado) Economic Integration in Central America, 1978; (ed.) Policy Alternatives for a New International Economic Order: An Economic Analysis, Overseas Development Council, 1979; (ed. with S. Weintraub) Economic Stabilization in Developing Countries, 1981; (with others) World Inflation and the Developing Countries, 1981; An International Debt and the Stability of the World Economy, 1983; International Debt: Systemic Risk and Policy Response, 1984; Exports of Manufactures from Developing Countries: Performance and Prospects for Market Access, 1984; (ed.) Trade Policy in the 1980s, 1984; The Future of World Trade in Textiles and Apparel, 1987, 2nd ed, 1990; Mobilizing Bank Lending to Debtor Countries, 1987; American Trade Adjustment: The Global Impact, 1989; United States External Adjustment and the World Economy, 1989; The Economics of Global Warming, 1992; Global Warming: The Economic Stakes, 1992; Third World Debt: A Reappraisal, 1992; International Debt Re-Examined, 1994; Trade and Income Distribution, 1994. **Address:** Institute for International Economics, 1750 Massachusetts Ave NW, Washington, DC 20036-1903, U.S.A.

CLINTON, Catherine. American, b. 1952. **Genres:** History, Women's studies and issues. **Career:** University of Benghazi, Libya, lecturer in history, 1974; Union College, Schenectady, NY, assistant professor of history, 1979-83; Harvard University, Cambridge, MA, assistant professor of history, 1983-1988; Brandeis University, assistant professor of history, 1988-1990, Harvard University, Dept. of Afro-American Studies, 1990-93, W.E.B. DuBois Institute, 1993-. **Publications:** The Plantation Mistress, 1982; The Other Civil War, 1984; (comp. with G.J. Barker-Benfield) Portraits of American Women, 1991; Tara Revisited, 1995; Life in Civil War America, 1996; We the People (textbook series), 1997; Civil War Stories, 1998; Public Women and the Confederacy, 1999; The Scholastic Encyclopedia of the Civil War, 1999; The Black Soldier, 2000; (with C. Lunardini) The Columbia Guide to American Women in the Nineteenth Century, 2000; A Poem of Her Own, 2003. EDITOR: (with N. Silber) Divided Houses, 1992; Half-Sisters of History, 1994; (with M. Gillespie) The Devil's Lane, 1997; (with M. Gillespie) Taking off the White Gloves, 1998; I, Too, Sing America, 1998; Southern Families at War, 2000; (and author of intro.) Fanny Kemble's Journals, 2000. **Address:** c/o Kris Dahl, ICM, 40 W 57th St Fl 16, New York, NY 10019-4001, U.S.A.

CLINTON, Hillary Rodham. American, b. 1947. **Genres:** Human relations/Parenting, Law. **Career:** Admitted to the bars of the State of Arkansas, U.S. District Court (east and west districts) of Arkansas, U.S. Court of Appeals (8th circuit), 1973, admitted to the bar of the U.S. Supreme Court, 1975; Children's Defense Fund, Cambridge, MA, and Washington, DC, attorney, 1973-74; Carnegie Council on Children, New Haven, CT, legal consultant, 1973-74; Judiciary Committee of the U.S. House of Representatives, Washington, DC, counsel for the impeachment inquiry staff, 1974; University of Arkansas, Fayetteville, assistant professor of law, 1974-77, Little Rock, lecturer at law school, 1979-80; U.S. District Court (east district) of Arkansas, reporter for federal court speedy trial planning group, 1975-79; Rose Law Firm, Little Rock, AR, partner, 1977-92; First Lady of the United States, Washington, DC, 1993-2001; Committee on Health Care, committee head, Washington, 1993-; Senator from New York, 2001-. **Publications:** NONFICTION: It Takes a Village: And Other Lessons Children Teach Us, 1996; An Invitation to the White House: At Home with History, 2000; Living History (memoir), 2003; Handbook on Legal Rights for Arkansas Women. **Address:** United States Senate, Washington, DC 20510, U.S.A.

CLINTON, James H(armon). American, b. 1946. **Genres:** Poetry. **Career:** Louisiana Division of Administration, Baton Rouge, assistant commissioner, 1973-77, 1978-80; Gulf South Research Institute, Baton Rouge, director of administration to president, 1980-88; Louisiana Partnership for Technology and Innovation, Baton Rouge, president, 1988-97; Mercatus LLC, Baton Rouge, president, 1997-98. **Publications:** What Is Fair, 1997. **Address:** 375 Wesley Ct, Chapel Hill, NC 27516, U.S.A. **Online address:** JHC1@concentric.net

CLINTON, James W(illiam). American, b. 1929. **Genres:** Politics/Government, Autobiography/Memoirs. **Career:** Department of the Air Force, navigator, operations analyst, project officer, 1951-55, 1959-77; Procter & Gamble, Cincinnati, OH, staff assistant in advertising, 1955; Brown & Haley, Tacoma, WA, assistant to sales manager, 1955-56; U.S. Civil Service Commission, Los Angeles, CA, field investigator, 1956-59; University of Wisconsin-Whitewater, assistant professor of management, 1977-80; University of Northern Colorado, Greeley, professor of management, 1980-99. **Publications:** The Loyal Opposition, 1997. Contributor to periodicals. **Address:** 1720 Highland Dr. SE, Puyallup, WA 98372, U.S.A.

CLINTON, Kate. American, b. 1951. **Genres:** Humor/Satire. **Career:** Comedian and writer, 1981-. Worked as a high school English teacher, 1973-81. **Publications:** Don't Get Me Started, 1998; Comedy You Can Dance To, 1998. **Address:** c/o Greg Phillips, CStar, 89 Melville, San Anselmo, CA 94960, U.S.A. **Online address:** greg@cstartists.com

CLIPPER SETHI, Robbie. American, b. 1951. **Genres:** Novels. **Career:** Rider University, Lawrenceville, NJ, professor of English and former department chair, 1985-. **Publications:** The Bride Wore Red, 1996; Fifty-Fifty, 2003. Contributor of stories, poems, articles, and reviews to periodicals. **Address:** Dept of English, Rider University, 2083 Lawrenceville Rd, Lawrenceville, NJ 08648, U.S.A. **Online address:** sethi@rider.edu

CLOAKE, John (Cecil). British, b. 1924. **Genres:** History, Local history/Rural topics, Biography. **Career:** British Diplomatic Service, London, England, assigned to Foreign Office, 1948-49, third secretary at embassy in Baghdad, Iraq, 1949-51, second secretary at legation in Saigon, Vietnam, 1951-54, assigned to Foreign Office, 1954-56, private secretary to permanent under-secretary, 1956-57, and parliamentary under-secretary, 1957-58, commercial consul in New York City, 1958-62, first secretary at embassy in Moscow, USSR, 1962-63, assigned to Foreign Office and Diplomatic Service Administration Office, 1963-68, commercial counselor at embassy in Tehran, Iran, 1968-72, head of trade relations and exports department at Foreign and Commonwealth Office, 1973-76, ambassador to Bulgaria, 1976-80; appointed Companion of the Order of St. Michael and St. George, 1979. Writer, 1980-. Visiting fellow, London School of Economics and Political Science, 1972-73. Fellow, Society of Antiquaries of London, 1998. **Publications:** Templer: Tiger of Malaya (biography), 1985; (ed.) Richmond in Old Photographs, 1990; Richmond Past, 1991; Royal Bounty: The Richmond Parish Lands Charity 1786-1991, 1992; Palaces and Parks of Richmond and Kew, 2 vols., 1995, 1996; Richmond Past and Present, 1999; Cottages and Common Fields of Richmond and Kew, 2001. Many articles and monographs on history of Richmond. **Address:** 4 The Terrace, 140 Richmond Hill, Richmond, Surrey TW10 6RN, England.

CLOS, Charles. See STOKOE, E(dward) G(eorge).

CLOTFELTER, Beryl E. American, b. 1926. **Genres:** Astronomy, Physics. **Career:** Professor Emeritus of Physics, Grinnell College, IA, 1996- (joined faculty, 1963; S.S. Williston Professor of Physics, 1973-96); Research

Physicist, Phillips Petroleum Co., Bartlesville, OK, 1953-55; Assistant Professor of Physics, University of Idaho, Moscow, 1955-56; Assistant Professor to Professor of Physics, Oklahoma Baptist University, Shawnee, 1956-63. **Publications:** Reference Systems and Inertia, 1970; The Universe and Its Structure, 1976. **Address:** Dept. of Physics, Grinnell College, Grinnell, IA 50112, U.S.A.

CLOTFELTER, Charles T. American, b. 1947. **Genres:** Economics, Politics/Government. **Career:** University of Maryland, College Park, assistant professor affiliated with Bureau of Business and Economic Research and department of economics, 1974-79; U.S. Treasury Office of Tax Analysis, Washington, DC, financial economist and Brookings economic policy fellow, 1978-79; Duke University, Durham, NC, associate professor, 1979-84, director of graduate studies at Institute of Policy Sciences and Public Affairs, 1979-81, 1989-90, vice provost for academic policy and planning, 1983-85, professor of public policy studies and economics, 1984-, vice chancellor of university, 1985-88, director of Center for the Study of Philanthropy and Voluntarism, 1986-, vice provost for academic programs, 1993-94, Z. Smith Reynolds Professor of Public Policy, 1996-, professor of economics and law, 1996-. National Bureau of Economic Research, research associate, 1982-; University of North Carolina at Chapel Hill, visiting scholar at Institute for Research in Social Science, 1982; member and/or chair of committees at Duke University; consultant; contributor of testimony regarding economic issues. **Publications:** Federal Tax Policy and Charitable Giving, 1985; (with P.J. Cook) Selling Hope: State Lotteries in America, 1989; (with R. Ehrenderg, M. Getz, and J. Siegfried) Economic Challenges in Higher Education, 1991; (ed.) Who Benefits from the Nonprofit Sector?, 1992; Buying the Best: Cost Escalation in Elite Higher Education, 1996. **Address:** Box 90245, Duke University, Durham, NC 27708-0245, U.S.A. **Online address:** Charles. clotfelter@duke.edu

CLOUDSLEY-THOMPSON, John (Leonard). British (born India), b. 1921. **Genres:** Novels, Biology, Children's non-fiction, Environmental sciences/Ecology, Natural history, Zoology. **Career:** Professor of Zoology Emeritus, Birkbeck College, University of London, 1986- (Reader, 1971-72; Professor of Zoology, 1972-86). Ed-in-Chief, Journal of Arid Environments, 1978-97. Lecturer in Zoology, King's College, University of London, 1950-60; Professor of Zoology, University of Khartoum, and Keeper, Sudan Natural History Museum, 1960-71; took part in Cambridge Iceland Expedition, 1947, expedition to Southern Tunisia, 1954, and univ. expeditions to various parts of Africa, 1960-73, including Trans-Sahara crossing, 1967. Vice-President, Linnean Society, 1975-76 and 1977-78; President, British Arachnological Society, 1982-85, British Society for Chronobiology, 1985-87, and British Herpetological Society, 1991-96. **Publications:** (ed.) Biology of Deserts, 1954; Spiders, Scorpions, Centipedes and Mites, 1958; Animal Behaviour, 1960; (with J. Sankey) Land Invertebrates, 1961; Rhythmic Activity in Animal Physiology and Behaviour, 1961; (with M.J. Chadwick) Life in Deserts, 1964; Desert Life, 1965; Animal Conflict and Adaptation, 1965; Animal Twilight, 1967; Microecology, 1967; The Zoology of Tropical Africa, 1969; Animals of the Desert, 1969; (with F.T. Abushama) A Guide to the Physiology of Terrestrial Arthropods, 1970; The Temperature and Water Relations of Reptiles, 1971; Spiders and Scorpions, 1973; Bees and Wasps, 1974; The Ecology of Oases, 1975; Crocodiles and Alligators, 1975; Terrestrial Environments, 1975; Insects and History, 1976; Man and the Biology of Arid Zones, 1976; (ed. with J. Bligh and A.G. Macdonald) Environmental Physiology of Animals, 1976; The Size of Animals, 1976; Dietary Adaptations of Animals, 1976; Evolutionary Trends in the Mating of Arthropods, 1976; The Water and Temperature Relations of Woodlice, 1976; Tortoises and Turtles, 1976; The Desert, 1977; Form and Function in Animals, 1978; Animal Migration, 1978; Why the Dinosaurs Became Extinct, 1978; Wildlife of the Desert, 1979; Camels, 1980; Biological Clocks, 1980; Tooth and Claw, 1980; Seals and Sea Lions, 1981; Vultures, 1981; (with D.G. Applin) Biological Periodicities, 1982; (ed.) Sahara Desert, 1984; Guide to Woodlands, 1985; Living in the Desert, 1985; Evolution and Adaptation of Terrestrial Arthropods, 1988; Adaptations of Desert Organisms series, 1989-2000; Ecophysiology of Desert: Arthropods and Reptiles, 1991; Invertebrate Animals, 1992; The Diversity of Desert Life, 1993; The Nile Quest (novel), 1994; Predation and Defence amongst Reptiles, 1994; Biotic Interactions in Arid Lands, 1996; Teach Yourself Ecology, 1998; The Diversity of Amphibians and Reptiles, 1999. **Address:** 10 Battishill St, London N1 1TE, England.

CLOUSE, Robert Gordon. American, b. 1931. **Genres:** History, Theology/Religion. **Career:** Professor of History, Indiana State University, Terre Haute, 1963-. Minister, First Brethren Church, Cedar Rapids, Iowa, 1957-60; Visiting Professor, Indiana University, Bloomington, 1965-66, 1966-68. **Publications:** (with others) Puritans, the Millennium and the Future of Israel, 1970; (with R.D. Linder and R.V. Pierard) The Cross and the Flag (social criticism), 1972; (with others) Christ and the Modern Mind, 1972; The Meaning of the Millennium: Four Views, 1977; The Church in the Age of Orthodoxy and the Enlightenment, 1980; (with R.V. Pierard) Streams of Civilization: The Modern World to the Nuclear Age, 1980; War: Four Christian Views, 1981; Wealth & Poverty, Four Christian Views, 1984; (with B. Clouse) Women in Ministry: Four Views, 1989; (with R.V. Pierard and E.M. Yamauchi) Two Kingdoms: The Church and Culture through the Ages, 1993; (with R.N. Hosak and R.V. Pierard) The New Millennium Manual, A Once and Future Guide, 1999; The Story of the Church, 2002. **Address:** 2122 South 21st St, Terre Haute, IN 47802, U.S.A. **Online address:** hiclous@ ruby.indstate.edu

CLOUSER, Roy A. American, b. 1937. **Genres:** Theology/Religion, Philosophy. **Career:** Rutgers University, Camden, NJ, instructor in symbolic logic, 1965-66; La Salle College, Philadelphia, PA, instructor in philosophy, 1966-68; College of New Jersey, Trenton, NJ, professor of philosophy and religion, 1968-, department head, 1979-82, 1985-86, 1996-98; writer. Staley Distinguished Christian Scholar Lecture Foundation, fellow. **Publications:** The Myth of Religious Neutrality: An Essay on the Hidden Role of Religious Belief in Theories, 1991; Knowing With the Heart: Religious Experience and Belief in God, 1999. Contributor of articles and reviews to academic journals and anthologies. **Address:** Dept of Philosophy and Religion, College of New Jersey, Ewing, NJ 08628, U.S.A. **Online address:** royclouser@home.com

CLOUTIER, Cecile. Canadian, b. 1930. **Genres:** Poetry. **Career:** Professor, poet, essayist, playwright. **Publications:** Mains de sable, 1960; Cuivre et soies, suivi de Mains de sable, 1964; Cannelles et craies, 1969; Paupieres, 1970; Cablogrammes, 1972; Chaleuils, 1978, trans. by A. Amprimoz as Springtime of Spoken Words, 1979; L'Echangeur, 1985; L'Ecoute: Poemes 1960-1983, 1986; Lampees, 1990; Ancres d'encre: poesie, 1993; Ostraka: poesie, 1994; Le poaimier: poemes, 1996. Contributor to books and periodicals. **Address:** 44 Farm Greenway, Don Mills, Toronto, ON, Canada M3A 3M2.

CLOVER, Peter. (born England). **Genres:** Children's fiction. **Career:** Writer and illustrator. Formerly worked in an advertising agency. **Publications:** Drawing Horses and Ponies, 1994; The Best Pony for Me!, 1995; The Phantom Pony, 1999; The Storm Pony, 2000; Dead Cool, 2003. SHELTIE THE SHETLAND PONY SERIES: Sheltie the Shetland Pony, 1996; Sheltie Saves the Day!, 1996; Sheltie and the Runaway,1996; Sheltie Finds a Friend, 1996; Sheltie in Danger, 1997; Sheltie to the Rescue, 1997; Sheltie Rides to Win, 1998; Sheltie in Trouble, 1998; Sheltie and the Saddle Mystery, 1998; Sheltie Leads the Way, 1998; Sheltie the Hero, 1998; Sheltie on Parade, 1999; Sheltie the Snow Pony, 1999; The Big Adventure, 1999; Sheltie on Patrol, 1999; Sheltie Goes to School, 1999; Sheltie Gallops Ahead, 1999; The Big Show, 1999; Sheltie: The Big Surprise, 1999; Sheltie in Double Trouble, 1999; Sheltie Forever, Puffin, 1999; The Big Present, 1999; Sheltie in Peril, 2000; Sheltie and the Foal, 2000; Sheltie: The Big Wish, 2000; Sheltie by the Sea, 2000; Sheltie Races On, 2000; Sheltie at the Funfair, 2001. RESCUE RIDERS SERIES: Race against Time, 1998; Fire Alert, 1998; Ghost Pony, 1998. HERCULES SERIES: New Pup on the Block, 2000; Operation Snowsearch, 2000; Treasure Hound, 2000. DONKEY DIARIES SERIES: Donkey Danger, 2001; Donkey Disaster, 2001; Donkey Drama, 2001; Donkey in Distress, 2002. **Address:** c/o Aladdin, Simon & Schuster, 1230 Avenue of the Americas, New York, NY 10020, U.S.A.

CLOW, Barbara Hand. American, b. 1943. **Genres:** Crafts, Science fiction/Fantasy, Medicine/Health. **Career:** Bear and Co., Inc. (publisher), Santa Fe, NM, executive vice-president, 1983-. Public speaker in the United States, Europe, and the Far East. **Publications:** Stained Glass: A Basic Manual, 1976; Eye of the Centaur, 1986; Chiron: Rainbow Bridge, 1987; Heart of the Christos, 1989; Liquid Light of Sex: Understanding Your Key Life Passages, 1991; Signet of Atlantis: War in Heaven Bypass, 1992; The Pleiadian Agenda: A New Cosmology for the Age of Light, 1996.

CLUBBE, John L(ouis) E(dwin). American, b. 1938. **Genres:** Architecture, Art/Art history, Literary criticism and history, Music, Urban studies, Biography. **Career:** University of Munster, Germany, lektor, 1965-66; Duke University, Durham, NC, assistant professor, 1966-70, associate professor of English, 1970-75; University of Kentucky, Lexington, professor of English, 1975-99, professor emeritus, 1999-. **Publications:** Victorian Forerunner: The Later Career of Thomas Hood, 1968; (co-author) English Romanticism: The Grounds of Belief, 1983; (with others) The English Romantic Poets: A Review of Research and Criticism, 1985; Cincinnati Observed: Architecture and History, 1992; Byron, Sully, and the Power of Portraiture, forthcoming. EDITOR/CO-EDITOR: Selected Poems of Thomas Hood, 1970; The Collected Letters of Thomas and Jane Welsh Carlyle, 9 vols., 1970, 1977, 1981;

Two Reminiscences of Thomas Carlyle, 1974; Nineteenth-Century Literary Perspectives, 1974; Carlyle and His Contemporaries, 1976; Froude's Life of Carlyle, 1979; Victorian Perspectives: Six Essays, 1989. **Address:** 1266 Canyon Rd, Santa Fe, NM 87501-6128, U.S.A. **Online address:** jclubbe@ newmexico.com

CLUNIS, D. Merilee. American. **Genres:** Gay and lesbian issues. **Career:** Psychotherapist and author. **Publications:** WITH G.D. GREEN: Lesbian Couples, 1988; revised as Lesbian Couples: Creating Healthy Relationships for the 90s, 1993; The Lesbian Parenting Book: A Guide to Creating Families and Raising Children, 1995. **Address:** c/o Seal Press, PMB 375, 300 Queen Anne Ave N, Seattle, WA 98109-4512, U.S.A.

CLUYSENAAR, Anne (Alice Andrée). Irish (born Belgium), b. 1936. **Genres:** Poetry, Songs/Lyrics and libretti, Inspirational/Motivational Literature, Literary criticism and history, Natural history, Autobiography/ Memoirs, Biography. **Career:** Director, Wentwood Forest Writers' Retreat, S. Wales. Tutor in creative writing, poet, librettist, critic, editor. Taught at Manchester University, 1957-58, Trinity College, Dublin, 1961-62, King's College, Aberdeen, 1963-65, University of Lancaster, 1965-71, Huddersfield Polytechnic, 1972-73, University of Birmingham, 1973-76, and Sheffield City Polytechnic, 1976-87. Founding director, Verbal Arts Association, 1983-86; co-founder and secretary, Usk Valley Vaughan Association, 1995-. Editor, Scintilla, 1997-. **Publications:** A Fan of Shadows, 1967; Nodes, 1969; An Introduction to Literary Stylistics: A Discussion of Dominant Structure in Verse and Prose (in U.S. as Aspects of Literary Stylistics), 1976; Double Helix, 1982; Timeslips: New and Selected Poems, 1997. EDITOR/CO-EDITOR: Selected Poems of James Burns Singer, 1977; The Hare That Hides Within, 2004; Henry Vaughan, Selected Poems, 2004. Contributor to books and periodicals. **Address:** Little Wentwood Farm, Llantrisant, Usk, Gwent NP15 1ND, Wales. **Online address:** anne.cluysenaar@virgin.net

CLYBOURN, Craig. See **HENSLEY, Dennis.**

CLYNES, Michael. See **DOHERTY, P(aul) C.**

COAN, Richard W. American, b. 1928. **Genres:** Novels, Psychology. **Career:** Professor Emeritus of Psychology, University of Arizona, 1989- (Assistant Professor, 1957-60; Associate Professor, 1960-64; Professor, 1964-89). Research Associate in Psychology, University of Illinois, Urbana, 1955-57. **Publications:** The Optimal Personality: An Empirical and Theoretical Analysis, 1974; Hero, Artist, Sage, or Saint?: A Survey of Views on What Is Variously Called Mental Health, Normality, Maturity, Self-Actualization, and Human Fulfillment, 1977; Psychologists: Personal and Theoretical Pathways, 1979; Psychology of Adjustment: Personal Experience and Development, 1983; Human Consciousness and Its Evolution: A Multidimensional View, 1987; A Princess for Larkin, 2001. **Address:** 2992 W Royal Copeland Dr, Tucson, AZ 85745, U.S.A.

COATES, Carrol F(ranklin). American, b. 1930. **Genres:** Literary criticism and history, Translations. **Career:** Ohio University, Athens, OH, instructor, 1960-62; Lycoming College, Williamsport, PA, assistant professor, 1962-63; Binghamton University-State University of New York, Binghamton, NY, assistant professor to associate professor to professor, 1963-. Universite D'Aix-Marseille I, exchange lecturer, 1980, 1983-84. **Publications:** TRANSLATOR AND AUTHOR OF INTRODUCTION: R. Depestre, The Festival of the Greasy Pole (novel), 1990; P. Anvers, Of Rice and Blood (novel), 1994; J.-B. Aristide, Dignity, 1996; J.S. Alexis, General Sun, My Brother (novel), 1999; A. Kourouma, Waiting for the Vote of the Wild Animals (novel), 2001; (with E.Danticat) J.S. Alexis, In the Flicker of an Eyelid, 2002. **Address:** Dept of Romance Languages & Literatures, Binghamton University-State University of New York, Binghamton, NY 13902-6000, U.S.A. **Online address:** ccoates@binghamton.edu

COATES, Charles (K.). American, b. 1929. **Genres:** Communications/ Media, Politics/Government, Writing/Journalism. **Career:** Nashville Tennesseean, Nashville, TN, reporter and editor, 1956-61; National Broadcasting Company (NBC), NYC, writer, editor, and producer of NBC News, 1961-72, 1975, 1980-81, including work for The Huntley-Brinkley Report, Nightly News and Today; University of New Mexico, Albuquerque, associate professor, 1972-96. **Publications:** Professional's TV News Handbook, 1994. **Address:** PO Box 1387, Kitty Hawk, NC 27949-1387, U.S.A. **Online address:** chascoates@msn.com

COATES, Ken. British, b. 1930. **Genres:** Business/Trade/Industry, Industrial relations, International relations/Current affairs, Money/Finance, Politics/ Government, Social commentary. **Career:** Coal miner, 1948-56; special

professor in adult education, University of Nottingham (member of the faculty 1960-2004). European Parliament, member, 1989-99. **Publications:** (with R. Silburn) Poverty, Deprivation, and Morale in a Nottingham Community, 1967; (with T. Topham) Industrial Democracy in Great Britain, 1967; (with R. Silburn) Poverty, 1970, rev. ed., 1983; The Crisis of British Socialism, 1971; Essays on Industrial Democracy, 1971; (with T. Topham) The New Unionism, 1972; Socialists and the Labour Party, 1975; New Worker Co-operatives, 1976; Beyond Wage Slavery, 1977; Democracy in the Labour Party, 1977; (with T. Topham) The Shop Steward's Guide to the Bullock Report, 1977; Industrial Development and Economic Planning, 1978; The Case of Nikolai Bukharin, 1978; European Nuclear Disarmament, 1980; (with T. Topham) Trade Unions in Britain, 1980; (with R. Silburn) Beyond the Bulldozer, 1980; Eleventh Hour for Europe, 1981; Work-Ins, Sit-Ins, and Industrial Democracy, 1981; Deterrence: Why We Must Think Again, 1981; Heresies: Resist Much, Obey Little, 1982; An Alternative Economy Strategy, 1982; The Social Democrats, 1983; The Most Dangerous Decade, 1984; (with T. Topham) Trade Unions and Politics, 1986; Think Globally, Act Locally, 1988; (with T. Topham) The Making of the Transport and General Workers Union, 1991; Human Rights in the World, 1992; (with S. Holland) Full Employment in Europe, 1995; Dear Commissioner, 1996; (with M.B. Brown) The Blair Revelation, 1996; Community under Attack, 1998; (with M.B. Brown) Third Way ...Where To?, 2001; Tony Blair-The Old New Goes to War, 2003; Worker's Control-Another Word Is Possible, 2003; Dealing with the Hydra?, 2003; Empire No More!, 2004; (with others) The Social Europe We Need, 2004. EDITOR: Democracy in the Mines, 1974; China and the Bomb, 1986; Civil and Academic Freedom in the U.S.S.R. and Eastern Europe, 1988. **Address:** Bertrand Russell House, Bulwell Ln, Nottingham NG6 0BT, England.

COATES, Robert Crawford. American, b. 1937. **Genres:** Food and Wine, Social commentary. **Career:** City of San Diego, CA, civil engineer and administrative analyst in city manager's office, 1959-63; Coates & Miller (attorneys), San Diego, partner, 1971-82; currently judge for San Diego Superior Court. University of San Diego and Western State University College of Law of San Diego, adjunct professor, 1981-. San Diego Ecology Center, president, 1985-86; San Diego County Law Library, member of board of trustees, 1985-, president, 1992; San Diego Natural History Museum, first vice-president, 1989-90; Seven Seas Exploration, Inc., treasurer, 1990-. Chair, S.D. Alcohol & Drug Abuse Prevention Task Force, 1996. **Publications:** Ships Crossing at the Dead of Night (poems), 1984; A Street Is Not a Home: Solving America's Homeless Dilemma, 1990; The Guys Who Can't Cook Cookbook, 1992. **Address:** San Diego Superior Court, Dept. S-45, 220 W Broadway, San Diego, CA 92101-3877, U.S.A.

COATS, Wendell John, Jr. American, b. 1947. **Genres:** Politics/ Government. **Career:** U.S. House of Representatives, Washington, DC, legislative assistant, 1979; Connecticut College-New London, professor of government and department chair, 1984-. **Publications:** The Activity of Politics and Related Essays, 1989; A Theory of Republican Character and Related Essays, 1994; Statesmanship: Six Modern Illustrations of a Modified Ancient Ideal, 1995; Oakeshott and His Contemporaries, 2000; Political Theory and Practice, 2003; Montaigne's Essais, 2004. Contributor to periodicals. **Address:** Dept of Government, Connecticut College, PO Box 5425, New London, CT 06320, U.S.A. **Online address:** wjcoa@conncoll. edu

COATSWORTH, John H(enry). American, b. 1940. **Genres:** Economics, History. **Career:** University of Chicago, IL, assistant professor, 1969-77, associate professor, 1977-80, professor of history, 1980-92; Harvard University, Cambridge, MA, professor of history and Monroe Gutman Professor of Latin American Affairs, 1992-. Visiting professor, guest lecturer and senior Fulbright lecturer at North and South American colleges and universities. **Publications:** Growth against Development: The Economic Impact of Railroads in Porfirian Mexico, 1981; Los origenes del atraso: Nueve ensayos de historia economica de Mexico, siglos XVIII y XIX, 1990; Central America and the United States: The Clients and the Colossus, 1994. EDITOR & CONTRIBUTOR: (with C.M. Rico) Images of Mexico in the United States, 1989; (with A.M. Taylor) Latin America and the World Economy since 1800, 1998. Contributor to books. Contributor of articles and reviews to history, economic, and Latin American studies journals. **Address:** David Rockefeller Center for Latin American Studies, Harvard University, 61 Kirkland St, Cambridge, MA 02138, U.S.A.

COBALT, Martin. See **MAYNE, William.**

COBB, Clifford W(illiam). American, b. 1951. **Genres:** Education, Economics. **Career:** National Association of Counties, Washington, DC, research associate, 1976-78; Palmore Institute, Kobe, Japan, English teacher, 1979-81; Claremont School District, Claremont, CA, substitute teacher, 1984-89; Institute for Educational Choice, Sacramento, CA, executive director, 1991-93; California Futures, Sacramento, researcher, 1991-93; Redefining Progress, San Francisco, CA, senior fellow, 1994-. **Publications:** Responsive Schools, Renewed Communities, 1992; (with J.B. Cobb, Jr.) The Green National Product: A Proposed Index of Sustainable Economic Welfare, 1994. Contributor to books and periodicals. **Address:** Redefining Progress, 1904 Franklin St., Oakland, CA 94612, U.S.A.

COBB, James H(arvey). American, b. 1953. **Genres:** Mystery/Crime/Suspense. **Career:** Writer. Member of U.S. Naval Institute and Museum of the Rockies. **Publications:** Choosers of the Slain (suspense novel), 1996; Stormdragon, in press. **Address:** c/o Henry Morrison Inc., PO Box 235, Bedford Hills, NY 10507, U.S.A.

COBB, Nancy (Howard). American, b. 1949. **Genres:** Adult non-fiction, Children's non-fiction. **Career:** Teacher at a primary school in New Haven, CT, 1970-71; actress and documentary film producer in New York City, 1975-82; writer, 1982-. Public Radio Show Host, Connecticut Voices; Sunken Garden Poetry series, public radio, interviewer/host, 1994-96. **Publications:** How They Met, 1992; Letter Writer Book for Kids, 1994; In Lieu of Flowers: A Conversation for the Living, 2000.

COBB, Thomas. American, b. 1947. **Genres:** Novels, Novellas/Short stories. **Career:** Rhode Island College, Providence, RI, professor of English, 1987-; writer. **Publications:** We Shall Curse the Dead (poems), 1976; Crazy Heart (novel), 1987; Acts of Contrition (stories), 2003. **Address:** Dept. of English, Rhode Island College, Providence, RI 02908, U.S.A.

COBB, Vicki. American, b. 1938. **Genres:** Children's non-fiction. **Publications:** Logic, 1969; (ed.) Biology Study Prints, 1970; Cells, 1970; Gases, 1970; Making Sense of Money, 1971; Sense of Direction, 1972; Science Experiments You Can Eat, 1972, rev. ed., 1994; Heat, 1973; The Long and Short of Measurement, 1973; How the Doctor Knows You're Fine, 1973; Arts and Crafts You Can Eat, 1974; Supersuits, 1975; Magic…Naturally!, 1976; More Science Experiments You Can Eat, 1979; Truth on Trial: The Story of Galileo, 1979; (with K. Darling) Bet You Can't, 1980; How to Really Fool Yourself, 1980; Lots of Rot, 1981; The Secret Life of School Supplies, 1981; The Secret Life of Hardware, 1982; Fuzz Does It!, 1982; Gobs of Goo, 1983; The Monsters Who Died, 1983; (with K. Darling) Bet You Can!, 1983; Brave in the Attempt, 1983; Chemically Active, 1984; The Secret Life of Cosmetics, 1985; The Scoop on Ice Cream, 1986; Sneakers Meet Your Feet, 1986; More Power to You, 1986; The Trip of a Drip, 1986; Inspector Bodyguard Patrols the Land of U, 1986; Skyscraper Going Up!, 1987; Scraps of Wraps, 1988; Why Doesn't the Earth Fall Up?, 1988; This Place Is Cold, 1989; This Place Is Dry, 1989; This Place Is High, 1989; This Place Is Wet, 1989; Why Can't You Unscramble an Egg?, 1989; Feeding Yourself, 1989; For Your Own Protection, 1989; Getting Dressed, 1989; Keeping Clean, 1989; Writing It Down, 1989; Natural Wonders, 1990; Why Doesn't the Sun Burn Out?, 1990; Fun & Games, 1991; This Place Is Lonely, 1991; This Place's Crowded, 1992; (with K. Darling) Wanna Bet!, 1993; (with J. Cobb) Light Action!, 1993; Why Can't I Live Forever, 1996; Blood and Gore, Like You've Never Seen, 1997; Dirt and Grime, Like You've Never Seen, 1998; (with K. Darling) Don't Try This at Home, 1998; This Place Is Wild: East Africa, 1998; Your Tongue Can Tell, 2000; Bangs and Twangs, 2000; Follow Your Nose, 2000; See for Yourself, 2001; Feeling Your Way, 2001; Perk Up Your Ears, 2001; Whirlers and Twirlers, 2001; Open Your Eyes, 2002; Sources of Forces, 2002; I See Myself, 2002; I Get Wet, 2002; I Face the Wind, 2003; I Fall Down, 2004; Fireworks, 2005; Junk Food, 2005; Sneakers, 2005; On Stage, 2005; Houdini, 2005. **Address:** 302 Pondside Dr, White Plains, NY 10607, U.S.A. **Online address:** email@vickicobb.com

COBBS, Elizabeth Anne. See **COBBS HOFFMAN, Elizabeth.**

COBBS HOFFMAN, Elizabeth. Also writes as Elizabeth Anne Cobbs. American, b. 1956. **Genres:** International relations/Current affairs. **Career:** Center for Women's Studies and Services, San Diego, CA, staff member, 1972-83, member of board of directors and president, 1983-94; University of California, San Diego, lecturer, 1988-89; University of San Diego, associate professor, 1989-. **Publications:** The Rich Neighbor Policy: Rockefeller and Kaiser in Brazil, 1992. AS ELIZABETH COBBS HOFFMAN: All You Need Is Love, 1998. **Address:** Dept of History, San Diego State University, 5500 Campanile Dr, San Diego, CA 92182-8147, U.S.A. **Online address:** ehoffman@mail.sdsu.edu

COBEN, Harlan. American, b. 1962. **Genres:** Mystery/Crime/Suspense. **Career:** Author of mystery novels. **Publications:** MYSTERY NOVELS: Play Dead, 1990; Miracle Cure, 1991. MYRON BOLITAR MYSTERY NOVELS: Deal Breaker, 1995; Dropshot, 1996; Fade Away, 1996; Back Spin, 1997; One False Move, 1997; Darkest Fear, 2000; Tell No One, 2001; Gone for Good, 2002; No Second Chance, 2003. **Address:** c/o Aaron Priest Literary Agency, 708 Third Ave., New York, NY 10017, U.S.A. **Online address:** Bolitar@aol.com

COBURN, Andrew. American, b. 1932. **Genres:** Novels, Mystery/Crime/Suspense, Writing/Journalism. **Career:** Feature Writer, and later Police Reporter, Suburban Ed., and City Ed., Eagle-Tribune, Lawrence, Massachusetts, 1963-73; Book Reviewer and Part-time Copy Ed., Boston Globe, 1973-78; political columnist for several Massachusetts newspapers, 1978-81; Full-time writer since 1978. **Publications:** The Trespassers, 1974; The Babysitter, 1979; Off Duty, 1980; Company Secrets, 1982; Widow's Walk, 1984; Sweetheart, 1985; Love Nest, 1987; Goldilocks, 1989; No Way Home, 1992; Voices in the Dark, 1994; Birthright, 1997. **Address:** 3 Farrwood Dr, Andover, MA 01810, U.S.A. **Online address:** Andrew1Coburn@aol.com

COBURN, Ann. British. **Genres:** Young adult fiction. **Career:** Freelance writer, 1991-. **Publications:** JUVENILE NOVELS: The Granite Beast, 1991; Welcome to the Real World, 1992; The Domino Effect, 1994. BORDERLANDS SERIES: Worm Songs, 1996; Web Weaver, 1997; Dark Water, 1998. **Address:** c/o Random House UK/Bodley Head, 20 Vauxhall Bridge Rd., London SW1V 2SA, England.

COBURN, L. J. See **HARVEY, John B.**

COCHRAN, Robert B(rady). American, b. 1943. **Genres:** Novels, Poetry, Literary criticism and history, Local history/Rural topics. **Career:** Ball State University, Muncie, IN, instructor, 1969-70; University of Southern Mississippi, Hattiesburg, assistant professor, 1970-71; National Endowment for the Humanities, lecturer/performer, 1971-72; University of Indiana at South Bend, assistant professor, 1973-76; University of Arkansas, Fayetteville, assistant professor, 1976-79, associate professor, 1979-87, professor, 1987-, director of Center for Arkansas and Regional Studies, 1989-. National Endowment for the Humanities Summer Seminar for School Teachers, project director, 1993, 1995; public speaker at universities and conferences. **Publications:** (with M. Luster) For Love and for Money: Vance Randolph, An Annotated Bibliography, 1979; Vance Randolph: An Ozark Life, 1985; Samuel Beckett: A Study of the Short Fiction, 1991; Our Own Sweet Sounds: A Celebration of Popular Music in Arkansas, 1996; Singing in Zion: Music and Song in the Life of an Arkansas Family, 1999; A Photographer of Note: Arkansas Artist Geleve Grice, 2002. FILMS: Beautiful Thing: Rugs by Jean Will; A Mountain Life: Walter Williams of Newton County, Arkansas; Music's Easier: Arkansas Fiddler and Stonemason Frankie Kelly. **Address:** Department of English, KH 333, University of Arkansas, Fayetteville, AR 72701, U.S.A.

COCHRANE, Peggy. American, b. 1926. **Genres:** Plays/Screenplays, Architecture, Medicine/Health. **Career:** Architect in private practice, 1960-. Association of Women in Architecture, President, 1970-72. **Publications:** Mayaland (musical), 1967; Witch Doctor's Cookbook, 1980; Witch Doctor's Manual, 1980; Cable Car (musical), 1986; Harry, Go Home! (play), 1990; Winning from Rejection, 1991; How to Con a Con Artist, 1991; The Sorcerers' Guide to Health, 1993; Finding Your Dream Home, forthcoming. **Address:** 15030 Ventura Blvd #19, Ste 626, Sherman Oaks, CA 91403, U.S.A.

COCKBURN, Patrick. British, b. 1950. **Genres:** International relations/Current affairs. **Career:** Journalist. Financial Times, London, England, Moscow correspondent, 1984-88; Independent, London, England, Middle East correspondent. **Publications:** Getting Russia Wrong: The End of Kremlinology, 1990; (with A. Cockburn) Out of the Ashes: The Resurrection of Saddam Hussein, 1999. **Address:** c/oIndependent, Independent House, 191 Marsh Wall, London E14 9RS, England.

COCKER, Mark. British, b. 1959. **Genres:** Biography. **Career:** Writer. **Publications:** (with C. Inskipp) A Himalayan Ornithologist: The Life and Work of Brian Houghton Hodgson, 1988; Richard Meinertzhagen: Soldier, Scientist, and Spy, 1989; Loneliness and Time: British Travel Writing in the Twentieth Century, 1992; Rivers of Blood, Rivers of Gold, 1998; Birders: Tales of a Tribe, 2001. **Address:** The Hollies, The Street, Claxton, Norfolk NR14 7AA, England.

COCKERILL, A(rthur) W(illiam). British, b. 1929. **Genres:** Plays/Screenplays, History, Writing/Journalism, Biography. **Career:** Metropolitan-

Vickers Electrical Co., Manchester, England, contracts engineer, 1951-54; British Timkin Ltd., Northampton, England, applications engineer, 1954-57; Iron Ore Company of Canada, Menihek, Labrador, operating manager, 1957-60; Twin Falls Power Corp., Twin Falls, Labrador, operations manager, 1960-64; Mathews Conveyer Co., Port Hope, Ontario, contracts international installation engineer, 1964-79; Spectrum Engineering Corp. Ltd., Peterborough, Ontario, consultant, 1979-85; Delta Tech Systems, Inc., Peterborough, technical publisher, 1984-93. Member of National Technical Committee on Quality Assurance Military service: British Army, Corps of Royal Engineers, 1939-51; commissioned officer. **Publications:** (Author and composer) "The Yukon Trail" (three-act musical play), first produced in Schefferville, Labrador, at Guild Theatre, September, 1960. "Benjamin" (one-act play), first produced in November, 1971. Sir Percy Sillitoe (biography), W. H. Allen, 1975. Airport Baggage-Handling, Rexnord, Inc., 1978. Sons of the Brave, Leo Cooper, 1984. Energy Management Handbook, Department of National Defence, 1985. Handbook of Technical Writing, Delta Tech Systems, 1986. (With Jack Nissen) Winning the Radar War, Macmillan (Canada), 1987. Handbook of A-C Maintenance, Transport Canada, 1990. **Address:** c/o Writers Union of Canada, 90 Richmond St E Ste 200, Toronto, ON, Canada M5C 1P1.

COCKRELL, Thomas D(errell). American, b. 1949. **Genres:** History, Biography. **Career:** Louisville Police Department, Louisville, MS, police officer, 1971-78; high school social studies teacher in Mississippi, 1974-75; activities director at a Methodist church, Philadelphia, MS, 1976-77; Mississippi Farm Bureau Insurance Co., Winston County, salesperson, 1978-79; Louisville Fire Department, firefighter, 1979-89; Louisiana State University in Shreveport, librarian, archivist and assistant professor of history and political science, 1989-90; Mississippi State University, lecturer in history, 1990-92; Blue Mountain College, Blue Mountain, MS, professor of history and head of social science, 1992-. East Mississippi Community College, instructor, 1983-87. Tippah County Historical Museum, member of executive committee, 1996-; guest on local television and radio programs. **Publications:** The Descendants of William Jasper Cockrell and Martha Ann Crowson, 1982; (ed. with M.B. Ballard) A Mississippi Rebel in the Army of Northern Virginia: The Civil War Memoirs of Private David Holt, 1995. Contributor to books. Contributor of articles and reviews to journals. **Address:** Department of Social Sciences, Blue Mountain College, PO Box 160, Blue Mountain, MS 38610, U.S.A.

COCKS, Nancy L. American. **Genres:** Design. **Career:** Writer, teacher, deputy warden, and Presbyterian minister on the Isle of Iona, Scotland. **Publications:** ADVENTURES OF FERGIE THE FROG SERIES: Fearless Fergie, 1996; Fergie Feels Left Out, 1996; Fergie Goes Moose Hunting, 1996; Fergie Hogs the Lily Pad, 1996; Fergie Fails a Test, 1997; Fergie, Frog Scout, 1997; Fergie Loses a Friend, 1997; Welcome Home, Fergie, 1997. OTHER: Growing Up with God: Using Stories to Explore a Child's Faith and Life, 2003. **Address:** 50 Wynford Dr., Toronto, ON, Canada M3C 1J7.

COCQUYT, Kathryn Marie. American, b. 1960. **Genres:** Novels, Children's fiction. **Career:** Writer. **Publications:** Little Freddie at the Kentucky Derby (juvenile), 1992; Little Freddie's Legacy (juvenile), 1994; The Celtic Heart (novel), 1994. **Address:** 14378 Delaware Dr, Moorpark, CA 93021-3557, U.S.A.

CODD. See SOMMERS, Robert (Thomas).

CODRESCU, Andrei. American (born Romania), b. 1946. **Genres:** Novels, Poetry, Autobiography/Memoirs, Novellas/Short stories. **Career:** Director, Institute for Paleo-Cybernetic Research, Palo Alto, California, 1967-73; Louisiana State University, professor of English. Columnist on National Public Radio; Exquisite Corpse, editor. **Publications:** ESSAYS: Secret Training, 1973; Raised by Puppets only to be Killed by Research, 1987; Craving for Swan, 1988; The Disappearance of the Outside, 1990; The Hole in the Flag: a Romanian Exile's Story of Return and Revolution, 1991; Road Scholar: Coast to Coast Late in the Century, 1993; Zombification: Essays from NPR, 1995; The Muse is Always Half-Dressed in New Orleans, 1995; The Dog With the Chip in His Neck, 1996; Hail Babylon!, 1998; The Devil Never Sleeps and Other Essays, 2000. NOVELS: The Repentance of Lorraine, 1994; The Blood Countess, 1995; Messiah, 1999. POETRY: License to Carry a Gun, 1970; The Here What Where, 1971; Grammar and Money, 1972; A Serious Morning, 1973; The History of the Growth of Heaven, 1973; A Mote Suite for Jan and Anselm, 1976; For the Love of a Coat, 1978; The Lady Painter, 1979; Diapers on the Snow, 1981; Necrocorrida, 1980; Selected Poems 1970-1980, 1983; Comrade Past and Mister Present, 1991; Belligerence, 1993; Alien Candor: Selected Poems, 1970-1995, 1996. TRANSLATIONS: At the Court of Yearning: Poems by L. Blaga, 1989.

SCREENPLAYS: Road Scholar, 1994. OTHER: Why I Can't Talk on the Telephone (short stories), 1972; (with A. Saroyan) San Francisco, 1973; The Life and Times of an Involuntary Genius (autobiography), 1974; Travels of a Vigilante, 1975; For Max Jacob, 1975; (with Alice Notley) Three Zero, Turning Thirty, 1982; In America's Shoes, 1983; Ectoplasm Is My Hobby: Blackouts and Dramatic Objects 1971 and 1986, 1987; Monsieur Teste in America and Other Instances of Realism, 1987; Land of the Free, 1999. EDITOR: American Poetry Since 1970: Up Late, 1987; The Stiffest of the Corpse: An Exquisite Corpse Reader, 1988; Reframing America, 1995; Thus Spake the Corpse, 1999; American Poets Say Goodbye to the Twentieth Century, 2001. **Address:** English Department, Louisiana State University, Baton Rouge, LA 70803, U.S.A.

CODY, James R. See ROHRBACH, Peter Thomas.

CODY, Jeffrey W. American, b. 1950. **Genres:** Architecture. **Career:** Educator. Cornell University, Ithaca, NY, visiting assistant professor, 1989-95; Chinese University of Hong Kong, member of architecture faculty. Antiquities Advisory Board of Hong Kong, member, 2000-. **Publications:** Building in China, 2001; Exporting American Architecture, 1870-2000, 2002. **Address:** Residence 14, Flat 2A, Chinese University of Hong Kong, Shatin, New Territories, Hong Kong. **Online address:** jwcody@cuhk.edu.hk

CODY, Liza. British, b. 1944. **Genres:** Mystery/Crime/Suspense. **Career:** Has worked as a painter, a studio technician at Madame Tussauds, London, and a graphic designer. Recipient, Crime Writers Association John Creasey Award, 1980; Silver Dagger, 1993; Anthony Bouchercon, 1993. **Publications:** Dupe, 1980; Bad Company, 1982; Stalker, 1984; Headcase, 1985; Under Contract, 1986; Rift, 1988; Backhand, 1992; Bucket Nut, 1993; Monkey Wrench, 1994; Musclebound, 1997. **Address:** c/o Felicity Bryan, 2A N. Parade, Banbury Rd, Oxford OX2 6PE, England.

CODY, Paul. American, b. 1953. **Genres:** Novels. **Career:** Free-lance writer, 1976-. Perkins School for the Blind, Watertown, MA, child-care worker, 1983-85; Cornell University, Ithaca, NY, lecturer in English, 1987-89; Cornell magazine, Ithaca, NY, associate editor and staff writer, 1991-96. Visiting professor of writing, Cornell University, 1997-. **Publications:** NOVELS: The Stolen Child, 1995; Eyes like Mine, 1996. Contributor to periodicals. **Address:** 901 North Tioga St., Ithaca, NY 14850, U.S.A.

CODY, Robin. American, b. 1943. **Genres:** Local history/Rural topics, Travel/Exploration. **Career:** Writer. **Publications:** Umbrella Guide to Bicycling the Oregon Coast (travel guide), 1990; Ricochet River (fiction), 1992; Voyage of a Summer Sun: Canoeing the Columbia River (travelogue), 1995.

COE, Jonathan. British, b. 1961. **Genres:** Novels, Biography. **Career:** University of Warwick, Coventry, England, tutor in English poetry, 1984-85; semiprofessional musician, 1985-87, legal proofreader, 1987-88, and free-lance writer and journalist, 1988-, all in London, England. **Publications:** NOVELS: The Accidental Woman, 1987; A Touch of Love, 1989; The Dwarves of Death, 1990; What a Carve Up!, 1994 in the U.S. as The Winshaw Legacy, 1995. BIOGRAPHIES: Humphrey Bogart: Take It and Like It, 1991; James Stewart: Leading Man, 1994. **Address:** Peake Associates, 14 Grafton Crescent, London NW1 8SL, England.

COE, Michael (Douglas). American, b. 1929. **Genres:** Anthropology/Ethnology, Food and Wine. **Career:** Yale University, New Haven, CT, instructor, 1960-62, assistant professor, 1962-63; professor, 1968-94, emeritus professor of anthropology, 1994-. **Publications:** La Victoria, 1961; Mexico, 1962; The Jaguar's Children: Preclassic Central Mexico, 1965; The Maya, 1966, rev. ed., 1993; (with K.V. Flannery) Early Cultures and Human Ecology in South Coastal Guatemala, 1967; America's First Civilization, 1968; The Maya Scribe and His World, 1973; Classic Maya Pottery at Dumbarton Oaks, 1975; The Lords of the Underworld: Masterpieces of Classic Maya Ceramics, 1978; (with R.A. Diehl) In the Land of the Olmec, 1980; Old Gods and Young Heroes: The Pearlman Collection of Maya Ceramics, 1982; (with G. Whittaker) Aztec Sorcerers in Seventeenth Century Mexico: The Treatise on Superstitions by Hernando Ruiz de Alarcon, 1983; (with D. Snow and E. Benson) Atlas of Ancient America, 1987; Breaking the Maya Code, 1992; (with S.D. Coe) The True History of Chocolate, 1996; (with J. Kerr) The Art of the Maya Scribe, 1997; (with M. Van Stone) Reading the Maya Glyphs, 2001; Angkor and the Khmer Civilization, 2003. **Address:** 376 St Ronan St, New Haven, CT 06511, U.S.A. **Online address:** OlmecC@aol.com

COE, Tucker. See WESTLAKE, Donald E.

COERR, Eleanor Beatrice. Also writes as Eleanor Hicks. American (born Canada), b. 1922. **Genres:** Children's non-fiction. **Career:** Lecturer, Chapman College, Orange, CA, and Monterey Peninsula College, CA. Reporter and Ed., Edmonton Journal, Canada, 1944-49; Ed. and Illustrator, syndicated weekly column in the Manila Times, Philippines, 1958-61; Contract Writer for USIS in Taiwan, 1960-62, and for Voice of America Special English Division, Washington, DC, 1963-65; Librarian, Davis Library, Bethesda, MD, 1971-72. **Publications:** (as Eleanor Hicks) Circus Day in Japan, 1953; The Mystery of the Golden Cat, 1968, 1973; Twenty-Five Dragons, 1971; Biography of a Giant Panda, 1975; The Mixed-Up Mystery Smell, 1975; The Biography of Jane Goodall, 1976; Biography of a Red Kangaroo, 1976; Sadako and the Thousand Paper Cranes, 1977; Waza at Windy Gulch, 1977; Gigi, a Whale Borrowed for Science and Returned to Sea, 1980; The Big Balloon Race, 1980; The Bell Ringer and the Pirates, 1983; The Josefina Story Quilt, 1986; Lady with a Torch, 1986; Chang's Paper Pony, 1988; Mieko and the Fifth Treasure, 1993; Sadako, 1993; Buffalo Bill and the Pony Express, 1995; S Is for Silver: A Nevada Alphabet, 2004. **Address:** Putnam Pub Group, 375 Hudson, New York, NY 10014, U.S.A. **Online address:** ecoerr@hotmail.com

COERS, Donald V. American, b. 1941. **Genres:** Literary criticism and history. **Career:** Sam Houston State University, Huntsville, TX, professor of English, 1969-, coordinator of graduate studies, 1992-95, associate vice president for academic affairs, 1995-2000; Angelo State University, San Angelo, TX, vice president for academic affairs, 2000-. **Publications:** John Steinbeck as Propagandist: "The Moon Is Down" Goes to War, 1991; (co-ed. with R. Demott and P. Ruffin), After The Grapes of Wrath: Essays on John Steinbeck, 1995. **Address:** Vice President for Academic Affairs, Angelo State University, San Angelo, TX 76909, U.S.A. **Online address:** Don.Coers@Angelo.edu

COETZEE, J(ohn) M(ichael). South African, b. 1940. **Genres:** Novels, Novellas/Short stories, Translations. **Career:** State University of New York, Buffalo, assistant professor, 1968-71, Butler Professor of English, 1984, 1986; University of Cape Town, lecturer, 1972-83, professor of general literature, 1984-99, distinguished professor of literature, 1999-; Johns Hopkins University, Baltimore, Hinkley Professor of English, 1986, 1989; Harvard University, visiting professor of English, 1991; University of Chicago, professor of social thought, 1998-. Recipient: Nobel Prize in Literature, 2003. **Publications:** Dusklands (2 novellas), 1974; (trans.) M. Emants, A Posthumous Confession, 1976; In the Heart of the Country (in US as From the Heart of the Country), 1977; Waiting for the Barbarians, 1980; (trans.) W. Stockenstrom, The Expedition to the Baobab Tree, 1983; Life and Times of Michael K, 1983; Foe, 1986; White Writing: On the Culture of Letters in South Africa, 1988; Age of Iron, 1990; Doubling the Point: Essays and Interviews, 1992; The Master of Petersburg, 1994; Giving Offense: Essays on Censorship, 1996; Boyhood, 1997; Disgrace, 1999 (Booker Prize); (with others) The Lives of Animals, 1999; Stranger Shores (essays), 2001; The Humanities in Africa = Die Geisteswissenschaften in Afrika, 2001; Youth, 2002; Elizabeth Costello, 2003; Elizabeth Costello, 2003. **Address:** PO Box 3090, Newton, SA 5074, Australia.

COFER, Judith Ortiz. Puerto Rican, b. 1952. **Genres:** Novels, Poetry, Autobiography/Memoirs, Young adult fiction, Novellas/Short stories. **Career:** Professor of English. **Publications:** Reaching for the Mainland (poetry), 1984; Peregrina, 1986; Terms of Survival: Poems, 1987; The Line of the Sun: A Novel, 1989; Silent Dancing: A Partial Remembrance of a Puerto Rican Childhood, 1990; The Latin Deli (prose & poetry), 1993; An Island Like You: Stories of the Barrio, 1995. **Address:** PO Box 2599, Athens, GA 30612, U.S.A.

COFFEY, Brian. See **KOONTZ, Dean R(ay).**

COFFEY, Michael. British, b. 1926. **Genres:** Classics. **Career:** University College London, London, England, assistant lecturer, 1951-54, lecturer, 1954-66, senior lecturer, 1966-76, reader in Greek and Latin, 1977-91, research fellow, 1991-; writer. **Publications:** Roman Satire, 1976, 2nd ed., 1989; (ed. with R. Mayer) Seneca, Phaedra, 1990. **Address:** Department of Greek and Latin, University College London, London WC1 6BT, England.

COFFIN, Tristram Potter. American, b. 1922. **Genres:** Mythology/Folklore, Sports/Fitness. **Career:** Professor Emeritus of English, University of Pennsylvania, Philadelphia, 1984- (Assistant Instructor of English, 1946-49; Associate Professor of English, 1958-64; Professor of English, 1964-84; Vice-Dean, Graduate School of Arts and Sciences, 1965-68). Instructor, English, 1949-50, Assistant Professor of English, 1950-56, and Associate Professor of English, 1956-58, Denison University, Granville, OH; Lecturer

in Folk Studies, Providence College, RI, 1984-90. **Publications:** The British Traditional Ballad in North America, 1950, 3rd ed., 1968; An Analytical Index to Journal Folklore, 1958; (with H.H. Flanders and B. Nettl) Ancient Ballads Traditionally Sung in New England, 4 vols., 1960; Uncertain Glory: Folklore and the American Revolution, 1971; The Old Ball Game: Baseball in Folklore and Fiction, 1971; The Book of Christmas Folklore, 1973; The Female Hero in Folklore and Legend, 1975; The Proper Book of Sexual Folklore, 1978; Great Game for a Girl, 1980; How to Play Tennis with What You Already Have, 1997; My Own Trumpet, 2001. EDITOR: (with M. Leach) The Critics and the Ballad, 1961; Indian Tales of North America, 1961; (with H. Cohen) Folklore in America, 1966; Our Living Traditions, 1968; (with H. Cohen) Folklore from the Working Folk of America, 1972; (with H. Cohen) The Parade of Heroes, 1978; (with H. Cohen) Folklore of the American Holidays, 1985, rev. ed., 1999; (with H. Cohen) America Celebrates, 1991; Born Again, 2003. **Address:** Box 509, Wakefield, RI 02880-0509, U.S.A. **Online address:** tpcoffin@aol.com

COFFMAN, Edward M. American, b. 1929. **Genres:** History. **Career:** Memphis State University, TN, instructor, to assistant professor, 1957-60; G.C. Marshall Research Foundation, Arlington, VA, research associate, 1960-61 (Guggenheim Fellow, 1973-74); University of Wisconsin, Madison, assistant professor, 1961-66, associate professor, 1966-68, professor, 1968-92, professor emeritus, 1992-; Kansas State University, Visiting Professor, 1969-70; U.S. Military Acad., Visiting Professor, 1977-78; U.S. Air Force Acad., Visiting Professor, 1982-83; U.S. Army Military History Institute, Visiting Professor, 1986-87; U.S. Army Command and General Staff College, Visiting Professor, 1990-91. Dept. of the Army Historical Advisory Committee, member, 1972-76, 1987-93, chair, 1989-93; National Historical Publications and Records Commission, Member, 1972-76. **Publications:** The Hilt of the Sword: The Career of Peyton C. March, 1966; The War to End All Wars: The American Military Experience in World War I, 1968; The Old Army: A Portrait of the American Army in Peacetime 1784-1898, 1986; The Regulars: The United States Army 18981941. **Address:** 1089 Lakewood Dr, Lexington, KY 40502, U.S.A.

COGCAVE, Serge O. See **CEVASCO, G(eorge) A(nthony).**

COHEN, Allan R(ay). American, b. 1938. **Genres:** Business/Trade/Industry. **Career:** Harvard University, Harvard Business School, Boston, MA, Ford Foundation research associate in the Philippines, 1961-62, Ford Foundation consultant in India, 1963-65; University of New Hampshire, Durham, assistant professor to J.L. Carter Professor of Management, 1966-82; Babson College, Babson Park, MA, professor, W. Carpenter Professor of Management, 1982-91, academic vice-president and dean of faculty, 1991-98, Edward A. Madden Distinguished Professor of Global Leadership, 1998-. **Publications:** Tradition, Change, and Conflict in Indian Family Business, 1974; (with S.L. Fink, H. Gadon, and Willits) Effective Behavior in Organizations, 1976, 7th ed. (with S.L. Fink), 2000; (with H. Gadon) Alternative Work Schedules, 1978; (with D.L. Bradford) Managing for Excellence, 1984; (with D.L. Bradford) Influence without Authority, 1990, 2nd ed., 2005; (ed.) The Portable MBA in Management, 1993; (with D.L. Bradford) Power Up: Transforming Organizations through Shared Leadership, 1998. **Address:** Babson College, Babson Park, MA 02457, U.S.A.

COHEN, Allen. American, b. 1940. **Genres:** Novellas/Short stories, Poetry, Social commentary. **Career:** Poet, 1957-; preschool owner and teacher, 1989-. **Publications:** Childbirth Is Ecstasy (poetry), 1970; Reagan Poems, 1981; (ed.) The San Francisco Oracle (facsimile edition; contents originally published 1966-68), 1991; Book of Hats (poetry), 1997. **Address:** 399 Orange St, Oakland, CA 94610, U.S.A. **Online address:** sforacle@prodigy.net

COHEN, Alvin. American, b. 1931. **Genres:** Economics, Money/Finance. **Career:** Lehigh University, Bethlehem, PA, assistant professor, 1962-65, associate professor, 1965-71, professor of economics, 1971-, director of Guatemala summer program. Universidad Nacional de San Marcos, Fulbright professor, 1961-62; University Nacional de El Salvador, visiting professor, 1962; Universidad Catolica de Cordoba, Fulbright professor, 1971; Universidad Francisco Marroquin, visiting professor, 1980. U.S. Department of State, assigned to Bolivia, 1968, 1969, and 1970. **Publications:** Economic Change in Chile, 1929-1959, 1960; Ensayos sobre la teoria del desarrollo economico, 1965; Desarrollo economico, 1971; (ed. with F.R. Gunter) The Colombian Economy: Issues of Trade and Development, 1992. Contributor to books. Contributor of articles and reviews to economic and Latin American studies journals. **Address:** 37 Rauch Business Center, Lehigh University, 621 Taylor St., Bethlehem, PA 18015, U.S.A.

COHEN, Andrew (Z.). Canadian, b. 1955. **Genres:** Documentaries/Reportage. **Career:** Ottawa Citizen, Ottawa, Ontario, staff writer, 1977-80;

United Press International, parliamentary correspondent in Ottawa, 1980-84, editor, foreign desk, Washington, DC, 1983; Financial Post, Toronto, Ontario, political writer, 1984-87, foreign editor, 1987-90, foreign affairs columnist, 1989-93, senior editor and columnist 1990-91, national affairs columnist, 1993-94. Cambridge University, visiting fellow, 1991-93. National Correspondent, Saturday Night Magazine, 1993-94, The Editorial Board, The Globe and Mail, 1994-; radio & television commentator on national and foreign affairs. **Publications:** (Ed.) Patrick Gossage, Close to the Charisma, 1986; A Deal Undone: The Making and Breaking of the Meech Lake Accord, 1990; essays, book reviews, monographs. **Address:** Beverly Slopen, 131 Bloor St W, Toronto, ON, Canada M5S 1S3.

COHEN, Anthea. (Doris Simpson). British, b. 1913. **Genres:** Novels, Mystery/Crime/Suspense, Medicine/Health. **Career:** State Registered Nurse, worked in hosps. in Leics., Chelsea, and Ryde, Isle of Wight, until 1970. **Publications:** CRIME FICTION: Angel without Mercy, 1982; Angel of Vengeance, 1983; Angel of Death, 1983; Fallen Angel, 1984; Guardian Angel, 1985; Hell's Angel, 1986; Ministering Angel, 1987; Destroying Angel, 1988; Angel Dust, 1989; Recording Angel, 1991; Angel in Action, 1992; Angel in Love, 1993; Angel in Autumn, 1995; Poison Pen, 1996; Dedicated Angel, 1997; Angel of Retribution, 1998; Dream On, 1999; Angel and the French Widow, 2000; Angel and the Deadly Secret, 2003; Better Dead, 2004. OTHER: Be Patient: Your Life in Their Hands, 1967; Popular Hospital Misconceptions, 1969; The Green Girl (novel), 1982; Dangerous Love (novel), 1984; Substance and Shadows, 1986. **Address:** c/o Vanessa Holt Assoc., 59 Crescent Rd, Leigh-on-Sea, Essex, Essex, England.

COHEN, Avner. Israeli, b. 1951. **Genres:** Military/Defense/Arms control. **Career:** Writer, philosopher, and historian. Tel Aviv University, Tel Aviv, Israel, philosophy instructor, 1983-1991; Center for International and Security Studies at Maryland, College Park, MD, senior research fellow; National Security Archive, Washington, DC, senior research fellow. **Publications:** Doubt, Anxiety, and Salvation: A Study of Meta-philosophical and Psychological Themes in the History of Skepticism (Ph.D. thesis), 1981; (ed. with S. Lee) Nuclear Weapons and the Future of Humanity: The Fundamental Questions, 1986; (ed. with M. Dascal) The Institution of Philosophy: A Discipline in Crisis?, 1989; (with M. Miller) Nuclear Shadows in the Middle East: Prospects for Arms Control in the Wake of the Gulf Crisis, 1990; Israel and the Bomb, 1998. Contributor to academic journals. **Address:** The National Security Archive, Gelman Library Suite 701, 2130 H St. N.W., Washington, DC 20037, U.S.A. **Online address:** acohen@gwis2.circ.gwu.edu

COHEN, Bernard. American, b. 1963. **Genres:** Novels. **Career:** Writer of fiction and non-fiction. **Publications:** Tourism, 1992; The Blindman's Hat, 1997; Snowdome, 1998. **Address:** 47 Clissold St., Katoomba, NSW 2780, Australia. **Online address:** bernard_cohen@hotmail.com

COHEN, Brenda. See ALMOND, Brenda.

COHEN, Cary. American. **Genres:** Administration/Management. **Career:** Caldwell Consulting Associates, president. **Publications:** Effective Contract Administration; The Complete Company Manual of Policies and Procedures; Federal Contract Management; The Executive Secretary's Handbook; Tha Handbook of Effective Contract Administration; The Manual of Financial Policies and Procedures; The Manual of Purchasing Policies and Procedures; The Manual of Personnel Policies and Procedures; The Manual of Sales Policies and Procedures. **Address:** Caldwell Consulting Associates, PO Box 29143, Richmond, VA 23242-0143, U.S.A.

COHEN, Daniel A. American, b. 1957. **Genres:** History, Literary criticism and history. **Career:** College of William and Mary, Williamsburg, VA, visiting assistant professor of history and fellow at Commonwealth Center for the Study of American Culture, 1988-90; Florida International University, Miami, assistant professor of history, 1990-94, associate professor, 1994-. **Publications:** Pillars of Salt, Monuments of Grace: New England Crime Literature and the Origins of American Popular Culture, 1674-1860, 1993; (ed.) The Female Marine and Related Works: Narratives of Cross-Dressing and Urban Vice in America's Early Republic, 1997. Contributor to history and American Studies journals. **Address:** Department of History, Florida International University, Miami, FL 33199, U.S.A.

COHEN, Elliot D. American, b. 1951. **Genres:** Philosophy. **Career:** Providence College, RI, lecturer in philosophy of law, 1974-77; University of Florida, Gainesville, instructor in behavioral studies, 1978-79; Florida Atlantic University, Boca Raton, assistant professor of philosophy, 1979-80; Indian River Community College, Fort Pierce, FL, assistant professor, 1980-

82, associate professor, 1983-88, professor of philosophy, 1989-; Barry University, professor, 1986-92. Alpha Health Services, marriage and family counselor, 1986-; Institute of Critical Thinking, director, 1990-. Leader of medical ethics workshops. **Publications:** Making Value Judgments: Principles of Sound Reasoning, 1985; Improving Your Thinking and Decision Making Skills: A Handbook of Fallacies, 1990; Caution: Faulty Thinking Can Be Harmful to Your Happiness, 1991; (with G. Cohen) The Virtuous Therapist, 1999; What Would Aristotle Do? Self-Control through the Power of Reason, 2003. EDITOR: Philosophers at Work: An Introduction to the Issues and Practical Uses of Philosophy, 1989, 2nd ed., 2000; Philosophical Issues in Journalism, 1992; (with M. Davis, and contrib.) AIDS: Crisis in Professional Ethics, 1993. Work represented in anthologies. Contributor to philosophy and psychology journals. **Address:** Dept of Social Science, Indian River Community College, 3209 Virginia Ave, Fort Pierce, FL 34981, U.S.A.

COHEN, Henry. American, b. 1933. **Genres:** Criminology/True Crime, Demography, Economics, Film, History, Psychology. **Career:** Loyola University, Chicago, assistant professor, 1969-71, associate professor, 1971-80, professor, 1980-93. **Publications:** Business and Politics in America from the Age of Jackson to the Civil War, 1971; Brutal Justice: Ordeal of an American City, 1980. EDITOR: Criminal Justice History: An International Annual, 1980-83; The Public Enemy, 1981. **Address:** 491 Utah St, San Francisco, CA 94110-1434, U.S.A.

COHEN, Hubert I. American, b. 1930. **Genres:** Film, Biography. **Career:** University of Michigan, Ann Arbor, College of Engineering, instructor in English, 1965-70, Department of Humanities, assistant professor, 1970-75, associate professor, 1975-85, professor, 1995-, film and video program director, 1978-80, Residential College and Film and Video Program, 1985-. **Publications:** Ingmar Bergman: The Art of Confession, 1993. Contributor of articles to periodicals. **Address:** Residential College, University of Michigan, Ann Arbor, MI 48109, U.S.A. **Online address:** hicohen@umich.edu

COHEN, Jason. American, b. 1967. **Genres:** Humor/Satire. **Career:** WNUR Radio, Evanston, IL, music director, 1987-89; Fire Records, London, England, United States co-manager, 1989-90; self-employed journalist, 1990-. **Publications:** (with M. Krugman) Generation Ecch!: The Backlash Starts Here, 1994. Contributor to publications. **Address:** 815-A Brazos, Apt. 223, Austin, TX 78701, U.S.A.

COHEN, Jeffrey A. American, b. 1952. **Genres:** Architecture, Art/Art history. **Career:** Drexel University, Philadelphia, PA, lecturer in architecture, 1977-80; Philadelphia Historic Sites Survey, researcher, surveyor, and photographer, 1977-80; University Museum Expedition, Cyrene, Libya, architectural draftsman and surveyor, summers 1978, 1979; Muhlenberg College, instructor, 1979; Papers of Benjamin Henry Latrobe, American Philosophical Society, Philadelphia, assistant editor for Architectural History, 1981-86, associate editor, 1986-94; Bryn Mawr College, lecturer, 1995-, director, Digital Media and Visual Resources Center; Goucher College, Baltimore, adjunct instructor, 1996. **Publications:** (asst. ed.) The Correspondence and Miscellaneous Papers of Benjamin Henry Latrobe: Vol. 1, 1784-1804, 1984; (assoc. ed.) The Correspondence and Miscellaneous Papers of Benjamin Henry Latrobe: Vol. 2, 1805-10, 1986, Vol. 3, 1811-20, 1988; (with J.F. O'Gorman, G.E. Thomas, and G. Holmes Perkins) Drawing toward Building: Philadelphia Architectural Graphics, 1732-1986, 1986; (with G.E. Thomas and M.J. Lewis) Frank Furness: The Complete Works, 1991, rev. ed., 1996; (with C.E. Brownell) The Architectural Drawings of Benjamin Henry Latrobe, 2 vols, 1995. Work represented in anthologies. Contributor of reviews and reports to professional journals. Developer of digital projects for the world wide web. **Address:** Growth and Structure of Cities Program, Bryn Mawr College, 101 N. Merion Ave., Bryn Mawr, PA 19010-2899, U.S.A.

COHEN, Jeremy. American/Israeli, b. 1953. **Genres:** Cultural/Ethnic topics, Theology/Religion, History. **Career:** Cornell University, Ithaca, NY, instructor, 1977-78, assistant professor of Jewish history and coordinator of program of Jewish studies, 1978-81; Ohio State University, Columbus, Melton Associate Professor, 1982-89, Melton Professor of Jewish History, 1989-97; Methodist Theological School in Ohio, Delaware, OH, adjunct associate professor, 1983-88, adjunct professor of church history, 1988-91; Tel Aviv University, Israel, professor in Jewish history, 1989-. Goldstein-Goren Diaspora Research Center, director, 2002-. **Publications:** The Friars and the Jews: The Evolution of Medieval Anti-Judaism, 1982; "Be Fertile and Increase, Fill the Earth and Master It": The Ancient and Medieval Career of a Biblical Text, 1989; Essential Papers on Judaism and Christianity in Conflict, 1991; From Witness to Witchcraft: Jews and Judaism in Medieval Christian Thought, 1997; Living Letters of the Law: Ideas of the Jews in

Medieval Christianity, 1999; Sanctifying the Name of God: Jewish Martyrs and Jewish Memories of the First Crusade, 2004. **Address:** Department of Jewish History, Tel Aviv University, 69978 Tel Aviv, Israel. **Online address:** jecohen@post.tau.ac.il

COHEN, Judith Love. American, b. 1933. **Genres:** Children's non-fiction, Self help, Young adult non-fiction. **Career:** TRW-Aerospace, Redondo Beach, CA, project manager, 1959-90; Command Systems Group-Aerospace, Torrance, CA, project manager, 1990-92; freelance consulting engineer, 1993-; writer. **Publications:** A Passover to Remember (play), 1985; You Can Be a Woman Engineer, 1991; (with M. Siegel) You Can Be a Woman Architect, 1992; (with F. McAlary) You Can Be a Woman Marine Biologist, 1992; (with B. Bryan) You Can Be a Woman Egyptologist, 1993; (with D. Gabriel) You Can Be a Woman Paleontologist, 1993; (with V. Thompson) You Can Be a Woman Zoologist, 1993; (with S. Franks) You Can Be a Woman Oceanographer, 1994; (with A. Ghez) You Can Be a Woman Astronomer, 1995; (with R. Redberg) You Can Be a Woman Cardiologist, 1996; (with K. Bozak) You Can Be a Woman Botanist, 1999; (with T. Dixon) You Can Be a Woman Basketball Player, 1999; (with S. Douty) You Can Be a Woman Softball Player, 2000; (with T. Venturini) You Can Be a Woman Soccer Player, 2000; (with D. Katz) Lessons in Love, 2001; (with K. Perez) You Can Be a Woman Meteorologist, 2002; (with D. Underwood) You Can Be a Woman Entomologist, 2002; (with M. Gosling, P. Weinstein, and M. McLaglan) You Can Be a Woman Movie Maker, 2003. **Address:** c/o Cascade Pass, 4223 Glencoe Ave Ste C-105, Marina Del Rey, CA 90292-8801, U.S.A. **Online address:** jlc@cascadepass.com

COHEN, Karl F. American, b. 1940. **Genres:** Film. **Career:** San Francisco State University, San Francisco, CA, assistant professor of cinema studies. Lecturer at film festivals throughout the world. **Publications:** Forbidden Animation: Censored Cartoons and Blacklisted Animators, 1997. **Address:** 478 Frederick, San Francisco, CA 94117, U.S.A. **Online address:** karlcohen@earthlink.net

COHEN, Laurence Jonathan. British, b. 1923. **Genres:** Philosophy. **Career:** Fellow Emeritus, Queen's College, Oxford, since 1990 (Fellow and Praelector, 1957-90). Fellow, British Academy, since 1973. Assistant in Logic and Metaphysics, Edinburgh, 1947-50; Lecturer in Philosophy, University of St. Andrews at Dundee, 1950-57; Visiting Professor, Columbia University, 1967-68; Yale University, 1972-73; President, British Society of Philosophy of Science, 1977-79; Co-President, International Union for History and Philosophy of Science, 1987-91; Visiting Professor, Northwestern University Law School, 1988; Secretary General, International Council of Scientific Unions, 1993-96; Chairman, Philosophy Section, British Academy, 1993-96. **Publications:** The Principles of World Citizenship, 1954; The Diversity of Meaning, 1962, 1966; The Implications of Induction, 1970; The Probable and the Provable, 1977; (co-ed.) Applications of Inductive Logic, 1980; (co-ed.) Logic, Methodology, and Philosophy of Science, 1981; The Dialogue of Reason, 1986; An Introduction to the Philosophy of Induction and Probability, 1989; An Essay on Belief and Acceptance, 1992. **Address:** Sturt House, East End, North Leigh, Oxon. OX8 6QA, England.

COHEN, Leah Hager. American. **Genres:** Adult non-fiction, Novels. **Career:** Educator and author. Emerson College, professor, c. 1990s. **Publications:** Train Go Sorry: Inside a Deaf World (nonfiction), 1994; Glass, Paper, Beans: Revelations on the Nature and Value of Ordinary Things (nonfiction), 1997; Heat Lightning (novel), 1997. **Address:** c/o Avon Books, 1350 Avenue of the Americas, New York, NY 10019, U.S.A.

COHEN, Lenard J. Canadian. **Genres:** International relations/Current affairs, Area studies. **Career:** Simon Fraser University, Burnaby, British Columbia, professor. **Publications:** (with P. Warwick) Political Cohesion in a Fragile Mosaic: The Yugoslav Experience, 1983; (with P. Warwick and P. Smith) The Vision and the Game: Making the Canadian Constitution, 1987; The Socialist Pyramid: Elites and Power in Yugoslavia, 1989; Regime Transition in a Disintegrating Yugoslavia: The Law-of-Rule vs. The Rule-of-Law, 1992; Broken Bonds: The Disintegration of Yugoslavia, 1993; Serpent in the Bosom: The Rise and Fall of Slobodan Milosevic, 2001. EDITOR: (with J.P. Shapiro) Communist Systems in Comparative Perspective, 1974; (with A. Moens and A.G. Sens) Alliance Politics in the Euro-Atlantic Community: NATO from the Cold War's End to the Age of Terrorism, 2002. **Address:** Simon Fraser University, 8888 University Dr., Burnaby, BC, Canada V5A 1S6. **Online address:** cohen@sfu.ca

COHEN, Leonard. Canadian, b. 1934. **Genres:** Novels, Plays/Screenplays, Poetry, Songs/Lyrics and libretti. **Career:** Professional composer and singer. **Publications:** Let Us Compare Mythologies, 1956; The Spice-Box of Earth, 1961; The Favorite Game (novel), 1963; Flowers for Hitler, 1964; Parasites of Heaven, 1966; Beautiful Losers (novel), 1966; Selected Poems, 1956-68, 1968; Leonard Cohen's Song Book, 1969; The Energy of Slaves, 1972; The Next Step (play), 1972; Death of a Lady's Man, 1979; Two Views (poetry), 1980; Book of Mercy (poetry), 1984; Leonard Cohen Anthology (songs), 1991; Stranger Music: Selected Poems & Songs, 1993; Dance Me to the End of Love, 1995; You Do Not Have to Love Me, 1996; God Is Alive, Magic Is Afoot, 2000. **Address:** c/o Stranger Mgmt., 419 N Larchmont Blvd Ste 91, Los Angeles, CA 90004-3000, U.S.A.

COHEN, Lizabeth (Ann). (born United States), b. 1952. **Genres:** History. **Career:** Fine Arts Museum, San Francisco, CA, assistant curator, 1975-77; Camron-Stanford House Museum, Oakland, CA, director, 1976-78; museum and history consultant; Carnegie-Mellon University, history department faculty, beginning 1986; New York University, New York, NY, member of faculty, 1992-97; Harvard University, Cambridge, MA, currently Howard Mumford Jones Professor of American Studies, Department of History. **Publications:** Making a New Deal: Industrial Workers in Chicago, 1919-1939, 1990; (with Thomas A. Bailey and David M. Kennedy) The American Pageant: A History of the Republic, 2002; A Consumer's Republic: The Politics of Mass Consumption in Postwar America, 2003. Contributor to professional journals. **Address:** Harvard University, History Department, 201 Robinson Hall, Cambridge, MA 02138, U.S.A. **Online address:** cohen3@fas.harvard.edu

COHEN, Lynne. (born United States), b. 1944. **Genres:** Art/Art history. **Career:** Photographer, with work exhibited at group shows throughout North America and Europe, including Museum of Modern Art, Victoria and Albert Museum and Serpentine Gallery, London, England, Corcoran Gallery of Art, San Francisco Museum of Modern Art, National Museum of Women in the Arts, and New York Public Library. University of Ottawa, Ottawa, Ontario, Canada, faculty member; also taught at Eastern Michigan University, Art Institute of Chicago, and Ecole des Beaux-Arts de Bordeaux; visiting artist at such institutions as Light Work, Syracuse University, Ecole Nationale de la Photographie, Arles, France, Wexner Center for the Arts, Museum voor Fotografie, Antwerp, Belgium, and University of Valencia. **Publications:** Occupied Territory, 1988; L'endroit du décor/Lost and Found, 1992; No Man's Land, 2001. Work also represented in exhibition catalogs and other publications. Contributor of photographs to periodicals. **Address:** Author Mail, Thames & Hudson Inc., 500 Fifth Ave., New York, NY 10110, U.S.A. **Online address:** lcohen@uottawa.ca

COHEN, Marcel. French, b. 1937. **Genres:** Novels. **Career:** Worked as a military correspondent, 1960-61; journalist, 1961-. **Publications:** Du desert au livre: Entretiens avec Edmond Jabes, 1981, trans. as From the Desert to the Book, 1990; Miroirs, 1981, trans. as Mirrors, 1997; Le grand paon-de-nuit, 1990, trans. as The Peacock Emperor Moth, 1995. UNTRANSLATED WORKS: Galpa (novel), 1969; Malestroit: Chroniques du silence, 1973; Voyage a Waizata, 1976; Murs, 1979; Je ne sais pas le nom, 1986; Assassinat d'un Garde, 1998; Faits, 2002. **Address:** 197 rue de Grenelle, 75007 Paris, France.

COHEN, Morton N(orton). Also writes as John Moreton. American (born Canada), b. 1921. **Genres:** Children's fiction, Literary criticism and history, Travel/Exploration, Biography. **Career:** Professor Emeritus of English, City College and Graduate School, City University of New York, 1981- (Associate Professor, 1952-71; Professor, 1971-81). Visiting Professor, Syracuse University, New York, 1965-66, 1967-68. Royal Society of Literature, Fellow, 1996-. **Publications:** Rider Haggard: His Life and Works, 1960, 1968; (as John Moreton) Punky: Mouse for a Day, 1962; Rudyard Kipling to Rider Haggard: The Record of a Friendship, 1965; (reteller as John Moreton) The Love for Three Oranges, by Sergei Prokofiev, 1966; Lewis Carroll, Photographer of Children: Four Nude Studies, 1979; Lewis Carroll and the Kitchins, 1980; Lewis Carroll and Alice 1832-1982, 1982, 1990; Lewis Carroll: A Biography, 1995; Reflections in a Looking Glass: A Centennial Celebration of Lewis Carroll, 1998. EDITOR: The Letters of Lewis Carroll, 1979; The Russian Journal-II: A Record Kept by Henry Parry Liddon of a Tour Taken with C.L. Dodgson in the Summer of 1867, 1979; Selected Letters of Lewis Carroll, 1982, 1996; (co-) Lewis Carroll and the House of Macmillan, 1987; Lewis Carroll: Interviews and Recollection, 1989; (with E. Wakeling) Lewis Carroll & His Illustrators, 2003. **Address:** 55 E 9th St Apt 10-D, New York, NY 10003, U.S.A.

COHEN, Norman J. American, b. 1943. **Genres:** Information science/Computers. **Career:** Hebrew Union-Jewish Institute of Religion, professor of Medrash, 1975-, Provost, 1996-; Rabbinic School in New York, director, 1986-; New York School, dean, 1987-95;. **Publications:** Self, Struggle, and

Change: Family Conflict Stories in Genesis and Their Healing Insights for Our Lives, 1995; Voices from Genesis: Guiding Us through the Stages of Life, 1998; The Way into Torah, 2000. EDITOR: The Fundamentalism Phenomenon: A View from Within, A Response from Without, 1990; (with R.M. Seltzer) The Americanization of the Jews, 1995. **Address:** Hebrew Union College, 1 West 4th St., New York, NY 10012, U.S.A. **Online address:** ncohen@huc.edu

COHEN, Paul (M.). American, b. 1955. **Genres:** Politics/Government. **Career:** Lawrence University, Appleton, WI, assistant professor, 1985-90, associate professor, 1990-99, department chair, 1998-, professor of history, 1999-, Patricia Hamar Boldt Professor of Liberal Studies, 2003-. Newberry Library Program in the Humanities, director, 1992. **Publications:** Piety and Politics: Catholic Revival and the Generation of 1905-1914 in France, 1987; Freedom's Moment: An Essay on the French Idea of Liberty from Rousseau to Foucault, 1997. Author of articles. **Address:** Box 599, Lawrence University, Appleton, WI 54912, U.S.A. **Online address:** paul.m.cohen@lawrence.edu

COHEN, Peter Zachary. American, b. 1931. **Genres:** Children's fiction, Plays/Screenplays. **Career:** Kansas State University, Manhattan, instructor, then assistant professor, 1961-85, associate professor of English, 1985-92. County Planning Commission, secretary, 1969-. **Publications:** The Muskie Hook, 1969; The Bull in the Forest, 1969; Morena, 1970; Foal Creek, 1972; Authorized Autumn Charts of the Upper Red Canoe River Country, 1972; Bee, 1975; The Cannon in the Park (play), 1975; Deadly Game at Stony Creek, 1978; Calm Horse, Wild Night, 1982; The Great Red River Raft, 1984; Brave Men in Wooden Boats, 1989. **Address:** 38382 Sycamore Creek Rd, Alta Vista, KS 66834, U.S.A.

COHEN, Ralph. American, b. 1917. **Genres:** Literary criticism and history. **Career:** University of Virginia, Charlottesville, Kenan Professor of English, 1978-, director of Commonwealth Center for Literary and Cultural Change, 1988-95. William Andrew Clark Memorial Library, research professor, 1980-81. **Publications:** The Art of Discrimination, 1964; The Unfolding of the Seasons, 1970. EDITOR: Studies in Eighteenth-Century British Art and Aesthetics, 1985; The Future of Literary Theory, 1989; Studies in Historical Change, 1992. **Address:** Department of English, 219 Bryan, University of Virginia, Charlottesville, VA 22903, U.S.A.

COHEN, Rich. American, b. 1968. **Genres:** Documentaries/Reportage. **Career:** Rolling Stone magazine, contributing editor. **Publications:** Tough Jews, 1998. **Address:** c/o Rolling Stone Magazine, 1290 Avenue of the Americas, New York, NY 10001, U.S.A.

COHEN, Richard. American, b. 1952. **Genres:** Novels, Novellas/Short stories, Education, Writing/Journalism. **Career:** Manuscript reader for a literary agency, 1973-76 and 1977-79; homemaker, 1979-87; University of Wisconsin-Madison, lecturer in creative writing, 1988; free-lance writer, 1987-. **Publications:** NOVELS: Domestic Tranquility, 1981; Don't Mention the Moon, 1983; Say You Want Me, 1988. STORIES: Pronoun Music, 2001. NON-FICTION: Writer's Mind: Crafting Fiction, 1994. Contributor of short stories to periodicals. **Address:** c/o Trident Media Group., 41 Madison Ave Fl 36, New York, NY 10010, U.S.A.

COHEN, Richard M(artin). American, b. 1941. **Genres:** Documentaries/Reportage. **Career:** United Press International, reporter, 1967-68; Washington Post, Washington, DC, general assignment reporter, 1968-76, syndicated columnist, 1976-; author. **Publications:** (with J. Witcover) A Heartbeat Away: The Investigation and Resignation of Vice President Spiro T. Agnew, 1974. **Address:** Washington Post, 1150 15th St. NW, Washington, DC 20071, U.S.A.

COHEN, Robert. American, b. 1957. **Genres:** Novels. **Career:** Writer; journalist. State University of New York at Stony Brook, adjunct professor of English, 1984-88; visiting assistant professor of creative writing at Rice University, Spring 1989, at University of Houston, 1989-90; Iowa Writers Workshop, Fall 1991. Harvard University - Briggs Copeland Professor in Fiction, Fall 1993- (5 years). **Publications:** NOVELS: The Organ Builder, 1988; The Here and Now, 1996; Inspired Sleep, 2001. STORIES: Varieties of Romantic Experience, 2002. **Address:** 270 Foote St., Middlebury, VT 05753, U.S.A.

COHEN, Robin. British (born Republic of South Africa), b. 1944. **Genres:** Politics/Government, Race relations, Sociology. **Career:** University of Ibadan, Nigeria, lecturer in politics, 1967-69; University of Birmingham, England, research fellow, 1969-71, lecturer, 1971-75, senior lecturer in sociology, 1975-77; University of the West Indies, St. Augustine, Trinidad, professor of sociology, 1977-79; University of Warwick, Coventry, England, professor of sociology, 1979-, executive director of Centre for Research in Ethnic Relations, 1984-89; University of Cape Town, South Africa, dean of humanities, 2001-03. Consultant to Council of Europe, UK Government Home Office and UNHCR. **Publications:** Labour and Politics in Nigeria, 1974, rev. ed., 1982; Endgame in South Africa, 1986; The New Helots, 1987; Contested Domains, 1991; Frontiers of Identity, 1994; Global Diasporas, 1997; (with P. Kennedy) Global Sociology, 2000. EDITOR: (with R. Sandbrook) The Development of an African Working Class, 1975; (with P. Gutkind) African Labor History, 1978; (with Gutkind) Peasants and Proletarians, 1979; Forced Labour in Colonial Africa, 1979; African Islands and Enclaves, 1983; (with F. Ambursley) Crisis in the Caribbean, 1983, rev. ed., 1984; (with R. Boyd) International Labour and the Third World, 1987; (with W. Cobbett) Popular Struggles in South Africa, 1988; (with H. Goulbourne) Democracy and Socialism in Africa, 1991; The Cambridge Survey of World Migration, 1995; Theories of Migration, 1996; (with S. Rai) Global Social Movements, 2000; (with P. Kennedy) Global Sociology, 2001; (with S. Vertovec) Conceiving Cosmopolitanism, 2003. **Address:** Dept of Sociology, University of Warwick, Coventry CV4 7AL, England.

COHEN, Selma Jeanne. American, b. 1920. **Genres:** Dance/Ballet. **Career:** Ed., International Encyclopedia of Dance; Dance Ed., World Encyclopaedia of Contemporary Theatre. Visiting professor of dance history, University of California, since 1983. Teacher of Dance History and Aesthetics, School of Performing Arts, NYC, 1953-55, Connecticut College School of Dance, New London, 1963-72, and New York University, NYC, 1968-70 and 1974-75; Teacher, University of Chicago, 1974-76. Managing Ed., 1959-65, and Ed., 1965-76, Dance Perspectives, NYC. **Publications:** The Modern Dance: Seven Statements of Belief, 1966; Doris Humphrey: An Artist First, 1972; Dance as a Theatre Art: Source Readings in Dance History, 1974; Next Week, Swan Lake: Reflections on Dance and Dances, 1982. **Address:** 29 E. 9th St, New York, NY 10003, U.S.A.

COHEN, Sholom. American, b. 1951. **Genres:** Children's fiction, Humor/Satire. **Career:** University of Western Ontario, London, Canada, music librarian, 1974-78; Columbia University, NYC, systems librarian, 1979-81; McDonnell Douglas Corp., St. Louis, MO, software engineer, 1982-88; Carnegie-Mellon University, Pittsburgh, PA, software consultant, 1988-; University of Pittsburgh, instructor, 2000-02. **Publications:** YITZ BERG FROM PITTSBURGH SERIES: Yitzy and the G.O.L.E.M., 1992; The Lopsided Yarmulke, 1995. **Address:** Software Engineering Institute, Carnegie-Mellon University, Pittsburgh, PA 15213, U.S.A. **Online address:** sgc@sei.cmu.edu

COHEN, Stanley I. American, b. 1928. **Genres:** Novels, Novellas/Short stories, Mystery/Crime/Suspense. **Publications:** NOVELS: Taking Gary Feldman (in U.K. as The Abduction), 1970; Tell Us Jerry Silver, 1973; The Diane Game, 1973; 330 Park, 1977; Angel Face, 1982. SHORT STORY COLLECTION: A Night in the Manchester Store, 2002. **Address:** 322 Pine Tree Dr, Orange, CT 06477, U.S.A.

COHEN, Stephen F(rand). American, b. 1938. **Genres:** History, Politics/Government. **Career:** Research Institute of Communist Affairs, Instructor and Jr. Fellow, 1965-68; Princeton University, New Jersey, Assistant Professor, 1968-73, Associate Professor, 1973-80, Director of Russian Studies, 1973-94, Professor of Politics, 1980-98; Columbia University, NYC, Russian Institute, Sr. Fellow, 1970-71, 1972-73, 1976-77, Visiting Professor of History, 1973-75; New York University, Professor of Russian Studies and History, 1998-; Post Soviet Affairs, Member of Editorial Board. **Publications:** Bukharin and the Bolshevik Revolution: A Political Biography 1888-1938, 1973; (with A. Rabinowitch and R. Sharlet) The Soviet Union since Stalin, 1980; Rethinking the Soviet Experience: Politics and History since 1917, 1985; Sovieticus: American Perceptions and Soviet Realities, 1985; (with K. vanden Heuvel) Voices of Glasnost: Interviews with Gorbachev's Reformers, 1989; Failed Crusade: America and the Tragedy of Post-Communist Russia, 2000, rev. ed., 2001. EDITOR: (with R.C. Tucker) The Great Purge Trial, 1965; An End to Silence: Uncensored Opinion in the Soviet Union, 1982. **Address:** Dept of Russian Studies, New York University, 19 University Pl, New York, NY 10003-4556, U.S.A.

COHEN, Stuart. American, b. 1958. **Genres:** Novels. **Career:** Novelist. Paititi Woolens Co., Juneau, AK, owner, 1984-96. Also worked as a cab driver. Invisible World, 2001-. **Publications:** Invisible World (novel), 1998. Naughty Logs; The Stone Angels, 2003. **Address:** 725 5th Street, Juneau, AK 99801, U.S.A. **Online address:** invworld@alaska.net

COHEN, Youssef. Italian (born Egypt), b. 1947. **Genres:** Politics/Government, Area studies. **Career:** University of Michigan, Ann Arbor, instructor at Inter-University Consortium for Political and Social Research, 1977-81, lecturer in political science, 1979-82; University of Pennsylvania, Philadelphia, assistant professor of political science, 1982-88; New York University, NYC, associate professor of politics, 1988-, director of graduate studies in politics, 1989-90, 1994-. **Publications:** (with A.F.K. Organski, J. Kugler, T. Johnson) Births, Deaths and Taxes: The Demographic and Political Transitions, 1984; The Manipulation of Consent: The State and Working-Class Consciousness in Brazil, 1989; Radicals, Reformers and Reactionaries: The Prisoners' Dilemma and the Collapse of Democracy in Latin America, 1994. Contributor to political science journals. **Address:** Department of Politics, New York University, 726 Broadway Ste 766, New York, NY 10003, U.S.A.

COHN, David. American, b. 1954. **Genres:** Architecture. **Career:** Journalist. Expansion (Spanish newspaper), architecture critic; international freelance correspondent. **Publications:** Manuel Gallego, 1998; Young Spanish Architects, 2000. Contributor to periodicals. **Address:** Tres Peles, 14 Estudio, E-28012 Madrid, Spain.

COHN, Henry S. American, b. 1945. **Genres:** History, Law, Biography. **Career:** Admitted to the Connecticut Bar and the bars of the District Court of Connecticut and the Second Circuit Court of Appeals, all 1970, and the U.S. Supreme Court, 1975; District of Connecticut, law clerk for U.S. District Judge T. Emmet Clarie, 1970-71; University of Connecticut School of Law, lecturer and adjunct professor, 1970-; assistant U.S. attorney in Hartford, CT, 1971-75; Office of the Secretary of the State, Hartford, elections attorney, 1975-78, deputy secretary of state, 1978-79, secretary of state, 1978-79; Fleischmann, Sherbacow, McWeeny and Cohn, Hartford, partner, 1979-82; Siegel, O'Connor and Kainen, Hartford, associate, 1982-83; Connecticut Attorney General's Office, Hartford, assistant attorney general, 1983-. **Publications:** (with David Bollier) The Great Hartford Circus Fire: Creative Resolution of Mass Disasters, 1991; Remembrances of Judge Clarie by His Clerks, 1993. Contributor to periodicals. **Address:** University of Connecticut, School of Law, 55 Elizabeth Street, Hartford, CT 06105, U.S.A. **Online address:** cpilj@law.uconn.edu

COHN, Norman. British, b. 1915. **Genres:** History, Mythology/Folklore, Theology/Religion. **Career:** Professor of French, University of Durham, 1960-63; Professor, University of Sussex, Brighton, 1966-80. **Publications:** (trans.) Gold Khan and Other Siberian Legends, 1946; The Pursuit of the Millennium, 1957, 4th ed., 2001; Warrant for Genocide, 1967, 3rd ed., 1981; Europe's Inner Demons, 1975; Cosmos, Chaos and the World to Come, 1993, 2nd ed., 2001; Noah's Flood, 1996. **Address:** Orchard Cottage, Wood End, Ardeley, Herts. SG2 7AZ, England.

COHN-SHERBOK, Dan. American, b. 1945. **Genres:** Theology/Religion. **Career:** Ordained rabbi; University of Kent at Canterbury, England, lecturer in theology, 1975-, chairman of Board of Theology and Religious Studies, 1980-82, director of Centre for the Study of Religion and Society, 1982-90, convener of Canterbury Theological Network, 1992-; University of Wales, Lampeter, professor of Judaism, 1997-. Visiting professor, University of Essex, 1993-94, Middlesex University, 1994. TV and radio broadcaster. **Publications:** NONFICTION: The Jewish Community of Canterbury, 1984; On Earth as It Is in Heaven, 1987; The Jewish Heritage, 1988; Jewish Petitionary Prayer, 1989; Holocaust Theology, 1989; Rabbinic Perspectives on the New Testament, 1990; Issues in Contemporary Judaism, 1991; A Dictionary of Judaica, 1992; A Dictionary of Judaism and Christianity, 1992; The Crucified Jew, 1992; Israel: The History of an Idea, 1992; Exodus: An Agenda for Jewish-Christian Dialogue, 1992; Atlas of Jewish History, 1993; Judaism and Other Faiths, 1994; The Future of Judaism, 1994; The American Jew, 1994; Jewish and Christian Mysticism, 1994; A Short History of Judaism, 1994; A Popular Dictionary of Judaism, 1994; God and the Holocaust, 1996; Modern Jewish Philosophy, 1996; (with A. Linzey) After Noah, 1996; The Hebrew Bible, 1996; 50 Key Jewish Thinkers, 1997; The Jewish Messiah, 1997; A Short Introduction to Judaism, 1997; Judaism, 1998; Jews, Christians and Religious Pluralism, 1999; Jesa, Christians and Religious Pluralism, 1999; Understanding the Holocaust, 1999; The Palestine-Israel Conflict, 2001; Messianic Judaism, 2001; Interfaith Theology, 2001; The Wisdom of the Kabbalah, 2002; AntiSemitism, 2002. EDITOR/CO-EDITOR: (and contrib.) Exploring Reality, 1987; (and contrib.) The Canterbury Papers (essays), 1990; (and contrib.) The Salman Rushdie Controversy in Interreligious Perspective, 1990; (and contrib.) Tradition and Unity: Sermons in Honour of Robert Runcie, 1990; (and contrib.) A Traditional Quest: Essays in Honour of Louis Jacobs, 1991; The Sayings of Moses, 1991; Using the Bible Today, 1991; (and contrib.) Islam in a World of Diverse Faiths, 1991; (and contrib.) The World's Religions and Human Liberation, 1992; Anti-Semitism in Our Time, 1992; Religion in Public Life, 1992; Problems in Contemporary Jew-

ish Theology, 1992; Torah and Revelation, 1992; Beyond Death, 1992; Many Mansions: Interfaith and Religious Intolerance, 1992; Glimpses of God, 1993; Divine Intervention and Miracles, 1996; Modern Judaism, 1996; Biblical Hebrew for Beginners, 1996; Medieval Jewish Philosophy, 1996; Holocaust Theology, 2002; Judaism: History Belief and Practice, 2004; The Vision of Judaism, 2004. **Address:** Dept of Theology & Religious Studies, University of Wales, Lampeter SA48 7ED, Wales.

COKAL, Susann. American, b. 1965. **Genres:** Novellas/Short stories. **Career:** California Polytechnic State University, San Luis Obispo, CA, assistant professor of creative writing and modern literature, 2001-. **Publications:** Mirabilis, 2001. Contributor of short stories to anthologies and journals. Contributor of essays about contemporary writers to journals. **Address:** California Polytechnic State University, 1 Grand Avenue, San Luis Obispo, CA 93407, U.S.A. **Online address:** scokal@calpoly.edu

COKER, Christopher. British. **Genres:** Economics, Politics/Government, Military/Defense/Arms control, Young adult non-fiction. **Career:** London School of Economics and Political Science, lecturer in international relations. **Publications:** NONFICTION: U.S. Military Power in the 1980s, 1983; The Future of the Atlantic Alliance, 1984; The Soviet Union, Eastern Europe, and the New International Economic Order, 1984; NATO, the Warsaw Pact, and Africa, 1985; A Nation in Retreat?: Britain's Defence Commitment, 1986; The United States and South Africa, 1968-1985: Constructive Engagement and Its Critics, 1986; British Defence Policy in the 1990s: A Guide to the Defence Debate, 1987; South Africa's Security Dilemmas, 1987; Reflections on American Foreign Policy since 1945, 1989; War and the Twentieth Century: A Study of War and Modern Consciousness, 1994. JUVENILE NONFICTION: Terrorism, 1986; Terrorism and Civil Strife, 1987. EDITOR: The United States, Western Europe, and Military Intervention Overseas, 1988; Drifting Apart?: The Superpowers and Their European Allies, 1989; Shifting into Neutral?: Burden Sharing in the Western Alliance in the 1990s, 1990. **Address:** London School of Economics and Politics, Houghton St., London WC2A 2AE, England.

COLALILLO-KATES, Isabella. Canadian (born Italy), b. 1948. **Genres:** Poetry. **Career:** Rainbow Light and Co., Toronto, Ontario, Canada, holistic education consultant, 1984-. Centennial College, professor of English, 1987-; University of Toronto, writing instructor, 1990-99, organizer of holistic education conferences at Ontario Institute for Studies in Education, 1997-, and member of Joint Centre for Teacher Development. Storytellers School of Toronto, member; Caduceus Institute (England), member of Triangles in Education. **Publications:** Recipes for Relaxation and Creativity, 1992; Tasting Fire (poetry and prose), 1999; Woman Falling Lightly to Earth (poetry), 2003. Contributor of short story to audio recordings. Contributor to books. Contributor of articles, short stories, and poetry to periodicals. **Address:** 431 Whitmore Ave., Toronto, ON, Canada H6E 2N6. **Online address:** isa@axxent.ca

COLBECK, Maurice. British, b. 1925. **Genres:** Children's fiction, Children's non-fiction, Travel/Exploration, Biography, Humor/Satire. **Career:** Ed., Yorkshire Life, 1956-88. **Publications:** Jungle Rivals; White God's Fury; Four Against Crime, 1959; Mosquitoes!: A Biography of Ronald Ross, 1964; Sister Kenny of the Outback, 1965; How to Be a Family Man, 1970; Yorkshire, 1976; Yorkshire Historymakers, 1977; Queer Folk, 1977; Yorkshire Laughter, 1978; Queer Goings On, 1979; Yorkshire: The Dales, 1980; Yorkshire Moorlands, 1983; (ed.) The Calendar Year, 1983; Village Yorkshire, 1987; Made in Yorkshire, What's Funny About Yorkshire?, 1992; My Yorkshire Life, 1993. **Address:** 164 Soothill Lane, Batley, W. Yorkshire WF17 6HP, England.

COLDSMITH, Don(ald C.). American, b. 1926. **Genres:** Novels, Novellas/Short stories, Romance/Historical, Westerns/Adventure, Essays. **Career:** Congregational minister, gunsmith, YMCA youth director. Bethany Hospital, Kansas City, intern, 1958-59, then physician in family practice, Emporia, Kansas; Emporia State University, adjunct associate professor of English, 1981; Western Writers of America, president, 1983-84. **Publications:** Horsin' Around, 1975; Trail of the Spanish Bit, 1980; Buffalo Medicine, 1981; Horsin' around Again, 1981; The Elk-Dog Heritage, 1982; Follow the Wind, 1983; Man of the Shadows, 1983; Daughter of the Eagle, 1984; Moon of Thunder, 1985; The Sacred Hills, 1985; Pale Star, 1986; River of Swans, 1986; Return to the River, 1987; The Medicine Knife, 1988; Flower in the Mountains, 1988; Trail from Taos, 1989; Rivers West: The Smoky Hill, 1989; Song of the Rock, 1989; The Changing Wind, 1990; Fort de Chastaigne, 1990; Quest for the White Bull, 1990; The Traveler, 1990; Return of the Spanish, 1991; Bride of the Morning Star, 1991; Walks in the Sun, 1992; World of Silence, 1992; Thunderstick, 1993; Track of the Bear,

1994; Child of the Dead, 1995; Runestone, 1995; Bearer of the Pipe, 1996; Tallgrass, 1997; South Wind, 1998; Medicine Hat, 1998; The Lost Band, 2000; The Long Journey Home, 2001; Raven Mocker, 2001; Still Horsin' Around, 2002; The Pipestone Quest, 2004.

COLE, Allan. American, b. 1943. **Genres:** Science fiction/Fantasy, Romance/Historical. **Career:** Journalist and editor in Los Angeles, CA; also worked as a chef in Los Angeles. **Publications:** SCIENCE FICTION NOVELS WITH CHRIS BUNCH: Sten, 1982; The Wolf Worlds, 1984; The Court of a Thousand Suns, 1985; Fleet of the Damned, 1988; Revenge of the Damned, 1989; The Return of the Emperor, 1990; Vortex, 1992; Empire's End, 1993. FANTASY NOVELS: The Far Kingdoms, 1993; The Warrior's Tale, 1994; (Coauthor) Kingdoms of the Night, 1995; The Warrior Returns, 1996; When the Gods Slept, Del Rey, in press. HISTORICAL NOVELS: A Daughter of Liberty, 1993; A Reckoning for Kings: A Novel of Tet. Writer for television. **Address:** c/o Russ Galen, Scovil Chichat Miller, 381 Park Ave. South No. 1020, New York, NY 10016, U.S.A.

COLE, Barry. British, b. 1936. **Genres:** Novels, Poetry, Travel/Exploration. **Career:** Worked in the Central Office of Information, London, 1965-70, 1974-94; Fellow in Literature, Univs. of Durham and Newcastle upon Tyne, 1970-72. **Publications:** POETRY: Blood Ties, 1967; Ulysses in the Town of Coloured Glass, 1968; Moonsearch, 1968; The Visitors, 1970; Vanessa in the City, 1971; Pathetic Fallacies, 1973; The Rehousing of Scaffardi, 1976; Dedications, 1977; Inside Outside: New and Selected Poems, 1997; Ghosts Are People Too, 2003. NOVELS: A Run across the Island, 1968; Joseph Winter's Patronage, 1969; The Search for Rita, 1970; The Giver, 1971; Doctor Fielder's Common Sense, 1972; The Edge of the Common, 1989. **Address:** 68 Myddelton Sq, London EC1R 1XP, England. **Online address:** barryh.cole@virgin.net

COLE, Betsy. American, b. 1940. **Genres:** Animals/Pets. **Career:** First and second grade teacher at elementary schools in Danville, VA, 1962-63, and Martinsville, VA, 1963-65; reading teacher in Martinsville, 1971-72, 1975-76; author and lecturer at schools and conferences. **Publications:** Green Creatures Ten to One, 1988; Is Aetosaur a Dinosaur?, 1992. **Address:** 1510 White Oak Ct., Martinsville, VA 24112, U.S.A.

COLE, Brock. American, b. 1938. **Genres:** Children's fiction, Young adult fiction. **Career:** University of Minnesota, instructor in English composition; University of Wisconsin, instructor in philosophy, until 1975; writer and illustrator, 1975-. **Publications:** SELF-ILLUSTRATED FOR CHILDREN: The King at the Door, 1979; No More Baths, 1980; Nothing but a Pig, 1981; The Winter Wren, 1984; The Giant's Toe, 1986; Alpha and the Dirty Baby, 1991. YOUNG ADULT NOVELS: The Goats, 1987; Celine, 1989; Buttons, 2000; Larky Mavis, 2001. OTHER: The Facts Speak for Themselves, 1997. Illustrator of books by L.R. Banks, J.P. Walsh. **Address:** 309 Highland Ave, Buffalo, NY 14222, U.S.A.

COLE, Bruce. American, b. 1938. **Genres:** Art/Art history. **Career:** Distinguished Professor of Fine Art, Indiana University, Bloomington, since 1988 (Associate Professor, 1973-77; Professor of Art History, 1977-88). Assistant Professor, University of Rochester, New York, 1969-73. **Publications:** Giotto and Florentine Painting 1280-1375, 1976; Agnolo Gaddi, 1977; Sienese Painting from Its Origins to the Fifteenth Century, 1980; Masaccio and the Art of Early Renaissance Florence, 1980; The Renaissance Artist at Work, 1983; Sienese Painting in the Age of the Renaissance, 1985; Italian Art, 1250-1550: The Relation of Art to Life and Society, 1987; (with Adelheid Gealt) Art of the Western World, 1989; Piero della Francesca: Tradition and Innovation in Renaissance Art, 1991; Giotto: The Scrovegni Chapel, 1993; Studies in the History of Italian Art, 1250-1550, 1996. **Address:** National Endowment for Humanities, 1100 Pennsylvania Ave NW, Washington, DC 20506, U.S.A.

COLE, Diane. American, b. 1952. **Genres:** Adult non-fiction, Biography. **Career:** National Jewish Monthly, Washington, DC, assistant editor, 1976-77; University of Pennsylvania Almanac, Philadelphia, PA, editor, 1978-79; free-lance writer, 1979-; Savvy magazine, New York City, contributing editor, 1983-87; Psychology Today, New York City, contributing editor, 1988-90; In Touch, book editor, 1999-. **Publications:** Hunting the Headhunters: A Woman's Guide, 1988; After Great Pain: A New Life Emerges, 1992; (coauthor) Is It You, Or Is It Me? How We Turn Our Emotions Inside Out and Blame Each Other, 1998. Work represented in anthologies. Contributor to periodicals. **Address:** 305 E 86th St., Apt. 7J-West, New York, NY 10028, U.S.A. **Online address:** djcole86@aol.com

COLE, Edmund Keith. Australian, b. 1919. **Genres:** Anthropology/ Ethnology, History, Biography, Novellas/Short stories. **Career:** Historian,

Church Missionary Society, since 1968. Principal, St. Paul's United Theological College, Limuru, Kenya, 1954-60; Archdeacon of Central Kenya, 1961-63; Vice-Principal, Ridley College, University of Melbourne, 1964-73; Principal Nungalinya College, Darwin, 1973-78; Director of Theological Education, Bendigo, Vic., 1978-84; Rector, Broome, W. A., until 1985. **Publications:** Mau Mau Mission, 1954; After Mau Mau, 1956; Kenya, Hanging in the Middle Way, 1959; Roper River Mission, 1968; Commissioned to Care, 1969; Cross Over Mount Kenya, 1970; Sincerity My Guide, 1970; Groote Eylandt Pioneer, 1971; Groote Eylandt Mission, 1971; History of CMS Australia, 1971; Oenpelli Stories, 1972; Perriman in Arnhem Land, 1973; Totems and Tamarinds, 1973; Groote Eylandt, 1975; History of Oenpelli, 1975; Oenpelli Jubilee, 1975; Outlines of Christian Doctrine, 1976; Life of Christ, 1976; Winds of Fury, 1977; Worship, 1978; Introducing the Old Testament, 1978; The Aborigines of Arnhem Land, 1979; Cole Family History, 1980; Arnhem Land: Places and People, 1980; Dick Harris: Missionary to the Aborigines, 1980; Seafarers of the Groote Archipelago, 1980; Aborigines: Towards Dignity and Identity, 1981; Aborigines and Mining on Groote Eylandt, 1981; A History of Numbulwar, 1982; The Aborigines of Victoria, 1982; Through Hardship to the Stars, 1984; The Lake Condah Mission, 1984; Fred Gray of Umbakumba, 1985; The Aborigines of Western Australia, 1985; From Mission to Church: The CMS Mission to the Aborigines of Arnhem Land, 1908-1985, 1985; Pethy, Lee, and Mary: Three CMS Missionaries in East Africa, 1986; Crusade Hymns: Their Stories and Their Meanings, 1987; Beneath the Southern Cross: Sacred Hymns, Poetry and Readings, 1988; Letters from China, 1893-1895: The Story of the Sister Martyrs of Ku Cheng, 1988; Groote Eylandt: Aborigines and Mining, 1988; Robert Harkness: The Bendigo Hymnwriter, 1988; But I Will Be with You: An Autobiography, 1988; Men of Faith and Vision: Archdeacon A. Crawford and Dean J. C. MacCullagh, 1989; A History of All Saints Church, Bendigo: The Rise and Demise of a Cathedral, 1990; A History of Holy Trinity Church, Bendigo, 1990; A History of Christ Church, Echuca, 1990; A History of Christ Church, East Bendigo, 1990; The Bendigo Crusade Choir, 1990; A History of the Diocese of Bendigo: an Anglican diocese in rural Victoria, 1991; Sharing in Mission: The centenary history of the Victorian Branch of the Church Missionary Society, 1892-1992, 1992; Servants for Jesus' Sake: Long-serving Victorian CMS Missionaries, 1993. EDITOR: Groote Eylandt Stories, 1972; A Taste of Salt: A selection of sermons and articles by Bishop Oliver Heyward, 1991. **Address:** 28 Woodbury St, Bendigo, VIC 3550, Australia.

COLE, Johnnetta B(etsch). American, b. 1936. **Genres:** Anthropology/ Ethnology. **Career:** Washington State University, Pullman, assistant professor of anthropology and director of black studies, 1967-70; University of Massachusetts-Amherst, professor of anthropology and Afro-American studies, 1970-83; provost of undergraduate education, 1981-83; Hunter College of the City University of New York, NYC, Russell Sage Visiting Professor of Anthropology, 1983, professor of anthropology, 1983-87; director of Latin American and Caribbean studies, 1984-87; Spelman College, Atlanta, GA, president, 1987-97; writer. Founding member of board of directors of Points of Light Foundation. **Publications:** Conversations: Straight Talk with America's Sister President, 1993; Dream the Boldest Dreams: And Other Lessons of Life, 1997. EDITOR: Anthropology for the Eighties: Introductory Readings, 1982; All-American Women: Lines that Divide, Ties that Bind, 1986; Anthropology for the Nineties: Introductory Readings, 1988. OTHER: (author of intro) M. Nkomo, Student Culture and Activism in Black South African Universities: The Roots of Resistance, 1984; (author of intro) D. Jegede, Art by Metamorphosis: Selections of African Art from the Spelman College Collection, 1988. Contributor to journals. **Address:** Office of the President, Bennett College, 900 E Washington St, Greensboro, NC 27401-3239, U.S.A.

COLE, Nora (Marie). American, b. 1953. **Genres:** Plays/Screenplays. **Career:** Actor and playwright. **Publications:** PLAYS: Olivia's Opus, 1993. **Address:** c/o Bret Adams Agency, 448 West 44th St., New York, NY 10036, U.S.A.

COLE, Phyllis (Blum). American, b. 1944. **Genres:** Literary criticism and history. **Career:** Wellesley College, Wellesley, MA, assistant professor of English, 1973-83, visiting research scholar at Center for Research on Women, 1983-89; Harvard University, Cambridge, MA, lecturer in women's studies and the history of Christianity and research associate at Divinity School, 1984-85, lecturer in Extension Division, 1987-88; Pennsylvania State University, Delaware County, Media, associate professor of English and women's studies, 1989-99, professor of English, women's studies, and American studies, 1999-. Lecturer at US colleges and universities. **Publications:** The American Writer and the Condition of England, 1815-60, 1987; Mary Moody Emerson and the Origins of Transcendentalism: A Family History, 1998. Contributor to books. Contributor of articles and reviews to periodicals. **Address:** Department of English, Pennsylvania State University, Delaware County, 25 Yearsley Mill Rd, Media, PA 19063, U.S.A. **Online address:** pbc2@psu.edu

COLE, Robert. American, b. 1939. **Genres:** History, Travel/Exploration, Bibliography. **Career:** Utah State University, Logan, professor of history, 1970-. **Publications:** (ed.) The Dissenting Tradition, 1975; A Traveller's History of France, 1988, 6th ed., 1999; Britain and the War of Words in Neutral Europe, 1939-45, 1990; A.J.P. Taylor: The Traitor within the Gates, 1993; A Traveller's History of Paris, 3rd ed., 2000; Twentieth-Century Political and War Propaganda: An Annotated Bibliography, 1995; (ed.) The Encyclopedia of Propaganda, 1998. **Address:** Department of History, Utah State University, Logan, UT 84322-0710, U.S.A. **Online address:** rcole@hass.usu.edu

COLE, Sheila R. American (born Canada), b. 1939. **Genres:** Novels, Children's fiction, History, Psychology, Sociology. **Career:** Reviewer of children's books, New York Times Sunday Book Review. Reporter, Sunnyvale Daily Standard, 1963-64, and Newport Beach Pilot, 1966-67. **Publications:** Meaning Well, 1974; (ed. with M. Cole) The Making of Mind: A Personal Account of Soviet Psychology by A. R. Luria, 1979; Working Kids on Working, 1980; When the Tide Is Low, 1985; (with M. Cole and C. Lightfoot) The Development of Children, 1989, 5th ed., 2000; The Dragon in the Cliff: A Novel Based on the Life of Marg Anning, 1991; When the Rain Stops, 1992; The Canyon (middle-grade novel), 1992; The Hen That Crowed, 1993; What Kind of Love? The Diary of a Pregnant Teenager, 1995; To Be Young in America: Growing Up with the Country, 1776-1940 (juvenile nonfiction), 2005.

COLE, Simon A. American. **Genres:** History. **Career:** Cornell University, Ithaca, NY, Department of Science and Technology Studies, instructor, 1995; City University of New York, Borough of Manhattan Community College, adjunct lecturer, 1997; Rutgers University, Camden, NJ, Institute for Health, Health Care Policy, and Aging Research, postdoctoral fellow, 1997-1999; Visual Networks, Inc., Rockville, MD, visualization architect, 2000; Harvard University, Cambridge, MA, instructor at the Kennedy School of Government; Cornell University, Ithaca, NY, Department of Science and Technology Studies, consultant, 2001; City University of New York, New York, NY, John Jay College of Criminal Justice, visiting scientist, 2001-2002; University of California, Irvine, Department of Criminology, Law and Society, School of Social Ecology, assistant professor, 2002-. **Publications:** Suspect Identities: A History of Fingerprinting and Criminal Identification, 2001. Contributor of scholarly articles to journals, book chapters, and encyclopedia entries. Contributor of commentary, book reviews, and magazine articles. **Address:** Department of Criminology, 2357 Social Ecology II, University of California, Irvine, CA 92697, U.S.A. **Online address:** scole@uci.edu

COLE, Stephen A. American, b. 1955. **Genres:** Local history/Rural topics. **Career:** Maine State Planning Office (economic and environmental policy development), Augusta, senior planner, 1991-98; CEI (a community development corporation), Wiscasset, ME, project manager, 1998-. **Publications:** I Was Content and Not Content, 2000. **Address:** 80 Bristol Rd., Damariscotta, ME 04543, U.S.A. **Online address:** scole@celmaine.org

COLE, Susan Letzler. American, b. 1940. **Genres:** Theatre. **Career:** Cleveland State University, Cleveland, OH, assistant professor of English, 1968-69; Southern Connecticut State College, New Haven, lecturer in English, 1969; Yale University, New Haven, tutor in English, 1969-70; Quinnipiac College, New Haven, assistant professor of English, 1970-71; Albertus Magnus College, New Haven, assistant professor, 1971-76, associate professor and department head, 1977-83, professor of English, academic coordinator of drama concentration in English, and director of concentration in creative writing, 1983-, dramaturg for college plays, 1988-. University of Virginia, Northern Virginia Center, instructor, summers, 1964, 1966; Yale University, visiting fellow, 1978-79, 1980-81; lecturer at colleges and universities. **Publications:** The Absent One: Mourning Ritual, Tragedy, and the Performance of Ambivalence, 1985; Directors in Rehearsal: A Hidden World, 1992; Playwrights in Rehearsal: The Seduction of Company, 2001. Contributor to books and journals. **Address:** Department of English, 318 Aquinas Hall, Albertus Magnus College, 700 Prospect St, New Haven, CT 06511, U.S.A.

COLE, Terrence (Michael). American, b. 1953. **Genres:** History. **Career:** State of Alaska, research analyst, 1975, historian, 1979, historical consultant, 1980-82; Alaska Northwest Publishing Company, Edmonds, WA, research editor, 1981-83, editor of Alaska Journal, 1983-86; National Bank of Alaska, Anchorage, corporate historian, 1986-88; University of Alaska, Fairbanks,

assistant professor, 1988-91, associate professor, 1991-95, professor of history, 1995-, Department of History, chair, 1992-98, chair of Library and Information Technology User's Committee, 1989-94. Governor's Advisory Council on Libraries, member, 1987-90. **Publications:** Ghost of the Gold Rush: A Historical Walking Tour of Fairbanks (monograph), 1977, rev. ed, 1987; E.T. Barnette: The Strange Story of the Man Who Founded Fairbanks, 1981, reprinted as Crooked Past: The History of Frontier Fairbanks, 1991; Nome: City of the Golden Beaches, 1984; The Cornerstone on College Hill: A History of the University of Alaska Fairbanks, 1994; Banking on Alaska: A History of the National Bank of Alaska, 2000. **Address:** Department of History, University of Alaska, Fairbanks, AK 99775, U.S.A.

COLE, Thomas R(ichard). American, b. 1949. **Genres:** Gerontology/Senior issues, Biography, Race relations, History, Humanities. **Career:** University of Texas Medical Branch, Galveston, professor at the Institute for the Medical Humanities, 1982-, director of medical humanities graduate program, 1983-93; University of Houston, Houston, TX, adjunct professor. Hospice of Galveston County, member of ethics committee, 1989-; National Council on Aging, member of advisory board, 1992. **Publications:** STAGE PLAYS: (as Tom Cole with B. Monroe) Primary Care, 1992. OTHER: The Journey of Life, 1992; No Color Is My Kind, 1997; The Strange Demise of Jim Crow: How Houston Desegregated Its Public Accommodations, 1959-1963 (documentary film). EDITOR: (with S. Gadow) What Does It Mean to Grow Old?, 1986; (with D.P. Van Tassel and R. Kastenbaum) Handbook of the Humanities and Aging, 1992; (with W.A. Achenbaum, P. Jakobi and R. Kastenbaum) Voices and Visions of Aging: A Critical Gerontology, 1993; (with M. Winkler) The Oxford Book of Aging, 1994; (with H.R. Moody) Aging and the Human Spirit, 1996. **Address:** University of Texas Medical Branch, 2.210 Ashbel Smith Bldg, Galveston, TX 77555-1311, U.S.A.

COLE, Wayne S. American, b. 1922. **Genres:** History, International relations/Current affairs, Biography. **Career:** University of Arkansas, Fayetteville, instructor and assistant professor, 1950-54; Iowa State University, Ames, assistant professor, associate professor, and professor of history, 1954-65; University of Maryland, College Park, professor of history emeritus, professor of history, 1965-92, 1992-. **Publications:** America First, 1953; Senator Gerald P. Nye and American Foreign Relations, 1962; An Interpretive History of American Foreign Relations, 1968, 1974; Charles A. Lindbergh and the Battle against American Intervention in World War II, 1974; Roosevelt and the Isolationists 1932-1945, 1983; Norway and the United States, 1905-1955, 1989; Determinism and American Foreign Relations during the Franklin D. Roosevelt Era, 1995; A Life in Twentieth Century America, 2002. **Address:** Dept. of History, University of Maryland, College Park, MD 20742, U.S.A. **Online address:** wc14@umail.umd.edu

COLEGATE, Isabel. British, b. 1931. **Genres:** Novels. **Career:** Novelist and essayist. **Publications:** The Blackmailer, 1958; A Man of Power, 1960; The Great Occasion, 1962; Statues in a Garden, 1964; Orlando King, 1968; Orlando at the Brazen Threshold, 1971; Agatha, 1973; News from the City of the Sun, 1979; The Shooting Party, 1980; The Orlando Trilogy, 1984; A Glimpse of Sion's Glory, 1985; Deceits of Time, 1988; The Summer of the Royal Visit, 1991; Winter Journey, 1995; A Pelican in the Wilderness: Hermits, Solitaires and Recluses, 2002. **Address:** c/o PFD, Drury House, 34-43 Russell St, London WC2B 5HA, England.

COLEMAN, A(llan) D(ouglass). American, b. 1943. **Genres:** Communications/Media, Photography, Art/Art history. **Career:** Vice-President, Photography Media Institute, NYC, since 1977. Ed. Emeritus, VIEWS: A New England Journal of Photography, Boston, since 1982 (Founding Ed., 1979-81). Photography Critic, New York Observer, since 1988. Senior Contributing Editor, Camera & Darkroom, 1990-95; Columnist, Photo Metro, 1989-, and Photography In New York, 1990-. Member, Board of Dirs., Center for Photography in Woodstock, since 1982, and Los Angeles Center for Photographic Studies, since 1982. Executive Vice-President, and Chairman of the Membership Committee, International Association of Art Critics, 1987-92. Photography Critic, The Village Voice, NYC, 1968-73, and the New York Times, 1970-74; Contributing Ed., Camera 35, 1975-82; Assistant Professor, Dept. of Photography, Tisch School of Arts, New York University, NYC, 1979-93. Member, Board of Dirs., Photographic Resource Center, Boston, 1978-82; Member, Board of Dirs., and Chairman of the Committee on Censorship and Freedom of Vision, Society for Photographic Education, 1982-84. **Publications:** The Grotesque in Photography, 1977; Light Readings: A Photography Critic's Writings 1968-1978, 1979; Lee/Model/Parks/Samaras/Turner: Five Interviews Before the Fact, 1979; (with Patricia Grantz and Douglas Sheer) The Photography A-V Program Directory, 1980; Tarnished Silver, 1996; Available Light, 1997; Depth of Field: Essays on Photography, Mass Media and Lens Culture, 1998. **Address:** 465 Van Duzer St, Staten Island, NY 10304-2029, U.S.A.

COLEMAN, C. Norman. American, b. 1945. **Genres:** Medicine/Health. **Career:** National Cancer Institute, Bethesda, MD, clinical associate in oncology, 1972-74; Stanford University, Stanford, CA, teacher of medical and radiation oncology, 1975-85; Harvard University, Harvard Medical School, Boston, MA, professor and chairperson of Joint Center for Radiation Therapy, 1985-99; National Cancer Institute, director of Radiation Oncology Sciences Program, 1999-. International Foundation for Cancer, president. **Publications:** Understanding Cancer: A Patient's Guide to Diagnosis, Prognosis, and Treatment, 1998. **Address:** 5710 Warwick Pl., Chevy Chase, MD 20815, U.S.A. **Online address:** ccoleman@mail.nih.gov

COLEMAN, James A. American, b. 1921. **Genres:** Physics, Astronomy. **Career:** Professor of Physics and Chairman of Dept. of Physics, American International College, Springfield, Massachusetts, since 1957. Instructor in Physics and Astronomy, Connecticut College for Women, New London, 1950-57. **Publications:** Relativity for the Layman, 1954; Modern Theories of the Universe, 1963; Early Theories of the Universe, 1967; The Circle (novel), 1970. **Address:** American International College, Springfield, MA 01109, U.S.A.

COLEMAN, Jane Candia. American, b. 1939. **Genres:** Novels, Novellas/Short stories, Poetry, Essays. **Career:** University of Pittsburgh, technical writer for medical school, 1960-65; Carlow College, Pittsburgh, director of women's creative writing center, 1980-85; writer, 1985-. **Publications:** No Roof but Sky: Poetry of the American West, 1990; Deep in His Heart J.R. Is Laughing at Us (poems), 1991; Stories from Mesa Country, 1991; Discovering Eve (stories), 1993; Shadows in My Hands (essays), 1993; Doc Holliday's Woman, 1995; The Red Drum (poetry), 1994; Moving On (stories) 1997; I, Pearl Hart, 1998; The O'Keefe Empire, 1999; Doc Holliday's Gone, 1999; Borderlands, 2000; The Italian Quartet, 2001; Desperate Acts, 2001; Mountain Time, 2001; Country Music, 2002; Matchless (novel), 2003; Tombstone Travesty (novel), 2004. Contributor to periodicals. **Address:** 1702 E Lind Rd, Tucson, AZ 85719, U.S.A.

COLEMAN, Jonathan (Mark). American, b. 1951. **Genres:** Adult nonfiction, Documentaries/Reportage. **Career:** New Review (magazine), London, England, editorial assistant, 1974; U.S. representative, 1975; Alfred A. Knopf Inc., New York City, publicity writer, 1975-77; Simon & Schuster, NYC, associate editor, 1977-78, senior editor, 1978-81, member of editorial board, 1980-81; Columbia Broadcasting System Inc., NYC, associate producer of network news, 1981-83; University of Virginia, Charlottesville, lecturer in advanced nonfiction writing, 1986-93; adviser to President Clinton's Race Initiative, 1997; writer. **Publications:** At Mother's Request: A True Story of Money, Murder, and Betrayal, 1985; Exit the Rainmaker, 1989; Long Way to Go: Black and White in America, 1997. Contributor to periodicals. **Address:** 801 Park St, Charlottesville, VA 22902-4317, U.S.A. **Online address:** jonacoles@aol.com

COLEMAN, Loren. American, b. 1947. **Genres:** Paranormal, Adult nonfiction, Animals/Pets, Communications/Media, Psychology, Film, Social sciences, Mythology/Folklore, Children's non-fiction, Natural history, Social work, Anthropology/Ethnology, Zoology, Biography, Sports/Fitness. **Career:** Little Grassy Outdoor Laboratory, Carbondale, IL, counselor and activity therapist, 1967-70; TARGET Program Youth Home, Urbana, IL, supervisor, 1971-74; Behavioral Foundation for Children, San Francisco, CA, treatment team leader and group counselor, 1974-75; Walker School for Children, Needham, MA, weekend program and assistant intake coordinator, 1975-78; Framingham Youth Guidance Clinic, Framingham, MA, group program coordinator and psychiatric social worker, 1978-80; Department of Social Services, Charlestown, MA, supervisor and administrator, 1980-83; University of Southern Maine, Portland, Muskie Institute, research Associate, 1983-96; Youth Alternatives, Portland, ME, program director, 1996-; writer. Instructor and associate professor in social work, sociology, and anthropology at Boston University and Bunker Hill Community College, Boston, MA, 1981-83, and in cryptozoology, documentary film and social science at University of Southern Maine, 1990-. **Publications:** NONFICTION: (with J. Clark) The Unidentified: Notes toward Solving the UFO Mystery, 1975; (with Clark) Creatures of the Outer Edge, 1978, as Creatures of the Goblin World, 1984; Mysterious America, 1983; Curious Encounters: Phantom Trains, Spooky Spots and Other Mysterious Wonders, 1985; Suicide Clusters, 1987; (with S. Partridge and R. Partridge) Unattended Children, 1987; (ed. with K. Tilbor, H. Hornby, and C. Boggis) Working with Older Adoptees, 1988; Tom Slick and the Search for the Yeti, 1989. Author of articles. **Address:** PO Box 360, Portland, ME 04112, U.S.A.

COLEMAN, Mary Ann. American, b. 1928. **Genres:** Children's fiction, Poetry. **Career:** Pompano Elementary School, Pompano, FL, first grade teacher, 1950-51; Fulton County, Atlanta, GA, welfare worker, 1951; Harris Street School, East Point, GA, third grade teacher, 1952-55; University of Georgia Continuing Education, Athens, teacher of poetry workshops for adults, 1970-91; poetry specialist in public and private schools in Georgia, 1980-. **Publications:** disappearances (poetry), 1978; Secret Passageway (mystery for children), 1989; Recognizing the Angel (poetry), 1991; The Dreams of Hummingbirds: Poems from Nature, 1993. Contributor to anthologies and textbooks. Contributor of poetry to periodicals. **Address:** 3736 Atlanta Highway, Athens, GA 30606, U.S.A.

COLEMAN, Mary DeLorse. American, b. 1954. **Genres:** Law, Public/Social administration. **Career:** Jackson State University, Jackson, MS, professor of political science and chairperson of department. Consultant to Blackside Inc.; US Dept of Health & Human Services, research scientist. **Publications:** Legislators, Law, and Public Policy, 1993. Work represented in anthologies. **Address:** Department of Political Science, Jackson State University, 1400 Jr. Lynch St., Jackson, MS 39217, U.S.A.

COLEMAN, Michael. See **JONES, Allan Frewin.**

COLEMAN, Terry. British, b. 1931. **Genres:** Novels, History, Politics/Government, Transportation, Biography, Documentaries/Reportage. **Career:** Arts correspondent, then Chief Feature Writer, The Guardian newspaper, London, 1961-74; Special Writer, Daily Mail newspaper, London, 1974-76; Chief Feature Writer, 1976-79, New York Correspondent, 1981, and Special Correspondent, 1982-89, The Guardian; Associate Editor, The Independent, London 1989-91. Feature Writer of the Year, British Press Awards, 1981; Journalist of the Year, Granada Awards, 1988. **Publications:** The Railway Navies, 1965; (co-author) Providence and Mr. Hardy, 1966; The Only True History, 1969; Passage to America (in US as Going to America), 1972; The Pantheretti (poems), 1973; (ed.) T. Hardy, The Poor Man and the Lady, 1974; The Liners, 1976; The Scented Brawl, 1978; Movers and Shakers: Collected Interviews, 1987; Thatcher's Britain, 1987; Nelson: Man and Legend (biography; in US as The Nelson Touch), 2001; Olivier: The Authorised Biography, 2005. NOVELS: A Girl for the Afternoons, 1965; Southern Cross, 1979; Thanksgiving, 1981; Empire, 1994. **Address:** c/o PFD, Drury House, 34-43 Russell St, London WC2B 5HA, England.

COLEMAN, Verna (Scott). Australian. **Genres:** Literary criticism and history, Biography. **Career:** Librarian at Mitchell Library, Sydney, and at other libraries in Australia and in England; writer. **Publications:** Miles Franklin in America: Her Unknown Brilliant Career, 1981; The Last Exquisite: A Portrait of Frederic Manning, 1990; Adela Pankhurst: The Wayward Suffragette, 1996. Contributor to books. **Address:** 4/311 B Edgecliff Rd, Woollahra, NSW 2025, Australia.

COLEMAN, William Oliver. Australian. **Genres:** Economics. **Career:** University of Exeter, England, tutorial fellow, 1987-88; Victoria University of Wellington, New Zealand, lecturer, 1988-91; University of Tasmania, Hobart, Australia, senior lecturer, 1991-. **Publications:** Money and Finance in the Australian Economy, 1994; Rationalism and Anti-Rationalism in the Origins of Economics, 1995; Exasperating Calculators, 2001. **Address:** University of Tasmania, GPO Box 252C, Sandy Bay, Hobart, Tasmania 7001, Australia. **Online address:** William.Coleman@utas.edu.au

COLERIDGE, Nicholas (David). British, b. 1957. **Genres:** Novels, Documentaries/Reportage. **Career:** Tatler, associate editor, 1979-81; London Evening Standard, columnist, 1981-84; Harpers & Queen, features editor, 1985-86, editor, 1986-89; Conde Nast Publications, editorial director, 1989-91, managing director, 1992-. **Publications:** Tunnel Vision (collection of journalism), 1981; (with N. Miles) The Long Weekend Book, 1983; Shooting Stars (novel), 1984; Around the World in Seventy-eight Days, 1984; (ed. with S. Quinn) The Sixties in Queen, 1987; The Fashion Conspiracy: A Remarkable Journey through the Empires of Fashion, 1988; How I Met My Wife and Other Stories, 1991; Paper Tigers: The Latest, Greatest Newspaper Tycoons and How They Won the World, 1993; With Friends Like These, 1997; StreetSmart, 1999; Godchildren, 2002. Contributor and columnist for periodicals. **Address:** Conde Nast Publications, Vogue House, Hanover Square, London WI5 1JU, England.

COLES, Don. Canadian, b. 1928. **Genres:** Novels, Poetry. **Career:** York University, Toronto, professor of humanities and creative writing, 1965-, and director of Program in Creative Writing, 1979-85. Banff Centre for the Fine Arts, Alberta, poetry editor, 1984-94. **Publications:** Sometimes All Over, 1975; Anniversaries, 1979; The Prinzhorn Collection, 1982; Landslides: Selected Poems, 1975-1985; K. in Love, 1987; Little Bird, 1992; Forests of the Medieval World, 1993; Someone Has Stayed in Stockholm, 1994; (trans.)

For the Living and the Dead, by Tomas Transtromer, 1996; Kurgan, 2000; Doctor Bloom's Story (novel), 2004. **Address:** 122 Glenview Ave, Toronto, ON, Canada M4R 1P8.

COLES, John Morton. Canadian/British, b. 1930. **Genres:** Archaeology/Antiquities. **Career:** University of Cambridge, lecturer and professor of European prehistory, 1960-86; Fitzwilliam College, Cambridge, fellow. **Publications:** (with E.S. Higgs) Archaeology of Early Man, 1968; Field Archaeology in Britain, 1972; Archaeology by Experiment, 1973; (with A.F. Harding) The Bronze Age in Europe, 1978; Experimental Archaeology, 1979; (with B. Orme) Prehistory of the Somerset Levels, 1980; The Archaeology of Wetlands, 1984; (with B. Coles) Sweet Track to Glastonbury, 1986; Meare Village East: The Excavation of A. Bulleid and H. S. G. Gray 1932-1956, 1987; (with B. Coles) People of the Wetlands, 1989; Images of the Past, 1990; From the Waters of Oblivion, 1991; (with A. Goodall and S. Minnitt) Arthur Bulleid and the Glastonbury Lake Village 1892-1992, 1992; (with D. Hall) Fenland Survey, 1994; The Rock Carvings of Uppland, 1994; (with S. Minnitt) Industrious and Fairly Civilized: The Glastonbury Lake Village, 1995; (with B. Coles) Enlarging the Past, 1996; (with S. Minnitt) The Lake Villages of Somerset, 1996; (with D. Hall) Changing Landscapes: the Ancient Fenland, 1998; Patterns in a Rocky Land: Rock Carvings in South-West Uppland, Sweden, 2000. EDITOR: (with D.D.A. Simpson) Studies in Ancient Europe, 1968; (with A.J. Lawson) European Wetlands in Prehistory, 1987; (with V. Fenwick and G. Hutchinson) A Spirit of Enquiry, 1993; (with R. Bewley and P. Mellars) World Prehistory, 1999; (with B. Coles and M. Jorgensen) Bog Bodies, Sacred Sites and Wetland Archaeology, 1999; (with T. Lane) Through Wet and Dry, 2002. **Address:** Fursdon Mill Cottage, Thorverton, Devon, England. **Online address:** johnmcoles@aol.com

COLES, Robert. American, b. 1929. **Genres:** Poetry, Paranormal, Psychiatry, Psychology, Social commentary, Sociology, Biography, Novellas/Short stories. **Career:** Research Psychiatrist, Harvard University, Cambridge, Massachusetts, since 1964. Chief, Neuropsychiatry Service, Biloxi, Mississippi Air Force Base, 1958-60. **Publications:** Children of Crisis: vol. I: A Study in Courage and Fear, 1967, vol. II: Migrants, Sharecroppers, Mountaineers, 1972, vol. III: The South Goes North, 1972, vol. IV: Eskimos, Chicanos, Indians, 1978, vol. V: Privileged Ones: The Well Off and Rich in America, 1978; Dead End School, 1968; Still Hungry in America, 1968; The Grass Pipe, 1969; The Image Is You, 1969; Uprooted Children: The Early Lives of Migrant Farmers, 1970; Drugs and Youth, 1970; Erik H. Erikson: The Growth of His Work, 1970; The Middle Americans, 1971; The Geography of Faith, 1971; A Spectacle unto the World, 1973; The Darkness and the Light, 1974; The Buses Roll, 1974; Irony in the Mind's Life, 1974; Headsparks, 1975; William Carlos Williams, 1975; The Mind's Fate, 1975; A Festering Sweetness (poetry), 1978; Women of Crisis: vol. I: Lives of Struggle and Hope, 1978, vol. II: Lives of Work and Dreams, 1980; The Last and First Eskimos, 1978; Walker Percy: An American Search, 1978; Flannery O'Connor's South, 1980; Dorothea Lange: Photographs of a Lifetime, 1982; The Old Ones of New Mexico, 1984; (with R. Spears) Agee, 1985; (with G. Stokes) Sex and the American Teenager, 1985; The Moral (and Political) Life of Children, 2 vols., 1986; (with H. Levitt) In the Streets, 1987; Simone Weil: A Modern Pilgrimage, 1987; Dorothy Day: A Radical Devotion, 1987; The Call of Stories: Teaching and the Moral Imagination, 1989; Rumors of Separate Worlds, 1989; The Spiritual Life of Children, 1990; Their Eyes Meeting the World: The Drawings and Paintings of Children, 1992; The Call of Service, 1993; The Secular Mind, 1999; Lives of Moral Leadership, 2000. **Address:** Box 674, Concord, MA 01742, U.S.A.

COLFAX, David (John). Also writes as J. David Colfax. American, b. 1936. **Genres:** Education, Politics/Government, Urban studies. **Career:** University of Connecticut, Storrs, CT, associate professor, 1963-69; Washington University, St. Louis, MO, associate professor, 1969-72; Colfax Associates, Boonville, CA, partner, 1972-; National Center for Appropriate Technology (NCAT), Boonville, regional director, 1977-81; Mountain House Press, Philo, CA, publisher and editor, 1988-; 5th District supervisor, Mendocino County, CA, 1999-. **Publications:** (with M. Colfax) Homeschooling for Excellence, 1987; (ed. with M. Colfax) J. Crepin, La Chevre, 1990; (with M. Colfax) Hard Times in Paradise: An American Family's Struggle to Carve Out a Homestead in California's Redwood Mountains, 1992. AS J. DAVID COLFAX: The Big City Voter: A Study of Political Participation in Chicago, 1964; (with I.L. Allen and H.G. Stetler) Metropolitan Connecticut: A Demographic Profile, 1965; (with Allen) Urban Sample Survey Field Procedures: Materials and Strategies, 1967; (with Allen) The Inner City in Crisis: The Case of Connecticut, 1968; (with Allen) Urban Problems and Public Opinion in Four Connecticut Cities, 1968; (with A.K. Cohen and M.L. Farber) A Panel Discussion of Urban Demonstrations, 1968; (ed. with J.L. Roach) Radical Sociology, 1971. **Address:** PO Box 246, Boonville, CA 95415, U.S.A.

COLFAX, J. David. *See* **COLFAX, David (John).**

COLISH, Marcia L(illian). American, b. 1937. **Genres:** History, Philosophy. **Career:** Skidmore College, Saratoga Springs, NY, instructor in history, 1962-63; Oberlin College, Oberlin, OH, instructor, 1963-65, assistant professor, 1965-69, associate professor, 1969-75, professor, 1975-2001, Frederick B. Artz Professor of History, 1985-2001, department head, 1973-74, 1978-81, 1985-86; NEH Fellow, 1968-69, 1986-87; Institute for Advanced Studies, member, 1986-87; University of Wisconsin, Institute for Research in the Humanities, fellow, 1974-75; Guggenheim Fellow, 1989-90; Woodrow Wilson Center, fellow, 1994-95; Yale University, visiting fellow, 2001-, visiting professor of history and religious studies, 2002-03; lecturer in history, 2004-05. **Publications:** The Mirror of Language: A Study in the Medieval Theory of Knowledge, 1968, rev. ed., 1983; The Stoic Tradition from Antiquity to the Early Middle Ages, Vol. I: Stoicism in Classical Latin Literature, Vol. II: Stoicism in Latin Christian Thought through the Sixth Century, 1985, rev. ed., 1990; Peter Lombard, 2 vols., 1994; Medieval Foundations of the Western Intellectual Tradition, 400-1400, 1997; Ambrose's Patriarchs, 2005. Contributor to books. Contributor of articles and reviews to periodicals. **Address:** 80 Seaview Terrace #29, Guilford, CT 06437, U.S.A. **Online address:** marcia.colish@yale.edu

COLL, Steve. American, b. 1958. **Genres:** Documentaries/Reportage. **Career:** KCET-TV, Los Angeles, CA, staff reporter on Community Information Project, 1982-83; California, Los Angeles, contributing editor, 1983-84; Inc., Washington, DC, contributing editor, 1984-85; Washington Post, Washington, DC, 1985-, staff writer in Washington and NYC, chief of New York financial bureau, 1987-89, South Asia bureau chief, 1989-92; managing editor, 1998-. International investigative correspondent, London, 1992-. The Washington Post Magazine, editor, 1995, editor and publisher, 1996-. **Publications:** The Deal of the Century: The Breakup of AT&T, 1986; The Taking of Getty Oil, 1987; (with D.A. Vise) Eagle on the Street, 1991; On The Grand Trunk Road, 1994; Ghost Wars, 2004. **Address:** c/o Washington Post, 1150 15th St. N.W., Washington, DC 20071, U.S.A.

COLLARD, Sneed B., III. American, b. 1959. **Genres:** Children's fiction, Young adult fiction, Children's non-fiction. **Career:** Freelance writer, 1984-. California Dept of Agriculture, dutch elm disease project, agricultural aide, 1980; University of California, Santa Barbara, lab assistant, 1981, Neuroscience Research Institute, director of computer laboratory, 1986-92; University of California, Berkeley, zoology dept research assistant and research diving program assistant instructor, 1982-83; California Department of Fish and Game, wild trout program, seasonal aide, 1983; Woodward-Clyde Consultants, environmental consultant, 1984. **Publications:** CHILDREN'S NONFICTION: Sea Snakes, 1993; Do They Scare You? Creepy Creatures, 1993, as Creepy Creatures, 1997; Green Giants, 1994; Tough Terminators, 1994; Smart Survivors, 1994; Our Natural Homes, 1996; Alien Invaders, 1996; Animal Dads, 1997; Monteverde, 1997; Our Wet World, 1998; Animal Dazzlers, 1998; Birds of Prey, 1999; 1,000 Years Ago on Planet Earth, 1999; Acting for Nature, 2000; Making Animal Babies, 2000; Forest in the Clouds, 2000; The Polar Bear and the Jaguar, 2000; A Whale Biologist at Work, 2000; Lizard Island, 2000; A Firefly Biologist at Work, 2001; Leaving Home, 2002; Beaks!, 2002; The Deep-Sea Floor, 2003; Animals Asleep, 2004; Teeth!, 2006; Platypus Probably, 2005; One Night in the Coral Sea, 2005; The Prairie Builders, 2005; Science Adventures series (4 books), 2005; Wings!, 2006; Shep, 2006; Biography series (6 books), 2006. CHILDREN'S FICTION: California Fire, 1999; Butterfly Count, 2002; Dog Sense (novel), 2005. Contributor to periodicals. **Address:** c/o Charlesbridge Publishing, 85 Main St, Watertown, MA 02472, U.S.A. **Online address:** collard@bigsky.net; www.sneedbcollardiii.com

COLLECTOR, Stephen. American, b. 1951. **Genres:** Photography. **Career:** Free-lance photographer, Boulder, CO, 1975-; writer. Worked as carpenter in Boulder, surveyor in New Mexico. **Publications:** Law of the Range: Portraits of Old-Time Brand Inspectors, 1991. **Address:** 4209 North 26th St., Boulder, CO 80304, U.S.A. **Online address:** stephenc@indra.com

COLLEE, John (Gerald). British, b. 1955. **Genres:** Novels, Plays/Screenplays. **Career:** Cambridge, England, medical doctor, 1979-82; radio scriptwriter, England, 1983-84; Amoco Corporation, Madagascar, doctor; writer, 1983-. **Publications:** NOVELS: Kingsley's Touch, 1984; A Paper Mask, 1989; The Rig, 1992. SCREENPLAYS: Dragon; author of television and radio plays. **Address:** 31 Linden Gardens, London W2, England.

COLLETTE, Christine. British, b. 1947. **Genres:** History, Women's studies and issues. **Career:** Local government officer in social services, 1964-80; Edge Hill College of Higher Education, Lancashire, England, reader, 1994-

2002. Candidate for Parliament, 1987. **Publications:** For Labour and for Women: The Women's Labour League, 1906-1918, 1989; The International Faith: British Labour Attitudes to Europe 1918-1939, 1998. EDITOR: (with F. Montgomery) Into the Melting Pot: Teaching Women's Studies in the New Millennium, 1997; (with S. Bird) Jews, Labour and the Left, 2000. Contributor to anthologies and journals. **Address:** Chez Jean de Beaulieu, 16350 Chassiecq, France. **Online address:** Christine.Collette@wanadoo.fr

COLLEY, Barbara. Also writes as Anne Logan. American, b. 1947. **Genres:** Mystery/Crime/Suspense, Romance/Historical. **Career:** Minden Press & Herald, Minden, LA, classified advertisement receptionist, 1966-67; Sperry Rand Corp., Minden, line dispatcher, 1967-68; Ebasco Services, Taft, LA, receptionist and filing and dispatch clerk, 1977-78; temporary clerical worker, Norco, LA, 1984-85; Ormond Country Club, Destrehan, LA, secretary and receptionist, 1985-87, 1989-91; temporary clerical worker, Luling, LA, 1987-89. writer, 1991-. **Publications:** MYSTERIES: Maid for Murder: A Squeaky Clean Charlotte LaRue Mystery, 2002; Death Tidies Up, 2003; A Dance with the Devil, 1997; Polished Off, 2004; Wiped Out, 2005. ROMANCE NOVELS: Dangerous Memories, 2004. ROMANCE NOVELS AS ANNE LOGAN: Gulf Breezes, 1992; Twin Oaks, 1993; Dial "D" for Destiny, 1994; That Old Devil Moon, 1996; Finding Kendall, 1997. **Address:** c/o Evan Marshall Agency, 6 Tristam Pl, Pinebrook, NJ 07058, U.S.A. **Online address:** adcoiii@aol.com

COLLEY, Linda. British, b. 1949. **Genres:** History, Politics/Government. **Career:** Cambridge University, UK, research fellow and lecturer in history, 1975-82; Yale University, Richard M. Colgate professor of history, director of Lewis Walpole Library, 1982-98; London School of Economics, Leverhulme Research Professor in History, 1998-2003; Princeton University, Shelby M.C. Davis Professor of History, 2003-. Fellow: British Academy; Royal Society of Literature. **Publications:** In Defiance of Oligarchy: The Tory Party, 1714-1760, 1982; Namier, 1989; Britons: Forging the Nation, 1707-1837, 1992; Captives: Britain, Empire and the World 1600-1850, 2002; Journalism and Political Writing. **Address:** Dept of History, Princeton University, Princeton, NJ 08544-1017, U.S.A.

COLLICOTT, Sharleen. Also writes as Sharleen Pederson. American, b. 1937. **Genres:** Children's fiction. **Career:** Writer, illustrator, ceramist, sculptor, and educator. Duntog Foundation, artist in residence, 1983; Otis/Parson Design Institute, teacher, 1983; California State University, Long Beach, teacher, 1983-84; National Endowment for the Arts, panelist, 1985; affiliated with India Ink Galleries, 1985-86, and Every Picture Tells a Story (art gallery), 1991-95; exhibitor at galleries in Los Angeles, CA. **Publications:** SELF-ILLUSTRATED: Seeing Stars, 1996; Toestomper and the Caterpillars, 1999; Mildred and Sam, 2003; Toestomper and the Bad Butterflies, 2003. Illustrator of books (some as Sharleen Pederson) by J. Barrett, K.R. Greenfield, M. Hallward, S. Klein, S. Lucky, L. Numeroff, Elementary Math Series. Contributor of illustrations to periodicals. **Address:** 2960 Bel Air Dr, Las Vegas, NV 89109-1581, U.S.A. **Online address:** rubincolli@aol.com

COLLIER, Christopher. American, b. 1930. **Genres:** Young adult fiction, Children's non-fiction, History, Local history/Rural topics. **Career:** Julian Curtiss School, Greenwich, CT, teacher, 1955-58; New Canaan High School, CT, teacher, 1959-61; Columbia University, Teachers College, NYC, instructor, 1958-59; University of Bridgeport, CT, instructor, 1961-64, assistant professor, 1964-67, associate professor, 1967-71, professor of history, 1971-78, David S. Day Professor of History, 1978-84, chairman of department, 1978-81; University of Connecticut, Storrs, professor, 1984-2000, professor of history emeritus, 2000-. Visiting professor, New York University, 1974; visiting lecturer, Yale University, 1977, 1981; chairman, Columbia University Seminar on Early American History, 1978-79. Consultant to public and private organizations, including museums, historical societies, law firms, public utilities, and text, trade, and scholarly publishers. Connecticut State Historian, 1985-. **Publications:** HISTORICAL NOVELS FOR YOUNG ADULTS (with J.L. Collier): My Brother Sam Is Dead, 1974; The Bloody Country, 1976; The Winter Hero, 1978; Jump Ship to Freedom, 1981; War Comes to Willy Freeman, 1983; Who Is Carrie?, 1984; The Clock, 1992; With Every Drop of Blood, 1994. NONFICTION FOR YOUNG ADULTS: (with J.L. Collier) The Drama of American History Series (middle school), 23 vols., 1996-2001. NONFICTION FOR ADULTS: (ed.) The Public Records of the State of Connecticut, 1802-03, Vol. 11, 1967; Roger Sherman's Connecticut: Yankee Politics and the American Revolution, 1971; Connecticut in the Continental Congress, 1973; Roger Sherman: Puritan Politician, 1976; (with B.B. Collier) The Literature of Connecticut History, 1983; (with J.L. Collier) Decision in Philadelphia: The Constitutional Convention of 1787, 1986; All Politics Is Local: Family and Provincial Interests in the Creation of the Constitution, 2003. Contributor to books and history and legal journals. **Address:** 344 W River Rd, Orange, CT 06477, U.S.A.

COLLIER, Gary. Canadian (born United States), b. 1947. **Genres:** Psychology. **Career:** University of Alberta, Edmonton, research associate in psychiatry, 1977-78; St. Mary's University, Halifax, NS, assistant professor of psychology, 1978-79; University College of Cape Breton, Sydney, NS, assistant professor to professor of psychology, 1978-, member of board of governors, 1982-84, chair of The Department of Psychology, 1987-90, 1992-93. Universite de Paris (VII), Laboratoire de Psychologie Sociale, chercheur invite, 1984-85; Emory University, visiting scholar, 1990. **Publications:** Emotional Expression, 1985; (with Henry L. Minton and Graham Reynolds) Currents of Thought in American Social Psychology, 1991; Social Origins of Mental Ability, 1994. **Address:** Department of Behavioural and Life Science, University College of Cape Breton, P.O. Box 5300, Sydney, NS, Canada B1P 6L2.

COLLIER, Graham. British, b. 1937. **Genres:** Music. **Career:** Self-employed composer, musician, bandleader, and writer, 1963-. Former director of Jazz Studies, Royal Academy of Music, London. **Publications:** Inside Jazz, 1973; Jazz: A Guide for Teachers and Students, 1975; Compositional Devices, 1975; Cleo and John, 1976; Jazz Workshop: The Blues, 1988; Interaction, Opening Up the Jazz Ensemble, 1996. **Address:** c/o Arpartado 477, 29400 Ronda, Malaga, Spain. **Online address:** graham@jazzcontinuum.com; www.jazzcontinuum.com

COLLIER, James Lincoln. Also writes as Charles Williams. American, b. 1928. **Genres:** Novels, Children's fiction, Children's non-fiction, History, Music, Social commentary, Biography, Humor/Satire. **Publications:** CHILDREN'S FICTION: The Teddy Bear Habit, 1967; Rock Star, 1970; Why Does Everybody Think I'm Nutty?, 1971; It's Murder at St. Basket's, 1972; (with C. Collier) My Brother Sam Is Dead, 1974; Rich and Famous, 1975; (with C. Collier) The Bloody Country, 1976; Give Dad My Best, 1976; (with C. Collier) The Winter Hero, 1978; (with C. Collier) Jump Ship to Freedom, 1981; Planet Out of the Past, 1983; (with C. Collier) War Comes to Willie Freeman, 1983; (with C. Collier) Who Is Carrie?, 1984; When the Stars Begin to Fall, 1986; Outside Looking In, 1987; The Winchesters, 1988; (with C. Collier) My Crooked Family, 1991; (with C. Collier) The Clock, 1992; With Every Drop of Blood, 1992; The Jazz Kid, 1994. CHILDREN'S NON-FICTION: Battleground: The U.S. Army in World War II, 1965; A Visit to the Firehouse, 1967; Which Musical Instrument Shall I Play?, 1969; Danny Goes to the Hospital, 1970; Practical Musical Theory, 1970; The Hard Life of the Teenager, 1972; Inside Jazz, 1973; Jug Bands and Handmade Music 1973; The Making of Man, 1974; Making Music for Money, 1976; CB, 1977; The Great Jazz Artists, 1977; Louis Armstrong: An American Success Story, 1985; Jazz: An American Saga, 1997; (with C. Collier) The Paradox of Jamestown, 1998; (with C. Collier) The French and Indian War, 1998; (with C. Collier) The American Revolution, 1998; (with C. Collier) Creating the Constitution, 1998; (with C. Collier) Building a New Nation, 1998; (with C. Collier) Pilgrims and Puritans, 1998; (with C. Collier) Andrew Jackson's America, 1998; (with C. Collier) The Cotton South and the Mexican War, 1998; (with C. Collier) The Jeffersonian Republicans; (with C. Collier) The Civil War, 1998; (with C. Collier) The Road to the Civil War, 1998; (with C. Collier) Reconstruction and the Rise of Jim Crow, 1864-1896, 1998; (with C. Collier) A Century of Immigration: 1820-1924, 1999; (with C. Collier) The Rise of Industry: 1860-1900, 1999; The Corn Raid, 1999; The Worst of Times, 1999; Chipper, 2001; Wild Boys, 2002. ADULT NOVELS: Somebody Up There Hates Me, 1962; (as Charles Williams) Fires of Youth, 1968. ADULT NON-FICTION: Cheers, 1960; The Hypocritical American, 1964; (with others) Sex Education U.S.A., 1968; The Making of Jazz, 1978; Louis Armstrong: An American Genius, 1983 (in U.K. as Louis Armstrong: A Biography), 1984); (with C. Collier) Decision in Philadelphia, 1986; Duke Ellington, 1987; The Reception of Jazz in America, 1988; Benny Goodman and the Swing Era, 1989; The Rise of Selfishness in America, 1991; Jazz: The American Theme Song, 1993. **Address:** S Quaker Hill Rd, Pawling, NY 12564, U.S.A.

COLLIER, Jane. See COLLIER, Zena.

COLLIER, Michael. American, b. 1953. **Genres:** Literary criticism and history, Poetry. **Career:** Folger Shakespeare Library, Washington, DC, director of poetry programs, 1983-84; University of Maryland at College Park, professor and director of creative writing, 1984-. Johns Hopkins University, visiting lecturer, 1985-89, director of Summer Writers' Conference, 1987; Yale University, visiting lecturer, 1990, associate fellow of Timothy Dwight College, 1991-; Warren Wilson College, instructor, 1991; Bread Loaf Writers' Conference, staff associate, 1992, director, 1994-. **Publications:** The Clasp and Other Poems, 1986; The Folded Heart, 1989; The Wesleyan Tradition: Four Decades of American Poetry, 1993; The Neighbor, 1995; The New Bread Loaf Anthology of Contemporary American Poetry, 1999; The Ledge,

2000; The New American Poets: A Bread Loaf Anthology, 2000. Contributor of poems and reviews to periodicals. **Address:** Department of English, University of Maryland at College Park, College Park, MD 20742, U.S.A.

COLLIER, Zena. (Zena Hampson). Also writes as Jane Collier, Zena Shumsky. American (born England), b. 1926. **Genres:** Novels, Novellas/Short stories, Young adult fiction. **Career:** Writers Workshop in Continuing Education, Nazareth College, part-time teacher; full-time writer. Resident fellow, Yaddo, MacDowell, Saltonstall Foundation, and Virginia Center for the Creative Arts. **Publications:** ADULT NOVELS: A Cooler Climate, 1990; Ghost Note, 1992. Contributor of short stories and essays to journals and magazines. YOUNG ADULT FICTION: (as Zena Shumsky with L. Shumsky) First Flight, 1962; (as Jane Collier) The Year of the Dream, 1962; (as Zena Shumsky with L. Shumsky) Shutterbug, 1963; (as Jane Collier) A Tangled Web, 1967; (as Zena Collier) Next Time I'll Know, 1981. YOUNG ADULT NON-FICTION: Seven for the People, 1979. **Address:** c/o Harvey Klinger, 301 W 53rd St, New York, NY 10019-5766, U.S.A. **Online address:** zcollier@earthlink.net

COLLIGNON, Jeff. Also writes as Borto Milan. American, b. 1953. **Genres:** Mystery/Crime/Suspense, Humor/Satire. **Career:** Writer. Worked as bartender, waiter, beekeeper, roofer, probation officer, teacher, window cleaner, janitor, desk clerk, and various other jobs. **Publications:** MYSTERIES: Her Monster, 1992. OTHER: (art work and text) Tropical Dark, 2001. MYSTERIES AS BORTO MILAN: In the Drift, 1996; Riding towards Home, 1997. **Address:** PO Box 451, Naples, FL 34106, U.S.A.

COLLIGNON, Rick. American, b. 1948. **Genres:** Novels. **Career:** Novelist. Worked as a roofer for twenty years. **Publications:** NOVELS: The Journal of Antonio Montoya, 1996; Perdido, 1997. **Address:** c/o MacAdam/Cage Publicity, 820 16th St., Ste 331, Denver, CO 80231, U.S.A.

COLLIN, Marion (Cripps). British, b. 1928. **Genres:** Romance/Historical, Literary criticism and history, Medicine/Health. **Career:** Student nurse, Isle of Wight, 1945-48; medical secty., London, 1948-52; Fiction Ed., Woman's Own mag., London, 1952-56; Lecturer in further education, 1972-89. **Publications:** FICTION: (with A. Britton) Romantic Fiction, 1960; Nurse Maria, 1963; Nurse at the Top, 1964; Doctors Three, 1964; Nurse in the Dark, 1965; The Doctor's Delusion, 1967; The Shadow of the Court, 1967; The Man on the Island, 1968; Sun on the Mountain, 1969; Nurse on an Island, 1970; Calling Dr. Savage, 1970; House of Dreams, 1971; Sawdust and Spangles, 1972; Nurses in the House, 1989. NON-FICTION: Hospital Office Practice, 1981; (with M. Drury) The Medical Secretary's and Receptionist's Handbook, 1986. **Address:** 20 Eridge Rd., Tunbridge Wells, Kent TN4 8HJ, England.

COLLIN, Matthew. British. **Genres:** Sociology. **Career:** Style magazine writer. **Publications:** (with J. Godfrey) Altered State: The Story of Ecstasy Culture and Acid House, 1997; Blimey!: The British Art Scene from Francis Bacon to Damien Hirst, 1998. **Address:** c/o Pete Aryton, Serpent's Tail Publishing, 4 Blackstock Mews, London N42BT, England.

COLLINGE, William B. American, b. 1949. **Genres:** Medicine/Health, Psychology. **Career:** Private practice of psychotherapy, 1977-. Pittsburg State University, Pittsburg, KS, assistant professor, 1975-78; University of Kansas, Lawrence, instructor, 1979-81; Cancer Support and Education Center, Menlo Park, CA, clinical supervisor, 1987-96; part-time teacher at University of Alaska, University of Nevada, University of California, Berkeley, and Omega Institute. **Publications:** Recovering from Chronic Fatigue Syndrome: A Guide to SelfEmpowerment, 1993; The American Holistic Health Association Complete Guide to Alternative Medicine, 1996; Subtle Energy: Awakening to the Unseen Forces in Our Lives, 1998; The Mind/Body Medicine Audio Library, 1998. Books have been published in many languages. **Address:** PO Box 263, Kittery Point, ME 03905-0263, U.S.A. **Online address:** wcollinge@comcast.net

COLLINGS, Gillian. Also writes as Frances Gilbert. British, b. 1939. **Genres:** Education, Children's fiction. **Career:** Trumbull Board of Education, Trumbull, CT, special education teacher and chairperson of special education, 1980-. **Publications:** (with others) Language Chain, Language Connection, 1989; Teaching Guide (teacher's companion to Turtle on a Summer's Day and Celeste and Regine in the Rain Forest), 1997. CHILDREN'S BOOKS (as Frances Gilbert): Turtle on a Summer's Day, 1994; Celeste and Regine in the Rain Forest, 1997. **Address:** 117 Williams Rd., Trumbull, CT 06611, U.S.A.

COLLINGS, I. J. (Jillie). Australian. **Genres:** Novels, Environmental sciences/Ecology, Paranormal. **Career:** Astrologer, Woman Magazine, 1975-85; Health/ecology columnist, The Guardian, 1987-90; Investigative writer/broadcaster, currently. **Publications:** The Malevolent Despot, 1968; Astrology and Your Child, 1980; Around the Next Corner, 1990; Life Forces: Guidelines for Living on an Increasingly Polluted Planet, 1991; The Ordinary Person's Guide to Extraordinary Health, 1993; Beat Heart Disease without Surgery, 1995; Colonic Irrigation, 1995. **Address:** 14 Highbourne House, 13-15 Marylebone High St, London W1U 4NS, England. **Online address:** jilliecollings@enterprise.net; jillie@wanadoo.es

COLLINGS, Matthew. (born England), b. 1955. **Genres:** Art/Art history. **Career:** Art critic and artist. Former editor of Artscribe magazine; art critic, British Broadcasting Corp. (BBC), 1988-97. **Publications:** Blimey! From Bohemia to Britpop: The London Artworld from Francis Bacon to Damien Hirst, 1997, 3rd edition, 1997; It Hurts: New York Art from Warhol to Now, 1998; (with Neal Brown and Sarah Kent) Tracey Emin. I Need Art Like I Need God (exhibition catalog), 1998; This Is Modern Art, edited by Sarah Fass, 1999; 2000; (Author of introduction) British Abstract Painting 2001 (exhibition catalog), 2001; Art Crazy Nation: The Post-Blimey! Art World, 2001; Sarah Lucas, 2003. Author of scripts for television series. **Address:** c/o Author Mail, Harry N. Abrams, 100 Fifth Ave., New York, NY 10011, U.S.A.

COLLINGS, Michael R(obert). American, b. 1947. **Genres:** Horror, Science fiction/Fantasy, Plays/Screenplays, Poetry, Literary criticism and history. **Career:** Instructor in English, San Bernardino Valley College, CA, 1976-79, and the University of California at Los Angeles, 1978-79; Pepperdine University, Malibu, CA, professor of English, 1979-. **Publications:** (with J. Collings) Whole Wheat Harvest, 1981; Brian W. Aldiss: A Reader's Guide, 1985; Piers Anthony: A Reader's Guide, 1985; Stephen King as Richard Bachman, 1985; The Shorter Works of Stephen King, 1985; The Many Facets of Stephen King, 1986; The Films of Stephen King, 1986; The Annotated Guide to Stephen King, 1986; The Stephen King Phenomenon, 1987; In the Image of God: Theme, Characterization and Landscape in the Fiction of Orson Scott Card, 1990; The Work of Stephen King: An Annotated Bibliography and Guide, 1996; The Art and Craft of Poetry, 1996; He's Scaring Us to Death, 1997. NOVEL: The House beyond the Hill, 1996. POETRY: A Season of Calm Weather, 1974; Naked to the Sun: Dark Visions of Apocalypse, 1985; Dark Transformations (poetry), 1990; All Calm, All Bright, 1995; (ed. with S.E. Gratner) Retooling for the Renaissance in the 3rd Millennium, 1995; Haiku, 1995; Matrix, 1995; Nestlings of a Dark God, 1996; Tales through Time, 1996; Still Secrecies of Love, 1996; Poetry, Especially for Children, 1996; The Nephiad, 1996; Epyllion in Anamnesis, 1996. **Address:** Pepperdine University, Humanities/Teachers Education Division, Cultural Arts Center 305, Malibu, CA 90263, U.S.A. **Online address:** mcolling@pepperdine.edu

COLLINS, Ace. (Andrew J). American, b. 1953. **Genres:** Novels, Adult non-fiction, Children's non-fiction. **Career:** Free-lance writer. **Publications:** YOU CAN DO IT SERIES FOR CHILDREN: You Can Do It Running, 1993; You Can Do It Dog Training, 1993; You Can Do It Juggling, 1993; You Can Do It Sidewalk Art and Games, 1993; You Can Do It Balloon Shapes and Animals, 1993. HOLIDAY ADVENTURE SERIES FOR CHILDREN (with L. Mandrell): Runaway Thanksgiving, 1992; Jonathan's Gifts, 1992; Peril in Evans Woods, 1993; All in a Day's Work, 1993; Eddie Finds a Hero, 1993; Best Man for the Job, 1993; A Mission for Jenny, 1993; Sunrise over the Harbor, 1993; Bond of Trust; Kimi's American Dream; Candy's Frog Prince; Abe's Hard Lesson; The End of the Rainbow; Twin Disasters; The Eyes of an Eagle; The Parade. ADULT NONFICTION: (with Mandrell) The Mandrell Family Album, 1983; The Christian Executive, 1984; (with L. Chapin as Andrew Collins) Father Does Know Best, 1989; Bette Midler, 1989; Sigourney Weaver, 1989; After the Storm, 1992; I Saw Him in Your Eyes, Vol I, 1993, Vol II, 1995, Vol III, 1995; Lassie, a Dog's Life: The First Fifty Years, 1993; Tanya Tucker: A Biography, 1994. ADULT FICTION: Darkness before Dawn, 1994; The Cutting Edge, 1994; Saving Grace, 1995; The Image of Truth, 1995. OTHER: wrote the 1940s segment of The Spirit of Christmas, scripted the play American Spirit, and wrote script and original song lyrics for A Christian Carol. **Address:** P.O. Box 644, Hillsboro, TX 76645, U.S.A.

COLLINS, Billy. American, b. 1941. **Genres:** Poetry. **Career:** Herbert H. Lehman College of the City University of New York, Bronx, NY, professor. US Poet Laureate. **Publications:** POETRY: The Apple That Astonished Paris, 1988; Questions about Angels, 1991; The Art of Drowning, 1995; Picnic, Lightning, 1997; Taking off Emily Dickinson's Clothes, 2000; Sailing Alone around the Room, 2001; Nine Horses, 2002; (ed.) Poetry 180: A Turning Back to Poetry. **Address:** c/o Chris Calhoun, Sterling Lord Literistic, 65 Bleecker St, New York, NY 10012, U.S.A.

COLLINS, Bud. (Arthur Worth , Jr). American, b. 1929. **Genres:** Sports/Fitness. **Career:** Boston Herald, Boston, MA, sports writer, 1955-63; Boston Globe, sports and general columnist, 1963-. Freelance writer, 1955-. Sportscaster for PBS, 1963-84,NBC, 1964-, CBS, 1968-72. Varsity tennis coach at Brandeis University, 1959-63. **Publications:** (with R. Laver) The Education of a Tennis Player, 1973; (with E. Goolagong) Evonne! On the Move, 1975; My Life with the Pros, 1989. EDITOR: (with R. Laver) Rod Laver's Tennis Digest, 1973; (with Z. Hollander) Bud Collins' Modern Encyclopedia of Tennis, 1980, 3rd ed., 1997. **Address:** c/o Sharf Marketing Group Inc, 822 Boylston St Ste 203, Chestnut Hill, MA 02467, U.S.A.

COLLINS, Catherine Fisher. American. **Genres:** Medicine/Health. **Career:** Model City Agency and Human Resource Department, Buffalo, NY, component manager, 1971-73; Comprehensive Health Planning Council of Western New York Inc., Tonawanda, coordinator of federal funds, 1973-76; Health Systems Agency, Tonawanda, director of quality assurance, 1976-86; Erie County Medical Center, Buffalo, director of ambulatory care, 1986-89; worked as an assistant academic dean, 1989-90; Erie Community College, Buffalo, professor and department head, 1990-92; State University of New York Empire State College, Buffalo, associate professor of community health and human services, 1992-. Medaille College, professor, 1980-82; State University of New York at Buffalo, assistant professor, 1984-90; Erie Community College, adjunct assistant professor, 1988-90; Buffalo State College of the State University of New York, adjunct assistant professor, 1998-. **Publications:** (ed.) African American Health and Social Issues, 1996; The Imprisonment of African American Women: Causes, Conditions, and Future Implications, 1997; Stress and the African American Female, 1998. **Address:** Department of Community Health and Human Services, State University of New York Empire State College, 617 Main St., Buffalo, NY 14203, U.S.A. **Online address:** ccollins@sescua.esc.edu

COLLINS, David. American, b. 1962. **Genres:** Autobiography/Memoirs. **Career:** Gale, Farmington Hills, MI, editor; writer. **Publications:** My Louise: A Memoir, 2002. **Address:** c/o Gale, 27500 Drake Rd, Farmington Hills, MI 48331-3535, U.S.A.

COLLINS, David R. See Obituaries.

COLLINS, Harold R(eeves). American, b. 1915. **Genres:** Literary criticism and history. **Career:** Retired Professor of English, Kent State University, Ohio, since 1955. Assistant Professor of English, Wilkes College, Wilkes-Barre, Pa., 1945-47; Instructor in English, University of Connecticut at Waterbury, 1947-55. **Publications:** Amos Tutuola, 1969.

COLLINS, Helen (Frances). American. **Genres:** Novels, Science fiction/Fantasy. **Career:** Nassau Community College, Garden City, NY, professor of English, 1967-. Member of East Lyme Land Conservation Trust, 1977-, Coalition to Save the Coastline, 1977-84, and East Lyme Tidal Wetlands Committee, 1977-84. **Publications:** Mutagenesis (science fiction), 1993; Egret (novel), 2002. Contributor to periodicals. **Address:** 22 Fairhaven Rd, Niantic, CT 06357, U.S.A.

COLLINS, Hugh. British, b. 1953. **Genres:** Law. **Career:** Brasenose College, Oxford, England, fellow and tutor in law. **Publications:** (author of revisions) T.S. Humphreys, Humphreys' Notes on District Registry, 16th ed, 1966; (ed.) R.B. Orange, Reminders on County Court Costs, 7th ed, 1970; (author of revisions) T.S. Humphreys, Humphreys' Notes on Matrimonial Causes Proceeding in County Courts and District Registries, 12th ed, 1974; (author of revisions) J.L. Robinson, County Court Costs, 4th ed, 1971, revised as Robinson's County Court Costs, 5th ed, 1976; (author of revisions) T.S. Humphreys, Weaving's Notes on Bankruptcy Practice and Procedure in County Courts, 5th ed, 1972; Notes on County Court Practices and Procedures, 1967, 5th ed., 1978; Marxism and Law, 1982; The Law of Contract, 1986; County Court Practice Handbook, 1992; Justice in Dismissal: The Law of Termination of Employment, 1992. **Address:** Professor of English Law, Law Dept, London School of Economics, Houghton St, London WC2A 2AE, England.

COLLINS, Irene. British, b. 1925. **Genres:** History. **Career:** University of Liverpool, England, lecturer to reader, 1947-86, honorary senior fellow, 1986-. **Publications:** The Government and the Newspaper Press in France, 1814-81, 1959; The Age of Progress: Europe, 1789-1870, 1964; Napoleon and His Parliaments, 1800-1815, 1979; Jane Austen and the Clergy, 1994; Jane Austen, The Parson's Daughter, 1998.

COLLINS, Jackie. British. **Genres:** Novels. **Publications:** The World Is Full of Married Men, 1968; The Stud, 1969; Sunday Simmons and Charlie Brick, 1971, as Sinners, 1981; Lovehead, 1974, as The Love Killers, 1977; The World Is Full of Divorced Women, 1975; The Hollywood Zoo, 1975; Lovers and Gamblers, 1977; The Bitch, 1979; Chances, 1981; Hollywood Wives, 1983; Lucky, 1985; Hollywood Husbands, 1986; Rock Star, 1988; Lady Boss, 1990; American Star, 1993; Hollywood Kids, 1994; Vendetta: Lucky's Revenge, 1997; Thrill, 1998; L.A. Connections, 1998; Dangerous Kiss, 1999; Lethal Seduction, 2000; Hollywood Wives: The New Generation, 2001.

COLLINS, Joan. British, b. 1933. **Genres:** Novels, Fashion/Costume, Biography. **Career:** Actress and writer. Has appeared in films, on the London stage, and in television series. London stage debut, in A Doll's House, 1945; starred as Alexis in the TV series Dynasty, 1981-90. **Publications:** Past Imperfect: An Autobiography, 1978; Katy: A Fight for Life (biography), 1982; Second Act, 1997. BEAUTY: The Joan Collins Beauty Book, 1980; My Secrets, 1994; Friends Secrets, 1999. NOVELS: Prime Time, 1988; Love and Desire and Hate, 1990; Too Damn Famous, 1995; My Star Quality, 2002. **Address:** c/o Paul Keylock, 16 Bulbecks Walk, S Woodham Ferrers, Chelmsford, Essex CM3 5ZN, England. **Online address:** PKeylock@aol.com (contact details)

COLLINS, Josie. See BENTLEY, Joyce.

COLLINS, Julie (Hubbard). American, b. 1959. **Genres:** Adult non-fiction. **Career:** Self-employed in Alaska as a handcrafter, 1975-, trapper, 1976-, and writer and photographer, 1979-. **Publications:** NONFICTION WITH M. COLLINS: Trapline Twins, 1989; Dog Driver: A Guide for the Serious Musher, 1991; Riding the Wild Side of Denali: Alaska Adventures with Horses and Huskies, 1998. **Address:** c/o Alpine Publications, PO Box 7027, Loveland, CO 80537, U.S.A.

COLLINS, Larry. American, b. 1929. **Genres:** Novels, Politics/Government, Social commentary. **Career:** Correspondent, U.P.I., Paris, Rome, and Beirut, 1957-59; Middle East Correspondent, Newsweek mag., Beirut, 1959-61; Bureau Chief, Newsweek mag., Paris, 1961-65. **Publications:** (with D. Lapierre) Is Paris Burning?, 1965; (with D. Lapierre) Or I'll Dress You in Mourning, 1968; (with D. Lapierre) O Jerusalem, 1972; (with D. Lapierre) Freedom at Midnight, 1975; (with D. Lapierre) The Fifth Horseman (novel), 1980; Fall from Grace (novel), 1985; Maze (novel), 1989; Black Eagles (novel), 1993; Tomorrow Belongs to Us, 1999. **Address:** La Biche Niche, 83350 Ramatuelle, France. **Online address:** larcollins@aol.com

COLLINS, Max Allan. Also writes as Peter Brackett. American, b. 1948. **Genres:** Mystery/Crime/Suspense, Graphic Novels. **Career:** Writer, the comic strips Dick Tracy, 1977-93, Mike Mist, 1979, and Ms. Tree, 1981, for newspapers and magazines. Musician, with Daybreakers group, 1966-71, and Cruisin' group, 1976-79, and 1986; songwriter, Tree International, Nashville, 1967-71; reporter, Muscatine Journal, 1968-70; instructor in English, Muscatine Community College, 1971-77. **Publications:** MYSTERY NOVELS: Bait Money, 1973; Blood Money, 1973; The Broker, 1976, as Quarry, 1985; The Broker's Wife, 1976, as Quarry's List, 1985; The Dealer, 1976, as Quarry's Deal, 1986; The Slasher, 1977, as Quarry's Cut, 1986; Fly Paper, 1981; Hush Money, 1981; Hard Cash, 1981; Scratch Fever, 1982; The Baby Blue Rip-Off, 1983; No Cure for Death, 1983; True Detective, 1983; Kill Your Darlings, 1984; True Crime, 1984; A Shroud for Aquarius, 1985; The Million-Dollar Wound, 1986; Nice Weekend for a Murder, 1986; Midnight Haul, 1986; Spree, 1987; Primary Target, 1987; Neon Mirage, 1988; Stolen Away, 1991; Carnal Hours, 1994; Blood and Thunder, 1995; Damned in Paradise, 1996; Flying Blind, 1999; Majic Man, 1999; Mourn the Living, 1999; Kisses of Death, 2001; Angel in Black, 2001; Chicago Confidential, forthcoming; The Lusitania Mysteries, 2002. NOVELIZATIONS OF FILMS: Dick Tracy, 1990; In the Line of Fire, 1994; (as Peter Brackett) I Love Trouble, 1994; Waterworld, 1995; Daylight, 1996; Air Force One, 1997; U.S. Marshals, 1998; Saving Private Ryan, 1998; The Mummy, 1999; U-571, 2000. SCREENPLAYS: The Expert, 1995; Mommy, 1995; Mommy's Day, 1995; Mike Hammer's Mickey Spillane (documentary), 1999; Real Time, 2000. OTHER: Dick Tracy Meets Angeltop, 1980; Dick Tracy Meets the Punks, 1980; The Mike Mist Minute Mist-eries, 1981; (co-ed.) M. Spillane, Mike Hammer: The Comic Strip, Vol. 1, 1982, Vol. 2, 1985; (with E. Gorman) Jim Thompson: The Killers inside Him, 1983; (with J.L. Traylor) One Lonely Knight: Mickey Spillane's Mike Hammer, 1984; (with T. Beatty) The Files of Ms. Tree, 3 vols., 1984-86; (with D. Locher) Dick Tracy: Tracy's Wartime Memories, 1986; The Dark City, 1987; Butcher's Dozen, 1988; (with J. Javna) The Best of Crime and Detective TV, 1988; Bullet Proof, 1989; Dick Tracy Goes to War, 1991; Dying in the Postwar World (short stories), 1991; Dick Tracy Meets His Match, 1992; Murder by the Numbers, 1993; Maverick (adventure), 1994; NYPD Blue: Blue Beginning, 1995; The Mystery Scene

Movie Guide, 1996; Earl MacPherson, 1997; NYPD Blue: Blue Blood, 1997; Mommy, 1997; Gil Elvgren, 1997; Pin-up Poster Book, 1997; Road to Perdition (graphic novel), 1998; Mommy's Day, 1998; (with D. Elvgren) Elvgren, 1998; Swimsuit Sweeties, 1999; Varga Girls I & II, 1999; Elvgren Girls I & II, 1999; Exotic Ladies, 1999; The Titanic Murders, 1999; (with B. Collins) Regeneration, 1999; For the Boys!, 2000; Indian Maidens, 2001; Pirate & Gypsy Girls, 2001; Pin-up Nudes, 2001, vol. 2, 2002; Seaside Sweethearts, 2001; Blue Christmas and Other Holiday Homicides, 2001; (with B. Collins) Murder: His and Hers (short stories), 2001; The History of Mystery, 2001; Patriotic Pin-ups, 2002; Cowgirl Pin-ups, 2002; Playful Pinups, 2002. EDITOR: M. Spillane, Tomorrow I Die, 1984; (with D. Locher) The Dick Tracy Casebook, 1990; (with D. Locher) Dick Tracy: The Secret Files, 1990; (with D. Locher) Dick Tracy's Fiendish Foes, 1991; (with M. Spillane) Murder Is My business, 1994; (and author of intro.) B. Collins, Too Many Tomcats and Other Feline Tales of Suspense, 2000; (with J. Gelb) Flesh and Blood, 2001; (and author of intro.) M. Spillane, Together We Kill, 2001; (with M. Spillane) A Century of Noir, 2002. **Address:** 301 Fairview Ave, Muscatine, IA 52761, U.S.A.

COLLINS, Merle. (born Aruba), b. 1950. **Genres:** Novels, Novellas/Short stories, Poetry. **Career:** Writer and educator, 1985-. **Publications:** POETRY: Because the Dawn Breaks! Poems Dedicated to the Grenadian People, 1985; Rotten Pomerack, 1992. NOVELS: Angel, 1987; The Color of Forgetting, 1995. SHORT STORIES: Rain Darling: Stories, 1990. EDITOR:(with R. Cobham) Watchers and Seekers: Creative Writing by Black Women in Britain, 1987; N. Payne and J. Buffong, Jump-Up-and-Kiss Me: Two Stories of Grenadian Childhood, 1990. Contributor to anthologies and periodicals. **Address:** Dept of Comparative Literature, 4136 Susquehanna Hall, University of Maryland, College Park, MD 20742, U.S.A. **Online address:** mc188@umail.umd.edu

COLLINS, Michael. See **LYNDS, Dennis.**

COLLINS, Michael. Irish, b. 1964. **Genres:** Novels. **Career:** Writer and computer programmer. Northwestern University, Chicago, IL, head of computer lab, creative writing teacher;. **Publications:** The Meat Eaters, 1992, in US as The Man Who Dreamt of Lobsters, 1993; The Life and Times of a Teaboy, 1994; The Feminists Go Swimming, 1996; The Emerald Underground, 1998; The Keepers of Truth, 2001; The Resurrectionists, 2002. **Address:** c/o Author Mail, Simon & Schuster, 1230 Avenue of the Americas, New York, NY 10020, U.S.A.

COLLINS, Miki (Dickey). American, b. 1959. **Genres:** Adult non-fiction, Animals/Pets. **Career:** Self-employed writer and photographer in Alaska, 1974-, handcrafter, 1975-, and trapper, 1976-. **Publications:** NONFICTION WITH J. COLLINS: Trapline Twins, 1989; Dog Driver: A Guide for the Serious Musher, 1991; Riding the Wild Side of Denali, 1998. **Address:** c/o Alpine Publications, PO Box 7027, Loveland, CO 80537, U.S.A.

COLLINS, Nancy A. American, b. 1959. **Genres:** Novels, Mystery/Crime/Suspense, Horror. **Career:** Writer. **Publications:** Sunglasses after Dark (novel), 1989; Tempter, 1990; In the Blood, 1992; Cold Turkey, 1992; Wild Blood, 1993; Paint It Black, 1994; Midnight Blue, 1995; Walking Wolf, 1995; Lynch: A Gothik Western, 1998; Angels on Fire, 1998; Nameless Sins, 1994; Avenue X, 2000; Knuckles and Tales, 2001. **Address:** c/o Donald Maas Literary Agency, 160 W 95th St Ste 1B, New York, NY 10025, U.S.A.

COLLINS, Patricia Hill. American, b. 1948. **Genres:** Women's studies and issues, Race relations. **Career:** Educator and sociologist. Harvard U.T.T.T. program, teacher, 1970-73; St. Joseph Community School, curriculum specialist, 1973-76; African American Center, Tufts University, director, 1976-80; University of Cincinnati, Cincinnati, OH, assistant, then associate professor, 198793, professor of African American studies, 1993-, Charles Phelps Taft Professor of Sociology, 1996, chair, minority fellowship program committee, 1992-. **Publications:** Black Feminist Thought: Knowledge, Consciousness, and the Politics of Empowerment, 1990; (ed. with M.L. Andersen) Race, Class, and Gender: An Anthology, 1992, 2nd ed., 1994. Contributor to books and periodicals. **Address:** Department of African American Studies, University of Cincinnati, ML 370, Cincinnati, OH 45221, U.S.A.

COLLINS, Philip Arthur William. British, b. 1923. **Genres:** Literary criticism and history, Bibliography. **Career:** Warden of Vaughan College, 1954-62, Sr. Lecturer, 1962-64, and Professor of English, 1964-82, University of Leicester. Member, Board of Dirs., The National Theatre, 1976-82. **Publications:** James Boswell, 1956; Dickens and Crime, 1962; Dickens and Education, 1963; The Impress of the Moving Age, 1965; Thomas Cooper the

Chartist: Byron and the Poets of the Poor, 1969; A Dickens Bibliography, 1970; Bleak House: A Commentary, 1971; Reading Aloud: A Victorian Metier, 1972; Charles Dickens: David Copperfield, 1977; Tennyson, Poet of Lincolnshire, 1985. EDITOR: English Christmas, 1956; Dickens: A Christmas Carol: The Public Reading Version, 1971; Dickens: The Critical Heritage, 1971; Charles Dickens: The Public Readings, 1975; Charles Dickens: Hard Times, 1978; Dickens: Interviews and Recollections, 1981; Thackeray: Interviews and Recollections, 1982; (with E. Giuliano) The Annotated Dickens, 1986; Tennyson: Seven Essays, 1992. **Address:** 26 Knighton Dr, Leicester LE2 3HB, England.

COLLINS, Robert O(akley). American, b. 1933. **Genres:** History. **Career:** Williams College, Williamstown, MA, lecturer in history, 1961, assistant professor of history, 1963-65; University of California at Santa Barbara, associate professor, 1965-69, professor of history, 1969-94, emeritus, 1994-. Columbia University, NYC, visiting assistant professor of history, 1962-63; International Academy, Santa Barbara, Board of Dirs., 1968-81; Journal of African Studies, Editorial Board. **Publications:** The Southern Sudan 1883-1898, 1962; (with R.L. Tignor) Egypt and the Sudan, 1967; King Leopold, England and the Upper Nile, 1968; Land beyond the Rivers: The Southern Sudan 1898-1918, 1971; African History: Text and Readings, 1971; Europeans in Africa, 1971; The Southern Sudan in Historical Perspective, 1975; (with R. Nash) The Big Drops: Legendary Rapids of the West, 1978; Shadows in the Grass: Britain in the Southern Sudan 1918-1956, 1983; The Waters of the Nile: Hydropolitics of the Nile and the Jonglei Canal, 1989; Western African History, 1990; Eastern African History, 1990; Central and South African History, 1990; Problems in African History: The Pre-Colonial Centuries, 1994; Problems in the History of Imperial Africa, 1994; Requiem for the Sudan: War, Drought and Disaster Relief on the Nile, 1994; Africa's Thirty Years War: Chad, Libya, and the Sudan, 1963-1993; The Historical Dictionary of PreColonial Africa, 2001; The Nile, 2002. EDITOR: Sir Richard Burton, The Nile Basin, 1967; Problems in African History, 1968; The Partition of Africa, 1969; Sir Gilbert Clayton, An Arabian Diary, 1969; Problems in the History of Colonial Africa, 1970; (with F. Deng) Britain in the Sudan 1898-1956, 1984. **Address:** Dept. of History, University of California, Santa Barbara, Santa Barbara, CA 93106-9410, U.S.A. **Online address:** rcollins@history.ucsb.edu

COLLINS, Ronald K. L. American, b. 1949. **Genres:** Law. **Career:** Temple University, Philadelphia, PA, professor of law, 1988-90; George Washington University, Washington, DC, professor of law, 1992-95; Seattle University, Tacoma, WA, professor of law, 1995-. **Publications:** (ed.) Constitutional Government in America, 1981; (ed.) G. Gilmore, The Death of Contract, 1995; (with D.M. Skover) The Death of Discourse, 1996. Contributor to books and periodicals. **Address:** School of Law, Seattle University, 900 Broadway, Seattle, WA 98122-4338, U.S.A.

COLLINS, Stephen. American, b. 1947. **Genres:** Novels, Plays/Screenplays. **Career:** Actor, director, and writer. **Publications:** Super Sunday (play), 1988; Eye Contact (novel), 1994; Double Exposure (novel), 1998. **Address:** c/o Frankel Lodgen Lacher Golditch Sardi & Howard, 16530 Ventura Blvd. #305, Encino, CA 91436, U.S.A.

COLLINS, Stephen L. American (born England), b. 1949. **Genres:** Intellectual history. **Career:** Shimer College, Mount Carroll, IL, member of humanities faculty, 1975-78; Boston University, Boston, MA, assistant professor of social science, 1978-83; Babson College, Babson Park, MA, assistant professor, 1983-88, associate professor of history, 1988-, William R. Dill Term Chair Holder in History and Society, 1992-. **Publications:** From Divine Cosmos to Sovereign State: An Intellectual History of Consciousness and the Idea of Order in Renaissance England, 1989. **Address:** Department of History, Babson College, Babson Park, MA 02457, U.S.A.

COLLINS, Tess. American. **Genres:** Plays/Screenplays, Novels. **Career:** Curran Theatre, San Francisco, CA, manager. Freelance writer, c. 1997-. **Publications:** Tossing Monte (play), c. 1997; The Law of Revenge (novel), 1997. **Address:** Curran Theatre, 445 Geary Blvd., San Francisco, CA 94102, U.S.A.

COLLINSON, Alan S. Also writes as Stan Freedman. British, b. 1934. **Genres:** Biology, Botany, Geography, Novels. **Career:** Teacher and head of geography and biology at school in Northallerton, Yorkshire, England, 1957-67; Trent Park College and Middlesex Polytechnic, London, England, lecturer, 1967-72; principal lecturer in fine art, Sunderland Polytechnic, 1972-88. **Publications:** Introduction to World Vegetation, 1978, 2nd ed, 1988; Choosing Health, 1991; Renewable Energy, 1991; Mountains, 1991;

Grasslands, 1992; Pollution, 1992; Working with Oceans, Polar Lands, and Space; He Fell Among Artists, 1995. **Address:** 54 Bolton Ave., Richmond, N. Yorkshire DL10 4BA, England.

COLLINSON, Roger (Alfred). British, b. 1936. **Genres:** Children's fiction. **Career:** School teacher, Essex Co. Council, Leigh-on-Sea, since 1975. **Publications:** A Boat and Bax, 1967; Butch and Bax, 1970; Four Eyes, 1976; Get Lavinia Goodbody!, 1983; Paper Flags and Penny Ices, 1984; Hanky-Panky, 1986; Willy and the Sumolin of Pudding and Other Stories, 1994; Willy and the UFO, 1995; Sticky Fingers, 1996; Butterfingers, 1997; Grisel and the Tooth Fairy, 1998. **Address:** c/o Anderson Press Ltd, Random Century House, 20 Vauxhall Bridge Rd, London SW1V 2SA, England.

COLLINSON, Sarah. British, b. 1965. **Genres:** International relations/ Current affairs. **Career:** European Commission, Brussels, Belgium, trainee and researcher, 1990-91; Royal Institute of International Affairs, London, England, research fellow, 1991-. European affairs consultant. **Publications:** Europe and International Migration, 1993, 2nd ed, 1994; Beyond Books: West European Migration Policy Towards the Twenty-First Century, 1993; (with H. Miall and A. Michalski) A Wider European Union? Integration and Cooperation in the New Europe, 1993. **Address:** Politics Dept, University of Reading, Reading, Berks. RG6 6AH, England.

COLLIS, Louise (Edith). British, b. 1925. **Genres:** Novels, Art/Art history, History, Biography. **Career:** Freelance writer and art critic. **Publications:** Without a Voice, 1951; A Year Passed, 1952; After the Holiday, 1954; The Angel's Name, 1955; Seven in the Tower, 1958; The Apprentice Saint (US title: Memoirs of a Medieval Woman), 1964; Soldier in Paradise, 1965; The Great Flood, 1966; A Private View of Stanley Spencer, 1972; Maurice Collis Diaries, 1978; Impetuous Heart: The Story of Ethel Smyth, 1984. Contributor to periodicals. **Address:** 65 Cornwall Gardens, London SW7 4BD, England.

COLLIS, Rose. (born England), b. 1959. **Genres:** Biography. **Career:** Singer, songwriter, journalist, and writer. **Publications:** Portraits to the Wall: Historic Lesbian Lives Unveiled, 1994; (editor) Lesbian Pillow Book, 1995; A Trouser-wearing Character: The Life and Times of Nancy Spain, 1995; k. d. lang, 1999; (editor) Mammoth Book of Lesbian Erotica, 2000; Colonel Barker's Monstrous Regiment: A Tale of Female Husbandry, 2001. **Address:** c/o Author Mail, Carroll & Graf Publishers, 161 William Street, Floor 16, New York, NY 10038, U.S.A.

COLLISON, Gary. American, b. 1947. **Genres:** History. **Career:** Pennsylvania State University at York, professor of American studies and English, 1975-. Has reviewed grant proposals and appeared as a guest on radio and television programs. **Publications:** Shadrach Minkins: From Fugitive Slave to Citizen, 1997. Contributor to books and periodicals. **Address:** Penn State York, 1031 Edgecomb Ave, York, PA 17403, U.S.A. **Online address:** glc@psuvm.psu.edu

COLLISON, Kerry B(oyd). Australian, b. 1944. **Genres:** Novels. **Career:** Entrepreneur, novelist, and civil servant. Business owner in Indonesia, c. 1967-; consultant to foreign investors in Indonesia, 1970-76; project developer and supervisor for construction of villa estate of Coolibah, Puncak, Indonesia, 1976-81; founder or cofounder of more than twenty businesses in Indonesia; Topaz Satellite Network Ltd., Hong Kong, chief executive officer, 1989-95; co-founder of Australian educational institutions, including Beaufort College, Perth; freelance novelist, 1995-; government consultant. **Publications:** NOVELS. Indonesian Gold; The Fifth Season, 1998. ASIAN TRILOGY SERIES: The Tim-Tim Man, 1996, as The Timor Man, 1999; Merdeka Square, 1997, 2nd ed, Freedom Square, 1999; Jakarta, 1998; The Asian Trilogy (boxed set), 1999. OTHER: In Search of Recognition: The Leo Stach Story, 2000; (ed with P. Barrett) The Happy Warrior (poetry). **Address:** PO Box 1102, Hartwell, VIC 3124, Australia. **Online address:** author@sidharta.com.au

COLLUM, Danny Duncan. American, b. 1954. **Genres:** History. **Career:** Abraham Lincoln Brigade Archives, NYC, executive director, 1988-93; Rust College, Holly Springs, MS, assistant professor of English, 1999-. Abraham Lincoln Brigade Archives, member of board of governors. **Publications:** African Americans in the Spanish Civil War, 1992; Black and White Together, 1996. Work represented in anthologies. **Address:** Department of Humanities, Rust College, 150 Rust Ave., Holly Springs, MS 38635, U.S.A. **Online address:** pdcollum@dixie-net.com

COLLURA, Mary-Ellen Lang. Canadian, b. 1949. **Genres:** Young adult fiction. **Career:** Author of young-adult novels and educator. Schoolteacher,

District 72, Campbell River, British Columbia, Canada, 1972-; North Island Wildlife Rehabilitation Association, director, 1990-92; Transition House, director, 1994-96. **Publications:** YA NOVELS: Winners, 1985, as Jordy, 1988; Sunny, 1988; Dreamers, 1995. Author of a grade-seven study guide of Native American communities as portrayed in her novel Winners and in the novels Sweetgrass, by J. Hudson, and Brothers of the Heart, by J. Blos. **Address:** 4068 Barclay Rd., Campbell River, BC, Canada V9N 4Y6.

COLLVER, Michael. American, b. 1953. **Genres:** Music. **Career:** Longy School of Music, Cambridge, MA, faculty member. **Publications:** A Catalog of Music for the Cornett, 1996. **Address:** 14 King St., Lexington, MA 02421-6035, U.S.A.

COLMAN, Andrew. See PINE, Nicholas.

COLMAN, Carol. American. **Genres:** Adult non-fiction. **Publications:** Love and Money: What Your Finances Say about Your Personal Relationships-and How to Improve Them, 1983; (with Michael A. Perelman) Late Bloomers: How to Achieve Your Potential at Any Age, 1985; (with Stefan Semchyshyn) How to Prevent Miscarriage and Other Crises of Pregnancy, foreword by Frederick P. Zuspan, 1989; (with Marianne J. Legato) The Female Heart: The Truth about Women and Coronary Artery Disease, 1991; (with Carol J. Eagle) All That She Can Be: Helping Your Daughter Achieve Her Full Potential and Maintain Her Self-Esteem during the Critical Years of Adolescence, 1993. (with Robin Dibner) The Lupus Handbook for Women: Up-to-Date Information on Understanding and Managing the Disease Which Affects One in 500 Women, 1994; (with Walter Pierpaoli and William Regelson) The Melatonin Miracle: Nature's Age-reversing, Disease-fighting, Sex-enhancing Hormone, 1995; (with W. Norman Scott) Dr. Scott's Knee Book: Symptoms, Diagnosis, and Treatment of Knee Problems, Including Torn Cartilage, Ligament Damage, Arthritis, Tendinitis, Arthroscopic Surgery, and Total Knee Replacement, illustrations by Johanna Warshaw, 1996; (with William Regelson) The Superhormone Promise: Nature's Antidote to Aging, 1996; (with Marianne Legato) What Women Need to Know: From Headaches to Heart Disease and Everything in Between, 1997. (with Julian Whitaker) Shed Ten Years in Ten Weeks, 1997; (with Erika Schwartz) Natural Energy: From Tired to Terrific in Ten Days, 1998; (with Richard Brown and Teodoro Bottiglieri) Stop Depression Now: SAM-e, the Breakthrough Supplement That Works as Well as Prescription Drugs in Half the Time, with No Side Effects, 1999; (with Lester Packer) The Antioxidant Miracle: Put Lipoic Acid, Pycnogenol, and Vitamins E and C to Work for You, 1999; (with Lester Packer) The Antioxidant Miracle: Your Complete Plan for Total Health and Healing, 1999; (with Robert Rountree) Immunotics: A Revolutionary Way to Fight Infection, Beat Chronic Illness, and Stay Well, 2000; (with A. Scott Connelly) Body Rx: Dr. Scott Connelly's Six-Pack Prescription: Six Meals a Day, Six Weeks to Strength, Six Weeks to Sculpt, Six Weeks to Burn Fat, Six Weeks to Maintain = Six Months to a Great Body, 2001; (with Raphael Kellman) Gut Reactions: A Radical New Four-Step Program for Treating Chronic Stomach Distress and Unlocking the Secret to Total Body Wellness, 2002; (Gary Hevin) Curves: Permanent Results without Permanent Dieting, 2003; (with Gary Heavin) Curves on the Go, 2004. **Address:** c/o Author Mail, Putnam, 375 Hudson St., New York, NY 10014, U.S.A.

COLMAN, Clay. See PINE, Nicholas.

COLMAN, E. Adrian M. Australian (born Scotland), b. 1930. **Genres:** Literary criticism and history. **Career:** Professor Emeritus of English, University of Tasmania, since 1990 (Professor, 1978-90). Lecturer in English, University of New South Wales, 1962-70; Research Associate, The Shakespeare Institute, University of Birmingham, 1968-69; Sr. Lecturer, 1970-74, and Associate Professor, 1974-78, University of Sydney. Chairman of Board, Australian Theatre for Young People, 1975-78. **Publications:** Shakespeare's Julius Caesar, 1965; The Structure of Shakespeare's Antony and Cleopatra, 1971; The Dramatic Use of Bawdy in Shakespeare, 1974; Horizon Study of Shakespeare's Henry IV Part I, 1990. EDITOR: Poems of Sir Walter Raleigh, 1977; King Lear, 1982; Henry IV Part I, 1987; Romeo and Juliet, 1993.

COLMAN, Hila (Crayder). Also writes as Teresa Crayder. American. **Genres:** Novels, Young adult fiction, Documentaries/Reportage, Essays. **Career:** Writer, 1949-. Publicity/promotion officer, National War Relief Agency, NYC, 1940-45; Executive Director, Labor Book Club, NYC, 1945-47. **Publications:** YOUNG ADULT FICTION: The Big Step, 1957; A Crown for Gina, 1958; Julie Builds Her Castle, 1959; The Best Wedding Dress, 1960; The Girl from Puerto Rico, 1961; Mrs. Darling's Daughter, 1962; Watch That Watch, 1963; Peter's Brownstone House, 1963; Phoebe's First Campaign, 1963; Classmates by Request, 1964; The Boy Who Couldn't Make Up His Mind, 1965; Christmas Cruise, 1965; Bride at Eighteen, 1966;

Dangerous Summer, 1966; Car-Crazy Girl, 1967; Thoroughly Modern Millie (novelization of screenplay), 1967; Mixed-Marriage Daughter, 1968; Something Out of Nothing, 1968; Andy's Landmark House, 1969; Claudia, Where Are You?, 1969; The Happenings at North End School, 1970; Daughter of Discontent, 1971; End of the Game, 1971; The Family and the Fugitive, 1972; Benny the Misfit, 1973; Chicano Girl, 1973; Diary of a Frantic Kid Sister, 1973; Friends and Strangers on Location, 1974; After the Wedding, 1975; Ethan's Favorite Teacher, 1975; That's the Way It Is, Amigo, 1975; The Amazing Miss Laura, 1976; Nobody Has to Be a Kid Forever, 1976; The Case of the Stolen Bagels, 1977; Sometimes I Don't Love My Mother, 1977; Rachel's Legacy, 1978; The Secret Life of Harold, the Bird Watcher, 1978; Tell Me No Lies, 1978; Ellie's Inheritance, 1979; Accident, 1980; What's the Matter with the Dobsons?, 1980; Confessions of a Storyteller, 1981; The Family Trap, 1982; Not for Love, 1983; Just the Two of Us, 1984; Nobody Told Me What I Need to Know, 1984; Weekend Sisters, 1985; Suddenly, 1987; The Double Life of Angela Jones, 1988; Rich and Famous Like My Mom, 1988; Forgotten Girl, 1990. NON-FICTION FOR YOUNG ADULTS: Beauty, Brains and Glamour: A Career in Magazine Publishing, 1988; A Career in Medical Research, 1968; Making Movies: Student Films to Features, 1969; City Planning: What It's All About-In the Planners' Own Words, 1971. FOR ADULTS: The Country Weekend Cookbook, 1961; Hanging On, 1977. AS TERESA CRAYDER: Sudden Fame, 1966; Cathy and Lisette, 1964; Cleopatra, 1969. **Address:** 76 Hemlock Rd, Bridgewater, CT 06752, U.S.A.

COLMAN, Penny (Morgan). American, b. 1944. **Genres:** Young adult fiction, Young adult non-fiction, Biography. **Career:** Freelance writer and editor, 1975-; seminar leader and speaker, 1975-; United Presbyterian Church, NYC, program developer, 1977-81; Granger Galleries, NYC, founder and president, 1981-85; Center for Food Action, Englewood, NJ, executive director, 1986-87; Queens College, CUNY, distinguished lecturer, 2003-. Appointed to New Jersey Commission on Hunger, 1986, and New Jersey State Women Infant Children Advisory Council, 1987. Has appeared on radio and television programs. **Publications:** JUVENILE NONFICTION: Breaking the Chains: The Crusade of Dorothea Lynde Dix, 1992; Spies! Women and the Civil War, 1992; Fannie Lou Hamer and the Fight for the Vote, 1993; A Woman Unafraid: The Achievements of Frances Perkins, 1993; 101 Ways to Do Better in School, 1994; Madame C.J. Walker: Building a Business Empire, 1994; Mother Jones and the Children's Crusade, 1994; Toilets, Bathtubs, Sinks and Sewers: The History of the Bathroom, 1994; Rosie the Riveter, 1995; Corpse, Coffins, and Crypts, 1997; Girls: A History of Growing Up Female, 2000; Where the Action Was, 2002. JUVENILE FICTION: I Never Do Anything Bad, 1988; Dark Closets and Noises in the Night, 1991. ADULT NONFICTION: (ed.) Spiritual Disciplines for Everyday Living, 1982; Grand Canyon Magic, 1987; This Is Bergen County Where People Make a Difference, 1989; (with S. Chess and A. Thomas) Fifty Years Together: Researchers, Psychiatrists, Professors, and Parents, 1993; Equal Rights Amendment: A Curriculum Guide, 1993. OTHER: Dare to Seek (one-act play), 1976; Education Is the Key (script for videotape), 1988. Author and editor of human resource manuals. Contributor to periodicals. **Address:** 138 Knickerbocker Rd, Englewood, NJ 07631, U.S.A. **Online address:** www.pennycolman.com

COLODNY, Len. (Leonard). American, b. 1938. **Genres:** Politics/Government. **Career:** Private investigator and businessman. Colodny's Inc. (a liquor brokerage), Washington, DC, vice president, 1960-73, president, 1973-75; Colodny's of Maryland Inc., Landover, MD, president, 1973-79; Prince George's County Human Relations Commission, Maryland, member, 1973-78; private consultant, 1979-; political analyst and lecturer, 1991-; consultant for the television documentary John Ehrlichman-In the Eye of the Storm, American International Television, 1996-. **Publications:** (with R. Gettlin) Silent Coup: The Removal of a President, 1991, in UK as Silent Coup: The Removal of Richard Nixon, 1991. **Address:** 6909 Lake Place Ct., Tampa, FL 33634, U.S.A. **Online address:** len@colodny.com

COLOGNE-BROOKES, Gavin (John). British, b. 1961. **Genres:** Literary criticism and history. **Career:** University of Evansville, Harlaxton College, Grantham, England, assistant professor of English, 1988-92; Bath Spa University College, Bath, England, senior lecturer in English and creative studies, 1993-. **Publications:** The Novels of William Styron: From Harmony to History, 1995; (ed. with N. Sammells and D. Timms) Writing and America, 1996; Dark Eyes on America: The Novels of Joyce Carol Oates, 2005. **Address:** Dept of English, Bath Spa University College, Newton Park, Bath BA2 9BN, England. **Online address:** gcologne-brookes@bathspa.ac.uk

COLOMBO, John Robert. Canadian, b. 1936. **Genres:** Poetry, Literary criticism and history, Local history/Rural topics, Paranormal, Social com-

mentary, Bibliography. **Career:** Author and editor of books for Canadian publishing houses, 1960-; CBC-TV, host Colombo's Quotes, 1979; columnist for newspapers and periodicals; author, compiler, translator. **Publications:** Mostly Monsters, 1977; Variable Cloudiness, 1977; Private Parts, 1978; Colombo's Book of Canada, 1978; The Poets of Canada, 1978; (with others) CDN SF&F: A Bibliography of Canadian Science Fiction and Fantasy, 1979; Blackwood's Books, 1981; (with M. Richardson) Not to Be Taken at Night, 1981; Poems of the Inuit, 1981; Friendly Aliens, 1981; Years of Light, 1982; Selected Poems, 1982; Colombo's Canadiana Quiz Book, 1983; Rene Levesque Buys Canada Savings Bonds and Other Great Canadian Graffiti, 1983; Colombo's 101 Canadian Places, 1983; The Toronto Puzzle Book, 1984; Canadian Literary Landmarks, 1984; Great Moments in Canadian History, 1984; (with M. Richardson) We Stand on Guard, 1985; 1001 Questions about Canada, 1986; Colombo's New Canadian Quotations, 1987; Off Earth (poetry), 1987; Mysterious Canada, 1988; 999 Questions about Canada, 1989; Extraordinary Experiences, 1989; Songs of the Great Land, 1989; Mysterious Encounters, 1990; Quotations from Chairman Lamport, 1990; Mackenzie's Ghost, 1991; The Dictionary of Canadian Quotations, 1991; Walt Whitman's Canada, 1992; The Canadian Global Almanac, 1993, 1992; The Little Blue Book of Canadian UFOs, 1993; The Mystery of the Shaking Tent, 1993; Haunted Toronto, 1996; Shapely Places, 1996; Mysteries of Ontario, 1998; Ghost Stories of Canada, 2000; Colombo's Famous Lasting Words, 2000; Yet More Iron Curtains, 2000; Canadian Capers, 2000; Ghosts in Our Past, 2000; Half a World Away, 2000; Impromptus: 1,000 Poems, 2000; Incredible Canadiana, 2000; Open Secrets, 2000; Small Wonders, 2000; Three Mysteries of Nova Scotia, 2000; Weird Stories from 19th-Century Canadian Newspapers, 2000; Briefs, 2001; Far Star, 2001; The Humour of Us, 2001; Many Mysteries, 2001; 1000 Questions about Canada, 2001; The Penguin Book of Canadian Jokes, 2001; Half Life, 2002; Foundlings, 2002; Only in Canada, 2002; The Ukrainian and the Tractor and Other Canadian Jokes and Anecdotes, 2002; The Penguin Treasury of Popular Canadian Poems and Songs, 2002; Making Light, 2002; Say It Again, Sam, 2003; More or Less, 2003; True Canadian Ghost Stories, 2003; 100 Poems, 2003; O Rare Denis Saurat, 2003; The Denis Saurat Reader, 2004; The Native Series, 2004; The Monster Book of Canadian Monsters, 2004. EDITOR: Colombo's Canadian Quotations, 1974; Colombo's Little Book of Canadian Proverbs, Graffiti, Limericks, and Other Vital Matters, 1975; Colombo's Canadian References, 1976; (and trans. with N. Roussanoff) The Balkan Range: A Bulgarian Reader, 1976; East and West: Selected Poems by George Faludy, 1978; Colombo's Names and Nicknames, 1978; The Great Cities of Antiquity, 1979; Other Canadas: An Anthology of Science Fiction and Fantasy, 1979; Colombo's Hollywood, 1979; Colombo's Book of Marvels, 1979; The Canada Colouring Book, 1980; 222 Canadian Jokes, 1981; Colombo's Last Words, 1982; Colombo's Laws, 1982; Windigo, 1982; Songs of the Indians, 1983. TRANSLATOR: (with N. Roussanoff) Under the Eaves of a Forgotten Village: 60 Poems from Contemporary Bulgaria, 1975; (with N. Roussanoff) The Left-Handed One: Poems by Lyubomir Levchev, 1977; (with N. Roussanoff) Remember Me Well: Poems by Andrei Germanov, 1978; (with N. Roussanoff) Depths: Poems by Dora Gabe, 1978; Dark Times: Poems of Waclaw Iwaniuk, 1979; Such Times: Poems of Ewa Lipska, 1981; Far from You: Poems of Pavel Javor, 1981; Selected Translations, 1982; Beyond Labels: Poems of Robert Zend, 1982; Symmetries: Poems of Marin Sorescu, 1982; Learn This Poem of Mine by Heart: Poems of George Faludy, 1983. **Address:** 42 Dell Park Ave, Toronto, ON, Canada M6B 2T6. **Online address:** jrc@ca.inter.net; www.colombo.ca

COLQUHOUN, Keith. British, b. 1937. **Genres:** Novels. **Publications:** The Money Tree, 1959; Point of Stress, 1961; The Sugar Coating, 1973; St. Petersburg Rainbow, 1975; Goebbels and Gladys, 1981; Filthy Rich, 1982; Kiss of Life, 1983; Foreign Wars, 1985; Mad Dog, 1992; Killing Stalin, 2002. **Address:** The Old Rectory, East Mersea, Essex, Essex C05 8SZ, England.

COLSON, Charles W(endell). American, b. 1931. **Genres:** Theology/Religion, Autobiography/Memoirs. **Career:** Prison Fellowship Ministries, Washington, D.C., Founder and Chairman of the board, 1976-. Admitted to the Bar of Virginia, 1959, Washington, D.C., 1961, and Massachusetts, 1964; Assistant to the Assistant Secretary of the U.S. Navy, 1955-56; Administration Assistant to U.S. Senator Leverett Saltonstall, 1956-61; Partner, Gadsby and Hannah, Boston, 1961-69; Special Counsel to the President of the United States, Richard Nixon, 1969-73; Partner, Colson and Shapiro, Washington, D.C., 1973-74; Associate, Fellowship House, Washington, D.C., 1975-76. BreakPoint, radio commentator. **Publications:** Born Again, 1976; Life Sentence, 1979; Loving God, 1983; Who Speaks for God: Confronting the World with Real Christianity, 1985; Dare to Be Different, Dare to Be Christian, 1986; Presenting Belief in an Age of Unbelief, 1986; The Role of Church in Society, 1986; The Struggle for Men's Hearts and Minds, 1986; (with others) Christianity in Conflict: The Struggle for Christian Integrity and Freedom in Secular Culture, 1986; Kingdoms in Conflict, 1987; Against the Night, 1989; (with D. Van Ness) Convicted: New Hope for Ending America's Crime Crisis, 1989; (co-author) Christ in Easter, 1990; God of Stones and Spiders, 1990; (with J. Eckerd) Why America Doesn't Work, 1991; (with E.S. Vaughn) The Body, 1992; A Dance with Deception, 1993; (with N. Pearcey) A Dangerous Grace, 1994; (with E.S. Vaughn) Gideon's Torch, 1995; How Shall We Now Live, 2000. Contributor to newspapers. **Address:** c/o Prison Fellowship, 1856 Old Reston Ave, Reston, VA 20190, U.S.A.

COLSON, Elizabeth. American, b. 1917. **Genres:** Anthropology/Ethnology. **Career:** Rhodes-Livingstone Institute, Director, 1948-51; University of Manchester, England, Sr. Lecturer, 1951-53; Goucher College, Towson, MD, Associate Professor, 1953-55; Boston University, Massachusetts, African Studies Program, Research Associate and Associate Professor, 1955-59; Brandeis University, Waltham, MA, Professor, 1959-63; University of California at Berkeley, Professor, 1964-84, Professor Emeritus of Anthropology, 1984-. Visiting Professor, Northwestern University, Illinois, 1963-64 and University of Zambia, 1987. **Publications:** (with M. Gluckman) Seven Tribes of Central Africa, 1951; The Makah, 1953; Marriage and the Family among the Plateau Tonga, 1958; Social Organization of Gwembe Tonga, 1960; The Plateau Tonga, 1962; Social Consequences of Resettlement, 1971; Tradition and Contract, 1974; (with T. Scudder) Secondary Education and the Formation of an Elite, 1980; (with L. Ralston and J. Anderson) Voluntary Efforts in Decentralized Management, 1983; (ed. with S. Morgan) People in Upheaval, 1987; (with T. Scudder) For Prayer and Profit, 1988; History of Nampeyo, 1991. **Address:** Dept. of Anthropology, University of California, Berkeley, CA 94720, U.S.A. **Online address:** gwembe@uclink.berkeley.edu

COLT, George Howe. (born United States). **Genres:** Autobiography/Memoirs. **Career:** Life, former staff writer. **Publications:** The Enigma of Suicide, 1991; The Big House: A Century in the Life of an American Summer Home, 2003. Contributor to publications. **Address:** 160 Chestnut Plain Road, Whately, MA 01093, U.S.A.

COLTER, Dale. See BROOMALL, Robert W(alter).

COLTON, Clarence Eugene. American, b. 1914. **Genres:** Theology/Religion. **Career:** Pastor Emeritus, Royal Haven Baptist Church, Dallas, Texas, since 1987 (Pastor, 1939-87). Former Head of Bible Dept., Wayland Baptist College, Plainview, Texas. **Publications:** The Minister's Mission, 1951; Expository Studies of the Life of Christ, 1957; The Sermon on the Mount, 1960; Questions Christians Ask, 1969; As the Pendulum Swings, 1970; Meditations on the 23rd Psalm, 1978; Revelation: Book of Mystery and Hope, 1979; The Faithfulness of Faith, 1985; How to Be a Good Christian, 1986; A Good God and an Evil World, 1993; What's Next, 1994; A Twenty-first Century New Testament Church, 1998. **Address:** 8302 Midway Rd, Dallas, TX 75209, U.S.A.

COLTON, Joel. American, b. 1918. **Genres:** History. **Career:** Duke University, Durham, NC, Professor Emeritus, Dept. of History, 1989- (Professor, 1947-89; Chairman of Dept., 1967-74). Member, International Commission on the History of Social Movement and Social Structures, 1975- (Co-President, 1985-90). Fellow, American Academy of Arts and Sciences, 1979-. Director for Humanities, Rockefeller Foundation, 1974-81. Member, Board of Eds., Journal of Modern History, 1968-71; Member, Board of Eds., French Historical Studies, 1985-88; Advisory Board, Historical Abstracts, 1982-. **Publications:** Compulsory Labor Arbitration in France 1936-1939, 1951; (with R.R. Palmer) A History of the Modern World, 2nd ed., 1956, 9th ed. (with R.R. Palmer and L. Kramer), 2002; Leon Blum: Humanist in Politics, 1966, 1987; Time-Life Great Ages of Man series, Twentieth Century, 1968, rev. ed., 1980; (ed.) The Contemporary Humanities in International Context, 1976; The Search for a Value Consensus, 1978; The Restoration of the Liberal Arts Curriculum, 1979; (ed. with S. Bruchey) Technology, the Economy, and Society: The American Experience, 1986; (with others) The Academic's Handbook, 1988, 2nd ed., 1995; The French and Spanish Popular Fronts: Comparative Perspectives, 1989.

COLUMBUS, Chris(topher). American, b. 1959. **Genres:** Plays/Screenplays. **Career:** Screenwriter. Director of motion pictures. **Publications:** SCREENPLAYS: Reckless, 1984; Gremlins, 1984; Young Sherlock Holmes, 1985; The Goonies, 1985; Heartbreak Hotel, 1988; Only the Lonely, 1991; (with R. Outten) Little Nemo: Adventures in Slumberland, 1992; Nine Months, 1995; Jingle All the Way, 1996. TELEPLAYS: (with others) Galaxy High School (series), 1986. **Address:** c/o Jack Rapke, Creative Artists Agency, 9830 Wilshire Blvd., Beverly Hills, CA 90212, U.S.A.

COLVILE, Georgiana M. M. American. **Genres:** Literary criticism and history. **Career:** Writer. **Publications:** Vers un Langage des Arts Autour des Annees Vingt, 1977; Beyond and Beneath the Mantle: On Thomas Pynchon's The Crying of Lot 49, 1988; Blaise Cendrars Ecrivain Proteiforme, 1994. EDITOR: Contemporary Women Writing in the Other Americas: Contemporary Women Writing in the Caribbean, Vol. 2, 1996; Contemporary Women Writing in the Other Americas: Contemporary Women Writing in Canada and Quebec, Vol. 3, 1996. **Address:** c/o Edwin Mellen Press, PO Box 450, 415 Ridge St., Lewiston, NY 14092, U.S.A.

COLVIN, Sir H(oward) M(ontagu). British, b. 1919. **Genres:** Architecture, History. **Career:** Fellow Emeritus, St. John's College, Oxford, since 1987 (Fellow, 1948-87; Reader in Architectural History, Oxford University, 1965-87). Assistant Lecturer, University College, London, 1946-48. Member, Royal Fine Art Commission, 1962-72, Royal Commission on Historical Monuments, England, 1963-76, Historic Bldgs. Council for England, 1970-84, Royal Commission on Ancient and Historical Monuments of Scotland, 1977-89, Royal Commission on Historical Manuscripts, 1981-88, and Historic Bldgs. and Monuments Commission, 1984-85; President, Society of Architectural Historians of Great Britain, 1979-81. **Publications:** The White Canons in England, 1951; A Biographical Dictionary of English Architects 1660-1840, 1954; A History of Deddington, 1963; Catalogue of Architectural Drawings in Worcester College Library, 1964; (with M. Craig) Architectural Drawings in the Library of Elton Hall, 1964; Building Accounts of King Henry III, 1971; A Biographical Dictionary of British Architects 1600-1840, 1978, rev. ed., 1995; Unbuilt Oxford, 1983; Calke Abbey, Derbyshire, 1985; The Canterbury Quadrangle, St. John's College, Oxford, 1988; (with J.S.G. Simmons) All Souls: An Oxford College and Its Buildings, 1989; Architecture and the After-Life, 1991; Essays in English Architectural History, 1999. EDITOR: The History of the King's Works, 6 vols., 1963-82; (co-) The Country Seat, 1970; (co-) Of Architecture, by R. North, 1981. **Address:** 50 Plantation Rd, Oxford, England.

COLVIN, James. See MOORCOCK, Michael (John).

COMAROFF, Jean. American (born Scotland), b. 1946. **Genres:** Anthropology/Ethnology, Sociology. **Career:** University of Wales, University College of Swansea, research fellow in sociology and anthropology, 1971-73; Bolton Institute of Technology, Victoria University of Manchester, England, lecturer in anthropology, 1973-74, senior research fellow in medical sociology and anthropology, 1976-78; University of Chicago, Chicago, IL, assistant professor, 1978-84, associate professor, 1984-87, professor of anthropology and social sciences, 1987-, Nuveen Lecturer at Divinity School, 1989, Wirzup Lecturer at Woodward Court, 1992, Bernard E. & Ellen C. Sunny Distinguished Service Professor & Chairman, 1996. Harvard University, fellow of Bunting Institute, 1981-82; Ecole des Hautes Etudes en Sciences Sociales (Paris), director of studies, 1988; Duke University, visiting professor, 1989; University of Washington, Seattle, Olson Lecturer, 1989; Cornell University, Messenger Lecturer, 1991; University of Helsinki, Westermarlk Memorial Lecturer, 1993. Conducted field work among the Barolong boo Ratshidi of the South Africa-Botswana borderland, 1969-70, 1974-75. **Address:** Department of Anthropology, University of Chicago, 1126 East 59th St., Chicago, IL 60637, U.S.A.

COMBES, Simon. See Obituaries.

COMFORT, B(arbara). American, b. 1916. **Genres:** Mystery/Crime/Suspense. **Career:** Artist, with solo exhibitions of her work. Comfort Inc., designer of acrylics; Portraits Inc., member; Landgrove Press, director. **Publications:** MYSTERY NOVELS: Vermont Village Murder, 1982; Green Mountain Murder, 1986; Phoebe's Knee, 1986; Grave Consequences, 1989; The Cashmere Kid, 1993; Elusive Quarry, 1995; A Pair for the Queen, 1998. **Address:** RR1, 43 Uphill Rd 219, Londonderry, VT 05148, U.S.A.

COMFORT, Philip W(esley). American, b. 1950. **Genres:** Poetry, Theology/Religion. **Career:** Ohio State University, Columbus, instructor in English, 1983-84; Tyndale House Publishers, Wheaton, IL, senior editor of Bible reference works, 1984, and member, New Testament bible translation committee. College of DuPage, lecturer, 1984-87; Wheaton College, Wheaton, IL, visiting professor, 1987-98; North Park College, visiting professor, 1992-93; Trinity Episcopal Seminary, Pawleys Island, SC, adjunct professor, 1997-2000; Coastal Carolina University, instructor, 1998-; Columbia International University, Columbia, SC, professor, 1999-. International Greek New Testament Project: Gospel of John, American member. **Publications:** Early Manuscripts and Modern Translations of the New Testament, 1990, 2nd ed., 1996; (trans. with R. Brown) The New Greek-English Interlinear New Testament, 1990; The Complete Guide to Bible Versions, 1991, rev. ed.,

1996; The Quest for the Original Text of the New Testament, 1992; (with G. Comfort) Dying to Live, 1992; (with W. Hawley) Opening the Gospel of John, 1994; I Am the Way: A Spiritual Journey through the Gospel of John, 1994; The Books of the New Testament, 1999; Essential Guide to Bible Versions, 2000; Selected Poems, 2001; The Text of the Earliest New Testament Greek Manuscripts, 2001; (with E. Carpenter) Holman Treasury of Key Bible Words. POETRY WITH WIPF & STOCK: Oceanic, 2004; Spirit Journey, 2004; Jesus Speaks, 2004. EDITOR: (New Testament) New Living Translation, 1996; (with D. Barrett) The Complete Text of the Earliest New Testament Manuscripts, 1999; Life Application New Testament Commentary, 2001. EDITOR & CONTRIBUTOR: A New Commentary on the Whole Bible, 1990; The Origin of the Bible, 1992; (with J.D. Douglas) Who's Who in Christian History, 1992; (with D. Partner) The One Year Book of Poetry, 1999; (with W. Elwell) Tyndale Bible Dictionary, 2001. Contributor to reference books and periodicals. **Address:** 307 Hagley Rd, Pawleys Island, SC 29585, U.S.A. **Online address:** philcomfort@verizon.net

COMFORT, Ray. American (born New Zealand), b. 1949. **Genres:** Novels, How-to books, Philosophy, Theology/Religion, Autobiography/Memoirs, Humor/Satire. **Career:** Living Waters Publications, Bellflower, director. **Publications:** Hell's Best Kept Secret, 1989; How to Win Souls and Influence People; How to Prove the Existence of God; The Power of Darkness; The Key to Heaven, 1993; God Doesn't Believe in Atheists, 1993; Revival's Golden Key, 1993; Everyday Evangelism, 1995; The Secrets of Nostradamus Exposed, 1996; 101 Things Men Do to Annoy Their Wives; Comfort, the Feebleminded, 1997; The Undertaker's Nightmare; Life, Liberty and the Pursuit of Righteousness; The Mystery (novel); Miracle in the Making, 2002. **Address:** Living Water Publications, PO Box 1172, Bellflower, CA 90706, U.S.A. **Online address:** ray@raycomfort.com

COMINI, Alessandra. American, b. 1934. **Genres:** Art/Art history, History, Autobiography/Memoirs, Biography. **Career:** Columbia University, NYC, assistant professor, 1969-74; Southern Methodist University, Dallas, TX, university distinguished professor of art history, 1974-. **Publications:** Schiele in Prison, 1973; Gustav Klimt, 1975; Egon Schiele's Portraits, 1974; Egon Schiele, 1976; The Fantastic Art of Vienna, 1978; The Changing Image of Beethoven, 1987; Kathe Kollwitz, 1992; Egon Schiele Nudes, 1994; In Passionate Pursuit: A Memoir, 2004. Contributor to books. **Address:** Div. of Art History, Meadows School of the Arts, Southern Methodist University, PO Box 750356, Dallas, TX 75275, U.S.A. **Online address:** acomini@smu.edu

COMMONER, Barry. American, b. 1917. **Genres:** Environmental sciences/Ecology, Sciences, Social commentary. **Career:** Professor Emeritus of Earth and Environmental Sciences, 1987-, and Director, Center for the Biology of Natural Systems, 1981-, Queens College, Flushing, New York (Professor, 1981-87). Assistant in Biology, Harvard University, Cambridge, MA, 1938-40; Instructor, Queens College, NYC, 1940-42; Lt., U.S. Naval Reserve, 1942-46; Associate Ed., Science Illustrated, 1946-47. With Washington University, St. Louis: Associate Professor of Plant Physiology, 1947-53; Professor, 1953-81; Director, Center for the Biology of Natural Systems, 1965-81; Chairman, Dept. of Botany, 1965-69. Visiting Professor of Community Health, Albert Einstein College of Medicine, NYC, 1981-87; Visiting Distinguished Professor of Industrial Policy, University of Massachusetts Lowell, 1992. **Publications:** Science and Survival, 1966; The Closing Circle, 1971; Ecology and Social Action, 1973; (ed. with H. Boksenbaum) Energy and Human Welfare: A Critical Analysis, 3 vols., 1975; The Poverty of Power, 1976; Energy, 1976; The Politics of Energy, 1979; Making Peace with the Planet, 1990; also books in Italian. **Address:** CBNS, Queens College, H Harding 401, Flushing, NY 11367, U.S.A. **Online address:** barry_commoner@qc.edu

COMNENA, Anna. See SONNENBERG, Ben.

COMPESTINE, Ying Chang. Chinese, b. 1963. **Genres:** Food and Wine. **Career:** Teacher and author of cookbooks and children's literature. Former English teacher and government interpreter in China. **Publications:** Secrets of Fat-free Chinese Cooking, 1997; Cooking with Green Tea, 2000; The Runaway Rice Cake, 2001; The Story of Chopsticks, 2001; The Story of Noodles, 2001; Secrets from a Healthy Asian Kitchen, 2002; The Story of Kites, 2003; The Story of Paper, 2003. **Address:** c/o Sheldon Fogelman Agency Inc., 10 East 40th St., New York, NY 10016, U.S.A. **Online address:** yingc@csd.net

COMPTON, D(avid) G(uy). Also writes as Guy Compton, Frances Lynch. British, b. 1930. **Genres:** Mystery/Crime/Suspense, Romance/Historical, Science fiction/Fantasy. **Career:** Worked as stage electrician, furniture maker, salesman, docker, and postman; Ed., Reader's Digest Condensed Books,

London, 1969-81. **Publications:** The Quality of Mercy, 1965, 1970; Farewell, Earth's Bliss, 1966; The Silent Multitude, 1966; Synthajoy, 1968; The Palace, 1969; The Electric Crocodile (in U.S. as The Steel Crocodile), 1970; Chronocules, 1970, in U.K. as Hot Wireless Sets, Aspirin Tablets, The Sandpaper Sides of Used Matchboxes, and Something That Might Have Been Castor Oil, 1971; The Missionaries, 1972; The Unsleeping Eye, 1973, in U.K. as The Continuous Katherine Mortenhoe, 1974; A Usual Lunacy, 1978; Windows, 1979; Ascendancies, 1980; Scudder's Game, 1985; Ragnarok, 1991; Nomansland, 1993; Stammering: Its Nature, History, Causes & Cures (non-fiction), 1993; Justice City, 1994; Back of Town Blues, 1995. MYSTERY NOVELS AS GUY COMPTON: Too Many Murderers, 1962; Medium for Murder, 1963; Dead on Cue, 1964; Disguise for a Dead Gentleman, 1964; High Tide for a Hanging, 1965; And Murder Came Too, 1966. ROMANCE NOVELS AS FRANCES LYNCH: Twice Ten Thousand Miles, 1974, as Candle at Midnight, 1977; The Fine and Handsome Captain, 1975; Stranger at the Wedding, 1977; A Dangerous Magic, 1978; In the House of Dark Music, 1979. **Address:** 4 New St., Whitstable, Kent CT5 1HF, England.

COMPTON, Guy. See COMPTON, D(avid) G(uy).

COMPTON, James V(incent). American, b. 1928. **Genres:** History, International relations/Current affairs. **Career:** Professor of History, San Francisco State University, since 1969. Konrad Adenauer Fellow in History, University of Munich, 1954-55; Lecturer in History and Government, University of Maryland, College Park, 1956-64; Lecturer in History, and Chairman, Program of North American Studies, University of Edinburgh, 1964-68. **Publications:** The Swastika and the Eagle: Hitler, the United States, and the Origins of World War II, 1967; (ed.) America and the Origins of the Cold War, 1972; (consulting ed. with Orville Bullitt) For the President: Personal and Secret Correspondence between Ambassador William C. Bullitt and President Franklin D. Roosevelt, 1973; Anticommunism in American Life since World War II, 1973; (ed.) The New Deal, 1974. **Address:** 170 Diamond St, San Francisco, CA 94114, U.S.A.

COMPTON, Patricia A. American, b. 1936. **Genres:** Novels. **Career:** Laguna Salada School District, Pacifica, CA, art teacher, 1969-75; Pyramid Alternatives, Pacifica, art therapist, 1974-76; Laguna Salada Union School District, director and teacher at the Alternative School, 1975-76; Golden Gate University, San Francisco, CA, lecturer, 1976; J. F. Kennedy University, Orinda, CA, lecturer, 1977-78; City of Walnut Creek Civic Arts, supervisor of arts education, 1977-79; Montalvo Center for the Arts, Saratoga, CA, executive director, 1979-82; free-lance illustrator, textile designer, and writer, 1989-; The Art Scene, Valley Scene, columnist, 1997; Commonwealth Club/Silicon Valley, executive director, 1997-. **Publications:** The Terrible Eek, 1991. **Address:** 15040 Oriole Rd., Saratoga, CA 95070, U.S.A.

COMSTOCK, Gary D(avid). American, b. 1945. **Genres:** Gay and lesbian issues, Sociology, Theology/Religion. **Career:** Wesleyan University, Middletown, CT, university Protestant chaplain and visiting professor of sociology, 1990-. **Publications:** Violence against Lesbians and Gay Men, 1991; Gay Theology without Apology, 1993; Unrepentant, Self-Affirming, Practicing: Lesbian/Bisexual/Gay People within Organized Religion, 1996; (with S.E. Henking) Que(e)rying Religion: A Critical Anthology, 1997; A Whosoever Church: Welcoming Lesbians and Gay Men into African-American Congregations, 2001; The Work of a Gay College Chaplain: Becoming Ourselves in the Company of Others, 2002. **Address:** Wesleyan University, 171 Church St, Middletown, CT 06459, U.S.A.

CONANT, Michael. American, b. 1924. **Genres:** Economics, Law. **Career:** Practiced law in Chicago, IL, 1951-54; University of California, Berkeley, professor at Haas School of Business, 1954-. University of Singapore, visiting professor, 1964-65. Consultant economist in antitrust litigation. **Publications:** Antitrust in the Motion Picture Industry, 1960; Railroad Mergers and Abandonments, 1964; The Constitution and Capitalism, 1974; The Constitution and the Economy: Objective Theory and Critical Commentary, 1991; Constitutional Structure and Purposes, 2001. Contributor of articles and reviews to law and business journals. **Address:** Haas School of Business, 545 Student Services #1900, University of California, Berkeley, CA 94720, U.S.A. **Online address:** conant@haas.berkeley.edu

CONARD, Rebecca. American, b. 1946. **Genres:** History, Intellectual history, Regional/Urban planning. **Career:** American River College, Sacramento, CA, English faculty, 1976-78; Wichita State University, Wichita, KS, assistant professor of history and director of Public History Program, 1992-98; Middle Tennessee State University, associate professor, 1998-2003, co-director of Public History Program, 1998-, professor of history, 2003-. Tallgrass Historians, Iowa City, IA, co-founder, 1993, principal, 1993-.

Publications: (with C. Nelson) Santa Barbara: El Pueblo Viejo, 1986; Places of Quiet Beauty: Parks, Preserves, and Environmentalism, 1997; Benjamin Shambaugh and the Intellectual Foundations of Public History, 2002. Contributor to encyclopedias. Contributor to history journals and other academic periodicals. **Address:** Department of History, Box 23, Middle Tennessee State University, Murfreesboro, TN 37132, U.S.A. **Online address:** rconard@mtsu.edu

CONATI, Marcello. Italian, b. 1928. **Genres:** Music. **Career:** Pianist, composer, music teacher, and author. Director of the Centro Internazionale di Ricerca sui Periodici Musicali, Parma-Colorno; music teacher at the Conservatorio A. Boito, Parma; Comitato di Redazione Rivista Italiana di Musicologia, Bologna; Commissione Artistica Orchestra Sinfonica A Toscanini, Parma; Comitato Direttivo Instituto Gramsci, Parma; Consiglio d'Amministrazione Conservatorio A. Boito, Parma. **Publications:** Canti popolari della Val d'Enza e Val Cedra Palatina, 1976; (ed. with M. Medici) Carteggio Verdi-Boito, 1978, trans. by W. Weaver as The Verdi-Boito Correspondence, 1994; (ed.) Interviste e incontri con Verdi, 1980, trans. by R. Stokes as Interviews and Encounters with Verdi, 1984, also as Encounters with Verdi, 1984; La bottega della musica, 1983; Verdi: Rigoletto, Guida, 1983; La Musica, 1855. La Musica, 1857-1859, 1989; La Musica, 1876-1878. La Musica, 1883-1885, 1989; Strenna teatrale europea, 1838-1848, 1989; L'Italia musicale, 1847-1859, 1992; Rigoletto: Un'analisi drammatico-musicale (music criticism), 1992; Simon Boccanegra di Giuseppe Verdi, 1993; Verdi 2001: Vita e opere narrate ai giovani, 1999. **Address:** CIRPM, via Conservatorio 31/B, 43100 Parma, Italy. **Online address:** mconati@netvalley.it

CONES, John W. American, b. 1945. **Genres:** Film, Philosophy. **Career:** Radio and television news reporter in Texas, 1968-74; association manager and lobbyist in Texas and Chicago, IL, 1974-80; securities lawyer in Houston, TX, 1981-86; attorney, writer, and lecturer in Los Angeles, CA, 1987-. University of California, Los Angeles, adjunct professor of film and television; lecturer at colleges and institutes. **Publications:** Film Finance and Distribution: A Dictionary of Terms, 1992; 43 Ways to Finance Your Feature Film: A Comprehensive Analysis of Film Finance, 1995; Film Industry Contracts, 1996; Hollywood Corruption, 1996; How the Movie Wars Were Won, 1996; Legacy of the Hollywood Empire, 1996; Movie Picture Biographies: The Hollywood Spin on Historical Figures, 1996; Motion Picture Industry Reform, 1996; Patterns of Bias in Motion Picture Content, 1996; Politics, Movies and the Role of Government, 1996; A Study in Motion Picture Propaganda: Hollywood's Preferred Movie Messages, 1996; Who Really Controls Hollywood?, 1996; What's Really Going on in Hollywood, 1997; The Feature Film Distribution Deal: A Critical Analysis of the Single Most Important Film Industry Agreement, 1997; The Book of Secular Wisdom, 2003. **Address:** 5325 Residencia, Newport Beach, CA 92660, U.S.A. **Online address:** jwc6774@cox.net; www.mecfilms.com/guide4.htm

CONEY, Michael G(reatrex). British, b. 1932. **Genres:** Science fiction/Fantasy, Humor/Satire, Novellas/Short stories. **Career:** Auditor, Russell and Co., Birmingham, 1949-56; Sr. Clerk, Pearce Clayton Maunder, Dorchester, Dorset, 1958-61; Accountant, Pontins, Bournemouth, 1962; Tenant, Plymouth Breweries, Totnes, Devon, 1963-66; Accountant, Peplow Warren Fuller, Newton Abbot, Devon, 1966-69; Manager, Jabberwock Hotel, Antigua, W. Indies, 1969-72; Mgmt. Specialist, British Columbia Forest Service, 1973-89. **Publications:** Mirror Image, 1972; Syzygy, 1973; Friends Come in Boxes, 1973; The Hero of Downways, 1973; Winter's Children, 1974; Monitor Found in Orbit (short stories), 1974; The Jaws That Bite, The Claws That Catch (in U.K. as The Girl with a Symphony in Her Fingers), 1975; Hello Summer, Goodbye (in U.S. as Rax), 1975; Charisma, 1975; Brontomek!, 1976; The Ultimate Jungle, 1979; Neptune's Cauldron, 1981; Cat Karina, 1982; Forest Ranger, Ahoy!, 1983; The Celestial Steam Locomotive, 1983; Gods of the Greataway, 1984; Fang, the Gnome, 1988; King of the Scepter'd Isle, 1989; A Tomcat Called Sabrina, 1992; No Place for a Sealion, 1992. **Address:** 2082 Neptune Rd, North Saanich, BC, Canada V8L 5J5. **Online address:** mconey@islandnet.com

CONEY, Sandra. New Zealander, b. 1944. **Genres:** History, Area studies, Women's studies and issues. **Career:** Broadsheet (feminist magazine), founder, 1972, editor, 1972-85; freelance writer, 1985-. Auckland Medical Aid Centre, counselor, 1974-84; Women's Health Action Trust, director, 1986-; Expert Group on Cervical Cancer Screening, member, 1989-91; also worked with Auckland Fertility Action, 1985, and Auckland Women's Health Clinic, 1988. Member of Women's Health Committee and Health Research Council of New Zealand. **Publications:** Every Girl: A Social History of Women and the YWCA in Auckland, 1986; The Unfortunate Experiment, 1988; (Supervising editor) Salute to New Zealand, 1989; Out of the Frying Pan: Inflammatory Writings, 1972-1989, 1990; (with L. Potter) Hysterectomy,

1990; The Menopause Industry, 1991; The Great New Zealand Diary, 1992; (ed.) Unfinished Business: What Happened to the Cartwright Report?, 1993; Standing in the Sunshine: A History of New Zealand Women since They Won the Vote, 1993; I Do: 125 Years of Weddings in New Zealand, 1995. Contributor to books and periodicals. **Address:** P.O. Box 46148, Herne Bay, Auckland, New Zealand.

CONFER, Dennis W. American, b. 1941. **Genres:** How-to books, Recreation, Travel/Exploration, Autobiography/Memoirs. **Career:** U.S. Air Force, career officer, working as chaplain services supervisor, budget officer, auditor, and comptroller, 1959-80, retiring as major; Wily Ventures (outfitters of big game hunters and fishers), owner, manager, publisher, hunting and business consultant, 1981-; Alyeska Pipeline, budget analyst, 1981-82; Municipality of Anchorage, worked as controller, management analyst, and executive. **Publications:** Wily Ventures Equipment List, 1982; Hunt Alaska Now, 1982; Hunt Alaska Now: Self-Guiding for Trophy Moose and Caribou, 1997, rev. ed., 1999; Adventures of an Alaskan, 2003. Contributor to periodicals. **Address:** 2509 Kilkenny Circle, Anchorage, AK 99504, U.S.A. **Online address:** WilyV@gci.net

CONFIANT, Raphael. Martiniquian (born Guadeloupe), b. 1951. **Genres:** Poetry, Novels, Language/Linguistics, Plays/Screenplays. **Career:** Comparative linguist, poet, playwright, author, educator, and editor. English teacher, 1977-96; University of Antilles and Guyana, lecturer in languages and regional cultures, 1997-. Active in trade union activities. Founding member of newspapers and periodicals. **Publications:** Jou Bare (poems), 1979; Jik Deye do Bondye, 1979; Bitako-a, 1985; Kod Yanm, 1986; Marisose, 1987, trans. by L. Coverdale as Mamzelle Dragonfly, 2000; Le Negre et l'amiral, 1988; (with others) L'Éloge de la Creolite, 1989; Eau de café, 1991, trans. by J. Ferguson, 1999; (with P. Chamoiseau) Lettres Creoles: Tracées Antillaise et Continentales de la litterature, 1655-1975, 1991; Aime Cesaure: Une traverse paradoxale du siècle, 1993; Barrancos del alba: literature francocaribea novella, 1993; Ravines du devant-jour: Récit, 1993; (trans) J. Berry, A Robber in the Village, 1993; L'Allée des soupirs: Roman, 1994; Bassin des ouragans, 1994; Commandeur du sucre: Récit, 1994; Contes Creoles des Amériques, 1995; Les Maitres de la parole Creole, 1995; La Savane des petrifications, 1995; La Vièrge du grande rétour, 1996; La Dernière Java de Mama Josepha, 1997; Le Meurtre du Samedi-Gloria, 1997; (trans) E. Jones, Adventure on the Knos Plant, 1998; L'archet du Colonel: Roman, 1998; (ed.) Dictionnaire des Titim et Sirandes, 1998; Regisseur du Rhum: Récit, 1999; Cahier de romances, 2000; (with D. Damoison) Le Galion, 2000; (author of intro) L. Hearn, Two Years in the French West Indies, 2000; (ed.) Dictionnaire des Nelogismes Creoles, 2001; Brin d'Amour, 2001. Translator of work from English into Jamaican. **Address:** University of Antilles and Guyana, Campus Fouillole, Pointe a Pitre, Guyana. **Online address:** raphael. confiant@martinique.univag.fr

CONFORD, Ellen. American, b. 1942. **Genres:** Children's fiction. **Publications:** Impossible Possum, 1971; Why Can't I Be William?, 1972; Dreams of Victory, 1973; Felicia the Critic, 1973; The Luck of Pokey Bloom, 1974; Me and the Terrible Two, 1974; Just the Thing for Geraldine, 1975; Dear Lovey Hart, I Am Desperate, 1975; The Alfred G. Graebner Memorial High School Handbook of Rules and Regulations, 1976; And This Is Laura, 1977; Eugene the Brave, 1978; Hail, Hail Camp Timberwood, 1978; Anything for a Friend, 1979; We Interrupt This Semester for an Important Bulletin, 1979; The Revenge of the Incredible Dr. Rancid and His Youthful Assistant Jeffrey, 1980; Seven Days to a Brand-New Me, 1981; To All My Fans with Love from Sylvie, 1982; Lenny Kandell, Smart Aleck, 1983; If This Is Love, I'll Take Spaghetti, 1983; You Never Can Tell, 1984; Strictly for Laughs, 1985; Why Me?, 1985; A Royal Pain, 1986; A Job for Jenny Archer, 1988; A Case for Jenny Archer, 1988; Jenny Archer, Author, 1989; Genie with the Light Blue Hair, 1989; What's Cooking, Jenny Archer?, 1989; Jenny Archer to the Rescue, 1990; Can Do, Jenny Archer, 1990; Loving Someone Else, 1990; Dear Mom, Get Me Out of Here!, 1992; Nibble, Nibble, Jenny Archer, 1993; I Love You, I Hate You, Get Lost, 1994; Get the Picture, Jenny Archer?, 1994; Norman Newman: My Sister the Witch, 1995; Norman Newman & The Werewolf of Walnut Street, 1995; The Frog Princess of Pelham, 1997; Crush (stories), 1998; Diary of a Monster's Son, 1999. ANNABEL THE ACTRESS SERIES: Starring in: Gorilla My Dreams, 1999; Just a Little Extra, 2000; Hound of the Barkervilles, 2002; Camping It Up, 2005.

CONGDON, Kristin G. American, b. 1948. **Genres:** Art/Art history, Education. **Career:** Booth Residential Treatment Center, Wauwatosa, WI, education coordinator, 1978-79; Community Relations and Social Development Commission, Milwaukee, WI, coordinator, 1979; University of Oregon, Eugene, instructor, 1981-83; Bowling Green State University, Bowling Green, OH, assistant professor of art education, 1984-87; University of Central

Florida, Orlando, Jenkins Eminent Scholar in Community Arts, 1988-93, professor of art, 1996-2000, professor of art and philosophy, 2000-. Maude Kerns Art Center, member of education committee, 1981-83; Crealde Art Center, ArtReach advisory board, 1988-93. Executive producer of Memory Painting: The Art of Bernadine Stetzel, broadcast by WBGU-TV, 1987. **Publications:** Uncle Monday and Other Traditional Tales form Florida, 2001; Artists from Latin American Cultures, 2002. CO-EDITOR: Art in a Democracy, 1987; Pluralistic Approaches to Art Education, 1991; Women Art Educators III, 1993; Evaluating Art Education Programs in Community Centers, 1998; Remembering Others: Making Invisible Histories of Art Education Visible, 2000. **Address:** Art Department, Visual Arts Bldg., University of Central Florida, Orlando, FL 32816, U.S.A. **Online address:** kcongdon@pegasus.cc.ucf.ed

CONGDON, Lee (Walter). American, b. 1939. **Genres:** History, Intellectual history. **Career:** Encyclopaedia Britannica, Chicago, IL, editorial assistant, 1965, writer, 1967-68; James Madison University, Harrisonburg, VA, assistant professor, 1972-78, associate professor, 1978-83, professor of history, 1983-, Fulbright-Hays fellow in Hungary, 1977-78. Field reader for Fulbright-Hays Doctoral Dissertation Research Abroad and Faculty Research Abroad programs, 1978, 1980, 1982, 1984, 1987-88, 1992, 1994-95, 1997, 1999, 2002. Fulbright-Hays Group Projects Abroad and Foreign Curriculum Consultants programs, 1983, 1998. **Publications:** The Young Lukacs, 1983; Exile and Social Thought: Hungarian Intellectuals in Germany and Austria, 1919-1933, 1991; Seeing Red: Hungarian Intellectuals in Exile and the Challenge of Communism, 2001. Contributor to books on history. **Address:** Department of History, James Madison University, Harrisonburg, VA 22807, U.S.A. **Online address:** congdolw@jmu.edu

CONGER, Jay A. American, b. 1952. **Genres:** Business/Trade/Industry. **Career:** Solarex Corp., Rockville, MD, manager of international marketing, 1977-80; Harbridge House, Boston, MA, associate consultant, 1982-85; McGill University, Montreal, Quebec, assistant professor, 1985-90, associate professor of organizational behavior, 1990-93, professor, 1994-95; Jay A. Conger and Associates, president; Harvard Business School, visiting associate professor, 1992-93; University of Southern California, The Leadership Institute, chairman, 1995-. **Publications:** (with R.N. Kanungo) Charismatic Leadership, 1988; The Charismatic Leader: Behind the Mystique of Exceptional Leadership, 1989; Learning to Lead, 1992; Spirit at Work, 1994; Winning 'Em Over, 1998; The Leader's Change Handbook, 1998; (with R.N. Kanungo) Charismatic Leadership in Organizations, 1998; Building Leaders, 1999; (with E. Lawler and D. Finegold) Corporate Boards, 2001; (with C. Pearce) Shared Leadership, 2002. **Address:** Bridge Hall 2nd Fl, School of Business Administration, University of Southern California, Los Angeles, CA 90089-1421, U.S.A. **Online address:** jconger@london.edu

CONGER, John Janeway. American, b. 1921. **Genres:** Psychology. **Career:** Professor Emeritus of Clinical Psychology and Psychiatry, University of Colorado Health Sciences Center, Denver (joined faculty as Professor, 1953; Associate Dean, 1961-63; Vice President for Medical Affairs; Dean, 1963-70; Acting Chancellor, 1984-85). President, American Psychological Association, 1981. Vice Chairman, National Motor Vehicle Safety Advisory Council, U.S. Dept. of Transport, 1967-70; President's Commission on Mental Health, 1978-79; John D. and Catherine T. MacArthur Foundation, vice president and director, Health Program, 1980-83. **Publications:** Child Development and Personality, 1956, 7th ed., 1990; Readings in Child Development, 1964; Personality, Social Class and Delinquency, 1967; Adolescence and Youth: Psychological Development in a Changing World, 1977, 5th ed., 1997; Basic and Contemporary Issues in Developmental Psychology, 1975; Adolescence: Generation under Pressure, 1979; Essentials of Child Development and Personality, 1980; Readings in Child and Adolescent Development, 1980; The Shape of the Tree, 1993. **Address:** 130 S Birch St., Denver, CO 80246-1017, U.S.A.

CONGER, Syndy McMillen. American, b. 1942. **Genres:** Literary criticism and history. **Career:** Western Illinois University, Macomb, professor of English, and director of graduate studies in English, 1972-. **Publications:** Matthew G. Lewis, Charles Robert Maturin, and the Germans, 1977; (ed. with J.R. Welsch) Narrative Strategies: Original Essays in Film and Prose Fiction, 1980; (ed.) Sensibility in Transformation: Creative Resistance to Sentiment from the Augustans to the Romantics, 1989; Mary Wollstonecraft and the Language of Sensibility, 1989; (ed. with C. Hay) The Past as Prologue, 1994; (ed. with G. Olsen and F. Frank) Iconoclastic Departures: Mary Shelley after Frankenstein, 1997. **Address:** Department of English, Western Illinois University, Macomb, IL 61455, U.S.A. **Online address:** syndy_conger@wiu.edu

CONGRESS, Richard. American, b. 1943. **Genres:** Novellas/Short stories. **Career:** City University of New York System, New York, NY, teacher of

English as a second language at schools including Bronx Community College and LaGuardia Community College, 1988-93; Random Chance Records, New York, NY, owner, 1999-. **Publications:** Blues Mandolin Man, 2001. **Address:** 20 East Ninth St., Apt. 15B, New York, NY 10003, U.S.A. **Online address:** agnosticcat@yahoo.com

CONIGLIARO, Vincenzo. American (born Italy), b. 1928. **Genres:** Psychiatry, Psychology. **Career:** Fordham University, NYC, assistant professor, 1961-66, associate professor of psychiatry, 1967-86, professor, 1986-. Catholic Charities, Brooklyn, NY, senior psychiatrist and director of training at Guidance Clinics, 1961-63; St. Francis Monastery, co-founder and instructor at Institute of Pastoral Counseling, 1961-63; School of Theology for Laymen, lecturer, 1961-63; Roman Catholic Archdiocese of New York, member of professional advisory board, Family Life Bureau and Family Consultation Service, 1966-74; lecturer at seminaries and medical centers; consultant to Academy of the Sacred Heart and to Roman Catholic religious orders. Postgraduate Center for Mental Health, lecturer and staff psychiatrist in community mental health and public education, 1963-66; Iona College, assistant professor, 1963-66, associate professor, 1966-68, co-founder of Graduate School of Pastoral Counseling and staff member, 1963-68; Metropolitan Consultation Center, lecturer, 1963-68, medical director, 1966-; Training Institute for Mental Health Practitioners, training analyst, senior supervisor, medical director, and member of board of trustees and board of directors, all 1968-, dean and president, 1978-; lecturer at colleges and universities; guest on television and radio programs. **Publications:** Dreams as a Tool in Psychodynamic Psychotherapy: The Royal Road to the Unconscious, 1997. Contributor to medical journals, popular magazines, and religious periodicals in the United States and Italy. **Address:** 22 W 21st St Fl 10, New York, NY 10010-6904, U.S.A.

CONKLIN, John E. American, b. 1943. **Genres:** Art/Art history, Criminology/True Crime, Sociology. **Career:** Harvard Law School, Center for Criminal Justice, Cambridge, MA, research associate, 1969-70; Tufts University, Medford, MA, professor of sociology, 1970-. **Publications:** Robbery and the Criminal Justice System, 1972; The Impact of Crime, 1975; Illegal But Not Criminal: Business Crime in America, 1977; Criminology, 1981, 8th ed., 2004; Sociology: An Introduction, 1984, 1987; Art Crime, 1994; Why Crime Rates Fell, 2003. EDITOR: The Crime Establishment: Organized Crime and American Society, 1973; New Perspectives in Criminology, 1996. **Address:** Dept of Sociology, Eaton Hall, Tufts University, Medford, MA 02155, U.S.A. **Online address:** john.conklin@tufts.edu

CONLEY, Carolyn A. American. **Genres:** Criminology/True Crime, History. **Career:** University of Alabama at Birmingham, assistant professor, 1985-92, associate professor, 1992-99, director of graduate studies in history, 1993-2002, professor of history, 1999-. **Publications:** The Unwritten Law: Criminal Justice in Victorian Kent, 1991; Melancholy Accidents: The Meaning of Violence in Post-Famine Ireland, 1999. Contributor of articles and reviews to academic journals. **Address:** Department of History, University of Alabama at Birmingham, 1530 3rd Ave S, Birmingham, AL 35294-3350, U.S.A. **Online address:** cconley@uab.edu

CONLEY, Tom (Clark). American, b. 1943. **Genres:** Film, Literary criticism and history, Translations. **Career:** University of Minnesota-Twin Cities, assistant professor, 1971-75, associate professor, 1975-79, professor of French, 1979-95; University of Minnesota, head of Department of French and Italian, 1983-88; Harvard University, Cambridge, MA, professor of Romance languages, 1995-. Visiting professor and lecturer at colleges and universities. **Publications:** Film Hieroglyphs: Ruptures in Classical Cinema, 1991; The Graphic Unconscious in Early Modern French Writing, 1992; The Self Made Map: Cartographic Writing in Early Modern France, 1996; A Map in a Movie, 2005. CO-EDITOR: Rethinking Technologies, 1993; (with S. Ungar) Identity Papers: Contested Nationhood in Twentieth-Century France, 1996. TRANSLATOR: (and author of intro.) M. de Certeau, The Writing of History, 1988; (and author of intro.) G. Deleuze, The Fold: Leibniz and the Baroque, 1993; (and author of intro.) J.L. Schefer, The Deluge, the Plague: Paolo Uccello, 1994; R. Bensmaia, A Year of Passages (novel), 1995; de Certeau, The Abduction of Speech, 1997; de Certeau, Culture in the Plural, 1997; C. Sacib, The Sovereign Map, 2005. Contributor to books. Contributor of articles and reviews to periodicals. **Address:** Dept of Romance Languages, 201 Boylston Hall, Harvard University, Cambridge, MA 02138, U.S.A. **Online address:** tconley@far.harvard.edu

CONLIN, Diane Atnally. American. **Genres:** History. **Career:** University of Michigan, Ann Arbor, former instructor in Roman art and archeology; University of Colorado, currently assistant professor of classics and archaeology. **Publications:** The Artists of the Ara Pacis: The Process of Hellenization in Roman Relief Sculpture, 1997. **Address:** University of Colorado, Department of Classics and Fine Arts, Boulder, CO 80309, U.S.A. **Online address:** Conlind@Colorado.edu

CONLON, Evelyn. Irish, b. 1952. **Genres:** Novels, Novellas/Short stories. **Career:** Writer-in-residence at Dublin City Library, Dublin, Ireland, and in County Kilkenny and County Cavan, both Ireland; worked as a reviewer and a broadcaster. Founder of a creche (nursery), Maynooth, Ireland, and founding member of the Dublin Rape Crisis Centre, Dublin, Ireland. **Publications:** SHORT STORIES: My Head Is Opening, 1987; Taking Scarlet As a Real Colour, 1993; (author of intro) M. Lavin, Tales from Bective Bridge, 1996; Telling: New and Selected Stories, 2000. NOVELS: Stars in the Daytime, 1989; A Glassful of Letters, 1998. OTHER: Where Did I Come From? (for children), 1982; author of film scripts. **Address:** c/o Blackstaff Press, Blackstaff House, Wildflower Way, Apollo Rd., Belfast BT12 6TA, Northern Ireland. **Online address:** mail@evelynconlon.com

CONLON, Kathleen (Annie). Also writes as Kate North. British, b. 1943. **Genres:** Novels. **Career:** Writer. **Publications:** Apollo's Summer Look, 1968; Tomorrow's Fortune, 1971; My Father's House, 1972; A Twisted Skein, 1975; A Move in the Game, 1979; A Forgotten Season, 1980; Consequences, 1981, in US as Developments, 1982; The Best of Friends, 1984; Face Values, 1985; Distant Relations, 1989; Unfinished Business, 1990; (as Kate North) Land of My Dreams, 1997. **Address:** 26A Brighton Rd, Birkdale, Southport PR8 4DD, England.

CONLON-MCKENNA, Marita. Irish, b. 1956. **Genres:** Children's fiction, Picture/board books, Novels. **Publications:** CHILDREN'S FICTION: My First Holy Communion, 1990; Under the Hawthorn Tree: Children of the Famine, 1990; Wildflower Girl, 1992; The Blue Horse, 1993; Little Star, 1993; The Very Last Unicorn, 1994; No Goodbye, 1994; Safe Harbour, 1995; Fields of Home, 1996; In Deep Dark Wood, 1999; Granny Macginty, 1999. NOVELS: The Magdalen, 1999; Promised Land, 2000; Miracle Woman, 2002. **Address:** Homewood, 50 Stillorgan Grove, Blackrock, Dublin, Ireland.

CONN, Didi. (born United States), b. 1951. **Genres:** Film. **Career:** Actress. Actress in films, television., and stage productions. **Publications:** Mommy, Give Me a Drinka Water (recording; for children), 1995; Frenchy's Grease Scrapbook: We'll Always Be Together!, 1998. **Address:** William Morris Agency, 151 South El Camino Dr., Beverly Hills, CA 90212, U.S.A.

CONN, Stewart. British (born Scotland), b. 1936. **Genres:** Plays/Screenplays, Poetry, Essays. **Career:** BBC Scotland, sr. radio drama producer, 1972-92; freelance writer and reviewer, 1992-. Poet laureate of Edinburgh, 2002. **Publications:** POETRY: Thunder in the Air: Poems, 1967; The Chinese Tower, 1967; Stoats in the Sunlight: Poems (in U.S. as Ambush and Other Poems), 1968; An Ear to the Ground, 1972; Under the Ice, 1978; In the Kibble Palace, 1987; The Luncheon of the Boating Party, 1992; In the Blood, 1995; At the Aviary, 1995; Stolen Light, 1999; L'anima del teixidor, 2000; Ghosts at Cockcrow, 2005. PLAYS: The Burning, 1971; Thistlewood, 1975; The Aquarium & Other Plays, 1976; Play Donkey, 1977; Hugh Miller, 2002. ESSAYS: Distances, 2000. **Address:** 1 Fettes Row, Edinburgh EH3 6SF, Scotland. **Online address:** stewart@jsconn.freeserve.co.uk

CONNELL, Evan S(helby). American, b. 1924. **Genres:** Novels, Novellas/Short stories, Biography. **Career:** Contact mag., Sausalito, CA, editor, 1960-65. **Publications:** The Anatomy Lesson and Other Stories, 1957; Mrs. Bridge, 1959; The Patriot, 1960; Notes from a Bottle Found on the Beach at Carmel, 1963; At the Crossroads: Stories, 1965; The Diary of a Rapist, 1966; Mr. Bridge, 1969; Points for a Compass Rose, 1973; The Connoisseur, 1974; Double Honeymoon, 1976; A Long Desire, 1979; The White Lantern, 1980; St. Augustine's Pigeon, 1980; Son of the Morning Star: Custer and the Little Bighorn, 1984; The Alchymist's Journal, 1991; Collected Stories of Evan S. Connell, 1995; Mesa Verde, 1992; Deus Lo Volt! Chronicle of the Crusades, 2000; The Aztec Treasure House, 2001. EDITOR: I Am a Lover, by Jerry Stoll, 1961; Woman by Three, 1969; Francisco Goya, 2004. **Address:** Fort Marcy 13, 320 Artist Rd, Santa Fe, NM 87501, U.S.A.

CONNELL, George B(oyce), (II). American, b. 1957. **Genres:** Philosophy. **Career:** Mercer University, Macon, GA, visiting instructor in philosophy, 1982; North Carolina State University, Raleigh, visiting associate professor of philosophy, 1984; North Carolina Wesleyan College, Rocky Mount, assistant professor of philosophy, 1984-86; Concordia College, Moorhead, MN, assistant professor, 1986-90, associate professor, 1990-. **Publications:** To Be One Thing: Personal Unity in Kierkegaard's Thought, 1985; (ed. with C. Stephen Evans, and contrib.) Foundations of Kierkegaard's Vi-

sion of Community: Kierkegaard on Religion, Ethics, and Politics, 1992. Contributor of articles and reviews to philosophy journals and religious magazines. **Address:** Department of Philosophy, Concordia College, Moorhead, MN 56562, U.S.A.

CONNELL, John. Australian (born United Kingdom), b. 1946. **Genres:** Anthropology/Ethnology, Area studies, Geography. **Career:** Geographer, educator, author. Sydney University, Australia, professor of geography. Directed the South Pacific Commission-International Labor Organization project on Migration, Employment and Development in the South Pacific. **Publications:** Migration from Rural Areas, 1976; (with M. Lipton) Assessing Village Labour Situations in Developing Countries, 1977; The End of Tradition, 1978; Taim Bilong Mani, 1978; Remittances and Rural Development, 1980; (with R. Howitt) Mining and Indigenous Peoples in Australasia, 1991; (with J. Lea) Planning the Future: Melanesian Cities in 2010, 1993; (with J. Lea) Pacific 2010: Urbanisation in Polynesia, 1995; Papua New Guinea: The Struggle for Development, 1997; (with R. Aldrich) The Last Colonies, 1998; (wih J. Lea) Urbanisation in the Island Pacific, 2002; (with C. Gibson) Sound Tracks: Popular Music, Identity and Place, 2003; (with C. Gibson) Music Tourism: On the Road Again, 2005. EDITOR: Local Government Councils in Bougainville, 1977; Traditional Medicine in Bougainville, 1980; (with M. Spencer and A. Ward) New Caledonia: Essays in Nationalism and Dependency, 1988; (with R. Aldrich) France in World Politics, 1989; (with R. King and P. White) Writing across Worlds, 1995; (with Howitt and P. Hirsch) Resources, Nations, and Indigenous Peoples, 1996; (with R. King) Small Worlds, Global Lives: Islands and Migration, 1999; Sydney, the Emergence of a World City, 2000. **Address:** Division of Geography, Madsen 475, University of Sydney, Sydney, NSW 2006, Australia. **Online address:** jconnell@mail.usyd.edu.au

CONNELLY, Frances S(usan). American. **Genres:** Art/Art history. **Career:** Ithaca College, Ithaca, NY, assistant professor of art history, 1983-88; University of Missouri-Kansas City, assistant professor, 1988-94, associate professor of art history, 1994-, head of department, 1995-. **Publications:** The Sleep of Reason: Primitivism in Modern European Art and Aesthetics, 1995. Contributor to scholarly journals. **Address:** Department of Art History, University of Missouri-Kansas City, Kansas City, MO 64110, U.S.A.

CONNELLY, Joe. American, b. 1963. **Genres:** Novels. **Career:** Writer. Worked ten years as a paramedic. **Publications:** Bringing Out the Dead, 1998. **Address:** c/o Alfred A. Knopf Inc., 201 East 50th St., New York, NY 10022, U.S.A.

CONNELLY, Karen. Canadian, b. 1969. **Genres:** Poetry, Travel/Exploration. **Career:** Writer. Writer in residence at University of New Brunswick, Fredericton, 1994-. **Publications:** The Small Words in My Body (poetry), 1990; Touch the Dragon: A Thai Journal, 1993; This Brighter Prison: A Book of Journeys, 1993; One Room in a Castle; The Disorder of Love; Dawn without Breaking, 1999. Work represented in anthologies. **Address:** c/o Turnstone Press, 607-100 Arthur St., Winnipeg, MB, Canada R3B 1H3.

CONNELLY, Michael. American, b. 1956. **Genres:** Novels. **Career:** Worked as a newspaper reporter in Florida and for Los Angeles Times; became a full-time novelist. **Publications:** NOVELS: The Black Echo, 1992; The Black Ice, 1993; The Concrete Blonde, 1994; The Last Coyote, 1995; The Poet, 1996; Trunk Music, 1997; Void Moon, 2000; A Darkness More Than Night, 2001; City of Bones, 2002; Chasing the Dime, 2002; Lost Light, 2003; The Narrows, 2004. **Address:** c/o Philip G. Spitzer Literary Agency, 50 Talmage Farm Lane, East Hampton, NY 11937, U.S.A.

CONNER, Patrick (Roy Mountifort). British, b. 1947. **Genres:** Art/Art history, Social sciences. **Career:** Director, Martyn Gregory Gall., since 1986. Keeper of Fine Art, The Royal Pavilion, Art Gallery and Museums, Brighton, 1975-86. **Publications:** Savage Ruskin, 1979; Oriental Architecture in the West, 1979; People at Home, 1982; People at Work, 1982; (ed.) The Inspiration of Egypt, 1983; Michael Angelo Rooker 1746-1801, 1984; The China Trade, 1986; Hilda May Gordon: A Colourist Abroad, 1987; George Chinnery (1774-1852), Artist of India and the China Coast, 1993. **Address:** Martyn Gregory Gallery, 34 Bury St, London SW1, England. **Online address:** mgregory@dircon.co.uk

CONNOLLY, John. Irish, b. 1968. **Genres:** Mystery/Crime/Suspense. **Career:** Author and journalist. Worked as a bartender, waiter, and government official. **Publications:** Bad Men, 2003. CHARLIE PARKER SERIES: Every Dead Thing, 1999; Dark Hollow, 2000; The Killing Kind, 2001; The White

Road, 2002. Contributor to periodicals. **Address:** c/o Author Mail, Hodder & Stoughton, 338 Euston Rd., London NW1 3BH, England. **Online address:** www.johnconnolly.co.uk

CONNOLLY, Joseph. British, b. 1950. **Genres:** Novels, Design, Fashion/Costume, Recreation, Writing/Journalism, Bibliography, Humor/Satire. **Career:** Free-lance writer, 1970-. Affiliated with Hutchinson Publishing Group, Ltd., London, England, 1968-70; owner and manager of Flask Bookshop, London, 1974-89. Regular feature writer for British newspapers. **Publications:** Collecting Modern First Editions, 1977; P.G. Wodehouse: An Illustrated Biography, with Complete Bibliography and Collector's Guide, 1979, rev. ed., 1987; Jerome K. Jerome: A Critical Biography, 1982; Modern First Editions: Their Value to Collectors, 1984, 4th ed., 1993; Children's Modern First Editions: Their Value to Collectors, 1988; The Book Quiz Book, 1985; Poor Souls, 1995; This Is It, 1996; Stuff, 1997; Summer Things, 1998; Beside the Seaside, 1999; Winter Breaks, 1999; It Can't Go On, 2000; All Shook Up, 2000; S.O.S., 2001. **Address:** c/o Giles Gordon, Curtis Brown, Haymarket, London W1, England.

CONNOLLY, Paul. *See* WICKER, Tom.

CONNOLLY, Peter. British, b. 1935. **Genres:** History. **Career:** Hon. Research Fellow, Institute of Archaeology, London, since 1986. Member, Society for Promotion of Roman Studies, since 1963, and Society for Promotion of Hellenic Studies, since 1974. Fellow, Society of Antiquaries, London, since 1985. **Publications:** The Roman Army, 1976; The Greek Armies, 1977; Hannibal and the Enemies of Rome, 1978; Pompeii, 1979; Greece and Rome at War, 1980; Living in the Time of Jesus of Nazareth, 1983; The Legend of Odysseus, 1986; Tiberius Claudius Maximus, 2 vols., 1988; The Roman Fort, 1991; Greek Legends, 1993; The Ancient City, 1998.

CONNOLLY, Ray. British, b. 1940. **Genres:** Novels, Plays/Screenplays, Biography. **Career:** Journalist. **Publications:** A Girl Who Came to Stay: That'll Be the Day (screenplay), 1973; Stardust (screenplay), 1974; Trick or Treat?, 1975; James Dean: The First American Teenager (documentary film), 1975; Newsdeath, 1978; A Sunday Kind of Woman, 1980; Honky Tonk Heroes (TV trilogy), 1980; John Lennon 1940-1980 (biography), 1981; The Sun Place, 1981; Stardust Memories (anthology of journalism), 1983; Forever Young (screenplay), 1984; Lytton's Diary (TV series), 1985-86; Defrosting the Fridge (screenplay), 1989; Perfect Scoundrels (TV series), 1990; Sunday Morning, 1992; Shadows on a Wall, 1994; (ed.) In the Sixties (anthology of journalism), 1995. **Address:** c/o Rogers, Coleridge & White Ltd, 20 Powis Mews, London W11 1JN, England.

CONNOLLY, S(ean) J. Irish, b. 1951. **Genres:** History. **Career:** Public Record Office of Ireland, archivist, 1977-80; St. Patrick's College, Dublin, Ireland, lecturer in history, 1980-81; University of Ulster, Coleraine, Northern Ireland, lecturer, 1981-89, reader in history, 1989-96; Queen's University of Belfast, professor of Irish History, 1996-. Irish Economic and Social History, Editor, 1983-89. **Publications:** Priests and People in Pre-Famine Ireland, 1982; Religion, Law, and Power: The Making of Protestant Ireland, 1660-1760, 1992; (gen. ed.) The Oxford Companion to Irish History, 1998. **Address:** School of History, Queen's University, Belfast BT7 1NN, Northern Ireland.

CONNOLLY, William E(ugene). American, b. 1938. **Genres:** Politics/Government. **Career:** Ohio University, Athens, assistant professor of political science, 1965-68; University of Massachusetts, Amherst, associate professor, 1968-; currently professor and chair of political science department, Johns Hopkins University, Baltimore, MD. University of Michigan, visiting assistant professor, 1968; Amherst College, visiting associate professor, 1972. **Publications:** Political Science and Ideology, 1967; (comp. with G. Gordon) Social Structure and Political Theory, 1974; The Terms of Political Discourse, 1974, 3rd ed, 1993; (with M.H. Best) The Politicized Economy, 1976, 2nd ed. 1982; Appearance and Reality in Politics, 1981; Politics and Ambiguity, 1987; Political Theory and Modernity, 1988, new ed, 1993; Identity/Difference: Democratic Negotiations of Political Paradox, 1991; The Augustine Imperative: A Reflection on the Politics of Morality, 1993; The Ethos of Pluralization, 1995; Why I Am Not a Secularist, 1999; Neuropolitics: Thinking, Culture, Speed, 2002. EDITOR: The Bias of Pluralism, 1969; Legitimacy and the State, 1984; (with A. Botwinick) Democracy and Vision: Sheldon Wolin and the Vicissitudes of the Political, 2001. Contributor to journals. **Address:** Department of Political Science, 338 Mergenthaler Hall, Johns Hopkins University, Baltimore, MD 21218, U.S.A. **Online address:** pluma@jhu.edu

CONNON, Bryan (James Milne). British, b. 1927. **Genres:** Plays/Screenplays, Literary criticism and history, Theatre, Biography. **Career:**
Researcher, 1954-61, public relations, 1962-68; National Westminster Bank, London, publicity manager, 1969-71; Joint Credit Card Company, London, advertising manager, 1971-73; National Westminster Bank, head of advertising and publicity, 1975-82. Lecturer on theater and cinema. Scriptwriter, critic, and broadcaster. **Publications:** Beverley Nichols, a Life (biography), 1991; W. Somerset Maugham and the Maugham Dynasty, 1997. Contributor to books. **Address:** Sudbrook Edge, 14 Arlington Rd, Eastbourne, Sussex BN21 1DJ, England. **Online address:** Connon@Sudbrookedge.freeserve.co.uk

CONNOR, Joan. American, b. 1954. **Genres:** Novellas/Short stories. **Career:** Vermont Department of Public Health, representative of Women's Health Outreach Program, 1977-79; English teacher at schools in Woodstock, VT, 1979, 1980, and Philadelphia, PA, 1980-83; Ohio University, Athens, visiting professor, 1995-96, associate professor of English, 1996-. Vermont League of Writers, leader of fiction writing workshop, 1994-95; judge of fiction contests; gives readings from her works. **Publications:** Here on Old Route 7, 1997; We Who Live Apart, 2000; History Lessons, 2003. Work represented in anthologies. Contributor of articles, poems, and reviews to magazines. **Address:** Department of English, 327 Ellis Hall, Ohio University, Athens, OH 45701, U.S.A. **Online address:** connor@ohiou.edu

CONNOR, Steven. British, b. 1955. **Genres:** Literary criticism and history. **Career:** University of London, Birkbeck College, England, professor of modern literature & theory, 1979-. **Publications:** Charles Dickens, 1985; Samuel Beckett: Repetition, Theory, and Text, 1988; Postmodernist Culture: An Introduction to Theories of the Contemporary, 1989; Theory and Cultural Value, 1992; The English Novel in History, 1950 to the Present, 1995; James Joyce, 1996; Dumbstruck: A Cultural History of Ventriloquism, 2000; The Book of Skin, 2004s. **Address:** School of English and Humanities, Birkbeck College, University of London, Malet St, London WC1E 7HX, England. **Online address:** s.connor@bbk.ac.uk

CONNOR, Tony. (John Anthony Augustus Connor). American (born England), b. 1930. **Genres:** Plays/Screenplays, Poetry, Translations. **Career:** Professor of English, Wesleyan University, Middletown, Conn., since 1971 (Visiting Poet and Lecturer, 1968-69). Textile designer, Manchester, 1944-60; Assistant in Liberal Studies, Bolton Technical College, Lancs., 1961-64; Visiting Poet, Amherst College, Massachusetts, 1965-68. **Publications:** POETRY: With Love Somehow: Poems, 1962; Lodgers: Poems, 1965; (with A. Clarke and C. Tomlinson) Poems: A Selection, 1964; 12 Secret Poems, 1965; Kon in Springtime: Poems, 1968; In the Happy Valley: Poems, 1971; The Memoirs of Uncle Harry, 1974; Seven Last Poems from the Memoirs of Uncle Harry, 1974; New and Selected Poems, 1982; Metamorphic Adventures (poems), 1996. PLAYS: Billy's Wonderful Kettle, 1971; I Am Real and So Are You, A Visit from the Family, and Crewe Station at 2 A.M., 1971; The Last of the Feinsteins, 1973; Dr. Crankenheim's Mixed-up Monster (play), 1974; David's Violin, 1976; Explorations, 1982. OTHER: (trans. with G. Gomori) Love of the Scorching Wind, by L. Nagy, 1973; Twelve Villanelles, 1977; Spirits of the Place, 1986. **Address:** 44 Brainerd Ave, Middletown, CT 06457, U.S.A.

CONNOR, William S. P. American, b. 1958. **Genres:** Essays. **Career:** WCSH-TV, Portland, ME, reporter and news anchor, 1986-94; Hearst Television, Washington, DC, White House correspondent, 1994-97; Evergreen Media Counselors, Washington, DC, senior consultant, 1997-. **Publications:** (with C. Hacinli) Romantic Days and Nights in Washington, DC, 1998. **Address:** Evergreen Media Counselors, 1100 17th St. N.W. Suite 1200, Washington, DC 20036, U.S.A. **Online address:** bconnor@mediatrainer.com

CONNORS, Bruton. (Edward Rohen). British, b. 1931. **Genres:** Novels, Novellas/Short stories, Poetry. **Career:** Served in Korea, 1952-54; Ministry of Supply machine gun inspector, 1954-56; Art Teacher, Ladysmith Jr.-Sr. High School, Canada, 1956-57; Head of the Art Dept., St. Bonaventure's School, 1958-73; Art Teacher, Ilford County High School, 1973-82. **Publications:** Nightpriest, 1965; Bruised Concourse, 1973; Old Drunk Eyes Haiku, 1974; Scorpio Broadside 15, 1975; Poems/Poemas, 1976. **Address:** 57 Kinfauns Rd, Goodmayes, Ilford, Essex IG3 9QH, England.

CONOVER, Roger L(loyd). American, b. 1950. **Genres:** Poetry, Literary criticism and history, Biography. **Career:** Worked as a milkman, theater manager, and lobster fisherman, 1970-75; writing instructor at University of Minnesota, 1976; acquisition editor in art, architecture, photography, and design for MIT Press, 1977-93. Member of boards and commissions. Member of writers' organizations. **Publications:** (ed. and author of intro) M. Loy, The Last Lunar Baedeker (poetry), 1982, new ed., 1996; Insel (novel), 1991; Arthur Cravan: Poete et Boxeur, 1992; Four Dada Suicides (criticism), 1995;

Boxes: An Anthology of Writings on Boxing and Visual Culture (criticism), 1996. Author of poems, essays, and articles. **Address:** 55 Lambert Rd., Freeport, ME 04032, U.S.A.

CONQUEST, Ned. (Edwin Parker Conquest, Jr). American, b. 1931. **Genres:** Novels, Plays/Screenplays, Songs/Lyrics and libretti, Poetry. **Career:** Lieutenant, ROTC Commission in U.S. Army Field Artillery, Germany, 1955-57; Associate, Milbank, Tweed, Hadley & McCloy, law firm, NYC, 1960-64; Assistant Professor of English Literature, Georgetown University, Washington, D.C., 1967-73. **Publications:** The Gun and Glory of Granite Hendley, 1969; Achilles and Company, 1988; Virginia, the Gray and the Green, 1990; The Way of the Eagle, 1994; The Widow's Might, 1997. **Address:** 1547 33rd St. NW, Washington, DC 20007, U.S.A.

CONQUEST, (George) Robert (Acworth). Also writes as Ted Pauker, Victor Gray. American/British, b. 1917. **Genres:** Science fiction/Fantasy, Poetry, History, International relations/Current affairs, Literary criticism and history. **Career:** Sr. Research Fellow, Hoover Institution, Stanford, CA, 1977-79, 1981-. With U.K. Army, 1939-46; Diplomatic Service, 1946-56; Fellow, London School of Economics, 1956-58; Literary Ed., The Spectator, London, 1962-63; Fellow, Columbia University, NYC, 1964-65; and Woodrow Wilson International Center, 1976-77. **Publications:** A World of Difference (novel), 1955; Poems, 1955; Common Sense About Russia, 1960; Courage of Genius: The Pasternak Affair, 1961; Between Mars and Venus (poetry), 1962; Power and Policy in the U.S.S.R., 1962; (with K. Amis) The Egyptologists (novel), 1965; Russia after Khrushchev, 1965; The Great Terror, 1968; Arias from a Love Opera (poetry), 1969; The Nation Killers, 1970; Lenin, 1972; Kolyma, 1978; Forays (poetry), 1979; Present Danger: Towards a Foreign Policy, 1979; The Abomination of Moab, 1979; We and They, 1980; (with Jon Manchip White) What to Do When the Russians Come: A Survivor's Guide, 1984; Inside Stalin's Secret Police: NKVD Politics 1936-39, 1985; The Harvest of Sorrow: Soviet Collectivization and the Terror Famine, 1986; New and Collected Poems, 1988; Stalin and the Kirov Murder, 1989; Tyrants and Typewriters, 1989; The Great Terror: A Reassessment, 1990; Stalin: Breaker of Nations, 1991; Reflections on a Ravaged Century, 1999; Demons Don't (poetry), 1999. EDITOR: New Lines I, 1956; Back to Life, 1958; (with K. Amis) Spectrum: A Science Fiction Anthology, 5 vols., 1961-65; New Lines II, 1963; Soviet Studies Series, 7 vols., 1968; The Last Empire: Nationality and the Soviet Future, 1986. **Address:** 52 Peter Coutts Circle, Stanford, CA 94305, U.S.A.

CONRAD, Jean. See MARTINEZ, Nancy C.

CONRAD, Margaret R. Canadian, b. 1946. **Genres:** History. **Career:** Clarke, Irwin Publishing, Toronto, ON, Canada, editor, 1968-69; Acadia University, Wolfville, NS, Canada, member of faculty, 1969-87, professor of history, 1987-2002, department head, 1992-95, founding member of planter studies committee, beginning 1984; University of New Brunswick, Fredericton, Canada Research Chair in Atlantic Canada Studies, 2002-; visiting lecturer; Dalhousie University, adjunct professor, 1991-2002; Mount Saint Vincent University, Nancy Rowell Jackman Chair of Women's Studies, 1996-98; speaker at educational institutions. Jury member for history and creative or scholarly writing competitions. Producer of video programs on contemporary Canada and the Atlantic region of Canada; workshop coordinator and presenter; guest on media programs. Royal Society of Canada, fellow, 1995; Officer of the Order of Canada, 2004. **Publications:** (with J. Ricker) Twentieth-Century Canada, 1974; George Nowlan: Maritime Conservative in National Politics, 1986; (with T. Laidlaw and D. Smyth) No Place Like Home: The Diaries and Letters of Nova Scotia Women, 1771-1938, 1988; (with others) History of the Canadian Peoples, 2 vols., 1993, 3rd ed., 2002; (with J. Hiller) Atlantic Canada, 2001; Canada: A National History, 2002. EDITOR: They Planted Well: New England Planters in Maritime Canada, 1988; Making Adjustments: Change and Continuity in Planter Nova Scotia, 1759-1800, 1991; (supervising) J.A. Norton, comp., New England Planters in Maritime Canada, 1759-1800: Bibliography of Sources, 1993; Intimate Relations: Family and Community in Planter Nova Scotia, 1759-1800, 1995; Saturday's Child: The Memoirs of Ellen Louks Fairclough, 1995; Looking into Acadie: 3 Illustrated Lectures, 1999; (and contrib.) Active Engagements: A Collection of Lectures by the Holders of Nancy's Chair in Women's Studies, 1986-1998, 2001; (with B. Moody) Planter Links: Culture and Community in Colonial Nova Scotia, 2001. Contributor to books. Contributor of articles and reviews to professional journals and newspapers. **Address:** Dept of History, University of New Brunswick, Fredericton, NB, Canada E3B 5A3. **Online address:** mconrad@unb.ca

CONRAD, Peter. American, b. 1945. **Genres:** Sociology. **Career:** Drake University, Des Moines, IA, assistant professor of sociology, 1975-78; Bran-

deis University, Waltham, MA, professor of sociology, 1979-. Gadjah Mada University, visiting scholar, 1989-90; McMaster University, Hooker Distinguished Visiting Professor, 1992; Queen's University of Belfast, Distinguished Fulbright Scholar, 1997. **Publications:** Identifying Hyperactive Children, 1976; (with J.W. Schneider) Deviance and Medicalization: From Badness to Sickness, 1980, rev. ed., 1992; Sociology of Health and Illness: Critical Perspectives, 1981, 6th ed., 2001; (with J.W. Schneider) Having Epilepsy, 1983; (with E. Gallagher) Health and Health Care in Developing Countries, 1993; (co-ed.) Handbook of Medical Sociology, 5th ed., 2000. **Address:** Department of Sociology, Brandeis University, MS-71, PO Box 9110, Waltham, MA 02454, U.S.A. **Online address:** conrad@brandeis.edu

CONRADI, Peter J(ohn). British, b. 1945. **Genres:** Literary criticism and history. **Career:** Kingston University, Kingston on Thames, England, professor of English, 1981-97, emeritus, 1997-. University of Colorado, Boulder, visiting professor of English, 1978-80; University of East Anglia, visiting lecturer, 1981; British Council reader in English at Jagiellonian University, Krakow, 1990-92; University College London, honorary research fellow, 1998; Magdalen College, Oxford, visiting fellow, 1999. **Publications:** John Fowles, 1982, rev. ed., 1983; Iris Murdoch: The Saint and the Artist, 1986, 2nd ed., 1989; Dostoevsky, 1988; Angus Wilson, 1997; (ed.) I. Murdoch, Existentialists & Mystics, 1997; Iris Murdoch: A Life, 2001; Going Buddhist, 2004. **Address:** c/o Bill Hamilton, A.M. Heath & Co, 79 St Martin's Ln, London WC2N 4AA, England.

CONRAN, Shirley (Ida). British, b. 1932. **Genres:** Novels, Design, Women's studies and issues, Adult non-fiction. **Career:** Co-Founder and Co-Owner, Conran Fabrics Ltd., 1957-. Editorial Adviser, Sidgwick and Jackson Ltd., London. Home Ed., Daily Mail, London, 1962; Women's Ed., London 1963-68; Women's Ed., Daily Mail, 1968; Design and Promotion Consultant, Westinghouse Kitchens, London, 1969; Columnist, Vanity Fair mag., 1970-71; Life and Styles Ed., Over 21 mag., 1972; Wrote "Survival" series, Daily Mirror, 1974. Handled publicity for Women in Media Equal Rights campaigns, 1972-74. **Publications:** Superwoman, 1975; Superwoman Yearbook, 1976; Superwoman 2 (in U.S. as Superwoman in Action), 1977; (with E. Sidney) Futures: How to Survive Life after Thirty, 1979; Lace (novel), 1982; The Magic Garden, 1983; Lace 2, 1985; Savages, 1987; Down with Superwoman, 1990; The Amazing Umbrella Shop, 1990; Crimson, 1992; Tiger Eyes, 1994; Starstruck, 1998. **Address:** 19 Regent's Park Terr, London NW1 7ED, England.

CONROY, John. American, b. 1951. **Genres:** History, Politics/Government. **Career:** Chicago Guide (now Chicago), Chicago, IL, senior editor, 1974-76; Reader, Chicago, staff writer, 1978-; writer. **Publications:** NONFICTION: Belfast Diary: War as a Way of Life, 1987; Unspeakable Acts, Ordinary People: The Dynamics of Torture, 2000. **Address:** c/o Wendy Weil, 232 Madison Ave Ste 1300, New York, NY 10016, U.S.A.

CONROY, (Donald) Pat(rick). American, b. 1945. **Genres:** Novels, Plays/Screenplays, Education, Autobiography/Memoirs, Biography. **Publications:** The Boo, 1970; The Water Is Wide, 1972; The Great Santini, 1976; The Lords of Discipline, 1980; The Prince of Tides, 1986; Beach Music, 1995; My Losing Season, 2002. SCREENPLAYS: Invictus (for TV), 1988; (with B. Johnson) The Prince of Tides, 1991; Beach Music 1997. **Address:** c/o Nan A. Talese/Doubleday Publicity, 1745 Broadway, New York, NY 10019, U.S.A. **Online address:** www.patconroy.com

CONSTABLE, Giles. American (born England), b. 1929. **Genres:** History. **Career:** Harvard University, Cambridge, MA, assistant professor, became associate professor, 1958-66; Lea Professor of medieval history, 1966-77; professor of history, 1977-. Dumbarton Oaks Research Library and Collection, Washington, DC, member of board of scholars, 1973-80; director, 1977-; senior fellow, 1980-. Center for Advanced Studies in Medieval Civilization, Poitiers, France, lecturer, 1961; Catholic University of America, visiting professor, 1978-. Speculum, assistant editor, 1958-78. Writer and editor. **Publications:** Monastic Tithes from Their Origins to the Twelfth Century, 1964; (ed.) The Letters of Peter the Venerable, 2 vols, 1967; (ed. with B. Smith) Libellus De Diversis Ordinibus et Professionibus Qui Sunt in Aecclesia: Orders and Callings of the Church, 1972; Medieval Monasticism: A Select Bibliography, 1976; Cluniac Studies, 1980; Attitudes Toward Self-Inflicted Suffering in the Middle Ages, 1982; (with A.P. Kazhdan) People and Power in Byzantium: An Introduction to Modern Byzantine Studies, 1982; (ed. with R.L. Benson and C.D. Lanham) Renaissance and Renewal in the Twelfth Century, 1982; (author of intro) Apolgiae Duae, edited by R.B.C. Haygens, 1985; Monks, Hermits, and Crusaders in Medieval Europe, 1988; (ed. with T. Evergates) The Cartulary and Charters of Notre-Dame of Homblieres, 1990; (ed. with E.H. Beatson and L. Dainelli) The Letters between

Bernard Berenson and Charles Henry Coster, 1993; Three Studies in Medieval Religious and Social Thought, 1995. Editor of scholarly journals. **Address:** 506 Quaker Rd., Princeton, NJ 08540, U.S.A.

CONSTANT, Stephen. (Stephen Constantine Daneff). British (born Bulgaria), b. 1931. **Genres:** Biography. **Career:** Special Correspondent for the Daily Express, London, 1956-61, and for the Daily Telegraph, London, 1961-73. **Publications:** Foxy Ferdinand, Tsar of Bulgaria, 1979. **Address:** 66 Earlsfield Rd, London SW18, England.

CONSTANTELOS, Demetrios J. American (born Greece), b. 1927. **Genres:** History, Human relations/Parenting, Humanities, Theology/Religion. **Career:** Charles Cooper Townsend Distinguished Professor of History and Religious Studies, Richard Stockton College of New Jersey, Pomona, 1971-, now emeritus. Assistant Professor, and Associate Professor of History, Hellenic College, Brookline, MA, 1965-71; Ed., Greek Orthodox Theological Review, Brookline, 1966-71; Boston College, visiting professor, 1967-68; New York University, 1992. **Publications:** The Greek Orthodox Church, 1967; Byzantine Philanthropy and Social Welfare, 1968, 1991; Marriage, Sexuality and Celibacy, 1975; Understanding the Greek Orthodox Church, 1982, 1990; Poverty, Society, and Philanthropy in the Late Medieval Greek World, 1992; Vizantine Kleronomia, 1990; Ethnike Tautoteta kai Threskeutike Idiaiteroteta tou Hellenismou, 1993; The Greeks: Their Heritage and Its Value Today, 1996; Christian Hellenism, 1998. EDITOR: Encyclicals and Documents of the Greek Orthodox Archdiocese 1922-1972, 1976; Orthodox Theology and Diakonia, 1981; Visions and Expectations for a Living Church, 1998; Anemizoda Rasa, 2 vols., 1999; The Torch Bearer, Vol. 1, 1999, Vol. 2, 2001; Paterika meletemata Kai Ekklesiastika Themata, 1999; Paideia, 2001. **Address:** 304 Forest Dr, Linwood, NJ 08221, U.S.A. **Online address:** Demetrios.Constantelos@stockton.edu; Djconstantelos@aol.com

CONSTANTINE, David (John). British, b. 1944. **Genres:** Novels, Novellas/Short stories, Poetry, Literary criticism and history, Translations. **Career:** University of Durham, lecturer, then sr. lecturer in German, 1969-81; Queens College, Oxford, fellow in German, 1981-2000. **Publications:** POETRY: A Brightness to Cast Shadows, 1980; Watching for Dolphins, 1983; (with R. Pybus) Talitha Cumi, 1983; Mappa Mundi, 1984; Madder, 1987; Selected Poems, 1992; Caspar Hauser (long poem), 1994; The Pelt of Wasps, 1998; Something for the Ghosts, 2002; A Poetry Primer, 2004; Collected Poems, 2004. TRANSLATOR: Selected Poems of Holderlin, 1990; (with H. Constantine) H. Michaux: Deplacements Degagements, 1990; J.W. von Goethe, Die Wahlverwandtschaften, 1994; (with M. Treharne) P. Jaccottet, Under Clouded Skies, 1994; Selected Writings of Heinrich von Kleist, 1997; H.M. Enzensberger, Lighter than Air, 2002. OTHER: The Significance of Locality in the Poetry of Friederich Holderlin, 1976; (ed.) German Short Stories 2, 1976; Early Greek Travellers and the Hellenic Ideal, 1984; Davies (novel), 1985; Holderlin, 1988; Back at the Spike (short stories), 1994; A Living Language, 2004. **Address:** 1 Hill Top Rd, Oxford OX4 1PB, England.

CONSTANTINE, Storm. British, b. 1956. **Genres:** Science fiction/Fantasy, Novels. **Career:** Freelance writer, c. 1987; finance officer in Staffordshire, England, 1990. **Publications:** "WRAETHTHU" NOVELS: The Enchantments of Flesh and Spirit, 1987; The Bewitchments of Love and Hate, 1988; The Fulfillments of Fate and Desire, 1989. OTHER NOVELS: The Monstrous Regiment, 1989; Hermetech, 1991; Aleph, 1991; Burying the Shadow, 1992; Sign for the Sacred, 1993; Calenture, 1994; Stalking Tender Prey, 1995; Scenting Hallowed Blood, 1996. **Address:** 35 Ingestre Rd., Stafford ST17 4DJ, England.

CONSTANTINE-SIMMS, Delroy. (born England), b. 1964. **Genres:** Sex. **Career:** Open University, Milton Keynes, England, tutor and counselor, 1990-92; University of Kingston, London, England, research assistant, 1994-95; University of Hertfordshire, Aldenham, England, research fellow, 1995-96; Barnet College of Further Education, London, lecturer, 1997-2000; Multi-cultural Media Foundation, London, news editor, 2000-. University of North Carolina-Chapel Hill, research associate at Sonja Haynes Black Cultural Center, 1996. **Publications:** (editor, with V. Showunmi, and contrib.) Teachers for the Future, 1995; (editor and contriutor.) The Greatest Taboo: Homosexuality in Black Communities, 2001; Hitler's Forgotten Black Victims, forthcoming. Contributor to periodicals. **Address:** Multi-cultural Media Foundation, POB 13258, London E1 2RR, England. **Online address:** delroysimms@yahoo.com

CONTEH-MORGAN, Earl. American (born Sierra Leone), b. 1950. **Genres:** Politics/Government, International relations/Current affairs. **Career:** Northwestern University, Evanston, IL, instructor in political science, 1981-82 and 1985; University of South Florida, Tampa, visiting assistant

professor, 1985-88, assistant professor, 1988-92, associate professor, 1993-98, professor of international studies, 1998-. Oakton Community College, adjunct professor, 1985; Eckerd College, adjunct professor, 1989; guest on media programs; consultant on development, peace, and war issues. **Publications:** American Foreign Aid and Global Power Projection: The Geopolitics of Resource Allocation, 1990; Japan and the United States: Global Dimensions of Economic Power, 1992; Democratization in Africa: The Theory and Dynamics of Political Transitions, 1997; (ed. with K. Magyar, and contrib.) Peacekeeping in Africa: ECOMOG in Liberia, 1998; (with M. Dixon-Fyle) Sierra Leone at the End of the Twentieth Century: History, Politics, and Society, 1999. Contributor to books. Contributor of articles and reviews to academic journals. **Address:** Department of Government and International Affairs, University of South Florida, 4202 East Fowler Ave., SOC 107, Tampa, FL 33620, U.S.A. **Online address:** conteh-m@luna.cas.usf.edu

CONTI, Gregory. Italian. **Genres:** Translations. **Career:** University of Perugia, Italy, professor of English; translator. **Publications:** TRANSLATOR: E. Deaglio, The Banality of Goodness: The Story of Giorgio Perlasca, 1998; R. Loy, First Words: A Childhood in Fascist Italy, 2000. Contributor to periodicals. **Address:** Borgo XX, Gingno S4, 06121 Perugia, Italy.

CONVERSE, Philip E. American, b. 1928. **Genres:** Politics/Government. **Career:** Assistant Professor, 1960-63, Associate Professor, 1963-65, Professor of Sociology and Political Science, 1965-75, Robert C. Angell Distinguished Professor of Political Science and Sociology, 1975-89, Director of Center for Political Studies, 1982-86, and Director of Institute for Social Research, 1986-89, University of Michigan, Ann Arbor; Director, Center for Advanced Study in the Behavioral Sciences, Stanford, California, 1989-94. President, International Society of Political Psychology, 1980-81; President, American Political Science Association, 1983-84. **Publications:** The American Voter, 1960; The Nature of Belief Systems in Mass Publics, 1964; Elections and the Political Order, 1966; The Human Meaning of Social Change, 1972; The Quality of American Life, 1976; Political Representation in France, 1986.

CONWAY, Alan. British, b. 1920. **Genres:** History. **Career:** Professor of American History, University of Canterbury, Christchurch, since 1967, now Emeritus. **Publications:** The Welsh in America, 1961; (co-author) Hanes yr Unol Daleithiau, 1965; The Reconstruction of Georgia, 1966; History of the Negro in the United States, 1968; (co-author) Soldier-Surgeon: The Crimean War Letters of Douglas A. Reid 1855-56, 1968. **Address:** 11 Clissold St, Christchurch, New Zealand.

CONWAY, Diana C(ohen). American, b. 1943. **Genres:** Children's fiction. **Career:** Anchorage Community College, Anchorage, AK, Spanish teacher, 1971-87; University of Alaska, Anchorage, professor of Spanish, 1987-89. **Publications:** Northern Lights: A Hanukkah Story, 1994; Darren's Work, 1998. Contributor of stories to children's periodicals. **Address:** Box 6461, Halibut Cove, AK 99603, U.S.A.

CONWAY, Jill Ker. American (born Australia), b. 1934. **Genres:** Women's studies and issues, Administration/Management, Humanities. **Career:** University of Sydney, Sydney, Australia, lecturer in history, 1958-60; Harvard University, Cambridge, Mass., teaching fellow, 1961-63; University of Toronto, Toronto, Ontario, lecturer, 1964-68, assistant professor, 1968-70, associate professor of history, 1970-75, vice-president of internal affairs, 1973-75; Smith College, Northampton, Mass., president and Sophia Smith Professor of History, 1975-85; Massachusetts Institute of Technology, Cambridge, visiting scholar in Program in Science, Technology, and Society, 1985-. **Publications:** The Female Experience in Eighteenth- and Nineteenth-Century America: A Guide to the History of American Women, 1982; The First Generation of American Women Graduates, 1987; (ed. with S. Bourque and J. Scott) Learning about Women, 1989; The Road from Coorain: An Autobiography, 1989; (ed.) Written By Herself, 1992, vol. II, 1996; (ed. with S.C. Bourque) The Politics of Women's Education, 1993; True North, 1994; A Woman's Education, 2001. **Address:** Massachusetts Institute of Technology, Building E-51, Room 209, Cambridge, MA 02139, U.S.A.

CONWAY, Martha. American. **Genres:** Adult non-fiction. **Career:** Author; writes a regular column for the Web site Enterzone. **Publications:** 12 Bliss Street, 2003. Contributor to anthologies. **Address:** c/o Matt Williams, The Gernet Co., 136 East 57th. St., New York, NY 10022, U.S.A. **Online address:** twelvebliss@yahoo.com

COOGAN, Michael D(avid). American, b. 1942. **Genres:** Archaeology/Antiquities, Theology/Religion. **Career:** Educator and author. Fordham University, adjunct summer instructor, 1966, 1969; Wilfrid Laurier

University, Waterloo, Ontario, Canada, adjunct assistant professor, 1972-74; St. Jerome's College, University of Waterloo, Waterloo, Ontario, Canada, assistant professor, 1971-74; W. F. Albright Institute of Archaeological Research, Jerusalem, Israel, professor of archaeology, 1975-76; Harvard University, Cambridge, MA, visiting lecturer, 1976-77, assistant professor, 1977-80, associate professor, 1980-85, visiting professor, 1989-90, 1994-95, 1997-98, director of publications, Harvard Semitic Museum, 1998-; Wellesley College, Wellesley, MA, visiting professor, 1986-89; Stonehill College, Easton, MA, associate professor, 1985-88, professor, 1988-. Archaeological expeditions include Tell Gezer, Israel, volunteer, 1968; Tell el-Hesi, Israel, area supervisor, 1970-71, field supervisor, 1973-75; Idalion, Cyprus, field supervisor, 1974; Wadi Tumilat Project, Egypt, associate director, 1977; and Southeast Dead Sea Plain, Jordan, field director, 1979-83. **Publications:** West Semitic Personal Names in the Murasu Documents, 1976; Stories from Ancient Canaan, 1978. EDITOR: (with B.M. Metzger, and contrib.) The Oxford Companion to the Bible, 1993; (with J.C. Exum and L.E. Stager) Scripture and Other Artifacts: Essays on the Bible and Archaeology in Honor of Philip J. King, 1994; (and contrib.) The Oxford History of the Biblical World, 1998; (and author of intro) The Illustrated Guide to World Religions, 1998; (with L.E. Stager and J.A. Greene) The Archaeology of Jordan and Beyond: Essays in Honor of James A. Sauer, 2000; (with M.Z. Brettler and C.A. Newsom) The New Oxford Annotated Bible with the Apocrypha, 3rd ed, 2001; (with B.M. Metzger) Oxford Guide to Ideas and Issues of the Bible, 2001; (with B.M. Metzger) The Oxford Guide to People and Places of the Bible, 2001. Contributor to books and journals. **Address:** 15 Whittemore St, Concord, MA 01742, U.S.A. **Online address:** mdcoogan@aol.com

COOGAN, Tim(othy) Pat(rick). Irish, b. 1935. **Genres:** Area studies, History. **Career:** Irish Press (newspaper), Dublin, Ireland, editor; freelance author, 1966-. Has also worked as a television interviewer. **Publications:** Ireland since the Rising, 1966; The I.R.A., 1970, rev ver, 1993; The Irish: A Personal View, 1975; On the Blanket: The H Block Story, 1980; (ed.) Ireland and the Arts, 1983; Disillusioned Decades: Ireland 1966-87, 1987; Michael Collins: A Biography, 1990 (in the US as The Man Who Made Ireland: The Life and Death of Michael Collins, 1992). **Address:** c/o Irish Press, Tara House, Tara St., Dublin 2, Ireland.

COOK, Sir Alan (Hugh). *See* Obituaries.

COOK, Bob. British, b. 1961. **Genres:** Novels. **Career:** Writer. **Publications:** Disorderly Elements, 1985; Questions of Identity, 1987; Faceless Mortals, 1988; Paper Chase (novel), 1989; Fire and Forget, 1990. **Address:** Richard Scott Simon Ltd, 43 Doughty St, London WC1N 2LF, England.

COOK, Chris(topher). British, b. 1945. **Genres:** History, Politics/Government, Reference. **Career:** Magdalen College, Oxford, lecturer in politics, 1969-70; London School of Economics, sr. research officer, 1970-80, British Library of Political and Economic Science, visiting research fellow, 1990-; Polytechnic of N. London, head of School of History, 1980-89. **Publications:** (ed. with D. McKie) The Decade of Disillusion, 1972; (ed. with J. Ramsden) By-Elections in British Politics, 1973, 2nd ed., 1997; (ed.) Pears Cyclopaedia, 1974-; (with J. Paxton) European Political Facts 1918-1973, 1975, 1900-1996, 1997; (ed. with G. Peele) The Politics of Reappraisal 1918-1973, 1975; (with B. Keith) British Historical Facts 1830-1900, 1975; (with P. Jones) Sources in British Political History, 6 vols., 1975-85; The Age of Alignment: Electoral Politics in Britain 1922-1929, 1975; A Short History of the Liberal Party 1900-76, 1976, 5th ed. (1900-2001), 2002; (with A. Sked) Post-War Britain: A Political History, 1979; (with J. Stevenson) The Slump: Society and Politics during the Depression, 1980; (with J. Stevenson) Longman Handbook of Modern British History, 1714-1980, 1983, 4th ed. (1714-2001), 2001; (with G. Pugh) Sources in European Political History, vol. I: The European Left, 1987; Dictionary of Historical Terms, 1989; Facts on File World Political Almanac, 1989; Facts on File Asia Political Almanac, 1994; Longman Guide to Sources in Contemporary British History, 2 vols, 1993-94; (with D. Bewes) What Happen Where, 1997; (with J. Stevenson) Longman Handbook of the Modern World, 1998. **Address:** Modern Archives Survey, London School of Economics, British Library of Political and Economic Science, Houghton St, Aldwych, London WC2, England.

COOK, David. British, b. 1940. **Genres:** Novels. **Career:** Professional actor since 1961. Writer-in-Residence, St. Martin's College, Lancaster, 1982-83. **Publications:** Albert's Memorial, 1972; Happy Endings, 1974; Walter, 1978; Winter Doves, 1979; Sunrising, 1983; Missing Persons, 1986; Crying Out Loud, 1988; Second Best, 1991. **Address:** Flat 17, Ockham Court, Bardwell Rd, Oxford OX2 6SR, England.

COOK, Deanna F. American, b. 1965. **Genres:** Food and Wine. **Career:** Scholastic Inc., NYC, associate editor, 1989-92; Family Fun Magazine,

Northampton, MA, senior editor, 1992-. **Publications:** Kids' Multicultural Cookbook: Food & Fun around the World, 1995; Disney's Family Cookbook, 1996; Kids' Pumpkin Projects; Family Fun's Crafts; Family Fun's Cookies for Christmas; Family Fun's Parties. **Address:** 57 Norwood Ave, Northampton, MA 01060, U.S.A.

COOK, Ferris. American, b. 1950. **Genres:** Homes/Gardens. **Career:** Gear, NYC, product designer, 1987; Fred C. Gloeckner Co. (horticultural brokerage), NYC, customer service representative, 1987-88; Smithsonian Guide to Historic America, assistant photographic editor, 1988-89; illustrator and writer, 1989-. American Museum of Natural History, assistant to the manager of special publications, 1991. Work exhibited at solo and group shows. **Publications:** (and illustrator) The Garden Trellis, 1996. EDITOR: Invitation to the Garden, 1992. EDITOR & ILLUSTRATOR: Garden Dreams, 1991; Remembered Gardens, 1993; P. Neruda, Odes to Common Things, 1994; P. Neruda, Odes to Opposites, 1995; Rilke, The Rose Window (And Other Verse from New Poems), 1997; E. Dickinson, A Murmur in the Trees, 1998; The Sonnets of Shakespeare, 1998; Gifts of Love: A Selection of Love Poetry, 2000; Bark: A Selection of Poetry about Dogs, 2000; Yowl: A Selection of Poetry about Cats, 2001. Contributor of articles and reviews to periodicals. **Address:** 438 Mohonk Rd, High Falls, NY 12440, U.S.A.

COOK, Glen (Charles). Also writes as Greg Stevens. American, b. 1944. **Genres:** Novels, Science fiction/Fantasy. **Career:** Worked at General Motors, St. Louis, starting 1965, now retired. **Publications:** SCIENCE FICTION NOVELS: The Heirs of Babylon, 1972; A Shadow of All Night Failing, 1979; October's Baby, 1980; All Darkness Met, 1980; The Swordbearer, 1982; Shadowline, 1982; Starfishers, 1982, Stars' End, 1982; The Fire in His Hands, 1984; The Black Company, 1984; Shadows Linger, 1984; Passage at Arms, 1985; A Matter of Time, 1985; With Mercy toward None, 1985; The White Rose, 1985; Doomstalker, 1986; Warlock, 1986; Ceremony, 1986; Reap the East Wind, 1987; Sweet Silver Blues, 1987; An Ill Fate Marshalling, 1988; Bitter Gold Hearts, 1988; Cold Copper Tears, 1988; The Dragon Never Sleeps, 1988; Shadow Games, 1989; Old Tin Sorrows, 1989; The Silver Spike, 1989; The Tower of Fear, 1989; Dread Brass Shadows, 1990; Dreams of Steel, 1990; Sung in Blood, 1990; Red Iron Nights, 1991; Deadly Quicksilver Lies, 1994; Petty Pewter Gods, 1995; Bleak Seasons, 1996; She Is the Darkness, 1997; Water Sleeps, 1998; Faded Steel Heat, 1999; Soldiers Live, 2000; Angry Lead Skies, 2002. AS GREG STEVENS: The Swap Academy (novel), 1970. **Address:** 4106 Flora Pl, St. Louis, MO 63110, U.S.A.

COOK, James L(ister). British, b. 1932. **Genres:** Engineering, Money/Finance. **Career:** Sybron/Balfour, Leven, Scotland, senior design draftsman, 1965-69; Munro & Millar, Edinburgh, Scotland, pipe design engineer, 1969-71; Sybron/Balfour, research engineer, 1971-79; Rank Strand Electric Ltd. (now Strand Lighting Ltd.), Kirkcaldy, Scotland, senior mechanical design engineer, 1979-81; C.E. Lummus Co., Houston, TX, senior designer and checker in vessels department, 1981-82; Howard Doris Ltd., senior planning engineer, 1982; Cooxint Ltd., director, 1983-86; Prime Actuator Control Systems Ltd., chief engineer, 1986-88; Lewis C. Grant Ltd., product design engineer, 1988-89; Ardmel Auto Ltd., contract design engineer, 1989; Glenrothes College, adjunct lecturer, 1990-91. University of Salford, lecturer, 1977. Inventor and computer programmer. **Publications:** Conversion Factors, 1991; Property Loans, 1999. Contributor to magazines.

COOK, Jean Thor. American, b. 1930. **Genres:** Children's non-fiction, Children's fiction. **Career:** Writer. St. Mary College, Kansas City, KS, publicity director for an inner-city adult baccalaureate program, 1978-80. **Publications:** Hugs for Our New Baby, 1987; Butterflies for Grandpa, 1990; Audrey and the Nighttime Skies, 1994; Sam, the Terror of Westbrook Elementary, 1994; Jesus Calms the Storm, 1994; Room for a Stepdaddy, 1995. **Address:** 325 Jack Boot Rd, Monument, CO 80132, U.S.A. **Online address:** jthorcook1@aol.com

COOK, Mark. British, b. 1942. **Genres:** Human relations/Parenting, Psychology, Sex. **Career:** University of Aberdeen, assistant lecturer in psychology, 1968-69; Oxford University, research officer, 1969-73; University College of Swansea, lecturer in psychology, 1973-. **Publications:** Interpersonal Perception, 1971; (with M. Argyle) Gaze and Mutual Gaze, 1976; (with R. McHenry) Sexual Attraction, 1978; Perceiving Others: The Psychology of Interpersonal Perception, 1979; Levels of Personality, 1984, 2nd ed., 1993; Personnel Selection and Productivity, 1988, 4th ed., 2003. EDITOR: (with G. Wilson) Love and Attraction, 1979; (with K. Howells) Adult Sexual Interest in Children, 1980; The Bases of Human Sexual Attraction, 1981; Issues in Person Perception, 1984. **Address:** Dept. of Psychology, University of Wales-Swansea, Singleton Park, Swansea SA2 8PP, Wales.

COOK, Paul. American, b. 1950. **Genres:** Science fiction/Fantasy. **Career:** Arizona State University, Tempe, senior lecturer in English, 1987-. **Publications:** SCIENCE FICTION: Duende Meadow, 1985; Halo, 1986; On the Rim of the Mandala, 1987; Fortress on the Sun, 1997. **Address:** Department of English, Arizona State University, Tempe, AZ 85287, U.S.A. **Online address:** pcook@dancris.com

COOK, Philip J. American, b. 1946. **Genres:** Politics/Government. **Career:** Duke University, Durham, NC, assistant professor, 1973-79, associate professor, 1979-84, professor, 1984-, director of Sanford Institute of Public Policy, 1985-89, 1997-99. **Publications:** (with C.T. Clotfelter) Selling Hope: State Lotteries in America, 1989; (with R.H. Frank) The Winner-Take-All Society, 1995; (with J. Ludwig) Gun Violence: The Real Costs, 2000. **Address:** Sanford Institute of Public Policy, Duke University, Durham, NC 27708, U.S.A. **Online address:** cook@pps.duke.edu

COOK, Rebecca J. American/Canadian, b. 1946. **Genres:** Law. **Career:** Legal scholar and educator, author and editor of books on human rights, and international lecturer. Admitted to bar, Washington, DC, 1982. International Planned Parenthood Federation, London, England, director of law program, 1973-78; Beveridge, Fairbanks and Diamond (law firm), associate, 1980; consultant to U.S. Congress, 1978-81; Columbia University, NYC, assistant professor of clinical public health, 1983-87, staff attorney for developmental law and policy program at Center for Population and Family Health, 1983-87; International Women's Human Rights Action Watch, deputy director, 1986-87; University of Toronto, ON, faculties of law and medicine, professor, 1987-. professor, 1987-. **Publications:** Abortion Laws in Commonwealth Countries, 1979; Emerging Issues in Commonwealth Abortion Laws, 1982; Women's Health and Human Rights: The Promotion and Protection of Women's Health through International Human Rights Law, 1994; Reproductive Health and Human Rights: Integrating Medicine, Ethics and Law, 2003. EDITOR: (with P. Senanayake) The Human Problem of Abortion: Medical and Legal Dimensions, 1979; Human Rights of Women: National and International Perspectives, 1994. Contributor to professional journals and periodicals. **Address:** Faculty of Law, University of Toronto, Toronto, ON, Canada M5S 2C5. **Online address:** rebecca.cook@utoronto.ca

COOK, Robert. British, b. 1958. **Genres:** History. **Career:** University of Sheffield, England, senior lecturer in American history, 1990-. **Publications:** Baptism of Fire: The Republican Party in Iowa, 1838-1878, 1994; Sweet Land of Liberty? The African-American Struggle for Civil Rights in the Twentieth Century, 1998; Civil War America: Making a Nation 1848-1877, 2003. **Address:** Department of History, University of Sheffield, Sheffield S10 2TN, England. **Online address:** rob.cook@shef.ac.uk

COOK, Roger F. (born United States), b. 1948. **Genres:** Literary criticism and history. **Career:** University of Missouri-Columbia, Columbia, MO, professor of German and chair of Department of German and Russian Studies, 1986-. **Publications:** The Demise of the Author: Autonomy and the German Writer, 1770-1848, 1993; The Cinema of Wim Wenders: Image, Narrative, and the Postmodern Condition, 1996; By the Rivers of Babylon: Heinrich Heine's Late Songs and Reflections, 1998; (editor) A Companion to the Works of Heinrich Heine, 2002. **Address:** 206 Spring Valley Rd., Columbia, MO 65203, U.S.A. **Online address:** cookrf@missouri.edu

COOK, Stephen L(loyd). American, b. 1962. **Genres:** Theology/Religion. **Career:** Yale University, New Haven, CT, instructor in Hebrew at Divinity School, summers, 1990-91; Union Theological Seminary, NYC, assistant professor of Old Testament, 1992-96; Virginia Theological Seminary, Alexandria, assistant professor, 1996-99, associate professor of Old Testament, 1999-. American Schools of Oriental Research, corporation representative, 1996-; Society of Biblical Literature, program unit chair, 1996-. Volunteer with joint archaeological expedition to Tell el-Hesi, Israel, 1983. **Publications:** Prophecy and Apocalypticism: The Postexilic Social Setting, 1995; The Apocalyptic Literature, 2003. CO-EDITOR: On the Way to Nineveh, 1999; The Whirlwind, 2001. Contributor of articles and reviews to periodicals. **Address:** Biblical Field, Virginia Theological Seminary, 3737 Seminary Rd, Alexandria, VA 22304, U.S.A. **Online address:** SCook@vts.edu

COOK, Timothy E. American, b. 1954. **Genres:** Communications/Media. **Career:** Williams College, Williamstown, MA, assistant professor, 1981-88, associate professor, 1988-92, professor, 1993-. Harvard University, adjunct professor at Kennedy School of Government, 1998-. **Publications:** Making Laws and Making News, 1989; (with M. Just and others) Crosstalk, 1996; Governing with the News, 1998. **Address:** Stetson Hall, Williams College, Williamstown, MA 01267, U.S.A. **Online address:** timothy.cook@williams.edu

COOK, William A. (born United States), b. 1944. **Genres:** Sports/Fitness. **Career:** Writer. North Brunswick Township, North Brunswick, NJ, member of township council, 1991-93. **Publications:** The 1919 World Series: What Really Happened?, 2001; The Summer of '64: A Pennant Lost, 2002; Pete Rose: Baseball's All-Time Hit King, 2004. **Address:** 3 Claremont, North Brunswick, NJ 08902, U.S.A.

COOKE, Bernard. American, b. 1922. **Genres:** Theology/Religion. **Career:** Professor of Religious Studies, University of Calgary, 1976-. Professor of Theology, and Chairman, Dept. of Theology, Marquette University, Milwaukee, Wisconsin, 1957-69; Professor of Religious Studies, University of Windsor, Ont., 1970-76; Professor of Theology, College of the Holy Cross, Worcester, MA, 1980-92; Professor of Theology, Incarnate Word College, San Antonio, TX, 1992-98; Professor of Theology, University of San Diego, 1999-. **Publications:** Christian Sacraments and Christian Personality, 1965; Formation of Faith, 1965; New Dimensions in Catholic Life, 1967; Beyond Trinity, 1969; God of Space and Time, 1969; Christian Community: Response to Reality, 1970; Theology in an Age of Revolution, 1971; Rethinking the Faith, 1972; Ministry to Word and Sacraments, 1976; Sacraments and Sacramentality, 1983; Reconciled Sinners: Healing Human Brokenness, 1986; (ed.) The Papacy and the Church in the United States, 1989; The Distancing of God: The Ambiguity of Symbol in History and Theology, 1990; God's Beloved, 1992; The Future of Eucharist, 1997. **Address:** 854 S Clearview Pky, New Orleans, LA 70123, U.S.A.

COOKE, Carolyn. American, b. 1959. **Genres:** Novellas/Short stories. **Career:** Writer. **Publications:** The Bostons (short stories), 2001. Work represented in anthologies and periodicals. **Address:** 25524 Ten Mile Cutoff, PO Box 462, Point Arena, CA 95468, U.S.A. **Online address:** redtag@mcn.org

COOKE, Jacob Ernest. American, b. 1924. **Genres:** History, Biography. **Career:** John H. MacCracken Professor Emeritus of History, Lafayette College, Easton, PA, 1990- (John H. MacCracken Professor, 1963-90). Assistant Professor, Columbia University, NYC, 1956-62; Professor and Head of History Dept., Carnegie-Mellon University, Pittsburgh, 1962-63. **Publications:** Frederick Bancroft: Historian, 1956; A History of the U.S. 1946-1960, 1965; Tench Coxe and the Early American Republic, 1977; Alexander Hamilton, 1982. EDITOR: The Federalist, 1962; (assoc.) The Papers of Alexander Hamilton, vols. I-XV, 1963-72; Reports of Alexander Hamilton, 1965; Alexander Hamilton, 1965; The Challenge of History, 1965; A History of the American Colonies, 13 vols., 1973-86; Encyclopedia of the North American Colonies, 3 vols., 1993. **Address:** Dept. of History, Lafayette College, Easton, PA 18042, U.S.A. **Online address:** Cookeje@cs.com

COOKE, John Peyton. American, b. 1967. **Genres:** Novels. **Publications:** NOVELS: The Lake, 1989; Out for Blood, 1991; Torsos, 1993; The Chimney Sweeper, 1994; Haven, 1996. Contributor to anthologies. Contributor of fiction to periodicals. **Address:** c/o William Morris Agency Inc., 1325 Ave of the Americas 15th Fl, New York, NY 10019, U.S.A. **Online address:** jpcooke@verizon.net

COOKE, Nathalie. Canadian (born India), b. 1960. **Genres:** Literary criticism and history. **Career:** McGill University, Montreal, QC, assistant professor, 1991-97, associate professor, 1997-. **Publications:** (ed. with R. Brown and D. Bennett) An Anthology of Canadian Literature in English, 1990; Margaret Atwood: A Biography, 1998; Margaret Atwood: A Critical Companion, 2004. Contributor of literary criticism to journals. **Address:** English Dept, McGill University, 853 Sherbrooke St W, Montreal, QC, Canada H3A 2T6. **Online address:** Nathalie.Cooke@McGill.ca

COOKE, William. British, b. 1942. **Genres:** Novellas/Short stories, Poetry, Literary criticism and history, Biography, Humor/Satire, Writing/Journalism. **Career:** Lecturer, Stoke-on-Trent College of Further and Higher Education, 1979-95. Member of faculty, Thistley Hough School, 1968-70, and City of Stoke-on-Trent Sixth Form College, 1970-79. **Publications:** Edward Thomas: A Critical Biography, 1970; Edward Thomas: A Portrait, 1978; Builder (poetry), 1980; Small Ads (poetry), 1980; Business English, 1990. EDITOR: Anvil, 1979; Howlers, 1988; Edward Thomas, 1997.

COOK-LYNN, Elizabeth. American, b. 1930. **Genres:** Novels, Novellas/Short stories, Poetry, Cultural/Ethnic topics, History, Literary criticism and history. **Career:** High school teacher in South Dakota and New Mexico; Eastern Washington University, Cheney, associate professor of Native American studies to associate professor emerita, 1971-; Arizona State University, Tempe, visiting professor. Member of Council of Editors of Learned Journals; Association for American Indian Research, trustee, 1994.

Publications: POETRY: Then Badger Said This, 1983; Seek the House of Relatives, 1985; I Remember the Fallen Trees, 1998. STORIES: The Power of Horses and Other Stories, 1990; From the River's Edge (novella), 1991. ESSAYS: Why I Can't Read Wallace Stegner and Other Essays, 1996; The Politics of Hallowed Ground: Wounded Knee and the Struggle for Indian Sovereignty, 1998. OTHER: A Crow Creek Trilogy (fiction), 1999; Anti-Indianism in Modern America (essays), 2001.

COOLEY, Martha S. American, b. 1955. **Genres:** Novels. **Career:** Writer. **Publications:** FICTION: The Archivist, 1998. **Address:** c/o Gelfman Schneider, 250 West 57th Street, New York, NY 10107, U.S.A.

COOLEY, Nicole (Ruth). American, b. 1966. **Genres:** Poetry. **Career:** Emory University, Atlanta, GA, instructor in English, 1992-95; writer, 1995-. Gives readings from her works. **Publications:** Resurrection (poems), 1996. Work represented in anthologies. Contributor of stories, poems, articles, and reviews to periodicals. **Address:** 1431 Emory Rd., Atlanta, GA 30306, U.S.A.

COOLEY, Thomas (Winfield). American, b. 1942. **Genres:** Literary criticism and history. **Career:** Ohio State University, Columbus, OH, assistant professor, 1970-79, associate professor, 1980-98, professor of English, 1999-; formerly director of the Writing Skills Laboratory at Ohio State University. **Publications:** Educated Lives: The Rise of Modern Autobiography in America, 1976; The Norton Sampler: Short Essays for Composition, 1979, 6th ed, 2002; The Norton Guide to Writing, 1992; (ed.) The Adventures of Huckleberry Finn: An Authoritative Text, Contexts and Sources, Criticism, 1998; The Ivory Leg in the Ebony Cabinet: Madness, Race, and Gender in the American Consciousness, 2001. Author of articles and reviews on American literature. **Address:** Department of English, Ohio State University, 511 Denney Hall, 164 West 17th Avenue, Columbus, OH 43210, U.S.A. **Online address:** Cooley.1@osu.edu

COOLIDGE, Olivia. (Mrs. Archibald C. Coolidge). American (born England), b. 1908. **Genres:** Children's fiction, History, Biography. **Career:** English Teacher, Potsdam-Hermannswerder, Germany, 1931-32; Classics Teacher, Wimbledon High School, London, 1932-37; Secretary, Education Service, Bureau of Camps, NYC, 1938; English Teacher, Low- Heywood School, Stamford, Conn., 1939, and Winsor School, Boston, 1940-46. Member, Board of Trustees, Mills College of Education, 1956-61. **Publications:** Greek Myths, 1949; Legends of the North, 1951; The Trojan War, 1952; Egyptian Adentures, 1954; Cromwell's Head, 1955; Roman People, 1959; Winston Churchill and the Story of Two World Wars, 1960; Caesar's Gallic War, 1961; Men of Athens, 1962; Makers of the Red Revolution, 1963; Edith Wharton, 1964; Lives of the Famous Romans, 1965; People in Palestine, 1965; The King of Men, 1966; Women's Rights, 1966; Eugene O'Neill, 1966; Marathon Looks on the Sea, 1967; George Bernard Shaw, 1968; The Golden Days of Greece, 1968; Tom Paine, Revolutionary, 1969; The Maid of Artemis, 1969; Tales of the Crusades, 1970; Come by Here, 1970; Gandhi, 1971; The Three Lives of Joseph Conrad, 1972; The Apprenticeship of Abraham Lincoln, 1974; The Statesmanship of Abraham Lincoln, 1977.

COOLING, Wendy. British. **Genres:** Children's fiction, Bibliography. **Career:** United Kingdom Year of Literature festival, Swansea, Wales, coordinator, 1995; WORDPLAY children's festival, organizer, c. 1995-; Book House Training Centre, director of course on children's publishing, c. 1995-; Disney Consumer Products, director of course on children's publishing, 1997; National Literacy Strategy and National Year of Reading, contact person, c. 1999. Former member of the civil service; English teacher, London, England; book consultant and advisor to schools, libraries, and parents; library director; bookstore manager; book promoter; advisory teacher with the ILEA Resources Support Group; head of the Children's Book Foundation; judge of children's literature awards; researcher for literary organizations; freelance book consultant and reviewer; appeared on radio programs. **Publications:** Finding Out...How to Find Out, 1989; Fame!: Who's Who in History at Madame Tussaud's, 1992; Sandy the Seal, 1994; (with P. Kropp) The Reading Solution, 1995; Books to Enjoy, 12-16 (guide), 1996. Writer of children's guides for the National Trust. Contributor to periodicals. EDITOR: Thirteen! Unpredictable Tales from Paul Jennings, 1995; The Great Automatic Grammatizator and Other Stories by Roald Dahl, 1996; The Puffin Book of Stories for Eight-Year-Olds, 1996; The Puffin Book of Stories for FiveYear-Olds, 1996; The Puffin Book of Stories for Seven-Year-Olds, 1996; The Puffin Book of Stories for Six-Year-Olds, 1996; Farmyard Tales from Far and Wide, 1998; Read Me a Story Please, 1998; Centuries of Stories, 1999; R. Dahl, Skin and Other Stories, 1999; It's Christmas; Simply Spooky; Surprise Surprise. EDITOR QUIDS FOR KIDS SERIES: Aliens to Earth, 1997;

Animal Stories, 1997; Bad Dreams, 1997; Ghost Stories, 1997; Go for Goal, 1997; Horror Stories, 1997; On the Run, 1997; Soccer Stories, 1997; Spine Chillers, 1997; Stars in Your Eyes, 1997; Stories of Growing Up, 1997; Stories of Hopes and Dreams, 1997; Stories of Past and Future, 1997; Stories of Strange Visitors, 1997; Stories of the Unexpected, 1997; Stories to Keep You Guessing, 1997; Time Watch, 1997; Top Secret, 1997; Weird and Wonderful, 1997; Wild and Free, 1997. **Address:** c/o Barefoot Books, 413 Sacket St., Brooklyn, NY 11231, U.S.A. **Online address:** WendyCooling@Bookconsult.freeserve.co.uk

COOMBS, Patricia. American, b. 1926. **Genres:** Children's fiction. **Publications:** Dorrie series, 20 vols., 1962-92; Waddy and his Brother, 1963; The Lost Playground, 1963; Lisa and the Grompet, 1970; Mouse Café, 1972; Molly Mullett, 1975; The Magic Pot, 1977; Tilabel, 1978; The Magician and McTree, 1983. Illustrator of books by others. **Address:** 178 Oswegatchie Rd, Waterford, CT 06385, U.S.A.

COOMBS, Philip (Hall). American, b. 1915. **Genres:** Education. **Career:** Williams College, Williamstown, MA, faculty, 1940-41; U.S. Office of Price Controls, economist, 1941-43; Office of Strategic Services, U.S. Army and Air Force, 1943-45; Amherst College, MA, professor of economics, 1947-49; Economic Adviser to Gov. Chester Bowles of Connecticut, 1948-50; President's Materials Policy Commission, executive director and editor of 4-vol. public report, 1950-52; Fund for the Advancement of Education, secretary and director of research, and the Ford Foundation, program director of education, 1952-60; Dept. of State, Washington, assistant secretary of state for international and cultural affairs, 1961-62; fellow of the Council on Foreign Relations, and the Brookings Institution, Washington, DC, 1962-63; International Institute for Educational Planning (affiliated with UNESCO), Paris, founding director, 1963-68; International Council for Educational Development, co-founder, vice-chairman, later chairman, 1970-95. **Publications:** The Fourth Dimension of Foreign Policy, 1964; Education and Foreign Aid, 1965; (with W. Schramm) The New Media, 1967; The World Educational Crisis, 1968; (with C. Beeby) The Qualitative Aspects of Educational Planning, 1969; (with others) International Development Targets, 1970; What Is Educational Planning?, 1970; Educational Cost Analysis, 1971; (with J. Hallak) Managing Educational Costs, 1972; New Paths to Learning for Rural Children and Youth, 1973; Attacking Rural Poverty, 1974; The World Crisis in Education, 1985; (with J. Hallak) Cost Analysis in Education, 1987. EDITOR/CO-EDITOR: Education for Rural Development, 1975; Meeting the Basic Needs of the Rural Poor, 1980; A Strategy to Improve the Quality of Mexican Higher Education, 1992; A Productive Future for the Benemerita Universidad Autonoma de Puebla (Mexico), 1994. **Address:** 317 W Main St, Chester, CT 06412, U.S.A.

COOMER, Joe. American, b. 1958. **Genres:** Novels, Adult non-fiction. **Career:** Full-time Writer. **Publications:** The Decatur Road, 1983; Kentucky Love, 1985; A Flatland Fable, 1986; Dream House, 1992; The Loop, 1992; Beachcombing for a Shipwrecked God, 1995; Sailing in a Spoonfull of Water, 1997; Apologizing to Dogs, 1999; One Vacant Chair, 2003. **Address:** 1951 NW Parkway, Azle, TX 76020, U.S.A.

COONEY, Ellen. American, b. 1952. **Genres:** Poetry. **Career:** Writer and educator. Taught writing at the Massachusetts Institute of Technology, Boston College, University of Maine, and Harvard University/Radcliffe College. **Publications:** Small-Town Girl (young adult), 1983; All the Way Home, 1984; The Old Ballerina, 1999; The White Palazzo, 2002; Gun Ball Hill, 2004; A Private Hotel for Gentle Ladies, 2005. Contributor to periodicals. **Address:** c/o Author Mail, University Press of New England, 1 Court St Ste 250, Lebanon, NH 03766, U.S.A. **Online address:** ellencooney@gwi.net

COONEY, Ray(mond George Alfred). British, b. 1932. **Genres:** Plays/Screenplays. **Career:** Actor, 1946-. Theatre dir. and producer, 1965-. Director, Ray Cooney Productions Ltd., 1966-. Founding artistic dir., Theatre of Comedy, 1983-. **Publications:** (sometimes in collaboration): One for the Pot, 1963; Chase Me, Comrade, 1966; My Giddy Aunt, 1970; Bang Bang Beirut, or Stand by Your Bedouin, 1971; Not Now, Darling, 1971; Charlie Girl, 1972; Move Over, Mrs. Markham, 1972; Why Not Stay for Breakfast?, 1974; There Goes the Bride, 1975; Run for Your Wife, 1984; Two into One, 1985; Wife Begins at Forty, 1986; It Runs in the Family, 1987; Out of Order, 1990; Funny Money, 1994; One Good Turn, 1994; Caught in the Net, 2001; Tom, Dick and Harry, 2003. **Address:** 29 Salmons Rd, Chessington, Surrey KT9 2JE, England.

COONTS, Stephen (Paul). Also writes as Eve Adams. American, b. 1946. **Genres:** Novels. **Career:** Naval officer, 1968-77; attorney in private practice, Buckhannon, WV, 1980-81; Petro-Lewis Corporation (oil and gas company),

Denver, CO, in-house counsel, 1981-86; full-time writer, 1986-. **Publications:** NOVELS: Flight of the Intruder, 1986; Final Flight, 1988; The Minotaur, 1989; Under Siege, 1990; The Red Horseman, 1993; The Intruders, 1994; Fortunes of War, 1998; Cuba, 1999; Hong Kong, 2000; America, 2001; Saucer, 2002; Liberty, 2003; Liars and Thieves, 2004; Saucer: The Conquest, 2004. OTHER: The Cannibal Queen, 1992; War in the Air, 1996; Combat, 2001; Victory, 2003; On Glorious Wings, 2003. AS EVE ADAMS: The Garden of Eden, 2005. **Address:** c/o Robert Gottlieb, Trident Media Group., 41 Madison Ave Fl 36, New York, NY 10010-2257, U.S.A.

COONTZ, Stephanie. American, b. 1944. **Genres:** Social commentary. **Career:** Evergreen State College, Olympia, WA, faculty member affiliated with department of History and Women's Studies, 1975-. Exchange professor, Kobe University of Commerce, 1986; lecturer, Washington Humanities Commission, 1989-91; Visiting Scholar, The National Faculty, 1990-; Exchange Professor, University of Hawaii at Hilo, 1992; Visiting Associate Professor of Sociology, University of Hawaii at Hilo, 1994. **Publications:** (with P. Henderson) Women's Work, Men's Property: On the Origins of Gender and Class, 1986; The Social Origins of Private Life: A History of American Families, 1988; The Way We Never Were: American Families and the Nostalgia Trap, 1992, rev. ed., 2000; The Way We Really Are: Coming to Terms with America's Changing Families, 1997; American Families: A Multicultural Reader, 1999. **Address:** Department of History and Women's Studies, Evergreen State College, Olympia, WA 98505, U.S.A.

COOPER, Ann (Catharine). American (born England), b. 1939. **Genres:** Children's non-fiction. **Career:** Bedford College, University of London, and Hammersmith Hospital, London, England, medical research, 1960-65; homemaker, 1965-84; Prosound Music, Boulder, CO, computing, 1984-86; writer, 1988-. **Publications:** FOR CHILDREN: (with A. Armstrong and C. Kampert) The Wildwatch Book: Ideas, Activities, and Projects for Exploring Colorado's Front Range, 1990; Eagles: Hunters of the Sky, 1992; Bats: Swift Shadows in the Twilight, 1994; Owls: On Silent Wings, 1994; Above the Treeline, 1996; In the Forest, 1996; Along the Seashore, 1997; In the Desert, 1997; Around the Pond, 1998; In the City, 2000. **Address:** 2839 3rd St, Boulder, CO 80304, U.S.A. **Online address:** wordswild@att.net

COOPER, Barry (Anthony Raymond). British, b. 1949. **Genres:** Music. **Career:** University of St. Andrews, Scotland, lecturer, 1973; University of Aberdeen, Scotland, lecturer, 1974-90; University of Manchester, England, senior lecturer, 1990-2000, reader, 2000-03, professor, 2003-. **Publications:** English Solo Keyboard Music of the Middle and Late Baroque, 1989; Beethoven and the Creative Process, 1990, 2nd ed., 1992; (gen. ed. and contrib.) The Beethoven Compendium, 1991, 2nd ed., 1996; Beethoven's Folksong Settings: Chronology, Sources, Style, 1994; Beethoven, 2000. Contributor of articles and reviews to musicology journals. Contributor to books. **Address:** Martin Harris Bldg (Music), University of Manchester, Coupland St, Manchester M13 9PL, England.

COOPER, Brian (Newman). British, b. 1919. **Genres:** Mystery/Crime/Suspense, History. **Career:** Sr. History Master, Moorfield School, Bolsover, Derbyshire, 1955-79. **Publications:** FICTION: Where the Fresh Grass Grows (in U.S. as Maria), 1955; A Path to the Bridge (in U.S. as Giselle), 1958; The Van Langeren Girl, 1960; A Touch of Thunder, 1961; A Time to Retreat, 1963; Genesis 38 (in U.S. as The Murder of Mary Steers), 1965; A Mission for Betty Smith (in U.S. as Monsoon Murder), 1967; Messiter's Dream, 1990; The Cross of San Vincente, 1991; The Singing Stones, 1993; Covenant with Death, 1994; Shadows on the Sand, 1995; The Travelling Dead, 1997; The Blacknock Woman, 1999; The Norfolk Triangle, 2000; The Murder Column, 2003. NON-FICTION: Transformation of a Valley, 1983. **Address:** 43 Parkland Close, Mansfield, Notts. NG18 4PP, England.

COOPER, C. Everett. *See* **REGINALD, Robert.**

COOPER, Carolyn (Joy). Also writes as Georgia Riley. Jamaican, b. 1950. **Genres:** Literary criticism and history. **Career:** Interim English teacher at a high school in Kingston, Jamaica, 1970; Atlantic Union College, South Lancaster, MA, assistant professor, 1975-80, associate professor of English, 1980, director of All-College Cultural Study of the Caribbean and coordinator of study-abroad research visit to Jamaica, 1977-78, member of executive committee of Adult Degree Program, 1978-80, director of program, 1980, head of Honors Core Curriculum Program, 1979-80; University of the West Indies, Kingston, lecturer, 1980-90, senior lecturer in English, 1990-. Visiting and guest professor at universities. **Publications:** Noises in the Blood: Orality, Gender, and the "Vulgar" Body of Jamaican Popular Culture, 1993. Contributor to books. Contributor of articles and reviews to periodicals.

Some writings appear under the pseudonym Georgia Riley. **Address:** Department of Literatures in English, University of the West Indies, Mona, Kingston 7, Jamaica.

COOPER, Cary L. American, b. 1940. **Genres:** Administration/Management, Business/Trade/Industry, Medicine/Health. **Career:** University of Manchester, Institute of Science and Technology, UK, professor, 1974-2003, pro vice chancellor, 1995-2000, deputy vice chancellor, 2000-2003; Lancaster University, professor and pro-vice-chancellor, 2003-. Robertson Cooper Ltd., director, 1999-. Also worked as a social worker in Los Angeles, CA. **Publications:** (with I.L. Mangham) T-Groups, 1971; (with J. Marshall) Understanding Executive Stress, 1978; (with J. Marshall) Executives under Pressure, 1979; The Executive Gypsy, 1979; Learning from Others in Groups, 1979; (with A. Jones) Combatting Managerial Obsolescence, 1980; The Stress Check, 1981; Executive Families under Stress, 1982; (with others) Introducing Organisational Behaviour, 1982; (with M. Davidson) High Pressure, 1982; (with M. Davidson) Stress and the Woman Manager, 1983; (with I. Robertson) Human Behaviour in Organisations, 1983; Public Faces, Private Lives, 1984; (with P. Hingley) The Changemakers, 1985; (with V. Sutherland) Man and Accidents Offshore, 1986; (with P. Hingley) Stress and the Nurse Manager, 1986; (with S. Sloan) Airline Pilots under Pressure, 1986; (with C. Cox) High Flyers, 1988; (with J. Wills) Pressure Sensitive, 1988; (with S. Sloan & S. Williams) Occupational Stress Indicator, 1988; (with R. Cooper & L. Eaker) Living with Stress, 1988; (with A. McGoldrick) Early Retirement, 1989; (with P. Makin & C. Cox) Managing People at Work, 1989; (with S. Lewis) Career Couples, 1989; (with V. Sutherland) Understanding Stress, 1990; (with J. Arnold & I. Robertson) Work Psychology, 1991, 3rd ed., 1998; (with V. Sutherland) Stress and Accidents in the Offshore Oil and Gas Industry, 1991; Cary Cooper on Stress, 1991; (with B. Dale) Total Quality and Human Resources, 1991; (with M. Davidson) The Stress Survivors, 1992; (with S. Cartwright) Mergers and Acquisitions, 1992; (with M. Davidson) Shattering the Glass Ceiling, 1992; (with M. Watts) Relax, 1992; (with B. White & C. Cox) Women's Career Development, 1992; (with H. Kahn) Stress in the Dealing Room, 1993; (with A. Straw) Successful Stress Management in a Week, 1993; (with S. Lewis) The Workplace Revolution, 1993; (with S. Cartwright) No Hassle!, 1994; (with R. Jennings & C. Cox) Business Elites, 1994; (with C. Travers) Teachers under Pressure, 1995; (with P. Makin & C. Cox) Organizations and the Psychological Contract, 1995; (with S. Cartwright) Managing Mergers, Acquisitions, and Strategic Alliances, 1995; (with J. Earnshaw) Stress and Employer Liability, 1996; (with S. Cartwright) Mental Health and Stress in the Workplace, 1996; (with P. Liukkonen & S. Cartwright) Stress Prevention in the Workplace, 1996; (with J. Berridge & C. Highley) Employee Assistance Programmes, 1997; (with V. Sutherland) Dealing with Difficult People, 1997; (with B. Dale & A. Wilkinson) Managing Quality and Human Resources, 1997; (with M. Watts) Stop the World, 1997; (with N. Holden) Management Cultures in Collision, 1998; (with S. Lewis) Balancing Career, Family, and Life, 1998; (with J. Quick) Stress and Strain, 1999; (with S. Palmer) Conquer Your Stress, 2000; (with V. Sutherland) Strategic Stress Management, 2000; (with S. Cartwright) HR Know-How in Mergers and Acquisitions, 2000; (with S. Cartwright) Organizational Stress, 2001; Organizational Health Psychology, 2001; (with Rayner & Hoel) Workplace Bullying, 2001; (with J. Quick) FT Guide to Executive Health, 2002; (with S. Palmer & K. Thomas) Creating a Balance, 2003; (with P. Sparrow) The Employment Relationship, 2003; (with S. Clarke) Managing the Risk of Workplace Stress, 2004; (with T. Theobold) Shut Up and Listen, 2004; (with P. Dewe) Stress: A Brief History, 2004; (with S. Lewis) Work-Life Integration, 2005. EDITOR: Theories of Group Processes, 1975; Developing Social Skills in Managers, 1976; OD in the US and the UK, 1977; (with C. Alderfer) Advances in Experiential Social Processes, Vol. 1, 1978, Vol. 2, 1980; (with R. Payne) Stress at Work, 1978; Behavioural Problems in Organisations, 1979; (with E. Mumford) The Quality of Working Life in Western and Eastern Europe, 1979; Developing Managers for the '80s, 1980; (with R. Payne) Current Concerns in Occupational Stress, 1980; (with J. Marshall) White Collar and Professional Stress, 1980; (with R. Payne) Groups at Work, 1981; (with J. Marshall) Coping with Stress at Work, 1981; Psychology and Management, 1981; Improving Interpersonal Relations, 1981; (with D. Torrington) After Forty, 1982; (with R.D. Freedman and S. A. Stumpf) Management Education, 1982; Stress Research, 1983; Practical Approaches to Women's Career Develo. **Address:** Vice-Chancellor's Office, Lancaster University, Lancaster LA1 4YW, England. **Online address:** c.cooper1@lancaster.ac.uk

COOPER, Charles. British (born Republic of South Africa), b. 1936. **Genres:** Economics, Environmental sciences/Ecology, Technology. **Career:** Organization for Economic Cooperations and Development, Paris, France, permanent member of secretariat, 1962-69; University of Sussex, Brighton, England, senior research in Science Policy Research Unit, 1969-70, professor and deputy director, Institute of Development Studies, 1977-80; Institute of

Social Studies, The Hague, Netherlands, professor of technology and development economics, 1980-, deputy rector, 1980-94. United Nations University, Maastricht, Netherlands, director of Institute for New Technologies, 1990-. University of Linburg, professor, 1991-. **Publications:** Science, Technology and Development, 1972; Economics and the Environment, 1982; (ed.) Technology and Innovation in the International Economy, 1990.

COOPER, David A. American, b. 1939. **Genres:** Theology/Religion. **Career:** Political consultant; Rabbi; Heart of Stillness Hermitage, Boulder, CO, director. **Publications:** The Heart of Stillness: The Elements of Spiritual Practice, 1992; Silence, Simplicity, and Solitude: A Guide for Spiritual Retreat, 1992; Entering the Sacred Mountain: A Mystical Odyssey, 1994; Renewing Your Soul: A Guided Retreat for the Sabbath and Other Days of Rest, 1995; God is a Verb: Kabbalah and the Practice of Mystical Judaism, 1997. AUDIO CASSETTES: The Mystical Kabbalah, 1994; Kabbalah Meditation: Judaism's Ancient System for Mystical Exploration Through Meditation and Contemplation, 1997; The Holy Chariot, 1998. Contributor to books. **Address:** c/o Sounds True, PO Box 8010, Boulder, CO 80306, U.S.A.

COOPER, David Brandt. *See* EVENSON, Brian.

COOPER, David D. American, b. 1948. **Genres:** Literary criticism and history. **Career:** University of California, Santa Barbara, lecturer in English, 1978-88; Michigan State University, East Lansing, assistant professor to associate professor of American thought and language, 1988-. Berea College, Eli Lilly distinguished visiting professor of religion and American culture, 1991. **Publications:** Thomas Merton's Art of Denial: The Evolution of a Radical Humanist, 1989; (ed.) James Laughlin and Thomas Merton: Selected Letters, 1997. **Address:** Department of American Thought and Language, Michigan State University, 229 Bessey Hall, East Lansing, MI 48824, U.S.A.

COOPER, Derek (Macdonald). British, b. 1925. **Genres:** Food and Wine, Transportation. **Career:** Free-lance writer and presenter for radio and television since 1961. Founder member and first Chairman, Guild of Food Writers. Producer, Radio Malaya and Radio Singapore, 1950-60, and Independent Television News, London, 1960-61. OBE, 1997. **Publications:** The Bad Food Guide, 1967; The Beverage Report, 1970; Skye, 1970, 1977; The Gullibility Gap, 1974; Hebridean Connection, 1977, 1991; A Guide to the Whiskies of Scotland, 1978; Road to the Isles, 1979, 1990; (with D. Pattullo) Enjoying Scotch, 1980; Wine with Food, 1980, 1986; (with F. Godwin) The Whisky Roads of Scotland, 1982; Skye Remembered, 1983; The Century Companion to Whiskies, 1983; The World of Cooking, 1983; The Road to Mingulay, 1985; The Gunge File, 1986; A Taste of Scotch, 1989; The Little Book of Malt Whiskies, 1992; The Balvenie, 1993; Snail Eggs and Samphire, 1999. **Address:** 4 St. Helena Terrace, Richmond, Surrey TW9 1NR, England.

COOPER, Dominic (Xavier). British, b. 1944. **Genres:** Novels, Novellas/Short stories, Essays, Music. **Career:** Clockmaker, 1974-. **Publications:** The Dead of Winter (novel), 1975, (Somerset Maugham Award, 1976); Sunrise (novel), 1977; Jack Fletcher, 1978; Will Stringer, 1980; The Country of the Gull, 1981; Men at Axlir (novel), 1978; The Horn Fellow, 1987; (ed.) Judgements of Value, 1988; Shadow of Heaven, 1989. **Address:** 9 Swordle Chorrach, Achateny, Acharacle, Argyll PH36 4LG, Scotland.

COOPER, Elisha. American, b. 1971. **Genres:** Children's non-fiction, Documentaries/Reportage. **Career:** New Yorker magazine, messenger, 1993-95; writer and artist, 1995-. **Publications:** FOR CHILDREN: Country Fair, 1997; Ballpark, 1998; Building, 1999; Dance!, 2001; Ice Cream, 2002; Magic Thinks Big, 2004. OTHER: A Year in New York, 1995; Off the Road: An American Sketchbook, 1997; A Day at Yale, 1996; Henry, 1999; California: A Sketchbook, 2000. **Address:** c/o Darhansoff & Verrill Literary Agency, 236 W 26th St Rm 802, New York, NY 10001-6736, U.S.A. **Online address:** elisha@aya.yale.edu

COOPER, Floyd. American. **Genres:** Biography, Illustrations. **Career:** Author and illustrator. Worked in advertising and for a greeting card company in Missouri; freelance illustrator, 1984-. **Publications:** SELF-ILLUSTRATED: Coming Home: From the Life of Langston Hughes, 1994; Mandela: From the Life of the South African Statesman, 1996; Cumbayah, in press. Illustrator of books by M. Davidson, E. Greenfield, E.F. Howard, K.O. Galbraith, J. Woodson, K.L. Williams, D. Eaton, D. Burden-Patmon, J. Merrill, V.M. Fleming, J.C. Thomas, W. Hudson, S. Belton, G. Hausman, J. Gorog, N. Grimes, K.D. Jones, C.D. Boyd, C.J. Farley, J. Haskins and K. Benson, V. Hamilton, J. Kurtz, M. DeGross, V.L. Kroll, A. Schroeder, N. Lamb, P.C. McKissack, J.C. Collins, J. Yolen. **Address:** c/o William Morrow, 1350 Avenue of the Americas, New York, NY 10019, U.S.A.

COOPER, Hannah. *See* SPENCE, William John Duncan.

COOPER, Helen. British, b. 1963. **Genres:** Children's fiction, Illustrations, Picture/board books. **Career:** Author and illustrator. Member of the author committee for a proposed Centre for the Children's Book. **Publications:** AND ILLUSTRATOR: Kit and the Magic Kite, 1987; (with M. Miller) Lucy and the Egg Witch, 1989; Ella and the Rabbit, 1990; Chestnut Grey: A Folktale from Russia, 1993; The Bear under the Stairs, 1993; The House Cat, 1993; The Tale of Bear, The Tale of Duck, The Tale of Pig, The Tale of Frog (board books), 1994; Little Monster Did It!, 1995; The Baby Who Wouldn't Go to Bed, 1996, in US as The Boy Who Wouldn't Go to Bed, 1997; Pumpkin Soup, 1998; Tatty Ratty, 2001; Sandmare, 2001. Illustrator of books by E. Johns, E. Lear, S. Pirotta. **Address:** c/o Hilary Delemere, The Agency, 24 Pottery Lane, Holland Park, London W11 4LZ, England. **Online address:** www.wormworks.com

COOPER, Henry. *See* KAYE, Barrington.

COOPER, Ilene. American, b. 1948. **Genres:** Novels, Young adult fiction, Young adult non-fiction. **Career:** Writer and editor. Winnetka Public Library, Winnetka, IL, children's librarian, 1976-80; Booklist, Chicago, IL, children's book editor, 1985-. Consultant to ABC Afterschool Specials, ABC-TV, 1976-82. **Publications:** NOVELS. The Winning of Miss Lynn Ryan, 1987; Buddy Love-Now on Video, 1995; I'll See You in My Dreams, 1997; Sam I Am, 2004. KIDS FROM KENNEDY MIDDLE SCHOOL SERIES: Queen of the Sixth Grade, 1988; Choosing Sides, 1990; Mean Streak, 1991; The New, Improved Gretchen Hubbard, 1992. FRANCES IN THE FOURTH GRADE SERIES: Frances Takes a Chance, 1991; Frances Dances, 1991; Frances Four-Eyes, 1991; Frances and Friends, 1991. HOLLYWOOD WARS SERIES: Lights, Camera, Attitude, 1993; My Co-Star, My Enemy, 1993; Seeing Red, 1993; Trouble in Paradise, 1993. HOLIDAY FIVE SERIES: Trick or Trouble, 1994; The Worst Noel, 1994; Stupid Cupid, 1995; Star Spangled Summer, 1996; No-Thanks Thanksgiving, 1996. YOUNG ADULT NONFICTION: Jewish Holidays All Year 'Round, 2002; Jack: The Early Years of John F. Kennedy, 2003. OTHER: Susan B. Anthony (biography), 1984; (ed. with D. Wilms) Guide to Non-Sexist Children's Books, Vol. II: 1976-1985, 1987; The Dead Sea Scrolls, 1997. Also writer for television series. **Address:** c/o Booklist, American Library Association, 50 E Huron, Chicago, IL 60611, U.S.A. **Online address:** Icooper@ALA.org

COOPER, Jane (Marvel). American, b. 1924. **Genres:** Poetry. **Career:** Member, Dept. of Literature and Writing, and Poet-in-Residence, Sarah Lawrence College, Bronxville, NY, 1950-87; Fellow, Bunting Institute of Radcliffe College, 1988-89; State Poet of New York, 1995-97; Grants and fellowships from Guggenheim and Ingram Merrill Foundations, National Endowment for the Arts. **Publications:** The Weather of Six Mornings, 1969; Maps & Windows, 1974; Threads: Rosa Luxemburg from Prison, 1979; Scaffolding: New and Selected Poems, 1984, reissued as Scaffolding: Selected Poems, 1993; Green Notebook, Winter Road, 1994; The Flashboat: Poems Collected and Reclaimed, 2000. **Address:** Pennswood Village K-103, 1382 Newtown-Langhorne Rd, Newtown, PA 18940-2401, U.S.A.

COOPER, Jilly (Sallitt). British, b. 1937. **Genres:** Romance/Historical, Children's fiction, Young adult fiction, Human relations/Parenting, Humor/Satire. **Career:** Middlesex Independent newspaper, Brentford, reporter, 1957-59; Sunday Times, columnist, 1969-82; Mail on Sunday, columnist, 1982-87. **Publications:** How to Stay Married, 1969; How to Survive from 9 to 5, 1970; Jolly Super, 1971; Men and Super Men, 1972; Jolly Super Too, 1973; Women and Super Women, 1974; Jolly Superlative, 1975; Super Men and Super Women (omnibus), 1976; Work and Wedlock (omnibus), 1977; Superjilly, 1977; Class: A View from Middle England, 1979; Supercooper, 1980; Little Mabel series (juvenile), 4 vols., 1980-85; (ed. with T. Hartman) Violets and Vinegar: An Anthology of Women's Writings and Sayings, 1980; (ed.) The British in Love, 1980; Love and Other Heartaches, 1981; Intelligent and Loyal, 1981; Jolly Marsupial, 1982; Animals in War, 1983; The Common Years, 1984; Leo and Jilly Cooper on Rugby, 1984; Riders, 1985; Hotfoot to Zabriskie Point, 1985; Leo and Jilly Cooper on Cricket, 1985; Horse Mania, 1986; How to Survive Christmas, 1986; Turn Right at the Spotted Dog, 1987; Rivals, 1988; Angels Rush In, 1990; Polo, 1991; The Man Who Made Husbands Jealous, 1993; Araminta's Wedding, 1993; Appassionata, 1996; Score!, 1999; Pandora, 2002. ROMANCE NOVELS: Emily, 1975; Bella, 1976; Harriet, 1976; Octavia, 1977; Imogen, 1978; Prudence, 1978. **Address:** c/o Vivienne Schuster, Curtis Brown, Haymarket House, 28/29 Haymarket, London SW1Y 4SP, England.

COOPER, Kenneth H(ardy). American, b. 1931. **Genres:** Medicine/Health, Sports/Fitness. **Career:** U.S. Army, 1957-60; U.S. Air Force Medical Corps,

1960-70, became lieutenant colonel, physician in aerospace medicine program at Brooks Air Force Base, San Antonio, TX, 1963-64, director of aerospace medical laboratory clinic at Lackland Air Force Base, San Antonio, TX, 1964-70. Certified as diplomate by American Board of Preventive Medicine, 1966. Aerobics Center, Dallas, TX, founder and physician, 1970-; consultant and lecturer on preventive medicine; writer. National Defense University, visiting lecturer, 1973-90; University of California, Los Angeles, regent's lecturer, 1980; Mayo Clinic, visiting lecturer, 1981. **Publications:** Aerobics, 1968; The New Aerobics, 1970; (with M. Cooper) Aerobics for Women, 1972; The Aerobics Way, 1977; The Aerobics Program for Total Well-Being, 1982; Running without Fear, 1985; Controlling Cholesterol, 1988; (with M. Cooper) The New Aerobics for Women, 1988; Preventing Osteoporosis, 1989; Overcoming Hypertension, 1990; Kid Fitness, 1991; Dr. Kenneth H. Cooper's Antioxidant Revolution, 1994; Regaining the Power of Youth at Any Age, 2000. **Address:** Cooper Aerobic Center, 12200 Preston Rd, Dallas, TX 75230, U.S.A.

COOPER, Lee Pelham. *See* **ROWE, Lee Pelham.**

COOPER, Leon N. American, b. 1930. **Genres:** Physics. **Career:** Physicist and neural scientist. University of Illinois, Urbana, research associate in physics, 1955-57; Ohio State University, Columbus, assistant professor, 1957-58; Brown University, Providence, RI, associate professor, 1958-62, professor of physics, 1962-66, Henry Ledyard Goddard university professor, 1966-74, co-chair of Center for Neural Sciences, 1973-, Thomas J. Watson, Sr. Professor of Science, 1974-; Institute for Brain and Neural Systems, 1992-. Visiting professor at universities and summer schools; consultant to government agencies, industrial and educational organizations. **Publications:** (with B.B. Schwartz) The Physics and Application of Superconductivity, 1968; An Introduction to the Meaning and Structure of Physics, 1968, short ed, 1970; Physics: Structure and Meaning, 1992; How We Learn, How We Remember: Toward an Understanding of Brain and Neural Systems, 1995. Contributor to journals and periodicals. **Address:** Department of Physics, Brown University, Providence, RI 02912, U.S.A.

COOPER, M. E. *See* **WAGNER, Sharon Blythe.**

COOPER, Melrose. *See* **KROLL, Virginia L(ouise).**

COOPER, Paulette. American (born Belgium), b. 1942. **Genres:** Animals/Pets, Travel/Exploration. **Career:** Writer. **Publications:** The Scandal of Scientology, 1972; (ed.) Growing up Puerto Rican, 1972; Let's Find Out about Halloween, 1972; The Medical Detectives, 1974; Reward, 1994; 277 Secrets Your Dog Wants You to Know, 1995; 277 Secrets Your Cat Wants You to Know, 1997; 277 Secrets Your Snake and Lizard Wants You to Know, 1999. **Address:** 401 E 74th St, New York, NY 10021, U.S.A. **Online address:** PauletteC@aol.com

COOPER, Polly Wylly. (born United States), b. 1940. **Genres:** History. **Career:** Potter and gallery owner. Crabettes (music group), founding member. **Publications:** A Visitor's Guide to Savannah, 1995; Savannah Safari Walking Tour, 1998; Savannah Movie Memories, 2000; Isle of Hope, Wormsloe, and Bethesda, 2002; Images of America: Beaufort, 2003. **Address:** 519 Parkersburg Rd., Savannah, GA 31406, U.S.A.

COOPER, R(obert) C(ecil). New Zealander, b. 1917. **Genres:** Botany. **Career:** New Zealand Public Service, New Zealand, worked as cadet, clerk, and section head in education, audit, state advances, and rehabilitation departments, 1934-48; Auckland War Memorial Museum, Auckland, New Zealand, botanist, 1948-68, assistant director, 1968-71; Science teacher at a high school in Te Kao, New Zealand, 1971-75. Washington University, St. Louis, MO, university fellow and research assistant at Missouri Botanic Garden, 1951-53; Auckland Cancer Research Unit, collected plant samples in New Zealand and the Pacific, including New Guinea, 1953-58. **Publications:** (with S.G. Brooker and R.C. Cambie) New Zealand Medicinal Plants, 1981, 3rd ed. 1991; (with Brooker and Cambie) Economic Native Plants of New Zealand, 1988; (with Cambie) New Zealand's Economic Native Plants, 1991. Contributor to professional journals. **Address:** 1/117 Cambridge Rd., Hamilton, New Zealand.

COOPER, Richard Newell. American, b. 1934. **Genres:** Economics, International relations/Current affairs. **Career:** Yale University, New Haven, CT, Assistant Professor, 1963-65, Frank Altschul Professor of Economics, 1966-77, Provost, 1972-74; U.S. Deputy Assistant Secretary of State, 1965-66, and Under Secretary of State for Economic Affairs, 1977-81; Harvard University, Cambridge, MA, Boas Professor of International Economics, 1981-. Federal Reserve Bank of Boston, Chairman, 1990-92; National Intel-

ligence Council, Chairman, 1995-97. **Publications:** The Economics of Interdependence, 1968; (with others) Britain's Economic Prospects, 1968; Currency Devaluation in Developing Countries, 1971; (with M. Kaji and C. Segre) Toward a Renovated International Monetary System, 1973; Economic Mobility and National Economic Policy, 1974; (with K. Kaiser and M. Kosaka) Towards a Renovated International System, 1977; Economic Policy in an Independent World, 1986; The International Monetary System, 1987; (with others) Can Nations Agree?, 1989; Economic Stabilization and Debt in Developing Countries, 1992; (with others) Boom, Crisis, and Adjustment, 1993; Environment and Resource Policies for the World Economy, 1994; (with others) Macroeconomic Policy and Adjustment in Korea, 1994; (with others) What the Future Holds, 2002. EDITOR & CONTRIBUTOR: A Reordered World: Emerging International Economic Problems, 1973; The International Monetary System under Flexible Exchange Rates, 1982. **Address:** Harvard University, Cambridge, MA 02138, U.S.A.

COOPER, Roger. British, b. 1935. **Genres:** Area studies. **Career:** McDermott, New Orleans, LA, agent in Iran, c. 1985; Tehran University, Tehran, Iran, instructor of English; worked as a translator, a speechwriter, journalist, and consultant, all in Iran. **Publications:** NONFICTION: The Baha'is of Iran, 1982, rev ed, 1985; Death Plus Ten Years (memoir), 1993. **Address:** c/o HarperCollins, 77-85 Fulham Palace Rd., Hammersmith, London W6 8JB, England.

COOPER, Ron L. American, b. 1960. **Genres:** Philosophy, Bibliography. **Career:** Adjunct instructor in philosophy. **Publications:** Heidegger and Whitehead: A Phenomenological Examination Into the Intelligibility of Experience, 1993. Contributor to philosophy journals. **Address:** 830 Elk Run, Jacksonville, FL 32259-8318, U.S.A.

COOPER, Susan Lewis. American, b. 1947. **Genres:** Psychology. **Career:** South Boston and Dorchester Orientation Centers, Boston, MA, counselor, 1969-70; supervisor and counselor of prison inmates and exoffenders associated with Employability and Counseling Center at Brooke House, Boston, Massachusetts Correctional Institute in Framingham, and Suffolk County House of Correction, all 1970-73; Somerville Community Youth Agency, Somerville, MA, counseling supervisor, 1973-76; Boston University, Boston, clinical intern in psychological services, 1976-77; Cambridge Women's Center, Cambridge, MA, clinical intern, 1977-78; Focus Counseling and Consultation Inc., Cambridge, psychologist and codirector, 1978-. Reproductive Science Center, Waltham, MA, psychologist, 1989-; Community Training Resources, Cambridge, teacher and workshop leader, 197681; Resolve Inc., support group leader, 1983-. **Publications:** (with C. Heenan) Preparing, Designing, and Leading Workshops: A Humanistic Approach, 1980; (with E. Glazer) Without Child: Experiencing and Resolving Infertility, 1988; (with Glazer) Beyond Infertility: The New Paths to Parenthood, 1994; (with Glazer) Choosing Assisted Reproduction: Social, Emotional, and Ethical Considerations, 1998. Contributor to books and newsletters. **Address:** Focus Counseling and Consultation Inc., 186-1/2 Hampshire St., Cambridge, MA 02139, U.S.A. **Online address:** mlc@world.std.com

COOPER, Terry L. American, b. 1938. **Genres:** Administration/Management, Public/Social administration. **Career:** University of Southern California, Los Angeles, lecturer, 1971-72, instructor in religion, 1972-73, assistant professor of social ethics and urban affairs, 1973-75, assistant professor, 1975-82, associate professor, 1982-91, professor of public administration, 1991-. Yonsei University, visiting professor, 1983; University of Kansas, visiting professor, 1984; Chinese University of Hong Kong, Fulbright professor, 1988-89. Member of Los Angeles County Sheriff's Special Advisory Committee, 1991, and Los Angeles Police Chief's Professional Advisory Committee, 1993. Gives seminars and workshops; guest on radio programs; consultant to film producer Arthur Hoyle, Prison Industry Relation Project of Los Angeles, Health Systems Agency Coalition of Los Angeles, and the Command College of the Peace Officers Standards and Training Commission of the State of California. **Publications:** The Responsible Administrator: An Approach to Ethics for the Administrative Role, 1982, 4th ed., 1998; An Ethic of Citizenship for Public Administration, 1990; (ed. with N.D. Wright) Exemplary Public Administrators: Character and Leadership in Government, 1992; Handbook of Public Administration Ethics, 1994, 2nd ed., 2000. Work represented in anthologies. Contributor of articles and reviews to public administration journals. **Address:** School of Policy, Planning, and Development, University of Southern California, University Park, RGL 302, Los Angeles, CA 90089-0626, U.S.A. **Online address:** tlcooper@usc.edu

COOPER, Wendy. *See* Obituaries.

COOPERRIDER, Allen Y(ale). American, b. 1944. **Genres:** Environmental sciences/Ecology. **Career:** U.S. Department of the Interior, Bureau of Land

Management, Washington, DC, wildlife biologist throughout the western US, 1974-90; Big River Associates (consultants in conservation biology), Ukiah, CA, partner, 1991-94; US Fish and Wildlife Service, Ecosystem Restoration Office, Ukiah, senior biologist, 1994-98; Ukiah Brewing Co., general manager, 1999-. **Publications:** (ed. with R. Boyd and H. Stuart) The Inventory and Monitoring of Wildlife Habitats, 1967; (with R. Noss) Saving Nature's Legacy: Protecting and Restoring Biodiversity, 1994; (with D. Wilcove) Defending the Desert, 1995. **Address:** 18451 Orr Springs Rd, Ukiah, CA 95482, U.S.A.

COOTES, Jim E. Australian, b. 1950. **Genres:** Horticulture. **Career:** Australian Department of Defense, Sydney, New South Wales, Australia, engraver, 1966-97; Australia Post, Sydney, delivery officer, 2001. **Publications:** The Orchids of the Philippines, 2001. Contributor to orchid magazines in Australia and around the world. **Address:** c/o Author Mail, Timber Press, 133 Southwest Second Ave. Suite 450, Portland, OR 97204, U.S.A. **Online address:** jecootes@ozemail.com.au

COOVER, Robert. American, b. 1932. **Genres:** Novels, Novellas/Short stories, Plays/Screenplays. **Career:** Brown University, Providence, RI, distinguished professor, 1979-. **Publications:** The Origin of the Brunists, 1966; The Universal Baseball Association, Inc., J. Henry Waugh, Prop., 1968; Pricksongs and Descants (short stories), 1969; A Theological Position (plays), 1972; The Public Burning, 1977; Hair o' the Chine, 1979; Charlie in the House of Rue, 1980; A Political Fable, 1980; Spanking the Maid, 1982; In Bed One Night and Other Brief Encounters, 1983; Gerald's Party, 1986; A Night at the Movies, 1987; Whatever Happened to Gloomy Gus of the Chicago Bears?, 1987; Pinocchio in Venice, 1991; John's Wife, 1996; Briar Rose, 1996; Ghost Town: A Novel, 1998.

COPE, David. American, b. 1948. **Genres:** Poetry. **Career:** Faculty member, Grand Rapids Community College, 1986-; Western Michigan University, 1997. **Publications:** Quiet Lives, 1983; On the Bridge, 1986; (ed.) Nada Poems, 1988; Fragments from the Stars, 1990; Coming Home, 1993; Silences for Love, 1997. **Address:** 2782 Dixie, S. W, Grandville, MI 49418, U.S.A.

COPE, Wendy. British, b. 1945. **Genres:** Poetry. **Career:** Freelance writer, 1986-. Teacher, Portway Jr. School, London, 1967-69, Keyworth Jr. School, London, 1969-73, Cobourg Primary School, 1973-81, and Brindishe Primary School, 1984-86; ILEA Contact teachers' newspaper, arts editor, 1982-84. **Publications:** Across the City, 1980; Hope and the 42, 1984; Making Cocoa for Kingsley Amis, 1986; Poem from a Colour Chart of Housepaints, 1986; Men and Their Boring Arguments, 1988; Does She Like Word-Games?, 1988; Twiddling Your Thumbs (for children), 1988; The River Girl (poem), 1991; Serious Concerns (poems), 1992; If I Don't Know (poems), 2001. EDITOR: Is That the New Moon?: Poems by Women Poets, 1989; The Orchard Book of Funny Poems, 1993; The Funny Side, 1998; The Faber Book of Bedtime Stories, 2000; Heaven on Earth: 101 Happy Poems, 2001; George Herbert: Verse and Prose, 2002. **Address:** c/o Faber & Faber, 3 Queen Sq, London WC1N 3AU, England.

COPELAND, Gary A. American, b. 1952. **Genres:** Communications/Media. **Career:** Public schools of Modesto, CA, teacher in Regional Occupational Program, 1974-77; Modesto Junior College, Modesto, instructor, 1976-77; California State University, Fresno, instructor in speech communication, 1977-79; Pennsylvania State University, University Park, instructor in continuing education, 1980-82; University of Alabama, Tuscaloosa, assistant professor, 1982-89, associate professor of telecommunication and film, 1989-, graduate coordinator, 1989-, chair of Institutional Review Board for the Protection of Human Subjects, 1991-. General Electric News and Information Exchange, assistant system operator for Showbiz Roundtable, 1990-93. Impression Management Consulting, senior research associate; Alabama Radio Reading Service, reader. **Publications:** (with J. Dominick and B. Sherman) Broadcasting/Cable and Beyond: An Introduction to Modern Electronic Media, 1990; (with K. Johnson-Cartee) Negative Political Advertising, 1991; (ed. with W. Nothstine and C. Blair) Critical Questions: Invention, Creativity, and the Criticism of Discourse and Media, 1993; (with others) Inside Political Campaigns, 1997; (with others) Manipulation of the American Voter, 1997. Work represented in anthologies. Contributor of articles and reviews to political science and communication journals. **Address:** Department of Telecommunication and Film, University of Alabama, PO Box 870152, Tuscaloosa, AL 35487, U.S.A. **Online address:** copeland@tcf.ua.edu

COPELAND, Pala. American, b. 1950. **Genres:** Fashion/Costume. **Career:** Lecturer, writer, and teacher, 1997-. **Publications:** (with Al Link) Soul Sex:

Tantra for Two, 2003. Contributor to newspapers and magazines. **Address:** 4 Freedoms Tantra, POB 144, Pembroke, ON, Canada K8A 6X1. **Online address:** 4freedoms@tantraloving.com

COPELAND, Peter. American, b. 1957. **Genres:** Autobiography/Memoirs, Biography. **Career:** Worked for City News Bureau of Chicago, Chicago, IL, 1980-82; El Paso Herald Post, El Paso, TX, reporter, 1982-84; Scripps Howard News Service, Mexico City, Latin America correspondent, 1984-88, Washington, DC, defense and foreign affairs correspondent, 1989-96, assistant managing editor/news, 1996-99, editor and general manager, 1999-. **Publications:** (with Rhonda Cornum) She Went to War: The Rhonda Cornum Story, 1992; (with Dean Hamer) The Science of Desire, 1994; The Heidi von Beltz Story, 1995; (with D. Hamer) Living With Our Genes. **Address:** Scripps Howard News Service, 1090 Vermont Ave NW 10th Fl, Washington, DC 20005, U.S.A.

COPELAND, Rebecca L. American (born Japan), b. 1956. **Genres:** Biography, Translations. **Career:** Washington University, St. Louis, MO, associate professor of Japanese literature, 1991. **Publications:** The Sound of the Wind: The Life and Work of Uno Chiyo (biography), 1992, in UK as The Sound of the Wind: A Biography of Uno Chiyo with Three Novellas, 1992. TRANSLATOR: Aru hitori no onna no hanashi, by Uno Chiyo, published as The Story of a Single Woman, 1992. Contributor to anthologies, reference books, and language texts. Contributor to periodicals. Also author of articles written in Japanese. **Address:** Washington University, Dept. of Anell, St. Louis, MO 63130, U.S.A. **Online address:** copeland@artsci.wustl.edu

COPEMAN, George Henry. British, b. 1922. **Genres:** Administration/Management, Economics. **Career:** Managing Director, 1964-69, and Chairman, 1969-74, Business Intelligence Services Ltd., London; Chmn, Copeman Paterson Ltd., 1977-87; Chairman, Wider Share Ownership Council, 1990-92; chairman, Wider Share Ownership Educational Trust, 1992-98. **Publications:** Leaders of British Industry, 1955; Promotion and Pay for Executives, 1957; The Challenge of Employee Shareholding, 1958; The Role of the Managing Director, 1959; Laws of Business Management, 1963; (with F. Hanika) How the Executive Spends his Time, 1964; The Chief Executive and Business Growth, 1971; (with Tony Rumble) Capital as an Incentive, 1972; Employee Share Ownership and Industrial Stability, 1975; The Managing Director, 1978; (co-author) Shared Ownership, 1984; International Employee Share Ownership: Why? How? Where?, 1989; Employee Share Ownership, 1991; Employee Share Ownership Accountants Digest No. 325, 1994. **Address:** Moonraker, Batts Lane, Marehill, Pulborough, W. Sussex RH20 2ED, England.

COPENHAVER, John D., Jr. American, b. 1949. **Genres:** Theology/Religion. **Career:** Kings Canyon National Park, student pastor, 1975; pastor of United Methodist churches in Virginia, 1977-80; Harrisonburg Area Wesley Foundation, campus minister for four colleges, including James Madison University, 1981-83; pastor of United Methodist church in Salem, VA, 1983-87; Shenandoah University, Winchester, VA, chaplain, 1987-89, assistant professor, 1987-92, associate professor, 1992-99, head of Department of Religion and Philosophy, 1989, professor of religion, 1999-. **Publications:** Prayerful Responsibility: Prayer and Social Responsibility in the Religious Thought of Douglas Steere, 1992. Contributor to periodicals. **Address:** Dept of Religion, Shenandoah University, 1460 University Dr, Winchester, VA 22601-1595, U.S.A. **Online address:** jcopenha@su.edu

COPLAN, David B. American, b. 1948. **Genres:** Music. **Career:** State University of New York College at Old Westbury, associate professor of social anthropology, 1981-92; University of Cape Town, Cape Town, South Africa, associate professor of social anthropology, 1993-. U.S. Foreign Service Institute, occasional lecturer in African studies, 1981-92; New York University, adjunct graduate faculty member in performance studies, 1990; University of the Western Cape, Fulbright professor, 1991; Rice University, visiting professor, 1994-95. Guest on radio programs in the United States and abroad. **Publications:** In Township Tonight! South Africa's Black City Music and Theatre, 1990; In the Time of Cannibals: Word Music of South Africa's Basotho Migrants, 1994; Lyrics of the Basotho Migrants: Translations of African Historical Documents, 1995. Contributor to books and periodicals. **Address:** Department of Social Anthropology, University of Cape Town, Rondebosch 7700, Cape Town, Republic of South Africa.

COPPA, Frank John. American, b. 1937. **Genres:** Communications/Media, History, Theology/Religion, Urban studies, Biography. **Career:** St. John's University, NYC, assistant professor, 1965-70, associate professor, 1971-79, professor of history, 1979-; also writer for television. **Publications:** Planning Protectionism and Politics in Liberal Italy: Economics and Politics in the Giolittian Age, 1971; Camillo di Cavour, 1973; Pope Pius IX: Crusader in a Secular Age, 1979; Dictionary of Modern Italian History, 1985; Cardinal Giacomo Antonelli and Papal Politics in European Affairs, 1990; The Origins of the Italian Wars of Independence, 1992; The Modern Papacy since 1789, 1998; The Papacy Confronts the Modern World, 2003. EDITOR: (with W. Griffin and B. Bast) From Vienna to Vietnam: War and Peace in the Modern World, 1969; (with P. Dolce) Cities in Transition: From the Ancient World to Urban America, 1974; Religion in the Making of Western Man, 1974; The Immigrant Experience in America, 1976; Screen and Society: The Impact of Television upon Aspects of Contemporary Civilization, 1979; (with R. Harmond) Technology in the Twentieth Century, 1983; Studies in Modern Italian History, 1986; (with W. Roberts) Modern Italian History: An Annotated Bibliography, 1990; (with M. Repetto) The Formation of the Italian Republic, 1993; Encyclopedia of the Vatican and Papacy, 1999; Controversial Concordats: The Vatican's Relations with Napoleon, Mussolini, and Hitler, 1999; (in chief) Great Popes through History: An Encyclopedia, 2 vols., 2002. **Address:** Dept of History, St. John's University, Jamaica, NY 11439, U.S.A.

COPPEL, Alfred. Also writes as Robert Cham Gilman, Alfred Marin. American, b. 1921. **Genres:** Novels, Mystery/Crime/Suspense, Science fiction/Fantasy. **Publications:** Hero Driver, 1952; Night of Fire and Snow, 1957; Dark December, 1960; A Certainty of Love, 1966; The Gate of Hell, 1968; (as Alfred Marin) The Clash of Distant Thunder, 1968; (as Robert Cham Gilman) The Rebel of Rhada (science fiction), 1968; Order of Battle, 1969; (as Alfred Marin) Rise with the Wind, 1969; (as Robert Cham Gilman) The Navigator of Rhada (science fiction), 1969; A Little Time for Laughter, 1970; (as Alfred Marin) A Storm of Spears, 1970; Between the Thunder and the Sun, 1971; (as Robert Cham Gilman) The Starkhan of Rhada (science fiction), 1971; The Landlocked Man, 1972; Thirty Four East, 1973; The Dragon, 1977; The Hastings Conspiracy, 1980; The Apocalypse Brigade, 1981; The Burning Mountain, 1983; The Marburg Chronicles, 1985; (as Robert Cham Gilman) The Warlock of Rhada, 1985; The Fates Command Us, 1986; Show Me a Hero, 1987; A Land of Mirrors, 1988; Glory, 1993; Wars and Winters, 1993; The Eighth Day of the Week, 1994; Glory's War, 1995. **Address:** The Wallace Lit. Agency, 177 E. 70th St., New York, NY 10021, U.S.A.

COPPER, Basil. British, b. 1924. **Genres:** Novels, Novellas/Short stories, Mystery/Crime/Suspense, Romance/Historical, Science fiction/Fantasy. **Career:** Former journalist and editor. Crime Writers Association of Great Britain, chairman, 1981-82. **Publications:** The Dark Mirror, 1966; Night Frost, 1966; No Flowers for the General, 1967; Scratch on the Dark, 1967; Die Now, Live Later, 1968; Don't Bleed on Me, 1968; The Marble Orchard, 1969; Dead File, 1970; No Letters from the Grave, 1971; The Vampire in Legend, Fact and Art, 1971; Strong Arm, 1972; The Big Chill, 1972; The Phantom, 1972; The Phantom and the Scorpia Menace, 1972; The Phantom and the Slave Market of Mucar, 1972; The Breaking Point, 1973; A Great Year for Dying, 1973; Shock Wave, 1973; A Voice from the Dead, 1974; Feedback, 1974; Ricochet, 1974; The High Wall, 1975; Impact, 1975; A Good Place to Die, 1975; The Lonely Place, 1976; Crack in the Sidewalk, 1976; Tight Corner, 1976; The Year of the Dragon, 1977; Death Squad, 1977; The Werewolf: In Legend, Fact and Art, 1977; Murder One, 1978; A Quiet Room in Hell, 1978; The Big Rip-Off, 1979; The Caligari Complex, 1979; The Further Adventures of Solar Pons, 1979; The Secret Files of Solar Pons, 1979; The Exploits of Solar Pons, 1993; Flip-Side, 1980; The Long Rest, 1981; The Empty Silence, 1981; Dark Entry, 1981; Hang Loose, 1982; Shoot-Out, 1982; The Far Horizon, 1982; Trigger-Man, 1982; Pressure-Point, 1983; The Narrow Corner, 1983; Hard Contract, 1983; The Hook, 1984; You Only Die Once, 1984; Tuxedo Park, 1984; The Far Side of Fear, 1985; Jet-Lag, 1986; Blood on the Moon, 1986; Snow-Job, 1986; Heavy Iron, 1987; Turn Down an Empty Glass, 1987; Bad Scene, 1987; House-Dick, 1988; Print-Out, 1988; Exploits of Solar Pons, 1993; The Recollections of Solar Pons, 1995; Cold Hand on My Shoulder, 2002. GOTHIC: Necropolis, 1975; The Curse of the Fleers, 1976; The House of the Wolf, 1982; The Black Death, 1992. FANTASY: The Great White Space, 1975; The Horror on Planet X, 1975; Into the Silence, 1983. SHORT STORIES: Not after Nightfall, 1967; From Evil's Pillow, 1973; When Footsteps Echo, 1975; And Afterward, the Dark, 1977; Here Be Daemons, 1978; The Dossier of Solar Pons, 1978; Voices of Doom, 1980; Whispers in the Night, 1999.

COPUS, Julia. British, b. 1969. **Genres:** Poetry. **Career:** Tim Aston Design Ltd., London, England, copywriter, 1990-91; Libri (second-hand book store), co-owner, 1991-92; Pearson Young Ltd., Kent, England, editorial assistant, 1992-93; teacher of English as a foreign language, 1993-. **Publications:** POETRY: Walking in the Shadows, 1995; The Shuttered Eye, 1995. **Address:** 5 Thomas Rd., North Baddesley, Southampton, Hampshire SO52 9EW, England.

COQUERY-VIDROVITCH, Catherine. French, b. 1935. **Genres:** Area studies. **Career:** Universite Paris 7, Paris, France, professor of modern African history, 1972-. State University of New York at Binghamton, adjunct professor, 1981-. **Publications:** IN ENGLISH TRANSLATION: Afrique Noire: Permanences et Ruptures, 1985, rev. ed, 1993, trans. as Africa: Endurance and Change South of the Sahara, 1988; Les Africaines: Histoire des Femmes d'Afrique Noire du XIXe au XXe Siecle, 1994, trans. as African Women: A Modern History, 1997. IN FRENCH: La Decouverte de l'Afrique: L'Afrique Noire Atlantique, des Origines au XVIIIe Siecle, 1965, 2nd ed., 1971; Brazza et la Prise de Possession du Congo: La Mission de l'Ouest Africain, 1883-1885, 1969; (coauthor) Histoire Economique du Congo, 1880-1968, 1970; Le "Congo Francais" au Temps des Grandes Compagnies Concessionnaires, 1898-1930, 1972, rev. ed., 2001; (with H. Moniot) L'Afrique Noire de 1800 a Nos Jours, 1974; (coauthor) Histoire de la France Coloniale, 1991; Histoire des Villes d'Afrique Noire des Origines a la Colonisation, 1993; Histoire des Africans au 19e Siecle, 1999. Contributor to books and professional journals. **Address:** Universite Paris 7, Denis Diderot Case 7017, 2 Place Jussieu, 75251 Paris, Cedex 5, France. **Online address:** coqueryv@ext.jussieu.fr

CORBETT, Patricia. American, b. 1951. **Genres:** Art/Art history. **Career:** Author, editor, and art historian. Former editor of European edition of Connoisseur; contributor of monthly column to Italian edition of the New York Times Book Review. **Publications:** (with Caroline Lebeau) Fabrics: The Decorative Art of Textiles, 1994; Verdura: The Life and Work of a Master Jeweler, 2002. Contributor to periodicals. **Address:** c/o Author Mail, Harry N. Abrams Inc., 100 Fifth Avenue, New York, NY 10011, U.S.A.

CORBETT, Richard (Graham). British, b. 1955. **Genres:** Politics/Government. **Career:** Intl Youth Organizations, European Coordination Bureau, secretary general, Brussels, Belgium, 1977-81; European Parliament, Brussels, member of Secretariat, 1981-89, political adviser to Socialist Group, 1989-95, deputy secretary general, 1995-96; MEP for Merseyside West, 1996-99; MEP for Yorkshire & Humber, 1999-; spokesman on EU constitutional affairs. **Publications:** (with F. Jacobs and M. Shackleton) The European Parliament, 1990, 5th ed., 2003; The Treaty of Maastricht, 1993; The European Parliament's Role in Closer EU Integration, 1998. Contributor to periodicals. **Address:** European Parliament, rue Wiertz, 1047 Brussels, Belgium. **Online address:** richard@richardcorbett.org.uk

CORBETT, Scott. American, b. 1913. **Genres:** Novels, Children's fiction, Children's non-fiction. **Career:** Served as correspondent, US Army, 42nd (Rainbow) Infantry Division, 1943-46. **Publications:** The Reluctant Landlord, 1950; Sauce for the Gander, 1951; We Chose Cape Cod, 1953; Cape Cod's Way: An Informal History, 1955; The Sea Fox: The Adventures of Cape Cod's Most Colorful Rumrunner, 1956; Susie Sneakers, 1956; Midshipman Cruise, 1956; Tree House Island, 1959; Dead Man's Light, 1960; The Lemonade Trick, 1960; The Mailbox Trick, 1961; Cutlass Island, 1962; Danger Point: The Wreck of the "Birkenhead," 1962; What Makes a Car Go?, 1963; The Disappearing Dog Trick, 1963; The Limerick Trick, 1964; The Baseball Trick, 1965; One by the Sea, 1965; The Cave above Delphi, 1965; What Makes TV Work?, 1965; Pippa Passes, 1966; The Case of the Gone Goose, 1966; What Makes a Light Go On?, 1966; Diamonds Are Trouble, 1967; What Makes a Plane Fly?, 1967; The Turnabout Trick, 1968; Cop's Kid, 1968; Ever Ride a Dinosaur?, 1969; The Hairy Horror Trick, 1969; Rhode Island, 1969; The Case of the Fugitive Firebug, 1969; Diamonds Are More Trouble, 1969; What Makes a Boat Float?, 1970; Steady, Freddie, 1970; The Baseball Bargain, 1970; The Mystery Man, 1970; The Case of the Ticklish Tooth, 1971; The Hateful Plateful Trick, 1971; The Big Joke Game, 1972; The Red Room Riddle, 1972; Dead before Docking, 1972; Run for the Money, 1973; The Home Run Trick, 1973; Dr. Merlin's Magic Shop, 1973; What about the Wankel Engine?, 1974; Take a Number, 1974; The Hockey Trick, 1974; Here Lies the Body, 1974; The Case of the Silver Skull, 1974; The Great Custard Pie Panic, 1974; The Boy with Will Power, 1975; The Case of the Burgled Blessing Box, 1975; The Boy Who Walked on Air, 1975; The Great McGoniggle's Gray Ghost, 1975; The Great McGoniggle's Key Play, 1976; The Black Mask Trick, 1976; The Hockey Girls, 1976; Captain Bucher's Body, 1976; The Great McGoniggle Rides Shotgun, 1977; The Hangman's Ghost Trick, 1977; The Foolish Dinosaur Fiasco, 1978; The Discontented Ghost, 1978; Bridges, 1978; The Donkey Planet, 1979; The Mysterious Zetabet, 1979; Jokes to Read in the Dark, 1980; Home Computers, 1980; The Great McGoniggle Switches Pitches, 1980; The Deadly Hoax, 1981; Grave Doubts, 1982; Jokes to Tell Your Worst Enemy, 1984; Down with Wimps, 1984; The Trouble with Diamonds, 1985; Witch Hunt, 1985. **Address:** 149 Benefit St, Providence, RI 02903, U.S.A.

CORBETT, William. American, b. 1942. **Genres:** Poetry, Literary criticism and history. **Career:** Poet, author and educator. Massachusetts Institute of

Technology, currently lecturer of writing. **Publications:** POETRY: Columbus Square Journal, 1976; Runaway Pond, 1981; City Nature: Collected Poems, 1986; On Blue Note, 1989; Don't Think, Look, 1991; New and Selected Poems, 1995. NON-FICTION: Literary New England: A History and Guide, 1993; Philip Guston's Late Work: A Memoir, 1994; Furthering My Education, 1997; New York Literary Lights, 1998. Contributor of poetry to periodicals. **Address:** 9 Columbus Sq., Boston, MA 02116, U.S.A.

CORBIN, Alain. French, b. 1936. **Genres:** History. **Career:** University of Limoges, assistant lecturer, 1968-69; University of Tours, senior lecturer, 1969-72, assistant professor, 1973-85, professor of history, 1985-86; Universite Paris I, Pantheon-Sorbonne, professor of history, 1987-; Institut Universitaire de France, professor of history, 1992. **Publications:** The Foul and the Fragrant: Odor and the French Social Imagination, 1986; (with M. Perrot) A History of Private Life, Vol 4: From the Fires of Revolution to the Great War, ed. by G. Duby, 1990; Le Village des Cannibales, 1990, trans. as The Village of Cannibals: Rage and Murder in France, 1870, 1991; Women for Hire: Prostitution and Sexuality in France after 1850, 1992; Time, Desire and Horror, 1996; Village Bells: Sound and Meaning in the 19th-Century Countryside, 1998; The Life of an Unknown: The Rediscovered World of a Clog Maker in 19th Century France, 2001. **Address:** Universite Paris I, Pantheon-Sorbonne, 17 rue de la Sorbonne, 75005 Paris, France.

CORBIN, Jane. British, b. 1954. **Genres:** Documentaries/Reportage. **Career:** ITN-TV, foreign correspondent for Channel 4 News, c. 1983-88; British Broadcasting Corp., London, England, current affairs and investigative journalist for BBC-TV, senior foreign correspondent for the television program Panorama, c. 1988-, presenter of the live debate program Behind the Headlines, c. 1991-. Also worked for Thames Television and Granada Television. **Publications:** The Norway Channel, 1994. Contributor to periodicals in England and abroad. **Address:** British Broadcasting Corp., 201 Wood Ln., London W12, England.

CORCORAN, Neil (Cornelius). British (born Ireland), b. 1948. **Genres:** Literary criticism and history. **Career:** University of Sheffield, Sheffield, England, lecturer, beginning in 1974, senior lecturer in English literature, 1991-; University of Wales Swansea, Professor of English, 1994-96; Professor of English, University of St. Andrews, 1996-. **Publications:** The Song of Deeds: A Study of The Anathemata of David Jones, 1982; Seamus Heaney, 1986; (ed.) The Chosen Ground: Essays on the Contemporary Poetry of Northern Ireland, 1991; English Poetry since 1940, 1992; After Yeats and Joyce, 1997; The Poetry of Seamus Heany: A Critical Study, 1998; Poets of Modern Ireland, 1999. **Address:** School of English, University of St. Andrews, St. Andrews KY16 9AL, England. **Online address:** cdc4@st-andrews.ac.uk

CORDAIRE, Christina. See KINGSTON, Christina.

CORDEIRO, Patricia (A.). British, b. 1944. **Genres:** Education, Language/Linguistics. **Career:** Elementary schoolteacher, Colchester, CT, 1965-66, and Provincetown, MA, 1968-72 and 1974-90; Rhode Island College, Providence, assistant professor, 1990-93, associate professor of education and human development, 1993-. Norwich University, field faculty adviser for Vermont College, 1987-92; Whitman Institute, fellow, 1988; University of Massachusetts at Boston, adjunct faculty member, 1988-, fellow of Lucretia Crocker Academy, 1989-; Lesley College, adjunct faculty member, 1990; French River Education Center, instructor, 1990; Learning Center (St. Louis, MO), instructor, 1991. Educational Developmental Corp., curriculum developer and evaluator, 1988-89. **Publications:** (with C. Cazden, M.E. Giacobbe, and others) Whole Language Plus: Essays on Literacy in the United States and New Zealand, 1992; Whole Learning: Whole Language and Content in the Upper Elementary Grades, 1992. Work represented in books. Contributor to language and education journals and to newspapers. **Address:** School of Education and Human Development, 216 Mann Hall, Rhode Island College, Providence, RI 02908, U.S.A.

CORDEN, Warner Max. Australian (born Germany), b. 1927. **Genres:** Economics. **Career:** Nuffield Reader in International Economics, Oxford University, 1967-76; Professor, Australian National University, Canberra, 1976-88; International Monetary Fund, 1986-88; Professor, Paul H. Nitze School of Advanced International Studies, Johns Hopkins University, Washington, DC, 1989-2002; University of Melbourne, professorial fellow, 2002-. **Publications:** The Theory of Protection, 1971; Trade Policy and Economic Welfare, 1974, 2nd ed., 1997; Inflation, Exchange Rates, and the World Economy, 1977, 3rd ed., 1985; Protection, Trade and Growth, 1985; International Trade Theory and Policy, 1992; Economic Policy, Exchange Rates, and the International System, 1994; The Road to Reform, 1997; Too

Sensational, 2002. **Address:** Department of Economics, University of Melbourne, Melbourne, VIC 3010, Australia.

CORDING, Robert. American, b. 1949. **Genres:** Poetry. **Career:** Poet. Holy Cross College, professor of English. **Publications:** Life-list, 1987; What Binds Us to This World, 1991; Heavy Grace, 1996; Against Consolation, 2002. **Address:** College of the Holy Cross, English Department, Worcester, MA 01610, U.S.A. **Online address:** rcording@holycross.edu

CORDINGLY, David. British, b. 1938. **Genres:** Art/Art history, History. **Career:** Freelance writer. Peter Hatch Partnership, graphic designer, 1963-65; British Museum, exhibition designer, 1967-71; Art Gallery and Museum, Brighton, keeper, 1971-78; Museum of London, assistant director, 1978-80; National Maritime Museum, London, keeper of pictures, head of exhibitions, 1980-93. **Publications:** Marine Painting in England 1700-1900, 1974; Painters of the Sea, 1979; The Art of the Van de Veldes, 1982; Nicholas Pocock, 1986; Captain James Cook, Navigator, 1988; Pirates, Fact and Fiction, 1992; Under the Black Flag, the Romance and Reality of Life among the Pirates, 1995; Pirates, an Illustrated History, 1996; Ships and Seascapes: An Introduction to Maritime Prints, Drawings and Watercolours, 1997; Women Sailors and Sailors' Women, 2001; Billy Ruffian: The Bellerophon and the Downfall of Napoleon. **Address:** 2 Vine Pl, Brighton, Sussex BN1 3HE, England. **Online address:** d.cordingly@btinternet.com

CORDLE, Thomas. American, b. 1918. **Genres:** Literary criticism and history. **Career:** Duke University, Durham, NC, instructor to professor of romance studies, 1950-86. **Publications:** Andre Gide, Twayne, 1969, revised edition, 1993. **Address:** 916 West Markham Ave., Durham, NC 27701, U.S.A.

COREN, Alan. British, b. 1938. **Genres:** Novellas/Short stories, Children's fiction, Plays/Screenplays, Humor/Satire. **Career:** Columnist, The Times, London, 1988- (TV Critic, 1972-78). Literary Ed., 1967-69, Deputy Ed., 1969-73, and Ed., 1978-87, Punch mag., London; Columnist, Daily Mail, 1974-77; Ed., The Listener mag., 1988-89. **Publications:** (co-author) Introduction (short stories), 1961; The Dog It Was That Died, 1965; All Except the Bastard, 1969; The Collected Bulletins of Idi Amin, 1974; The Sanity Inspector, 1974; The Further Bulletins of Idi Amin, 1975; Golfing for Cats, 1975; The Peanut Papers, 1977; The Lady from Stalingrad Mansions, 1977; The Arthur Books (for children), 1973-81; The Rhinestone as Big as the Ritz, 1979; Tissues for Men, 1980; The Best of Alan Coren, 1980; The Cricklewood Diet, 1982; Bumf, 1984; Something for the Weekend, 1986; Bin Ends, 1987; Seems Like Old Times, 1989; More Like Old Times, 1991; A Year in Cricklewood, 1992; Toujours Cricklewood, 1993; Sunday Best, 1994; A Bit on the Side, 1995; The Alan Coren Omnibus, 1996; The Cricklewood Dome, 1998; The Cricklewood Tapestry, 2000. EDITOR: The Punch Book of Kids, 1974; Punch in the Country, 1976; Present Laughter, 1982; The Penguin Book of Modern Humour, 1983. **Address:** c/o Robson Books, 10 Blenheim Court, Brewery Rd, London N7 9NT, England.

COREN, Stanley. Canadian (born United States), b. 1942. **Genres:** Psychology, Animals/Pets. **Career:** University of British Columbia, Vancouver, professor of psychology, 1973-. SC Psychological Enterprises Ltd. (consultants), director; Royal Society of Canada, fellow. Also assistant professor, New School for Social Research; chairperson, Psychological Laboratories; member, Program for Visual Perception. Vancouver Dog Obedience Training Club, dog trainer. **Publications:** (with L.M. Ward, A. Gruft, and J.B. Collins) The Behavioral Basis of Design, Volume I, Dowden, 1976; (with J.S. Girgus) Seeing Is Deceiving: The Psychology of Visual Illusions, 1978; (with C. Porac) Lateral Preferences and Human Behavior, 1981; (with L.M. Ward) Sensation and Perception, 3rd ed. with instructor's manual, 1989, 5th ed. (with L.M. Ward and J.T. Enns), 1999; (ed.) Left-Handedness: Behavioral Implications and Anomalies, 1990; The Left-Hander Syndrome: The Causes and Consequences of Left-Handedness, 1992; The Intelligence of Dogs, 1994; Sleep Thieves, 1996; What Do Dogs Know?, 1997; Why We Love the Dogs We Do, 1999; The Pawprint of History, 2002. **Address:** Department of Psychology, University of British Columbia, 2136 West Mall, Vancouver, BC, Canada V6T 1Z4. **Online address:** scoren@psych.ubc.ca

COREY, Deborah Joy. Canadian, b. 1958. **Genres:** Novels. **Career:** Worked in modeling and promotion for several years in Toronto, Ontario, Canada, during the late 1970s and early 1980s; freelance writer, c. 1983-. **Publications:** NOVELS: Losing Eddie, 1993; The Skating Pond, 2003. Contributor to periodicals. **Address:** c/o Algonquin Books/Workman Publishing, 708 Broadway, New York, NY 10003, U.S.A.

CORIOLANUS. See MCMILLAN, James.

CORK, Richard (Graham). British, b. 1947. **Genres:** Art/Art history. **Career:** Art Critic, Evening Standard, London, 1969-77, 1980-83; Ed., Studio International, London, 1975-79; Art Critic, The Listener, London, 1984-90; Slade Professor of Fine Art, Cambridge University, 1989-90; Chief Art Critic, The Times, London, 1991-2001; Henry Moore Senior Research Fellow at the Courtauld Institute of Art, London, 1992-95; Art Critic, The New Statesman, 2003-. Member, Art Advisory Group, South Bank Board, London, 1987-93; Trustee, Public Art Development Trust, 1988-96; Member, British Council Visual Art Committee, 1992-96; Chairman of Visual Arts Panel, Arts Council of England, 1995-98; Member, Advisor Council, Paul Mellon Centre; Syndic of Fitzwilliam Museum, Cambridge. **Publications:** Vorticism and Abstract Art in the First Machine Age, 2 vols., 1975 and 1976; The Social Role of Art, 1979; Art Beyond the Gallery in Early 20th Century England, 1985; David Bomberg, 1987; (with E. Rosenberg) Architect's Choice, 1992; A Bitter Truth: Avant-Garde Art and the Great War, 1994; Bottle of Notes: Claes Oldenburg/Coosje van Bruggen, 1997; Jacob Epstein, 1999; Everything Seemed Possible: Art in the 1970s, 2003; New Spirit, New Sculpture, New Money: Art in the 1980s, 2003; Breaking down the Barriers: Art in the 1990s, 2003; Annus Mirabilis? Art in the Year 2000, 2003. **Address:** 24 Milman Rd, London NW6 6EG, England.

CORLETT, Mary Lee. American, b. 1957. **Genres:** Adult non-fiction, Art/Art history. **Career:** Cleveland Museum of Art, Cleveland, OH, assistant to the registrar, 1985-88; Smithsonian Institution, Washington, DC, research assistant in print department of National Portrait Gallery, 1988-89; National Gallery of Art, Washington, DC, research associate in Dept of Modern Prints and Drawings, 1989-2002, research associate in Dept of Special Projects in Modern Art, 2002-. **Publications:** (with R.E. Fine) Graphicstudio: Contemporary Art from the Collaborative Workshop at the University of South Florida, 1991; Prints of Roy Lichtenstein, 1994, rev. ed., 2002. Work represented in anthologies. **Address:** Dept of Special Projects in Modern Art, National Gallery of Art, Fourth St and Constitution Ave NW, Washington, DC 20565, U.S.A.

CORLEY, Ernest. See BULMER, (Henry) Kenneth.

CORLEY, Thomas Anthony Buchanan. British, b. 1923. **Genres:** Business/Trade/Industry, Economics, History, Biography. **Career:** Sr. Lecturer in Economics, University of Reading, 1968-88 (Lecturer, 1962-68), currently part-time; Bank of England, 1950-56 (Central Bank of Iraq, Baghdad, Director of Issue Dept., 1953-55); Dept. of Applied Economics, University of Cambridge, 1956-58; Assistant Lecturer and Lecturer, Queen's University, Belfast, 1958-62. **Publications:** True Book about Napoleon, 1958; Democratic Despot: A Life of Napoleon III, 1961; (ed.) Otto Wolff: Ouvrard, Speculator of Genius, 1962; Domestic Electrical Appliances, 1966; Quaker Enterprise in Biscuits: Huntley & Palmers of Reading 1822-1972, 1972; History of the Burmah Oil Company, 2 vols., 1983, 1988. **Address:** University of Reading Business School, Centre for International Business History, Department of Management, PO Box 218, Reading RG6 6AA, England. **Online address:** t.a.b.corley@reading.ac.uk

CORLISS, Richard (Nelson). American, b. 1944. **Genres:** Film. **Career:** National Review, NYC, film critic, 1966-70; Museum of Modern Art, NYC, staff member of film department, 1968-70; Film Comment, NYC, editor, 1970-89; New Times, NYC, film critic, 1975-78; Soho Weekly News, New York, film critic, 1980; Time, NYC, associate editor, 1980-85, senior writer, 1985-. Member of the selection committee for the New York Film Festival, 1971-87. **Publications:** (ed.) The Hollywood Screenwriters (biography), 1972; Greta Garbo (biography), 1974; Talking Pictures: Screenwriters in the American Cinema (nonfiction), 1974; Lolita (monograph), 1994. Contributor of articles to periodicals. **Address:** Time Magazine, Time-Life Building, Rockefeller Center, New York, NY 10020, U.S.A.

CORMACK, Sir Patrick (Thomas). British, b. 1939. **Genres:** Architecture, History, Politics/Government, Social commentary. **Career:** Member of Parliament (Conservative) for Staffordshire SW 1974- (Member for Cannock, 1970-74). Chairman, Parliamentary Heritage Group; Member, Royal Commission on Historic Manuscripts. Schoolmaster, St. James School, Grimsby, Wrekin College, Shropshire, and Brewood Grammar School, 1961-70; Editor, House Magazine, 1983-; Visiting Fellow, St. Antony's College, Oxford, 1994-95; Vice President, Society of Antiquaries, 1994-98; International President, First Magazine, 1996-. **Publications:** Heritage in Danger, 1976; (ed.) Right Turn, 1978; Westminster: Palace and Parliament, 1981; Castles of Britain, 1982; Wilberforce: The Nation's Conscience, 1983; English Cathedrals, 1984. **Address:** House of Commons, London SW1, England.

CORMACK, Robert J. Scottish, b. 1946. **Genres:** Education, Public/Social administration. **Career:** Queen's University, Belfast, Northern Ireland, lecturer, 1973-87, senior lecturer, 1987-92, reader in sociology, 1992-94, dean of the faculty of economics and social sciences, 1992-94, professor of sociology, 1994-, pro-vice-chancellor, 1995-; UHI Millennium Institute, Inverness, principal, 2001-. Belfast Citizens Advice Bureau, chairperson, 1989-92. **Publications:** (with R.D. Osborne) Religion, Education, and Employment, 1983; (with R.D. Osborne and R.L. Miller) Education and Policy in Northern Ireland, 1987. EDITOR (with R.D. Osborne): Discrimination and Public Policy in Northern Ireland, 1991; (and A.M. Gallaher) After the Reforms: Education and Policy in Northern Ireland, 1993. **Address:** UHI Millennium Institute, Executive Office, Ness Walk, Inverness IV3 5SQ, Scotland. **Online address:** www.uhi.ac.uk

CORN, Alfred. American, b. 1943. **Genres:** Novels, Poetry, Literary criticism and history. **Career:** Columbia College, NYC, preceptor, 1968-70; University Review, NYC, associate ed., 1970; DaCapo Press, NYC, Staff writer, 1971-72; Connecticut College, New London, assistant professor, 1978; Yale University, New Haven, CT, visiting lecturer, 1977-79, 1986-87, 1992; Columbia University, adjunct associate, 1983-93, adjunct professor, 1994-97; CUNY, 1984-85; University of Cincinnati, 1989; UCLA, 1990; Ohio State University, 1990; adjunct professor, Lang College, New School, 1991; Columbia University, 1997-2001; Hofstra University, 1998-2000, Godard College, 1999, University of Tulsa, 2001-02. **Publications:** All Roads at Once, 1976; A Call in the Midst of the Crowd, 1978; The Various Light, 1980; Notes from a Child of Paradise, 1984; The Metamorphoses of Metaphor: Essays in Poetry and Fiction, 1987; The West Door, 1988; (ed.) Incarnation: Contemporary Writers on the New Testament, 1990; Autobiographies, 1992; Part of His Story, 1997; Present, 1997; The Poem's Heartbeat: A Manual of Prosody, 1997; Stake: Selected Poems, 1972-2001; Contradictions (poetry), 2002. **Address:** c/o Author Mail, Copper Canyon Press, Fort Worden State Park, PO Box 271 Bldg 313, Port Townsend, WA 98368, U.S.A.

CORN, Charles. American, b. 1936. **Genres:** History. **Career:** George Washington University, Washington, DC, instructor in English, beginning in 1964; American University, Washington, DC, instructor in English, until 1969; executive with publishing companies in Boston, MA and NYC. **Publications:** Distant Islands: Travels across Indonesia, 1991; The Scents of Eden: A Narrative of the Spice Trade, 1998. **Address:** 1711 Jones St., San Francisco, CA 94109, U.S.A. **Online address:** corn@pacbell.net

CORN, David. American, b. 1959. **Genres:** Documentaries/Reportage, Mystery/Crime/Suspense. **Career:** Nation, Washington, DC, Washington editor, 1987-; writer. **Publications:** Blond Ghost: Ted Shackley and the CIA's Crusades, 1994; Deep Background (political thriller), 1999. Contributor to periodicals. **Address:** Nation, 110 Maryland Ave. NE #308, Washington, DC 20002, U.S.A.

CORNELL, Gary. American. **Genres:** Information science/Computers. **Career:** Professional computer programmer, author, and University of Connecticut professor. **Publications:** (with W. Abikoff) The Basic Adam, 1984; (with W. Abikoff) The Basic Apple IIc: A Self-Teaching Guide, 1985; ProDOS and Beyond, 1985; Basics for DOS, 1991; QuickBASIC 4.5, 1991; Visual Basic for Windows Inside & Out, 1992; Visual Basic 3 for Windows Handbook, 1993; Teach Yourself Word for Windows, 1994; (with C.S. Horstmann and T. Strain) Delphi Nuts & Bolts: For Experienced Programmers, 1995; (with T. Strain) Visual Basic 4 Nuts & Bolts: For Experienced Programmers, 1995; (with C.S. Horstmann and J. Cuthbertson) The Visual Basic 4 for Windows 95 Handbook, 1995; (with C.S. Horstmann and D. Jezak) Activex: Visual Basic 5 Control Creation Ed., 1997; (with C.S. Horstmann) Core Java 1.1: Fundamentals, 1997; (with C.S. Horstmann) Core Java 1.1: Advanced Features, 1997; (with C.S. Horstmann and D. Jezak) Core Visual Basic 5, 1997; (with C.S. Horstmann and T. Strain) Visual Basic 5 From the Ground Up, 1997; (with C.S. Horstmann and K. Abdali) Cgi Programming With Java, 1998; (with C.S. Horstmann and K. Topley) Core Java Foundation Classes, 1998; (with P. Patel) Core NT Web Server With CDROM, 1998; (with C.S. Horstmann and J.L. Traub) Core Visual J, 1998; Learn Microsoft Visual Basic Scripting Editor Now, 1998. EDITOR: (with J.H. Silverman) Arithmetic Geometry, 1986; (with J.H. Silverman and G. Stevens) Modular Forms and Fermat's Last Theorem. **Address:** c/o Apress LP, 2560 9th St Ste 219, Berkeley, CA 94710, U.S.A. **Online address:** cornell@math.uconn.edu

CORNELL, Jennifer C. American, b. 1967. **Genres:** Novellas/Short stories. **Career:** Oregon State University, Corvallis, OR, assistant professor of English, 1994-. Youth and community worker in Belfast, Northern Ireland. **Publications:** Departures (short stories), 1995, in Ireland as All There Is, 1995. Contributor to anthologies. **Address:** English Department, Oregon State University, 238 Moreland Hall, Corvallis, OR 97331, U.S.A.

CORNELL, Judith. American, b. 1941. **Genres:** Inspirational/Motivational Literature. **Career:** Holos University Graduate School, assistant professor of spiritual healing and energy medicine; California Institute of Integral Studies, San Francisco, CA, adjunct professor; speaker and seminar leader. **Publications:** Mandala: Luminous Symbols for Healing, 1994; Drawing the Light from Within: Keys to Awaken Your Creative Power, 1990; Amma: Healing the Heart of the World, 2001. Contributor to periodicals.

CORNER, James. British, b. 1961. **Genres:** Horticulture. **Career:** Robert Camlin Associates, Manchester, England, drafter, 1980-82; Maurice Wrangell Associates, NYC, landscape architectural intern, 1982; William Gillespie and Partners, Manchester, landscape architectural assistant, 1982-84; Robert Fleming and Associates, Philadelphia, PA, landscape architect, 1984-86; Wallace, Roberts & Todd, Philadelphia, landscape architect, 1987; University of Pennsylvania, Philadelphia, studio critic, 1987, lecturer, 1987-90, assistant professor, 1990-96, associate professor of landscape architecture and regional planning, 1996-, Ian McHarg Honorary Lecturer, 1997. University of Norway, visiting professor, 1993; Harvard University, Daniel Urban Kiley Lecturer, 1993; University of Chicago, visiting lecturer, 1994; University of Illinois at Chicago Circle, Jens Jensen Professor of Landscape and Urbanism, 1997; Royal Danish Academy of Art, visiting professor, 1997; Yale University, Timothy Egan Memorial Lecturer, 1997; speaker at colleges and universities. Work exhibited in traveling shows and group exhibitions. **Publications:** (with A.S. MacLean) Taking Measures across the American Landscape: Essays, Photographs, Drawings, 1996; Landscape Architectural Theory: Anthology, 1960-1996, 1997; (ed. with A. Balfour, and contrib.) Reconstructing Landscape: Essays in the Theory and Practice of Contemporary Landscape Architecture, 1998. Contributor to books. Contributor of articles and reviews to professional journals. **Address:** Graduate School of Fine Arts, University of Pennsylvania, Philadelphia, PA 19104, U.S.A. **Online address:** corner@pobox.upenn.edu

CORNGOLD, Stanley. American, b. 1934. **Genres:** Literary criticism and history. **Career:** Princeton University, lecturer, 1966-67, assistant professor, 1967-72, associate professor, 1972-81, professor of German and comparative literature, 1981-. **Publications:** The Commentators' Despair: The Interpretation of Kafka's Metamorphosis, 1973; The Fate of the Self: German Writers and French Theory, 1986, 2nd. ed., 1994; Franz Kafka: The Necessity of Form, 1988; (with I. Giersing) Borrowed Lives, 1991; (trans.) Goethe's Elective Affinities, 1997; Complex Pleasure: Forms of Feeling in German Literature, 1998; Lambent Traces: Franz Kafka, 2004. EDITOR: Ausgewaehlte Prosa of Max Frisch, 1968; (and trans.) The Metamorphosis, by F. Kafka, 1972; (with R. Ludwig) Thomas Mann, 1875-1975, 1975; (with M. Curschmann and T. Ziolkowski) Aspekte der Goethezeit, 1977. **Address:** Department of German, 219 E Pyne Bldg, Princeton University, Princeton, NJ 08544, U.S.A. **Online address:** corngold@princeton.edu

CORNWELL, Anita (R.). American, b. 1923. **Genres:** Novels, Children's fiction. **Career:** Free-lance writer and novelist. Pennsylvania State Department of Public Welfare employee. **Publications:** Black Lesbian in White America, Naiad Press, 1983; The Girls of Summer (juvenile), illustrated by Kelly Caines, New Seed Press, 1989. **Address:** 3220 Powelton Ave., Philadelphia, PA 19104, U.S.A.

CORP, Edward. British, b. 1948. **Genres:** History, Biography. **Career:** University of Toulouse, professor. **Publications:** (with J. Sanson) La cour des Stuarts a Saint-Germain-en-Laye au temps de Louis XIV, 1992; (with S. Crowe) Our Ablest Public Servant: Sir Eyre Crowe, 1864-1925, 1993; L'autre exil: Les Jacobites en France au debut du XVIIIe siecle, 1993; (with E. Cruickshanks) The Stuart Court in Exile and the Jacobites, 1994; Lord Burlington: The Man and His Politics, 1998; The King over the Water, 2001; The Stuart Court in Rome: The Legacy of Exile, 2003; A Court in Exile: The Stuarts in France, 2004. **Address:** 15 rue Des Arts, 31000 Toulouse, France. **Online address:** e.corp@wanadoo.fr

CORRADO, Anthony. American, b. 1957. **Genres:** Politics/Government. **Career:** Colby College, Waterville, ME, instructor, 1986-89, assistant professor, 1989-94, associate professor, 1994-2000, professor of government, 2001-. **Publications:** Creative Campaigning, 1992; Paying for Presidents, 1993; Let America Decide, 1995; (with H. Alexander) Financing the 1992 Election, 1996; (with others) Campaign Finance Reform: A Sourcebook, 1997; Campaign Finance Reform, 2000. **Address:** Department of Government, Colby College, Waterville, ME 04901, U.S.A.

CORRAN, Mary. British, b. 1953. **Genres:** Science fiction/Fantasy. **Career:** Trainee system analyst, Reading, Berkshire, 1980-82; oil analyst, various stockbroking companies, banks and financial institutions, City of London, 1982-92; writer. **Publications:** FANTASY NOVELS: Imperial Light, 1994; Fate, 1995; Darkfell, 1996. Contributor to books. **Address:** 19 Park Close, Eastbourne, E. Sussex BN20 8AG, England.

CORRICK, James A. American, b. 1945. **Genres:** Young adult non-fiction, Air/Space topics, Novellas/Short stories, Sciences, Science fiction/Fantasy. **Career:** Writer and editor, Tucson, AZ, 1979-; University of Arizona, Tucson, tutor, 1981-82; L5 Society, Tucson, editor, 1985-87; National Space Society, Washington, DC, editor, 1987; Muscular Dystrophy Association, Tucson, science writer, 1991-92. **Publications:** The Human Brain: Mind and Matter, 1983; Recent Revolutions in Chemistry, 1986; Recent Revolutions in Biology, 1987; Career Preparation, 1988; Double Your Pleasure: The Ace SF Double, 1989; The World of Nature: Farm Animals, 1991; Mars, 1991; Muscular Dystrophy, 1992; The Early Middle Ages, 1995; The Late Middle Ages, 1995. Contributor to books. Has also published articles and short stories. **Address:** 4402 East Cooper Circle, Tucson, AZ 85711, U.S.A.

CORRIGAN, John R. (born United States), b. 1970. **Genres:** Mystery/Crime/Suspense. **Career:** Maine School of Science and Mathematics, Limestone, teacher of English literature and writing, 1998-. **Publications:** Cut Shot (mystery novel), 2001; Snap Hook (mystery novel), 2004. **Address:** c/o Giles Anderson, Literary Agency, 395 Riverside Dr., Suite 12AH, Presque Isle, ME 04769, U.S.A. **Online address:** corriganj@mssm.org

CORRINGTON, Robert S. American, b. 1950. **Genres:** Administration/Management. **Career:** Drew University, Casperson School of Graduate Studies, Madison, NJ, professor of philosophical theology. Previously professor at Pennsylvania State University. **Publications:** (editor, with Carl Hausman and Thomas M. Seebohm) Pragmatism Considers Phenomenology, 1987; The Community of Interpreters: On the Hermeneutics of Nature and the Bible in the American Philosophical Tradition, 2nd edition, 1995; (editor, with Armen Marsoobian and Kathleen Wallace) Justus Buchler, Metaphysics of Natural Complexes, 1990; (editor, with Armen Marsoobian and Kathleen Wallace) Nature's Perspective: Prospects of Ordinal Metaphysics, 1991; Nature and Spirit: An Essay in Ecstatic Naturalism, 1992; An Introduction to C. S. Pierce: Philosopher, Semiotician, and Ecstatic Naturalist, 1993; Ecstatic Naturalism: Signs of the World, 1994; Nature's Self: Our Journey from Origin to Spirit, 1996; Nature's Religion, 1997; A Semiotic Theory of Theology and Philosophy, 2000; Wilhelm Reich: Psychoanalyst and Radical Naturalist, 2003; Riding the Windhorse: Manic Depressive Disorder and the Quest for Wholeness, 2003. Contributor to numerous academic journals. **Address:** Drew University, 36 Madison Avenue, Madison, NJ 07940, U.S.A. **Online address:** rcorring@drew.edu

CORTEN, Irina H. American (born Russia), b. 1941. **Genres:** Education, Language/Linguistics, Area studies. **Career:** University of Wisconsin-Madison, instructor in Russian, 1973-74; University of Kansas, Lawrence, visiting assistant professor of Russian, 1974-75; University of Minnesota-Twin Cities, Minneapolis, associate professor of Russian, 1975-. Guest on national television and radio programs. **Publications:** Vocabulary of Soviet Society and Culture: A Selected Guide to Russian Words, Idioms, and Expressions of the Post-Stalin Era, 1992. Author of scholarly and journalistic articles. **Address:** Russian Program, 253 Elliot Hall, University of Minnesota Twin Cities, 75 E. River Rd S.E., Minneapolis, MN 55455, U.S.A.

CORUM, James S(terling). American (born France), b. 1953. **Genres:** History. **Career:** Queen's University, Kingston, ON, instructor in history, 1988-91; U.S. Air Force School of Advanced Air and Space Studies, Maxwell Air Force Base, AL, professor of comparative military studies, 1991-2004; Oxford University, All Souls College, visiting fellow, 2005; U.S. Army Command and General Staff College, professor, 2005-. **Publications:** The Roots of Blitzkrieg: Hans von Seeckt and German Military Reform, 1992; (with R. Muller) The Luftwaffe's Way of War, 1997; The Luftwaffe: Creating the Operational Air War 1918-1940, 1998; (with W. Johnson) Airpower in Small Wars: Fighting Insurgents and Terrorists, 2003. Contributor to periodicals. **Address:** U.S. Army Command and General Staff College, Leavenworth, KS 66048, U.S.A.

CORY, Charlotte. British, b. 1956. **Genres:** Novels. **Career:** Artist, specializing in woodcuts for Dragonfly Press; writer. **Publications:** NOVELS: The Unforgiving, 1991; The Laughter of Fools, 1993; The Guest, 1996. **Address:** c/o David Godwin Associates, 355 Monmouth St, London WC2H 9DG, England.

CORYELL, Janet L(ee). American, b. 1955. **Genres:** History, Biography. **Career:** University of Dayton, Dayton, OH, assistant professor of history, 1986-89; Auburn University, Auburn, AL, assistant professor of history,

1989-91; Western Michigan University, Kalamazoo, assistant professor of history, 1991-92; associate professor, 1992-. **Publications:** Neither Heroine nor Fool: Anna Ella Carroll of Maryland, Kent State University Press, 1990. (Editor with James Greiner and James R. Smither) A Surgeon's Civil War: The Letters & Diary of Daniel M. Holt, M.D., Kent State University Press, 1994. **Address:** Department of History, 4406 Friedmann Hall, Western Michigan University, Kalamazoo, MI 49008, U.S.A.

COSBY, Bill. American, b. 1937. **Genres:** Children's non-fiction, Human relations/Parenting, Humor/Satire. **Career:** Began career as stand-up comic, 1962; television and film actor. **Publications:** You Are Somebody Special, ed. by Charlie W. Shedd (for children), 1978; Fatherhood, 1986; Time Flies, 1988; Love and Marriage, 1989; Childhood, 1991; The Wit and Wisdom of Fat Albert; Bill Cosby's Personal Guide for Power Tennis; Congratulations! Now What?, 1999. **Address:** c/o The Brokaw Company, 9255 Sunset Blvd., Suite 804, Los Angeles, CA 90069, U.S.A.

COSENTINO, Frank. Canadian, b. 1937. **Genres:** History, Sports/Fitness. **Career:** Salesman, 1960-63; Canadian Football League, professional football player (quarterback) in Hamilton, 1960-66, Edmonton, AB, 1967-68, and Toronto, ON, 1969; high school teacher in Hamilton, ON, 1963-65; University of Western Ontario, London, assistant professor, 1970-74, associate professor of physical education, 1975-76, chairman of department, 1975-76, head football coach, 1970-74; York University, Toronto, professor of physical education, recreation, and athletics, 1976-81, chairman and director of department, 1976-81, head football coach, 1978-80, 1984-87, professor emeritus and senior scholar, 1999-. **Publications:** Canadian Football: The Grey Cup Years, 1969; (with M.L. Howell) A History of Physical Education in Canada, 1970; (with G. Leyshon) Olympic Gold, 1975; Ned Hanlan, 1978; (with D. Morrow) Lionel Conacher, 1981; (with G. Leyshon) Winter Gold, 1983; (with M. Dinning, K. Jones, and G. Malszecki) A History of Physical Education, 1985; (with D. Morrow, M. Keyes, and others) A Concise History of Sport in Canada, 1989; Not Bad, Eh? Prose and Poetry in Canadian Sport, 1990; Renfrew Millionaires: The Valley Boys of Winter, 1910, 1990; A Passing Game: A History of the CFL, 1995; Almonte's Brothers of the Wind: R. Tait McKenzie and James Naismith, 1996; Afros, Aboriginals and Amateur Sport in Pre WWI Canada, 1998; Almonte, 2000. **Address:** 25 Maple Ridge Dr, Box 316, Eganville, ON, Canada K0J 1T0. **Online address:** frankc@yorku.ca

COSGROVE, Denis (Edmund). British, b. 1948. **Genres:** Geography, Horticulture. **Career:** Oxford Polytechnic, Oxford, England, lecturer, 1972-75, senior lecturer, 1975-79, principal lecturer in geography, 1979-80; Loughborough University of Technology, England, lecturer, 1980-84, senior lecturer, 1984-88, reader in cultural geography, 1988-93; University of London, Royal Holloway College, England, professor of human geography, 1994-99; University of California, Los Angeles, Alexander von Humboldt Professor of Geography, 2000-. Landscape Research Group Ltd., director, 1980-87. Visiting professor/lecturer at colleges and universities worldwide. **Publications:** Social Formation and Symbolic Landscape, 1984; The Palladian Landscape: Geographical Change and Its Cultural Representations in Sixteenth-Century Italy, 1993; Mappings, 1999; Apollo's Eye: A Cartographic Genealogy of the Globe in the Western Imagination. EDITOR & CONTRIBUTOR: (with S.J. Daniels) The Iconography of Landscape: Essays on the Symbolic Representation, Design, and Use of Past Environments, 1988; (with G.E. Petts) Water, Engineering, and Landscape: Water Control and Landscape Transformation in the Modern Period, 1990. Contributor to books. Contributor of articles and reviews to geography and education journals. **Address:** Dept of Geography, 1170 Bunche Hall, University of California, Los Angeles, 405 Hilgard Ave, Los Angeles, CA 90095, U.S.A. **Online address:** cosgrove@geog.ucla.edu

COSIC, Dobrica. Yugoslav, b. 1921. **Genres:** Novels, Essays. **Career:** Novelist, essayist, and politician. Yugoslav Communist Youth League, member, beginning in 1939; Yugoslav National Liberation Movement, member, beginning in 1941; League of Communists of Yugoslavia, member, until 1968; worked as a journalist; served as political commissioner of Partisans' Battalion Two in central Serbia during World War II. Held several political, administrative, and cultural posts in the Yugoslav Communist government after World War II, including member of League of Communists of Serbia Central Committee, 1965-68; people's deputy from Serbia to the Yugoslav Assembly, 1945-68; and Marshal Tito's courtly poet. Founder, with Liubomin Tadic, of the scholarly journal Javnost (title means "Public Opinion"). **Publications:** Daleko je sunce (novel), 1951, trans by Muriel Heppell and Milica Mihajlovic as Far Away Is the Sun (also known as The Sun Is Far Away), 1963; Koreni (novel; title means: Roots), 1954; Deobe (title means: Divisions), three vols, 1961; Akcija: zapici, povodi, odgovori,

1955-1964 (essays), 1964; Locitve (fiction), 1964; Prilike: Akcija 1, 1966; Odgovornosti: Akcija 2, 1966; Sabrana dela, 1966; Bajka (novel; title means: A Fairy Tale), 1966; Moc i strepnje (essays; title means: Power and Foreboding), 1971; Vreme smrti (fiction), four vols, 1972-79, trans by Heppell in three volumes as Vol 1: A Time of Death, 1978, Vol 2: Reach to Eternity, 1980, Vol 3: South to Destiny, 1981, trans by Heppell in four volumes as This Land, This Time, Vol 1: Into the Battle, Vol 2: A Time of Death, Vol 3: Reach to Eternity, Vol 4: South to Destiny, 1983; Stvarno I moguce: clanci i ogledi, 1982; Vreme zla (title means: A Time of Evil), three vols, Vol 1: Gresnik (title means: The Sinner), 1985, Vol 2: Otpadnik (title means: The Apostate), 1986, Vol 3, Vernik (title means: A Believer), 1990. Work represented in anthologies of Yugoslav literature. Cosic's novels have been translated into English, Russian, German, Czech, Slovak, Finnish, Bulgarian, and Arabic. **Address:** c/o Harcourt Brace, 525 B St, Suite 1900, San Diego, CA 92101-4495, U.S.A.

COSKRAN, Kathleen. American, b. 1943. **Genres:** Novellas/Short stories. **Career:** University of Minnesota-Twin Cities, Minneapolis, adjunct faculty, 1988-; Hamline University, St. Paul, MN, adjunct faculty, 1989-. **Publications:** The High Price of Everything (stories), 1988; (ed.) Tanzania on Tuesday; (ed.) An Inn Near Kyoto. Work represented in anthologies. Contributor to periodicals. **Address:** 1804 McKinley St NE, Minneapolis, MN 55418, U.S.A.

COSMAN, Mark. American, b. 1945. **Genres:** How-to books. **Career:** Volunteers of America (VOA), Los Angeles, CA, President of Friends of VOA, 1984-. **Publications:** In the Wake of Death: Surviving the Loss of a Child, 1996. **Address:** Volunteers of America, 3600 Wilshire Blvd. No. 1500, Los Angeles, CA 90010, U.S.A.

COSSOLOTTO, Matthew. American, b. 1953. **Genres:** Plays/Screenplays, Advertising/Public relations, Communications/Media, How-to books, Politics/Government, Self help, Technology, Ghost Writer. **Career:** U.S. House of Representatives, Washington, DC, legislative assistant to Congressman Leon E. Panetta, 1977-81, special assistant to Speaker James C. Wright Jr., 1983-88; served in the Peace Corps, Sierra Leone, West Africa, 1981-82; MCI Communications Corp., Washington, DC, senior manager of the Corporate Communications Department and speechwriter for William G. McGowan, 1988-92; PepsiCo Foods & Beverages International, Somers, NY, director of communications, 1992-95; GTE Corp., Stamford, CT, director of communications, 1995-96; Ovations International, Inc., Yorktown Heights, NY, founder and president, 1996-. President and board chair of the Center for Voting and Democracy, 1991-96. Has appeared on television and radio news programs. **Publications:** NONFICTION: Almanac of Transatlantic Politics, 1991; Almanac of European Politics: 1995, 1995; Habit Force! How to Kick the Habits of F.A.I.L.U.R.E and Adopt the Habits of S.U.C.C.E.S.S., 2004. Contributor to periodicals.

COSTA, Manuel J(oseph). American, b. 1933. **Genres:** Inspirational/Motivational Literature. **Career:** Roman Catholic priest, 1961-75; pastor of St. Bernard's parish in Eureka, CA, 1968-74; College of Notre Dame, Belmont, CA, assistant professor of religious studies and director of campus ministry, 1974-75; Bridge Counseling Center, Morgan Hill, CA, executive director, 1975-79; Miramonte Mental Health Services, Palo Alto, CA, executive director, 1979-88; psychotherapist in private practice, 1989-. Guild for Psychological Studies, seminar leader, 1981-. **Publications:** (with M. Eussen) Life and Love, 1969; Tackling Life Head On: Lessons for Kids' Lives with Ronnie Lott as Coach, 1997. **Address:** 5570 Harvard Dr., San Jose, CA 95118-3418, U.S.A.

COSTER, Graham. British, b. 1960. **Genres:** Novels, Travel/Exploration. **Career:** Granta, assistant editor, 1983-87; worked as editor at publishing house. **Publications:** Train, Train: A Novel, 1989; A Thousand Miles from Nowhere: Trucking Two Continents, 1995; (ed. and author of intro) The Wild Blue Yonder: The Picador Book of Aviation, 1997; Corsairville: The Lost Domain of the Flying Boat, 2000. Contributor to periodicals. **Address:** c/o Viking, Author Mail, 27 Wrights Lane, London W8 5TZ, England.

COSTIGAN, Daniel M. Also writes as Ned Negitsoc. American, b. 1929. **Genres:** Art/Art history, Engineering, History, Information science/Computers, Technology, Humor/Satire. **Career:** Information Systems Designer, 1962-. Ed./Columnist, Rahway, New Jersey News-Record/Clark Patriot, 1987-97. Chairman, Publs. Committee, National Micrographics Association, 1978-80. **Publications:** FAX: The Principles and Practice of Facsimile Communication, 1971; Micrographic Systems, 1975, 1980; (ed.) Guide to Micrographic Equipment, 1977-79; Electronic Delivery of Documents and Graphics 1978; Encore for a Worthy Performer, 1984; Never Trust a Columnist Who Uses a Pen Name, 1990; Showplace, 1993; Beyond Barbizon, 2000; The Collected Works of Otis DeNigalnac. **Address:** 8 Wyndmoor Way, Edison, NJ 08820, U.S.A. **Online address:** negitsoc@aol.com

COSTLEY, Bill. (William Kirkwood Costley, Jr). Also writes as Boles Kulik. American, b. 1942. **Genres:** Plays/Screenplays, Poetry, Advertising/Public relations, Communications/Media, Writing/Journalism, Documentaries/Reportage. **Career:** Communications consultant, 1976-. Formerly, medical technician, library asst., English instr., technical editor/writer, journalist, publicist. **Publications:** POETRY: Knosh I Cir, 1975; R(A)G(A)S, 1978; A(Y)S(H)A, 1988; Terrazzo, 1993; Siliconia, 1995. PLAYS/SCREENPLAYS: Hard Currency, 1985; The 4th, 1986; Death of a Realtor, 1996; Mothers to Wolves (screenplay), 1999. **Address:** c/o Arts End Books, PO Box 441, West Dover, VT 05356, U.S.A. **Online address:** billcostley@newsguy.com; billcostley@yahoo.com

COTE, Richard N. American, b. 1945. **Genres:** Genealogy/Heraldry, History, Local history/Rural topics. **Career:** Freelance writer, 1971-; freelance photographer and historical researcher in Manitowoc, WI, 1971-79; South Carolina Historical Society, Charleston, project director, field archivist, and historical writer, 1979-80; County of Charleston, SC, director of micrographics, 1982-85; writer. **Publications:** (comp.) Local and Family History in South Carolina: A Bibliography, 1981; (comp.) The Dictionary of South Carolina Biography, 1983; Ports, Power, and Trade: A History of the South Carolina State Ports Authority, 1991; Love by Mail: The International Guide to Personal Advertising, 1992; Jewel of the Cotton Fields: An Architectural and Social History of Secessionville Manor, 1995; Safe House: The Compelling Memoirs of the Only CIA Spy to Seek Asylum in Russia, 1995; Rice and Ruin: The William Bull Pringles and the Death of the South Carolina Rice Culture, 1800-1884, 1995. Author of "Calumet County Ancestors" and "Manitowoc County Ancestors," genealogy columns in Wisconsin newspapers. Contributor to periodicals. **Address:** P.O. Box 1898, Mount Pleasant, SC 29465-1898, U.S.A.

COTHRAN, James R(obert). American, b. 1940. **Genres:** Homes/Gardens. **Career:** South Carolina State Highway Department, Columbia, landscape designer, 1965; Lyles, Bissette, Carlisle & Wolfe, Columbia, site planner, 1966; Robert and Marvin Associates, Walterboro, SC, landscape architect, 1967; U.S. Dept of Housing and Urban Development, Atlanta, GA, site planner and landscape architect, 1968-70; Robert and Co., Atlanta, landscape architect and planner, 1970-78, assistant vice president, 1978-81, vice president, 1981-, head of planning and landscape architecture department, 1978-. Georgia State University, instructor, 1990-; University of Georgia, instructor, 2002-; frequent lecturer throughout the Southeast. American Society of Landscape Architects, fellow, 2002. **Publications:** Gardens of Historic Charleston, 1995; Gardens and Historic Plants of the Antebellum South, 2003. **Address:** 96 Poplar St, Atlanta, GA 30303, U.S.A. **Online address:** J.Cothran@Robertco.com

COTMAN, John Walton. American, b. 1954. **Genres:** Area studies, International relations/Current affairs, Politics/Government, Third World. **Career:** Howard University, Washington, DC, instructor, 1990-91, assistant professor of political science, 1991-96, associate professor, 1996-. American University, visiting assistant research professor, School of International Service, 1994-95. **Publications:** Birmingham, JFK, and the Civil Rights Act of 1963: Implications for Elite Theory, 1989; The Gorrion Tree: Cuba and the Grenada Revolution, 1993; (ed. with E. Linger) Cuban Transitions at the Millennium, 2000. Contributor to books and political science and Caribbean studies journals. **Address:** Department of Political Science, MSC 590536, Howard University, 2400 6th St NW, Washington, DC 20059, U.S.A. **Online address:** jcotman@fac.howard.edu

COTT, Nancy F(alik). American, b. 1945. **Genres:** History, Women's studies and issues. **Career:** Professor of History and American Studies, Yale University, New Haven, Conn. (Member of Faculty since 1975). Instructor in History, Wheaton College, Norton, Massachusetts, 1971, Clark University, Worcester, Massachusetts, 1972, and Wellesley College, Massachusetts, 1973-74. **Publications:** Root of Bitterness: Documents of the Social History of American Women, 1972, rev. ed. 1996; The Bonds of Womanhood: "Woman's Sphere" in New England, 1780-1835, 1977; (with ed. Elizabeth H. Pleck) A Heritage of Her Own: Families, Work and Feminism in America, 1979; The Grounding of Modern Feminism, 1987; (ed.) Women in U.S. History (20 vols.), 1993-94; A Woman Making History: Mary Ritter Beard Through Her Letters, 1991. **Address:** American Studies Program, P.O. Box 208236, New Haven, CT 06520, U.S.A.

COTTER, James Finn. American, b. 1929. **Genres:** Literary criticism and history. **Career:** Professor of English, Mount Saint Mary College, New-

burgh, New York, since 1963. Contr. writer for The Hudson Review. Fulbright-Hays Lecturer, Algeria, 1970-71. **Publications:** Inscape: The Christology and Poetry of Gerard Manley Hopkins, 1972; (trans.) Divine Comedy, 1988; Beginnings, 1988. **Address:** 372 Grand St, Newburgh, NY 12550, U.S.A.

COTTERRELL, Roger (B. M.). British, b. 1946. **Genres:** Law, Music. **Career:** University of Leicester, England, lecturer in law, 1969-74; University of London, Queen Mary and Westfield College, England, lecturer, 1974-78, senior lecturer, 1978-85, reader, 1985-90, professor of legal theory, 1990-, head of department, 1989-91, dean of Faculty of Laws, 1993-96. **Publications:** The Sociology of Law: An Introduction, 1984, rev. ed., 1992; The Politics of Jurisprudence, 1989, rev. ed., 2003; Law's Community: Legal Theory in Sociological Perspective, 1995; Emile Durkheim-Law in a Moral Domain, 1999; (with C. Goode) Bass Lines: A Life in Jazz, 2002. EDITOR: (with B. Bercusson) Law, Democracy, and Social Justice, 1988; Law and Society, 1994; Sociological Perspectives on Law, 2 vols., 2001. **Address:** Dept of Law, Queen Mary and Westfield College, University of London, Mile End Rd, London E1 4NS, England. **Online address:** r.b.m.cotterrell@gmul.ac.uk

COTTINGHAM, John (Graham). British, b. 1943. **Genres:** Philosophy. **Career:** University of Washington, Seattle, lecturer in philosophy, 1967-68; Oxford University, Oxford, England, lecturer in philosophy at Exeter College, 1968-71; University of Reading, Reading, England, lecturer, 1971-87, reader, 1987-90, professor of philosophy, 1990-, department head, 1989-93. Scholar in residence, Randolph-Macon Woman's College, 1987. Consultant to publishers. **Publications:** Descartes' Conversation with Burman, 1976; Rationalism: A Selective Critical Survey of Rationalist Thought from Plato to the Present Day, 1984; Descartes, 1986; A History of Western Philosophy, vol. 4: The Rationalists, 1989; A Descartes Dictionary, 1993; Philosophy and the Good Life: Reason and the Passions in Greek Cartesian and Psychoanalytic Ethics, 1998; On the Meaning of Life, 2003. EDITOR: The Cambridge Companion to Descartes, 1992; Reason, Will and Sensation: Studies in Cartesian Metaphysics, 1994; Western Philosophy (anthology), 1996; Descartes, 1998. TRANSLATOR: (with Stoothoff and Murdoch) Descartes: Selected Philosophical Writings, 1988. EDITOR & TRANSLATOR: (with R. Stoothoff and D. Murdoch) The Philosophical Writings of Descartes, 2 vols., 1985, 3rd vol. (with R. Stoothoff, D. Murdoch, and A. Kenny), 1991; Descartes: Meditations on First Philosophy and Selections from the Objections and Replies, 1986; (with R. Ariew and T. Sorell) Descartes' Meditations, Background Source Materials, 1998. **Address:** Department of Philosophy, University of Reading, Reading RG6 6AA, England. **Online address:** J.G.Cottingham@Reading.AC.UK

COTTLE, Thomas J. American, b. 1937. **Genres:** Education, Psychology, Sociology. **Career:** Research sociologist and practicing psychotherapist. Consultant, ABC-TV, since 1972. Assistant Professor of Social Relations, Harvard University, Cambridge, Massachusetts, 1965-69; Fellow, Center for Advanced Study, University of Illinois, Urbana, 1969-70; Research Sociologist, Massachusetts Institute of Technology, Cambridge, 1970-73. **Publications:** Time's Children: Impressions of Youth, 1971; The Prospect of Youth: Contexts for Sociological Inquiry, 1972; (with C. R. Eisendrath) Out of Discontent: Visions of the Contemporary University, 1972; The Abandoners: Portraits of Loss, Separation and Neglect, 1973; The Voices of School: Educational Issues Through Personal Accounts, 1973; (with S. L. Klineberg) The Present of Things Future: Explorations of Time in Human Experience, 1974; Black Children, White Dreams, 1974; A Family Album: Portraits of Intimacy and Kinship, 1974; Lovers From Denver, 1974; The Horizons of Time: Inquiries and Speculations, 1974; Busing, 1976; Barred from School, 1976; Perceiving Time, 1976; Children in Jail, 1977; College: Reward and Betrayal, 1977; (ed.) Readings in Adolescent Psychology, 1977; Private Lives and Public Accounts, 1977; (co-ed.) Psychotherapy, 1979; Black Testimony, 1980; Children's Secrets, 1981; Divorce and the Jewish Child, 1981; Like Fathers, Like Sons, 1981; Hidden Surivors, 1981. **Address:** c/o WCVB, 5 TV Place, Needham, MA 02494, U.S.A.

COTTONWOOD, Joe. American, b. 1947. **Genres:** Children's fiction, Novels, Poetry. **Career:** Writer. Computer operator, 1968-76; self-employed building contractor, 1976-. Worked as a dishwasher, fry cook, and bus driver. **Publications:** FOR CHILDREN: The Adventures of Boone Barnaby, 1990; Danny Ain't, 1992; Quake!, 1995; Babcock, 1996. FOR ADULTS: Famous Potatoes, 1976; Frank City (Goodbye), c. 1977. POETRY: Son of a Poet. **Address:** PO Box 249, La Honda, CA 94020, U.S.A.

COTTRELL, Sir Alan (Howard). British, b. 1919. **Genres:** Environmental sciences/Ecology, Physics. **Career:** Professor of Physical Metallurgy,

University of Birmingham, 1949-55; Deputy Head of Metallurgy Division, Atomic Research Establishment, Harwell, 1955-58; Goldsmiths' Professor of Metallurgy, University of Cambridge, 1958-65; Chief Adviser, Studies, Ministry of Defence, 1965-67; Deputy Chief Scientific Adviser, 1968-71, and Chief Scientific Adviser to H. M. Government, 1971-74; Master of Jesus College, Cambridge, 1974-86. **Publications:** Theoretical Structural Metallurgy, 1948; Dislocations and Plastic Flow in Crystals, 1953; The Mechanical Properties of Matter, 1964; Theory of Crystal Dislocations, 1964; An Introduction to Metallurgy, 1967; Portrait of Nature, 1975; Environmental Economics, 1978; How Safe Is Nuclear Energy?, 1981; Introduction to the Modern Theory of Metals, 1988; Concepts in the Electron Theory of Alloys, 1998. **Address:** Jesus College, Cambridge, England.

COTTRELL, Richard. British, b. 1936. **Genres:** Plays/Screenplays, Translations. **Career:** Oxford Playhouse, Oxford, England, front of house manager, 1960-63; Allied Filmmakers, London, England, reader, 1963; British Broadcasting Corp., London, reader and scriptwriter in Sound Drama Department, 1963-64; Hampstead Theatre, London, general manager, 1964-66; Prospect Theatre Company, London, associate director, 1966-69; Cambridge Theatre Company, Cambridge, England, founder and director, 1970-75; Bristol Old Vic Theatre, Bristol, England, director, 1975-80; freelance director and playwright, 1980-85; Nimrod Theatre, Sydney, Australia, director, 1985-87. **Publications:** PLAYS Deutsches Haus (2 act), 1959; (coauthor of adaptation) Howards End (3 act), 1965; (adapter) A Room with a View (3 act), 1967. TRANSLATIONS: G. Feydeau, The Birdwatcher, 1963; A. Chekhov, The Cherry Orchard, 1967; A. Chekhov, The Seagull, 1970; A. Chekhov, The Three Sisters, 1971; G. Feydeau, Ruling the Roost, 1972; E. Westphal, You and Your Clouds, 1972; E. Ionesco, Aunt Sally; or, The Triumph of Death, 1973; A. Chekhov, Uncle Vanya, 1982; J. Racine, Britannicus, 1994. **Address:** c/o Casarotto Ramsay & Associates Ltd, National House, 60-66 Wardour St, London W1V 3HP, England.

COTTRELL, Robert C. American, b. 1950. **Genres:** Biography, Civil liberties/Human rights, History, Intellectual history, Politics/Government, Theology/Religion. **Career:** South Oklahoma City Community College, Oklahoma City, adjunct professor, 1980-84; University of Oklahoma, Norman, instructor, 1983-84; California State University, Chico, assistant professor, 1984-89, associate professor, 1989-94; Professor, 1994-. **Publications:** Izzy: A Biography of I.F. Stone, 1992; The Social Gospel of E. Nicholas Comfort: Founder of the Oklahoma School of Religion, 1997; Roger N. Baldwin and American Civil Liberties, forthcoming. Contributor to books. **Address:** 219 Trinity Hall, Department of History, California State University, Chico, CA 95929, U.S.A.

COTTRET, Bernard. French, b. 1951. **Genres:** History. **Career:** Oxford University, Merton College, Oxford, England, lecturer in French, 1972-73; University of Paris IV, Sorbonne, Paris, France, assistant professor, 1981-89; University of Lille III, Lille, France, professor of British Studies, 1989-92; University of Versailles-Saint-Quentin-en-Yvelines, Versailles, France, professor, 1992-, and chairman of humanities department, 1992-96; Universitaire de France, senior member of institute, 1998-. **Publications:** Terre d'exil, 1985; La Glorieuse Revolution, 1988; Le Christ des Lumieres, 1990; The Huguenots in England, 1991; Cromwell, 1992; Bolingbroke, 1992; Calvin, 1995; Histoire d'Angleterre, 1996; (with M. Cottret) Histoire politique de l'Europe, 1996; Bolingbroke's Political Writings, 1997; 1598. L'edit de Nantes, 1997; Henri VIII, 1999; La Renaissance, 2000; Histoire de la Reforme protestante, 2001; Le Revolution Americaine, 2003. Contributor to periodicals. **Address:** Universite de Versailles-Saint-Quentin-en-Yvelines, 47 Boulevard Vauban, 78280 Guyancourt, France. **Online address:** bernard.cottret@wanadoo.fr

COTTRINGER, Anne. Canadian, b. 1952. **Genres:** Children's fiction. **Career:** Freelance cinematographer and director for films and television, 1980-. **Publications:** Ella and the Naughty Lion, 1996; Movie Magic, 1999; Danny and the Great White Bear, 1999; Gordon, 1999; Buster's Bark, 2001; Buster's Bone, 2002; Bruna, 2003; Rosa & Galileo, 2003; Hot Dog, 2004; Mary Is Scary, 2005. Contributor to magazines.

COULMAS, Florian. German, b. 1949. **Genres:** Language/Linguistics, Social sciences, Documentaries/Reportage. **Career:** University of Duesseldorf, West Germany, assistant professor, 1980-88, professor of linguistics, 1988; Chuo University, Tokyo, Japan, professor of general linguistics, 1988; Duisburg University, Germany, professor of Japanese studies; Georgetown University, Visiting professor. **Publications:** A Festschrift for Native Speaker, 1980; Conversational Routine, 1981; Sprache und Staat, 1985; Direct and Indirect Speech, 1986; The Writing Systems of the World, 1989; Language Adaptation, 1990; Language and Economic Policy, 1992; A Language Policy for the European Community, 1991; Das Land der rituellen Harmonie, 1993; The Blackwell Encyclopedia of Writing Systems, 1996; Gewahlte Worte, 1996; Handbook of Sociolinguistics, 1997; Writing Systems, 2002; Die Kultur Japans, 2003. **Address:** Modernes Japan, University Duisburg-Essen, 47048 Duisburg, Germany.

COULSON, Juanita. American, b. 1933. **Genres:** Romance/Historical, Science fiction/Fantasy, Westerns/Adventure. **Career:** Publr., Forum mag., Science Fiction Writers of America, 1971-72. **Publications:** SCIENCE FICTION: Crisis on Cheiron, 1967; The Singing Stones, 1968; Unto the Last Generation, 1975; Space Trap, 1976; Tomorrow's Heritage, 1981; Outward Bound, 1982; Legacy of Earth, 1989; The Past of Forever, 1989; Star Sister, 1990. FANTASY: The Web of Wizardry, 1978; The Death God's Citadel, 1980; Cold, Hard Silver, 1994; A Matter of Faith, 1995; Shadows over Scorpio, 2004; Avenger, 2004. OTHER: The Secret of Seven Oaks, 1972; Door into Terror, 1972; Stone of Blood, 1975; Fear Stalks the Bayou, 1976; Intersection Point, 1976; Dark Priestess, 1977; Fire of the Andes, 1979. **Address:** 227 Toland St, London, OH 43140-1556, U.S.A.

COULTER, Catherine. American. **Genres:** Romance/Historical. **Career:** Writer. Worked in human resources for firms in NYC and San Francisco, CA. **Publications:** ROMANCE NOVELS: The Autumn Countess, 1978; The Rebel Bride, 1979; Lord Harry's Folly, 1980, as Lord Harry, 1995; Lord Deverill's Heir, 1980, as The Heir, 1996; An Honorable Offer, 1981, as The Offer, 1997; The Generous Earl, 1981, as The Duke, 1995; Devil's Embrace, 1982; An Intimate Deception, 1983, as The Deception, 1998; Chandra, 1984; Sweet Surrender, 1984; Devil's Daughter, 1985; Fire Song, 1985; Aftershocks, 1985; The Aristocrat, 1986; Midnight Star, 1986; Wild Star, 1986; Jade Star, 1987; Afterglow, 1987; Midsummer Magic, 1987; Moonspun Magic, 1988; Calypso Magic, 1988; False Pretenses, 1988; Night Shadow, 1989; Night Fire, 1989; Night Storm, 1990; Impulse, 1990; Earth Song, 1990; Secret Song, 1991; Season of the Sun, 1991; Beyond Eden, 1992; Sherbrooke Bride, 1992; Hellion Bride, 1992; The Heiress Bride, 1993; Lord of Hawkfell Island, 1993; Lord of Raven's Peak, 1994; The Wyndham Legacy, 1994; The Nightingale Legacy, 1994; Lord of Falcon Ridge, 1995; The Valentine Legacy, 1995; Rosehaven, 1996; The Wild Baron, 1997; Mad Jack, 1999. SUSPENSE NOVELS: The Cove, 1996; The Maze, 1997; The Target, 1998; The Edge, 1999; Eleventh Hour, 2002.

COULTER, Harris L. American, b. 1932. **Genres:** Medicine/Health. **Career:** United Nations, New York City, simultaneous interpreter, 1961-63; U.S. Department of State, Washington, DC, translator and interpreter, 1964-66; free-lance translator and interpreter, 1966-; writer. **Publications:** Homoeopathic Medicine, 1973; Homoeopathic Influences in Nineteenth-Century Allopathic Therapeutics, 1973; Divided Legacy: A History of the Schism in Medical Thought, Vol. I: The Patterns Emerge: Hippocrates to Paracelsus, 1975, 2nd ed 1994, Vol. II: The Origins of Modern Western Medicine: J.B. Van Helmont to Claude Bernard, 1988, Vol. III: The Conflict Between Homeopathy and the American Medical Association, 2nd ed., 1982, Vol. IV, Twentieth-Century Medicine: The Bacteriological Era, 1994; Homeopathic Science and Modern Medicine: The Physics of Healing with Microdoses, 1981; (with B.L. Fisher) DPT: A Shot in the Dark, 1985; AIDS and Syphilis: The Hidden Link, 1987; Vaccination, Social Violence, and Criminality: The Medical Assault on the American Brain, 1990; The Controlled Clinical Trial: An Analysis, Center for Empirical Medicine and Project Care, 1990. **Address:** c/o Claudia Menza Literary Agency, 1170 Broadway Ste 807, New York, NY 10001, U.S.A.

COUNSEL, June. British, b. 1926. **Genres:** Children's fiction, Young adult fiction, Novellas/Short stories, Illustrations. **Career:** Worked as a clerk in the Senate House of London University, secretary, free-lance writer of articles and radio scripts, and teacher specializing in remedial work and adult education. Full-time writer, 1981-. Lecturer, Peterborough Arts Council Celebration of Writing, 1988. **Publications:** Mostly Timothy, 1971; A Dragon in Class 4, 1984; But Martin!, 1984; The Quest for the Golden Dragon, 1987; A Dragon in Spring Term, 1988; A Dragon in Summer, 1988; Now You See It, Now You Don't, 1991; Dragon in Top Class, 1994; The Secrets Tree, 1995; Steggie's Way, 1998; Once upon Our Time, 2000. Also author of short stories. **Address:** 17 Andrew Close, Ailsworth, Peterborough PE5 7AD, England.

COUPER, Stephen. See GALLAGHER, Stephen.

COUPLAND, Douglas. Canadian, b. 1961. **Genres:** Novels. **Career:** Author. **Publications:** Generation X: Tales for an Accelerated Culture, 1991; Shampoo Planet, 1992; Life after God, 1994; Microserfs, 1995; Polaroids from the Dead, 1996; Girlfriend in a Coma, 1997; Miss Wyoming, 2000; All

Families are Psycotic, 2001; City of Glass, 2002; Hey Nostradamus!, 2003. Contributor to periodicals. **Address:** c/o HarperCollins, 10 E. 53rd St., Author Mail, 7th Floor, New York, NY 10022, U.S.A.

COURNOS, Francine. American, b. 1945. **Genres:** Medicine/Health. **Career:** Writer, editor, educator, and psychiatrist. Montefiore Medical Center, Bronx, NY, intern, 1971-72, non-psychiatric residency, 1972-73; New York State Psychiatric Institute, NYC, psychiatric residency, 1973-76, director of community service unit, 1976-78, director of Washington Heights Community Service, 1978-; private practice as psychiatrist, 1976-; New York State Office of Mental Health, NYC, chief medical officer, 1982-86; consultant, 1986-89. Columbia University, NYC, assistant professor of clinical psychiatry, 1979-, professor, 1995-. **Publications:** Frequently Asked Questions about HIV/AIDS and People with Mental Illness (booklet), 1998; City of One: A Memoir, 1999. EDITOR: (with N. Bakalar) AIDS and People with Severe Mental Illness: A Handbook for Mental Health Professionals, 1996; (with M. Forstein) What Mental Health Practitioners Need to Know about HIV and AIDS, 2000. Contributor to books and psychiatric journals. **Address:** New York State Psychiatric Institute, 1051 Riverside Dr Unit 112, New York, NY 10032, U.S.A. **Online address:** fc15@columbia.edu

COURT, Wesli. See TURCO, Lewis (Putnam).

COURTENAY, Bryce. Australian (born Republic of South Africa), b. 1933. **Genres:** Novels, Biography, Documentaries/Reportage, Essays. **Career:** McCann-Erickson (advertising agency), Sydney, Australia, advertising writer, 1956-66, board member, 1959-66, creative director and southeast Asia chair, 1960-66; J. Walter Thompson Advertising Agency, Sydney, creative director and southeast Asia chair, 1966-71; Courtenay Beirnstein, partner, 1971-76; Harrison, Robinson & Courtenay Ltd. (advertising agency) founder, 1976-87; writer. **Publications:** The Eleven Powers (documentary), 1986; The Power of One (novel), 1989; Tandia (novel), 1990; The Pitch (essays), 1992; April Fools' Day (biography), 1993; Potato Factory, 1995; Family Frying Pan, 1997; Jessica, 1998; Night Country, 1998; Tommo & Hawk, 1998; Solomon's Song, 1999; Four Fires, 2001; Smoky Joe's Cafe, 2001; Matthew Flinders's Cat, 2002; Brother Fish, 2004. **Address:** 6/104 Balfour Rd, Rose Bay, NSW 2029, Australia. **Online address:** www.brycecourtenay.com

COURTER, Gay (Eleanor). American, b. 1944. **Genres:** Novels, Food and Wine, Homes/Gardens, Civil liberties/Human rights. **Career:** Secty-Treasurer, Courter Films and Assocs., Crystal River, Florida, 1972-. President, Courter Media Corp., Crystal River, 1978-. Documentary scriptwriter, PBS. **Publications:** The Beansprout Book, 1973; The Midwife (novel), 1981; River of Dreams (novel), 1984; Code Ezra (novel), 1986; Flowers in the Blood (novel), 1990; The Midwife's Advice (novel) 1992; I Speak for this Child (non-fiction), 1995.

COURTNEY, D. G. See GURR, David.

COURTNEY, Dayle. See POSNER, Richard.

COURTNEY, Robert. See ROBINSON, Frank M(alcolm).

COUSINEAU, Phil. American, b. 1952. **Genres:** Plays/Screenplays, History. **Career:** Writer, film director, film producer, and script consultant. Seminar leader/guest lecturer at film institutes, Centers, and universities. Writer-in-residence, Shakespeare and Co. Bookstore, 1987. Co-director of film, The Peyote Road, 1993. **Publications:** SCREENPLAYS: (co-author) The 1932 Ford V8, 1986; The Presence of the Goddess, 1987; (co-author) The Hero's Journey: The World of Joseph Campbell, 1987; (co-author) Forever Activists: Stories of the Abraham Lincoln Brigade, 1990; (co-author) Eritrea: A Portrait of the Eritrean People, 1990; (co-author) Wiping the Tears of Seven Generations, 1991; The Peyote Road, 1993; Ecological Design, 1994; The Red Road to Sobriety, 1995; Your Humble Serpent, 1996; Wayfinders, 1999; A Seat at the Table, 2003. EDITOR: (and author of intro.) The Hero's Journey: Joseph Campbell on His Life and Work, 1990; (and author of intro.) The Soul of the World, 1993; (and contrib.) Soul: An Archaeology, 1994; Prayers at 3 A.M., 1995; Design Outlaws, 1997; Riddle Me This, 1999, as A World Treasury of Riddles, 2001; The Soul Aflame, 2000; The Way Things Are, 2003. OTHER: Deadlines: A Rhapsody on a Theme of Famous Last Words, 1991; (with J. Densmore, and ed.) Riders on the Storm: My Life with Jim Morrison, 1991; Burning the Midnight Oil, 1995; UFOs, 1995; Soul Moments, 1997, rev. ed. as Coincidence or Destiny, 2002; The Art of Pilgrimage, 1998; The Book of Roads, 2000; Once and Future Myths, 2001; The Olympic Odyssey, 2003. Contributor to books. Contributor of articles, reviews, and poetry to newspapers and periodicals. **Address:** c/o HarperSanFrancisco Pubs, 353 Sacramento St, San Francisco, CA 94111, U.S.A. **Online address:** cous@philcousineau.net

COUTO, Nancy Vieira. American, b. 1942. **Genres:** Poetry. **Career:** Elementary schoolteacher in Dartmouth, MA, 1964-65; National Academy of Sciences, Washington, DC, staff assistant, 1967-68; General-American Life Insurance Co., San Francisco, CA, claims representative, 1968-72; SperryUnivac, San Francisco, secretary, 1972-73; WTEV-6, New Bedford, MA, executive secretary, 1975-78; Cornell University, Ithaca, NY, lecturer in English, 1980-82; Cornell University Press, Ithaca, secondary rights assistant, 1981-82, subsidiary rights manager, 1982-94; Leatherstocking Literary Services, Ithaca, NY, owner, 1994-; poet. Gives readings of her works. **Publications:** The Face in the Water, 1990. **Address:** 508 Turner Place, Ithaca, NY 14850, U.S.A.

COVENEY, Peter (Vivian). British, b. 1958. **Genres:** Sciences. **Career:** Oxford University, Oxford, England, junior research fellow, 1984-87; University of Wales, Bangor, lecturer, 1987-90; Schlumberger Cambridge Research Laboratory, Cambridge, England, program leader, 1990-. **Publications:** (With Roger Highfield) The Arrow of Time: A Voyage through Science to Solve Time's Greatest Mystery, 1990; Frontiers of Complexity: The Search for Order in a Chaotic World, 1995. **Address:** Schlumberger Cambridge Research, High Cross, Madingley Road, Cambridge CB3 0EL, England.

COVIN, David L. American, b. 1940. **Genres:** Cultural/Ethnic topics, Area studies. **Career:** California State University, Sacramento, assistant professor of government and ethnic studies, 1970-74, associate dean of general studies, 1972-74, associate professor of government and ethnic studies, 1975-79, professor of government and ethnic studies, 1979, director of Pan African Studies. Union Graduate School, adjunct professor, 1979. **Publications:** Brown Sky, 1987. Contributor of short stories and articles to periodicals. **Address:** Director of Pan African Studies, California State University, 6000 J St., Sacramento, CA 95819, U.S.A. **Online address:** covind@CSUS.edu

COVINGTON, Dennis. American. **Genres:** Novels. **Career:** New York Times, NYC, journalist; University of Alabama-Birmingham, Birmingham, AL, currently professor and director of creative writing program; writer and freelance journalist. **Publications:** Lizard, 1991; Lasso the Moon, 1995; Salvation on Sand Mountain: Snake Handling and Redemption in Southern Appalachia, 1995; (with V. Covington) Cleaving: The Story of a Marriage, 1999. **Address:** English Department, University of Alabama, University Station, Birmingham, AL 35294, U.S.A.

COVINGTON, James W. American, b. 1917. **Genres:** History. **Career:** Emeritus Dana Professor of History, 1989-, Dana Professor of History, University of Tampa, Florida, 1976 (Associate Professor, 1950-53; Dean, Evening Division, 1961-64; Professor, 1954-89). Historian, Apollo History, National Aeronautics and Space Administration, Kennedy Space Center, 1968-70. **Publications:** (co-author) Story of the University of Tampa, 1955; Story of Southwestern Florida, 1957; The British Meet the Seminoles, 1961; (ed.) Pirates, Indians and Spaniards, 1963; Under the Minarets, 1982; The Billy Bowlegs War, 1983; Plant's Palace, 1991; The Seminole Indians of Florida, 1993. **Address:** 2901 S. Beach Dr, Tampa, FL 33629, U.S.A.

COVINGTON, Linda. See WINDSOR, Linda.

COVINGTON, Vicki. American, b. 1952. **Genres:** Novels. **Career:** University of Alabama in Birmingham, social worker in substance abuse programs, 1978-88; writer, 1988-. **Publications:** Gathering Home (novel), 1988; Bird of Paradise (novel), 1990; The Last Hotel for Women (novel), 1996. **Address:** Amanda Urban, International Creative Management, 40 West 57th St, New York, NY 10019, U.S.A.

COWAN, Edward (James). British, b. 1944. **Genres:** History, Biography. **Career:** University of Edinburgh, Lecturer in Scottish History, 1967-79; University of Guelph, Ont., Associate Professor, 1979-83, Professor of History, 1983-93; Glasgow University, chair department of Scottish history, 1993-. **Publications:** Montrose: For Covenant and King, 1977; The People's Past: Scottish Folk in Scottish History, 1980. **Address:** Glasgow University, Department of Scottish History, 9 University Gardens, Glasgow G12 8QH, Scotland.

COWAN, Gordon. British, b. 1933. **Genres:** Education, Sports/Fitness. **Career:** Teacher in Liverpool Secondary Schools, 1955-65; Lecturer in Education, 1965-68, and Head of Education Dept., 1968-72, C. F. Mott College of Education; Deputy Acting Principal, Manchester College of Education, 1972-77; Assistant Principal, Manchester College of Higher Education, 1977-83; Head of Student Services, Manchester Metropolitan University, 1983-95. MBE. **Publications:** Project Work in the Secondary School, 1967;

A Centennial History of Sale Moor Cricket Club, 1987; Cricket Coaching Series, 1986; Step by Step Soccer Skills, 1994; Step by Step Cricket Skills, 1994. **Address:** 39 Barwell Rd, Sale, Cheshire M33 5EE, England.

COWAN, Henry (Jacob). Australian, b. 1919. **Genres:** Engineering, Technology. **Career:** University of Sydney, Dept. of Architectural Science, professor and head, 1953-84, professor emeritus, 1984-. Architectural Science Review, editor, 1958-. **Publications:** The Theory of Prestressed Concrete Design, 1956; (with P.R. Smith) Design of Reinforced Concrete, 1963, 3rd ed., 1976; Reinforced and Prestressed Concrete in Torsion, 1965; An Historical Outline of Architectural Science, 1966, 2nd ed., 1976; (with P.R. Smith) The Design of Prestressed Concrete, 1966; (with J.S. Gero, G.D. Ding, and R.W. Muncey) Models in Architecture, 1968; Architectural Structures, 1971, 2nd ed., 1976; Dictionary of Architectural Science, 1973; (with J.S. Gero) Design of Building Frames, 1976; The Master Builders, 1977, 2nd ed., 1985; Science and Building, 1978; (with J.F. Dixon) A Building Science Laboratory Manual, 1978; Solar Energy Applications in the Design of Buildings, 1980; (with F. Wilson) Structural Systems, 1981, 2nd ed., 1995; Design of Reinforced Concrete Structures, 1982, 2nd ed., 1989; (with P.R. Smith) Environmental Systems, 1983; Predictive Methods for the Energy Conserving Design of Buildings, 1983; Energy Conservation in the Design of Multi-Story Buildings, 1984; (with P.R. Smith) Dictionary of Architectural and Building Technology, 2nd ed., 1986, 4th ed., 2004; Encyclopedia of Building Technology, 1987; (with P.R. Smith) The Science and Technology of Building Materials, 1988; Handbook of Architectural Technology, 1991; A Contradiction in Terms, 1993; From Wattle and Daub to Concrete and Steel, 1998; The World's Greatest Buildings, 2000. **Address:** Faculty of Architecture, University of Sydney, Sydney, NSW 2006, Australia.

COWAN, James C. American, b. 1927. **Genres:** Literary criticism and history, Psychology, Sex, Bibliography. **Career:** Instructor, 1963-64, and Assistant Professor, 1964-66, Tulane University, New Orleans; Assistant Professor, 1966-67, Associate Professor, 1967-72, and Professor, 1972-83, University of Arkansas, Fayetteville; Adjunct Professor of English, University of North Carolina, Chapel Hill, 1983-99. Ed., D.H. Lawrence Review, 1968-83. **Publications:** D.H. Lawrence's American Journey: A Study in Literature and Myth, 1970; D.H. Lawrence: An Annotated Bibliography of Writings about Him, 2 vols., 1982, 1985; D.H. Lawrence and the Trembling Balance, 1990; D.H. Lawrence: Self and Sexuality, 2002. **Address:** 302 N Estes Dr, Chapel Hill, NC 27514, U.S.A.

COWARD, Barry. British, b. 1941. **Genres:** History, Biography. **Career:** University of London, Birkbeck College, London, England, reader in history, 1966-. **Publications:** The Stuart Age: A History of England, 1609-1714, 1980, 2nd ed., 1994; The Stanleys, Lords Stanley and Earls of Derby, 1385-1672: The Origins, Wealth, and Power of a Landowning Family, 1983; Social Change and Continuity in Early Modern England, 1550-1750, 1988, 2nd ed., 1997; Oliver Cromwell, 1991, 2nd ed., 2000; Stuart England, 1603-1714, 1997; (with C. Durston) The English Revolution, 1997. **Address:** School of History, Classics & Archaeology, Birkbeck College, University of London, Malet St, London WC1E 7HX, England. **Online address:** b.coward@bbk.ac.uk

COWART, Jack. American, b. 1945. **Genres:** Art/Art history. **Career:** National Gallery of Art, Washington, D.C., head of 20th-Century Art Dept. and curator, 1983-92; Wadsworth Atheneum, Hartford, CT, assistant curator of paintings, 1972-74; St. Louis Museum, MO, curator of 19th- and 20th-Century Art, 1974-83; Corcoran Gallery of Art, Washington, D.C., deputy director/chief curator, 1992-99; Roy Lichtenstein Foundation, founding executive director, 1999-. **Publications:** Henri Matisse Paper Cut-Outs, 1977; Arts International, 1979; Connaissance des Arts, 1977; Roy Lichtenstein, 1970-80, 1981; American Artist, 1981; Expressions: New Art from Germany, 1983; Henri Matisse: The Early Years in Nice 1916-1930, 1986; Georgia O'Keeffe 1977-1986, 1987; Matisse in Morocco, 1990; Ellsworth Kelly: The Years in France 1948-54, 1992; Manuel Neri: A Sculptor's Drawings, 1994. **Address:** Roy Lichtenstein Foundation, 745 Washington St, New York, NY 10014, U.S.A.

COWASJEE, Saros. Canadian (born India), b. 1931. **Genres:** Novels, Novellas/Short stories, Plays/Screenplays, Literary criticism and history. **Career:** Professor of English, University of Regina, SK, 1971-, now Emeritus (joined faculty, 1963). General Ed., Arnold Publishers (New Delhi) "Literature of The Raj" series, 1984-2000. Assistant Ed., Times of India Press., Bombay, 1961-63; Managing Ed., Wascana Review, 1966-70; Research Associate, University of California, Berkeley, 1970-71; University of Aarhus, Visiting Commonwealth Professor, 1974-75. **Publications:** Sean O'Casey: The Man behind the Plays, 1963; O'Casey, 1966; Stories and Sketches, 1970; Goodbye to Elsa (novel), 1974; Coolie: An Assessment, 1976; So Many Freedoms: A Study of the Major Fiction of Mulk Raj Anand, 1977; Nude Therapy (short stories), 1978; The Last of the Maharajas (screenplay), 1980; Suffer Little Children (novel), 1982; Studies in Indian and Anglo-Indian Fiction (criticism), 1993; The Assistant Professor (novel), 1996. EDITOR: Author to Critic: The Letters of Mulk Raj Anand, 1973; (with V. Shahane) Modern Indian Fiction, 1981; Stories from the Raj, 1982; (with S.K. Kumar) Modern Indian Short Stories, 1982; The Raj and After (fiction anthology), 1986; More Stories from the Raj and After (anthology), 1986; (with K.S. Duggal) When the British Left (fiction anthology), 1987; Women Writers of the Raj: Short Fiction (anthology), 1990; (with K.S. Duggal) Orphans of the Storm: Stories on the Partition of India, 1995; The Best Short Stories of Flora Annie Steel, 1995; The Oxford Anthology of Raj Stories, 1998; A Raj Collection, 2005; The Mulk Raj Anand Omnibus, 2004. Introductions to the reprint editions of several Raj novels, and the novels of Mulk Raj Anand. **Address:** Dept. of English, Regina University, Regina, SK, Canada S4S 0A2. **Online address:** saros.cowasjee@uregina.ca

COWDEN, Robert H. American, b. 1934. **Genres:** Music, Bibliography. **Career:** University of Rochester, NY, instructor, summers, 1961, 1964-65; Jacksonville University, FL, assistant professor of music and director of Opera Workshop, 1966-68; Wayne State University, Detroit, MI, assistant professor, 1968-72, adjunct professor of music, 1972-74, director of graduate program in lyric theater, 1968-72, director of fine and applied arts, College of Lifelong Learning, 1972-74, executive producer of television adult education activities, 1972-74, director of Hilberry Classic Theatre, 1969-70, and Lyric Theatre, 1970-71; University of Nebraska, Omaha, J.J. Isaacson Professor of Music and department head, 1974-76; San Jose State University, CA, professor of music, 1976-, department head, 1976-82. Chautauqua Opera Company, director and coordinator of Apprentice Artist Program, 1968; California State Summer School for the Arts, member of music faculty and head of Music Division, 1987-. Michigan Opera Theatre, director, 1969-70; Detroit Symphony Orchestra, director, 1969-72; Banff School of Fine Arts, director, 1971; University of Windsor, director, 1972; performer; consultant. **Publications:** The Chautauqua Opera Association, 1929-1958: An Interpretive History, 1974; (ed. in chief) Opera Companies of the World, 1992; Classical Singers of the Operatic and Recital Stages, 1994; Popular Singers of the 20th Century, 1999. COMPILER: Concert and Opera Singers: A Bibliography of Biographical Materials, 1985; Concert and Opera Conductors: A Bibliography of Biographical Materials, 1987; Instrumental Virtuosi: A Bibliography of Biographical Materials, 1989. TRANSLATOR: G. Verdi, Un Ballo in Maschera, 1970; Lortzing, Der Wildschuetz; Brecht and Weill, Der Jasager; Pergolesi, La Serva Padrona. Contributor of articles and reviews to music journals. **Address:** School of Music and Dance, San Jose State University, 1 Washington Sq, San Jose, CA 95192-0095, U.S.A. **Online address:** rcowden@email.sjsu.edu

COWELL, Cressida. British, b. 1966. **Genres:** Children's fiction. **Career:** Children's author and illustrator. **Publications:** Little Bo Peep's Library Book, 1998; Don't Do That, Kitty Kilroy!, 1999; What Shall We Do with the Boo-Hoo Baby?, 2000; Hiccup, the Viking Who Was Seasick, 2000, in US as Hiccup, the Seasick Viking, 2001; One Too Many Tigers, 2002; Claydon Was a Clingy Child, 2002; How to Train Your Dragon, 2003; Super Sue (pop-up book), in press. **Address:** c/o Caroline Walsh, David Higham Associates Ltd., 5-8 Lower John St., London W1R 4HA, England.

COWELL, Stephanie. American, b. 1943. **Genres:** History, Translations. **Career:** Singer, writer, and historical lecturer. **Publications:** Nicholas Cooke: Actor, Soldier, Physician, Priest, 1993; The Physician of London, 1995; The Players, 1997; In the Chambers of the King, forthcoming. Translator of Wolfgang Amadeus Mozart's La clemenza di Tito, for Strawberry opera ensemble. **Address:** 585 West End Ave., New York, NY 10024-1715, U.S.A. **Online address:** stephanie@cowell-clay.com; www.cowell-clay.com

COWEN, Ron(ald). American, b. 1944. **Genres:** Plays/Screenplays. **Publications:** Summertree, 1968; Saturday Adoption, 1969; The Book of Murder, 1974; (with D. Lipman) An Early Frost, 1985; (with D. Lipman) The Love She Sought, 1990; (with D. Lipman) Sisters, 1991, 1996. **Address:** c/o William Morris Agency, 1 William Morris Place, Beverly Hills, CA 90212, U.S.A.

COWEN, Zelman. Australian, b. 1919. **Genres:** Law. **Career:** Professor of Public Law, and Dean of Faculty of Law, University of Melbourne, 1951-66; Vice-Chancellor, University of New England, 1967-70; Vice Chancellor, University of Queensland, 1970-77; Governor-General of Australia, 1977-82; Provost, Oriel College, Oxford, 1982-90; Chairman, British Press Council, 1983-88; Chairman, John Fairfax Holdings Ltd, 1992-94; Chairman, National

Academy of Music, 1995-2000. **Publications:** (specialist ed.) Dicey: Conflict of Laws, 6th ed., 1949; Australia and the United States: Some Legal Comparisons, 1954; (with P.B. Carter) Essays on the Law of Evidence, 1956; American-Australian Private International Law, 1957; Federal Jurisdiction in Australia, 1959, rev. ed. (with L. Zines), 2002; (with D. Mendes da Costa) Matrimonial Causes Jurisdiction, 1961; The British Commonwealth of Nations in a Changing World, 1964; Sir John Latham and Other Papers, 1965; Sir Isaac Isaacs, 1967, 2nd ed., 1993; The Private Man, 1969; Individual Liberty and the Law, 1975; The Virginia Lectures, 1984; Reflections on Medicine, Biotechnology and the Law, 1986; A Touch of Healing, 3 vols., 1986 vols., 1986. **Address:** 4 Treasury Pl., East Melbourne 3002, Australia.

COWIE, Colin. Zambian, b. 1962. **Genres:** Food and Wine. **Career:** Colin Cowie Lifestyle (an event planning, catering, and design company), Los Angeles and New York, founder, 1985-. Has designed china, crystal and silverware for Lenox. **Publications:** Effortless Elegance with Colin Cowie: Menus, Tips, Strategies, and More Than 200 Recipes for Easy Entertaining, 1996; Weddings, 1998. Contributor to periodicals. **Address:** c/o Colin Cowie Lifestyle, 80 5th Ave Ste 1004, New York, NY 10011, U.S.A.

COWIE, Hamilton Russell. Australian (born New Zealand), b. 1931. **Genres:** History. **Career:** Associate Professor of Education, University of Queensland, St. Lucia, since 1972, now retired. Assistant to Headmaster, Church of England Grammar School, Brisbane, 1970-72. **Publications:** Frankfurt to Fra Mauro: A Thematic History of the Modern World, 1975; Revolutions in the Modern World, 1979; Crossroads: Nationalism and Internationalism in the Modern World, Economic Trends in the Modern World, Asia and Australia in World Affairs, The Historical Background to Problems of Contemporary Society, Imperialism and Race Relations, 5 vols., 1979-82; (with K. Cowie) Discovering Brisbane, 1981; Obedience or Choice: The Major Issues of the Modern World, 1987; Legacies: The Modern State, Nationalism and Internationalism, Australia and Asia, a Changing Relationship, Imperialism, Racism and re-assessments, 3 vols., 1992-94; The Essential Collection: Bastille to Sarajevo, Versailles to Bosnia, 2 vols., 1993-94; Modern Revolutions: Their Character and Influence, 1996. **Address:** PO Box 1588, Milton BCPO, QLD 4064, Australia.

COWLES, Fleur. American. **Genres:** Art/Art history, Autobiography/Memoirs, Biography. **Career:** Freelance painter and writer. Assistant Ed., Look mag U.S.A., 1949-55; Founder and Ed., Flair mag., 1950-51; Ed., Flairbook U.S.A., 1952. **Publications:** Bloody Precedent, 1951; The Case of Salvador Dali, 1959; The Hidden World of Hadhramoutt, 1964; I Can Tell It Now, 1965; Treasures of the British Museum, 1966; Tiger Flower, 1969; Lion and Blue, 1974; Friends and Memories, 1975; Romany Free, 1977; The Love of Tiger Flower, 1980; All Too True, 1980; The Flower Game, 1983; Flowers, 1985; People as Animals, 1985; To Be a Unicorn, 1986; People as Animals, 1986; An Artist's Journey, 1988; The History of the Rose, 1992; She Made Friends and Kept Them, 1996; The Best of FLAIR, 1996. **Address:** A5 Albany, Piccadilly, London W1, England. **Online address:** fleur@fleurcowles.com

COWLEY, (Cassia) Joy. New Zealander, b. 1936. **Genres:** Novels, Novellas/Short stories, Children's fiction, Children's non-fiction, Theology/Religion, Picture/board books. **Career:** Pharmacist's apprentice, 1953-56. **Publications:** FOR CHILDREN. FICTION: The Duck in the Gun, 1969; The Silent One, 1981; London, Methuen, 1982; The Terrible Taniwha of Timberditch, 1982; Two of a Kind: Stories, 1984; Salmagundi, 1985; Captain Felonius, 1986; Brith the Terrible, 1986; The Lucky Feather, 1986; My Tiger (stories), 1986; Pawprints in the Butter: A Collection of Cats, 1991; Bow Down, Shadrach, 1991; Happy Birthday, Mrs. Felonius, 1992; The Day of the Rain, 1993; Little Unicorn Library: The Park Street Playground, 1993; The Screaming Mean Machine, 1993; Beep and the Telephone, 1994; Beyond the River, 1994; The Day of the Snow, 1994; Gladly Here I Come, 1994; Song of the River, 1994; The Cheese Trap, 1995; Babysitter Bother, Chicken Dinners, and Croack-a-roo-roo-roo ("The Happy Hens Series"), 1995; The Day of the Wind, 1995; The Mouse Bride, 1995; Brave Mama Puss, Papa Puss to the Rescue, Mabel and the Marvellous Meow, and Oscar in Danger ("Puss Quartet"), 1995-96; The Sea Daughter, 1995; Tulevai and the Sea, 1995; Gracias the Thanksgiving Turkey, 1996; Nicketty-Nacketty-Noo-Noo-Noo, 1996; Snake and Lizard, 1996; Elephant Rhymes, 1997; The Great Bamboozle, 1997; A Haunting Tale, 1997; The Hitchhikers: Stories from Joy Cowley, 1997; Singing Down the Rain, 1997; Ticket to the Sky Dance, 1997; The Bump, 1997; Agapanthus Hum and the Eyeglasses, 1998; Starbright and the Dream Eater, 1998; Wild West Gang, 1998; Big Moon Tortilla, 1998; Dragon Slayer, 1999; The Day the Truck Got Stuck, 1999; The Rusty, Trusty Tractor, 1999; Red-eyed Tree Frog, 1999; More of the Wild Wests, 1999; The Video Shop Sparrow, 1999; Agapanthus Hum and Major Bark, 2000;

Apple, Banana, Cherry, 2000; Cricket's Storm, 2000; Eating Plums in Bed, 2000; Pip the Penguin, 2000; Wild Wests and Pong Castle, 2000; Wild Wests and the Haunted Fridge, 2000; Shadrach Girl, 2000; Mrs Goodstory, 2001; Pudding, 2001; Brodie, 2001; JOY Chapter Books (30), 2001; Agapanthus Hum and the Angel Hoot, 2002; Froghopper, 2002; Weta, 2002; Froghopper and the Paua Poachers, 2003; Mrs Wishy Washy Farm, 2003; The Wishing of Biddie Malone, 2003; A Nice Little Tractor, 2003; Mr Wishy Washy, 2003; Mrs Wishy Washy Makes a Splash, 2003. NONFICTION: Write On!, 1994 in US as A Guide for Young Authors, 1995; Joy Cowley Answers Kids' Questions, 1995. READERS: More than 500 vols., including: Mrs Wishy Washy; The Meanies; Huggles. FOR ADULTS. NOVELS: Nest in a Falling Tree, 1967; Man of Straw, 1970; Of Men and Angels, 1972; The Mandrake Root, 1975; The Growing Season, 1978; Classical Music, 1999; Holy Days, 2001. SHORT STORIES: Heart Attack and Other Stories, 1985; The Complete Short Stories, 1997. OTHER: (ed. with T. France) Women Writers of New Zealand 1932-1982, 1982; Aotearoa Psalms: Prayers of a New People, 1989; Whole Learning: Whole Child, 1994; Psalms Down-Under, 1996; Everything 'round Us Is Praise, 1997; Psalms for the Road, 2002. **Address:** Fish Bay, Kenepuru, RD2, Picton 7372, New Zealand.

COWLEY, Marjorie. American, b. 1925. **Genres:** Children's fiction, Young adult fiction, Mythology/Folklore. **Career:** University of California, Los Angeles, director of Host Family Program at International Student Center, 1961-68; teacher at a morning school in Venice, CA, 1970-72; University of California, Los Angeles, lecturer on prehistoric archaeology at Museum of Cultural History, 1973-87. Graphic designer and calligrapher, 1973-93; teacher of prehistoric archaeology at public and private schools, 1975-88. **Publications:** FOR CHILDREN: Dar and the Spear-Thrower, 1994; Anooka's Answer, 1998. **Address:** 535 Ocean Ave #1A, Santa Monica, CA 90402, U.S.A. **Online address:** MHCowley@aol.com

COX, Alex. British, b. 1954. **Genres:** Plays/Screenplays. **Career:** Actor, director, editor, and writer. **Publications:** SCREENPLAYS: Sleep Is for Sissies (also known as Edge City), 1980; Repo Man, 1984; Sid and Nancy (also known as Sid and Nancy: Love Kills), 1986; Straight to Hell, 1987; Death and the Compass (also known as La Muerte y la brujula), 1996; Fear and Loathing in Las Vegas, 1998. **Address:** Exterminating Angel Products, School of Art & Design, 42 Hope St, Liverpool L1 9HW, England.

COX, Archibald. See Obituaries.

COX, Charles Brian. British, b. 1928. **Genres:** Poetry, Education, Literary criticism and history. **Career:** Emeritus Professor, 1993-, Professor of English Literature, 1966-93, and Pro-Vice Chancellor, 1987-91, University of Manchester. Co-Ed., Critical Quarterly, 1959-; Director, Manchester Poetry Centre, 1971. Lecturer, and Sr. Lecturer, University of Hull, 1954-66; Visiting Professor, King's College, London and Sheffield Hallam University, 1993-98. Honorary Fellow, Westminster College, Oxford, 1993. Chair, North West Arts, and Chair, Arvon Foundation, 1994-2000. **Publications:** The Free Spirit, 1963; (with A.E. Dyson) Modern Poetry, 1963; Conrad's Nostromo, 1964; (with A.E. Dyson) The Practical Criticism of Poetry, 1965; Joseph Conrad: The Modern Imagination, 1974; Conrad, 1977; Every Common Sight (verse), 1981; Two Headed Monster (verse), 1985; Cox on Cox: An English curriculum for the 1990s, 1991; The Great Betrayal, 1992; Collected Poems, 1993; The Battle for the English Curriculum, 1995; Emeritus (verse), 2001. EDITOR: (with A.E. Dyson) Poems of This Century, 1968; (with A.E. Dyson) Word in the Desert, 1968; (with A.P. Hinchliffe) The Waste Land: A Casebook, 1968; (with A.E. Dyson) The Black Papers on Education, 1971; (with A.E. Dyson) The Twentieth Century Mind, 3 vols., 1972; Conrad: Youth, Heart of Darkness, and The End of the Tether, 1974; (with R. Boyson) Black Paper 1975, 1975; (with R. Boyson) Black Paper 1977, 1977; African Writers, 2 vols., 1997; Literacy Is Not Enough, 1998. **Address:** 20 Park Gates Dr, Cheadle Hulme, Stockport, Cheshire SK8 7DF, England.

COX, Christopher Barry. British, b. 1931. **Genres:** Botany, Earth sciences, Geography, Marine sciences/Oceanography, Zoology. **Career:** Professor, 1976-96, and Assistant Principal, 1989-96, King's College, London (Lecturer, 1956-66; Sr. Lecturer, 1966-69; Reader, 1969-76; Head of Biology Dept., 1984-88). **Publications:** Prehistoric Animals, 1969; (with P.D. Moore) Biogeography: An Ecological and Evolutionary Approach, 1973, 7th ed., 2005; Prehistoric World, 1985; Macmillan Illustrated Encyclopedia of Dinosaurs and Prehistoric Animals, 1988; Atlas of the Living World, 1989. **Address:** Forge Cottage, 11 Blacksmith Close, Ashtead KT21 2BD, England.

COX, Gary W(alter). American, b. 1955. **Genres:** Politics/Government. **Career:** University of Texas at Austin, professor of government, 1982-87; University of California, San Diego, La Jolla, professor of political science,

1987-. **Publications:** The Efficient Secret, 1987; (ed. with S. Kernell) The Politics of Divided Government, 1991; Legislative Leviathan, 1992; Making Votes Count, 1997. **Address:** Dept of Political Science, University of California-San Diego, 9500 Gilman Dr, La Jolla, CA 92093-0521, U.S.A.

COX, Sir Geoffrey (Sandford). British (born New Zealand), b. 1910. **Genres:** History. **Career:** Reporter, Foreign and War Correspondent, News Chronicle, 1935-37, and Daily Express, 1937-40; Political Correspondent, News Chronicle, 1945; Assistant Ed., News Chronicle, 1954; Regular Contributor, BBC radio and T. V., 1945-56; Ed. and Chief Executive, Independent Televison News, 1956-68; Deputy Chairman, Yorkshire Television, 1968-71; Chairman, Tyne-Tees Television, 1971-74 and London Broadcasting Co., 1977-81. **Publications:** Defence of Madrid, 1937; Red Army Moves, 1941; Road to Trieste, 1946; Race for Trieste, 1977; See It Happen, 1983; A Tale of Two Battles, 1987; Countdown to War, 1988; Pioneering Television News, 1995; Eyewitness, 1999. **Address:** Edgehill, Deepdene Park Rd, Dorking, Surrey RH5 4AW, England.

COX, Gordon. Welsh, b. 1942. **Genres:** Music. **Career:** School teacher, 1964-80; University of Reading, Reading, England, lecturer in education, 1980-. **Publications:** Folk Music in a Newfoundland Outport, 1980; A History of Music Education in England, 1872-1928, 1993. Contributor of articles on music education to academic journals. **Address:** 18 New Road, Reading RG1 5JD, England.

COX, Jim. (born United States). **Genres:** Classics. **Career:** Writer and educator. McKendree College, Lebanon, IL, professor, retired. **Publications:** The Great Radio Soap Operas, 1999; The Great Radio Audience Participation Shows: Seventeen Programs from the 1940s and 1950s, 2001; Radio Crime Fighters: Over 300 Programs from the Golden Age, 2002; Say Goodnight, Gracie: The Last Years of Network Radio, 2002; Frank and Anne Hummert's Radio Factory: The Programs and Personalities of Broadcasting's Most Prolific Producers, 2003; Mr. Keen, Tracer of Lost Persons, 2004. **Address:** Drew University, POB 611, Jefferson, NC 28640, U.S.A.

COX, Kevin Robert. British, b. 1939. **Genres:** Geography, Politics/Government, Urban studies. **Career:** Professor of Geography, Ohio State University, Columbus, since 1971 (Assistant Professor 1965-68; Associate Professor 1968-71). **Publications:** (co-ed. with R.G. Golledge) Behavioral Problems in Geography: A Symposium, 1969; Man, Location and Behavior: An Introduction to Human Geography, 1972; Conflict, Power and Politics in the City: A Geographic View, 1973; (co-ed. with D. Reynolds and S. Rokkan) Locational Approaches to Power and Conflict, 1974; (ed.) Urbanization and Conflict in Market Societies, 1978; Location and Public Problems: A Political Geography of the Contemporary World, 1979; (ed. with R. G. Golledge) Behavioral Problems in Geography Revisited, 1981; (ed. with R. J. Johnston) Conflict, Politics and the Urban Scene, 1982; (ed.) Spaces of Globalization, 1997. **Address:** 7179 Lorine Ct., Columbus, OH 43235-5125, U.S.A. **Online address:** kcox@geography.ohio-state.edu

COX, Madison. American, b. 1958. **Genres:** Homes/Gardens. **Career:** Madison Cox Garden Design, NYC, owner, 1989-. **Publications:** Private Gardens of Paris, 1989; (coauthor) Gardens of the World, 1991; Artists' Gardens, 1993; Majorelle Gardens, 1999. **Address:** Madison Cox Design, 220 W 19th St, New York, NY 10011, U.S.A.

COX, Patsi Bale. (Patricia Bale). Also writes as G. F. Bale. American. **Genres:** Biography, Mystery/Crime/Suspense. **Career:** Writer. **Publications:** NONFICTION:(ed. with C. Pelletier and J. Glaser) A Country Music Christmas, 1996; (with J. Jones) Jenny Jones: My Story, 1997; (with T. Tucker) Nickel Dreams: My Life, 1997; (with R. Emery) The View from Nashville, 1998. NOVELS WITH G.B. WELLBROCK AS G.F. BALE: If Thoughts Could Kill, 1990; Cry, Baby, Cry, 1991. **Address:** c/o William Morrow & Company, 1350 Avenue of the Americas, New York, NY 10019, U.S.A.

COX, Paul(us). Dutch, b. 1940. **Genres:** Plays/Screenplays, Photography. **Career:** Photographer, screenwriter, and director of motion pictures. Worked as teacher of photography and cinematography, 1971-82; Illumination Films, Melbourne, VIC, Australia, cofounder (with Tony Llewellyn-Jones), producer, and director, c. 1975-. Photographs exhibited at institutions. Actor in motion pictures. **Publications:** (with U. Beier) Home of Man, 1971; (photographer) Ulli Beier, 1980; Reflections (autobiography). SCREENPLAYS; AND DIRECTOR: (with J. Larkin) The Journey, 1972; Illuminations, 1976; (with S.H. Jones) Inside Looking Out, 1977; (with J. Clarke) Lonely Hearts, 1981; (with B. Ellis) Man of Flowers, 1983; Death and Destiny, 1984; (adaptor with B. Ellis) My First Wife, 1984; (with E. and N. Kaye) Cactus, 1986;

Vincent, 1988; Island, 1989; (with B. Dickins) Golden Braid, 1990; (with B. Dickins) A Woman's Tale, 1991; The Nun and the Bandit, 1992; Exile, 1993; (with B. Dickens and M. Wilburd) Touch Me, 1994; (with J. Clarke) Lust and Revenge, 1996; (with J. Larkin) Homecoming; Innocence, 1999; Molokai, 1999. SHORT FILMS: Matuta, 1965; Time Past, 1966; Skindeep, 1968; Marcel, 1969; Symphony, 1969; Mirka, 1970; Phyllis, 1971; Island, 1975; We Are All Alone, My Dear, 1975; Ways of Seeing, 1977; Ritual, 1978. DOCUMENTARY FILMS: Calcutta, 1970; All Set Backstage, 1974; For a Child Called Michael, 1979; The Kingdom of Nek Chand, 1980; Underdog, 1980; Death and Destiny 1984; Handle with Care, 1985; (with others) The Hidden Dimension, 1997; The Diaries of Vaslav Nijinsky, 2001. JUVENILE TELEPLAYS; AND DIRECTOR: The Secret Life of Trees, 1986; The Gift, 1988. **Address:** Illumination Films, 1 Victoria Ave, Albert Park, Melbourne, VIC 3206, Australia.

COX, Richard (Hubert Francis). Also writes as R. Heber. British, b. 1931. **Genres:** Novels, International relations/Current affairs, Travel/Exploration. **Career:** Novelist, 1974-; journalist. Defence Correspondent, Daily Telegraph, London, 1966-72. **Publications:** Pan Africanism in Practice, 1964; Kenyatta's Country, 1965; Traveller's Guide to East Africa, 1966, 9th ed. as Traveller's Guide to Kenya and Northern Tanzania, 1997; Sealion: The German Invasion of Britain, 1940; Sam 7, 1977; Auction, 1979; The Time It Takes, 1980; The KGB Directive, 1981; The Ice Raid, 1983; Ground Zero, 1984; The Columbus Option, 1986; An Agent of Influence, 1988; Park Plaza, 1991; Eclipse, 1995; (as R. Heber) Murder at Wittenham Park, 1998; (with L. Fitzgerald) How to Meet a Puffin, 2004. **Address:** 18 Haukeville, Alderney, Channel Islands GY9 3UA, United Kingdom.

COX, Robert H(enry). American, b. 1961. **Genres:** Politics/Government. **Career:** Indiana University-Bloomington, associate instructor in political science, 1984-89; University of Oklahoma, Norman, assistant professor of political science, 1989-. Erasmus University (Rotterdam, Netherlands), research assistant in public administration, 1987. Radio commentator on European affairs. **Publications:** The Development of the Dutch Welfare State: From Workers' Insurance to Universal Entitlement, 1993. Contributor to books. Contributor of articles and reviews to political science journals. **Address:** Department of Political Science, University of Oklahoma, Norman, OK 73019, U.S.A.

COX, Roger (Kenneth). British, b. 1936. **Genres:** Business/Trade/Industry, Marketing. **Career:** Retail Development Manager, John Menzies, 1968-71; Group Marketing Officer, Development, ADA Halifax, 1973-75; Marketing Consultant, 1977-. **Publications:** Retail Site Assessment, 1968; Retail Development, 1971; Retailing, 1978; Running Your Own Shop, 1985; (with J.P.R. Brittain) Retail Management, 1988. **Address:** 30 London Rd, Westerham, Kent TN16 1BD, England.

COX, Roger L. American, b. 1931. **Genres:** Literary criticism and history. **Career:** Bates College, Lewiston, ME, instructor in English, 1958-61; DePauw University, Greencastle, IN, assistant professor, 1961-65, associate professor of English, 1965-71; University of Delaware, Newark, associate professor, 1971-75, professor of English, 1975-98, professor emeritus, 1998-. **Publications:** Between Earth and Heaven: Shakespeare, Dostoevsky, and the Meaning of Christian Tragedy, 1969; Shakespeare's Comic Changes: The Time-Lapse Metaphor as Plot Device, 1991. **Address:** 726 Loveville Rd Apt 309, Hockessin, DE 19707, U.S.A.

COX, Stephen (LeRoy). American (born Canada), b. 1966. **Genres:** Communications/Media, Film. **Career:** Comedy Magazine, Tampa, FL, writer, 1987-88; St. Louis Post-Dispatch, MO, columnist, 1989-90; contributor to L.A. Times, 1992-. Guest on radio and television programs. **Publications:** The Beverly Hillbillies, 1988; The Munchkins Remember the Wizard of Oz and Beyond, 1989; The Munsters, 1989; (with John Lofflin) The Official Abbott and Costello Scrapbook, 1990; The Addams Chronicles, 1991; Here's Johnny!, 1992; The Hooterville Handbook: A Viewer's Guide to Green Acres, 1993; (with R. Johnson) Here on Gilligan's Isle, 1993; The Munchkins of Oz, 1996; Dreaming of Jeannie: TV's Prime Time in a Bottle, 1997; The Addams Chronicles, 1998. **Address:** 1918 Grismer Ave, Suite B, Burbank, CA 91504, U.S.A.

COX, Steve. British, b. 1962. **Genres:** History, Documentaries/Reportage. **Career:** Free-lance photojournalist. Giles Smith Photography, advertising and industrial photographer, 1981-86; Steve Bicknell Photography, senior photographer, 1986-87; University of Birmingham, photographer for archaeological expeditions in Oman, 1986, 1988; work exhibited at Oxford Museum of Modern Art and in Portugal, U.S., and Australia; contributor to television programs. Guest on radio and television programs; public speaker.

Publications: (with P. Carey) Generations of Resistance, 1995. Contributor to magazines and newspapers. **Address:** 30 Instow Rd., Earley, Reading, Berkshire RG6 5QJ, England.

COX, Vic. American, b. 1942. **Genres:** Children's non-fiction, Environmental sciences/Ecology, Travel/Exploration. **Career:** Westways magazine, Los Angeles, CA, writer/editor, 1971-75; California State University, Department of Journalism, Long Beach, CA, instructor, 1977-78; Los Angeles Times, Los Angeles, copyeditor, 1979-83; Santa Barbara News-Press, Santa Barbara, CA, copyeditor, 1982-88; University of California, Santa Barbara, public information representative, 1989, 1991-92, senior editor, 1996-. Freelance writer and editor, 1976-. University of Southern California Sea Grant, consultant, 1982-83; Santa Barbara City College Journalism Department, assistant adviser, 1989-91. Also worked in Brazil for the U.S. Peace Corps, 1964-66; has served on boards of environmental and educational groups. **Publications:** Whales & Dolphins, 1989; Ocean Life: Beneath the Crystal Seas, 1990; The Challenge of Immigration, 1995; Guns, Violence, & Teens, 1997. Contributor to books and reference works.

COX-JOHNSON, Ann. See **SAUNDERS, Ann Loreille.**

COYLE, Beverly (Jones). American, b. 1946. **Genres:** Novels, Plays/Screenplays. **Career:** University of Newcastle, New South Wales, Australia, instructor in English, 1974-77; Vassar College, Poughkeepsie, NY, assistant professor, 1977-85, associate professor of English, 1985, professor of English, 1991, Mary Augusta Scott Chair of Literature, now emeritus. **Publications:** A Thought to Be Rehearsed: Aphorism in Wallace Stevens' Poetry, 1983; (ed. with A. Filreis) Secretaries of the Moon: The Letters of Wallace Stevens and Jose Rodriguez Feo, 1986; The Kneeling Bus, 1990; In Troubled Waters, 1993; Taken In, 1998; Parallel Lives (play). **Address:** c/o Biff Liff, William Morris Agency, 1325 Ave of the Americas, New York, NY 10019, U.S.A. **Online address:** bevcoyle1@nyc.rr.com

COYNE, James K(itchenman). American, b. 1946. **Genres:** Politics/Government. **Career:** Coyne Chemical Co., Philadelphia, PA, president, 1971-80, currently director; U.S. Congress, Washington, DC, representative from Pennsylvania, 1980-82; White House, Washington, DC, special assistant, 1983-85; American Consulting Engineers Council, Washington, DC, chief executive officer, 1985-86; American Tort Reform Association, Washington, DC, president, 1987-88; Roy F. Woston, Inc., Washington, DC, vice president and director, 1988-90; Americans to Limit Congressional Terms, Washington, DC, president, 1991-92; First Washington Management Group, McLean, VA, chair, 1992-94; National Air Transportation Assn., president, 1994-. **Publications:** (with John H. Fund) Cleaning House: America's Campaign for Term Limits, Regnery Gateway, 1992; Kick the Bums Out, Natural Press Books, 1992. **Address:** 1007 Turkey Run Rd., Mc Lean, VA 22101, U.S.A.

COYNE, Michael. American. **Genres:** Film. **Career:** Historian and writer. **Publications:** The Crowded Prairie: American National Identity in the Hollywood Western, 1996. **Address:** c/o I. B. Tauris & Co. Ltd., 6 Salem Rd, London W2 4BU, England.

COZZENS, Peter. American, b. 1957. **Genres:** History, Military/Defense/Arms control. **Career:** U.S. Department of State, Washington, DC, foreign service officer, 1983-, U.S. consul in Tijuana, Mexico, 1994. **Publications:** No Better Place to Die: The Battle of Stones River, 1990; This Terrible Sound: The Battle of Chickamauga, 1992; The Shipwreck of Their Hopes: The Battles for Chattanooga, 1994; The Darkest Days of the War: The Battles of Iuka and Corinth, forthcoming. Contributor to Civil War Times Illustrated and Illinois Historical Journal. **Address:** c/o University of Illinois Press, 1325 S Oak St, Champaign, IL 61820-6903, U.S.A.

CRAATS, Rennay. Canadian, b. 1973. **Genres:** Area studies, History, Sports/Fitness, Travel/Exploration. **Career:** Freelance writer and editor for institutions including the Calgary Board of Education and Calgary Catholic School Board. **Publications:** Canada through the Decades: The 1970s, 2000; Canada through the Decades: The 1940s, 2000; Canada through the Decades: The 1910s, 2000; Living Science: The Science of Fire, 2000; Living Science: The Science of Sound, 2000; Great Canadian Prime Ministers, 2000; Twentieth-Century U.S.A.: History of the 1900s, 2002; Canadian Provinces: Quebec, 2002; Canadian Cities: Toronto, 2002; E.B. White, 2002; Roald Dahl, 2002; Canadian History: Canada in the Global Age, 2003; American Cities: New Orleans, 2003; War and Peace: The American Civil War, 2003. FOR THE LOVE OF... SERIES: Baseball, 2001; Basketball, 2001; Karate, 2002; Judo, 2002; Skateboarding, 2002; Snowboarding, 2002; Cycling, 2002; In-line Skating, 2002. AMERICAN STATES ... SERIES: Indiana, 2001; Arizona,

2002; Illinois, 2002; New Mexico, 2002; New Hampshire, 2002; Maryland, 2002; Michigan, 2002. Contributor to periodicals. **Address:** 331 Citadel Hills Place NW, Calgary, AB, Canada T3G 2X1. **Online address:** boomerang-com@shaw.ca

CRABTREE, Adam. American, b. 1938. **Genres:** Psychology. **Career:** Psychotherapist in private practice, 1966-. Centre for Training in Psychotherapy, Toronto, ON, Canada, cofounder, 1986, training psychotherapist and lecturer, 1986-; founder and director of Willow Workshops; cofounder of Stress Analysis Consultants. Open International University, clinical teacher, 1993-; lecturer at St. John's University, Humber College, and McMaster University. Narrator of radio documentary series The Enchanted Boundary, CBC-Radio; The Splitting of the Mind, CBC-Radio; Mysteries of the Mind, CJRT-Radio; and In Sickness and in Health, CJRT-Radio; guest on radio and television programs throughout Canada. Former Benedictine monk and Roman Catholic priest. **Publications:** Multiple Man: Explorations in Possession and Multiple Personality, 1985; Animal Magnetism, Early Hypnotism, and Psychical Research from 1766 to 1925: An Annotated Bibliography, 1988; From Mesmer to Freud: Magnetic Sleep and the Roots of Psychological Healing, 1993; Trance Zero: Breaking the Spell of Conformity, 1997. RADIO DOCUMENTARY SERIES: The Enchanted Boundary; The Splitting of the Mind; Mysteries of the Mind; In Sickness and in Health. Work represented in anthologies. Contributor to psychology journals. **Address:** 344 Dupont St Ste 401, Toronto, ON, Canada M5R 1V9. **Online address:** adamcrabtree@rogers.com

CRABTREE, John. British, b. 1950. **Genres:** Area studies, History, Politics/Government. **Career:** Freelance researcher and consultant, specialist in the Andean countries. Oxford Analytica (consulting firm), Oxford, England, Latin America editor, 1985-97; Oxford University, senior associate member of St. Antony's College, 1987-90, 1994-95, 2000-04. Universidade de Sao Paulo, visiting professor, 1990; University of London, Institute of Latin American Studies, visiting fellow. **Publications:** El fraude electoral en Bolivia, 1978; (with G. Duffy and J. Pearce) The Great Tin Crash, 1987; Peru Under Garcia: An Opportunity Lost, 1992; Fujimori's Peru: The Political Economy, 1998; (with L. Whitehead) Towards Democratic Viability: The Bolivian Experience, 2001; Peru: The Background, 2002. **Address:** 11 Walton St, Oxford, England.

CRACE, Jim. British, b. 1946. **Genres:** Novels. **Career:** Sudanese Educational Television, Khartoum, volunteer producer and writer, 1968-69; Kgosi Kgari Sechele Secondary School, Molepolole, Botswana, teacher of English, 1969-70; free-lance radio and feature journalist, 1970-86; full-time novelist, 1986-. Midlands Arts Centre, writer-in-residence, 1981-83; Birmingham Festival of Readers and Writers, founder and director, 1983; West Midlands Arts, chair of literature panel, 1984-85. **Publications:** NOVELS: Continent, 1986; The Gift of Stones, 1988; Arcadia, 1992; Signals of Distress 1994; Quarantine, 1997; Being Dead, 2000; The Devil's Larder, 2001. **Address:** c/o David Godwin Associates, 44 Monmouth St., London WC2H 9DG, England.

CRACKNELL, Basil Edward. British, b. 1925. **Genres:** Agriculture/Forestry, Local history/Rural topics, Third World. **Career:** Economist, Ministry of Agriculture, 1952-65; Sr. Research Fellow, University of Nottingham, 1966-69; Sr. Economic Adviser, Overseas Development Administration, London, 1969-85; Economic consultant, 1985-. **Publications:** Canvey Island: The Story of a Marshland Community, 1958; Portrait of London River: The Tidal Thames from Teddington to the Sea, 1968; (with D.K. Britton) Cereals in the United Kingdom: Production, Marketing, and Utilisation, 1969; Portrait of Surrey, 1970, 3rd ed, 1980; Dominica, 1973; The West Indians: How They Live and Work, 1974; The Evaluation of Aid Projects and Programmes, 1983; Evaluating Development Aid: Issues, Problems and Solutions, 2000. **Address:** 1 Hyde Close, Kingston-nr-Lewes, E. Sussex BN7 3PA, England. **Online address:** basil@borachnell.fanet.co.uk

CRAFT, Michael. (Michael Craft Johnson). American, b. 1950. **Genres:** Young adult fiction. **Career:** Chicago Tribune, Chicago, IL, art director, 1976-87. **Publications:** MARK MANNING SERIES: Flight Dreams, 1997; Eye Contact, 1998; Body Language, 1999; Name Games, 2000; Boy Toy, 2001; Hot Spot, 2002. CLAIRE GRAY SERIES: Rehearsing, 1993; Desert Autumn, 2001; Desert Winter, 2003. **Address:** c/o Author Mail, St. Martin's Press/Minotaur, 175 Fifth Ave., New York, NY 10010, U.S.A.

CRAGG, (Albert) Kenneth. British, b. 1913. **Genres:** Theology/Religion, Translations. **Career:** Warden, St. Augustine's College, Canterbury, 1960-67; Honorary Fellow, Jesus College, Oxford; Bye Fellow, Gonville and Caius College, Cambridge, 1969-73; Reader in Religious Studies, University of

Sussex, Brighton, 1973-78. **Publications:** The Call of the Minaret, 1956; Sandals at the Mosque, 1958; The Dome and the Rock, 1964; Counsels in Contemporary Islam, 1965; Christianity in World Perspective, 1968; The Privilege of Man, 1968; The House of Islam, 1969; Alive to God; The Event of the Quran, 1970; The Mind of the Quran, 1973; The Christian and Other Religion, 1977; Islam from Within, 1980; This Year in Jerusalem, 1982; Muhammad and the Christian, 1984; The Pen and the Faith, 1985; Jesus and the Muslim, 1985; The Christ and the Faiths, 1986; Readings in the Qur'an, 1988; What Decided Christianity, 1989; The Arab Christian, 1991; Troubled by Truth, 1992; To Meet and to Greet 1992; Faith and Life Negotiate, 1994; Returning to Mount Hira, 1994; The Lively Credentials of God, 1995; Palestine: The Prize and Price of Zion, 1997; With God in Human Trust, 1998; The Weight in the Word, 1999; The Education of Christian Faith, 2000; Muhammad in-the-Qur'an, 2002; The Christian Jesus, 2003. TRANSLATOR: K. Husain, City of Wrong, 1959; M. Abduh, The Theology of Unity, 1964; Passage to France, 1977; The Hallowed Valley, 1977. **Address:** 3 Goring Lodge, White House Rd, Oxford, Oxon. OX1 4QE, England.

CRAGGS, Stewart R. British, b. 1943. **Genres:** Music. **Career:** University of Sunderland, England, technical services librarian, 1973-81, reader services librarian, 1981-92, development services librarian, 1992-95, professor of music bibliography, 1993; freelance researcher and bibliographer, 1995-. Justice of the peace, 1974-2000. **Publications:** William Walton: A Thematic Catalogue, 1977; William Alwyn: A Catalogue, 1985; Arthur Bliss: A Bio-Bibliography, 1988; Richard Rodney Bennett: A Bio-Bibliography, 1989; William Walton: A Catalogue, 1990; John McCabe: A Bio-Bibliography, 1991; William Walton: A Source Book, 1993; John Ireland: A Catalogue, Discography, and Bibliography, 1993; Alun Hoddinott: A Bio-Bibliography, 1993; (compiler) Edward Elgar: A Source Book, 1995; William Mathias: A Bio-Bibliography, 1995; Arthur Bliss: A Source Book, 1995; Soundtracks: An International Dictionary of Composers for Film, 1998; Malcolm Arnold: A Bio-Bibliography, 1998; (ed.) William Walton: Music and Literature, 1999; Lennox Berkeley: A Source Book, 2000; Benjamin Britten: A Bio-Bibliography, 2001; Peter Maxwell Davies: A Source Book, 2002; Arthur Bliss: Music and Literature, 2003. **Address:** 106 Mount Rd, High Barnes, Sunderland SR4 7NN, England. **Online address:** stewcraggs@aol.com

CRAIG, Alisa. See **MACLEOD, Charlotte (Matilda)** in the Obituaries.

CRAIG, Amanda. British (born Republic of South Africa), b. 1959. **Genres:** Novels. **Career:** Free-lance writer, 1988-. **Publications:** Foreign Bodies, 1990; A Private Place, 1991; A Vicious Circle, 1996; In a Dark Wood, 2000. Contributor to periodicals.

CRAIG, Brian. See **STABLEFORD, Brian M(ichael).**

CRAIG, Colleen. American. **Genres:** Adult non-fiction. **Career:** Writer for stage and film; Stott pilates trainer, Toronto, Ontario, Canada. **Publications:** Pilates on the Ball: The World's Most Popular Workout Using the Exercise Ball, 2001; Abs on the Ball: A Pilates Approach to Building Abdominals, 2003. Producer of videotapes. **Address:** Pilates on the Ball Studio, 315 Albany Avenue, Toronto, ON, Canada M5R 3E2. **Online address:** info@pilatesontheball.com

CRAIG, David. See **TUCKER, (Allan) James.**

CRAIG, G(illian) M(ary). Welsh, b. 1949. **Genres:** Agriculture/Forestry. **Career:** Commonwealth Bureau of Pastures and Field Crops, Hurley, England, information scientist, 1970-76; University of Reading, Reading, England, research officer for Agricultural Extension and Rural Development Centre, 1976-78, research fellow at Centre for Agricultural Strategy, 1985-93; freelance consultant for agricultural information, 1993-. **Publications:** Information Systems in United Kingdom Agriculture, 1979; Information Systems for the Communication of UK Agriculture and Rural Land Use Information, 1995. EDITOR: (with J.L. Jollans and A. Korbey) The Case for Agriculture: An Independent Assessment, 1986; The Agriculture of the Sudan, 1991; The Agriculture of Egypt, 1993. **Address:** Centre for Agricultural Strategy, University of Reading, 1 Early Gate, Reading RG6 2AT, England.

CRAIG, Gordon (Alexander). American (born Scotland), b. 1913. **Genres:** History, Military/Defense/Arms control, Politics/Government. **Career:** Sterling Professor Emeritus of Humanities, Stanford University, California, 1980- (Professor of History, 1961-69, Sterling Professor of Humanities, 1969-79). Professor, Free University, Berlin, 1962-. Instructor in History, Yale University, New Haven, CT, 1939-41; Instructor to Professor of History, Princeton University, NJ, 1941-61. Visiting Professor, Columbia University,

NYC, 1947-48, 1949-50. Guggenheim Fellow, 1969-70, 1982-83. Recipient: Goethe Medal, 1987; German-American Academic Council, Benjamin Franklin-Wilhelm von Humboldt Prize, 1999. **Publications:** (ed. with E.M. Earle and F. Gilbert) Makers of Modern Strategy: Military Thought from Machiavelli to Hitler, 1943; (co-author) The Second Chance: America and Peace, 1944; (ed. with Gilbert) The Diplomats 1919-1939, 1953; NATO and the New German Army, 1955; The Politics of the Prussian Army, 1640-1945, 1955; From Bismarck to Adenauer: Aspects of German Statecraft, 1958; Europe since 1815, 1961, 3rd. ed. 1971; The Battle of Koeniggraetz: Prussia's Victory over Austria 1866, 1964; War, Politics and Diplomacy: Selected Essays, 1966; (co-author) World War I: A Turning Point in Modern History, 1967; Military Policy and National Security, 1972; (ed.) History of Germany in the Nineteenth Century, 1975; (ed.) Economic Interest, Militarism and Foreign Policy: Essays of Eckart Kehr, 1977; Germany, 1866-1945, 1978; Germany and the West: The Ambivalent Relationship, 1982; The Germans, 1982; (with A.L. George) Force and Statecraft, 1983; The End of Prussia, 1984; The Triumph of Liberalism: Zurich in the Golden Age, 1830-1869, 1989; The Politics of the Unpolitical, 1995; Theodor Fontane, 1999; Politics and Culture in Modern Germany, 1999. **Address:** Dept of History, Stanford University, Stanford, CA 94305, U.S.A. **Online address:** GCRA@Leland.Stanford.edu

CRAIG, Jonathan. See **POSNER, Richard.**

CRAIG, Lee A(llen). American. **Genres:** Economics. **Career:** Center for Econmetric Model Research, School of Business, Indiana University, Bloomington, research associate, 1985-89; North Carolina State University, Raleigh, assistant professor, 1989-94, associate professor of economics, 1994-. Duke University, postdoctoral fellow at Center for Demographic Studies, 1991-94. **Publications:** To Sow One Acre More: Childbearing and Farm Productivity in the Antebellum North, 1993; (with D. Fisher) The Integration of the European Economy, 1850-1913, 1997. Contributor of articles and reviews to economic, statistics, and history journals. **Address:** Department of Economics, North Carolina State University, 310D Hillsborough Bldg. Box 7506, Raleigh, NC 27695, U.S.A. **Online address:** craig@econbus2.econ.ncsu.edu

CRAIG, Patricia. British, b. 1948. **Genres:** Literary criticism and history, Novellas/Short stories. **Career:** Freelance writer. Formerly, Children's Books Ed., The Literary Review, London. **Publications:** Elizabeth Bowen, 1986; (with M. Cadogan) You're a Brick, Angela! A New Look at Girls' Fiction 1839-1975, 1976; Women and Children First: The Fiction of Two World Wars, 1978; The Lady Investigates: Women Detectives and Spies in Fiction, 1981; The Oxford Book of English Detective Stories, 1990; The Penguin Book of British Comic Stories, 1990; The Penguin Book of British Comic Writing, 1992; The Rattle of the North: an anthology of Ulster prose, 1992; The Oxford Book of Schooldays, 1994; The Oxford Book of Modern Women's Stories, 1994; The Oxford Book of Travel Stories, 1996. **Address:** 2 Cresswell Pk., Blackheath, London SE3 9RD, England.

CRAIG, Robert H. American, b. 1942. **Genres:** History, International relations/Current affairs, Travel/Exploration, Ethics, Third World. **Career:** National University of Costa Rica, San Jose, professor of religion, 1978-82; Bucknell University, Lewisburg, PA, associate professor of religion and political science, 1983-86; College of the Holy Cross, Worcester, MA, assistant professor of social ethics, 1986-90; Mount Union College, Alliance, OH, associate professor of religious studies, 1990-96; College of St. Scholastica, Duluth, MN, Professor of History & International Studies, 1996-. Latin American Biblical Seminary, professor, 1980-82. **Publications:** (with J.M. Bonino and C. Alvarez) Protestantismo y Liberalismo en America Latina, 2nd ed., 1985; Religion and Radical Politics: An Alternative Christian Tradition in the United States, 1992. **Address:** Department of History/Dept of Languages & Internat'l Studies, The College of St. Scholastica, 1200 Kenwood Avenue, Duluth, MN 55811-4199, U.S.A. **Online address:** RCRAIG@css.edu

CRAIG, Ruth. American, b. 1922. **Genres:** Children's fiction. **Career:** Humpty Dumpty's Magazine, NYC, editor, 1972-76; Institute of Children's Literature, West Redding, CT, instructor, 1976-. Worked as a reporter for local weekly newspapers. **Publications:** Malu's Wolf, 1995. **Address:** 712 Powell St., Williamsburg, VA 23185, U.S.A.

CRAIG, Stephen C. American, b. 1948. **Genres:** Politics/Government. **Career:** Texas Tech University, Lubbock, visiting assistant professor, 1977-78; University of New Mexico, Albuquerque, visiting assistant professor, 1978-79; University of Florida, Gainesville, assistant professor, 1979-85, associate professor, 1985-94, director of Graduate Program in Political Campaigning, 1985-, professor of political science, 1994-. Florida Campaign

Associates, partner and political consultant. **Publications:** The Malevolent Leaders: Popular Discontent in America, 1993. EDITOR & CONTRIBUTOR: Broken Contract?: Changing Relationships Between Americans and Their Government, 1995; After the Boom: The Politics of Generation X, 1997. **Address:** Department of Political Science, 3324 Turlington Hall, University of Florida, Gainesville, FL 32611, U.S.A.

CRAIK, Elizabeth M(ary). Scottish, b. 1939. **Genres:** History, Classics. **Career:** University of Birmingham, England, research fellow in Greek, 1963-64; University of St. Andrews, Scotland, assistant lecturer to senior lecturer in Greek, 1967-97; Kyoto University, professor in classics, 1997-. **Publications:** The Dorian Aegean, 1980; (ed.) Marriage and Property, 1984; Euripides, Phoenician Women, 1988; (ed.) Owls to Athens, 1990; Hippocrates, Places in Man, 1998. **Address:** Department of Greek, University of St. Andrews, St. Andrews KY16 9AL, Scotland. **Online address:** ec@st-and.ac.uk

CRAIK, T(homas) W(allace). British, b. 1927. **Genres:** Literary criticism and history. **Career:** Professor of English, University of Durham, 1977-89, prof emeritus, 1989-. Assistant Lecturer, 1953-55, and Lecturer, 1955-65, University of Leicester; Lecturer, 1965-67, and Sr. Lecturer, 1967-73, University of Aberdeen; Professor of English, University of Dundee, 1973-77. **Publications:** The Tudor Interlude: Stage, Costume and Acting, 1958, 3rd ed., 1967; The Comic Tales of Chaucer, 1964. EDITOR: Massinger, A New Way to Pay Old Debts, 1964; Massinger, The City Madam, 1964; Selected Poetry and Prose of Sir Philip Sidney, 1965; Marlowe, The Jew of Malta, 1966; Minor Elizabethan Tragedies, 1974; (with J.M. Lothian) Shakespeare, Twelfth Night, 1975; (with C. Leech and L. Potter) The "Revels" History of Drama in English, 6 vols., 1975-83; (with R.J. Craik) John Donne: Selected Poetry and Prose, 1986; Beaumont and Fletcher, The Maid's Tragedy, 1988; Shakespeare, The Merry Wives of Windsor, 1989; Shakespeare, King Henry V, 1995.

CRAIS, Clifton C(harles). American, b. 1960. **Genres:** History, Race relations. **Career:** Kenyon College, Gambier, OH, visiting instructor, 1987-88, assistant professor, 1988-93, associate professor of history, 1993-, founder and chairperson of Kenyon Seminar, 1990-93. University of London, member of Institute of Commonwealth Studies, London School of Oriental and African Studies, 1985-, member of Institute of Historical Research, 1985-86; Rhodes University, South Africa, university research scholar at Institute of Social and Economic Research, 1985, 1992; University of Cape Town, South Africa, visiting assistant professor, 1988-89, visiting associate of Centre for African Studies, 1988-89, 1991-92; Stanford University, Stanford Humanities Center, fellow, 1994-95; guest on radio programs. Conducted field work in Ciskei and Transkei, South Africa, 1992, 1993. **Publications:** White Supremacy and Black Resistance in Pre-Industrial South Africa: The Making of the Colonial Order in the Eastern Cape, 1770-1865, 1992; (ed. with Nigel Worden, and contrib.) Breaking the Chains: Slavery and Its Legacy in Nineteenth-Century South Africa, 1993. Contributor of articles and reviews to periodicals. **Address:** Department of History, Seitz House, Kenyon College, Gambier, OH 43022, U.S.A.

CRAM, David L. American, b. 1934. **Genres:** Medicine/Health. **Career:** Wisconsin General Hospital, Madison, research assistant, 1955-58; U.S. Air Force, career officer, 1958-70, flight surgeon based at Mather Air Force Base, 1960-63, chief of medicine at a tactical hospital, 1966-70, retiring as lieutenant colonel; University of California, San Francisco, assistant professor, 1971-75, associate professor, 1975-79, associate clinical professor, 1979-81, clinical professor of dermatology and of oral medicine and hospital dentistry, 1981-91, clinical professor emeritus, 1991-, vice chair of department, 1977-86, chief of Dermatology Clinic at Ralph K. Davies Medical Center, 1971-84, director of Psoriasis Day Care Center, 1974-86, chief of inpatient service, 197880. Board certified in dermatology and in laser medicine and surgery; American Board of Dermatology, diplomat. **Publications:** The Healing Touch: Keeping the Doctor-Patient Relationship Alive under Managed Care, 1997; Understanding Parkinson's Disease: A Self-Help Guide, 1999; Coping with Psoriasis: A Patient's Guide to Treatment, 2000; Answers to Frequently Asked Questions in Parkinson's Disease: A Resource Book for Patients and Families, 2001. Contributor to medical books and journals. **Address:** 84 King Ave, Piedmont, CA 94611, U.S.A.

CRAMER, Clayton E. American, b. 1956. **Genres:** History, Military/Defense/Arms control, Reference. **Career:** Harris Digital Telephone Systems, Novato, CA, software engineer, 1982-84; Kontron Electronics, Mountain View, CA, software engineer, 1984-87; DSC, Petaluma, CA, software engineer, 1987-96; Nokia High Speed Access Products, Petaluma, software engineer, 1996-2000; American Communications Technologies Intl, software engineer, 2000-01; Hewlett-Packard Corp, software engineer, 2001-. **Publications:** (ed.) By the Dim and Flaring Lamps: The Civil War Diary of Samuel McIlvaine, 1990; For the Defense of Themselves and the State: The Original Intent and Judicial Interpretation of the Right to Keep and Bear Arms, 1994; Firing Back! Defending Your Right to Keep and Bear Arms, 1995; Black Demographic Data, 1790-1860: A Sourcebook, 1997; Concealed Weapon Laws of the Early Republic: Dueling, Southern Violence, and Moral Reform, 1999. Contributor to periodicals. **Address:** 13284 W Redwick Dr, Boise, ID 83713, U.S.A. **Online address:** clayton@claytoncramer.com

CRAMER, John G(leason), Jr. American, b. 1934. **Genres:** Physics. **Career:** Indiana University, Bloomington, postdoctoral fellow, 1961-63, assistant professor, 1963-64; University of Washington, Seattle, assistant professor, 1964-68, associate professor, 1968-74, professor, 1974-, director of nuclear physics lab, 1983-90. West German Bundesministerium and University of Munich, guest professor, 1971-72; Los Alamos Meson Physics Facility and Los Alamos National Laboratory, member program advisory committee, 1976-78, National Superconducting Cyclotron Lab., 1983-87; University of British Columbia, TRIUMF, 1985-88; Lawrence Berkeley Lab., CA, program advisor-consultant, 1979-82; CERN Experiments NA 35 and NA 49, 1991-; Hahn-Meitner Institute, Berlin, guest professor, 1982-83; Max-Planck-Institute fuer Physik, Munich, Germany, guest professor, 1994-95. **Publications:** Twistor, 1989; Einstein's Bridge, 1997. Contributor to physics and popular periodicals. **Address:** University of Washington, Department of Physics, Box 351560, Seattle, WA 98195, U.S.A.

CRAMER, Richard Ben. American, b. 1950. **Genres:** Biography, Politics/Government. **Career:** Sun, Baltimore, MD, reporter, 1973-76; Philadelphia Inquirer, Philadelphia, PA, reporter, 1976-78, foreign correspondent in Europe, Africa, and the Middle East, beginning in 1978; free-lance journalist and writer. Has worked as a contributing editor for Esquire. **Publications:** Ted Williams: The Season of the Kid, 1991; What It Takes: The Way to the White House, 1992; Bob Dole, 1995; Joe DiMaggio: The Hero's Life, 1999. Contributor to newspapers and periodicals. **Address:** c/o Sterling Lord Literistic Inc., 65 Bleeker St., New York, NY 10012-2420, U.S.A.

CRAMER, Stanley H. American, b. 1933. **Genres:** Education, Psychology. **Career:** State University of New York at Buffalo, professor, 1965-2001. **Publications:** (with E.L. Herr) Guidance of the College Bound: Problems, Practices, and Perspectives, 1968; (with E.L. Herr, C.N. Morris and T.T. Frantz) Research and the School Counselor, 1970; (ed. with J.D. Hansen) Group Guidance and Counseling in the Schools, 1971; (with E.L. Herr) Vocational Guidance and Career Development in the Schools: Toward a Systems Approach, 1972; (with E.L. Herr) Career Guidance through the Lifespan, 1979, 6th ed. (with E.L. Herr and S. Niles), 2004; (with E.L. Herr) Controversies in the Mental Health Professions, 1987; (with J.C. Hansen and R.H. Rossberg) Counseling: Theory and Process, 1993. **Address:** 1676 Starling Dr, Sarasota, FL 34231, U.S.A. **Online address:** staroz1676@aol.com

CRANDELL, Rachel. (born United States), b. 1943. **Genres:** Children's non-fiction. **Career:** Worked at Smithsonian Institution, Washington, DC, 1965, and Girl Scouts of Nation's Capital Council, 1966; nursery school teacher in Monrovia, IN, 1972-81; elementary school teacher in St. Louis, MO, 1981-2001; writer, 2001-. Wild Canid Survival and Research Center, board president, 1985-95; St. Louis Rainforest Advocates, president and board member, 1989-2002; Monteverde Conservation League, president, 2002; also worked as an environmental coordinator for a bilingual school in Costa Rica. Earthkeeper trainer for children; rainforest advocate and leader of trips to the tropics; public speaker and workshop presenter. **Publications:** Six Inches to England: An Anthology of International Children's Stories, 2001; (And photographer) Hands of the Maya: Villagers at Work and Play, 2002. **Address:** 1128 Weidman Rd, Town and Country, MO 63017, U.S.A. **Online address:** rwcrandell@aol.com

CRANE, Caroline. Also writes as Carolyn Wesley. American, b. 1930. **Genres:** Mystery/Crime/Suspense, Young adult fiction. **Publications:** Lights down the River, 1963; Pink Sky at Night, 1964; A Girl Like Tracy, 1966; Wedding Song, 1967; Don't Look at Me that Way, 1970; Stranger on the Road, 1971; Summer Girl, 1979; The Girls Are Missing, 1980; Coast of Fear, 1981; Wife Found Slain, 1981; The Foretelling, 1982; The Third Passenger, 1983; Trick or Treat, 1983; Woman Vanishes, 1984; Something Evil, 1984; Someone at the Door, 1985; Circus Day, 1986; Man in the Shadows, 1987; (as Carolyn Wesley) King's Castle, 1987; The People Next Door, 1988; Whispers from Oracle Falls, 1991; Night Memories, 1994; The Love Detective, 1994; Land of Glory, 2003. **Address:** 62 Herschel Dr, Wurtsboro, NY 12790-4502, U.S.A. **Online address:** ckiyabu@hvc.rr.com

CRANE, Conrad C(harles). American, b. 1952. **Genres:** History, Military/Defense/Arms control. **Career:** U.S. Army, career officer, 1974-2000, platoon leader and battery executive officer for 2nd Battalion, 52nd Air Defense Artillery, 1975-77, assistant battalion operations officer and battery commander for 2nd Battalion, 61st Air Defense Artillery in Korea, 1977-79, battery commander of 1st Battalion, 65th Air Defense Artillery, 1980-81, assistant professor at U.S. Military Academy, West Point, NY, 1983-86, branch chief and military historian at U.S. Army Air Defense Artillery School, Fort Bliss, TX, 1986-88, battalion executive officer, 2nd Battalion, 6th Air Defense Artillery, 1988-90, professor of American and military history at U.S. Military Academy, 1990-2000, U.S. Army War College, research professor of military strategy, 2000-03; U.S. Army Military History Institute, director, 2003-. **Publications:** (with C. Kirkpatrick) The Prudent Soldier, the Rash Old Fighter, and the Walking Whiskey Keg: The Battle of Valverde, New Mexico, 13-21 February, 1862, 1987; Bombs, Cities, and Civilians: American Airpower Strategy in World War II, 1993; American Airpower Strategy in Korea, 1950-1953, 2000; Landpower and Crises: Army Roles and Missions in Smaller-Scale Contingencies during the 1990s, 2001; Reconstructing Iraq: Insights, Challenges, and Missions for Military Forces in a Post Conflict Scenario, 2003. Work represented in anthologies. Contributor of articles and reviews to history and military journals. **Address:** U.S. Army Military History Institute, U.S. Army War College, Carlisle Barracks, PA 17013, U.S.A. **Online address:** conrad.crane@carlisle.army.mil

CRANE, Hamilton. *See* MASON, Sarah J.

CRANE, Peter R(obert). American, b. 1954. **Genres:** Natural history, Botany. **Career:** University of Reading, Reading, England, lecturer in botany, 1978-81; Indiana University-Bloomington, postdoctoral researcher in biology, 1981-82; Field Museum of Natural History, Chicago, IL, assistant curator of paleobotany, 1982-85, associate curator, 1985-90, curator, 1990-92, MacArthur Curator, 1992-94, chairperson, Department of Geology, 1991-92, vice-president of Center for Evolutionary and Environmental Biology, 1992-93, vice-president for academic affairs, 1994-, A. Watson Armour III Curator, 1994-, director of the museum, 1995-. University of Chicago, lecturer, 1984-, professor, 1992-, research associate in geophysical sciences, 1989-92; speaker at dozens of universities in the United States and abroad. **Publications:** (with P. Kenrick) The Origin and Early Diversification of Land Plants, 1997. EDITOR: (with E.M. Friis and W.G. Chaloner, and contrib.) The Origins of Angiosperms and Their Biological Consequences, 1987; (with Blackmore, and contrib.) The Evolution, Systematics, and Fossil History of the Hamamelidae, 2 vols, 1989; (with S. Lidgard) The Fifth North American Paleontological Convention: Abstracts and Program, 1992. **Address:** Field Museum of Natural History, Roosevelt Rd. at Lake Shore Dr., Chicago, IL 60605-2496, U.S.A. **Online address:** pcrane@fmnh.org

CRANE, Richard (Arthur). British, b. 1944. **Genres:** Plays/Screenplays, Songs/Lyrics and libretti. **Career:** Writer of plays for theater, television, and radion, in Bradford, Brighton, Edinburgh, London, Moscow, and New York, and actor, in London, NY, and in repertory, on TV, and in films, 1970-. Fellow in Theatre, University of Bradford, Yorkshire, 1972-74; Board of Dirs., Edinburgh Festival Fringe Society, 1973-89; Resident Dramatist, National Theatre, London, 1974-75; Fellow in Creative Writing, University of Leicester, 1976; Literary Manager, Royal Court Theatre, London, 1978-79; Associate Director, Brighton Theatre, 1980-85; Dramaturge, Tron Theatre, Glasgow, 1983-84; Visiting Writer, University of E. Anglia, 1988; Lecturer in English, University of Maryland, 1990; Writer-in-Residence, Birmingham Polytechnic, 1990-91; Tutor in Playwriting, University of Birmingham, 1990-91; Writer-in-Residence, H.M. Prison, Bedford, 1993-94; Lecturer in Creative Writing, University of Sussex, 1994-. **Publications:** Thunder: A Play of the Brontes, 1976; Gunslinger: A Wild West Show, 1978; Mutiny (recording), 1983, 1985; Crippen, 1990; Under the Stars, 1994. **Address:** c/o Casarotto Ramsay & Associates Ltd, National House, 60-66 Wardour St., London W1V 3ND, England.

CRANEFIELD, Paul F. American, b. 1925. **Genres:** Medicine/Health, Sciences, Biography. **Career:** Rockefeller University, NYC, professor, 1966-. **Publications:** (ed. with C. McBrooks) The Historical Development of Physiological Thought, Stechert Hafner, 1959; (with B.F. Hoffman) Electrophysiology of the Heart, McGraw, 1960; The Way In and the Way Out, Futura, 1974; Conduction of the Cardiac Impulse, Futura, 1975; (with R.S. Aronson) Cardiac Arrhythmias, Futura, 1988; Science and Empire, Cambridge University Press, 1990; Born Wanderer: The Life of Stanley Portal Hyatt Futura, 1995. **Address:** c/o Rockefeller University, 1230 York Ave, New York, NY 10021, U.S.A.

CRANFIELD, Charles Ernest Burland. British, b. 1915. **Genres:** Theology/Religion. **Career:** Emeritus Professor, University of Durham, since 1980 (Lecturer in Theology, 1950-62; Sr. Lecturer, 1962-66; Reader, 1966-78; Professor of Theology, 1978-80). Joint General Ed., International Critical Commentary, new series, since 1966. Ordained, Methodist Church, 1941; Minister in Shoeburyness, 1940-42; Forces Chaplain, 1942-46; Minister in Cleethorpes, 1946-50; admitted to Presbyterian Church of England (now part of United Reformed Church), 1954. **Publications:** The First Epistle of Peter, 1950; The Gospel According to St. Mark, 1959; I and II Peter and Jude, 1960; A Critical and Exegetical Commentary on the Epistle to the Romans, 2 vols., 1975-79; Romans: A Shorter Commentary, 1985; The Bible and Christian Life (essays), 1985; If God Be For Us (sermons), 1985; The Apostles' Creed: A Faith to Live By, 1993; On Romans and Other New Testament Essays, 1998. **Address:** 30 Western Hill, Durham DH1 4RL, England.

CRANFIELD, Ingrid. British (born Australia), b. 1945. **Genres:** Architecture, Art/Art history, Children's non-fiction, Geography, Natural history, Recreation, Travel/Exploration, Reference, Translations. **Career:** International Wool Secretariat, London, England, research asst, 1966-68; Royal Geographical Society, London, senior asst, 1968-72; freelance writer, editor, translator, and consultant, 1972-; Dictionary of Art, London, senior desk editor, 1991-96. Endeavour Training Ltd., council, 1978-, executive board, 1984-, director, 1998-. Governor of comprehensive secondary school in London Borough of Barnet, 1988-2003, and of primary school in London Borough of Enfield, 1999-, chair of governors, 2004-; West Herts College, lecturer, tutor, and course leader, Professional Development Diploma in Publishing course, 2002-. **Publications:** The Challengers: British and Commonwealth Adventure since 1945, 1976; Skiing Down Everest and Other Crazy Adventures, 1983; Q Challenge Quiz Books, 4 vols., 1988; Animal World, 1991; 100 Greatest Natural Wonders, 1996; Georgian House Style, 1997; The Archeology Kit, 1998; Art Deco House Style, 2001. TRANSLATOR: (with P. Adler) H.J. Hansen, The Ships of the German Fleets, 1848-1945, 1974; M. Hoang, Genghis Khan, 1990. EDITOR: (with R. Harrington) Off the Beaten Track, 1977; (with R. Harrington) The Independent Traveller's Handbook, 1980; (with R. Harrington) The International Traveler's Handbook (in UK as The Traveller's Handbook), 1982; The Age of the Dinosaurs, 12 vols., 2000; The Illustrated Directory of Dinosaurs and Other Prehistoric Creatures, 2000. Contributor of articles, compilations, puzzles, and reviews to periodicals and encyclopedias. **Address:** 16 Myddelton Gardens, Winchmore Hill, London N21 2PA, England. **Online address:** ingrid_cranfield@hotmail.com

CRARY, Elizabeth (Ann). American, b. 1942. **Genres:** Human relations/Parenting, Children's non-fiction. **Career:** Educator, author, publisher, and parenting consultant. Food Research Institute, University of Wisconsin, Madison, research assistant, 1966-70, food science department, 1971-77; Parenthood Education Programs, Madison, WI, founder and director, 1974-77; North Seattle Community College, instructor in parent education, 1977; Parenting Press, publisher, 1978; Parent Education Associates, codirector, 1980. **Publications:** NONFICTION: Without Spanking or Spoiling: A Practical Approach to Toddler and Preschool Guidance, 1979; Kids Can Cooperate, 1984; Pick Up Your Socks-and Other Skills Growing Children Need, 1990; 365 Wacky, Wonderful Ways to Get Your Children to Do What You Want, 1994; Love and Limits: Guidance Tools for Creative Parenting, 1994; Magic Tools for Raising Kids, 1994. CHILDREN'S PROBLEM SOLVING SERIES: I Can't Wait, 1982; I Want It, 1982; I Want to Play, 1982; My Name Is Not Dummy, 1983; I'm Lost, 1985; Mommy Don't Go, 1986; Finders, Keepers?, 1987. DEALING WITH FEELINGS SERIES: I'm Proud, 1991; I'm Frustrated, 1992; I'm Mad, 1992. **Address:** 2132 N 115th St., Seattle, WA 98133, U.S.A.

CRATTY, Bryant J. American, b. 1929. **Genres:** Education, Psychology, Sports/Fitness. **Career:** University of California, Los Angeles, instructor, 1958-61, assistant professor, 1961-65, associate professor, 1965-67, professor of kinesiology, and director, Perceptual-Motor Learning Laboratory, 1967-91, professor emeritus, 1991-. Research Quarterly: The Journal of Motor Behavior, editor. **Publications:** Movement Behavior and Motor Learning, 1967, 3rd ed., 1973; Motor Activity and the Education of Retardates, 1969; Psychology and the Superior Athlete, 1969; Perceptual and Motor Development of Infants and Children, 1970, 3rd ed., 1989; Children and Youth in Competitive Sport; Movement and Spatial Awareness in Blind Children and Youth, 1971; Active Learning, 1971; Physical Expressions of Intelligence, 1972; (with J.S. Breen) Educational Activities for the Physically Handicapped, 1972; Psychology in Contemporary Sport, 1973, 3rd ed., 1989; Teaching Motor Skills, 1973; Intelligence in Action, 1973; Psychomotor Behavior in Education and Sport: Selected Papers, 1974; Teaching Human Behavior via Active Games, 1975; Remedial Motor Activity for Children: Theory, Evaluation and Remediation, 1975; The Athlete in the Sports Team, 1980; Social Psychology in Athletics, 1980; Adapted Physical Education for Handicapped

Children and Youth, 1980; Psychological Preparation and Athletic Excellence, 1984; (with R. Piggot) Student Projects in Sports Psychology, 1984; Active Learning, 1985; From Scribbling to Printing, a Teaching Guide for Parents and Teacher, 1987; Physical Development for Children, 1987; Clumsy Child Syndromes, 1997. **Address:** 21901 Burbank Blvd #182, Woodland Hills, CA 91367, U.S.A. **Online address:** www.bjcbms@aol.com

CRAVENS, Hamilton. American, b. 1938. **Genres:** History. **Career:** Iowa State University, Ames, instructor, 1968-80, professor of history, 1980-. Associated with University of Maryland, College Park; Ohio State University, Columbus; Goettingen University, Germany, Bonn University, Cologne University, and Heidelberg University. **Publications:** The Triumph of Evolution, 1978, rev. ed., 1988; Ideas in America's Cultures, 1982; Before Head Start, 1993, rev. ed., 2002; Technical Knowledge in American Culture, 1996; Health Care Policy in Modern America, 1997; The Social Sciences Go to Washington, 2003. **Address:** 615 Ross Hall, Dept. of History, Iowa State University, Ames, IA 50011, U.S.A. **Online address:** hcravens@iastate.edu

CRAVEY, Pamela J. (born United States), b. 1945. **Genres:** Librarianship. **Career:** Florida State University, Tallahassee, instructor and librarian, 1968-69; University of Georgia, Athens, instructor and librarian, 1972-75; Georgia Stage University, Atlanta, associate professor and librarian, 1975-2000, associate professor emeritus, 2000-; self-employed consultant, 2000-. Council on Library Resources, project librarian for library service enhancement program; consultant to American Academy of Religion. **Publications:** Protecting Library Staff, Users, Collections, and Facilities: A How-to-Do-It Manual, 2001. Contributor to books and periodicals. **Address:** 2103 North Decatur Rd., Suite 308, Decatur, GA 30033, U.S.A.

CRAWFORD, Alan. British, b. 1943. **Genres:** Architecture, Crafts, Design. **Career:** Research Fellow, Victorian Studies Centre, University of Leicester, 1970-72; Lecturer in History of Design, Birmingham Polytechnic, 1972-78; part-time consultant to English Heritage, 1989-. Chairman Victorian Society, 1982-86; South Square Fellow, Royal College of Art, London, 1992-93. **Publications:** (with Robert Thorne) Birmingham Pubs 1890-1939, 1975; (ed.) By Hammer and Hand: The Arts and Crafts Movement in Birmingham, 1984; C. R. Ashbee: Architect, Designer and Romantic Socialist, 1985; (with Robert Thorne and Michael Dunn) Birmingham Pubs 1880-1939, 1986; Charles Rennie Mackintosh, 1995. **Address:** 58 Cecile Park, London N8 9AU, England.

CRAWFORD, Gary W(illiam). American, b. 1953. **Genres:** Poetry, Reference. **Career:** Gothic Press, Baton Rouge, LA, editor, 1979-. **Publications:** Ramsey Campbell, 1988; Poems of the Divided Self, 1992; J. Sheridan Le Fanu: A Bio-Bibliography, 1995; In Shadow Lands (poems), 1998. **Address:** 1701 Lobdell Ave. No. 32, Baton Rouge, LA 70806, U.S.A.

CRAWFORD, Mark. American, b. 1954. **Genres:** Earth sciences, Environmental sciences/Ecology, History, Marketing, Military/Defense/Arms control. **Career:** Mining geologist, 1977-95; freelance writer, 1995-. **Publications:** Toxic Waste Sites, 1997; Physical Geology, 1997; Encyclopedia of the Mexican-American War, 1998; Courage on Lesser Fields, 1998; Endangered Habitats and Ecosystems, 1998. **Address:** 5101 Violet Ln, Madison, WI 53714, U.S.A. **Online address:** giltedge@chorus.net

CRAWFORD, Mary. American, b. 1942. **Genres:** Psychology, Women's studies and issues. **Career:** University of Illinois at Urbana-Champaign, Urbana, visiting instructor, 1973-74; Buena Vista College, Storm Lake, IA, assistant professor, 1974-78; West Chester University of Pennsylvania, West Chester, assistant professor, 1978-81, associate professor, 1981-84, professor of psychology and women's studies, 1984-93; University of South Carolina, Columbia, professor of psychology and graduate director of women's studies, 1993-. Hamilton College, visiting professor, 1981, Jane Watson Irwin Visiting Professor of Psychology and Women's Studies, 1986-88; Trenton State College, distinguished visiting scholar, 1989-90. Iowa Humanities Board, academic humanist for Women 2000, 1975-76; Women's College Coalition, research director, 1991-94. **Publications:** (with M. Gentry) Gender and Thought: Psychological Perspectives, 1989; (with R. Unger) Women and Gender: A Feminist Psychology, with instructor's manual (with Unger and A. Stark), 1992; Talking Difference: Gender and Conversational Style, 1995; (with Unger) Readings for a Feminist Psychology, in press. Work represented in anthologies. Contributor of articles and reviews to psychology and women's studies journals, and to popular magazines. **Address:** 2211 Laurel Street, Columbia, SC 29204-1021, U.S.A.

CRAWFORD, Robert. See **RAE, Hugh C(rawford).**

CRAWFORD, T. Hugh. American, b. 1956. **Genres:** Literary criticism and history. **Career:** Virginia Military Institute, Lexington, associate professor of English. **Publications:** Modernism, Medicine, and William Carlos Williams, 1993. **Address:** Literature Communication & Culture, Georgia Institute of Technology, Atlanta, GA 30332, U.S.A. **Online address:** hugh.crawford@lcc.gatech.edu

CRAWFORD, Tad. American, b. 1946. **Genres:** Art/Art history, Law, Money/Finance, Mythology/Folklore, Psychology, Writing/Journalism. **Career:** Attorney in New York City, 1971-; School of Visual Arts, New York City, instructor in humanities, 1973-; Allworth Press, New York City, publisher, 1989-. **Publications:** The Writer's Legal Guide, 1977, 4th ed. (with K. Murray), 2002; Legal Guide for the Visual Artist, 1977, 4th ed., 1999; The Visual Artist's Guide to the New Copyright Law, 1978; (with A. Kopelman) Selling Your Photography, 1980; (with Kopelman) Selling Your Graphic Design and Illustration, 1981; (with S. Mellon) The Artist-Gallery Partnership: A Practical Guide to Consignment, 1981, rev. ed., 1998; Business and Legal Forms for Fine Artists, 1990, rev. ed., 1999; Business and Legal Forms for Authors and Self-Publishers, 1990, rev. ed., 1999; Business and Legal Forms for Illustrators, 1990, rev. ed., 1998; (with E.D. Bruck) Business and Legal Forms for Graphic Designers, 1990, rev. ed., 2003; Business and Legal Forms for Photographers, 1991, rev. ed., 1997; The Secret Life of Money, 1995; Business and Legal Forms for Crafts, 1998; The Money Mentor, 2001; (with E.D. Bruck) Business and Legal Forms for Interior Designers, 2001. **Address:** c/o Jean V. Naggar, Jean V. Naggar Literary Agency, 216 E 75th St, New York, NY 10021, U.S.A.

CRAWLEY, Harriet. British, b. 1948. **Genres:** Novels. **Career:** Writer. Conservative candidate for Brent East in general election, 1987, and for London Central in European elections, 1989. Has also worked as a television presenter and interviewer. **Publications:** Degree of Defiance, 1969. NOVELS: The Goddaughter, 1975; The Lovers and the Loved, 1990; Painted Lady, 1994. **Address:** c/o PFD, Drury House, 34-43 Russell St, London WC2B 5HA, England.

CRAY, Edward. American, b. 1933. **Genres:** Civil liberties/Human rights, Law, Mythology/Folklore, Social commentary. **Career:** American Civil Liberties Union of Southern California, director of publications, 1965-70; Southern California Symphony, Hollywood Bowl Association, director of publicity, 1970-71; University of Southern California, Los Angeles, School of Journalism, sr. lecturer, 1976-82, associate professor, 1982-90, professor, 1982-. **Publications:** The Big Blue Line, 1967; (ed.) The Erotic Muse, 1968, 2nd ed. 1992; In Failing Health, 1971; The Enemy in the Streets, 1972; Burden of Proof, 1973; Levi's, 1978; Chrome Colossus, 1980; General of the Army, 1990; (with J. Kotler and M. Beller) American Datelines, 1991; Chief Justice, 1997; Ramblin' Man, 2004. **Address:** 647 Raymond Ave No 2, Santa Monica, CA 90405, U.S.A. **Online address:** cray@usc.edu

CRAYDER, Teresa. See **COLMAN, Hila (Crayder).**

CREAGER, Clara. American, b. 1930. **Genres:** Crafts. **Career:** Professor Emeritus, Dept. of Art, Ohio State University, Columbus. **Publications:** Weaving: A Creative Approach for Beginners, 1974; All About Weaving, 1984. **Address:** 75 W. College Ave, Westerville, OH 43081, U.S.A.

CREAMER, Robert W. American, b. 1922. **Genres:** Sports/Fitness, Biography, Ghost Writer. **Career:** Spec. Contributor, Sports Illustrated mag., NYC, since 1985 (Sr. Ed., 1954-84). **Publications:** (ghost writer) Mickey Mantle: The Quality of Courage, 1964; (with J. Conlan) Jocko, 1967; (with R. Barber) Rhubarb in the Catbird Seat, 1968; Babe: The Legend Comes to Life, 1974; (co-author) The Yankees, 1979; Stengel: His Life and Times, 1984; (with R. Houk) Season of Glory: The Amazing Saga of the 1961 New York Yankees, 1988; Baseball in '41, 1991; (co-author) Mantle Remembered, 1995. **Address:** c/o Sterling Lord Literistic Inc., 65 Bleeker St, New York, NY 10012-2420, U.S.A.

CREAN, Susan M. Canadian, b. 1945. **Genres:** Art/Art history, Communications/Media, Cultural/Ethnic topics, History, Intellectual history, Organized labor, Race relations, Women's studies and issues, Autobiography/Memoirs, Biography. **Career:** Editor, critic, broadcaster, television producer, arts consultant, and journalist in Toronto, Ontario, Canada, 1970-. Served as a research and tutorial assistant at universities and colleges; lectured and presented papers on Canadian, feminist, and television issues. **Publications:** NONFICTION: Who's Afraid of Canadian Culture?, 1976; (with M. Rioux) Deux Pays Pour Vivre: Un plaidoyer, 1980; (with M. Rioux) Two Nations: An Essay on the Culture and Politics of Canada and Quebec in a World of American Pre-Eminence, 1983; Newsworthy: The Lives of Media Women,

1985; In the Name of the Fathers, c. 1989; Grace Hartman: A Woman for Her Time (biography), c. 1996; The Laughing One: A Journey to Emily Carr, 2001. Contributor of articles, editorials, and reviews to periodicals. **Address:** 17 Coady Ave, Toronto, ON, Canada M4M 2Y9. **Online address:** smc@istar.ca

CRECELIUS, Daniel. American, b. 1937. **Genres:** Area studies, History, Translations. **Career:** California State University, Los Angeles, assistant professor to professor of Middle East history, 1964-2001, emeritus, 2002-. **Publications:** The Roots of Modern Egypt: A Study of the Regimes of 'Ali Bey al-Kabir and Muhammad Bey Abu al-Dhahab, 1760-1775, 1981; Fihris Waqfiyyat al-'Asr al-'Uthmani al-Mahfuthah bi Wizarat al-Awqaf wa Dar al-Watha'iq al-Ta'rikhiyyah al-Qawmiyyah bi al-Qahirah, 1992. EDITOR: (and contrib.) Eighteenth Century Egypt: The Arabic Manuscript Sources, 1990; (and trans., with 'Abd al-Wahhab Bakr) Al-Damurdashi's Chronicle of Egypt, 1688-1755, 1991; (with 'Abd al-Wahhab Bakr) Makhtutat al-Durrah al-Musanah fi Akhbar al-Kinanah, 1992; (and trans., with H. Badr) A Short Manuscript History of the Mamluk Amir Murad Bey; (with H. Badr and Husam al-Din Ismail) Ta'rikh al-Wazir Muhammad Ali Basha li al-Shaykh Khalil ibn Ahmad al-Rajabi, 1997; and others. Work also represented in anthologies. Contributor of articles to scholarly journals and chapters to topical studies. **Address:** Middle East History, California State University, 5151 State University Dr, Los Angeles, CA 90032, U.S.A. **Online address:** dcrecel@calstatela.edu

CRECY, Jeanne. *See* **WILLIAMS, Jeanne.**

CREECH, Sharon. Also writes as Sharon Rigg. American, b. 1945. **Genres:** Young adult fiction. **Career:** Federal Theater Project Archives, Fairfax, VA; Congressional Quarterly, Washington, DC, editorial assistant; TASIS England American School, Surrey, England, teacher of American and British literature, 1979-82, 1984-, and TASIS (The American School in Switzerland), Lugano, Switzerland, 1983-85. **Publications:** FOR YOUNG PEOPLE: Absolutely Normal Chaos, 1990; Walk Two Moons, 1994; Pleasing the Ghost, 1996, in UK as The Ghost of Uncle Arvie; Chasing Redbird, 1997; Bloomability, 1998; Fishing in the Air, 2000; The Wanderer, 2000 (Newbery Honor); A Fine, Fine School, 2001; Love That Dog, 2001; Ruby Holler, 2002. OTHER: The Center of the Universe: Waiting for the Girl (play), 1992. AS SHARON RIGG: The Recital, 1990; Nickel Malley. **Address:** c/o HarperCollins Children's Books, 1350 Ave of the Americas, New York, NY 10019, U.S.A.

CREED, William S. (born United States). **Genres:** Science fiction/Fantasy. **Career:** Writer. Formerly served as a member of a city council. Served in U.S. Air Force. **Publications:** Comes the End: A Futuristic Thriller, 2003. **Address:** 64155 Van Dyke Ave, Suite 270, Washington, MI 48095, U.S.A. **Online address:** wscreed@comcast.net

CREEDEN, Sharon. American, b. 1938. **Genres:** Mythology/Folklore. **Career:** Storyteller, 1983-95. Served as a deputy prosecuting attorney. **Publications:** Fair Is Fair: World Folktales of Justice, 1995. **Address:** 2536 Alki S.W., Seattle, WA 98116, U.S.A.

CREELEY, Robert (White). American, b. 1926. **Genres:** Novels, Novellas/Short stories, Plays/Screenplays, Poetry, Literary criticism and history. **Career:** Capen Professor of Poetry and Humanities, State University of New York, Buffalo, 1990- (visiting professor, 1966-67; professor of English, 1967-78; Gray Professor of Poetry and Letters, 1978-89). Operated Divers Press, Palma de Mallorca, 1953-55; ed., Black Mountain Review, NC, 1954-57; visiting lecturer, 1961-62, lecturer, 1963-66, 1968-69, University of New Mexico, Albuquerque; lecturer, University of British Columbia, Vancouver, 1962-63. **Publications:** Le Fou, 1952; The Kind of Act of, 1953; The Immoral Proposition, 1953; Ferrini and Others, 1953; The Gold Diggers (short stories), 1954; A Snarling Garland of Xmas Verses, 1954; All That Is Lovely in Men, 1955; If You, 1956; The Whip, 1957; A Form of Women, 1959; For Love: Poems 1950-60, 1962; The Island (novel), 1963; Distance, 1964; Two Poems; Mister Blue (short stories), 1964; Hi There!, 1965; Words, 1965; About Women, 1966; Poems, 1950-65, 1966; For Joel, 1966; A Sight, 1967; Words, 1967; Robert Creeley Reads, 1967; The Finger, 1968; 5 Numbers, 1968; The Charm (poetry), 1968; The Boy, 1968; Numbers, 1968; Divisions and Other Early Poems, 1968; Pieces, 1968; Contexts of Poetry, 1968; Mazatlan: Sea, 1969; Hero, 1969; A Wall, 1969; Mary's Fancy, 1970; In London, 1970; The Finger: Poems 1966-69, 1970; For Betsy and Tom, 1970; For Benny and Sabina, 1970; As Now It Would Be Snow, 1970; America, 1970; Christmas: May 10, 1970, 1970; A Quick Graph: Collected Notes and Essays, 1970; Sea, 1971; 1,2,3,4,5,6,7,8,9,0, 1971; For the Graduation, 1971; Listen (play), 1972; Change, 1972; One Day after Another, 1972; A Day Book, 1972; For My Mother, 1973; Kitchen, 1973; The

Creative, 1973; A Sense of Measure (essays), 1972; His Idea, 1973; Inside Out, 1973; Contexts of Poetry: Interviews 1961-71, 1973; Sitting Here, 1974; Thirty Things, 1974; Presences: A Text for Marisol, 1976; Mabel: A Story and Other Prose, 1976; Selected Poems, 1976, 1991; Myself, 1977; Hello, 1978; Later: A Poem, 1978; Desultory Days, 1978; Was That a Real Poem and Other Essays, 1979; Charles Olson and Robert Creeley: The Complete Correspondence, 9 vols., 1980-89; Mother's Voice, 1981; Echoes, 1982; The Collected Poems of Robert Creeley 1945-1975, 1982; Mirrors, 1983; The Collected Prose of Robert Creeley, 1984; A Calendar: 12 Poems, 1984; Memory Gardens, 1986; Collected Essays, 1989; The Essential Burns, 1989; Jane Hammond, 1989; Windows, 1990; Autobiography, 1990; Have a Heart, 1990; (with I. Layton) The Complete Correspondence, 1990; Places, 1990; The Old Days, 1991; Gnomic Verses, 1991; Tales Out of School, 1993; Life and Death, 1993; Echoes, 1994; Daybook of a Virtual Poet, 1998; (with M. Gimblett) The Dogs of Auckland, 1998; So There: Poems 1976-1983, 1998; (with J. Millei) Personal: Poems, 1998; (with E. Dorfman) En Famille (poem), 1999; (with A. Katz) Edges, 1999; Thinking, 2000; Clemente's Images, 2000; For Friends, 2000; Just in Time: Poems, 1984-1994, 2001; (with A. Rand) Drawn & Quartered, 2001; Just in Time: Poems, 1984-1994, 2001. EDITOR: C. Olson, Mayan Letters, 1953; (with D. Allen) New American Story, 1965; Selected Writings of Charles Olson, 1966; (with D. Allen) The New Writing in the USA, 1967; Whitman: Selected Poems, 1973. **Address:** State University of New York, Buffalo, 420 Capen, Buffalo, NY 14260, U.S.A.

CREGAN, David (Appleton Quartus). British, b. 1931. **Genres:** Novels, Plays/Screenplays. **Career:** Head of English Dept., Palm Beach Private School, Florida, 1955-57; Assistant English Master, Burnage Boys' Grammar School, Manchester, 1957; Mouse poison salesman, 1957-58; Assistant English Master and Head of Drama Dept., 1958-62, and Part-time Drama Teacher, 1962-67, Hatfield School, Herts.; Salesman and Clerk at the Automobile Association, 1958; has worked with Cambridge Footlights, 1953, 1954, The Royal Court Theatre Studio, London, 1964, 1968, and the Midlands Arts Centre, Birmingham, 1971; conducted 3-week studio at the Royal Shakespeare Company Memorial Theatre, Stratford upon Avon, 1971; Co-founder and Director, New Theatre Workshops, Gulbenkian Foundation, 1979-84. Member, Drama Panel, West Midlands Arts Association, 1972-75, Eastern Arts, 1981-85, 1990-. **Publications:** Ronald Rossiter (novel), 1959; Miniatures, 1965; Transcending, and The Dancers, 1966; Three Men for Colverton, 1966; The Houses by the Green, 1968; How We Held the Square: A Play for Children, 1973; The Land of Palms and Other Plays, 1973; Poor Tom and Tina, 1976; Play Nine, 1980; Sleeping Beauty, 1984; Red Riding Hood, 1985; Jack and the Beanstalk, 1987; Beauty and the Beast, 1988; Cinderella, 1989; Best Radio Plays of 1990, 1991; Aladdin, 1991; On the Green Rock, 2001; Three Plays (Whisper along the Patio; Nice Dorothy; The Last Thresh), 2001; The Difficult Unicorn, 2002. **Address:** 76 Wood Close, Hatfield, Herts., England.

CREIGHTON, Kathleen. (born United States), b. 1943. **Genres:** Romance/Historical. **Career:** Writer. **Publications:** ROMANCE FICTION: Demon Lover, 1985; Delilah's Weakness, 1986; Angel's Walk, 1986; Double Dealings, 1986; Still Waters, 1986; Gypsy Dancer, 1987; In Defense of Love, 1987; Katie's Hero, 1987; The Prince and the Patriot, 1988; Winter's Daughter, 1988; The Sorcerer's Keeper, 1988; Rogue's Valley, 1988; Tiger Dawn, 1989; Love and Other Surprises, 1990; The Heartmender, 1990; In from the Cold, 1991; Wolf and the Angel, 1992; A Christmas Love, St. 1992; A Wanted Man, 1994; Eyewitness, 1995; One Good Man, 1995; Men of Steel, 1995; Never Trust a Lady, 1997; One Christmas Knight, 1997; One More Knight, 1998; One Summer's Knight, 1999; Eve's Wedding Knight, 1999; The Cowboy's Hidden Agenda, 2000; The Awakening of Dr. Brown, 2001; The Seduction of Goody Two-Shoes, 2001; The Virgin Seduction, 2002.; The Black Sheep's Baby, 2002; Shooting Starr, 2003; The Top Gun's Return, 2003. Work represented in anthologies. Some writings appear under the pseudonym Kathleen Carrol. **Address:** c/o Patricia Teal, Patricia Teal Literary Agency, 2036 Vista Del Rosa, Fullerton, CA 92831, U.S.A. **Online address:** katecreighton@wctel.net

CREIGHTON, Linn. American (born China), b. 1917. **Genres:** Novels, Theology/Religion. **Career:** Newton Trust Co., Newton, MA, clerk, 1940-41; South Kent School, teacher of French and Latin, 1941-42; pastor of Presbyterian Church in Flemington, NJ, 1950-82; writer. **Publications:** Bicentennial History of the Presbyterian Church in Flemington, NJ, 1991; Beyond This Darkness (novel), 1993; Plays of the Passion, 1998. **Address:** 17 Kendal Dr, Kennett Square, PA 19348-2321, U.S.A.

CREMO, Michael (A.). Also writes as Drutakarma Dasa. American, b. 1948. **Genres:** Adult non-fiction. **Career:** Initiated as a disciple of A.C.

Bhaktivedanto, Swami Prabheyada, 1976; Bhaktivedanta Book Trust, San Diego, CA, writer and editor, 1980-86; Bhaktivedanta Institute, San Diego, research associate, 1984-. International Society for Krishna Consciousness (ISKCON), teacher of bhakti-yoga, 1973-, member of governing body of Philosophical Research Group, 1991-; public affairs consultant for ISKCON Communications, 1980-; Govardhan Hill, director, 1988-. **Publications:** (with R.L. Thompson) Forbidden Archeology: The Hidden History of the Human Race, 1993; Hidden History of the Human Race, 1994; Divine Nature, 1995; Forbidden Archaeology's Impact, 1998; Human Devolution, 2000. AS DRUTAKARMA DASA (with others): Coming Back: The Science of Reincarnation, 1982; Chant and Be Happy: The Power of Mantra Meditation, 1982; The Higher Taste: A Guide to Gourmet Vegetarian Cooking and a Karma-Free Diet, 1983. Contributor to spiritual periodicals and to newspapers, under the pseudonym Drutakarma Dasa. **Address:** Bhaktivedanta Institute, 2334 Stuart St, Berkeley, CA 94705, U.S.A. **Online address:** mcremo@cs.com

CRENSHAW, James L. American, b. 1934. **Genres:** Theology/Religion. **Career:** Robert L. Flowers Professor of Old Testament, 1993-, Professor of Old Testament, 1987-, Duke University, Durham, NC. Assistant Professor of Religion, Atlantic Christian College, Wilson, NC, 1964-65; Assistant Professor to Associate Professor, Mercer University, Macon, GA, 1965-69; Assistant Professor to Professor, Vanderbilt Divinity School, Nashville, TN, 1970-87. Associate Ed., 1976-78, and Ed., 1978-84, Society of Biblical Literature Monograph Series. Editorial Board of Catholic Biblical Quarterly, 1993-99. **Publications:** Prophetic Conflict: Its Effect Upon Israelite Religion, 1971; (co-author) Old Testament Form Criticism, 1974; Hymnic Affirmation of Divine Justice, 1975; Studies in Ancient Israelite Wisdom, 1976; Gerhard von Rad, 1978; Samson: A Secret Betrayed, A Vow Ignored, 1978; Old Testament Wisdom, 1981, rev. ed., 1998; A Whirlpool of Torment, 1984; Story and Faith, 1986; Ecclesiastes, 1987; Trembling at the Threshold of a Bibical Text, 1994; Joel, 1995; Urgent Advice and Probing Questions, 1995; Sirach, 1997; Education in Ancient Israel, 1998; The Psalms: An Introduction, 2001. EDITOR/CO-EDITOR: Essays in Old Testament Ethics, 1974; The Divine Helmsman, 1980; Theodicy in the Old Testament, 1983; Perspectives on the Hebrew Bible, 1988; Personalities of the Old Testament, 8 vols. **Address:** 8 Beckford Pl, Durham, NC 27705, U.S.A. **Online address:** jcrenshaw@div.duke.edu

CRENSON, Victoria. American, b. 1952. **Genres:** Children's non-fiction. **Career:** Staff writer for educational foundation involved in adolescent literacy. Has also worked as a science writer, children's book editor, book reviewer for children's literature, book marketing director, and as a freelance writer and editor. Volunteer work for several nature centers. **Publications:** FOR CHILDREN: Discovering Dinosaurs: An Up-to-Date Guide Including the Newest Theories, 1988; Butterflies and Moths, 1993; The Nutcracker, 1993; Bay Shore Park: The Death and Life of an Amusement Park, 1995; Horseshoe Crabs and Shorebirds: The Story of a Food Web, 2003. Author of other books. THE SENSES SERIES WITH K. SMITH: Hearing, 1988; Seeing, 1988; Smelling, 1988; Tasting, 1988; Thinking, 1988; Touching, 1988. HOW AND WHY SERIES: Prehistoric Life, 1989; Sea Creatures, 1989; Snakes, 1989; Wild Animals, 1989. LEARNING FUN BOOK SERIES: Insects, 1990; Space, 1990; Strange Creatures, 1990. ADVENTURES IN COURAGE SERIES: Abraham Lincoln, 1992; George Washington, 1992; Martin Luther King, Jr., 1992. FOR ADULTS: Norman Rockwell's Portrait of America, 1989. OTHER: Creator of text and activities for three children's multimedia series. **Address:** 2223 Sulgrave Ave, Baltimore, MD 21209, U.S.A.

CRERAR, Duff (Willis). Canadian, b. 1955. **Genres:** History, Military/Defense/Arms control, Theology/Religion. **Career:** Queen's University, instructor, 1981-90; Grande Prairie Regional College, instructor, 1990-. Department of National Defense, Chaplain General's Branch, historical consultant, 1991-. **Publications:** Padres in No-Man's-Land: Chaplains of the Canadian Expeditionary Force and the Great War, 1995. Contributor to periodicals and editor of volumes on chaplain history. **Address:** 10706 92c St, Grande Prairie, AB, Canada T8V 3W3. **Online address:** duff.crerar@gprc.ab.ca

CRESSWELL, Helen. British, b. 1936. **Genres:** Novellas/Short stories, Children's fiction, Plays/Screenplays. **Publications:** Sonya-by-the-Shore, 1960; Jumbo Spencer, 1963; The White Sea Horse, 1964; Jumbo Back to Nature, 1965; Pietro and the Mule, 1965; Where the Wind Blows, 1966; Jumbo Afloat, 1966; The Pie Makers, 1967; A Day on Big O, 1967; A Tide for the Captain, 1967; The Signposters, 1968; The Sea Piper, 1968; Jumbo and the Big Dig, 1968; Rug Is a Bear, 1968; Rug Plays Tricks, 1968; The Night Watchmen, 1969; A Game of Catch, 1969; A Gift from Winklesea, 1969; A House for Jones, 1969; Rug Plays Ball, 1969; Rug and a Picnic, 1969; The Outlanders, 1970; The Wilkses, 1970; Rainbow Pavement, 1970; John's First Fish, 1970; Up the Pier, 1971; The Weather Cat, 1971; The Bird Fancier, 1971; At the Stroke of Midnight, 1971; The Beachcombers, 1972; Jane's Policeman, 1972; The Long Day, 1972; Short Back and Sides, 1972; Blue Birds over Pit Row, 1972; Roof Fall, 1972; Lizzie Dripping series, 6 vols., 1972-91; The White Sea Horse and Other Tales of the Sea, 1972; The Bongleweed, 1973; The Bower Bird, 1973; The Key, 1973; The Trap, 1973; The Beetle Hunt, 1973; The Two Hoots series, 7 vols., 1974-77; Cheap Day Return, 1974; Shady Deal, 1974; Butterfly Chase, 1975; The Winter of the Birds, 1975; Jumbo Spencer (TV play), 1976; Bagthorpe series, 10 vols., 1977-99; Donkey Days, 1977; Absolute Zero, 1978; The Flyaway Kite, 1979; My Aunt Polly by the Sea, 1980; Dear Shrink, 1982; The Secret World of Polly Flint, 1982; Ellie and the Hagwitch, 1984; Whodunnit?, 1986; Moondial, 1987; Time Out, 1987; Dragon Ride, 1987; Fox in a Maze, 1988; Greedy Alice, 1989; Rosie and the Boredom Eater, 1989; The Story of Grace Darling, 1989; Whatever Happened in Winklesea?, 1989; Almost Goodbye Guzzler, 1990; Meet Posy Bates, 1990; Posy Bates Again, 1991; The Return of the Psammead (book & TV series), 1992; (ed.) The Puffin Book of Funny Stories, 1992; Posy Bates and the Bag Lady, 1993; The Watchers: Mystery at Alton Towers, 1993; Stonestruck, 1995; Mystery Stories, 1996; Mister Maggs, 1996; Bag of Bones, 1997; Sophie and the Seawolf, 1997; Rumpelstiltskin, 1997; The Phoenix and the Carpet, 1997; Collins Treasury of Fairy Tales, 1997; The Little Grey Donkey, 1998; Garlunk, 1998; Snatchers, 2000. **Address:** Old Church Farm, Eakring, Newark, Notts. NG22 0DA, England.

CRESSWELL, Stephen. American, b. 1956. **Genres:** History. **Career:** Mount Vernon College, Washington, DC, reference librarian, 1980-81; University of Virginia, Charlottesville, instructor in history, 1985; West Virginia Wesleyan College, Buckhannon, professor of history, 1986-. **Publications:** Mormons and Cowboys, Moonshiners and Klansmen: Federal Law Enforcement in the South and West, 1870-1893, 1991; (ed.) We Will Know What War Is: The Civil War Diary of Sirene Bunten, 1993; Multiparty Politics in Mississippi, 1877-1902, 1995. **Address:** Department of History, West Virginia Wesleyan College, Buckhannon, WV 26201, U.S.A.

CREVIER, Daniel. Canadian, b. 1947. **Genres:** Information science/Computers. **Career:** Writer. **Publications:** AI: The Tumultuous History of the Search for Artificial Intelligence, 1993. **Address:** Opthalmos Inc., 280 Victoria, Longueuil, QC, Canada J4H 2J6.

CREW, Danny O(liver). American, b. 1947. **Genres:** Music, Politics/Government. **Career:** City of Boca Raton, Boca Raton, FL, assistant city manager, 1982-84; City of Pompano Beach, Pompano Beach, FL, assistant city manager, 1984-90; St. Lucie County, Fort Pierce, FL, assistant county manager, 1990-92; City of Gastonia, Gastonia, NC, city manager, 1993-. **Publications:** Presidential Sheet Music: An Illustrated Catalogue of Published Music Associated with the American Presidency and Those Who Sought the Office, 2001. **Address:** PO Box 189, Gastonia, NC 28053, U.S.A. **Online address:** weetabix@quik.com

CREW, Gary. Australian, b. 1947. **Genres:** Novels, Novellas/Short stories, Children's fiction. **Career:** McDonald, Wagner, & Priddle, Brisbane, Queensland, Australia, senior draftsman and drafting consultant, 1962-72; Everton Park State High School, Brisbane, English teacher, 1974-78; Mitchelton State High School, Brisbane, English teacher, 1978-81; Aspley High School, Brisbane, subject master in English, 1982; Albany Creek High School, Brisbane, subject master in English and head of English department, 1983-88; Queensland University of Technology, Brisbane, creative writing lecturer, 1989-; Heinemann Octopus, series editor, 1990-. **Publications:** NOVELS: The Inner Circle, 1985; The House of Tomorrow, 1988; Strange Objects, 1990; No Such Country, 1991; Angel's Gate, 1993; Gothic Hospital, 2000. CHILDREN'S STORY BOOKS: Tracks, 1992; Lucy's Bay, 1992; The Figures of Julian Ashcroft, 1993; First Light, 1993; Gulliver in the South Seas; The Watertower, 1996; Bright Star, 1999; Caleb, 1998. Contributor of short stories to anthologies. Contributor to books and periodicals. **Address:** PO Box 440, Maleny, QLD 4552, Australia. **Online address:** crewg@ozemail.com.au

CREW, Linda. American, b. 1951. **Genres:** Novels, Children's fiction, Young adult fiction. **Career:** Farmer and writer. Worked as receptionist, florist, and substitute mail carrier. **Publications:** FOR CHILDREN: Nekomah Creek, 1991; Nekomah Creek Christmas, 1994. FOR ADULTS: Ordinary Miracles, 1993. FICTION FOR YOUNG ADULTS: Children of the River (novel), 1989; Someday I'll Laugh about This, 1990; Fire on the Wind, 1995; Long Time Passing, 1997; Brides of Eden: A True Story Imagined, 2001. **Address:** c/o Robin Rue, Writers House, 21 W 26th St, New York, NY 10010, U.S.A. **Online address:** LJCI@earthlink.net

CREW, Louie. Also writes as Li Min Hua. American, b. 1936. **Genres:** Poetry, Gay and lesbian issues, Essays. **Career:** Master of English and Bible, Darlington School, Rome, GA, 1959-62; Master of English and Sacred Studies, St. Andrew's School, Middletown, DE, 1962-65; Instructor of English, Penge Secondary Modern School, London; 1965-66; Instructor of English, University of Alabama, Tuscaloosa, 1966-70; Director, Independent Study in England for Experiment in International Living, 1970-71; Professor of English, Claflin College, Orangeburg, SC, 1971-73; Associate Professor of English, Fort Valley State Col., GA, 1973-79; Associate Professor of English, University of Wisconsin at Stevens Point, 1979-84; Director of Writing Program, Chinese University of Hong Kong, 1984-87; freelance writer, 1987-88; Rutgers University, Newark, NJ, Associate Professor, 1989-2001, Professor Emeritus, 2002-. Founder, Integrity: International Ministry of Lesbian and Gay Anglicans, 1974-. Member of Board, Journal of Homosexuality, 1978-83, 1990-. Member of Board, National Gay Task Force, 1976-78; and National Council of Teachers of English, 1976-80. **Publications:** POETRY: Sunspots, 1976; Midnight Lessons, 1987; Quean Lutibelle's Pew, 1990. ESSAYS: The Gay Academic, 1978; E-Natter of Quean Lufibelle, 1990; A Book of Revelations, 1991. OTHER: (comp.) 101 Reasons to Be an Episcopalian, 2003. **Address:** 377 S Harrison St, East Orange, NJ 07018, U.S.A. **Online address:** lcrew@newark.rutgers.edu

CREWS, Donald. American, b. 1938. **Genres:** Children's fiction, Illustrations. **Career:** Illustrator and author; free-lance artist, photographer, and designer. Assistant art director, Dance (magazine), NYC, 1959-60; staff designer, Will Burton Studios, NYC, 1961-62. **Publications:** SELF ILLUSTRATED PICTURE BOOKS: We Read: A to Z, 1967; Ten Black Dots, 1968, rev ed, 1986; Freight Train, 1978; Truck, 1980; Light, 1981; Harbor, 1982; Carousel, 1982; Parade, 1982; School Bus, 1984; Bicycle Race, 1985; Flying, 1986; Bigmama's, 1991; Shortcut, 1992; Sail Away, 1995; Night at the Fair, 1998. Illustrator of books by: H. Milgrom, J.R. Dennis, F.M. Branley, R. Kalan, D. de Wit, P. Giganti, Jr., P. Lillie, G. Shannon, M. Schlein. **Address:** Greenwillow Books, 1350 Avenue of the Americas, New York, NY 10019, U.S.A.

CREWS, Frederick C(ampbell). American, b. 1933. **Genres:** Literary criticism and history, Psychology. **Career:** Center for Advanced Study in the Behavioral Sciences, fellow, 1965-66; University of California, Berkeley, instructor, 1958-60, assistant professor, 1960-63, associate professor, 1963-66, professor, 1966-94 professor emeritus of English, 1994-. **Publications:** The Tragedy of Manners: Moral Drama in the Later Novels of Henry James, 1957; E.M. Forster: The Perils of Humanism, 1962; The Pooh Perplex: A Freshman Casebook (parodies), 1963; The Sins of the Fathers: Hawthorne's Psychological Themes, 1966; The Patch Commission (satire), 1968; The Random House Handbook, 1974, 6th ed., 1992; Out of My System: Psychoanalysis, Ideology, and Critical Method, 1975; (with S. Schor) The Borzoi Handbook for Writers, 1985, 3rd ed., 1993; (with S. Schor and M. Hennessy) Skeptical Engagements, 1986; The Critics Bear It Away: American Fiction and the Academy, 1992; (with others) The Memory Wars: Freud's Legacy in Dispute, 1995; Postmodern Pooh (satire), 2001. EDITOR: Great Short Works of Nathaniel Hawthorne, 1967; (with O. Schell) Starting Over: A College Reader, 1970; Psychoanalysis and Literary Process, 1970; The Random House Reader, 1981; Unauthorized Freud: Doubters Confront a Legend, 1998. **Address:** 636 Vincente Ave, Berkeley, CA 94707-1524, U.S.A. **Online address:** Fredc@berkeley.edu

CREWS, Gordon A(rthur). American, b. 1964. **Genres:** Criminology/True Crime. **Career:** State constable, 1985-86; criminal investigator, 1986; Richland County Sheriff's Office, Columbia, deputy sheriff, 1986-88, training and officer of bloodhounds for dog team, 1987-88; South Carolina Department of Corrections, Watkins Pre-Release Center, Columbia, accreditation and training manager, 1988-89; Central Carolina Technical College, Criminal Justice Dept, head and faculty, 1990-94; Midlands Technical College, criminal justice faculty, 1994-97; University of South Carolina, Beaufort, director of criminal justice and military programs, 1997-99; Valdosta State University, criminal justice faculty, 1999-2000; Jacksonville State University, Alabama, associate professor and department head, 2000-2003; Roger Williams University, School of Justice Studies, associate dean and associate professor, 2003-. **Publications:** (with R.H. Montgomery Jr. and W.R. Garris) Faces of Violence in America, 1996; (with M.R. Counts) The Evolution of School Violence in America: Colonial Times to Present Day, 1997; (with Montgomery) A History of Correctional Violence: An Examination of Reported Causes of Riots and Disturbances, 1998; (with Montgomery) Chasing Shadows: Confronting Juvenile Violence in America, 2001. Developer of distance education and computer-based training programs. Contributor to books and periodicals. **Address:** School of Justice Studies, Roger Williams University, 1 Old Ferry Rd, Bristol, RI 02809, U.S.A. **Online address:** gordoncrews@yahoo.com

CREWS, Harry (Eugene). American, b. 1935. **Genres:** Novels, Autobiography/Memoirs. **Career:** Broward Junior College, Fort Lauderdale, FL, English teacher, 1962-68; University of Florida, Gainesville, associate professor, 1968-74, professor of English, 1974-. **Publications:** The Gospel Singer, 1968; Naked in Garden Hills, 1969; This Thing Don't Lead to Heaven, 1970; Karate Is a Thing of the Spirit, 1971; Car, 1972; The Hawk Is Dying, 1973; The Gypsy's Curse, 1974; A Feast of Snakes, 1976; A Childhood: The Biography of a Place, 1978; Blood and Grits (non-fiction), 1979; Florida Frenzy, 1982; Two, 1984; All We Need of Hell, 1987; The Knockout Artist, 1988; Blood Issue (play), 1989; Body, 1990; Scar Lover, 1992; Classic Crews: A Harry Crews Reader, 1993; Celebration: A Novel, 1998; Getting Naked with Harry Crews (interviews), 1999.

CREWS, Nina. American (born Germany), b. 1963. **Genres:** Children's fiction. **Career:** Author and illustrator of children's books; animator; freelance animation artist/coordinator, 1986-94, and illustrator, 1991-; Ink Tank (animation studio), NYC, producer, 1995-97. **Publications:** One Hot Summer Day, 1995; I'll Catch the Moon, 1996; Snowball, 1997; You Are Here, 1998; A High, Low, Near, Far, Loud, Quiet Story, 1999; A Ghost Story, 2001; The Neighborhood Mother Goose, 2004. Illustrator of books by E.F. Howard, B. Katz. Contributor of illustrations to periodicals. **Address:** c/o Greenwillow Books, 1350 Avenue of the Americas, New York, NY 10019, U.S.A.

CRIBB, Robert (Bridson). Australian, b. 1957. **Genres:** Area studies, History, Politics/Government. **Career:** Griffith University, Brisbane, Queensland, Australia, lecturer in Indonesian politics, 1983-86; Australian National University, Canberra, Australian Capital Territory, research fellow, 1987-90; Netherlands Institute for Advanced Study, Wassenaar, fellow in residence, 1988-89; University of Queensland, St. Lucia, Australia, lecturer in Southeast Asian history, 1990-92, senior lecturer, 1993-96, reader, 1996-; Nordic Institute of Asian Studies, Copenhagen, research professor, 1996-97, director, 1997-99; writer. **Publications:** Gejolak revolusi di Jakarta 1945-1949: Pergulatan antara otonomi dan hegemoni (title means: The Outbreak of Revolution in Jakarta 1945-1949: The Struggle between Autonomy and Hegemony; translated by H. Basari), 1990; Gangsters and Revolutionaries: The Jakarta People's Militia and the Indonesian Revolution, 1945-1949, 1991; Historical Dictionary of Indonesia, 1992; (with C. Brown) Modern Indonesia: A History since 1945, 1995; Historical Atlas of Indonesia, 2000. EDITOR & CONTRIBUTOR: (with C. Mackerras and A. Healy) Contemporary Vietnam: Perspectives from Australia, 1988; The Indonesian Killings of 1965-1966: Studies from Java and Bali, 1990; (with M. Bocquet Siek) Islam and the Panca Sila, 1991; The Late Colonial State in Indonesia, 1994. Works appear in anthologies. Contributor to political science and Asian studies journals. **Address:** Division of Pacific & Asian History, Research School of Pacific and Asian Studies, Australian National University, Canberra, ACT 0200, Australia. **Online address:** robert.cribb@anu.edu.au

CRICHTON, (John) Michael. Also writes as Michael Douglas, Jeffrey Hudson, John Lange. American, b. 1942. **Genres:** Novels, Science fiction/Fantasy, Plays/Screenplays, Medicine/Health. **Career:** Post-doctoral fellow, Salk Institute, La Jolla, 1969-70; visiting writer, Massachusetts Institute of Technology, Cambridge, 1988; physician, currently. **Publications:** The Andromeda Strain, 1969; Five Patients: The Hospital Explained, 1970; The Terminal Man, 1972; The Great Train Robbery, 1975; Eaters of the Dead, 1976; Jasper Johns, 1977; Congo, 1980; Electronic Life: How to Think about Computers, 1983; Sphere, 1987; Travels, 1988; Jurassic Park, 1990, screenplay, 1993; Rising Sun, 1992, screenplay, 1993; Disclosure, 1994; The Lost World, 1995; Airframe, 1996; Michael Crichton's Jurassic World, 1997; Timeline, 1999; Prey, 2002. SCREENPLAYS: Westworld, 1973; Looker, 1981; Runaway, 1984; (with A.-M. Martin) Twister, 1996. AS MICHAEL DOUGLAS: (with D. Crichton) Dealing: or, The Berkeley-to-Boston Forty-Brick Lost-Bag Blues, 1972. AS JEFFREY HUDSON: A Case of Need, 1968. AS JOHN LANGE: Odds On, 1966; Scratch One, 1967; Easy Go, 1968; Zero Cool, 1969; The Venom Business, 1969; Drug of Choice, 1970; Grave Descend, 1970; Binary, 1972. **Address:** c/o Page & Jenkins Financial Services, 433 N Camden Dr Ste 500, Beverly Hills, CA 90210-4443, U.S.A.

CRICHTON, Robin. British, b. 1940. **Genres:** Children's fiction, Plays/Screenplays, History. **Career:** Edinburgh Film and Video Productions, Scotland, producer and director; screenwriter; author. **Publications:** Who Is Santa Claus? (juvenile), 1987; Christmas Mouse, Ladybird, 1991; Sara, 1996. Author of screenplays. **Address:** Traquair House, Innerleithen, Peeblesshire EH44 6PW, Scotland.

CRICK, Bernard. British, b. 1929. **Genres:** Politics/Government, Social commentary, Biography, Essays, Humor/Satire. **Career:** Political writer and journalist. Birkbeck College, University of London, professor of politics, 1971-84. Political Quarterly, London, joint ed., 1967-80; University College London, honorary fellow, 1998-. Knighted, 2002. **Publications:** The American Science of Politics, 1958; In Defence of Politics, 1962, 5th ed., 2000; The Reform of Parliament, 1964; Theory and Practice: Essays in Politics, 1972; Basic Forms of Government, 1973; Crime, Rape, and Gin: Reflections on Contemporary Attitudes to Violence, Pornography, and Addiction, 1977; George Orwell: A Life, 1980, 3rd. ed., 1992; Socialism, 1987; (with T. Crick) What Is Politics? 1987; Politics and Literature, 1989; Political Thoughts and Polemics, 1990; (with D. Millar) To Make the Parliament of Scotland a Model for Democracy, 1999; Essays on Citizenship, 2000; Crossing Borders, 2001; Democracy, 2002. EDITOR: Essays on Reform, 1967; Protest and Discontent, 1970; Machiavelli: The Discourses, 1971; Taxation Theory, 1973; (with W. Robson) China in Transition, 1975; (with A. Porter) Political Education and Political Literacy, 1978; Unemployment, 1981; (with A. Coppard) Orwell Remembered, 1984; National Identities and the Constitution, 1990. **Address:** 8A Bellevue Terrace, Edinburgh EH7 4DT, Scotland. **Online address:** Bernard.Crick@ed.ac.uk

CRICK, F(rancis) H(arry) C(ompton). *See* Obituaries.

CRIDDLE, Byron. British, b. 1942. **Genres:** Politics/Government. **Career:** University of Aberdeen, Scotland, Department of Politics, reader. **Publications:** Socialists and European Integration, 1969; (with D.S. Bell) The French Socialist Party: Resurgence and Victory, 1984; (with D.S. Bell) The French Socialist Party: Emergence of a Party of Government, 1988; (with D.S. Bell) The French Communist Party in the Fifth Republic, 1994; (with R. Waller) The Almanac of British Politics, 5th ed., 1995, 7th ed., 2002; (with A. Roth) The New MPs of '97, 1997; (with A. Roth) Parliamentary Profiles, A to D, 1998, rev. ed., 2003, E to K, 1999, L to R, 2000; S to Z, 2000; (with A. Roth) The New MPs of '01, 2001. **Address:** Dept of Politics, University of Aberdeen, Aberdeen AB24 3FX, Scotland.

CRIDER, (Allen) Bill(y). Also writes as Nick Carter, Jack MacLane. American, b. 1941. **Genres:** Novels, Mystery/Crime/Suspense, Westerns/Adventure, Children's fiction. **Career:** Corsicana High School, Texas, teacher, 1963-65; Howard Payne University, Brownwood, TX, associate professor, 1971-76, professor and chair of English dept., 1977-83; Alvin Community College, Alvin, TX, chair of English dept., 1984-. **Publications:** WESTERN NOVELS: Ryan Rides Back, 1988; Galveston Gunman, 1988; A Time for Hanging, 1989; Medicine Show, 1990. CRIME NOVELS: (with J. Davis, as Nick Carter) The Coyote Connection, 1981; Too Late to Die, 1986; Shotgun Saturday Night, 1987; Cursed to Death, 1988; One Dead Dean, 1988; Death on the Move, 1989; Dying Voices, 1989; Evil at the Root, 1990. MYSTERIES: Blood Marks, 1991; Dead on the Island, 1991; Booked for a Hanging, 1992; Gator Kill, 1992; The Texas Capitol Murders, 1992; Murder Most Fowl, 1994; When Old Men Die, 1994; A Dangerous Thing, 1994. OTHER: (ed.) Mass Market American Publishing, 1982; A Vampire Named Fred (for children), 1990; (with W. Scott) Murder under Blue Skies, 1998. NOVELS AS JACK MacLANE: Keepers of the Beast, 1988; Goodnight Moom, 1989; Blood Dreams, 1989; Rest in Peace, 1990; Just Before Dark, 1990. **Address:** 1606 S. Hill, Alvin, TX 77511, U.S.A. **Online address:** abc@wt.net

CRIMMINS, G(erald) Garfield. Also writes as Jerry Crimmins. American, b. 1940. **Genres:** Art/Art history. **Career:** Moore College of Art, Philadelphia, PA, professor of art, 1968-99. Artist, with solo and group exhibitions in major U.S. cities and Europe; art represented in private and institutional collections nationally and international. **Publications:** Anatomical Notes, 1975; Thicker Than Blood, 1976; The Song of the Fair Haired, 1977; A Visitor's Guide to La Republique de Reves, 1980; The Secret History of La Republique de Reves, 1984; The Republic of Dreams, 1998. **Address:** 153 Roberts Ave, Glenside, PA 19038, U.S.A. **Online address:** revesguy@earthlink.net

CRIMMINS, Jerry. *See* CRIMMINS, G(erald) Garfield.

CRISPO, John. Canadian, b. 1933. **Genres:** Business/Trade/Industry, Economics, Humanities, Industrial relations. **Career:** Professor of Political Economy, Faculty of Mgmt. and Dept. of Economics, University of Toronto, since 1965 (Assistant Professor, 1961-64; Associate Professor, 1964-65; Founding Director, Centre for Industrial Relations, 1965-72; First Dean, Faculty of Management Studies, 1970-75); C.D. Howe Policy Analysis Institute; International Trade Advisory Council; North American Committee. **Publications:** International Unionism: A Study in Canadian-American Relations, 1967; The Role of International Unionism, 1967; (co-author) Construction Labour Relations, 1969; (co-author) Canadian Industrial Relations: The Report of the Prime Minister's Task Force on Labour Relations, 1969; Fee-

setting by Independent Practitioners, 1972; The Public Right to Know: Accountability in the Secretive Society, 1975; The Canadian Industrial Relations System, 1978; Industrial Democracy in Western Europe, 1978; Mandate for Canada, 1978; National Consultation: Problems and Prospects, 1985; Free Trade: The Real Story, 1988; Can Canada Compete, 1990; Making Canada Work: Competing in the Global Economy, 1992. EDITOR: Industrial Relations: Challenges and Responses, 1966; Collective Bargaining and the Professional Employee, 1966. **Address:** c/o Rotman School of Management, University of Toronto, 105 St. George St, Toronto, ON, Canada M5S 3E6.

CRIST, Judith. American, b. 1922. **Genres:** Film. **Career:** Adjunct Professor, Graduate School of Journalism, Columbia University, NYC, 1958-. Reporter, 1945-60, Arts Ed., 1960-63, and Film Critic, 1963-66, New York Herald Tribune; Film and Theatre Critic, NBC-TV Today Show, 1963-73; Film Critic, New York Magazine, 1968-75, Saturday Review, 1975-78, 1980-84 and, 50 Plus, 1978-83. Contributing Ed. and Film Critic, TV Guide, 1966-88; Arts Critic, WWOR-TV, 1981-87; Critical Columnist, Coming Attractions, 1985-93. **Publications:** The Private Eye, the Cowboy, and the Very Naked Girl: Movies from Cleo to Clyde, 1968; Judith Crist's TV Guide to the Movies, 1974; Take 22: Moviemakers on Moviemaking, 1984, rev. ed., 1991. **Address:** Crist Associates Ltd, 180 Riverside Dr, New York, NY 10024, U.S.A.

CRITCHLOW, Donald T. American, b. 1948. **Genres:** History, Politics/Government. **Career:** University of California-Berkeley, teaching assistant, 1974; University of California, Institute of Industrial Relations, research assistant, 1975; San Francisco State University, acting instructor in History, 1976; University of California-Berkeley, acting instructor in Environmental Studies, 1977; North Central College, Napierville, IL, assistant professor of History, 1978-81; University of Dayton, assistant professor of History, 1981-83; University of Notre Dame, assistant professor, associate professor, both of History, 1983-91; Saint Louis University, department of history chair, professor, 1991-. **Publications:** The Brookings Institution, 1916-1952, Expertise and the Public Interest in a Democratic Society, 1985; (with W. Rorabaugh) America! A Concise History, 1994; Studebaker: The Life and Death of an American Corporation, 1996; The Serpentine Way: Family Planning Policy in Postwar America: Elites, Agendas, and Political Mobilization, 1997. EDITOR: Socialism in the Heartland: The Midwestern Experience, 1890-1920, 1986; (with E. Hawley) Federal Social Policy: The Historical Dimension, 1989; (with Hawley) Poverty and Public Policy in Modern America, 1989; A History of the United States, 1995; The Politics of Abortion and Birth Control in Historical Perspective, 1996. **Address:** 2623 Colston, Chevy Chase, MD 20815, U.S.A.

CRITTENDEN, Ann. American, b. 1937. **Genres:** Economics. **Career:** Southern Methodist University, Dallas, TX, lecturer, 1960-62; Rutgers University, New Brunswick, NJ, lecturer, 1963-66; Fortune, New York, NY, reporter, 1967-71; Newsweek, New York, NY, finance writer and associate editor, 1971-72, foreign correspondent in Asia and South America, 1972-74; New York Times, New York, NY, economics reporter, 1975-83, author and lecturer, 1983-. Fund for Investigative Reporting, executive director, 1982-88; Aspen Institute, project director, 1985. **Publications:** Sanctuary: A Story of American Conscience and the Law in Collision, 1988; Killing the Sacred Cows: Bold Ideas for a New Economy, 1993; The Price of Motherhood: Why the Most Important Job in the World Is Still the Least Valued, 2001. Contributor to periodicals. **Address:** 3412 Lowell St. NW, Washington, DC 20016, U.S.A.

CRNOBRNJA (TSERNOBERNYA), Mihailo. Yugoslav, b. 1946. **Genres:** Politics/Government, Economics. **Career:** University of Belgrade, Belgrade, Yugoslavia, professor of political science, 1975-89; Government of Yugoslavia, Belgrade, ambassador to the European Community, Brussels, Belgium, 1989-92; McGill University, Montreal, Quebec, faculty lecturer in political science, 1993-. **Publications:** (with M. Karr) Business and Investment Opportunities in Yugoslavia, 1982; (ed.) Information as an Economic Resource, 1985; (ed.) Europe 1992 and Beyond, 1991; Le drame Yougoslave, 1992, trans as The Yugoslav Drama, 1994; (with Z. Papic) A Programme for Economic Reconstruction and Modernization in Countries of Former Yugoslavia, 1995. Contributor to books and periodicals. UNTRANSLATED WORKS: Reciklaza petro-dolara i finansijska pozicija Jugoslavije (title means: The Recycling of Petro-Dollars and the Financial Position of Yugoslavia), 1981; Zivotna sredina i ekonomski razvoj (title means: The Environment and Economic Development), 1982; Socijalna politika u Beogradu (title means: Social Policy in Belgrade), 1985. Contributor of articles and reviews to periodicals. **Address:** Department of Political Science, McGill University, 855 Sherbrooke St. W., Montreal, QC, Canada H3A 2T7.

CROALL, Jonathan. British, b. 1941. **Genres:** Children's fiction, Education, Environmental sciences/Ecology, History, Local history/Rural topics,

Medicine/Health, Self help, Biography. **Career:** Cassell & Co., London, England, editor, 1964-65; Penguin Books, London, editor, 1965-66; Oxford University Press, London, editor, 1966-69; Penguin Education, London, managing editor, 1969-71, commissioning editor, 1971-74; Times Educational Supplement, London, features editor, 1975-82; Arts Express, London, editor, 1983-87; Bedford Square Press, managing director, 1987-90; freelance writer, 1990-2001; National Theatre, Stagewrite magazine, editor, 1991-2001. **Publications:** Don't Shoot the Goalkeeper, 1974; The Parents' Day School Book, 1976; Neill of Summerhill: The Permanent Rebel, 1983; All the Best, 1983; Don't You Know There's a War On? The People's Voice, 1939-1945, 1989; Sent Away, 1992; Dig for History, 1992; Helping to Heal, 1993; Preserve or Destroy: Tourism and the Environment, 1995; Let's Act Locally, 1997; Gielgud: A Theatrical Life, 2000; Hamlet Observed, 2001; Inside the Molly House, 2001; Peter Hall's Bacchai, 2002. **Address:** c/o A.P. Watt Ltd., 20 John St, London WC1N 2DR, England.

CROCE, Paul Jerome. American, b. 1957. **Genres:** History. **Career:** Brown University, Providence, RI, tutor and teaching assistant, 1976-85; Georgetown University, Washington, DC, visiting assistant professor, 1985-87; Rollins College, visiting professor, 1987-89; Stetson University, DeLand, FL, instructor in social science, 1988, assistant professor, 1989-95, associate professor and chair of American studies, 1995-. Has presented papers at many conferences and lectured in several academic arenas; appeared on radio talk shows. **Publications:** Science and Religion in the Era of William James, Vol. 1: Eclipse of Certainty, 1820-1880, 1995. Contributor to books. Contributor of articles and reviews to periodicals. **Address:** Dept of American Studies, Stetson University, DeLand, FL 32720, U.S.A.

CROCOMBE, Ronald Gordon. New Zealander, b. 1929. **Genres:** Anthropology/Ethnology, Area studies, Cultural/Ethnic topics, Politics/Government. **Career:** University of the South Pacific, Suva, Professor, 1969-88, Director of Institute of Pacific Studies, 1975-86, Professor Emeritus of Pacific Studies, 1988-. Research Fellow, Australian National University, Canberra, 1961-64; Visiting Professor, University of California, 1964-65; Director, New Guinea Research Unit, 1965-69. **Publications:** Land Tenure in the Cook Islands, 1963; Improving Land Tenure, 1968; (with M. Crocombe) The Works of Ta'unga, 1968; Land Tenure in the Pacific, 1971; The South Pacific, 1973, 6th ed., 2001; Voluntary Service and Development, 1990; Pacific Neighbours, 1992; Post Secondary Education in the South Pacific: Land Issues in the Pacific, 1994; The Pacific Islands and the USA, 1996. EDITOR: Holy Torture in Fiji, 1975; Cook Islands Politics, 1978; Pacific Indians, 1980; Politics of the Pacific Islands Series, 1982-87; Pacific Universities, 1988; Culture & Democracy in the South Pacific, 1992. Author of other books. Contributor to professional journals. **Address:** Box 309, Rarotonga, Cook Islands. **Online address:** ronc@oyster.net.ck

CROFT, Barbara. American, b. 1944. **Genres:** Novels, Novellas/Short stories. **Career:** Writer. Has also worked as a teacher, editor, journalist, public relations writer, and out-of-print book dealer. **Publications:** Primary Colors and Other Stories, 1991; Necessary Fictions, 1998; Moon's Crossing, 2003. Contributor to periodicals. **Address:** 202 N Kenilworth Ave, Oak Park, IL 60302, U.S.A.

CROFT, Robert W(ayne). American, b. 1957. **Genres:** Literary criticism and history. **Career:** Teacher of English and gifted education classes at public schools in Tifton, GA, 1978-89; Gainesville College, Gainesville, GA, associate professor of English, 1993-. **Publications:** Anne Tyler: A Biobibliography, 1995; An Anne Tyler Companion, 1998. **Address:** Department of English, Gainesville College, PO Box 1358, Gainesville, GA 30503, U.S.A.

CROLL, Elisabeth J(oan). British (born New Zealand), b. 1944. **Genres:** Anthropology/Ethnology, History, Women's studies and issues. **Career:** University of London, School of Oriental and African Studies, professor of Chinese anthropology, and vice-principal. **Publications:** Feminism and Socialism in China, 1978; The Politics of Marriage in Contemporary China, 1981; The Family Rice Bowl: Food and the Domestic Economy in China, 1982; Chinese Women since Mao, 1983; Wise Daughters from Foreign Lands: European Women Writers in China, 1989; Women and Rural Development: The Case of the People's Republic of China, 1979; Women and Rural Development in China, 1986; From Heaven to Earth: Images and Experiences of Development in China, 1994; Changing Identities of Chinese Women: Rhetoric, Experience and Self-Perception in Twentieth-Century China, 1995; Endangered Daughters: Discrimination and Development in Asia, 2000. EDITOR: The Women's Movement in China: A Selection of Readings, 1974, 1976; (co-) China's One-Child Family Policy, 1985; (with Gordon White) Agriculture and Socialist Development, 1985; (with D. Parkin) Bush Base: Forest Farm and Culture, Environment and Develop-

ment, 1992. **Address:** School of Oriental and African Studies, University of London, London WC1E 7HP, England.

CROMER, Alan (Herbert). American, b. 1935. **Genres:** Physics. **Career:** Harvard University, Cambridge, MA, research fellow, 1959-61; Northeastern University, Boston, MA, assistant professor, 1961-65, associate professor, 1965-70, professor of physics, 1970-. EduTech Inc., founder, 1980, president, 1980-86. **Publications:** (with E. Saletan) Theoretical Mechanics, 1970; Physics for the Life Sciences, 2nd ed, 1977; Physics in Science and Industry, 1980; Computer-Simulated Physics Experiments, with software, 1980; AstroLab, with software, 1980; Experiments in Physics, 3rd ed, 1984; Uncommon Sense: The Heretical Nature of Science, 1993; (with C. Zahopoulos) Sourcebook of Demonstrations, Activities, and Experiments (laboratory manual), 1994; Experiments in Introductory Physics (laboratory manual), 1994. Contributor to books, magazines and newspapers. **Address:** Department of Physics, Northeastern University, Boston, MA 02115, U.S.A.

CROMPTON, Louis. American (born Canada), b. 1925. **Genres:** Gay and lesbian issues. **Career:** University of Nebraska at Lincoln, assistant professor, 1955-60, associate professor, 1960-64, professor, 1964-88, professor emeritus of English, 1989-. **Publications:** Shaw the Dramatist, 1969; Byron and Greek Love: Homophobia in 19th Century England, 1985; Homosexuality and Civilization, 2003. EDITOR: C. Dickens, Great Expectations, 1964; B. Shaw, The Road to Equality: Ten Unpublished Lectures and Essays, 1884-1918, 1971; B. Shaw, The Great Composers, 1978. **Address:** 6816 Blake St, El Cerrito, CA 94530, U.S.A. **Online address:** louiscrompton@hotmail.com

CROMWELL, Rue L(eVelle). American, b. 1928. **Genres:** Medicine/Health, Psychology. **Career:** George Peabody College for Teachers, Nashville, TN, assistant professor to professor, 1955-61; Vanderbilt University, Nashville, professor, 1961-69; Lafayette Clinic, Detroit, MI, chief of Division of Psychology, 1969-72; University of Rochester, NY, professor of psychiatry, pediatrics, and psychology, 1972-86; University of Kansas, Lawrence, E. Wright Distinguished Professor, 1986-2001, professor emeritus, 2001-. **Publications:** Acute Myocardial Infarction: Reaction and Recovery, 1977; The Nature of Schizophrenia, 1978; Schizophrenia: Origins, Processes, Treatment, and Outcome, 1993. **Address:** Department of Psychology, University of Kansas, Lawrence, KS 66045, U.S.A. **Online address:** cromwell@ku.edu

CRONIN, Mary J. American, b. 1947. **Genres:** Business/Trade/Industry, Information science/Computers. **Career:** Boston College, Chestnut Hill, MA, professor of management. **Publications:** Doing Business on the Internet: How the Electronic Highway Is Transforming American Companies, 1993; Doing More Business on the Internet, 1995; (ed.) The Internet Strategy Handbook: Lessons from the New Business Frontier, 1995; Global Advantage on the Internet: From Corporate Connectivity to International Competitiveness, 1995. **Address:** Carroll School of Management, Boston College, Chestnut Hill, MA 02467, U.S.A.

CRONIN, Mike. British, b. 1967. **Genres:** Area studies, Local history/Rural topics. **Career:** De Montfort University, Leicester, England, lecturer and senior research fellow. **Publications:** The Blueshirts and Irish Politics, 1997; Sport and Nationalism in Ireland: Gaelic Games, Soccer, and Irish Identity since 1884, 1999; (with J.M. Regan) Ireland: The Politics of Independence, 1922-49, 2000; A History of Ireland, 2001; (with T. Chandler and W. Vamplew) Sport and Physical Education: The Key Concepts, 2002; (with D. Adair) The Wearing of the Green: A History of St. Patrick's Day, 2002. EDITOR: The Failure of British Fascism: The Far Right and the Fight for Political Recognition, 1996; (with D. Mayall) Sporting Nationalisms: Identity, Ethnicity, and Assimilation, 1998. **Address:** Department of Historical and International Studies, De Montfort University, The Gateway, Leicester LE1 9BH, England. **Online address:** mjcronin@dmu.ac.uk

CRONISH, Nettie. Canadian, b. 1954. **Genres:** Food and Wine. **Career:** Chef, educator, and author. **Publications:** Nettie's Vegetarian Kitchen, 1996; Vegetarian Cooking (CD-ROM), 1996, as World Cuisine Vegetarian, 1996; New Vegetarian Basics, 1999; (with B. Selley and S. Havala) The Complete Idiot's Guide to Being Vegetarian in Canada, 2000. **Address:** 11 Dunloe Rd., Toronto, ON, Canada M4V 2W4. **Online address:** cronurq@idirect.com

CRONKITE, Walter (Leland), (Jr.). American, b. 1916. **Genres:** Communications/Media, International relations/Current affairs, Autobiography/Memoirs. **Career:** United Press, war and foreign correspondent, 1941-49; CBS News, correspondent, 1950-81, special correspondent, 1981-. **Publications:** Eye on the World, 1971; South by

Southeast, 1984; North by Northeast, 1986; Westwind, 1990; A Reporter's Life, 1996. **Address:** CBS, 51 W. 52nd St, New York, NY 10019, U.S.A.

CRONON, William. American, b. 1954. **Genres:** History. **Career:** University of Wisconsin-Madison, Frederick Jackson Turner Professor of History, Geography, and Environmental Studies, 1992-. **Publications:** Changes in the Land: Indians, Colonists, and the Ecology of New England, 1983, 2nd ed., 2003; Nature's Metropolis: Chicago and the Great West, 1991; (co-ed.) Under an Open Sky: Rethinking America's Western Past, 1992; (ed.) Uncommon Ground, 1995. Contributor to professional journals and textbooks. **Address:** Dept. of History, 5103 Humanities Bldg., University of Wisconsin-Madison, 455 N Park St, Madison, WI 53706, U.S.A. **Online address:** wcronon@wisc.edu

CROOK, Joseph Mordaunt. British, b. 1937. **Genres:** Architecture, Art/Art history. **Career:** Architectural Historian. Institute of Historical Research, London, research fellow, 1961-62; Leicester University, assistant lecturer, 1963-65; Royal Holloway and Bedford New College, University of London, research fellow, 1962-63, lecturer, 1965-75, reader, 1975-81, professor, 1981-99. University of Oxford, Slade Professor, 1979-80, Waynflete Lecturer, Magdalen College, 1984-85, Supernumerary Fellow, Brasenose College, 2002-; Fellow of the British Academy, 1988. **Publications:** The British Museum, 1971; Victorian Architecture: A Visual Anthology, 1972; The Greek Revival: Neo-Classical Attitudes in British Architecture 1760-1870, 1972; (with M.H. Port) The History of the King's Works, vol. VI, 1782-1851, 1973; (with H.M. Colvin, J. Newman and K. Downes) The History of the King's Works, vol. V, 1660-1782, 1976; William Burges and the High Victorian Dream, 1981; (with C.A. Lennox-Boyd) Axel Haig and the Victorian Vision of the Middle Ages, 1983; The Dilemma of Style: Architectural Ideas from the Picturesque to the Post Modern, 1987; John Carter and the Mind of the Gothic Revival, 1995; The Rise of the Nouveaux Riches: Style and Status in Victorian and Edwardian Architecture, 1999; The Architect's Secret: Victorian Critics and the Image of Gravity, 2003. EDITOR: C.L. Eastlake, History of the Gothic Revival, 1970; J.T. Emmett, Six Essays, 1972; R. Kerr, The Gentleman's House, 1972; K. Clark, The Gothic Revival, 1995. **Address:** 55 Gloucester Ave, London NW1 7BA, England.

CROOK, Marion. Canadian, b. 1941. **Genres:** Young adult fiction, Young adult non-fiction. **Career:** Writer. Public health nurse, 1963-82. **Publications:** FICTION: Payment in Death, 1987; Stone Dead, 1987; The Hidden Gold Mystery, 1987; No Safe Place, 1988; Crosscurrents, 1988; Island Feud, 1991; Riptide!, 1992; Summer of Madness, 1995; Riding Scared, 1996. NONFICTION: Teenagers Talk about Adoption, 1986; Please Listen to Me: Your Guide to Understanding Teenagers and Suicide, 1988; Suicide: Teens Talk to Teens, 1988, repr., 1997; The Body Image Trap: Understanding and Rejecting Body Image Myths, 1992; The Trials of Eve: A Viewers' Guide to the Film, 1992; Looking Good: Teenagers and Eating Disorders, 1992; My Body: Women Speak Out about Their Health Care, 1995; (with N. Wise) How to Self-Publish and Make Money, rev ed, 1996. OTHER: Fingerprints: Crime Writers of Canada, 1984; The Face in the Mirror (video), 1986; The Capitalist (radio play), 1987; Writing Mystery Stories, Writers on Writing, 1989. **Address:** 1680 Cornell Avenue, Coquitlam, BC, Canada V3J 3A1.

CROSBY, Alfred W., Jr. American, b. 1931. **Genres:** History. **Career:** Professor of American Studies, University of Texas at Austin, 1977-. Associate Professor of History, Washington State University, Pullman, 1966-77. **Publications:** America, Russia, Hemp and Napoleon, 1965; The Columbian Exchange: Biological and Cultural Consequences of 1492, 1972; Epidemic and Peace 1918, 1976, as America's Forgotten Pandemic: The Influenza of 1918, 1989; Ecological Imperialism: The Biological Expansion of Europe 900-1900, 1986; Germs, Seeds, and Animals: Studies in Ecological History, 1994; The Measure of Reality, 1997; Throwing Fire: Projectile Technology through History, 2002. **Address:** 67 N Centre St, Nantucket, MA 02554, U.S.A. **Online address:** acrosby@nantucket.net

CROSBY, Donald G(ibson). American, b. 1928. **Genres:** Chemistry, Environmental sciences/Ecology, Medicine/Health. **Career:** Union Oil Co., San Pedro, CA, chemist, 1946-51; Union Carbide, South Charleston, WV, chemist, 1954-61; University of California, Davis, professor of environmental toxicology, 1961-91, professor emeritus, 1991-. **Publications:** (with M. Jacobson) Naturally-Occurring Insecticides, 1972; Environmental Toxicology and Chemistry, 1998; The Poisoned Weed: Plants Toxic to Skin, 2003. EDITOR: (with G. Helz and R. Zepp) Aquatic and Surface Photochemistry, 1994; (with J.J. Cech and B. Wilson) Multiple Stresses in Ecosystems, 1998; Contributor to scientific journals. **Address:** 1107 Oak Ave, Davis, CA 95616, U.S.A.

CROSBY, Harry W(illiams). American, b. 1926. **Genres:** Novels, Local history/Rural topics, Travel/Exploration. **Career:** Teacher of biology and

chemistry at public schools in San Diego, CA, 1951-63; photographer, 1964-75; historian and writer, 1974-. Cinematographer and voiceover narrator for the television documentary The Mystery Murals of Baja California, aired by the Public Broadcasting System, 1975, 1978. **Publications:** The King's Highway in Baja California, 1974; The Cave Paintings of Baja California, 1975, rev. ed., 1998; Last of the Californios, 1981; Doomed to Fail, 1989; Antigua California: Mission and Colony on the Peninsular Frontier, 1697-1768, 1994; Portrait of Paloma (novel), 2001; Tijuana 1964, 2000. Contributor to magazines. **Address:** 1277 Silverado, La Jolla, CA 92037, U.S.A. **Online address:** harrywcrosby.com

CROSLAND, Margaret. British. **Genres:** Literary criticism and history, Biography, Translations. **Publications:** Madame Colette, 1953; Ballet Carnival, 1955; Jean Cocteau, 1955; Home Book of Opera, 1957; Louise of Stolberg, 1962; (ed.) Marquis de Sade, Selected Letters, 1965; (ed.) A Traveller's Guide to Literary Europe (in U.S. as A Guide to Literary Europe), 1965; Colette: The Difficulty of Loving, 1973; Women of Iron and Velvet, 1976; Raymond Radiguet, 1976; (ed.) C. Pavese, The Leather Jacket, 1980; Beyond the Lighthouse, 1981; Piaf, 1985; Simone de Beauvoir, The Woman and Her Work, 1992; Sade's Wife, 1995; The Enigma of Giorgio de Chirico, 1999; Madame de Pompadour, 2000. TRANSLATOR: M. Drouet, First Poems, 1956; (with S. Road) J. Cocteau, Opium, 1957; M. Drouet, Then There Was Fire, 1957; M. Genevoix, The Story of Renard, 1959; Donatella, M. Drouet, 1969; G. de Chirico, Hebdomeros; Colette, The Other Woman, 1971; (with D. Le Vay) Colette, The Thousand and One Mornings, 1973; P. Barbier, The World of the Castrati, 1996; G. de Gaulle Anthonioz, God Remained Outside: An Echo of Ravensbruck, 1999; (with E. Powell) D. Manotti, Rough Trade, 2001; P. Barbier, Vivaldi's Venice, 2003. TRANSLATOR AND EDITOR: Selected Writings of De Sade, 1953, 1984; J. Cocteau, My Contemporaries, 1967; C. Pavese, A Mania for Solitude, 1969; Memoirs of Giorgio de Chirico, 1971; Cocteau's World, 1972; Colette, Retreat from Love, 1974; Colette, Duo, 1974; The Gothic Tales of the Marquis de Sade, 1990; E. Piaf, My Life, 1990; The Passionate Philosopher: A Marquis de Sade Reader, 1992. **Address:** 25 Thornton Meadow, Wisborough Green, Billingshurst RH14 0BW, England.

CROSLAND, Maurice P. British, b. 1931. **Genres:** History, Sciences. **Career:** Lecturer, 1963-69, and Reader in the History of Science, 1969-74, University of Leeds. Professor of the History of Science, and Director of the Unit for History, Philosophy and Social Relations of Science, University of Kent at Canterbury, 1974-94. Visiting professor; University of California, Berkeley 1967, Cornell University, 1967-68, University of Pennsylvania, 1971. President, British Society for the History of Science, 1974-76. **Publications:** Historical Studies in the Language of Chemistry, 1962, 1978; The Society of Arcueil: A View of French Science at the Time of Napoleon I, 1967; Gay-Lussac, Scientist and Bourgeois, 1978, 1991; Science under Control: The French Academy of Sciences, 1795-1914, 1992; In the Shadow of Lavoisier: The Annales de chimie and the Establishment of a New Science, 1994; Studies in the Culture of Science in France and Britain since the Enlightenment, 1995. EDITOR: Science in France in the Revolutionary Era, Described by Thomas Bugge, 1969; The Science of Matter: A Historical Survey, 1971, 1992; The Emergence of Science in Western Europe, 1975. **Address:** School of History, Rutherford College, University of Kent, Canterbury, Kent CT2 7NX, England.

CROSS, Anthony Glenn. British, b. 1936. **Genres:** History, Literary criticism and history, Bibliography. **Career:** University of East Anglia, Norwich, lecturer, 1964-69, sr. lecturer, 1969-72, reader in Russian, 1972-81; University of Leeds, professor of Russian, 1981-85; Cambridge University, professor of Slavonic studies, 1985-. Harvard University, Cambridge, MA, Frank Knox Memorial Fellow, 1960-61; visiting fellow, Center for Advanced Study, University of Illinois, 1968-69, and All Souls College, Oxford, 1978-79. Journal of European Studies, co-editor, 1971-; Newsletter of the Study Group on 18th Century Russia, editor, 1973-. British Academy, fellow, 1989-. **Publications:** N.M. Karamzin: A Study of His Literary Career, 1783-1803, 1971; Anglo-Russian Relations in the 18th Century, 1977; By the Banks of the Thames, 1980; The 1780s: Russia under Western Eyes, 1981; The Tale of the Russian Daughter and Her Suffocated Lover, 1982; (with G.S. Smith) 18th Century Russian Literature, Culture and Thought, 1984; The Russian Theme in English Literature, 1985; Anglophilia on the Throne, 1992; Engraved in the Memory, 1993; Anglo-Russica, 1993; By the Banks of the Neva, 1997; Peter the Great through British Eyes, 2000; Catherine the Great and the British, 2001. EDITOR: (gen. ed.) Russia through European Eyes, 1553-1917 (series), 1968-72; Russia under Western Eyes, 1517-1825, 1971; Russian Literature in the Age of Catherine the Great (essays), 1976; Great Britain and Russia in the 18th Century, 1978; Russian and the West in the 18th Century, 1983; (co) Russia and the World of the 18th Century, 1988;

An Englishwoman at the Court of Catherine the Great: The Journal of Baroness Elizabeth Dimsdale, 1781, 1989; (co) Literature, Lives, and Legality in Catherine's Russia, 1994; (co) Britain and Russia in the Age of Peter the Great, 1998; Russia in the Reign of Peter the Great, 1998; St Petersburg, 1703-1825, 2003. **Address:** Dept of Slavonic Studies, Sidgwick Ave, Cambridge CB3 9DA, England.

CROSS, (Margaret) Claire. British, b. 1932. **Genres:** Genealogy/Heraldry, History, Theology/Religion. **Career:** County Archivist, Cambs., 1958-61; International Fellow, American Association of University Women, 1961-62; Research Fellow, Reading University, 1962-65; University of York, lecturer to Professor in History, 1965-. **Publications:** The Free Grammar School of Leicester, 1953; The Puritan Earl: The Life of Henry Hastings, Third Earl of Huntingdon 1536-1595, 1966; The Royal Supremacy in the Elizabethan Church, 1969; Church and People 1450-1660, 1976; Urban Magistrates and Ministers; Religion in Hull and Leeds from the Reformation to the Civil War, 1985; The Elizabethan Religious Settlement, 1558-1575, 1992; The End of Medieval Monasticism in the East Riding of Yorkshire, 1993. EDITOR: The Letters of Sir Francis Hastings, 1574-1604, 1969; Youk Clergy Wills 1520-1600: 1 The Minister Clergy, 1984; York Clergy Wills 1520-1600: 2 The City Clergy, 1989; (with N. Vickers) Monks, Friars and Nuns in Sixteenth Century Yorkshire, 1995; (with D. Loades and J. Scarisbrick, and contrib.) Law and Government under the Tudors: Essays Presented to Sir Geoffrey Elton on His Retirement, 1988. **Address:** Centre for Medieval Studies, University of York, The King's Manor, York Y01 7EP, England. **Online address:** mcc1@york.ac.uk

CROSS, Gillian (Clare). British, b. 1945. **Genres:** Children's fiction, Young adult fiction. **Career:** LA Carnegie Medal, Wolf, 1990; winner overall, Smarties Prize, The Great Elephant Chase, 1992; Whitbread Children's Novel Award for The Great Elephant Chase, 1992. **Publications:** The Runaway, 1979; The Iron Way, 1979; Revolt at Ratcliffe's Rags, 1980; Save Our School, 1981; A Whisper of Lace, 1981; The Dark behind the Curtain, 1982; The Demon Headmaster, 1982; The Mintyglo Kid, 1983; Born of the Sun, 1983; On the Edge, 1984; The Prime Minister's Brain, 1985; Swimathon, 1986; Chartbreak, 1986; Roscoe's Leap, 1987; A Map of Nowhere, 1988; Rescuing Gloria, 1989; Twin and Super-Twin, 1990; Wolf, 1990; The Monster from Underground, 1990; Gobbo the Great, 1991; Rent-a-Genius, 1991; The Great Elephant Chase, 1992; Furry Maccaloo, 1993; Beware Olga!, 1993; The Tree House, 1993; Hunky Parker Is Watching You, 1994; What Will Emily Do?, 1994; New World, 1994; The Crazy Shoe Shuffle, 1995; Posh Watson, 1995; The Roman Beanfeast, 1996; The Demon Headmaster Strikes Again, 1996; Pictures in the Dark, 1996; The Demon Headmaster Takes Over, 1997; The Goose Girl, 1998; Tightrope, 1999; Down with the Dirty Danes!, 2000; Calling a Dead Man, 2001, in US as Phoning a Dead Man, 2002; Beware of the Demon Headmaster, 2002; Facing the Demon Headmaster, 2002; The Dark Ground, 2004. **Address:** c/o Children's Books Dept., Oxford University Press, Great Clarendon St, Oxford OX2 6DP, England.

CROSS, Ian (Robert). New Zealander, b. 1925. **Genres:** Novels, Plays/Screenplays. **Career:** Freelance writer, c. 1957-; New Zealand Listener, Wellington, New Zealand, 1973-77; New Zealand on Air, Wellington, chair and chief executive, 1977-. **Publications:** NOVELS: The God Boy, 1957; The Backward Sex, 1960; After Anzac Day, 1961. OTHER: The City of No (teleplay), 1970; The Unlikely Bureaucrat: My Years in Broadcasting (autobiography), 1988; The Family Man, 1993. Contributor of short stories to periodicals. **Address:** 115 Somerset Rd., Wanganui, New Zealand.

CROSS, K. Patricia. American, b. 1926. **Genres:** Education. **Career:** University of Illinois, Urbana, Assistant Dean of Women, 1953-59; Cornell University, Ithaca, NY, Dean of Students, 1959-63; Educational Testing Service, Director, College and University Progs., 1963-66, Sr. Research Psychologist, 1963-80; University of California, Berkeley, Research Educator, Center for Research and Development in Higher Education, 1967-77, Elizabeth and Edward Conner Professor of Higher Education, 1988-98, Professor of Higher Education Emerita, 1998-; Harvard University, Cambridge, MA, Professor of Education and Dept. Chair, 1980-88. **Publications:** The Junior College Student: A Research Description, 1968; Beyond the Open Door: New Students to Higher Education, 1971; Explorations in Nontraditional Study, 1972; (with S. Gould) New Students and New Needs in Higher Education, 1972; Integration of Earning and Learning: Cooperative Education and Nontraditional Study, 1973; Planning for Nontraditional Programs: An Analysis of the Issues, 1974; (with J. Valley) Accent on Learning: Improving Instruction and Reshaping the Curriculum, 1976; The Missing Link, 1978; Adults as Learners, 1981; (with A.M. McCartan) Adult Learning: State Policies and Institutional Practices, 1984; (with T.A. Angelo)

Classroom Assessment Techniques, 1988, 2nd ed., 1993; (with M. Steadman) Classroom Research: Implementing the Scholarship of Teaching, 1996. **Address:** 904 Oxford St, Berkeley, CA 94707, U.S.A. **Online address:** patcross@socrates.berkeley.edu

CROSS, Richard K. American, b. 1940. **Genres:** Literary criticism and history. **Career:** Dartmouth College, Hanover, NH, instructor, 1966-68; University of California at Los Angeles, Assistant Professor, 1968-74, Associate Professor 1974-80, Professor of English, 1980-83; University of Maryland, College Park, Professor of English, 1983-, Chairman of the Dept., 1983-88. Visiting Professor of English and American Literature, University of Wuerzburg, 1971-72, University of Goettingen, 1990-91, University of Freiburg, 1997-98, and University of Mannheim, 1998. **Publications:** Flaubert and Joyce: The Rite of Fiction, 1971; Malcolm Lowry: A Preface to His Fiction, 1980. **Address:** Dept. of English, University of Maryland, College Park, MD 20742, U.S.A. **Online address:** rcross@wam.umd.edu

CROSSAN, G(regory) D(ixon). New Zealander, b. 1950. **Genres:** Literary criticism and history. **Career:** Sr. Lecturer in English, Massey University, Palmerston North, 1977-. Assistant Lecturer in English, University of Canterbury, Christchurch, 1973-76. **Publications:** A Relish for Eternity (on the poetry of John Clare), 1976; various articles. **Address:** School of English and Media Studies, Massey University, Palmerston North, New Zealand. **Online address:** G.D.Crossan@massey.ac.nz

CROSSEN, Cynthia. American. **Genres:** Adult non-fiction. **Career:** Wall Street Journal, senior editor, reporter, 1983-. **Publications:** Tainted Truth: The Manipulation of Fact in America, 1994; The Rich and How They Got That Way: How the Wealthiest People of All Time-from Genghis Khan to Bill Gates-Made Their Fortunes, 2000. Contributor to newspapers. **Address:** Wall Street Journal, 1155 Avenue of the Americas, New York, NY 10036, U.S.A. **Online address:** cynthia.crossen@wsj.com

CROSSETTE, Barbara. American. **Genres:** Area studies, Travel/Exploration. **Career:** New York Times United Nations bureau chief, 1994-, Washington correspondent, 19911993, bureau chief (New Delhi, India) 1988-1991 and (Bangkok) 1984-1988. Fulbright Professor of Journalism at Punjab University and at the Indian Institute for Mass Communications, New Delhi, 1980. Columbia University, Southern Asia Institute, research associate. **Publications:** India: Facing the Twenty-First Century, 1993; So Close to Heaven: The Vanishing Buddhist Kingdoms of the Himalayas, 1995; The Great Hill Stations of Asia, 1998. EDITOR: America's Wonderful Little Hotels and Inns, 1980; (with W. Lowe) America's Wonderful Little Hotels and Inns: Eastern Region, 1984; (with W. Lowe) America's Wonderful Little Hotels and Inns: Western Region, 1984. **Address:** The New York Times, UN Secretarial Building, Room 453, New York, NY 10017, U.S.A.

CROSSLEY, Pamela Kyle. American, b. 1955. **Genres:** History, Area studies. **Career:** Dartmouth College, Hanover, NH, assistant professor, 1985-90, associate professor, 1990-93, professor of history, 1993-. **Publications:** Orphan Warriors: Three Manchu Generations and the End of the Qing World, 1990; The Manchus, 1996; (with R. Bullier, D. Headrick, S. Hirsch, and others) The Earth and Its Peoples: A Global History, 1996; A Translucent Mirror: History and Identity in Qing Imperial Ideology, 1997. Contributor to books. Contributor of articles and reviews to journals and newspapers. **Address:** Department of History, Dartmouth College, Hanover, NH 03755, U.S.A.

CROSSLEY-HOLLAND, Kevin (John William). British, b. 1941. **Genres:** Children's fiction, Poetry, History, Mythology/Folklore, Travel/Exploration, Translations. **Career:** Macmillan, London, editor, 1962-69; Gregory Fellow in Poetry, 1969-71; BBC, London, talks producer, 1972; Victor Gollancz, London, editorial director, 1972-77; Boydell and Brewer, Ltd., editorial consultant, 1983-89; St. Olaf College, MN, visiting professor of English, 1987, 1988, Fulbright scholar, 1989; University of St. Thomas, MN, endowed chair and professor of humanities and fine arts, 1991-96. **Publications:** Havelok the Dane, 1964; King Horn, 1965; (trans.) The Battle of Maldon and Other Old English Poems, 1965; The Green Children, 1966; The Callow Pit Coffer, 1968; Beowulf, 1968; (with J. Paton Walsh) Wordhoard, 1969; (trans.) Storm and Other Old English Riddles, 1970; Norfolk Poems, 1970; The Pedlar of Swaffham, 1972; Pieces of Land, 1972; The Rain-Giver and Other Poems, 1972; The Sea-Stranger, 1973; The Fire-Brother, 1974; Green Blades Rising: The Anglo-Saxons, 1975; The Wildman, 1976; The Dream-House, 1976; (trans.) The Exeter Riddle Book, 1978; The Norse Myths, 1981; Between My Father and My Son, 1982; The Dead Moon, 1982; The Anglo-Saxon World, 1982; Time's Oriel (poetry), 1983; (with G. Thomas) Tales from the Mabinogion, 1984; Axe-Age, Wolf-Age: A Selection for

Children from the Norse Myths, 1985; Storm, 1985; Waterslain and Other Poems, 1986; British Folk Tales, 1987; (with G. Thomas) The Quest for Olwen, 1988; Wulf, 1988; Old English Elegies, 1988; The Painting-Room (poetry), 1988; Under the Sun and over the Moon, 1989; Sleeping Nanna, 1989; The Stones Remain, 1989; New and Selected Poems, 1965-1990, 1991; Sea Tongue, 1991; Tales from Europe, 1991; Long Tom and the Dead Hand, 1992; (with G. Thomas) The Tale of Taliesin, 1992; The Labours of Herakles, 1993; Norse Myths, 1993; The Wildman (libretto), 1995; The Language of Yes, 1996; Poems from East Anglia, 1997; Short! A Book of Very Short Stories, 1998; East Anglian Poems, 1998; World of King Arthur and His Court, 1999; The Wuffings (play), 1999; Enchantment, 2000; The Seeing Stone, 2000; Selected Poems, 2001; At the Crossing-Places, 2001; The Ugly Duckling: From the Story by Hans Christian Andersen, 2001; Viking!, 2002; King of the Middle March, 2003. EDITOR: Running to Paradise: An Introductory Selection of the Poems of W.B. Yeats, 1968; Winter's Tales for Children 3, 1969; The Faber Book of Northern Legends, 1977; The Faber Book of Northern Folk-Tales, 1980; The Riddle Book, 1982; Folk-Tales of the British Isles, 1985; Oxford Book of Travel Verse, 1986; Northern Lights: Legends, Sagas and Folk-Tales, 1987; Medieval Lovers, 1988; Medieval Gardens, 1990; (with L. Sail) The New Exeter Book of Riddles, 1998; Young Oxford Book of Folk Tales, 1998. **Address:** Chalk Hill, Burnham Market, Norfolk PE31 8JR, England. **Online address:** kevin@crossley-holland.com

CROUCH, Stanley. American, b. 1945. **Genres:** Poetry, Race relations, Essays. **Career:** Playwright and actor under Jayne Cortez, 1965-67; drummer with pianist Raymond King, 1966; drummer and bandleader with groups including Quartet and Black Music Infinity, 1967-; Claremont College, Claremont, CA, instructor in drama, literature, and jazz history, 1969-75. Columnist for Los Angeles Free Press, The Cricket, and SoHo Weekly News; Village Voice, jazz critic; New Republic, contributing editor, 1990-; writer. **Publications:** Ain't No Ambulances for No Nigguhs Tonight (poems), 1972; Notes of a Hanging Judge: Essays and Reviews, 1979-1989, 1990; The All-American Skin Game, 1995; Always in Pursuit: Fresh American Perspectives, 1995-1997, 1998; Don't the Moon Look Lonesome: A Novel in Blues and Swing, 2000. Works represented in anthologies. Contributor to periodicals. Composer of musical pieces. **Address:** c/o Lincoln Center for the Performing Arts, Jazz Program, 70 Lincoln Center Plaza, New York, NY 10023-6548, U.S.A.

CROUCH, Tanja L. American, b. 1958. **Genres:** Film, Inspirational/Motivational Literature, Music, Self help. **Career:** Triad Artists Inc., Los Angeles, CA, agent, 1987-91; Lib Hatcher Agency, Nashville, TN, agent, 1991-92; Turn Key Management, Nashville, TN, partner and artist manager, 1992-94; Barbara Orbison Productions, Nashville, TN, vice president, 1994-99; freelance writer and producer, 1999-; Right Brain Films and Lux Edit, account representative, 2003-. **Publications:** This Joint Is Jumpin' (television documentary), 2000, as book, 2001; One Hundred Careers in the Music Business, 2001; One Hundred Careers in Film and Televison, 2002; Truth or DareDo You Have the Courage to Change Your Life?, 2003. **Address:** 1012 Meandering Way, Franklin, TN 37067, U.S.A. **Online address:** Tanja@RightBrainFilms.com

CROW, Bill. American, b. 1927. **Genres:** Music. **Career:** Jazz musician, 1945-; Broadway theater musician, NYC, 1975-90; writer. **Publications:** Jazz Anecdotes, 1990; From Birdland to Broadway, 1992. Author of column "The Band Room" in Allegro, 1983-. Contributor to periodicals. **Address:** c/o Oxford University Press, 198 Madison Ave, New York, NY 10016-4308, U.S.A.

CROW, Mary. American. **Genres:** Poetry, Literary criticism and history, Translations. **Career:** Colorado State University, Fort Collins, professor of English, director of Creative Writing Program, 1988-91; National Endowment for the Arts Fellowship, 1984; Colorado Book Award, 1992; Colorado Council on the Arts Poetry Fellowship, 2000; Poet Laureate of Colorado, 1996. **Publications:** POETRY: Going Home, 1979; The Business of Literature, 1981; Borders, 1989; I Have Tasted the Apple, 1996; The High Cost of Living, 2002. EDITOR: Woman Who Has Sprouted Wings: Poems by Contemporary Latin American Women Poets, 1984. TRANSLATOR: From the Country of Nevermore: Selected Poems of Jorge Teillier, 1990; Vertical Poetry: Recent Poems of Roberto Juarroz, 1992; Homesickness: Selected Poems of Enrique Lihn, 2000; Engravings Torn from Insomnia: Selected Poems of Olga Orozco, 2002. **Address:** 1707 Homer Dr, Fort Collins, CO 80521, U.S.A. **Online address:** mcrow@lamar.colostate.edu

CROWDER, Ashby Bland, (Jr.). American, b. 1941. **Genres:** Literary criticism and history, Bibliography. **Career:** University of Tennessee, Knoxville,

instructor in English, 1965; Centre College of Kentucky, Danville, instructor in English, 1965-67; Middle Tennessee State University, Murfreesboro, assistant professor of English, 1968; Eastern Kentucky University, Richmond, assistant professor of English, 1969-72; Hendrix College, Conway, AR, associate professor, 1974-82, M.E. and Ima Graves Peace Professor of English, American Literature and the Humanities, 1982-, department head, 1983-86, 1994-2001. Baylor University, lecturer, 1993. **Publications:** Writing in the Southern Tradition: Interviews with Five Contemporary Authors, 1990; Poets and Critics: Their Means and Meanings, 1993; (ed.) The Complete Works of Robert Browning, Vol. XIII: The Inn Album and Pacchiarotto and How He Worked in Destemper with Other Poems, 1995; Wakeful Anguish: A Critical Biography of William Humphrey, 2004. Contributor to books. Contributor of articles, poems and reviews to journals. **Address:** Hendrix College, 1600 Washington Ave, Conway, AR 72032, U.S.A. **Online address:** crowder@hendrix.edu

CROWDER, George. New Zealander, b. 1956. **Genres:** Politics/Government. **Career:** Department of Justice, Wellington, New Zealand, legal adviser, 1978-80; Oxford University, Oxford, England, tutor in political theory, 1985-90; California State University, Fullerton, lecturer in political science, 1991; Vytantas Magnus University, Kaunas, Lithuania, lecturer in political theory, 1992-93; Bernard M. Baruch College of the City University of New York, NYC, assistant professor of political science, 1993-. Hunter College of the City University of New York, assistant professor, 1993-. **Publications:** Classical Anarchism: The Political Thought of Godwin, Proudhon, Bakunin, and Kropotkin, 1991. **Address:** Department of Political Science, Bernard M. Baruch College of CUNY, 17 Lexington Ave., Box 333, New York, NY 10010, U.S.A.

CROWE, John. See **LYNDS, Dennis.**

CROWE, Michael (J.). American, b. 1936. **Genres:** History, Sciences. **Career:** University of Notre Dame, IN, instructor, 1961-65, assistant professor, 1965-68, associate professor, 1968-73, professor, 1973-2000, Rev. John J. Cavanaugh Professor in the Humanities, 2000-02, professor emeritus, 2002-, chair, Program of Liberal Studies and Graduate Program in History and Philosophy of Science, 1967-73. University of Cambridge, visiting scholar, 1986-87; University of Louisville, distinguished scholar in residence, 2002. **Publications:** A History of Vector Analysis: The Evolution of the Idea of a Vectorial System, 1967, new ed, 1994; The Extraterrestrial Life Debate 1750-1900: The Idea of a Plurality of Worlds from Kant to Lowell, 1986, new ed. as The Extraterrestrial Life Debate 1750-1900, 1999; Theories of the World from Antiquity to the Copernican Revolution, 1990, 2nd ed., 2001; Modern Theories of the Universe from Herschel to Hubble, 1994. EDITOR: The Letters and Papers of Sir John Herschel: A Guide to the Manuscripts and Microfilm, 1991; (with D.R. Dyck and J.J. Kevin) Calendar of the Correspondence of Sir John Herschel, 1998. Author of booklets, scholarly papers, reviews, and other writings. **Address:** Program of Liberal Studies, 215 O'Shaughnessy Hall, University of Notre Dame, Notre Dame, IN 46556, U.S.A. **Online address:** crowe.1@nd.edu

CROWE, Norman. American, b. 1938. **Genres:** Architecture, Environmental sciences/Ecology, Urban studies. **Career:** Walter Weber, Architect and Lusk and Wallace Associates Architects, Colorado Springs, architect, 1964-66, 1967-68; Arkitekt I. Hammarskjold-Reiz and Stadsarkitektkontoret (Town Architect and Planning Agency), Lund, Sweden, architect, 1966-67; Anton J. Egner and Associates Architects, Ithaca, NY, architect, 1969-72; Ohio University, School of Architecture, assistant professor of architecture, 1972-74; University of Notre Dame, IN, School of Architecture, assistant professor of architecture, 1974-81, instructor in the Rome Studies Program in Italy, 1974-75, associate professor of architecture, 1981-93, director of graduate program in architecture, 1987-96, 2000-, professor of architecture, 1993-; self-employed architect and consultant, 1974-. Has taken part in group exhibitions; Guest lecturer at colleges and universities; speaker at professional conferences, etc. **Publications:** (with P. Laseau) Visual Notes: For Architects and Designers, 1984; Nature and the Idea of a Man-Made World: An Investigation into the Evolutionary Roots of Form and Order in the Built Environment, 1995; (ed. with R. Economakis and M. Lykoudis) Building Cities: Towards a Civil Society and a Sustainable Environment, 1999. Contributor to books and periodicals. **Address:** School of Architecture, 110 Bond Hall, University of Notre Dame, Notre Dame, IN 46556, U.S.A. **Online address:** ncrowe@nd.edu

CROWE, Thomas Rain. American, b. 1949. **Genres:** Poetry, Translations. **Career:** Beatitude Magazine and Press, San Francisco, CA, editor, 1974-78; Katuah Journal, Asheville, NC, founding editor, 1983-87; New Native Press, Cullowhee, NC, publisher, 1988-; Sylva Herald, press operator, 1989-93;

Fern Hill Records, founder and producer, 1994-; Asheville Poetry Review, Asheville, editor-at-large, 1995-2000; reviewer feature writer, Bloomsbury Review, Jazz News, Smoky Mountain News, 1995-; The Boatrockers (performance group), founder and performer, 1996-. **Publications:** Learning to Dance, 1985; Poems for Che Guevara's Dream, 1991; The Sound of Light (poems and music), 1991; Night Sun, 1993; The Laugharne Poems, 1997; (ed. with G. Denez and T. Hubbard) Writing the Wind: A Celtic Resurgence, 1997. TRANSLATOR: H.-A. Dal, Why I Am a Monster, 1991; Hafiz, In Wineseller's Street, 1998; Hafiz, Drunk on the Wine of the Beloved, 2001; 10,000 Dawns: Love Poems of Yvan & Claire Goll, 2004; Zoro' s Field: My Life in the Appalachian Woods (memoir), 2005. **Address:** 407 Canada Rd, Tuckasegee, NC 28783, U.S.A. **Online address:** newnativepress@hotmail.com

CROWE, William J., Jr. American, b. 1925. **Genres:** Autobiography/Memoirs. **Career:** U.S. Navy, 1946-89: commissioned ensign, 1946, lieutenant junior grade, 1949, lieutenant, 1952, lieutenant commander, 1958, commander, 1962, captain, 1972, rear admiral (two star), 1974, vice admiral (three star), 1977, admiral (four star), 1980; retired as admiral, 1989. Assistant to the naval aide to the president, 1954-55; head of East Asia and Pacific Branch of Politico-Military Policy Division, Washington, DC, 1967-70; director of Office of Micronesian Status Negotiations (MSN) and deputy to President's Personal Representative for MSN, Washington, DC, both 1971-73; deputy director of Strategic Policy Office of Chief of Naval Operations, Washington, DC, 1973-74; director of East Asia and Pacific Region, Office of Assistant Secretary of Defense, Washington, DC, 1974-76; commander of Middle East Force, Bahrain, 1976-77; deputy chief of Naval Operations Plans and Policy and senior Navy member, United Nations Military Staff Committee, Washington, DC, 1977-80; commander in chief, Allied Forces Southern Europe, 1980-83; commander in chief, United States Pacific Command, 1983-85; chair of Joint Chiefs of Staff, Washington, DC, 1985-89. University of Oklahoma, Norman, professor of geopolitics, 1990-94; Center for Strategic and International Studies, counselor, 1990-94; chair of the President's Foreign Intelligence Advisory Board, 1993-94, U.S. Ambassador to U.K., 1994-97. **Publications:** (with D. Chanoff) The Line of Fire, 1993; (with M. Bundy and S. Drell) Reducing Nuclear Danger: The Road Away from the Brink. **Address:** 1406 Coventry Ln, Alexandria, VA 22304, U.S.A.

CROWELL, Jenn(ifer). American, b. 1978. **Genres:** Novels. **Career:** Writer. **Publications:** NOVELS: Necessary Madness, 1997; Letting the Body Lead, 2002. **Address:** c/o Jane Gelfman, Gelfman Schneider Literary Agents, 250 W 57th St, New York, NY 10107, U.S.A.

CROWL, Samuel. American, b. 1940. **Genres:** Literary criticism and history. **Career:** Ohio University, Athens, assistant professor, 1970-75, associate professor, 1975-80, professor of English, 1980-92, trustee professor of English, 1992-, dean of University College, 1981-92. Member of Ohio Student Loan Commission, 1985-88, and Ohio Humanities Council, 1985-91. **Publications:** Shakespeare Observed, 1992; Shakespeare at the Cineplex, 2003. Contributor of articles and reviews to Shakespeare journals. **Address:** Department of English, Ellis Hall, Ohio University, Athens, OH 45701, U.S.A.

CROWLEY, David. British, b. 1966. **Genres:** Art/Art history. **Career:** University of Brighton, Brighton, England, lecturer, 1991-. University of Staffordshire, lecturer. Consultant to Fitzroy Dearborn's Encyclopedia of Interior Design. **Publications:** Victorian Style, 1990; National Style and Nation-State: Design in Poland from the Vernacular Revival to the International Style, 1992. **Address:** University of Brighton, 11 Pavilion Parade, Brighton BN2 1RA, England.

CROWLEY, William R. American, b. 1946. **Genres:** Reference. **Career:** Shell Chemical, 1968-71; Apollo Chemical, 1971-74; Nalco Chemical, 1974-80; Amoco Chemicals, 1980-93; Competitive Analysis Technologies, Cypress, TX, president, 1993-. **Publications:** Oil and Gas on the Internet: 650 Energy-Industry Addresses at Your Fingertips (directory), 1996; (ed.) Chemicals on the Internet: A Directory of Industry Sites, Vol 1: Organic and Petrochemicals, Vol 2: Inorganic Chemicals and Minerals, 1997. **Address:** 11702-B Grant Rd, Ste. 333, Cypress, TX 77429, U.S.A. **Online address:** COMPETE@CONCEMTRIC.NET

CROWLEY-MILLING, Michael C. British (born Wales), b. 1917. **Genres:** Physics. **Career:** Metropolitan Vickers Electrical Co. Ltd., Manchester, England, research engineer, 1938-66; Daresbury Nuclear Physics Laboratory, near Warrington, England, member of directorate, 1966-71; European Organization for Nuclear Research, Geneva, Switzerland, group leader to the director for the accelerator program, 1971-83. Holder of 30 British and foreign patents; consultant to laboratories in Europe and the United States. **Publications:** John Bertram Adams, Engineer Extraordinary: A Tribute, 1993. EDITOR: Accelerator Control Systems, 1986; Accelerator and Experimental Physics Control Systems, 1990. Contributor to scientific journals. **Address:** 15 Les Ruches, 1264 St. Cerque, Switzerland.

CROWN, Alan D(avid). Australian (born England), b. 1932. **Genres:** Theology/Religion, Bibliography. **Career:** Schoolmaster at secondary schools, Leeds, England, 1957-59, Melbourne, Australia, 1959-62; University of Sydney, Australia, lecturer, 1962-67, senior lecturer, 1968-84, associate professor, 1984-90, professor, 1990-96, head of dept, 1984-96, honorary research associate, 1997-98, emeritus professor of Semitic studies, 1999-, project director for Archive of Australian Judaica, Mandelbaum House, joint honorary master and chairman, 1996-. University of California, Los Angeles, postdoctoral fellow, 1968; Hebrew University of Jerusalem, visiting lecturer, 1973-74; Oxford University, teacher at Oriental Institute, 1979-80, visiting scholar at Oxford Centre for Post-Graduate Hebrew Studies, 1979-80, 1983, administrator of International Qumran Project, 1988-, senior associate fellow, 1992-; University of New England, honorary associate, 1983-85; Annenberg Research Institute, fellow, 1988; guest lecturer at colleges and universities worldwide. Order of Australia, 1996. **Publications:** A Descriptive Checklist of Hebrew Manuscripts and Rare Printed Books in Fisher Library, 1973, 2nd ed., 1984; Biblical Studies Today, 1975; (trans.) Y. Gamzu, In the Midst of the Night in the Midst of Jerusalem, 1977; (trans. and author of intro. and notes) Israel Weissbrem and His Work, 1983, 2nd ed., as The World of Israel Weissbrem, Part 1, 1993; A Bibliography of the Samaritans, 1984, 2nd ed., 1993. EDITOR: (co) Essays Presented to E.C.B. MacLaurin, 1973; (and trans.) Zimrat Haares, 2 vols., 1977; (and contrib.) The Samaritans: Their Religion, Literature, Society, and Culture, 1989; (with R. Pummer and A. Tal, and contrib.) A Companion to Samaritan Studies: An Encyclopaedic Dictionary of the Samaritans, 1993. Work represented in anthologies. Contributor of articles and reviews to scholarly journals. **Address:** Mandelbaum House, 385 Abercrombie St, Darlington, NSW 2008, Australia. **Online address:** acrown@mail.usyd.edu.au

CROWN, David Allan. American, b. 1928. **Genres:** Criminology/True Crime. **Career:** US Postal Inspection Service, Identification Laboratory, San Francisco, CA, assistant director, 1957-67; US Dept. of the Army, Questioned Documents Laboratory, Washington, DC, director, 1967-72; Dept. of State, Questioned Documents Staff, INR/DDC, Washington, director, 1972-77; Office of Technical Services, Questioned Documents Laboratory, Washington, chief, 1977-82. American University, Washington, adjunct professor, 1971-75; Antioch School of Law, Washington, adjunct professor, 1977-81; Crown Forensic Labs. Inc., Fairfax, VA, president. **Publications:** The Forensic Examination of Paints and Pigments, 1968; (co-author) Forensic Sciences, 1982; (co-author) Legal Medicine Annual, 1985; (co-ed.) Forensische Handschritenuntersuchung, 1993. **Address:** 3344 Twin Lakes Ln, Sanibel, FL 33957, U.S.A.

CROWTHER, Hal. Canadian, b. 1945. **Genres:** Essays. **Career:** Time, staff writer; Newsweek, associate editor; Buffalo News, Buffalo, NY, media columnist, film and drama critic; Humanist, columnist; Free Inquiry, columnist; Spectator, columnist, 1981-, executive editor, 1986-1989; also columnist for Independent Weekly, Durham, NC, Oxford American, Progressive Populist, and North Carolina Independent. Author. **Publications:** Unarmed but Dangerous: Withering Attacks on All Things Phony, Foolish, and Fundamentally Wrong with America Today, 1995; Cathedrals of Kudzu: A Personal Landscape of the South, 2000. Contributor to books, periodicals and newspapers. **Address:** c/o The Independent Weekly, 2810 Hillsborough Rd., Durham, NC 27705, U.S.A.

CROWTHER, Harold Francis. American, b. 1920. **Genres:** Novels, Psychology, Music. **Career:** Retired Lawyer, Salina, Kansas, since 1983. With U.S. Navy, 1939-45; Probation Officer, Salina County Juvenile Court, 1956-59. **Publications:** The Oblique Equalizer or Some for Me, 1965. **Address:** 312 E. 12th St., Apt. 1, Joplin, MO 64801, U.S.A.

CROWTHER, Nick. Also writes as Nick Hassam. British, b. 1949. **Genres:** Novels. **Career:** Leeds Permanent Building Society, Leeds, England, communications manager, 1980-95; freelance writer and consulting editor, 1995-. **Publications:** (ed.) Narrow Houses, 1992; Touch Wood, 1993; Blue Motel, 1994; Heaven Sent, 1995; (with Ed Kramer) Tombs, 1995; (with J. Lovegrove) Escardy Gap, 1996; (with Kramer) Dante's Disciples, 1996. Some writings appear under the pseudonym Nick Hassam. **Address:** P.S. Publishing LLP, Hamilton House, 4 Park Ave, Harrogate HG2 9BQ, England.

CROYDEN, Margaret. American. **Genres:** Art/Art history. **Career:** New Jersey City University, Jersey City, NJ, former professor of English literature;

Columbia Broadcasting System, Inc. (CBS), former host of Camera Three; New York Theatre Wire, commentator and reviewer; theater critic; lecturer and speaker. **Publications:** Lunatics, Lovers, and Poets: The Contemporary Experimental Theatre, 1974; In the Shadow of the Flame: Three Journeys, 1993; Conversations with Peter Brook: 1970-2000, 2003. Contributor of articles to publications. **Address:** c/o Author Mail, Faber & Faber, 19 Union Square W., New York, NY 10003, U.S.A.

CROZIER, Andrew. British, b. 1943. **Genres:** Poetry. **Career:** Reader in English, University of Sussex, Brighton. **Publications:** Loved Litter of Time Spent, 1967; Train Rides, 1968; Walking on Grass, 1969; (with John James and Tom Phillips) In One Side and Out the Other, 1970; Neglected Information, 1973; The Veil Poem, 1974; Printed Circuit, 1974; (with Ian Potts) Seven Contemporary Sun Dials, 1975; Pleats, 1975; Duets, 1976; High Zero, 1978; Were There, 1978; Residing, 1976; Utamaro Variations, 1982; All Where Earth Is, 1985; (ed. with Tim Longville) A Various Art (anthology), 1987. **Address:** Arts Building, University of Sussex, Brighton, Suffolk BN1 9NQ, England.

CROZIER, Brian. Also writes as John Rossiter. British (born Australia), b. 1918. **Genres:** Novels, International relations/Current affairs, Third World, Biography. **Career:** Distinguished Visiting Fellow, Hoover Institution, Stanford, CA, 1996-2002. Contributing Editor, National Review, NY, since 1978. Staff member: Reuters, 1943-44; News Chronicle, 1944-48; Sydney Morning Herald, 1948-51, Reuters-AAP, 1951-52, Straits Times, 1952-53, The Economist, 1954-64, BBC, 1954-65; Forum World Features, chairman, London, 1965-75; Director, Institute for the Study of Conflict, London, 1970-79. **Publications:** The Rebels: A Study of Post-War Insurrections, 1960; The Morning After: A Study of Independence, 1963; Neo-Colonialism, 1964; South-East Asia in Turmoil, 1965; The Struggle for the Third World, 1966; Franco, 1967; The Masters of Power, 1969; The Future of Communist Power (in U.S. as After Stalin), 1970; De Gaulle, 2 vols., 1973-74, in U.S., 1 vol., 1973; A Theory of Conflict, 1974; The Man Who Lost China: A Biography of Chiang Kai-shek, 1978; Strategy of Survival, 1978; The Minimum State, 1979; Franco: Crepusculo de un Hombre, 1980; The Price of Peace, 1980; (co-author) Socialism Explained, 1984; (co-author) This War Called Peace, 1984; (as John Rossiter) The Andropov Deception (novel), 1984, U.S. ed. as Brian Crozier, 1986; Socialism: Dream and Reality, 1987; The Gorbachev Phenomenon, 1990; Communism: Why Prolong Its Death Throes?, 1990; Free Agent: The Unseen War 1941-1991, 1993; (co-author) Le Phénix Rouge, 1995; The KGB Lawsuits, 1995; The Rise and Fall of the Soviet Empire, 1999. EDITOR: We Will Bury You: A Study of Left-wing Subversion Today, 1970; The Grenada Documents, 1987. **Address:** 18 Wickliffe Ave., London N3 3EJ, England.

CROZIER, Lorna. Also writes as Lorna Uher. Canadian, b. 1948. **Genres:** Poetry, Adult non-fiction. **Career:** High sch. English teacher, Glaslyn, SK, 1970-72, and Swift Current, 1972-77; Saskatchewan Summer School of the Arts, Fort San, creative writing teacher, 1977-81; writer-in-residence, Cypress Hills Community College, Swift Current, 1980-81, Regina Public Library, SK, 1984-85, and University of Toronto, 1989-90; Saskatchewan Dept. of Parks, Culture, and Recreation, Regina, director of communications, 1981-83; CBC Radio, broadcaster and writer, 1986; Banff School of the Fine Arts, Alberta, guest instr., 1986, 1987; University of Saskatchewan, special lectr., 1986-91; University of Victoria, Dept of Writing, professor, 1991-. **Publications:** AS LORNA UHER: Inside Is the Sky, 1976; Crow's Black Joy, 1978; (with P. Lane) No Longer Two People, 1979; Animals of Fall, 1979; Humans and Other Beasts, 1980. AS LORNA CROZIER: The Weather, 1983; The Garden Going on without Us, 1985; (ed. with G. Hyland) A Sudden Radiance: Saskatchewan Poetry, 1987; Angels of Flesh, Angels of Silence, 1988; Inventing the Hawk, 1992; Everything Arrives at the Light, 1995; A Saving Grace, 1996; What the Living Won't Let Go, 1999; (ed.) Desire in Seven Voices, 1999; (ed. with P. Lane) Addicted: Notes from the Belly of the Beast, 2001; The Apocrypha of Light, 2002; Bones in Their Wings: Ghazals, 2003.

CROZIER, Michael (Paul). Australian, b. 1956. **Genres:** Cultural/Ethnic topics, History, Politics/Government, Social sciences, Sociology. **Career:** Monash University, tutor in political science, 1981; Victoria College, Toorak, Australia, lecturer in sociology, 1986; University of Melbourne, Parkville, Australia, senior lecturer in political science, 1987-. **Publications:** (ed. with P. Murphy) The Left in Search of a Center, 1996; (with A. Capling and M. Considine) Australian Politics in the Global Era, 1998. Contributor to periodicals. **Address:** Department of Political Science, University of Melbourne, VIC 3010, Australia. **Online address:** m.crozier@ unimelb.edu.au

CRUMBLEY, Paul. American (born Uruguay), b. 1952. **Genres:** Literary criticism and history. **Career:** English teacher at a school in Seattle, WA,

1980-86, department head, 1984-86; University of North Carolina at Wilmington, lecturer in English, 1986-87; University of North Carolina at Chapel Hill, instructor in English, 1987-93, director of Writing Center, 1990-92; Niagara University, Niagara University, NY, assistant professor of English, 1993-95; Utah State University, Logan, lecturer, 1995-96, assistant professor of English, 1996-, faculty coordinator for American studies, 1997-. Oxford University, Lincoln College, assistant to the director of Bread Loaf School of English, summers, 1987-91. **Publications:** Inflections of the Pen: Dash and Voice in Emily Dickinson, 1997. Contributor to books. Contributor of articles and reviews to academic journals. **Address:** Department of English, Utah State University, Logan, UT 84322, U.S.A. **Online address:** PCrumbley@ English.usu.edu

CRUMMEY, Michael. Canadian. **Genres:** Novels. **Career:** Poet and writer. **Publications:** Arguments with Gravity, 1996; Hard Light, 1998; Flesh and Blood: Stories, 1998; River Thieves, 2001; Salvage, 2002. **Address:** c/o Author Mail, Random House of Canada Ltd., One Toronto St. Unit 300, Toronto, ON, Canada M5C 2V6.

CRUMP, William D(rake). American, b. 1949. **Genres:** Reference. **Career:** Reference Pathology, Nashville, TN, pathologist, 1982-86, 1990-95; Roche Biomedical, Monroe, LA, pathologist, 1986-89; Loyola University, Chicago, IL, fellow at Medical Center, 1989-90; writer. Church organist, 1998-2002. **Publications:** The Christmas Encyclopedia, 2001, 2nd ed., 2005; Was the First Gift Really Gold?, 2003. **Address:** 757 Howse Ave, Madison, TN 37115, U.S.A. **Online address:** cootum@earthlink.net

CRUNK, Tony. American, b. 1956. **Genres:** Children's fiction, Poetry. **Career:** University of Montana, visiting assistant professor of English, 1995-98; Murray State University, Murray, KY, visiting assistant professor of English, 1998-99; University of Alabama-Birmingham, assistant professor of creative writing and literature, 2000-. **Publications:** Two Towns and the People Who Lived in Them, 1978; Living in the Resurrection (poetry), 1995; Big Mama, 2000; Grandpa's Overalls, 2001. **Address:** Dept of English, University of Alabama at Birmingham, HB217, 1530 3rd Ave, South, Birmingham, AL 35294-1260, U.S.A. **Online address:** tcrunk@uab.edu

CRUSE, Howard. (born United States), b. 1944. **Genres:** Graphic Novels. **Career:** Writer, graphic artist, illustrator, comix creator. WAPI-TV (now WVTM-TV), Birmingham, AL, assistant to art director, 1964-65; Birmingham News, Birmingham, staff artist, 1967; Mag Computer Corporation, New York, NY, paste-up artist, 1969; WBMG-TV, Birmingham, art director and puppeteer, 1969-72; Atlanta Children's Theatre, Atlanta, GA, actor and scenic design assistant, 1972-72; Art Service, Inc., Atlanta, staff artist, 1973-74; Luckie & Forney Advertising, Birmingham, staff artist, 1975-76; Starlog, New York, art director, 1977-78; freelance writer and artist, 1963-; Gay Comix, founding editor, 1980-84. **Publications:** (Illustrator) H. William Stine and Megan Stine, How to Succeed in Sports without Ever Playing, 1981; (Illustrator) Steven Bloom, Video Invaders, 1982; Wendel (collection),1985; Howard Cruse's Barefootz (collection), 1986; (Illustrator) Delaney and Goldblum, Strategies for Survival, 1987; Dancin' Nekkid with the Angels: Comic Strips and Stories for Grownups, 1987; Wendel on the Rebound (collection), 1989; Early Barefootz (collection), 1990; Stuck Rubber Baby (graphic novel), 1995; Wendel All Together (collection), 2001. Swimmer with a Rope in His Teeth, 2004. Creator of cartoon strips and contributor of cartoons and illustrations to periodicals. **Address:** POB 100, North Adams, MA 01247, U.S.A. **Online address:** howard@howardcruse.com

CRUSH, Jonathan. British/Canadian, b. 1953. **Genres:** Geography, Area studies. **Career:** National University of Lesotho, Roma, lecturer in human geography, 1979-81; Queen's University, Kingston, ON, research fellow and assistant professor of geography, 1983-85, research fellow, 1987-92, associate professor, 1987-93, professor of geography, 1993-, director of IDRC Migrant Labour Project, 1990-93, director of Southern African Migration Project, 1996-2004, director of Southern African Research Centre, 2000-; University of Alberta, Edmonton, Mactaggart fellow and assistant professor of geography, 1985-87. University of Natal, visiting research fellow in development studies, 1984; University of the Witwatersrand, visiting scholar, 1987, visiting research fellow, 1989; University of Cape Town, research fellow and visiting scholar, 1989, 1997-98. **Publications:** The Struggle for Swazi Labour, 1890-1920, 1987; (with A. Jeeves and D. Yudelman) South Africa's Labor Empire: A History of Black Migrancy to the Gold Mines, 1991. EDITOR: (with C. Ambler, and contrib.) Liquor and Labour in Southern Africa, 1992; Power of Development, 1995; (with W. James) Crossing Boundaries, 1995; (with A. Jeeves, and contrib.) White Farms, Black Labor, 1997; Beyond Control: Immigration and Human Rights in a Democratic South Africa, 1998. Work represented in anthologies. Contributor of articles and reviews to geography and African studies journals. **Address:** Southern Africa Research Centre, Queen's University, Kingston, ON, Canada K7L 3N6. **Online address:** crushj@post.queensu.ca

CRUSIE, Jennifer. (Jennifer Smith). American, b. 1949. **Genres:** Romance/Historical. **Career:** Novelist and educator. Taught elementary and high school art and high school English in Beavercreek, OH. **Publications:** Sizzle (novella), 1992; Manhunting, 1993; Getting Rid of Bradley, 1994; Strange Bedpersons, 1994; What the Lady Wants, 1995; Charlie All Night, 1996; Anyone but You, 1996; The Cinderella Deal, 1996; Trust Me on This, 1997; Tell Me Lies, 1998; Crazy for You, 1999; Welcome to Temptation, 2000; Fast Women, 2001; Faking It, 2002. Contributor of articles and reviews to publications. **Address:** c/o Author Mail, St. Martin's Press, 175 Fifth Ave., New York, NY 10010, U.S.A. **Online address:** JenniferCrusie@POBoxes.com

CRUSIUS, Timothy Wood. American, b. 1950. **Genres:** Philosophy. **Career:** University of North Carolina at Greensboro, assistant professor of English, 1978-80; Texas A&M University, College Station, assistant professor, 1980-85, associate professor of English, 1986-90; Southern Methodist University, Dallas, TX, associate professor, 1990-99, professor of English, 1999-, director of discursive writing, 1990-95, coordinator of SMU-in-Legacy, 1998-, member of executive board of Robert Beavers Family Study Center. **Publications:** Discourse: A Critique and Synthesis of Recent Theories, 1989; A Teacher's Introduction to Philosophical Hermeneutics, 1991; (with C. Channell) The Aims of Argument: A Rhetoric and Reader, 1995, 3rd ed, 2000; Kenneth Burke and the Conversation after Philosophy, 1999. Contributor to books and periodicals. **Address:** Department of English, Southern Methodist University, Dallas, TX 75275, U.S.A. **Online address:** tcrusius@post.cis.smu.edu

CRUTCHER, Chris(topher C.). American, b. 1946. **Genres:** Young adult fiction. **Career:** Kennewick Dropout School, Kennewick, WA, teacher, 1970-73; Lakeside School, Oakland, CA, teacher, 1973-76, director of school, 1976-80; Community Mental Health, Spokane, WA, child protection team specialist, 1980-82; child and family therapist, 1982-. **Publications:** YOUNG ADULT FICTION: Running Loose, 1983; Stotan!, 1986; The Crazy Horse Electric Game, 1987; Chinese Handcuffs, 1989; Staying Fat for Sarah Byrnes, 1993; Ironman: A Novel, 1995; Whale Talk, 2001; King of the Mild Frontier, 2003. OTHER: Athletic Shorts: Six Short Stories, 1991; The Deep End, 1992. **Address:** East 3405 Marion Ct., Spokane, WA 99223, U.S.A. **Online address:** STOTAN717@aol.com

CRUZ, Victor Hernandez. Puerto Rican, b. 1949. **Genres:** Poetry, Essays. **Career:** Former Ed., Umbra mag., NYC; visiting professor: University of California, Berkley, and San Diego, University of Michigan. **Publications:** Papo Got His Gun, 1966; Snaps: Poems, 1969; (ed. with H. Kohl) Stuff: A Collection of Poems, Visions and Imaginative Happenings from Young Writers in Schools-Opened and Closed, 1970; Mainland, 1973; Tropicalization, 1976; By Lingual Wholes, 1982; Rhythm, Content and Flavor: New and Selected Poems, 1989; Red Beans, 1991; Panaramas, 1997. **Address:** P. O. Box 1047, Aguas Buenas, PR 00703, U.S.A.

CRYSTAL, David. British, b. 1941. **Genres:** Poetry, Children's non-fiction, Language/Linguistics, Medicine/Health, Speech/Rhetoric, Theology/Religion, Reference. **Career:** College of North Wales, assistant lecturer, 1963-65; University of Reading, lecturer and reader, 1965-75, professor of linguistic science, 1976-85; University College of Wales, Bangor, professorial fellow, 1985-; Crystal Reference, chairman, 2002-. Child Language Teaching and Therapy, editor, 1985-96; Linguistics Abstracts, editor, 1985-96; English Today, consulting editor, 1986-94. OBE, 1995. **Publications:** (with R. Quirk) Systems of Prosodic and Paralinguistic Features in English, 1964; Linguistics, Language and Religion, 1965; What Is Linguistics?, 1968, 5th ed., 1985; (with D. Davy) Investigating English Style, 1969; Prosodic Systems and Intonation in English, 1969; Linguistics, 1971; The English Tone of Voice, 1975; (with D. Davy) Advanced Conversational English, 1975; (with P. Fletcher and M. Garman) The Grammatical Analysis of Language Disability, 1976; Child Language, Learning, and Linguistics, 1976; Working with LARSP, 1979; Eric Partridge: In His Own Words, 1980; A First Dictionary of Linguistics and Phonetics, 1980, 5th ed., 2002; Introduction to Language Pathology, 1980, 4th ed. (with R. Varley), 1998; Clinical Linguistics, 1981; Directions in Applied Linguistics, 1981; Linguistic Controversies, 1981; Profiling Linguistic Disability, 1982; Linguistic Encounters with Language Handicap, 1984; Language Handicap in Children, 1984; Who Cares about English Usage?, 1984, 2nd ed., 2000; Listen to Your Child, 1986; Cambridge Encyclopedia of Language, 1987, 2nd ed., 1997; Rediscover Grammar, 1988, 2nd ed., 1996; Pilgrimage, 1988; The English Language, 1988, 2nd ed.,

2002; Convent, 1989; Language A to Z, 1991; Making Sense of English Usage, 1991; Nineties Knowledge, 1992; Introducing Linguistics, 1992; An Encyclopedic Dictionary of Language and Languages, 1992, rev. ed. as The Penguin Dictionary of Language, 1999; The Cambridge Paperback Encyclopedia, 1993, 3rd ed., 1999; Cambridge Encyclopedia of the English Language, 1995, 2nd ed., 2003; Discover Grammar, 1996; John Bradburne: Songs of the Vagabond, 1996; English as a Global Language, 1997, 2nd ed., 2003; Language Play, 1998; (with H. Crystal) Words on Words, 2000; (with H. Crystal) John Bradburne's Mutemwa, 2000; Language Death, 2000; Happenings, 2000; Language and the Internet, 2001. EDITOR: (with W. Bolton) The English Language, 1969; The Cambridge Encyclopedia, 1990, 4th ed., 2000; The Cambridge Concise Encyclopedia, 1992, 2nd ed., 1995; The Cambridge Biographical Encyclopedia, 1994, 2nd ed., 1998; The Cambridge Biographical Dictionary, 1996; New Penguin Encyclopedia, 2002; New Penguin Factfinder, 2003; New Penguin Concise Encyclopedia, 2003. CHILDREN'S NON-FICTION: (with J. Bevington) Skylarks, 1975; (with J. Foster) Heat, Light, Sound, Roads, Railways, Canals, Monasteries, Manors, Castles, Money, Parliament, Newspapers, The Romans, The Greeks, The Ancient Egyptians, Air, Food, Volcanoes, Deserts, Electricity, Motorcycles, Computers, Horses and Ponies, The Normans, The Vikings, The Celts, The Anglo-Saxons, The Stone Age, Fishing, 29 vols., 1979-85; Air and Breathing, Heating and Cooling, Light and Seeing, Sound and Hearing, 1991. **Address:** Akaroa, Gors Ave, Holyhead LL65 1PB, Wales.

CSABA, László. Hungarian, b. 1954. **Genres:** Economics. **Career:** Institute for World Economy, Budapest, Hungary, junior fellow to senior fellow, 1976-87; Kopint-Datorg Economic Research, Budapest, senior economist, 1988-2000; College of Foreign Trade, professor of international economics; Budapest University of Economics, professor of economics, 1997-; Universitas Debrecen, professor and head of doctoral program, 1999-; Central European University, visiting professor, 1998, professor of economics and European Studies, 2000-. Adviser to the Hungarian minister of finance, 1991-95. Visiting professor at European universities. European Assn for Comparative Economic Studies, president, 1999-2000; Hungarian Academy of Sciences, Committee on Economics, co-chair, 1996-2002, chair, 2003-05. **Publications:** Eastern Europe in the World Economy, 1990; The Capitalist Revolution in Eastern Europe, 1995. EDITOR: Systemic Change and Stabilization in Eastern Europe, 1993; Privatization, Liberalization, and Destruction, 1994; The Hungarian Small Business in Comparative Perspective, 1998; (with W. Andreff and M. Dimitrov) Economies in Transition and the Varieties of Capitalism, 1999; (with Z. Bara) Small Economies' Adjustment to Global Tendencies, 2000. Contributor to books and periodicals. **Address:** IRES Dept, Central European University, Nador u. 9, H-1051 Budapest, Hungary. **Online address:** csabal@ceu.hu

CSEPELI, Gyorgy. Hungarian, b. 1946. **Genres:** Politics/Government. **Career:** Eotvos Lorand University, Budapest, Hungary, assistant professor of sociology, 1972-80, chairperson of Department of Social Psychology, Institute of Sociology. **Publications:** Structures and Contents of Hungarian National Identity, 1990; (with E.A. Orkeny) Ideology and Political Beliefs in Hungary: The Twilight of State Socialism, 1992; Contemporary Hungarian National Identity, 1997. **Address:** Pazmany Peter setany 1/a, 1116 Budapest, Hungary. **Online address:** csgyun@ludens.elte.hu

CSOORI, Sandor. Hungarian, b. 1930. **Genres:** Novels, Plays/Screenplays, Poetry. **Career:** Staff member of Papai Neplap (Papa Popular News), from 1949; Veszprem Megyei Nepujsag (Veszprem County Popular Newspaper), from 1949; Szabad Ifjusag (Free Youth), from 1952; and Irodalmi Ujsag (Literary News), 1953-54. Uj Hang (New Voice), head of poetry section, 1955-56; Hungarian Film Studio, dramaturge, from 1971. Joined opposition movement, 1980; Hungarian Democratic Forum, founding member, 1987. **Publications:** POETRY: Felroppen a madar (title means: The Bird Takes Wing), 1954; Ordogpille (title means: Devil's Moth), 1957; Menekules a maganybol (title means: Flight from Solitude), 1962; (with F. Hidas) Szigoru korban elunk (title means: We Live in Harsh Times), 1967; Masodik szuletesem (title means: My Second Birth), 1967; Lekvarcirkusz bohocai (title means: Clowns of a Jam Circus), 1969; Parbeszed, sotetben (title means: Dialogue, in the Dark), 1973; A latogato emlekei (title means: The Memories of a Visitor), 1977; Joslas a te idodrol (title means: Predictions About Your Time), 1979; A tizedik este (title means: The Tenth Evening), 1980; Wings of Knives and Nails, edited and trans. by I.L. Halasz de Beky, 1981; Elma-radt lazalom (title means: Nightmare Postponed), 1982; Varakozas a tavaszban (title means: Waiting in the Spring), 1983; Memory of Snow, trans. N. Kolumban, 1983; Kezemben zold ag (title means: In My Hand a Green Branch), 1985; Labon jaro verofeny (title means: Bright Sunshine on Foot), 1987; Csoori Sandor breviarium (includes prose; title means: Breviary), 1988; A vilag emlekmuvei (title means: Monuments of the World),

1989; Barbarian Prayer: Selected Poems, 1989; Selected Poems of Sandor Csoori, trans. L. Roberts, 1992. SCREENPLAYS: (with F. Kosa) Itelet (title means: Sentence), 1967; (with Kosa) Nincs ido (title means: There Is No Time), 1972; (with Kosa) Forradas (title means: Scars), 1972; (with S. Sara) 80 huszar (title means: Eighty Hussars), 1980; (with Sara) Tuske a korom alatt (title means: Thorn Under the Fingernail), 1987. FICTION: Faltol falig (title means: From Wall to Wall), 1969; Utazas, felalomban (title means: Journey While Half-Asleep), 1974; Iszapeso (title means: Mud-Rain), 1981. OTHER: Tudositas a toronybol (title means: Report from the Tower), 1963; Kubai naplo (title means: Cuban Diary), 1965; A kolto es a majompofa (title means: The Poet and the Monkey Face), 1966; Biztato (title means: Reassurance), 1973; Nomad naplo (title means: The Wanderer's Diary), 1979; (ed.) Szarny es piramis (title means: Wing and Pyramid), by L. Nagy, 1980; Tenger es diolevel (title means: The Sea and the Walnut Leaf), 1982; (ed.) Mert szemben ulsz velem (title means: Because You Sit Opposite Me), by G. Illyes, 1982; Keszulodes a szamadasra (title means: Preparation for the Day of Reckoning), 1987; Nappali hold (title means: Moon at Daylight), 1991. **Address:** c/o Magveto Konyvkiado, Vorosmarty ter 1, 1806 Budapest V, Hungary.

CUA, Antonio S. American (born Philippines), b. 1932. **Genres:** Philosophy. **Career:** University of California, Berkeley, teaching assistant, 1955-58; Ohio University, Athens, instructor to assistant professor, 1958-62; Oswego College, State University of New York, Dept. of Philosophy, professor and chairman, 1962-68; Catholic University of America, Washington, DC, professor, 1969-95, emeritus, 1996-. Co-editor, Journal of Chinese Philosophy; associate editor, International Journal of Philosophy of Religion; editorial consultant, American Philosophical Quarterly, and Philosophy East and West. President, Society for Asian and Comparative Philosophy, 1978-79; president, Intl. Society for Chinese Philosophy, 1984-85. **Publications:** Reason and Virtue, 1966; Moral Vision and Tradition, 1977, rev. ed., 1998; Dimensions of Moral Creativity, 1978; The Unity of Knowledge and Action, 1982; Ethical Argumentation, 1985; Two Lectures on Confucian Ethics, 1998. EDITOR: Encyclopedia of Chinese Philosophy, 2003. **Address:** School of Philosophy, Catholic University of America, Washington, DC 20064, U.S.A. **Online address:** cua@cua.edu

CUDMORE, Dana (D.). American, b. 1954. **Genres:** Travel/Exploration. **Career:** Media Services, advertising consultant; newspaper editor, writer, Cobleskill, NY. **Publications:** The Remarkable Howe Caverns Story, 1990. **Address:** 565 Patrick Rd, Cobleskill, NY 12043, U.S.A.

CUERVO, Talía. See VEGA, Ana Lydia.

CUETARA, Mittie. American, b. 1957. **Genres:** Children's fiction. **Career:** Freelance illustrator in Boston, MA, and San Francisco, CA, 1985-90; founder, art director, and principal illustrator at a greeting card company, San Francisco, 1990-93; writer and illustrator of children's books, 1993-. **Publications:** AND ILLUSTRATOR: Terrible Teresa and Other Very Short Stories, 1997; The Crazy Crawler Crane and Other Very Short Truck Stories, 1998; Baby Business, 2003.

CUEVAS, Judy. See IVORY, Judith.

CULBERT, Steven (Tye). (Comes-In-Backwards). American, b. 1950. **Genres:** Novels. **Career:** Writer. Worked as a carpenter, truck driver, laborer, editor of scientific and legal documents, and visiting professor at universities and colleges including Texas Christian University, Fort Worth, TX, c. 1975-85, University of San Francisco, San Francisco, CA, 1979, and Occidental College, Los Angeles, CA, c. 1989. Taught at community colleges in Dallas and Fort Worth, TX. **Publications:** The Beautiful Woman without Mercy, 1993; The King of Scarecrows, 1993; (with G.S. Peoples) Responsibilities (essays and poems), 1993; Lovesong for the Giant Contessa (novel); Bob Steel (screenplay), 1999. Author of unpublished poetry collections. Author of poems in periodicals and anthologies. **Address:** MSMR Program, University of Texas, 701 S. Nedderman Dr., Arlington, TX 76019, U.S.A.

CULHANE, John (William). American, b. 1934. **Genres:** Film, Plays/Screenplays, Science fiction/Fantasy. **Career:** St. Louis Globe Democrat, St. Louis, MO, reporter, 1955; Rockford Register-Republic, Rockford, IL, daily columnist and reporter, 1956-61; Chicago Daily News, IL, reporter and foreign correspondent, 1962-66; Newsweek, correspondent in Chicago bureau, 1966-69, and associate editor, NYC, 1969-71; freelance journalist, 1971-85; Reader's Digest, Pleasantville, NY, roving editor, 1985-93; Johimith Robidoux Productions, roving writer, 1994-. Performed as a clown with Ringling Brothers and Barnum & Bailey circus, 1974-84; mousetro-of-ceremonies for Mickey Mouse's fiftieth-birthday retrospective and whistle-

stop train tour across the United States, 1978; provided the voice of the dragon for the animated television special The Last of the Red-Hot Dragons, 1980; moderator of Forum on Animation and Fantasy Filmmaking, North American college campuses, 1981; co-producer of the television documentary Circus!, 1984. **Publications:** BOOKS: (with M.K. Frith and B. Johnson) The Art of the Muppets, 1980; Special Effects in the Movies: How They Do It, 1981; Walt Disney's Fantasia, 1983; The American Circus: An Illustrated History, 1990; Disney's Aladdin: The Making of the Animated Film, 1992; A Taz Thanksgiving, 1994. Contributor to books and periodicals. TELEVISION SCREENPLAYS: (with S. Culhane) Noah's Animals, 1974; (with Culhane) King of the Beasts, 1976; (with Culhane) The Last of the Red-Hot Dragons, 1980; Backstage at Disney's, 1983; Disney's Aladdin: A Whole New World, 1992. Contributed "Statue of Liberty speech" to David Copperfield Vanishes the Statue of Liberty, 1983; (commentator) Frank and Ollie (documentary), 1995; (with others) Arabian Knight, 1995. **Address:** c/o Carl D. Brandt, Brandt and Brandt Literary Agents, Inc., 1501 Broadway, New York, NY 10036, U.S.A.

CULLEN, Bill. Irish, b. 1942. **Genres:** Autobiography/Memoirs. **Career:** Author and businessman. Began selling fruits, flowers, newspapers, toys, and balloons on the streets of Dublin at age six; Walden Motor Corporation, office messenger to director general, 1956-65; Firlane Motor Company, director; Glencullen Group, founder, chairman, and chief executive officer, 1986-. Lifetime Success Institute, founder; Irish Youth Foundation, director. **Publications:** It's a Long Way from Penny Apples, 2001. **Address:** Glencullen Group, Kylemore Road, Ballyfermot, Dublin, Ireland.

CULLEN, Mark. Canadian, b. 1956. **Genres:** Horticulture. **Career:** Weall & Cullen Nurseries Ltd., Markham, Ontario, president, 1990-. CFRB-Radio (Toronto), host of the weekly live garden show Anything Grows; Right in Your Own Backyard, TV series, host; Canada AM, weekly gardening segment, co-host; Sunday Sun, columnist. **Publications:** A Greener Thumb, 1990; The Real Dirt, 1992; The All Seasons Gardener, Getting More from Your Canadian Garden, 1995; The Complete Gardener. **Address:** Weall & Cullen Nurseries Ltd., 784 Sheppard Ave., E., Willowdale, ON, Canada M2K 1C3.

CULLEN, Robert (B.). American, b. 1949. **Genres:** Criminology/True Crime, Law, Mystery/Crime/Suspense, Sports/Fitness. **Career:** New York Times, New York City, copy boy, summer, 1969; Evening News, Newark, NJ, reporter, 1970-71; Associated Press, reporter in Charlotte, NC, 1971-72, and Raleigh, NC, 1972-73, chief of Raleigh bureau, 1974-76, reporter in Washington, DC, 1976-82; Newsweek, bureau chief in Moscow, U.S.S.R., 1982-85, general editor in New York City, 1985-86, diplomatic correspondent from Washington, DC, 1986-88; free-lance writer and editor, 1988-. **Publications:** (Ed. and contrib.) The Post-Containment Handbook, 1990; Soviet Sources (novel), 1990; Twilight of Empire: Inside the Crumbling Soviet Bloc, 1991; The Killer Department, 1993; Cover Story (novel), 1994; (with B. Rotella) Golf Is Not a Game of Perfect, 1995; Dispatch from a Cold Country (novel), 1996; (with B. Rotema) Golf Is a Game of Confidence, 1996. **Address:** c/o Raphael Sagalyn Agency, 7201 Wisconsin Ave, Ste 675, Bethesda, MD 20814-7213, U.S.A.

CULLINGWORTH, J(ohn) Barry. See Obituaries.

CULP, Stephanie (Anne). American, b. 1947. **Genres:** Administration/Management, Design, Homes/Gardens, Self help. **Career:** The Culp Organization (consulting firm), Temecula, CA, owner, 1982-; Copley News Service, syndicated columnist, 1995-99. White House Conference on Small Business, delegate from southern California, 1986. Guest on television and radio programs; National Organization of Professional Organizers, founding member, past president. **Publications:** How to Get Organized When You Don't Have the Time, 1986; (with J.R. Reed) Authentic Craftsmanship in Interior Design, 1989; How to Conquer Clutter, 1989; Conquering the Paper Pile-Up, 1990; Organized Closets and Storage for Every Room in the House, 1990; Streamlining Your Life, 1991; You Can Find More Time for Yourself Every Day, 1994; Stephanie Culp's 12 Month Organizer and Project Planner, 1995; 611 Ways to Do More in a Day, 1998. Contributor to periodicals. **Address:** The Culp Organization, PO Box 890700, Temecula, CA 92589-0700, U.S.A.

CULPER, Felix. See MCCAUGHREAN, Geraldine (Jones).

CULVER, Timothy J. See WESTLAKE, Donald E.

CULYER, A(nthony) J(ohn). British, b. 1942. **Genres:** Economics, Medicine/Health, Bibliography. **Career:** Professor of Economics, University of York, since 1979 (Lecturer and Reader, 1969-79; Deputy Director, Institute of Social and Economic Research, 1971-82). Tutor and Assistant Lecturer, Exeter University, 1965-69; Visiting Professor at Queen's University, Kingston, Ont., 1976, Otago University, NZ, 1979, Australian National University, Canberra, 1979, and Trent University, Peterborough, Ont., 1985-86; professor, University of Toronto, 1989-; Pro-Vice-Chancellor, University of York, 1992-94, Deputy, 1994-; Institut fur Medizinische Informatic und Systemforschung, Munich, 1990. **Publications:** The Economics of Social Policy, 1973; (with M.H. Cooper) Health Economics, 1973; Economic Policies and Social Goals, 1974; Need and the National Health Service, 1976; (with J. Wiseman and A. Walker) Annotated Bibliography of Health Economics, 1977; (with V. Halberstadt) Human Resources and Public Finance, 1977; Measuring Health: Lessons for Ontario, 1978; The Political Economy of Social Policy, 1980; (with B. Horisberger) Economic and Medical Evolution of Health Care Technologies, 1983; (with others) The International Bibliography of Health Economics, 1986; Health Care Expenditure in Canada: Myth and Reality, Past and Future, 1988; The Economics of Health, 2 vols., 1991; The Political Economy of Social Policy, 1991; Svensk Sjukvard: Basti Varlden?, 1992; Equity in Health Care, 1992. EDITOR: (with K. Wright) Economic Aspects of Health Services, 1978; Health Indicators, 1983; (with G. Terny) Public Finance and Social Policy, 1985; Economics, 1985; (with B. Jonsson) Public and Private Health Services, 1986; Standards for Socioeconomic Evaluation of Health Care Products and Services, 1990; (co-) Competition in Health Care: Reforming the NHS, 1990; (with A. Wagstaff) Reforming Health Care Systems: Experiments with the NHS, 1996. **Address:** The Laurels, Barmby Moor, York YO42 4EJ, England.

CUMBERLEGE, Marcus (Crossley). (Claude Michael Bulstrode). British (born France), b. 1938. **Genres:** Poetry. **Career:** English teacher, British Council, Lima, Peru, 1957-58, 1962-63; advertising executive, Ogilvy & Mather, London, 1964-67; English teacher, Lycee International, St. Germain, 1968-70; lecturer, University of Lugano, 1978-82. Free-lance translator, Bruges, Belgium, 1982-97. **Publications:** Oases, 1968; Poems for Quena and Tabla, 1970; Running towards a New Life, 1973; The Poetry Millionaire, 1977; Firelines, 1977; La Nuit Noire, 1977; Twintig Vriendelijke Vragen, 1977; (with O. Davis) Bruges, Brugge, 1978; Northern Lights, 1981; Life Is a Flower, 1981; Flemish Fables, 1982; Sweet Poor Hobo, 1984; Things I Cannot Change, 1993; The Best Is Yet to Be, 1997; The Moon, the Blackbird and the Falling Leaf, 1999; Once I Had a Secret Love, 2000; Angels at Work, 2002. **Address:** Eekhoutstraat 42, 8000 Brugge, Belgium. **Online address:** marcuscumberlege@easynet.be

CUMMING, Carman. Canadian, b. 1932. **Genres:** Writing/Journalism. **Career:** Canadian Press, Toronto, Ontario, Canada, editor, 1955-60, New York, NY, editor, 196062, United Nations correspondent and feature writer, New York, 1962-65; parliamentary correspondent and editor, Ottawa, 1966-69; Ottawa Journal, copy editor, summer, 1970; CBC News, reporter/editor, summer, 1971; CBC Radio program Capital Report, press analyst, 1971-73; Carleton University, sessional lecturer, 1968-69, assistant professor, 1969-71, associate professor, 1971-83, acting director of School of Journalism, 1971-72, professor, 1983-91, adjunct professor, 1991-97. Exchange professor, University of Western Ontario, 1973-74. **Publications:** (with M. Cardinal and P. Johansen) Canadian News Services, 1981; Secret Craft: The Journalism of Edward Farrer, 1992; Sketches from a Young Country: The Images of Grip Magazine, 1999; Devil's Game: The Civil War Intrigues of Charles A. Dunham, 2004. **Address:** 22 Harvard Ave, Ottawa, ON, Canada K1S 4Z3. **Online address:** Carmancumming@aol.com

CUMMING, Elizabeth (Skeoch). Scottish, b. 1948. **Genres:** Art/Art history. **Career:** Dundee City Art Gallery, Dundee, Scotland, assistant keeper of fine art, 1972-75; Edinburgh City Art Centre, Edinburgh, Scotland, keeper of fine art collections, 1975-84; free-lance art historian, 1984-92, 2000-; Edinburgh College of Art, Edinburgh, lecturer in design history, 1992-2000. University of Dundee, part-time lecturer, 1973-75; University of Edinburgh, lecturer, 1990-91; organizer of exhibitions for Scottish Arts Council and Glasgow Museums and Art Galleries. **Publications:** (with W. Kaplan) The Arts and Crafts Movement, 1991; Glasgow 1900, 1992; Phoebe Anna Traquair, 1993; (with N.G. Bowe) Arts and Crafts Movements in Dublin and Edinburgh, 1998. Contributor to essay collections and periodicals. **Address:** 29 Liberton Brae, Edinburgh EH16 6AG, Scotland. **Online address:** e_cumming@lineone.net

CUMMINGS, Pat (Marie). American, b. 1950. **Genres:** Young adult fiction, Illustrations. **Career:** Freelance author and illustrator, 1974-; adjunct professor of illustration, Parsons School of Design. **Publications:** SELF-ILLUSTRATED FOR CHILDREN: Jimmy Lee Did It, 1985; C.L.O.U.D.S., 1986; Clean Your Room, Harvey Moon!, 1991; Petey Moroni's Camp

Runamok Diary, 1992; Carousel, 1994; Dear Mabel!, 1996; The Blue Lake, 1997; My Aunt Came Back, 1998; Purrrrr, 1999; Angel Baby, 2000; Ananse and the Lizard, 2002. EDITOR & COMPILER: Talking with Artists, 1991, rev. ed., 1999; Talking with Artists 2, 1995; (with L.C. Minor) Talking with Adventurers, 1998. Illustrator of books by J.D. Barrett, J. Caines, E. Greenfield, N. Grimes, E. Howard, C. Jameson, M.R. MacDonald, T. MacDougall, A.S. Medearis, M. Stolz, M.P. Walter, C. Warren, E. Winthrop. **Address:** c/o Author Mail, HarperCollins, 1350 Avenue of the Americas, New York, NY 10019-4703, U.S.A.

CUMMINGS, Sally (Nikoline). American. **Genres:** Business/Trade/Industry. **Career:** Educator, editor, and author. Keele University, Staffordshire, England, temporary lecturer, 1995; University of Edinburgh, Edinburgh, Scotland, temporary lecturer in politics, 1998-1999, lecturer in politics, 1999-2003; St. Andrews University, St. Andrews, Scotland, lecturer in politics, 2003-. Held research posts with NATO and the European Union. **Publications:** (with Clifford Chance and Nigel Peters) Doing Business in Kazakstan, 1995; Kazakhstan: Centre-Periphery Relations, 2000; (editor, with Mary Buckley) Kosovo: Perceptions of War and Its Aftermath, 2001; (editor and contriributor) Power and Change in Central Asia, 2002; (editor and contributor) Oil, Transition, and Security in Central Asia, 2003; Understanding Central Asia, 2003. Author of various scholarly papers. **Address:** School of International Relations, University of St. Andrews, St. Andrews, Fife KY16 9AL, Scotland. **Online address:** snc@and.ac.uk

CUMMINS, C. Lyle, Jr. American, b. 1930. **Genres:** History, Technology, Biography. **Career:** H.J. Brunnier, San Francisco, CA, structural engineer, 1951-54; C.L. Cummins, Sausalito, CA, designer, development engineer, and marketing representative, 1956-63; Jacobs Manufacturing Co., West Hartford, CT, product engineer, 1963-67; product manager for Buehler Corp., Indianapolis, IN, and American Bosch Corp., Springfield, MA, 1967-70; University of Portland, OR, assistant professor of mechanical engineering, 1970-72; Servojet Electronic Systems, director. Society of Automotive Engineers, fellow, 1994. **Publications:** Internal Fire, 1976, 3rd ed., 2000; Diesel's Engine, Vol. I, 1993; The Diesel Odyssey of Clessie Cummins, 1998. **Address:** Carnot Press, PO Box 301, Wilsonville, OR 97070-0301, U.S.A. **Online address:** clessie88@aol.com

CUNLIFFE, Barry. British, b. 1939. **Genres:** Archaeology/Antiquities. **Career:** Bristol University, lecturer in archaeology, 1963-66; Southampton University, professor of archaeology, 1966-72; University of Oxford, professor of European archaeology, 1972-. **Publications:** Roman Bath Discovered, 1971, rev. ed., 1985; Fishbourne: Roman Palace and Its Gardens, 1971; The Cradle of England, 1973; The Making of the English, 1973; The Regni, 1973; Iron Age Communities in Britain, 1974, rev. ed., 1991; Rome and the Barbarians, 1975; Iron Age Sites in Central South Britain, 1976; (with T. Rowley) The Origins of Urbanization in Barbarian Europe, 1976; Hengistbury Head, 1978; Rome and Her Empire, 1978; The Celtic World, 1979; Danebury: Anatomy of an Iron Age Hillfort, 1983; Heywood Sumner's Wessex, 1985; The City of Bath, 1986; Greeks, Romans and Barbarians, 1988; Danebury, 1993; Wessex to A.D. 1000, 1993; The Oxford Illustrated Prehistory of Europe, 1994; The Book of Iron Age Britain, 1995; The Ancient Celts, 1997; Facing the Ocean, 2001; The Extraordinary Voyage of Pytheas the Greek, 2001.

CUNNINGHAM, Dru. American. **Genres:** Children's fiction. **Career:** Author, journalist, and teacher. Celina School System, Celina, OH, and Bellefontaine School System, Bellefontaine, OH, elementary teacher, c. 1970s; Bowling Green Christian Academy, Bowling Green, OH, elementary teacher, 1992-. **Publications:** It's Fun to Choose, 1988; The Most Wonderful Place to Live, 1995. Contributor of interviews, articles, and poems to magazines and newspapers. **Address:** 418 North Main St., Bowling Green, OH 43402, U.S.A.

CUNNINGHAM, Frank R. American, b. 1937. **Genres:** Film, Humanities, Intellectual history, Literary criticism and history, Essays. **Career:** Elwyn Institute, Media, PA, instructor, Haverford College, director of tutoring, summer, 1966; Lehigh University, Bethlehem, PA, instructor in English, 1966-68; Franklin and Marshall College, Lancaster, PA, assistant professor of English, 1968-69; Fordham University, Bronx, NY, assistant professor of English, 1970-71; Kansas State University, Manhattan, assistant professor of English, 1971-73; San Jose State University, CA, assistant professor of English, 1973-76, assistant professor of writing, 1977-78; Jagiellonian University, Cracow, Poland, senior Fulbright lecturer in American literature & civilization, 1976-77; University of South Dakota, Vermillion, associate professor, 1978-84, professor of American literature & civilization, 1984-. Summer visiting scholar at Yale University, 1980, Princeton University,

1981, and University of California, Berkeley, 1990, 1991; research associate, University of Nebraska, Lincoln, 1984-86, and University of Minnesota-Twin Cities, 1986-88; Yale University, visiting fellow, 1999-2000, 2004-. South Dakota Public Radio, host of an educational jazz program, 1982-84. **Publications:** Sidney Lumet: Film and Literary Vision, 1991, 2nd ed., 2001; Lumet's Fail Safe, 2005. Work represented in anthologies. Contributor of articles and reviews to journals and magazines.

CUNNINGHAM, Hugh. British, b. 1942. **Genres:** History. **Career:** University of Sierra Leone, Freetown, lecturer in history, 1963-66; University of Kent at Canterbury, lecturer, 1969-84, senior lecturer, 1984-91, professor of social history, 1991-2001, emeritus professor, 2001-. **Publications:** The Volunteer Force: A Political and Social History, 1859-1908, 1975; Leisure in the Industrial Revolution, 1980; The Children of the Poor: Representations of Childhood since the Seventeenth Century, 1991; Children and Childhood in Western Society since 1500, 1996, 2nd ed., 2005; The Challenge of Democracy: Britain 1832-1918, 2001. **Address:** School of History, Rutherford College, University of Kent at Canterbury, Canterbury CT2 7NX, England. **Online address:** H.Cunningham@kent.ac.uk

CUNNINGHAM, James V. American, b. 1923. **Genres:** Civil liberties/Human rights, Cultural/Ethnic topics, Economics, Human relations/Parenting, Institutions/Organizations, Local history/Rural topics, Money/Finance, Politics/Government, Public/Social administration, Race relations, Regional/Urban planning, Social commentary, Social work, Sociology, Urban studies. **Career:** Independent Voters of Illinois, Chicago, organizer, 1951-56; Hyde Park Kenwood Community Conference, Chicago, organizer, 1956-59; Action-Housing, Inc., Pittsburgh, PA, organizer, 1959-66; University of Pittsburgh, professor, 1966-97, professor emeritus, 1997-; writer. **Publications:** The Resurgent Neighborhood, 1965; Urban Leadership in the Sixties, 1970. WITH OTHERS: A New Public Policy in Neighborhood Preservation, 1979; Building Neighborhood Organizations, 1983; Organizing for Community Controlled Development: Renewing Civil Society, 2003. **Address:** University of Pittsburgh, 2117 CL, Pittsburgh, PA 15260, U.S.A.

CUNNINGHAM, Keith. American, b. 1939. **Genres:** Cultural/Ethnic topics. **Career:** Northern Arizona University, Flagstaff, instructor, 1969-72, assistant professor, 1972-78, associate professor, 1978-81, professor of English, 1981-. Library of Congress, American Folklife Center, field worker for Nevada Folklife Project, 1979-80; Arizona Commission on the Arts, folklorist in residence, 1990-. **Publications:** (ed.) The Oral Tradition of the American West, 1990; American Indians' Kitchen-Table Stories, 1992; Two Zuni Artists, 1998. Contributor to anthologies and professional journals. **Address:** Dept of English, Box 6032, Northern Arizona University, Flagstaff, AZ 86011, U.S.A. **Online address:** keith.cunningham@nau.edu

CUNNINGHAM, Marion (Elizabeth). American, b. 1922. **Genres:** Food and Wine. **Career:** Cookbook author and restaurant consultant. **Publications:** (ed.) The Fannie Farmer Cookbook, 13th ed. 1990; The Fannie Farmer Baking Book, 1984; The Breakfast Book, 1987; The Supper Book, 1992; Cooking with Children, 1995. **Address:** 1147 Northgate Rd, Walnut Creek, CA 94598, U.S.A.

CUNNINGHAM, Patricia (A.). American. **Genres:** Fashion/Costume, Women's studies and issues. **Career:** Bowling Green State University, Bowling Green, OH, professor, 1979-85; University of Connecticut, Storrs, associate professor, 1984-95; Ohio State University, Columbus, associate professor, 1996-. **Publications:** Reforming Women's Fashion: 1850-1920, 2002; Politics Health and Art, 2003. EDITOR: (with S.V. Lab) Dress and Popular Culture, 1990; (with S.V. Lab) Dress in American Culture, 1993. **Address:** 265 Campbell Hall, 1787 Neil Ave, Ohio State University, Columbus, OH 43210, U.S.A.

CUNNINGHAM, Valentine. American, b. 1944. **Genres:** Adult non-fiction. **Career:** Professor, author. St. John's College, Oxford, junior resident fellow, 1969-72; University of Oxford, lecturer in English, 1972-, chairman of English faculty, 1984-87, professor of English language and literature, 1996-; Corpus Christi College, Oxford, England, fellow and tutor in English, beginning 1972, dean, 1980-91; senior tutor, 1991-94; professor of English, fellow. University of Konstanz, Germany, visiting professor; BBC broadcaster. Judge for literary prizes, including Booker Prize, 1992, 1998, and Commonwealth Writers Prize, 2000-01. **Publications:** Everywhere Spoken Against: Dissent in the Victorian Novel, 1975; British Writers of the Thirties, 1988; In the Reading Gaol: Postmodernity, Texts, and History, 1994; Reading after Theory, 2002. EDITOR: The Penguin Book of Spanish Civil War Verse, 1980; Spanish Front: Writers on the Civil War, 1986; Adam Bede/George Eliot, 1996; The Victorians: An Anthology of Poetry and Poetics,

2000. Contributor to journals, newspapers and books. **Address:** Corpus Christi College, Oxford OX1 4JF, England. **Online address:** valentine.cunningham@ccc.ox.ac.uk

CUNO, Kenneth M. American, b. 1950. **Genres:** Area studies. **Career:** American University, Cairo, Egypt, visiting assistant professor of history, 1985-90; University of Illinois at Urbana-Champaign, assistant professor of history, 1990-96, associate professor, 1996-; has conducted extracurricular discussions on Middle Eastern topics, and has presented papers at seminars and conferences. **Publications:** The Pasha's Peasants: Land, Society, and Economy in Lower Egypt, 1740-1858, 1992. Contributor to books. Contributor of articles and reviews to periodicals. **Address:** The University of Illinois, Department of History, 309 Gregory Hall, 810 South Wright St., Urbana, IL 61801, U.S.A.

CUOMO, George (Michael). American, b. 1929. **Genres:** Novels, Poetry, Novellas/Short stories, Criminology/True Crime. **Career:** Professor of English, University of Massachusetts at Amherst, 1973-94, Emeritus, 1994. Professor of English, California State University at Hayward, 1965-73. **Publications:** Becoming a Better Reader, 1960; Jack Be Nimble (novel), 1963; Bright Day, Dark Runner (novel), 1964; Among Thieves (novel), 1968; Sing, Choirs of Angels (short stories), 1970; The Hero's Great Great Great Great Great Grandson (novel), 1971; Geronimo and the Girl Next Door (poetry), 1974; Pieces from a Small Bomb (novel), 1976; Becoming a Better Reader and Writer, 1978; Family Honor (novel), 1983; Trial by Water (novel), 1993; A Couple of Cops (non-fiction), 1995. **Address:** 121A Brattle St., Cambridge, MA 02138, U.S.A. **Online address:** JGCUOMO@AOL.COM

CUOMO, Mario (Matthew). American, b. 1932. **Genres:** Politics/Government, Urban studies. **Career:** Lawyer: Corner, Finn, Cuomo & Charles, NYC, partner, 1963-75; St. John's University School of Law, Jamaica, NY, professor of law, 1963-73; secretary of state, New York, 1975-78; lt. governor of New York, 1979-82; governor of New York, 1983-94. **Publications:** The Forest Hills Controversy, 1972; Forest Hills Diary: The Crisis of Low-Income Housing, 1974; Diaries of Mario M. Cuomo: The Campaign for Governor, 1984; (with H. Holzer) Lincoln on Democracy: An Anthology, 1990; More Than Words: The Speeches of Mario M. Cuomo, 1993; The New York Idea, An Experiment in Democracy, 1994; Reason to Believe, 1995; Blue Spruce, 1999; Why Lincoln Matters: Today More than Ever, 2004.

CURL, James Stevens. British, b. 1937. **Genres:** Architecture, Art/Art history, Design, History, Humanities, Urban studies, Biography, Reference. **Career:** Survey of London, architectural ed., 1970-73; Scottish Civic Trust, European Architectural Heritage Year, architectural adviser, 1973-75; Herts. County Council, sr. planning officer, 1975-78; Leicester School of Architecture, sr. lecturer, 1978-87, professor of architectural history and sr. research fellow, 1987-98; Centre for Conservation Studies, Leicester, emeritus professor of architectural history, 1998-2000; Queen's University of Belfast, professor of architectural history and senior research fellow, 2000-02. **Publications:** The Victorian Celebration of Death, 1972, rev. ed., 2004; The Erosion of Oxford, 1977; English Architecture: An Illustrated Glossary, 1977; Mausolea in Ulster, 1978; Moneymore and Draperstown, 1979; Classical Churches in Ulster, 1980; The History, Architecture, and Planning of the Estates of the Fishmongers Company in Ulster, 1981; The Life and Work of Henry Roberts (1803-76), Architect, 1983; The Londonderry Plantation, 1609-1914, 1986; English Architecture, 1987; Victorian Architecture, 1990; The Art and Architecture of Freemasonry, 1991, rev. ed., 2002; Classical Architecture, 1992, rev. ed., 2001; Encyclopaedia of Architectural Terms, 1993; Georgian Architecture, 1993, rev. ed., 2003; Egyptomania, 1994; Oxford Dictionary of Architecture, 1999-2000; The Honourable the Irish Society 1608-2000, 2000; Kensal Green Cemetery, 2001; Death and Architecture, 2002; Piety Proclaimed, 2002; The Egyptian Revival, 2005; The Oxford Dictionary of Architecture and Landscape Architecture, 2005. **Address:** 15 Torgrange, Holywood, Down BT18 0NG, Northern Ireland. **Online address:** jscurl@btinternet.com

CURLEE, Lynn. American, b. 1947. **Genres:** Children's fiction. **Career:** Exhibiting gallery artist, 1973-; freelance writer, 1991-. **Publications:** SELF-ILLUSTRATED FOR CHILDREN: Ships of the Air, 1996; Into the Ice: The Story of Arctic Explorations, 1997. Illustrator of books by D. Haseley. **Address:** PO Box 699, Jamesport, NY 11947, U.S.A.

CURLEY, Marianne. New Zealander, b. 1959. **Genres:** Children's fiction. **Career:** Author. Electricity Commission of New South Wales, New South Wales, Australia, senior legal stenographer, 1976-81; Benchmark Frames and

Trusses, secretary/receptionist, 1991; Skillshare Coffs Harbour, part-time trainer, 1992; part-time teacher, 1992-96; word processing operator, 1997; private computer instructor, 1997. **Publications:** Old Magic, 2000; The Named, 2002. **Address:** 43 Nariah Crescent, Toormina, NSW 2452, Australia. **Online address:** mcurley@austrais.aunz.com

CURNOW, Jonathan. *See* **SHARP, Clifford Henry.**

CURRAN, Charles E. American, b. 1934. **Genres:** Philosophy, Theology/Religion. **Career:** Assistant Professor to Professor of Moral Theology, Catholic University of America, Washington, DC, 1965-89; Elizabeth Scurlock University Professor of Human Values, Southern Methodist University, Dallas, 1991-. President, Catholic Theological Society of America, 1969-70, American Society of Christian Ethics, 1971-72, and American Theological Society, 1989-90; Sr. Research Scholar, Kennedy Center for Bioethics, Georgetown University, Washington, DC, 1972. **Publications:** Christian Morality Today, 1966; A New Look at Christian Morality, 1968; (co-author) Dissent in and for the Church, 1969; (co-author) The Responsibility of Dissent, 1969; Contemporary Problems in Moral Theology, 1970; Catholic Moral Theology in Dialogue, 1972; Crisis in Priestly Ministry, 1972; Politics, Medicine and Christian Ethics: A Dialogue with Paul Ramsey, 1973; New Perspectives in Moral Theology, 1974; Ongoing Revision: Studies in Moral Theology, 1975; Themes in Fundamental Moral Theology, 1977; Issues in Sexual and Medical Ethics, 1978; Transition and Tradition in Moral Theology, 1979; American Catholic Social Ethics, 1982; Moral Theology, 1982; Critical Concerns in Moral Theology, 1984; Directions in Catholic Social Ethics, 1985; Directions in Fundamental Moral Theology, 1985; Faithful Dissent, 1986; Toward an American Catholic Theology, 1988; Sexualitat und Ethik, 1988; Tensions in Moral Theology, 1988; Catholic Higher Education, Theology and Academic Freedom, 1990; The Living Tradition of Catholic Moral Theology, 1992; The Church and Morality, 1993; History and Contemporary Issues, 1996; The Origins of Moral Theology in the United States, 1997; The Catholic Moral Tradition Today, 1999; Moral Theology at the End of the Century, 1999; Catholic Social Teaching 1891-Present, 2002; The Moral Theology of Pope John Paul II, 2005. EDITOR: Absolutes in Moral Theology?, 1968; Contraception: Authority and Dissent, 1969; (with G.J. Dyer) Shared Responsibility in the Local Church, 1970; (with R.A. McCormick and others) Readings in Moral Theology, 14 vols., 1979-2004; Moral Theology: Challenges for the Future, 1990. **Address:** 317 Dallas Hall, PO Box 750317, Southern Methodist University, Dallas, TX 75275-0317, U.S.A.

CURREY, Richard. American, b. 1949. **Genres:** Autobiography/Memoirs, Novels, Novellas/Short stories, Adult non-fiction. **Career:** Writer. D. H. Lawrence Fellow in Literature, 1981; National Endowment for the Arts Fellow, 1982, 1987. Recipient of Santa Fe Festival of the Arts Poetry Prize, 1979, Associated Writing Progs; Pushcart Prize, 1991; writers Film Project, 1996-97. Short Fiction Prize, 1984, O. Henry Prize, 1988, and Vietnam Veterans of American Excellence in the Arts Award, 1989; Western States Arts Federation Grantee, 1992. **Publications:** Crossing Over: A Vietnam Journal, 1980; Fatal Light (novel), 1988 (Ernest Hemingway Foundation Special Citation); The Wars of Heaven (short stories), 1990; Crossing Over: The Vietnam Stories, 1993; Lost Highway (novel), 1997; Rio Grande (nonfiction), 1998. **Address:** 160 Washington, S.E., #185, Albuquerque, NM 87108, U.S.A.

CURRIE, Dwight. American, b. 1953. **Genres:** Inspirational/Motivational Literature. **Career:** Taught high school English in Iowa for three years; in advertising and public relations in New York, NY and surrounding area for ten years; co-owner of Misty Valley Books. **Publications:** How We Behave at the Feast: Reflections on an Age of Plenty, 2000, as An Invitation to the Feast: Celebrating Life in an Age Plenty, 2001. **Address:** 308 Bayside Parkway, Nokomis, FL 34275, U.S.A.

CURRIE, Edwina. British, b. 1946. **Genres:** Novels, Humor/Satire. **Career:** British Parliament, London, England, Conservative member of House of Commons for Derbyshire, 1983-. Conservative Group for Europe, chairperson, 1995-; European Movement, vice-chairperson of British branch, 1995-. **Publications:** Lifelines (nonfiction), 1989; What Women Want (essays), 1990; Three-Line Quips (humor), 1991; A Parliamentary Affair (novel), 1994; A Woman's Place (novel), 1996. **Address:** House of Commons, London SW1A 0AA, England.

CURRIE, Katy. *See* **KYLE, Susan S(paeth).**

CURRIE, Philip J(ohn). Canadian, b. 1949. **Genres:** Earth sciences, Zoology. **Career:** Redpath Museum, Montreal, Quebec, geology technician, 1974-76; Provincial Museum, Edmonton, Alberta, curator of paleontology,

1976-81; Tyrrell Museum of Palaeontology, Drumheller, Alberta, curator of dinosaurs, 1981-. **Publications:** (ed. with K. Carpenter) Dinosaur Systematics: Approaches and Perspectives, 1990; The Flying Dinosaurs, 1991; Dinosaur Renaissance (in Japanese), 1994; (with Z.V. Spinar) The Great Dinosaurs: A Story of the Giants' Evolution, 1994; (with E.B. Koppelhus) Questions about Dinosaurs, 1996; (with K. Padian) Encyclopedia of Dinosaurs, 1997; (with E. Felber and J. Sovak) A Moment in Time with Troodon, 1997; (with Felber and Sovak) A Moment in Time with Albertosaurus, 1997; (with J. Sovak) Yazawa Handbook Series (in Japanese), 1997; (with E.B. Koppelhus and J. Sovak) A Moment in Time with Centrosaurus, 1998; (with C. Mastin) The Newest and Coolest Dinosaurs, 1998; (with E.B. Koppelhus and J. Sovak) A Moment in Time with Sinosauropteryx, 1999; (with E.B. Koppelhus, M. Shugar, and J. Wright) Feathered Dragons, 2004. **Address:** Tyrrell Museum of Palaeontology, PO Box 7500, Drumheller, AB, Canada T0J 0Y0. **Online address:** philip.currie@gov.ab.ca

CURRIE, Stephen. (Tristan Howard). American, b. 1960. **Genres:** History, Children's fiction, Children's non-fiction, Education, Reference. **Career:** Poughkeepsie Day School, Poughkeepsie, NY, teacher, 1982-. Dutchess Community College, Saturday Enrichment Program teacher, 1986-89. **Publications:** Music in the Civil War, 1992; Problem Play, 1993; Birthday-a-Day, 1995; We Have Marched Together, 1995; Adoption, 1997; Issues in Sports, 1998; Slavery, 1998; Life in a Wild West Show, 1998; The Olympics, 1999; Abortion, 1999; The Polynesians, 2000; Life of a Slave on a Southern Plantation, 2000; The Liberator, 2000; Immigration, 2001; Women Inventors, 2001; Thar She Blows, 2001. Forthcoming: Sweet Betsy; Life in the Trenches in World War I; Polar Explorers. Contributor to periodicals; author of math, science, and social studies educational materials; book reviewer; author of Leftovers series and other juvenile series fiction. **Address:** 14 Oakwood Blvd, Poughkeepsie, NY 12603-4112, U.S.A. **Online address:** sacurrie@idsi.net

CURRY, Constance (Winifred). American, b. 1933. **Genres:** History. **Career:** Collegiate Council for the United Nations, NYC, national field representative, 1957-59; US National Student Association, Atlanta, GA, director of Southern Student Human Relations Project, 1960-64; American Friends Service Committee, Atlanta, southern field representative, 196475; Atlanta Office of Human Services, Atlanta, director, 1975-90; writer, 1990-. **Publications:** Silver Rights: One Family's Struggle for Justice in America, 1995; (with A. Henry) The Fire Ever Burning, 2000; (ed. and contrib.) Deep in Our Hearts: Nine White Women in the Freedom Movement, 2000. Contributor to journals. **Address:** 930 Myrtle St NE, Atlanta, GA 30309, U.S.A.

CURRY, G(len) David. American, b. 1948. **Genres:** Military/Defense/Arms control, Social commentary. **Career:** University of South Alabama, Mobile, assistant professor, 1976-79, associate professor of sociology, 1979-83; SPSS, Inc., Chicago, IL, statistical writer, 1987-88; University of Chicago, Chicago, lecturer in statistical methods and director of National Gang Intervention and Suppression Project, 1988-89; West Virginia University, Morgantown, associate professor of sociology, 1989-94; University of Missouri-St. Louis, associate professor of Criminology, 1994-; writer. University of Notre Dame, research fellow at Center for Civil Rights, 1977-80; University of Chicago, lecturer, 1981; Safer Foundation, research associate, 1984-87; research associate and analyst at Ogburn Stouffer Center for Social Research, Center for the Study of Social Policy, and National Opinion Research Center; lecturer at Loyola University of Chicago. Mobile Rape Crisis Center, volunteer counselor, 1977-80; Penelope House (shelter for battered women), volunteer data processor and statistician, 1979-83, member of advisory board, 1981-82; Gulf Coast Vietnam-Era Veterans Readjustment Counseling Center, team leader, 1981-82; Chicago Intervention Network, member of long range planning committee, 1986-87; Operation PUSH, member of international veterans committee, 1986-88. Military service: U.S. Army, 1969-72; served in Vietnam; became captain. **Publications:** Sunshine Patriots: Punishment of the Vietnam Offender, University of Notre Dame Press, 1985. (With Irving A. Spergel) A Survey of Fifty-four Communities and Six Sites: Gang Problems and Responses, Volume 2, U.S. Government Printing Office, forthcoming. **Address:** Department of Criminology & Criminal Justice, University of Missouri-St. Louis, 8001 Natural Bridge Rd., St. Louis, MO 63121, U.S.A.

CURRY, Jane (Louise). American, b. 1932. **Genres:** Children's fiction, Young adult fiction, Mythology/Folklore. **Career:** Writer, 1965-; Lecturer, Stanford University, CA, 1987-88 (Teaching Assistant, 1959-61, 1964-65; Acting Instructor, 1967-68; Instructor, 1983-84). Art Instructor, Los Angeles City Schools, CA, 1955-59. Fulbright Fellow, Royal Holloway College, 1961-62, and Leverhulme Fellow, University College, 1965-66, University of

London. **Publications:** Down from the Lonely Mountain: California Indian Tales, 1965; Beneath the Hill, 1967; The Sleepers, 1968; The Change-Child, 1969; The Daybreakers, 1970; Mindy's Mysterious Miniature, (in UK as the Housenapper), 1970; Over the Sea's Edge, 1971; The Ice Ghosts Mystery, 1972; The Lost Farm, 1974; Parsley Sage, Rosemary and Time, 1975; The Watchers, 1975; The Magical Cupboard, 1976; Poor Tom's Ghost, 1977; The Birdstones, 1977; The Bassumtyte Treasure, 1978; Ghost Lane, 1979; The Wolves of Aam, 1981; The Shadow Dancers, 1983; The Great Flood Mystery, 1985; The Lotus Cup, 1986; Back in the Beforetime: Tales of the California Indians, 1987; Me, Myself and I, 1987; The Big Smith Snatch, 1989; Little Little Sister, 1989; What the Dickens!, 1991; The Great Smith House Hustle, 1993; The Christmas Knight, 1993; Robin Hood and His Merry Men, 1994; Robin Hood in the Greenwood, 1995; Moon Window, 1996; Dark Shade, 1998; Turtle Island: Stories of the Algonquin Peoples, 1999; A Stolen Life, 1999; (reteller) The Wonderful Sky Boat, 2001; The Egyptian Box, 2002; Hold up the Sky, 2003; Brave Cloelia, 2004; The Black Canary, 2005. **Address:** c/o Simon & Schuster Children's Publishing Division, 1230 Avenue of the Americas, New York, NY 10020, U.S.A.

CURRY, Neil. British, b. 1937. **Genres:** Poetry. **Career:** University of Guelph, Ontario, lecturer, 1964-65; schoolteacher in England, 1967-72; high school English teacher and department head in Ulverston, England, 1972-89; Chetwynde School, Cumbria, England, English teacher and department head, 1989-95. **Publications:** POETRY: Between Root and Sky, 1962; The Trojan Women, Helen, and the Bacchae, 1981; Ships in Bottles, 1988; Walking to Santiago, 1992; The Bending of the Bow, 1993; (ed.) N. Nicholson, Collected Poems, 1994; Tidelines, 2000; The Road to the Gunpowder House, 2003. **Address:** 2 Trinity Gardens, Ulverston, Cumbria LA12 7UB, England.

CURRY, Richard O(rr). American, b. 1931. **Genres:** History, Politics/Government. **Career:** University of Connecticut, Storrs, American History, assistant professor, 1963-66, associate professor, 1966-71, professor, 1971-92, professor emeritus, 1992-; instructor, Pennsylvania State University, University Park, 1960-62; assistant professor, University of Pittsburgh, 1962-63. **Publications:** A House Divided: A Study of Statehood Politics and the Copperhead Movement in West Virginia, 1964; (with J. Sproat and K. Cramer) The Shaping of America, 1972; (with J. Sproat and K. Cramer) The Shaping of American Civilization, 2 vols., 1972; An Uncertain Future: Thought Control and Repression during the Reagan-Bush Era, 1992. EDITOR: The Abolitionists: Reformers or Fanatics?, 1965, as The Abolitionists, 1973; (and contrib.) Radicalism, Racism and Party Realignment: The Border States during Reconstruction, 1969, 1973; (co- and contrib) Conspiracy: The Fear of Subversion in American History, 1972; (co-) Slavery in America: Theodore Weld's American Slavery as It Is, 1972, 1979; (and co-author) Freedom at Risk: Secrecy, Censorship and Repression in the 1980s, 1988; (co- and contrib.) American Chameleon: Individualism in Trans-National Context, 1991. **Address:** 106 Windham St., Willimantic, CT 06226-2212, U.S.A.

CURTEIS, Ian (Bayley). British, b. 1935. **Genres:** Plays/Screenplays. **Career:** Acted and directed in theatres around Britain, 1956-64; Director, BBC and I.T.V. television, 1963-66. **Publications:** TELEVISION PLAYS: Beethoven; Sir Alexander Fleming, 1972; Mr. Rolls and Mr. Royce; Long Voyage Out of War (trilogy); The Folly; Second Time Around; Inferno, 1973; Philby, Burgess, and Maclean; Hess; Churchill and the Generals; Suez, 1956; Miss Morrison's Ghosts, 1982; Berenson and Duveen (trilogy), 1982; The Falklands Play, 1984; also various series. SCREENPLAYS: The Spaghetti House Siege, 1978; Man's Estate, 1982; The Man Within, 1983; Lost Empires, 1984; The Nightmare Years, 1992; The Zimmerman Telegram, 1992; Yalta, 1994. OTHER: The State Visit, 1974; A Personal Affair, 1982. **Address:** c/o Coutts and Co., Campbell's Office, 440 Strand, London WC2R 0QS, England.

CURTIN, Deane. American, b. 1951. **Genres:** Food and Wine, Philosophy. **Career:** Gustavus Adolphus College, St. Peter, MN, professor of philosophy, 1978-. **Publications:** Cooking, Eating, Thinking: Transformative Philosophies of Food, 1992; Chinnagrounder's Challenge, 1999. **Address:** Dept of Philosophy, Gustavus Adolphus College, St. Peter, MN 56082-1498, U.S.A. **Online address:** curtin@gac.edu

CURTIS, Anthony. British, b. 1926. **Genres:** Literary criticism and history. **Career:** Sunday Telegraph, London, literary ed., 1961-69; Financial Times, London, freelance writer and reviewer, 1990- (literary ed., 1970-90). **Publications:** New Developments in the French Theatre: Sartre, Camus, de Beauvoir and Anouilh, 1948; The Pattern of Maugham, 1974; Somerset Maugham, 1977; Spillington and the Whitewash Clowns, 1981; Somerset Maugham (Writers and Their Work), 1982; Before Bloomsbury: The 1890s Diaries of

Three Kensington Ladies, 2002. EDITOR: (and contrib.) The Rise and Fall of the Matinee Idol, 1974; (with J. Whitehead) Somerset Maugham: The Critical Heritage, 1987; W.S. Maugham, The Nonesuch Storytellers, 1990; (lit. ed.) On Reviewing and Reviewers, 1998. **Address:** 9 Essex Villas, London W8 7BP, England. **Online address:** anticurtis@aol.com

CURTIS, Brian. American, b. 1971. **Genres:** Adult non-fiction. **Career:** Worked as a sports reporter and anchor in Ohio; Sports Conversation (radio talk show), Virginia, former host; worked in athletic departments at University of Virginia, University of Delaware, and Ohio University; former soccer coach at collegiate and high-school levels; Fox Sports Net, Los Angeles, CA, former sports reporter and broadcaster. **Publications:** The Men of March: A Season inside the Lives of Basketball Coaches, 2003. **Address:** c/o Author Mail, Taylor Trade, 4501 Forbes Blvd, Suite 200, Lanham, MD 20706, U.S.A.

CURTIS, C(hristopher) Michael. American, b. 1934. **Genres:** Novels, Novellas/Short stories. **Career:** Atlantic Monthly, Boston, MA, senior editor, 1963-. Military service: U.S. Army, 1957. **Publications:** EDITOR: American Stories, 1990; American Stories II: Fiction from the Atlantic Monthly, 1991.

CURTIS, Christopher (Paul). American, b. 1954. **Genres:** Young adult fiction, Children's fiction. **Career:** Writer. Has worked as factory worker. **Publications:** The Watsons go to Birmingham-1963, 1995; Bud, Not Buddy, 1999 (Newbery Medal, King Medal). **Address:** c/o Charlotte Sheedy, Charlotte Sheedy Literary Agency, 65 Bleecker St., 12th Floor, New York, NY 10012, U.S.A.

CURTIS, Glade B. American, b. 1950. **Genres:** Medicine/Health. **Career:** University of Rochester, Rochester, NY, resident in obstetrics and gynecology at university-affiliated hospitals, 1979-83, chief resident at Strong Memorial Hospital, 1982-83; private practice of obstetrics and gynecology, Sandy, UT, 1983-. National Board of Medical Examiners, diplomate; American Board of Obstetrics and Gynecology, board certified. Alta View Hospital, member of active medical staff, 1983-, chief of obstetrics and gynecology, 1986-90; Jordan Valley Hospital, member of active medical staff, 1983-. University of Utah, clinical instructor. American Academy of Professional Coders, member of physician advisory board. Public speaker. **Publications:** My Body, My Decision: Common Female Surgeries, 1986; Your Pregnancy Week-by-Week, 1989, 3rd ed, 1998; (foreword) Drugs, Vitamins, and Minerals in Pregnancy, 1989; Your Pregnancy: Questions and Answers, 1995; Your Pregnancy over Thirty, 1997; Your Pregnancy, 1999; Your Pregnancy Recovery Guide, 1999. **Address:** 1667 Haven Glen Lane, Salt Lake City, UT 84121, U.S.A.

CURTIS, J(ulie) A. E. British, b. 1955. **Genres:** Literary criticism and history. **Career:** University of Leeds, Leeds, England, teaching assistant, 1983-86; Cambridge University, Cambridge, England, research fellow, 1986-91; Oxford University, Wolfson College, Oxford, England, lecturer in Russian, 1991-. **Publications:** Bulgakov's Last Decade: The Writer as Hero, 1987; Manuscripts Don't Burn: Mikhail Bulgakov, a Life in Letters and Diaries, 1991. **Address:** Wolfson College, Oxford University, Oxford OX2 6UD, England.

CURTIS, Jamie Lee. American, b. 1958. **Genres:** Children's fiction, Children's non-fiction. **Career:** Actress on television and in films, 1977-. **Publications:** When I Was Little: A Four-Year-Old's Memoir of Her Youth, 1993; Tell Me Again about the Night I Was Born, 1995; Today I Feel Silly and Other Moods that Make My Day, 1998. **Address:** c/o Rick Kurtzman, Creative Artists Agency, 9830 Wilshire Blvd., Beverly Hills, CA 90212-1804, U.S.A.

CURTIS, Richard. New Zealander, b. 1956. **Genres:** Plays/Screenplays. **Career:** Writer for television and motion pictures; wrote and acted as coexecutive producer of Four Weddings and a Funeral, Gramercy, 1994. **Publications:** (with S. Bell and H. Fielding) Who's Had Who: An Historical Register Containing Official Lay Lines of History from the Beginning of Time to the Present Day, 1987; Four Weddings and a Funeral: Four Appendices and a Screenplay, 1994. SCREENPLAYS: The Tall Guy, 1989; Bernard and the Genie, 1992; Four Weddings and a Funeral, 1994. TELEVISION SCRIPTS: (with others) Not the Nine O'Clock News, 1981; Blackadder's Christmas Carol (special), 1989; Rowan Atkinson: Not Just Another Pretty Face, 1992; Mr. Bean, Tiger Television, 1992; (with B. Elton) Blackadder episodes. **Address:** c/o PFD, Drury House, 34-43 Russell Street, London WC2B 5HA, England.

CURTIS, Susan. American, b. 1956. **Genres:** Social commentary, Biography, Cultural/Ethnic topics. **Career:** Florida International University,

Miami, assistant professor of U.S. history, 1986-89; Purdue University, West Lafayette, IN, professor of U.S. intellectual and religious history and American Studies, 1989-; American Studies Program, director, 1999-. **Publications:** A Consuming Faith: The Social Gospel and Modern American Culture, 1991; Dancing to a Black Man's Tune: A Life of Scott Joplin, 1994; The First Black Actors on the Great White Way, 1998. **Address:** Department of History, Purdue University, West Lafayette, IN 47907, U.S.A. **Online address:** curtis@purdue.edu

CURTIS, Tony. Welsh, b. 1946. **Genres:** Novels, Poetry, Art/Art history, Literary criticism and history. **Career:** Wilmslow Grammar School, Cheshire, teacher, 1969-71; Maltby Grammar School, Yorkshire, teacher, 1971-74; University of Glamorgan, Pontypridd, professor of poetry, 1974-. Yr Academi Gymreig (National Association of Writers in Wales), executive member, 1977-90, chairman, 1984-89; Royal Society of Literature, fellow, 2000. **Publications:** Walk down a Welsh Wind, 1972; Album, 1974; (with D. Bush and N. Jenkins) Three Young Anglo-Welsh Poets, 1974; Out of the Dark Wood (fiction), 1977; The Deer Slayers, 1978; Carnival, 1978; Preparations, 1980;Letting Go, 1983; Dannie Abse, 1985; Wales-The Imagined Nation: Essays in Cultural and National Identity, 1986; Selected Poems 1970-1985, 1986; Poems: Selected and New, 1986; The Last Candles (poems), 1989; How to Study Modern Poetry, 1989; Taken for Pearls, 1993; War Voices, 1996; The Arches, 1997; Welsh Painters Talking, 1997; Welsh Artists Talking, 2000; Heaven's Gate, 2001. EDITOR: Pembrokeshire Poems, 1975; The Art of Seamus Heaney, 1983, 4th ed., 2000; The Poetry of Pembrokeshire, 1989; The Poetry of Snowdonia, 1989; (with S. James) Love from Wales, 1991; J. Herman, Related Twilights, 2nd ed., 2002. **Address:** School of Humanities and Social Sciences, University of Glamorgan, Pontypridd, M. Glam CF37 1DL, Wales. **Online address:** profcurtis@btinternet.com

CURTISS, A(rlene) B. American, b. 1934. **Genres:** Children's fiction. **Career:** Author. Has worked as a psychotherapist, a hypnotherapist, and a family therapist. **Publications:** In the Company of Bears (picture book), 1994; Children of the Gods, 1995; Hallelujah, a Cat Comes Back, 1995. Has published essays in newspapers and has had her poetic fiction quoted in greeting cards. **Address:** 3415 Laredo Ln., Escondido, CA 92025, U.S.A.

CURZON, Clare. (Eileen-Marie Duell). Also writes as Marie Buchanan, Rhona Petrie. British, b. 1922. **Genres:** Novels, Novellas/Short stories, Mystery/Crime/Suspense, Romance/Historical. **Career:** Full-time writer. Worked as a teacher, probation officer, interpreter, translator, and social secty. **Publications:** MYSTERIES: A Leaven of Malice, 1979; Special Occasion, 1981; I Give You Five Days, 1983; Masks and Faces, 1984; The Trojan Horse, 1985; The Quest for K, 1986; Trail of Fire, 1987; Shot Bolt, 1988; Three-Core Lead, 1988; The Face in the Stone, 1989; The Blue-Eyed Boy, 1990; Cat's Cradle, 1991; First Wife, Twice Removed, 1992; Death Prone, 1992; Nice People, 1993; Past Mischief, 1996; Close Quarters, 1997; All Unwary, 1997; Guilty Knowledge, 1999; The Colour of Blood, 2000; Don't Leave Me, 2001; Dangerous Practice, 2002; A Meeting of Minds, 2003; Flawed Light, 2003; Last to Leave, 2005; The Glass Wall, 2005. CRIME FICTION AS RHONA PETRIE: Death in Deakins Wood, 1963; Murder by Precedent, 1964; Dead Loss, 1966; Foreign Bodies, 1967; MacLurg Goes West, 1968; Despatch of a Dove, 1969; Come Hell and High Water (stories), 1970; Thorne in the Flesh, 1971. MYSTERIES AS MARIE BUCHANAN: Greenshards (in U.S. as Anima), 1972; An Unofficial Breath, 1973; The Dark Backward, 1975; Morgana, 1977; The Countess of Sedgwick, 1980. **Address:** c/o David Grossman Literary Agency, 118B Holland Park Ave, London W11 4UA, England.

CURZON, David. Australian, b. 1941. **Genres:** Poetry, Theology/Religion. **Career:** United Nations, New York City, staff member, 1974-2001, chief of Central Evaluation Unit, 1988-2001. Commission of European Communities, special adviser; National Aeronautics and Space Administration, consultant; also professor of economics. **Publications:** Midrashim, 1991; Confession of Faith, 1991; Modern Poems on the Bible: An Anthology of Twentieth Century Poetry Based on Biblical Texts, 1992; The Gospels in Our Image: An Anthology of Twentieth Century Poetry Based on Biblical Texts, 1995; The View from Jacob's Ladder: One Hundred Midrashim, 1996; Dovchik (Poems, 1975-1990), 1996. Contributor to periodicals. **Address:** 254 W 82nd St Apt 2B, New York, NY 10024, U.S.A.

CUSHMAN, Karen. American, b. 1941. **Genres:** Young adult fiction. **Career:** Writer, 1990-. **Publications:** Catherine, Called Birdy, 1994; The Midwife's Apprentice, 1995; The Ballad of Lucy Whipple, 1996; Matilda Bone, 2000; Rodzina, 2003. **Address:** 5480 College Ave, Oakland, CA 94618, U.S.A.

CUSIC, Don. American, b. 1948. **Genres:** Music, Biography. **Career:** Country Music Association, staff writer, 1973-74; Record World, country and

gospel editor, 1974-76; Monument Records, director of artist development, 1976-77; New Horizon Management, co-president, 1978-79; Cashbox, country and gospel editor, 1979-80; Middle Tennessee State University, Murfreesboro, professor of recording industry, 1982-94; Belmont University, Nashville, TN, professor of music business, 1994-. **Publications:** Sandi Patti: The Voice of Gospel, 1988; The Sound of Light: A History of Gospel Music, 1990; Randy Travis: King of the New Traditionalists, 1990; The Poet as Performer, 1991; Reba McEntire: Country Music's Queen, 1991; Cowboys and the Wild West: An A-Z Guide from the Chisholm Trail to the Silver Screen, 1994; Hank Williams: The Complete Lyrics, 1994; Willie Nelson: Lyrics, 1995; Music in the Market, 1996; Eddy Arnold, 1997; Merle Haggard: Poet of the Common Man, 2002. Contributor to magazines. **Address:** Belmont University, 1900 Belmont Blvd, Nashville, TN 37212, U.S.A. **Online address:** cusicd@mail.Belmont.edu

CUSICK, Heidi Haughy. Also writes as Sandra Lee. American, b. 1946. **Genres:** Food and Wine. **Career:** Handley Cellars, Philo, CA, in charge of public relations and hospitality, 1992-95; freelance writer, 1995-. Owner of several businesses, including Brannon's Bay View Restaurant, Village Market and Deli. College of the Redwoods, culinary arts coordinator. **Publications:** Soul and Spice: African Cooking in the Americas, 1995; Sonoma: The Ultimate Winery Guide, 1995; Mendocino: The Ultimate Wine and Food Guide, in press; Bold International Pantry, in press. EDITOR: Picnics: A Country Garden 1995; Scones, Muffins, and Teacakes, 1996. Some writings appear under the pseudonym Sandra Lee. **Address:** PO Box 301, Redwood Valley, CA 95470-0301, U.S.A.

CUSK, Rachel. British (born Canada), b. 1967. **Genres:** Novels. **Publications:** NOVELS: Saving Agnes, 1992; The Temporary, 1995; The Country Life, 1997. OTHER: A Life's Work: On Becoming a Mother, 2001. **Address:** c/o The Wylie Agency, 17 Bedford Sq, London WC1B 3JA, England.

CUSSLER, Clive (Eric). American, b. 1931. **Genres:** Novels. **Career:** Discoverer of more than 60 historical shipwrecks. Bestgen & Cussler Advertising, Newport Beach, CA, owner, 1961-65; Darcy Advertising, Hollywood, CA, copy director; Mefford, Wolff and Weir Advertising, Denver, vice-president and creative director of broadcast, 1970-73. National Underwater and Marine Agency, chairman. New York Explorers Club, fellow; Royal Geographic Society, fellow. **Publications:** The Mediterranean Caper, 1973; Iceberg, 1975; Raise the Titanic, 1976; Vixen O-Three, 1978; Night Probe, 1981; Pacific Vortex, 1983; Deep Six, 1984; Cyclops, 1986; Treasure, 1988; Dragon, 1990; Sahara, 1992; Inca Gold, 1994; Shock Wave, 1995; The Sea Hunters, 1996; Flood Tide, 1997; Atlantis Found, 1999; Deep Encounter, 2001.

CUTHBERT, Margaret. American. **Genres:** Novels. **Career:** Obstetrician, gynecologist, and novelist. **Publications:** The Silent Cradle (novel), 1998. Contributor to books. **Address:** c/o Pocket Books, Simon & Schuster Bldg., 1230 Avenue of the Americas, New York, NY 10020, U.S.A.

CUTLER, Jane. American, b. 1936. **Genres:** Children's fiction. **Career:** Writer and editor. Taught writing at University of California Extension, San Francisco, and at San Francisco State University. **Publications:** JUVENILE: Family Dinner (novel), 1991; No Dogs Allowed (short stories), 1992; Darcy and Gran Don't Like Babies (picture book), 1993; My Wartime Summers (novel), 1994; Mr. Carey's Garden (picture book), 1996; Spaceman (novel), 1997; Rats! (short stories), 1996; The Song of the Molimo (novel), 1998; 'Gator Aid (novel), 1999; The Cello of Mr. O (picture book), 1999; The Birthday Doll (picture book), 2002; Leap, Frog!, 2002; Easy-to-Read Series, 2003. Contributor of short stories to periodicals. Also developed and edited reading material for children, grades K-8.

CUTLER, Stan. American. **Genres:** Novels, Plays/Screenplays, Mystery/Crime/Suspense. **Career:** Television writer and novelist beginning in 1956. Writer and producer for television series and movies. **Publications:** Best Performance by a Patsy, 1991; The Face on the Cutting Room Floor (novel), 1991; Shot on Location, 1993; Rough Cut, 1994; Cold Reading, 1997. **Address:** c/o Jane Gelfman, Gelfman Schneider Literary Agency, 250 W 57th St., New York, NY 10107, U.S.A.

CUTTER, Charles. American, b. 1936. **Genres:** Theology/Religion, Bibliography. **Career:** Jewish Theological Seminary of America, NYC, technical services librarian, 1965-68; Ohio State University, Columbus, Jewish studies bibliographer and cataloger at university library and coordinator of international programs, 1969-76; Brandeis University, Waltham, MA, lecturer in Near Eastern and Judaic studies, 1976-, head of Judaica department of University Libraries, 1976-, head of special collections department,

1988-. Hunter College of the City University of New York, reference librarian, 1967-68; American Jewish Historical Society, archival cataloger, 1979-82. **Publications:** (with M. Oppenheim) Jewish Reference Sources, 1982; (with Oppenheim) Judaica Reference Sources: A Selective, Annotated Bibliographic Guide, 1993. Contributor to library journals. **Address:** University Libraries, Brandeis University, Waltham, MA 02454, U.S.A.

CUTTING, Linda Katherine. American, b. 1954?. **Genres:** Autobiography/Memoirs. **Career:** Concert pianist for the Boston Symphony Orchestra, soloist for orchestras in the United States, and music teacher. Third Annual to Tell the Truth Conference (Long Island Regional Conference), Smithtown, NY, keynote speaker, 1998. **Publications:** Memory Slips: A Memoir of Music and Healing, 1997; In Sanctuary (novel). Contributor to books and periodicals. **Address:** c/o HarperCollins, 10 East 53rd St., New York, NY 10022, U.S.A.

CYR, Mary. American/Canadian, b. 1946. **Genres:** Music. **Career:** University of Guelph, ON, Canada, professor of music, 1992-, chairperson of department, 1992-98, director, School of Fine Art and Music, 1998-2002. Viola da gambist. **Publications:** Performing Baroque Music, 1992. **Address:** School of Fine Art and Music, University of Guelph, Guelph, ON, Canada N1G 2W1. **Online address:** mcyr@uoguelph.ca

CYTOWIC, Richard E(dmund). American, b. 1952. **Genres:** Medicine/Health, Psychology, Autobiography/Memoirs. **Career:** North Carolina Baptist Hospital/Bowman Gray, Winston-Salem, intern in medicine, ophthalmology, and neurology, 1977-78, resident in neurology, 1978-79, fellow in neurology, neuropsychology, and cerebral blood flow, 1979-80; George Washington University, Washington, DC, chief resident in neurology, 1980-81; Capitol Neurology, Washington, DC, physician and president, 1981-. Wake Forest University, assistant in neurology at Bowman Gray School of Medicine, 1978-80; Washington Hospital Center, attending physician, 1981-; Capitol Hill Hospital, chief of neurology section, 1985-88; Hambidge Center for Creative Arts and Sciences, resident fellow, 1987-89; Virginia Center for the Creative Arts, resident, 1991-92; Med-Scene Teleconferences, medical adviser, 1984-; guest on television and radio programs. **Publications:** Synesthesia: A Union of the Senses, 1989, 2nd ed., 2002; Nerve Block for Common Pains: A Manual for Primary Practitioners, 1990; The Man Who Tasted Shapes: A Neurologist Reveals the Illusion of the Rational Mind, 1993, rev. ed., 2003; The Neurological Side of Neuropsychology: Understanding and Assessing Higher Brain Functions, 1994. Work represented in anthologies. Contributor to medical journals, popular magazines. **Address:** Capitol Neurology, 4720 Blagden Terrace NW, Washington, DC 20011-3720, U.S.A. **Online address:** richard@cytowic.net

CZEKANOWSKA, Anna. Polish, b. 1929. **Genres:** Music, Essays. **Career:** University of Warsaw, Poland, associate professor, 1976-86, professor, 1986-, director of the Institute of Musicology, 1976-90, chair of department of ethnomusicology. **Publications:** Polish Folk Music: Slavonic Heritage, Polish Tradition, 1990; Studien Lum National Stil poluischer Musikgeschichte, 1990; Pathways in Ethnomusicology (essays), 2002. Also author of a textbook and scholarly books in Polish. Contributor to books. **Address:** Institute of Musicology, University of Warsaw, 01-541 Warsaw, Poland. **Online address:** czekan@mercury.ci.uw.edu.pl

CZERNEDA, Julie E(lizabeth). Canadian, b. 1955. **Genres:** Education, Science fiction/Fantasy. **Career:** University of Waterloo, Waterloo, Ontario, senior demonstrator in biology, 1979-82; writer and editor, 1985-. Czerneda Publishing Inc., president, 1991-98. **Publications:** SCIENCE FICTION: A Thousand Words for Stranger, 1997; Beholder's Eye, 1998. Work represented in anthologies. NONFICTION: Science Probe 9, with teacher's guide, 1986, 2nd ed, 1993, as Science Probe 1, 1996; Science Explorations 10, 1987, teacher's guide, 1988; Science Dimensions 8, 1991; Science Dimensions 9, 1992; Science Dimensions 9 Investigations, 1993; Career Connections: Careers for People Interested in Living Things, 1993; Career Connections: Teacher Resource Bank, Vol I, 1993, Vol II, 1995, Vol III, 1997; Career Connections: Careers for People Who Like to Work with Their Hands, 1994; Career Connections: Careers for People Interested in Communications Technology, 1995; Career Connections: Careers for People Fascinated by Government and the Law, 1995; By Design: Technology, Integration, and Exploration, 1996; All Aboard: CrossCurricular Design and Technology Activities and Strategies, 1996; Take a Technowalk to Learn about Structures and Materials, 1996; (ed. and contrib) Packing Fraction and Other Tales of Science and Imagination, 1998; No Limits: Developing Scientific Literacy Using Science Fiction, 1998. Author of teacher's materials. **Address:** 4008 Martindale Crescent, Orillia, ON, Canada L3V 6H2. **Online address:** julie.czerneda@sff.net; www.sff.net/people/Julie.Czerneda

CZIGÁNY, Lóránt (György). Hungarian, b. 1935. **Genres:** Literary criticism and history. **Career:** British Museum, London, England, special assistant, 1962-69; Szepsi Csombor Literary Circle, London, general editor, 1967-92; University of California, Berkeley, lecturer in Hungarian Studies, 1969-73; member of board of Hungarian studies at University of London, 1977-88. Writer for Radio Free Europe and British Broadcasting Corp. **Publications:** The Béla Iványi-Grünwald Collection of Hungarica, 1967; A magyar irodalom fogadtatása a viktoriánus Angliában (title means: The Reception of Hungarian Literature in Victorian England), 1976; The Oxford History of Hungarian Literature: From the Earliest Times to the Present, 1984; Nézz vissza haraggal: Államosított irodalom Magyarországon 1946-88; (title means: Look Back in Anger: Literature under State-Control, 1946-88), 1990; Gyökértelen, mint a zászló nyele (title means: Rootless like a Flagpole), 1994. **Address:** 15 Temple Fortune Lane, London NW11 7UB, England.

D

D., Joey. *See* MACAULAY, Teresa (E.).

DAALDER, Ivo H. Dutch, b. 1960. Genres: Military/Defense/Arms control. Career: Harvard University Center for Science and International Affairs, Cambridge, MA, Harvard-MacArthur pre-doctoral fellow, 1985-87, member of study group on international implications of ethnic conflict, 1994-95; International Institute for Strategic Studies, research associate, 1987-88, senior research fellow, 1988-89; National Security Council, director for global affairs, 1995-96, director for European affairs, 1996-97; Center for International and Security Studies at Maryland, College Park, research fellow, 1989-91, director of research, 1991-88; University of Maryland, School of Public Affairs, College Park, adjunct professor, 1991, visiting assistant professor, 1991-93, assistant professor, 1993-95, associate professor and director of international security and economic policy, 1995-98; Brookings Institution, Washington, DC, senior fellow in foreign policy studies. Publications: The SDI Challenge to Europe, 1987; Strategic Defences in the 1990s: Criteria for Deployment, 1991; The CFE Treaty: An Overview and an Assessment, 1991; The Nature and Practice of Flexible Response: NATO Strategy and Theater Nuclear Forces since 1967, 1991; Cooperative Arms Control: A New Agenda for the Post-Cold War Era, 1992; Stepping down the Thermonuclear Ladder: How Low Can We Go?, 1993; The Clinton Administration and Multilateral Peace Operations, 1995; Anthony Lake and the War in Bosnia, 1995; Prospects for Global Leadership Sharing, 1996; Getting to Dayton: The Making of America's Bosnia Policy, 2000; (with M.E. O'Hanlon) Winning Ugly: NATO's War to Save Kosovo, 2000; (with I.M. Destler) The National Security Council: Its Past, Present, and Future, in press; (with P.B. Starnes) Force, Order, and Global Governance, in press. EDITOR: (with T. Terriff) Rethinking the Unthinkable: New Directions in Nuclear Arms Control, 1993; (with F.G. Burwell) The United States and Europe in the Global Arena, 1998. Contributor to periodicals and newspapers. Author of policy reports, conference papers, and book reviews. Address: 9119 Cricklewood Court, Vienna, VA 22182, U.S.A.

DABNEY, Joseph Earl. American, b. 1929. Genres: Food and Wine, History, Air/Space topics, Military/Defense/Arms control, Mythology/Folklore. Career: Newspaperman in Georgia and South Carolina, 1949-65; Lockheed Aeronautical Systems Co., Marietta, Georgia, public relations officer, 1965-90. Publications: Mountain Spirits: A Chronicle of Corn Whiskey from King James' Ulster Plantation to America's Appalachians, 1974, vol. 2, Mountain Spirits II, 1980, reissued as More Mountain Spirits, 1986; HERK, Hero of the Skies, 1979, 3rd ed., 2003; Smokehouse Ham, Spoon Bread & Scuppernong Wine: The Folklore and Art of Southern Appalachian Cooking, 1998 (James Beard Cookbook of the Year Award). Address: 3966 St Clair Ct NE, Atlanta, GA 30319-1846, U.S.A. Online address: joedabney@aol.com

DABYDEEN, Cyril. Canadian (born Guyana). Genres: Novels, Novellas/Short stories, Poetry. Career: Writer and editor. Taught in Guyana, 1961-70; Algonquin College, communications lecturer, 1975-81; University of Ottawa, professor of creative writing and English, 1982-. Ottawa Journal, reviewer, 1975-78; World Literature Today, reviewer. Also worked as a community activist and govt. consultant on race relations and human rights in Canada. Gives readings across Canada, the US, UK/Europe, Asia, and the Caribbean. Publications: NOVELS: Dark Swirl, 1989; The Wizard Swami, 1989; Sometimes Hard, 1994. POETRY: Poems in Recession, 1972; Goatsong, 1977; Distances, 1977; Heart's Frame, 1979; This Planet Earth, 1980;

Elephants Make Good Stepladders, 1982; Islands Lovelier Than a Vision, 1987; Coastland: New and Selected Poems, 1989; (with S. Mayne et al) Six Ottawa Poets, 1990; Stoning the Wind, 1994; Born in Amazonia, 1996; Hemisphere of Live, 2003; Discussing Columbus, 2004. STORIES: Still Close to the Island, 1980; Monkey Jungle, 1988; Jogging in Havanna, 1992; Berbice Crossing, 1996; Black Jesus and Other Stories, 1997; My Brahmin Days and Other Stories, 2000; North of the Equator, 2001; Play a Song Somebody, 2004. EDITOR: A Shapely Fire: Changing the Literary Landscape, 1987; Another Way to Dance, 1990, 2nd ed., 1997. Works appear in anthologies and literary magazines. Address: 295 Somerset E, Ottawa, ON, Canada K1N 6V9. Online address: cdabydeen@ncf.ca

DABYDEEN, David. British (born Guyana), b. 1956. Genres: Novels, Poetry, Art/Art history, Literary criticism and history. Career: Community Education Officer, Wolverhampton, 1982-84; Warwick University, Coventry, Professor of Literature, 1984-. Association for the Teaching of Caribbean, African and Asian Literature, President, 1985-87. Publications: (ed.) The Black Presence in English Literature, 1983, 1985; Slave Song (poetry), 1984; Coolie Odyssey (poetry), 1985; Hogarth's Blacks: Images of Blacks in Eighteenth-Century English Art, 1988; (ed. with B. Samaroo) India in the Caribbean, 1987; (ed.) A Handbook for Teaching Caribbean Literature, 1988; (ed.) Rented Rooms, 1988; Hogarth, Walpole and Commercial Britain, 1988; The Intended (novel), 1990; Disappearance (novel), 1993; Turner (poetry), 1994; The Counting House (novel), 1996; A Harlot's Progress (novel), 1999. Address: Centre for Caribbean Studies, University of Warwick, Coventry CV4 7AL, England. Online address: d.dabydeen@warwick.ac.uk

DACE, Tish. American, b. 1941. Genres: Literary criticism and history, Theatre, Writing/Journalism. Career: Kansas State University, instructor in speech and associate director of theatre, 1967-71; John Jay College of Criminal Justice, City University of New York, assistant professor, 1971-74, associate professor of speech, drama and English, 1975-80, chairman, Dept. of Speech and Theatre, 1979-80; University of Massachusetts Dartmouth, dean, College of Arts and Sciences, 1980-86, professor of English and drama, 1986-97, chancellor professor, 1997-2002, chancellor professor emerita, 2002-. Greenwich Village News, NYC, theatre editor, 1976-77; theatre critic: Soho Weekly News, NYC, 1977-82, Other Stages, NYC, 1978-82, The Villager, 1982-83, Plays and Players, London, 1984-86, Back Stage, 1992-2002, and Plays International, London, 1986-; American Theatre Wing Design Awards, chair, 1986-2002; Best Plays, editorial board, 2000-. Publications: LeRoi Jones (Imamu Amiri Baraka): A Checklist of Works by and about Him, 1971; (co-author) The Theatre Student: Modern Theatre Drama, 1973; (co-author) Black American Writers, 1978; Langston Hughes: The Contemporary Reviews, 1997. Contributor to periodicals and books. Address: Kaya Mars 12, Belnem, Bonaire, Netherlands Antilles. Online address: tdace@umassd.edu

DACEY, Philip. American, b. 1939. Genres: Poetry. Career: Member of the English Dept., now Professor of English, Southwest State University, Marshall, Minnesota, since 1970. Publications: The Beast with Two Backs, 1969; Fish, Sweet Giraffe, The Lion, Snake, and Owl, 1970; Four Nudes, 1971; How I Escaped from the Labyrinth and Other Poems, 1977; The Condom Poems, 1979; Men at Table, 1979; The Boy under the Bed, 1981; Gerard Manley Hopkins Meets Walt Whitman in Heaven and Other Poems, 1982; Fives, 1984; (ed. with D. Jauss) Strong Measures: Contemporary American Poetry in Traditional Forms, 1985; The Man with Red Suspenders,

1986; The Condom Poems II, 1989; Night Shift at the Crucifix Factory, 1991; What's Empty Weighs the Most: 24 Sonnets, 1997; The Deathbed Playboy, 1999; The Paramour of the Moving Air, 1999. **Address:** English Dept, Southwest State University, Marshall, MN 56258, U.S.A. **Online address:** dacey@ssu.southwest.msus.edu

D'ADAMO, Peter J. American. **Genres:** Medicine/Health. **Career:** Naturopathic physician, writer. **Publications:** (with C. Whitney) Eat Right 4 Your Type: The Individualized Diet Solution to Staying Healthy, Living Longer and Achieving Your Ideal Weight, 1997. **Address:** c/o Putnam Berkeley Group Inc., 375 Hudson St., New York, NY 10014, U.S.A.

DADLEZ, E(va) M(aria). American, b. 1956. **Genres:** Philosophy. **Career:** BRS, Latham, NY, technical writer, 1982-84; Syracuse University, Syracuse, NY, instructor in philosophy and English, between 1984 and 1992; Ithaca College, Ithaca, NY, assistant professor of philosophy, 1992-93; University of Central Oklahoma, Edmond, associate professor of philosophy, 1993-. Mountain Plains Philosophy Conference, member of executive committee. Guest speaker at universities. **Publications:** What's Hecuba to Him? Fictional Events and Actual Emotions, 1997. **Address:** Department of Humanities and Philosophy, University of Central Oklahoma, 100 N University Dr, Edmond, OK 73034, U.S.A. **Online address:** edadlez@ucok.edu

DA FONSECA, Eduardo Giannetti. Brazilian, b. 1957. **Genres:** Economics. **Career:** Cambridge University, Cambridge, England, research fellow at St. John's College, 1984-87; University of Sao Paulo, Sao Paulo, Brazil, lecturer in economics, 1988-. Cambridge University, Joan Robinson Memorial Lecturer, 1992-93; Instituto Fernand Brandel de Economia Mundial, Octavio Gouvea de Bulhoes Professor, 1992-. **Publications:** Liberalismo x Pobreza, 1989; Livre para Crescer, 1990; Beliefs in Action, 1991; Vícios privadoe, benefícios públicos?, 1993; As partes e o todo, 1995. **Address:** Faculdade de Economia, Universidade de Sao Paulo, Caixa Postal 11498, Sao Paulo, SP, Brazil.

DAFTARY, Farhad. Iranian (born Belgium), b. 1938. **Genres:** Cultural/ Ethnic topics. **Career:** Yekom Consultants, Tehran, Iran, founder, 1974, director, 1974-80; Institute of Ismaili Studies, London, England, professor of history, 1988-, Academic Department, head, 1991; writer. Plan Organization of Iran, senior adviser, 1972; Central Bank of Iran, director of Research Department, 1973. **Publications:** The Isma'ilis: Their History and Doctrines, 1990; The Assassin Legends: Myths of the Isma'ilis, 1994; Mediaeval Isma'ili History and Thought, 1996; A Short History of the Ismailis, 1998; Intellectual Traditions in Islam, 2000; Culture and Memory in Medieval Islam, 2003. Contributor to professional journals and encyclopedias. **Address:** Institute of Ismaili Studies, 42-44 Grosvenor Gardens, London SW1 W0EB, England. **Online address:** fdaftary@iis.ac.uk

DAHL, Arlene. American, b. 1928. **Genres:** Adult non-fiction. **Career:** Actress, designer, cosmetic executive, advertising executive, and author. Arlene Dahl Enterprises, president, 1951-75; A. N. Saab & Co., sleepwear designer, 1952-57; Kenyon & Eckhart Advertising Company, vice president, then president of Woman's World division, 1967-72; Sears, Roebuck & Co., national beauty director, 1970-75; O.M.A., fashion consultant, 1975-78; Dahlia Perfumes Inc., president, 1975-80; Vogue Patterns, designer, 1978-85; president and chief executive officer, Dahlia Productions, 1978-81, and Dahlmark Productions, 1981-; Lasting Beauty Ltd., president and chair, 1986-; Broadway Walk of Stars Foundation, founder/president, 1998-. Also author of internationally syndicated beauty column "Let's Be Beautiful," 1950-70 "Arlene Dahl's Lucky Stars" column, 1985-90, "Beauty Scopes and Scoops," 1988-90; and "Arlene Dahl's Astrological Forecast" magazine, 1991-, and syndicated astrological column, 1990-. **Publications:** Always Ask a Man, 1965; Your Beautyscope, 12 vols., 1969, rev., 1978; Arlene Dahl's Secrets of Skin Care, 1971; Arlene Dahl's Secrets of Hair Care, 1978; Beyond Beauty: A Three-Part Journey, 1980; Arlene Dahl's Lovescopes, 1983. **Address:** Dahlmark Productions, PO Box 116, Sparkill, NY 10976, U.S.A.

DAHL, Curtis. American, b. 1920. **Genres:** Literary criticism and history. **Career:** S. V. Cole Professor of English Literature, Emeritus, Wheaton College, Norton, Massachusetts, since 1966 (Assistant Professor, 1948-53; Associate Professor, 1953-58; Professor 1958-91). President, New England College English Association, 1951-52, and New England American Studies Association, 1962-64. **Publications:** Robert Montgomery Bird, 1963. EDITOR: There She Blows: A Narrative of a Whaling Voyage, 1971; Around the World in 500 Days, 2000. **Address:** 189 N Washington St, Norton, MA 02766, U.S.A.

DAHL, John. American, b. 1956. **Genres:** Plays/Screenplays. **Career:** Storyboard artist; music video director; director and screenwriter. Director of films and rock-musicals. **Publications:** SCREENPLAYS: (with R. Dahl; also director) Kill Me Again, 1989; (with R. Dahl; also director) Red Rock West, 1992; Private Investigations, 1996; (with R, Dahl; also director) Blackout, 1998. **Address:** c/o United Talent Agency, 560 Wilshire Blvd. Suite 500, Beverly Hills, CA 90212, U.S.A.

DAHL, Robert (Alan). American, b. 1915. **Genres:** Economics, Politics/ Government. **Career:** Sterling Professor of Political Science, Yale University, New Haven, 1964-, now emeritus (joined faculty, 1946; Eugene Meyer Professor of Political Science, 1955-64). Mgmt. Analyst, US Dept. of Agriculture, Washington, DC, 1940; Economist, Office of Production Management, War Production Board, 1940-42; with US Army, 1943-45. **Publications:** Congress and Foreign Policy, 1950; (with R. Brown) Domestic Control of Atomic Energy, 1951; (with C.E. Lindblom) Politics, Economics Welfare, 1953; A Preface to Democratic Theory, 1956; (with Haire and Lazarsfeld) Social Science Research on Business, 1959; Who Governs? Democracy and Power in an American City, 1961; Modern Political Analysis, 1963, 5th ed. 1990; Political Oppositions in Western Democracies, 1966; Pluralist Democracy in the United States, 1967, 4th ed., 1981; After the Revolution, 1970, 1990; Polyarchy: Participation and Opposition, 1971; (with E.R. Tufte) Size and Democracy, 1973; Dilemmas of Pluralistic Democracy, 1983; A Preface to Economic Democracy, 1985; Controlling Nuclear Weapons, 1985; Democracy, Liberty and Equality, 1986; Democracy and Its Critics, 1989; The New American Political (Dis)order, 1994; Toward Democracy: A Journey, Reflections, 1940-1997, 1997; On Democracy, 1998; How Democratic Is the American Constitution, 2001. **Address:** 17 Cooper Rd, North Haven, CT 06473, U.S.A. **Online address:** robert.dahl@yale.edu

DAHLEN, Beverly. American, b. 1934. **Genres:** Poetry. **Publications:** Out of the Third, 1974; A Letter at Easter: To George Stanley, 1976; The Egyptian Poems, 1983; A Reading (1-7), 1985; A Reading (11-17), 1989; A Reading (8-10), 1992; AReading Spicer and Eighteen /Sonnets, 2004. **Address:** 15 1/2 Mirabel Ave, San Francisco, CA 94110, U.S.A.

DAHLIE, Hallvard. Canadian (born Norway), b. 1925. **Genres:** Literary criticism and history. **Career:** Professor Emeritus of English, University of Calgary, since 1990 (Professor, 1967-90; Head of Dept., 1974-79). **Publications:** Brian Moore, 1969, 1981; (ed. with R. Chadbourne) The New Land as Literary Theme, 1978; Alice Munro and Her Works, 1985; Varieties of Exile: The Canadian Experience, 1986; Isolation and Commitment: Frederick Philip Grove's Settlers of the Marsh, 1993. **Address:** 3639 7A St., SW, Calgary, AB, Canada T2T 2Y6.

DAHRENDORF, Lord Ralf. British (born Germany), b. 1929. **Genres:** Sociology. **Career:** University Lecturer, Saarbrucken, 1957; Fellow, Center for Advanced Study in the Behavioral Sciences, Stanford University, CA, 1957-58; Professor of Sociology, Hamburg, 1958-60; Visiting Professor, Columbia University, NYC, 1960; Professor of Sociology, Tubingen, 1960-64; Parliamentary Secretary of State, Foreign Office, W. Germany, 1969-70; Member, Commission of the European Communities, Brussels, 1970-74; Director, London School of Economics, 1974-84; Warden, St. Antony's College, Oxford, 1987-97; Member, House of Lords, 1993-, Chairman, Delegated Powers Select Committee, 2002-. **Publications:** Marx in Perspective, 1953; Industrie und Betriebssoziologie, 1956; Soziale Klassen und Klassenkonflikt, 1957; Homo Sociologicus, 1959; Sozialstruktur des Betriebes, 1959; Gesellschaft und Freiheit, 1961; Uber den Ursprung der Ungleichheit, 1961; Die Angewandte Aufklarung, 1963; Das Mitbestimmungsproblem in der Deutschen Sozialforschung, 1963; Arbeiterkinder an Deutschen Universituaten, 1965; Bildung ist Burgerrecht, 1965; Gesellschaft und Demokratie in Deutschland, 1965; Markt und Plan, 1966; Confict after Class, 1967; Essays in the Theory of Society, 1967; Pfade aus Utopia, 1967; Die Soziologie und der Soziologe, 1967; Fur eine Erneuerung der Demokratie in der Bundesrepublik, 1968; Konflikt und Freiheit, 1972; Pluadoyer fuur die Europuaische Union, 1973; The New Liberty, 1975; Life Changes, 1979; On Britain, 1982; Die Chancender Krise, 1983; Reisen nach innen und aussen, 1984; Law and Order, 1985; The Modern Social Conflict, 1988; Reflections on the Revolution in Europe, 1990; LSE: A History of the London School of Economics, 1895-1995, 1995; Morals, Revolution and Civil Society, 1997; After 1989, 1997; Liberal und unabhangig, Gerd Bucerius und sein Zeit, 2000; Universities after Communism, 2000; Uber Grenzen, 2002. **Address:** House of Lords, London SW1A 0PW, England.

DAICHES, David. British, b. 1912. **Genres:** History, Literary criticism and history, Biography. **Career:** Assistant in English, Edinburgh University, 1935-36; Andrew Bradley Fellow, Balliol College, Oxford, 1936-37; Assistant Professor, University of Chicago, 1939-43; Second Secretary, British Embassy, Washington, 1944-46; Professor, Cornell University, Ithaca, New

York, 1945-51; Lecturer, Cambridge University, 1951-61; Fellow, Jesus College, Cambridge, 1957-62; Dean, School of English and American Studies, 1961-67, and Professor of English, 1961-77, University of Sussex; Director Institute for Advanced Studies, Edinburgh University, 1980-86. **Publications:** The Place of Meaning in Poetry, 1935; New Literary Values, 1936; Literature and Society, 1938; The Novel and the Modern World, 1939, 1960; Poetry and the Modern World, 1940; The King James Version of the Bible: A Study of Its Sources and Development, 1941; Virginia Woolf, 1942; Robert Louis Stevenson, 1947; A Study of Literature, 1948; (ed.) Poems in English, 1950; Robert Burns, 1951; (ed.) A Century of the Essay, 1951; Willa Cather, 1951; Two Worlds, 1956; Critical Approaches to Literature, 1956; Literary Essays, 1956; Milton, 1957; The Present Age, 1958; A Critical History of English Literature, 1960; George Eliot's Middlemarch, 1963; English Literature, 1964; (ed.) The Idea of a New University, 1964; The Paradox of Scottish Culture, 1964; More Literary Essays, 1968; Scotch Whisky, 1969; Some Late Victorian Attitudes, 1969; A Third World, 1971; (ed.) Penguin Companion to Literature: Great Britain and the Commonwealth, 1971; Sir Walter Scott and His World, 1971; Robert Burns and His World, 1971; Charles Edward Stuart, 1973; Robert Louis Stevenson and His World, 1973; Was, 1975; Moses: Man in the Wilderness (in U.S. as Moses: The Man and His Vision), 1975; James Boswell and His World, 1976; Scotland and the Union, 1977; Glasgow, 1977; Edinburgh, 1978; Literary Landscapes of the British Isles, 1979; (ed.) Fletcher of Saltoun: Selected Writings, 1979; Literature and Gentility in Scotland, 1982; Robert Fergusson, 1982; God and the Poets, 1984; Edinburgh: A Travellers' Companion, 1986; A Weekly Scotsman and Other Poems, 1994. **Address:** 22 Belgrave Crescent, Edinburgh EH4 3AL, Scotland.

DAIGON, Ruth. American (born Canada), b. 1923. **Genres:** Plays/Screenplays. **Career:** Vancouver Symphony, British Columbia, Canada, soprano soloist, 1946-48; Temple Emanuel, NYC, soloist, 1949-54; New York Pro Musica, NYC, soprano soloist, 1950-54; Columbia Records, recording artist, 1950-56; Community Church, Great Neck, NY, soloist, 1952-63; Camera Three, CBS-TV, regular appearances, 1954-56; University of Connecticut at Storrs, recital and television artist, 1963-70. Editor, Poets On: (a poetry journal), 1976-96; organizer, poetry activities, Hartford CT Festival of Arts, 1980; organizer of poetry programs for Public Broadcasting Service, 1984-86; regular participant in Bay Area poetry readings, and in the Marin Summer Poetry Festivals, 1990-; participant in international poetry festival, BBC, 1991; guest artists on KPFA Radio Poetry Hour, Berkeley, CA. **Publications:** Learning Not To Kill You (poems), 1976; (ed. with A. Daigon and M. Levine) Put It in Writing (anthology), 1978; On My Side of the Bed, 1980; A Portable Past, 1986; Between One Future and the Next, 1994; About a Year, 1996. Contributor of verse to poetry journals. Work represented in anthologies. Has published extensively on the internet. **Address:** 29 Loring Ave., Mill Valley, CA 94941, U.S.A.

DAILEY, Janet. American, b. 1944. **Genres:** Romance/Historical, Westerns/Adventure. **Publications:** No Quarter Asked, 1974; Savage Land, 1974; Something Extra, 1975; Fire and Ice, 1975; Boss Man from Ogallala, 1975; After the Storm, 1975; Land of Enchantment, 1975; Sweet Promise, 1976; The Homeplace, 1976; Dangerous Masquerade, 1976; Show Me, 1976; Valley of the Vapours, 1976; The Night of the Cotillion, 1976; Fiesta San Antonio, 1977; Bluegrass King, 1977; A Lyon's Share, 1977; The Widow and the Wastrel, 1977; The Ivory Cane, 1977; Six White Horses, 1977; To Tell the Truth, 1977; The Master Fiddler, 1977; Giant of Medabi, 1978; Beware of the Stranger, 1978; Darling Jenny, 1978; The Indy Man, 1978; Reilly's Woman, 1978; For Bitter or Worse, 1978; Tidewater Lover, 1978; The Bride of the Delta Queen, 1978; Green Mountain Man, 1978; Sonora Sundown, 1978; Summer Mahogany, 1978; The Matchmakers, 1978; Big Sky Country, 1978; Low Country Liar, 1979; Strange Bedfellow, 1979; For Mike's Sake, 1979; Sentimental Journey, 1979; Bed of Grass, 1979; That Boston Man, 1979; Kona Winds, 1979; A Land Called Deseret, 1979; Touch the Wind, 1979; Difficult Decision, 1980; Enemy in Camp, 1980; Heart of Stone, 1980; Lord of the High Lonesome, 1980; The Mating Season, 1980; Southern Nights, 1980; The Thawing of Mara, 1980; One of the Boys, 1980; The Rogue, 1980; Wild and Wonderful, 1980; Ride the Thunder, 1981; A Tradition of Pride, 1981; The Travelling Kind, 1981; Dakota Dreamin', 1981; The Hostage Bride, 1981; Night Way, 1981; Lancaster Men, 1981; For the Love of God, 1981; Calder saga: This Calder Sky, 1981, This Calder Range, 1982, Stands a Calder Man, 1982; Northern Magic, 1982; With a Little Luck, 1982; That Carolina Summer, 1982; Terms of Surrender, 1982; Wildcatter's Woman, 1982; Calder Born, Calder Bred, 1983; Foxfire Light, 1982; The Second Time, 1982; Mistle Toe and Holly, 1982; Separate Cabins, 1983; Western Man, 1983; Best Way to Lose, 1983; Leftover Love, 1984; Silver Wings, Santiago Blue, 1984; The Pride of Hannah Wade, 1985; The Glory Game, 1985; The Great Alone, 1986; Heiress, 1987; Rivals, 1989; Masquerade, 1990; Aspen Gold, 1991; Tangled Vines: A Novel, 1992; With a

Little Luck, 1993; The Proud and the Free, 1994; The Healing Touch, 1994; Legacies, 1996; Notorious, 1996; A Spring Bouquet, 1996; Flower Girls, 1997; Illusions, 1997; Homecoming, 1998; Calder Pride, 1999; A Capital Holiday, 2001; (with S. Steffen and K. Adams) The Only Thing Better Than Chocolate, 2001; Scrooge Wore Spurs, 2002; Green Calder Grass, 2002; Shifting Calder Wind, 2003; Calder Promise, 2004.

DAITCH, Susan. American, b. 1954. **Genres:** Novels, Novellas/Short stories. **Career:** Writer. Has taught at Sarah Lawrence College and Barnard College. Teacher at Iowa Writers Workshop, 1990. **Publications:** Storyland, USA (short stories), 1984; The Colorist (novella), 1985, rev. and expanded into novel, The Colorist, 1990; L.C. (novel), c. 1987; Disorderly Conduct: The Voice Literary Supplement Fiction Reader, 1991; Storytown: Stories, 1996. Contributor to periodicals. **Address:** c/o Dalkey Archive, Campus Box 4241, Illinois State University, Normal, IL 61790, U.S.A. **Online address:** sed372@aol.com

DALBY, Liza Crihfield. American. **Genres:** Anthropology/Ethnology, Novels. **Career:** Anthropologist and author. Worked as a geisha in Japan. **Publications:** Geisha, 1983; Kimono: Fashioning Culture, 1993; The Tale of Murasaki (novel), 2000. Contributor to books. **Address:** c/o Author Mail, Nan A. Talese Books, 1540 Broadway, 18th Floor, New York, NY 10036, U.S.A.

DALCOURT, Gerard Joseph. American, b. 1927. **Genres:** Philosophy. **Career:** University of Kansas, Lawrence, Librarian, 1954-56; Villanova University, PA, Instructor, 1957-62; Seton Hall University, South Orange, NJ, Assistant Professor, 1962-66, Associate Professor, 1966-75, Professor, 1975-97, Dept. Chairman, 1988-91, Professor Emeritus, 1997-. **Publications:** The Philosophy of St. Thomas Aquinas, 1965; (ed. and trans.) The Great Dialogue of Nature and Space, 1970; The Methods of Ethics, 1983. **Address:** 579 Prospect, Maplewood, NJ 07040, U.S.A.

DALE, Peter. British, b. 1938. **Genres:** Plays/Screenplays, Poetry, Education, Literary criticism and history, Translations. **Career:** Head of English Dept., Hinchley Wood School, Esher, Surrey, 1972-93; Co-ed., Agenda, London, 1982-96; full-time writer, 1993-. **Publications:** Walk from the House, 1962; The Storms, 1968; Mortal Fire, 1970; Mortal Fire: New and Selected Poems and Translations, 1976; Cross Channel, 1977; One Another (sonnets), 1978, rev. ed., 2002; Too Much of Water: Poems 1976-82, 1983; (with W.S. Milne and R. Richardson) A Set of Darts: Epigrams, 1990; Earth Light: New Poems, 1991; Edge to Edge, New & Selected Poems, 1996; Da Capo: A Sequence, 1997; Under the Breath: New Poems, 2002; Peter Dale in Conversation with Cynthia Haven, 2005. TRANSLATOR: The Legacy and Other Poems of Francois Villon, 1971, rev. ed. as Poems of Francois Villon, 2001; (with K. Subbiah) The Seasons of Cankam, 1975; Francois Villon, 1978; Narrow Straits, 1985; The Poems of Jules Laforgue, 1986, rev. ed., 2001; The Divine Comedy, 1996; T. Corbiere, Way-Blue Loves and Other Poems, 2005. PLAYS: Cell, 1975; Sephe, 1981; The Dark Voyage, 1991. PROSE: Michael Hamburger in Conversation with Peter Dale, 1998; An Introduction to Rhyme, 1998; Anthony Thwaite in Conversation with Peter Dale and Ian Hamilton, 1999; Richard Wilbur in Conversation with Peter Dale, 2000.

DALE, Richard. American, b. 1932. **Genres:** International relations/Current affairs, Politics/Government. **Career:** University of New Hampshire, Durham, Dept. of Government, instructor, 1962-63; Northern Illinois University, DeKalb, assistant professor of political science, 1963-66; Southern Illinois University, Carbondale, Dept. of Political Science, adjunct professor, 1966-67, assistant professor, 1967-71, associate professor, 1971-97, associate professor emeritus, 1997-. Member of the Council, South African Institute of Race Relations, 1974-81; Member, Advisory Board, University Press of America, Washington, DC, 1976-81; Member, Editorial Advisory Board, Journal of Contemporary African Studies, 1980-85; Member, Editorial Advisory Board, Conflict Quarterly, 1992-. **Publications:** (ed. with C.P. Potholm) Southern Africa in Perspective: Essays in Regional Politics, 1972; Botswana's Search for Autonomy in Southern Africa, 1995. MONOGRAPHS: Botswana and Its Southern Neighbor: The Patterns of Linkage and the Options in Statecraft, 1970; The Racial Component of Botswana's Foreign Policy, 1971; The Racial Component of Botswana's Foreign Policy, 1971. Author of articles in professional journals and book chapters. **Address:** PO Box 18635, Fountain Hills, AZ 85269-8635, U.S.A. **Online address:** Rnmidale@aol.com

DALE, Rodney A. M. British. **Genres:** Medicine/Health, Music, Mythology/Folklore, Technology, Biography, Reference. **Career:** Writer & editor. **Publications:** BIOGRAPHY: Louis Wain: The Man Who Drew Cats, 1968, rev.

ed., 1991; Catland, 1977; The Sinclair Story, 1985; (ed.) Walter Wilson: Portrait of an Inventor, 1986; Cats in Books, 1997. TECHNOLOGY: Bridges, 1973; Inland Waterways, 1974; Iron Roads, 1974; From Ram Yard to Milton Hilton: A History of Cambridge Consultants Ltd 1960-1979, 1979; (with J. Gray) Edwardian Inventions 1901-1905, 1979; (with I. Williamson) BASIC Programming, 1979; (co-author) Understanding Microprocessors with the Science of Cambridge MK-14, 1980; The Myth of the Micro, 1980; (ed. and co-author) The Discoveries & Inventions Series for the British Library (Machines in the Home; Early Flying Machines; The Industrial Revolution; Timekeeping; Home Entertainment; Machines in the Office: Early Railways; Early Cars), 1992-94; (with C. Fiddy) The Fern House Design & Technology Pack, 1995. CAREERS: (ed.) Hobsons Engineering Casebook, 1979; (ed.) Hobsons Computing Casebook, 1980; Becoming an Architect, 1983; (ed.) Hobsons Sixth Form Science, Technology and Engineering Casebook, 1985. FOLKLORE: The Tumour in the Whale, 1978; It's True...It Happened to a Friend, 1984. MUSIC: The World of Jazz, 1980; A History of Jazz, 1983; Teach Yourself Jazz, 1997, rev. ed., 2004. COSMOLOGY: (with G. Sassoon): The Manna Machine, 1978; (co-ed.) The Kabbalah Decoded, 1978. OTHER: (ed.) O-level English (textbook), 1982; (with Dr. J. Starkie) Understanding AIDS (medicine), 1988; Puss in Boots (pantomime), 1990, verse, 2001; The Tinder Box (pantomime), 1993; About Time (novel), 1995; (with S. Puttick) The Wordsworth Dictionary of Abbreviations & Acronyms (reference), 1997; Hello, Mrs Fish (humor), 1997; Halcyon Days (autobiography), 1999; The Wordsworth Dictionary of Culinary & Menu Terms (reference), 2000; A Treasury of Love Poems, 2003; A Treasury of Proverbs, 2003. **Address:** Fern House, 19 High St, Haddenham, Ely, Cambs. CB6 3XA, England. **Online address:** info@fernhouse.com

DALEY, Robert (Blake). American, b. 1930. **Genres:** Novels. **Career:** Publicity Director, New York Giants, 1953-58; Foreign and War Correspondent in Europe and N. Africa, New York Times, 1959-64; Deputy Commissioner, New York Police Dept., 1971-72. Photographs exhibited at Baltimore Museum, Art Institute of Chicago, and New York Gallery of Modern Art, 1968-69. **Publications:** The World beneath the City, 1959; Cars at Speed, 1961; The Bizarre World of European Sports, 1963; The Cruel Sport, 1963; The Swords of Spain, 1965; The Whole Truth, 1967; Only a Game, 1967; A Priest and a Girl, 1969; A Star in the Family, 1971; Target Blue, 1973; Strong Wine Red as Blood, 1974; To Kill a Cop, 1976; Treasure, 1977; The Fast One, 1978; Prince of the City, 1979; An American Saga, 1980; Year of the Dragon, 1981; The Dangerous Edge, 1983; Hands of a Stranger, 1985; Man with a Gun, 1988; A Faint Cold Fear, 1990; Portraits of France, 1991; Tainted Evidence, 1993; Wall of Brass, 1994; Nowhere to Run, 1996; The Innocents Within, 1999; The Enemy of God, 2005. **Address:** c/o Esther Newburg, ICM, 40 W 57th St, New York, NY 10019, U.S.A.

DALITZ, Richard Henry. British (born Australia), b. 1925. **Genres:** Physics, Biography. **Career:** Fellow Emeritus, All Souls College, and Professor Emeritus, Rudolf Peierls Centre for Theoretical Physics, Oxford University, 1990- (Fellow and Professor, 1964-90). Reader in Mathematical Physics, University of Birmingham, 1955-56; Professor of Physics, Enrico Fermi Institute for Nuclear Studies, University of Chicago, 1956-66; Research Professor, Royal Society, London, 1963-90. **Publications:** Strange Particles and Strong Interactions, 1962; Nuclear Interactions of the Hyperons, 1965; (co-author) Nuclear Energy Today and Tomorrow, 1971; (co-author) Dr. Paul Dirac: A Biographical Memoir, 1987; (co-author) A Breadth of Physics, 1988; The Collected Works of P.A.M. Dirac 1924-1948, 1995; (co-author) Selected Scientific Papers of Sir Rudolf Peierls, 1997; (co-author) The Foundations of Newtonian Scholarship, 1997. **Address:** 28 Jack Straw's Lane, Oxford OX3 0DW, England. **Online address:** r.dalitz@physics.ox.ac.uk

DALLAS, Gregor. French (born England), b. 1948. **Genres:** History. **Career:** Writer and historian. **Publications:** The Imperfect Peasant Economy: The Loire Country, 1800-1914, 1982; At the Heart of a Tiger-Clemenceau and His World, 1841-1929, 1993; 1815: The Roads to Waterloo, 1996, in US as The Final Act: The Roads to Waterloo, 1997; 1918: War and Peace, 2000. **Address:** c/o Author Mail, Overlook Press, 141 Wooster St. Apt 4B, New York, NY 10012, U.S.A. **Online address:** gregor.dallas@free.fr

DALLAS, Roland. American. **Genres:** Biography. **Career:** Journalist. Foreign Report, England, editor, 1982-; former Reuters correspondent. **Publications:** The Economist Pocket Africa, 1994; Pocket Latin America: Profiles, Facts, and Figures about Latin America, 1994; Pocket Middle East and North Africa, 1995; King Hussein: A Life on the Edge, 1998; Fromm International, 1999. **Address:** Foreign Report, Jane's Information Group, Sentinel House, 163 Brighton Rd., Coulsdon, Surrey CR5 2YH, England.

DALLEK, Robert. American, b. 1934. **Genres:** History, International relations/Current affairs, Biography. **Career:** Columbia University, NYC,

Instructor in History, 1960-64; University of California at Los Angeles, Professor of History (joined faculty as Assistant Professor, 1964); Oxford, Harmsforth Visiting Professor, 1994-95; Boston University, Professor of History, 1996-2003; Dartmouth College, Montgomery Fellow and Visiting Professor of History, 2004. Fellow, Society of American Historians; Member, Board, of Editors, Reviews in American History; Member of the Council, Society for Historians of American Foreign Relations, and Committee on the History of the Second World War; American Academy of Arts & Sciences, Fellow. **Publications:** Democrat and Diplomat: The Life of William E. Dodd, 1968; Franklin D. Roosevelt and American Foreign Policy 1932-45, 1979; The American Style of Foreign Policy: Cultural Politics and Foreign Affairs, 1983; Ronald Reagan: The Politics of Symbolism, 1984; (co-author) The Great Republic: A History of the American People, 3rd ed., 1985, 4th ed., 1991; Lone Star Rising: Lyndon Johnson and His Times, 1908-1960, 1991; Hail to the Chief: The Making and Unmaking of American Presidents, 1996; Flawed Giant: Lyndon Johnson and His Times, 1961-1973, 1998; An Unfinished Life: John F. Kennedy, 1917-1963, 2003. EDITOR: The Roosevelt Diplomacy and World War II (reader), 1970; Western Europe, vol. I of Dynamics of World Power: A Documentary History of American Foreign Policy 1945-1973, 1973. **Address:** 2138 Cathedral Ave NW, Washington, DC 20008-1502, U.S.A. **Online address:** RDallek@aol.com

DALLY, Ann. British, b. 1926. **Genres:** History, Medicine/Health, Psychiatry, Psychology, Social commentary, Women's studies and issues, Biography. **Career:** Psychiatrist in private practice, London, now retired. Research Fellow, Wellcome Institute for the History of Medicine. **Publications:** A-Z of Babies, 1961; (with R. Sweering) A Child Is Born, 1965 (in U.S. as The Birth of a Baby, 1969); Intelligent Person's Guide to Modern Medicine, 1967; Cicely: The Story of a Doctor, 1968; Mothers: Their Power and Influence, 1976; The Morbid Streak (in U.S. as Understanding), 1978; Why Women Fail, 1979; Inventing Motherhood, 1982; A Doctor's Story, 1990; Women under the Knife, 1991; Fantasy Surgery, 1996; The Trouble with Doctors, 2003. **Address:** Wiblings Farm, Graffham, Petworth, W. Sussex GU28 0PU, England.

DALOZ, Laurent A. Parks. American, b. 1940. **Genres:** Education. **Career:** U.S. Peace Corps, Washington, DC, trainer in Missouri and Washington and volunteer in Nepal, 1963-65; PACE Curriculum Center, Parkersburg, WV, language arts consultant, 1966; Konawaena High School, Kealakekua Kona, HI, social studies teacher, 1966-67; Port Moresby, Papua New Guinea, educational planner, 1969-71; Community College of Vermont, Montpelier, founding academic dean, 1972-76; Johnson College, Johnson, VT, faculty mentor for external degree program, 1977-84; Vermont College, Montpelier, faculty adviser for adult degree program, 1980-85; Harvard University, Cambridge, MA, faculty member of Harvard Institute for the Management of Lifelong Education, 1987-88, consultant on faculty development for the Harvard Graduate School of Education, 1989-90; Lesley College, Cambridge, MA, instructor, 1988-96, professor, 1996; Teachers College, Columbia University, NYC, adjunct professor, 1996, 2001, 2003; Whidbey Institute, Clinton, WA, core faculty member and associate director, 1997-. Has presented papers and keynote addresses on a number of topics and has worked as a consultant. **Publications:** Effective Teaching and Mentoring: Realizing the Transformational Power of Adult Learning Experiences, 1986; (with C. Keen, J. Keen, and S. Daloz Parks) Common Fire: Lives of Commitment in a Complex World, 1996; Mentor: Guiding the Journey of Adult Learners, 1999. Contributor to books and periodicals. **Address:** The Whidbey Institute, PO Box 57, Clinton, WA 98236, U.S.A.

DALRYMPLE, G. Brent. American, b. 1937. **Genres:** Earth sciences. **Career:** Geologist. U.S. Geological Survey, Menlo Park, CA, Branch of Theoretical Geophysics, research geologist, 1963-70, Branch of Isotope Geology, 1970-81, 1984-94, research geologist, assistant chief geologist, western region, 1981-84; College of Oceanic and Atmospheric Science, Oregon State University, Corvallis, professor and dean, 1994-. Stanford University, visiting professor, lecturer, research associate, and consulting professor since the 1970s; principle investigator for moon rocks collected by Apollo missions. **Publications:** (with M.A. Lanphere) Potassium-Argon Dating: Principles, Techniques, and Applications to Geochronology, 1969; Irradiation Samples for 40Ar/39Ar Dating Using the Geological Survey TRIGA Reactor, 1981; The Age of the Earth, 1991; 49Ar/39Ar Age Spectra and Total-Fusion Ages of Tektites from Cretaceous-Tertiary Boundary Sedimentary Rocks in the Beloc Formation, Haiti, 1993; (with Lanphere and B.D. Turrin) Abstracts of the Eighth International Conference on Geochronology, Cosmochronology, and Isotope Geology, 1994; (with J.W. M'Gonigle) 40Ar/39Ar Ages of Some Challis Volcanic Group Rocks and the Initiation of Tertiary Sedimentary Basins in Southwestern Montana, 1995. Contributor to journals and periodicals. **Address:** Oregon State University, College of Oceanic & Atmospheric Science, Corvallis, OR 97331, U.S.A.

DALTON, Annie. British, b. 1948. **Genres:** Science fiction/Fantasy, Children's fiction. **Career:** Writer. **Publications:** FANTASY NOVELS: Out of the Ordinary, 1988; Night Maze, 1989. The Afterdark Princess, 1990; The Witch Rose, 1990; The Alpha Box, 1991; Naming the Dark, 1992; Swan Sister, 1992; The Real Tilly Beany, 1993; Tilly Beany and the Best Friend Machine, 1993; Ugly Mug, 1994; Tilly Beany Saves the World, 1997; Space Baby, 1998; Tyler and the Talkstalk, 1998; Dozy Rosy, 1999; The Dreamsnatcher, 1998; Paradise High, 1999. **Address:** c/o Laura Cecil, 27 Alwyne Villas, London N1 2HG, England.

DALTON, Joe. See MAYER, Bob.

DALTON, Sheila. Canadian (born England). **Genres:** Children's fiction, Young adult fiction, Novels, Poetry. **Career:** Freelance writer and poet, 1982-. Freelance editor and reference librarian. Previous positions include, bartender and art gallery assistant. **Publications:** Bubblemania (picture book), 1992; Blowing Holes Through the Everyday (poetry), 1993; Tales of the Ex Fire-Eater: A Novel, 1994; Doggerel (picture book), 1996; Catalogue (picture book), 1998; Trial by Fire (young adult), 1998. **Address:** c/o The Writers' Union of Canada, 40 Wellington Street East Third Floor, Toronto, ON, Canada M5E 1C7. **Online address:** sagespirit@hotmail.com

DALY, Brenda O. American, b. 1941. **Genres:** Literary criticism and history, Women's studies and issues. **Career:** High school English teacher in Hopkins, MN, Melrose, MA, and Bloomington, MN, 1964-71, 1980; University of Minnesota-Twin Cities, Minneapolis, visiting assistant professor of English and women's studies, 1985, instructor in English, 1985-86, affiliated scholar of Center for Advanced Feminist Studies, 1986-88; Macalester College, lecturer, 1985-86; St. Olaf College, visiting assistant professor, 1986-87; Iowa State University, Ames, associate professor of English, 1987-. **Publications:** (ed. with M. Reddy) Narrating Mothers: Theorizing Maternal Subjectivities, 1991; Lavish Self-Divisions: The Novel of Joyce Carol Oates, 1996; Authoring a Life, 1998. Contributor to literature journals and books. **Address:** Department of English, 253 Ross Hall, Iowa State University, Ames, IA 50011, U.S.A. **Online address:** bdaly@iastate.edu

DALY, Cardinal Cahal Brendan. Irish, b. 1917. **Genres:** Ethics, Theology/Religion. **Career:** Ordained priest, 1941; ordained bishop, 1967; Archbishop of Armagh, 1990-; Roman Catholic Cardinal, 1991-. Chairman, Christus Rex. Society, 1941-66; Lecturer, then Reader in Scholastic Philosophy, Queen's University, Belfast, 1946-67; Canon of Diocesan Chapter of Down and Connor, 1966; R.C. Bishop of Ardagh and Clonmacnois, 1967-82; Bishop of Down and Connor, 1982-90; Archbishop of Armagh and Primate of All Ireland, 1990-96; Archbishop Emeritus, 1996-. **Publications:** Morals, Law and Life, 1962; Natural Law Morality Today, 1965; Violence in Ireland and Christian Conscience, 1973; Peace: The Work of Justice, 1979; The Price of Peace, 1991; Morals and Law, 1993; Tertullian the Puritan and His Influence, 1993; Northern Ireland - Peace - Now Is the Time, 1994; Love Begins at Home, 1995; Moral Philosophy in Britain from Bradley to Wittgenstein, 1996; Steps on My Pilgrim Journey, 1998; The Minding of Planet Earth, 2003. **Address:** Ard Mhacha, 23 Rosetta Ave, Belfast BT7 3HG, Northern Ireland. **Online address:** card_daly@btinternet.com

DALY, Leo (Arthur). Irish, b. 1920. **Genres:** Novels, Novellas/Short stories, Plays/Screenplays, Area studies, Literary criticism and history, Travel/Exploration. **Career:** Radio-Telefis-Eireann, broadcaster. **Publications:** The Aran Islands, 1975; James Joyce and the Mullingar Connection, 1975; Titles, 1981; The Rock Garden (novel), 1984; The Stone-Cutter's Daughter (novel), 1991; James Joyce at the Cross Keys, 1991; Only Two and Six Return (radio play), 1993; Island Lovers (short stories), 1993; Austin Friars, 1994; The Jealous Wall (play), 1995. EDITOR: The Midlands, 1979; The Westmeath Examiner Centenary Edition, 1982; Life of Colman of Lynn, 1999. **Address:** 10 Mary St, Mullingar, Westmeath, Ireland.

DALY, M(artin) W. American, b. 1950. **Genres:** Area studies. **Career:** New England College, England, lecturer in history, 1978-79; University of Durham, Durham, England, research fellow in arts, 1980-83; University of Khartoum, Khartoum, Sudan, Fulbright visiting professor at Institute of African and Asian studies, 1984-85; Arkansas State University, State University, assistant professor of history, 1985-87; Memphis State University, Memphis, TN, assistant professor, 1987-89, associate professor, 1989-91, professor of history, 1991-92, fellow at Humanities Center, 1989; University of Tennessee at Chattanooga, professor of history, 1992-97, head of department, 1992-95; Kettering University, Flint, MI, professor of humanities and social science and head of department, both 1997-. Richmond College, England, lecturer, 1978-79; Woodrow Wilson International Center for Scholars, fellow, 1986; Oxford University, senior associate member of St.

Antony's College, 1987; University of Durham, Leonard Slater Lecturer, 1989; Tel Aviv University, Fulbright visiting professor, 1994-95; University of East Anglia, archival researcher for Saudi history project; guest speaker at universities. **Publications:** (with P.M. Holt) The History of the Sudan: From the Coming of Islam to the Present Day, 3rd ed, 1979, 4th ed., as A History of the Sudan, 1988; British Administration and the Northern Sudan, 1917-1924, 1980; Sudan, 1983, 2nd ed, 1992; Empire on the Nile: The Anglo-Egyptian Sudan, 1898-1934, 1986; (with Deng) Bonds of Silk: The Human Factor in the British Administration of the Sudan, 1990; Imperial Sudan: The Anglo-Egyptian Condominium, 1934-1956, 1991; On Trek in Kordofan: Diaries of a British District Officer in the Sudan, 1931-33, 1994; (with L.E. Forbes) The Sudan, 1994; The Sirdar: Sir Reginald Wingate and the British Empire in the Middle East, 1997. EDITOR: The Road to Shaykan: Letters of Major-General William Hicks Pasha Written during the Sennar and Kordofan Campaigns, 1883, 1983; Modernization in the Sudan: Studies in Honor of Richard Hill, 1985; Al-Majdhubiyya and al-Mikashfiyya: Two Sufi Tariqas in the Sudan, 1985; (with G. Benavides, and contrib) Religion and Political Power, 1989; (with A.A. Sikainga, and contrib) Civil War in the Sudan, 1993; The Cambridge History of Egypt, Vol II: Modern Egypt, 1998; (general ed) The Cambridge History of Egypt (series), 1998. Contributor to books. Contributor of articles and reviews to scholarly journals. **Address:** Department of Humanities and Social Science, Kettering University, 1700 West Third Ave., Flint, MI 48504, U.S.A. **Online address:** mdaly@kettering.edu

DALY, Maureen. Also writes as Maureen Daly McGivern. American (born Northern Ireland), b. 1921. **Genres:** Novels, Plays/Screenplays, Writing/Journalism, Novellas/Short stories, Film, Young adult fiction. **Career:** Freelance journalist and script writer. Journalist and columnist, The Desert Sun, 1987-. Police Reporter and Columnist, Chicago Tribune, 1946-48; Associate Ed., Ladies' Home Journal, Philadelphia, 1948-54; Editorial Consultant, Saturday Evening Post, Philadelphia, 1960-69. **Publications:** Seventeenth Summer, 1942; Smarter and Smoother: A Handbook on How to Be That Way, 1944; The Perfect Hostess: Complete Etiquette and Entertainment for the Home, 1948; What's Your P.Q. (Personality Quotient)?, 1952; Twelve Around the World, 1957; (as Maureen Daly McGivern, with W.P. McGivern) Mention My Name in Mombasa: The Unscheduled Adventures of an American Family Abroad, 1958; Patrick series, 4 vols., 1959-63; Spanish Roundabout, 1960; Moroccan Roundabout, 1961; Sixteen and Other Stories, 1961; The Ginger Horse, 1964; The Small War of Sergeant Donkey, 1966; Rosie, The Dancing Elephant, 1967; (with W. McGivern) The Seeing, 1981; Acts of Love, 1986; First a Dream, 1990. EDITOR: My Favorite Stories, 1948; Profile of Youth, 1951; My Favorite Mystery Stories, 1966; My Favorite Suspense Stories, 1968. **Address:** 73-305 Ironwood St, Palm Desert, CA 92260, U.S.A.

DALY, Niki. South African, b. 1946. **Genres:** Children's fiction, Illustrations. **Career:** Singer and songwriter, CBS Record Company, London, 1970-72; junior art director, Advertising Agency, London, 1973-75; free-lance illustrator, 1975-, author, 1978-; graphics teacher, East Ham College of Technology, London, 1976-79; head of graphic design, Stellenbosch University, 1983-89; head of Songololo Books division, David Philip Publishers, 1989-92. **Publications:** SELF-ILLUSTRATED FOR CHILDREN: The Little Girl Who Lived Down the Road, 1978; Vim the Rag Mouse, 1979; Joseph's Other Red Sock, 1982; Leo's Christmas Surprise, 1983; Not So Fast, Songololo, 1985. WALKER STORYTIME SERIES: Ben's Gingerbread Man, 1985; Teddy's Ear, 1985; Monsters Are Like That, 1985; Just Like Archie, 1986; Look at Me!, 1986; Thank You Henrietta, 1986. OTHER: (with I. Mennen) Ashraf of Africa, 1991 in UK and US as Somewhere in Africa, 1992; Mama, Papa and Baby Joe, 1991; Mary Malloy and the Baby Who Wouldn't Sleep, 1991 in UK as Mary Malloy, the Crescent Moon and the Baby Who Couldn't Sleep, 1993; Papa Lucky's Shadow, 1991; (with W. Hartmann) All the Magic in the World, 1993; Why the Sun and Moon Live in the Sky, 1994; (with I. Mennen) One Round Moon and a Star for Me, 1994; My Dad: Story and Pictures, 1995; (with N. Turkington) The Dancer, 1996; (with W. Hartmann) The Dinosaurs are Back and it's All Your Fault Head, 1996; Zan Angelo, 1998. Illustrator of books by K. Hersom, C. Gregorowski, L. Baum, R. Craft, R. Shermbrucker, C. Best. **Address:** c/o Laura Cecil, 17 Alwyne, London N1 2HG, England. **Online address:** inkman@iafrica.com

DALYELL, Tam. Scottish, b. 1932. **Genres:** History, International relations/Current affairs, Politics/Government, Sciences. **Career:** Worked as a teacher at Bo'ness High School, 1956-62; deputy director of studies at Dunera Ship School, 1961-62; British Parliament, Labour member for West Lothian, Scotland, 1962-, opposition spokesman on science, 1980-82; writer. Secretary of the Labour Party's Standing Conference on the Sciences, 1962-64; chair of Parliamentary Labour Party's Education Committee, 1964-65, Sports Group, 1964-74, and Foreign Affairs Group, 1974-75; vice chair of

Parliamentary Labour Party's Defense and Foreign Affairs Groups, 1972-74, and Scottish Labour Group's Members of Parliament, 1973-75; member of House of Commons's Public Accounts Committee, 1962-66, and Select Committee on Science and Technology, 1967-69; member of Cabinet-Parliamentary Labour Party Liaison Committee, 1974-76. Member of European Parliament, 1975-79, including Budget Committee, 1976-79, and Energy Committee, 1979. Council member of National Trust of Scotland. Author of "Thistle Diary" column in New Scientist, 1967-. University of Edinburgh, rector, 2003-; Royal Society of Edinburgh, fellow, 2003-. **Publications:** The Case of Ship-Schools, 1960; Ship-School Dunera, 1963; Devolution: The End of Britain?, 1977; A Science Policy for Britain, 1983; Thatcher's Torpedo, 1983; One Man's Falklands, 1983; Thatcher: Patterns of Deceit, 1986; Misrule: How Mrs. Thatcher Has Misled Parliament from the Sinking of the Belgrano to the Wright Affair, 1987; Dick Crossman: A Portrait, 1989. **Address:** Binns, Linlithgow EH49 7NA, England.

DALZELL, Alexander. Canadian (born Northern Ireland), b. 1925. **Genres:** Literary criticism and history, Translations. **Career:** University of London, King's College, assistant lecturer in classics, 1951-53; University of Sheffield, Sheffield, England, assistant lecturer in classics, 1953-54; Trinity College, Toronto, ON, lecturer to professor of classics, 1954-88. **Publications:** (trans.) The Correspondence of Erasmus, Vol. 10 (with R. Mynors and J. Estes), 1992, Vol. 11 (with C. Nauert), 1994, Vol. 12 (with C. Nauert), 2003 ; The Criticism of Didactic Poetry, 1996. **Address:** 344 Saunders St, Fredericton, NB, Canada E3B 1N8. **Online address:** adalzell@nbnet.nb.ca.

DAMAS, David (John). American, b. 1926. **Genres:** Anthropology/Ethnology, History, Environmental sciences/Ecology. **Career:** National Museums of Canada, Ottawa, ON, Arctic ethnologist, 1962-69; McMaster University, Hamilton, ON, associate professor, 1969-73, professor of anthropology, 1973-90, professor emeritus, 1991-. **Publications:** Igluligmiut Kinship and Local Groupings: A Structural Approach, 1963. EDITOR & CONTRIBUTOR: Band Societies, 1969; Ecological Essays, 1969; Handbook of North American Indians, Volume V: The Arctic, 1984; Bountiful Island: A Study of Land Tenure on a Micronesion Atoll, 1994; Arctic Migrants/Arctic Villagers: The Transformation in Inuit Settlement in the Central Arctic, 2002. **Address:** Dept of Anthropology, McMaster University, 1280 Main St W, Hamilton, ON, Canada L8S 4L9.

DAMASIO, Antonio R. American (born Portugal), b. 1944. **Genres:** Medicine/Health, Psychology. **Career:** University of Iowa, Iowa City, associate professor, 1976-80, chief of division of behavioral neurology and cognitive neuroscience, 1977-, professor of neurology, 1980-, head of department, 1986-, Van Allen Distinguished Professor, 1989; writer. Adjunct professor at Salk Institute, 1989-. **Publications:** (with H. Damasio) Lesion Analysis in Neuropsychology, 1989; Descartes's Error: Emotion, Reason, and the Human Brain, 1994; The Feeling of What Happens: Body and Emotion in the Making of Consciousness, 1999; Looking for Spinoza: Joy, Sorrow, and the Feeling Brain, 2003. Contributor to periodicals. **Address:** Department of Neurology, University of Iowa College of Medicine, 200 Hawkins Dr, Iowa City, IA 52242, U.S.A.

D'AMATO, Anthony. American, b. 1937. **Genres:** Plays/Screenplays, Law, Philosophy, Politics/Government. **Career:** Northwestern University, Chicago, Assistant Professor to Associate Professor, Leighton Professor of Law, 1968-. **Publications:** (ed. with W.C. Beal) The Realities of Vietnam, 1968; The Concept of Custom in International Law, 1971; (with R.M. O'Neil) The Judiciary and Vietnam, 1972; (co-author) The Politics of Ecosuicide, 1972; (co-author) The Political Calculus (philosophy), 1972; (co-author) International Law and Vietnam, vol. 3, 1973; The Magic Man (play), 1974; (with others) Desegregation from Brown to Alexander, 1978; (with B. Weston and R. Falk) International Law and World Order, 1980; R.S.V.P. Broadway (musical play), 1981; Assyrian Case for Autonomy, 1982; Jurisprudence: A Descriptive and Normative Analysis of Law, 1984; International Law: Process and Prospect, 1987; (with A. Jacobson) Justice and the Legal System, 1992; International Law Coursebook, 1994; (ed.) International Law Anthology, 1994; International Law and Political Reality, 1995; (co-ed.) International Environmental Law Anthology, 1996; (co-ed.) International Intellectual Property Anthology, 1996; (co-ed.) International Environmental Property Law, 1997; International Law Studies, 1997; Introduction to Law and Legal Thinking, 1996; (with D.E. Long) Coursebook in International Intellectual Property, 2000. **Address:** School of Law, Northwestern University, 357 E. Chicago Ave, Chicago, IL 60611, U.S.A. **Online address:** a-damato@northwestern.edu

D'AMBROSIO, Charles. American, b. 1960. **Genres:** Novellas/Short stories. **Career:** Freelance writer. **Publications:** The Point (short stories),

1995. Contributor of stories to anthologies and periodicals. **Address:** Little Brown, 3 Center Plaza, Floor 3, Boston, MA 02108, U.S.A.

DAMMAN, Gregory C. American. **Genres:** Law. **Career:** Hecht, Sweet, Alesio, Morrow, Poppe & Otte (law firm), Lincoln, NE, associate attorney, 1989-91; attorney in general practice, Lincoln, 1991-96, and Seward, NE, 1996-. Damman Legal Research, owner and operator, 1991-96. **Publications:** How to Form and Operate a Limited Liability Company, 1995, 2nd ed, 1998; Collecting Child Support: Twelve Effective Strategies, 1997. Contributor to periodicals. **Address:** Blevens & Damman, 129 N. 5th St., Seward, NE 68434-2100, U.S.A. **Online address:** gd42805@navix.net

DAMON, William. American, b. 1944. **Genres:** Psychology, Human relations/Parenting. **Career:** Clark University, Worcester, MA, professor of psychology and graduate dean, 1974-89; Brown University, Providence, RI, professor of education and human development and department head, 1989-. Center for Advanced Study in Behavioral Sciences (Palo Alto, CA), fellow; consultant to Children's Television Workshop. **Publications:** The Social World of the Child, 1977; Social and Personality Development, 1983; Self-Understanding in Childhood and Adolescence, 1988; The Moral Child, 1990; (with A. Colby) Some Do Care, 1992; Greater Expectations, 1995. **Address:** Center for Human Development, Box 1938, Brown University, Providence, RI 02912, U.S.A.

DAMS, Jeanne M(artin). American, b. 1941. **Genres:** Mystery/Crime/Suspense. **Career:** Writer. **Publications:** MYSTERY NOVELS: The Body in the Transept, 1995; Trouble in the Town Hall, 1996; Holy Terror in the Hebrides, 1997; Malice in Miniature, 1998; Death in Lacquer Red, 1999; Victim in Victoria Station, 1999; Red, White, & Blue Murder, 2000; Killing Cassidy, 2000; Green Grow the Victims, 2001; To Perish in Penzance, 2001; Silence Is Golden, 2002; Sins Out of School, 2003; Winter of Discontent, 2004. **Address:** c/o Kimberley Cameron, Reece Halsey North, 98 Main St Ste 704, Tiburon, CA 94920, U.S.A. **Online address:** jdams@jeannedams.com

DANA, Robert (Patrick). American, b. 1929. **Genres:** Poetry, Literary criticism and history, Writing/Journalism. **Career:** Cornell College, Mt. Vernon, IA, joined faculty, 1953, Professor and Poet-in-Residence, 1968-94, Professor Emeritus of English 1994-. Contributor Ed.: American Poetry Review, 1973-88, New Letters, 1980-83, and North American Review, 1991-. Ed., Hillside Press, 1957-67, and North American Review, 1964-68. **Publications:** My Glass Brother and Other Poems, 1957; The Dark Flags of Waking, 1964; Journeys from the Skin: A Poem in Two Parts, 1966; Some Versions of Silence, 1967; The Power of the Visible, 1971; In a Fugitive Season, 1980; What the Stones Know, 1984; Blood Harvest, 1986; Against the Grain: Interviews with Maverick American Publishers, 1986; Starting Out for the Difficult World, 1987; What I Think I Know: New and Selected Poems, 1991; Yes, Everything, 1994; Hello, Stranger, 1996; A Community of Writers: Paul Engle and The Iowa Writers' Workshop, 1999; Summer, 2000. **Address:** 1466 Westview Dr., Coralville, IA 52241, U.S.A.

DANAKAS, John. Canadian, b. 1963. **Genres:** Young adult fiction. **Career:** Winnipeg Sun, Winnipeg, Manitoba, journalist, 1986-91; University of Manitoba, Winnipeg, media relations officer, 1996-. Dal's Restaurant, restaurateur. **Publications:** Curve Ball, 1993; Lizzie's Soccer Showdown, 1994; Hockey Night in Transcona, 1995. **Address:** Public Affairs Office, University of Manitoba, 423 University Cres., Winnipeg, MB, Canada R3T 2N2.

DANCE, Daryl Cumber. American, b. 1938. **Genres:** Cultural/Ethnic topics, Mythology/Folklore, Bibliography. **Career:** Virginia State College (now University), Petersburg, instructor in English, 1963-72; Virginia Commonwealth University, Richmond, associate professor, 1972-85, professor of English, 1985-92. Visiting professor of black studies at University of California, Santa Barbara, 1986-87; University of Richmond, VA, 1992-. **Publications:** Shuckin and Jivin: Folklore from Contemporary Black Americans, 1978; Folklore from Contemporary Jamaica, 1985; Fifty Caribbean Writers: A Bio-Bibliographical-Critical Casebook, 1986; Long Gone: The Mecklenburg Six and the Theme of Escape in Black Folklore, 1987; New World Adams: Conversations with West Indian Writers, 1992; Honey, Hush! An Anthology of African American Women's Humor, 1998; The Lineage of Abraham: The Biography of a Free Black Family in Charles City, VA, 1999; From My People: Four Hundred Years of African American Folklore, 2002. **Address:** Department of English, University of Richmond, Richmond, VA 23173, U.S.A.

DANCER, J. B. See HARVEY, John B.

DANCER, J. B. See WELLS, Angus.

D'ANCONA, Matthew. British, b. 1968. **Genres:** Theology/Religion. **Career:** Times, London, England, assistant editor, 1990-95; Sunday Telegraph, London, deputy editor and political columnist, 1996-. Oxford University, fellow of All Souls College, 1989-96. **Publications:** (coauthor) Eyewitness to Jesus, 1996 (also published as The Jesus Papyrus); The Ties That Bind Us, 1996; The Quest for the True Cross, 2000. **Address:** Sunday Telegraph, 1 Canada Sq., Canary Wharf, London E14 5DT, England.

DANDRIDGE, Rita B(ernice). American. **Genres:** Literary criticism and history, Cultural/Ethnic topics, Bibliography. **Career:** Morgan State University, Baltimore, MD, instructor to assistant professor of English, 1964-71; University of Toledo, Toledo, OH, assistant professor of English, 1971-74; Norfolk State University, Norfolk, VA, associate professor to professor of English, 1974-, member of editorial board, 1986. Fellow in residence, University of Virginia Center for the Humanities, 1987. **Publications:** Ann Allen Shockley: An Annotated Primary and Secondary Bibliography, 1987; Black Women's Blues: A Literary Anthology, 1934-1988, 1992; The Oxford Companion to African American Literature, 1997. Contributor of critical articles and reviews to periodicals. **Address:** Department of English, Norfolk State University, 700 Park Ave, Norfolk, VA 23504, U.S.A. **Online address:** rbdandridge@nsu.edu

DANER, Paul. See STOKOE, E(dward) G(eorge).

DANESH, Abol Hassan. Iranian, b. 1952. **Genres:** Sociology. **Career:** Plan and Budget Organization, Tehran, Iran, migration expert, 1982-84; University of California, Riverside, associate in sociology, 1981, 1984; Colby College, Waterville, ME, visiting assistant professor of sociology, 1985-89; University of Rhode Island, Kingston, assistant professor, 1989-92, associate professor of sociology, 1992-. **Publications:** An Introduction to a Theory of Irregular Rural-Urban Migration, 1983; Causes of Unproductive Jobs in the Third World, 1984; Rural Exodus and Squatter Settlements in the Third World, 1987; The Informal Economy: A Research Guide, 1991; The Informal Economy and Informalization in Photography, 1994; Corridor of Hope, 1999. Contributor to periodicals. **Address:** 51 Pepper Bush Trail, Saunderstown, RI 02874-2368, U.S.A. **Online address:** Hassan@uri.edu

DANFORTH, John C(laggett). American, b. 1936. **Genres:** History. **Career:** Davis, Polk, Wardwell, Sunderland and Kiendl (law firm), New York, tax lawyer, 1964-66; Bryan, Cave, McPheeters and McRoberts (law firm), St. Louis, MO, in private law practice, 1966-68; attorney general of Missouri, 1969-76; United States senator from Missouri, 1976-95; Bryan Cave (law firm), St. Louis, lawyer, 1995-. Former ranking member of Senate Commerce, Science, and Transportation Committee. Ordained Episcopal deacon, 1963, and priest, 1964; assistant rector, New York, 1963-66; associate rector, in Clayton, MO, 1966-68, and Grace Church, Jefferson City, MO, 1969; St. Alban's, Washington, DC, associate rector, 1977-94; Church of the Holy Communion, St. Louis, associate priest, 1995-. Chair of Missouri Law Enforcement Assistance Council, 1973-74. Assistant chaplain, Memorial Sloan-Kettering Cancer Center, NYC; assistant rector, Church of Epiphany, New York, and Church of St. Michael and St. George, Clayton. **Publications:** Resurrection: The Confirmation of Clarence Thomas, 1994. **Address:** Bryan Cave LLP, 1 Metropolitan Square, 211 North Broadway Suite 3600, St. Louis, MO 63102, U.S.A.

DANFORTH, Paul M. See ALLEN, John E(lliston).

DANGAREMBGA, Tsitsi. Zambian, b. 1959. **Genres:** Novels, Plays/Screenplays. **Career:** Author and filmmaker. **Publications:** The Lost of the Soil (screenplay), 1983; She No Longer Weeps (play), 1987; Nervous Conditions (novel), 1989; (with J. Riber and A. Whaley; and director) Everyone's Child (screenplay), 1996. **Address:** c/o The Women's Press, 34 Great Sutton St., London EC1V ODX, England.

DANIEL, Colin. See WINDSOR, Patricia.

DANIEL, Pete. American, b. 1938. **Genres:** History. **Career:** Curator, National Museum of American History, Washington, D.C., since 1982. Assistant Professor 1971-73, Associate Professor, 1973-78, and Professor, 1978-79, University of Tennessee, Knoxville. Assistant Ed., Booker T. Washington Papers, 1969-70. **Publications:** The Shadow of Slavery: Peonage in the South 1901-69, 1972; (with R. Smock) A Talent for Detail, 1974; Deep'n as It Come: The 1927 Mississippi River Flood, 1977; Breaking the Land: The Transformation of Cotton, Tobacco and Rice Cultures since 1880, 1985; Standing at the Crossroads: Southern Life in the Twentieth Century, 1986; (with others) Official Images: New Deal Photography, 1987; Carry Me Home, 1990; Lost Revolutions, 2000.

DANIEL, Tony. American, b. 1963. **Genres:** Novels, Science fiction/Fantasy. **Career:** Seattle Pacific University, Seattle, WA, teacher, 1991; Vashon High School, Vashon Island, WA, assistant debate coach, 1992-93; Clarion West Writers' Workshop, member of board of directors, 1992-93; writer, 1989-. **Publications:** NOVELS: Warpath, 1993; Earthling, 1997; Robot's Twilight Companion, 1999; Metaplanetary, 2001. Contributor of novellas, stories, poems, articles, and reviews to magazines and newspapers. **Address:** c/o John A. Ware Literary Agency, 392 Central Park W, New York, NY 10025, U.S.A.

DANIEL, Wayne W. American, b. 1929. **Genres:** Mathematics/Statistics, Medicine/Health, Music. **Career:** Elementary schoolteacher in Haralson County, GA, 1949-50; high school teacher of English and mathematics in Villa Rica, GA, 1954-57; Georgia Department of Public Health, Atlanta, statistical research assistant, 1957-58, research statistician, 1959-60, chief of mental health statistics section, Biostatistics Service, 1965-67, director of Biostatistics Service, 1967-68; Milledgeville State Hospital, Milledgeville, GA, biostatistical analyst, 1960-63; Georgia State University, Atlanta, assistant professor to professor of decision sciences, 1968-91. Member of Citizens Advisory Council, Georgia Senate Music Industry Committee, 1985-96. **Publications:** Biostatistics: A Foundation for Analysis in the Health Sciences, 1974; (with J.C. Terrell) Business Statistics: Basic Concepts and Methodology, 1975; Introductory Statistics with Applications, 1977; Applied Nonparametric Statistics, 1978; Essentials of Business Statistics, 1984; Pickin' on Peachtree: A History of Country Music in Atlanta, Georgia, 1990. Author of articles. **Address:** 2943 Appling Dr, Chamblee, GA 30341-5113, U.S.A. **Online address:** wwdaniel@gsu.edu

DANIELS, Anthony. British, b. 1949. **Genres:** Travel/Exploration. **Career:** Psychiatrist and, under a pseudonym, medical journalist. **Publications:** Coups and Cocaine: Two Journeys in South America, 1986; Fool or Physician: The Memoirs of a Sceptical Doctor, 1987; Zanzibar to Timbuktu, 1988; Sweet Waist of America: Journeys around Guatemala, 1990; Utopias Elsewhere: Journeys in a Vanishing World, 1991, in UK as The Wilder Shores of Marx: Journeys in a Vanishing World; Monrovia Mon Amour: A Visit to Liberia, 1992. **Address:** c/o John Murray Publishers Ltd., 50 Albemarle St., London W1X 4BD, England. **Online address:** ADan530211@aol.com

DANIELS, Elizabeth Adams. American, b. 1920. **Genres:** Biography. **Career:** Professor Emeritus of English, Vassar College, Poughkeepsie, New York (Instructor 1948-54; Assistant Professor 1954-60; Associate Professor 1960-65; Professor from 1965); Vassar Historian, 1986-. **Publications:** Jessie White Mario: Risorgimento Revolutionary, 1973; Posseduta dall'angelo, 1977; (ed.) Vassar: The Remarkable Growth of a Man and His College, 1984; Main to Mudd, 1987; Matthew Vassar, More Than a Brewer, 1992; Bridges to the World: Henry Noble MacCracken and Vassar College, 1994; Main to Mudd, and More, 1996; (with M. Bruno) Vassar College, 2001; (with C. Griffen) "Full Steam Ahead in Poughkeepsie," The Story of Coeducation at Vassar, 2001. **Address:** Vassar College, Poughkeepsie, NY 12601, U.S.A.

DANIELS, Karen. American, b. 1957. **Genres:** Science fiction/Fantasy. **Career:** Novelist. **Publications:** ZADDACK TALES SERIES: Dancing Sun, 2000; Mentor's Lair, 2000. **Address:** c/o Author Mail, 2 Neptune Road, Poughkeepsie, NY 12601, U.S.A. **Online address:** kdauthor@aol.com

DANIELS, Lucy. See OLDFIELD, Jenny.

DANIELS, Lucy. See WELFORD, Sue.

DANIELS, Mark R. American, b. 1952. **Genres:** Politics/Government. **Career:** Slippery Rock University, Slippery Rock, PA, professor of government and public affairs. **Publications:** Terminating Public Programs: An American Political Paradox, 1997; Medicaid Reform and the American States: Case Studies on the Politics of Managed Care, 1998; Creating Sustainable Community Programs, 2001. **Address:** Department of Government and Public Affairs, Slippery Rock University, Slippery Rock, PA 16057, U.S.A. **Online address:** mark.daniels@sru.edu

DANIELS, Mary. American, b. 1937. **Genres:** Animals/Pets, Art/Art history. **Career:** Feature Writer and Columnist, Chicago Tribune, 1969-. Recipient of various awards. **Publications:** Morris: An Intimate Biography: The Nine Lives of Morris the Cat, 1974; Cat Astrology, 1976; (with D. Barbier) Dressage for the New Age, 1990. EDITOR: Robert Vavra's Classic Book of Horses, 1992; The Arts & Crafts of Morrocco, 1995. **Address:** Chicago Tribune, 435 N. Michigan Ave, Chicago, IL 60611, U.S.A. **Online address:** mdaniels@tribune.com

DANIELS, Max. See GELLIS, Roberta (Leah Jacobs).

DANIELS, Olga. See SINCLAIR, Olga (Ellen).

DANIELS, Philip. See CHAMBERS, Peter.

DANIELS, Rebecca. American, b. 1949. **Genres:** Plays/Screenplays, Theatre. **Career:** National Onion Singing Telegram Service, public relations manager, branch manager, and performer in San Francisco and Los Angeles, CA, and Portland, OR, 1977-79; Murphy, Symonds & Stowell (management recruiters), Portland, executive recruiter, 1979-82; Artists Repertory Theatre, Portland, founder, 1982, producing director and artistic director, 1982-88; Pacific Lutheran University, Tacoma, WA, visiting assistant professor of communication arts, 1988-89; University of Portland, adjunct instructor in theater, 1989-90; Seattle Pacific University, visiting lecturer, 1989-90; St. Lawrence University, Canton, NY, assistant professor, 1992-98, department head, 1997-, associate professor of speech and theater, 1998-. **Publications:** Women Stage Directors Speak: Exploring the Effects of Gender on Their Work, 1996; The Famous Mrs. Beach (play), 2001 Contributor to journals. **Address:** Department of Speech and Theatre, St. Lawrence University, Canton, NY 13617, U.S.A. **Online address:** rdaniels@stlawu.edu

DANIELS, Robert (Vincent). American, b. 1926. **Genres:** History, Politics/Government, International relations/Current affairs, Language/Linguistics. **Career:** Professor Emeritus of History, University of Vermont, Burlington, since 1988 (joined faculty, 1956). State Senator, Vermont, 1973-82; President, American Assn. for the Advancement of Slavic Studies, 1992. **Publications:** The Conscience of the Revolution, 1960, 1988; The Nature of Communism, 1962; Understanding Communism, 1964; Russia, 1964; Studying History, 1966; Red October, 1967, 1984; Europe Talking, 1975; Russia: The Roots of Confrontation, 1985; Is Russia Reformable?, 1988; Year of the Heroic Guerilla, 1989; Trotsky, Stalin, and Socialism, 1991; The End of the Communist Revolution, 1993; Russia's Transformation, 1997. EDITOR: A Documentary History of Communism, 1960, 2nd ed. 1984, 3rd ed, 1993-94; The Stalin Revolution, 1965, 4th ed. 1996; Marxism and Communism, 1966; The Russian Revolution, 1972; (co-) The Dynamics of Soviet Politics, 1976; The University of Vermont: The First Two Hundred Years, 1991; Soviet Communism from Reform to Collapse, 1994. **Address:** 195 S. Prospect St, Burlington, VT 05401, U.S.A. **Online address:** rdaniels@zoo.uvm.edu

DANIELS, Sarah. British, b. 1956. **Genres:** Plays/Screenplays. **Career:** Writer-in-Residence, 1983-84, and Associate Writer, 1984-85, Royal Court Theatre, London; Resident Writer, Albany Empire, 1989-90. **Publications:** Masterpieces, 1984, 1986; Ripen Our Darkness and The Devil's Gateway, 1986; Neaptide, 1986; Byrthrite, 1987; The Gut Girls, 1989; Beside Herself, 1990; Headrot Holiday, 1992; The Madness of Esme and Shaz, 1994. **Address:** c/o Judy Daish Associates, 83 Eastbourne Mews, London W2 6lQ, England.

DANIELS, Zoe. See LAUX, Constance.

D'ANIERI, Paul J. D. American, b. 1965. **Genres:** Politics/Government. **Career:** L'viv State University, Ukraine, Fulbright visiting scholar, 1993-94; University of Kansas, associate professor of political science, Russian, and East European studies, 1991-, associate dean of international programs. **Publications:** Economic Interdependence in Ukrainian-Russian Relations, 1999; (with R. Kravchuk and T. Kuzio) Politics and Society in Ukraine, 1999; (ed., with R. Kravchuk and T. Kuzio) State and Institution Building in Ukraine, 1999. Contributor to periodicals. **Address:** Department of Political Science, 504 Blake Hall, University of Kansas, Lawrence, KS 66045, U.S.A. **Online address:** p-danieri@ukans.edu

DANKO, William D(avid). American, b. 1952. **Genres:** Biography. **Career:** School of Business, State University of New York, Albany, professor of marketing, 1976-. **Publications:** (with T.J. Stanley) The Millionaire Next Door: The Surprising Secrets of America's Wealthy, 1996. **Address:** State University of New York at Albany, 1400 Washington Ave., Albany, NY 12222, U.S.A.

DANLEY, John R(obert). American, b. 1948. **Genres:** Economics. **Career:** Southern Illinois University at Edwardsville, department of philosophy, 1976-. **Publications:** The Role of the Modern Corporation in a Free Society, 1994. **Address:** Department of Philosophy, Box 1433, Southern Illinois University at Edwardsville, Edwardsville, IL 62026-1433, U.S.A.

DANN, Colin (Michael). British, b. 1943. **Genres:** Children's fiction, Natural history. **Career:** Writer. Winner of Arts Council of Great Britain

National Book Award for Children's Literature, 1979. **Publications:** (with C. Guthrie) Looking at Insects, 1978; The Animals of Farthing Wood, 1979; In the Grip of Winter, 1981; Fox's Feud, 1982; Fox Cub Bold, 1983; The Siege of White Deer Park, 1985; Ram of Sweetriver, 1986; King of The Vagabonds, 1987; The Beach Dogs, 1988; Just Nuffin, 1989; In the Path of the Storm, 1989; A Great Escape, 1990; A Legacy of Ghosts, 1991; The City Cats, 1991; Battle for the Park, 1992; Farthing Wood: The Adventure Begins, 1994; Copycat, 1997; Nobody's Dog, 1999; Journey to Freedom, 1999; Lion Country, 2000; Pride of the Plains, 2002. **Address:** Castle Oast, Ewhurst Green, Robertsbridge, E. Sussex, England.

DANN, Jack. American, b. 1945. **Genres:** Novels, Novellas/Short stories, Romance/Historical, Science fiction/Fantasy, Poetry. **Career:** Freelance writer and lectr. Broome Community College, Binghamton, NY, instructor of writing and science fiction, 1972, 1990, 1991; Cornell University, Ithaca, NY, assistant professor, 1973. SFWA Bulletin, managing ed., 1970-75. **Publications:** Starhiker (novel), 1977; Christs and Other Poems, 1978; Junction (novel), 1981; The Man Who Melted (novel), 1984; (with J.C. Haldeman II) Echoes of Thunder (novel), 1991; (with J.C. Haldeman II) High Steel, 1993; The Memory Cathedral, 1995; The Silent, 1998; Counting, 2001; (with R. Campbell and D. Etchison) Gathering the Bones, 2003; The Rebel, 2004; Nebula Awards 39, forthcoming. SHORT STORIES: Timetipping, 1980; (co-author) Slow Dancing through Time, 1990; Jubilee, 2001; Visitations, 2003. EDITOR: Wandering Stars (anthology), 1974; (with G. Zebrowski) Faster Than Light (anthology), 1976; Immortal, 1977; More Wandering Stars, 1981; (with J.V.B. Dann) In the Field of Fire, 1987; (with P. Sargent and G. Zebrowski) Three in Time: White Wolf Rediscovery Trio, vol. 1, 1997; (with P. Sargent and G. Zebrowski) Three in Space: White Wolf Rediscovery Trio #2, vol. 1, 1998; (with J. Webb) Dreaming Down-Under, 1998; (with G. Davidson) Everybody Has Somebody in Heaven, 2000. EDITED WITH G. DOZOIS: Future Power, 1976; Aliens!, 1980; Unicorns! 1984; Magicats! 1984; Bestiary!, 1985; Mermaids!, 1986; Sorcerers!, 1986; Demons!, 1987; Dogtails!, 1988; Seaserpents!, 1989; Dinosaurs!, 1990; Little People!, 1991; Magicats II, 1991; Unicorns II, 1992; Dragons!, 1993; Invaders!, 1993; Horses!, 1994; Angels!, 1995; Dinosaurs II, 1995; Hackers!, 1996; Timegates, 1997; Immortals!, 1998; Nanotech!, 1998; Armegeddons, 1999; Aliens among Us, 2000; Genometry, 2001; Space Soldiers, 2001; Future Sport, 2002; Beyond Flesh, 2002; Future Crime, 2003. **Address:** PO Box 101, Foster, VIC 3960, Australia. **Online address:** jackmdann@aol.com

DANNER, Mark (David). American, b. 1958. **Genres:** Documentaries/Reportage, Adult non-fiction. **Career:** New York Review of Books, NYC, editorial assistant, 1981-84; Harper's, NYC, senior editor, 1984-86; New York Times Magazine, NYC, story editor, 1986-90; New Yorker, NYC, staff writer, 1990-. American Broadcasting Co., writer and producer for the ABC-TV program Peter Jennings Reports. New York University, fellow of New York Institute for the Humanities. University of California, Berkeley, visiting professor, 1998-. Guest on television programs. MacArthur Fellow, 1999. **Publications:** The Massacre at El Mozote: A Parable of the Cold War, 1994; Beyond the Mountains: The Legacy of Duvalier, 2000; The Saddest Story; America, the Balkans and the Post-Cold War World, 2000. Television news documentaries include specials, House on Fire: America's Haitian Crisis and While America Watched: The Bosnia Tragedy, both 1994. Contributor to books and periodicals. **Address:** c/o New Yorker, 4 Times Square, New York, NY 10036, U.S.A. **Online address:** mardanner@aol.com

DANO, Linda. Also writes as Felicia Gallant. American, b. 1943. **Genres:** Romance/Historical, Fashion/Costume, Homes/Gardens. **Career:** Actress in films and television series, model, fashion consultant, and author. Fashion designer and owner, Strictly Personal (a fashion consulting business). **Publications:** (as Felicia Gallant, with R. Flanders) Dreamweaver (romance novel), 1984; (with A. Kyle) Looking Great: Daytime Television Star Linda Dano Shares Her Fashion, Beauty, and Style Secrets to Help You Look Your Best, 1997; (with A. Kyle) Living Great: Style Expert and Television Star Linda Dano Shows You How to Bring Style Home with Her Easy, Affordable Decorating Ideas and Techniques, 1998. **Address:** c/o VSMP, The Marketing Group, 1010 Nautilus, Mamaroneck, NY 10543, U.S.A.

DANOPOULOS, Constantine P. American (born Greece), b. 1948. **Genres:** Military/Defense/Arms control. **Career:** Southwest Missouri State University, Springfield, faculty member, 1978-81; Ball State University, Muncie, IN, faculty member, 1981-82; San Jose State University, San Jose, CA, faculty member, 1983-. Guest speaker at educational institutions throughout the world; guest on media programs; speaker for civic organizations. Election observer in Bosnia, 1996. **Publications:** Warriors and Politicians in Modern Greece, 1984. EDITOR & CONTRIBUTOR: The Decline of Military Regimes: The Civilian Influence, 1988; Military Disengagement from

Politics, 1988; From Military to Civilian Rule, 1992; Civilian Rule in the Developing World, 1992; (with K.P. Magyar) Prolonged Conflicts: A Post-Nuclear Challenge, 1994; (with C. Watson) The Political Role of the Military: An International Handbook, 1996; (with D. Zirker) Civil-Military Relations in the Soviet and Yugoslav Successor States, 1996; (with K. Messas) Crises in the Balkans: Views from the Participants, 1997; (with Zirker, and author of intro.) The Military and Society in the Former Eastern Bloc, 1998. Contributor to books. Contributor of articles and reviews to academic journals. **Address:** 6188 Northland Terr, Fremont, CA 94555, U.S.A.

DANOW, David K. American, b. 1944. **Genres:** Literary criticism and history. **Career:** University of California, Riverside, professor of Russian and comparative literature. **Publications:** The Thought of Mikhail Bakhtin: From Word to Culture, 1991; The Dialogic Sign: Essays on the Major Novels of Dostoevsky, 1991; Models of Narrative: Theory and Practice, 1992, rev. ed., 1997; The Spirit of Carnival: Magical Realism and the Grotesque, 1995; Transformation as the Principle of Literary Creation from the Homeric Epic to the Joycean Novel, 2003. **Address:** Department of Comparative Literature, University of California, Riverside, CA 92521, U.S.A.

DANQUAH, Meri Nana-Ama. Ghanaian, b. 1967. **Genres:** Autobiography/Memoirs. **Career:** Writer, poet, and performance artist. **Publications:** Willow Weep for Me (memoir), 1998; (ed. and author of intro) Becoming American: Personal Essays by First Generation Immigrant Women, 2000. Contributor to periodicals. **Address:** 7095 Hollywood Blvd., #447, Los Angeles, CA 90028, U.S.A. **Online address:** mdanquah@hotmail.com

DANTICAT, Edwidge. American (born Haiti), b. 1969. **Genres:** Novels, Novellas/Short stories. **Career:** Novelist, short story writer, 1994-. **Publications:** Breath, Eyes, Memory (novel), 1994; Krik? Krak! (short stories), 1995; The Farming of Bones (novel), 1998; The Dew Breaker, 2004. **Address:** c/o Soho Press, 853 Broadway No. 1903, New York, NY 10003, U.S.A.

DANTO, Arthur C(oleman). American, b. 1924. **Genres:** Philosophy. **Career:** Johnsonian Professor Emeritus of Philosophy, Columbia University, NYC (joined faculty, 1951). Art Critic, The Nation Magazine, NYC. **Publications:** Analytical Philosophy of History, 1965; Nietzsche as Philosopher, 1965; Analytical Philosophy of Knowledge, 1968; What Philosophy Is, 1968; Mysticism and Morality, 1972; Analytical Philosophy of Action, 1974; Jean-Paul Sartre, 1975; The Transfiguration of the Commonplace, 1981; Narration and Knowledge, 1985; The Philosophical Disenfranchisement of Art, 1986; The State of the Art, 1987; Connections to the World, 1989; Encounters and Reflections: Art in the Historical Present, 1990; Beyond the Brillo Box: The Visual Arts in Post-Historical Perspective, 1992; Embodied Meanings: Critical Essays and Aesthetic Meditations, 1994; After the End of Art: Contemporary Art and the Pale of History, 1997; The Body/Body Problem, 1999; Madonna of the Future: Essays in a Pluralistic Art World, 2000. **Address:** 420 Riverside Dr, New York, NY 10025, U.S.A. **Online address:** acd1@columbia.edu

D'ANTONIO, Michael. American, b. 1955. **Genres:** Theology/Religion. **Career:** Dover Democrat, Dover, NH, reporter, 1976-77; Portland Press Herald, Portland, ME, reporter, 1977-78, correspondent in Washington, DC, 1978-83; Newsday, NYC, writer, 1983-90. **Publications:** Fall from Grace: The Failed Crusade of the Christian Right, 1990; Heaven on Earth: Dispatches from America's Spiritual Frontier, 1992; Atomic Harvest, 1993; Best Medicine, 1999; Tin Cup Dreams, 2000; Mosquito, 2002. **Address:** c/o Hyperion Editorial Dept, 77 W 66th St 11th Fl, New York, NY 10023, U.S.A.

DANTZER, Robert. French, b. 1944. **Genres:** Medicine/Health, Psychology. **Career:** National Institute of Agronomic Research, France, 1968-. National Institute of Health and Medical Research, Bordeaux, France, director of Laboratory of Integrative Neurobiology, 1994-. Consultant to pharmaceutical companies. **Publications:** Le stress en elevage intensif, 1979; Les emotions, 1988, 2nd ed., 1994; The Psychosomatic Delusion: Why the Mind Is Not the Soul of All Our Ills, 1993. Contributor to books. Contributor to scientific journals. **Address:** Laboratory of Integrative Neurobiology, National Institute of Health and Medical Research, INSERM U394, rue Camille Saint-Saens, 33077 Bordeaux, France. **Online address:** robert.dantzer@bordeaux.inserm.fr

DANZ, Harold P. American, b. 1929. **Genres:** Animals/Pets. **Career:** U.S. Department of the Interior, National Park Service, 1955-74, associate regional director in Lakewood, CO, 1974-91; Danz and Associates, Lakewood, owner, 1991-92; American Bison Association, Denver, CO, executive director, 1992-

93; writer, 1993-. **Publications:** Of Bison and Man, 1997; Cougar!, 1999. Contributor to periodicals. **Address:** 6751 S. Callaway Dr., Chandler, AZ 85249-4451, U.S.A.

DANZIGER, Charles. American, b. 1962. **Genres:** Adult non-fiction. **Career:** Museum of Modern Art, NYC, assistant general counsel, 1990-94; Danziger & Danziger (law firm), NYC, partner and specialist in art law, 1994-. **Publications:** The American Who Couldn't Say Noh: Almost Everything You Need to Know about Japan, 1994. Contributor to magazines and newspapers. **Address:** Danziger & Danziger, 405 Park Ave. Suite 1104, New York, NY 10022, U.S.A.

DANZIGER, Paula. See Obituaries.

DAOUST, Jean-Paul. Canadian, b. 1946. **Genres:** Poetry. **Career:** Writer, teacher, and editor. Cegep Edouard-Montpetit, Quebec, Canada, professor. **Publications:** POETRY: Oui, cher: Recit (title means: Yes, Dear: A Narrative), 1976; Chaise longues (title means: Lounge Chairs), 1977; Portrait d'interieur (title means: Portrait of an Interior), 1981; Poemes de Babylone (title means: Babylon Poems), 1982; Taxi, 1984; Dimanche apres-midi (title means: Sunday Afternoon), 1985; La peau du coeur et son opera (title means: Heart Skin and Its Opera), 1985; Les garcons magiques (title means: Magic Boys), 1986; Suite contemporaine (title means: Contemporary Suite), 1987; Rituels d'Ameriques (title means: Rituals of the Americas), 1990; Les cendres bleues (title means: Blue Ashes), 1990, rev. ed., 2001; Black Diva: Selected Poems, 1982-1986, 1991; Du Dandysme (title means: On Dandyism), 1991; Les chambres de la mer, 1991; Les poses de la lumiere (title means: Poses of Light), 1991; L'Amerique, 1993; Levres ouvertes, 1993, rev. ed., 2001; Fusions, 1994; (with L. Desjardins and M. Latif-Ghattas) Poemes faxes (title means: Faxed Poems), 1994; 111 Wooster Street, 1996; Taxi pour Babylone, 1996; Les saisons de l'Ange, 1997, vol. 2, 1999; Le poeme deshabille, 2000; Versets Amoureux, 2001; Roses labyrinthes, 2002. OTHER: Soleils d'acajou (novel; title means: The Mahogany Suns), 1983; Le Desert rose (novel), 2000. **Address:** 151 chemin Champoux, Ste-Melanie, QC, Canada J0K 3A0. **Online address:** mesanges@pandore.qc.ca

DARABONT, Frank. American (born France), b. 1959. **Genres:** Plays/Screenplays. **Career:** Screenwriter, director, and producer. **Publications:** SCREENPLAYS: (with W. Craven, C. Russell, and B. Wagner) A Nightmare on Elm Street 3: Dream Warriors, 1987; (with C. Russell) The Blob, 1988; (with M. Garris, J. Wheat, and K. Wheat) The Fly II, 1989; (with S. Lady) Mary Shelley's Frankenstein, 1994; The Shawshank Redemption, 1994; The Green Mile, 1999; The Adventures of Young Indiana Jones, 1999. TELEVISION SCRIPTS: The Ventriloquist's Dummy, 1990; Showdown, 1992; Two-Fisted Tales, 1992; Young Indiana Jones: Travels with Father, 1996; Black Cat Run, 1998. Contributing writer to screenplays. **Address:** c/o William Morris Agency, 151 El Camino Dr., Beverly Hills, CA 90212, U.S.A.

DARBY, Catherine. See PETERS, Maureen.

DARBY, John. British, b. 1940. **Genres:** History, Social sciences. **Career:** Chairman, Ethnic Studies Network, 1998-; Visiting Professor, University of Notre Dame, 1999-; Senior Research Fellow, The Initiative on Conflict Resolution and Ethnicity (INCORE) for the United Nations University and the University of Ulster, Professor of Ethnic Studies, 1984-88; University of Ulster, Coleraine, 1974-90 (Lecturer in Social Administration, 1974-84; Dir of the Centre for the Study of Conflict, 1984-90); Research-Publications Officer, Northern Ireland Community Relations Commission, 1971-74. **Publications:** Conflict in Northern Ireland, 1976; Violence and the Social Services in Northern Ireland, 1978; Northern Ireland: Background to the Conflict, 1983; Dressed to Kill: Cartoonists and the Northern Irish Conflict, 1983; Intimidation and the Control of Conflict in Northern Ireland, 1986; Political Violence: Northern Ireland in a Comparative Setting, 1990; Scorpions in a Bottle, 1997; The Management of Peace Processes, 2000. **Address:** Incore, University of Ulster, Coleraine, Northern Ireland. **Online address:** John@incore.ulst.ac.uk

DARBY, Mary Ann. American, b. 1954. **Genres:** Bibliography. **Career:** High school teacher of English and social studies, Corvallis, MT, 1976-77, Klamath Falls, OR, 1978-82, and Seattle, WA, 1982-88; middle-school teacher of language arts, Renton, WA, 1993-98, and Los Altos, CA, beginning 1998; Jefferson State Community College, Birmingham, AL, English teacher. University of Washington, Seattle, guest lecturer, 1997. City of Bellevue, part-time employee, 1990-92. **Publications:** (with Miki Pryne) Hearing All the Voices: Multicultural Books for Adolescents, 2002. Contributor of articles and reviews to periodicals. **Address:** 2233 Rockcreek Trail, Hoover, AL 35226, U.S.A. **Online address:** bkwoman2@yahoo.com

DARBY, William D(uane). American, b. 1942. **Genres:** Film. **Career:** Davenport University, professor in English, 1991-. **Publications:** Necessary American Fictions, 1987; (with J. DuBois) American Film Music, 1991; Masters of Lens and Light, 1992; (with D.F. Darby) Major League Baseball, 1979-1992, 1993; John Ford's Westerns, 1996. **Address:** 13168 E Outer Dr, Detroit, MI 48224-2735, U.S.A.

DARDEN, Robert. American, b. 1954. **Genres:** Documentaries/Reportage, Ghost Writer. **Career:** Waco Tribune-Herald, Waco, TX, arts and entertainment editor, 1978-86; Door, Waco, senior editor, 1987-; Baylor University, assistant professor of English, 1999-. **Publications:** December Champions; Drawing Power; Fast Forward; Handel's Young Messiah; Into the Endzone; Mad Man in Waco; There's Always a Way: The Story of Kevin Saunders; The Option Play; (with P.J. Richardson) The Way of an Eagle; I, Jesus, 1996; (with P.J. Richardson) Wheels of Thunder, 1996; (with P.J. Richardson) Corporate Giants, 2002; People Get Ready: A New History of Black Gospel Music, 2004. EDITOR: What a World! The Collected Essays of Dr. Ralph Lynn; The Door Compilation. Contributor to books and periodicals. **Address:** PO Box 1444, Waco, TX 76703-1444, U.S.A. **Online address:** dooreditor@earthlink.net

DARKE, Marjorie (Sheila). British, b. 1929. **Genres:** Children's fiction. **Career:** Textile designer, John Lewis Partnership, London, 1951-54: Writer 1962-. **Publications:** Ride the Iron Horse, 1973; The Star Trap, 1974; Mike's Bike, 1974; A Question of Courage, 1975; What Can I Do?, 1975; The Big Brass Band, 1976; Kipper's Turn, 1976; My Uncle Charlie, 1977; The First of Midnight, 1977; A Long Way to Go, 1978; Kipper Skips, 1979; Carnival Day, 1979; Comeback, 1981; Tom Post's Private Eye, 1983; Messages: A Collection of Shivery Tales, 1984; Imp, 1985; The Rainbow Sandwich, 1989; A Rose from Blighty, 1990; Night Windows, 1990; Emma's Monster, 1992; Just Bear and Friends, 1996. **Address:** c/o Rogers Coleridge and White Ltd, 20 Powis Mews, London W11 1JN, England.

DARLING, David J. British, b. 1953. **Genres:** Adult non-fiction, Astronomy, Children's non-fiction, Philosophy, Physics, Sciences, Theology/Religion, Young adult non-fiction. **Career:** Cray Research, Minneapolis, MN, manager of applications software, 1978-82; free-lance writer, 1983-. **Publications:** JUVENILE NONFICTION. DISCOVERING OUR UNIVERSE SERIES: Comets, Meteors, and Asteroids, 1984; The Moon: A Spaceflight Away, 1984; The Planets: The Next Frontier, 1984; The Sun: Our Neighborhood Star, 1984; Where Are We Going in Space?, 1984; Other Worlds: Is There Life Out There?, 1985; The Galaxies: Cities of Stars, 1985; The New Astronomy, 1985; The Stars, 1985; The Universe, 1985. WORLD OF COMPUTERS SERIES: Computers at Home, 1986; Faster, Faster, Fastest: The Story of Supercomputers, 1986; Inside Computers, 1986; The Microchip Revolution, 1986; Robots and the Intelligent Computer, 1986. COULD YOU EVER... SERIES: Build a Time Machine?, 1990; Dig a Hole to China?, 1990; Fly to the Stars?, 1990; Meet an Alien?, 1990; Speak Chimpanzee?, 1990; Could You Ever?, 1991; Live Forever?, 1991. OTHER: Diana, the People's Princess (biography), 1984. EXPERIMENT SERIES: Making Light Work: The Science of Optics, 1991; Up, Up, and Away: The Science of Flight, 1991; Spiderwebs to Skyscrapers: The Science of Structures, 1991; Sounds Interesting: The Science of Accoustics, 1991; Between Fire and Ice: The Science of Heat, 1992; From Glasses to Gases: The Science of Matter, 1992. BEYOND 2000 SERIES: Genetic Engineering, 1995; Micromachines and Nanotechnology, 1995; Computers of the Future, 1996; The Health Revolution: Surgery and Medicine in the 21st Century, 1996. ADULT NONFICTION: Deep Time, 1989; Equations of Eternity, 1993; Soul Search, 1995; Zen Physics, 1996; The Extraterrestrial Encyclopedia, 2000: Life Everywhere: The Maverick Science of Astrobiology, 2001; The Complete Book of Spaceflight, 2002. Contributor of articles and reviews to periodicals. **Address:** 8776 Dorothy Ave, Brainerd, MN 56401-7084, U.S.A. **Online address:** daviddarling@angelfire.com; www.daviddarling.info

DARLING, Diana. American, b. 1947. **Genres:** Novels. **Career:** Sculptor. Worked at Studio Nicoli, Carrara, Italy, 1973-75, 1979-80, Cite Internationale des Arts, Paris, France, 1976-78, and Meridian Sculpture Founders, Melbourne, Australia, periodically throughout the 1980s. **Publications:** The Painted Alphabet (novel), 1992; Marc Jurt, 1997. **Address:** Tegalsuci, Tegallalang, Gianyar Bali, Indonesia.

DARLING, Julia. British, b. 1956. **Genres:** Poetry, Novellas/Short stories, Novels. **Career:** Community arts worker in Sunderland, England, 1980-86; writer, 1988-. **Publications:** Sauce (poems), 1993; Bloodlines (stories),

1995; Crocodile Soup (novel), 1998. PLAYS: Black Gold; Raffert's Cafe. **Address:** 5 Charlotte Sq., Newcastle upon Tyne NE1 4XF, England. **Online address:** J.Darl14134@aol.com

DARLING, T. H. *See* **HARRIS, Thomas Walter.**

DARLINGTON, Ralph. British, b. 1954. **Genres:** History, Industrial relations, Organized labor. **Career:** University of Salford, Salford, England, lecturer, 1991-; writer. **Publications:** The Dynamics of Workplace Unionism: Shop Stewards' Organization in Three Merseyside Plants, 1994; The Political Trajectory of J.T. Murphy, 1998; (with D. Lyddon) Glorious Summer: Class Struggle in Britain, 1972, 2001. **Address:** School of Management, University of Salford, Salford M5 4WT, England. **Online address:** r.r.darlington@salford.au.uk

DARNAY, Arsen J. American (born Hungary). **Genres:** Science fiction/Fantasy, Environmental sciences/Ecology, Information science/Computers, Mathematics/Statistics. **Career:** Government and industry executive, writer, publisher; Editorial Code and Data, Inc, president, 1990-. **Publications:** (with W.E. Franklin) The Role of Packaging in Solid Waste Management 1966 to 1970, 1971; (with W.E. Franklin) Salvage Markets for Materials in Solid Wastes, 1972; A Hostage for Hinterland, 1976; The Karma Affair, 1978; The Siege of Faltara, 1978; The Purgatory Zone, 1981; The Splendid Freedom, 1983; Manufacturing USA, 1989; Market Share Reporter, 1990; American Salaries and Wages Survey, 1990; Services Industry USA, 1991; Economic Indicateors Handbook; Statistical Record of the Environment, 1991; Finance, Insurance, Real Estate USA, 1992; Transportation and Public Utilities USA, 997; Agriculture, Mining and Construction USA, 1998. **Address:** 259 McKinley, Grosse Pointe Farms, MI 48236, U.S.A.

DARNELL, Regna (Diebold). American/Canadian, b. 1943. **Genres:** Anthropology/Ethnology, Biography, Language/Linguistics. **Career:** Professor of Anthropology, University of Western Ontario. **Publications:** Readings in the History of Anthropology, 1974; Daniel Garrison Brinton: The Fearless Critic of Philadelphia, 1988; Edward Sapir: Linguist, Anthropologist, Humanist, 1990; (ed. with J. Irvine) Collected Works of Edward Sapir 4: Ethnology, 1994; And Along Came Boas: Continuity and Revolution in Americanist Anthropology, 1998; (ed. with J. Irvine and R. Handler) Collected Works of Edward Sapir 3: Ethnology, 1999; (ed. with L. Valentine) Theorizing the Americanist Tradition, 1999; Invisible Genealogies: A History of Americanist Anthropology, 2001. **Address:** Dept. of Anthropology, University of Western Ontario, Social Science Centre, London, ON, Canada N6A 5C2. **Online address:** rdarnell@julian.uwo.ca

DARNTON, Robert. American, b. 1939. **Genres:** History, Literary criticism and history. **Career:** Princeton University, NJ, Shelby Collum Davis Professor of European History. **Publications:** Mesmerism and the End of the Enlightenment in France, 1968; The Business of Enlightenment: A Publishing History of the Encyclopaedie, 1979; The Literary Underground of the Old Regime, 1982; The Great Cat Massacre and Other Episodes in French Cultural History, 1984; The Kiss Lamourette: Reflections in Cultural History, 1989; Edition and sedition: L'universe de la litterature clandestine au XVIIe siecle, 1991; Berlin Journal, 1989-1990, 1991; Gens de lettres, gens du livre, 1992; The Forbidden Best-Sellers of Pre-Revolutionary France, 1994; The Corpus of Clandestine Literature in France, 1994; J.-P. Brissot, His Career and Correspondence (1779-1878), 2001; Pour les Lumieres: Defense, illustration, methode, 2020. EDITOR: (with D. Roche) Revolution in Print, 1989; (with O. Duhamel) Democratie, 1998. **Address:** Dept. of History, Princeton University, Princeton, NJ 08540, U.S.A.

DARRIEUSSECQ, Marie. French, b. 1970?. **Genres:** Novels. **Career:** Writer; employed as a professor of literature in France. **Publications:** Truismes, 1996, trans. by L. Coverdale as Pig Tales: A Novel of Lust and Transformation, 1997. **Address:** c/o The Fund for Independent Publishing, 38 Greene St., Floor 4, New York, NY 10013-2505, U.S.A.

DARROCH, James L. Canadian, b. 1951. **Genres:** Economics. **Career:** McMaster University, Hamilton, Ontario, Canada, lecturer in European history, 1979; Queen's University, Kingston, Ontario, assistant professor of European history, 1980-82; Wilfrid Laurier University, Waterloo, Ontario, assistant professor of business policy, 1985-86; York University, North York, Ontario, sessional assistant professor, 1986-88, assistant professor, 1988-93, associate professor of policy studies and director of entrepreneurial studies, both 1993-. **Publications:** Canadian Banks and Global Competitiveness, 1994. Contributor to books. Contributor of articles and reviews to business management and banking journals. **Address:** 204 Policy Area, Faculty of Administrative Studies, York University, 4700 Keele St., North York, ON, Canada M3J 1P3.

DART, Iris Rainer. American. **Genres:** Novels. **Career:** Writer. **Publications:** NOVELS: The Boys in the Mail Room, 1980; Beaches, 1985; 'Til the Real Thing Comes Along, 1987; I'll Be There, Little, 1991; The Stork Club, 1992; Show Business Kills, 1995. Collaborated on episode of television series That Girl. **Address:** c/o Elaine Markson Literary Agency, 44 Greenwich Ave, Fl 3, New York, NY 10011, U.S.A.

DARTON, Eric. American, b. 1950. **Genres:** Novels, History. **Publications:** Radio Tirane (fiction), 1991; Free City (novel), 1996; Divided We Stand (history), 2000. **Address:** c/o Watkins Loomis Agency Inc., 133 E 35th St, New York, NY 10016, U.S.A.

DARVILLE, Helen (Fiona). Also writes as Helen Demidenko. Australian, b. 1971. **Genres:** Novels. **Career:** Writer and lecturer. Appeared on radio broadcasts. **Publications:** NOVELS: (As Helen Demidenko) The Hand That Signed the Paper, 1994; republished as Helen Darville, 1996. Contributor to books and periodicals. **Address:** c/o Allen & Unwin, PO Box 8500, St. Leonards, NSW, Australia.

DARWISH, Adel. British (born Egypt), b. 1945. **Genres:** Politics/Government, Cultural/Ethnic topics, International relations/Current affairs, History, Military/Defense/Arms control, Third World, Area studies, Translations, Writing/Journalism. **Career:** Free-lance writer, 1966-84; Asharq Al-Awsat, London, England, editor, 1984; Independent, London, reporter on foreign affairs, 1986-. Middle East consultant and commentator to television and radio stations and to strategic studies centers, 1988-. **Publications:** Secret Diplomacy and Islamic Fundamentalism in Egypt, 1983; The Muslim Brotherhood and Britain in the 1950s, 1984; Iraqi Defence Strategy in the Gulf War, 1987; Between the Quill and the Sword: The Political Background to the Satanic Verses Affair, 1989; (with G. Alexander) Unholy Babylon: The Secret History of Saddam's War, 1991; (with J. Bulloch) Water Wars: Coming Conflicts in the Middle East, 1993. **Address:** The Independent, 1 Canada Square, Canary Wharf, London E14, England. **Online address:** adeld@mideastnews.com

DARY, David Archie. American, b. 1934. **Genres:** Communications/Media, History, Social commentary, Bibliography. **Career:** Reporter and Ed., CBS News 1960-63; Manager of Local News, NBC News, Washington D.C., 1963-67; Professor of Journalism, University of Kansas, Lawrence, 1969-89; Professor of Journalism, University of Oklahoma, Norman, and Director, School of Journalism and Mass Communication, 1989-2000, now retired. President, Western Writers of America, 1989-90. **Publications:** Radio News Handbook, 1967, 1970; TV News Handbook, 1971; How to Write News for Broadcast and Print Media, 1973; The Buffalo Book, 1974; Tales of the Old-Time Plains, 1979; Cowboy Culture, 1981; True Tales of Old-Time Kansas, 1984; Entrepreneurs of the Old West, 1986; More True Tales of Old Time Kansas, 1987; Kanzana, 1854-1900: A Selected Bibliography of Books, Pamphlets and Ephemera of Kansas, 1986; Lawrence, Douglas County Kansas: An Informal History, 1982; Pictorial History of Lawrence, Douglas County Kansas, 1992; Seeking Pleasure in the Old West, 1995; Red Blood and Black Ink: Journalism in the Old West, 1998; The Santa Fe Trail: Its History, Legends, and Lore, 2000; The Oregon Trail: An American Saga, 2004. **Address:** 1113 Robin Hood Ln, Norman, OK 73072, U.S.A.

DAS, Lama Surya. American, b. 1950. **Genres:** Inspirational/Motivational Literature. **Career:** English teacher, Kyoto, Japan, 1973-74; Karma Triyana Dharma Chakra monastery, Woodstock, NY, founder, 1977, director, 1977-80; Lama in the Non-Sectarian Practice Lineage of Tibetan Buddhism; meditation workshop and retreat teacher in Dzogchen, Vajrayana, and Mahayana Buddhism; worker with Cambodian and Vietnamese boat people; organizer of the Western Buddhist Teachers Network with Dalai Lama and its teachers' conferences, Dharamsala, India; founding board member of the Seva Foundation; founder of the Dzogchen Foundation, Cambridge, MA. Talks by Lama Surya Das have been recorded on audio cassettes; Beliefnet, online columnist. **Publications:** The Snow Lion's Turquoise Mane: Wisdom Tales from Tibet, 1992; (with N.K. Rinpoche; and trans.) Natural Great Perfection: Dzogchen Teachings and Vajra Songs, 1995; Dancing with Life: Dzogchen View, Meditation, and Action, 1996; Awakening the Buddha Within: Eight Steps to Enlightenment, 1997; The Facts of Life from a Buddhist Perspective; Awakening to the Sacred; Awakening the Buddhist Heart; Letting Go of the Person You Used to Be. Translator, editor, and publisher of Buddhist works. Contributor of articles and poetry to periodicals. **Address:** c/o Cambridge Dzogchen Center, 5 Longfellow Park, Cambridge, MA 02138-4896, U.S.A. **Online address:** surya@surya.org

DAS, Suranjan. Indian, b. 1954. **Genres:** Civil liberties/Human rights, Cultural/Ethnic topics, Local history/Rural topics, Politics/Government.

Career: Visva-Bharati University, Santiniketan, India, lecturer in history, 1978-81; University of Calcutta, Calcutta, India, reader in history, 1981-, member of university senate. **Publications:** Communal Riots in Bengal, 1905-1947, 1991; The Goondas, 1996; Kashmir & Sindh, 2002. EDITOR: (with S. Bandopadhyay) Caste and Communal Politics in India, in press; Electoral Politics in South Asia, 2000. Work represented in anthologies. Contributor of articles and reviews to scholarly journals and Indian newspapers. **Address:** University of Calcutta, Department of History, 5 1/2 Hazra Road, Calcutta 700 019, India.

DASA, Drutakarma. See CREMO, Michael (A.).

DASCAL, Marcelo. Israeli (born Brazil), b. 1940. **Genres:** Language/Linguistics, Philosophy, Speech/Rhetoric. **Career:** University of Sao Paulo, Brazil, instructor, 1964; Hebrew University of Jerusalem, researcher and lecturer, 1967-72; Ben Gurion University of the Negev, Beer-Sheva, Israel, 1967-76, began as lecturer, became senior lecturer, chair of department of philosophy, 1969-73; Tel Aviv University, began as instructor, became professor of philosophy, 1967-; Universidade Estadual de Campinas, Campinas, Brazil, professor, 1974-85; Young Persons Institute for Arts and Sciences, Tel Aviv, teacher, 1975-92; writer. University of Massachusetts, visiting lecturer, 1973-74; University of California at Berkeley, visiting associate professor of philosophy, 1980. Manuscrito, editor, 1982-99; Pragmatics & Cognition, editor, 1991-. **Publications:** Filosofia das Ciencias (title means: Philosophy of Science), 1964; La Semiologie de Leibniz (Leibniz's Semiotics), 1978; Pragmatics and the Philosophy of Mind, Vol. 1: Thought in Language, 1983; Leibniz: Language, Signs, and Thought, 1987; Interpretaton and Understanding, 2003; Mashav Haruach (The Gust of the Wind), 2004. EDITOR: (with A. Parush) Harationali Vehairatzionali (The Rational and the Irrational), 1975; Fundamentos Metodologicos da Linguistica (Methodological Foundations of Linguistics), 4 vols., 1978-82; (with M. Brinker and D. Nesher) Baruch de Spinoza: Kovetz ma'amarim al mishnato (Baruch de Spinoza: A Collection of Essays on His Thought), 1979; Tekstim Filosofi'im, 1979-; (with J. Gracia, E. Rabossi, and E. Villanueva) Philosophical Analysis in Latin America, 1984; Dialogue: An Interdisciplinary Approach, 1985; (with cooperation of O. Zimmermann) M. Buber, Sobre Comunidade (On Community), 1987; Ma? Da!, 1987-; (with O. Gruengard) Knowledge and Politics, 1989; (with A. Cohen) The Institution of Philosophy, 1989; Conhecimento, Linguagm, Ideologia (Knowledge, Language, Ideology), 1989; Cultural Relativism and Philosophy, 1991; (with D. Gerhardus, K. Lorenz, and G. Meggle) Philosophy of Language, 2 vols., 1993-95; (with E. Yakira) Leibniz and Adam, 1993; (with R. Gibbs and J. Nuyts) Human Cognitive Processes, 1996-; (with others) Eucuentros and Desencuenbros: Spanish-Jewish Cultural Interactions, 2000: (with E. Weigand) Negotiation and Power in Dialogic Interaction, 2001. Contributor to professional journals. **Address:** Dept of Philosophy, Tel Aviv University, 69978 Tel Aviv, Israel. **Online address:** dascal@post.tau.ac.il

DASGUPTA, Shamita Das. American (born India), b. 1949. **Genres:** Psychology. **Career:** Franklin University, Columbus, OH, member of adjunct faculty of behavioral sciences, 1982-83; Rutgers University, Newark Campus, Newark, NJ, teacher of psychology and women's studies, 1985-90, director of honors program, 1989-90; Women's Resources of Monroe County, Stroudsburg, PA, executive director, 1990-92; Rutgers University, Newark Campus, lecturer, 1992-95, assistant professor of psychology, 1996-. Kean College of New Jersey, member of adjunct faculty, 1987-90; New School for Social Research, faculty member in Adult Division, 1989-90; lecturer at colleges and universities, including Cornell University, Yale University, University of Illinois at Urbana-Champaign, Columbia University, and Wiliams College. Manavi (organization for South Asian women in the United States), cofounder, 1985, coordinator, 1985-; consultant to Health Research and Educational Trust of New Jersey, U.S. Marine Corps, and Bell Laboratories. **Publications:** (with S. Warrier) In Visible Terms: Domestic Violence in the Asian Indian Context, 1995, rev ed, 1997. EDITOR & CONTRIBUTOR: (with S. DasGupta) The Demon Slayers and Other Stories: Bengali Folk Tales, 1995; A Patchwork Shawl: Chronicles of South Asian Women in America, 1998. Contributor to books and periodicals. **Address:** c/o Sage Publications, 2455 Teller Rd, Thousand Oaks, CA 91320, U.S.A. **Online address:** Sddas@andromeda.rutgers.edu

DASGUPTA, Subrata. Canadian (born India), b. 1944. **Genres:** Novels, Information science/Computers, Intellectual history, Psychology. **Career:** International Business Machines World Trade Corp., Calcutta, India, programmer and systems analyst, 1967-71; Simon Fraser University, Burnaby, BC, assistant professor of computer science, 1975-79; Ohio State University, Columbus, assistant professor of computer science and information science, 1979-80; University of Alberta, Edmonton, associate professor of computer science, 1980-82; University of Southwestern Louisiana, Lafayette, associate professor, 1982-84, professor, 1984-86, Edmiston Professor of Computer Science, 1986-92; Victoria University of Manchester, England, Dowty Professor of Computer Systems Engineering at Institute of Science and Technology, 1992-93; University of Louisiana at Lafayette, eminent scholar endowed chair in computer science, 1993-, professor of history, 1993-, director of Institute of Cognitive Science, 2000-. Lecturer at colleges and universities around the world. **Publications:** The Design and Description of Computer Architectures, 1984; Computer Architecture: A Modern Synthesis, Vol I: Foundations, Vol II: Advanced Topics, 1989; Design Theory and Computer Science, 1991; Creativity in Invention and Design, 1994; Technology and Creativity, 1996; Jagadis Chandra Bose and the Indian Response to Western Science, 1999; Three Times a Minority (novel), 2003. Contributor to books. Contributor to scientific journals. **Address:** Institute of Cognitive Science, University of Louisiana at Lafayette, PO Box 43772, Lafayette, LA 70504-3772, U.S.A. **Online address:** subrata@louisiana.edu

DASH, Julie. American. **Genres:** Plays/Screenplays. **Career:** Screenwriter, producer, and director. Motion Picture Association of America, Los Angeles, CA, member of Classifications and Ratings Administration, 1978-80; Geechee Girls Multimedia Productions Inc., founder. Director of documentaries, films, and music videos. **Publications:** SCREENPLAYS: Working Models of Success, 1973; Diary of an African Nun, 1977; Four Women, 1975; Illusions, 1983; Daughters of the Dust, 1992, published with memoir as Daughters of the Dust: The Making of an African American Woman's Film, 1992, novel adaptation as Daughters of the Dust, 1997. **Address:** c/o Dutton, 375 Hudson St., New York, NY 10014, U.S.A. **Online address:** geecheegirl@pacificnet.net

DASSANOWSKY, Robert. (Robert von Dassanowsky). American/Austrian, b. 1960. **Genres:** Plays/Screenplays, Poetry, Literary criticism and history, Documentaries/Reportage, Translations. **Career:** University of Colorado, Colorado Springs, assistant professor of German, 1993-99, head of German studies and director of film studies, 1993-, associate professor of German and film, 1999-, interim chair of Dept of Visual and Performing Arts, 2000-01, chair of Dept of Languages and Cultures, 2001-. Professional actor, 1976-83; writer/researcher for Stone-Stanley Television Productions and Disney Channel, Los Angeles, 1990-92; consultant/translator, J. Paul Getty Conservation Institute, Los Angeles, 1991-93; University of California-Los Angeles, visiting assistant professor of German, 1992-93; Colorado P.E.N., founding president, 1994-99; Austrian American Film Assn, founding vp, 1997-; Intl Alexander Lernet-Holenia Society, founding vp, 1998-. Belvedere Film, co-head, 1999-; producer or executive producer, films: Semmelweis, 2001; The Nightmare Stumbles Past, 2002; Believe, 2003; Wilson Chance, 2005. Celluloid magazine, columnist, 2002-. **Publications:** Phantom Empires: The Novels of Alexander Lernet-Holenia and the Question of Postimperial Austrian Identity, 1996; (trans.) H. Raimund, Verses of a Marriage, 1996; Telegrams from the Metropole: Selected Poetry 1999; (trans.) A. Lernet-Holenia, Mars in Aries, 2003; Austrian Cinema, 2005. PLAYS: The Birthday of Margot Beck, 1980; Briefly Noted, 1981; Vespers, 1982; Tristan in Winter, 1986; Songs of a Wayfarer, 1986; Coda, 1991. Author of television scripts. Contributor to books. Contributor of poetry, reviews, and critical articles on literature, film and sociopolitics to periodicals, anthologies, and collections. **Address:** Dept of Languages and Cultures, University of Colorado, PO Box 7150, Colorado Springs, CO 80933, U.S.A. **Online address:** belvederefilm@yahoo.com

DATES, Jannette L. American. **Genres:** Writing/Journalism, Race relations, Social commentary. **Career:** Baltimore City Public School System, MD, classroom demonstration teacher, 1958-63, television demonstration teacher, 1964-69, producer and writer of elementary and secondary school telecourses, 1964-71; Goucher College, Baltimore, instructor in department of education, 1970-72; Morgan State University, Baltimore, instructor in department of education, 1970-72, instructor, 1972-77, assistant professor in department of communication and theater arts, 1977-80, coordinator of university television projects, 1973-80; Howard University, Washington, DC, assistant professor in department of radio, television, and film and sequence coordinator for broadcast management/policy, 1981-85, associate dean for educational affairs in school of communications, 1987-92, associate professor, 1990-99, professor in department of radio, television and film, 1999-; Coppin State College, Baltimore, associate professor in department of languages, literature, and journalism and director of video production service, 1985-87. **Publications:** (ed. with W. Barlow, and contrib.) Split Image: African Americans in the Mass Media, 1990, rev. ed., 1993. Contributor to books. Contributor to periodicals. **Address:** School of Communications, Howard University, Washington, DC 20059, U.S.A.

D'ATH, Justin. Australian (born New Zealand), b. 1953. **Genres:** Novels, Science fiction/Fantasy, Children's fiction, Young adult fiction. **Career:**

TAFE, Bendigo Regional Institute, teacher of professional writing. Teaches literacy and mathematics classes at a women's prison. Also managed a club at an Aborigine mission and worked as forklift driver, car builder, ranch worker, fruit picker, iron miner, sugar mill worker, store clerk, laboratory technician, and electrical worker. **Publications:** The Initiate (novel), 1989. FOR CHILDREN: Infamous, 1996; Humungous, 1997; Fantabulous, 1998; Why Did the Chykkan Cross the Galaxy?, 1998; SNIWT, 1999; The Upside Down Girl, 2000; Topsy and Turvy, 2001; Koala Fever, 2001; Goldfever, 2001; Echidna Mania, 2001; Snowman Magic, 2002; Astrid Spark, Fixologist, 2002. FOR YOUNG ADULTS: Hunters and Warriors, 2001; Shaedow Master, 2003. Contributor of adult stories and articles to magazines.

DAUBER, Philip M. American, b. 1942. **Genres:** Plays/Screenplays, Documentaries/Reportage. **Career:** Alameda High School, Alameda, CA, teacher of physics and astronomy, 1994-. **Publications:** The Search for Anti-worlds (documentary film), 1976; Spaceborne (short film), 1977; (with R.A. Muller) The Three Big Bangs, 1996. Contributor to magazines. **Address:** Alameda High School, 2201 Encinal Ave., Alameda, CA 94501, U.S.A.

DAUDEYOS, Armand. See SALMON, John (Hearsey McMillan) in the Obituaries.

DAUER, Lesley. American, b. 1965. **Genres:** Poetry. **Career:** University of Massachusetts at Amherst, instructor in English and creative writing, 1989-91; Johns Hopkins University, Baltimore, MD, instructor in English at Center for Talented Youth, 1993-97; Foothill College, Los Altos Hills, CA, instructor in English and creative writing, 1996-. Cabrillo College, instructor, 1996-97; private writing tutor; Foothill Writers' Conference, associate director; Project Read Literacy Program, volunteer teacher, 1987-88. **Publications:** The Fragile City (poems), 1996. Work represented in anthologies. Contributor of poems to journals. **Address:** 488 University Ave. No. 310, Palo Alto, CA 94301, U.S.A.

DAUGHARTY, Janice. American, b. 1944. **Genres:** Novels, Novellas/Short stories. **Career:** Homemaker; worked briefly as a librarian; freelance writer, 1994-. **Publications:** NOVELS: Dark of the Moon, 1994; Necessary Lies, 1995; Pawpaw Patch, 1996; Earl in the Yellow Shirt, 1997; Whistle, 1998; Like a Sister, 1999; Just Doll, 2004. OTHER: Going through the Change (short stories), 1994.

DAUGHERTY, Greg(ory Ash). American, b. 1953. **Genres:** Money/Finance. **Career:** Success, NYC, articles editor in Chicago, IL, 1981-84, managing editor, 1984-85; Sylvia Porter's Personal Finance, NYC, managing editor, 1985-86, executive editor, 1986-89; Consumer Reports, Yonkers, NY, economics editor, 1989-. Contributing editor, World: The Magazine for Decision Makers, 1987-. Correspondent, Writer's Digest, 1987-. **Publications:** The Consumer Reports Mutual Funds Book, 1994. Contributor to magazines and newspapers. **Address:** Consumer Reports, 101 Truman Ave., Yonkers, NY 10703, U.S.A.

DAUGHTREY, Anne Scott. American. **Genres:** Administration/Management, Business/Trade/Industry, Economics. **Career:** Old Dominion University, Norfolk, VA, assistant professor, 1959-63, associate professor, 1963-66, professor, 1966-79, Eminent Professor of Management, 1979-88, Emerita 1988-. **Publications:** Basic Business and Economic Education, 1965, 4th ed. (with Ristau), 1991; (with S. J. DeBrum, P. Haines and D. Malsbary) General Business for Economic Understanding, 11th ed. 1976, 12th ed. (with Ristau and DeBrum), 1981; (with Ristau and Eggland) Introduction to Business, 1986, 3rd ed. (with Ristau, Eggland, Dlabay, and Burrow), 1996; (with B. Ricks) Contemporary Supervision: Managing People and Technology, 1989, 2nd ed. (with Ricks and Ginn), 1995; papers in professional journals, plus monographs and chapters.

DAUGHTRY, Herbert D(aniel), (Sr.). American, b. 1931. **Genres:** Theology/Religion. **Career:** House of the Lord Churches, national presiding Pentecostal minister, c. 1960-. **Publications:** A Special Message to Men of African Ancestry, 1981; Seize the Future: Two Speeches, 1981; No Monopoly on Suffering: Blacks and Jews in Crown Heights (and Elsewhere), 1997; My Beloved Community: Sermons, Speeches, and Lectures, 2001; The House of the Lord Pentecostal Church: Official Orientation Material; Jesus Christ: African in Origin, Revolutionary in Action; Inside the Storm; From Magnificence to Wretchedness: The Sad Saga of Black Humanity. **Address:** House of the Lord Churches, 415 Atlantic Ave., Brooklyn, NY 11217, U.S.A.

D'AVENI, Richard. American. **Genres:** Adult non-fiction. **Career:** Educator and author. University of North Carolina at Chapel Hill, assistant professor of business, 1986-88; Amos Tuck School of Business Administration,

Dartmouth College, Hanover, NH, professor of strategic management, 1988-; CEO and founder, RadStrat.com. Consultant to Fortune 500 corporations; regular speaker at executive education programs, including Wharton School of Business. **Publications:** (with Richard E. Gunther) Hypercompetition: Managing the Dynamics of Strategic Maneuvering, 1994; Hypercompetitive Rivalries, 1995; (with Robert E. Gunther and Joni Cole) Strategic Supremacy: How Industry Leaders Create Growth, Wealth, and Power through Spheres of Influence, 2001. Contributor to journals. **Address:** Tuck School of Business at Dartmouth, 100 Tuck Hall, Hanover, NH 03755, U.S.A. **Online address:** richard.a.daveni@dartmouth.edu

DAVENPORT, Guy (Mattison), (Jr.). *See* Obituaries.

DAVENPORT, John (Chester). British, b. 1938. **Genres:** Medicine/Health. **Career:** In general dental practice, Cambridge, 1963-64; Bristol Dental School, sr. house officer, 1964, registrar, 1965-66;, University of Birmingham, lecturer, 1966-79, sr. lecturer in dental prosthetics, 1979-95, professor of primary dental care, 1995-2000; Birmingham Area Health Authority, sr. registrar, 1966-79, consultant, 1979-95. **Publications:** (with R.M. Basker and H.R. Tomlin) Prosthetic Treatment of the Edentulous Patient, 1976, 4th ed., 2002; A Colour Atlas of Removable Partial Dentures, 1988; Clinical Guide to Removable Partial Dentures, 2000; Clinical Guide to Removable Partial Denture Design, 2000. **Address:** Dental School, St. Chad's Queensway, Birmingham B4 6NN, England.

DAVENPORT, Paul. Canadian (born United States), b. 1946. **Genres:** Economics. **Career:** McGill University, Montreal, Quebec, professor of economics, 1973-89; University of Alberta, president and vice-chancellor, 1989-94; University of Western Ontario, president and vice-chancellor, 1994-; writer. **Publications:** University Education in Quebec: An Economic Perspective, 1979; (with C. Green, B. Watson, and others) Industrial Policy in Ontario and Quebec, 1982; (ed. with R.T. Leach, and contrib.) Reshaping Confederation: The 1982 Reform of the Canadian Constitution, 1984. **Address:** President & Vice-Chancellor, University of Western Ontario, 1151 Richmond St, London, ON, Canada N6A 3K7. **Online address:** pdavenpo@uwo.ca

DAVENPORT, Roger (Hamilton). British, b. 1946. **Genres:** Children's fiction, Young adult fiction. **Career:** Worked as actor, 1967-80, advertising executive, 1980-82, and theater manager, 1983-84; writer, TV and radio scripts, 1985-. **Publications:** JUVENILE NOVELS: Onlooker, 1989; Pieces of the Game, 1993; Out of His Mind, 1996; Lowlake, 2000; Ortho's Brood, 2001.

DAVENPORT-HINES, Richard (Peter Treadwell). British, b. 1953. **Genres:** Art/Art history, Literary criticism and history, Sex, Biography. **Career:** University of London, London School of Economics and Political Science, England, research officer, 1982-86; writer. Radio broadcaster. **Publications:** Dudley Docker, 1984; Sex, Death, and Punishment: Attitudes to Sex and Sexuality in Britain since the Renaissance, 1990; Glaxo: A History to 1962, 1992; The Macmillans, 1992; Vice, 1993; Auden, 1995; Gothic: 400 Years of Excess, Horror, Evil and Ruin, 1998; The Pursuit of Oblivion: A Global History of Narcotics, 2001; A Night at the Majestic, 2005. EDITOR: Speculators and Patriots, 1986; Markets and Bagmen, 1986; Business in the Age of Reason, 1987; The End of Insularity, 1988; British Business in Asia since 1860, 1989; Business in the Age of Depression and War, 1990. **Address:** 51 Elsham Rd, London W14 8HD, England. **Online address:** jdavenp225@aol.com

DAVEY, H. E. American. **Genres:** Art/Art history. **Career:** Teacher of Japanese arts, including martial arts, yoga, and calligraphy. Sennin Foundation, Inc., Albany, CA, president; also founder and director of Center for Japanese Cultural Arts. Kokusai Budoin, councilor at headquarters in Tokyo, Japan, director of U.S. branch, and teacher of nihon jujutsu and kobudo. Art work in the form of brush writing is exhibited annually in Japan. **Publications:** The Way of the Universe, 1985; Unlocking the Secrets of Aiki-jujutsu, 1997; Brush Meditation: A Japanese Way to Mind and Body Harmony, 1999; (with Ann H. Kameoka) The Japanese Way of the Flower: Ikebana as Moving Meditation, 2000; Japanese Yoga: The Way of Dynamic Meditation, 2001; Living the Japanese Arts and Ways: Forty-five Paths to Meditation and Beauty, 2003. Contributor of articles and art work to periodicals. **Address:** Tuck School of Business at Dartmouth, Albany, CA 94706, U.S.A.

DAVID, Catherine. American, b. 1949. **Genres:** Biography. **Career:** Nouvel Observateur, Paris, France, journalist. **Publications:** BIOGRAPHIES: Simone Signoret, trans S. Sampson, 1992. NOVELS: L'ocean miniature, 1983; Beaute du geste, 1994, trans A. Anderson as The Beauty of Gesture: The

Invisible Keyboard of Piano and T'ai Chi, 1996; Passage de l'ange, 1995; Egyptes, 1997; Little Bang, 1999; Homme qui savait tout, 2001. **Address:** c/o North Atlantic Books, 1456 Fourth St., Berkeley, CA 94710, U.S.A.

DAVID, Catherine. French, b. 1954. **Genres:** Art/Art history. **Career:** Musee National d'Art Moderne, Centre Georges Pompidou, Paris, France, curator, 1981-90; Ecole du Louvre, Paris, professor of contemporary art, 1989-91; University of Paris, Paris, professor of anthropology and aesthetics, 1990-93; Galerie Nationale de Jeu de Paume, Paris, 1990-; Documenta X, Kassel, Germany, curator of exhibit, 1994-97. **Publications:** Gilberto Zorio, 1986; (with B. Blistene and A. Pacquement) L'Epoque, la mode, la morale, la passion: aspects de l'art d'aujourd'hui, 1977-1987, 1987; (with J-F Chevrier) Suzanne Lafont, 1991; (with C. Merewether and L.S. Sims) Wifredo Lam: A Retrospective of Works on Paper, 1992; (with M-C MendesFrance) L'esprit de liberte, 1992; Art & Language, 1993; (with A. Barzel) Raymundo Sesma: Dies solis, estudio para una Ultima cena: video installazione, 1993; Day After Day, 1994; Bordering on Fiction, 1995; Documenta X: The Book, 1997. Contributor to books. **Address:** Galerie nationale de Jeu de Paume, 1 place de la Concorde, Jardin des Tuileries, 75008 Paris, France.

DAVID, James F. American. **Genres:** Science fiction/Fantasy. **Career:** Author and professor of psychology. **Publications:** Footprints of Thunder, 1995; Fragments, 1997; Ship of the Damned, 2000. **Address:** c/o Tor Books, 175 Fifth Ave., New York, NY 10010, U.S.A. **Online address:** jfoster@georgefox.edu

DAVID, Jonah M. *See* JONES, David Martin.

DAVID, Larry. (born United States), b. 1947. **Genres:** Humor/Satire. **Career:** Writer, producer, director, actor, and comedian. Worked variously as a cab driver, chauffeur, and bra salesman. **Publications:** TELEVISION SCRIPTS: Fridays, 1980-82; Saturday Night Live, 1984-85; The Original Talking Max Headroom Show, 1987; The Seinfeld Chronicles (pilot), 1989; (And executive producer) Seinfeld, 1989-96, 1998; (And executive producer) Larry David: Curb Your Enthusiasm (special), 1999; (And executive producer) Curb Your Enthusiasm (series), 2000. SCREENPLAYS: (And director) Sour Grapes, 1998. **Address:** Endeavor Entertainment, 9460 Wishire Blvd, 10th Fl., Beverly Hills, CA 90212, U.S.A.

DAVID, Thomas. Hungarian, b. 1940. **Genres:** Travel/Exploration. **Career:** Oesterreichisches Zellkultur-Forschungslabor, Vienna, Austria, president and chief scientist. Conducted research on polygonal pelvic osteotomy, 1969-86, ethnomedicine (cancer and immunodeficiency) and biotherapy against cancer, 1986-. **Publications:** Griechenland (art and photography), 1982; Istria (art and photography), 1983; Crete (art and photography), 1984; Salzburg (art and photography), 1986; Miracle Medicines of the Rainforest, 1997. **Address:** Oesterreichisches Zellkultur-Forschungslabor, Margaretenstrasse 2-4/III/14, A-1040 Vienna, Austria. **Online address:** codtea-nutritional@mail.xpoint.at

DAVIDAR, David. Indian, b. 1959?. **Genres:** Novels. **Career:** Gentleman magazine, Bombay, India, executive editor until 1985; Penguin Books India, New Delhi, India, chief executive officer and publisher, 1985-; Dorling Kindersley India, managing director, 2000-. **Publications:** The House of Blue Mangoes, 2002. **Address:** c/o Author Mail, HarperCollins, 10 East 53rd Street, 7th Floor, New York, NY 10022, U.S.A.

DAVIDOFF, Leonore. American, b. 1932. **Genres:** History, Sociology, Women's studies and issues. **Career:** University of Birmingham, England, research officer, 1956-57; University of London, tutor, 1956-60; Lucy Cavendish College, Cambridge, England, senior member, 1962-68; University of Essex, Colchester, England, research officer, 1969-74, lecturer, 1975-88, senior lecturer, 1988-90, research professor, 1990-; visiting professor at universities. **Publications:** The Best Circles: Society, Etiquette and The Season, 1973, reprinted, 1986; (ed. with B. Westover) Our work, Our Lives, Our Words: Women's History and Women's Work, 1986; (with C. Hall) Family Fortunes: Men and Women of the English Middle Class 1780-1850, 1987, repr, 1996; Worlds Between: Historical Perspectives on Gender and Class, 1995; (with M. Doolittle, J. Fink, and K. Holden) The Family Story: Blood, Contract and Intimacy 1830-1960, 1998. **Address:** Department of Sociology, University of Essex, Wivenhoe Park, Colchester C04 3SQ, England. **Online address:** davidoff@essex.ac.uk

DAVIDSON, Basil. British, b. 1914. **Genres:** History, International relations/Current affairs. **Career:** Writer and Historian. Paris Correspondent, 1945-47, and Chief Foreign Leader Writer, 1947-49, The Times, London; Special Correspondent, New Statesman, London, 1949-53; Leader Writer, Daily Mirror, London, 1959-61; professorships in Europe, Africa, and USA, 1962-. **Publications:** Partisan Picture, 1946; Germany: From Potsdam to Partition, 1950; Report on Southern Africa, 1952; Daybreak in China, 1953; (ed. with A. Ademola) The New West Africa, 1953; The African Awakening, 1954; Turkestan Alive, 1957; Old Africa Rediscovered, 1959; Black Mother: The African Slave Trade, 1961; (with P. Strand) Tir a Mhurain: The Outer Hebrides, 1962; A Guide to African History, 1963; Which Way Africa?, 1964; The African Past, 1964; A History of West Africa to 1800, 1965; Africa: History of a Continent, 1966, rev. ed. as Africa in History, 1968; A History of Eastern and Central Africa to the Late 19th Century, 1967; The Africans: An Entry to Cultural History (in US as The African Genius), 1969; The Liberation of Guinea, 1969; Discovering Our African Heritage, 1971; In the Eye of the Storm: Angola's People, 1972; Black Star: View of the Life and Times of Nkrumah, 1973; Can Africa Survive? Arguments against Growth without Development, 1974; (with P. Strand) Ghana: An African Portrait, 1976; Discovering Africa's Past, 1978; Africa in Modern History, 1978 (in US as Let Freedom Come); Special Operations Europe, 1980; The People's Cause, 1981; The Story of Africa, 1984; The Fortunate Isles, 1989; The Black Man's Burden, 1992; Modern Africa, 1993; The Search for Africa: Essays on Culture and Politics, 1994; West Africa before the Colonial Era: A History to 1850, 1998. NOVELS: Highway Forty, 1949; Golden Horn, 1952; The Rapids, 1955; Lindy (in US as Ode to a Young Love), 1958; The Andrassy Affair (novel), 1966.

DAVIDSON, Diane Mott. American. **Genres:** Mystery/Crime/Suspense. **Career:** Writer; prep school teacher, volunteer counselor, tutor and licensed lay preacher in the Episcopal church. **Publications:** MYSTERIES: Catering to Nobody, 1990; Dying for Chocolate, 1992; The Cereal Murders, 1993; The Last Suppers, 1994; Killer Pancake, 1995; The Main Corpse, 1996; The Grilling Season, 1997; Prime Cut, 1998; Tough Cookie, 2000; Sticks and Scones, 2001; Chopping Spree, 2002; Double Shot, 2004. **Address:** c/o Sandra Dijkstra Literary Agency, PMB 515, 1155 Camino Del Mar, Del Mar, CA 92014-3115, U.S.A.

DAVIDSON, Gordon. American, b. 1944. **Genres:** Theology/Religion, Human relations/Parenting. **Career:** U.S. Peace Corps, Washington, DC, volunteer in India; investment adviser, 1991-94; lecturer and writer, 1994-. Sirius Educational Resources, cofounder; Sirius School of Spiritual Science, cofounder. **Publications:** (with C. McLaughlin) Builders of the Dawn: Community Lifestyles in a Changing World, 1985, 3rd ed, 1993; (with C. McLaughlin) Spiritual Politics: Changing the World from the Inside Out, 1994. **Address:** Sirius Educational Resources, P.O. Box 1101, Greenbelt, MD 20768, U.S.A.

DAVIDSON, Jeff. American, b. 1951. **Genres:** Business/Trade/Industry, How-to books, Human relations/Parenting, Self help, Ghost Writer. **Career:** Author. Profiles Inc., Vernon, CT, project manager, 1975-77; Emay Corp, Washington, DC, sr project manager, 1977-80; IMR Systems, Falls Church, VA, vice-president, marketing, 1980-84; Breathing Space Institute, founder, 1984. **Publications:** Checklist Management, 1987; (with D. Beveridge), How to Be a 10 in Business, 1987; The Marketing Sourcebook for Small Business, 1989; Marketing for the Home-Based Business, 1990, 2nd ed., 1999; Marketing Your Consulting & Professional Services, 1990, 3rd ed., 1997; (with D. Yoho), How to Have a Good Year Every Year, 1991; Selling to the Giants, 1991; Avoiding the Pitfalls of Starting Your Own Business, 1991; Power and Protocol for Getting to the Top, 1991; You Can Start Your Own Business, 1991; Marketing to Home-Based Business, 1991; (with D. Vlcek), The Domino Effect, 1992; Your Bank, 1992; Cash Traps, 1992; Getting New Clients, 1993; Breathing Space, 1993, 2nd ed., 1999; Marketing on a Shoestring, 2nd ed., 1994; The Complete Idiot's Guide to Managing Stress, 1997, 2nd ed., 1999; The Complete Idiot's Guide to ... series: ...Assertiveness, 1997, ...Reaching Your Goals, 1998, ...Managing Your Time, 2nd ed., 1999, ...Reinventing Your Life, 2001, ...Change Management, 2001, ...Getting Things Done, 2005; Marketing Your Career and Yourself, 1999; The Joy of Simple Living, 1999; The Ten Minute Guide to Project Management, 2000; 101 Internet Marketing Tips, 2002; The Complete Guide to Public Speaking, 2003; The Christian Family Guide to Organizing, 2003; The 60-Second Procrastinator, 2004; The 60-Second Organizer, 2005. **Address:** Breathing Space Institute, 2417 Honeysuckle Rd Ste 2A, Chapel Hill, NC 27514-6819, U.S.A. **Online address:** Jeff@BreathingSpace.com; www.BreathingSpace.com

DAVIDSON, Lionel. Also writes as David Line. British, b. 1922. **Genres:** Novels, Mystery/Crime/Suspense, Children's fiction. **Publications:** The Night of Wenceslas, 1960; The Rose of Tibet, 1962; A Long Way to Shiloh (in U.S. as The Menorah Men), 1966; Making Good Again, 1968; Smith's Gazelle, 1971; The Sun Chemist, 1976; The Chelsea Murders (in U.S. as

Murder Games), 1978; Kolymsky Heights, 1994; children's fiction as David Line-Soldier and Me, 1965; Run for Your Life, 1966; Mike and Me, 1974; (as Lionel Davidson) Under Plum Lake, 1980; Screaming High, 1985. **Address:** c/o Curtis Brown Ltd, 28/29 Haymarket, London SW1Y 4SP, England.

DAVIDSON, Michael. American, b. 1944. **Genres:** Poetry, Literary criticism and history. **Career:** San Diego State University, lecturer, 1973-76; University of California at San Diego, assistant professor, 1976-81, Archive for New Poetry, curator, 1976-85, professor of literature, 1981-. **Publications:** Exchanges, 1972; Two Views of Pears, 1973; The Mutabilities and the Foul Papers, 1976; Summer Letters, 1976; Grillwork, 1980; Discovering Motion, 1980; The Prose of Fact, 1981; The Landing of Rochambeau, 1985; Analogy of the Ion, 1988; The San Francisco Renaissance and Postmodern Poetics, 1989; Post Hoc, 1990; Ghostlier Demarcations: Modern Poetry and the Material Word, 1997; The Arcades, 1999; (ed.) The New Collected Poems of George Open, 2002. **Address:** Dept. of Literature, University of California at San Diego, La Jolla, CA 92093, U.S.A. **Online address:** rdavidson@ucsd.edu

DAVIDSON, Nicole. See JENSEN, Kathryn.

DAVIDSON, Osha Gray. American, b. 1954. **Genres:** Urban studies, Politics/Government. **Career:** The County magazine, Des Moines, IA, assistant editor, 1972; The Grapevine (a boycott information newsletter), Iowa City, IA, publisher, 1982-85; author and freelance writer, 1984-. **Publications:** Broken Heartland: The Rise of America's Rural Ghetto, 1990; Under Fire: The NRA and the Battle for Gun Control, 1993. Contributor to periodicals. **Address:** c/o Alison Picard, P.O. Box 2000, Cotuit, MA 02635, U.S.A.

DAVIDSON, Pamela. British (born Netherlands), b. 1954. **Genres:** Literary criticism and history. **Career:** University of Birmingham, England, lecturer in Russian, 1981-84; University of Surrey, Guildford, England, lecturer in Russian, 1984-93; University College London, School of Slavonic and East European Studies, 1993-, senior lecturer, 1996-, reader in Russian literature, 2001-; freelance translator; consultant on Russian culture. **Publications:** (with J. Norman) Russian Phrase Book, 2nd ed., 1980, 3rd. ed., 1989; The Poetic Imagination of Vyacheslav Ivanov: A Russian Symbolist's Perception of Dante, 1989; (comp. with I. Tlusty; author of intro. and notes) Posviashchaetsia Akhmatovoi: Stikhi raznykh poetov, posvyashchennye Akhmatovoi (Dedicated to Akhmatova: Anthology of Poems), 1990; Viacheslav Ivanov: A Reference Guide, 1996; (ed. and contrib.) Russian Literature and Its Demons, 2000. **Address:** School of Slavonic and East European Studies, Senate House, University College London, Malet St, London WC1E 7HU, England. **Online address:** p.davidson@ssees.ucl.ac.uk

DAVIDSON, Robyn. Australian, b. 1950. **Genres:** Novels, Travel/Exploration. **Career:** Writer. **Publications:** TRAVEL BOOKS: Tracks, 1981; (with P. Adam-Smith and T. Keneally) Australia: Beyond the Dreamtime, 1987; Traveling Light, 1989; From Alice to Ocean: Alone across the Outback, 1992; (ed.) The Picador Book of Journeys, 2001; Desert Places, 1996. OTHER: Ancestors (novel), 1989. Contributor to periodicals. **Address:** c/o Pat Kavanagh, PFD, Drury House, 34-43 Russell St, London WC2B 5HA, England. **Online address:** robyn@dircon.co.uk; robyn@vsnl.net

DAVIDSON, Roger H(arry). American, b. 1936. **Genres:** Politics/Government, Public/Social administration. **Career:** Professor of Government and Politics, University of Maryland, College Part, since 1987. Co-ed., Encyclopedia of the U.S. Congress, 1989-95. Assistant Professor of Government, Dartmouth College, Hanover, New Hampshire, 1962-68; Research Associate, W. E. Upjohn Institute for Employment Research, 1965-66; Scholar in Residence, National Manpower Policy Task Force, Washington, D.C., 1970-71; Staff member, Select Committee on Cttees., U.S. House of Reps., Washington, D.C., 1973-74; Associate Professor, 1968-71, Professor of Political Science, 1971-83, Chairman, 1976-78, and Associate Dean, 1978-80, Univ of California, Santa Barbara; Sr. Specialist, American Government and Public Administration, Congressional Research Service, Library of Congress, Washington, D.C., 1980-88. **Publications:** (with D. M. Kovenock and M. K. O'Leary) Congress in Crisis: Politics and Congressional Reform, 1966; (with J. F. Bibby) On Capitol Hill: Studies in the Legislative Process, 1967, 1972; The Role of the Congressman, 1969; The Politics of Comprehensive Manpower Legislation, 1972; (with W. J. Oleszek) Congress Against Itself, 1977; (with S. P. Patterson and R. B. Ripley) A More Perfect Union, 1979, 4th ed. 1989; (with W. J. Oleszek) Congress and Its Members, 1981, 6th ed. 1997; (with W. J. Oleszek) Governing, 1987, 2nd ed. 1992; The Postreform Congress, 1992; (with R.A. Baker) First among Equals: Senate Leaders in The Twentieth Century, 1992; (with J.A. Thurber) Remaking

Congress, 1995; (with J.P. Pfiffner) Understanding the Presidency, 1996. **Address:** 1140 B Tydings Hall, College Park, MD 20742, U.S.A.

DAVIDSON, Sol M. American, b. 1924. **Genres:** Children's fiction, Young adult fiction, Administration/Management, Education, History, Human relations/Parenting, Mythology/Folklore, Social commentary, Cartoons, Humor/Satire. **Career:** President, Davidson, Wyatt & Associates, mgmt. consultants, Des Moines, 1976-. Vice-President, and Director of Operations, Dial Finance Co., Des Moines, 1959-74. Assistant to the President, Northwestern Bell Telephone Co., Des Moines, 1974-76. The Sandpiper, editor in chief, 1999-2002. **Publications:** Culture and the Comic Strips, 1959; The Cultivation of Imperfection, 1965; The Value of Friction, 1968; Philbert the Flea, 1989; Wild Jake Hiccup: America's First Frontiersman, 1992. **Address:** PO Box 2974, Palm Beach, FL 33480, U.S.A.

DAVIES, Christie. (John Christopher Hughes Davies). British, b. 1941. **Genres:** Children's fiction, Criminology/True Crime, Ethics, Sociology, Humor/Satire. **Career:** Professor of Sociology, University of Reading, 1985- (Lecturer and St Lecturer, 1972-81; Reader, 1981-85). Radio Producer, BBC Third Program, 1967-69; Lecturer in Sociology, University of Leeds, Yorks., 1969-72. **Publications:** (with R. Brandon) Wrongful Imprisonment, Mistaken Convictions and Their Consequences, 1973; (with R. Lewis) The Reactionary Joke Book, 1973; Permissive Britain: Social Change in the 60s and 70s, 1975; Welsh Jokes, 1978; (with R. Dhavan) Censorship and Obscenity, 1978; Ethnic Humor around the World: A Comparative Analysis, 1990; Jokes and Their Relation to Society, 1998; (with M. Neal) The Corporation Under Siege, 1998; The Mirth of Nations, 2003; The Strange Death of Moral Britain, 2004; The Right to Joke, 2004; Dewi the Dragon Finds a Wife, 2005. **Address:** Dept of Sociology, University of Reading, Whiteknights, Reading, Berks. RG6 6AA, England. **Online address:** J.C.H.Davies@Reading.ac.uk

DAVIES, Horton (Marlais). American (born Wales), b. 1916. **Genres:** Literary criticism and history. **Career:** Theology/Religion. Professor Emeritus, Princeton University, New Jersey, since 1984 (Professor of Religion, 1956-59; Putnam Professor, 1959-84). Professor and Dean, Faculty of Divinity, Rhodes University, Grahamstown, S. Africa, 1946-53; Sr. Lecturer, and Head of Dept., Mansfield and Regent's Park Colls., Oxford University, 1953-56; Member, Center of Theological Inquiry, Princeton, New Jersey, 1987-91. **Publications:** The English Free Churches, 1952, 1964; Christian Deviations, 1954, 4th rev. ed., 1974; A Mirror of the Ministry in Modern Novels, 1959; Worship and Theology in England, 6 vols., 1961-95; (with Hugh Davies) Sacred Art in a Secular Century, 1978; (with M.H. Davies) Holy Days and Holidays, 1982; Catching the Conscience, 1985; Like Angels on a Cloud, 1985; The Worship of the American Puritans, 1990; The Vigilant God: Providence in the Thought of Augustine, Aquinas, Calvin, and Barth, 1991; Bread of Life and Cup of Joy: Newer Ecumenical Perspectives on the Eucharist, 1993; A Church Historian's Odyssey on Three Continents: A Memoir, 1993; The Communion of Saints, 1990; (with M.H. Davies) Huguenots in English-Speaking Lands, 2000. **Address:** 120 McCosh Circle, Princeton, NJ 08544, U.S.A. **Online address:** Daviesh@Princeton.edu

DAVIES, Hunter. Scottish, b. 1936. **Genres:** Novels, Children's fiction, Travel/Exploration, Biography. **Career:** Journalist. Writer, Sunday Times, London, 1960-84; Columnist, Punch, 1979-89; Presenter, Bookshelf, BBC, 1983-86; The Independent, 1989-. **Publications:** Here We Go Round the Mulberry Bush, 1966, screenplay, 1967; The Other Half, 1966; The New London Spy, 1966; The Beatles, 1968; The Rise and Fall of Jake Sullivan, 1969; I Knew Daisy Smuten, 1970; A Very Loving Couple, 1971; The Glory Game, 1972; Body Charge, 1972; A Walk Along the Wall, 1974; George Stephenson, 1975; The Creighton Report, 1976; The Sunday Times Book of Jubilee Year, 1977; A Walk Around the Lakes, 1979; The Book of British Lists, 1980; William Wordsworth, 1980; The Grades, 1981; Father's Day, 1981; A Walk Along the Tracks, 1982; Great Britain: A Celebration, 1982; Flossie Teacake's Fur Coat, 1982; A Walk Round London's Parks, 1983; The Joy of Stamps, 1983; The Good Guide to the Lakes, 1984; Flossie Teacake Strikes Back, 1984; Come On Ossie, 1985; The Grand Tour, 1986; Ossie Goes Supersonic, 1986; The Good Quiz Book to the Lakes, 1987; Back in the USSR, 1987; Beatrix Potter's Lakeland, 1988; Saturday Night, 1989; S.T. A. R. S., 1989; My Life in Football, 1990; In Search of Columbus, 1991; Striker, 1992; Teller of Tales, 1992; Wainwright, 1995; Living on the Lottery, 1996. **Address:** 11 Boscastle Rd, London NW5, England.

DAVIES, J(ohn) D(avid). Welsh, b. 1957. **Genres:** Military/Defense/Arms control, History. **Career:** History teacher at a school in Cornwall, 1979-82, and at a secondary school in Horsham, England, 1985-86; Bedford Modern

School, Bedford, England, history teacher and senior master (curriculum) 1987-. **Publications:** Gentlemen and Tarpaulins: The Officers and Men of the Restoration Navy, Clarendon Press, 1991; Work also represented in anthologies. Contributor to history and nautical journals. **Address:** Bedford Modern School, Manton Lane, Bedford MK41 7NT, England. **Online address:** j.d.davies@net.ntl.com

DAVIES, Jennifer (Eileen). British, b. 1950. **Genres:** Homes/Gardens, Education, Local history/Rural topics. **Career:** Writer and free-lance television producer. Member of a committee formed to create a living museum of Perry pear trees at Malvern, in Worcestershire, England. **Publications:** The Victorian Kitchen Garden, 1987; The Victorian Kitchen Garden Companion, 1988; The Victorian Kitchen, 1989; The Victorian Flower Garden, 1991; Harry Dodson's Practical Kitchen Garden, 1992; The Wartime Kitchen and Garden, 1993; Safe in Print, 1994; Tales of the Old Country Horseman, 1997; Tales of the Old Gypsies, 1999; Saying It with Flowers: The History of the Flower Shop, 2000. Contributor to education journals and popular magazines. **Address:** Park Barn near Parkway, Ledbury, Herefordshire HR8 2JB, England.

DAVIES, Linda. American, b. 1963. **Genres:** Novels. **Career:** Has worked in financial trading in both New York City and London, England; writer. **Publications:** NOVELS: A Nest of Vipers, 1994; Wilderness of Mirrors, 1995. **Address:** c/o David Black, Black Literary Agency, 156 Fifth Ave. Suite 608, New York, NY 10010, U.S.A.

DAVIES, Martin (Brett). British, b. 1936. **Genres:** Psychology, Social work, Sociology. **Career:** Research Officer, Home Office, London 1964-71; Sr. Lecturer, University of Manchester, 1971-75; University of East Anglia, Norwich, Director of Social Work Program, 1975-79, Professor of Social Work, 1979-. Ed., Social Work Monographs, 1982-2000. **Publications:** Probationers in Their Social Environment, 1969; Financial Penalties and Probation, 1970; Social Enquiry Reports and the Probation Service, 1973; An Index of Social Environment, 1973; Social Work in the Environment, 1974; Prisoners of Society, 1974; Support Systems in Social Work, 1977; The Essential Social Worker, 1980, 1994; Towards a Classification of Unemployment, 1986; Skills, Knowledge and Qualities in Probation Practice, 1988; The Sociology of Social Work, 1991; Contemporary Probation Practice, 1993; Blackwell Companion to Social Work, 1997; Blackwell Encyclopaedia of Social Work, 2000. **Address:** School of Social Work & Psychosocial Studies, University of East Anglia, Norwich NR4 7TJ, England. **Online address:** m.davies@uea.ac.uk

DAVIES, Martin L. British, b. 1948. **Genres:** Literary criticism and history. **Career:** University of Leicester, lecturer, 1975-. **Publications:** Identity or History? Marcus Herz and the End of the Enlightenment, 1995; (ed. and author of epilogue) M. Herz, Philosophisch-medizinische Aufsaetze, in press. Contributor to books. Contributor of articles and reviews to journals and periodicals. Contributor to German-language books and periodicals. Translator of stories for books. **Address:** School of Modern Languages, Leicester University, University Road, Leicester LEI 7RH, England.

DAVIES, Nicola. Also writes as Stevie Morgan. British, b. 1958. **Genres:** Novels, Children's non-fiction. **Career:** Freelance broadcaster and writer. **Publications:** Big Blue Whale, 1997; Bat Loves the Night, 2001; One Tiny Turtle, 2001; Wild about Dolphins, 2001; Currants Pats and Poops, 2003; Unexpected Sharks, 2003. AS STEVIE MORGAN: Delphinium Blues, 1999; Fly Away Peter, 2000; Checking Out, 2002. **Address:** c/o Ed Victor, 6 Bayley St, London WC1B 3HB, England. **Online address:** nicola.davies@btinternet.com

DAVIES, Oliver. American, b. 1956. **Genres:** Theology/Religion. **Career:** University of Wales, Lampeter, reader in systematic theology. **Publications:** God Within: The Mystical Tradition of Northern Europe, 1988; Meister Eckhart: Mystical Theologian, 1991; Celtic Christianity in Early Medieval Wales: The Origins of the Welsh Spiritual Tradition, 1996; A Theology of Compassion: Metaphysics of Difference and the Renewal of Tradition, 2003; The Creativity of God: World, Eucharist, Reason, 2004. OTHER: (trans.) Beguine Spirituality: Mystical Writings of Mechthild of Magdeburg, Beatrice of Nazareth, and Hadewijch of Brabant, 1989; (editor, translator, and author of introduction) The Rhineland Mystics: Writings of Meister Eckhart, Johannes Tauler, and Jan van Ruusbroec and Selections from the Theologica Germanica and the Book of Spiritual Poverty, 1990; (editor and author of introduction, with Fiona Bowie) Mystical Writings, with new translations by Robert Carver, 1990; (editor) Gateway to Paradise: Basil the Great, 1991; (editor) Born to New Life, 1992; (editor and translator, with Alun Idris Jones) Promise of Good Things: The Apostolic Fathers, 1993; (Selector and translator) Selected Writings, 1994; (editor,with Fiona Bowie) Celtic Christian Spirituality: An Anthology of Medieval and Modern Sources, 1999; (translator and author of introduction) Celtic Spirituality, with the collaboration of Thomas O'Loughlin, preface by James Mackey, 1999; (editor,with Denys Turner) Silence and the Word: Negative Theology and Incarnation, 2002. Contributor of translations. **Address:** Dept of Theology, Religious, and Islamic Studies, University of Wales, Lampeter, Ceredigion SA48 7ED, Wales. **Online address:** o.davies@lamp.ac.uk

DAVIES, Peter Ho. American (born England), b. 1966. **Genres:** Novellas/ Short stories. **Career:** Author. Emory University, Atlanta, GA, lecturer, 1996-97; University of Oregon, Eugene, assistant professor, 1997-99; University of Michigan, Ann Arbor, assistant professor, 1999-. Fine Arts Work Center fellow, 1996-; National Endowment for the Arts fellow, 1998. **Publications:** STORIES: The Ugliest House in the World, 1997; Equal Love, 2000. Contributor to anthologies and publications. **Address:** English Language and Literature, 4200 Angell Hall, 435 S. State St., Ann Arbor, MI 48109, U.S.A. **Online address:** phdavies@umich.edu

DAVIES, Peter J. Australian, b. 1937. **Genres:** Medicine/Health, Music, Psychiatry, Psychology, Biography. **Career:** St. Vincent's Hospital, Melbourne, Australia, physician in internal medicine and gastroenterology, 1971-86; private practice of medicine in Melbourne, 1971-98. Lecturer in the United States, England, and Australia. **Publications:** Mozart in Person: His Character and Health, 1989; Mozart's Health Illnesses and Death, in The Pleasures and Perils of Genius: Mostly Mozart, 1993; Beethoven in Person: His Deafness, Illnesses and Death, 2001; Beethoven in Person: The Character of a Genius, 2001.

DAVIES, Philip John. British, b. 1948. **Genres:** Area studies, Politics/ Government. **Career:** University of Maryland, College Park, 1972-74; Lanchester (Coventry) Polytechnic, lecturer, 1975-76; Manchester University, lecturer, 1976-91; De Montfort University, professor of American studies, 1991-; British Library, Eccles Centre for American Studies, director, 2001-. Visiting professor/visiting fellow: University of Massachusetts, Boston, John W. McCormack Institute of Public Affairs, 1984-85; Creighton University, Omaha, 1996; Wartburg College, Iowa, 1996. Fellow: Salzburg Seminar, 2000; Institute for US Studies, 2000-; Study of the Americas, London, 2000-; Royal Historical Society; Royal Society of the Encouragement of the Arts. British Association for American Studies, chair, 1998-2004; UK Council of Area Studies Associations, chair, 2004-; Social Sciences, academician. Guest lecturer at universities in UK and abroad. Guest appearances on TV and radio in UK and abroad. **Publications:** Metropolitan Mosaic, 1980; The History and Evolution of the Constitution, 1989; Elections: USA, 1992; US Elections Today, 1999. EDITOR & CONTRIBUTOR: (with B. Neve) Cinema, Politics, & Society in America, 1981; (with F. Waldstein) Political Issues in America Today, 1988; Science Fiction, Social Conflict, & War, 1990; (with Waldstein) Political Issues in America: The 1990s, 1991; An American Quarter Century, 1995; Political Issues in America Today: The 1990s Revisited, 1996; Representing and Imagining America, 1996; History Atlas of North America, 1998; (with J.K. White) Political Parties and the Collapse of Old Orders, 1999; (with P. Wells) American Film and Politics from Reagan to Bush Jr., 2002; (with G.C. Edwards) New Challenges for the American Presidency, 2004. Contributor to books and journals. **Address:** Eccles Centre for American Studies, British Library, London NW1 2DB, England. **Online address:** Philip.Davies@bl.uk

DAVIES, Piers Anthony David. New Zealander (born Australia), b. 1941. **Genres:** Plays/Screenplays, Poetry, Law. **Career:** Wackrow, Smith & Davies, Auckland, barrister and solicitor (qualified 1965). New Zealand Film Commission, Short Film Fund, chairman, 1987-91; International Law Association, Cultural Heritage Law Committee, member, 1997-. **Publications:** East and Other Gong Songs, 1967; Day Trip from Mount Meru, 1969; Diaspora, 1974; Bourgeois Homage to Dada, 1974; (ed.) Central Almanac, 1974; Jetsam, 1984. SCREENPLAYS: (with P. Weir) Life and Flight of Rev. Buck Shotte, 1969; (with P. Weir) Homesdale, 1971; (with P. Weir) The Cars That Ate Paris, 1973; Skin Deep, 1978; R.v. Huckleberry Finn (documentary), 1979; Olaf's Coast (documentary), 1982; The Lamb of God, 1985; A Fair Hearing, 1995. Contributor to books. **Address:** 16 Crocus Pl, Remuera, Auckland 5, New Zealand.

DAVIES, R(obert) R(ees). Welsh, b. 1938. **Genres:** History. **Career:** University of Wales, University College of Swansea, Swansea, lecturer in history, 1961-63; University of London, London, England, lecturer in history, 1963-76; University of Wales, University College of Wales, Aberystwyth, professor of history, 1976-95; All Souls College, Oxford, Chichele Professor of Medieval History, 1995-; writer. **Publications:** Lordship and Society in

the March of Wales, 1282-1400, 1978; Conquest, Coexistence, and Change: Wales, 1063-1415, 1987, reprinted as The Age of Conquest, 1991; Domination and Conquest, 1990; Revolt of Owain Glyn Dwr, 1995; The First English Empire: Power and Identities in the British Isles 1093-1343, 2000. **Address:** All Souls College, Oxford OX1 4A1, England.

DAVIES, Robert William. British, b. 1925. **Genres:** Area studies, Economics, History, Politics/Government. **Career:** University of Birmingham, Centre for Russian and East European Studies, Research Fellow, 1956-59; Lecturer, 1959-62; Sr. Lecturer, 1962-63, Director, 1963-79, Professor of Soviet Economic Studies, 1965-89, Professor Emeritus, 1989-. **Publications:** The Development of the Soviet Budgetary System, 1958; (with E.H. Carr) Foundations of a Planned Economy 1926-1929, vol. I, 1969; (with E. Zaleski and others) Science Policy in the U.S.S.R., 1969; The Socialist Offensive: The Collectivization of Soviet Agriculture, 1929-1930, 1980; The Soviet Collective Farm 1929-1930, 1980; The Soviet Economy in Turmoil 1929-1930, 1989; Soviet History in the Gorbachev Revolution, 1989; Crisis and Progress in the Soviet Economy, 1931-1933, 1996; Soviet History in the Yeltsin Era, 1997; Soviet Economic Development from Lenin to Khrushchev, 1998; (with S.G. Wheatcroft) The Years of Hunger: Soviet Agriculture, 1931-1933, 2004. EDITOR/CO-EDITOR: The Technological Level of Soviet Industry, 1977; The Soviet Union, 1978, 1989; Soviet Investment for Planned Industrialisation 1929-37, 1984; Materials for a Balance of the Soviet National Economy 1928-30, 1985; E.H. Carr's What Is History?, 2nd ed., 1986; From Tsarism to the New Economic Policy, 1990; (with M. Harrison and S.G. Wheatcroft) The Economic Transformation of the Soviet Economy, 1913-1945, 1993; (with O. Khlevniuk and E.A. Rees) The Stalin-Kaganovich Correspondence 1931-1936, 2004; Introduction to E.H. Carr's The Russian Revolution from Lenin to Stalin, 2004. **Address:** Centre for Russian and East European Studies, University of Birmingham, Birmingham B15 2TT, England.

DAVIES, Stephanie. Also writes as Stevie Davies. British, b. 1946. **Genres:** Novels, Literary criticism and history. **Career:** Victoria University of Manchester, Manchester, England, member of English Language and Literature faculty, 1971-74; full-time author, 1984-94; Roehampton Institute, senior research fellow, 1994-. Royal Society of Literature, fellow, 1998. **Publications:** EDITOR: The Bronte Sisters: Selected Poems, 1976; Renaissance, 1978; Anne Bronte, The Tenant of Wildfell Hall, 1996. NONFICTION AS STEVIE DAVIES: Images of Kingship in "Paradise Lost": Milton's Politics and Christian Liberty, 1983; Emily Bronte: The Artist as a Free Woman, 1983; The Idea of Woman in Renaissance Literature: The Feminine Reclaimed, 1987; Shakespeare: Twelfth Night, 1993; John Donne, 1994; Emily Bronte Heretic, 1994; Henry Vaughan, 1995; Shakespeare, The Taming of the Shrew, 1995; Emily Bronte, 1998; Unbridled Spirit: Women of the English Revolution, 1998. FICTION AS STEVIE DAVIES: Boy Blue, 1987; Primavera, 1990; Arms and the Girl, 1992; Closing the Book, 1994; Four Dreamers and Emily, 1996; The Web of Belonging, 1997. Contributor to periodicals. **Address:** Dept of English, University of Wales Swansea, Singleton Park, Swansea SA2 8PP, Wales. **Online address:** stephanie. davies@swansea.ac.uk

DAVIES, Stevie. See **DAVIES, Stephanie.**

DAVIES-MITCHELL, Margaret (Constance). (Lady Mitchell). British, b. 1923. **Genres:** Novels, Literary criticism and history. **Career:** Professor of French, University of Reading, 1974-88, emeritus, 1988- (Lecturer, 1964-70; Reader in French Studies, 1970-74); University of Nottingham, visiting professor, 1988-92. **Publications:** Two Gold Rings (novel), 1958; Colette, 1961; Apollinaire, 1964; Une Saison en Enfer, 1974. Author of articles on French poetry.

DAVILA, Arlene M. Portuguese, b. 1965. **Genres:** Anthropology/Ethnology. **Career:** Harvard University, Cambridge, MA, curatorial intern at Peabody Museum of Archaeology and Ethnology, 1985-86; Brooklyn Museum, Brooklyn, NY, curatorial intern in Department of African, Oceanic, and New World Art, 1988; Museum of Contemporary Hispanic Art, NYC, director of education, 1989; El Museo del Barrio, NYC, curatorial assistant, 1990-93; Hunter College of the City University of New York, NYC, adjunct lecturer in anthropology, 1994-95; Syracuse University, Syracuse, NY, assistant professor of anthropology, 1995-. Herbert H. Lehman College of the City University of New York, adjunct lecturer in Puerto Rican studies, 1992-93; University of Connecticut, guest speaker, 1997; Colgate University, guest speaker, 1998; New York University, visiting research associate at Center for Media, Culture, and History, 1998-. **Publications:** Sponsored Identities: Cultural Politics in Puerto Rico, 1997. Contributor to books. Contributor of articles and reviews to scholarly journals. **Address:** Department of

Anthropology, 204 Maxwell Hall, Syracuse University, Syracuse, NY 13244, U.S.A. **Online address:** ardavila@maxwell.syr.edu

DAVIS, Alan (R.). American, b. 1950. **Genres:** Novellas/Short stories. **Career:** Parish Library, Lafayette, LA, reference librarian, 1974-77; Louisiana Department of Corrections, counselor/technical writer, 1975-77; Loyola University, Chicago, IL, lecturer, 1980-81; University of North Carolina, lecturer, 1981-85; Charlotte Business Quarterly and Charlotte Business and Finance, Charlotte, NC, editorial assistant, 1984; Minnesota State University, Moorhead, MN, started as assistant professor, became professor of English, 1985-, M.F.A. coordinator, chair of English department, 1991-97, co-director of creative writing, 1991-97. Has led workshops on contemporary fiction and creative writing at universities, writing centers and writing conferences in Ireland, Slovenia, Canada, and the U.S.; has served as artist mentor and literature panelist on state and regional arts councils. New Rivers Press, senior editor, 2002. **Publications:** STORIES: Rumors from the Lost World: Stories, 1993; Alone with the Owl, 2000. EDITOR WITH M.C. WHITE: American Fiction: The Best Unpublished Short Stories by Emerging Writers (annual anthology), 1987-99. Contributor of book reviews, short stories and articles to periodicals. **Address:** Minnesota State University, PO Box 38, Moorhead, MN 56563, U.S.A. **Online address:** davisa@mnstate.edu

DAVIS, Albert Belisle. American, b. 1947. **Genres:** Novels, Poetry. **Career:** Nicholls State University, Thibodaux, LA, distinguished service professor of English and novelist in residence. **Publications:** Leechtime (novel), 1989; What They Wrote on the Bathhouse Walls: Yen's Marina, Chinese Bayou, Louisiana (poems), 1989; Marquis at Bay (novel), 1992; Virginia Patout's Parish (poetry), 1999. Work represented in anthologies. Contributor to literary journals. **Address:** Dept of English, Nicholls State University, PO Box 2023, Thibodaux, LA 70310, U.S.A. **Online address:** albert.davis@nicholls.edu

DAVIS, Allen F. American, b. 1931. **Genres:** History, Biography. **Career:** Emeritus Professor of History, Temple University, Philadelphia, PA, 1999(Professor of History, 1968-99). Instructor, Wayne State University, Detroit, MI, 1959-60; Associate Professor of History, University of Missouri, Columbia, 1960-68. Executive Secretary, 1972-77, President, 1989-90, American Studies Association; Visiting Professor, University of Texas at Austin, 1983. John Adams Chair, University of Amsterdam, 1986-87. **Publications:** (with J. Cooke and R. Daly) March of American Democracy, vol. 5, 1965; Spearheads for Reform, 1967, 2nd ed., 1984; American Heroine: The Life and Legend of Jane Addams, 1973, 2nd ed., 2000; (with J. Watts) Generations, 1974, rev. ed., 1983; (co-author) Still Philadelphia, 1983; (co-author) The American People, 1986, 6th ed., 2003; (co-author) Philadelphia Stories, 1988; (with M.L. McCree Bryant) One-Hundred Years at Hull House, 1990; Postcards from Vermont, 2002. EDITOR: (with H. Woodman) Conflict and Consensus in American History, 1966, 9th ed., 1997; (with M. McCree) Eighty Years at Hull House, 1969; (with M. Haller) The Peoples of Philadelphia, 1973, rev. ed., 1998; Jane Addams on Peace, War and International Understanding, 1976; For Better or Worse, 1981. **Address:** 2032 Waverly St, Philadelphia, PA 19146, U.S.A.

DAVIS, Anita (Grey) P(rice). (born United States), b. 1943. **Genres:** Adult non-fiction. **Career:** Teacher at public schools in Shelby, NC, 1963-67, and Browns Mills, NJ, 1967-68; Converse College, Spartanburg, SC, instructor, 1969-72, assistant professor, 1972-76, associate professor, 1976-83, professor, 1983-88, Charles A. Dana Professor of Education, 1988-, department chair, 1978-83, 1986-2000. Rutherford County Historical Committee, chair, 2003. Public speaker; workshop presenter; guest on media programs. **Publications:** HISTORY AND BIOGRAPHY MATERIALS: The South in the American Revolutionary War, 1993; (with others) Harriet Quimby: An Activity Book for Children, 1993; Harriet Quimby: America's First Lady of the Air-A Biography for Intermediate Readers, 1998; Walnut Grove Plantation: A Fun and Learn Book, 2000; Real Heroes: Rutherford County Men Who Made the Supreme Sacrifice during World War II, 2002; (with Barry Hambright) Chimney Rock and Rutherford County, 2002; North Carolina during the Great Depression: A Documentary Portrait of a Decade, 2003; Rutherford County, North Carolina, in World War II, 2003. Contributor to periodicals. EDUCATION AND TEST PREPARATION MATERIALS: (with others) The Graduate Management Admission Test: The Best and Most Comprehensive in Test Preparation,, 3rd edition published as The Graduate Management Admission Test: The Best and Most Comprehensive in Test Preparation, 1997; (with others) The Best Test Preparation for the Graduate Record Examination, 1990, 2nd edition, 1992; (with others) The Best Test Preparation for the Scholastic Aptitude Test, 1990, 2nd edition published as The Best Test Preparation for the New Scholastic Aptitude Test, 1993; (with others) The Best Test Preparation for the NTE Core Battery (and Tests of

Professional Knowledge), 1991; (with others) The Best Test Preparation for the Medical College Admission Test, 1991; (with others) The Best Test Preparation for the Law School Admissions Test, 1992; (with others) Verbal Skill Builder, 1992; (with others) The Best Test Preparation for the New PSAT/NMSQT: The Preliminary SAT/National Merit Scholarship Qualifying Test, 1994; Max Notes: To Kill a Mockingbird, 1994; Max Notes: I Know Why the Caged Bird Sings, 1994; (with others) Focus on Women, 1995; Max Notes: The Inferno, 1995; (with others) The Best Test Preparation for the ACT Test, 1995; (with Katharine Preston) Discoveries, 1996; (with others) The Best Test Preparation for the CLEP Exam, 1996; Reading Instruction Essentials, 1996, 2nd edition, 1998; (with others) SAT I, 1997; (with others) The Best CLEP Review, 1997; (with others) Regents Test for Reading in the Elementary School, 1997; Max Notes: Sula, 1998; The Best Test Preparation for the High School Proficiency Test, 1999; (Author of revision) NTE Study Guide, 1999; (Author of revision) LSAT Study Guide, 1999; (editor) Max Notes: Tar Baby, 1999; Florida Teacher Certification Exam Study Guide, 1999; Children's Literature Essentials, 2000; The Best Test Preparation for the PRAXIS II, 2000; (with others) The Best Test Preparation for the Cooperative Admissions Examination and the High School Placement Test, 2001; The Best Teachers' Test Preparation for the PRAXIS PLT Test: K-6, 2002; (editor, with others, and contributor) ACT Assessment: The Very Best Coaching and Study Course for the ACT, with CD-ROM, 2002; (editor, with others, and contribributor) CLEP General Examinations: The Best Review for the College Level Examination Program General Examinations, 2002; (editor, with others, and contributor.) FCTE: The Best Test Preparation for the Florida Teacher Certification Examination, 2002; (ed., with others, and contrib.) GMAT CAT: The Best Test Preparation for the Graduate Management Admission Test, Computer-Adaptive Testing, with CD-ROM, 2002; The Best Teachers' Test Preparation for the PRAXIS PLT Test: 5-9, 2002; The Best Teachers' Test Preparation for the PRAXIS PLT Test: 7-12, 2002; (editor, with others, and contributor) LSAT with CD-ROM: The Very Best Test Preparation for the Law School Admission Test, 2002; (editor, with others, and contributor) MCAT with CD-ROM: The Very Best Test Preparation for the Medical College Admission Test, 2002; The Best Test Preparation for the COOP and HSPT, 2002; (editor, with others, and contributor) PSAT/NMSQT Assessment: The Best Coaching and Study Course for the Preliminary Scholastic Test/National Merit Scholarship Qualifying Test, 2002. Author of instructional materials related to historic U.S. battlegrounds. Contributor to books and to articles and reviews to periodicals. **Address:** 205 Mansfield Dr., Spartanburg, SC 29307, U.S.A. **Online address:** anita13@charter.net

DAVIS, Ann. Canadian, b. 1946. **Genres:** Art/Art history. **Career:** Winnipeg Art Gallery, Winnipeg, MB, staff member, 1973-76, administrative curator, 1976-79; National Museum of Singapore, Singapore, museum adviser, 1983; La Ribambelle, member of board of directors, 1985-87; London Regional Art and Historical Museums, director of education, 1990-91; Nickle Arts Museum, Calgary, AB, director, 1992-; University of Calgary, director of Museum and Heritage Studies, 1996-. University of Winnipeg, associate professor, 1976-79; member of faculty, Carleton University, 1980, and University of Western Ontario, 1982-91. **Publications:** Somewhere Waiting: The Life and Art of Christiane Pflug, 1991; The Logic of Ecstasy: Canadian Mystical Painting, 1920-1940, 1992. Author of exhibition catalogs. Contributor to Canadian Encyclopedia and to history and art journals. **Address:** 33 Maryland Pl SW, Calgary, AB, Canada T2V 2E5. **Online address:** adavis@ucalgary.ca

DAVIS, Burke. American, b. 1913. **Genres:** Novels, Children's non-fiction, History, Biography. **Career:** Ed., Feature Writer and Sports Ed., Charlotte News, North Carolina, 1937-47; Reporter, Baltimore Evening Sun, Maryland, 1947-52; Reporter Greensboro News, North Carolina, 1951-60; Writer and Historian, Colonial Williamsburg, Virginia, 1960-78. **Publications:** Whisper My Name, 1949; The Ragged Ones, 1951; Yorktown, 1952; They Called Him Stonewall, 1954; Gray Fox, 1956; Roberta E. Lee, 1956; Jeb Stuart, The Last Cavalier, 1957; To Appomattox, 1959; Our Incredible Civil War, 1960; Marine!, 1961; The Guilford Courthouse-Cowpens Campaign, 1962; America's First Army, 1962; Appomattox: Closing Struggle of the Civil War, 1963; The Summer Land, 1965; (co-author) Rebel Raider, 1966; The Billy Mitchell Affair, 1967; A Williamsburg Galaxy, 1967; (co-author) The World of Currier & Ives, 1968; Get Yamamoto, 1969; Yorktown: The Winning of American Independence, 1969; Billy Mitchell Story, 1969; The Campaign That Won America: Yorktown, 1970; Heroes of the American Revolution, 1971; Jamestown, 1971; Thomas Jefferson's Virginia, 1971; Amelia Earhart, 1972; Three for Revolution, 1975; Biography of a Kingsnake, 1975; George Washington and the American Revolution, 1975; Newer and Better Organic Gardening, 1976; Biography of a Fish Hawk, 1976; Black Heroes of the American Revolution, 1976; Old Hickory: A Life of Andrew Jackson, 1977; Mr. Lincoln's Whiskers, 1978; Sherman's March,

1980; The Long Surrender, 1985; The Southern Railway, 1985; War Bird: The Life and Times of Elliott White Springs, 1986.

DAVIS, Christopher. American, b. 1928. **Genres:** Novels, Plays/Screenplays. **Career:** Teacher of writing, Bryn Mawr College, Pa., 1977-96. **Publications:** Lost Summer, 1958; First Family, 1959; A Kind of Darkness, 1962; Belmarch, 1964; Sad Adam-Glad Adam (children's fiction), 1966; The Shamir of Dachau, 1966; Ishmael, 1967; A Peep into the 20th Century, 1971; The Producer (theatre), 1972; The Sun in Mid-Career, 1975; Suicide Note, 1977; Waiting for It (on the death penalty), 1980; Private Territory (play), 1984; A Peep into the 20th Century (play), 1988; Dog, Horse, Rat, 1990. **Address:** c/o Curtis Brown, 10 Astor Pl, New York, NY 10003, U.S.A. **Online address:** sallywarner@earthlink.net

DAVIS, (Elvis) Clark, (III). American, b. 1964. **Genres:** Literary criticism and history. **Career:** Northeast Louisiana University, Monroe, assistant professor of English, 1992-. **Publications:** After the Whale: Melville in the Wake of Moby-Dick, 1995. **Address:** Department of English, Northeast Louisiana University, Monroe, LA 71209, U.S.A.

DAVIS, David (Howard). American, b. 1941. **Genres:** Politics/Government. **Career:** Rutgers University, NJ, assistant professor of political science, 1971-77; Environmental Protection Agency, member of staff, 1973-74; Cornell University, Ithaca, NY, associate professor of government, 1977-78; Library of Congress, Congressional Research Service, member of staff, 1979-80; deputy assistant secretary of Interior, Energy and Minerals, Washington, DC, 1980-81; International Energy Associates, Limited, Washington, DC, senior associate consultant, 1981-84; University of Wyoming, Laramie, associate professor of political science, 1984-89; University of Toledo, OH, Dept. of Political Science and Public Administration, associate professor, 1989-92, professor of political science, 1992-. Social Science Journal, editor, 1986-89; PA Times, commentary page editor, 1993-95. **Publications:** How the Bureaucracy Makes Foreign Policy, 1972; Energy Politics, 1974, 4th ed., 1982; American Environmental Politics, 1998. **Address:** Dept of Political Science and Public Administration, University of Toledo, Toledo, OH 43606, U.S.A. **Online address:** David.Davis@utoledo.edu

DAVIS, David Brion. American, b. 1927. **Genres:** History, Literary criticism and history, Race relations. **Career:** Sterling Professor of History, Yale University, New Haven, CT, 1978-, now Emeritus (Professor and Farnum Professor, 1969-78). Ernest I. White Professor of History, Cornell University, Ithaca, NY, 1963-69; Harold Vyvyan Harmsworth Professor, Oxford University, 1969-70; Chair in American Civilization, Ecole de Hautes Etudes en Sciences Sociales, Paris, 1980-81; Director, Gilder Lehrman Center for the Study of Slavery, Resistance, and Abolition, 1998-2001. **Publications:** Homicide in American Fiction, 1957; The Problem of Slavery in Western Culture, 1967; The Slave Power Conspiracy and the Paranoid Style, 1969; The Problem of Slavery in the Age of Revolution, 1975; (with others) The Great Republic, 1977; Slavery and Human Progress, 1984; From Homicide to Slavery: Studies in American Culture, 1986; Slavery in the Colonial Chesapeake, 1986; Revolutions: Reflections on American Equality and Foreign Liberations, 1990; (with others) The Antislavery Debate, 1992; (with others) The Boisterous Sea of Liberty: A Documentary History of American from Discovery through the Civil War, 1998; In the Image of God: Religion, Moral Values, and Our Heritage of Slavery, 2001; Challenging the Boundaries of Slavery, 2003. EDITOR: Ante-bellum Reform, 1967; The Fear of Conspiracy, 1971; Antebellum American Culture, 1979. **Address:** Rm 214 Allwin Hall, 31 Hillhouse Ave, PO Box 208206, Yale University, New Haven, CT 06520-8353, U.S.A. **Online address:** david.b.davis@yale.edu

DAVIS, David R. American, b. 1948. **Genres:** Humor/Satire. **Career:** Writer and political cartoonist. **Publications:** A Redneck Night before Christmas, 1997. Former political cartoonist for Madison County Journal. Contributor of articles and cartoons to periodicals. **Address:** 704 Parker Dr., Clinton, MS 39056, U.S.A. **Online address:** ddavis7@bellsouth.net

DAVIS, Dick. British, b. 1945. **Genres:** Poetry, Translations. **Career:** Assistant Professor of Persian, 1988-93, Associate Professor, 1993-, Ohio State University, Columbus. Teacher in Italy, Greece, England, and Iran, 1970-87. Poet-in-Residence, 1985-87 and Visiting Associate Professor, 1987-88, University of California, Santa Barbara. **Publications:** (with Clive Wilmer and Robert Wells) Shade Mariners, 1970; In the Distance, 1975; Seeing the World, 1980; (ed.) The Selected Writings of Thomas Traherne, 1980; Wisdom and Wilderness: The Achievement of Yvor Winters, 1983; What the Mind Wants, 1984; The Covenant, 1984; (trans.) The Conference of the Birds, by Attar, 1984; (trans.) The Little Virtues, by Natalia Ginzburg, 1985; (trans.)

The City and the House, by Ginzburg, 1987; (ed. with David Williams) New Writing from the North, 1988; (ed.) The Ruba'iyaat of Omar Khayyaam, 1989; Devices and Desires: New and Selected Poems 1967-1987, 1989; A Kind of Love: New & Selected Poems, 1991; Epic and Sedition: The Case of Ferdowsi's Shahnameh, 1992; The Legend of Seyarash, by Ferdowsi, 1992; (trans.) My Uncle Napoleon, 1996; Touchwood, 1996; (trans.) Borrowed Ware, 1996. **Address:** Dept. of Judaic and Near Eastern Languages, Ohio State University, 203 Jennings Hall, Columbus, OH 43210, U.S.A. **Online address:** davis77@osu.edu

DAVIS, Donald. American, b. 1944. **Genres:** Novellas/Short stories. **Career:** Western North Carolina, United Methodist minister, 1967-88; nationwide storyteller, 1967-. Featured storyteller at Smithsonian Institution, the World's Fair, festivals, and concerts. National Association for the Preservation and Perpetuation of Storytelling, chairperson, 1983-88. Producer of books and tapes of his works; master teacher of workshops and storytelling courses; guest host for the National Public Radio program Good Evening. **Publications:** My Lucky Day, 1983; Listening for the Crack of Dawn, 1990; Barking at a Fox-Fur Coat, 1991; Jack Always Seeks His Fortune, 1992; Telling Your Own Stories, 1993; Thirteen Miles from Suncrest, 1994; See Rock City, 1996; Writing as a Second Language, 2000; Ride the Butterflies, 2000. Contributor of articles and fiction to periodicals. RECORDED STORIES: Storytelling Festival, 2 vols., 1983; American Storytelling Series, Vol. 8: "The Crack of Dawn" and "Twelve Huntsmen," 1980s; Listening for the Crack of Dawn, 1991; Rainy Weather, 1992; Jack's First Job, 1992; Uncle Frank Invents the Electron Microphone, 1992; Party People, 1993; Miss Daisy, 1993; Christmas at Grandma's, 1994; The Southern Bells, 1994; Walking through Sulphur Springs, 1995; Jack and the Animals, 1995. **Address:** PO Box 397, Ocracoke, NC 27960, U.S.A.

DAVIS, Francis. American, b. 1946. **Genres:** Cultural/Ethnic topics, Music. **Career:** Philadelphia Inquirer, jazz critic, 1982-93; Atlantic Monthly, music writer, 1984-, contributing editor, 1991-. Producer and host of weekly jazz show, WHYY-FM Radio, Philadelphia, 1978-81. **Publications:** In the Moment: Jazz in the 1980s, 1986; Outcats, 1990; The History of the Blues, 1995; Bebop and Nothingness, 1996; Like Young, 2001; Afterglow, 2002; Jazz and Its Discontents, 2004. **Address:** c/o The Atlantic Monthly, 77 N Washington St Ste 5, Boston, MA 02114-1908, U.S.A.

DAVIS, Hank. American, b. 1941. **Genres:** Psychology. **Career:** Professor and author. Naval Medical Research Institute, MD, psychologist, 1965-67; California State University at Los Angeles, assistant professor of psychology, 1968-70; University of Guelph, ON, Canada, associate professor of psychology to professor of psychology, 1971-. Co-founder of the Centre for the Study of Animal Welfare, University of Guelph. Music and baseball journalist; former recording artist; annotator, producer, and compiler of record albums. **Publications:** Small-Town Heroes: Images of Minor League Baseball, 1997. EDITOR: (with H.M.B. Hurwitz) Operant-Pavlovian Interactions, 1977; (with D. Balfour) The Inevitable Bond: Examining Scientist-Animal Interactions, 1992. Author of scientific papers on experimental psychology and animal behavior and cognition. **Address:** Department of Psychology, University of Guelph, Guelph, ON, Canada N1G 2W1. **Online address:** hdavis@uoguelph.ca

DAVIS, Hope Hale. See Obituaries.

DAVIS, Jon. American, b. 1952. **Genres:** Poetry. **Career:** Fine Arts Work Center, Provincetown, MA, managing editor of Shankpainter, 1986-87, coordinator of writing program, 1987-88; Salisbury State University, Salisbury, MD, visiting assistant professor of creative writing, 1988-89, visiting assistant professor of American literature, 1989-90; Institute of American Indian Arts, Santa Fe, NM, professor of creative writing and literature, 1990-, department head, 1990-91, 1993-94. National Endowment of the Arts Poetry Fellowship, 1987; College of Santa Fe, NM, Countermeasures, co-editor, 1995-. **Publications:** POETRY: West of New England, 1983; Dangerous Amusements, 1987; The Hawk. The Road. The Sunlight after Clouds, 1995; Local Color, 1995; Scrimmage of Appetite, 1995. Work represented in anthologies. Contributor of poems, stories, essays, and reviews to periodicals. **Address:** Creative Writing Program, Institute of American Indian Arts, 83 Avon Nu Po, Santa Fe, NM 87508-1300, U.S.A. **Online address:** jdavis@iaiancad.org

DAVIS, Keith. See Obituaries.

DAVIS, Kenneth C. American. **Genres:** Cultural/Ethnic topics, History, Social commentary. **Career:** Writer. **Publications:** Two-Bit Culture: The Paperbacking of America, 1984. DON'T KNOW MUCH ABOUT...: History,

1990; Geography, 1992; the Civil War, 1996; the Bible, 1998; the Solar System, 2001; the Universe, 2001; Space, 2001; the Fifty States, 2001; the Pilgrims, 2001; the Planet Earth (for Kids!), 2001; the Presidents, 2002; the Kings and Queens of England, 2002; the Pioneers, 2002; the Dinosaurs, 2003. Contributor to periodicals. **Address:** c/o Nat Sobel, Sobel Weber Associates, 146 E 19th St, New York, NY 10003-2404, U.S.A.

DAVIS, Linda W. American, b. 1945. **Genres:** Biology, Horticulture. **Career:** Kansas State University, Manhattan, KS, instructor, 1988-. **Publications:** Weed Seeds of the Great Plains, 1993. **Address:** 3419 Womack Way, Manhattan, KS 66503, U.S.A.

DAVIS, Lindsey. British, b. 1949. **Genres:** Romance/Historical. **Career:** Formerly a civil servant; full-time writer. **Publications:** HISTORICAL MYSTERIES: The Silver Pigs, 1989; Shadows in Bronze, 1990; Venus in Copper, 1991; The Iron Hand of Mars, 1992; Poseidon's Gold, 1993; Last Act in Palmyra, 1994; Time to Depart, 1995; A Dying Light in Corduba, 1996; The Course of Honour, 1997; Three Hands in the Fountain, 1997; Two for the Lions, 1998; One Virgin Too Many, 1999; Ode to a Barker, 2000; A Body in the Bath House, 2001; The Jupiter Myth, 2002; The Accusers, 2030; Scandal Takes a Holiday, 2004. **Address:** c/o Century Publishing Ltd., Random House, 20 Vauxhall Bridge Rd, London SW1V 2SA, England.

DAVIS, Margaret (Thomson). British (born Scotland). **Genres:** Novels. **Publications:** The Breadmakers, 1972; A Baby Might Be Crying, 1973; A Sort of Peace, 1973; The Prisoner, 1974; The Prince and the Tobacco Lords, 1976; Roots of Bondage, 1977; Scorpion in the Fire, 1977; The Dark Side of Pleasure, 1981; The Making of a Novelist, 1982; A Very Civilized Man, 1982; Light and Dark, 1984; Rag Woman, Rich Woman, 1987; Mothers and Daughters, 1988; Wounds of War, 1989; A Woman of Property, 1991; A Sense of Belonging, 1993; Hold Me Forever, 1994; Kiss Me No More, 1995; A Tangled Web, 1999; Clydesiders, 1999; The Gourlay Girls, 2000; Clydesides at War, 2002. **Address:** 11 Hanover Gardens, Keir Hardie Court, Bishopbriggs G64 1AQ, Scotland.

DAVIS, Mark H. American, b. 1953. **Genres:** Psychology. **Career:** Eastern Illinois University, Charleston, assistant professor of psychology, 1983-86; Eckerd College, St. Petersburg, FL, assistant professor to associate professor of psychology, 1986-. **Publications:** Empathy: A Social Psychological Approach, 1996. **Address:** Department of Psychology, Eckerd College, St. Petersburg, FL 33733, U.S.A. **Online address:** davismh@eckerd.edu

DAVIS, Martyn P(aul). British, b. 1929. **Genres:** Communications/Media, Advertising/Public relations. **Career:** Marketing Communications Consultant, 1989-. Trustee, Inter-Varsity Club. Publicity Controller, Buland Publishing Co., 1953-56; Associate Director, Robert Brandon & Partners, 1956-58, and Sr. Executive, T. Booth Waddicor and Partners, 1958-60; Head of Marketing Services, College for the Distributive Trades, London, 1960-88. **Publications:** (ed.) Impact Yellow Book, 1957; A Career in Advertising, 1963; Handbook for Media Representatives, 1967; Business to Business Marketing and Promotion, 1990; The Effective Use of Advertising Media, 5th ed., 1996; Successful Advertising: Key Alternative Approaches, 1998. **Address:** 1 Park Steps, St. George's Fields, Albion St., London W2 2YQ, England.

DAVIS, Mary Byrd. British/American (born Wales), b. 1936. **Genres:** Environmental sciences/Ecology. **Career:** Northern Michigan University, Marquette, acquisitions librarian, 1974-75; Georgetown College, KY, assistant librarian for reader services, 1975-78; University of Kentucky Libraries, Lexington, librarian in public and technical service sections, 1978-83; freelance writer, editor, and translator, 1983-; Sierra Club's Energy Report newsletter, editor, 1986-87; Earth First! Journal, Canton, NY, office manager and staff writer, 1990; Wild Earth, Canton, co-founder and publisher 1991-92, associate editor, 1992-97; Uranium Enrichment News, editor, 1999-2001. **Publications:** NONFICTION: James Elroy Flecker: A Critical Study, 1977; The Military-Civilian Nuclear Link: A Guide to the French Nuclear Industry, 1988; Guide de l'industrie nucleaire francaise: De la mine aux dechets, du reacteur a la bombe, 1988; The Ecologist's Guide to France, 1988; (trans) The Scientific Mission of the Calypso at the Site of French Nuclear Testing on Mururoa, 1989; The Green Guide to France, 1990; (as Mary Dymond Davis) From Walden Pond to Muir Woods: Alternative Ways across America, 1990; Going off the Beaten Path: An Untraditional Travel Guide to the U.S., 1991; Old Growth in the East, 1993, rev. ed., 2003; (with B. Barrillot) Les Dechets militaires nucleaires francais, 1994; (ed.) Eastern Old-Growth Forests: Prospects for Rediscovery and Recovery, 1996; La France nucleaire: matieres et sites, 1997, rev. ed., 2002. Contributor of articles, including

translations from the French, to periodicals. **Address:** Yggdrasil Institute, PO Box 131, Georgetown, KY 40324, U.S.A. **Online address:** yggdrasili@yahoo.org

DAVIS, Mildred (B.). American, b. 1930. **Genres:** Mystery/Crime/Suspense. **Publications:** The Room Upstairs, 1948; They Buried a Man, 1953; The Dark Place, 1955; The Voice on the Telephone, 1964; The Sound of Insects, 1966; Strange Corner, 1967; Walk into Yesterday, 1967, as Nightmare of Murder, 1969; The Third Half, 1969; Three Minutes to Midnight, 1972; The Invisible Border, 1974; Tell Them What's-Her-Name Called, 1975; Scorpion, 1977; (with Katherine Davis) Lucifer Land (non-mystery novel), 1977.

DAVIS, Nancy Yaw. American, b. 1936. **Genres:** Anthropology/Ethnology, Literary criticism and history. **Career:** Alaska Methodist University, Anchorage, instructor, 1960-62; Anchorage Community College, lecturer, 1963-67, 1970, assistant professor, 1971-72; University of Alaska, Anchorage, assistant professor, 1972-75; Cultural Dynamics, Anchorage, president, 1976-89, sole proprietor, 1989-. **Publications:** Steps toward Understanding Rapid Culture Change in Native Rural Alaska, 1976; Historical Indicators of Alaska Native Culture Change, 1978; Kodiak Native Sociocultural Impacts, 1979; A Sociocultural Description of Small Communities in the Kodiak-Shumagin Region, 1986; (ed. with W.E. Davis) Adventures through Time: Readings in the Anthropology of Cook Inlet, Alaska, 1996; The Zuni Enigma: A Native American People's Possible Japanese Connection, 2000. Author of reports for federal and regional governments and articles in scholarly journals and collections. **Address:** Cultural Dynamics, 719 N St. Suite 3, Anchorage, AK 99501, U.S.A.

DAVIS, Ossie. See Obituaries.

DAVIS, Patrick. British, b. 1925. **Genres:** Travel/Exploration, Autobiography/Memoirs. **Career:** Publs. Officer, London School of Economics and Political Science, 1964-91. **Publications:** A Child at Arms, 1970, 1986; An Experience of Norway, 1974: (with S. Gilmore) A Connecticut Yankee in the 8th Gurkha Rifles: A Burma Memoir, 1995. **Address:** 6 Mt. Harry Rd, Sevenoaks, Kent TN13 3JH, England. **Online address:** mary.patrick.davis@talk21.com

DAVIS, Peter G(raffam). American, b. 1936. **Genres:** Music. **Career:** New York Times, staff writer, 1969-81; New York (magazine), music critic, 1981-. **Publications:** The American Opera Singer: The Lives and Adventures of America's Great Singers in Opera and Concert, From 1825 to the Present, 1997. **Address:** c/o New York Magazine, 444 Madison Ave 14th Fl, New York, NY 10022, U.S.A. **Online address:** Pgdavis@aol.com

DAVIS, R(oland) P(arker) Stephen, Jr. American, b. 1951. **Genres:** Archaeology/Antiquities. **Career:** Wright State University, Dayton, OH, instructor for archaeological field school, 1975; University of Tennessee, Knoxville, archaeological field supervisor, 1976; West Virginia Antiquities Commission, Morgantown, staff archaeologist, 1976-77; West Virginia Geological Survey, Morgantown, staff archaeologist, 1977-78; U.S. Forest Service, Elkins, WV, cultural resource paraprofessional training instructor, 1979; University of Tennessee, research associate in archaeology, 1980-82; University of North Carolina at Chapel Hill, research archaeologist, 1983-. **Publications:** (with Ward, P.C. Livingood, and V.P. Steponaitis) Excavating Occaneechi Town: Archaeology of an Eighteenth-Century Indian Village in North Carolina, 1998; (with Ward) Time before History: The Archaeology of North Carolina, 1999. Contributor to books and scholarly journals. **Address:** Research Laboratories of Archaeology, University of North Carolina at Chapel Hill, Chapel Hill, NC 27599, U.S.A. **Online address:** rpsdavis@unc.edu

DAVIS, Richard A., (Jr.). American, b. 1937. **Genres:** Earth sciences. **Career:** Affiliated with the department of geology at Western Michigan University, Kalamazoo, MI, 1965-73; affiliated with department of geology at University of South Florida, Tampa, 1973-. **Publications:** Principles of Oceanography, 1972, 2nd ed, 1981; Deposition of Systems, 1983, 2nd ed, 1992; Oceanography, 1987, 2nd ed, 1991; The Evolving Coast, 1994. **Address:** Department of Geology, University of South Florida, Tampa, FL 33620, U.S.A.

DAVIS, Richard Whitlock. American, b. 1935. **Genres:** History, Biography. **Career:** Emeritus Professor, Washington University, St. Louis, MO, 2003- (Associate Professor, 1969-73; Dept. Chairman, 1974-77; Professor of History and Director of Center for the History of Freedom, 1973-2003). General Ed., The Making of Modern Freedom. Supvr. in History, Christ's College, Cambridge, 1960-62; Instructor, University of Rhode Island, Kingston, 1962-

64; Assistant Professor, University of California at Riverside, 1964-69. Distinguished Visiting Professor, Christ's College, Cambridge, England, 1981-82. **Publications:** Dissent in Politics 1760-1830, 1971; Political Change and Continuity 1760-1885: A Buckinghamshire Study, 1972; Disraeli, 1976; The English Rothschilds, 1983. EDITOR: Religion and Irreligion in Victorian Society, 1992; Lords of Parliament, 1717-1914, 1995; The Origins of Modern Freedom, 1995; Leaders in the Lords, 1765-1902, 2003. **Address:** 7106 Waterman Ave, St. Louis, MO 63130, U.S.A. **Online address:** rwdavis@artsci. wustl.edu

DAVIS, Robin W(orks). American, b. 1962. **Genres:** Education. **Career:** Richardson Public Library, TX, youth services librarian, 1987-91; Hurst Public Library, TX, youth services librarian, beginning 1991. Consultant and workshop presenter. **Publications:** Creature Features, 1989; Camp Wanna Read, 1991; Promoting Reading with Reading Programs, 1992; An Alphabet of Books: Literature-Based Activities for Schools and Libraries, 1995; An Alphabet of Authors, 1995; Art Information through Children's Literature, 1995; Big Books for Little Readers, 1996. **Address:** 901 Precinct Line Rd, Hurst, TX 76053, U.S.A.

DAVIS, Rose Parkman. Also writes as Rose Parkman Marshall. American, b. 1947. **Genres:** Poetry, Education, Librarianship, Bibliography. **Career:** Jackson State University, MS, teacher of English, 1970-72; high school English teacher in Boston, MA, freelance consultant, and legal secretary, 1972-78; Tougaloo College, MS, instructor in English and director of Writing Center, 1979-84; freelance writer and consultant, Jackson, 1984-88; Mary Holmes College, West Point, MS, reference and technical services librarian, 1989-91; Mississippi State University, Mississippi State, branch librarian and assistant professor, 1991-95; Winthrop University, Rock Hill, SC, coordinator of library instruction and assistant professor, 1996-2000; University of South Carolina, Columbia, coordinator of library instruction, 2000-. **Publications:** Black History Every Month: Puzzles for Learning, 1982; A Guide to Training Peer Tutors, 1983; Women's Studies: Bibliographic Essay and List of Electronic Resources, 1994-95, 1995; Zora Neale Hurston: An Annotated Bibliography and Reference Guide, 1997; Possession! (poems), forthcoming. Work represented in anthologies. Contributor of articles, stories, poems, and reviews to periodicals. **Address:** PO Box 4528, Columbia, SC 29240-4528, U.S.A. **Online address:** rosem@gwm.sc.edu

DAVIS, Shelley L(orraine). American, b. 1956. **Genres:** History. **Career:** Historian and author. Office of Air Force History, Washington, DC, historian, 1979; Air Force Communications Command, Belleville, IL, historian, 1980-82; Air Force Logistics Command, Sacramento, CA, historian, 1982-83; Air Force Space Communications Division, Colorado Springs, CO, historian, 1983-84; Tactical Air Command, Austin, TX, historian, 1984-87; Defense Mapping Agency, Washington DC, historian, 1987-88; Internal Revenue Service, Washington, DC, historian, 1988-95 (resigned in protest); freelance writer, 1996-2000; Stars & Stripes, Arlington, VA, historian, 2000-. Member, executive leadership demonstration program, U.S. Department of Defense, Washington, DC, 1987-88. **Publications:** History of the Memphis Service Center: Yesterday, Today, and Tomorrow, 1972-1992, 1992; Unbridled Power: Inside the Secret Culture of the IRS, 1997. CO-AUTHOR AND DESIGNER: History of McClellan Air Force Base, 1983; Air Force Communications Command, 1938-1981. **Address:** 323 E Greystone Ave, Monrovia, CA 91016-2368, U.S.A. **Online address:** shelley@stripes.com

DAVIS, Steven J(oseph). American, b. 1957. **Genres:** Business/Trade/Industry. **Career:** University of Chicago, Chicago, IL, assistant professor, 198589, associate professor, 1989-94, professor of economics, 1994-. University of Maryland at College Park, visiting associate professor, 1990; Massachusetts Institute of Technology, visiting associate professor, 1993-94; Milken Institute for Job and Capital Formation, visiting scholar, 1994. National Bureau of Economic Research, organizer of Group on Labor Market Dynamics and Aggregate Fluctuations, 1988-92, became research associate; U.S. Bureau of the Census, research associate of Center for Economic Studies; Institute for Fiscal Studies, London, England, international research associate; Northwestern/Chicago Joint Center for Poverty Research, faculty affiliate and member of executive committee. Chicago Partners (consulting firm), principal; Chicago Economics and Finance Experts, president; Federal Reserve Bank of Chicago, consultant and research associate of Corporate Studies Group, 1991-93. **Publications:** (with J. Haltiwanger and S. Schuh) Job Creation and Destruction, 1996; (with M. Henrekson) Foeretagandets Villkor: Spelregler foer sysselsaettning och tillvaext (title means: Entrepreneurial and Business Conditions: The Rules of the Game for Employment and Growth), 1996. Contributor to books. Contributor of articles and reviews to professional journals. **Address:** Graduate School of Business, University of Chicago, 1101 East 58th St., Chicago, IL 60637, U.S.A. **Online address:** sjd@gsbsjd.uchicago.edu

DAVIS, (Edmund) Wade. Irish/Canadian, b. 1953. **Genres:** Anthropology/Ethnology, Biology, Adult non-fiction. **Career:** Jardin Botanico Antonio Uribe, Medellin, Colombia, plant collector, 1974-75; plant explorer for US Department of Agriculture, 1974-75; MacMillan Bloedel, Queen Charlotte Islands, British Columbia, axman and topographer, 1977-78; ethnobotanical researcher and writer, 1982-; honorary research associate in ethnobiology at Institute of Economic Botany, Bronx, NY, 1986-, and at Instituto Caribe de Antropologia y Sociologia, 1990-. Guest lecturer at universities. Guest on radio and televison programs, 1985-; host of radio and televison programs, 1991-. Scientific expeditions in Colombia, Panama, Ecuador, Peru, Bolivia, Canada, Brazil, Haiti, Guatemala, Jamaica, Borneo, Tibet, China, Malaysia, and Venezuela, 1974-. **Publications:** The Serpent and the Rainbow (nonfiction), 1986; Passage of Darkness: The Ethnobiology of the Haitian Zombie (nonfiction), 1988; Penan: Voice for the Borneo Rain Forest, 1990; Shadows in the Sun, 1992; Nomads of the Dawn, 1995; One River, 1996. **Address:** Institute of Economic Botany, New York Botanical Garden, Bronx, NY 10458, U.S.A.

DAVIS, Wendi. See HOLDER, Nancy L.

DAVISON, Liam. Australian, b. 1957. **Genres:** Novels, Novellas/Short stories. **Career:** Freelance writer, c. 1988-. **Publications:** NOVELS: The Velodrome, 1988; Soundings, 1993; The White Woman, 1994; The Betrayal, 1999. OTHER: The Shipwreck Party (short stories), 1989; Collected Stories, 2000. **Address:** 21 Canadian Bay Rd, Mt. Eliza, VIC 3930, Australia.

DAVISON, Peter (Hobley). British, b. 1926. **Genres:** Literary criticism and history. **Career:** University of Birmingham, England, lecturer, 1965-70, senior lecturer, 1970-73; St. David's University College, Lampeter, Dyfed, U.K., professor of English, 1973-79; University of Kent, professor of English and American literature, 1979-85; writer. Fellow at University of Birmingham's Shakespeare Institute, 1964-65 and 1971-72; Cecil Oldman Lecturer at University of Leeds, 1984; visiting professor in performing arts at Westfield College, London, 1986-89; De Montfort University, Leicester, research professor, 1992-2001; NEW1, Wrexham, 2001-. OBE, 1999. **Publications:** Futures Valuing of Greasy Wool Clips, 1961; The Rocks (screenplay), 1963; The Contexts of English (monograph), 1975; The Seven Deceits (dance drama), 1978; Henry V in the Context of the Popular Dramatic Tradition (monograph), 1981; Contemporary Drama and the Popular Dramatic Tradition in England, 1982; Popular Appeal in English Drama to 1850, 1982; Hamlet: Text and Performance, 1983; Sheridan: A Case Book, 1986; Henry V: Masterguide, 1986; (comp. of bib. and contrib.) Pelican Guide to American Literature, 1987; Othello: The Critical Debate, 1988; George Orwell: A Literary Life, 1996. EDITOR: Songs of the British Music Hall, 1971; (and contrib.) New Cambridge Bibliography of English Literature, 1900-1950, 1972; (and contrib.) Theatrum Redivivum, 17 vols., 1972; (and contrib.) Year's Work in English Studies, 1984-85; The First Quarto of King Richard III, 1996; The Complete Works of George Orwell, 20 vols., 1998; (specialist ed.) G. Orwell, Letters and Documents in UK Libraries and Archives (microfilm), 2004. EDITOR WITH R. MEYERSOHN AND E. SHILS: Literary Taste, Culture and Mass Communication, 14 vols., 1978-80; Orwell in Spain, 2001; Orwell and Politics, 2001; Orwell and the Dispossessed, 2001; Orwell's England, 2001; Service for Worship, 2001. Editor of editions of various works including William Shakespeare's plays. Contributor to periodicals. **Address:** 1 Hughes Close, Marlborough SN8 1TN, England.

DAVISON, Peter (Hubert). See Obituaries.

DAVOLLS, Linda. British, b. 1966. **Genres:** Zoology. **Career:** Zoological Society of London, Regents Park, London, England, Journal of Zoology and Animal Conservation, scientific journals, assistant editor, 1988-. **Publications:** Tano and Binti: Two Chimpanzees Return to the Wild, 1994; Suli and the Pandas, 1996. **Address:** 15 Berens Rd., Kensal Green, London NW10 5DX, England. **Online address:** linda.davolls@zsl.org

DAWE, (Donald) Bruce. Australian, b. 1930. **Genres:** Poetry, Novellas/Short stories. **Career:** Freelance writer, Queensland. Formerly worked as laborer, gardener, and postman. **Publications:** No Fixed Address, 1962; A Need of Similar Name, 1965; An Eye for Tooth: Poems, 1968; Beyond the Subdivision: Poems, 1969; Heat Wave, 1970; Condolences of the Season, 1971; Just a Dugong at Twilight, 1975; Sometimes Gladness: Collected Poems 1954-1978, 1978, 5th ed., 1997; Over Here, Harv! and Other Stories, 1983; Towards Sunrise: Poems 1979-1986, 1986; This Side of Silence: Poems, 1987-1990, 1990; Bruce Dawe: Essays and Opinions, 1990; Mortal Instruments: Poems, 1990-1995, 1995; A Poet's People, 1999. EDITOR: Dimensions, 1974; Speaking in Parables: A Reader, 1987. **Address:** Colundria, QLD, Australia.

DAWE, Margaret. American, b. 1957. **Genres:** History. **Career:** East Hampton Star, Long Island, NY, reporter, 1981-86; Brooklyn College, Brooklyn, NY, adjunct lecturer, 1986-93; Wichita State University, Wichita, KS, assistant professor, 1993-99, associate professor, 1999-, chair, 2001-. **Publications:** Nissequott, 1992. **Address:** English Department, Wichita State University, Wichita, KS 67260, U.S.A.

DAWE, R(oger) D(avid). British, b. 1934. **Genres:** Classics, Literary criticism and history. **Career:** Cambridge University, England, research fellow of Caius College, 1957-63, teaching fellow at Trinity College, beginning in 1963, senior research fellow, 1998-2001; author and editor. **Publications:** Collation and Investigation of the Manuscripts of Aeschylus, 1964; A Repertory of Conjectures on Aeschylus, 1965; Studies on the Text of Sophocles, Vols. I-II, 1973, Vol. III, 1978; Sophocles: The Classical Heritage, 1996. EDITOR: Sophocles, Vol. I, 1975, 3rd ed., 1995, Vol. II, 1979, 3rd ed., 1996; Sophocles, Oedipus Rex, 1982; (and trans.) Homer, The Odyssey: Translation and Analysis, 1993; Philogelos, 2000. contributor of articles to learned journals. **Address:** Trinity College, Cambridge University, Cambridge CB2 1TQ, England.

DAWICK, John. New Zealander, b. 1934. **Genres:** Biography. **Career:** Massey University, Palmerston North, New Zealand, lecturer, senior lecturer in English, 1964-95. **Publications:** Pinero: A Theatrical Life, 1993. Contributor to periodicals. **Address:** 130 Acaster Lane, Bishopthorpe, York YO2 1TD, England. **Online address:** dawickjohn@hotmail.com

DAWID, Annie. American, b. 1960. **Genres:** Novels, Novellas/Short stories. **Career:** Lewis and Clark College, Portland, OR, professor of English, 1990-, director of Creative Writing Program. Participant in public readings; photographer; Hawthornden Castle Intl. Retreat for Writers, Midlothian, Scotland, fellowship, 1996. **Publications:** York Ferry (novel), 1993; Lily in the Desert (short stories), 2001. Contributor of reviews to periodicals. **Address:** Department of English, Box 58, Lewis and Clark College, 0615 SW Palatine Hill Rd, Portland, OR 97219-7899, U.S.A.

DAWN, Marva J. American, b. 1948. **Genres:** Theology/Religion. **Career:** University of Idaho, Moscow, instructor in English, 1970-72, campus minister, 1972-75; director of special ministries at a Lutheran church in Olympia, WA, 1976-79; Christians Equipped for Ministry, Vancouver, WA, co-founder, 1979, director of teaching and writing ministry, 1979-; Regent College, Vancouver, BC, teaching fellow in spiritual theology. **Publications:** To Walk and Not Faint, 1980, rev. ed., 1997; To Walk in the Kingdom, 1982; I'm Lonely, LORD-How Long?, 1983, rev. ed., 1998; Keeping the Sabbath Wholly, 1989; The Hilarity of Community, 1992, as Truly the Community, 1997; Sexual Character, 1993; Joy in Our Weakness, 1994, rev. ed., 2002; Reaching Out without Dumbing Down, 1995; Is It a Lost Cause?, 1997; A Royal "Waste" of Time, 1999; The Unnecessary Pastor, 1999; Powers, Weakness, and the Tabernacling of God, 2001; Morning by Morning, 2001; How Shall We Worship, 2003; Unfettered Hope, 2003; Corrupted Words Reclaimed, 2005. EDITOR & TRANSLATOR: G. von Rad, Holy War in Ancient Israel, 1991; Sources and Trajectories: 8 Early Articles by Jacques Ellul that Set the Stage, 1997. Work represented in anthologies. Contributor to periodicals. **Address:** Christians Equipped for Ministry, 304 N Fredericksburg Way, Vancouver, WA 98664, U.S.A.

DAWSON, Carol. American, b. 1951. **Genres:** Novels, Poetry. **Career:** Writer. Painter, with work exhibited in galleries in Seattle, WA, and New Mexico; jeweler, 1965-79. **Publications:** Job (poems), 1975. NOVELS: The Waking Spell, 1992; Meeting the Minotaur, 1997; The Mother-in-Law Diaries, 1999; Body of Knowledge, in press. Contributor to magazines. **Address:** Witherspoon Associates, 235 E 31st St, New York, NY 10016, U.S.A.

DAWSON, Elizabeth. *See* GEACH, Christine.

DAWSON, George Glenn. American, b. 1925. **Genres:** Economics. **Career:** Emeritus Professor of Economics and Dean, Empire State College, State University of New York, Old Westbury, 1975- (Professor 1970-75). Assistant Professor 1959-64, Associate Professor 1964-65, and Professor and Head, Division of Social Studies, and Director, Center for Economic Education 1965-70; New York University, NYC. **Publications:** (ed.) Communism (readings), 1962; (ed.) Freedom (readings), 1962; (with R. McClain) Guide to Economics, 1963; Economics: Book One, 1965, Book Two, 1965; (with McClain) Economics for Businessmen and Investors, 1966; (ed.) Economic Education Experiences of Enterprising Teachers, vols. 4-15, 1966-78; College Level Economics, 1968; Our Nation's Wealth, 1968; Foundations of the American Economy, 1969; (with S. Gordon and J. Witchel) The American Economy, 1969; (with Gordon) Introductory Economics, 1972, 7th ed., 1991;

(with E. Prehn) Teaching Economics in American History, 1973, 1984; (with L. Leamer) Suggestions for a Basic Economics Library, 1973; (ed.) Economics and Our Community, 1973; (ed.) Government and the Economy, 1974. **Address:** 2292 Arby Ct, Wantagh, NY 11793, U.S.A. **Online address:** GDawsonNabad@aol.com

DAWSON, Janet. American, b. 1949. **Genres:** Mystery/Crime/Suspense. **Career:** Writer. Has worked as a newspaper reporter. **Publications:** Kindred Crimes, 1990; Till the Old Men Die, 1993; Take a Number, 1993; Don't Turn Your Back on the Ocean, 1994; Nobody's Child, 1995; A Credible Threat, 1996; Witness to Evil, 1997. Author of short stories. **Address:** c/o Charlotte Sheedy Literary Agency, 65 Bleecker St. 12th Fl., New York, NY 10012, U.S.A.

DAWSON, Roger. American (born England), b. 1940. **Genres:** Business/Trade/Industry, How-to books. **Career:** Real estate broker, 1976-82; speaker and writer, 1982-. **Publications:** You Can Get Anything You Want: Secrets of Power Negotiating, 1987; Secrets of Power Persuasion, 1992; The Confident Decision Maker: How to Make the Right Business and Personal Decisions Every Time, 1993; The 13 Secrets of Power Performance, 1994; Secrets of Power Negotiations, 1995. **Address:** 214 San Carlos Way, Placentia, CA 92870-2222, U.S.A. **Online address:** Rogdawson@aol.com

DAY, A(rthur) Colin. British, b. 1935. **Genres:** Information science/Computers, Reference. **Career:** Wycliffe Bible Translators, translator in Vietnam, India, and Nepal, 1959-67; University College London, Computer Centre, London, England, head of applications, 1967-92; writer, 1992-. **Publications:** Fortran Techniques, 1972; A London Fortran Course, 1972; Compatible Fortran, 1978; Illustrating Computers, 1982; Text Processing, 1984; Using Ventura Publisher, 1988, rev. ed., 1990; Roget's Thesaurus of the Bible, 1992, rev. ed. as Collins Thesaurus of the Bible, 2002. **Address:** Hillcroft, Thornton Rust, Leyburn, North Yorkshire DL8 3AW, England. **Online address:** acolinday@aol.com

DAY, Aidan. British, b. 1952. **Genres:** Literary criticism and history. **Career:** University of Hull, Hull, England, research fellow, 1978-79, lecturer in English, 1979-82; University of Edinburgh, Edinburgh, Scotland, lecturer in English literature, 1984-92, reader in English Literature, 1992-99, professor of Nineteenth Century and Contemporary Literature, 1999-. **Publications:** Jokerman: Reading the Lyrics of Bob Dylan, 1988; Romanticism, 1996; Angela Carter: The Rational Glass, 1998. EDITOR: (with C. Ricks) The Tennyson Archive (facsimile edition of complete poetical manuscripts), 31 vols., 1987-93; (and author of intro) Robert Browning: Selected Poetry and Prose, 1991; Alfred Lord Tennyson: Selected Poems, 1991. **Address:** Department of English Literature, University of Edinburgh, David Hume Tower, George Sq, Edinburgh EH8 9JX, Scotland. **Online address:** Aidan.Day@ed.ac.uk

DAY, Alan. British, b. 1932. **Genres:** History, Archaeology/Antiquities, Bibliography. **Career:** Oxford City Libraries, Oxford, England, central lending librarian, 1962-65; Leeds Polytechnic, Leeds, England, senior lecturer and principal lecturer, 1965-79; Manchester Polytechnic, Manchester, England, head of department of library and information studies, 1979-90. **Publications:** History: A Reference Book, 1977; Archaeology: A Reference Book, 1978; Discovery and Exploration: A Reference Handbook, 1980; J.B. Priestley: An Annotated Bibliography, 1980; Search for the Northwest Passage: An Annotated Bibliography, 1986; The British Library: A Guide to Its Structure, Publications, Collections, and Services, 1988; (ed. with P. Lea) Printed Reference Material and Related Sources of Information, 3rd ed, 1990; (ed. with J.M. Harvey) Walfords Guide to Reference Material, Vol II: Social and Historical Sciences, 1990, 6th ed, 1994; (comp.) England, 1993; The New British Library, 1994; The Falkland Islands, South Georgia, and the South Sandwich Islands, 1995. Contributor to library and education journals. **Address:** c/o ABC-Clio Press, P.O. Box 1911, Santa Barbara, CA 93116, U.S.A.

DAY, Alexandra. (Sandra Woodward Darling). American. **Genres:** Children's fiction. **Career:** Green Tiger Press (children's book publishing company), San Diego, CA, founder and owner with Harold Darling, 1970-86; Blue Lantern Studio, Seattle, owner with H. Darling; children's writer and illustrator. Designer of note cards and stationery. **Publications:** The Teddy Bears' Picnic, 1983; The Blue Faience Hippopotamus, 1984; Good Dog, Carl, 1985; when You Wish upon a Star, 1987; Frank and Ernest, 1988; Paddy's Pay-Day, 1989; Carl Goes Shopping, 1989; Frank and Ernest Play Ball, 1990; Carl's Christmas, 1990; (with A. Darling) Teddy Bear's Picnic Cookbook, 1991; Carl's Afternoon in the Park, 1991; Carl's Masquerade, 1992; Carl Goes to Daycare, 1993; Frank and Ernest on the Road, 1994; Carl

Makes a Scrapbook, 1994; My Puppy's Record Book, 1994; Carl Pops Up, 1994; Carl's Birthday, 1995; Carl's Baby Journal, 1996; The Mirror, 1997; (with C. Edens) The Christmas We Moved to the Barn, 1997; Follow Carl, 1998, Boswell Wide Awake, 1999; Darby, the Special Order Pup, 2000; Special Deliveries, 2001. OTHER: (ed. with W. Poltarnees) A.B.C. of Fashionable Animals, 1989. Illustrator of books by J. Kennedy, J.M. Grant, C. Edens, N. Washington. **Address:** 4649 Sunnyside Ave N, Seattle, WA 98103, U.S.A.

DAY, Edward C. American, b. 1932. **Genres:** Novels, Children's fiction, Travel/Exploration, Young adult fiction, Humor/Satire. **Career:** Harvard University Press, assistant sales manager to advertising manager, 1957-69; Itek Corp., Lexington, MA, public relations representative, 1969-70; Bates College, Lewiston, ME, part-time staff writer, 1970-72; Bath Art Shop and Gallery, Bath, ME, owner and operator, 1973-74; Whitcoulls Publishers, Christchurch, New Zealand, assistant publishing manager, 1974-77 and 1979-80; Alaska Northwest Publishing Co., Edmonds, WA, associate editor, 1977-78; Summer Street Studios, Rockport, ME, landscape photographer, 1980-83; Wooden-Boat (magazine), Brooklin, ME, merchandise manager, 1983-85; Colby College, Waterville, ME, development writer and director of corporate and foundation relations, 1985-90; free-lance writer, 1990-92; Vermont Foodbank, director of development, 1993-94, executive director, 1995-97. **Publications:** John Tabor's Ride, 1989. Contributor to magazines and newspapers. **Address:** 1670 Center Rd, Montpelier, VT 05602-8534, U.S.A.

DAY, Holliday T. American, b. 1936. **Genres:** Art/Art history. **Career:** Free-lance art critic, 1975-80; Joslyn Art Museum, Omaha, NE, curator of American art, 1980-85; Indianapolis Museum of Art, Indianapolis, IN, senior curator of contemporary art, 1985-2000. Consortium of Indianapolis Universities, lecturer, spring, 1987. Panelist, lecturer, and juror for art exhibitions, 1978-94. **Publications:** Seven Sculptors, 1978; Europe in the Seventies (bibliography), 1979; Stacked, Packed, and Hung, 1980; Dennis Kowalski, 1980; I-80 Series, 1980-82; The Shape of Space: The Sculpture of George Sugarman, 1981; (with Adrian, Cathcart, and Flood) Ed Paschke: Selected Works, 1982; New Art of Italy: Chia Clemente Cucchi Paladino, 1983; Elyn Zimmerman, 1985; Painting and Sculpture Today, 1986; Art of the Fantastic: Latin America, 1920-1987, 1987; (with Sturges) Joslyn Art Museum: Painting and Sculpture from the European and American Collections, 1987; (ed.) Indianapolis Museum of Art: Collections Handbook, 1988; Joseph Cantor: Connoisseur, 1988; Rick Paul, 1989; Power: Its Myths and Mores in American Art, 1961-1991, 1991; Forefront Series, 1991-2000; (with Harris and Waller) The Poetry of Form: Richard Tuttle Drawings from the Vogel Collection, 1993; Felrath Hines, 1995; Crossroads of American Sculpture, 2000. Contributor to books; contributor of articles and reviews to periodicals. **Address:** 1207 Golden Hill Dr, Indianapolis, IN 46208, U.S.A.

DAY, Laura (Globus). American, b. 1959. **Genres:** How-to books, Psychology. **Career:** Teacher of practical intuition at seminars throughout the United States and Europe, c. 1982-; private consultant. Active in community and private healing therapy. **Publications:** Practical Intuition: How to Harness the Power of Your Instinct and Make It Work for You, 1996; Practical Intuition for Success: A Step-by-Step Program to Increase Your Wealth Today, 1997; Practical Intuition in Love, 1997; The Circle: How the Power of a Single Wish Can Change Your Life, 2001. **Address:** Canal Street Station, PO Box 2061, New York, NY 10013, U.S.A. **Online address:** healingday@aol.com

DAY, Marele. Australian, b. 1947. **Genres:** Mystery/Crime/Suspense, Writing/Journalism. **Career:** Has worked picking fruit, and as a researcher, trademark searcher, and academic searcher; teacher in New South Wales, 1984-87; teacher of English as a second language; freelance editor and writer, c. 1988-. Has served as a judge in writing contests. **Publications:** FICTION: Shirley's Song, 1984; The Life and Crimes of Harry Lavender, 1988; The Case of the Chinese Boxes, 1990; The Last Tango of Dolores Delgado, 1992; The Disappearances of Madalena Grimaldi, 1994; Lambs of God, 1998. NONFICTION: The Art of Self-Promotion for Writers, 1993; (ed.) How to Write Crime, 1996. Contributor to anthologies. **Address:** c/o Allen and Unwin, 9 Atchison St., PO Box 8500, St. Leonards, NSW 2065, Australia.

DAY, Michael Herbert. British, b. 1927. **Genres:** Anthropology/Ethnology, Archaeology/Antiquities. **Career:** Sr. lecturer in anatomy, 1964-69, and reader in physical anthropology, 1969-72, Middlesex Hospital Medical School, London; professor of anatomy, United Medical and Dental Schools, St. Thomas's Campus, London, 1972-89; senior research fellow, The Natural History Museum; professor, Dept. of Palaeontology, British Museum (natural

history), London, 1989-. **Publications:** Guide to Fossil Man, 1965, rev. ed., 1986; (ed.) Human Evolution, 1973. **Address:** 26 Thurlow Rd, Hampstead, London NW3 57PP, England. **Online address:** m.day@mailbox.ulcc.ac.uk

DAY, Nancy. American, b. 1953. **Genres:** Young adult non-fiction. **Career:** Writer and marketing consultant. BBL Microbiology Systems, Cockeysville, MD, advertising manager, 1976-79; M.A. Bioproducts, Walkersville, MD, director of marketing communications, 1979-81; West Company, Phoenixville, PA, business development manager, 1982-83; CooperBiomedical, Malvern, PA, director of marketing communications, 1983-85; freelance marketing consultant, 1985-2000; Sakaduski Marketing Solutions, Northport, NY, president, 2000-. **Publications:** The Horseshoe Crab, 1992; Animal Experimentation: Cruelty or Science?, 1994, rev. ed., 2000; Abortion: Debating the Issue, 1995; Sensational TV: Trash or Journalism?, 1996; Violence in Schools: Learning in Fear, 1996; Advertising: Information or Manipulation?, 1999; The Death Penalty for Teens: A Pro/Con Issue, 2000; Killer Superbugs: The Story of Drug-resistant Diseases, 2001; Malaria, West Nile, and Other Mosquito-borne Diseases, 2001; Censorship, or Freedom of Expression? 2001. PASSPORT TO HISTORY SERIES; Your Travel Guide to Renaissance Europe, 2001; Your Travel Guide to Colonial America, 2001; Your Travel Guide to Ancient Greece, 2001; Your Travel Guide to Civil War America, 2001; Your Travel Guide to Ancient Maya Civilization, 2001; Your Travel Guide to Ancient Egypt, 2001. Contributor to periodicals. Author of business booklets, articles, and other publications. **Address:** 136 Woodbine Ave., Northport, NY 11768, U.S.A. **Online address:** nancy@ sakaduskimarketing.com

DAY, Stacey B. American (born England), b. 1927. **Genres:** Novels, Plays/ Screenplays, Poetry, Medicine/Health, Philosophy, Sociology, Autobiography/ Memoirs. **Career:** Physician, medical administrator, and educator. Former conservator, and head, Bell Museum of Pathobiology; former associate professor of pathology and laboratory medicine, University of Minnesota Medical School, Minneapolis; former professor, Cornell University Medical College, NYC, University of Calabar (Nigeria), and University of Arizona; former Fulbright professor, Prague; former dir., WHO Center, and Meharry Medical College, Nashville; former member and head, Biosciences Communications and Medical Education, Sloan Kettering Institute, NYC. Ed.-in-chief, Biosciences Communication, Karger, Basel, Switzerland, 1975-80; producer, TV and radio health film and education programmes, Nigerian TV (Calabar), West Africa, 1981-85; permanent visiting professor of medical education, Oita Medical University and Japan, 1990-99. President, International Foundation for Biosocial Development and Human Health. **Publications:** Collected Lines, 1966; By the Waters of Babylon, 1966; American Lines, 1967; The Music Box, 1967; Rosalita, 1968; Poems and Etudes, 1968; The Idle Thoughts of a Surgical Fellow, 1968; Edward Stevens, 1969; Bellechasse, 1970; (with B.G. MacMillan and W.A. Altmeier) Curling's Ulcer, 1971; Ten Poems and a Letter from America, 1971; (with R.A. Good) Membranes and Viruses in Immunopathology, 1972; Tuluak and Amaulik, 1974; (with R.A. Good and J. Yunis) Molecular Pathology, 1975; East of the Navel and Afterbirth: 1976; Cancer Invasion and Metastasis, 1977; The American Biomedical Network, 1978; A Companion to the Life Sciences, vol. I, 1978; Health Communications, 1979; (with J. Tachae and H. Selye) Cancer, Stress, and Death, 1979; Integrated Medicine, 1980; Biopsychosocial Health, 1981; The Biopsychosocial Imperative, 1981; The Way of a Physician, 1982; Creative Health and Health Enhancement, 1982; Man in Search of Health, 1983; Primary Health Care Guide Lines, 1984; Health and Quality of Life in Central Europe in the Year 2000, 1992; The Spirit of Bushido, 1993; (with K. Inokuchi) The Wisdom of Hagakure, 1995; Developing Health in the West African Bush, 2 Parts, 1995; (with M. Kobayashi and K. Inokuchi) The Medical Student and the Mission of Medicine in the 21st Century (in Japanese), 1996; Letters of Owen Wangensteen to a Surgical Fellow, 1996; Man and Mu, 1997; Selected Poems and Embers of a Medical Life, 1997; The Surgical Treatment of Ischemic Heart Disease, 1999; Introduction to Katsutaro Nagata-Comprehensive Medicine, 1999; Introduction to the Davenfoot Foundation Grammar School, 2000; W. Von Humboldt, Ueber die unter dem namen Bhagavadgita, 2001; A Vitae Sophia of Integral Humanism and Japanese Lectures, 1990-2000, 2001; Letters to Ivana from Calabar, 2001; The Klacelka in a Slavic Woodland, 2003. EDITOR: Death and Attitudes towards Death, 1972; Ethics in Medicine in a Changing Society, 1973; Trauma, 1975; Communication of Scientific Information, 1975; (series ed. with R.A Good) Comprehensive Immunology, 1975; Readings in Oncology, 1980; Computers for Medical Office and Patient Management, 1982; Life Stress, 1982; (with T.A. Lambo) Contemporary Issues in International Health, 1989. **Address:** 6 Lomond Ave, Chestnut Ridge, NY 10977-6901, U.S.A. **Online address:** biosocmed@aol.com

DAY-LEWIS, Sean (Francis). British, b. 1931. **Genres:** Biography. **Career:** Local newspapers in England, 1952-60; Daily Telegraph, London, 1960-86, television and radio editor, 1970-86; London Daily News, television editor, 1986-87; freelance writer and commentator on television, 1987-. **Publications:** Bulleid: Last Giant of Steam, 1963, 2nd ed., 1968; C. Day Lewis: An English Literary Life, 1980; One Day in the Life of Television, 1989; TV Heaven, 1992; Talk of Drama: Views of the Television Dramatist Now and Then, 1998. **Address:** Restorick Row, Rosemary Lane, Colyton, Devon EX24 6LW, England. **Online address:** seandaylewis@tesco.net

DAYTON, Charles (W.). American, b. 1943. **Genres:** Education. **Career:** Cayuga Community College, Auburn, NY, English teacher, 1968-71; American Institutes for Research, Palo Alto, CA, research scientist, 1972-84; Stanford Urban Coalition, director of Peninsula Academies, 1982-84; Foothill Associates, Nevada City, CA, education consultant, 1984-; University of California, Berkeley, Graduate School of Education, Career Academy Support Network, coordinator 1998-. **Publications:** (with J.A. Hamilton, J.M. Wolff, and S.M. Jung) Safeguarding Your Education, 1977; (with R.J. Rossi and K.J. Gilmartin) Agencies Working Together: A Guide to Coordination and Planning, 1982; (with D. Stern and M. Raby) Career Academies: Partnerships for Reconstructing American High Schools, 1992; (with D. Stern and M. Raby) Career Academies and High School Reform, 1998; (with others) Issues in Schoolwide Application of Career Academies, 2000; (with D. Stern and M. Raby) Career Academies: Building Blocks for Reconstructing American High Schools, 2000; (with others) Implementing Career Academies Schoolwide, 2001. Work represented in anthologies. Contributor to periodicals. **Address:** Foothill Associates, 230 Main St, Nevada City, CA 95959, U.S.A.

DEÀK, Erzsi. American, b. 1959. **Genres:** Children's fiction. **Career:** Journalist, editor, and writer. **Publications:** (editor, with Kristin Embry Litchman) Period Pieces: Stories for Girls, 2003. **Address:** c/o Author Mail, HarperCollins, 10 East 53rd St., 7th Floor, New York, NY 10012, U.S.A. **Online address:** erzsideak@hotmail.com

DEAK, Istvan. American (born Hungary), b. 1926. **Genres:** History. **Career:** Columbia University, NYC, instructor, 1963-64, assistant professor, 1964-67, associate professor, 1967-71, director, Institute on East Central Europe, 1967-78, Seth Low Professor of History, 1971-2000, Seth Low Professor Emeritus of History, 2000-. **Publications:** Weimar Germany's Left-Wing Intellectuals: A Political History of the Weltbuhne and Its Circle, 1968; The Lawful Revolution: Louis Kossuth and the Hungarians 1848-49, 1979; Beyond Nationalism: A Social and Political History of the Habsburg Officer Corps, 1848-1914, 1990; Essays on Hitler's Europe, 2001. EDITOR: Eastern Europe in the 1970's, 1972; (with A. Mitchell) Everyman in Europe: Essays in Social History, 2 vols., 1974, 1981; The Politics of Retribution in Europe: World War II and Its Aftermath, 2000. **Address:** 410 Riverside Dr, New York, NY 10025, U.S.A. **Online address:** id1@columbia.edu

DEAN, Bradley P. American (born Philippines), b. 1954. **Genres:** Environmental sciences/Ecology, Literary criticism and history, Natural history. **Career:** Thunderbird-Red Lion Motor Inns, executive assistant manager at locations in Oregon, Washington, and northern California, 1976-78; Eastern Washington University, Cheney, lecturer in English, 1982-84; University of Connecticut, Storrs, lecturer in English, 1984-87; University of Connecticut, Greater Hartford Campus, West Hartford, lecturer in English, 1988; TransPacific Communications, Ayden, NC, owner and consultant, 1988-98; Sunstar, Inc., international business communications coordinator, 1988-98; Rhode Island College, lecturer in English, 1989; University of Montana, faculty affiliate, 1989-91; East Carolina University, visiting assistant professor, 1990-91; adjunct professor, 1993-97; Thoreau Institute, Lincoln, MA, director of Media Center. Hellgate Writers, Inc. and Northern Lights Institute, project humanist, 1989; Walden Woods Project, member of advisory board, 1992-97; member of Thoreau Society and Thoreau Country Conservation Alliance. **Publications:** EDITOR: H.D. Thoreau, Faith in a Seed: The Dispersion of Seeds and Other Late Natural History Writings, 1993; H.D. Thoreau, Wild Fruits, 2000. Work represented in anthologies. Contributor of articles to periodicals. **Address:** PO Box 70, West Peterborough, NH 03468-0070, U.S.A. **Online address:** brad.dean@walden.org

DEAN, Eric T., Jr. American, b. 1950. **Genres:** History. **Career:** U.S. Peace Corps, Washington, DC, tuberculosis control worker in Hahm Pyong and Seoul, South Korea, 1972-75; Legal Services of Northern Indiana, attorney in Lafayette, Kokomo, and Fort Wayne, 1978-81; attorney in private practice, Crawfordsville, IN, 1981-89; Purdue University, West Lafayette, IN, instructor in history, 1989; Yale University, New Haven, CT, instructor in history, 1993 and 1995; Marcus Law Firm, New Haven, real estate attorney, 1996-. **Publications:** Shook over Hell: Post-Traumatic Stress, Vietnam, and the Civil War, 1997. Contributor to law and history journals. **Address:** Marcus Law Firm, 111 Whitney Ave, New Haven, CT 06510, U.S.A. **Online address:** edean@marcuslawfirm.com

DEAN, Martin. American, b. 1962. **Genres:** History. **Career:** Historian. Center for Advanced Holocaust Studies, U.S. Holocaust Memorial Museum, Washington, DC, Pearl Resnick post-doctoral fellow, 1997-98, applied research scholar, 1998-. **Publications:** Collaboration in the Holocaust: Crimes of the Local Police in Belorussia and Ukraine, 1941-44, 1999. **Address:** c/o St. Martin's Press, 175 Fifth Ave., New York, NY 10010, U.S.A.

DEAN (DYER-BENNETT), Pamela (Collins). American, b. 1953. **Genres:** Science fiction/Fantasy. **Career:** Writer. **Publications:** FANTASY NOVELS: The Secret Country, 1985; The Hidden Land, 1986; The Whim of the Dragon, 1989; Tam Lin, 1991; The Dubious Hills, 1994. **Address:** c/o Tor Publications, 175 Fifth Ave, New York, NY 10010, U.S.A.

DEAN, William Denard. American, b. 1937. **Genres:** Intellectual history, Philosophy, Social commentary, Theology/Religion. **Career:** Northland College, Ashland, WI, assistant professor of philosophy and religion, 1966-68; Gustavus Adolphus College, St. Peter, MN, assistant professor, 1968-73, associate professor, 1973-80, professor of religion, 1980-96, Florence and Raymond Sponberg Chair in Ethics, 1996; University of Chicago, Institute for Advanced Study of Religion, research scholar, 1984-85; Indiana University, Center on Philanthropy, scholar in residence, 1991-93; Iliff School of Theology, Denver, CO, professor of constructive theology, 1996-2004. **Publications:** Coming to: A Theology of Beauty, 1972; Love before the Fall, 1976; American Religious Empiricism, 1986; (co-ed.) The Size of God: The Theology of Bernard Loomer in Context, 1987; History Making History: The New Historicism in American Religious Thought, 1988; The Religious Critic in American Culture, 1994; The American Spiritual Culture: And the Invention of Jazz, Football, and the Movies, 2002. **Address:** 4565 E Mexico #9, Denver, CO 80222, U.S.A. **Online address:** wdean@Iliff.edu

DEANE-DRUMMOND, Anthony (John). British, b. 1917. **Genres:** International relations/Current affairs, Autobiography/Memoirs. **Career:** With the British Army until 1971 (Major General); Director, Paper and Paper Products Ltd., Potters Bar, Herts., 1971-79; Director, Cotswold Conversions, 1983-88. **Publications:** Return Ticket, 1955; Riots, 1974; Arrows of Fortune, 1991. **Address:** Royal Bank of Scotland, 67 Lombard St, London EC3, England.

DE ANGELIS, Angela. See BROWNE-MILLER, Angela.

DE ANGELIS, Lissa G. American, b. 1954. **Genres:** Food and Wine. **Career:** Chef, teacher, and company president in Amity Harbor, NY, 1975-82; Natural Gourmet Cookery School, NYC, associate director and professor, 1981-91; freelance nutritionist, chef, and writer, 1991-2002; in-your-home chef, certified culinary professional, and writer. **Publications:** Recipes for Change, 1996; The Arthritis Cure Cookbook, 1998; SOS for PMS, 1999. Contributor to periodicals. **Address:** PO Box 72, Lindenhurst, NY 11757-0072, U.S.A. **Online address:** lissad@optonline.net

DEANS, Sis Boulos. American, b. 1955. **Genres:** Novellas/Short stories, Children's fiction, Young adult fiction, Biography. **Career:** Mercy Hospital, Portland, ME, surgical technician, 1985-. Worked as lifeguard, waitress, writing instructor, and nine years as an animal medical technician for veterinarians. **Publications:** CHILDREN'S FICTION: Chick-a-dee-dee-dee: A Very Special Bird, 1987; Emily Bee and the Kingdom of Flowers, 1988; The Legend of Blazing Bear, 1992. YOUNG ADULT NOVELS: BrickWalls, 1996; Racing the Past, 2001; Every Day and All the Time, 2003. OTHER: Decisions and Other Stories (adult short stories), 1995; His Proper Post: A Biography of Gen. Joshua Lawrence Chamberlain, 1996. Contributor of adult short fiction, poetry, and plays to periodicals. **Address:** 260 Gray Rd, Gorham, ME 04038, U.S.A.

DE ARAUGO, Tess (S.). Also writes as Tess De Araugo-O'Mullane. Australian, b. 1930. **Genres:** Novellas/Short stories, Children's fiction, Cultural/Ethnic topics, History, Autobiography/Memoirs, Biography. **Career:** Assistant and secretary in family businesses in Melbourne, Australia, 1945-51, and Barham, New South Wales, Australia, 1954-57; co-owner of a business in Essendon, Victoria, Australia, 1956-60; proprietor of a plant nursery in Mount Waverley, Victoria, Australia, 1968-78; co-owner of a taxicab business in Chelsea, Victoria, Australia, 1978-84; Peninsula Taxi Cooperative, co-owner, 1984-89; Rose Publishing House, Rosebud, owner/publisher, 1993-2002; writer. **Publications:** (ed. with P. Pepper), You Are What You Make Yourself to Be: The Story of a Victorian Aboriginal Family, 1842-1980, 1980, rev. ed., 1989; (with P. Pepper) What Did Happen to the Aborigines of Victoria? Volume I: The Kurnai of Gippsland, 1985; Boonoorong on the Mornington Peninsula, 1993; Dear Fethers, 2000. Contributor to books and periodicals. **Address:** 19 Grenville Grove, Rosebud West, VIC 3940, Australia.

DE ARAUGO-O'MULLANE, Tess. *See* **DE ARAUGO, Tess (S.).**

DEARDEN, James Shackley. British, b. 1931. **Genres:** Literary criticism and history. **Career:** Curator, Ruskin Galleries, Isle of Wight, 1957-96; printer, Yellowsands Press, Bembridge School, 1958-94; curator, Brantwood, Coniston, Cumbria, 1959-96. Ed., Ruskin Newsletter, 1969-89; ed., Ruskin Research Series, 1979-86; director, Guild of St. George, 1979-; co-general editor, Whitehouse Edition of John Ruskin, 1994-2000. **Publications:** A Short History of Brantwood, 1967; Facets of Ruskin, 1970; (with K.G. Thorne) Ruskin and Coniston, 1971; John Ruskin: An Illustrated Life, 1973, rev. ed., 2004; Turner's Isle of Wight Sketchbook, 1979; John Ruskin's Camberwell, 1990; John Ruskin and Victorian Art, 1993; Ruskin, Bembridge and Brantwood, 1994; Hare Hunting on the Isle of Wight, 1996; John Ruskin, a Life in Pictures, 1999; Centenary Edition of John Ruskin's King of the Golden River, 1999; John Ruskin's Dogs, 2003. EDITOR: The Professor: Arthur Severn's Memoir of John Ruskin, 1967; J. Ruskin, Iteriad, or Three Weeks among the Lakes, 1969; (with V.A. Burd) John Ruskin's Diary for 1830, 1990. **Address:** 4 Woodlands, Foreland Rd, Bembridge, Isle of Wight, England.

DEARIE, John. (born United States). **Genres:** Young adult fiction. **Career:** Writer and finance professional. Federal Reserve Bank of New York, held various positions in Banking Studies, Foreign Exchange, and Policy and Analysis for nine years; Financial Services Forum, vice president and chief policy officer; Financial Services Volunteer Corps (FSVC), managing director. **Publications:** Love and Other Recreational Sports, 2003. **Address:** Financial Services Volunteer Corps, 10 East 53rd St., New York, NY 10022, U.S.A.

DEARMOND, Dale. American, b. 1914. **Genres:** Children's fiction, Children's non-fiction, Illustrations. **Career:** City and Borough of Juneau, AK, city librarian, 1958-79; author and illustrator of children's books. Woodcuts featured in solo shows in Los Angeles, CA; The Dalles, OR; Boston, MA; Seattle, WA; Anchorage, Fairbanks, Juneau, Ketchikan, and Sitka, AK; and Whitehorse, Yukon Territory, Canada. **Publications:** SELF-ILLUSTRATED: Juneau: A Book of Woodcuts, 1973; Raven: A Collection of Woodcuts, 1975; Dale DeArmond: A First Collection of Prints, c. 1979; Berry Woman's Children, 1985; The Seal Oil Lamp, 1988; The First Man, 1990; The Boy Who Found the Light: Eskimo Folktales, 1990; Sun Signs from a Polar Star, 1993; Tales from the Four Winds of the North, 1996; Raven Charm, 1998. Illustrator of books by: S.B. Nickerson. **Address:** 120 Katlian St, Sitka, AK 99835, U.S.A.

DEATHRIDGE, John (William). British, b. 1944. **Genres:** Music. **Career:** Performed concerts and conducted research in Munich, West Germany (now Germany), 1972-83; Cambridge University, Cambridge, England, reader in music and fellow of King's College, 1983-96; King's College, London, King Edward Professor of Music, 1996-. **Publications:** Wagner's Rienzi: A Reappraisal Based on a Study of the Sketches and Drafts, 1977; (with C. Dahlhaus) The New Grove Wagner, 1984; (with M. Geck and E. Voss) Verzeichnis der musikalisohn Werke, 1986. EDITOR: The Family Letters of Richard Wagner, 1991; (with U. Muler and P. Wapnewski), The Wagner Handbook, 1992; R. Wagner: Lohengrin WWV75, 1996-2000. Contributor to books and professional journals. **Address:** Dept of Music, King's College, The Strand, London WC2R 2LS, England. **Online address:** john.deathridge@kcl.ac.uk

DEATS, Richard L. American, b. 1932. **Genres:** Human relations/Parenting, International relations/Current affairs, Theology/Religion, Third World. **Career:** Editor, Fellowship magazine, Fellowship of Reconciliation, Director of Inter-Faith Activities, 1972-79, 1984-93, Executive Secretary, 1979-84. Professor of Social Ethics, Union Theological Seminary, Manila, Philippines 1959-72, and Southeast Asia Graduate School of Theology, 1968-72. **Publications:** The Story of Methodism in the Philippines, 1964; Nationalism and Christianity in the Philippines, 1967; (co-ed. and contrib.) The Filipino in the Seventies: An Ecumenical Perspective, 1973; Ambassador of Reconciliation, 1991; How to Keep Laughing Even Though You've Considered All the Facts, 1994; Martin Luther King, Jr.: Spirit-Led Prophet, 1999; Mahatma Gandhi: Non-Violent Liberator, 2005. **Address:** Box 271, Nyack, NY 10960, U.S.A. **Online address:** editor@forusa.org

DEAVER, Jeffery Wilds. Also writes as William Jefferies. American, b. 1950. **Genres:** Mystery/Crime/Suspense. **Career:** Worked as an attorney; freelance writer, c. 1984-. **Publications:** MYSTERY AND SUSPENSE NOVELS: Manhattan Is My Beat, 1989; Death of a Blue Movie Star, 1990; Hard News, 1991; Mistress of Justice, 1992; The Lesson of Her Death, 1993; Praying for Sleep, 1994; A Maiden's Grave, 1995; The Bone Collector, 1997; The Empty Chair, 2000; Speaking in Tongues, 2000; The Blue

Nowhere, 2001; The Stone Monkey, 2002; The Vanished Man, 2003. OTHER: (as Jeff Deaver) The Complete Law School Companion (nonfiction), c. 1984, rev version as The Complete Law School Companion: How to Excel at America's Most Demanding Post-Graduate Curriculum, 1992. LOCATION SCOUT MYSTERIES AS WILLIAM JEFFERIES: Shallow Graves, c. 1992; Bloody River Blues, c. 1993. **Address:** c/o Deborah Schneider, Gefman Schneider Literary Agents Inc., 250 West 57th Street, New York, NY 10101, U.S.A. **Online address:** JWD258@aol.com

DEAVER, Julie Reece. American, b. 1953. **Genres:** Young adult fiction, Communications/Media. **Career:** Writer for television series, 1973; teacher's aide in special education, Pacific Grove, California, 1978-88; illustrator for magazines. **Publications:** Say Goodnight, Gracie, 1988; First Wedding, Once Removed, 1990; You Bet Your Life, 1993; Chicago Blues, 1995; The Night I Disappeared, 2002.

DEBAKEY, Michael Ellis. American, b. 1908. **Genres:** Medicine/Health. **Career:** Baylor College of Medicine, Chairman, Dept. of Surgery, 1948-93, Distinguished Service Professor, 1968-, President, 1969-79, Chancellor, 1978-96, Olga Keith Wiess Professor of Surgery, 1981-, Chancellor Emeritus, 1996-; DeBakey Medical Foundation, Houston, President, 1961-; DeBakey Heart Center, Director, 1985-. Journal of Vascular Surgery, Founding Ed.; Cardiovascular Research Center Bulletin, Editorial Committee, Chairman; Contemporary Therapy, Ed., Section on Cardiovascular Surgery, Contemporary Surgery, and Surgical Section on Cardiovascular Disease; Year Book Publishers, Year Book of General Surgery, Chicago, Ed., 1957-71. **Publications:** The Blood Bank and the Technique and Therapeutics of Transfusions, 1942; (co-author) Battle Casualties: Incidence, Mortality, and Logistic Considerations, 1952; Christopher's Minor Surgery, 7th ed., 1955, 8th ed. (co-ed.), 1959; (co-author) Cold Injury: Ground Type, 1958; (co-author) Buerger's Disease, 1963; A Surgeon's Diary of a Visit to China, 1974; The Living Heart, 1977; (ed.) Advances in Cardiac Valves, 1983; (co-ed.) Factors Influencing the Course of Myocardial Ischemia, 1983; The Living Heart Diet, 1984; The Living Heart Brand Name Shopper's Guide, 1992; The Living Heart Guide to Eating Out, 1993; The New Living Heart Diet, 1996; The New Living Heart, 1997. Contributor to professional books and journals. **Address:** Baylor College of Medicine, One Baylor Plaza, Houston, TX 77030, U.S.A.

DE BECKER, Gavin. American. **Genres:** How-to books. **Career:** Consultant on violence and threat assessment. Gavin de Becker & Associates Inc. (consulting firm), Los Angeles, CA, founder and chief executive. Has served as a presidential adviser, expert witness, and trainer; designed the MOSAIC threat assessment used by U.S. Supreme Court, CIA, U.S. Marshals Service, and other agencies. Served two terms on the President's Advisory Board at the U.S. Department of Justice; served at the U.S. Department of State; principal adviser on a federal research project into mentally ill people who stalk public figures; served two years on the Governor's Advisory Board at the California Department of Mental Health; co-chairperson of the Domestic Violence Advisory Board. Director of Special Services Group, selected by President Ronald Reagan, 1980. UCLA School of Public Policy and Social Research, senior fellow. **Publications:** The Gift of Fear: Survival Signals That Protect Us from Violence, 1997; Protecting the Gift: Keeping Children and Teenagers Safe (and Parents Sane), 1999; Fear Less: Real Truth about Risk, Safety and Security in a Time of Terrorism. Contributor of introductions and essays for several books. **Address:** Gavin de Becker & Associates, 11684 Ventura Blvd. Suite 440, Studio City, CA 91604, U.S.A. **Online address:** infoline@gavindebecker.com

DEBERG, Betty A. American, b. 1953. **Genres:** Theology/Religion. **Career:** Vanderbilt University, Nashville, TN, director of admissions and financial aid for Divinity School, 1980-88; Valparaiso University, Valparaiso, IN, assistant professor, 1988-94, associate professor of theology, 1994-96; University of Northern Iowa-Cedar Falls, professor of religion and head of Department of Philosophy and Religion, 1997-. Speaker at colleges and universities. **Publications:** Ungodly Women: Gender and the First Wave of American Fundamentalism, 1990, new ed., 2000; Women and Women's Issues in North American Lutheranism: A Bibliography, 1992; (with C. Cherry and A. Porterfield) Religion on Campus, 2001. Contributor to books. Contributor of articles and reviews to journals. **Address:** Dept of Philosophy and Religion, University of Northern Iowa, Cedar Falls, IA 50614-0501, U.S.A. **Online address:** deberg@uni.edu

DE BERNIERES, Louis. British, b. 1954. **Genres:** Novels, History. **Career:** Landscape gardener in Surrey, England, 1972-73; schoolteacher in Colombia, 1974; mechanic, 1980; teacher in London, England, 1981-. Commonwealth Writers Prize, 1995; Lannan Award, 1995. **Publications:** The War of Don

Emmanuel's Nether Parts (novel), 1990; Senor Vivo and the Coca Lord, 1991; The Troublesome Offspring of Cardinal Guzman, 1992; Captain Corelli's Mandolin, 1994; Red Dog, 2001. **Address:** c/o Lavinia Trevor, 6 The Glass House, 49A Goldhawk Rd, London W12 8QP, England.

DEBIN, David. Also writes as Bill Doe, Smith & Doe. American, b. 1942. **Genres:** Mystery/Crime/Suspense, Adult non-fiction, Plays/Screenplays. **Career:** Antioch University, Santa Barbara, CA, instructor in creative writing. Author of screenplays and television scripts, 1970-. **Publications:** MYSTERY NOVELS: Nice Guys Finish Dead, 1992; The Big O, 1994; Murder Live at Five, 1995. ADULT NON-FICTION, WITH M. SMITH, AS SMITH AND DOE: What Men Don't Want Women to Know, 1998; The Book of Horrible Questions, 1999; The Ultimate Sex Test, 2000; Worst Case Scenarios: A Survivalist Guide to Love, Sex, and Romance, 2001. **Address:** 651 Para Grande Ln, Santa Barbara, CA 93108-2019, U.S.A. **Online address:** albmarx@aol.com

DE BLIJ, Harm J(an). American (born Netherlands), b. 1935. **Genres:** Environmental sciences/Ecology, Geography. **Career:** Michigan State University, E. Lansing, African Studies Center, professor and associate director, 1961-69, distinguished professor of geography, 1999-; University of Miami, professor of geography, 1969-94; Association of American Geographers, councillor, 1970-72, secretary, 1972-75; National Geographic Research, ed., 1984-90; ABC Television, geography correspondent, 1989-96; Georgetown University, distinguished professor, 1989-94; NBC Television, geography analyst, 1996-98. **Publications:** Africa South, 1962; Dar es Salaam: A Study in Urban Geography, 1963; A Geography of Subsaharan Africa, 1964; Systematic Political Geography, 1967, 4th ed. 1988; Mombasa: An African City, 1968; Geography: Regions and Concepts, 1971, 9th ed., 2000; Essentials of Geography, 1973; Man Shapes the Earth, 1974; (with D. Greenland) The Earth in Profile: A Physical Geography, 1977; (with A.C.G. Best) African Survey, 1977; Human Geography: Culture, Society, and Space, 1977, 6th ed., 1999; The Earth: A Topical Geography, 1980, 4th ed., 1995; (with E.B. Martin) African Perspectives, 1981; Wine: A Geographic Appreciation, 1983; Wine Regions of the Southern Hemisphere, 1985; World Geography, 1989; Physical Geography of the Global Environment, 1991; (with P.O. Muller) Nature on the Rampage, 1994; Harm de Blij's Geography Book, 1995; Wartime Encounter with Geography, 2000. **Address:** PO Box 608, Boca Grande, FL 33921, U.S.A.

DE BONDT, Gabe J. Dutch, b. 1969. **Genres:** Economics, Money/Finance. **Career:** Nederlandsche Bank, staff member, 1994-2000; European Central Bank, Frankfurt am Main, Germany, staff member, 2001-. **Publications:** Financial Structure and Monetary Transmission in Europe, 2000. **Address:** European Central Bank, Kaiserstrasse 29, D-60311 Frankfurt am Main, Germany. **Online address:** gabe.de_bondt@ecb.int

DEBONIS, Steven. American, b. 1949. **Genres:** History. **Career:** Taxicab driver in NYC, 1969-72; U.S. Refugee Program, Phanat Nikhom, Thailand, instructor, 1980-81; U.S. Refugee Program, Bataan, Philippines, educational supervisor, 1982-92; St. Ursula High School, Hachinohe, Japan, English teacher, 1993-. Allen College, Kuji, Japan, English teacher, 1995. **Publications:** Children of the Enemy: Oral Histories of Vietnamese Amerasians, 1995. **Address:** 133 Egret Circle, West Palm Beach, FL 33413, U.S.A. **Online address:** harp88@yahoo.com

DE BONO, Douglas. (born United States), b. 1957. **Genres:** Young adult fiction. **Career:** Database administrator and consultant in Minneapolis, MN; also worked as a technical writer. **Publications:** THE TERROR WAR SERIES: Point of Honor, 2002; Blood Covenant, 2002; Reap the Whirlwind, 2002; Rogue State, 2002; Firewall, 2003. Author of research articles and opinion pieces. **Address:** c/o Author Mail, Metropolis Ink, 11 Ingalls St., Keene, NH 03431, U.S.A. **Online address:** info@pointofhonor.com

DE BONO, Edward (Francis Charles). British (born Malta), b. 1933. **Genres:** Administration/Management, Education, Philosophy, Psychology, Technology. **Career:** University of Cambridge, Dept. of Investigative Medicine, assistant director of research, 1964-. Cognitive Research Trust, director. **Publications:** The Five Day Course in Thinking, 1967; The Use of Lateral Thinking (in US as New Think), 1967; The Mechanism of Mind, 1969; Lateral Thinking, 1972; Lateral Thinking for Management, 1972; The Dog Exercising Machine, 1972; Po: Beyond Yes and No, 1972; Children Solve Problems, 1973; Practical Thinking, 1973; The Case of the Disappearing Elephant, 1974; The Greatest Thinkers, 1976; The Happiness Purpose, 1977; Opportunities: A Handbook of Business Opportunity Search, 1978; Future Positive, 1979; Atlas of Management Thinking, 1981; DeBono's Course in Thinking, 1982; Tactics: The Art and Science of Success, 1984;

Conflicts: A Better Way to Resolve Them, 1985; Six Thinking Hats, 1985; Masterthinker's Handbook, 1985; Letters to Thinkers, 1987; CORT Thinking Program, 1987; Thinking: Skills for Success, 1990; Word Power, 1990; I Am Right You Are Wrong, 1991; Six Action Shoes, 1991; Sur Petition, 1992; Serious Creativity, 1992; Edward de Bono's Six Thinking Hats, 1992; Teach Your Child How to Think, 1993; Parallel Thinking, 1994; Teach Yourself to Think, 1995; Mind Pack, 1995; The Creative Force: Operations Handbook, 1995; Edward de Bono's Textbook of Wisdom, 1996; How to Be More Interesting, 1997; Edward de Bono's Direct Attention Thinking Tools, 1997; Simplicity, 1998; Edward de Bono's Thinking for Action, 1998; Why I Want to Be King of Australia, 1999; How You Can Be More Interesting, 2000; New Thinking for the New Millennium, 2000. EDITOR: Technology Today, 1972; Eureka!: History of Inventions, 1974.

DE BOTTON, Alain. Swiss, b. 1969. **Genres:** Sex. **Career:** Novelist and journalist. Worked as a television reviewer for New Statesman; Sunday Telegraph, journalist. **Publications:** Essays in Love, 1993, in US as On Love; The Romantic Movement: Sex, Shopping, and the Novel, 1994; Kiss & Tell, 1995; How Proust Can Change Your Life, 1997; The Consolations of Philosophy, 2000; The Art of Travel, 2002; Status Anxiety, 2004. Contributor of articles and book and television reviews to periodicals.

DE BREADUN, Deaglan. Irish. **Genres:** Novellas/Short stories, History, Politics/Government. **Career:** Irish Times, Dublin, Ireland, Belfast bureau chief, now foreign affairs correspondent. **Publications:** Scealloga (in Irish), 1990; The Far Side of Revenge: Making Peace in Northern Ireland, 2001. **Address:** Irish Times, 10-16 D'Olier St, Dublin 2, Ireland. **Online address:** ddebreadun@irish-times.ie

DEBRECZENY, Paul. American (born Hungary), b. 1932. **Genres:** Novels, History, Literary criticism and history, Novellas/Short stories. **Career:** Tulane University, New Orleans, assistant to associate professor of Russian, 1960-67; University of North Carolina, Chapel Hill, associate professor, 1967-74, professor, 1974-83, Alumni Distinguished Professor of Russian and Comparative Literature, 1983-99, professor Emeritus, 1999-. **Publications:** Nikolay Gogol and his Contemporary Critics, 1966; The Other Pushkin: A Study of Alexander Pushkin's Prose Fiction, 1983, 2nd ed. (in Russian) 1996; Temptations of the Past (historical novel), 1982; (trans.) Alexander Pushkin: The Captain's Daughter and Other Stories, 1992; Social Functions of Literature: Alexander Pushkin and Russian Culture, 1997. EDITOR: (and trans. with J. Zeldin) Literature and National Identity: Nineteenth-Century Russian Critical Essays, 1970; Chekhov's Art of Writing: A Collection of Critical Essays, 1977; (and trans.) Alexander Pushkin: Complete Prose Fiction, 1983; American Contributions to the Ninth International Congress of Slavists Kiev, vol. II: Literature, Poetics, History, 1983; (with R. Anderson) Russian Narrative and Visual Art: Varieties of Seeing, 1994. **Address:** 304 Hoot Owl Lane, Chapel Hill, NC 27514, U.S.A. **Online address:** pdebrecz@email.unc.edu

DEBRIX, François. French, b. 1968. **Genres:** Politics/Government. **Career:** Florida International University, Miami, professor of international relations, 1998-. **Publications:** Re-Envisioning Peacekeeping, 1999. EDITOR: (with C. Weber) Rituals of Mediation: International Politics and Social Meaning, 2003; Language, Agency, and Politics in a Constructed World, 2003. **Address:** Department of Political Science, DM432, Florida International University, University Park, Miami, FL 33199, U.S.A. **Online address:** debrix@fiu.edu

DEBRY, Roger K. American, b. 1942. **Genres:** Information science/Computers, Children's fiction. **Career:** IBM Corporation, Boulder, CO, member of senior technical staff, 1972-. Instructor in technology management program, Denver University. **Publications:** Communicating with Display Terminals, 1985; Bartholomew's Christmas Adventure: A Bear's Tale (children's fiction), 1995. Contributor of technical articles to journals. **Address:** Department of Computing & Networking Sciences, Utah Valley State College, 800 West University Parkway, Orem, UT 84058-5999, U.S.A.

DEBS, Victor, Jr. American, b. 1949. **Genres:** Sports/Fitness. **Career:** Board of Education, NYC, teacher, 1970-92. Rutgers University, instructor in baseball history. **Publications:** They Kept Me Loyal to the Yankees, 1993; Baseball Tidbits, 1997; Still Standing after All These Years, 1997; Missed It by That Much, 1998. **Address:** 175 Lewiston St., Staten Island, NY 10314, U.S.A. **Online address:** TKMLTY7@aol.com

DEBURON, Nicole. French (born Tunisia). **Genres:** Novels. **Career:** Writer. **Publications:** Drole de Sahara, 1956, trans. V. Graham as Sahara Boom-de-ay, 1957; Et vogue la gondole!, 1957, trans. V. Graham as To the Gondolas,

1958, as The Bride and the Bugatti, 1959; Les pieds sur le bureau, trans. V. Graham as Say I'm in Conference, 1959; Meisjes van Parijs (in Dutch), 1961, trans. J. MacGibbon as Girls of Paris, 1962; Sainte Chérie, 1964, new ed. as Les saintes chéries, 1995; Sainte Chérie en vacances, 1967; Vas-y, maman!, 1978; Go-y Mom (screenplay), 1978; Dix-jours-de-rêve (novel), 1982; Qui c'est ce garçon? (novel), 1985; Où sont mes lunettes?, 1991; Arrêtez de piquer mes sous!, 1992; Arrête ton cinéma!, 1995; Mais t'as-tout pour-être heureuse!, 1996; Chéri, tu m'écoutes? Alors, répète ce que je viens de dire, 1998; Mon coeur, tu penses à quoi: A rien, 2000. Erotissimo (screenplay). **Address:** 7 rue Daru, 8 Paris, France.

DEBUS, Allen George. American, b. 1926. **Genres:** Chemistry, History, Intellectual history, Medicine/Health, Music, Philosophy, Sciences. **Career:** University of Chicago, asst professor, 1961-65, associate professor, 1965-68, professor, 1968-78, director, Morris Fishbein Center, 1971-77, Morris Fishbein Professor of the History of Science and Medicine, 1978-96, Emeritus, 1996-. **Publications:** The English Paracelsians, 1965; (with R. Multhauf) Alchemy and Chemistry in the 17th Century, 1966; The Chemical Dream of the Renaissance, 1968; (with B. Rust) The Complete Entertainment Discography, 1973; Chemical Philosophy: Paracelsian Science & Medicine in the 16th and 17th Centuries, 2 vols., 1977; Man and Nature in the Renaissance, 1978; Robert Fludd and His Philosophical Key, 1979; Music of Victor Herbert, 1979; Science and History, 1984; Chemistry, Alchemy and the New Philosophy, 1550-1700, 1987; The French Paracelsians, 1991; Paracelso e la Tradizione Paracelsiana, 1996; Chemistry and Medical Debate, 2001. EDITOR: reprint of E. Ashmole, Theatrum Chemicum Britannicum (1652), 1967; World Who's Who in Science, 1968; Science and Education in the 17th Century, 1970; (and contrib.) Science, Medicine and Society in the Renaissance, 2 vols., 1972; (and contrib.) Medicine in 17th Century England, 1974; reprint of J. Dee, The Mathematicall Praeface to the Elements of Geometrie of Euclid of Megara (1570), 1975; (with I. Merkel, and contrib.) Hermeticism and the Renaissance, 1988; (with M. Walton, and contrib.) Reading the Book of Nature, 1998; Alchemy and Early Modern Chemistry: Papers from Ambix, 2004. **Address:** Social Sciences 206, University of Chicago, 1126 E 59th St, Chicago, IL 60637, U.S.A. **Online address:** adebus@midway.uchicago.edu

DECANDIDO, Keith R. A. American. **Genres:** Science fiction/Fantasy. **Career:** Library Journal, assistant editor, 1990-93; Byron Preiss Visual Publications and Multimedia Company, New York, NY, associate editor, then editor, of science fiction, fantasy, and horror, starting in 1993. **Publications:** (with J.R. Nieto) Spider-Man: Venom's Wrath, 1998; (with C. Golden and N. Holder) Buffy the Vampire Slayer: The Watcher's Guide, 1998; Buffy: The Vampire Slayer: The Xander Years, 1999; (with Nieto) Spider-Man: Venom's Rage, in press. EDITOR: (with B. Preiss and J.G. Betancourt) The Ultimate Alien, 1995; (with Preiss and Betancourt) The Ultimate Dragon, 1995; (with Preiss and R. Silverberg) Virtual Unrealities: The Short Fiction of Alfred Bester, 1997; (with J. Sherman) Urban Nightmares (short stories), 1997. Author of episodes for Marvel Comics. Short stories published in anthologies. Contributor of reviews, interviews, and articles to periodicals. **Address:** 21 West 100th St., New York, NY 10025, U.S.A. **Online address:** krad@ix. netcom.com

DE CARVALHO, Mario. Portuguese, b. 1944. **Genres:** Novels. **Career:** Lawyer in Lisbon, Portugal, 1975-. **Publications:** IN ENGLISH TRANSLATION: Um deus passeando pela brisa da tarde (novel), 1994, trans as A God Strolling in the Cool of the Evening. OTHER: Contos da'setima esfera, 1981; Casos do beco das sardinheiras, 1981; O livro grande de tebas navio e mariana, 1982; A inaudita guerra da avenida gago coutinho, 1983; Fabulario & etc., 1984; Era uma vez um alferes, 1984; Contos soltos, 1986; (with C.P. Correia) E se tivesse a bondade de me dizer porque, 1986; A paixao do conde de frois, 1986; Os alferes, 1989; Quatrocentos mil sestercios, 1991; Agua em pena de pato, teatro do quotidiano, 1991; Era bom que trocassemos umas ideias sobre o assunto, 1995; Haja harmonia, 1997; Contos Vagabundo, 1999; Fantasia, 2003. **Address:** Av. Eng Arantes E Oliveira, 6-8-C, 1900 Lisbon, Portugal. **Online address:** mariodecarvalho@mail.telefac.ht

DECK, Allan Figueroa. American, b. 1945. **Genres:** Literary criticism and history. **Career:** Entered Societas Jesu (Society of Jesus; Jesuits; S.J.), 1963, ordained Roman Catholic priest, 1976; Pontifical University of Comillas, Madrid, Spain, lecturer in Latin American literature, 1972; St. Louis University, St. Louis, MO, lecturer in Brazilian literature, 1972-73; University of Santa Clara, Santa Clara, CA, lecturer in Mexican American history, 1973-75; pastor of a Roman Catholic church in Santa Ana, CA, 1976-79; Diocese of Orange, CA, director of Hispanic ministry, 1979-85, member of board of directors, Catholic Community Agencies, 1980-81; Jesuit School of Theology at Berkeley, Berkeley, CA, assistant professor of Hispanic ministry

and missiology, 1988-92; Loyola Marymount University, Los Angeles, CA, lecturer in Chicano studies and theology, 1992-93, coordinator of Hispanic pastoral studies, 1992-, associate professor of theological studies, 1993-. **Publications:** Francisco Javier Alegre: A Study of Mexican Literary Criticism, 1976; The Second Wave: Hispanic Ministry and the Evangelization of Culture, 1989; (ed.) Frontiers of Hispanic Theology in the United States, 1992; (ed. with Jay P. Dolan) The Notre Dame History of Hispanic Catholics in the U.S., Volume III: Hispanic Catholic Culture in the U.S.: Issues and Concerns, 1994; (ed. with Y. Tarango and T. Matovina) Perspectivas: Hispanic Ministry, 1995. Contributor to books. Contributor of articles and reviews to periodicals. **Address:** 480 S. Batavia St., Orange, CA 92868, U.S.A.

DE COSTA, Elena M. American, b. 1949. **Genres:** Cultural/Ethnic topics, Literary criticism and history, Language/Linguistics, Theatre, Third World. **Career:** University of Wisconsin-Madison, instructor in Spanish, 1975-76; College of Wooster, Wooster, OH, assistant professor of Spanish, 1977-82; Indiana University of Pennsylvania, Indiana, PA, assistant professor of Spanish language and Hispanic and comparative literature, 1982-85; Santa Clara University, Santa Clara, CA, assistant professor of Spanish, 1987-. Santa Clara County Unified School District, instructional aide for migrant education program, 1988. **Publications:** Collaborative Latin American Popular Theatre: From Theory to Form, From Text to Stage, 1992. Work represented in anthologies. Contributor of articles and reviews to academic journals. **Address:** Department of Foreign Languages, Carroll College, 100 N. East Ave., Waukesha, WI 53186-3103, U.S.A. **Online address:** edecosta@carroll1.cc. edu

DECOSTA-WILLIS, Miriam. American, b. 1934. **Genres:** Cultural/Ethnic topics, Race relations, Women's studies and issues, Language/Linguistics, Literary criticism and history, Local history/Rural topics. **Career:** Associated with LeMoyne College, Memphis, TN, 1957-58; Owen College, Memphis, instructor, 1960-65; Memphis State University, Memphis, associate professor of Spanish, 1966-70; Howard University, Washington, DC, associate professor of Romance Languages, 1970-74, professor and chair of department, 1974-76; LeMoyne-Owen College, Memphis, professor of English and director of DuBois Scholars Program, 1979-89; George Mason University, Fairfax, VA, Commonwealth Professor of Spanish, 1989-91; University of Maryland, Baltimore County, professor in Africana Studies. **Publications:** EDITOR: (and author of intro) Blacks in Hispanic Literature: Critical Essays, 1977; (with F.P. Delk and P. Dotson) Homespun Images: An Anthology of Black Memphis Writers and Artists, 1989; (with P. Bell-Scott, B. Guy-Sheftall, J.J. Royster, J. Sims-Wood, and L.P. Fultz) Double Stitch: Black Women Write about Mothers and Daughters, 1991; (with R.P. Bell and R. Martin) Erotique Noire/Black Erotica, 1992; The Memphis Diary of Ida B. Wells, 1995; Singular Like a Bird: The Art of Nancy Morejon, 1999. Contributor to books and periodicals. **Address:** Department of Africana Studies, University of Maryland, Baltimore County, Baltimore, MD 21250, U.S.A. **Online address:** decosta2@umbc.edu

DECREDICO, Mary A. American, b. 1959. **Genres:** History, Local history/Rural topics. **Career:** U.S. Naval Academy, Annapolis, MD, professor of history, 1986-; writer, 1991-. **Publications:** Patriotism for Profit: Georgia's Urban Entrepreneurs and the Confederate War Effort, 1990; Mary Boykin Chesnut: A Confederate Woman's Life, 1996. **Address:** Department of History, U.S. Naval Academy, Annapolis, MD 21402-5044, U.S.A.

DE CRESPIGNY, (Richard) Rafe (Champion). Australian, b. 1936. **Genres:** History. **Career:** Reader in Chinese since 1973, Master of University House since 1991, Australian National University, Canberra (Lecturer, 1964-70, and Sr. Lecturer, 1970-73). **Publications:** The Biography of Sun Chien, 1966; (with H.H. Dubs) Official Titles of the Former Han Dynasty, 1967; The Last of the Han, 1969; The Records of the Three Kingdoms, 1970; China: The Land and Its People, 1971; China This Century: A History of Modern China, 1975, 2nd ed., 1992; Portents of Protest, 1976; Northern Frontier, 1984; Emperor Huan and Emperor Ling, 1989; Generals of the South, 1990; To Establish Peace, 1996.

DECROW, Karen. American, b. 1937. **Genres:** Education, Law, Women's studies and issues, Civil liberties/Human rights, Social commentary. **Career:** Lawyer. Golf Digest mag., Norwalk, CT, Fashion and Resorts Editor, 1959-60; American Society of Planning Officials, Chicago, Zoning Digest, Editor, 1960-61; Center for the Study of Liberal Education for Adults, Chicago, Writer and Editor, 1961-64; Holt, Rinehart and Winston Inc., NYC, Social Studies and Adult Education, Editor, 1965; L.W. Singer Co. Inc., NYC, Textbook Editor, 1965-66; Eastern Regional Institution for Education, Syracuse, NY, Writer, 1967-69; Syracuse New Times, NY, Columnist, 1985-;

World Woman Watch, Co-founder, 19881974-77. **Publications:** (with R. DeCrow) University Adult Education: A Selected Bibliography, 1967; (ed.) The Pregnant Teenager, by H. Osofsky, 1968; The Young Woman's Guide to Liberation, 1971; (ed.) Corporate Wives, Corporate Casualties, by R. Seidenberg, 1973; Sexist Justice, 1974; (with R. Seidenberg) Women Who Marry Houses: Panic and Protest in Agoraphobia, 1983; (with J. Kammer) Good Will toward Men, 1994. **Address:** 7599 Brown Gulf Rd, Jamesville, NY 13078, U.S.A.

DEDMAN, Stephen. American. **Genres:** Science fiction/Fantasy. **Career:** Has worked as an actor, an experimental subject, a used dinosaur salesman, and a manager of a science fiction book store; Australian Physicist, Australia, editorial assistant; Eidolon, associate editor; freelance writer, c. 1977-. **Publications:** The Art of Arrow Cutting, 1997. Contributor of fiction to periodicals. **Address:** c/o Tor Books, 175 Fifth Ave., 14th Fl., New York, NY 10010, U.S.A.

DEE, Ed(ward J.), (Jr.). American, b. 1940. **Genres:** Novels, Novellas/Short stories, Mystery/Crime/Suspense, Criminology/True Crime. **Career:** New York Police Department, NYC, police officer, 1962-82, retiring as lieutenant; writer. **Publications:** 14 Peck Slip, 1994; Bronx Angel, 1995; Little Boy Blue, 1997; Nightbird, 1999; The Con Man's Daughter, 2003. **Address:** 96 Henlopen Gardens, Lewes, DE 19958, U.S.A. **Online address:** edee58@cs.com; www.edwarddee.com

DEE, Jonathan. American. **Genres:** Adult non-fiction. **Career:** Paris Review, New York, NY, senior editor, 1987-90; teacher of creative writing at New School University and Young Men's Hebrew Association's Unterberg Poetry Center, New York, NY. **Publications:** The Lover of History, 1990; The Liberty Campaign, 1993; St. Famous, 1996; Palladio, 2002. Contributor to publications. **Address:** c/o Doubleday Publicity, 1540 Broadway, New York, NY 10036, U.S.A.

DEEM, James M(organ). American, b. 1950. **Genres:** Children's fiction, Young adult fiction, Archaeology/Antiquities, Children's non-fiction, Education, History, Paranormal, Writing/Journalism. **Career:** Detroit Institute of Technology, Detroit, MI, director of Learning Center, 1976-78; Mohawk Valley Community College, Utica, NY, assistant professor and department chair of developmental studies, 1979-84; John Jay College of Criminal Justice, New York City, associate professor of communication skills, 1984-2003. **Publications:** YOUNG ADULT NOVELS: Frog Eyes Loves Pig, 1988; Frogburger at Large, 1990; 3 NBs of Julian Drew, 1994. MIDDLE GRADE NOVELS: The Very Real Ghost Book of Christina Rose, 1996. MIDDLE-GRADE NONFICTION: How to Find a Ghost, 1988; How to Catch a Flying Saucer, 1991; How to Hunt Buried Treasure, 1992; Ghost Hunters, 1992; How to Travel through Time, 1993; How to Read Your Mother's Mind, 1994; How to Make a Mummy Talk, 1995; Bodies from the Bog, 1998; Zachary Taylor, 2002; Millard Fillmore, 2002; The Vikings, 2004; El Salvador, 2004. OTHER: Study Skills in Practice (college textbook), 1993. Contributor to books and periodicals. **Address:** c/o Houghton Mifflin Co, 222 Berkeley St, Boston, MA 02116, U.S.A. **Online address:** jamesmdeem@yahoo.com; www.jamesmdeem.com; www.mummytombs.com

DEENA, Seodial F(rank) H(ubert). (born Guyana), b. 1956. **Genres:** Adult non-fiction. **Career:** East Carolina University, Greenville, NC, associate professor of English, 1994-, and coordinator of Multicultural Literature Program. **Publications:** Canonization, Colonization, Decolonization: A Comparative Study of Political and Critical Works by Minority Writers, 2001; Situating Caribbean Literature and Criticism in Multicultural and Post-colonial Studies, 2003. **Address:** 900 Maple Ridge Rd., Greenville, NC 27858, U.S.A. **Online address:** deenas@mail.ecu.edu

DE FERRARI, Gabriella. Peruvian, b. 1941. **Genres:** Adult non-fiction. **Career:** Institute of Contemporary Art, Boston, MA, director, 1975-77; Harvard University, Cambridge, MA, acting curator of the Busch Reisinger Museum, 1978-79, assistant director of curatorial affairs for the Fogg Art Museum, 1979-82; freelance writer and editor. **Publications:** A Cloud on Sand, 1990; Gringa Latina, 1995. Contributor to periodicals. **Address:** 10 Jay St., New York, NY 10013, U.S.A.

DEFFAA, Chip. American, b. 1951. **Genres:** Music. **Career:** New York Post, NYC, jazz critic, 1986-. **Publications:** Swing Legacy, 1989; Voices of the Jazz Age: Profiles of Eight Vintage Jazz Men, 1990; In the Mainstream: Eighteen Portraits in Jazz, 1992; Traditionalists and Revivalists in Jazz, 1993; (with D. Cassidy) C'Mon Get Happy … Fear and Loathing on the Partridge Family Bus, 1994; Blue Rhythms: Six Lives in Rhythm and Blues,

1996; Jazz Veterans: A Portrait Gallery, 1996; (ed.) F. Scott Fitzgerald: The Princeton Years, 1996. Contributor to periodicals. **Address:** 50 Quartz Lane, Paterson, NJ 07501-3345, U.S.A.

DEFORD, Frank. American, b. 1938. **Genres:** Novels, Social commentary, Sports/Fitness. **Career:** Sports Illustrated mag., NYC, senior writer, 1964-89, 1998-; The National, daily sports newspaper, NYC, editor-in-chief, 1990-91; Newsweek, columnist, 1992-98. NPR, sports commentator. **Publications:** (with D. Budge) A Tennis Memoir, 1968; Five Strides on the Banked Track, 1971; There She Is: The Life and Times of Miss America, 1971; Cut 'n' Run, 1973; (with A. Ashe) Portrait in Motion, 1975; Big Bill Tilden, 1976; The Owner, 1976; (with J. Kramer) The Game, 1980; Everybody's All-American, 1981; (with B.J. King) The Autobiography, 1982; Alex: The Life of a Child, 1983; The Spy in the Deuce Court, 1986; The World's Tallest Midget, 1987; Casey on the Loose, 1989; Love and Infamy, 1993; The Best of Frank Deford, 2000; The Other Adonis, 2001; An American Summer, 2002. **Address:** PO Box 1109, 73 Clapboard Hill Rd, Greens Farms, CT 06838-1109, U.S.A.

DEFRANK, Thomas M. American, b. 1945. **Genres:** Politics/Government, Documentaries/Reportage. **Career:** Bryan Daily Eagle, Bryan, TX, reporter; Fort Worth Star-Telegram, TX, reporter; Minneapolis Star, MN, reporter; Newsweek, Washington, DC, intern to deputy bureau chief and senior White House correspondent, 1968-95; freelance writer, 1995-96; New York Daily News, Washington Bureau chief, 1996-. Guest on television programs. **Publications:** (with P. Goldman, M. Miller, A. Murr, and T. Mathews) Quest for the Presidency 1984, 1985; (with Goldman, Miller, Murr, and Mathews) Quest for the Presidency 1988, 1989; (with Goldman, Miller, Murr, and Mathews) Quest for the Presidency 1992, 1994; (with J.A. Baker III) The Politics of Diplomacy (memoir), 1995; (with E. Rollins) Bare Knuckles and Back Rooms (autobiography), 1996. **Address:** 608 South Carolina Ave SE, Washington, DC 20003, U.S.A.

DEFREES, Madeline. Also writes as Sister Mary Gilbert, Sister Mary Gilbert. American, b. 1919. **Genres:** Novellas/Short stories, Poetry, Writing/Journalism, Autobiography/Memoirs, Essays. **Career:** With Holy Names College, Spokane, WA, 1950-67; University of Montana, Missoula, associate professor, 1967-71, professor of English, 1971-79; University of Massachusetts, Amherst, professor of English, 1979-85, director of MFA Writing Program, 1980-83, professor emeritus, 1985-; full-time writer. Wichita State University, distinguished poet-in-residence, 1993. **Publications:** AS SISTER MARY GILBERT: Springs of Silence (autobiography), 1953; Later Thoughts from the Springs of Silence, 1962; From the Darkroom (poetry), 1964. AS MADELINE DEFREES: When Sky Lets Go, 1978; Imaginary Ancestors, 1978; Magpie on the Gallows, 1982; The Light Station on Tillamook Rock (poetry), 1989; Imaginary Ancestors (poetry), 1990; Possible Sibyls, 1991; Blue Dusk: New & Selected Poems, 1951-2001.

DEGEORGE, Richard T(homas). American, b. 1933. **Genres:** Philosophy, Bibliography. **Career:** University of Kansas, Lawrence, assistant professor, 1959-62, associate professor, 1962-64, professor, 1964-72, university distinguished professor of philosophy, 1972-. **Publications:** Patterns of Soviet Thought, 1966; (co-author) Science and Ideology in Soviet Society, 1967; The New Marxism, 1968; Soviet Ethics and Morality, 1969; Guide to Philosophical Bibliography and Research, 1971; The Philosopher's Guide, 1980; Business Ethics, 1982, 5th ed. 1999; The Nature and Limits of Authority, 1985; Competing with Integrity in International Business, 1993; Freedom and Tenure: Ethical Issues, 1997; The Ethics of Information Technology and Business, 2003. EDITOR: Classical and Contemporary Metaphysics, 1962; (co) Reflections on Man, Part II: Dialectical Thought, 1966; Ethics and Society, 1966; (with F.M. DeGeorge) The Structuralists from Marx to Levi-Strauss, 1972; (with J. P. Scanlan) Marxism and Religion in Eastern Europe, 1976; (with J. Pichler), Ethics, Free Enterprise and Public Policy, 1978; Semiotic Themes, 1981. **Address:** Dept. of Philosophy, University of Kansas, 1445 Jayhawk Blvd Rm 3090, Lawrence, KS 66045-7590, U.S.A. **Online address:** degeorge@ku.edu

DEGRAAFF, Robert M(ark). American, b. 1942. **Genres:** Animals/Pets, Poetry. **Career:** St. Lawrence University, Canton, NY, instructor, 1966-69, assistant professor, 1972-76, associate professor, 1976-85, professor of English, 1985-, coordinator of London Program, 1981-83. St. Lawrence University Chorus, tenor; St. Lawrence University Catch Club (singing group), leader. **Publications:** The Book of the Toad, Park Street Press, 1991. Contributor of articles and reviews to academic journals. **Address:** Department of English, St. Lawrence University, Canton, NY 13617, U.S.A.

DE GRAVE, Kathleen. American, b. 1950. **Genres:** Novels, Novellas/Short stories, Literary criticism and history, Women's studies and issues. **Career:**

Pittsburg State University, KS, professor of English, 1989-, director of Writing across the Curriculum program, 1989-, co-director of creative writing, 2000-. **Publications:** Company Woman (novel), 1995; Swindler, Spy, Rebel: The Confidence Woman in Nineteenth Century America (literary study), 1995; (author of intro.) The Jungle, 2003. Contributor of short stories to periodicals. **Address:** English Dept, Pittsburg State University, Pittsburg, KS 66762, U.S.A. **Online address:** kdegrave@pittstate.edu

DEGRAZIA, Emilio. American, b. 1941. **Genres:** Novels, Novellas/Short stories. **Career:** Winona State University, Winona, MN, assistant professor, 1969-79, associate professor, 1979-86, professor of English, 1986-; writer. **Publications:** Enemy Country (short stories), 1984; (with others) Today's Gift (prose meditations), 1985; Billy Brazil (novel), 1991; Seventeen Grams of Soul (short stories), 1994; A Canticle for Bread and Stones (novel), 1997; Winona: A Romantic Tragedy (play).

DE GRUCHY, John W(esley). South African, b. 1939. **Genres:** Area studies, Theology/Religion, Humanities. **Career:** Ordained minister of United Congregational Church, 1961; pastor of United Congregational Church in Durban, South Africa, 1961-68, and Johannesburg, South Africa, 1968-73; University of Cape Town, South Africa, lecturer, 1973-75, senior lecturer, 1975-80, associate professor, 1980-86, professor of Christian studies, 1986-, director of the Graduate School in Humanities, 1999-. South African Council of Churches, director, 1968-73; United Congregational Church, moderator, 1980-81. **Publications:** The Church Struggle in South Africa, 1979, 2nd ed., 1986; Bonhoeffer and South Africa, 1985; Cry Justice!, 1986; Theology and Ministry in Context and Crisis, 1987; Dietrich Bonhoeffer: Witness to Jesus Christ, 1987; Liberating Reformed Theology, 1991; Christianity and Democracy, 1995. EDITOR: E. Bethge, Bonhoeffer: Exile and Martyr, 1975; (with C. Villa-Vicencio) Apartheid Is a Heresy, 1983; (with C. Villa-Vicencio) Resistance and Hope: South African Essays in Honour of Beyers Naude, 1985; (with L. Rasmussen) Reinhold Niebuhr, 1988; (with C. Green) Karl Barth: Theologian of Freedom, 1989; (with G. Kelly) Karl Rahner: Theologian of the Graced Search for Meaning, 1989; (with H.M. Rumscheidt) Adolf Von Harnack: Liberal Theology at Its Height, 1989; (with M. Prozesky) A South African Guide to World Religions, 1991; (with C. Villa-Vicencio) Doing Theology in Context, 1994; Bonhoeffer for a New Day, 1997; (with J. Cochrane and S. Martin) Facing the Truth, 1999; The Cambridge Companion to Dietrich Bonhoeffer, 1999; Christianity, Art and Transformation: Theological Aesthetics in the Struggle for Justice, 2001. **Address:** Graduate School in Humanities, University of Cape Town, Private Bag Rondebosch 7701, Cape Town, Republic of South Africa. **Online address:** jdeg@humanities.uct.ac.za

DE HAAS, Margaret. British, b. 1954. **Genres:** Law. **Career:** Barrister, called to the bar in 1977. Queen's counsel, 1998, recorder, 1999; circuit judge, 2004. **Publications:** WITH I.S. GOLDREIN: Property Distribution on Divorce, 1983, rev. ed., 1989; Butterworths Personal Injury Litigation Service. 1985-; Structured Settlements, 1993, 2nd ed., 1997; (with C. Bispham) Domestic Injunctions, 2nd ed., 1997; Medical Negligence, 1997; (co-ed.) Personal Injury: Major Claims Handling, 2000. **Address:** Queen Elizabeth II Law Courts, Derby Sq, Liverpool L2, England. **Online address:** goldhaas@netcomuk.co.uk

DE HAMEL, Joan (Littledale). British/New Zealander, b. 1924. **Genres:** Children's fiction. **Career:** Lecturer in French, Dunedin Teachers College, 1967-80. **Publications:** X Marks the Spot, 1973; Take the Long Path, 1978; Hemi's Pet, 1985; The Third Eye, 1987; Hideaway, 1992; Hemi and The Shortie Pyjamas, 1996. **Address:** 25 Howard St, Macandrew Bay, Dunedin, New Zealand.

DE HAVEN, Tom. American, b. 1949. **Genres:** Novels, Novellas/Short stories, Graphic Novels. **Career:** Magazine Associates, New York City, managing editor, 197376; free-lance magazine editor, 1977-80; Hofstra University, Hempstead, NY, adjunct professor of creative writing, 1981-87; Rutgers University, New Brunswick, NJ, assistant professor of American studies, 1987-90; Virginia Commonwealth University, Richmond, associate professor of American studies and creative writing, 1990-. **Publications:** Freaks' Amour (novel), 1978; Jersey Luck (novel), 1980; Funny Papers (novel), 1985; U.S.S.A., Book 1 (young adult novel), 1987; Sunburn Lake: A Trilogy (novellas; contains Clap Hands! Here Comes Charley; He's All Mine; and Where We'll Never Grow Old), 1988; Joe Gosh (young adult novel), 1988; Neuromancer, Volume 1. (graphic fantasy novel; adapted from William Gibson's novel), edited by David Harris, 1989; Chronicle of the King's Tramp (fantasy novels), Book 1: Walker of Worlds, 1990, Book 2: The End-of-Everything Man, 1991, Book 3: The Last Human, 1992; Pixie Meat (fiction), 1990; Derby Dugan's Depression Funnies, 1996; The Orphan's Tent, 1996; Green Candles (graphic novel), 1997. **Address:** 14106 Huntgate Woods Rd., Midlothian, VA 23112-4355, U.S.A.

DE HERRERA, Nancy Cooke. American. **Genres:** Autobiography/Memoirs. **Career:** Writer. Served as U.S. Ambassador of Fashion for U.S. Information Service. As Nancy Cooke, presenter of lecture series A Travelogue through Fashion; or, Around the World with Nancy Cooke. **Publications:** Beyond Gurus: A Woman of Many Worlds (memoir), 1993, new. ed., as The Socialite & the Holyman, 1999; All You Need Is Love, 2003.

DEHN, Olive. British, b. 1914. **Genres:** Children's fiction. **Publications:** Tales of Sir Benjamin Bulbous, Bart, 1935; The Basement Bogle, 1935; The Nixie from Rotterdam, 1937; Tales of the Taunus Mountains, 1937; The Well-Behaved Witch, 1937; Come In, 1946; Higgly-Piggly Farm, 1957; The Pike Dream, 1958; The Caretakers (and the Poacher, and the Gipsy, to the Rescue, and of Wilmhurst), 5 vols., 1960-67; Spectacles for the Mole, 1968; Good-bye Day, 1980. **Address:** Lear Cottage, Colemans Hatch, Hartfield, Sussex, England.

DEICHMANN, Ute. German, b. 1951. **Genres:** Biology, Chemistry, History. **Career:** Schoolteacher, 1975-87; University of Cologne, Cologne, Germany, research fellow and lecturer, 1987-96; Beckman Center for the History of Chemistry, Philadelphia, PA, Edelstein international fellow in the history of the chemical sciences, 1996-97; Hebrew University of Jerusalem, Jerusalem, Israel, research fellow, 1997; University of Cologne, research fellow and lecturer, 1997-2000, assistant professor, 2000-. **Publications:** Biologen unter Hitler: Vertreuburg, 1992, trans. as Biologists under Hitler, 1996; Chemiker und Biochemiker im Nationalsozialismus, 2001. Contributor to journals. **Address:** Institut fur Genetik, University of Cologne, Weyertal 121, D-50931 Cologne, Germany. **Online address:** ute.deichmann@uni-koeln.de

DEIGHTON, Len. British, b. 1929. **Genres:** Novels, Mystery/Crime/Suspense, Food and Wine, History, Novellas/Short stories. **Publications:** The Ipcress File, 1962; Horse Under Water, 1963; Funeral in Berlin, 1964; Action Cook Book (in U.S. as Cookstrip Cook Book), 1965; Ou est le Garlic, 1965, rev. ed. as Basic French Cooking, 1979; Billion Dollar Brain, 1966; An Expensive Place to Die, 1967; (ed.) Len Deighton's London Dossier, 1967; (co-author) The Assassination of President Kennedy, 1967; Only When I Larf, 1968; Bomber, 1970; Declarations of War (stories), 1971; Close-Up, 1972; Spy Story, 1974; Yesterday's Spy, 1975; Twinkle, Twinkle, Little Spy (in U.S. as Catch a Falling Spy), 1976; Fighter, 1977; SS-GB, 1978; (with A. Schwartzman) Airshipwreck, 1978; Blitzkrieg, 1979; (co-author) Battle of Britain, 1980; XPD, 1981; Goodbye Mickey Mouse, 1982; Berlin Game, 1983; Mexico Set, 1984; London Match, 1985; Winter, 1987; Spy Hook, 1988; ABC of French Food, 1989; Spy Line, 1989; Spy Sinker, 1990; Basic French Cookery Course, 1990; MAMista, 1991; City of Gold, 1992; Violent Ward, 1993; Blood, Tears & Folly, 1993; Faith, 1994; Hope, 1995; Charity, 1997. **Address:** c/o Jonathan Clowes Ltd, 10 Ironbridge House, Bridge Approach, London NW1 8BD, England.

DEITZ, Tom. (Thomas Franklin). American, b. 1952. **Genres:** Science fiction/Fantasy. **Career:** Writer. **Publications:** FANTASY NOVELS. DAVID SULLIVAN SERIES: Windmaster's Bane, 1986; Fireshaper's Doom, 1987; Darkthunder's Way, 1989; Sunshaker's War, 1990; Stoneskin's Revenge, 1991; Ghostcountry's Wrath, 1995; Dreamseeker's Road, 1995. SOULSMITH SERIES: Soulsmith, 1991; Dreambuilder, 1992; Wordwright, 1993. OTHER FANTASY NOVELS: The Gryphon King, 1989; Above the Lower Sky, 1994; The Demons in the Green, 1996. **Address:** c/o Avon Books, 1350 Avenue of the Americas, New York, NY 10019, U.S.A.

DE JONGE, Alex. British, b. 1938. **Genres:** Literary criticism and history, Sports/Fitness, Biography, Translations. **Publications:** (with others) Nineteenth Century Russian Literature, 1973; Nightmare Culture, Lautreamont and Les Chants de Maldoror, 1973, 2nd ed., 2005; Dostoevsky and the Age of Intensity, 1975; Prince of Clouds: A Biography of Baudelaire, 1976; The Weimar Chronicle: Prelude to History, 1977; Napoleon's Last Will and Testament, 1977; Fire and Water: A Life of Peter the Great, 1979; The Life and Times of Grigorii Rasputin, 1982; Stalin and the Shaping of the Soviet Union, 1986; (trans.) The Godolphin Arabian, 2003. **Address:** Dept of Foreign Languages, James Madison University, 800 S Main St, Harrisonburg, VA 22807-0002, U.S.A.

DE JOUVENEL, Hugues Alain. French (born Switzerland), b. 1946. **Genres:** Institutions/Organizations, International relations/Current affairs, Sciences, Technology, Translations. **Career:** Affiliated with the International Center of Research and Training on the Future, Paris, France, 1969-71; United Nations Institute for Training and Research, New York, NY, visiting scholar and research associate, 1972-73; Futuribles International, general delegate, 1974-; Futuribles Group, director, 1974-; professor at National

School of Public Administration. Secretary and acting director of Center for Economic, Industrial, and Social Studies and Documentation, 1974. News editor and press attache for French Ministry of Defense, 1972. **Publications:** (with others) The United Nations and the Future, 1972; Sciences, Technology, and the Future, 1979; Le Point critique, 1980; Europe's Ageing Population, 1989; Cataluna en el Horizonte 2010, 1994; La France a l'Horizon 2010, 1995; The Knowledge Base of Future Studies, 1996; Changing Europe, 1996; Vers une prospective des retraites en France a l'horizon 2030, 1998; (with V. Gollain and A. Sallez) Emploi et Territoires en Ile-de-France: Prospective, 1999; La Tour d'Aigues, 1999; Decision, Prospective, autoorganisation, 2000. TRANSLATOR: C. A. Doxiades, Between Dystopia and Utopia; J.S. Coleman, Changes in Educational Structures. **Address:** Futuribles, 55, rue de Varenne, F-75341 Paris Cedex 07, France.

DEKA, Connie. See **LAUX, Constance.**

DE KERCKHOVE, Derrick. Belgian, b. 1944. **Genres:** Information science/Computers. **Career:** University of Toronto, St. Michael's College, professor of French, 1967-, McLuhan Program in Culture and Technology, started as co-director, became director, 1991-. **Publications:** Connected Intelligence: The Arrival of the Web Society, 1997. EDITOR: (with C.H. Lumsden) The Alphabet and the Brain: The Lateralization of Writing, 1988; (with C. Dewdney) The Skin of Culture: Investigating the New Electronic Reality, 1995. Contributor to books. **Address:** St. Michael's College, 81 St. Mary St., Toronto, ON, Canada M5S 1J4.

DEKKER, Carl. See **LYNDS, Dennis.**

DEKKER, George. American, b. 1934. **Genres:** Literary criticism and history. **Career:** Professor of English since 1974, and Atha Professor in Humanities since 1988, Stanford University, California.(Associate Professor, 1972-74). Lecturer, University College, Swansea, Wales, 1962-64; Lecturer, 1964-66, Sr. Lecturer, 1966-70, and Reader in Literature, 1970-72, University of Essex, Colchester. **Publications:** Sailing After Knowledge: The Cantos of Ezra Pound, 1963; James Fenimore Cooper: The Novelist, 1967; (ed. with Larry Johnston) The American Democrat, by James Fenimore Cooper, 1969; (ed. with John McWilliams) James Fenimore Cooper: The Critical Heritage, 1973; Coleridge and the Literature of Sensibility, 1978; (ed.) Donald Davie and the Responsibilities of Literature, 1984; The American Historical Romance, 1987. **Address:** Dept. of English, Stanford University, Stanford, CA 94305, U.S.A.

DE LA BILLIERE, Sir Peter (Edgar de la Cour). British, b. 1934. **Genres:** Autobiography/Memoirs. **Career:** British Army, career officer, 1952-92. **Publications:** Storm Command: A Personal Story, 1992; Looking for Trouble (autobiography), 1994. Contributor to periodicals. **Address:** Curtis Brown, 28/29 Haymarket, London SW1Y 4SP, England.

DE LA CRUZ, Melissa. Filipino, b. 1971. **Genres:** Novels, Young adult fiction, Popular Culture, Adult non-fiction. **Career:** Freelance magazine writer. **Publications:** NOVELS: Cat's Meow, 2001; The Au Pairs, 2004; Fresh Off the Boat, 2005. NON-FICTION: How to Become Famous in Two Weeks or Less, 2003; The Fashionista Files, 2004. Contributor to periodicals and anthologies. **Address:** c/o Author Mail, Ballantine Books, 1745 Broadway, New York, NY 10019, U.S.A.

DELAGE, Denys. Canadian, b. 1942. **Genres:** Sociology. **Career:** Laval Universite, Quebec, professor of sociology, 1981-, chair of department, 1991-95. **Publications:** The Bitter Feast: Amerindians and Europeans in Northeastern North America, 1600-64, 1985; La religion dans l'alliance franco-amerindienne, 1991; L'influence des Amerindiens sur les Canadiens et les Francais au temps de la Nouvelle-France, 1992; Les Traites des Sept Feux avec les Britanniques, 2001. **Address:** Department of Sociology, Laval Universite, Quebec City, QC, Canada G1K 7P4. **Online address:** denys.delage@soc.ulaval.ca

DELAHAYE, Michael (John). British, b. 1946. **Genres:** Mystery/Crime/Suspense. **Career:** Full-time writer and broadcast journalist. Teacher of English, British Institute, Florence, 1968-69; Television Reporter and Correspondent, BBC, News and Current Affairs Dept., London, 1969-79; Reporter and Producer, BBC TV, London, 1988-98. **Publications:** The Sale of Lot 236, 1981; On the Third Day (in U.K. as The Third Day), 1984; Stalking-Horse, 1987. **Address:** c/o David Higham Assocs, 5-8 Lower John St, London W1R 4HA, England.

DELAHUNT, Meaghan. Australian/Irish (born Australia), b. 1961. **Genres:** Novels. **Career:** Novelist; creative writing lecturer; freelance journalist.

Worked as car detailer, socialist organizer, aerobics instructor, English-as-a-second-language instructor. **Publications:** In the Blue House, 2001. Contributor to anthologies and periodicals. **Address:** c/o Author Mail, Bloomsbury Publishing, 38 Soho Sq, London W1V 5DF, England.

DE LA ISLA, José. American, b. 1944. **Genres:** Adult non-fiction. **Career:** Public policy analyst and writer. Commentator for World Radio Morning News, broadcast by National Public Radio/KPFT-FM Radio, and for Cable News Network. Taught at University of Oregon and University of California-Berkeley. **Publications:** The Rise of Hispanic Political Power, 2003. Contributor to newspapers. **Address:** c/o Author Mail, Archer Books, POB 1254, Santa Maria, CA 93456, U.S.A. **Online address:** isla@trip.net

DELANEY, Denis. See **GREEN, Peter (Morris).**

DELANEY, Gayle (M. V.). American, b. 1949. **Genres:** Psychology, Self help, Sex. **Career:** Founding President, Association for the Study of Dreams; dream psychologist in private practice, 1979-; California Institute of Integral Studies, San Francisco, CA, assistant professor, 1980-85; Delaney and Flowers Dream and Consultation Center, San Francisco, co-director, 1981-. Institute of Transpersonal Psychology, visiting associate professor, 1987; Princeton University, member of alumni council, 1988-92; guest on television talk shows; dream analyst on television stations; radio host. Lecturer on dreaming and sleep deprivation around the world, in English, French, and Italian. **Publications:** Living Your Dreams, 1979, rev. ed., 1996; Breakthrough Dreaming: How to Tap the Power of Your 24-Hour Mind, 1991; (ed.) New Directions in Dream Interpretation, 1992; Sexual Dreams, 1994, as Sensual Dreaming, 1995; The Dream Kit, 1995; In Your Dreams, 1997; All about Dreams, 1998. Contributor to books. Contributor of articles on dream psychology to periodicals. **Address:** Delaney & Flowers Dream & Consultation Center, PO Box 27173, San Francisco, CA 94127, U.S.A. **Online address:** gayle@gdelaney.com; www.gdelaney.com

DELANEY, Michael. American, b. 1955. **Genres:** Children's fiction, Illustrations. **Career:** Writer and illustrator. Gourmet magazine, freelance illustrator, 1981-96; J. Walter Thompson, advertising copywriter, 1985-90. **Publications:** The Marigold Monster, 1983; Henry's Special Delivery, 1984; Not Your Average Joe, 1990. SELF-ILLUSTRATED: Deep Doo Doo, 1996. Cartoons and illustrations published in magazines. **Address:** c/o Author Mail, Dutton Publicity, 345 Hudson St, New York, NY 10014, U.S.A. **Online address:** chauck@discovernet.net

DELANEY, Norman Conrad. American, b. 1932. **Genres:** History, Biography. **Career:** Del Mar College, Corpus Christi, TX, professor, 1967-. **Publications:** John McIntosh Kell of the Raider Alabama, 1973, repr., 2003; Ghost Ship, 1989; An Oral History of Naval Air Station Corpus Christi during World War II, 1997; (co-author) Raiders and Blockaders, 1998. **Address:** 3747 Aransas St, Corpus Christi, TX 78411, U.S.A. **Online address:** ndelaney@delmar.edu

DELANEY, Shelagh. British, b. 1939. **Genres:** Plays/Screenplays. **Publications:** Sweetly Sings the Donkey (short stories), 1963; Writing Woman, 1984. PLAYS: A Taste of Honey, 1959, (screenplay), 1962; The Lion in Love, 1961; The House that Jack Built, 1977; Don't Worry about Matilda, 1987. SCREENPLAYS: The White Bus, 1966; Charlie Bubbles, 1968; The Raging Moon, 1970; Dance with a Stranger, 1985. TELEVISION: Did Your Nanny Come from Bergen?, 1970; St. Martin's Summer, 1974; Find Me First, 1979; Rape, 1981. RADIO PLAYS: So Does the Nightingale, 1980; Don't Worry About Matilda, 1983. **Address:** c/o Tessa Sayle Agency, 11 Jubilee Place, London SW3 3TE, England.

DELANO, Anthony. British (born Australia), b. 1930. **Genres:** Novels, Education, Writing/Journalism, Documentaries/Reportage. **Career:** Managing Ed., Daily Mirror, London, 1978-84; Director, Mirror Group, 1984-87 (Rome Correspondent, 1956-60; Paris Correspondent, 1960-63; American Correspondent, 1963-70; London Diary Ed., 1970-74; Roving Correspondent, 1970-74; Chief American Correspondent, 1974-78); Senior Lecturer, University of Queensland, 1989-1992; Visiting Professor in Journalism, London Institute, 2003-. **Publications:** Breathless Diversions (novel), 1975; Slip-Up (documentary), 1977; Manacled Mormon, 1978; Maxwell, 1988; The News Breed, 1995. **Address:** 4 Moscow Mansions, 224 Cromwell Rd, London SW5 OSP, England. **Online address:** t.delano@lcp.liust.ac.uk

DELANY, Samuel R(ay). American, b. 1942. **Genres:** Science fiction/Fantasy. **Publications:** The Jewels of Aptor, 1962, unabridged ed., 1968; The Fall of the Towers, vol. I, Captives of the Flames, 1963, as Out of the Dead City, 1968, vol. II, The Towers of Toron, 1964, vol. III, City of a Thousand

Suns, 1965; The Ballad of Beta-2, 1965; Empire Star, 1966; Babel-17, 1966; The Einstein Intersection, 1967; Nova, 1968; Driftglass: Ten Tales of Speculative Fiction, 1971; Dhalgren, 1975; Triton, 1976; The Jewel-Hinged Jaw: Notes on the Language of Science Fiction, 1977; The American Shore, 1978; (with H. Chaynkin) Empire, 1978; (ed.) Nebula Award Winners 13, 1979; Tales from Neveryon, 1979; Heavenly Breakfast: An Essay on the Winter of Love, 1979; Distant Stars, 1981; Neveryon: Or the Tale of Signs and Cities, 1982; Stars in My Pocket Like Grains of Sand, 1984; Starboard Wine: More Notes on the Language of Science Fiction, 1984; Flight from Neveryon, 1985; The Bridge of Lost Desire, 1987; The Motion of Light in Water, 1988; The Straits of Messina, 1988; Wagner-Artaud: A Play of 19th and 20th Century Critical Fictions, 1988; They Fly at Ciron, 1993; Silent Interviews, 1994; Equinox, 1994; Atlantis: Three Tales, 1995; Longer Views: Extended Essays, 1996; Trouble on Triton, 1996; Bread and Wine: An Erotic Tale of New York City, 1998; Hogg, 1998; Times Square Red, Times Square Blue, 1999; Shorter Views: Queer Thoughts & the Politics of the Paraliterary, 1999; 1984: Selected Letters, 2000. **Address:** c/o Henry Morrison, Inc, PO Box 235, Bedford Hills, NY 10507, U.S.A.

DE LA PEDRAJA, René. American (born Cuba), b. 1951. **Genres:** History, Military/Defense/Arms control. **Career:** Universidad de los Andes, Bogota, Colombia, research professor of economics, 1976-85; business consultant in Bogota, 1984-86; Kansas State University, Manhattan, assistant professor of history, 1986-89; Canisius College, Buffalo, NY, assistant professor, 1989-92, associate professor of history, 1992-97, professor of history, 1997-, member of faculty senate, 1993-. **Publications:** Historia de la Energia en Colombia, 1985; FEDEMETAL y la industrializacion de Colombia, 1986; Energy Politics in Colombia, 1989; The Rise and Decline of U.S. Merchant Shipping in the Twentieth Century, 1992; Historical Dictionary of the U.S. Merchant Marine, 1994; Oil and Coffee: The Merchant Shipping of Latin America, 1998; Latin American Merchant Shipping in the Age of Global Competition, 1999. Contributor to periodicals. **Address:** Dept of History, Canisius College, 2001 Main St, Buffalo, NY 14208-1098, U.S.A. **Online address:** delapedr@canisius.edu

DELARA, Ellen. American, b. 1949. **Genres:** Human relations/Parenting. **Career:** Educator, therapist, and researcher. Cornell University, Ithaca, NY, Family Life Development Center faculty fellow. **Publications:** (with J. Garbarino) And Words Can Hurt Forever: How to Protect Adolescents from Bullying, Harassment, and Emotional Violence, 2002. Contributor to books. **Address:** Cornell University, Family Life Development Center, 118 Original Mann Bldg., Ithaca, NY 14853, U.S.A. **Online address:** ewj2@cornell.edu

DE LAS CASAS, Walter. American (born Cuba), b. 1947. **Genres:** Poetry, Education. **Career:** Sarah J. Hale High School, Brooklyn, NY, Spanish teacher, 1979-93; Science Skill Center High School, Brooklyn, teacher of Spanish language and literature, 1994-96. **Publications:** POEMS: La Ninez Que Dilata, 1986; Libido (in Spanish), 1989; Tributes, 1993; Discourse, 1999; Human, 2004. **Address:** 323 Dahill Rd Apt 1A, Brooklyn, NY 11218, U.S.A. **Online address:** delascasis2@netzero.net

DELBANCO, Nicholas F(ranklin). American (born England), b. 1942. **Genres:** Novels, Novellas/Short stories, Plays/Screenplays, Autobiography/Memoirs. **Career:** Bennington College, Vermont, member of faculty, Dept. of Language and Literature, 1966-; University of Michigan, Ann Arbor, Robert Frost Collegiate Professor of English, 1985-. Visiting professor, Columbia and Iowa Univs., Skidmore, Trinity and Williams Colleges. **Publications:** The Martlet's Tale, 1966, screenplay, 1970; Grasse, 3/23/66, 1968; Consider Sappho Burning, 1969; News, 1970; In the Middle Distance, 1971; Fathering, 1973; Small Rain, 1975; Possession, 1977; Sherbrookes, 1978; Stillness, 1980; Group Portrait: Conrad, Crane, Ford, James, and Wells, 1982; About My Table and Other Stories, 1983; The Beaux Arts Trio: A Portrait, 1985; Running in Place: Scenes from the South of France (memoir), 1989; The Writers' Trade and Other Stories, 1990; In the Name of Mercy, 1995; Old Scores, 1997; The Lost Suitcase: Reflections on the Literary Life, 2000; What Remains, 2000; The Countess of Stanlein Restored, 2001; The Vagabonds, 2004. **Address:** 428 Concord St, Ann Arbor, MI 48104-1706, U.S.A.

DELBLANC, Sven (Axel Herman). Swedish (born Canada), b. 1931. **Genres:** Novels, Plays/Screenplays. **Career:** Worked as farmhand and manual laborer; University of Uppsala, Uppsala, Sweden, educator; writer. Visiting professor at University of California, Berkeley, 1968-69. **Publications:** NOVELS IN ENGLISH TRANSLATION: Homunculus, 1965 trans by V. Moberg as Homunculus: A Magical Tale, 1969; Kastrate: En romantisk berattelser, 1975, trans by C.W. Williams as The Castrati: A Romantic Tale, 1979; Speranza, 1980, trans by P.B. Austin, 1983. HEDEBY NOVELS:

Aminne (title means: Remembrance), 1970; Stenfagel: En berattelse fran Sormland (title means: Stone Bird), 1973; Vinteride: En berattelse fran Sormland (title means:Winter Ride), 1974; Stadsporten: En berattelse fran Sormland (title means: The City Gate), 1976. OTHER: Asnebrygga (novel; title means: Donkey Bridge), 1970; Zahak, 1971; Primavera: En konstnarlig berattelse, 1973; Grottmannen (novel; title means: The Cave Man), 1977; Morgenstjarnan (teleplay; title means: The Morning Star), 1977; Gunnar Emmanuel: En tidlos berattelse, 1978; Grona vintern, 1978; Un man pa havet, 1979; Treklover: Hjalmer Bergman, Birger Sjoberg, Vilhelm Moberg, 1980; Samuels bok (title means: Samuel's Book), 1981; Samuels dottrar (title means: Samuel's Daughter), 1982; Kanaans land, 1984; Fagelfro: Narande och giftigt fran tre decennier, 1986; (with L. Lonnroth) Den Svenska litteraturen, 1987; Dant, osett: En overlick av Reinhold Ljunggrens bilvarld, 1990; Livets ax: Barndomsminnen, 1991; Ragnar Johansson, 1991; Slutord, 1991; Homerisk hemkomst: Tva essaer om Iliaden och Odysseen (essay), 1992. PLAYS: Robotbas (title means: Robot Base), 1963; Ariadne och pafageln (title means: Ariadne and the Peacock), 1964; Den arme Richard: En melodram i va akter (title means: Poor Richard), 1978. NOVELS: Eremitkraftan (title means: The Hermit Crab), 1962; Prastkappan (title means: The Cossack), 1963; Ara och minne, 1965; Nattresa (title means: Night Journey), 1967; Trampa vatten, 1972; Kara farmor (title means: Dear Grandmother), 1979; Stormhatten, 1979; Senecas dod, 1982; Jerusalems natt, 1983; Marie ensam (title means: Maria Alone), 1985; Moria land, 1987; Ankan; Ifigenia: Berattelse i tva upptag. Writer for Dagens Nyheter. **Address:** Askvagen 23, 75252 Uppsala, Sweden.

DEL CARO, Adrian. American, b. 1952. **Genres:** Humanities, Intellectual history, Literary criticism and history, Philosophy. **Career:** University of California, Riverside, lecturer in German and comparative literature, 1979-80; Louisiana State University, Baton Rouge, assistant professor, 1980-83, associate professor, 1983-89, professor of German, 1989-92; University of Colorado, Boulder, professor and chair, Germanic and Slavic Languages and Literatures, 1992. **Publications:** Dionysian Aesthetics, 1981; Nietzsche contra Nietzsche, 1989; (trans.) Puntigam, or, The Art of Forgetting, 1990; Hoelderlin: The Poetics of Being, 1991; Hugo von Hofmannsthal: Poets and the Language of Life, 1993; The Early Poetry of Paul Celan: In the Beginning Was the Word, 1997; (ed. with J. Ward) German Studies in the Post-Holocaust Age, 2000. Contributor to language and literature, humanities, and philosophy journals. **Address:** Department of Germanic and Slavic Languages, University of Colorado, Boulder, Box 276, Boulder, CO 80309, U.S.A.

DELEON, Peter. American, b. 1943. **Genres:** Criminology/True Crime, Politics/Government. **Career:** University of Colorado at Denver, professor of public affairs, 1985-, director of Office of International Education, 1994-. Also worked for Rand Corp. as a senior researcher. Invited lecturer in China and Mexico; consultant to European Center for Social Welfare, Swedish Colloquium for Advanced Study in the Social Sciences, and Science Center, Berlin, Germany. **Publications:** (Co-author) The Prosecution of Adult Felony Defendants in Los Angeles County, 1976; The Development and Diffusion of the Nuclear Power Reactor: A Comparative Analysis, 1979; (with G.D. Brewer) The Foundations of Policy Analysis, 1983; (with H. Nowotny and B. Wittrock) Choosing Futures: Evaluating the Secretariat for Futures Studies, 1985; The Altered Strategic Environment: Towards the Year 2000, 1987; Advice and Consent: The Development of the Policy Sciences, 1988; Thinking about Political Corruption, 1993; Democracy and the Policy Sciences, in press. Work represented in books. Contributor to policy and administration journals. **Address:** Box 142, LW 500, PO Box 173364, Denver, CO 80217-3364, U.S.A.

DELERM, Philippe. French, b. 1950. **Genres:** Novels, Children's fiction. **Career:** Writer and schoolteacher. **Publications:** La cinquième saison, 1983; Un été pour mémoire, 1985; Le bonheur: tableux et bavardages, 1986; Rouen, 1987; Le buveur de temps, 1987; Le miroir de ma mère, 1988; Autumn, 1990; C'est bien, 1991, trans. by S. Hamp as A Little List of Favourite Things: How I Like to Spend My Time, 1999; Les amoureux de l'Hôtel de Ville (novel), 1993; Mister Mouse, ou, La Métaphysique du terrier, (novel), 1994; En pleine lucarne, 1995; L'envol, 1996; Sundborn, ou, les jours de lumière (novel) 1996; Sortilège au Muséum, 1996; La première gorgée de bière et autres plaisirs minisucles (title means: The First Mouthful of Beer and Other Small Pleasures, 1997, trans. by S. Hamp as The Small Pleasures of Life, 1998, as We Could Almost Eat Outside: An Appreciation of Life's Small Pleasures, 1999; Les chemins nous inventent (title means: The Paths Invent Us), 1997; La malédiction des ruines, 1997; Il avait plu tout le dimanche (novel; title means: It Rained All Sunday), 1998; Panier de fruits, 1998; Elle s'appelait Marine (children's stories), 1998; L'enoil, 1999; Quiproquo, 1999; La portique (novel), 1999; La sieste assassinée, 2001; Interiéur: Vilhelm Hammershoi, 2001. **Address:** c/o Editions Gallimard, 5 rue Sebastien-Bottin, 75328 Paris cedex 07, France.

DELESSERT, Jacquine. *See* **REITER, Victoria (Kelrich).**

DELFATTORE, Joan. American. **Genres:** Education, Civil liberties/Human rights, Law. **Career:** University of Delaware, Newark, professor of English, 1979-. **Publications:** What Johnny Shouldn't Read: Textbook Censorship in America, Yale University Press, 1992. **Address:** Department of English, University of Delaware, 204 Memorial Hall, Newark, DE 19716-2537, U.S.A.

DELGADO, Hector L. American, b. 1949. **Genres:** Sociology. **Career:** Rutgers University, Camden Campus, Camden, NJ, assistant director of admissions services and coordinator of Latino student recruitment, 1971-73, vice-chairperson of academic foundations department and coordinator of Hispanic affairs, 1978-80; Princeton University, Princeton, NJ, assistant dean of student affairs, 1980-83; University of Michigan, Ann Arbor, instructor in sociology and Latino studies, 1984-86; Occidental College, Los Angeles, CA, assistant professor of sociology and anthropology, 1988-92; University of Arizona, Tucson, assistant professor of sociology and assistant research social scientist at Mexican-American Studies and Research Center, 1993-. **Publications:** New Immigrants, Old Unions: Organizing Undocumented Workers in Los Angeles, 1993. Contributor to books. Contributor of articles and reviews to sociology journals. **Address:** 1736 E. Elizabeth St., Pasadena, CA 91104, U.S.A.

DELILLO, Don. American, b. 1936. **Genres:** Novels, Plays/Screenplays. **Publications:** Americana, 1971; End Zone, 1972; Great Jones Street, 1973; Ratner's Star, 1976; Players, 1977; Running Dog, 1978; The Names, 1982; White Noise, 1985; The Day Room (play), 1987; Libra, 1988; Mao II, 1991; Underworld, 1997; Valparaiso (play), 1999; The Body Artist, 2001; Pafko at the Wall: A Novella, 2001; Cosmopolis: A Novel, 2003. **Address:** c/o Wallace Literary Agency, 177 E 70th St, New York, NY 10021, U.S.A.

DELINSKY, Barbara (Ruth Greenberg). Also writes as Billie Douglass, Bonnie Drake. American, b. 1945. **Genres:** Novels. **Career:** Children's Protective Services, Boston, sociological researcher, 1968-69; Dover-Sherborn School System, Massachusetts, instructor in photography, 1978-82. **Publications:** Bronze Mystique, 1984; A Special Something, 1984; Fingerprints, 1984; Secret of the Stone, 1986; First, Best and Only, 1987; Twelve Across, 1987; Twilight Whispers, 1987; T.L.C., 1988; Commitments, 1988; Fulfillment, 1988; Through My Eyes, 1989; Heart of the Night, 1989; Montana Man, 1989; Having Faith, 1990; Crosslyn Rise: The Dream, 1990; Crosslyn Rise: The Dream Unfolds, 1990; Crosslyn Rise: The Dream Comes True, 1990; Facets, 1990; A Woman Betrayed, 1991; With this Ring: Father of the Bride, 1991; The Stud, 1991; The Outsider, 1992; The Passions of Chelsea Kane, 1992; More Than Friends, 1993; Suddenly, 1994; For My Daughters, 1994; Together Alone, 1995; Shades of Grace, 1996; A Woman's Place, 1997; Three Wishes, 1997; Coast Road, 1998; Lake News, 1999; Rekindled, 1999; Vineyard, 2000; Woman Next Door, 2001; Uplift, 2001; An Accidental Woman, 2002; Flirting with Pete, 2003. AS BILLIE DOUGLASS: A Time to Love, 1982; Knightly Love, 1982; Search for a New Dawn, 1982; An Irresistible Impulse, 1983; Beyond Fantasy, 1983; Fasting Courting, 1983; Flip Side of Yesterday, 1983; Sweet Serenity, 1983; The Carpenter's Lady, 1983; Variation on a Theme, 1984. AS BONNIE DRAKE: Sensuous Burgundy, 1981; Surrender by Moonlight, 1981; Sweet Ember, 1981; The Passionate Touch, 1981; Amber Enchantment, 1982; Lilac Awakening, 1982; The Ardent Protector, 1982; Whispered Promise, 1983; Gemstone, 1983; Lover from the Sea, 1983; Passion and Illusion, 1983; Moment to Moment, 1984 Moment to Moment, 1984. **Address:** c/o Writers House Inc., 21 W 26th St., New York, NY 10010, U.S.A. **Online address:** www.barbaradelinsky.com

DE LISLE, Harold F. American, b. 1933. **Genres:** Botany, Biology. **Career:** University of Pasadena, Pasadena, CA, assistant professor of biology, 1979-89; Moorpark College, Moorpark, CA, professor of biology, 1989-. **Publications:** Common Plants of the Southern California Mountains, 1961; Wildlife of the Southern California Mountains, 1983; (ed) Proceedings of the Conference on California Herpetology, 1989; Natural History of Monitor Lizards, 1996. **Address:** Moorpark College, Biology Department, Moorpark, CA 93021, U.S.A.

DELLER, John J. American, b. 1931. **Genres:** Gerontology/Senior issues. **Career:** US Army, career officer, 1956-76, retiring as colonel; served as chief of medicine, Letterman General Hospital, San Francisco, 1966, 1977; University of California, San Francisco, associate clinical professor, 1976-77; Eisenhower Medical Center, Rancho Mirage, CA, physician, 1978-, chief of staff, 1992-93, director of diabetes program, 1989-2003; retired, 2004. Writer. Lecturer on cruise ships, 1981-. Doctor Talk, TV show, co-host. **Publica-** tions: Achieving Agelessness, 1991; The Palm Springs Formula for Staying Healthier and Living Longer, 1995. **Address:** 346 Crest Lake Dr, Palm Desert, CA 92211-1704, U.S.A.

DE LOMELLINI, C. A. *See* **KELLEY, (Kathleen) Alita.**

DE LONG, David G. American, b. 1939. **Genres:** Architecture. **Career:** John Carl Warnecke and Associates (architects and planners), NYC, associate, 1971-75; University of Pennsylvania, Philadelphia, professor of architecture, 1984-, chair of Graduate Program in Historic Preservation, 1984-97, associate dean of Graduate School of Fine Arts, 1992-94. Getty Center for the History of Art and Humanities, visiting scholar, 1989; American Academy in Rome, James Marston Fitch Resident in Historic Preservation, 1997-98; Guggenheim Fellow, 1997-98. **Publications:** The Architecture of Bruce Goff: Buildings and Projects, 1916-1974, 2 vols., 1977; (ed.) Historic American Buildings, 14 vols., 1977-80; Bruce Goff: Toward Absolute Architecture, 1988; (with D.B. Brownlee, S. Geldin, and E.A. Smith) Louis I. Kahn: In the Realm of Architecture, 1991; (ed. and primary author) Frank Lloyd Wright: Designs for an American Landscape, 1996; (ed. and primary author) Frank Lloyd Wright and the Living City, 1998; (with others) Out of the Ordinary: Robert Venturi and Denise Scott Brown, 2001. **Address:** Meyerson Hall, University of Pennsylvania, Philadelphia, PA 19104, U.S.A.

DEL PASO, Fernando. Mexican, b. 1935. **Genres:** Poetry, Novels. **Career:** Novelist, diplomat, painter, and journalist. British Broadcast Corporation (BBC), London, England, publicist and newscaster, 1970-; worked in advertising in Mexico; Radio France Internationale, Paris, France, member of staff, 1985-; Mexican Embassy, Paris, cultural attaché, then general consul until 1986; Bibliotheca Iberoamericana Octavio Paz, Guadalajara, Mexico, director. Painter. Work has been exhibited at galleries in Mexico, Spain and elsewhere. **Publications:** Sonetos del amor y de lo diario (poetry), 1958; José Trigo, 1966; Palinuro de México, 1977, trans. E. Plaister as Palinuro of Mexico, 1989; Noticias del imperio (title means: News from the Empire), 1987; La loca de Miramar (monolog), 1988; De la A a la Z por un poeta (for children), 1990; Paleta de diez colores (for children), 1992; (prologue) Flores en México, 1992; Palinuro en las escalera (play), 1992; Memoria y olvido de Juan José Arreola, 1920-1947 (biography), 1994, 2nd ed, 1996; Linda 67. Historia ed un crimen, 1996; (with M.L. Portilla) Yo soy un hombre de letras: discurso (speech), 1996; La muerte se va a Granada: poema dramático en dos actos, 1998; Cuentos dispersos (stories), 1999; Obras (collected works), two vols, 2000; Ensayo y obra periodística, 2002. Contributor to periodicals. Works have been translated into English, French, German, Portuguese, Dutch, and Chinese. **Address:** c/o Author Mail, Random House Mondadori, Homero 544, 11570 Col. Chapultepec Morales, DF, Mexico.

DEL RE, Giuseppe. Italian, b. 1932. **Genres:** Chemistry, Education, Philosophy. **Career:** University of Naples, Italy, assistant professor of chemistry, 1956-58, associate professor of spectroscopy, 1963-68, professor of theoretical chemistry, 1969-; RIAS, Baltimore, MD, research group leader, 1959-62; University of Paris VI, invited researcher at Institut de Biologie Physico-Chimique, 1963-70; University of Montreal, visiting professor, 1971; University of Waterloo, visiting professor, 1973, 1976, 2001; University of Erlangen, visiting professor, 1981-; Ecole Normale Superieure, Paris, 1997; lecturer in Peru and Hungary. Member of Education Committees of the Italian government. Creator of the Del Re method for determining atom charges in molecules and the process of introducing maximum localization hybrids in the molecular orbital method. **Publications:** (with G. Berthier and J. Serre), Electronic States of Molecules and Atom Clusters, 1980; The Cosmic Dance: Science Discovers the Mysterious Harmony of the Universe, 2000. EDITOR: Brain Research and the Mind-Body Problem: Epistemological and Metaphysical Issues, 1992; Scienza moderna e sense del divino, trans. T.F. Torrance, 1992. Contributor to books and scientific journals. **Address:** Via della Giuliana 58, I-00195 Rome, Italy. **Online address:** giuseppe.delre@unina.it

DELRIO, Martin. *See* **DOYLE, Debra.**

DELRIO, Martin. *See* **MACDONALD, James D.**

DEL RIO, Nikki. *See* **GORDON, Lewis Ricardo.**

DELSOHN, Gary. American, b. 1952. **Genres:** Adult non-fiction. **Career:** Writer. Denver Post, Denver, CO, reporter; Sacramento Bee, Sacramento, CA, senior writer, 1989-. **Publications:** (with Alex English) The English Language, 1986; The Prosecutors: A Year in the Life of a District Attorney's

Office, 2003. Contributor to periodicals and Web sites. **Address:** c/o Author Mail, Dutton, 375 Hudson St., New York, NY 10014, U.S.A. **Online address:** gdelsohn@sacbee.com

DEL VALLE, Teresa. Spanish, b. 1937. **Genres:** History, Anthropology/Ethnology, Urban studies, Women's studies and issues. **Career:** Mercedarian Missionary Sisters, missionary in Guam; University of Guam, Mangilao, lecturer in history, 1969-72; East-West Center, Honolulu, HI, research assistant at Communications Institute, 1972-73, lecturer in anthropology, 1974-75; Universidad del Pais Vasco (University of the Basque Country), Donostia-San Sebastian, Spain, assistant professor, 1980-84, professor of social anthropology, 1984-, head of Dept of Social Anthropology, 1981-85, director of women's studies seminar, 1981-85, 1992-94. University of Nevada, Reno, research associate in Basque Studies Program, 1985-86, visiting professor, 1994; Princeton University, visiting fellow, 1986; University of Guam, associate member of Micronesian Area Research Center, 1989-. Conducted field studies in Guam, Micronesia, and Spain; script writer and field consultant for ethnographic documentary productions; public speaker. **Publications:** Social and Cultural Change in the Community of Umatac, Southern Guam, 1979; The Importance of the Mariana Islands to Spain at the Beginning of the Nineteenth Century, 1992; (ed.) Gendered Anthropology, 1993; Korrika Basque Ritual for Ethnic Identity, 1993. UNTRANSLATED WORKS: Mujer vasca, 1985; Una introduccion a las culturas oceanicas: Micronesia, 1987; (with others) La mujer y la palabra, 1987; Korrika: Rituales de la lengua en el espacio, 1988; (ed.) W.A. Douglass, Cultura vasca y su diaspora: Ensayos teoricos y descriptivos, 1991; (with C. Sanz) Genero y sexualidad, 1991; Mujeres en la ciudad, 1991; Andamios para una nueva ciudad. Lecturas desde le antropolegia, 1997; (ed.) Perspectivas feministas desde la antropologia social, 2000; Emakumeak Euskal Herrian, 2001; (with others) Modelos emergentes en los sistemas y en las relaciones de genero, 2002. Contributor to books and professional journals. **Address:** Facultad de Filosofia y Ciencias de la Educacion, Universidad del Pais Vasco, Apartado 1249, 20018 Donostia-San Sebastian, Spain. **Online address:** yvpvamut@sf.ehu.es

DELVES, Peter J(ohn). British, b. 1951. **Genres:** Medicine/Health. **Career:** University of London, England, reader in immunology. **Publications:** Encyclopedia of Immunology (ed. with I.M. Roitt), 1992, 2nd ed. (ed.-in-chief), 1998; (with I.M. Roitt) Slide Atlas of Essential Immunology, 1992; (ed.) Cellular Immunology Labfax, 1994; Essential Techniques: Antibody Applications, 1995; Essential Techniques: Antibody Production, 1997. **Address:** Department of Immunology, University College London, Windeyer Bldg, 46, Cleveland St, London W1P 6DB, England. **Online address:** p.delves@ucl.ac.uk

DELZELL, Charles F. American, b. 1920. **Genres:** History. **Career:** Professor Emeritus, Vanderbilt University, Nashville, Tennessee, since 1989 (Professor of History, 1952-89; Chairman, Dept. of History, 1970-73, 1983, 1986; Acting Director, Center for European Studies, 1985-86). Assistant Professor of History, University of Hawaii, Honolulu, 1949-50; Instructor in History, University of Oregon, Eugene, 1950-51. **Publications:** The Meaning of Yalta: Big Three Diplomacy and the New Balance of Power, 1956, 3rd ed. 1965; Mussolini's Enemies: The Italian Anti-Fascist Resistance, 1961, 1974; Italy in Modern Times, 1964; (ed.) The Unification of Italy, 1959-1961, 1965; Mediterranean Fascism, 1919-1945, 1970; (with H. A. Schmitt) Historians of Modern Europe, 1971; (with W. S. Sworakowski) World Communism: A Handbook 1918-1965, 1973; (ed.) The Papacy and Totalitarianism Between The Two World Wars, 1974; (ed.) The Future of History, 1977; Italy in the Twentieth Century, 1980. **Address:** Dept. of History, Vanderbilt University, Nashville, TN 37235, U.S.A.

DEMARAY, Donald E(ugene). American, b. 1926. **Genres:** Theology/Religion, Biography. **Career:** Seattle First Free Methodist Church, minister of youth, 1952-53; Seattle Pacific College, WA, School of Religion, dean, 1959-66; Asbury Theological Seminary, Wilmore, KY, associate professor, 1966-67, professor of preaching & speech, 1966-92, dean of students, 1967-75, Senior Beeson Professor of Preaching, 1992-, now emeritus. **Publications:** Basic Beliefs, 1958, rev. ed., 1996; Loyalty to Christ, 1958; Amazing Grace, 1958; The Acts, 1959; Questions Youth Ask, 1961; Acts (in Aldersgate series), 2 vols., 1961; Layman's Guide to the Bible, 1964, as Sourcebook of the Bible, 1971; Alive to God through Prayer, 1965, rev. ed. as How Are You Praying?, 1986; Preacher Aflame!, 1972; Pulpit Giants, 1973; An Introduction to Homiletics, 1974, rev. ed., 1991; A Guide to Happiness, 1974; The Minister's Ministries, 1974; The Practice of the Presence of God (paraphrase), 1975, 2nd ed., 1997; Near Hurting People: The Pastoral Ministry of Robert Moffat Fine, 1978; Proclaiming the Truth, 1980, rev. ed., 2001; Watch Out for Burnout, 1983; Snapshots, 1985; Laughter, Joy, and Healing, 1986, rev. ed., 1995; The Innovation of John Newton 1725-1807,

1988; Listen to Luther, 1989; The Little Flowers of St. Francis (paraphrase), 1992; The Daily Wesley, 1994, rev. ed., 1996; The Daily Roberts, 1996; Experiencing Healing and Wholeness, 1998; Prayers and Devotions of John Wesley, 1998; Wesley's Daily Prayers, 1998; Healing and Wholeness, 1999; With His Joy: The Life and Ministry of David McKenna, 2000. EDITOR: Prayers and Devotions of John Wesley, 1957; A Pulpit Manual, 1959; Prayers and Devotions of C. H. Spurgeon, 1960; Blow, Wind of God (anthology), 1975; Thomas a Kempis' Imitation of Christ, 1996; The Wesleys' Hymns & Poetry, 2003; (with K. Pickerill) A Robust Ministry, 2004. **Address:** Asbury Theological Seminary, Wilmore, KY 40390, U.S.A. **Online address:** don_demaray@asburyseminary.edu

DE MARINIS, Marco. Italian, b. 1949. **Genres:** Theatre. **Career:** University of Bologna, Italy, scholar in Degree Program in the Discipline of the Arts, Music, and Performance, 1972-80, researcher, 1981-87, associate professor, 1992-2000, professor of theater, 2000-; University of Macerata, associate professor of theater, 1988-91. International School of Theater Anthropology, staff scientific collaborator. **Publications:** Mimo e mimi, 1980; Semiotica del teatro, 1982, 2nd ed., 1992; Al limite del teatro, 1983; Il nuovo teatro, 1947-1970, 1987, 4th ed., 2000; Capire il teatro, 1988, 4th ed., 2000; Mimo e teatro nel 1900, 1993; The Semiotics of Performance, 1993; Drammaturgia dell'attore, 1997; La danza alla rovescia di Artaud, 1999; In cerca dell'attore, 2000. **Address:** Department of Music and Performance, University of Bologna, Via Barberia 4,40123, 40121 Bologna, Italy. **Online address:** demarinis@muspe.unibo.it

DE MARINIS, Rick. American, b. 1934. **Genres:** Novels, Novellas/Short stories. **Career:** University of Montana, Missoula, instructor in English, 1967-69; San Diego State University, California, associate professor of English, 1969-76; University of Texas, El Paso, professor of English, 1988-. Arizona State University, Tempe, visiting writer, 1980-81; Wichita State University, Kansas, distinguished writer-in-residence, 1986. Recipient, Drue Heinz Literature Prize, 1986, and American Academy and Institute of Arts and Letters Award in Literature, 1990. **Publications:** A Lovely Monster: The Adventures of Claude Rains and Dr. Tellenbeck, 1976; Scimitar, 1977; Cinder, 1978; Jack and Jill: Two Novellas and a Short Story, 1979; The Burning Women of Far Cry, 1986; Under the Wheat (stories), 1986; The Coming Triumph of the Free World (stories), 1988; The Year of the Zinc Penny, 1989; The Voice of America (stories), 1991; The Mortician's Apprentice (novel), 1994; Borrowed Hearts, 1999; The Art & Craft of the Short Story, 2000; A Clod of Wayward Marl, 2001; Sky Full of Sand, 2003; Apocalypse Then (stories), 2004. **Address:** 5612 Gharrett Ave, Missoula, MT 59803, U.S.A.

DEMARR, Mary Jean. American, b. 1932. **Genres:** Literary criticism and history, Bibliography. **Career:** Junior high school English and German teacher in Wausau, WI, 1955-56; Willamette University, Salem, OR, visiting assistant professor of English, 1964-65; Indiana State University, Terre Haute, assistant professor, 1965-70, associate professor, 1970-75, professor of English and women's studies, 1975-95, professor emerita, 1995-. **Publications:** (with J.S. Bakerman) Adolescent Female Portraits in the American Novel, 1961-1981: An Annotated Bibliography, 1983; (with Bakerman) The Adolescent in the American Novel since 1960, 1986; (ed. and contrib.) In the Beginning: First Novels in Mystery Series, 1995; Colleen McCullough: A Critical Companion, 1996; Barbara Kingsolver: A Critical Companion, 1999; Kaye Gibbons: A Critical Companion, 2003. Contributor to books. Contributor of articles and reviews to periodicals. **Address:** 594 Woodbine, Terre Haute, IN 47803, U.S.A. **Online address:** mjd594@msn.com

DE MEDICI, Lorenza. Italian, b. 1926. **Genres:** Food and Wine, Children's non-fiction. **Career:** Novita, Italy, editor of living section, 1949-54; writer, 1954-; Vogue Italia, food editor, 1962-66. Owner and operator of an antique shop and a weaving fabric store in Milan, 1972-82; host of "The de'Medici Kitchen" (fourteen-part television series), Public Broadcasting Service (PBS), beginning in 1982. Founder and teacher of "The Villa Table" (cooking classes), 1984-; makes annual tours of the United States to present cooking classes and demonstrations; guest on radio and television programs. **Publications:** I mille menu, 3 vols., 1967-68; La cucina dello zodiaco, 1968; I jolly della cucina, 12 vols., 1970-72; Tutto in tavola, 6 vols., 1980-82; La cucina Mediterranea, 1986; La cucina della badia, 1986; Il grande libro dei dolci, 1988, in US as Great Desserts, 1989; The Renaissance of Italian Cooking, 1989; Italy the Beautiful Cookbook, 1989; The Heritage of Italian Cooking, 1990; The Renaissance of Italian Gardens, 1990; The de Medici Kitchen, 1992; Tuscany the Beautiful Cookbook, 1992; Pasta, 1992; Pizza, 1993; Florentines: A Tuscan Feast, 1993; The Villa Table, 1993; Lorenza's Pasta, 1995. CHILDREN'S BOOKS: Giochiamo alla cucina, 1966; Giochiano con i fiori, 1966; Giochiamo con un filo, 1966; Giochiamo con gli animali, 1966. Contributor to periodicals. **Address:** Badia a Coltibuono, 53013 Gaiole in Chianti, Siena, Italy.

DEMERS, David (Pearce). American, b. 1953. **Genres:** Writing/Journalism, Communications/Media. **Career:** University of Wisconsin-River Falls, assistant professor of communication, 1991-95; University of Minnesota-Twin Cities, Minneapolis, assistant professor of communications, 1995-96; Washington State University, Pullman, assistant professor of communications, 1996-. **Publications:** The Menace of the Corporate Newspaper. **Address:** School of Communication, Washington State University, Pullman, WA 99164, U.S.A. **Online address:** ddemers@wsu.edu

DEMIDENKO, Helen. See DARVILLE, Helen (Fiona).

DEMIJOHN, Thom. See DISCH, Thomas M(ichael).

D'EMILIO, John. American, b. 1948. **Genres:** Civil liberties/Human rights, Gay and lesbian issues, History, Sex. **Career:** University of North Carolina at Greensboro, professor of U.S. history and gay history, 1983-; writer. National Gay and Lesbian Task Force, co-chair of board of directors, 1989-91; Center for Advanced Studies in the Behavioral Sciences, fellow, 1990-91; Humanities Research Centre, Australian National University, fellow, 1993. **Publications:** The Civil Rights Struggle: Leaders in Profile, 1979; Sexual Politics, Sexual Communities: The Making of a Homosexual Minority in the United States, 1940-1970, 1983; (with E. Freedman) Intimate Matters: A History of Sexuality in America, 1988; Making Trouble: Essays on Gay History, Politics, and the University, 1992; (ed. with others) Creating Change, 2000; The World Turned, 2002. **Address:** Department of Gender & Women's Studies (M/C 360), 1152A Behavioral Sciences Bldg, University of Illinois at Chicago, 1007 W Harrison St, Chicago, IL 60607-7137, U.S.A. **Online address:** demilioj@uic.edu

DEMILLE, Nelson (Richard). American, b. 1943. **Genres:** Novels, Mystery/Crime/Suspense. **Career:** Has had a variety of jobs, including carpenter, electrician's apprentice, house painter, art dealer, army officer, insurance investigator, and editorial asst. Free-lance writer, 1973-. **Publications:** By the Rivers of Babylon, 1978; Cathedral, 1981; The Talbot Odyssey, 1984; Word of Honor, 1985; The Charm School, 1988; The Gold Coast, 1990; The General's Daughter, 1992; Spencerville, 1994; Plum Island, 1997; The Lion's Game, 1999; Up Country, 2002; Night Fall, 2004. OTHER: (with T.H. Block) Mayday, 1979. Short stories appear in anthologies.

DE MILLE, Richard. American, b. 1922. **Genres:** Science fiction/Fantasy, Anthropology/Ethnology, Children's non-fiction, Philosophy, Biography. **Career:** Writer, 1953-. Television Director, KTLA, 1946-50; Psychometrician, University of Southern California, 1961-62; Lecturer in Psychology, University of California, Santa Barbara, 1962-65; Scientist, General Research Corp., 1967-70; Consulting Ed., 1973-84. **Publications:** Put Your Mother on the Ceiling: Children's Imagination Games, 1967; Castaneda's Journey, 1976, rev. ed., 2000; The Don Juan Papers, 1990, rev. ed., 2001; My Secret Mother: Lorna Moon, 1998. **Address:** 960 Lilac Dr, Montecito, CA 93108, U.S.A.

DEMING, Alison Hawthorne. American, b. 1946. **Genres:** Poetry, Essays. **Career:** Worked in public and women's health care for fifteen years; University of Southern Maine, Portland, instructor, 1983-87; Fine Arts Work Center, Provincetown, MA, coordinator of writing fellowship program, 1988-90; University of Arizona, Tucson, director of Poetry Center, 1990-2000, associate professor of creative writing, 1998-. Visiting lecturer in writing at Vermont College, 1983-85; guest lecturer. **Publications:** Science and Other Poems, 1994; Temporary Homelands (essays), 1994; (ed.) Poems of the American West: A Columbia Anthology, 1995; The Monarchs: A Poem Sequence, 1997; The Edges of the Civilized World, 1998; Writing the Sacred into the Real, 2000. Contributor of poems and essays to periodicals and anthologies. **Address:** Dept of English, University of Arizona, Tucson, AZ 85721, U.S.A. **Online address:** aldeming@aol.com

DEMOS, John Putnam. American, b. 1937. **Genres:** History. **Career:** Brandeis University, Waltham, MA, assistant professor, 1968-72, professor, 1972-86, chairman of department of history, c. 1984-86; Center for Psychosocial Studies, Chicago, IL, director, 1974-75; Yale University, New Haven, CT, professor of history, 1986-. Has served as a consultant to other private and governmental organizations. **Publications:** A Little Commonwealth: Family Life in Plymouth Colony, 1970; (ed.) Remarkable Providences, 1600-1760, 1972; (ed. with S.S. Boocock) Turning Points: Historical and Sociological Essays on the Family, 1978; Entertaining Satan: Witchcraft and the Culture of Early New England, 1982; Past, Present, and Personal, 1986; The Unredeemed Captive: A Family Story from Early America, 1994. Contributor of articles and book reviews to professional journals and other periodicals. **Address:** Department of History, Yale University, PO Box 208324, New Haven, CT 06520, U.S.A.

DEMOTT, Robert (James). American, b. 1943. **Genres:** Poetry, Literary criticism and history. **Career:** Ohio University, Athens, assistant professor, 1969-74, associate professor, 1974-79, professor of American literature, 1979-, Edwin and Ruth Kennedy Distinguished Professor, 1998-. **Publications:** (author of revision) H. and E. Landry, A Concordance to the Poems of Hart Crane, 1973; (ed. with S.E. Marovitz) Artful Thunder: Versions of the Romantic Tradition in American Literature in Honor of Howard P. Vincent, 1975; Robinson Jeffers' Tamar, In: The Twenties, 1975; Steinbeck's Reading: A Catalogue of Books Owned and Borrowed, 1984; (ed.) J. Steinbeck, Working Days: The Journals of the Grapes of Wrath, 1938-1941, 1989; (author of intro.) J. Steinbeck, The Grapes of Wrath, 1992; Poetry: News of Loss, 1995; Steinbeck's Typewriter, 1996; Dave Smith, 2000; The Weather in Athens: Poems, 2001. Contributor to periodicals. **Address:** Department of English, 331 Ellis Hall, Ohio University, Athens, OH 45701, U.S.A. **Online address:** demott@ohio.edu

DEMOTT, Wes. American, b. 1952. **Genres:** Mystery/Crime/Suspense. **Career:** Federal Bureau of Investigation, Washington, DC, special agent, 1982-85; independent businessperson in Virginia, Florida, and Ohio, 1985-95; writer, 1995-. Aetna (insurance company), worked as a property claims representative. **Publications:** SUSPENSE NOVELS: Walking K, 1998; Vapors, 1999; Jasperville, forthcoming. **Address:** 4281 7th Ave SW, Naples, FL 34119-4029, U.S.A. **Online address:** WDeMott@aol.com

DEMPSEY, Charles (Gates). American, b. 1937. **Genres:** Art/Art history. **Career:** Educator and art historian. American Academy, Rome, Italy, fellow in the history of art; Bryn Mawr College, Bryn Mawr, PA, 1965-80, began as assistant professor, became professor of history of art, chair, 1975-80; Johns Hopkins University, Baltimore, MD, professor of Italian Renaissance and Baroque art, 1980-; Johns Hopkins Center for Italian Studies, Florence, Italy, director of studies, 1980-85. Visiting professor in the United States, France, and Australia; served on boards and advisory panels. **Publications:** Annibale Carracci and the Beginnings of Baroque Style, 1977, rev. ed, 2000; La galerie des Carrache, 1984; The Portrayal of Love: Botticelli's Primavera and Humanist Culture at the Time of Lorenzo the Magnificent, 1992; Annibale Carracci, the Farnese Gallery, 1995; (with E. Cropper) Nicolas Poussin: Friendship and the Love of Painting, 1996; (ed. and author of intro) Quattrocento Adriatico: Fifteenth-century Art of the Adriatic Rim (colloquium), 1996; Inventing the Renaissance Putto, 2001. Contributor of articles and reviews to periodicals and journals. Contributor to English and foreign-language books. **Address:** Dept. of the History of Art, Mergenthaler Hall, Johns Hopkins University, 3400 North Charles St., Baltimore, MD 21218, U.S.A. **Online address:** charles.dempsey@jhu.edu

DEMSKI, Joel S. American, b. 1940. **Genres:** Business/Trade/Industry. **Career:** Columbia University, NYC, research associate, 1966-67, assistant professor of business, 1967-68; Stanford University, Stanford, CA, assistant professor, 1968-70, associate professor, 1970-73, professor of information and accounting systems, 1973-79, Paul Holden Professor, 1979-84, Joan E. Horngren Professor, 1984-85; Yale University, New Haven, CT, Milton Steinback Professor of Information and Accounting Systems, 1985-94; University of Florida, Gainesville, Frederick E. Fisher Eminent Scholar in Accounting, 1994-. Visiting faculty member, University of Chicago, 1974-75, University of Michigan, 1981-82, and Odense University, 1990. **Publications:** Information Analysis, 1972, 2nd ed, 1980; (with N. Dopuch and J. Birnberg) Cost Accounting: Accounting Data for Management's Decisions, 2nd ed, 1974, 3rd ed, 1982; (with G. Feltham) Cost Determination: A Conceptual Approach, 1976; (ed. with Dopuch and S. Zeff) Essays in Honor of William A. Paton, 1979; Managerial Uses of Accounting Information, 1994. Contributor to books. Contributor to accounting and business journals. **Address:** P.O. Box 117160, Fisher School of Accounting, University of Florida, Gainesville, FL 32611, U.S.A.

DE MUNCK, Victor C. American (born Netherlands), b. 1948. **Genres:** Anthropology/Ethnology. **Career:** University of New Hampshire, Durham, assistant professor, 1993-98; State University of New York College at New Paltz, assistant professor of anthropology, 1998-. **Publications:** Seasonal Cycles, 1993; (ed. and contrib.) Romantic Love and Sexual Behavior: Perspectives from the Social Sciences, 1998; Methods in the Field, 1998; Contemporary Issues in Psychological Anthropology, in press. **Address:** Department of Anthropology, State University of New York College at New Paltz, New Paltz, NY 12561, U.S.A. **Online address:** victor@bestweb.net

DE NEUFVILLE, Richard. American, b. 1939. **Genres:** Engineering, Technology, Transportation. **Career:** White House Fellow, Washington, DC, 1965-66; Massachusetts Institute of Technology, Cambridge, Assistant to Associate Professor, 1966-75, Professor and Chairman, Technology and Policy

Program, 1975-; Visiting professor: London Graduate School of Business, 1973-74, University of California, Berkeley, 1974-75, 1978, Ecole Centrale de Paris, 1981-82; Ecole Nationale des Ponts et Chaussees, Paris, 1986-; U.S. Japan Leadership Fellow, Tokyo, 1990-91; University of Bristol, 1992-99; Oxford University, 2001; University of Cambridge, 2002-. **Publications:** (with J. Stafford) Systems Analysis for Engineers and Managers, 1971; (with D.H. Marks) Systems Planning and Design, 1974; Airport Systems Planning, 1976; Applied Systems Analysis, 1990; Airport Systems Planning, Design and Management, 2003. **Address:** Room E40-245, MIT, Cambridge, MA 02139, U.S.A. **Online address:** ardent@mit.edu

DENG, Francis Mading. Sudanese, b. 1938. **Genres:** Area studies, History. **Career:** Sudanese Ambassador to Scandinavia, 1972-74; Sudanese Ambassador to the United States, 1974-76; Minister of State for Foreign Affairs (Sudan) Khartoum, Sudan, 1976-80; Sudanese Ambassador to Canada (Minister of State), 1980-83; The Brookings Institution, Washington, DC, senior fellow, 1988-. Yale Law School, visiting lecturer; representative of the United Nations Secretary-General on Internally Displaced Persons, 1992-. **Publications:** Tradition and Modernization: a Challenge for Law among the Dinka of the Sudan, 1971; The Dinka of the Sudan, 1972; The Dinka and Their Songs, 1973; Dynamics of Identification: A Basis for National Integration in the Sudan, 1973; Dinka Folktales: African Stories from the Sudan, 1974; Africans of Two Worlds: The Dinka in Afro-Arab Sudan, 1978; Dinka Cosmology, 1980; Security Problems: An African Predicament, 1981; Recollections of Babo Nimir, 1982; Seed of Redemption: A Political Novel, 1986; The Man Called Deng Majok: A Biography of Power, Polygyny, and Change, 1986; Cry of the Owl (novel), 1989; (with M.W. Daly) Bonds of Silk: The Human Factor in the British Administration of the Sudan, 1990; (with L. Minear) The Challenges of Famine Relief: Emergency Operations in the Sudan, 1992; Protecting the Dispossessed: A Challenge for the International Community, 1993; War of Visions: Conflict of Identities in the Sudan, 1995; Sovereignty as Responsibility: Conflict Management in Africa, 1996. EDITOR: (with R.O. Collins) The Britain in the Sudan, 1898-1956: The Sweetness and the Sorrow, 1984; (with P. Gifford) The Search for Peace and Unity in the Sudan, 1987; (with A. An-Naim) Human Rights in Africa: Cross-Cultural Perspectives, 1990; (with I.W. Zartman) Conflict Resolution in Africa, 1991. Contributor to periodicals. **Address:** The Brookings Institution, 1775 Massachusetts Ave. NW, Washington, DC 20036, U.S.A.

DENG XIAOHUA. Also writes as Can Xue. Chinese, b. 1953. **Career:** Writer. **Publications:** TRANSLATED BY R.R. JANSSEN & JIAN ZHANG: Dialogues in Paradise, 1989; Old Floating Cloud: Two Novellas, 1991; A Perfromance of Breakthrough (novel), 1988; The Embroiderd Shoes, 1997. **Address:** room 1512, Mu Dan Bei Li 5#, Hai Dian Qu, Beijing 100083, People's Republic of China. **Online address:** dengxiaohua2001@sina.com.cn

DENHAM, Andrew. British. **Genres:** Politics/Government. **Career:** University of Nottingham, England, faculty member of law and social sciences. **Publications:** Think-Tanks of the New Right, 1996; (with M. Garnett) British Think-Tanks and the Climate of Opinion, 1998; (with M. Garnett) Keith Joseph (biography), 2001. EDITOR: (with D. Stone and M. Garnett) Think-Tanks across Nations: A Comparative Approach, 1998; (with D. Stone) Think Tank Traditions, 2004. Contributor to periodicals. **Address:** School of Politics, University of Nottingham, Nottingham NG7 2RD, England. **Online address:** andrew.denham@nottingham.ac.uk

DENHAM, James M. American, b. 1957. **Genres:** History. **Career:** Georgia Southern University, instructor, 1987; Limestone College, Gaffney, SC, assistant professor of history, 1987-91; Florida Southern College, professor of history, 1991-, director of Center for Florida History, 2001-. Summer institutes/fellowships: University of SC, 1990; US Military Academy, West Point, 1993; W.E.B. DuBois Institute, Harvard University, 1999; National Humanities Center, Research Triangle Park, NC, 2000; Columbia University. **Publications:** A Rogue's Paradise: Crime and Punishment in Antebellum Florida, 1821-1861, 1997; (with C. Brown Jr.) Cracker Times and Pioneer Lives: The Florida Reminiscences of George Gillette Keen and Sarah Pamela Williams, 2000; (with W.W. Rogers) Florida Sheriffs: A History, 1821-1945, 2001; (ed. with K. Huneycutt) Echoes from a Distant Frontier: The Brown Sisters' Correspondence in Antebellum Florida, 2004. Contributor to books. Contributor of articles and reviews to journals and periodicals. **Address:** History Dept, Florida Southern College, 111 Lake Hollingsworth Dr, Lakeland, FL 33801-5698, U.S.A. **Online address:** jdenham@flsouthern.edu

DEN HARTOG, Kristen. (born Canada), b. 1965. **Genres:** Adult non-fiction. **Career:** Author, florist. **Publications:** Water Wings (novel), 2001; The Perpetual Ending (novel), 2002. Work represented in anthologies and contributor to periodicals. **Address:** c/o Author Mail, MacAdam/Cage, 1900 Wazee St., Suite 210, Denver, CO 80202, U.S.A.

DENIS, Rafael Cardoso. (born Brazil), b. 1964. **Genres:** Novels. **Career:** Universidade do Estado do Rio de Janeiro, Rio de Janeiro, Brazil, adjunct professor, 1996-2000; Pontifícia Universidade Católica, Rio de Janeiro, assistant professor, 2000-. **Publications:** (editor, with Colin Trodd, and contributor) Art and the Academy in the Nineteenth Century, 2000; Uma introdução à história do design, 2000; A maneira negra (fiction), 2000; Controle remoto (novel), 2002. Some writings appear under the name Rafael Cardoso. **Address:** c/o Author Mail, Editora Record, Rua Argentina 171, 20921-380 Rio de Janeiro, Brazil. **Online address:** rafaelcd@dsg.puc-rio.br

DENKER, Henry. American, b. 1912. **Genres:** Novels, Plays/Screenplays. **Career:** Member of the Council, Dramatists' Guild, 1970-73, Author's League, 1984-89. **Publications:** I'll Be Right Home, Ma, 1947; My Son, the Lawyer, 1949; Salome: Princess of Galilee, 1951; The First Easter, 1951; Time Limit! (play), 1957; Far Country (play), 1961; A Case of Libel (play), 1963; What Did We Do Wrong? (play), 1967; The Director, 1970; The Kingmaker, 1972; A Place for the Mighty, 1974; The Physicians, 1975; The Experiment, 1976; The Headhunters (play), 1976; The Starmaker, 1977; The Scofield Diagnosis, 1977; The Second Time Around (play), 1977; The Actress, 1978; Error of Judgment, 1979; Horowitz and Mrs. Washington, 1979, as play, 1980; The Warfield Syndrome, 1981; Outrage, 1982, as play, 1983, as film, 1985; The Healers, 1983; Kincaid, 1984; Robert, My Son, 1985; Judge Spencer Dissents, 1986; The Choice, 1987; The Retreat, 1988; Gift of Life, 1989; Payment in Full, 1991; Doctory on Trial, 1992; Mrs. Washington and Horowitz, Too, 1993; Labyrinth, 1994; This Child Is Mine, 1995; To Marcy, with Love, 1996; A Place for Kathy, 1997; Tea with Madame Bernhardt (play), 1998; Clarence, 1998; Curtain Call (play), 1999; Class Action, 2000; Benjie (novel), 2001. **Address:** 241 Central Park W, New York, NY 10024, U.S.A.

DENNETT, Nolan A. American, b. 1950. **Genres:** Novels. **Career:** St. Louis Conservatory and School for the Arts, St. Louis, MO, director of dance, 1974-78; Chicago Moving Company, Chicago, IL, artist in residence, 1978-81; University of California, Santa Barbara, teacher of drama and dance, 1981-88; San Jose State University, San Jose, CA, associate professor of dance, 1988-89; Western Washington University, Bellingham, movement specialist and member of theater arts faculty, 1989-. Metro Theater Circus, principal performer and choreographer, 1975-78; Dance Kaleidium of St. Louis, artistic director, 1976-78; Repertory-West Dance Company, principal dancer, 1981-88, artistic director, 1987-88; San Francisco Moving Company, principal dancer, 1988-89; National Ballet of Peru, guest choreographer, 1989; writer. DePaul University, faculty member at Goodman School of Drama, 1980-81; Wright State University, guest faculty member, 1981; Western Washington University, guest faculty member, summers, 1982-86. Producer and director of videotape documentaries. **Publications:** Place of Shelter (novel), 1994. Work represented in anthologies. Contributor of articles and stories to periodicals. **Address:** Dance Program, Western Washington University, Bellingham, WA 98225, U.S.A.

DENNEY, Robert (Eugene). American, b. 1929. **Genres:** History. **Career:** U.S. Marine Corps, 1947-50, served in China, then as squad leader and later platoon sergeant in Guam, beginning in 1948, stationed in Quantico, VA, until 1950; U.S. Army, 1950-67, drill instructor at Fort Knox, KY, 1950, staff sergeant, c. 1950, during Korean War served in intelligence unit operating in North Korea, 1951-52, first sergeant, 1953-54, sergeant major, 1954-55, warrant officer, 1956, chief warrant officer, mid-1950s, assistant operations officer in Hanau, Hesse, West Germany, 1957, deputy director, helicopter navigation systems test, 1958-60, captain, signal corps, project officer, at Fort Huachuca, AZ, 1960-63, project officer at Fort Benning, GA, early 1964-65, during Vietnam War served as project officer in Vietnam, 1966, as major, operations officer at Fort Belvoir, VA, 1967, retired, 1967; worked in computer industry as project manager, systems designer, systems integrator, developer, and configuration management specialist, for twenty-two years; writer. **Publications:** The Civil War Years: A Daily Account of the Life of a Nation, 1992; Civil War Prisons Escapes: A Day-by-Day Chronicle, 1993; Civil War Medicine: Care & Comfort of the Wounded, 1994. **Address:** 6106 Cloud Dr., Springfield, VA 22150, U.S.A.

DENT, David J. American. **Genres:** Air/Space topics. **Career:** Journalist, educator, and author. Has worked as a television reporter for the American Broadcasting Companies, Inc. (ABC); New York University, New York, NY, associate professor of journalism and mass communication. Contributing correspondent to Black Entertainment Television News; has also appeared as a commentator on Court TV. **Publications:** In Search of Black America: Discovering the African American Dream, 2000. Contributor to magazines and newspapers. **Address:** New York University, Department of Journalim, Arthur Carter Hall, 10 Washington Pl., New York, NY 10003, U.S.A. **Online address:** dd2@nyu.edu

DENT, Richard J. American, b. 1951. **Genres:** Anthropology/Ethnology. **Career:** American University, Washington, DC, associate professor of anthropology and head of department, 1988-. **Publications:** Chesapeake Prehistory, 1995. **Address:** Department of Anthropology, American University, Washington, DC 20016, U.S.A. **Online address:** potomac@american.edu

DE PALCHI, Alfredo. Italian, b. 1926. **Genres:** Poetry. **Career:** Poet. Chelsea and Chelsea Editions, editor and publisher. **Publications:** POETRY: Sessioni con l'analista, 1967, trans by I.L. Salomon as Sessions with My Analyst, 1970; Mutazioni, 1988; The Scorpion's Dark Dance, trans. by S. Raiziss, 1993, 2nd ed., 1995; Costellazione Anonima, 1998; Anonymous Constellation, trans. by S. Raiziss, 1997; Addictive Aversions, trans. by S. Raiziss and others, 1999; Paradigma, 2001. EDITOR: (of Italian section, with S. Raiziss) Modern European Poetry, 1966; (with M. Palma) The Metaphysical Streetcar Conductor: Sixty Poems by Luciano Erba, 1998. Contributor of poems to magazines.

DEPAOLA, Tomie. (Thomas Anthony dePaola). American, b. 1934. **Genres:** Novellas/Short stories, Children's fiction, Children's non-fiction. **Career:** Freelance artist and designer, 1956-. Instructor, 1962-63, and Assistant Professor of Art, 1963-66, College of the Sacred Heart, Newton, MA; Assistant Professor of Art, San Francisco College for Women, 1967-70; Instructor in Art, Chamberlayne Jr. College, Boston, 1972-73; Associate Professor in Speech and Theatre, Colby-Sawyer College, New London, NH, 1973-76; Associate Professor of Art, 1976-78, and Artist-in-Residence, 1978-79, New England College, Henniker, NH. **Publications:** The Wonderful Dragon of Timlin, 1966; Fight the Night, 1968; Joe and the Snow, 1968; Parker Pig, Esquire, 1969; The Journey of the Kiss, 1970; The Monsters' Ball, 1970; The Wind and the Sun, 1972; Andy, That's My Name, 1973; Charlie Needs a Cloak, 1973; Nana Upstairs and Nana Downstairs, 1973; The Unicorn and the Moon, 1973; Watch Out for the Chicken Feet in Your Soup, 1974; The Cloud Book, 1975; Michael Bird-Boy, 1975; Strega Nona, 1975; Things to Make and Do for Valentine's Day, 1976; When Everyone Was Fast Asleep, 1976; Four Stories for Four Seasons, 1977; Helga's Dowry, 1977; The Quicksand Book, 1977; Bill and Pete, 1978; The Christmas Pageant, 1978; The Clown of God, 1978; Criss-Cross, Applesauce, 1978; Pancakes for Breakfast, 1978; The Popcorn Book, 1978; Big Anthony and the Magic Ring, 1979; Flicks, 1979; The Kids' Cat Book, 1979; Oliver Button Is a Sissy, 1979; Songs of the Fog Maiden, 1979; The Family Christmas Tree Book, 1980; The Knight and the Dragon, 1980; The Lady of Guadalupe, 1980; The Legend of Old Befana, 1980; The Prince of the Dolomites, 1980; Fin M'Coul, 1981; The Hunter and the Animals, 1981; Now One Foot, Now the Other, 1981; Francis, the Poor Man of Assisi, 1982; Giorgio's Village, 1982; Strega Nona's Magic Lessons, 1982; The Legend of the Bluebonnet, 1983; Marianna May and Nursey, 1983; Noah and the Ark, 1983; Sing, Pierrot, Sing, 1983; The Story of the Three Wise Kings; Tomie dePaola's Country Farm, 1984; Tomie dePaola's Mother Goose Story Streamers, 1984; The Mysterious Giant of Barletta, 1984; David and Goliath, 1984; The First Christmas, 1984; Tomie dePaola's Mother Goose, 1985; Tomie dePaola's Favorite Nursery Tales, 1986; Merry Christmas, Strega Nona, 1986; Queen Esther, 1986; Katie, Kit and Cousin Tom, 1986; Pajamas for Kit, 1986; Bill and Pete Go Down the Nile, 1987; Tomie dePaola's Book of Christmas Carols, 1987; An Early American Christmas, 1987; The Parables of Jesus, 1987; The Miracles of Jesus, 1987; The Legend of the Indian Paintbrush, 1988; Tomie dePaola's Book of Poems, 1988; Baby's First Christmas, 1988; Haircuts for the Woolseys, 1989; Too Many Hopkins, 1989; The Art Lesson, 1989; Tony's Bread, 1989; My First Chanukah, 1989; Little Grunt and the Big Egg, 1990; Tomie dePaola's Book of Bible Stories, 1990; My First Easter, 1991; My First Passover, 1991; Bonjour, Mr. Satie, 1991; My First Halloween, 1991; My First Thanksgiving, 1992; Jamie O'Rourke and The Big Potato, 1992; Jingle the Christmas Clown, 1992; Patrick, Patron Saint of Ireland, 1992; Stega Nona, 1993; Tom The Legend of the Persian Carpet, 1993; The Legend of the Poinsettia, 1994; Kit & Kat, 1994; Christopher, the Holy Giant, 1994; Country Angel Christmas, 1995; Strega Nona Meets Her Match, 1996; Get Dressed, Santa, 1996; The Baby Sister, 1996; The Bubble Factory, 1996; Days of the Blackbird, 1997; Antonio the Bread Boy, 1997; Bill and Pete to the Rescue, 1998; Big Anthony, 1998; Erandi's Braids, 1999; 26 Fairmont Avenue, 1999; The Night of Las Posadas, 1999; Jamie O'Rourke and the Pooka, 2000; Tomie dePaola's Mother Goose Favorites, 2000; Tomie dePaola's Rhyme Time, 2000; Here We All Are, 2000; Strega Nona Takes a Vacation, 2000; On My Way, 2001; Meet the Barkers, 2001; Boss for a Day, 2001; What a Year, 2002; Tomie's Little Christmas Pageant, 2002; T-Rex Is Missing!, 2002; New Barker in the House, 2002; Hide-and-Seek All Week, 2002; Four Friends at Christmas, 2002; Adelita, 2002; Trouble in the Barkers' Class, 2003; Things Will Never Be the Same, 2003; Marcos, 2003; Marcos Counts, 2003; Four Friends in Summer, 2003; Tomie's Little Book of Poems, 2004; Pascual and the Kitchen Angels, 2004; Guess Who's Coming to Santa's for Dinner?, 2004; Four Friends in Autumn, 2004. Illustrator of books by M. Frith, A. Prager. **Address:** c/o Author Mail, Penguin Young Readers Group, 345 Hudson St, New York, NY 10014, U.S.A. **Online address:** www.tomie.com

DE PAOR, Louis. Irish, b. 1961. **Genres:** Poetry, Literary criticism and history. **Career:** Poet, songwriter, editor, and educator. Three Words for Green (group of musicians and dancers), Australia, founder, 1987-96; National University of Ireland, Galway, director of Irish studies. **Publications:** Próca solais is luatha: dánta 1980-87, 1988; Innti 13 (poems), 1990; (with S.O. Tuama) Coiscéim na haoise seo (poems), 1991; Faoin mblaoisc bheag sin (criticism), 1991; 30 dán, 1992; Aimsir bhreicneach/Freckled Weather (poems), 1993; Seo., siúd., agus uile. (poems), 1996; Goban cré is cloch/Sentences of Earth and Stone (poems), 1996; (with S.O. Tuama) Leabhar Sheáin Uí Thuama (poems), 1997; Corcach agus Dánta Eile, 1999; An Illuminated Celtic Book of Days, 1999; (ed.) M. Davitt, Freacnairc mhearcair: rogha dánta 1970-1998/The Oomph of Quicksilver: Selected Poems 1970-1998, 2000. Author of songs in Irish with J. Spillane. Contributor to books and periodicals. **Address:** National University of Ireland, Centre for Irish Studies, Galway, Ireland. **Online address:** louis.depaor@nuigalway.ie

DERBY, Sally. American, b. 1934. **Genres:** Children's fiction, Picture/board books. **Career:** Teacher (retired), writer. **Publications:** The Mouse Who Owned the Sun, 1993; Jacob and the Stranger, 1994; King Kenrick's Splinter, 1994; My Steps, 1996; Taiko on a Windy Night, 2001; Hannah's Bookmobile Christmas, 2001; Two Fools and a Horse, 2003; The Wacky Substitute, 2005. **Address:** 770 Southmeadow Circle, Cincinnati, OH 45231, U.S.A. **Online address:** derbymiller@fuse.net

DER DERIAN, James (Arthur). American, b. 1955. **Genres:** Politics/Government. **Career:** University of Massachusetts at Amherst, professor of political science, 1984-. Oxford University, lecturer, 1982-83, visiting fellow of St. Antony's College, 1995; Columbia University, lecturer, 1984; teacher at Gardner and Lancaster State Prisons, 1986-91; University of Southern California, senior research fellow at Center for International Studies, 1988; Massachusetts Institute of Technology, visiting scholar at Center for International Studies, 1991-92; guest lecturer at colleges and universities in the United States and abroad. Producer and moderator of a radio and television series Great Decisions, broadcast by college and community networks, 1985-90; consultant to 60 Minutes; guest on television and radio programs in the United States and Australia. **Publications:** On Diplomacy: A Genealogy of Western Estrangement, 1987; (ed. with M. Shapiro, and contrib.) International/Intertextual Relations: Postmodern Readings of World Politics, 1989; Antidiplomacy: Spies, Speed, Terror, and War, 1992; (ed. and contrib.) International Theory: Critical Investigations, 1995; Virtual Security, 1996; The Virilio Reader, in press. Contributor to books. Contributor of articles and reviews to periodicals. **Address:** Department of Political Science, Thompson Hall, University of Massachusetts at Amherst, Amherst, MA 01003, U.S.A.

DERESKE, Jo. American, b. 1947. **Genres:** Mystery/Crime/Suspense, Children's fiction. **Career:** Freelance writer; author of mystery novels and children's books; librarian. Western Washington University, Bellingham, WA, interlibrary loan librarian, 1978-88; Corridor Information Services, owner-operator, 1983-87; Whatcom Community College, Bellingham, WA, librarian. **Publications:** CHILDREN'S BOOKS: Glom Gloom, 1985; The Lone Sentinel, 1989; My Cousin, the Poodle, 1991. MYSTERY NOVELS: Miss Zukas and the Library Murders, 1994; Miss Zukas and the Island Murders, 1995; Miss Zukas and the Stroke of Death, 1996; Miss Zukas and the Raven's Dance, 1996; Savage Cut, 1996; Cut and Dry, 1997; Out of Circulation, 1997; Final Notice, 1998; Short Cut, 1998; Miss Zukas in Death's Shadow, 1999; Miss Zukas Shelves the Evidence, 2001. Contributor of articles and short stories to periodicals. **Address:** 4943 Reese Hill Rd., Sumas, WA 98295-8602, U.S.A.

DERFLER, (Arnold) Leslie. American, b. 1933. **Genres:** History. **Career:** Professor of History, Florida Atlantic University, Boca Raton, since 1969. Member of faculty, Carnegie Mellon University, Pittsburgh, 1962-68, and University of Massachusetts, Amherst, 1968-69. **Publications:** (ed.) The Dreyfus Affair: Tragedy of Errors, 1963; The Third French Republic 1870-1940, 1966; Socialism since Marx, 1973; Alexandre Millerand: The Socialist Years, 1977; (ed.) Hindi, 1977; President and Parliament: A Short History of the French Presidency, 1984; (ed.) An Age of Conflict, 1990, rev. ed., 1995; Paul Lafargue and the Founding of French Marxism, 1991; Paul Lafargue and the Flowering of French Socialism, 1998. **Address:** Dept. of History, Florida Atlantic University, Boca Raton, FL 33431, U.S.A. **Online address:** derflerl@fau.edu

DERKSEN, Jeff. Canadian, b. 1958. **Genres:** Poetry. **Career:** Artspeak Gallery, Vancouver, BC, founding board member, 1986-95; The New Gallery,

Calgary, AB, board member, 1994-95; Writing magazine, Vancouver, BC, editor, 1989-93; Kootenay School of Writing, Vancouver, BC, founding board member, 1984-. **Publications:** POETRY: Memory Is the Only Thing Holding Me Back, 1984; Until (chapbook), 1987; Down Time, 1990; Selfish (chapbook), 1993; Dwell, 1994. **Address:** c/o Kootenay School of Writing, 201-505 Hamilton St, Vancouver, BC, Canada V6B 2R1.

DE ROMILLY, Jacqueline (David). French, b. 1913. **Genres:** Classics. **Career:** Schoolteacher; University of Lille, professor of ancient Greek, 1949-57; University of Paris, France, professor of ancient Greek, 1957-73; College de France, 1973-84; Academie francaise, 1988-. Harvard University, Jackson Lecturer; University of Michigan, Jerome Lecturer; Cornell University, Messenger Lecturer, 1967. **Publications:** Thucydide et l'imperialisme athenien, 1947, trans. as Thucydides and Athenian Imperialism, 1973; Time in Greek Tragedy, 1968; Magic and Rhetoric in Ancient Greece, 1975; The Rise and Fall of States according to Greek Authors, 1977; Precis de Litterature grecque, 1980, trans. as A Short History of Greek Literature, 1985; Les grands sophistes dans l'Athenes de Pericles, 1988, trans. as The Great Sophists in Periclean Athens, 1992. UNTRANSLATED WORKS: Histoire et raison chez Thucydide, 1956; La crainte et l'angoisse dans le theatre d'Eschyle, 1958; L'evolution du pathetique, 1960; Nous autres professeurs, 1969; La tragedie grecque, 1970; La loi dans la pensee grecque, 1971; Problemes de la democratie grecque, 1975; La douceur dans la pensee grecque, 1979; "Patience mon coeur": L'essor de la psychologie dans la litterature grecque classique, 1984; L'enseignement en detresse, 1984; Homere, 1985; La modernite d'Euripide, 1986; Sur les chemins de Sainte-Victoire, 1987, rev. ed., 2002; La Grece antique a la decouverte de la liberte, 1989; (ed., trans., and author of notes) Thucydide: La guerre du Peloponnese, 5 vols., Belles Lettres, 1953-79, 1990; La construction de la Verite chez Thucydide, 1990; Ouverture a coeur, 1990; Ecrits sur l'enseignement, 1991; Pourquoi la Grece? 1992; Les oeufs de Paques (stories), 1993; Lettre aux parents sur les choix scolaires, 1993; Rencontres avec la Grece antique, 1995; Tragedies grecques au fil des ans, 1995; Alcibiade, 1995; Hector, 1997; Le Tresor des Savoirs oublies, 1998; Laisse flotter les rubans (short stories), 1999; La Grece antique contre la violence, 2000; Heros tragiques, heros lyriques, 2000; Sous de dehors si calmes (short stories), 2002; Une certaine idee de la Grece, 2003; De la flute a la lyre, 2004. **Address:** Academie francaise, 23 quai Conti, 75006 Paris, France.

DE ROSSO, Diana. British, b. 1921. **Genres:** Novels, Autobiography/Memoirs, Biography. **Career:** Writer since 1982. Opera and concert singer in Dublin, London, Italy, Yugoslavia, Scandinavia, and Austria, 1941-62; Restaurateur in Sussex, 1972-88. **Publications:** A Personal Biography of James Mason, 1989; A Life of Intrigue (autobiography), 1991.

DERR, Mark (Burgess). American, b. 1950. **Genres:** History, Biography. **Career:** Writer. **Publications:** NONFICTION: Some Kind of Paradise, 1989, repr., 1998; Over Florida, 1992; The Frontiersman: The Real Life and Many Legends of Davy Crockett (biography), 1993; Dog's Best Friend: Annals of the Dog-Human Relationship, 1997; A Dog's History of America: How Our Best Friend Explored, Conquered, and Settled a Continent, 2004. Contributor to periodicals.

DERRETT, (John) Duncan (Martin). British, b. 1922. **Genres:** Law, Theology/Religion. **Career:** Lecturer in Hindu Law, School of Oriental and African Studies, 1949-56, Reader in Oriental Laws, 1956-65, and Professor of Oriental Laws, 1965-82, University of London; Lecturer in Hindu Law, Inns of Court School of Law, London, 1965-79; Wilde Lecturer in Natural and Comparative Religion, University of Oxford, 1978-81. **Publications:** The Hoysalas, 1957; Hindu Law Past and Present, 1957; Introduction to Modern Hindu Law, 1963; (ed. and co-author) Studies in the Law of Succession in Nigeria, 1965; Religion, Law and the State in India, 1968; (ed. and co-author) Introduction to Legal Systems, 1968; Law in the New Testament, 1970; Critique of Modern Hindu Law, 1970; Jesus's Audience, 1973; (trans. and ed.) R. Lingat, Classical Law of India, 1973; Henry Swinburne 1551-1624, 1973; Dharmasastra and Juridical Literature, 1973; Bharuci's Commentary on the Manusmrti, 1975; Essays in Classical and Modern Hindu Law, 4 vols., 1976-78; Studies in the New Testament, 6 vols., 1977-95; Death of a Marriage Law, 1978; (ed. and co-author) The Concept of Duty in South Asia, 1978; Beitrage zu Indischem Rechtsdenken, 1979; The Anastasis, 1982; A Textbook for (Buddhist) Novices, 1983; The Making of Mark, 1985; New Resolutions of Old Conundrums (on Luke), 1986; The Ascetic Discourse, 1989; The Victim, the Johannine Passion Narrative, 1993; The Sermon on the Mount, 1994; Prophecy in the Cotswolds, 1803-1947, 1994; Two Masters: The Buddha and Jesus, 1995; Some Telltale Words in New Testament, 1996; Law and Morality, 1998; The Bible and the Buddhists, 2000. **Address:** Half Way House, High St, Blockley, Moreton-in-Marsh, Glos. GL56 9EX, England.

DERRY, John (Wesley). British, b. 1933. **Genres:** History, Biography. **Career:** Emmanuel College, Cambridge, Research Fellow, 1959-61; London School of Economics, assistant lecturer, 1961-63, lecturer, 1963-65; Downing College, Cambridge, Director of Studies in History, and Fellow, 1965-70; University of Newcastle upon Tyne, lecturer, 1970-73, Sr. lecturer, 1973-77, Reader 1977-92, professor, 1992-98, Emeritus professor of Modern British History, 1998-. **Publications:** William Pitt, 1962; Reaction and Reform, 1963, 3rd ed. 1970; The Regency Crisis and the Whigs, 1963; Parliamentary Reform, 1966; The Radical Tradition, 1967; Political Parties, 1968; (ed.) Cobbett's England. 1968; Charles James Fox, 1972; Castlereagh, 1976; English Politics and the American Revolution, 1976; Politics in the Age of Fox, Pitt and Liverpool, 1990; Charles, Earl Grey 1992. **Address:** Dept. of History, University of Newcastle upon Tyne, Newcastle NE1 7RU, England.

DERSHOWITZ, Alan M. American, b. 1938. **Genres:** Civil liberties/Human rights, Criminology/True Crime, Law, Psychiatry. **Career:** Civil liberties lawyer since 1963; Professor of Law, Harvard University, Cambridge, Massachusetts, since 1967 (Associate Professor, 1964-67). Consultant, National Institute of Mental Health; syndicated columnist, United Features Syndicate; Columnist ("Justice"), Penthouse mag. **Publications:** (with J. Katz and others) Psychoanalysis, Psychiatry and the Law, 1967; (with J. Goldstein and R. Schwartz) Criminal Law: Theory and Process, 1974; (with others) Fair and Certain Punishment: Report of the Twentieth-Century Fund Task Force on Criminal Sentencing, 1976; (with T. Taylor) Courts of Terror, 1976; The Best Defense, 1982; Reversal of Fortune: Inside the Von Bulow Case, 1986; Taking Liberties: A Compendium of Hard Cases, Legal Dilemmas and Bum Raps, 1988; Chutzpah, 1991; Contrary to Popular Opinion, 1992; The Abuse Excuse, 1994; The Advocate's Devil, 1994; Reasonable Doubts, 1996; The Vanishing American Jew, 1997; Sexual McCarthyism, 1998; Just Revenge, 1999; The Genesis of Justice, 2000; Supreme Injustice, 2001; Why Terrorism Works, 2002. **Address:** Harvard Law School, 1575 Massachusetts Ave, Cambridge, MA 02138, U.S.A. **Online address:** alder@law.harvard.edu

DERVAES, Claudine. American, b. 1954. **Genres:** Travel/Exploration. **Publications:** The Travel Training Series, 6 volumes including International Travel, Selling Cruises, and Sales and Marketing, 1994-96, rev. ed., 2000; The Travel Dictionary, 1996, rev. ed., 2000; Teaching Travel: A Handbook for the Educator, 1998; The U.K. to U.S.A. Dictionary, 2004. **Address:** c/o Solitaire Publishing, 1090 S Chateau Pt, Inverness, FL 34450-3565, U.S.A. **Online address:** PSolitaire@aol.com

DERY, Mark. American, b. 1959. **Genres:** Information science/Computers. **Career:** Full-time cultural critic and freelance journalist. **Publications:** Culture Jamming: Hacking, Slashing, and Sniping in the Empire of Signs (political monograph), 1993; (ed.) Flame Wars: The Discourse of Cyberculture (nonfiction anthology), 1995; Escape Velocity: Cyberculture at the End of the Century (nonfiction), 1996. Contributor to books and periodicals. Contributor to Beyond Cyberpunk, a hypercard database of essays and esoterica. **Address:** c/o Linda Chester, Linda Chester Literary Agency, 630 5th Ave., New York, NY 10111, U.S.A.

DESAI, Anita. Indian, b. 1937. **Genres:** Novels, Children's fiction. **Publications:** Cry, The Peacock, 1963; Voices in the City, 1965; Bye-Bye, Blackbird, 1971; The Peacock Garden, 1974; Where Shall We Go This Summer?, 1975; Cat on a Houseboat, 1976; Fire on the Mountain, 1977; Games at Twilight, 1978; Clear Light of Day, 1980; A Village by the Sea, 1982; In Custody, 1984; Baumgartner's Bombay, 1988; Journey to Ithaca, 1995; Fasting, Feasting, 1999; Diamond Dust: Stories, 2000. **Address:** MIT Program in Writing & Humanistic Studies, Rm 14E-303, Massachusetts Institute of Technology, Cambridge, MA 02139-4307, U.S.A.

DESAI, Boman. American (born India), b. 1950. **Genres:** Novels, Essays. **Career:** Writer; beginning in 1976, worked as a part- and full-time telephone interviewer and demographics researcher, currently works as a secretary for Sears, Roebuck and Co. Worked as a musician, farmhand, bartender, dishwasher, bookstore clerk, and telephone operator, while a student until 1976. **Publications:** The Memory of Elephants (novel), 1988; Asylum, USA, 2000. **Address:** 567 W Stratford No. 305, Chicago, IL 60657, U.S.A.

DESAI, Kiran. Indian, b. 1971. **Genres:** Novels. **Career:** Writer. **Publications:** Hullabaloo in the Guava Orchard, 1998. Contributor to anthologies and periodicals. **Address:** c/o ARAGI, 143 W 27th #4F, New York, NY 10001, U.S.A.

DESALLE, Rob. American. **Genres:** Environmental sciences/Ecology. **Career:** American Museum of Natural History, New York, NY, associate curator of entomology, 1991-; Columbia University, New York, NY, adjunct associate professor; City University of New York, New York, NY, adjunct professor. **Publications:** (with D. Lindley) The Science of Jurassic Park and the Lost World; or, How to Build a Dinosaur, 1997. EDITOR: (with B. Schierwater) Molecular Approaches to Ecology and Evolution, 1998; Epidemic!: The World of Infectious Diseases, 1999; (with M. Yudell) The Genomic Revolution: Unveiling the Unity of Life, 2002. Contributor to academic journals. **Address:** Center for Biodiversity and Conservation, American Museum of Natural History, Central Park West at 79th St., New York, NY 10024, U.S.A. **Online address:** desalle@amnh.org

DESANTIS, Vincent P. American, b. 1916. **Genres:** History. **Career:** Professor of American History, University of Notre Dame, Indiana, since 1949 (Chairman, Dept. of History, 1963-71); now emeritus. **Publications:** Republicans Face the Southern Question: The New Departure Years 1877-1897, 1959; (co-author) Our Country, 1960; (co-author) Roman Catholicism and the American Way of Life, 1960; (co-author) America's Ten Greatest Presidents, 1961; (co-author) The Gilded Age: A Reappraisal, 1963; (co-author) The Democratic Experience, 1963, 5th ed. 1981; (co-author) America Past and Present, 2 vols., 1968; (co-author) American Foreign Policy in Europe, 1969; (co-author) America's Eleven Greatest Presidents, 1971; (compiler) The Gilded Age, 1973; The Shaping of Modern America 1877-1914, 1973, 2nd ed. 1877-1920, 1989, 3rd ed, 1998; (co-author) Six Presidents from the Empire State, 1974; (co-author) The Heritage of 1776, 1976; (co-author) The Impact of the Cold War: Reconsiderations, 1977; (co-author) A History of United States Foreign Policy, 4th ed. 1980; (co-author) Region, Race and Reconstruction, 1982; (co-author) Popular Images of American Presidents, 1988. **Address:** Dept. of History, University of Notre Dame, Notre Dame, IN 46556, U.S.A. **Online address:** NOTREDAMEHISTORY.1@nd.edu

DESARTHE, Agnès. French, b. 1966. **Genres:** Children's fiction, Novels. **Career:** Author of books for children and adults and translator. Worked as a teacher of English. **Publications:** Les peurs de Conception, 1992; Quelques minutes de bonheur absolu, 1993; Un secret sans importance, 1996; Cinq photos de ma femme, 1998, trans. by A. Hunter as Five Photos of My Wife, 2001; Les bonnes intentions, 2000, trans. by A. Hunter as Good Intentions, 2001. **Address:** c/o Author Mail Flamingo Books, HarperCollins Publishers, 77-85 Fulham Palace Rd., Hammersmith, London W6 8JB, England.

DESAUTELS, Denise. Canadian, b. 1945. **Genres:** Poetry, Literary criticism and history. **Publications:** Comme miroirs en feuilles (poems), 1975; Marie, tout s'eteignait en moi, 1977; La promeneuse et l'oiseau suivi de Journal de la promeneuse, 1980; L'ecran, precede de, Aires du tempts, 1983; (with A-M Alonzo and R. April) Nous en reparlerons sans doute, 1986; Un livre de Kafka a la main, suivi de La Blessure, avec huit photographies de Jocelyne Alloucherie, 1987; Lecons de Venise, 1990; Mais la menace est une belle extravagance suivi de Le Signe Discret, avec huit photographies d'Ariane Theze, 1991; Le Saut de l'ange: autour de quelques objets de Martha Townsend, 1992; (with A-M Alonzo) Lettres a Cassandre, 1994. **Address:** c/o Ed.s de Noirot, 1835 boul des Hauteurs, St. Hippolyte, QC, Canada J0R 1P0.

DESCOLA, Philippe. French, b. 1949. **Genres:** Anthropology/Ethnology. **Career:** Cambridge University, Cambridge, England, visiting scholar at King's College, 1981; Ecole des Hautes Etudes en Sciences Sociales, Paris, France, temporary lecturer, 1981-84, assistant professor, 1984-89, professor of anthropology, 1989-. Cambridge University, visiting scholar at King's College, 1991-92. **Publications:** La nature domestique: Symbolisme et praxis dans l'ecologie des Achuar, 1986, trans. as In the Society of Nature: A Native Ecology in Amazonia, 1994; Les lances du crepuscule: Relations jivaros, 1993, trans. as The Spears of Twilight, 1996; (ed. with G. Palsson, and contrib.) Nature and Society: Anthropological Perspectives, 1996. Contributor to books and periodicals. IN FRENCH: (with G. Lenclud, C. Severi, and A.C. Taylor) Les idees de l'anthropologie, 1988; (ed. with M. Abeles, P. Bonte, J.-P. Digard, and others) Dictionnaire de l'ethnologie et de l'anthropologie, 1991. Contributor to books and anthropology journals. **Address:** Laboratoire d'Anthropologie Sociale, Ecole des Hautes Etudes en Sciences Sociales, 52 rue du Cardinal-Lemoine, F-75005 Paris, France.

DESENA, Carmine. American, b. 1957. **Genres:** Humor/Satire, Writing/Journalism. **Career:** Vocational Rehab Services, Bayside, NY, manager of Intensive Psychological Rehabilitation Treatment program, 1979-. OK, So We Lied (comedy troupe), cofounder. **Publications:** Lies: The Whole Truth (humor), 1993; The Comedy Source (writers' handbook), 1996; Satan's Little Instruction Book (humor), 1996; (coauthor) The Air down Here: True Tales from a South Bronx Boyhood. Contributor to magazines, newspapers, radio, and the Web.

DESGUIN, Guillard. *See* **HUMEZ, Nicholas (David).**

DESHPANDE, Chris. British, b. 1950. **Genres:** Children's non-fiction. **Career:** Teacher for children ages four to eighteen in Nottingham, London, and Birmingham, England, 1972-; became head of learning support department in a Birmingham 11-18 comprehensive school, 1985-. Lecturer in schools and at conferences. **Publications:** Diwali, 1985; Finger Foods, 1988; Five Stones and Knuckle Bones, 1988; Scrape, Rattle and Blow, 1988; Tea, 1989; Bangles, Badges and Beads, 1990; Silk, 1991. COMPILER (with J. Eccleshare): Spring Tinderbox, 1992; Celebrations, Food, 1993. **Address:** A. & C. Black Ltd., 35 Bedford Row, London WC1R 4JH, England.

DESJARLAIS, John. American (born Germany), b. 1953. **Genres:** Novels, Writing/Journalism, Essays. **Career:** 2100 Productions, Madison, WI, associate producer, 1984-92; University of Wisconsin-Madison, instructor in writing, 1990-; Illinois State University, instructor in writing, 1993-95; Wisconsin Public Radio, producer, 1992-93; Kishwaukee College, journalism/English instructor, 1995-; writer. **Publications:** The Throne of Tara, 1990; Relics, 1993. **Address:** Kishwaukee College, 21193 Malta Rd, Malta, IL 60150, U.S.A. **Online address:** jdesjar@kishwaukeecollege.edu

DESMANGLES, Leslie G. American (born Haiti), b. 1941. **Genres:** Theology/Religion. **Career:** Assistant minister of Baptist church in Mount Holly, NJ, 1965-66, and United Methodist church in Ardmore, PA, 1966-67; campus minister at Methodist church in Philadelphia, PA, 1967-68; Eastern College, St. Davids, PA, lecturer in religion, 1968-69; Ohio Wesleyan University, Delaware, OH, assistant professor of religion, 1970-76; DePaul University, Chicago, IL, assistant professor of religion, 1976-78; Trinity College, Hartford, CT, assistant professor, 1978-82, associate professor, 1982-93, professor of religion, 1993-, director of Intercultural Studies Program, 1982-88, and Area Studies Program, 1988-89, acting affirmative action officer, 1992-. Ohio University at Marion, visiting lecturer, 1975-76; Union Theological Seminary, NYC, visiting lecturer, 1980; University of Connecticut, visiting lecturer, 1989; Hartford College for Women, visiting associate professor, 1989-91. **Publications:** The Faces of the Gods: Vodou and Roman Catholicism in Haiti, 1992. Work represented in anthologies. Contributor of articles and reviews to scholarly journals. **Address:** Department of Religion, Trinity College, Hartford, CT 06106, U.S.A. **Online address:** leslie.desmangles@trincoll.edu

DESMOINAUX, Christel. French, b. 1967. **Genres:** Children's fiction. **Career:** Illustrator, 1988-. **Publications:** SELF-ILLUSTRATED FOR CHILDREN: Comme Il Rougit, M. Souris!, 1989; Julia N'En Rate Pas Une!, 1991; Panique dans L'Ascenseur, 1992; Henri, Tete-en-L'Air, 1992; L'Oeuf de Madame Poule (title means: Mrs. Hen's Egg), 1998; Rosa veut maigrie (Rosie, the Cow Who Wanted to Be Slim), 1999; Marius le minus, 1999; Emile et Lucette, 1999; Prends-moi dans te bras, 2000; Le Meilleur ami de Suzette, 2000; Mrs. Hen's Big Surprise, 2000; Courage Gaston, 2001; Aldo au marriege, 2001; Aldo prend son bain, 2001; Aldo est grognon, 2001; Aldo est malade, 2001; Aldo et son doudou, 2002; Aldo au square, 2002; L'anniversaire d'Aldo, 2002; Aldo au supermarche, 2002; Lucie la raleux, 2002; Plouk, 2002; Hallo-What?, 2003; Arsene le glouton, 2003; Lolotte la marmotte, 2003; L'elephant qui voulait etre papa, 2004. Illustrator of books by S. Bellosguardo, C. Clement, J. Delaroche, A. Dena, J. and W. Grimm, O. Hellmann-Hurpoil, D. Mora, F. Rotillon, E. Tharlet, A. Vandewiele. Illustrator of the cartoon series Bravo la Famille (television), 1993. **Address:** c/o Children's Division Editorial Dept, Simon & Schuster, 1230 Avenue of the Americas, New York, NY 10020, U.S.A. **Online address:** desmoino@free.fr

DE SOUZA, Eunice. Indian, b. 1940. **Genres:** Poetry, Children's non-fiction. **Career:** Lecturer in English, since 1969, and Head of Dept. of English, since 1990, St. Xavier's College, Bombay. Arts Columnist, Economic Times, Bombay, 1973-84; Literary Ed., Indian Post, Bombay, 1987. **Publications:** All about Birbal, 1969; Himalayan Tales, 1973; (ed. with Adil Jussawalla) Statements: An Anthology of Indian Prose in English, 1976; Fix (poetry), 1979; Women in Dutch Painting (poetry), 1988; Ways of Belonging: Selected Poems, 1990; Selected and New Poems, (poetry), 1994. **Address:** St. Xavier's College, Bombay 400 001, India.

DESPAIN, Pleasant. American, b. 1943. **Genres:** Mythology/Folklore. **Career:** University of Massachusetts, Amherst, instructor in literature and speech, 1966-68; University of Washington, Seattle, instructor in literature and speech, 1970-72; KING-TV, Seattle, producer/writer and host of children's storytelling show, 1975-80. Professional storyteller/author (including school workshops), 1972-. Consultant/author for Rose Studios (computer software development for interactive children's story games),

1994-. **Publications:** Twenty-two Splendid Tales to Tell from around the World, vols. 1-2, 1993 (originally as Pleasant Journeys, 1979); Thirty-three Multicultural Tales to Tell, 1993; Eleven Turtle Tales: Adventure Tales from around the World, 1994; Strongheart Jack and the Beanstalk, 1995; The Mystery Artist, 1995; Eleven Nature Tales, 1996; The Emerald Lizard: 15 Latin American Tales, 1999; Sweet Land of Story: 36 American Tales to Tell, 2000; Books of Nine Lives, vols. 1-9, 2001-03. **Address:** 405 Third St #2, Troy, NY 12180, U.S.A. **Online address:** pleasant@att.net

DESPLECHIN, Marie. French, b. 1959. **Genres:** Children's fiction, Young adult fiction. **Career:** Freelance journalist; author of children's and young adult books, 1994-. **Publications:** Et Dieu dans tout ça? (novel; title means: And God in All That?), 1994; (with others) Trésors des galions, 1994; Tu seras un homme, mon neveu, 1995; Trop sensibles, 1995, as Taking It to Heart, 2001; Verte (title means Green), 1996; J'envie ceux qui sont dans ton coeur (title means: I Envy Those Who Are in Your Heart), 1997; Un vague d'amour sur un lac d'amitié, 1997; La prédication de Nadia, 1999; Copie double, Bayard, 2000; Sans moi (title means: Without Me), 1998, trans. W. Hobson, 2001; Le monde Joseph (title means: Joseph's World), 2000; Le coup du kiwi, 2000. **Address:** c/o Author Mail, St. Martin's Press, 175 5th Ave., New York, NY 10010, U.S.A.

DESPRES, Loraine. American. **Genres:** Novels, Plays/Screenplays. **Career:** Writer. University of California at Los Angeles, instructor; international screenwriting consultant. Wrote television scripts for primetime shows for NBC, CBS, and ABC. Worked as a writer of educational radio, film, and advertising in Chicago, Paris, and New Orleans. **Publications:** NOVELS: The Scandalous Summer of Sissy LeBlanc, 2001; The Southern Belle's Handbook: Sissy LeBlanc's Rules to Live By, 2003. Author of television scripts for Dynasty; The Equalizer; Crime Story; Knots Landing; The Love Boat; Family; The Highlander; The Waltons; Chips;"Who Shot J.R.?" episode of Dallas. Contributor of feature articles and interviews to magazines. **Address:** c/o Author Mail 7th Floor, HarperCollins Publishers, 10 East 53rd St., New York, NY 10022, U.S.A.

DESPUTEAUX, Helene. Canadian, b. 1959. **Genres:** Children's fiction, Illustrations. **Career:** Illustrator. Educator and art specialist for schools. Also worked as a puppeteer. Selected illustrations have appeared at the Bologna Children's Art Fair (Bologna, Italy), 1983 and 1986, the Otani Memorial Art Museum (Nishinomya, Japan), 1983, and the Ward Museum of Art (Tokyo, Japan), 1983. **Publications:** SELF-ILLUSTRATED LOLLYPOP SERIES (in English): Lollypop: My Clothes, 1991; Lollypop: My Food, 1991; Lollypop: My House, 1991; Lollypop's Animals, 1992; Lollypop's Colors, 1992; Lollypop's Numbers, 1992; Lollypop's Playtime, 1992; Lollypop's Baby Book, 1993; Lollypop's Travels, 1995; Lollypop's Farm, 1996; Lollypop's Music, 1996; Lollypop's Zoo, 1996. Also writes in French. Illustrator of books in the Lollypop series by M. Chartrand, N. Nadeau, and J. Sanschagrin. Illustrator of other books by M. Aubin, M-F Laurent, L. Casson, R. Tregebov, G. Chislett, R. Munsch, C. MacAulay, K. Frasier, D. McVeity. **Address:** 80 rue Bourgeois, Beloeil, QC, Canada J3G 2X6.

DES RIVIÈRES, Jim. Canadian, b. 1953. **Genres:** Information science/Computers. **Career:** Carleton University, Ottawa, Ontario, programmer at Computer Centre, 1972-83, assistant professor of computer science, 1981-82; Xerox Palo Alto Research Center, Palo Alto, CA, computer scientist, 1982-84, 1989-93; Object Technology International, Inc., Ottawa, computer scientist, 1993-. **Publications:** (with G. Kiczales) The Art of the Metaobject Protocol, 1991. **Address:** Object Technology International Inc., 2670 Queensview Dr., Ottawa, ON, Canada K2B 8K1. **Online address:** jeem@acm.org

DESROCHERS, Diane. American, b. 1937. **Genres:** Novels, Science fiction/Fantasy, Civil liberties/Human rights, Paranormal, Theology/Religion, Writing/Journalism. **Career:** Resident geriatric care manager; private practice of pastoral and psychic counseling and crisis intervention. **Publications:** Walker between the Worlds (novel), 1995. **Address:** 40 Great River Dr, Sound Beach, NY 11789-2034, U.S.A. **Online address:** firstAmendmt@aol.com

DESSAIX, Robert. Australian, b. 1944. **Genres:** Literary criticism and history. **Career:** University professor, literary interviewer and commentator, and broadcaster. Australian National University, Canberra, teacher, until 1985; ABC Radio National's Books and Writing Program, producer and presenter, 1985-95. **Publications:** Turgenev: The Quest for Faith (criticism), 1980; (trans, with Ulman) The Sheepskin Coat & An Absolutely Happy Village (novellas), by B. Vakhtin, 1990; A Mother's Disgrace (autobiography), 1994; Night Letters (fiction), 1996. EDITOR: (and trans, with M. Ulman) A History of Post-War Soviet Writing: The Literature of Moral Opposition (criticism), by G. Svirski, 1981; Australian Gay and Lesbian Writing: An Anthology, 1993; (with H. Daniel) Picador New Writing (anthology), 1993. **Address:** c/o Lyn Tranter, Australian Literary Management, 2-A Booth St., Balmain, NSW 2041, Australia.

DESSART, George Baldwin, Jr. American (born Germany), b. 1925. **Genres:** Communications/Media. **Career:** Station WCAU-TV, Philadelphia, 1953-65 as director, writer, and producer of television broadcasts and series, director of public affairs, 1952-54; executive producer, documentary unit for WCBSTV, NYC, 1965-67; director of community services, 1967-71, executive assistant to the general manager, 1971-. Lecturer in charge of TV labs, Annenberg School of Communications, University of Pennsylvania, 1961-69; adjunct associate professor of education, Lehmann College, City University of New York, 1969-72, adjunct professor, 1972-. **Publications:** Television in the Real World, 1978; (with W.F. Baker) Down the Tube: An Inside Account of the Failure of American Television, 1998. **Address:** 1320 St. Charles St. #2, Alameda, CA 94501-3926, U.S.A.

DESSER, David. American, b. 1953. **Genres:** Film. **Career:** University of Illinois at Urbana-Champaign, Urbana, professor of cinema studies, 1981-. **Publications:** The Samurai Films of Akira Kurosawa, 1983; Eros Plus Massacre: An Introduction to the Japanese New Wave Cinema, 1988; (ed. with A. Nolletti, Jr.) Reframing Japanese Cinema: Authorship, Genre, History, 1992; (with L. Friedman) American-Jewish Filmmakers: Traditions and Trends, 1993; (ed. with G. Studlar) Reflections in a Male Eye: John Huston and the American Experience, 1993; (ed. with L. Ehrlich) Cinematic Landscapes: The Visual Arts and Cinema in China and Japan, 1994. **Address:** Department of Speech Communication, University of Illinois at Urbana-Champaign, Urbana, IL 61801, U.S.A.

D'ESTE, Carlo. American, b. 1936. **Genres:** Military/Defense/Arms control, Bibliography. **Career:** Military historian and biographer, 1978-. Formerly, lieutenant colonel with the United States Army. **Publications:** Decision in Normandy: The Unwritten Story of Montgomery and the Allied Campaign, 1983; Bitter Victory: The Battle for Sicily, 1943, 1988; World War II in the Mediterranean, 1942-1945, 1990; Fatal Decision: Anzio and the Battle for Rome, 1991; Patton: A Genius for War, 1995. **Address:** c/o HarperCollins, 1000 Keystone Industrial Park, Scranton, PA 18512, U.S.A.

DE SYON, Guillaume. French, b. 1966. **Genres:** History. **Career:** Albright College, Reading, PA, teacher of history. **Publications:** (ed. with others) The Collected Papers of Albert Einstein, Volumes 8A and 8B: Correspondence, 1914-1918, 1998; Zeppelin! Germany and the Airship, 1900-1939, 2001. **Address:** Albright College, 13th and Bern Sts., Reading, PA 19612, U.S.A. **Online address:** gp_desyon@fandm.edu

DETTMAR, Kevin J(ohn) H(offmann). American, b. 1958. **Genres:** Language/Linguistics. **Career:** Loyola Marymount University, Los Angeles, CA, visiting assistant professor of English, 1990-91; Clemson University, Clemson, SC, began as assistant professor, became associate professor of English, 1991-. **Publications:** EDITOR & CONTRIBUTOR: Rereading the New: A Backward Glance at Modernism, 1992; (with S. Watt) Marketing Modernisms: Fates and Fortunes of the Literary Text in Commodity Culture, in press. Work represented in anthologies. Contributor of articles and reviews to literature journals. **Address:** Department of English, Clemson University, P.O. Box 341503, Clemson, SC 29634, U.S.A.

DETWEILER, Robert. American, b. 1932. **Genres:** Literary criticism and history. **Career:** Professor of Comparative Literature, Emory University, Atlanta, since 1973. Assistant Professor of English, University of Florida, Gainesville, 1963-65; Assistant Professor of English, Hunter College of City University of New York, 1965-66; Associate Professor of Literature, Florida Presbyterian College, St. Petersburg, 1966-70; Fulbright Professor of American Studies, University of Salzburg, Austria, 1971-72; University of Regensburg, Germany, 1989; University of Copenhagen, Denmark, 1993. **Publications:** Four Spiritual Crises in Mid-Century American Fiction, 1964; Saul Bellow, 1967; Iris Murdoch's The Unicorn, 1969; John Updike, 1973, 1984; Story, Sign and Self: Phenomenology and Structuralism as Literary Critical Methods, 1978; (ed. with G. Meeter) Faith and Fiction: The Modern Story, 1979; (ed.) Derrida and Biblical Studies, 1982; (ed.) Art/Literature/Religion: Life on the Borders, 1983; (ed.) Reader Response Approaches to Biblical and Secular Texts, 1985; Breaking the Fall: Religious Readings of Contemporary Fiction, 1989; Uncivil Rites: America Fiction, Religion and the Public Sphere, 1996. **Address:** Graduate Institute of Liberal Arts, Emory University, Atlanta, GA 30322, U.S.A.

DETZ, Joan (Marie). American. **Genres:** Speech/Rhetoric, Writing/Journalism. **Career:** Director, Joan Detz Speechwriting, Coaching, 1985-.

Teacher, James Blair School, Williamsburg, Virginia, 1974-76; Writer and Researcher, Wells, Rich and Greene Advertising, NYC, 1976-80; Speechwriter, Brooklyn Union Gas, New York, 1980-85. **Publications:** How to Write and Give a Speech, 1984, 1992; You Mean I Have to Stand Up and Say Something?, 1986; Can You Say a Few Words?, 1991.

DEUKER, Carl. American, b. 1950. **Genres:** Children's fiction, Young adult fiction. **Career:** Saint Luke School, Seattle, WA, teacher, 1977-90; Northshore School District, Bothell, WA, teacher, 1991-. Seattle Sun (daily newspaper), film and book critic, 1980-85. **Publications:** On the Devil's Court, 1988; Heart of a Champion, 1993; Painting the Black, 1997; Night Hoops, 2000; High Heat, 2003; Runner, 2005. **Address:** 2827 NW 62nd St, Seattle, WA 98107-2513, U.S.A. **Online address:** cdeuker@nsd.org

DEUTSCH, Sarah (Jane). American, b. 1955. **Genres:** History. **Career:** Educator, historian. Massachusetts Institute of Technology, Cambridge, MA, 1985-89, began as assistant professor, became associate professor of history; Clark University, Worcester, MA, associate professor of history; University of Arizona, associate professor to professor of history. **Publications:** No Separate Refuge: Culture, Class, and Gender On an Anglo-Hispanic Frontier in the American Southwest, 1880-1940, 1987; From Ballots to Breadlines: American Women, 1920-1940, 1994; Women and the City: Gender, Space, and Power in Boston, 1870-1940, 2000. Contributor to books and periodicals. **Address:** University of Arizona, History Dept., Box 210027, Tucson, AZ 85721, U.S.A. **Online address:** sdeutsch@u.arizona.edu

DEUTSCHER, Irwin. American, b. 1923. **Genres:** Sociology. **Career:** Community Studies Inc., Kansas City, MO, Director of Research in Health and Welfare, 1954-59; Syracuse University, NY, Director, Youth Development Center, and professor of Sociology, 1959-68; Case Western Reserve University, Cleveland, professor of Sociology, 1968-75; University of Akron, OH, professor, 1975-83, professor Emeritus of Sociology, 1983-. **Publications:** (with E.C. and H.M. Hughes) Twenty Thousand Nurses Tell Their Story, 1958; (ed. with E.J. Thompson) Among the People: Encounters with the Poor, 1968; What We Say/What We Do: Sentiments and Acts, 1973; (with F.P. & H.F. Pestello), Sentiments & Acts, 1993; Making a Difference: The Practice of Sociology, 1999; Accommodating Diversity: National Policies That Prevent Ethnic Conflict, 2002; (with L. Lindsey) Preventing Ethnic Conflict: Successful CrossNational Strategies. **Address:** 4740 Connecticut Ave NW No 1007, Washington, DC 20008, U.S.A. **Online address:** IrwinD@juno.com

DEVALLE, Susana B(eatriz) C(ristina). Argentine. **Genres:** Cultural/Ethnic topics. **Career:** Buenos Aires National University, Buenos Aires, Argentina, researcher at Institute of Anthropology, 1966-67; El Colegio de Mexico, Mexico City, researcher at Center for Asian and African Studies, 1970-72, professor and researcher of Asian and African studies, 1973-, director of research group on ethnicity and nationalisms in Asia, Africa, and Latin America, and coordinator of research group on the culture of violence, coexistence, and human rights, both 1994-. Australian National University, visiting fellow in Asian studies, 1983, 1984; University of Hawaii at Manoa, visiting fellow in ethnic studies, 1990; lecturer at Universidad Iberoamericana. Mexican Ministry of Education, national researcher in the social sciences, Sistema Nacional de Investigadores, 1987-; consultant to the Australian Parliament (foreign affairs). **Publications:** (with P. Mukherjee, C. Aguero, and others) Movimientos Agrarios y Cambio Social en Asia y Africa (title means: Agrarian Movements and Social Change in Asia and Africa), 1974; La Palabra de la Tierra: Protesta Campesina en India, siglo XIX (title means: The Word of the Land: Peasant Protest in India, Nineteenth Century), 1977; (ed. with C. Aguero and M. Tanaka, and contrib.) Peasantry and National Integration, 1981; (ed. and contrib.) La Diversidad Prohibida: Resistencia Etnica y Poder de Estado (title means: Forbidden Diversity: Ethnic Resistance and State Power), 1989; Discourses of Ethnicity: Culture and Protest in Jharkhand, 1992. Work represented in anthologies. Contributor to of to academic journals. **Address:** Center for Asian and African Studies, El Colegio de Mexico, Camino al Ajusco No. 20, 01000 Mexico City, DF, Mexico. **Online address:** sdevalle@colmex.mx

DEVANE, Terry. See HEALY, Jeremiah.

DE VARONA, Frank J. Cuban, b. 1943. **Genres:** Area studies, History. **Career:** Miami Senior High Adult Education Center, Miami, FL, assistant principal, 1973-75; Miami Coral Park Senior High Adult Education Center, Miami, principal, 1975-77; West Miami Junior High School, Miami, principal, 1977-79; Miami Edison Senior High School, Miami, principal, 1979-82; Dade County Public Schools, Miami, South Central Area director, 1982-85, area superintendent, 1985-87, associate superintendent of Bureau of

Education, 1987-91, region I superintendent, 1991-. Taught social studies in three junior high schools, 1967-70, and a senior high school, 1970-72; served as a consultant for elementary, junior/middle, and senior high school textbooks on subjects relating to social studies; producer, director, and host of weekly television program in Miami, 1990-92. **Publications:** (Coauthor) Hispanics in United States History: Through 1865, Vol I, 1989; (Coauthor) Hispanics in United States History: 1865 to the Present, Vol II, 1989; (And series editor) Bernardo de Galvez, 1990; (ed.) Hispanic Presence in the United States: Historical Beginnings, 1993; Florida Government Activities, 1993; Simon Bolivar: Latin American Liberator, 1993; Benito Juarez, President of Mexico, 1993; Miguel Hidalgo y Costilla: Father of Mexican Independence, 1993; (Coauthor) The Cuban Educational System: Past, Present and Future, 1993. Contributor to newspapers, magazines, and books in the US and in Spain. **Address:** Region I, Dade County Public Schools, 733 East 57 St., Hialeah, FL 33013, U.S.A.

DE VASCONCELOS, Erika. Canadian, b. 1965. **Genres:** Novels. **Career:** Novelist and short story writer. **Publications:** My Darling Dead Ones, 1997. Author of short stories. **Address:** c/o Author Mail, Random House Canada, 1 Toronto St Unit 300, Toronto, ON, Canada M5C 2V6.

DEVASHISH, Donald Acosta. American, b. 1956. **Genres:** Novels, Translations. **Career:** Writer. **Publications:** (trans.) Shabda Cayanika, Part 1, 1995, Part 2, 1996, Part 3, in press; Felicitavia: A Spiritual Journal (novel), 1997; Conversations, 1998. **Address:** PNS 265, PO Box 5075, San German, PR 00683, U.S.A. **Online address:** Devashisa@igc.org

DEVAUX, Claudia. American, b. 1946. **Genres:** Inspirational/Motivational Literature, Bibliography. **Career:** Formerly: Hewlett-Packard Co., Cupertino, CA, marketing executive; minister to separated, divorced, and widowed Roman Catholics. Currently: Teacher and researcher; webmaster; lector/Eucharistic minister; Enneagram teacher. **Publications:** (with others) Bamboo Swaying in the Wind, 2000.

DE VECCHI, Nicolo. Italian, b. 1943. **Genres:** Economics. **Career:** University of Trento, Italy, professor of economics, 1972-74; University of Pavia, Italy, professor of political economy, 1974-. **Publications:** Entrepreneurs, Institutions, and Economic Change: The Economic Thought of J.A. Schumpeter (1905-1925), 1995. UNTRANSLATED WORKS: Valore e distribuzione nell'economia politica classica (title means: Value and Distribution in the Classical Political Economy), 1976; Jevons: il calcolo logico in economia politica (title means: Jevons: Logical Calculus in Political Economy), 1976. Contributor to books and periodicals.

DE VILLIERS, Marq. Canadian (born Republic of South Africa), b. 1940. **Genres:** History. **Career:** Writer and journalist. WHERE Magazines International, editorial director. **Publications:** White Tribe Dreaming: Apartheid's Bitter Roots as Witnessed by Eight Generations of an Afrikaner Family, 1987, 1989; White Tribe Dreaming: Apartheid's Bitter Roots: Notes of an Eighth-Generation Afrikaner, 1987; Down the Volga in a Time of Troubles: A Journey Revealing the People and Heartland of Post-Perestroika Russia, 1991; Down the Volga: A Journey Through Mother Russia in a Time of Troubles, 1992; The Heartbreak Grape: A California Winemaker's Search for the Perfect Pinot Noir, 1994; (with G. Drabinsky) Closer to the Sun: An Autobiography, 1995; (with S. Hirtle) Blood Traitors, 1997; (with Hirtle) Into Africa: A Journey through the Ancient Empires, 1997; The Water Wars: The Looming Crisis in Global Fresh Water, 1999. **Address:** Box 801, Lunenburg, NS, Canada B0J 2C0. **Online address:** jacobus@fox.nstn.ca.

DEVINCENT-HAYES, Nan. (Gianni). American. **Genres:** Novels, Novellas/Short stories, Horror, Romance/Historical, Science fiction/Fantasy, Young adult fiction, Plays/Screenplays, Adult non-fiction, Communications/Media, Cultural/Ethnic topics, Education, Humanities, Politics/Government, Women's studies and issues, Writing/Journalism. **Career:** Writer. Salisbury State University, adjunct professor, 1985-90, assistant professor of English, 1989-92, adjunct professor of communications, 1995-; Wor-Wic College, adjunct professor of English, 1985-89; Mount Aloysius College, associate professor of English and chair of dept, 1989-91; University of Maryland Eastern Shore, visiting lecturer and adjunct professor of English, 1992-94. **Publications:** Move It, 1988; The Last of the Wallendas, 1993; Images of America: Ocean City, 2 vols., 1999; Images of America: Assateague and Chincoteague, 2000; Wallops Island, 2001; Thy Brothers' Reaper (screenplay), 2001; Rehobeth and the Quiet Resorts, 2002; Zambelli: The First Family of Fireworks, 2003. NOVELS: 22 Friar Street, 2001; Thy Brothers' Reaper, 2001; Jacob's Trouble, 2001; Heartbroken Love, 2002. TEXTBOOKS: Troublesome Grammar; Grammar & Sentence Diagramming, 1998. Fiction and nonfiction represented in anthologies. Contributor to periodicals, literary magazines, and scholarly works. **Address:** 5736 Royal Mile Blvd, Salisbury, MD 21801, U.S.A. **Online address:** ndhayes@att.net; www.ezy.net/~wrtrbloc

DE VINCK, (Baron) José M. G. A. Also writes as John Pynson. Belgian, b. 1912. **Genres:** Poetry, Human relations/Parenting, Philosophy, Sex, Theology/Religion, Translations. **Career:** Owner, Alleluia Press, Allendale, NJ. Seton Hall University, professor of philosophy, 1950-54; St. Anthony Guild Press, Paterson, NJ, ed., trans. and designer, 1955-70; Tombrock College, Paterson, NJ, professor of philosophy and theology, 1967-74; Sunday Publs., Fairfield, NJ, associate ed., 1974; self-employed, 1975-. **Publications:** Images, 1940; (with E. du Bus de Warnaffe) Le Cantique de la Vie, 1943; (ed. and trans. with J. Raya) Byzantine Missal for Sundays and Feast Days, 1958; (trans.) The Works of Bonaventure, 5 vols., 1960-70; The Virtue of Sex, 1966; (with J. T. Catoir) The Challenge of Love, 1969; (ed. and trans. with J. Raya) Byzantine Daily Worship, 1969; The Yes Book: An Answer to Life, 1972; The Words of Jesus, 1977; (ed.) Byzantine Altar Gospel, 1979; (ed.) Byzantine Altar Epistles, 1980; Revelations of Women Mystics, 1985; (with A.L. Contos) The Septuagint Psalms, 1993; The Quest for the Golden Dove: Thoughts on Love Human and Divine, 1994; Faith in The New Age, A Critical Survey, 1997 Critical Survey, 1997. **Address:** c/o Alleluia Press, PO Box 103, Allendale, NJ 07401-0103, U.S.A.

DEVITO, Joseph A. American, b. 1938. **Genres:** Communications/Media, Speech/Rhetoric. **Career:** Queens College of City University of New York, professor, 1972-85; Hunter College of City University of New York, professor, 1985-, now professor emeritus. **Publications:** The Psychology of Speech and Language, 1970; General Semantics, 1971; Psycholinguistics, 1971; The Interpersonal Communication Book, 1976, 10th ed., 2004; Human Communication: The Basic Course, 1978, 9th ed., 2003; Elements of Public Speaking, 1981, 7th ed., 2000; Communication Handbook: A Dictionary, 1986; The Nonverbal Communication Workbook, 1989; Messages: Building Interpersonal Communication Skills, 1990, 6th ed., 2005; Essentials of Human Communication, 1993, 5th ed., 2005; Studying Communication, 1995; The Interpersonal Challenge III, 1997 Interpersonal Challenge 28, 1995. Interpersonal Challenge 28, 1995; The Essential Elements of Public Speaking, 2003. EDITOR: Communication, 1971, 3rd ed., 1981; Language, 1973; The Nonverbal Communication Reader, 1990. **Address:** 140 Nassau St (3C), New York, NY 10038, U.S.A. **Online address:** jadevito@earthlink.net

DEVLIN, Albert J. American. **Genres:** Administration/Management. **Career:** Writer. University of Missouri-Columbia, professor of English. Academic advisor for PBS television. **Publications:** Eudora Welty's Chronicle: A Story of Mississippi Life, 1983. EDITOR: Conversations with Tennessee Williams, 1986; Welty: A Life in Literature, 1987; (with N.M. Tischler) The Selected Letters of Tennessee Williams, Vol 1: 1920-1945, 2000. **Address:** Department of English, University of Missouri, 309 University Hall, Columbia, MO 65211, U.S.A.

DEVLIN, Anne. Irish, b. 1951. **Genres:** Novellas/Short stories, Plays/Screenplays. **Career:** Royal Court Theatre, London, writer associate, 1985-; University of Birmingham, visiting lecturer in playwriting, 1987-; University of Lund, Sweden, writer in residence, 1990; Trinity College, Dublin, writers fellowship, 2004. **Publications:** PLAYS: Ourselves Alone and Other Plays, 1986; Heartlanders, 1989; After Easter, 1994. OTHER: The Way Paver (short stories), 1986; Titanic Town (screenplay), 1998. **Address:** English Dept, Arts Bldg, Trinity College, Dublin 2, Ireland. **Online address:** anne.devlin@virgin.net

DEVLIN, Dean. American, b. 1962. **Genres:** Plays/Screenplays. **Career:** Actor, producer, and screenwriter. Also worked as a musician. **Publications:** SCREENPLAYS: (with R. Rothstein and C. Leitch) Universal Soldier, 1992; (with R. Emmerich) Stargate, 1994; (with R. Emmerich and S. Molstad) Independence Day (also known as ID4), 1996, (novel, 1996); (with R. Emmerich and T. Elliott) Godzilla, 1998. TELEPLAYS: SERIES: The Visitor, 1997-98. **Address:** c/o Creative Artists Agency, 9830 Wilshire Blvd, Astaire Bldg. Suite 2610, Beverly Hills, CA 90212-1825, U.S.A.

DEVLIN, Keith. British, b. 1947. **Genres:** Mathematics/Statistics, Sciences. **Career:** University of Oslo, scientific visitor, 1971, scientific assistant in mathematics, 1972, 1973; Victoria University of Manchester, temporary lecturer in mathematics, 1973; University of Heidelberg, scientific assistant in mathematics, 1974; University of Bonn, scientific assistant in mathematics, 1974-76; University of Toronto, assistant professor of mathematics, 1976; University of Lancaster, lecturer, 1977-79, reader in mathematics, 1979-87; Stanford University, visiting associate professor of mathematics, 1987-88, associate professor of mathematics and philosophy, 1988-89; Colby

College, Carter Professor and chair of Dept of Mathematics and Computer Science, 1989-93; St. Mary's College of California, professor of mathematics and dean of School of Science, 1993-. **Publications:** Aspects of Constructibility, 1973; (with H. Johnsbraaten) The Souslin Problem, 1974; The Axiom of Constructibility: A Guide for the Mathematician, 1977; Fundamentals of Contemporary Set Theory, 1979, 2nd ed., 1993; Sets, Functions, and Logic, 1981, 2nd ed., 1992; Constructibility, 1984; Microchip Mathematics, 1984; Micro Maths, 1984; Mathematics: The New Golden Age, 1988, 2nd ed., 1999; Logic and Information, 1991; The Joy of Sets, 1993; All the Math That's Fit to Print, 1994; Mathematics: The Science of Patterns, 1994; (with D. Rosenberg) Language at Work-Analyzing Communication Breakdown in the Workplace to Inform Systems Design, 1996; Goodby Descartes-The End of Logic and the Search for a New Cosmology of the Mind, 1997; Life by the Numbers, 1998; The Language of Mathematics, 1998; The Math Gene, 2000.

DEVNEY, Darcy C(ampion). American, b. 1960. **Genres:** Administration/Management, How-to books, Public/Social administration. **Career:** Affiliated with Harvard University, Cambridge, MA, 1979-2001; writer. **Publications:** Organizing Special Events and Conferences: A Practical Guide for Busy Volunteers and Staff, 1990; The Volunteer's Survival Manual: The Only Practical Guide to Giving Your Time and Money, 1992. **Address:** Practical Press, PO Box 382296, Cambridge, MA 02238-2296, U.S.A.

DEVON, Paddie. Irish, b. 1953. **Genres:** Children's fiction, Plays/Screenplays. **Career:** Writer. Photographic and fashion model, 1967-74; Tudor Publications, Belfast, Northern Ireland, graphic artist and art director, until 1982; Sweet Inspirations, Bangor, Ireland, interior design consultant, 1984-. Youth leader in local church; helps with riding for the disabled on a voluntary basis. **Publications:** (self-illustrated) The Grumpy Shepherd, 1995. **Address:** Ballywooley Cottage, 175 Crawfordsburn Rd., Bangor, County Down BT19 1BT, Ireland.

DEVOR, Aaron H. Also writes as Holly Devor. Canadian (born United States), b. 1951. **Genres:** Sociology. **Career:** Simon Fraser University, Burnaby, BC, instructor in women's studies for Prison Education Program, 1986-88, instructor in women's studies, 1988-89; University of Victoria, BC, visiting lecturer, 1989-90, assistant professor, 1990-94, associate professor, 1994-97, professor of sociology, 1997-, associate dean of social sciences, 2001-02, dean of Faculty of Graduate Studies, 2002-07. Society for the Scientific Study of Sexuality, fellow; Society for Teaching & Learning in Higher Education, 3M fellow. Lecturer at colleges and universities. Guest on television and radio programs in Canada, US, and Japan; consultant. **Publications:** Gender Blending: Confronting the Limits of Duality, 1989; FTM: Female-to-Male Transsexuals in Society, 1997. Contributor to books. Contributor of articles and reviews to professional journals. **Address:** Dept of Sociology, University of Victoria, Box 3050, Victoria, BC, Canada V8W 3P5. **Online address:** ahdevor@uvic.ca

DEVOR, Holly. *See* DEVOR, Aaron H.

DE VORSEY, Louis, Jr. American, b. 1929. **Genres:** Geography. **Career:** University of Georgia, Athens, professor of geography, 1967-, now emeritus. **Publications:** The Indian Boundary in the Southern Colonies, 1763-1775, 1966; De Brahm's Report of the General Survey in the Southern District of North America, 1971; The Georgia-South Carolina Boundary, 1982; Keys to the Encounter: A Library of Congress Resource Guide for the Study of the Age of Discovery, 1992; (with M.J. Rice) The Plantation South, 1992; (with W.P. Cumming) The Southeast in Early Maps, 1998. EDITOR: The Atlantic Pilot, 1974; (with J. Parker) In the Wake of Columbus, 1985; (with D. Dallmeyer) Rights to Oceanic Resources, 1989. **Address:** 587 Harris Rd, Lexington, GA 30648, U.S.A. **Online address:** loudev@aol.com

DE VOS, Susan. American (born Japan), b. 1953. **Genres:** Demography. **Career:** University of Wisconsin-Madison, associate scientist. University of Zimbabwe, visiting lecturer. **Publications:** Household Composition in Latin America, 1995. Contributor to academic journals. **Address:** 626 Gately Terrace, Madison, WI 53711, U.S.A.

DEVRIES, Kelly. American, b. 1956. **Genres:** History. **Career:** University of British Columbia, Vancouver, sessional lecturer, 1988-89; Wilfrid Laurier University, Waterloo, ON, assistant professor of history, 1989-91; Loyola College, Baltimore, MD, assistant professor, 1991-96, associate professor of history, 1996-. **Publications:** Medieval Military Technology, 1992; Infantry Warfare in the Early Fourteenth Century, 1996; The Norwegian Invasion of England in 1066, 1999; Joan of Arc: A Military Leader, 1999; A Comprehensive Bibliography of Medieval Military History and Technology, 2002. **Ad-**

dress: Department of History, Loyola College, 4501 N Charles St, Baltimore, MD 21210, U.S.A. **Online address:** kdevries@loyola.edu

DE VRIES, Rachel (Guido). American, b. 1947. **Genres:** Novels, Poetry, Essays, Gay and lesbian issues. **Career:** Syracuse University, Humanistic Studies Center, instructor of creative writing; Community Writers' Project, Syracuse, co-founder and co-director, 1984-. Alternate Literary Programs in the Schools, poet-in-residence, 1984-. Nurse, in the U.S. and in Kenya, 1968-78; Women's Writers' Center, Cazenovia, NY, resident faculty member and co-director, 1978-82. **Publications:** An Arc of Light, 1978; (with others) Learning Our Way: Essays in Feminist Education, 1983; Tender Warriors, 1986; Anthology: The Voices We Carry: Recent Italian American Women's Fiction, 1994; How to Sing to DAGO (poetry), 1995; The Gambler's Daughter, 2001. **Address:** c/o Firebrand Books, 141 The Commons, Ithaca, NY 14850, U.S.A.

DE WAAL, Ronald Burt. American, b. 1932. **Genres:** Literary criticism and history, Autobiography/Memoirs, Bibliography. **Career:** Special Collections Librarian, University of New Mexico, Albuquerque, 1958-59; Head Librarian, New Mexico Military Institute, Roswell, 1959-60, Sperry Utah Co., Salt Lake City, 1961-64, and Westminster College, Salt Lake City, 1964-66; Humanities Librarian, and Exhibits Coordinator, Colorado State University, Fort Collins, 1966-88. **Publications:** The World Bibliography of Sherlock Holmes and Dr. Watson: A Classified and Annotated List of Materials Relating to Their Lives and Adventures, 1887-1972, 1974; The International Sherlock Holmes, 1980; The Universal Sherlock Holmes, 5 vols., 1994; Pages from the Journal of Ron De Waal, 1993-2002, 2003. Contributor to periodicals. **Address:** 638 12th Ave, Salt Lake City, UT 84103, U.S.A.

DEWALD, Paul A. American, b. 1920. **Genres:** Psychiatry. **Career:** Private practitioner of psychoanalysis, St. Louis, Missouri, 1961-; Clinical Professor of Psychiatry, School of Medicine, St. Louis University, 1969-; Medical Director, St. Louis Psychoanalytic Institute, 1972-83. **Publications:** Psychotherapy: A Dynamic Approach, 1964, 1969; The Psychoanalytic Process, 1972; Learning Process in Psychoanalytic Supervision, 1987; The Supportive and Active Psychotherapies: A Dynamic Approach, 1994; (ed. with R.W. Clark) Ethics Case Book of the American Psychoanalytic Association. **Address:** 8000 Delmar Blvd 3H, St. Louis, MO 63124, U.S.A. **Online address:** padewald@mindspring.com

DEWALT, Gary W(eston). American. **Genres:** Plays/Screenplays, Documentaries/Reportage. **Career:** Freelance journalist, investigative filmmaker, and author. **Publications:** SCREENPLAYS: (also director and producer) Genbaku Shi: Killed by the Atomic Bomb, 1985. NONFICTION: (with A. Boukreev) The Climb: Tragic Ambitions on Mt. Everest, 1997. **Address:** c/o St. Martin's Press, 175 Fifth Ave. Rm. 1715, New York, NY 10010, U.S.A.

DEWART, Gilbert. American, b. 1932. **Genres:** Travel/Exploration. **Career:** Arctic Institute of North America, Washington, DC, geophysicist and glaciologist, 1956-58; Seismological Laboratory, Pasadena, CA, research engineer and field geophysicist, 1958-63; Byrd Polar Research Center, Columbus, OH, research associate and fellow, 1963-71; ESD Geophysics (consultants), Pasadena, CA, proprietor, 1972-85; Moorpark College, Moorpark, CA, lecturer, 1986-; writer. Field investigator with U.S. Geological Survey; joint venturer with Cave Research Foundation; prospector for Geophysical Service, Inc.; adviser on natural disasters to American Red Cross; lecturer at universities and colleges; earthquake information lecturer. **Publications:** Antarctic Comrades, 1989. **Address:** Moorpark College, 7075 Campus Rd, Moorpark, CA 93021-1695, U.S.A. **Online address:** dewartg@hotmail.com

DEWBERRY, Elizabeth. Also writes as Elizabeth Dewberry Vaughn. American, b. 1962. **Genres:** Plays/Screenplays, Novels. **Career:** Emory University, instructor of English, 1987-88, visiting assistant professor of English, 1989-90; Samford University, adjunct lecturer of English, 1991-92; Ohio State University, assistant professor of English, 1992-94; Wesleyan Writers' Conference, teaching fellow, 1993; University of Southern California, visiting lecturer of creative writing, 1993; Sewanee Writers' Conference, faculty member, 1994; Bread Loaf Writers' Conference, faculty member, 1994; University of the South, Tennessee Williams Fellow, 1995. **Publications:** PLAYS: (Adaptor with Tom Key from Vaughn's novel) Many Things Have Happened since He Died, 1993; Head On (one-act), 1995; Flesh and Blood, 1996. NOVELS AS ELIZABETH DEWBERRY VAUGHN: Many Things Have Happened Since He Died and Here Are the Highlights, 1990; Break the Heart of Me, 1994. Contributor to books. Contributor to

periodicals. **Address:** c/o Elaine Markson, Elaine Markson Literary Agency, 44 Greenwich Ave., New York, NY 10011, U.S.A.

DEWDNEY, A(lexander) K(eewatin). Canadian, b. 1941. **Genres:** Biology, Information science/Computers, Mathematics/Statistics. **Career:** University of Western Ontario, London, associate professor of computer science, 1968-97, professor of computer science emeritus, 1997-. Omnibus Research, Inc., president. **Publications:** The Planiverse, 1984, rev. ed., 2000; The Armchair Universe, 1986; The Turing Omnibus, 1988; The Magic Machine, 1990; Two Hundred Percent of Nothing, 1993; The New Turing Omnibus, 1993; The Tinkertoy Computer, 1993; Introductory Computer Science, 1996; Yes, We Have No Neutrons, 1997; Hungry Hollow, 1998; A Mathematical Mystery Tour, 1999; Beyond Reason, 2004. **Address:** Department of Computer Science, University of Western Ontario, London, ON, Canada N6A 5B7. **Online address:** akd@julian.uwo.ca

DEWDNEY, John Christopher. British, b. 1928. **Genres:** Geography. **Career:** Professor of Geography, Fourah Bay College, University of Sierra Leone, 1965-67; University of Durham, Lecturer, 1953-68, Sr. Lecturer, 1968-71, Reader, 1971-86, Professor of Geography, 1986-92, emeritus, 1992-. **Publications:** (with H. Bowen-Jones and W.B. Fisher) Malta-Background for Development, 1961; A Geography of the Soviet Union, 1965, 1971, 1979; Turkey, 1971; The U.S.S.R., 1976, 1979; (with others) People in Britain: A Census Atlas, 1980; U.S.S.R. in Maps, 1982; (with G.H. Blake and J. Mitchell) Cambridge Atlas of the Middle East and North Africa, 1987. EDITOR: Durham County and City with Teesside, 1970; (with D. Rhind) People in Durham: A Census Atlas, 1976. **Address:** 48 South St., Durham City DH1 4QP, England.

DEWEESE, Gene. (Thomas Eugene DeWeese). Also writes as Jean DeWeese, Thomas Stratton, Victoria Thomas. American, b. 1934. **Genres:** Novellas/Short stories, Mystery/Crime/Suspense, Horror, Romance/Historical, Science fiction/Fantasy, Children's fiction, Young adult fiction, Crafts. **Career:** Delco Radio, Kokomo, IN, electronics technician, 1954-59; Delco Electronics, Milwaukee, technical writer, 1959-74. **Publications:** NOVELS: Jeremy Case, 1976; The Wanting Factor, 1980; Something Answered, 1983; King of the Dead, 1996; Lord of the Necropolis, 1997; The Vault, 1999; Murder in the Blood (mystery), 2002. STAR TREK NOVELS: Chain of Attack, 1987; The Peacekeepers, 1988; The Final Nexus, 1988; Renegade, 1991; Into the Nebula, 1995; Engines of Destiny, 2005. JUVENILE SCIENCE FICTION: Major Corby and the Unidentified Flapping Object, 1979; Nightmares from Space, 1981; Adventures of a Two-Minute Werewolf, 1983; Black Suits from Outer Space, 1985; The Dandelion Caper, 1986; The Calvin Nullifier, 1987; Whatever Became of Aunt Margaret?, 1990; Firestorm, 1997. WITH ROBERT COULSON: Gates of the Universe, 1975; Now You See It/Him/Them..., 1975; Charles Fort Never Mentioned Wombats, 1977; Nightmare Universe, 1985. WITH ROBERT COULSON AS THOMAS STRATTON: The Invisibility Affair, 1967; The Mind-Twisters Affair, 1967. GOTHIC NOVELS AS JEAN DeWEESE: The Reimann Curse, 1975, rev. ed. as A Different Darkness, 1982; The Moonstone Spirit, 1975; The Carnelian Cat, 1975; Cave of the Moaning Wind, 1976; Web of Guilt, 1976; The Doll with Opal Eyes, 1976; Nightmare in Pewter, 1978; Hour of the Cat, 1980; The Backhoe Gothic, 1981. OTHER: (with G. Rogowski) Making American Folk Art Dolls (non-fiction), 1975; Computers in Entertainment and the Arts (non-fiction), 1984; (with C. Kugi as Victoria Thomas) Ginger's Wish, 1987. Contributor of short stories to periodicals. **Address:** 2718 N Prospect, Milwaukee, WI 53211, U.S.A. **Online address:** gdeweese@wi.rr.com

DEWEESE, Jean. See DEWEESE, Gene.

DEWEESE, Pamela J. American, b. 1951. **Genres:** Literary criticism and history. **Career:** College of Charleston, SC, assistant professor, 1987-90; Sweet Briar College, VA, assistant professor, 1990-93, associate professor, 1993-99, professor of Spanish, 1999-. **Publications:** Approximations to Luis Goytisolo's Antagonia, 2000. Contributor to books and periodicals. **Address:** Dept of Modern Languages and Literatures, Sweet Briar College, Sweet Briar, VA 24595, U.S.A. **Online address:** deweese@sbc.edu

DEWEY, Donald O(dell). American, b. 1930. **Genres:** History. **Career:** Professor of History, 1969-, and Dean of Natural and Social Sciences, 1983-, now Emeritus, California State University, Los Angeles (Assistant Professor, 1962-65; Associate Professor, 1966-69). Assistant Ed., 1960, and Associate Ed., 1960-62, The Papers of James Madison. Ashland (OR) Daily Tidings, city editor, 1953-54. **Publications:** Marshall versus Jefferson: The Political Background of Marbury v. Madison, 1970; That's a Good One: Cal State LA at Fifty, 1997. CO-AUTHOR: Becoming Informed Citizens: Lessons on the

Constitution for Junior High School Students, 1988; Invitation to the Dance: An Introduction to Social Dance, 1991; Becoming Informed Citizens: Lessons on the Bill of Rights and Limited Government, 1994; Controversial Presidential Elections, 2001; The Federalists & Anti-Federalists, 2001. CO-EDITOR: The Papers of James Madison, 3 vols., 1962-64; The Continuing Dialogue, 2 vols., 1964-65. EDITOR: Union and Liberty: Documents in American Constitutionalism, 1969; The Federalist and Anti-Federalist Papers, 1998. **Address:** Dept of History, California State University, Los Angeles, CA 90032, U.S.A. **Online address:** ddewey@calstatela.edu

DEWEY, Joseph (Owen). American, b. 1957. **Genres:** Literary criticism and history. **Career:** University of Pittsburgh at Johnstown, PA, assistant professor, 1987-91, associate professor of American literature, 1991-. Workshop coordinator; seminar presenter. **Publications:** In a Dark Time: The Apocalyptic Temper of the American Novel in the Nuclear Age, 1992; Novels from Reagan's America: A New Realism, 2000; Understanding Richard Powers, 2003. EDITOR & CONTRIBUTOR: (with B. Horvath) The Finer Thread, the Tighter Weave: Perspectives on the Short Fiction of Henry James, 2002; (with S.G. Kellman) Under/Words: Perspectives on Don DeLillo's Underworld, 2003. Contributor to books. Contributor of articles and reviews to periodicals. **Address:** Department of English, Biddle Hall, University of Pittsburgh at Johnstown, Johnstown, PA 15904, U.S.A. **Online address:** dewey@pitt.edu; JDeweyjoe@aol.com

DEWHIRST, Ian. British, b. 1936. **Genres:** Poetry, History, Novellas/Short stories. **Career:** Reference Librarian, Keighley Public Library, 1967-91 (Library Assistant, 1960-65; Lending Librarian, 1965-67). Member Committee of Yorkshire Dialect Society, 1964-2001. Member, Editorial Board, Orbis, 1970-75. **Publications:** The Handloom Weaver and Other Poems, 1965; The Haworth Water-Wolf, and Other Yorkshire Stories, 1967; Scar Top, and Other Poems, 1968; Gleanings from Victorian Yorkshire, 1972; A History of Keighley, 1974; Yorkshire Through the Years, 1975; The Story of a Nobody, 1980; You Don't Remember Bananas, 1985; Keighley in Old Picture Postcards, 1987; Keighley in the 1930s and 1940s, 1989; Victorian Keighley Characters, 1990; In the Reign of the Peacemaker, 1993; Down Memory Lane, 1993; Images of Keighley, 1996. EDITOR: A Poet Passed...Poems by Alfred Holdsworth, 1968; A Century of Yorkshire Dialect, 1997. COMPILER: Old Keighley in Photographs, 1972; More Old Keighley in Photographs, 1973. **Address:** 14 Raglan Ave, Fell Lane, Keighley, W. Yorkshire BD22 6BJ, England.

DEWHURST, Eileen (Mary). British, b. 1929. **Genres:** Mystery/Crime/Suspense. **Career:** Held administrative posts in London and Liverpool universities and Liverpool Chamber of Commerce, 1953-64; freelance journalist, 1964-90; official guide to the Lady Lever Art Collection, Port Sunlight, 1976-82. **Publications:** Death Came Smiling, 1975; After the Ball, 1976; Curtain Fall, 1977; Drink This, 1980; Trio in Three Flats, 1981; Whoever I Am, 1982; The House that Jack Built, 1983; There Was a Little Girl, 1984; Playing Safe, 1985; A Private Prosecution, 1986; A Nice Little Business, 1987; The Sleeper, 1988; Dear Mr. Right, 1990; The Innocence of Guilt, 1991; Death in Candie Gardens, 1992; Now You See Her, 1995; The Verdict on Winter, 1996; Alias the Enemy, 1997; Roundabout, 1998; Death of a Stranger, 1999; Double Act, 2000; Closing Stages, 2001; No Love Lost, 2002; Easeful Death, 2003; Naked Witness, 2003. **Address:** c/o Gregory & Company, 3 Barb Mews, London W6 7PA, England.

DEWITT, Calvin B. American, b. 1935. **Genres:** Environmental sciences/Ecology, Ethics, Theology/Religion. **Career:** University of Michigan-Dearborn, assistant professor, 1963-66, associate professor, 1966-69, professor of biology, 1969-71; University of Wisconsin-Madison, honorary fellow in zoology, 1970, professor of environmental studies, 1972-. Calvin College, fellow of Calvin Center for Christian Scholarship, 1977-78; Au Sable Institute, director, 1980-2004, president, 2004-. Former town chairman in Dunn, WI. **Publications:** The Environment and the Christian, 1991; (with L. Wilkinson and others) Earthkeeping in the Nineties, 1991; (with G.T. Prance) Missionary Earthkeeping, 1992; Earth-Wise: A Biblical Response to Environmental Issues; Caring for Creation: Responsible Stewardship of God's Handiwork, 1998. **Address:** 2508 Lalor Rd, Oregon, WI 53575, U.S.A. **Online address:** cbdewitt@wisc.edu

DEWITT, Helen. American, b. 1957. **Genres:** Novels. **Career:** Author. **Publications:** The Last Samurai, 2000. **Address:** c/o Author Mail, Hyperion, 77 West 66th St., 11th Floor, New York, NY 10023, U.S.A.

DEXTER, (Norman) Colin. British, b. 1930. **Genres:** Mystery/Crime/Suspense. **Career:** Assistant Classics Master, Wyggeston School, Leicester, 1954-57; Sixth Form Classics Master, Loughborough Grammar School,

1957-59; Sr. Classics Master, Corby Grammar School, Northants, 1959-66; Sr. Assistant Secretary to the University of Oxford Delegacy of Local Examinations, Summertown, 1966-88. **Publications:** Last Bus to Woodstock, 1975; Last Seen Wearing, 1976; The Silent World of Nicholas Quinn, 1977; Service of All the Dead, 1979; The Dead of Jericho, 1981; The Riddle of the Third Mile, 1983; The Secret of Annexe 3, 1986; The Wench Is Dead, 1989; The Jewel That Was Ours, 1991; The Way through the Woods, 1992; Morse's Greatest Mystery, 1993; The Daughters of Cain, 1994; Death Is Now My Neighbour, 1996; The Remorseful Day, 2000. **Address:** 456 Banbury Rd, Oxford OX2 7RG, England.

DEXTER, Pete. American, b. 1943. **Genres:** Novels, Plays/Screenplays. **Career:** West Palm Beach Post, Palm Beach, Fla., reporter, 1971-72; Philadelphia Daily News, Philadelphia, Pa., columnist, 1972-84; Sacramento Bee, Sacramento, Calif., columnist, 1985-; novelist. Worked as a truck driver, gas station attendant, mail sorter, construction laborer, and salesman. **Publications:** NOVELS: God's Pocket, 1984; Deadwood, 1986; Paris Trout, 1988; Brotherly Love, 1991; The Paperboy, 1995; Train, 2003. SCREENPLAYS: Rush, 1991; (with others) Michael, 1996. **Address:** Sacramento Bee, PO Box 15779, Sacramento, CA 95852, U.S.A.

DEXTER, Ross. *See* **STOKOE, E(dward) G(eorge).**

DE ZEGHER, M. Catherine. Dutch, b. 1955. **Genres:** History. **Career:** Kanaal Art Foundation, Kortrijk, Belgium, co-founder, 1985, director, 1987-. Institute of Contemporary Art, Boston, MA, visiting curator, 1995-97; lecturer at University of Leeds, Royal College of Art, London, and University of London. Participated in archaeological excavations in Greece and Belgium; curator of art exhibits around the world. **Publications:** Inside the Visible: An Elliptical Traverse of TwentiethCentury Art, in, of, and from the Feminine, 1996; The Precarious: Art and Poery of Cecilia Vicuna and Quipoem, 1997; Mona Hatoum, 1997; Martha Rosler: Rights of Passage, 1997. Contributor to books. Author of exhibition catalogs. **Address:** Kanaal Art Foundation, Pottelberg 73A, 8500 Kortrijk, Belgium.

DHAMI, Narinder. (born England), b. 1958. **Genres:** Children's fiction. **Career:** Worked as a primary school teacher in London, England, c. 1980-90; full time writer, 1990-. **Publications:** (with Kate Rogers) A Medal for Malina, 1990; (with Julie Park) Cat's Eyes, 1993; Angel Face, 1995; My Secret Love by Andy Brown, 1995; Starring Alice Mackenzie, 1996; Me and My Big Mouth, 1997; Oh Brother!, 1998; Spotlight on Sunita, 1998; The Cool Rule, 1998; (Adapter) The Case of the Disappearing Dragon (screenplay novelization),1998; Who's Who?, 1998; Annie's Game, 1999; Animal Crackers, 2000; Genius Games, Hyperion (New York, NY), 2001; (Adapter) Charles Dickens, Christmas Carol: The Movie, 2001; (Adapter) Gurinder Chadha, Guljit Bindra, and Paul Mayeda Berges, Bend It Like Beckham (screenplay novelization), 2002; Changing Places, 2002; (Adapter) Cinderella, 2003; (Adapter) Disney's The Lion King, 2003; (Adapter) Disney's The Jungle Book, 2003; (Adapter) Disney's The Aristocats, 2003; (Adapter) Disney's Lady and the Tramp, 2003; (Adapter) Sleeping Beauty, 2003; Bindi Babes, 2003, 2004; Bollywood Babes, 2005. ANIMAL STARS SERIES; ILLUSTRATED BY STRAWBERRIE DONNELLY: Harry's Starring Role, 1999; Casper in the Spotlight, 1999; Spike's Secret, Hodder 1999; Midnight the Movie Star, 1999; Casper in the Spotlight, 1999; Trixie's Magic Trick, 1999. SLEEPOVER CLUB SERIES: Starring the Sleepover Club, 1997; The Sleepover Club Sleeps Out, 1997; Sleepover in Spain, 1998; Sleepover Girls and Friends, 1999; Sleepover Girls Go Designer, 1999; Vive le Sleepover Club!, 2000; Sari Sleepover, 2000; Sleepover Club Down Under, 2000; Sleepover Girls Go Karting, 2001; Sleepoverclub.com, 2001; Sleepover Girls on the Ball (summer special), 2001. Contributor to Writers News. **Address:** Rosemary Canter, PFD, Drury House, 34-43 Russell Street, London WC2B 5HA, England.

DHAVAMONY, Mariasusai. Indian, b. 1925. **Genres:** Philosophy, Theology/Religion. **Career:** Gregorian University, professor of history of religions and Hinduism, 1966-, now emeritus. Chief Ed., Studia Missionalia periodical, and Chief Director-Ed., Documenta Missionalia series, 1968-. **Publications:** Subjectivity and Knowledge according to St. Thomas Aquinas, 1965; Love of God according to Saiva Sidhanta, 1971; (with C. Papali and P. Fallon) For Dialogue with Hinduism, 1972; Phenomenology of Religion, 1973; Classical Hinduism, 1982; La luce di Dio nell'Induismo, 1987; L'Induismo, 1991; (with others) Le grandi figure dell'Induismo, 1992; L'Hindouisme et Foi Chretienne, 1995; Christian Theology of World Religions, 1997; Teologia delle religioni, 1997; Christian Theology of Inculturation, 1997; La Spiritualite Hindoue, 1997; La teologia de las religiones, 1998; Pluralismo Religioso e Missione della Chiesa, 2001; Madre Teresa, 2002; The Kingdom of God and World Religions, 2004; World Religions in the History of Salvation, 2004; Il Dialogo indu-cristiano e Missione della Chiesa, 2004. EDITOR: Evangelization, Dialogue and Development, 1972; Prospettive di Missiologia oggi, 1982; La meditazione nelle grandi religioni, 1989; Teologia Cristiana delle religioni e della Missione Ad Gentes, 2002. Contributor to books and periodicals. **Address:** Gregorian University, Piazza della Pilotta 4, 00187 Rome, Italy. **Online address:** dhavamony@unigre.it

DI, Zhu Xiao. American (born People's Republic of China), b. 1958. **Genres:** Autobiography/Memoirs, Education. **Career:** Jiangsu Education College, Nanjing, China, assistant professor of English, supervisor of field education, liaison officer, and interpreter, 1982-87; Harvard University, Cambridge, MA, research assistant at Fairbank Center for East Asian Research, 1987-89; Cognetics Inc., research assistant, 1989-90; Management Strategies Inc., assistant to the president, 1991-92; University of Massachusetts at Boston, assistant study director at Center for Survey Research, 1992-93, senior assistant director, 1993-97; Harvard University, research associate at Joint Center for Housing Studies, 1997-. Consultant. **Publications:** (with JinMin Chen) English-Speaking Nations (textbook), 1984; Thirty Years in a Red House: A Memoir of Childhood and Youth in Communist China, 1998. Contributor to Chinese management journals and other periodicals. **Address:** 357 Commercial St. No. 619, Boston, MA 02109, U.S.A. **Online address:** zhu_xiao_di@ksg.harvard.edu

DIAL-DRIVER, Emily. American, b. 1946. **Genres:** Education, Writing/Journalism, Plays/Screenplays. **Career:** Ohio State University, Columbus, dietary interviewer for Children's Hospital Research Foundation, 1968-69; Rogers State University, Claremore, OK, instructor, 1971-74, instructor, then professor of English, 1980-, coordinator of ACHIEVE Program and chairperson of curriculum committee, both 1996-99. National speaker on topics related to distance education, educational media, and curriculum development; developer of "telecourses"; also gives poetry readings. **Publications:** Composition II: Multiple Learning Opportunities, 1989; Write Right, 1993; College Writing: Discovering the Writing Spiral, 1994; A Guide to College Writing, 1996. PLAYS: Beauty and the Beast, 1987; The Three Little Pigs, 1988; Hansel and Gretel, 1989. EDITOR: (and author of intro) Maggie Fry, The Cherokee Female Seminary Years: A Cherokee National Anthology, 1990; (and contrib) The Competitive Edge II, 1992. Scriptwriter for television courses. Contributor of articles and poems to periodicals. **Address:** Department of Communications and Fine Arts, Rogers State University, 1701 West Will Rogers Blvd., Claremore, OK 74017, U.S.A. **Online address:** edial-driver@rsu.edu

DIALLO, Kadiatou. (born Guinea), b. 1959. **Genres:** Autobiography/Memoirs. **Career:** Public speaker and former gem dealer. Also founder of the Amadou Diallo Foundation. **Publications:** (with Craig Wolff) My Heart Will Cross This Ocean: My Story, My Son, Amadou, 2003. **Address:** c/o Author Mail, Ballantine Books, 1745 Broadway, New York, NY 10019, U.S.A.

DIAMANT, Anita. American, b. 1951. **Genres:** Novels, How-to books, Essays. **Career:** Writer. Boston Phoenix, columnist and staff writer, 1980-83; Boston, senior staff writer, 1986-88; WBUR-FM Radio, commentator, 1981-82, 1994. Columnist, Boston Globe magazine, 1988-94, and Parenting, 1993-95. **Publications:** The New Jewish Wedding, 1985, rev. ed., 2001; The Jewish Baby Book, 1988, as The New Jewish Baby Book: Names, Ceremonies, Customs-A Guide for Today's Families, 1994; What to Name Your Jewish Baby, 1989; (with H. Cooper) Living a Jewish Life, 1991; Bible Baby Names, 1996; Choosing a Jewish Life: A Handbook for People Converting to Judaism, 1997; Saying Kaddish, 1998; How to Mourn as a Jew; (with K. Kishner) How to be a Jewish Parent, 2000; Pitching My Tent: On Marriage, Motherhood, Friendship and Other Leaps of Faith (essays), 2003. NOVELS: The Red Tent, 1997; Good Harbor, 2001. **Address:** c/o Amanda Urban, ICM Agency, 40 W 57th St 17th Fl, New York, NY 10019, U.S.A.

DIAMOND, Arthur. American, b. 1957. **Genres:** Children's non-fiction, Biography, History. **Career:** Writer. St. John's University, Queens, NY, adjunct professor of English, 1990-91; corporate sales communications, 1991-2000. **Publications:** The Romanian Americans, 1988; Paul Cuffe, 1989; The Bhopal Chemical Leak, 1990; Smallpox and the American Indian, 1991; Alcoholism, 1992; Jackie Robinson, 1992; Egypt: Gift of the Nile, 1992; Prince Hall: Social Reformer, 1992; Malcolm X, 1993; Anwar Sadat, 1994; Charlie Chaplin, 1995. **Address:** 80-17 209th St, Queens Village, NY 11427, U.S.A. **Online address:** aidiamondfamily@aol.com

DIAMOND, Jared (Mason). American, b. 1937. **Genres:** Environmental sciences/Ecology, Geography. **Career:** Physiologist, ecologist, geographer, and author, specializing in evolutionary biology, ecology, bird faunas of New Guinea and other southwest Pacific islands, biological membranes, and comparative environmental history. Harvard Medical School, Cambridge, MA., associate in biophysics, 1965-66; University of California Medical School, Los Angeles, associate professor of physiology, 1966-68, professor, 1968-. American Museum of Natural History, Department of Ornithology, research associate, 1973-; Los Angeles County Museum of Natural History, research associate, 1985-. National Science Foundation, fellow, 1958-61, 1961-62; Trinity College, Cambridge, fellow in physiology, 1961-65; Harvard University Society of Fellows, junior fellow, 1962-65. **Publications:** NONFICTION: Avifauna of the Eastern Highlands of New Guinea, 1972; (with M. Lecroy) Birds of Karkar and Bagabag Islands, New Guinea, 1979; The Third Chimpanzee: The Evolution and Future of the Human Animal, 1992 in UK as The Rise and Fall of the Third Chimpanzee; Guns, Germs, and Steel: The Fates of Human Societies, 1997. EDITOR: (with M.L. Cody) Ecology and Evolution of Communities, 1975; (with T.J. Case) Community Ecology, 1986. Contributor to nature magazines. Author of research papers on physiology, ecology, and ornithology. **Address:** Department of Geography, University of California, Los Angeles, CA 90095-1524, U.S.A.

DIAMOND, Jed. American, b. 1943. **Genres:** Psychology. **Career:** Psychotherapist and author. Director of MenAlive (health center for men); member of boards of advisors. **Publications:** Looking for Love in All the Wrong Places: Romantic and Sexual Addictions, 1988; The Warrior's Journey Home: Healing Men, Healing Planet, 1994; Male Menopause, 1997; Surviving Male Menopause: A Guide for Women and Men, 2000; The Whole Man Program: Reinvigorating Your Body and Spirit after Forty, 2002. **Address:** 34133 Shimmins Rd, Willits, CA 95490, U.S.A. **Online address:** Jed@menalive.com

DIAMOND, Petra. See SACHS, Judith.

DIAMOND, Rebecca. See SACHS, Judith.

DIAMOND, Rickey Gard. American, b. 1946. **Genres:** Novels, Novellas/Short stories, Environmental sciences/Ecology, Women's studies and issues, Essays. **Career:** Central Vermont Community Action Council, Barre, director of communications, 1981-85; Vermont Woman, Burlington, founding editor, 1985-88; Central Vermont Community Action Council, director of development, 1988-93; Norwich University, Vermont College Campus, Montpelier, part-time adjunct faculty member, 1990-95, assistant professor of liberal studies, 1995-2001; Union Institute & University, professor, 2001-. Multicultural Media (music distributors and producers), co-owner; Community College of Vermont, instructor, 1984, 1985; Johnson State College, tutorial instructor, 1987, instructor, 1993. **Publications:** Vermont Odysseys: Essays on the New Vermont, 1991; Second Sight (novel), 1997. Contributor of stories, articles, and reviews to periodicals. **Address:** 56 Browns Mill Rd, Montpelier, VT 05602-9565, U.S.A.

DIAMOND, Sara. American, b. 1958. **Genres:** Politics/Government. **Career:** Writer. **Publications:** Spiritual Warfare: The Politics of the Christian Right, 1989; Roads to Dominion: Right-Wing Movements and Political Power in the United States, 1995; Facing the Wrath: Confronting the Right in Dangerous Times, 1996; Not by Politics Alone: The Enduring Influence of the Christian Right, 1998. **Address:** PO Box 6006, Albany, CA 94706-0006, U.S.A.

DIAZ, Tony. American, b. 1968. **Genres:** Novels. **Career:** Author, teacher, political activist. Assistant director of the Central American Resource Center; affiliated with The Houston Immigration and Refugee Coalition, La Coordinator 2000, and other community groups. Has held teaching positions with the University of Houston, Inprint Houston, St. Charles Church, the High School for the Performing and Visual Arts, and the Chicano Family Center. **Publications:** The Aztec Love God (novel), 1998; (ed.) Latino Heretics, Fiction Collective Two, 1999. Contributor to anthologies and periodicals. **Address:** Red Lat Writings, PO Box 540181, Houston, TX 77245, U.S.A. **Online address:** AztecMuse@aol.com

DIAZ-STEVENS, Ana Maria. American, b. 1942. **Genres:** Cultural/Ethnic topics, Theology/Religion. **Career:** New York Catholic Archdiocese, NYC, administrative coordinator of Spanish-speaking apostolate, 1969-72; Brooklyn Catholic Diocese, Brooklyn, NY, member of Board of Catholic Charities, 1973-76; Centro de Evangelizacion, Ministerio e Investigacion, Jamaica, NY, co-founder, editor, and investigator, 1974-78; Queens College of the City University of New York, Flushing, NY, adjunct assistant professor of modern languages, sociology, and Puerto Rican studies, 1978-86; Fordham University, NYC, assistant professor of social science, 1986-87; Rutgers University, New Brunswick, NJ, assistant professor of Puerto Rican and Hispanic studies, 1989-93; Union Theological Seminary, NYC, associate professor of church and society, 1993-. **Publications:** Oxcart Catholicism on Fifth Avenue: The Impact of the Puerto Rican Migration upon the Archdiocese of New York, 1993; The Religious Experience of Latinos in the United States: An Interdisciplinary Perspective, 1994; An Enduring Flame: Popular Religiosity of Latinos, 1994; Recognizing the Latino Resurgence in U.S. Religion, 1997. Contributor to books and academic journals. **Address:** Union Theological Seminary, 3041 Broadway, New York, NY 10027, U.S.A. **Online address:** dstevens@uts.columbia.edu

DIBARTOLOMEO, Albert. American, b. 1952. **Genres:** Novels. **Career:** Philadelphia School Board, Philadelphia, PA, library assistant, 1975-80; self-employed cabinetmaker, Philadelphia, 1980-89; Temple University, instructor, 1986-88; Delaware County Community College, instructor, 1990; Community College of Philadelphia, Philadelphia, instructor in creative writing and expository writing, 1990; Drexel University, Philadelphia, adjunct assistant professor of English, 1990-95, auxiliary faculty, instructor of English, 1996-; Philadelphia College of Pharmacy and Science, adjunct faculty, instructor of English, 1994-96; University of Pennsylvania, visiting lecturer, creative writing, 1995-. Gives readings of his works. **Publications:** The Vespers Tapes (novel), 1991, as Blood Confessions, 1992; Fool's Gold (novel), 1993. Contributor of short stories to periodicals. **Address:** c/o Diana Finch, Trident Media Group, 41 Madison Ave., #36, New York, NY 10010-2257, U.S.A.

DIBBERN, Mary. American, b. 1951. **Genres:** Music, Translations. **Career:** Pianist, working in the field of classical vocal music. Performed with many French opera companies also worked in the United States, China, and other European countries. **Publications:** The Tales of Hoffmann: A Performance Guide, 2001; (with C. Kimball and P. Choukroun) Interpreting the Songs of Jacques Leguerney, 2001; Carmen: A Performance Guide; Faust/Romeo et Juliette: A Performance Guide. **Address:** c/o Author Mail, Pendragon Press, 52 Whitehill Ln, PO Box 190, Hillsdale, NY 12529-0190, U.S.A. **Online address:** MaryDibbern@aol.com

DIBBLE, J(ames) Birney. American, b. 1925. **Genres:** Novels, Travel/Exploration, Mystery/Crime/Suspense, Biography, Novellas/Short stories, Poetry. **Career:** Surgeon, Eau Claire, Wisconsin, since 1957. **Publications:** In This Land of Eve, 1964; The Plains Brood Alone, 1973; Pan (fiction), 1980; Brain Child (fiction), 1987; Outlaw for God, 1991; The Taking of Hill 1052 (novel), 1995. **Address:** W 4290 Jene Rd, Eau Claire, WI 54701, U.S.A.

DIBDIN, Michael. British, b. 1947. **Genres:** Mystery/Crime/Suspense. **Career:** English teacher, International House, Perugia, 1980-82; language asst., University of Perugia, 1982-84. Recipient, Crime Writers Association Golden Dagger Award, 1988. **Publications:** The Last Sherlock Holmes Story, 1978; A Rich Full Death, 1986; Ratking, 1988; The Tryst, 1989; Vendetta, 1990; Dirty Tricks, 1991; Cabal, 1992; The Dying of the Light, 1993; Dead Lagoon, 1994; Dark Spectre, 1995; Così Fan Tutti, 1996; A Long Finish, 1998; Blood Rain, 1999; Thanksgiving, 2000. **Address:** c/o PFD, Drury House, 34-43 Russell St, London WC2B 5HA, England.

DI BLASI, Debra. American, b. 1957. **Genres:** Novellas/Short stories, Plays/Screenplays. **Career:** Robert Half of Northern California, San Francisco, advertising manager, 1986-89; MacWeek, San Francisco, advertising production manager, 1989; Accessible Arts Inc., Kansas City, KS, assistant to the executive director, 1990-92; Sprint Communications, Kansas City, MO, senior secretary in International Network Design and Engineering Department, 1992-95; Kansas City Art Institute, Kansas City, MO, writing tutor, 1994, writing instructor, 1995-. National and international fiction and poetry competitions, judge, 1997-; SOMA, associate guest editor; lectures on writing, teaches writing workshops, reads from her works. **Publications:** Drought and Say What You Like (novellas), 1997; Prayers of an Accidental Nature (short stories), 1999. SCREENPLAYS: The Season's Condition, 1993; Drought, 1997. Author of short stories, represented in anthologies and periodicals. Contributor of essays, articles, and reviews to periodicals. **Address:** Kansas City Art Institute, 4415 Warwick Blvd, Kansas City, MO 64111, U.S.A. **Online address:** ddiblasi@excite.com

DI CERTO, J(oseph) J(ohn). American, b. 1933. **Genres:** Novels, Children's fiction, Communications/Media, Air/Space topics, Social commentary. **Career:** Director of Communications, CBS Broadcast International, 1981- (Director of Sales Promotions, CBS TV stations, 1978-80; Director of Communications, CBS Cable, 1980-81). Sr. Technical Writer, Curtiss Wright Corp., 1956-59; Technical Writer and Ed., American Machine and Foundry, 1959-62; Publs. Engineer, Sperry Gyroscope, 1962-66;

Advertising Supvr., Sylvania Electric Products, NYC, 1966-74; Manager of Special Projects, Sperry Rand Corp., Advertising Agencies, NYC 1974-78. **Publications:** Planning and Preparing Data Flow Diagrams, 1963; Missile Base beneath the Sea, 1967; The Electric Wishing Well: The Energy Crisis, 1976; From Earth to Infinity, 1980; Star Voyage, 1981; Looking into TV, 1983; The Wall People, 1985, rev. ed., 2004; Hoofbeats in the Wilderness, 1988; The Pony Express, 2002.

DICK, Bernard F. American, b. 1935. **Genres:** Film, Literary criticism and history. **Career:** Iona College, New Rochelle, NY, instructor to associate professor and chairman, Classics Dept., 1961-70; Fairleigh Dickinson University, Teaneck, NJ, associate professor, 1970-73, professor of English and comparative literature, 1973-95, professor of communication and English, 1995-, director, School of Communication Arts, 1996-97. **Publications:** William Golding, 1967; The Hellenism of Mary Renault, 1972; The Apostate Angel: A Critical Study of Gore Vidal, 1974; Anatomy of Film, 1978, 5th ed., 2004; Billy Wilder, 1980, rev. ed., 1996; (ed.) Dark Victory (screenplay), 1981; Hellman in Hollywood, 1982; Joseph L. Mankiewicz, 1983; The Star-Spangled Screen, 1985; Radical Innocence: A Critical Study of the Hollywood Ten, 1989; Columbia Pictures: Portrait of a Studio, 1992; The Merchant Prince of Poverty Row: Harry Cohn of Columbia Pictures, 1993; City of Dreams: The Making and Remaking of Universal Pictures, 1997; Engulfed: The Death of Paramount Pictures and the Birth of Corporate Hollywood, 2001; Hal Wallis: Producer to the Stars, 2004. **Address:** 580 Wyndham Rd, Teaneck, NJ 07666, U.S.A. **Online address:** BernardFD5666729@aol.com

DICK, David. American, b. 1930. **Genres:** Novels, Local history/Rural topics. **Career:** WHAS-Radio and Television, Louisville, KY, journalist, 1959-66; CBS Inc., correspondent in Washington, DC, Atlanta, GA, Caracas, Venezuela, and Dallas, TX, 1966-85; Bourbon Times, Paris, KY, publisher, 1988-91; Plum Lick Publishing Inc., North Middletown, KY, president, 1992-. University of Kentucky, professor, 1985-96. **Publications:** NONFICTION: The View from Plum Lick, 1992; Follow the Storm, 1993; Peace at the Center, 1994; The Quiet Kentuckians, 1996; Home Sweet Kentucky, 1999; Rivers of Kentucky, 2001. OTHER: A Conversation with Peter P. Pence (fiction), 1995; The Scourges of Heaven (historical novel), 1998. **Address:** Plum Lick Publishing Inc., PO Box 68, North Middletown, KY 40357, U.S.A. **Online address:** ddick@uky.campus.mci.net

DICKASON, Olive Patricia. Canadian, b. 1920. **Genres:** Anthropology/Ethnology, History. **Career:** High school history teacher in Wilcox, Saskatchewan, 1943-44; Leader-Post, Regina, Saskatchewan, general and city hall reporter, 1944-46; Winnipeg Free Press, Winnipeg, Manitoba, reporter and subeditor, 1946-47; free-lance writer, 1947-50; Gazette, Montreal, Quebec, reporter, subeditor, and women's editor, 1950-55; Globe and Mail, Toronto, Ontario, associate women's editor, 1955-57, women's editor of Globe magazine, 1957-62; women's editor, 1962-67; chief of information services for National Gallery of Canada, 1967-70; University of Alberta, Edmonton, sessional lecturer, 1975-76, assistant professor, 1976-79, associate professor, 1979-85, professor of history, 1985-92, professor emeritus, 1992-; University of Ottawa, adjunct professor, 1997-. **Publications:** Indian Arts in Canada, 1972; The Myth of the Savage and the Beginnings of French Colonialism in the Americas, 1984; (with L.C. Green) The Law of Nations and the New World, 1989; Canada's First Nations: A History of Founding Peoples from Earliest Times, 1992, 3rd ed., 2001. EDITOR: (& comp.) The Native Imprint, vol. 1, To 1815, 1995; (with D.A. Long) Visions of the Heart, 1996. Contributor to books and periodicals. **Address:** 500 Laurier Ave W Apt 808, Ottawa, ON, Canada K1R 5E1. **Online address:** dickason@uottawa.ca

DICKE, Thomas S(cott). American, b. 1955. **Genres:** History. **Career:** High school teacher of history, geography, and American government in Hebron, IL, 1979-81; Ohio State University, Columbus, instructor, 1987-88, lecturer, 1988-89; University of Georgia, Athens, temporary assistant professor, 1989-90; Southwest Missouri State University, Springfield, assistant professor, 1990-93, associate professor of history, 1993-. **Publications:** Franchising in America: The Development of a Business Method, 1840-1980, 1992. Contributor of articles and reviews to history and business journals. **Address:** Department of History, Southwest Missouri State University, 901 S National Ave, Springfield, MO 65804, U.S.A. **Online address:** TomDicke@smsu.edu

DICKERSON, Dennis C. American, b. 1949. **Genres:** History. **Career:** Williams College, Williamstown, MA, Stanfield Professor of History and head of department, 1976-. African Methodist Episcopal Church, historiographer. **Publications:** Out of the Crucible: Black Steelworkers in

Western Pennsylvania, 1875-1980, 1986; Militant Mediator: Whitney M. Young, Jr., 1998. Work represented in anthologies. Contributor to scholarly journals. **Address:** Department of History, Stetson Hall, Williams College, Williamstown, MA 01267, U.S.A. **Online address:** dennis.c.dickerson@ williams.edu

DICKEY, Eric Jerome. American. **Genres:** Novels, Plays/Screenplays. **Career:** Writer. Worked for Rockwell (now Boeing), TN, computer systems technology. Employed at Federal Express; Lowenstein's, Memphis, TN, as a bill collector; Memphis State University (now University of Memphis), in the college game room; as a stand-up comedian, Seattle, WA, and San Antonio, TX; as an actor; and as a substitute teacher. **Publications:** NOVELS: Sister, Sister, 1996; Friends and Lovers, 1997; Milk in My Coffee, 1998; Cheaters: Caught Up in the Game, 1999. MYSTERIES: Thieves' Paradise, 2002; The Other Woman, 2003. SCREENPLAY: Cappuccino, 1998. **Address:** c/o Dutton, 375 Hudson St., New York, NY 10014, U.S.A. **Online address:** edickey142@aol.com

DICKEY, Page. American, b. 1940. **Genres:** Homes/Gardens. **Career:** Garden designer, author, columnist, and lecturer. **Publications:** Duck Hill Journal: A Year in a Country Garden, 1991; Breaking Ground: Portraits of Ten Garden Designers, 1997; Inside Out: Relating Garden to House, 2000; Dogs in Their Gardens, 2001; Cats in Their Gardens, 2002. **Address:** 23 Baxter Rd, North Salem, NY 10560, U.S.A. **Online address:** pdickey@ optonline.net

DICKIE, Matthew W(allace). Scottish, b. 1941. **Genres:** Classics. **Career:** Swarthmore College, instructor, 1967-68, associate professor of classics, 1972-78; University of Illinois, Chicago, professor of classics, 1978-. **Publications:** (ed., with O. Anderson) Homer's World: Fiction, Tradition, Reality, 1995; Magic and Magicians in the Greco-Roman World, 2001. Contributor to professional journals. **Address:** Department of Classics and Mediterranean Studies, University of Illinois, Chicago Circle, Box 4348, Chicago, IL 60680, U.S.A. **Online address:** theurgy@uic.edu

DICKINSON, Don(ald Percy). Canadian, b. 1947. **Genres:** Novels, Novellas/Short stories. **Career:** British Columbia, English teacher. **Publications:** (with B. Dempster and D. Margoshes) Third Impressions, 1982; Fighting the Upstream (stories), 1987; Blue Husbands (stories), 1991; The Crew (novel), 1993; Robbiestime (novel), 2000. Work represented in anthologies. **Address:** 554 Victoria St, PO Box 341, Lillooet, BC, Canada V0K 1V0.

DICKINSON, Harry Thomas. British, b. 1939. **Genres:** History, Biography. **Career:** Professor of History, Edinburgh University, 1980- (Lecturer and Reader, 1966-80); concurrently, Professor of History, Nanjing University, China, 1987-. History Master, Washington Grammar School, Co. Durham, 1961-64; Earl Grey Research Fellow, University of Newcastle upon Tyne, 1964-66. **Publications:** Bolingbroke, 1970; Walpole and the Whig Supremacy, 1973; Liberty and Property, 1977; British Radicalism and the French Revolution, 1985; Caricatures and the Constitution 1760-1832, 1986; The Politics of the People in Eighteenth-Century Britain, 1995. EDITOR: Correspondence of Sir James Clavering, 1967; Politics and Literature in the 18th Century, 1974; The Political Works of Thomas Spence, 1982; Britain and the French Revolution 1789-1815, 1989; Britain and the American Revolution, 1998; (with M. Lynch) The Challenge to Westminster, 2000; A Companion to Eighteenth-Century Britain, 2002. **Address:** History Dept, University of Edinburgh, Edinburgh EH8 9JY, Scotland. **Online address:** Harry.Dickinson@ed.ac.uk

DICKINSON, Janice. American, b. 1955. **Genres:** Autobiography/Memoirs. **Career:** Model and photographer. **Publications:** No Lifeguard on Duty: The Accidental Life of the World's First Supermodel (memoir), 2002; Everything about Me Is Fake-I'm Perfect, 2004. **Address:** 9972 West Wanda Dr., Beverly Hills, CA 90210, U.S.A.

DICKINSON, Margaret. See **MUGGESON, Margaret Elizabeth.**

DICKINSON, Matt. British. **Genres:** Documentaries/Reportage. **Career:** Writer and filmmaker. British Broadcasting Corporation, member of staff, 1984-1988; freelance producer-director, 1988-. **Publications:** The Death Zone: Climbing Everest through the Killer Storm, 1997, in US as The Other Side of Everest: Climbing the North Face through the Killer Zone, 1999; Black Ice, 2002. **Address:** c/o Author Mail, Hutchinson Random House, 20 Vauxhall Bridge Rd., London SW1V 2SA, England. **Online address:** MDickinson@literati.net

DICKINSON, Peter. British (born Zambia), b. 1927. **Genres:** Novels, Mystery/Crime/Suspense, Science fiction/Fantasy, Children's fiction, Young adult fiction, Poetry. **Career:** Punch mag., London, assistant editor, 1952-69. Society of Authors, chairman, 1979-80. **Publications:** Skin Deep, 1968 (in US as The Glass-Sided Ants' Nest); The Weathermonger, 1968; A Pride of Heroes (in US as The Old English Peep-Show), 1969; Heartsease, 1969; The Seals (in US as The Sinful Stones), 1970; The Devil's Children, 1970; Sleep and His Brother, 1971; Emma Tupper's Diary, 1971; The Lizard in the Cup, 1972; The Dancing Bear, 1972; The Green Gene, 1973; The Gift, 1973; The Iron Lion, 1973; The Poison Oracle, 1974; Chance, Luck and Destiny, 1975; The Lively Dead, 1975; The Blue Hawk, 1976; King and Joker, 1976; Annerton Pit, 1977; Walking Dead, 1977; Hepzibah, 1978; One Foot in the Grave, 1979; Tulku, 1979; The Flight of the Dragons, 1979; City of Gold, 1980; A Summer in the Twenties, 1981; The Last House-Party, 1982; Healer, 1983; Hindsight, 1983; Death of a Unicorn, 1984; A Box of Nothing, 1985; Tefuga, 1986; Perfect Gallows, 1988; Merlin Dreams, 1988; Eva, 1988; Skeleton-in-Waiting, 1989; AK, 1990; Play Dead, 1991; A Bone from a Dry Sea, 1992; Time and the Clock-mice, etc, 1993; The Yellow Room Conspiracy, 1996; Shadow of a Hero, 1994; Chuck and Danielle, 1996; The Lion Tamer's Daughter and Other Supernatural Stories, 1997; The Kin, 4 vols., 1998; Some Deaths before Dying, 1999; The Ropemaker, 2001; The Tears of the Salamander, 2003; The Gift Boat (in US as Inside Grandad).

DICKINSON, Terence. Canadian, b. 1943. **Genres:** Children's non-fiction, Young adult non-fiction, Astronomy. **Career:** Science writer, 1976-. Ontario Ministry of Transportation and Communications, Toronto, Ontario, technician, 1964-1967; McLaughlin Planetarium, Royal Ontario Museum, Toronto, scientific assistant, 19671970; Stasenburgh Planetarium, Rochester, NY, assistant director, 19701973; editor, Astronomy, 1973-1975; Ontario Science Centre, Toronto, editor of publications, 1975-1976; Whig-Standard, Kingston, Ontario, astronomy columnist, 1976-1982; St. Lawrence College, Kingston, Ontario, part-time teaching master, 1977-. Astronomy commentator for Quirks and Quarks, CBC Radio, 1978-1994, and Discovery Channel, 1994-. Consultant to museums, science centers, educational institutions, and Hollywood science fiction films. Ghost writer of many of the astronomy and space questions for the Trivial Pursuit board game. Frequent speaker at professional societies, universities and colleges, and astronomy conventions throughout North America. Regular interview guest on Canadian radio and television. **Publications:** CHILDREN'S AND YOUNG ADULT NONFICTION: Exploring the Night Sky: The Equinox Astronomy Guide for Beginners, 1987; Exploring the Sky by Day: The Equinox Guide to Weather and the Atmosphere, 1988; From the Big Bang to Planet X: The Fifty Most-asked Questions about the Universe-and Their Answers, 1993; (with A. Schaller) Extraterrestrials: A Field Guide for Earthlings, 1994; Other Worlds: A Beginner's Guide to Planets and Moons, 1995. ADULT NONFICTION: Exploring the Moon and the Solar System, 1971; (with S. Brown) Sky Guide, 1977; (with G. Chaple and V. Costanzo) The Edmund Mag 6 Star Atlas, 1982; Nightwatch: An Equinox Guide to Viewing the Universe, 1983, rev ed, 1995; Halley's Comet: Mysterious Visitor from Outer Space, 1985; The Universe and Beyond, 1986, rev ed, 1995; (with A. Dyer) Backyard Astronomer's Guide, 1991, rev ed, 1995; Summer Stargazing: A Practical Guide for Recreational Astronomers for Use Anywhere in North America through 2010, 1996; (with J. Newton) Splendors of the Universe: A Practical Guide to Photographing the Night Sky, 1997. Contributor to magazines and newspapers. **Address:** PO Box 10, Yarker, ON, Canada K0K 3N0.

DICKINSON, W(illiam) Calvin. American, b. 1938. **Genres:** Local history/ Rural topics. **Career:** Chowan College, instructor, 1961-63, department head, 1965-71; Tennessee Technological University, Cookeville, associate professor, 1971-76, professor of history, 1976-. Macalester College, visiting lecturer, 1971; College of Charleston, visiting lecturer, 1986. Upper Cumberland Humanities and Social Sciences Institute, associate director, 1982-; Tennessee Historical Commission, associate director of Architectural Survey Program, 1983-. **Publications:** James Harrington's Republic, 1983; (ed. with L. Whiteaker and others) Lend an Ear: Heritage of the Tennessee Upper Cumberland, 1983; History of Morgan County, 1987; (with Whiteaker) Tennessee in American History, 1989; (with Whiteaker) Letters of Cornelius Tenure, Civil War Soldier, 1989; Sidney Godolphin, Lord Treasurer, 1990; (with H. Neufeldt) History of Tennessee Tech University, 1991; Cumberland County, Tennessee, 1800-1985, 1992; (with Whiteaker) Tennessee: State of the Nation, 1994, 2nd ed., 1995; (with E. Hitchcock) The War of the Spanish Succession, 1702-1713: A Bibliography, 1996; Bibliography of Tennessee History, 1973-1996, 1998. Contributor to books. Contributor of articles and reviews to scholarly journals and other periodicals. **Address:** 876 Pen Oak Dr, Cookeville, TN 38501, U.S.A.

DICKMAN, Thomas. American, b. 1955. **Genres:** Translations. **Career:** Writer. Licensed clinical social worker. **Publications:** (trans. with A. Lefebvre) M. Beaud, A History of Capitalism, 1500-1980, 1983; (trans.)

Socialism in the Crucible of History; Inside the Millennium (novel). **Address:** 1784 South 800 E., Salt Lake City, UT 84105, U.S.A.

DICKS, Shirley. American, b. 1940. **Genres:** Criminology/True Crime, Military/Defense/Arms control. **Career:** Leader of a death row ministry, 1986-; writer. **Publications:** Death Row: Interviews with Inmates, Their Families, and Opponents of Capital Punishment, 1990; From Vietnam to Hell: Interviews with Victims of Post-Traumatic Stress Disorder, 1990; Victims of Crime and Punishment: Interviews with Victims, Convicts, Their Families, and Support Groups, 1991; They Want to Kill My Son, 1992; Easy Guide for Beginner Writers, 2000; Poison Passion, 2000. EDITOR: Congregation of the Condemned: Voices against the Death Penalty, 1992; Young Blood, 1995. Contributor to magazines. **Address:** c/o Jeff Dicks Medical Coalition, PO Box 343, Beechgrove, TN 37018, U.S.A. **Online address:** sdicks@bloomand.net

DICKSON, Athol. American, b. 1955. **Genres:** Inspirational/Motivational Literature. **Career:** Writer and architect. **Publications:** Whom Shall I Fear? 1996. **Address:** c/o Zondervan Publishing House, 5300 Patterson Ave. SE, Grand Rapids, MI 49530, U.S.A.

DICKSON, (W.) Michael. American, b. 1968. **Genres:** Mathematics/ Statistics. **Career:** Educator and author. Indiana University, Bloomington, assistant professor, 1996-98, associate professor of history, 1998-2000, Ruth N. Halls Professor of history and philosophy of science, 2002-04; University of South Carolina, professor of philosophy of science, 2004-. Visiting scholar, University of Cambridge, 1995, and Oxford University, 2002-03; University of Chicago, adjoint professor, 2000. **Publications:** Quantum Chance and Nonlocality, 1998; (with R. Clifton) Structuring Reality: Mathematica and Philosophical Foundations of Quantum Theory, in press. Contributor to encyclopedias, books, and professional journals. **Address:** Department of History and Philosophy of Science, 1011 East Third St., Indiana University, Bloomington, IN 47405, U.S.A. **Online address:** michael@mdickson.com; midickso@indiana.edu

DICKSON, Paul. American, b. 1939. **Genres:** History, Recreation, Social commentary, Speech/Rhetoric, Sports/Fitness, Humor/Satire. **Career:** McGraw-Hill Publs., NYC, editor, 1964-69. **Publications:** Think Tanks, 1971; The Great American Ice Cream Book, 1972; The Future of the Workplace, 1975 (in UK as Work Revolution, 1977); The Electronic Battlefield, 1976; The Mature Person's Guide to Kites, Yo-Yo's, Frisbees and Other Childlike Diversions, 1977; The Future File, 1977; Out of This World: American Space Photography, 1977; Chow: A Cook's Tour of Military Food, 1978; The Official Rules, 1980; The Official Explanations, 1980; Toasts, 1981; Words, 1982; (with J.C. Goulden) There Are Alligators in Our Sewers, 1983; Jokes, 1984 (as Too Much Saxon Violence, 1986); On Our Own, 1985; Names, 1986; The Library in America, 1986; Family Words, 1988; The New Official Rules, 1989; The Dickson Baseball Dictionary, 1989; Timelines, 1990; What Do You Call a Person from..., 1990; Slang!, 1990; (ed.) Baseball's Greatest Quotations, 1991; (with D. Evelyn) On This Spot, 1992; Dickson Word Treasury, 1992; (with J.C. Goulden) Myth Informed, 1992; (with P. Clancy) The Congress Dictionary, 1993; (with W.B. Mead) Baseball: The President's Game, 1993; The Worth Book of Softball, 1994; War Slang, 1994; The Book of Thanksgiving, 1995; (with R. Skole) The Volvo Guide to Halls of Fame, 1996; The Joy of Keeping Score, 1996; The Official Rules at Home, 1996; The Official Rules for Lawyers, 1996; The Official Rules at Work, 1997; The Official Rules of Golfers, 1997; Labels for Locals, 1997; The New Dickson Baseball Dictionary, 1999; The Official Rules for Life, 2000; Sputnik: The Shock of the Century, 2001; The Hidden Language of Baseball, 2003; (with T.B. Allen) The Bonus Army: An American Epic, 2005. **Address:** Box 80, Garrett Park, MD 20896, U.S.A. **Online address:** newdefiner@aol.com; www.pauldicksonbooks.com

DIDION, Joan. American, b. 1934. **Genres:** Novels, Social commentary, Novellas/Short stories. **Publications:** Run River, 1963; Slouching Towards Bethlehem (essays), 1968; Play It as It Lays (novel), 1970; A Book of Common Prayer (novel), 1977; Telling Stories, 1978; The White Album, 1979; Salvador, 1983; Democracy (novel), 1984; Miami, 1987; After Henry (in U.K. as Sentimental Journeys), 1992; The Last Thing He Wanted, 1996; Political Fictions (essays), 2001; Where I Was From, 2003. **Address:** c/o Janklow and Nesbit, 445 Park Ave., Fl 13, New York, NY 10022, U.S.A.

DIEBOLD, John. American, b. 1926. **Genres:** Administration/Management, Technology, Information science/Computers. **Career:** Founder, and Chairman of Board, Diebold Group Inc., mgmt. consultants, NYC, since 1954. Founder, and Chairman, John Diebold Inc., mgmt. and investment, since 1967. Chairman, DCL Inc., holding co. of Diebold Computer Leasing Inc.,

since 1967. Director, Genesco. With Griffenhagen and Assocs., mgmt. consultants, NYC and Chicago, 1951-60: Owner, 1957-60. **Publications:** Automation: The Advent of the Automatic Factory, 1952; Beyond Automation, 1964; Man and the Computer: Technology as an Agent of Social Change, 1969; Business Decisions and Technological Change, 1970; (ed.) World of the Computer, 1973; Management, 1973; Automation, 1983; Making the Future Work, 1985; Managing Information, 1985; Business in the Age of Information, 1985; The Innovators, 1990. **Address:** John Diebold Inc., PO Box 515, Bedford Hills, NY 10507, U.S.A.

DIEHL, Huston. American, b. 1948. **Genres:** Literary criticism and history. **Career:** State University of New York College at Geneseo, assistant professor of English, 1975-79; University of Oklahoma, Norman, assistant professor, 1979-82, associate professor of English, 1982-85, Associates' Distinguished Lecturer, 1984-85; University of Iowa, Iowa City, associate professor, 1985-95, professor of English, 1995-. Colorado College, visiting professor, 1982 and 1984. **Publications:** An Index of Icons in English Emblem Books, 1986; Staging Reform, Reforming the Stage: Protestantism and Popular Theater in Early Modern England, 1997. Contributor to books and periodicals. **Address:** Department of English, University of Iowa, Iowa City, IA 52242, U.S.A. **Online address:** huston-diehl@uiowa.edu

DIEHN, Gwen. American, b. 1943. **Genres:** Art/Art history, Communications/Media, Crafts, Children's non-fiction. **Career:** Teacher of grades K-8 in public school systems in New Orleans, LA, and San Antonio, TX, 1965-78; Indiana Vocational Technical Community College, South Bend, instructor of oral and written communications, 1979-84; Asheville City Schools, Asheville, NC, teacher of grades 3-5, 1985-89; Warren Wilson College, Asheville, professor of fine arts, 1989-. **Publications:** (with J. Comeau) Communication on the Job (textbook), 1986; (with T. Krautwurst) Nature Crafts for Kids: Fifty Fantastic Things to Make with Mother Nature's Help, 1992. SELF-ILLUSTRATED FOR CHILDREN: (with S. Griesmaier) Streamwalking with Kids, 1988; Mt. Mitchell, 1991; (with T. Krautwurst) Science Crafts for Kids: 50 Fantastic Things to Invent and Create, 1994; (with T. Krautwurst) Kids' Style Nature Crafts, 1995; (with Al Anderson and T. Krautwurst) Geology Crafts, 1996; Making Books that Fly, Fold, Wrap, Hide, Pop Up, Twist, and Turn: Books for Kids to Make, 1998; Simple Printmaking, 2001; The Decorated Page, 2002; The Decorated Journal, 2005. **Address:** 154 College View Dr, Swannanoa, NC 28778, U.S.A. **Online address:** gdiehn@mindspring.com

DIEM, Max. German, b. 1947. **Genres:** Chemistry. **Career:** Hunter College of the City University of New York, instructor in chemistry. **Publications:** Introduction to Modern Vibrational Spectroscopy, 1993. Contributor to scientific journals. **Address:** Department of Chemistry, Hunter College of the City University of New York, New York, NY 10021, U.S.A.

DIERKER, Larry. (born United States), b. 1946. **Genres:** Humor/Satire. **Career:** Sports commentator and former professional baseball player and manager. Houston Astros, (originally Houston Colt .45s until 1964), pitcher, 1964-76, director of group and season sales office, 1977-79, radio and television color analyst, 1979-97, manager, 1997-2001; St. Louis Cardinals, pitcher, 1977; MLB.com, guest columnist, 2004-. Owner of Larry's Big Bamboo (restaurant), Minute Maid Stadium, Houston. **Publications:** This Ain't Brain Surgery: How to Win the Pennant without Losing Your Mind, 2003. Contributor to numerous sports columns. **Address:** MLB Advanced Media, L.P., 75 Ninth Avenue, Fifth Floor, New York, NY 10011, U.S.A.

DIETERICH, Michele M. American, b. 1962. **Genres:** Recreation, Sports/ Fitness. **Career:** Artist and writer. Freelance commercial artist in Newport Beach, CA; Mountain Biker International, London, England, itinerant correspondent; Happenings Magazine, Bozeman, MT, staff writer and art critic. Contributing photographer to Mountain Biker International. **Publications:** Skiing, 1991. Contributor of photographs to books and periodicals. **Address:** 410 N. Ida Ave., Bozeman, MT 59715-3015, U.S.A.

DIETRICH, William S. American, b. 1951. **Genres:** Novels, Environmental sciences/Ecology. **Career:** Bellingham Herald, Bellingham, WA, political reporter, 1973-76; Gannett News Service, Washington, DC, reporter, 1976-78; Vancouver Columbian, Vancouver, WA, reporter and columnist, 1978-82; Seattle Times, Seattle, WA, science reporter, 1982-. **Publications:** The Final Forest: The Battle for the Last Great Trees of the Pacific Northwest, 1992; Northwest Passage: The Great Columbia River, 1995; Ice Reich, 1998; Getting Back, 2000; Dark Winter, 2001; Natural Grace: Plants and Animals of the Pacific Northwest, 2003; Hadrian's Wall, 2004.

DIETZ, Peter (John). British, b. 1924. **Genres:** Autobiography/Memoirs, Military/Defense/Arms control, History. **Career:** Royal Marine Corps, 1943-

46, became captain; British Army, Royal Army Educational Corps, career officer, 1951-80, retiring as brigadier general; department head, Royal Military College of Science, Shrivenham, 1968-71; lecturer, Open University, 1982-89. Adjudicator, Guild of Adjudicators, 1964-68. **Publications:** (ed.) Garrison, 1986; The Last of the Regiments: Their Rise and Fall, 1990; The British in the Mediterranean, 1995. **Address:** Kernow, Pannier Lane, Carbis Bay, St. Ives, Cornwall TR26 2RF, England.

DI FILIPPO, Paul. Also writes as Philip Lawson. American, b. 1954. **Genres:** Novels, Novellas/Short stories. **Career:** Writer. **Publications:** SHORT STORIES: The Steampunk Trilogy, 1995; Ribofunk, 1996; Destroy All Brains!, 1996; Fractal Paisleys, 1997; Lost Pages, 1998; Strange Trades, 2001; Little Doors, 2002; Babylon Sisters, 2002; Neutrino Drag, 2004. NOVELS: Ciphers, 1997; Would It Kill You to Smile?, 1998; Joe's Liver, 2000; (with M. Bishop as Philip Lawson) Muskrat Courage, 2000; A Year in the Linear City, 2002; A Mouthful of Tongues, 2002; Fuzzy Dice, 2003. Work represented in anthologies. Contributor of stories and articles to magazines. **Address:** 2 Poplar St, Providence, RI 02906, U.S.A. **Online address:** pgdf@earthlink.net

DIGBY-JUNGER, Richard. American, b. 1954. **Genres:** Literary criticism and history. **Career:** Worked at radio and television stations throughout the upper Midwest, 1974-89; Northern Illinois University, DeKalb, assistant professor, 1989-96; Western Michigan University, Kalamazoo, associate professor of English, 1996-, and director of journalism program. **Publications:** The Journalist as Reformer: Henry Demarest Lloyd and Wealth against Commonwealth, 1996. **Address:** Department of English, Western Michigan University, Kalamazoo, MI 49008, U.S.A. **Online address:** richard.digby-junger@wmich.edu

DIGGES, Deborah. American, b. 1950. **Genres:** Poetry. **Career:** Writer and poet. **Publications:** POETRY: Vesper Sparrows, 1986; Late in the Millennium, 1989; Rough Music, 1995; (ed. and trans. with M. Cruz-Bernal) Ballad of the Blood: The Poems of Maria Elena Cruz Varela, 1996. OTHER: Fugitive Spring: Coming of Age in the '50s and '60s (memoir), 1992; The Stardust Lounge: Stories from a Boy's Adolescence, 2001. **Address:** English Department, East Hall, Tufts University, Medford, MA 02155, U.S.A. **Online address:** deborah.digges@tufts.edu

DI GREGORIO, Mario A(urelio Umberto). Italian, b. 1950. **Genres:** Natural history. **Career:** Milan Conservatoire, Milan, Italy, teacher of Italian, Latin, and history, 1974; Cambridge University, Cambridge, England, research fellow at Darwin College, 1978-81, lecturer in history, 1979-92; University of L'Aquila, Italy, professor of the history of science, 1992-. Guest lecturer at universities worldwide; visiting professor at Hiram College, Hiram, Ohio, 1989. **Publications:** T.H. Huxley's Place in Natural Science, 1984; Charles Darwin's Marginalia, Vol. 1: Books, 1990. **Address:** Dipartimento di Culture Comparate, Piazza S. Margherita 2, 67100 L'Aquila, Italy.

DIGREGORIO, Mario J. American. **Genres:** Horticulture. **Career:** U.S. Government, park ranger for National Park Service (in Massachusetts, New Jersey, and Colorado) and park resource manager for U.S. Army Corps of Engineers (in Massachusetts and Illinois), 1976-86; Town of Brewster, MA, municipal conservation administrator, 1986-88; Sabatia Inc. (environmental consultants), Hatchville, MA, professional wetland scientist and botanist, 1983-. New England Plant Conservation Program, member of Endangered Species Task Force; Commonwealth of Massachusetts, consulting ecologist and rare plant specialist for Natural Heritage and Endangered Species Program; expert witness in superior, district, and land courts on issues related to wetlands and wildlife. **Publications:** (with J. Wallner) Wildflowers of the Cape Cod Canal: An Annotated Checklist, 1985; (with Wallner) A Vanishing Heritage: Cape Cod's Wildflowers, 1989; (coauthor) A Guide to the Natural History of Cape Cod and the Islands, 1990; (with Wallner) New England's Mountain Flowers: A High Country Heritage, 1997. Author of natural history booklets. Contributor to periodicals. **Address:** 107 Goeletta Dr., Hatchville, MA 02536, U.S.A. **Online address:** sabatia@aol.com

DI LELLA, Alexander Anthony. American, b. 1929. **Genres:** Language/Linguistics, Theology/Religion. **Career:** Andrews-Kelly-Ryan Distinguished Professor of Biblical Studies, Catholic University of America, Washington, D.C., 1976- (Associate Professor of Semitic Languages, 1966-76). Fellow, American School of Oriental Research, 1962-63; Guggenheim Fellow, 1972-73; President, Catholic Biblical Association of America, 1975-76. **Publications:** The Hebrew Text of Sirach: A Text-Critical and Historical Study, 1966; (with L. F. Hartman) The Book of Daniel, 1978; Proverbs, in The Old Testament in Syriac, 1979; (with P. W. Skehan) The Wisdom of Ben Sira, 1987; (ed.) New Revised Standard Version of the Bible: Catholic Edtion,

1993; Il libro di Daniele, 1-6, 1995, 7-14, 1996; Daniel: A Book for Troubling Times, 1997. **Address:** Curley Hall, Catholic University of America, Washington, DC 20064, U.S.A. **Online address:** dilella@cua.edu

DILLARD, Annie. American, b. 1945. **Genres:** Novels, Poetry, Literary criticism and history, Autobiography/Memoirs, Essays. **Career:** Wesleyan University, Middletown, CT, professor, 1979-99, writer-in-residence, 1987-99, emeritus, 1999-. Harper's Magazine, contributing editor, 1973-82. Recipient of Pulitzer Prize, 1975. **Publications:** Tickets for a Prayer Wheel, 1974; Pilgrim at Tinker Creek, 1974; Holy the Firm, 1977; Living by Fiction, 1978; Encounters with Chinese Writers, 1984; An American Childhood, 1987; The Writing Life, 1989, The Living, 1992; Mornings Like This, 1995; For the Time Being, 1999. **Address:** c/o Russell & Volkening, 50 W 29th, New York, NY 10001, U.S.A.

DILLARD, R(ichard) H(enry) W(ilde). American, b. 1937. **Genres:** Literary criticism and history, Novels, Plays/Screenplays, Poetry. **Career:** Chair of Graduate Program in Contemporary Literature and Creative Writing, since 1971, and Professor of English, since 1974, Hollins College, Virginia (Assistant Professor, 1964-68; Associate Professor, 1968-74). Vice President, The Film Journal, NYC, since 1973. Instructor in English, University of Virginia, Charlottesville, 1961-64. Contributor Ed., The Hollins Critic, 1966-77. Editor-in-Chief, Children's Literature, 1992-; Editor, The Hollins Critic, 1996-. **Publications:** The Day I Stopped Dreaming About Barbara Steele and Other Poems, 1966; (with G. Garrett and J. Rodenbeck) Frankenstein Meets the Space Monster (screenplay), 1966; (ed. with L. D. Rubin) The Experience of America: A Book of Readings, 1969; News of the Nile (poetry), 1971; (ed. with G. Garrett and J. R. Moore) The Sounder Few: Essays from "The Hollins Critic," 1971; After Borges (poetry), 1972; The Book of Changes (novel), 1974; Horror Films, 1976; The Greeting: New and Selected Poems, 1981; The First Man on the Sun (novel), 1983; Understanding George Garrett (criticism), 1988; Just Here, Just Now (poetry), 1994; Omniphobia (short fiction), 1995. **Address:** Box 9671, Hollins College, VA 24020, U.S.A.

DILLENBERGER, John. American, b. 1918. **Genres:** Art/Art history, Theology/Religion. **Career:** Professor Emeritus, Graduate Theological Union, Berkeley, CA, 1983- (Dean, 1963-69, Professor of Historical Theology, 1963-78, and President, 1967-72, 1998-99). Assistant Prof of Religion, 1949-52, Dept. Representative, Columbia College, 1949-54, Associate Professor, 1952-54, and Assistant Secretary, Ph.D. Program, 1951-54, Columbia University and Union Theological Seminary, NYC; Associate Professor of Theology, 1954-57, and Parkman Professor of Theology, 1957-58, Divinity School, and Chairman, Professor in History and Philosophy of Religion, Faculty of Arts and Sciences, 1955-58, Harvard University, Cambridge, MA; Ellen S. James Professor of Systematic and Historical Theology, Drew University, Madison, NJ, 1958-62; Dean of Graduate Studies, Dean of Faculty, and Professor of Historical Theology, San Francisco Theological Seminary, CA, 1962-64; President, Hartford Seminary, 1978-83. **Publications:** God Hidden and Revealed, 1953; (with C. Welch) Protestant Christianity, 1954; Protestant Thought and Natural Science, 1960; Contours of Faith, 1969; (with J. Dillenberger) Perceptions of the Spirit in 20th Century American Art, 1977; Benjamin West: The Context of His Life's Work, 1977; The Visual Arts and Christianity in America, 1984; A Theology of Artistic Sensibilities, 1986; Images and Relics: Theological Perceptions and Visual Images in 16th Century Europe, 1999; From Fallow Fields to Hallowed Halls: A Theologian's Journey, 2004. EDITOR: Martin Luther: Selections from His Writings, 1961; John Calvin: Selections from His Writings, 1971. **Address:** 727 Gelston Pl, El Cerrito, CA 94530, U.S.A. **Online address:** JohnDillenberger@comcast.net

DILLER, Harriett. American, b. 1953. **Genres:** Adult non-fiction. **Career:** Freelance writer, 1979-. **Publications:** Celebrations That Matter, 1990; Grandaddy's Highway, 1993; The Waiting Day, 1994. **Address:** 590 East King St., Chambersburg, PA 17201, U.S.A.

DILLINGHAM, William B. American, b. 1930. **Genres:** Literary criticism and history, Education, Humanities. **Career:** Charles Howard Candler Professor of American Literature, 1986-96, emeritus, 1996-, Emory University, Atlanta. **Publications:** Frank Norris: Instinct and Art, 1969; An Artist in the Rigging: The Early Work of Herman Melville, 1972; Practical English Handbook, 1973, 10th ed, 1996; Humor of the Old Southwest, 2nd ed., 1975, 3rd ed. 1994; Melville's Short Fiction, 1853-1856, 1978; Melville's Later Novels, 1986; Melville and His Circle: The Last Years, 1996. **Address:** 1416 Vistaleaf Dr, Decatur, GA 30033, U.S.A. **Online address:** wdillin@emory.edu

DILLON, Kathleen M. (Hynek). American, b. 1947. **Genres:** Psychology. **Career:** Western New England College, Springfield, MA, professor of psychology, 1968-. Massachusetts Department of Mental Health, psychiatric social worker, 1969; licensed psychologist in private clinical practice, 1981-. Springfield College, adjunct faculty member, 1970-74; University of Massachusetts at Amherst, adjunct faculty member, 1982. **Publications:** Living with Autism: The Parents' Stories, 1995: Living with Pain, 2002. Contributor to journals. **Address:** Department of Psychology, Box 5058, Western New England College, 1215 Wilbraham Rd, Springfield, MA 01119, U.S.A. **Online address:** kdillon@wnec.edu

DILLON, M(artin) C. American, b. 1938. **Genres:** Philosophy. **Career:** Washington and Lee University, Lexington, VA, instructor in philosophy, 1964-65; State University of New York at Binghamton, instructor, 1968-70, assistant professor, 1970-74, associate professor, 1974-88, professor of philosophy, 1988-93, distinguished teaching professor, 1993-, director of undergraduate studies in philosophy, 1978-90, acting chair of department, 1982, acting director of Law and Society Program, 1987-88. Yale University fellow, 1966-67, 1967-68; International Business Machines (IBM) Inc., instructor, 1986-93; lecturer at colleges and universities. **Publications:** Merleau-Ponty's Ontology, 1988; Semiological Reductionism, 1995; Beyond Romance, 2001. EDITOR & CONTRIBUTOR: Merleau-Ponty Vivant, 1991; Ecart & Differance, 1997. Contributor to periodicals. **Address:** Department of Philosophy, State University of New York at Binghamton, Binghamton, NY 13902-6000, U.S.A. **Online address:** mdillon355@aol.com

DILLON, Stuart. See STUART, Sally E(lizabeth).

DILLON, Wilton Sterling. American, b. 1923. **Genres:** Anthropology/ Ethnology, Area studies. **Career:** Sr. Scholar Emeritus, Smithsonian Institution, Washington, D.C., 1995- (Director of Symposia and Seminars, 1969-85, Director of Interdisciplinary Studies, 1986-90, Sr. Scholar-in-Residence, 1990-95). President, Literary Society of Washington, 1990. Trustee Emeritus, Phelps-Stokes Fund of New York (Executive Secretary and Director of Research, 1957-63). Member of Editorial Board, Alabama Heritage Political Communication and Persuasion. Secretary-Treasurer, Institute for Psychiatry and Foreign Affairs. Pres Emeritus, Institute for Intercultural Studies, NYC. **Publications:** Gifts and Nations, 1968; (ed. with J.F. Eisenberg) Man and Beast: Comparative Social Behavior, 1972; (ed.) The Cultural Drama: Modern Identities and Social Ferment, 1974; (ed. with N.G. Kotler) The Statue of Liberty Revisited: Making a Universal Symbol, 1994. **Address:** Smithsonian Institution, Washington, DC 20560, U.S.A. **Online address:** mcelroym@op.si.edu

DILLOW, Gordon. American. **Genres:** Money/Finance. **Career:** Writer and Journalist. Orange County Register, Santa Ana, CA, regional reporter, Metro columnist, war correspondent embedded with the First Marine Division stationed in Kuwait and Iraq, 2003; Los Angeles Herald Examiner, Los Angeles, CA, reporter, war correspondent in Nicaragua, 1980s; Los Angeles Times, Los Angeles, reporter; Brownsville Herald, Brownsville, TX, reporter; Missoulian, Missoula, MT, reporter. **Publications:** (with William J. Rehder) Where the Money Is: True Tales from the Bank Robbery Capital of the World, 2003. **Address:** Orange County Register, 625 N. Grand Avenue, Santa Ana, CA 92701, U.S.A. **Online address:** gldillow@aol.com

DILS, Tracey E. Also writes as Tracey Herrold. American, b. 1958. **Genres:** Children's fiction, Writing/Journalism. **Career:** Frontier Press, Columbus, OH, associate editor, 1980-81; Merrill Publishing Company, Columbus, production editor, 1982-84, developmental editor, 1984-86; Willowisp Press, Worthington, OH, managing editor/editorial project manager, 1986-89, editor-in-chief, 1989-90; Ohio State University Press, Columbus, marketing manager, 1990-93; A Writer's Place, Columbus, manager, director, author, 1993-. Instructor at Southern Ohio Writers Conference, Romance Writers of America National Convention, and Thurber House, all 1989; Suncoast Writers' Conference and Society for Children's Book Writers, Southwest Texas Chapter, both 1990; Ohio State University Summer Writing Series, 1991-93, and Rockport Writing Series, 1992; faculty member, Institute of Children's Literature, 1993-. **Publications:** Words, Words, Words, 1988; (as Tracey Herrold) The Puppy Who Needed a Friend, 1989; The Scariest Stories You've Ever Heard, Part III, 1990; Grandpa's Magic, 1990; Whatever I Do, the Monster Does Too, 1991; George Washington: Country Boy, Country Gentleman, 1992; Boytalk: How to Talk to Your Favorite Guy, 1992; A Look around Coral Reefs, 1995; Annabelle's Awful Waffle, in press. CONTRIBUTOR: How to Write a Novel for Young Readers and Get it Published, edited by K. Falk and C. Savage, 1990. **Address:** 1759 Bedford Rd., Columbus, OH 43212, U.S.A.

DIMARCO, Cris K. A. Also writes as Cris Newport. American, b. 1960. **Genres:** Novels. **Career:** Freelance book reviewer and editor, 1988-; New

Hampshire Technical Institute, Concord, associate professor of English, 1991-97; Windstorm Creative Ltd, Port Orchard, WA, senior editor, 1996-. Colby Sawyer College, adjunct faculty; Women of Power magazine, managing editor; Into Print & Beyond (seminar on publishing), co-creator and teacher. **Publications:** NOVELS: Sparks Might Fly, 1994; The White Bones of Truth, 1996; Queen's Champion: The Legend of Lancelot Retold (fantasy), 1997; Virtual Rock, 2002. OTHER: 1001 Nights: Exotica 1, 2000. Contributor of book reviews to periodicals. **Address:** c/o Windstorm Creative, 7419 Ebbert Dr SE, Port Orchard, WA 98367-9753, U.S.A. **Online address:** crisnewport@aol.com

DIMAURO, Louis F. American, b. 1953. **Genres:** Physics. **Career:** American Telephone and Telegraph, Bell Laboratories, Murray Hill, NJ, member of technical staff, 1981-84; Louisiana State University-Baton Rouge, assistant professor, 1984-88; Brookhaven National Laboratory, Upton, NY, scientist, 1988-. Lawrence Livermore National Laboratory, guest physicist, 1994-. State University of New York at Stony Brook, adjunct professor, 1988-. **Publications:** Application of High Field and Short Wavelength Sources, 1998; Multiphoton Processes, 2000. **Address:** 12 Block Island Dr., Sound Beach, NY 11789, U.S.A. **Online address:** dimauro@bnl.gov

DIMBLEBY, Jonathan. British, b. 1944. **Genres:** International relations/ Current affairs, Biography. **Career:** Freelance journalist, broadcaster and writer. Voluntary Service Overseas, president; Soil Association, president; Council for the Protection of Rural England, vice-president; Bath Festivals Trust, chairman; Forum for the Future, Richard Dimbleby Cancer Fund, trustee. **Publications:** Richard Dimbleby, 1975; The Palestinians, 1979; The Prince of Wales: A Biography, 1994; The Last Governor, 1997. **Address:** c/o David Higham Assocs. Ltd, 5-8 Lower John St, Golden Sq, London W1R 4HA, England.

DIMMICK, Barbara. American, b. 1954. **Genres:** Novels. **Career:** Writer. **Publications:** In the Presence of Horses: A Novel, 1998; Heart-Side Up, 2002. **Address:** c/o Author Mail, Graywolf Press, 2402 University Avenue Suite 203, St. Paul, MN 55114, U.S.A.

DIMOND, Peter. British. **Genres:** Music. **Career:** Classics teacher at a grammar school in England, 1951-65; Somerset Education Authority, Somerset, England, music adviser, 1965-82; Open University, lecturer, 1971-2004; Trinity College, London, England, examiner in music, 1982-92. **Publications:** Music Made Simple, 1982; The Art of Beethoven, 1993; A Mozart Diary, 1997. **Address:** Golden Pheasant, Stocklinch, Ilminster, Somerset TA19 9JF, England. **Online address:** ptrdmnd@aol.com

DINELLO, Paul. American. **Genres:** Science fiction/Fantasy. **Career:** Comedian, actor, writer. Worked for Allstate Insurance Co. and at the Chicago Mercantile Exchange; performed with Second City. **Publications:** (with Amy Sedaris and Stephen Colbert) Wigfield: The Can-Do Town That Just May Not, 2003. **Address:** c/o Author Mail, Hyperion Editorial Dept., 77 West 66th St., 11th Fl., New York, NY 10023, U.S.A.

DINERMAN, Beatrice. American, b. 1933. **Genres:** Medicine/Health, Politics/Government, Urban studies. **Career:** Public Administration Analyst, Bureau of Governmental Research, 1956-62, and Research Associate, School of Public Health, 1966-67, University of California, Los Angeles; Director, Ford Foundation Project on Priority Planning, Welfare Planning Council of Los Angeles, 1962-65; Social Science Research Analyst, Economic and Youth Opportunities Agency, Los Angeles, 1965-66; Consultant, Health Planning Association of Southern California, Los Angeles, 1967-68; Research Associate, School of Public Administration, 1968-69, and Research Consultant, Regional Research Institute in Social Welfare, 1970-72, University of Southern California, Los Angeles; Chief, Research and Information, Comprehensive Health Planning Council of Los Angeles County, 1972-75; Director, Dept. of Health Planning, Pacific Health Resources, 1975-80; Independent Mgmt. Consultant, 1980-81, 1995; Director, Program Planning, Cedars-Sinai Medical Center, Los Angeles, 1982-95. **Publications:** Chambers of Commerce in the Modern Metropolis, 1958; Hospital Development and Communities, 1961; Administrative Decentralization in City and County Government, 1961; Structure and Organization of Local Government in the United States, 1961; (co-author) Southern California Metropolis, 1963; Citizen Participation in the Model Cities Program, 1971; various articles.

DINH, Linh. American (born Vietnam), b. 1963. **Genres:** Novellas/Short stories, Poetry. **Career:** Writer and artist; Art in General, New York, NY, critic-in-residence, 1994; Levy Gallery for the Arts, Moore College of Art and Design, Philadelphia, PA, Toys and Incense guest curator, 1994; The Fabric Workshop, Philadelphia, PA, artist-in-residence, 1994; cofounder and editor of The Drunken Boat (bimonthly journal devoted to art and literature), 1991-93. **Publications:** FICTION: (ed.) Night, Again: Contemporary Fiction from Vietnam (short story anthology), 1996; Fake House and Other Stories (short stories), 2000. POETRY: Drunkard Boxing, 1998; A Small Triumph Over Lassitude (chapbook), 2001; All Around That Empties Out, 2002. OTHER: (ed. and trans) Three Vietnamese Poets, 2001; Vietnam Postcards, 2002. Contributor of poetry to anthologies and journals; contributor of freelance articles to Web journals. **Address:** c/o Author Mail, Seven Stories Press, 140 Watts St., New York, NY 10013, U.S.A. **Online address:** linhdinh99@yahoo.com

DINNERSTEIN, Leonard. American, b. 1934. **Genres:** History. **Career:** New York Institute of Technology, NYC, Instructor, 1960-65; Fairleigh Dickinson University, Teaneck, NJ, Assistant Professor, 1967-70; University of Arizona, Tucson, Associate Professor, 1970-72, Professor of American History, 1972-, Director, Committee on Judaic Studies, 1993-. **Publications:** The Leo Frank Case, 1968; (with D.M. Reimers) Ethnic Americans: A History of Immigration and Assimilation, 1975, 4th ed., 1999; (with R.L. Nichols and D.M. Reimers) Natives and Strangers, 1979, 4th ed., 2003; America and the Survivors of the Holocaust, 1982; Uneasy at Home, 1987; Antisemitism in America, 1994. EDITOR: (with F.C. Jaher) The Aliens, 1970, as Uncertain Americans, 1977; (with K.T. Jackson) American Vistas, 1971, 7th ed., 1995; Antisemitism in the United States, 1971; (with M.D. Palsson) Jews in the South, 1973; (with J. Christie) Decisions and Revisions, 1975. **Address:** 1981 E Miraval Cuarto, Tucson, AZ 85718, U.S.A. **Online address:** Dinnerst@u.arizona.edu

DINTENFASS, Mark. American, b. 1941. **Genres:** Novels. **Career:** Professor of English, Lawrence University, Appleton, Wisconsin, since 1968. **Publications:** Make Yourself an Earthquake, 1969; The Case Against Organization, 1970; Figure 8, 1974; Montgomery Street, 1978; Old World, New World, 1982; The Loving Place, 1986. **Address:** PO Box 599, Appleton, WI 54912-0599, U.S.A.

DINTRONE, Charles V. American, b. 1942. **Genres:** Communications/Media. **Career:** Fresno State University, CA, assistant government publications librarian, 1968-72; San Diego State University, CA, head of government publications at university library, 1972-89, coordinator of library instruction, 1989-92, reference librarian for political science, communication, and European history, 1992-, head, general reference division at university library, 1999-. **Publications:** Television Program Master Index, 1996. Contributor to Government Publications Review. **Address:** Library, San Diego State University, 5500 Campanile Dr, San Diego, CA 92182, U.S.A. **Online address:** charles.dintrone@sdsu.edu

DIOGUARDI, Joseph J. American, b. 1940. **Genres:** Politics/Government. **Career:** Arthur Andersen & Co., NYC, certified public accountant, 1962-84, partner; U.S. House of Representatives, congressman from Westchester district, NY, 1985-89; Truth in Government, Ossining, NY, chair, 1989-; writer, speaker, and human rights activist, 1989-. **Publications:** House of Ill Repute, 1987; Unaccountable Congress: It Doesn't Add Up, 1992. **Address:** Truth in Government, PO Box 70, Ossining, NY 10562, U.S.A. **Online address:** jjd@aacl.com

DIONNE, E(ugene) J., Jr. American, b. 1952. **Genres:** Adult non-fiction, Politics/Government. **Career:** Journalist and writer. Has worked as a reporter for New York Times; currently employed as a columnist for Washington Post, Washington, DC. **Publications:** Why Americans Hate Politics, 1991, rev. ed., 1992; They Only Look Dead: Why Progressives Will Dominate the Next Political Era, 1996, rev. ed., 1997. **Address:** c/o Washington Post, 1150 Fifteenth St. NW, Washington, DC 20071, U.S.A.

DI PIERO, W(illiam) S(imone). American, b. 1945. **Genres:** Poetry, Art/Art history, Essays, Translations. **Career:** Stanford University, Stanford, CA, professor of English, 1982-. **Publications:** Solstice, 1982; Memory and Enthusiasm: Essays, 1975-1985, 1989; Out of Eden: Essays on Modern Art, 1991; Shooting the Works: On Poetry and Pictures (essays), 1996. POETRY: The First Hour, 1982; The Only Dangerous Thing, 1984; Early Light, 1985; The Dog Star, 1990; The Restorers, 1992; Shadows Burning, 1995; Skirts and Slacks, 2001; Brother Fire, 2004. TRANSLATOR: Giacomo Leopardi, Pensieri, 1981; This Strange Joy: The Collected Poems of Sandro Penna, 1982; The Ellipse: Selected Poems of Leonardo Sinisgalli, 1983; Ion, by Euripides, 1996. Contributor of poems and essays to periodicals. **Address:** 225 Downey St Apt 5, San Francisco, CA 94117-4456, U.S.A.

DIPPEL, John V(an) H(outen). American, b. 1946. **Genres:** History. **Career:** Stevens Institute of Technology, Hoboken, NJ, adjunct professor of

humanities, 1978-80; Jan Krukowski and Associates, NYC, senior associate and promotional writer, 1981-. **Publications:** Two Against Hitler, 1992; Bound upon a Wheel of Fire: Why So Many German Jews Made the Tragic Decision to Remain in Nazi Germany, 1996. Contributor to magazines and newspapers. **Address:** 333 Hudson Terr., Piermont, NY 10968, U.S.A.

DI PRIMA, Diane. American, b. 1934. **Genres:** Novels, Plays/Screenplays, Poetry, Autobiography/Memoirs, Translations, Novellas/Short stories, Women's studies and issues, Literary criticism and history. **Career:** Poet, prose writer, playwright, and teacher. Instructor, New College of California, San Francisco, 1980-87, California College of Arts & Crafts, 1990-93, SF Art Institute, 1992, California Institute of Integral Studies, 1993-95. Contributor Ed., Kulchur mag., NYC, 1961-62; Co. Ed., Floating Bear mag., NYC, 1961-69; Ed. and Publr., Poets Press, NYC, 1964-69; Publr., Eidolon Editions, San Francisco, publisher, editor, 1974-; Director, New York Poets Theatre, 1961-65; Naropa Institute, School of Poetics, faculty, 1974-; Mama Bear's News and Notes, columnist, 1987-92; Harbin Quarterly, columnist, 1992-93. **Publications:** This Kind of Bird Flies Backward, 1958; Dinners and Nightmares (short stories), 1961, (expanded ed.), 1998; The New Handbook of Heaven, 1962; The Man Condemned to Death (trans.), 1963; Poets Vaudeville, 1964; Seven Love Poems from the Middle Latin, 1965; Haiku, 1966; New Mexico Poem, 1967; Earthsong, 1968; Hotel Albert, 1968; Memoirs of a Beatnik (novel), 1969, rev. ed., 1988; L.A. Odyssey, 1969; The Book of Hours, 1970; Kerhonkson Journal, 1971; Revolutionary Letters, 1971; The Calculus of Variation (novel), 1972; Loba, Part 1, 1973; Freddie Poems, 1974; Brass Burnace Going Out, 1975; Selected Poems, 1956-75, 1975; Loba, Part 2, 1976; The Loba As Eve, 1977; Loba, Parts 1-8, 1978; Wyoming Series, 1988; The Mysteries of Vision, 1988; Pieces of a Song: Selected Poems, 1990; Seminary Poems 1991; The Mask Is the Path of the Star, 1993; Loba, Parts 1-16, 1998; Recollections of My Life as a Woman, the New York Years: A Memoir, 2001. EDITOR: Various Fables from Various Places, 1960; War Poems, 1968; The Floating Bear: A Newsletter, 1973. Works appear in anthologies, magazines, and newspapers. **Address:** 78 Niagra Ave., San Francisco, CA 94112, U.S.A.

DIRENZO, Anthony. American, b. 1960. **Genres:** Novels, Novellas/Short stories, Administration/Management, Advertising/Public relations, Business/Trade/Industry, Cultural/Ethnic topics, Literary criticism and history, Cartoons, Essays, Humor/Satire. **Career:** Syracuse University, Syracuse, NY, adjunct professor of English, 1990-93; Ithaca College, Ithaca, NY, associate professor in writing program, 1990-. Worked as a copywriter, public relations agent, broadcaster, lector, cantor, and Eucharistic minister. **Publications:** American Gargoyles: Flannery O'Connor and the Medieval Grotesque, 1993; If I Were Boss: The Early Business Stories of Sinclair Lewis, 1997; After the Fair Is Over (novel). Contributor of stories and essays to literary journals. **Address:** Dept of Writing, Ithaca College, Park 223, Ithaca, NY 14850, U.S.A. **Online address:** direnzo@ithaca.edu

DISALVO, Jackie. (Jacqueline). American, b. 1943. **Genres:** History, Literary criticism and history, Military/Defense/Arms control, Politics/Government, Theology/Religion. **Career:** Antioch College (now University), Yellow Springs, OH, instructor in English, summer, 1969; Rutgers University, New Brunswick, NJ, assistant professor of English at Livingston College, 1972-83; Bernard M. Baruch College of the City University of New York, NYC, associate professor of English, 1984-. Graduate Center of the City University of New York, associate professor, 1990-. **Publications:** War of Titans: Blake's Critique of Milton and the Politics of Religion, 1984; (co-ed.) Blake, Politics and History, 1998. Work represented in anthologies. Contributor of articles, poems, and reviews to magazines. **Address:** Department of English, Bernard M. Baruch College of the City University of New York, 17 Lexington Ave, New York, NY 10010, U.S.A. **Online address:** Jacqueline_Disalvo@baruch.cuny.edu

DISCH, Thomas M(ichael). Also writes as Thom Demijohn, Leonie Hargrave, Cassandra Knye. American, b. 1940. **Genres:** Literary criticism and history, Science fiction/Fantasy, Plays/Screenplays, Poetry, Songs/Lyrics and libretti, Novels, Novellas/Short stories. **Career:** Freelance writer and lectr., 1964-. Theatre Critic, The Nation, New York Daily News, NYC. Formerly, draftsman and copywriter. **Publications:** The Genocides, 1965; Mankind Under the Leach, 1966, later as Puppies of Terra; One Hundred and Two H-Bombs (short stories), 1966 as White Fang Goes Dingo, 1971; (as Cassandra Knye) The House That Fear Built (novel), 1966; Echo Round His Bones, 1967; Camp Concentration, 1968; Under Compulsion (short stories), 1968, in U.S. as Fun with Your New Head, 1971; (as Thom Demijohn) Black Alice (suspense novel), 1968; The Prisoner, 1969; (with M. Hacker and C. Platt) Highway Sandwiches (poetry), 1970; The Right Way to Figure Plumbing (poetry), 1971; 334, 1972; Getting into Death (short stories), 1973; (as Leonie Hargrave) Clara Reeve, 1975; On Wings of Song, 1979; Triplicity (omnibus), 1980; Fundamental Disch (short stories), 1980; (with C. Naylor) Neighboring Lives (historical novel), 1981; ABCDEFGHIJKLM-NOPQRSTUVWXYZ (poetry), 1981; Orders of the Retina (poetry), 1982; Burn This (poetry), 1982, 1996; The Man Who Had No Idea (short stories), 1982; Frankenstein (libretto for opera by Gregory Sandow), 1982; Ringtime, 1983; The Businessman: A Tale of Terror, 1984; Torturing Mr Amberwell, 1985; The Brave Little Toaster (children's book), 1986; Amnesia (computer-interactive novel), 1986; The Tale of Dan De Lion (children's book), 1986; The Silver Pillow, 1984; The Brave Little Toaster Goes to Mars, 1988; Yes, Let's: New and Selected Poems, 1989; Ben Hur (play), 1990; The M.D.: A Horror Story, 1991; Dark Verses and Light (poetry), 1991; The Cardinal Detoxes (play), 1991; The Priest: A Gothic Romance, 1995; The Castle of Indolence, 1995; The Dark Old House (poetry), 1996; The Child's Garden of Grammar, 1997; The Dreams Our Stuff Is Made Of, 1998; Sub: A Study in Witchcraft, 1999; Castle of Perseverence, 2002 EDITOR: The Ruins of Earth: An Anthology of the Immediate Future, 1971; Bad Moon Rising, 1973; The New Improved Sun; An Anthology of Utopian Science Fiction, 1975; (with C. Naylor) New Constellations, 1976; (with C. Naylor) Strangeness, 1977. **Address:** Box 226, Barryville, NY 12719, U.S.A.

DISKI, Jenny. British, b. 1947. **Genres:** Novels. **Career:** Teacher in London, England, 1973-82; writer. **Publications:** NOVELS: Nothing Natural, 1986; Rainforest, 1987; Like Mother, 1988; Then Again, 1990; Happily Ever After, 1991; Monkeys Uncle, 1994; Vanishing Princess, 1995; Don't, 1998; then Again, 1998; Skating to Antarctica, 1998; The Dream Mistress, 1999; Only Human, 2000; The View from the Bed (essays), 2003. **Address:** c/o Derek Johns, A.P. Watt Ltd., 20 John St, London WC1N 2DR, England.

DITCHOFF, Pamela J. American, b. 1950. **Genres:** Novels, Poetry. **Career:** WFSL-TV, Lansing, MI, copywriter and creative consultant, 1982-84; Quality Dairy, Lansing, MI, advertising agent, 1984-85; ASAP Copywriting, East Lansing, MI, owner and sole operator, 1985-87; Haslett Middle School and elementary schools, Haslett, MI, instructor in Quest Program for Gifted Children, 1985-89; Lansing Community College, instructor in communication and business, 1986-87; Michigan State University, East Lansing, graduate teaching assistant, 1986-89; Instructor in Creative Writers in Schools Program, Michigan, 1989-93; author. **Publications:** Poetry: One, Two, Three (textbook), 1989; Lexigram Learns America's Capitals (textbook), 1994; The Mirror of Monsters and Prodigies (novel), 1995; 7 Days & 7 Sins (novel), 2002. Contributor of short stories to anthologies; contributor of poetry to periodicals. **Address:** c/o Jane Dystel Literary Management, 1 Union Square W, New York, NY 10003, U.S.A.

DIVAKARUNI, Chitra Banerjee. Indian, b. 1956. **Genres:** Poetry, Novels, Novellas/Short stories. **Career:** Diablo Valley College, professor of creative writing, 1987-89; Foothill College, Los Altos, CA, professor of creative writing, 1989-. MidPeninsula Support Network for Battered Women, 1990-; President, MAITRI (help-line for South Asian women), 1991-. **Publications:** POETRY: Dark Like the River, 1987; The Reason for Nasturtiums, 1990; Black Candle, 1991; Leaving Yuba City: New and Selected Poems, 1997. STORIES: Arranged Marriage, 1995; The unknown errors of our lives : stories, 2001. NOVELS: The Mistress of Spices, 1997; Sister of My Heart, 1999; Neela, victory song, 2002; The Vine of Desire, 2002. EDITOR: Multitude, 1993; We, Too, Sing America, 1998. Contributor to periodicals. **Address:** Foothill College, English Department, 12345 El Monte Rd., Los Altos, CA 94022, U.S.A.

DIVALE, William T(ulio). American, b. 1942. **Genres:** Anthropology/Ethnology, Autobiography/Memoirs. **Career:** Professor of Anthropology and Chairman of Social Sciences, York College of City University of New York (joined faculty, 1973). **Publications:** I Lived inside the Campus Revolution, 1970; Warfare in Primitive Societies, 1973; Matrilocal Residence in Pre-literate Society, 1984. **Address:** Dept. of Anthropology, York College, City University of New York, 94-20 Guy Brewer Blvd, Jamaica, NY 11451, U.S.A. **Online address:** Divale@york.cuny.edu

DIVINE, Robert A(lexander). American, b. 1929. **Genres:** History. **Career:** George W. Littlefield Professor Emeritus in American History, University of Texas at Austin, 1996- (Instructor, 1954-57; Assistant Professor, 1957-61; Associate Professor, 1961-63; Professor of History, 1963-80; Littlefield Professor, 1981-96). Fellow, Institute for Advanced Study in the Behavioral Sciences, Stanford, CA, 1962-63. **Publications:** American Immigration Policy 1924-52, 1957; The Illusion of Neutrality, 1962; The Reluctant Belligerent, 1965; Second Chance, 1967; Roosevelt and World War II, 1969; Foreign Policy and U.S. Presidential Elections 1940-1960, 2 vols., 1974; Blowing on the Wind, 1978; Eisenhower and the Cold War, 1981; (with T.H.

Breen, G.M. Frederickson and R.H. Williams) America: Past and Present, 1984, 6th ed., 2002; The Sputnik Challenge, 1993; Perpetual War for Perpetual Peace, 2000. EDITOR: American Foreign Policy, 1960; The Age of Insecurity, 1968; (with J.A. Garraty) Twentieth Century America, 1968; Causes and Consequences of World War II, 1969; American Foreign Policy since 1945, 1969; The Cuban Missile Crisis, 1971; Exploring the Johnson Years, 1981; The Johnson Years, vol. 2, 1987, vol. 3, 1994. **Address:** Dept of History, University of Texas, Austin, TX 78712, U.S.A. **Online address:** divine@austin.rr.com

DIVINSKY, Nathan (Joseph). Canadian, b. 1925. **Genres:** Mathematics/Statistics, Recreation. **Career:** University of Manitoba, Winnipeg, assistant professor in mathematics, 1951-59; University of British Columbia, Vancouver, began in 1959, became professor of mathematics. Canadian delegate to International Chess Federation, 1987. Member of Vancouver School Board, 1974-80; city alderman, 1980-81. **Publications:** Rings and Radicals, 1965; Around the World in 80 Years, 1965; Linear Algebra, 1975; (with R. Keene) Warriors of the Mind: A Quest for the Supreme Genius of the Chess Board, 1989; Chess Encyclopedia, 1990; Life Maps of the Great Chess Master, 1993. **Address:** 5689 McMaster Rd, Vancouver, BC, Canada V6T 1K1.

DIXON, Ann R. American, b. 1954. **Genres:** Children's fiction, Poetry, Young adult non-fiction, Essays. **Career:** Hoedads Inc., Eugene, OR, reforestation contractor, 1977-81; freelance writer, Willow, AK, 1982-; Matanuska-Susitna Borough, Willow, AK, librarian, 1987-97. **Publications:** How Raven Brought Light to People, 1992; The Sleeping Lady, 1994; Merry Birthday, Nora Noel, 1997; Trick-or-Treat, 1998; Blueberry Shoe, 1999; Waiting for Noel, 2000; Alone across the Arctic, 2001; Winter Is, 2002; Big-Enough Anna, 2003. **Address:** PO Box 1009, Willow, AK 99688, U.S.A. **Online address:** www.anndixon.com

DIXON, Bernard. British, b. 1938. **Genres:** Medicine/Health, Sciences. **Career:** European Ed., American Society for Microbiology News, 1996-; European Ed., Biotechnology, New York, 1980-96. Research Fellow, University of Newcastle upon Tyne, 1965; Assistant Ed., and Deputy Ed., World Medicine, London, 1965-68; Deputy Ed., 1968-69, and Ed., 1969-79, New Scientist, London. Chairman, Association of British Science Writers, 1971-72; medical science research, ed., 1989-2003. **Publications:** What Is Science For?, 1973; Magnificent Microbes, 1976; Invisible Allies, 1976; Beyond the Magic Bullet, 1979; Ideas of Science, 1984; Health and the Human Body, 1986; Engineered Organisms in the Environment, 1988; How Science Works, 1989; Science and Society, 1989; Power Unseen: How Microbes Rule the World, 1994. EDITOR: Journeys in Belief, 1968; From Creation to Chaos, 1989. **Address:** 130 Cornwall Rd, Ruislip Manor, Middlesex HA4 6AW, England.

DIXON, Dougal. British, b. 1947. **Genres:** Science fiction/Fantasy, Earth sciences, Natural history. **Career:** Freelance writer, 1980-. Researcher and editor, Mitchell Beazley Ltd., 1973-78, and Blandford Press, 1978-80; Open University, part-time tutor in earth sciences, 1976-78. Bournemouth Science Fiction and Fantasy Group, chairman, 1981-82; part-owner and chief projectionist of an independent cinema, 1988-. **Publications:** Doomsday Planet (comic strip), 1980; After Man, 1981; Discovering Earth Sciences, 1982; Science World: Geology, 1982, Geography, 1983; Picture Atlas: Mountains, 1984, Forests, 1984, Deserts, 1984; Find Out about Prehistoric Reptiles, 1984; Find Out about Jungles, 1984; (with J. Burton) The Age of Dinosaurs (in US as Time Exposure), 1984; Nature Detective Series: Minerals, Rocks, and Fossils, 1984; Time Machine 7: Ice Age Explorer, 1985; Secrets of the Earth, 1986; Find Out about Dinosaurs, 1986; The First Dinosaurs, 1987; Hunting the Dinosaurs, 1987; The Jurassic Dinosaurs, 1987; The Last Dinosaurs, 1987; Be a Dinosaur Detective, 1987; The New Dinosaurs, 1988; Dino Dots, 1988; (ed.) The Macmillan Illustrated Encyclopedia of Dinosaurs and Prehistoric Animals, 1988; My First Dinosaur Library, 1989; When Dinosaurs Ruled the Earth, 1989; Air and Oceans, 1990; The Changing Landscape, 1990; Man after Man, 1990; The Giant Book of Dinosaurs, 1990; The Big Book of Prehistoric Life, 1990; Equinox Junior Animals Series, Animal Evolution, 1992; The Big Book of the Earth, 1991; The Practical Geologist, 1992; Explore the World of Prehistoric Life on Earth, 1992; Dinosaurs: Giants of the Earth, 1992; Dinosaurs: The Real Monsters, 1992; Dinosaurs: All Shapes and Sizes, 1992; Dinosaurs: The Fossil Hunters, 1992; Geography Facts, 1992; Earth Facts, 1992; Young Geographer: The Changing Earth, 1992; Dougal Dixon's Dinosaurs, 1993; Tell Me about Dinosaurs, 1993; Spotlights: Prehistoric Life, 1993; Questions and Answers about Dinosaurs, 1995; Digging up the Past, 1995; Ladybird Discovery, 1995; Collins Gem, Dinosaurs, 1996; The Earth, Its Wonders, Its Secrets: Natural Disasters, 1996; Amazing Dinosaurs, 2000; The Atlas of Evolution, vol. 2, 2001; Dinosaurs, 4 vols., 2001; My First Book of

Dinosaurs, 2001; Megabytes, Dinosaurs, 2001; The Magic Facet Machine: Dinosaurs, 2002; History Hunters: The Dinosaur Skull, 2003; History Hunters: The Mammoth's Tomb, 2003; The Future Is Wild, 2003. **Address:** 55 Mill Ln, Wareham, Dorset BH20 4QY, England. **Online address:** Dougal. Dixon@ukgateway.net

DIXON, Larry. American, b. 1966. **Genres:** Science fiction/Fantasy. **Career:** Artist and novelist. **Publications:** FANTASY NOVELS (WITH M. LACKEY). The Free Bards, 1997. SERRATED EDGE SERIES: Born to Run, 1987; Chrome Circle, 1994; The Chrome Borne, 1999. MAGE WARS SERIES: The Black Gryphon, 1994; The White Gryphon, 1995; The Silver Gryphon, 1996. OWL TRILOGY: Owlflight, 1997; Owlsight, 1998; Owlknight, 1999. **Address:** c/o Author Mail, Baen Publishing, PO Box 1403, Riverdale, NY 10471, U.S.A.

DIXON, Stephen. American, b. 1936. **Genres:** Novels, Novellas/Short stories, Bibliography. **Career:** Worked at various jobs, including bartender, waiter, jr. high school teacher, technical writer, news ed., etc., 1953-79; New York University School of Continuing Education, lecturer, 1979-80; Johns Hopkins University, Baltimore, assistant professor, 1980-83, associate professor, 1984-89, professor of fiction, 1990-. **Publications:** SHORT STORIES: No Relief, 1976; Quite Contrary: The Mary and Newt Story, 1979; 14 Stories, 1980; Movies, 1983; Time to Go, 1984; The Play and Other Stories, 1988; Love and Will, 1989; All Gone, 1990; Friends: More Will and Magna Stories, 1990; Long Made Short, 1993; The Stories of Stephen Dixon, 1994; Sleep, 1999. NOVELS: Work, 1977; Too Late, 1978; Fall & Rise, 1985; Garbage, 1988; Frog (novel, novellas, and stories), 1991; Interstate, 1995; Gould, 1997; 30, 1999; Tisch, 2000; I., 2002; Old Friends, 2004. OTHER: Man on Stage (play stories), 1996. **Address:** Writing Seminars, Gilman 135, Johns Hopkins University, Baltimore, MD 21218, U.S.A.

DIZIKES, John. American, b. 1932. **Genres:** History. **Career:** University of California, Santa Cruz, professor of history and American Studies. **Publications:** Britain, Roosevelt, and the New Deal: British Opinion, 1932-1938, 1979; Sportsmen and Gamesmen: American Sporting Life in the Age of Jackson, 1981; Opera in America: A Cultural History, 1993; Yankee Doodle Dandy: The Life and Times of Tod Sloan, 2000. **Address:** Department of American Studies, University of California Santa Cruz, 1156 High St., Santa Cruz, CA 95064, U.S.A.

DJERASSI, Carl. American (born Austria), b. 1923. **Genres:** Novels, Novellas/Short stories, Plays/Screenplays, Poetry, Chemistry, Sex, Autobiography/Memoirs. **Career:** Ciba Pharmaceutical Products, Summit, NJ, research chemist, 1942-43, 1945-49; Syntex, Mexico City, associate director of research, 1949-52, research vice president, 1957-60; Wayne State University, Detroit, MI, professor of chemistry, 1952-59; Stanford University, CA, professor of chemistry, 1959-2002; Syntex Labs., Palo Alto, CA, vice president, 1960-62; Syntex Research, vice president, 1962-68, president, 1968-72; Zoecon Corp., president, 1968-83, chairman of the board, 1968-86. **Publications:** Optical Rotary Dispersion: Applications to Organic Chemistry, 1960; Steroid Reactions: An Outline for Organic Chemists, 1963; Structure Elucidation of Natural Products by Mass Spectrometry (2 vols.), 1964; (co-author) Interpretation of Mass Spectra of Organic Compounds, 1964; (co-author) Mass Spectrometry of Organic Compounds, 1967; The Politics of Contraception, 1979, 1981; The Futurist and Other Stories, 1988; Cantor's Dilemma (novel), 1989, 1991; Steroids Made It Possible (autobiography), 1990; The Clock Runs Backward (poetry), 1991; The Pill, Pygmy Chimps, and Degas' Horse (autobiography), 1992; From the Lab into the World (collected essays), 1994; The Bourbaki Gambit (novel), 1994; Marx, deceased (novel), 1996; Menachem's Seed (novel), 1996; NO (novel), 1998; An Immaculate Misconception (play), 19980; (with R. Hoffmann) Oxygen (play), 2001; This Man's Pill (memoir), 2001; Calculus (play), 2002; Ego-Three on a Couch (play), 2004; Phallacy (play), 2005. **Address:** Dept of Chemistry, Stanford University, Stanford, CA 94305-5080, U.S.A. **Online address:** djerassi@stanford.edu; www.djerassi.com

DJOLETO, (Solomon Alexander) Amu. Ghanaian, b. 1929. **Genres:** Adult non-fiction, Children's fiction, Poetry, Novels. **Career:** Ghana Ministry of Education, Government Secondary Technical School, Takoradi, education officer, 1958, became both senior education officer and head of the English department, 1963, assistant headmaster, 1964; affiliated with a publishing firm, London, England, 1965-66; Ghana Ministry of Education, editor of Ghana Teachers Journal, 1966, became principal education officer in charge of information, public relations, and publications, 1967, deputy chief education officer and head of the planning division, 1973, executive director of the Ghana Book Development Council, 1975-89; Ghana Publishing Corporation, board member, beginning 1968; Authorship Development Fund, vice-

chairperson of board; United Nations Educational, Scientific and Cultural Organization, consultant on book development councils to several African countries, 1981-88; United Nations University, consultant, 1988-89; Ghana Ministry of Education, textbooks consultant, 1989-. **Publications:** NONFICTION: (co-ed. with T.H.S. Kwami) West African Prose Anthology, 1974; English Practice for the African Student (textbook), 1967, rev. and updated as English Practice, 1990. EDITOR: Ten Stories from Chaucer, 1979; Books and Reading in Ghana, 1985; Chaucer's Prologue and Five Stories, 1987. FICTION: The Strange Man, 1967; Money Galore, 1975; Hurricane of Dust, 1988. POETRY: Amid the Swelling Act, 1992. CHILDREN'S BOOKS: Obodai Sai (novel), 1990; Twins in Trouble, 1991; The Frightened Thief, 1992; Kofi Loses His Way, 1996; The Girl Who Knows about Cars, 1996; Akos and the Fire Ghost, 1997. Contributor to books. **Address:** PO Box C2217, Cantonments Communications Centre, Accra, Ghana.

DJWA, Sandra (Ann). Canadian, b. 1939. **Genres:** Poetry, Literary criticism and history, Biography, Essays. **Career:** Simon Fraser University, Burnaby, BC, professor of English, 1980-, chairwoman of English department, 1986-94, member of board of governors, 1990-95. **Publications:** E.J. Pratt: The Evolutionary Vision, 1974; (with M.G. Flitton) An Inventory of Research-in-Progress and Suggested Research Projects in English-Canadian Literature, 1978-1979, 1979; The Politics of the Imagination: A Life of F.R. Scott, 1987; F.R. Scott and His Works, 1989; F.R. Scott: Une Vie, 2001; Professing English: A Life of Roy Daniells, 2001. EDITOR: (and author of intro.) Charles Heavysege, Saul and Selected Poetry of Charles Heavysege, 1976; (with R. St. J. Macdonald) On F.R. Scott: Essays on His Contributions to Law, Literature, and Politics, 1983; (with R.G. Moyles) E.J. Pratt: Complete Poems, 2 vols, 1989; Giving Canada a Literary History: A Memoir by Carl F. Klinck, 1991. **Address:** Department of English, Simon Fraser University, 8888 University Dr, Burnaby, BC, Canada V5A 1S6. **Online address:** djwa@sfu.ca

DOAK, Wade (Thomas). New Zealander, b. 1940. **Genres:** Anthropology/Ethnology, Children's non-fiction, Environmental sciences/Ecology, History, Marine sciences/Oceanography, Natural history, Young adult non-fiction, Zoology. **Career:** Dive South Pacific Underwater Magazine, publisher; filmmaker, currently. **Publications:** Elingamite and Its Treasure, 1969; Beneath New Zealand Seas, 1971; Fishes of the New Zealand Region, 1972, rev. ed., 1978; Sharks and Other Ancestors, 1975; Islands of Survival, 1976; The Cliffdwellers, 1979; Dolphin, Dolphin, 1981; The Burning of the Boyd, 1984; Ocean Planet, 1984; Encounters with Whales and Dolphins, 1988; Wade Doak's World of New Zealand Fishes, 1991; Swimming with Dolphins in New Zealand, 1994; Friends in the Sea: Solo Dolphins in New Zealand & Australia, 1995; Deep Blue, 1996; I Am a Fish, 1999. **Address:** PO Box 20, Whangarei, New Zealand. **Online address:** www.wadedoak.com

DOAN, Eleanor Lloyd. American, b. 1914. **Genres:** Children's non-fiction, Crafts, Theology/Religion, Novellas/Short stories. **Career:** Merchandising Manager, 1945-75, Editorial Director, 1951-66, Marketing Research Manager, 1966-71, Manager of Special Projects, 1971-75, and Promotional Publicist, 1975-85, Gospel Lights Publs., Ventura, Ca. **Publications:** Fascinating Finger Fun, 1951; Teaching Twos and Threes, 1951; Series I: Twos and Threes, 1951; 261 Crafts and Fun, 1953; How to Plan a Junior Church, 1954; Series II: Twos and Threes, 1956; Fun to Do Handcrafts, 1957; Hobby Fun, 1958; Sourcebook for Speakers, 1960; Handcraft Encyclopedia, 1961; (co-author) How to Plan a Primary Church, 1961; Equipment Encyclopedia, 1962; Pattern Encyclopedia, 1962; (co-author) Missy Stories for Preschoolers, 1962; (co-author) Missy Stories for Primaries, 1962; (co-author) Missy Stories for Juniors, 1962; (co-author) Missy Stories for Youth, 1962; Teaching Juniors, 1962; Teaching Junior Highs, 1962; Teaching Adults, 1962; Fun and Food Crafts, 1963; Teaching Fours and Fives, 1963; Teaching Primaries, 1964; More Handicrafts, 1966; Visual Aid Encyclopedia, 1966, Sourcebook for Mothers, 1969; New Sourcebook for Speakers, 1969; Kid Stuff, 1970; Treasury of Inspiration, 1970; Bible Story Picture Book, 1971; 145 Fun to Do Crafts, 1972; Creative Crafts for Young Children, 1973; Creative Crafts for Children, 1973; Creative Crafts for Juniors, 1973; Creative Crafts for Youth, 1973; 157 More Fun to Do Crafts, 1973; Mothers Treasury Inspiration, 1973; Treasury of Verse for Children, 1978, 1987; Find the Words Search Puzzle Book, 1990; The Complete Speakers Sourcebook, 1995. WORK IN PROGRESS: (biographical fiction novel) Heritage.

DOANE, Janice (L.). American, b. 1950. **Genres:** Literary criticism and history, Women's studies and issues. **Career:** State University of New York College at Buffalo, instructor in English, 1980-83; St. Mary's College of California, Moraga, assistant professor, 1984-89, associate professor of English, 1989-, department head, 1993-. Instructor at Canisius College, 1980-82, and Medaille College, 1981. **Publications:** Silence and Narrative:

The Early Novels of Gertrude Stein, 1986; (with D. Hodges) Nostalgia and Sexual Difference: The Resistance to Contemporary Feminism, 1987; (with Hodges) From Klein to Kristeva: Psychoanalytic Feminism and the Search for the "Good Enough" Mother, 1992. Contributor to books and literature journals. **Address:** Department of English, St. Mary's College of California, Moraga, CA 94575, U.S.A.

DOBBIN, Murray. Canadian, b. 1945. **Genres:** Economics, Politics/Government, Biography. **Career:** Free-lance writer and broadcaster, 1971-. Lecturer in native studies, 1978-86; public relations officer and organizer, 1986-. **Publications:** The One-and-a-Half Men, 1981; Preston Manning and the Reform Party, 1991; The Politics of Kim Campbell, 1993; Taxes: The Second Certainty, (radio documentary), 1992; The Remaking of New Zealand, (radio documentary), 1994; The Mythof the Good Corporate Citizen, 1998. **Address:** 803-1340 12th Ave W, Vancouver, BC, Canada V6H 1M5.

DOBBS, Michael. British, b. 1948. **Genres:** Mystery/Crime/Suspense. **Career:** Boston Globe, Boston, MA, editorial assistant and political feature writer, 1971-75; Saatchi & Saatchi Advertising, deputy chairperson, 1983-86 and 1988-91, director of Worldwide Corporate Communications, 1987-88; Conservative Party, England, chief of staff, 1986-87, deputy chairman, 1994-95; writer, broadcaster. Government adviser, 1981-87. **Publications:** NOVELS: House of Cards, 1989; Wall Games, 1990; Last Man to Die, 1991; To Play the King, 1992; The Touch of Innocents, 1994; The Final Cut, 1995; Goodfellowe M.P., 1997; The Buddha of Brewer Street, 1998; Whispers of Betrayal, 2000. **Address:** 18 Bruton Place, Mayfair, London W1J 6LY, England. **Online address:** michldobbs@aol.com

DOBIE, Kathy. American. **Genres:** Autobiography/Memoirs. **Career:** Writer. **Publications:** The Only Girl in the Car: A Memoir, 2003. Contributor to periodicals and Web sites. **Address:** Author Mail, Dial Press, Bantam Dell Publishing Group, Random House, 1745 Broadway, New York, NY 10019, U.S.A.

DOBREZ, Patricia. Australian, b. 1943. **Genres:** Biography. **Career:** Writer and scholar. Australian Catholic University, teacher; independent scholar. **Publications:** (with P. Herbst) The Art of the Boyds: Generations of Artistic Achievement, 1990; Michael Dransfield's Lives: A Sixties Biography, 1999. **Address:** Australian Catholic University, Signadou Campus, PO Box 256, Dickson, ACT 2602, Australia.

DOBRIN, Lyn. American, b. 1942. **Genres:** Children's fiction, Civil liberties/Human rights, Food and Wine, Homes/Gardens, Medicine/Health, Travel/Exploration. **Career:** U.S. Peace Corps, Washington, DC, volunteer in Kenya, 1965-67; World Hunger Year, New York City, editor, 1976-80; Adelphi University, Garden City, NY, director of community relations, School of Social Work, 1981-95; public relations consultant and freelance writer, 1995-. **Publications:** (with J. Ibongia) The Magic Stone, 1967; (with T. Liotti and A. Dobrin) Convictions: Political Prisoners; Their Stories, 1981; Look to This Day: Voices Affirming the Human Spirit, 1988. **Address:** 613 Dartmouth St, Westbury, NY 11590, U.S.A. **Online address:** lyndobrin@erols.com

DOBSON, Alan P. British, b. 1951. **Genres:** Politics/Government, History, International relations/Current affairs. **Career:** University of Wales, University College of Swansea, lecturer, 1978-91, senior lecturer in politics, 1991-96, reader, 1996; University of Dundee, Politics Department, professor, 1999-. Norwegian Nobel Institute, Oslo, senior research fellow, 1997. **Publications:** U.S. Wartime Aid to Britain, 1986; Politics of the Anglo-American Economic Special Relationship, 1988; Peaceful Air Warfare: The USA, Britain, and the Politics of International Aviation, 1991; Flying in the Face of Competition: The Policies and Diplomacy of Airline Regulatory Reform in Britain, the USA and the European Community 1968-94, 1995; Anglo-American Relations in the Twentieth Century: Of Friendship, Conflict and the Rise and Decline of Superpowers, 1995; (ed.) Deconstructing and Reconstructing the Cold War, 1999; (with S. Marsh) U.S. Foreign Policy since 1945, 2000; U.S. Economic Statecraft for Survival 1933-1991: Of Sanctions, Embargoes and Economic Warfare, 2002. **Address:** Department of Politics, University of Dundee, Dundee DD1 4HN, Scotland. **Online address:** A.P.Dobson@dundee.ac.uk

DOBSON, Andrew (Nicholas Howard). British, b. 1957. **Genres:** Philosophy, Politics/Government. **Career:** University of Keele, England, lecturer in politics, 1987-, professor of politics, 1993-; Open University, professor of politics. **Publications:** An Introduction to the Politics and Philosophy of Jose Ortega y Gasset, 1989; Green Political Thought: An Introduction, 1990, 2nd ed., 1995; Jean-Paul Sartre and the Politics of

Reason, 1993; Justice and the Environment, 1998. EDITOR/CO-EDITOR: The Green Reader, 1991; The Politics of Nature: Explorations in Green Political Theory, 1993; Fairness and Futurity, 1999; Citizenship and Environment, 2003; Citizenship, Environment, Economy, 2005; Environmental Citizenship, 2005; Political Theory and the Ecological Challenge, 2005. **Address:** Dept of Government and Politics, Open University, Walton Hall, Milton Keynes, Staffs MK7 6AA, England.

DOBSON, James C. American, b. 1936. **Genres:** Medicine/Health, Psychology, Women's studies and issues, Human relations/Parenting. **Career:** Hudson School District, Hacienda Heights, CA, teacher, 1960-63, psychometrist, 1962-63; Charter Oak Unified School District, Covina, CA, psychometrist-counselor, 1963-64; school psychologist and coordinator of pupil personnel services, 1964-66; University of Southern California, School of Medicine, Department of Medical Genetics and Child Development, Children's Hospital of Los Angeles, assistant professor, 1969-77, associate clinical professor of pediatrics, 1978-83; Focus on the Family, president and founder, 1977-. **Publications:** Dare to Discipline, 1970; (ed. with R. Koch) The Mentally Retarded Child and His Family: A Multidisciplinary Handbook, 1971, rev. ed., 1976; Hide or Seek, 1974; What Wives Wish Their Husbands Knew about Women, 1975; The Strong-Willed Child, 1978; Preparing for Adolescence, 1978; Straight Talk to Men and Their Wives, 1980; Emotions: Can You Trust Them?, 1980; Dr. Dobson Answers Your Questions, 1982; Love Must Be Tough, 1983; Love for a Lifetime, 1987; Parenting Isn't for Cowards, 1987; Children at Risk, 1990; The New Dare to Discipline, 1992; When God Doesn't Make Sense, 1993; Life on the Edge, 1996; Solid Answers, 1997; Night Light, 2000; Bringing up Boys, 2001; Night Light for Parents, 2002. **Address:** c/o James Dobson, Inc, 1755 Telstar Dr #203, Colorado Springs, CO 80920-0500, U.S.A. **Online address:** backpacker18@juno.com

DOBSON, Jill. British, b. 1969. **Genres:** Young adult fiction. **Career:** Author and editor. Worked as a vegetarian caterer, kibbutz farmer, volunteer archaeologist, English teacher in Japan and Russia, copyeditor for The Moscow Times, and Australian Department of Defence employee. **Publications:** YOUNG ADULT FICTION: The Inheritors, 1988; Time to Go, 1991; A Journey to Distant Mountains, 2001. **Address:** c/o Author Mail, University of Queensland Press, PO Box 42, St. Lucia, QLD 4067, Australia.

DOBSON, Joanne. American, b. 1942. **Genres:** Novels, Literary criticism and history. **Career:** Amherst College, Amherst, MA, visiting professor of English and American studies, 1985-86; Tufts University, Medford, MA, visiting assistant professor of English, 1986-87; Fordham University, Bronx, NY, assistant professor, 1987-92, associate professor of English, 1992-. **Publications:** (ed.) E.D.E.N. Southworth, The Hidden Hand, 1988; Dickinson and the Strategies of Reticence: The Woman Writer in Nineteenth-Century America, 1989. NOVELS: Quieter than Sleep, 1997; The Northbury Papers, 1998; The Raven and the Nightingale, 1999; Cold and Pure and Very Dead, 2000; The Maltese Manuscript, 2003. Contributor to books and periodicals. **Address:** Department of English, Fordham University, Bronx, NY 10458, U.S.A. **Online address:** dedcons@aol.com

DOBSON, Julia. See TUGENDHAT, Julia.

DOBSON, R(ichard) Barrie. British, b. 1931. **Genres:** History. **Career:** Cambridge University, Professor of Medieval History, 1988-99. University of St. Andrews, Scotland, Lecturer in Mediaeval History, 1958-64; University of York, Lecturer, 1964-68, Sr. Lecturer, 1968-71, Reader, 1971-76, Professor of History, 1976-88, Honorary Professor of History, 1999-. British Academy, Fellow, 1988. **Publications:** Selby Abbey and Town, 1969; (with M.J. Angold) The World of the Middle Ages, 1970; Durham Priory 1400-1450, 1973; The Jews of Medieval York and the Massacre of March 1190, 1974; (with J. Taylor) Rymes of Robyn Hood: An Introduction to the English Outlaw, 1976; York City Chamberlains' Account Rolls 1396-1500, 1981; (with S. Donaghey) The Nunnery of Clementhorpe, 1984; Preserving the Perishable: Contrasting Communities in Medieval England, 1990; Church and Society in the Medieval North of England, 1996. EDITOR: The Peasants' Revolt of 1381, 1970; The Church, Politics, and Patronage in the Fifteenth Century, 1984. **Address:** 15 St Olave's Rd, York Y030 7AL, England.

DOCHERTY, James C(airns). Australian, b. 1949. **Genres:** History. **Career:** Australian National University, Canberra, research assistant for Australian Dictionary of Biography, 1974, research assistant in political science, 1974, 1977; Australian federal government, Australian Bureau of Statistics, 1978-79, Department of Industrial Relations, Canberra, 1984-96, Department of Immigration and Multicultural Affairs, 1996-2004. Monash

University, honorary research associate at National Centre for Australian Studies, 1990-96. **Publications:** Selected Social Statistics of New South Wales, 1861-1976 (monograph), 1982; Newcastle: The Making of an Australian City, 1983; (consultant and contrib.) Australians: Historical Statistics, ed. by W. Vamplew, 1987; Historical Dictionary of Australia, 1992, rev. ed., 1999; (ed. with D. Peetz and A. Preston, and contrib.) Workplace Bargaining in the International Context: First Report of the Workplace Bargaining Research Project, 1993; A Historical Dictionary of Organized Labor, 1996, rev. ed., 2004; Historical Dictionary of Socialism, 1997. **Address:** 59 Devonport St, Lyons, ACT 2606, Australia.

DOCKREY, Karen. American, b. 1955. **Genres:** Theology/Religion, Inspirational/Motivational Literature. **Career:** Youth minister, 1980-; writer, 1984-. **Publications:** Getting to Know God, 1984, study guide, 1986; Friends: Finding and Keeping Them, 1985; Dating: Making Your Own Choices, 1987; What's Your Problem?, 1987; Family Survival Guide (leader's and student's versions), 1988; Living until Jesus Comes, 1989; When Everyone's Looking at You, 1989; Junior High Retreats and Lock-Ins, 1990; (with J. Hall) Holiday Specials and Boredom Busters, 1990; Youth Workers and Parents: Sharing Resources for Equipping Youth, 1990; Why Does Everybody Hate Me?, 1991; The Youth Worker's Guide to Creative Bible Study, 1991; Does Anybody Understand? Devotions for Teens on Family Survival, 1992; What's a Kid like Me Doing in a Family like This?: Leader's Book, 1992; From Frustration to Freedom, 1992; It's Not Fair!: Through Grief to Healing, 1992; (with J. Godwin and P. Godwin) Holman Student Bible Dictionary, 1993; Will I Ever Feel Good Again?: When You're Overwhelmed by Grief and Loss, 1993; Are You There, God?, with leader's guide, 1993; When a Hug Won't Fix the Hurt, 1993; I Thought You Were My Friend!, with leader's guide, 1994; (with B. Matthews and A. Adams) I Only See My Dad on Weekends: Kids Tell Their Stories about Divorce and Blended Families, 1994; (with others) Ready for Life, 1994; Tuned-Up Parenting: Eight Studies to Invite Harmony in Your Home, 1994; (with E. Dockrey) You'll Never Believe What They Told Me: Trusting God through Cancer and Other Serious Illness, 1994; Alone but Not Lonely, 1994; Curing the Self Hate Virus, 1994; Growing a Family Where People Really Like Each Other, 1996; Fun Friend-Making Activities for Adult Groups, 1997; Am I in Love? Twelve Youth Studies on Guy/Girl Relationships, 1997; YouthCare: Giving Real Help That Makes a Real Difference, 1997; Facing Down the Tough Stuff, 1998. Contributor to books and periodicals. **Address:** 8CPH, 3558 South Jefferson Ave., St. Louis, MO 63118, U.S.A. **Online address:** kdockrey@mindspring.com

DOCTOROW, E(dgar) L(awrence). American, b. 1931. **Genres:** Novels, Novellas/Short stories, Plays/Screenplays, Essays. **Career:** Glucksman Professor of English and American Letters, New York University, NYC, 1982-; Publr., 1969, Dial Press, NYC; Writer-in-Residence, University of California at Irvine, 1969-70; Creative Writing Fellow, School of Dramas, Yale University, New Haven, CT, 1974-75. Member of Faculty, Sarah Lawrence College, Bronxville, New York, 1971-78. **Publications:** Welcome to Hard Times, 1960; Big as Life, 1966; The Book of Daniel, 1971; Ragtime, 1975; Drinks before Dinner (play), 1979; Loon Lake, 1980; Daniel (screenplay), 1983; Lives of the Poets: Six Stories and a Novella, 1984; World's Fair, 1985; Billy Bathgate, 1988; Jack London, Hemingway, and the Constitution: Selected Essays 1977-92, 1993; The Waterworks, 1994; City of God, 2000; Sweetland Stories, 2004. **Address:** Dept of English, New York University, 19 University Pl, New York, NY 10003, U.S.A.

DODD, Lynley Stuart (Weeks). New Zealander, b. 1941. **Genres:** Children's fiction, Illustrations. **Career:** Full-time writer and illustrator. **Publications:** (with E. Sutton) My Cat Likes to Hide in Boxes, 1974. SELF-ILLUSTRATED: The Nickle Nackle Tree, 1976; Titimus Trim, 1979; The Smallest Turtle, 1982; The Apple Tree, 1982; Hairy Maclary from Donaldson's Dairy, 1983; Hairy Maclary's Bone, 1984; Hairy Maclary, Scattercat, 1985; Wake Up, Bear, 1986; Hairy Maclary's Caterwaul Caper, 1987; A Dragon in a Wagon, 1988; Hairy Maclary's Rumpus at the Vet, 1989; Slinky Malinki, 1990; Find Me a Tiger, 1991; Hairy Maclary's Showbusiness, 1991; The Minister's Cat ABC, 1992; Slinky Malinki, Open the Door, 1993; Schnitzel Von Krumm's Basketwork, 1994; Sniff-Snuff-Snap!, 1995; Schnitzel Von Krumm, Forget-Me-Not, 1996; Hairy Maclary, Sit, 1997; Slinky Malinki Catflaps, 1998; Hairy Maclary and Zachary Quack, 1999; Hedgehog Howdedo, 2000; Scarface Claw, 2001; Schnitzel Von Krumm, Dogs Never Climb Trees, 2002; The Other Ark, 2004; Zachary Quack, Minimonster, 2005. **Address:** Edward Ave, RD 3, Tauranga, New Zealand.

DODD, Wayne. Also writes as Donald Wayne. American, b. 1930. **Genres:** Novels, Children's fiction, Poetry, Literary criticism and history. **Career:** Distinguished Professor of English, Ohio University, Athens. Ed., The Ohio Review and Ohio Review Books. **Publications:** (as Donald Wayne) The Adventures of Little White Possum, 1970; We Will Wear White Roses, 1974; Made in America, 1975; A Time of Hunting, 1975; The Names You Gave It, 1980; The General Mule Poems, 1980; Sometimes Music Rises, 1986; Echoes of the Unspoken, 1990; Toward the End of the Century; Essays into Poetry, 1992; Of Desire and Disorder, 1993; The Blue Salvages, 1997; Is, 2003. **Address:** 11292 Peach Ridge Rd, Athens, OH 45701, U.S.A.

DODDS, Bill. American, b. 1952. **Genres:** Young adult fiction, Human relations/Parenting, Humor/Satire. **Career:** Catholic Youth Organization, Seattle, WA, retreat leader, 1974-76; King County Advocates for Retarded Citizens, Seattle, WA, recreation center assistant director, 1976-78; The Progress, Seattle, WA, reporter and editor, 1978-88. Freelance writer of fiction and nonfiction for adults and children, 1988-. **Publications:** JUVENILE: The Hidden Fortune, 1991; My Sister Annie, 1993; Bedtime Parables, 1993. OTHER: (Coauthor) Speaking Out, Fighting Back: Personal Experiences of Women Who Survived Childhood Sexual Abuse in the Home, 1985; O Father: A Murder Mystery, 1991; How I Flunked Penmanship and Other Tales of Growing up Catholic, 1991. HUMOR: The Parents' Guide to Dirty Tricks, 1989, reprinted as How to Outsmart Your Kids: The Parents' Guide to Dirty Tricks, 1993; How to Be a Catholic Mother, 1990; Dads, Catholic Style (inspirational), 1990; How to Survive Your 40th Birthday, 1990; Contributor to books. Columnist for and contributor to periodicals. **Address:** c/o Boyds Mills Press, 815 Church St., Honesdale, PA 18431, U.S.A.

DODGE, Peter. American, b. 1926. **Genres:** History, Sociology. **Career:** Associate Professor of Sociology, University of New Hampshire, Durham, 1964-96. Instructor, 1958-61, and Assistant Professor, 1961-64, Harpur College, State University of New York, Binghamton; Social Science Research Council Grantee to Brazil, 1968-69. **Publications:** Beyond Marxism: The Faith and Works of Hendrik de Man, 1966; (ed. and trans.) Hendrik de Man, Socialist Critic of Marxism: A Documentary Study, 1979. **Address:** 14 Runnymede Dr, North Hampton, NH 03862, U.S.A. **Online address:** peterdodge@comcast.net

DODGE, Tom. American, b. 1939. **Genres:** Sports/Fitness, Adult nonfiction. **Career:** High school English teacher in Mansfield, TX, 1965-68; Blinn College, Brenham, TX, instructor in English, 1968-70; Mountain View College, Dallas, TX, professor of English, 1970-94. KERA-Radio, commentator for the affiliate of National Public Radio, 1988-. **Publications:** (trans.) A Generation of Leaves (poems), 1977; A Literature of Sports (anthology), 1980; Oedipus Road (nonfiction), 1996; Tom Dodge Talks about Texas (nonfiction), 2000. **Address:** 302 Stiles Dr., Midlothian, TX 76065, U.S.A. **Online address:** tom_dodge1@yahoo.com

DODGSHON, Robert A(ndrew). British, b. 1941. **Genres:** Geography, History. **Career:** Museum of English Rural Life, University of Reading, assistant keeper, 1966-70; University of Wales, Aberystwyth, professor of geography (joined faculty, 1970). HGRG Research Monograph Series, editor, 1978-82. **Publications:** (ed. with R.A. Butlin) An Historical Geography of England and Wales, 1978; The Origins of British Field Systems, 1980; Land and Society in Early Scotland, 1981; The European Past: Social Evolution and Spatial Order, 1987; (ed.) Historical Geography of Europe, 1998; From Chiefs to Landlords, 1998; Society in Time and Space, 1998; Age of the Clans, 2002. Contributor to professional journals. **Address:** Inst. of Geography and Earth Studies, University of Wales, King St, Ceredigion, Aberystwyth SY23 3DB, Wales. **Online address:** rad@aber.ac.uk

DODMAN, Nicholas H. American (born England), b. 1946. **Genres:** Animals/Pets. **Career:** Tufts University School of Veterinary Medicine, Professor, Section Head and Program Director, Animal Behavior. **Publications:** The Dog Who Loved Too Much, 1996; The Cat Who Cried for Help, 1997; (ed) Psychopharmacology of Animal Behavior Disorders, 1998; Dogs Behaving Badly, 1999; If Only They Could Speak, 2002. **Address:** Department of Clinical Sciences, Tufts University School of Veterinary Medicine, 200 Westboro Rd, North Grafton, MA 01536, U.S.A. **Online address:** nicholas.dodman@tufts.edu

DODMAN, Nicholas H. (born England), b. 1946. **Genres:** Adult non-fiction. **Career:** Veterinarian, educator, and author. Tufts University School of Veterinary Medicine, North Grafton, MA, professor and director of Tufts University Animal Behavior Clinic, 1982-; PetPlace.com, consultant; Veterinary Center PETFAX, consultant. **Publications:** The Dog Who Loved Too Much: Tales, Treatments, and the Psychology of Dogs, 1995; The Cat Who Cried for Help: Attitudes, Emotions, and the Psychology of Cats, 1997; (editor, with Louis Shuster) Psychopharmacology of Animal Behavior Disorders, 1998; Dogs Behaving Badly: An A to Z Guide to Understanding and Curing Behavior Problems in Dogs, 1999; *If Only They Could Speak: Stories about Pets and Their People*, 2002. Author of scientific studies. **Address:** 200 Westboro Rd., North Grafton, MA 01536, U.S.A. **Online address:** Nicholas.Dodman@Tufts.edu

DOE, Bill. *See* **DEBIN, David.**

DOEBLER, Bettie Anne. American. **Genres:** Poetry, Literary criticism and history. **Career:** Dickinson College, Carlisle, PA, instructor to associate professor of English, 1961-70; Arizona State University, Tempe, associate professor to professor of English, 1971-94, director of Interdisciplinary Humanities Program, 1982-92, professor emeritus, 1995-; Grand Canyon University, visiting professor of English, 2004-05. **Publications:** The Quickening Seed: Death in the Sermons of John Donne, 1970; "Rooted Sorrow": Dying in Early Modern England, 1994; (with R. Slotten and J. Thiem) The Book of the Mermaid, 2001; (with R. Slotten and J. Thiem) Nine Waves (poems), 2003. EDITOR/CO-EDITOR & AUTHOR/CO-AUTHOR OF INTRODUCTION: Willet, Sacrorum Emblematum Centura Una, 1984; W. Harrison, Deaths Advantage Little Regarded, 1993; (with R.M. Warnicke) Taylor's The Pilgrim's Profession, 1995; (with R.M. Warnicke) Death's Sermon unto the Living, 1999; (with R.M. Warnicke) H. Gamon, The Praise of a Godly Woman, 2001; (with R.M. Warnicke and J. Barlow) A True Guide to Glory, 2004. Contributor of poems to periodicals. **Address:** 6102 E Calle del Norte, Scottsdale, AZ 85251, U.S.A. **Online address:** bettieadoebler@aol.com

DOERR, Anthony. American, b. 1973. **Genres:** Novellas/Short stories. **Career:** Associated with Bowling Green State University, Bowling Green, OH; Boise State University, Boise, ID, distinguished writer-in-residence, 2002-03. **Publications:** The Shell Collector: Stories, 2002. Contributor of short fiction to periodicals. **Address:** 881 W Sandstone Ln, Boise, ID 83702, U.S.A.

DOERR, Juergen C. *See* Obituaries.

DOGNIEZ, Cecile. French, b. 1953. **Genres:** Theology/Religion. **Career:** Centre Lenain de Tillemont, Paris, France, instructor. **Publications:** Bibliography of the Septuagint (1970-1993), 1995. WITH M. HARL: Le Deuteronome (title means: Deuteronomy), 1992; Les Douze Prophetes, 1999; Le Pentataique d'Alexandre, 2001. **Address:** Centre Lenain de Tillemont, CNRS Sorbonne, 1 rue Victor Cousin, 75005 Paris, France. **Online address:** cecile.dogniez@wanadoo.fr

DOHERTY, Berlie. British, b. 1943. **Genres:** Novels, Children's fiction, Plays/Screenplays, Poetry. **Career:** Social worker, 1968; English teacher, 1978-80; full-time writer, 1983-. **Publications:** How Green You Are!, 1982; The Making of Fingers Finnigan, 1983; Tilly Mint Tales, 1984; White Peak Farm, 1984; Children of Winter, 1985; Granny Was a Buffer Girl, 1986 (Carnegie Medal); Tough Luck, 1987; Tilly Mint and the Dodo, 1988; Paddiwak and Cosy, 1988; Spellhorn, 1989; Requiem, 1991; Dear Nobody, 1991 (Carnegie Medal); Snowy, 1992; Walking on Air, 1993; Street Child, 1993; Old Father Christmas, 1993; Willa and Old Miss Annie, 1994; The Vinegar Jar, 1994; The Golden Bird, 1995; The Snake-Stone, 1995; The Magical Bicycle, 1995; Our Field, 1996; Daughter of the Sea, 1996; Running on Ice, 1997; Bella's Den, 1997; The Midnight Man, 1998; Tales of Wonder and Magic, 1997; The Forsaken Merman, 1998; The Sailingship Tree, 1998; Fairy Tales, 2000; Y garreg neidr, 2000; The Famous Adventures of Jack, 2001; Zzaap and the Wordmaster, 2001; Holly Starcross, 2001; The Nutcracker, 2002; Blue John, 2003; Tricky Nelly's Birthday Treat, 2003; Coconut Comes to School, 2003; Jeannie of white Peak Farm, 2003; Deep Secret, 2003; The Starburster, 2004. PLAYS: Dear Nobody, 1995; Morgan's Field, 1996; Street Child, 2000; Lorna Doone, 2001; Granny Was a Buffer Girl. **Address:** c/o David Higham Associates Ltd., 5-8 Lower John St, Golden Sq, London, Derbyshire W1R 4HA, England.

DOHERTY, Craig A. American, b. 1951. **Genres:** Children's non-fiction, Architecture. **Career:** Berlin High School, Berlin, NH, English teacher, 1987-. Writer. **Publications:** COAUTHOR WITH K.M. DOHERTY: The Apaches and Navajos, 1989; The Iroquois, 1989; Benazir Bhutto, 1990; Arnold Schwarzenegger: Larger than Life, 1993; The Zunis, 1993. NATIVE AMERICAN PEOPLE SERIES WITH K.M. DOHERTY: The Cahuilla, 1994; The Chickasaw, 1994; The Crow, 1994; The Huron, 1994; The Narragansett, 1994; The Ute, 1994. BUILDING AMERICA SERIES WITH K.M. DOHERTY: The Gateway Arch, 1995; The Golden Gate Bridge, 1995; Hoover Dam, 1995; Mount Rushmore, 1995; Sears Tower, 1995; The Washington Monument, 1995; The Astrodome, 1996; The Erie Canal, 1996; The Statue of Liberty, 1996. **Address:** RFD-1, Box 572, Milan, NH 03588, U.S.A.

DOHERTY, Justin (Francis). British, b. 1960. **Genres:** Literary criticism and history. **Career:** Queen's University of Belfast, Belfast, Northern Ireland, lecturer in Russian, 1989-95; Trinity College, Dublin, Ireland, lecturer in Russian, 1995-. **Publications:** The Acmeist Movement in Russian Poetry, 1995. **Address:** Department of Russian, Trinity College, Dublin 2, Ireland. **Online address:** jdoherty@tcd.ie

DOHERTY, Katherine M(ann). American, b. 1951. **Genres:** Children's non-fiction, Architecture. **Career:** New Hampshire Community Technical College, Berlin, NH, director of library resources, 1986-. Writer. **Publications:** COAUTHOR WITH C.A. DOHERTY: The Apaches and Navajos, 1989; The Iroquois, 1989; Benazir Bhutto, 1990; Arnold Schwarzenegger: Larger than Life, 1993; The Zunis, 1993. NATIVE AMERICAN PEOPLE SERIES WITH C.A. DOHERTY: The Cahuilla, 1994; The Chickasaw, 1994; The Crow, 1994; The Huron, 1994; The Narragansett, 1994; The Ute, 1994. BUILDING AMERICA SERIES WITH C.A. DOHERTY: The Gateway Arch, 1995; The Golden Gate Bridge, 1995; Hoover Dam, 1995; Mount Rushmore, 1995; Sears Tower, 1995; The Washington Monument, 1995; The Astrodome, 1996; The Erie Canal, 1996; The Statue of Liberty, 1996. **Address:** New Hampshire Community Technical College, 2020 Riverside Dr, Berlin, NH 03570, U.S.A.

DOHERTY, P(aul) C. Also writes as Paul Harding, Michael Clynes, Anna Apostolou, Ann Dukthas, C. L. Grace. British, b. 1946. **Genres:** Mystery/Crime/Suspense. **Career:** School headmaster in England, 1981-; writer, 1985-. **Publications:** HUGH CORBETT NOVELS: Satan in St. Mary's, 1987; The Crown in Darkness, 1988; Spy in Chancery, 1988; The Angel of Death, 1990; The Prince of Darkness, 1993; The Assassin in the Greenwood, 1993; Murder Wears a Cowl, 1994; The Song of a Dark Angel, 1995; Satan's Fire, 1996; The Devil's Hunt, 1996; The Treason of the Ghosts, 2000; The Demon Archer, 2001; Corpse Candle, 2001; The Magician's Death, 2004. CANTERBURY TALES/NICHOLAS CHIRKE NOVELS: An Ancient Evil, Being the Knight's Tale, 1994; A Tapestry of Murders, Being the Man of Law's Tale, 1996; A Tournament of Murders, Being the Franklin's Tale, 1997; Ghostly Murders, Being the Priest's Tale, 1998; A Haunt of Murder, 2003; The Hangman's Hymn, 2003. BROTHER ATHELSTAN NOVELS (most as Paul Harding): The Nightingale Gallery, 1991; The House of the Red Slayer, 1992, in US as Red Slayer, 1994; Murder Most Holy, 1993; Anger of God, 1993; By Murder's Bright Light, 1994; House of Crows, 1995; Assassin's Riddle, 1996; The Devil's Domain, 1998; The Field of Blood, 1999; The Houre of Shadows, 2004. EGYPTIAN NOVELS: The Mask of Ra, 1999; The Horus Killing, 2000; The Anubis Slayings, 2001; The Slayers of Seth, 2002; The Assassins of Isis, 2004. ALEXANDER OF MACEDON NOVELS: The House of Death, 2001; The Godless Man, 2002; The Gates of Hell, 2003. OTHER: The Death of a King, 1985; The Masked Man, 1991; King Arthur (juvenile biography), 1987; The Whyte Harte, 1988; The Fate of Princes, 1990; The Serpent among the Lilies, 1990; The Rose Demon, 1997; (as Anna Apostolou) Murder in Macedon, 1997; (as Anna Apostolou) A Murder in Thebes, 1998; The Haunting, 1998; The Soul Slayer, 1998; The Song of the Gladiator, 2004. NONFICTION: Isabella and Edward, 2002; The Mysterious Death of Tutankhamun, 2002; Isabella and the Strange Death of Edward II; The Death of a God: The Death of Alexander the Great. SIR ROGER SHALLOT NOVELS AS MICHAEL CLYNES: The White Rose Murders, 1991; The Poisoned Chalice, 1992; The Grail Murders, 1993; A Brood of Vipers, 1994; The Gallows Murders, 1996; The Relic Murders, 1997. NICHOLAS SEGALLA NOVELS AS ANN DUKTHAS; A Time for the Death of a King, 1994; The Prince Lost to Time, 1995; The Time of Murder at Mayerling, 1996; In the Time of the Poisoned Queen, 1998. KATHRYN SWINBROOKE NOVELS AS C.L. GRACE: A Shrine of Murders, 1993; The Eye of God, 1994; The Merchant of Death, 1995; The Book of Shadows, 1996; Saintly Murders, 2001; A Maze of Murders, 2003. **Address:** Trinity, 14 Mornington Rd., Woodford Green, Essex IG8 0TP, England. **Online address:** pdoherty.trinity.redbridge@lgfl.net

DOHERTY, Paul (Michael). American, b. 1948. **Genres:** Sciences. **Career:** Writer and educator. Oakland University, Oakland, CA, professor of physics, 1974-86; Exploratorium Teacher Institute, San Francisco, CA, staff physicist, 1986-, codirector, 1990-, senior staff scientist, 1997-. Tom Tits Experiment, Sweden, visiting scientist; San Francisco State University, adjunct professor of physics. **Publications:** Atlas of the Planets, 1980; Building and Using an Astronomical Observatory, 1986; The Arrival of Halley's Comet, 1986; (with J. Cassidy) The Klutz Book of Magnetic Magic, 1994; (with D. Rathjen and the Exploratorium Teach Institute) The Cheshire Cat and Other Eye-popping Experiments on How We See the World, 1995; (with D. Rathjen and the Exploratorium Teacher Institute) The Magic Wand and Other Bright Experiments on Light and Color, 1995; (with D. Rathjen and the Exploratorium Teacher Institute) The Cool Hot Rod and Other Electrifying Experiments on

Energy and Matter, 1996; (with D. Rathjen and the Exploratorium Teacher Institute) The Spinning Blackboard and Other Dynamic Experiments on Force and Motion, 1996; The Photographic Atlas of the Stars, 1997; (with J. Cassidy and P. Murphy) Zap Science, 1998; (with K. Pottner) The Best Paper Airplanes You'll Ever Fly, 1998; (with P. Murphy) Traces of Time, 2000; (with D. Rathjen and the Exploratorium Teacher Institute) Square Wheels and Other Easy-to-Build, 2002. Illustrator of books by P. Moore. Contributor to periodicals. **Address:** Exploratorium Teacher Institute, 3601 Lyon, San Francisco, CA 94123, U.S.A. **Online address:** Pauld@exploratorium.edu

DOHERTY, Robert. See **MAYER, Bob.**

DOIG, Ivan. American, b. 1939. **Genres:** Novels, Communications/Media, Social commentary, Autobiography/Memoirs. **Career:** Full-time writer, 1969-. Lindsay-Schaub Newspapers, Decatur, IL, editorial writer, 1963-64; The Rotarian, Evanston, IL, assistant editor, 1964-66. **Publications:** (with C.M. Doig) News: A Consumer's Guide, 1972; The Streets We have Come Down (non-fiction), 1975; Utopian America: Dreams and Realities (non-fiction), 1976; This House of Sky: Landscapes of a Western Mind (non-fiction), 1978; Winter Brothers: A Season at the Edge of America (non-fiction), 1980; The Sea Runners, 1982; (with D. Kelso) Inside This House of Sky (non-fiction), 1983; English Creek, 1984; Dancing at the Rascal Fair, 1987; Ride with Me, Mariah Montana, 1990; Heart Earth (non-fiction), 1993; Bucking the Sun, 1996; Mountain Time, 1999; Prairie Nocturne, 2003.

DOKEY, Cameron. American, b. 1956. **Genres:** Children's fiction, Young adult fiction. **Career:** Oregon Shakespeare Festival, Ashland, actor, 1977-81; Pacific Science Center, Seattle, WA, exhibit copywriter, 1989-93; novelist, 1993-. **Publications:** YOUNG ADULT NOVELS: Eternally Yours, 1994; The Talisman, 1994; Love Me, Love Me Not, 1995; Blue Moon, 1995; Heart's Desire, 1995; Katherine, Heart of Freedom; Charlotte, Heart of Fire; Stephanie, Heart of Gold; Carrie, Heart of Courage; Together Forever, 1997; Lost and Found, 1999; Hindenburg, 1937, 1999; Washington Avalanche, 1910, 2000; Here Be Monsters, 2000; Charmed Haunted by Desire, 2000. SHORT STORIES (CO-AUTHOR): New Year, New Love, 1996; Be Mine, 1997; How I Survived My Summer Vacation, vol. 1, 2000. OTHER: Midnight Mysteries (children's), 1997; Graveside Tales (children's), 1997; Winning Is Everything (middle grades), 1997. Co-author of educational materials based on the cable television series Beakman's World. **Address:** c/o Fran Lebowitz, Writers House Inc, 21 W 26th St, New York, NY 10010, U.S.A.

DOLAN, David. American, b. 1955. **Genres:** Area studies, Novels. **Career:** IMS News, Washington, DC, correspondent, 1984-87; Middle East Television, Jerusalem, Israel, reporter, 1987; CBS Radio News, NYC, correspondent, 1988-. **Publications:** Holy War for the Promised Land, 1991, 3rd ed. as Israel at the Crossroads, 1998; The End of Days (novel), 1997. Contributor to magazines and newspapers;. **Address:** Jerusalem Capital Studios, Jaffa Rd., Jerusalem, Israel.

DOLAN, Frederick Michael. American, b. 1955. **Genres:** Adult non-fiction, Essays, Humanities, Philosophy, Literary criticism and history, Politics/Government. **Career:** University of California, Berkeley, assistant professor, 1988-94, associate professor of rhetoric, 1994-. **Publications:** (ed. with T.L. Dumm) Rhetorical Republic: Governing Representations in American Politics, 1993; Allegories of America: Narratives, Metaphysics, Politics, 1994. Contributor of articles and reviews to academic journals. **Address:** Department of Rhetoric, 7325 Dwinelle Hall, University of California, Berkeley, CA 94720, U.S.A. **Online address:** FMDolan@SOCRATES.BERKELEY.EDU

DOLAN, Sean J. American, b. 1958. **Genres:** Biography. **Career:** Chelsea House, NYC, senior editor, 1986-. **Publications:** Chiang Kai-shek, 1989; Robert F. Kennedy, 1989; Christopher Columbus: The Intrepid Mariner, Columbine, 1990; Lewis and Clark, 1990; Daniel Boone, 1990; Matthew Henson, 1991; Junipero Serra, 1991; West Germany: On the Road to Reunification, 1991; James Beckwourth, 1992; The Polish Americans, 1992; Roald Amundsen, 1992; Gabriel Garcia Marquez, 1993; The Irish-American Experience, 1993; Ray Charles, 1993; Thurgood Marshall, 1993; W.E.B. DuBois, 1993; Earvin "Magic" Johnson, 1993; Michael Jordan, 1994; Lady Bird, 1994; Pursuing the Dream, 1965-1971, 1995; Johnny Cash, 1995; Juan Ponce de Leon, 1995; Charles Barkley, 1996; Bob Marley, 1997; Germany, 1999; Everything You Need to Know about Cults, 2000; Mexico, 2002; Canada, 2002. **Address:** c/o Chelsea House Publishers, 2080 Cabot Blvd., Ste. 201, Langhorne, PA 19047-1813, U.S.A.

DOLIN, Eric Jay. American. **Genres:** Biology. **Career:** Independent scholar and freelance writer. National Marine Fisheries Service, fishery-policy

analyst. Also worked for the U.S. Environmental Protection Agency as environmental consultant and program manager. **Publications:** The U.S. Fish and Wildlife Service, 1989; (editor, with Lawrence E. Susskind and J. William Breslin) International Environmental Treaty Making, 1992; (with Bob Dumaine) The Duck Stamp Story: Art, Conservation, History, 2000; (Author of text) Smithsonian Book of National Wildlife Refuges, 2003; Snakehead: A Fish Out of Water, 2003; Political Waters: The Long, Dirty, Contentious, Incredibly Expensive but Eventually Triumphant History of Boston Harbor; A Unique Environmental Success Story, 2004; Publisher of numerous articles on environmental topics in journals, magazines, and newspapers. **Address:** c/o Author Mail, University of Massachusetts, POB 429D, Amherst, MA 01004, U.S.A.

DOLIN, Sharon. American, b. 1956. **Genres:** Poetry. **Career:** Poet, editor and educator. Teaches at Cooper Union and New York University, both in NYC. **Publications:** POETRY: Mind Lag, 1982; Heart Work, 1995; Climbing Mount Sinai, 1996. Contributor of poems to literary journals. **Address:** Faculty of Humanities, Cooper Union, 41 Cooper Sq., New York, NY 10003, U.S.A.

DOLL, Mary A(swell). American, b. 1940. **Genres:** Literary criticism and history, Mythology/Folklore, Women's studies and issues. **Career:** Garrison Forest School, Garrison, MD, teacher, 1962-65; Sidwell Friends School, Washington, DC, teacher, 1965-66; Park School, Brooklandville, MD, teacher and chair of senior program, 1966-70; Community College of Baltimore, MD, teacher, 1970-71; State University of New York College at Oswego, instructor, 1978-82, assistant professor of English, 1982-84; University of Redlands, CA, instructor in English, 1985-88; California State University, San Bernardino, instructor in writing and supervisor of student teachers, 1986-88; Loyola University, New Orleans, LA, instructor in English, 1988; Tulane University, New Orleans, visiting assistant professor of literature, 1988-89; Holy Cross College, New Orleans, associate professor and chair of English department, 1989-94, professor, 1995-2000; Savannah College of Art & Design, professor, 2000-. Frequent lecturer at conferences and symposia. **Publications:** Beckett and Myth: An Archetypal Approach, 1988; (ed. with C. Stites) In the Shadow of the Giant: Thomas Wolfe, 1988; Joseph Campbell and the Ecological Imperative, Joseph Campbell, Uses of Comparative Mythology, 1992; Tom Stoppard and the Theatre of Unknowing, British Literature since 1960, 1993; Ghosts of Themselves: The Demeter Myth in Beckett, Images of Persephone in Literature, 1993; To the Lighthouse & Back: Writings on Teaching and Living, 1996; Like Letters in Running Water: A Mythopoetics of Curriculum, 1999. **Address:** Savannah College of Art and Design, Savannah, GA 31405, U.S.A. **Online address:** mdoll4444@aol.com

DOLLE, Raymond F. American, b. 1952. **Genres:** Literary criticism and history, Writing/Journalism, Travel/Exploration. **Career:** Pennsylvania State University, University Park, lecturer in English, 1985-86; Indiana State University, Terre Haute, assistant professor, 1986-90, associate professor of English, 1990-. Bi-monthly column, "The Technical Writer," in the Journal of Environmental Health. **Publications:** Anne Bradstreet: A Reference Guide, 1990. Contributor to books and periodicals. **Address:** Department of English, Indiana State University, A-286 Root Hall, Terre Haute, IN 47809, U.S.A.

DOLLIMORE, Jonathan. British, b. 1948. **Genres:** Literary criticism and history. **Career:** Farm worker, 1962-64; engineering apprentice in an automobile factory, 1963-64; free-lance journalist and correspondent, 1964-69; University of Sussex, Brighton, England, professor in English; writer. **Publications:** (ed. with A. Sinfield) The Selected Plays of John Webster, 1983; Radical Tragedy: Religion, Ideology, and Power in the Drama of Shakespeare and His Contemporaries, 1984, 2nd ed., 1989; (ed. with A. Sinfield) Political Shakespeare: New Essays in Cultural Materialism, 1985, 2nd ed., 1994; Sexual Dissidence: Augustine to Wilde, Freud to Foucault, 1991; Death, Desire and Loss in Western Culture, 1998; Sex, Literature and Censorship, 2001. **Address:** Dept of English & Related Literature, University of York, Heslington, York YO10 5DD, England. **Online address:** jonathan.dollimore@york.ac.uk

DOLLING-MANN, Patricia May. British, b. 1939. **Genres:** Romance/Historical. **Career:** Novelist. Formerly worked as a registered nurse. **Publications:** WESSEX CHRONICLES (historical fiction): Weatherbury Farm, 1999; A Claim to Kin, 2000; The d'Urberville Inheritance, 2001. **Address:** 27 Cottingham Grove Bletchley, Buckinghamshire MK3 5AA, England. **Online address:** patmann@ouvip.com

DOLNICK, Barrie. American, b. 1960. **Genres:** Administration/Management. **Career:** Writer, consultant, astrologer, and tarot card reader.

Worked in marketing in London, England, and New York, NY; founder of Executive Mystic Services, 1993. **Publications:** Simple Spells for Love: Ancient Practices for Emotional Fulfillment, 1994; Simple Spells for Success: Ancient Practices for Creating Abundance and Prosperity, 1996; (with Julia Condon and Donna Limoges) Sexual Bewitchery: And Other Ancient Feminine Wiles, 1998; The Executive Mystic: Psychic Power Tools for Success, 1998; (with Donald Baack) How to Write a Love Letter: Putting What's in Your Heart on Paper, 2000; Simple Spells for Hearth and Home: Ancient Practices for Creating Harmony, Peace, and Abundance, 2000; (Illustrator) Vivienne Flesher, Zodiac Memory Book of Days, 2001; Instructions for Your Discontent: How Bad Times Can Make Life Better, 2003. Minerva Rules Your Future: Goddess-Given Advice for Smart Moves at Work, 2003. **Address:** c/o Author Mail, Harmony Books, 1745 Broadway, New York, NY 10019, U.S.A. **Online address:** execmystic@aol.com

DOMAN, Glenn. American, b. 1919. **Genres:** Education, Medicine/Health, How-to books. **Career:** Founder, 1955, and Chairman of the Board, 1980-89, Institutes for the Achievement of Human Potential, Philadelphia. Associate Director, Centro de Reabilitacao Nossa Senhora da Gloria, Rio de Janeiro, since 1959. Staff Member, Temple University Hospital, Philadelphia, 1941, and Pennsylvania Hospital, 1945-48; Director, Norwood Rehabilitation Center, Philadelphia, 1948-55; Professor of Human Development, University of Plano, 1965-72. President, International Rehabilitation Forum, 1959, and World Organization for Human Potential, 1968-72. **Publications:** How to Teach Your Baby to Read, 1964, 1979; Nose Is Not Toes (children's book), 1964; What to Do About Your Brain-Injured Child, 1974; Teach Your Baby Math, 1979; (with J. Michael Armentrout) The Universal Multiplication of Intelligence, 1980; How to Give Your Baby Encyclopedic Knowledge, 1984; How to Multiply Your Baby's Intelligence, 1984; How to Teach Your Baby to Be Physically Superb, 1988. **Address:** Institutes for the Achievement of Human Potential, 8801 Stenton Ave, Wyndmoor, PA 19038, U.S.A.

DOMBROWSKI, Daniel A. American, b. 1953. **Genres:** Philosophy. **Career:** St. Joseph's University, Philadelphia, PA, assistant professor of philosophy, 1978-82; Creighton University, Omaha, NE, associate professor of philosophy, 1983-87; Seattle University, Seattle, WA, professor of philosophy, 1988-. **Publications:** Plato's Philosophy of History, 1981; The Philosophy of Vegetarianism, 1984; Thoreau the Platonist, 1986; Hartshorne and the Metaphysics of Animal Rights, 1988; Christian Pacifism, 1991; St. John of the Cross, 1992; Analytic Theism, Hartshorne and the Concept of God, 1996; Babies and Beasts: The Argument from Marginal Cases, 1997; Kazantzakis and God, 1997; A Brief, Liberal, Catholic Defense of Abortion, 2000; Not Even a Sparrow Falls: The Philosophy of Stephen R.L. Clark, 2000; Rawls and Religion: The Case for Political Liberalism, 2001; Divine Beauty: The Aesthetics of Charles Hartshorne, 2003. **Address:** Department of Philosophy, Seattle University, Seattle, WA 98122, U.S.A. **Online address:** ddombrow@seattleu.edu

DOMINIAN, Jack. British (born Greece), b. 1929. **Genres:** Human relations/Parenting, Psychology, Theology/Religion. **Career:** Central Middlesex Hospital, London, consultant physician, 1965-88. **Publications:** Psychiatry and the Christian, 1962; Christian Marriage, 1967; Marital Breakdown, 1968; The Future of Christian Marriage, 1969; The Church and the Sexual Revolution, 1971; Cycle of Affirmation, 1975; The Marriage Relationship Today, 1974; Depression, 1976; Authority: A Christian Interpretation, 1976; Marital Pathology, 1980; Marriage, Faith, and Love, 1981; The Growth of Love and Sex, 1982; Make or Break, 1984; The Capacity to Love, 1985; Sexual Integrity: The Answer to AIDS, 1987; Passionate and Compassionate Love, 1991; Marriage, 1995; One Like Us: A Psychological Interpretation of Jesus, 1998; Let's Make Love, 2001; Living Love, 2004. **Address:** Pefka, 19 Clements Rd, Chorleywood, Herts. WD3 5JS, England.

DONAGHY, Michael. See Obituaries.

DONALD, Diana. British, b. 1938. **Genres:** Art/Art history. **Career:** Department of History of Art and Design, Manchester Metropolitan University, Manchester, England, department head, 1986-97; professor of history of art and design, 1990-. Yale University, visiting fellow at Center for British Art, 1987. **Publications:** The Age of Caricature: Satirical Prints in the Reign of George III, 1996; (trans. and ed. with C. Banerji) Gillray Observed: The Earliest Account of His Caricatures in "London and Paris," 1999. Contributor to journals. **Address:** Department of Art History and Design, Manchester Metropolitan University, Manchester M15 6BG, England. **Online address:** dianadonald@ukonline.co.uk

DONALD, Merlin (Wilfred). Canadian, b. 1939. **Genres:** Psychology. **Career:** Yale University, New Haven, CT, postdoctoral research fellow at

School of Medicine, 1968-70, clinical research psychologist and assistant professor of neurology, 1970-72; Queen's University, Kingston, ON, assistant professor to professor of psychology, 1972-. University of London, visiting professor, 1980-81, 1988-89; reviewer for agencies and journals. **Publications:** Origins of the Modern Mind, 1991. Contributor of many articles and reviews to scientific and scholarly journals. Also has published poetry in Canadian journals & magazines. **Address:** Department of Psychology, Queen's University, Kingston, ON, Canada K7L 3N6.

DONALD, Peter (Harry). Scottish, b. 1962. **Genres:** History. **Career:** University of London, Institute of Historical Research, England, research fellow, 1986-87; Church of Scotland, assistant minister, 1990-91, parish minister, 1991-. Affiliated with the Centre of Theology and Public Issues. **Publications:** An Uncounselled King: Charles I and the Scottish Troubles, 1637-1641, 1990; God in Society: Doing Social Theology in Scotland Today, 2003. Contributor of essays to periodicals. **Address:** Crown Manse, 39 Southside Rd, Inverness IV2 4XA, Scotland. **Online address:** pdonald7@aol.com

DONALDSON, Gary A. American. **Genres:** History. **Career:** Xavier University of Louisiana, New Orleans, associate professor of history. **Publications:** The History of African Americans in the Military: Double V, 1991; America at War since 1945: Politics and Diplomacy in Korea, Vietnam, and the Gulf War, 1996; Abundance and Anxiety: America, 1945-1960, 1997; Truman Defeats Dewey, 1999. Contributor to periodicals. **Address:** Dept. Of History, Xavier University of Louisiana, 1 Drexel Dr., New Orleans, LA 70125, U.S.A.

DONALDSON, Islay (Eila) Murray. Scottish, b. 1921. **Genres:** Biography, Local history/Rural topics. **Career:** Kirkby Stephen Grammar School, Westmoreland, teacher of English, 1947-48; Queen's University, Belfast, Northern Ireland, assistant lecturer in English, 1948-49; Workers' Educational Association, Belfast, teacher, beginning in 1949; University of Edinburgh, Edinburgh, Scotland, parttime lecturer and courier, 1971-79. Scottish Arts Council, lecturer on graveyards and Staffordshire portrait figures. **Publications:** The Life and Work of Samuel Rutherford Crockett, 1989; East Lothian Gravestones, 1991; Midlothian Gravestones, 1994. **Address:** 7 Custom House Square, Dunbar EH42 1HY, Scotland.

DONALDSON, Joan. American, b. 1953. **Genres:** Children's fiction, Essays. **Career:** Organic fruit farmer, 1975-. Hope College, Hope, MI, teaching associate of dance, 1981-84. Michigan Literacy Tutor, folk dance instructor with Community Education, and musician for church services, 1982-87. Quiltmaker, creating commissioned pieces of folk art. **Publications:** The Real Pretend, 1992; Great American Quilts 1994, 1994; A Pebble & a Pen (young adult novel), 2000. Contributor to periodicals. **Address:** Pleasant Hill Farm, Fennville, MI 49408, U.S.A.

DONALDSON, Julia. British, b. 1948. **Genres:** Children's fiction, Plays/Screenplays. **Career:** Writer. **Publications:** A Squash and a Squeeze, 1993; Birthday Surprise (play), 1994; Names and Games (play), 1995; Turtle Tug, 1995; The Magic Twig 1995; The Boy Who Cried Wolf, 1995; The Three Billly Goats Gruff, 1995; Mr Snow, 1996; Strange Sue, 1996; The Town Mouse and the Country Mouse, 1996; Counting Chickens, 1996; The King's Porridge, 1996; Top of the Mops, 1997; The Wonderful Smells, 1997; The False Tooth Fairy, 1998; All Gone, 1998; Books and Crooks, 1998; Waiter! Waiter!, 1998; The Brownie in the Teapot, 1998; The Gruffalo, 1999; Clever Katya, 1999; The Noises Next Door, 1999; The King's Ears, 2000; The Strange Dream, 2000; The Boy Who Talked to the Birds, 2000; Monkey Puzzle, 2000; Follow the Swallow, 2000; Steve's Sandwiches, 2000; One Piece Missing, 2000; Jumping Jack, 2000; Cat Whispers, 2000; The Giant Jumperee, 2000; Problem Page, 2000; Fox's Socks, 2000; Hide and Seek Pig, 2000; Rabbit's Nap, 2000; Postman Bear, 2000; The Gruffalo Song, 2000; Stop Thief!, 2001; The Monster in the Cave, 2001; Room on the Broom, 2001; The Smartest Giant in Town, 2002; Night Monkey Day Monkey, 2002; Spinderella, 2002; The Dinosaur's Diary, 2002; Hamlet, 2002; Midsummer Dream, 2002; The Trial of Wilf Wolf, 2002; Conjuror Cow, 2003; The Head in the Sand, 2003; Bombs and Blackberries, 2003; Brick-a-Breck, 2003; I Don't Want To, 2003; The Magic Paintbrush, 2003; Princess Mirror-Belle, 2003; The Snail and the Whale, 2003. Author of songs, scripts, and stories for television and radio (mainly children's programs). Author of unpublished musicals, King Grunt's Cake and Pirate on the Pier. **Address:** 2 Chapelton Ave, Glasgow G61 2RE, Scotland.

DONALDSON, Loraine. American. **Genres:** Demography, Economics, Third World. **Career:** Georgia State University, Atlanta, assistant professor, 1964-66, associate professor, 1966-70, professor of economics, 1970-94.

Economic consultant. **Publications:** Development Planning in Ireland, 1966; Economic Development, 1984; Fertility Transition, 1991. **Address:** 703 Holly Dr, Fairhope, AL 36532, U.S.A.

DONALDSON, Molla S(loane). American, b. 1944. **Genres:** Medicine/Health. **Career:** George Washington University, Washington, DC, research assistant, 1972-76, research instructor, 1976-78, assistant research professor of health care sciences, 1978-83; CIMA, Risk Control Services, Washington, DC, risk control consultant, 1984-86; George Washington University, senior health services researcher at Medical Decision Center, 1985-88; National Academy of Sciences, Institute of Medicine, Washington, DC, senior staff officer, 1988-. George Washington University, associate professor, 1988-90, adjunct professor, 1994-; speaker at Virginia Commonwealth University and Medical College of Virginia, 1998. **Publications:** (with B. Means, A. Nigam, and others) Autobiographical Memory for Health-Related Events: Enhanced Memory for Recurring Incidents, 1988. EDITOR: (with K.L. Lohr) Health Data in the Information Age: Use, Disclosure, and Privacy, 1994; (with K.N. Lohr, K.D. Yordy, and N.A. Vanselow) Primary Care: America's Health in a New Era, 1996. Contributor to books and periodicals. **Address:** Outcomes Research Branch/ARP/DCCPS, National Cancer Institute, 6130 Executive Blvd., EPN Room 4028, Bethesda, MD 20892-7344, U.S.A. **Online address:** molla.donalsdon@nih.gov

DONALDSON, Scott. American, b. 1928. **Genres:** Literary criticism and history, Social commentary, Biography. **Career:** College of William and Mary, Williamsburg, VA, assistant professor, 1966-69, associate professor, 1969-74, professor 1974-84, Louise G.T. Cooley Professor of English, 1984-, now emeritus. Sun newspapers, Minnesota, executive ed., 1961-64. **Publications:** The Suburban Myth, 1969; Poet in America: Winfield Townley Scott, 1972; By Force of Will: The Life and Art of Ernest Hemingway, 1977; (with A. Massa) American Literature: Nineteenth and Early Twentieth Centuries, 1978; Fool for Love, F. Scott Fitzgerald, 1983; John Cheever: A Biography, 1988; Archibald MacLeish: An American Life, 1992; Hemingway vs. Fitzgerald: The Rise and Fall of a Literary Friendship, 1999. EDITOR: J. Kerouac, On the Road, 1979; Critical Essays on F. Scott Fitzgerald's The Great Gatsby, 1984; Conversations with John Cheever, 1987; New Essays on A Farewell to Arms, 1990; The Cambridge Companion to Hemingway, 1996. **Address:** 10040 E Happy Valley Rd, Desert Highlands 303, Scottsdale, AZ 85255, U.S.A. **Online address:** scottd10@mac.com

DONALDSON, Thomas. American, b. 1945. **Genres:** Ethics, Business/Trade/Industry, Essays, Philosophy. **Career:** Loyola University of Chicago, Chicago, IL, assistant professor, 1976-81, associate professor, 1981-84, Henry J. Wirtenberger Professor of Ethics, 1984-88, chair of core curriculum committee for Arts and Sciences, 1980-81, director of Graduate Program in Philosophy, 1982-84; University of Virginia, Charlottesville, C. Stewart Sheppard Visiting Professor of Business Administration, 1988-89, and senior fellow of Olsson Center for Ethics; Georgetown University, Washington, DC, John F. Connelly Professor of Business Ethics, 1990-96, adjunct professor of philosophy, and senior research fellow of Kennedy Institute for Ethics; University of Pennsylvania, Wharton School, Mark O. Winkelman Professor, 1996-, director of the Wharton Ethics Program. **Publications:** (ed. with P. Werhane, and contrib.) Ethical Issues in Business: A Philosophical Approach, 1979, 6th ed., 1999; Corporations and Morality, 1982; (ed. and contrib.) Case Studies in Business Ethics, 1984; (ed.) Issues in Moral Philosophy, 1985; Ethics in International Business, 1989; (with T.W. Dunfee) Ethics in Business and Economics, 2 vols., 1998; (with T.W. Dunfee) The Ties that Bind, 1999. Work represented in anthologies. Contributor of articles and reviews to professional journals. **Address:** Wharton School, University of Pennsylvania, Philadelphia, PA 19104, U.S.A. **Online address:** donaldst@wharton.upenn.edu

DONEGAN, Greg. See MAYER, Bob.

DONGALA, Emmanuel Boundzeki. Congolese, b. 1941. **Genres:** Poetry. **Career:** Writer and educator. Instructor, Institut de Chimie, Strasbourg, 1973-75; research assistant, école Nationale Supérieure de Chimie, Montpellier, France, 1976-78; professor of chemistry, Université de Brazzaville, Republic of the Congo, 1979-98; professor of chemistry and French, Simon's Rock College, Great Barrington, MA, 1998-; professor of French, Bard College, Annandale-on-Hudson, NY, 1998-. Founder, Théatre de l'éclair, Republic of the Congo, 1981. **Publications:** Un fusil dans la main, un poeme dans la poche (title means: A Gun in Hand, a Poem in the Pocket), 1973; Jazz et vin de palme (title means: Jazz and Palm Wine), 1982; Le feu des origines, 1987, trans. by L. Corti as The Fire of Origins, 2001; Les petits garçons naissent aussi des étoiles, 1998, trans. by J. Réjouis and V. Vinokurov as Little Boys Come from the Stars, 2001. Contributor of articles on

chemistry to professional journals. **Address:** Simon's Rock College of Bard, 84 Alford Road, Great Barrington, MA 01230, U.S.A. **Online address:** edongala@simons-rock.edu

DONIA, Robert J(ay). American, b. 1945. **Genres:** History. **Career:** University of Michigan, lecturer in Russian & Eastern European Studies, 1977; University of Windsor, assistant professor of history, 1977-78; Ohio State University, assistant professor of history, 1978-. **Publications:** Islam under the Double Eagle: The Muslims of Bosnia and Hercegovina, 1878-1914, 1981; (with J.V.A. Fine Jr.) Bosnia and Hercegovina: A Tradition Betrayed, 1994. **Address:** Department of History, Ohio State University, 4300 Campus Dr., Lima, OH 45804, U.S.A.

DONKER, Marjorie. American, b. 1926. **Genres:** Language/Linguistics, Literary criticism and history. **Career:** Western Washington University, Bellingham, instructor, 1967-70, assistant professor, 1970-73, associate professor, 1973-82, professor of English, 1982-. **Publications:** (with G. Muldrow) A Dictionary of Literary-Rhetorical Conventions of the English Renaissance, 1982; Shakespeare's Proverbial Themes, 1992. **Address:** Department of English, Western Washington University, Bellingham, WA 98225, U.S.A.

DONKIN, Nance (Clare). Australian, b. 1915. **Genres:** Children's fiction, Novellas/Short stories, History. **Career:** Recipient: Member, Order of Australia, 1986, and Alice Award, Society of Women Writers Australia, 1990; Journalist, Daily Mercury, Maitland, and Morning Herald, Newcastle. President, Children's Book Council, Victoria, 1968-76. **Publications:** Araluen Adventures, 1946; No Medals for Meg, 1947; Julie Stands By, 1948; Blue Ribbon Beth, 1951; (ed.) The Australian Children's Annual, 1963; Sheep, 1967; Sugar, 1967; An Emancipist, 1968; A Currency Lass, 1969; House by the Water, 1969; An Orphan, 1970; Johnny Neptune, 1971; The Cool Man (anthology), 1973; A Friend for Petros, 1974; Margaret Catchpole, 1974; Patchwork Grandmother, 1975; Green Christmas, 1976; Yellowgum Girl, 1976; A Handful of Ghost (anthology), 1976; The Best of the Bunch, 1978; The Maidens of Pefka, 1979; Nini, 1979; Stranger and Friend (for adults), 1983; We of the Never Never Retold for Children, 1983; Two at Sullivan Bay, 1985; Blackout, 1987; A Family Affair: The Women Were There (for adults), 1988; Always a Lady (for adults), 1990. **Address:** Rm 75 Chatham Lea Hostel, 13 Chatham Rd, Canterbury, VIC 3126, Australia.

DONLEAVY, J(ames) P(atrick). Irish (born United States), b. 1926. **Genres:** Novels, Novellas/Short stories, Plays/Screenplays, Social commentary. **Publications:** The Ginger Man, 1955, complete ed., 1963; The Ginger Man (play), 1961, in UK as What They Did in Dublin, with the Ginger Man, 1962; Fairy Tales of New York (play), 1961; A Singular Man, 1963; A Singular Man (play), 1965; Meet My Maker the Mad Molecule (short stories), 1964; The Saddest Summer of Samuel S., 1966; The Beastly Beatitudes of Balthazar B., 1968; The Onion Eaters, 1971; The Collected Plays of J.P. Donleavy, 1972; A Fairy Tale of New York, 1973; The Unexpurgated Code: A Complete Manual of Survival and Manners, 1975; The Destinies of Darcy Dancer, Gentleman, 1977; Schultz, 1979; Leila, 1983; De Alfonce Tennis, 1984; J.P. Donleavy's Ireland, 1986; Are You Listening, Rabbi Low, 1987; A Singular Country, 1989; That Darcy, That Dancer, That Gentleman, 1990; The History of the Ginger Man (memoirs), 1994; The Lady Who Liked Clean Rest Rooms (novella), 1996; Wrong Information Is Being Given Out at Princeton (novel), 1997; The Author and His Image (short stories), 1997; Letter Marked Personal, 2000. **Address:** Levington Pk, Mullingar, Westmeath, Ireland.

DONNACHIE, Ian. Scottish, b. 1944. **Genres:** Economics, History. **Career:** Strathclyde University, dept. of history, research assistant, 1967-68; Napier University, Edinburgh, lecturer in history, 1968-70; Open University in Scotland, staff tutor in history, 1970-85, sr. lecturer, 1985-; Deakin University, Vic., lecturer in social sciences, 1982; University of Dundee, hon. lecturer in history, 1998-. Visiting fellow, Deakin University, and University of Sydney, NSW, 1985. Assistant ed., Industrial Archaeology, 1968-73, and Industrial Archaeology Review, 1975-78. **Publications:** (with J. Butt and J. Hume) Industrial History: Scotland, 1968; (with J. Butt) The Industries of Scotland, 1969; Industrial Archaeology of Galloway, 1971; War and Economic Growth in Britain 1793-1815, 1973; (with I. Macleod) Old Galloway, 1974; Roads and Canals, 1976; (with A. Hogg) The War of Independence and the Scottish Nation, 1976; (with J. Hume and M. Moss) Historic Industrial Scenes: Scotland, 1977; A History of the Brewing Industry in Scotland, 1979; (with J. Butt) Industrial Archaeology in the British Isles, 1979; (with I. Macleod) Victorian and Edwardian Scottish Lowlands in Old Photographs, 1979; (with G. Hewitt) Scottish History 1560-1980, 1982; (with C. Harvie and I.S. Wood) Forward! Labour Politics in Scotland 1888-1988, 1989; (with G. Hewitt) Companion to Scottish History, 1989; (with C. Whatley) The

Manufacture of Scottish History, 1991; (with G. Hewitt) Historic New Lanark, 1993, 2nd ed., 1999; Robert Owen, 2000; (with G. Hewitt) Collins Dictionary of Scottish History, 2001. EDITOR: (with J. Butt) Industrial Archaeology, 5 vols., 1969-73; Studying Scottish History, Literature and Culture, 1996; Modern Scottish History 1707 to the Present, 5 vols., 1998. **Address:** Open University in Scotland, Jennie Lee House, 10 Drumsheugh Gardens, Edinburgh EH3 7QJ, Scotland. **Online address:** I.Donnachie@ open.ac.uk

DONNELLY, Deborah. American. **Genres:** Science fiction/Fantasy. **Career:** University librarian, corporate speech writer, nanny, and science-fiction writer. **Publications:** Veiled Threats, 2002; Died to Match, 2002. Contributor of short stories to science fiction magazines and translated into Italian, Portuguese, Polish, and Lithuanian. **Address:** 1101 N 19th St, Boise, ID 83702, U.S.A. **Online address:** veiledthreats@pobox.com

DONNELLY, Jane. British. **Genres:** Romance/Historical. **Career:** Former journalist; television critic. **Publications:** A Man Apart, 1968; Don't Walk Alone, 1969; Shadows from the Sea, 1970; Take the Far Dream, 1970; Halfway to the Stars, 1971; Never Turn Back, 1971; The Man in the Next Room, 1971; The Mill in the Meadow, 1972; A Stranger Came, 1972; The Long Shadow, 1973; Rocks Under Shining Water, 1973; A Man Called Mallory, 1974; Collision Course, 1975; The Man Outside, 1975; Ride Out the Storm, 1975; Dark Pursuer, 1976; The Silver Cage, 1976; Dear Caliban, 1977; Four Weeks in Winter, 1977; The Intruder, 1977; Forest of the Night, 1978; Love for a Stranger, 1978; Spell of the Seven Stones, 1978; The Black Hunter, 1978; Touched by Fire, 1978; A Man to Watch, 1979; A Savage Sanctuary, 1979; Behind a Closed Door, 1979; No Way Out, 1980; When Lightning Strikes, 1980; Flash Point, 1981; So Long a Winter, 1981; The Frozen Jungle, 1981; Diamond Cut Diamond, 1982; A Fierce Encounter, 1983; Call Up the Storm, 1983; Face the Tiger, 1983; Moon Lady, 1984; Ring of Crystal, 1985; To Cage a Whirlwind, 1985; Force Field, 1987; The Frozen Heart, 1987; Ride a Wild Horse, 1987; No Place to Run, 1988; Fetters of Gold, 1988; When We're Along, 1989; The Devil's Flower, 1990; The Jewels of Helen, 1991; Once a Cheat, 1991; Hold Back the Dark, 1993; The Trespasser, 1994; Shadow of a Tiger, 1994; Cover Story, 1994; Sleeping Beauty, 1995; Living with Marc, 1996. **Address:** c/o Harlequin Mills and Boon Ltd, Eton House, 18-24 Paradise Rd, Richmond, Surrey TW9 1SR, England.

DONNELLY, Joe. Scottish, b. 1950. **Genres:** Horror. **Career:** Editor and columnist with local weekly papers, 1968-75; Evening Times, Glasgow, Scotland, staff writer, 1976-80; Sunday Mail, Scotland, 1980-. Worked previously as a whisky taster. **Publications:** Bane, 1989; Stone, 1990; The Shee, 1992; Still Life, 1993; Shrike, 1994; Havock Junction, 1995; Incubus, 1996; Twitchy Eyes, 1997. **Address:** c/o Vivienne Schuster, Curtis Brown Ltd., Haymarket House, 28-29 Haymarket, London SW1Y 4SP, England.

DONNER, Rebecca. (born Canada). **Genres:** Adult non-fiction. **Career:** Writer. New Yorker, New York, NY, intern; KGB Sunday Fiction Series, New York, literary director, 1998-2002. **Publications:** (editor and author of introduction) On the Rocks: The KGB Bar Fiction Anthology, 2002; Sunset Terrace (novel), 2003. **Address:** c/o Author Mail, MacAdam/Cage Publishing, 1900 Wazee St., Ste. 210, Denver, CO 80202, U.S.A. **Online address:** ridonner@yahoo.com

DONNISON, David Vernon. British (born Myanmar), b. 1926. **Genres:** Regional/Urban planning, Social sciences. **Career:** London School of Economics, Professor of Social Administration, 1961-69; Centre for Environmental Studies, Director, 1969-75; Supplementary Benefits Commission, Chairman, 1975-80; University of Glasgow, Professor of Town and Regional Planning, 1980-90, Honorary Research Fellow, 1990-. **Publications:** The Neglected Child and the Social Services, 1954; Welfare Services in a Canadian Community, 1958; The Government of Housing, 1965; Social Policy and Administration Revisited, 1975; (with P. Soto) The Good City: A Study of Urban Development and Policy in Britain, 1979; The Politics of Poverty, 1982; (with C. Ungerson) Housing Policy, 1982; A Radical Agenda, 1991; Act Local, 1994; Policies for a Just Society, 1998. EDITOR: (with D. Eversley) London: Urban Patterns, Problems and Policies, 1973; (with A. Middleton) Regenerating the Inner City: Glasgow's Experience, 1987; (with D. Maclennan) The Housing Service of the Future, 1991. **Address:** 23 Bank St, Glasgow G12 8JQ, Scotland.

DONNITHORNE, Audrey Gladys. (Dong Yu-de). British/Australian (born People's Republic of China), b. 1922. **Genres:** Economics. **Career:** Honorary Research Fellow, Centre for Asian Studies, University of Hong Kong, 1985-. Taught English at Yenching University-in-Chengdu, 1942; Junior Civil Assistant, War Office London, 1943-44; Worker on Smallholding, Kent, U.K., 1945; Research Assistant, 1948-51, Lecturer in Political Economy, 1951-66, and Reader in Chinese Economic Studies, 1966-68, University College, University of London; Professorial Fellow, 1969-85, and Foundation Head, Contemporary China Centre, 1970-77, Australian National University, Canberra; Director, AITECE Ltd., Hong Kong, 1988-2000. **Publications:** (with G.C. Allen) Western Enterprise in Far Eastern Economic Development: China and Japan, 1954; (with G.C. Allen) Western Enterprise in Indonesia and Malaya, 1957; British Rubber Manufacturing, 1958; China's Economic System, 1967; China's Grain: Output, Procurement, Transfers and Trade, 1970; The Budget and the Plan in China: Central-Local Economic Relations, 1972; Centre-Provincial Economic Relations in China, 1981. Contributor to periodicals. **Address:** Flat A3, 18th Fl, Kingsfield Tower, 73 Bonham Rd, Hong Kong. **Online address:** agd@netvigator.com

DONNITHORNE, Larry. American, b. 1944. **Genres:** Military/Defense/Arms control, Administration/Management. **Career:** U.S. Army, career officer, 1966-93, retiring as colonel; College of the Albemarle, Elizabeth City, NC, president. U.S. Military Academy, teacher of leadership and moral philosophy. **Publications:** The West Point Way of Leadership, Doubleday, 1994. **Address:** College of the Albemarle, P.O. Box 2327, Elizabeth City, NC 27906, U.S.A.

DONOGHUE, Emma. Irish, b. 1969. **Genres:** Literary criticism and history, Gay and lesbian issues. **Career:** Writer. **Publications:** NOVELS: Stir-Fry, 1994; Hood, 1995; Slammerkin, 2000. OTHER: Passions between Women: British Lesbian Culture, 1668-1801 (nonfiction) 1993; I Know My Own Heart: A Lesbian Regency Romance (play), 1994. **Address:** 37 Victoria Rd., Cambridge CB4 3BW, England.

DONOGHUE, Mildred R(ansdorf). American, b. 1929. **Genres:** Education, Language/Linguistics. **Career:** California State University, Fullerton, assistant professor, 1962-66, associate professor, 1966-71, professor of education and reading, 1971-. **Publications:** Foreign Languages and the Schools, 1967; Foreign Languages and the Elementary School Child, 1968; The Child and the English Language Arts, 1971, 5th ed., 1990; Second Languages in Primary Education, 1979; Using Literature Activities to Teach Content Areas to Emergent Readers, 2001. **Address:** California State University, PO Box 6868, Fullerton, CA 92834, U.S.A.

DONOHUE, Gail. See STOREY, Gail Donohue.

DONOHUE, William A. American, b. 1947. **Genres:** Civil liberties/Human rights, Politics/Government. **Career:** Schoolteacher in NYC, 1973-77; La Roche College, Pittsburgh, PA, professor of sociology, 1977-87; Heritage Foundation, Washington, DC, resident scholar, 1987-88; La Roche College, professor of sociology, 1988-93. Member of board of advisers, Washington Legal Foundation and Rockford Institute's Center on the Family; Heritage Foundation, adjunct scholar. Military service: U.S. Air Force. **Publications:** The Politics of the American Civil Liberties Union, Transaction Books, 1985; The New Freedom: Individualism and Collectivism in the Social Lives of Americans, Transaction Books, 1990; Twilight of Liberty: The Legacy of the ACLU, Transaction Books, 1994. **Address:** Catholic League, 1011 First Ave., New York, NY 10022, U.S.A.

DONOUGHUE, (Baron) Bernard. British, b. 1934. **Genres:** Politics/Government, Biography. **Career:** Member, Editorial Staff, The Economist, London, 1959-60; Sr. Research Officer, Political and Economic Planning (PEP), London, 1960-63; Sr. Lecturer in Politics, London School of Economics, 1963-74; Sr. Policy Adviser to the Prime Minister, 1974-79; Director, Economist Intelligence Unit, London, 1979-81; Assistant Ed., The Times, London, 1981-82; Head of Research, Kleinwort Grieveson & Co., 1982-88; Minister of Agriculture, 1997-99. **Publications:** (ed) Oxford Poetry 1956, 1956; British Politics and the American Revolution, 1963; (co-author) The People into Parliament, 1964; (co-author) Herbert Morrison: Portrait of a Politician, 1973; Prime Minister, 1987. **Address:** 71 Ebury Mews East, London SW1W 9QA, England.

DONOVAN, Katie. Irish, b. 1962. **Genres:** Poetry, Literary criticism and history, Essays. **Career:** Teacher of English to foreign students in Dublin, Ireland, 1986-87, and at a secondary school in Hungary, 1987-88; Irish Times, Dublin, features writer, editor, and literary critic, 1988-2002. Samaritans, member, 1981-83. Gives readings from her works. **Publications:** Irish Women Writers (essay), 1988. POEMS: Watermelon Man, 1993; Entering the Mare, 1997; Day of the Dead, 2002. EDITOR: (with B. Kennelly and A.N. Jeffares) Ireland's Women: Writings Past and Present, 1994; (with Kennelly) Dublines, 1996. **Address:** An Tigh Thuas, Torca Rd., Dalkey, Dublin, Ireland.

DOOLEY, Allan C(harles). American, b. 1943. **Genres:** Humanities, Literary criticism and history, Bibliography. **Career:** Kent State University, Kent, OH, assistant professor, 1969-77, associate professor, 1978-92, professor of English, 1992-. **Publications:** (gen. ed.) The Complete Works of Robert Browning, Vol. V, 1981, Vol. VII, 1985, Vol. VIII, 1987, Vol. IX, 1989, Vol. XIII, 1995; Vol. VI, 1996; Vol. 16, 1998, Vol. X, 1999; Author and Printer in Victorian England, 1992. Work represented in anthologies. Contributor of articles and reviews to periodicals. **Address:** Department of English, Kent State University, Main Campus, PO Box 5190, Kent, OH 44242-0001, U.S.A. **Online address:** adooley@kent.edu

DOOLEY, Brian J. American, b. 1954. **Genres:** Information science/Computers. **Career:** Technical writer and editor. Datapro Corp., Deran, NJ, senior analyst and senior associate editor, 1983-88; Okidata Corp., Mt. Laurel, NJ, senior technical writer, 1988-89; Unisys Corp., Flemington, NJ, senior product information analyst, 1989-92; Aoraki Corp., Christchurch, New Zealand, senior technical writer, 1993-94; B. J. Dooley Technical Information Services, Leithfield Beach, New Zealand, director, 1994-. **Publications:** Desktop Publishing for WordPerfect for Windows, 1992; Learn Windows in a Day: For Versions 3.0 and 3.1, 1992; Learn OS/2 2.1 in a Day, 1993; (revision) J. Christy, The Complete Guide to Single-Engine Cessnas, 4th ed., 1993; Learn Microsoft Powerpoint 4.0 for Windows in a Day, 1995. Contributor to periodicals and research reports. **Address:** 28A McBratneys Rd, Christchurch 8006, New Zealand. **Online address:** bjdtis@yahoo.com

DOOLEY, Maura. British, b. 1957. **Genres:** Novellas/Short stories, Poetry, Adult non-fiction. **Career:** Arvon Foundation, Lumb Bank, Yorkshire, England, director of writing center, 1982-87; South Bank Board, London, England, director of literature program, 1987-93; freelance literature consultant, 1993-97; consultant to performing arts labs, 1994-2002; Jim Henson Films, London, script adviser, 1997-2000; University of London, Goldsmiths College, convener of MA in creative writing, 2000-. Southern Arts Literature Panel, chair, 1988-90; Arvon Foundation Management Committee, council member, 1989-; London Arts, Board Literature Panel, advisory member, 1992-93; board member, 1999-2001; Poetry Book Society, chair, 1999-2003. **Publications:** POETRY: Ivy Leaves and Arrows, 1986; Turbulence, 1988; Explaining Magnetism, 1991; Kissing a Bone, 1996. EDITOR: (with D. Hunter) Singing Brink, 1987; (with D. Morley and P. Callow) Northern Stories II, 1990; Making for Planet Alice: New Women Poets, 1996; How Novelists Work, 2000; The Honey Gatherers: Love Poetry, 2003; Sound Barrier: Selected Poems, 2002. **Address:** c/o Bloodaxe Books, PO Box 1SN, Newcastle NE99 1SN, England.

DOOLING, Richard (Patrick). American, b. 1954. **Genres:** Novels, Novellas/Short stories. **Career:** Attorney and writer. Bryan, Cave, McPheeters & McRoberts, St. Louis, MO, law associate, 1987-91. Also worked as a respiratory technician and respiratory therapist in the 1980s. **Publications:** Critical Care (novel), 1992; White Man's Grave, 1994; Bush Pigs (short story), 1994; Blue Streak, 1996; Brainstorm, 1998; Bet Your Life, 2002. **Address:** 816 S 95th St, Omaha, NE 68114-5072, U.S.A. **Online address:** rpdooling@yahoo.com

DORAN, David K. British, b. 1929. **Genres:** Engineering. **Career:** G. Wimpey, London, England, chief structural engineer, 1965-85; consulting civil and structural engineer in London, 1985-. **Publications:** EDITOR: Construction Materials Reference Book, 1992; Construction Materials Pocket Book, 1994; Eminent Civil Engineers: Their 20th Century Life and Times, 1999; Site Engineers Manual, 2004. **Address:** 17 Blake Hall Cres, London E11 3RH, England. **Online address:** David.Doran@btinternet.com

DORAN, Robert. Australian, b. 1940. **Genres:** Theology/Religion. **Career:** Amherst College, Amherst, MA, professor of religion, 1978-. **Publications:** Temple Propaganda: The Purpose and Characters of 2 Maccabees, 1982; (trans.) Lives of Simeon Stylites, 1992; Birth of a Worldview, 1995. **Address:** Department of Religion, Amherst College, Amherst, MA 01002, U.S.A.

DOREMUS, Paul N. American, b. 1960. **Genres:** Business/Trade/Industry. **Career:** Office of Technology Assessment, Washington, DC, former analyst; National Institute of Standards and Technology, Gaithersburg, MD, strategic planning analyst. **Publications:** (with W.W. Keller, L.W. Pauly, and S. Reich) The Myth of the Global Corporation, 1998. Author of articles on technology-related topics, including multinational corporations, international trade, and intellectual property rights in high technology industries. **Address:** 100 Bureau Dr., Gaithersburg, MD 20899, U.S.A. **Online address:** paul.doremus@nist.gov

DORF, Fran. American, b. 1953. **Genres:** Novels, Mystery/Crime/Suspense. **Career:** Esquire, NYC, 1976-77; International Playtex, Stamford, CT, 1978-81; writer. **Publications:** A Reasonable Madness, 1991; Flight, 1992. **Address:** William Morris Agency, 1325 Avenue of the Americas, New York, NY 10019, U.S.A.

DORFER, Ingemar (Nils Hans). Also writes as Harry Winter. Swedish (born Germany), b. 1939. **Genres:** Air/Space topics, Communications/Media, Technology, Military/Defense/Arms control, Novels. **Career:** Ministry of Defense, Stockholm, Sweden, special assistant for national security affairs, 1971-75; National Defense Research Institute, Stockholm, senior research associate, 1975-; head of international program, 1987-, head of research, 1993-. Ministry for foreign affairs, Sweden, special adviser to the foreign minister, 1992-94. Uppsala University, Uppsala, Sweden, associate professor of government, 1974-. Guest scholar at Stockholm International Peace Research Institute, 1968, Norwegian Institute for International Affairs, 1972, Washington Center for Foreign Policy Research, 1976, and Woodrow Wilson International Center for Scholars, Smithsonian Institution, 1978, 1995; fellow of International Institute of Strategic Studies, London, England, 1980. Consultant with C & L Associates, Potomac, MD. **Publications:** Communication Satellites, 1969; System 37 Viggen: Arms, Technology, and the Domestication of Glory, 1973; Arms Deal: The Selling of the F16, 1983; The Nordic Nations in the New Western Security Regime, 1997. NOVELS co-author as HARRY WINTER: Operation Garbo I, 1988; Garbo II, 1989; Garbo III, 1991; Operation Narva, 1993; Operation Poltava, 1996. **Address:** Radmansgatan 69, 11360 Stockholm, Sweden.

DORFLINGER, Carolyn. American, b. 1953. **Genres:** Children's fiction. **Career:** Spanish and French teacher at Branchburg Central School, Branchburg, NJ, 1975-80, Shenendehowa Schools, Clifton Park, NY, 1988-89, and Harding Township School, New Vernon, NJ, 1995-. Writer. **Publications:** Tomorrow Is Mom's Birthday, 1994. Contributor to Guideposts for Kids. **Address:** 131 Chatham St., Chatham, NJ 07928, U.S.A.

DORIANI, Beth Maclay. American, b. 1961. **Genres:** Literary criticism and history. **Career:** Religion and Literature, staff member, 1986-88; Northwestern College, Orange City, IA, assistant professor to associate professor of English, 1990-98; Malone College, Canton, OH, Academic Dean, 1998-2000; Montreat College, Montreat, NC, Vice Pres and Dean of Academics, associate professor, 2000-. **Publications:** Emily Dickinson: Daughter of Prophecy, 1996; For All You're Worth: Getting That Academic Job in Today's Market, 1999. Contributor to books. Contributor of articles and reviews to journals. **Address:** Box 1267, Montreat College, Montreat, NC 28757, U.S.A.

DORKIN, Evan. (born United States). **Genres:** Graphic Novels. **Career:** Comic book artist and writer. **Publications:** (Illustrator) Jason Cohen and Michael Krugman, Generation Ecch!, 1994; Superman & Batman: World's Funnest, 2000. SELF-ILLUSTRATED: Fun with Milk and Cheese (collection of Milk and Cheese issues), 1997; Hectic Planet, Book One: Dim Future (collection of Hectic Planet issues), 1998; Hectic Planet, Book Two: Checkered Past (collection of Hectic Planet issues), 1998; Hectic Planet, Book Three: The Young and the Reckless (collection of Hectic Planet issues), 2001; Dork!: Who's Laughing Now? (collection of Dork! issues), 2001; Circling the Drain (includes stories from Dork! issues 7-10 plus new material), 2003. Adapted Eltingville Club stories for proposed animated television series. Author of scripts and contributor to various comics titles. **Address:** c/o Author Mail, SLG Publishing, 577 S. Market St., San Jose, CA 95113, U.S.A. **Online address:** evandorkin@aol.com

DORMAN, Michael L. American, b. 1932. **Genres:** Politics/Government, Adult non-fiction, Civil liberties/Human rights, Criminology/True Crime, History, Law, Race relations, Writing/Journalism. **Career:** Newspaper reporter and ed., 1950-64. **Publications:** We Shall Overcome, 1964; The Secret Service Story, 1967; The Second Man, 1968; King of the Courtroom, 1969; Under 21, 1970; Payoff: The Role of Organized Crime in American Politics, 1972; The Making of a Slum, 1972; Confrontation, 1974; Vesco: The Infernal Money-Making Machine, 1975; Witch Hunt, 1976; The George Wallace Myth, 1976; Detectives of the Sky, 1976; Dirty Politics: From 1776 to Watergate, 1979; Blood and Revenge, 1991. **Address:** 7 Lauren Ave S, Dix Hills, NY 11746, U.S.A.

DORMENT, Richard. American, b. 1946. **Genres:** Art/Art history. **Career:** Philadelphia Museum of Art, assistant curator of European painting, 1973-76; Royal Academy of Arts, London, England, guest curator "Alfred Gilbert" exhibition, 1986; Daily Telegraph, art critic, 1987-. **Publications:** Alfred Gilbert, 1985; Alfred Gilbert, Sculptor of Eros, 1986; British Painting in the

Philadelphia Museum of Art, 1986. Contributor to periodicals. **Address:** 10 Clifton Villas, London W9 2PH, England.

DORNENBURG, Andrew. American. **Genres:** Food and Wine. **Career:** Rosemarie's (restaurant), NYC, sous-chef; host (with Karen Page) of online show on the electronic Gourmet Guide (eGG), America Online, 1995-; contributor, to YearbookNews.com (search engine). **Publications:** NONFICTION (WITH K. PAGE): Becoming a Chef: With Recipes and Reflections from America's Leading Chefs, 1995; The Becoming a Chef Journal, 1996; Culinary Artistry, 1996; Dining Out: Secrets from America's Leading Critics, Chefs, and Restaurateurs, 1998. **Address:** 527 Third Ave. Suite 130, New York, NY 10016, U.S.A. **Online address:** KarenAPage@aol.com

DORNER, Marjorie. American, b. 1942. **Genres:** Novels, Plays/Screenplays, Novellas/Short stories. **Career:** Wisconsin State University-Oshkosh (now University of Wisconsin-Oshkosh), instructor in English, 1965-66; St. Norbert College, Depere, WI, instructor in English, 1966-68; Winona State University, Winona, MN, professor of English, 1971-. **Publications:** NOVELS: Nightmare, 1987; Family Closets, 1989; Freeze Frame, 1990; Blood Kin, 1992; Seasons of Sun and Rain, 1999. OTHER: The Hundredth Battle (play), 1976; Winter Roads, Summer Fields (short story collection), 1992.

DORRELL, Linda M. American, b. 1962. **Genres:** Novels. **Career:** Writer, 1984-. Bakery worker, 1981-82; News Journal, Florence, SC, news editor, 1984-88; self-employed typist, 1989-. **Publications:** NOVELS: True Believers, 2001; Face to Face, 2002. **Address:** 5620 South Irby St., Effingham, SC 29541, U.S.A. **Online address:** Lindorrell@aol.com

DORRESTEIN, Renate. Dutch, b. 1954. **Genres:** Novels. **Career:** Journalist, 1972-. Established Anna Bijns Foundation, 1986; University of Michigan, writer-in-residence, 1987. **Publications:** Buitenstaanders, 1983; Vreemde streken, 1984; Noorderzon, 1986; Een nacht om te vliegeren, 1987; Het perpetuum mobile van de liefde, 1988; Korte metten, 1988; Vóór alles een dame: een vrolijke geschiedenis in dagelijkse afleveringen, 1989; Het hemelse gerecht, 1991; Heden ik, 1993; Een sterke man, 1994; Ontaarde moeders, 1992, trans. W. Boeke as Unnatural Mothers, 1992; Verborgen gebreken, 1996; Want dit is mijn lichaam, 1997; Een hart van steen, 1998, trans. as A Heart of Stone, 2000; Het geheim van de schrijver, 2000; Zonder genade, 2001, trans. as Without Mercy; Het duister dat ons scheidt, 2003. **Address:** c/o Author Mail, Veen Uitgevers Groep, PO Box 14095, 3508 SC Utrecht, Netherlands.

DORRIEN, Gary J. American, b. 1952. **Genres:** Philosophy, Politics/Government, Theology/Religion. **Career:** Parsons Center (school for emotionally disturbed children), Albany, NY, teacher, 1979-82; ordained Episcopal priest, 1982; St. Andrew's Episcopal Church, Albany, assistant pastor, 1982-87; Doane Stuart School, Albany, chaplain, 1982-87; Kalamazoo College, Kalamazoo, MI, professor of religion, dean of Stetson Chapel, chair of religious studies, and chair of humanities, 1987-2000, Parfet Distinguished Professor, 2000-. **Publications:** Logic and Consciousness: The Dialectics of Mind, 1985; The Democratic Socialist Vision, 1986; Reconstructing the Common Good: Theology and the Social Order, 1990; The Neoconservative Mind: Politics, Culture and the War of Ideology, 1993; Soul in Society: The Making and Renewal of Social Christianity, 1995; The Word as True Myth: Interpreting Modern Theology, 1997; The Remaking of Evangelical Theology, 1998; The Barthian Revolt in Modern Theology, 2000; The Making of American Liberal Theology: Imagining Progressive Religion, 2001; The Making of American Liberal Theology: Idealism, Realism and Modernity, 2003; Imperial Designs: The New Pax Americana, 2004. **Address:** Parfet Distinguished Professor, Kalamazoo College, 1200 Academy St, Kalamazoo, MI 49007, U.S.A. **Online address:** dorrien@kzoo.edu

DORROS, Arthur (M.). American, b. 1950. **Genres:** Children's fiction, Young adult fiction, Children's non-fiction, Young adult non-fiction. **Career:** Writer and illustrator, 1979-. Worked as a builder, carpenter, drafter, photographer, horticultural worker, and dockhand; teacher in elementary and junior high schools and adult education in Seattle, WA, and NYC for six years; artist in residence for NYC public schools, running programs in creative writing, bookmaking, and video; University of Washington, teacher of courses on writing in the classroom; consultant in libraries and schools; director of Children's Writing Workshop; presents seminars and workshops on writing to students, teachers, and administrators in schools, libraries, and at conferences internationally. **Publications:** JUVENILE FICTION: Alligator Shoes, 1982; Yum Yum (board book), 1987; Splash Splash (board book), 1987; Abuela, 1991; Tonight Is Carnaval, 1991; Radio Man/Don Radio, 1993; Isla, 1995; The Fungus That Ate My School, 2000; Ten Go Tango,

2000; When the Pigs Took Over, 2002. JUVENILE NONFICTION: Pretzels, 1981; Ant Cities, 1987; Feel the Wind, 1989; Rain Forest Secrets, 1990; Me and My Shadow, 1990; Follow the Water from Brook to Ocean, 1991; This Is My House, 1992; Animal Tracks, 1992; Elephant Families, 1994; A Tree Is Growing, 1997. Contributor of articles and illustrations to periodicals. **Address:** c/o HarperCollins, Author Mail, 1350 Avenue of the Americas, New York, NY 10019-4703, U.S.A. **Online address:** arthur@arthurdorros.com; arthurdorros.com

DORSEN, Norman. American, b. 1930. **Genres:** Civil liberties/Human rights, Law. **Career:** Dewey, Ballantine, Bushby, Palmer & Wood, NYC, Law Associate, 1958-60; New York University School of Law, NYC, Stokes Professor of Law, 1961-. Society of American Law Teachers, president, 1972-73; American Civil Liberties Union, president, 1976-91; Lawyers Committee for Human Rights, chairman, 1995-; US Assn of Constitutional Law, president, 1996-. Visiting professor at universities. **Publications:** (with others) Political and Civil Rights in the U.S., 3rd ed., 1967, 4th ed., 1979, supplement, 1982; Frontiers of Civil Liberties, 1968; Discrimination and Civil Rights, 1969; (with L. Friedman) Disorder in the Court, 1973; (with S. Gillers) Regulation of Lawyers, 1985; (with D. Rudovsky and L. Whitman) Human Rights in Northern Ireland, 1991. EDITOR: The Rights of Americans, 1971; (with S. Gillers) None of Your Business-Government Secrecy in America, 1974; Our Endangered Rights: The ACLU Report on Civil Liberties Today, 1984; The Evolving Constitution, 1987; (with F. Gifford) Democracy and the Rule of Law, 2001; The Unpredictable Constitution, 2002. **Address:** New York University, School of Law, 40 Washington Sq S, New York, NY 10012, U.S.A. **Online address:** Norman.Dorsen@nyu.edu

DORSET, Phyllis (Flanders). American, b. 1924. **Genres:** Novels, Novellas/Short stories, History, Military/Defense/Arms control, Autobiography/Memoirs. **Career:** Technical Writer and Ed., SRI International, California, 1956-65, 1966-. Technical Writer and Ed., Sandia Corp., 1952-56, Technical Operations, 1963-66, Arthur D. Little Inc., 1964-66, and Physics International Inc., 1968-74. **Publications:** Historic Ships Afloat, 1967; The New Eldorado: The Story of Colorado's Gold and Silver Rushes, 1970; (ed.) My Life at Fort Ross, 1987; A Finite Difference: The Short History of the Stanford Research Institute Physics Division, 2003. **Address:** 460 Sherwood Way, Menlo Park, CA 94025, U.S.A.

DORSEY, Candas Jane. Canadian, b. 1952. **Genres:** Poetry, Novels, Novellas/Short stories. **Career:** Edmonton Bullet, Edmonton, Alberta, Canada, freelance writer and editor, 1980-. Has also worked in theatre and as a social worker. **Publications:** POETRY: This Is for You, 1973; Orion Rising, 1974; Results of the Ring Toss, 1976; Leaving Marks, 1992. NOVELS: (with N. Abercrombie) Hardwired Angel, 1987; Black Wine, 1997; (with R. Deegan) Dark Earth Dreams, 1995. SHORT STORIES: Machine Sex and Other Stories, 1988; (ed., with G. Truscott) Tesseracts Three: Canadian Science Fiction, 1990. Contributor of short fiction to books. **Address:** c/o Porcepic Books, 4252 Commerce Circle, Victoria, BC, Canada V8Z 4M2.

D'ORSO, Michael. American, b. 1953. **Genres:** Essays, Humor/Satire. **Career:** Journalist. Commonwealth Magazine, Richmond, VA, staff writer, 1981-84; Virginian-Pilot, Norfolk, VA, features writer, 1984-. **Publications:** (with D.S. Redford) Somerset Homecoming: Recovering a Lost Heritage, 1988; (As Mike D'Orso) Fast Takes: Slices of Life through a Journalist's Eye, 1990; (with C. Elliott) The Cost of Courage: The Journey of an American Congressman, 1992; (with M. Cartwright) For the Children: Lessons from a Visionary Principal-How We Can Save Our Public Schools, 1993; (with D. Byrd) Rise and Walk: The Trial and Triumph of Dennis Byrd, 1993; (As Mike D'Orso) Pumping Granite, and Other Portraits of People at Play, 1994; Like Judgment Day: The Ruin and Redemption of a Town Called Rosewood, 1996; (with D. Hakala) Thin is Just a Four-Letter Word, 1997; (with J.L. Lieberman) In Praise of Public Life, 2000. Contributor to periodicals. **Address:** 515 Mayflower Rd., Norfolk, VA 23508, U.S.A.

DOSS, Erika. American. **Genres:** Art/Art history. **Career:** Minneapolis College of Art and Design, Minneapolis, MN, instructor in art history, 1981-83; Carleton College, Northfield, MN, visiting assistant professor of art history, 1983-84; Cleveland State University, Cleveland, OH, assistant professor of art history, 1984-86; University of Colorado, Boulder, assistant professor, 1986-91, director of London Study Abroad Program, 1988, associate professor of art history and director of American Studies Program, 1991-. University of Minnesota-Twin Cities, instructor, 1983; University of Oregon, visiting assistant professor, 1984; University of Sydney, senior Fulbright lecturer, 1996; lecturer at universities and institutes worldwide. **Publications:** Benton, Pollock, and the Politics of Modernism: From Regionalism to Abstract Expressionism, 1991; Spirit Poles and Flying Pigs: Public Art and

Cultural Democracy in American Communities, 1995; (ed. and contrib.) Looking at LIFE: Cultural Essays on America's Favorite Magazine, in press. Contributor to books. Contributor of articles and reviews to academic journals. **Address:** Department of Fine Arts, Campus Box 318, University of Colorado, Boulder, CO 80309, U.S.A. **Online address:** erika.doss@colorado.edu

DOSS, Margot P(atterson). Also writes as Mary Baltimore, Silas Factor, Francisco Shunpike. American, b. 1920. **Genres:** Poetry, Earth sciences, Travel/Exploration. **Career:** Columnist, San Francisco Chronicle, 1961-91. Lecturer in Natural History, California Acad. of Science. Commissioner, Golden Gate National Recreation Area, 1976-. Lecturer, University of California, 1970-83; Performer and Outdoor Ed., KPIX-TV Evening mag., 1977-83; Pt Reyes Light, Garden Gallivanting column; KWMR radio, Margot's Dossier. **Publications:** San Francisco at Your Feet, 1964, 4th ed., 1991; Walks for Children in San Francisco, 1970; Bay Area at Your Feet, 1970, 3rd ed., 1986; Golden Gate Park at Your Feet, 1970; Paths of Gold, 1974; There, There, 1978; A Walker's Yearbook, 1984; Full Moon Haiku, 1992; A Reminiscence of #9 Brighton, 1998. **Address:** Box 220, Bolinas, CA 94924, U.S.A.

DOS SANTOS, Joyce Audy. Also writes as Joyce Audy Zarins. American, b. 1949. **Genres:** Children's fiction, Young adult fiction, Art/Art history, Children's non-fiction, Illustrations. **Career:** Writer and illustrator, 1976-; ATSA Associates, Haverhill, MA, designer, 1980-81; Merrimack Publishers Circle, Topsfield, MA, designer, 1982-84; Ayer Publishing Co., Salem, NH, designer, 1985-86. Worked at Andover Bookstore, Andover, MA, 1988. Workshop leader, Northern Essex Community College, 1987-98; Middlesex Community College, drawing teacher; University of New Hampshire, teacher of writing and illustrating children's books; sculptor, welded steel. **Publications:** SELF-ILLUSTRATED FOR CHILDREN: Sand Dollar, Sand Dollar, 1980; The Diviner, 1980; Henri and the Loup-Garou, 1982; Giants of Smaller Worlds: Drawn in Their Natural Sizes, 1983; (as Joyce Audy Zarins) Toasted Bagels: A Break-of-the-Day Book, 1988. Illustrator of books by B.J. Adams, S. Climo, B.H. Costikyan, M. Dionetti, J.L. Henry, L. Lawlor, S. Mooser, K. Morgan, J. Oppenheim, R. Roy, J. Thayer. Contributor of articles on art to periodicals. **Address:** 19 Woodland St, Merrimac, MA 01860, U.S.A. **Online address:** joyce.zarins@verizon.net

DOSSEY, Larry. American, b. 1940. **Genres:** Medicine/Health. **Career:** Medical doctor; author of books on spirituality and medicine. Dallas Diagnostic Association, physician (Internal Medicine); Medical City Dallas Hospital, chief of staff; Isthmus Institute of Dallas, president; National Institutes of Health, Office of Alternative Medicine, Panel on Mind/Body Interventions, co-chair; Alternative Therapies, executive editor. **Publications:** Space, Time, and Medicine, 1982; Beyond Illness: Discovering the Experience of Health, 1984; Recovering the Soul: A Scientific and Spiritual Search, 1989; Meaning and Medicine: Lessons from a Doctor's Tales of Breakthrough and Healing, 1991; Healing Words: The Power of Prayer and the Practice of Medicine, 1993; Prayer Is Good Medicine: How to Reap the Healing Benefits of Prayer, 1996; Be Careful What You Pray for... You Just Might Get It: What We Can Do about the Unintentional Effects of Our Thoughts, Prayers, and Wishes, 1997. Contributor to periodicals. **Address:** c/o author Mail, 7th Floor, HarperCollins Publishers, 10 East 53rd St., New York, NY 10022, U.S.A.

DOTI, Lynne Pierson. American, b. 1948. **Genres:** Economics, Money/Finance. **Career:** Chapman University, Orange, CA, professor of economics, 1971-. **Publications:** Banking in the American West, 1991; California Bankers 1848-1993, 1994; Banking in an Unregulated Environment: California 1879-1905, 1995. Contributor to periodicals. **Address:** Argyros School of Business and Economics, Chapman University, 1 University Dr, Orange, CA 92866-1099, U.S.A. **Online address:** ldoti@chapman.edu

DOTSON, Bob. (Robert Charles Dotson). American, b. 1946. **Genres:** Documentaries/Reportage, Communications/Media. **Career:** Television journalist. KMBC-TV, Kansas City, MO, reporter, photographer, and documentary producer, 1967-68; WKY-TV, Oklahoma City, OK, director of special projects, 1969-75; WKYC-TV, Cleveland, OH, correspondent, 1975-77; NBC-TV news bureau, Dallas, TX, correspondent, 1977-79; correspondent for Today Show, 1978-85; correspondent in Atlanta, GA, for "...In Pursuit of the American Dream" (now called Assignment America) segments of NBC-TV's Nightly News with Tom Brokaw, 1985-. Visiting professor at University of Oklahoma, 1969-73; correspondent for Now with Tom Brokaw and Katie Couric, 1993; correspondent for Dateline NBC, Today Show, and NBC Nightly News, 1994. **Publications:** "...In Pursuit of the American Dream"

(nonfiction vignettes), 1985; Make it Memorable, 2000. **Address:** c/o Ron Konecky, 488 Madison Ave., 9th Floor, New York, NY 10022, U.S.A.

DOTY, Mark. American, b. 1953. **Genres:** Poetry, Autobiography/Memoirs. **Career:** Poet and memoirist. University of Houston, teacher of creative writing. Worked at temporary jobs in NYC, c. 1970s and early 1980s. National Book Critics Circle Award, 1993. **Publications:** POETRY: Turtle, Swan, 1987; Bethlehem in Broad Daylight, 1991; My Alexandria, 1993; Atlantis, 1995; Sweet Machine, 1998; Source, 2001; School of the Arts, 2005. NONFICTION: Heaven's Coast: A Memoir, 1996; Firebird: A Memoir, 1999; Still Life with Oysters and Lemon, 2001. **Address:** 148 W 16th St #4, New York, NY 10011, U.S.A. **Online address:** markdoty@earthlink.net

DOUCET, Julie. (born Canada), b. 1965. **Genres:** Graphic Novels. **Career:** Independent cartoonist and artist; worked for various magazines. **Publications:** GRAPHIC NOVELS: Lift Your Leg, My Fish Is Dead!, 1993; My Most Secret Desire: A Collection of Dream Stories, 1995; My New York Diary, 1999; The Madame Paul Affair, 2000; Long-Term Relationship, 2001; Contributor of stories, periodicals, and art to anthologies. **Address:** c/o Author Mail, Drawn & Quarterly, POB 48056, Montreal, Quebec, Canada H2V 4S8.

DOUGHERTY, James E(dward). American, b. 1923. **Genres:** International relations/Current affairs, Military/Defense/Arms control, Area studies. **Career:** St. Joseph's University, Philadelphia, PA, 1951-97, began as instructor, became professor, 1960-97, executive vice-president, 1968-73, 1976-77, emeritus professor of political science, 1997-; Foreign Policy Research Institute, research associate, 1955-68; National War College, professor, 1964-65; Institute for Foreign Policy Analysis, senior member of staff, 1976-89. **Publications:** (with others) Protracted Conflict, 1959; (with others) Building the Atlantic World, 1963; (with A.J. Cottrell) The Politics of the Atlantic Alliance, 1964, in UK as The Atlantic Alliance, 1964; (ed. with J.F. Lehman Jr.) The Prospects for Arms Control, 1965; Arms Control and Disarmament, 1966; (with Lehman) Arms Control for the Late Sixties, 1967; (with R.L. Pfaltzgraff Jr.) Contending Theories of International Relations, 1971, 5th ed., 2001; How to Think about Arms Control and Disarmament, 1973; (coauthor) SALT: Arms Control in the 1970s, 1973; Security through World Law and World Government: Myth or Reality?, 1974; British Perspectives on a Changing Global Balance, 1975; (with D.K. Pfaltzgraff) Eurocommunism and the Atlantic Alliance, 1977; (with Cottrell) Iran's Quest for Security: U.S. Arms Transfers and the Nuclear Option, 1977; (with P.H. Nitze and F.X. Kane) The Fateful Ends and Shades of SALT: Past...Present... and Yet to Come?, 1979; The Horn of Africa: A Map of Political-Strategic Conflict, 1982; The Bishops and Nuclear Weapons, 1984; (coauthor) Ethics, Deterrence, and National Security, 1985; (ed. with R.L. Pfaltzgraff Jr.) Shattering Europe's Defense Consensus, 1985; (with R.L. Pfaltzgraff Jr.) American Foreign Policy: FDR to Reagan, 1986; Joint Chiefs of Staff Reorganization and U.S. Arms Control Policy, 1986. **Address:** 374 Freedom Blvd, Coatesville, PA 19320, U.S.A.

DOUGLAS, Ann. Also writes as Ann (Douglas) Wood. American, b. 1942. **Genres:** Literary criticism and history, Women's studies and issues. **Career:** Columbia University, NYC, professor of English and comparative literature 1974-. **Publications:** The Feminization of American Culture, 1977; Terrible Honesty: Mongrel Manhattan in the 1920s, 1994. EDITOR & AUTHOR OF INTRODUCTION: H.B. Uncle Tom's Cabin, 1981; S. Rowson and L. Temple, Charlotte Temple, 1991. Contributor to periodicals. Has written as Ann (Douglas) Wood. **Address:** 420 Lewis Ohn Hall, Columbia University, Broadway 116th St., New York, NY 10027, U.S.A.

DOUGLAS, Arthur. See HAMMOND, Gerald (Arthur Douglas).

DOUGLAS, Edward. See AMBURN, Ellis.

DOUGLAS, Garry. See KILWORTH, Garry.

DOUGLAS, John (Frederick James). British, b. 1929. **Genres:** Geography, Photography, Third World, Travel/Exploration. **Career:** Army Officer, 1952-; Photographer and travel consultant, 1965-; Library Director, Geoslides Photo Agency, London, 1969-; Director, Geo Group and Associates, 1989-; Managing Director Geo Aerial Photography, 1993-; Director, Nyala Publishing, 1996-. **Publications:** South Downs, 1969; The Arctic Highway, 1972; Town and Village in Northern Ghana, 1973; Water Problems in the Third World, 1973; Kampong Tengah, a Malay Village, 1974; Kuala Lumpur, A Third World City, 1974; A Dyak Longhouse in Borneo, 1975; Environmental Viewpoint: Water, 1976; Shelter and Subsistence, 1976; Ice and Snow, 1976; Expedition Photography, 1979; Creative Techniques in Travel Photography,

1982; (with K. White) Spectrum Guide to Malawi, 2003; Norway's Arctic Highway, 2003. **Address:** Geo Group & Associates, 4 Christian Fields, London SW16 3JZ, England. **Online address:** jd@geo-group.co.uk

DOUGLAS, Kirk. American, b. 1918. **Genres:** Novels, Autobiography/ Memoirs. **Career:** Actor, motion picture producer. **Publications:** MEMOIRS: The Ragman's Son, 1998; Climbing the Mountain, 1997; My Stroke of Luck, 2002. NOVELS: Dance with the Devil, 1990; The Gift, 1992; Last Tango in Brooklyn, 1994. OTHER: The Broken Mirror (children), 1997; Young Heroes of the Bible, 1998. **Address:** The Bryna Co, 141 S El Camino Dr Ste 209, Beverly Hills, CA 90212-2731, U.S.A.

DOUGLAS, L. Warren. American, b. 1943. **Genres:** Novels, Science fiction/Fantasy. **Career:** Toledo University, Toledo, OH, archaeology field crew supervisor, 1967; University of Alberta, Edmonton, Alberta, Canada, anthropology and prehistory instructor, beginning in 1972; regional planning commission artist, beginning c. 1973; woodcarver, beginning c. 1973. **Publications:** NOVELS: A Plague of Change, 1992; Bright Islands in a Dark Sea, 1993; Cannon's Orb, 1994. ARBITER SERIES: Stepwater, 1995; Glaice, 1996; The Wells of Phyre, 1996. **Address:** c/o Roc Publicity, 375 Hudson St., New York, NY 10014, U.S.A.

DOUGLAS, Michael. See CRICHTON, (John) Michael.

DOUGLAS, Richard. See WHITING, Charles (Henry).

DOUGLAS, Susan J(eanne). American, b. 1950. **Genres:** Communications/ Media. **Career:** Hampshire College, Amherst, MA, professor of media and American studies; affiliated with the University of Michigan, Ann Arbor, MI. Media critic for The Progressive. **Publications:** Inventing American Broadcasting, 1899-1922, 1987; Where the Girls Are: Growing up Female with the Mass Media, 1994; Listening in: Radio and the American Imagination, 1999. Contributor to periodicals. **Address:** University of Michigan Department of Communications, 2020 Friezer, 105 South State St., Ann Arbor, MI 48109, U.S.A.

DOUGLAS-HAMILTON, (Lord) James Alexander. British, b. 1942. **Genres:** History. **Career:** Practising Scots Advocate, 1968-77; MP for Edinburgh West, 1974-97; Opposition then Government Whip, 1977-81; Parliamentary Private Secretary to Malcolm Rifkind MP, 1983-87; Parliamentary Under Secretary at the Scottish Office, 1987-95; Minister of State at the Scottish Office, 1995-97; Director, Douglas-Hamilton "D" Co. Ltd, 1997-; Life Peer, 1998; Lead Spokesman for Home Affairs, 2000-03; Spokesman for Education, 2003-. **Publications:** Motive for a Mission: The Story behind Hess's Flight to Britain, 1971; (ed.) The Air Battle for Malta, 1981; Roof of the World, 1983; The Truth about Rudolf Hess, 1993. Contributor to books. **Address:** Scottish Parliament, George IV Bridge, Edinburgh EH99 1SP, Scotland. **Online address:** james.douglas-hamilton. msp@scottish.parliament.uk

DOUGLASS, Billie. See DELINSKY, Barbara (Ruth Greenberg).

DOUGLASS, Sara. See WARNEKE, Sara.

DOVE, Rita (Frances). American, b. 1952. **Genres:** Novels, Novellas/Short stories, Plays/Screenplays, Poetry. **Career:** Arizona State University, Tempe, assistant professor of creative writing, 1981-84, associate professor, 1984-87, professor of English, 1987-89; University of Virginia, professor of English, 1989-93, Commonwealth Professor of English, 1989-93. Poet Laureate of the US, 1993-95, and special consultant to the Library of Congress, 1999-2000; Poet Laureate of Virginia, 2004-. Recipient: Pulitzer Prize, 1987. **Publications:** POETRY: Ten Poems, 1977; The Only Dark Spot in the Sky, 1980; The Yellow House on the Corner, 1980; Mandolin, 1982; Museum, 1983; Thomas and Beulah, 1986; The Other Side of the House, 1988; Grace Notes, 1989; Selected Poems, 1993; Lady Freedom among Us, 1994; Mother Love, 1995; On the Bus with Rosa Parks, 1999; American Smooth, 2004. OTHER: Fifth Sunday (stories), 1985; The Siberian Village (play), 1991; Through the Ivory Gate (novel), 1992; The Darker Face of the Earth (play), 1994, The Poet's World (essays), 1995; Seven for Luck (song cycle) 1998; (ed.) The Best American Poetry 2000, 2000. Poems, short stories, and essays appear in anthologies and other publications. **Address:** Dept of English, University of Virginia, 219 Bryan Hall, PO Box 400121, Charlottesville, VA 22904-4121, U.S.A.

DOVER, Sir K(enneth) J(ames). British, b. 1920. **Genres:** Classics, Autobiography/Memoirs. **Career:** Chancellor, University of St. Andrews,

Scotland, 1981- (Professor of Greek, 1955-76). Fellow and Tutor, Balliol College, Oxford, 1948-55; President, Corpus Christi College, Oxford, 1976-86. Co-Ed., Classical Quarterly, 1962-68; President, Hellenic Society, 1971-74, Classical Association, 1976, and British Academy, 1978-81; Professor of Classics (winter quarter), Stanford University, California, 1987-92. **Publications:** Greek Word Order, 1960; (ed.) Thucydides Book VI, 1965; (ed.) Thucydides Book VII, 1965; (ed.) Aristophanes' Clouds, 1968; Lysias and the Corpus Lysiacum, 1968; (with A.W. Gomme and A. Andrewes) Historical Commentary on Thucydides, vol. IV, 1970; vol. V, 1980; (ed.) Theocritus: Select Poems, 1971; Aristophanic Comedy, 1972; Greek Popular Morality, 1975; Greek Homosexuality, 1978; The Greeks, 1980; (co-author) Ancient Greek Literature, 1980; Greek and the Greeks (Collected Papers, vol. I), 1987; The Greeks and Their Legacy, 1989; (ed.) Aristophanes' Frogs, 1993; Marginal Comment (memoirs), 1994; The Evolution of Greek Prose Style, 1997. **Address:** 49 Hepburn Gardens, St. Andrews, Fife KY16 9LS, Scotland.

DOWDEN, Anne Ophelia Todd. American, b. 1907. **Genres:** Botany, Natural history. **Career:** Head of Art Dept., Manhattanville College, New York, 1932-53; Drapery and wallpaper design, 1934-52; Freelance botanical artist and author, 1952-. **Publications:** The Little Hill, 1961; Look at a Flower, 1963; The Secret Life of the Flowers, 1964; Roses, 1965; Wild Green Things in the City: A Book of Weeds, 1972; The Blossom on the Bough: A Book of Trees, 1975; State Flowers, 1978; This Noble Harvest: A Chronicle of Herbs, 1979; From Flower to Fruit, 1984; The Clover and the Bee: A Book of Pollination, 1990; Poisons in Our Path: Plants that Harm and Heal, 1993. Researched and designed books on plants and flowers. **Address:** 350 Ponca Pl, Boulder, CO 80303, U.S.A.

DOWER, John W(illiam). American, b. 1938. **Genres:** Area studies, Cultural/Ethnic topics, Design, History, Photography, Race relations, Bibliography. **Career:** John Weatherhill (publishers), Tokyo, Japan, book editor and designer, 1963-65; University of Wisconsin-Madison, professor of history, 1971-86; University of California, San Diego, La Jolla, Joseph Naiman Professor of History and Japanese Studies, 1986-91; Massachusetts Institute of Technology, Cambridge, Henry R. Luce Professor of International Cooperation and Global Stability, 1991-96, Elting E. Morison Professor of History, 1996-; writer. Executive producer of Hellfire: A Journey from Hiroshima (documentary film), 1986. **Publications:** The Elements of Japanese Design: A Handbook of Family Crests, Heraldry, and Symbolism, 1971; Empire and Aftermath: Yoshida Shigeru and the Japanese Experience, 1878-1945, 1979; A Century of Japanese Photography, 1980; Japanese History and Culture from Ancient to Modern Times: Seven Basic Bibliographies, 1985; War without Mercy: Race and Power in the Pacific War, 1986; Japan in War & Peace, 1993; Embracing Defeat: Japan in the Wake of World War II, 1999 (Pulitzer Prize for general nonfiction, 2000). EDITOR: Origins of the Modern Japanese State: Selected Writings of E.H. Norman, 1975; (with J. Junkerman) The Hiroshima Murals: The Art of Iri Maruki and Toshi Maruki, 1985. Contributor to books. **Address:** Dept of History, Massachusetts Institute of Technology, 77 Massachusetts Ave Bldg E51-287, Cambridge, MA 02139, U.S.A.

DOWLAH, Caf. Bangladeshi, b. 1958. **Genres:** Politics/Government. **Career:** State University of New York Agricultural and Technical Institute at Canton, assistant professor of economics and government, 1991-96; World Bank, Dhaka Office, Dhaka, Bangladesh, policy economist for Private Sector Development and Rural Development Units, 1997-. Speaker at universities; consultant to U.S. Agency for International Development, United Nations Development Program, and Bangladesh Ministry of Industries. **Publications:** Perestroika: Historical and Intellectual Roots, 1990; Soviet Political Economy in Transition: From Lenin to Gorbachev, 1992; (as Alex F. Dowlah, with J.E. Elliott) The Life and Times of Soviet Socialism, 1997. Contributor to books. Contributor of articles and reviews to periodicals. Some writings appear under the names Caf Dowlah or A. F. Dowlah. **Address:** Third Floor, House 4/5, Block E, Lalmatia, Dhaka 1207, Bangladesh. **Online address:** cdowlah@ worldbank.org

DOWLING, Terry. Australian, b. 1947. **Genres:** Science fiction/Fantasy, Novellas/Short stories. **Career:** Science fiction author and editor. Worked as a communications instructor and lecturer, an actor, and a songwriter. **Publications:** SCIENCE FICTION. (ed., with R. Delap and G. Lamont) The Essential Ellison: A 35-Year Retrospective (fiction anthology), 1987; The Mars You Have in Me (short stories), 1992; (ed., with V. Ikin), Mortal Fire: Best Australian Science Fiction (anthology), 1993; The Man Who Lost Red (novellas), 1994; An Intimate Knowledge of the Night, 1995. RYNOSSEROS SHORT STORY SERIES: Rynosseros, 1990; Wormwood, 1991; Blue Tyson, 1992; Twilight Beach, 1993. Contributor to periodicals and anthologies. **Address:** 11 Everard St., Hunters Hill, NSW 2110, Australia.

DOWNER, Lesley. British, b. 1949. **Genres:** Travel/Exploration, Women's studies and issues, Autobiography/Memoirs, Biography. **Career:** Gifu Women's University, Gifu, Japan, lecturer in English, 1978-81; Tokyo Broadcasting System, London, England, personal assistant, 1984-; free-lance writer, journalist, and broadcaster, 1986-. **Publications:** (with M. Yoneda) Step-by-Step Japanese Cooking, 1985; Japanese Vegetarian Cookery, 1986; (contrib. and consulting ed.) The "Economist" Business Traveller's Guide to Japan, 1987, rev. ed., 1990; Japanese Food and Drink, 1987; Japan, 1989; On the Narrow Road to the Deep North: Journey into a Lost Japan, 1989; A Taste of Japan, 1991; The Brothers: The Hidden World of Japan's Richest Family, 1994; Hard Currency in Amazonian: Penguin Book of Women's New Travel Writing, 1998; Women of the Pleasure Quarters: The Secret History of the Geisha, 2001. **Address:** c/o Bill Hamilton, A.M. Heath, St Martins Lane, London, England. **Online address:** lesleydowner@email.msn.com

DOWNES, Bryan T(revor). American (born Canada), b. 1939. **Genres:** Local history/Rural topics, Politics/Government, Public/Social administration, Urban studies. **Career:** San Francisco State College, California, Assistant Professor, 1966-67; Michigan State University, East Lansing, Assistant Professor, 1967-70, Associate Professor 1970-71; University of Missouri, St. Louis, Associate Professor of Political Science, 1971-76; University of Oregon, Eugene, Associate Professor, 1976-78, Associate Dean and Professor of Community Service and Public Affairs, 1978-80, Professor of Public Affairs, 1981-2001, Dept Head, 1996-2000, Professor Emeritus, 2001-. **Publications:** (ed.) Cities and Suburbs: Selected Readings in Local Politics and Public Policy, 1971; Politics, Change, and Urban Crisis, 1975. **Address:** Dept. of Planning, Public Policy and Management, University of Oregon, Eugene, OR 97403-1209, U.S.A. **Online address:** downesb@oregon.uoregon.edu

DOWNES, David A(nthony). American, b. 1927. **Genres:** Novels, Literary criticism and history, Autobiography/Memoirs. **Career:** Seattle University, WA, chairman, Dept. of English, 1964-68; California State University, Chico, dean of humanities, 1968-72, professor, 1972-91, director of graduate studies, 1977-78, chairman of English Dept., 1978-84, emeritus professor of English, 1991-. University Journal, editor, 1974-78. **Publications:** Gerard Manley Hopkins: A Study of His Ignatian Spirit, 1960; Victorian Portraits: Hopkins and Pater, 1965; The Temper of Victorian Belief: Studies in the Religious Novels of Pater, Kingsley and Newman, 1972; Ruskin's Beatific Landscapes, 1980; The Great Sacrifice, 1983; Hopkins' Sanctifying Imagination, 1985; The Ignatian Personality of G.M. Hopkins, 1990; (co-ed.) Saving Beauty: Further Studies in Hopkins, 1994; Hopkins' Achieved Self, 1996, rev. ed., 2002; Rereading Hopkins: Selected New Essays, 1996; G.M. Hopkins: An Inventory of the Anthony Bischoff Research Collection at Gonzaga University, 2001; Hopkins Variations: Standing Round a Waterfall, 2002; The Belle of Cripple Creek Gold, 2001. **Address:** 1076 San Ramon Dr, Chico, CA 95973, U.S.A. **Online address:** ddownes@mail.csuchico.edu

DOWNIE, Leonard, Jr. American, b. 1942. **Genres:** Law, Urban studies, Writing/Journalism. **Career:** Washington Post, on staff, 1964-, managing ed., 1984-91, executive ed., 1991-. **Publications:** Justice Denied: The Case for Reform of the Courts, 1971; Mortgage on America, 1974; The New Muckrakers, 1976; (with R.G. Kaiser) The News about the News, 2002. **Address:** The Washington Post, 1150 15th St NW, Washington, DC 20071, U.S.A.

DOWNIE, Mary Alice. Canadian (born United States), b. 1934. **Genres:** Westerns/Adventure, Children's fiction, Young adult fiction, Poetry, Songs/Lyrics and libretti, Botany, Children's non-fiction, Homes/Gardens, Local history/Rural topics, Mythology/Folklore, Picture/board books, Translations. **Career:** Writer and editor. **Publications:** (with B. Robertson) The Wind Has Wings: Poems from Canada, 1968; Scared Sarah, 1974; (trans.) The Magical Adventures of Pierre, 1974; Dragon on Parade, 1974; The Witch of the North: Folktales from French Canada, 1975; The King's Loon, 1980; The Last Ship, 1980; (with M. Hamilton) And Some Brought Flowers: Plants in a New World, 1980; (with J. Downie) Honor Bound, 1971; (with G. Rawlyk) A Proper Acadian, 1981; (with J.H. Gilliland) Seeds and Weeds: A Book of Country Crafts, 1981; The Wicked Fairy Wife, 1983; (with J. Downie) Alison's Ghosts, 1984; Jenny Greenteeth, 1984; (with J.H. Gilliland) Stones and Cones: Country Crafts for Kids, 1984; (with B. Robertson) The New Wind Has Wings, 1984; (with E. Greene and M.A. Thompson) The Window of Dreams, 1986; (with B. Robertson) The Well-Filled Cupboard: Everyday Pleasures of Home and Garden, 1987; How the Devil Got His Cat, 1988; (with Mann Hwa Huang-Hsu) The Buffalo Boy and the Weaver Girl, 1989; (ed. with B. Robertson) Doctor Dwarf and Other Poems for Children by A.M. Klein, 1990; Cathal the Giant Killer and the Dun Shaggy Filly, 1991; (with M.A. Thompson) Written in Stone: A Kingston Reader, 1993; The Cat Park, 1993; Snow Paws, 1996; Bright Paddles, 1999; (with J. Downie)

Danger in Disguise, 2000. LIBRETTOS: The Kingdom, 1998; The Winter Children, 1999. **Address:** 190 Union St, Kingston, ON, Canada K7L 2P6. **Online address:** downiej@post.queensu.ca

DOWNIE, R(obert) S(ilcock). British, b. 1933. **Genres:** Education, Ethics, Humanities, Medicine/Health, Philosophy, Biography. **Career:** University of Glasgow, Lecturer, 1959-67, Sr. Lecturer, 1968-69, Professor of Moral Philosophy, 1969-, Stevenson Lecturer in Medical Ethics, 1985-88. University of Syracuse, New York, Visiting Professor of Philosophy, 1963-64. **Publications:** Government Action and Morality, 1964; (co-author) Respect for Persons, 1969; Roles and Values: An Introduction to Social Ethics, 1971; (co-author) Education and Personal Relationships, 1974; (co-author) Values in Social Work, 1976; (co-author) Caring and Curing, 1980; Healthy Respect: Ethics in Health Care, 1987; Health Promotion: Models and Values, 1990; The Making of a Doctor: Medical Education in Theory and Practice, 1992; Francis Hutcheson, 1994; The Healing Arts: An Illustrated Oxford Anthology, 1994; Palliative Care Ethics, 1996; Clinical Judgment: Evidence in Practice, 2000. **Address:** Dept. of Moral Philosophy, University of Glasgow, Glasgow G12 8QQ, Scotland. **Online address:** R.Downie@philosophy.arts.gla.ac.uk

DOWNING, David A(lmon). Also writes as Russell Almon. American, b. 1958. **Genres:** Novels. **Career:** University of Washington Extension, Seattle, instructor in fiction writing, 1990-; CNA Companies (an architectural and engineering firm), Kirkland, WA, marketing writer, 1992-. **Publications:** (with W.R. Clevenger as Russell Almon) The Kid Can't Miss!, 1992. **Address:** 143 Northwest 79th St., Seattle, WA 98117, U.S.A.

DOWNING, David C(laude). American, b. 1951. **Genres:** Education, Literary criticism and history, Biography. **Career:** Westmont College, Santa Barbara, CA, 1977-94; Elizabethtown College, Elizabethtown, PA, Ralph W. Schlosser Professor of English, 1994-. **Publications:** What You Know Might Not Be So, 1987; Imagine Yourself a Perfect Speller, 1990; Planets in Peril: A Critical Study of C.S. Lewis's Ransom Trilogy, 1992; The Most Reluctant Convert: C.S. Lewis's Journey to Faith, 2002. **Address:** 608 Antler Dr, Lewisberry, PA 17339, U.S.A. **Online address:** Downindc@etown.edu

DOWNING, Michael (Bernard). American, b. 1958. **Genres:** Novels, Plays/Screenplays. **Career:** Novelist, editor, and educator. Harvard College, Shrewsbury, England, Harvard-Shrewsbury Fellow, 1980-81; Oceanus (periodical), Woods Hole, MA, senior editor, 1983-84; FMR (periodical), Milan, Italy, senior editor, 1984-86; Bentley College, Waltham, MA, instructor in English, 1987-88; Wheelock College, Boston, MA, instructor, 1988-91, assistant professor of humanities and director of writing program, 1992-. **Publications:** A Narrow Time, 1987; Mother of God, 1990; Perfect Agreement, 1997; Breakfast With Scot, 1999. PLAY: The Last Shaker, 1995. Work represented in anthologies. Contributor of stories, poems, essays, and reviews to periodicals. **Address:** Wheelock College, 200 Riverway, Boston, MA 02215, U.S.A. **Online address:** downing58@aol.com

DOWNS, Dorothy. American, b. 1937. **Genres:** Art/Art history. **Career:** University of Miami, Coral Gables, FL, registrar at Lowe Art Museum, 1977-78, director of New Gallery, 1986-87, instructor in art history, 1996; Four Corners Gallery, Coral Gables, director, 1978-79; art dealer, consultant, and appraiser, 1979-80; Center for the Fine Arts, Dade County, FL, manager of Center Art Store, 1982-84; Guest curator and consultant; has appeared on television programs. **Publications:** Art of the Florida Seminole and Miccosukee Indians, 1995. TELEVISION DOCUMENTARY: Patterns of Power, 1991. Author of exhibition catalogs. Contributor to magazines and newspapers. **Address:** 5650 SW 87th St, Miami, FL 33143, U.S.A. **Online address:** dordow@earthlink.net

DOWNS, Robert C. S. American, b. 1937. **Genres:** Novels, Novellas/Short stories, Plays/Screenplays. **Career:** Instructor in English, Phillips Exeter Academy, Exeter, NH, 1962-63; Lecturer in English, Hunter College, City University, NYC, 1965-66; Sales Promotion Writer, Life mag., NYC, 1966-68; Assistant Professor of English, Colby Jr. College, New London, NH, 1968-73; Associate Professor of English, University of Arizona, Tucson, 1973-79; Professor of English, 1980-98, Emeritus, 1998- Pennsylvania State University. **Publications:** Going Gently, 1973; Peoples, 1974; Country Dying, 1976; White Mama, 1980; Living Together, 1983; White Mama (screenplay) CBS-TV, 1980; The Fifth Season, 2000. Contributor of short fiction to periodicals. **Address:** 764 W Hamilton Ave, State College, PA 16801, U.S.A. **Online address:** rcd4@psu.edu

DOWTY, Alan K. American, b. 1940. **Genres:** International relations/Current affairs, Politics/Government. **Career:** Hebrew University of Jerusalem, lecturer 1972-75, chairman of the Intl. Relations Dept., 1974-75; University of Notre Dame, Indiana, associate professor, 1975-78, professor of political science, 1978-2004; University of Calgary, Kahanoff Chair Professor of Israel Studies, 2003-. **Publications:** The Limits of American Isolation, 1971; The Role of Great Power Guarantees in International Peace Agreements, 1974; Middle-East Crisis: U.S. Decision-Making in 1958, 1970, and 1973, 1984; Closed Borders: The Contemporary Assault on Free Movement, 1987; (co-author) The Arab-Israeli Conflict: Perspectives, 1984, 2nd ed., 1991; The Jewish State: A Century Later, 1998; (ed.) Critical Issues in Israeli Society, 2004; Israel/Palestine, 2005. **Address:** 615 S Greenlawn Ave, South Bend, IN 46615, U.S.A. **Online address:** dowty.1@nd.edu

DOYLE, Brian. Canadian, b. 1935. **Genres:** Children's fiction, Young adult fiction. **Career:** Glebe Collegiate Institute, teacher and head of English dept., now retired. **Publications:** Hey Dad!, 1978; You Can Pick Me up at Peggy's Cove, 1979; Up to Low, 1982; Angel Square, 1984; Easy Avenue, 1988; Covered Bridge, 1990; Spud Sweetgrass, 1992; Spud in Winter, 1995; Uncle Ronald, 1996; The Low Life, 1999; Mary Ann Alice, 2001; Boy O'Boy, 2003. **Address:** 118 Ossington Ave, Ottawa, ON, Canada K1S 3B8.

DOYLE, Charles (Desmond). Also writes as Mike Doyle. Canadian (born England), b. 1928. **Genres:** Poetry, Literary criticism and history, Politics/ Government, Biography. **Career:** University of Victoria, BC, professor of English, now emeritus; Tuatara mag., ed., 1969-74. **Publications:** A Splinter of Glass: Poems 1951-55, 1956; Distances: Poems 1956-61, 1963; Messages for Herod, 1965; A Sense of Place: Poems, 1965; (as Mike Doyle) Noah, 1970; R.A.K. Mason, 1970; Earth Meditations, 1971; Abandoned Sofa, 1971; Earthshot, 1972; Preparing for the Ark, 1973; Planes, 1975; Stonedancer, 1976; James K. Baxter, 1976; William Carlos Williams and the American Poem, 1982; A Steady Hand, 1983; Richard Aldington: A Biography, 1989; The Urge to Raise Hats, 1989; Separate Fidelities, 1991; Intimate Absences: Selected Poems, 1993; Trout Spawning at Lardeau River, 1997; Living Ginger. EDITOR/CO-EDITOR: Recent Poetry in New Zealand, 1965; William Carlos Williams: The Critical Heritage, 1980; The New Reality: The Politics of Restraint in British Columbia, 1984; Wallace Stevens: The Critical Heritage, 1985; After Bennett: A New Politics for British Columbia, 1986; Richard Aldington: Reappraisals, 1990. **Address:** 641 Oliver St, Victoria, BC, Canada V8S 4W2. **Online address:** doylec@uvic.ca

DOYLE, Dale. *See* **DOYLE, Paul A.**

DOYLE, Debra. Also writes as Nicholas Adams, Victor Appleton, Martin DelRio, Robyn Tallis. American, b. 1952. **Genres:** Science fiction/Fantasy. **Career:** Science fiction and fantasy novelist. Computer Assisted Learning Center, teacher of fiction writing. **Publications:** ALL WITH J. D. MACDONALD. CIRCLE OF MAGIC SERIES: School of Wizardry, 1990; Tournament and Tower, 1990; City by the Sea, 1990; The Prince's Players, 1990; The Prisoners of Bell Castle, 1990; The High King's Daughter, 1990. MAGEWORLDS SERIES: The Price of the Stars, 1992; Starpilot's Grave, 1993; By Honor Betray'd, 1994; The Gathering Flame, 1995; The Long Hunt, 1996. BAD BLOOD SERIES: Bad Blood, 1993; Hunters' Moon, 1994; Judgment Night, 1995. OTHER NOVELS: Timecrime Inc., 1991; Night of the Living Rat, 1992; Knight's Wyrd, 1992; Groogleman, 1996. NOVELS AS ROBYN TALLIS: Night of Ghosts and Lightning, 1989; Zero-Sum Games, 1989. NOVELS AS NICHOLAS ADAMS: Pep Rally, 1991. NOVELS AS VICTOR APPLETON: Monster Machine, 1991; Aquatech Warriors, 1991. NOVELS AS MARTIN DELRIO: Mortal Kombat (movie novelizations: adult and young adult versions), 1995; Spider-Man Super-Thriller: Midnight Justice, 1996; Spider-Man SuperThriller: Global War, 1996; Prince Valiant (movie novelization), 1997. Contributor of short stories to anthologies. **Address:** 127 Main St, Colebrook, NH 03576, U.S.A.

DOYLE, Dennis M(ichael). (born United States), b. 1952. **Genres:** Theology/Religion. **Career:** Educator. University of Dayton, Dayton, OH, professor of religious studies, 1984-. **Publications:** The Church Emerging from Vatican II: A Popular Approach to Contemporary Catholicism, 1992, revised edition, 2002; Communion Ecclesiology, 2000; (with son, Patrick Doyle) Rumors at School, 2000; Contributor to periodicals. **Address:** 362 Marathon Ave., Department of Religious Studies, Dayton, OH 45406, U.S.A. **Online address:** Dennis.Doyle@notes.udayton.edu

DOYLE, Mike. *See* **DOYLE, Charles (Desmond).**

DOYLE, Paul A. Also writes as Dale Doyle. American, b. 1925. **Genres:** Novellas/Short stories, Poetry, Literary criticism and history, Bibliography. **Career:** Fordham University, Bronx, NY, Assistant Professor of English, 1948-60; St. John's University, Jamaica, NY, Associate Professor, 1960-62;

State University of New York, Nassau College, Professor of English, 1962-. Best Sellers, Contributing Ed., 1962-84; Choice, Consultant, 1966-94; Evelyn Waugh Newsletter and Studies, Managing Editor, 1967-98, Editor Emeritus, 2002-; NASSAU Review, Managing Editor, 1970-; literary critic. **Publications:** (co-author) Basic College Skills, 2 vols., 1958; Pearl S. Buck, 1965; (co-author) How to Read More Effectively, 1966; Evelyn Waugh: An Introduction, 1968; Sean O'Faolain, 1968; Liam O'Flaherty, 1971; Paul Vincent Carroll: A Critical Introduction, 1972; Guide to Basic Bibliography in English Literature, 1976; A Reader's Companion to Evelyn Waugh's Novels and Short Stories, 1989; (co-author) Early American Trains, 1993. EDITOR/ CO-EDITOR: Alexander Pope's Iliad: An Examination, 1960; Readings in Pharmacy, 1962; A Concordance to the Collected Poems of James Joyce, 1966; Henry David Thoreau: Studies and Commentaries, 1972; Liam O'Flaherty: An Annotated Bibliography, 1972; Evelyn Waugh: A Checklist of Primary and Secondary Criticism, 1972; A Bibliography of Evelyn Waugh, 1986. Contributor to reference books and periodicals. **Address:** 161 Park Ave, Williston Park, NY 11596, U.S.A.

DOYLE, Paul I(gnatius). American, b. 1959. **Genres:** Business/Trade/ Industry. **Career:** Delta Management Group, Portland, OR, vice-president, 1987-92; Donnelly Corp., Holland, MI, operations development manager, 1992-. **Publications:** (with R.J. Doyle) Gain-Management: A Process for Building Teamwork, Productivity, and Profitability throughout Your Organization, 1991. Contributor to periodicals. **Address:** 743 Crestview St., Holland, MI 49423-7317, U.S.A.

DOYLE, Robert C. American, b. 1946. **Genres:** History, Military/Defense/ Arms control, Documentaries/Reportage. **Career:** Professional musician and band leader, 1972-86; Bob Doyle Talent Agency, owner, 1978-86; Pennsylvania State University, University Park, American studies program, department of English, lecturer, 1987-94; Wilhelms University, Munster, Germany, department of English, Fulbright lecturer, 1994-95; Marc Bloch University, Strasbourg, France, American studies, visiting professor, 1995-98; Franciscan University, Steubenville, OH, associate professor of history, 2000-; guest on radio and television programs. **Publications:** Voices from Captivity: Interpreting the American POW Narrative, 1994; A Prisoner's Duty: Great Escapes in U.S. Military History, 1997. Contributor of articles and reviews to periodicals. **Address:** 1317 Ridge Ave, Steubenville, OH 43952, U.S.A. **Online address:** bdoyle@uov.net

DOYLE, Robert J. American, b. 1931. **Genres:** Administration/ Management. **Career:** Ford Motor Co., Cincinnati, OH, personnel administrator, 1957-64; Wolverine World Wide, Rockford, MI, training director, 1964-67; Donnelly Mirrors Inc., Holland, MI, director of human resources, 1967-74; Precision Castparts Corp., Portland, OR, director of personnel, 1974-75; Hay Associates, Seattle, WA, principal, 1975-77; Delta Management Group, Portland, OR, president, 1977-. Scanlon Plan Associates, co-founder and past president. **Publications:** Gainsharing and Productivity, 1983; (with P.I. Doyle) Gain-Management: A Process for Building Teamwork, Productivity, and Profitability throughout Your Organization, 1992. **Address:** 3617 224th Pl SE, Issaquah, OR 98029, U.S.A. **Online address:** rjd@aol.com

DOYLE, Roddy. Irish, b. 1958. **Genres:** Novels, Plays/Screenplays. **Career:** Lecturer at universities, playwright, screenwriter, and novelist. **Publications:** NOVELS: The Commitments, 1988; The Snapper, 1990; The Van, 1991; Paddy Clarke Ha Ha Ha, 1993 (Booker Prize); The Woman Who Walked into Doors, 1996. THE LAST ROUNDUP SERIES: A Star Called Henry, 1999. SCREENPLAYS: (with D. Clement and I. La Frenais) The Commitments, 1991; The Snapper, 1993. PLAYS: Brown Bread, 1992; USA, 1992. FOR CHILDREN: Giggler Treatment, 2000; Rover Saves Christmas, 2001. **Address:** c/o Secker and Warburg, 20 Vauxhall Bridge Rd, London SW1V 2SA, England.

DOYLE, William. British, b. 1942. **Genres:** History. **Career:** University of York, Lecturer, 1967-78, Sr. Lecturer in History, 1978-81; University of Nottingham, Professor of History, 1981-85, Dept. Head, 1982-85; University of Bristol, Professor of History, 1986-, Dept. Head, 1986-90. British Academy, Fellow, 1998. **Publications:** The Parlement of Bordeaux and the End of the Old Regime, 1771-1790, 1974; The Old European Order, 1660-1800, 1978, 2nd ed., 1992; Origins of the French Revolution, 1980, rev. ed., 1998; (trans.) The French Nobility in the Eighteenth Century: From Feudalism to Enlightenment, by Guy Chaussinand-Nogaret, 1985; The Ancien Regime, 1986; The Oxford History of the French Revolution, 1989; Officers, Nobles and Revolutionaries, 1995; Venality, The Sale of Offices in Eighteenth Century France, 1996; Jansenism, 2000; Old Regime France, 2001; The French Revolution: A Very Short Introduction, 2001. CO-EDITOR: The

Blackwell Dictionary of Historians, 1988; The Impact of the French Revolution on European Consciousness, 1989. **Address:** Department of Historical Studies, University of Bristol, 13 Woodland Rd, Bristol BS8 1TB, England. **Online address:** william.doyle@bristol.ac.uk

DOZIER, Zoe. *See* **BROWNING, Dixie Burrus.**

DRABBLE, Margaret. British, b. 1939. **Genres:** Novels, Young adult fiction, Plays/Screenplays, Literary criticism and history, Biography. **Publications:** A Summer Bird-Cage, 1963; The Garrick Year, 1964; The Millstone, 1965; Wordsworth, 1966; Jerusalem the Golden, 1967; The Waterfall, 1969; Bird of Paradise (play), 1969; Touch of Love (screenplay), 1969; The Needle's Eye, 1972; Arnold Bennett, 1974; The Realms of Gold, 1975; The Ice Age, 1977; For Queen and Country (juvenile), 1978; A Writer's Britain, 1979; The Middle Ground, 1980; (ed.) The Oxford Companion to English Literature, 1985, rev. ed., 2000; The Radiant Way, 1987; A Natural Curiosity, 1989; The Gates of Ivory, 1991; Angus Wilson: A Biography, 1995; The Witch of Exmoor (novel), 1996; The Peppered Moth (novel), 2001; The Seven Sisters, 2002. **Address:** c/o PFD, Drury House, 34-43 Russell St, London WC2B 5HA, England.

DRACKETT, Phil(ip Arthur). Also writes as Paul King. British, b. 1922. **Genres:** Novellas/Short stories, Westerns/Adventure, Children's fiction, Children's non-fiction, Sports/Fitness, Theatre, Travel/Exploration, Biography. **Career:** Royal Automobile Club, Press and Public Relations, director; local and national newspapers and magazines, writer and broadcaster. **Publications:** Fighting Days, 1942; (with M. Wells) Come Out Fighting, 1944; Speedway, 1951; Motor Racing, 1952; Motoring, 1955; (with L. Webb) You and Your Car, 1958; Great Moments in Motoring, 1958; (with A. Thompson) You and Your Motorcycle 1959; Automobiles Work Like This, 1960; Veteran Cars, 1961; Motor Rallying, 1963; Passing the Test, 1964; Young Car Drivers' Companion, 1964; (as Paul King) Taking Your Car Abroad, 1965; Let's Look at Cars, 1966; Slot Car Racing, 1968; Like Father, Like Son, 1969; Rally of the Forests, 1970; Car Care Tips, 1973; Book of the Veteran Car, 1973; Purnell Book of Great Disasters, 1978; Purnell Book of Dangermen, 1979; Wonderful World of Cars, 1979; Inns and Harbours of North Norfolk, 1980; The Car Makers, 1980; The Story of the RAC International Rally, 1980; Vintage Cars, 1981; The Classic Mercedes-Benz, 1983; Brabham: Story of a Racing Team, 1985; Flashing Blades: The Story of British Ice Hockey, 1987; They Call It Courage: Story of the Segrave Trophy, 1990; Benetton-Ford: A Racing Partnership, 1990, rev. ed., 1992; Vendetta on Ice, 1993; (with J. Kemsley) Just Another Incident, 1994; Champions on Ice, 2000. EDITOR: International Motor Racing, 4 vols., 1969-72; Motor Racing Champions, 2 vols., 1973-74; Encyclopaedia of the Motor Car, 1979. Contributor to sports and other encyclopedias. **Address:** Seafret Cottage, 9 Victoria Rd, Mundesley-on-Sea, Norwich NR11 8JG, England.

DRACUP, Angela. Also writes as Caroline Sibson, Angela Drake. British, b. 1943. **Genres:** Novels, Romance/Historical, Young adult fiction. **Career:** Freelance chartered educational psychologist. Educational psychologist in Bradford, England, 1964-72, in Leeds, England, 1975-78, and in North Yorkshire, England, 1981-. Senior lecturer at the College of Ripon and York St. John, 1975-78. **Publications:** AS CAROLINE SIBSON: The Chosen One, 1988; Birds of a Feather, 1990. AS ANGELA DRACUP: The Placing, 1991; The Split, 1993; The Ultimate Gift, 2000; Voices from the Past, 2000. RAINBOW ROMANCE SERIES: An Independent Spirit, 1984; Bavarian Overture, 1986; A Tender Ambition, 1986; A Man to Trust, 1987; Dark Impulse, 1987; Star Attraction, 1988; Dearest Pretender, 1989; Venetian Captive, 1989. AS ANGELA DRAKE: The Mistress Woman of Dreams, 1996; Mozart's Darling, 1996; Master of Destiny, 2000; Stay Very Close, 2001. **Address:** 6 Lancaster Rd, Harrogate, N. Yorkshire HG2 0EZ, England. **Online address:** frank@fdracup.freeserve.co.uk

DRAKE, Albert (Dee). American, b. 1935. **Genres:** Novels, Novellas/Short stories, Poetry. **Career:** Oregon Research Institute, Eugene, research assistant, 1963-64; University of Oregon, teaching assistant, 1965-66; Michigan State University, East Lansing, professor emeritus of English (joined faculty, 1966). **Publications:** (ed.) Michigan Signatures, 1969; Three Northwest Poets, 1970; Riding Bike, 1973; The Postcard Mysteries, 1976; Tillamook Burn, 1977; In the Time of Surveys, 1978; One Summer, 1979; Beyond the Pavement, 1981; The Big Little GTO Book, 1982; Street Was Fun in '51, 1982; I Remember the Day James Dean Died and Other Stories, 1983; Homesick, 1987; Herding Goats, 1989; Hot Rodder!, 1992; Flat Out, 1994; Fifties Flashback, 1997; Overtures to Motion, 2003. **Address:** 9727 SE Reedway St, Portland, OR 97266-3738, U.S.A.

DRAKE, Angela. *See* **DRACUP, Angela.**

DRAKE, Bonnie. *See* **DELINSKY, Barbara (Ruth Greenberg).**

DRAKE, Charles D. British, b. 1924. **Genres:** Law. **Career:** Professor of English Law, University, of Leeds, since 1972 (Dean, Faculty of Law, 1974-78; Head of Dept., 1979-82). Visiting Professor, University of South Carolina, Columbia, 1978-79, and Vanderbilt University, Nashville, Tennessee, 1981, 1985-86; ILO Expert, Mission to Fiji Islands, 1981. **Publications:** Law of Partnership, 1972, 1976; Labour Law, 2nd ed., 1973, 3rd ed. 1981; (with B. Bercusson) The Employment Acts 1974-1980, 1981; (with F. Wright) Law of Health and Safety at Work, 1982; Trade Union Acts, 1985. **Address:** 4 North Lane, Roundhay, Leeds LS8 2QJ, England.

DRAKE, David A. American, b. 1945. **Genres:** Novels, Novellas/Short stories, Science fiction/Fantasy. **Career:** Freelance writer, 1981-. Assistant town attorney, Chapel Hill, 1972-80. **Publications:** The Dragon Lord, 1979; Time Safari, 1982; Skyripper, 1983; The Forlorn Hope, 1984; Cross the Stars, 1984; Birds of Prey, 1984; (with K.E. Wagner) Killer, 1984; (with J. Morris) Active Measures, 1985; Bridgehead, 1985; At Any Price, 1985; Ranks of Bronze, 1986; Counting the Cost, 1987; (with J. Morris) Kill Ratio, 1987; Fortress, 1987; Dagger, 1988; The Sea Hag, 1988; Rolling Hot, 1989; (with J. Morris) Target, 1989; (with J. Morris) Explorers in Hell, 1989; Northworld, 1990; Surface Action, 1990; (with J. Kjelgaard) The Hunter Returns, 1991; Vengeance, 1991; The Warrior, 1991; The Jungle, 1991; Old Nathan, 1991; Justice, 1992; Starliner, 1992; The Square Deal, 1992; The Sharp End, 1993; The Voyage, 1994; Igniting the Reaches, 1994; Through the Breach, 1995; (with J. Morris) Arc Riders, 1995; Fireships, 1996; (with J. Morris) The Fourth Rome, 1996; Redliners, 1996; Patriots, 1996; Lord of the Isles, 1997; With the Lightnings, 1998; Queen of Demons, 1998; Servant of the Dragon, 1999; Lt. Leary, Commanding, 2000; Mistress of the Catacombs, 2001; Paying the Piper, 2002; Goddess of the Ice Realm, 2003; The Far Side of the Stars, 2003. STORIES: Hammer's Slammers, 1979; From the Heart of Darkness, 1983; Lacey and His Friends, 1986; Vettius and His Friends, 1989; The Military Dimension, 1991; All the Way to the Gallows, 1996; Grimmer than Hell, 2003. EDITOR: Men Hunting Things, 1988; Things Hunting Men, 1988; (with B. Fawcett) The Fleet, 1988; (with B. Fawcett) Counterattack, 1988; (with B. Fawcett) Breakthrough, 1989; (with S. Miesel) A Separate Star, 1989; (with M.H. Greenberg and C. Waugh) Space Gladiators, 1989; (with S. Miesel) Heads to the Storm, 1989; (with M.H. Greenberg and C. Waugh) Space Infantry, 1989; (with M.H. Greenberg and C. Waugh) Space Dreadnaughts, 1990; Bluebloods, 1990; (with B. Fawcett) Sworn Allies, 1990; (with B. Fawcett) Total War, 1990; (with M.H. Greenberg and C. Waugh) The Eternal City, 1990; (with B. Fawcett) Crisis, 1991; (with B. Fawcett) Battlestation, 1992; (with B. Fawcett) Vanguard, 1993; Dogs of War, 2002. **Address:** Box 904, Chapel Hill, NC 27514, U.S.A. **Online address:** DAD@david_drake.com

DRAKE, Jane. Canadian, b. 1954. **Genres:** Children's non-fiction, Recreation, Environmental sciences/Ecology. **Career:** Author of nonfiction books for children. **Publications:** (with A. Love) Take Action: An Environmental Book for Kids, 1992; (with Love) The Kids' Cottage Book, 1993, in UK as The Kids' Summer Handbook, 1994. **Address:** 95 Ridge Dr., Toronto, ON, Canada M4T 1B6. **Online address:** jane.drake@sympatico.ca

DRAKE, Timothy A. Also writes as Lance Haataja, Robert Pierce. American, b. 1967. **Genres:** Theology/Religion. **Career:** Circle Media, North Haven, CT, features correspondent, 1999-, managing editor, 2001-; Envoy Magazine, Hebron, OH, contributing editor, 2000-. Spirit '93 Fund, chairman of advisory board, 2001-. **Publications:** (with P. Madrid) Suprised by Truth 2, 2000; (with L. Nordhagen) When Only One Converts, 2001; There We Stood, Here We Stand: Eleven Lutherans Rediscover Their Catholic Roots, 2001. EDITOR: (with H. Graham) Where We Got the Bible, 1997; (with C. Hartman) Physicians Healed, 1998; (with P. Madrid) Where Is That in the Bible?, 2001. Contributor to magazines and publications. Also uses pseudonyms Lance Haataja and Robert Pierce. **Address:** 2009 13th Street South, Saint Cloud, MN 56301, U.S.A. **Online address:** timd@astound.net

DRAKULIĆ, Slavenka. Croatian (born Yugoslavia), b. 1949. **Genres:** Novels, History. **Career:** Journalist and writer. **Publications:** Smrtni grijesi feminizma: ogled o mudologiji, 1984; Hologrami straha (novel), 1988, trans. as Holograms of Fear, 1992; Mramorna koža (novel), 1989, trans. as Marble Skin, 1994; How We Survived Communism and Even Laughed, 1991; Balkan Express: Fragments from the Other Side of War, 1993; Café Europa, 1996; Boeanska Glad trans. as The Taste of a Man, 1997; S: A Novel about the Balkans, 2000. **Address:** c/o W. W. Norton, 500 Fifth Ave., New York, NY 10110, U.S.A.

DRAPER, Alfred Ernest. British, b. 1924. **Genres:** Novels, Biography, History. **Career:** Formerly journalist, Daily Herald, Daily Mail, BBC, and

Daily Express, London. **Publications:** Swansong for a Rare Bird, 1969; The Death Penalty, 1972; Smoke Without Fire (biography), 1974; The Prince of Wales, 1975; The Story of the Goons, 1976; Operation Fish, 1978; Amritsar, 1981; Grey Seal, 5 vols., 1981-85; The Con Man, 1987; Dawns Like Thunder, 1987; Scoops and Swindles, 1988; Tanky Challenor: SAS and The Met, 1989; A Crimson Splendour, 1991; Operation Midas, 1993. **Address:** 31 Oakridge Ave, Radlett, Herts. WD7 8EW, England.

DRAPER, Hastings. *See* **JEFFRIES, Roderic.**

DRAPER, Maureen McCarthy. American, b. 1941. **Genres:** Music, Medicine/Health. **Career:** Hillsborough, CA, English and Latin teacher, 1971-73; Palo Alto, CA, piano teacher, 1973-98; San Francisco and Cupertino, CA, music and poetry seminar and retreat leader, 1980-; Fine Arts Museum, San Francisco, art docent, 1987-92; Stanford Hospital, Palo Alto, coordinator of music for healing, 2001-; music consultant. **Publications:** The Nature of Music: Beauty, Sound, and Healing, 2001; The Nature of Music (companion CDs), Vol. 1: Morning Music, Vol. 2: After Hours, 2001. **Address:** 18800 Montebellow Rd., Cupertino, CA 95014, U.S.A. **Online address:** modraper@ridgewine.com

DRAPER, Robert. American, b. 1959?. **Genres:** Biography. **Career:** Writer and editor, Texas Monthly; staff writer, GQ. **Publications:** ZZ Top, 1985; Huey Lewis and the News, 1986; Rolling Stone Magazine: The Uncensored History, 1990; Hadrian's Walls (novel), 1999. **Address:** c/o Author Mail, Knopf Publishing, 1745 Broadway, New York, NY 10019, U.S.A.

DRAPER, Sharon Mills. American. **Genres:** Children's fiction, Young adult fiction, Social sciences. **Career:** Walnut Hills High School, Cincinnati, OH, English teacher and head of the English Department, 1970-; associate at Mayerson Academy for professional development of teachers. **Publications:** Tears of a Tiger, 1994; Ziggy and the Black Dinosaurs, 1994; Ziggy and the Black Dinosaurs: Lost in the Tunnel of Time, 1996; Forged by Fire, 1997; Shadows of Caesar's Creek, 1997; Romiette and Julio, 1999; Jazzimagination, a Journal to Read and Write, 2000; Teaching from the Heart (essays), 2000; Not Quite Burned Out but Crispy around the Edges (essays), 2001; Darkness before Dawn, 2001; Double Dutch, 2002. Contributor to books. **Address:** c/o Janell Agyeman, Marie Brown Associates Inc., 990 NE 82 Terrace, Miami, FL 33138, U.S.A.

DRAPER, Theodore. American, b. 1912. **Genres:** History, International relations/Current affairs, Military/Defense/Arms control, Politics/Government. **Career:** Writer. **Publications:** The Six Weeks' War, 1944; The 84th Infantry Division in the Battle of Germany, 1946; The Roots of American Communism, 1957; American Communism and Soviet Russia, 1960; Castro's Revolution: Myths and Realities, 1962; Castroism, Theory and Practice, 1965; Abuse of Power, 1967; Israel and World Politics: The Roots of the Third Arab-Israeli War, 1968; The Dominican Revolt, 1968; The Rediscovery of Black Nationalism, 1970; Present History, 1983; A Present of Things Past, 1990; A Very Thin Line: The Iran-Contra Affair, 1991; A Struggle for Power: The American Revolution, 1996. **Address:** 35 Linwood Circle, Princeton, NJ 08540, U.S.A.

DRAWE, D. Lynn. American, b. 1942. **Genres:** Botany, Environmental sciences/Ecology. **Career:** Texas A & I University, Kingsville, assistant professor of agriculture, 1970-74; Welder Wildlife Foundation, Sinton, TX, assistant director, 1974-98, director, 1999-. Private rancher; consultant on rangeland ecology and ecosystem management. **Publications:** (with J. Everitt) Trees, Shrubs, and Cacti of South Texas, 1993; (with S. Hatch and J. Schuster) Grasses of the Texas Gulf Coastal Prairies and Marshes, 1999; (with J. Everitt and R. Lonard) Broad-Leaved Herbaceous Plants of South Texas, 1999. Contributor to scientific journals. **Address:** Welder Wildlife Foundation, PO Box 1400, Sinton, TX 78387, U.S.A. **Online address:** welderwf@aol.com

DRAY, Philip. American. **Genres:** Documentaries/Reportage. **Career:** Educator and historian. New School University, New York, NY, professor of African-American history. **Publications:** (with S. Cagin) Hollywood Films of the Seventies: Sex, Drugs, Violence, Rock 'n' Roll, and Politics, 1984, as Born to Be Wild: Hollywood and the Sixties Generation, 1994; (with S. Cagin) We Are Not Afraid: The Story of Goodman, Schwerner, and Chaney and the Civil Rights Campaign for Mississippi, 1988; (with S. Cagin) Between Earth and Sky: How CFCs Changed Our World and Endangered the Ozone Layer, 1993; At the Hands of Persons Unknown: The Lynching of Black America, 2002. Contributor to periodicals. **Address:** c/o Author Mail, Random House, 1745 Broadway, New York, NY 10019, U.S.A.

DRAZIN, Israel. American, b. 1935. **Genres:** Theology/Religion. **Career:** Ordained rabbi, 1957; weekend rabbi of Jewish congregations in Randallstown, MD, Baltimore, MD, and Columbia, MD, until mid 1970s. Drazin & Drazin (law firm), Columbia, senior partner, 1974-98. **Publications:** Targumic Studies, 1981; Targum Onkelos to Deuteronomy, 1983; Targum Onkelos to Exodus, 1988; (ed.) Nathan Drazin, Legends Worth Living, 1991; Targum Onkelos to Leviticus, 1993; (with C. Curey) For God and Country, 1995; Targum Onkelos to Numbers, 1996. Contributor to scholarly and popular magazines. **Address:** Ikon Building Ste 100, 10420 Little Patuxent Parkway, Columbia, MD 21044, U.S.A. **Online address:** IDDrazin@aol.com

DR. BASEBALL. *See* **BJARKMAN, Peter C(hristian).**

DREHER, Henry. American, b. 1955. **Genres:** Medicine/Health, Administration/Management, Psychology, Social commentary, Sports/Fitness, Autobiography/Memoirs. **Career:** Health and medical writer in NYC. **Publications:** Your Defense against Cancer, 1989; (with L. Temoshok) The Type C Connection: The Mind-Body Links to Cancer and Your Health, 1992; The Immune Power Personality: Seven Traits You Can Develop to Stay Healthy, 1995; (with A.D. Domar) Healing Mind, Healthy Woman, 1996; (with J. Torre) Joe Torre's Ground Rules for Winners, 1999; (with A.D. Domar) Self-Nurture, 1999; (with S. Chiel) For Thou Art with Me: The Healing Power of Psalms, 2000. CHILDREN'S BOOKS: Great Sports Thrills; Beware: This House Is Haunted!. Contributor to periodicals. **Address:** 84 E. Third St. No. 2C, New York, NY 10003, U.S.A.

DRESSER, Norine. Also writes as Jessie Lattimore, Margaret N. Stone. American, b. 1931. **Genres:** Novellas/Short stories, Cultural/Ethnic topics, Mythology/Folklore. **Career:** California State University, Los Angeles, (retired) teacher of American folklore, American pop culture, basic writing, freshman composition, and American food ways, 1972-; Research associate at Center for the Study of Comparative Folklore and Mythology, University of California, Los Angeles, 1985-91. **Publications:** (as Margaret N. Stone with G.I. Sugarman) Your Hyperactive Child, 1974; (as Jessie Lattimore with M. Fontes) High Contrast, 1988; American Vampires, 1989; Our Own Stories: Cross-Cultural Communication Practice, 1993; I Felt Like I was from Another Planet, 1993. **Address:** Multicultural Issues, Los Angeles Times, 202 W 1st St, Los Angeles, CA 90012, U.S.A. **Online address:** mickeyimc@aol.com

DRESSLER, Alan (Michael). American, b. 1948. **Genres:** Air/Space topics. **Career:** Hale Observatory, Pasadena, CA, Carnegie Institution of Washington fellow, 1976-78, Las Campanas fellow, 1978-81; Carnegie Institution of Washington, member of scientific staff at Mt. Wilson and Las Campanas observatories, 1981-, acting associate director, 1988-89. **Publications:** Voyage to the Great Attractor: A Journey through Intergalactic Space, 1994. **Address:** Carnegie Observatory, 813 Santa Barbara St., Pasadena, CA 91101, U.S.A.

DRESSLER, Joshua. American, b. 1947. **Genres:** Law. **Career:** Hamline University, St. Paul, MN, professor of law, 1977-82; Wayne State University, Detroit, MI, professor of law, 1982-93; McGeorge School of Law, Sacramento, CA, professor of law, 1993-2001; Ohio State University, Columbus, Frank R. Strong Chair in Law, 2001-. Ohio State Journal of Criminal Law, managing editor. **Publications:** Understanding Criminal Law, 1987, 3rd ed., 2001; Understanding Criminal Procedure, 1991, 3rd ed., 2002; Cases and Materials on Criminal Law, 1994, 3rd ed., 2003; Criminal Procedure: Principles, Policies and Perspectives, 1999, 2nd ed., 2003. Contributor to legal journals. **Address:** Moritz College of Law, Ohio State University, 55 W 12th St, Columbus, OH 43210, U.S.A. **Online address:** dressler.11@osu.edu

DREW, Bettina. American, b. 1956. **Genres:** Literary criticism and history. **Career:** City College of the City University of New York, NYC, lecturer in English, 1981-90; New York University, NYC, lecturer in humanities, 1990-93; writer, 1993-. West Side Young Men's Christian Association (YMCA), workshop instructor at Writer's Voice, 1994-95; Yale University, instructor, 1995; lecturer at Mercy College, Bronx Community College, and New York Technical College; gives readings from her works. **Publications:** Nelson Algren: A Life on the Wild Side, 1989; (ed.) The Texas Stories of Nelson Algren, 1995; Travels in Expendable Landscapes (essays), in press. Author of the unpublished screenplay "My Own Simone." Contributor of poems, articles, and reviews to magazines and newspapers. **Address:** 2 Mayflower Cir., Shrewsbury, MA 01545-2863, U.S.A.

DREW, Horace R., III. Also writes as Red Rabbit. British, b. 1955. **Genres:** Medicine/Health. **Career:** Medical Research Council Laboratory, Cambridge,

England, staff member, 1981-86; CJIRA Molecular Science, New South Wales, Australia, principal research scientist, 1987-. **Publications:** Understanding DNA, 1992, 2nd ed., 1996. Author of magazine articles. Some writings appear under the pseudonym Red Rabbit. **Address:** 125 Charles St., Putney, NSW 2112, Australia.

DREW, Philip. Australian, b. 1943. **Genres:** Architecture, Cultural/Ethnic topics, Design, Regional/Urban planning. **Career:** Australian Correspondent, Architecture and Urbanism, Tokyo, since 1978. Technical Ed., The Architectural Press., London, 1970-71; Sr. Lecturer in Architecture, University of Newcastle, N. S. W., 1974-82; Associate Professor, Washington University, St. Louis, 1982-83; Fellow, Literature Board of Australia Council, 1989-90; Philip Drew is the design critic, Business Review Weekly magazine, currently. **Publications:** Third Generation: The Changing Meaning of Architecture, 1973; Frei Otto: Form and Structure, 1976; Tensile Architecture, 1979; Two Towers: Harry Seidler, 1980; The Architecture of Arata Isozaki, 1982; Leaves of Iron: Glenn Murcutt, Pioneer of an Australian Architectural Form, 1985; (with K. Frampton) Harry Seidler: Four Decades of Architecture, 1992; Veranda: Embracing Place, 1992; Real Space: The Architecture of Martorell, Bohigas, Mackay, Puigdomenech, 1993; The Coast Dwellers: Australians Living on the Edge, 1994; Sydney Opera House, 1995; Edward Suzuki: Buildings & Projects, 1996; Church of the Light, Church on the Water, Tadao Ando, 1996; The Museum of Modern Art, Gunma, Arata Isozaki, 1996; Touch this Earth Lightly: Glenn Murcutt, in His Own Words, 1999; The Masterpiece: Jorn Utzon, a Secret Life, 1999. Author of articles and lectures on tensile, contemporary and Australian architecture. **Address:** 12 View St, Annandale, NSW 2038, Australia.

DREW, Simon. British, b. 1952. **Genres:** Art/Art history. **Career:** Art gallery director and writer. **Publications:** Camp David, 1994; Handel's Warthog Music, 1995; Great Mistakes of Civilisation, 1996; Dogsbodies, 1998. **Address:** 13 Foss St., Dartmouth TQ6 9DR, England. **Online address:** simondrew@co.uk

DREWE, Robert. Australian, b. 1943. **Genres:** Novels, Plays/Screenplays, Novellas/Short stories. **Career:** Journalist: cadet reporter, Perth West Australian, 1961-64; Reporter, 1964-65, and Head of the Sydney Bureau, 1965-70, The Age, Melbourne; daily columnist, 1970-73, Features Ed., 1971-72, and Literary Ed., 1972-74, The Australian, Sydney; Special Writer, 1975-76, and Contributing Ed., 1980-82, The Bulletin, Sydney; Management Committee, Australian Society of Authors, 1973-74; Writer-in-Residence, University of Western Australia, Perth, 1976, 1979; Columnist, Mode, Sydney, 1981-82, and Sydney City Monthly, 1981-83; Writer-in-Residence, La Trobe University, Melbourne, 1986; Literature Board member, Australia Council, 1989-92; Australian Creative Fellow, 1993-96; Who Weekly, film critic, 1992-94. **Publications:** NOVELS: The Savage Crows, 1976; A Cry in the Jungle Bar, 1979; Fortune, 1986; Our Sunshine, 1991; The Drowner, 1995; The Shark Net, 2000. SHORT STORIES: The Bodysurfers, 1983; The Bay of Contented Men, 1989; (ed.) The Picador Book of The Beach, 1993. PLAYS/SCREENPLAYS: The Bodysurfers, 1989; Sweetlip, 1990; South American Barbecue, 1991; Machete, 1993. **Address:** c/o Hickson Assocs. Pty. Ltd, P. O. Box 271, Woollahra, NSW 2025, Australia.

DREWES, Athena A. American, b. 1948. **Genres:** Psychology, Bibliography. **Career:** Maimonides Hospital, Division of Parapsychology and Psychophysics, research assistant, 1969-75; Jewish Board of Family and Children's Services, NYC, Child Development Center, play therapist and psychometrician, 1974-82; Child Study Center, Goshen, NY, play therapist and psychometrician, 1982-85; Warwick Special Education Preschool, Warwick, NY, play therapist and psychometrician, 1985-91; Astor Home for Children, Rhinebeck, NY, senior psychologist/clinical coordinator, 1992-. Guest on radio talk shows. **Publications:** (with S.A. Drucker) Parapsychological Research with Children: An Annotated Bibliography, 1991. Contributor to psychology journals and newspapers. **Address:** Astor Home for Children, 6339 Mill St, PO Box 5005, Rhinebeck, NY 12572, U.S.A. **Online address:** jimbridg@frontiernet.net

DREXLER, Rosalyn. Also writes as Julia Sorel. American. **Genres:** Novels, Plays/Screenplays, Writing/Journalism, Film. **Career:** Painter, sculptor, singer, journalist, currently. **Publications:** NOVELS: I Am the Beautiful Stranger, 1965; One or Another, 1970; To Smithereens, 1972; The Cosmopolitan Girl, 1975; Starburn, 1979; Bad Guy, 1982, 1988; Art Does Not Exist, 1996. AS JULIA SOREL: Unwed Widow, 1975; Rocky, 1976; Dawn, Story of a Teenage Runaway, 1976; Alex, The Other Side of Dawn, 1977; See How She Runs, 1978. ANTHOLOGIES: The Bold New Women, 1966; New American Review, 1969; Wonder, 1980; Black Ice #8, 1992. PLAYS: The Line of Least Existence and Other Plays, 1967; The Investiga-

tion and Hot Buttered Roll, 1969; Transients Welcome, 1984; Dear, 1997. **Address:** c/o Georges Borchardt Inc, 136 E. 57th St, New York, NY 10022, U.S.A.

DREYER, Eileen. (born United States), b. 1952. **Genres:** Novels. **Career:** Author. Sixteen years' experience as a trauma and forensic nurse death investigator. **Publications:** CRIME NOVELS: A Man to Die For, 1991; If Looks Could Kill, 1992; Nothing Personal, 1993; Bad Medicine, 1995; Brain Dead, 1997; With a Vengeance, 2003; Head Games (sequel to Bad Medicine), 2004. ROMANCE NOVELS; UNDER PSEUDONYM KATHLEEN KORBEL: Playing the Game, 1986; A Stranger's Smile, 1986; Worth Any Risk, 1987; A Prince of a Guy, 1987; Edge of the World, 1988; The Princess and the Pea, 1988; The Road to Mandalay, 1989; Perchance to Dream, 1989; The Ice Cream Man, 1989; Hotshot, 1990; Lightening Strikes, 1990; A Rose for Maggie, 1991; A Fine Madness, 1991; Jake's Way, 1992; Isn't It Romantic?, 1992; Walk on the Wild Side, 1992; Simple Gifts, 1994; A Soldier's Heart, 1995; Don't Fence Me In, 1996; Sail Away, 1998; Some Men's Dreams, 2003. Contributor of stories to anthologies. **Address:** POB 8614, East 51st. St., St. Louis, MO 63126, U.S.A. **Online address:** eileendreyer@eileendreyer.com

DREZ, Ronald J(oseph). American, b. 1940. **Genres:** History. **Career:** Bonded Carbon and Ribbon Co. Inc., New Orleans, LA, salesperson, 1969-72; Dockside Elevators, New Orleans, operations manager, 1973-82; Delta Transload, New Orleans, general manager, 1982-86; self-employed, 1987-. University of New Orleans Metro College Eisenhower Center, assistant director, 1987-; Stephen Ambrose Tours, president, 1999-. **Publications:** Voices of D-Day, 1994; Twenty Five Yards of War, 2001. **Address:** 8516 Fordham Ct, New Orleans, LA 70127, U.S.A.

DREZE, Jean. Indian (born Belgium), b. 1959. **Genres:** Economics, Politics/Government, Third World. **Career:** University of London, London School of Economics and Political Science, England, lecturer in economics, 1987-88; free-lance development economist, 1988-. **Publications:** (with A. Sen) Hunger and Public Action, 1989; (with A. Sen) India: Economic Development and Social Opportunity, 1995; (with A. Sen) India: Development and Participation, 2002. EDITOR: (with A. Sen) The Political Economy of Hunger, 3 vols., 1990; (with A. Sen) Indian Development: Selected Regional Perspectives, 1997. **Address:** c/o Delhi School of Economics, Delhi 110 007, Delhi, India.

DRIEDGER, Leo. Canadian. **Genres:** Area studies, Cultural/Ethnic topics, Sociology. **Career:** University of Manitoba, Winnipeg, professor of ethnic relations, urban sociology, and sociology of religion, 1966-, now emeritus. Elizabethtown College, fellow at Young Center for the Study of Anabaptist and Pietist Groups, 1991. Royal Society of Canada, fellow. **Publications:** (with N. Chappell) Aging and Ethnicity, 1987; Ethnic Canada, 1987; Mennonite Identity in Conflict, 1988; The Ethnic Factor, 1989; Mennonites in Winnipeg, 1990; (with S. Halli and Trovato) Ethnic Demography, 1990; The Urban Factor, 1991; (with H. Kauffman) The Mennonite Mosaic: Identity and Modernization, 1991; (with D. Kraybill) Mennonite Peacemaking: From Quietism to Activism, 1994; Multi-Ethnic Canada, 1996; (with S. Halli) Immigrant Canada, 1999; Mennonites in the Global Village, 2000; Race and Racism, 2000; Race and Ethnicity; Finding Identities and Equalities, 2003. Contributor to 30 journals. **Address:** Department of Sociology, University of Manitoba, Winnipeg, MB, Canada R3T 2N2.

DRINKWATER, Penny. British, b. 1929. **Genres:** Food and Wine. **Career:** Speaker, writer, critic, currently. **Publications:** To Set Before a King; Time for a Party; Making and Mixing Drinks; Basic Cookery; (with Elaine Self) A Passion for Garlic, 1980. **Address:** 59 Maresfield Gardens, Hampstead, London NW3 5TE, England.

DRISKILL, J. Lawrence. (Larry). American, b. 1920. **Genres:** Children's non-fiction, Cultural/Ethnic topics, Gerontology/Senior issues, Theology/Religion. **Career:** Presbyterian minister and author. Missionary to Japan (Osaka area), 1949-72; Highland Presbyterian Church, Maryville, TN, pastor, 1973-82; interim pastor at Madison Square Presbyterian Church, San Antonio, TX, 1973, Grace Presbyterian Church, Long Beach, CA, 1984-85, and Christ Presbyterian Church, Los Angeles, CA, 1987-89; Nichigo (Japanese-speaking) pastor at First Presbyterian Church, Altadena, CA, 1990-99. Visiting professor, University of Dubuque seminary, 1961-62, and Trinity University, San Antonio, TX, 1972-73; part-time professor, Maryville College, 1974-75. Volunteer with Asian American churches in the Los Angeles area and mission advocate for the San Gabriel Presbytery. **Publications:** Mission Adventures in Many Lands, 1992; (with L.C. Driskill) Japan Diary of Cross-Cultural Mission, 1993; Mission Stories from Around the World,

1994; Cross-Cultural Marriages and the Church: Living the Global Neighbor-hood, 1995; Worldwide Mission Stories for Young People, 1996; (ed. and contrib.) Christmas Stories from Around the World, 1996; Adventures in Senior Living, 1997; (co-author) Kingship in the Bible and Japan's Emperor System, 1998. **Address:** 1420 Santo Domingo Ave, Duarte, CA 91010, U.S.A.

DRIVER, C(harles) J(onathan). British (born Republic of South Africa), b. 1939. **Genres:** Novels, Poetry. **Career:** Full-time writer. President, National Union of South African Students, 1963-64; housemaster, International Sixth Form Centre, Sevenoaks School, Kent, 1968-73; director of sixth-form studies, Matthew Humberstone Comprehensive School, 1973-77; principal, Island School, Hong Kong, 1978-83; headmaster, Berkhamsted School, Hertford-shire, 1983-89; master, Wellington College, Berks., 1989-2000. Member, Literature Panel, Arts Council, 1975-77; chairman, Literature Panel, Lincs. and Humberside Arts Council, 1977; editor, Conference & Common Room, 1993-2000. **Publications:** Elegy for a Revolutionary, 1969; Send War in Our Time, O Lord, 1970; Death of Fathers, 1972; A Messiah of the Last Days, 1974; Patrick Duncan (biography), 1980; Shades of Darkness, 2004. POETRY: (with J. Cope) Occasional Light, 1979; I Live Here Now, 1979; Hong Kong Portraits, 1986; In the Water-Margins, 1994; Holiday Haiku, 1996; Requiem, 1998; So Far, Selected Poems 1960-2004, 2005. Contributor to periodicals. **Address:** Apple Yard Cottage, Mill Ln, Norltiam, London, E. Sussex TN31 6JU, England. **Online address:** jontydriver@hotmail.com

DRLICA, Karl. American, b. 1943. **Genres:** Medicine/Health, Ethics. **Career:** University of California, Davis, postdoctoral fellow in plant pathology and molecular biology, 1971-73; Princeton University, Princeton, NJ, post-doctoral fellow in biochemistry, 1973-76; University of Rochester, NY, assistant professor to associate professor, 1977-85; Public Health Research Institute, NYC, associate member, member, 1985-. New York University, associate research professor, research professor, 1985-; lecturer at colleges and universities. **Publications:** Understanding DNA and Gene Cloning: A Guide for the Curious, 1984, 3rd ed., 1996; Double-Edged Sword: Risks and Opportunities of the Genetic Revolution, 1994. Contributor to books and scientific journals. **Address:** Public Health Research Institute, 455 First Ave., New York, NY 10016, U.S.A.

DROSNIN, Michael. American, b. 1946. **Genres:** Documentaries/Reportage. **Career:** Washington Post, Washington, DC, staff reporter, 1966-68; Wall Street Journal, NYC, staff reporter, 1969-70; freelance journalist, 1970-. **Publications:** NONFICTION: Citizen Hughes, 1985; The Bible Code, 1997; Bible Code II: The Countdown, 2002. **Address:** c/o John Brockman, Brockman Inc., 5 East 59th St., New York, NY 10022, U.S.A.

DRUCKER, Johanna. American, b. 1952. **Genres:** Art/Art history. **Career:** University of Texas at Dallas, assistant professor, 1986-88; Harvard University, Cambridge, MA, faculty fellow in art history, 1988-89; Columbia University, NYC, assistant professor of modern art, 1989-94; Yale University, New Haven, CT, associate professor of contemporary art, 1994-. Feminist Art and Art History Conference, coordinator, 1995-96; work represented in special collections in the United States and abroad. **Publications:** Dark, the Bat Elf, 1972; As No Storm, 1975; Twenty-Six '76 Let Hers, 1976; From A to Z: The Our An Bibliography, 1977; Fragile, 1977; The Surprize Party, 1977; Netherland: (How) So Far, 1978; Experience of the Medium, 1978; Kidz, 1980; Jane Goes Out W' the Scouts, 1980; 'S Crap 'S Ample, 1980; Italy, The Figures, 1980; Dolls of the Spirit, 1981; It Happens Pretty Fast, 1982; Tongues, 1982; Just As, 1983; Against Fiction, 1983; Spectacle, 1984; Through Light and the Alphabet, 1986; (with E. McVarish) Sample Dialogue, 1989; The Word Made Flesh, 1989; Simulant Portrait, 1990; The History of the/My Wor(l)d, 1990; (with B. Freeman) OTHERSPACE: Martian Ty/opography, 1993; Theorizing Modernism, 1994; The Visible Word, 1994; Dark Decade (fiction), 1994; Narratology, 1994; Three Early Fictions, Potes and Poets Press, 1994; The Alphabetic Labyrinth, 1995; The Century of Artists' Books, 1995; The Current Line, 1996. Work represented in anthologies. Contributor to periodicals. **Address:** Department of the History of Art, Yale University, PO Box 208272, New Haven, CT 06515, U.S.A.

DRUCKER, Mort. American, b. 1929. **Genres:** Humor/Satire, Illustrations, Picture/board books. **Career:** National Periodicals, New York City, staff artist, 1948-50; free-lance commercial artist, 1951-. Mad magazine, contributing artist, 1956-. Humorous illustrations represented in permanent collections. Guest on television programs. Speaker at colleges and universities. **Publications:** (with P. Laikin) The JFK Coloring Book, 1961; Mort Drucker's Show-stoppers, 1985; (with P. Laikin) The Ollie North Coloring Book, 1987; Familiar Faces: The Art of Mort Drucker, 1988; (with P. Laikin) The Ronald Reagan Coloring Book, 1988; (with L.J. Ames) Draw Fifty Famous Caricatures, 1990. ILLUSTRATOR: Whitefish Will Rides Again, 1994; Tomatoes from Mars, 1999.

DRUCKER, Olga Levy. American (born Germany), b. 1927. **Genres:** Autobiography/Memoirs. **Career:** Audio Video Engineering Company, Merrick, NY, president, 1989-2004. Lecturer at schools, libraries, and synagogues. **Publications:** Kindertransport (young adult autobiography), 1992. Contributor of articles and poetry to periodicals. **Address:** 1 Pineapple Ln, Stuart, FL 34996-6341, U.S.A. **Online address:** odrucker@gate.net

DRUCKER, Peter (Ferdinand). American (born Austria), b. 1909. **Genres:** Novels, Public/Social administration. **Career:** Mgmt. Consultant (own firm), 1940-. Clarke Professor of Social Science and Management, Claremont Graduate School, California, 1971-. Professor of Politics and Philosophy, Bennington College, Vermont, 1942-49; Professor of Mgmt., 1950-72, and Chairman of the Dept., 1956-62, New York University President, Society of History of Technology, 1965-66. **Publications:** The End of Economic Man, 1939; The Future of Industrial Man, 1942; Concept of the Corporation, 1946; The New Society, 1950; The Practice of Management, 1954; America's Next Twenty Years, 1959; The Landmarks of Tomorrow, 1960; Managing for Results, 1964; The Effective Executive, 1966; The Age of Discontinuity, 1969; Technology, Management and Society, 1970; Men, Ideas and Politics, 1971; Management: Tasks, Responsibilities, Practices, 1974; The Unseen Revolution, 1976, as The Pension Fund Revolution, 1995; People and Performance, 1977; Adventures of a Bystander, 1979; Managing in Turbulent Times, 1980; Toward the Next Economics, 1981; The Changing World of the Executive, 1982; The Last of All Possible Worlds (novel), 1982; The Temptation to Do Good (novel), 1984; Innovation and Entrepreneurship, 1986; Frontiers of Management, 1986; The New Realities, 1989; Managing the Nonprofit Organization, 1990; Managing for the Future, 1992; The Ecological Vision, 1992; Post Capitalist Society, 1993; Managing in a Time of Great Change, 1995; Drucker on Asia: A Dialogue with Isao Nakauchi, 1996; Peter Drucker on the Profession of Management, 1998; Management Challenges for the 21st Century, 1999; The Essential Drucker, 2001; The Daily Drucker, 2004.

DRUCKER, Peter. American, b. 1958. **Genres:** Biography. **Career:** National Mobilization for Survival, NYC, program coordinator, 1989-91; International Institute for Research and Education, Amsterdam, Netherlands, co-director, 1993-. Lecturer in history and political science at Polytechnic Institute of New York and New College of California. National Campaign for Peace in the Middle East, co-founder and leader, 1990-91. **Publications:** Max Schachtman and His Left: A Socialist's Odyssey through the "American Century," 1994; (trans.) Catherine Samary, Yugoslavia Dismembered, 1995. Contributor to periodicals. **Address:** International Institute for Research and Education, Willemspark weg 202, 1071 HW Amsterdam, Netherlands.

DRUM, Alice. American, b. 1935. **Genres:** Education. **Career:** American University, Washington, DC, instructor in English, 1976; Antioch University, Columbia, MD, adjunct professor of general studies, 1976-78; Gettysburg College, Gettysburg, PA, adjunct assistant professor of English, 1977-80; Georgetown University, Washington, DC, lecturer in general studies, 1980-81; Hood College, Frederick, MD, assistant professor of English, 1981-85, coordinator of writing program, 1981-83, assistant director of Learning Center, 1982-83, associate dean of academic affairs, 1983-85; Franklin and Marshall College, Lancaster, PA, adjunct associate professor of English, 1985-, dean of freshmen, 198588, vice president of the college, 1988-, dean of educational services, 1988-94. University of Maryland at College Park, lecturer, 1980-83. **Publications:** (with R. Kneedler) Funding a College Education, 1996. Contributor to books. Contributor of articles and poems to periodicals. **Address:** Office of the Vice President, Franklin and Marshall College, Lancaster, PA 17604, U.S.A.

DRUMM, D. B. See **NAHA, Ed.**

DRUMMOND, Edward H. American, b. 1953. **Genres:** Medicine/Health. **Career:** Seacoast Mental Health Center, Portsmouth, NH, associate medical director, 1986-. **Publications:** Overcoming Anxiety without Tranquilizers: A Groundbreaking Program for Treating Chronic Anxiety (also published as Benzo Blues), 1997; The Complete Guide to Psychiatric Drugs: Straight Talk for Best Results, 2000. **Address:** 43 Pine St., Rye, NH 03870, U.S.A. **Online address:** tedd@seacoastmentalhealth.org

DRUMMOND, June. South African, b. 1923. **Genres:** Mystery/Crime/Suspense, Romance/Historical. **Career:** Journalist, Woman's Weekly and Natal Mercury, both in Durban, 1946-48; secretary in London, 1948-50, and with the Durban Civic Orchestra, 1950-53; Assistant Secretary, Church Adoption Society, London, 1954-60; Chairman, Durban Adoption Committee, Indian Child Welfare Society, 1963-74. **Publications:** The Black Unicorn, 1959; Thursday's Child, 1961; A Time to Speak, 1962; A Cage of Humming-

Birds, 1964; Welcome, Proud Lady, 1964; Cable-Car, 1965; The Saboteurs, 1967; The Gantry Episode (in U.S. as Murder on a Bad Trip), 1968; The People in Glass House, 1969; Farewell Party, 1971; Bang! Bang! You're Dead, 1973; The Boon Companions, 1974 (in U.S. as Drop Dead, 1976); Slowly the Poison, 1975; Funeral Urn, 1976; The Patriots, 1979; I Saw Him Die, 1979; Such a Nice Family, 1980; The Trojan Mule, 1982; The Bluestocking, 1985; Junta, 1989; The Unsuitable Miss Pelham, 1990; Burden of Guilt, 1991; The Impostor, 1992; Hidden Agenda, 1993; Loose Cannon, 2003; The Meddlers, 2004. **Address:** W9 Robert Storm House, North Ridge Rd., Durban 4001, Republic of South Africa.

DRURY, John. British, b. 1936. **Genres:** Theology/Religion. **Career:** Cambridge University, Cambridge, England, dean of King's College, 1981-91; Oxford University, Oxford, England, dean of Christ Church, 1991-2003. Writer. **Publications:** Angels and Dirt, 1972; Tradition and Design in Luke's Gospel, 1976; Parables in the Gospels: History and Allegory, 1985; The Burning Bush, 1990; (ed.) Critics of the Bible, 1724-1873, 1990; Painting the Word, 1999. **Address:** All Souls College, Christ Church, Oxford University, Oxford OX1 4AL, England.

DRURY, Sally. British, b. 1960. **Genres:** Homes/Gardens, Horticulture. **Career:** Haymarket Publishing, Teddington, England, technical editor of magazines, 1982-88, London, England, Horticulture Week, technical editor, 2000-; Institute of Horticulture, The Horticulturist, consultant editor, 2000-. **Publications:** (with F. Gapper and P. Gapper) Gardens of England, 1991. Contributor to horticultural periodicals. **Address:** 2 Kia-Ora Villas, Barwis Hill, Penzance, Cornwall TR18 2AN, England. **Online address:** sally.drury@dial.pipex.com

DRURY, Tom. American. **Genres:** Novels, Novellas/Short stories. **Career:** Novelist, short-story writer, and educator. Wesleyan University, Middletown, CT, visiting lecturer, 2001-. Speaker at writer's conferences; has also taught at Yale University and the University of Southern Mississippi. **Publications:** The End of Vandalism, 1994; The Black Brook, 1998; Hunts in Dreams, 2000. Contributor of short stories and essays to periodicals and anthologies. **Address:** c/o Author Mail, Houghton Mifflin, 222 Berkeley, Boston, MA 02116, U.S.A. **Online address:** tdrury@wesleyan.edu

DRYFOOS, Joy G. American, b. 1925. **Genres:** Psychology. **Career:** Community organizer for public schools in Hastings-on-Hudson, NY, 1959-60; Research, Writing, and Editing Associates, research associate, 1960-66; Planned Parenthood Federation of America, research associate, 1967-68; Alan Guttmacher Institute, director of research and planning, fellow, and consultant, 1969-81; independent researcher, writer, and lecturer, 1981-. Sarah Lawrence College, research associate for National Commission on Community Health Services, 1981-; lecturer at universities; guest on television programs. Member of panels and committees; consultant. **Publications:** Putting Boys in the Picture: A Review of Programs to Promote Sexual Responsibility among Male Adolescents, 1988; Adolescents-at-Risk: Prevalence and Prevention, 1990; Full Service Schools: A Revolution in Health and Social Services for Children, Youth, and Families, 1994; Safe Passage: Making It through Adolescence in a High Risk Society, 1998; Inside Full Service Community Schools, 2002. **Address:** 32 Russell St, Brookline, MA 02446-2414, U.S.A. **Online address:** jdryf65322@aol.com

DUBBER, Markus Dirk. American. **Genres:** Essays. **Career:** Chambers of Gerald B. Tjoflat, U.S. Court of Appeals for the Eleventh Judicial Circuit, Jacksonville, FL, judicial clerk, 1991-92; University of Chicago Law School, Chicago, IL, Bigelow teaching fellow and lecturer in law, 1992-93; State University of New York at Buffalo School of Law, associate professor, 1993-99, professor of law, 1999-. Buffalo Criminal Law Review, editor, 1996-; University of Michigan Law School, visiting professor, 2001; Law and History Review, board of editors, 2001-; Association of American Law Schools, chair of Comparative Law Section, 2001-02; Buffalo Criminal Law Center, director, 1996-. **Publications:** (ed., with Bernd Schunemann) Die Stellung des Opfers im Strafrechtssystem: Neue Entwicklungen im deutschen und amerikanischen Recht, 2000; Criminal Law: Model Penal Code, 2002; Victims in the War on Crime: The Use and Abuse of Victims' Rights, 2002; Einfuhrung in das US-amerikanische Strafrecht, 2004; (with Mark Kelman) American Criminal Law: Cases, Statutes, and Comments, 2005; The Police Power: Patriarchy and the Foundations of American Government, 2005. Author of numerous articles, essays, and book reviews for periodicals. **Address:** University at Buffalo Law School, University of New York, 712 O'Brian Hall, North Campus, Buffalo, NY 14260, U.S.A. **Online address:** dubber@buffalo.edu

DUBENS, Eugene (M.). British, b. 1957. **Genres:** Novels. **Career:** Fiction writer. **Publications:** The Hypnotist, 2000. **Address:** 73 Wagner Close, Basingstoke RJ24 7JB, England. **Online address:** eugeneathome@hotmail.com

DUBERMAN, Martin. American, b. 1930. **Genres:** Plays/Screenplays, Gay and lesbian issues, History, Literary criticism and history. **Career:** Harvard University, Cambridge, MA, tutor, 1955-57; Yale University, New Haven, CT, instructor and assistant professor, 1957-62; Princeton University, NJ, assistant professor, 1962-65, associate professor, 1965-67, professor of history, 1967-71; City University of New York, Graduate Center and Lehman College, distinguished professor, 1971-. Founder/director, Center for Lesbian and Gay Studies (CLAGS), CUNY Graduate School. **Publications:** Charles Francis Adams, 1807-1886, 1961; In White America, 1964; James Russell Lowell, 1966; Metaphors, 1968; The Colonial Dudes, 1969; The Uncompleted Past (essays), 1969; The Memory Bank, 1970; Guttman Ordinary Scale, 1972; Black Mountain: An Exploration in Community (non-fiction), 1972; Male Armor: Selected Plays 1968-1974, 1975; Visions of Kerouac, 1977; About Time: Exploring the Gay Past, 1986, 1991; Paul Robeson, 1989; Hidden from History: Reclaiming Gay and Lesbian Past, 1989; Cures, 1991, rev. ed., 2002; Mother Earth, 1991; Stonewall, 1993; Midlife Queer, 1996; Left Out: The Politics of Exclusion/Essays 1964-99, rev. ed., 2002. EDITOR: The Antislavery Vanguard: New Essays on the Abolitionists, 1965; A Queer World, 1997; Queer Representations, 1997. **Address:** History Dept, Lehman College, Bronx, NY 10468, U.S.A.

DUBERSTEIN, Helen (Laura). American, b. 1926. **Genres:** Plays/Screenplays, Poetry, Novellas/Short stories, Novels, Women's studies and issues, Illustrations, Autobiography/Memoirs, Songs/Lyrics and libretti. **Career:** Artistic Director, Theatre for the New City, 1974-75; President, Playwrights Group, Inc., 1974-76; Playwright-in-Residence, Hartford University, Conn., 1977-78. **Publications:** PLAYS: Street Scene, 1971; The Affair, 1973; The Guillotine, 1978. POETRY: Succubus/Incubus, 1972; The Human Dimension, 1972; The Voyage Out, 1978; Changes, 1978; The Shameless Old Lady, 1995. NOVELS: A Thousand Wives Dancing, 2002; Roma, 2002. OTHER: Shadow Self & Other Tales, 1997. Works appear in anthologies and periodicals. **Address:** 463 West St #904D, New York, NY 10014, U.S.A. **Online address:** Ghohel@aol.com

DUBERSTEIN, Larry. American, b. 1944. **Genres:** Novels, Novellas/Short stories, Essays. **Career:** Carpenter and cabinetmaker, 1971-; writer. Affiliated with Darkhorse Builders, and Squarehorse Builders. **Publications:** NOVELS: The Marriage Hearse, 1987; Carnovsky's Retreat, 1988; Postcards from Pinsk, 1991; The Alibi Breakfast, 1995; The Handsome Sailor, 1998; The Mt. Monadnock Blues, 2003. STORIES: Nobody's Jaw, 1979; Eccentric Circles, 1992. **Address:** PO Box 390609, Cambridge, MA 02139, U.S.A.

DUBIN, Michael J. American, b. 1938. **Genres:** Politics/Government. **Career:** John F. Kennedy High School, Long Island, NY, social teacher, 1965-96; writer. **Publications:** (with S.B. Parsons and W.W. Beach) US Congressional Districts and Data, 1843-1883, 1986; (with S.B. Parsons and K.T. Parsons) US Congressional Districts, 1883-1913, 1988; US Congressional Elections, 1788-1997: The Official Results, 1998; US Presidential Elections 1788-1860: The Official Results by County and State, 2002; US Gubernatorial Elections 17761860: The Official Results by State and County, 2003. **Address:** 14507 Black Gold Ln, Sun City West, AZ 85375, U.S.A. **Online address:** MIK323@aol.com

DUBOIS, Ellen Carol. American, b. 1947. **Genres:** Women's studies and issues. **Career:** University of California at Los Angeles, professor, 1988-; State University of New York at Buffalo, assistant professor, 1971-78, associate professor of history, 1978-. **Publications:** Feminism and Suffrage: The Emergence of an Independent Women's Movement in America, 1848-1869, 1978; (ed. and author of critical commentary) Elizabeth Cady Stanton, Susan B. Anthony: Correspondence, Writings, Speeches, 1981; (with others) Feminist Scholarship: Kindling in the Groves of Academe, 1985; Unequal Sisters, 1987; Harriet Stanton Blatch and the Winning of Woman Suffrage, 1997; Woman Suffrage Womens Right, 1998. **Address:** Dept of History, University of California, Los Angeles, 405 Hilgard Ave, Los Angeles, CA 90024-1473, U.S.A.

DUBOSARSKY, Ursula. Australian. **Genres:** Children's fiction, Young adult fiction. **Career:** Government Public Service, Canberra, Australia, research officer; researcher for Readers Digest books and magazines. **Publications:** YOUNG ADULT FICTION: High Hopes, 1990; Zizzy Zing, 1991; The Last Week in December, 1993; The White Guinea-Pig, 1994; The First Book of Samuel, 1995; Bruno and the Crumhorn, 1996; Black Sails, White Sails, 1997; My Father Is not a Comedian, 1999; The Game of the Goose, 2000; Abyssinia, 2003; How to Be a Great Detective, 2004. CHILDREN'S FICTION: Maisie and the Pinny Pig, 1989; The Strange Adventures of Isador Brown, 1998; Honey and Bear, 1998; The Two Gorillas, 1999; The Even Stranger Adventures of Isador Brown, 2001; Fairy Bread, 2001; The Magic

Wand, 2002; Special Days for Honey and Bear, 2002; Isador Brown's Strangest Adventures of All, 2003. **Address:** c/o Penguin Books Australia Ltd., 487 Maroondah Highway, Ringwood, VIC 3134, Australia. **Online address:** dubosar@optusnet.com.au; www.ursuladubosarsky.com

DUBOSE, Lou(is H.). American, b. 1948. **Genres:** Politics/Government. **Career:** Austin Chronicle, Austin, TX, politics editor; Texas Observer, Austin, editor, 1987-. **Publications:** (with Molly Ivins) Shrub: The Short but Happy Life of George W. Bush, 2000. (with Molly Ivins) Bushwhacked: Life in George W. Bush's America, 2003; (with Jan Reid and Carl Cannon) Boy Genius: Karl Rove, the Brains behind the Remarkable Political Triumph of George W. Bush, 2003; (with Jan Reid) The Hammer, PublicAffairs (New York, NY), 2004. Contributor to periodicals. **Address:** Texas Observer, 307 West 7th St., Austin, TX 78701, U.S.A.

DUBOST, Thierry. French, b. 1958. **Genres:** Literary criticism and history. **Career:** Schoolteacher in France, 1985-93; University of Caen, France, assistant professor, 1993-94, associate professor, 1994-2001, professor of English, 2001-, dean of Distance Learning Centre. **Publications:** (trans.) W. Soyinka, Death and the King's Horseman, 1986; Struggle, Defeat or Rebirth: Eugene O'Neill's Vision of Humanity, 1997; Le Theatre de Thomas Kilroy, 2001. EDITOR: (with A. Mills) La femme Noire americaine: Aspects d'une crise d'identite (title means: Black American Women: Aspects of an Identity Crisis), 1997; (with P. Brennan) Regards croises sur G.B. Shaw (title means: G.B. Shaw: Crossing Lines), 1998. **Address:** Departement d'anglais, Universite de Caen, Esplanade de la Paix, Cdx 14032 Caen, France. **Online address:** Dubost@cte.unicaen.fr

DU BRUL, Jack B. (born United States), b. 1968. **Genres:** Novels. **Career:** Writer. Worked variously as a bartender and carpenter. **Publications:** PHILIP MERCER SERIES: Vulcan's Forge, 1998; Charon's Landing, 1999; The Medusa Stone, 2000; Pandora's Curse, 2001; River of Ruin, 2002. **Address:** c/o Author Mail, Onyx Books, Penguin Group, 375 Hudson St., New York, NY 10014, U.S.A. **Online address:** jack@jackdubrul.com

DUBUS, Andre, III. American, b. 1959. **Genres:** Novels, Novellas/Short stories. **Career:** Writer. Boulder Community Treatment Center, Boulder, CO, counselor in a correctional facility, 1982-83; worked as a bartender throughout the 1980s; carpenter, 1988-. Part-time writing instructor at Emerson College, Boston, MA. **Publications:** The Cage Keeper and Other Stories, 1989; Bluesman, 1993; House of Sand and Fog, 1999; Dancing after Hours, 2003. **Address:** 24 Allen St, Newburyport, MA 01950, U.S.A.

DUCHAC, Joseph. American, b. 1932. **Genres:** Literary criticism and history. **Career:** Long Island University, Brooklyn, NY, member of library staff, including periodicals librarian and head of public services, head reference librarian, 1964-95. **Publications:** The Poems of Emily Dickinson: An Annotated Guide to Commentary Published in English, 1890-1977, 1979; The Poems of Emily Dickinson: An Annotated Guide to Commentary Published in English, 1978-1989, 1993. Contributor to periodicals. **Address:** 25 Parade Pl, Brooklyn, NY 11226-1003, U.S.A.

DUCHÊNE, Louis-François. British/Swiss, b. 1927. **Genres:** Economics, Literary criticism and history, Politics/Government. **Career:** The Economist, London, Leader Writer, 1963-67; International Institute for Strategic Studies, Director, 1969-74; Sussex University, Brighton, Sussex European Research Centre, Director, 1974-82. **Publications:** The Case of the Helmeted Airman: A Study of W.H. Auden's Poetry, 1972; New Limits on European Agriculture, 1985; Jean Monnet: the First Statesman of Interdependence, 1994. EDITOR/CO-EDITOR: The Endless Crisis: America in the Seventies, 1970; Europe's Industries, 1983; Managing Industrial Change in Western Europe, 1987. **Address:** 3 Powis Villas, Brighton, Sussex BN1 3HD, England.

DUCKWORTH, Eleanor. Canadian, b. 1935. **Genres:** Education. **Career:** Harvard University, Cambridge, MA, associate professor, 1981-89, professor of education, 1989-. **Publications:** (trans.) Jean Piaget, Genetic Epistemology, 1971; Learning with Breadth and Depth, 1979; The Having of Wonderful Ideas and Other Essays on Teaching and Learning, 1987, 2nd ed., 1995; (with others) Science Education: A Minds-On Approach for the Elementary Years, 1989; (with others) Teacher to Teacher: Learning from Each Other, 1997; (ed.) "Tell Me More": Listening to Learners Explain, 2001. **Address:** Harvard University, Appian Way, Cambridge, MA 02138, U.S.A.

DUCKWORTH, Marilyn. New Zealander, b. 1935. **Genres:** Novels, Novellas/Short stories, Poetry, Autobiography/Memoirs. **Career:** Worked in public relations, nursing, factory work, and library work. **Publications:** NOVELS: A Gap in the Spectrum, 1959; The Matchbox House, 1960; A

Barbarous Tongue, 1963; Over the Fence Is Out, 1969; Disorderly Conduct, 1984; Married Alive, 1985; Rest for the Wicked, 1986; Pulling Faces, 1987; A Message from Harpo, 1989; Unlawful Entry, 1992; Seeing Red, 1993; Leather Wings, 1995; Studmuffin, 1997; Swallowing Diamonds, 2003. OTHER: Other Lover's Children (poems), 1975; Explosions from the Sun (stories), 1989; Fooling (novella), 1994; Camping on the Faultline (memoir), 2000. Contributor of short stories to periodicals and anthologies. Contributor to periodicals. **Address:** 41 Queen St, Mt Victoria, Wellington, New Zealand. **Online address:** marilynduckworth@paradise.net.nz

DUCKWORTH, William (Ervin). American, b. 1943. **Genres:** Music. **Career:** Atlantic Christian College, Wilson, NC, instructor to associate professor of music, 1966-73; Bucknell University, Lewisburg, PA, professor of music, 1973-, past department head, founder of The Gallery Series of performance art and experimental music. Media Press, president, 1969-72; Ringling Museum of Art, artistic director of Sounds in the Gallery concert series, 1986-88; Internationale Ferienkurse fur Neue Musik, member of composition faculty, 1988. **Publications:** (with E. Brown) Theoretical Foundations of Music, 1978; A Creative Approach to Music Fundamentals, 1981, 2nd ed., 1995; Talking Music, 1995. Composer of over 30 musical works. Contributor to books. **Address:** 6109 Boulevard East, West New York, NJ 07093, U.S.A.

DUDER, Tessa. New Zealander, b. 1940. **Genres:** Children's fiction, Young adult fiction, Plays/Screenplays, Marine sciences/Oceanography. **Career:** Spirit of Adventure Trust, Auckland, 1986-; Children's Literature Foundation of New Zealand, 1991-; Waikato University, writer-in-residence, 1991; NZ Society of Authors (PEN NZ Inc.), national president, 1996-98; Meridian Energy Katherine Mansfield Fellowship to Merton, France, 2003. **Publications:** Kawau, 1980; Night Race to Kawau, 1982; The Book of Auckland, 1985; Spirit of Adventure, 1985; Jellybean, 1985; Play It Again, Sam, 1987; Dragons, 1987; Alex, 1988; Simply Messing about in Boats, 1988; Waitemata: Harbour of Sail, 1989; Alex in Winter, 1989; Alessandra: Alex in Rome, 1990; Songs for Alex, 1992; The Making of Alex: The Movie, 1993; (with M. Baynton) The Warrior Virgin (play), 1995; Mercury Beach, 1997; The Tiggie Tompson Show, 1999;(with W. Taylor) Hot Mail, 2000; Tiggie Tompson All at Sea, 2001; Tiggie Tompson's Longest Journey, 2003. EDITOR: Nearly Seventeen, 1993; Crossings, 1995; Falling in Love, 1995; A Book of Pacific Lullabies, 1998; Salt beneath the Skin, 1999; Seduced by the Sea, 2002; Spirit of Youth, 2003; Storylines, 2003. **Address:** 2/126 Selwyn Ave, Mission Bay, Auckland, New Zealand. **Online address:** tessa.duder@ihug.co.nz

DUDLEY, Ellen. American, b. 1938. **Genres:** Travel/Exploration, Recreation. **Career:** Worked as media relations director, Union for Concerned Scientists, Washington, DC. **Publications:** (with E. Seaborg) Hiking and Backpacking, 1994; (with E. Seaborg) American Discoveries: Scouting the First Coast-to-Coast Recreational Trail, 1996. **Address:** c/o Mountaineers Books, 1001 SW Klickitat Way, Ste. 201, Seattle, WA 98134, U.S.A.

DUDLEY-SMITH, Timothy. British, b. 1926. **Genres:** Songs/Lyrics and libretti, Theology/Religion, Bibliography, Biography. **Career:** Crusade mag., 1954-59; Archdeacon of Norwich, 1973-81; Bishop of Thetford, 1981-91. **Publications:** Christian Literature and the Church Bookstall, 1963; What Makes a Man a Christian?, 1965; A Man Named Jesus, 1971; Someone Who Beckons, 1978; Lift Every Heart, 1984; A Flame of Love, 1987; Songs of Deliverance, 1988; Praying with the English Hymn Writers, 1989; A Voice of Singing, 1993; Authentic Christianity, 1995; John Stott: A Comprehensive Bibliography, 1995; Great Is the Glory, 1997; John Stott: The Making of a Leader, 1999; John Stott: A Global Ministry, 2001; Beneath a Travelling Star, 2001; A House of Praise, 2003. **Address:** 9 Ashlands Ford, Salisbury, Wilts. SP4 6DY, England.

DUE, Tananarive. American, b. 1966. **Genres:** Novels. **Career:** Novelist. Columnist for the Miami Herald; former intern at the New York Times and Wall Street Journal. Has performed with the Rockbottom Remainders, a rock band that includes authors Stephen King, Dave Barry, and Amy Tan, as keyboardist/vocalist/dancer. **Publications:** NOVELS: The Between, 1995; My Soul to Keep, 1997; The Black Rose, 2001; Living Blood, 2001; The Good House, 2003. Contributor to Naked Came the Manatee, a comic thriller written by thirteen southern writers, each contributing a chapter. MEMOIRS: (with P.S. Due) Freedom in the Family, 2002. **Address:** 2909 Maryland St, Longview, WA 98632, U.S.A. **Online address:** tdue@tananarivedue.com

DUECK, Adele. Canadian, b. 1955. **Genres:** Young adult fiction. **Career:** Freelance writer; also serves the family farm as an accountant and secretary.

Publications: Anywhere But Here (young adult novel), 1996. Author of Homefront, a column in Western People, 1986-90. **Address:** PO Box 152, Lucky Lake, SK, Canada S0L 1Z0.

DUEY, Kathleen. American, b. 1950. **Genres:** Children's fiction, Young adult fiction, Children's non-fiction, Young adult non-fiction. **Career:** Writer. **Publications:** AMERICAN DIARIES SERIES: Emma Eileen Grove: Mississippi, 1865, 1996; Mary Alice Peale: Philadelphia, 1777, 1996; Sarah Anne Hartford: Massachusetts, 1651, 1996; Anisett Lundberg: California, 1851, 1996; Willow Chase: Kansas Territory, 1847, 1997; Ellen Elizabeth Hawkins: Mobeetie, Texas, 1886, 1997; Evie Peach: St. Louis, 1857, 1997; Alexia Ellery Finsdale: San Francisco, 1905, 1997; Celou Sudden Shout: Idaho, 1826, 1998; Summer MacCleary: Virginia, 1749, 1998; Agnes May Gleason: Walsenberg, Colorado, 1933, 1998; Amelina Carrett: Bayou Grand Coeur, Louisiana, 1863, 1999; Josie Poe: Palouse, Washington, 1943, 1999; Rosa Moreno: Hollywood, California, 1928, 1999; Nell Dunne: Ellis Island, 1904, 2000; Maddie Retta Lauren: Sandersville, Georgia, C.S.A, 1864, 2000; Francesca Vigilucci: Washington, DC, 1913, 2000; Janey G. Blue: Pearl Harbor, 1941, 2001; Zellie Blake: Massachusetts, 1836, 2002. SURVIVAL! SERIES (with K.A. Bale): Earthquake, 1906, 1998; Cave-In: St. Claire, Pennsylvania, 1859, 1998; Stranded: Death Valley, 1850, 1998; Flood: Mississippi, 1927, 1998; Blizzard: Estes Park, Colorado, 1886, 1998; Fire: Chicago, 1871, 1998; Titanic: April 14, 1912, 1998; Hurricane: Open Seas, 1844, 1999; Train Wreck: Kansas, 1892, 1999; Swamp: Bayou Teche, Louisiana, 1851, 1999; Forest Fire: Hinckley, Minnesota, 1894, 1999; Hurricane: New Bedford, Massachusetts, 1784, 1999; San Francisco Earthquake, 1906, 1999; Louisiana Hurricane, 1860, 2000. SPIRIT OF THE CIMARRON SERIES: Esperanza, 2002; Bonita, 2002; Sierra, 2002; Spirit: Stallion of the Cimarron (adaptation), 2002. UNICORN'S SECRET SERIES: Moonsilver, 2001; The Silver Thread, 2001; The Silver Bracelet, 2002; Mountains of the Moon, 2002; Beyond the Sunset, 2002; True Heart, 2002; Castle Avamin, 2003; The Journey Home, 2003. OTHER: Double-Yuck Magic, 1991; Mr. Stumpguss Is a Third-Grader, 1992; The Third Grade's Skinny Pig, 1993; (with K.A. Bale) Three of Hearts, 1998; Nowhere to Run, Nowhere to Hide!, 2000; Stay Out of the Graveyard!, 2000; Bogeyman in the Basement!, 2000; Beware the Alien Invasion!, 2000; (with M. Barnes) Freaky Facts about Natural Disasters, 2000; (with M. Barnes) More Freaky Facts about Natural Disasters, 2001. **Address:** c/o Publicity, Penguin/Putnam, 345 Hudson St, New York, NY 10014, U.S.A. **Online address:** kathleen@kathleenduey.com

DUFAULT, Peter Kane. American, b. 1923. **Genres:** Poetry. **Career:** Journalist, 1950-64; musician (fiddle, banjo, etc.) and teacher, 1964-2000. Williams College, Williamstown, MA, Critic-in-Residence, 1968-69; Cheltenham Festival of Literature, England, Poet-in-Residence, 1978, 1993. **Publications:** Angel of Accidence, 1953; For Some Stringed Instrument, 1957; On Balance, 1978; Memorandum to the Age of Reason, 1988; New Things Come into the World, 1993; Looking in All Directions, 2000. Contributor to anthologies and magazines. **Address:** RD2 56 Hickory Hill Rd, Hillsdale, NY 12529, U.S.A. **Online address:** peterkanedufault@hotmail.com; www.webjogger.net/poetrydufault

DUFAULT, Roseanna Lewis. American, b. 1954. **Genres:** Literary criticism and history. **Career:** University of Colorado, Boulder, instructor in French, 1979-85; Colorado State University, Fort Collins, assistant professor of French, 1986-89; Ohio Northern University, Ada, assistant professor, 1989-92, associate professor of French, 1992-. Alliance Francaise, instructor, 1980-83; Universite de Bordeaux III, lecturer, 1985-86. Ohio Council on World Affairs, representative, 1989; Ohio Northern Academic Alliance, member, 1990-. **Publications:** Metaphors of Identity: The Treatment of Childhood in Selected Quebecois Novels, 1991. EDITOR: Women by Women, 1997; Doing Gender, 2001. Work represented in anthologies. Contributor to scholarly journals. **Address:** Department of Modern Languages, 200N Dukes Memorial Bldg, Ohio Northern University, 525 S Main St, Ada, OH 45810-1599, U.S.A. **Online address:** r-dufault@onu.edu

DUFF, Alan. New Zealander, b. 1950. **Genres:** Novels. **Career:** Syndicated newspaper columnist, 1971-. **Publications:** Once Were Warriors, 1994; One Night Out Stealing, 1995. **Address:** 51 Busby Hill, Havelock North, New Zealand.

DUFFEY, Betsy (Byars). American, b. 1953. **Genres:** Children's fiction. **Publications:** The Math Wiz, 1990; A Boy in the Doghouse, 1991; The Gadget War, 1992; Lucky in Left Field, 1992; Puppy Love , 1992; How to Be Cool in the Third Grade, 1993, in UK as How to Be Cool in Junior School, 1996; Lucky on the Loose, 1993; Wild Things, 1993; Throw-Away Pets , 1993; Lucky Christmas, 1994; Coaster, 1994; Utterly Yours, Booker

Jones, 1995, in UK as Buster and the Black Hole, 1996; Hey, New Kid!, 1996; Camp Knock Knock, 1996; The Camp Knock Knock Mystery, 1997; Virtual Cody, 1997; Cody's Secret Admirer, 1998; Spotlight on Cody, 1998; Alien for Rent, 1999; Cody Unplugged, 1999; (with B. Byars and L. Myers) My Dog, My Hero, 2000; Fur-Ever Yours, Booker Jones, 2001. **Address:** 4825 Franklin Pond Rd., Atlanta, GA 30342, U.S.A.

DUFFIELD, Gervase E. British, b. 1935. **Genres:** Ethics, History, Intellectual history, Theology/Religion. **Career:** Ed., News Today, 1980-; Ed., News Extra, 1964-79, 1985-. Member, General Synod of Church of England for Oxford Diocese, 1960-80. Ed., The Churchman, 1967-72. **Publications:** The Work of William Tyndale, 1963; The Work of Thomas Cranmer, 1965; Admission to Holy Communion, 1964; Martin Bucer's Psalter of David 1530, 1973; Bunyan of Bedford, 1978; The Work of Peter Martyr, 1990; Tyndale's 1525 New Testament Fragment, 1994. EDITOR: The Paul Report Considered, 1964; Why Not? Priesthood and the Ministry of Women, 1978; Across the Divide, 1978; The Prayer Book Noted 1550, by John Marbeck, 1982; William Barlowe's Dialogue of Lutheran Factions 1531, 1983. **Address:** Appleford House, Abingdon, Oxford OX14 4PB, England.

DUFFY, Bruce. American, b. 1953?. **Genres:** Novels. **Career:** Writer. **Publications:** NOVELS: The World As I Found It, 1987; Last Comes the Egg, 1997. Contributor to periodicals. **Address:** Simon & Schuster, 1230 Avenue of the Americas, New York, NY 10020, U.S.A.

DUFFY, Eamon. American. **Genres:** Theology/Religion. **Career:** Magdalene College, Cambridge University, university lecturer in ecclesiastical history. **Publications:** Peter and Jack: Roman Catholics and Dissent in Eighteenth Century England, 1982; The Stripping of the Altars: Traditional Religion in England, c1400-c1580, 1992; Saints and Sinners: A History of the Popes, 1997; The Voices of Morebath, 2001. EDITOR: Challoner and His Church: A Catholic Bishop in Georgian England, 1981; (with B. Bradshaw) Humanism, Reform, and Reformation: The Career of John Fisher, Bishop of Rochester, 1989. Contributor to books. **Address:** Magdalene College, Cambridge CB3 0AG, England.

DUFFY, James H(enry). Also writes as Haughton Murphy. American, b. 1934. **Genres:** Novels, Mystery/Crime/Suspense, Politics/Government. **Career:** Cravath, Swaine & Moore (law firm), New York, NY, associate lawyer, 1959-67, partner, 1968-88; full-time writer, 1989-. **Publications:** Domestic Affairs: American Programs and Priorities, 1979; Dog Bites Man: City Shocked! (novel), 2001. REUBEN FROST MYSTERY NOVEL SERIES AS HAUGHTON MURPHY: Murder for Lunch, 1986; Murder Takes a Partner, 1987; Murders and Acquisitions, 1988; Murder Keeps a Secret, 1989; Murder Times Two, 1990; Murder Saves Face, 1991; A Very Venetian Murder, 1992. **Address:** 116 E 68th St, New York, NY 10021, U.S.A. **Online address:** jduffy@attglobal.net

DUFFY, Margaret. British, b. 1942. **Genres:** Mystery/Crime/Suspense. **Career:** Clerical officer for Inland Revenue in Worthing, England, 1958-66, and for Ministry of Defence, Bath, 1969-74; writer. **Publications:** A Murder of Crows, 1987; Death of a Raven, 1988; Brass Eagle, 1988; Who Killed Cock Robin?, 1990; Rook-Shoot, 1990; Man of Blood, 1992; Gallows Bird, 1993; Dressed to Kill, 1994; Corpse Candle, 1995; Prospect of Death, 1995; Music in the Blood, 1997; A Fine Target, 1998; A Hanging Matter, 2002; Dead Trouble, 2004; So Horrible a Place, 2004. **Address:** The Crossing, Iron Mine Lane, Dousland, Devon PL20 6NA, England.

DUFFY, Maureen (Patricia). Also writes as D. M. Cayer. British, b. 1933. **Genres:** Novels, Plays/Screenplays, Poetry, History, Biography, Translations. **Career:** Teacher, 1951-53, 1956-60. **Publications:** That's How It Was, 1962; (trans.) D. Rea, A Blush of Shame, 1963; The Single Eye, 1964; The Microcosm, 1966; The Paradox Players, 1967; Lyrics for the Dog Hour: Poems, 1968; Wounds, 1969; Lovechild, 1971; The Venus Touch (poetry), 1971; I Want to Go to Moscow, 1973; Capital, 1975; Evesong (poetry), 1976; The Passionate Shepherdess, 1977; House-spy, 1978; Memorials of the Quick and the Dead (poetry), 1979; The Erotic World of Faery, 1980; Inherit the Earth, 1980; Gorsaga, 1981; Men and Beasts, 1984; Collected Poems 1949-84, 1985; A Thousand Capricious Chances (history), 1989; Henry Purcell, 1994; England: The Making of the Myth (history), 2001. NOVELS: Change, 1987; Illuminations, 1991; Occam's Razor, 1993; Restitution, 1998. **Address:** 18 Fabian Rd, London SW6 7TZ, England.

DUFFY, Susan. American, b. 1951. **Genres:** Bibliography. **Career:** Writer and educator. California Polytechnic State University, San Luis, Obispo, currently professor of liberal studies. **Publications:** Shirley Chisholm: A Bibliography of Writings by and about Her, 1988; (ed., with M. Slann)

Morality and Conviction in American Politics: A Reader, 1990; The Political Left in the American Theatre of the 1930s: A Bibliographic Sourcebook, 1992; American Labor on Stage: Dramatic Interpretations of the Steel and Textile Industries in the 1930s, 1996; (with P.T. Adalian, Jr.) A Comprehensive Index to Artist and Influence: The Journal of Black American Cultural History, 1981-1999, 1999; (introduction and analyses) The Political Plays of Langston Hughes, 2000. **Address:** College of Liberal Arts, California Polytechnic State University, 1 Grand Ave, San Luis Obispo, CA 93407, U.S.A. **Online address:** sduffy@calpoly.edu

DUFRESNE, Jim. American, b. 1955. **Genres:** Travel/Exploration. **Career:** Booth Newspapers, Lansing, MI, outdoor writer, 1987-. **Publications:** Isle Royale National Park: Foot Trails and Water Routes, 1984, 2nd ed., 1991; Voyageurs National Park: Water Routes, Foot Paths, and Ski Trails, 1986; (with K. Leghorn) Glacier Bay National Park: A Backcountry Guide to the Glaciers and Beyond, 1987; Michigan: Off the Beaten Path, 1988, 4th ed, 1996; Michigan State Parks: A Complete Guide for Campers, Boaters, Anglers, Hikers, and Skiers, 1989; Michigan's Best Outdoor Adventures with Children, 1990; Fifty Hikes in Lower Michigan: The Best Walks, Hikes, and Backpacks from Sleeping Bear Dunes to the Hills of Oakland County, 1991; Wild Michigan, 1992; Porcupine Mountains Wilderness State Park: A Backcountry Guide for Hikers, Campers, Backpackers, and Skiers, 1993; Alaska: A Travel Survival Kit, 4th ed., 1994; Backpacking in Alaska: A Lonely Planet Walking Guide, 1995; Trekking in Alaska: A Walking Guide, 1995; (with J. Williams) Tramping in New Zealand: A Walking Guide, 1995. **Address:** PO Box 852, Clarkston, MI 48347, U.S.A.

DUFRESNE, John. American, b. 1948. **Genres:** Novels, Novellas/Short stories, Writing/Journalism. **Career:** Northeast Louisiana University, Monroe, instructor in composition and creative writing, 1984-87; Augusta College, Augusta, GA, instructor in composition, creative writing, and humanities, 1988-89; Florida International University, North Miami, associate professor in creative writing, 1989-98, professor, 1999-; writer. Employed as a social worker and crisis intervention counselor; served as a draft counselor during the Vietnam War; worked as cab driver, bartender, janitor, house painter, and in a plastics factory. **Publications:** STORIES: The Way That Water Enters Stone, 1991. NOVELS: Louisiana Power & Light, 1994; Love Warps the Mind a Little, 1997; Deep in the Shade of Paradise, 2002. OTHER: The Freezer Jesus (screenplay), 2002; The Lie That Tells a Truth, 2003. **Address:** Dept of English, Florida International University, North Miami, FL 33181, U.S.A. **Online address:** johndufresne@mindspring.com

DUGGAN, Christopher. British, b. 1957. **Genres:** Area studies, History. **Career:** Wolfson College, Oxford, England, junior research fellow, 1983-85; All Soul's College, Oxford, fellow, 1985-97; University of Reading, England, lecturer in Italian history and director of the Centre for the Advanced Study of Italian Society (CASIS), 1987-, reader in Italian history, 1994-2002, professor of modern Italian history, 2002-. **Publications:** (with M.I. Finley and D.M. Smith) A History of Sicily, 1986; Fascism and the Mafia, 1989; A Concise History of Italy, 1994; Francesco Crispi: From Nation to Nationalism, 2002. Contributor of articles and reviews to journals and newspapers. **Address:** Department of Italian Studies, University of Reading, Reading, England. **Online address:** c.j.h.duggan@reading.ac.uk

DUGGLEBY, John. American, b. 1952. **Genres:** Art/Art history, Business/Trade/Industry, Children's non-fiction, Communications/Media, Education, History, Marketing, Popular Culture, Travel/Exploration, Zoology, Biography, Ghost Writer. **Career:** Allstate Insurance, Northbrook, IL, magazine editor, 1976-78; American Telephone & Telegraph, Chicago, IL, member of corporate communications staff, 1978-81; Burson-Marsteller Public Relations, Chicago, member of creative staff, 1981-84; Duggleby Communications, McFarland, WI, owner, 1984-. **Publications:** The Sabertooth Cat, 1989; Pesticides, 1990; Doomed Expeditions, 1990; Impossible Quests, 1990; Artist in Overalls: The Life of Grant Wood, 1996; Story Painter: The Life of Jacob Lawrence, 1998. Contributor to periodicals and educational media. **Address:** Duggleby Communications, 5322 Norma Rd, Mc Farland, WI 53558, U.S.A. **Online address:** duggleby@mailbag.com

DUHL, Leonard J. American, b. 1926. **Genres:** Medicine/Health, Psychiatry, Urban studies, Regional/Urban planning. **Career:** Physician. Professor of Urban Social Policy and Public Health, University of California, Berkeley, 1968-. Chief, Office of Planning, National Institute of Mental Health, Bethesda, Maryland, 1964-66; Special Assistant to the Secretary, Dept. of Housing and Urban Development, Washington, D.C., 1966-68. **Publications:** Approaches to Research in Mental Retardation, 1959; The Urban Condition: People and Policy in the Metropolis, 1963; Urban America and the Planning of Mental Health Services, Symposium No. 10, 1964;

Mental Health and Urban Social Policy, 1968; (ed.) A Symposium on the Urban Crisis, 1969; (with M. Myerson, C. Rapkin and J. Collins) The City and the University, 1969; Making Whole: Health for a New Epoch, 1980; The Mental Health Complex: It's a New Ball Game, 1985; Healthy Social Change, 1985; Health Planning and Social Change, 1986; (co-ed.) The Future of Mental Health Care, 1987; The Social Entrepreneurship of Change, 1990; The Urban Condition-20 Years Later, 1993. Contributor to professional periodicals. **Address:** c/o School of Public Health, Warren Hall, University of California, Berkeley, CA 94720, U.S.A. **Online address:** len-duhl@socrates.berkeley.edu

DUIGAN, John. British, b. 1949. **Genres:** Plays/Screenplays, Novels. **Career:** Screenwriter, director, actor, and novelist. University of Melbourne, Melbourne, Australia, teacher; La Trobe University, Australia, teacher. **Publications:** SCREENPLAYS: The Firm Man (short), 1974; The Trespassers, 1976; (with J. Sainken) Mouth to Mouth, 1978; Winter of Our Dreams, 1981; Far East, 1983; One Night Stand, 1984; Vietnam (television miniseries), 1986; Room to Move (television), 1987; The Year My Voice Broke, 1987; Flirting, 1990; (with J. Sharp and C. Angier) Wide Sargasso Sea, 1993; Sirens, 1994. NOVELS: Badge, 1975; Room to Move (novelization of screenplay), 1985; Players. **Address:** 54A Tite St., London SW3 4JA, England.

DUINA, Francesco G. American, b. 1969. **Genres:** Politics/Government. **Career:** Harvard University, Cambridge, MA, lecturer, Committee on Degrees in Social Studies. Monitor Co., management consultant. **Publications:** Harmonizing Europe: Nation-States within the Common Market, 1999. **Address:** Department of Social Studies, 8 Hilles Library, Harvard University, Cambridge, MA 02138, U.S.A. **Online address:** duina@fas.harvard.edu

DUKE, Anna Marie. Also writes as Patty Duke, Patty Duke Astin. American, b. 1946. **Genres:** Women's studies and issues, Autobiography/Memoirs. **Career:** Actress on stage, television, and in films. **Publications:** (as Patty Duke Astin; with Los Angeles Commission on Assaults Against Women) Surviving Sexual Assault, 1983; (with K. Turan) Call Me Anna: The Autobiography of Patty Duke, 1987; (with G. Hochman) A Brilliant Madness: Living with Manic-Depressive Illness, 1992. **Address:** c/o Creative Artists Agency, 9830 Wilshire Blvd, Beverly Hills, CA 90212-1825, U.S.A.

DUKE, Donald. Also writes as Roger Valentine. American, b. 1929. **Genres:** Transportation. **Career:** Golden West Books Alhambra, CA, publisher, 1964-. Westerners Branding Iron Quarterly, editor, 1972-78, 1987-. **Publications:** Southern Pacific Steam Locomotives, 1955; The Pacific Electric Railway, 1955; Night Train, 1961; Santa Fe: Steel Rails to California, 1963; George Westinghouse and Electric Traction, 1967; Trails of the Iron Horse, 1975; American Narrow Gauge, 1978; Water Trails West, 1980; RDC: The Budd Rail-Diesel Car, 1990; The American West in Postage Stamps, 1992; Mount Washington: Its Hotel and Cable Railway, 1994; Fred Henry Harvey: Civilizer of the American West, 1994; Santa Fe: The Railroad Gateway to the American West, vol. 1, 1995, vol. 2, 1997; Incline Railways of Los Angeles & Southern California, 1999; Electric Railways around San Francisco Bay, 2 vols., 1999; The Pacific Electric Railway, Vol. 1: Northern Division, 2002, Vol. 2: Eastern Division, 2003, Vol. 3: Southern Division, 2003. **Address:** PO Box 80250, San Marino, CA 91118-8250, U.S.A.

DUKE, Martin. American (born England), b. 1930. **Genres:** Medicine/Health, Essays. **Career:** Manchester Memorial Hospital, Manchester, CT, director of medical education, 1963-84; self-employed internist and cardiologist in Connecticut, 1963-93; writer. **Publications:** The Development of Medical Techniques and Treatments, 1991; Tales My Stethoscope Told Me, 1998. Work represented in anthologies. Contributor to medical journals. **Address:** PO Box 967, Manchester, CT 06045, U.S.A.

DUKE, Michael S. American/Canadian, b. 1940. **Genres:** Novellas/Short stories, Literary criticism and history, Translations. **Career:** George Washington University, Washington, DC, assistant professor of Chinese, 1974-76; University of Vermont, Burlington, assistant professor of Chinese, 1976-77; National Taiwan University, Taipei, assistant professor of European literature, 1979-80; University of Wisconsin-Madison, visiting assistant professor of Chinese, 1980-81; University of British Columbia, Vancouver, assistant professor, 1982-85, associate professor, 1985-90, professor of Asian studies, 1990-, head of department, 1991-96. Oberlin-in-Taiwan Program, resident director, 1978-80; resident director of Council on International Educational Exchange at Peking University, 1986-87; New York Times, cultural informant for Beijing Bureau, 1986-87; guest on radio and TV programs. **Publications:** Lu You, 1977; Blooming and Contending: Chinese

Literature in the Post-Mao Era, 1985; The Iron House: A Memoir of the Chinese Democracy Movement and the Tiananmen Massacre, 1990; (trans.) Raise the Red Lantern: 3 Novellas by Su Tong, 1993. EDITOR, AUTHOR OF INTRODUCTION & CONTRIBUTOR: Contemporary Chinese Literature: An Anthology of Post-Mao Fiction and Poetry, 1985; Modern Chinese Women Writers: Critical Appraisals, 1989; Worlds of Modern Chinese Fiction: Short Stories and Novellas from the People's Republic, Taiwan, and Hong Kong, 1991. **Address:** Dept of Asian Studies, University of British Columbia, 1871 West Mall, Vancouver, BC, Canada V6T 1Z2. **Online address:** aihua@shaw.ca

DUKE, Patty. *See* DUKE, Anna Marie.

DUKE, Steven B. American, b. 1934. **Genres:** Law. **Career:** Yale University, New Haven, CT, professor of law, 1961-. Criminal defense lawyer. **Publications:** (with Albert C. Gross) America's Longest War: Rethinking Our Tragic Crusade Against Drugs, J. P. Tarcher (Los Angeles), 1993. Contributor to law journals, magazines, and newspapers. **Address:** P.O. Box 208215, New Haven, CT 06520, U.S.A.

DUKERT, Joseph M(ichael). American, b. 1929. **Genres:** Economics, Environmental sciences/Ecology, Technology, International relations/Current affairs. **Career:** Independent energy consultant, 1965-. **Publications:** Atompower, 1962; This Is Antarctica, 1965, rev. ed., 1971; Nuclear Ships of the World, 1973; A Short Energy History of the United States and Some Thoughts about the Future, 1980; High Energy Costs: Uneven, Unfair, Unavoidable?, 1981; The Evolution of the North American Energy Market, 1999. **Address:** 4709 Crescent St, Bethesda, MD 20816, U.S.A. **Online address:** dukert@erols.com

DUKES, Paul. British, b. 1934. **Genres:** Area studies, History. **Career:** University of Aberdeen, professor of history. **Publications:** Catherine the Great and the Russian Nobility, 1967; The Emergence of the Super-Powers, 1970; A History of Russia, 1974; (ed.) Russia Under Catherine the Great, 2 vols., 1977-78; October and the World, 1979; The Making of Russian Absolutism, 1982; A History of Europe, 1985; The Last Great Game: USA versus USSR, 1989; History and World Order, 1996; The Superpowers, 2000. **Address:** History Dept, University of Aberdeen, Aberdeen AB24 3FX, Scotland. **Online address:** p.dukes@abdn.ac.uk

DUKORE, Bernard F. American. **Genres:** Literary criticism and history, Theatre, Bibliography. **Career:** Hunter College, Bronx, NY, instructor of speech and drama, 1957-60; University of Southern California, Los Angeles, assistant professor of drama, 1960-62; California State University at Los Angeles, associate prof of drama, 1962-66; Stanford University, CA, visiting associate professor of drama, 1965-66; professor of drama, City University of New York, 1966-72, and University of Hawaii, Honolulu, 1972-86; Virginia Tech, Blacksburg, university distinguished professor of theatre and humanities, 1986-97, university distinguished professor emeritus, 1997-. **Publications:** Bernard Shaw, Director, 1971; Bernard Shaw, Playwright, 1973; Where Laughter Stops, 1976; Money and Politics in Ibsen, Shaw and Brecht, 1980; The Theatre of Peter Barnes, 1981; (comp.) Bernard Shaw's Arms and the Man, 1982; Harold Pinter, 1982, 2nd ed., 1985; American Dramatists 1918-1945, 1984; Death of a Salesman and The Crucible, 1989; Alan Ayckbourn: A Casebook, 1991; Barnestorm, 1995; Bernard Shaw and Gabriel Pascal, 1996; Sam Peckinpah's Feature Films, 1999; Shaw's Theatre, 2000. EDITOR: The Man of Mode (play), 1962; A Bibliography of Theatre Arts Publications in English, 1963; (with R. Cohn) Twentieth Century Drama: England, Ireland, the U.S. (anthology), 1966; (with M. Rohrberger and S.H. Woods Jr.) Introduction to Literature, 1968; Saint Joan: A Screenplay by Bernard Shaw, 1968; (with R. O'Brien) Tragedy (anthology), 1969; (with D.C. Gerould) Avant-Garde Drama (anthology), 1969; (with J. Gassner) A Treasury of the Theatre: vol. II, 1970; Drama and Revolution (anthology), 1971; Documents for Drama and Revolution (anthology), 1971; Dramatic Theory and Criticism, 1974; Seventeen Plays, 1976; The Collected Screenplays of Bernard Shaw, 1980; B. Shaw, The Drama Observed, 4 vols., 1992; Shaw and the Last Hundred Years, 1994; Not Bloody Likely!, 1997; Bernard Shaw on Cinema, 1997. **Address:** 2510 Plymouth St, Blacksburg, VA 24060-8256, U.S.A. **Online address:** bdukore@vt.edu

DUKTHAS, Ann. *See* DOHERTY, P(aul) C.

DULANEY, W. Marvin. American, b. 1950. **Genres:** History, Race relations. **Career:** Wittenberg University, Springfield, OH, Upward Bound instructor, 1978, academic and career counselor, 1978-81; Texas Christian University, Fort Worth, intercultural affairs adviser, 1981-83; University of Texas at Arlington, assistant director of Upward Bound program, 1983-85;

St. Olaf College, Northfield, MN, assistant professor of history, 1985-86; University of Texas at Arlington, assistant professor, 1986-93, associate professor of history, 1993-94, Walter Prescott Webb Lecturer, 1991; College of Charleston, SC, director of African-American studies and Avery Research Center, 1994-, chair, Dept of History, 1998-. African American Museum, Dallas, TX, curator of history, 1987-94, and director of annual African-American History Fairs. Lecturer at colleges and universities; guest on media programs. Juanita Jewel Craft House Civil Rights Museum, curator, 1993; Charleston Civil War Re-Enactor Regiment, member of Company I, 54th Massachusetts Infantry Regiment, 1994-96; moderator of annual Know Your Heritage Quiz Shows. **Publications:** (ed. with K. Underwood, and contrib.) Essays on the American Civil Rights Movement, 1993; Black Police in America, 1996. Contributor to books. Contributor of articles and reviews to periodicals.

DULLES, Cardinal Avery. American, b. 1918. **Genres:** Theology/Religion, Bibliography. **Career:** Woodstock College, Maryland, systematic theology, assistant professor, 1960-62, associate professor, 1962-69, professor, 1969-74; Catholic University of America, Washington, DC, professor, 1974-88, professor emeritus of systematic theology, 1988-; Fordham University, NYC, McGinley Professor of Religion and Society, 1988-. **Publications:** Princeps Concordiae, 1941; A Testimonial to Grace, 1946; (with J.M. Demske and R.J. O'Connell) Introductory Metaphysics, 1955; Apologetics and the Biblical Christ, 1963; The Dimensions of the Church, 1967; Revelation and the Quest for Unity, 1968; Revelation Theology: A History, 1969; (with W. Pannenberg and C.E. Braaten) Spirit, Faith, and Church, 1970; The Survival of Dogma, 1971; A History of Apologetics, 1971; Models of the Church, 1974; Church Membership as a Catholic and Ecumenical Problem, 1974; The Resilient Church, 1977; A Church to Believe In, 1982; Models of Revelation, 1983; (with P. Granfield) The Church: A Bibliography, 1985; The Catholicity of the Church, 1985; The Reshaping of Catholicism, 1988; The Craft of Theology, 1992; The Assurance of Things Hoped For, 1994; A Testimonial to Grace and Reflections on a Theological Journey, 1996; The Priestly Office, 1997; (with P. Granfield) The Theology of the Church: A Bibliography, 1999; The Splendor of Faith: The Theological Vision of Pope John Paul II, 1999; The New World of Faith, 2000; Newman, 2002. **Address:** Spellman Hall, Fordham University, Bronx, NY 10458, U.S.A. **Online address:** mcgchair@fordham.edu

DUMBRELL, John. British, b. 1950. **Genres:** Politics/Government, History. **Career:** Manchester Metropolitan University, Manchester, England, lecturer in American studies, 1978-94; Keele University, Staffordshire, England, senior lecturer in American studies, 1994-. Also served as a tutor for the Open University. **Publications:** (ed.) Vietnam and the Antiwar Movement, 1989; The Making of US Foreign Policy, 1990; Vietnam, 1992; The Carter Presidency: A Re-Evaluation, 1993, 2nd ed., 1995; American Foreign Policy: Carter to Clinton, 1996; A Special Relationship: Anglo-American Relations in the Cold War and After, 2000. Contributor to periodicals. **Address:** Department of American Studies, Keele University, Staffordshire 5T5 5BG, England. **Online address:** asa09@ams.keele.ac.uk

DUMMETT, (Agnes Margaret) Ann. Also writes as Ann Chesney. British, b. 1930. **Genres:** Civil liberties/Human rights, Plays/Screenplays. **Career:** Local Voluntary Organisation for Race Equality, Oxford, England, community relations officer, 1966-69; College of Further Education, Oxford, English teacher, 1969-71; Institute of Race Relations, London, England, researcher on the teaching of history, 1971-73; Joint Council for Welfare of Immigrants, London, researcher, 1978-84; Runnymede Trust, London, director, 1984-87; writer. Served on committees of justice, British branch of International Commission of Jurists, 1978-80 and 1988-90; member of Government Committee of Inquiry into Education of Ethnic Minority Groups, 1979-84; contributes to Council of Europe Community Relations Project, 1989-; consultant to Commission for Racial Equality, 1990-99. **Publications:** A Portrait of English Racism, 1973; Citizenship and Nationality, 1976; (with I. Martin) British Nationality: A Guide to the New Law, 1982; (ed.) Towards a Just Immigration Policy, Cobden Trust, 1986; (with A. Nicol) Subjects, Citizens, Aliens, and Others, 1990; Racially Motivated Crime, 1997. **Address:** 54 Park Town, Oxford OX2 6SJ, England.

DUMMETT, Michael (Anthony Eardley). British, b. 1925. **Genres:** Philosophy, Politics/Government, Race relations, Recreation. **Career:** Birmingham University, assistant lecturer, 1950-51; All Souls College, Oxford, fellow, 1950-79; Oxford University, reader in the philosophy of mathematics, 1962-74, New College, fellow, 1979-92, Wykeham Professor of Logic, 1979-92. Knighted, 1999. **Publications:** Frege: Philosophy of Language, 1973; The Justification of Deduction, 1973; Elements of Intuitionism, 1977, rev. ed., 2000; Truth and Other Enigmas, 1978; Immigration:

Where the Debate Goes Wrong, 1978; Catholicism and the World Order, 1979; The Game of Tarot, 1980; Twelve Tarot Games, 1980; The Interpretation of Frege's Philosophy, 1981; Voting Procedures, 1984; The Visconti-Sforza Tarot Cards, 1986; Ursprunge der analytischen Philosophie, 1988; Frege and Other Philosophers, 1991; The Logical Basis of Metaphysics, 1991; Frege: Philosophy of Mathematics, 1991; Origins of Analytical Philosophy, rev. ed., 1993; Grammar and Style, 1993; The Seas of Language, 1993; Il Mondo e l'Angelo, 1993; I Tarocchi Siciliani, 1995, rev. ed., 2002; (with R. Decker and T. Depauls) A Wicked Pack of Cards, 1996; Principles of Electoral Reform, 1997; La Natura e il Futuro di Filosofia, 2001; On Immigration and Refugees, 2001; (with R. Decker) A History of the Occult Tarot 1870-1970, 2002. **Address:** 54 Park Town, Oxford OX2 6SJ, England.

DUMONT, Ninda. *See* **FRANKLIN, Linda Campbell.**

DUNANT, Sarah. British, b. 1950. **Genres:** Mystery/Crime/Suspense, Essays, Plays/Screenplays. **Career:** BBC-Radio, London, England, producer, 1974-76; free-lance writer and broadcaster, 1977-; Presentor/Anchor Woman, T.V. BBC 2 Cultural Magazine "The Late Show," Currently. **Publications:** NOVELS: (with P. Dunant) Exterminating Angels, 1983; (with P. Dunant) Intensive Care, 1986; Snow Storms in a Hot Climate, 1988; Under My Skin, 1996; Transgressions, 1997; Mapping the Edge, 2000; The Birth of Venus, 2004. OTHER: Thin Air (television serial), 1988; Birthmarks, 1991; Fatlands, 1993. EDITOR: The War of the Words (essays), 1994; The Age of Anxiety (essays), 1997. **Address:** c/o Gillon Aitken, 29 Fernshaw Rd, London SW10 0TG, England.

DUNBAR, Gary S(eamans). American, b. 1931. **Genres:** Geography. **Career:** Longwood College, Farmville, VA, instructor in geography and history, 1956-57; University of Virginia, Charlottesville, visiting assistant professor, 1957-58, assistant professor, 1958-62, associate professor of geography, 1962-67, department chair, 1963-67; University of California, Los Angeles, visiting associate professor, 1967, associate professor, 1968-70, professor of geography, 1970-88, professor emeritus, 1988-; Ahmadu Bello University, Nigeria, visiting professor, 1965-67; member of summer faculty, University of Manitoba, 1961, Queen's University, Kingston, ON, 1962, McMaster University, 1963, and York University, 1968; State University of New York, College at Oneonta, adjunct lecturer, 1997; New York State Historical Association, member of editorial board, 1997-. **Publications:** Historical Geography of the North Carolina Outer Banks, 1958; Elisee Reclus, Historian of Nature, 1978; (comp.) A Biographical Dictionary of American Geography in the Twentieth Century, 1992, 2nd ed., 1996; The History of Geography: Collected Essays, 1996. EDITOR: The History of Geography: Translations of Some French and German Essays, 1983; The History of Modern Geography: An Annotated Bibliography of Selected Works, 1985; Modern Geography: An Encyclopedic Survey, 1991; Geography: Discipline, Profession and Subject since 1870, 2001. Contributor of articles and reviews to geography and history journals. **Address:** 13 Church St, Cooperstown, NY 13326, U.S.A. **Online address:** gdunbar1@stny.rr.com

DUNBAR, Joyce. British, b. 1944. **Genres:** Children's fiction. **Career:** Writer. Worked as an English teacher, 1968-89, the last ten years in the drama department at the college at Stratford-on-Avon; teaches writing workshops in Skyros, Greece; visits schools. **Publications:** Jugg, 1980; The Magic Rose Bough, 1984; Mundo and the Weather-Child, 1985, 1993; A Bun for Barney, 1987; The Raggy Taggy Toys, 1987; Software Superslug, 1987; Tomatoes and Potatoes, 1988; Billy and the Brolly Boy, 1988; Mouse Mad Madeline, 1988; One Frosty Friday Morning, 1989; Joanna and the Bean-Bag Beastie, 1989; Software Superslug and the Great Computer Stupor, 1989; Ollie Oddbin's Skylark, 1989; I Wish I Liked Rice Pudding, 1989; Software Superslug and the Nutty Novelty Knitting, 1990; Ten Little Mice, 1990; Five Mice and the Moon, 1990; The Scarecrow, 1991; Giant Jim and Tiny Tim, 1991; I Want a Blue Banana, 1991; Why Is the Sky Up?, 1991; Lollopy, 1991; Four Fierce Kittens, 1991; Can Do, 1992; Mouse and Mole, 1993; Mouse and Mole Have a Party, 1993; Seven Sillies, 1993; My First Read Aloud Story Book, 1993; The Spring Rabbit, 1993; The Wishing Fish Tree, 1994; Brown Bear, Snow Bear, 1994; Doodling Daniel (x4), 1994; Little Eight John (retelling), 1994; Oops-A-Daisy, 1995; Indigo and the Whale, 1996; This Is the Star, 1996; Freddie the Frog, 1996; Happy Days for Mouse and Mole, 1996; A Very Special Mouse and Mole, 1996; The Selfish Snail, 1997; If you Want to Be a Cat..., 1997; Baby Bird, 1997; Hansel and Gretel, 1997; Tell Me Something Happy before I Go to Sleep, 1998; The Pig Who Wished, 1998; The Sand Children, 1998; Panda & Gander, 1999; The Glass Garden, 1999; Eggday, 1999; The Very Small, 2000; Hip-Dip-Dip with Mouse & Mole, 2000; The Ups and Downs of Mouse & Mole, 2001; Magic Lemonade, 2001. Author of many stories for children's educational series. Contributor of stories to anthologies.

DUNBAR, Leslie W(allace). American, b. 1921. **Genres:** Philosophy, Politics/Government, Race relations. **Career:** Assistant Professor of Political Science, Emory University, Atlanta, GA, 1948-51; Atomic Energy Commission Chief of Community Affairs, Savannah River Plant, Aiken, SC, 1951-54; Guggenheim Fellow, 1954-55; Assistant Professor of Political Science, Mt. Holyoke College, South Hadley, MA, 1955-58; Director of Research, 1958-61, and Executive Director, 1961-65, Southern Regional Council, Atlanta; Executive Director and Secretary, Field Foundation, NYC, 1965-80; Visiting Professor, University of Arizona, Tucson, 1981. Consultant for National Urban League, 1980-83, Fund for Peace, 1980-83; Senior Associate, Ford Foundation, 1985-87. United Negro College Fund Scholar-at-Large, 1984-85, Book Review Editor, Southern Changes, 1989-93. **Publications:** A Republic of Equals, 1966; Puerto Ricans in the U.S., 1983; (ed.) Minority Report: What Happened to Blacks, Hispanics, American Indians and Other American Minorities in the Eighties, 1984; The Common Interest: How Our Social Welfare Policies Don't Work and What We Can Do about Them, 1988; Reclaiming Liberalism, 1990; Collected Essays, 2002. **Address:** 3050 Military Rd NW, Washington, DC 20015, U.S.A.

DUNBOYNE, Lord. *See* Obituaries.

DUNCAN, A(rchibald) A(lexander) M(cBeth). Scottish, b. 1926. **Genres:** History, Biography. **Career:** Professor of Scottish History and Literature, University of Glasgow, 1962-93 (Dean, Faculty of Arts, 1973-76; Clerk of Senate, 1978-83). Governor, Morrison's Academy, Crieff, Scotland, 1963-93; Commissioner, Royal Commission on Ancient and Historical Monuments, Scotland, 1969-92; Lecturer, Balliol College, Oxford, 1950-51, Queen's University, Belfast, 1951-53, and University of Edinburgh, 1953-62; President, Scottish History Society, 1976-81, 1997-2000. **Publications:** Scotland: The Making of the Kingdom, 1975; The Kingship of the Scots, 842-1292: Succession and Independence, 2020. EDITOR: (with J.M. Webster) Regality of Dumfermline Court Book 1531-1538, 1953; Scottish Independence 1100-1328, 1971; Formulary E: Scottish Letters and Brieves, 1286-1424, 1976; W.C. Dickinson, Scotland from the Earliest Times to 1603, 3rd. ed., 1977; Regesta Regum Scottorum, V: The Acts of Robert I, 1306-29, 1988; J. Barbour, The Bruce, 1997. **Address:** 17 Campbell Dr, Bearsden, Glasgow G61 4NF, Scotland.

DUNCAN, Alexandra. *See* **MOORE, Ishbel (Lindsay).**

DUNCAN, Alice Faye. American, b. 1967. **Genres:** Children's non-fiction, Civil liberties/Human rights. **Career:** School librarian, 1993-. **Publications:** The National Civil Rights Museum Celebrates Everyday People, 1995; Willie Jerome, 1995; Miss Viola and Uncle Ed Lee, 1999; Honey Baby Sugar Child, 2003. **Address:** PO Box 9595, Memphis, TN 38190, U.S.A. **Online address:** AFDuncan@aol.com

DUNCAN, Andy. American, b. 1964. **Genres:** Science fiction/Fantasy. **Career:** Educator and fiction writer. News & Record, Greensboro NC, features writer and copy editor, 1986-93; University of Alabama, Tuscaloosa, assistant director of student media, 2002-. **Publications:** Beluthahatchie and Other Stories, 2000. Contributor of short fiction to periodicals. **Address:** University of Alabama Office of Student Media, Box 870170, Tuscaloosa, AL 35487, U.S.A.

DUNCAN, Carol Greene. American, b. 1936. **Genres:** Art/Art history. **Career:** Ramapo College of New Jersey, Mahwah, professor of art history, 1972-. **Publications:** The Pursuit of Pleasure, 1976; The Aesthetics of Power (essays), 1993; Civilizing Rituals: Inside Public Art Museums, 1995.

DUNCAN, Christine H. (born United States). **Genres:** Mystery/Crime/Suspense. **Career:** Writer. **Publications:** Safe Beginnings (mystery novel), 2002. **Address:** c/o Author Mail, Treble Heart Books, 1284 Overlook Dr., Sierra Vista, AZ 85635, U.S.A. **Online address:** CHDuncan100@cs.com

DUNCAN, Colin A(drien) M(acKinley). Canadian, b. 1954. **Genres:** Agriculture/Forestry, Environmental sciences/Ecology, History. **Career:** University of Edinburgh, Edinburgh, Scotland, research technician in microbiology, 1979-81; Queen's University, Kingston, Ontario, historian of England and of the environment, postdoctoral research fellow, instructor, and assistant professor, 1987-98; McGill University, Montreal, Quebec, assistant professor of history of the environment, 1997-. **Publications:** (ed. with D.W. Tandy) From Political Economy to Anthropology: Situating Economic Life in Past Societies, 1994; The Centrality of Agriculture: Between Humankind and the Rest of Nature, 1996. Contributor to periodicals. **Address:** McGill School of Environment, 3534 University St, Montreal, QC, Canada H3A 2A7. **Online address:** colin.duncan@sympatico.ca

DUNCAN, Cynthia M. American. **Genres:** Sociology. **Career:** Educator and author. Mountain Association for Community Economic Development, Berea, KY, research director; Aspen Institute, director of Rural Economic Policy Program, until 1989; University of New Hampshire, Durham, associate professor, then professor of sociology and department chair, 1989-2000. **Publications:** (ed.) Rural Poverty in America, 1992; (with N. Lamborghini and E. Pank) Young Families and Youth in the North Country: A Report to the Northern New Hampshire Foundation, 1993; Worlds Apart: Why Poverty Persists in Rural America, 1999. Contributor to journals. **Address:** Department of Community and Resource Development, Ford Foundation, 320 East 43rd St., New York, NY 10017, U.S.A.

DUNCAN, Dave. Also writes as Sarah B. Franklin. Canadian (born Scotland), b. 1933. **Genres:** Science fiction/Fantasy. **Career:** Worked as geologist, 1955-76; manager of geological consulting business, 1976-86; writer. **Publications:** THE SEVENTH SWORD FANTASY SERIES: The Reluctant Swordsman, 1988; The Coming of Wisdom, 1988; The Destiny of the Sword, 1988. "A MAN OF HIS WORD" FANTASY SERIES: Magic Casement, 1990; Faery Lands Forlorn, 1991; Perilous Seas, 1991; Emperor and Clown, 1992. A HANDFUL OF MEN FANTASY SERIES: The Cutting Edge, 1992; Upland Outlaws, 1993; The Stricken Field, 1993; The Living God, 1994. THE GREAT GAME FANTASY SERIES: Past Imperative, 1995; Present Tense, 1996; Future Indefinite, 1997. OTHER FANTASY: A Rose-Red City, 1987; The Reaver Road, 1992; The Hunters' Haunt, 1995; The Cursed, 1995; Past Imperative, 1995; Present Tense, 1996; Future Indefinite, 1997; The Gilded Chain, 1998; Lord of the Fire Lands, 1999; Sky of Swords, 2000. SCIENCE-FICTION NOVELS: Shadow, 1987; West of January, 1989; Strings, 1990; Hero!, 1991. HISTORICAL NOVEL: (as Sarah B. Franklin) Daughter of Troy, 1998. **Address:** c/o Richard Curtis, Richard Curtis Associates, Inc, 171 E. 74th St., New York, NY 10021, U.S.A. **Online address:** himself@daveduncan.com

DUNCAN, David Douglas. American, b. 1916. **Genres:** Photography. **Career:** Has worked as a boxer, deep-sea diver, and airline publicity photographer; freelance photojournalist, 1938-39; photographer for the American Museum-Michael Lerner expeditions in Chile and Peru, 1940-41; coordinator for Interamerican affairs in Mexico and Central America, 1941-42; photographer for Life magazine, 1946-56; self-employed as photojournalist in Europe, the Middle East, Africa, and Asia, 1956-; photo-correspondent in Vietnam for Life and American Broadcasting Corporation (ABC) television, 1967-68; photographed the 1968 Republican and Democratic conventions for National Broadcasting Company (NBC) television. Photographs exhibited in one person shows and collections. **Publications:** ALSO PHOTOGRAPHER, EXCEPT WHERE NOTED: This Is War!: A Photo-Narrative in Three Parts, 1951; The Private World of Pablo Picasso, 1958; The Kremlin, 1960; Picasso's Picassos, 1961; Yankee Nomad: A Photographic Odyssey (autobiography), 1966; I Protest: Khe Sanh, Vietnam, 1968; Self-Portrait: U.S.A., 1969; War without Heroes, 1970; Prismatics: Exploring a New World, 1973; Goodbye Picasso, 1974; The Silent Studio, 1976; Magic Worlds of Fantasy, 1978; The Fragile Miracle of Martin Gray, 1979; Great Treasures of the Kremlin, 1979; Viva Picasso: A Centennial Celebration, 1881-1981, 1980; The World of Allah, 1982; New York, New York: Masterworks of a Street Peddler, photographs by George Forss, 1984; Sunflowers for Van Gogh, 1986; Picasso and Jacqueline, 1988; A Secret Garden, 1992; Thor, 1993; Picasso Paints a Portrait, 1996; Yo-Yo: Kidnapped in Providence, 2000; Photo Nomad, 2004.

DUNCAN, David James. American, b. 1952. **Genres:** Novellas/Short stories. **Career:** Writer, conservationist, father, fly fisherman, contemplative. **Publications:** The River Why, 1983; The Brothers K, 1992; River Teeth: Stories and Writings, 1995. **Address:** c/o Doubleday Adult Trade, 1540 Broadway, New York, NY 10036, U.S.A.

DUNCAN, Lois. Also writes as Lois Kerry. American, b. 1934. **Genres:** Novels, Mystery/Crime/Suspense, Children's fiction, Young adult fiction, Poetry, Songs/Lyrics and libretti, Paranormal, Young adult non-fiction, Essays, Children's non-fiction. **Career:** University of New Mexico, Journalism Dept., instructor, 1970-82; Woman's Day, contributing editor; freelance writer. **Publications:** Debutante Hill, 1958; The Littlest One in the Family, 1960; The Middle Sister, 1961; Game of Danger, 1962; Silly Mother, 1962; Giving Away Suzanne, 1963; Season of the Two-Heart, 1964; Ransom, 1966; Point of Violence, 1966; They Never Came Home, 1969; Major Andre, Brave Enemy, 1969; Peggy, 1970; A Gift of Magic, 1971; Hotel for Dogs, 1971; I Know What You Did Last Summer, 1973; When the Bough Breaks, 1973; Down a Dark Hall, 1974; Summer of Fear, 1976; Killing Mr. Griffin, 1978; Daughters of Eve, 1979; How to Write and Sell Your Personal Experiences, 1979; Stranger with My Face, 1981; Chapters: My Growth as a Writer, 1982; From Spring to Spring, 1982; The Terrible Tales of Happy Days School, 1983; The Third Eye, 1984; Locked In Time, 1985; Horses of Dreamland, 1985; The Twisted Window, 1987; Wonder Kid Meets the Evil Lunch Snatcher, 1988; Songs from Dreamland, 1989; Don't Look Behind You, 1989; The Birthday Moon, 1989; Who Killed My Daughter?, 1992; The Circus Comes Home, 1993; Psychic Connections: A Journey into the Mysterious World of Psi, 1995; The Magic of Spider Woman, 1995; Gallows Hill, 1997; The Longest Hair in the World, 1999; I Walk at Night, 2000; Song of the Circus, 2002. AS LOIS KERRY: Love Song for Joyce, 1958; A Promise for Joyce, 1959. EDITOR: Night Terrors (anthology), 1996; Trapped, 1998; On the Edge, 2000. **Address:** c/o Random House Inc, Juvenile Dept, 1540 Broadway, New York, NY 10030, U.S.A. **Online address:** loisduncan@arquettes.com

DUNCAN, Patrick Sheane. American. **Genres:** Novels, Plays/Screenplays. **Career:** Screenplay writer, director, and novelist. **Publications:** SCREENPLAYS: Eighty-four Charlie Mopic, 1989; Live! From Death Row (teleplay), 1992; A Home of Our Own, 1993; The Pornographer, 1994; Nick of Time, 1995; Mr. Holland's Opus, 1996; Courage under Fire, 1997. NOVELS: Courage under Fire, 1996. **Address:** c/o Putnam Berkley Publicity, 375 Hudson St., New York, NY 10014, U.S.A.

DUNCAN, Terence. See NOLAN, William F(rancis).

DUNCAN, William (Robert). British, b. 1944. **Genres:** Business/Trade/Industry, Marketing, Travel/Exploration. **Career:** University College Northampton, senior lecturer in marketing, 1990-; information officer and travel writer and tour manager, mainly concerning the Far East 1966-70; Egon Ronay Organisation, editor, 1971-75; managing editor, Kluwer Publishing, 1975-79, and Oyez Publishing, 1979-80; Export Times, regular contributor on Japan, 1980-92; Duncan Publishing, founder, principal, 1980-93. **Publications:** A Guide to Japan, 1970; Japanese Markets Review, 1974; Doing Business with Japan, 1976; Thailand: A Complete Guide, 1976; (co-author) The Operating Environment (textbook), 1999. Author of articles on Japan and Southeast Asia for newspapers and journals. **Address:** 40 Bonham Court, Kettering, Northants NN16 8NJ, England. **Online address:** william.duncan@northampton.ac.uk

DUNCKER, Patricia. British (born Jamaica), b. 1951. **Genres:** Literary criticism and history. **Career:** Educator. University of Wales, Aberystwyth, teacher of writing and 19th and 20th century literature, 1991-2002; University of East Anglia, UK, professor of prose fiction, 2002-. **Publications:** Strangers and Sisters: An Introduction to Contemporary Feminist Fiction, 1992; Hallucinating Foucault, 1996; Monsieur Shoushana's Lemon Trees, 1997; James Miranda Barry, 1999; The Deadly Space Between, 2002; Writing on the Wall (essays), 2002; Seven Tales of Sex and Death, 2003. EDITOR: In and Out of Time: Lesbian Feminist Fiction, 1990; (with V. Wilson, and contrib.) Cancer through the Eyes of Ten Women, 1996; (with J. Thomas) The Woman Who Loved Cucumbers, 2002; (with J. Thomas) Mirror, Mirror, 2004. **Address:** School of English & American Studies, University of East Anglia, Norwich, Norfolk NR4 7TJ, England.

DUNDY, Elaine. American, b. 1927. **Genres:** Novels, Plays/Screenplays, Biography. **Publications:** The Dud Avocado, 1958; My Place (play), 1962; The Old Man and Me, 1964; The Injured Party, 1974; Finch, Bloody Finch (biography), 1980; Elvis and Gladys (biography), 1985; Ferriday, Louisiana (biography), 1991. In progress: Extraordinary Combinations (memoirs). **Address:** c/o John Johnson Ltd., Clerkenwell House, 45/47 Clerkenwell Green, London EC1R 0HT, England.

DUNHAM, William. American, b. 1947. **Genres:** Mathematics/Statistics. **Career:** Ohio State University, Columbus, lecturer in mathematics, 1974-75; visiting associate professor, 1987-89; Hanover College, Hanover, IN, assistant professor, 1975-81; associate professor, 1981-90; professor of mathematics, 1990-92; Muhlenberg College, Truman Koehler Professor of Mathematics, 1992-. **Publications:** Journey through Genius: The Great Theorems of Mathematics, 1990; The Mathematical Universe, 1994; Euler: The Master of Us All, 1999. **Address:** Department of Mathematical Sciences, Muhlenberg College, Allentown, PA 18104, U.S.A. **Online address:** wdunham@muhlenberg.edu

DUNK, Thomas W. Canadian, b. 1955. **Genres:** Anthropology/Ethnology, Sociology. **Career:** Lakehead University, Thunder Bay, ON, Canada, professor, 1989-. **Publications:** It's a Working Man's Town, 1991; Social Relations in Resource Hinterlands, 1991; (ed. with S. McBride and R.W. Nelsen) The Training Trap: Ideology, Training, and the Labour Market, 1996. **Address:** Department of Sociology, Lakehead University, Thunder Bay, ON, Canada P7B 5E1.

DUNKERLEY, James. British, b. 1953. **Genres:** Politics/Government, Cultural/Ethnic topics. **Career:** Latin America Bureau, London, England, researcher, 1979-80, 1983-84; University of London, research fellow at Institute of Latin American Studies, 1981-82, professor in politics at Queen Mary and Westfield College and Institute of Latin American Studies, 1992-; University of Liverpool, England, research fellow at Centre for Latin American Studies, 1982-83; University of Notre Dame, IN, faculty fellow at Kellogg Institute, 1985. **Publications:** (with C. Whitehouse) Unity Is Strength: Trade Unions in Latin America, 1980; Bolivia: Coup d'Etat, 1980; The Long War: Dictatorship and Revolution in El Salvador, 1982; Rebellion in the Veins: Political Struggle in Bolivia, 1952-1982, 1984; (with F. Amburseley) Granada: Whose Freedom?, 1984; Origenes del poder militar en Bolivia, 1879-1935, 1987; Power in the Isthmus: A Political History of Central America, 1988; Political Suicide in Latin America, 1992; The Pacification of Central America, 1987-93, 1994; (ed. with V. Bulmer-Thomas) The United States and Latin America, 1999; Americana: The Americas in the World around 1850, 2001; Warriors and Scribes, 2001. **Address:** Institute of Latin American Studies, 31 Tavistock Square, London WCH1 9HA, England. **Online address:** j.dunkerley@sas.ac.uk

DUNKLEY, Graham (Royce). Australian, b. 1946. **Genres:** Economics. **Career:** Victoria University of Technology, Melbourne, Australia, research associate in economics, 1975-. **Publications:** The Greening of the Red: Socialism, Sustainability, and the Environmental Crisis, 1992; The Free Trade Adventure: The Uruguay Round and Globalism-a Critique, 1997, rev. ed., 2000; Free Trade: Myth, Reality and Alternatives, 2004; The Americanisation of Australia, 2005. **Address:** Dept of Economics, Victoria University of Technology, PO Box 14438, Melbourne, VIC 8001, Australia.

DUNLAP, Julie. American, b. 1958. **Genres:** Children's fiction, Children's non-fiction, Marine sciences/Oceanography, Natural history, Biography. **Career:** University of Missouri, Kansas City, MO, Biology Department, teaching assistant, 1978-79; Yale University, New Haven, CT, Biology Department, teaching fellow, 1980; Yale University Forestry School, post-doctoral researcher, 1987-88; Humane Society of the United States, Washington, DC, associate director of higher education, 1989-90; freelance writer. **Publications:** BIOGRAPHIES: Aldo Leopold: Living with the Land, 1993; Parks for the People: A Story about Frederick Law Olmstead, 1994; Eye on the Wild: A Story about Ansel Adams, 1995; Birds in the Bushes: A Story about Margaret Morse Nice, 1996. OTHER: Extraordinary Horseshoe Crabs (natural history), 1999; (with M. Lorbiecki) Louisa May and Mr. Thoreau's Flute (historical fiction picture book), 2002; (with M. Lorbiecki) John Muir and Stickeen (historical fiction picture book), 2004. Contributor to periodicals. Author of academic publications. **Address:** 6371 Tinted Hill, Columbia, MD 21045, U.S.A.

DUNLAP, Susan D. (Sullivan). American, b. 1943. **Genres:** Mystery/Crime/Suspense. **Career:** Social worker, Dept. of Social Services, Baltimore, 1966-67, NYC, 1967, and Contra Costa County, California, 1968-84; President, Sisters in Crime, 1990-91. **Publications:** Karma, 1981; As a Favor, 1984; An Equal Opportunity Death, 1984; Not Exactly a Brahmin, 1985; The Bohemian Connection, 1985; The Last Annual Slugfest, 1986; Too Close to the Edge, 1987; A Dinner to Die For, 1987; Pious Deception, 1989; Diamond in the Buff, 1990; Rogue Wave, 1991; Death and Taxes, 1992; Time Expired, 1993; High Fall, 1994; Sudden Exposure, 1996; Cop Out, 1997; No Immunity, 1998. **Address:** c/o Dominick Abel, 146 W 82nd St, New York, NY 10024, U.S.A.

DUNLEAVY, Deborah. Canadian, b. 1951. **Genres:** Music, Songs/Lyrics and libretti. **Career:** Children's performer, 1980-. Drama teacher in Toronto, Canada, 1979-80. Storytellers Group, 1998-. **Publications:** The Language Beat, 1992; Jumbo Book of Music (juvenile), 2001; Jumbo Book of Drama (juvenile), 2002. RECORDED SONGS: Jibbery Jive, 1984; Tick Tock Rock, 1986; Talking on the Telephone, 1989; Kidstreet, 1993; Strike up the Band, 2001. Composed songs for an English-as-a-foreign-language series for Japanese television, Jim Henson Productions. **Address:** PO Box 205, Brockville, ON, Canada K6V 5V2. **Online address:** kgp@recorder.ca; www.deborahdunleavy.com

DUNLOP, Eileen (Rhona). British, b. 1938. **Genres:** Children's fiction, History, Mythology/Folklore, Travel/Exploration, Biography. **Career:** Head Teacher, Preparatory School of Dollar Academy, Clackmannan, 1980-90. **Publications:** CHILDREN'S FICTION: Robinsheugh, 1975; A Flute in Mayferry Street, 1976; Fox Farm, 1978; The Maze Stone, 1982; Clementina, 1985; The House on the Hill, 1987; The Valley of Deer, 1989; The Chip Shop Ghost, 1991; Finn's Island, 1991; Green Willow's Secret, 1993; Finn's Roman Fort, 1994; Stones of Destiny, 1994; Websters' Leap, 1995; Waters of

Life, 1996; The Ghost by the Sea, 1996; Tales of St. Patrick, 1996; A Royal Ring of Gold, 1999; Ghoul's Den, 2000; The Haunting of Alice Fairlie, 20011 Nicholas Moonlight, 2002; Weerdwood, 2003. OTHER: (with A. Kamm) Edinburgh, 1982; (ed. with A. Kamm) A Book of Old Edinburgh, 1983; (with A. Kamm) Kings and Queens of Scotland, 1984; (with A. Kamm) Scottish Heroes and Heroines of Long Ago, 1984; (with A. Kamm) The Story of Glasgow, 1984; (with A. Kamm) Scottish Homes through the Ages, 1985; (ed. with A. Kamm) The Scottish Collection of Verse to 1800, 1985; (ed.) Scottish Traditional Rhymes, 1985; Saints of Scotland, 1996. **Address:** 46 Tarmangie Dr, Dollar, Clackmannan FK14 7BP, Scotland.

DUNLOP, Ian (Geoffrey David). British, b. 1925. **Genres:** Architecture, Biography. **Career:** Chaplain, Westminster School, 1959-62; Vicar of Bures, Suffolk, 1962-72; Canon and Chancellor of Salisbury Cathedral, 1972-92. **Publications:** Versailles, 1956; Palaces and Progresses of Elizabeth I, 1962; Chateaux of the Loire, 1969; Collins Companion Guide to the Ile de France, 1979, 2nd ed. as The Country round Paris; The Cathedrals' Crusade, 1982; Royal Palaces of France, 1985; Thinking It Out: Christianity in Thin Slices, 1986; Burgundy, 1990; Marie-Antoinette: A Portrait, 1993; Louis XIV, 1999; Edward VII and the Entente Cordiale, 2004. **Address:** Gowanbrae, The Glebe, Selkirk TD7 5AB, Scotland.

DUNMORE, John. New Zealander (born France), b. 1923. **Genres:** Education, History, Autobiography/Memoirs, Biography. **Career:** Executive Member, New Zealand Playwrights' Association; Sr. Lecturer, 1961-66, and Professor of French, 1966-84, Massey University, Palmerston North. President, Australasian Language and Literature Association, 1980-82. **Publications:** Le Mystere d'Omboula; French Explorers in the Pacific, 2 vols., 1965; Aventures dans le Pacifique; Success at University: Success at School, 1969; The Fateful Voyage of the St. Jean Baptiste, 1969; Norman Kirk: A Portrait, 1972; (trans.) In Search of the Maori; Meurtre a Tahiti; How to Succeed as an Extra-Mural Student; Pacific Explorer: The Life of Jean-Francois de la Perouse, 1985; New Zealand: The North Island, 1988; New Zealand: The South Island; Who's Who in Pacific Navigation, 1991; Around the Shining Waters; Visions and Realities, 1997; I Remember Tomorrow, 1998; Chronology of Pacific History, 2000; Playwrights in New Zealand, 2001; Monsieur Baret: First Woman Around the World, 2002; Louis de Bougainville's Pacific Jornal 1767-68, 2003; Storms and Dreams: The Life of L.A. de Bougainville, 2004. EDITOR: The Map Drawn by the Chief Tukitahua, 1964; An Anthology of French Scientific Prose; (and trans) The Expedition of the St. Jean-Baptiste to the Pacifique, 1769-70, 1981; New Zealand and The French, 1990; The French and the Maori, 1992; (and trans) The Journal of Jean-Francois de la Perouse, 2 vols., 1994. **Address:** 9B Pounamu Ave, Greenhithe, Auckland, New Zealand. **Online address:** john_dunmore@hotmail.com

DUNN, Charles W(illiam). American (born Scotland), b. 1915. **Genres:** Language/Linguistics, Literary criticism and history. **Career:** Emeritus Professor, Harvard University, Cambridge, Massachusetts, since 1984 (Chairman, Dept. of Celtic Languages and Literatures, 1963-84). Instructor in English, Cornell University, Ithaca, New York, 1943-46; Professor of English, University of Toronto, Ont., 1946-56, and New York University, NYC, 1956-63. **Publications:** A Chaucer Reader: Selections from the Canterbury Tales, 1952; Highland Settler: A Portrait of the Scottish Gael in Nova Scotia, 1953; The Foundling and the Werwolf: A Literary-Historical Study of Guillaume de Palerne, 1960; (with E. Byrnes) Middle English Literature, 1973; (with M. W. Bloomfield) The Role of the Poet in Early Societies, 1989. **Address:** 25 Longfellow Rd, Cambridge, MA 02138, U.S.A. **Online address:** charles.dunn@netscape.com

DUNN, Douglas (Eaglesham). Scottish, b. 1942. **Genres:** Novellas/Short stories, Poetry. **Career:** Library assistant, Renfrew County Library, Paisley, 1959-62, and Andersonian Library, Glasgow, 1962-64; assistant librarian, Akron Public Library, OH, 1964-66, and Brynmor Jones Library, University of Hull, 1969-71; freelance writer, 1971-91; University of Dundee, hon. professor, 1987-89; University of St. Andrews, professor of English, 1991-; St. Andrews Scottish Studies Center, director, 1993-. **Publications:** Terry Street, 1969; Backwaters, 1971; Night, 1971; The Happier Life, 1972; Love or Nothing, 1974; Barbarians, 1979; St. Kilda's Parliament, 1981; Europa's Lover, 1982; Elegies, Secret Villages (short stories), 1985; Selected Poems, 1986; Northlight, 1988; New and Selected Poems 1966-1988, 1989; Poll Tax: The Fiscal Fake, 1990; (trans.) Andromache, 1990; Dante's Drum-Kit, 1993; Boyfriends and Girlfriends (short stories), 1995; The Donkey's Ears, 2000; The Year's Afternoon, 2000; New Selected Poems, 2003. EDITOR: New Poems 1972-73, 1973; A Choice of Byron's Verse, 1974; Two Decades of Irish Writing, 1975; What Is to Be Given: Selected Poems of Delmore Schwartz, 1976; The Poetry of Scotland, 1979; Scotland: An Anthology,

1991; Faber Book of 20th Century Scottish Poetry, 1992; Oxford Book of Scottish Short Stories, 1995; The Faber Browning, 2004. **Address:** School of English, University of St. Andrews, St. Andrews, Fife KY16 9AL, Scotland. **Online address:** ded@st-andrews.ac.uk

DUNN, Durwood. American, b. 1943. **Genres:** Local history/Rural topics. **Career:** Hiwassee College, Madisonville, TN, instructor in history and political science, 1970-74; University of Tennessee, Knoxville, instructor in history, 1975; Tennessee Wesleyan College, Athens, instructor, 1975-77, assistant professor, 1977-79, associate professor, 1979-81, professor of history and political science, 1981-, head of department, 1976-. United Methodist Church, member of Holston Conference Commission on Archives and History, 1984-92. **Publications:** Cades Cove: The Life and Death of a Southern Appalachian Community, 1818-1937, 1988; (ed.) These Are Our Lives: McMinn Countians in the Twentieth Century, 1992; An Abolitionist in the Appalachian South: Ezekiel Birdseye on Slavery, Capitalism, and Separate Statehood in East Tennessee, 1841-1486, 1997; (ed.) Appalachian Echoes Series, 1997-. Contributor of articles and reviews to periodicals. **Address:** Dept of History and Political Science, Tennessee Wesleyan College, Athens, TN 37371, U.S.A.

DUNN, John (Montfort). British, b. 1940. **Genres:** Politics/Government. **Career:** University of Cambridge, professor of political theory, 1987-, fellow of Kings College, Cambridge, 1966- (fellow, Jesus College, 1965-66; director of Studies in History, 1966-72; lecturer in political science, 1972-77; reader in politics, 1977-87). **Publications:** The Political Thought of John Locke, 1969; Modern Revolutions: An Introduction to the Analysis of a Political Phenomenon, 1972; (co-author) Dependence and Opportunity: Political Change in Ahafo, 1973; Western Political Theory in the Face of the Future, 1979; Political Obligation in Its Historical Context, 1980; Locke, 1984; The Politics of Socialism, 1984; Rethinking Modern Political Theory: Essays 1979-83, 1985; Interpreting Political Responsibility: Essays 1981-89, 1990; The History of Political Theory, 1995; The Cunning of Unreason: Making Sense of Politics, 2000; Pensare la politica, 2002; Locke: A Very Short Introduction, 2003. EDITOR: West African States: Failure and Promise, 1978; The Economic Limits to Modern Politics, 1989; Contemporary West African States, 1989; Democracy: The Unfinished Journey, 508 BC-1993 AD, 1992; Contemporary Crisis of the Nation State, 1994; Great Political Thinkers, 1997. **Address:** Dept. of History and Politics, Kings College, Cambridge CB2 1ST, England.

DUNN, John M., (III). American, b. 1949. **Genres:** History. **Career:** Writer, educator. Paulding Country Junior High School, Dallas, Georgia, English teacher, 1972-76; U.S. Department of Defense American Junior High School, Stuttgart, West Germany, English teacher, 1976-80; Asheville-Buncombe County Technical College, Asheville, NC, instructor in adult education and writing, 1980-81; Osceola Middle School, Ocala, FL, English teacher, 1981-82; Forest High School, Ocala, teacher of history, sociology, law, and ethics, 1982-. Central Florida Community College, part-time instructor for Elder Hostel and Senior Institute programs, 199096. **Publications:** The Russian Revolution, 1994; The Relocation of the North American Indian, 1995; The Spread of Islam, 1996; Issues in Advertising, 1997. FOR YOUNG ADULTS: The Civil Rights Movement, 1998; The Enlightenment, 1999; Life during the Black Death, 2000; The Vietnam War: A History of U.S. Involvement, 2001. Contributor to newspapers and periodicals. **Address:** 222 SE 29th Terrace, Ocala, FL 34471, U.S.A.

DUNN, Mark (Rodney). American, b. 1956. **Genres:** Novels, Plays/Screenplays, Geography, Language/Linguistics. **Career:** Writer. Thirteenth Street Repertory Co., New York, NY, playwright in residence, 1988-97; New Jersey Repertory Co., Long Branch, NJ, playwright in residence, 1998-; Community League, Williamsport, PA, playwright in residence, 1999-. **Publications:** NOVELS: Ella Minnow Pea: A Progressively Lipogrammatic Epistolary Fable, 2001; Welcome to Higby, 2002; Ibid: A Life, 2004. PLAYS: Belles (two-act), 1990; Minus Some Buttons (two-act), 1991; Sandpies and Scissorlegs (two-act), 1992; Frank's Life, 1992; Five Tellers Dancing in the Rain (two-act), 1994; Judge and Jury (two-act), 1994; Oh Revoir, 1996; Elvis and Eleanor, 1996; Gendermat (one-act), 1999; Cabin Fever: A Texas Tragicomedy, 2000; The Deer and the Antelope Play, 2001; TJ or, The Public and Private Intrigues of Thomas Jefferson and His Illustrious Circle; Volley Boys; Armistice Day; Judy Garland Slept Here; Octet; Dix Tableaux, 2005. NONFICTION: United States Counties, 2004; Zounds! A Browser's Dictionary of Interjections, 2005. **Address:** Albuquerque, NM 87107, U.S.A. **Online address:** Montydunn@aol.com

DUNN, Peter Norman. American/British, b. 1926. **Genres:** Literary criticism and history. **Career:** University of Aberdeen, Assistant Lecturer, and Lecturer in Spanish, 1949-65; University of Rochester, New York, Professor of Spanish Literature, 1966-77; Wesleyan University, Middletown, Conn., Professor of Romance Languages, 1977-97. **Publications:** Castillo Solorzano and the Decline of the Spanish Novel, 1952; (ed.) Calderon, El alcalde de Zalamea, 1966; Fernando de Rojas, and La Celestina, 1975; The Spanish Picaresque Novel, 1979; Spanish Picaresque Fiction: A New Literary History, 1993. Contributor of articles of criticism and literary history. **Address:** Dept of Romance Languages, Wesleyan University, Middletown, CT 06459, U.S.A. **Online address:** pdunn@wesleyan.edu

DUNN, Stephen. American, b. 1939. **Genres:** Poetry, Essays. **Career:** Professor, and Poet-in-Residence, Stockton State College, Pomona, New Jersey (began as Associate Professor, 1974). Assistant Professor, Southwest Minnesota State College, Marshall, 1970-73; Visiting Lecturer Syracuse University, New York, 1973-74; Visiting Professor, University of Washington, 1981; Adjunct Professor of Poetry, Columbia University, NYC, 1984-87. **Publications:** Five Impersonations, 1971; Looking for Holes in the Ceiling, 1974; Full of Lust and Good Usage, 1976; (ed.) A Cat of Wind, an Alibi of Gifts (poetry), 1977; (ed.) Silence Has a Rough, Crazy Weather (poetry), 1978; A Circus of Needs, 1978; Work and Love, 1981; Not Dancing, 1984; Local Time, 1986; Between Angels, 1989; Landscape at the End of the Century, 1991; Walking Light: Essays & Memoirs, 1993; New & Selected Poems, 1974-1994, 1994; Loosestrife (poetry), 1996; Riffs & Reciprocities, 1998; Different Hours, 2000. **Address:** 790 Piney Run Rd., Frostburg, MD 21532-4241, U.S.A. **Online address:** sdunn55643@aol.com

DUNN, Suzannah. British, b. 1963. **Genres:** Novels. **Career:** Writer. Course director in novel-writing, University of Manchester. **Publications:** Darker Days than Usual (short fiction), 1990; Quite Contrary, 1991; Blood Sugar, 1994; Past Caring, 1995; Venus Flaring, 1996; Tenterhooks, 1998; Commencing Our Descent, 1999. **Address:** c/o Deborah Rogers, Rogers Colgridge & White, 20 Powis Mews, London W11 1JN, England.

DUNNAGE, Jonathan (Michael). British, b. 1963. **Genres:** History. **Career:** University of Wales, Swansea, lecturer in Italian, 1993-. **Publications:** The Italian Police and the Rise of Fascism: A Case-Study of the Province of Bologna, 1897-1925, 1997; (ed.) After the War: Violence, Justice, Continuity and Renewal in Italian Society, 1999; Twentieth Century Italy: A Social History (monograph), 2002. Contributor to books and periodicals. **Address:** Department of Italian, University of Wales, Swansea, Swansea SA2 8PP, Wales. **Online address:** j.dunnage@swansea.ac.uk

DUNNE, Gillian A(nne). Irish, b. 1956. **Genres:** Gay and lesbian issues. **Career:** Anglia Polytechnic University, Cambridge, England, lecturer in human geography, 199295; Cambridge University, Cambridge, senior research associate in social and political sciences, 1994-98; University of London, London School of Economics and Political Science, London, England, research fellow at Gender Institute, 1998-. Lecturer at institutions of higher learning; guest on television and radio programs. **Publications:** Lesbian Lifestyles: Women's Work and the Politics of Sexuality, 1997; (ed.) Living Difference: Lesbian Perspectives on Work and Family Life, 1998. Contributor to books and periodicals. **Address:** Gender Institute, London School of Economics and Political Science, University of London, Houghton St., London WC2A 2AE, England. **Online address:** gdunne@jasmine.u-net.com

DUNNE, John S(cribner). American, b. 1929. **Genres:** Theology/Religion. **Career:** University of Notre Dame, Indiana, instructor, 1957-60, assistant professor, 1960-65, associate professor, 1965-69, professor of theology, 1969-, and John A. O'Brien Chair, 1988-. Visiting Lecturer, and holder of Riggs Chair, Yale University, New Haven, CT, 1972-73; Sarum Lecturer, Oxford University, 1976-77. **Publications:** The City of the Gods, 1965; A Search for God in Time and Memory, 1969; The Way of All the Earth, 1972; Time and Myth, 1973; The Reasons of the Heart, 1978; The Church of the Poor Devil, 1982; The House of Wisdom, 1985; The Homing Spirit, 1987; The Peace of the Present, 1991; Love's Mind, 1993; The Music of Time, 1996; The Mystic Road of Love, 1999; Reading the Gospel, 2000; The Road of the Heart's Desire, 2002; A Journey with God in Time, 2003. **Address:** Theology Dept, Corby Hall, University of Notre Dame, Notre Dame, IN 46556, U.S.A.

DUNNE, Pete. American, b. 1951. **Genres:** Natural history. **Career:** Cape May Bird Observatory, Cape May, NJ, sanctuary director, 1976-99; vice president of natural history information, New Jersey Audubon Society; founder, World Series of Birding, 1984, and Operation Flight Path (protects habitats of migratory birds), 1987. Keynote speaker at Watchable Wildlife Conference, Huntington Beach, CA, 1996, and at Texas Tropics Nature '99 Festival, McAllen, TX. **Publications:** Tales of a Low-Rent Birder, 1986;

(with D. Sibley and C. Sutton) Hawks in Flight: The Flight Identification of North American Migrant Raptors, 1988; (with R. Kane and P. Kerlinger; and editor) New Jersey at the Crossroads of Migration, 1989; The Feather Quest: A North American Birder's Year, 1992; More Tales of a Low-Rent Birder, 1994; Before the Echo: Essays on Nature, 1995; The Wind Masters: The Lives of North American Birds of Prey (fiction), 1995; Small-Headed Flycatcher, Seen Yesterday, He Didn't Leave His Name, and Other Stories, 1998. Contributor to periodicals. **Address:** Cape May Bird Observatory, 701 East Lake Dr., PO Box 3, Cape May Point, NJ 08212, U.S.A. **Online address:** cmbol@njaudubon.org

DUNNING, John H. British, b. 1927. **Genres:** Business/Trade/Industry, Economics, International relations/Current affairs. **Career:** University of Reading, foundation professor of economics, 1964-74, Esmee Fairbairn Professor of Intl Investment and Business Studies, 1975-87, ICI research professor in intl investment and business studies, 1987-92, emeritus professor of intl business, 1992-. Rutgers University, Newark, state of NJ professor of intl business; University of Intl Business and Economics, Beijing, honorary professor of intl business, 1995-2001. Economists Advisory Group, London, chairman and director, 1982-2002. University of Southampton, former lecturer. Adviser, National Economic Development Office, England, 1973, UN, 1973-74, OECD, 1974-85, European Commission, 1995-96. Sr. economic adviser to UN Centre on Transnational Corporations and UNCTAD, 1987-. **Publications:** American Investment in British Manufacturing Industry, 1958, rev. ed., 1998; Studies in International Investment, 1970; United Kingdom Multinationals and Trade Flows of Less Developed Countries, 1976; (with T. Houston) United Kingdom Industry Abroad, 1976; United States Industry in Britain, 1976; International Production and the Multinational Enterprise, 1981; (with R.D. Pearce) The World's Largest Industrial Companies, 1985; Multinational Enterprises, Economic Structure, and International Competitiveness, 1985; Japanese Participation in British Industry, 1986; Explaining International Production, 1988; Multinationals: Technology and Competitiveness, 1988; Multinational Enterprises and the Global Economy, 1993; Global Business and the Challenge of the 1990s, 1993; Alliance Capitalism and Global Business, 1997. EDITOR/CO-EDITOR: Readings in International Investment, 1972; Economic Analysis and the Multinational Enterprise, 1974; International Capital Movements, 1982; The IRM Directory of Statistics on International Investment and Production, 1987; Structural Change in the World Economy, 1990; Governments, Globalization and International Business, 1997; Regions, Globalization and the Knowledge Based Economy, 2000; Global Capitalism at Bay, 2001; Theories and Paradigms of International Business Activity, 2002; Making Globalization Good, 2003. **Address:** Holly Dell Satwell Close, Rotherfield Greys, Henley on Thames RG9 4QT, England. **Online address:** j.m.turner@reading.ac.uk

DUNSTAN, G(ordon) R(eginald). British, b. 1917. **Genres:** Biography, Theology/Religion, Medicine/Health. **Career:** Ordained priest of Church of England, 1942, Chaplain to the Queen, 1976-87. Curate of Churches of England in Halifax, 1942-45, and Huddersfield, England, 1945-46; St. Deiniol's Library, Hawarden, England, sub-warden, 1946-49; vicar of Sutton Courtney with Appleford, England, 1949-55; minor canon of St. George's Chapel, Windsor Castle, England, 1955-59, and at Westminster Abbey, 1959-67; University of London, England, fellow of King's College and F.D. Maurice Professor of Moral and Social Theology, 1967-82, professor emeritus, 1982-. Canon theologian of Leicester Cathedral, 1966-82. Lecturer at William Temple College, 1947-49, and Ripon Hall, Oxford, 1953-55; Prideaux Lecturer at University of Exeter, 1968; Gresham's Professor in Divinity at City University, 1969-71; Moorhouse Lecturer at University of Melbourne, 1973; Stephenson Lecturer at University of Sheffield, 1980; honorary research fellow of University of Exeter, 1982-. Deputy priest in ordinary to The Queen, 1959-64, priest in ordinary, 1964-76; select preacher at Cambridge University, 1960, and University of Leeds, 1970; Hulsean Preacher, 1977. **Publications:** The Sacred Ministry, 1970; The Artifice of Ethics, 1974; A Moralist in the City, 1974; The Status of the Human Embryo: Perspectives from Moral Tradition, 1988. EDITOR: The Episcopal Register of Edmund Lacy, Bishop of Exeter, 1420-1455, 5 vols., 1963-72; Duty and Discernment, 1975; (with A.S. Duncan and R.B. Welbourn) Dictionary of Medical Ethics, 1977, rev. ed., 1983; (with M.J. Seller) Consent in Medicine, 1983; (with E.A. Shinebourne) Doctors' Decisions: Ethical Conflicts in Medical Practice, 1989; The Human Embryo: Aristotle and the Arabic and European Traditions, 1990; (with P.J. Lachmann) Death, Dying, and the Medical Duty, 1996. **Address:** 208 Kingsgate, Pennsylvania Rd, Exeter EX4 6DH, England.

DUNSTER, Julian A. British/Canadian, b. 1954. **Genres:** Agriculture/Forestry. **Career:** Clogwyn Climbing Gear and Troll Products, United Kingdom, technical consultant, 1973-77; Pugh-Lewis Ltd., United Kingdom,

forestry manager, 1979-80; participated in contract claim staking, prospecting, and exploration for gold and tungsten, British Columbia, Canada, and Yukon Territory, Canada, 1980-81; British Columbia Ministry of Forests, Golden Forest District, district planning forester, 1981-84; Dunster and Associates Ltd. (environmental consulting firm), principal, 1984-; University of Toronto, sessional lecturer in department of geography, 1988; Simon Fraser University, assistant professor in natural resources management program, 1989-90; registered professional forester, 1984-; University College of North Wales, Bangor, visiting scientist in department of forestry and wood science, 1986. **Publications:** (with R.B. Gibson) Forestry and Assessment: Development of the Class Environmental Assessment for Timber Management in Ontario, 1989; (with K. Dunster) Dictionary of Natural Resource Management, 1996; (with S.M. Murray) Arboriculture and the Law in Canada, 1997. Contributor to periodicals. **Address:** PO Box 109, Bowen Island, BC, Canada V0N 1G0.

DUNTEMANN, Jeff. (born United States), b. 1952. **Genres:** Technology. **Career:** Programmer, writer, and editor. Xerox Corporation, programmer; PC Tech Journal, senior technical editor; Borland, creator of programming magazine Turbo Technix; Coriolis Group, Scottsdale, AZ, cofounder and editorial director of book publishing division, 1989-2002; Paraglyph Press, Scottsdale, cofounder, 2002-. **Publications:** Complete Turbo Pascal, Scott, 1986, revised and enlarged edition, 1989; Turbo Pascal Solutions, Scott, 1988; Assembly Language from Square One: For the PC AT and Compatibles 1990; Assembly Language: Step-by-Step, 1992, revised and published as Assembly Language Step-by-Step: Programming with DOS and Linux, 2000; (with Keith Weiskamp) PC Techniques C/C++ Power Tools: HAX, Techniques, and Hidden Knowledge, 1992; (editor) Paul S. Cilwa, Borland Pascal 7 Insider 1993; (editor) Jim Mischel, Macro Magic with Turbo Assembler, 1993; (with Ron Pronk) Inside the PowerPC Revolution, 1994; (with Paul S. Cilway) Windows Programming Power with Custom Controls, 1994; (editor) Scott Jarol, Visual Basic Multimedia Adventure Set, 1994; (editor) Jim Mischel, The Developer's Guide to WinHelp.Exe: Harnessing the Windows Help Engine, 1994; (with Urban A. LeJeune) Mosaic and Web Explorer 1995; (with Urban A. LeJeune) Netscape and HTML Explorer, 1995, revised and published as The New Netscape and HTML Explorer, 1996; (with Ron Pronk and Patrick Vincent) Web Explorer Pocket Companion, 1995; (with Ron Pronk and Patrick Vincent) Mosaic Explorer Pocket Companion, 1995; All-in-One Web Surfing and Publishing Kit (includes CD-ROM), 1995; (with Jim Mischel and Don Taylor) Delphi Programming Explorer, 1995, published with CD-ROM as Delphi Starter Kit, 1995, revised and published as The New Delphi 2 Programming Explorer, 1996; (with Jim Mischel) Borland C++Builder Programming Explorer 1997; Jeff Duntemann's Drive-by Wi-Fi Guide, 2003. Contributor of articles to periodicals and of short fiction to science-fiction anthologies. **Address:** c/o Paraglyph Press Inc, 238 East Cambridge Ave, Phoenix, AZ 85006, U.S.A. **Online address:** jeff@duntemann.com

DUPLESSIS, Rachel Blau. American, b. 1941. **Genres:** Poetry, Literary criticism and history, Essays. **Career:** Columbia University, Columbia, NY, preceptor at School of General Studies, 1966, preceptor at Columbia College, 1967-70; Rijksuniversiteit te Gent, Ghent, Belgium, supplant, 1970-71; Universite de Lille III, France, maitre de conference associe, 1970-72; Trenton State College, NJ, assistant professor, 1972-73; Rutgers University, New Brunswick, NJ, Douglass College, lecturer, 1973-74; Temple University, Philadelphia, PA, assistant professor, 1974-83, associate professor, 1983-87, professor, 1987-; writer. **Publications:** POETRY: Wells, 1980; Gypsy/Moth, 1984; Tabula Rosa, 1987; Draft X: Letters, 1991; Drafts (3-14), 1991; Essais: quatres poemes, 1996; Drafts 15-XXX, The Fold, 1997; Drafts 1-38, Toll, 2001; Draft, Unnumbered: Precis, 2003. OTHER: Writing beyond the Ending: Narrative Strategies of Twentieth-Century Women Writers (literary criticism), 1985; H.D.: The Career of That Struggle (criticism), 1986; The Pink Guitar: Writing as Feminist Practice (essays), 1990; Genders, Races and Religious Cultures in Modern American Poetries, 1908-1934 (criticism), 2001. EDITOR: (with S.S. Friedman) Signets: Reading H.D. (critical essays), 1990; The Selected Letters of George Oppen, 1990; (with A. Snitow) The Feminist Memoir Project, 1998; (with P. Quartermain) The Objectivist Nexus, 1999. Work represented in anthologies. Contributor to periodicals. **Address:** English Department, Anderson Hall, Temple University, 1114 S Berks Mall, Philadelphia, PA 19122-6090, U.S.A.

DUPRAU, Jeanne. American, b. 1944. **Genres:** Adult non-fiction. **Career:** Teacher, editor, and technical writer in California and New York. Volunteer work includes teaching computer classes for seniors, community garden projects, and grief counseling. **Publications:** Adoption: The Facts, Feelings, and Issues of a Double Heritage, 1981; (with M. Tyson) The Apple IIgs Book, 1986; The Earth House: There Is Nothing to Fear in This Moment,

1992; Cloning, 2000; Cells, 2002; The American Colonies, 2002; The City of Ember, 2003. **Address:** 237 Santa Margarita Ave., Menlo Park, CA 94025, U.S.A. **Online address:** jduprau@aol.com

DUPRÉ, Louis. American (born Belgium). **Genres:** Philosophy, Theology/Religion. **Career:** Professor in the Philosophy of Religion, Yale University, New Haven, CT, 1973-. Instructor, 1958-59, Assistant Professor, 1959-64, Associate Professor, 1964-67, and Professor in Philosophy, Georgetown University, Washington, D.C. **Publications:** Het Vertrekpunt der Marxistische Wijsbegeerte, 1954; Kierkegaard as Theologian, 1963; Contraception and Catholics, 1964; The Philosophical Foundations of Marxism, 1966; The Other Dimension, 1972; Transcendent Selfhood, 1976; A Dubious Heritage, 1977; The Deeper Life, 1981; Terugkeer naar Innerlijkheid, 1981; Marx's Social Critique of Culture, 1983; The Common Life, 1984; Passage to Modernity, 1993; Metaphysics and Culture, 1994; Religious Mystery and Rational Refection, 1998; Symbols of the Sacred, 2000. EDITOR: Faith and Reflection, 1969; Light from Light, 1987; Christian Spirituality: Post-Reformation and Modern, 1989. **Address:** 67 N Racebrook Rd, Woodbridge, CT 06525, U.S.A. **Online address:** louis.dupre@yale.edu

DUPREE, Nathalie. American, b. 1939. **Genres:** Food and Wine. **Career:** Professional chef. Restaurant chef in Majorca, Spain; then opened a country restaurant in Georgia; founder, chef, and teacher of Rich's Cooking School, 1975-84. Hosted half-hour shows for PBS, TVFN, and the Learning Channel, 1986-. Appeared on television and radio shows. **Publications:** COOKBOOKS: New Southern Cooking with Nathalie Dupree, 1988; Nathalie Dupree's Matters of Taste, 1990; Nathalie Dupree Cooks for Family and Friends, 1991; Nathalie Dupree's Southern Memories, 1993; Nathalie Dupree Cooks Great Meals for Busy Days, 1994; Nathalie Dupree Cooks Everyday Meals from a Well-Stocked Pantry, 1995; Nathalie Dupree Cooks Quick Meals for Busy Days, 1996; Nathalie Dupree's Comfortable Entertaining, 1999. Contributor to periodicals. **Address:** 100 Queen St, Charleston, SC 29401, U.S.A. **Online address:** nathalie@nathalie.com

DUPREE, Sherry Sherrod. American, b. 1946. **Genres:** Education, History, Librarianship, Bibliography, Biography, Reference. **Career:** Ann Arbor Public Schools, Tappan Junior High School Media Center, MI, instructional media specialist and dept chair, 1970-76; University of Michigan Hospital, Ann Arbor, summer dietetic supervisor, 1970-73; University of Florida Libraries, Gainesville, associate Afro-American and religion specialist, 1977-83; University of Florida, Institute of Black Culture, Gainesville, project director, 1982-93; Santa Fe Community College, Gainesville, reference librarian, 1983-; Bethune Cookman College, Daytona Beach, FL, extension professor of teacher education, 1986-89. Visiting professor, Eastern Michigan University, Ypsilanti, MI, 1975. Founder and organizer, DuPree African-American Pentecostal and Holiness Collection (materials on African American Pentecostal churches, etc.), New York Public Library's Schomburg Center for Research in Black Culture. PNEUMA, associate editor, 1985-. **Publications:** NONFICTION: Biographical Dictionary of African-American, Holiness-Pentecostals: 1880-1990, c. 1990; (with H.C. DuPree) African-American (Good News) Music, 1993; African-American Pentecostals Movement: An Annotated Bibliography, 1996. Author or co-author of booklets. Contributor to books, reference books, and periodicals. **Address:** Santa Fe Community College Library, Building Y-225, 3000 NW 83rd St, Gainesville, FL 32606, U.S.A. **Online address:** sherry.dupree@santafe.cc.fl.us

DUPUIS, Robert. American, b. 1926. **Genres:** Music, Biography. **Career:** Detroit Public Schools, Detroit, MI, worked as teacher, counselor, assistant principal, and principal, 1950-84; volunteer tutor for Detroit school children, 1991-. **Publications:** Bunny Berigan: Elusive Legend of Jazz, 1993. Work represented in books. **Address:** 725 Lincoln Rd., Grosse Pointe, MI 48230, U.S.A. **Online address:** bunnyrob@aol.com

DURAC, Jack. See RACHMAN, Stanley Jack.

DURAN, Jane. American, b. 1947. **Genres:** Education. **Career:** Rutgers University, New Brunswick, NJ, coadjutant, 1981; Trenton State College, Trenton, NJ, visiting assistant professor, 1982-83; Hamilton College, Clinton, NY, visiting assistant professor, 1983-84; University of California, Santa Barbara, fellow in education, 1984-85; affiliated scholar in philosophy, 1985-87; Mount St. Mary's College, Los Angeles, CA, assistant professor, 1987-88; University of California, Santa Barbara, research associate and lecturer in philosophy, 1988-98, member of Sociology Network Theory Seminar, 1990-97, and Science, Culture, Technology, and Society Discussion Group, 1995-98. California Polytechnic State University, San Luis Obispo, lecturer, 1985 and 1986; Johns Hopkins University, associate of Center for Research on Students Placed at Risk, 1995-98; guest lecturer at colleges and universities.

Publications: Epistemics, 1989; Toward a Feminist Epistemology, 1991; Knowledge in Context, 1994; Philosophies of Science/Feminist Theories, 1997. Contributor to books. Contributor to philosophy journals. **Address:** University of California at Santa Barbara, Graduate School of Education, Santa Barbara, CA 93106, U.S.A. **Online address:** jduran@education.ucsb.edu

DURANG, Christopher. American, b. 1949. **Genres:** Plays/Screenplays. **Publications:** (with Albert Innaurato) The Idiots Karamazov (musical play), 1974; A History of the American Film, 1978; The Vietnamization of New Jersey, 1978; The Nature and Purpose of the Universe/Death Comes to Us All, Mary Agnes/'dentity Crisis: Three Short Plays, 1979; Sister Mary Ignatius Explains It All for You, 1980; Christopher Durang Explains It All for You, 1983; Baby with the Bathwater, 1984; The Marriage of Bette and Boo, 1985; Laughing Wild, 1988; Durang/Durang (evening of one-acts), 1994; Christopher Durang-27 Short Plays, 1995; Christopher Durang-Complete Full Length Plays, 1997. **Address:** c/o Patrick Herold, Helen Merrill Ltd., 295 Lafayette St, Ste 915, New York, NY 10012-2700, U.S.A.

DURBAN, Pam. American, b. 1947. **Genres:** Novels, Novellas/Short stories. **Career:** Editor and writer, Atlanta Gazette, 1974-75; visiting assistant professor of creative writing, State University of New York at Geneseo, 1979-80; assistant professor of creative writing, 1980-81, Murray State University; associate professor of creative writing, Ohio University, 1981-86. **Publications:** (ed.) Cabbagetown Families, Cabbagetown Food, 1976; All Set About with Fever Trees and Other Stories, 1985; The Laughing Place (novel), 1993; So Far Back, 2000. **Address:** Department of English, Georgia State University, Atlanta, GA 30303, U.S.A.

DURDEN, Robert F(ranklin). American, b. 1925. **Genres:** History, Biography. **Career:** Duke University, Durham, NC, professor of history, 1952-, chairman of the dept., 1974-80. **Publications:** James Shepherd Pike: Republicanism and the American Negro, 1850-1882, 1957; Reconstruction Bonds and Twentieth-Century Politics: South Dakota and North Carolina (1904), 1962; The Climax of Populism: The Election of 1896, 1965; (ed.) The Prostrate State: South Carolina under Negro Government, 1968; The Gray and the Black: The Confederate Debate on Emancipation, 1972; The Dukes of Durham, 1865-1929, 1975; (co-author) Maverick Republican in the Old North State: Political Biography of Daniel L. Russell, 1977; The Self-Inflicted Wound: Nineteenth Century Southern Politics, 1985; The Launching of Duke University, 1924-49, 1993; Lasting Legacy to the Carolinas: The Duke Endowment, 1924-1994, 1998; Electrifying the Piedmont Carolinas: The Duke Power Company, 1904-1997, 2001; Bold Entrepreneur: A Life of James B. Duke, 2003. **Address:** History Dept, Box 90719, Duke University, Durham, NC 27708, U.S.A.

DURFEE, Mary. American, b. 1951. **Genres:** Philosophy. **Career:** Worked for NCR Corp., 1980-81; Colgate University, Hamilton, NY, lecturer, 1983-84; Canisius College, Buffalo, NY, assistant professor, 1985-86; Antioch College, Center for Adult Learning, Yellow Springs, OH, adjunct assistant professor, 1987-89; Wittenberg University, Springfield, OH, visiting assistant professor, 1990-91; University of Dayton, Dayton, OH, adjunct assistant professor, 1992; Michigan Technological University, Houghton, assistant professor of social sciences, 1992-. University of Dayton, adjunct assistant professor, 1987-90. **Publications:** (with J.N. Rosenau) Thinking Theory Thoroughly: Coherent Approaches to an Incoherent World, 1995. Contributor to periodicals. **Address:** Department of Social Sciences, Michigan Technological University, 1400 Townsend Dr., Houghton, MI 49931, U.S.A.

DURGIN, Doranna. American, b. 1960. **Genres:** Science fiction/Fantasy. **Career:** Author. Columbus Metroparks, OH, park naturalist, from 1982; worked homestead and old farm in Appalachian mountains in the 1980s; worked as a groomer at pet stores in Rochester, NY, 1992-95; freelance technical writer, Rochester, NY, 1996-. Currently managing editor at Wordwright Critique Service; owner and operator of author web page service, Blue Hound Visions. Has done animal rescue work in Kentucky and Virginia. **Publications:** FANTASY NOVELS: Dun Lady's Jess, 1994; Changespell, 1996; Touched by Magic, 1996; Barrenlands, 1998; Wolf Justice, 1998; Wolverine's Daughter, 2000; Seer's Blood, 2000; Tooth and Claw, 2001; A Feral Darkness, 2001; Gene Roddenberry's Earth: Final Conflict-Heritage, 2001. **Address:** PO Box 31123, Flagstaff, AZ 86003-1123, U.S.A. **Online address:** doranna@sff.net

DURHAM, Walter T. American, b. 1924. **Genres:** History, Local history/Rural topics, Biography. **Career:** Durham Manufacturing Co. Inc., partner, 1948-73, chairperson, 1973-. Gallatin Aluminum Products Co. Inc., cofounder, treasurer, 1958-63, president, 1963-73. Tennessee Library

Advisory Council, chairperson, 1991-93; White House Conference on Library and Information Services, member of task force, 1991-. **Publications:** The Great Leap Westward: A History of Sumner County, Tennessee, from Its Beginnings to 1805, 1969; Old Sumner: A History of Sumner County, Tennessee, from 1805 to 1861, 1972; A College for This Community, 1974; Daniel Smith, Frontier Statesman, 1976; The Building Supply Dealer in Tennessee: A History of the Tennessee Building Material Association, 1925-1976, 1976; James Winchester, Tennessee Pioneer, 1979; Rebellion Revisited: A History of Sumner County, Tennessee, from 1861 to 1870, 1982; Nashville, the Occupied City: The First 17 Months, 1985; (with J.W. Thomas) A Pictorial History of Sumner County, Tennessee, 1796-1986, 1986; Reluctant Partners: Nashville and the Union, July 1, 1863 to June 30, 1865, 1987; Before Tennessee: The Southwest Territory, 1790-1796, 1990; Wynnewood, Bledsoe's Lick, Castalian Springs, Tennessee, 1994; (with T. and J.F. Creasy) A Celebration of Houses Built before 1900 in Sumner County, Tennessee, 1996; Volunteer 49ers: Tennessee and the California Gold Rush, 1997; The Life of William Trousdale, Soldier, Statesman, Diplomat, 2001; (with G. Milliken) Gallatin 200: A Time Line History Celebrating the Bicentennial of Gallatin, Tennessee, 2002; Josephus Conn Guild and Rosemont: Politics and Plantation in 19th Century Tennessee, 2002; Bailie Peyton of Tennessee: 19th Century Politics and Thoroughbreds, 2004. Contributor to books and history journals. **Address:** 1010 Durham Dr, Gallatin, TN 37066, U.S.A. **Online address:** WTDurham@bellsouth.net

DURNBAUGH, Donald F. American, b. 1927. **Genres:** History, Theology/Religion. **Career:** Director of Program Brethren Service Commission, Austria, 1953-56; Juniata College, PA, Assistant Professor of History, 1958-62, Archivist, 1992-; Bethany Theological Seminary, Oak Brook, IL, Associate Professor, 1962-69, Professor of Church History, 1970-88; Brethren Colls. Abroad, Marburg and Strasburg, Germany, Director in Europe, 1964-65; Northern Baptist Theological Seminary, Adjunct Professor, 1968-71; Center for Reformation and Free Church Studies, Chicago Theological Seminary, Associate, 1966-78; Church of the Brethren, Moderator, 1985-86; Elizabethtown College, PA, Zeigler Professor of Religion and History, 1989-93; Communal Societies, editor, 1995-98. **Publications:** The Believers' Church, 1968; Pragmatic Prophet: The Life of Michael Robert Zigler, 1989; Brethren Beginnings, 1992; Fruit of the Vine: A History of the Brethren, 1708-1995, 1997. EDITOR: (and trans.) European Origins of the Brethren, 1958; (and trans.) The Brethren in Colonial America, 1967; (and co-author) Die Kirche der Brueder, 1971; (and co-author) The Church of the Brethren Past and Present, 1971; (and trans.) Every Need Supplied, 1974; To Serve the Present Age, 1975; On Earth Peace, 1978; The Brethren Encyclopedia, 3 vols., 1983-84; Meet the Brethren, 1984; (and co-author) Church of the Brethren: Yesterday and Today, 1986; (co) The Day Book/Account Book of Alexander Mack, Jr. (1712-1803), 2004. **Address:** Juniata College, PO Box 948, Huntingdon, PA 16652-2119, U.S.A. **Online address:** durnbaughd@juniata.edu

DURO, Paul. British/Australian, b. 1953. **Genres:** Art/Art history. **Career:** Newcastle upon Tyne Polytechnic, Newcastle upon Tyne, England, associate senior lecturer, 1984-88; Australian National University, Canberra, lecturer in art history, 1989-95, senior lecturer, 1995-99; University of Rochester, NY, professor of art history, 2000-. **Publications:** (ed.) Perspectives on Academic Art, Canberra, 1991; (with M. Greenhalgh) The Essential Art History, 1992; (ed. and author of introduction) The Rhetoric of the Frame, 1996; The Academy and the Limits of Painting in 17th-Century France, 1997. Contributor of articles and reviews to art journals. **Address:** Department of Art and Art History, 424 Morey Hall, University of Rochester, Rochester, NY 14627, U.S.A. **Online address:** duro@mail.rochester.edu

DURRANT, Lynda. American, b. 1954. **Genres:** Novels. **Career:** Writer and teacher. **Publications:** Echohawk, 1996. **Address:** PO Box 123, Bath, OH 44210, U.S.A.

DURRELL, Julie. American, b. 1955. **Genres:** Children's fiction, Illustrations. **Career:** Writer and illustrator. **Publications:** SELF-ILLUSTRATED FOR CHILDREN: Mouse Tails, 1985; Tickety-Tock, What Time Is It?, 1990; It's My Birthday!, 1990; Little Mouse's Book of Colors, 1991. Illustrator of books by others including C. Haywood, J. Ryder, D.R. Parnell, N. Wing. **Address:** c/o Paige Gillies, Publisher's Graphics, 251 Greenwood Ave., Bethel, CT 06801, U.S.A.

DURRENBERGER, E. Paul. American, b. 1943. **Genres:** Anthropology/Ethnology, Archaeology/Antiquities. **Career:** Archaeological researcher and field worker for Texas Archaeological Research Laboratory, Texas Memorial Museum, Smithsonian Institution, and Washington State University, 1962-65; Eastern New Mexico University, Portales, instructor in anthropology, 1966;

Antioch College, assistant professor of anthropology, 1971-72; University of Iowa, Iowa City, assistant professor, 1972-76, associate professor, 1976-82, professor of anthropology, 1982-. University of Iceland, Fulbright professor, 1984; University of South Alabama, visiting professor, 1987-89. Conducted field work in Thailand and Iceland; consultant to University of Chiangmai. National Public Radio, commentator for the series All Things Considered, 1995-96. **Publications:** A Socio-Medical Study of the Lisu of Northern Thailand, 1970; A SocioEconomic Study of a Shan Village in Maehongson Province, 1977; Agricultural Production and Household Budgets in a Shan Peasant Village in Northwestern Thailand: A Quantitative Description, 1978; Lisu Religion (monograph), 1989; (with N. Tannenbaum) Analytical Perspectives on Shan Agriculture and Village Economics, 1990; (with D. Durrenberger) The Saga of Gunnlaugur Snake's Tongue, with an Essay on the Structure and Translation of the Saga, 1992; It's All Politics: South Alabama's Seafood Industry, 1992; The Dynamics of Medieval Iceland: Political Economy and Literature, 1992; Icelandic Essays: Explorations in the Anthropology of a Modern Nation, 1995; Gulf Coast Soundings: People and Policy in the Mississippi Shrimp Industry, 1996; (with D. Durrenberger) The Saga of Havardur of Isafjordur, with an Essay on the Political, Economic, and Cultural Background of the Saga, 1996. EDITOR: (and contrib.) Chayanov, Peasants, and Economic Anthropology, 1984; (with G. Palsson, and contrib.) The Anthropology of Iceland, 1989; (with L. Maril and J.S. Thomas) Marine Resource Utilization, 1989; (with Palsson, and contrib.) Images of Contemporary Iceland: Everyday Lives and Global Contexts, 1996; State Power and Culture in Thailand: An Historical View, 1996. Contributor to books. Contributor of articles and reviews to professional journals. **Address:** Department of Anthropology, University of Iowa, Iowa City, IA 52242, U.S.A.

DURSCHMIED, Erik. Canadian (born Austria), b. 1930. **Genres:** Plays/Screenplays, History, Autobiography/Memoirs, Documentaries/Reportage. **Career:** Canadian Broadcasting Corp., Toronto, ON, camera operator, 1956-60; British Broadcasting Corp., London, England, camera operator for Panorama, 1960-72; independent film producer in Paris, France, 1973-80; Columbia Broadcasting System, NYC, film director and camera operator, 1981-86; independent film producer in Paris and Los Angeles, CA, 1987-; filmmaker and writer. Austrian Military Staff College, lecturing professor. Lecturer at institutions in the U.S. and Canada. **Publications:** Don't Shoot the Yanqui: The Life of a War Cameraman (autobiography), 1990; Armee Rouge: Le dernier Combat, 1991. DOCUMENTARY SCREENPLAYS: Castro, 1958; Guy Burgess: The Super Spy, 1959; Algiers: A Day of Killing, 1961; North Korea: Portrait of a Country, 1962; Yemen Story, 1963; The Seven Hundred Million: First-Ever Look at China, 1964; Vietnam: Trilogy of Combat, 1964; The Mills of the Gods, 1965; Hill 943, 1968; Army of the Holy Land, 1969; Belfast Weekend: A Bomb and a Pub Crawl, 1969; Amazonian Indians, 1969; Dacca Massacre, 1971; De Gaulle Funeral, 1971; Aetna Eruption, 1972; The France I Love, 1973; Those Who Are Lost, 1974; Dubai Army, 1975; Day in the Life of an Oil Sheikh, 1975; Dollars Like Sand, 1975; A Short Street in Belfast, 1975; Rhodesia White, 1976; Tear for the Sea: Amoco Dadiz Oil Spill, 1977; Apartheid, 1977; Cobra and Co., 1978; Defense of Europe, 1979; Battle of the Skies: Airbus versus Boeing, 1980; Firebreak: World War III Rehearsal, 1980; Help!! Cambodia's Killing Fields, 1980; Vietnam: Bitter Victory, 1981; Beirut (news reports), 1981; Under the Soviet Gun-Afghanistan, 1983; A Trial in Kabul: Dr. Augoyard, 1983; Iraq: Portrait of a Country at War, 1984-86; North Korea: A Portrait of Isolation, 1985; The Day the Reindeer Died, 1986; The Storm, 1987; Mystery of the Pyramid, 1988. MILITARY HISTORY: The Hinge Factor, 1999; The Weather Factor, 2000; Whisper of the Blade, 2001; The Blood of Revolution (in UK as Whisper of the Blade), 2001; The Hinges of Battle, 2002; From Armageddon to the Fall of Rome, 2002; Unsung Heroes, 2003. **Address:** 14 Rue Rambuteau, 75003 Paris, France. **Online address:** erikfrance@aol.com

DUSSEL PETERS, Enrique. German (born France), b. 1965. **Genres:** Economics, Area studies. **Career:** Universidad Nacionál Autónoma de México, Mexico City, professor of economics, 1993-. Consultant to Mexican and international institutions. **Publications:** (ed. with M. Piore and C.R. Durán) Pensar globalmente y actuar regionalmente: Hacia un nuevo paradigma industrial para el siglo XXI, 1997; (with C.R. Durán and T. Taniura) Changes in Industrial Organization of the Mexican Automobile Industry by Economic Liberalization, 1997; La economía de la polarización: Teoría y evolución del cambio estructural de las manufacturas mexicanas, 1982-1996, 1997; (with C.R. Durán) El reto de la educación superior en la sociedad del conocimiento, 1997; (with C.R. Durán) Dinámica Regional y Competitividad Industrial, 1999; Las industrias farmacéutica y farmoquímica en México y el distrito federal, 1999; El tratado de libre comercio de Norteamérica y el desempeño de la economía en México, 2000; Polarizing Mexico: The Impact of Liberalization Strategy, 2000; Estrategias y políticas de competitividad en Centroamérica: De la integración externa a la integración interna, 2001.

Contributor to periodicals. **Address:** Faculty of Economics, City University, Universidad Nacional Autonoma de Mexico, 04510 Mexico City, Mexico. **Online address:** dussel@servidor.unam.mx

DUSSLING, Jennifer. American, b. 1970. **Genres:** Children's fiction. **Career:** Writer. **Publications:** Finger Painting, 1995; In a Dark, Dark House, 1995; Under the Sea, 1995; Bossy Kiki, 1996; Stars, 1996; Creep Show, 1996; A Very Strange Dollhouse, 1996; Don't Call Me Names!, 1996; Muppet Treasure Island, 1996; Top Knots!: The Ultimate Bracelet and Hair-Wrapping Kit, 1996; The Bunny Slipper Mystery, 1997; A Simple Wish, 1997; Bug Off!, 1997. **Address:** 14 Redcliffe Ave., Highland Park, NJ 08904-1641, U.S.A.

DUTKINA, Galina (Borisovna). Russian, b. 1952. **Genres:** Essays. **Career:** Moscow Radio, Japanese Section, Moscow, USSR, editor and announcer, 1974-79; Progress Publishing House, Moscow, senior editor in Oriental department, 1980-83; Raduga Publishing House, Moscow, Russia, expert editor in foreign literature department, 1983-93; Center for Postgraduate Training of High School Professors, Moscow, professor, 1993-95; freelance journalist and translator, 1995-. **Publications:** Misuteri Mosukuwa (in Japanese; title means: Mysterious Moscow: The Diary of Galya-san), 1993; Moscow Days (essays), 1996. Contributor to books and periodicals. Translator of books into Russian from Japanese and English. **Address:** 116 Leningradskoe shosse, Flat 90, 125445 Moscow, Russia.

DUTOIT, Ulysse. French, b. 1944. **Genres:** Art/Art history. **Career:** Educator, filmmaker, producer, and author. Taught film studies at Ecole Normale, University of Lausanne, Rutgers University, and Hunter College; University of California at Berkeley, Berkeley, lecturer in French cinema, 1975-. Producer of educational television programs in France. **Publications:** WITH L. BERSANI: The Forms of Violence: Narrative in Assyrian Art and Modern Culture, 1985; Arts of Impoverishment: Beckett, Rothko, Resnais, 1993; Caravaggio's Secrets, 1998; Caravaggio, 1999. **Address:** Department of French, 4216 Dwinelle, 642-4519, University of California, Berkeley, CA 94720, U.S.A.

DÜTTMANN, Martina (Friederike). Also writes as Martina Schneider. German, b. 1938. **Genres:** Architecture. **Career:** Bauwelt (architectural weekly), Berlin, Germany, editor, 1966-70; free-lance writer, 1970-72; Free University of Berlin, curriculum planner, 1972-74; University of Stuttgart, lecturer, 1972-74; Hochschuele fuer Bildende Kuenste, Berlin, lecturer, 1974-75; Abakon, Berlin, publisher, 1975-79; Archibook, Berlin, publisher, 1979-. Birkhaeuser Verlag, architectural editor, 1988-95; Bauwelt Berlin Annual, editor, 1996-2000. **Publications:** (as Martina Schneider) Abenteuerspielplaetze (title means: Adventure Playgrounds), 1972; (as Martina Schneider) Information ueber Gestalt (title means: Information on Gestalt), 1975, 2nd ed., 1986; Johannes Uhl: Zeichnen und Bauen 1987; (ed. with F. Schneider) Morris Lapidus: The Architect of the American Dream, 1992; Wie die Architektur zur Sprache kommt (title means: How Architecture Finds Its Language), 1992. **Address:** Archibook, Westendallee 97 f, 14052 Berlin, Germany. **Online address:** bauwelt-berlin-annual@t-online.de

DUTTON, Michael R. Australian (born England), b. 1957. **Genres:** Politics/Government, Area studies, Humanities. **Career:** University of Adelaide, Adelaide, Australia, lecturer in Chinese politics and language at Asian Studies Centre, 1988-90; University of Melbourne, Melbourne, Australia, lecturer, 1990-93, senior lecturer in Chinese politics and social theory, 1994-. **Publications:** Policing and Punishment in China: From Patriarchy to "the People," 1992; Streetlife China, 1998. **Address:** Department of Political Science, University of Melbourne, Melbourne, VIC, Australia. **Online address:** m.dutton@politics.unimelb.edu.au

DUTTON, Paul Edward. Canadian, b. 1952. **Genres:** History. **Career:** Simon Fraser University, Burnaby, British Columbia, Canada, professor of medieval history, 1983-. **Publications:** The "Glosae super Platonem" of Bernard of Chartres, 1991; Carolingian Civilization: A Reader, 1993, 2nd ed., 2004; The Politics of Dreaming in the Carolingian Empire, 1994; (with E. Jeauneau) The Autograph of Eriugena, 1996; (with H.L. Kessler) The Poetry and Paintings of the First Bible of Charles the Bald, 1997; Charlemagne's Courtier: The Complete Einhard, 1998; Charlemagne's Mustache and Other Cultural Clusters of a Dark Age, 2004. **Address:** Dept of Humanities, Simon Fraser University, Burnaby, BC, Canada V5A 1S6.

DUVAL, Aimee. *See* THURLO, Aimee.

DUVOISIN, Roger C(lair). American, b. 1927. **Genres:** Medicine/Health. **Career:** Lenox Hill Hospital, NYC, rotating intern, 1954-55, assistant

resident in neurology, 1955-56; Columbia Presbyterian Medical Center, NYC, assistant resident at Neurological Institute, 1956-58; Columbia University, NYC, research associate at College of Physicians and Surgeons, 1962-64, assistant professor, 1964-69, associate professor, 1969-72, professor of neurology, 1972-73; Mount Sinai School of Medicine of the City University of New York, NYC, professor of neurology, 1973-79; University of Medicine and Dentistry of New Jersey, professor of neurology and chairman of department at Rutgers Medical School, Piscataway, 1979-, William Dow Lovett Professor of Neurology at Robert Wood Johnson Medical School, New Brunswick, 1990-96, Professor Emeritus, 1996-. Diplomate of American Board of Medical Examiners; certified in neurology by American Board of Psychiatry and Neurology. Visiting scientist at King's College Hospital and Institute of Psychiatry, University of London, 1973. Presbyterian Hospital, NYC, assistant attending neurologist, 1962-69, associate attending neurologist, 1969-72, attending neurologist, 1972-73, member of executive committee of Neurological Institute, 1962-68; attending neurologist at Mount Sinai Hospital, NYC, 1973-79; consulting neurologist at Helen Hayes Hospital, West Haverstraw, NY, 1965-73; Robert Wood Johnson University Hospital, New Brunswick, chief of Neurology Service, 1979-95; chairman of Prognosis Committee, 1980-87, chairman of ad hoc committee on brain death certification, 1983-84. Member of medical advisory panel of Federal Aviation Administration, 1966-70, and Neurological Disease Panel of U.S. Pharmacopeia, 1971-78; member of medical advisory board of Parkinson's Disease Foundation, 1969-89, and Dystonia Medical Research Foundation, 1988-93; member of Research Commission on Extrapyramidal Disease, World Federation of Neurology, 1969-; member of scientific advisory board of National Amyotrophic Lateral Sclerosis Association, 1982-86; chair, Scientific Advisory Board, American Parkinson's Disease Assn, 1995-; member, Board of Scientific Counsellors; Natl Inst Neurological Diseases & Stroke, National Institutes of Health, 1991-96. **Publications:** Parkinson's Disease: A Guide for Patient and Family, 1978, 4th ed. (with J. Sage), 1996; (ed. with A. Plaitakis and contrib.) The Olivopontocerebellar Atrophies, 1985. **Address:** Department of Neurology, University of Medicine and Dentistry of New Jersey, Robert Wood Johnson Medical School, 1 Robert Wood Johnson Place, CN-19, New Brunswick, NJ 08901-1928, U.S.A.

DUYFHUIZEN, Bernard. American, b. 1953. **Genres:** Literary criticism and history. **Career:** University of Tulsa, OK, assistant instructor, 1980-83, visiting lecturer in English, 1983-84; University of Wisconsin-Eau Claire, assistant professor, 1984-89, associate professor, 1989-92, professor of English, 1992-, director of graduate studies, 1987-93, head of department, 1992-98, College of Arts & Sciences, associate dean, 1998-, interim dean, 2003-. University of Wisconsin System, member of Working Group on Remedial English Placement, 1994. King Alfred's College, faculty exchange teacher in Winchester, England, 1992. Pynchon Notes (journal), editor. **Publications:** Narratives of Transmission, 1992. Work represented in books. Contributor of articles and reviews to periodicals. **Address:** College of Arts & Sciences, University of Wisconsin-Eau Claire, Eau Claire, WI 54702-4004, U.S.A. **Online address:** pnotesbd@uwec.edu

DVORETZKY, Edward. American, b. 1930. **Genres:** Poetry, Literary criticism and history, Translations. **Career:** Teaching Fellow in German, Harvard University, Cambridge, Massachusetts, 1954-56; Instructor 1956-59, Assistant Professor 1959-64, and Associate Professor 1964-67, Rice University, Houston, Texas. Professor, Dept. of German, University of Iowa, Iowa City, 1967-92. **Publications:** The Enigma of Emilia Galotti, 1963; The Eighteenth-Century English Translations of Emilia Galotti, 1966; Der Teufel und sein Advokat: Gedichte und Prosa, 1981; Tief im Herbstwald (poetry), 1983; (co-author) Windfuesse (poetry), 1984; (co-author) Im Osten wie im Westen (poetry), 1987; (co-author) Fische, Huehnerschlachtlieder und die Leidenschaften (poetry), 1989; (compiler) Lessing Yearbook Index, 1994 TRANSLATOR: G.E. Lessing, Emilia Galotti, 1962; G.E. Lessing, Philotas, 1979. EDITOR: Lessing: Dokumente zur Wirkungsgeschichte 1755-1968, 2 vols., 1971, 1972; Lessing Heute: Beitraege zur Wirkungsgeschichte, 1981. **Address:** 1314 Nails Creek Dr, Sugar Land, TX 77478-5320, U.S.A.

DWORKIN, Andrea. American, b. 1946. **Genres:** Novels, Novellas/Short stories, Politics/Government, Women's studies and issues. **Career:** Writer and lecturer. **Publications:** Woman Hating: A Radical Look at Sexuality, 1974; Our Blood: Prophecies and Discourses on Sexual Politics, 1976; Marx and Gandhi Were Liberals: Feminism and the "Radical" Left, 1977; Why So-Called Radical Men Love and Need Pornography, 1978; The New Woman's Broken Hearts (short stories), 1980; Pornography: Men Possessing Women, 1981; Right-Wing Women: The Politics of Domesticated Females, 1983; Ice and Fire (novel), 1986; Intercourse, 1987; (with C.A. MacKinnon) Pornography and Civil Rights: A New Day for Women's Equality, 1988; Letters from a War Zone, 1989; Mercy, 1990; Life and Death, 1997; (ed. with

C.A. MacKinnon) In Harm's Way: The Pornography Civil Rights Hearings, 1997; Scapegoat, 2000; Heartbreak, 2002. **Address:** c/o Elaine Markson, 44 Greenwich Ave, New York, NY 10011, U.S.A.

DWYER, Augusta (Maria). Canadian, b. 1956. **Genres:** Environmental sciences/Ecology. **Career:** Marquee (music and life-styles weekly), London, England, staff writer, 1977; worked throughout Europe, North Africa, and South America as English teacher, hotel clerk, secretary, shop assistant, waitress, and bartender, 1977-82; free-lance writer, translator, and broadcaster, 1982-85; Maclean's (magazine), researcher and reporter, 198587; free-lance writer, 1987-. Correspondent from Central America and Mexico, 1984, and Haiti and the Dominican Republic, 1985. Volunteer social worker at Centrepoint Soho, London, and with abandoned children in Paraiso, Costa Rica. **Publications:** Into the Amazon: Chico Mendes and the Struggle for the Rain Forest, 1990; On the Line: Life on the US-Mexican Border, 1994. **Address:** c/o Cook, Livingston Curtis Brown, 200 First Ave, Toronto, ON, Canada M4M 1X1.

DWYER, Deanna. See KOONTZ, Dean R(ay).

DWYER, Jim. Also writes as Rev. Junkyard Moondog. American, b. 1949. **Genres:** Poetry, Environmental sciences/Ecology, Literary criticism and history, Bibliography. **Career:** State University of New York at Albany, librarian, 1973-76; University of Oregon, Eugene, librarian, 1976-82; Northern Arizona University, Flagstaff, librarian, 1982-86; Meriam Library, California State University, Chico, head of bibliographic services, 1986-. Sacramento River Preservation Trust, member of board of directors and secretary, 1989-; Chico Natural Foods Board, vice-president, 1992-93, president, 1993-94. **Publications:** Earth Works: Recommended Fiction and Nonfiction about Nature and the Environment for Adults and Young Adults, 1996; Where the Wild Books Are: A Guide to Ecofiction, forthcoming. Poet, under the pseudonym Rev. Junkyard Moondog. Contributor of articles and poems to periodicals. **Address:** Meriam Library, California State University, Chico, CA 95929-0295, U.S.A. **Online address:** jrdwyer@csuchico.edu

DWYER, K. R. See KOONTZ, Dean R(ay).

DWYER, Richard A. American, b. 1934. **Genres:** History, Biography. **Career:** Purdue University, West Lafayette, IN, instructor to assistant professor, 1964-66; University of Florida, Gainesville, assistant professor to associate professor, 1966-71; Florida International University, Miami, professor of English, 1971-90; writer. **Publications:** WITH RICHARD E. LINGENFELTER: The "Nonpareil" Press of T.S. Harris, 1957; The Songs of the Gold Rush, 1964; Songs of the American West, 1968; Lying on the Eastern Slope: James Townsend's Comic Journalism on the Mining Frontier, 1984; Death Valley Lore, 1988; Dan De Quille, the Washoe Giant, 1990; Sagebrush Trilogy: Idah Meacham Strobridge and Her Works, 1990. **Address:** University of Nevada Press, Mail Stop 166, Reno, NV 89557, U.S.A. **Online address:** rdwyer@networld.com

DYAL, Donald H(enriques). American, b. 1947. **Genres:** Bibliography, Reference, History. **Career:** Texas A&M University, College Station, TX, serials acquisitions librarian, 1973-76, serials and separates acquisitions librarian, 1976-77, head of special collections division, 1977-91, adjunct professor of history, 1985, head of special collections, manuscripts and archives, 1992-94, associate university librarian director of the Cushing Memorial Library, 1994-. Has served as a member of many academic committees and a consultant. **Publications:** (with S. Smith) Texas Library Journal Index, 1924-1975, 1977; (with H. Dethloff) A Special Kind of Doctor: A History of Veterinary Medicine in Texas, 1991; (with M.P. Kelsey) The Courthouses of Texas, 1993; Historical Dictionary of the Spanish American War, 1996; I Am My Work; My Work Is Me (monograph); (ed.) American Book and Magazine Illustrators to 1920. Contributor to books and periodicals. **Address:** Cushing Memorial Library, Texas A&M University, College Station, TX 77843, U.S.A.

DYCHTWALD, Maddy Kent. (born United States), b. 1952. **Genres:** Advertising/Public relations. **Career:** Consultant and speaker. Actress, 1974-83; Dychtwald & Associates (marketing consultants), Emeryville, CA, director of special projects, 1983-86; Age Wave, Inc. (generational marketing consultants), Emeryville, cofounder (with husband), 1986-, director of communications, 1986, vice president of communications, 1987-90, senior vice president of communications, 1990-95, business development. **Publications:** Cycles: How We Will Live, Work, and Buy, 2003. Contributor to journals. **Address:** Age Wave Inc., 2000 Powell St, Ste. 1680, Emeryville, CA 94608, U.S.A. **Online address:** mdychtwald@maddydychtwald.com

DYCK, Ian. Canadian, b. 1954. **Genres:** Biography, History. **Career:** University of Saskatchewan, Saskatoon, Saskatchewan, Canada, instructor, 1985-87; University of Lethbridge, Lethbridge, Alberta, Canada, assistant professor, 1987-88; Simon Fraser University, Burnaby, British Columbia, Canada, associate professor of history, 1988-. **Publications:** William Cobbett and Rural Popular Culture, 1992. EDITOR: Citizen of the World: Essays on Thomas Paine, 1988; (with M. Chase) Living and Learning: Essays in Honour of J.F.C. Harrison, 1996. **Address:** Department of History, Simon Fraser University, 8888 University Drive, Burnaby, BC, Canada V5A 1S6.

DYCK, Peter J. Canadian (born Russia), b. 1914. **Genres:** Theology/Religion. **Career:** Writer. Lecturer at schools, churches, and retreats. **Publications:** A Leap of Faith, 1990; The Great Shalom, 1990; (with E. Dyck) Up from the Rubble, 1991; Shalom at Last, 1992; Story Time Jamboree, 1993. **Address:** 1 Woodcrest Circle, Scottdale, PA 15683, U.S.A.

DYEN, Isidore. American, b. 1913. **Genres:** Language/Linguistics. **Career:** Professor Emeritus, Yale University, New Haven, Conn, since 1984 (Research Fellow 1939-42; Instructor in Malay, 1942-43; Assistant Professor of Malayan Languages, 1943-57; Professor, 1957-58; Professor of Malayopolynesian and Comparative Linguistics, 1958-73; Professor of Comparative Linguistics and Austronesian Languages, 1973-84). Vice-President, American Oriental Society, 1965-66. Adjunct Research Professor, University of Hawaii-Manoa, 1985-89. **Publications:** Spoken Malay, 1945; The Proto-Malayo-Polynesian Laryngeals, 1953; (with E. Schafer, H. Fernald and H. Glidden) Index to Journal of the American Oriental Society, vols. 21-60, 1955; A Lexicostatistical Classification of the Austronesian Languages, 1965; A Sketch of Trukese Grammar, 1965; Beginning Indonesian, 4 vols., 1967; A Descriptive Indonesian Grammar, 1967; (ed.) Lexicostatistics in Genetic Linguistics: Proceedings of the Yale Conference, 1973; (with D. Aberle) Lexical Reconstruction: The Case of the Athapaskan Kinship System, 1974; Linguistic Subgrouping and Lexicostatistics, 1975; (with J.B. Kruskal and P. Black) An Indoeuropean Classification: A Lexicostatistical Experiment, 1992. **Address:** Dept. of Linguistics, University of Hawaii, Honolulu, HI 96822, U.S.A.

DYER, Charles (Raymond). British, b. 1928. **Genres:** Plays/Screenplays. **Career:** Freelance actor and dir.; Playwright, Royal Shakespeare Co. **Publications:** Time, Murderer, Please, 1956; Wanted, One Body, 1956; Rattle of a Simple Man, 1962, novel, 1964; Staircase (play), 1966, novel as Charlie Always Told Harry Almost Everything (in U.S. as Staircase: or, Charlie Always Told Harry Almost Everything), 1969; Mother Adam, 1971; Lovers Dancing, 1984; Loving Leopold (play), 1987; Loving George, 1993. **Address:** Old Wob, Gerrards Cross, Bucks. SL9 8SF, England.

DYER, Donald R(ay). American, b. 1918. **Genres:** Area studies, Psychology. **Career:** University of Florida, Gainesville, assistant professor to associate professor, 1950-62; U.S. Department of State, Washington, DC, foreign service officer in Rio de Janeiro, Brazil, Mexico City, Mexico, and New Delhi, India, 1962-79. Visiting professor at Universidad de la Habana, 1953, and Universidad Nacional San Marcos, 1958-60. **Publications:** Lesser Antilles, 1959; (coauthor) The Caribbean, 1961; (coauthor) Modern Brazil, 1971; Cross-Currents of Jungian Thought, 1991; Jung's Thoughts on God, 2000. **Address:** 510 Caswell Rd, Chapel Hill, NC 27514, U.S.A.

DYER, James (Frederick). British, b. 1934. **Genres:** Children's fiction, Archaeology/Antiquities, Children's non-fiction, History, Local history/Rural topics. **Career:** Freelance archaeologist, writer and broadcaster. Archaeological Ed., Shire Publs., Princes Risborough, Bucks. Ed., The Bedfordshire Magazine, 1965-74; Principal Lecturer in Archaeology, Putteridge Bury College of Education, Luton, 1966-76. **Publications:** (with J. Dony) The Story of Luton, 1964, 3rd ed., 1975; Discovering Archaeology in England and Wales, 1969, 6th ed., 1997; Discovering Archaeology in Denmark, 1972; Southern England: An Archaeological Guide, 1973; Your Book of Prehistoric Britain, 1974; (ed.) From Antiquary to Archaeologist: William Cunnington 1754-1810, 1974; Worthington Smith 1835-1917, 1978; The Penguin Guide to Prehistoric England and Wales, 1981; Hillforts of England and Wales, 1981, 2nd ed., 1992; Teaching Archaeology in Schools, 1983; Shire Guide to Bedfordshire, 1987, 2nd ed., 1995; Ancient Britain, 1990, 2nd ed., 1995; The Ravens, 1990; Discovering Prehistoric England, 1993, 2nd ed., 2001; The Stopsley Book, 1998; The Stopsley Picture Book, 1999; Rhubarb and Custard: The Luton Modern School History, 2004. **Address:** 6 Rogate Rd, Luton, Beds. LU2 8HR, England.

DYER, Joel. American, b. 1958. **Genres:** Documentaries/Reportage. **Career:** Boulder Weekly, Boulder, CO, editor in chief, c. 1992-. **Publications:** Harvest of Rage, 1997; Crime or Punishment, 1998. Contributor to magazines and newspapers. **Address:** c/o Boulder Weekly, 690 South Lashley Lane, Boulder, CO 80303, U.S.A. **Online address:** bweditor@tesser.com

DYER, Joyce. American, b. 1947. **Genres:** Literary criticism and history, Autobiography/Memoirs, Essays. **Career:** Hiram College, Hiram, OH, professor of English and director of writing, 1991-. **Publications:** The Awakening: A Novel of Beginnings (criticism), 1993; In a Tangled Wood: An Alzheimer's Journey (memoir), 1996; (ed.) Bloodroot: Reflections on Place by Appalachian Women Writers (essays), 1998; Gum-Dipped: A Daughter Remembers Rubber Town (memoir), 2003. Contributor to scholarly journals and popular magazines. **Address:** Hinsdale Hall, PO Box 67, Hiram College, Hiram, OH 44234, U.S.A. **Online address:** dyerja@hiram.edu

DYER, Wayne W(alter). American, b. 1940. **Genres:** Novels, Psychology. **Career:** Resource Teacher and Counselor, Pershing High School, Detroit, 1965-67; Instructor in Counselor Education and Practicum Supvr., Wayne State University, Detroit, 1969-71; Director of Guidance and Counseling, Mercy High School, Farmington, Michigan, 1967-71; Education Counselor and Assistant Professor, 1971-74, and Associate Professor, 1974-77, St. John's University, Jamaica, New York; Staff Consultant, Drug Information and Service Center, Board of Cooperative Educational Services, Dix Hills, New York, 1972-75; Staff Consultant, Mental Health Association of Nassau Co. and Nassau Co. Dept. of Drug and Alcohol Addiction, 1973-75; Trainer and Staff Consultant of Guidance and School Psychological Personnel, Half Hollow School District, Huntington, New York, 1973-75; Staff Consultant, Detroit Hospital Drug Treatment Program, Herman Kiefer Hospital, Detroit, 1974-75; Member of the Teaching Staff and Adjunct Consultant, Drug Treatment and Education Center, North Shore University Hospital, Manhasset, New York, 1974-75. **Publications:** (with J. Vriend) Counseling Effectively in Groups, 1973; (with J. Vriend) Counseling Techniques That Work: Application to Individual and Group Counseling, 1974; Your Erroneous Zones: Bold But Simple Techniques for Eliminating Unhealthy Behavior Patterns, 1976; Pulling Your Own Strings, 1977; The Sky's the Limit, 1980; Gifts from Eykis (novel), 1982; Group Counseling for Personal Mastery, 1980; What Do You Really Want for Your Children, 1985; Happy Holidays, 1986; You'll See It When You Believe It, 1989; Real Magic: Creating Miracles in Everyday Life, 1992; Your Sacred Self, 1994; Everyday Wisdom, 1994; Staying on the Path, 1995; A Promise Is a Promise, 1995; Manifest Your Destiny, 1997. **Address:** Hay House Inc., PO BOX 5100, Carlsbad, CA 92018-5100, U.S.A.

DYKEMAN, Therese B(oos). American, b. 1936. **Genres:** Poetry, Philosophy, Biography. **Career:** University of Bridgeport, CT, adjunct professor, 1981-90; Fairfield University, CT, adjunct professor, 1985-. Adjunct professor at other New England community colleges and universities. **Publications:** EDITOR: American Women Philosophers, 1650-1930: Six Exemplary Women Thinkers, 1993; The Neglected Canon: Nine Women Philosophers, 1997; The Social, Political and Philosophical Works of Catharine Beecher, 2002. Contributor of articles and poems to periodicals. **Address:** 47 Woods End Rd, Fairfield, CT 06824, U.S.A. **Online address:** TDykeman@fair1.fairfield.edu

DYRNESS, William A. American, b. 1943. **Genres:** Art/Art history, Cultural/Ethnic topics, Theology/Religion. **Career:** Hinson Memorial Baptist Church, Portland, OR, minister to students, 1971-73; Regent College, Vancouver, guest instructor, 1972-74; Asian Theological Seminary, Manila, professor of theology, 1972-82; New College, Berkeley, CA, president, 1982-86, professor of theology, 1986-89; Fuller Theological Seminary, School of Theology, Pasadena, CA, dean, 1990-2000, professor of theology and culture, 1990-. **Publications:** Rouault: A Vision of Suffering and Salvation, 1971; Christian Critique of American Culture, 1974; Themes of Old Testament Theology, 1979; Christian Art in Asia, 1979; Let the Earth Rejoice! 1983; A Christian Apologetics in a World Community, 1983; How Does America Hear the Gospel?, 1989; Learning about Theology from the Third World, 1990; Invitation to Cross-Cultural Theology, 1992; The Earth Is God's: A Theology of American Culture, 1997; Visual Faith: Art Theology and Worship in Dialogue, 2001; Reformed Theology and Visual Culture, 2004. **Address:** School of Theology, Fuller Theological Seminary, 135 N Oakland Ave, Pasadena, CA 91182, U.S.A.

DYSON, Esther. Swiss, b. 1951. **Genres:** Information science/Computers. **Career:** Computer newsletter publisher, journalist, venture capitalist. Forbes magazine, reporter, 1974-77, columnist, 1987-; New Court Securities, securi-

ties analyst, 1977-79; Oppenheimer & Co., president, 1980-82; Rosen Electronics Newsletter; Release 1.0, editor and publisher, 1982-; EDventure Holdings, owner and president, 1982-; Computer Industry Daily, editor and publisher, 1985; Mayfield Software Partners, limited partner; Guardian Magazine (United Kingdom), columnist; Content Magazine, columnist; National Public Radio, commentator. **Publications:** Release 2.0: A Design for Living in the Digital Age, 1997. Contributor to professional journals and periodicals. **Address:** Edventure Holdings Inc., 104 5th Ave, 20th Fl, New York, NY 10011, U.S.A.

DYSON, Freeman (John). American (born England), b. 1923. **Genres:** Physics, Autobiography/Memoirs. **Career:** RAF Bomber Command, High Wycombe, Bucks., Civilian Scientist, 1943-45; Cornell University, Ithaca, NY, Professor of Physics, 1951-53; Institute for Advanced Study, Princeton, NJ, Professor of Physics, 1953-. Recipient of National Book Critics Circle Award for Non-fiction, 1984. **Publications:** Disturbing the Universe (autobiography), 1979; Weapons and Hope, 1984; Origins of Life, 1986; Infinite in All Directions, 1988; From Eros to Gaia, 1992; Imagined Worlds, 1997; The Sun, the Genome and the Internet, 1999. **Address:** 105 Battle Rd. Circle, Princeton, NJ 08540, U.S.A. **Online address:** dyson@ias.edu

DYSON, John. New Zealander, b. 1943. **Genres:** Travel/Exploration, History, Children's fiction, Children's non-fiction, Sports/Fitness, Recreation. **Career:** Reporter and writer for newspapers and magazines in New Zealand, Hong Kong, and England, 1959-72; free-lance journalist and author, 1972-; roving editor for Reader's Digest Magazine, 1988-. **Publications:** NONFICTION: (with others) The Magnificent Continent, 1976; Business in Great Waters, 1977; The Hot Arctic, 1979; The South Seas Dream: An Adventure in Paradise, 1982; (with J. Fitchett) Sink the Rainbow!: An Enquiry into the "Greenpeace Affair", 1986; Spirit of Sail: On Board the World's Great Sailing Ships, 1987; Columbus: For Gold, God, and Glory, 1991; FICTION: The Prime Minister's Boat Is Missing, 1974; Blue Hurricane, 1983; China Race, 1984; JUVENILE: Yachting the New Zealand Way, 1965; Behind the Wheel, 1974; In a Garage, 1974; (with K. Dyson) Fun with Kites, 1976; The Pond Book, 1976; The Motorcycling Book, 1977; The Young Yachtsman, 1978; Westward with Columbus, 1991. **Address:** 27 The Terrace, Barnes, London SW13 ONR, England.

DYSON, Michael Eric. American, b. 1958. **Genres:** Essays. **Career:** Mathy College, Princeton University, Princeton, NJ, assistant master; Hartford Seminary, faculty member; Chicago Theological Seminary, instructor, later assistant professor; Brown University, Providence RI, assistant professor; University of North Carolina, Chapel Hill, professor of African and Afro-American studies. **Publications:** Reflecting Black: African-American Cultural Criticism (essays), 1993; Making Malcolm: The Myth and Meaning of Malcolm X, 1995; Between God and Gangsta Rap: Bearing Witness to Black Culture (essays), 1996; I May Not Get There with You: The True Martin Luther King Jr., 2000; Holler if You Can Hear Me, 2001. **Address:** 84 14th Street SE, Hickory, NC 28602, U.S.A.

DZIELSKA, Maria. Polish, b. 1942. **Genres:** Classics. **Career:** Jagiellonian University, Cracow, Poland, assistant, 1967-73, assistant professor, 1973-87, dozent, 1987-92, professor of Byzantine history, 1992-. **Publications:** Apollonius of Tyana, 1986; Hypatia of Alexandria, 1995. **Address:** Department of Byzantine History, Jagiellonian University, Studencka 3, 31-116 Cracow, Poland.

DZUBACK, Mary Ann. American, b. 1950. **Genres:** Education, Women's studies and issues, Social sciences. **Career:** Washington University, St. Louis, MO, assistant professor of education, 1987-94, associate professor of education and history, 1994-. writer. **Publications:** Robert M. Hutchins: Portrait of an Educator, 1991. Author of articles. **Address:** Department of Education, Washington University, Campus Box 1183, St. Louis, MO 63130, U.S.A.

DZUNG WONG, Baoswan. Swiss, b. 1949. **Genres:** Mathematics/Statistics, Translations. **Career:** Christ-Koenig Kolleg, Nuolen, Switzerland, instructor, 1973-76; Kantonsschule, Wettingen, Switzerland, instructor, 1982-86, 1991-; Antares Consulting, Nussbaumen, Switzerland, software engineer, 1987-88; Oekreal Schools of Business, instructor, 1988-94. **Publications:** (trans.) Group Theoretical Methods and Their Applications, 1992; Bezierkurven, gezeichnet und gerechnet, 2003. **Address:** Wegaecherstrasse 3, 5417 Untersiggenthal, Switzerland.

E

EADY, Cornelius. American, b. 1954. **Genres:** Poetry. **Career:** Poet and playwright. State University of New York at Stony Brook, associate professor of English, director of Poetry Center. Founder, with poet Toi Derricote, of Cave Canem (summer workshop/retreat for emerging African-American poets). **Publications:** POETRY: Kartunes, 1980; Victims of the Latest Dance Craze, 1985; The Autobiography of a Jukebox: Poems, 1985; BOOM BOOM BOOM, 1988; The Gathering of My Name, 1991; You Don't Miss Your Water, 1995; Brutal Imagination, 2001. Contributor to anthologies. **Address:** 39 Jane St, New York, NY 10014, U.S.A.

EAGLE, Kin. *See* **ADLERMAN, Daniel.**

EAGLE, Kin. *See* **ADLERMAN, Kimberly M.**

EAGLES, Charles W. American, b. 1946. **Genres:** Civil liberties/Human rights, History, Race relations. **Career:** Research Triangle Institute, Research Triangle Park, NC, district supervisor, 1969-71; North Carolina State University, Raleigh, assistant professor of history, 1977-80; Southeast Missouri State University, Cape Girardeau, assistant professor of history, 1980-82; Vanderbilt University, Nashville, TN, assistant professor of history, 1982-83; University of Mississippi, University, professor of history, 1983-. **Publications:** Jonathan Daniels and Race Relations: The Evolution of a Southern Liberal, 1982; Democracy Delayed: Congressional Reapportionment and Urban-Rural Conflict in the 1920s, 1990; Outside Agitator: Jon Daniels and the Civil Rights Movement in Alabama, 1993. EDITOR: The Civil Rights Movement in America, 1986; The Mind of the South: Fifty Years Later, 1992; Is There a Southern Political Tradition?, 1996. **Address:** Department of History, University of Mississippi, PO Box 1848, University, MS 38677-1848, U.S.A. **Online address:** eagles@olemiss.edu

EAGLETON, Terry. (Terence Francis). British, b. 1943. **Genres:** Novels, Plays/Screenplays, Literary criticism and history, Politics/Government. **Career:** Cambridge University, Jesus College, tutor in English, 1964-69; Oxford University, tutor in English, Wadham College, 1969, lecturer in critical theory, 1988, Thomas Warton Professor of English Literature, 1993; University of Manchester, professor of cultural theory, 2001-. Poetry reviewer, Stand mag. **Publications:** Shakespeare and Society, 1966; The New Left Church, 1966; Exiles and Emigres, 1970; The Body as Language, 1970; Myths of Power: A Marxist Study of the Brontes, 1974; Marxism and Literary Criticism, 1976; Criticism and Ideology, 1976; Brecht and Company (play), 1979; Walter Benjamin: or, Towards a Revolutionary Criticism, 1981; The Rape of Clarissa, 1982; Literary Theory, 1983; The Function of Criticism, 1984: William Shakespeare, 1985; Against the Grain, 1986; Saints and Scholars (novel), 1987; Saint Oscar (play), 1989; The Ideology of the Aesthetic, 1990; Ideology: An Introduction, 1992; The White, the Gold and the Gangrene (play), 1993; Wittgenstein (film), 1993; Heathcliff and the Great Hunger, 1995; Marxist Literary Theory, 1996; The Illusions of Postmodernism, 1996; Saint Oscar and Other Plays, 1997; The Eagleton Reader, 1998; Crazy John and the Bishop and Other Essays on Irish Culture, 1998; Marx, 1999; Scholars and Rebels in 19th-Century Ireland, 1999; The Idea of Culture, 2000; Modernity, Modernism, Postmodernism (essays), 2000; The Truth about the Irish, 2000; The Gatekeeper: A Memoir, 2001; Sweet Violence: The Idea of the Tragic, 2002; The English Novel: An Introduction, 2004.

EAKINS, Patricia. (born United States), b. 1942. **Genres:** Adult non-fiction. **Career:** Freelance writer, editor, and book coach, 1974-; New York Institute of Technology, instructor, 1979-86, adjunct assistant professor, 1986-; Trinity College, Hartford, CT, visiting assistant professor, 1990-94; New School, New York, NY, instructor, 1992-97. Catskill Reading Society, guest readings coordinator, 1985-. **Publications:** Oono (chapbook), 1982; The Hungry Girls and Other Stories, 1988; The Marvelous Adventures of Pierre Baptiste: Father and Mother, First and Last (novel), 1999; Writing for Interior Design, 2004. Contributor to periodicals. **Address:** 1200 Broadway, New York, NY 10001, U.S.A. **Online address:** marmillink@aol.com

EARL, Maureen. British (born Egypt), b. 1944. **Genres:** Novels, Plays/Screenplays. **Career:** Worked as a newspaper reporter, television reporter, documentary filmmaker, screenwriter, and writer for television dramas. **Publications:** NOVELS: Gulliver Quick, 1992; Boat of Stone, 1993. Author of screenplays. Contributor to magazines and newspapers. **Address:** Aldama I, San Miguel Allende, 37700 GTO, Mexico.

EARL, Riggins R., Jr. American, b. 1942. **Genres:** History. **Career:** University of Tennessee, Knoxville, assistant professor of religious studies, 1974-82; Interdenominational Theological Center, Atlanta, GA, professor of ethics and theology, 1990-. Berea College, Martin L. King, Jr. Lecturer; guest lecturer at other institutions; consultant and teacher at urban youth academies. **Publications:** (ed.) To You Who Teach in the Black Church, 1972; Dark Symbols, Obscure Signs: God, Self, and Community in the Slave Mind, 1995; Dark Salutations: Rituals, God, and Greetings in the Black Community, 2001. Contributor to books and periodicals. **Address:** Interdenominational Theological Center, 700 Martin L. King, Jr. Dr. SW, Atlanta, GA 30314, U.S.A.

EARLE, Sylvia A. American, b. 1935. **Genres:** Marine sciences/Oceanography. **Career:** Research marine biologist and oceanographer. Resident director for Cape Haze Marine Laboratories, Sarasota, FL, 1966; research scholar, Radcliffe Institute; research fellow, Farlow Herbarium, Harvard University, 1975; research biologist and curator, California Academy of Sciences, 1976; fellow, Natural History Museum, University of California, Berkeley, 1976; chief scientist, National Oceanic and Atmospheric Administration (NOAA), 1990-92; founder, president, CEO Deep Ocean Technology and Deep Ocean Engineering, Oakland, CA, 1981-90. **Publications:** Humbrella, a New Red Alga of Uncertain Taxonomic Position From the Juan Fernandez, 1969; (with J.R. Young) Siphonoclathrus, A New Genus of Chlorophyta (Siphonales: Codiaceae) from Panama, 1972; (with A. Giddings) Exploring the Deep Frontier: The Adventure of Man in the Sea, 1980; Sea Change: A Message of the Oceans, 1995. EDITOR: (with B.C. Collette) Results of the Tektite Program: Ecology of Coral Reef Fishes, 1972; (with R.J. Lavenberg) Results of the Tektite Program, Coral Reef Invertebrates and Plants, 1975. **Address:** Deep Ocean Engineering, 1431 Doolittle Drive, San Leandro, CA 94577, U.S.A.

EARLEY, Pete. American. **Genres:** Documentaries/Reportage. **Career:** Writer. Enid News & Eagle, Enid, OK, intern, 1969-73; Washington Post, Washington, DC, investigative reporter. **Publications:** Family of Spies: Inside the John Walker Spy Ring, 1988; Prophet of Death: The Mormon Blood-Atonement Killings, 1991; The Hot House: Life Inside Leavenworth Prison, 1992; Circumstantial Evidence: Death, Life, and Justice in a Southern Town, 1995; Confessions of a Spy: The Real Story of Aldrich Ames, 1996. **Address:** c/o Putnam & Berkley Group, 375 Hudson St., New York, NY 10014, U.S.A.

EARLEY, Tom. *See* Obituaries.

EARLEY, Tony. American, b. 1961. **Genres:** Novels, Novellas/Short stories. **Career:** Instructor, University of the South, Carnegie-Mellon University, University of Alabama; columnist and sports editor, Daily Courier, Forest City, North Carolina; Professsor, Vanderbilt University. **Publications:** Here We Are in Paradise (stories), 1994; Jim the Boy (novel), 1999; Somehow Form a Family: Stories that are Mostly True, 2001. **Address:** c/o Gordon Kato, 133 West 75th Street Suite 1-A, New York, NY 10023, U.S.A.

EARLS, Nick. Irish, b. 1963. **Genres:** Novellas/Short stories, Novels, Young adult fiction. **Career:** Writer. Medical practitioner in Brisbane, Queensland, 1987-1994; freelance writer, 1988-. **Publications:** Passion (short stories), 1992; After January (young adult novel), 1996; Zigzag Street (novel), 1996. Contributor of short fiction to anthologies. **Address:** c/o Curtis Brown, PO Box 19, Paddington, NSW 2021, Australia. **Online address:** nickearls@peg.apc.org

EARLY, Jack. *See* SCOPPETTONE, Sandra.

EARLY, Tom. *See* KELTON, Elmer.

EARNSHAW, Micky. (Spencer Wright Earnshaw). American, b. 1939. **Genres:** Music. **Career:** Drummer with Ian Underwood, Berkeley, CA, 1963-65; University of Vermont, Burlington, VT, mathematics instructor, 1969-73; drum-set instructor, Vancouver, British Columbia, 1974-84; freelance musician, Vancouver, 1974; Courtenay Youth Music Center, Courtenay, British Columbia, drum instructor, 1976-90. Instructor at drum-set clinics; touring musician with Eddie "Lockjaw" Davis. **Publications:** The Essence of Rhythm, 1994; Eighth-Note Rhythms in Common Time; Developing Rhythmic Independence. **Address:** 78-216 Makolea St #32, Kailua Kona, HI 96740-4427, U.S.A. **Online address:** mickyearnshaw@hotmail.com

EARNSHAW, Steven. (born England), b. 1962. **Genres:** History. **Career:** University of Leicester, Leicester, England, part-time lecturer, 1990-94; Nene College, Northampton, England, lecturer, 1994-95; Sheffield Hallam University, Sheffield, England, senior lecturer in English, 1995-. **Publications:** (editor, with Jane Dowson) Postmodern Subjects/Postmodern Texts, 1995; The Direction of Literary Theory: Generations of Meaning, 1996; (editor) Just Postmodernism, 1997; The Pub in Literature: England's Altered State, 2000. **Address:** Department of English, Sheffield Hallam University, Collegiate Cres, Sheffield S10 2BP, England. **Online address:** s.l.earnshaw@shu.ac.uk

EAST, Churchill. *See* HARNER, Stephen M.

EASTERBROOK, Gregg. American, b. 1953. **Genres:** Novels. **Career:** Writer, 1977-. **Publications:** This Magic Moment: A Love Story for People Who Want the World to Make Sense (novel), 1987; A Moment on the Earth (nonfiction), 1995; The Progress Paradox, 2004. **Address:** Newsweek Ste. 1220, 1750 Pennsylvania Ave. NW, Washington, DC 20006-4578, U.S.A.

EASTERMAN, Daniel. *See* MACEOIN, Denis.

EASTON, David. Canadian, b. 1917. **Genres:** Politics/Government, Social sciences. **Career:** University of Chicago, assistant professor, 1947-53, associate professor, 1953-55, professor 1955-84, Andrew MacLeish Distinguished Service Professor Emeritus, Dept. of Political Science, 1984-. University of California at Irvine, Distinguished Research Professor of Political Science, 1982-. Member Board of Eds., Behavioral Science, 1956-, Youth and Society, 1970-83, Journal of Political Methodology, 1972-83, International Political Science Abstracts, 1972-80, Journal of Politics and the Life Sciences, 1986-92, Journal of Political Systems, 1986-, Journal of Theoretical Politics, 1986-, International Series in Social and Political Thought, 1986-. Jointly, Sir Edward Peacock Professor of Political Science, Queen's University, Canada, 1971-80. President, American Political Science Association, 1968-69; President, International Committee on Social Science Documentation, 1969-71; Vice-President, American Academy of Arts and Sciences, 1985-90. **Publications:** The Political System: An Inquiry into the State of Political Science, 1953; A Framework for Political Analysis, 1965; A Systems Analysis of Political Life, 1965; (with J. Dennis) Children in the Political System; Origins of Political Legitimacy, 1969; The Analysis of Political Structure, 1990. EDITOR: Varieties of Political Theory, 1966; (with J. Gunnell and L. Graziano) The Development of Political Science: A Comparative Survey, 1991; (with C. Schelling) Divided Knowledge: Across Disciplines, Across Cultures, 1991; (with J. Gunnell and M. Stein) Regime

and Discipline: Democracy and the Development of Political Science, 1995. **Address:** Dept of Political Science, University of California, 3151 Social Science Plaza, Irvine, CA 92697-5100, U.S.A. **Online address:** d2easton@orion.oac.uci.edu

EASTON, Elizabeth Wynne. American, b. 1956. **Genres:** Art/Art history. **Career:** Brooklyn Museum, Brooklyn, NY, assistant curator of European paintings, 1988-91, associate curator, 1992-98, curator, 1998-. **Publications:** The Intimate Interiors of Edouard Vuillard, 1989. **Address:** Brooklyn Museum, 200 Eastern Parkway, Brooklyn, NY 11238, U.S.A. **Online address:** eweaston@hotmail.com

EASTON, Jane. *See* Obituaries.

EASUM, William M. American, b. 1939. **Genres:** Theology/Religion. **Career:** United Methodist church in San Antonio, TX, senior pastor, 1969-93; 21st Century Strategies Inc., Port Aransas, TX, founder, president, and senior consultant, 1993-99; Easum, Bandy & Associates, Port Aransas, president and senior consultant, 1999-. **Publications:** The Church Growth Handbook, 1990; How to Reach the Baby Boomer, 1991; Dancing with Dinosaurs, 1993; Sacred Cows Make Gourmet Burgers, 1995; The Complete Ministry Audit, 1996; (with T. Bandy) Growing Spiritual Redwoods, 1997; Leadership on the Other Side, 2000; Unfreezing Moves, 2002. **Address:** 554 Bayside Dr., Port Aransas, TX 78373, U.S.A. **Online address:** easum@easum.com

EATON, Charles Edward. American, b. 1916. **Genres:** Novels, Novellas/Short stories, Poetry, Art/Art history, Autobiography/Memoirs, Biography, Essays. **Career:** Instructor of Creative Writing, University of Missouri, Columbia, 1940-42; Vice Consul, American Embassy, Rio de Janeiro, 1942-46; Professor of Creative Writing, University of North Carolina, Chapel Hill, 1946-51. **Publications:** The Bright Plain, 1942; The Shadow of the Swimmer, 1951; The Greenhouse in the Garden, 1956; Write Me from Rio (stories), 1959; Countermoves, 1963; The Edge of the Knife, 1970; Karl Knaths, 1971; The Girl from Ipanema (stories), 1972; Karl Knaths: Five Decades of Painting, 1973; The Man in the Green Chair, 1977; The Case of the Missing Photographs (stories), 1978; Colophon of the Rover, 1980; The Thing King, 1983; The Work of the Wrench, 1985; New and Selected Poems, 1942-1987, 1987; New and Selected Stories 1959-1989, 1989; A Guest on Mild Evenings, 1991; A Lady of Pleasure (novel), 1993; The Country of the Blue, 1994; The Fox and I, 1996; The Scout in Summer, 1999; The Jogger by the Sea, 2000; The Man from Buena Vista: Selected Nonfiction, 1944-2000, 2001; Between the Devil and the Deep Blue Sea, 2002; The Work of the Sun: New and Selected Poems, 1991-2002. **Address:** 808 Greenwood Rd, Chapel Hill, NC 27514, U.S.A.

EATON, Jack. British, b. 1947. **Genres:** Administration/Management, Organized labor. **Career:** Vanden Berghs, Bromborough, England, personnel management trainee; Oxford University, Oxford, England, research associate and senior research fellow at St. Edmund Hall, 1971-72; University of Wales, Aberystwyth, lecturer in human resource management, 1972-. Lecturer at institutions. **Publications:** (with C.G. Gill and R. Morris) Industrial Relations in the Chemical Industry, 1978; (with C.G. Gill) Trade Union Directory: A Guide to All TUC Unions, 1981; Judge Bryn Roberts: A Biography, 1989; (with W. Maksymiw and C.G. Gill) British Trade Union Directory, 1990; (with M.F. Bott, A. Coleman, and D. Rowland) Professional Issues in Software Engineering, 2nd ed., 1994, 3rd ed., 2000; Globalization and Human Resource Management in the Airline Industry, 1996, 2nd ed., 2001; Comparative Employment Relations, 2000; (with N. Fuller-Love) Rheolaeth Adnoddau Dynol (distance learning materials; title means "Human Resource Management"). Contributor to books. Contributor of articles and reviews to periodicals. **Address:** 48 Maesceinion, Aberystwyth, Wales. **Online address:** jke@aber.ac.uk

EATON, John Herbert. British, b. 1927. **Genres:** Animals/Pets, Theology/Religion. **Career:** St. George's Upper School, Jerusalem, teacher, 1953-56; University of Birmingham, assistant lecturer, 1956-59, lecturer, 1959-69, sr. lecturer, 1969-77, reader, Dept., of Theology, 1977-92, retired, 1992. **Publications:** Obadiah, Nahum, Habakkuk and Zephaniah: Introduction and Commentary, 1961; Psalms: Introduction and Commentary, 1967; Kingship and the Psalms, 1976, 1986; Festal Drama in Deutero-Isaiah, 1979; First Studies in Biblical Hebrew, 1980; Vision in Worship, 1981; Readings in Biblical Hebrew, 1982; The Psalms Come Alive, 1984; Job, 1985; The Contemplative Face of Old Testament Wisdom, 1989; Interpreted by Love: Expositions of Great Old Testament Passages, 1994; Psalms of the Way and the Kingdom, 1995; The Circle of Creation: Animals in the Light of the Bible, 1995; Mysterious Messengers: A Course on Hebrew Prophecy from Amos Onwards,

1998; A Historical and Spiritual Commentary on the Psalms, with a New Translation, 2003; Meditating on the Psalms, 2004. **Address:** 19 Sandhills Lane, Barnt Green, Birmingham B45 8NU, England.

EATON, Richard M. American, b. 1940. **Genres:** History, Area studies. **Career:** U.S. Peace Corps, Washington, DC, volunteer in Tabriz, Iran; University of Arizona, Tucson, assistant professor, 1972-78, associate professor, 1978-94, professor of history, 1994-. **Publications:** Sufis of Bijapur, 1300-1700: Social Roles of Sufis in Medieval India, 1978; Islamic History as Global History (pamphlet), 1990; (with G. Michell) Firuzabad: Palace City of the Deccan, 1990; The Rise of Islam and the Bengal Frontier, 1204-1760, 1993; Essays on Islam and Indian History, 2000. **Address:** Department of History, University of Arizona, Tucson, AZ 85721, U.S.A. **Online address:** reaton@u.arizona.edu

EATON, Trevor (Michael William). British, b. 1934. **Genres:** Language/Linguistics, Literary criticism and history. **Career:** University of Erlangen, Germany, Lecturer in English, 1958-60; University of New South Wales, Newcastle, Lecturer in English Language, 1961-65; Norton Knatchbull School, Teacher, 1965-87, Head of the Philosophy Dept., 1974-87; Linguistics Association of Great Britain, Linguistics and Literature Section, Section Convener, 1972-76; Journal of Literary Semantics, Founder and Editor, 1972-2002; Professional Performer of Chaucer's works as The Chaucer Man, 1988-; Founder, International Association of Literary Semantics, 1992-. Has recorded Chaucer's works for Pearl Records, 1986-; Double CD Recording of Beowulf in Anglo-Saxon for Pearl Records, 1996. **Publications:** The Semantics of Literature, 1966; The Foundations of Literary Semantics, 1970; Theoretical Semics, 1972; (ed.) I.A. Richards, Poetries: Their Media and Ends, 1974; (ed.) Essays in Literary Semantics, 1978. **Address:** Honeywood Cottage, 35 Seaton Ave, Hythe, Kent CT21 5HH, England.

EATWELL, Roger. British, b. 1949. **Genres:** Politics/Government. **Career:** University of Bath, England, professor of politics. **Publications:** POLITICAL SCIENCE: The 1945-1951 Labour Governments, 1979; Fascism: A History, 1995; European Political Cultures, 1996; Fascismo: verson un modello nuovo, 1999. EDITOR: (with N. O'Sullivan and contrib.) The Nature of the Right: European and American Politics and Political Thought since 1789, 1989; (with A. Wright) Contemporary Political Ideologies, 1999; (with C. Mudde) Western Democracies and the New Extreme Right Challenge, 2003. **Address:** European Studies, University of Bath, Bath BA2 7AY, England. **Online address:** R.Eatwell@bath.ac.uk

EBAUGH, Helen Rose (Fuchs). American, b. 1942. **Genres:** Theology/Religion. **Career:** University of Houston, Houston, TX, assistant professor, 1973-79, associate professor, 1979-89, professor of sociology, 1993-, chairman of department, 1985-87. **Publications:** Out of the Cloister: A Study of Organizational Dilemmas, 1977; Becoming an Ex: The Process of Role Exit, 1988; (ed., with J.S. Chafetz) Women in the Vanishing Cloister: Organizational Decline in Catholic Religious Orders in the United States, 1993; Religion and the New Immigrants: Continuities and Adaptations in Immigrant Congregations, 2000; (ed., with J.S. Chafetz) Religion across Borders: Transnational Immigrant Networks, 2002. Contributor of articles to scholarly journals. **Address:** Department of Sociology, University of Houston, 496 Philip G. Hoffman Hall, Houston, TX 77204, U.S.A.

EBBETT, Eve. Also writes as Eva Burfield. New Zealander (born England), b. 1925. **Genres:** Novels, History, Novellas/Short stories. **Career:** After high school, worked as an advertising clerk at a provincial newspaper, then as a bank clerk for 6 years, then part-time work for another provincial paper, including book reviews. **Publications:** AS EVA BURFIELD: Yellow Kowhai, 1957; A Chair to Sit On, 1958; The Long Winter, 1964; Out of Yesterday, 1965; After Midnight, 1965; The White Prison, 1966; The New Mrs. Rainier, 1967; The Last Day of Summer, 1968. AS EVE EBBETT: Give Them Swing Bands, 1969; To the Garden Alone, 1970; In True Colonial Fashion, 1977; Victoria's Daughters: New Zealand Women of the Thirties, 1981; When the Boys Were Away, 1984. **Address:** 908 Sylvan Rd, Hastings, New Zealand.

EBEL, Roland H. American, b. 1928. **Genres:** Politics/Government. **Career:** Republican State Central Committee, Lansing, MI, assistant publicity director, 1956 and 1958; Western Michigan University, Kalamazoo, MI, assistant professor, 1960-64; Tulane University, New Orleans, LA, associate professor of political science, 1964-93. **Publications:** (ed.) Proceedings of the VI Inter-American University Seminar on Municipal Affairs, 1968; Political Modernization in Three Guatemalan Indian Communities, 1969; (ed. and contrib.) Cambio politico en tres comunidades indigenas de Guatemala, 1969; (ed. and contrib.) Perspectives on the Energy Crisis, 1976; (with J.D. Cochrane and R. Taras) Political Culture and Foreign Policy in Latin America: Case Studies from the Circum-Caribbean, 1991; Misunderstood Caudillo: Miguel Ydigoras Fuentes and the Failure of Democracy in Guatemala, 1998. **Address:** Department of Political Science, Tulane University, New Orleans, LA 70118, U.S.A. **Online address:** tanglewild@juno.com

EBEL, Suzanne. *See* **GOODWIN, Suzanne.**

EBERHART, Richard (Ghormley). American, b. 1904. **Genres:** Plays/Screenplays, Poetry. **Career:** Tutor to son of King Prajadhipik of Siam, 1930-31; English Teacher, St. Mark's School, Southboro, MA, 1933-41, and Cambridge School, Kendal Green, MA, 1941-42; Assistant Manager to Vice-President, Butcher Polish Co., Boston, 1946-52; Visiting Professor, University of Washington, Seattle, 1952-53, 1967, 1972; Professor of English, University of Connecticut, Storrs, 1953-54; Visiting Professor, Wheaton College, Norton, MA, 1954-55; Resident Fellow and Gauss Lecturer, Princeton University, NJ, 1955-56; Consultant in Poetry, 1959-61, and Hon. Consultant in American Letters, 1963-69, Library of Congress, Washington, DC. Dartmouth College, Hanover, NH, Professor and Poet-in-Residence, 1956-68, Class of 1925 Professor, 1968-70, Professor of English Emeritus, 1970-. Director, Yaddo Corp., 1964-; Hon. President, Poetry Society of America, 1972-. **Publications:** A Bravery of Earth, 1931; Reading the Spirit, 1936; Song and Idea, 1940; Poems, New and Selected, 1944; Burr Oaks, 1947; Brotherhood of Men, 1949; An Herb Basket, 1950; The Apparition (play), 1951; Selected Poems, 1951; The Visionary Farms (play), 1952; Undercliff: Poems 1946-1953, 1953; Triptych (play), 1955; Great Praises, 1957; The Oak: A Poem, 1957; Collected Poems, 1930-1960, Including 51 New Poems, 1960; The Mad Musician, and Devils and Angels (plays), 1962; Collected Verse Plays, 1962; The Quarry: New Poems, 1964; The Bride from Mantua (play), 1964; The Vastness and Indifference of the World, 1965; Fishing for Snakes, 1965; Selected Poems 1930-1965, 1965; Thirty One Sonnets, 1967; Shifts of Being: Poems, 1968; The Achievement of Richard Eberhart: A Comprehensive Selection of His Poems, 1968; Three Poems, 1968; The Groundhog Revisiting, 1972; Fields of Grace, 1972; Two Poems, 1975; Collected Poems 1930-1976, 1976; Poems to Poets, 1976; Hour, Gnats, 1977; Of Poetry and Poets, 1979; Survivors, 1979; Ways of Light, Poems, 1972-1980, 1980; Richard Eberhart: A Celebration (festschrift), 1980; Four Poems, 1980; New Hampshire: Nine Poems, 1980; Chocorua, 1981; Florida Poems, 1981; The Long Reach: New and Uncollected Poems, 1948-1984, 1984; Spite Fence, 1984; Throwing Yourself Away, 1984; Snowy Owl, 1984; Richard Eberhart Symposium, Negative Capability, 1986; Collected Poems 1930-1986, 1988; Maine Poems, 1989; New and Selected Poems, 1930-1990, 1990; Richard Eberhart New and Selected Poems, 1930-1990, 1995. EDITOR: (with S. Rodman) War and the Poet: An Anthology of Poetry Expressing Man's Attitude to War from Ancient Times to the Present, 1945; Dartmouth Poems, 12 vols., 1958-59, 1962-71. **Address:** 80 Lyme Rd, #161, Hanover, NH 03755-1226, U.S.A.

EBERLE, Gary. American, b. 1951. **Genres:** Novels, Novellas/Short stories, Social commentary, Theology/Religion. **Career:** Aquinas College, Grand Rapids, MI, professor of English, 1981-; judge of poetry competitions. **Publications:** The Geography of Nowhere: Finding One's Self in the Postmodern World, 1994; Angel Strings (novel), 1995; A City Full of Rain: Collected Stories, 2001; Sacred Time and the Search for Meaning, 2003. Work represented in anthologies. Contributor of stories, poems, and articles to periodicals. **Address:** Department of English, Aquinas College, 1607 Robinson Rd SE, Grand Rapids, MI 49506, U.S.A. **Online address:** eberlgar@aquinas.edu

EBERSTADT, Nicholas (Nash). American, b. 1955. **Genres:** Politics/Government. **Career:** American Enterprise Institute for Public Policy Research, Washington, DC, visiting scholar, 1985-99, Henry Wenelt Chair in Political Economy, 1999-. Harvard University, visiting fellow, 1980-2002; consultant to government and private organizations. **Publications:** Poverty in China, 1979; (ed.) Fertility Decline in the Less Developed Countries, 1981; Foreign Aid and American Purpose, 1988; The Poverty of Communism, 1988; (with J. Banister) The Population of North Korea, 1992; Korea Approaches Reunification, 1995; The Tyranny of Numbers, 1995; The End of North Korea, 1999; Prosperous Paupers and Other Population Problems, 2000; Korea's Future and the Great Powers, 2001. **Address:** American Enterprise Institute for Public Policy Research, 1150 17th St NW, Washington, DC 20036, U.S.A. **Online address:** eberstadt@aei.org

EBERT, James I(an). American, b. 1948. **Genres:** Archaeology/Antiquities. **Career:** Ebert and Associates Inc., Albuquerque, NM, vice-president, 1983-. **Publications:** Distributional Archaeology, 1992, 2nd ed., 2001. **Address:** Ebert and Associates Inc., 3700 Rio Grande Blvd NW Ste 3, Albuquerque, NM 87107, U.S.A. **Online address:** jebert@ebert.com

EBERT, Roger (Joseph). American, b. 1942. **Genres:** Plays/Screenplays, Film, History. **Career:** Film critic. News-Gazette, Champaign-Urbana, IL, staff writer, 1958-66; Daily Illinois, Chicago, editor, 1963-64; Chicago City College, instructor in English, 1967-68; Chicago Sun Times, film critic, 1967-; University of Chicago Fine Arts Program, lecturer on film, 1969-; Sneak Previews, PBS-TV, co-host, 1977-82; At the Movies, co-host, 1982-86; Ebert and Roeper (formerly Siskel and Ebert), syndicated TV prog., co-host, 1986-. U.S. Student Press Association, president, 1963-64; Art Institute of Chicago, Film Center, member, board of advisers, 1973-; University of Illinois Alumni Association, member, board of directors, 1975-77. **Publications:** An Illini Century, 1967; Beyond the Valley of the Dolls (screenplay), 1970; A Kiss Is Still a Kiss: Roger Ebert at the Movies, 1984; The Perfect London Walk, 1986; Two Weeks in the Midday Sun, 1987; Roger Ebert's Movie Home Companion, 1990; Roger Ebert's Movie Yearbook, 1991-; Behind the Phantom's Mask, 1993; Ebert's Little Movie Glossary, 1994; Roger Ebert's Book of FIlm, 1996; Questions for the Movie Answer Man, 1997; Roger Ebert's Bigger Little Movie Glossary, 1999; I Hated, Hated, Hated This Movie, 2000; The Great Movies, 2002. **Address:** Chicago Sun-Times, 401 N Wabash Rm 110, Chicago, IL 60611, U.S.A.

EBLE, Connie. American, b. 1942. **Genres:** Language/Linguistics. **Career:** University of Kentucky, Lexington, instructor, 1968-71; University of North Carolina at Chapel Hill, assistant professor to professor of English, 1971-. **Publications:** College Slang 101, 1989; Slang and Sociability, 1996. **Address:** Department of English, CB 3520, University of North Carolina at Chapel Hill, Chapel Hill, NC 27599, U.S.A. **Online address:** cceble@email.unc.edu

ECHENOZ, Jean. French, b. 1947. **Genres:** Novels, Plays/Screenplays. **Career:** Writer. **Publications:** Le meridien de Greenwich (novel), 1979; Cherokee (novel), 1983, trans by M. Polizzotti, 1987; Nous trois, 1992; Equipee malaise (novel), trans by M. Polizzotti as Double Jeopardy, 1993; Le rose et le blanc (screenplay); Lac (novel); I'm Gone, 2001. Contributor to newspapers and periodicals. **Address:** c/o Editions de Minuit, 7 rue Bernard-Palissy, 75006 Paris, France.

ECHERUO, Michael (Joseph Chukwudalu). Nigerian, b. 1937. **Genres:** Poetry, Literary criticism and history, Language/Linguistics. **Career:** Founding President, Nigerian Association for African and Comparative Literature. Lecturer, Nigerian College of Arts and Technology, Enugu, 1960-61; Lecturer, 1961-70, Sr. Lecturer, 1970-73, and Professor, 1973-74, University of Nigeria, Nsukka; Professor of English, 1974-80, and Dean of the Postgrad. School, 1978-80, University of Ibadan; Imo State University, Okigwe, Vice-Chancellor, 1981-88; Syracuse University, William Safire Professor of English, 1990-. **Publications:** Mortality: Poems, 1968; (ed.) Igbo Traditional Life, Literature, and Culture, 1972; Joyce Cary and the Novel of Africa, 1973; Distances: New Poems, 1975; Victorian Lagos, 1977; The Conditioned Imagination from Shakespeare to Conrad, 1978; Joyce Cary and the Dimensions of Order, 1979; (ed.) Shakespeare's The Tempest, 1980; Igbo-English Dictionary: Comprehensive Dictionary of the Igbo Language, 1998. **Address:** Department of English, 410 Hall of Languages, Syracuse University, Syracuse, NY 13244, U.S.A.

ECHEVARRIA, Jana. (born United States), b. 1956. **Genres:** Cultural/Ethnic topics. **Career:** California State University-Long Beach, Long Beach, professor of bilingual special education, 1992-2003, department chair, 2002-. SIOP Institute, writer and consultant; National Center for Learning Disabilities, member of professional advisory board. **Publications:** (with R. McDonough) Instructional Conversations in Special Education Settings: Issues and Accommodations, 1993; Instructional Conversations: Understanding through Discussion Training Manual, 1995; (with A. Graves) Sheltered Content Instruction: Teaching Students with Diverse Abilities, 2nd edition, 2003; (with A. Pickett and L. Safarik) A Core Curriculum and Training Program to Prepare Paraeducators to Work with Learners Who Have Limited English Proficiency,1998; (with M. E. Vogt and D. Short) Making Content Comprehensible for English Language Learners: The SIOP Model, 2000. Contributor to books. **Address:** 7030 Seawind Dr., Long Beach, CA 90803, U.S.A. **Online address:** jechev@csulb.edu

ECKART, Gabriele. German, b. 1954. **Genres:** Novellas/Short stories, Poetry. **Career:** Havelobst (agricultural cooperative), Werder, East Germany, cultural worker, 1979-82; free-lance writer in Berlin, East Germany, 1982-86; University of Texas at Austin, writer in residence, 1988; University of Minnesota-Twin Cities, Minneapolis, teaching assistant, 1988-93; Spring Hill College, assistant prof., 1994-97. **Publications:** Per Anhalter, 1982, trans. as Hitchhiking: Twelve German Tales, 1992; Tagebuch (title means: Diary), 1979; So sehe ick die Sache (title means: That's How I See It), 1984; Wie

mag ich alles, was beginnt (title means: How Much Do I Like Everything, That Begins), 1987; Seidelstein (title means: Seidel Rock), 1988; Frankreich heisst Jeanne (title means: France Is Called Jeanne), 1989; Der gute fremde Blick (title means: The Good Foreign View), 1992; Sprachtraumata in den Texten Wolfgang Hilbigs (title means: Language Trauma in the Texts of Wolfgang Hilbig), 1995. Author of poems and short stories, primarily about life in the former East Germany. **Address:** Dept of Foreign Languages & Anthropology, Southeast Missouri State University, 1 University Plaza, Cape Girardeau, MO 63701, U.S.A.

ECKBLAD, Edith Berven. American, b. 1923. **Genres:** Children's fiction, Children's non-fiction, Poetry, Songs/Lyrics and libretti, Inspirational/Motivational Literature. **Career:** Teacher of creative writing, Gateway Technological Institute, Racine, Wisconsin, 1972-74, 1976-78; received: Council for Wisconsin Writers juvenile picture book award, 1975; Archer/Eckblad Award. **Publications:** Just Marty, 1947; Living with Jesus, 1955; Something for Jesus, 1959; Danny's Straw Hat, 1962; Kindness Is a Lot of Things, 1965; Various Songs, 1967; A Smile Is to Give, 1969; Danny's Orange Christmas Camel, 1970; Soft as the Wind, 1974; Qu'Est-ce Qui Est Doux?, 1976; God Listens and Knows, 1981. **Address:** 7020 Mariner Dr Unit 102, Racine, WI 53406-3867, U.S.A.

ECKERT, Kathryn Bishop. (Kathryn Bishop Omoto). American, b. 1935. **Genres:** Architecture. **Career:** Michigan Department of State, Michigan Historical Center, Lansing, worked as architectural historian, deputy state historic preservation officer, and acting state historic preservation officer, 1974-92, state historic preservation officer, 1992-97. **Publications:** Buildings of Michigan, 1993; Sandstone Architecture of the Lake Superior Region, 2000; The Campus Guide: Cranbrook, 2001. Contributor to periodicals. **Address:** PO Box 525, Leland, MI 49654, U.S.A. **Online address:** katheckert@charter.net

ECKLAR, Julia (Marie). American, b. 1964. **Genres:** Science fiction/Fantasy. **Career:** Secretary; data processor; freelance writer, 1987-. **Publications:** Star Trek: The Kobayashi Maru, 1989; Regenesis, 1995. Contributor of novellas to magazines. **Address:** c/o Karen Cercone, 521 7th St, Trafford, PA 15085-1052, U.S.A.

ECKSTEIN, Rick. American, b. 1960. **Genres:** Sociology. **Career:** Villanova University, Villanova, PA, associate professor of sociology, 1990-, associate director of Center for Peace and Justice Education, 1992-. **Publications:** Nuclear Power and Social Power, 1997. **Address:** Department of Sociology, Villanova University, Villanova, PA 19085, U.S.A. **Online address:** reckstei@email.vill.edu

ECONOMOU, George. American, b. 1934. **Genres:** Poetry, Literary criticism and history, Translations. **Career:** Lecturer, Wagner College, NYC, 1958-60; Ed., Chelsea Review, NYC, 1958-60, and Trobar, NYC, 1960-64; Professor of English, Long Island University, Brooklyn, New York, 1961-83; Professor of English, University of Oklahoma, Norman, 1983-2000, Emeritus Professor, 2000-. **Publications:** The Georgics, 1968; Landed Natures, 1969; Poems for Self-Therapy, 1972; The Goddess Natura in Medieval Literature, 1972; (ed.) Geoffrey Chaucer: A Collection of Criticism, 1975; Ameriki: Book One and Selected Earlier Poems, 1977; Voluntaries, 1984; (ed.) Proensa: An Anthology of Troubadour Poetry, 1986; Harmonies and Fits, 1987; (trans.) William Langland's Piers Plowman, The C Version, a Verse Translation, 1996; Century Dead Center and Other Poems, 1998. **Address:** 1401 Magnolia, Norman, OK 73072, U.S.A. **Online address:** gero@mymailstation.com

EDDIE, David. Canadian, b. 1961. **Genres:** Documentaries/Reportage. **Career:** Writer. Newsweek magazine, New York, NY, held position in the letters department; East Hampton Star, former reporter; Canadian Broadcasting Corporation (CBC), Toronto, former television news writer and former later producer for CBC Radio's Sunday Morning. **Publications:** Chump Change, 1996; Housebroken: Confessions of a Stay-at-Home Dad, 1999. Contributor to periodicals. **Address:** c/o Riverhead Books Publicity, 375 Hudson St., New York, NY 10014, U.S.A.

EDDINGS, David. American, b. 1931. **Genres:** Novels, Young adult fiction. **Career:** Writer; has worked as a buyer for Boeing Co., Seattle, as a grocery clerk, and as a college English teacher. **Publications:** YOUNG ADULT FICTION: Pawn of Prophecy, 1982; Queen of Sorcery, 1982; Magician's Gambit, 1984; Castle of Wizardry, 1984; Enchanter's Endgame, 1984; Guardians of the West, 1987; King of the Murgos, 1988; Demon Lord of Karanda, 1988; Sorceress of Darshiva, 1989; The Diamond Throne, 1989; The Ruby Knight, 1990; The Seeress of Kell, 1991; The Sapphire Rose, 1991; Domes of Fire,

1993; The Shining Ones, 1993; The Hidden City, 1994; (with L. Eddings) Belgarath the Sorcerer, 1995; (with L. Eddings) Polgara the Sorceress, 1997; The Rivan Codex, 1998; The Redemption of Althalus, 2000; The Elder Gods, 2003; The Treasured One, 2004. ADULT FICTION: High Hunt, 1973; The Losers, 1992. **Address:** c/o Eleanor Wood, Spectrum Literary Agency, 320 Central Park W #1D, New York, NY 10025, U.S.A.

EDDINS, Dwight L. American, b. 1939. **Genres:** Poetry, Literary criticism and history. **Career:** University of Alabama, instructor, 1966-67, assistant professor, 1967-70, associate professor, 1972-76, professor of English, 1976-. **Publications:** Yeats: The Nineteenth Century Matrix, 1971; Of Desire, and the Circles of Hell, 1980; The Gnostic Pynchon, 1990; (ed.) Emperor Redressed, 1995. **Address:** Dept of English, Box 870244, University of Alabama, Tuscaloosa, AL 35487-0244, U.S.A. **Online address:** deddins@ english.as.ua.edu

EDEL, Abraham. American, b. 1908. **Genres:** Philosophy. **Career:** City University of New York, City College, joined faculty, 1931, Distinguished Professor, 1970-73, Professor Emeritus of Philosophy, 1973-, and Distinguished Professor Emeritus of Philosophy, Graduate School, 1973-; University of Pennsylvania, Philadelphia, Research Professor of Philosophy, 1974-. **Publications:** Theory and Practice of Philosophy, 1946; Ethical Judgment: The Use of Science in Ethics, 1955; (with M. Edel) Anthropology and Ethics, 1959, rev. ed. as Anthropology and Ethics: The Quest for Moral Understanding, 2000; Science and the Structure of Ethics, 1961, rev. ed., 1998; Method in Ethical Theory, 1963, rev. ed., 1994; Analyzing Concepts in Social Science, 1979; Exploring Fact and Value, 1980; Aristotle and His Philosophy, 1982; Interpreting Education, 1985; (with E. Flower and F.W. O'Connor) Morality, Philosophy, and Practice: Historical and Contemporary Readings and Studies, 1989; The Struggle for Academic Democracy, 1990; Relating Humanities and Social Thought, 1990; In Search of the Ethical, 1993; (with E. Flower and F.W. O'Connor) Critique of Applied Ethics, 1994; The Evolution of John Dewey's Ethical Theory, 1908-1932, 2001. EDITOR: (with Y.H. Krikorian) Contemporary Philosophic Problems: Selected Readings, 1959; (and contrib.) Aristotle, 1967; (and author of introd.) The Chiga of Uganda, 2nd ed., 1996. **Address:** 104 N Shedwick St, Philadelphia, PA 19104-4912, U.S.A.

EDELHEIT, Abraham J. American, b. 1958. **Genres:** Cultural/Ethnic topics, History, International relations/Current affairs, Politics/Government, Social commentary, Bibliography. **Career:** Kingsborough Community College of the City University of New York, Manhattan Beach Campus, Brooklyn, NY, adjunct professor of Holocaust studies, 1985-86, associate professor of history, currently; Touro College, NYC, adjunct professor of history in Flatbush Evening Program, 1987-90, visiting professor of history, 1991-93; Macmillan Publishing Co., Inc., NYC, editorial consultant in Reference Book Division, 1988-89; U.S. Holocaust Memorial Museum, Washington, DC, researcher and writer, 1990-91. Edelheit Research Institute for Contemporary History, cofounder and assistant director, 1985-; Csengeri Institute Holocaust Lecture Series, City University of New York, moderator, 1988-90. **Publications:** (with H. Edelheit) Bibliography of Holocaust Literature, 1986, supplement, 1990, 2nd supplement, 1993; (with H. Edelheit) The Jewish World in Modern Times: A Selected, Annotated Bibliography, 1988; (with H. Edelheit) A World in Turmoil: An Integrated Chronology of the Holocaust and World War II, 1991; (with H. Edelheit) The Rise and Fall of the Soviet Union: A Selected Annotated Bibliography of Sources in English, 1993; (with H. Edelheit) The History of the Holocaust: A Handbook and Dictionary, 1994; The Yishuv in the Shadow of the Holocaust: Zionist Politics and the Policy of Rescue Aliya, 1933-1939; (with H. Edelheit) Israel and the Jewish World, 1948-1993, 1995; (with H. Edelheit) East European Jewry, 1919-1939, 1996; (with H. Edelheit) History of Zionism: A Handbook and Dictionary; (with H. Edelheit) Jewry throughout the Ages: A Dictionary of Terms. Contributor to periodicals. **Address:** 2020 Ave V, Brooklyn, NY 11229, U.S.A.

EDELMAN, Marian Wright. American, b. 1939. **Genres:** Civil liberties/ Human rights. **Career:** National Association for the Advancement of Colored People (NAACP), Legal Defense and Education Fund Inc., NYC, staff attorney, 1963-64, director of office in Jackson, MS, 1964-68; partner of Washington Research Project of Southern Center for Public Policy, 1968-73; Children's Defense Fund, Washington, DC, founder and president, 1973-. W.E.B. Du Bois Lecturer at Harvard University, 1986. Member of numerous committees, projects, presidential commissions, etc. Recipient of numerous grants, awards, and honorary degrees. **Publications:** School Suspensions: Are They Helping Children?, 1975; Portrait of Inequality: Black and White Children in America, 1980; Families in Peril: An Agenda for Social Change, 1987; The Measure of Our Success: A Letter to My Children and Yours,

1992; Guide My Feet: Prayers and Meditations on Loving and Working for Children, 1995; Stand for Children, 1998; Lanterns: A Memoir of Mentors, 1999. Contributor to books. **Address:** Children's Defense Fund, 25 E St. NW, Washington, DC 20001, U.S.A.

EDELSTEIN, Terese. American, b. 1950. **Genres:** Translations. **Career:** String teacher at public schools in St. Louis, MO, 1972-75; Duke University String School, Durham, NC, violin teacher, 1977-80; Detroit Institute of Music and Dance, Detroit, MI, violin teacher, 1984-87. **Publications:** TRANSLATIONS: (with I. Smidt) C. Asscher-Pinkhof, Star Children, 1986; (with Smidt) I. Vos, Hide and Seek, 1991; (with Smidt) I. Vos, Anna Is Still Here, 1993; (with Smidt) I. Vos, Dancing on the Bridge of Avignon, 1995; I. Vos, The Key Is Lost, 2000; G. Spillebeen, Kipling's Choice, 2005. **Address:** 1342 Devonshire, Grosse Pointe Park, MI 48230, U.S.A.

EDGAR, David. British, b. 1948. **Genres:** Plays/Screenplays. **Career:** Telegraph and Argus, Bradford, Yorkshire, lecturer reporter, 1969-72; Leeds University, creative writing fellow, 1972-74; Birmingham Repertory Theatre, resident playwright, 1974-75; University of Birmingham, playwriting tutor, 1975-78, sr. research fellow, 1988-, hon professor, 1992-95, professor, 1995-99. **Publications:** Dick Deterred, 1974; Destiny, 1976; The Jail Diary of Albie Sachs, 1978; Ball Boys, 1978; Mary Barnes, 1979; (with S. Todd) Teendreams, 1979; Nicholas Nickleby, 1982; Maydays, 1983; Entertaining Strangers, 1985; That Summer, 1987; The Second Time as Farce, 1988; (with N. Grant) Vote for Them, 1989; Heartlanders, 1989; The Shape of the Table, 1990; Dr Jekyll and Mr Hyde, 1991; Pentecost, 1995; Albert Speer, 2000; Edgar: Shorts, 2000; The Prisoner's Dilemma, 2001. **Address:** c/o Alan Brodie Representation, 6th Fl, Fairgate House, 78 New Oxford St, London WC1A 1HB, England. **Online address:** DavidEdgar@compuserve. com

EDGAR, Stacey L. American, b. 1940. **Genres:** Information science/ Computers, Philosophy. **Career:** General Electric Co., Syracuse, NY, computer programmer and analyst, 1960-67; State University of New York College at Geneseo, instructor in computer science and philosophy, 1969-75, lecturer, 1976-91, assistant professor of philosophy, 1991-97, associate professor of philosophy, 1997-. **Publications:** Advanced Problem Solving with FORTRAN 77, 1989; (with W.J. Edgar, and E. Daly) Introduction to Logic, 1992; Fortran for the Nineties, 1992; Morality and Machines, 1995. **Address:** Department of Philosophy, 103 Welles, State University of New York College at Geneseo, Geneseo, NY 14454, U.S.A. **Online address:** edgar@geneseo.edu

EDGERTON, Clyde. American, b. 1944. **Genres:** Novels. **Career:** Teacher of English and Education, 1972-89; writer, 1978-; University of North Carolina at Wilmington, Creative Writing Dept, professor, 1998-. **Publications:** Raney, 1985; Walking across Egypt, 1987; The Floatplane Notebooks, 1988; Killer Diller, 1991; In Memory of Junior, 1992; Redeye, 1995; Where Trouble Sleeps, 1997; Lunch at the Piccadilly, 2003.

EDGERTON, David. British (born Uruguay), b. 1959. **Genres:** History. **Career:** Victoria University of Manchester, Manchester, England, lecturer in the economics of science and technology, 1984-85, lecturer at Institute for Science and Technology, 1985-88, lecturer in the history of science and technology, 1988-92; Imperial College of Science and Technology, University of London, London, England, faculty member, 1993-. **Publications:** England and the Aeroplane: An Essay on a Militant and Technological Nation, 1991; Science, Technology and the British Industrial Decline, 1996. Contributor to journals. **Address:** Imperial College of Science and Technology, University of London, London SW7 2AZ, England.

EDGERTON, Teresa (Ann). American, b. 1949. **Genres:** Science fiction/ Fantasy. **Career:** Writer. **Publications:** FANTASY NOVELS: GREEN LION SERIES: Child of Saturn, 1989; The Moon in Hiding, 1989; The Work of the Sun, 1990. GOBLIN SERIES: Goblin Moon, 1991; The Gnome's Engine, 1991. CHRONICLES OF CELYDONN TRILOGY: The Castle of the Silver Wheel, 1993; The Grail and the Ring, 1994; The Moon and the Thorn, 1995. **Address:** c/o Ace Publishing, Berkeley Publishing Group, 375 Hudson, New York, NY 10014, U.S.A.

EDGHILL, Rosemary. See **BES-SHAHAR, Eluki.**

EDLOW, Jonathan A. (born United States), b. 1952. **Genres:** History. **Career:** Physician. Practicing emergency medicine, 1981-; Beth Israel Deaconess Hospital, Boston, MA, vice chair of the department of emergency medicine; Harvard Medical School, Boston, assistant professor of medicine. **Publications:** Bull's-Eye: Unraveling the Medical Mystery of Lyme Disease,

2003. Contributor of medical detective stories to periodicals. **Address:** c/o Author Mail, Yale University Press, POB 209040, New Haven, CT 06520, U.S.A.

EDMISTEN, Patricia Taylor. American, b. 1939. **Genres:** International relations/Current affairs. **Career:** University of West Florida, Pensacola, professor of sociology of education, educational psychology, and special education, 1977-. Peace Corps volunteer in Peru, 1962-64. **Publications:** Nicaragua Divided: La Prensa and the Chamorro Legacy, 1990; (ed. and trans.) Autobiography of Maria Elena Moyano, 2000; The Mourning of Angels, 2001. **Address:** 518 N Baylen St, Pensacola, FL 32501-3904, U.S.A.

EDMONSON, Munro S. American, b. 1924. **Genres:** Anthropology/Ethnology. **Career:** Tulane University, New Orleans, professor of anthropology, 1951-, now emeritus. Middle America Research Institute, associate, 1952-. **Publications:** Los Manitos, 1957; Status Terminology, 1958; (ed. with J.H. Rohrer) The Eighth Generation, 1959; Quiche-English Dictionary, 1965; Lore (folklore), 1971; (trans.) The Book of Counsel (Mayan mythology), 1971; (ed.) Meaning in Mayan Languages, 1973; (ed.) Sixteenth-Century Mexico, 1974; (trans.) The Ancient Future of the Itza, 1982; (trans.) Heaven Born Merida and Its Destiny, 1986; The Book of the Year, 1988; Quiche Dramas and Divinatory Calendars, 1997. **Address:** Tulane University, College of Arts and Sciences, Dept. of Anthropology, New Orleans, LA 70118, U.S.A.

EDMUNDS, R(ussell) David. American, b. 1939. **Genres:** Anthropology/Ethnology, History, Bibliography. **Career:** University of Wyoming, Laramie, instructor, 1971-72, assistant professor of history, 1972-75; Texas Christian University, Fort Worth, assistant professor, 1975-78, associate professor, 1978-81, professor of American history, 1982-; writer. Visiting professor at University of California, Berkeley, 1978, and at San Diego State University, 1984. Michael Burris Lecturer at Macalester College, 1979. Consultant to projects, institutions, and organizations. **Publications:** The Otoe-Missouria People, 1976; The Potawatomis: Keepers of the Fire, 1978; Shawnee Prophet, 1983; Tecumseh and the Quest for Indian Leadership, 1984; Kinsmen through Time: An Annotated Bibliography of Potawatomi History, 1987; (with J.L. Peyser) The Fox Wars: The Mesquakie Challenge to New France, 1993. EDITOR: American Indian Leaders: Studies in Diversity, University of Nebraska Press, 1980. Contributor to anthologies. Contributor to reference books. Contributor to periodicals. **Address:** Department of History, Texas Christian University, Fort Worth, TX 76129, U.S.A.

EDSON, J(ohn) T(homas). British, b. 1928. **Genres:** Westerns/Adventure. **Publications:** FLOATING OUTFIT SERIES: Trail Boss, 1961; The Ysabel Kid, 1962; Quiet Town, 1962; Rio Guns, 1962; The Texan, 1962; Waco's Debt, 1962; The Hard Riders, 1962; The Half Breed, 1963; Gun Wizard, 1963; The Rio Hondo Kid, 1963; Gunsmoke Thunder, 1963; Wagons to Backsight, 1964; Trigger Fast, 1964; The Rushers, 1964; The Rio Hondo War, 1964; Troubled Range, 1965; The Wildcats, 1965; The Trouble Busters, 1965; The Peacemakers, 1965; The Fortune Hunters, 1965; The Man from Texas, 1965; A Town Called Yellowdog, 1966; The Law of the Gun, 1966; Return to Backsight, 1966; Guns in the Night, 1966; Sidewinder, 1967; The Fast Gun, 1967; The Floating Outfit, 1967; Terror Valley, 1967; The Hooded Raiders, 1968; Rangeland Hercules, 1968; McGraw's Inheritance, 1968; The Bad Bunch, 1968; The Making of a Lawman, 1968; Goodnight's Dream, 1969; From Hide and Horn, 1969; Cuchilo, 1969; The Small Texan, 1969; The Town Tamers, 1969; A Horse Called Mogollon, 1971; Hell in the Palo Duro, 1971; Go Back to Hell, 1972; The South Will Rise Again, 1972; .44 Calibre Man, 1973; Set Texas Back on Her Feet (in U.S. as Viridian's Trail), 1973; The Hide and Tallow Men, 1974; The Quest for Bowie's Blade, 1974; Beguinage, 1978; Beguinage Is Dead!, 1978; Viridian's Trail, 1978; The Gentle Giant, 1979; Master of Triggernometry, 1981; White Indian, 1981; Old Moccasins on the Trail, 1981; Diamonds, Emeralds, Cards and Colts, 1986; No Finger on the Trigger, 1987. WACO SERIES: Sagebrush Sleuth, 1962; Arizona Ranger, 1962; The Drifter, 1963; Waco Rides In, 1964; Hound Dog Man, 1967; Doc Leroy, M.D., 1977; Waco's Badge, 1991. CIVIL WAR SERIES: The Fastest Gun in Texas, 1963; The Devil Gun, 1966; The Colt and the Sabre, 1966; Comanche, 1967; The Rebel Spy, 1968; The Bloody Border, 1969; Back to the Bloody Border, (in U.S. as Renegade), 1970; Kill Dusty Fog!, 1970; Under the Stars and Bars, 1970; You're in Command Now, Mr. Fog, 1973; The Big Gun, 1973; A Matter of Honour, 1981; Decision for Dusty Fog, 1986; The Code of Dusty Fog, 1988. CALAMITY JANE SERIES: The Bull Whip Breed, 1965; Trouble Trail, 1965; The Cow Thieves, 1965; The Big Hunt, 1967; Calamity Spells Trouble, 1968; Cold Deck, Hot Lead, 1969; White Stallion, Red Mare, 1970; The Remittance Kid, 1978; The Whip and the War Lance, 1979. ROCKABYE COUNTY SERIES: The Professional Killers, 1968; The 1/4 Second Draw, 1969; The

Deputies, 1969; Point of Contact, 1970; The Owlhoot, 1970; Run for the Border, 1971; Bad Hombre, 1971; The Sixteen Dollar Shooter, 1974; The Sheriff of Rockabye County, 1981; The Lawmen of Rockabye County, 1982. OLD DEVIL HARDIN SERIES: Young Ole Devil, 1975; Get Urrea, 1975; Old Devil and the Caplocks, 1976; Old Devil and the Mule Train, 1976; Old Devil at San Jacinto, 1977; Old Devil's Hands and Feet, 1982. CAP FOG SERIES: Cap Fog, Meet Mr. J.G. Reeder, 1977; You're a Texas Ranger, Alvin Fog, 1979; Rapido Clint, 1980; The Justice of Company "Z," 1981; The Return of Rapido Clint and Mr J.G. Reeder, 1984; Decision for Dusty Fog, 1987. BUNDUKI SERIES: Bunduki and Dawn, 1975; Sacrifice for the Quagga God, 1975; Bunduki, 1975; Fearless Master of the Jungle, 1978. OTHER: Slaughter's Way, 1965; Slip Gun, 1971; Two Miles to the Border, 1972; Blonde Genius, 1973; J.T.'s Hundredth, 1979; J.T.'s Ladies, 1980; The Hide and Horn Saloon, 1983; Cut One, They All Bleed, 1983; Wanted! Belle Starr, 1983; Buffalo Are Coming, 1984; Is-A-Man, 1985; More J.T.'s Ladies, 1987; Mark Counter's Kin, 1989; Rapid Clint Strikes Back, 1989; Texas Kidnappers, 1996; Mississippi Raider, 1996; Cure the Texas Fever, 1996; Wedge Goes to Arizona, 1996; Arizona Range War, 1996; Arizona Gun Law, 1996. **Address:** 1 Cottesmore Ave, Melton Mowbray, Leics. LE13 0HY, England.

EDSON, Russell. American, b. 1935. **Genres:** Novels, Plays/Screenplays, Poetry, Essays. **Publications:** Appearances: Fable and Drawings, 1961; A Stone Is Nobody's: Fables and Drawings, 1961; The Boundry, 1964; The Very Thing That Happens: Fables and Drawings, 1964; The Brain Kitchen: Writings and Woodcuts, 1965; What a Man Can See, 1969 The Childhood of an Equestrian, 1973; The Clam Theater, 1973; The Falling Sickness (plays), 1975; The Intuitive Journey, 1976; The Reason Why the Closet-Man Is Never Sad, 1977; The Wounded Breakfast: Ten Poems, 1978; With Sincerest Regrets, 1980; Wuck Wuck Wuck!, 1984; Gulping's Recital, (novel) 1984; The Wounded Breakfast (full book, 60 prose poems), 1985; Ticktock, 1992; The Song of Percival Peacock (novel), 1992; The Tunnel: Selected Poems, 1994; The Tormented Mirror, 2001. **Address:** 29 Ridgeley St, Darien, CT 06820, U.S.A. **Online address:** russedson@earthlink.net

EDWARDS, Allen Jack. American, b. 1926. **Genres:** Psychology. **Career:** Emeritus Professor of Psychology, Southwest Missouri State University, Springfield, 1973-. Assistant Professor, 1958-62, and Associate Professor of Education, 1962-63, University of Kansas, Lawrence; Associate Professor, Southern Illinois University, Carbondale, 1963-65; Associate Professor and subsequently Professor of Education, University of Missouri-Columbia, 1965-72. **Publications:** (co-author) Educational Psychology: The Teaching-Learning Process, 1968; Individual Mental Testing: part I: History and Theories, 1971, part II: Measurement, 1972; (ed. and contrib.) Selected Writings of David Wechser, 1974; Dementia, 1993; When Memory Fails: Helping the Alzheimer's and Dementia Patient, 1994. **Address:** 110 Russell Blvd, Columbia, MO 65203-1708, U.S.A.

EDWARDS, Anne. American, b. 1927. **Genres:** Novels, Romance/Historical, Children's non-fiction, Autobiography/Memoirs, Biography, Documentaries/Reportage, Young adult fiction, Film, History, Theatre. **Career:** Member of Council, 1978-81, and President, 1981-85, The Authors Guild; Authors League, council. **Publications:** (adaptor) A Child's Bible, 1967; The Survivors, 1968; Miklos Alexandrovitch Is Missing (in U.K. as Alexandrovitch Is Missing), 1969; Shadow of a Lion, 1971; Haunted Summer, 1972; The Hesitant Heart, 1974; Judy Garland: A Biography, 1974; (with Stephen Citron) The Inn and Us (reminiscences), 1975; Child of Night (in U.K. as Ravenwings), 1975; P.T. Barnum (juvenile), 1976; The Great Houdini (juvenile), 1977; Vivien Leigh: A Biography, 1977; Sonya: The Life of the Countess Tolstoy, 1981; The Road to Tara: The Life of Margaret Mitchell, 1983; Matriarch: Queen Mary and the House of Windsor, 1984; Road to Tara: The Life of Margaret Mitchell, 1985; A Remarkable Woman: Katherine Hepburn, 1986; Early Reagan, 1987; Shirley Temple: American Princess, 1988; The DeMilles: An American Family, 1989; Royal Sisters: Queen Elizabeth and Princess Margaret, 1990; Wallis: The Novel, 1991; The Grimaldis of Monaco: Centuries of Scandal, Years of Grace, 1992; La Divina, 1993; Streisand, 1997; Ever After, 2000; Maria Callas, 2001. **Address:** c/o International Creative Mgmt. Inc, 40 W. 57th St, New York, NY 10019, U.S.A.

EDWARDS, Anne K. *See* **EMMONS, Mary L.**

EDWARDS, Clive D. British, b. 1947. **Genres:** Antiques/Furnishings, Art/Art history, History, Business/Trade/Industry. **Career:** Perrings Furnishings, London, England, retail manager, 1965-85; Loughborough University, Loughborough, England, lecturer in art and design, 1991-. **Publications:** (author of revision) J. Gloag, Dictionary of Furniture, 1990; Victorian Furniture:

Technology and Design, 1993; Twentieth-Century Furniture: Its Materials, Manufacture, and Markets, 1994; Eighteenth-Century Furniture, 1996; Encyclopedia of Furniture-Making Materials, Trades and Techniques, 2000. Contributor to books. Contributor of articles and reviews to periodicals. **Address:** School of Art and Design, Loughborough University, Epinal Way, Loughborough LE11 0QE, England. **Online address:** c.edwards@lboro.ac.uk

EDWARDS, F. E. See **NOLAN, William F(rancis).**

EDWARDS, Frank B. Canadian, b. 1952. **Genres:** Children's fiction, Children's non-fiction, How-to-books. **Career:** Writer. Canadian Geographic, Ottawa, ON, assistant editor, 1975-78; Harrowsmith Magazine, Camden East, ON, associate editor, 1979-82; Equinox Magazine, Camden East, executive editor, 1981-85; Bungalo Books, Kingston, ON, and Tucson, AZ, publisher, 1986-. Camden House Books, publisher and editorial director, 1985-89; Hedgehog Productions (book packagers and consultants), president. St. Lawrence College, instructor, 1996. **Publications:** FOR CHILDREN: Mortimer Mooner Stopped Taking a Bath!, 1990; Melody Mooner Stayed Up All Night, 1991; Snow: Learning for the Fun of It, 1992; (with L. Aziz) Close Up: Microscopic Photographs of Everyday Stuff, 1992; Grandma Mooner Lost Her Voice, 1992; (with Aziz) Ottawa: A Kid's Eye View, 1993; A Dog Called Dad, 1994; Mortimer Mooner Makes Lunch, 1995; Melody Mooner Takes Lessons, 1996; Downtown Lost & Found, 1997; The Zookeeper's Sleepers, 1997; Peek-a-boo at the Zoo, 1997; Snug as a Big Red Bug, 1999; Crowded Ride in the Countryside, 1999; Nightgown Countdown, 1999; Robin Hood with Lots of Dogs, 1999; Treasure Island with Lots of Dogs, 1999; Frogger, 2000; Bug, 2002. FOR ADULTS: The Smiling Wilderness, 1984; (ed.) The Cottage Book: A Collection of Practical Advice for Lakeside Living, 1991, rev. ed., 1994; (with T. Carpenter) Kids, Computers, and You, 1995. **Address:** Pokeweed Press, Suite 337 829 Norwest Rd, Kingston, ON, Canada K7P 2N3. **Online address:** edwards@pokeweed.com

EDWARDS, Hank. See **BROOMALL, Robert W(alter).**

EDWARDS, Harvey. American, b. 1929. **Genres:** Plays/Screenplays, Children's non-fiction, Education, Recreation, Sports/Fitness, Travel/Exploration. **Career:** Owner, Edwards Films, Eagle Bridge, New York Freelance writer, journalist and filmmaker. Former European Ed., Skiing mag., NYC, and Correspondent for Ski mag., NYC, and Mountain Gazette, Denver, Colorado; Assistant to Director, Jewish Braille Institute, NYC, 1956-58. **Publications:** Scandinavia: The Challenge of Welfare, 1968; Lars Olav: A Norwegian Boy, 1969; Leise: A Danish Girl from Dragoer, 1970; France and the French, 1972; Skiing to Win, 1973; 100 Hikes in the Alps, 1979; 2nd ed., 1994; A Day in the Life of Sammy the Trainman (screenplay), 2003. DOCUMENTARY FILMS: Ten Days around Mont Blanc, 1974; The Great Traverse, 1975; High Route Adventure, 1975; Personnalite Rossignol, 1976; If You Can Walk, 1976; Free and Easy, 1977; Race Day, 1978; Skiing across the French Alps, 1978; Powder Hound, 1979; The Return of Powder Hound, 1980; Marathon Fever, 1981; Marathon Symphony, 1982; Winners/Losers, 1982; Bicycle Racing USA, 1983; Life among the BMXers, 1984; Bicycle Dancin', 1985; Skating and Striding: Cross Country Skiing in America, 1986; Why We Love Cross Country Skiing, 1986; Last Ride, 1987; Living Poetry, 1988, II: Yes, with Lemon, 1996; Teaching Kids to Write Poetry, 1990; Kids' Poetry, 1990; Let the Mountains Speak, 1992; Pagan Rites in Vermont's Northeast Kingdom, 1993; The Metro Group, 1994; The Greening of Vermont, 1997; Tree, 1999; The Rabbi's Dilemma, 2001; Between Summer & Winter, 2005. **Address:** 203 Center Rd, Eagle Bridge, NY 12057, U.S.A. **Online address:** edfilms@worldnet.att.net

EDWARDS, June. See **FORRESTER, Helen.**

EDWARDS, Larry. American, b. 1957. **Genres:** Novels, Film, Food and Wine, Music, Biography, Reference. **Career:** Writer. Relim Publishing, feature writer; Infonent, Inc., entertainment editor. **Publications:** Blood on the Streets (fiction), 1989; Buster: A Legend in Laughter, 1995; Bela Lugosi: Master of the Macabre, 1997. Contributor to magazines. **Address:** 2554 Alemany Blvd, San Francisco, CA 94112, U.S.A. **Online address:** lae21657@yahoo.com

EDWARDS, Louis. American, b. 1962. **Genres:** Novels. **Career:** Writer. **Publications:** NOVELS: Ten Seconds, 1991; N: A Romantic Mystery, 1997. **Address:** c/o Dutton, 375 Hudson St., New York, NY 10014, U.S.A.

EDWARDS, (Kenneth) Martin. British, b. 1955. **Genres:** Novels, Novellas/Short stories, Mystery/Crime/Suspense, Law. **Career:** Booth and Co. (solicitors), Leeds, England, trainee, 1978-80; Mace & Jones (solicitors),

Liverpool, England, solicitor, 1980-84, partner, 1984-. **Publications:** Understanding Computer Contracts, 1983; Understanding Dismissal Law, 1984; Managing Redundancies, 1986; Careers in the Law, 1988, 7th ed., 1995; Executive Survival, 1989, 2nd ed., as How to Get the Best Deal from Your Employer, 1991; Dismissal Law, 1991; All the Lonely People (novel), 1991; (ed.) Northern Blood, 1992; Suspicious Minds (novel), 1992; I Remember You (novel), 1993; Yesterday's Papers (novel), 1994; Anglian Blood, 1995; (ed.) Northern Blood 2, 1995; Eve of Destruction (novel), 1996; Know-How for Employment Lawyers, FT Law and Tax, 1996; (ed.) Perfectly Criminal, 1996; (ed.) Whydunit?, 1997; The Devil in Disguise (novel), 1998; (ed.) Northern Blood 3, 1998; (ed.) Past Crimes, 1998; First Cut Is the Deepest (novel), 1999; (ed.) Missing Persons, 1999. Contributor of articles and stories to periodicals. **Address:** Mace & Jones, 19 Water St., Liverpool, Merseyside L2 0RP, England.

EDWARDS, Michael. British, b. 1938. **Genres:** Poetry, Art/Art history, Literary criticism and history. **Career:** Professor, College de France. Formerly, Reader, Dept. of Literature, University of Essex, Colchester; Formerly, Professor of English, University of Warwick. Visiting Professor, 1997, European Chair, 2000-01, College de France; Visiting Professor, University of the Witwaterstand, 1997, Ecole Normale Superieure, 1998. Co-Ed., Prospice Review, 1973-82. **Publications:** La Thebaide de Racine, 1965; La Tragedie racinienne (criticism), 1972; Eliot/Language, 1975; Towards a Christian Poetics, 1984; Poetry and Possibility, 1988; Of Making Many Books, 1990; Raymond Mason, 1994; Eloge de l'attente, 1996; De Poetica Christiana, 1997; Beckett ou le don des langues, 1998; Lecons de poesie, 2001; Ombres de lune, 2001; Sur un vers d'Hamlet, 2001; Un monde meme et autre, 2002; Shakespeare et la comedie, 2003; Terre de poesie, 2003; Racine et Shakespeare, 2004. POETRY: Commonplace, 1971; To Kindle the Starling, 1972; Where, 1975; The Ballad of Mobb Conroy, 1977; The Magic, Unquiet Body, 1985; Rivagemobile, 2003. EDITOR: French Poetry Now, 1975; (co) Directions in Italian Poetry, 1975; Raymond Queneau, 1978; Words/Music, 1979; Languages, 1981. **Address:** College de France, 11 place Marcelin Berthelot, Cedex 05, 75231 Paris, France. **Online address:** michael.edwards@college-de-france.fr

EDWARDS, P. D. Australian, b. 1931. **Genres:** Literary criticism and history. **Career:** University of Queensland, Brisbane, Australia, lecturer in English, 1954-58, 1961; University of Sydney, Australia, lecturer to senior lecturer in English, 1962-68; University of Queensland, professor of English, 1969-96, pro-vice-chancellor for humanities, 1985-90. **Publications:** Anthony Trollope, 1968; Anthony Trollope: His Art and Scope, 1978; Anthony Trollope's Son in Australia, 1982; Idyllic Realism from Mary Russell Mitford to Hardy, 1988; Dickens's Young Men, 1997. **Address:** Department of English, University of Queensland, St. Lucia, Brisbane, QLD 4072, Australia. **Online address:** p.edwards@uq.net.au

EDWARDS, Philip (Walter). British, b. 1923. **Genres:** Literary criticism and history, Travel/Exploration. **Career:** Professor of English Literature, Trinity College, Dublin, 1960-66; Professor of Literature, University of Essex, 1966-74; King Alfred Professor of English Literature, University of Liverpool, 1974-90. **Publications:** Sir Walter Raleigh, 1953; Thomas Kyd and Early Elizabethan Tragedy, 1966; Shakespeare and the Confines of Art, 1968; Person and Office in Shakespeare's Plays, 1970; (with C.A. Gibson) Plays and Poems of Philip Massinger, 1976; Threshold of a Nation, 1979; Shakespeare: A Writer's Progress, 1986; Last Voyages, 1988; The Story of the Voyage, 1994; Sea-Mark, 1997. EDITOR: Thomas Kyd: The Spanish Tragedy, 1959; Shakespeare, Pericles Prince of Tyre, 1976; Shakespeare, Hamlet, 1985; The Journals of Captain Cook, 1999. **Address:** High Gillinggrove, Gillinggate, Kendal, Cumbria LA9 4JB, England. **Online address:** pedwards@gilling.edi.co.uk

EDWARDS, Ronald George. Australian, b. 1930. **Genres:** Mythology/Folklore, Music, Cultural/Ethnic topics, Crafts, Travel/Exploration, Children's fiction. **Career:** Founded in 1950, The Rams Skull Press, still publishing to the present day; President, Australian Folklore Society; President, Australian Whipmakers Plaiters Association. **Publications:** Overlander Songbook, 1956; Index to Australian Folksong, 1970; Australian Folk Songs, 1972; Australian Bawdy Ballads, 1974; Australian Traditional Bush Crafts, 1975; The Big Book of Australian Folk Songs, 1976; Australian Yarns, 1977; Skills of the Australian Bushman, 1979; The Stock Saddle, 1980; Yarns and Ballads of the Australian Bush, 1981; (with Lin Wei-Nao) Mud Brick and Earth Building the Chinese Way, 1984; Bush Leatherwork, 1984; The Convict Maid, 1987; Wild Master and the Bongo Multiwagon, 1987; Bushcraft 3, 1988; A Handful of Oranges, 1988; Fred's Crab and Other Bush Yarns, 1989; More Bush Leatherwork, 1989; Cant Hook and Broad Axe, 1989; Camping Prohibited and Other Folklore, 1989; The Gentle

Rain on Shikoku, 1989; Walking on Yellow Radish, 1990; Cats, 1990; The Wealthy Roo, 1990; Underground Goldfish, 1991; The Lass Who Rode the Rover, 1991; Bushcraft 4, 1992; Bushcraft 5, 1992; An Impractical Guide to Andros, 1992; Australian Folk Song, Part A, 1992; (ed.) The Australian Whipmaker, 1992; Bushcraft 6, 1993; Australian Folk Song (12 vols.), 1994; Deliver Us from Eagles, 1994; Bushcraft 7, 1995; Snow in Sicily, 1995; Bushcraft 8, 1996; Some Songs from the Torres Strait, 2001. **Address:** 12 Fairyland Rd, Kuranda, QLD 4872, Australia. **Online address:** ramskull@tpg.com.au

EDWARDS, Sarah (Anne). American, b. 1943. **Genres:** Novels, Business/Trade/Industry. **Career:** Clinical social worker and writer. Office of Economic Opportunity Regional Office, Kansas City, KS, community representative, 1966-68; Dept of Health, Education, and Welfare, Kansas City, social services/parent involvement and resource specialist, 1968-73; private practice in psychotherapy, training and consulting in personal, interpersonal, organizational behavior, Sierra Madre, CA, 1973-80; University of Kansas Medical Center, children's rehabilitation unit, social services department, director of training, 1975-76; Cathexis Institute, Glendale, CA, co-director, 1976-77; CompuServe Information Service, Working from Home Forum, co-founder and manager, 1983-97; Pine Mountain Institute, Pine Mountain, CA, co-founder. Co-host, Working from Home, Business Radio Network, 1987-2001, and Home and Garden cable TV network, 1994-98; commentator, CNBC, 1996-99, NPR Marketplace, 1996-97. Senior fellow, Center for the New West, Denver, CO. **Publications:** WITH P. EDWARDS: How to Make Money with Your Personal Computer, 1984; Working from Home, 1985, 5th ed., 1999; The Best Home Business for the 90s, 1991, rev. ed. as The Best Home Business for the 21st Century, 1994; (and with L.C. Douglas) Getting Business to Come to You, 1991, rev. ed., 1998; Making It on Your Own, 1991, rev. ed., 1996; Making Money with Your Computer at Home, 1993, rev. ed., 1997; Finding Your Perfect Work, 1996; (and with W. Zooi) Home Business You Can Buy, 1997; (and with R. Benzel) Teaming Up, 1997; (and with L. Rohrbough) Making Money in Cyberspace, 1998; (and with W. Zooi) Outfitting Your Home Business for Much Less, 2000; The Practical Dreamer's Handbook, 2000; (and with P. Economy) Home-Based Business for Dummies, 2000; Changing Directions without Losing Your Way, 2001; (and with M. Nemko) Cool Careers for Dummies, 2001; (and with L.M. Roberts) The Entrepreneurial Parent, 2002; (and with P. Economy) Why Aren't You Your Own Boss, 2003. NOVELS: Sitting with the Enemy, 2002. **Address:** Box 6775, 2624 Teakwood Ct, Pine Mountain Club, CA 93222, U.S.A. **Online address:** sedwards@frazmtn.com

EDWARDS, Thomas R(obert). American, b. 1928. **Genres:** Literary criticism and history. **Career:** Rutgers University, New Brunswick, NJ, associate professor, 1964-66, professor, 1966-93, emeritus professor of English, 1993-. Raritan: A Quarterly Review, executive editor, 1981-2002. **Publications:** This Dark Estate: A Reading of Pope, 1963; Imagination and Power, 1971; Over Here: Criticizing America 1968-1989, 1991. **Address:** 1240 Rahway Rd, Scotch Plains, NJ 07076, U.S.A.

EFIMOVA, Alla. American (born Russia), b. 1961. **Genres:** Art/Art history. **Career:** State University of New York College at Brockport, instructor in foreign languages and literatures, 1990-91; University of Rochester, Rochester, NY, instructor in art history, 1991-92; University of California Irvine, visiting lecturer in art history, 1995; University of California, Santa Cruz, lecturer in art history, 1996-. Guest lecturer at colleges and universities. **Publications:** (with L. Manovich) Tekstura: Russian Essays on Visual Culture, 1993. Contributor of articles and reviews to books and journals. **Address:** 61 Fairlawn Dr., Berkeley, CA 94708, U.S.A.

EGAN, Desmond. Irish, b. 1936. **Genres:** Poetry. **Career:** Poet. Editor and founder of the literary magazine, Era, 1974-84; full-time writer, 1987-. **Publications:** Midland, 1973; Leaves, 1974; Siege!, 1976; The Death of Metaphor: Collected Prose, 1986; Snapdragon, 1993; In the Holocaust of Autumn, 1996; Famine, 1998; Prelude, 1999; Music, 2000; The Hill of Allen, 2001. POETRY: Woodcutter, 1978; Athlone?, 1980; Collected Poems, 1983; Seeing Double, 1983; Poems for Peace, 1985; A Song for My Father, 1989; Peninsula: Poems of the Dingle Peninsula, 1992; Selected Poems, 1992; In the Holocaust of Autumn, 1994; Poems for Eimear (sequence), 1994. EDITOR: (with M. Hartnett) Choice (poetry anthology), 1973. TRANSLATOR: Medea/Euripides, 1991; Philoctetes, 1999. Contributor to magazines and anthologies. **Address:** Great Connell, Newbridge, Kildare, Ireland.

EGAN, Ferol. American, b. 1923. **Genres:** Novels, History, Biography. **Career:** Writer, three-time Commonwealth Medal winner for: The El Dorado Trial, Sand In a Whirlwind, and Fremont: Explorer for a Restless Nation;

and Fremont Award for contributions to the history of the American Frontier West. **Publications:** The El Dorado Trail: The Story of the Gold Rush Routes Across Mexico, 1970; Sand in a Whirlwind: The Paiute Indian War of 1860, 1972; Fremont: Explorer for a Restless Nation, 1977; The Taste of Time, 1977; Last Bonanza Kings: The Bourns of San Francisco, 1998. EDITOR: Incidents of Travel in New Mexico, 1969; A Sailor's Sketch of the Sacramento Valley in 1842, 1971; California, Land of Gold, or, Stay At Home and Work Hard, 1971; A Dangerous Journey, 1972; Overland Journey to Carson Valley and California, 1973; Across the Rockies with Fremont, 1975. **Address:** 1199 Grizzly Peak Blvd, Berkeley, CA 94708, U.S.A.

EGAN, Greg. Australian, b. 1961. **Genres:** Novels, Novellas/Short stories. **Career:** Writer and computer programmer. **Publications:** NOVELS: An Unusual Angle, 1983; Quarantine, 1995; Permutation City, 1995; Distress, 1997; Diaspora, 1998; Teranesia, 1999. SHORT STORIES: Our Lady of Chernoble, 1995; Axiomatic, 1997; Luminous, 1998. Contributor of short stories to magazines. **Address:** c/o Peter Robinson, Curtis Brown, Haymarket House, 28/29 Haymarket, London SWIY 4SP, England. **Online address:** gregegan@netspace.net.au

EGAN, Jennifer. American, b. 1962. **Genres:** Novels, Novellas/Short stories. **Career:** Free-lance writer, 1991-. **Publications:** The Invisible Circus (novel), 1995; Emerald City and Other Stories (short stories), 1996; Look at Me (novel), 2001. Contributor to periodicals and anthologies. **Address:** c/o ICM, 40 W 57th St 17th Fl, New York, NY 10001, U.S.A. **Online address:** JEgan8@hotmail.com

EGAN, Kieran. Irish, b. 1942. **Genres:** Education. **Career:** Simon Fraser University, Burnaby, British Columbia, professor of education, 1972-. **Publications:** The Tudor Peace, 1969; Structural Communication, 1976; Educational Development, 1979, with new intro. and foreword as Individual Development and the Curriculum, 1986; (with D.A. Nyberg) The Erosion of Education: Socialization and the Schools, 1981; Education and Psychology: Plato, Piaget, and Scientific Psychology, 1983; Teaching as Story Telling, 1986; Primary Understanding: Education in Early Childhood, 1988; Romantic Understanding: The Development of Rationality and Imagination, Ages Eight through Fifteen, 1990; Imagination in Teaching and Learning, 1992; The Educated Mind: How Cognitive Tools Shape Our Understanding, 1997. EDITOR: (with K.A. Strike) Ethics and Educational Policy, 1978; (with S. de-Castell and A. Luke) Literacy, Society, and Schooling, 1986; (with D. Nadaner) Imagination and Education, 1988; (with H. McEwan) Narrative in Teaching, Learning, and Research, 1995. **Address:** Department of Education, Simon Fraser University, Burnaby, BC, Canada V5A 1S6. **Online address:** Kieran_Egan@sfu.ca

EGAN, Linda. American, b. 1945. **Genres:** Literary criticism and history. **Career:** High school Spanish teacher at a private school, Santa Barbara, CA, 1970-78; Santa Barbara News-Press, Santa Barbara, reporter, 1980-82, editorial page editor, 1983-88; Los Rios Community College District, Sacramento, CA, public information manager, 1982-83; Santa Barbara City College, Santa Barbara, lecturer, 1974-83 instructor in Spanish and chair of journalism department, 1988-90, director of Summer in Salamanca study program, 1999; University of California-Davis, associate professor of Spanish, 1993-. California Polytechnic State University, guest lecturer for editor-in-residence program, 1997; resident Spanish teacher for private tour to Peru, 1989; teaches writing in Santa Barbara area. **Publications:** Diosas, demonios y debate: las armas metafísicas de Sor Juana, 1997; Carlos Monsiváis: Culture and Chronicle in Contemporary Mexico, 2001. Contributor to books. Contributor of articles and reviews to periodicals. **Address:** Department of Spanish and Classics, University of California-Davis, 1 Shields Ave., Davis, CA 95616, U.S.A. **Online address:** lindadeeegan@attbi.com; ldegan@ucdavis.edu

EGAN, Lorraine Hopping. American, b. 1960. **Genres:** Children's fiction, Young adult fiction, Children's non-fiction, Information science/Computers, Young adult non-fiction. **Career:** Teaching and Computers, associate editor, 1983-86; freelance writer, 1986-; Scholastic Inc., NYC, magazine editor of Futures, 1988, editor of SuperScience Blue, 1988-91; Aristoplay Ltd, Ann Arbor, MI, product development director, 1991-96; Hall of Fame Sports Books, Ann Arbor, owner, 1993-95; Smithsonian Press, editor of The Story of Science, 2003-05; adviser. Author of computer software and online materials; creator of games, card decks, and puzzles for companies. Contributor of four drama scripts to radio program Kinetic City Super Crew, 1994; inventor of Mars 2020 board game, Aristoplay, 1996. **Publications:** NONFICTION: Wild Weather (for young adults): Tornadoes, Hurricanes, Lightning, Floods, Blizzards, 1994-2003; Wild Earth (for young adults): Avalanche, Volcano, Earthquake, 1999-2003; Bone Detective and Space Rocks, Women's

Adventures in Science, 2002-05. Contributor of articles to periodicals. Author of educational materials. **Address:** 5606 N Dixboro Rd, Ann Arbor, MI 48105, U.S.A. **Online address:** mail@hoppingfun.com

EGAN, Tim. American, b. 1957. **Genres:** Children's fiction, Illustrations. **Career:** Egan Design, Canoga Park, CA, art director; Recycled Paper Greetings, Chicago, IL, writer and illustrator; also works as a free-lance illustrator. **Publications:** SELF-ILLUSTRATED FOR CHILDREN: Friday Night at Hodges' Cafe, 1994; Chestnut Cove, 1995; Metropolitan Cow, 1996; Burnt Toast on Davenport Street, in press. **Address:** 7453 Jordan Ave., Canoga Park, CA 91303, U.S.A.

EGAN, Timothy. American, b. 1954. **Genres:** Criminology/True Crime, Travel/Exploration. **Career:** New York Times, NYC, correspondent based in and chief of Seattle, WA, bureau, 1987-. **Publications:** NONFICTION: Seattle, 1986; The Good Rain: Across Time and Terrain in the Pacific Northwest, 1990; Breaking Blue, 1992; Lasso the Wind, 1998. **Address:** 4834 53rd Ave S, Seattle, WA 98118, U.S.A.

EGBUNA, Obi (Benedict). Nigerian, b. 1938. **Genres:** Novels, Plays/Screenplays, Race relations, Novellas/Short stories. **Career:** Essayist, critic, novelist, playwright, visiting professor, visiting writer. **Publications:** Wind Versus Polygamy (novel), 1964, republished as Elina, 1978; The Anthill, 1965; The Wind; The Murder of Nigeria, 1968; Daughters of the Sun and Other Stories, 1970; Destroy This Temple, 1971; Emperor of the Sea and Other Stories, 1973; Menace of the Hedgehog, 1973; The ABC of Black Power Thought, 1973; Emperor of the Sea and Other Stories, 1974; The Minister's Daughter (novel), 1975; Dem Say; Diary of a Homeless Prodigal (essays), 1976; The Hoe; Divinity; Black Candle for Christmas (short story), 1980; The Rape of Lysistrata (novel), 1980; The Madness of Didi (novel), 1980; The Dialectical Process in Modern African Literature: A Study in the Epistemology of Decolonization, 1986.

EGGERS, Kerry. American, b. 1953. **Genres:** Sports/Fitness. **Career:** Oregonian, Portland, sports writer, 1975-2000; Portland Tribune, sportswriter, 2001-. **Publications:** Blazers Profiles, 1991; Against the World, 1992; Wherever You May Be...The Bill Schonely Story, 1999; Clyde the Glide: The Clyde Drexler Story, 2004. **Address:** 620 SW 5th Ave Ste 400, Portland, OR 97204, U.S.A. **Online address:** keggers@portlandtribune.com

EGGINTON, Joyce. British/American. **Genres:** Documentaries/Reportage. **Career:** Worked for British newspapers and magazines; Observer, London, England, New York correspondent, 1964-84; New York University, New York City, adjunct professor of journalism, 1986-90; full-time writer. **Publications:** Excursion to Russia, 1955; They Seek a Living, 1957; (with C. Smith) Duet for Three Hands, 1958; The Poisoning of Michigan, 1980, also published as Bitter Harvest, 1980; From Cradle to Grave: The Short Lives and Strange Deaths of Marybeth Tinning's Nine Children, 1989; Day of Fury, 1991, as Too Beautiful a Day to Die, 1992; Circle of Fire, 1994. Contributor to periodicals.

EGIELSKI, Richard. American, b. 1952. **Genres:** Children's fiction. **Career:** Illustrator, 1973-. **Publications:** AUTHOR AND ILLUSTRATOR: Buz, 1995; The Gingerbread Boy, 1997; Jazper, 1998. Illustrator of works by F.N. Monjo, J. Bellairs, M. Chaikin, I.L. Cusack, J. Aylesworth, G. Burgess, R. Kennedy, P. Conrad, W.J. Brooke, B. Martin, Jr., W. Wise, A. Arkin, A. Yorkins. **Address:** 27 Amsterdam Rd, Milford, NJ 08848, U.S.A.

EGLER, Claudio A(ntonio) G(oncalves). Brazilian, b. 1951. **Genres:** Economics. **Career:** Federal University of Paraiba, Joao Pessoa, Paraiba, Brazil, professor of economic geography, 1978-87; Federal University of Rio de Janeiro, Rio de Janeiro, Brazil, professor of economic geography, 1987-. Consultant to National Council of Technological and Scientific Development and Inter-American Institute for Agricultural Cooperation. **Publications:** (with others) Geographie et Ecologie de la Paraiba, 1980; (with B.K. Becker) Brazil: A New Regional Power in the World Economy, 1992; (with others) Innovation Technogiques et Mutations Industrielles en Amerique Latine, 1993. **Address:** Department of Geography, Federal University of Rio de Janeiro, Cidade Universitaria, Ilha do Fundao 21941-590, Rio de Janeiro, Brazil. **Online address:** egler@ufrj.br

EGLETON, Clive. Also writes as Patrick Blake, John Tarrant. British, b. 1927. **Genres:** Mystery/Crime/Suspense. **Career:** Served in the British Army, rising to the rank of Lt. Col., 1945-75. Civilian desk officer, Directorate of Security (Army), 1981-89. **Publications:** A Piece of Resistance, 1970; Last Post for a Partisan, 1971; The Judas Mandate, 1972; Seven Days to a Killing, 1973 (in U.S. as The Black Windmill, 1974); The October Plot (in U.S. as The Bormann Brief), 1974; Skirmish, 1975; State Visit, 1976; (as John Tarrant) The Rommel Plot, 1977; The Mills Bomb, 1978; (as John Tarrant) The Clauber Trigger, 1978; Backfire, 1979; (as Patrick Blake) Escape to Athena, 1979; The Winter Touch (in U.S. as The Eisenhower Deception), 1981; A Falcon for the Hawk, 1982; (as John Tarrant) China Gold, 1982; (as Patrick Blake) Double Griffin, 1982; The Russian Enigma, 1982; A Conflict of Interests, 1983; Troika, 1984; A Different Drummer, 1985; Picture of the Year, 1987; Gone Missing (in US as Missing from the Record), 1988; Death of a Sahib, 1989; In the Red, 1990; Last Act, 1991; A Double Deception, 1992; Hostile Intent, 1993; A Killing in Moscow, 1994; Death Throes, 1994; A Lethal Involvement, 1996; Warning Shot, 1996; Blood Money, 1997; Dead Reckoning, 1999; The Honey Trap, 2000; One Man Running, 2001; Cry Havoc, 2002; Assassination Day, 2004. **Address:** Dolphin House, Beach House Rd, Bembridge, Isle of Wight PO35 5TA, England.

EGLI, Ida Rae. American, b. 1946. **Genres:** Literary criticism and history, Poetry, Novellas/Short stories. **Career:** Santa Rosa Junior College, Santa Rosa, CA, instructor, English Dept., 1985-. **Publications:** EDITOR: No Rooms of Their Own: Women Writers of Early California, 1991; Women of the Gold Rush: The New Penelope and Other Stories, by F.F. Victor. Contributor of stories, poems, and articles to periodicals. **Address:** Department of English, Santa Rosa Junior College, 1501 Mendocino Ave, Santa Rosa, CA 95401, U.S.A.

EGOFF, Sheila A. Canadian (born United States), b. 1918. **Genres:** Literary criticism and history. **Career:** Galt Public Library, Galt, ON, children's librarian, 1938-42; Toronto Public Library, children's librarian, 1942-52, reference librarian, 1952-57; Canadian Library Association, editor, 1957-61; affiliated with University of British Columbia, Vancouver, beginning in 1961, became professor of librarianship, served as May Hill Arbuthnot Honorary Lecturer, 1979; Officer, Order of Canada, 1994. **Publications:** The Republic of Childhood: A Critical Guide to Canadian Children's Literature, 1968, 2nd ed., 1975; (with A. Belisle) Notable Canadian Children's Books/Un choix de livres canadiens pour la jeunesse, 1973; Thursday's Child: Trends and Patterns in Contemporary Children's Literature, 1981; Worlds Within: Fantasy from the Middle Ages to Today, 1988; Canadian Children's Books 1799-1939, 1992; Books That Shaped Our Minds, 1998. EDITOR: (with G.T Stubbs and L.F. Ashley) Only Connect: Readings on Children's Literature, 1969, 2nd ed., 1980; One Ocean Touching: Papers from the First Pacific Rim Conference on Children's Literature, 1979. **Address:** 3687 W 16th Ave, Vancouver, BC, Canada V6R 3C3.

EGOLF, Tristan. American, b. 1971. **Genres:** Adult non-fiction. **Career:** Writer. **Publications:** Lord of the Barnyard: Killing the Fatted Calf and Arming the Aware in the Corn Belt, 1998; Skirt and the Fiddle, 2002. **Address:** c/o Author Mail, Grove Press, 175 Fifth Avenue, New York, NY 10010, U.S.A.

EGOYAN, Atom. Canadian (born Egypt), b. 1960. **Genres:** Plays/Screenplays. **Career:** Director for stage, screen and television, producer, film editor, actor, and writer. Associated with Playwrights Unit in Toronto, Ontario, Canada. Director of Ego Film Arts in Toronto, 1982-. **Publications:** SCREENPLAYS: Next of Kin, 1984; Family Viewing, 1987; Speaking Parts, 1989; A Fortified City, 1990; The Adjuster, 1991; Calendar, 1992; Exotica, 1994. SHORT FILMS: Howard in Particular, 1979; Open House, 1982. Director and writer of the segment "En passant" for the film Montreal vu par, 1992. OTHER: Speaking Parts (essays, interviews, and script), 1993; Exotica, 1995. PLAYS: The Doll. **Address:** Ego Film Arts, 80 Niagara St., Toronto, ON, Canada M5V 1C5.

EHLE, John. American, b. 1925. **Genres:** Novels, Biography, Plays/Screenplays, History, Race relations. **Career:** Member of the faculty, University of North Carolina, Chapel Hill, 1951-64. Member, Executive Committee, National Book Committee, 1972-75. **Publications:** Move Over Mountain, 1957; The Survivor, 1958; Kingstree Island, 1959; Shepherd of the Streets, 1960; Lion on the Hearth, 1961; The Land Breakers, 1964; The Free Men, 1965; The Road, 1967; Time of Drums, 1970; The Journey of August King, 1971; The Cheeses and Wines of England and France with Notes on Irish Whiskey, 1972; The Changing of the Guard, 1975; The Winter People, 1982; Last One Home, 1984; Trail of Tears: The Rise and Fall of the Cherokee Nation, 1988; The Widow's Trial, 1989; Dr. Frank: Living with Frank Porter Graham, 1993. **Address:** 125 Westview Drive NW, Winston-Salem, NC 27104, U.S.A.

EHLER, R(ichard) L. American, b. 1930. **Genres:** Communications/Media. **Career:** General Electric Co., manager of technical communications in New York, Massachusetts, Illinois, and California, 1955-63; Motorola, Phoenix,

AZ, supervisor of technical communications, 1963-64; Lennon & Newell, Inc., San Francisco, CA, account executive, 1964-65; ChaceCo Advertising, Inc., Santa Barbara, CA, vice president, 1965-72; Larson/Bateman, Inc., Santa Barbara, account executive, 1972-79; Richler and Co., Inc., Santa Barbara, owner, 1979-; writer. **Publications:** The Print Media Planning Manual, 1991; Directory of Print Media Advertising Resources, 1992; Media Analysis Tools, 1992; Checklists for Print Media Advertising, Planning, and Buying, 1992. Contributor to periodicals. **Address:** Richler and Co. Inc., 754 Palermo Dr Ste A, Santa Barbara, CA 93105, U.S.A. **Online address:** Richlerandco@worldnet.att.net

EHLERT, Lois (Jane). American, b. 1934. **Genres:** Children's fiction, Illustrations. **Career:** Writer, illustrator, teacher, and graphic designer. **Publications:** SELF-ILLUSTRATED FOR CHILDREN: Growing Vegetable Soup, 1987; Planting a Rainbow, 1988; Color Zoo, 1989; Eating the Alphabet: Fruits and Vegetables from A to Z, 1989; Color Farm, 1990; Feathers for Lunch, 1990; Fish Eyes: A Book You Can Count On, 1990; Red Leaf, Yellow Leaf, 1991; Circus, 1992; Moon Rope: A Peruvian Folktale/Un lazo a la luna: una layenda peruana, 1992; Nuts to You!, 1993; Mole's Hill: A Woodland Tale, 1994; Snowballs, 1995; Under My Nose, 1996; Cuckoo: A Mexican Folktale/Cucu: Un cuento folklorico mexicano, 1997; Hands, 1997; Top Cat, 1998; Market Day, 2000; Waiting for Wings, 2001; In My World, 2002. Illustrator of books by J. Archambault, G. Baer, B. Martin Jr., S. Murphy, A. Turner, S. Weeks. **Address:** c/o Children's Books, Harcourt Brace Inc, 525 B St Ste 1900, San Diego, CA 92101, U.S.A.

EHRENBERG, John. American, b. 1944. **Genres:** Politics/Government. **Career:** University of New Mexico, Albuquerque, assistant professor of political science, 1972-77; St. John's University, NYC, assistant professor of political science, 1977-80; Long Island University, Brooklyn, NY, associate professor, 1980-85, professor of political science, 1985-. **Publications:** The Dictatorship of the Proletariat, 1992; Proudhon and His Age, 1996. Contributor to scholarly journals. **Address:** Department of Political Science, Lond Island University, Brooklyn, NY 11201, U.S.A. **Online address:** jehrenbe@hornet.liunet.edu

EHRET, Christopher. American, b. 1941. **Genres:** History, Language/Linguistics. **Career:** University of California, Los Angeles, associate professor, then professor, 1968-. **Publications:** Southern Nilotic History: Linguistic Approaches to the Study of the Past, 1971; Ethiopians and East Africans: The Problem of Contacts, 1974; The Historical Reconstruction of Southern Cushitic Phonology and Vocabulary, 1980; (with M. Posnansky) The Archaeological and Linguistic Reconstruction of African History, 1982; Reconstructing Proto-Afroasiatic: Vowels, Tone, Consonants, and Vocabulary, 1995; An African Classical Age, 1998; A HistoricalComparative Reconstruction of Nilo-Saharan, 2001; The Civilizations of Africa: A History to 1800, 2002. **Address:** Dept. of History, University of California, 405 Hilgard Ave, Los Angeles, CA 90024, U.S.A.

EHRET, Terry. American, b. 1955. **Genres:** Poetry. **Career:** High school teacher of English, psychology, and art history in Salinas, Belmont, and San Francisco, CA, 1977-90; California Poets in the Schools, poet-teacher, 1990-; Santa Rosa Junior College, Santa Rosa, CA, English instructor, 1991-; Sonoma State University, lecturer, 1993-; San Francisco State University, lecturer, 1996-2000; Sixteen Rivers Press, San Francisco, founding member, 1999-; private workshops through the Sitting Room, Cotati, CA, 1998-. **Publications:** (with S. Gilmartin and S.H. Sibbet) Suspensions (poems), 1990; Lost Body (poems), 1993; Travel/How We Go on Living, 1995; Translations from the Human Language, 2001. Contributor of poems, essays, and reviews to periodicals. **Address:** 924 Sunnyslope Rd, Petaluma, CA 94952, U.S.A. **Online address:** tehret@home.com

EHRLER, Brenda. American, b. 1953. **Genres:** How-to books. **Career:** Accounting clerk in Salt Lake City, UT, 1977-85; office administrator in Sumas, WA, 1985-91; Williams Energy Service, Salt Lake City, budget and procedure assistant, 1991-93, budget and procedure specialist, 1993-96, senior coordination specialist, 1996-98; writer and motivational speaker, 1998-. **Publications:** Learning to Be You: It's an Inside Job; Recovery and Healing for the Loved Ones of the Substance-Addicted, 1999. **Address:** 746 East Rosemore Ct., Salt Lake City, UT 84107, U.S.A. **Online address:** brendae@gateway.net

EHRLICH, Amy. American, b. 1942. **Genres:** Children's fiction, Young adult fiction, Young adult non-fiction. **Career:** Worked as a teacher in a day care center, fabric colorist, and hospital receptionist; Family Circle magazine, NYC, roving editor, 1976-77; Delacorte Press, NYC, senior editor, 1977-78; Dial Books for Young Readers, NYC, senior editor, 1978-82, executive edi-

tor, 1982-84; Candlewick Press, Cambridge, MA, vice president, editor-in-chief, 1991-96, editor at large, 1996-. **Publications:** FOR YOUNG ADULTS. FICTION: Where It Stops, Nobody Knows, 1988; The Dark Card, 1991. OTHER: (ed.) When I Was Your Age: Original Stories about Growing Up, 1996, vol. 2, 2003. FOR CHILDREN: Zeek Silver Moon, 1972; The Everyday Train, 1977; Leo, Zack, and Emmie, 1981; Annie and the Kidnappers, 1982; Annie Finds a Home, 1982; Buck-Buck the Chicken, 1987; Leo, Zack, and Emmie Together Again, 1987; Emma's New Pony, 1988; The Story of Hanukkah, 1989; Lucy's Winter Tale, 1991; Parents in the Pigpen: Pigs in the Tub, 1993; Maggie and Silky Joe, 1994; Hurry Up, Mickey, 1996; Rachel: The Story of Rachel Carson, 2003. ADAPTER: Wounded Knee: An Indian History of the American West, 1974; Annie: The Storybook Based on the Movie, 1982; Bunnies All Day Long, 1985; Bunnies and Their Grandma, 1985; Cinderella, 1985; The Ewoks and the Lost Children, 1985; (and ed.) The Random House Book of Fairy Tales, 1985; Bunnies On Their Own, 1986; Bunnies at Christmastime, 1986; Pome and Peel: A Venetian Tale, 1989; Rapunzel, 1989. RETELLER: Thumbelina, 1979; The Wild Swans, 1981; The Snow Queen, 1982.

EHRLICH, Eugene. American, b. 1922. **Genres:** Language/Linguistics, Writing/Journalism. **Career:** Senior Lecturer, Dept. of English, Columbia University, NYC, 1948-85. **Publications:** How to Study Better, 1960, 1976; (with D. Murphy) The Art of Technical Writing, 1962; (with D. Murphy) Researching and Writing Term Papers and Reports, 1964; (with D. Murphy and D. Pace) College Developmental Reading, 1966; (with D. Murphy) Basic Grammar for Writing, 1970; (with D. Murphy) Concise Index to English, 1974; Basic Vocabulary Builder, 1975; English Grammar, 1976, 3rd ed., 2000; Punctuation, Capitalization, and Spelling, 1977; (with others) Oxford American Dictionary, 1980; (with G. Carruth) The Oxford Illustrated Literary Guide to the United States, 1982; (with G. Hawes) Speak for Success, 1984; Amo, Amas, Amat, & More, 1985; The Bantam Concise Handbook of English, 1986; The Harper Dictionary of Foreign Terms, 3rd ed., 1987; (with G. Carruth) The Harper Book of American Quotations, 1988; Superwordpower, 1989; (with David H. Scott) Mene, Mene, Tekel: A Lively Lexicon of Words and Phrases from the Bible, 1990; Collins Gem Thesaurus, 1990; Collins Gem Webster's Dictionary, 1990; Funk & Wagnalls Standard Dictionary, 2nd ed., 1993; (with S.I. Hayakawa) Choose the Right Word, 2nd ed., 1994; Veni, Vidi, Vici, 1995; The Highly Selective Thesaurus for the Extraordinarily Literate, 1996; The Highly Selective Dictionary for the Extraordinarily Literate, 1997; Les Bons Mots, 1997; What's in a Name?, 1999; You've Got Ketchup in Your Muumuu, 2000. **Address:** 1166 Old White Plains Rd., Mamaroneck, NY 10543, U.S.A.

EHRLICH, Jack. (John Gunther Ehrlich). American, b. 1930. **Genres:** Mystery/Crime/Suspense, Westerns/Adventure. **Career:** Lawyer: district attorney, Suffolk County, NY, bureau chief, retired; reporter, Newsday, NYC, 1955-60. **Publications:** Revenge, 1958; Court-Material, 1959; Parole, 1960; Slow Burn, 1961; Cry, Baby, 1962; The Girl Cage, 1967; The Drowning, 1970; The Fastest Gun in the Pulpit, 1972; Bloody Vengeance, 1973; The Laramie River Crossing, 1973; The Chatham Killing, 1976; Rebellion at Cripple Creek, 1979; Command Influence, 2000. **Address:** c/o Theron Raines, Raines & Raines, 103 Kenyon Rd, Medusa, NY 12120-1404, U.S.A.

EHRLICH, Linda C. American, b. 1952. **Genres:** Film. **Career:** Southern Illinois University, Carbondale, instructor in English as a second language, 1982-83; Urawa Women's College, Tokyo, Japan, visiting instructor, 1984; University of Hawaii at Manoa, Honolulu, coordinator of international conferences at East-West Center, 1984-85; University of Tennessee, assistant professor, 1989-95, associate professor of Japanese and cinema, 1995-96, guest scholar, 1993-94; Case Western Reserve University, Cleveland, OH, associate professor of Japanese, comparative literature, and cinema, 1996-, fellow at Summer Institute in Teaching Ethics, 1997. John Carroll University, visiting instructor, 1988, 1989, and 1992; University of Pittsburgh, visiting professor in Semester-at-Sea Program, 1998; guest lecturer at educational institutions; public speaker. Freelance translator and interpreter, 1979-; Sony Corp., Tokyo, Japan, copywriter, 1984. **Publications:** EDITOR: (with D. Desser) Cinematic Landscapes: Observations on the Visual Arts and Cinema of China and Japan, 1994, 2nd ed, 2000; An Open Window: The Cinema of Victor Erice, 2001. Contributor to books. Contributor of articles, poetry, translations, and reviews to periodicals. **Address:** Department of Modern Languages and Literatures, Case Western Reserve University, Cleveland, OH 44106, U.S.A. **Online address:** lce2@po.cwru.edu

EHRLICH, Paul. American, b. 1932. **Genres:** Biology, Environmental sciences/Ecology. **Career:** Bing Professor of Population Studies, Stanford University, California, 1976- (Assistant Professor and Associate Professor, 1959-66; Professor, 1966-76). Consulting Ed. in Population in Biology,

McGraw-Hill Book Co., NYC, 1966-75 (Adviser in the Biological Sciences, 1966-75). Hon. President, Zero Population Growth, 1970- (President, 1969-70). Member, National Acad. of Sciences. Fellow, American Acad. of Arts and Sciences, American Philosophical Society. **Publications:** How to Know the Butterflies, 1961; Process of Evolution, 1963; Principles of Modern Biology, 1968; Population Bomb, 1968; Population, Resources, Environment: Issues in Human Ecology, 1970; How to Be a Survivor, 1971; The Bomb, 1977; Ecoscience: Population, Resources, Environment, 1977; Golden Door: International Migration, Mexico and the United States, 1980; Extinction, 1981; (with others) The Cold and the Dark: The World after Nuclear War, 1984; The Machinery of Nature, 1986; Earth, 1987; The Science of Ecology, 1987; The Birder's Handbook, 1988; New World, New Mind, 1989; The Population Explosion, 1990; Healing the Planet, 1991; Birds in Jeopardy, 1992; The Stork and the Plow, 1995; Betrayal of Science and Reason, 1996; A World of Wounds, 1997; Human Natures, 2000; Wild Solutions, 2001. **Address:** Dept. of Biological Sciences, Stanford University, Stanford, CA 94305, U.S.A.

EHRMAN, Bart D. American. **Genres:** Theology/Religion. **Career:** Rutgers University, New Brunswick, NJ, lecturer and instructor, 1984-88; University of North Carolina, Chapel Hill, Chapel Hill, NC, professor of religious studies, 1988-. Duke University, visiting assistant professor, 1991. **Publications:** Didymus the Blind and the Text of the Gospels, 1986; (with G.D. Fee and M.W. Holmes) The Text of the Fourth Gospel in the Writings of Origen, 1992; The Orthodox Corruption of Scripture: The Effect of Early Christological Controversies on the Text of the New Testament, 1993; (ed., with M.W. Holmes) The Text of the New Testament in Contemporary Research: Essays on the Status Quaestionis, 1995; The New Testament: A Historical Introduction to the Early Christian Writings, 1997; The New Testament and Other Early Christian Writings: A Reader, 1998; After the New Testament: A Reader in Early Christianity, 1999; Jesus, Apocalyptic Prophet of the New Millennium, 1999. **Address:** University of North Carolina, Department of Religious Studies, 105 Saunders Hall, Chapel Hill, NC 27599, U.S.A. **Online address:** behrman@email.unc.edu

EHRMAN, John (Patrick William). British, b. 1920. **Genres:** History, Biography. **Career:** Chairman, National Manuscripts Conservation Trust, 1989-94. Member, Royal Commission on Historical Manuscripts, 1973-94. Fellow, Trinity College, Cambridge, 1947-52; Historian, Cabinet Office, 1948-56; Lees Knowles Lecturer, Cambridge University, 1957-58; Vice President, Navy Records Society, 1968-70 and 1974-76; Member, Reviewing Committee on Export of Works of Art, 1970-76; Trustee, National Portrait Gallery, London, 1971-85; Chairman, Advisory Committee, British Library Reference Division, 1975-84; James Ford Special Lecturer, Oxford University, 1976-77. Chairman, Panizzi Foundation Selection Council, 1983-89. **Publications:** The Navy in the War of William III, 1689-1697, 1953; Grand Strategy, 1943-1944, 1956; Grand Strategy, 1944-45, 1956; Cabinet Government and War, 1890-1940, 1958; The British Government and Commercial Negotiations with Europe, 1783-1793, 1962; The Younger Pitt, The Years of Acclaim, 1969; The Reluctant Transition, 1983; The Consuming Struggle, 1996. **Address:** The Mead Barns, Taynton, Burford, Oxon. OX18 4UH, England.

EHRMAN, John. American, b. 1959. **Genres:** Politics/Government. **Career:** George Washington University, Washington, DC, lecturer in history, 1992-. **Publications:** The Rise of Neoconservatism, 1995. **Address:** c/o Carl Brandt, Brandt & Brandt, 1501 Broadway, New York, NY 10036, U.S.A.

EIBEL, Deborah. Canadian, b. 1940. **Genres:** Poetry. **Career:** Walnut Hill School, Natick, MA, teacher of English literature, 1962-63; University of North Carolina, Greensboro, teacher, 1963-65; Haifa University, Israel, teacher of English literature, 1966-67; Johns Hopkins University, Baltimore, MD, instructor, 1970-71; Concordia University, Loyola and Sir George Williams campuses, Montreal, Quebec, teacher of English literature and creative writing, 1972-78; McGill University Continuing Education, Montreal, Quebec, teacher of creative writing, 1977; College Marie-Victorin, Montreal, teacher of English literature, 1987-88; Concordia University, Sir George Williams campus, teacher of poetry, 1991; writer. **Publications:** POETRY: Kayak Sickness, 1972; Streets Too Narrow for Parades, 1985; Making Fun of Travellers, 1991; Gold Rush, 1992; Purple Passages, 1998; A Poet's Notebook, 1997; Poems for the Twenty-First Century. Contributor to anthologies. **Address:** 5795 Caldwell Ave, Montreal, QC, Canada H4W 1W3.

EICHNER, Hans. Canadian (born Austria), b. 1921. **Genres:** Novels, Literary criticism and history. **Career:** Professor, 1967-88, Chairman, 1973-88, and Professor Emeritus, 1988-, Dept. of German, University of Toronto, ON.

General Ed., Canadian Studies in German Language and Literature, 1970-. Assistant Lecturer, Bedford College, University of London, 1948-50; Assistant Professor, 1950-56, Associate Professor, 1956-62, and Prof. and Head of Dept. of German, 1962-67, Queen's University, Kingston, ON. **Publications:** Thomas Mann: Eine Einfuehrung in sein Werk, 1953, 1961; Friedrich Schlegel: Literary Notebooks 1797-1801, 1957; (with H. Hein) Reading German for Scientists, 1959; Four Modern German Authors: Mann, Rilke, Kafka, Brecht, 1964; Friedrich Schlegel, 1970; Deutsche Literatur im klassisch-romantischen Zeitalter, 1789-1805, vol. I, 1990; Kahn & Engelmann (novel), 2000; Against the Grain: Selected Essays, 2003. EDITOR: Kritische Friedrich Schlegel-Ausgabe, vols. II-VI, 1959-74, vol. XVI, 1981; (with L. Kahn) Studies in German in Memory of Robert L. Kahn, 1971; Romantic and Its Cognates: The European History of a Word, 1972; (with E. Behler) F. Schlegel, Studienausgabe, 6 vols., 1988; Hamann, Ausgewaehlte Schriften, 1994. **Address:** PO Box 41, Rockwood, ON, Canada N0B 2K0.

EICHORN, Rosemary D. American, b. 1943. **Genres:** Architecture. **Career:** Artist, teacher, and lecturer in Soquel, CA, 1964-. **Publications:** The Art of Fabric Collage, 2000. **Address:** c/o Author Mail, Taunton Press, 63 South Main St., Newtown, CT 06470, U.S.A. **Online address:** rosemary@sewjourn.com

EICKHOFF, Randy Lee. American, b. 1945. **Genres:** Novels, Theatre. **Career:** Lincoln Star, Lincoln, NE, columnist and journalist; University of Texas, El Paso, English Graduate School, faculty member. **Publications:** NOVELS: A Hand to Execute, 1987; The Gombeen Man, 1992; The Fourth Horseman, 1998; (with L.C. Lewis) Bowie, 1998; Fallon's Wake, 2000; Return to Ithaca: A Confessional Novel, 2001; The Destruction of the Inn, 2001; Then Came Christmas, 2002; He Stands Alone, 2002; And Not to Yield, 2003. ULSTER CYCLE SERIES: The Raid, 1997; The Feast, 1999; The Sorrows, 2000; The Destruction of the Inn, 2001; He Stands Alone, 2002; The Red Branch Tales, 2003. OTHER: Exiled: The Tigua Indians of Ysleta del Sur (nonfiction), 1996; (as R.L. Eickhoff) The Odyssey: A Modern Translation of Homer's Classic Tale, 2001; Falstaff: A Comic Foil to Bolinbroke and The American Canon. PLAYS: A Christmas Carol for the Experimental Theatre; Albé; Twelve Loaves of Bread; The Rest Is Silence. Contributor of drama and poetry to magazines, journals, and anthologies. Contributor of reviews, articles, criticism, and academic essays to magazines and professional journals. **Address:** J.M. Hanks High School, 2001 Lee Trevino, El Paso, TX 79925, U.S.A. **Online address:** randyeickhoff@aol.com

EIDSON, Thomas. American, b. 1944. **Genres:** Novels. **Career:** Hill & Knowlton (public relations), president and chief executive officer. **Publications:** St. Agnes' Stand, 1994; The Last Ride, 1995; All God's Children, 1996; Hannah's Gift, 1998. **Address:** c/o Dutton/Penguin USA, 375 Hudson St., New York, NY 10014, U.S.A.

EILBERG-SCHWARTZ, Howard. American, b. 1956. **Genres:** Theology/Religion. **Career:** Indiana University-Bloomington, assistant professor of religious studies, 1986-89; Temple University, Philadelphia, PA, assistant professor of religious studies, 1989-90; Stanford University, Stanford, CA, assistant professor of religious studies, 1990-94; San Francisco State University, San Francisco, CA, associate professor of religious studies and director of Jewish studies, both 1994-. **Publications:** The Human Will in Judaism, 1988; The Savage in Judaism, 1990; (ed.) People of the Body: Jews and Judaism from an Embodied Perspective, 1992; God's Phallus: And Other Problems for Men and Monotheism, 1994; (ed.) Off with Her Head: The Denial of Female Identity in Religion, Myth and Culture, 1995. **Address:** Jewish Studies Program, San Francisco State University, 1600 Holloway Ave., San Francisco, CA 94132, U.S.A.

EILON, Samuel. British, b. 1923. **Genres:** Administration/Management, Economics, Money/Finance, Technology. **Career:** Chief Ed., OMEGA, International Journal of Mgmt. Science 1971-1993; Sr. Research Fellow, Imperial College, London (Head, Dept. of Mgmt. Science, 1963-87); Member of the Monopolies and Mergers Commission, 1990-97. **Publications:** Industrial Engineering Tables, 1962; Elements of Production Planning and Control, 1962; (with J.R. King and R.I. Hall) Exercises in Industrial Management: A Series of Case Studies, 1966; (with J.R. King) Industrial Scheduling Abstracts, 1967; (with W. Lampkin) Inventory Control Abstracts, 1968; (with C.D.T. Watson-Gandy and N. Christofides) Distribution Management-Mathematical Modelling and Practical Analysis, 1971; Management Control, 1971, 1979; (with T.R. Fowkes) Applications of Management Science in Banking and Finance, 1972; (with B. Gold and J. Soesan) Applied Productivity Analysis for Industry, 1976; Aspects of Management, 1977, 1979; The Art of Reckoning: Analysis of Performance Criteria 1984; Management Assertions and Aversions, 1985; (with B. Blackwell) The Global Challenge of

Innovation, 1991; Management Practice and Mispractice, 1992; Anthology of Management Science, 1996; Management Strategies: A Critique of Theories and Practices, 1999. **Address:** 1 Meadway Close, London NW11 7BA, England.

EINHORN, Barbara. New Zealander, b. 1942. **Genres:** Politics/Government. **Career:** University of Sussex, Brighton, England, lecturer and convenor, 1995-. **Publications:** Cinderella Goes to Market (monograph), 1993; (ed. with E.J. Yeo) Women in Market Societies: Crisis and Opportunity, 1995; (ed. with M. Kaldor and Z. Kavan) Citizenship and Democracy in Contemporary Europe, 1996. **Address:** Research Centre in Women's Studies, University of Sussex, Brighton BN1 9RQ, England.

EISEN, Sydney. American/Canadian (born Poland), b. 1929. **Genres:** Education, History, Humanities, Intellectual history, Theology/Religion, Bibliography. **Career:** Williams College, Williamstown, MA, instructor, 1955-58, assistant professor, 1958-61; City College of the City University of New York, assistant professor, 1961-65; York University, North York, ON, associate professor, 1965-68, professor of history and humanities, 1968-96, chair of department of history, 1970-72, founding member and member of coordinating committee of Victorian Studies Option, 1972-88, dean of faculty of arts, 1973-78, director of Centre for Jewish Studies, 1989-95, Vanier College, university professor, 1993-96, emeritus university professor, 1996-; writer. University of Toronto, visiting associate professor, 1965-66. National Humanities Faculty, member of faculty, 1972-85, member of board of trustees and executive committee, 1974-81, president and chairman of board of directors, 1976-80. **Publications:** (with M. Filler) The Human Adventure: Readings in World History, 2 vols, 1964; (with B. Lightman) Victorian Science and Religion: A Bibliography with Emphasis on Evolution, Belief, and Unbelief, Comprised of Works Published from c. 1900-75, 1984; (author of intro.) R. Helmstadter and B. Lightman, eds., Victorian Faith in Crisis, 1990. EDITOR: (general) The West and The World (various books and pamphlets), 1967-80; (consulting) A. Haberman, The Making of the Modern Age, 1987; (general) A. Haberman and A. Shubert, The West and the World. **Address:** Vanier College 237, York University, 4700 Keele St, North York, ON, Canada M3J 1P3. **Online address:** seisen@yorku.ca

EISENBERG, Deborah. American, b. 1945. **Genres:** Novellas/Short stories, Plays/Screenplays. **Career:** Currently teaching in the Master of Fine Arts Creative Writing program at the University of Virginia. **Publications:** STORIES: Transactions in a Foreign Currency, 1986; Under the 82nd Airborne, 1992; The Stories (So Far) of Deborah Eisenberg, 1996; All around Atlantis, 1997. PLAYS: Pastorale, 1982. OTHER: Air, 24 Hours: Jennifer Bartlett (monograph), 1994. Contributor to periodicals. **Address:** c/o Lynn Nesbit, Johnlow Nesbit & Associates, 445 Park Ave Fl 13, New York, NY 10022, U.S.A.

EISENBERG, Ellen M. American, b. 1962. **Genres:** History, Local history/Rural topics. **Career:** Willamette University, Salem, OR, assistant professor, 1990-95, associate professor, 1995-2001, professor of history, 2001-, Dwight & Margaret Lear Professor of History, 2003-. **Publications:** Jewish Agricultural Colonies in New Jersey, 1882-1920, 1995. Contributor to periodicals. **Address:** Dept of History, Willamette University, 900 State Ave, Salem, OR 97301, U.S.A.

EISENBERG, John S. American, b. 1956. **Genres:** Autobiography/Memoirs. **Career:** Sportswriter, author. Baltimore Sun, Baltimore, MD, sportswriter. **Publications:** The Longest Shot: Lil E. Tee and the Kentucky Derby, 1996; Cotton Bowl Days: Growing Up with Dallas and the Cowboys in the 1960s, 1997; From 33rd Street to Camden Yards: An Oral History of the Baltimore Orioles, 2001; Native Dancer: The Grey Ghost: Hero of a Golden Age, 2003. **Address:** c/o Author Mail, Warner Books, 1271 Avenue of the Americas, New York, NY 10020, U.S.A. **Online address:** John.Eisenberg@baltsun.com

EISENBERG, Robert. American, b. 1956. **Genres:** Documentaries/Reportage. **Career:** Investor, journalist. **Publications:** Boychiks in the Hood: Travels in the Hasidic Underground (nonfiction), 1995. **Address:** 1101 Harney St., Omaha, NE 68131, U.S.A.

EISENHOWER, John S(heldon) D(oud). American, b. 1922. **Genres:** History, Autobiography/Memoirs. **Career:** U.S. Army, officer, 1944-63, reserve officer, 1963-, Brigadier general, U.S. Army Reserves, 1974-. Assistant staff secty. at the White House, Washington D.C., 1958-61; U.S. Ambassador to Belgium, 1969-71. **Publications:** The Bitter Woods: The Battle of the Bulge, 1944-1945, 1969; Strictly Personal (memoir), 1974; Allies: Pearl Harbor to D-Day, 1982; So Far from God: The U.S. War with Mexico, 1846-1848,

1989; Intervention! The United States and the Mexican Revolution, 1913-1917, 1993; Agent of Destiny: The Life and Times of General Winfield Scott, 1997; (with J.T. Eisenhower) Yanks: The Epic Story of the American Army in World War I, 2001; General Ike, 2003. **Address:** PO Box 778, Kimberton, PA 19442, U.S.A.

EISENMAN, Stephen F. American, b. 1956. **Genres:** Art/Art history, Anthropology/Ethnology. **Career:** Writer. Occidental College, Los Angeles, CA, professor of art history. **Publications:** Le Fantastique Reel: Graphic Works by Odilon Redon, 1990; The Temptation of Saint Redon: Biography, Ideology, and Style in the Noirs of Odilon Redon, 1992; Nineteenth-Century Art: A Critical History, 1994; Gauguin's Skirt, 1997. **Address:** Department of Art History and the Visual Arts, Occidental College, 1600 Campus Rd., Los Angeles, CA 90041, U.S.A.

EISENSON, Marc. American, b. 1943. **Genres:** Economics, Money/Finance, Self help. **Career:** Good Advice Press, Elizaville, NY, partner, 1984-. **Publications:** The Banker's Secret Credit Card Software, 1990; The Banker's Secret, 1991; The Banker's Secret Loan Software, 1992; (with A. Eisenson) The Peanut Butter and Jelly Game (juvenile), 1996; Stop Junk Mail Forever, 1997, rev. ed., 2001; (with G. Detweiler) Debt Consolidation 101, 1997; (with G. Detweiler and N. Castleman) Invest in Yourself: Six Secrets to a Rich Life, 1998; (with G. Detweiler and N. Castleman) Slash Your Debt: Save Money and Secure Your Future, 1999. **Address:** PO Box 78, Elizaville, NY 12523, U.S.A. **Online address:** goodadvice@ulster.net; marc@investinyourself.com

EISENSTADT, Shmuel Noah. Israeli (born Poland), b. 1923. **Genres:** Social sciences, Sociology. **Career:** Hebrew University, Jerusalem, professor of sociology, 1959-, now Rose Isaacs Professor Emeritus of Sociology (lecturer, 1951-57; associate professor, 1957-59). **Publications:** The Absorption of Immigrants, 1954; From Generation to Generation, 1956; Essays on Sociological Aspects of Political and Economic Development, 1961; The Political Systems of Empires, 1963; Essays on Compative Institutions, 1965; Modernization, Protest and Change, 1966; Israeli Society, 1968; The Protestant Ethic and Modernization, 1968; Political Sociology of Modernization, 1968; Social Differentiation and Stratification, 1972; Tradition, Change and Modernity, 1973; Post-Traditional Societies, 1974; (with M. Curelaru) The Forms of Sociology, 1976; Revolution and the Transformation of Societies, 1978; (co) Patrons, Clients, and Friends, 1984; Transformation of Israeli Society, 1985; (co) Society, Culture, and Urbanisation, 1986; (with M. Abitbol and N. Chazan) The Origins of the State Reconsidered, 1986; (with others) Social Change in Latin American Societies, 1986; (with A. Shachar) Society, Culture and Urbanization, 1987; European Civilization in a Comparative Perspective, 1987; Civilita Comparate, 1990; Jewish Civilization: The Jewish Historical Experience in a Comparative Perspective, 1992; Fundamentalismo e Modernita, 1994; Power, Trust and Meaning (essays), 1995; Japanese Civilization, 1996; Paradoxes of Democracy, 1999. EDITOR: Comparative Perspectives on Social Change, 1968, Charisma and Institution Building, 1968; Political Sociology, 1971; (with S. Rokkan) Building States and Nations, 1973; (with S. Graubard) Intellectuals and Traditions, 1973; (with Y. Atzmon) Socialism and Tradition, 1975; (with L. Roniger and A. Seligman) Centre Formation, Protest Movements and Class Structure in Europe and the United States, 1987; Patterns of Modernity, 2 vols., 1987; (with M. Abitbol and N. Chazan) The Early State in African Perspective, 1988; (with I. Silber) Knowledge and Society: Studies in the Sociology Culture, Past and Present, 1988; (with E. Ben-Ari) Japanese Models of Conflict Resolution, 1990; (with W. Schluchter and B. Wittrock) Public Spheres and Collective Identities, 2001; Multiple Modernities, 2002; (with M. Hoexter and N. Levtzion) The Public Sphere in Muslim Societies, 2002. **Address:** Rechov Radak 30, Jerusalem, Israel. **Online address:** miriamb@vanleer.org.il

EISENSTEIN, Hester. American, b. 1940. **Genres:** Sociology, Women's studies and issues. **Career:** Yale University, New Haven, CT, acting instructor, 1966-68, instructor, 1967-68, assistant professor of history, 1968-70; Columbia University, Barnard College, NYC, assistant professor of history and coordinator of Experimental College, 1970-77, lecturer in experimental education, 1977-79, senior lecturer, 1977-79, coordinator of Experimental Studies Program, 1977-80; Office of the Director of Equal Opportunity in Public Employment in New South Wales, Australia, senior equal employment opportunity adviser, 1981-84, assistant director, 1984-85; Dept of Education of NSW, leader and chief education officer in Equal Employment Opportunity Unit, 1985-88; State University of New York at Buffalo, visiting associate professor, 1988-89, visiting professor of women's studies, 1989-90, professor of American studies, 1990-96; City University of New York, Queens College and Graduate Center, professor of sociology, 1996-, director, women's studies program, 1996-2000. **Publications:** (gen. ed.) The Scholar and the Feminist (series), 1979-80; (ed. with A. Jardine) The Future of Difference, 1980; Contemporary Feminist Thought, 1983; Gender Shock: Practising Feminism on Two Continents, 1991; Inside Agitators, 1996. Work represented in anthologies. Contributor of articles and reviews to education and women's studies journals. **Address:** Department of Sociology, Queens College CUNY, 65-30 Kissena Blvd, Flushing, NY 11367, U.S.A. **Online address:** hester_eisenstein@qc.edu

EISENSTEIN, Phyllis (Kleinstein). American, b. 1946. **Genres:** Science fiction/Fantasy, Medicine/Health. **Career:** Teacher, Clarion Workshop in Science Fiction and Fantasy Writing, Michigan State University, East Lansing, 1983. Anthology Trustee, Science Fiction Writers of America, 1976-80; Co-Founder and Director, Windy City SF Writers Conference, Chicago, 1972-77; Columbia College, Chicago, also teacher, of popular fiction writing, 1992-; Teacher of Science fiction/Fantasy, Columbia College, Chicago, 1979-80, 1989-. **Publications:** Born to Exile, 1978; Sorcerer's Son, 1979; Shadow of Earth, 1979; In the Hands of Glory, 1981; The Crystal Palace, 1988; In the Red Lord's Reach, 1989; Overcoming the Pain of Inflammatory Arthritis, 1997; The Book of Elementals: The Saga of the Sorcerer's Son, 2003; Night Lives: Nine Stories of the Dark Fantastic, 2003. **Address:** 6208 N Campbell, Chicago, IL 60659, U.S.A. **Online address:** phyllis@ripco.com

EISGRUBER, Christopher L(udwig). American, b. 1961. **Genres:** Adult non-fiction. **Career:** Law clerk to Judge Patrick E. Higginbotham, Dallas, TX, 1988-89, and to Justice John Paul Stevens, Washington, DC, 1989-90; New York University, New York, NY, assistant professor, 1990-93, associate professor, 1993-95, professor of law, 1995-2001; Princeton University, Princeton, NJ, faculty research fellow, 2000-01, Laurance S. Rockefeller Professor of Public Affairs and director of Program in Law and Public Affairs, 2001-. Member of Pennsylvania State Bar; testified before committees and subcommittees of the U.S. Senate and House of Representatives. **Publications:** Constitutional Self-Government, 2001. Contributor to books. **Address:** Program in Law and Public Affairs, Woodrow Wilson School, Princeton University, Princeton, NJ 08544, U.S.A. **Online address:** eisgrube@princeton.edu

EISIMINGER, Sterling, (Jr.). American, b. 1941. **Genres:** Poetry, Humanities, Language/Linguistics, Essays. **Career:** Clemson University, Clemson, SC, professor of English, 1968-. Member of board of advisers for Camp Alert (for handicapped children) and Clemson Public Library. **Publications:** (with J. Idol) Why Can't They Write?, 1975; (with C. Burden, E. Burden and L. Ganim) Business in Literature, 1977; Wordspinner, 1991; Consequence of Error, 1991; (with Idol and R. Gollin) Prophetic Pictures, 1991; Nonprescription Medicine, 1995; Integration with Dignity, 2003. **Address:** Department of English, Clemson University, Clemson, SC 29634, U.S.A. **Online address:** esterli@clemson.edu

EISLER, Barry. American, b. 1964. **Genres:** Novels. **Career:** Attorney, author. Hamada and Matsumoto, Tokyo, Japan, attorney; Matsushita Electric and Industrial Co. Ltd., Osaka, Japan, counsel; three years with the U.S. State Department. **Publications:** JOHN RAIN SERIES: Rain Fall, 2002; Hard Rain, 2003; Rain Storm, 2004. **Address:** c/o Author Mail, G. P. Putnam's Sons, 375 Hudson St., New York, NY 10014, U.S.A. **Online address:** barry@barryeisler.com

EISLER, Benita. American, b. 1937. **Genres:** Biography. **Career:** Writer. WNET-TV, New York, NY, producer, 1975-78; Princeton University, Princeton, NJ, part-time lecturer in French. **Publications:** (Ed.) The Lowell Offering: Writings by New England Mill Women, 1840-1845, 1978; Class Act: America's Last Dirty Secret, 1983; Private Lives: Men and Women of the Fifties, 1986; O'Keeffe and Stieglitz: An American Romance, 1991; Bryon: Child of Passion, Fool of Fame, 1999. **Address:** c/o Watkins Loomis Agency Inc., 133 E. 35th St., New York, NY 10016-3886, U.S.A.

EISNER, Gisela. British (born Germany), b. 1925. **Genres:** Economics. **Career:** Manchester University, member of staff, 1951-56. **Publications:** Jamaica 1830-1930: A Study in Economic Growth, 1961. **Address:** 69 Macclesfield Rd, Buxton, Derbyshire, England. **Online address:** eisner@btinternet.com

EISNER, Michael Alexander. American. **Genres:** Novels. **Career:** Writer; U.S. State Department, Washington, DC, attorney, 1997; Morrison & Foerster, Los Angles, CA, attorney. **Publications:** The Crusader, 2001. **Address:** c/o Doubleday, 1540 Broadway, New York, NY 10036, U.S.A.

EITNER, Lorenz E. A. American, b. 1919. **Genres:** Art/Art history. **Career:** Chairman, Art Dept., Stanford University, California, and Director, Stanford

University Museum, 1963-. Professor, Art Dept., University of Minnesota, Minneapolis, 1949-63. **Publications:** Neoclassicism and Romanticism, 2 vols., 1970; Gericault's Raft of the Medusa, 1972; (ed.) Gericault, etude Biographique et critique, 1973; Gericault: His Life & Work, 1982; An Outline of Nineteenth Century Painting, 1987; The Drawing Collection: Stanford University Museum of Art, 1993; French Nineteenth Century Paintings, 2000. **Address:** 684 Mirada, Stanford, CA 94305, U.S.A.

EKWENSI, Chief Cyprian D. Nigerian, b. 1921. **Genres:** Novels, Children's fiction, Novellas/Short stories. **Career:** Director of Information Services, Federal Ministry of Information, Enugu, 1966- (Director of Information, Lagos, 1961-66). Lecturer in Pharmacognosy and Pharmaceutics, School of Pharmacy, Lagos, 1949-56; Pharmacist, Nigerian Medical Service, and Head of Features, Nigerian Broadcasting Corp., 1956-61; Managing Director, Star Printing and Publishing Co. Ltd., 1974-79; Managing Director, Ivory Trumpet Publishing Co. Ltd., 1981-83. Chairman, East Central State Library Board, 1972; Chairman, Hosps. Mgmt. Board, 1986. **Publications:** When Love Whispers, 1947; Ikolo the Wrestler, 1947; The Leopard's Claw, 1950; People of the City, 1954; The Drummer Boy, 1960; The Passport of Mallam Ilia, 1960; Jagua Nana, 1961; Burning Grass: A Story of the Fulani of Northern Nigeria, 1962; An African Night's Entertainment: A Tale of Vengeance, 1962; Yaba Round-about Murder, 1962; Beautiful Feathers, 1963; Great Elephant Bird, 1965; The Rainmaker and Other Stories, 1965; Iska, 1966; Lokotown and Other Stories, 1966; Trouble in Form Six, 1966; The Boa Suitor, 1966; Juju Rock, 1966; Restless City and Christmas Gold, 1975; The Rainbow-Tinted Scarf and Other Stories, 1975; Samankwe and the Highway Robbers, 1975; Survive the Peace, 1976; (ed.) Festac Anthology of Nigerian New Writing, 1977; Motherless Baby, 1980; Divided We Stand, 1980; Jagua Nana's Daughter, 1986; For a Roll of Parchment, 1987; Behind the Convent Wall, 1987; Gone to Mecca, 1991; King Forever!, 1992; Masquerade Time, 1992; The Red Flag, 1993. **Address:** 14 Hillview, Independence Layout, PO Box 317, Enugu, Anambra, Nigeria.

ELAD, Amikam. Israeli, b. 1946. **Genres:** Theology/Religion, History, Architecture. **Career:** Hebrew University of Jerusalem, Jerusalem, Israel, head of department of Islamic and Middle Eastern history. **Publications:** Medieval Jerusalem and Islamic Worship: Holy Places, Ceremonies, and Pilgrimage, 1995. Contributor to academic journals. **Address:** Department of Islamic and Middle East Studies, Hebrew University of Jerusalem, Mount Scopus, Jerusalem, Israel.

ELBIRT, Paula M. Also writes as Dr. Paula. American, b. 1954. **Genres:** Medicine/Health. **Career:** MDS4KIDS, PC, New York, NY, president, 1984-99; drpaula.com Inc,, Washington, NJ, medical director, 1997-2001; Children's Aid Society of New York, medical director, 2002-. Worked in pediatric pulmonology and was director of pediatric primary care education, Brooklyn Hospital, Brooklyn, NY. **Publications:** (with L. Small) A New Mother's Home Companion, 1993; (with S. Solin) The Seventeen Guide to Sex and Your Body, 1996; Dr. Paula's House Calls to Your Newborn: Birth through Six Months, 2000; Dr. Paula's Good Nutrition Guide for Babies, Toddlers, and Preschoolers, 2001; 365 Ways to Get Your Child to Sleep, 2001; Ask Dr. Paula, 2002; Johnson's Mother and Baby, 2003. **Address:** 150 E. 77th St., New York, NY 10021, U.S.A. **Online address:** pelbirt@nac.net

ELBORN, Andrew. *See* **CLEMENTS, Andrew.**

ELBOZ, Stephen. (born England), b. 1956. **Genres:** Children's fiction. **Career:** Writer. Previously worked as a primary school teacher; presently part-time junior-school teacher in Corby, England. **Publications:** The House of Rats, 1991; The Games Board Map, 1993; Bottle Boy, 1994; The Byzantium Bazaar, 1996, published as A Store of Secrets, 2000; Ghostlands, 1996; Temmi and the Flying Bears, 1998; The Tower at Moonville, 1999; Temmi and the Frost Dragon (sequel to Temmi and the Flying Bears), 2002. FOR YOUNG READERS: Captain Skywriter and Kid Wonder (stories), 1995; Kid Wonder and the Terrible Truth, 1999; Kid Wonder and the Half-hearted Hero, 2000; Kid Wonder and the Sticky Skyscraper, 2000; (with Dee Schulman) Clever Monkey, 2002; KIT STIXBY SERIES: A Handful of Magic, 2000; A Land without Magic, 2001; A Wild Kind of Magic, 2001. **Address:** c/o Author Mail, Oxford University Press, Great Clarendon St., Oxford OX2 6DP, England.

ELCOCK, Howard (James). British, b. 1942. **Genres:** Public/Social administration, History, Politics/Government. **Career:** Professor of Government, University of Northumbria, 1984. Lecturer and Sr. Lecturer in Politics, University of Hull, 1966-81; Visiting Professor of Political Science, State University of New York College at Fredonia, 1993-94. Member, Humberside County council, 1973-81. **Publications:** Administrative Justice, 1969; Portrait of a Decision: The Council of Four and the Treaty of Versailles, 1972; Political Behaviour, 1976; (with S. Haywood) The Buck Stops Where? Accountability and Control in the NHS, 1980; (with M. Wheaton) Local Government, 1982, 1994; (ed. with G. Jordan) Learning from Local Authority Budgeting, 1987; (with G. Jordon and A. Midwinter) Budgeting in Local Government: Managing the Margins, 1989; Change and Decay: Public Administration in the 1990s, 1991; Political Leadership, 2001. **Address:** Social Sciences Research Centre, University of Northumbria, Newcastle-upon-Tyne NE1 8ST, England. **Online address:** howard.elcock@unn.ac.uk

ELDER, John. American, b. 1947. **Genres:** Natural history, Essays. **Career:** Middlebury College, Middlebury, VT, professor of English, 1973-; Bread Loaf School of English, Ripton, VT, teacher, 1983-. **Publications:** Imagining the Earth, 1985, 2nd ed., 1996; Following the Brush, 1993; Reading the Mountains of Home, 1998; The Frog Run, 2002. EDITOR/CO-EDITOR: The Norton Book of Nature Writing, 1990; Spirit and Nature, 1992; American Nature Writers, 1996. **Address:** Department of English, Middlebury College, Middlebury, VT 05753, U.S.A. **Online address:** elder@middlebury.edu

ELDER, Michael Aiken. See Obituaries.

ELDIN, Raymond. See MORTON, James (Severs).

ELDON, Kathy. American, b. 1946. **Genres:** Travel/Exploration, Food and Wine. **Career:** Freelance journalist, film producer, author, art teacher, broadcaster, lecturer, media consultant, mother. **Publications:** (Compiler, with J. Kane and N. Swanborg) Nairobi, All You Need to Know, But Don't Know Who to Ask: A Guide for Visitors and Residents in Kenya, 1979; (with E. Mullan) Tastes of Kenya: Epicurean Cuisine, 1981; Making Music in Kenya, 1981; Kathy Eldon's Eating Out Guide to Kenya, 1983; (Collector) Specialties of the House from Kenya's Finest Restaurants, 1985; (Collector) More Specialties of the House, 1987; (with A. Eldon) Angel Catcher: A Journal of Loss and Remembrance, 1998; (with A. Eldon) Soul Catcher: A Journal to Help You Become Who You Really Are, 1999; (with M. Eldon) Kitchens and Cooking; The Story of Medicine; Tom-Tom to Television. EDITOR: D. Eldon, The Journey Is the Destination: The Journals of Dan Eldon, 1997; The Art of Life, 2000. **Address:** c/o Jane Dustel, 1 Union Square West, New York, NY 10003, U.S.A. **Online address:** kathykenya@aol.com.

ELDRIDGE, Colin Clifford. British, b. 1942. **Genres:** History. **Career:** University of Edinburgh, post-doctoral fellow, 1966-68; University of Wales, Saint David's University College, Lampeter, lecturer, 1968-75, senior lecturer, 1975-92, reader in history, 1992-99, professor of history, 1999-. **Publications:** England's Mission: The Imperial Idea in the Age of Gladstone and Disraeli, 1868-80, 1973; Victorian Imperialism, 1978; The Zulu War: Origins, Course and Aftermath, 1996; Disraeli and the Rise of a New Imperialism, 1996; The Imperial Experience: From Carlyle to Forster, 1996. EDITOR: Essays in Honour of C.D. Chandaman, 1980; British Imperialism in the Nineteenth Century, 1984; From Rebellion to Patriation, 1989; Empire, Politics and Popular Culture, 1990; Kith and Kin: Canada, Britain and the United States from the Revolution to the Cold War, 1997. **Address:** Tanerdy, Ciliau Aeron, Lampeter, Ceredigion, Wales. **Online address:** c.eldridge@lamp.ac.uk

ELDRIDGE, John E. T. British, b. 1936. **Genres:** Sociology. **Career:** University of York, lecturer and sr. lecturer, 1964-69; University of Bradford, professor, 1969-72; University of Glasgow, professor of sociology, 1972-. **Publications:** Industrial Disputes: Essays in the Sociology of Industrial Relations, 1968; (ed.) Max Weber: The Interpretation of Social Reality, 1971; Sociology and Industrial Life, 1971; (with A. D. Crombie) Sociology of Organizations, 1974; (with Glasgow University Media Group) Bad News, 1976; (with Glasgow University Media Group) More Bad News, 1980; Recent British Sociology, 1980; C. Wright Mills, 1983; (with Glasgow University Media Group) War and Peace News, 1985; (co-author) Just Managing, 1985; (co-author) Industrial Society and Economic Crisis, 1991; (co-author) Targetting Moscow: Talking about Trident, 1991; (ed.) Getting the Message: News, Truth and Power, 1993; (with L. Eldridge) Raymond Williams: Making Connections, 1994; (ed.) The Glasgow University Media Group Reader, 1995; The Mass Media and Power in Modern Britain, 1997; (ed. with J. Macinnes, S. Scott, C. Warhurst, and A. Witz) For Sociology: Legacies and Prospects, 2000. **Address:** Dept. of Sociology & Anthropology, 61 S. Park Ave., University of Glasgow, Glasgow G12 8QQ, Scotland. **Online address:** J.E.T.Eldridge@socsci.gla.ac.uk

ELDWORTH, R. See PERRETT, Bryan.

ELEGANT, Robert (Sampson). British/American (born United States), b. 1928. **Genres:** Novels, History, International relations/Current affairs, Language/Linguistics, Biography, Documentaries/Reportage. **Career:** Novelist; Journalist: War Correspondent, Korea, Overseas News Agency, International News Service, 1951-53; South Asian Correspondent and Chief of New Delhi Bureau, 1956-57, Southeast Asian Correspondent, and Chief of Hong Kong Bureau, 1958-61, and Chief, Central European Bureau, Bonn, 1962-64, Newsweek mag.; Chief, Hong Kong Bureau, 1965-69; Foreign Affairs Columnist, 1970-76, Los Angeles Times. **Publications:** China's Red Masters (in U.K. as China's Red Leaders), 1951; The Dragon's Seed, 1959; The Center of the World, 1963; Mao's Great Revolution, 1971; Mao vs. Chiang: The Battle for China, 1972; Hong Kong, 1977; Pacific Destiny: The Rise of the East, 1990. NOVELS: A Kind of Treason, 1966; The Seeking, 1969; Dynasty, 1977; Manchu, 1980; Mandarin, 1983; White Sun, Red Star (in U.S. as From a Far Land), 1986; Bianca, 1992; The Everlasting Sorrow, 1994; The Big Brown Bears, 1995; Last Year in Hong Kong, 1997; Cry Peace, 2005. **Address:** 10 Quick St, London N1 8H2, England. **Online address:** relegant@yahoo.com

ELEGANT, Simon. American. **Genres:** Novels. **Career:** China scholar and novelist. Far Eastern Economic Review, arts and society editor. **Publications:** A Floating Life: The Adventures of Li Po, 1997. **Address:** c/o Author Mail, 7th Fl, Ecco Press/HarperCollins Publishers, 10 E 53rd St, New York, NY 10022, U.S.A.

ELEVELD, Mark. American. **Genres:** Art/Art history. **Career:** Teacher, publisher, editor, and freelance writer. Joliet West High School, Joliet, IL, English teacher; University of St. Francis, IL, philosophy instructor; EM Press, Joliet, cofounder and copublisher; press agent for poet Marc Smith, 1993-1996. **Publications:** (editor) The Spoken Word Revolution: Slam, Hip-Hop, and the Poetry of a New Generation, 2003. **Address:** EM Press, 305 Brooks Ave., Joliet, IL 60435, U.S.A.

ELEY, Beverley. Australian. **Genres:** Novels. **Career:** Nonfiction writer. Angus & Robertson Bookshops, Australia, publicity and advertising manager, c. 1970s; Cassell Australia Collier Macmillan, worked as marketing manager; Australia Consumers Association, worked as marketing manager and spokesperson; author, 1995-. **Publications:** Ion Idriess, 1995; The Book of David, 1996. **Address:** c/o HarperCollins Publishers, 10 East 53rd St, Author Mail, 7th Floor, New York, NY 10022, U.S.A.

ELFSTROM, Gerard. American, b. 1945. **Genres:** Ethics. **Career:** Morris Brown College, Atlanta, GA, assistant professor of philosophy and head of department, 1976-80; Emory University, Atlanta, visiting assistant professor of philosophy, 1981-84; Agnes Scott College, Decatur, GA, assistant professor of philosophy, 1985-88; Auburn University, Auburn, AL, assistant professor, 1988-92, associate professor of philosophy, 1992-97, professor, 1997-. **Publications:** (with N. Fotion) Military Ethics, 1986; Ethics for a Shrinking World, 1989; Moral Issues and Multinational Corporations, 1991; (with Fotion) Toleration, 1992; New Challenges for Political Philosophy, 1997; International Ethics: A Reference Handbook, 1998. Contributor of articles and reviews to periodicals. **Address:** Department of Philosophy, 6080 Haley Center, Auburn University, Auburn, AL 36849-5210, U.S.A.

ELFWOOD, Christiana. See SOURVINOU-INWOOD, Christiane.

ELGIN, (Patricia Anne) Suzette Haden (Wilkins). American, b. 1936. **Genres:** Science fiction/Fantasy, Language/Linguistics, Self help. **Career:** San Diego State University, began as Assistant Professor, 1972, Associate Professor Emeritus, 1980-. Publisher, producer and writer, Linguistics & Science Fiction newsletter (formerly The Lonesome Node), 1981-. Formerly TV folk music performer, instr. of music and guitar, and instr. of linguistics. **Publications:** The Communipaths, 1970; Furthest, 1971; At the Seventh Level, 1972; (with J.T. Grinder) Guide to Transformational Grammar: History, Theory, Practice, 1973; What Is Linguistics?, 1973, 1979; A Primer of Transformational Grammar for Rank Beginners, 1975; Pouring Down Words, 1975; Star-Anchored, Star-Angered, 1979; The Gentle Art of Verbal Self-Defense, 1980; Ozark Fantasy Trilogy, 3 vols., 1981, 2000; More on the Gentle Art of Self-Defense, 1983; Native Tongue, 1984; Yonder Comes the Other End of Time, 1986; The Last Word on the Gentle Art of Self-Defense, 1987; Native Tongue II: The Judas Rose, 1987; Success with the Gentle Art of Verbal Self-Defense, 1989; Staying Well with the Gentle Art of Verbal Self-Defense, 1990; The Gentle Art of Written Self-Defense, 1993; Genderspeak: Men, Women, and the Gentle Art of Verbal Self-Defense, 1993; Native Tongue III: Earth Song, 1994; You Can't Say That to Me!, 1995; BusinessSpeak, 1995; The Gentle Art of Communicating with Kids, 1996; Try to Feel It My Way, 1997; How to Disagree without Being Disagreeable, 1997; How to Turn the Other Cheek and Still Survive in Today's World, 1997; The Grandmother Principles, 1998; The Language Imperative, 2000; Language in

Emergency Medicine, 2000; Peacetalk 101, 2003. **Address:** PO Box 1137, Huntsville, AR 72740-1137, U.S.A. **Online address:** ocls@madisoncounty. net

ELIAS, Jason. American, b. 1947. **Genres:** Medicine/Health. **Career:** Self-employed in NYC, 1970-; Tri State Institute for Traditional Chinese Acupuncture, teacher, 1984-88. **Publications:** (Co-author) Feminine Healing, 1995; The A-Z Guide to Herbal Healing Remedies, 1995; Chinese Medicine for Maximum Immunity, 1998. **Address:** c/o Integral Health Associates, 3 Paradies Lane, New Paltz, NY 12561, U.S.A. **Online address:** www. jasonelias1@aol.com

ELIAS, Ruth. Israeli (born Czech Republic), b. 1922. **Genres:** Autobiography/Memoirs. **Career:** Writer. **Publications:** Die Hoffnung erhielt mich am Leben: mein Weg von Theresienstadt und Auschwitz nach Israel, 1988, trans. by M.B. Dembo as Triumph of Hope: From Theresienstadt and Auschwitz to Israel, 1998. **Address:** c/o Author Mail, John Wiley & Sons Inc, 111 River St, Hoboken, NJ 07030-5773, U.S.A.

ELIAS, Scott A. American, b. 1953. **Genres:** Zoology, Earth sciences. **Career:** University of Bern, Bern, Switzerland, visiting professor, 1981; University of Colorado, Boulder, CO, research associate, 1982-94, fellow, 1994-95; University of Alaska, Fairbanks, AK, visiting professor, 1991. **Publications:** Quaternary Insects and Their Environments, 1994; Ice Age Environments of Alaskan National Parks, 1995; Ice Age Environments of National Parks in the Rocky Mountains, 1995. **Address:** INSTAAR, CB450, University of Colorado, Boulder, CO 80309, U.S.A.

ELIAS, Victor J. Argentine, b. 1937. **Genres:** Economics, Agriculture/Forestry. **Career:** National University of Tucuman, Tucuman, Argentina, professor of econometrics, 1965-88, director of the magister of economics, 1988-. **Publications:** Government Expenditures on Agriculture and Agricultural Growth in Latin American Countries, 1985; Sources of Growth: A Study of Seven Latin American Economies, 1992. **Address:** Casilla de Correo 209, 4000 Tucuman, Argentina.

ELIE, Lolis Eric. American, b. 1963. **Genres:** Essays. **Career:** Atlanta Journal, Atlanta, GA, staff writer, 1986-89; Callaloo, Charlottesville, VA, assistant managing editor, 1989-90; University of Virginia, Charlottesville, instructor of English, 1989-90; freelance journalist, 1986-; Wynton Marsalis Enterprises Inc., NYC, road manager, 1991-93; The Times-Picayune, New Orleans, LA, metro columnist, 1995-. **Publications:** Smokestack Lightning: Adventures in the Heart of Barbecue Country, 1995. Contributor to anthologies and periodicals. **Address:** 3800 Howard Ave., New Orleans, LA 70140, U.S.A. **Online address:** TPElie@aol.com

ELIE, Paul. (born United States), b. 1965. **Genres:** Adult non-fiction. **Career:** Writer and editor. Farrar, Straus, and Giroux, New York, NY, 1993-, became a senior editor. **Publications:** (editor) A Tremor of Bliss: Contemporary Writing on the Saints, introduction by Robert Coles, 1994; The Life You Save May Be Your Own: An American Pilgrimage, 2003. Contributor to periodicals. **Address:** EM Press, Union Square West, New York, NY 10003, U.S.A.

ELISHA, Ron. Australian (born Israel), b. 1951. **Genres:** Children's fiction, Plays/Screenplays. **Career:** General practitioner of medicine, Melbourne, Australia, 1977-. **Publications:** FOR CHILDREN: Pigtales, 1994; Too Big, 1997. PLAYS: In Duty Bound, 1983; Two, 1985; Einstein, 1986; The Levine Comedy, 1987; Safe House, 1989; Esterhaz, 1990; Pax Americana, 1990; Choice, 1994; The Goldberg Variations, 2000. Contributor to periodicals. **Address:** 2 Malonga Ct, North Caulfield, VIC 3161, Australia. **Online address:** relisha@bigpond-net.au

ELIUM, Don. American, b. 1954. **Genres:** Human relations/Parenting. **Career:** Psychotherapist, author, speaker. John F. Kennedy University, member of psychology faculty, 1986-. Los Medanos College, instructor, 1989-. **Publications:** (with J. Elium) Raising a Son: Parents and the Making of a Healthy Man, 1992; Raising a Daughter: The Awakening of a Healthy Woman, 1993; Raising a Family: Living on Planet Parenthood, 1997. **Address:** 2168 Norris Rd., Walnut Creek, CA 94596, U.S.A.

ELIUM, Jeanne (Ann). American, b. 1947. **Genres:** Education, Human relations/Parenting, Psychology. **Career:** Writer, 1965-; elementary schoolteacher in Eudora, KS, 1969-71; Planned Parenthood, patient educator in Boise, ID, and Concord, CA, 1972-84; group facilitator for growth and support groups in Boise, and San Francisco, CA, 1979-; parent educator in

and around San Francisco, 1988-. **Publications:** ALL WITH D. ELIUM: Raising a Son: Parents and the Making of a Healthy Man, 1992; Raising a Daughter: Parents and the Awakening of a Healthy Woman, 1994; Raising a Family, 1997; Raising a Teenager, 1999. **Address:** 2168 Norris Rd, Walnut Creek, CA 94596-5839, U.S.A. **Online address:** jeanneelium@aol.com

ELIZONDO, Virgil P. (born United States), b. 1935. **Genres:** Cultural/Ethnic topics. **Career:** Ordained Roman Catholic priest, 1965; Assumption Seminary, San Antonio, TX, dean of students, beginning 1969, organizer of Mexican American Cultural Center, 1972-. San Fernando Cathedral, rector and presenter of the weekly televised mass Misa de las Américas. **Publications:** A Search for Meaning in Life and Death, 1971, published as The Human Quest: A Search for Meaning through Life and Death, 1978; Christianity and Culture: An Introduction to Pastoral Theology and Ministry for the Bicultural Community, 1975; Mestizaje: The Dialectic of Cultural Birth and the Gospel; A Study in the Intercultural Dimension of Evangelization, three volumes, Mexican American Cultural Center, 1978; (with Angela Erevia) Our Hispanic Pilgrimage, Mexican-American Cultural Center, 1980; La Morenita, evangelizadora de las Américas, 198;. Galilean Journey: The Mexican-American Promise, 1983, revised edition, 2000. The Future Is Mestizo: Life Where Cultures Meet, 1988, revised edition, 2000; Guadalupe, Mother of the New Creation, 1997; (with Timothy M. Matovina) Mestizo Worship: A Pastoral Approach to Liturgical Ministry, 1998; (with Timothy M. Matovina) San Fernando Cathedral: Soul of the City, 1998; Beyond Borders: Writings of Virgilio Elizondo and Friends, 2000; (with Bernard J. Lee, William V. D'Antonio, and others) The Catholic Experience of Small Christian Communities, 2000. EDITOR: (with Norbert Greinacher) Women in a Men's Church, 1980; (with Norbert Greinacher) Tensions between the Churches in the First World and the Third World, 1981; (with Norbert Greinacher) Churches in Socialist Societies of Eastern Europe, 1982; (with Norbert Greinacher) Church and Peace, 1983; (with Claude Geffré and Gustavo Gutiérrez) Difference Theologies, Common Responsibility: Babel or Pentecost?, 1984; (with Leonardo Boff) The People of God Amidst the Poor, 1984; (with Norbert Greinacher) The Transmission of the Faith to the Next Generation, 1984; (with Leonardo Boff) Option for the Poor: Challenge to the Rich Countries, 1986; (with Leonardo Boff) Convergences and Differences, 1988; (with Leonardo Boff) 1492-1992: The Voice of the Victims, 1990; Way of the Cross: The Passion of Christ in the Americas, 1992; (with Leonardo Boff) Any Room for Christ in Asia?, 1993; (with Leonardo Boff; and contrib.) Ecology and Poverty: Cry of the Earth, Cry of the Poor, 1995; (with Sean Freyne) Pilgrimage, 1996. **Address:** Mexican American Cultural Center, Assumption Seminary, 3000 West French Pl., San Antonio, TX 78228, U.S.A.

ELIZUR, Joel. Israeli, b. 1952. **Genres:** Psychology, Psychiatry, Human relations/Parenting. **Career:** Kibbutz Child and Family Clinic, Israel, director of medical psychology, 1975-; Hebrew University of Jerusalem, Jerusalem, Israel, department of psychology, 1991-. **Publications:** (With Salvador Minuchin) Institutionalizing Madness: Families, Therapy, and Society, Basic Books, 1989. **Address:** Department of Psychology, Hebrew University of Jerusalem, Mount Scopus, Israel.

ELKINS, Charlotte. American, b. 1948. **Genres:** Mystery/Crime/Suspense, Romance/Historical. **Career:** Self-employed artist, 1972-73; secondary school teacher, 1974-76; M. H. DeYoung Museum, San Francisco, CA, librarian of American art, 1980-81; writer, 1982-. **Publications:** MYSTERY NOVELS (with A. Elkins) A Wicked Slice, 1989; Rotten Lies, 1995; Nasty Breaks, 1997. Contributor to anthologies, periodicals, and the internet. **Address:** c/o Nat Sobel, Sobel Weber Associates, 146 E 19th St, New York, NY 10003-2404, U.S.A.

ELKINS, Dov Peretz. American, b. 1937. **Genres:** Education, Psychology, Theology/Religion. **Career:** Temple Bethel, Rochester, NY, rabbi, 1972-76; Growth Assocs., Princeton, NJ, founder and director, 1976-; Park Synagogue, Cleveland, sr. rabbi, 1987-92; Princeton NJ Jewish Center, rabbi, 1992-. **Publications:** (with A. Eisenberg) Worlds Lost and Found (biblical archaeology), 1964; So Young to Be a Rabbi, 1969; (with A. Eisenberg) Treasures from the Dust (biblical archaeology), 1972; A Tradition Reborn (sermons and essays), 1972; God's Warriors, Stories of Military Chaplains (children), 1974; Glad to Be Me, 1976; Teaching People to Love Themselves, 1977; Clarifying Jewish Values, 1977; Jewish Consciousness Raising, 1979; Self Concept Sourcebook, 1979; Loving My Jewishness, 1978; Experiential Programs for Jewish Groups, 1979; 12 Pathways to Feeling Better about Yourself, 1980; My 72 Friends, 1989; Prescription for a Long and Happy Life, 1993; Jewish Guided Imagery, 1996; Hasidic Wisdom, 1997; A Shabbat Reader, 1998; Forty Days of Transformation, 1999; Meditations for the Days of Awe, 1999; New & Old Prayers for the High Holy Days, 2000; Chicken

Soup for the Jewish Soul, 2001; The Bible's Top 50 Ideas: The Essential Concepts Everyone Should Know, 2005. EDITOR: Rejoice with Jerusalem (reading and prayers), 1972; Moments of Transcendence, vol. 1: Rosh Hashanah, vol. 2: Yom Kippur, 1992. **Address:** 212 Stuart Rd E, Princeton, NJ 08540-1946, U.S.A. **Online address:** dpe@JewishGrowth.org

ELLENBECKER, Todd S. American, b. 1962. **Genres:** Medicine/Health, Sports/Fitness. **Career:** Lincoln Institute for Athletic Medicine, Phoenix, AZ, staff physical therapist, 1986-89; Healthsouth Sports Medicine and Rehabilitation, Scottsdale, AZ, clinical director of sports medicine and coordinator of clinical education, 1989-95; Physiotherapy Associates, Scottsdale, AZ, clinic director, 1995-. Presenter of seminars and training courses; consultant. **Publications:** The Elbow in Sport: Mechanism of Injury, Evaluation, and Treatment, 1996; (with P. Roetert) Complete Conditioning for Tennis, 1998; Knee Ligament Rehabilitation, 2000; Closed Kinetic Chain Exercise, 2001; The Scientific & Clinical Application of Elastic Resistance, 2003; Clinical Examination of the Shoulder, 2004; Strength Band Training, 2005. Contributor to books and professional journals. **Address:** Physiotherapy Associates, Scottsdale Sports Clinic, 9449 N 90th St Ste 100, Scottsdale, AZ 85258, U.S.A.

ELLENBERG, Jordan S. (born United States), b. 1971. **Genres:** Novels. **Career:** Mathematician and writer. Princeton University, Princeton, NJ, instructor, 1998-2001, assistant professor, 2001-. **Publications:** The Grasshopper King (novel), 2003; Contributor to scientific journals and to periodicals. **Address:** Dept. of Mathematics, Princeton University, 808 Fine Hall, Washington Rd., Princeton, NJ 08544, U.S.A. **Online address:** ellenber@math.princeton.edu

ELLERBECK, Rosemary. (Anne L'Estrange). Also writes as Anna L'Estrange, Nicola Thorne, Katherine Yorke. British (born Republic of South Africa). **Genres:** Novels. **Career:** Full-time writer, 1975-. Formerly, publisher and editor. **Publications:** Inclination to Murder, 1965; Hammersleigh, 1976; Rose, Rose Where Are You?, 1977; (as Anna L'estrange) Return to Wuthering Heights, 1978. AS NICOLA THORNE: The Girls, 1967; Bridie Climbing, 1969; In Love, 1973; A Woman Like Us, 1979; The Perfect Wife and Mother, 1980; The Daughters of the House, 1981; Where the Rivers Meet, 1982; Affairs of Love, 1983; The Askham Chronicles, 1898-1967: Never Such Innocence, 1985, Yesterday's Promises, 1986, Bright Morning, 1986, A Place in the Sun, 1987; Pride of Place, 1988; Champagne, 1989; Bird of Passage, 1990; The People of This Parish, 1991; The Rector's Daughter, 1992; Champagne Gold, 1992; A Wind in Summer, 1993; Silk, 1993; Profit and Loss, 1994; Trophy Wife, 1995; Repossession, 1996; Worlds Apart, 1996; Old Money, 1997; Rules of Engagement, 1997; In This Quiet Earth, 1998; The Good Samaritan, 1998; Past Love, 1998; Class Reunion, 1999; A Time of Hope, 1999; In Time of War, 2000; My Name Is Martha Brown, 2000; In Search of Martha Brown (nonfiction), 2000; The Broken Bough, 2001; The Blackbird's Song, 2001; A Friend of the Family, 2002; The Water's Edge, 2002; Oh Happy Day!, 2003. **Address:** c/o Juliet Burton Literary Agency, 2 Clifton Ave, London W12 9DR, England. **Online address:** Rosemary@ellerbeck01fsnet.co.uk

ELLINGHAM, Lewis. American, b. 1933. **Genres:** Poetry, Genealogy/Heraldry, Biography. **Career:** Writer and editor. Gay Writers Conference of the United States, member of organizing committee, 1990-91. **Publications:** The Jefferson Airplane (poetry), 1971; (with E.J. Rose) The Heymanns of Kaltenholzhausen, 1995; The Ancestors of David Miller and Clarissa Moore, 1995; Ellingham Index in North America, 1998; (with K. Killian) Poet Be like God (biography), 1998. **Address:** c/o Wesleyan University Press, 110 Mt Vernon St, Middletown, CT 06459, U.S.A.

ELLIOT, Alistair. British, b. 1932. **Genres:** Poetry, Theatre, Translations. **Career:** Freelance writer, 1983-. Actor and Stage Manager, English Children's Theatre, London, 1957-59; Assistant Librarian, Kensington, London, 1959-61; Cataloguer, Keele University Library, 1961-65; Accessions Librarian, Pahlavi University Library, Shiraz, Iran, 1965-67; Special Collections Librarian, University of Newcastle upon Tyne, 1967-82. **Publications:** POETRY: Air in the Wrong Place, 1968; Contentions, 1978; Kisses, 1978; Talking to Bede, 1982; Talking Back, 1982; On the Appian Way, 1984; My Country: Collected Poems, 1989; Turning the Stones, 1993; Facing Things, 1997; Roman Food Poems, 2003. TRANSLATOR: Euripides, Alcestis, 1965; Aristophanes, Peace, in Greek Comedy, 1965; Verlaine, Femmes/Hombres, Women/Men, 1979; H. Heine, The Lazarus Poems, 1979; French Love Poems, 1991; Italian Landscape Poems, 1993; Euripides, Medea, 1993; Valéry, La Jeune Parque, 1997. EDITOR: Poems by James I and Others, 1970; Lines on the Jordan, 1971; Virgil, The Georgics with John Dryden's Translation, 1981. **Address:** 27 Hawthorn Rd, Newcastle upon Tyne NE3 4DE, England.

ELLIOT, Bruce. See **FIELD, Edward.**

ELLIOT, Jeffrey M. American, b. 1947. **Genres:** International relations/Current affairs, Politics/Government, Bibliography, Autobiography/Memoirs. **Career:** Professor of Political Science and Director of the Graduate Program, North Carolina Central University, Durham, since 1981. Ed., Journal of Black Political Studies, since 1985. Adviser on Foreign Affairs, U.S. House of Representatives, Washington, D.C., since 1985. Assistant Professor of History and Political Science, University of Alaska, Anchorage, 1972-74; Assistant Dean of Academic Affairs, Miami-Dade Community College, 1974-76; Assistant Professor of Political Science, Wesleyan College, Norfolk, Virginia, 1978-79; Sr. Curriculum Specialist, Educational Development Center, Newton, Massachusetts, 1979-81. **Publications:** Keys to Economic Understanding, 1977; Literary Voices, 1980; Political Ideals, Policy Dilemmas, 1981; Fantasy Voices, 1981; Deathman Pass Me By, 1983; Tempest in a Teapot: The Falkland Islands War, 1983; Kindred Spirits, 1984; The Presidential-Congressional Political Dictionary, 1984; Black Voices in American Politics, 1985; Urban Society, 1985; Fidel Castro: Nothing Can Stop the Course of History, 1985; The Work of R. Reginald: An Annotated Bibliography and Guide, 1985; The Analytical Congressional Directory, 1986; Discrimination in America: An Annotated Resource Guide, 1986; Fidel Castro: Resources on Contemporary Persons, 1986; The State and Local Government Political Dictionary, 1986; The Third World, 1987; The Arms Control, Disarmament, and Military Security Dictionary, 1988; Dictionary of American Government, 1988; Fidel, 1988; Conversations with Maya Angelou, 1988; Voices of Zaire: Rhetoric or Reality?, 1990; The Work of Pamela Sargent: An Annotated Bibliography and Guide, 1990; The Work of Jack Dann: An Annotated Bibliography and Guide, 1990; The Work of George Zebrowski: An Annotated Bibliography and Guide, 1990; The Trilemma of World Oil Politics, 1991; The Brown and Benchmark Reader in American Government, 1992; The Brown and Benchmark Reader in International Relations; Into the Flames: The Life Story of a Righteous Gentile, 1992; Adventures of a Freelancer: The Literary Exploits and Autobiography of Stanton A. Coblentz, 1993; After All These Years: Sam Moskowitz on His Science Fiction Career, 1994; Fidel by Fidel, 1996; The Historical Dictionary of OPEC, 1997. **Address:** 511 N. Water's Edge Dr., Durham, NC 27703-6722, U.S.A.

ELLIOT, Kate. See **RUBINSKY, Holley.**

ELLIOTT, Charles. American, b. 1951. **Genres:** Biography, History. **Career:** Air France, New York City, accountant, 1975-80; Jean Cocteau Repertory Theatre, New York City, costume designer, 1977-80; real estate salesperson, Cape Town, South Africa, 1980; Alta Plaza Bar, San Francisco, CA, bartender and manager, 1980-90; writer. **Publications:** Princesse de Versailles, The Life of Marie Adelaide of Savoy, 1992; The Diamond Necklace, in press. **Address:** 335 Stoneridge Ln., San Francisco, CA 94134, U.S.A.

ELLIOTT, Clark A. American, b. 1941. **Genres:** History, Librarianship, Sciences, Biography, Reference. **Career:** Simmons College, Boston, MA, assistant professor of library science, 1969-71; Harvard University Archives, Cambridge, MA, associate curator for archives administration and research, 1971-97; MIT, Dibner Institute for the History of Science and Technology, Burndy Library, Cambridge, MA, librarian, 1997-2000; American Academy of Arts and Sciences, consultant (archives and history), 2000-05. Founder and editor of History of Science in America: News and Views, 1980-87. **Publications:** Biographical Dictionary of American Science: The Seventeenth through the Nineteenth Centuries, 1979; (comp.) Biographical Index to American Science: The Seventeenth Century to 1920, 1990; (ed. with M.W. Rossiter) Science at Harvard University: Historical Perspectives, 1992; History of Science in the United States: A Chronology and Research Guide, 1996; (ed. with P.G. Abiv-Am) Commemorative Practices in Science: Historical Perspectives on the Politics of Collective Memory, 1999. **Address:** 105 Beech St #2, Belmont, MA 02478, U.S.A. **Online address:** claelliott@earthlink.net

ELLIOTT, Elaine M. American, b. 1931. **Genres:** Romance/Historical. **Career:** Worked as an animal groomer for twelve years and in animal welfare for thirty-five years; also works as family counselor. **Publications:** Love's Sweet Fire, 1984; Daughter of the Reservation, 1998; Cranberries, 1999; Peaches, Pears, & Plums, 1999. **Address:** 377 Dominion View Rd, Colville, WA 99114, U.S.A. **Online address:** Jackpot@plix.com

ELLIOTT, Joey. See **HOUK, Randy.**

ELLIOTT, John Huxtable. British, b. 1930. **Genres:** History. **Career:** Lecturer in History, Cambridge University, 1957-67; Professor of History,

King's College, University of London, 1968-73; Professor, School of Historical Studies, Institute for Advanced Study, Princeton, New Jersey, 1973-90; Regius Professor of Modern History, Oxford University, 1990-97. **Publications:** Imperial Spain, 1963; The Revolt of the Catalans, 1963; Europe Divided, 1559-1598, 1968; The Old World and the New, 1492-1650, 1970; (with H.G. Koenigsberger) The Diversity of History, 1970; Memoriales y Cartas del Conde Duque de Olivares, 1978-80; (with J. Brown) A Palace for a King, 1980; Richelieu and Olivares, 1984; The Count-Duke of Olivares, 1986; Spain and Its World, 1500-1700, 1989; The Hispanic World, 1991. EDITOR: (with L. Brockliss) The World of the Favourite, 1999; (with J. Brown) The Sale of the Century, 2002. **Address:** Oriel College, Oxford OX1 4EW, England.

ELLIOTT, Kate. *See* **RASMUSSEN, Alis A.**

ELLIOTT, Marianne. Irish, b. 1948. **Genres:** History. **Career:** West London Institute of Higher Education, London, lecturer in history, 1975-77; University of Wales, University College, Swansea, research fellow and lecturer in history, 1977-82; Iowa State University, Ames, honorary visiting professor of history, 1983; University of South Carolina at Columbia, visiting professor of history, 1984; University of Liverpool, England, research fellow in history, 1984-87, Andrew Geddes and John Rankin Professor of Modern History, 1993-, director, Institute of Irish Studies, 1997-. Victoria University of Manchester, England, Simon senior research fellow, 1988-89; Birkbeck College, University of London, lecturer in history, 1991-93; Oxford University, Ford Lecturer, 2005. Conference of Irish Historians in Britain, co-founder, 1976-2004; OBE, 2000; British Academy, fellow, 2002. **Publications:** Partners in Revolution: The United Irishmen and France, 1982; Watchmen in Sion: The Protestant Idea of Liberty, 1985; (trans.) R.C. Cobb, The People's Armies, 1987; Wolfe Tone: Prophet of Irish Independence, 1989; (with others) A Citizens' Inquiry: The Opsahl Report on Northern Ireland, 1993; The Catholics of Ulster: A History, 2000; (ed.) The Long Road to Peace in Northern Ireland, 2002; Robert Emmet: The Making of a Legend, 2003. **Address:** Institute of Irish Studies, University of Liverpool, PO Box 147, Liverpool L64 3BX, England.

ELLIOTT, Melinda. American, b. 1947. **Genres:** History, Archaeology/Antiquities. **Career:** Writer, journalist, licensed massage therapist. **Publications:** The School of American Research: A History: The First Eighty Years, 1987; (with R. Dillingham) Acoma and Laguna Pottery, 1992; Great Excavations: Tales of Early Southwestern Archaeology, 1888-1939, 1995. Contributor to periodicals. **Address:** 2442 Cerrillos Rd., Ste. 262, Santa Fe, NM 87505, U.S.A.

ELLIOTT, Odette. British, b. 1939. **Genres:** Children's fiction. **Career:** International Voluntary Service, Leicester, England, secretary and assistant administrator of overseas work camp exchange scheme, 1980-83; University College London, London, England, secretary and administrator, 1984-87; Centre for Policy on Ageing, London, secretary and administrator, 1988-92; Horizon House Publications, London, secretary, 1993-. School governor. Founder of a Save the Children fund group in Gateshead, England. **Publications:** Under Sammy's Bed, 1989; Sammy Goes Flying, 1990; Sammy and the Telly, 1991; Sammy's Christmas Workshop, 1992; Nightingale News, 1996. **Address:** 35 Meyrick Rd., Willesden, London NW10 2EL, England.

ELLIS, Albert. American, b. 1913. **Genres:** Human relations/Parenting, Psychology, Sex. **Career:** Psychotherapist and president, Albert Ellis Institute, NYC, 1959-. Adjunct professor of psychology, Pittsburg State University, KS. Private practice, psychotherapy, and marriage and family counseling, NYC, 1943-68; chief psychologist, New Jersey State Diagnostic Center, 1949-50, and New Jersey State Dept. of Instns. and Agencies, 1950-52. **Publications:** Introduction to the Scientific Principles of Psychoanalysis, 1950; Folklore of Sex, 1951; (ed. with A.P. Pillay) Sex, Society and the Individual, 1953; American Sexual Tragedy, 1954; (ed. and contrib.) Sex Life of the American Woman and the Kinsey Report, 1955; (with R. Brancale) Psychology of Sex Offenders, 1956; How to Live with a "Neurotic," 1957; Sex without Guilt, 1958; The Art and Science of Love, 1960; (with R.A. Harper) Creative Marriage, 1961, as A Guide to Successful Marriage, 1966; (with R.A Harper) A Guide to Rational Living, 1961, rev. ed., 1997; (with A. Abarbanel) The Encyclopedia of Sexual Behavior, 1961; Reason and Emotion in Psychotherapy, 1962, rev. ed., 1994; The Intelligent Woman's Guide to Man-Hunting, 1963; Sex and the Single Man, 1963; The Origins and Development of the Incest Taboo, 1963; If This Be Sexual Heresy, 1963; (with E. Sagarin) Nymphomania, 1964; Homosexuality, 1965; Suppressed, 1965; The Case for Sexual Liberty, 1965; The Search for Sexual Enjoyment, 1966; (with J.L. Wolfe and S. Moseley) How to Prevent Your Child from Becoming a Neurotic Adult, 1966; (with R.O. Conway) The Art

of Erotic Seduction, 1967; Is Objectivism a Religion?, 1968; (with J.M. Gullo) Murder and Assassination, 1971; Growth through Reason, 1971; Executive Leadership, 1972; The Civilized Couple's Guide to Extramarital Adventure, 1972; How to Master Your Fear of Flying, 1972; (with F. Seruya and S. Losher) Sex and Sex Education, 1972; Humanistic Psychotherapy, 1973; (with R.A. Harper) A New Guide to Rational Living, 1975; Sex and the Liberated Man, 1976; (with W. Knaus) Overcoming Procrastination, 1977; (with R. Grieger) Handbook of Rational Emotive Therapy, 1977, vol. 2, 1986; (with E. Abrams) Brief Psychotherapy in Medical and Health Practice, 1978; The Intelligent Woman's Guide to Dating and Mating, 1979; Theoretical and Empirical Foundations of Rational-Emotive Therapy, 1979; (with I. Becker) A Guide to Personal Happiness, 1982; (with M.E. Bernard) Rational-Emotive Approaches to the Problems of Childhood, 1983; (with M.E. Bernard) Clinical Applications of Rational-Emotive Therapy, 1985; Overcoming Resistance, 1985; (with W. Dryden) The Practice of Rational-Emotive Therapy, 1987; (with others) Rational-Emotive Treatment of Alcoholism and Substance Abuse, 1988; (with R. Yeager) Why Some Therapies Don't Work, 1989; (with others) Rational-Emotive Couples Therapy, 1989; (with W. Dryden) The Essential Albert Ellis, 1990; (with P. Hunter) Why Need I Be Broke?, 1991; (with W. Dryden) A Dialogue with Albert Ellis, 1991; (with E. Velten) When AA Doesn't Work for You, 1992; (with M. Abrams and L. Dengelegi) The Art and Science of Rational Eating, 1992; (with A. Lange) How to Keep People from Pushing Your Buttons, 1994; (with M. Abrams) How to Cope with a Fatal Disease, 1994; Better and Deeper Brief Therapy, 1996; (with others) Stress Counseling, 1997; (with R.C. Tafrate) How to Control Your Anger before It Controls You, 1997; (with W. Drydon) The Practice of Rational Emotive Behavior Therapy, 1997; (with C. MacLaren) Rational Emotive Behavior Therapy, 1998; How to Control Your Anxiety before It Controls You, 1998; (ed. with S. Blau) The Albert Ellis Reader, 1998; (with E. Velten) Optimal Aging, 1998; How to Make Yourself Happy and Remarkably Less Disturbable, 1999; (with T. Crawford) Making Intimate Connections, 2000; (with M.G. Powers) The Secret of Coping with Verbal Abuse, 2000; Feeling Better, Getting Better, Staying Better, 2001; Overcoming Destructive Beliefs, Feelings, and Behaviors, 2001; (with J. Wilde) Case Studies in Rational Emotive Behavior Therapy with Children and Adolescents, 2001; (with R.A. Harper) Dating, Mating and Relating, 2001; (with S. Nielsen and W.B. Johnson) Counseling and Psychotherapy with Religious Persons, 2001; (with I. Reiss) From the Dawn of the Sex Revolution, 2001; Overcoming Resistance, 2002; Anger: How to Live with and without It, rev. ed., 2002; Ask Dr. Ellis, 2003; (with W. Dryden) Albert Ellis Live!, 2003; Sex without Guilt in the Twenty-first Century, 2003. **Address:** 45 E 65th St, New York, NY 10021, U.S.A. **Online address:** aiellis@aol.com

ELLIS, Alec (Charles Owen). British, b. 1932. **Genres:** Education, History, Librarianship. **Career:** Deputy Director, Academic Affairs, School of Information Science and Technology, Liverpool Polytechnic, 1988-91 (Lecturer 1965-68; Sr. Lecturer 1968-72; Principal Lecturer, 1972-78; Head of Dept., School of Librarianship and Information Studies, 1978-88). Assistant Librarian, Liverpool City Libraries, 1949-61; Librarian, St. Katharine's College of Education, Liverpool, 1961-64. **Publications:** How to Find Out about Children's Literature, 1966, 3rd ed., 1973; A History of Children's Reading and Literature, 1968; Library Services for Young People in England and Wales 1830-1970, 1971; Books in Victorian Elementary Schools, 1971; Public Libraries and the First World War, 1975; The Parish of All Hallows Allerton, 1976; (co-author) Chosen for Children, 1977; Public Libraries at the Time of the Adams Report, 1978; Educating Our Masters, 1985; Librarianship on the Mersey, 1987; The Parish of All Hallows Allerton: A History, 2000; The Bibby Family and All Hallows Church, Allerton, 2001. **Address:** 32 Gipsy Lane, Calderstones, Liverpool L18 3HL, England.

ELLIS, Alice Thomas. Also writes as Anna Margaret Haycraft. British, b. 1932. **Genres:** Novels, Food and Wine, Humor/Satire. **Career:** Columnist (Home Life): The Spectator, London, 1984-90; The Universe, 1989-91; The Catholic Herald, 1991-96, 1998-2001; The Oldie, 1996-. **Publications:** COOKBOOKS: Natural Baby Food: A Cookery Book, 1977; (as Anna Haycraft; with C. Blackwood) Darling, You Shouldn't Have Gone to So Much Trouble, 1980. NOVELS: The Sin Eater, 1977; The Birds of the Air, 1980; The 27th Kingdom, 1982; The Other Side of the Fire, 1983; Unexplained Laughter, 1985; The Clothes in the Wardrobe, 1987; The Skeleton in the Cupboard, 1988; The Fly in the Ointment, 1989; The Inn at The Edge of The World, 1990; Pillars of Gold, 1992; Serpent on the Rock, 1994; Fairy Tale, 1996. ESSAYS: Home Life, 1986; More Home Life, 1987; Home Life Three, 1988; Home Life Four, 1989; Cat among the Pigeons, 1994. OTHER: (ed.) M. Keene, Mrs. Donald, 1983; (with T. Pitt-Aikens) Secrets of Strangers (psychology), 1986; Loss of Good Authority, 1989; A Welsh Childhood (autobiography), 1990; Wales: An Anthology, 1991; The Evening of Adam (stories), 1994; (ed. and story) Valentine's Day, 2000. **Address:** c/o Robert Kirby, PFD, Drury House, 34-43 Russell St, London WC2B 5HA, England.

ELLIS, Barbara W. American, b. 1953. **Genres:** Adult non-fiction, Environmental sciences/Ecology, Homes/Gardens. **Career:** Fred C. Gloeckner Co., NYC, executive assistant and producer and editor of horticultural supply catalogs, 1978-79; American Horticultural Society, Mount Vernon, VA, associate editor, 1980-83, publications director and editor, 1983-87; freelance writer and editor in Alexandria, VA, 1987-88; Rodale Press, Emmaus, PA, editor of garden books, 1988-89, senior editor, 1989-93, managing editor, 1993-94; freelance writer, 1994-. **Publications:** (with S.R. Frey) Outdoor Living Spaces, 1992; (with J. Benjamin and D.L. Martin) Rodale's Low-Maintenance Gardening Techniques, 1995; Attracting Birds & Butterflies, 1997; Easy Practical Pruning, 1997; Taylor's Guide to Growing North America's Favorite Plants, 1998; (with J. Benjamin and D.L. Martin) Rodale's Low-Maintenance Landscaping Techniques, 1999; Taylor's Guide to Annuals, 1999; Taylor's Guide to Perennials, 2000; Complete Gardener's Dictionary, 2000; Taylor's Guide to Bulbs, 2001; Deckscaping, 2002; 20 Plans for Colorful Shady Retreats, 2003. EDITOR: Rodale's Illustrated Encyclopedia of Gardening and Landscaping Techniques, 1990; (with F.M. Bradley) Rodale's All-New Encyclopedia of Organic Gardening, 1992; (with F.M. Bradley) Organic Gardener's Handbook of Natural Insect and Disease Control, 1992; Safe & Easy Lawn Care, 1997; (with J. Benjamin) Rodale's No-Fail Flower Garden, 1994; Organic Pest & Disease Control, 1997. Contributor to garden magazines. **Address:** Walnut Hill Farm, 25 E Adams Ln, Alburtis, PA 18011-2622, U.S.A. **Online address:** bwe@fast.net

ELLIS, Bret Easton. American, b. 1964. **Genres:** Novels. **Career:** Writer. **Publications:** Less Than Zero, 1985; The Rules of Attraction, 1987; American Psycho, 1991; The Informers, 1994; Glamoramama, 1998. **Address:** c/o Amanda Urban, International Creative Management, 40 W. 57th St, New York, NY 10019, U.S.A.

ELLIS, Ella Thorp. American, b. 1928. **Genres:** Novels, Children's fiction, Autobiography/Memoirs. **Career:** Instructor in Creative Writing, San Francisco State University, and University of California Extension, Berkeley. **Publications:** Roam the Wild Country, 1967; Riptide, 1969; Celebrate the Morning, 1972; Where the Road Ends, 1974; Hallelujah, 1976; Sleepwalter's Moon, 1980; Hugo and the Princess Nena, 1983; Swimming with the Whales, 1995; The Year of My Indian Prince, 2001. **Address:** 1438 Grizzly Peak Blvd, Berkeley, CA 94708, U.S.A. **Online address:** ellathorpellis@hotmail.com

ELLIS, Evelyn. British, b. 1948. **Genres:** Law. **Career:** Barrister. University of Birmingham, England, lecturer, 1972-88, senior lecturer in law, 1988-93, reader in public law, 1993-96, professor of public law, 1996-. Boston College, visiting fellow, 1977-78. **Publications:** Sex Discrimination Law, 1988; European Community Sex Equality Law, 1991, 2nd ed., 1998; (with T. Tridimas), Public Law of the European Community, 1995; (ed.) The Principle of Proportionality in the Laws of Europe, 1999. **Address:** School of Law, University of Birmingham, Edgbaston, Birmingham B15 2TT, England. **Online address:** E.D.Ellis@bham.ac.uk

ELLIS, Gwen. American, b. 1938. **Genres:** Children's fiction, Children's non-fiction, Film, Inspirational/Motivational Literature, Picture/board books. **Career:** Focus on Family, Colorado Springs, CO, managing editor of books, 1991-95; Servant Publications, Ann Arbor, MI, acquisitions editor, 1996-98; Zondervan, Grand Rapids, MI, gift product director, 1998-99, children's acquisitions editor, 1999-; Seaside Creative Services, Inc., founder, 2003-. **Publications:** 101 Ways to Make Money at Home, 1995; Decorating on a Shoestring, 2000; Big Book of Family Fun, 2000.

ELLIS, Gwynn Pennant. British. **Genres:** Chemistry. **Career:** Reader, University of Wales, Cardiff, since 1962. Found and Co-ed., Progress in Medicinal Chemistry, since 1961. Research Chemist, I.C.I., 1953-57; Head of Chemistry Research, Fisons Pharmaceuticals, 1957-62. **Publications:** Modern Textbook of Organic Chemistry, 1966; (co-author) Qualitative Organic Chemical Analysis, 1967; Medicinal Chemistry Reviews, 1972; Spectral and Chemical Characterisation of Organic Compounds, 1976, 3rd ed. 1990; Chromenes, Chromanones, and Chromones, 1977; Chromans and Tocopherols, 1981; Synthesis of Fused Heterocycles, Part 1, 1987, Part 2, 1992. **Address:** 6 Ffordd Gwyndy, Penrhos Garnet, Bangor, Gwynedd LL57 2EX, Wales.

ELLIS, Harold. British, b. 1926. **Genres:** Medicine/Health. **Career:** Professor Emeritus of Surgery, University of London, 1989- (Professor, Westminster Medical School, 1961-89). University Clinical Anatomist, University of Cambridge, 1989-93; Guy's Hospital, 1993-. Surgical Tutor, University of Oxford, 1959-61. **Publications:** Clinical Anatomy, 1960; Anatomy for Anaesthetists, 1963; History of the Bladder Stone, 1968; (with S. Feldman) Principles of Resuscitation, 1969; (with R. Calne) Lecture Notes on General Surgery, 1974; Intestinal Obstruction, 1982; Maingot's Abdominal Operations, 1985; Famous Operations, 1985; Spot Diagnosis in General Surgery, 1990; Research in Medicine, 1990; Human Cross-Sectional Anatomy: Atlas of Body Sections and CT Images, 1992; Surgical Case Histories from the Past; (with R. Savalgi) Clinical Anatomy for Laparoscopic and Thoracoscopic Surgery, 1995; Index of Differential Diagnosis, 1996; History of Surgery, 2001. **Address:** Dept of Anatomy, Kings College (Guy's Campus), London Bridge, Hodgkin Bldg, London SE1 1UL, England.

ELLIS, Harry Bearse. *See* Obituaries.

ELLIS, Jamellah. (born United States). **Genres:** Dance/Ballet. **Career:** Writer and attorney. U.S. District Court for the District of Maryland, judicial clerk to the Honorable Andre M. Davis; Arnold & Porter, Washington, DC, attorney; Saul Ewing LLP, Baltimore, MD, attorney, 2003-. Cofounder of All the While Reconcile (publishing company). **Publications:** That Faith, That Trust, That Love (novel), 2001. **Address:** c/o Strivers Row Publicity, 1745 Broadway, New York, NY 10019, U.S.A. **Online address:** jamellahellis@msn.com

ELLIS, Jerry. American, b. 1947. **Genres:** Travel/Exploration, History. **Career:** Writer, lecturer and Native American folk artist. **Publications:** Walking the Trail: One Man's Journey along the Cherokee Trail of Tears, 1991; Bareback! One Man's Journey along the Pony Express Trail, 1993; Marching through Georgia: My Walk with Sherman, 1995; (compiler) In Short: A Collection of Brief Creative Non-Fiction, 1996. **Address:** 1714 Smith Gap Rd. N.W., Fort Payne, AL 35968, U.S.A. **Online address:** tanager@peop.tds.net

ELLIS, Julie. Also writes as Alison Lord, Jeffrey Lord, Susan Marino, Julie Marvin, Susan Marvin, Susan Richard. American, b. 1933. **Genres:** Novels, Mystery/Crime/Suspense, Romance/Historical. **Career:** Author. **Publications:** The Women around R.F.K., 1967; (as Alison Lord) DeeDee, 1969, as The Strip in London, 1970; (as Julie Marvin) Revolt of the Second Sex, 1970; (as Jeffrey Lord) Jeb, 1970; Evil at Hillcrest, 1971; (as Susan Marino) Vendetta Castle, 1971; The Jeweled Dagger, 1973; Walk into Darkness, 1973; Kara, 1974; Eden, 1975; Walk a Tightrope, 1975; Eulalie, 1976; The Magnolias, 1976; The Girl in White, 1976; Rendezvous in Vienna, 1976; Wexford, 1976; Savage Oaks, 1977; Long Dark Night of the Soul, 1978; The Hampton Heritage, 1978; The Hampton Women, 1980; Glorious Morning, 1982; East Wind, 1983; Maison Jennie, 1984; Rich Is Best, 1985; The Only Sin, 1986; The Velvet Jungle, 1987; A Daughter's Promise, 1988; Loyalties, 1989; No Greater Love, 1991; Trespassing Heart, 1992; Lasting Treasures, 1993; Commitment, 1994; Far to Go, 1995; Avenged, 1995; Deadly Obsession, 1995; Nine Days to Kill, 1996; An Uncommon Woman (in UK as Passionate Obsession), 1997; Geneva Rendezvous, 1997; Second Time Around, 1997; When the Summer People Have Gone, 1998; A Woman for All Seasons, 1998; Single Mother, 1999; A Sacred Obligation, 2000; Best Friends, 2000; House on the Lake, 2000; The Hampton Passion, 2001; A Town Named Paradise, 2001; Another Eden, 2002; When Tomorrow Comes, 2003; A Turn in the Road, 2003; Small Town Dreams, 2004; One Day at a Time, 2005. NOVELS AS SUSAN MARVIN: The Secret of the Villa Como, 1966; Chateau in the Shadows, 1969; Summer of Fear, 1971; The Secret of Chateau Laval, 1973; Where Is Holly Carleton?, 1974; Chateau Bougy-Villars, 1975. NOVELS AS SUSAN RICHARD: Ashley Hall, 1967; Intruder at Maison Benedict, 1967; The Secret of Chateau Kendall, 1967; Chateau Saxony, 1970; Terror at Nelson Woods, 1973; Secret of the Chateau Leval, 1975. **Address:** c/o Vanessa Holt Ltd, 59 Crescent Rd, Leigh-on-Sea, Essex SS9 2PF, England. **Online address:** Julieellisnyc@aol.com

ELLIS, Kate. British, b. 1953. **Genres:** Mystery/Crime/Suspense. **Career:** Teacher, 1974-77; P.A., 1977-81; trainee accountant, 1981-84; mother and aspiring writer, 1984-98; novelist, 1998-. **Publications:** WESLEY PETERSON CRIME NOVELS: The Merchant's House, 1999; The Armada Boy, 2000; An Unhallowed Grave, 2001; The Funeral Boat, 2001; The Bone Garden, 2001; A Painted Doom, 2002; The Skeleton Room, 2003; The Plague Maiden, 2003. Author of short stories. **Address:** c/o Piatkus Books, 5 Windmill St, London WIT 2JA, England. **Online address:** Kateellis_Bullock@ntlworld.com; www.kateellis.co.uk

ELLIS, Keith. British, b. 1927. **Genres:** Mathematics/Statistics, Money/Finance. **Career:** Staff Writer, John Bull mag., London, 1950-60; freelance writer, 1960-. **Publications:** How to Make Money in Your Spare Time, 1967;

The American Civil War, 1971; Warriors and Fighting Men, 1971; The Making of America, 1973; Man and Measurement, 1973; Man and Money, 1973; Prediction and Prophecy, 1973; Thomas Telford, 1974; Thomas Edison, 1974; Science and the Supernatural, 1974; Number Power, 1977; How to Cope with Insomnia, 1983. **Address:** 3 Belmont Hill, St. Albans, Herts. AL1 1RD, England.

ELLIS, Mark (Karl). British, b. 1945. **Genres:** Novels, Language/Linguistics. **Career:** University of Libya, assistant lecturer in English, 1970-73; Asian Institute of Technology, Bangkok, assistant lecturer in English, 1973-78; Language Training Services, Bath, sr. partner, 1980-. **Publications:** Bannerman, 1973; A Fatal Charade, 1974; The Adoration of the Hanged Man, 1975; Survivors Beyond Babel, 1979; (co-author) Language Guide to the Economist, 1982; Nelson Reading Skills Series, 1982-84; Professional English, 1984; (co-author) Counterpoint, 4 vols., 1985; Longman Business Skills Series, 1987, 1992; (co-author) Marathon 1 & 2, 1991, 1993; (co-author) Pyramid, 1993; (co-author) Teaching Business English, 1994; Kiss in the Dark, 1997; Functional English, 2005. **Address:** 39 St. Martin's, Marlborough, Wilts., England. **Online address:** Mark@printha.com

ELLIS, Peter Berresford. Also writes as Peter MacAlan, Peter Tremayne. British, b. 1943. **Genres:** Novels, Mystery/Crime/Suspense, Horror. **Career:** Brighton Herald (weekly newspaper), England, junior reporter, 1960-62; worked as newspaper reporter, and then assistant editor of publishing trade weeklies, 1963-70; Irish Post, deputy editor, 1970; Newsagent & Bookshop, editor, 1974-75; full-time writer, 1975-. Celtic League, intl chairperson, 1988-90; London Assn for Celtic Education, chairperson and vicepresident; columnist, Irish Democrat, 1987, and Irish Post, 2000. Fellow, Royal Historical Society; Royal Society of Antiquaries of Ireland. **Publications:** Wales-A Nation Again!, 1968; (with S. Mac a'Ghobhainn) The Scottish Insurrection of 1820, 1970; (with Mac a'Ghobhainn) The Problem of Language Revival, 1971; A History of the Irish Working Class, 1972; (ed. and author of intro.) J. Connolly: Selected Writings, 1973; The Cornish Language and Its Literature, 1974; Hell or Connaught!: The Cromwellian Colonisation of Ireland, 1652-1660, 1975; The Boyne Water, 1976; The Great Fire of London, 1976; Caesar's Invasion of Britain, 1978; A Voice from the Infinite: The Life of Sir Henry Rider Haggard, 1856-1925, 1978; MacBeth: High King of Scotland, 1040-57 A.D., 1979; (with P. Williams) By Jove, Biggles!: The Life of Captain W.E. Johns, 1981, repr.as Biggles!: The Life of Captain W.E. Johns, with J. Scholfield, 1993; The Liberty Tree (novel), 1982; The Last Adventurer: The Life of Talbot Mundy, 1879-1940, 1984; Celtic Inheritance, 1985; The Celtic Revolution, 1985; The Rising of the Moon, 1987; A Dictionary of Irish Mythology, 1987; 1989; The Celtic Empire, 1990; A Guide to Early Celtic Remains in Britain, 1991; A Dictionary of Celtic Mythology, 1992; Celt and Saxon, 1993; The Celtic Dawn, 1993; The Book of Deer, 1994; The Druids, 1994; Celtic Women, 1996; Celt and Greek, 1997; Celt and Roman, 1998; The Chronicles of the Celts, 1999; Erin's Blood Royal, 1999; Eyewitness to Irish History, 2004. Author of six pamphlets on Celtic history and linguistics. Contributor to periodicals and academic journals. AS PETER MacALAN: The Judas Battalion, 1983; Airship, 1984; The Confession, 1985; Kitchener's Gold, 1986; The Valkyrie Directive, 1987; The Doomsday Decree, 1988; Fireball, 1991; The Windsor Protocol, 1993. AS PETER TREMAYNE: The Hound of Frankenstein, 1977; Dracula Unborn, 1977, in US as Bloodright: A Memoir of Mircea, Son of Vlad Tepes of Wallachia, Also Known as Dracula, 1979; (ed. and author of intro.) Masters of Terror: William Hope Hodgson, Vol. 1, 1977; The Vengeance of She, 1978; The Revenge of Dracula, 1978; The Ants, 1979; The Curse of Loch Ness, 1979; (ed.) Irish Masters of Fantasy, 1979, as The Wondersmith and Other Tales, 1988; The Fires of Lan-Kern, 1978; Dracula, My Love, 1980; Zombie!, 1981; The Return of Raffles, 1981; The Morgow Rises!, 1982; The Destroyers of Lan-Kern, 1982; The Buccaneers of Lan-Kern, 1983; Snowbeast!, 1983; Raven of Destiny, 1984; Kiss of the Cobra, 1984; Swamp!, 1985; Angelus!, 1985; My Lady of Hy-Brasil and Other Stories, 1987; Nicor!, 1987; Trollnight!, 1987; Ravenmoon, 1988, in US as Bloodmist, 1988; Island of Shadows, 1991; Aisling and Other Irish Tales of Terror, 1992; Dracula Lives!, 1993; (with P. Haining) The Un-Dead: The Legend of Bram Stoker and Dracula, 1997; The Sister Fidelma Mysteries: Murder by Absolution, 1994; Shroud for the Archbishop, 1995; Suffer Little Children, 1995; The Subtle Serpent, 1996; The Spider's Web, 1997; Valley of the Shadow, 1998; The Monk Who Vanished, 1999; Act of Mercy, 1999; Hemlock at Vespers, 2000; Our Lady of Darkness, 2000; Smoke in the Wind, 2001; The Haunted Abbot, 2002; Badger's Moon, 2003; Whispers of the Dead, 2004; The Leper's Bell, 2004; Master of Souls, 2005. As Peter Tremayne, contributor of short stories to magazines and anthologies in Britain and the United States. **Address:** c/o A. M. Heath and Co. Ltd, 79 St. Martin's Ln, London WC2N 4AA, England. **Online address:** www.sisterfidelma.com

ELLIS, Ralph D. American. **Genres:** Philosophy. **Career:** Philosopher and educator. Clark Atlanta University, Atlanta, GA, professor of philosophy;

editor of Consciousness and Emotion (academic journal). **Publications:** An Ontology of Consciousness, 1986; (with C.S. Ellis) Theories of Criminal Justice: A Critical Reappraisal, 1989; Coherence and Verification in Ethics, 1992; Questioning Consciousness: The Interplay of Imagery, Cognition, and Emotion in the Human Brain, 1995; Eros in a Narcissistic Culture: An Analysis Anchored in the Life-World, 1996; Just Results: Ethical Foundations for Policy Analysis, 1998; (with N. Newton) The Caldron of Consciousness: Motivation, Affect, and Self-Organization: An Anthology, 1999. **Address:** Clark Atlanta University, 223 James P. Brawley Dr. SW, Atlanta, GA 30314, U.S.A. **Online address:** ralphellis@mindspring.com

ELLIS, Reuben. American, b. 1955. **Genres:** Novels. **Career:** Teikyo Lorretto Heights University, Denver, CO, assistant professor of English, 1991-94; Hope College, Holland, MI, associate professor of English, 1994-99; Prescott College, Prescott, AZ, associate professor of English, 1999-. **Publications:** Beyond Borders, 1996; Stories and Stone, 1997; Vertical Margins, 2001. **Address:** Prescott College, 301 Grove Ave., Prescott, AZ 86301, U.S.A. **Online address:** rellis@prescott.edu

ELLIS, Richard (J.). American (born England), b. 1960. **Genres:** History, Politics/Government. **Career:** University of California, Santa Cruz, visiting lecturer in political science, 1989; Willamette University, Salem, OR, assistant professor, 1990-95; associate professor, 1995-99; Mark O. Hatfield Professor of Politics, 1999-; writer. **Publications:** (with A. Wildavsky) Dilemmas of Presidential Leadership: From Washington Through Lincoln, 1989; (with M. Thompson and Wildavsky) Cultural Theory, 1990; American Political Cultures, 1993; Presidential Lightning Rods: The Politics of Blame Avoidance, 1994; The Dark Side of the Left, 1998; Speaking to the People, 1998; Founding the American Presidency, 1999; Democratic Delusions: The Initiative Process in America, 2002; To the Flag: The Unlikely History of the Pledge of Allegiance, 2005. **Address:** Dept of Political Science, Willamette University, Salem, OR 97301, U.S.A. **Online address:** rellis@willamette.edu

ELLIS, Royston. Also writes as Richard Tresillian. British, b. 1941. **Genres:** Novels, Romance/Historical, Poetry, Antiques/Furnishings, Business/Trade/Industry, Food and Wine, Travel/Exploration, Biography, Humor/Satire. **Career:** Freelance poet, lectr., and TV and radio interviewer, 1956-61; Jersey News and Features Agency, assistant ed., 1961-63; Canary Island Sun, associate ed., 1963-66; project director, Emerald Hillside Estates, and agent and attorney for Marquis of Bristol, Dominica, W. Indies, 1966-74; Radio Dominica, producer and broadcaster, 1973-76; Educator, Dominica, associate ed., 1974-76; Dominica Broadcasting Services, director, 1976-78; Wordsman Ltd., Guernsey, ed., 1977-86; freelance travel writer, 1986-; cruise lecturer 1994-; humor and restaurant columnist, 1997-. Editorial consultant: Explore Sri Lanka, Colombo, 1990-96, 2000-; Wordsman Ltd, Maldives, 1996-97; President's Office, Maldives, 1999-2001. **Publications:** Jiving to Gyp, 1959; Drifting with Cliff Richard, 1959; Rave, 1960; Rainbow Walking Stick, 1961; The Big Beat Scene, 1961; The Shadows by Themselves, 1961; Rebel, 1962; The Seaman's Suitcase, 1963; Myself for Fame, 1964; The Flesh Merchants, 1966; The Rush at the End, 1967; The Cherry Boy, 1967; The Small Business Institute Guide to Import/Export, 1976; The Bondmaster, 1977; Blood of the Bondmaster, 1977; Bondmaster Breed, 1979; Fleur, 1979; Bondmaster Fury, 1982; The Bondmaster's Revenge, 1983; Bondmaster Buck, 1984; Master of Black River, 1984; Black River Affair, 1985; Black River Breed, 1985; Bloodheart, 1985; Bloodheart Royal, 1986; Bloodheart Feud, 1987; Giselle, 1988; Guide to Mauritius, 1988, rev. ed., 2002; India by Rail, 1989; The Grand Hotel, 1991; Sri Lanka by Rail, 1994; (with G. Amarasinghe) Guide to Maldives, 1995, rev. ed., 2000; (with G. Amarasinghe) A Maldives Celebration, 1997; Seeing Sri Lanka by Train, 1997; History of the Bandarawela Hotel, 1998; History of the Tea Factory Hotel, 1998; Festivals of the World: Madagascar, 1998; A Man for All Islands (biography), 1998; On Freedom's Wings, 1998; STO: On the Move, 1999; Festivals of the World: Trinidad, 1999; My Story: Toni the Maldive Lady, 1999; A Hero in Time, 2001; Sri Lanka: An Insight Guide, 2000, rev. ed., 2002; Sri Lanka: The Bradt Travel Guide, 2002; Maldives: An Insight Guide, 2002; The Sri Lanka Story, 2003; The Growing Years, 2004. "Bondmaster" and "Bloodheart" books published in UK as Richard Tresillian. **Address:** Horizon Cottage, Kaikawala, Induruwa, Sri Lanka. **Online address:** royston@roystonellis.com; www.roystonellis.com

ELLIS, Sarah. Canadian, b. 1952. **Genres:** Children's fiction, Young adult fiction, Adult non-fiction, Children's non-fiction. **Career:** Toronto Public Library, librarian, c. 1975; Vancouver Public Library, BC, children's librarian, 1976-81; North Vancouver District Library, BC, children's librarian, 1981-. **Publications:** CHILDREN'S FICTION: The Baby Project, 1986 in US as A Family Project, 1988; Next-Door Neighbours, 1989 in US as Next-Door Neighbors, 1990; Pick-Up Sticks, 1991; Out of the Blue, 1994; Next

Stop, 2000; A Prairie as Wide as the Sea, 2001; Big Ben, 2001. YOUNG ADULT FICTION: Putting Up with Mitchell, 1989; Back of Beyond, 1996. OTHER: The Young Writers' Companion (children's non-fiction), 1999; From Reader to Writer (adult non-fiction), 2000. **Address:** 4432 Walden St, Vancouver, BC, Canada V5V 3S3.

ELLIS, Steven G. British, b. 1950. **Genres:** History. **Career:** National University of Ireland, Galway, research assistant, 1976-77, junior lecturer, 1977-84, statutory lecturer, 1984-91, professor of history, 1991-. **Publications:** Tudor Ireland, 1985; Reform and Revival: English Government in Ireland, 1470-1534, 1986; Tudor Frontiers and Noble Power, 1995; (ed. with S. Barber) Conquest and Union: Fashioning a British State, 1485-1725, 1995; Ireland in the Age of the Tudors, 1998. **Address:** Department of History, National University of Ireland Galway, Galway, Ireland. **Online address:** steven.ellis@nuigalway.ie

ELLIS, Trey. Also writes as Tom Ricostranza. American, b. 1962. **Genres:** Novels, Plays/Screenplays. **Career:** Writer. **Publications:** Platitudes, 1988; Home Repairs, 1993; (as Tom Ricostranza) The Inkwell (screenplay), 1994; Cosmic Slop (teleplay); Tuskegee (teleplay). Contributor to periodicals. **Address:** c/o Publicity Department, Simon & Schuster, 1230 Avenue of the Americas, New York, NY 10020, U.S.A. **Online address:** TEllis@literati.net; http://literati.net/Ellis/

ELLIS, Walter M. American, b. 1943. **Genres:** History, Novels. **Career:** University of California, Los Angeles, 1979-87; Loyola Marymount University, Los Angeles, CA, visiting assistant professor of history, 1988-91; University of North Dakota, assistant professor, 1992-; writer. National Teacher Corps, instructor, 1967-69; teacher of English, history, and humanities at a university school, 1971-79; University of California, visiting lecturer, summer, 1989; Pepperdine University, visiting lecturer, autumn, 1989. **Publications:** Alcibiades, 1989; Ptolemy of Egypt, 1994; Prince of Darkness (novel), 1998. Contributor to history journals. **Address:** University of North Dakota, Department of History, PO Box 8096, Grand Forks, ND 58202-8096, U.S.A.

ELLIS, William E. American, b. 1940. **Genres:** Novellas/Short stories, History. **Career:** High school teacher and coach in Harrodsburg, KY, 1962-63, and Shelbyville, KY, 1963-66; Lees Junior College, Jackson, KY, instructor in history, 1967-70; Eastern Kentucky University, Richmond, professor of history, 1970-99, university historian, 1999-. Kentucky Monthly, columnist. **Publications:** A Man of Books and a Man of the People: E.Y. Mullins and the Crisis of Moderate Southern Baptist Leadership, 1985; Patrick Henry Callahan: Progressive Layman in the American South, 1989; River Bends and Meanders: Stories, Sketches, and Tales of Kentucky (fiction), 1992; Dog Days and Other Stories (fiction), 1996; Robert Worth Bingham and the Southern Mystique: From the Old South to the New South and Beyond, 1997; The Kentucky River, 2000.

ELLISON, Harlan (Jay). Also writes as Paul Merchant. American, b. 1934. **Genres:** Novels, Novellas/Short stories, Science fiction/Fantasy, Plays/Screenplays, Graphic Novels. **Career:** Freelance screenwriter, author and lectr. President, Kilmanjaro Corp., 1979-. Co-founder, Science Fiction Writers of America. Ed., Rogue mag., Chicago, 1959-60; Founding Ed., Regency Books, publrs., Chicago, 1960-61; television series and movie scriptwriter, 1962-77; Weekly Columnist. "The Glass Teat" TV column, 1968-71, and "Harlan Ellison Hornbook," 1972-73, Los Angeles Free Press newspaper; Book Critic, Los Angeles Times, 1969-82; Instructor, Clarion Writers Workshops, Michigan State University, East Lansing, 1969-77, 1984; Editorial Commentator, CBC-TV, 1972-78; Creator and Ed., Harlan Ellison Discovery Series of First Novels, Pyramid Books, 1973-77; Creative Consultant, Writer and Director, The Twilight Zone, CBS-TV, 1984-85, and Cutter's World, 1987-88. **Publications:** SCIENCE FICTION NOVELS: The Man with Nine Lives, 1960; Doomsman, 1967; (with E. Bryant) Phoenix without Ashes, 1975; The City on the Edge of Forever (novelization of TV play), 1977. SCIENCE FICTION SHORT STORIES: A Touch of Infinity, 1960; Ellison Wonderland, 1962, as Earthman, Go Home, 1964, rev. ed., 1984; Paingod and Other Delusions, 1965, rev. ed., 1975; I Have No Mouth, and I Must Scream, 1967; From the Land of Fear, 1967; Love Ain't Nothing but Sex Misspelled, 1968, rev. ed., 1976; The Beast That Shouted Love at the Heart of the World, 1969, rev. ed., 1984, 1994; Over the Edge: Stories from Somewhere Else, 1970; (with others) Partners in Wonder, 1971; Alone against Tomorrow, 1971, in U.K. as All the Sound of Fear, and The Time of the Eye, 2 vols., 1973-74; De Helden van de Highway, 1973; Approaching Oblivion, 1974; Deathbird Stories, 1975, rev. ed., 1991; No Doors, No Windows, 1976, rev. ed, 1991; Hoe Kan Ik Schreeuwen Zonder Mond, 1977; Strange Wine, 1978; The Illustrated Harlan Ellison, 1978; The Fantasies of Harlan Ellison

(omnibus), 1979; Shatterday, 1980; Stalking the Nightmare, 1982; The Essential Ellison, 1987, rev. ed., 2001; Angry Candy, 1988; Footsteps, 1989; Dreams with Sharp Teeth (omnibus), 3 vols, 1991; Run for the Stars, 1991; Ensamvark, 1992; Mind Fields, 1994; Jokes without Punchlines, 1995; Slippage, 1996; Troublemakers, 2001. GRAPHIC NOVELS: Demon with a Glass Hand, 1986; Night and the Enemy, 1987; Vic and Blood, 1989; Harlan Ellison's Dream Corridor, 1995. SCIENCE FICTION PLAYS: The City on the Edge of Forever, 1967; I, Robot, 1994. NOVELS: Rumble, 1958, rev. ed. as Web of the City, 1975; Rockabilly, 1961, rev. ed. as Spider Kiss, 1975; All the Lies That Are My Life, 1980; Run for the Stars, 1991; Mefisto in Onyx, 1993. SHORT STORIES: The Deadly Streets, 1958; (as Paul Merchant) Sex Gang, 1959; Gentleman Junkie and Other Stories of the Hung-up Generation, 1961, rev. ed., 1975; Children of the Streets, 1961; All the Sounds of Fear, 1973; The Time of the Eye, 1974. PLAYS: The Oscar (screenplay), 1966; Harlan Ellison's Movie, 1991; Episodes for Burke's Law Series, The Outer Limit Series, and others. OTHER: Memos from Purgatory (non-fiction), 1961; The Glass Teat, 1970; The Other Glass Teat, 1975; The Book of Ellison, 1978; Sleepness Nights in the Procrustean Bed: Essays, 1984; An Edge in My Voice, 1985; Harlan Ellison's Watching, 1989; The Harlan Ellison Hornbook (essays), 1990. EDITOR: Dangerous Visions, 1967; Nightshade and Damnations, 1968; Again, Dangerous Visions, 1972; J. Sutherland, Stormtrack, 1975; A.B. Cover, Autumn Angels, 1975; T. Carr, The Light at the End of th4e Universe, 1976; M. Randall, Islands, 1976; B. Sterling, Involution Ocean, 1978; Medea: Harlan's World, 1985. **Address:** c/o The Harlan Ellison Recording Collection, PO Box 55548, Sherman Oaks, CA 91413, U.S.A. **Online address:** www.harlanellison.com

ELLISON, Joan Audrey. Also writes as Elspeth Robertson. British, b. 1928. **Genres:** Food and Wine, Translations, Music. **Career:** Microbiologist, 1948-50; Lecturer, Queen Elizabeth College, Univ of London. 1950-54; Information Officer, Norway Food Centre, London, 1966-72; Ed. with M. Costa, Time-Life Foods of the World series, 1970-72; Food Consultant, food industries in U.K. and Scandinavia; Head, Dept. of Nutrition and Home Economics, Flour Advisory Bureau Ltd., London, 1972-78; Secretary, Royal Society of Health, London, 1980-82; International Artists' Management, concert agent, 1987-. **Publications:** (trans. and ed.) The Great Scandinavian Cook Book, 1966; (as Elspeth Robertson) The Findus Book of Fish Cookery, 1968; (trans.) The Best of Scandinavian Cookery; (trans. and ed.) Norway's Delights, 1969; (co-author) Growing for the Kitchen, 1978; The Colman Book of British Traditional Cooking, 1980; The Bread Book, 1987; Patisserie of Scandinavia, 1989. **Address:** International Artists' Management, 135 Stevenage Rd, Fulham, London SW6 6PB, England. **Online address:** audreyelectricalison-intl.freeserve.co.uk

ELLISON, Joan Jarvis. American, b. 1948. **Genres:** Autobiography/Memoirs. **Career:** University of Texas at Galveston, research associate, 1974-76; freelance writer, 1980-; shepherd, Pelican Rapids, MN, 1984-. **Publications:** Shepherdess: Notes from the Field (nonfiction), 1995. **Address:** 20740 410th St, Pelican Rapids, MN 56572, U.S.A. **Online address:** dellison@loretel.net

ELLROY, James. American, b. 1948. **Genres:** Mystery/Crime/Suspense. **Career:** Writer. Has held a variety of jobs, including country club caddy, 1965-84. **Publications:** Brown's Requiem, 1981; Clandestine, 1982; Blood on the Moon, 1984; Because the Night, 1985; Killer on the Road, 1986; Suicide Hill, 1986; Silent Terror, 1986; The Black Dahlia, 1987; The Big Nowhere, 1988; L.A. Confidential, 1990; White Jazz, 1992; Brown's Requium, 1994; Hollywood Nocturnes, 1994; American Tabloid, 1995; My Dark Places, 1996; L.A. Noir, 1998; Crime Wave, 1999; The Cold 6,000, 2001. **Address:** c/o Nat Sobel, Sobel Weber Associates Inc., 146 E 19th St., New York, NY 10003, U.S.A.

ELLWOOD, Sheelagh (Margaret). British, b. 1949. **Genres:** History, Politics/Government. **Career:** Freelance writer in Madrid, Spain, 1975-88; Foreign and Commonwealth Office, London, England, principal research officer for Iberia, 1988-95, assistant deputy governor of Gibraltar, 1995-98, senior principal research officer (Iberia), 1998-. **Publications:** Prietas las filas, 1983; Spanish Fascism in the Franco Era, 1987; The Spanish Civil War, 1991; Profiles in Power: Franco, 1994. Contributor to books. **Address:** Research Analysts (WSERG), Foreign and Commonwealth Office, King Charles St, London SW1A 2AH, England. **Online address:** Sheelagh.Ellwood@fco.gov.uk

ELLYARD, David. Australian, b. 1942. **Genres:** Astronomy, Meteorology/Atmospheric sciences, Technology. **Career:** Physicist in Antarctica, 1965-67; science teacher and senior master at a school in Sydney, Australia, 1969-72; Australian Broadcasting Co., Sydney, radio and television broadcaster, 1972-

87; public servant in Sydney, 1988-; New South Wales Department of State and Regional Development, Sydney. University of New England, member of board of governors, 1990-93. **Publications:** Oliphant, 1981; The Proud Arch, 1982; Quantum, 1987; Sky Watch, 1988, rev. ed., 1998; Handbook of Southern Sky Astronomy, 1993; Droughts and Flooding Plains, 1994; (coauthor) The Southern Sky Guide, 1994, 2nd ed., 2000; Weatherwise, 1999. **Address:** 9 Redgrove Ave, Beecroft, NSW 2119, Australia. **Online address:** ellyard@one.net.au

ELMER, Robert. American, b. 1958. **Genres:** Novels, Novellas/Short stories, Romance/Historical, Children's fiction, Young adult fiction. **Career:** Olympia News, WA, reporter, 1981-82; Simpson College, San Francisco, CA, director of admissions, 1982-83; Westside Alliance Church, Olympia, WA, assistant pastor, 1983-84; Goldendale Sentinel, WA, editor, 1985-87; Baron & Co., Bellingham, WA, senior copywriter, 1988-; author/speaker, 1994-. **Publications:** FOR CHILDREN: A Way through the Sea, 1994; Beyond the River, 1994; Into the Flames, 1995; Far from the Storm, 1995; Chasing the Wind, 1996; A Light in the Castle, 1996; Follow the Star, 1997; Touch the Sky, 1997; Escape to Murray River, 1997; Captive at Kangaroo Springs, 1997; Rescue at Boomerang Bend, 1998; Dingo Creek Challenge, 1998; Race to Wallaby Bay, 1998; Firestorm at Kookaburra Station, 1999; Koala Beach Outbreak, 1999; Panic at Emu Flat, 1999; Promise Breaker, 2000; Peace Rebel, 2000; Great Galaxy Goof, 2000; Zero-G Headache, 2000; Refugee Treasure, 2001; Brother Enemy, 2001; Wired Wonder Woof, 2001; Miko's Muzzy Mess, 2001; About-Face Space Race, 2001; Cosmic Camp Caper, 2001; Freedom Trap, 2002; The Super-Duper Blooper, 2002; AstroBall Free-4-All, 2002; Mid-Air Zillionaire, 2002; Tow-Away Stowaway, 2002; True Betrayer, 2002. YOUTH NOVELS: Digital Disaster, 2004; Fudge Factor, 2004; Webjam, 2004. FOR ADULTS: The Duet (novel), 2004. Contributor of short stories to books. **Address:** c/o WaterBrook Press, 2375 Telstar Dr Ste 160, Colorado Springs, CO 80920, U.S.A.

EL-MOSLIMANY, Ann P(axton). American, b. 1937. **Genres:** Children's fiction. **Career:** Teacher, elementary to university levels, 1959-83; Kuwait University, Kuwait, 1984-86; Seattle Central Community College, Seattle, WA, 1986-1990; Islamic School of Seattle, Seattle, principal and teacher, 1989-. Palynological Consultants, paleoecological research, 1987-. **Publications:** Zaki's Ramadan Fast, 1994. Contributor to scientific journals. **Address:** Islamic School of Seattle, 720 25th Ave, Seattle, WA 98122, U.S.A. **Online address:** annelmoslimany@yahoo.com

ELMSLIE, Kenward. Also writes as Lavinia Sanchez. American, b. 1929. **Genres:** Novels, Novellas/Short stories, Plays/Screenplays, Poetry, Songs/Lyrics and libretti. **Publications:** Power Plant Poems, 1967; Lizzie Borden (libretto), 1967; Miss Julie (libretto), 1967; The Champ, 1968; Album, 1969; Circus Nerves, 1971; Motor Disturbance, 1971; City Junket (play), 1972; The Grass Harp (musical), 1972; The Orchid Stories, 1973; The Sweet Bye and Bye (libretto), 1973; Penguin Modern Poets 24, 1974; The Seagull (libretto), 1974; Tropicalism, 1975; Washington Square (libretto), 1976; The Alphabet Work, 1977; Communications Equipment, 1979; Moving Right Along, 1980; Bimbo Dirt, 1982; Lola (libretto), 1982; Three Sisters (libretto), 1986; 26 Bars, 1987; Sung Sex, 1989; Paydirt, 1991; The Lavinia Sanchez Festschrift, 1992; Postcards on Parade (musical), 1993; Champ Dust, 1994; Bare Bones, 1995; Champ Dust Spinoff: Ten Collages, 1995; Routine Disruptions, 1998; Nite Soil, 2000; Cyberspace, 2000; Blast from the Past, 2001; Snippets, 2002; (with M. Kite) Spilled Beans, 2002; Agenda Melt, 2004; Lingoland (musical), 2005. **Address:** Poet's Corner, Calais, VT 05648, U.S.A. **Online address:** www.kenwardelmslie.com

ELON, Amos. Israeli, b. 1926. **Genres:** Novels, Plays/Screenplays, History. **Career:** Author and journalist. Foreign corresp., editorial writer, and columnist, Ha'aretz (newspaper), Tel Aviv, 1952-83. Regular contributor: The New Yorker Magazine, New York Review of Books. **Publications:** Journey through Haunted Land, 1966; The Israelis: Founders and Sons, 1971; (with S. Hassan) Between Enemies: A Compassionate Dialogue Between an Israeli and an Arab, 1974; Herzl (biography), 1975, (play), 1976; Understanding Israel: A Social Studies Approach, 1976; Timetable (novel), 1980; Flight into Egypt (history), 1980; (with R. Nowitz) The Holy Land from the Air, 1987; Jerusalem: City of Mirrors, 1989; A Certain Panic, 1990; A Blood-Dimmed Tide: Dispatches from the Near East, 1994; Founder: The Life and Times of Mayer Amschel Rothschild, 1996; A Blood-Dimmed Tide II, 2000. **Address:** c/o Author Mail, Henry Holt & Co, 115 W 18th St, New York, NY 10011, U.S.A. **Online address:** b_elon@netvision.net.il

ELROD, P(at) N. American. **Genres:** Science fiction/Fantasy. **Career:** Writer. **Publications:** THE VAMPIRE FILES SERIES: Bloodlist, 1990; Lifeblood, 1990; Bloodcircle, 1990; Art in the Blood, 1991; Fire in the

Blood, 1991; Blood on the Water, 1992. THE JONATHAN BARRETT VAMPIRE SERIES: Red Death, 1993; Death and the Maiden, 1994; Death Masque, 1995; Dance of Death, 1996. OTHER: I, Strahd, 1993; Dark Sleep, 1996; The Wind Breathes Cold, 1996; (ed. with M.H. Greenberg) Time of the Vampires, 1996. Work represented in anthologies. Contributor to magazines. **Address:** P.O. Box 100362, Fort Worth, TX 76185, U.S.A.

EL-SHAZLY, Nadia El-Sayed. Egyptian, b. 1936. **Genres:** International relations/Current affairs, Military/Defense/Arms control. **Career:** Al-Mossawar (weekly magazine), trainee, 1956; Al-Ahram (daily newspaper), correspondent, 1957-58; researcher and writer. Project for Democracy Studies in the Arab World, Oxford, England, member, 1991-. Volunteer work includes membership in Muhammad Awad Society (for underprivileged females), 1975-, al-Mustaqbal Society (for wounded war veterans), 1973-77, al-Nour wal-Amal Society (for the blind), 1973-77, and al-Hilal al-Ahmar Society, 1973-85; Umm al-Bahariyah Society (for Egyptian sailors' families), founder, 1972, member of board of directors, 1972-80; United Seamen's Services-Egypt, founder, 1976, member of board of directors, 1976-88; Imhotep Society (for the physically disabled), founder, 1979, president, 1979-87. **Publications:** The Gulf Tanker War: Iran's and Iraq's Maritime Swordplay, 1998. Contributor to periodicals. **Address:** PO Box 13326, London W5 2FS, England. **Online address:** NESelshazly@aol.com

ELSON, R. N. See **NELSON, Ray.**

ELSY, (Winifred) Mary. British. **Genres:** Children's fiction, Travel/Exploration. **Career:** Producer's Assistant, Realist Film Unit, 1957-58, and Associate-Rediffusion, Television, London, 1958-59; Writer and Sub-Ed., Fleetway Publs., 1960-62, B.R.C. Publishing Co., 1963-64, and Evans Bros., 1965-66; Children's Book Ed., Abelard-Schuman Ltd., London, 1967-68. **Publications:** Travels in Belgium and Luxembourg, 1966; Brittany and Normandy, 1974; Travels in Normandy, 1988; Travels in Brittany, 1988; Travels in Alsace and Lorraine, 1989; Travels in Burgundy, 1989; Pedals and Petitticoats, 2005. **Address:** 519C Finchley Rd, Hampstead, London NW3 7BB, England. **Online address:** melsy_trav_chnwtr@btopenworld.com; maryelsy.trav@btopenworld.com

ELTIS, Walter (Alfred). British (born Czech Republic), b. 1933. **Genres:** Economics. **Career:** Oxford University, England, lecturer in economics, 1961-88, fellow of Exeter College, 1963-88, emeritus fellow, 1988-; National Economic Development Office, London, England, economic consultant, 1963-66, economic director, 1986-88, director general, 1988-92; Department of Trade and Industry, London, chief economic adviser to the president of the Board of Trade, 1992-95; visiting professor at University of Toronto, 1976-77, European University, Florence, Italy, 1979, University of Reading, 1992-. Economic and financial consultant with Rowe & Pitman, London, 1976-86; consultant bank credit analyst in Montreal, Quebec, 1983-88, 1995-. **Publications:** Economic Growth: Analysis and Policy, 1966; Growth and Distribution, 1973; (with R. Bacon) Britain's Economic Problem: Too Few Producers, 1976; The Classical Theory of Economic Growth, 1984, 2nd ed., 2000; Classical Economics, Public Expenditure and Growth, 1993; (with R. Bacon) Britain's Economic Problem Revisited, 1996; Britain, Europe and EMU, 2000. EDITOR: (with P.J.N. Sinclair) The Money Supply and the Exchange Rate, 1981; (with P. Sinclair) Keynes and Economic Policy, 1988; (with S.M. Eltis) Condillac: Commerce and Government, 1997. **Address:** Danesway, Jarn Way, Boars Hill, Oxford OX1 5JF, England.

ELTON, Hugh. British, b. 1964. **Genres:** History. **Career:** Oxford University, Oxford, England, tutor in classics at Lincoln College, 1988; participated in archaeological field studies in Italy, Turkey, and France, 1991; Cambridge University, England, site assistant with Cambridge Archaeological Unit, 1991-92; Rice University, Houston, TX, visiting assistant professor of history, 1993-94; Trinity College, Hartford, CT, visiting assistant professor of history, 1994-. Conducted field studies in England, Greece, and Israel. Speaker at colleges and universities. **Publications:** (ed. with J.F. Drinkwater and contrib.) Fifth-Century Gaul: A Crisis of Identity?, 1992; Warfare in Roman Europe, A.D. 350-425, 1996; Frontiers of the Roman Empire, 1996. Contributor to books. Contributor of articles and reviews to classical studies journals. **Address:** Department of History, Trinity College, Hartford, CT 06106, U.S.A.

ELTRINGHAM, S(tewart) K(eith). British/Canadian, b. 1929. **Genres:** Environmental sciences/Ecology, Marine sciences/Oceanography, Natural history, Zoology. **Career:** Pilot-biologist, The Wildfowl Trust, Slimbridge, Glos., 1957-61; Lecturer in Zoology, King's College, University of London, 1962-67; Director, Nuffield Unit of Tropical Animal Ecology, Queen Elizabeth National Park, Uganda, 1967-71; Director, Uganda Institute of

Ecology Queen Elizabeth National Park, Uganda, and Chief Research Officer, Uganda National Parks, 1971-73; University Lecturer in Applied Biology, 1973-89, University Lecturer in Zoology, 1989-96, Cambridge University. **Publications:** Life in Mud and Sand, 1971; The Ecology and Conservation of Large African Mammals, 1979; Elephants, 1982; Wildlife Resources and Economic Development, 1984; The Hippos, 1999. EDITOR: (with E.G. Jones) Marine Borers, Fungi and Fouling Organisms of Wood, 1971; The Illustrated Encyclopedia of Elephants, 1991. **Address:** Dept of Zoology, Cambridge University, Downing St, Cambridge CB2 3EJ, England. **Online address:** ske1000@cam.ac.uk

ELVENSTAR, Diane C. *See* **MEDVED, Diane.**

ELY, David. American, b. 1927. **Genres:** Novels, Novellas/Short stories. **Career:** Reporter, St. Louis Post-Dispatch, Missouri, 1949-50, 1952-54 and 1955-56; Administrative Assistant, Development and Resources Corp., NYC, 1956-59. **Publications:** Trot, 1963; Seconds, 1963; The Tour, 1967; Time Out (short stories), 1968; Poor Devils, 1970; Walking Davis, 1972; Mr. Nicholas, 1974; Always Home (short stories), 1991; A Journal of the Flood Year, 1992 (novel). **Address:** P. O. Box 1387, East Dennis, MA 02641, U.S.A.

ELY, Melvin Patrick. American, b. 1952. **Genres:** Cultural/Ethnic topics, History. **Career:** Huguenot High School, Richmond, VA, teacher, 1973-75; Granby High School, Granby, MA, teacher, 1975-76; University of Virginia, Charlottesville, postdoctoral fellow of Carter G. Woodson Institute, 1985-86; Yale University, New Haven, CT, assistant professor, 1986-92, associate professor of history and Afro-American studies, 1992-95; College of William and Mary, Williamsburg, VA, associate professor, 1995-96, professor of history and black studies, 1996-. **Publications:** The Adventures of Amos 'n' Andy: A Social History of an American Phenomenon, 1991; Israel on the Appomattox: A Southern Experiment in Black Freedom from the 1790s through the Civil War, 2004. **Address:** Dept of History, College of William and Mary, PO Box 8795, Williamsburg, VA 23187-8795, U.S.A. **Online address:** mpelyx@wm.edu

EMANUEL, James A(ndrew). American, b. 1921. **Genres:** Poetry, Songs/Lyrics and libretti, Literary criticism and history, Autobiography/Memoirs, Essays. **Career:** Civilian Chief, Pre-Induction Section, Army and Air Force Induction Station, Chicago, 1951-53; Instructor, Harlem YWCA Business School, NYC, 1954-56; Instructor, 1957-62, Assistant Professor, 1962-70, Associate Professor, 1970-72, and Professor of English, 1972-84, City College of New York; Fulbright Professor of American Literature, University of Grenoble, France, 1968-69; Visiting Professor of English, University of Toulouse, France, 1971-73, 1979-81. **Publications:** Langston Hughes, 1967; (ed. with T. L. Gross) Dark Symphony: Negro Literature in America, 1968; The Treehouse and Other Poems, 1968; At Bay, 1969; Panther Man, 1970; (with M. Kantor and L. Osgood) How I Write 2, 1972; Black Man Abroad: The Toulouse Poems, 1978; A Chisel in the Dark, 1980; The Broken Bowl: New and Uncollected Poems, 1983; A Poet's Mind, 1983; Deadly James and Other Poems, 1987; The Quagmire Effect, 1988; Whole Grain: Collected Poems, 1958-1989, 1991; De la rage au coeur, 1992; (with G. Simons) Blues in Black and White, 1992; Reaching for Mumia: 16 Haiku, 1995; JAZZ from the Haiku King, 1999; The Force and the Reckoning, 2001. **Address:** B.P. 339, 75266 Paris Cedex 06, France.

EMBERLEY, Peter C. Canadian, b. 1956. **Genres:** Education, Theology/Religion. **Career:** Carleton University, Ottawa, ON, professor of political science and philosophy, 1984-. **Publications:** Bankrupt Education: The Decline of Liberal Education in Canada, 1994; Values Education and Technology: The Ideology of Dispossession, 1995; Zero Tolerance: Hot Button Politics in Canada's Universities, 1996; Divine Hunger: Canadians on Spiritual Walkabout, 2002. **Address:** Department of Political Science, Carleton University, 1125 Colonel By Dr, Ottawa, ON, Canada K1S 5B6. **Online address:** pemberle@ccs.carleton.ca

EMBEY, Philip. *See* **PHILIPP, Elliot Elias.**

EMECHETA, (Florence Onye) Buchi. British (born Nigeria), b. 1944. **Genres:** Novels, Sociology, Autobiography/Memoirs. **Career:** British Museum, London, Library Officer, 1965-69; Inner London Education Authority, Youth Worker and Sociologist, 1969-. **Publications:** In the Ditch, 1972; Second Class Citizen, 1974; The Bride Price, 1976; The Slave Girl, 1977; Titch the Cat, 1979; Joys of Motherhood, 1979; Nowhere to Play, 1980; The Moonlight Bride, 1981; Destination Biafra, 1982; Naira Power, 1982; Double Yoke, 1982; The Rape of Shavi, 1983; The Wrestling Match, 1983; Head above Water (autobiography), 1986; A Kind of Marriage, 1986; Gwendolyn,

1989 in US as The Family, 1990; Kehinde, 1994; The New Tribe, 2000. **Address:** 7 Briston Grove, Crouch End, London N8 9EX, England.

EMENEAU, Murray Barnson. American (born Canada), b. 1904. **Genres:** Anthropology/Ethnology, Language/Linguistics, Mythology/Folklore. **Career:** Professor Emeritus, University of California, Berkeley, since 1971 (Assistant Professor of Sanskrit and General Linguistics, 1940-43; Associate Professor, 1943-46; Professor, 1946-71). **Publications:** Jambhaladatta's Version of Vetalapancavinsati, 1934; A Union List of Printed Indic Texts and Translations in American Libraries, 1935; Kota Texts, 1944-46; Studies in Vietnamese Grammar, 1951; Sanskrit Sandhi and Exercises, 1952; 4th ed. 1968; Kolami, a Dravidian Language, 1955; (with T. Burrow) A Dravidian Etymological Dictionary, 1961, 1966, supplement 1968, 2nd ed. 1984; (with T. Burrow) Dravidian Borrowing from Indo-Aryan, 1962; Brahui and Dravidian Comparative Grammar, 1962; India and Historical Grammar, 1965; Dravidian Linguistics, Ethnology, and Folktales: Collected Papers, 1967; Dravidian Comparative Phonology: A Sketch, 1970; Toda Songs, 1971; Ritual Structure and Language Structure of the Todas, 1974; Language and Linguistic Area: Selected Essays, 1980; Toda Grammer and Texts, 1984; Sanskrit Studies: Selected Papers, 1988; Dravidian Studies: Selected Papers, 1994. **Address:** 909 San Benito Rd, Berkeley, CA 94707-2436, U.S.A.

EMERSON, Earl W. American, b. 1948. **Genres:** Mystery/Crime/Suspense. **Career:** Seattle Fire Dept., Wash., lieutenant, 1978-. **Publications:** The Rainy City, 1985; Poverty Bay, 1985; Nervous Laughter, 1986; Fat Tuesday, 1987; Black Hearts and Slow Dancing, 1988; Deviant Behavior, 1988; Help Wanted: Orphans Preferred, 1990; Yellow Dog Party, 1991; Morons and Madmen, 1993; The Portland Laugher, 1994; The Vanishing Smile, 1995; Going Crazy in Public, 1996; The Million-Dollar Tattoo, 1996; The Dead Horse Paint Company, 1997; Catfish Cafe, 1098; Vertical Burn, 2002; Into the Inferno, 2003. **Address:** c/o Jane Rotrosen Agency, 318 E 51st St, New York, NY 10022, U.S.A. **Online address:** ewemerson@comcast.net

EMERSON, Ken. American, b. 1948. **Genres:** Sociology. **Career:** Boston Phoenix, Boston, MA, writer and editor, 1968-77; New York Times Magazine, NYC, editor; Newsday, NYC, New York viewpoints editor, 1990-95. **Publications:** NONFICTION: Doo-dah!: Stephen Foster and the Rise of American Popular Culture, 1997. Contributor to periodicals. **Address:** The Century Foundation, 41 E. 70th St., New York, NY 10021, U.S.A. **Online address:** Emersonrk@aol.com

EMERSON, Thomas E. American, b. 1945. **Genres:** Anthropology/Ethnology, Archaeology/Antiquities. **Career:** Illinois Historic Preservation Agency, chief archaeologist, 198494; University of Illinois at Urbana-Champaign, director of Illinois Transportation Archaeological Research Program and adjunct assistant professor of anthropology, 1994-. Upper Mississippi Valley Archaeological Research Foundation, director, 1973-76; Northeastern Archaeological Foundation, director, 1974-77; Council of South Dakota Archaeologists, member, 1978-80; Illinois Archaeological Survey, research member, 1973-75, member, 1979-, member of board of directors, 1993-94; Illinois Interagency Coal Mining Committee, member, 1986-94; Landmark Preservation Council of Illinois, regional representative, 1998-. In addition to ongoing archaeological field work in the Midwest, also participated in studies in Tromso, Norway. **Publications:** (with G. Milner and D. Jackson) The Florence Street Site, 1983; (with Jackson) The BBB Motor Site, 1984; The Dyroff and Levin Sites (published with The Go-Kart North Site by A. Fortier), 1984; (with Jackson) Emergent Mississippian and Early Mississippian Homesteads at the Marcus Site, 1987; Cahokia and the Archaeology of Power, 1997. EDITOR & CONTRIBUTOR: (with K. Farnsworth) Early Woodland Archeology, 1986; (with R.B. Lewis) Cahokia and the Hinterlands: Middle Mississippian Cultures of the Midwest, 1991; (with J. Walthall) Calumet and Fleur-dy-Lys: French and Indian Interaction in the Midcontinent, 1992; (with T. Pauketat) Cahokia: Ideology and Domination in the Mississippian World, 1997. Contributor to books. Contributor to archaeology and anthropology journals. **Address:** 109 Davenport Hall, Department of Anthropology, University of Illinois, Urbana, IL 61801, U.S.A.

EMERY, Clayton. Also writes as Ian Hammell. American, b. 1953. **Genres:** Science fiction/Fantasy, Young adult fiction. **Career:** Writer. Worked as a blacksmith, dishwasher, schoolteacher in Australia, carpenter, zookeeper, farmhand, land surveyor, and volunteer firefighter. **Publications:** MAGIC: THE GATHERING SERIES: Whispering Woods, 1995; Shattered Chains, 1995; Final Sacrifice, 1995. ARCANE AGE: NETHERIL TRILOGY: Sword Play, 1996; Dangerous Games, 1996; Mortal Consequences, 1997. OTHER: (with E. Wajenberg) The 4D Funhouse, 1985; Tales of Robin Hood, 1988; Runesword: Outcasts, 1990; Cardmaster, 1997; The Secret World of Alex Mack: FatherDaughter Disaster!, 1997; Are You Afraid of the Dark? The

Tale of the Campfire Vampires, 1997. Contributor to books and periodicals. SHADOW WORLD SERIES (as Ian Hammell): The Burning Goddess, 1994; Clock Strikes Sword, 1995; City of Assassins, 1996. **Address:** 155 Grove Rd., Rye, NH 03870, U.S.A.

EMERY, Robert Firestone. American, b. 1927. **Genres:** Economics. **Career:** International economic consultant, 1992-; economist, Federal Reserve System, Washington, D.C., 1955-92. Professor Emeritus of Finance, Southeastern University, Washington, D.C., 1988- (Chairman, Dept. of Financial Administration, 1963-65; Dean, Sr. Division, 1965-68; Adjunct Professor, 1960-88). **Publications:** The Financial Institutions of Southeast Asia: A Country-by-Country Study, 1970; The Japanese Money Market, 1984; The Money Markets of Developing East Asia, 1991; The Bond Markets of Developing East Asia, 1997; Korean Economic Reform: Before & Since the 1997 Crisis, 2001. **Address:** 3421 Shepherd St, Chevy Chase, MD 20815, U.S.A.

EMERY, Robert J. (born United States), b. 1941. **Genres:** Adult non-fiction. **Career:** Media Entertainment, Inc., Tampa, FL, president and chief executive officer, c. 1977-. Film and television producer and director; executive producer, director, and editor for the documentary television series The Directors, broadcast by Encore and Starz! cable networks, beginning c. 1998. U.S. Air Force, 1958-61. **Publications:** (And creator) The Directors (documentary television series), broadcast by Encore and Starz! cable networks, 1998; The Directors-Take One (based on the television series), 2001; The Directors-Take Two: In Their Own Words (based on the television series), 2002; The Directors-Take Three (based on the television series), 2003; The Directors-Take Four (based on the television series), 2003. Author of screenplays. **Address:** c/o Author Mail, Allworth Press, 10 East 23rd St. Suite 510, New York, NY 10010, U.S.A. **Online address:** me@mediaent.net

EMERY, Tom. American, b. 1971. **Genres:** History, Biography. **Career:** Blackburn College, Carlinville, IL, sports information director, 1993-94; Monterey Coal Co., journalist, 1994-95; Macoupin County Enquirer, Carlinville, reporter, 1994-96; History in Print, Carlinville, owner and general manager, 1997-. **Publications:** Richard Rowett: Thoroughbreds, Beagles, and the Civil War, 1997; The Other John Logan: Col. John Logan and the 32nd Illinois, 1998; The Beagle: Its Beginnings in America, 2000; Hold the Fort: The Battle of Allatoona Pass, 2001; Eddie: Lincoln's Forgotten Son, 2002; Gustave Loehr: Rotary's Forgotten Founder, 2003. **Address:** Carlinville, IL 62626, U.S.A. **Online address:** tomemery11@yahoo.com

EMMERICH, André. American (born Germany), b. 1924. **Genres:** Art/Art history. **Career:** President, Andre Emmerich Gallery, NYC, 1954-96. President, Art Dealers of America, 1972-74, 1991-94. **Publications:** Art before Columbus, 1963; Sweat of the Sun and Tears of the Moon: Gold and Silver in Pre-Columbian Art, 1965. **Address:** 30 E 72nd St, New York, NY 10021, U.S.A. **Online address:** NIPE@pipeline.com

EMMERIJ, Louis (Johan). Dutch, b. 1934. **Genres:** Economics. **Career:** University of Paris, France, associate of Institut d'Etudes Economiques et Sociales, 1961-62; Organization for Economic Cooperation and Development, Paris, associate of Directorate of Scientific Affairs, 1962-70, president of Development Center, 1986-92; United Nations, International Labor Office, Geneva, Switzerland, director of World Employment Program, 1971-76; Institute of Social Studies, The Hague, Netherlands, rector, 1976-85; Inter-American Development Bank, Washington, DC, special adviser to the president, 1993-99. **Publications:** (primary author) Education, Human Resources, and Development in Argentina, 1967; (primary author) Occupational and Educational Structure of the Labour Force and Levels of Economic Development, 2 vols, 1970; Can the School Build a New Social Order?, 1974; (primary author) Employment, Growth, and Basic Needs, 1976; Volledige Werkgelegenheid door Creatief Verlof (title means: Full Employment through Creative Leave), 1978; From the Old to a New Global Order, 1979; Internationale Economische Herstructurering (title means: International Economic Restructuring), 1982; Nord-Sud: La Grenade Degoupillee, 1992; (lead author) Ahead of the Curve?, 2001. CO-AUTHOR: The Mediterranean Regional Project, Spain, 1965, Yugoslavia, 1965; De Crisis te Lijf: (title means: Fighting the Crisis), 1981; Science, Technology, and Science Education in the Development of the South, 1989; Limits to Competition, 1995; UN Contributions to Development Thinking and Practice, 2004. EDITOR: Schade en Herstel (title means: Damage and Repair), 1984; Development Policies and the Crisis of the 1980's, 1987; One World or Several?, 1989; (with E. Iglesias) Financial Flows to Latin America, 1991; (and contrib.) Economic and Social Development into the XXI Century, 1997. Contributor to books and professional journals. **Address:** 4200 Massachusetts Ave NW Apt 306A, Washington, DC 20016, U.S.A. **Online address:** Emmerij@netzero.net

EMMET, Alan. American. **Genres:** Novels, Homes/Gardens, Horticulture, History. **Career:** Historic Landscape Preservation, Harvard University Graduate School of Design, Cambridge, MA, course assistant, 1978-81; Society for the Preservation of New England Antiquities, consultant, 1982-92; National Trust for Historic Preservation, consultant, 1993-94; full time writer, 1994-. **Publications:** (with D.C. Allen and others) Cambridge, Massachusetts, the Changing of a Landscape, 1978; So Fine a Prospect: Historic Gardens of New England, 1996; The Mr. and Mrs. Club, 2001. Contributor to periodicals. **Address:** 224 Concord Rd, Westford, MA 01886, U.S.A.

EMMETT, Ayala. American (born Israel), b. 1935. **Genres:** Anthropology/Ethnology. **Career:** University of Rochester, Rochester, NY, research associate, 1981-87, assistant professor, 1981-84, lecturer, 1984-87, assistant professor, 1987-94, associate professor of anthropology, 1994-. Empire State College of the State University of New York, mentor, 1981-83; Haifa University, visiting professor, 1990. Conducted anthropological field work in Israel. **Publications:** Our Sisters' Promised Land: Women's Peace Politics and the Israeli Palestinian Conflict, 1996. Contributor of articles and reviews to periodicals. **Address:** Department of Anthropology, University of Rochester, Rochester, NY 14627, U.S.A. **Online address:** aemt@mail.rochester.edu

EMMONS, Mary L. Also writes as Anne K. Edwards. American, b. 1940. **Genres:** Novels, e-Books. **Career:** Novelist. **Publications:** Death on Delivery (e-book), 2001. NOVEL AS ANNE K. EDWARDS: Journey into Terror, 2001. Contributor of monthly columns and reviews to online sources. **Address:** PO Box 3402, Gettysburg, PA 17325, U.S.A. **Online address:** Marbob00@earthlink.net; AnneKEdwards@Yahoo.com

EMMONS, Phillip. *See* **LITTLE, Bentley.**

EMMONS, Shirlee. American, b. 1923. **Genres:** Music, Biography. **Career:** Professional singer, speaker, teacher, and writer. Columbia University, Barnard College, adjunct teacher, 1963-66; private teacher of vocal technique, 1964-; Princeton University, adjunct teacher, 1966-81; Tanglewood Institute, voice teacher, 1982; American Institute of Musical Studies, Graz, Austria, voice teacher, 1983 and 1985; State University of New York, State University College at Purchase, adjunct teacher, 1980-91; Boston University, associate professor, 1981-87; Rutgers University, adjunct teacher, 1987-90; Queens College, adjunct teacher, 1988-; Hunter College, visiting professor, 1991-98. **Publications:** (with S. Sonntag) The Art of the Song Recital, 1979; Tristanissimo: The Authorized Biography of Heroic Tenor Lauritz Melchior, 1990; (with A. Thomas) Power Performance for Singers, 1998. Contributor to professional journals. **Address:** 12 W 96th St, New York, NY 10025, U.S.A. **Online address:** voiceperformance@aol.com

EMORY, Jerry. American, b. 1957. **Genres:** Young adult non-fiction, Natural history, Travel/Exploration. **Career:** Writer. Golden Gate Audubon Society, Berkeley, CA, executive director, 1979-81; Mono Lake Coalition, San Francisco, CA, steward, 1981-85; Charles Darwin Research Station/The Nature Conservancy, Galapagos Islands, Ecuador, director of public relations, 1985-86; Conservation International, Quintana Roo, Mexico, communications consultant, spring, 1987; columnist, "Pacific Beat," for Pacific Discovery, California Academy of Sciences, San Francisco, 1988-90. **Publications:** NONFICTION FOR YOUNG ADULTS. GREENPATCH SERIES: Nightprowlers: Everyday Creatures under Every Night Sky, 1994; Dirty, Rotten, Dead? A Worm's Eye View of Death, Decomposition...and Life, 1996. OTHER: San Francisco Bay Shoreline Guide, 1995; Bay Area Backroads, 1999; The Monterey Bay Shoreline Guide, 1999. **Address:** 740 Summit Ave, Mill Valley, CA 94941, U.S.A. **Online address:** jeremory@pacbell.net

EMSHWILLER, Carol (Fries). American, b. 1921. **Genres:** Novels, Science fiction/Fantasy, Westerns/Adventure. **Career:** NY State Creative Artists Public Service Grant, 1975; National Endowment for Arts Grant, 1980; NY State Foundation for the Arts Grant, 1988. **Publications:** NOVELS: Carmen Dog, 1988; Leaping Man Hill, 1999; The Mount, 2002. OTHER: Joy in Our Cause, 1974; Verging on Pertinent, 1989; Start of the End of It All, 1990; Ledoyt, 1995; Report to the Men's Club and Other Stores, 2002. **Address:** 210 E 15th St Apt 12E, New York, NY 10003, U.S.A. **Online address:** cemsh@aol.com

EMSLEY, John. British, b. 1938. **Genres:** Chemistry. **Career:** University of London, England, lecturer at King's College, 1967-82, reader, 1982-90, science writer in residence at Imperial College of Science and Technology, 1990-97; University of Cambridge, Chemistry Dept, science writer in residence, 1997-. **Publications:** The Inorganic Chemistry of the Non-Metals, 1971; (with D. Hall) The Chemistry of Phosphorus, 1976; The Elements,

1989; The Consumer's Good Chemical Guide, 1994; Molecules at an Exhibition, 1998; Was It Something You Ate?, 1999; The 13th Element, 2000; Nature's Building Blocks, 2002; Vanity, Vitality, and Virility, 2004. **Address:** Dept of Chemistry, University of Cambridge, Lensfield Road, Cambridge CB2 1EW, England. **Online address:** je218@cam.ac.uk

ENCINIAS, Miguel. American, b. 1923. **Genres:** Cultural/Ethnic topics, History. **Career:** U.S. Air Force, career officer as a fighter pilot, 1940-71, serving during World War II and in Korea and Vietnam, retiring as lieutenant colonel; prisoner of war in Germany. University professor of Hispanic literature and French. Founder of Compania de Teatro and La Zarzuela de Albuquerque. **Publications:** (ed. and trans. with A. Rodriguez) G.P. de Villagra, Historia de la Nueva Mexico, 1610, 1992; Two Lives for Onate, 1997. **Address:** 1009 Green Valley Rd NW, Albuquerque, NM 87107-6321, U.S.A.

ENER, Guener. Turkish, b. 1935. **Genres:** Novellas/Short stories, Mystery/Crime/Suspense. **Career:** Translator for a state bank in Ankara, Turkey, 1967; Yuekselis College, Ankara, teacher of painting, 1968-69; Cem Yayinevi, Istanbul, Turkey, illustrator of book covers, 1972-78; freelance painter, 1978-. Presented her tales for children on a radio program in Helsinki, Finland, 1985. **Publications:** Tired of September (stories), 1969; Blue of the Broken Glass (stories), 1972; The Bald-Headed Girl (children's stories), 1990; (trans.) Sister Shako and Kolo the Goat, 1994. Contributor to art magazines and newspapers. **Address:** ICBS/IBIS, Skindergade 3B, K Copenhagen, Denmark.

ENG, David L. American. **Genres:** Social commentary. **Career:** Columbia University, New York, NY, teacher of English and comparative literature. **Publications:** (editor, with Alice Y. Hom) Q & A in Asian America, 1998; Racial Castration: Managing Masculinity in Asian America, 2001; (editor, with David Kazanjian) Loss: The Politics of Mourning, 2003. **Address:** Department of English and Comparative Literature, Columbia University, 1150 Amsterdam Ave, New York, NY 10027, U.S.A. **Online address:** dle8@columbia.edu

ENGDAHL, Sylvia L(ouise). American, b. 1933. **Genres:** Science fiction/Fantasy, Children's fiction, Young adult fiction, Young adult non-fiction. **Publications:** Enchantress from the Stars, 1970, new ed., 2001; Journey between Worlds, 1970; The Far Side of Evil, 1971, rev. ed., 2003; This Star Shall Abide (in U.K. as Heritage of the Star), 1972; Beyond the Tomorrow Mountains, 1973; The Planet-Girded Suns: Man's View of Other Solar Systems, 1974; (with R. Roberson) The Subnuclear Zoo: New Discoveries in High Energy Physics, 1977; (with R. Roberson) Tool for Tomorrow: New Knowledge about Genes, 1979; Our World Is Earth, 1979; The Doors of the Universe, 1981; Children of the Star (omnibus), 2000. EDITOR: (with R. Roberson) Universe Ahead: Stories of the Future, 1975; Anywhere, Anywhen: Stories of Tomorrow, 1976.

ENGEL, Bernard F. American, b. 1921. **Genres:** Literary criticism and history. **Career:** Michigan State University, East Lansing, Dept. of American Thought and Language, professor, 1957-89, chairman, 1967-77, professor emeritus, 1990-. **Publications:** Marianne Moore, 1964, 1989; The Achievement of Richard Eberhart, 1970; Richard Eberhart, 1972. EDITOR: History of the 413th Infantry, 1946, reissued 1993; A New Voice for a New People: Midwestern Poetry 1800-1910, 1985. **Address:** 6193 Captains Way, East Lansing, MI 48823-1612, U.S.A.

ENGEL, Cindy. British. **Genres:** Animals/Pets. **Career:** Open University, Milton Keynes, England, professor of environmental science. Also worked as a conservationist, animal researcher, biologist, and science adviser to documentary filmmakers. **Publications:** Wild Health: How Animals Keep Themselves Well and What We Can Learn from Them, 2002. Contributor to periodicals. **Address:** c/o Houghton Mifflin, Adult Editorial, 8th Floor, 222 Berkeley Street, Boston, MA 02116, U.S.A.

ENGEL, Howard. Also writes as F. X. Woolf. Canadian, b. 1931. **Genres:** Novels, Criminology/True Crime, Mystery/Crime/Suspense, Plays/Screenplays, Novellas/Short stories. **Career:** Full-time novelist, 1985-. Freelance broadcaster, 1956-67, radio producer, 1967-68, Executive Producer, 1968-80, and Literary Ed., 1980-85, CBC, Toronto. Co-founder, 1982, Treasurer, 1982-85, Ed. of Fingerprints, 1985-86, and Chairman, 1986-87, Crime Writers of CA; Canadian Give the Gift of Literacy Foundation, director, 1992. **Publications:** NOVELS: The Suicide Murders, 1980, (screenplay), 1984; The Ransom Game, 1981; Murder on Location, 1982; Murder Sees the Light, 1984, (screenplay), 1985; (with J. Hamilton, as F.X. Woolf) Murder in Space, 1985; A City Called July, 1986; A Victim Must Be Found, 1988; Dead and Buried, 1990; Murder in Montparnasse, 1992; There Was an Old

Woman, 1993; Getting Away with Murder, 1995; Mr Doyle & Dr Bell, 1997; The Cooperman Variations, 2001; also radio plays. OTHER: The Whole Megillah (novella), 1992; (ed. with E. Wright) Criminal Shorts (short stories), 1992; Lord High Executioner (nonfiction), 1996. **Address:** c/o Beverley Slopen Agency, 131 Bloor St W Ste 711, Toronto, ON, Canada M5S 2L5.

ENGEL, Joel. American, b. 1952. **Genres:** Human relations/Parenting, Film. **Career:** Journalist. New York Times, New York, NY, entertainment writer; Los Angeles Times, Los Angeles, CA, staff writer. **Publications:** It's O.K. to Be Gifted or Talented!: A Parent/Child Manual, 1987; It's O.K. to Grow Up!: A Parent/Child Manual, 1987; Addicted: Kids Talking about Drugs in Their Own Words, 1989; Rod Serling: The Dreams and Nightmares of Life in the Twilight Zone, 1989; (Coauthor) C. Carroll, Surf-Dog Days and Bitchen' Nights, 1989; Gene Roddenberry: The Myth and the Man behind Star Trek, 1994; Oscar-winning Screenwriters on Screenwriting: The Award-winning Best in the Business Discuss Their Craft, 1995, rev. ed, 2002; (Coauthor) G. Foreman, By George: The Autobiography of George Foreman, 1995; (Coauthor) J. Youngblood, Blood, 1998; (Coauthor) J. Morris, The Oldest Rookie: Big-League Dreams from a Small-Town Guy, 2001. **Address:** c/o Author Mail, Hyperion Books, 77 West 66th St. 11th Floor, New York, NY 10023, U.S.A.

ENGEL, Margorie L(ouise). American, b. 1943. **Genres:** Business/Trade/Industry, How-to books, Human relations/Parenting, Law, Sociology. **Career:** Educational program developer in Virginia, California, and Connecticut, 1965-76; Fairfield University, CT, public relations, 1976-78; Siebert Associates, partner, new business development, 1978-85; Hamilton-Forbes Associates, Boston, MA, president, 1985-; Manhattanville College, professor, 1987-88; Northeastern University, Brudnick Center for the Study of Conflict and Violence, fellow, 1998-. Stepfamily Association of America, president/CEO, 1998; Your Stepfamily magazine, senior editorial adviser, 2002-. Guest lecturer at colleges and universities; guest on television and radio programs. **Publications:** A Guide to Mergers and Acquisitions, 1984; The Divorce Decisions Workbook, 1992; (with D. Gould) Weddings for Complicated Families, 1993, 2nd ed. as Weddings: A Family Affair, 1998; Divorce Help Sourcebook, 1994; (with J.D. Payne and M. Payne) The Canadian Divorce Decisions Workbook, 1994; Stepfamilies Business Decisions Booklet Series, 2001. Contributor to books and periodicals. **Address:** 25 Walnut St, Boston, MA 02108, U.S.A. **Online address:** engel@saafamilies.org; www.stepfamilies-international.org

ENGEL, Monroe. American, b. 1921. **Genres:** Novels, Literary criticism and history. **Career:** Sr. Lecturer in English, Harvard University, Cambridge, Massachusetts, 1955-89, Retired. Associate Ed., Reynal & Hitchcock, 1946-47, and Viking Press, NYC, 1947-51; Lecturer, Princeton University, New Jersey, 1954-55. **Publications:** NOVELS: A Length of Rope, 1952; Visions of Nicholas Solon, 1959; Voyager Belsky, 1962; Fish, 1981; Statutes of Limitations, 1988. OTHER: The Maturity of Dickens, 1959; (ed.) The Uses of Literature, 1974. **Address:** 167 Pemberton St, Cambridge, MA 02140, U.S.A. **Online address:** miengel@comcast.net

ENGELBERG, Alan (D.). American, b. 1941. **Genres:** Novels. **Career:** Physician in private practice in Los Angeles, CA, 1974-; writer. **Publications:** Variant (novel), 1989. **Address:** 9615 Wendover Dr., Beverly Hills, CA 90210, U.S.A.

ENGELHARD, Jack. American (born France), b. 1940. **Genres:** Novels, Plays/Screenplays, Adult non-fiction. **Career:** Suburban Newspaper Group, Cherry Hill, NJ, reporter, mid1960s; Willingboro Suburban, Willingboro, NJ, editor, mid1960s; Burlington County Times, Willingboro, reporter and feature writer, early 1970s; Philadelphia Inquirer, Philadelphia, PA, humor columnist and racing reporter, ten years beginning in 1970s; Westinghouse Broadcasting, KYWRadio, Philadelphia, editor in charge of newsroom, early 1980s; free-lance writer. Military service: Israel Defense Forces. **Publications:** The Horsemen (non-fiction), 1974; No Visitors, Please (play), 1970s; The Laughing Man (play), 1970s; Clark Street (play), 1970s; Indecent Proposal (novel), 1988. **Address:** 419 Cherry Hill Blvd., Cherry Hill, NJ 08002, U.S.A.

ENGELHARDT, H(ugo) Tristram, Jr. American, b. 1941. **Genres:** Ethics, Medicine/Health, Philosophy. **Career:** University of Texas Medical Branch at Galveston, assistant professor, 1972-75, associate professor, 1975-77; Georgetown University, School of Foreign Service, faculty, 1977-78, professor of philosophy, professor of health and humanities, Rosemary Kennedy Professor of the Philosophy of Medicine, and senior research scholar at Kennedy Institute of Ethics, all 1977-82; Baylor College of Medicine, Houston, professor of community medicine, 1983-, professor of medical ethics and professor of obstetrics and gynecology, both 1990-2001, professor emeritus, 2001-; Institute of Religion, Houston, adjunct research fellow, 1983-2001; Rice University, professor, 1983-; Centro Oncologico de Excelencia, Buenos Aires, member of consulting medical staff, 1987-94; University of Adelaide, M.S. McLeod Visiting Professor, 1987. Lecturer at colleges and universities in the United States and abroad. **Publications:** Mind-Body, 1973; (trans. with R.M. Zaner) A. Schutz and T. Luckmann, The Structures of the Life-World, 1973; The Foundations of Bioethics, 1986, 2nd ed., 1996; (with B.A. Brody) Bioethics, 1987; Bioethics and Secular Humanism, 1991; The Foundations of Christian Bioethics, 2000. EDITOR AND CONTRIBUTOR: (with S.F. Spicker) Evaluation and Explanation in the Biomedical Sciences, 1975; (with Spicker) Philosophical Dimensions of the Neuro-Medical Sciences, 1976; (with D. Callahan) Science, Ethics, and Medicine, 1976; (with Spicker) Philosophical Medical Ethics, 1977; (with Callahan) Knowledge, Value, and Belief, 1977; The Encyclopedia of Bioethics, 1978; (with Callahan) Morals, Science, and Sociality, 1978; (with Callahan) Knowing and Valuing, 1980; (with J.M. Healey and Spicker) The Law-Medicine Relation, 1981; (with W.B. Bondeson, Spicker, and J.M. White) New Knowledge in the Biomedical Sciences, 1982; (with others) Abortion and the Status of the Fetus, 1983, 2nd ed., 1984; (with R.C. McMillan and Spicker) Euthanasia and the Newborn, 1987; (with Spicker and Bondeson) The Contraceptive Ethos, 1987; (with others) The Use of Human Beings in Research, 1988; (with T. Pinkard) Hegel Reconsidered, 1994. EDITOR WITH OTHERS: Mental Health, 1978; Clinical Judgment, 1979; Mental Illness, 1980; Concepts of Health and Disease, 1981; The Roots of Ethics, 1981; Scientific Controversies, 1987; Sicherheit und Freiheit, 1991. Work represented in anthologies. Contributor to medical and philosophy journals. **Address:** 2802 Lafayette, Houston, TX 77005-3038, U.S.A.

ENGELL, James. American, b. 1951. **Genres:** Education, Literary criticism and history. **Career:** Harvard University, Cambridge, MA, assistant professor, 1978-80, associate professor, 1980-82, Gurney Professor of English and Professor of Comparative Literature, 1983-; writer. Emerson Hospital and Health System, corporator, 1989-94. **Publications:** The Creative Imagination: Enlightenment to Romanticism, 1981; Forming the Critical Mind: Dryden to Coleridge, 1989; Coleridge, The Early Family Letters, 1994; The Committed Word: Literature and Public Values, 1999; Saving Higher Education in the Age of Money, 2005. EDITOR: (with W.J. Bate) Samuel Taylor Coleridge, Biographia Literaria; or, Biographical Sketches of My Literary Life and Opinions, 2 vols, 1983; (and contrib.) Johnson and His Age, 1984; (with D. Perkins, and contrib.) Teaching Literature: What Is Needed Now, 1988. **Address:** Dept of English and American Literature and Language, Barker Center, Harvard University, Cambridge, MA 02138, U.S.A.

ENGELS, John (David). American, b. 1931. **Genres:** Poetry. **Career:** St. Michael's College, Winooski Park, VT, assistant professor, 1962-70, professor of English, 1970-. **Publications:** (with N. Engels) Writing Techniques, 1962; (with N. Engels) Experience and Imagination, 1965; Vivaldi in Early Fall (collection), 1981; Walking to Cootehill, 1992; House and Garden, 2001. POETRY: The Homer Mitchell Place, 1968; Signals from the Safety Coffin, 1975; Vivaldi in Early Fall, 1977; Blood Mountain, 1977; The Seasons in Vermont, 1982; Weather-Fear: New and Selected Poems 1958-1982, 1983; Cardinals in the Ice Age, 1987; Big Water, 1995; Sinking Creek, 1998. EDITOR: The Merrill Guide to William Carlos Williams, 1969; The Merrill Checklist of William Carlos Williams, 1969; The Merrill Studies in Paterson, 1971. **Address:** Dept. of English, St. Michael's College, 1 Winooski Park, Colchester, VT 05439, U.S.A. **Online address:** jengels@smcvt.edu

ENGER, Leif. American, b. 1961. **Genres:** Novels. **Career:** Novelist. Minnesota Public Radio, reporter and producer, 1984-2000. **Publications:** NOVELS. Peace like a River, 2001. WITH LIN ENGER AS L.L. ENGER: Sacrifice, 1993; The Sinners' League: A Gun Pedersen Mystery, 1994; Swing; Comeback; Strike. **Address:** c/o Paul Cirone, Aaron M. Priest Literary Agency, 708 3rd Ave 23rd Fl, New York, NY 10017-4103, U.S.A.

ENGLADE, Ken(neth Francis). American, b. 1938. **Genres:** Criminology/True Crime, Mystery/Crime/Suspense. **Career:** LaFourche Comet (newspaper), Thibodaux, LA, reporter, 1960-63; United Press International, reporter, bureau manager, correspondent, Baton Rouge, LA, 1963-64, New Orleans, LA, 1964-67, Edinburgh, TX, 1967-68, Albuquerque, NM, 1968-71, New York, NY, 1971-72, Saigon, Vietnam, 1972-73, Hong Kong, 197375, and Dallas, TX, 1975-77; freelance writer, 1977-79; Florida Times Union, Georgia capital correspondent 1980-83; freelance writer, 1983-. **Publications:** CRIME NONFICTION: Cellar of Horror, 1989; Murder in Boston, 1990; Beyond Reason: The True Story of a Shocking Double Murder, a Brilliant and Beautiful Virginia Socialite, and a Deadly Psychotic Obsession, c. 1990; Deadly Lessons, 1991; A Family Business, 1992; To Hatred Turned: A

True Story of Love and Death in Texas, c. 1993; Blood Sister, 1994; Hot Blood: The Millionairess, the Money, and the Horse Murders, 1996. NOVELS IN TONY HILLERMAN'S FRONTIER, PEOPLE OF THE PLAINS SERIES: People of the Plains, 1996; The Tribes, 1996; The Soldiers, 1996; Battle Cry, 1997. OTHER: Hoffa (film novelization), c. 1993. **Address:** 3228 Renaissance Dr. SE, Rio Rancho, NM 87124-7934, U.S.A.

ENGLAND, Chris. British, b. 1961. **Genres:** Plays/Screenplays, Sports/Fitness, Travel/Exploration. **Career:** Actor, director, playwright, and author. **Publications:** (with A. Smith) An Evening with Gary Lineker (play), 1992, as TV movie, 1994; (with N. Hancock) What Didn't Happen Next, 1997; Bostock's Cup (TV movie), 1999; Balham to Bollywood, 2002; No More Buddha, Only Football, 2003.

ENGLE, Margarita. American, b. 1951. **Genres:** Novels, Children's fiction, Young adult fiction, Poetry. **Career:** California State Polytechnic University, Pomona, associate professor of agronomy, 1978-82; writer in Clovis, CA. **Publications:** Singing to Cuba, 1993; Skywriting, 1995. Work represented in anthologies. Contributor to literary journals.

ENGLEHART, Bob. (Robert Wayne Englehart, Jr). American, b. 1945. **Genres:** Cartoons. **Career:** Chicago Today, Chicago, IL, staff artist, 1966-72; Fort Wayne Journal Gazette, Fort Wayne, IN, editorial cartoonist, 1972-75; Journal Herald, Dayton, OH, editorial cartoonist, 1975-80; Hartford Courant, Hartford, CT, editorial cartoonist under name Bob Englehart, 1981-. Owner of art studio Englehart and Associates, 1972-75. **Publications:** Never Let the Facts Get in the Way of a Good Cartoon (cartoons), Journal Herald, 1979. A Distinguished Panel of Experts (cartoons), Hartford Courant, 1985. **Address:** Hartford Courant, 285 Broad St, Hartford, CT 06115, U.S.A.

ENGLEMAN, Paul. Also writes as Paul Francis. American, b. 1953. **Genres:** Mystery/Crime/Suspense. **Career:** Playboy (magazine), Chicago, IL, publicity manager, 1977-83, publicity director, 1984-85; writer. **Publications:** Dead in Center Field, 1983; Catch a Fallen Angel, 1986; Murder-in-Law, 1987; Who Shot Longshot Sam?, 1989; (as Paul Francis with D. Clark) Murder on Tour, 1989; The Man with My Name, 1994; Left for Dead, 1995; The Man With My Cat, 2000. **Address:** c/o James Trupin, Jet Literary Associates, Inc., 2570 Camino San Patricio, Santa Fe, NM 87505, U.S.A.

ENGLISH, Barbara (Anne). British, b. 1933. **Genres:** History, Bibliography. **Career:** Lecturer, Sr. Lecturer, Reader, and Professor of History University of Hull, since 1982 (Research Fellow, 1980-82) Archivist, National Register of Archives, West Riding (Northern Section), Yorks., 1958-62; Assistant Ed., Thomas Nelson & Sons Ltd., publrs., Edinburgh, 1962-64. **Publications:** John Company's Last War (in U.S. a The War for a Persian Lady), 1971; The Lords of Holderness, 1980; (co-author) Beverley: An Archaeological and Architectural Study, 1982; (co-author) Strict Settlement: A Guide for Historians, 1983; Yorkshire Enclosure Awards, 1985; The Great Landowners of East Yorkshire, 1990; Royal Historical Society's Annual Bibliography, 1987-92; Yorkshire Hundred and Quo Warranto Rolls, 1996. **Address:** Westwood Close, Beverley, East Yorkshire HU17 8EL, England.

ENGLISH, John A(lan). Canadian, b. 1940. **Genres:** Military/Defense/Arms control. **Career:** Canadian Army, career officer, beginning in 1962; present rank, lieutenant colonel; U.S. Naval War College, Newport, RI, professor of strategy, 1997-. Queen's University, Kingston, Ontario, visiting defense fellow, 1984-85, postdoctoral fellow and assistant professor, 1992-95, adjunct assistant professor, 1995-97; Canadian Land Forces Command and Staff College, directing staff instructor, 1985-86 and 1988-90; International Institute for Strategic Studies, research associate, 199091. **Publications:** A Perspective on Infantry, 1981, as On Infantry, 1984, rev ed (with B.I. Gudmundsson), 1994; (ed. with J. Addicott and P.J. Kramers) The Mechanized Battlefield: A Tactical Analysis, 1984; The Canadian Army and the Normandy Campaign: A Study of Failure in High Command, 1991, as Failure in High Command: The Canadian Army and the Normandy Campaign, 1995; Marching through Chaos: The Descent of Armies in Theory and Practice, 1996; Lament for an Army: The Decline of Canadian Military Professionalism, 1998. Contributor to books. Contributor of articles and reviews to professional journals. **Address:** Strategy and Policy Department, U.S. Naval War College, 686 Cushing Rd., Newport, RI 02841, U.S.A. **Online address:** englishj@nwc.navy.mil

ENGLISH, Lyn D. Australian. **Genres:** Education, Mathematics/Statistics. **Career:** Classroom teacher at state primary schools in Queensland, Australia, 1974-78; Open Access Unit, Brisbane, Australia, mathematics curriculum coordinator, 1979-85; Queensland University of Technology, Brisbane, lecturer, 1982-88, senior lecturer, 1988-92, associate professor, 1992-2000, professor of mathematics education, 2000-, assistant director, Centre for Mathematics and Science Education, 1993-. **Publications:** (with A.R. Baturo) Sunshine Maths, Years 1-7, 1983-85; (with G.S. Halford) Mathematics Education: Models and Processes, 1995. EDITOR: (and contrib.) Mathematical Reasoning: Analogies, Metaphors, and Images, 1998; Handbook of International Research in Mathematics Education, 2002; Mathematical and Analogical Reasoning of Young Learners, forthcoming; (with S. Goodchild) Classroom Research in Mathematics: A Critical Examination of Methodology. Contributor to books and professional journals. **Address:** Queensland University of Technology, Victoria Park Rd, Kelvin Grove, Brisbane, QLD 4059, Australia. **Online address:** L.English@qut.edu.au

ENGS, Ruth C(lifford). American, b. 1939. **Genres:** History, Medicine/Health. **Career:** Dalhousie University, Halifax, NS, assistant professor, 1970; Indiana University-Bloomington, assistant professor, 1973-79, associate professor, 1980-92, professor of applied health science, 1992-. University of Queensland, Brisbane, Australia, visiting professor, 1980. **Publications:** Responsible Alcohol and Drug Use, 1978; Alcohol and Other Drugs: Self Responsibility, 1987; Clean Living Movements: American Cycles of Health Reform, 2000; The Progressive Era's Health Reform Movement: A Historical Dictionary, 2003; The Eugenics Movement: An Encyclopedia, 2005. EDITOR: Controversies in the Addiction Field, 1990; Women: Alcohol and Other Drugs, 1991. Contributor to professional journals. **Address:** IU Research Park, 501 N Morton, Showers Bldg, Ste 101, Indiana University, Bloomington, IN 47404, U.S.A. **Online address:** engs@indiana.edu

ENGSTER, Daniel (Albert). American, b. 1965. **Genres:** Politics/Government. **Career:** Tulane University, New Orleans, LA, visiting professor of political science, 1997-98; University of Texas-San Antonio, assistant professor of political science, 1998-. **Publications:** Divine Sovereignty: The Origins of Modern State Power, 2001. **Address:** Department of Political Science, University of Texas-San Antonio, 6900 North Loop 1604 W., San Antonio, TX 78249, U.S.A.

ENGSTROM, Elizabeth. American, b. 1951. **Genres:** Mystery/Crime/Suspense. **Career:** Suspense writer, 1984-; writing instructor, 1990-; director of Maui Writers School Department of Continuing Education. **Publications:** NOVELS: When Darkness Loves Us, 1985; Black Ambrosia, 1988; Lizzie Borden, 1991; Lizard Wine, 1995; Black Leather, 2003. SHORT STORIES: Nightmare Flower, 1992; The Alchemy of Love, 1998; Suspicions, 2002. **Address:** 598 Brookside Dr, Eugene, OR 97405, U.S.A. **Online address:** liz@elizabethengstrom.com

ENNALS, Peter. Canadian, b. 1943. **Genres:** Architecture, Geography, Local history/Rural topics. **Career:** Queen's University, Kingston, ON, Canada, lecturer in geography, 1972-74; Mount Allison University, Sackville, NB, Canada, member of geography faculty, 1974-, vicepresident for academics and research, 1998-2002. Kwansei Gakuin University, Japan, visiting professor of Canadian studies. **Publications:** Homeplace: The Making of the Canadian Dwelling over Three Centuries, 1998. Contributor to scholarly journals. **Address:** Department of Geography, Mount Allison University, 144 Main St, Sackville, NB, Canada E4L 1A7. **Online address:** pennals@mta.ca

ENNULAT, Egbert M. American (born Germany), b. 1929. **Genres:** Art/Art history, Music. **Career:** Musician, teacher, and writer. Methodist College, Frankfurt am Main, Germany, and Jugendmusikschule, Frankfurt, teacher, ending 1961; Oberlin College, OH, instructor, 1963-64; College of Wooster, OH, instructor, 1964-65; University of Georgia, Athens, assistant professor, 1965-72, associate professor, 1972-79, professor of music, 1979-2000, Josiah Meigs Professor, 1994-2000, professor emeritus, 2000-. Sandy Beaver Professor for Excellence in Teaching, 1988-91. Guest professor at University of Erlangen-Nuremberg, Germany, 1978, Keimyung University, Korea, 1982, and State University Port Alegre, Brazil, 1994. Music performer in concert, on recordings, and television and radio programs worldwide. **Publications:** EDITOR: Arnold Schoenberg Correspondence: A Collection of Translated and Annotated Letters with Guido Adler, Pablo Casals, Emanuel Feuermann, and Olin Downes, 1991; Collected Works by Johann Fossa. Contributor to musical periodicals.

ENQUIST, Per Olov. Swedish, b. 1934. **Genres:** Novels, Novellas/Short stories, Plays/Screenplays. **Career:** Uppsala, Sweden Nya Tidning, literary and theater critic, 1960-63; Svenska Dagbladet, literary and theater critic, 1966-67; Expressen, literary and theater critic, 1967-. University of California at Los Angeles, visiting professor, 1973. **Publications:** FICTION: Kristallögat (title means: The Crystal Eye), 1961; Färdvägen (title means: The Route), 1963; (with T. Ekbom and P. Husberg) Broderna Casey (title means: The Casey Brothers), 1964; Magnetisörens femte vinter, 1964, trans. by P.B. Austei

as The Magnetist's Fifth Winter, 1989; Hess, 1966; Legionärerna, 1968, trans. by A. Blair as The Legionnaires: A Documentary Novel, 1973; Sekonden, 1971; Berättelser fran de inställda upprorens tid (stories; title means: Tales from the Age of Cancelled Rebellions), 1974; Musikanternas uttag, 1978, trans. by J. Tate as The March of the Musicians, 1985; (with A. Ehnmark) Doktor Mabuses nya testamente (title means: Dr. Mabuse's New Will), 1982; Nedstörtad ängel: en kärleksroman, 1985, trans. by A. Paterson as Downfall: A Love Story, 1986; (with Ehnmark) Protagoras sats: pa spaning efter det politiska förnuftet (title means: Protagora's Theory: On the Hunt for Political Sense), 1987; Kapten Nemos bibliotek, 1991, trans. by Paterson as Captain Nemo's Library, 1992; Kartritarna, 1992; Livläkarens besok, 1999. PLAYS: Tribadernas natt, 1975, trans. by R. Shideler as The Night of the Tribades, 1977; 1977; (with Ehnmark) Chez nous: bilder fran svenskt församlingsliv (title means: Chez Nous: Pictures from Swedish Community Life), 1976; (with Ehnmark) Mannen pa trottoaren (title means: Man on the Pavement), 1979; Till Fedra (title means: To Phaedra), 1980; Fran regnormarnas liv, 1981, trans. as The Rain Snakes; En triptyk, 1981; I lodjurets timma, 1988, trans. by Shideler as The Hour of the Lynx, 1990; Tre pjäser, 1994; Bildmakarna (title means: The Picture Makers), 1998; Systrarna (title means: Sisters), 2000. OTHER: (ed.) Sextiotalskritik: en antologi (title means: Criticism of the Sixties: An Anthology), 1966; De misstolkade legionärerna (nonfiction), 1970; Katedralen i München och andra berättelser (stories; title means: The Cathedral in Munich and Other Stories), 1972; Strindberg-ett liv (television screenplay, title means: Strindberg-A Life), 1984; Mannen i baten (title means: Man in the Boat), 1985; Tva reportage om idrott (title means: Two Report on Sport), 1986; Hamsun: en fortaelling (film script), 1996; Jakten pa den forlorade själen, 1997. Enquist's writings have been translated into more than twenty languages. **Address:** c/o Norstedts Forlag, Box 2052, 103 12 Stockholm 2, Sweden.

ENRIQUEZ DE SALAMANCA, Cristina. Spanish, b. 1952. **Genres:** Bibliography, Literary criticism and history. **Career:** Law office of Rafael Burgos, Madrid, Spain, associate, 1976-77; law office of Jaime Miralles and Manuel Miralles, Madrid, Spain, partner, 1978-79; U.S. Federal Government, Fort Macoy, WI, bilingual interpreter, 1980; Hata Reservations Inc., Madison, WI, bilingual interpreter, 1980-82; Institutos Eurocentres Barcelona, Barcelona, Spain, teacher of Spanish as a second language, 1983, 1984, 1992-94; Universidad Autonoma de Barcelona, Barcelona, independent research associate at Women's Studies Center, 198488; Sanyo Spain, Spain, teacher of Spanish for foreign employees, 1984-85; Yale University, New Haven, CT, visiting assistant professor of Spanish and Portuguese, 1995-96; Middlebury College, Middlebury, VT, professor of Spanish, 1996; University of California, San Diego, lecturer in Spanish literature, 1996-. **Publications:** EDITOR: (with K. McNerney) Double Minorities of Spain: A Bio-Bibliographical Guide to Women Writers of Catalonia, Galicia, and the Basque Country, 1994; (with C. Jagoe and A. Blanco and contrib.) La mujer en los discursos de genero del siglo XIX: Textos y contextos, 1997. Contributor to books. Contributor of articles and reviews to periodicals. Translator of books from English into Spanish. **Address:** Marmella 4-6, Atico 2-A, 08023 Barcelona, Spain.

ENSLIN, Theodore (Vernon). American, b. 1925. **Genres:** Poetry. **Career:** Author, poet. **Publications:** The Work Proposed, 1958; New Sharon's Prospect, 1962; The Place Where I Am Standing, 1964; This Do (and The Talents), 1966; New Sharon's Prospect and Journals, 1966; To Come to Have Become, 1966; The Four Temperaments, 1966; Characters in Certain Places, 1967; The Diabelli Variations and Other Poems, 1967; 2/30-6/31; Poems 1967, 1967; Agreement and Back: Sequences, 1969; The Poems, 1970; Forms, 4 vols., 1970-73; Views 1-7, 1970; The Country of Our Consciousness, 1977; Etudes, 1972; Views, 1973; Sitio, 1973; In the Keepers House, 1973; With Light Reflected, 1973; The Swamp Fox, 1974; The Mornings, 1974; Fever Poems, 1974; The Last Days of October, 1974; The Median Flow: Poems 1943-1973, 1974; Synthesis 1-24, 1975; Mahler, 1975; Landler, 1975; Papers, 1976; The July Book, 1976; Ranger, 2 vols., 1979-81; Markings, 1983; Music for Several Occasions, 1985; The Waking of the Eye, 1986; The Weather Within, 1986; Case Book, 1987; Little Wandering Flake of Snow, 1990; Love and Science, 1991; Gamma Ut, 1992; From near the Great Pine, 1993; Communitas, 1995; Propositions for John Taggart, 1996; Thumbprint on Landscape, 1998; Then, and Now, 1999; Sequentiae, 1999; The Roads around Jenkins, 2000; Ring, 2001; Keep Sake, 2001; In Tandem, 2003. **Address:** 379 Kansas Rd, Milbridge, ME 04658, U.S.A.

ENSLOW, Sam. American, b. 1946. **Genres:** Plays/Screenplays, Art/Art history, History, Archaeology/Antiquities, Travel/Exploration. **Career:** ITT Sheraton Corp. of America, held management positions in Washington, DC, and New York City, 1968-73; Green Retreat Nursery, Fort Lauderdale, FL, owner and operator, 1974-80; independent arts consultant and appraiser,

1980-International representative, Dagmar, Inc., Bogata, Colombia, 1979-86; La Ventana (ranch in Puerto Carreño, Colombia), general partner, 1980-90. Coordinator of a special field school for Northern Virginia Community College and Fort Lauderdale's Museum of Archaeology, 1989; leader of study group to the Middle Orinoco on the border of Colombia and Venezuela, 1989-. International Executive Service Corps, volunteer, 1991; Royal Geographical Society, fellow, 1990; Broward County Archaeological Society, president, chairman, 1991-94. **Publications:** (with F. Smith and G. Graves) Romancing the Gold: Pre-Columbian Ceramics and Gold from Private Collections, 1986; The Art of Prehispanic Colombia: An Illustrated Cultural and Historical Survey, 1990; Prehistoric Florida (script), 1992; Anna's Journey (script). Contributor to periodicals including Georgian and Russian publications. **Address:** 5449 NE Fifth Ave, Fort Lauderdale, FL 33334, U.S.A. **Online address:** a004915t@bc.setlin.org

ENSMINGER, Peter A. American, b. 1957. **Genres:** Biology, Botany, Medicine/Health, Natural history. **Career:** Research associate at universities, including Syracuse University, Freiburg University, and Cornell University, until 1994; medical consultant, writer, and editor, 1994-. **Publications:** Life under the Sun, 2001. **Address:** 256 Greenwood Pl, Syracuse, NY 13210, U.S.A.

ENSOR, Robert. American, b. 1922. **Genres:** Children's fiction, Illustrations. **Career:** Engineer, writer. Barnes Engineering Company, Stamford, CT, head of field research special instrument section, 1952-85. Marshall Point Lighthouse Museum, director, 1990-97. **Publications:** SELF-ILLUSTRATED FOR CHILDREN: Nellie the Lighthouse Dog, 1993; Nellie the Flying Instructor, 1995; Good Golly Miss Molly and the 4th of July Parade, 1997. **Address:** Marshall Pt. Rd., PO Box 269, Port Clyde, ME 04855, U.S.A.

ENYEART, James L. American, b. 1943. **Genres:** Photography. **Career:** Albrecht Gallery of Art, St. Joseph, MO, charter director, 1967-68; University of Kansas, Lawrence, associate professor, Dept of Art History, Spencer Museum of Art, curator of photography, 1969-76; Friends of Photography, Carmel, CA, executive director, 1976-77; University of Arizona, Tucson, ed., The Archive, director, Centre for Creative Photography, and adjunct professor of art, 1977-89; Intl. Museum of Photography and Film, George Eastman House, Rochester, NY, Image, ed., and director, 1989-95; College of Santa Fe, Marion Center, director, 1995-2003, Anne and John Marion Professor of Photographic Arts, 1995-. **Publications:** Francis Bruguiere, 1977; George Fiske, Yosemite Photographer, 1980; Photography of the Fifties: An American Perspective, 1980; Heinecken, 1980; W. Eugene Smith: Master of the Photographic Essay, 1981; Jerry Uelsmann: 25 Years, A Retrospective, 1982; Aaron Siskind: Terrors and Pleasures 1931-1980, 1982; (with R.D. Monroe and P. Stoker) Three Classic American Photographs: Texts and Contexts, 1982; (with others) Edward Weston Omnibus, 1984; Edward Weston's California Landscapes, 1984; (co-author) Henry Holmes Smith: Collected Writings 1935-1985, 1986; Judy Dater: 20 Years, 1986; Andreas Feininger: A Retrospective, 1986; Decade by Decade, 1989; Ansel Adams in Color, 1994; Tarnished Silver, 1996; Land, Sky, and All That Is Within, 1998; Photographers, Writers and the American Scene, 2002; Harmony of Reflected Light: Photography of Arthur Wesley Dow. EDITOR: Kansas Album, 1977. CATALOGS: Karsh, 1970; Kansas Landscape, 1971; Invisible in America, 1973; Language of Light, 1974; No Mountains in the Way, 1975. Contributor to books and periodicals. **Address:** 46 Bonanza Trail, Santa Fe, NM 87505, U.S.A. **Online address:** enyeartcsf@cnsp.com

EOYANG, Eugene Chen. American (born Hong Kong), b. 1939. **Genres:** Literary criticism and history, Translations. **Career:** Doubleday and Co., NYC, editorial trainee, 1960-61, editor of Anchor Books, 1961-66; Indiana University-Bloomington, lecturer, 1969-71, assistant professor, 1971-74, associate professor, 1974-78, professor of comparative literature, 1978-, associate dean of research and graduate development, 1977-80, chair of Department of East Asian Languages and Cultures, 1982-84, resident and founding director, East Asian Summer Language Institute, 1984-89; Lingnan College (University), Hong Kong, chair/professor of English, 1996-. University of Illinois at Urbana-Champaign, visiting professor, 1987; Royal Society or the Promotion of Arts, Merchandise, and Commerce, fellow; lecturer at colleges and universities. **Publications:** The Transparent Eye: Translation, Chinese Literature, and Comparative Poetics, 1993; Coat of Many Colors: Reflections on Diversity by a Minority of One, 1995; Borrowed Plumage: Polemical Essays on Translation, 2003. EDITOR: (and trans., and author of intro. and notes) Ai Qing: Selected Poems, 1982; (regional ed. for China) HarperCollins World Reader; (co-) Translating Chinese Literature.

EPANOMITIS, Fotini. Australian, b. 1969. **Genres:** Novels. **Career:** Writer. University of Canberra, Australia, writer-in-residence, 1996;. **Publications:**

The Mule's Foal, 1993. **Address:** c/o Allen & Unwin, 9 Atchison St., PO Box 8500, St. Leonards, Sydney, NSW 2065, Australia.

EPHRON, Delia. Also writes as Delia Brock. American, b. 1944. **Genres:** Children's fiction, Children's non-fiction. **Career:** New York magazine, NYC, writer, 1975-78; writer. **Publications:** How to Eat Like a Child, and Other Lessons in not Being a Grown-up, 1978; Teenage Romance: Or How to Die of Embarrassment, 1981; Santa and Alex, 1983; Funny Sauce: Us, The Ex, the Ex's New Mate, the New Mate's Ex & the Kids, 1986; Do I Have to Say Hello?, 1988; The Girl Who Changed the World, 1993; Hanging Up, 1995; Big City Eyes, 2000. SCREENPLAYS: (with N. Ephron) This Is My Life (adaptation), 1990; (with N. Ephron) Mixed Nuts, 1994; (with N. Ephron, P. Dexter, and J. Quinlan) Michael, 1996; (with N. Ephron) You've Got Mail, 1998; (with N. Ephron) Hanging Up, 2000. WITH L. BODGER: (as Delia Brock) The Adventurous Crocheter, 1972; (as Delia Brock) Gladrags, 1975; Crafts for All Seasons, 1980. **Address:** c/o Lynn Nesbit, Janklow & Nesbit Associates, 445 Park Ave., Fl 13, New York, NY 10022, U.S.A.

EPHRON, Nora. American, b. 1941. **Genres:** Novels, Plays/Screenplays. **Career:** New York Post, reporter, 1963-68; free-lance journalist, 1968-72; Esquire magazine, columnist and contrib. ed., 1972-73, senior ed. and columnist, 1974-76; New York magazine, contrib. ed., 1973-74; author and screenwriter. **Publications:** Wallflower at the Orgy (articles), 1970; Crazy Salad: Some Things about Women (articles), 1975; Perfect Gentleman (television movie), 1978; Scribble, Scribble: Notes on the Media (columns), 1979; Heartburn (novel), 1983; (with D. Ephron) This Is My Life, 1992. SCREENPLAYS: Heartburn, 1986; (with A. Arlen) Silkwood, 1983; When Harry Met Sally, 1989; (with A. Arlen) Cookie, 1989; My Blue Heaven, 1990; (with J. Arch and D.S. Ward and director) Sleepless in Seattle, 1993; (with D. Ephron and director) Mixed Nuts, 1994; (with D. Ephron and director) Michael, 1996. **Address:** c/o Sam Cohn, International Creative Management, 40 West 57th St., New York, NY 10019, U.S.A.

EPPLE, Anne Orth. American, b. 1927. **Genres:** Children's non-fiction, Crafts, Natural history, Botany. **Publications:** Nature Quiz Book, 1955; Modern Science Quiz Book, 1958; The Beginning Knowledge Book of Ants, 1969; The Beginning Knowledge Book of Fossils, 1969; The Lookalikes, 1971; Nature Crafts, 1974; Something from Nothing Crafts, 1976; The Amphibians of New England, 1983; A Field Guide to the Plants of Arizona, 1995. **Address:** 1927 Leisure World, Mesa, AZ 85206, U.S.A. **Online address:** lepple@aol.com

EPPS, Bradley S. American, b. 1958. **Genres:** Literary criticism and history. **Career:** Emory University, Atlanta, GA, assistant professor, 1989-91; Harvard University, assistant professor to professor of Romance languages and literatures, 1991-, John L. Loeb Professor of Humanities, 1996-98; guest lecturer at colleges and universities. **Publications:** Significant Violence: Oppression and Resistance in the Narratives of Juan Goytisolo, 1970-1990, 1996. Contributor to books. Contributor of articles and reviews to periodicals. **Address:** 401 Marlborough, Boston, MA 02115-1501, U.S.A. **Online address:** bsepps@fas.harvard.edu

EPSHTEIN, Mikhail N. *See* **EPSTEIN, Mikhail N.**

EPSTEIN, Eric Joseph. American, b. 1959. **Genres:** Reference. **Career:** Tri-County OIC, Harrisburg, PA, lead instructor and adult basic education instructor at Loysville Secure Treatment Unit, State Correctional Institute-Camp Hill, and Dauphin County Prison, 1985-. Pennsylvania State University, visiting assistant professor of humanities in Harrisburg and Middletown, 1992-. Certified corrections officer, Pennsylvania Department of Corrections, 1989; certified in solid-waste recycling management, Pennsylvania State University, 1990. Speaker on the Holocaust and on nuclear power issues. **Publications:** (co-author) Dictionary of the Holocaust: Biography, Geography, and Terminology, 1997. **Address:** 4100 Hillsdale Rd, Harrisburg, PA 17112-1419, U.S.A. **Online address:** eepstein@igc.apc.org

EPSTEIN, Joseph. American, b. 1937. **Genres:** Social commentary, Essays. **Career:** Northwestern University, Evanston, IL, visiting lecturer in literature and writing, 1974-2003; American Scholar, Washington, DC, editor, 1975-. **Publications:** Divorced in America: Marriage in an Age of Possibility, 1974; Familiar Territory: Observations on American Life, 1979; Ambition: The Secret Passion, 1980; (ed.) Masters: Portraits of Great Teachers, 1981; The Middle of My Tether: Familiar Essays, 1983; Plausible Prejudices: Essays on American Writing, 1985; Once More around the Block: Familiar Essays, 1987; Partial Payments: Essays Arising from the Pleasures of Reading, 1989; The Goldin Boys & Other Stories, 1992; With My Trousers Rolled, 1993; Pertinent Players, 1995; Life Sentences, 1997; Narcissus Leaves the Pool,

1999; Snobbery, 2002; Fabulous Small Jews (stories), 2003; Envy, 2004. **Address:** American Scholar, United Chapters of Phi Beta Kappa, 1811 Q St NW, Washington, DC 20009, U.S.A. **Online address:** j.epstein@northwestern.edu

EPSTEIN, Lawrence J(effrey). American, b. 1946. **Genres:** Popular Culture. **Career:** Suffolk Community College, Selden, NY, professor of English, 1974-, chairperson of Humanities Division, 1985-90. District representative to U.S. Congressman William Carney, 1982-86. President of Suffolk Division of the American Jewish Congress, 1980-86. **Publications:** Samuel Goldwyn, 1981; Zion's Call, 1984; A Treasury of Jewish Anecdotes, 1989; A Treasury of Jewish Inspirational Stories, 1993; The Haunted Smile: The Story of Jewish Comedians in America, 2001. **Address:** English Department, Suffolk Community College, 533 College Rd, Selden, NY 11784, U.S.A.

EPSTEIN, Leslie (Donald). American, b. 1938. **Genres:** Novels. **Career:** Queens College, City University of New York, Flushing, professor of English, 1965-78; Boston University, director of Graduate Creative Writing Program, 1978-. **Publications:** NOVELS: P.D. Kmerakov, 1975; King of the Jews (in U.K. as The Elder), 1979; Regina, 1982; Pinto and Sons, 1990; Pandaemonium, 1997; Ice Fire Water, 1999; San Remo Drive, 2003. OTHER: Steinway Quintet Plus Four (stories), 1976; Stanley the Starfish, 1980; Goldkorn Tales (novellas), 1985. **Address:** 23 Parkman St, Brookline, MA 02446, U.S.A. **Online address:** lesliep@bu.edu

EPSTEIN, Mikhail N. Also writes as Mikhail N. Epshtein. American (born Russia), b. 1950. **Genres:** Cultural/Ethnic topics, Literary criticism and history, Philosophy, Essays. **Career:** Wesleyan University, Middletown, CT, visiting professor, 1990; Emory University, Atlanta, GA, asst professor, 1990-95, associate professor, 1995-2000, Samuel Candler Dobbs Professor of Cultural Theory and Russian Literature, 2000-. World Literature Institute of the Academy of Sciences of the USSR, researcher, 1973-78; director of interdisciplinary Image and Thought Association, Moscow, 1986-88; Experimental Center of Creativity, director of the Laboratory of Contemporary Culture, Moscow, 1988-90. **Publications:** Novoe v klassike, Derzhavin, Pushkin, Blok v sovremennom vospriiatii (title means: The Classics Renovated: Derzhavin, Pushkin, and Blok in Contemporary Perception), 1982; Paradoksy novizny (title means: The Paradoxes of Innovation), 1988; Priroda, mir, tainik vselennoi… (title means: Nature, the World, the Mystery of the Universe…), 1990; Relativistic Patterns in Totalitarian Thinking, 1991; Ottsovstvo (title means: Fatherhood), 1992; Novoe sektantstvo (title means: New Sectarianism), 1993; Velikaia Sov (title means: Great Soviet Land), 1994; Vera i obraz (title means: Faith and Image), 1994; Na granitsakh kul'tur (title means: On the Borders of Cultures), 1995; After the Future: The Paradoxes of Postmodernism and Contemporary Russian Culture, 1995; Bog detalie (title means: A Deity of Details), 1997, 2nd ed., 1998; (with A. Genis and S. Vladiv-Glover) Russian Postmodernism, 1999; (with E. Berry) Transcultural Experiments, 1999; Postmodern v Rossii (title means: The Postmodern in Russia), 2000; Filosofice zozarozuogo (title means: The Philosophy of the Possible), 2001. Contributor to books and periodicals. **Address:** Emory University, REALC, 1707 N Decatur Rd, Atlanta, GA 30322, U.S.A. **Online address:** russmae@emory.edu

EPSTEIN, Rachel S. American, b. 1941. **Genres:** Documentaries/Reportage. **Career:** J. C. Penney, NYC, training writer, 1981-84; International Council of Shopping Centers, NYC, writer, 1984-94; New York Observer, NYC, shopping columnist, 1989-94. **Publications:** (with N. Liebman) BizSpeak, 1986; Alternative Investments, 1988; Careers in the Investment World, 1988; Investment Banking, 1988; Investments and the Law, 1988; Careers in Health Care, 1989; Eating Habits and Disorders, 1990; Anne Frank, 1997. **Address:** c/o Robin Straus, 229 East 79th St., New York, NY 10021, U.S.A.

EPSTEIN, Richard A(llen). American, b. 1943. **Genres:** Law. **Career:** Admitted to the bar of California, 1969; University of California School of Law, Los Angeles, assistant professor, 1968-70, associate professor, 1970-73; University of Chicago Law School, visiting associate professor, 1972-73, professor, 1973-82, James Parker Hall professor, 1982-88, James Parker Hall Distinguished Service professor of law, 1988-. **Publications:** NONFICTION: (with C.O. Gregory and H. Kalven, Jr.; sole revisor of 5th and 6th eds) Cases and Materials on Torts, 1977, 6th ed., 1995; Modern Products Liability Law: A Legal Revolution, 1980; A Theory of Strict Liability: Toward a Reformulation of Tort Law, c. 1980; Takings: Private Property and the Power of Eminent Domain, 1985; Forbidden Grounds: The Case Against Employment Discrimination Laws, 1992; Bargaining with the State, c. 1993; Simple Rules for a Complex World, 1995; Mortal Peril: Our Inalienable Right to Health Care, 1997. EDITOR: (with J. Paul) Labor Law and the Employment Market:

Foundations and Applications, 1985; (with G.R. Stone and C.R. Sunstein) The Bill of Rights in the Modern State, 1992. Contributor to periodicals. **Address:** University of Chicago Law School, 1111 East 60th St., Chicago, IL 60637, U.S.A.

EPSTEIN, Robert M(orris). American, b. 1948. **Genres:** Military/Defense/Arms control. **Career:** Substitute teacher at elementary and secondary schools in Philadelphia, PA, 1973; Community College of Philadelphia, Philadelphia, instructor in history, 1978-80; U.S. Army Command and General Staff College, Fort Leavenworth, KS, associate professor, 1981-84, professor of history, 1984-. Drexel University, instructor, 1979; University of Kansas, adjunct professor, 1995-; speaker at colleges and universities. **Publications:** Prince Eugene at War, 1809, 1984; Napoleon's Last Victory and the Emergence of Modern War, 1994. Contributor to books. Contributor of articles and reviews to history and military studies journals. **Address:** School of Advanced Military Studies, U.S. Army Command and General Staff College, Fort Leavenworth, KS 66027, U.S.A.

EPSTEIN, Seymour. American, b. 1917. **Genres:** Novels. **Career:** Professor Emeritus, University of Denver, Colorado. **Publications:** Pillar of Salt, 1960; The Successor, 1961; Leah, 1964; A Penny for Charity, 1964; Caught in That Music, 1967; The Dream Museum, 1971; Looking for Fred Schmidt, 1973; Love Affair, 1979; A Special Destiny, 1986; September Faces, 1987; Light, 1989. **Address:** 480 S. Marion Parkway #901A, Denver, CO 80209, U.S.A. **Online address:** Contemplit@aol.com

EPSTEIN, Stephan R. American, b. 1960. **Genres:** Economics, Politics/Government. **Career:** University of London, London School of Economics and Political Science, London, England, Reader in Economic History. Research Fellow, Trinity College, Cambridge. **Publications:** Alle origini, della fattoria toscana, 1986; An Island for Itself, 1992; Potere e mercati nella Sicilia medievale, 1995; Freedom and Growth, 1999. **Address:** Department of Economic History, London School of Economics and Political Science, University of London, London WC2A 2AE, England.

ERDRICH, Louise. American, b. 1954. **Genres:** Novels, Poetry. **Career:** Writer. **Publications:** Jacklight (poems), 1984; Love Medicine, 1984 (National Book Critics Award); The Beet Queen, 1986; Tracks, 1988; Baptism of Desire (poems), 1989; (with M. Dorris) Route Two, 1990; (with M. Dorris) The Crown of Columbus (novel), 1991; The Bingo Palace, 1994; The Falcon: A Narrative of the Captivity and Adventures of John Tanner, 1994; The Bluejay's Dance, 1995; Tales of Burning Love, 1996; Grandmother's Pigeon, 1996; The Antelope Wife, 1998; The Birchbark House, 1999; Last Report on the Miracles at Little No Horse, 2001; The Master Butchers Singing Club, 2003; Books and Islands in Ojibwe County, 2003; Four Souls, 2004; The Painted Drum, 2005. **Address:** c/o Wylie Agency, 250 W 57th St Ste 2114, New York, NY 10107-2199, U.S.A.

EREIRA, Alan. British, b. 1943. **Genres:** Anthropology/Ethnology, History. **Career:** British Broadcasting Corporation, London, England, producer, 1965-96; Sunstone Films Ltd, director, 1996-. Founder, Tairona Heritage Trust, London, 1991-. **Publications:** The People's England, 1981; The Invergordon Mutiny, 1981; The Heart of the World, 1990, as The Elder Brothers: A Lost South American People and Their Message about the Fate of the Earth, 1992; (with T. Jones) Crusades, 1995; (with T. Jones) Terry Jones' Medieval Lives, 2004. **Address:** 90 Summerlee Ave, London N2 9QH, England.

ERHARD, Tom. American, b. 1923. **Genres:** Novels, Plays/Screenplays, Literary criticism and history. **Career:** Albuquerque Public Schools, New Mexico, Information Director, 1953-57; National Education Association, Washington, DC, Assistant Director, for Press and Radio, 1957-58; New Mexico State University, Las Cruces, Professor of English and Drama, 1960-99, Emeritus, 1999-. **Publications:** For the Love of Pete, 1954; The High White Star, 1957; Rocket in His Pocket, 1960, 1964; The Electronovac Gasser, 1963; A Wild Fight for Spring, 1966; In Search of Leaders, 1967; Stress and Campus Response, 1968; The Agony and Promise, 1969; The Cataclysmic Loves of Cooper and Looper and Their Friend Who Was Squashed by a Moving Van, 1969; The Troubled Campus, 1970; Lynn Riggs: Southwestern Playwright, 1970; The New Decade, 1971; 900 Plays: A Synopsis-History of American Theatre, 1978; Pomp and Circumstances, 1982; I Saved a Winter Just for You, 1984; A Merry Medieval Christmas, 1985; Laughing Once More, 1986.

ERICKSON, Betty J(ean). American, b. 1923. **Genres:** Children's fiction, Children's non-fiction, Education. **Career:** Educator and writer. Master teacher at public schools in Stockton, CA, and Alhambra, CA, 1945-51;

Mills College, demonstration teacher, summers, 1947-51, teaching fellow, 1951-52; elementary teacher, Bellevue, NE, 1966-68; Prince William County Schools, VA, Title I teacher, reading specialist, Reading Recovery Teacher, 1968-94; Springwoods Elementary School, Woodbridge, VA, reading specialist, 1994-. **Publications:** Oh, No, Sherman!, 1996; Play Ball, Sherman!, 1996; Use Your Beak, 1998; Big Bad Rex, 1998; Where's the Snow?, 1998; Look in My Book, 1998; Sherman, 1999; The Little Rabbit Who Wanted Red Wings (retelling), 2000; In Search of Something Delicious, 2003; Why Do Worms Come up When It Rains?, 2003; Sherman's Lost and Found, 2004; Sherman in the Talent Show, 2004. Contributor to periodicals. **Address:** 14611 Anderson St, Woodbridge, VA 22193-1213, U.S.A. **Online address:** BettyEri@comcast.net

ERICKSON, Carolly. American, b. 1943. **Genres:** Biography. **Career:** six years as a college professor, then to a career as a full-time writer. **Publications:** Medieval Vision (essays), 1976; Civilization and Society in the West, 1978; Our Tempestuous Day, 1986; Arc of the Sorrow, 1998. BIOGRAPHIES: Bloody Mary, 1978; Great Harry, 1980; The First Elizabeth, 1983; Mistress Anne, 1984; Bonnie Prince Charlie, 1989; To the Scaffold, 1991; Great Catherine, 1994; Her Little Majesty, 1997; Josephine, 1999; Alexandra, 2001; The Girl from Botany Bay, 2004; Lillibet, 2004. EDITOR: Records of Medieval Europe, 1971. **Address:** St. Martin's Press, Attn: Publicity Dept, 175 Fifth Avenue, New York, NY 10010, U.S.A.

ERICKSON, Charlotte J(oanne). American, b. 1923. **Genres:** History. **Career:** Instructor, Vassar College, Poughkeepsie, New York, 1950-52; Research Fellow, National Institute of Economic and Social Research, 1952-55; Assistant Lecturer, 1955-58, Lecturer, 1958-66, Sr. Lecturer, 1966-75, Reader, 1975-79, and Professor of Economic History, 1979-82, London School of Economics; Paul Mellon Professor of American History, 1983-90, and Professor Emerita, 1990-, Cambridge University. MacArthur Prize Fellow, 1990-95. **Publications:** American Industry and the European Immigrant, 1860-1885, 1957, 1969; British Industrialists, Steel and Hosiery 1850-1950, 1958, 1986; Invisible Immigrants, 1972, rev. ed., 1990; Emigration from Europe 1815-1914, 1976; Leaving England: Essays on British Emigration, 1994. **Address:** 8 High St, Chesterton, Cambridge CB4 1NG, England.

ERICKSON, Darlene (E.) Williams. American, b. 1941. **Genres:** Literary criticism and history. **Career:** Central Ohio Technical College, Newark, 1980-82, coordinator of gifted programs, 1984-89; Ohio State University-Newark, instructor, 1988; Ohio Dominican College, Columbus, professor, 1989-, chair of Freshman Year Experience, 1990-91; chair of Faculty Development Committee, 1991-92, chair of department of English, 1991-98, coordinator of Council of Independent Colleges grant, 1992-99. Miami University, teaching fellow, 1985-86; Ashland-Otterbein College, adjunct professor, 1987-88. **Publications:** Illusion Is More Precise than Precision: The Poetry of Marianne Moore, 1992. Reviewer for periodicals. **Address:** Ohio Dominican College, 1216 Sunbury Rd, Rm 226 Erskine Hall, Columbus, OH 43219, U.S.A. **Online address:** ericksod@odc.edu

ERICKSON, Hal. American, b. 1950. **Genres:** Communications/Media, Film. **Career:** Great American Children's Theatre, Milwaukee, WI, actor, lecturer, and author of "in-school" touring program, 1978-84; writer, 1985-. Aldrich Chemical Co., customer service assistant, 1987-94; All-Music and Video Guide, contributing writer/editor, 1994-. Actor with Milwaukee Opera Company, Milwaukee Repertory Theater, and summer stock productions in West Virginia and Arkansas. **Publications:** Syndicated Television: The First Forty Years, 1947-1987, 1989; Baseball in the Movies: A Comprehensive Reference, 1915-1991, 1992; Religious Radio and Television in the United States, 1921-1991: The Programs and Personalities, 1992; Television Cartoon Shows: An Illustrated Encyclopedia, 1949-1993, 1995; Sid and Marty Krofft: A Critical Study of Saturday Morning Children's Television, 1969-93, 1998; "From Beautiful Downtown Burbank": A Critical History of Rowan and Martin's Laugh-In, 1968-73; The Baseball Filmography 1915-2001, 2002. Contributor to encyclopedias. **Address:** 6731 W Moltke Ave, Milwaukee, WI 53210, U.S.A. **Online address:** hle3@execpc.com

ERICKSON, Raymond (F.). American, b. 1941. **Genres:** Music. **Career:** Yale University, New Haven, CT, acting instructor in music, 1968-70; International Business Machines (IBM) Systems Research Institute, NYC, research fellow, 1970-71; Queens College of the City University of New York, Flushing, NY, assistant professor, 1971-75, associate professor, 1975-81, professor of music, 1981-, department head, 197881, appointed director of Aaron Copland School of Music, 1981, dean of faculty of arts and humanities, 1993-, and past member of board of directors of Godwin-Ternbach Museum. Aston Magna Foundation for Music and the Humanities Inc., academy director and lecturer, 1978-, and past member of board of directors.

Yale University, associate fellow of Pierson College, 1972-; State University of New York at Binghamton, adjunct professor at Watson School of Engineering, 1983-87; lecturer at colleges and universities. Concert pianist and harpsichordist; consultant to Library of Congress. **Publications:** DARMS: A Reference Manual, 1976; (trans. and author of intro) C.V. Palisca, editor, "Musica Enchiriadis" and "Scolica Enchiriadis," 1995; (ed. and author of intro) Schubert's Vienna: Viennese Culture in the Reign of Francis I (1792-1835), 1997. Contributor to books. Contributor of articles and reviews to academic journals. **Address:** 76 Laight St. No. 1, New York, NY 10013, U.S.A. **Online address:** raymond_erickson@qc.edu

ERICKSON, Steve. American, b. 1950. **Genres:** Novels. **Publications:** Days Between Stations, 1985; Rubicon Beach, 1986; Tours of the Black Clock, 1989; Leap Year, 1989; Arc d'X, 1993; Amnesiascope, 1996; American Nomad, 1997; The Sea Came in at Midnight, 1999. **Address:** c/o Melanie Jackson Agency, 41 W 72nd St Apt 3F, New York, NY 10023, U.S.A.

ERICSON, David F. American, b. 1950. **Genres:** Politics/Government. **Career:** Detroit News, Detroit, MI, copy editor, 1977-80; Oberlin College, Oberlin, OH, instructor in political science, 1986-87; Washington University, St. Louis, MO, visiting professor of political science, 1987-89; Wichita State University, Wichita, KS, assistant professor, 1992-98, associate professor of political science, 1998-. **Publications:** The Shaping of American Liberalism: The Debates over Ratification, Nullification, and Slavery, 1993; (co-ed.) The Liberal Tradition in American Politics: Reassessing the Legacy of American Liberalism, 1999; The Debates over Slavery: Antislavery and Proslavery Liberalism in Antebellum America, 2000. **Address:** Department of Political Science, Wichita State University, Wichita, KS 67260-0017, U.S.A. **Online address:** david.ericson@wichita.edu

ERICSON, Richard V(ictor). Canadian, b. 1948. **Genres:** Business/Trade/Industry, Communications/Media, Criminology/True Crime, Law, Politics/Government, Sociology, Writing/Journalism. **Career:** Cambridge University, England, instructor in sociology at Churchill College, 1971-73; University of Alberta, Edmonton, assistant professor of sociology, 1973-74; University of Toronto, ON, assistant professor, 1974-79, associate professor, 1979-82, professor of criminology and sociology, 1982-93, director of Centre of Criminology, 1992-93; University of British Columbia, Vancouver, professor of sociology and law and principal of Green College, all 1993-2003; University of Toronto, professor of criminology, 2004-. Visiting professor and lecturer at colleges and universities worldwide. **Publications:** Young Offenders and Their Social Work, 1975; Criminal Reactions, 1975; Making Crime, 1981, rev. ed., 1993; Reproducing Order, 1982; (with P. Baranek) The Ordering of Justice, 1982; (with Baranek and Chan) Visualizing Deviance, 1987; (with Baranek and Chan) Negotiating Control, 1989; (with K. Carriere) Crime Stoppers, 1989; (with Baranek and Chan) Representing Order, 1991; (with K. Haggerty) Policing the Risk Society, 1997; (with A. Doyle and D. Barry) Insurance as Governance, 2003; (with A. Doyle) Uncertain Business, 2004. MONOGRAPHS: (with B. Burtch) The Silent System, 1979; (with J. Chan) Decarceration and the Economy of Penal Reform, 1981; (with M. McMahon) Policing Reform, 1984; (with S. Voumvakis) News Accounts of Attacks on Women, 1984. EDITOR & CONTRIBUTOR: (with J. Gladstone and C. Shearing) Criminology: A Reader's Guide (monograph), 1991; (with Stehr) The Culture and Power of Knowledge (monograph), 1992; Crime and the Media (monograph), 1995; (with Stehr) Governing Modern Societies (monograph), 2000; (with A. Doyle) Risk and Morality, 2003; (with K. Haggerty) The New Politics of Surveillance and Visibility, 2005. Contributor to books and academic journals. **Address:** Centre of Criminology, University of Toronto, 130 St George St Rm 8001, Toronto, ON, Canada M5S 3H1.

ERIKSON, Robert. Swedish, b. 1938. **Genres:** Sociology. **Career:** Stockholm University, Sweden, Department of Sociology, professor, 1981-; Swedish Institute for Social Research, 1986-. **Publications:** (with J.H. Goldthorpe) The Constant Flux: A Case Study of Class Mobility in Industrial Societies, 1992. EDITOR: (with R. Aberg) Valfard i forandring: levnadsvillkor i Sverige 19681981, c. 1984, trans. as Welfare in Transition: A Survey of Living Conditions in Sweden, 1968-1981, 1987; (with others) The Scandinavian Model: Welfare States and Welfare Research, 1987; (with others) Welfare Trends in the Scandianian Countries, 1993; (with J.O. Jonsson) Can Education Be Equalized?: The Swedish Case in Comparative Perspective, 1996. **Address:** Swedish Council for Working Life and Social Research, Box 2220, S-10315 Stockholm, Sweden. **Online address:** RE@sofi.su.se

ERKKILA, Betsy. American, b. 1944. **Genres:** Cultural/Ethnic topics, Gay and lesbian issues, Literary criticism and history, Women's studies and issues, Biography, International relations/Current affairs, Politics/Government.

Career: University of Amiens, France, Fulbright lecturer in American studies, 1972-74; University of Pennsylvania, Philadelphia, assistant professor, 1980-86, associate professor, 1986-90, professor of English, from 1990, director of Walt Whitman Conference, 1992; Northwestern University, Henry Sanborn Noyes Professor of Literature, 1995; California State University, Chico, visiting assistant professor of English, 1974-80; California State University, director of London and Paris Travel-Study Program, 1977, 1978; Columbia University, adjunct associate professor, 1988; Princeton University, adjunct professor, 1990. **Publications:** Walt Whitman among the French: Poet and Myth, 1980; Whitman the Political Poet, 1989; The Wicked Sisters: Women Poets, Literary History, and Discord, 1992; Mixed Blood and Other Crosses: Rethinking Literature from the Revelution to the Culture Wars, 2005. EDITOR: (with J. Grossman) Breaking Bounds: Whitman and American Cultural Studies, 1996; Ezra Pound: The Contemporary Reviews, fotthcoming. **Address:** Department of English, Northwestern University, Evanston, IL 60208-2240, U.S.A.

ERLBACH, Arlene. Also writes as Max Taylor. American, b. 1948. **Genres:** Children's fiction, Young adult fiction, Children's non-fiction, Young adult non-fiction. **Career:** Writer. Schoolteacher in Illinois. **Publications:** YOUNG ADULT NOVELS: Does Your Nose Get in the Way, Too?, 1987; Guys, Dating, and Other Disasters, 1987; Drop-Out Blues, 1988; Dial 555-Love, 1991; A Little More to Love, 1994. MIDDLE GRADE NOVEL: The Herbie Hummerston Homework Haters' Club, 1995. MIDDLE GRADE NOVELS AS MAX TAYLOR: The Halloween Hex, 1990; My Brother, the Droid, 1990; Short Circuit, 1990. CHILDREN'S NONFICTION: Bicycles, 1994; Floods, 1994; Hurricanes, 1993; Peanut Butter, 1994; Soda Pop, 1994; Tornadoes, 1994; The Best Friends Book, 1995; Blizzards, 1995; Forest Fires, 1995; Video Games, 1995; The Families Book, 1996; Happy Birthday Everywhere, 1997; Sidewalk Games around the World, 1996; Wonderful Wolves of the Wild, 1996; Teddy Bears, 1997; My Pet Rat, 1998; The Kids' Business Book, 1998; The Kids' Invention Book, 1998; The Kids' Volunteer Book, 1998; The Welfare System, 1998; Kent State, 1998; Worth the Risk, 1999; Happy New Year Everywhere, 1999; Merry Christmas Everywhere, 2002; Hanukkah, Celebrating the Holiday of Lights, 2001; Christmas, Celebrating Life, Giving & Kindness, 2002; The Middle School Survival Guide, 2003; Valentine's Day Crafts, 2003. **Address:** 5829 Capulina Ave, Morton Grove, IL 60053, U.S.A. **Online address:** tbears48@comcast.net

ERLINE, N. T. See **RAGEN, Naomi.**

ERLMANN, Veit. German, b. 1951. **Genres:** Cultural/Ethnic topics, Music. **Career:** University of Natal, Durban, South Africa, professor of ethnomusicology, 1981-85; University of the Witwatersrand, Johannesburg, South Africa, professor of ethnomusicology, 1986-87; Free University of Berlin, Germany, professor of ethnomusicology, 1987-. **Publications:** African Stars: Studies in Black South African Performance, 1991; Nightsong: Power, Performance and Practice in South Africa, 1995; Music, Modernity and the Global Imagination, 1999. **Address:** School of Music, University of Texas at Austin, 1 University Station E3100, Austin, TX 78712-0435, U.S.A. **Online address:** erlmann@mail.utexas.edu

ERNAUX, Annie. French, b. 1940. **Genres:** Novels, Autobiography/Memoirs. **Career:** French novelist and memoirist. Has worked as a secondary school teacher of French in Haute-Savoie and the Paris region, 1966-77; Centre National d'Enseignement par Correspondance, professor, 1977-. **Publications:** Les armoires vides, 1974, trans. as Cleaned Out, 1990; Ce qu'ils disent ou rien, 1977; La femme gelee, 1981, trans. as A Frozen Woman, 1995; La place, 1984, trans. as A Man's Place, 1992; Une femme, 1987, trans. as A Woman's Story, 1991; Passion simple, 1991, trans. as Simple Passion, 1993; I Remain in Darkness, 1999; L'evenement, 2000, trans. as Happening, 2001; La vie exterieure, 2000; Se Perdre, 2001; L'occupation, 2002; L'ecriture comme un couteou, 2003.

ERNST, Carl W. American, b. 1950. **Genres:** Theology/Religion. **Career:** Pomona College, Claremont, CA, assistant professor, 1981-87, associate professor of religion, 1987-92, department head, 1991-92; University of North Carolina at Chapel Hill, professor of religious studies, 1992-, department head, 1995-, member of faculty advisory board, Ackland Art Museum, 1995-. **Publications:** Words of Ecstasy in Sufism, 1984; Eternal Garden: Mysticism, History, and Politics at a South Asian Sufi Center, 1992; (associate ed, with G.M. Smith) Manifestations of Sainthood in Islam, 1993; Ruzbihan Baqli: Mystical Experience and the Rhetoric of Sainthood in Persian Sufism, 1996; (trans.) R. Baqli, The Unveiling of Secrets: Diary of a Sufi Master, 1997; The Shambhala Guide to Sufism, 1997. **Address:** Department of Religious Studies, University of North Carolina at Chapel Hill, Chapel Hill, NC 27599, U.S.A. **Online address:** cernst@email.unc.edu

EROFEEV, Viktor V. Russian, b. 1947. **Genres:** Novels. **Career:** Gorky Institute of Literature, Moscow, Russia, researcher, until 1992; writer, 1992-. **Publications:** Russian Beauty: A Novel, 1990; V labirinte prokliatykh voprosov, 1990; Zhizn s idiotom, 1991; Izbrannoe, ili, Karmannyi apokalipsis, 1993; Russkaia krasavitsa, 1994; (ed. with A. Reynolds) Penguin Book of New Russian Writing, 1995; Strashnyi sud, 1996; Muzhchiny, 1997; Russkie tsvety zla, 1997; Piat rek zhizni, 1998; Entsiklopediia russkoi dushi, 1999. **Address:** 9 First Smolensky Lane, 121099 Moscow, Russia.

ERSPAMER, Peter R(oy). American, b. 1959. **Genres:** Intellectual history, Literary criticism and history, Philosophy. **Career:** Winona State University, MN, visiting assistant professor of German, 1992-93; University of Missouri-Columbia, visiting assistant professor of German, 1993-94; Fort Hays State University, KS, visiting assistant professor of German, 1994-96, organizer of Holocaust Symposium, 1996; Indiana University/Purdue University, lecturer in German, 1997-98. Boston University, visiting scholar, 1997; Marquette University, visiting assistant professor German, 1999; Carroll College, Waukesha, WI, visiting lecturer in German, 2000; Mount Senario College, Hales Corners, WI, adjunct professor of English and history, 2000-02; Rochester Community and Technical College, MN, adjunct instructor in English, 2003-. National Association for the Advancement of Colored People, tutor for summer tutorial project, 1986. **Publications:** The Elusiveness of Tolerance: The "Jewish Question" from Lessing to the Napoleonic Wars, 1997. Contributor to books. **Address:** 521 NW 19th St Apt 11, Rochester, MN 55901-2490, U.S.A. **Online address:** perspamer@yahoo.com; peter.erspamer@roch.edu

ERTELT, Justin P. American, b. 1978. **Genres:** Business/Trade/Industry, Money/Finance. **Career:** Advanced Fire Protection, Fargo, ND, licensed fire sprinkler journeyman, 1997-; Just-in Time Publishing, Fargo, president and chief executive officer, 2000-. **Publications:** Saving Your Way to Success, 2000. **Address:** Just-in Time Publishing, PO Box 86, Fargo, ND 58107, U.S.A. **Online address:** justin@savingyourwaytosuccess.com; www.savingyourwaytosuccess.com

ERWIN, Douglas H. American, b. 1958. **Genres:** Earth sciences. **Career:** Michigan State University, East Lansing, assistant professor, 1985-90, associate professor of geology, 1990; Smithsonian Institution, National Museum of Natural History, Washington, DC, research paleobiologist, 1990-, associate curator, 1990-93, curator of paleobiology, 1993-. International Geological Correlation Program, coleader of project on biotic recoveries from mass extinctions, 199397. **Publications:** The Great Paleozoic Crisis: Life and Death in the Permian, 1993; (with D.E.G. Briggs and F. Collier) The Fossils of the Burgess Shale, 1994. EDITOR: (with R.L. Anstey) New Approaches to Speciation in the Fossil Record, 1995; (with D. Jablonski and J. Lipps) Evolutionary Paleobiology: Essays in Honor of James W. Valentine, 1996. Contributor to books. Contributor of articles and reviews to scientific journals. **Address:** Dept of Paleobiology, MRC-121, Smithsonian Institution, Washington, DC 20560, U.S.A. **Online address:** erwin.d@si.edu

ESEKIE, Bruno. See **MPHAHLELE, Es'kia.**

ESHBACH, Lloyd Arthur. American, b. 1910. **Genres:** Science fiction/Fantasy. **Career:** Worked for dept. stores, 1925-41; Advertising Copywriter, Glidden Paint Co., Reading, Pa., 1941-50; Publisher, Fantasy Press, Reading, 1950-58, and Church Center Press, Myerstown, Pa., 1958-63; Advertising Manager, 1963-68, and Sales Representative, 1968-75, Moody Press, Chicago; Clergyman, for 3 small churches in eastern Pa., 1975-78. **Publications:** (ed.) Of Worlds Beyond: The Science of Science-Fiction Writing, 1947; The Tyrant of Time, 1955; Over My Shoulder, Reflections on a Science Fiction Era, 1983; The Land Beyond the Gate, 1984; The Armlet of the Gods, 1986; The Sorceress of Scath, 1988; The Scroll of Lucifer, 1989.

ESHLEMAN, Clayton. American, b. 1935. **Genres:** Poetry, Translations. **Career:** Professor English Dept., Eastern Michigan University, Ypsilanti, since 1986. Ed., Sulfur Magazine, since 1981. Instructor, in English, Matsushita Electric Corp., Osaka, 1962-64; Instructor, New York University American Language Institute, NYC, 1966-68; Ed. and Publr., Caterpillar mag., NYC, 1967-70, and Sherman Oaks, California, 1970-73; Member, School of Critical Studies, California Institute of the Arts, Valencia, 1970-72; taught at the University of California at Los Angeles, 1974-77; Dreyfus Poet in Residence and Lecturer in Creative Writing, California Institute of Technology, 1979-84, Ed., Caterpillar Magazine, 1967-73. **Publications:** Mexico and North, 1962; The Chavin Illumination, 1965; Lachrymae Mateo: 3 Poems for Christmas 1966, 1966; Walks, 1967; The Crocus Bud, 1967; Brother Stones, 1968; Cantaloups and Splendour, 1968; T'ai, 1969; The House of Okumura, 1969; Indiana: Poems, 1969; The House of Ibuki: A

Poem, New York City, 14 March-30 Sept. 1967, 1969; The Yellow River Record, 1969; A Pitchblende, 1969; (ed.) A Caterpillar Anthology: A Selection of Poetry and Prose from Caterpillar Magazine, 1971; The Wand, 1971; Bearings, 1971; Altars, 1971; The Sanjo Bridge, 1972; Coils, 1973; Human Wedding, 1973; Aux Morts, 1974; Realignment, 1974; Portrait of Francis Bacon, 1975; The Gull Wall: Poems and Essays, 1975; Cogollo, 1976; The Woman Who Saw Through Paradise, 1976; Grotesca, 1977; Core Meander, 1977; What She Means, 1978; Our Lady of the Three-Pronged Devil, 1981; Hades in Manganese, 1981; Foetus Graffiti, 1981; Fracture, 1983; Visions of the Fathers of Lascaux, 1983; The Name Encanyoned River: Selected Poems 1960-85, 1986; Conductors of the Pit: Major Works by Rimbaud, Ballejo, Cesaire, Artaud and Holan, 1988; Antiphonal Swing: Selected Prose 1962-1987, 1989; Novices: A Study of Poetic Apprenticeship, 1989, 2nd ed, 1996; Hotel Cro-Magnon, 1989; Under World Arrest, 1994; Nora's Roar, 1996. TRANSLATOR: Residence on Earth, by Pablo Neruda, 1962; (with D. Kelly) State of the Union, by Aime Cesaire 1966; Poemas Humanos Human Poems, by Cesar Vallejo, 1968; (with J.R. Barcia) Spain, Take This Cup from Me, by Cesar Vallejo, 1974; (with N. Glass) Four Texts, by Artaud, 1982; (with A. Smith) The Collected Poetry, by Aime Cesaire, 1983; Sea-Urchin Hara-kiri, by Bernard Bador, 1984; Given Giving: Selected Poems of Michel De-guy, 1984; (with A. Smith) Lost Body, by Aime Cesaire, 1986; (with A. Smith) Lyric and Dramatic Poetry 1946-1982, by Aime Cesaire, 1990; Trilce, by Cesar Vallejo, 1992; (with B. Bador) Antonin Artaud, Watchfriends & Rack Screams, 1995. **Address:** 210 Washtenaw Ave, Ypsilanti, MI 48197, U.S.A. **Online address:** ceshleman@comcast.net

ESKEW, Glenn T. American, b. 1962. **Genres:** History, Race relations. **Career:** E.B. Construction Corp., Birmingham, AL, plumbing apprentice, 1978-83; Meridian Star, Meridian, MS, reporter, 1984-85; Georgia Historical Quarterly, editorial assistant, 1987-88; Albert Einstein Institution, Cambridge, MA, fellow, 1991-92, 1992-93; Georgia State University, Atlanta, assistant professor of history, 1993-. Georgia Humanities Council, associate. Georgia Heritage Association, member of U.S; 441 Heritage Corridor Commission. **Publications:** But for Birmingham: The Local and National Movements in the Civil Rights Struggle, 1997; (ed. with E. Cashin) Paternalism in a Southern City: Race, Religion, and Gender in Augusta, Georgia, in press. Contributor to books. Contributor of articles and reviews to periodicals. **Address:** Department of History, Georgia State University, PO Box 4117, Atlanta, GA 30302, U.S.A. **Online address:** hisgte@gsu.edu

ESKRIDGE, Ann E. American, b. 1949. **Genres:** Novels, Plays/Screenplays. **Career:** WXYZ-TV, Detroit, MI, reporter, 1972-76; freelance public relations agent, Detroit, 1976-78; Lieutenant Governor of Michigan, executive assistant, 1978-79; Michigan State Treasurer, administrator, 1979-81; Statewide Nutrition Commission, administrator, 1982-83; Detroit Council President Erma Henderson, administrative assistant, 1983; Golightly Vocational Technical Center, Detroit, instructor in mass media, 1983-90; freelance writer and teaching consultant, Detroit, 1990-92; Michigan Consolidated Gas Company, speechwriter, 1992-95; freelance writer, 1995-. Chicago Daily Defender, reporter, summers, 1968-69; Oklahoma Daily, reporter, 1970; Oklahoma Journal, reporter, 1970; KWTV (Oklahoma City), reporter, 1970-71; WBEN-TV (Buffalo, NY), reporter, 1971-72. Conducts workshops, lectures and demonstrations on scriptwriting at colleges. **Publications:** The Sanctuary, 1994; The Sanctuary (play), 1995. SCREENPLAYS: Brother Future, 1991; Echoes across the Prairie...The Vanishing Black West (documentary). Contributor to periodicals. **Address:** 17217 Fairfield, Detroit, MI 48221, U.S.A.

ESKRIDGE, Kelley. American, b. 1960. **Genres:** Novels. **Career:** Former business executive; novelist and short fiction writer. Wizards of the Coast, vice president of project management. **Publications:** Solitaire, 2002. Contributor of short fiction to periodicals. Work has appeared in collections. **Address:** c/o Shawna McCarthy, McCarthy Literary Agency, 7 Allen St., Rumson, NJ 07760, U.S.A. **Online address:** info@kelleyeskridge.com

ESKRIDGE, William N(ichol), Jr. American, b. 1951. **Genres:** Law. **Career:** U.S. District Court, New York, NY, law clerk to judge Edward Weinfeld, 1978-79; Shea & Gardner, Washington, DC, associate, 1979-82; University of Virginia Law School, Charlottesville, assistant professor, 1982-86; Georgetown University Law Center, Washington, DC, associate professor, 1987-90, professor, 1990-; visiting professor at US law schools. **Publications:** (with P. Frickey) Cases and Materials on Legislation: Statutes and the Creation of Public Policy, 1988; (with P. Frickey and D. Farber) Constitutional Law: Themes for the Constitution's Third Century, 1993; (with P. Frickey) Dynamic Statutory Interpretation, 1994; (with P. Frickey and H. Hart) The Legal Process: Basic Problems in the Making and Application of Law, 1994; The Case for Same-Sex Marriage: From Sexual Liberty to Civilized Com-

mitment, 1996; (with N. Hunter) Sexuality, Gender, and the Law, 1997; Equality Practice: Civil Unions and the Future of Gay Rights, 2001. EDITOR: A Dance along the Precipice: The Political and Economic Dimensions of the International Debt Problem, 1985; (with S. Levinson) Constitutional Stupidities, Constitutional Tragedies, 1998; Gaylaw: Challenging the Apartheid of the Closet, 1999. **Address:** Georgetown University Law Center, 600 New Jersey Avenue NW, Washington, DC 20001, U.S.A.

ESLER, Anthony James. American, b. 1934. **Genres:** Novels, History. **Career:** Professor of History, College of William & Mary, Williamsburg, VA, 1972-99 (Assistant Professor, 1962-67; Associate Professor, 1967-72). Fulbright Post-doctoral Research Fellow, University of London, 1961-62; American Council of Learned Societies Research Fellow, Chicago, 1969-70; William and Mary Research Fellow, 1975-76; Fulbright Travel Grant, Ivory Coast and Tanzania, 1983. **Publications:** The Aspiring Mind of the Elizabethan Younger Generation, 1966; Bombs, Beards and Barricades: 150 Years of Youth in Revolt, 1971; The Blade of Castlemayne, 1974; Hellbane, 1975; Lord Libertine, 1976; Forbidden City, 1977; The Freebooters, 1979; Generational Studies: A Basic Bibliography, 1979; Babylon, 1980; Bastion, 1980; Generations in History: An Introduction to the Concept, 1982; The Generation Gap in Society and History: A Select Bibliography, 2 vols., 1984; The Human Venture: A World History, 2 vols., 1986, 5th ed., 2004; (co-author) A Survey of Western Civilization, 1987; The Western World: A History, 2 vols., 1994, 2nd ed., 1997; (co-author) Connections: A World History, 1997, 3rd ed., 2004. EDITOR: The Youth Revolution: The Conflict of Generations in Modern History, 1974. **Address:** Dept. of History, College of William and Mary, Williamsburg, VA 23185, U.S.A. **Online address:** Anthonyesler@aol.com

ESPADA, Martin. American, b. 1957. **Genres:** Poetry. **Career:** Has worked as an attorney; University of Massachusetts, Amherst, English instructor. **Publications:** POETRY: The Immigrant Iceboy's Bolero, 1982; Trumpets From the Islands of Their Eviction, 1987, expanded ed, 1994; Rebellion Is the Circle of a Lover's Hands, 1990; City of Coughing and Dead Radiators: Poems, 1993; (ed.) Poetry Like Bread: Poets of the Political Imagination From Curbstone Press, 1994; Imagine the Angels of Bread: Poems, 1996. Contributor to periodicals. **Address:** Dept. of English, Bartlett Hall, University of Massachusetts, Amherst, MA 01003, U.S.A.

ESPAILLAT, Rhina P. American (born Dominican Republic), b. 1932. **Genres:** Novellas/Short stories, Poetry, Essays. **Career:** Teacher and poet. NYC public schools, teacher, 1953-54; Jamaica High School, NY, teacher, 1965-80; NYC Board of Education, consultant, 1984-89. **Publications:** Lapsing to Grace: Poems and Drawings, 1992; Where Horizons Go, 1998; Rehearsing Absence, 2001; The Shadow I Dress In, 2004. CHAPBOOKS: Mundo y Palabra/The World and the Word, 2001; Rhina P. Espaillat: Greatest Hits, 1942-2001, 2003; The Story-Teller's Hour, 2004. Contributor of poetry to anthologies and textbooks. Contributor of poetry, essays, and short stories to publications. **Address:** 12 Charron Dr, Newburyport, MA 01950, U.S.A. **Online address:** espmosk@verizon.net

ESPOSITO, Mary Ann. American, b. 1942. **Genres:** Food and Wine. **Career:** Public Broadcasting Service (PBS), host and creator of Ciao Italia, Durham, NH, 1989-; Mary Ann Esposito, Inc., president, 1996-; author of cookbooks. University of New Hampshire, Portsmouth, instructor in Italian cooking, 1985-90; European Heritage Institute, Richmond, VA, lecturer and cook, 1990-91; Visiting and guest chef to culinary institutes, including Boston University; has been a guest cook at Tre Vaselle in Torgiano, Italy, and La Cucina d'Edgardo in Montalcino, Tuscany. **Publications:** COOKBOOKS: Ciao Italia, 1991; Nella Cucina, 1993; Celebrations Italian Style, 1995; What you Knead, 1997; Mangia Pasta, 1998; Ciao Italia: Bringing Italy Home, 2001; Ciao Italia in Umbria, 2002; Ciao Italia in Tuscany, 2003. **Address:** Mary Ann Esposito, Inc., PO Box 891, Durham, NH 03824, U.S.A.

ESPOSITO, Phil(ip Anthony). (born Canada), b. 1942. **Genres:** Autobiography/Memoirs. **Career:** Professional ice hockey player, broadcaster, executive, and author. Chicago Black Hawks, center, 1964-1967; Boston Bruins, center, 1968-1976; New York Rangers, center, 1976-1981; general manager, 1986-1989; Tampa Bay Lightning, president and general manager, 1992-1999; Fox Sports Net, analyst, 1999-. **Publications:** (with Tony Esposito and Tim Moriarty) The Brothers Esposito, 1971; (with Gerald Eskenazi) Hockey Is My Life, 1972; (with Tony Esposito and Kevin Walsh) We Can Teach You to Play Hockey, 1972; (with Dick Drew) Phil Esposito's Winning Hockey for Beginners, 1976; Thunder and Lightning: A No-B.S. Hockey Memoir, 2003. **Address:** c/o Triumph Books, 601 S. LaSalle, St. Suite 500, Chicago, IL 60605, U.S.A.

ESSED, Philomena. Dutch, b. 1955. **Genres:** Race relations. **Career:** University of Amsterdam, Amsterdam, the Netherlands, scholar at the Amsterdam Research Institute for Global Issues and Development Studies (AGIDS), member of the Diversity working group in the Emancipation Committee for Women, affiliated with other working groups at the university; external researcher and associate faculty member in the social sciences at the University of East London, England. **Publications:** NONFICTION: Alledags Racisme, 1984, trans. by C. Jaffe as Everyday Racism: Reports from Women of Two Cultures, 1990; Understanding Everyday Racism: An Interdisciplinary Theory, 1991; Diversiteit: Vrouwen, Kleur en Cultuur, 1994, trans. by R. Gircour as Diversity: Gender, Color, and Culture, 1996. **Address:** AGIDS, Faculty of Social and Behavioural Sciences, Department of Geography and Planning, Nieuwe Prinsengracht 130, 1018 VZ Amsterdam, Netherlands. **Online address:** Essed@antenna.nl

ESSEX, Karen. American. **Genres:** Biography, Novels. **Career:** Journalist, writer, and producer. Blake Edwards Entertainment, Los Angeles, CA, former vice president; Force Ten Productions, former senior vice president. **Publications:** (with J.L. Swanson) Bettie Page: The Life of a Pin-up Legend (biography), 1996; Kleopatra (fiction), 2001; Pharoah: Volume II of Kleopatra, 2002. Contributor to periodicals and online literary magazines. **Address:** c/o Author Mail, Warner Books, 1271 Avenue of the Americas, New York, NY 10020, U.S.A.

ESSEX-CATER, Antony John. British, b. 1923. **Genres:** Medicine/Health, Mystery/Crime/Suspense. **Career:** Vice-President, National Association for Maternal and Child Welfare, since 1988 Deputy Medical Officer of Health, City of Manchester, 1961-68; County Medical Officer, Monmouthshire County Council, 1968-74; Medical Officer of Health and Consultant Venereologist, Jersey, Channel Islands, 1974-88; Chairman, National Association for Maternal and Child Welfare, London, 1976-88. **Publications:** Synopsis of Public Health and Social Medicine, 1961, 1967, 3rd ed. as Manual of Public and Community Medicine, 1979. **Address:** c/o Honfleur, Mont Cambrai, St. Lawrence, Jersey, Channel Islands JE3 1JP, United Kingdom.

ESTERBERG, Kristin G. American, b. 1960. **Genres:** Gay and lesbian issues, Sociology. **Career:** Houghton Mifflin Co., Boston, MA, editorial assistant to associate editor and editor in College Division, 1982-85; freelance editor, Boston, 1985-89; University of Missouri-Kansas City, assistant professor, 1991-96, associate professor of sociology, 1996-97, director of women's studies, 1991-97; University of Massachusetts at Lowell, assistant professor, 1997-2001, associate professor of sociology, 2001-, department chair, 2002-04, associate provost, 2004-. **Publications:** Lesbian and Bisexual Identities: Creating Communities, Creating Selves, 1997; Qualitative Methods in Social Research, 2002. Contributor to books. Contributor of articles and reviews to periodicals. **Address:** Dept of Sociology, University of Massachusetts at Lowell, 850 Broadway Ste 5, Lowell, MA 01854, U.S.A. **Online address:** Kristin_Esterberg@uml.edu

ESTERHAMMER, Angela. Canadian, b. 1961. **Genres:** Humanities, Literary criticism and history. **Career:** University of Western Ontario, London, assistant professor, 1989-94, associate professor, 1994-2000, professor of English and comparative literature, 2000-. **Publications:** Creating States: Studies in the Performative Language of John Milton and William Blake, 1994; (trans. and author of intro.) R.M. Rilke, Two Stories of Prague, 1994; The Romantic Performative: Language and Action in British and German Romanticism, 2000; (ed.) Romantic Poetry, 2002. Work represented in anthologies. Contributor of articles, translations, and reviews to literature journals. **Address:** Department of English, University of Western Ontario, London, ON, Canada N6A 3K7. **Online address:** angelae@uwo.ca

ESTERHAZY, Peter. Hungarian, b. 1950. **Genres:** Novels. **Career:** Freelance writer. **Publications:** FICTION: Fancsiko and Pinta, 1976; Production-Novel, 1979; Indirect, 1981; Who Can Guarantee the Lady's Safety?, 1982; Transporters, 1983; Little Hungarian Pornography, 1984; Daisy (play), 1984; Helping Verbs of the Heart, 1985; 17 Swans, 1987; Certain Adventure, 1989; The Book of Hrabal, 1990; The Glance of Countess Hahn-Hahn, 1991; Farewell Symphony, 1994; A Woman, 1995; She Loves Me, 1995; Harmonia Caelestis, 2000. OTHER: The Stuffed Swan, 1988; The Wonderful Life of the Little Fish, 1991; From the Ivory Tower, 1991; Notes of a Blue Stocking, 1994. **Address:** Hungarian Writers Federation, Bajza-utca 18, H-1062 Budapest, Hungary.

ESTES, Clarissa Pinkola. American, b. 1943. **Genres:** Songs/Lyrics and libretti, Psychology, Women's studies and issues. **Career:** Poet; psychoanalyst; clinical practice, Denver, CO, 1971-. Developer and teacher of "Writing as Liberation of the Spirit" program in state and federal prisons throughout the U.S., 1971-; Women in Transition Safe House, Denver, co-coordinator, 1973-75; C. G. Jung Center for Education and Research, executive director; founder, Guadelupe Foundation (human rights organization); trustee, Union Institute and University, and Vermont College; Bloomsbury Review, contributing editor; educational posttrauma specialist. **Publications:** Women Who Run with the Wolves: Myths and Stories of the Wild Woman Archetype, 1992; The Gift of Story: A Wise Tale about What Is Enough, 1993; The Faithful Gardener: A Wise Tale about That Which Can Never Die, 1995. Contributor to books. **Address:** PO Box 970, Boulder, CO 80306-0970, U.S.A.

ESTES, Daniel J(ohn). American, b. 1953. **Genres:** Theology/Religion. **Career:** Dallas Theological Seminary, Dallas, TX, instructor at Lay Institute, 1977; Clintonville Baptist Church, Columbus, OH, assistant pastor, 1978-84, 1989-93; Cedarville University, Cedarville, OH, assistant professor, 1984-90, associate professor, 1990-95, professor of Bible, 1995-, assistant academic vice-president, 1993-2001, director of Honors Program, 1995-99, associate academic vice president, 2001-. **Publications:** Hear, My Son: Wisdom and Pedagogy in Proverbs 1-9, 1997. Contributor to books and periodicals. **Address:** Cedarville University, 251 N Main St, Cedarville, OH 45314, U.S.A. **Online address:** estesd@cedarville.edu

ESTES, William (Kaye). American, b. 1919. **Genres:** Psychology. **Career:** Professor of Psychology, Harvard University, Cambridge, Massachusetts, 1979. Ed., Psychological Science, 1990-94. Member of Faculty, 1946-62, Professor of Psychology, 1955-60, and Research Professor, 1960-62, University of Indiana, Bloomington; Professor of Psychology, and Member of Institute of Mathematical Studies in Social Sciences, Stanford University, California, 1962-68; Professor of Psychology, Rockefeller University, NYC, 1968-79. President, Midwestern Psychological Association, 1956-57; President, Division of Experimental Psychology, American Psychological Association, 1958-59; Associate Ed., Journal of Experimental Psychology, 1958-62; Ed., Journal of Comparative and Physiological Psychology, 1962-68; Ed., Psychological Review, 1977-82. **Publications:** An Experimental Study of Punishment, 1944; (co-author) Modern Learning Theory, 1954; (co-ed.) Studies in Mathematical Learning Theory, 1959; Stimulus Sampling Theory, 1967; Learning Theory and Mental Development, 1970; Handbook of Learning and Cognitive Processes, 6 vols., 1975-78; Models of Learning, Memory, and Choice, 1982; Statistical Models in Behavioral Research, 1991; Classification and Cognition, 1994. **Address:** Harvard University, W. James Hall, 33 Kirkland St., Cambridge, MA 02138-2044, U.S.A.

ESTEY, Ralph H(oward). Canadian, b. 1916. **Genres:** Agriculture/Forestry, Botany, History. **Career:** Elementary schoolteacher prior to World War II; Wartime Emergency Training, teacher, 1942-43; vocational agriculture teacher in Woodstock, New Brunswick; University of Connecticut, Storrs, botany teacher, 1956-57; McGill University, Montreal, Quebec, associate professor, 1961-72, professor of mycology, history of plant pathology, and nematology, 1972-82, department head, beginning in 1970, professor emeritus, 1982-. **Publications:** Essays on the Early History of Plant Pathology and Mycology in Canada, 1994. **Address:** 91 Devon Rd, Baie d'Urfe, QC, Canada H9X 2X3. **Online address:** rhestey@videotron.ca

ESTLEMAN, Loren D. American, b. 1952. **Genres:** Mystery/Crime/Suspense, Westerns/Adventure, Novellas/Short stories. **Career:** The Press, Ypsilanti, reporter, 1973; Community Foto-News, Pinckney, MI, editor, 1975-76; Ann Arbor News, special writer, 1976-77; Dexter Leader, staff writer, 1977-80. Western Writers of America, vice president, 1998-2000, president, 2000-02. **Publications:** The Oklahoma Punk, 1976; Sherlock Holmes versus Dracula, or The Adventure of the Sanguinary Count, 1978; Dr. Jekyll and Mr. Holmes, 1979; The Wister Trace (non-fiction), 1987; Red Highway, 1988; Peeper, 1989; Sudden Country, 1991; The Rocky Mountain Moving Picture Association, 1999; White Desert, 2000; The Master Executioner, 2001. DETROIT SERIES: Whiskey River, 1990; Motown, 1991; King of the Corner, 1992; Edsel, 1995; Stress, 1996; Jitterbug, 1998; Thunder City, 1999. AMOS WALKER MYSTERIES: Motor City Blue, 1980; Angel Eyes, 1981; The Midnight Man, 1982; The Glass Highway, 1983; Sugartown, 1984; Every Brilliant Eye, 1985; Lady Yesterday, 1987; Downriver, 1988; General Murders: 7 Amos Walker Mysteries, 1988; Silent Thunder, 1989; Sweet Women Lie, 1990; Never Street, 1997; The Witchfinder, 1998; The Hours of the Virgin, 1999; A Smile on the Face of the Tiger, 2000; Sinister Heights, 2002; Poison Blonde, 2003. PETER MACKLIN MYSTERIES: Kill Zone, 1984; Roses Are Dead, 1985; Any Man's Death, 1986; Something Borrowed, Something Black, 2002. WESTERNS: The Hider, 1978; Aces and Eights, 1981; The Wolfer, 1981; Mister St. John, 1983; This Old Bill, 1984; Gun Man, 1985; Bloody Season, 1988; Best Western Stories of Loren D. Estleman, 1989; Billy Gashade, 1997; Journey of the Dead, 1998; (ed.) American West: 20 New Stories, 2001; Black Powder, White Smoke, 2002. PAGE MURDOCK WESTERNS: The High

Rocks, 1979; Stamping Ground, 1980; Murdock's Law, 1982; The Stranglers, 1984; City of Widows, 1994; White Desert, 2000; Port Hazard, 2003. **Address:** c/o Morgan and Associates, PO Box 2967, Ann Arbor, MI 48106, U.S.A. **Online address:** www.lorenestleman.com

ESTOW, Clara. American (born Colombia), b. 1945. **Genres:** History. **Career:** University of Massachusetts at Boston, instructor, 1968-71, assistant professor, 1974-82, associate professor, 1982-94, professor of Hispanic studies, 1994-, department head, 1989-92, department head at Harbor Campus, Boston, 1995-, director of Latin American studies program, 1995-98, chair, Faculty Council, 1999-2001, member of executive committee, Center for World Languages and Cultures. International Institute Foundation in Spain, secretary of executive committee; Massachusetts Foundation for the Humanities, workshop leader, 1992-95. Camp Hemlock Hill, director, 1968. **Publications:** Pedro the Cruel of Castile, 1350-1369, 1995. Contributor to books. Contributor of articles and reviews to periodicals. **Address:** Department of Hispanic Studies, University of Massachusetts, Boston, MA 02125, U.S.A. **Online address:** clara.estow@umb.edu

ESTRADA, Rita Clay. Also writes as Rita Clay, Tira Lacy. American. **Genres:** Novels, Romance/Historical, Westerns/Adventure, Reference. **Career:** Writer, 1980-. **Publications:** ROMANCE NOVELS: The Will and the Way, 1985; A Woman's Choice, 1985; The Best Things in Life, 1986; Something to Treasure, 1986; The Ivory Key, 1987; A Little Magic, 1988; Second to None, 1989; Trust, 1989; To Buy a Groom, 1990; The Lady Says No, 1990; Twice Loved, 1991; To Have and to Hold, 1992; One More Time, 1993; Forms of Love, 1994; Conveniently Yours, 1994; The Colonel's Daughter, 1994; The Twelve Gifts of Christmas, 1994; Interlude in Time, 1994; The Stormchaser, 1996; Love Me, Love My Bed, 1996; Wishes, 1997; Dreams, 1998; Everything about Him, 1999; Bedazzled, 2002. ROMANCE NOVELS AS RITA CLAY: Wanderer's Dream, 1981; Sweet Eternity, 1981; Wise Folly, 1982; Yesterday's Dreams, 1982; Experiment in Love, 1983; Summer Song, 1983; Recapture the Love, 1984. ROMANCE NOVELS AS TIRA LACY: With Time and Tenderness, 1983; Only for Love, 1984. OTHER: Valentine Sampler, 1993; (ed. with R. Gallagher) Writing Romances: A Handbook, 1997; Blissful (western), 2000; Too Wicked to Love (western), 2001; You Can Write a Romance!, 1999. **Address:** PO Box 73686, Houston, TX 77273-3686, U.S.A. **Online address:** rcestrada1@juno.com

ESTRIDGE, Robin. Also writes as Philip Loraine, Robert York. British, b. 1920. **Genres:** Novels, Mystery/Crime/Suspense, Plays/Screenplays. **Publications:** NOVELS AS ROBIN ESTRIDGE: The Future Is Tomorrow, 1947; The Publican's Wife, 1948; Meeting on the Shore, 1949; Return of a Hero (in US as Sword without Scabbard), 1950; The Olive Tree, 1953; A Cuckoo's Child, 1969. NOVELS AS ROBERT YORK: The Swords of December, 1978; My Lord the Fox, 1985. MYSTERY NOVELS AS PHILIP LORAINE: White Lie the Dead (in US as And to My Beloved Husband), 1950; Exit with Intent: The Story of a Missing Comedian, 1950; The Break in the Circle, 1951 (in US as Outside the Law, 1953); The Dublin Nightmare (in US as Nightmare in Dublin), 1952; The Angel of Death, 1961; Day of the Arrow, 1964 (in UK as The Eye of the Devil, 1966); W. I. L. One to Curtis, 1967; The Dead Men of Sestos, 1968; A Mafia Kiss, 1969. Photographs Have Been Sent to Your Wife, 1971; Voices in an Empty Room, 1973; Ask the Rattlesnake (in US as Wrong Man in the Mirror), 1975; Lions' Ransom, 1980; Sea Change, 1982; Death Wishes, 1983; Loaded Questions, 1985; Last Shot, 1986; Crackpot, 1993; In the Blood, 1994; Ugly Money, 1996. **Address:** c/o Rochelle Stevens, 2 Terrets Place, Upper Street, London N1 1QZ, England.

ESTY, Daniel C. American, b. 1959. **Genres:** Environmental sciences/Ecology. **Career:** Arnold & Porter, Washington, DC, attorney, 1986-89; U.S. Environmental Protection Agency, Washington, DC, special assistant to the administrator, 1989-90, deputy chief of staff, 1990-91, deputy assistant administrator for policy, 1991-93; Institute for International Economics, Washington, DC, senior fellow, 1993-94; Yale University, New Haven, CT, professor of law and director of Center for Environmental Law and Policy, 1994-, associate dean of School of Forestry and Environmental Studies, 1998-. **Publications:** Greening the GATT, 1994; (ed. with M.R. Chertow) Thinking Ecologically: The Next Generation of Environmental Policy, 1997; Sustaining the Asia Pacific Miracle, 1997. **Address:** Center for Environmental Law and Policy, Yale University, PO Box 208215, New Haven, CT 06520, U.S.A. **Online address:** daniel.esty@yale.edu

ETINGER, Almog. See ALMOG, Ruth.

ETLIN, Richard A. American, b. 1947. **Genres:** Architecture, Art/Art history, Environmental sciences/Ecology. **Career:** University of Kentucky, Lexington, assistant professor of architectural history, 1975-81; University of Maryland at College Park, faculty member, 1981-, professor of architectural history, 1989-, Distinguished University Professor, 2000-. Johns Hopkins University, visiting associate professor, 1987; Columbia University, visiting professor, 1991. Council for the International Exchange of Scholars, chairperson of discipline screening committee for Fulbright awards in architecture and city planning, 1985-88. **Publications:** The Architecture of Death: The Transformation of the Cemetery in Eighteenth-Century Paris, 1984; Modernism in Italian Architecture, 1890-1940, 1991; Frank Lloyd Wright and Le Corbusier: The Romantic Legacy, 1994; Symbolic Space: French Enlightenment Architecture and Its Legacy, 1994; In Defense of Humanism: Value in the Arts and Letters, 1996. EDITOR: Studies in the History of Art, vol. 29: Nationalism in the Visual Arts, 1991; (series) Modern Architecture and Cultural Identity, 1994-; Art, Culture, and Media under the Third Reich, 2002. **Address:** School of Architecture, Planning & Preservation, University of Maryland, College Park, MD 20742-1411, U.S.A. **Online address:** retlin@umd.edu

ETTER, Dave. (David Pearson Etter). American, b. 1928. **Genres:** Poetry. **Career:** Former writer for the Encyclopedia Britannica, Chicago. **Publications:** Go Read the River, 1966; The Last Train to Prophetstown, 1968; Strawberries, 1970; (with J. Knoepfle and L. Mueller) Voyages to the Inland Sea, 1971; Crabtree's Woman, 1972; Well You Needn't, 1975; Bright Mississippi, 1975; Central Standard Time: New and Selected Poems, 1978; Alliance, Illinois, 1978; Open to the Wind, 1978; Riding the Rock Island through Kansas, 1979; Cornfields, 1980; West of Chicago, 1981; Boondocks, 1982; Alliance, Illinois, 1983; Home State, 1985; Live at the Silver Dollar, 1986; Selected Poems, 1987; Midlanders, 1988; Electric Avenue, 1988; Carnival, 1990; Sunflower County, 1994; I Want to Talk about You, 1995; How High the Moon, 1996; Next Time You See Me, 1997; The Essential Dave Etter, 2001; Greatest Hits 1960-2000, 2002. **Address:** 628 E Locust St, Lanark, IL 61046, U.S.A.

ETTINGER, Elżbieta. American (born Poland), b. 1925. **Genres:** Novels, Translations, Autobiography/Memoirs. **Career:** Professor, Massachusetts Institute of Technology, Cambridge, Massachusetts, from 1973. With Radcliffe Seminars, Harvard Extension, Cambridge, Massachusetts, from 1970 (Sr. Fellow, Radcliffe Institute, 1972-74). **Publications:** Kindergarten, 1970; (trans.) Nullum Crimen Sine Lege, 1975; (ed. and trans.) Comrade and Lover: Rosa Luxemburg's Letters to Leo Jogiches, 1979; Rosa Luxemburg: A Life, 1986; Hannah Arendt/Martin Heidegger, 1995.

ETZIONI, Amitai. American (born Germany), b. 1929. **Genres:** Sociology. **Career:** Director, Center for Policy Research, 1968-. Sponsor, The Atlantic Council of the United States, 1964-; Member of the Board, Canadian Peace Research Institute, since 1964; Member, Editorial Board, Administration and Mental Health, since 1972; Member, Governing Council of the American Jewish Congress, and the National Advisory Board of the National Alliance for Safer Cities, since 1973; Member, Advisory Panel of the Population Society, and the International Society for Research in Aggression, 1973-. Instructor to Professor, Columbia University, NYC, 1958-80; Professor, George Washington University, 1980-87, 1989-; Thomas Henry Carroll Ford Foundation Professor, Graduate School of Business, Harvard University, 1987-89. Associate Ed., American Sociological Review, 1964-68; Associate Ed. Sociological Abstracts, 1968-71; President, American Sociological Association, 1994-95. **Publications:** A Diary of a Commando Soldier, 1951; A Comparative Analysis of Complex Organizations, 1961, 1975; (ed.) Complex Organizations: A Sociological Reader, 1961, 3rd ed. 1980; The Hard Way to Peace: A New Strategy, 1962; Winning Without War, 1964; Modern Organizations, 1964; The Moon-Doggie: Domestic and International Implications of the Space Race, 1964; Political Unification: A Comparative Study of Leaders and Forces, 1965; Studies in Social Change, 1966; (ed.) International Political Communities, 1966; The Active Society: A Theory of Societal and Political Processes, 1968; (ed.) Readings on Modern Organizations, 1969; (ed.) The Semi-Professions and Their Organization: Teachers, Nurses, Social Workers, 1969; Demonstration Democracy, 1971; Genetic Fix, 1973; Social Problems, 1976; The Organizational Structure of the Kibbutz, 1980; Capital Corruption: An Assault on American Democracy, 1984; The Moral Dimension, 1988; (ed.) Socio-Economics: Towards a New Synthesis, 1990; The Spirit of Community, 1993; Public Policy in a New Key, 1993; The New Golden Rule, 1997. **Address:** c/o M. E. Sharpe, Inc, 80 Business Park Dr, Armonk, NY 10504, U.S.A.

EUBA, Femi. British (born Nigeria), b. 1941. **Genres:** Novels, Plays/Screenplays, Theatre. **Career:** University of Ibadan, Nigeria, lecturer, 1975-76; University of Ife, Ile-Ife, Nigeria, senior lecturer, 1976-86; College of William and Mary, Williamsburg, VA, visiting professor, 1986-88; Louisiana

State University, Baton Rouge, professor, 1988-. Playwright; theater director and actor; consultant to African Theatre. **Publications:** Archetypes, Imprecators and Victims of Fate: Origins and Developments of Satire in Black Drama, 1989; Camwood at Crossroads (novel), 1993. PLAYS: The Gulf, 1992; Eye of Gabriel, 1993; Riddles on Greed: Three One-Act Plays (A Riddle of the Palms, Crocodiles, The Cameleon); Dionysus of the Holocaust, 1996. RADIO PLAYS: The Yam Debt, 1964; The Telegram, 1965; Down by the Lagoon, 1965; The Game, 1966; Tortoise, 1967; Chameleon, 1968; The Devil, 1970; The Wig and the Honeybee, 1976. Work represented in anthologies. Contributor of essays to periodicals. **Address:** Louisiana State University, PO Box 16352, Baton Rouge, LA 70893, U.S.A. **Online address:** theuba@lsu.edu

EUCHNER, Charles C. American, b. 1960. **Genres:** Politics/Government. **Career:** Education Week, Washington, DC, staff writer, 1982-84; St; Mary's College of Maryland, St. Mary's City, visiting instructor, 1989-90; College of the Holy Cross, Worcester, MA, assistant professor of political science, 1990-97; Boston Redevelopment Authority, Boston, MA, coordinator, 1997-. Boston Cares, volunteer. **Publications:** Extraordinary Politics, 1998. **Address:** John F. Kennedy School of Government, 79 John F. Kennedy St., Cambridge, MA 02138, U.S.A. **Online address:** Charles.Euchner.bra@ci.boston.ma.us

EUGENIDES, Jeffrey. American, b. 1960. **Genres:** Novels. **Career:** Writer. **Publications:** The Virgin Suicides, 1993; Middlesex, 2002 (Pulitzer Prize, 2003). Contributor to periodicals. **Address:** c/o Farrar, Straus and Giroux, 19 Union Sq W, New York, NY 10003, U.S.A.

EULA, Michael J(ames). American, b. 1957. **Genres:** History. **Career:** El Camino College, Torrance, CA, professor of history, 1989-. University of California, Irvine, visiting assistant professor, 1991; Chapman University, visiting lecturer in history, 1993-2002; St. Thomas University School of Law, adjunct lecturer in international tax law, 2002Riverside County, CA, administrative law judge, 1999-. Historical consultant to Rymel Multimedia Inc., and Gateway Educational Products. **Publications:** (ed. with A. Wrobel, and contrib.) American Ethnics and Minorities: Readings in Ethnic History, 1990; Between Peasant and Urban Villager: Italian-Americans of New Jersey and New York, 1880-1980; The Structures of Counter-Discourse, 1993. Contributor to books. Contributor of articles and reviews to history, religious studies journals, and law reviews. **Address:** Department of History, El Camino College, Torrance, CA 90506, U.S.A. **Online address:** historylb@aol.com

EVANOVICH, Janet. Also writes as Steffie Hall. American. **Genres:** Mystery/Crime/Suspense, Romance/Historical. **Publications:** DETECTIVE NOVELS STEPHANIE PLUM SERIES: One for the Money, 1994; Two for the Dough, 1996; Three to Get Deadly, 1997; Four to Score, 1998; High Five, 1999; Hot Six, 2000; Seven Up, 2001; Hard Eight, 2002; Visions of Sugar Plums, 2002; To the Nines, 2003; Ten Big Ones, 2004. ROMANCE NOVELS: The Grand Finale, 1988; Thanksgiving, 1988; Manhunt, 1988; Ivan Takes a Wife, 1989; Back to the Bedroom, 1989; Wife for Hire, 1990; Smitten, 1990; The Rocky Road to Romance, 1991; Naughty Neighbor, 1992. FULL SERIES (with S. Hall): Full Tilt, 2003; Full Speed, 2003; Full Blast, 2004. METRO GIRL SERIES: Metro Girl, 2004. NOVELS AS STEFFI HALL: Hero at Large, 1987; Full House, 1989, new ed as Evanovich, 2002; Foul Play, 1989. **Address:** PO Box 5487, Hanover, NH 03755, U.S.A. **Online address:** janet@evanovich.com

EVANS, Alan. (Alan Stoker). British, b. 1930. **Genres:** Novels, Children's fiction, Young adult fiction. **Career:** Civil Servant, H. M. Government. **Publications:** The End of the Running, 1966; Mantrap, 1967; Bannon, 1968; Vicious Circle, 1970; The Big Deal, 1971; Running Scared (juvenile), 1975; Kidnap!, 1977; Escape at the Devil's Gate (juvenile), 1978; Thunder at Dawn, 1978; Ship of Force, 1979; Dauntless, 1980; Seek Out and Destroy, 1982; Deed of Glory, 1984; Audacity, 1985; Eagle at Taranto, 1987; Night Action, 1989; Orphans of the Storm, 1990; Sink or Capture, 1993; Sword at Sunrise, 1994.

EVANS, Brendan. British, b. 1944. **Genres:** Education, Politics/Government. **Career:** Various school and further education governorships. **Publications:** Radical Adult Education: A Political Critique, 1987; The Politics of the Training Market: from Manpower Services Commission to Training and Enterprise Councils, 1992; From Salisbury to Major: Continuity and Change in Conservative Politics, 1996; Thatcherism and British Politics, 2001. **Address:** Vice-Chancellors Office, University of Huddersfield, Queensgate, Huddersfield HDA 3DH, England. **Online address:** bjevans@hud.ac.uk

EVANS, Calvin (Donald). Canadian, b. 1931. **Genres:** History, Bibliography. **Career:** Halifax Citadel Museum, Halifax, NS, Canada, secretary, 1954; minister of United Church of Canada in Saskatchewan, Newfoundland, Ontario, Quebec, and Nova Scotia, Canada, 1955-66; Memorial University of Newfoundland, St. John's, NL, Canada, cataloger, 1967-68, head of Periodicals Division at university library, 1968-73; University of Guelph, ON, Canada, head of humanities and social sciences at university library, 1973-79; University of Alberta, Edmonton, Canada, assistant librarian for public services, 1979-83, assistant librarian for planning and personnel, 1983-84; McGill University, Montreal, QC, Canada, area librarian at Humanities and Social Sciences Library, 1984-93, branch services coordinator, 1993-. **Publications:** For Love of a Woman: The Evans Family and a Perspective on Shipbuilding in Newfoundland, 1992; Soren Kierkegaard Bibliographies: Remnants, 1944-1980, and the Multimedia, 1925-1991, 1993. Contributor to library journals. **Address:** PO Box 569, 13 Marine Dr, Botwood, NL, Canada A0H 1E0.

EVANS, David Ellis. British, b. 1930. **Genres:** Archaeology/Antiquities, Classics, Language/Linguistics, Literary criticism and history. **Career:** University College of Swansea, Wales, assistant lecturer, 1957-59, lecturer, 1960-68, reader, 1968-74, professor of Welsh, 1974-78; University of Oxford, Jesus Professor of Celtic, 1978-96, professor emeritus of Celtic and honorary fellow, Jesus College, 1996-. Language and Literature Section, The Bulletin of the Board of Celtic Studies, ed., 1972-88, chief ed., 1989-93; Studia Celtica, chief ed., 1994-95. **Publications:** Gaulish Personal Names: A Study of Some Continental Celtic Formations, 1967; The Labyrinth of Continental Celtic, 1981. EDITOR: Cofiant Agricola, lywodraethwr Prydain, 1974; Proceedings of the Seventh International Congress of Celtic Studies, Oxford 1983, 1986; Cofio'r Dafydd, 1987. **Address:** Jesus College, Oxford, England.

EVANS, David Stanley. See Obituaries.

EVANS, Douglas. American, b. 1953. **Genres:** Children's fiction, Education. **Career:** Writer, educator. Teacher of second grade at an elementary school in Veneta, OR, 1976-83; International School of Helsinki, Helsinki, Finland, teacher of second grade, 1983-84; American School of London, England, teacher of second grade, 1984-85; Orinda School District, Orinda, CA, teacher of second grade, 1987-97. **Publications:** Classroom at the End of the Hall, 1996; So What Do You Do?, 1997; The Truth about Teachers, 1998; The Elevator Family, 2000; Math Rashes and Other Classroom Tales, 2000; MVPassistant (Magellan Voyage Project), 2004. **Address:** 2819 Piedmont Ave, Berkeley, CA 94705-2313, U.S.A. **Online address:** devans@utmelon.com

EVANS, Earlene Green. American, b. 1938. **Genres:** Education. **Career:** Elementary school teacher in Richmond, VA, 1964-74; library media specialist, 1974-97; Virginia State Senate, Richmond, VA, assistant page supervisor, 1998-99 sessions; auditor of testing standards for state of Virginia, 1999-; notary public. **Publications:** WITH M. BRANCH: Hidden Skeletons and Other Funny Stories, 1995; (ed.) A Step Beyond: Multimedia Activities for Learning American History, 1995; 3-D Displays for Libraries, Schools, and Media Centers, 2000. Contributor to periodicals and newspapers.

EVANS, Eric J(ohn). British, b. 1945. **Genres:** History. **Career:** University of Stirling, lecturer in history, 1969-70; University of Lancaster, lecturer, 1970-80, sr. lecturer, 1980-84, reader in modern British history, 1984-85, professor of social history, 1985-. Lancaster Pamphlets, Routledge, joint ed., 1983-; Making of the Contemporary World, Routledge, joint ed., 1994-; Longman Advanced History, 1995-. Social History Society of U.K., chairman, 1991-98. **Publications:** Tillicoultry: A Centenary History 1871-1971, 1971; The Contentious Tithe: The Tithe Problem and English Agriculture, 1976; Social Policy 1830-1914, 1978; A Social History of Britain in Postcards 1870-1930, 1980; The Forging of the Modern State: Early Industrial Britain, 1783-1870, 1983, 3rd ed., 2001; The Great Reform Act of 1832, 2nd ed., 1994; Political Parties in Britain 1783-1867, 1985; Britain before the Reform Act: Politics and Society 1815-32, 1989; Liberal Democracies, 1990; Sir Robert Peel: Statesmanship, Power and Party, 1991; The Birth of Modern Britain, 1780-1914, 1997; Thatcher and Thatcherism, 1997, 2nd ed., 2004. **Address:** Dept. of History, University of Lancaster, Bailrigg, Lancaster LA1 4YG, United Kingdom. **Online address:** E.Evans@lancaster.ac.uk

EVANS, Francesca. See SCOTTI, R. A.

EVANS, Greg. American, b. 1947. **Genres:** Cartoons. **Career:** High school art teacher in California and Australia, 1970-74; radio and television station promotion manager in Colorado Springs, CO, 1975-80; author and artist of comic strip Luann, 1985-. **Publications:** Meet Luann, 1986; Why Me?,

1986; Is It Friday Yet?, 1987; Who Invented Brothers Anyway?, 1989; School and Other Problems, 1989; Homework Is Ruining My Life, 1989; So Many Malls, So Little Money, 1990; Pizza Isn't Everything but It Comes Close, 1991; Dear Diary: The Following Is Top Secret, 1991; Will We Be Tested on This?, 1992; There's Nothing Worse than First Period P.E., 1992; If Confusion Were a Class I'd Get an A, 1992; School's OK if You Can Stand the Food, 1992; I'm Not Always Confused, I Just Look that Way, 1993; My Bedroom and Other Environmental Hazards, 1993; Luann-The Plunge; Passion, Betrayal, Outrage, Revenge. **Address:** c/o United Media, 200 Madison Ave., New York, NY 10016, U.S.A.

EVANS, Ivan. *See* **WELLS, Angus.**

EVANS, James Allan S. Canadian, b. 1931. **Genres:** Classics, History, Writing/Journalism. **Career:** McMaster University, professor of history, 1962-72; University of British Columbia, Vancouver, professor of classics, 1972-96, head of dept., 1986-93, professor emeritus, 1996-. Commentator, literary editor, 1967-71; Vergilius, editor, 1963-73; Studies in Medieval and Renaissance History, editor, 1978-; Association of Ancient Historians Newsletters, secretarytreasurer, 1979-82. University of Washington, visiting professor of history, 1997; American School of Classical Studies, Athens, Whitehead Visiting Professor, 1998-99. Royal Society of Canada, fellow, 1992. **Publications:** Social and Economic History of an Egyptian Temple in Greco-Roman Egypt, 1961; Procopius, 1972; (ed.) Polis and Imperium: Studies in Honour of Edward Togo Salmon, 1974; Herodotus, 1982; Herodotus, Explorer of the Past: Three Essays, 1991; The Age of Justinian: The Circumstances of Imperial Power, 1996; The Empress Theodora, 2002; The Power Game in Byzantium, 2003; Arts and Humanities through the Eras: Ancient Greece and Rome, 2004; The Emperor Justinian and the Byzantine Empire, 2005. **Address:** Dept of Classical, Near Eastern & Religious Studies, University of British Columbia, Vancouver, Canada V6T 1W5. **Online address:** jaxevans@cablelan.net

EVANS, James H., Jr. American. **Genres:** Literary criticism and history, Theology/Religion. **Career:** Ordained Baptist minister, 1973; Southern Connecticut State College, New Haven, student chaplain, 1974-75; associate pastor of Baptist church in NYC, 1975-79; Colgate Rochester Divinity School/Bexley Hall/Crozer Theological Seminary, Rochester, NY, lecturer, 1979, assistant professor, 1980-84, associate professor of theology and black church studies and Martin Luther King, Jr., Memorial Professor, 1984, acting director of Program of Black Church Studies and Alternate Education Program, 1982, dean of Black Church Studies, 1989, Ayer Lecturer, 1989, president, 1990-. Malcolm-King College, faculty member, 1977; Empire State College of the State University of New York, 1979; University of Rochester, adjunct assistant professor, 1983, visiting associate professor, 1988, adjunct associate professor, 1989-90; Princeton Theological Seminary, visiting professor, 1984-85; Colgate University, University Professor of the Humanities in Philosophy and Religion, 1990; Eastern Baptist Theological Seminary, Frank B. Mitchell Lecturer, 1991-. New Haven Afro-American Historical Society, research assistant, 1975. **Publications:** Spiritual Empowerment in Afro-American Literature: Frederick Douglass, Booker T. Washington, Rebecca Jackson, Richard Wright, and Toni Morrison, 1987; Black Theology: A Critical Assessment and Annotated Bibliography, 1987; We Have Been Believers: Faith, Freedom, and Black Theology, 1992. Work represented in anthologies. Contributor of articles and reviews to education and religious studies journals. **Address:** Colgate Rochester Divinity School, Bexley Hall/Crozer Theological Seminary, 1100 South Goodman St., Rochester, NY 14620, U.S.A.

EVANS, Jonathan. *See* **FREEMANTLE, Brian (Harry).**

EVANS, Laurence Chubb. (Larry Evans). American, b. 1939. **Genres:** Children's fiction, Illustrations. **Career:** Illustrator, graphic artist, and freelance writer. **Publications:** FOR CHILDREN (as Larry Evans): 3-Dimensional Mazes, Vols 1 and 2, 1976-77, as 3-D Mazes, 1995; 3-Dimensional Monster Mazes, 1977; 3-D Maze Art, 1977; Maze Cubes, 1977; 3-Dimensional Optical Illusions to Color and Construct, 1977; How to Draw Monsters, 1977; InVisibles: Hidden Picture Puzzles, Vol 1, 1977, as Adventures with InVisibles, 1995; InVisibles: Hidden Picture Puzzle, Vol 2, 1978, as Imaginary InVisibles, 1995; World of Nature InVisibles, 1978, as Nature's Treasures InVisibles, 1995; Gross and Gruesome Games and Puzzles, 1978; Space Warp Color and Story, 1979; Victorian Puzzles, 1979; How to Draw Prehistoric Monsters, 1979; Pyramid Puzzles, 1979; (with E. Gorey) Gorey Games, 1979; Gnomes Games, 1980; Optricks, 1995; Oceans of InVisibles, 1995; Lateral Logic Mazes for the Serious Puzzler, 1996; A Super-Sneaky Double-Crossing Up, Down Round & Round Maze Book, 1998. OTHER: Illustration Guide for Architects, Vols 1 and 2, 1982; Illustrator's Resource File, 1984; The Complete Illustration Guide for Architects, 1993. Creator of puzzles. Creator of 3-dimensional maze calendars and posters as well as a maze designer and illustrator for Klutz Press. Contributor of article on 3-dimensional mazes to Omni magazine. **Address:** c/o Gallery One, 209 Western Ave, Petaluma, CA 94952, U.S.A. **Online address:** levans1234@aol.com

EVANS, Mary Anna. American. **Genres:** Mystery/Crime/Suspense. **Career:** Mystery writer. Has also worked as an environmental consultant, university administrator, community college instructor, and a roustabout on an offshore natural gas platform. **Publications:** Artifacts, 2003. **Address:** 8321 SW 23rd Place, Gainesville, FL 32607, U.S.A. **Online address:** maryannaevans@yahoo.com

EVANS, Ray. *See* **GILL, Anton.**

EVANS, Richard. British. **Genres:** Science fiction/Fantasy. **Career:** Science-fiction novelist and author of short fiction. Former musician; guitarist and songwriter for band St. Vitus Dancers; keyboardist for Playing in Trains and James. Freelance writer, 1995-. **Publications:** Machine Nation, 2002. Contributor of short fiction to periodicals. **Address:** c/o Author Mail, Writers Club Press, 5220 South 16th St. Ste. 200, Lincoln, NE 68512, U.S.A. **Online address:** info@richardevansonline.com

EVANS, Richard I(sadore). American, b. 1922. **Genres:** Psychology, Documentaries/Reportage, Education. **Career:** University of Tennessee, Knoxville, visiting professor of psychology, 1947-48; Michigan State College (now University), East Lansing, faculty member, 1948-50; University of Houston, Central Campus, Houston, TX, professor of psychology, 1950-, director, Social Psychology/Behavioral Medicine Research and Graduate Training Group, 1979-, Distinguished University Professor of Psychology, 1989-, director, Social Psychology Program, 1992. **Publications:** Conversations with Carl Jung and Reactions from Ernest Jones, 1964, rev. ed. as Jung on Elementary Psychology, 1976, as Dialogue with C.G. Jung, 1981; Dialogue with Erich Fromm, 1966; Dialogue with Erik Erikson, 1967; B.F. Skinner: The Man and His Ideas, 1968, as Dialogue with B.F. Skinner, 1981; (with P.K. Leppmann) Resistance to Innovation in Higher Education, 1968; Psychology and Arthur Miller, 1969; (with J. Bierer) Innovations in Social Psychiatry, 1969; Gordon Allport: The Man and His Ideas, 1971, as Dialogue with Gordon Allport, 1981; Jean Piaget: The Man and His Ideas, 1973, as Dialogue with Jean Piaget, 1981; Carl Rogers: The Man and His Ideas, 1975, as Dialogue with Carl Rogers, 1981; Konrad Lorenz: The Man and His Ideas, 1975; The Making of Psychology, 1976; R.D. Laing: The Man and His Ideas, 1976, as Dialogue with R.D. Laing, 1981; Albert Bandura: The Man and His Ideas, 1989. EDITOR: (with R.M. Rozelle) Social Psychology in Life, 1970, 2nd ed., 1973; The Making of Social Psychology, 1980. Author of research articles and book chapters. **Address:** Department of Psychology, University of Houston, 4800 Calhoun Blvd, 4800 Calhoun Blvd, Houston, TX 77204-5341, U.S.A. **Online address:** rievans@uh.edu

EVANS, Richard J(ohn). British, b. 1947. **Genres:** Women's studies and issues, History, Politics/Government, Autobiography/Memoirs, Biography. **Career:** Stirling University, Scotland, lecturer in history, 1972-76; University of East Anglia, Norwich, England, lecturer, 1976-83, professor of European history, 1983-89; Columbia University, visiting associate professor of European history, 1980; University of London, Birkbeck College, professor of history, 1989-98, vice-master, 1993-98, acting master, 1997; Cambridge University, professor of modern history, 1998-; Gonville and Caius College, Cambridge, fellow, 1998-. **Publications:** The Feminist Movement in Germany, 1894-1933, 1976; The Feminists: Women's Emancipation Movements in Europe, America, and Australasia, 1840-1920, 1977; Sozialdemokratie und Frauenemanzipation im Deutschen Kaiserreich, 1979; Comrades and Sisters, 1987; Steam Cars, 1987; Rethinking German History, 1987; Death in Hamburg: Society and Politics in the Cholera Years, 1830-1910, 1987; Kneipengesprache im Kaiserreich, 1989; In Hitler's Shadow, 1989; Proletarians and Politics, 1990; Rituals of Retribution: Capital Punishment in Germany 1600-1989, 1996; Rereading German History: From Unification to Reunification, 1800-1995, 1997; In Defence of History, 1997; Tales from the German Underworld, 1998; Lying about Hitler: History, Holocaust and the David Irving Trial, 2001; The Coming of the Third Reich, 2003. EDITOR: Society and Politics in Wilhelmine Germany, 1978; (with W.R. Lee) The German Family (essays), 1981; The German Working Class, 1888-1933, 1982; (with Lee) The German Peasantry, 1985; (with D. Geary) The German Unemployed, 1986; The German Underworld, 1988; (with D. Blackbourn) The German Bourgeoisie, 1991.

EVANS, Robert C. American, b. 1955. **Genres:** History, Literary criticism and history. **Career:** Auburn University at Montgomery, AL, instructor,

1982-84, assistant professor, 1984-86, associate professor, 1986-94, professor of English, 1994-, Distinguished Research Professor, 1994-97, University Alumni Professor, 1998-2001, Distinguished Teaching Professor, 2001-. **Publications:** Ben Jonson and the Poetics of Patronage, 1989; Jonson, Lipsius, and the Politics of Renaissance Stoicism, 1992; Jonson and the Contexts of His Time, 1994; Habits of Mind: Evidence and Effects of Ben Jonson's Reading, 1995; (comp. with others) Ben Jonson's Major Plays: Summaries of Modern Monographs, 2000; Close Readings: Analyses of Short Fiction, 2000; Kate Chopin's Short Fiction: A Critical Companion, 2001. EDITOR: (with B. Wiedemann) "My Name Was Martha": A Renaissance Woman's Autobiographical Poem, 1993; (with A.C. Little) "The Muses Females Are": Martha Moulsworth and Other Women Writers of the English Renaissance, 1995; (with A. Depas-Orange) "The Birthday of My Self": Martha Moulsworth, Renaissance Poet, 1996; (with A.C. Little and B. Wiedemann) Short Fiction: A Critical Companion, 1997; (with R. Harp) Frank O'Connor: New Perspectives, 1998; (with R. Harp) Brian Friel: New Perspectives, 2002. Contributor to books. Contributor of articles and reviews to literary journals. **Address:** Dept of English and Philosophy, Box 2444023, Auburn University Montgomery, Montgomery, AL 36124-4023, U.S.A. **Online address:** litpage@aol.com

EVANS, Sara M(argaret). American, b. 1943. **Genres:** History, Politics/Government, Women's studies and issues. **Career:** Chair, Dept. of History, University of Minnesota, 1991-94, Professor of History since 1989, Associate and Assistant Professor, 1976-89; Instructor in History, University of North Carolina, Greensboro, 1974, and Duke University, Durham, North Carolina, 1974-75; Assistant Professor of History, University of North Carolina, Chapel Hill, 1975-76. **Publications:** Personal Politics: The Roots of Women's Liberation in the Civil Rights Movement and the New Left, 1979; (with Harry C. Boyte) Free Spaces: The Sources of Democratic Change in America, 1986; (with Barbara J. Nelson) Wage Justice: Comparable Worth and the Paradox of Technocratic Reform, 1989; Born for Liberty: A History of Women in America, 1989. **Address:** Dept. of History, University of Minnesota, Minneapolis, MN 55455, U.S.A.

EVANS, Stephen S(tewart). American, b. 1954. **Genres:** History, Literary criticism and history. **Career:** Social studies teacher at public schools in Aston, PA, 1979-81; Marine Corps University, Command and Staff College, Quantico, VA, educational adviser, 1996-, lecturer, 1997-. **Publications:** The Lords of Battle: Image and Reality of the Comitatus in Dark Age Britain, 1997; The Heroic Poetry of Dark-Age Britain: An Introduction to Its Dating, Composition, and Use as a Historical Source, 1997. **Address:** 4 Wellington Dr., Stafford, VA 22554, U.S.A.

EVANZZ, Karl. (Karl E. Anderson). American, b. 1953. **Genres:** History, Biography. **Career:** Lowe, Mark & Moffett, Alexandria, VA, law clerk, 1976-77; law clerk to Harry T. Alexander, 1977-81; Washington Post, Washington, DC, on-line editor, 1980-. St. Louis Argus, Washington correspondent, 1981-83. **Publications:** The Judas Factor: The Plot to Kill Malcolm X, 1992; The Messenger: The Rise and Fall of Elijah Muhammad, 1999. **Address:** Washington Post, News Dept., 1150 Fifteenth St. N.W. 4th fl, Washington, DC 20071, U.S.A.

EVELEIGH, Victoria. British, b. 1959. **Genres:** Children's fiction. **Career:** Worked for Exmoor National Park Authority for 3 years; now farming and writing on Exmoor. **Publications:** Katy's Exmoor: The Story of an Exmoor Pony, 2002; Katy's Exmoor Adventures: The Sequel to Katy's Exmoor, 2003. **Address:** West Ilkerton Farm, Lynton, Exmoor, Devon EX35 6QA, England. **Online address:** salas@tortoise-publishing.co.uk

EVELING, (Harry) Stanley. British, b. 1925. **Genres:** Plays/Screenplays, Theatre, Philosophy, Novellas/Short stories. **Career:** Fellow, Edinburgh University Assistant Lecturer, Dept. of Logic and Metaphysics, King's College Aberdeen University, 1955-57; Lecturer, Dept. of Philosophy, University College of Wales, Aberystwyth, 1957-60; visiting professor, Dartmouth College and Santa Cruz. **Publications:** PLAYS: The Lunatic, the Secret Sportsman and the Woman Next Door, and Vibrations, 1970; The Balachites, and The Strange Case of Martin Richter, 1970; Come and Be Killed, and Dear Janet Rosenberg, Dear Mr. Kooning, 1970; Mister, in A Decade's Drama, 1980; The Buglar Boy and His Swish Friend, 1983; The Albrighi Fellow, 1995; Running on the Spot, 1998; 147, 2000. OTHER: Poems, 1956; The Total Theatre (non-fiction), 1972. **Address:** 30 Comely Bank, Edinburgh EH4 1AJ, Scotland. **Online address:** hseveling@ednet.co.uk

EVENBACH, Anton. See STEINER, Evgeny.

EVENSON, Brian. Also writes as David Brandt Cooper. American, b. 1966. **Genres:** Novellas/Short stories, Novels. **Career:** University of Washington,

Seattle, lecturer in English, 1990-93, assistant director of computer integrated class, 1991-93; Magic Realism, contributing editor, 1992-97; Brigham Young University, Provo, UT, assistant professor of English, 1993-95; Rough Draft, editor, 1994-; Oklahoma State University, Stillwater, visiting assistant professor of English, 1995-99; Conjunctions magazine, senior editor, 1998-; University of Denver, assistant professor of English, 1999-; writer. **Publications:** STORIES: Altmann's Tongue: Stories and a Novella, 1994; The Din of Celestial Birds, 1997; Prophets and Brothers, 1997; Contagion, 2000. NOVEL: Father of Lies, 1998. Contributor to periodicals. **Address:** Dept of English, University of Denver, 200 E Asbury, Denver, CO 80208, U.S.A. **Online address:** bevenson@du.edu

EVERDELL, William R(omeyn). American, b. 1941. **Genres:** Poetry, History, Intellectual history, Politics/Government, Sciences. **Career:** Lycee Arago, Paris, assistant in English, 1963-64; St. Ann's School, Brooklyn, NY, chair of history department, 1972-73, head of upper school, 1973-75, co-chair of history department, 1975-84, dean of humanities, 1984-. New York University, adjunct instructor, 1984-89. **Publications:** (co-author) Rowboats to Rapid Transit, 1974; The End of Kings: A History of Republics and Republicans, 1983, 2nd ed., 2000; Christian Apologetics in France, 1730-1790: The Roots of Romantic Religion, 1987; The First Moderns: Profiles in the Origins of Twentieth-Century Thought, 1997. Contributor to periodicals. **Address:** St Ann's School, 129 Pierrepont St, Brooklyn, NY 11201, U.S.A. **Online address:** everdell@aol.com

EVERETT, Douglas Hugh. British, b. 1916. **Genres:** Chemistry. **Career:** Emeritus Professor of Physical Chemistry, University of Bristol, since 1982 (Leverhulme Professor of Physical Chemistry 1954-82). Professor of Chemistry, Dundee University, 1948-54, FRS, 1980. **Publications:** (trans. and co-author) Chemical Thermodynamics, 1954; (ed. with F. S. Stone) Colston Papers Volume X: Structure and Properties of Porous Materials, 1958; Introduction to the Study of Chemical Thermodynamics, 1959, 1971; (trans. and co-author) Surface Tension and Adsorption, 1966; (ed. with R. H. Ottewill) Surface Area Determination, 1970; Basic Principles of Colloid Science, 1988; (with W. Rudzinski) Adsorption of Gases on Heterogeneous Surfaces, 1992. **Address:** School of Chemistry, University of Bristol, Cantock's Close, Bristol BS8 1TS, England.

EVERITT, Alan Milner. British, b. 1926. **Genres:** History, Local history/Rural topics. **Career:** Professor and Head of Dept. of English Local History, University of Leicester, 1968-84 (Research Fellow in Urban History, 1960-65; Lecturer in Local History, 1965-68). **Publications:** Suffolk and the Great Rebellion 1640-60, 1961; The Community of Kent and the Great Rebellion, 1640-60, 1966; The Local Community and the Great Rebellion, 1969; Perspectives in English Urban History, 1973; The Pattern of Rural Dissent: The Nineteenth Century, 1972; Landscape and Community in England, 1985; Continuity and Colonization: The Evolution of Kentish Settlement, 1986; (with J. Chartres) Agricultural Markets and Trade, 1500-1750, 1990. Contributor to journals and books. **Address:** Fieldedge, Poultney Lane, Kimcote, Nr. Lutterworth, Leics. LE17 5RX, England.

EVERITT, James H. American. **Genres:** Horticulture. **Career:** Range scientist and author. Kika De La Garza Agricultural Center, Weslaco, TX, range scientist, 1974-. **Publications:** (with R.I. Leonard and F.W. Judd) Woody Plants of the Lower Rio Grande Valley, 1991; (with D.L. Drawe) Trees, Shrubs, and Cacti of South Texas, 1993, rev. ed, 2002; (ed.) Proceeding of the Sixteenth Biennial Workshop on Videographing Color Photography in Resource Assessment, 1997; (with D.L. Drawe and R.I. Lonard) Field Guide to the Broad-leaved Herbaceous Plants of South Texas: Used by Livestock and Wildlife, 1999. **Address:** U.S.D.A. A.R.S. Kika de la Garza, Subtropical Agricultural Research Service, Integrated Farming and Natural Resources Unit, 2413 East Hwy. 83, Weslaco, TX 78596, U.S.A. **Online address:** jeveritt@weslaco.ars.usda.gov

EVERS, Larry. American, b. 1946. **Genres:** Anthropology/Ethnology, Cultural/Ethnic topics, Mythology/Folklore. **Career:** University of Chicago, Chicago, IL, postdoctoral fellow in department of anthropology, 1972-73; University of Arizona, Tucson, assistant professor, 1974-80, associate professor, 1980-86, professor of English, 1986-, director of graduate study, 1991-94; writer. Member of El Presidio Historic District advisory board. **Publications:** South Corner of Time, University of Arizona Press, 1980. (With Felipe S. Molina) Yaqui Deer Songs, University of Arizona Press, 1987. (With Molina) Coyote Songs, CHAX Press, 1991. **Address:** Department of English, University of Arizona, Tucson, AZ 85721, U.S.A.

EVERSZ, Robert (McLeod). American, b. 1954. **Genres:** Mystery/Crime/Suspense. **Career:** Earl Wilson and Associates (marketing consultants), Los

Angeles, CA, vice president for operations, 1981-84; Robert Eversz and Associates (marketing consultants), Los Angeles, CA, 1984-88. Writer, 1988-. Central European University, Prague, Czech Republic, instructor in Summer Writers' Workshop. **Publications:** NOVELS: The Bottom Line Is Murder, 1988; False Profit, 1989; Shooting Elvis: Confessions of an Accidental Terrorist, 1996; Gypsy Hearts, 1997; Killing Paparazzi, 2002. **Address:** c/o A.L. Hart, Fox Chase Agency, PO Box 61903, King of Prussia, PA 19406-0119, U.S.A.

EVIOTA, Elizabeth Uy. Filipino, b. 1946. **Genres:** Area studies, Economics, History, Social sciences, Sociology, Third World, Women's studies and issues. **Career:** Institute of Philippine Culture, Quezon City, project director, 1976-79; UNICEF, NYC, research associate in Family Welfare, People's Participation, and Women in Development Division, 1980-81; Ateneo de Manila University, Manila, Philippines, lecturer in sociology and anthropology, 1985-, coordinator of Gender Studies Committee, 1988-90. University of Sussex, visiting fellow at Institute of Development Studies, 1990; consultant to Canadian International Development Agency, 1988, 1994-96, Asian Development Bank, 1987, 1991, and Economic Development Institute of the World Bank, 1991-93. **Publications:** Philippine Women and Development: An Annotated Bibliography, 1978; The Political Economy of Gender: Women and the Sexual Division of Labour in the Philippines, 1992. Work represented in anthologies. Contributor to sociology journals. **Address:** Department of Sociology and Anthropology, Ateneo de Manila University, PO Box 154, Manila, Philippines.

EWING, David Walkley. American, b. 1923. **Genres:** Administration/Management. **Career:** Assistant Ed., 1949-64, Associate Ed., 1964-68, Sr. Associate Ed., 1968-72, Executive Ed., 1974-80, and Managing Ed., 1980-85, Harvard Business Review, Boston, Massachusetts. **Publications:** The Managerial Mind, 1964; The Practice of Planning, 1968; The Human Side of Planning, 1969; Writing for Results: In Business, Government, and the Professions, 1974; Freedom Inside the Organization, 1977; Do It My Way or You're Fired!, 1983; Justice on the Job, 1989; Inside the Harvard Business School, 1990. EDITOR: Long-Range Planning for Management, 1964; Effective Marketing Action, 1958; Incentives for Executives, 1962; (and contrib) Long-Range Planning for Management, 1964, 1972; Technological Change and Management, 1970; Science Policy and Business, 1973. **Address:** 195 Cambridge St, Winchester, MA 01890, U.S.A.

EXETASTES. See HARAKAS, Stanley Samuel.

EXTON, Clive (Jack Montague). British, b. 1930. **Genres:** Plays/Screenplays. **Career:** Worked in advertising, 1946-48; Actor, 1951-59. **Publications:** SCREENPLAYS: Night Must Fall, 1963; (with M. Bragg) Isadora, 1968; Entertaining Mr. Sloane, 1969; Ten Rillington Place, 1970; Doomwatch, 1971; (with D. Hemmings) Running Scared, 1971; (with T. Nation) Nightmare Park, 1973; Legacies, 1973. PLAYS: No Fixed Abode, 1959; Have You Any Dirty Washing, Mother Dear, 1969; Twixt, 1991; Murder Is Easy (Agatha Christie's novel), 1993; Jeeves and the Last of the Woosters, (characters by P.G. Wodehouse), 1993; Dressing Down, 1997. FOR TELEVISION: When Greek Meets Greek, 1975; The Root of All Evil, 1975; A Chance for Mr. Lever, 1976; The Overnight Bag, 1976; Killers series, 1976; The Crezz series, 1976; Stigma, 1977; Henry Intervening, 1978; Agatha Christie's Poirot series, 1989-93; Jeeves and Wooster series, 1990-93, (Writers' Guild Award, 1992); The Long Run Home, 1997. **Address:** c/o Rochelle Stevens & Co., 2, Terret's Place, London N1 1QZ, England.

EYCK, Frank. Canadian (born Germany), b. 1921. **Genres:** History, Theology/Religion. **Career:** Exeter University, UK, Lecturer in Modern European History, 1959-68; University of Calgary, AB, Professor, 1968-87, Professor Emeritus of History, 1987-. Vice-Chairman of Council, Inter-University Centre of Post-Graduate Studies, Dubrovnik, 1974-79. **Publications:** The Prince Consort: A Political Biography, 1959; The Frankfurt Parliament 1848-49, 1968; G.P. Gooch: A Study in History and Politics, 1982; Religion and Politics in German History, 1998. EDITOR: The Revolutions of 1848-49, 1972; Frederick Hertz: The German Public Mind in the Nineteenth Century, 1975. **Address:** Dept. of History, University of Calgary, Calgary, AB, Canada T2N 1N4. **Online address:** feyck@telusplanet.net

EYER, Diane E(lizabeth). American, b. 1944. **Genres:** History, Psychology, Sociology, Women's studies and issues. **Career:** Institute of Pennsylvania Hospital, poetry therapist, 1971-73; Philadelphia Institute for Gestalt Therapy, counselor, 1971-75; Rutgers University, New Brunswick, NJ, instructor, 1985-89; University of Pennsylvania, Philadelphia, teaching assistant, 1983-85, research assistant, 1984-87, lecturer, 1991-; Temple University, Philadelphia, PA, instructor, 1986-87, assistant professor of psychology,

1994-. Therapist in private practice; producer, narrator, and editor of documentary and educational films; editorial consultant to publications. **Publications:** Studying Literacy in Morocco: A Model (documentary film script), 1988; Mother-Infant Bonding: A Scientific Fiction, 1992; Motherguilt, 1996; (with K. Hirsh-Pasek and R. Golinhoff) Einstein Never Used Flashcards, 2003. Contributor to books and periodicals. **Address:** c/o Beth Vesel, Sanford J. Greenburger Associates, 55 5th Ave, New York, NY 10003, U.S.A.

EYNON, Robert. (Bob). British, b. 1941. **Genres:** Novellas/Short stories, Westerns/Adventure. **Career:** Full-time writer, 1987-. Language teacher, The High School, Bedford, 1963-65; teacher of English, Lycee Foch, Rodez, France, 1965-66, and Ecole de La Salle, Lille, France, 1966-67; language teacher, Peter Symond's School, Winchester, Hants., 1967-69, and Girls' Grammar School, Pontypridd, Glamorgan, 1968-72; Lecturer in Education, University College, Cardiff, Glamorgan, 1972-84; Visiting Lecturer, Ibadan University, Nigeria, 1975; Parks labourer, Rhondda Borough Council, 1985-86. **Publications:** Bitter Waters, 1988; Texas Honour, 1988; Johnny One-Arm, 1989; Gunfight at Simeon's Ridge, 1991; Gun-Law Legacy, 1991; Sunset Reckoning, 1993; Anderton Justice, 1997; Pecos Vengeance, 1998; Brothers till Death, 1999; Arizona Payback, 2001; Poison Valley, 2003. Author of novels and stories in Welsh as Bob Eynon. **Address:** 5 Troedyrhiw Terrace, Treorchy, M. Glam CF42 6PG, Wales.

EYRE, Annette. See WORBOYS, Anne.

EYRE, Elizabeth. See STAYNES, Jill.

EYRE, Elizabeth. See STOREY, Margaret.

EYRE, Peter. American, b. 1942. **Genres:** Translations. **Career:** Professional actor, 1960-, and director. Worked with Royal Shakespeare Company and Old Vic Theatre; Broadway, off Broadway; worked in regional theater, films, television, and radio. **Publications:** (trans. with T. Alexander) K. Mann, Siblings: The Children's Story, 1992; Chere Maitre, 2002.

EYRE, S. Robert. British, b. 1922. **Genres:** Environmental sciences/Ecology. **Career:** Lecturer, 1952-66, and Sr. Lecturer, 1966 until retirement 1982, University of Leeds. President, Geography Section, British Association for the Advancement of Science, 1970-71. **Publications:** (author and ed. with G. R. J. Jones) Geography as Human Ecology, 1966; Vegetation and Soils: A World Picture, 2nd ed. 1968; (ed.) World Vegetation Types, 1971; (with J. Palmer) The Face of North East Yorkshire, 1973; The Real Wealth of Nations, 1978. **Address:** Rokeby Cott, Husthwaite, York, England.

EYSENCK, Michael (William). British, b. 1944. **Genres:** Psychology. **Career:** University of London, Birkbeck College, London, England, lecturer, 1965-80, reader in psychology, 1981-87; University of London, Royal Holloway and Bedford New College, Egham, Surrey, England, professor of psychology, 1987-. **Publications:** Human Memory: Theory, Research, and Individual Differences, 1977; Attention and Arousal: Cognition and Performance, 1982; (with H. Eysenck) Mindwatching: Why People Behave the Way They Do, 1983; A Handbook of Cognitive Psychology, 1984; (with H. Eysenck) Personality and Individual Differences, 1985; Happiness: Facts and Myths, 1990; (co-author) Cognitive Psychology: A Student's Handbook, 1990; Anxiety: The Cognitive Perspective, 1992; Principles of Cognitive Psychology, 1993; Individual Differences: Normal and Abnormal, 1994; Perspectives on Psychology, 1994; Simply Psychology, 1996; Anxiety and Cognition: A Unified Theory, 1997; Psychology: An Integrated Approach, 1998; Psychology: A Student's Handbook, 2000. **Address:** Department of Psychology, Royal Holloway, University of London, Egham, Surrey TW20 0EX, England. **Online address:** m.eysenck@rhul.ac.uk

EZELL, Lee. American. **Genres:** Inspirational/Motivational Literature. **Career:** Author and inspirational speaker. Ezell Communications, Newport Beach, CA, director. **Publications:** The Cinderella Syndrome: Discovering God's Plan When Your Dreams Don't Come True, 1985; The Missing Piece: Finding God's Peace for Your Past, 1986; Private Obsessions, 1991; Pills for Parents in Pain, 1992; (with L. Gilbert) Iron Jane: It's Time for a Lasting, Loving Ceasefire in the Battle of the Sexes, 1994; Will the Real Me Please Stand Up!, 1998; Porcupine People: Learning to Love the Unlovable, 1998; Finding God When Life's Not Fair: Surviving Soul-Shakers and Aftershocks, 2001; What Men Understand about Women. Ezell's books have been translated into thirteen languages:. **Address:** Ezell Communications, Box 7475, Newport Beach, CA 92658, U.S.A.

EZELL, Margaret J. M. American, b. 1955. **Genres:** Literary criticism and history, Women's studies and issues. **Career:** Texas A&M University, College Station, professor of English, 1982-, and fellow of Interdisciplinary Group for History Literary Studies. Folger Shakespeare Library and Institute, visiting lecturer, 1991. **Publications:** The Patriarch's Wife: Literary Evidence and the History of the Family, 1987; Writing Women's Literary History, 1993. EDITOR: The Poetry and Prose of Mary, Lady Chudleigh, 1993; (with K.O'B. O'Keeffe) Cultural Artifacts and the Production of Meaning: The Page, the Body, and the Image, 1994. Contributor to magazines and newspapers. **Address:** Department of English, Texas A&M University, College Station, TX 77843, U.S.A.

EZRAHI, Yaron. Israeli. **Genres:** Communications/Media, Cultural/Ethnic topics, Politics/Government, Sciences. **Career:** Hebrew University of Jerusalem, Israel, professor of political science; peace activist. Appeared on radio programs. **Publications:** NONFICTION: (ed. with E. Tal) Science Policy and Development; The Case of Israel, 1972; The Descent of Icarus: Science and the Transformation of Contemporary Democracy, 1990; (ed. with E. Mendelsohn and H. Segal) Technology, Pessimism, and Postmodernism, 1994; Rubber Bullets: Power and Conscience in Modern Israel, 1997. Contributor to periodicals. **Address:** Dept of Political Science and Social Sciences, Mount Scopus, Hebrew University of Jerusalem, 91905 Jerusalem, Israel. **Online address:** msezrahi@mscc.huji.ac.il

F

FAAS, Ekbert. German, b. 1938. **Genres:** Novels, Literary criticism and history. **Career:** Professor of Humanities and English, York University, Toronto, 1976-. Lecturer, Goethe Institute, Madrid and London, 1961-64; Assistant Professor of English, 1965-68, and Privat-Dozent, 1971-72, University of Wuerzburg. **Publications:** (trans.) Ted Hughes, 1971; Poesie als Psychogramm. Die dramatisch-monologische Versdichtung im Viktorianischen Zeitalter, 1974; Offene Formen in der moderneu Kunst und Literatur, 1975; Towards a New American Poetics, 1978; Ted Hughes: The Unaccommodated Universe, 1980; Young Robert Duncan: Portrait of the Poet as Homosexual in Society, 1983; Tragedy and After: Euripides, Shakespeare, Goethe, 1984; Shakespeare's Poetics, 1986; Retreat into the Mind: Victorian Poetry and the Rise of Psychiatry, 1988; Woyzeck's Head (novel), 1991; La tete de Woyzeck (novel), 1995; (with M. Trombacco) Robert Creeley: A Biography, 2001; The Genealogy of Aesthetics, 2002. EDITOR: Kenneth Rexroth: Excerpts from a Life, 1981; (with S. Reed) Irving Layton and Robert Creeley: The Complete Correspondence, 1989. **Address:** 242 Winters College, York University, Toronto, ON, Canada M3J 1P3.

FABRICANT, Michael B. American, b. 1948. **Genres:** Adult non-fiction. **Career:** Community Service Society, NYC, research associate, 1975-80; Hunter College, NYC, assistant professor, 1980-85, associate professor, 1985-88, professor of social work, 1988-. Member of board of directors for National Coalition for the Homeless, Union County Legal Services, Elizabeth Coalition to House the Homeless, and St. Joseph's Social Service Center; consultant to American Red Cross, Henry Street Settlement, and John Jay College of Criminal Justice of the City University of New York. **Publications:** Deinstitutionalizing Delinquent Youth, 1980; Juveniles in the Family Court, 1983; (with S. Burghardt) Working Under the Safety Net, 1987; (with S. Burghardt) The Welfare State Crisis and the Transformation of Social Service Work, 1992. **Address:** 118 Lincoln Ave., Elizabeth, NJ 07208, U.S.A. **Online address:** mbfabric@webspan.net

FABRIZIO, Timothy C(harles). American, b. 1948. **Genres:** Antiques/Furnishings. **Career:** National Pantomime Theater, Boston, MA, actor and technician, 1968-71; Lift Bridge Book Shops, Brockport, NY, co-owner, 1972-84; Terra Firma Books and Antiques, Rochester, NY, owner, 1985-. Library of Congress, consultant in music machine and record acquisition. **Publications:** (with G.F. Paul) The Talking Machine, 1997; Antique Phonograph Gadgets, Gizmos and Gimmicks, 1999; Discovering Antique Phonographs, 2000; Phonographs with Flair, 2001; Antique Phonograph Advertising, 2002; Antique Phonograph Accessories and Contraptions, 2003; Phonographica: The Early History of Recorded Sound Observed, 2004. **Address:** Phonophan, PO Box 747, Henrietta, NY 14467, U.S.A. **Online address:** phonophan@aol.com.

FACTOR, Silas. *See* DOSS, Margot P(atterson).

FADIMAN, Anne. American, b. 1953. **Genres:** Documentaries/Reportage. **Career:** Literary journalist and editor. American Scholar, editor, 1998-; worked nine years as an editor and staff writer for Life magazine; worked for three years as editor-at-large and columnist for Civilization. **Publications:** The Spirit Catches You and You Fall Down: A Hmong Child, Her American Doctors, and the Collision of Two Cultures, 1997; Ex Libris: Confessions of a Common Reader, 1998. Contributor to periodicals. **Address:** c/o Steven Barclay Agency, 12 Western Ave, Petaluma, CA 94952, U.S.A.

FAGAN, Brian Murray. American/British (born United Kingdom), b. 1936. **Genres:** Anthropology/Ethnology, Archaeology/Antiquities, History, Travel/ Exploration. **Career:** British Institute in Eastern Africa, former director, Bantu Studies project; Livingstone Museum, Zambia, keeper of prehistory, 1959-65; University of Illinois, visiting associate professor, 1965-66; University of California, Santa Barbara, associate professor, 1967-69, professor of anthropology, 1969-. **Publications:** Southern Africa during the Iron Age, 1966; (with S.G.H. Daniels and D.W. Phillipson) Iron Age Cultures in Zambia, vol. 1, 1967, vol. 2, 1969; (with F. Van Noten) The Hunter-Gatherers of Gwisho, 1971; In the Beginning, 1972, 10th ed., 2001; Men of the Earth, 1974, 11th ed. as People of the Earth, 2003; The Rape of the Nile, 1975; Elusive Treasure, 1977; Quest for the Past, 1978; Return to Babylon, 1979; World Prehistory, 1979, 5th ed., 2001; The Aztecs, 1984; Clash of Cultures, 1984; The Adventure in Archaeology, 1985; Bareboating, 1985; Anchoring, 1985; The Great Journey, 1987; The Journey from Eden, 1991; Archaeology: A Brief Introduction, 1978, 8th ed., 2002; Ancient North America, 1991, 3rd ed., 2000; Kingdoms of Gold, Kingdoms of Jade, 1992; Cruising Guide to Southern California's Offshore Islands, 1992; Cruising Guide: San Francisco to Ensenada, Mexico, 1994; Time Detectives, 1995; From Black Land to Fifth Son, 1998; Floods, Famines, and Emperors, 1999; Little Ice Age, 2001; Ancient Lives, 2000, 2nd ed., 2003; Cruising Guide to Central and Southern California, 2001; Before California, 2003; The Long Summer, 2004; Chaco Canyon, 2005. EDITOR: Victoria Falls Handbook, 1964; A Short History of Zambia, 1966; Oxford Companion to Archaeology, 1996; Eyewitness to Discovery, 1997.

FAGAN, Louis J. American, b. 1971. **Genres:** Novels. **Career:** Listener, editorial assistant, 1995-96; State University of New York at Cobleskill, adjunct instructor in English, 1997-. Gives readings of his stories. **Publications:** New Boots (novel), 1999. Contributor to periodicals. **Address:** 612 W 6th St, Jamestown, NY 14701, U.S.A.

FAGAN, Thomas K(evin). American, b. 1943. **Genres:** Psychology. **Career:** Western Illinois University, Macomb, assistant professor to associate professor of psychology, 1969-76; University of Memphis, TN, professor of psychology, 1976-. **Publications:** School Psychology: Past, Present, and Future, 1994, rev. ed., 2000; (co-ed.) Historical Encyclopedia of School Psychology, 1996. Some writings appear under the name Tom Fagan. **Address:** 202 Psychology, University of Memphis, Memphis, TN 38152-3230, U.S.A. **Online address:** tom-fagan@mail.psyc.memphis.edu

FAGGEN, Robert. American. **Genres:** Literary criticism and history. **Career:** Claremont McKenna College, Claremont, CA, currently associate professor of literature; Claremont Graduate School, currently adjunct associate professor. **Publications:** Robert Frost and the Challenge of Darwin, 1997; (ed.) Striving Towards Being: The Letters of Thomas Merton and Czeslaw Milosz, 1997; (ed. and author of intro) E.A. Robinson, Selected Poems, 1997; (ed.) R. Frost, Early Poems, 1998. Contributing editor to the Paris Review. **Address:** Athenaeum 214, Claremont McKenna College, Claremont, CA 91711, U.S.A. **Online address:** r_faggen@benson.mckenna.edu

FAGLES, Robert. American, b. 1933. **Genres:** Poetry, Literary criticism and history, Translations. **Career:** Translator from ancient Greek, poet, and educator. Yale University, New Haven, CT, instructor of English, 1959-60; Princeton University, Princeton, NJ, instructor of English, 1960-62, assistant professor, 1962-65, associate professor of English and comparative literature, 1965-70, professor of comparative literature, 1970-2002, emeritus, 2002-; Program in Comparative Literature, director, 1965-, founding chair of department, 1975-94. **Publications:** TRANSLATIONS: Bacchylides, Complete Poems, 1961; (author of introductory essays, notes, and glossary with W.B. Stanford) Aeschylus, The Oresteia, 1975; Sophocles, The Three Theban Plays, 1984; Homer, The Iliad, 1990; Homer, The Odyssey, 1996. POETRY: I, Vincent: Poems from the Pictures of Van Gogh, 1978. OTHER: (co-ed.) Homer: A Collection of Critical Essays, 1962; (co-ed.) Pope's Iliad and Odyssey, 1967; Sophocles: Antigone & Oedipus the King: A Companion to the Penguin Translation of Robert Fagles, 1987. **Address:** Program in Comparative Literature, Princeton University, Princeton, NJ 08544, U.S.A.

FAHEY, David (Allen). American, b. 1948. **Genres:** Art/Art history. **Career:** G. Ray Hawkins Gallery, Los Angeles, Calif., director, 197586; Fahey/Klein Gallery, Los Angeles, co-owner and codirector, 1986-. Instructor at Compton College, 1974-84; instructor and lecturer at University of California, Los Angeles, 1982-84, and University of Southern California, 1985. Co-founder of Hollywood Photographers Archive, 1985-86; project coordinator for Herb Ritts Pictures, Twelve Trees Press, 1988. Military service: U.S. Army, 1969-71; served in Vietnam. **Publications:** Masters of Starlight, Ballantine, 1987. **Address:** Fahey/Klein Gallery, 148 North La Brea, Los Angeles, CA 90046, U.S.A.

FAHEY, David M(ichael). American, b. 1937. **Genres:** History. **Career:** Assumption College, Worcester, MA, instructor, 1963-65, assistant professor of history, 1965-66; Indiana University, Gary, IN, assistant professor, 1966-69; Miami University, Oxford, OH, associate professor, 1969-82, professor of history, 1982-; writer. Social History of Alcohol and Drugs: An Interdisciplinary Journal, editor in chief, 2003-04. **Publications:** (with others) The English Heritage (textbook), 1978; Temperance and Racism: John Bull, Johnny Reb, and the Good Templars, 1996. EDITOR: The Collected Writings of Jessie Forsyth, 1988; The Black Lodge in White America: "True Reformer" Browne and His Economic Strategy, 1994; (co-) Alcohol and Temperance in Modern History: An International Encyclopedia, 2003; The Alabama, British Neutrality, and the American Civil War by the Late Frank J. Merli, 2004. Contributor to periodicals. **Address:** Dept of History, Miami University, Oxford, OH 45056, U.S.A. **Online address:** Faheydm@muohio.edu

FAHLMAN, Clyde. American, b. 1931. **Genres:** Humor/Satire. **Career:** Pacific Northwest Bell, Portland, OR, district manager for the western United States, 1955-86; Portland Community College, Portland, adjunct faculty member, 1986-. **Publications:** Laughing Nine to Five: The Quest for Humor in the Workplace, 1997. **Address:** 685 Southwest 84th Ave., Portland, OR 97225, U.S.A. **Online address:** cfahlman@teleport.com

FAHN, Abraham. Israeli (born Austria), b. 1916. **Genres:** Botany. **Career:** Professor Emeritus of Botany, Hebrew University of Jerusalem, since 1986 (joined faculty, 1945; Instructor, 1949-52; Lecturer, 1952-55; Sr. Lecturer, 1955-60; Associate Professor, 1960-65; Dean of the Faculty of Science, 1963-65; Professor, 1965-76; Head, Dept. of Botany, 1965-72; Pro-Rector, 1969-70; Otto Warburg Professor, 1976-86). President, Botanical Society of Israel, 1981-84. Recipient, Israel Prize for Natural Sciences, 1963. **Publications:** (with M. Zohary) Cultivated Plants of Israel (in Hebrew), 1957, (with D. Heller and M. Avishai) 1998; Plant Anatomy, 1967, 4th ed., 1990; Secretory Tissues in Plants, 1979; (with E. Werker and P. Baas) Wood Anatomy and Identification of Trees and Shrubs from Israel and Adjacent Regions, 1986; (with D.F. Cutler) Xerophytes, 1992;. **Address:** Dept. of Botany, Hebrew University of Jerusalem, 91904 Jerusalem, Israel. **Online address:** fahn@vms.huji.ac.il

FAIG, Kenneth W(alter), Jr. American, b. 1948. **Genres:** Literary criticism and history. **Career:** North American Company for Life and Health Insurance, Chicago, IL, actuary, 1973-87; Allstate Life Insurance Co., Northbrook, IL, actuary, 1987-89; PolySystems, Chicago, actuary, 1989-. Moshassuck Press, publisher, 1987-. **Publications:** H.P. Lovecraft: His Life, His Work, 1979; The Parents of H.P. Lovecraft, 1990; Some of the Descendants of Asaph Phillips and Esther Whipple, 1993; Tales of the Lovecraft Collectors (fiction), 1995; Big Heart: Remembering Robert Earl Hughes, 2001. EDITOR: E. Miniser, Going Home, 1995; F.C. Clark, Susan's Obituary, 1996; H.P. Lovecraft, Criticism of Amateur Verse, 1998; E. Miniser, The Coast of Bohemia, 2000. **Address:** 2311 Swainwood Dr, Glenview, IL 60025, U.S.A. **Online address:** moshasuk@interaccess.com

FAIGLEY, Lester. American, b. 1947. **Genres:** Writing/Journalism. **Career:** University of Texas at Austin, professor of English and founding director of Division of Rhetoric and Composition, 1979-. National University of Singapore, senior fellow, 1986-87; Pennsylvania State University, visiting professor, 1990; Oxford University, visiting professor at Brasenose College, 1992.

Publications: (with S. White) Evaluating College Writing Programs, 1983; (with R. Cherry, D. Jolliffe, and A. Skinner) Assessing Writers' Knowledge and Processes of Composing, 1985; Fragments of Rationality, 1992; (with J. Selzer) Good Reasons, 2000, 2nd ed., 2003; The Longman Guide to the Web, 2000; (with J. Selzer) Good Reasons with Contemporary Arguments, 2001, 2nd ed., 2004; The Penguin Handbook, 2003; The Brief Penguin Handbook, 2003; (with D. George, A. Palchik, C. Selfe) Picturing Texts, 2004. **Address:** Division of Rhetoric and Composition, University of Texas at Austin, Austin, TX 78712, U.S.A.

FAILING, Patricia. American, b. 1944. **Genres:** Art/Art history. **Career:** University of Washington, Seattle, guest lecturer, 1982-89, assistant professor, 1989-92, associate professor of art history, 1992-. Lewis and Clark College, lecturer in philosophy, 1985; Reed College, visiting associate professor, 1986; lecturer at art museums, colleges, and universities. **Publications:** America's Best-Loved Art, 1983; Doris Chase, Artist in Motion, with videotape, 1992; Howard Kottler: Face to Face, 1995. Contributor to books. Contributor of articles and reviews to periodicals. **Address:** Department of Art History, Box 353440, University of Washington, Seattle, WA 98195, U.S.A.

FAIN, Michael. Also writes as Judith Michael. American, b. 1936. **Genres:** Novels, Romance/Historical. **Career:** Writer and photographer. Worked as an optical engineer. **Publications:** NOVELS AS JUDITH MICHAEL (with J. Barnard): Deceptions, 1982; Possessions, 1984; Private Affairs, 1986; Inheritance, 1988; A Ruling Passion, 1990; Sleeping Beauty, 1991; Pot of Gold, 1993; A Tangled Web, 1995; Acts of Love, 1997; A Certain Smile, 1999. Contributor to periodicals. **Address:** c/o Jane Rotrosen Agency, 318 E 51st St, New York, NY 10022, U.S.A.

FAINLIGHT, Ruth. American, b. 1931. **Genres:** Novellas/Short stories, Poetry, Songs/Lyrics and libretti, Translations. **Career:** Vanderbilt University, Nashville, TN, poet-in-residence, 1985, 1990. **Publications:** A Forecast, a Fable, 1958; Cages, 1966; 18 Poems from 1966, 1967; To See the Matter Clearly, 1968; (with A. Sillitoe and T. Hughes) Poems, 1971; Daylife and Nightlife (short stories), 1971; The Region's Violence, 1973; 21 Poems, 1973; Another Full Moon, 1976; Two Fire Poems, 1977; The Function of Tears, 1979; Sibyls and Others, 1980; Climates, 1983; Fifteen to Infinity, 1983; Selected Poems, 1988; The Knot, 1990; This Time of Year, 1993; Dr. Clock's Last Case (short stories), 1994; Selected Poems, 1995; Sugar-Paper Blue, 1997; Burning Wire, 2002. TRANSLATOR: (with A. Sillitoe) All Citizens Are Soldiers (play), 1967; S. de Mello Breyner Andresen, Navigacions, 1983; S. de Mello Breyner Andresen, Marine Rose, 1987. **Address:** 14 Ladbroke Terr, London W11 3PG, England.

FAIR, David. American, b. 1952. **Genres:** Children's fiction. **Career:** Carroll County Public Library, Westminster, MD, librarian, 1977-. Performer in rock 'n' roll bands. **Publications:** The Fabulous Four Skunks, 1996. **Address:** 1 Black Oak Ln, Westminster, MD 21157, U.S.A.

FAIRBAIRN, Brett. Canadian, b. 1959. **Genres:** Economics, History. **Career:** University of Saskatchewan, Saskatoon, assistant professor to professor of history, 1986-, director of graduate studies in history, 1996-99. Saskatchewan Archives Board, chairperson, 1997-99. Government of Saskatchewan, special adviser to department of post-secondary education, 1996. **Publications:** Building a Dream: The Co-operative Retailing System in Western Canada, 1928-1988, 1989; (with J. Bold, M. Fulton, and others) Co-operatives and Community Development: Economics in Social Perspective, 1991; (ed. with H. Baker and J. Draper) Dignity and Growth: Citizen Participation in Social Change, 1991; Democracy in the Undemocratic State: The German Reichstag Elections of 1898-1903, 1997; (ed. with I. MacPherson and N. Russell) Canadian Cooperatives in the Year 2000: Memory, Mutual Aid and the Millennium, 2001. **Address:** Department of History, University of Saskatchewan, 101 Diefenbaker Pl, Saskatoon, SK, Canada S7N 5B8. **Online address:** brett.fairbairn@usask.ca

FAIRBANKS, Nancy. See HERNDON, Nancy.

FAIRCHILD, B(ertram) H., (Jr.). American, b. 1942. **Genres:** Poetry, Literary criticism and history. **Career:** Poet, 1972-. C&W Machine Works, Liberal, Kansas, until 1966; Hercules Inc., Lawrence, Kansas, 1966-67; Kearney State College, Kearney, Nebraska, instructor, 1968-70; University of Tulsa, teaching fellow, 1970-73; Southwest Texas State University, assistant professor, 1973-76; Texas Woman's University, associate professor, 1976-83; California State University, San Bernardino, professor, 1983-. **Publications:** Such Holy Song: Music as Idea, Form, and Image in the Poetry of William Blake (literary criticism), 1980. POETRY: Arrival of the Future, 1985; The

Art of the Lathe: Poems, 1998; Local Knowledge, 1991; Early Occult Memory Systems of the Lower Midwest, 2003. Contributor of poetry, essays, and articles to periodicals. **Address:** California State University, 5500 University Parkway, San Bernardino, CA 92407, U.S.A. **Online address:** Bhfairchil@aol.com; fairchld@csusb.edu

FAIRFAX, John. British, b. 1930. **Genres:** Poetry, Literary criticism and history. **Career:** Director, Phoenix Press, Newbury, Berks, 1967-. Director, Writers Studio, Newbury, Berks. Co-Founding Director, Arvon Foundation, Devon, 1968-. School teacher, 1955-62; Arvon Foundation, creative writing centres, co-founder, 1968. Corporate commissioned poems, 2000-. **Publications:** POETRY: This I Say: Twelve Poems, 1967; Adrift on the Star Brow of Taliesin, 1975; Bone Harvest Done, 1980; Wild Children, 1986; 100 Poems, 1992; Zuihitsu, 1996; Poems '99, 2000; Poems in Virtual Reality, 2004. OTHER: The 5th Horseman of the Apocalypse, 1969; (with M. Baldwin and B. Patten) Double Image, 1972; (with J. Moat) The Way to Write, 1981; Creative Writing, 1989. EDITOR: Listen to This: A Contemporary Anthology, 1967; Stop and Listen: An Anthology of Thirteen Living Poets, 1969; Frontier of Going: An Anthology of Space Poetry, 1969; Horizons, 1971. **Address:** The Thatched Cottage, Hermitage, Newbury, Berks., England.

FAIRFIELD, John D. American, b. 1955. **Genres:** Urban studies. **Career:** University of Rochester, Rochester, lecturer in history, 1980; Wells College, Aurora, NY, lecturer in history, 1981; Rochester Institute of Technology, Rochester, NY, lecturer in history, 1982-83; Alfred University, Alfred, NY, lecturer in history, 1983-84; Xavier University, Cincinnati, OH, assistant professor, 1984-90, associate professor of history, 1990-. **Publications:** The Mysteries of the Great City: The Politics of Urban Design, 1877-1937, 1993. Contributor to history and planning journals. **Address:** Department of History, Xavier University, 3800 Victory Parkway, Cincinnati, OH 45207, U.S.A.

FAIRFIELD, Paul. Canadian, b. 1966. **Genres:** Philosophy. **Career:** Queen's University, Kingston, Ontario, Canada, adjunct assistant professor of philosophy, 2001-. **Publications:** (with G.B. Madison and I. Harris) Is There a Canadian Philosophy? Reflections on the Canadian Identity, 2000; Moral Selfhood in the Liberal Tradition: The Politics of Individuality, 2000; Theorizing Praxis: Studies in Hermeneutical Pragmatism, 2000; Death and Life, 2001; The Ways of Power: Hermeneutics, Ethics, and Social Criticism, 2002; (ed and contrib) Working through Postmodernity, in press. Contributor to books and periodicals. **Address:** Department of Philosophy, Queen's University, Kingston, ON, Canada K7L 3N6. **Online address:** paulfairfield@hotmail.com

FAIRLEY, James S(tewart). British, b. 1940. **Genres:** Animals/Pets, Natural history, Zoology. **Career:** Queen's University, Belfast, research fellow, 1966-68; University College, Galway, Ireland, lecturer in zoology, 1968-91, associate professor, 1991-99, now retired. **Publications:** Irish Wild Mammals: A Guide to the Literature, 1972, 1992; An Irish Beast Book, 1975, 1984; (ed.) The Experienced Huntsman, 1977; Irish Whales and Whaling, 1981; A Basket of Weasels, 2001. **Address:** 15 Luxor Gardens, Belfast BT5 5NB, Northern Ireland.

FAIRMAN, Joan Alexandra. (Mrs. George T. Mitchell, Jr). American, b. 1935. **Genres:** Children's fiction. **Career:** Consultant, Towers, Perrin, Forster & Crosby, Inc. (mgmt. consultants), Philadelphia, 1970-91; Executive Secretary, Curtis Publishing Co., Philadelphia, 1953-70. **Publications:** (contri) Widening Circles, 1970, 1974; A Penny Saved, 1971. **Address:** 430 Wayland Rd, Cherry Hill, NJ 08034, U.S.A.

FAIRSTEIN, Linda A. American, b. 1947. **Genres:** Mystery/Crime/Suspense, Law. **Career:** New York County District Attorney's Office, appointed to staff, 1972, chief of sex crimes prosecution unit, 1976-, deputy chief of trial division, 1981-. Member of the board of directors for several non-profit organizations. National Lecturer on such topics as violence against women, domestic violence, and aspects of the criminal justice system to professional organizations, colleges and universities, health care professionals, and women's groups. **Publications:** Sexual Violence: Our War against Rape, 1993; Final Jeopardy, 1996; Likely to Die, 1997; Cold Hit, 1999; The Deadhouse, 2001; The Bone Vault, 2003. **Address:** Office of the District Attorney, Sex Crimes Prosecution Unit, 1 Hogan Place, New York, NY 10013, U.S.A.

FAITH, Nicholas. British, b. 1933. **Genres:** Business/Trade/Industry, Economics, Documentaries/Reportage. **Career:** Writer. Sunday Times, London, England, business news editor. **Publications:** The Infiltrators: The European Business Invasion of America, 1971; Money Matters, 1973;

Wankel: The Curious Story behind the Revolutionary Engine, 1975, in UK as The Wankel Engine: The Story of the Revolutionary Rotary Engine, 1976; The Winemasters, 1978; Safety in Numbers: The Mysterious World of Swiss Banking, 1982; Victorian Vineyard: Chateau Loudenne and the Gilbeys, 1983; Sold: The Rise and Fall of the House of Sotheby, 1985; Cognac, 1986; The Simon & Schuster Pocket Guide to Cognac and Other Brandies, 1987; The Story of Champagne: The History and Pleasures of the Most Celebrated of Wines, 1989; The World the Railways Made, 1990; Château Margaux, 1991; Château Beychevelle, 1991; Classic Trucks, 1995; Classic Ships: Romance and Reality, 1996; Black Box: The Air-Crash Detectives: Why Air Safety Is No Accident, 1997; (with I. Wisniewski) Classic Vodka, 1997; Classic Trains, 1998; Crash: The Limits of Car Safety, 1998; Blaze: The Forensics of Fire, 2000; Classic Brandy, 2000; Derail: Why Trains Crash, 2001; A Very Different Country: A Typically English Revolution, 2002. **Address:** c/o Author Mail, Prion Books, Imperial Works, Perren St., London NW5 3ED, England.

FALCK, Colin. British, b. 1934. **Genres:** Poetry, Literary criticism and history, Philosophy, Theology/Religion. **Career:** Lecturer in Sociology, London School of Economics, 1961-62; Lecturer in Humanities, Chelsea College, London, 1964-84; Adjunct Professor of English Literature, Syracuse University London Centre, 1985-89; Associate Professor in Modern Literature, York College, PA, 1989-99. Associate Ed., The Review, Oxford and London, 1962-72; Poetry Ed., The New Review, London, 1974-78. **Publications:** The Garden in the Evening (poetry adaptations), 1964; Promises, 1969; Backwards into the Smoke, 1973; In This Dark Light, 1978; Myth, Truth and Literature: Towards a True Post-Modernism, 1989, 2nd ed., 1994; Memorabilia, 1992; Post-Modern Love, 1997; America and British Verse in the Twentieth Century: The Poetry that Matters, 2003. EDITOR: (with I. Hamilton) Poems since 1900: An Anthology, 1975; Robinson Jeffers: Selected Poems, 1987; Edna St. Vincent Millay: Selected Poems, 1991;. **Address:** 20 Thurlow Rd, London NW3 5PP, England.

FALCO, Edward. American, b. 1948. **Genres:** Novels, Plays/Screenplays, Poetry, Novellas/Short stories. **Career:** Syracuse University, Syracuse, NY, part-time instructor in English, 1979-84; Virginia Polytechnic Institute and State University, Blacksburg, instructor, 1984-88, assistant professor, 1988-90, associate professor of English, 1990-, chair of Creative Writing Committee, 1989-. Adjunct instructor in English, Onondaga Community College, 1979-82, and LeMoyne College, 1982-84. **Publications:** Concert in the Park of Culture (prose poems), 1984; Plato at Scratch Daniel's and Other Stories, 1990; Winter in Florida (novel), 1990; Acid (short stories), 1996. **Address:** Department of English, Virginia Polytechnic Institute and State University, Blacksburg, VA 24061-0112, U.S.A.

FALCON, Mark. (Eileen Marion Pickering). British, b. 1940. **Genres:** Westerns/Adventure. **Career:** Publisher and writer. **Publications:** Reluctant Outlaw, 1979; The Yellow Bandana, 1979; Lightning Hits Glory Town, 1980; The Outlaw's Woman, 2003; Outlaws' Loot, 2004; Kinsella's Revenge, 2004. **Address:** 121 Highbury Grove, Clapham, Beds. MK41 6DU, England.

FALCONER, Delia. Australian, b. 1966. **Genres:** Novels, Novellas/Short stories. **Career:** Royal Melbourne Institute of Technology, Melbourne, Victoria, Australia, creative writing teacher. **Publications:** The Service of Clouds (novel), 1998. Contributor of stories to magazines. **Address:** c/o AMC Pty. Ltd., PO Box 1034, Carlton, VIC 3052, Australia. **Online address:** agency@amcaust.com.au

FALCONIERI, John V(incent). American, b. 1920. **Genres:** Plays/Screenplays, Anthropology/Ethnology, Theatre. **Career:** Bowling Green State University, Bowling Green, Ohio, assistant professor of romance literature, 1952-58; Western Reserve (now Case Western Reserve) University, Cleveland, Ohio, associate professor of romance literature, 1958-64; State University of New York at Albany, professor of romance literature, 1964-72, chairman of department, 1968-72; John Cabot International College, Rome, Italy, president, 1972-78; American University of Rome, Rome, president and provost, 1978-89. Editor, Theatre Annual. **Publications:** Historia de la Commedia dell'Arte en Espana (title means: History of the Commedia dell'Arte in Spain), 1957; (trans) A History of Hispanic American Literature: E. Anderson Imbert, 1964; Columbus Discovers America, (one-act play); The Maculate Conception (novel), 1998; Creationism and Evolutionism Reconciled, 2000. EDITOR: (with A.M. Pasquariello) Jose Lopez-Rubio, La Otra Orilla: Comedia en Tres Actos (title means: The Other Shore), 1977; Fuga, 1980; Mi Adorado Juan, 1983; Gabriel de Corral: Life and Works, 1983; D. Prado y Tovar, Hir buscando a quien me busca (play); Mira de Amescua, Callar en buena ocasion (plays). **Address:** 7865 E Mississippi Ave #301, Denver, CO 80231, U.S.A. **Online address:** difalcon@prodigy.net

FALES-HILL, Susan. (born Italy), b. 1962. **Genres:** Autobiography/Memoirs. **Career:** Writer and television producer. Cocreator of the television show Lincs's, 1998; has written and produced television shows. Board member of Harvard University Alumni Association, Studio Museum of Harlem, and Eastside House Settlement. **Publications:** Always Wear Joy: My Mother Bold and Beautiful, 2003. Contributor to magazines. **Address:** c/o Author Mail, HarperCollins Publishers, 10 East Fifty-third Street, Seventh Floor, New York, NY 10022, U.S.A.

FALK, Avner. Israeli (born Palestine), b. 1943. **Genres:** History, Politics/Government, Psychiatry, Psychology, Biography. **Career:** Jerusalem Psychiatric Hostel and Halfway House, Israel, psychologist, 1966; Washington University, St. Louis, MO, trainee at Child Guidance Clinic, 1966-67; St. Louis State Hospital, intern, 1967-68; Missouri Institute of Psychiatry, intern, 1967-68; Jewish Hospital of St. Louis, intern, 1968-69; City of St. Louis, staff psychologist at Child Guidance Clinic, 1970-71; Talbiyeh Mental Health Center, Jerusalem, clinical psychologist in outpatient services, 1971-72; private practice of psychotherapy, 1971-95; Sarah Herzog Mental Health Center, Jerusalem, supervising clinical psychologist, 1972-82; Kfar Shaul Mental Health Center, supervising clinical psychologist, 1973-75; Etanim Mental Health Center, supervising clinical psychologist, 1975-83. Lecturer and visiting scholar at universities and institutes worldwide. **Publications:** Moshe Dayan, halsh veha Agadah: Biographia Psychoanalytith (Moshe Dayan, the Man and the Myth: A Psychoanalytic Biography), 1985; David Melech Yisrael: Biographia Psychoanalytith shel David Ben-Gurion (David King of Israel: A Psychoanalytic Biography of David Ben-Gurion), 1987; Herzl, King of the Jews: A Psychoanalytic Biography of Theodor Herzl, 1993; A Psychoanalytic History of the Jews, 1996; Fratricide in the Holy Land, 2004; A Psychobiography of Napoleon Bonaparte, 2005. Contributor to books and periodicals. **Address:** 6 Caspi St, 93554 Jerusalem, Israel. **Online address:** avner.falk@usa.net

FALK, Candace. American, b. 1947. **Genres:** History, Politics/Government, Social commentary, Women's studies and issues, Biography. **Career:** The Emma Goldman Papers, National Historical Publications and Records Commission of the National Archives and University of California at Berkeley, editor and director, 1980-. **Publications:** Love, Anarchy, and Emma Goldman, a Biography, 1984, rev. ed., 1999; The Emma Goldman Papers (microfilm ed.), 1991; Emma Goldman: A Guide to Her Life and Documentary Sources, 1994; Emma Goldman: Selections from the American Years-A Documentary Edition, 4 vols., 2002-05. **Address:** c/o Emma Goldman Papers, University of California, 2372 Ellsworth St, Berkeley, CA 94720-6030, U.S.A. **Online address:** emma@uclink.berkeley.edu

FALK, Peter H(astings). American, b. 1950. **Genres:** Art/Art history. **Career:** Sound View Press, Madison, CT, publisher, 1985-. Independent art historian, researcher, writer, and publisher 1976-. **Publications:** EDITOR: Who Was Who in American Art; The Exhibition Record Series; monographs on American artists. **Address:** Falk Art Reference, 70 Wall St, PO Box 833, Madison, CT 06443, U.S.A.

FALK, Stanley Lawrence. American, b. 1927. **Genres:** History, International relations/Current affairs, Military/Defense/Arms control. **Career:** Historical Consultant, 1982-. Historian, Office of Chief of Military History, Dept. of the Army, 1949-54, Bureau of Social Science Research, American University, 1954-56, and Historical Division, Joint Chiefs of Staff, 1956-59; Sr. Historian, Office of Chief of Military History, Dept. of the Army, 1959-62, all in Washington, DC; Educational Specialist, 1962-65, Associate Professor of National Security Affairs, 1965-70, and Professor of International Relations, Resident School, 1970-74, Industrial College of the Armed Forces, Washington, DC; Chief Historian, US Air Force, Washington, DC 1974-80; Deputy Chief Historian for Southeast Asia, US Army Center of Military History, Washington, DC, 1980-82. **Publications:** Bataan: The March of Death, 1962; (co-author) Organization for National Security, 1963; The International Arena, 1964; Human Resources for National Strength, 1966; Decision at Leyte, 1966; The National Security Structure, 1967, rev. ed., 1972; The Environment of National Security, 1968, rev. ed., 1973; Defense Military Manpower, 1970; The Liberation of the Philippines, 1971; Bloodiest Victory: Palaus, 1974; Seventy Days to Singapore: The Malayan Campaign, 1975. EDITOR: The World in Ferment: Problem Areas for the United States, 1970; FOO: A Japanese-American Prisoner of the Rising Sun, 1993; (co) MIS in the War against Japan, 1995. Contributor to books. **Address:** 2310 Kimbro St, Alexandria, VA 22307, U.S.A.

FALK, Thomas H(einrich). American (born Germany), b. 1935. **Genres:** Literary criticism and history. **Career:** University of Southern California, Los Angeles, instructor in German, 1961-67; North Texas State University, instructor, 1964-65; Michigan State University, East Lansing, instructor, 1965-70, assistant professor, 1970-79, associate professor of German and interdisciplinary studies, 1979-92, associate professor emeritus, 1992-. **Publications:** Elias Canetti: A Critical Study, 1993. Contributor of articles and reviews to academic journals. **Address:** 8939 Caminito Verano, La Jolla, CA 92037, U.S.A. **Online address:** thfalk@san.rr.com

FALKINGHAM, Jane (Cecelia). British, b. 1963. **Genres:** Demography, Economics, Social sciences. **Career:** City University, London, England, tutor in economics, 1985-86; London School of Economics and Political Science, London, research officer on the economics of retirement, 1986-88, and on the welfare state, Suntory Toyota International Centre for Economics and Related Disciplines, 1988-92, research fellow, 1991-93, lecturer in population studies, 1993-2002; University of Southampton, professor of demography and international social policy, 2002-. Consultant to World Bank, European Union, and the British government. **Publications:** (with P. Johnson) Ageing and Economic Welfare, 1992; Household Welfare in Central Asia, 1997; Women in Tajihistan, 2000; Health Care in Central Asia, 2002. EDITOR: (with S. Baldwin, and contrib.) Social Security and Social Change: New Challenges to Beveridge, 1993; (with J. Hills) The Dynamics of Welfare, 1995. Work represented in anthologies. Contributor to journals in the social sciences. **Address:** University of Southampton, Highfield, Southampton SO17 1BJ, England. **Online address:** j.c.falkingham@soton.ac.uk

FALLON, Ivan (Gregory). Irish, b. 1944. **Genres:** Business/Trade/Industry, Biography. **Career:** Irish Times, writer, 1964-66; Thompson Provincial Newspaper Group, writer, 1966-67; Daily Mirror, London, England, writer, 1967-68; Sunday Telegraph, London, city editor, 1968-70 and 1971-84, deputy editor, 1984-; Sunday Express, London, deputy city editor, 1970-71. University of Buckingham, council member. **Publications:** (with J.L. Srodes) Dream Maker: The Rise and Fall of John Z. DeLorean, 1983, in UK as De-Lorean: The Rise and Fall of a Dream-maker; (with C. Monckton) The Laker Story, 1984; (with Srodes) Takeovers, 1987; The Brothers: The Rise and Rise of Saatchi & Saatchi, 1988; Billionaire: The Life and Times of Sir James Goldsmith, 1991; The Player: The Life of Tony O'Reilly, 1994. **Address:** iTouch PLC, 57-63 Scrutton St., London EC2A 4PF, England.

FALLON, Peter. Irish, b. 1951. **Genres:** Poetry, Novellas/Short stories. **Career:** Poet, reader, and lecturer. Gallery Press, Dublin, Ireland, founder, editor, and publisher, 1970-. Deerfield Academy, poet in residence, 1976-77, 1996-97; O'Brien Press, fiction editor, 1979-. **Publications:** POETRY: Among the Walls, 1971; Co-incidence of Flesh, 1972; The First Affair, 1974; The Speaking Stones, 1978; Finding the Dead, 1978; Winter Work, 1983; The News and Weather, 1988; Eye to Eye, 1992; The Deerfield Stories, 1992; News of the World, 1993, rev. ed., 1998. EDITOR: B. Kennelly, New and Selected Poems, 1976; M. Hartnett, A Farewell to English, 1978; (with D. O'Driscoll) The First Ten Years: Dublin Arts Festival Poetry, 1979; D. O'Grady, The Headgear of the Tribe, 1979; (with S. Golden) Soft Day: A Miscellany of Contemporary Irish Writing, 1980; (with A. Carpenter) The Writers: A Sense of Ireland-New Work by 44 Irish Writers, 1980; B. Behan, After the Wake: 21 Prose Works, 1981; P. Boyle, The Port Wine Stain: Patrick Boyle's Short Stories, 1983; B. Friel, The Diviner: Brian Friel's Best Short Stories, 1983; (with P. Egan) Padraig Siochfhradha, Jimeen: Lucky Tree Books for Children (new ed. of Egan's Jimin Mhaire Thaidhg), 1984; S. O'Kelly, The Weaver's Grave, 1985; E. Ni Chuilleanain, The Second Voyage, 1986; (with D. Mahon) The Penguin Book of Contemporary Irish Poetry, 1990. **Address:** Gallery Press, Loughcrew, Oldcastle, Meath, Ireland. **Online address:** gallery@indigo.ie

FALLOWELL, Duncan (Richard). British, b. 1948. **Genres:** Novels, Songs/Lyrics and libretti, Travel/Exploration. **Career:** Writer. **Publications:** (ed.) Drug Tales (stories), 1979; (with A. Ashley) April Ashley's Odyssey (memoir), 1982; Satyrday (novel), 1986; The Underbelly (novel), 1987; To Noto; or, London to Sicily in a Ford (travel), 1989; One Hot Summmer in St. Petersburg (travel) 1994; 20th Century Characters (profiles) 1994; Gormenghast (libretto), 1996; A History of Facelifting (novel), 2003. Lyricist for musical compositions. Contributor to periodicals. **Address:** c/o Gillon Aitken Associates Ltd, 29 Fernshaw Rd, London SW10 0TG, England. **Online address:** duncanfallowell@hotmail.com

FALLOWS, James Mackenzie. American, b. 1949. **Genres:** Economics, Environmental sciences/Ecology, Military/Defense/Arms control, Politics/Government, Biography. **Career:** Washington Monthly, staff editor, 1972-74; free-lance magazine writer, 1972-76; Texas Monthly, associate editor, 1974-76; chief speech writer for President Jimmy Carter, 1977-79; Atlantic (formerly Atlantic Monthly), Boston, Washington editor, 1979-. Rhodes Scholar, 1970-72. **Publications:** The Water Lords, 1971; (with M.J. Green and D. Zwick) Who Runs Congress?, 1972; Warren G. Magnuson: Democratic Senator from Washington, 1972; (ed. with C. Peters) The System, 1976; (ed. with Peters) Inside the System, 1976; Old Capital and a New President, 1979; National Defense, 1981; More Like Us, 1989; Looking at the Sun: The Rise of the New East Asian Economic and Political System, 1994; Breaking the News, 1996; Free Flight, 2001. **Address:** c/o The Atlantic, 77 N Washington St Ste 5, Boston, MA 02114-1908, U.S.A. **Online address:** www.jamesfallows.com

FALOLA, Toyin. Nigerian, b. 1953. **Genres:** History, Area studies. **Career:** Elementary schoolteacher in Pahayi, Nigeria, 1970-71; high school teacher in Ibadan, Nigeria, 1973; Government College, Makurdi, Nigeria, high school teacher, 1976-77; Public Service Commission of Oyo State, Nigeria, administrative officer, 1977; University of Ife (now Obafemi Awolowo University), Nigeria, lecturer, 1981-85, senior lecturer, 1985-88; Cambridge University, England, research fellow, 1988-89; Nigerian Institute of International Affairs, Lagos, senior research fellow and coordinator of a project in oral documentation, 1989; York University, Downsview, Ontario, professor of history, 1990-91; University of Texas at Austin, professor of African history, 1991-; guest lecturer at colleges and universities worldwide. **Publications:** (with others) Islam and Christianity in West Africa, 1983; (with others) Summary of West African History, 1983; The Political Economy of a Pre-Colonial African State: Ibadan, 1830-1900, 1984; (with others) The Military in Nineteenth-Century Yoruba Politics, 1984; (with others) The Rise and Fall of Nigeria's Second Republic, 1979-1984, 1985; Politics and Economy in Ibadan, 1893-1945, 1989; (coauthor) A History of Nigeria, Vol. I: Nigeria Before 1800, 1989, Vol. II: Nigeria in the Nineteenth Century, 1991, Vol. III: Nigeria in the Twentieth Century, 1992; Yoruba Historiography, African Studies Program, 1991; (with others) The Military Factor in Nigeria, 1994; (with others) Religious Impact on the Nation State: The Nigerian Predicament, 1995; Development Planning and Decolonization in Nigeria, 1996. EDITOR: (co-) Rural Development Problems in Nigeria, 1992; (and author of intro.) Pioneer, Patriot, and Patriarch: Samuel Johnson and the Yoruba People, 1993. EDITOR/CO-EDITOR & CONTRIBUTOR: Nigeria: Peoples, States, and Culture, 1986; Transport Systems in Nigeria, 1986; A History of West Africa, 1987; Britain and Nigeria: Exploitation or Development?, 1987; (with Ihonvbere) Nigeria and the International Capitalist System, 1988; Obafemi Awolowo: The End of an Era?, 1988; Modern Nigeria, 1990; (with Olupona) Religion and Society in Nigeria: Historical and Comparative Perspectives, 1991; (with Ityavyar) The Political Economy of Health in Africa (monograph), 1992; (with Law) Warfare and Diplomacy in Pre-Colonial Nigeria, 1992; Child Health in Nigeria: The Impact of a Depressed Economy, 1994; Pawnship in Africa: Debt Bondage in Historical Perspective, 1994. Contributor to books. Contributor to history and African studies journals. **Address:** Department of History, University of Texas at Austin, Austin, TX 78712, U.S.A.

FALUDI, Susan. American, b. 1959. **Genres:** Women's studies and issues, Civil liberties/Human rights. **Career:** Worked as a copy clerk for the New York Times; previously a reporter at Miami Herald, Atlanta Constitution, and Mercury News; affiliated with Wall Street Journal, beginning in 1990. Writer. **Publications:** Backlash: The Undeclared War against American Women, 1991; Stiffed: The Betrayal of the Modern Man, 1999. Contributor of articles to periodicals. **Address:** Sandra Dijkstra, Sandra Dijkstra Literary Agency, 1155 Camino del Mar Suite 515, Del Mar, CA 92014, U.S.A.

FALZEDER, Ernst. Austrian, b. 1955. **Genres:** Psychology. **Career:** Austrian Society for Sexological Research, founding and board member, 1979; University of Salzburg, Psychological Institute, assistant, 1979-85, lecturer, 1985-, assistant professor, 1986-87; Verein Lebenshilfe, Salzburg, work with mentally and physically disabled children, 1983; Lebensberatung (Counseling Center), Salzburg, psychotherapist, 1985; University of Innsbruck, Psychological and Pedagogical Institutes, lecturer, 1985-; community improvement program, Salzburg, psychologist, 1986-87; Verein Beratung und Unterbringung Unterkunftsloser (program to aid the homeless), 1988-89; University of Geneva, research fellow, 1989-97; Woodrow Wilson International Center for Scholars, Washington, DC, research fellow, 1997; Cornell Medical School, NYC, research associate, 1997-98; Harvard University, visiting scholar, 1998-99; writer. **Publications:** Die "Sprachverwirrung" und die "Grundstorung:" Die Untersuchungen S. Ferenczis und Michael Balints uber Entstehung und Auswirkungen fruher Objektbeziehungen, 1986. EDITOR: (with A. Papst, and contrib.) Wie Psychoanalyse wirksam wird-Sepp Schindler zum 65. Geburtstag, 1987; (with E. Brabant and P.G. Deutsch) Sigmund Freud-Sandor Ferenczi, Correspondence, Tomes 1-3, 1992-99 (trans. as The Correspondence of Sigmund Freud and Sandor Ferenczi, Vols. 1-3, 1994-99); (with A. Haynal and contrib.) 100 Years of Psychoanalysis, 1994; The Complete Correspondence of S. Freud and K.

Abraham, 2002. Contributor to professional books and periodicals dealing with the theory, technique, and history of psychoanalysis. **Address:** Nr. 290, A-4582 Spital Am Pyhrn, Austria. **Online address:** falzeder@yahoo.com

FANCHER, Jane S(uzanne). American, b. 1952. **Genres:** Science fiction/ Fantasy, Graphic Novels. **Career:** Science fiction writer and illustrator;. **Publications:** NOVELS. GRAPHIC NOVELS: Gate of Ivrel: Claiming Rites, 1987; Gate of Ivrel: Fever Dreams, 1988. CANTRELL SERIES: Groundties, 1991; Uplink, 1992; Harmonies of the 'Net, 1992. OTHER Ring of Lightning, 1995. Contributor of short stories to books. Contributor to periodicals. **Address:** c/o DAW Publicity, 375 Hudson St., 3rd Floor, New York, NY 10014, U.S.A.

FANCHI, John R(ichard). American, b. 1952. **Genres:** Novels, Earth sciences, Engineering, Mathematics/Statistics, Physics, Sciences. **Career:** Writer and teacher. **Publications:** Parametrized Relativistic Quantum Theory, 1993; Principles of Applied Reservoir Simulation, 1997, 2nd ed., 2001; Math Refresher for Scientists and Engineers, 1997, 2nd ed., 2000; Integrated Flow Modeling, 2000; Flashpoint: Sakhalin, 2001; Shared Earth Modeling, 2002; Energy: Technology and Directions for the Future, 2004; Energy in the 21st Century, 2005. **Address:** 1884 Parfet Estates Dr, Golden, CO 80401, U.S.A. **Online address:** jfanchi@mines.edu

FANCUTT, Walter. British, b. 1911. **Genres:** History, Theology/Religion. **Career:** Baptist Minister 1933-; Editorial Consultant, Leprosy Mission, London, since 1970 (Editorial Secretary, 1957-70). General Secretary, Southern Baptist Association Baptist Minister, London and Hampshire, 1934-57. **Publications:** Then Came Jesus, 1943; From Vision to Advance, 1951; Whitchurch Baptist Church 1652-1952, 1952; In This Will I Be Confident, 1957; Beyond the Bitter Sea, 1959; Present to Heal, 1962; Daily Remembrance, 1966; The Imprisoned Splendour, 1973; The Southern Baptist Association, 1974; With Strange Surprise, 1974; The Luminous Cloud, 1980; His Excellent Greatness, 1982; East Dene, 1982; With William Carey in Ryde, 1993. EDITOR: Kingsgate Pocket Poets, 9 vols., 1943; Escaped as a Bird, 1963. **Address:** St. Josephs Residential Home, Madiera Road, Ventnor, Isle of Wight PO38 1Q5, England.

FANE, Bron. See **FANTHORPE, R(obert) Lionel.**

FANE, Julian. British, b. 1927. **Genres:** Novels. **Career:** Royal Society of Literature, fellow, 1974; contributor to newspapers, magazines, etc. **Publications:** Morning; A Letter; Memoir in the Middle of the Journey; Gabriel Young; Tug-of-War; Hounds of Spring, 1976; Happy Endings, 1979; Revolution Island, 1979; Gentleman's Gentleman, 1981; Memories of My Mother, 1987; Rules of Life, 1987; Cautionary Tales for Women, 1988; Hope Cottage, 1990; Best Friends, 1990; Small Change, 1992; Eleanor, 1993; The Duchess of Castile, 1994; His Christmas Box, 1995; Money Matters, 1996; The Social Comedy, 1998; Evening, 1999; Tales of Love and War, 2002; Byron's Diary, 2003; The Stepmother, 2003. OTHER: The Collected Works of Julian Fane, 5 vols.; The Harlequin Editions (15 small books). **Address:** Rotten Row House, Lewes, Sussex BN7 1TN, England.

FANTHORPE, R(obert) Lionel. Also writes as Erle Barton, Lee Barton, Thornton Bell, Leo Brett, Bron Fane, Mel Jay, Marston Johns, Victor La Salle, Robert Lionel, John E. Muller, Phil Nobel, Lionel Roberts, Neil Thanet, Trebor Thorpe, Pel Torro, Olaf Trent, Karl Zeigfreid. British, b. 1935. **Genres:** Novels, Novellas/Short stories, Horror, Science fiction/Fantasy, Plays/Screenplays, Poetry, Songs/Lyrics and libretti, Children's non-fiction, Criminology/True Crime, History, Inspirational/Motivational Literature, Mythology/Folklore, Paranormal, Theology/Religion, Documentaries/ Reportage. **Career:** Worked as a machine operator, farm worker, warehouseman, journalist, salesman, TV personality, and storekeeper during the 1950s; schoolteacher in Dereham, 1963-67; education tutor, Cambridgeshire, 1967-69; Phoenix Timber Co., Rainham, industrial training officer, 1969-72; Hellesdon High School, Norfolk, English teacher, 1972-79; Glyn Derw High School, headmaster, 1979-89; Church-in-Wales, priest, 1988-; writer, lecturer, broadcaster, tutor, consultant, 1989-. **Publications:** SCIENCE FICTION NOVELS: The Waiting World, 1958; Alien from the Stars, 1959; Hyperspace, 1959; Space-Borne, 1959; Fiends, 1959; Doomed World, 1960; Satellite, 1960; Asteroid Man, 1960; Out of the Darkness, 1960; Hand of Doom, 1960; Flame Mass, 1961; The Golden Chalice, 1961; Space Fury, 1962; Negative Minus, 1963; Neuron World, 1965; The Triple World, 1965; The Unconfined, 1965; The Watching World, 1966; (with P. Fanthorpe) The Black Lion, 1979. SCIENCE FICTION STORIES: Resurgam, 1957; Secret of the Snows, 1957; The Flight of the Valkyries, 1958; Watchers of the Forest, 1958; Call of the Werewolf, 1958; The Death Note, 1958; Mermaid Reef, 1959; The Ghost Rider, 1959; The Man Who Couldn't Die, 1960;

Werewolf at Large, 1960; Whirlwind of Death, 1960; Fingers of Darkness, 1961; Face in the Dark, 1961; Devil from the Depths, 1961; Centurion's Vengeance, 1961; The Grip of Fear, 1961; Chariot of Apollo, 1962; Hell Has Wings, 1962; Graveyard of the Damned, 1962; The Darker Drink, 1962; Curse of the Totem, 1962; Goddess of the Night, 1963; Twilight Ancestor, 1963; Sands of Eternity, 1963; Moon Wolf, 1964; Avenging Goddess, 1964; Death Has Two Faces, 1964; The Shrouded Abbott, 1964; Bitter Reflection, 1964; Call of the Wild, 1965; Vision of the Damned, 1965; The Sealed Sarcophagus, 1965; Stranger in the Shadow, 1966; Curse of the Khan, 1966. POETRY: Earth, Sea and Sky, 2000. OTHER: (all with P.A. Fanthorpe) Spencer's Metric and Decimal Guide, 1970; Metric Conversion Tables, 1970; Spencer's Office Guide, 1971; Spencer's Metric Decimal Companion, 1971; Decimal Payroll Tables, 1971; The Black Lion, 1979; The Holy Grail Revealed, 1982; God in All Things, 1987; The Story of St. Francis of Assisi, 1989; Birds and Animals of the Bible, 1990; The Christmas Story, 1990; Rennes-le-Chateau: its Mysteries and Secrets, 1991 (in US as Secrets of Rennes-le-Chateau, 1992); Joseph: Dreamer, Prisoner and Provider, 1992; Noah and the Great Flood, 1992; Children of the Bible, 1994; The Oak Island Mystery, 1994; Down the Badger Hole: an Anthology of Lionel Fanthorne's Early Badger Books, 1996; The World's Greatest Unsolved Mysteries, 1997; The World's Most Mysterious People, 1998; The World's Most Mysterious Places, 1999; Mysteries of the Bible, 1999; Death: The Final Mystery, 2000; The World's Most Mysterious Objects, 2002; The World's Most Mysterious Murders, 2003; Unsolved Mysteries of the Sea, 2004; Mysteries of Templar Treasure and the Holy Grail, 2004. THOUGHTS AND PRAYERS... series: ...for Troubled Times, 1989; ...for Lonely Times, 1992; ...for Special Occasions, 1992; ...Week by Week, 1992; ...for the Bereaved, 1995; ...for Healing Times, 1995; ...with the Bible, Vol 1: Old Testament, Vol 2: New Testament, 1995; ...for Stressful Times, 2001; ...for Families, 2001; ...for Changing Times, 2001; ...for Growing Christians, 2001. SCIENCE FICTION NOVEL AS ERLE BARTON: The Planet Seekers, 1964. SCIENCE FICTION NOVELS AS LEE BARTON: The Unseen, 1964; The Shadow Man, 1966. SCIENCE FICTION NOVELS AS THORNTON BELL: Space Trap, 1964; Chaos, 1964. SCIENCE FICTION AS LEO BRETT (novels unless otherwise indicated): The Druid (stories), 1959; The Return (stories), 1959; Exit Humanity, 1960; The Microscopic Ones, 1960; Faceless Planet, 1960; March of the Robots, 1961; Wind Force, 1961; Black Infinity, 1961; Nightmare, 1962; Face in the Night, 1962; The Immortals, 1962; They Never Came Back, 1962; The Frozen Tomb (stories), 1962; The Forbidden, 1963; From Realms Beyond, 1963; The Alien Ones, 1963; Power Sphere, 1963; Phantom Crusader (stories), 1963. SCIENCE FICTION AS BRON FANE (novels unless otherwise indicated): Juggernaut, 1960 (in US as Blue Juggernaut, 1965); Last Man on Earth, 1960; The Crawling Fiend (stories), 1960; Rodent Mutation, 1961; Storm God's Fury (stories), 1962; The Intruders, 1963; Somewhere Out There, 1963; The Thing from Sheol (stories), 1963; Softly by Moonlight, 1963; Unknown Destiny, 1964; Nemesis, 1964; Suspension, 1964; The Macabre Ones!, 1964; The Walking Shadow (stories), 1964; U.F.O. 517, 1966. SCIENCE FICTION NOVELS AS VICTOR LA SALLE: Menace from Mercury, 1954. SCIENCE FICTION NOVELS AS JOHN E. MULLER: The Ultimate Man, 1961; The Uninvited, 1961; Crimson Planet, 1961; The Venus Venture, 1961 (in US as Marston Johns, 1965); Forbidden Planet, 1961; The Return of Zeus, 1962; Perilous Galaxy, 1962; Uranium 235, 1962; The Man Who Conquered Time, 1962; Orbit One, 1962 (in US as Mel Jay, 1966); The Eye of Karnak, 1962; Micro Infinity, 1962; Beyond Time, 1962 (in US as Marston Johns, 1966); Infinity Machine, 1962; The Day the World Died, 1962; Vengeance of Siva, 1962; The X-Machine, 1962; Reactor Xk9, 1963; Special Mission, 1963; Dark Continuum, 1964; Mark of the Beast, 1964; The Exorcists, 1965; The Man from Beyond, 1965; Beyond the Void, 1965; Spectre of Darkness, 1965 Out of the Night, 1965; Phenomena X, 1966; Survival Project, 1966. SCIENCE FICTION AS PHIL NOBEL: The Hand from Gehenna (stories), 1964. SCIENCE FICTION AS LIONEL ROBERTS (novels unless otherwise indicated): The Incredulist (stories), 1954; Guardians of the Tomb (stories), 1958; The Golden Warrior (stories), 1958; Dawn of the Mutants, 1959; Time-Echo, 1959 (in US as Robert Lionel, 1964); Cyclops in the Sky, 1960; The In-World, 1960; The Face of X, 1960 (in US as Robert Lionel, 1965); The Last Valkyrie, 1961; The Synthetic Ones, 1961; Flame Goddess, 1961. SCIENCE FICTION NOVELS AS NEIL THANET: Beyond the Veil, 1964; The Man Who Came Back, 1964. SCIENCE FICTION AS TREBOR THORPE: The Haunted Pool (stories), 1958; Five Faces of Fear (novel), 1960; Lightning World (novel), 1960; Voodoo Hell Drums (stories), 1961. SCIENCE FICTION NOVELS AS PEL TORRO: Frozen Planet, 1960; World of the Gods, 1960; The Phantom Ones, 1961; Legion of the Lost, 1962; The Strange Ones, 1963; Galaxy 666, 1963; Formula 29X, 1963 (in US as Beyond the Barrier of Space, 1969); Through the Barrier, 1963; The Timeless Ones, 1963; The Last Astronaut, 1962; The Face of Fear, 1963; The Return, 1964 (in US as Exiled in Space, 1968); Space No Barrier, 1964 (in US as Man of Metal, 1970); Force 97X, 1965. SCIENCE FICTION AS OLAF TRENT: Roman Twilight,

1964. SCIENCE FICTION NOVELS AS KARL ZEIGFREID: Walk through Tomorrow, 1962; Android, 1962; Gods of Darkness, 1962; Atomic Nemesis, 1962; Zero Minus X, 1962; Escape to Infinity, 1963; Radar Alert, 1963; World of Tomorrow, 1963 (in US as World of the Future, 1964); The World That Never Was, 1963; Projection Barrier, 1964; No Way Back, 1964; Barrier 346, 1965; The Girl from Tomorrow, 1966. **Address:** Rivendell, 48 Claude Rd, Roath, Cardiff CF24 3QA, Wales. **Online address:** Fanthorpe@ aol.com; www.lionel-fanthorpe.com

FANTHORPE, U(rsula) A(skham). British, b. 1929. **Genres:** Poetry. **Career:** Assistant English Teacher, 1954-62, and Head of English, 1962-70, Cheltenham Ladies College; clerk in businesses in Bristol, 1972-74; hospital clerk and receptionist, Bristol, 1974-89; Arts Council Creative Writing Fellow, St. Martin's College, Lancaster, 1983-85; Northern Arts Fellow, Univs. of Durham & Newcastle, 1987; Hawthornden Fellowships, 1987, 1997, 2002; Fellow, Royal Society of Literature, 1988. CBE, for services to poetry, 2001; Queen's Gold Medal for Poetry, 2003. **Publications:** Side Effects, 1978; Four Dogs, 1980; Standing To, 1982; Voices Off, 1984; Selected Poems, 1986; A Watching Brief, 1987; Neck Verse, 1992; Safe as Houses, 1995; Consequences, 2000; Queueing for the Sun, 2003. **Address:** Culverhay House, Wotton under Edge, Glos. GL12 7LS, England.

FANTONI, Barry (Ernest). Also writes as Sylvie Krin, E. J. Thribb. Italian (born England), b. 1940. **Genres:** Mystery/Crime/Suspense, Plays/Screenplays, Humor/Satire. **Career:** Assistant Ed., Private Eye mag., London. Chairman, Chelsea Arts Club, London, 1978-80; Cartoonist, The Times Diary, 1983-89. **Publications:** (with R. Ingrams) Bible for Motorists, 1967; (with R. Ingrams; as Sylvie Krin) Love in the Saddle, 1974; Private Eye Cartoons, 1975; (with J. Wells) Lional (musical), 1977; (as E. J. Thribb) So Farewell Then, and Other Poems, 1977; Mike Dime (crime novel), 1980; (as Sylvie Krin) Born to Be Queen, 1981; (with G. Melly) The Media Mob, 1981; Stickman (crime novel), 1982; The Times Cartoons, 1984; Chinese Horoscopes, 1985; Barry Fantoni Cartoons, 1987; The Royal Chinese Horoscopes, 1988; Colemanballs 4, 1988; (as Sylvie Krin) Heir of Sorrows, 1988; Chinese Horoscopes, Love Signs, 1989; The Best of Barry Fantoni Cartoons, 1990; Complete Chinese Horoscopes, 1991; Colemanballs 6, 1992; Colemanballs 7, 1994; Colemanballs 8, 1996; Colemanballs 9, 1998; Modigliani, My Love (play), 1998; Colemanballs 10, 2000; Rooms of the House (play), 2000. EDITOR: Colemanballs, 3 vols., 1982-86; Colemanballs 5, 1990. **Address:** 3 Franconia Rd, London SW4 9NB, England. **Online address:** bazfan@lineone.net

FAQIH, Ahmed. Lybian, b. 1942. **Genres:** Novels, Plays/Screenplays. **Career:** Worked for twenty-five years as a journalist and literary editor for journals in Arab countries such as Libya; Azure, editor in chief. **Publications:** Gardens of the Night (trilogy of novels), 1995; The Gazelles (play). Author of novels, short stories, and essays in Arabic, some of which appear in English-language periodicals. **Address:** 5 Porchester Square Mews, The Colonnades, London W2, England.

FARAGHER, John Mack. American, b. 1945. **Genres:** History, Biography. **Career:** Department of Public Social Services, Los Angeles, CA, social worker, 1968-69; Yale University, New Haven, CT, instructor in American studies, 1975-77; University of Hartford, West Hartford, CT, assistant professor of history, 1977-78; Mount Holyoke College, South Hadley, MA, assistant professor, 1978-83, associate professor of history, 1983-. **Publications:** Women and Men on the Overland Trail, 1979; Sugar Creek: Life on the Illinois Prairie, 1987; Daniel Boone: The Life and Legend of an American Pioneer, 1992; (with others) Out of Many: A History of the American People, 1994. EDITOR: (with F. Howe) Women and Higher Education in American History: Essays from the Mount Holyoke College Sesquicentennial Symposia, 1988; The Encyclopedia of Colonial and Revolutionary America, 1990; Rereading Frederick Jackson Turner: The Significance of the Frontier in American History, and Other Essays, 1994. Contributor to books and periodicals. **Address:** Department of History, Mount Holyoke College, South Hadley, MA 01075, U.S.A.

FARBER, Barry J. American, b. 1959. **Genres:** Business/Trade/Industry. **Career:** Farber Training Systems Inc., Livingston, NJ, president. Diamond Group (radio and television producers), president; also president of a literary agency. Diamonds in the Rough (television program), host; guest on radio and television programs; seminar presenter. **Publications:** State-of-the-Art Selling, 1994; Sales Secrets from Your Customers, 1995; Superstar Sales Secrets, 1995; Superstar Sales Manager's Secrets, 1995; Diamonds in the Rough, 1995; Diamonds under Pressure: Five Steps to Turning Adversity into Success, 1998; Dive Right In, 1999. **Address:** Farber Training Systems Inc., 66 East Sherbrooke Parkway, Livingston, NJ 07039, U.S.A. **Online address:** barryjfarber@erols.com

FARBMAN, Albert I. American, b. 1934. **Genres:** Biology. **Career:** New York University, NYC, instructor in anatomy, 1962-64; Northwestern University, Chicago, IL, assistant professor, 1964-67, associate professor, 1967-72, professor of anatomy, 1972-81; Northwestern University, Evanston, IL, professor of neurobiology, 1981-. **Publications:** Cell Biology of Olfaction, 1992. **Address:** Department of Neurobiology, Northwestern University, Evanston, IL 60208, U.S.A.

FARCAU, Bruce. *See* **GRACE, Alexander M.**

FARICY, Robert. American, b. 1926. **Genres:** Theology/Religion. **Career:** Professor, Gregorian University, Rome, 1971-. **Publications:** Teilhard de Chardin's Theology of the Christian in the World, 1967; Building God's World, 1976; Spirituality for Religious Life, 1976; Praying, 1979; Praying for Inner Healing, 1979; (with M. Flick and G. O'Collins) The Cross Today, 1978; All Things in Christ: The Spirituality of Teilhard de Chardin, 1981; Christian Faith in My Everyday Life, 1981; The End of the Religious Life, 1983; Wind and Sea Obey Him, 1983; Seeking Jesus in Contemplation and Discernment, 1983; (with L. Rooney) Mary, Queen of Peace: Is Our Lady Appearing at Medjugorje?, 1984; (with L. Rooney) Medjugorje Unfolds, 1985, in U.S. as Medjugorje Up Close, 1986; (with S. Blackborow) The Healing of the Religious Life, 1985; (with L. Rooney) The Contemplative Way of Prayer, in U.K. as Personal Prayer, 1986; (with R. Wicks) Contemplating Jesus, 1986; (with L. Rooney) Medjugorje Journal, 1988; The Lord's Dealing: The Primacy of the Feminine in Christian Spirituality, 1988; (with L. Rooney) Lord Jesus, Teach Me to Pray, 1989; (with L. Rooney) Medjugorje Retreat, 1989; A Pilgrim's Journal, 1989; (with L. Pecoraio) Mary among Us, 1989; The Scottsdale Apparitions, 1992; Praying with Teilhard de Chardin, 1995; (with L. Rooney) Your Wounds I Will Heal, 1999; (with L. Rooney) Praying with Mary, 2000. **Address:** 1404 W Wisconsin Ave, Milwaukee, WI 53233, U.S.A. **Online address:** bobfaricy@yahoo.com

FARISH, Terry. American, b. 1947. **Genres:** Novels, Children's fiction, Young adult fiction, Writing/Journalism. **Career:** Worked for American Red Cross in Vietnam, 1969-70; Ralston Public Library, Ralston, NE, director, 1976-82; Leominster Public Library, Leominster, MA, head of children's services, 1986-90; Cambodian Mutual Assistance Association, Lowell, MA, director of Young Parent Program, 1990-92; Rivier College, Nashua, NH, faculty, 1993-99; Salt Institute for Documentary Studies, Portland, ME, faculty, 2001-. Salt Magazine, editor, 2001-. **Publications:** Why I'm Already Blue (young adult novel), 1989; Shelter for a Seabird (young adult novel), 1990; Flower Shadows (novel), 1992; If the Tiger (novel), 1995; Talking in Animal (children's novel), 1996; A House in Earnest, 2000; The Cat Who Liked Potato Soup, 2003.

FARKAS, George. American, b. 1946. **Genres:** Economics, Business/Trade/Industry. **Career:** Yale University, New Haven, CT, assistant professor of sociology and Institution for Social and Policy Studies, 1972-78; Abt Associates, Inc., Cambridge, MA, senior analyst, 1978-82; University of Texas at Dallas, associate professor, 1982-87, professor of sociology and political economy, 1987-, head of Graduate Program in Political Economy, 1989-94, founder and director of Center for Education and Social Policy, 1993-. **Publications:** (ed. with E.W. Stromsdorfer) Evaluation Studies Review Annual, Vol V, 1980; (with P. England) Households, Employment, and Gender: A Social, Economic, and Demographic View, 1986; (ed. with England, and contrib.) Industries, Firms, and Jobs: Sociological and Economic Approaches, 1988, expanded ed, 1994; Human Capital or Cultural Capital? Ethnicity and Poverty Groups in an Urban School District, 1996. Contributor to books. Contributor of articles and reviews to scholarly journals. **Address:** School of Social Sciences, University of Texas at Dallas, Box 830688, GR.3.1, Richardson, TX 75083, U.S.A. **Online address:** Farkas@utdallas.edu

FARLOW, James O(rville), (Jr.). American, b. 1951. **Genres:** Earth sciences, Sciences. **Career:** Indiana University-Purdue University at Fort Wayne, lecturer in geology, 1978-79; Hope College, Holland, MI, assistant professor of geology, 1979-81; Indiana University-Purdue University at Fort Wayne, assistant professor, 1982-87, associate professor, 1987-90, professor of geology, 1990-. Consultant to Texas Department of Parks and Wildlife, 1985-. **Publications:** (intro. and annotations) Bones for Barnum: Adventures of a Dinosaur Hunter, by R.T. Bird, 1985; A Guide to Lower Cretaceous Dinosaur Footprints and Tracksites of the Paluxy River Valley, Somervell County, Texas (guidebook), 1987; On the Tracks of Dinosaurs: A Study of Dinosaur Footprints (children's book), 1991; The Dinosaurs of Dinosaur Valley State Park, Texas Department of Parks and Wildlife, 1993; (with R.E. Molnar) Meat-Eating Dinosaurs (children's book), 1995. Contributor to books. Contributor of science fiction short stories to Analog Science Fiction/Science Fact, and scientific articles to journals and magazines. **Address:**

Department of Geosciences, Indiana University-Purdue University at Fort Wayne, 2101 Coliseum Blvd. E., Fort Wayne, IN 46805, U.S.A.

FARMAN FARMAIAN, Sattareh. American (born Iran), b. 1921. **Genres:** Education, Social work, Urban studies, Women's studies and issues, Autobiography/Memoirs, Biography. **Career:** International Institute of Los Angeles, Los Angeles, CA, social worker, 1947-49; Travellers Aid Society, Los Angeles, social worker, 1949-51; Cities Service Oil Company, New York City, consultant, 1951-54; United Nations, social welfare expert for Arab states, Baghdad, Iraq, 1954-58; Community Welfare Centers of Iran, founder and executive director, 1958-79; Family Planning Association of Iran, founder, executive director, and chair, 1958-79; Tehran School of Social Work, Iran, founder and dean, 1958-79; County of Los Angeles, department of social services, children's services worker, 1980-92; United Way of Los Angeles, consultant for social welfare planning on priorities, 1980-. Researcher for Tehran University, faculty of social sciences, 1958-79; adviser to United Nations, 1969-79; representative at international conferences, 1974-76; University of Chicago Annual Workshop on Population Communication, Education, and Research, annual lecturer for Community and Family Study Center, 1979-; International Association of Schools of Social Work, former board member; former adviser to South Korean government on media's role in population and social development. **Publications:** The Social Problems of Urbanization in Iraq, 1958; Children's Needs, 1960; County Profile of Iranian Family Planning and Social Welfare, 1965; Children and Teachers, 1966; Prostitution Problems in the City of Tehran, 1969; On the Other Side of the China Wall, 1977; (with D. Munker) Daughter of Persia: A Woman's Journey from Her Father's Harem through the Islamic Revolution, 1992. Contributor of articles about human development to periodicals. **Address:** 10687 Wilkins Ave No 4, Los Angeles, CA 90024, U.S.A.

FARMER, Nancy. American, b. 1941. **Genres:** Children's fiction. **Career:** Worked in the Peace Corps in India, 1963-65; University of California at Berkeley, lab technician, 1969-72; Loxton, Hunting and Associates, Songo, Mozambique, chemist and entomologist, 1972-74; University of Zimbabwe, Rukomeche, lab technician and entomologist, 1975-78; freelance scientist and writer in Harare, Zimbabwe, 1978-88; Stanford University Medical School, Palo Alto, CA, lab technician, 1991-92. Freelance writer, 1992-. **Publications:** JUVENILE FICTION: Lorelei, 1988; Tsitsi's Skirt (picture book), 1988; The Ear, the Eye and the Arm, 1989, 1994; Tapiwa's Uncle, 1992; Do You Know Me, 1993; The Warm Place, 1995; Runnery Granary, 1996; A Girl Named Disaster, 1996; The House of the Scorpion, 2002 (Newbery Honor, 2003). **Address:** c/o Michelle Fadlalla, Simon & Schuster, 1230 Avenue of the Americas, New York, NY 10020, U.S.A.

FARMER, Penelope (Jane). British, b. 1939. **Genres:** Novels, Children's fiction, Young adult fiction. **Career:** Teacher, London, 1961-63. **Publications:** FOR ADULTS: Standing in the Shadow, 1984; Eve: Her Story, 1985; Away from Home, 1987; Glasshouses, 1988; Snakes and Ladders, 1993; Penelope, 1996. FOR CHILDREN: Daedalus and Icarus, 1971; Serpent's Teeth: The Story of Cadmus, 1971; The Story of Persophone, 1972; Heracles, 1974; August the Fourth, 1974; The Coal Train, 1977; The Runaway Train, 1980. FOR YOUNG ADULTS: The China People, 1960; The Summer Birds, 1962; The Magic Stone, 1964; Saturday Shillings, 1965; The Seagull, 1965; Emma in Winter, 1966; Charlotte Sometimes, 1969; The Dragonfly Summer, 1971; A Castle of Bone, 1972; William and Mary, 1974; Year King, 1977; Thicker than Water, 1989; Stone Croc, 1991. OTHER: (ed.) Beginnings: Creation Myths of the World, 1978; (trans.) Soumchi, 1980; Two, or, The Book of Twins and Doubles, 1996; (ed.) Sisters: An Anthology, 1999; The Virago Book of Grandmothers: An Autobiographical Anthology, 2000. **Address:** c/o Deborah Owen Ltd, 78 Narrow St., London E14 8BP, England.

FARMER, Philip José. Also writes as Kilgore Trout. American, b. 1918. **Genres:** Novels, Novellas/Short stories, Science fiction/Fantasy, Autobiography/Memoirs. **Career:** Freelance writer, 1969-. Electromechanical technical writer for defense-space industry: General Electric Co., Syracuse, NY, 1956-58; Motorola, Scottsdale, AZ, 1959-62, Phoenix, 1962-65; Bendix, Ann Arbor, MI, 1962; and McDonnell-Douglas, Santa Monica, CA, 1965-69. **Publications:** The Green Odyssey, 1957; Flesh, 1960; A Woman a Day, 1960, as The Day of Timestop, 1968, in UK as Timestop!, 1974; The Lovers, 1961; Cache from Outer Space, 1962; The Celestial Blueprint and Other Stories, 1962; Fire and the Night (novel), 1962; Inside Outside, 1964; Tongues of the Moon, 1964; Dare, 1965; The Maker of Universes, 1962, 1980; The Gate of Time, 1966, as Two Hawks from Earth, 1979; The Gates of Creation, 1966; Night of Light, 1966; The Image of the Beast, 1968; A Private Cosmos, 1968; Blown, 1968; A Feast Unknown, 1969; Behind the Walls of Terra, 1970; Lord Tyger, 1970; Lord of the Trees, the Mad Goblin, 1970; The Stone God Awakens, 1970; Love Song (novel),

1970; To Your Scattered Bodies Go, 1971; The Fabulous Riverboat, 1971; The Wind Whales of Ishmael, 1971; Tarzan Alive, 1972; Time's Last Gift, 1972; The Other Log of Phineas Fogg, 1973; Traitor to the Living, 1973; Doc Savage, 1973;The Adventure of the Peerless Peer by John H. Watson, M.D., 1974; Hadon of Ancient Opar, 1974; (as Kilgore Trout) Venus on the Half-Shell, 1974; (ed.) Mother Was a Lovely Beast, 1974; Flight to Opar, 1976; The Dark Design, 1977; The Lavalite World, 1977; Dark Is the Sun, 1979; Jesus on Mars, 1979; The Magic Labyrinth, 1979; Riverworld and Other Stories, 1979; A Barnstormer in Oz, 1982; Greatheart Silver, 1982; Stations of the Nightmare, 1982; The Purple Book, 1982; Father to the Stars, 1982; The Unreasoning Mask, 1983; River of Eternity, 1983; Gods of Riverworld, 1983; Dayworld, 1983; Two Hawks from Earth, 1985; Traitor to the Living, 1985; Dayworld Rebel, 1987; Escape from Loki, 1991; Red Orc's Rage, 1991; Dayworld Breakup, 1991; Riders of the Purple Wage, 1992; Tales of Riverworld, 1992; (with P. Anthony) The Caterpillar's Question, 1992; More Than Fire, 1993; (ed.) Quest to Riverworld, 1993; The World of Tiers, Vol. 1, 1996; Nothing Burns in Hell, 1998; (with others) Naked Came the Farmer, 1998; The Dark Heart of Time: A Tarzan Novel, 1999. SHORT STORIES: Strange Relations, 1960; The Alley God, 1960; Down in the Black Gang, and Others, 1971; The Book of Philip Jose Farmer, 1973; Riverworld War, 1980; The Grand Adventure, 1984. **Address:** c/o Ted Chichak, Scovil Chichak Galen Literary Agency, 381 Park Ave S Ste 1020, New York, NY 10016, U.S.A.

FARMILOE, Dorothy. Canadian, b. 1920. **Genres:** Poetry, Adult nonfiction, Writing/Journalism. **Career:** St. Clair College, Windsor, ON, teacher, 1969-78; The Elk Lake Explorer, publisher, 1979-. **Publications:** The Lost Island, 1966; (co-author) 21 x 3, 1967; Poems for Apartment Dwellers, 1970; (ed.) Contraverse, 1971; Winter Orange Mood, 1972; Blue Is the Colour of Death, 1973; And Some in Fire, 1974; Creative Communication, 1974; Elk Lake Diary Poems, 1976; Adrenalin of Weather, 1978; How to Write a Better Anything, 1979; Words for My Weeping Daughter, 1980; Communication for Business Students, 1981; Elk Lake Lore and Legend, 1984; Isabella Valancy Crawford: The Life and the Legends, 1984; Dragons and Dinosaurs and Other Poems, 1988; The Legend of Jack Munroe, 1994; Mothers and Daughters, 1998; Cobalt in Retrospect & Rhyme, 2003. **Address:** PO Box 94, Elk Lake, ON, Canada P0J 1G0.

FARNSWORTH, Clyde. American, b. 1931. **Genres:** International relations/ Current affairs. **Career:** Reporter for the New York Times for thirty-five years, for the New York Herald Tribune for three, and for United Press International (U.P.I.) for five. **Publications:** No Money Down, 1963; Out of This Nettle: A History of Postwar Europe, 1974; Shadow Wars (fiction), 1998. **Address:** 3207 Macomb Street, Washington, DC 20008, U.S.A. **Online address:** chfarnsworth@compuserve.com

FARNSWORTH, Stephen J(ames). (born United States), b. 1961. **Genres:** Politics/Government. **Career:** Kansas City Star and Times, Kansas City, MO, staff reporter, 1985-90; Fairchild News Service, Washington, DC, national economics correspondent, 1990-93; Center for the Study of Responsive Law, Washington, DC, researcher, 1993-94; Georgetown University, Washington, DC, lecturer in political science, 1994-95; Mary Washington College, Fredericksburg, VA, senior lecturer, 1995, instructor, 1996-97, assistant professor, beginning 1997, now associate professor of political science. **Publications:** (with S. Robert Lichter) The Nightly News Nightmare: Network Television's Coverage of U.S. Presidential Elections, 1988-2000, 2003. Contributor to periodicals. **Address:** Department of Political Science, Mary Washington College, 1301 College Ave., Fredericksburg, VA 22401, U.S.A. **Online address:** sfarnswo@mwc.edu

FAROGHI, Suraiya. German, b. 1941. **Genres:** History. **Career:** University of Munich, Germany, professor of Middle Eastern and Turkish studies, 1988-. University of the Bosporus, member of visiting faculty, 1998 and 2001; University of Minnesota-Twin Cities, Union Pacific Visiting Professor, 1998; Charles University, member of visiting faculty, 2000-01; Wissenschaftskolleg, Berlin, Germany, fellow, 2001-02. International Institute for Social History, member of international advisory board, 1994-98. **Publications:** Towns and Townsmen of Ottoman Anatolia: Trade, Crafts, and Food Production in an Urban Setting, 1520-1650, 1984; Men of Modest Substance: House Owners and House Property in 17th-Century Ankara and Kayseri, 1987; Herrscher uber Mekka: die Geschichte der Pilgerfahrt, 1990, English trans, 1994; Kultur und Alltag im Osmanischen Reich, 1995, English trans, 2000; Coping with the State: Political Conflict and Crime in the Ottoman Empire, 1550-1720 (collected articles), 1995; Making a Living in the Ottoman Lands, 1480-1820 (collected articles), 1995; Approaching Ottoman History: An Introduction to the Sources, 1999; Geschichte des Osmanischen Reiches, 2000; Stories of Ottoman Men and Women: Establishing Status, Establishing Control (collected articles), 2002; Subjects of the Sultan. Contributor to books. **Address:** Institut fur Geschichte und Kultur des Nahen Orients, sowie fur Turkologie, University of Munich, Veterinarstrasse 1, 80539 Munich, Germany. **Online address:** suraiya@lrz.uni-muenchen.de

FARON, Fay. American, b. 1949. **Genres:** Criminology/True Crime. **Career:** Rat Dog Dick Detective Agency, San Francisco, CA, owner, 1982-; Elder Angels, founder, 1997; author of "Ask Rat Dog," a column syndicated by Creighton-Morgan Publishing, 1994-. **Publications:** The Instant National Locator Guide, 1991-; A Private Eye's Guide to Collecting a Bad Debt, 1995; Missing Persons, 1997; Rip-Off, 1998. **Address:** Rat Dog Dick Detective Agency, 500 Pelican Ave Ste 209, New Orleans, LA 70114, U.S.A. **Online address:** ratdog@sprintmail.com

FARQUHAR, Mary Ann. Chinese, b. 1949. **Genres:** Bibliography. **Career:** Educator and author. Griffith University, Queensland, Australia, currently associate professor of Asian studies. **Publications:** Children's Literature in China: From Lu Xun to Mao Zedong, 1999. Contributor to books. **Address:** School of International Business and Asian Studies, Griffith University, Kessels Rd., Nathan, QLD 4111, Australia. **Online address:** M.Farquhar@mailbox.gu.edu.au

FARR, Diana. See **PULLEIN-THOMPSON, Diana.**

FARR, Diane. (born United States). **Genres:** Romance/Historical. **Career:** Writer. **Publications:** ROMANCE NOVELS: Fair Game, 1999; The Nobody, 1999; Falling for Chloe, 2000; Once upon a Christmas, 2000; Duel of Hearts, 2002; The Fortune Hunter, 2002; Under the Wishing Star, 2003; Under a Lucky Star, 2004. **Address:** Irene Goodman, Irene Goodman Literary Agency, 80 Fifth Ave. Suite 1101, New York, NY 10011, U.S.A.

FARR, Jory. American, b. 1952. **Genres:** Music. **Career:** Press-Enterprise, Riverside, CA, popular culture critic and columnist, c. 1987-. **Publications:** Moguls and Madmen: The Pursuit of Power in Popular Music, 1994. **Address:** c/o Ken Sherman, 9507 Santa Monica Blvd Ste 211, Beverly Hills, CA 90210, U.S.A.

FARRAN, Roy Alexander. Canadian (born England), b. 1921. **Genres:** Novels, Military/Defense/Arms control. **Career:** Alderman, City of Calgary, 1961-71; Minister of Telephones and Utilities, Government of Alberta, 1973-75; Solicitor-General, Government of Alberta, 1975-79; Columnist, Edmonton Journal and Calgary Herald, 1979-89; Chairman, Alberta Racing Commission, 1979-95. **Publications:** Winged Dagger, 1948; History of the Calgary Highlanders; Jungle Chase, 1951; Winged Dagger, 1954; The Day After Tomorrow, 1956; The Search, 1958; Operation Tombola, 1960; Never Had a Chance, 1968; The Wild Colonial Boy, 1999.

FARRAR, Ronald T(ruman). American, b. 1935. **Genres:** Communications/ Media, Biography. **Career:** Indiana University, Bloomington, assistant professor then associate professor, 1964-70; Southern Methodist University, Dallas, TX, Dept. of Journalism, professor and chairman, 1970-73; University of Kentucky, Lexington, School of Journalism, professor and director, 1977-86; University of South Carolina, Columbia, Reynolds-Faunt Professor of Journalism, 1986-. **Publications:** Reluctant Servant: The Story of Charles G. Ross, 1968; (co-author) Mass Media and the National Experience, 1971; College 101, 1984; Mass Communication: An Introduction to the Field, 1988, 3rd ed., 1996; (with J.F. Worthington) Ultimate College Survival Guide, 1995; Creed for My Profession, 1998; (with others) Advertising and Public Relations Law, 1998. **Address:** 105 Holly Ridge Lane, West Columbia, SC 29169-3723, U.S.A.

FARRELL, Ben. See **CEBULASH, Mel.**

FARRELL, David. See **SMITH, Frederick E(screet).**

FARRELL, David M. Irish, b. 1960. **Genres:** Politics/Government. **Career:** Dublin Institute of Technology, Dublin, Ireland, lecturer, 1986-87; University College, Dublin, lecturer, 1987-88; University of Manchester, Manchester, England, lecturer, 1988-89; University of Wales-Cardiff, lecturer 1989-90; University of Manchester, Manchester, Jean Monnet lecturer, 1991-97, senior Jean Monnet lecturer, 1997-00, Jean Monnet Professor in European politics, 2000-. **Publications:** Comparing Electoral Systems, 1997; Electoral Systems: A Comparative Introduction, 2001. EDITOR: (with S. Bowler) Electoral Strategies and Political Marketing, 1992; (with D. Broughton, D. Denver, and C. Rallings), British Elections and Parties Yearbook, 1994, 1995; (with C. Rallings, D. Broughton, and D. Denver) British Elections and Parties

Yearbook, 1995, 1996; (with J. Fisher, D. Broughton, and D. Denver) British Elections and Parties Yearbook, 1996, 1996; (with S. Bowler and R.S. Katz) Party Discipline and Parliamentary Government, 1999; (with R. Schmitt-Beck) Do Political Campaigns Matter? Campaign Effects in Elections and Referendums, in press; (with P. Webb and I. Holliday and contrib) Political Parties in Advanced Industrial Democracies, in press. Contributor to books and journals. **Address:** Department of Government, University of Manchester, Manchester M13 9PL, England. **Online address:** david.farrell@man. ac.uk

FARRELL, Harry (Guy). American, b. 1924. **Genres:** Criminology/True Crime, Local history/Rural topics, Documentaries/Reportage. **Career:** San Jose Mercury News, San Jose, CA, reporter, 1946-54, political editor, 1954-74, columnist, 1974-81, staff writer, 1981-86. Correspondent for Oakland Tribune, 1949-52; Fairchild Publications, 1953-56; and Long Beach Press-Telegram, 1959. Lecturer at San Jose State University, 1987. **Publications:** NONFICTION: Recon Diary: Combat History of the 79th Cavalry Reconnaissance Troop, 1946; San Jose-And Other Famous Places, 1983; The San Felipe Story, 1987; Swift Justice: Murder and Vengeance in a California Town, 1992; Shallow Grave in Trinity County, 1997. **Address:** 3138 Allenwood Dr, San Jose, CA 95148, U.S.A. **Online address:** hairyferal@aol.com

FARRELL, Warren (Thomas). American, b. 1943. **Genres:** Business/Trade/Industry, How-to books, Human relations/Parenting, Law, Politics/Government, Psychology, Sex, Sociology, Women's studies and issues. **Career:** Author. Lecturer and consultant on gender, male-female relationships and men's issues, 1969-. **Publications:** The Liberated Man, 1975; Why Men Are the Way They Are, 1986; The Myth of Male Power: Why Men Are the Disposable Sex-Fated for War, Programmed for Work, Divorced from Emotion, 1993; Women Can't Hear What Men Don't Say, 1999; Father & Child Reunion, 2001; The Pay Paradox: What Women Aren't Told about Why Men Earn More, 2004. **Address:** 2982 Las Olas Ct, Carlsbad, CA 92009-9534, U.S.A. **Online address:** warren@warrenfarrell.com; www. warrenfarrell.com

FARRELL-BECK, Jane. American. **Genres:** Fashion/Costume. **Career:** Clothing and personal appearance historian. Iowa State University, Ames, professor of textiles and clothing. **Publications:** (with B. Payne and G. Winakor) The History of Costume from Ancient Mesopotamia through the Twentieth Century, 2nd ed, 1992; (with C. Gau) Uplift: The Bra in America, 2001. Contributor to periodicals. **Address:** Textiles and Clothing Program, 1072 LeBaron, Iowa State University, Ames, IA 50011, U.S.A. **Online address:** jfarrell@iastate.edu

FARRER-HALLS, Gill. British, b. 1958. **Genres:** Theology/Religion. **Career:** Meridian Trust, administrator of Buddhist Film and Video Archive and videotape producer, 1991-98. Also works as aroma therapy teacher. **Publications:** The World of the Dalai Lama, 1998; Handbook of Buddhist Wisdom, 1999. **Address:** 29a Miranda Rd., London N19 3RA, England.

FARRINGTON, David P. British, b. 1944. **Genres:** Criminology/True Crime. **Career:** Cambridge University, England, professor of psychological criminology, 1969-. **Publications:** (with D.J. West) Who Becomes Delinquent?, 1973; (with D.J. West) The Delinquent Way of Life, 1977; (with L. Ohlin and J.Q. Wilson) Understanding and Controlling Crime, 1986; (with M. Tonry and L.E. Ohlin) Human Development and Criminal Behavior, 1991; (with R. Loeber, M. Stouthamer-Loeber, and W.B. Van Kammen) Antisocial Behavior and Mental Health Problems, 1998; (with E.G. Cohn and R.A. Wright) Evaluating Criminology and Criminal Justice, 1998. EDITOR: (with K. Hawkins and S. Lloyd-Bostock) Psychology, Law and Legal Processes, 1979; (with J. Gunn) Abnormal Offenders, Delinquency and the Criminal Justice System, 1982; (with J. Gunn) Reactions to Crime, 1985; (with J. Gunn) Aggression and Dangerousness, 1985; (with R. Tarling) Prediction in Criminology, 1985; (with S. Walklate) Offenders and Victims, 1992; (with R.J. Sampson and P.O.H. Wikstrom) Integrating Individual and Ecological Aspects of Crime, 1993; Psychological Explanations of Crime, 1994; (with M. Tonry) Building a Safer Society, 1995; (with A. Raine, P.A. Brennan, and S.A. Mednick) Biosocial Bases of Violence, 1997; (with R. Loeber) Serious and Violent Juvenile Offenders, 1998; (with B.C. Welsh and L.W. Sherman) Costs and Benefits of Preventing Crime, 2001; (with R. Loeber) Child Delinquents, 2001; (with G.A. Bernfeld and A.W. Leschied) Offender Rehabilitation in Practice; (with C.R. Hollin and M. McMurran) Sex and Violence, 2001; (with L.W. Sherman, B.C. Welsh, and D.L. Mackenzie) Evidence-Based Crime Prevention, 2002. **Address:** Institute of Criminology, 7 West Rd., Cambridge CB3 9DT, England.

FARRIS, William Wayne. American, b. 1951. **Genres:** History. **Career:** Harvard University, Cambridge, MA, instructor, 1980-81; University of Tennessee, Knoxville, assistant professor, 1981-88, associate professor, 1988-94, professor, 1994-. **Publications:** Population, Disease, and Land in Early Japan, 645-900, 1985; Heavenly Warriors, 1992; Sacred Texts and Buried Treasures, 1998. **Address:** 2630 Dunford Hall, University of Tennessee, Knoxville, TN 37996-4065, U.S.A.

FARROW, James S. See TUBB, E(dwin) C(harles).

FARTHING-KNIGHT, Catherine. Australian, b. 1933. **Genres:** Autobiography/Memoirs, Children's fiction. **Career:** C.S.I.R.O., Melbourne, Victoria, Australia, map drawing, 1953; writer, painter, and poet. Girl Guide leader in Papua New Guinea, 1967-71, and in Melbourne, 1972-84; "Meal on Wheels" district commissioner in Papua New Guinea, 1967-71. Pianist for Spastic Society, 1972-86, and for Villa Maria School for the Blind, 1994-96. Silk paintings exhibited in 1996. **Publications:** Days with Gran, 1995. **Address:** 34 College St., Hawthorn, VIC 3122, Australia.

FARWELL, Edith F. American, b. 1960. **Genres:** Communications/Media. **Career:** Association for Progressive Communications, San Francisco, CA, executive director, 1991-. **Publications:** (as Edie Farwell with A.H. Maiden) The Tibetan Art of Parenting, 1997; Women @ Internet, 1999. **Address:** Association for Progressive Communications, Presidio Bldg 1012, Torney Ave Box 29904, San Francisco, CA 94129, U.S.A. **Online address:** efarwell@ igc.apc.org

FASCHING, Darrell J. American, b. 1944. **Genres:** Ethics, Theology/Religion. **Career:** Syracuse University, Syracuse, NY, assistant dean of Hendricks Chapel, 1975-80; LeMoyne College, Syracuse, assistant professor of religious studies, 1980-82; University of South Florida, Tampa, assistant professor, 1982-85, associate professor, 1985-89, professor of religious studies, 1989-, affiliate assistant professor of medical ethics, 1983-, director of graduate religious studies, 1984-89, associate dean, arts & sciences, 1991-93, department head, 1993-98. **Publications:** The Thought of Jacques Ellul, 1981; (ed. and contrib.) The Jewish People in Christian Preaching, 1984; Narrative Theology after Auschwitz: From Alienation to Ethics, 1992; The Ethical Challenge of Auschwitz and Hiroshima: Apocalypse or Utopia?, 1993; The Coming of the Millennium, 1996; (with D. de Chant) Comparative Religious Ethics: A Narrative Approach, 2001; (with J. Esposito and T. Lewis) World Religions Today, 2002. Work represented in anthologies. Contributor to academic journals. **Address:** Dept of Religious Studies, Cooper Hall, University of South Florida, 4202 E Fowler Ave., Tampa, FL 33620-5550, U.S.A. **Online address:** Fasching@cas.usf.edu

FASCHINGER, Lilian. Austrian, b. 1950. **Genres:** Novels, Novellas/Short stories, Poetry. **Career:** Austrian novelist, short story writer, and poet. **Publications:** NOVELS: Die neue Scheherazade, 1986; Lustspiel, 1989; Magdalena Suenderin, 1995, trans. by S. Whiteside as Magdalena the Sinner, 1996; trans. by E. McCown as Magdalena the Sinner, 1997. SHORT STORIES: Frau mit drei Flugzeugen, 1993. POETRY: Ortsfremd: Gedichte, 1994. **Address:** c/o HarperCollins, 10 E. 53rd St, Author Mail, 7th Floor, New York, NY 10022, U.S.A.

FASOLT, Constantin. American (born Germany), b. 1951. **Genres:** History. **Career:** Columbia University, NYC, lecturer in history, 1981-83; University of Chicago, IL, assistant professor, 1983-90, associate professor, 1990-98, professor of history, 1999-, chair of History of Western Civilization program, 1989-95. Lecturer at colleges, universities, and national and international conferences. **Publications:** Council and Hierarchy: The Political Thought of William Durant the Younger, 1991; Visions of Order in the Canonists & Civilians, 1995; Blindsided by the Evidence, 2000; The Limits of History, 2003. Work represented in anthologies. Contributor of articles and reviews to history and German studies journals. **Address:** Department of History, University of Chicago, 1126 E 59th St, Chicago, IL 60637, U.S.A. **Online address:** icon@uchicago.edu

FASSETT, John D. American, b. 1926. **Genres:** History, Autobiography/Memoirs, Biography. **Career:** US Supreme Court, Washington, DC, law clerk, 1954-55; Yale University, New Haven, CT, lecturer, 1955-56; Wiggin and Dana, New Haven, partner, 1954-73; United Illuminating Co., New Haven, president and chair of board, 1973-85; associated with many commissions and boards in New England. **Publications:** United Illuminating: History of an Electric Company (corporate history), 1990; New Deal Justice: The Life of Stanley Reed of Kentucky (biography), 1994; The Shaping Years: A Memoir of My Youth and Education (autobiography), 2000. Contributor to periodicals. **Address:** 2600 Croasdaile Farm Pkwy Apt 354, Durham, NC 27705, U.S.A. **Online address:** jdfass@highstream.net

FASSMANN, Heinz. Austrian (born Germany), b. 1955. **Genres:** Demography, Geography. **Career:** Austrian Academy of Sciences, Vienna, researcher, 1981-92, director, 1992-96; Technical University, Munich, professor, 1996-2000; University of Vienna, professor, 2000-. **Publications:** (ed. with R. Muenz) European Migration in the Late Twentieth Century, 1994. UNTRANSLATED WORKS: (with P. Meusburger) Arbeitsmarktgeographie, 1997; (ed. with J. Kohlbacher and U. Reeger) Zuwanderung und Segregation, 2002. **Address:** Sebastian Kneipp-Gasse 52, A-2380 Perchtoldsdorf, Austria.

FATCHEN, Max. Australian, b. 1920. **Genres:** Novellas/Short stories, Children's fiction, Poetry. **Career:** Journalist, Adelaide News and Sunday Mail, Adelaide, 1946-55; Literary Ed., The Advertiser, Adelaide, 1971-81. **Publications:** POETRY: Driver and Trains, 1963; Keepers and Lighthouses, 1963; The Plumber, 1963; The Electrician, 1963; The Transport Driver, 1965; The Carpenter, 1965; Peculia Australia: Verses, 1965; Just Fancy, Mr. Fatchen! A Collection of Verse, Prose and Fate's Cruel Blows, 1967; Songs for My Dog and Other People (nonsense verse), 1980; Wry Rhymes for Troublesome Times, 1983; A Paddock of Poems, 1987; A Pocketful of Rhymes, 1989; Peculiar Rhymes & Lunatic Lines, 1995; Australia at the Beach, 1999; Terrible Troy, 2000; The Very Long Nose of Jonathan Jones, 2000. FICTION: The River Kings, 1966; Conquest of the River, 1970; The Spirit Wind, 1973; Chase through the Night, 1977; The Time Wave, 1979; Closer to the Stars, 1981. OTHER: Forever Fatchen, 1983; Had Yer Jabs (short stories), 1987; A Country Christmas, 1990; Mostly Max, 1995. **Address:** Box 6, Smithfield, SA 5114, Australia.

FAULCON, Robert. See **HOLDSTOCK, Robert.**

FAULKNER, Charles Herman. American, b. 1937. **Genres:** Anthropology/Ethnology, Archaeology/Antiquities. **Career:** St. Lawrence University, Canton, New York, instructor of sociology and anthropology, 1963-64; University of Tennessee, Knoxville, assistant professor, 1964-70, associate professor, 1971-76, professor of anthropology, 1976-, distinguished professor of humanities, 1999-. **Publications:** An Archaeological Survey of Marshall County, Indiana, 1961; (with J. Graham), Excavations in the Nickajack Reservoir, 1965; The Old Stone Fort: Exploring an Archaeological Mystery, 1968; The Late Prehistoric Occupation of Northwestern Indiana, 1972; (with C.R. McCollough) Excavations of the Higgs and Doughty Sites: I-75 Salvage Archaeology, 1973; Introductory Report of the Normandy Reservoir Salvage Project, 1972, 3rd to 6th reports, 1976-78; (with C.K. Buckles) Glimpses of Southern Appalachian Folk Culture: Papers in Memory of Norbert F. Riedl, 1978; (with G.W. Kline and G.D. Crites) The McFarland Project: Early Middle Woodland Settlement and Subsistence in the Upper Duck River Valley in Tennnessee, 1982. EDITOR: The Prehistoric Native American Art of Mud Glyph Cave, 1986; The Bat Creek Stone, 1992; (with A. Young) Proceedings of the Tenth Symposium on Ohio Valley Urban and Historic Archaeology, 1993; Rock Art of the Eastern Woodlands, 1996. **Address:** Dept. of Anthropology, University of Tennessee, 252 S Stadium Hall, Knoxville, TN 37996, U.S.A. **Online address:** cfaulkne@utk.edu

FAULKNER, Howard J. American, b. 1945. **Genres:** Autobiography/Memoirs, Biography. **Career:** Washburn University, Topeka, KS, instructor, 1972-73, assistant professor, 1973-78, associate professor, 1981-82, professor of American literature, 1982-; University of Skopje, Macedonia, Fulbright professor, 1979-80; University of Metz, visiting professor, 1987-88; Sofia University, Bulgaria, Fulbright professor, 1995-96. **Publications:** (ed. with V. Pruitt) The Selected Correspondence of Karl A. Menninger, 1919-1945, 1989; re-issued with vol. 2, The Selected Correspondence of Karl A. Menninger, 1946-1965, 1995; Dear Dr. Menniger: Women's Voices from the Thirties, 1997; The Rules of the Game: An Introductory English Grammar, 2001. **Address:** Department of English, Washburn University, Topeka, KS 66621, U.S.A. **Online address:** zzfaul@washburn.edu

FAUSETT, David. New Zealander, b. 1950. **Genres:** Literary criticism and history, History. **Publications:** Writing the New World: Imaginary Voyages and Utopias of the Great Southern Land, 1993; The Strange Surprizing Sources of Robinson Crusoe, 1994; Images of the Antipodes in the Eighteenth Century: A Study in Stereotyping, 1995. EDITOR: (and trans.) G. de Foigny, The Southern Land, Known, 1993; H. Smeeks, The Mighty Kingdom of Krinke Kesmes, 1994. **Address:** 4 Wilding Ave., Epsom, Auckland 3, New Zealand.

FAUST, Irvin. American, b. 1924. **Genres:** Novels, Novellas/Short stories. **Career:** Director, Guidance and Counseling, Garden City High School, New York, since 1960, now retired. Guidance Counselor, Lynbrook High School, NY, 1956-60. **Publications:** Roar Lion Roar, 1965; The Steagle, 1966; The File on Stanley Patton Buchta, 1970; Willy Remembers, 1971; Foreign Devils, 1973; A Star in the Family, 1975; Newsreel, 1980; The Year of the Hot Jock, 1985; Jim Dandy, 1994. **Address:** 417 Riverside Dr, New York, NY 10025, U.S.A.

FAUST, Jeff. American, b. 1966. **Genres:** Sports/Fitness. **Career:** Manpower Temporary Services, Rochester, NY, office worker, 198896; Toycrafter, Rochester, press operator, 1996-. Classic Adventures, Hamlin, NY, tour leader, 1992-94. **Publications:** Greenberg's American Flyer Track Plans, 1989; Rochester by Bike, 1992; Mountain Bike! New Hampshire, 1998. **Address:** 55 Oakland St, Rochester, NY 14620, U.S.A.

FAUST, John R. American, b. 1930. **Genres:** International relations/Current affairs. **Career:** University of Southwestern Louisiana, Lafayette, assistant professor of political science, 1960-62; Illinois Wesleyan University, Bloomington, associate professor of political science, 1962-66; Eastern Illinois University, Charleston, visiting associate professor, summers, 1963-65, associate professor, then professor of political science, 1966-. Institute of Developmental Administration, Bangkok, Thailand, visiting professor, 1993. Consultant on Sino-American relations, 1988-. **Publications:** (with J.E. Kornberg) China in World Politics, 1995. Contributor to books. Contributor to professional journals. **Address:** Department of Political Science, Eastern Illinois University, Charleston, IL 61920, U.S.A.

FAUSTO-STERLING, Anne. American, b. 1944. **Genres:** Biology. **Career:** Brown University, Providence, RI, assistant professor, 1971-76, associate professor, 1976-86, professor of biology, 1986-, curricular consultant on gender and the sciences. **Publications:** Myths of Gender: Biological Theories about Women and Men, 1985, 2nd ed., 1992; Sexing the Body, 2000. Contributor to journals. **Address:** Division of Biology and Medicine, Box G-160J, Brown University, Providence, RI 02912, U.S.A. **Online address:** Anne.Fausto-Sterling@brown.edu

FAVREAU, Jon. (born United States), b. 1966. **Genres:** Business/Trade/Industry. **Career:** Actor in films and television. Director of films and executive producer of television programs. **Publications:** SCREENPLAYS: Swingers, 1996; Hollywood Tales (television pilot), 1997; To the Moon, 1999; Marshall of Revelation, 1999; Smog (television movie), 1999; Made, 2001;. **Address:** Endeavor, 9701 Wilshire Blvd, 10th floor, Beverly Hills, CA 90212, U.S.A.

FAWCETT, Quinn. See **YARBRO, Chelsea Quinn.**

FAY, Jim. American, b. 1934. **Genres:** Education, How-to books, Human relations/Parenting. **Career:** Worked as a public schoolteacher for 14 years and an elementary school principal for 17 years; School Consultant Services Inc., Golden, CO, president. Cline-Fay Institute Inc., co-founder, president, and chief executive officer. **Publications:** Who Says You're So Great?, 1982; Principally Speaking, 1985; (with F.W. Cline) Parenting with Love and Logic, 1990; (with Cline) Parenting Teens with Love and Logic, 1992; Parenting Solutions, 1993; Tickets to Success, 1994; I've Got What It Takes, 1994; Helicopters, Drill Sergeants, and Consultants, 1994; (with Cline) Grandparenting with Love and Logic, 1994; Taking Control of the Classroom with Love and Logic, 1994; (with D. Funk) Teaching with Love and Logic, 1995; The Love and Logic Journal, 1995; (with C. Fay) Love and Logic Magic for Early Childhood, 2000; (with C. Fay) Love and Logic Teacherisms, 2001; (with C. Fay) The Pearls of Love and Logic for Parents and Teachers Disruptions, 2001; (with C. Fay) Love and Logic Magic When Kids Leave You Speechless Disruptions, 2001; (with C. Fay) Love and Logicisms, 2001; Meeting the Challenge, 2001. **Address:** Cline-Fay Institute Inc., 2207 Jackson St, Golden, CO 80401, U.S.A.

FAYER, Steve. American, b. 1935. **Genres:** Novels, Novellas/Short stories, Plays/Screenplays, Civil liberties/Human rights, History, Race relations, Documentaries/Reportage. **Career:** Independent screen and television writer, Boston, MA, 1977-. **Publications:** (with H. Hampton and S. Flynn) Voices of Freedom: An Oral History of the Civil Rights Movement from the 1950s through the 1980s, 1990. TELEVISION DOCUMENTARIES: After The Crash, 1991; (with O. Bagwell) Malcolm X: Make It Plain, 1994; Frederick Douglass: When the Lion Wrote History, 1994. TELEVISION DOCUMENTARY SERIES: Eyes on the Prize: America's Civil Rights Years, 1954-1965, 1987; Eyes on the Prize II: America at the Racial Crossroads, 1990; The Great Depression, 1993; Africans in America, 1998; (with D. McCabe and P. Stekler) George Wallace: Settin' the Woods on Fire, 2000. **Address:** 189 Bay State Rd, Boston, MA 02215, U.S.A.

FEARNLEY-WHITTINGSTALL, Jane. British, b. 1939. **Genres:** Botany, Cultural/Ethnic topics, History, Homes/Gardens, Horticulture, How-to books.

Career: Self-employed landscape/garden designer and consultant, 1980-. Lecturer on garden design and history; presentor on radio and TV programs. **Publications:** Rose Gardens: Their History and Design, 1989; Historic Gardens, 1990; Ivies, 1992; Jane Fearnley-Whittingstall's Gardening Made Easy, 1995; Jane Fearnley-Whittingstall's Garden Plants Made Easy, 1996; Peonies: The Imperial Flower, 1999; The Garden: An English Love Affair, 2002. Contributor to periodicals. **Address:** Merlin Haven House, Wotton-under-Edge, Glos. GL12 7BA, England.

FEAVER, William (Andrew). British, b. 1942. **Genres:** Art/Art history. **Career:** University of Newcastle upon Tyne, James Knott Research Fellow, 1971-73; art critic, The Listener, and the Financial Times; Sunday Times mag., London, art adviser; The Observer, London, art critic, 1975-98; curator, broadcaster. **Publications:** The Art of John Martin, 1975; When We Were Very Young, 1977; Masters of Caricature, 1981; Pitmen Painters: The Ashington Group, 1943-1984, 1990; Lucian Frend, 2002. **Address:** 1 Rhodesia Rd, London SW9 9EJ, England.

FEDDER, Norman Joseph. American, b. 1934. **Genres:** Plays/Screenplays, Literary criticism and history, Theatre. **Career:** Kansas State University, Manhattan, associate professor, 1970-80, professor, 1980-89, distinguished professor of theatre, 1989-99, distinguished professor emeritus of theatre, 1999-. Nova Southeastern University, Ft Lauderdale, FL, adjunct professor of playwriting, 2002-. Coalition for the Advancement of Jewish Education, Drama Network, Coordinator. Elected to Kansas Theatre Hall of Fame, 1990. Registered drama therapist, 1899; board certified trainer in drama therapy, 1994. **Publications:** The Eternal Kick, 1963; The Influence of D.H. Lawrence on Tennessee Williams, 1966; My Old Room, 1967; A Thousand at the Branches, 1969; We Can Make Our Lives Sublime, 1969; Some Events Connected with the Early History of Arizona, 1969; The Planter May Weep, 1970; Earp!, 1971; (with M. McCarthy) Monks, 1972; PUBA, 1973; The Betrayal, 1974; The Decision, 1974; The Matter with Kansas, 1975; The Kansas Character, 1976; Tennessee Williams' Dramatic Technique, 1977; A Jew in Kansas, 1978; American Jewish Theatre, 1979; Next Thing to Kinfolks, 1980; Beyond Absurdity and Sociopolitics: The Religious Theatre Movement in the Seventies, 1980; (with R. Lippman) The Buck Stops Here, 1982; (with R. Lippman) Abraham! Abraham! 1985; No Other Gods: A Midrash on Moses, 1987; Never Let 'Em Catch You at It: An Evening with Milburn Stone, 1989; A Light to the Nations, 1990; The Tailor and the Cloth, 1991; Facing Sudden Success: Philip Roth's Zuckerman Unbound, 1992; The Reed and the Cedar, 1992; Dramatizing the Torah: Plays about Moses, 1992; Custody, 1993; (with A. Aharoni) Inbar, 1996; Out of the Depths, 1998; Arthur Miller and the Holocaust, 2002. **Address:** 7966B Lexington Club Blvd, Delray Beach, FL 33446-3423, U.S.A. **Online address:** fedder@ksu.edu

FEDER, Bernard. American, b. 1924. **Genres:** History, Medicine/Health, Sciences, Social sciences. **Career:** Teacher of Social Studies, secondary schs. in NYC, 1949-66; Assistant Professor 1966-69, and Associate Professor of Education 1969-70, Hofstra University, Hempstead, NY; Professor of Education, University of Sarasota, Florida, 1975-90. **Publications:** (author and ed.) Viewpoints: US, 1967, 1972; (author and ed.) Viewpoints in World History, 1967, 1974; The Process of American Government, 1972; Bucking the System: Politics of Dissent, 1973; Price of Maintaining Poverty: Politics of Welfare, 1973; A Matter of Life and Breath, 1973; Walking the Straight Line: Politics of Drug Control, 1973; Policeman and Citizen: Politics of Law and Order, 1973; Then and Now: Cases in the American Experience, 1974; The Complete Guide to Taking Tests, 1979; (with E. Feder) The Expressive Arts Therapies, 1981, 1984; (ed.) Medguide, 1984; (with Dr. D. Stutz) The Savvy Patient: How to Be an Active Participant in Your Medical Care, 1990; (with E. Feder) The Art and Science of Evaluation in the Arts Therapies, 1998; Cleopatra's Nose: Historical Accidents That Helped Shape Our World, forthcoming. **Address:** 21 NW 101 Court, Gainesville, FL 32607, U.S.A. **Online address:** Federb@atlantic.net

FEDER, Chris Welles. American, b. 1938. **Genres:** Poetry, Education. **Career:** Encyclopaedia Britannica, Chicago, IL, Vienna, Austria, and NYC, foreign language editor, 1964-68; Ludi Education Inc., NYC, managing editor, 1968-73; freelance writer and textbook author, 1974-. Educational consultant; has helped develop elementary school texts in reading, language arts, and social studies; has developed materials to help illiterate adults achieve literacy. **Publications:** (with S. Margulies) Developing Everyday Reading Skills, 1988; (with S. Margulies) Century 21 Reading Program, 1989; (with G. Sesso) New York City Story, Then and Now (for children), 1991, rev. ed., 1999; Brain Quest (Grades 1-7), 1992, rev. ed., 1999; Brain Quest (Preschool), 1993, rev. ed., 1999; Brain Quest (Kindergarten), 1993, rev. ed., 1999; Brain Quest for Threes (Ages 3-4), 1994, rev. ed., 1999; My

First Brain Quest (Ages 2-3), 1994, rev. ed., 1999; The Movie Director: Dramatic Monologues and Poems, 2002. Contributor to textbook series and literary anthologies for children. Contributor of poetry to literary magazines. **Address:** c/o Raines & Raines, 103 Kenyon Rd, Medusa, NY 12120, U.S.A.

FEDER, Martin E(lliott). American, b. 1951. **Genres:** Biology. **Career:** University of Chicago, Chicago, IL, assistant professor, 1979-85, associate professor, 1985-89, professor of organismal biology and anatomy, 1989-, associate dean of Division of Biological Sciences, 1988-91. **Publications:** CO_EDITOR: (with G.V. Lander) Predator-Prey Relationships: Perspectives and Approaches from the Study of Lower Vertebrates, 1986; New Directions in Ecological Physiology, 1988; (with W.W. Burggren) Environmental Physiology of the Amphibians, 1992. Contributor to biology journals. **Address:** Department of Organismal Biology and Anatomy, University of Chicago, 1027 East 57th St., Chicago, IL 60637, U.S.A.

FEDERMAN, Raymond. American (born France), b. 1928. **Genres:** Novels, Poetry, Literary criticism and history, Translations. **Career:** Jazz saxophonist, 1947-50; University of California, Santa Barbara, 1959-64; State University of New York, Buffalo, assoc. professor of French, 1964-68, professor of French and Comparative Literature, 1968-73, professor of English and Comparative Literature, 1973-90, Melodia E. Jones Distinguished Professor of English and Comparative Literature, 1990-. **Publications:** Journey to Chaos: Samuel Beckett's Early Fiction, 1965; (trans) Y. Caroutch, Temporary Landscapes, 1965; Among the Beasts (poetry), 1967; Samuel Beckett: His Work and His Critics, 1970; (ed.) Cinq Nouvelles Nouvelles, 1971; Double or Nothing, 1971; Amer Eldorado, 1974; (ed.) Surfiction: Fiction Now and Tomorrow, 1975, 1981; Take It or Leave It, 1976; Me Too (poetry), 1976; (ed. with T. Bishop) Samuel Beckett, 1976; (ed. with L. Graver) Samuel Beckett: The Critical Heritage, 1979; The Voice in the Closet, 1979; The Twofold Vibration, 1982; Smiles on Washington Square (novel), 1985; To Whom It May Concern (novel), 1990; Duel (poetry), 1990; Now Then (poetry), 1992; Critifiction (essays), 1993; The Supreme Indecision of the Writer (essays), 1995; La Fourrure de ma tante Rachel (novel), 1996; The Precipice and Other Catastrophes (plays), 1999. **Address:** 16576 Calle Pulido, San Diego, CA 92128-3251, U.S.A. **Online address:** moinous@aol.com

FEDOROFF, Nina (V.). American, b. 1942. **Genres:** Sciences. **Career:** Biological Abstracts, Philadelphia, PA, assistant manager of Translational Bureau, 1962-63; free-lance translator and abstracter from Russian to English, 1963-66; Syracuse Symphony Orchestra, Syracuse, NY, flutist, 1964-66; University of California, Los Angeles, acting assistant professor of biology, 1972-74; Carnegie Institution of Washington, Baltimore, MD, staff scientist, 1974-95. Johns Hopkins University, professor of biology, 1978-95; University of Maryland at College Park, member of scientific advisory board, Center for Agricultural Biotechnology, 1987-; Pennsylvania State University, Willaman Professor of Life Sciences, 1995-. **Publications:** (ed. with D. Botstein) The Dynamic Genome: Barbara McClintock's Ideas in the Century of Genetics, 1992. Work represented in scientific anthologies. Contributor to scientific journals and newspapers. **Address:** Biotechnology Institute, 0519 Wartik Laboratory, Pennsylvania State University, University Park, PA 16802, U.S.A. **Online address:** nvf1@psu.edu

FEELEY, Gregory. American, b. 1955. **Genres:** Novels, Science fiction/Fantasy, Literary criticism and history. **Career:** Writer. **Publications:** The Oxygen Barons (science fiction), 1990. Author of essays/reviews and short fiction.

FEELEY, Malcolm M(cCollum). American, b. 1942. **Genres:** Law. **Career:** New York University, Dept of Politics, NYC, instructor to assistant professor, 1968-72; Russell Sage Foundation Fellow in Law and Social Science, NYC, 1972-; Yale University, New Haven, CT, Law School research associate; Institution for Social and Policy Studies, lecturer until 1977; University of Wisconsin-Madison, Dept of Political Science, assistant professor to professor, 1977-84; University of California, Berkeley, School of Law, visiting professor, 1982-83, professor and chair at Center for the Study of Law and Society, 1984-. Consultant for foundations, professional agencies, and government agencies. **Publications:** The Process Is the Punishment: Handling Cases in a Lower Court, 1979; (with A. Sarat) The Policy Dilemma: Federal Crime Policy and the Law Enforcement Assistance Administration, 1980; Court Reform on Trial, 1983; (with S. Krislov) Casebook in Constitutional Law, 1985; (with Krislov) Constitutional Law, 1990; (with J. Kaplan and J.H. Skolnick) Criminal Justice: Introductory Cases and Materials, 1991; (with E. Rubin) Judicial Policy Making and the Modern State, 1998; (with S. Miyazawa) The Japanese Adversary Process in Context, 2002. EDITOR: (with R. Hill) Affirmative School Integration, 1968; (with T.L. Becker) The

Impact of Supreme Court Decisions, 1973; (with R. Tomasic) Neighborhood Justice, 1982; (with H.N. Scheiber) Power Divided: Essays on the Theory and Practice of Federalism, 1989. Contributor to books and professional journals and author of reports for foundations and government agencies. **Address:** School of Law (Boalt Hall), University of California, Berkeley, CA 94720, U.S.A.

FEENEY, Don J(oseph), Jr. American, b. 1948. **Genres:** Psychology. **Career:** Champaign Council on Alcoholism, Champaign, IL, clinical director, 1976-79; private practice of psychology, hypnotherapy, and family services, Chicago, IL, 1979-80; Tri-County Mental Health Center, East Chicago, IN, psychologist, 1980-82; Psychological Consulting Services, Downers Grove, IL, consultant, 1985-, chief executive officer, 1998-. Christ Hospital, Oak Lawn, IL, psychologist with alcohol treatment program, 1982-; private practice of psychology, hypnotherapy, and family services, Downers Grove; developer and presenter of self-hypnosis and wellness programs; guest on television programs. **Publications:** Entrancing Relationships: Exploring the Hypnotic Framework of Addictive Relationships, 1999. Contributor to psychology journals. **Address:** Psychological Consulting Services, 6900 Main St. Suite 54, Downers Grove, IL 60516, U.S.A.

FEHRENBACH, T(heodore) R(eed). Also writes as Thomas Freeman. American, b. 1925. **Genres:** History, Military/Defense/Arms control, Money/Finance. **Career:** Royal Poinciana Corp., San Antonio, TX, president, 1971-93. Texas Historical Commission, chairman, 1987-91; Princeton University, Dept. of History, Advisory Council, 1992-96. **Publications:** Battle of Anzio, 1962; U.S. Marines in Action, 1962; (as Thomas Freeman) Crisis in Cuba, 1963; This Kind of War, 1963; Swiss Banks, 1966; Crossroads in Korea, 1966; This Kind of Peace, 1967; F.D.R.'s Undeclared War, 1967; Lone Star, 1968; Greatness to Spare, 1968; UN in War and Peace, 1968; Fight for Korea, 1969; Fire and Blood, 1973; Comanches, 1974; The San Antonio Story, 1978; Seven Keys to Texas, 1983; Texas: A Salute from Above, 1985. Author of columns and editorials. **Address:** PO Box 6698, San Antonio, TX 78209, U.S.A.

FEIFER, George. American, b. 1934. **Genres:** History, International relations/Current affairs, Novels. **Career:** CBS News, NYC, news writer, 1964. Freelance writing and lecturing 1965-. **Publications:** NONFICTION: Justice in Moscow, 1964; The Challenge of Change, 1967; Message from Moscow, 1969; Russia Close-Up, 1973, in US as Our Motherland, and Other Ventures in Russian Reportage, 1974; (with B. and B. Rosen) The Destined Hour: The Hostage Crisis and One Family's Ordeal, 1982; Tennozan: The Battle of Okinawa and the Atomic Bomb, 1992; Divorce: An Oral Portrait, 1995; Red Files, 2000; The Battle of Okinawa: The Blood and the Bomb, 2001. NOVELS: The Girl from Petrovka, 1971; Moscow Farewell, 1976. OTHER: (with D. Burg) Solzhenitsyn (biography), 1972; (with V. Panov) To Dance (autobiography), 1978. Work represented in anthologies. Contributor to books and periodicals. **Address:** 48 Cross Brook Rd, Roxbury, CT 06783-1211, U.S.A.

FEIFFER, Jules. American, b. 1929. **Genres:** Novels, Novellas/Short stories, Plays/Screenplays, Humor/Satire. **Career:** Village Voice, NYC, cartoonist, 1956-97; freelance cartoonist, 1951-; syndicated cartoonist, 1959-. Yale University Drama School, New Haven, CT, faculty member, 1973-74; Northwestern University, adjunct professor of writing, 1997; Southhampton College, adjunct professor of writing, 1999-. Member, Dramatist Guild Council; member, American Academy of Arts & Letters. Recipient: Academy Award for animated cartoon, Munro, 1962; Special George Polk Memorial Award, 1963; Pulitzer Prize for Editorial Cartooning, 1986. **Publications:** Sick, Sick, Sick, 1958; Passionella and Other Stories, 1959; The Explainers, 1960, Boy, Girl, Boy, Girl, 1961; Munro (animated cartoon), 1961; Hold Me!, 1963; Feiffer's Album, 1963; Harry, the Rat with Women (novel), 1963; The Unexpurgated Memoirs of Bernard Mergendeiler, 1965; The Great Comic Book Heroes, 1965; The Penguin Feiffer, 1966; Feiffer on Civil Rights, 1966; Little Murders, 1968; Feiffer's Marriage Manual, 1967; The White House Murder Case (play), 1970; Carnal Knowledge: A Screenplay, 1971; Pictures at a Prosecution: Drawings and Text from the Chicago Conspiracy Trial, 1971; Feiffer on Nixon, 1974; Knock, Knock (play), 1977; Hold Me (play), 1977; Ackroyd (novel), 1977; Tantrum (cartoon novel), 1979; Popeye (screenplay), 1980; Grown Ups (play); Jules Feiffer's America from Eisenhower to Reagan, 1982; Marriage Is an Invasion of Privacy and Other Dangerous Views, 1984; Feiffer's Children, 1986; Ronald Reagan in Movie America, 1988; Elliot Loves, 1989, (play), 1990; I Want to Go Home (screenplay), 1989; Anthony Rose (play), 1989; The Collected Works, vols. 1-4, 1989-92; Selected from Contemporary American Plays: An Anthology, 1990. FOR CHILDREN: Man in the Ceiling, 1993; A Barrel of Laughs, a Vale of Tears, 1995; Meanwhile..., 1999; I Lost My Bear, 1998; Bark George,

1999; I'm not Bobby!, 2000; Somethings Are Scary, 2000; By the Side of the Road, 2001; The House across the Street, 2002. **Address:** c/o Universal Press Syndicate, 4900 Main St, Kansas City, MO 64112, U.S.A. **Online address:** www.julesfeiffer.com

FEIGON, Lee. American, b. 1945. **Genres:** International relations/Current affairs, Biography. **Career:** Professor of History, since 1976, and Director of East Asian Studies, since 1978, Colby College, Waterville, Maine. **Publications:** Chen Duxiu: Founder of the Chinese Communist Party, 1984; China Rising: The Meaning of Tianammen, 1990; Demystifying Tibet: Unlocking the Secrets of the Land of Snow, 1996. **Address:** Dept. of East Asian Studies, Colby College, Waterville, ME 04901, U.S.A.

FEILER, Bruce. American, b. 1964. **Genres:** Documentaries/Reportage. **Career:** Taught English and American culture at a junior high school in Sano, Japan, 1987-88; Kyodo News Service, Tokyo, Japan, reporter, 1988-89; writer, 1991-; Clyde Beatty-Cole Bros. Circus, clown, 1993-. **Publications:** Learning to Bow: Inside the Heart of Japan, 1991; Looking for Class: Seeking Wisdom and Romance at Oxford and Cambridge, 1993; Under the Big Top: A Season with the Circus, 1995; Walking the Bible, 2001; Abraham, 2002. Contributor to periodicals. **Address:** 120 Habersham St., Savannah, GA 31401, U.S.A.

FEIN, Richard J. American, b. 1929. **Genres:** Poetry, Literary criticism and history. **Career:** State University College of New York at New Paltz, professor emeritus of English. **Publications:** Robert Lowell, 1971; The Dance of Leah, 1986; (trans.) Selected Poems of Yankev Glatshteyn, 1987; Kafka's Ear, 1990; At the Turkish Bath, 1994; To Move into the House, 1996; Ice Like Morsels, 1999; I Think of Our Lives, 2002; Mother Tongue, 2004. **Address:** 46 Irving St, Cambridge, MA 02138-3007, U.S.A.

FEINBERG, Leonard. American (born Russia), b. 1914. **Genres:** Literary criticism and history. **Career:** Iowa State University, Ames, professor of English, 1957-82, distinguished professor emeritus in humanities, 1982-. University, of Ceylon, Fulbright lecturer, 1957-58. **Publications:** The Satirist, 1963; Introduction to Satire, 1967; (ed.) Asian Laughter, 1971; The Secret of Humor, 1978; The ET Visitor's Guide to the U.S.A., 2001; Hypocrisy: Don't Leave Home without It, 2002; Where the Williwaw Blowe, 2003. **Address:** 2404 Loring St F-25, San Diego, CA 92109-2347, U.S.A.

FEINBERG, Richard. American, b. 1947. **Genres:** Anthropology/Ethnology, Language/Linguistics. **Career:** Roosevelt University, Chicago, IL, temporary instructor, 1974; Kent State University, Kent, OH, assistant professor, 1974-80, associate professor, 1980-86, acting coordinator of American studies program, 1980-81, professor of cultural anthropology, 1986-, president of Kent Research Group, 1997-98, faculty senate, chair, 1997-98. Central States Anthropological Society, 1st vice president, 2003-04; Association for Social Anthropology in Oceania, board of directors. Has conducted field research on the Navajo Indian reservation, in the Solomon Islands, in Papua New Guinea, and in Brady Lake, OH. Has served as a reviewer for publishers and granting agencies and as a contributor to conferences, meetings, symposia, and workshops. **Publications:** The Anutan Language Reconsidered, 2 vols, 1977; Anutan Concepts of Disease: A Polynesian Study (monograph), 1979; Social Change in a Navajo Community, 1979; Anuta: Social Structure of a Polynesian Island, 1981; Polynesian Seafaring and Navigation: Ocean Travel in Anutan Culture and Society, 1988; Oral Traditions of Anuta: A Polynesian Outlier in the Solomon Islands, 1998; Anuta: Polynesian Lifeways for the 21st Century, 2003. EDITOR: (and contrib.) Tempest in a Tea House: American Attitudes toward Breast-Feeding, 1980; (and comp. with S. Win) ASAO Bibliography, 1991; (and contrib.) Seafaring in the Contemporary Pacific Islands: Studies in Continuity and Change, 1995; (with K.A. Watson-Gegeo, and contrib.) Leadership and Change in the Western Pacific: Essays in Honor of Sir Raymond Firth (monograph), 1996; (with M. Ottenheimer) The Cultural Analysis of Kinship. Contributor to books and periodicals. **Address:** Dept of Anthropology, Kent State University, Kent, OH 44242, U.S.A. **Online address:** rfeinber@kent.edu

FEINBERG, Rosa Castro. (born United States), b. 1939. **Genres:** Language/Linguistics. **Career:** Teacher of reading, Spanish, science, adult classes in English as a second language, and other subjects at public high schools, Quincy, FL, 1960, Miami, FL, 1960-61, and Tallahassee, FL, 1961-63; Dade County Public Schools, Miami, FL, high school English teacher and debate coach, 1963-64, junior high school teacher of Spanish, social studies, English as a second language, and bilingual classes, 1964-72; University of Miami, Coral Gables, FL, staff member at Florida School Race Desegregation Consulting Center, 1973-75, assistant director of National

Origin Desegregation Assistance Center, 1975-76, associate director, 1977-80, director, 1980-90, director of Bilingual Education Training Program for Administrators, 1983-87, director of Institute for Cultural Innovation, 1986-90, research professor of educational and psychological studies, 1988-90; Florida International University, University Park Campus, Miami, visiting associate professor, 1990-92, associate professor, 1992-2002, adjunct professor, 2003. St. Thomas University, guest lecturer, 1987; University of Chicago, Joyce Lecturer, 1991; guest speaker at other educational institutions, including Arizona State University; workshop coordinator and presenter; public speaker. National Network of Hispanic Educators, chair, 1981-82; Center for Applied Linguistics, member of board of trustees, 1991-96; National Educational Equity Working Group, member, 1993-95; National Coalition of Advocates for Students, member of board of trustees, 1995-98; Coalition for Quality Education, member of board of directors, 1998-. Florida State Task Force on Bilingual Education, member, 1977-79; Florida Post-Secondary Education Planning Commission, member, 1982-87; Florida State Advisory Council on Bilingual Education, chair, 1983-89; Florida State Task Force on Migrant Education, member, 1984-85; Florida State Task Force on Multicultural Education, member, 1991-95. Testified before U.S. Commission on Civil Rights, National Conference on the Education of Hispanics, and White House Initiative on Excellence in Education for Hispanics; consultant to U.S. Department of Health, Education, and Welfare, U.S. Agency for International Development, and Government of Spain. National Conference of Puerto Rican Women, member, 1976-; Spanish American League against Discrimination, member of board of directors, 1976-94, member of executive committee, 1983-86, member of advisory board, 1994-; Coalition of Hispanic American Women, member, 1980-2000. Dade County Housing Finance Authority, commissioner, 1984-86; Miami Capital Development Corp., member of executive committee and board of directors, 1984-86; Dade County Value Adjustment Board, member, 1986-96; Dade County League of Cities, member of board of directors and executive committee, 1988-95, liaison to Florida League of Cities, 1993-94; Coalition for Quality Education in Dade County, honorary cochair, 1989-95, member of board of directors, 1996-; Dade County Hispanic Heritage Council, member of board of directors, 1992-93. Holmes Braddock Adult Education Center, volunteer, 1998. Member of board of directors, ASPIRA of Florida, 1980-88, ARISE Foundation, 1987-96, and Public Broadcasting System, 1989-96. **Publications:** (editor, with L. Valverde and E. Marquez) Educating Spanish Speaking Hispanics, 1980; Bilingual Education: A Reference Handbook, 2002. Contributor to books, articles and reviews to periodicals. **Address:** c/o Department of Educational Foundations, University Park Campus, Florida International University, Miami, FL 33199, U.S.A. **Online address:** rcastro@ fiu.edu

FEINGOLD, Eugene. *See* Obituaries.

FEINGOLD, S. Norman. *See* Obituaries.

FEINSTEIN, David. American, b. 1946. **Genres:** Psychology. **Career:** Johns Hopkins University, School of Medicine, Baltimore, MD, instructor in psychiatry, 1973-75; clinical psychologist; writer. **Publications:** Rituals for Living and Dying, 1990; (with P.E. Mayo) Mortal Acts, 1992; (with S. Krippner) The Mythic Path, 1997; (with D. Eden) Energy Medicine, 1999; Energy Psychology Interactive, 2003. **Address:** 777 E Main St, Ashland, OR 97520, U.S.A.

FEINSTEIN, Edward. American, b. 1954. **Genres:** Adult non-fiction. **Career:** Rabbi. Ordained, Jewish Theological Seminary of America, New York, NY, 1981; Solomon Schechter Academy, Dallas, TX, founding director; Congregation Shearith Israel, Dallas, associate rabbi; Camp Ramah, CA, executive director, 1990-93; Valley Beth Shalom, Encino, CA, rabbi; Ziegler Rabbinical School, University of Judaism, Los Angeles, CA, lecturer; on the faculties of the Wexner Heritage Foundation and the Whizen Institute on the Family. Former board member of various religious organizations. **Publications:** Tough Questions Jews Ask: A Young Adult's Guide to Building a Jewish Life, 2003. Columnist and contributing editor. **Address:** Valley Beth Shalom, 15739 Ventura Blvd, Encino, CA 91436, U.S.A. **Online address:** efeinstein@vbs.org

FEINSTEIN, Elaine. British, b. 1930. **Genres:** Novels, Novellas/Short stories, Poetry, Biography. **Career:** Editorial staff member, Cambridge University Press, 1960-62; Lecturer in English, Bishop's Stortford Training College, Herts., 1963-66; Assistant Lecturer in Literature, University of Essex, Wivenhoe, 1967-70; Fellow, Royal Society of Literature, 1990. **Publications:** In a Green Eye, 1966; The Magic Apple Tree, 1971; At the Edge, 1972; Matters of Chance (short stories), 1972; The Celebrants and Other Poems, 1973; Some Unease and Angels, 1977; Selected Poems, 1977; The

Silent Areas (short stories), 1980; The Feast of Euridice (poems), 1980; Bessie Smith (biography), 1986; Badlands, 1987; A Captive Lion: The Life of Marina Tsvetayeva (biography), 1987; City Music (poems), 1990; Lawrence and the Women (biography), 1993; Selected Poems, 1994; Daylight, 1997; Pushkin, 1998; After Pushkin, 1999; Gold, 2000; Ted Hughes: The Life of a Poet, 2001. NOVELS: The Circle, 1970; The Amberstone Exit, 1972; The Glass Alembic (in US as The Crystal Garden), 1973; The Children of the Rose, 1975; The Ecstasy of Miriam Garner, 1976; The Shadow Master, 1978; The Survivors, 1982; The Border, 1984; Mother's Girl, 1988; All You Need, 1989; Loving Brecht, 1992; Dreamers, 1994; Lady Chatterley's Confession, 1996; Dark Inheritance, 2001. EDITOR: Selected Poems of John Clare, 1968; (with F. Weldon) New Stories 4, 1979; PEN New Poetry 2, 1988. TRANSLATOR: The Selected Poems of Marina Tsvetayeva, 1971; Three Russian Poets, 1978; (co-) N. Turbina, First Draft: Poems, 1987. **Address:** c/o Gil Coleridge, Rogers, Coleridge, & White, 20 Powis Mews, London W11, England. **Online address:** Elainefeinstein@ compuserve.com; www.elainefeinstein.com

FEINSTEIN, John. American, b. 1956. **Genres:** Sports/Fitness, Mystery/Crime/Suspense. **Career:** Staff writer, The National, NYC, 1989-91. Staff writer, Washington Post, 1977-88, and Sports Illustrated mag., NYC, 1988-89; Contract columnist: Washington Post Sunday Magazine, Golf Magazine; Commentator: National Public Radio. **Publications:** A Season on the Brink: A Year with Bobby Knight and the Indiana Hoosiers, 1986; A Season Inside: One Year in College Basketball, 1988; Forever's Team: One Team's Journey Through Life, 1989; Hard Courts: Real Life on the Pro Tennis Tours, 1991; Running Mates (mystery), 1992; Play Ball: The Life and Troubled Times of Major League Baseball, 1993; A Good Walk Spoiled: Days and Nights on the PGA Tour, 1995; Winter Games (mystery), 1995; A Civil War: Army vs. Navy, a Year Inside College Football's Purest Rivalry, 1996; A March to Madness - The View From the Floor in the ACC, 1997; The Majors, 1999; Last Amateurs, 2000; Punch, 2002; Open, 2003. **Address:** 9200 Town Gate Lane, Bethesda, MD 20817, U.S.A.

FEINSTEIN, Sascha. American, b. 1963. **Genres:** Poetry, Bibliography, Literary criticism and history. **Career:** Poet, anthologist, journal editor, and educator. Lycoming College, assistant professor, 1995-99, codirector of creative writing program, 1996-, associate professor, 1999-; Brilliant Corners, editor, 1996-. **Publications:** POETRY: Misterioso, 2000. ANTHOLOGIES: (ed. with Y. Komunyakaa) The Jazz Poetry Anthology, 1991; (ed. with Y. Komunyakaa) The Second Set: The Jazz Poetry Anthology, Vol. 2, 1996. CRITICAL STUDIES: Jazz Poetry: From the 1920s to the Present, 1997; A Bibliographic Guide to Jazz Poetry, 1998. Contributor to literary journals. **Address:** Department of English, Lycoming College, Williamsport, PA 17701, U.S.A. **Online address:** feinstei@lycoming.edu

FEIST, Raymond E(lias). American, b. 1945. **Genres:** Science fiction/Fantasy. **Career:** Writer. **Publications:** FANTASY NOVELS: RIFTWAR SERIES: Magician, 1982, published in 2 vols as Magician: Apprentice and Magician: Master, 1986, rev. ed., 1992; Silverthorn, 1985; A Darkness at Sethanon, 1986; Prince of the Blood, 1989; The King's Buccaneer, 1992. EMPIRE SERIES: (with J. Wurts) Daughter of the Empire, 1987; (with Wurts) Servant of the Empire, 1990; (with Wurts) Mistress of the Empire, 1992. THE SERPENTWAR SAGA: Shadow of a Dark Queen, 1994; Rise of a Merchant Prince, 1995. OTHER NOVELS: Faerie Tale, 1988. **Address:** c/o Doubleday, 1540 Broadway, New York, NY 10036, U.S.A.

FELDER, David W. American, b. 1945. **Genres:** Philosophy. **Career:** Florida Agricultural and Mechanical University, Tallahassee, professor of philosophy, 1971. Boston University, visiting scholar, 1991; University of Chicago, visiting scholar, 1995; Tallahassee World Federalists, chair. **Publications:** The Best Investment: Land in a Loving Community, 1983; How to Work for Peace, 1991; From Conflict to Consensus: An Introduction to Logic, 1996. **Address:** 9601-30 Miccosukee Rd, Tallahassee, FL 32309, U.S.A. **Online address:** FelderDave@aol.com

FELDHERR, Andrew. American, b. 1963. **Genres:** Literary criticism and history. **Career:** Princeton University, Princeton, NJ, assistant professor of classics. **Publications:** Spectacle and Society in Livy's History, 1998. **Address:** 109 East Pyne, Department of Classics, Princeton University, Princeton, NJ 08544, U.S.A. **Online address:** feldherr@princeton.edu

FELDHUSEN, John F. American, b. 1926. **Genres:** Education, Psychology. **Career:** Wisconsin School for Boys, counselor, 1949-51; teacher at a private school in Lake Geneva, WI, 1951-54; Madison Business College, WI, instructor, 1955-58; University of Wisconsin-Madison, instructor, 1958-59; Wisconsin State University (now University of Wisconsin-Eau Claire), assistant professor, 1959-61, associate professor, 1961-62; Purdue University, West Lafayette, IN, associate professor, 1962-65, professor, 1965-, Robert B. Kane Distinguished Professor of Education, 1990-, now emeritus. United Arab Emirates University, leader of team to evaluate the College of Education, 1989-91. National Institute on Professional Training in Gifted Education, director, 1980-84. **Publications:** (with D.J. Treffinger and S.J. Moore) Global and Componential Evaluation of Creativity Instructional Materials, 1970; (with W. Kryspin) Writing Behavioral Objectives, 1974; (with W. Kryspin) Developing Classroom Tests, 1974; (with D.J. Treffinger) Teaching Creative Thinking and Problem Solving, 1977, 2nd ed. as Creative Thinking and Problem Solving in Gifted Education, 1980; (with R.L. Hohn and D.J. Treffinger) Reach Each You Teach, 1979, vol. 2, 1989; ; The Three-Stage Model of Course Design, 1980; (with W.B. Richardson) Leadership Education: Developing Skills for Youth, 1984; (with K.A. Heller) Identifying and Nurturing the Gifted, 1986; (with W.W. Haeger) Developing a Mentor Program, 1989; (with J.L. VanTassel-Baska and K.R. Seeley) Excellence in Educating the Gifted, 1989; (with S.M. Hoover and M.F. Sayler) Identification and Education of the Gifted and Talented at the Secondary Level, 1990; (with R. Jenkins-Friedman and E.S. Richert) Special Populations of Gifted Learners, 1991; TIDE: Talent Identification and Development in Education, 1995; (with D.J. Treffinger) Planning for Productive Thinking and Learning, 2000. EDITOR: (and contrib.) Toward Excellence in Gifted Education, 1985; (with others, and contrib.) Comprehensive Curriculum for Gifted Learners, 1988; (with N.K. Buchanan) Conducting Research and Evaluation in Gifted Education, 1991. Contributor to books. Contributor of articles and reviews to education and psychology journals. **Address:** Beering Hall 1446, Purdue University, West Lafayette, IN 47906, U.S.A. **Online address:** feldhusenjf@aol.com

FELDMAN, Daniel L(ee). American, b. 1949. **Genres:** Politics/Government. **Career:** Olwine, Connelly, Chase, O'Donnell & Weyher (law firm), NYC, associate, 1973-74; executive assistant to Congresswoman Elizabeth Holtzman, 1974-77; New York State Assembly, Albany, counsel to a subcommittee, 1977-78, and a committee, 1979-80, assemblyman from 45th Assembly District, 1981-98, chair of Committee on Correction, 1987-98. Adjunct professor at John Jay College of Criminal Justice of the City University of New York, 1977-79, Long Island University, 1982-86, New York University, 1985-89, Brooklyn Law School, 1990-94, Baruch College, 1995-98, Fordham Law School, 2003-; visiting professor at Oxford University, 1982, 1990, and Holy Cross College, 1987-88. **Publications:** Reforming Government: Winning Strategies Against Waste, Corruption, and Mismanagement, 1981; The Logic of American Government, 1990; (co-author and legislative ed.) New York Criminal Law, 1996. **Address:** Assistant Deputy Attorney General, 120 Broadway, New York, NY 10271, U.S.A.

FELDMAN, David Lewis. American, b. 1951. **Genres:** Environmental sciences/Ecology. **Career:** Missouri Department of Natural Resources, resources planner, 1980; West Virginia State College, Institute, assistant professor, 1980-82; Moorhead State University, Moorhead, MN, associate professor and acting chair, 1982-88; Oak Ridge National Lab, Oak Ridge, TN, policy analyst, 1988-93; University of Tennessee, Knoxville, senior research staff. **Publications:** Water Resources Management: In Search of an Environmental Ethic, 1991; Global Climate Change and Public Policy, 1994; The Energy Crisis: Unresolved Issues & Enduring Legacies, 1996. **Address:** Energy, Environment, and Resources Center, University of Tennessee, Conference Center Bldg., Ste. 311, Knoxville, TN 37996-4134, U.S.A. **Online address:** feldman@utk.edu

FELDMAN, Ellen. Also writes as Elizabeth Villars. American, b. 1941. **Genres:** Novels. **Career:** Writer. **Publications:** NOVELS: a.k.a. Katherine Walden, 1982; Conjugal Rites, 1986; Looking for Love, 1990; Too Close for Comfort, 1994; Rearview Mirror, 1996; God Bless the Child, 1996; Lucy, 2003; The Boy Who Loved Anne Frank, 2005. Contributor of book reviews to newspapers and nonfiction articles to magazines. Has ghostwritten several fiction and nonfiction books for professionals and celebrities.

FELDMAN, Gayle. American, b. 1951. **Genres:** How-to books, Human relations/Parenting, Psychology. **Career:** Publishers Weekly, NYC, book news editor, 1989-. **Publications:** You Don't Have to Be Your Mother, 1994. **Address:** c/o Molly Friedrich, Aaron M. Priest Literary Agency, 708 3rd Ave 23rd Fl, New York, NY 10017-4103, U.S.A.

FELDMAN, Gerald D(onald). American, b. 1937. **Genres:** History. **Career:** University of California, Berkeley, Professor of History, 1963-. **Publications:** Army, Industry and Labor in Germany, 1914-1918, 1966; (ed.) German Imperialism, 1914-1918: The Development of an Historical Debate, 1972; (ed. with T.G. Barnes) A Documentary History of Modern Europe, 4

vols., 1972; Iron and Steel in the German Inflation 1916-1923, 1977; (with H. Homburg) Industrie und Inflation: Studien und Dokumente zur Politik der Deutschen Unternehmer 1916-1923, 1977; (ed. with O. Busch) Historische Prozesse der Deutschen Inflation, 1978; Vom Weltkrieg zur Weltwirtschaftskrise: Studien zur deutschen Wirtschafts-und Sozialgeschichte 1914-1932, 1984; (with I. Steinisch) Industrie und Gewerkschaften 1918-1924; Die uberforderte Zentralartbeitsgemeinschaft, 1985; Armee, Industrie und Arbeiterschaft in Deutschland 1914 bis 1918, 1985; (ed.) Die Nachwirkungen der Inflation auf die deutsche Geschichte 1924-1933, 1985; (with K. Tenfelde) Workers, Owners and Politics in Coal Mining: An International Comparison of Industrial Relations, 1990; The Great Disorder: Politics, Economics and Society in the German Inflation, 1914-1924, 1993; Hugo Stinnes, Biographie eines Industriellen 1871-1924, 1998. **Address:** Dept. of History, University of California, Berkeley, CA 94720, U.S.A. **Online address:** gfeld@socrates.berkeley.edu

FELDMAN, Irving (Mordecai). American, b. 1928. **Genres:** Poetry. **Career:** Distinguished Professor of English, State University of New York, Buffalo, 1964-. Member of faculty, University of Puerto Rico, Rio Piedras, 1954-56, University of Lyons, France, 1957-58, and Kenyon College, Gambier, OH, 1958-64. **Publications:** Work and Days and Other Poems, 1961; The Pripet Marshes and Other Poems, 1965; Magic Paper and Other Poems, 1970; Lost Originals, 1972; Leaping Clear and Other Poems, 1976; New and Selected Poems, 1979; Teach Me, Dear Sister, 1983; All of Us Here, 1986; The Life and Letters, 1994; Beautiful False Things, 2000; Collected Poems 1954-2004, 2004. **Address:** Dept of English, State University of New York, Buffalo, NY 14260, U.S.A. **Online address:** feldman@buffalo.edu

FELDMAN, Lynne B. Canadian, b. 1956. **Genres:** Business/Trade/Industry, Cultural/Ethnic topics, History, Race relations, Travel/Exploration, Biography. **Career:** Gage Publishing Co., Toronto, ON, editor, 1986-88; freelance writer and researcher in Toronto, 1988-. **Publications:** (with J.N. Ingham) Contemporary American Business Leaders, 1990; (with J.N. Ingham) African American Business Leaders: A Biographical History, 1992; A Sense of Place: Birmingham's Black Middle-Class Community, 1890-1930, 1999. Contributor to books. **Address:** 90 Farnham Ave, Toronto, ON, Canada M4V 1H4. **Online address:** lynfeling@yahoo.com

FELDMAN, Noah (R.). (born United States), b. 1970. **Genres:** Administration/Management. **Career:** Legal scholar and author. Yale University, New Haven, CT, visiting lecturer, 1996; New York University School of Law, assistant professor, 2001-04, associate professor of law, 2004-. Visiting associate professor of law at Yale Law School, 2004, and Harvard Law School, 2005. Has also served as a law clerk to Chief Judge Harry T. Edwards, U.S. Court of Appeals for the DC Circuit, and to Associate Justice David H. Souter, U.S. Supreme Court; New America Foundation, Washington, DC, adjunct fellow; chief U.S advisor for the writing of Iraq's new constitution, 2003. **Publications:** After Jihad: America and the Struggle for Islamic Democracy, 2003; What We Owe Iraq: War and the Ethics of Nation Building, 2004; Author of scholarly articles on topics such as constitutional law, law and religion, and legal theory. **Address:** New York University School of Law, Vanderbilt Hall, 40 Washington Square S, Room 411C, New York, NY 10012-1099, U.S.A. **Online address:** noah.feldman@nyu.edu

FELICIANO, Hector. American, b. 1952?. **Genres:** History, Documentaries/Reportage. **Career:** Editor in chief of the World Media Network (newspaper syndicate), NYC. Worked for the City of Paris Cultural Affairs Bureau, Paris, France; journalist for the Washington Post, Washington, DC, and the Los Angeles Times, Los Angeles, CA; also worked as an investigator of stolen art and a lecturer. **Publications:** NONFICTION: (with D. Senecal and others) A New York, 1988; Musee disparu, 1995, trans. as The Lost Museum: The Nazi Conspiracy to Steal the World's Greatest Works of Art, 1997. Contributor to periodicals. **Address:** c/o Basic Books, 10 East 53rd St., New York, NY 10022, U.S.A.

FELINTO (BARBOSA DE LIMA), Marilene. Brazilian, b. 1957. **Genres:** Novels. **Career:** College of Literature, Sao Paulo, Brazil, assistant professor of Portuguese language, 1983-87; Folha de Sao Paulo, Sao Paulo, journalist, 1989-. University of California, Berkeley, visiting writer, 1992; translator from English into Portuguese; Haus der Kulturen der Welt (Berlin), visiting lecturer, 1994. **Publications:** As Mulheres de Tijucopapo (novel), 1982, 2nd ed., 1992, trans. as The Women of Tijucopapo, 1994. UNTRANSLATED WORKS: Outros Herois e Este Graciliano (nonfiction), 1983; O Lago Encantado de Grongonzo (novel), 1987, 2nd ed., 1991; Postcard (stories), 1992. Work represented in anthologies. **Address:** Secret. Admins., Al. Barao de Limeira 425, 01290-001 Sao Paulo, Brazil.

FELIX, Antonia. American. **Genres:** Sciences, Natural history, Children's non-fiction. **Career:** Writer and opera singer. **Publications:** (with S. Christian) Can It Really Rain Frogs?: The World's Strangest Weather Events, 1997; (with S. Christian) Shake, Rattle, and Roll: The World's Most Amazing Volcanoes, Earthquakes, and Other Forces, 1997; (with S. Christian) Is There a Dinosaur in Your Backyard?: The World's Most Fascinating Fossils, Rocks, and Minerals, 1998; (with S. Christian) What Makes the Grand Canyon Grand?: The World's Most Awe-Inspiring Natural Wonders, 1998; Wild about Harry: The Illustrated Biography of Harry Connick, Jr., 1995; Christie Todd Whitman: People's Choice, 1996; Prayers and Meditations for Children, 1997; Christmas in America, 1999; Silent Soul: The Miracles and Mysteries of Audrey Santo, 2001; Andrea Bocelli: A Celebration, 2000;(Compiler, with the editors of the New York Post) The Post's New York: Celebrating 200 Years of NYC through the Pages and Pictures of the New York Post, 2001; Laura: America's First Lady, First Mother, 2002. EDITOR: L. Mendelson, A Charlie Brown Christmas: The Making of a Tradition, 2000; (with L. Sunshine) Pearl Harbor: The Movie and the Moment, 2001. **Address:** c/o Author Mail, Thomas Dunne Books, St. Martin's Press, 175 Fifth Ave., New York, NY 10010, U.S.A.

FELIX, Christopher. *See* MCCARGAR, James (Goodrich).

FELL, Alison. Scottish, b. 1944. **Genres:** Novels, Poetry. **Career:** Welfare State Theatre, Leeds/Bradford, co-founder, 1970; Women's Street Theatre, London, co-founder, 1971; Underground Press, journalist, 1971-75; Spare Rib, fiction editor, 1975-79; London Borough of Brent, C. Day Lewis Fellow, 1978; London Borough of Walthamstow, writer in residence, 1981-82; New South Wales Institute of Technology, Sydney, writer in residence, 1986; The Female Eye Conference, Hudders Field, guest writer, 1996; New Blood (new writers competition), Institute of Contemporary Arts, co-judge and presenter, 1996; University of East Anglia, writing fellow, 1998; University College, London, Royal Literary Fund Fellow, 2002; University of Middlesex, research fellow, 2003. Leads writing workshops. Gives readings from works at Art Centers, literature festivals, and universities. **Publications:** NOVELS: The Grey Dancer, 1981; Every Move You Make, 1984; The Bad Box, 1987; The Shining Mountain, 1989; Mer de Glace, 1991; The Pillow Boy of the Lady Onogoro, 1994; The Mistress of Lilliput, 1999; Tricks of the Light, 2003. POETRY: Kisses for Mayakovsky, 1984; The Crystal Owl, 1988; Dionysus Day (prose poem), 1992; Dreams, Like Heretics, 1997. FILMS: The Weaver, 1993; One Green Bottle, 1994. OTHER: Medea: Mapping the Edge (play), 2001. Contributor to books, periodicals, and anthologies. **Address:** c/o Tony Peake, Peake Associates, 14 Grafton Crescent, London N1G 9BT, England.

FELSKE, Coerte V. W. American, b. 1960. **Genres:** Horror. **Career:** Screenwriter and author. **Publications:** The Shallow Man, 1995; Word, 1998; The Millennium Girl, 1999. **Address:** c/o Crown Publishing Group, 201 East 50th St., New York, NY 10022, U.S.A.

FELSTEIN, Ivor. Also writes as Frank Steen, Philip McCann. British. b. 1933. **Genres:** Novellas/Short stories, Medicine/Health, Psychology, Sex. **Career:** Private psychotherapist, Sr. Physician, Bolton Health Authority, 1963-98. Medical Registrar, Kingston Group Hosps., Surrey, 1960-63; Medical Columnist: Bolton Evening News, 1966-70 and Liverpool Echo, 1974-76; Consulting Editor, British Journal of Sexual Medicine, 1973-86. Book reviewer, Reed Publications. **Publications:** Later Life: Geriatrics Today and Tomorrow, 1969; Snakes and Ladders: Medical and Social Aspects of Modern Management, 1971; A Change of Face and Figure, 1971; Living to Be a Hundred, 1973; Sex in Later Life, 1973; (with J. Mitson and M. Barnard) The Medical Shorthand Typist, 1974; Sexual Pollution: The Fall and Rise of Venereal Diseases; Looking at Retirement, 1977; (with others) B.M.A. Book of Executive Health, 1979; Sex in Later Life, 1980; (co-author) Well Being, 1982; Understanding Sexual Medicine, 1986; (co-author) Foot Health, 1989; (co-author) Care of the Elderly, 1995. Contributor of short stories to periodicals. Contributor to encyclopedia and periodicals. **Address:** Consulting Rooms, 11 Chorley New Rd, Bolton, Lancs. BL1 4QR, England. **Online address:** ivor@felstein1826.freeserve.co.uk

FELSTINER, Mary Lowenthal. American, b. 1941. **Genres:** History, Medicine/Health, Women's studies and issues. **Career:** Stanford University, lecturer in history, 1971; Sonoma State College, lecturer, 1971-72; San Francisco State University, San Francisco, CA, assistant professor, 1973-76, associate professor, 1976-81, professor of history, 1981-. **Publications:** (co-ed. and contrib.) Chanzeaux: A Village in Anjou, 1966; To Paint Her Life: Charlotte Salomon in the Nazi Era, 1994. Contributor to periodicals. **Address:** Department of History, San Francisco State University, 1600 Holloway Ave, San Francisco, CA 94132, U.S.A.

FENBY, Jonathan. British, b. 1942. **Genres:** History. **Career:** Journalist. Reuters World Service, Reuters Ltd., correspondent and editor, 1963-77; Economist, correspondent in France and Germany, 1982-86; Independent, London, home editor and assistant editor, 1986-88; Guardian, London, deputy editor, 1988-93; Observer, London, editor, 1993-95; South China Morning Post, Hong Kong, editor, 1995-; Sunday Morning Post, Hong Kong, editor, 1995-. **Publications:** (with L. Chester) Fall of the House of Beaverbrook, 1979; Piracy and the Public: Forgery, Theft, and Exploitation, 1983; International News Services, 1986; France on the Brink, 1998. **Address:** South China Morning Post, 28th Floor, Dorset House, 979 King's Road, Quarry Bay, Hong Kong.

FENDRICH, James Max. American, b. 1938. **Genres:** Sociology. **Career:** Florida State University, Tallahassee, FL, assistant professor, 1965-68, associate professor, 1968-74, professor, 1974-94. Former consultant, President's Advisory Commission on Civil Disorders; worked for U.S. Commission on Civil Rights, Veterans Administration, U.S. Army Behavioral and Social Science, and Sociological Resources for Secondary Schools. President and director, Committee on Political Education (C.O.P.E.); member, Big Bend Labor Council and Florida AFL-CIO. **Publications:** (with L.M. Killian and C.U. Smith) Leadership in American Society: A Case Study of Black Leadership, 1969; Ideal Citizens: The Legacy of the Civil Rights Movement, 1993. **Address:** Department of Sociology, Florida State University, Tallahassee, FL 32306, U.S.A.

FENNER, Frank John. Australian, b. 1914. **Genres:** Environmental sciences/Ecology, Medicine/Health. **Career:** Australian National University, Canberra, Professor of Microbiology, 1949-73, Director, John Curtin School of Medical Research, 1967-73, Director, Centre for Resource and Environmental Studies, 1973-79, Visiting Fellow, 1980-. **Publications:** (with F.M. Burnet) The Production of Antibodies, 1949; (with F.N. Ratcliffe) Myxomatosis, 1965; The Biology of Animal Viruses, 1968, (with others) 1974; (with D.O. White) Medical Virology, 1970, 4th ed., 1994; Classification and Nomenclature of Viruses, 1976; (with others) Veterinary Virology, 1987, 2nd ed., 1993; (with others) Smallpox and Its Eradication, 1988; (with R. Wittek and K.R. Dumbell) The Orthopoxviruses, 1988; (with Z. Jezek) Human Monkeypox, 1988; (with B. Fantini) Biological Control of Vertebrate Pests: The History of Myxomatosis-An Experiment in Evolution, 1999; (with D.R. Curtis) The John Curtin School of Medical Research-The First Fifty Years: 1948-1998. EDITOR: (with A.L.G. Rees) The Australian Academy of Science: The First Twenty-Five Years, 1980; (with A. Gibbs) Portraits in Virology, 1988; History of Microbiology in Australia, 1990; The Australian Academy of Science: The First Forty Years, 1995. **Address:** John Curtin School of Medical Research, Box 334, GPO, Canberra, ACT 2601, Australia. **Online address:** Frank.Fenner@anu.edu.au

FENNER, James R. *See* TUBB, E(dwin) C(harles).

FENNER, Roger T(heedham). British, b. 1943. **Genres:** Engineering, Technology. **Career:** Professor of Engineering Computation, Imperial College, University of London, 1991- (Reader 1979-91; Lecturer, 1968-79). Technical Officer, Imperial Chemical Industries Ltd., Plastics Division, Welwyn Garden City, 1965-68. **Publications:** Extruder Screw Design, 1970; Computing for Engineers, 1974; Finite Element Methods for Engineers, 1975; Principles of Polymer Processing, 1979; Engineering Elasticity, 1986; Mechanics of Solids, 1989. **Address:** Mechanical Engineering Dept, Imperial College, Exhibition Rd, London SW7 2BX, England. **Online address:** r.fenner@ic.ac.uk

FENNO, Jack. *See* CALISHER, Hortense.

FENTEN, D. X. American, b. 1932. **Genres:** Information science/Computers, Homes/Gardens. **Career:** Author and columnist, Weekend Gardener, 1974-; Newsday Newspaper, Garden Ed., 1978-91; Syndicated newspaper columnist, Computer Bits. **Publications:** Better Photography for Amateurs, 1960; Electric Eye Still Camera Photography, 1961; Flower and Garden Photography, 1966; Aviation Careers, 1969; Greenhorn's Guide to Gardening, 1969; Harvesting the Sea, 1970; Sea Careers, 1970; The Clear and Simple Gardening Guide, 1971; Making of a Police Officer, 1972; (with Barbara Fenten) The Organic Grow It, Cook It, Preserve It Guidebook, 1972; Gardening Naturally, 1973; Ms-M. D., 1973; (with Barbara Fenten) The Concise Guide to Natural Foods, 1974; First Book of Indoor Gardening, 1974; Ins and Outs of Gardening, 1974; Ms-ATT'Y, 1974; The Concise Guide to TV and Radio Careers, 1975; The Concise Guide to Volunteer Work, 1975; Strange Differences, 1975; The Weekend Gardener, 1976; Greenhousing for Purple Thumbs, 1976; (with Fenten) Careers in the Sports Industry, 1977; The Children's Complete How Does Your Garden Grow

Guide to Plants and Planting, 1977; Ms-Architect, 1977; (with Fenten) Tourism and Hospitality Careers Unlimited, 1978; Behind the Scenes, 10 vols., 1980; Easy to Make House Plants, 1981; (with Fenten) The Team Behind the Great Parades, 1981. **Address:** 27 Bowdon Road, Greenlawn, NY 11740, U.S.A.

FENTON, Alexander. Scottish, b. 1929. **Genres:** Anthropology/Ethnology. **Career:** Scottish National Dictionary, Edinburgh, senior assistant editor, 1955-59; National Museum of Antiquities of Scotland, Edinburgh, assistant keeper, 1959-75, deputy keeper, 1975-78, director, 1978-85; National Museums of Scotland, research director, 1985-89; European Ethnological Research Centre, director, 1989-. University of Edinburgh, lecturer, 1958-60, 1974-80, professor of Scottish ethnology and director, School of Scottish Studies, 1990-. **Publications:** The Various Names of Shetland, 1973, 2nd ed., 1977; Scottish Country Life, 1976, new ed., 1999; The Island Blackhouse: A Guide to the Blackhouse at 42 Arnol, Lewis, 1978; The Northern Isles: Orkney and Shetland, 1978, new ed., 1997; Continuity and Change in the Building Tradition of Northern Scotland, 1979; (with B.D. Walker) The Rural Architecture of Scotland, 1981; The Shape of the Past, 2 vols., 1985-86; Wirds an' wark 'e seasons roon on an Aberdeenshire Farm, 1987; Country Life in Scotland: Our Rural Past, 1987; The Turra Coo, 1989; Scottish Country Life, 1989; On Your Bike: 13 Years of Travelling Curators, 1990; Craiters or 20 Buchan Tales, 1995. EDITOR & CONTRIBUTOR: (with A. Gailey) The Spade in Northern and Atlantic Europe, 1970; (with J. Podolak and H. Rasmussen) Land Transport in Europe, 1973; (with B.D. Walker and G. Stell) Building Construction in Scotland, 1976; (with H. Palsson) The Northern and Western Isles in the Viking World, 1984; (with G. Stell) Loads and Roads in Scotland and Beyond, 1984; (with E. Kisban) Food in Change, 1986; (with J. Myrdal) Food and Drink and Travelling Accessories: Essays in Honour of Goesta Berg, 1988. Contributor to books and periodicals. **Address:** European Ethnological Research Centre, c/o National Museums of Scotland, Queen St, Edinburgh EH2 1JF, Scotland. **Online address:** a.fenton@nms.ac.uk

FENTON, John Charles. British, b. 1921. **Genres:** Theology/Religion. **Career:** Canon, Christ Church, Oxford, 1978-92; Principal, Lichfield Theological College, 1958-65; Principal, St. Chad's College, Durham, 1965-78. **Publications:** Preaching the Cross, 1958; The Passion According to John, 1961; The Gospel of St. Matthew, 1963; The Gospel According to John, 1970; (with M.H. Duke) Good News, 1976; Finding the Way through John, 1988; Sunday Readings, 1991; Affirmations, 1993; Finding the Way through Mark, 1995; The Matthew Passion, 1995; Galatians, 1996; Galatians and 1 & 2 Thessalonians, 1999; More about Mark, 2001. **Address:** 8 Rowland Close, Lower Wolvercote, Oxford OX2 8PW, England.

FENTON, Julia. See FENTON, Robert L.

FENTON, Kate. British, b. 1954. **Genres:** Novels. **Career:** House of Commons, London, England, researcher and secretary to Anthony Steen, 1977-78; British Broadcasting Corporation (BBC-Radio), Cardiff, Wales, producer of radio features, 1978-82; BBC-Radio, London, producer of radio features, 1982-85; writer, 1985-. Yorkshire Theatre Company, touring musical director, 1974-76; free-lance pianist. **Publications:** NOVELS: The Colours of Snow, 1990; Dancing to the Pipers, 1993; Lions and Liquorice, 1995; Balancing on Air, 1996; Too Many Godmothers, 2000; Picking Up, 2002. **Address:** c/o John Johnson Ltd., Clerkenwell House, 45-47 Clerkenwell Green, London EC1R 0HT, England. **Online address:** office@KateFenton.com

FENTON, M(elville) Brockett. Canadian, b. 1943. **Genres:** Biology. **Career:** Carleton University, Ottawa, Ontario, Biology faculty, 1969-86; York University, North York, Ontario, professor of biology, 1986-, head of department, 1986-94. Rockefeller University, visiting associate professor, 1976; Cornell University, visiting professor, 1985-86. **Publications:** Just Bats, 1983; Communication in the Chiroptera, 1985; (Co-editor) Recent Advances in the Study of Bats, 1987; Bats, 1992. **Address:** Department of Biology, York University, North York, ON, Canada M3J 1P3.

FENTON, Robert L. Also writes as Julia Fenton. American, b. 1929. **Genres:** Novels, Romance/Historical. **Career:** Fenton, Nederlander, Tracy & Dodge (entertainment law firm), senior partner; writer, worked as literary agent for 20 years, as film producer with Universal Studios and Twentieth Century Fox for several years. Producer of Movie of the Week, Double Standard, NBC-TV, 1988, and Woman on the Ledge, 1993. Marygrove College, Detroit, MI, adjunct professor of creative writing. **Publications:** NOVELS AS JULIA FENTON: Black Tie Only, 1990; Blue Orchids, 1992; Royal Invitation, 1995; Speakeasy, forthcoming. **Address:** 31800 Northwestern Highway No 390, Farmington Hills, MI 48334, U.S.A. **Online address:** fenent@msn.com; robertlfenton.com

FERDER, Fran. American. **Genres:** Theology/Religion. **Career:** Franciscan Sister of Perpetual Adoration and licensed clinical psychologist. Part-time faculty member at Seattle University, School of Theology and Ministry; co-director of Therapy and Renewal Associates (ministerial counseling center); author, speaker, and workshop leader. **Publications:** Called to Break Bread?: A Psychological Investigation of 100 Women Who Feel Called to Priesthood in the Catholic Church, c. 1978; Word Made Flesh: Scripture, Psychology, and Human Communication, 1986; (with J. Heagle) Partnership: Women and Men in Ministry, 1989; (with J. Heagle) Your Sexual Self: Pathway to Authentic Intimacy, 1992; (with J. Heagle) Tender Fires: The Spiritual Promise of Sexuality, 2002. Contributor to books. **Address:** c/o School of Theology & Ministry, Seattle University, 901 12th Ave, PO Box 222000, Seattle, WA 98122-1090, U.S.A.

FERGUSON, Alane. American, b. 1957. **Genres:** Children's fiction. **Career:** Writer. **Publications:** That New Pet!, 1987; Show Me the Evidence, 1989; Cricket and the Crackerbox Kid, 1990; The Practical Joke War, 1991; Overkill, 1992; Stardust, 1993; Poison, 1994; A Tumbleweed Christmas, 1995; Secrets, 1995. **Address:** 1460 Conifer Trail, Elizabeth, CO 80107, U.S.A.

FERGUSON, Brad. American, b. 1953. **Genres:** Science fiction/Fantasy, Horror. **Career:** Columbia Broadcasting System (CBS) Radio News, NYC, journalist, writer, editor, and producer; freelance writer, 1986-. **Publications:** Crisis on Centaurus, 1986; A Flag Full of Stars, 1991; The Last Stand, 1995; (with Kathi Ferguson) The Haunted Starship, 1997. Contributor to anthologies. Contributor of fiction to periodicals. **Address:** c/o Pocket Books, Simon & Schuster Bldg., 1230 Avenue of the Americas, New York, NY 10020, U.S.A. **Online address:** thirteen@fred.net

FERGUSON, Everett. American, b. 1933. **Genres:** Theology/Religion. **Career:** Abilene Christian University, Texas, professor, 1962-98, distinguished scholar in residence, 1998-. The Second Century, editor, 1981-92; Journal of Early Christian Studies, co-editor, 1993-99. **Publications:** Early Christians Speak, 1971, 3rd ed., 1999, vol. 2, 2002; (with A.J. Malherbe) Gregory of Nyssa: The Life of Moses, 1978; Demonology of the Early Christian World, 1984; Backgrounds of Early Christianity, 1987, 3rd ed., 2003; (ed.) Encyclopaedia of Early Christianity, 1990, 2nd ed., 1997; Church of Christ: A Biblical Ecclesiology for Today, 1996. **Address:** 609 East North 16th St, Abilene, TX 79601, U.S.A. **Online address:** eferguson29@cox.net

FERGUSON, Gary. American, b. 1956. **Genres:** Travel/Exploration, Local history/Rural topics. **Career:** Author, naturalist, and public speaker. Interpretive naturalist for the U.S. Forest Service at Sawtooth National Recreation Area, ID. **Publications:** Freewheeling: Bicycling the Open Road, 1984; Walks of California, 1987; (with H. Wolinsky) The Heart Attack Recovery Handbook, 1988; Walks of the Rockies, 1988; Walks of the Pacific Northwest, 1991; Rocky Mountain Walks, 1993; Walking down the Wild: A Journey Through the Yellowstone Rockies, 1993; (with K. Wall) Lights of Passage: Rituals and Rites of Passage for the Problems and Pleasures of Modern Life, 1994; New England Walks, 1995; Northwest Walks, 1995; Spirits of the Wild: The World's Great Nature Myths, 1996; The Sylvan Path: A Journey through America's Forests, 1997, as Through the Woods: A Journey through America's Forests, 1998; (with K. Wall) Rites of Passage: Celebrating Life's Changes, 1998; Shouting at the Sky: Troubled Teens and the Promise of the Wild, 1999; (with J. Clayton and M.B. Keilty) Guide to America's Outdoors: Southern Rockies, 2001; Hawks Rest: A Season in the Remote Heart of Yellowstone, 2003; Folklore of Medicinal Plants and Herbs. Contributor to magazines and newspapers. **Address:** c/o C. S. Lewis & Co. Publicists, 196 Van Dale Rd., Woodstock, NY 12498, U.S.A. **Online address:** ferguson@wildwords.net

FERGUSON, Kathy E. American, b. 1950. **Genres:** Women's studies and issues. **Career:** Siena College, Albany, NY, professor of political science, 1976-85; University of Hawaii at Manoa, Honolulu, professor of political science and women's studies, 1985-. **Publications:** Self, Society, and Womankind, 1980; The Feminist Case against Bureaucracy, 1984; The Man Question, 1993; Kibbutz Journal, 1995; (with P. Turnbull) Oh, Say Can You See? The Semiotics of the Military in Hawaii, 1999. **Address:** Women's Studies Program, University of Hawaii at Manoa, Honolulu, HI 96822, U.S.A. **Online address:** kferguso@hawaii.edu

FERGUSON, Mark W. J. British (born Northern Ireland), b. 1955. **Genres:** Biology, Medicine/Health, Natural history, Zoology. **Career:** Queen's University of Belfast, Belfast, Northern Ireland, lecturer in anatomy, 1978-84; Victoria University of Manchester, Manchester, England, professor of biological sciences, 1984-. University of Southern California, research fellow, 1981. Winston Churchill Fellow, 1978. **Publications:** The Structure, Development, and Evolution of Reptiles, 1984; (with others) Alligators and Crocodiles: An Illustrated Encyclopedic Account by International Experts, 1990; (with A. Huddart) Cleft Lip and Palate: Long Term Results and Future Prospects, 1991. EDITOR: (with C. Deeming) Egg Incubation: Its Effects on Embryonic Development in Birds and Reptiles, 1992; (with others) Gray's Anatomy, 38th ed., 1996. **Address:** Faculty of Life Sciences, University of Manchester, 3.239 Stopford Bldg, Oxford Rd, Manchester M13 9PT, England.

FERGUSON, R. Brian. American, b. 1951. **Genres:** Anthropology/Ethnology, Bibliography. **Career:** Drew University, Madison, NJ, lecturer, 1977; Hunter College of the City University of New York, NYC, lecturer, 1980; John Jay College of Criminal Justice of the City University of New York, NYC, lecturer, 1982-83; Rutgers University, Newark Campus, Newark, NJ, instructor, 1983-85, assistant professor, 1985-91, associate professor, 1991-99, professor of anthropology, 1999-, member, Center on Global Change and Governance, 1996-. Conducted ethnographic field research in Puerto Rico, 1980-96. New York Academy of Sciences, Board of Governors, 2002-. **Publications:** (with L.E. Farragher) The Anthropology of War: A Bibliography, 1988; Yanomami Warfare: A Political History, 1995. EDITOR & CONTRIBUTOR: Warfare, Culture, and Environment, 1984; (with N. Whitehead) War in the Tribal Zone: Expanding States and Indigenous Warfare, 1992; The State, Identity and Violence: Political Disintegration in the Post Cold War World, 2003. Contributor to books. Contributor of articles and reviews to professional journals and popular magazines. **Address:** Dept of Sociology and Anthropology, Rutgers University, Newark Campus, 360 King Blvd Rm 603, Newark, NJ 07102-1897, U.S.A.

FERGUSON, Robert (Thomas). British, b. 1948. **Genres:** Biography. **Career:** Writer. **Publications:** Best Radio Drama 1984, 1985; Best Radio Drama 1986, 1987; Enigma: The Life of Knut Hamsun, 1987; Henry Miller: A Life, 1991; Henrik Ibsen: A New Biography, 1996; The Short Sharp Life of T.E. Hulme, 2002. **Online address:** robert.ferguson@c2i.net

FERGUSON, Ron. Scottish, b. 1939. **Genres:** Novels, Sports/Fitness, Technology, Theology/Religion, Autobiography/Memoirs, Biography. **Career:** Minister of the Church of Scotland; leader of Iona Community, 1981-88; writer, 1988-; St. Magnus Cathedral, Kirkwall, Scotland, minister, 1990-2001, writer, 2001-. Worked as a journalist. **Publications:** Geoff (biography), 1979; Grace and Dysentery, 1986; Chasing the Wild Goose, 1988; George Macleod: Founder of the Iona Community, 1990; Black Diamonds and the Blue Brazil, 1993; Technology at the Cross Roads, 1994; Love Your Crooked Neighbor, 1999; Donald Dewar Ate My Hamster!, 1999; Hitler Was a Vegetarian, 2001; The Reluctant Reformation of Clarence McGonigall, 2002; Fear and Loathing in Lochgelly, 2002. **Address:** Vinbreck, Orphir, Orkney KW17 2RE, Scotland. **Online address:** ronferguson@clara.co.uk

FERGUSON, Sarah (Margaret). Also writes as Sarah, Duchess of York. British, b. 1959. **Genres:** Children's fiction. **Career:** Worked for public relations agencies, publishing firms, and art galleries in London, England; Weight Watchers, spokesperson. **Publications:** AS SARAH, DUCHESS OF YORK: Budgie the Little Helicopter, 1989; Budgie at Bendick's Point, 1989; Budgie Goes to Sea, 1991; Budgie and the Blizzard, 1991; My Story, 1996; Dining with the Duchess, 1998; Winning the Weight Game, 2000; What I Know Now, 2003. **Address:** c/o Publicity Dept, Simon & Schuster, 1230 Avenue of the Americas Fl Conc 1 Ste C3A, New York, NY 10020-1586, U.S.A.

FERGUSON, Will. Canadian. **Genres:** Adult non-fiction. **Career:** Writer and syndicated columnist; spent five years in Japan, c. 1990-95. **Publications:** NONFICTION: Why I Hate Canadians, 1997; The Hitchhiker's Guide to Japan, 1998; Hokkaido Highway Blues: Hitchhiking Japan, 1998. **Address:** c/o Douglas & McIntyre Publishing Group, 2323 Quebec St., Suite 201, Vancouver, BC, Canada V5T 4S7.

FERGUSON, William M. American, b. 1917. **Genres:** Archaeology/Antiquities. **Career:** Historian and writer. **Publications:** (with J.Q. Royce) Maya Ruins in Central America in Color: Tikal, Copan, and Quirigua, 1977; (with J.Q. Royce) Maya Ruins of Mexico in Color, 1984; (with A.H. Rohn and R. Woodbury) Anasazi Ruins of the Southwest in Color, 1987; (with J.Q. Royce and A.H. Rohn) Mesoamerica's Ancient Cities: Aerial Views of Precolumbian Ruins in Mexico, Guatemala, Belize, and Honduras, 1990, rev. ed. (with R.E.W. Adams), 2001; The Anasazi of Mesa Verde and the Four Corners, 1996. **Address:** PO Box 236, 101 N Washington, Wellington, KS 67152, U.S.A.

FERLING, John E. American, b. 1940. **Genres:** History, Bibliography, Biography. **Career:** Morehead State University, Morehead, KY, assistant

professor of history, 1965-68; West Chester State University, West Chester, PA, associate professor of history, 1970-71; State University of West Georgia, Carrollton, professor of history, 1971-. **Publications:** The Loyalist Mind, 1977; A Wilderness of Miseries, 1981; The First of Men: A Life of George Washington, 1988; John Adams: A Life, 1992; Struggle for a Continent, 1993; John Adams: A Bibliography, 1993; Setting the World Ablaze, 2000. **Address:** Department of History, State University of West Georgia, Carrollton, GA 30118, U.S.A. **Online address:** jferling@westga.edu

FERLINGHETTI, Lawrence. American, b. 1920. **Genres:** Novels, Plays/Screenplays, Poetry, Art/Art history. **Career:** Principal owner and ed.-in-chief, City Lights Books, San Francisco, CA; also painter; first poet laureate of San Francisco, 1998-2000. Member, American Academy of Arts & Letters. **Publications:** Pictures of the Gone World, 1955, rev. ed., 1995; A Coney Island of the Mind, 1958; (trans.) J. Prevert, Selections from Paroles, 1958; Tentative Description of a Dinner to Promote the Impeachment of President Eisenhower, 1958; (ed.) Beatitude Anthology, 1960; Her (novel), 1960; One Thousand Fearful Words for Fidel Castro, 1961; Berlin, 1961; Starting from San Francisco: Poems, 1961, 1967; Unfair Arguments with Existence: Seven Plays for a New Theatre, 1963; (with others) Penguin Modern Poets 5, 1963; Routines (play and short pieces), 1964; Where Is Vietnam?, 1965; An Eye on the World: Selected Poems, 1967; After the Cries of the Birds, 1967; Moscow in the Wilderness, Segovia in the Snow, 1967; The Secret Meaning of Things, 1969; Tyrannus Nix?, 1969; The Mexican Night: Travel Journal, 1970; Back Roads to Far Places, 1971; Love Is No Stone on the Moon, 1971; Open Eyes, Open Heart, 1973; Who Are We Now?, 1976; Northwest Ecolog, 1978; Landscape of Living and Dying, 1979; Endless Life: Selected Poems, 1981; A Trip to Italy and France, 1981; Mule Mountain Dreams, 1981; The Populist Manifestos, 1981; (with N.J. Peters) Literary San Francisco, 1981; Leaves of Life, 1983; Seven Days in Nicaragua Libre, 1984; European Poems and Transitions, 1984; Love in the Days of Rage (novel), 1988; When I Look at Pictures (poems and paintings), 1990; These Are My Rivers: New and Selected Poems, 1993; The Cool Eye, 1993; A Far Rockaway of the Heart: New Poems, 1997; How to Paint Sunlight: New Poems, 2001. **Address:** City Lights Books, 261 Columbus Ave, San Francisco, CA 94133, U.S.A.

FERLITA, Ernest. American, b. 1927. **Genres:** Plays/Screenplays, Songs/Lyrics and libretti, Film, Theatre, Theology/Religion, Translations. **Career:** Jesuit Priest, 1962-. Loyola University, New Orleans, professor of drama and speech, 1969-, now emeritus (chairman, 1970-88). **Publications:** Songs of Hiroshima, 1970; The Theatre of Pilgrimage, 1971; (with J.R. May) Film Odyssey, 1976; The Way of the River, 1977; (with J.R. May) The Parables of Lina Wertmuller, 1977; (verse trans.) The Spiritual Marriage of the Shepherd Peter and the Mexican Church, 1977; Quetzal, 1979; (with others) Religion in Film, 1982; Gospel Journey, 1982; Introduction to Poems of Gerard Manley Hopkins, 1986; The Uttermost Mark: The Dramatic Criticism of Gerard Manley Hopkins, 1990; Performance: Hopkins' Sine Qua Non (essay), 1991; The Paths of Life: Cycle A, 1992; Cycle B, 1993; Cycle C, 1994; Advent/Christmas Season, 1999; A Third Remove: Hopkins and St. Patrick (essay), 1996; The Road to Bethlehem: The Use of the Imagination in the Spiritual Exercises (essay), 1997; The Playwright as Theologian Confronting Evil (essay), 1997; In the Light of the Lord, 2003. PLAYS: New Fire, 1968; The Hills Send off Echoes, 1968; The Stones Cry Out, 1968; The Krewe of Dionysus, 1974; The Mask of Hiroshima, 1989; Two Cities, 1999; Ma-Fa, 2000. **Address:** Loyola University, 6363 St. Charles Ave, New Orleans, LA 70118, U.S.A. **Online address:** ferlita@loyno.edu

FERMI, Rachel. American, b. 1964. **Genres:** Photography. **Career:** Camden County College, Blackwood, NJ, assistant professor of photography, 1990-. **Publications:** (with E. Samra) Picturing the Bomb, 1995. **Address:** Camden County College, Blackwood, NJ 08012, U.S.A.

FERMINE, Maxence. (born France), b. 1968. **Genres:** Poetry. **Career:** Author and poet. **Publications:** Neige, 1999, translation by Chris Mulhern published as Snow, 2003; L'apiculteur, 2000; (with Olivier Besson) Sagesses et malices de Confucius, le roi sans royaume, 2001; Opium, 2002; Le violon noir, translation by Chris Mulhern published as The Black Violin, 2003; Billiard Blues: suivi de Jazz blanc et Poker, 2003. **Address:** c/o Author Mail, Atria Books, Simon & Schuster, 1230 Avenue of the Americas, New York, NY 10020, U.S.A.

FERNÁNDEZ-ARMESTO, Felipe (Fermin Ricardo). British, b. 1950. **Genres:** History, Travel/Exploration, Biography. **Career:** St. John's College, Oxford, England, senior scholar, 1974-76; Charterhouse, Surrey, England, master, 1976-81; Warwick University, Coventry, England, visiting lecturer, 1981-82; Oxford University, fellow and director of Iberian studies at St. Antony's College, 1981-90, member of faculty of Modern History, 1983-; University of London, Queen Mary, professor, 2000-. Visiting lecturer. Contributor to radio and TV programs. **Publications:** Columbus and the Conquest of the Impossible (biography), 1974; Ferdinand and Isabella (biography), 1975; The Canary Islands after the Conquest, 1982; Sadat and His Statecraft (biography), 1983; Before Columbus: Exploration and Colonization from the Mediterranean to the Atlantic, 1229-1492, 1987; The Spanish Armada, 1988; Columbus, 1991; Edward Gibbon's Atlas of the World, 1991; Barcelona: A Thousand Years of the City's Past, 1992; Columbus on Himself, 1992; The Times Atlas of European History, 1994; Millennium, 1995; Truth: A History, 1997; Civilizations: Culture, Ambition, and the Transformation of Nature, 2001; Food: A History, 2001. EDITOR: The Times Atlas of World Exploration, 1991; The Times Guide to the Peoples of Europe, 1994; England, 1945-2000, 2001. Contributor to books, periodicals, and journals. Translator of books. **Address:** Dept of History, Queen Mary, University of London, London E1 4NS, England.

FERNANDEZ-SHAW, Carlos M(anuel). Spanish, b. 1924. **Genres:** Cultural/Ethnic topics, Music, History. **Career:** Spanish Diplomatic Service, worked at Ministry of Foreign Affairs in Madrid, 1949-51, secretary of embassies in Copenhagen, Denmark, 1951-52, Stockholm, Sweden, 1952-53, and Asuncion, Paraguay, 1953-56, head of Department of Institutions and Publications, Cultural Relations Division, Madrid, 1956-58, consul in Montreal, QC, 1958-61, in charge of cultural affairs at embassies in Washington, DC, 1961-65, and Rome, Italy, 1965-70, assistant secretary of Cultural Affairs Division, Madrid, 1970-73, ambassador to Paraguay, 1973-77, Australia, 1977, New Zealand, 1978, Fiji and Papua New Guinea, both 1979, and Tonga and the Solomon Islands, both 1981, inspector general in Madrid, 1983-85, consul general in Miami, FL, 1986-89. University of Madrid, assistant lecturer in public international law, 1949-51; Institute of Spanish Culture, head of Department of Cultural Exchange, 1956-58. **Publications:** Presencia Espanola en los Estados Unidos, 1972, 3rd ed., 1991, trans. as The Hispanic Presence in North America from 1492 to Today, 1991; The Spanish Contributions to the Independence of the U.S.A., 1976; Ventura y tribulaciones de un padre recien Estrenado (title means: The Joys and Anxieties of a Brand-New Father), 1976; Los Estados Independientes de Norteamerica (title means: The Independent States of North America), 1977; El Primer Consul de Espana en Australia: Antonio Arrom (title means: The First Consul of Spain in Australia: Antonio Arrom), 1988; La Florida Contemporanea: Siglos XIX y XX (title means: Contemporary Florida: The Nineteenth and Twentieth Centuries), 1992; El arpa en el contexto musical del Paraguay (title means: The Harp in the Musical Landscape of Paraguay), 1992; Spain and Australia: Five Centuries of History, 2000; Espana y Australia: Quinientos anos de relaciones, 2001. **Address:** Claudio Coello 60, 28001 Madrid, Spain.

FERRARI, R(onald) L(eslie). British, b. 1930. **Genres:** Engineering, Sciences. **Career:** GEC Ltd., Wembley, England, research officer at Hirst Research Centre, 1956-65; Cambridge University, Cambridge, England, lecturer in engineering, 1965-90, fellow of Trinity College, 1966-; writer. Cornell University, visiting professor, 1964-65; McGill University, visiting professor, 1972-73; Netherhall School, governor, 1986-90. **Publications:** (ed. with A.K. Jonscher) Problems in Physical Electronics, 1973; Introduction to Electromagnetic Fields, 1975; (with P.P. Silvester) Finite Elements for Electrical Engineers, 1983, 3rd ed., 1996. **Address:** Trinity College, Cambridge University, Cambridge CB2 1TQ, England. **Online address:** rlf1@cam.ac.uk

FERRARO, Barbara. American, b. 1943. **Genres:** Women's studies and issues. **Career:** Entered the Order of the Sisters of Notre Dame de Namur (a Roman Catholic religious order for women) in 1962; took final vows, 1965, left the order, 1988; teacher, parish minister, 1966-81; codirector of Covenant House (a shelter and counseling center for the homeless), Charleston, WV, 1981-. **Publications:** The Inside Stories: Thirteen Valiant Women Challenging the Church, 1987; (with P. Hussey and J. O'Reilly) No Turning Back: Two Nuns' Battle with the Vatican over Women's Right to Choose, 1990. **Address:** 600 Shrewsbury St, Charleston, WV 25301-1211, U.S.A. **Online address:** covhsjust@aol.com

FERRARO, Susan (Lyons). American, b. 1946. **Genres:** Romance/ Historical, Literary criticism and history. **Career:** Freelance writer. Teacher of classes in literature and journalism at State University of New York College at Purchase, Marymount College, Tarrytown, NY, College of New Rochelle, and local colleges in Westchester County, NY. **Publications:** Remembrance of Things Past, 1990; Responsible Writing, 1994; Sweet Talk: The Language of Love, 1995. Work represented in anthologies. Contributor to periodicals. **Address:** c/o Molly Friedrich, Aaron Priest Literary Agency, 708 Third Ave., New York, NY 10017, U.S.A.

FERRÉ, Frederick. American, b. 1933. **Genres:** Philosophy. **Career:** Dana Professor of Philosophy, Dickinson College, Carlisle, Pa., 1962-80; University of Georgia, Athens, Head of Dept. of Philosophy and Religion, 1980-88; Research Professor of Philosophy, 1988-. **Publications:** Language, Logic and God, 1961, 3rd ed. 1981; (with K. Bendall) Exploring the Logic of Faith: A Dialogue on the Relation of Modern Philosophy to Christian Faith, 1962; (ed.) William Paley's Natural Theology, 1963; Basic Modern Philosophy of Religion, 1967; (ed.) Comte: Introduction to Positive Philosophy, 1970; Shaping the Future, 1976; (with J. Kockelmans & J. E. Smith) The Challenge of Religion, 1982; (ed. with Rita H. Mataragnon) God and Global Justice: Religion and Poverty in an Unequal World, 1985; Philosophy of Technology, 1988; Concepts of Nature and God: Resources for College and University Teaching, 1989; Hellfire and Lightning Rods: Liberating Science, Technology, and Religion, 1993; (ed. with P. Hartel) Ethics and Environmental Policy: Theory Meets Practice, 1994; Being and Value: Toward a Constructive Postmodern Metaphysics, 1996; Knowing and Value: Toward a Constructive Postmodern Epistemology, 1998; Living and Value: Toward a Constructive Postmodern Ethics, 2001. **Address:** 148 S Stratford Dr., Athens, GA 30605-3024, U.S.A. **Online address:** FFerre@uga.edu

FERRÉ, John P. American, b. 1956. **Genres:** Communications/Media, Ethics, Theology/Religion. **Career:** Purdue University-Calumet, Hammond, IN, visiting instructor in English and philosophy, 1979-80; University of Louisville, Louisville, KY, assistant professor, 1985-90, associate professor, 1990-98, professor of communication, 1998-. **Publications:** Merrill Guide to the Research Paper, 1983; A Social Gospel for Millions: The Religious Bestsellers of Charles Sheldon, Charles Gordon, and Harold Bell Wright, 1988; (with S.C. Willihnganz) Public Relations and Ethics: A Bibliography, 1991; (with C.G. Christians and P.M. Fackler) Good News: Social Ethics and the Press, 1993. EDITOR: (with S.E. Pauley) Rhetorical Patterns: An Anthology of Contemporary Essays, 1981; (and contrib.) Channels of Belief: Religion and American Commercial Television, 1990. Work represented in anthologies. Contributor of articles and reviews to professional journals. **Address:** Department of Communication, University of Louisville, Louisville, KY 40292, U.S.A. **Online address:** ferre@louisville.edu

FERREE, Myra Marx. American, b. 1949. **Genres:** Sociology, Women's studies and issues. **Career:** University of Connecticut, Storrs, professor of sociology and women's studies, 1976-2000; University of Wisconsin, Madison, professor of sociology, 2000-. Guest professor, University of Frankfurt, 1985, Flinders University, 1993, and University of Bochum, 2003. **Publications:** (with B. Hess) Controversy and Coalition, 1985, 3rd ed., 2000; (co-ed.) Feminist Organizations, 1995; (with Gamson, Gerhards, and Rucht) Shaping Abortion Discourse, 2002. **Address:** Dept of Sociology, 1180 Observatory Dr, University of Wisconsin, Madison, WI 53706-1393, U.S.A.

FERRELL, Carolyn. American. **Genres:** Novels. **Career:** Writer. **Publications:** Don't Erase Me, 1997. **Address:** c/o Houghton Mifflin Company, 222 Berkeley St., Boston, MA 02116, U.S.A.

FERRELL, Frank. American, b. 1940. **Genres:** Social sciences. **Career:** Square Sales and Service, Bala Cynwyd, PA, president and chief executive officer, 1962-84. Ferrell Family Endeavors, Inc., senior partner. Affiliated with Trevor's Campaign, Ardmore, PA. **Publications:** (with J. Ferrell and E. Wakin) Trevor's Place: The Story of the Boy Who Brings Hope to the Homeless, 1985; Trevor's Place: A Decade Later, 1996; Trevor's Place: Year 2000, So What Happens Now?!. **Address:** PO Box 21, Gladwyne, PA 19035, U.S.A.

FERRELL, Jeff. American. **Genres:** Criminology/True Crime. **Career:** Regis University, Denver, CO, 1982-95, assistant professor of sociology to associate professor; Northern Arizona University, Flagstaff, associate professor to professor of criminal justice, 1995-2001; Southern Methodist University, Dallas, TX, visiting professor of sociology, 2002-. **Publications:** NONFICTION: Crimes of Style: Urban Graffiti and the Politics of Criminality, 1993, rev. ed, 1996; (ed. with C.R. Sanders) Cultural Criminology, 1995; (ed. with M.S. Hamm) Ethnography at the Edge: Crime, Deviance, and Field Research, 1998; (ed. with N. Websdale) Making Trouble: Cultural Constructions of Crime, Deviance, and Control, 1999; Tearing down the Streets: Adventures in Urban Anarchy, 2001. Contributor to books and periodicals. **Address:** Southern Methodist University, Department of Anthropology, Division of Sociology, PO Box 750336, Dallas, TX 75275, U.S.A. **Online address:** ferrelltdts@earthlink.net

FERRELL, Nancy Warren. American, b. 1932. **Genres:** Adult non-fiction, Children's non-fiction, Education. **Career:** Bureau of Indian Affairs Schools,

Sitka, AK, elementary teacher at Mount Edgecumbe Hospital, 1958-61; Department of Labor, Juneau, AK, writer of course studies for Manpower Development and Training Agency (MDTA) programs, 1963, writer and editor of Trends magazine, 1964-66, director of Alaska bureau of labor statistics, 1964-67; Juneau Public Library, Juneau, part-time technician, 1980-96; freelance writer and editor. Lecturer at jails and for panels, community groups, and religious organizations; teacher at workshops for young writers. **Publications:** NONFICTION CHILDREN'S BOOKS: The Fishing Industry, 1984; Passports to Peace, 1986; New World of Amateur Radio, 1986; Camouflage, Nature's Defense, 1989; U.S. Coast Guard, 1989; U.S. Air Force, 1990; Alaska: A Land in Motion, 1994; Battle of the Little Bighorn, 1996; Destination Valdez, 1998. ADULT NONFICTION: Barrett Willoughby: Alaska's Forgotten Lady, 1994; Early Years of Juneau, Alaska, 1997; Alaska's Heroes, 2002. Contributor of fiction and nonfiction to periodicals. **Address:** Box 20005, Juneau, AK 99802, U.S.A. **Online address:** NancyF@ptialaska.net

FERRER, Elizabeth. American, b. 1955. **Genres:** Art/Art history. **Career:** South Street Seaport Museum, NYC, exhibitions coordinator, 1980-82; Brooklyn Educational and Cultural Alliance, Brooklyn, NY, research and educational programs director, affiliated with Brooklyn Rediscovery, 1982-83; Pictogram (contemporary art gallery), NYC, founder and director, 1984-86; Columbia University, NYC, curatorial consultant and administrator affiliated with Miriam and Ira D; Wallach Art Gallery, 1987-89; Americas Society, NYC, curator and exhibitions coordinator, 1989-94, director of visual arts department and curator of art gallery, 1994-97; Austin Museum of Art, Austin, TX, director, 1997-. Lecturer at universities and museums. **Publications:** (Coeditor) Wifredo Lam: Works on Paper, 1992; A Shadow Born of Earth: New Photography in Mexico, 1993; (Coeditor) Latin American Artists of the Twentieth Century, 1993; (Coeditor) Space of Time: Contemporary Art in the Americas, 1993; (foreword) C. Puerto, A Selective Bibliography on Twentieth-Century Latin American Women Artists, 1996; The True Poetry: The Art of Maria Izquierdo, 1997. Author of exhibition catalogs. Contributor of articles and reviews to periodicals. **Address:** Austin Museum of Art, 823 Congress Ave., Ste 100, Austin, TX 78701-2435, U.S.A. **Online address:** eferrer@amoa.org

FERRIGNO, Robert. American, b. 1948. **Genres:** Novels. **Career:** Writer. Instructor in English and literature in Seattle, WA, 1971-73; feature writer for Orange County Register, until 1988; instructor in journalism at California State University, Fullerton. **Publications:** NOVELS: The Horse Latitudes, 1990; The Cheshire Moon, 1993; Dead Man's Dance, 1995; Dead Silent, 1996; Heartbreaker, 1999; Visible Man, 2001; Scavenger Hunt, 2003. **Address:** PO Box 934, Kirkland, WA 98083, U.S.A. **Online address:** rcferrigno@aol.com; www.robertferrigno.com

FERRIS, Jean. American, b. 1939. **Genres:** Young adult fiction. **Career:** Clinical audiologist, Veterans Administration Hospital, San Francisco, CA, 1962-63, San Diego Speech and Hearing Association, San Diego, CA, 1963-65, and in a doctor's office, San Diego, 1975-76; free-lance writer, 1977-; secretary and office assistant, San Diego, 1979-84. **Publications:** YOUNG ADULT FICTION: Amen, Moses Gardenia, 1983; The Stainless Steel Rule, 1986; Invincible Summer, 1987; Looking for Home, 1989; Across the Grain, 1990; Relative Strangers, 1993; Signs of Life, 1995; All That Glitters, 1996; Into the Wind, 1996; Song of the Sea, 1996; Weather the Storm, 1996; Bad, 1998; Love among the Walnuts, 1998; Eight Seconds, 2000; Of Sound Mind, 2001; Once upon a Marigold, 2002. **Address:** 605 W Walnut Ave, San Diego, CA 92103, U.S.A.

FERRIS, Jeri Chase. American, b. 1937. **Genres:** Children's non-fiction, Biography. **Career:** Worked as a secretary; Los Angeles Unified School District, Los Angeles, CA, teacher, 1967-93; writer. **Publications:** Go Free or Die: A Story about Harriet Tubman, 1988; Walking the Road to Freedom: A Story about Sojourner Truth, 1988; What Are You Figuring Now?: A Story about Benjamin Banneker, 1988; What Do You Mean?: A Story about Noah Webster, 1988; Arctic Explorer: The Story of Matthew Henson, 1989; Native American Doctor: The Story of Susan LaFlesche Picotte, 1991; What I Had Was Singing: The Story of Marian Anderson, 1994. **Address:** c/o Lerner Publications, 241 First Ave. North, Minneapolis, MN 55401, U.S.A.

FERRIS, John (Stephen). British, b. 1937. **Genres:** Environmental sciences/Ecology, Social sciences, Urban studies. **Career:** British Home Office, London, England, administrative officer, 1963-69; University of Nottingham, England, lecturer in social studies, 1972-. Visiting research scholar or research associate, University of Bielefeld, 1988, University of Bremen, 1989, and Czech Academy of Sciences, 1992. **Publications:** Participation in Urban Planning: The Barnsbury Case, 1973. EDITOR: (with D. Whynes and P.T. Bean, and contrib.) The Defence of Welfare, 1986; (with R. Page) Social

Policy in Transition: Anglo-German Perspectives, 1992; Realism in Green Politics, 1993; (with M. Morris, C. Norman, and J. Sempik, and contrib.) People, Land & Sustainability, 2000. Work represented in anthologies. Contributor to periodicals. **Address:** c/o Community Policy Research, 90 Denison St, Beeston, Notts. NG9 1DQ, England. **Online address:** john.ferris4@ntlworld.com

FERRIS, Paul. British, b. 1929. **Genres:** Novels, Plays/Screenplays, Medicine/Health, Biography. **Career:** Freelance writer. **Publications:** A Changed Man, 1958; The City, 1960; Then We Fall, 1960; The Church of England, 1962; A Family Affair, 1963; The Doctors, 1965; The Destroyer, 1965; The Nameless: Abortion in Britain Today, 1966; The Dam, 1967; Men and Money: Financial Europe Today (in U.S. as The Money Men of Europe), 1968; The House of Northcliffe, 1971; The New Militants: Crisis in the Trade Unions, 1972; Very Personal Problems, 1973; The Cure, 1974; The Detective (in U.S. as High Places), 1976; Dylan Thomas, 1977; Talk to Me about England, 1979; Richard Burton, 1981; A Distant Country, 1983; Gentlemen of Fortune (in U.S. as The Master Bankers), 1984; (ed.) Collected Letters of Dylan Thomas, 1985, rev. ed., 2000; Children of Dust, 1988; Sir Huge: The Life of Huw Weldon, 1990; Sex and the British: A Twentieth Century History, 1993; Caitlin, 1993; The Divining Heart, 1995; Dr. Freud, 1997; Infidelity, 1999; Dylan Thomas the Biography, 1999; Cora Crane, 2003. TELEPLAYS: The Revivalist, 1975; Dylan, 1978; Nye, 1982; The Extremist, 1983; The Fasting Girl, 1984.

FERRIS, Timothy. American/Irish, b. 1944. **Genres:** Astronomy, Sciences, Writing/Journalism. **Career:** United Press International, NYC, reporter, 1967-69; New York Post, reporter, 1969-71; Rolling Stone mag., NYC, associate editor, 1971-73, contributing editor, 1973-80; Brooklyn College of the City University of New York, professor, 1974-82; University of Southern California, Los Angeles, professor of journalism, 1982-89; University of California, Berkeley, professor of journalism, 1989-. **Publications:** The Red Limit: The Search for the Edge of the Universe, 1977, rev. ed., 2001; Galaxies, 1980; Spaceshots: The Beauty of Nature beyond Earth, 1984; (with B. Porter) The Practice of Journalism: A Guide to Reporting and Writing the News, 1988; Coming of Age in the Milky Way, 1988; World Treasury of Physics, Astronomy, and Mathematics, 1991; The Mind's Sky, 1992; The Universe and Eye, 1993; The Whole Shebang: A State-of-the-Universe(s) Report, 1997; Life beyond Earth, 2001; (ed.) Best American Science Writing 2001, 2001; Seeing in the Dark, 2002. **Address:** University of California, Graduate School of Journalism, Berkeley, CA 94720, U.S.A. **Online address:** mail@timothyferris.com

FERRIS, William (R.). American, b. 1942. **Genres:** Local history/Rural topics, Cultural/Ethnic topics, Mythology/Folklore, Bibliography. **Career:** Jackson State University, Jackson, MS, assistant professor of English, 1970-72; Yale University, New Haven, CT, associate professor of American and Afro-American studies, 1972-79; University of Mississippi, Oxford, professor of anthropology and director of Center for the Study of Southern Culture, 1979-97; National Endowment for the Humanities, chairman, 1997-; writer. Stanford University, Stanford Humanities Center, visiting fellow, 1989-90; lecturer at colleges and universities in the United States and abroad. Worked on documentary films; Center for Southern Folklore, cofounder and president, 1972-84; The Blues (documentary), Mississippi Authority for Educational Television, producer and host, 1972; guest on television and radio programs; film consultant. Photographer with exhibitions throughout the United States and Germany. **Publications:** Blues from the Delta, 1970, rev. ed., 1978; Mississippi Black Folklore: A Research Bibliography and Discography, 1971; Black Prose Narrative from the Mississippi Delta, 1974-75; Images of the South: Visits with Eudora Welty and Walker Evans, 1978; Local Color, 1982; Ray Lum: Mule Trader and Storyteller, 1992. EDITOR: Afro-American Folk Arts and Crafts, 2 vols, 1978, rev. ed., 1983; (with S. Hart) Folk Music and Modern Sound, 1982; (with C.R. Wilson) Encyclopedia of Southern Culture, 1989. **Address:** The Wendy Weil Agency Inc, 232 Madison Ave., Suite 1300, New York, NY 10016, U.S.A.

FESHBACH, Murray. American, b. 1929. **Genres:** Environmental sciences/Ecology, Medicine/Health, Demography. **Career:** Affiliated with National Bureau of Economic Research Inc., NYC, 1955-56; U.S. Bureau of the Census, Foreign Demographic Analysis Division, Washington, DC, analyst, 1957-67, chief of U.S.S.R. branch, 1967-68, chief of U.S.S.R./East Europe branch, 1969-78, chief of U.S.S.R. population, employment, and research and development branch, 1978-79; Georgetown University, Washington, DC, senior research scholar at the Center for Population Research and professorial lecturer in demography, 1981-84, research professor of demography, 1984-. Columbia University, adjunct professor, 1983-85; North Atlantic Treaty Organization (NATO) Headquarters, Office of the Secretary General,

Sovietologist-in-residence, 1986-87; lecturer at universities and other institutions. **Publications:** (with A. Friendly, Jr.) Ecocide in the USSR: Health and Nature under Siege, 1992; Ecological Disaster: Cleaning Up The Hidden Legacy of The Soviet Regine, 1995. EDITOR: National Security Issues in the USSR, 1987; (in-chief) Enviromental and Health Atlas of Russia, 1995. **Address:** Georgetown University, Department of Demography, Washington, DC 20057-1214, U.S.A.

FETHERSTON, Drew. American. **Genres:** Documentaries/Reportage. **Career:** Wall Street Journal, NYC, reporter; Newsday, Melville, NY, reporter. **Publications:** The Chunnel: The Amazing Story of the Undersea Crossing of the English Channel, 1997. Contributor to periodicals. **Address:** c/o Newsday Business Staff, 235 Pinelawn Rd., Melville, NY 11747, U.S.A. **Online address:** fetherst@newsday.com

FETTERS, Thomas T. (born United States), b. 1938. **Genres:** Children's fiction. **Career:** Crown Cork and Seal, Alsip, IL, consultant in packaging performance, 1961-. **Publications:** (with Peter Swanson) Piedmont & Northern, 1968; Palmetto Traction, 1975; Logging Railroads of South Carolina, 1985; The Lustron Home: The History of a Postwar Pre-fabricated Housing Experiment, 2001; Bears, Balds, and Sidewinders, Timber Times, forthcoming. **Address:** 545 South Elizabeth Dr, Lombard, IL 60148, U.S.A. **Online address:** tfetters@attbi.com

FEUERSTEIN, Georg. German, b. 1947. **Genres:** Cultural/Ethnic topics, Philosophy, Social commentary, Theology/Religion, Translations. **Career:** University of Durham, Yoga Research Centre, England, director, 1975-80; Integral Publishing, Lower Lake, CA, director, 1986-; Yoga World, editor, 1997-2001; Yoga Research and Education Center, Santa Rosa, CA, director, 1997-; International Journal of Yoga Therapy, editor, 1999-. **Publications:** Yoga: Sein Wesen und Werden, 1969; (with J. Miller) A Reappraisal of Yoga (essays), 1969, as Yoga and Beyond, 1972; The Essence of Yoga, 1974, rev. ed. as Wholeness or Transcendence?, 1992; The Bhagavad-Gita: Its Philosophy and Cultural Setting, 1974, as The Bhagavad-Gita: An Introduction, 1983; Textbook on Yoga, 1975; Yoga-Sutra: An Exercise in the Methodology of Textual Analysis, 1979; The Bhagavad-Gita: A Critical Rendering, 1980; The Philosophy of Classical Yoga, 1980; Structures of Consciousness: The Genius of Jean Gebser, 1987; Yoga: The Technology of Ecstasy, 1989; Jean Gebser: What Color Is Your Consciousness?, 1989; Encyclopedic Dictionary of Yoga, 1990, rev. ed. as The Shambhala Encyclopedia of Yoga, 1997; Holy Madness, 1991; The Shambhala Guide to Yoga, 1996; Sacred Paths: Essays on Wisdom, Love, and Mystical Realization, 1991; Sacred Sexuality, 1992;The Mystery of Light: The Life and Teaching of Omraam Mikhael Aivanhov, 1994; Spirituality by the Numbers, 1994; (with S. Kak and D. Frawley) In Search of the Cradle of Civilization, 1995; Lucid Waking, 1997; Tantra: The Path of Ecstasy, 1998; The Yoga Tradition, 1998; (with L. Payne) Yoga for Dummies, 1999; Yoga Gems, 2002. EDITOR: (and trans.) The Yoga-Sutra of Patanjali, 1980; Enlightened Sexuality (essays), 1989; (with S. Bodian) Living Yoga, 1993; (with T. Feuerstein) Voices on the Threshold of Tomorrow, 1993; Teachings of Yoga, 1997. **Address:** Yoga Research and Education Center, PO Box 426, Manton, CA 96059, U.S.A. **Online address:** mail@yrec.org; www.yrec.org

FEUERWERKER, Albert. American, b. 1927. **Genres:** History. **Career:** University of Michigan, Ann Arbor, associate professor, 1960-63, Director, Center for Chinese Studies, 1961-67, 1972-84, professor of history, 1963-86, A.M. and H.P. Bentley Professor of History, 1986-96, A.M. and H.P. Bentley Professor Emeritus of History, 1996-. **Publications:** China's Early Industrialization, 1958; (with S. Cheng) Chinese Communist Studies of Modern Chinese History, 1961; The Chinese Economy, circa 1870-1911, 1969; Rebellion in Nineteenth Century China, 1975; State and Society in Eighteenth-Century China: The Ching Empire in Its Glory, 1976; The Foreign Establishment in China in the Early Twentieth Century, 1976; Economic Trends in the Republic of China 1912-1949, 1977; Studies in the Economic History of Late Imperial China, 1995; The Chinese Economy, 1870-1949, 1995. EDITOR & CONTRIBUTOR: Modern China, 1964; (with R. Murphey and M.C. Wright) Approaches to Modern Chinese History, 1967; History in Communist China, 1968; Chinese Social and Economic History from the Song to 1900, 1982; (with J.K. Fairbank) Cambridge History of China, vol. 13, 1986. **Address:** Center for Chinese Studies, University of Michigan, Suite 3668, 1080 S. University, Ann Arbor, MI 48109-1106, U.S.A. **Online address:** afeuer@umich.edu

FFORDE, Jasper. British, b. 1961. **Genres:** Novels. **Career:** Novelist. Former focus puller (assistant cameraman) for films. **Publications:** The Eyre Affair, 2001; Lost in a Good Book, 2002. **Address:** c/o Janklow and Nesbit UK Ltd., 29 Adam & Eve Mews, London W8 6UG, England.

FFORDE, Katie. British, b. 1952. **Genres:** Romance/Historical. **Publications:** Living Dangerously, 1955; The Rose Revived, 1996; Stately Pursuits, 1997; Wild Designs, 1997; Life Skills, 1999; Thyme Out, 2000 in US as Second Thyme Around, 2001; Artistic Licence, 2002; Highland Fling, 2002; Paradise Fileds, 2003; Restoring Grace, 2004. **Address:** c/o Sarah Molloy, A.M. Heath, 79 St Martin's Lane, London WC2N 4AA, United Kingdom. **Online address:** kf@katiefforde.com; www.katiefforde.com

FIALKA, John J. American, b. 1938. **Genres:** Documentaries/Reportage, Economics, Technology, Military/Defense/Arms control. **Career:** Wall Street Journal, Washington Bureau, Washington, DC, reporter, 1981-. Founder of SOAR! a charity for retired religious people, primarily Roman Catholic nuns. **Publications:** Hotel Warriors: Covering the Gulf War, 1992; War by Other Means: Economic Espionage in America, 1997. **Address:** Wall Street Journal, 1025 Connecticut Ave. N.W., Washington, DC 20036, U.S.A.

FICKERT, Kurt J. American (born Germany), b. 1920. **Genres:** Poetry, Literary criticism and history, Essays. **Career:** Professor Emeritus, Wittenberg University, Springfield, OH, (Chairman of the Dept. of Foreign Languages, 1969-75; Professor, 1956-86). Instructor in German, Hofstra University, Hempstead, NY, 1947-53; Assistant Professor of German, Florida State University, Tallahassee, 1953-54, and Kansas State University, Fort Hays, 1954-56. **Publications:** To Heaven and Back: The New Morality in the Plays of Friedrich Durrenmatt, 1972; Herman Hesse's Quest: The Evolution of the Dichter Figure in His Work, 1978; Kafka's Doubles, 1979; Signs and Portents: Myth in the Work of Wolfgang Borchert, with a Translation of His Poems, 1980; Franz Kafka: Life, Work and Criticism, 1984; Neither Left nor Right: The Politics of Individualism in Uwe Johnson's Work, 1987; "Zwei gemeinsame Ansichten" in Johnson: Ansichten-EinsichtenAussichten, 1989; End of a Mission: Kafka's Search for Truth in His Last Stories, 1993; Dialogue with the Reader: The Narrative Stance in Uwe Johnson's Fiction, 1996. Contributor to periodicals. **Address:** 33 S Kensington Pl, Springfield, OH 45504, U.S.A. **Online address:** kfickert@wittenberg.edu

FIDO, Martin (Austin). British, b. 1939. **Genres:** Bibliography, Criminology/True Crime. **Career:** University of Leeds, Oxford, England, lecturer in English, 1966-72; University of West Indies, Barbados, reader in English and head of the Department of English and Linguistics, 1973-83; Hoevec Investors Ltd., Barbados, actor, 1981-83; writer, broadcaster, courier, guide-lecturer, 1983-. **Publications:** NONFICTION: Charles Dickens, 1968; Charles Dickens: An Authentic Account of His Life and Times, 1970; Oscar Wilde, 1973; Rudyard Kipling, 1974; Shakespeare, 1978; Oscar Wilde: An Illustrated Biography, 1985; Shakespeare, 1985; Murder Guide to London, 1986; The Crimes, Detection, and Death of Jack the Ripper, 1987; Bodysnatchers: A History of the Resurrectionists, 1742-1832, 1989; Murders after Midnight, 1990; (with K. Skinner) The Peasenhall Murder, 1990; (with P. Begg and K. Skinner) The Jack the Ripper A to Z, 1991; The Chronicle of Crime: The Infamous Felons of Modern History and Their Hideous Crimes, 1993; Deadly Jealousy, 1993; (with P. Begg) Great Crimes and Trials of the Twentieth Century, 1994; Twentieth Century Murder, 1995; (with K. Fido) The World's Worst Medical Mistakes, 1996; (with K. Fido) Our Family, 1997; The World of Charles Dickens, 1997. PLAYS: Let's Go Bajan!, 1983. AUDIOTAPES, WRITER AND READER: Silence of the Lambs: The True Stories, 1992; Guilty or Insane?, 1992; The Kennedys, 1992; On the Trail of Jack the Ripper, 1992; Son of Sam, 1992; Hell Hath No Fury, 1992; 10 Rillington Place, 1993; Shady Ladies and Wicked Women, 1993; The Yorkshire Ripper, 1993; The Krays, 1993; Classic Murders, 1994; The Manson Family, 1994, reissued as A Passion for Killing, 1995; The Truth about Jack the Ripper, 1994; Serial Killers, 1995; The Mob, 1996; Who Killed JFK?, 1996; Cults that Kill, 1996. Contributor of reviews to periodicals. **Address:** c/o Richard Jeffs, Roger Hancock Ltd., 4 Water Lane, London NW1 8NZ, England.

FIEDLER, Fred E. American (born Austria), b. 1922. **Genres:** Administration/Management, Psychology. **Career:** University of Illinois, Urbana, professor of psychology, 1951-69; University of Washington, Seattle, professor of psychology, and professor of mgmt. and organization, 1969-, now professor of psychology emeritus. **Publications:** Leader Attitudes and Group Effectiveness, 1958; (with E.P. Godfrey and D.M. Hall) Boards, Management and Company Success, 1959; A Theory of Leadership Effectiveness, 1967; (with M.M. Chemers) Leadership and Effective Management, 1974; (ed. with others) Managerial Control and Organizational Democracy, 1976; (with others) Improving Leadership Effectiveness: The Leader Match Concept, 1977, 1984; (with J.E. Garcia) New Approaches to Effective Leadership: Cognitive Resources and Organizational Performance, 1987; (with J.E. Garcia and C.T. Lewis) People, Management, and Productivity, 1985. **Address:** Dept. of Psychology, University of Washington, Seattle, WA 98195, U.S.A.

FIELD, D. M. *See* GRANT, Neil.

FIELD, David (McLucas). American, b. 1944. **Genres:** Plays/Screenplays. **Career:** Columbia Pictures Industries, Inc., West Coast story editor, 1973-75; American Broadcasting Companies, Inc. (ABC-TV), "Movies of the Week" manager, 1973-75; Twentieth Century-Fox Film Corp., vice president of creative affairs, 1975-78, executive vice president of worldwide production, 1980-83; United Artists Corp., senior vice president, 1978-80; motion picture producer and screenwriter. Tri-Star Pictures, consultant. **Publications:** Amazing Grace and Chuck (screenplay), 1987. **Address:** 2501 Colorado Ave, Suite 350, Santa Monica, CA 90404, U.S.A.

FIELD, Dorothy. American/Canadian, b. 1944. **Genres:** Plays/Screenplays, Poetry, Children's non-fiction, Women's studies and issues. **Career:** Freelance artist, using artist-made paper as a medium for sculptural work and books. **Publications:** FOR CHILDREN: In the Street of the Temple Cloth Printers, 1996. OTHER: Meditations at the Edge: Paper and Spirit, 1996; (with C.G. Chudley) Between Gardens, 1999; Leaving the Narrow Place (poetry), 2004. Author of articles and reviews on papermaking and traditional Asian culture.

FIELD, Edward. Also writes as Bruce Elliot. American, b. 1924. **Genres:** Novels, Poetry. **Career:** Former Lecturer, YM-YWHA Poetry Center, NYC. **Publications:** Stand Up, Friend, with Me, 1963; Variety Photoplays, 1967; (ed. and trans.) Eskimo Songs and Stories, 1973; Sweet Gwendolyn and the Countess, 1977; A Full Heart, 1977; Stars in My Eyes, 1978; (ed.) A Geography of Poets, 1979; (co-author) Village (novel), 1982; (co-author) The Office (novel), 1987; New and Selected Poems, 1987; Counting Myself Lucky, Selected Poems, 1963-1992, 1992; (co-ed.) A New Geography of Poets, 1992; A Frieze for a Temple of Love, 1998; (trans.) Magic Words, 1998; (co-author) The Villagers (novel), 2000. Writes fiction with N. Derrick as Bruce Elliot. **Address:** 463 West St A323, New York, NY 10014, U.S.A. **Online address:** fieldinski@yahoo.com

FIELD, Genevieve. American, b. 1970. **Genres:** Documentaries/Reportage. **Career:** Writer and editor. Connie Clausen & Associates, former literary agent; Cader Books, former editor; Melcher Media, former executive editor of MTV Books; Nerve (online magazine), NYC, executive editor, 1997-. **Publications:** MTV's Road Rules, Road Trips, 1996; (ed., with R. Griscom) Nerve: Literate Smut: Fiction, Essays, and Photographs from Some of Today's Most Provocative Writers and Artists, 1998; (ed.) Smart Sex, 1998. **Address:** c/o Pocket Books, Simon & Schuster, 1230 Avenue of the Americas, New York, NY 10020, U.S.A. **Online address:** genevieve@nerve.com

FIELD, J. V. British, b. 1943. **Genres:** History. **Career:** University of London, Birkbeck College, London, England, honorary visiting research fellow. **Publications:** (with J. Brody) A Catalogue of Books Printed before 1641 in the Science Museum Library, 1979; (with D.R. Hill and M.T. Wright) Byzantine and Arabic Mathematical Gearing, 1985; (with Wright) Early Gearing: Geared Mechanisms in the Ancient and Mediaeval World (exhibition catalog), 1985; (with J.J. Gray) The Geometrical Work of Girard Desargues, 1987; Kepler's Geometrical Cosmology, 1988; (ed. with F.A.J.L. James) Renaissance and Revolution: Humanists, Craftsmen, and Natural Philosophers in Early Modern Europe, 1993; (intro. and notes) L.B. Alberti, De la Pintura, trans. by J.R. Martinez, 1996; The Invention of Infinity: Mathematics and Art in the Renaissance, 1997; (trans. and author of intro. and notes, with E.J. Aiton and A.M. Duncan) J. Kepler, Memoirs of the American Philosophical Society, Vol. 209: The Harmony of the World, 1997; (with James) Science in Art: Works in the National Gallery That Illustrate the History of Science and Technology (monograph), 1997. Contributor to books and scholarly journals. **Address:** Department of History of Art, Birkbeck College, University of London, 43 Gordon Sq., London WC1H 0PD, England. **Online address:** jv.field@hart.bbk.ac.uk

FIELD, Mark G(eorge). American (born Switzerland), b. 1923. **Genres:** Medicine/Health, Sociology. **Career:** Boston University, MA, professor of sociology, 1962-, now emeritus. Senior sociologist, Dept of Psychiatry, Massachusetts General Hospital, Boston. Davis Center for Russian and Eurasian Studies, fellow, associate, 1962-, and adjunct professor, 1988-, School of Public Health, Harvard University, Cambridge, MA (associate, Russian Research Center, 1959-61; lecturer in sociology, Harvard Medical School, 1971-72). **Publications:** Doctor and Patient in Soviet Russia, 1957; The Social Environment and Its Effect on the Soviet Scientist, 1959; Soviet Socialized Medicine: An Introduction, 1967; Technology, Medicine and Society: Effectiveness, Differentiation and Depersonalization, 1968; (with R.E. Berry Jr., D. Koch-Weser, J. Karefa-Smart, and M. Thompson) Evaluat-

ing Health Program Impact: The U.S.-Yugoslav Cooperative Research Effort, 1974; Soviet Infant Mortality: A Mystery Story, 1986; (with A. d'Houtaud) La Sante: Approche Psychosociologique, 1989; Success and Crisis in National Health Systems, 1989; Soviet Health Problems and the Convergence Hypothesis, 1991; Soviet Medicine before and after the Fall, 1992; Post-Communist Medicine: Morbidity, Mortality and the Deteriorating Health Situation, 1994; The Health Crisis in the Former Soviet Union: A Report from the "Post-War Zone," 1995; Turf Battles on Medicine Avenue, 1996. EDITOR: The Social Consequences of Modernization in Communist Societies, 1976; (with M. Rosenthal and I. Butler) The Political Dynamics of Physician Manpower Policy, 1990; (with J.L. Twigg) Russia's Torn Safety Nets, 2000. **Address:** 40 Peacock Farm Rd, Lexington, MA 02421, U.S.A. **Online address:** mfield@hsph.harvard.edu

FIELD, Ophelia. (born Australia). **Genres:** Autobiography/Memoirs. **Career:** Policy analyst, writer. Human Rights Watch, London, England, policy analyst; Sunday Telegraph, London, books consultant. **Publications:** The Favourite: Sarah, Duchess of Marlborough, 2002, published as Sarah Churchill, Duchess of Marlborough: The Queen's Favourite, 2003. Author of policy reports and contributor to periodicals. **Address:** c/o Author Mail, St. Martin's Press, 175 Fifth Ave., New York, NY 10010, U.S.A.

FIELD, Thalia. American. **Genres:** Poetry, Songs/Lyrics and libretti. **Career:** Writer. Has worked as an instructor for Teachers and Writers Collaborative Theater for a New Audience, Brown University, and Bard College; Naropa University, Boulder, CO, currently a faculty member. Co-founded an interdisciplinary arts program in Juneau, AK. **Publications:** Point and Line (poems), 1999; The Pompeii Exhibit (opera libretto). Contributor of poetry to periodicals. **Address:** c/o Author Mail, New Directions Publishing Group, 80 Eighth Ave., New York, NY 10011, U.S.A.

FIELDHOUSE, David K(enneth). British, b. 1925. **Genres:** History, Third World. **Career:** History teacher, Haileybury College, 1950-52; Lecturer, University of Canterbury, Christchurch, New Zealand, 1953-57; Beit Lecturer in Commonwealth History, 1958-81, and Fellow, Nuffield College, 1966-81, Oxford University; Fellow, Jesus College, Cambridge, and Vere Harmsworth Professor of Imperial and Naval History, Cambridge University, 1981-92. **Publications:** The Colonial Empires, 1966, 1982; The Theory of Capitalist Imperialism, 1967, 1969; Economics and Empire, 1973; Unilever Overseas, 1978; Colonialism 1870-1945, 1981; Black Africa 1945-1980, 1986; Merchant Capital and Economic Decolonization, 1994; The West and the Third World, 1999. **Address:** Jesus College, Cambridge, England. **Online address:** dkf1000@cam.ac.uk

FIELDING, Helen. British, b. 1959?. **Genres:** Novels, Humor/Satire. **Career:** BBC-TV, England, producer, 1979-89; freelance writer, c. 1989-; columnist for the London Independent, 1995-. **Publications:** (with S. Bell and R. Curtis) Who's Had Who, In Association with Berk's Rogerage: An Historical Register Containing Official Lay Lines of History from the Beginning of Time to the Present Day, 1987, reissued as Who's Had Who: An Historical Register Containing Official Lay Lines of History from the Beginning of Time to the Present Day, 1990; Cause Celeb (novel), 1994; Bridget Jones's Diary (novel), 1996. Contributor to magazines. **Address:** c/o The Independent, 1 Canada Sq., Canary Wharf, London E14 5DL, England.

FIELDING, Kate. *See* OLDFIELD, Jenny.

FIELDING, Nigel G(oodwin). British, b. 1950. **Genres:** Criminology/True Crime, Law, Sociology. **Career:** Metropolitan Police College, London, England, lecturer in law, 1972-73; Lewes Technical College, Sussex, England, part-time lecturer in sociology, 1973-77; Ealing College of Higher Education, London, lecturer in criminology, 1977-78; University of Surrey, Guildford, England, lecturer in criminology, 1978-89, senior lecturer in sociology, 1989-, reader in sociology, 1992-95; consultant to Home Office, Economic and Social Research Council, and Police Training Council, Professor of Sociology, 1995-. **Publications:** The National Front, 1981; The Probation Practice, 1984; Linking Data, 1986; Joining Forces, 1988; Actions and Structure, 1988; Investigating Child Sexual Abuse, 1990; The Police and Social Conflict, 1991; Using Computers in Qualitative Research, 1991; Negotiating Nothing: Police Decision-making in Disputes, 1992; Community Policing, 1995; Computer Analysis and Qualitative Research, 1998; The Economic Dimensions of Crime, 2000; Interviewing, 2001. **Address:** Dept of Sociology, University of Surrey, Guildford, Surrey GU2 5XH, England. **Online address:** n.fielding@surrey.ac.uk

FIELDING, Raymond. American, b. 1931. **Genres:** Plays/Screenplays, Film. **Career:** Dean, School of Motion Picture, Television and Recording

Arts, Florida State University, Tallahassee, 1990-. Lecturer, 1957-61, Assistant Professor, 1961-65, and Associate Professor, 1965-66, University of California at Los Angeles; Associate Professor, University of Iowa, Iowa City, 1966-69; Professor of Communications, Temple University, Philadelphia, 1969-78; Professor, 1978-90, and Director of the School of Communications, 1985-90, University of Houston. Trustee, University Film Foundation, 1981-. Fellow, Society of Motion Picture and Television Engineers, 1976-. Member, Academy of Motion Picture Arts and Sciences, 1981-. President, University Film Association, 1967-68, and Society for Cinema Studies, 1972-74; awarded the Eastman Kodak Gold Medal of the Society of Motion Picture and Television Engineers, 1991. "From Newsreels to Televison News," TV series, senior consultant, 1997. **Publications:** The Honorable Mountain (screenplay), 1956; The Technique of Special Effects Cinematography, 1965, 4th ed., 1985; (ed.) A Technological History of Motion Pictures and Television, 1967; The American Newsreel, 1911-67, 1972, screenplays, 1975, 1978; The March of Time 1935-1951, 1978. **Address:** School of Motion Picture, Television and Recording Arts, Florida State University, Tallahassee, FL 32306-2350, U.S.A. **Online address:** fielding@earthlink.net

FIELDS, Hillary. American. **Genres:** Romance/Historical. **Career:** Writer. Formerly literary agent's assistant. **Publications:** HISTORICAL ROMANCES: The Maiden's Revenge, 2000; Marrying Jezebel, 2000; Heart of a Lion, 2001. Contributor to periodicals. **Address:** c/o St. Martin's Press, 175 Fifth Ave., New York, NY 10010, U.S.A. **Online address:** hillymeg@bellatlantic.net

FIELDS, Jennie. American, b. 1953. **Genres:** Novels. **Career:** Affiliated with Foote, Cone, and Belding (advertising agency), Chicago, IL, 1977-79; affiliated with Needham, Harper, and steers, Chicago, 1979-82; Young and Rubicam (advertising agency), NYC, senior vice president, 1982-85, senior vice president and creative director, 1989-93; Leo Burnett, Chicago, senior vice president, 1985-89; Lowe and Partners, senior vice president and creative director, 1993-95; Bozell, senior vice president, creative director, 1995-98; Robert A. Becker Inc, 1999-. **Publications:** Lily Beach, 1993; Crossing Brooklyn Ferry, 1997; The Middle Ages, 2002. Contributor of short stories to periodicals. **Address:** 452 8th St, Brooklyn, NY 11215, U.S.A. **Online address:** LilyBeach@aol.com

FIENBERG, Anna. Australian (born England), b. 1956. **Genres:** Children's fiction, Young adult fiction. **Career:** New South Wales School Magazine, staff, 1980-90, editor 1988-90; national book club consultant. **Publications:** CHILDREN'S FICTION: Billy Bear and the Wild Winter, 1988; The Champion, 1988; Wiggy and Boa, 1988, as Pirate Trouble for Wiggy and Boa, 1996; The 9 Lives of Balthazar, 1989; The Magnificent Nose, and Other Marvels, 1991; Ariel, Zed and the Secret of Life, 1992; The Hottest Boy Who Ever Lived, 1993; Madeline the Mermaid and Other Fishy Tales, 1995; Power to Burn, 1995; Dead Sailors Don't Bite, 1996; The Doll's Secret, 1997; (reteller) Snugglepot and Cuddlepie, 1997; Minton Goes Flying, 1998; Minton Goes Sailing, 1998; Tashi and the Demons, 1999; Minton Goes Driving, 1999; Minton Goes Trucking, 1999; Borrowed Light, 2000; Tashi and the Big Stinker, 2000; Minton Goes Under, 2000; Minton Goes Home, 2000; Tashi and the Dancing Shoes, 2001; The Big, Big, Big Book of Tashi, 2001; Joseph, 2001; The Witch in the Lake, 2001. WITH B. FIENBERG: Tashi, 1995; Tashi and the Giants, 1995; Tashi and the Ghosts, 1997; Tashi and the Genie, 1997; Tashi and the Baba Yaga, 1998. **Address:** c/o Allen & Unwin Pty Ltd, PO Box 8500, St Leonards, NSW 1590, Australia. **Online address:** afienberg@bigpond.com

FIENNES, Sir Ranulph (Twisleton-Wykeham-). British, b. 1944. **Genres:** Military/Defense/Arms control, Travel/Exploration, Autobiography/Memoirs. **Career:** Explorer: led British expeditions to the White Nile, 1969; Jostedalsbre Glacier, 1970; Headless Valley, 1971; toward North Pole, 1977; Transglobe Expedition, 1979-82; first polar circumnavigation of Earth; became first man to reach both poles. Executive Consultant to Chairman of Occidental Petroleum, Inc., 1984-87; discovered Omani, lost city of Ubar, 1992; first unsupported crossing of antarctic continent, 1993, longest unsupported polar journey in history, 1993. **Publications:** A Talent for Trouble, 1970; Icefall in Norway, 1972; The Headless Valley, 1973; Where Soldiers Fear to Tread, 1975; Hell on Ice, 1979; To the Ends of the Earth, 1983; Bothie, the Polar Dog, 1984; Living Dangerously, 1987; The Feather Men, 1991; Atlantis of the Sands, 1992; Mind over Matter, 1993; The Sett, 1996; Fit for Life, 1999; Beyond the Limits, 2000; The Secret Hunters, 2001; Captain Scott, 2003. **Address:** Greenlands, Somerset TA24 7NU, England.

FIENUP-RIORDAN, Ann. American, b. 1948. **Genres:** History, Anthropology/Ethnology, Film. **Career:** University of Alaska, Anchorage,

instructor in anthropology, 1973-74; Mud Inc., owner and operator, 1974; Nelson Island School of Design, researcher and publication designer, 1975; Alaska State Council on the Arts, Anchorage, instructor, 1978; Yukon Kuskokwim Health Corp., Bethel, AK, interviewer and research consultant, 1978-80; Alaska Pacific University, Anchorage, assistant professor of social science, 1980-83; University of Alaska, assistant professor of anthropology, 1983-84; US Department of the Interior, Minerals Management Service, Yukon Delta specialist, 1986-88; Yupiit Nation, consulting anthropologist, 1988-89; Anchorage Museum of History and Art, curator of exhibit "Agaiyuliyurallput: The Living Tradition of Yup'ik Masks," 1994-96. Nelson Island Oral History Project, consulting humanist; National Science Foundation, research grants, 2000; Arctic Anthropology, associate editor; Smithsonian Institution, Arctic Studies Center, Anchorage, research associate. **Publications:** Maraiurivik Nunakauiami, 1975; Shape Up with Baby, 1980; The Nelson Island Eskimo, 1983; The Yup'ik Eskimos as Described in the Travel Journals and Ethnographic Accounts of John and Edith Kilbuck, 1885-1900, 1988; Eskimo Essays, 1990; The Real People and the Children of Thunder, 1991; Boundaries and Passages, 1994; Freeze Frame, 1995; The Living Tradition of Yup'ik Masks, 1996; Where the Echo Began and Other Oral Traditions from Southwestern Alaska Recorded by Hans Himmelheber, 1999; Hunting Tradition in a Changing World, 2000. Contributor to books. Contributor of articles and reviews to professional journals and regional magazines. **Address:** 9951 Prospect Dr, Anchorage, AK 99516, U.S.A. **Online address:** riordan@alaska.net

FIERSTEIN, Harvey (Forbes). American, b. 1954. **Genres:** Plays/Screenplays. **Career:** Gay activist, actor, playwright, 1971-. **Publications:** Torch Song Trilogy, 1981, as film, 1988; La Cage aux Folles, 1983; Forget Him, 1984; Safe Sex, 1987; Spookhouse, 1987; In Search of the Cobra Jewels, 1975; Freaky Pussy, 1976; Flatbush Tosca, 1977; Cannibals Just Don't Know No better, 1978; HBO Showcase of "Tidy Endings," 1988; (co-author) Legs Diamond, 1988; The Sissy Duckling, 1999; Common Ground, 2000. **Address:** c/o RF Entertainment, 29 Haines Road, Bedford Hills, NY 10507, U.S.A. **Online address:** Ron@rfent.com

FIFIELD, Christopher G(eorge). British, b. 1945. **Genres:** Music, Biography. **Career:** Glyndebourne Festival Opera, Lewes, England, member of music staff, 1971-72, 1977-86; University of London, England, director of music at University College, 1980-90; Lambeth Orchestra, music director, 1982-; Jubilate Choir, conductor, 1988-2001; Northampton Symphony Orchestra, conductor, 1990-96; Central Festival Opera, music director, 1990-96; Reigate and Redhill Choral Society, conductor, 1992-96. **Publications:** Max Bruch: His Life and Works, 1988; True Artist and True Friend: A Biography of Hans Richter, 1993; Letters and Diaries of Kathleen Ferrier, 2003. **Address:** 162 Venner Rd, London SE26 5JQ, England. **Online address:** christopherfifield@ntlworld.com

FIGES, Eva. British (born Germany), b. 1932. **Genres:** Novels, Novellas/Short stories, Literary criticism and history, Women's studies and issues, Writing/Journalism, Autobiography/Memoirs. **Publications:** Equinox, 1966; Winter Journey, 1967; The Banger, 1968; Konek Landing, 1969; Patriarchial Attitudes: Women in Society, 1970; Scribble Sam, 1971; B, 1972; Days, 1974; Tragedy and Social Evolution, 1975; Nelly's Version, 1977; Little Eden: A Child at War, 1978; Waking, 1981; Sex and Subterfuge, 1982; Light, 1983; The Seven Ages, 1986; Ghosts, 1988; The Tree of Knowledge, 1990; The Tenancy, 1993; The Knot, 1996. **Address:** c/o Rogers, Coleridge & White Ltd, 20 Powis Mews, London W11 1JN, England.

FIGES, Kate. British. **Genres:** Women's studies and issues. **Career:** Journalist and author. Mail on Sunday (newspaper), London, England, books editor for You magazine. **Publications:** Because of Her Sex: The Myth of Equality for Women in Britain, 1994; (with J. Zimmerman) Life after Birth: What Even Your Friends Won't Tell You about Motherhood, 2001. EDITOR: The Best of Cosmopolitan Fiction, 1991; The Cosmopolitan Book of Short Stories, 1995; (Selector and author of intro) The Penguin Book of International Women's Stories, 1996; Childhood (anthology), 1998. Contributor to newspapers. **Address:** c/o The Guardian, 119 Farringdon Rd., London EC1R 3ER, England.

FIGES, Orlando (G.). British, b. 1959. **Genres:** History. **Career:** Trinity College, Cambridge University, Cambridge, university lecturer in history and fellow. **Publications:** Peasant Russia, Civil War: The Volga Countryside in Revolution, 1917-1921, 1989; A People's Tragedy: The Russian Revolution, 1891-1924, 1996; Natasha's Dance, 2002. **Address:** Trinity College, Trinity St., Cambridge CB2 1TQ, England. **Online address:** ogf1000@cam.ac.uk

FIGIEL, Sia. American Samoan, b. 1967. **Genres:** Essays. **Career:** Writer. Has worked as an au pair in Europe, as a performance and graphic artist, and as a journalist in American Samoa. Artist-in-residence at University of the South Pacific, Suva, Fiji; University of Technology, Sydney, Australia; and Arts in Education Program, American Samoa, 1996. **Publications:** Where We Once Belonged, 1996; The Girl in the Moon Circle, 1996; To a Young Artist in Contemplation: Poetry and Prose, 1998; They Who Do Not Grieve, 1999. **Address:** c/o Author Mail, Pasifika Press, 283 Karangahape Rd., Auckland, New Zealand.

FIGLEY, Marty Rhodes. American, b. 1948. **Genres:** Biography, Theology/Religion. **Career:** Writer, 1990-. **Publications:** The Story of Zacchaeus, 1995; Mary and Martha, 1995; Noah's Wife, 1996; Lydia, 1996; the School Children's Blizzard, 2003; Saving the Liberty Bell, 2004; Washington Is Burning, 2005. Has also written fiction for periodicals. **Address:** 3913 Keith Pl, Annandale, VA 22003, U.S.A. **Online address:** marthafigley@hotmail.com

FIGUEIRA, Thomas J. American, b. 1948. **Genres:** Archaeology/Antiquities, Classics, History. **Career:** Stanford University, Stanford, CA, acting assistant professor, 1977-78; Dickinson College, Carlisle, PA, assistant professor, 1978-79; Rutgers University, New Brunswick, NJ, professor (II) of classics and ancient history, 1979-. **Publications:** Aegina, 1981; (ed. with G. Nagy) Theognis of Megara, 1985; Athens and Aigina in the Age of Imperial Colonization, 1991; Excursions in Epichoric History, 1993; The Power of Money, 1998; Wisdom of the Ancients, 2001. **Address:** Department of Classics, Rutgers University, 131 George St, New Brunswick, NJ 08903-0270, U.S.A. **Online address:** figueira@rci.rutgers.edu

FIKES, Jay C(ourtney). American, b. 1951. **Genres:** Anthropology/Ethnology, Social sciences, Theology/Religion. **Career:** Palomar Community College, San Marcos, CA, bilingual tutor in chemistry at Pala Indian Reservation, 1974; Allan Hancock Community College, Vandenberg Air Force Base Center, instructor in anthropology, 1975-76; Navajo Nation, Window Rock, AZ, land use planner, 1983; U.S. International University, Oceanside, CA, adjunct professor of anthropology, 1985; Marmara University, Istanbul, Turkey, professor of social science research methods, 1985-87; freelance researcher and writer, 1988-89; Highlands University, Las Vegas, NM, adjunct professor of anthropology, 1989; Friends Committee on National Legislation, legislative secretary specializing in Native American issues, 1990; Smithsonian Institution, postdoctoral fellow in anthropology, 1991-93; consultant to filmmakers, 1992-93; Institute of Intercultural Issues, president, 1993-96; Yeditepe University, Istanbul, Turkey, professor of anthropology, 1999-. Appeared in the documentary series Coming and Going, 1994; guest on radio talk shows. **Publications:** (with N. Nix) Step inside the Sacred Circle: Aboriginal American Animal Allegories, 1989; Carlos Castaneda: Academic Opportunism and the Psychedelic Sixties, 1993; Reuben Snake: Your Humble Serpent, 1996; Huichol Mythology, 2002; (with J. Gonzalez Mercado) The Man Who Ate Honey, 2003. Contributor to books. Contributor of articles and reviews to periodicals. **Address:** PO Box 517, Carlsbad, CA 92018-0517, U.S.A.

FILDERMAN, Diane E(lizabeth). American, b. 1959. **Genres:** Children's fiction. **Career:** Children's book author. **Publications:** Mickey Steals the Show, 1995. **Address:** 1 Chicago St., Dewey Beach, DE 19971, U.S.A.

FILES, Meg. American, b. 1946. **Genres:** Novellas/Short stories. **Career:** Author. Pima Community College, Tucson, AZ, English Dept, chair, 1988-; Ohio State University, Thurber House, writer-in-residence. **Publications:** Meridian 144, 1991; Home Is the Hunter: And Other Stories, 1996; Life Stories, 2002. Contributor of short stories and articles to periodicals. **Address:** PO Box 85394, Tucson, AZ 85754, U.S.A. **Online address:** megfiles@compuserve.com

FILEY, Mike. Canadian. **Genres:** Travel/Exploration, History. **Career:** Toronto Sunday Sun, Toronto, Ontario, Canada, columnist; freelance writer, c. 1970-. Also public speaker and tour guide. **Publications:** A Toronto Album: Glimpses of the City That Was, 1970; Toronto: Reflections of the Past, 1972; Toronto: The Way We Were: A Collection of Photos and Stories About North America's Greatest City, c. 1974; Trillium and Toronto Island, 1976; Toronto City Life: Old and New, 1979; I Remember Sunnyside: The Rise and Fall of a Magical Era, 1981, 1996; Not a One-Horse Town: 125 Years of Toronto and Its Streetcars, 1986; Mount Pleasant Cemetery: An Illustrated Guide, c. 1990; Toronto Sketches 3: The Way We Were, c. 1994; Toronto Sketches 4: The Way We Were, 1995; The TTC Story: The First Seventy-Five Years; Like No Other in the World: The Story of Toronto's SkyDome; From Horse Power to Horsepower; Toronto Sketches; More Toronto Sketches. Contributor to periodicals. **Address:** c/o The Toronto Sunday Sun, 333 King St. East, Toronto, ON, Canada M5A 3X5.

FILIPACCHI, Amanda. American/French, b. 1967. **Genres:** Novels. **Career:** Novelist, 1993-. **Publications:** NOVELS: Nude Men, 1993; Vapor, 1999. **Address:** c/o Melanie Jackson, 41 W 72nd St #3F, New York, NY 10023, U.S.A.

FILKINS, Peter. American, b. 1958. **Genres:** Poetry, Translations. **Career:** Writer and teacher. Parnassus: Poetry in Review, assistant editor, 1981-83; Schottengymnasium, Vienna, Austria, teaching assistant, 1984-85; North Adams State College, Department of English, adjunct instructor, 1986, 1988-89; Hiram College, Department of English, visiting instructor, 1986-87; Williams College, instructor, 1990-93, 1996; Simon's Rock College of Bard, Division of Languages & Literature, associate professor, 1988-, coordinator of Poetry Fiction Series, 1990-. Artist-in-residence, Yaddo Artists Colony, 1989, Millay Colony for the Arts, 1993, and MacDowell Colony, 1997. **Publications:** What She Knew (poems), 1998; After Homer (poems), 2002. TRANSLATOR: Songs in Flight: The Collected Poems of Ingeborg Bachmann, 1994; A. Hotschnig, Leonardo's Hands, 1999; The Book of Franza and Requiem for Fanny Goldmann, 1999. Contributor of poetry, translations, and criticism to periodicals. **Address:** Simon's Rock College of Bard, Great Barrington, MA 01230, U.S.A. **Online address:** pfilkins@simons-rock.edu

FINCH, Annie (Ridley Crane). American, b. 1956. **Genres:** Plays/Screenplays, Poetry, Songs/Lyrics and libretti, Literary criticism and history. **Career:** Natural History, editorial assistant, 1981-82; Sequoia, general editor and poetry editor, 1987-91; New College of San Francisco, CA, lecturer in poetry writing, 1991-92; University of Northern Iowa, Cedar Falls, poet-in-residence and assistant professor of English, 1992-95; Miami University, Oxford, OH, assistant professor of English, 1995-99, associate professor of English and creative writing, 1999-2004; University of Southern Maine, director of Stonecoast lowresidency MFA in creative writing, 2004-. Gives poetry workshops and readings from her works. Magic Theatre, San Francisco, CA, assistant to literary manager, 1989-90; theatrical director, producer, and actress. **Publications:** POETRY: The Encyclopedia of Scotland, 1982; The Furious Sun in Her Mane (song cycle), 1994; Catching the Mermother, 1995; Eve, 1997; Season Poems, 2001; Calendars, 2003; Home Birth, 2004; The Encyclopedia of Scotland, 2004; (trans.) The Complete Poems of Louise Lebe, 2005. PLAYS: The Mermaid Tragedy, 1986; The Moon and the Snake, 1989; Life by the Ocean, 1990. CRITICISM: The Ghost of Meter: Culture and Prosody in American Free Verse, 1993; The Body of Poetry, 2005. LIBRETTI: A Captive Spirit, 1999; Merina, 2003. EDITOR/CO-EDITOR: (and contrib.) A Formal Feeling Comes: Poems in Form by Contemporary Women, 1994; After New Formalism (essays), 1999; An Exaltation of Forms: Contemporary Poets Celebrate the Diversity of Their Art, 2001; Carolyn Kizer: Perspectives on Her Life & Work, 2001. Work represented in anthologies. Contributor to books. Contributor of poems, articles, and reviews to periodicals. **Address:** Stonecoast MFA, University of Southern Maine, 120 Bedford St, Portland, ME 04104, U.S.A. **Online address:** afinch@usm.maine.edu

FINCH, Caleb E(llicott). American (born England), b. 1939. **Genres:** Gerontology/Senior issues, Zoology. **Career:** Rockefeller University, NYC, guest investigator, 1969-70; Cornell University, School of Medicine, NYC, assistant professor of anatomy, 1970-72; University of Southern California, Los Angeles, assistant professor, 1972-75, associate professor, 1975-78, professor of gerontology and biological sciences, 1978-, ARCO and William F. Kieschnick Professor of Neurobiology of Aging, 1985-, university professor, 1989, and adjunct professor of neurology, physiology, and biophysics, also associate director for neurogerontology at Research Institute of Ethel Percy Andrus Gerontology Center, 1984-; writer. Visiting lecturer at U.S. colleges and institutions. **Publications:** Cellular Activities during Ageing in Mammals, 1969; Longevity, Senescence, and the Genome, 1990; (with R.E. Ricklefs) Aging, 1995; (with T.B.L. Kirkwood) Chance, Development, and Aging, 2000. EDITOR: (with L. Hayflick, and contrib.) Handbook of the Biology of Aging, 1977, 2nd ed. (with E.L. Schneider), 1985; (with A.C. Adelman and D. Gibson, and contrib.) Development of the Rodent as a Model for Aging, Vol. II, 1978; (with J.A. Behnke and G.B. Moment) The Biology of Aging, 1978; (with D.E. Potter and A.D. Kenny, and contrib.) Parkinson's Disease, Vol. II: Aging and Neuroendocrine Relationships, 1978; (with A. Cherkin, N. Kharasch, T. Makinodan, and others, and contrib.) Aging, Vol. VIII: Physiology and the Cell Biology of Aging, 1979; (with P. Davies, and contrib.) Molecular Neuropathology of Aging, 1987; (with P. Davies, and contrib.) The Molecular Biology of Alzheimer's Disease, 1988; (with T.E. Johnson) The Molecular Biology of Aging, 1990; (with M.R. Rose) Genetics and Evolution of Aging, 1994; (with K.W. Wachter) Between Zeus and the Salmon, 1997; Clusterin in Normal Brain Functions and during Neurodegeneration, 1999; (with J.W. Vaupel and K. Kinsella) Cells and Surveys, 2001. Work represented in anthologies. Contributor to periodicals.

Address: Ethel Percy Andrus Gerontology Center, University of Southern California, 3715 McClintock, Los Angeles, CA 90089-0191, U.S.A. **Online address:** cefinch@usc.edu

FINCH, Christopher. British, b. 1939. **Genres:** Art/Art history, Film, Biography. **Career:** Curator, Walker Art Center, Minneapolis, 1968-69. **Publications:** Pop Art: Object and Image, 1968; Image as Language, 1968; Patrick Caulfield (art), 1971; The Art of Walt Disney, 1973, rev. ed. 1995; Rainbow: The Stormy Life of Judy Garland, 1975; Norman Rockwell's America, 1976; Walt Disney's America, 1978; (with Linda Rosenkrantz) Gone Hollywood, 1979; Norman Rockwell's 332 Magazine Covers, 1979; Of Muppets and Men, 1981; The Making of The Dark Crystal, 1983; Special Effects, 1984; American Watercolors, 1986; Twentieth-Century Watercolours, 1988; Beer: A Connoisseur's Guide to the World's Best, 1989; Nineteenth-Century Watercolors, 1991; Highways to Heaven, 1992; Jim Henson: The Works, 1993; The Art of the Lion King, 1994; America's Best Beers, 1994. **Address:** c/o Jane Dystel Literary Management, PO Box 2080, New York, NY 10025-1552, U.S.A.

FINCH, Matthew. See FINK, Merton.

FINCH, Merton. See FINK, Merton.

FINCH, Peter. Welsh, b. 1947. **Genres:** Poetry, Language/Linguistics, Literary criticism and history. **Career:** Second Aeon Publs., editor, 1966-; Association of Little Presses, treasurer, 1970-; Arts Council of Wales, Oriel Bookshop, manager, 1973-98; Yr Academi Gymreig, Welsh National Literature Promotion Agency, treasurer, 1978-81, head of academi, 1998-. **Publications:** (with S. Morris) Wanted, 1968; Pieces of the Universe, 1969; Cycle of the Suns, 1970; Beyond the Silence, 1970; An Alteration in the Way I Breathe, 1970; (with J.W. Rushton) The Edge of Tomorrow, 1971; The End of the Vision, 1971; Whitesung, 1972; Blats, 1973; Anatarktika, 1973; Trowch Eich Radio Ymlaen, 1977; How to Learn Welsh, 1978; Connecting Tubes, 1980; Blues and Heartbreakers, 1981; Big Band Dance Music, 1981; Collected Visual Poetry 1930-50, 1981; Between 35 and 42, 1982; Dances Interdites, 1983; Some Music and a Little War, 1984; On Criticism, 1985; How to Publish Your Poetry, 1985; Reds in the Bed, 1986; Selected Poems, 1987; How to Publish Yourself, 1988; Peter's Leeks, 1988; The Cheng Man Ching Variation, 1990; Publish Yourself: Not too Difficult after All, 1990; Make, 1990; Poems for Ghosts, 1991; Five Hundred Cobbings, 1993; The Poetry Business, 1994; The Spell, 1995; Useful, 1997; Antibodies, 1997; Dauber, 1997; Food, 2001; Real Cardiff, 2002; Vizet-Water, 2003; Real Cardiff Two, 2005. EDITOR: Typewriter Poems, 1973; (with M. Stephens) The Green Horse, 1978. **Address:** 19 Southminister Rd, Roath, Cardiff CF23 5AT, Wales. **Online address:** peter.finch@dial.pipex.com; www.peterfinch.co.uk

FINCH, Robert (Charles). American, b. 1943. **Career:** Oregon State University, Corvallis, instructor in English, 1969-71; carpenter in Brewster, MA, 1971-75; free-lance writer, 1975-; Cape Cod Museum of Natural History, Cape Cod, MA, director of publications, 1982-86. Orion Nature Quarterly, advisory board member; Brewster Conservation Commission, co-chair, 1980-87; Brewster Land Acquisition Commission, co-chair, 1984-87; Cape Cod Community College, West Barnstable, MA, part-time instructor, 1972-74, 1995; Emerson College, part-time instructor, 1995; Friends of the Cape Cod National Seashore, director, 1995-96. **Publications:** Common Ground: A Naturalist's Cape Cod (essays), 1981; The Primal Place, 1983; Outlands: Journeys to the Outer Edges of Cape Cod (essays), 1986; (advisory ed and contrib) On Nature: Essays on Nature, Landscape, and Natural History, edited by Daniel Halpern, 1987; (ed. with J. Elder) The Norton Book of Nature Writing, 1990; The Cape Itself, 1991; (ed.) A Place Apart, an anthology of Cape Cod literature, 1993; Cape Cod National Seashore Handbook, 1994; Smithsonian Guide to Natural America: Southern New England, 1996. Contributor to anthologies. Author of introductions to books. Author of weekly columns for several Cape Cod Newspapers, 1975-82, 1995-; editor of The Cape Naturalist, 1973-82. Contributor to periodicals. **Address:** Old Country Rd., Wellfleet, MA 02667, U.S.A.

FINCHLER, Judy. American, b. 1943. **Genres:** Children's fiction. **Career:** Educator, librarian, writer. Schoolteacher in Paterson, NJ, 1964-67; supplemental instructor in Parsippany, NJ, 1977-81; Paterson Board of Education, teacher, 1981-86, teacher-librarian, 1986-2004, now retired. **Publications:** Miss Malarkey Doesn't Live in Room 10, 1995; Miss Malarkey Won't Be in Today, 1998; Testing Miss Malarkey, 2000; You're a Good Sport, Miss Malarkey, 2002; Miss Malarkey's Field Trip, 2004. **Address:** 23 Trouville Dr, Parsippany, NJ 07054, U.S.A. **Online address:** Jfinchler@optonline.net

FINE, Anne. British, b. 1947. **Genres:** Novels, Children's fiction, Young adult fiction. **Career:** Teacher, Cardinal Wiseman Secondary School, Coventry, 1968-69, and Saughton Prison, Edinburgh, 1971-72; Oxfam, Oxford, information officer, 1969-71. Royal Society of Literature, fellow, 2003; OBE, 2003. **Publications:** CHILDREN/YA FICTION: The Summer-House Loon, 1978; The Other, Darker Ned, 1979; The Stone Menagerie, 1980; Round behind the Ice-House, 1981; The Granny Project, 1983; Scaredy-Cat, 1985; Anneli the Art Hater, 1986; Madame Doubtfire, 1987; Crummy Mummy & Me, 1987; A Pack of Liars, 1988; Goggle-Eyes, 1989; Bill's New Frock, 1989; Stranger Danger, 1989; The Country Pancake, 1989; A Sudden Puff of Glittering Smoke, 1989; A Sudden Swirl of Icy Wind, 1990; Only a Show, 1990; Design-a-Pram, 1991; A Sudden Glow of Gold, 1991; Poor Monty, 1991; The Worst Child I Ever Had, 1991; The Angel of Nitshill Road, 1991; The Book of the Banshee, 1991; Flour Babies, 1992; Same Old Story Every Year, 1992; The Chicken Gave It to Me, 1992; The Haunting of Pip Parker, 1992; Press "Play," 1994; The Diary of a Killer Cat, 1994; Step by Wicked Step, 1995; How to Write Really Badly, 1996; The Tulip Touch, 1996; Keep It in the Family, 1996; Jennifer's Diary, 1996; Countdown, 1996; Care of Henry, 1996; Telling Liddy, 1998; Bad Dreams, 2000; Very Different, 2001; Up on Cloud Nine, 2002; The More the Merrier, 2003. ADULT FICTION: The Killjoy, 1986; Taking the Devil's Advice, 1990; In Cold Domain, 1994; All Bones and Lies, 2001. **Address:** c/o David Higham Associates, 5-8 Lower John St, Golden Sq, London W1R 4HA, England.

FINE, Doris Landau. German, b. 1949. **Genres:** Education. **Career:** Columbia Point Health Center, Dorchester, MA, physical therapist, 1971-73; Kinderschool of United Cerebral Palsy, South Natick, MA, staff member, 1973-75; Eunice Kennedy Shriver Center, Waltham, MA, assistant director of physical therapy, 1975-77; University of Massachusetts, adjunct faculty member, 1979-80; Waltham Public Schools, Waltham, physical therapist, 1980-82; Northeastern University, Boston, MA, lecturer in physical therapy, 1985-88; Youville Hospital, Cambridge, MA, member of pediatric evaluation team, 1988-90; Education Development Center, Inc., Newton, MA, training specialist, 1992-93; Boston University, Boston, lecturer at Sargent College of Allied Health Professionals, 1993-96; Education Development Center, Inc., consultant, 1995-. Kids Are People Elementary School, physical therapist and staff trainer; Wheelock College, instructor, 1984. **Publications:** (with K. Blenk) Making School Inclusion Work: A Guide to Everyday Practices, 1995. Contributor of articles and reviews to journals. **Address:** Education Development Center Inc., 55 Chapel St., Newton, MA 02458, U.S.A.

FINE, Jonathan. Canadian, b. 1949. **Genres:** Language/Linguistics. **Career:** Hebrew University of Jerusalem, Jerusalem, Israel, visiting scholar at Center for Applied Linguistics, 1977-78; Ontario Institute for Studies in Education, Toronto, research officer in applied psychology, 1979-80; Educational Testing Service, Princeton, NJ, collaborator and consultant, 1980-81; University of Medicine and Dentistry of New Jersey, Rutgers Medical School, Piscataway, instructor in psychiatry, 1981-82; Tel Aviv University, Tel Aviv, Israel, visiting senior lecturer in linguistics, 1983; Hebrew University of Jerusalem, visiting senior lecturer in English, 1983-85; Bar-Ilan University, Ramat-Gan, Israel, senior lecturer, 1983-94, associate professor of English, 1994-, coordinator of linguistics, 1986-91, head of Department of English, 1991-93, coordinator of undergraduate program in linguistics, 1993-. St. Joseph's Hospital, Hamilton, Ontario, research associate at McMaster Psychiatric Unit, 1978-80; Hospital for Sick Children, Toronto, visiting scientist, 1989-90, 1996-97; consultant. **Publications:** How Language Works: Cohesion in Normal and Nonstandard Communication, 1994. EDITOR & CONTRIBUTOR: (with R. Freedle) Developmental Issues in Discourse, 1983; Second Language Discourse, 1988. Contributor to books. Contributor of articles and reviews to language and linguistics journals. **Address:** Department of English, Bar-Ilan University, 52900 Ramat-Gan, Israel. **Online address:** finejo@mail.biu.ac.il

FINE, Marshall. American, b. 1950. **Genres:** Film. **Career:** Clarion Ledger, Jackson, MS, entertainment editor/film, theater and music critic, 1977; Argus Leader, Sioux Falls, SD, entertainment editor/film, theater, and music critic, 1978-1983; Times-Union, Rochester, NY, entertainment writer/film, theater, and music critic, 1983-86; Marin Independent Journal, San Rafael, CA, entertainment writer/film and theater critic, 1986-87; Gannett Westchester Newspapers, White Plains, NY, entertainment writer and film critic, 1987-. Member of prototype team, USA Today, 1981; faculty member, National Critics Institute's Eugene O'Neill Theater Center, 1988-89, 2001-02. Chairman, New York film Critics Circle, 1992, 2002; Jacob Burns Film Center, Journal NewsFilm Club, creator, 2001, host/producer, 2001-; FloFox's Dicthology, documentary short film, director, 2002. **Publications:** Bloody Sam: The Life and Films of Sam Peckinpah, 1991; Harvey Keitel: The Art of

Darkness, 1997. Contributor to newspapers and periodicals. **Address:** Gannett Newspapers, 1 Gannett Dr, White Plains, NY 10604, U.S.A.

FINE, Richard. American, b. 1951. **Genres:** Writing/Journalism. **Career:** Virginia Commonwealth University, Richmond, VA, assistant professor, 1979-86, associate professor, 1986-97, professor of English, 1997-, chair of English department, 1994-. Universite de Caen, Caen, France, Fulbright junior lecturer in American studies and American literature, 1981-82, visiting full professor at Institut d'Anglais, 1987-88. Publications director, Sabot School, Richmond. Manuscript reader for American Quarterly, 1986-88, and for University of Texas Press, 1992-. **Publications:** Hollywood and the Profession of Authorship, 1928-1940, 1985; reprinted with new preface as West of Eden: Hollywood and the Profession of Authorship, 1993; James M. Cain and the American Authors' Authority, 1992. Contributor to reference works. Contributor to professional journals. **Address:** Department of English, Box 842005, Virginia Commonwealth University, Richmond, VA 23284-2005, U.S.A.

FINE, Sidney. American, b. 1920. **Genres:** History, Industrial relations, Organized labor. **Career:** University of Michigan, Ann Arbor, instructor, 1948-51, assistant professor, 1951-55, associate professor, 1955-59, professor, 1959-74, Andrew Dickson White Distinguished Professor of History, 1974-2001, Andrew Dickson White Professor Emeritus of History, 2001-. **Publications:** Laissez Faire and the General Welfare State: A Study of Conflict in American Thought, 1865-1901, 1956; The Automobile under the Blue Eagle: Labor, Management and the Automobile Manufacturing Code, 1963; Sit-Down: The General Motors Strike of 1936-1937, 1969; Frank Murphy: The Detroit Years, 1975; Frank Murphy: The New Deal Years, 1979; Frank Murphy: The Washington Years, 1984; Violence in the Model City: The Cavanagh Administration, Race Relations, and the Detroit Riot of 1967, 1989; Without Blare of Trumpets: Walter Drew, the National Erectors Association and the Open Shop Movement, 1903-1957, 1995; Expanding the Frontiers of Civil Rights: Michigan, 1948-1968, 2000. EDITOR: The American Past: Conflicting Interpretations of the Great Issue, 1961, 4th ed., 1976; Recent America, 1962. **Address:** Dept. of History, University of Michigan, Ann Arbor, MI 48109, U.S.A. **Online address:** Sidneyf@umich.edu

FINELLO, Dominick. American, b. 1944. **Genres:** Literary criticism and history, Bibliography. **Career:** Rider University, Lawrenceville, NJ, faculty member. **Publications:** Analytical and Bibliographical Guide to Criticism on "Don Quixote", 1790-1893, 1987; Pastoral Themes and Forms in Cervantes' Fiction, 1994; Cervantes: Social and Literary Polemics, 1998. **Address:** Rider University, Lawrenceville, NJ 08648, U.S.A. **Online address:** finello@rider.edu

FINEMAN, Martha Albertson. American, b. 1943. **Genres:** Law, Women's studies and issues. **Career:** Law clerk, U.S. Court of Appeals (7th Circuit), 1975-76; University of Wisconsin Law School, Madison, WI, assistant professor then associate professor, 1976-86, professor, 1987-91; Columbia University School of Law, New York, NY, Maurice T. Moore professor, 1991-; Cornell University School of Law, Ithaca, NY, Dorothea S. Clarke Professor of Feminist Jurisprudence, 1991-. Columbia University, director of Feminism and Legal Theory Project, 1984-; University of Wisconsin Law School Institute of Legal Studies, director of family law and policy program, 1988-90; Columbia University, visiting professor, 1990-91. **Publications:** (with others) The Politics of Child Custody Decisionmaking, 1989; (with others) Child Advocacy, 1990; (ed., with N.S. Thomadsen) At the Boundaries of Law: Feminism and Legal Theory, 1991; The Illusion of Equality: The Rhetoric and Reality of Divorce Reform, 1991; (with others) Lawyering and Its Limits, 1991; (with others) Symbolism, Language and Politics, 1992; (ed., with R. Mykitiuk) The Public Nature of Private Violence: The Discovery of Domestic Abuse, 1994; The Neutered Mother, the Sexual Family, and Other Twentieth Century Tragedies, 1995; (ed., with I. Karpin) Mothers in Law: Feminist Theory and the Legal Regulation of Motherhood, 1995; (ed. with M. McCluskey) Feminism, Media and the Law, 1997; (with others) Justice and Power in Sociological Studies, 1997; (with others) Analyzing Law, 1998. Contributor of articles and book reviews to professional journals. **Address:** Columbia University School of Law, 435 West 116th St., New York, NY 10027, U.S.A. **Online address:** fineman@law.cornell.edu

FINGER, Seymour (Maxwell). American, b. 1915. **Genres:** International relations/Current affairs, Politics/Government, Essays. **Career:** Adjunct Professor, and Professor Emeritus of Political Science, Graduate School and the College of Staten Island, City University of New York, 1985- (Professor, College of Staten Island, 1971-85; Professor, Graduate School, 1973-85). Director Emeritus, Ralph Bunche Institute on the UN, 1985- (Director, 1973-

85). Adjunct Professor, New York University, NYC, 1986; Visiting Professor, Georgetown Univ, 1992-. Formerly, career officer in the US Foreign Service: Vice-Consul, Stuttgart, 1946-49; Second Secretary, American Embassy, Paris, 1949-51, American Legation, Budapest, 1951-53, and American Embassy, Rome, 1954-55; First Secretary, American Embassy, Laos, 1955-56; Sr. Adviser on Economics and Social Affairs, US Mission to the UN, 1956-65; Counselor of Mission, 1965-67; Ambassador and Sr. Adviser to the US Permanent Representative to the UN, 1967-71. **Publications:** Your Man at the U.N.: People, Politics and Bureaucracy in the Making of American Foreign Policy, 1980, rev. ed. as American Ambassadors at the U.N., 1986; American Jewry during the Holocaust, 1984; Bending with the Winds: Kurt Waldheim and the United Nations, 1991; Their Brother's Keepers: American Jewry and the Holocaust, 1991; Inside the World of Diplomacy, 2001. EDITOR: (and contrib.) The New World Balance and Peace in the Middle East, 1975; (with Y. Alexander) Terrorism: Interdisciplinary Perspectives, 1977; (with J.R. Harbert and contrib.) U.S. Policies in International Institutions, 1978.

FINGLETON, Eamonn. Irish, b. 1948. **Genres:** Business/Trade/Industry, Economics, Money/Finance, Politics/Government. **Career:** Financial Times, London, England, personal finance editor, 1979-81; Forbes, NYC, associate editor, 1981-83; Merrill Lynch Market Letter, NYC, senior financial editor, 1983-84; Euromoney, London, East Asia editor, 1985-87, deputy editor, 1987-89; author and freelance writer, 1989-; Unsustainable.org, editor, 2001-. **Publications:** Making the Most of Your Money, 1977; (with T. Tickell) The Penguin Money Book, 1981; Blindside: Why Japan Is Still on Track to Overtake the U.S. by the Year 2000, 1995; In Praise of Hard Industries: Why Manufacturing, Not the Information Economy, Is the Key to Future Prosperity, 1999; Unsustainable: How Economic Dogma Is Destroying American Prosperity, 2003. Contributor to periodicals. **Address:** Tsunamachi Condominium 201, Mita 2-18-3, Tokyo 108, Japan. **Online address:** efingleton@hotmail.com

FINK, Carole (Kapiloff). American, b. 1940. **Genres:** History, Biography. **Career:** Connecticut College, New London, instructor in history, 1964-65; Albertus Magnus College, New Haven, CT, lecturer in history, 1966-67; Canisius College, Buffalo, NY, assistant professor of history, 1968-71; State University of New York at Binghamton, assistant professor of history, 1971-78; University of North Carolina, Wilmington, professor of history, 1978-91; Ohio State University, Columbus, professor of history, 1991-. Cardin chair in the humanities, Loyola College, 1987-88. **Publications:** The Genoa Conference: European Diplomacy, 1921-1922, 1984; (ed. with Isabel V. Hull and MacGregor Knox) German Nationalism and the European Response, 1890-1945, 1985; (translator and author of introduction) Marc Bloch, Memoirs of War, 1914-15, 1988; Marc Bloch: A Life in History, 1989; (ed. with A. Frohn and J. Heideking) Genoa, Rapallo, and the Reconstruction of Europe in 1922, 1991. WORK IN PROGRESS: Research on the Polish minorities treaty of June, 1919. **Address:** Department of History, Ohio State University, Columbus, OH 43210, U.S.A. **Online address:** fink.24@osu.com

FINK, Deborah. American, b. 1944. **Genres:** Anthropology/Ethnology, Local history/Rural topics, Women's studies and issues. **Career:** Anthropologist and writer. Visiting professor at Grinnell College, 1980; Iowa State University, 1980, 1981, and 1983; and University of Iowa, 1984-85. **Publications:** Open Country, Iowa: Rural Women, Tradition and Change, 1986; Agrarian Women: Wives and Mothers in Rural Nebraska, 1880-1940, 1992; Meatpacking Lines: Workers in the Rural Midwest, 1998; Cutting into the Meatpacking Line: Workers and Change in the Rural Midwest, 1998. Contributor to other works and periodicals. **Address:** 222 S Russell, Ames, IA 50010, U.S.A. **Online address:** afink@iastate.edu

FINK, Karl J. American, b. 1942. **Genres:** Language/Linguistics, Intellectual history, Literary criticism and history. **Career:** Texas Lutheran College, Seguin, instructor in German, 1966-67; Luther College, Decorah, IA, instructor in German, 1967-69; University of Illinois at Urbana-Champaign, visiting assistant professor of German, 1974-77; Southern Illinois University, Carbondale, visiting assistant professor of German, 1977-78; University of Kentucky, Lexington, assistant professor of German, 1978-82; St. Olaf College, Northfield, MN, professor of German, 1982-. **Publications:** (ed. with James W. Marchand) The Quest for the New Science, Southern Illinois University Press, 1979; (ed. with Max L. Baeumer) Goethe as a Critic of Literature, University Press of America, 1984; Goethe's History of Science, Cambridge University Press, 1991; (ed. with Herbert Rowland) The German Book Review, Winter Verlag, 1994. **Address:** Department of German, St. Olaf College, Northfield, MN 55057, U.S.A.

FINK, Leon. American, b. 1948. **Genres:** Politics/Government, Social sciences, History. **Career:** City College of the City University of New York, part-time lecturer, 1972-74; University of North Carolina at Chapel Hill, assistant professor to professor of history, 1977-. Fulbright professor, University of Munich, 1983-84. **Publications:** Workingmen's Democracy: The Knights of Labor and American Politics, 1983; (with B. Greenberg) Upheaval in the Quiet Zone: The History of Hospital Workers Local 1199, 1989; Major Problems in the Gilded Age and the Progressive Era, 1993; In Search of the Working Class, 1994; (co-ed. with S.T. Leonard and D.M. Reid) Intellectuals and Public Life: Between Radicalism and Reform, 1996. **Address:** Department of History, University of North Carolina at Chapel Hill, Chapel Hill, NC 27599-3195, U.S.A.

FINK, Merton. Also writes as Matthew Finch, Merton Finch. British, b. 1921. **Genres:** Novels, Romance/Historical, Education, Humor/Satire. **Career:** Dental Surgeon, National Health Service, since 1952; Deputy Chairman, Bath Literary Society; Chairman, Service Committee, Bath Branch, Royal British Legion; Humorist, monthly column "Dental Practice," since 1968. **Publications:** AS MATTHEW FINCH: Dentist in the Chair, 1955; Teething Troubles, 1956; The Third Set, 1957; Hang Your Hat on a Pension, 1958; Empire Builder, 1959; Snakes and Ladders, 1960; Solo Fiddle, 1961; Beauty Bazaar, 1962; The Match Breakers, 1963; Five as the Symbols, 1964; Chew This Over, 1965; The Succubus, 1966; Eye with Mascara, 1967; A Fox Called Flavius, 1974; (with Bill Tidy) Open Wide. AS MERTON FINCH: Simon Bar Cochba, 1971. **Address:** Quill Cottage, 27 Harbutts, Bathampton, Bath BA2 6TA, England.

FINKEL, Alvin. Canadian, b. 1949. **Genres:** Business/Trade/Industry, History, Social sciences. **Career:** Athabasca University, Athabasca, Alberta, assistant professor, 1978-81, associate professor, 1981-86, professor of history, 1986-. **Publications:** Business and Social Reform in the Thirties, 1979; The Social Credit Phenomenon in Alberta, 1989; (with M. Conrad) History of the Canadian Peoples, Vol. 1: Origins to 1867, (with M. Conrad) Vol. 2: 1867 to the Present, 2nd ed., 1997, 3rd ed., 2001; (with C. Leibovitz) In Our Time: The Chamberlain-Hitler Collusion, 1997; Our Lives: Canada since 1945, 1997; (with M. Conrad) Canada: A National History, 2002. **Address:** Center for State and Legal Studies, Athabasca University, 1 University Dr, Athabasca, AB, Canada T9S 3A3. **Online address:** alvinf@athabascau.ca

FINKEL, Donald. American, b. 1929. **Genres:** Poetry. **Career:** Poet-in-Residence, Washington University, St. Louis, Missouri, 1960-92. Instructor, University of Iowa, Iowa City, 1957-58, and Bard College, Annandale-on-Hudson, New York, 1958-60; Visiting Lecturer, Bennington College, VT, 1966-67, and Princeton University, NJ, 1985; University of Missouri-St. Louis, 1998-99. **Publications:** The Clothing's New Emperor and Other Poems, 1959; The Jar (play), 1961; Simeon: Poems, 1964; A Joyful Noise: Poems, 1966; Answer Back, 1968; The Garbage Wars: Poems, 1970; Adequate Earth, 1972; A Mote in Heaven's Eye, 1975; Going Under and Endurance, 1978; What Manner of Beast, 1981; The Detachable Man, 1984; The Wake of the Electron, 1987; Selected Shorter Poems, 1987; (trans.) A Splintered Mirror, 1991; Beyond Despair, 1994; A Question of Seeing, 1998. **Address:** 2051 Park Ave, St. Louis, MO 63104, U.S.A. **Online address:** dfinkel@artsci.wustl.edu

FINKENSTAEDT, Rose L. H. American, b. 1927. **Genres:** Race relations. **Publications:** Face to Face: Blacks in America; White Perceptions and Black Realities, 1994. Contributor to periodicals. **Address:** 22 Quai de Bethune, 75004 Paris, France.

FINKLE, Derek. American. **Genres:** Documentaries/Reportage. **Career:** Writer. **Publications:** No Claim to Mercy: A Suburban Mystery (nonfiction), 1998. Contributor of fiction and nonfiction to periodicals. **Address:** c/o Penguin Books Canada Limited, 10 Alcorn Ave. Suite 300, Toronto, ON, Canada M4V 3B2.

FINLAY, Peter (Warren). Also writes as D. B. C. Pierre. Irish (born Australia), b. 1961. **Genres:** Novels. **Career:** Cartoonist, graphic designer, photographer, filmmaker, and writer. **Publications:** NOVEL AS D. B. C. PIERRE: Vernon God Little: A Twenty-first-Century Comedy in the Presence of Death, 2003 (Booker Prize). **Address:** c/o Author Mail, Faber & Faber Ltd., 3 Queen Square, London WC1N 3AU, England.

FINLAY, Richard J(ason). Scottish, b. 1962. **Genres:** Politics/Government, Area studies. **Career:** University of Strathclyde, Glasgow, Scotland, lecturer in history. **Publications:** Independent and Free: Scottish Politics and the Origins of the Scottish National Party, 1918-1945, 1993; A Partnership for Good: Scottish Politics and the Union, 1880-1992, 1995. EDITOR: (with D. Broon and M. Lynch) Scottish National Identity through the Ages, 1995;

(with T. Devine) Scotland in the Twentieth Century, in press. Contributor to books and history journals. **Address:** Department of History, University of Strathclyde, Glasgow, Scotland.

FINLAY, William. *See* MACKAY, James Alexander.

FINLAYSON, Iain (Thorburn). Scottish, b. 1945. **Genres:** Fashion/Costume, Biography, Cultural/Ethnic topics, Literary criticism and history, Local history/Rural topics, Novellas/Short stories. **Career:** Writer, 1974-. Home Office, London, England, civil servant, 1970-74. **Publications:** Winston Churchill, Hamish Hamilton, 1983; The Moth and the Candle, St. Martin's, 1984; The Sixth Continent, Atheneum, 1986, published in England as Writers in Romney Marsh, Severn House, 1987; The Scots, Atheneum, 1987; Denim: An American Legend, Fireside, 1990; Tangier: City of the Dream, HarperCollins, 1992. Author of short stories published in the Literary Review; contributor of book reviews and feature articles to national newspapers and magazines since 1974. Translator of poetry. **Address:** c/o Deborah Rogers, Rogers, Coleridge & White Ltd., 20 Powis Mews, London W11 1JN, England.

FINLEY, Glenna. American, b. 1925. **Genres:** Romance/Historical. **Career:** Announcer, KEVR-Radio, Seattle, 1941-42; Producer, NBC International Division, NYC, 1945-47; Film Librarian, March of Time newsreel series, NYC, 1947-48; News Bureau Staff Member, Time Inc., NYC, 1948-49; freelance writer, 1957-. **Publications:** Death Strikes Out, 1957; Career Wife, 1964, in paperback title as A Tycoon for Ann; Nurse Pro Tem, 1967; Journey to Love, 1970; Love's Hidden Fire, 1971; Treasure of the Heart, 1971; Love Lies North, 1972; Bridal Affair, 1972; Kiss a Stranger, 1972; Love in Danger, 1973; When Love Speaks, 1973; The Romantic Spirit, 1973; Surrender My Love, 1974; A Promising Affair, 1974; Love's Magic Spell, 1974; The Reluctant Maiden, 1975; The Captured Heart, 1975; Holiday for Love, 1976; Love for a Rogue, 1976; Storm of Desire, 1977; Dare to Love, 1977; To Catch a Bride, 1977; Master of Love, 1978; Beware My Heart, 1978; The Marriage Merger, 1978; Wildfire of Love, 1979; Timed for Love, 1979; Love's Temptation, 1979; Stateroom for Two, 1980; Affairs of Love, 1980; Midnight Encounter, 1981; Return Engagement, 1981; One Way to Love, 1982; Taken by Storm, 1982; A Business Affair, 1983; Wanted for Love, 1983; A Weekend for Love, 1984; Love's Waiting Game, 1985; A Touch of Love, 1985; Diamonds for My Love, 1986; Secret of Love, 1987; The Marrying Kind, 1989; Island Rendezvous, 1990; Stowaway for Love, 1992; The Temporary Bride, 1993. **Address:** 7868-F Rea Rd #312, Charlotte, NC 28277, U.S.A.

FINLEY, Karen. American, b. 1956. **Genres:** Plays/Screenplays. **Career:** Performance artist in NYC and elsewhere since the 1980s. Visual artist; has exhibited paintings, sculptures, and other installations. **Publications:** (and illustrator) Shock Treatment, 1990; (and illustrator) Enough Is Enough: Weekly Meditations for Living Dysfunctionally (aphorisms), 1993; A Certain Level of Denial, in press; Living It Up, in press; A Different Kind of Intimacy, 2001. PERFORMANCE PIECES: The Constant State of Desire, 1987; We Keep Our Victims Ready, 1990; A Certain Level of Denial, 1992. **Address:** c/o City Lights Books Inc., 261 Columbus Ave., San Francisco, CA 94133, U.S.A.

FINLEY, Michael. American, b. 1950. **Genres:** Business/Trade/Industry, Technology, Autobiography/Memoirs. **Career:** University of Minnesota-Twin Cities, Minneapolis, editor, 1973-78; Worthington Daily Globe, Worthington, MN, editor, 1978-80; Future Shoes (writing and consulting business), owner, 1980-. **Publications:** Techno-Crazed, 1995; (with H. Robbins) Why Teams Don't Work, 1995; (with H. Robbins) Why Change Doesn't Work 1996; (with H. Robbins) Transcompetition, 1998. **Address:** 1841 Dayton Ave., St. Paul, MN 55104, U.S.A. **Online address:** mfinley@mfinley.com

FINLEY, Mitch. American, b. 1945. **Genres:** Human relations/Parenting, Theology/Religion. **Career:** Roman Catholic Diocese of Spokane, WA, director of Family Life Office, 1977-82; free-lance writer, 1982-. **Publications:** Christian Families in the Real World, 1984; Catholic Spiritual Classics, 1987; Time Capsules of the Church, 1990; Your Family in Focus, 1993; Everybody Has a Guardian Angel, 1993; Catholic Is Wonderful!, 1994; Heavenly Helpers, 1994; Season of Promises, 1995; Whispers of Love, 1995; Gospel Truth, 1995; Season of New Beginnings, 1996; Joy of Being Catholic, 1996; (with K. Finley) Building Christian Families, 1996; 101 Ways to Nourish Your Soul, 1997; Seeker's Guide to Being Catholic, 1997; Let's Begin with Prayer, 1997; Surprising Mary, 1997; Joy of Being a Eucharistic Minister, 1998; Seeker's Guide to the Christian Story, 1998; For Men Only, 1998; Saints Speak to You Today, 1999; Catholic Virtues, 1999; Prayer for People Who Think Too Much, 1999; Your Are My Beloved, 1999; Ten Commandments, 2000; Seeker's Guide to Saints, 2000; Your One-Stop Guide to Mary, 2000; Joy of Being a Lector, 2000; Saint Anthony and Saint Jude, 2001; Understanding What Faith Is not, to Understand What Faith Is, 2001; Seven Gifts of the Holy Spirit, 2001; Corporal and Spiritual Works of Mercy, 2003; It's not the Same without You, 2003. **Address:** 1657 E Gordon Ave, Spokane, WA 99207-4651, U.S.A. **Online address:** FiveStrBanjo@aol.com

FINLEY, Randy. American, b. 1954. **Genres:** History. **Career:** Ashdown Public Schools, Ashdown, AR, high school history teacher, 1976-88; DeKalb College, Dunwoody, GA, assistant professor of history, 1992-. **Publications:** From Slavery to Uncertain Freedom (monograph), 1996. **Address:** Department of History, DeKalb College, 2101 Womack Rd., Dunwoody, GA 30338, U.S.A. **Online address:** rfinley@dekalb.dc.peachnet.edu

FINLEY, Robert. Canadian, b. 1957. **Genres:** Literary criticism and history. **Career:** Université canadienne en France, Villefranche-sur-mer, France, lecturer, 1989-94; Université Ste. Anne, Pointe d'Eglise, Nova Scotia, Canada, associate professor of literature and creative writing, 1994-. **Publications:** The Accidental Indies, 2000. Contributor of reviews and fiction to periodicals. **Address:** Université Ste. Anne, Pointe d'Eglise, NS, Canada B0A 1M0. **Online address:** finley@klis.com

FINLEY, Will. See FRY, William Finley, Jr.

FINN, Margot C. American, b. 1960. **Genres:** History. **Career:** Emory University, Atlanta, GA, assistant professor, 1989-94, associate professor of history, 1994-. **Publications:** After Chartism, 1993. **Address:** Department of History, Emory University, Atlanta, GA 30320, U.S.A.

FINN, R(alph) L(eslie). British, b. 1922. **Genres:** Novels, Sports/Fitness, Autobiography/Memoirs, Novellas/Short stories. **Career:** Freelance advertising and publicity consultant; Tutor in English. Feature writer, Reynolds News, 1937-40, People, 1941-47, Birmingham Daily Mail, and Daily Mail, London, 1953-55; Creative Director, advertising agencies, 1955-70; Principal, Ralfinn Sports International. **Publications:** Out of the Depths; Down Oxford Street; He Said, What's Blue?; Time Marches Sideways; Twenty Seven Stairs; The Peephole; After the Sickness; And the Ants Came; Freaks v. Supermen; Captive on a Flying Saucer: The Lunatic Lover and Poet; Waiting Room; And All Is Mist; Return to Earth; I Sent You Red Roses; Death of a Dream; Bleu (in French); My Greatest Game; World Cup 1954; Spurs Supreme; Spurs Go Marching On; Spurs Again; Arsenal: Chapman to Mee; Champions Again: Manchester United 1965; England World Champions 1966; London's Cup Final 1967; World Cup 1970; Official History of Tottenham Hotspur 1972; History of Chelsea; No Tears in Aldgate; Spring in Aldgate; Saturday Afternoon (screenplay); Punch Drunk (screenplay); Time Remembered, Grief Forgotten, 1985. Has written over 1,000 short stories appearing in major magazines and newspapers. **Address:** 7 Red Lodge, Red Road, Elstree, Herts. WD6 4SN, England.

FINNEGAN, William (Patrick). American, b. 1952. **Genres:** Race relations, International relations/Current affairs, Civil liberties/Human rights, Politics/Government, Third World, Writing/Journalism. **Career:** Grassy Park High School, South Africa, teacher, 1980; New Yorker, staff writer, 1987-. **Publications:** Crossing the Line: A Year in the Land of Apartheid, 1986; Dateline Soweto: Travels with Black South African Reporters, 1988; A Complicated War: The Harrowing of Mozambique, 1992; Cold New World: Growing Up in a Harder Country, 1998. **Address:** Amanda Urban, International Creative Management, 40 West 57 St, New York, NY 10019, U.S.A.

FINNEY, Ernest J. American. **Genres:** Novels, Novellas/Short stories. **Career:** Writer. **Publications:** NOVELS: Winterchill, 1989; Lady with the Alligator Purse, 1992; Words of My Roaring, 1993; California Time, 1998. STORIES: Birds Landing, 1986; Flights in the Heavenlies, 1996. **Address:** PO Box 6041, Visalia, CA 93290-6041, U.S.A.

FINNIGAN (MACKENZIE), Joan. Also writes as Michelle Bedard. Canadian, b. 1925. **Genres:** Novellas/Short stories, Children's fiction, Plays/Screenplays, Poetry, Area studies, Children's non-fiction, History, Travel/Exploration, Biography. **Career:** Poet, playwright, and oral historian. Former schoolteacher and journalist. **Publications:** POETRY: Through the Glass Darkly, 1963; A Dream of Lilies, 1965; Entrance to the Greenhouse, 1968; In the Brown Cottage on Loughborough Lake, 1970; It Was Warm and Sunny When We Set Out, 1970; Living Together, 1976; A Reminder of Familiar Faces, 1978; This Series Has Been Discontinued, 1980; The Watershed Collection, 1988; Wintering Over, 1992; Second Wind: Second Sight, 1998. PLAYS: The Best Damn Fiddler from Calabogie to Kaladar, 1969; Songs

from Both Sides of the River, 1987; Wintering Over, 1988. ORAL HISTORY: Some of the Stories I Told You Were True, 1981; Laughing All the Way Home, 1984; Legacies, Legends and Lies, 1985; Tell Me Another Story, 1988; Tallying the Tales of the Old-Timers, 1999. OTHER: (as Michelle Bedard) Canada in Bed, 1967; Kingston: Celebrate This City, 1976; I Come from the Valley, 1976; Canadian Colonial Cooking, 1976; Giants of Canada's Ottawa Valley, 1981; Look! The Land Is Growing Giants (children's), 1983; Finnigan's Guide to the Ottawa Valley, 1988; The Dog That Wouldn't Be Left Behind (children's), 1989; Old Scores; New Goals, a History of the Ottawa Senators, 1891-1992, 1992; Lisgar Collegiate Institute, 1843-1993 (history), 1993; Witches, Ghosts and Loups-Garous (scary tales), 1994; Dancing at the Crossroads (fiction), 1995; Down the Unmarked Roads (fiction), 1996; Life along the Opeongo Line (history), 2004. **Address:** Moore Farm, Hambly Lake, Hartington, ON, Canada K0H 1W0.

FINNIS, John M(itchell). Australian, b. 1940. **Genres:** Philosophy, Ethics, Law, Theology/Religion, Social sciences. **Career:** University of California, Berkeley, associate in law, 1965-66; University College, Oxford, England, fellow and praelector in jurisprudence, 1966-; Oxford University, Oxford, lecturer, 1967-72, reader in Commonwealth and U.S. law, 1972-89, professor of law and legal philosophy, 1989-; University of Malawi, professor of law and head of department, 1976-78; University of Notre Dame, Indiana, Biolchini professor of law, 1995-. Called to the Bar at Gray's Inn, 1970. **Publications:** Natural Law and Natural Rights, Oxford University Press, 1980. Fundamentals of Ethics, Georgetown University Press, 1983. (With Joseph M. Boyle, Jr. and Germain Grisez) Nuclear Deterrence, Morality and Realism, Oxford University Press, 1987. Moral Absolutes, Catholic University of America Press, 1991; Aquinas: Moral, Political, and Legal Theory, 1998. **Address:** University College, Oxford University, Oxford OX1 4BH, England.

FINSTAD, Suzanne. American, b. 1955. **Genres:** Mystery/Crime/Suspense, Adult non-fiction, Film, Genealogy/Heraldry, International relations/Current affairs, Law, Music, Theatre, Biography, Documentaries/Reportage. **Career:** Butler & Binion, Houston, Tex., legal assistant, 1976-78, law clerk, 1978-80, trial attorney, 1980-82; writer and legal consultant, 1982-. Special counsel to attorney ad litem in the heirship determination of Howard Hughes, 1981; Co-producer, "Sleeping with the Devil," CBS, 1997. **Publications:** Heir Not Apparent, 1984; Ulterior Motives: The Killing and Dark Legacy of Tycoon Henry Kyle, 1987; Sleeping with the Devil, 1991; (collaborator) Queen Noor Memoirs, 1994; Child Bride: The Untold Story of Priscilla Beaulieu Presley, 1997; Natasha: The Biography of Natalie Wood, 2001. **Address:** c/o Joel Gotler, 9200 Sunset Blvd, Los Angeles, CA 90069, U.S.A.

FINUCANE, Ronald C(harles). American, b. 1939. **Genres:** History. **Career:** Leverhulme Fellow, Oxford, 1970; University of Maryland, College Park, lecturer in overseas program in London, England, 1974-82; University of Puget Sound, Tacoma, WA, Chism Visiting Professor of Humanities, 1983-85, director of Chism Faculty Seminar in Medieval History, 1984-85; Georgia Southern College, Statesboro, assistant professor of history, 1985-88; Benedictine College, Atchison, KS, associate professor of history and chair of department, 1988-91; Oakland University, Rochester, MI, professor of history and chair of department, 1991-. University of Reading, UK, lecturer and research fellow at Graduate Centre for Medieval Studies, 1973-77; National Endowment for the Humanities, director of summer seminar for high school teachers on medieval and Renaissance autobiography, 1985; Oxford Research Services, director, 1975-88; engaged in historical research in and around Oxford, England. **Publications:** Miracles and Pilgrims: Popular Beliefs in Medieval England, 1977; Appearances of the Dead: A Cultural History, 1982; Soldiers of the Faith: Crusaders and Moslems at War, 1983; Rescue of the Innocents, 1997. **Address:** Department of History, Oakland University, 350 O'Dowd Hall, Rochester, MI 48309-4401, U.S.A. **Online address:** Finucane@oakland.edu

FIRCHOW, Peter. American, b. 1937. **Genres:** Novellas/Short stories, Literary criticism and history, Translations. **Career:** Professor of English and Comparative Literature, University of Minnesota, Minneapolis (joined faculty, 1967). Assistant Professor of English, University of Michigan, Ann Arbor, 1965-67. President, Midwest Modern Language Association, 1977-78; Visiting Professor, National Cheng Kung University, Taiwan, 1982-83; Jilin University, China, 1987, Ludwig-Maximillian University, Munich, 1988-89; Karl-Franzens University, Graz, Austria, 1989, 2003, University of Bonn, Germany, Fulbright Professor, 1995-96; National University of Costa Rica, Fulbright Professor, 2000. **Publications:** (trans. and author of intro.) Lucinde and the Fragments, 1971; Aldous Huxley, Satirist and Novelist, 1972; (ed. and interviewer) The Writer's Place, 1974; (ed. and trans. with E.S. Firchow) East German Short Stories: An Introductory Anthology, 1979; The End of Utopia: A Study of Huxley's Brave New World, 1984; The Death of the German Cousin: Variations on a Literary Stereotype, 1890-1920, 1986; (trans. with E.S. Firchow) A. Brandstetter, The Abbey, 1998; Envisioning Africa: Racism and Imperialism in Conrad's Heart of Darkness, 2000; W.H. Auden: Contexts for Poetry, 2002; Reluctant Modernists: Aldous Huxley and Some Contemporaries, 2002. **Address:** 135 Birnamwood Dr, Burnsville, MN 55337, U.S.A. **Online address:** pef@umn.edu

FIRESIDE, Harvey F. American (born Austria), b. 1929. **Genres:** History, Politics/Government, Young adult non-fiction. **Career:** New York Institute of Technology, NYC, assistant professor of social science, 1964-68; Ithaca College, NY, assistant professor, 1968-70, associate professor, 1970-74, professor, 1974-96, Charles A. Dana Professor of Politics Emeritus, 1996. Cornell University, visiting professor, 2002-. **Publications:** Icon and Swastika: The Russian Orthodox Church under Nazi and Soviet Control, 1971; Soviet Psychoprisons, 1979; Brown v. Board of Education: Equal Education for All, 1994; Young People from Bosnia Talk about War, 1996; Plessy v. Ferguson: Separate but Equal?, 1997; Fifth Amendment: The Right to Remain Silent, 1998; New York Times v. Sullivan: Expanding Freedom of the Press, 1999; Nuremberg Nazi War Crimes Trials, 2000; "Mississippi Burning" Civil Rights Murder Conspiracy Trial, 2002. **Address:** 322 N Aurora St, Ithaca, NY 14850, U.S.A. **Online address:** HFireside@juno.com

FIRKATIAN, Mari A. Armenian (born Bulgaria), b. 1959. **Genres:** Biography, History. **Career:** Auburn University, Auburn, AL, instructor in history, 1987-96; American University in Bulgaria, Blagoevgrad, Bulgaria, assistant professor of history, 1992-94; University of Hartford, Hartford, CT, instructor in history, 1996-; has given papers and presentations. **Publications:** The Forest Traveler: Georgi Stoikov Rakovski and Bulgarian Nationalism, 1996. Contributor to books. Contributor of articles and book reviews to periodicals. **Address:** Department of Humanities, Tunxis Community College, 271 Scott Swamp Rd, Farmington, CT 06032-3187, U.S.A. **Online address:** tx_firkatian@commnet.edu

FIROR, John (William). American, b. 1927. **Genres:** Meteorology/ Atmospheric sciences. **Career:** Senior Research Associate, National Center for Atmospheric Research, Boulder, CO, 1996-. Director of Advanced Study Program Center, 1980-96 (Director of High Altitude Observatory, 1961-68; Director of Center, 1968-74; Executive Director of Center, 1974-80). Member of staff, Dept. of Terrestrial Magnetism, Carnegie Institution, Washington, D.C., 1953-61. **Publications:** The Changing Atmosphere: A Global Challenge, 1990; (with J. Jacobsen) The Crowded Greenhouse, 2002. **Address:** National Center for Atmospheric Research, PO Box 3000, Boulder, CO 80307, U.S.A. **Online address:** firor@ucar.edu

FIRSCHING, F. Henry. American, b. 1923. **Genres:** Sciences, Theology/ Religion. **Career:** Diamond Alkali, Fairport Harbor, OH, senior research chemist, 1955-58; University of Georgia, Athens, assistant professor of chemistry, 1958-63; Southern Illinois University, Edwardsville, professor of chemistry, 1963-92; retired, 1992. Presenter of the radio program Think about It. **Publications:** The God Hypothesis: A Scientist Looks at Religion, 1997; The Most Intriguing Story Ever Told: A Summary of Scientific Studies about How We Got Here, 2002. Contributor to scientific journals. **Address:** 5205 Springfield Dr, Edwardsville, IL 62025-5833, U.S.A.

FIRST, Philip. See WILLIAMSON, Philip G.

FISCH, Harold. British/Israeli, b. 1923. **Genres:** Literary criticism and history, Theology/Religion. **Career:** Bar-Ilan University, Israel, emeritus professor, 1989, professor of English, 1964-89, associate professor, 1957-64, university rector, 1968-71; University of Leeds, lecturer, English language, literature, 1947-57. **Publications:** The Dual Image, 1959, 1971; Jerusalem and Albion (literary history), 1964; (trans.) Haggada, 1965, 1973; Hamlet and the Word, 1971; S.Y. Agnon, 1975; The Zionist Revolution, 1978; A Remembered Future, 1984; Poetry with a Purpose, 1988, 1990; New Stories for Old, 1998; The Biblical Presence in Shakespeare, Milton and Blake, 1999. EDITOR: The Five Books of the Tora and the Haftarot, 1967; Mans Mortalitie, by R. Overton, 1968; The Koren Jerusalem Bible, 1969. **Address:** 4 Shmaryahu Levin St, Jerusalem, Israel.

FISCHEL, Jack R. American, b. 1937. **Genres:** History. **Career:** Millersville University, Millersville, PA, teacher, 1965-2004, emeritus professor, 2004-. Lancaster County Human Relations Commission, member. **Publications:** Jewish American History: An Encyclopedia, 1992; The Holocaust, 1998; Historical Dictionary of the Holocaust, 1999. Contributor of articles and reviews to periodicals. **Address:** Emeritus Professor of History, Millersville University, Millersville, PA 17551, U.S.A. **Online address:** jackiefischel@aol.com

FISCHEL, William A. American, b. 1945. **Genres:** Economics, Law, Urban studies. **Career:** Dartmouth College, Hanover, NH, professor of economics, 1973-. **Publications:** The Economics of Zoning Laws, 1985; Regulatory Takings: Law, Economics, and Politics, 1995; The Homevoter Hypothesis, 2001. **Address:** Department of Economics, 6106 Rockefeller, Dartmouth College, Hanover, NH 03755, U.S.A. **Online address:** waf@dartmouth.edu

FISCHER, Dennis. Swiss/American (born Germany), b. 1960. **Genres:** Film. **Career:** Spotlight Cable, assistant traffic controller, 1982-83; Hollywood Reporter, Hollywood, CA, assistant editor, 1984-85; high school teacher, Los Angeles, CA, 1985-. **Publications:** Horror Film Directors, 1931 to 1990, 1991; Science Fiction Film Directors, 1895-1998, 2000. **Address:** 6820 Alondra Blvd., Paramount, CA 90723, U.S.A.

FISCHER, John. See FLUKE, Joanne.

FISCHER, Klaus P. German, b. 1942. **Genres:** History. **Career:** Fort Lewis College, Durango, CO, instructor in European history, 1968-69; Chapman College, Orange, CA, adjunct professor of history and philosophy, 1973-, director of school at Vandenberg Air Force Base, 1978-90; Allan Hancock College, Santa Maria, CA, professor of philosophy and history, 1990-, chairperson, Department of Social Science, 1994. Salier-Gymnasium, Waiblingen, Germany, exchange teacher, 1973; U.S. International University, adjunct professor, 1978. **Publications:** History and Prophecy: Oswald Spengler and the Decline of the West, 1989; Nazi Germany: A New History, 1995. Contributor to academic journals. **Address:** Department of Social Science, Allan Hancock College, 800 South College, Santa Maria, CA 93454, U.S.A.

FISCHER, Lucy Rose. American, b. 1944. **Genres:** Gerontology/Senior issues, Human relations/Parenting, Medicine/Health, Psychology, Sociology. **Career:** University of Minnesota, Minneapolis, assistant professor of sociology, 1979-87; St. Olaf College, Northfield, MN, associate professor, 1987-89; Wilder Research Center, St. Paul, MN, senior research scientist, 1989-92; HealthPartners Research Foundation, senior investigator, 1992-; writer, artist. Research consultant for several nonprofit organizations. Midwest Council for Social Research on Aging, newsletter editor; Healthy Outcomes, editor. **Publications:** Linked Lives: Adult Daughters and Their Mothers, 1986; (with D.P. Mueller, P.W. Cooper, and R.A. Chase) Older Minnesotans: What Do They Need? How Do They Contribute?, 1989; (with K. Schaffer) Older Volunteers: Time and Talent, 1993. Contributor to periodicals. **Address:** 2320 Parklands Rd., Minneapolis, MN 55416, U.S.A. **Online address:** Lucy. R.Fischer@healthpartners.com

FISCHER, Lynn. American, b. 1942. **Genres:** Food and Wine, Gerontology/ Senior issues, How-to books, Medicine/Health, Psychology, Sports/Fitness. **Career:** Healthy Living, Washington, DC, president. Fox Television, medical anchor, evening news, and host of Healthbeat, 1984-86; Discovery Channel, host and producer of The Low Cholesterol Gourmet, 1991-95; public broadcasting, host of Lynn Fischer's Healthy Indulgences, 1995-98; America on Line, Nutrition Expert, live chats weekly, 1997-. **Publications:** The Low Cholesterol Gourmet, 1989; The Quick Low Cholesterol Gourmet, 1992; Healthy Indulgences, 1995; The Better Sex Diet, 1996; Fabulous Fat Free, 1996; Lowfat Cooking for Dummies, 1998; Quick & Healthy for Dummies, 2000. **Address:** 3525 Barley Ln, Lakeland, FL 33803-5907, U.S.A. **Online address:** lowfatlife@aol.com

FISCHER, R. J. See FLUKE, Joanne.

FISCHER, Tibor. British, b. 1959. **Genres:** Novels. **Career:** Freelance journalist and novelist. **Publications:** Under the Frog, 1992, in US as Under the Frog: A Black Comedy, 1994; The Thought Gang, 1994; The Collector Collector, 1997; Don't Read This Book if You're Stupid, 2000; I Like Being Killed: Stories, 2001. **Address:** c/o Stephanie Cabot, William Morris Agency, 52153 Poland St, London W1F 7LX, England.

FISCHETTI, Mark. American. **Genres:** Adult non-fiction. **Career:** Writer. Scientific American, New York, NY, science writer and contributing editor. **Publications:** (editor) The Family Business Management Handbook, 1996; (with Tim Berners-Lee) Weaving the Web: The Original Design and Ultimate Destiny of the World Wide Web by Its Inventor, 1999; (with Elinor Levy) The New Killer Diseases: How the Alarming Evolution of Mutant Germs, 2003. Contributor to periodicals. **Address:** Scientific American Inc., 415 Madison Ave., New York, NY 10017, U.S.A.

FISCHLER, Alan. American, b. 1952. **Genres:** Literary criticism and history. **Career:** PTN Publishing Corp., Hempstead, NY, associate editor,

1973; Genesee Community College, Batavia, NY, instructor in English and journalism, 1975-77; Eisenhower College, Seneca Falls, NY, visiting instructor in rhetoric, 1977-78; Nazareth College of Rochester, Rochester, NY, instructor in English, 1977-81; Rochester Institute of Technology, Rochester, NY, member of faculty and chairman of humanities and international studies, 1981-84; Hartman Materials Handling Systems, Victor, NY, manager of technical communications, 1984-86; Rochester Institute of Technology, visiting assistant professor of language, literature, and communication, 1987-88; Le Moyne College, Syracuse, NY, assistant professor, 1988-91, associate professor, 1991-97, professor of English, 1997-. **Publications:** Modified Rapture: Comedy in W.S. Gilbert's Savoy Operas, 1991. Work represented in anthologies. Contributor to magazines and newspapers. **Address:** Department of English, Le Moyne College, Le Moyne Heights, Syracuse, NY 13214, U.S.A. **Online address:** fischlab@mail.lemoyne.edu

FISDEL, Steven A. American. **Genres:** History, Humanities, Self help, Theology/Religion. **Career:** Ordained rabbi. Temple Chai, Long Grove, IL, educational director, 1982-85; Beth Israel, congregational rabbi, Chico, CA, 1992-96; Katriel Enterprises (spiritual counseling practice), Burlingame, CA, proprietor, 1992-; Chochmat HaLev Institute, Berkeley, CA, core faculty member, 1995-; Bnai Torah, Antioch, CA, congregational rabbi, 1996-; Esalen Institute, Big Sur, CA, instructor, 1997-. **Publications:** The Practice of Kabbalah, 1996; The Dead Sea Scrolls: Understanding the Spiritual Message, 1998; The Tree of Life Meditations, Vol. 1, 2002; The Original Tarot of the Kabbalah, 2003. Contributor to books and periodicals. **Address:** Katriel Enterprises, PO Box 4841, Burlingame, CA 94011, U.S.A. **Online address:** fisdel@ix.netcom.com

FISH, Charles (K.). American, b. 1936. **Genres:** Local history/Rural topics, Agriculture/Forestry, Photography, Social commentary, Autobiography/Memoirs. **Career:** Princeton University, NJ, instructor to assistant professor of English, 1963-68; Windham College, Putney, VT, associate professor of English, 1968-76, academic dean, 1969-71, faculty trustee, 1971-72; Vermont Council on the Humanities and Public Issues, program development consultant to assistant director for the state, 1976-77; Martocci & Henry Real Estate, Inc., Brattleboro, VT, sales manager, 1982-87, principal broker, 1982-89, director of policy and operations, 1987-89; Western New England College, Springfield, MA, associate professor of English, 1989-2001, acting dean, School of Arts and Sciences, 1990-91, chair, department of English and humanities, 1998-2001. **Publications:** In Good Hands: The Keeping of a Family Farm, 1995; Blue Ribbons and Burlesque: A Book of Country Fairs, 1998. Contributor to literature journals. **Address:** 32 Bunker Rd, E Dummerston, VT 05346, U.S.A.

FISH, Stanley E(ugene). American, b. 1938. **Genres:** Law, Literary criticism and history. **Career:** University of California, Berkeley, Assistant Professor, 1963-67, Professor, 1967-74; University of Southern California, Los Angeles, Leonard S. Bing Visiting Professor, 1973-74; Johns Hopkins University, Baltimore, Professor of English, 1974-78, Kenan Professor of English and Humanities, 1978-85; University of Maryland Law School, Adjunct Professor, 1976-85; Columbia University, NYC, Visiting Professor, 1983; Duke University, Durham, Chairman of the Dept. of English, 1985-92, Arts and Sciences Distinguished Professor of English, Professor of Law, 1985-98; Duke Univ. Press, Executive Director, 1994-98; University of Illinois at Chicago, Dean, College of Liberal Arts and Sciences, 1999-. Member of the editorial board, Milton Quarterly, Milton Studies, Medievalia et Humanistica, Journal on Law and Literature, and Poetics Today. **Publications:** John Skelton's Poetry, 1965; Surprised by Sin: The Reader in Paradise Lost, 1967, rev. ed., 1997; Self-Consuming Artifacts: The Experience of Seventeenth-Century Literature, 1972; The Living Temple: George Herbert and Catechizing, 1978; Is There a Text in This Class? The Authority of Interpretive Communities, 1980; Doing What Comes Naturally: Change, Rhetoric, and the Practice of Theory in Legal and Literary Studies, 1989; There's No Such Thing as Free Speech, and It's a Good Thing, Too, 1994; Professional Correctness, 1995; The Trouble with Principle, 2000; How Milton Works, 2001. **Address:** Arts & Sciences, University of Illinois at Chicago, 601 S. Morgan St., MC 228, Chicago, IL 60607-7104, U.S.A.

FISHBACK, Mary. (born United States), b. 1954. **Genres:** Genealogy/Heraldry. **Career:** Loudoun Hospital Center, Leesburg, VA, nurse and phlebotomist, 1973-89; Graydon Manor, Leesburg, VA, nurse and phlebotomist, 1989-99; Town of Leesburg, Leesburg, VA, librarian, 2000-. Loudoun Library Foundation, member, 1990-2003, and coordinator of Book Center; Thomas Balch Library Commission, chair, 1994-99; Thomas Balch History and Genealogy Library, volunteer for nearly thirty years. Northern Virginia Hospice, nurse, 1980-87. **Publications:** 250 Years of Towns and Villages, 1999; People and Places, 2000; (with others) Middleburg Cemeteries, Loud-

oun County, Virginia, 2000; A Family Album, 2001; Northern Virginia's Equestrian Heritage, 2002; Leesburg, 2003. Contributor to periodicals. **Address:** 408 Madison Ct. S.E., Leesburg, VA 20176, U.S.A. **Online address:** mfishback@leesburgva.org

FISHBACK, Price V(anmeter). American, b. 1955. **Genres:** Economics. **Career:** Weyerhaeuser Co., economic researcher and forecaster, 1979-80; University of Georgia, Athens, temporary assistant professor, 1982-83, assistant professor, 1983-87, associate professor of economics, 1987-91; University of Arizona, Tucson, associate professor of economics, 1990-93, professor of economics, 1993-; National Bureau of Economic Research, research associate, 1994-; writer. University of Texas, visiting professor, 1987-89. Cliametrics Society, trustee, 1994-98. Journal of Economic History, member of editorial board, 1990-94; Explorations in Economic History, member of editorial board, 1998-. **Publications:** Soft Coal, Hard Choices: The Economic Welfare of Bituminous Coal Miners, 1890-1930, 1992; Prelude to the Welfare State: The Origins of Workers' Compensation, 2000. Work represented in anthologies. Contributor of articles and reviews to economic and history journals. **Address:** Department of Economics, University of Arizona, Tucson, AZ 85721, U.S.A. **Online address:** pfishback@bpa.arizona.edu

FISHBURN, Angela Mary. British, b. 1933. **Genres:** Crafts, Homes/Gardens. **Career:** Former part-time tutor in Adult Education, Herts. and Bucks. County Councils. **Publications:** Lampshades: Technique and Design, 1975; The Batsford Book of Soft Furnishings (Home Furnishings), 2 vols, 1978-82; Curtains and Window Treatments, 1982; Batsford Book of Lampshades, 1984; Creating Your Own Soft Furnishings, 1984; Soft Furnishings for the Bedroom, 1988. **Address:** Oak Farm, Ashley Green, Near Chesham, Bucks., England.

FISHER, Allen. British, b. 1944. **Genres:** Poetry. **Career:** Co-publisher, Aloes Books, London, 1972-, publisher of Spanner, London, 1974-, and co-publisher, New London Pride, 1975-81. **Publications:** Thomas Net's Tree-Birst, 1971; Before Ideas, Ideas, 1971; Spaces for Winter Solstice (Blueprint), 1972; Sicily, 1973; Place, 1974; Long Shout to Kernewek, 1975; 5 Plages 'shun, 1975; Paxton's Beacon, 1976; Gripping the Rail, 1976; "Der Verolene" Operation, 1976; Stane, 1977; Fire-Place (with Hearth-Work by Pierre Joris), 1977; Self-Portraits, Pink 149, 1977; Doing, 1977; Samuel Matthews, 1977; Docking, 1978; London Blight, 1978; Convergences, in Place, of the Play, 1978; Becoming, 1978; The Apocalyptic Sonnets, 1978; Intermediate Spirit Receiver, 1980; Hooks (Taken Out of Place 32), 1980; Eros, Father, Pattern, 1980; Imbrications, 1981; Unpolished Mirrors, 1981; The Art of Flight VI-IX, 1982; Poetry for Schools, Including Black Light, Shorting-Out, and Other Poems, 1982; Bending Windows, 1982; Defamiliarising, 1983; African Boog, 1983; Banda, 1983; Brixton Fractals, 1985; Buzzards and Bees, 1987; Camel Walk, 1988; Stepping Out, 1989; Convalescence, 1992; (with B. Catling and Bill Griffiths) Future Exiles, 1992; Dispossession and Cure, 1994; Scram, 1994; Fizz, 1994; Breadboard, 1994; Civic Crime, 1994; Emergent Manner, 1999; Topological Shovel, 1999; Ring Shout, 2000; Sojourns, 2001; Gravity, 2004; Entanglement, 2004. **Address:** Froebel College, Roehampton University, London SW15 5PJ, England. **Online address:** meeq03@dial.pipex.com

FISHER, Angela. Australian, b. 1947. **Genres:** Anthropology/Ethnology, Third World. **Career:** Social worker, Darwin, Australia, 1968-70; researcher of traditional jewelry and jewelry designer in African and Middle Eastern countries, 1970-77; photographer and writer, 1977-; jewelry designer, 1984-. **Publications:** Africa Adorned, 1984; (with C. Beckwith and G. Hancock) African Ark: People and Ancient Cultures of Ethiopia and the Horn of Africa, 1990; (with C. Beckwith) African Ceremonies, 2 vols., 1999, concise ed., 2002; (with C. Beckwith) Faces of Africa, 2004. **Address:** 42 Belsize Ave, London NW3 4AH, England. **Online address:** africanceremonies@btinternet.com

FISHER, David E. American, b. 1932. **Genres:** Novels, Plays/Screenplays, Sciences. **Career:** Professor, University of Miami, Florida, since 1966. **Publications:** The Courtesy Not to Bleed, 1970; Crisis, 1971; Compartments, 1972; A Fearful Symmetry, 1974; The Last Flying Tiger, 1976; The Creation of the Universe, 1977; The Creation of Atoms and Stars, 1979; The Ideas of Einstein, 1980; The Man You Sleep With, 1980; Variation on a Theme, 1981; Katie's Terror, 1982; Grace for the Dead, 1984; The Third Experiment: Is There Life on Mars?, 1985; The Birth of the Earth, 1987; A Race on the Edge of Time, 1987; The Origin and Evolution of Our Own Particular Universe, 1988; Hostage One, 1989; Fire and Ice, 1989; Across the Top of the World, 1992; The Wrong Man, 1993; The Scariest Place on Earth, 1994; Tube, 1996; A Brief History of Life on Other Worlds, 1997.

Address: Dept of Geological Sciences, University of Miami, PO Box 249176, Miami, FL 33176, U.S.A. **Online address:** dfisher@miami.edu

FISHER, Ernest F., Jr. American, b. 1918. **Genres:** Military/Defense/Arms control. **Career:** Career army reserve officer, 1944-84, retiring with rank of colonel. U.S. Army of Europe Headquarters, Heidelberg, West Germany, member of historical division, 1954-59; U.S. Army, Center of Military History, Washington, DC, 1960-83. Part-time instructor in history, University of Virginia, Northern Virginia Center, Arlington, VA, 1960-70. **Publications:** Cassino to the Alps, 1977; Guardians of the Republic: A History of the Noncommissioned Officer Corps of the U.S. Army, 1994. Contributor to periodicals and encyclopedias. **Address:** 1701 North Kent St. No. 402, Arlington, VA 22209, U.S.A.

FISHER, Franklin M. American, b. 1934. **Genres:** Economics. **Career:** University of Chicago, Assistant Professor of Economics, 1959-60; Massachusetts Institute of Technology, Cambridge, Assistant Professor, 1960-62, Associate Professor, 1962-65, Professor of Economics, 1965-, Jane Berkowitz Carlton and Dennis William Carlton Professor of Economics, 2000-. Journal of the American Statistical Association, Associate Ed.; Review of Economic Studies, American Ed., 1965-68; Econometrica, Ed., 1968-77. **Publications:** A Priori Information and Time Series Analysis, 1962; A Study in Econometrics: The Demand for Electricity in the United States, 1962; (with A. Ando and H.A. Simon) Essays on the Structure of Social Science Models, 1963; Supply and Costs in the United States Petroleum Industry, 1964; The Identification Problem in Econometrics, 1966; (with K. Shell) The Economic Theory of Price Indices, 1972; (with J. McGowan and J. Greenwood) Folded, Spindled, and Mutilated, 1983; (with R. Mancke and J. McKie) IBM and the U.S. Data Processing Industry, 1983; Disequilibrium Foundations of Equilibrium Economics, 1983; (ed.) Antitrust and Regulation: Essays in Memory of John J. McGowan, 1985; Industrial Organization, Economics and the Law, 1990; Econometrics: Essays in Theory and Applications, 1991; Aggregation: Aggregate Production Functions and Related Topics, 1992; (with K. Shell) The Economic Theory of Production Price Indexes, 1997; Microeconomics Essays in Theory and Applications: Collected Papers of Franklin M. Fisher, 1999; (with others) Did Microsoft Harm Consumers?, 2000. **Address:** Dept. of Economics, E52-359, Massachusetts Institute of Technology, Cambridge, MA 02139, U.S.A. **Online address:** ffisher@mit.edu

FISHER, Leonard Everett. American, b. 1924. **Genres:** Children's fiction, Young adult fiction, Children's non-fiction, Mythology/Folklore, Young adult non-fiction, Illustrations. **Career:** Paier College of Art, CT, dean emeritus, 1982- (joined faculty, 1966; professor of fine arts and dean of academic affairs, 1978-82). **Publications:** Pumpers, Boilers, Hooks and Ladders, 1961; Pushers, Spads, Jennies and Jets, 1961; Head Full of Hats, 1962; The Glassmakers, 1964; The Silversmiths, 1964; The Papermakers, 1965; The Printers, 1965; The Wigmakers, 1965; The Hatters, 1965; The Tanners, 1966; The Weavers, 1966; The Cabinetmakers, 1966; The Shoemakers, 1967; The Schoolmasters, 1967; The Peddlers, 1968; The Doctors, 1968; The Potters, 1969; The Limners, 1969; The Architects, 1970; Two if by Sea, 1970; Revolutionary War Heroes, 1970; The Shipbuilders, 1971; The Death of Evening Star, 1972; The Homemakers, 1973; The Art Experience: Oil Painting, 1973; The Warlock of Westfall, 1974; The Liberty Book, 1974; Sweeney's Ghost, 1975; Across the Sea from Galway, 1975; The Blacksmiths, 1976; Letters from Italy, 1977; Noonan, 1978; Alphabet Art, 1978; The Railroads, 1979; The Factories, 1979; The Hospitals, 1980; The Sports, 1980; A Russian Farewell, 1980; Storm at the Jetty, 1980; The Newspapers, 1981; The Seven Days of Creation, 1981; The Unions, 1982; Number Art, 1982; The Schools, 1983; Star Signs, 1983; Boxes! Boxes!, 1984; The Olympians, 1984; Symbol Art, 1985; The Statue of Liberty, 1985; Masterpieces of American Painting, 1985; The Great Wall of China, 1986; Ellis Island, 1986; Look Around, 1986; Remington and Russell, 1986; Calendar Art, 1987; The Tower of London, 1987; The Alamo, 1987; Theseus and the Minotaur, 1988; Pyramid of the Sun, Pyramid of the Moon, 1988; The White House, 1989; The Wailing Wall, 1989; The Oregon Trail, 1990; Prince Henry the Navigator, 1990; Jason and the Golden Fleece, 1990; The ABC Exhibit, 1991; Sailboat Lost, 1991; Cyclops, 1991; Galileo, 1992; Tracks across America, 1992; David and Goliath, 1993; Gutenberg, 1993; Stars and Stripes, 1993; Marie Curie, 1994; Kinderdike, 1994; Gandhi, 1995; Moses, 1995; Niagara Falls, 1996; William Tell, 1996; Anasazi, 1997; The Jetty Chronicles, 1997; Gods and Goddesses of Ancient Egypt, 1997; Alexander Graham Bell, 1998; To Bigotry, No Sanction, 1998; Gods and Goddesses of the Ancient Maya, 1999; Sky, Sea, the Jetty and Me, 2001; Gods and Goddesses of the Ancient Norse, 2002; The Gods and Goddesses of Ancient China, 2003. **Address:** 7 Twin Bridge Acres Rd, Westport, CT 06880-1028, U.S.A. **Online address:** L.E.Fisher@sbcglobal.net

FISHER, Louis. American, b. 1934. **Genres:** Politics/Government. **Career:** Sr. Specialist (Separation of Powers), Congressional Research Service, Library of Congress, Washington, D.C., 1988- (Analyst, 1970-74; Specialist, 1974-88). Assistant Professor of Political Science, Queens College, Flushing, NY, 1967-70; Professor of Political Science and Law, American University, Washington, DC, 1975-77, Georgetown University, Washington, DC, 1976-77, Catholic University, Washington, DC, 1990-95, School of Law, 1992-96, Indiana University, Bloomington, 1987, Johns Hopkins University, Baltimore, 1989, College of William and Mary (School of Law), Williamsburg, VA, 1990-92. **Publications:** President and Congress: Power and Policy, 1972; Presidential Spending Power, 1975; The Constitution Between Friends, 1978; The Politics of Shared Power: Congress and the Executive, 1981, 4th ed., 1998; Constitutional Conflicts between Congress and the President, 1985, 4th ed., 1997; Constitutional Dialogues: Interpretation as Political Process, 1988; American Constitutional Law, 1990, 6th ed., 2005; Encyclopedia of the American Presidency, 1994; Presidential War Power, 1995, 2nd ed., 2004; Political Dynamics of Constitutional Law, 1996, 3rd ed., 2001; Congressional Abdication on War and Spending, 2000; Religious Liberty in America: Political Safeguards, 2002; Nazi Saboteurs on Trial: A Military Tribunal & American Law, 2003; The Politics of Executive Privilege, 2004; Military Tribunals and Presidential Power: American Revolution to the War on Terrorism, 2005. **Address:** 520 Ridgewell Way, Silver Spring, MD 20902, U.S.A.

FISHER, Marshall Jon. American, b. 1963. **Genres:** Documentaries/Reportage. **Career:** Writer. **Publications:** The Ozone Layer (young adult), 1992; (with D.E. Fisher) Tube: The Invention of Television, 1996; (with D.E. Fisher) Strangers in the Night: A Brief History of Life on Other Worlds, 1998. **Address:** c/o Counterpoint, 387 Park Ave S 12th Fl, New York, NY 10016-8810, U.S.A. **Online address:** marshallfisher@juno.com

FISHER, Marvin. American, b. 1927. **Genres:** History, Literary criticism and history. **Career:** Professor of English, 1958-, now retired, Arizona State University, Tempe (Chairman of Dept., 1977-83); visiting professor: University of Minnesota; University of California, Davis; Aristotle University, Greece; University of Oslo, Norway; University of Tubingen, Germany. **Publications:** Workshops in the Wilderness: The European Response to American Industrialization 1830-1860, 1967; Going Under: Melville's Short Fiction and the American 1850's, 1977; Continuities: Essays and Ideas in American Literature, 1986; Herman Melville: Life, Work and Criticism, 1988. Contributor of articles, essays, and reviews to journals and books. **Address:** Dept. of English, Arizona State University, Tempe, AZ 85287, U.S.A.

FISHER, Nikki. See STRACHAN, Ian.

FISHER, Ralph Talcott, Jr. American, b. 1920. **Genres:** History, Politics/Government. **Career:** Professor Emeritus of History University of Illinois, Urbana, since 1988 (Associate Professor, 1958-60; Director, Russian and East European Center, 1959-87; Professor, 1960-88). Member, Editorial Board, Russian Review, since 1959, and Slavic Review, 1969-79. Assistant, Instructor, then Assistant Professor of History, Yale University, New Haven, Conn., 1950-58. Distinguished Visiting Professor, Arizona State University, Tempe, 1990. Secretary, 1960-69, Vice-President, 1978-79, and President, 1979-80, American Association for the Advancement of Slavic Studies. **Publications:** Pattern for Soviet Youth: A Study of the Congresses of the Komsomol 1918-1954, 1959; (ed. with G. Vernadsky) Dictionary of Russian Historical Terms, by Pushkarev, 1970; (co-ed.) Source Book for Russian History from the Early Times to 1917, 3 vols., 1972. **Address:** 2115 Burlison Dr, Urbana, IL 61801, U.S.A.

FISHER, Robert E. American, b. 1940. **Genres:** Art/Art history. **Career:** University of Redlands, Redlands, CA, professor of art history and head of department, 1971-72. California Private Colleges and Universities, resident director for year-in-Japan program at Waseda University, 1974-75, director of program for study in Japan, 1988-90; lecturer at colleges, universities, and museums. Korean Cultural Service, Los Angeles, cultural adviser, 1980-84. **Publications:** Buddhist Art and Architecture, 1993; Art of Tibet, 1997. Contributor to art books. Contributor to periodicals. **Address:** PO Box 2556, Carmel, CA 93921, U.S.A. **Online address:** bfisher@redshift.com

FISHER, Roger (Dummer). American, b. 1922. **Genres:** International relations/Current affairs. **Career:** Samuel Williston Professor Emeritus of Law, Harvard University, Cambridge, MA, 1976- (Lecturer, 1958-60; Professor, 1960-76). Director, Harvard Negotiation Project, 1980-. Sr. Consultant, and Director, Conflict Management, Inc., 1984-. Member, Board of Trustees, Hudson Institute, 1963-; Member, Board of Dirs., Council for a Livable

World, Washington, DC, 1969-. Assistant to the General Counsel, Economic Cooperation Administration, Paris, 1948-49; Associate, law firm of Covington and Burling, Washington, DC, 1950-56; Assistant to the Solicitor-General of the U.S., Dept. of Justice, Washington, 1956-58. Member, Executive Council, American Society of International Law, 1961-64, 1966-69; Originator and exec. Ed., The Advocates, TV series, 1969-70; Vice-President, World Affairs Council, Boston, 1972-74; Member, Governor's Commission on Citizen Participation, Massachusetts, 1973. **Publications:** (ed.) International Conflict and Behavioral Science, 1964; International Conflict for Beginners, 1969 (in U.K., as Basic Negotiating Strategy, 1971); Dear Israelis, Dear Arabs, 1972; Points of Choice, 1978; Improving Compliance with International Law, 1981; Getting to Yes, 1981, rev. ed., 1991; Getting Together, 1988; Beyond Machiavelli: Tools for Coping with Conflict, 1994; Getting It Done: How to Lead When You're Not in Charge, 1999. **Address:** Harvard University, Law School, Pound Hall 500, Cambridge, MA 02138, U.S.A.

FISHER, Roy. British, b. 1930. **Genres:** Poetry. **Career:** Freelance writer and musician, 1982-. School and coll. teacher, 1953-63; Principal Lecturer and Head of Dept. of English and Drama, Bordesley College of Education, Birmingham, 1963-71; Member, Dept. of American Studies, University of Keele, Staffs, 1971-82. **Publications:** City, 1961; Then Hallucinations: City 2, 1962; The Ship's Orchestra, 1966; Ten Interiors with Various Figures, 1967; The Memorial Fountain, 1967; Collected Poems 1968, 1969; Titles, 1969; (with T. Phillips) Correspondence, 1970; Matrix, 1971; Metamorphoses, 1971; The Cut Pages, 1971; (with D. Greaves) Also There, 1972; (with R. King) Bluebeard's Castle, 1972; (with I. Tyson) Cultures, 1975; (with R. King) Neighbours!, 1976; 19 Poems and an Interview, 1976; Barnardine's Reply, 1977; The Thing about Joe Sullivan: Poems, 1971-1977, 1978; Comedies, 1979; Poems 1955-1980, 1980; Talks for Words, 1980; Consolidated Comedies, 1981; (with R. King) The Half-Year Letters: An Alphabet Book, 1983; Turning the Prism, 1985; A Furnace, 1986; (with R. King) The Left-Handed Punch, 1986; (with P. Lester) A Birmingham Dialogue, 1986; Poems 1955-1987, 1988; (with T. Pickard) Birmingham's What I Think With (film), 1991; (with R. King) Anansi Company, 1992; Birmingham River, 1994; It Follows That, 1994; The Dow Low Drop: New and Selected Poems, 1996; (with I. Tyson) Roller, 1999; Interviews through Time and Selected Prose, 2000; (with R. King) Tabernacle, 2000. **Address:** Four Ways, Earl Sterndale, Buxton, Derbyshire SK17 0EP, England. **Online address:** mad.litt@btinternet.com

FISHER, Stephen L(ynn). American, b. 1944. **Genres:** Politics/Government, Local history/Rural topics. **Career:** Tulane University, New Orleans, LA, member of faculty, 1970-71; Emory and Henry College, Emory, VA, member of faculty, 1971-, currently Hawthorne Professor of Political Science, head of department, 1972-77, 1979-80, 1982-85, and director of the Appalachian Center for Community Service, 1995-. Guest lecturer at colleges and universities; public speaker; consultant to social agencies and educational institutions. Carnegie Foundation National Baccalaureate College Professor of the Year, 1999. **Publications:** The Minor Parties of the Federal Republic of Germany: Toward a Comparative Theory of Minor Parties, 1974; (ed.) A Landless People in a Rural Region: A Reader on Land Ownership and Property Taxation, 1979; (ed. and contrib.) Fighting Back in Appalachia: Traditions of Resistance and Change, 1993. Work represented in anthologies. Contributor of articles and reviews to professional journals, regional magazines, and newspapers. **Address:** Appalachian Center for Community Service, Emory and Henry College, PO Box 947, Emory, VA 24327, U.S.A. **Online address:** slfisher@ehc.edu

FISHKIN, Shelley Fisher. American, b. 1950. **Genres:** Literary criticism and history. **Career:** Freelance writer for newspapers and magazines, 1969-; Yale University, New Haven, CT, executive secretary of the Poynter Fellowship in Journalism, 1971-80, director of the Poynter Fellowship in Journalism, 1980-85, associate Chubb Fellow, 1974-85, visiting lecturer in American studies, 1981-84, director of the Gordon Grand Fellowship, 1984-85; University of Texas, Austin, senior lecturer, 1985-89, associate professor, 1989-93, professor of American studies, 1993-, professor of American studies and English, 1994-. Stanford University, visiting scholar at Institute for Research on Women and Gender, 1987-88; Cambridge University, visiting fellow, 1992-93. Lecturer at universities and embassies in Belgium, France, Italy, Mexico, and the Netherlands, 1992-93. Charlotte Perkins Gilman Society, cofounder and executive director, 1990-. **Publications:** From Fact to Fiction: Journalism and Imaginative Writing in America, 1985; Was Huck Black? Mark Twain and African-American Voices, 1993; (ed. with E. Hedges, and contrib.) Listening to Silences: New Essays in Feminist Criticism, 1994. Work represented in books and anthologies. Contributor to periodicals. **Address:** American Studies Program, GAR 303, University of Texas, Austin, TX 78712, U.S.A.

FISHLOCK, David Jocelyn. British, b. 1932. **Genres:** Administration/Management, Air/Space topics, Business/Trade/Industry, Education, Engineering, Medicine/Health, Physics, Politics/Government, Sciences, Technology. **Career:** Science Ed., The Financial Times, London, 1967-1991; Editor/Publisher, R&D Efficiency, 1991-2002. Technology Ed., New Scientist, London, 1962-67. **Publications:** Metal Colouring, 1962; (with K.W. Hards) New Ways of Working Metals, 1965; The New Materials, 1967; Taking the Temperature, 1967; Man Modified, 1969; The Business of Science, 1974; The Business of Biotechnology, 1982; (with E. Antebi) Biotechnology: Strategies for Life, 1986; (with S. Rippon) The Heart, 1990. EDITOR: A Guide to the Laser, 1967; A Guide to Superconductivity, 1969; A Guide to Earth Satellites, 1971; The New Scientists, 1971. **Address:** Traveller's Joy, Copse Lane, Jordans, Bucks. HP9 2TA, England.

FISHLOCK, Trevor. British, b. 1941. **Genres:** Travel/Exploration, Documentaries/Reportage. **Career:** Portsmouth Evening News, staff member, 1957-62; Freelance News Agency, reporter, 1962-68; London Times, staff correspondent, Wales and West England, 1968-78, South Asia, 1980-83, New York, 1983-86; Daily Telegraph, roving foreign correspondent, 1986-89 and 1991-, Moscow correspondent, 1989-91; Sunday Telegraph, roving foreign correspondent, 1991-93. **Publications:** Wales and the Welsh, 1972; Talking of Wales, 1976; Discovering Britain: Wales, 1979; Americans and Nothing Else, 1980; Gandhi's Children, 1983; India File, 1983; Indira Gandhi, 1986; The State of America, 1986; Out of Red Darkness: Reports From the Collapsing Soviet Empire, 1992; My Foreign Country: Trevor Fishlock's Britain, 1997. **Address:** Daily Telegraph, 1 Canada Square, Canary Wharf, London E14 5DT, England.

FISHMAN, Aryei. Israeli/American (born Poland), b. 1922. **Genres:** Theology/Religion, Sociology. **Career:** Affiliated with Kibbutz Yavne, 1946-47, and Jewish Agency, 1950; Bar-Ilan University, Ramat Gan, associate professor of sociology, 1969-. Military service: U.S. Army, 1943-46. Israel Defense Forces, 1948-49. **Publications:** (ed.) The Religious Kibbutz Movement, World Zionist Organization, 1957; Judaism and Modernization on the Religious Kibbutz, Cambridge University Press, 1992. **Address:** Department of Sociology, Bar-Ilan University, 52900 Ramat Gan, Israel.

FISHMAN, Cathy Goldberg. American, b. 1951. **Genres:** Picture/board books, Theology/Religion. **Career:** Elementary schoolteacher, 1973-75; day care director, 1976-78; children's bookstore owner, 1979-83; full-time mother and writer, 1983-. **Publications:** PICTURE BOOKS: On Rosh Hashanah and Yom Kippur, 1997; On Passover, 1997; On Hanukkah, 1998. **Address:** 1861 Central Ave., Augusta, GA 30904, U.S.A. **Online address:** catfishG@groupZ.net

FISHMAN, Katharine Davis. American. **Genres:** Cultural/Ethnic topics, Dance/Ballet, Education, Psychiatry, Psychology, Social sciences, Essays. **Career:** Vogue, New York, N.Y., copywriter, 1958-60; Mademoiselle, New York City, assistant travel editor, 1960-63; freelance writer, 1964-. **Publications:** The Computer Establishment, 1981; Behind The One-Way Mirror: Psychotherapy and Children, 1995; Attitude! Eight Young Dancers Come of Age at the Ailey School, 2004.

FISHMAN, Lisa. Also writes as Lee Fishman Morren. American, b. 1966. **Genres:** Poetry. **Career:** Beloit College, Beloit, WI, assistant professor of English, 1998-. **Publications:** The Deep Heart's Core Is a Suitcase (poems), 1996. Some writings appear under the name Lee Fishman Morren. **Address:** Department of English, Beloit College, Beloit, WI 53511, U.S.A.

FISHMAN, Steve. American, b. 1955. **Genres:** Business/Trade/Industry. **Career:** Journalist. Worked for Norwich Bulletin, Norwich, CT, and Miami Herald, Miami, FL; stringer for Christian Science Monitor, the Associated Press, and Newsweek; editor for United Press International. **Publications:** A Bomb in the Brain: A Heroic Tale of Science, Surgery, and Survival, 1988; Karaoke Nation; or, How I Spent a Year in Search of Glamour, Fulfillment, and a Million Dollars, 2003. Contributor to periodicals. **Address:** c/o Author Mail, Free Press, Simon & Schuster, 1230 Avenue of the Americas, New York, NY 10020, U.S.A.

FISK, Milton. American, b. 1932. **Genres:** Ethics. **Career:** University of Notre Dame, South Bend, IN, instructor to assistant professor, 1957-63; Yale University, New Haven, CT, assistant professor, 1963-66; Indiana University, Bloomington, associate professor to professor, 1966-97, professor emeritus, 1997-. **Publications:** Nature and Necessity, 1973; Ethics and Society, 1980; The State and Justice, 1989; Toward a Healthy Society, 2000; (ed.) Not for Sale: A Defense of Public Goods, 2001. **Address:** 4237 East Penn Ct., Bloomington, IN 47408, U.S.A.

FISK, Pauline. British, b. 1948. **Genres:** Children's fiction, Young adult fiction. **Career:** Writer. **Publications:** FOR YOUNG PEOPLE: Midnight Blue, 1990; Telling the Sea, 1992; Tyger Pool, 1994; The Beast of Whixall Moss, 1997; The Candle House, 1999; Sabrina Fludde, 2001; The Road Judge, 2005; The Mrs. Merridge Project, 2005. **Address:** c/o Laura Cecil Agency, 17 Alwyne Villas, London N1 2HG, England.

FISKE, Robert H(artwell). American, b. 1948. **Genres:** Writing/Journalism. **Career:** Writer. **Publications:** Guide to Concise Writing, 1990; Thesaurus of Alternatives to Worn-Out Words and Phrases, 1994; The Writer's Digest Dictionary of Concise Writing, 1996. **Address:** 4 Longwood Drive, Andover, MA 01810-1516, U.S.A. **Online address:** vocabula@aol.com

FISKE, Sharon. See **HILL, Pamela.**

FISS, Owen M(itchell). American, b. 1938. **Genres:** Law. **Career:** Sterling Professor of Law, Yale University, New Haven, CT, 1993- (Professor of Law, 1974-84; Alexander M. Bickel Professor of Public Law). Member, Editorial Board, Foundation Press, and Philosophy and Public Affairs, Law, Economics, and Organization, etc.; Member, Executive Board, Lawyers Committee for Civil Rights under Law. Law Clerk to Thurgood Marshall, then Judge of the U.S. Court of Appeals, Second Circuit, 1964-65; Law Clerk to Justice Brennan, U.S. Supreme Court, 1965-66; Special Assistant to John Doar, Assistant Attorney-General, U.S. Dept. of Justice, 1966-68; Professor of Law, University of Chicago, 1968-74. **Publications:** Injunctions, 1972, (with D. Rendleman) 1984; The Civil Rights Injunction, 1978; (with R.M. Cover) The Structure of Procedure, 1979; (with R.M. Cover and J. Resnik) Procedure, 1988; Troubled Beginnings of the Modern State, 1888-1910, 1993; Liberalism Divided, 1996; The Irony of Free Speech, 1996; A Community of Equals, 1999. **Address:** Yale Law School, New Haven, CT 06520, U.S.A.

FITCH, Noel Riley. American, b. 1937. **Genres:** Literary criticism and history, Travel/Exploration, Biography. **Career:** Moscow Junior High School, Moscow, ID, teacher of language arts, 1959-62; Moscow Senior High School, Moscow, ID, teacher of English, 1962-63; Washington State University, teaching assistant, 1963-66, part-time instructor, 1967-68; Eastern Nazarene College, assistant professor, 1966-67, 1968-71; California State University, San Diego, part-time associate professor, 1976-78; Point Loma College, professor of literature, 1971-87, chair of department of literature and modern languages, 1982-85. University of Southern California, lecturer, 1986-; American University of Paris, professor, 1987-. **Publications:** Sylvia Beach and the Lost Generation: A History of Literary Paris in the Twenties and Thirties, 1983; (ed. with R.W. Etulain) Faith and Imagination: Essays on Evangelicals and Literature, 1985; Literary Cafes of Paris, 1989; (author of intro.) In Transition: A Paris Anthology, 1990; Walks in Hemingway's Paris: A Guide to Paris for the Literary Traveler, 1990; Anais: The Erotic Life of Anais Nin, 1993; Appetite for Life: The Biography of Julia Child, 1997. Contributor of chapters to books. **Address:** 11829 Mayfield Ave, Los Angeles, CA 90049, U.S.A. **Online address:** noelriley@aol.com

FITCH, Sheree. Canadian, b. 1956. **Genres:** Poetry. **Career:** Children's author and performance poet. Worked as a government clerk; founder and president of Campus, a group for older, part-time students at St. Thomas University and the University of New Brunswick, while an undergraduate; founder and member of Enterprise Theatre, an alternative theatre troupe, while an undergraduate; performer and actress on stage, radio, film, and television. **Publications:** POETRY FOR CHILDREN: Toes in My Nose, And Other Poems, 1987; Sleeping Dragons All Around, (prose), 1989; Merry-Go-Day, 1991; There Were Monkeys in My Kitchen!, 1992; I Am Small, 1994; Mabel Murple, 1995; If You Could Wear My Sneakers!: Poems, 1997; There's a Mouse in My House, 1998; The Hullabaloo Bugaboo Day, 1998; The Other Author, Arthur, forthcoming; If I Were the Moon, forthcoming; Sun-Day, Moon-Day, Some Day Dreams, forthcoming. PLAYS: Light a Little Candle, 1996; Rummabubba, Lid-Maker of the Snufflewogs, 1997; The Monkeys are Back and We're Out of Bananas, 1998; The Hullabaloo Bugaboo Day, 1998. POETRY FOR ADULTS: In This House Are Many Women, 1996. Contributor of poems for adults to periodicals. **Address:** c/o Writer's Federation of Nova Scotia, 1113 Marginal Rd, Halifax, NS, Canada B3H 4P7.

FITES, Philip. Canadian (born United States), b. 1946. **Genres:** Information science/Computers. **Career:** Worked as a computer operator trainee; computer programmer for a bank in Denver, CO, 1966-67; University of Alberta, Edmonton, assistant analyst, 1967-70; Northwestern Utilities Ltd., programmer and analyst, 1971-72; City of Edmonton, analytical services officer, 1975-77; Computer Sciences Canada, customer consultant and financial products specialist, 1977-78; Noram Timesharing Development Ltd., owner,

director, and officer, 1978-79; Fites & Kulpa (consultants), partner, 1978-79; Fites and Associates Management Consultants Ltd., owner, 1979-; Northern Alberta Institute of Technology, instructor, 1984-85; Computer Career Institute, curriculum development coordinator, 1986; teacher at Athabasca University and Thebacha College, Northwest Territories; AEPOS Technologies, senior information security consultant, 1996-. Canadian Advisory Council on Information Technology Security, member of working groups, 1987-; International Information Security Systems Security Certification Consortium, founding member, 1989, president and chairman of board of directors, 1989-90; Information Security Exchange, member, 1990-92. **Publications:** (with P. Johnson and M. Kratz) The Computer Virus Crisis, 1989, 2nd ed. 1992; (with M. Kratz and A. Brebner) Control and Security of Computer Information Systems, 1989; (with M. Kratz) Information Systems Security: A Practitioner's Reference, 1993. Contributor to periodicals. **Address:** 200 Baseline Rd., Ottawa, ON, Canada K2C 0A2. **Online address:** fites@cyberus.ca

FITTER, Chris. British, b. 1955. **Genres:** Cultural/Ethnic topics. **Career:** Fairleigh Dickinson University, Wroxton College, Banbury, England, adjunct professor of English, 1983-85; University of Mississippi, Oxford, assistant professor of English, 1988-94; Rutgers University, Camden, NJ, assistant professor of English, 1994-. Central America Support Group, chapter organizer. **Publications:** Poetry, Space, Landscape (cultural history), 1995. Contributor to books and periodicals. **Address:** Department of English, Rutgers University, Camden, NJ 08102, U.S.A. **Online address:** fitter@crab.rutgers.edu

FITTER, Richard (Sidney Richmond). British, b. 1913. **Genres:** Natural history, Biography. **Career:** Chairman of the Steering Committee, 1975-88, Species Survival Commission, International Union for Conservation of Nature. Open Air Correspondent, Observer, London, 1958-66; Director, Intelligence Unit, Council for Nature, 1959-63; Trustee, World Wildlife Fund (UK), 1977-83; Chairman, Fauna and Flora Preservation Society, 1983-88. **Publications:** London's Natural History, 1945; London's Birds, 1949; Pocket Guide to British Birds, 1952; Pocket Guide to Nests and Eggs, 1954; (with D. McClintock) Pocket Guide to Wild Flowers, 1956; The Ark in Our Midst, 1959; Six Great Naturalists, 1959; Guide to Bird Watching, 1963; Wildlife in Britain, 1963; Britain's Wildlife: Rarities and Introductions, 1966; (with M. Fitter) The Penguin Dictionary of British Natural History 1967; Vanishing Wild Animals of the World, 1968; Finding Wild Flowers, 1971; (with H. Heinzel and J. Parslow) The Birds of Britain and Europe, with North Africa and the Middle East, 1972; (with A. Fitter and M. Blamey) The Wild Flowers of Britain and Northern Europe, 1974; The Penitent Butchers, 1978; Handguide to the Wild Flowers of Britain and Northern Europe, 1979; (with M. Blamey) Gem Guide to Wild Flowers, 1980; (with N. Arlott and A. Fitter) The Complete Guide to British Wildlife, 1981; (with J. Wilkinson and A. Fitter) Collins Guide to the Countryside, 1984; (with A. Fitter and A. Farrer) Guide to the Grasses, Sedges, Rushes, and Ferns of Britain and Northern Europe, 1984; Wildlife for Man, 1986; (with R. Manuel) Field Guide to the Freshwater Life of Britain and North-west Europe, 1986; (with A. Fitter) A Field Guide to the Countryside in Winter, 1988; (with M. Blamey and A. Fitter) Wild Flowers of Britain and Ireland, 2003;. **Address:** 9 Coppice Ave, Great Shelford, Cambridge CB2 5AQ, England.

FITZGERALD, Astrid. Swiss/American, b. 1938. **Genres:** Novels, Young adult fiction, Art/Art history, Philosophy, Travel/Exploration. **Career:** Freelance fine artist and writer, 1965-. Golden Mean (travel exhibition), member of board of advisers. Work exhibited in group and solo shows; represented in museums and corporate collections. **Publications:** (illustrator and photographer) Traveler's Key to Ancient Greece, 1989; An Artist's Book of Inspiration (quotations), 1996; Being Consciousness Bliss: A Seeker's Guide, 2002. **Address:** 650 West End Ave #1Bb, New York, NY 10025, U.S.A. **Online address:** astrid@bestweb.net

FITZGERALD, Carol. (born United States), b. 1942. **Genres:** Bibliography. **Career:** Broward County Commission, Broward County, FL, commission aide, 1978-2001; Broward County Library System, administrative coordinator for the director, 2001-. Cleveland Clinic Hospital, Fort Lauderdale, FL, trustee, 1987-98, chair, 1988-90, vice chair of executive board, 1990-97; Light of the World Clinic, director, 1996-. **Publications:** The Rivers of America: A Descriptive Bibliography, 2001. **Address:** 2100 South Ocean Ln., Apt. 706, Fort Lauderdale, FL 33316, U.S.A. **Online address:** riversgal@aol.com

FITZGERALD, Ernest Abner. American, b. 1925. **Genres:** Theology/Religion. **Career:** Bishop, The United Methodist Church Altanta Area, Georgia. **Publications:** There's No Other Way, 1970; The Structures of Inner

Peace, 1973; You Can Believe, 1975; Living under Pressure, 1976; A Time to Cross the River, 1977; How to Be a Successful Failure, 1978; God Writes Straight with Crooked Lines, 1980; Diamonds Everywhere, 1983; Keeping Pace: Inspirations in the Air, 1988. **Address:** 2536 Huntington Woods Dr., Winston-Salem, NC 27103, U.S.A.

FITZGERALD, Garret. Irish, b. 1926. **Genres:** Demography, Economics, International relations/Current affairs, Language/Linguistics, Politics/Government, Autobiography/Memoirs. **Career:** With Aer Lingus, Irish Airlines, 1947-58; Lecturer, Dept. of Political Economy, University College Dublin, 1959-73; Irish Times, weekly columnist, 1959-73, 1991-; Fine Gael Member of the Dail Eireann (Irish Parliament) for Dublin SE, 1969-92 (Member, Seanad Eireann, Irish Senate, 1965-69, and former Member, Senate Electoral Law Commission; Member, Dail Committee on Public Accounts, 1969-73; Minister for Foreign Affairs, 1973-77; President, Fine Gael Party, 1977-87; Prime Minister of Ireland, Taoiseach, 1981-82, 1982-87). Former director, Guinness Peat Aviation. Director: Trade Development Institute, Dublin. President, Council of Ministers of EEC, 1975, and of the European Council, 1984. **Publications:** State-Sponsored Bodies, 1961; Planning in Ireland, 1968; Towards a New Ireland, 1972; Unequal Partners, 1980; Estimates for Baronies of Minimum Level of Irish-Speaking Amongst Successive Decennial Cohorts 1771-1781 to 1861-1871, 1984; All in a Life (autobiography), 1991; Reflections on the Irish State, 2001; Irish-Speaking in the Pre-Famine Period, 2004. **Address:** 37 Annavilla, Dublin 6, Ireland. **Online address:** garretfg@iol.ie

FITZGERALD, Mary Anne. South African. **Genres:** Documentaries/Reportage. **Career:** Writer. Morgan, Orr and Associates, Nairobi, Kenya, public relations consultant; freelance foreign correspondent. **Publications:** Nomad: Journeys from Samburu, 1993; My Warrior Son, 1998. **Address:** c/o Michael Joseph Ltd., 80 Strand, London WC2R 0RL, England.

FITZMAURICE, Gabriel. Irish, b. 1952. **Genres:** Poetry, Literary criticism and history, Translations. **Career:** Irish Department of Education, schoolteacher, 1972-; writer. Writers' Week (Listowel, County Kerry), chair, 1982-85, 1991-92. **Publications:** POETRY: Rainsong, 1984; Road to the Horizon, 1987; Nocht, 1989; Dancing Through, 1990; The Father's Part, 1992; The Space Between: New and Selected Poems 1984-1992, 1993; Ag Siobshiul Chun An Rince, 1995; The Village Sings, 1996; Giolla na nAmhran: Danta 1988-1998, 1998; A Wrenboy's Carnival: Poems 1980-2000, 2000; I and the Village, 2002; The Boghole Boys, 2005. POETRY FOR CHILDREN: The Moving Stair, 1989, rev. ed., 1993; Nach Iontach Mar Ata, 1994; But Dad!, 1995; Puppy and the Sausage, 1998; Dear Grandad, 2001; A Giant Never Dies, 2002; The Oopsy Kid, 2003; Don't Squash Fluffy, 2004; I'm Proud to Be Me, 2005. OTHER: Kerry on My Mind (essays), 1999;. TRANSLATOR: M. O hAirtneide, The Purge, 1989; Poems I Wish I'd Written, 1996; G. Rosenstock, The Rhino's Specs, 2003; Poems from the Irish, 2004. EDITOR: (with D. Kiberd) An Crann Faoi Bhlath/The Flowering Tree, 1991; Between the Hills and Sea, 1991; Con Greaney, Traditional Singer, 1991; Homecoming/An Bealach'na Bhaile, 1993; Irish Poetry Now, 1993; Kerry through Its Writers, 1993; The Listowel Literary Phenomenon: North Kerry Writers, 1994; (with R. Dunbar) Rusty Nails and Astronauts, 1999; (with A. Cronin and J. Looney) "The Boro" and "The Cross," 2000; The Kerry Anthology, 2000; Come All Good Men and True, 2004; The World of Bryan Mac Mahon, 2005. **Address:** Moyvane, Kerry, Ireland.

FITZPATRICK, David. Australian, b. 1948. **Genres:** History. **Career:** Oxford University, England, research fellow at Nuffield College, 1975-77; University of Melbourne, Parkville, Australia, research fellow, 1977-79; Trinity College, Dublin, Ireland, lecturer, 1979-93, fellow, 1982-, associate professor, 1993-2000, professor of modern history, 2000-. "Irish Narratives" series, general editor, 1997-2003; University of Aberdeen, Research Institute of Irish and Scottish Studies, honorary professor, 2000-05. **Publications:** Politics and Irish Life, 1913-1921: Provincial Experience of War and Revolution, 1977, rev. ed., 1998; Irish Emigration, 1801-1921, 1984, rev. ed., 1989; Oceans of Consolation: Personal Accounts of Irish Migration to Australia, 1995; The Two Irelands, 1912-1939, 1998; Harry Boland's Irish Revolution, 2003. **Address:** Department of Modern History, Trinity College, Dublin 2, Ireland.

FITZPATRICK, Deanne. Canadian. **Genres:** Crafts. **Career:** Fiber artist, with work represented at Canadian museums. **Publications:** Hook Me a Story: The History and Method of Rug Hooking in Atlantic Canada, 2000; The Secrets of Designing Hooked Rugs. Contributor to periodicals. **Address:** R.R.5, Amherst, NS, Canada B4H 3Y3. **Online address:** hookingrugs@ns.eastlink.ca

FITZPATRICK, Mary Anne. American, b. 1949. **Genres:** Communications/Media, Human relations/Parenting. **Career:** O'Hara High School, social

studies teacher, 1971-72; Emerson College, Boston, MA, debate coach and instructor, 1972-73; West Virginia University, Morgantown, teaching assistant in educational psychology, 1973-74; University of Wisconsin-Milwaukee, assistant professor of communications, 1976-78; University of Wisconsin-Madison, assistant professor, 1978-81, associate professor, 1981-84, professor of communications, 1984-, director of Center for Communication Research, 1980-, department head, 1993-, Vilas Associate in social science, 1989-91. Visiting professor, University of Texas, 1983, University of Nebraska, 1984, George Washington University, 1987-88, University of California, Santa Barbara, 1988, University of Iowa, 1990, and University of Kansas, 1992; New Mexico State University, distinguished visiting professor, 1987; lecturer at colleges and universities in the United States and Australia. **Publications:** Between Husbands and Wives: Communication in Marriage, 1988; (with Noller) Communication in Family Relationships, 1993. EDITOR & CONTRIBUTOR: (with P. Noller) Perspectives on Marital Interaction (monograph), 1988; (with T. Edgar and V. Freimuth) AIDS: A Communication Perspective, 1992; Work represented in anthologies. Contributor of articles and reviews to communications and social science journals. **Address:** Department of Communication Arts, 6110 Vilas Communication Hall, University of Wisconsin-Madison, 821 University Ave., Madison, WI 53706, U.S.A.

FITZPATRICK, Tony. American, b. 1949. **Genres:** Environmental sciences/Ecology, Natural history, Essays, Novels. **Career:** Writing teacher at junior high, high school, and college levels, 1972-83; University of Illinois, Urbana, agriculture writer and editor, 1980-87; Washington University, St. Louis, MO, science editor, 1987-; writer. **Publications:** Signals from the Heartland, Walker, 1993. **Address:** Washington University, 1 Brookings Dr., P.O. Box 1070, St. Louis, MO 63130, U.S.A.

FITZPATRICK, Vincent (dePaul), (III). American, b. 1950. **Genres:** Biography, Literary criticism and history. **Career:** Enoch Pratt Free Library, Baltimore, Md., Curator of H. L. Mencken Collection, 1980-. **Publications:** H.L.M., The Mencken Bibliography: A Second Ten-Year Supplement, 1972-1981, 1986; H.L. Mencken, 1989; (with M.B. Ruscica and C.H. Fitzpatrick) The Complete Sentence Workout Book Alternate, 2nd ed., 1991; (co-editor) 35 Years of Newspaper Work: A Memoir by H.L. Mencken, 1994. Contributor to books. **Address:** Department of Humanities, Enoch Pratt Free Library, 400 Cathedral St, Baltimore, MD 21201, U.S.A.

FITZROY, Charles (Patrick Hugh). British, b. 1957. **Genres:** Travel/Exploration. **Career:** Fine Art Travel Ltd., London, England, director, 1984-; Robert Holder Ltd., director, 1984-; bellinitravel.com, director, 2000-. **Publications:** Italy: A Grand Tour for the Modern Traveller, 1991; Italy Revealed, 1994; Grafton Regis: The Portrait of a Northamptonshire Village, 2000. **Address:** c/o Sara Mengue, 4 Hatch Pl, Kingston upon Thames, Surrey KT2 5NB, England. **Online address:** cfitzroy@fineartravel.co.uk

FITZSIMONS, Cecilia (A. L.). British, b. 1952. **Genres:** Animals/Pets, Children's non-fiction, Illustrations, Picture/board books, Earth sciences, Environmental sciences/Ecology, Geography, How-to books, Marine sciences/Oceanography, Medicine/Health, Natural history, Sciences, Travel/Exploration, Zoology. **Career:** Author and illustrator. **Publications:** My First Birds, 1985; My First Butterflies, 1985; My First Fishes and Other Waterlife, 1987; My First Insects, Spiders and Crawlers, 1987; Seashore Life of North America, 1989; In the Field, 1990; In the Playground, 1990; In the Woods, 1990; At the Seaside, 1990; Sainsbury's Book of the Sea, 1991; Rivers and Ponds, 1992; The Seashore, 1992; Trees and Woodlands, 1992; Animals in Danger, 1993; Sainsbury's Book of Birds, 1994; Clever Clogs, Wild Animals, 1994; Sainsbury's Animals of the World, 1995; Step-by-Step 50 Nature Projects for Kids, 1995; Animal Habitats, 1996; Animal Lives, 1996; Creatures of the Past, 1996; Water Life, 1996; (with M. Elliot and P. Boase) 100 Things for Kids to Make and Do, 1996; Fruit, 1996; Vegetables and Herbs, 1997; Cereals, Nuts and Spices, 1997; Dairy Foods and Drinks, 1997; Sainsbury's Book of Dangerous Animals, 1997; Birds of Prey, 1997; Horses and Ponies of the World, 1998; Wildlife Explorer, 1998; The Giant Book of Bugs, 1998; Small Pets, 1999; The Wildlife of Valderrama, 1999; A Day in Donana, 1999; I Didn't Know That: Wolves Howl at the Moon, 2000; I Didn't Know That: Giant Pandas Eat All Day, 2000; Dinosaurs, 2000; Animal Friends, 2001. Illustrator of books by others including J. Charman, J. Cockrane, E. Fejer and S. Frampton, S. Finnie, H. Gee and S. McCormick, R. Harlow and Kuo Kang Chen, E. Lawrence, C. Littlejohn, L. Peake, S. Perry, P. Steele, R. Wilson.

FIX, Michael. American, b. 1950. **Genres:** Politics/Government, Urban studies. **Career:** Urban Institute, Washington, DC, principal research associate and director of Immigrant Policy Program, 1977-. Consultant to Equal

Opportunity Program, Rockefeller Foundation. **Publications:** (Coauthor) Relief or Reform? Reagan's Regulatory Dilemma, 1984; (Coeditor) Coping with Mandates: What Are the Alternatives?, 1990; (Coeditor) The Paper Curtain, 1991; (Coeditor) Clear and Convincing: The Measurement of Discrimination in America, 1993; (Coauthor) Immigration and Immigrants: Setting the Record Straight, 1994. **Address:** Urban Institute, 2100 M St. NW, Washington, DC 20037, U.S.A.

FLACK, Jerry D(avid). American, b. 1943. **Genres:** Education. **Career:** Teacher of U.S. history at public schools in Marshall, Mich., 1965-66; teacher of English, language arts programs, and programs for gifted language arts students at public schools in Kalamazoo, Mich., 1966-80, academic specialist for English, 1972-75, academic specialist for gifted/talented education, 1978-79; teacher and coordinator of Providing Learning Enrichment Through Differentiated Guided Exploration Program at public schools in Bridgman, Mich., 1980-81; teacher in Program for Academic and Creative Enrichment at a school in Lafayette, Ind., 1981-82; Purdue University, West Lafayette, Ind., instructor in education, 1982, guest lecturer at Indianapolis campus, 1983; University of Colorado, Colorado Springs, professor of gifted and talented education, 1983-. Instructor at University of Southern Maine, 1982; guest lecturer at Northern Michigan University, 1983, Purdue University, 1986 and 1988, and University of Arkansas, 1987. Chairman of Creativityfest: World Conference on Gifted Children, 1987. Member of Colorado State Board of Education Gifted and Talented Advisory Board, 1984-86, and Gifted and Talented Task Force, 1988. **Publications:** Once Upon a Time: Creative Problem Solving through Fairy Tales, 1985; Hey! It's My Future, 1986; Inventing, Inventions, and Inventors: A Teaching Resource Guide, 1989; Mystery and Detection: Thinking and Problem Solving with the Sleuths, 1990; Lives of Promise: Studies in Biography and Family History, 1992; TalentEd: Strategies for Developing the Talent in Every Learner, 1993; Odysseys: Personal Discoveries, 1993; Voyages: Extending Horizons, 1993; Distinations: Grand Visions, 1993. **Address:** School of Education, University of Colorado, 1861 Austin Bluffs Parkway, PO Box 7150, Colorado Springs, CO 80933-7150, U.S.A.

FLAHERTY, Liz. (born United States), b. 1950. **Genres:** Romance/ Historical. **Career:** Writer. **Publications:** Always Annie (romance fiction),1999; Because of Joe (fiction), 2003. Contributor to periodicals. **Address:** Jill Grosjean, Grosjean Literary Agency, 1390 Millstone Rd, Sag Harbor, NY 11963, U.S.A.

FLAHERTY, Michael G. American, b. 1952. **Genres:** Sociology. **Career:** Eckerd College, St. Petersburg, FL, assistant professor, 1980-87, associate professor, 1987-92, professor of sociology, 1992-. **Publications:** A Watched Pot: How We Experience Time, 1999. EDITOR (with C. Ellis): Investigating Subjectivity: Research on Lived Experience, 1992; Social Perspectives on Emotions, vol. 3, 1995.Contributor to sociology journals. **Address:** Department of Sociology, Eckerd College, 4200 54th Ave S, St. Petersburg, FL 33711, U.S.A.

FLAM, Jack D(onald). American, b. 1940. **Genres:** Art/Art history. **Career:** Rutgers University, New Brunswick, NJ, instructor in art, 1963-66; University of Florida, Gainesville, assistant professor, 1966-69, associate professor of art, 1969-72; City University of New York, NYC, professor of art history at Brooklyn College and Graduate Center, 1975-, distinguished professor of art history, 1991-. Art critic for the Wall Street Journal, 1984-92. **Publications:** (ed.) Matisse on Art, 1973; Zoltan Gorency (novel), 1974; Bread and Butter (novel), 1977; (with J. Cowart, D. Fourcade, and J.H. Neff) Henri Matisse Paper Cut Outs, 1978; (with D. Ashton) Robert Motherwell, 1981; Matisse: The Man and His Art, 1869-1918, 1986; (ed.) Matisse: A Retrospective, 1988; Motherwell, 1991; Richard Diebenkorn: Ocean Park, 1993; Matisse: The Dance, 1993; Western Artists/African Art, 1994; Judith Rothschild: An Artist's Search, 1998; Les peintures de Picasso: Un theatre mental, 1998; The Modern Drawing, 1999; Matisse in the Cone Collection, 2001; Matisse and Picasso: The Story of Their Rivalry and Friendship, 2003; Primitivism and Twentieth-Century Art: A Documentary History, 2003. Coeditor of Documents of 20th Century Art. Contributor to journals.

FLAMHAFT, Ziva. Israeli, b. 1944. **Genres:** International relations/Current affairs. **Career:** Office of the Prime Minister of Israel, public relations assistant and office manager in Department of Special Affairs, 1964-69; worked for Israeli government offices in NYC, 196973; Hunter College of the City University of New York, NYC, adjunct lecturer, 1984; Queens College of the City University of New York, Flushing, NY, adjunct lecturer, 1985-92, adjunct assistant professor, 1992-94, substitute instructor, 1994-96, instructor, 1996-. Speaker at colleges and universities workd wide; guest on television and radio programs. **Publications:** Israel on the Road to Peace: Accepting the Unacceptable, 1996. Contributor to books and periodicals. **Address:** Queens College of the City University of New York, Kissena Blvd., Flushing, NY 11367, U.S.A. **Online address:** zflamhaft@cuny.campus.mci.net

FLAMINI, Roland. American. **Genres:** Biography, Film. **Career:** Time magazine, NYC, correspondent; freelance writer, c. 1975-. **Publications:** NONFICTION: Scarlett, Rhett, and a Cast of Thousands: The Filming of Gone with the Wind, 1975; Pope, Premier, President: The Cold War Summit That Never Was, 1980; Ava: A Biography, 1983; Ten Years at Number 10: Images of a Decade in Office, 1989; Sovereign: Elizabeth II and the Windsor Dynasty, 1991; Thalberg: The Last Tycoon and the World of M-G-M, 1994; Passport Germany: Your Pocket Guide to German Business, Customs, and Etiquette, 1997. Contributor to periodicals. **Address:** c/o UPI, 1510 H St. NW, Washington, DC 20005, U.S.A.

FLANDERS, Rebecca. *See* **BALL, Donna.**

FLANNERY, Tim(othy Fridtjof). Australian, b. 1956. **Genres:** Environmental sciences/Ecology, Zoology. **Career:** Australian Museum, principal research scientist, 1984-98; Harvard University, chair of Australian studies, 1998-99; South Australian Museum, director. **Publications:** (with M. Archer and G. Grigg) The Kangaroo, 1985; (with P. Kendall) Australia's Vanishing Mammals, 1990; The Future Eaters: An Ecological History of the Australasian Lands and People, 1994; (with P. Schouten) Possums of the World: A Monograph of the Phalangeroidea, 1994; Mammals of New Guinea, 1995; Mammals of the South-West Pacific and Moluccan Islands, 1995; (with R. Martin, A. Szalay, and P. Schouten) Tree Kangaroos, 1996; Throwim 'Way Leg, 1997; (with P. Schouten) A Gap in Nature, 2001; The Eternal Frontier: An Ecological History of North America in 5 Acts, 2001; (with J. Long, M. Archer, and S. Hand) Prehistoric Mammals of Australia and New Guinea, 2002; Beautiful Lies: Population & Environment in Australia, 2003; (with P. Schouten) Astonishing Animals, 2004; Country, 2004. EDITOR: 1788 Watkin Tench, 1996; John Nicol: Mariner, 1997; Terra Australis: The Journals of Matthew Flinders, 2000; The Birth of Sydney, 2000; The Explorers, 2000; The Life and Adventures of William Buckley, 2002; The Birth of Melbourne, 2002; Sailing Alone around the World, 2003. **Address:** South Australian Museum, North Terrace, Adelaide, SA 5000, Australia. **Online address:** komar.vera@saugov.sa.gov.au

FLASTE, Richard (Alfred). American, b. 1942. **Genres:** Adult non-fiction, Documentaries/Reportage, Food and Wine. **Career:** New York Times, NYC, parent-child columnist, reporter, 1973-76, assistant style editor, 1976-80, deputy director of science news, 1980-82, director of science news, 1982-. **Publications:** NONFICTION: (with D.N. Flaste and E. Rodman) The New York Times Guide to Children's Entertainment: In New York, New Jersey, and Connecticut, c. 1976; (with P. Franey) Pierre Franey's Kitchen, 1982; (with Franey) Pierre Franey's Low-Calorie Gourmet, c. 1984; (with others) The New York Times Guide to the Return of Halley's Comet, c. 1985; (with Franey) The New York Times 60-Minute Gourmet's Low Calorie Cooking, 1989; (ed.) The New York Times Book of Science Literacy: What Everyone Needs to Know From Newton to the Knuckleball, c. 1991; (with Franey) Pierre Franey's Cooking in America, 1992; (with others) Medicine's Great Journey: One Hundred Years of Healing, 1992; (with Franey) Pierre Franey's Cooking in France, 1994; (with Franey and B. Miller) A Chef's Tale: A Memoir of Food, France, and America, 1994; (with J.E. Brody) Jane Brody's Good Seafood Book, 1994; (with E.L. Deci) Why We Do What We Do: The Dynamics of Personal Autonomy, c. 1995; (with L. Abramson) The Defence Is Ready: Life in the Trenches of Criminal Law, 1997. **Address:** New York Times, 229 West 43rd St., New York, NY 10036, U.S.A.

FLATH, Carol Apollonio. American, b. 1955. **Genres:** Language/ Linguistics, Literary criticism and history, Translations. **Career:** Duke University, Durham, NC, instructor, 1980-83, lecturer, 1985-89, assistant professor, 1989-95, associate professor of the practice of Slavics, 1995-. University of Virginia, instructor, 1982; North Carolina State University, lecturer in Japanese, 1987-88; contract conference interpreter of Russian, 1989-. **Publications:** (with E. Andrews, J. Van Tuyl, E. Maksimova, and I. Dolgova) S mesta v kar'er: Leaping into Russian: A Systematic Introduction to Contemporary Russian Grammar, 1993. TRANSLATOR FROM JAPANESE: S. Kizaki, The Phoenix Tree and Other Stories, 1990; S. Kizaki, The Sunken Temple (novel), 1993. TRANSLATOR FROM RUSSIAN: T. Lahusen, V. Garros, and N. Korbanevskaya, eds., Intimacy and Terror: Soviet Diaries of the 1930s, 1995; G. Ivanova, Labor Camp Socialism: The Gulag in the Soviet Totalitarian System, 2000. Contributor of articles and translations to periodicals. **Address:** Box 90259, Slavic, Duke University, Durham, NC 27708, U.S.A. **Online address:** flath@acpub.duke.edu

FLAYHART, William Henry, (III). American, b. 1944. **Genres:** History. **Career:** Delaware State University, Dover, professor of history, 1970-, department head, 1993-2000. University of Leiden, visiting professor, 1994-95; Netherlands Maritime Museum, visiting lecturer. Cunard Line and Clipper Cruises, scholar in residence, 1964-; Steamship Historical Society of America, director, 2002-. **Publications:** (with J.H. Shaum Jr.) Majesty at Sea: The Four-Stackers, 1981; (with R.W. Warwick) QE2, 1985; Counterpoint to Trafalgar: The Anglo-Russian Invasion of Naples, 1805-1806, 1992; The American Line, 2000; Perils of the Atlantic, 2003. **Address:** 39 Stuart Dr, Dover, DE 19901, U.S.A. **Online address:** wFlayhar@dseu.edu

FLEETWOOD, Hugh (Nigel). British, b. 1944. **Genres:** Novels, Plays/Screenplays, Novellas/Short stories. **Career:** Writer, 1972-. **Publications:** NOVELS: A Painter of Flowers, 1972; The Girl Who Passed for Normal, 1973; Foreign Affairs, 1973, 1974; A Conditional Sentence, 1974; A Picture of Innocence, 1975; The Order of Death, 1976; An Artist and a Magician, 1977; Roman Magic, 1978; The Beast, 1978, 1979; The Godmother, 1979; The Redeemer, 1979; A Young Fair God, 1982; Paradise, 1986; The Past, 1987; The Witch, 1989; The Mercy Killer, 1990; OTHER: Fictional Lives (stories), 1980; A Dance to the Glory of God (stories), 1983; (with E. de Concini and R. Faenza) Corrupt (screenplay; based on Fleetwood's novel, The Order of Death), 1984; A Dangerous Place (nonfiction), 1986; The Man Who Went Down with His Ship (stories), 1988; (with Roberto Faenza) The Bachelor (screenplay based on Schnitzler's short story). Contributor to Transatlantic Review. **Address:** Flat 3, 10 Carlingford Rd., London NW3 1RX, England.

FLEISCHMAN, Paul. American, b. 1952. **Genres:** Novellas/Short stories, Children's fiction, Young adult fiction. **Career:** Has worked as janitor, bagel baker, bookstore clerk, and proofreader. **Publications:** The Birthday Tree, 1979; The Half-a-Moon Inn, 1980; Graven Images: Three Stories, 1982; Animal Hedge, 1983; Finzel the Farsighted, 1983; Path of the Pale Horse, 1983; Phoebe Danger, Detective, in the Case of the Two-Minute Cough, 1983; Coming-and-Going Men: Four Tales of Itinerants, 1985; I Am Phoenix: Poems for Two Voices, 1985; Rear-View Mirrors, 1986; Rondo in C, 1988; Joyful Noise: Poems for Two Voices, 1988; Saturnalia, 1990; Shadow Play, 1990; The Borning Room, 1991; Time Train, 1991; Townsend's Warbler, 1992; Bull Run, 1993; Copier Creations, 1993; A Fate Totally Worse than Death, 1995; Dateline: Troy, 1996; Seedfolks, 1997; Whirligig, 1998; Weslandia, 1999; Mind's Eye, 1999; (ed.) Cannibal in the Mirror, 2000; Big Talk: Poems for Four Voices, 2000; Lost!: A Story in String, 2000; Seek, 2001; Animal Hedge, 2003; Breakout, 2003; Sidewalk Circus, 2004.

FLEISCHMAN, Paul R. American, b. 1945. **Genres:** Essays, Medicine/Health, Inspirational/Motivational Literature, Psychiatry, Theology/Religion. **Career:** Yale University School of Medicine, psychiatry residency, 1971-74, chief resident in psychiatry, 1973-74, later member of clinical faculty, supervisor of psychotherapy, and seminar leader in psychiatry and religion. Consultant to hospitals, clinics, colleges, and drug treatment centers; lecturer in religion, psychology, and psychiatry at universities; conference speaker and lecturer. Guest lecturer, Jaipur Medical College, India, and Bombay Psychiatric Society, India; Williamson Lecturer in Religion and Medicine, University of Kansas Medical School. **Publications:** Therapeutic Action of Vipassana Meditation (essays), 1986; Why I Sit, 1986; Healing the Healer and the Experience of Impermanence (essays), 1991; Spiritual Aspects of Psychiatric Practice, 1993; The Healing Spirit, 1990, rev. ed., 1994; Cultivating Inner Peace, 1997; Karma & Chaos, 1999. Contributor to periodicals. **Address:** 1394 South East St, Amherst, MA 01002, U.S.A.

FLEISCHMAN, (Albert) Sid(ney). American, b. 1920. **Genres:** Novels, Children's fiction, Plays/Screenplays, Autobiography/Memoirs. **Career:** Magician in vaudeville and night clubs, 1938-41; San Diego Daily Journal, reporter, 1949-50; Point mag., San Diego, associate editor, 1950-51. **Publications:** The Straw Donkey Case, 1948; Murder's No Accident, 1949; Shanghai Flame, 1951; Look Behind You, Lady (in U.K. as Chinese Crimson), 1952; Danger in Paradise, 1953; Counterspy Express, 1954; Malay Woman (in U.K. as Malayan Manhunt), 1954; Blood Alley (novel and screenplay), 1955; Good-bye My Lady (screenplay), 1956; Lafayette Escadrille (screenplay), 1958; Yellowleg, 1960; The Deadly Companions (screenplay), 1961; The Abracadabra Kid, a Writer's Life, 1996. CHILDREN'S FICTION: Mr. Mysterious and Company, 1962; By the Great Horn Spoon!, 1963, as Bullwhip Griffin, 1967; The Ghost in the Noonday Sun, 1965; McBroom series, 9 vols., 1966-80; Chancy and the Grand Rascal, 1966; Longbeard the Wizard, 1970; Jingo Django, 1971; The Wooden Cat Man, 1972; The Ghost on a Saturday Night, 1974; Mr. Mysterious's Secret of Magic (in U.K. as Secrets of Magic), 1975; Me and the Man on the Moon-Eyed Horse, 1977; Humbug Mountain, 1978; The Hey Hey Man, 1979; The Case of the Cackling Ghost (Princess Tomorrow, Flying Clock, Secret Message), 4 vols., 1981; The Case of the 264-Pound Burglar, 1982; McBroom's Almanac, 1984; The Whipping

Boy, 1986; The Scarebird, 1988; Midnight Horse, 1990; Jim Ugly, 1992; The 13th Floor, 1995; Bandit's Moon, 1998; McBroom's Ghost, 1998; McBroom Tells the Truth, 1998; A Carnival of Animals, 2000; Bo and Mzzz Mad, 2001; Disappearing Act, 2003.

FLEISCHNER, Jennifer. American, b. 1956. **Genres:** Children's non-fiction, Literary criticism and history, Young adult non-fiction, Biography. **Career:** Dover Publications Inc., publicity director, 1977-78; State University of New York at Albany, lecturer, 1986-88, assistant professor, 1988-96, associate professor of English, 1996-, director of undergraduate studies, 1996-, affiliated faculty member in women's studies, 1988-, Diversity Lecturer, 1995. College of Mount St. Vincent, visiting assistant professor, 1989-90; Hartwick College, Babcock Lecturer, 1992; Harvard University, Andrew W. Mellon faculty fellow in Afro-American studies, 1993-94; Columbia University, visiting scholar in English, 1994-95. **Publications:** FOR YOUNG READERS: The Inuit: People of the Arctic, 1995; The Dred Scott Case: Testing the Right to Live Free, 1996; I Was Born a Slave: The Life of Harriet Jacobs as Told in Her Own Words, 1997. FOR ADULTS: Book Group Guide to the Work of Barbara Kingsolver, 1994; Book Group Guide to the Work of Louise Erdrich, 1995; Book Group Guide to the Work of Doris Lessing, 1995; Mastering Slavery: Memory, Family, and Identity in Women's Slave Narratives, 1996; Mrs. Lincoln and Mrs. Keckly: The Remarkable Story of the Friendship between a First Lady and a Former Slave, 2003. EDITOR & CONTRIBUTOR: The American Experience, 1990; The Apaches: People of the Southwest, 1994; Scholastic Encyclopedia of American Presidents, 1994; (with S.O. Weisser) Feminist Nightmares: Women at Odds, Feminism and the Problem of Sisterhood, 1994. Contributor to books. Contributor of articles and reviews to magazines.

FLEISHER, Paul. American, b. 1948. **Genres:** Children's non-fiction, Education, Natural history, Young adult non-fiction, Essays. **Career:** Teacher at public schools in Providence, RI, 1970-72, Petersburg, VA, 1975-76, and Williamsburg, VA, 1976-78; Richmond Public Schools, Richmond, VA, teacher in programs for the gifted, 1978-; Virginia Commonwealth University, instructor, 1981-86; Johns Hopkins University, Center for Talented Youth, adjunct member of faculty, 1989-90; University of Richmond Adult Continuing Studies, instructor, 1998-. **Publications:** Secrets of the Universe, 1987; Understanding the Vocabulary of the Nuclear Arms Race, 1988; Write Now!, 1989; Tanglers, 1991; (with P. Keeler) Looking Inside (juvenile), 1991; Changing Our World: A Handbook for Young Activists, 1993; Ecology A-Z, 1994; Our Oceans: Experiments and Activities in Marine Science, 1995; Life Cycles of a Dozen Diverse Creatures, 1996; Brain Food: Games That Teach Kids to Think, 1997; Tanglers Too, 1998; Ice Cream Treats: The Inside Scoop, 2000; Gorilla, 2000; Ants, 2002; 21st Century Writing, 2003. WEBS OF LIFE SERIES: Tide Pool, Coral Reef, Saguaro Cactus, Oak Tree, 1997; Salt Marsh, Pond, Alpine Meadow, Mountain Stream, 1998. Contributor to magazines. **Address:** 2781 Beowulf Ct, Richmond, VA 23231, U.S.A. **Online address:** pfleishe@earthlink.net

FLEISHMAN, Avrom. American, b. 1933. **Genres:** Film, Literary criticism and history, Social commentary. **Career:** Instructor, Columbia University, NYC, 1958-59, and Hofstra University, Hempstead, NY, 1960-63; Assistant Professor, University of Minnesota, Minneapolis, 1963-66, and Michigan State University, East Lansing, 1966-67; Professor of English, Johns Hopkins University, Baltimore, MD, 1970-99 (Associate Professor, 1968-70). **Publications:** A Reading of Mansfield Park: An Essay in Critical Synthesis, 1967; Conrad's Politics: Community and Anarchy in the Fiction of Joseph Conrad, 1967; The English Historical Novel: Walter Scott to Virginia Woolf, 1971; Virginia Woolf: A Critical Reading, 1975; Fiction and the Ways of Knowing: Essays on British Novels, 1978; Figures of Autobiography: The Language of Self-Writing in Victorian and Modern England, 1983; Narrated Films: Storytelling Situations in Cinema History, 1992; The Condition of English: Literary Studies in a Changing Culture, 1998; New Class Culture: How an Emergent Class Is Transforming America's Culture, 2002. **Address:** 1123 Bellemore Rd, Baltimore, MD 21210, U.S.A.

FLEISHMAN, Lazar. American (born Ukraine), b. 1944. **Genres:** Literary criticism and history. **Career:** Hebrew University, Jerusalem, senior lecturer, 1974-81, associate professor of comparative literature and Slavic studies, 1981-85; Stanford University, Stanford, CA, professor of Slavic studies, 1985-, chair of department, 1992-94, writer. Visiting professor of Slavic studies at universities in the US, Russia, Latvia, and the Czech Republic. **Publications:** Stat'i o Pasternake (Essays on Pasternak), 1977; Boris Pasternak v dvadtsatye gody (Boris Pasternak in the '20s), 1981; (ed. with R. Hughes and O. Raevsky) Russkii Berlin, 1921-1923 (Russian Berlin), 1983; Boris Pasternak v tridtsatye gody (Boris Pasternak in the '30s), 1984; Poetry and Revolution in Russia, 1905-1930: An Exhibition of Books and

Manuscripts, 1989; Boris Pasternak: The Poet and His Politics, 1990; Materialy po istorii russkoi i svoetskoi kul'tury: Iz arkhiva Guverovskogo Instituta (From the History of Russian and Soviet Culture: Out of the Hoover Institution Archives), 1992; (with H.B. Harder S. Dorzweiler) Boris Pasternak's Lehrjahre, 1996; (with I. Abyzov and B. Ravdin) Russkaia pechat' v Rige (Russian Press in Riga, vols. 1-5), 1997; V tiskakh pzvokatsii: Opezatisch Trest I zusskaia zazubezhraia pechat, 2003. **Address:** Slavic Dept, Stanford University, Stanford, CA 94305, U.S.A.

FLEISSNER, Robert F. Also writes as Archibald Harris. American, b. 1932. **Genres:** Literary criticism and history. **Career:** Spring Hill College, Mobile, AL, instructor in English, speech, and drama, 1958-59; Ohio State University, Columbus, assistant instructor in English, 1960-61; City College of the City University of New York, lecturer in English, 1962-64; Dominican College, Blauvelt, NY, assistant professor of English, 1964-66; University of New Mexico, Albuquerque, instructor in English, 1966-67; Central State University, Wilberforce, OH, assistant professor to associate professor of English, 1967-. **Publications:** Dickens and Shakespeare, 1965; Resolved to Love, 1980; The Prince and the Professor, 1986; Ascending the Prufrockian Stair, 1988; A Rose by Another Name, 1989; Shakespeare and the Matter of the Crux, 1991; T.S. Eliot and the Heritage of Africa, 1992; Frost's Road Taken, 1996; (ed.) E.M. Fleissner, The Magic Key, 1996; Sources, Meaning, and Influences of Coleridge's "Kubla Khan," 2000; Names, Titles & Characters by Literary Writers, 2001; The Master Sleuth on the Trail of "Edwin Drood," 2002; Shakespearean and Other Literary Investigations with the Master Sleuth (and Conan Doyle), 2003; Shakespeare and Africa, 2005. **Address:** Dept of Humanities, Box 1004, Central State University, Wilberforce, OH 45384, U.S.A.

FLEM, Lydia. Belgian. **Genres:** Psychology. **Career:** Psychoanalyst and author. **Publications:** La vie quotidienne de Freud et ses patients (title means: The Daily Life of Freud and his Patients), 1986; L'homme Freud (title means: Freud the Man), 1991; Casanova, ou, L'exercise du bonheur, 1995, trans. by C. Temerson as Casanova: The Man Who Really Loved Women, 1997. **Address:** c/o Farrar Straus & Giroux, 19 Union Sq. W., New York, NY 10003, U.S.A.

FLEM-ATH, Rand. Canadian. **Genres:** Archaeology/Antiquities. **Career:** Writer, researcher, and librarian. **Publications:** (with R. Flem-Ath) When the Sky Fell: In Search of Atlantis, 1995; (with C. Wilson) The Atlantis Blueprint: Unlocking the Ancient Mysteries of a Long Lost Civilization, 2000. **Address:** c/o Author Mail, Delacorte Press, Bantam Dell Publishing Group, 1540 Broadway, New York, NY 10036, U.S.A. **Online address:** oncetherewasaway@hotmail.com

FLEMING, Alice (Carew Mulcahey). American, b. 1928. **Genres:** Children's fiction, Children's non-fiction, Social commentary. **Publications:** The Key to New York, 1960; Wheels, 1960; A Son of Liberty, 1961; Doctors in Petticoats, 1964; Great Women Teachers, 1965; The Senator from Maine, 1969; Alice Freeman Palmer: Pioneer College President, 1970; Reporters at War, 1970; General's Lady, 1971; Highways into History, 1971; Pioneers in Print, 1971; Ida Tarbell: First of the Muckrakers, 1971; Psychiatry: What's It All About?, 1972; Nine Months: An Intelligent Woman's Guide to Pregnancy, 1972; The Moviemakers, 1973; Trials That Made Headlines, 1974; Contraception, Abortion, Pregnancy, 1974; New on the Beat, 1975; Alcohol: The Delightful Poison, 1975; Something for Nothing, 1978; The Mysteries of ESP, 1980; What to Say When You Don't Know What to Say, 1982; Welcome to Grossville, 1985; The King of Prussia and a Peanut Butter Sandwich, 1988; George Washington Wasn't Always Old, 1991; What, Me Worry? How to Hang in When Your Problems Stress You Out, 1992; P.T. Barnum: The World's Greatest Showman, 1993; A Century of Service, 1997; Frederick Douglass: From Slave to Statesman, 2004. EDITOR: Hosannah the Home Run!, 1972; America Is Not All Traffic Lights, 1976. **Address:** c/o Raines & Raines, 103 Kenyon Rd, Medusa, NY 12120-1404, U.S.A.

FLEMING, Anne. British, b. 1928. **Genres:** Mystery/Crime/Suspense, Literary criticism and history, Medicine/Health. **Career:** Freelance writer, c. 1984-; founder of the Old Forge Press. Serves on the editorial board of the Byron Journal. **Publications:** NONFICTION: Bright Darkness: The Poetry of Lord Byron Presented in the Context of His Life and Times, 1984; In Search of Byron in England and Scotland, 1988; The Myth of the Bad Lord Byron, 1998. EDITOR: (and comp.) U. Fleming, The Desert and the Marketplace: Writings, Letters, Journals, 1995; (and comp. with C. Horrigan) The Fleming Method of Relaxation for Concentration, Stress Management, and Pain Relief: For Doctors, Nurses, and Therapists, 1996. CRIME NOVELS: There Goes Charlie, 1990; Sophie Is Gone, 1994; Death and Deconstruction, 1995; This Means Mischief, 1996. Contributor of articles and reviews to periodicals periodicals. **Address:** Cuckfield, Sussex, England.

FLEMING, Candace. American, b. 1962. **Genres:** Children's fiction. **Career:** Writer, 1990-. Harper College, Liberal Arts Department, Palatine, IL, adjunct professor, 1997-. **Publications:** Professor Fergus Fahrenheit and His Wonderful Weather Machine, 1994; Women of the Lights, 1996; Madame LaGrande and Her So High, to the Sky, Uproarious Pompadour, 1996; Gabriella's Song, 1997; Westward Ho, Carlotta!, 1998; The Hatmaker's Sign, 1998; When Agnes Caws, 1999; A Big Cheese for the White House, 1999; Who Invited You, 2001; Muncha! Muncha! Muncha!, 2002; Ben Franklin's Almanac: Being a True Account of the Good Gentlemen's Life, 2003; Boxes for Kathe, 2003; Smile, Lily!, 2004; Gator Gumbo, 2004; This Is the Baby, 2004. Contributor to magazines.

FLEMING, Jacky. British, b. 1955. **Genres:** Women's studies and issues, Cartoons, Humor/Satire. **Career:** Cartoonist. Cartoons represented in exhibitions. **Publications:** Be a Bloody Train Driver, 1991; Never Give Up, 1992; Falling in Love, 1993; Dear Katie 1994; Hello Boys, 1996. Contributor of cartoons to periodicals.

FLEMING, James Rodger. American, b. 1949. **Genres:** Environmental sciences/Ecology, History, Meteorology/Atmospheric sciences, Technology, Bibliography. **Career:** National Center for Atmospheric Research, Cloud Physics Division, meteorologist, 1973; University of Washington, Seattle, research meteorologist, 1973-74; private consulting meteorologist in Miami, FL, and NY, 1974-82; Smithsonian Institution, Washington, DC, fellow, Papers of Joseph Henry, 1985-87; American Meteorological Society, historical consultant, 1987-; Colby College, Waterville, ME, assistant professor, associate professor, then professor and director of science, technology, and society program, 1988-. Harvard University, history of science, research associate, 1992-93, visiting scholar, 1999-2000; Massachusetts Institute of Technology, visiting scholar, 1992-94; Pennsylvania State University, Center for Global Change Science, visiting professor, 1994; lecturer at colleges and universities. **Publications:** Guide to Historical Resources in the Atmospheric Sciences, 1989; Meteorology in America, 1800-1870, 1990; Historical Perspectives on Climate Change, 1998. EDITOR: (with H.A. Gemery) Science, Technology, and the Environment, 1994; (with R.E. Goodman, and contrib.) International Bibliography of Meteorology, 1994; (and contrib.) Historical Essays on Meteorology, 1919-1995, 1996; Weathering the Storm: Sverre Petterssen, the D-Day Forecast and the Rise of Modern Meteorology, 2001. Contributor to books. Contributor of articles and reviews to professional journals. **Address:** Science, Technology, and Society Program, Colby College, Waterville, ME 04901, U.S.A. **Online address:** jfleming@colby.edu

FLEMING, Justin. (born Australia), b. 1953. **Genres:** Documentaries/Reportage. **Career:** Office of the Attorney General, Sydney, New South Wales, Australia, judge's associate, 1974-79; Office of the Commonwealth Crown Solicitor, Sydney, New South Wales, Australia, legal officer, 1979-80; barrister at law in Sydney, New South Wales, Australia, 1980-92, and in Dublin Ireland, 1992. Called to the Bar at King's Inns, Ireland, 1992. Australian National Playwrights' Conference, board member. **Publications:** Hammer (play), 1981; Indian Summer (play), 1982; (Lyricist, with Stephen Edwards and Jonathan Alver) Crystal Balls (opera), 1995; Burnt Piano (play), 1998; Harold in Italy (play) 1998; The Cobra (play), 1998. (Lyricist) Tess of the d'Urbervilles (musical play), 1999; Coup d'Etat (play), 2002; Barbarism to Verdict (documentary television series), 2002. **Address:** 110 High St., North Sydney, New South Wales 2060, Australia.

FLEMING, Kate. British, b. 1946. **Genres:** Biography. **Publications:** The Churchills, Weidenfeld & Nicolson, 1975; Celia Johnson, Weidenfeld & Nicolson, 1991. **Address:** Andrew Hewson, 45 Clerkenwell Green, London EC1R 0EB, England.

FLEMING, Keith. American, b. 1960. **Genres:** History. **Career:** Writer, editor, and journalist. Served as editor of Chicago Literary Review. **Publications:** The Boy with a Thorn in His Side: A Memoir, 2000; Original Youth: The Real Story of Edmund White's Boyhood, 2003. **Address:** c/o Author Mail, HarperCollins Publishers, 10 East 53rd St., 7th Floor, New York, NY 10022, U.S.A.

FLEMING, Robert E. American, b. 1936. **Genres:** Literary criticism and history. **Career:** Teacher at a junior high school in Rockford, IL, 1959-60, and a high school, Rockford, 1960-64; University of New Mexico, Albuquerque, assistant professor, 1967-71, associate professor, 1971-76, professor of English, 1976-, associate dean, College of Arts and Sciences, 1988-. National Endowment for the Humanities-New Mexico Humanities Council, lecturer, 1978, 1980, 1985; lecturer at Gorky Institute, Moscow State University, and Kuban State University, 1993. **Publications:** Willard Motley, 1978; James Weldon Johnson and Arma Wendell Bontemps: A Reference Guide, 1978; Sinclair Lewis: A Reference Guide, 1980; Charles F. Lummis, 1981; James Weldon Johnson, 1987; The Face in the Mirror: Hemingway's Writers, 1994. Contributor of articles and reviews to academic journals. **Address:** Department of English, Humanities 217, University of New Mexico, Albuquerque, NM 87131, U.S.A.

FLEMING, Sally. *See* **WALKER, Sally M(acArt).**

FLEMING, Thomas. Also writes as Christopher Cain. American, b. 1927. **Genres:** Novels, History, Biography. **Career:** Full-time writer, 1961-. Cosmopolitan Magazine, associate ed., 1954, executive ed., 1958-61; Society of Magazine Writers, president, 1967-68; American Revolution Round Table, chairman, 1970-81; PEN, American Center, president, 1971-73. **Publications:** HISTORY: Now We Are Enemies, 1960; Beat the Last Drum, 1963; One Small Candle, 1964; West Point: The Man and Times of the U.S. Military Academy, 1969; The Forgotten Victory, 1973; 1776: Year of Illusions, 1975; New Jersey, 1977; The First Stroke, 1978; The Living Land of Lincoln, 1980; Downright Fighting: The Story of Cowpens, 1989; Liberty!: The American Revolution, 1997; Lights along the Way, 1999; Duel: Alexander Hamilton, Aaron Burr and the Future of America, 1999; The New Dealer's War: FDR and the War within World War II. NOVELS: All Good Men, 1961; The God of Love, 1963; King of the Hill, 1966; A Cry of Whiteness, 1967; Romans, Countrymen, Lovers, 1969; The Sandbox Tree, 1970; The Good Shepherd, 1974; Liberty Tavern, 1976; Rulers of the City, 1977; Promises to Keep, 1978; A Passionate Girl, 1979; The Officers' Wives, 1981; Dreams of Glory, 1983; The Spoils of War, 1984; Time and Tide, 1987; Over There, 1992; Loyalties: A Novel of World War II, 1994; Remember the Morning, 1997; The Wages of Fame, 1998; Hours of Gladness, 1999; When This Cruel War Is Over, 2001. BIOGRAPHY: First in Their Hearts, 1967; The Man from Monticello, 1969; The Man Who Dared the Lightning, 1971. EDITOR: Affectionately Yours, George Washington, 1967; Benjamin Franklin: A Biography in His Own Words, 1972. **Address:** 315 E 72nd St, New York, NY 10021-4625, U.S.A. **Online address:** TFlem37048@aol.com

FLEMING, Virginia (Edwards). American, b. 1923. **Genres:** Poetry, Children's fiction, Young adult fiction, Songs/Lyrics and libretti. **Career:** Writer. First Presbyterian Church, Pitman, NJ, nursery school teacher, 1973-83, deacon, 1976-80. **Publications:** So Tender the Spirit (poetry), 1985; Wellspring (poetry), 1986; Be Good to Eddie Lee, 1993. Contributor of stories and poems anthologies. **Address:** 516 McKinley Ave, Pitman, NJ 08071, U.S.A. **Online address:** nutool@juno.com

FLESCHER, Irwin. American, b. 1926. **Genres:** Human relations/Parenting, Psychology. **Career:** Clinical Psychologist, private practice, New York, 1959-. Counseling Psychologist, New York State Dept. of Labor, 1952-55; Psychologist, Bureau of Child Guidance, NYC, 1955-58; School and Research Psychologist, East Williston Public Schools, New York, 1960-86; Adjunct Associate Professor, Long Island University, New York, 1971-74. **Publications:** Children in the Learning Factory: The Search for a Humanizing Teacher, 1972; Wearing Thin: Rhymes from the Diet Jungle, 2001. **Address:** 33 Canterbury Lane, Roslyn Heights, NY 11577, U.S.A.

FLETCHER, Colin. American (born Wales), b. 1922. **Genres:** Poetry, Natural history, Recreation, Sports/Fitness, Travel/Exploration, Biography. **Career:** Served (from Marine to Captain) in the Royal Marines, 1940-47; Hotel Manager, Kenya, 1947-48; Farmer, Kenya, 1948-52; Prospector, Canada, 1954-56; Santa Claus, San Francisco dept. store, 1956; Janitor, Head Janitor, San Francisco hospital, 1957-58. **Publications:** The Thousand-Mile Summer, 1964; The Man Who Walked through Time, 1968; The Complete Walker, 1968; The Winds of Mara, 1973; The New Complete Walker, 1974; The Man from the Cave, 1981; The Complete Walker III, 1984; The Secret Worlds of Colin Fletcher, 1989; River: One Man's Journey down the Colorado, Source to Sea, 1997. **Address:** c/o Brandt and Hochner, 1501 Broadway, New York, NY 10036, U.S.A.

FLETCHER, John Walter James. British, b. 1937. **Genres:** Humanities, Literary criticism and history, Translations. **Career:** University of Toulouse, lecturer in English, 1961-64; University of Durham, lecturer in French, 1964-66; University of East Anglia, Norwich, lecturer in French, 1966-68, reader in French, 1968-69, professor of European and comparative literature, 1969-98, pro-vice-chancellor, 1974-79; University of Kent, Canterbury, honorary senior research fellow, 1998-. Calder & Boyars, London, Critical Appraisals series, editor, 1974-79. **Publications:** The Novels of Samuel Beckett, 1964, rev. ed., 1970; Samuel Beckett's Art, 1967; A Critical Commentary on Flaubert's Trois Contes, 1968; New Directions in Literature, 1968; (with R. Federman) Samuel Beckett: His Works and His Critics, 1970; (with J. Spurling) Beckett: A Study of His Plays, 1972, 3rd ed., 1985; Claude

Simon and Fiction Now, 1975; (with B. Fletcher) A Student's Guide to the Plays of Samuel Beckett, 1978; Novel and Reader, 1980; Alain Robbe-Grillet, 1983; (with C. Bove) Iris Murdoch: A Descriptive Primary and Annotated Secondary Bibliography, 1994; Samuel Beckett: A Faber Critical Guide, 2000; About Beckett: The Playwright and the Work, 2003. EDITOR: (with B. Fletcher) Samuel Beckett: Fin de partie, 1970; Samuel Beckett: Waiting for Godot, 1971; Forces in Modern French Drama, 1972. TRANSLATOR: (with B. Fletcher) C. Simon, The Georgics, 1989; (with B. Fletcher) J.-C. Favez, The Red Cross and the Holocaust, 1999; J.-P. Boule, Herve Guibert, Voices of the Self, 1999. **Address:** School of European Culture and Languages, University of Kent, Canterbury CT2 7NF, England. **Online address:** J.W.J.Fletcher@kent.ac.uk

FLETCHER, Ralph. American, b. 1953. **Genres:** Children's fiction, Poetry, Education. **Career:** Educational consultant, 1985-; author, 1990-. **Publications:** FOR CHILDREN: Fig Pudding, 1995; A Writer's Notebook: Unlocking the Writer Within You, 1996; Twilight Comes Twice, 1997; Spider Boy, 1997; Flying Solo, 1998; Live Writing: Breathing Life into Your Words, 1999. POETRY: Water Planet: Poems About Water, 1991; I Am Wings: Poems About Love, 1994; Ordinary Things: Poems from a Walk in Early Spring, 1996; Buried Alive: The Elements of Love, 1996; Room Enough for Love, 1998; Relatively Speaking: Poems About Family, 1999. OTHER: Walking Trees: Teaching Teachers in the NYC Schools, 1990; Walking Trees: Portraits of Teachers and Children in the Culture of Schools, 1995; What a Writer Needs, 1993; Breathing In, Breathing Out: Keeping a Writer's Notebook, 1996; (with J. Portalupi) Craft Lessons: Teaching Writing K8, 1998. **Address:** 6 Caverno Dr, Durham, NH 03824, U.S.A. **Online address:** fletcher17@earthlink.net

FLETCHER, Richard Alexander. *See* Obituaries.

FLETCHER, Susan (Clemens). American, b. 1951. **Genres:** Children's fiction. **Career:** Campbell-Mithun, Minneapolis, MN, and Denver, CO, media buyer, 1974-77, advertising copywriter, 1977-79; writer. **Publications:** The Haunting Possibility (mystery), 1988; Dragon's Milk (fantasy), 1989; The Stuttgart Nanny Mafia (novel), 1991; Flight of the Dragon Kyn (fantasy), 1993; Sign of the Dove (fantasy), 1996; Shadow Spinner (novel), 1998; Walk across the Sea (novel), 2001. Contributor to periodicals. **Address:** 32475 Armitage Rd, Wilsonville, OR 97070, U.S.A.

FLEURANT, Gerdes. American (born Haiti), b. 1939. **Genres:** Mythology/Folklore. **Career:** Salem State College, Salem, MA, professor of sociology, 1971-93; Wellesley College, Wellesley, MA, associate professor of music, 1993-, also chairperson of department and director of multicultural planning and policy. Vodun priest. **Publications:** Dancing Spirits: Rhythms and Rituals of Haitian Vodun, the Rada Rite, 1996. **Address:** Department of Music, Wellesley College, Wellesley, MA 02481, U.S.A. **Online address:** GFleurant@wellesley.edu

FLEW, Antony (Garrard Newton). British, b. 1923. **Genres:** Education, Philosophy, Psychology. **Career:** Emeritus Professor, University of Reading, 1983- (Professor of Philosophy, 1973-82). Professor, University of Keele, Staffs, 1954-72; Professor, University of Calgary, Alberta, 1972-73; Professor of Philosophy, York University, Toronto, 1983-85; Distinguished Research Fellow, Social Philosophy and Policy Center, Bowling Green State University, Ohio, 1986-91. **Publications:** A New Approach to Psychical Research, 1953; Hume's Philosophy of Belief, 1961; God and Philosophy, 1966; Evolutionary Ethics, 1967; An Introduction to Western Philosophy, 1971; Crime or Disease?, 1973; Thinking about Thinking, 1975; Sociology, Equality, and Education, 1976; The Presumption of Atheism, 1976; A Rational Animal, 1978; The Politics of Procrustes, 1981; Darwinian Evolution, 1984; David Hume: Philosopher of Moral Science, 1986; The Logic of Mortality, 1987; Power to the Parents: Reversing Educational Decline, 1987; Equality in Liberty and Justice, 1989; Thinking about Social Thinking, 1992; Atheistic Humanism, 1993; Shepard's Warning: Putting Schools Back on Course, 1994; Philosophic Essays, 1998; How to Think Straight, 1998; Social Life and Moral Judgment, 2003. EDITOR: Malthus on Population, 1971; Dictionary of Philosophy, 1979. **Address:** 26 Alexandra Rd, Reading RG1 5PD, England.

FLICKENGER, Rob. American. **Genres:** Communications/Media. **Career:** Computer systems administrator, writer, and editor. NDA, Burlingame, CA, Unix administrator, 1998-2000; O'Reilly & Associates, Sebastopol, CA, Internet systems administrator, 2000-02; freelance writer and editor, 2003-. Cofounded and operated independent Web services and consulting company, Las Vegas, NV, 1995-98; speaker at conferences, 2001-02; founder of NoCat. net. **Publications:** Building Wireless Community Networks: Implementing the Wireless Web, 2002, 2nd edition, 2003; Linux Server Hacks: 100 Industrial-Strength Tips and Tools, 2003; Wireless Hacks: 100 Industrial-Strength Tips and Tools, 2003. Contributor of articles to periodicals. **Address:** c/o Author Mail, O'Reilly Books, 1005 Gravenstein Hwy. N, Sebastopol, CA 95472, U.S.A. **Online address:** rob@oreillynet.com

FLIEGER, Verlyn. American, b. 1933. **Genres:** Young adult fiction, Literary criticism and history. **Career:** University of Maryland at College Park, professor of English, 1976-. **Publications:** Splintered Light, 1983, rev. ed., 2002; A Question of Time: J.R.R. Tolkien's Road to Faerie, 1997; Pig Tale, 2002. **Address:** 10221 Meredith Ave, Silver Spring, MD 20910, U.S.A. **Online address:** vf6@umail.umd.edu

FLIER, Michael S. American, b. 1941. **Genres:** Cultural/Ethnic topics, Language/Linguistics. **Career:** University of California, Los Angeles, assistant professor of Slavic languages, 1968-73, associate professor, 1973-79, chairman of dept., 1978-84, 1987-89, professor, 1979-91; Harvard University, Oleksandr Potebnja Professor of Ukrainian Philology, 1991-, chairman of Dept of Linguistics, 1994-98, chairman of Dept of Slavic Languages and Literatures, 1999-, director of Ukrainian Research Institute. Visiting professor at US colleges and universities. **Publications:** Aspects of Nominal Determination in Old Church Slavic, 1974; Slavic Forum: Essays in Linguistics and Literature, 1974; Say It in Russian, 1982. EDITOR: American Contributions to the Ninth International Congress of Slavists 1983, vol. I: Linguistics, 1983; (with H. Birnbaum) Medieval Russian Culture, 1984; (with R.D. Brecht) Issues in Russian Morphosyntax, 1985; (with A. Timberlake) The Scope of Slavic Aspect, 1985; (with D.S. Worth) Slavic Linguistics, Poetics, Cultural History, 1985; (with S. Karlinsky) Language, Literature, Linguistics: In Honor of Francis J. Whitfield, 1987; (with D. Rowland) Medieval Russian Culture, vol. II, 1994; (with R.P. Hughes) For SK: In Celebration of the Life and Career of Simon Karlinsky, 1994; (with H. Birnbaum) The Language and Verse of Russia: In Honor of Dean S. Worth, 1995; Ukrainian Philogy and Linguistics, 1996; (with H. Andersen) Francis J. Whitfield, Old Church Slavic Reader, 2004. **Address:** Dept. of Slavic Languages and Literatures, Harvard University, Barker Center, 12 Quincy St, Cambridge, MA 02138, U.S.A. **Online address:** flier@fas.harvard.edu

FLINDERS, Neil J. American, b. 1934. **Genres:** Education, Human relations/Parenting, Speech/Rhetoric, Theology/Religion. **Career:** Seminary Principal, 1960-62, Institute Instructor, and Teacher Trainer, 1963-67; 1968-70, Church of Jesus Christ of the Latter Day Saints, Provo, Utah; Director of Research and Long Range Planning Church Educational System, Salt Lake City, 1969-79; Professor of Education, Brigham Young University, Provo, Utah, 1979-95. **Publications:** Personal Communications: How to Understand and Be Understood, 1966; Leadership and Human Relations: A Handbook for Parents, Teachers and Executives, 1969; Continue in Prayer, 1975; Moral Perspective and Educational Practice, 1979; A Piece of Cowardice, 1982; My Decision: An Act of Faith or A Piece of Cowardice, 1984; Teach the Children: An Agency Approach to Education, 1990. Author of professional articles related to the foundations and philosophy of education. **Address:** 4326 No. 900 W, Pleasant Grove, UT 84062, U.S.A.

FLINN, Kelly. American, b. 1971. **Genres:** Autobiography/Memoirs. **Career:** United States Air Force, lieutenant, until 1997. Also an assistant at the Air Force Academy and a soccer coach. **Publications:** Proud to Be: My Life, the Air Force, the Controversy, 1997. **Address:** c/o Random House, 1745 Broadway, New York, NY 10019, U.S.A. **Online address:** kjfdefense@aol.com

FLINT, Betty Margaret. Canadian, b. 1920. **Genres:** Psychology. **Career:** Professor Emerita, Institute of Child Study, OISE, University of Toronto (joined faculty, 1948). **Publications:** The Security of Infants, 1958; The Child and the Institution: A Study of Deprivation and Recovery, 1968; The Flint Infant Security Scale for Infants 3-24 Months, 1974; New Hope for Deprived Children, 1978; Pathways to Maturity: Insights from a Thirty Year Study of Deprived Children, 1996. **Address:** 25 Cumberland Ln Unit 812, Ajax, ON, Canada L1S 7K1.

FLINT, James. British, b. 1968. **Genres:** Novels. **Career:** Times of India, New Delhi, general reporter, 1988; Independent, London, England, researcher and journalist, 1994-95; Wired magazine, editor, 1995-97; freelance writer, 1997-. **Publications:** NOVELS: Habitus, 1998; 52 Ways to Magic America, 2000; The Book of Ash, 2004. SHORT STORIES: Douce Apocalypse, 2004. Contributor to periodicals. **Address:** c/o Jonny Geller, Curtis Brown, Haymarket House, 28-29 Haymarket, London SW1Y 4SP, England.

FLINT, John Edgar. Canadian, b. 1930. **Genres:** History, Third World, Biography. **Career:** King's College, University of London, Assistant Lecturer, and Reader in Colonial History, 1954-67; University of Nigeria, History Dept., Professor and Head, 1963-64; Dalhousie University, Halifax, NS, Professor of History, 1967-92, Professor Emeritus, 1992-. **Publications:** Sir George Goldie and the Making of Nigeria, 1960; Mary Kingsley: A Reassessment, 1963; Nigeria and Ghana, 1966; Books on the British Empire and Commonwealth, 1968; (ed. with G. Williams) Perspectives of Empire: Essays Presented to Gerald S. Graham, 1973; Cecil Rhodes, 1974; (ed.) Cambridge History of Africa, vol. V, 1977. **Address:** Dept. of History, Dalhousie University, Halifax, NS, Canada. **Online address:** jflint@chat.carleton.ca

FLITTER, Marc. American. **Genres:** Autobiography/Memoirs. **Career:** Neurosurgeon, Miami, FL, 1976-87; Hamot Medical Center, Erie, PA, chief of neurosurgery. **Publications:** Judith's Pavilion: The Haunting Memories of a Neurosurgeon (memoirs), 1997. **Address:** 555 S Schwartz Ave, Farmington, NM 87401-5955, U.S.A. **Online address:** maflitter@aol.com

FLOEGSTAD, Kjartan. Also writes as Kjartan Villum. Norwegian, b. 1944. **Genres:** Poetry, Novels, Translations. **Career:** Freelance writer, c. 1968-. Also worked as a sailor, industrial worker, and a reader for a publishing house. **Publications:** POETRY: Valfart (Pilgrimage), 1968; Seremoniar (Ceremonies), 1968; Dikt og spelmannsmusikk 1968-1993 (Poems and Fiddler's Music), 1993. NONFICTION: Den hemmelege jubel (The Secret Cheering), 1970; Loven vest for Pecos, og andre essays om populoer kunst og kulturindustri (The Law West of Pecos, and Other Essays on Popular Art and the Culture Industry), 1981; Ordlyden (Wording), 1983; Tyrannosaurus Text, 1988; Portrett av eit magisk liv: Poeten Claes Gill (Portrait of a Magic Life: The Poet Claes Gill), 1988; Arbeidets lys (The Light of Work), 1990; Pampa Union: Latinamerikanske reiser (travel; Pampa Union: Travels in Latin America), 1994. NOVELS: Fangliner (Mooring Lines), 1972; Rasmus, 1974; (As Kjartan Villum) Doeden ikke heller (Not Even Death), 1975; (as Villum) Ein for alle (One for All), 1976; Dalen Portland, 1977, trans. by N. Christensen as Dollar Road, 1989; Fyr og flamme (Fire and Flame), 1980; U3, 1983; Det 7. klima: Salim Mahmood i Media Thule (The Seventh Climate: Salim Mahmood in Media Thule), 1986; Kniven pa strupen (The Knife at the Throat), 1991; Fimbul, 1994. TRANSLATIONS: De tre roevarane (The Three Robbers), by J.T. Ungerer, 1973; Litteratur i revolusjonen: Dikt fra Cuba (Literature and Revolution: Poetry From Cuba), 1973; Dikt i utval (Selected Poetry), by Pablo Neruda, 1973. **Address:** Maridalsvg. 265B, 0872 Oslo 8, Norway.

FLOKOS, Nicholas. American. **Genres:** Romance/Historical. **Career:** Writer and editor. University of Pittsburgh, former writing instructor. **Publications:** Nike: A Romance, 1998. **Address:** c/o Joseph Regal, Russell & Volkening Inc., 50 West 29th St., New York, NY 10001, U.S.A.

FLOOD, (Nancy) Bo. American, b. 1945. **Genres:** Mythology/Folklore. **Career:** Center for Retarded Children, Rolling Meadows, IL, teacher and therapist, 1968; University of Hawaii-Manoa, Honolulu, assistant professor of psychology, 1971-72; University of Minnesota-Twin Cities, Minneapolis, assistant professor of psychology, 1972-74; Colorado Mountain College, Glenwood Springs, instructor in psychology, 1974-95; Northern Marianas College, Saipan, instructor in psychology, 1989-91; instructor and counselor in education, arts, and humanities, 1995-, director of programs for persons with disabilities, 1995-97. Sopris Mental Health Center, staff psychologist, 1974-81; private practitioner of child and family counseling, 1981-90. Presenter of writing and psychology workshops and lectures. **Publications:** Working Together against World Hunger, 1995; (with L. Lafferty) Born Early: A Children's Story about Premature Birth, 1995; From the Mouth of the Monster Eel: Stories from Micronesia, 1996; I'll Go to School, If..., 1996; (with M. Nuckols) The Counseling Handbook: Practical Strategies to Help Children with Common Problems, 1998; (with B.E. Strong and W. Flood) Pacific Island Legends: Tales from Micronesia, Melanesia, Polynesia, and Australia (with teacher's resource guide), 1999; Mariana Island Legends: Myth and Magic (with teacher's resource guide and children's writing curriculum), 2001; (with B.E. Strong and W. Flood) Micronesian Legends: History and Culture, 2001; My Homes and Places (therapeutic game for counselors, teachers, and children). Contributor to scientific books. Contributor of articles and short stories to children's magazines and professional journals. **Address:** Box 5534, CHRB, Saipan, MP 96950, U.S.A. **Online address:** wflood@hotmail.com

FLOOD, Pansie Hart. American, b. 1964. **Genres:** Children's fiction. **Career:** Bertie County Schools, Windsor, NC, school health educator, 1986-87; Wake County Schools, Raleigh, NC, middle school and high school teacher, 1987-88; Pitt County Schools, Greenville, NC, middle school teacher, 1988-. **Publications:** Sylvia and Miz Lula Maye, 2001; Secret Holes, 2003. **Address:** PO Box 20614, Greenville, NC 27858, U.S.A. **Online address:** floodpan@earthlink.net

FLOOD, Phoebe. *See* **WHITWORTH, John.**

FLORA, Joseph M(artin). American, b. 1934. **Genres:** Literary criticism and history. **Career:** Professor of English, University of North Carolina, Chapel Hill, 1977- (Instructor, 1962-64; Assistant Professor, 1964-67; Associate Professor, 1967-77; Assistant Dean of Grad School, 1967-72; Associate Dean, 1977-78; Chairman of Dept., 1980-91). **Publications:** Vardis Fisher, 1965; William Ernest Henley, 1970; Frederick Manfred, 1974; Hemingway's Nick Adams, 1982; Ernest Hemingway: A Study of the Short Fiction, 1989; Vardis Fisher: Centennial Essays, 2000; The Companion to Southern Literature, 2002. CO-EDITOR: Southern Writers: A Biographical Dictionary, 1979; The English Short Story 1880-1945, 1985; Fifty Southern Writers before 1900, 1987; Fifty Southern Writers after 1900, 1987; Contemporary Novelists of the South, 1993; Contemporary Poets, Dramatists, Essayists of the South, 1994. **Address:** 505 Caswell Rd, Chapel Hill, NC 27514, U.S.A.

FLORES, Ivan. American, b. 1923. **Genres:** Information science/ Computers. **Career:** President, Flores Assocs., 1960-; Pace Institute, Adjunct Professor of Information Systems, 1997-; New Jersey Institute of Technology, Professor of Computer Information Systems, 1994-; Professor of Statistics and Computer Information Science, 1968-90, Baruch College, City University of New York. Ed., Modern Data, 1968-, and Journal of Computer Languages, since 1973. Adjunct Professor of Electrical Engineering, 1958-62, and Associate Professor, 1961-63, Polytechnic Institute of Brooklyn, New York; Ed., Journal of Association for Computing Machinery, 1963-67; Adjunct Professor of Electrical Engineering, New York University, NYC, 1963-64; Associate Professor of Electrical Engineering, Stevens Institute of Technology, Hoboken, New Jersey, 1965-67. **Publications:** Computer Logic, 1960; Logic of Computer Arithmetic, 1963; Computer Software, 1965; Computer Programming, 1966; Computer Design, 1967; Computer Sorting, 1969; Computer Organization, 1969; Data Structure and Management, 1970, 1977; BAL and Assemblers, 1971; JCL and File Definition, 1971; Computer Programming, 1971; The BAL Machine, 1972; OS/MVT, 1973; Peripheral Devices, 1973; Data Base Architecture, 1981; (with C. Terry) Microcomputer Systems, 1982; Word Processing Handbook, 1982; (with A. Seidman) The Handbook of Computers and Computing, 1984; The Professional Microcomputer Handbook, 1986. **Address:** 441 Redmond Rd, South Orange, NJ 07079, U.S.A. **Online address:** ivanfs@optonline.net

FLORIDA, Richard (L.). American, b. 1957. **Genres:** Business/Trade/ Industry, Economics. **Career:** Carnegie-Mellon University, Pittsburgh, PA, director of the Center for Economic Development, and associate professor of public policy and management at H. John Heinz III School of Urban and Public Affairs and faculty member of department of engineering and public policy, 1987-. Also taught at Ohio State University. Consultant to multinational corporations and government agencies. **Publications:** The Breakthrough Illusion: Corporate America's Failure to Move from Innovation to Mass Production, 1990; Beyond Mass Production: The Japanese System and Its Transfer to the United States, 1993; (co-ed.) Industrializing Knowledge, 1999. Coauthor or editor of other books. Contributor to scholarly journals. **Address:** H. John Heinz III School of Public Policy & Management, Hamburgh Hall 250, Carnegie-Mellon University, 5000 Forbes Ave, Pittsburgh, PA 15213-3890, U.S.A. **Online address:** florida@cmu.edu

FLORY, David A. (born United States), b. 1939. **Genres:** History. **Career:** Rutgers University, New Brunswick, NJ, assistant professor, 1970-75; Opera Theater of New Jersey, artistic director, 1979-81; Middlesex County Cultural and Heritage Commission, Middlesex County, NJ, public information officer, 1983-89; Purdue University, West Lafayette, IN, began as assistant professor, became associate professor, 1989-. **Publications:** El Conde lucanor: Don Juan Manuel en su contexto histórico, 1995; Marian Representations in the Miracle Tales of Thirteenth-Century Spain and France, 2000. **Address:** 711 Hillcrest Rd, West Lafayette, IN 47906, U.S.A. **Online address:** flory@purdue.edu

FLOWERS, Ronald B(ruce). American, b. 1935. **Genres:** Law, Theology/ Religion. **Career:** Minister at a Christian church (Disciples of Christ) in Crofton, KY, 1961-63; Texas Christian University, Fort Worth, assistant professor, 1966-73, associate professor, 1973-84, professor of religion, 1984-, department head, 1990-99, John F. Weatherly Professor of Religion, 1998-. **Publications:** Religion in Strange Times: The 1960s and 1970s, 1984; That

Godless Court?: Supreme Court Decisions on Church-State Relationships, 1994; (with R.T. Miller) Toward Benevolent Neutrality: Church, State, and the Supreme Court, 1977, 5th ed., 1996; To Defend the Constitution: Religion, Conscientious Objection, Naturalization, and the Supreme Court, 2003. Contributor to books. Contributor to theology journals and religious magazines. **Address:** Department of Religion, Texas Christian University, Box 298100, Fort Worth, TX 76129, U.S.A. **Online address:** r.flowers@tcu.edu

FLOWERS, Sarah. American, b. 1952. **Genres:** Air/Space topics, Children's non-fiction, History. **Career:** Santa Clara County Library, Morgan Hill, CA, librarian, 1991-93, adult program librarian, 1995-98, community librarian, 1998-2003, deputy county librarian, 2003-; Los Gatos Public Library, Los Gatos, CA, young adult librarian, 1993-95. **Publications:** The Reformation, 1995; Sports in America, 1996; Age of Exploration, 1999; Space Exploration, 2000. **Address:** Santa Clara County Library, 1095 N 7th St, San Jose, CA 95112, U.S.A. **Online address:** sflowers@scinet.co.santa-clara.ca.us

FLOYD, John E(arl). Canadian, b. 1937. **Genres:** Economics, Money/ Finance. **Career:** University of Washington, Seattle, assistant professor, 1962-66, associate professor, 1966-70, professor of economics, 1970-71; University of Toronto, Toronto, Ontario, professor of economics, 1970-. Graduate Center of the City University of New York, visiting professor, 1973-74; Australian National University, visiting fellow, summer, 1987. **Publications:** (with P. O'Donoghue, T. Roberts, and M. Eyesenbach) Microsets, 1981; On the Dollar, 1985; World Monetary Equilibrium: International Monetary Theory in an Historical-Institutional Context, 1985; (with T.J.O. Dick) Canada and the Gold Standard, 1992. Work represented in books. Contributor to economic journals. **Address:** Department of Economics, University of Toronto, 150 St. George St, Toronto, ON, Canada M5S 3G7.

FLUEHR-LOBBAN, Carolyn. American, b. 1945. **Genres:** Anthropology/ Ethnology, Area studies. **Career:** Rhode Island College, Providence, assistant professor, 1972-78, associate professor, 1978-84, professor of anthropology, 1984-. Conducted field research in the Sudan, Egypt, and Tunisia. **Publications:** Islamic Law and Society in the Sudan, 1986; (ed.) International Perspectives on Marxist Anthropology, 1989; (ed.) Ethics and the Profession of Anthropology: Dialogue for a New Era, 1991; (with R.A. Lobban and J.O. Voll) Historical Dictionary of the Sudan, 2nd ed., 1992, 3rd ed. (with R.A. Lobban and R. Teramer), 2000; Islamic Society in Practice, 1994; (ed.) Against Islamic Extremism: The Writings of Muhammad Said al-Ashmany, 1998. Contributor to journals. **Address:** Department of Anthropology, Rhode Island College, Providence, RI 02908, U.S.A.

FLUKE, Joanne. Also writes as Jo Gibson, John Fischer, R. J. Fischer, Chris Hunter, Gina Jackson, Kathryn Kirkwood. American. **Genres:** Novels, Mystery/Crime/Suspense, Romance/Historical, Young adult fiction. **Career:** Writer. **Publications:** NOVELS. The Stepchild, 1980; The Other Child, 1983; Winter Chill, 1984; Cold Judgment, 1985; Vengeance Is Mine, 1986; Video Kill, 1989; Final Appeal, 1989; Dead Giveaway, 1990; Fatal Identity, 1993; Deadly Memories, 1995. HANNAH SWENSON MYSTERIES: Chocolate Chip Cookie Murder, 2000; Strawberry Shortcake Murder, 2001; Blueberry Muffin Murder, 2002; Lemon Meringue Pie Murder, 2003; Fudge Cupcake Murder, 2004; Sugar Cookie Murder, 2004. AS JOHN FISCHER: High Stakes, 1986; Station Break, 1987. AS CHRIS HUNTER: Eyes, 1996. ROMANCES AS GINA JACKSON: Caitlyn's Cowboy, 1999; Cookies and Kisses 2000. ROMANCES AS KATHRYN KIRKWOOD: A Match for Melissa, 1998; A Season for Samantha, 1999; A Husband for Holly, 1999; A Valentine for Vanessa, 2000; A Townhouse for Tessa, 2001. YOUNG ADULT NOVELS AS JO GIBSON: The Dead Girl, 1993; The Crush, 1994; The Crush II, 1994; Slay Bells, 1994; My Bloody Valentine, 1995; The Seance, 1996; Wicked, 1996; Dance of Death, 1996. HUMOR AS R.J. FISCHER (coauthor): Baby's Guide to Raising Mom, 1997; Doggy Do's (and Don'ts), 1997; Where Would I Be without You, Mom?, 1998. Contributor to books.

FLUSFEDER, David (L.). (born United States), b. 1960. **Genres:** Biography. **Career:** Writer and journalist. Times, London, England, TV columnist, 1993-1996; taught creative writing at Birkbeck and Morley Colleges, University of London, Arvon Foundation, and Pentonville Prison, London. Also worked as cinema manager and projectionist. **Publications:** NOVELS: Man Kills Woman, 1993; Like Plastic, 1996; Morocco, 2000; The Gift, 2003. SHORT STORIES: (contributor) Fatherhood, 1997; (contrib.) The Agony and the Ecstasy: New Writing for the World Cup, 1998; (contributor) New Writing 8, 1999. Contributor of short stories to periodicals. **Address:** c/o HarperCollins Publishers, 77-85 Fulham Palace Road, Hammersmith, London W6 8JB, England.

FLYNN, James Robert. American/New Zealander, b. 1934. **Genres:** Philosophy, Politics/Government, Psychology. **Career:** University of Otago, Dunedin, Professor, 1967-96, Emeritus Professor, Political Studies Dept., 1996-. Assistant Professor of Political Science, Eastern Kentucky State University, Richmond, 1957-61, Wisconsin State College, Whitewater, 1961-62, and Lake Forest College, Illinois, 1962-63; Lecturer to Sr. Lecturer, University of Canterbury, Christchurch, 1963-67. **Publications:** American Politics: A Radical View, 1967; Humanism and Ideology, 1973; Race, IQ, and Jensen, 1980; Asian Americans: Achievement beyond IQ, 1991; How to Defend Humane Ideals, 2000. **Address:** Dept. of Political Studies, University of Otago, PO Box 56, Dunedin, New Zealand. **Online address:** jim.flynn@stonebow.otago.ac.nz

FLYNN, Joseph. (born United States). **Genres:** Film. **Career:** Writer. Worked variously as a copywriter at advertising agencies, including Foote, Cone, & Belding; J. Walter Thompson; Doyle, Dane, Bernbach; Ogilvy & Mather; and McCann-Erickson. **Publications:** The Concrete Inquisition, 1993; Digger, 1997; The Next President, 2000. **Address:** c/o Author Mail, Bantam Books, 1745 Broadway, New York, NY 10019, U.S.A. **Online address:** josephyflynn@josephflynn.com

FLYNN, Katie. *See* TURNER, Judith.

FLYNN, Leslie Bruce. American (born Canada), b. 1918. **Genres:** Theology/Religion. **Career:** Grace Baptist Church, Nanuet, New York, pastor, 1949-89, pastor emeritus, 1989-. Regional Ed., Christian Life Magazine, 1944-89. **Publications:** Did I Say That?, 1959, 1986; Serve Him with Mirth, 1960; Your God and Your Gold, 1961; The Power of Christ-like Living, 1962; Did I Say Thanks?, 1963; Christmas Messages, 1964; Day of Resurrection, 1965; How to Save Time in the Ministry, 1966; Your Influence is Showing, 1967; You Can Live Above Envy, 1970; A Source Book of Humorous Stories, 1973; 19 Gifts of the Spirit, 1974; It's about Time, 1974, rev. ed., 1999; Now a Word from Our Creator, 1976; Great Church Fights, 1976; Man: Ruined and Restored, 1978; God's Will: You Can Know It, 1979; Joseph: God's Man in Egypt, 1979; The Gift of Joy, 1980; From Clay to Rock, 1981; You Don't Have to Go It Alone, 1981; Dare to Care Like Jesus, 1982; The Twelve, 1982; Worship, Together We Celebrate, 1983; Your Inner You, 1984; The Sustaining Power of Hope, 1985; Holy Contradictions, 1987; Come Alive with Illustrations, 1987; Jesus in the Image of God, 1987, rev. ed., 1997; What the Church Owes the Jew, 1988, rev. ed., 1998; When the Saints Come Storming In, 1988; The Other Twelve, 1988; The Miracles of Jesus, 1990; Humorous Incidents and Quips, 1990; How to Survive in the Ministry, 1992; The Four Faces of Jesus, 1993; The Master Plan of Prayer, 1995; My Daughter a Preacher, 1996. **Address:** 32 Highview Ave, Nanuet, NY 10954, U.S.A.

FLYNN, Nancy L. American, b. 1956. **Genres:** Administration/Management. **Career:** Writer, consultant, speaker. Founder and executive director, ePolicy Institute; founder, Write to Business, writing, editing, and coaching service for public and private businesses. Ohio State University, Columbus, English department and School of Journalism, adjunct writing instructor. Frequent speaker on writing for business and technology matters. **Publications:** (with Tom Flynn) Writing Effective E-mail: Improving Your Electronic Communication, 1998; The $100,000 Writer: How to Make a Six-Figure Income As a Freelance Business Writer, 2000; The ePolicy Handbook: Designing and Implementing Effective E-Mail, Internet, and Software Policies, 2001; (with Randolph Kahn) E-Mail Rules: A Business Guide to Managing Policies, Security, and Legal Issues for E-Mail and Digital Communication, 2003; Networking for Success: The Art of Establishing Personal Contacts, 2003; Instant Messaging Rules: A Business Guide to Managing Policies, Security, and Legal Issues for Safe IM Communication, 2004. **Address:** c/o Write to Business, 2300 Walhaven Ct., Suite 100A, Columbus, OH 43220, U.S.A. **Online address:** nancy@epolicyinstitute.com

FLYNN, Robert (Lopez). American, b. 1932. **Genres:** Novels, Novellas/Short stories, Humor/Satire. **Career:** Gardner-Webb College, Boiling Springs, NC, instructor, 1957-59; Baylor University, Waco, TX, assistant professor, 1959-63; Trinity University, San Antonio, professor and novelist-in-residence, TX, 1963-. **Publications:** North to Yesterday, 1967; In the House of the Lord, 1969; The Sounds of Rescue, The Signs of Hope, 1970; Seasonal Rain and Other Stories, 1986; Wanderer Springs, 1987; A Personal War in Vietnam, 1989; When I Was Just Your Age, 1992; The Last Klick, 1994; Living with the Hyenas, 1995; The Devils Tiger, 2000; Tie-Fast Country, 2001; Growing up a Sullen Baptist, 2001; Paul Baker & the Integration of Abilities, 2002; Slouching toward Zion, 2004. **Online address:** RLFlynn@earthlink.net

FLYVBJERG, Bent. (born Denmark), b. 1952. **Genres:** Design. **Career:** Development and planning educator, consultant, and author. Aalborg University, Aalborg, Denmark, professor of planning. Two-time visiting Fulbright scholar in the United States; European University Institute, Florence, Italy, visiting fellow. **Publications:** Rationality and Power: Democracy in Practice, 1998; Making Social Science Matter: Why Social Inquiry Fails and How It Can Succeed Again, 2001; (with Nils Bruzelius and Werner Rothengatter) Megaprojects and Risk: An Anatomy of Ambition, 2003. Author of various scholarly articles in English and Danish; work has been translated into Albanian, Chinese, Czech, Dutch, French, German, Hebrew, Norwegian, Polish, Portuguese, Russian, Spanish, Swedish, and Thai. **Address:** Aalborg University, Department of Development and Planning, Fibigerstraede 11, 9220 Aalborg, Denmark.

FOER, Jonathan Safran. American, b. 1977. **Genres:** Novels, Ghost Writer. **Career:** Writer. Worked as receptionist at public relation's firm, morgue assistant, jewelry salesman, farm sitter, and ghostwriter. **Publications:** (ed.) A Convergence of Birds: Original Fiction and Poetry Inspired by the Work of Joseph Cornell, 2001; Everything Is Illuminated (novel), 2002. Contributor to magazines. **Address:** c/o Nicole Aragi, 245 Eighth Ave., Box 134, New York, NY 10011, U.S.A.

FOERSTEL, Herbert N. American, b. 1933. **Genres:** Reference. **Career:** Towson State University, Towson, MD, fine arts librarian, 1959-66; University of Maryland at College Park, science librarian, head of Engineering and Physical Sciences Library, head of branch libraries, 1967-96. **Publications:** Surveillance in the Stacks: The FBI's Library Awareness Program, 1991; Secret Science: Federal Control of American Science and Technology, 1993; Banned in the USA: A Reference Guide to Book Censorship in Schools and Public Libraries, 1994, rev. ed., 2002; (with K. Foerstel) Climbing the Hill: Gender Conflict in Congress, 1996; Free Expression and Censorship in America, 1997; Banned in the Media: A Reference Guide to Censorship in the Press, Motion Pictures, Broadcasting, and the Internet, 1998; Freedom of Information and the Right to Know: The Origins and Applications of the Freedom of Information Act, 1999; From Watergate to Monicagate: Ten Controversies in Journalism and Media, 2001; Refuge of a Scoundrel: The Patriot Act in Libraries, 2004. Contributor of articles and reviews to periodicals. **Address:** 5110 W Penfield Rd, Columbia, MD 21045, U.S.A. **Online address:** foerstel@aol.com

FOERSTEL, Karen. American, b. 1965. **Genres:** Women's studies and issues, Biography. **Career:** Roll Call, Washington, DC, reporter, 1989-95; Congressional Quarterly, Washington, DC, reporter, 1995-96, 1998-; New York Post, NYC, congressional correspondent from Washington, DC, 1996-98. **Publications:** (with H.N. Foerstel) Climbing the Hill: Gender Conflict in Congress, 1996; Biographical Dictionary of Congressional Women, 1999. **Address:** The Nature Conservancy, 4245 N Fairfax Dr Ste 100, Arlington, VA 22203-1606, U.S.A.

FOGEL, Robert William. American, b. 1926. **Genres:** Business/Trade/Industry, Economics, History. **Career:** Charles R. Walgreen Professor of American Institutions, University of Chicago, 1981- (Ford Foundation Visiting Research Professor, 1963-64; Associate Professor, 1964-65; Professor of Economics, 1965-69; Professor of Economics and History, 1970-75). Instructor, Johns Hopkins University, Baltimore, MD, 1958-59; Assistant Professor, 1960-61, and Professor of Economics and History, 1968-75, University of Rochester, NY; Taussig Research Professor, 1973-74, and Harold Hitchings Burbank Professor of Political Economy and Professor of History, 1975-81, Harvard University, Cambridge, MA, Pitt Professor of American History and Institutions, University of Cambridge, 1975-76. Prize in Economic Sciences in Memory of Alfred Nobel, 1993. **Publications:** The Union Pacific Railroad, 1960; Railroads and American Economic Growth, 1964; (co-author) The Reinterpretation of American Economic History, 1971; (co-ed.) Dimensions of Quantitative Research in History, 1972; (with S.L. Engerman) Time on the Cross: The Economics of American Negro Slavery, 1974; Ten Lectures on the New Economic History, 1977; (with G.R. Elton) Which Road to the Past? 1983; (co-ed.) Aging: Stability and Change in the Family, 1981; Trends in Nutrition, Labor Welfare, and Labor Productivity, 1982; Long-Term Changes in Nutrition and the Standard of Living, 1986; Without Consent or Contract: The Rise and Fall of American Slavery, 1989; Without Consent or Contract: The Rise and Fall of American Slavery: Evidence and Methods, 1992; Without Consent or Contract: The Rise and Fall of American Slavery: Markets and Production: Technical Papers, Vol. 1, 1992; Without Consent or Contract: The Rise and Fall of American Slavery: Conditions of Slave Life and the Transition to Freedom: Technical Papers, Vol. II, 1992; The Conquest of High Mortality and Hunger in Europe and America: Timing and Mechanisms, 1993; The Fourth Great Awakening & the Future of Egalitarianism, 2000. **Address:** Graduate School of Business, University of Chicago, 1101 E. 58th St Rm 118, Chicago, IL 60637, U.S.A. **Online address:** imok@cpe.uchicago.edu

FOGELMARK, Staffan. Swedish, b. 1939. **Genres:** Classics, Bibliography. **Career:** University of Lund, Lund, Sweden, reader in Greek, 1972, acting professor, 1976, 1978, and 1986; Harvard University Center for Hellenic Studies, fellow, 1973; University of Edinburgh, Charles Gordon Mackay Lecturer, 1979; University of Gothenburg, professor of Greek, 1997. **Publications:** Studies in Pindar with Particular Reference to Paean VI and Nemean VII, 1972; Chrysaigis IG 12:5, 611, 1975; Flemish and Related Panel-Stamped Bindings: Evidence and Principles, 1990. Contributor of articles to classical studies and philology journals in the United States and abroad. **Address:** Gerdagatan 8, S-223 62 Lund, Sweden. **Online address:** staffan.fogelmark@class.gu.se

FOGG, Gordon Elliott. *See* Obituaries.

FOGLE, Jeanne. American, b. 1949. **Genres:** History, Documentaries/Reportage. **Career:** A Tour de Force, Washington, DC, owner, 1984-; Smithsonian Institution, Washington, DC, tour leader and lecturer in the Resident Associate Program, 1985-; Northern Virginia Community College, Annandale, adjunct professor of history, 1990-. **Publications:** 200 Years: Stories of the Nation's Capital, 1991; Proximity to Power: Neighbors to the Presidents near Lafayette Square, 2000. Contributor to encyclopedias. **Address:** PO Box 2782, Washington, DC 20013, U.S.A. **Online address:** tdforce@aol.com; www.atourdeforce.com

FOLBRE, Nancy. American. **Genres:** Economics. **Career:** Bowdoin College, assistant professor of economics, 1980-83; New School for Social Research, assistant professor of economics, 1983-85; University of Massachusetts, associate professor of economics, 1984-91, professor of economics, 1991-. Visiting professor, visiting lecturer, visiting scholar at universities worldwide. Consultant. **Publications:** (ed.) Women's Work in the World Economy, 1991; Who Pays for the Kids?: Gender and the Structures of Constraint, 1994; (with the Center for Popular Economics) A Field Guide to the U.S. Economy, 1987, rev. expanded ed. as The New Field Guide to the U.S. Economy: A Compact and Irreverent Guide to Economic Life in America, 1995, as The Ultimate Field Guide to the U.S. Economy: A Compact and Irreverent Guide to Economic Life in America, 2000; (ed.) The Economics of the Family, 1996; (with R. Albelda and the Center for Popular Economics) The War on the Poor: A Defense Manual, 1996; The Invisible Heart: Economics and Family Values, 2001. Contributor of professional articles to periodicals. Contributor to books. **Address:** University of Massachusetts, Department of Economics, Amherst, MA 01003, U.S.A. **Online address:** folbre@econs.umass.edu

FOLDVARY, Fred E. Hungarian (born Israel), b. 1946. **Genres:** Economics, Politics/Government. **Career:** Federal Reserve Bank of San Francisco, CA, programmer analyst, 1978-81; American Topical Association, editor, 1981-87; Latvian University of Agriculture, Jelgava, associate professor of economics, 1992-93; Mary Washington College, instructor, 1994; Virginia Polytechnic Institute and State University, Blacksburg, visiting assistant professor of economics, 1994-95; Santa Clara University, 1998-. Citizens for a Sound Economy, adjunct scholar, 1988. **Publications:** The Soul of Liberty, 1980; Natural Rights, 1985; Public Goods and Private Communities, 1994; (ed. and contrib.) Beyond Neoclassical Economics: Heterodox Approaches to Economic Theory; Dictionary of Free Market Economics, 1998. Contributor to books. Contributor to economic, philosophy, and finance journals. **Address:** 1920 Cedar St, Berkeley, CA 94709, U.S.A. **Online address:** foldvary@pobox.com

FOLEY, Denise (M.). American, b. 1950. **Genres:** Music. **Career:** Bucks County Courier Times, Levittown, PA, reporter and columnist, 1977-83; Prevention (magazine), Emmaus, PA, senior editor, 1983-86; Children (magazine), Emmaus, managing editor, 1986-89; freelance writer, 1989-; Temple University, Philadelphia, PA, instructor in writing, 1990-. **Publications:** (with E. Nechas) What Do I Do Now?, 1992; (with Nechas) The Women's Encyclopedia of Health and Emotional Healing, 1993; (with Nechas, D. Salmon, and S. Perry) The Doctors' Book of Home Remedies for Children, 1994; (with Nechas) Unequal Treatment: What You Don't Know about How Women Are Mistreated by the Medical Community, 1994. Contributor to periodicals. **Address:** 528 Kingston Rd., Oreland, PA 19075, U.S.A.

FOLEY, Gaelen. American. **Genres:** Romance/Historical. **Career:** Writer. **Publications:** HISTORICAL ROMANCE: The Pirate Prince, 1998; Princess, 1999; Prince Charming, 2000; The Duke, 2000; Lord of Fire, 2002; Lord of Ice, 2002; Lady of Desire, 2003; Devil Takes a Bride, 2004; One Night of Sin, 2005. **Address:** PO Box 522, South Park, PA 15129, U.S.A. **Online address:** gaelenf@aol.com

FOLEY, Jack. American, b. 1940. **Genres:** Poetry. **Career:** Poet, writer, editor, and radio personality. Homemaker, c. 1974-85; KPFAFM, Berkeley, CA, host and executive producer-in-charge of poetry program, 1988-; Poetry USA, Oakland, CA, editor-in-chief, 1990-95; Poetry Flash, contributing editor, 1992-. Poetry: San Francisco, guest editor, winter 1988-89; Djerassi Program, resident artist, 1994. Worked briefly in Western Union telegraph office as young man. Performer of poetry with wife Adelle. **Publications:** POETRY: Letters/Lights-Words for Adelle, 1987; Gershwin, 1991; hypertext ed., 1995; Adrift, 1993; Exiles, 1996; Greatest Hits 1974-2003, 2004. Contributor of poetry to journals. PROSE: Inciting Joy (monograph), 1993; "O Her Blackness Sparkles!" The Life and Times of the Batman Art Gallery, 1960-65, 1995. Contributor to anthologies. Contributor of literary criticism and reviews to journals. Contributor of film criticism to periodicals. Contributor of art criticism to periodicals. RECORDINGS: Three Talkers, 1988; Adrift (audiotape version), 1992; Lou Harrison: A Birthday Celebration, 1994; Greatest Hits 1974-2003, 2004. **Address:** 2569 Maxwell Ave, Oakland, CA 94601, U.S.A. **Online address:** jasfoley@aol.com

FOLEY, (Mary) Louise Munro. American/Canadian, b. 1933. **Genres:** Novels, Mystery/Crime/Suspense, Children's fiction, Young adult fiction, Plays/Screenplays, Social work, Theology/Religion, Writing/Journalism. **Career:** California State University, Sacramento, Institute for Human Service Mgmt., editor of publs., 1975-80. **Publications:** The Caper Club, 1969; No Talking, 1970; Sammy's Sister, 1970; A Job for Joey, 1970; Somebody Stole Second, 1972; Tackle 22, 1978; The Train of Terror, 1982; The Sinister Studies of KESP-TV, 1983; The Lost Tribe, 1983; The Mystery of the Highland Crest, 1984; The Mystery of Echo Lodge, 1985; Danger at Anchor Mine, 1985; Forest of Fear, 1986; The Mardi Gras Mystery, 1987; Mystery of the Sacred Stones, 1988; Australia, 1988; The Cobra Connection, 1989; Ghost Train, 1992; Thief! said the Cat, 1992; Blood! said the Cat, 1992; Poison! said the Cat, 1992; In Search of the Hidden Statue, 1993; Moving Target, 1993; Stolen Affections, 1995; Running into Trouble, 1996; My Substitute Teacher's Gone Batty, 1996; The Bird-Brained Fiasco, 1996; The Phoney-Baloney Professor, 1996; The Catnap Cat-astrophe, 1997; Ordinary Sinners, 2003. EDITOR: Stand Close to the Door, 1976; Women in Skilled Labor, 1980. **Address:** 5010 Jennings Way, Sacramento, CA 95819, U.S.A.

FOLEY, Mick. (born United States), b. 1965. **Genres:** Autobiography/Memoirs. **Career:** Professional wrestler, writer. **Publications:** Mankind, Have a Nice Day! A Tale of Blood and Sweatsocks, 1999; Mick Foley's Christmas Chaos, 2000; Foley Is Good: . . . and the Real World Is Faker than Wrestling, 2001; Mick Foley's Halloween Hijinx, 2001; Tietam Brown: A Novel, 2003. **Address:** Luke Janklow, Janklow and Nesbit Associates, 445 Park Avenue, New York, NY 10022, U.S.A.

FOLGARAIT, Leonard. American. **Genres:** Art/Art history. **Career:** Educator and author. Vanderbilt University, Nashville, TN, professor of fine arts, director of graduate studies. **Publications:** So Far from Heaven: David Alfaro Siqueiros's The March of Humanity and Mexican Revolutionary Politics, 1987; Mural Painting and Social Revolution in Mexico, 1920-1940: Art of the New Order, 1998. Contributor to art periodicals. **Address:** Vanderbilt University, Fine Arts Department, 2200 West End Ave., Nashville, TN 37235, U.S.A. **Online address:** Leonard.Folgarait@vanderbilt.edu

FOLK, Thomas C. American, b. 1955. **Genres:** Literary criticism and history. **Career:** Rutgers University, Newark Campus, Newark, NJ, associate professor. **Publications:** The Pennsylvania Impressionists, 1997. **Address:** PO Box 501, Bernardsville, NJ 07924, U.S.A.

FOLKS, Jeffrey Jay. American, b. 1948. **Genres:** Poetry, Literary criticism and history. **Career:** Indiana University-Bloomington, lecturer in English, 1975-76; Tennessee Wesleyan College, Athens, instructor, 1977-79, assistant professor, 1979-82, associate professor, 1982-85, professor of English, 1985-. University of Skopje, senior Fulbright lecturer, 1986-87; Sofia University, senior Fulbright lecturer, 1994-95. **Publications:** Southern Writers and the Machine: Faulkner to Percy, 1993; The First of September: Poems, 1993; From Richard Wright to Toni Morrison, 2001. EDITOR/CO-EDITOR: (and trans. with the author) M. Jovanovski, Faceless Men and Other Stories, 1992; Remembering James Agee, 1997; Southern Writers at Century's End, 1997; The World Is Our Home, 2000. Work represented in anthologies. Contributor of articles, translations, and reviews to literature journals and literary magazines. **Address:** English Department, Doshisha University, Kamigyo, Kyoto 602-8580, Japan. **Online address:** jjfolks@usa.net

FOLLETT, CB. American, b. 1936. **Genres:** Poetry. **Career:** Poet. Arctos Press, publisher/owner. Peaceable Kingdom (manufacturer and distributor of sculpted animal ceramic jewelry), creator, owner, business manager, and designer, 1973-94; artist with group and solo shows throughout California; work represented in galleries. Worked as copy editor and proofreader for Cunningham & Walsh (advertising agency), McCann Erickson (public relations firm), International Business Relations, San Francisco, CA, and Stanford University. **Publications:** The Latitudes of Their Going (poems), 1993; Gathering the Mountains (poems), 1995; Bull Kelp, 1995; Nightmare Fish, 1997; Arms, 1997; Vallon-Pont'Arc, 1998; Visible Bones (poems), 1998; At the Turning of the Light (poems; National Poetry Book Award), 2001. EDITOR: Beside the Sleeping Maiden: Poets of Marin, 1997; Grrrrr: A Collection of Poems about Bears, 2000; (co) Runes: A Review of Poetry (annual), 2002-. Work represented in anthologies. Contributor of poems to magazines. **Address:** PO Box 401, Sausalito, CA 94966, U.S.A. **Online address:** Runes@aol.com

FOLLETT, Ken(neth Martin). Also writes as Symon Myles, Zachary Stone. British, b. 1949. **Genres:** Mystery/Crime/Suspense, Young adult fiction. **Career:** Full-time writer, 1977-. South Wales Echo, Cardiff, reporter and rock music columnist, 1970-73; London Evening News, reporter, 1973-74; Everest Books, London, editorial director, 1974-76, deputy managing director, 1976-77. **Publications:** (as Symon Myles) The Big Black, 1974; (as Symon Myles) The Big Needle, 1974; (as Symon Myles) The Big Hit, 1975; The Shakeout, 1975; The Bear Raid, 1976; The Secret of Kellerman's Studio (juvenile), 1976; (as Zachary Stone) The Modigliani Scandal, 1976, published in U.S. as by Ken Follett, 1985; (as Zachary Stone) Paper Money, 1977; Storm Island (in U.S. as Eye of the Needle), 1978; Triple, 1979; The Key to Rebecca, 1980; The Man from St. Petersburg, 1982; On Wings of Eagles, 1983; Lie Down with Lions, 1985; The Pillars of the Earth, 1989; The Mystery Hideout, 1990; The Power Twins, 1990; Night over Water, 1991; A Dangerous Fortune, 1993; Pillars of the Almighty, 1994; A Place Called Freedom, 1995; The Third Twin, 1996; The Hammer of Eden, 1998; Code to Zero, 2000; Jackdaws, 2001; Hornet Flight, 2002; Whiteout, 2004. **Address:** PO Box 4, Knebworth SG3 6UT, England. **Online address:** www.kenfollett.com

FOLLY, Martin H(arold). (born England), b. 1957. **Genres:** History. **Career:** Brunel University, Uxbridge, Middlesex, England, senior tutor for American studies, 1989-. **Publications:** People in History (juvenile), 1988; Churchill, Whitehall, and the Soviet Union, 1940-45, 2000. Contributor to periodicals. **Address:** 1 Tash Pl., New Southgate, London N11 1PA, England. **Online address:** martin.folly@lineone.net

FOLSOM, Allan (R.). American, b. 1941. **Genres:** Novels. **Career:** Worked in Los Angeles, CA, as a delivery driver, film editor, and camera operator; author of television scripts, screenplays, and novels. **Publications:** The Day after Tomorrow (novel), 1994; Day of Confession, 1998. Author of television scripts for series, and television film. Author of unproduced screenplays. **Address:** c/o Aaron M. Priest Literary Agency, 708 3rd Ave., 23rd Fl., New York, NY 10017, U.S.A.

FOLSTER, David. Canadian, b. 1937. **Genres:** Agriculture/Forestry, Film, Geography, History, Essays. **Career:** Daily Gleaner, Fredericton, New Brunswick, Canada, reporter and sports editor, 1960; Sprague Electric Co., North Adams, MA, technical writer, 1961-66; full-time writer, 1967-. **Publications:** (ed.) R.A. Tweedie, On with the Dance: A New Brunswick Memoir, 1935-1960, 1986; The Great Trees of New Brunswick, 1987; The Chocolate Ganongs of St. Stephen, 1990; New Brunswick in the Movies, forthcoming. **Address:** PO Box 21017, Fredericton, NB, Canada E3B 7A3. **Online address:** treehouse@fundy.net

FOMBRUN, Charles J. American, b. 1954. **Genres:** Administration/Management, Business/Trade/Industry. **Career:** Columbia University, NYC, instructor in management, 1978-79; University of Pennsylvania, The Wharton School, Philadelphia, lecturer, 1979-80, assistant professor of management, 1980-84; New York University, NYC, visiting associate professor, 1984-86, associate professor, 1986-91, professor of management, 1991-, and research professor, 1992-. Presents workshops on human resource management, implementing strategy, and managing strategic change. **Publications:** (with N.M. Tichy and M.A. Devanna) Strategic Human Resource Management, 1984; Turning Points: Creating Strategic Change in Corporations, 1992; Reputation: Realizing Value from the Corporate Image, 1996. Work represented in anthologies. Contributor of articles and reviews in business and management journals and in newspapers. **Address:** Leonard N. Stern School of Business, New York University, 44 West Fourth St., New York, NY 10012, U.S.A.

FOMIN. *See* **GOLOMSTOCK, Igor (Naumovitch).**

FONAGY, Peter. American, b. 1952. **Genres:** Psychology. **Career:** University of London, London, England, lecturer, 1977-87, senior lecturer, 1988-92, Freud Memorial Professor of Psychoanalysis, 1992-, founding member of Centre for Health in Society, and director of Psychoanalysis Unit. Anna Freud Centre, coordinator of research, 1989-. Royal Free Hospital, probationer clinical psychologist, 1976-78, honorary senior clinical psychologist and lecturer, 1981-85; North East Thames Regional Authority, probationer clinical psychologist, 1977-80; London Clinic of Psychoanalysis, staff member, 1982-85; private practice of psychoanalysis, 1986-; consultant to Council of Europe, National Institute of Mental Health of the United States, and University of Haifa. **Publications:** (with A. Higgitt) Personality Theory and Clinical Practice, 1985; (with Higgitt and M. Lader) The Natural History of Tolerance to the Benzodiazepines, 1988. EDITOR: (with J. Sandler and E. Person, and coauthor of intro) Freud's On Narcissism: An Introduction, 1991; (with E.S. Person and A. Hagelin) On Freud's Observations on Transference-Love, 1993; (with A. Cooper and R. Wallerstein) The Theory of Psychoanalytic Practice, 1994; (co) Contemporary Freud series. Work represented in anthologies. Contributor to professional journals. **Address:** Sub-Dept pf Clinical Psychology, University College London, Gower St., London WC1E 6BT, England.

FONDA, Peter. American, b. 1939. **Genres:** Plays/Screenplays. **Career:** Actor, screenwriter, film producer, film director. **Publications:** (with D. Hopper and T. Southern) Easy Rider (screenplay), 1969; (with A. Sharp) The Hired Hand (screenplay), 1971; Fatal Mission (screenplay), 1990; Don't Tell Dad (memoir), 1998. **Address:** Indian Hills Ranch, Route 38G, Box 2040, Livingston, MT 59047, U.S.A.

FONE, Byrne Reginald Spencer. American, b. 1936. **Genres:** Literary criticism and history. **Career:** New York University, assistant (English), 1960-1963; Queens College, New York, lecturer, 1963-1964; New York University, instructor, 1964-1965; City College of New York, 1965-1968, assistant professor, 1968-. **Publications:** (with G. Marcelle) Boswell's Life of Johnson, and Other Works, 1966; (with Marcelle) Melville's Moby Dick and Other Works, 1966; (ed.) C. Cibber, An Apology for the Life of Colley Cibber, with an Historical View of the State During His Own Time, 1968; Colley Cibber's Love's Last Shift, 1968; Love's Last Shift and Sentimental Comedy, 1969; The Augustan Translators, 1974; History of English Literature, 1974; (ed.) Hidden Heritage, History and the Gay Imagination: An Anthology, 1981; Masculine Landscapes: Walt Whitman and the Homoerotic Text, Southern 1992; A Road to Stonewall: Male Homosexuality and Homophobia in English and American Literature, 1750-1969, 1994. **Address:** City College of New York, Department of English, Convent Ave. at 138th St., New York, NY 10031, U.S.A.

FONER, Eric. American, b. 1943. **Genres:** History, Race relations. **Career:** Columbia University, NYC, instructor, and subsequently assistant professor and associate professor, 1969-73, Dewitt Clinton Professor of History, 1982-; City College, City University of New York, professor of history, 1973-82. **Publications:** Free Soil, Free Labor, Free Men: The Ideology of the Republican Party Before the Civil War, 1970; Tom Paine and Revolutionary America, 1976; Politics and Ideology in the Age of the Civil War, 1980; Nothing but Freedom, 1983; Reconstruction: America's Unfinished Revolution, 1988; A House Divided, 1990; Freedom's Lawmakers, 1993; America's Reconstruction, 1995; The Story of American Freedom, 1998; Who Owns History?, 2002. EDITOR: America's Black Past: A Reader in Afro-American History, 1970; Nat Turner, 1971; Thomas Paine, 1995. **Address:** 606 W 116th St, New York, NY 10027, U.S.A.

FONER, Naomi. American. **Genres:** Plays/Screenplays. **Career:** Served as media director of Eugene McCarthy's campaign for president, 1968; Public Broadcasting Service (PBS), production assistant and researcher on staff of Sesame Street, 1968-; creator and co-producer of television series, The Best of Families; screenwriter and film producer, 1986-. **Publications:** SCREENPLAYS: Violets Are Blue, 1986; Running on Empty, 1988; A Dangerous Woman, 1993; Losing Isaiah, 1995. TELEPLAY: Blackout. **Address:** c/o CAA, 9830 Wilshire Blvd, Beverly Hills, CA 90212, U.S.A.

FONG, Bobby. American, b. 1950. **Genres:** Literary criticism and history. **Career:** Berea College, KY, instructor to associate professor of English, 1978-89; Hope College, Holland, MI, professor of English, 1989-95, dean for arts and humanities, 1989-94; Hamilton College, Clinton, NY, professor of English, 1995-2001, dean of faculty, 1995-2000; Butler University, president, 2001-. **Publications:** EDITOR: (with D.A. Hoekema) Christianity and Culture in the Crossfire, 1997; (with K. Beckson) The Oxford English Text Edition of the Complete Works of Oscar Wilde, Vol. IV: Poems and Poems in Prose, 1998. Contributor to books. Contributor of articles and reviews to academic journals and popular magazines. **Address:** Office of the President, Butler University, 4600 Sunset Ave, Indianapolis, IN 46208, U.S.A. **Online address:** bfong@butler.edu

FONROBERT, Charlotte Elisheva. German, b. 1965. **Genres:** Theology/Religion. **Career:** Syracuse University, Syracuse, NY, staff member, 1995-96; University of Judaism, Los Angeles, CA, assistant professor of Rabbinic literature, 1996-2000; Stanford University, Stanford, CA, assistant professor of religious studies, 2000-. **Publications:** Menstrual Purity: Rabbinic and Christian Reconstructions of Biblical Gender, 2000. Contributor to periodicals. **Address:** Department of Religious Studies, Building 70, Stanford University, Stanford, CA 94305, U.S.A. **Online address:** fonrober@stanford.edu

FONSECA, James W(illiam). American, b. 1947. **Genres:** Demography. **Career:** George Mason University, Fairfax, VA, associate professor of geography, 1973-, acting dean of Graduate School, 1988-90, director of Prince William Institute, 1992-, and director of individualized studies. **Publications:** The Urban Rank-Size Hierarchy (monograph), 1989; (with A.C. Andrews) The Atlas of American Higher Education, 1993; (with Andrews) The Atlas of American Society, 1995. Contributor to geography journals. **Address:** Department of Geography, George Mason University, Fairfax, VA 22030, U.S.A.

FONTANEL, Beatrice. Moroccan, b. 1957. **Genres:** Fashion/Costume, History, Art/Art history. **Career:** Bayard-Presse, Paris, France, journalist, 1981-88; Gallimard Jeunesse (book publisher), Paris, editor, 1990-96; Herve de la Martiniere (publisher), writer, 1996-. **Publications:** Support and Seduction: A History of the Corset and Bra, 1997; Babies, History, Art, and Folklore, 1997; Babies Celebrated, 1998; Monsters: The Book of the Ugliest Animals, 1998. **Address:** 15 rue Littre, 75006 Paris, France.

FONTENAY, Charles L(ouis). American (born Brazil), b. 1917. **Genres:** Novels, Science fiction/Fantasy, Young adult fiction, Philosophy, Biography. **Career:** The Tennessean, political reporter, 1946-64, city ed., 1964-68, rewriter, 1968-87. **Publications:** Twice upon a Time, 1958; Rebels of the Red Planet, 1961; The Day the Oceans Overflowed, 1964; Epistle to the Babylonians, 1969; The Keyen of Fu Tze, 1977; Estes Kefauver: A Biography, 1980; The Kipton Chronicles, 21 vols., 1995-99; Target Grant: 1862, 1999; Here, There and Elswhen, 1999; Modal, 2000; Getting Back at Boo, 2002. **Address:** 1708 20th Ave N Apt D, St. Petersburg, FL 33713, U.S.A. **Online address:** cfontena@tampabay.rr.com

FONTES, Manuel D(a Costa). American (born Portugal), b. 1945. **Genres:** Mythology/Folklore. **Career:** Kent State University, Kent, OH, assistant professor, 1975-79, associate professor, 1975-85, professor of Spanish and Portuguese, 1985-. **Publications:** Romanceiro Português do Canadá, 1979; Romanceiro Português dos Estados Unidos, Vol 1: Nova Inglaterra, 1980, Vol 2: Califórnia, 1983; Romanceiro da Ilha de São Jorge, 1983; Romanceiro da Provincia de Trás-os-Montes (Distrito de Bragança), 2 vols, 1987; Portuguese and Brazilian Balladry: A Thematic and Bibliographic Index, 2 vols, 1997; (ed. with S.G. Armistead) Cancioneiro Tradicional de Trás-os-Montes, 1998; Folklore and Literature: Studies in the Portuguese, Brazilian, Sephardic, and Hispanic Oral Traditions, 2000. Contributor to periodicals worldwide. **Address:** Department of Modern and Classical Language Studies, Kent State University, Kent, OH 44242, U.S.A. **Online address:** mfontes@neo.rr.com

FONTES, Montserrat. Also writes as Jessie Lattimore. American, b. 1940. **Genres:** Novels, Literary criticism and history, Humanities. **Career:** Markham Junior High School, Los Angeles, CA, teacher of English, 1968-72; University High School, Los Angeles, teacher of English and journalism, 1973-; John Marshall High School, literature and journalism; writer. Leader of workshops at city, state, and national conventions on journalism, 1978-; consultant for American literature and journalism textbooks. **Publications:** (as Jessie Lattimore with N. Dresser) High Contrast, 1988; First Confession (novel), 1991; Dreams of the Centaur, 1996.

FOON, Dennis. Canadian/American, b. 1951. **Genres:** Children's fiction, Young adult fiction, Plays/Screenplays, Children's non-fiction. **Career:** University of British Columbia Centre for Continuing Education, instructor in playwriting, 1974-79; Green Thumb Theatre for Young People, Vancouver, co-founder and artistic director, 1975-88; Young People's Theatre, Toronto, playwright-in-residence, 1983-84; International Association of Theatres for Children and Youth, Canadian vice-president, 1979-82. **Publications:** PLAYS FOR CHILDREN: The Last Days of Paul Bunyan, 1978; The Windigo, 1978; Heracles, 1978; New Canadian Kid, 1982; (adapter of novel) V. Hugo,

The Hunchback of Notre Dame, 1983; (adapter of play) V. Ludwig, Trummi Kaput, 1983; Skin, 1988; Liars, 1988; Invisible Kids, 1989; War, 1995; Chasing the Money, 2000. OTHER, FOR CHILDREN: (with Knight) Am I the Only One?: A Young People's Book about Sex Abuse (non-fiction), 1985; The Short Tree and the Bird That Could Not Sing, 1986; Mirror Game, 1992; Seesaw, 1993. SCREENPLAYS: Little Criminals, 1996. NOVELS: Double or Nothing, 2000; Skud, 2002; The Dirteaters (science fiction), 2003; Freewalker (science fiction), 2004.

FOOS, Laurie. American, b. 1966. **Genres:** Novels. **Career:** Fisher College, Boston, MA, and Marlboro, MA, adjunct instructor, 1993-. **Publications:** Ex Utero (novel), 1995. Contributor to anthologies. **Address:** c/o Coffee House Press, 27 N. 4th St. Suite 400, Minneapolis, MN 55401, U.S.A.

FOOT, David. British, b. 1929. **Genres:** Horticulture, Sports/Fitness, Autobiography/Memoirs, Biography. **Career:** Western Gazette, Yeovil, England, journalist, 1946-55; Bristol Evening World, Bristol, England, journalist, 1955-62; freelance journalist, 1962-. Television and radio journalist, general feature writer, sports reporter, and columnist. **Publications:** Viv Richards, 1979; From Grace to Botham, 1980; Harold Gimblett: Tormented Genius of Cricket, 1982; Zed, 1983; (with R. Cousins) Skateaway, 1984; Cricket's Unholy Trinity, 1985; Sunshine, Sixes and Cider, a History of the Somerset County Cricket Club, 1986; Hungry Fighters of the West, 1988; 40 Years On: Story of Lord's Taverners, 1990; Country Reporter, 1990; Beyond Bat and Ball, 1993; Wally Hammond, the Reasons Why, 1996; Fragments of Idolatry, 2001; (with D. Shepherd) Shep, 2001. EDITOR: The Hand That Bowled Bradman, 1973; Ladies' Mile, 1977; Gardening My Way, 1978. **Address:** 20 Downs Cote View, Westbury-on-Trym, Bristol BS9 3TU, England.

FOOT, Michael Richard Daniell. British, b. 1919. **Genres:** Art/Art history, History, International relations/Current affairs, Biography. **Career:** Manchester University, professor of modern history, 1967-73. **Publications:** (with J.L. Hammond) Gladstone and Liberalism, 1952; British Foreign Policy since 1898, 1956; Men in Uniform, 1961; SOE in France, 1966, new ed., 2004; Resistance, 1976; Six Faces of Courage, 1978, new ed., 2003; (with J.M. Langley) MI9, 1979; SOE: An Outline History, 1984, new ed., 1999; Art and War, 1990; SOE in the Low Countries, 2003. EDITOR: Gladstone Diaries, vols. 1 & 2: 1825-1839, 1968, vols. 3 & 4: 1840-1855 (with H.C.G. Matthew), 1975; War and Society, 1973; Holland at War against Hitler, 1990; (with I.C.B. Dear) Oxford Companion to the Second World War, in U.S. as Oxford Companion to World War II, 1995, rev. ed., 2001. **Address:** Martins Cottage, Nuthampstead, Royston, Herts. SG8 8ND, England.

FOOT, Mirjam M(ichaela). British (born Netherlands), b. 1941. **Genres:** Art/Art history, Bibliography. **Career:** British Library, London, England, curator of rare books, 1965-85, head of acquisitions and Western European collections, 1985-90, and director of collections and preservation, 1990-99; University College London, professor of library and archive studies, 2000-. **Publications:** The Henry Davis Gift: Studies in the History of Bookbinding, Vol. 1, 1978, Vol. 2, 1983; Pictorial Bookbindings, 1986; (with H. Nixon) The History of Decorative Bookbinding in England, 1992; Studies in the History of Bookbinding, 1993; The History of Bookbinding as a Mirror of Society, 1998. Contributor to professional journals. **Address:** Martins Cottage, Bell Lane, Nuthampstead, Herts. SG8 8ND, England. **Online address:** m.foot@ucl.ac.uk

FOOTE, Horton. American, b. 1916. **Genres:** Novels, Plays/Screenplays. **Career:** Actor, 1939-42; workshop dir., King Smith School of Creative Arts, 1944, and mgr., Productions Inc., 1945-48, both in Washington D.C. **Publications:** PLAYS: The Chase, 1952; The Trip to Bountiful, 1954; The Traveling Lady, 1955; A Young Lady of Property: Six Short Plays, 1955; Harrison, Texas: Eight Television Plays, 1956; Flight (in Television Plays for Writers), 1957; The Midnight Caller, 1959; Three Plays, 1962; To Kill a Mockingbird (screenplay), 1964; The Roads to Home, 1982; Courtship, Valentine's Day 1918, 1987; Selected One-Act Plays, 1988; Roots in Parched Ground, Convicts, Lily Dale, and The Widow Claire, 1988; Cousins, and The Death of Papa, 1989; To Kill a Mockingbird, Tender Mercies, and The Trip to Bountiful: Three Screenplays, 1989; Four Plays, 1993; The Young Man From Atlanta, 1994 (Pulitzer Prize for Drama 1995). OTHER: The Chase (novel), 1956; Farewell: A Memoir of a Texas Childhood, 1999. **Address:** 505 N. Houston Street, Wharton, TX 77488, U.S.A.

FOOTITT, Hilary. British, b. 1948. **Genres:** History, Politics/Government, Women's studies and issues. **Career:** Lecturer in French studies, 1972-89, and head of languages, 1988-89, at Cambridgeshire College of Arts and Technology, England; University of Westminster, London, England, head of languages, 1990-. **Publications:** (with J. Simmonds) The Politics of Liberation: France, 1943-1945, 1988. **Address:** University of Westminster, 9-18 Euston Centre, London NW1 3ET, England.

FORBES, Anna. American, b. 1954. **Genres:** Medicine/Health. **Career:** Planned Parenthood of Southeastern Pennsylvania, family planning counselor, 1978-81; public affairs coordinator, 1981-82; National Abortion Rights Action League, regional coordinator, 1981-83; American Civil Liberties Union of Pennsylvania, development associate, 1983-85; Philadelphia AIDS Task Force, Philadelphia, PA, support services coordinator, 1985-86; ActionAIDS, co-founder, 1986, services coordinator and Buddy System coordinator, 1986-88, director of community relations, 1988-90; Philadelphia Department of Public Health, Philadelphia, public information and policy consultant in AIDS Activities Coordinating Office, 1990-94; independent consultant on AIDS and women's health policy, 1994-. Bryn Mawr College, teacher of a course on AIDS and public policy, 1996-; public speaker on women and AIDS; HIV Testing Action Coalition, founding member, 1995-. **Publications:** AIDS AWARENESS LIBRARY: What Is AIDS?, 1996; Where Did AIDS Come From?, 1996; Living in a World with AIDS, 1996; Myths and Facts about AIDS, 1996; What You Can Do about AIDS, 1996; Kids with AIDS, 1996; Heroes against AIDS, 1996; When Someone You Know Has AIDS, 1996. Contributor to Our Bodies, Ourselves, 3rd ed, 1998. Contributor to magazines. **Address:** 3017 Fayette Rd, Kensington, MD 20895-2748, U.S.A. **Online address:** aforbes@critpath.org

FORBES, Daniel. *See* **KENYON, Michael.**

FORCHÉ, Carolyn (Louise). American, b. 1950. **Genres:** Poetry. **Career:** Visiting Lecturer, Michigan State University, E. Lansing, 1974; Visiting Lecturer, 1975, and Assistant Professor, 1976-78, San Diego State University; Visiting Lecturer, University of Virginia, Charlottesville, 1979, 1982-83; Assistant Professor, 1980, and Assistant Professor, 1981, University of Arkansas, Fayetteville; Visiting Lecturer, New York University, 1983, Vassar College, Poughkeepsie, New York, 1984, and Columbia University, NYC, 1984-85; Writer-in-Residence, State University of New York, Albany, 1985. **Publications:** Gathering the Tribes, 1976; Undisclosed No. 24, 1977; The Country between Us, 1983; The Angel of History, 1994. **Address:** George Mason University, Department of English, MS 3E4, 4400 University Dr, Fairfax, VA 22030-4443, U.S.A. **Online address:** mattison@huskynet.com

FORD, Barbara. American, b. 1934. **Genres:** Children's fiction, Animals/Pets, Food and Wine. **Career:** American Museum of Natural History, writer, mid-1960s; free-lance writer, New York City, 1970-; Institute of Children's Literature, instructor, 1988-. **Publications:** FOR CHILDREN: Can Invertebrates Learn?, 1972; How Birds Learn to Sing, 1975; Katydids: The Singing Insects, 1976; Animals That Use Tools, 1978; (with R.R. Keiper) The Island Ponies: An Environmental Study of Their Life on Assateague, 1979; Why Does a Turtle Live Longer Than a Dog? A Report on Animal Longevity, 1980; Black Bear: The Spirit of the Wilderness, 1981; Alligators, Raccoons, and Other Survivors: The Wildlife of the Future, 1981; The Elevator, 1982; (with D.C. Switzer) Underwater Dig: The Excavation of a Revolutionary War Privateer, 1982; Keeping Things Cool: The Story of Refrigeration and Air Conditioning, 1986; Wildlife Rescue, 1987; Inventions That Changed Our Lives: The Automobile, 1987; St. Louis, 1989; Walt Disney: A Biography, 1989; The Eagles' Child, 1990; Howard Carter, 1995; Most Wonderful Movie in the World, 1996; Paul Revere, 1997. FOR ADULTS: Future Food: Alternate Protein for the Year 2000, 1978. **Address:** Pleasant Valley Rd, Mendham, NJ 07945, U.S.A.

FORD, Brian John. British, b. 1939. **Genres:** Biology, Physics, Sciences. **Career:** Research biologist, lecturer, writer, broadcaster, 1961-. Founding chmn., Scientific and Technical Authors' Committee, Society of Authors. Fellow of Court of Governors, Cardiff University; former president, Union of Science Journalists Assns, Brussels. Director of scientific and research agencies in UK & US. **Publications:** German Secret Weapons, Blueprint for Mars, 1969; Allied Secret Weapons, the War of Science, 1970; Microbiology and Food, 1970; Nonscience...or How to Rule the World (satire), 1971; V1, V2 (in Japanese), 1971; The Optical Microscope Manual, 1973; The Earth Watchers, 1973; The Revealing Lens, 1973; Microbe Power, 1976; Patterns of Sex, 1979; Cult of the Expert (satire), 1982; 101 Questions about Science, 1983; 101 More Questions about Science, 1984; Single Lens: The Story of the Simple Microscope, 1985; Compute: How, Why, Do I Really Need To?, 1985; The Food Book, 1986; The Human Body, 1990; Leeuwenhoek Legacy, 1991; Images of Science, 1992; The First Encyclopedia of Science, 1993; New Quiz Book, 1994; BSE: The Facts, 1996; Sensitive Souls: How Plants & Animals Communicate, 1997; Secret Language of Life, 2000; Future of Food, 2000; Using the Digital Microscope, 2002. COAUTHOR: The Recovery, Removal and Reconstruction of Human Skeletal Remains, 1970;

History of English-Speaking Peoples, 1971; The Cardiff Book, 1973; Viral Pollution of the Environment, 1983; Sex and Health, 1985; Walking in Britain, 1988. EDITOR: The First 50 Years: History of the Institute of Biology, 2000; GM Crops, the Scientists Speak, 2003. **Address:** Rothay House, Mayfield Rd, Eastrea, Cambs. PE7 2AY, England. **Online address:** mail@brianjford.com; www.brianjford.com

FORD, Carolyn (Mott). American, b. 1938. **Genres:** Children's fiction, Poetry. **Career:** Writer. Monmouth Medical Center, Long Branch, NJ, former guest services representative; also worked as library assistant, tax clerk, and stringer for a local radio station. **Publications:** Nothing in the Mailbox, 1996. Work represented in anthologies. Contributor of articles and reviews to periodicals, newsletters and newspapers;. **Address:** 548 Ocean Blvd. No. 20, Long Branch, NJ 07740, U.S.A.

FORD, David. *See* **GILMAN, George G.**

FORD, G. M. American, b. 1945. **Genres:** Mystery/Crime/Suspense. **Career:** Rogue Community College, Grants Pass, OR, English teacher, 1972-85; City University, Bellevue, WA, communications teacher, 1986-92. **Publications:** MYSTERY NOVELS: Who in Hell Is Wanda Fuca?, 1995; Cast in Stone, 1996; The Bum's Rush, 1997; Slow Burn, 1998; Last Ditch, 1999; The Deader the Better, 2000; Fury, 2001; Black River, 2002. **Address:** c/o Author Mail, 7th Fl, HarperCollins Publishers, 10 E 53rd St, New York, NY 10022, U.S.A. **Online address:** gmford@qwest.net

FORD, Gordon Buell, Jr. American, b. 1937. **Genres:** Classics, Language/Linguistics, Translations. **Career:** The Lybrand, Ross Brothers, and Montgomery Foundation Distinguished Professor of English, Linguistics, and TESOL, University of Northern Iowa, 1972-; Professor of Linguistics, The Southeastern Investment Trust, Inc. Research Foundation, Louisville, Kentucky, 1976-. The Yeager, Ford, and Warren Foundation Distinguished Professor of Indo-European Classical, Slavic and Baltic Linguistics, Sanskrit, and Medieval Latin, Northwestern University, Evanston, Illinois, 1965-; Professor of English, 1968-69 and Professor of Anthropology, 1971-72, Northwestern University, Chicago; University of Chicago, Visiting Professor of Medieval Latin, 1966-, Visiting Professor of Linguistics, 1966-. **Publications:** The Ruodlieb: The First Medieval Epic of Chivalry from Eleventh-Century Germany, 1965; The Ruodlieb: Facsimile Edition, 1965, 1967, 1968; The Wolfenbuttel Lithuanian Postile Manuscript of the Year 1573, vols. I-III, 1965-66; The Ruodlieb: Linguistic Introduction, Latin Text with a Critical Apparatus, and Glossary, 1966; Isidore of Seville's History of the Goths, Vandals, and Suevi, 1966, 1970; Baltramiejus Vilentas' Lithuanian Translation of the Gospels and Epistles (1579), vols. I-II, 1966; (trans.) Jan Gonda: A Concise Elementary Grammar of the Sanskrit Language with Exercises, Reading Selections, and a Glossary, 1966; (trans.) Antoine Meillet: The Comparative Method in Historical Linguistics, 1967; Old Lithuanian Texts of the Sixteenth and Seventeenth Centuries with a Glossary, 1969; The Old Lithuanian Catechism of Baltramiejus Vilentas (1579): A Phonological, Morphological, and Syntactical Investigation, 1969; The Letters of Saint Isidore of Seville, 1966, 1970; The Old Lithuanian Catechism of Martynas Mazvydas (1547), 1971; (trans.) Manfred Mayrhofer: A Sanskrit Grammar, 1972; Isidore of Seville: On Grammar, 1972, revision forthcoming. **Address:** 3619 Brownsboro Road, Louisville, KY 40207, U.S.A.

FORD, Herbert (Paul). American, b. 1927. **Genres:** History, Biography. **Career:** Professor Emeritus of Journalism, Pacific Union College, Angwin, California, since 1989 (Associate Professor of Journalism, 1974-84; Professor and Vice President of Development and Alumni Relations, 1984-89). Consultant in Development since 1990. Public Relations Director, Seventh-day Adventists' Conferences, 1954-69, and The Voice of Prophecy, 1969-74; Director, Corporate Communications, Adventist Health System-West, 1983. **Publications:** Wind High, Sand Deep, 1965; Flee the Captor, 1966; No Guns on Their Shoulders, 1968; Crimson Coats and Kimonos, 1968; Affair of the Heart, 1969; Rudo the Reckless Russian, 1970; Man Alive, 1971; For the Love of China, 1971; Pitcairn, 1972; The "Miscellany" of Pitcairn's Island, 1980; Island of Tears, 1990; Pitcairn - Port of Call, 1996. **Address:** 531 Sunset Dr, Angwin, CA 94508, U.S.A.

FORD, Hilary. *See* **YOUD, Sam.**

FORD, James Allan. Scottish, b. 1920. **Genres:** Novels, Essays. **Career:** Entered U.K. Civil Service, 1938; Assistant Secretary, Dept. of Agriculture for Scotland, Edinburgh, 1958-66; Registrar General for Scotland, 1966-69; Director of Establishments, Scottish Office, Edinburgh, 1969-79. President, Scottish Centre, International P.E.N., 1970-73, and 1983-86. **Publications:** The Brave White Flag, 1961; Season of Escape, 1963; A Statue for a Public

Place, 1965; A Judge of Men, 1968; The Mouth of Truth, 1971. **Address:** 6 Hillpark Court, Edinburgh EH4 7BE, Scotland.

FORD, Jennifer. American. **Genres:** Literary criticism and history. **Career:** Writer. **Publications:** Coleridge on Dreaming: Romanticism, Dreams, and the Medical Imagination, 1998. **Address:** c/o Cambridge University Press, Edinburgh Bldg., Shaftesbury Rd., Cambridge CB2 2RU, England.

FORD, Jerry. (Jerome W). American, b. 1949. **Genres:** Recreation. **Career:** Scottsdale Progress, Scottsdale, AZ, sports reporter, 1971-77; Arizona Daily Sun, Flagstaff, AZ, sports reporter, 1977-79; Logan Herald & Journal, Logan, Utah, entertainment/news reporter, 1979-84; Decatur Herald Review, Decatur, IL, news editor, 1984-88; Holland Sentinel, Holland, MI, managing editor, 1988-90. **Publications:** The Grand Slam Collection: Have Fun Collecting Baseball Cards, 1993. **Address:** c/o Publicity Director, Lerner Publications Co., 241 First Ave. N., Minneapolis, MN 55401, U.S.A.

FORD, Kirk. See **SPENCE, William John Duncan.**

FORD, Marjorie Leet. American, b. 1947. **Genres:** Novels. **Career:** Writer, producer. **Publications:** (with L. Hinrichs and N. Zurek) Cactus: A Prickly Portrait of a Desert Eccentric, 1995; Do Try To Speak As We Do: The Diary of an American Au Pair (novel), 2001, in UK as The Diary of an American Au Pair, 2001.Contributor to periodicals and Web sites. **Address:** c/o Author Mail, St. Martin's Press, 175 Fifth Ave., New York, NY 10010, U.S.A. **Online address:** leetford@ricochet.net

FORD, Melissa Mathison. See **MATHISON, Melissa.**

FORD, Michael Curtis. American. **Genres:** Novels. **Career:** Author, Romance linguistics scholar. Worked as a consultant, banker, and translator. **Publications:** NOVELS: The Ten Thousand: A Novel of Ancient Greece, 2001; Gods and Legions, 2002. **Address:** c/o Author Mail, St. Martin's Press, 175 Fifth Ave., New York, NY 10010, U.S.A.

FORD, Susan. (born United States), b. 1957. **Genres:** Mystery/Crime/ Suspense. **Career:** Writer, photographer, spokesperson. National Breast Cancer Awareness Month spokesperson in the 1990s; Betty Ford Center, board member. **Publications:** (with Laura Hayden) Double Exposure: A First Daughter Mystery, 2002; (with Laura Hayden) Sharp Focus: A First Daughter Mystery, 2003. Contributor to other magazines and newspapers. **Address:** c/o Author Mail, Thomas Dunne Books, St. Martin's Press, 175 Fifth Ave., New York, NY 10010, U.S.A.

FORDER, Anthony. British, b. 1925. **Genres:** Public/Social administration, Social work. **Career:** Probation Officer, London Probation Service, 1953-59; Lecturer London School of Economics, 1959-63; Sr. Lecturer, Oppenheimer College of Social Service, Zambia, and University of Zambia, 1963-66; Lecturer in Social Administration, Liverpool University, 1966-70; Head, Dept. of Applied Social Studies, Millbank College of Commerce, 1971-72; Principal Lecturer, 1972-76; and Head of the Dept. of Social Work, 1976-84; Liverpool Polytechnic. **Publications:** Social Casework and Administration, 1966, 1970; (ed. and co-author) Penelope Hall's Social Social Services of England and Wales, 7th ed. 1969, 10th ed. 1983; Concepts in Social Administration: A Framework for Analysis, 1974; (co-author) Theories of Welfare, 1984 (ed.) Working with Parents of Handicapped Children, 1985. **Address:** 26 Eric Rd, Wallasey CH44 5RQ, England.

FOREMAN, Amanda. British, b. 1968. **Genres:** Biography. **Career:** Researcher and writer. Lady Margaret Hall, Oxford, researcher, 1991-. **Publications:** Georgiana, Duchess of Devonshire (biography), 1998. Contributor of articles to London newspapers. **Address:** Lady Margaret Hall, Oxford OX2 6QA, England.

FOREMAN, Lelia Rose. American, b. 1952. **Genres:** Science fiction/ Fantasy. **Career:** Children's Orthopedic Hospital, Seattle, WA, medical technician, 1974. **Publications:** SCIENCE FICTION: Shatterworld, 1995. Work represented in anthologies. **Address:** 13111 Northeast 191st Cir., Battle Ground, WA 98604, U.S.A.

FOREMAN, Michael. British, b. 1938. **Genres:** Children's fiction. **Career:** Art director, Ambit, London, 1960-. Lecturer, St. Martin's School of Art, London, 1963-65, London School of Printing, 1967, Royal College of Art, 1968-70, and Central School of Art, London, 1971-72; art eirector, Playboy, Chicago, 1965, and King, London, 1966. **Publications:** The Perfect Present, 1967; The Two Giants, 1967; The Great Sleigh Robbery, 1968; Horatio (in

U.S. as The Travels of Horatio), 1970; Moose, 1971; Dinosaurs and All That Rubbish, 1972; War and Peas, 1974; All the King's Horses, 1976; Panda's Puzzle, 1977; Trick a Tracker, 1979; Winter's Tales, 1979; Panda and the Odd Lion, 1981; Land of Dreams, 1982; Panda and the Bunyips, 1984; Cat and Canary, 1984; Private Zoo, 1985; Panda and the Bushfire, 1986; Ben's Box, 1986; Ben's Baby, 1987; The Angel and the Wild Animal, 1988; One World, 1989; War Boy, 1989; World of Fairy Tales, 1990; Mother Goose, 1991; Jack's Fantastic Voyage, 1992; The Boy Who Sailed with Columbus, 1992; War Game, 1993; Grandfather's Pencil and the Room of Stories, 1993; Dad! I Can't Sleep, 1994; Surprise, Surprise!, 1995; After the War Was Over, 1995; Seal Surfer, 1996; The Little Reindeer, 1996; Look! Look!, 1997; Angel and the Box of Time, 1997; Jack's Big Race, 1998; Chicken Licken, 1998; Little Red Hen, 1999; Rock-a-Doodle-Do, 2000; Cat in the Manger, 2000; Saving Sinbad, 2001; Michael Foreman's Playtime Rhymes, 2002; Wonder Goal!, 2003; Trip to Dinosaur Time, 2003; Hello, World, 2003. **Address:** c/o John Locke, 15 East 76th St., New York, NY 10021, U.S.A.

FOREMAN, Richard. American, b. 1937. **Genres:** Plays/Screenplays, Novels. **Career:** Founding Director, Ontological-Hysteric Theatre, NYC, since 1968. **Publications:** Richard Foreman: Plays and Manifestos, 1976; Richard Foreman: Reverberation Machines, More Plays and Manifestos, 1985; Love and Science: Music Theater Texts, 1991; Unbalancing Acts: Foundations for a Theater, 1992; My Head Was a Sledgehammer and Other Plays, 1995; No-Body (novel), 1997; Paradise Hotel and other plays, 2000. **Address:** 152 Wooster St, New York, NY 10012, U.S.A.

FOREST, Jim. (James H). American/Dutch, b. 1941. **Genres:** Children's fiction, Biography. **Career:** Writer. **Publications:** Thomas Merton's Struggle with Peacemaking, 1986; Love Is the Measure: A Biography of Dorothy Day, 1987, rev. ed., 1994; Making Friends of Enemies (in UK as Making Enemies Friends), 1987; Pilgrim to the Russian Church (in UK as Finding God among the Russians), 1988; (with N. Forest) Four Days in February, 1989; The Tale of the Turnip, 1989; Religion in the New Russia: The Impact of Perestroika on Soviet Religious Life, 1990, in U.K. as Free at Last?, 1990; Living with Wisdom: A Life of Thomas Merton, 1991; The Whale's Tale, 1992; Praying with Icons, 1996; Ladder of the Beatitudes, 1998; Confession: Doorway to Forgiveness, 2002. **Address:** Kanisstraat 5, 1811 GJ Alkmaar, Netherlands. **Online address:** jhforest@cs.com

FORKER, Charles R(ush). American, b. 1927. **Genres:** Plays/Screenplays, Poetry, Literary criticism and history, Theatre, Bibliography. **Career:** University of Wisconsin-Madison, instructor in English, 1957-59; Indiana University-Bloomington, instructor, 1959-61, assistant professor, 1961-65, associate professor, 1965-68, professor of English, 1968-. Visiting professor at University of Michigan, 1969-70, Dartmouth College, 1982-83, and Concordia University, Montreal, Quebec, 1989. **Publications:** (with D.G. Calder) Edward Phillips's History of the Literature of England and Scotland: A Translation from the Compendiosa Enumeratio Poetarum with an Introduction and Commentary (monograph), 1973; (with J. Candido) Henry V: An Annotated Bibliography, 1983; Skull beneath the Skin: The Achievement of John Webster, 1986; Fancy's Images: Contexts, Settings, and Perspectives in Shakespeare and His Contemporaries, 1990. EDITOR: (and author of intro. and commentary) J. Shirley, The Cardinal, 1964; W. Shakespeare, Henry V, 1971; (assoc.) Visions and Voices of the New Midwest, 1978; C. Marlowe, Edward II, 1994; Richard II: The Critical Tradition, 1998; Richard the Second, 2002. **Address:** Department of English, Indiana University-Bloomington, Bloomington, IN 47405, U.S.A. **Online address:** forker@ indiana.edu

FORMAN, Joan. Also writes as Pamela F. Greene. British. **Genres:** Children's fiction, Young adult fiction, Plays/Screenplays, Poetry, Children's non-fiction, History, Natural history, Paranormal. **Career:** Contrib, The Sunday Times, London. Educational Administration and Bursar of teachers' training coll., Lancs., until 1953; Poetry Page Ed., John o'Londons, 1958-62, and Time and Tide, 1962-63. **Publications:** (ed.) Galaxy Anthology, 4 vols.; See for Yourself, 2 vols.; The Romans; The Wise Ones; The Old Girls; Night of the Fox; The Accusers; Midwinter Journey; Maid in Arms; Mr. Browning's Lady; The Pilgrim Women; Guests of Honour; Portrait of the Late; Ding Dong Belle; The End of a Dream; The Walled Garden; A Search for Comets; The Turning Tide; The Freedom of the House; (ed.) Look Through a Diamond; The Princess in the Dark, 1973; Haunted East Anglia, 1974; The Mask of Time, 1978; The Haunted South, 1978; Haunted Royal Homes, 1987; Royal Hauntings, 1987; The Golden Shore, 1988. **Address:** c/o Thelma Newman, 36 Talmena Ave, Wadebridge, Cornwall PL27 7RR, England.

FORMAN, Robert K. C. American, b. 1947. **Genres:** Theology/Religion. **Career:** Vassar College, Poughkeepsie, NY, faculty member, 1987-89; Hunter

College of the City University of New York, assistant professor to associate professor of religious studies, 1989-. **Publications:** Master Eckhart: Mystic as Theologian, 1992; The Innate Capacity, in press. EDITOR: The Problem of Pure Consciousness, 1990; Religions of the World, 3rd ed, 1993; Religions of Asia, 1993. **Address:** Program in Religion 1241 HW, Hunter College - CUNY, 695 Park Ave., New York, NY 10021, U.S.A.

FORNÉS, Maria Irene. American (born Cuba), b. 1930. **Genres:** Plays/ Screenplays. **Career:** Playwright-Director, Theater for the New City, Padua Hills Festival, INTAR, and American Place Theatre, 1965-87. **Publications:** The Widow, 1963; The Office, 1965; The Successful Life of Three, 1965; Promenade, 1965; Tango Place, 1965; A Vietnamese Wedding, 1967; The Annunciation, 1967; The Red Burning Light, 1968; Promenade and Other Plays, 1971; The Curse of Langston Hughes, 1972; Aurora, 1973; Dr. Kheal, 1973; Molly's Dream, 1973; Cap-a-Pie, 1975; Washing, 1976; Lolita in the Garden, 1977; In Service, 1978; Fefu and Her Friends, 1978; Eyes on the Harem, 1979; Evelyn Brown, 1980; Blood Wedding, 1980; Life Is a Dream, 1981; A Visit, 1981; Mud, 1983; Sarita, 1984; The Danube, 1984; The Conduct of Life, 1985; No Time, 1985; Drowning, 1985; Cold Air, 1985; Lovers and Keepers, 1986; Plays, 1986; Abington Square, 1986; The Trial of Joan of Arc on a Matter of Faith, 1986; Charley, 1986; Art, 1986; Uncle Vanya, 1987; Hunger, 1988; And What of the Night, 1988; La Plaza Chica, 1994. **Address:** 1 Sheridan Sq, New York, NY 10014, U.S.A.

FORNI, P(ier) M(assimo). American, b. 1951. **Genres:** Literary criticism and history, Poetry. **Career:** Istituto Gonzaga, Milan, Italy, instructor, 1976-78; University of California, Los Angeles, research assistant at Center for Medieval and Renaissance Studies, 1980-81, lecturer in Italian, 1981-82; University of Pittsburgh, Pittsburgh, PA, assistant professor of Italian, 1983-85; Johns Hopkins University, Baltimore, MD, assistant professor, 1985-90, associate professor, 1990-95, professor of Italian literature, 1995-. Visiting professor at universities. Gives readings from his works. **Publications:** (trans. from English) P. Fisk, La Collina degli Agrifogli (translation of Midnight Blue), 1991; Forme Complesse nel Decameron, 1992; Adventures in Speech: Rhetoric and Narration in Boccaccio's "Decameron," 1996; Hotel Pace dei Monti (poems), 1996. EDITOR: (with G. Cavallini) F. Chiappelli, Il Legame Musaico: Saggi di Letteratura Italiana, 1984; G. Boccaccio, Ninfale Fiesolano, 1991; (co) Forma e Parola: Studi in Memoria di Fredi Chiappelli, 1992; I Fioretti di San Francesco, 1993; (with R. Bragantini) Lessico Critico Decameroniano, 1993. **Address:** Hispanic and Italian Studies Program, Zanvyl Krieger School of Arts and Sciences, Johns Hopkins University, 3400 North Charles St., Baltimore, MD 21212, U.S.A. **Online address:** forni@ jhu.edu

FORREST, Katherine V(irginia). Canadian, b. 1939. **Genres:** Novels, Novellas/Short stories, Mystery/Crime/Suspense, Science fiction/Fantasy. **Career:** Naiad Press, senior fiction editor, formerly; writer, currently. **Publications:** CRIME FICTION: Amateur City, 1984; Murder at the Nightwood Bar, 1987; The Beverly Malibu, 1989; Murder by Tradition, 1991; Liberty Square, 1996; Apparition Alley, 1997; Sleeping Bones, 1999. OTHER NOVELS: Curious Wine, 1983; Daughters of a Coral Dawn, 1984; An Emergence of Green, 1986; Dreams and Swords (short stories), 1987; Flashpoint, 1994; Daughters of an Amber Noon, 2003; Hancock Park, 2004.

FORREST, Richard (Stockton). Also writes as Stockton Woods. American, b. 1932. **Genres:** Medicine/Health, Mystery/Crime/Suspense. **Career:** Full-time writer since 1972. Branch Manager, Lawyers Title Insurance Co., Hartford, Conn., 1958-68; Vice-President, Chicago Title Insurance Co., Hartford, 1968-72. **Publications:** Who Killed Mr. Garland's Mistress?, 1974; A Child's Garden of Death, 1975; The Wizard of Death, 1977; Death Through the Looking Glass, 1978; The Death in the Willows, 1979; The Killing Edge, 1980; Death at Yew Corner, 1981; Death Under the Lilacs, 1985; Lark, 1986; Death on the Mississippi, 1989; (with M. and C. Forrest) Nursing Homes: The Complete Guide, 1990; (with M. Forrest) Beyond Retirement: Alternative Housing for the Elderly, 1991; The Pied Piper of Death, 1997. AS STOCKTON WOODS: The Laughing Man, 1980; Game Bet, 1981; The Man Who Heard Too Much, 1983;. **Address:** 8912 Ewing Dr., Bethesda, MD 20817, U.S.A.

FORRESTER, Duncan B(aillie). Scottish, b. 1933. **Genres:** Ethics, Theology/Religion. **Career:** Minister, missionary, and teacher. University of Edinburgh, Scotland, part-time assistant in politics, 1957-58; professor of Christian ethics and practical theology, 1978-2001, director of Centre for Theology and Public Issues, 1984-2001, principal of New College, 1986-96, dean of Faculty of Divinity, 1996-2000; licensed by Presbytery of St. Andrews, 1960; Hillside Church Edinburgh, assistant minister, and leader of St. James Mission, 1960-61; Madras Christian College, Tambaram, South India,

1962-70, lecturer to professor of politics; ordained presbyter of Church of South India, 1962; University of Sussex, England, chaplain, and lecturer in politics and religious studies in School of African and Asian Studies, 1970-78. Edinburgh Council of Social Services, chairman 1983-86. **Publications:** Caste and Christianity, 1980; (with J.I.H. McDonald and G. Tellini) Encounter with God, 1983; (with D. Murray) Studies in the History of Worship in Scotland, 1983; Christianity and the Future of Welfare, 1985; Theology and Politics, 1988; (ed. and contrib.) Just Sharing, 1988; Beliefs, Values, and Policies: Conviction Politics in a Secular Age, 1989; (ed. and contrib.) Theology and Practice, 1990; The True Church and Morality, 1997; Christian Justice & Public Policy, 1997; Truthful Action: Explorations in Practical Theology, 2000; On Human Worth, 2001. **Address:** New College, University of Edinburgh, The Mound, Edinburgh EH1 2LX, Scotland. **Online address:** d.forrester@ed.ac.uk

FORRESTER, Helen. (Jamunadevi Bhatia). Also writes as June Edwards. British/Canadian, b. 1919. **Genres:** Novels, Autobiography/Memoirs. **Career:** Writer. **Publications:** Alien There Is None, 1959, retitled Thursday's Child; The Latchkey Kid, 1970; Twopence to Cross the Mersey, 1974; (as June Edwards) Most Precious Employee, 1976; Minerva's Stepchild, 1979; (fiction ed.) Anthology 80, 1979; Liverpool Daisy, 1979, as Liverpool Miss, 1982; By the Waters of Liverpool, 1981; Three Women of Liverpool, 1984; Lime Street at Two, 1985; The Moneylenders of Shahpur, 1987; Yes, Mama, 1987; The Lemon Tree, 1990; The Liverpool Basque, 1993; Mourning Doves, 1996; Madame Barbara, 1999; A Cuppa Tea and an Aspirin, 2003. **Address:** c/o The Writers' Union of Canada, 40 Wellington St E 3rd Fl, Toronto, ON, Canada M5E 1C7.

FORRESTER, John. British, b. 1949. **Genres:** Psychiatry, History. **Career:** Cambridge University, Cambridge, England, reader in history and philosophy of the science, 1984-. **Publications:** Language and the Origins of Psychoanalysis, 1980; (trans.) Jacques Lacan, The Seminars of Jacques Lacan: Freud's Writings on Technique 1953-1954, edited by Jacques-Alain Miller, Book I, 1988; The Seductions of Psychoanalysis: Freud, Lacan, and Derrida, 1990; (with L. Appignanesi) Freud's Women, 1992; Dispatches from the Freud Wars, 1997. **Address:** Department of History and Philosophy of Science, Cambridge University, Free School Lane, Cambridge CB2 3RH, England.

FORRESTER, Michael A. Scottish, b. 1953. **Genres:** Psychology. **Career:** Loughborough University, Leicestershire, England, research associate, 1986-87; University of Kent, Canterbury, England, lecturer, 1987-. **Publications:** The Development of Young Children's Social-Cognitive Skills, 1992. **Address:** Department of Psychology, University of Kent, Canterbury CT2 7LZ, England.

FORRESTER, Sandra. American, b. 1949. **Genres:** Young adult fiction. **Career:** Department of the Army, Alexandria, VA, occupational analyst, 1974-85, Falls Church, VA, management analyst, 1985-92; National Institute of Environmental Health Sciences, Research Triangle Park, NC, management analyst, 1992-. **Publications:** Sound the Jubilee (young adult novel), 1995. **Address:** National Institute of Environmental Health Sciences, 101 Alexander Dr., Research Triangle Park, NC 27709, U.S.A.

FORRESTER, Sibelan. American, b. 1961. **Genres:** Poetry, Language/ Linguistics, Literary criticism and history, Translations. **Career:** Oberlin College, Oberlin, OH, assistant professor of Russian, 1989-94; Swarthmore College, Swarthmore, PA, assistant professor, 1994-98, associate professor of Russian, 1998-. **Publications:** (ed. with P. Chester) Engendering Slavic Literature, 1996; (trans. with C. Hawkesworth) I. Vrkljan, The Silk, the Shears, 1999. **Address:** Department of Modern Languages and Literatures, Swarthmore College, 500 College Ave, Swarthmore, PA 19081, U.S.A. **Online address:** sforres1@swarthmore.edu

FORSTENZER, Thomas R. American, b. 1944. **Genres:** History. **Career:** Rutgers University, New Brunswick, NJ, professor of history, 1970-80; UNESCO, Paris, France, consultant, 1980-83, staff member to executive officer, 1984-. **Publications:** Youth in the 1980's, 1979; French Provincial Police and the Fall of the Second Republic: Social Fear and Counter Revolution, 1981; (as Tom Forstenzer with F. Mayor) The New Page, 1995. **Address:** UNESCO, 7 place de Fontenoy, 75700 Paris, France.

FORSTER, Marc R. American, b. 1959. **Genres:** History. **Career:** Harvard University, Cambridge, MA, lecturer in history, 1989-90; Connecticut College, New London, assistant professor of history, 1990-95, associate professor of history, 1995-. **Publications:** The Counter-Reformation in the Villages: Religion and Reform in the Bishopric of Speyer, 1560-1720, Cornell

University Press, 1992. **Address:** Department of History, Connecticut College, Box 5497, New London, CT 06320, U.S.A.

FORSTER, Margaret. British, b. 1938. **Genres:** Novels, Biography. **Career:** Fiction Reviewer, Evening Standard, London, 1977-80. **Publications:** Dames Delight, 1964; The Bogey Man; Fenella Fizackerly; Georgy Girl; Miss Owen-Owen Is at Home; Mr. Bone's Retreat; The Park; The Travels of Maudie Tipstaff; The Rash Adventurer; The Rise and Fall of Charles Edward Stuart, 1973; The Seduction of Mrs. Pendlebury, 1974; Thackeray: Memoirs of a Vistorian Gentleman, 1978; Mother, Can You Hear Me?, 1979; The Bride of Lowther Fell, 1980; Marital Rites, 1981; Significant Sisters: Active Feminism 1839-1939, 1984; Private Papers, 1986; Elizabeth Barrett Browning: A Biography, 1988; Have the Men Had Enough? (novel), 1989; Lady's Maid (novel), 1990; The Battle for Christabel (novel), 1991; Daphne du Maurier (biography), 1993; Hidden Lives (memoir), 1995; Mothers' Boys (novel), 1996. **Address:** 11 Boscastle Rd., London NW5, England.

FORSYTH, Frederick. British, b. 1938. **Genres:** Novels, Novellas/Short stories, Mystery/Crime/Suspense. **Career:** Staff member, BBC, London, 1965-67; freelance journalist in Nigeria, 1968-70; presenter, Soldiers television programme, 1985. Recipient: Mystery Writers of America Edgar Allan Poe award, 1971, 1983. **Publications:** The Biafra Story (non-fiction), 1969; Day of the Jackal, 1971; The Odessa File, 1972; The Dogs of War, 1974; The Shepherd, 1975; The Devil's Alternative, 1979; Forsyth's Three, 1980; No Comebacks: Collected Short Stories, 1982; The Fourth Protocol, 1984; The Negotiator, 1989; Deceiver, 1992; (ed.) Great Flying Stories, 1991; The Shepherd, 1992; The Fist of God, 1994; Icon, 1996; The Phantom of Manhattan, 1999; The Veteran, 2001; Avenger, 2003.

FORSYTH, James (Law). British, b. 1913. **Genres:** Plays/Screenplays, Poetry, Biography. **Career:** Dramatist-in-residence, Old Vic Co., London, 1946-48, and Howard University, Washington, D.C., 1961-62, and Florida State University, 1964; Director, Tufts University Program in London, 1967-71; Artistic Director, Forsyths' Barn Theatre, Ansty, Sussex, 1972-83. **Publications:** Emmanuel: A Nativity Play, 1952; Three Plays: The Other Heart, Heloise, Adelaise, 1957; The Road to Emmaus: A Play for Eastertide, 1958; Joshua, 1959; (adaptor) Brand, by Ibsen, 1960; Dear Wormwood, 1961, as Screwtape, 1973; (adaptor) Cyrano de Bergerac, by E. Rostand, 1968; The Last Journey, 1972; Defiant Island, 1975; Tyrone Guthrie: A Biography, 1976; Back to the Barn: The Story of a Country Theatre; On Such a Day as This (poetry), 1989; From Time to Time (poetry), 1990; also radio and TV plays: If My Wings Heal (play), 1968; A Woman There Will Be (poetry), 1991; The Clearing Where the Cuckoo Came (poetry), 1992. **Address:** Grainloft, Ansty, Near Haywards Heath, Sussex RH17 5AG, England.

FORSYTH, Kate. Also writes as Kate Humphrey. Australian, b. 1966. **Genres:** Science fiction/Fantasy. **Career:** Writer, poet, editor, and journalist. **Publications:** The Starthorn Tree (young adult), 2002; (as Kate Humphrey) Full Fathom Five, 2003. THE WITCHES OF EILEANAN SERIES: Dragonclaw, 1997, in US as The Witches of Eileannan, 1998; The Pool of Two Moons, 1998; The Cursed Towers, 1999; The Forbidden Land, 2000; The Skull of the World, 2001; The Fathomless Caves, 2002. Contributor of to periodicals. As Kate Humphrey, contributor of poetry to literary journals and newspapers. **Address:** c/o Curtis Brown Australia, Level 1, 2 Boundary St., Paddington, NSW 2021, Australia. **Online address:** kforsyth@ozemail.com.au

FORSYTH, Michael (de Jong). British, b. 1951. **Genres:** Architecture. **Career:** Architect in the U.S. Virgin Islands and in Gothenburg, Sweden, 1972-73; Arthur Erickson Architects and Parkin Partnership, Toronto, Ontario, architect, 1976-79; University of Bristol, Bristol, England, lecturer in architecture, 1979-84, research fellow in drama, 1984-90; special lecturer in theatre architecture, 1990-; writer. Visiting lecturer at University of Toronto, University of Wales, University of Bath, University of London, Brighton University, and Plymouth University. Forsyth Chartered Architects, director; Plato Consortium Lt., member of board of directors; University of Bath, director of studies, MSc in the conservation of historic buildings; British School at Rome, member of selection board for the Rome Prize in architecture; Friends of the Victoria Art Gallery, Bath, chairman of executive committee; Bath Preservation Trust, member of executive committee. Radio and television broadcaster for British Broadcasting Corporation; violinist. **Publications:** Buildings for Music: The Architect, the Musician, and the Listener from the Seventeenth Century to the Present Day, 1985; Auditoria: Designing for the Performing Arts, 1987. **Address:** Department of Architecture and Civil Engineering, University of Bath, Bath BA2 7AY, England. **Online address:** M.Forsyth@bath.ac.uk

FORSYTH, Phyllis Young. American, b. 1944. **Genres:** Classics. **Career:** University of Waterloo, Waterloo, Ontario, professor of classical studies,

1969-. **Publications:** Atlantis: The Making of Myth, 1980; Catullus: A Teaching Text, 1986; Catullus: Advanced Placement Ed., 1997; Thera in the Bronze Age, 1997. Contributor to academic journals. **Address:** Department of Classical Studies, University of Waterloo, Waterloo, ON, Canada N2L 3G1. **Online address:** forsyth@watarts.uwaterloo.ca

FORSYTHE, Ronald. See **TEAL, G. Donn.**

FORT, Ilene Susan. American, b. 1949. **Genres:** Art/Art history. **Career:** H.W. Wilson Co., Bronx, NY, indexer for Reader's Guide to Periodical Literature, 1971-73; Worldwide Books, Boston, MA, editor, 1975-79; consultant, 1979-83; Los Angeles County Museum of Art, Los Angeles, CA, assistant curator, 1983-87, associate curator, 1987-93, curator, 1993-96. **Publications:** The Flag Paintings of Childe Hassam, 1988; (co-author) American Art: A Catalogue of the Los Angeles County Museum of Art, 1991; Paintings of California, 1993; Childe Hassam's New York, 1993; The Figure in American Sculpture: A Question of Modernity, 1995; American Paintings in Southern California Collections, 1996. **Address:** Los Angeles County Museum of Art, 5905 Wilshire Blvd., Los Angeles, CA 90036, U.S.A. **Online address:** ifort@lacma.org

FORTE, Maurizio. Italian, b. 1961. **Genres:** Archaeology/Antiquities. **Career:** Archeologist, editor, and writer. Bologna University, Bologna, Italy, laurea in ancient history, 1985-; ICARUS Project, tutor; National Research Council, Italy, researcher; involved with multimedia, computer graphics, and virtual reality computer applications in relation to archaeology. **Publications:** Le terrecotte ornamentali dei templi lumensi: Catalogo delle terrecotte architettoniche a stampo conservate al Museo archeologico nazionale di Firenze, 1991; (with P. von Eles) La pianura bolognese nel villanviano: Insediamenti della prima eta del ferro, 1994; (with others; and editor with A. Siliotti) Virtual Archeology: Re-Creating Ancient Worlds, trans. by J. Toms and R. Skeates, 1997. Author of museum catalogues. **Address:** c/o Harry N. Abrams Inc., 100 Fifth Ave., New York, NY 10011, U.S.A. **Online address:** maurizio@sirio.cineca.it

FORTES (DE LEFF), Jacqueline. Mexican, b. 1952. **Genres:** Psychology, Sciences. **Career:** Universidad Nacional Autonoma de Mexico, Mexico City, assistant professor, 1973-74, associate researcher, 1980-84, professor of psychology, 1984-, family therapist and supervisor, Clinic of Psychological Services, 1984-89. Instituto de la Familia, professor, 1983-, family therapist and senior supervisor, 1991-, vice-president and chief of teaching programs, 1991-93, president and researcher, 1993-; National Institute of Cardiology, family therapist and supervisor of trainees, 1990-91; consultant to Institute of Research in Applied Mathematics and Systems and National Council of Science and Technology; Mexican Family Therapy Association, secretary 1998-99; Revista Psicoterapia y Familia, editor, 2002-. **Publications:** (with L. Lomnitz) La Formacion del Cientifico en Mexico: Adquiriendo una nueva Identidad, 1991, trans published as Becoming a Scientist in Mexico, 1994. Contributor to books published in Spanish. Contributor to periodicals. **Address:** Hegel 120-204, 11570 Mexico City, DF, Mexico. **Online address:** jfortes@prodigy.net.mx

FORTEY, Richard. British, b. 1946. **Genres:** Natural history. **Career:** Paleontologist and author. Natural History Museum, London, England, research fellow, 1970-77, became principal scientific officer and then merit researcher, 1978-. Lewis Thomas Prize, 2003. **Publications:** Fossils: The Key to the Past, 1982; The Dinosaurs' Alphabet, 1990; The Hidden Landscape: A Journey in to the Geological Past, 1993; Life: An Unauthorized Biography, 1997, in US as Life: A Natural History of the First Four Billion Years of Life on Earth, 1998. **Address:** 48 St Andrew's Rd, Henley on Thames, Oxon. RG9 1JD, England. **Online address:** raf@nhm.ac.uk

FOSSUM, Robert H. American, b. 1923. **Genres:** Poetry, Literary criticism and history. **Career:** Professor of English and American Literature, Claremont McKenna College, and Claremont Graduate School, California, since 1963, Emeritus since 1987. Associate Professor, Dept. of English, Beloit, Wisconsin, 1950-62; Associate Professor of English, California State University, Los Angeles, 1962-63. **Publications:** William Styron: A Critical Essay, 1968; Hawthorne's Inviolable Circle, 1972; (with Sy Kahn) Facing Mirrors, 1980; (with John Roth) The American Dream, 1981; (with John Roth) American Ground, 1988. **Address:** 403 University Circle, Claremont, CA 91711, U.S.A.

FOSTER, Alan Dean. American, b. 1946. **Genres:** Novellas/Short stories, Science fiction/Fantasy. **Career:** Headlines Ink Agency, Studio City, California, head copywriter, 1970-71; University of California at Los Angeles, instructor of English and film, intermittently, 1971-; Los Angeles

City College, instructor of English and film, 1972-76. **Publications:** FANTASY: Luana (novelization of screenplay), 1974; Clash of the Titans (novelization of screenplay), 1981; Spellsinger at the Gate (Spellsinger and The Hour at the Gate), 1983; Krull (novelization of screenplay), 1983; The Day of the Dissonance, 1984; The Moment of the Magician, 1984; Shadowkeep, 1984; Pale Rider (novelization of screenplay), 1985; The Paths of the Perambulator, 1985; The Time of the Transference, 1986; Son of Spellsinger, 1993; Chorus Skating, 1994. OTHER: The Tar-Aiym Krang, 1972; Bloodhype, 1973; Icerigger, 1974; Dark Star (novelization of screenplay), 1974; Star Trek Log One-Ten (novelization of TV scripts), 10 vols, 1974-78; Midworld, 1975; (as George Lucas) Star Wars (novelization of screenplay), 1976; Orphan Star, 1977; The End of the Matter, 1977; Splinter of the Mind's Eye, 1978; Mission to Moulokin, 1979; Alien (novelization of screenplay), 1979; The Black Hole (novelization of screenplay), 1979; Cachalot, 1980; Outland (novelization of screenplay), 1981; The Thing (novelization of screenplay), 1982; Nor Crystal Tears, 1982; For Love of Mother-Not, 1983; The Man Who Used the Universe, 1983; The I Inside, 1984; The Last Starfighter (novelization of screenplay), 1984; Slipt, 1984; Starman (novelization of screenplay), 1984; Voyage to the City of the Dead, 1984; Sentenced to Prism, 1985; Aliens (novelization of screenplay), 1986; Into the Out Of, 1986; The Deluge Drivers, 1987; Glory Lane, 1987; Flinx in Flux, 1988; Alien Nation (novelization of screenplay), 1988; To the Vanishing Point, 1988; Maori, 1988; Quozl, 1989; Cyber Way, 1990; A Call to Arms, 1991; Cat-a-lyst, 1991; Alien 3 (novelization of screenplay), 1992; Codgerspace, 1992; The False Mirror, 1992; The Spoils of War, 1993; Greenthieves, 1994; Ascending Whine, 1995; (with E.F. Russell) Design for Great Day, 1995. SHORT STORIES: With Friends Like These…, 1977; The Horror on the Beach, 1978; …Who Needs Enemies, 1984; The Metrognome and Other Stories, 1990. EDITOR: The Best of Eric Frank Russell, 1978; Animated Features and Silly Symphonies, 1980; (with M.H. Greenberg) Smart Dragons, Foolish Elves, 1991; (with Greenberg) Betcha Can't Read Just One, 1993. **Address:** c/o Thranx Inc, PO Box 12757, Prescott, AZ 86304, U.S.A. **Online address:** adf@alandeanfoster.com

FOSTER, Cecil (A.). West Indian, b. 1954. **Genres:** Race relations, Novels. **Career:** Caribbean News Agency, senior reporter and editor, 1975-77; Barbados Advocate News, reporter and columnist, 1977-79; Toronto Star, Toronto, Ontario, Canada, reporter, 1979-82; Contrast, Toronto, editor, 1979-82; Transportation Business Management, editor, 1982-83; Globe and Mail, Toronto, reporter, 1983-89; Financial Post, senior editor, 1989-. **Publications:** Distorted Mirror: Canada's Racist Face, 1991; No Man in the House (novel), 1991; Sleep On, Beloved (novel), 1995; A Place Called Heaven: The Meaning of Being Black in Canada. Contributor of articles and reviews to periodicals. **Address:** 125 Greenbush Cres., Thornhill, ON, Canada L4J 5M3.

FOSTER, David Manning. Australian, b. 1944. **Genres:** Novels. **Career:** U.S. Public Health Service, Philadelphia, PA, international postdoctoral research fellow, 1970-71; Medical School, University of Sydney, NSW, sr. research officer, 1971-72, Australian creative fellow, 1992-. **Publications:** North South West, 1973; The Pure Land, 1974; The Fleeing Atlanta (poetry), 1975; Escape to Reality, 1977; (with D. Lyall) The Empathy Experiment, 1977; Moonlite, 1981; Plumbum, 1983; Dog Rock, 1985; Christian Rosy Cross, 1986; Testostero, 1987; The Pale Blue Crochet Coathanger Cover, 1988; Hitting the Wall, 1989; Mates of Mars, 1991; (ed.) Self Portraits, 1991; A Slab of Fosters, 1994; The Glade within the Grove, 1996; The Ballad of Erinungarah (verse novel), 1997; In the New Country, 1999; Studs & Nogs (essays), 1999; The Land Where Stories End, 2001.

FOSTER, David William. American, b. 1940. **Genres:** Literary criticism and history, Bibliography. **Career:** University of Missouri, assistant professor of Spanish, 1964-66; Arizona State University, Tempe, professor, 1966-90, regents' professor of Spanish and women's studies, 1966-. Rocky Mountain Review of Language and Literature, editor, 1980-84. **Publications:** (co) Research on Language Teaching, 1962; Forms of the Novel in the Work of Camilo Jose Cela, 1967; Myth of Paraguay in the Fiction of Augusto Roa Bastos, 1969; (with V.R. Foster) Manual of Hispanic Bibliography, 1970; (with V.R. Foster) Research Guide to Argentine Literature, 1970; A Bibliography of the Works of Jorge Luis Borges, 1971; Christian Allegory in Early Hispanic Poetry, 1971; The Marques de Santillana, 1971; (with G.L. Bower) Haiku in Western Languages, 1972; Early Spanish Ballad, 1972; Unamuno and the Novel as Expressionist Conceit, 1973; (with V.R. Foster) Modern Latin American Literature, 1975; Currents in the Contemporary Argentine Novel, 1975; Twentieth Century Spanish-American Novel: A Bibliography, 1975; (with H.J. Becco) La nueva narrativa hispoamericana: Bibliograffa, 1976; Chilean Literature: A Working Bibliography, 1978; Augusto Roa Bastos, 1978; Studies in the Contemporary Spanish American

Short Story, 1979; Mexican Literature: A Bibliography of Secondary Sources, 1981, 2nd ed., 1992; Peruvian Literature: A Bibliography of Secondary Sources, 1981; (with R. Reis) A Dictionary of Contemporary Brazilian Authors, 1982; Para una lectura semiotica del ensayo latinoamericano, 1983; Jorge Luis Borges: An Annotated Primary and Secondary Bibliography, 1984; Estudios sobre teatro mexicano contemporaneo: semiologia de la competencia teatral, 1984; Cuban Literature, 1984; Alternate Voices in the Contemporary Latin American Narrative, 1985; The Argentine Teatro-Independiente, 1930-1955, 1986; Social Realism in the Argentine Narrative, 1986; Handbook of Latin American Literature, 1987; From Mafalda to Los Supermachos, 1989; The Argentine Generation of 1880, 1990; (with W. Rela) Brazilian Literature: A Research Bibliography, 1990; Gay and Lesbian Themes in Latin American Writing, 1991; Contemporary Argentine Cinema, 1992; Cultural Diversity in Latin American Literature, 1994; Latin American Writers on Gay and Lesbian Themes: A Bio-Critical Sourcebook, 1994; Violence in Argentine Literature, 1995; (with D. Altamiranda, G. Geirola, and C. de Urioste) Literatura espanola: una antologia, 1995; Sexual Textualities, 1997; Espacio escenico y lenguaje, 1998; Buenos Aires: Perspective on the City and Cultural Production, 1998; A Funny Dirty Little War, 1998; (with M.F. Lockhart and D.B. Lockhart) Culture and Customs of Argentina, 1998; (with D. Altamiranda and C. de Urioste) The Writer's Reference Guide to Spanish, 1999; Gender and Society in Contemporary Brazilian Cinema, 1999; Produccion cultural e identidades homoeroticas, 1999; Mexico City and Contemporary Mexican Fiilmmaking, 2002. EDITOR: A Dictionary of Contemporary Latin American Authors, 1975; Sourcebook of Hispanic Culture in the United States, 1982; Marques de Santillana: Poesia (selection), 1982; (with F.A. Rosales) Hispanics and the Humanities in the Southwest, 1983. **Address:** Dept of Languages and Literature, Arizona State University, Tempe, AZ 85287-0202, U.S.A. **Online address:** david.foster@asu.edu

FOSTER, Edward Halsey. Also writes as Samuel Retsov. American, b. 1942. **Genres:** Poetry, Literary criticism and history. **Career:** Stevens Institute of Technology, Hoboken, NJ, associate professor, 1975-84, professor of English and American literature, 1985-, director of programs in the humanities and social sciences, 2002-. Talisman House, Publishers, president, 1993-. University of Istanbul, Turkey, visiting Fulbright professor, 1985-86; Drew University, Graduate School of English, Madison, NJ, visiting professor, 1991, 1992, 1994, 1996; Beykent University, Istanbul, visiting professor, 2001. Talisman: A Journal of Contemporary Poetry and Poetics, editor, 1988-; Multi-Cultural Review, poetry editor, 1991-95. **Publications:** Catherine Maria Sedgwick, 1974; The Civilized Wilderness, 1975; Josia Gregg and Lewis H. Garrard, 1977; Susan and Anna Warner, 1978; Richard Brautigan, 1983; Cummington Poems, 1982; William Saroyan, 1984; Jack Spicer, 1991; William Saroyan: A Study of the Short Fiction, 1992; Understanding the Beats, 1992; The Space between Her Bed and Clock (poems), 1993; Understanding the Black Mountain Poets, 1994: Code of the West: A Memoir of Ted Berrigan, 1994; The Understanding (poems), 1994; All Acts Are Simply Acts, 1995; Adrian as Song, 1996; Boy in the Key of E, 1998; Answerable to None: Berrigan, Bronk, and the American Real, 1999; The Angelus Bell, 2001; Mahrem, 2002. EDITOR: (with G.W. Clark) Hoboken, 1976; (with D. Mesyats) The New Freedoms, 1994; (with L. Schwartz and J. Donahue) Primary Trouble, 1996; The White Tomb: Selected Poems of Stuart Merrill, 1999; Decadents, Symbolists, and Aesthetes in America, 2000; (with J. Donahue) The World in Time and Space, 2002. **Address:** c/o Talisman, PO Box 3157, Jersey City, NJ 07303-3157, U.S.A.

FOSTER, Frances Smith. American, b. 1944. **Genres:** History, Literary criticism and history, Women's studies and issues. **Career:** San Diego State University, San Diego, CA, professor of literature, 1971-88; University of California at San Diego, La Jolla, professor of literature, 1988-94; Emory University, Atlanta, 1994-; writer. **Publications:** Witnessing Slavery: The Development of Ante-Bellum Slave Narratives, 1979; Written by Herself: Literary Production of African American Women, 1746-1892, 1994. EDITOR: Minnie's Sacrifice, 1994; A Brighter Coming Day: A Frances Ellen Watkins Harper Reader, 1990; (co) Oxford Companion to African American Literature, 1997; Behind the Scenes, 2001; (co) Incidents in the Life of a Slave Girl, 2001; (co) Concise Oxford Companion to African American Literature, 2001. **Address:** Dept of English, Callaway Memorial Center, Emory University, Atlanta, GA 30322, U.S.A. **Online address:** ffoster@emory.edu

FOSTER, Iris. See POSNER, Richard.

FOSTER, Jeanne. See WILLIAMS, Jeanne.

FOSTER, Joanne Reckler. American, b. 1941. **Genres:** Autobiography/Memoirs. **Career:** Rocky Mountain News, Denver, CO, assistant to assistant city editor and general assignment reporter, specializing in urban affairs, 1963-67; National Observer, Silver Spring, MD, staff writer, 1967-69; Washington Post, Washington, DC, reporter, 1969; freelance writer, editor, and proofreader, 1978-. **Publications:** (with D.D. Dempsey) The Captain's a Woman: Tales of a Merchant Mariner (memoir), 1997. **Address:** 2380 Mosquito Point Rd., White Stone, VA 22578, U.S.A. **Online address:** whitetop@crosslink.net

FOSTER, John Bellamy. American, b. 1953. **Genres:** Economics. **Career:** Evergreen State College, Olympia, WA, faculty member, 1985; University of Oregon, Eugene, visiting assistant professor, 1985-87, assistant professor, 1987-91, associate professor of sociology, 1992-. York University, fellow of Bethune College, 1978-86; visiting lecturer at colleges and universities. **Publications:** (ed. with H. Szlajfer, and contrib.) The Faltering Economy: The Problem of Accumulation Under Monopoly Capitalism, 1984; The Theory of Monopoly Capitalism: An Elaboration of Marxian Political Economy, 1986; The Vulnerable Planet: A Short Economic History of the Environment, 1994; (ed. and author of intro.) E. Fischer, How to Read Karl Marx, 1996. Contributor to books. Contributor of articles and reviews to periodicals. **Address:** Department of Sociology, University of Oregon, Eugene, OR 97403, U.S.A.

FOSTER, John Wilson. (born Ireland), b. 1944. **Genres:** Botany. **Career:** University of British Columbia, Vancouver, Canada, beginning in 1974, began as assistant professor, became full professor of English; University of Ulster, Academy for Irish Cultural Heritages, Londonderry, Northern Ireland, Leverhulme Visiting Professor, 2004-. **Publications:** Forces and Themes in Ulster Fiction, 1974; Fictions of the Irish Literary Revival: A Changeling Art, 1987; Colonial Consequences: Essays in Irish Literature and Culture, 1991; (editor, with Gerald Dawe) The Poet's Place: Ulster Literature and Society; Essays in Honor of John Hewitt, 1907-87, 1991; (editor) The Idea of the Union: Statements and Critiques in Support of the Union of Great Britain and Northern Ireland, 1995; The Achievement of Seamus Heaney, 1995; The Titanic Complex: A Cultural Manifest, 1996; (Senior editor, with associate editor Helena C. G. Chesney) Nature in Ireland: A Scientific and Cultural History, 1997; (editor) Titanic Reader, 2000; Recoveries: Neglected Episodes in Irish Cultural History, 1860-1912, 2002; The Age of Titanic: Cross-Currents in Anglo-American Culture, 2002. **Address:** Academy for Irish Cultural Heritages, Aberfoyle House, University of Ulster, Magee Campus, Northland Rd, Londonderry BT48 7JL, Ireland.

FOSTER, (William) Lawrence. American, b. 1947. **Genres:** Sex, Theology/Religion. **Career:** Roosevelt University, Chicago, IL, instructor in American social history, 1976-77; Georgia Institute of Technology, Atlanta, assistant professor, 1977-82, associate professor of American history, 1982-. University of Sydney, visiting Fulbright professor, 1985. **Publications:** Religion and Sexuality: Three American Communal Experiments of the Nineteenth Century, 1981, as Religion and Sexuality: The Shakers, the Mormons, and the Oneida Community, 1984; Women, Family, and Utopia: Communal Experiments of the Shakers, the Oneida Community, and the Mormons, 1991; (ed.) Free Love in Utopia, 2000. Contributor to books.

FOSTER, M(ichael) A(nthony). American, b. 1939. **Genres:** Science fiction/Fantasy, Poetry, Novellas/Short stories. **Career:** Served in the U.S. Air Force, 1957-62, 1965-76: Captain. **Publications:** POETRY: Shards from Byzantium, 1969; The Vaseline Dreams of Hundifer Soames, 1970. SCIENCE FICTION: The Warriors of Dawn, 1975; The Gameplayers of Zan, 1977; The Day of the Klesh, 1979; Waves, 1980; The Morphodite, 1981; Transformer, 1983; Preserver, 1985; Owl Time (short stories), 1985. **Address:** 5409 Amberhill Dr, Greensboro, NC 27455, U.S.A.

FOSTER, Nora R(akestraw). American, b. 1947. **Genres:** Marine sciences/Oceanography. **Career:** University of Alaska Museum, Fairbanks, AK, coordinator of aquatic collection, 1981-. **Publications:** Intertidal Bivalves: A Guide to the Common Marine Bivalves of Alaska, University of Alaska Press, 1991; A Synopsis of the Marine Prosobranch Gastropod and Bivalve Mollusks in Alaskan Waters, University of Alaska, Institute of Marine Science. **Address:** University of Alaska Museum, 907 Yukon Dr., Fairbanks, AK 99775, U.S.A.

FOSTER, Richard. British, b. 1946. **Genres:** Art/Art history, Architecture, Biography. **Career:** British Broadcasting Corporation (BBC), London, England, television producer, 1970-72; producer and writer, 1972. **Publications:** Discovering English Churches, 1981; (with P. Tudor-Craig) The Secret Life of Paintings, 1986; The Parish Churches of Britain, 1988; Patterns of Thought: The Hidden Meaning of the Great Pavement of Westminster Abbey,

1991; William Morris: Broken Dreams, 1995. Contributor to magazines. **Address:** Rachel Calder, Tessa Sayle Agency, 11 Jubilee Place, London SW3 3TE, England.

FOSTER, Sam. *See* BOUNDS, Sydney J(ames).

FOSTER, Steven. American, b. 1957. **Genres:** Photography, Medicine/Health. **Career:** Shaker Community, Sabbathday Lake, ME, herbalist, 1974-78; Volunteers in Service to America (VISTA), director of Herb Garden Project in Santa Cruz, CA, 1979; Ozark Resources Center, Brixey, MO, research director of Ozark Beneficial Plant Project, 1983-87; free-lance writer, technical editor, photographer, and consultant in Eureka Springs, AR, 1987-. Izard Ozark Native Seeds, proprietor, 1983-88. Member of boards of directors and advisory boards. **Publications:** (and photographer) Herbal Bounty: The Gentle Art of Herb Culture, 1984; (with J.A. Duke and photographer) A Field Guide to Medicinal Plants: Eastern and Central North America, 1990; Echinacea: Nature's Immune Enhancer, Healing Arts Press, 1991; (with Yue Chongxi) Herbal Emissaries: Bringing Chinese Herbs to the West, 1992; (with R. Caras) A Field Guide to Venomous Animals and Poisonous Plants of North America, 1994. Photographer for books by B. Conrow and A. Hecksel. **Address:** Steven Foster Group, General Delivery, CR 158, Brixey, MO 65618, U.S.A.

FOTOPOULOS, Takis. Greek, b. 1940. **Genres:** Economics, Environmental sciences/Ecology, Philosophy, Politics/Government, Social sciences. **Career:** University of North London, England, lecturer, 1969-72, senior lecturer in economics, 1973-89; Society and Nature, editor, 1992-98; Democracy and Nature, editor, 1999-2003; International Journal of Inclusive Democracy, editor, 2004-. **Publications:** Dependent Development, 1985; The War in the Gulf, 1991; The Neoliberal Consensus, 1993; The New World Order and Greece, 1997; Towards an Inclusive Democracy, 1997; Inclusive Democracy, 1999; Drugs: An Alternative Approach, 1999; The New Order in the Balkans, 1999; Religion, Autonomy, Democracy, 2000; From Athenian Democracy to Inclusive Democracy, 2000; Globalisation, Left and Inclusive Democracy, 2002; The War against "Terrorism," 2003; Chomsky's Capitalism, 2004; The Multi-dimensional Crisis and Inclusive Democracy, 2004. Contributor to books and periodicals. **Address:** 20 Woodberry Way, London N12 0HG, England. **Online address:** takis@fotopoulos1.fsnet.co.uk

FOULKES, (Albert) Peter. British, b. 1936. **Genres:** Literary criticism and history, Travel/Exploration. **Career:** Assistant Professor of German, University of Mississippi, University, 1961-63, and University of Illinois, Urbana, 1963-65; Assistant Professor, 1965-67, Associate Professor, 1967-72, and Professor of German Studies, 1972-77, Stanford University, California; Alexander von Humboldt Sr. Research Fellow, University of Constance, 1972-74; Professor of German, University of Wales, Cardiff, 1977-90; Vice President, Institute of Linguists, London, 1990-99. **Publications:** The Reluctant Pessimist: A Study of Franz Kafka, 1967; The Search for Literary Meaning, 1976; Literature and Propaganda, 1983. EDITOR: (with E. Lohner) Deutsche Novellen von Tieck bis Hauptmann. 1969; (with Lohner) Das deutsche Drama von Kleist bis Hauptmann, 1973; The Uses of Criticism, 1977; Die Judenbuche, 1989; Tales from French Catalonia, 2001. **Address:** Clara, 66500 Prades, France.

FOULKES, Richard (George). British, b. 1944. **Genres:** Theatre. **Career:** University of Birmingham, England, administrator, 1967-73; University of Leicester, Leicester, England, lecturer, 1973-98, reader, 1998-. Northampton Repertory Players, director, 1990-96, chairman, 1995-96. New Dictionary of National Biography, associate editor; Society for Theatre Research, general editor of publications. **Publications:** The Shakespeare Tercentenary of 1864, 1984; The Calverts: Actors of Some Importance, 1992; Repertory at the Royal: Sixty-Five Years of Theatre in Northampton, 1992; Church and State in Victorian England, 1997; Performing Shakespeare in the Age of Empire, 2002. EDITOR: Shakespeare and the Victorian Stage, 1986; British Theatre in the 1890's: Essays on Drama and the Stage, 1992; Scenes from Provincial Stages, 1994. Contributor to journals. **Address:** Department of English, University of Leicester, Leicester LE1 7RH, England.

FOURIE, Corlia. South African, b. 1944. **Genres:** Children's fiction, Novellas/Short stories, Mythology/Folklore. **Career:** Journalist and writer, 1965-. **Publications:** Ganekwane and the Green Dragon: Four Stories from Africa, trans. by M. van Biljon, 1994; Tintinyane, the Girl Who Sang like a Magic Bird; The Magic Pouch and Other Stories. Author of short stories, plays, and books for children published in Afrikaans. **Address:** P.O. Box 1330, Rooseveltpark 2129, Republic of South Africa.

FOUST, Jeff. American, b. 1971. **Genres:** Information science/Computers. **Career:** Coola Inc., Woburn, MA, web developer, 1999-. **Publications:**

HTML 3 How-To, 1996; HTML 3.2 How-To, 1997; HTML 4 How-To, 1997; Astronomer's Computer Companion, 1999. Contributor to periodicals. **Address:** c/o Author Mail, No Starch Press Suite 250, 555 DeHaro St., San Francisco, CA 94107, U.S.A. **Online address:** jfoust@alum.mit.edu

FOWERS, Blaine J. American, b. 1956. **Genres:** Psychology. **Career:** Counseling and Psychological Services Center, University of Texas at Austin, counselor, 1984-85; State University of New York at Buffalo, University Counseling Service, counseling psychology intern, 1985-86; Falkirk Hospital, Central Valley, NY, staff psychologist, 1986-87; Department of Counseling and Family Studies, University of New Mexico, assistant professor, 1987-90, Counseling Psychology Program director of training, 1990; Family Center for Counseling and Education, clinical director, 1988-90; Department of Educational and Psychological Studies, University of Miami, assistant professor, 1990-95, associate professor, 1995-, director of training, 1997-, acting department chair, 1998. Presenter at professional workshops, conferences, and conventions. **Publications:** (with F.C. Richardson and C. Guignon) Re-Envisioning Psychology: Moral Dimensions of Theory and Practice, 1999; Beyond the Myth of Marital Happiness, 2000. Contributor to books and periodicals. **Address:** School of Education, Department of Educational and Psychological Studies, University of Miami, 312 Merrick Bldg., Coral Gables, FL 33124, U.S.A. **Online address:** bfowers@miami.edu

FOWLER, Alastair (David Shaw). Scottish, b. 1930. **Genres:** Poetry, Literary criticism and history. **Career:** Regius Professor Emeritus of Rhetoric and English Literature, University of Edinburgh. Jr. Research Fellow, Queen's College, Oxford, 1955-59; Fellow and Tutor in English, Brasenose College, Oxford, 1962-71; Professor, University of Virginia, Charlottesville, 1990-97 (Visiting Professor, 1985-90). **Publications:** Spenser and the Numbers of Time, 1964; Triumphal Forms, 1970; Seventeen (poetry), 1971; Conceitful Thought, 1975; Catacomb Suburb, 1976; Spenser, 1978; From the Domain of Arnheim, 1982; Kinds of Literature, 1982; A History of English Literature, 1987; The Country House Poem, 1994; Time's Purpled Masquers, 1996; Renaissance Realism, 2003. EDITOR: (and trans.) Richard Will's De Re Poetica, 1958; C.S. Lewis's Spenser's Images of Life, 1967; (with J. Carey) The Poems of John Milton, 1968; Silent Poetry, 1970; (with I.C. Butler) Topics in Criticism, 1971; The New Oxford Book of Seventeenth Century Verse, 1991; Paradise Lost, 1998. **Address:** Dept of English, University of Edinburgh, David Hume Tower, George Sq, Edinburgh EH8 9JX, Scotland.

FOWLER, Christopher. British, b. 1953. **Genres:** Novels, Novellas/Short stories, Humor/Satire. **Career:** Worked as copywriter for agencies in London, England, 1972-78; Creative Partnership (film marketing firm), London, founder and creative director, 1979-; writer. **Publications:** HUMOR: How to Impersonate Famous People, 1986; The Ultimate Party, 1987. NOVELS: Roofworld, 1988; Rune, 1990; Red Bride, 1992; Darkest Day, 1993; Spanky, 1994; Psychoville, 1995; Disturbia, 1997; Soho Black, 1999; Calabash, 2000. STORIES: City Jitters 1 (anthology), 1988; City Jitters 2 (anthology), 1988; The Bureau of Lost Souls, 1989; Sharper Knives, 1992; Flesh Wounds, 1995; Uncut, 1999; Personal Demons 1998: The Devil in Me, 2001; Full Dark House, 2003; Demonized, 2003. SCREENPLAYS: The Waiting Darkness; Breathe: First Born (for television). Contributor to periodicals. **Address:** Creative Partnership, 13 Bateman St, London W1D 3AF, England. **Online address:** chris@cfowler.demon.co.uk

FOWLER, Connie May. American, b. 1959. **Genres:** Novels. **Publications:** Sugar Cage, 1992; River of Hidden Dreams, 1994; Before Women Had Wings, 1996; Remembering Blue, 2000; When Katie Wakes: A Memoir, 2002. **Address:** c/o Joy Harris Literary Agency, 156 5th Ave., Ste 617, New York, NY 10010, U.S.A. **Online address:** conniemayhome@aol.com

FOWLER, Don D. American, b. 1936. **Genres:** Anthropology/Ethnology, History, Photography. **Career:** University of Nevada, Reno, assistant professor, 1964-67, associate research professor, 1968-72, research professor of anthropology, 1972-78, Mamie Kleberg Professor of Anthropology and Historic Preservation, 1978-2005. Smithsonian Institution, Washington, DC, research associate, 1970-2004. Society for American Archaeology, president, 1985-87. **Publications:** In a Sacred Manner We Live: Edward S. Curtis's Photographs of North American Indians, 1972; Myself in the Water: J.K. Hillers' Photographs 1871-1900, 1989; A Laboratory for Anthropology, Science and Romanticism in American Southwest, 1846-1930, 2000. EDITOR/CO-EDITOR: Down the Colorado: John Wesley Powell's Diary of the First Trip through the Grand Canyon, 1969; Photographed All the Best Scenery: Jack Hiller's Diary of the Powell Expedition, 1972; Anthropology of the Desert West: Essays in Honor of Jesse P. Jennings, 1986; American Archaeology Past & Future, 1986; H. Stansbury's Exploration of the Valley of the Great Salt Lake, 1988; Others Knowing Others: Perspectives on Ethnographic

Careers, 1994; Philadelphia and the Development of Americanist Archaeology, 2003; (with L. Cordell) Southwestern Archaeology in the Twentieth Century, 2005. **Address:** 1010 Foothill Rd, Reno, NV 89511, U.S.A.

FOWLER, Earlene. American, b. 1954. **Genres:** Mystery/Crime/Suspense. **Publications:** Fool's Puzzle, 1994; Irish Chain, 1995; Kansas Troubles, 1996; Goose in the Pond, 1997; Dove in the Window, 1998; Mariner's Compass, 1999; Seven Sisters, 2000; Arkansas Traveler, 2001; Steps to the Altar, 2002; Sunshine and Shadow, 2003; Broken Dishes, 2004; Delectable Mountains, 2005. **Address:** c/o Ellen Geiger, Curtis Brown Ltd, 10 Astor Pl, New York, NY 10003, U.S.A. **Online address:** www.earlenefowler.com

FOWLER, Gene. American, b. 1931. **Genres:** Poetry. **Career:** Writer. Served five years in San Quentin Prison, 1954-59. **Publications:** Field Studies, 1965; Quarter Tones, 1966; Shaman Songs, 1967; Her Majesty's Ship, 1969; Fires, 1971; Vivisection, 1974; Felon's Journal, 1975; Fires: Selected Poems 1963-1976, 1975; Return of the Shaman, 1981; Waking the Poet, 1981; The Quiet Poems, 1982. **Address:** 1432 Spruce St, Berkeley, CA 94709, U.S.A. **Online address:** acorioso@earthlink.net

FOWLER, Virginia C. American, b. 1948. **Genres:** Literary criticism and history. **Career:** Virginia Tech, Blacksburg, assistant professor, 1977-83, associate professor, 1983-96, director of graduate studies, 1985-91, professor of English, 1996-. **Publications:** Henry James's American Girl: The Embroidery on the Canvas, 1984; Nikki Giovanni, 1992; Conversations with Nikki Giovanni, 1992; Gloria Naylor: In Search of Sanctuary, 1996. Work represented in anthologies. Contributor of articles and reviews to scholarly journals. **Address:** Department of English, Virginia Tech, Blacksburg, VA 24061-0112, U.S.A. **Online address:** vfowler@vt.edu

FOWLES, John. British, b. 1926. **Genres:** Novels, Novellas/Short stories, Poetry, Translations. **Publications:** The Collector, 1958; The Aristos: A Self-Portrait in Ideas, 1964; The Magus, 1966; The French Lieutenant's Woman, 1969; The Ebony Tower: Collected Novellas, 1974; Poems, 1974; (trans.) Perrault: Cinderella 1974; Shipwreck, 1974; (trans.) Ourika, 1977; Daniel Martin, 1977; Islands, 1978; The Tree, 1979; The Enigma of Stonehenge, 1980; A Brief History of Lyme, 1981; (co-ed.) J. Aubrey, Monumenta Britannica, 2 vols., 1981-82; A Short History of Lyme Regis, 1982; Mantissa, 1982; Land, 1985; A Maggot, 1985; Lyme Regis Camera, 1990; I Write Therefore I Am, 1997; Wormholes: Essays and Occasional Writings, 1998. **Address:** c/o Anthony Sheil, Gillon Aitken Associates Ltd, 29 Fernshaw Rd, London SW10 0TG, England. **Online address:** www.fowlesbooks.com

FOWLKES, Diane L(owe). American, b. 1939. **Genres:** Politics/Government, Women's studies and issues. **Career:** Georgia State University, Atlanta, assistant professor, 1973-80, associate professor, 1980-92, professor, 1992-98, founding director of women's studies institute, 1992-98, professor emerita of political science, 1998-. Worked as a secretary, 1961-70. Diable Stable Inc. (breeders and racers of thoroughbred horses), president. Women's Policy Group/Women's Policy Education Fund, vice-president, 1992-94. **Publications:** How Feminist Theory Reconstructs American Government and Politics (monograph), 1983; (coed.) Feminist Visions: Toward a Transformation of the Liberal Arts Curriculum, 1984; White Political Women: Paths From Privilege to Empowerment, 1992. Work represented in books. Writer for the television series Democratic Government and Politics, BBC, 1987. Contributor to political science, social science, and women's studies journals. **Address:** PO Box 3806, Ocala, FL 34478, U.S.A.

FOX, Andrew Jay. (born United States), b. 1964. **Genres:** Young adult fiction. **Career:** Writer, administrator. Sagamore Children's Center, Long Island, NY, administrative intern, 1988-90; Hillel Jewish Students Center, New Orleans, LA, 1990-91; Louisiana Office of Public Health, New Orleans, Commodity Supplemental Food Program, manager, 1991-. Cofounder, New Year Coalition, New Orleans, to stop celebratory gunfire. **Publications:** Fat White Vampire Blues, 2003; Bride of the Fat White Vampire, 2004. **Address:** Louisiana Department of Public Health, POB 606030, Room 407, New Orleans, LA 70160, U.S.A. **Online address:** andrewfox@andrewfoxbooks.com

FOX, Anthony. See FULLERTON, Alexander (Fergus).

FOX, Barry. American. **Genres:** Biography. **Career:** Speaker and author; Business Report, former executive editor; Housecalls radio program, Los Angeles, CA, substitute host, 1995-2002; guest on radio and television programs. University of Integrative Studies, Sonora, CA, professor. Chair of the Consumer Advisory Council, American Nutraceutical Association. **Publications:** Foods to Heal By: An A-to-Z Guide to Medicinal Foods and Their

Curative Properties, 1996; To Your Health: The Healing Power of Alcohol, 1997; (with Jason Theodosakis and Brenda Adderly) The Arthritis Cure: The Medical Miracle that Can Halt, Reverse, and May Even Cure Osteoarthritis, 1997; (with Jason Theodosakis and Brenda Adderly) Maximizing the Arthritis Cure: A Step-by-Step Program to Faster, Stronger Healing during Any Stage of the Cure, 1998; (with Gabe Mirkin) The 20/30 Fat and Fiber Diet Plan, 1998; (with Selma Schimmel) Cancer Talk: Voices of Hope and Endurance from The Group Room, the World's Largest Cancer Support Group, 1999; (with Gerald Reaven and Terry Kristen) Syndrome X: Overcoming the Silent Killer that Can Give You a Heart Attack, 2000; (with Alexander Mauskop) What Your Doctor May Not Tell You about Migraines: The Breakthrough Program that Can Help End Your Pain, 2001; (with Frederic Vagnini) The Side Effects Bible: The Dietary Solution to Unwanted Side Effects of Common Medications, 2005. WITH ARNOLD FOX: DLPA to End Chronic Pain and Depression, 1985; Wake Up! You're Alive: MD's Prescription for Healthier Living through Positive Thinking, 1988; Immune for Life: Live Longer and Better by Strengthening Your Doctor Within, 1989; Making Miracles: Inspiring Mind-Methods to Supercharge Your Emotions and Rejuvenate Your Health, 1989; Beyond Positive Thinking: Putting Your Thoughts into Action, 1991; 14-Day Miracle Plan: Inspiring Mind Methods to Supercharge Your Emotions and Rejuvenate Your Health, 1991; The Healthy Prostate: A Doctor's Comprehensive Program for Preventing and Treating Common Problems, 1996; Alternative Healing, 1996; Boost Your Immune System Now!: Live Longer and Better by Strengthening Your Doctor Within, 1997. WITH WIFE, NADINE TAYLOR: (And with Rene Delorm) Diana and Dodi: A Love Story, 1998; Arthritis for Dummies, 2000; (And with Mark Houston) What Your Doctor May Not Tell You about Hypertension: The Revolutionary Nutrition and Lifestyle Program to Help Fight High Blood Pressure, 2003. Contributor of nearly 200 articles to periodicals. **Address:** 23679 Calabasas Rd., #223, Calabasas, CA 91302, U.S.A. **Online address:** TayFox@aol.com

FOX, Connie. *See* **FOX, Hugh (Bernard).**

FOX, Frank. American (born Poland), b. 1923. **Genres:** History. **Career:** Professor of history, nonfiction writer, editor, and translator. Temple University, Philadelphia, PA, teacher, 1963-67; West Chester University, West Chester, PA, professor, 1967-89; occasional classes taught at University of Delaware, Newark, and St. Joseph's University, Philadelphia, PA. Lecturer and speaker. Curator of Polish poster and film poster exhibits throughout the US. Interviewed on radio and television. Author, with S. Parker, of a series of articles on Watergate published in New York magazine, 1974-75; author of a series of articles on Polish art and culture. **Publications:** (ed. and trans.) C. Perechodnik, Am I a Murderer? Testament of a Jewish Ghetto Policeman (memoir), 1996; Polish Posters: Combat on Paper, 1960-1990 (exhibit catalog), 1996; God's Eye: Aerial Photography and the Katyn Forest Massacre, 1999. Contributor of history articles to periodicals; contributor of essays to anthologies. **Address:** 51 Merbrook Ln, Merion, PA 19066, U.S.A. **Online address:** fischele@aol.com

FOX, Hugh (Bernard). Also writes as Connie Fox. American, b. 1932. **Genres:** Novels, Plays/Screenplays, Poetry, Literary criticism and history, Autobiography/Memoirs. **Career:** Loyola University of Los Angeles, CA, member of faculty, 1958-68; Smith-Mundt Professor of American Studies, Institute Pedagogico and University Catolica, Caracas, Venezuela, 1964-66; Michigan State University, East Lansing, professor of American thought and language, 1968-. **Publications:** 40 Poems, 1966; A Night with Hugh Fox, 1966; Eye into Now, 1967; Soul Catcher Songs, 1967; Apotheosis of Olde Towne, 1968; Henry James, 1968; Permeable Man, 1969; Open Letter to a Closed System, 1969; Countdown of an Empty Streetcar, 1969; Charles Bukowski, 1969; Mind Shaft, 1969; Son of Camelot Meets the Wolfman, 1969; (with S. Schott) Ghost Dance: Portfolio I, 1969; (with A. Cortina) Ghost Dance: Portfolio II, 1970; Ecological Suicide Bus, 1970; (with E.A. Vigo) Handbook against Gorgons, 1971; (with G. Deisler) The Industrial Ablution, 1971; Paralytic Grandpa Dream Secretions, 1971; The Omega Scriptures, 1971; Icehouse, 1971; Kansas City Westport Mantras, 1971; Survival Handbook, 1972; Just, 1972; Caliban and Ariel, 1972; Peeple, 1973-74; Gods of the Cataclysm, 1975; Huaca, 1977; First Fire, 1978; Mom-Honeymoon, 1978; Leviathan: An Indian Ocean Whale Journal, 1981; The Dream of the Black Topaz Chamber (poetry), 1982; The Guernica Cycle: The Year Franco Died, 1982; Lyn Lifshin: A Critical Study, 1985; (as Connie Fox) Babishka: A Poem-cycle, 1985; Papa Funk (chapbook), 1986; The Mythological Foundations of the Epic Genre, 1988; (as Connie Fox) Our Lady of Laussel (poetry), 1991; (as Connie Fox) Skull Worship (poetry), 1991; Our Lady of Laussel (poetry), 1991; F. Richard (Dick) Thomas' 50th Birthday (poetry), 1991; Jamais Vu (poetry), 1991; The Sacred Cave (poetry collection), 1992; Entre Nous (poetry), 1992; The Ghost Dance Anthology: 25 Years of Poetry from Ghost Dance, 1968-1993; Other Kinds of Scores, 1994; The Last Summer (novel), 1995; The Living Underground: The Prose Anthology, 1995; Stairway to the Sun (anthology), 1995; Hugh Fox: The Greatest Hits (poetry), 2002; Boston: A Long Poem, 2002; The Book of Ancient Revelations, 2005; Our Gang: The Last Act, 2005. EDITOR: Anthology 2, 1969; The Living Underground, 1973; The Diamond Eye, 1975. **Address:** ATL/EBH, Michigan State University, East Lansing, MI 48823, U.S.A. **Online address:** hughfox@aol.com

FOX, John O. American, b. 1938. **Genres:** Money/Finance. **Career:** Sherman, Fox, Meehan & Canton, Washington, DC, founding partner, 1968-84, counsel, 1984-2000. Mount Holyoke College, South Hadley, MA, visiting lecturer, 1985-. **Publications:** If Americans Really Understood the Income Tax: Uncovering Our Most Expensive Ignorance, 2000. **Address:** 90 Fearing St., Amherst, MA 01002, U.S.A. **Online address:** jofox@attbi.com

FOX, Karl A(ugust). American, b. 1917. **Genres:** Economics, Environmental sciences/Ecology, Mathematics/Statistics, Social sciences. **Career:** Distinguished Professor of Economics Emeritus, Iowa State University, Ames, 1987- (Head, Dept. of Economics, 1955-72; Distinguished Professor of Economics, 1968-87). Associate Head, 1947-51, and Head, 1951-54, Division of Statistical and Historical Research, U.S. Bureau of Agricultural Economics. Chairman, Social Science Research Council Committee on Areas for Social and Economic Statistics, 1964-67. **Publications:** Econometric Analysis for Public Policy, 1958; (with M. Ezekiel) Methods of Correlation and Regression Analysis, 3rd ed., 1959; (with E. Thorbecke and J. Sengupta) The Theory of Quantitative Economic Policy, 1966; Intermediate Economic Statistics, 1968, 2nd ed. (with T. Kaul), 2 vols., 1980; (with J. Sengupta) Economic Analysis and Operations Research: Optimization Techniques in Quantitative Economic Models, 1969; (with W. Merrill) Introduction to Economic Statistics, 1970; Social Indicators and Social Theory: Elements of an Operational System, 1974; Social System Accounts, 1985; The Eco-Behavioral Approach to Surveys and Social Accounts for Rural Communities, 1990, 1994; Demand Analysis, Econometrics, and Policy Models: Selected Writings of Karl A. Fox, vol. 1, 1992; Urban-Regional Economics, Social System Accounts, and Eco-Behavioral Science: Selected Writings of Karl A. Fox, vol. 2, 1994. EDITOR: (with D. Johnson) Readings in the Economics of Agriculture, 1969; (with J. Sengupta and G. Narasimham) Economic Models, Estimation and Risk Programming: Essays in Honor of Gerhard Tintner, 1969; (and contrib.) Economic Analysis for Educational Planning, 1972; (with D.G. Miles) Systems Economics, 1987. **Address:** Dept. of Economics, Iowa State University, Ames, IA 50011, U.S.A. **Online address:** fox328L@aol.com

FOX, Les. American, b. 1947. **Genres:** Novels, Young adult non-fiction. **Career:** Writer and publisher, 1996-. **Publications:** WITH S. FOX: Return to Sender: The Secret Son of Elvis Presley; A Novel, 1996; The Beanie Baby Handbook, 1997; (with J. Long) The Beanie Baby Cookbook, 1998; Silver Dollar Fortune Telling; Washington Deceased; When the Cookie Crumbles; City Prey; January Fever. **Address:** West Highland Publishing Co. Inc., PO Box 36, Midland Park, NJ 07432, U.S.A.

FOX, Levi. British, b. 1914. **Genres:** History, Literary criticism and history. **Career:** Shakespeare Birthplace Trust, director, secretary, 1945-89, director emeritus, 1990-. Dugdale Society, general editor, 1945-88. **Publications:** Leicester Abbey, 1938; Administration of the Honour of Leicester in the Fourteenth Century, 1940; Leicester Castle, 1943; (with P. Russell) Leicester Forest, 1945; Coventry's Heritage, 1947, 1957; Stratford-upon-Avon, 1949; Shakespeare's Town, 1949; Oxford, 1951; Shakespeare's Stratford-upon-Avon, 1951; Shakespeare's Country, 1953; The Borough Town of Stratford-upon-Avon, 1953; (ed.) English Historical Scholarship in the 16th and 17th Centuries, 1956; Shakespeare's Town and Country, 1959, 1976; Stratford-upon-Avon: An Appreciation, 1963, 1976; The 1964 Shakespeare Anniversary Book, 1964; Celebrating Shakespeare, 1965; Correspondence of the Reverend Joseph Greene, 1965; A Country Grammar School, 1967; The Shakespeare Book, 1969; (ed.) Shakespeare's Sonnets, 1970; Shakespeare's England, 1972; In Honour of Shakespeare, 1972; (comp.) The Shakespeare Treasury, 1972; (comp.) The Stratford-upon-Avon Shakespeare Anthology, 1975; Stratford: Past and Present, 1975; Shakespeare's Flowers, 1978; Shakespeare's Birds, 1978; The Shakespeare Centre, 1982; Shakespeare in Medallic Art, 1982; Shakespeare's Magic, 1982; The Early History of King Edward VI School, Stratford-upon-Avon, 1984; Coventry Constables' Presentments, 1986; Historic Stratford-upon-Avon, 1986; Stratford-upon-Avon: Shakespeare's Town, 1986; Oxford in Colour, 1987; Discovering Shakespeare Country, 1987; Shakespeare's Town and Country, 1990; Minutes and Accounts of the Corporation of Stratford, 1990; The Shakespeare Birthplace Trust: A Personal Memoir, 1997. **Address:** The Shakespeare Center, Stratford-upon-Avon CV37 6QW, England.

FOX, M(ichael) W. British, b. 1937. **Genres:** Children's fiction, Agriculture/Forestry, Animals/Pets, Children's non-fiction, Environmental sciences/Ecology, Fashion/Costume, Food and Wine, Natural history, Philosophy. **Career:** Vice President, The Humane Society of the U.S., Washington, D.C., since 1976. Associate Professor of Psychology, Washington University, St. Louis, 1969-76. **Publications:** Canine Behavior, 1965; Canine Pediatrics, 1966; Integrative Development of Brain and Behavior in the Dog, 1971; Behavior of Wolves, Dogs and Related Canids, 1971; Understanding Your Dog, 1972; Understanding Your Cat, 1974; Concepts in Ethology: Animal and Human Behavior, 1974; Ramu and Chennai, 1975; What Is Your Cat Saying, 1977; Wild Dogs Three, 1977; Between Animal and Man, 1976; What Is Your Dog Saying, 1977; Understanding Your Pet, 1978; One Earth One Mind, 1980; Returning to Eden: Animal Rights and Human Responsibilities, 1980; The Soul of the Wolf, 1980; The Touchlings, 1981; How To Be Your Pet's Best Friend, 1981; Dr. Michael Fox's Massage Program for Cats and Dogs, 1981; Love Is a Happy Cat, 1982; The Healing Touch, 1983; Farm Animals: Husbandry, Behavior and Veterinary Practice, 1983; The Whistling Hunters, 1984; The Animal Doctor's Answer Book, 1984; Agricide: The Hidden Crisis that Affects Us All, 1986; Laboratory Animal Husbandry, 1986; The New Eden, 1989; Inhumane Society: The American Way of Exploiting Animals, 1990; Superdog: Raising the Perfect Canine Companion, 1990; Supercat: Raising the Perfect Feline Companion, 1991; You Can Save the Animals: 50 Things to Do Right Now, 1991; Superpigs and Wondercorn: The Brave New World of Biotechnology and Where It All May Lead, 1992; The Boundless Circle: Caring for Creatures and Creation, 1996; Eating with Conscience: the Bioethics of Food, 1997. FOR CHILDREN. FICTION: The Wolf, 1973; Vixie, The Story of a Little Fox, 1973; Sundance Coyote; Whitepaws: A Coyote-Dog, 1979; Fox's Fables: Lessons from Nature, 1980; The Way of the Dolphin, 1981. NON-FICTION: Animals Have Rights Too, 1991. EDITOR: Abnormal Behavior in Animals, 1968; The Wild Canids, 1974; On the Fifth Day: Animal Rights and Human Obligations, 1978; (with L.D. Mickley) Advances in Animal Welfare Science 1985, 1986; (with Mickley) Advances in Animal Welfare Science 1986-87, 1987. **Address:** c/o KLI Authors, Adolf Lorenz Gasse 2, A-3422 Altenberg, Austria.

FOX, Mem. Australian, b. 1946. **Genres:** Children's fiction, Adult non-fiction. **Career:** Teacher of English, Zimbabwe and Ruwanda, 1968-69; Cabra Dominican School, Adelaide, South Australia, drama teacher, 1970; South Australian Institute of Technology, English tutor, 1971-72; Flinders University of South Australia, lecturer, 1973-86, senior lecturer, 1987-1994, associate professor, 1994-. **Publications:** FOR CHILDREN: Possum Magic, 1983; Wilfrid Gordon McDonald Partridge, 1984; A Cat Called Kite, 1985; Hattie and the Fox, 1986; Sail Away, 1986; Arabella: The Smallest Girl in the World, 1986; Just Like That, 1986; Zoo Looking, 1987; Koala Lou, 1987; A Bedtime Story, 1987; The Straight Line Wonder, 1987; Night Noises, 1988; Guess What?, 1988; Feathers and Fools, 1988; Sophie, 1988; With Love, at Christmas, 1988; Shoes from Grandpa, 1989; Time for Bed, 1993; Tough Boris, 1994; Great Scott!, 1996; Wombat Divine, 1996; Whoever You Are, 1997; The Straight Line Wonder, 1997; Boo to a Goose, 1998. FOR ADULTS: Mem's the Word (autobiography), 1990; How to Teach Drama to Infants Without Really Crying, 1984 in US as Teaching Drama to Young Children, 1987; "Dear Mem Fox, I've Read All Your Books Even the Pathetic Ones," 1992; Articles of Faith, 1993; (with L. Wilkinson) English Essentials: The Wouldn't-Be-Without-It Handbook on Writing Well, 1993; Radical Reflections: Passionate Opinions on Teaching, Living, and Learning, 1993. Contributor of essays to anthologies and periodicals. **Address:** c/o Jenny Darling, PO Box 413, Toorak, VIC 3142, Australia.

FOX, Paula. American, b. 1923. **Genres:** Novels, Children's fiction, Young adult fiction. **Publications:** Maurice's Room, 1966; Poor George, 1966; A Likely Place, 1967; Dear Prosper, 1967; How Many Miles to Babylon, 1967; The Stone-Faced Boy, 1968; Portrait of Ivan, 1969; The King's Falcon, 1969; Desperate Characters, 1969; The Western Coast, 1972; Blowfish Live in the Sea, 1972; The Slave Dancer, 1973; The Widow's Children, 1976; The Little Swineherd and Other Tales, 1978; A Place Apart, 1980; A Servant's Tale, 1984; One-Eyed Cat, 1984; The Moonlight Man, 1986; Lily and the Lost Boy, 1987; The Village by the Sea, 1988; The God of Nightmares, 1990; Monkey Island, 1991; Western Wind, 1993; Amzat and His Brothers, 1993; The Eagle Kite, 1995; Radiance Descending, 1997; Borrowed Finery, 2001. **Address:** c/o Robert Lescher, Lescher & Lescher Ltd, 47 E 19th St Fl 3, New York, NY 10003-1323, U.S.A.

FOX, Richard Allan, Jr. American, b. 1943. **Genres:** Anthropology/Ethnology, Archaeology/Antiquities. **Career:** University of North Dakota, Grand Forks, instructor in anthropology, 1977-78, associate research archaeologist, 1977-82; Old Sun College, Gleichen, Alberta, instructor in education, 1983, 1984-85; University of Calgary, Calgary, Alberta, instructor in archaeology, 1988; University of North Dakota, research archaeologist, 1988-90, assistant professor of anthropology, 1988-91; University of South Dakota, Vermillion, assistant professor, 1991-93, associate professor of anthropology, 1994-, director of Archaeology Laboratory, 1991-. Conducted extensive archaeological field work at sites including Little Bighorn Battlefield National Monument, the Yankton Sioux Reservation, Fort Phil Kearny, Fort Abraham Lincoln, and White Buffalo Robe Village. **Publications:** (with E. Pease, A. Johnson, and T. Johnson) Grass, Tipis, and Black Gold, 1976; (with D.D. Scott) Archaeological Insights into the Custer Battle: An Assessment of the 1984 Field Season, 1987; (with Scott, M. Connor, and D. Harmon) Archaeological Perspectives on the Battle of the Little Big Horn, 1989; Archaeology, History, and Custer's Last Battle: The Little Big Horn Reexamined, 1993. Contributor to books. Contributor of articles and reviews to archaeology and history journals. **Address:** Department of Anthropology, University of South Dakota, Vermillion, SD 57069, U.S.A.

FOX, Robert. British, b. 1938. **Genres:** History, Sciences. **Career:** Professor of History of Science, Oxford University, 1988-. Lecturer, 1966-72, Sr. Lecturer, 1972-75, Reader, 1975-87, and Professor of History of Science, 1987-88, University of Lancaster. CRHST, director, Cite des Sciences et de l'Industrie CNRS, 1986-88; Science Museum, London, assistant director, 1988; Ed., The British Journal for the History of Science, 1971-77; President, British Society for the History of Science, 1980-82; President, Division of History of Science of the International Union of History and Philosophy of Science, 1994-97; President, International Union of History and Philosophy of Science, 1996-97. **Publications:** The Caloric Theory of Gases from Lavoisier to Regnault, 1971; The Culture of Science in France, 1700-1900, 1992; Science, Industry and the Social Order in Post-Revolutionary France, 1995; (co-author) Laboratories, Workshops and Sites, 1999. EDITOR/CO-EDITOR: S. Carnot, Reflexions sur la puissance motrice du feu, 1978; The Organization of Science and Technology in France 1808-1914, 1980; (and trans.) S. Carnot, Reflexions on the Motive Power of Fire, 1986; Education, Technology, and Industrial Performance in Europe, 1850-1939, 1993; Technological Change, 1996; Luxury Trades and Consumerism in Ancien Regime Paris, 1998; Natural Dyestuffs and Industrial Culture in Europe, 1750-1880, 1999; T. Harriot, An Elizabethan Man of Science, 2000. **Address:** Modern History Faculty, Broad St, Oxford OX1 3BD, England.

FOX, Robin. British, b. 1934. **Genres:** Anthropology/Ethnology. **Career:** University of Exeter, England, lecturer in sociology, 1959-62; London School of Economics and Political Science, University of London, England, lecturer in social anthropology, 1962-67, Malinowski Memorial Lecturer, 1967; Rutgers University, New Brunswick, NJ, professor of anthropology, 1967-84, university professor of social theory, 1984-; writer. Guggenheim Foundation, director of research, 1972-84; Oxford University, visiting professor of anthropology, 1973-74; University of New Mexico, Byron Harvey III Lecturer, 1975; Haverford College, William Pyle Phillips Lecturer, 1976; Ecole des Hautes Etudes en Sciences Sociales and Maison des Sciences de l'Homme, University of Paris VI, associate director of studies, 1979-80; visiting professor, Universidad de los Andes, 1981-82, and University of California, San Diego, 1982; Smith College, Neal B. De Nood Memorial Lecturer, 1982; St. John's College, Cambridge, visiting professor and senior overseas scholar, 1982-83. Conducted field work among the Pueblos of New Mexico and the Gaelic-speaking islanders of Donegal. **Publications:** The Keresan Bridge: A Problem in Pueblo Ethnography, 1967; Kinship and Marriage, 1967; (with L. Tiger) The Imperial Animal, 1971; Encounter with Anthropology, 1973; (ed. and contrib.) Biosocial Anthropology, 1975; The Tory Islanders: A People of the Celtic Fringe, 1978; The Red Lamp of Incest, 1980; (ed. and contrib. with J. Mehler) Neonate Cognition: Beyond the Blooming Buzzing Confusion, 1984; The Violent Imagination, 1989; The Search for Society: Quest for a Biosocial Science and Morality, 1989; Reproduction and Succession, 1993; The Challenge of Anthropology, 1994; Conjectures and Confrontations, 1997; The Passionate Mind: Sources of Destruction and Creativity, 2000. **Address:** Department of Anthropology, Douglass Campus, Rutgers University, New Brunswick, NJ 08903, U.S.A.

FOX, Roy F. American, b. 1948. **Genres:** Communications/Media. **Career:** Boise State University, ID, associate professor of English, 1978-91, director of writing, 1980-91, director of Technology in English Language and Literature Center, 1987-91; University of Missouri-Columbia, Dept of Learning, Teaching, and Curriculum, professor and chair, and director of Missouri Writing Project, 1991-, Maxine Christopher Shutz Lecturer, 1996, William T. Kemper fellow, 1998. Also worked as high school English teacher; consultant to MPI Media Group, Idaho Supreme Court, and Idaho Department of Vocational Rehabilitation. **Publications:** Images in Language, Media, and Mind, 1994; Technical Communication: Problems and Solutions, 1994;

Harvesting Minds: How TV Commercials Control Kids, 1996; MediaSpeak: Three American Voices, 2001. Contributor to books and periodicals. **Address:** Dept of Learning, Teaching, & Curriculum, 303 Townsend Hall, University of Missouri-Columbia, Columbia, MO 65211, U.S.A. **Online address:** foxr@missouri.edu

FOX, Ted. (Theodore J. Fox). American, b. 1954. **Genres:** Music. **Career:** Freelance writer. **Publications:** Showtime at the Apollo, 1983, rev. ed., 2003; In the Groove: The Men behind the Music, 1986.

FOX, William L. American, b. 1953. **Genres:** History, Theology/Religion. **Career:** Senior minister of Congregational church in Pomona, CA, 1988-92; Howard University, adjunct professor, 1992-99; Universalist National Memorial Church, Washington, DC, senior minister, 1993-98; Goucher College, Baltimore, MD, administrator. **Publications:** Willard L. Sperry: Quandaries of a Liberal Protestant Mind, 1991; Lodge of the Double-Headed Eagle: Two Centuries of Scottish Rite Freemasonry in America's Southern Jurisdiction, 1997; Valley of the Craftsmen: A Pictorial History. **Address:** 1021 Dulandy Valley Rd, Baltimore, MD 21204, U.S.A. **Online address:** wfox@goucher.edu

FOX-GENOVESE, Elizabeth. American, b. 1941. **Genres:** Area studies, History, Women's studies and issues, Translations, Literary criticism and history, Social commentary. **Career:** Eleonore Raoul Professor of the Humanities, Professor of History, Emory University, Atlanta, Georgia; Teaching fellow, Harvard University, Cambridge, Massachusetts, 1965-69; Assistant Ed. in History, Houghton Mifflin Co., NYC, 1966-67; Assistant Professor of History and Liberal Arts, 1973-76, and Associate Professor, 1976-80, University of Rochester, New York; formerly, Professor of History, State University of New York, Binghamton, from 1980. Director, Project on Integrating Materials on Women into Traditional Survey Courses; developer and Chairperson, Cluster on Interdisciplinary Study on Women in Culture and Society, 1978-80. **Publications:** The Origins of Physiocracy: Economic Revolution and Social Order in Eighteenth-Century France, 1976; (with others) Girondins et Montagnards, 1982; (with E.D. Genovese) Fruits of Merchant Capital: Slavery and Bourgeois Property in the Rise and Expansion of Capitalism, 1983; (trans. and co-ed.) The Autobiography of Pierre Samuel Du Pont De Nemours, 1983; Within the Plantation Household: Black and White Women of the Old South, 1988; Feminism without Illusions: A Critique of Individualism, 1991; (ed.) Augusta Evans, by Beulah, 1992; "Feminism Is Not the Story of My Life": How Today's Feminist Elite has Lost Touch with the Real Concerns of Women, 1996. **Address:** Dept. of History, Emory University, Atlanta, GA 30322, U.S.A.

FOXWORTHY, Jeff. American, b. 1958. **Genres:** Humor/Satire. **Career:** Performing and recording artist, comedian, and author, 1984-. IBM Corporation, GA, 1979-84. **Publications:** HUMOR: You Might Be a Redneck If..., 1989; Hick is Chic: A Guide to Etiquette for the Grossly Unsophisticated, 1990; Red Ain't Dead: 150 More Ways to Tell If You're a Redneck, 1991; Check Your Neck: More of You Might Be a Redneck If..., 1992; (with V. Henley) You're Not a Kid Anymore When..., 1993; Redneck Classic: The Best of Jeff Foxworthy, 1995; No Shirt. No Shoes. No Problem, 1996. **Address:** c/o Creative Artists Agency, 9830 Wilshire Blvd, Beverly Hills, CA 90212, U.S.A.

FOXX, Jack. See **PRONZINI, Bill.**

FRADIN, Judith (Bernette) Bloom. (born United States), b. 1945. **Genres:** Biography. **Career:** High school English and history teacher, 1967-75, 1982-90; Northeastern Illinois University, Chicago, writing instructor, 1975-82; photo researcher, 1985-; researcher and writer, 1990-. President, Southwest Evanston Associated Residents (SWEAR). **Publications:** FROM SEA TO SHINING SEA SERIES; WITH HUSBAND, DENNIS BRINDELL FRADIN: Montana, 1992; Arkansas, 1994; Delaware, 1994; Connecticut, 1994; Indiana, 1994; Maryland, 1994; North Dakota, 1994; Washington, 1994; West Virginia, 1994; Wyoming, 1994; Minnesota, 1995; Louisiana, 1995; Kansas, 1995; Mississippi, 1995; Nevada, 1995; Puerto Rico, 1995; Oklahoma, 1995; Oregon, 1995; Rhode Island, 1995; South Dakota, 1995. OTHER: (with Dennis Brindell Fradin) Ida B. Wells: Mother of the Civil Rights Movement, 2000; (with Dennis Brindell Fradin) Who Was Sacagawea?, 2002; (with Dennis Brindell Fradin) Fight On!: Mary Church Terrell's Battle for Integration, 2003; (with Dennis Brindell Fradin) The Power of One: Daisy Bates and the Little Rock Nine, 2004. Contributor of articles and photographs. **Address:** 2121 Dobson, Evanston, IL 60202, U.S.A.

FRAENKEL, Jack R. American, b. 1932. **Genres:** Criminology/True Crime, Education. **Career:** Professor of Interdisciplinary Studies in Education, since

1971, and Director of the Research and Development Center since 1987, San Francisco State University (Associate Professor, 1966-71). Series Ed., Inquiry into Crucial American Problems, Prentice-Hall, Englewood Cliffs, New Jersey, since 1970, and Crucial Issues in American Government, Allyn & Bacon Inc., Boston, Massachusetts. **Publications:** (ed.) The U.S. War with Spain 1898: Was Expansionism Justified?, 1969; (ed. with R.E. Gross and W. McPhie) Teaching the Social Studies: What, Why and How, 1969; Crime and Criminals, 1970; (with B. Reardon and M. Carter) Peacekeeping, 1970; (with H. Taba, A. McNaughton and M. Durkin) Teacher's Handbook to Elementary Social Studies, 1971; Helping Students Think and Value, 1973; (with B. Reardon and M. Carter) Human Rights: A Study of Values, 1974; How to Teach About Values: An Analytic Approach, 1977; Decision-Making in American Government, 1983; Civics, 1983; Toward Improving Research in Social Studies Education, 1988; How to Design and Evaluate Research in Education, 1990, rev. ed., 2000; Educational Research: A Guide to the Process, 1991, rev. ed., 2001. **Address:** College of Education, San Francisco State University, Research & Development Center, Burk Hall 522, San Francisco, CA 94132, U.S.A. **Online address:** jrf@sfsu.edu

FRAJLICH(-ZAJAC), Anna. American (born Kirgizstan), b. 1942. **Genres:** Poetry, Literary criticism and history. **Career:** Associate editor of a magazine for the blind, Warsaw, Poland, 1965-69; State University of New York at Stony Brook, instructor in Polish, 1970-71; Kimbell Research Institute, NYC, research assistant in epidemiology, 1971-75; New York University, NYC, instructor in Polish, 1977; freelance writer and broadcaster and interviewer for Radio Free Europe, 1977-81; Columbia University, NYC, lecturer to adjunct associate professor of Polish language and literature, 1982-. **Publications:** POETRY: Aby wiatr namalowac (title means: To Paint the Wind), 1976; Tylko ziemia (Just Earth), 1979; Indian Summer, 1982; Ktory las (Which Forest), 1986; Drzewo za oknem (The Tree behind the Window), 1991; Between Dawn and the Wind: Selected Poetry (in Polish and English), trans. R. Grol-Prokopczyk, 1991; Ogrodem i ogrodzeniem (The Garden and the Fence), 1993; Jeszcze w drodze (Still on Its Way), 1994; W sloncu listopada (In November's Sunshine), 2000; Znow szuka mnie wiatr (The Wind Seeks Me Again), 2001; Le vent, a nouveau me cherche (in Polish and French), trans. A.-C. Carls, 2003. OTHER: Living Language: Fast and Easy Polish (booklet), 1992; (ed.) Between Lvov New York and Ulysses' Ithaca: Jozef Wittlin-Poet, Essayist, Novelist, 2001. Work represented in anthologies. Contributor to books. Contributor of poetry, articles and reviews to periodicals and literary magazines. **Address:** Dept of Slavic Languages, Columbia University, New York, NY 10027, U.S.A. **Online address:** af38@columbia.edu

FRAKES, George Edward. American, b. 1932. **Genres:** Environmental sciences/Ecology, History, Race relations. **Career:** Emeritus Professor of History and Geography, Santa Barbara City College, California, 1994- (Instructor in History, 1962-65; Asst. Professor, 1967-69; Associate Professor, 1969-71; Professor of History and Geography, 1973-94; Chairman, Dept. of History, 1971-73, and 1986-87; Chairman, Social Science Division, 1973-76). Supvr. of Student Teachers, University of California Santa Barbara Campus, 1965-66. **Publications:** (with A. DeConde) Instructor's Manual for Patterns in American History, 1968; Laboratory for Liberty, 1970; (with W.R. Adams) Colombus to Aquarius: An Interpretive History, 2 vols., 1976; A Teacher's Life, 2002. EDITOR: (with C. Solberg) Pollution Papers, 1971; (with Solberg) Minorities in California History, 1971. Contributor to encyclopedias and historical journals. **Address:** 735 Willow Glen Rd, Santa Barbara, CA 93105-2439, U.S.A. **Online address:** gefsb@aol.com

FRAKES, William B. American, b. 1952. **Genres:** Information science/Computers. **Career:** American Telephone & Telegraph Bell Laboratories (AT&T), Holmdel, NJ, member of technical staff, 1982-87, distinguished member of technical staff, 1987, supervisor of Intelligent Systems Research Group, 1987-89; Software Productivity Consortium, Herndon, VA, manager of software reuse research, 1989-92; Virginia Polytechnic Institute and State University, Northern Virginia Graduate Center, Falls Church, Computer Science Dept., associate professor, 1992-. Software Engineering Guild, president. Adjunct faculty member, Rutgers University, 1986-87, and Columbia University, 1988-89. **Publications:** (with C.J. Fox and B.A. Nejmeh) Software Engineering in the UNIX/C Environment, 1991; (ed. with R. Baeza-Yates) Information Retrieval: Data Structures and Algorithms, 1992; (ed. with R. Prieto-Diaz) Advances in Software Reuse: Selected Papers from the Second International Workshop on Software Reuse, 1993. Work represented in books. Contributor to computer engineering and software journals. **Address:** Computer Science Department, Virginia Polytechnic Institute and State University, 7054 Haycock Rd., Falls Church, VA 22043-2311, U.S.A.

FRALEY, Tobin. American, b. 1951. **Genres:** Animals/Pets. **Career:** Writer and woodcarver. Restorer and collector of wooden carousel animals. **Publica-

tions: The Carousel Animal, 1983; (with Carol Bialkowski) Carousels: The Myth, the Magic, and the Memories, 1991; The Great American Carousel: A Century of Master Craftsmanship, 1994; A Humbug Christmas (children's book), 1998; Carousel Animals: Artistry in Motion, 2002. **Address:** c/o Author Mail, Chronicle Books, 85 Second St., Sixth Fl., San Francisco, CA 94105, U.S.A.

FRAME, J. Davidson. American, b. 1947. **Genres:** Administration/Management. **Career:** Computer Horizons Inc., Bethesda, MD, vice-president, 1973-79; George Washington University, Washington, DC, professor, 1979-98; Project Management Institute, Newtown Square, PA, director of certification, 1990-96, director of education services, 1996-98, member of board of directors, 2000-2003; University of Management and Technology, Arlington, VA, dean, 1998-. **Publications:** International Business and Global Technology, 1983; Managing Projects in Organizations, 1987, rev. ed., 2003; The New Project Management, 1994; The Project Office, 1998; Project Management Competence: Building Key Skills for Individuals, Teams, and Organizations, 1999; Managing Risk in Organizations, 2003; Project Finance: Tools and Techniques, 2003. **Address:** University of Management and Technology, 1925 N Lynn St Ste 306, Arlington, VA 22209, U.S.A. **Online address:** davidson.frame@umtweb.edu

FRAME, Ronald. Scottish, b. 1953. **Genres:** Novels, Novellas/Short stories, Plays/Screenplays. **Career:** Full-time writer, 1981-. Recipient of Samuel Beckett Prize, 1986, and Scottish Arts Council Spring Book Award, 1987. **Publications:** Winter Journey, 1984 (Betty Trask Prize for First Novel, 1984), radio play, 1986; Watching Mrs. Gordon and Other Stories, 1985; A Long Weekend with Marcel Proust, 1986; Sandmouth People, 1987; A Woman of Judah, 1987, radio play, 1993; Penelope's Hat, 1989; Bluette, 1990; Underwood and After, 1991; Mask and Shadow, 1992; Walking My Mistress in Deauville, 1992; The Sun on the Wall, 1994; Lantern Bearers (novel), 2001; Permanent Violet, 2002. Author of radio and television plays. **Address:** c/o Curtis Brown Ltd, Haymarket House, 28/29 Haymarket 4th Fl, London SWIY 4SP, England.

FRANCE, Linda. British, b. 1958. **Genres:** Poetry. **Career:** Workers' Educational Association, Newcastle upon Tyne, England, tutor, 1985-95. University of Newcastle upon Tyne, tutor at Centre for Continuing Education and School of English, 1987-. Tutor for Arvon Foundation. **Publications:** Acts of Love, 1990; Red, 1992; (ed.) Sixty Women Poets, 1993; (with B. Aris) Acknowledged Land, 1994; The Gentleness of the Very Tall, 1994; Diamonds in Your Pockets, 1996; Storyville, 1997; The Simultaneous Dress, 2002; I Am Frida Kahlo, 2002; Aerogramme, 2004; Wild, 2004; The Toast of the Kit Cat Club, 2005. Work represented in anthologies. **Address:** c/o Bloodaxe Books Ltd., High Green, Tarset, Northd. NE48 1RP, England.

FRANCE, Miranda. British, b. 1966. **Genres:** Travel/Exploration. **Career:** Freelance journalist, Edinburgh, Scotland, 1989-93; foreign correspondent from Buenos Aires, Argentina, 1993-95; freelance journalist, London, England, 1995-. University of Edinburgh, part-time teacher of Spanish literature, 1992-93. **Publications:** Bad Times in Buenos Aires (travel book), 1998; Don Quixote's Delusions, Travels in Castilian Spain (travel book), 2001. Contributor to magazines and newspapers. **Address:** c/o Derek Johns, A. P. Watt Ltd., 20 John St., London SC1N 2AR, England.

FRANCE, R(ichard) T(homas). British, b. 1938. **Genres:** Theology/Religion. **Career:** Tyndale Hall, Bristol, England, lecturer in biblical theology, 1963-65; assistant curate of Church of England, Cambridge, England, 1966-69; University of Ife, Nigeria, lecturer in biblical studies, 1969-73; Tyndale House, Cambridge, librarian, 1973-76, research fellow, 1977-78, warden, 1978-81; Ahmadu Bello University, Zaria, Nigeria, senior lecturer in religious studies, 1976-77; London Bible College, England, senior lecturer in New Testament, 1981-88, head of Department of Biblical Studies, 1982-88, vice-principal, 1983-88; Wycliffe Hall, Oxford, England, principal, 1989-95; rector of Church of England parishes in Shropshire, England, including parish of Wentnor, 1995-99. Visiting professor: Trinity Evangelical Divinity School, Deerfield, IL, 1975, Gordon-Conwell Theological Seminary, South Hamilton, MA, 1986. Cambridge University, member of faculty of divinity, 1979-81; Oxford University, chairperson of faculty of theology, 1994-95. St. James' Cathedral, Ibadan, Nigeria, hon. canon, 1994-; University of Wales, Bangor, hon. research fellow, 2004-. **Publications:** The Living God, 1970; Jesus and the Old Testament, 1971; The Man They Crucified, 1975, rev. ed. as Jesus the Radical, 1989; (with A.R. Millard and G.N. Stanton) A Bibliographical Guide to New Testament Research, 1979; Matthew: An Introduction and Commentary, 1985; The Evidence for Jesus, 1986; Matthew: Evangelist and Teacher, 1989; Divine Government, 1990; Jesus in a Divided Society, 1993; Women in the Church's Ministry, 1995; Mark: The

People's Bible Commentary, 1996; (with P. Jenson) Translating the Bible, 1997; A Slippery Slope? The Ordination of Women and Homosexual Practice, 2000; Timothy, Titus and Hebrews, 2001; The Gospel of Mark, 2002. EDITOR: (with D. Wenham, and contrib.) Gospel Perspectives, Vol I, 1980, Vol II, 1981, Vol III, 1983; (with A.E. McGrath) Evangelical Anglicans, 1993. Contributor to periodicals, books, and anthologies. **Address:** Tyn-y-Twll, Llangelynin, Llwyngwril, Gwynedd LL37 2QL, Wales.

FRANCESCHINI, Remo. American, b. 1932. **Genres:** Criminology/True Crime. **Career:** New York Police Department, NYC, commander of detectives, 1957-91. St. John's University, adjunct professor of criminal justice. **Publications:** A Matter of Honor: One Cop's Lifelong Pursuit of John Gotti and the Mob, Simon & Schuster, 1993. **Address:** 682 Tuckahoe Rd., Yonkers, NY 10710, U.S.A.

FRANCIS, C. D. E. *See* **HOWARTH, Patrick (John Fielding)** in the Obituaries.

FRANCIS, Clare. British, b. 1946. **Genres:** Novels, Travel/Exploration, Autobiography/Memoirs. **Publications:** Come Hell or High Water, 1977; Come Wind or Weather, 1978; The Commanding Sea, 1981; Night Sky, 1983; Red Crystal, 1985; Wolf Winter (in U.S. as The Killing Winds), 1987; Requiem, 1991; Deceit, 1993; Betrayal, 1995; A Dark Devotion, 1997; Keep Me Close, 1999; A Death Divided, 2001; Homeland, 2004. **Address:** c/o John Johnson, 45-47 Clerkenwell Green, London EC1R 0HT, England.

FRANCIS, Diane (Marie). American/Canadian, b. 1946. **Genres:** Economics. **Career:** Freelance newspaper writer, 1976-78; freelance magazine writer, 1978-81; Canadian Business, contributing editor, 1979-81; Quest, columnist, 1981-83; Toronto Star, financial columnist, 1981-87; CBC radio, commentator, 1985-95; Maclean's and Toronto Sun, columnist, 1987-98; Financial Post, Toronto, editor, 1991-98, editor-at-large, 1998-. Canadian Foundation for AIDS Research, director; CARE Canada, director; George Brown College, foundation board. **Publications:** Controlling Interest: Who Owns Canada?, 1986; Contrepreneurs, 1988; The Diane Francis Inside Guide to Canada's 50 Best Stocks, 1990; A Matter of Survival: Canada in the 21st Century, 1993; Underground Nation: The Secret Economy and the Future of Canada, 1994; Fighting for Canada, 1996; Bre-X: The Inside Story, 1997; Immigration: The Economic Case, 2002. **Address:** 300-1450 Don Mills Rd, Don Mills, ON, Canada M3B 3R5. **Online address:** dfrancis@nationalpost.com

FRANCIS, Dick. (Richard Stanley Francis). British, b. 1920. **Genres:** Novellas/Short stories, Mystery/Crime/Suspense, Autobiography/Memoirs. **Career:** Amateur steeplechase jockey, 1946-48; professional steeplechase jockey, 1948-57; Sunday Express, racing columnist, 1957-73. **Publications:** The Sport of Queens (autobiography), 1957; Dead Cert, 1962; Nerve, 1964; For Kicks, 1965; Odds Against, 1965; Flying Finish, 1966; Blood Sport, 1967; Forfeit, 1968; Enquiry, 1969; (with J. Welcome) Best Racing and Chasing Stories 2, 1969; Rat Race, 1970; Bonecrack, 1971; Smokescreen, 1972; Slay-Ride, 1973; Knock Down, 1974; High Stakes, 1975; In the Frame, 1976; Risk, 1977; Trial Run, 1978; Whip Hand, 1979; Reflex, 1980; Twice Shy, 1981; Banker, 1982; The Danger, 1983; Proof, 1984; Break In, 1985; Bolt, 1986; A Jockey's Life (biography of Lester Piggott), 1986; Hot Money, 1987; The Edge, 1988; Straight, 1989; Longshot, 1990; Comeback, 1991; Driving Force, 1992; Decider, 1993; Wild Horses, 1994; Come to Grief, 1995; To the Hilt, 1996; 10-lb. Penalty, 1997; Field of 13, 1998; Second Wind, 1999; Shattered, 2000; Break In, 2003. EDITOR (with J. Welcome): Best Racing and Chasing Stories, 1966; The Racing Man's Bedside Book, 1969; (and author of intro.) The Dick Francis Treasury of Great Racing Stories, 1990; (and author of intro.) Classic Lines: More Great Racing Stories, 1991; The Dick Francis Complete Treasury of Great Racing Stories, 2003. **Address:** c/o John Johnson Ltd, 45/47 Clerkenwell Green, London EC1R 0HT, England.

FRANCIS, Dorothy Brenner. Also writes as Sue Alden, Ellen Goforth, Pat Louis. American, b. 1926. **Genres:** Mystery/Crime/Suspense, Romance/Historical, Children's fiction, Adult non-fiction. **Career:** Writer. **Publications:** Adventure at Riverton Zoo, 1966; Mystery of the Forgotten Map, 1968; Laugh at the Evil Eye, 1970; Another Kind of Beauty, 1970; Hawaiian Interlude, 1970; Studio Affair, 1972; Blue Ribbon for Marni, 1973; Nurse on Assignment, 1973; Nurse under Fire, 1973; Murder in Hawaii, 1973; Nurse in the Caribbean, 1974; Golden Girl, 1974; Nurse of the Keys, 1974; Nurse at Spirit Lake, 1975; Keys to Love, 1975; Legacy of Merton Manor, 1976; Nurse at Playland Park, 1976; (as Sue Alden) The Magnificent Challenge, 1976; Two against the Arctic, 1976; The Flint Hills Foal, 1976; (as Sue Alden) Nurse of St. John, 1977; Piggy Bank Minds, 1977; Run of the Sea

Witch, 1978; The Boy with the Blue Ears, 1979; Shoplifting: The Crime Everybody Pays For, 1980; (as Ellen Goforth) Path of Desire, 1980; New Boy in Town, 1981; Special Girl, 1981; (as Ellen Goforth) A New Dawn, 1982; Say Please, 1982; Captain Morgana Mason, 1982; (as Pat Louis) Treasure of the Heart, 1982; Ghost of Graydon Place, 1982; A Secret Place, 1982; A Blink of the Mind, 1982; Just Friends, 1983; Promises and Turtle Shells, 1984; The Warning, 1984; The Magic Circle, 1984; Kiss Me Kit, 1984; Bid for Romance, 1985; Write On, 1986; Stop Thief!, 1986; The Tomorrow Star, 1986; Fellow Your Heart, 1986; Computer Crime, 1987; The Right Kind of Girl, 1987; Vonnie and Monique, 1987; Suicide: The Preventable Tragedy, 1989; Drift Bottles in History and Folklore, 1990; Metal Detecting for Treasure, 1992; Survival at Big Shark Key, 1999; The Toy Deer of the Florida Keys, 1999; Bigfoot in New York City?, 1999; Case of the Bad-Luck Bike Ride across Iowa, 2001; The Case of the Missing Emeralds, 2001; Cody Smith and the Holiday Mysteries, 2001; The Case of the Vanishing Cat, 2001; The Jayhawk Horse Mystery, 2001; The Case of the Disappearing Kidnapper, 2001; Sharks!, 2001; The American Alligator, 2001; Dolphins, 2001; Sea Turtles, 2001; Borderland Horse, 2001; Loess Hills Forever, 2002; Clara Barton, 2002; Our Transportation Systems, 2002; Courage on the Oregon Trail, 2003; Conch Shell Murder, 2003; Pier Pressure, 2005. **Address:** 1505 Brentwood Terr, Marshalltown, IA 50158, U.S.A. **Online address:** rdfran@ibm.net

FRANCIS, H(erbert) E(dward). American, b. 1924. **Genres:** Novellas/Short stories, Literary criticism and history, Translations. **Career:** Instructor of English, Pennsylvania State University, 1950-52, University of Tennessee, 1952-56, and Northern Illinois University, 1956-58; Emory University, Atlanta, GA, assistant professor of English, 1958-65; University of Alabama, Huntsville, professor of English, 1966-. Contributing Ed., Poem Magazine, Literary Review, and Manoa; Fulbright Visiting Professor to University Nacional de Cuyo, Mendoza, Argentina, 1964, 1965-66, and 1969, and to Cordoba, Argentina, 1969-70. **Publications:** The Itinerary of Beggars, 1973; Naming Things, 1980; A Disturbance of Gulls, 1983; The Sudden Trees, 1999; Goya, Are You with Me Now?, 1999; The Invisible Country, 2003. **Address:** 508 E Clinton Ave, Huntsville, AL 35801, U.S.A.

FRANCIS, James A. American, b. 1954. **Genres:** Classics, Theology/Religion. **Career:** St. John's University, Collegeville, MN, assistant director of Christian Humanism Project, 1978-81, instructor in liberal studies, 1980-81; Duke University, Durham, NC, lecturer in early Christian asceticism and monasticism, 1985; Rollins College, Winter Park, FL, visiting assistant professor of classics, 1991-95, program director, 1993-95; University of Kentucky, Lexington, assistant professor of classics, 1995-. Former member of the Roman Catholic Ordo Sancti Benedicti (Order of St. Benedict; Benedictines; O.S.B.), under the religious name J. Alcuin Francis. **Publications:** Early Monastic Rules: The Rules of the Fathers and the Regula Orientalis, 1982; Subversive Virtue: Asceticism and Authority in the Second-Century Pagan World, 1995. Contributor to books and journals. **Address:** Department of Classics, 1153 Patterson Office Tower, University of Kentucky, Lexington, KY 40506, U.S.A.

FRANCIS, Lesley Lee. American, b. 1931. **Genres:** Literary criticism and history. **Career:** Sweet Briar College, Sweet Briar, VA, assistant professor of Spanish, 1960-62; St. Edward's University, Austin, TX, assistant professor, 1966-69, associate professor of Spanish, 1969-74; American Association of University Professors, Washington, DC, associate secretary, 1974-. Escuela de la Tahona, La Granja, Spain, owner and director, summers, 1968-73, 1983-88. **Publications:** The Frost Family's Adventure in Poetry: Sheer Morning Gladness at the Brim, 1994. Contributor of articles and poems to periodicals. **Address:** 4904 Valley Oak Dr., Austin, TX 78731, U.S.A.

FRANCIS, Matthew (Charles). British, b. 1956. **Genres:** Novels, Poetry. **Career:** Hampshire County Council, Winchester, England, computer programmer, 1983-85; Metier Ltd., London, England, technical writer, 1985-86; Powell Duffryn Systems Ltd., Basingstoke, England, technical writer, 1986-87; free-lance technical writer, 1987-94; Southampton University, research student, 1994-98; freelance teacher of creative writing, 1998-99; University of Glamorgan, Pontypridd, Wales, lecturer in creative writing, 1999-. **Publications:** Whom (novel), 1989; Blizzard (poems), 1996; Dragons (poems), 2001. **Address:** Tessa Sayle Agency, 11 Jubilee Place, London SW3 3TE, England. **Online address:** matthew@7greenhill.freeserve.co.uk

FRANCIS, Paul. See ENGLEMAN, Paul.

FRANCIS, Richard. British, b. 1945. **Genres:** Novels, Intellectual history. **Career:** Professor of creative writing, Manchester University, since 1972. American Council of Learned Socs. Fellow, Harvard University, Cambridge,

Massachusetts, 1970-72; Lecturer in English, Tripoli University, Libya, 1976-77; Visiting Professor of American Literature and Creative Writing, University of Missouri, Columbia, 1987-88. **Publications:** Blackpool Vanishes, 1979; Daggerman, 1980; The Enormous Dwarf, 1982; The Whispering Gallery, 1984; Swansong, 1986; Revolution (novelization of screenplay), 1986; The Land Where Lost Things Go, by Olive Watson, 1990; Taking Apart the Polo Polo, 1995; Transcendental Utopias: Individual and Community at Brook Farm, Fruitlands and Walden, 1997; Fat Hen, 1999; Ann the Word, 2000. **Address:** 9 Glenfield Rd, Heaton Chapel, Stockport SK4 2QP, England.

FRANCIS, Samuel. American, b. 1947. **Genres:** Politics/Government. **Career:** Heritage Foundation, Washington, DC, policy analyst, 1977-81; U.S. Senate, Washington, DC, staff member, 1981-86; Washington Times, Washington, DC, editorial writer, 1986-91, deputy editorial page editor, 1987-91, columnist, 1991-. **Publications:** The Soviet Strategy of Terror, 1981; Power and History: The Political Thought of James Burnham, 1983; Beautiful Losers: Essays on the Failure of American Conservatism, 1993; Revolution from the Middle, 1997; Thinkers of Our Time, 1999. Contributor to periodicals. **Address:** c/o Creators Syndicate, 5777 W Century Blvd #700, Los Angeles, CA 90045, U.S.A. **Online address:** sam@samfrancis.net

FRANCISCO, Nia. American, b. 1952. **Genres:** Poetry, Cultural/Ethnic topics. **Career:** Has worked as an instructor at Navajo Community College, Tsaile, AR, 1976-78, in the Navajo Tribe Division of Education, Window Rock, AZ, 1977-79, in the Chinle School District, Chinle, AZ, 1979-80, at the Navajo Academy, Farmington, NM, 1981-83, and with the Fort Defiance Division of Child Development, Fort Defiance, AZ, 1983; member of Arizona Commission on Humanities, Phoenix, AZ, 1978-79. **Publications:** Blue Horses for Navajo Women, 1988; Carried Away by the Black River, 1994. Work represented in anthologies. **Address:** P.O. Box 794, Navajo, NM 87328, U.S.A.

FRANCK, Frederick. Also writes as Dr. Frank Fredericks. American (born Netherlands), b. 1909. **Genres:** Art/Art history, Theology/Religion. **Career:** Freelance writer and artist. **Publications:** (as Dr. Frank Fredericks) Open Wide, Please, 1957; (with L. Begue) Au Pays du Soleil, 1958; Days with Albert Schweitzer, 1959; My Friend in Africa, 1960; African Sketchbook, 1961; My Eye Is in Love, 1963; Outsider in the Vatican, 1965; Au Fil de l'Eau, 1965; I Love Life, 1967; Exploding Church, 1967; (with L. Begue) Openboek Croquis Parisiens, 1969; Simenon's Paris, 1970; Tussen Broek en Brooklyn, 1971; Tutte le Strade portano a Roma, 1970; The Zen of Seeing, 1973; Pilgrimage to Now/Here, Christ-Buddha and the True Self of Man, 1973; An Encounter with Oomoto, 1975; The Book of Angelus Silesius, 1976; Zen and Zen Classics, 1978; Everyone: The Timeless Myth of Everyman Reborn, 1978; The Awakened Eye, 1979; Art as a Way: A Return to the Spiritual Roots, 1981; The Buddha Eye: An Anthology of the Kyoto School, 1982; The Supreme Koan: Confessions of a Journey Inward, 1982; Messenger of the Heart: The Book of Angelus Silesius, 1982; De Zen Van het Zien, 1982; Echoes from the Bottomless Well, 1985; De Droomzolder, Oog in oog met Venetie, 1985; Life Drawing Life, 1989; Little Compendium on That which Matters, 1989, 1993; To Be Human against All Odds, 1991; Zen Seeing, Zen Drawing, 1993; Fingers Pointing towards the Sacred, 1994; Drawings of Lambarene, Albert Schweitzer's Hospital in Action, 1994; The Tao of the Cross, 1995; (co-ed.) What Does It Mean to Be Human?, 1998; Beyond Hiroshima, 1999; Watching the Vatican, 2000; Pacem in Terris: A Love Story, 2000; Moments of Seeing, 2000; Seeing Venice: An Eye in Love, 2002; A Passion for Seeing, 2003; A Zen Book of Hours, 2003. **Address:** Pacem in Terris, 96 Covered Bridge Rd, Warwick, NY 10990, U.S.A.

FRANCK, Thomas Martin. American (born Germany), b. 1931. **Genres:** International relations/Current affairs, Law, Politics/Government. **Career:** Professor of Law, School of Law, and Director, Center for International Studies, 1965-2002, New York University, NYC; on leave from NYU: Director of Research, UN Institute for Training and Research, 1980-82. Director, International Law Program, Carnegie Endowment for International Peace, 1975-79 (Acting Director, 1973-75); Visiting Professor Osgoode Hall Law School, York University, Toronto, 1972-76. **Publications:** Race and Nationalism, 1960; (co-author) The Role of the United Nations in the Congo, 1963; (co-author) African Law, 1963; East African Unity through Law, 1964; Comparative Constitutional Process, 1968; The Structure of Impartiality, 1968; (co-author) A Free Trade Association, 1968; (co-author) Why Federations Fail, 1968; (co-author) Word Politics, 1971; (co-ed.) Secrecy and Foreign Policy, 1974; (co-author) Resignation in Protest, 1975; (co-author) Foreign Policy by Congress, 1979; (co-author) U.S. Foreign Relations Law, vols. I-III, 1980-81, vols. IV-V, 1984; The Tethered Presidency, 1981; Human Rights in Third World Perspective, 3 vols., 1982; Nation against Nation,

1985; Judging the World Court, 1986; Foreign Relations and National Security Law, 1987, 2nd ed., 1993; The Power of Legitimacy among Nations, 1990; Political Questions/Judicial Answers, 1992; Fairness in the International Legal and Institutional Systems, 1993; Fairness in International Law and Institutions, 1995; (co-author) International Law Decisions in National Courts, 1996; The Empowered Self, 1999; (ed.) Delegating State Powers, 2000; Recourse to Force, 2002.

FRANCO, Betsy. American. **Genres:** Young adult fiction, Young adult nonfiction. **Career:** Writer and editor for children and adults; creator of educational materials. **Publications:** Japan, 1993; Mexico, 1993; Russia, 1993; India, 1994; Nigeria, 1994; China, 1994; Brazil, 1995; South Korea, 1995; Italy, 1995; Quiet Elegance: Japan through the Eyes of Nine American Artists, 1997; Sorting All Sorts of Socks, 1997; Fourscore and Seven, 1999; Grandpa's Quilt, 1999; Write and Read Math Story Books, 1999; Unfolding Mathematics with Unit Origami, 1999; Shells, 2000; Why the Frog Has Big Eyes, 2000; Caring, Sharing, and Getting Along, 2000; Thematic Poetry: On the Farm, 2000; Twenty Marvelous Math Tales, 2000; Thematic Poetry: Neighborhoods and Communities, 2000; Thematic Poetry: Creepy Crawlies, 2000; 201 Thematic Riddle Poems to Build Literacy, 2000; Thematic Poetry: All About Me!, 2000; The Tortoise Who Bragged: A Chinese Tale with Trigrams, 2000; My Pinkie Finger, 2001; Instant Poetry Frames for Primary Poets, 2001; Fifteen Wonderful Writing Prompt Mini-Books, 2001; Clever Calculator Cat, 2001; Funny Fairy Tale Math, 2001; Thematic Poetry: Transportation, 2001; Clever Calculations about Cats and Other Cool Creatures (teacher resource book), 2001; Adding Alligators and Other Easy-to-Read Math Stories, 2001; Five-Minute Math Problem of the Day for Young Learners, 2001; Twelve Genre Mini-Books, 2002; Instant Math Practice Pages for Homework-or Anytime!, 2002; Six Silly Seals and Other Read-Aloud Story Skits, 2002; Amazing Animals, 2002; Pocket Poetry Mini-Books, 2002; Silly Sally, 2002; Jake's Cake Mistake, 2002; (with Claudine Jellison and Johanna Kaufman) 2002; (with Denise Dauler) Math in Motion: Wiggle, Gallop, and Leap with Numbers, 2002; Many Ways to 100, 2002; A Bat Named Pat, 2002; Subtraction Fun, 2002; Time to Estimate, 2002; Marvelous Math Word Problem Mini-Books, 2002; What's Zero?, 2002; Going to Grandma's Farm, 2003; Word Families: Guess-Me Poems and Puzzles, 2003; Mathematickles!, 2003; Amoeba Hop, 2003; Alphabet: Guess-Me Poems and Puzzles, 2003; Counting Our Way to the 100th Day!: 100 Poems and 100 Pictures to Celebrate the 100th Day of School, 2004. EDITOR: You Hear Me?: Poems and Writing by Teenage Boys, 2000; Things I Have to Tell You: Poems and Writing by Teenage Girls, photographs by Nina Nickles, 2001; (with Annette Ochoa and Traci Gourdine) Night Is Gone, Day Is Still Coming: Stories and Poems by American Indian Teenagers and Young Adults, 2003. Author of numerous workbooks, easy level readers, easy mathematics resource books, and science resource books. **Address:** POB 60487, Palo Alto, CA 94306, U.S.A.

FRANEY, Ros(alind). British. **Genres:** Novels, Social commentary, Documentaries/Reportage. **Career:** IPC Magazines, London, journalist, 1972-74; UNICEF, Ethiopia, information officer, 1974-75; Shelter, London, journalist, 1977-82; freelance writer and journalist in London, 1982-85; Yorkshire Television, London, researcher, 1985-89, producer/director of documentaries, 1990-97; freelance executive producer, 1997-98, 2001-03; Channel 4 TV, UK, deputy commissioning editor, documentaries, 1998-2000; Mentorn TV, executive producer, 2003-. **Publications:** Poor Law: The Mass Arrest of Homeless Claimants in Oxford, 1983; Cry Baby (novel), 1987; (with G. McKee) Time Bomb: Irish Bombers, English Justice and the Guildford Four, 1988. **Address:** Mentorn, 43 Whitfield St, London W1T 4HA, England.

FRANK, Charles R(aphael), (Jr.). American, b. 1937. **Genres:** Economics, International relations/Current affairs. **Career:** Makerere University College, Kampala, Uganda, Lecturer, 1963-65; Yale University, New Haven, CT, Assistant Professor of Economics, 1965-67; Princeton University, NJ, Professor of Economics and International Affairs, 1967-74; Brookings Institution, Washington, DC, Sr. Fellow, 1972-74; Deputy Assistant Secretary of State, Washington, DC, 1974-78; Salomon Bros., Inc., NYC, Vice President, 1978-87; Frank and Co., Inc., President, 1987-88; G. E. Capital Corp, Stamford, CT, Vice President, 1988-97; European Bank for Reconstruction and Development, London, England, First Vice-President, 1997-. **Publications:** The Sugar Industry in East Africa, 1965; (with Van Arkadie) Economic Accounting and Development Planning, 1966; Production Theory and Indivisible Commodities, 1969; Statistics and Econometrics, 1971; Foreign Trade Regimes and Economic Development: The Case of Korea, 1975; Foreign Trade and Domestic Aid, 1977. **Address:** 33 Pout St, London SW1X 0BB, England.

FRANK, Dorothea Benton. (born United States). **Genres:** Fashion/Costume. **Career:** Author, fundraiser, advocate. Worked as a fashion buyer and representative; volunteer fundraiser for arts and education; advocate for literacy and women's issues. New Jersey Cultural Trust, New Jersey State Council on the Arts, and the Drumthwatchet Foundations, member; Montclair Art Museum, Montclair, NJ, and Margaret Mitchell House, Atlanta, GA, trustee. Former board member of American Stage Company, New Jersey Chamber Music Society, Bill T. Jones/Arnie Zane Dance Company, and the Community Foundation of New Jersey. **Publications:** Sullivan's Island: A Lowcountry Tale, 1999; Plantation: A Lowcountry Tale, 2001; Isle of Palms: A Lowcountry Tale, 2003; Shem Creek: A Lowcountry Tale, 2004. **Address:** c/o Author Mail, Berkley Publicity, 375 Hudson Street, New York, NY 10014, U.S.A. **Online address:** dot@dotfrank.com

FRANK, Frederick S. American, b. 1935. **Genres:** Horror, Romance/Historical, Writing/Journalism, Bibliography, Adult non-fiction. **Career:** English teacher at a public school in Middleburg, NY, 1959-60; Boston University, Boston, MA, assistant professor of English, 1964-70; Allegheny College, Meadville, PA, professor of English, 1970-, now emeritus; writer. **Publications:** Guide to the Gothic, 1984; The First Gothics, 1987; Gothic Fiction: A Masterlist, 1988; Montague Summers: A Bibliographical Portrait, 1988; Through the Pale Door: A Guide to and through the American Gothic, 1990; Guide to the Gothic II, 1995; The Poe Encyclopedia, 1997. Worked represented in anthologies. **Address:** 451 Sunnyside Ave, Meadville, PA 16335-1312, U.S.A. **Online address:** ffrank@toolcity.net; www.toolcity.net/~frank

FRANK, Helmut J. American (born Germany), b. 1922. **Genres:** Economics. **Career:** Professor Emeritus of Economics, University of Arizona, Tucson, since 1984 (Assistant Professor, 1961-63; Associate Professor, 1963-67; Professor, 1967-83; Director, Division of Economic and Business Research, 1978-80). Founding Ed., The Energy Journal, since 1990 (Ed., 1980-89). Economist, W. J. Levy Consultants, New York, 1950-56, and Paris, 1960-61, and University of Denver Research Institute, 1967-68. **Publications:** Crude Oil Prices in the Middle East, 1966; (with J. J. Schanz) U.S.-Canadian Energy Trade, 1978; (with J. H. Lichtblau) Outlook for World Oil in the 21st Century, 1978; Community Energy Assessment for the Tucson-Pima Metropolitan Area, 1994. **Address:** Dept. of Economics, University of Arizona, Tucson, AZ 85721, U.S.A.

FRANK, J. Suzanne. Also writes as Chloe Green. American, b. 1967. **Genres:** Novellas/Short stories, Mystery/Crime/Suspense, Romance/Historical. **Career:** Writer. **Publications:** Reflections in the Nile, 1997; Shadows on the Aegean, 1998; Sunrise on the Mediterranean, 1999; Twilight in Babylon, 2002. AS CHLOE GREEN: Going out in Style, 2000; Designed to Die, 2001; Fashion Victim, 2002. Work is represented in anthologies.

FRANK, Joan. American. **Genres:** Essays. **Career:** Writer. Teacher and lecturer at colleges and other venues; juror for fiction competitions; gives readings on radio broadcasts. **Publications:** Desperate Women Need to Talk to You (essays), 1994; Boys Keep Being Born (short stories), 2001. Work represented in anthologies. Contributor of essays and short stories to periodicals. **Address:** c/o Maria Massie, Witherspoon and Associates, 235 East 31st St., New York, NY 10016, U.S.A.

FRANK, Joseph (Nathaniel). American, b. 1918. **Genres:** Literary criticism and history. **Career:** Professor Emeritus, Princeton University, New Jersey, since 1983 (Lecturer in English, 1955-56; Professor of Comparative Literature, 1966-83; Director, Christian Gauss Seminars in Criticism, 1966-83). Ed., Bureau of National Affairs, Washington, D.C., 1942-50; Special Researcher, American Embassy, Paris, 1951-52; Assistant Professor of English, University of Minnesota, 1958-61; Associate Professor and Professor, Dept. of Comparative Literature, Rutgers-The State University, New Jersey, 1961-66; Professor of Comparative Literature and Slavic Languages and Literature, Stanford University, California, 1986. **Publications:** The Widening Gyre: Crisis and Mastery in Modern Literature, 1963; F.M. Dostoevsky: The Seeds of Revolt 1821-1849, 1976, The Years of Ordeal 1850-1859, 1983, The Stir of Liberation, 1860-1865, 1986; The Legacy of R.P. Blackmur, 1987; Through the Russian Prism, 1990; The Idea of Spatial Form, 1991; F.M. Dostoevsky, The Miraculous Years, 1865-1871. EDITOR: A Primer of Ignorance by R.P. Blackmur, 1967; Selected Letters of Fyodor Dostoevsky, 1987. **Address:** 78 Pearce-Mitchell Pl, Stanford, CA 94305, U.S.A.

FRANK, Larry. American, b. 1926. **Genres:** Art/Art history. **Career:** President of a company that buys and sells North American Indian art and New Mexico Spanish colonial art, Arroyo Hondo, NM, c. 1963-. **Publications:** Historic Pottery of the Pueblo Indians, 1974; Indian Silver Jewelry of the Southwest, 1978; New Kingdom of the Saints, 1994; Train Stops (stories),

1998; A Land So Remote, 3 vols., 2001; Fragments of a Mask (novel), 2002; Siftings (poetry), 2004. **Address:** PO Box 290, Arroyo Hondo, NM 87513, U.S.A.

FRANK, (A.) Scott. American, b. 1960?. **Genres:** Plays/Screenplays. **Career:** Screenwriter. **Publications:** SCREENPLAYS: (as A. Scott Frank) Plain Clothes, 1988; Dead Again, 1991; Little Man Tate, 1991; Malice, 1993; Get Shorty, 1995; Heaven's Prisoners, 1996; Out of Sight, 1998; Minority Report, 2001. TELEPLAYS: Fallen Angels; (with W.F. Parkes) Birdland. **Address:** c/o Beth Swofford, Creative Artists Agency, 9830 Wilshire Blvd, Beverly Hills, CA 90212, U.S.A.

FRANKE, William. American, b. 1956. **Genres:** Literary criticism and history. **Career:** Columbia College, adjunct faculty member in writing and English, 1984-86; Vanderbilt University, Nashville, TN, faculty member, 1991-, associate professor of comparative literature and Italian, 1996-, fellow of Alexander von Humboldt-Stiftung and Robert Penn Warren Center for the Humanities, 1995-96. Lecturer at educational institutions. **Publications:** Dante's Interpretive Journey, 1996. Contributor to books. Contributor of articles and poems to journals. **Address:** Program in Comparative Literature, Vanderbilt University, PO Box 1709, Station B, Nashville, TN 37235, U.S.A.

FRANKEL, Alona. Israeli (born Poland), b. 1937. **Genres:** Children's fiction, Autobiography/Memoirs, Illustrations, Picture/board books. **Career:** Graphic designer and illustrator, 1955-; author and illustrator of children's books, 1975-. Exhibitions in Israel and abroad. **Publications:** FOR CHILDREN (SELF-ILLUSTRATED): Once upon a Potty, 1975, in 2 vols as Once upon a Potty: His, 1975, and Once upon a Potty: Hers, 1978; The Family of Tiny White Elephants, 1978; The Goodnight Book, 1979; Let's Go from Head to Toe, 1979; Angela, the Little Devil, 1979; One, Two, Three, What Can a Mushroom Be?, 1980; A Book to Eat By, 1980; A True Story, 1981; The Clothes We Wear, 1983; The Moon Book, 1983; The Book of Numbers, 1983; The Book of Letters, 1983; The Princess of Dreams, 1984; A Fairy Tale, 1985; There Is No One Like Mother, 1985; The Ship and the Island, 1985; The Princess and the Caterpillar, 1987; A Lullaby, 1987; One Day... (a book of numbers), 1990; From Armadillo to Octopus (a book of the Hebrew alphabet), 1990; The Book of Manners, 1990; I Want My Mother, 1990; A Book to Babysit By, 1991; Prudence's Babysitter Book, 2000; Prudence's Book of Food, 2000; Prudence's Get-Well Book, 2000; Prudence's Good Night Book, 2000; Joshua's Counting Book, 2000; Moon and the Stars, 2000; On Grandparents' Farm, 2001. Illustrator of books by others. **Address:** c/o Child Matters, 155 Beech St, Boston, MA 02131-2714, U.S.A. **Online address:** www.alonafrankel.com

FRANKEL, Ellen. American, b. 1951. **Genres:** Novellas/Short stories, Children's fiction, Mythology/Folklore, Theology/Religion. **Career:** Teacher at Franklin and Marshall College, Lancaster, PA, Drexel University, Philadelphia, PA, and Millersville University, Millersville, PA, 1977-85; freelance writer, 1981-; B'nai B'rith Book Club, Washington, DC, editor, 1990; Jewish Publication Society of America, Philadelphia, editor in chief, 1991-, CEO, 1998-. Storyteller, 1988-. **Publications:** Choosing to Be Chosen (stories for children), 1985; George Washington and the Constitution, 1987; The Classic Tales: Four Thousand Years of Jewish Lore, 1989; (with B. Teutsch) The Encyclopedia of Jewish Symbols, 1992; The Five Books of Miriam: A Woman's Commentary on the Torah, 1996; The Jewish Spirit, 1998; The Illustrated Hebrew Bible, 1999. **Address:** Jewish Publication Society, 2100 Arch St 2nd Fl, Philadelphia, PA 19103, U.S.A. **Online address:** efrankel@juwishpub.org

FRANKEL, Glenn. American, b. 1949. **Genres:** International relations/Current affairs. **Career:** Journalist, nonfiction writer. Washington Post, Washington, DC, Richmond, VA, bureau chief, 1979-82, Southern Africa bureau chief, 1983-86, Jerusalem bureau chief, 1986-89, London bureau chief, 1989-92. **Publications:** Beyond the Promised Land: Jews and Arabs on the Hard Road to a New Israel, 1994. **Address:** Washington Post, 1150 15th St. NW, Washington, DC 20071, U.S.A.

FRANKEL, Sandor. American, b. 1943. **Genres:** Law. **Career:** Attorney, in private practice, New York, since 1971. Temporary Counsel to National Commission for Reform of Federal Criminal Laws, 1968. Staff member, White House Task Force on Crime, 1967; Assistant U.S. Attorney for District of Columbia, 1968-71. **Publications:** Beyond a Reasonable Doubt, 1972; The Aleph Solution, 1978; How To Defend Yourself Against the I. R. S., 1985. **Address:** 230 Park Ave., New York, NY 10169, U.S.A.

FRANKEL, Valerie. American, b. 1965. **Genres:** Novels. **Career:** New York Woman, NYC, 1987-89; Mademoiselle, NYC, 1990-99. **Publications:**

A Deadline for Murder, 1991; Murder on Wheels, 1992; Prime-Time for Murder, 1994; (with E. Tien) The Heartbreak Handbook, 1994; A Body to Die For, 1995; (with Tien) The I Hate My Job Handbook, 1995; Prime Time Style, 1996; Smart versus Pretty, 2000; The Accidental Virgin, 2003; The Not-So-Perfect Way, 2004. Work represented in anthologies.

FRANKENBERG, Dirk. American, b. 1937. **Genres:** Marine sciences/Oceanography. **Career:** University of Georgia, Athens, assistant professor to professor of zoology, 1962-74; University of North Carolina at Chapel Hill, professor of marine sciences and division director, 1974-. National Science Foundation, Washington, DC, program director, 1970, 1978-80; National Academy of Sciences, member of Ocean Sciences Board and Board on Science and Technology for International Development. **Publications:** (with R.J. Menzies) Handbook on the Common Marine Isopod Crustacea of Georgia, c. 1966; The Nature of the Outer Banks: Environmental Processes, Field Sites, and Development Issues, Corolla to Ocracoke, 1995; The Nature of North Carolina's Southern Coast: Barrier Islands, Coastal Waters, and Wetlands, 1997; Estuarine Interactions, in press. **Address:** Department of Marine Sciences, University of North Carolina at Chapel Hill, Chapel Hill, NC 27599, U.S.A. **Online address:** DF_berg@marine.unc.edu

FRANKL, Razelle. American, b. 1932. **Genres:** Theology/Religion, Institutions/Organizations, Communications/Media. **Career:** Philadelphia '76, Inc. (bicentennial corporation), Philadelphia, PA, coordinator for health programs, 1973-74; Glassboro State College, Glassboro, NJ, adjunct member of faculty, 1974-77 and 1981-82, assistant professor, 1982-88, associate professor of Management, 1988-95; Rowan University, professor of management, 1995. Instructor at Drexel University, 1972-73. Guest on television and radio programs. **Publications:** Televangelism: The Marketing of Popular Religion, 1987. Contributor to books and periodicals. **Address:** 536 Moreno Rd., Wynnewood, PA 19096-1121, U.S.A. **Online address:** frankl@rowan.edu

FRANKLAND, (Anthony) Noble. British, b. 1922. **Genres:** History, Military/Defense/Arms control, Biography. **Career:** Official Military Historian, 1951-60; Deputy Director of Studies, Royal Institute of International Affairs, London, 1956-60; Director, Imperial War Museum, London, 1960-82; Consultant, World at War television series, London, 1971-74. **Publications:** (ed.) Documents on International Affairs, 1955, 1956, 1957, 1958-60; Crown of Tragedy: Nicholas II (in U.S. as Imperial Tragedy: Nicholas II, Last of the Tsars), 1961; (with C. Webster) The Strategic Air Offensive Against Germany 1939-45, 4 vols., 1961; The Bombing Offensive Against Germany: Outlines and Perspectives, 1965; Bomber Offensive: The Devastation of Europe, 1970; (ed. with C. Dowling) The Politics and Strategy of the Second World War, 8 vols., 1974-78, and Decisive Battles of the 20th Century, 1976; Prince Henry, Duke of Gloucester, 1980; (gen. ed.) The Encyclopedia of Twentieth-Century Warfare, 1989; Witness of a Century, the Life and Times of Prince Arthur, Duke of Connaught, 1993; History at War: The Campaigns of an Historian, 1998. **Address:** 26/27 Riverview Terrace, Abingdon, Oxon. OX14 5AE, England.

FRANKLET, Duane. American, b. 1963. **Genres:** Information science/Computers. **Career:** Data Tracking Associates, Houston, partner, 1992-; writer, 1985-. **Publications:** Bad Memory, 1997. **Address:** 4200 Montrose Suite 300, Houston, TX 77006, U.S.A.

FRANKLIN, Allan (David). (born United States), b. 1938. **Genres:** Sciences. **Career:** Princeton University, Princeton, NJ, research associate, 1965-66, instructor, 1966-67; University of Colorado, Boulder, assistant professor, 1967-73, associate professor, 1973-82, professor of physics, 1982-. Visiting professor and lecturer at various institutions, including City University of New York, 1974-75; University of Campinas, Brazil, 1982; and University of London, 1982-92. **Publications:** The Principle of Inertia in the Middle Ages, 1976; The Neglect of Experiment, 1986; Experiment, Right or Wrong, 1990; The Rise and Fall of the Fifth Force: Discovery, Pursuit, and Justification in Modern Physics, 1993; Can That Be Right? Essays on Experiment, Evidence, and Science, 1999; Are There Really Neutrinos? An Evidential History, 2000; Selectivity and Discord: Two Problems of Experiment, 2002; No Easy Answers: Science and the Pursuit of Knowledge, 2005. Contributor to numerous academic journals. **Address:** 1911 Mariposa, Boulder, CO 80302, U.S.A. **Online address:** Allan.Franklin@colorado.edu

FRANKLIN, Caroline. British, b. 1949. **Genres:** Literary criticism and history. **Career:** Schoolteacher in Yorkshire and Worcestershire, England, and in Wales, 1972-84; Trinity College, Carmarthen, Wales, senior lecturer, 1989-. **Publications:** Byron's Heroines, 1992; Byron: A Literary Life, 2000. EDITOR: The Wanderings of Warwick, by C. Smith, 1992; Emmeline, by M.

Brunton, 1992; The History of Cornelia, by S. Scott, 1992. Work represented in anthologies. Contributor to books. **Address:** Deaprtment of English, University of Wales, Swansea, Singleton Park, Swansea SA2 8PP, Wales. **Online address:** c.franklin@ swansea.ac.uk

FRANKLIN, Cheryl J. American, b. 1955. **Genres:** Science fiction/Fantasy. **Career:** Boeing, Anaheim, CA, communications systems analyst, 1976-2001; writer. **Publications:** Fire Get, 1987; Fire Lord, 1989; The Light in Exile, 1990; Fire Crossing, 1991; Inquisitor, 1992; Sable, Shadow and Ice; 1994; Ghost Shadow, 1996.

FRANKLIN, Daniel P. American, b. 1954. **Genres:** Politics/Government. **Career:** Colgate University, Hamilton, NY, assistant professor of political science, 1985-91; Georgia State University, Atlanta, associate professor of political science, 1991-; Franklin Political Consulting, president. **Publications:** Extraordinary Measures, 1991; Making Ends Meet, 1993; Political Culture and Constitutionalism, 1994; Politics and Film, forthcoming. **Address:** Department of Political Science, Georgia State University, Atlanta, GA 30303, U.S.A. **Online address:** dfrankli@gsu.edu

FRANKLIN, David B. American, b. 1951. **Genres:** Anthropology/Ethnology, History. **Career:** Young Harris College, Young Harris, GA, professor of history and anthropology, 1979-. **Publications:** The Scottish Regency of the Earl of Arran: A Study in the Failure of Anglo-Scottish Relations, 1995; History Ireland, 2004. **Address:** Young Harris College, Young Harris, GA 30582, U.S.A.

FRANKLIN, Jane (Morgan). American, b. 1934. **Genres:** History, Politics/Government. **Career:** Historian. Tobacco worker on family farm, 1942-51; Bailey Library, Bailey, NC, part-time librarian, 1948-51; United Nations, NYC, public information representative, 1955-56; freelance typist, proofreader, editor, researcher, and writer, 1959-71; National Semiconductor, Santa Clara, CA, assembler, 1972; Heublein's Inc., Menlo Park, CA, bottler, 1972; Grossman, Ackerman & Peters (law firm), San Francisco, CA, legal secretary, 1973-74; WPOP, Hartford, CT, newswriter, 1974-75; WJDM, Elizabeth, NJ, "Jane Morgan at the Movies," 1975-76; freelance editor and indexer, 1977-79. Center for Cuban Studies, NYC, staff member, 1980-81; American Film Festival, Rutgers University, New Brunswick, NJ, prescreening juror, 1980-83, juror, 1983; Cuba Update, researcher and writer, 1981-83, co-editor, 1984-90, contributing editor, 1990-2002. Radio and television commentator about Cuba. Gives public speeches, participates in debates, and lectures about Cuba, Vietnam, Nicaragua, El Salvador, and Panama. **Publications:** Cuban Foreign Relations: A Chronology, 1959-1982, 1984; (ed., with M.E. Gettleman, H.B. Franklin, and M. Young) Vietnam and America: A Documented History, 1985, rev. ed., 1995; A Chronology of U.S. Panama Relations in the U.S. Invasion of Panama: The Truth behind Operation Just Cause, 1991; The Cuban Revolution and the United States: A Chronological History, 1992; Cuba and the United States: A Chronological History, 1997. Contributor to periodicals.

FRANKLIN, John H(ope). American, b. 1915. **Genres:** History, Race relations, Biography, Essays. **Career:** Instructor, Fisk University, Nashville, TN, 1936-37; professor of history, St. Augustine's College, Raleigh, NC, 1939-43; professor of history, North Carolina College, 1943-47; professor of history, Howard University, Washington, DC, 1947-56; professor and chairman, Dept. of History, Brooklyn College, NYC, 1956-64; professor of American history, 1964-82, and chairman of Dept. of History, 1967-70, University of Chicago; James Duke Professor of History, Duke University, Durham, NC, 1982-85, Emeritus, 1985-. **Publications:** The Free Negro in North Carolina, 1790-1860, 1943; From Slavery to Freedom, 1947, 8th ed., 2000; The Militant South 1800-1860, 1956; Reconstruction after the Civil War, 1961; The Emancipation Proclamation, 1963; (with J.W. Caughey and E.R. May) Land of the Free, 1966; Illustrated History of Black Americans, 1970; Racial Equality in America, 1976; Southern Odyssey, 1976; George Washington Williams: A Biography, 1985; Race and History: Selected Essays 1938-1988, 1990; The Color Line: Legacy for the Twenty-First Century, 1993; (with L. Schweninger) Runaway Slaves, 2000. EDITOR: The Civil War Diary of James T. Ayers, 1947; A. Tourgee, A Fool's Errand, 1961; T.W. Higginson, Army Life in a Black Regiment, 1962; Three Negro Classics, 1965; (with I. Star) The Negro in the Twentieth Century, 1967; Color and Race, 1968; W.E.B. Du Bois, The Suppression of the African Slave Trade, 1969; Reminiscences of an Active Life: The Autobiography of John R. Lynch, 1970; (with A. Meier) Black Leaders of the Twentieth Century, 1982. **Address:** Dept. of History, Duke University, Durham, NC 27708, U.S.A.

FRANKLIN, Kerry. See CALDWELL, Stratton F(ranklin).

FRANKLIN, Linda Campbell. Also writes as Ninda Dumont, Grace McFarland. American, b. 1941. **Genres:** Antiques/Furnishings, Design, Technology, Bibliography, Illustrations, Reference. **Career:** The Ephemera News quarterly, editor, 1981-83; Show Forth bimonthly, editor, 1983-84; Kitchen Collectibles News bimonthly, editor and publisher, 1984-86. **Publications:** From Hearth to Cookstove, 1976, rev. ed., 1979; Antiques and Collectibles: A Bibliography of Works in English, 1978; Our Old Fashioned Country Diary, 1980, 17th ed., 1996; Library Display Ideas, 1980; 300 Years of Kitchen Collectibles, 1981, 5th ed., 2003; Display and Publicity Ideas for Libraries, 1985; 300 Years of Housecleaning Collectibles, 1992; (ed. and illustrator), My Heart 2 Heart Diary, 1994; Heart 2 Heart Scraps & Scribbles, 1995; Heart 2 Heart Diary: Blue Dog, 1996; Heart 2 Heart Scraps & Pockets, 1997; Heart 2 Heart Girlfriends' Book, 1999; Heart 2 Heart Travel Diary, 1998; Girlfriends' Address Book, 1999; Girlfriends' Stationery, 2000; Big Crush, 2002; My Secrets, 2002; Pass-Note Diary, 2003. **Address:** 1412 Park Ave, Baltimore, MD 21217, U.S.A. **Online address:** barktok@mindspring.com

FRANKLIN, Michael J(ohn). Welsh, b. 1949. **Genres:** Biography, Literary criticism and history. **Career:** Worcester Girls' Grammar School, Worcester, England, English teacher, 1974-83; University of Birmingham, Birmingham, England, extra-mural lecturer, 1982-83; University of Wales, University College, Cardiff, Wales, extra-mural lecturer in continuing education, 1989-, part-time lecturer in English, 1992-95. Trinity College, Carmarthen, Wales, parttime lecturer, 1994-95; St. John's Comprehensive School, Mid Glamorgan, Wales, head of English department. **Publications:** Sir William Jones: A Critical Biography, 1995; (ed.) Sir William Jones: Selected Poetical and Prose Works (critical edition), 1995. Contributor to books and periodicals. **Address:** Department of English, St. John's Comprehensive School, Glan Rd., Aberdare, M. Glam, Wales.

FRANKLIN, Richard Langdon. Australian, b. 1925. **Genres:** Philosophy. **Career:** University of Western Australia, Perth, Lecturer, 1956-67; University of New England, Armidale, NSW, Professor, 1968-86, Emeritus Professor of Philosophy, 1986-. **Publications:** Freewill and Determinism, 1968; The Search for Understanding, 1995. **Address:** 8 Lambs Ave, Armidale, NSW 2350, Australia.

FRANKLIN, Robert M(ichael). American, b. 1954. **Genres:** Cultural/Ethnic topics, Theology/Religion. **Career:** St. Paul Church of God in Christ, Chicago, IL, assistant pastor, 1978-84; University of Chicago, Divinity School, instructor, and director of field education, 1981-83; Harvard University, Divinity School, Cambridge, MA, associate director of ministerial studies, 1984-85, visiting lecturer, 1986-88, visiting professor, 2003; Colgate Rochester/Bexley/Crozer Divinity School, Rochester, NY, assistant professor and dean of black church studies, 1985-89; Emory University, Candler School of Theology, Atlanta, GA, assistant professor, 1989-91, associate professor of ethics and society, 1991-, director of black church studies, 1989-, presidential distinguished professor, 2003-; Interdenominational Theological Center, president, 1997-2002; writer. Historical Commission of the Church of God in Christ, cochair; Urban League, member of board of directors; Georgia Department of Education, member of advisory board on teaching about religion in public schools; Ford Foundation, NY, program officer, 1995-97; National Public Radio, commentator, 2001-. **Publications:** Liberating Visions: Human Fulfillment and Social Justice in African-American Thought, Fortress, 1990; Another Day's Journey, 1997. **Address:** Emory University, Bishops Hall, Atlanta, GA 30322, U.S.A. **Online address:** rfrank222@aol.com

FRANKLIN, Samuel Harvey. New Zealander (born England), b. 1928. **Genres:** Geography, Sociology. **Career:** Victoria University of Wellington, Dept. of Geography, professor, 1967-. **Publications:** The European Peasantry, 1969; Rural Societies, 1971; Trade, Growth, and Anxiety: New Zealand beyond the Welfare State, 1978; Cul de Sac: The Question of New Zealand's Future, 1985. **Address:** Victoria University of Wellington, Dept. of Geography, Box 600, Wellington, New Zealand. **Online address:** harvey.franklin@vuw.ac.nz

FRANKLIN, Sarah B. See DUNCAN, Dave.

FRANKLIN, Yelena. American (born Yugoslavia), b. 1945. **Genres:** Essays. **Career:** Michigan Bell Telephone Company, Detroit, MI, editor, manager, writer, director, and producer, 1973-88; Editorial Services, Grosse Pointe, MI, partner, 1989-93; Video Monitoring Services, Southfield, MI, General Manager, 199394; Masco Corporation, Taylor, MI, Public Relations Manager, 1994-95. **Publications:** A Bowl of Sour Cherries, 1998. **Address:** c/o Author Mail, White Pine Press, PO Box 236, Buffalo, NY 14201, U.S.A. **Online address:** yelenavf@aol.com

FRANKS, Helen. British, b. 1934. **Genres:** Women's studies and issues, Medicine/Health, Self help. **Career:** Writer. **Publications:** Prime Time, 1981; Goodbye Tarzan, 1984; Remarriage, 1988; (ed.) What Every Woman Wants to Know about Retirement, 1988; Mummy Doesn't Live Here Any More: Why Women Leave Their Children, 1990; (with D. Moran) Bone Boosters: Natural Ways to Beat Osteoporosis, 1993; Getting Older Slowly: Your Guide to Successful Aging, 1995, in US as Breaking the Age Barrier, 1996; Hidden Fears: Self-Help for Anxieties and Phobias, 1996. **Address:** 19 Crediton Hill, London NW6 1HS, England.

FRANTZEN, Allen J. American, b. 1947. **Genres:** Gay and lesbian issues, Intellectual history, Literary criticism and history. **Career:** Oberlin College, Ohio, assistant professor of English, 1976-78; Loyola University of Chicago, assistant professor, 1978-82, associate professor, 1983-88, director, Graduate Progs. in English, 1984-89, professor of English, 1988-. **Publications:** The Literature of Penance in Anglo-Saxon England, 1983; King Alfred, 1986; Desire for Origins: New Languages, Old English, and Teaching the Tradition, 1990; Speaking Two Languages: Traditional Disciplines and Contemporary Theory in Medieval Studies, 1991; Troilus and Criseyde: The Poem and the Frame, 1993; Before the Closet: Same-Sex Love from Beowulf to Angels in America, 1998; Bloody Good: Chivalry, Sacrifice, and the Great War, 2003. **Address:** Dept. of English, Loyola University of Chicago, 6525 N Sheridan Rd, Chicago, IL 60626, U.S.A. **Online address:** afrantz@luc.edu

FRANTZICH, Stephen E. American, b. 1944. **Genres:** Politics/Government. **Career:** Denison University, Granville, OH, assistant professor of political science, 1971-73; Hamilton College, Clinton, NY, assistant professor of political science, 1973-77; U.S. Naval Academy, Annapolis, MD, professor of political science and department head, 1977-. Consultant to U.S. Congress and C-SPAN cable network. **Publications:** (with S. Percy) American Government: The Political Game, 1994; (with S. Schier) Congress: Games and Strategies, 1995, rev. ed., 2003; (with J. Sullivan) The C-SPAN Revolution, 1996; Citizen Democracy, 1999; Cyberage Politics 101, 2002. **Address:** Department of Political Science, U.S. Naval Academy, 589 McNair Rd, Annapolis, MD 21402, U.S.A. **Online address:** frantzic@usna.edu

FRANZONI, David (H.). American. **Genres:** Plays/Screenplays. **Career:** Screenwriter. **Publications:** SCREENPLAYS: Jumpin' Jack Flash, 1986; Citizen Cohn, 1992; Amistad, 1997; (with J. Logan) Gladiator, 1999. **Address:** c/o Leslie Barnes, Creative Artists Agency, 9830 Wilshire Blvd., Beverly Hills, CA 90212, U.S.A.

FRAPPIER-MAZUR, Lucienne. French, b. 1932. **Genres:** Literary criticism and history. **Career:** University of Pennsylvania, Philadelphia, assistant professor, 1962-71, associate professor, 1971-79, member of Graduate Group in Comparative Literature and Literary Theory, 1979-, professor of French, 1979-96, associate director of French Institute, 1995-96, professor emerita, 1996-. Visiting professor at University of California, Santa Barbara, 1987, Yale University, 1989, and Universite Paris VII, 1991; lecturer at colleges and universities throughout the US. **Publications:** L'Expression metaphorique dans La Comedie humaine, 1976; (ed. and author of intro. and notes) H. de Balzac, Les Chouans, La Comedie humaine, 1977; Sade et l'ecriture de l'orgie: Pouvoir et parodie dans L'Histoire de Juliette, 1991, trans. as Writing the Orgy: Power and Parody in Sade, 1996; (ed. with M. Donaldson-Evans and G. Prince) Autobiography, Historiography, Rhetoric: A Festschrift in Honor of Frank Paul Bowman, 1994. Contributor to books and periodicals. **Address:** Dept of Romance Languages, 521 Williams Hall, University of Pennsylvania, Philadelphia, PA 19104, U.S.A. **Online address:** frappier@sas.upenn.edu.

FRASER, Anthea. Also writes as Lorna Cameron, Vanessa Graham. British. **Genres:** Novels, Mystery/Crime/Suspense. **Career:** Crime Writers' Association, secretary, 1986-96. **Publications:** NOVELS: Designs of Annabelle, 1971; In the Balance, 1973; (as Vanessa Graham) Time of Trial, 1979; (as Lorna Cameron) Summer in France, 1981; (as Vanessa Graham) Second Time Around, 1982; (as Vanessa Graham) The Stand-In, 1984. MYSTERY/CRIME: Laura Possessed, 1974; Home through the Dark, 1974; Whistler's Lane, 1975; Breath of Brimstone, 1977; Presence of Mind, 1978; Island in Waiting, 1979; A Shroud for Delilah, 1984; A Necessary End, 1985; Pretty Maids All in a Row, 1986; Death Speaks Softly, 1987; The Nine Bright Shiners, 1987; Six Proud Walkers, 1988; The April Rainers, 1989; Symbols at Your Door, 1990; The Lily-White Boys, 1991; Three, Three, The Rivals, 1992; The Gospel Makers, 1994; The Seven Stars, 1995; The Macbeth Prophecy, 1995; I'll Sing You Two-O (The Lily-White Boys), 1996; One Is One and All Alone, 1996; Motive for Murder, 1996; The Ten Commandments, 1997; Dangerous Deception, 1998; Eleven That Went Up to Heaven, 1999; The Twelve Apostles, 1999; Past Shadows, 2001; Fathers and Daughters, 2002; Brought to Book, 2003; Jigsaw, 2004. **Address:** c/o Juliet Burton Literary Agency, 2 Clifton Ave, London W12 9DR, England.

FRASER, (Lady) Antonia. British, b. 1932. **Genres:** Mystery/Crime/Suspense, Children's fiction, History, Biography. **Career:** Member, Arts Council, 1970-72; Chairman, Committee of Mgmt., Society of Authors, London, 1974-75; General Ed., Kings and Queens of England series, Weidenfeld and Nicolson, publishers, London, 1974-75; Chairman, Crime Writers Association, 1985-86, 1986-87; President, English P.E.N., 1988-89. **Publications:** King Arthur, 1954; Robin Hood, 1955; Dolls, 1963; History of Toys, 1966; Mary, Queen of Scots, 1969; Cromwell: Our Chief of Men (in U.S. as Cromwell: The Lord Protector), 1973; Mary, Queen of Scots, and the Historians, 1974; King James VI and I, 1974; King Charles II (in U.S. as Royal Charles), 1979; The Weaker Vessel: Woman's Lot in Seventeenth Century England, 1984; Boadicea's Chariot: The Warrior Queens, 1988; The Six Wives of Henry VIII, 1992; More Women of Mystery, 1994; The Gunpowder Plot (in US as Faith and Treason), 1996; Marie Antoinette: The Journey, 2001. MYSTERIES: Quiet as a Nun, 1977; The Wild Island, 1978; A Splash of Red, 1981; Cool Repentance, 1982; Oxford Blood, 1985; Jemima Shore's First Case, 1986; Your Royal Hostage, 1987; The Cavalier Case, 1990; Jemima Shore at the Sunny Grave and Other Stories, 1991; Political Death, 1995. EDITOR: The Lives of the Kings and Queens of England, 1975; Scottish Love Poems, 1975; Love Letters, 1976; Heroes and Heroines, 1980; Mary, Queen of Scots in Poetry, 1981; Oxford and Oxfordshire in Verse, 1982; The Pleasure of Reading, 1992; Middle Ages, 2000; House of Windsor, 2000; The Tudors, 2000; The Stuarts, 2000; The Wars of the Roses, 2000; The Houses of Hanover and Saxe-Coburg-Gotha, 2000. **Address:** c/o Curtis Brown Group Ltd, Haymarket House, 28/29 Haymarket, London SW1Y 4SP, England.

FRASER, Conon. British, b. 1930. **Genres:** Children's fiction, Children's non-fiction, Environmental sciences/Ecology, Geography, History, Homes/Gardens, Travel/Exploration. **Career:** Freelance writer. Television Producer, New Zealand Broadcasting Corp., 1964-69; Film Producer and Director, New Zealand National Film Unit, 1969-86. **Publications:** CHILDREN'S FICTION: Dead Man's Cave, 1954; The Green Dragon, 1955; Shadow of Danger, 1956; The Underground Explorers, 1957; The Underground River, 1959; The Scoter Island Adventure, 1959; Lim of Hong Kong, 1960; Oystercatcher Bay, 1962; Brave Rescue, 1964. OTHER: With Captain Cook in New Zealand (children's non-fiction), 1963; Looking at New Zealand, 1969; (co-author) Gardens of New Zealand, 1975; Beyond the Roaring Forties, 1986; (co-ed.) Enderby Settlement Diaries (history), 2000. **Address:** 39A Henry Hill Rd, Taupo, New Zealand.

FRASER, George (C.). American, b. 1945. **Genres:** Business/Trade/Industry. **Career:** Procter & Gamble, Cincinnati, OH, unit marketing manager, 1972-84; United Way Services, Cleveland, OH, director of marketing and communications, 1984-87; Ford Motor Co., Dearborn, MI, minority dealership development program trainee, 1987-89; SuccessSource Inc., Cleveland, president and publisher, 1988-. Guest on television and radio talk shows. **Publications:** Success Runs in Our Race: The Complete Guide to Effective; Networking in the African American Community, 1989; The Networking Guide to Black Resources; Race for Success: The Ten Best Business Opportunities for Blacks in America, 1998. **Address:** Frasernet.com Inc, 2940 Noble Rd #103, Cleveland Heights, OH 44121, U.S.A. **Online address:** gfraser@frasernet.com

FRASER, George MacDonald. British, b. 1925. **Genres:** Novels, Plays/Screenplays. **Career:** Glasgow Herald newspaper, deputy editor, 1964-69. **Publications:** Flashman, 1969; Royal Flash, 1970, screenplay, 1975; The General Danced at Dawn, 1970; Flash for Freedom, 1971; Steel Bonnets, 1971; Flashman at the Charge, 1973; McAuslan in the Rough, 1974; Flashman in the Great Game, 1975; Flashman's Lady, 1977; Mr. American, 1980; Flashman and the Redskins, 1982; The Pyrates, 1983; Flashman and the Dragon, 1985; The Hollywood History of the World, 1988; The Sheikh and the Dustbin, 1988; Flashman and the Mountain of Light, 1990; Quartered Safe Out Here, 1992; The Candlemass Road, 1993; Flashman and the Angel of the Lord, 1994; Black Ajax, 1998; Flashman and the Tiger, 1999; The Light's on at Signpost, 2002. SCREENPLAYS: The Three Musketeers, 1973; The Four Musketeers, 1974; The Prince and the Pauper, 1976; Octopussy, 1983; Red Sonya, 1984; Casanova (for TV), 1987; The Return of the Musketeers, 1989.

FRASER, Gordon. British, b. 1943. **Genres:** Sciences. **Career:** IPC Business Press, London, England, journalist, 1970-72; self-employed publicist, London, 1972-75; Rutherford Laboratory, Chilton, England, information officer, 1975-77; CERN Courier, Geneva, Switzerland, editor, 1977-2001.

Visiting lecturer in science communication at British universities. **Publications:** (coauthor) Search for Infinity, 1995; The Quark Machines, 1997; (ed.) The Particle Century, 1998; Antimatter, 2000. **Address:** 14 La Chataigneraie, 01220 Divonne-les-Bains, France. **Online address:** gordon.fraser@ wanadoo.fr

FRASER, Harry. British, b. 1937. **Genres:** Crafts, How-to books, Technology. **Career:** Potclays Ltd., Stoke-on-Trent, Director 1976-, Joint Managing Director, 1983-96, Managing Director, 1996-. Production Manager, Twyfords Ltd., Etruria, Stoke-on-Trent, 1959-62; Manager Armitage-Shanks Ltd., Armitage, Rugeley, Staffs., 1962-65; Divisional Manager, Wengers Ltd., Etruria, 1965-66, and Podmore & Sons Ltd., Shelton, Stoke-on-Trent, 1966-73; Managing Director, Harry Fraser Ltd., 1973-77. **Publications:** Kilns and Kiln Firing for the Craft Potter, 1969; Glazes for the Craft Potter, 1973, rev. ed., 1999; Electric Kilns, 1974; Electric Kilns and Firing, 1978; Ceramic Faults and Their Remedies, 1986; Electric Kilns: A User's Manual, 1994. **Address:** Redferns, 12 Leyfield Rd, Trentham, Stoke-on-Trent, Staffs ST4 8HQ, England.

FRASER, Jane. See PILCHER, Rosamunde.

FRASER, Kathleen. American, b. 1935. **Genres:** Poetry, Essays, Women's studies and issues. **Career:** Professor of Creative Writing, San Francisco State University, since 1978 (Director of the Poetry Center, 1972-75, and Founder, American Poetry Archive, 1974; Associate Professor, 1975-78). Visiting Professor, Writers Workshop, University of Iowa, Iowa City, 1969-71; Writer-in-Residence, Reed College, Portland, Oregon, 1971-72. **Publications:** Change of Address and Other Poems, 1966; Stilts, Somersaults, and Headstands: Game Poems Based on a Painting by Peter Breughel (juvenile), 1968; In Defiance of the Rains, 1969; Little Notes to You from Lucas Street, 1972; What I Want, 1974; Magritte Series, 1978; New Shoes, 1978; Each Next (narratives), 1980; Something (even human voices) in the foreground, a lake, 1984; Boundayr, 1987; Notes Preceding Trust, 1987; When New Time Folds Up, 1993; Wing, 1995; il cuore: the heart Selected Poems, 1970-1995, 1997; Translating the Unspeakable: Poetry and the Innovative Necessity (eeay), 2000; 20th Century, 2000. **Address:** 1936 Leavenworth St, San Francisco, CA 94133, U.S.A. **Online address:** kfraser@sfsu.edu

FRASER, Laura (Jane). American, b. 1961. **Genres:** Adult non-fiction. **Career:** Freelance writer in San Francisco, CA, 1982-94; Graduate School of Journalism, University of California-Berkeley, instructor in magazine writing. **Publications:** The Animal Rights Handbook: Everyday Ways to Save Lives, 1990; Losing It: America's Obsession with Weight and the Industry That Feeds on It, 1997, as Losing It: False Hopes and Fat Profits in the Diet Industry, 1998; An Italian Affair (memoir), 2001. Contributor to periodicals. **Address:** c/o Author Mail, Pantheon Books, 1540 Broadway, New York, NY 10036, U.S.A.

FRASER, Margot. American, b. 1936. **Genres:** Novels, Novellas/Short stories. **Career:** Juvenile Probation Department of San Diego County, San Diego, CA, probation officer, 1958-68; Serra Reference Center, San Diego, reference librarian, 1969-70; U.S. International University, San Diego, reference librarian, 1970-72; Innisfree Books, Cannon Beach, OR, owner and manager, 1972-82; author. **Publications:** The Laying Out of Gussie Hoot (novel), 1990; Hardship (novella), 1993; Piedra Lumbre, (short story), 1993. **Address:** Southern Methodist University Press, PO Box 415, Dallas, TX 75275, U.S.A.

FRASER, Mary Ann. American, b. 1959. **Genres:** Children's fiction, Children's non-fiction, Illustrations. **Career:** Graphic artist, 1982-90; fine artist, 1983-. **Publications:** On Top of the World: The Conquest of Mount Everest, 1991; Ten Mile Day and the Building of the Transcontinental Railroad, 1993; One Giant Leap, 1993; Sanctuary: The Story of Three Arch Rocks, 1994; In Search of the Grand Canyon, 1994; I.Q. Goes to School, 2002; I.Q. Goes to the Library, 2003. Illustrator of books for children.

FRASER, Nicholas C(ampbell). British, b. 1956. **Genres:** Natural history. **Career:** University of Aberdeen, Scotland, assistant curator of paleontology at Geology Museum, 1979-81; Cambridge University, England, fellow of Girton College, 1985-90; Virginia Museum of Natural History, Martinsville, curator of vertebrate paleontology, 1990-, director of research and collections, 2004-; Virginia Polytechnic Institute and State University, adjunct professor of geology, 1993-. **Publications:** (ed. with H.D. Sues) In the Shadow of the Dinosaurs: Early Mesozoic Tetrapods, 1994. Contributor to books. Contributor of articles and reviews to paleontology and geology journals; contributor to popular magazines. **Address:** Virginia Museum of Natural History, 1001 Douglas Ave., Martinsville, VA 24112, U.S.A. **Online address:** nfraser@vmnh.net

FRASER, Robert (H.). British, b. 1947. **Genres:** Plays/Screenplays, Literary criticism and history. **Career:** University of Cape Coast, Ghana, lecturer in English, 1970-74; University of Leeds, England, lecturer in English, 1974-78; University of London, England, research associate at Royal Holloway and Bedford New College, 1986-91, School of Advanced Study, research fellow, 1997-99; Cambridge University, England, Trinity College, lecturer in English, 1991-93, director of Studies in English, 1992-93; Open University, England, senior research fellow, 1999-. Visiting professor, University of Kuwait, 1988, and University of Sao Paulo, 1990. **Publications:** The Novels of Ayi Kwei Armah, 1980; West African Poetry: A Critical History, 1986; The Making of The Golden Bough, 1990, rev. ed., 2001; Sir James Frazer and the Literary Imagination, 1990; Proust and the Victorians: The Lamp of Memory, 1993; Victorian Quest Romance: Stevenson, Haggard, Kipling and Conan Doyle, 1998; Lifting the Sentence: The Poetics of Postcolonial Fiction, 1999; The Chameleon Poet: A Life of George Barker, 2002; Ben Okri: Towards the Invisible City, 2002. PLAYS: Kwame's Aunt, 1972; Soul Brother, 1973; Life of Gesualdo, Prince of Venosa, 1975; January and May, 1976; Something in the Air, 1976; A Mistress Not So Coy, 1977; God's Good Englishman, 1984; Very Naughty O..., 1988; The Parisian Painter, 1989. EDITOR: The Collected Poems of George Barker, 1987; (and author of intro.) Sir J. Frazer: The Golden Bough, A New Abridgement from the Second and Third Editions, 1994; The Selected Poems of George Barker, 1995. **Address:** Walton Hall, Open University, Milton Keynes MK7 6AA, England. **Online address:** Fras999@yahoo.co.uk

FRASER, Ronald (Angus). British, b. 1930. **Genres:** History, Area studies, Autobiography/Memoirs. **Career:** Foreign correspondent for Reuters News Agency, 1952-57; editor of New Left Review; writer. **Publications:** (ed.) Work: Twenty Personal Accounts, Vol. 1, 1968, Vol. 2, 1969; In Hiding: The Life of Manuel Cortes, 1972; Tajos: The Story of a Village on the Costa del Sol (in U.K. as The Pueblo: A Mountain Village on the Costa del Sol), 1973; Blood of Spain: An Oral History of the Spanish Civil War (in U.K. as Blood of Spain: The Experience of Civil War, 1936-1939), 1979; (with P. Broue and P. Vilar) Metodologia historica de la guerra y revolucion espanolas, 1980; In Search of a Past: The Rearing of an English Gentleman, 1933-1945 (in U.K. as In Search of a Past: The Manor House, Amnersfield, 1933-1945), 1984; (with others) Nineteen Sixty-eight: A Student Generation in Revolt, 1988. **Address:** c/o Tessa Sayle, 11 Jubilee Pl, London SW3, England.

FRASER, Russell A(lfred). American, b. 1927. **Genres:** Literary criticism and history. **Career:** Instructor, University of California at Los Angeles, 1950; Assistant Professor, Duke University, Durham, North Carolina, 1951-56; Assistant Professor and Associate Professor, Princeton University, New Jersey, 1956-65 (Associate Dean, Graduate School, 1962-65); Professor and Chairman of English Dept., Vanderbilt University, Nashville, TN, 1965-68; Austin Warren Professor of English, University of Michigan, Ann Arbor, 1968-95; (Chairman, Dept. of English Language and Literature, 1968-73). **Publications:** The Court of Venus, 1955; The Court of Virtue, 1962; Shakespeare's Poetics, 1962; King Lear (criticism), 1963; The War Against Poetry, 1970; An Essential Shakespeare, Nine Plays and the Sonnets, 1972; The Dark Ages and the Age of Gold, 1973; (with N. Rabkin) Drama of the English Renaissance, 2 vols., 1976; The Language of Adam, 1976; A Mingled Yarn: The Life of R.P. Blackmur, 1981; The Three Romes, 1985; Young Shakespeare, 1988; Shakespeare: The Later Years, 1992; Singing Masters: Poets in English, 1500 to the Present, 1999. EDITOR: Selected Writings of Oscar Wilde, 1969; All's Well That Ends Well, 1985. **Address:** 2685 Geddes Ave., Ann Arbor, MI 48104, U.S.A. **Online address:** rafraser@umich.edu

FRASER, W. Hamish. British, b. 1941. **Genres:** History, Industrial relations, Urban studies. **Career:** University of Strathclyde, lecturer, 1966-77, reader, 1987-96, professor in history, 1996-2003, professor emeritus, 2003-. **Publications:** Trade Unions and Society: The Struggle for Acceptance 1850-1880, 1974; Workers and Employers: Documents on Trade Unions and Industrial Relations in Britain since the 18th Century, 1980; The Coming of the Mass Market 1850-1914, 1982; Conflict and Class: Scottish Workers 1700-1838, 1988; People and Society in Scotland 1830-1914, 1990; Glasgow Vol II 1830-1912, 1996; Alexander Campbell and the Search for Socialism, 1996; A History of British Trade Unionism 1700-1998, 1999; Scottish Popular Politics, from Radicalism to Labour, 2000; Aberdeen: A New History, 2000. **Address:** Dept. of History, University of Strathclyde, Glasgow G1 1XQ, Scotland. **Online address:** w.h.fraser@strath.ac.uk

FRASER, Wynnette (McFaddin). American, b. 1925. **Genres:** Children's fiction, Mystery/Crime/Suspense. **Career:** Spent twelve years in secretarial positions, including work for Shaw Air Base in South Carolina, Crippled Children's Society of South Carolina, Presbyterian churches in Florence and Darlington, SC, and assistant librarian in a high school; spent nineteen years as a caseworker at Darlington County Department of Social Services. Public speaker at schools, colleges, and workshops. **Publications:** CHILDREN'S MYSTERY-ADVENTURE BOOKS: Mystery on Mirror Mountain, 1989; Courage on Mirror Mountain, 1989; Mystery at Deepwood Bay, 1992; Invasion on Mirror Mountain, 1994. Contributor to periodicals.

FRATIANNI, Michele. American (born Italy), b. 1941. **Genres:** Business/Trade/Industry, Economics. **Career:** Commission of the European Communities, Brussels, Belgium, economic adviser, 1976-79; Indiana University-Bloomington, professor, 1979-93, W. George Pinnell Professor of Business Economics, 1993-. President's Council of Economic Advisers, senior staff economist, 1981-82. **Publications:** (with P. DeGrauwe and M. Nabli) Money, Output, and Exchange Rates: The European Experience, 1985; (with J. von Hagen) The European Monetary System and European Monetary Union, 1992; The Monetary History of Italy, 1997; Storia Monetaria d'Italia: La lira e la politica monetaria italiana dall'unitB all'Unione Europea (title means: Monetary History of Italy), 2001. EDITOR: One Money for Europe, 1978; (with D. Salvatore) Handbook of Monetary Policy, 1992; (with P. Savona and J. Kirton) Governing Global Finance, 2002. **Address:** School of Business, Indiana University-Bloomington, Tenth and Fee Lane, Bloomington, IN 47405, U.S.A. **Online address:** fratiann@indiana.edu

FRATKIN, Elliot. American, b. 1948. **Genres:** Anthropology/Ethnology. **Career:** University of Maryland, Baltimore County, Catonsville, instructor, 1979-85; University of Nairobi, Kenya, research associate, 1985-86; Duke University, Durham, NC, visiting assistant professor, 1987-89; Pennsylvania State University, University Park, assistant professor, 1989-94; Smith College, Northampton MA, assistant professor, 1994-. Associate editor of Human Ecology. **Publications:** Why Elephant Is an Old Woman, 1974; Herbal Medicine and Concepts of Disease in Samburu, 1975; Surviving Drought and Development, 1991; (ed. with K. Galvin and E.A. Roth) African Pastoralist Systems, 1994; Ariaal Pastoralists of Kenya, 1998; Cultural Anthropology, 1999. **Address:** Dept of Anthropology, 107 Wright Hall, Smith College, Northampton, MA 01063, U.S.A. **Online address:** efratkin@email.smith.edu

FRATTI, Mario. American (born Italy), b. 1927. **Genres:** Plays/Screenplays, Poetry. **Career:** Rubelli publrs., Venice, trans., 1953-63; drama critic, Sipario, Milan, 1963-66, Ridotto, Venice, Paese Sera, Rome, and L'Ora, Palermo, 1963-73; Adelphi College, NYC, professor, 1967-68; Hunter College, professor, 1967-; America Today, drama critic, 1986-. **Publications:** Il Ritorno (in U.S. and U.K. as The Return), 1961; Il Suicidio (in U.S. and U.K. as The Suicide), 1962; La Gabbia (in U.S. as The Cage), 1963; The Academy, 1963; Le Vedova Bianca (in U.S. as Mafia), 1963; Le Telefonata (in U.S. as The Gift), 1965; I Frigoriferi (in U.S. as The Refrigerators), 1965; Eleonora Duse, 1967; Il Ponte (in U.S. as The Bridge), 1967; The Victim, 1968; Four Plays, 1972; Races: Six New Plays, 1972; Birthday, 1978; American Scenes, 2 vols., 1980; Nine (Tony Award), 1982; Mario Fratti (biography), 1983; Young Wife, Mothers and Daughters, Three Beds, 1984; Paganini, 1985; Lovers, 1985; A.I.D.S., 1986; 500: A Musical about Columbus, 1988; Friends, 1989; Porno, 1990; Family, 1992; Leningrad Euthanasia, 1993; Beata, the Pope's Daughter, 1994; Sacrifice, 1995; Jurors, 1996; L'Imboscata (in U.S. as The Ambush), 2000; Erotic Adventures in Venice, 2001; Puccini: Passion and Music, 2002; Blindness, 2003; Terrorist, 2003; November 2004, 2004. **Address:** 145 W 55th St Apt 15D, New York, NY 10019, U.S.A.

FRAUSTINO, Lisa Rowe. American, b. 1961. **Genres:** Children's nonfiction, Plays/Screenplays. **Career:** Author. National Education Corporation, Scranton, PA, editor, 1985-86; University of Scranton, Scranton, PA, instructor, 1987-90, 1994; Dick Jones Communications, Dalton, PA, associate editor, 1989-91; Institute of Children's Literature, Redding Ridge, CT, instructor, 1989-94; Hollins College, Roanoke, VA, instructor, 1995. Speaker and workshop presenter. **Publications:** FOR CHILDREN: Grass and Sky, 1994; Ash, 1995; Junkyard Purple, 1996. SCREENPLAYS: The Olden Days, 1988; Empty Words. Contributor of short stories to children's magazines. Contributor to periodicals. **Address:** c/o Teenreads.com, 250 West 57th Street, Suite 1228, New York, NY 10107, U.S.A.

FRAYN, Michael. British, b. 1933. **Genres:** Novels, Plays/Screenplays, Humor/Satire, Translations. **Career:** Reporter, 1957-59, and Columnist, 1959-62, The Guardian, Manchester and London; Columnist, The Observer, London, 1962-68. **Publications:** COLLECTED COLUMNS/ESSAYS: The Original Michael Frayn, 1983; The Additional Michael Frayn, 2000. NOVELS: The Tin Men, 1965; The Russian Interpreter, 1966; Towards the End of the Morning (in U.S. as Against Entropy), 1967; A Very Private Life, 1968; Sweet Dreams, 1974; The Trick of It, 1989; A Landing on the Sun, 1991; Now You Know, 1992, (play) 1995; Headlong, 1999; Spies, 2002.

PLAYS/SCREENPLAYS: The Two of Us, 1970; Alphabetical Order, 1975; Clouds, 1976; Donkeys' Years, 1976; Make and Break, 1980; Noises Off, 1982; Benefactors, 1984; Plays One (collection), 1985; Clockwise, 1986; Balmoral, 1987; Look Look, 1990; Listen to This, 1990; Audience, 1991; Here, 1993; Copenhagen, 1998; Alarms and Excursions, 1998; Democracy, 2003. TRANSLATIONS: The Cherry Orchard, 1978; The Fruits of Enlightenment, 1979; Three Sisters, 1983; Wild Honey, 1984; The Seagull, 1986; Uncle Vanya, 1987; Chekhov: Plays, 1988; The Sneeze, 1989; Trifonov: Exchange, 1990. OTHER: Constructions, 1974; (with D. Burke) Celia's Secret, 2000. **Address:** c/o Greene & Heaton Ltd, 37 Goldhawk Rd, London W12 8QQ, England.

FRAZEE, Randy. American, b. 1961. **Genres:** Theology/Religion. **Career:** Pantego Bible Church, Fort Worth, TX, senior pastor, 1990-. **Publications:** The Comeback Congregation, 1995; The Connecting Church, 2001; Making Room for Life, 2004; The Christian Life Profile, 2004. **Address:** Pantego Bible Church, 8001 Anderson Blvd, Fort Worth, TX 76120, U.S.A. **Online address:** Randy@Pantego.org

FRAZER, Andrew. See MARLOWE, Stephen.

FRAZER, Timothy C. American, b. 1941. **Genres:** Language/Linguistics. **Career:** Millikin University, Decatur, IL, instructor in English, 1969-71; Western Illinois University, Macomb, assistant professor, 1972-76, associate professor, 1976-81, coordinator of writing program, 1982-83, professor of English, 1981-2002, emeritus, 2002-; Lincoln Land Community College, ESL instructor, 2003-05. **Publications:** Midland Illinois Dialect Patterns, 1987; (ed.) "Heartland" English: Variation and Transition in the American Midwest, 1993. Work represented in anthologies. Contributor of articles and reviews to academic journals. **Address:** 615 E Franklin, Macomb, IL 61455, U.S.A. **Online address:** tcf@macomb.com

FRAZIER, Arthur. See BULMER, (Henry) Kenneth.

FRAZIER, Charles (Robinson). American, b. 1950. **Genres:** Novels, Travel/Exploration. **Career:** Professor of English, University of Colorado, Professor of English, North Carolina State University. **Publications:** (with D. Seacrest) Adventuring in the Andes: The Sierra Club Guide to Peru, Bolivia, the Amazon Basin, and the Galapagos, 1985; Cold Mountain (novel), 1996. **Address:** c/o Darhansoff & Verrill Literary Agents, 236 W 26th St Rm 802, New York, NY 10001-6736, U.S.A.

FRAZIER, Donald S(haw). American, b. 1965. **Genres:** History. **Career:** Fort Worth Star-Telegram, TX, staff writer, 1983-87; General Dynamics Corp., technical publications analyst, 1987-88; Texas Christian University, Fort Worth, research assistant/graduate teaching assistant, 1990-92, visiting assistant professor of history, 1992-93; Tarrant County Junior College, Fort Worth, adjunct instructor, 1991; McMurry University, Abilene, TX, assistant professor, 1993-97, associate professor, 1997-98, chair of dept, 1998-2001, professor of history, 2001-. Longwood College, Francis B. Simpkins Memorial Lecturer, 1997; consultant to Palo Alto National Battlefield, History Channel, and the television documentary The Mexican-American War; McWhiney Foundation, executive director, 1996-. **Publications:** Blood and Treasure: Confederate Empire in the Southwest, 1995; The U.S. and Mexico at War: Nineteenth Century Expansionism and Conflict, 1998; Cottonclads! The Battle of Galveston and the Defense of the Texas Coast, 1996; Tom Green's Texans: The Civil War in Southwest Louisiana, 1861-1865, forthcoming. **Address:** Department of History, Box 637-McMurry Station, McMurry University, Abilene, TX 79697, U.S.A. **Online address:** dfrazier@mcm.edu

FRAZIER, Shirley George. American, b. 1957. **Genres:** Business/Trade/Industry, How-to books. **Career:** Sweet Survival, Paterson, NJ, president, 1989-. **Publications:** How to Start a Home-Based Gift Basket Business, 1998, 3rd ed., 2003; The Gift Basket Design Book, 2004. **Address:** Sweet Survival, PO Box 31, River Street Station, Paterson, NJ 07544, U.S.A. **Online address:** survival@sweetsurvival.com

FREDA, Joseph. American, b. 1951. **Genres:** Novels. **Career:** University of New Hampshire, Durham, instructor, 1977-81; Digital Equipment Corporation, Merrimack, NH, senior software writer, editor, and system manager, 1981-84; Tegra Inc., Billerica, MA, communications manager, 1984-88, product manager, 1988-92, manager of creative services, 1992-94; Prepress Solutions, East Hanover, NJ, creative director, 1994-99; Freda & Flaherty Creative, Kenoza Lake, NY, principal, 1999-. Freelance writer, 1995-. **Publications:** NOVELS: Suburban Guerrillas, 1995; The Patience of Rivers, 2003.

Contributor of short stories to journals. **Address:** PO Box 99, Kenoza Lake, NY 12750, U.S.A. **Online address:** jfreda@joefreda.com

FREDERICK, David C. American, b. 1961. **Genres:** Law. **Career:** U.S. Court of Appeals, Ninth Circuit, San Francisco, CA, law clerk, 1989-91; Supreme Court of the United States, Washington, DC, law clerk, 1991-92; Shearman & Sterling, Washington, DC, attorney, 1992-95; U.S. Department of Justice, Washington, DC, counselor to the inspector general, 1995-96, assistant to the solicitor general, 1996-. Everybody Wins Inc., Washington, DC, general counsel and director, 1995-97; First Presbyterian Church, Arlington, VA, elder, 1996-. **Publications:** Rugged Justice (legal history), 1994. Contributor to legal journals. **Address:** Office of the Solicitor General, Department of Justice, Washington, DC 20530, U.S.A.

FREDERICKS, Dr. Frank. *See* **FRANCK, Frederick.**

FREEBORN, Richard (Harry). British, b. 1926. **Genres:** Novels, Novellas/Short stories, History, Literary criticism and history, Translations. **Career:** University Lecturer in Russian, and Hulme Lecturer in Russian, Brasenose College, Oxford, 1954-64; Visiting Professor, University of California at Los Angeles, 1964-65; Sir William Mather Chair of Russian Studies, University of Manchester, 1965-67; Professor Emeritus of Russian Literature, University of London, 1988- (Professor, 1967-88). **Publications:** LITERARY CRITICISM: Turgenev: A Study, 1960; The Rise of the Russian Novel, 1974; The Russian Revolutionary Novel: Turgenev to Pasternak, 1982; Dostoevsky, 2003; Furious Vissarion, 2003. NOVELS: Two Ways of Life, 1962; The Emigration of Sergey Ivanovich, 1963; Russian Roulette, 1979; The Russian Crucifix, 1987. OTHER: A Short History of Modern Russia, 1966. TRANSLATOR: I. Turgenev: Sketches from a Hunter's Album, 1967; I. Turgenev: Home of the Gentry, 1970; I. Turgenev: Rudin, 1974; Love and Death: Six Stories by Ivan Turgenev, 1983; I. Turgenev: First Love and Other Stories, 1989; I. Turgenev: Fathers and Sons, 1991; I. Turgenev: A Month in the Country, 1991; Fyodor Dostoevsky: An Accidental Family, 1994. EDITOR: (and contrib.) Russian Literary Attitudes from Pushkin to Solzhenitsyn, 1976; (with C. Ward) Russian and Slavic Literature to 1917, vol. I, 1976; (with J. Grayson) Ideology in Russian Literature, 1990; (and intro.) Anton Chekhov: The Steppe and Other Stories, 1991; (and intro.) Ivan Goncharov: Oblomov, 1992; (adviser) Encyclopedia of the Novel, 1998; Reference Guide to Russian Literature, 1998; The Cambridge Companion to Tolstoy, 2002. Contributor to books. **Address:** School of Slavonic and East European Studies, University of London, Malet St, London WC1E 7HU, England. **Online address:** FzbRicha@aol.com

FREED, Anne O. American, b. 1917. **Genres:** Education, Gerontology/Senior issues, Social work, Autobiography/Memoirs. **Career:** War Relocation Authority, Washington, DC, assistant social science analyst, 1943-44; clinical social worker, supervisor, and field instructor in agencies offering family services, child welfare, mental health, child guidance, and geriatric services, 1952-73; Eastern Pennsylvania Psychiatric Institute, assistant director of Children's Unit, 1960-64, 1973-83; Family Service Association of Greater Boston, director of professional services and director of clinical services; Smith College, School for Social Work, assistant professor, 1965-70; Boston University, adjunct lecturer, 1965-82, adjunct professor of social work, 1964-93; Boston College, lecturer, adjunct associate, and adjunct professor, 1982-2000; Smith College, School for Social Work in International Program, adjunct faculty, 2000-. **Publications:** (ed. with D. Blau) Mental Health Education in Nursing Homes, 1980; The Changing Worlds of Older Women in Japan, Knowledge, Ideas, and Trends, 1993. Contributor of articles and reviews to professional journals. **Address:** 133 Del Pond Dr, Canton, MA 02021-2753, U.S.A. **Online address:** freedar@comcast.net

FREED, Curt R(ichard). American, b. 1943. **Genres:** Medicine/Health. **Career:** Physician, educator, and pioneer in fetal tissue transplantation. Los Angeles County Harbor General Hospital, Torrence, CA, intern to resident, 1969-71; Massachusetts General Hospital, Boston, resident, 1971-72; University of California, San Francisco, research fellow in clinical pharmacology, 1972-75; University of Colorado Health Sciences Center, 1975-, assistant professor to professor of medicine and pharmacology, 1987-, became head of Division of Clinical Pharmacology and Toxicology, 1993, became director of Neural Transplantation Program for Parkinson's Disease, 1988, and Parkinson's Center without Walls, 1997. **Publications:** (with S. LeVay) Healing the Brain: A Doctor's Controversial Quest for a Cell Therapy to Cure Parkinson's Disease, 2002. **Address:** University of Colorado Health Sciences Center, 4200 East Ninth Ave., Campus Box C-237, Denver, CO 80262, U.S.A. **Online address:** Curt.Freed@UCHSC.edu

FREED, Lynn. American (born Republic of South Africa). **Genres:** Novels, Novellas/Short stories, Travel/Exploration, Autobiography/Memoirs, Essays,

Humor/Satire. **Publications:** Heart Change, 1982; Home Ground, 1986; The Bungalow, 1993; The Mirror, 1997; House of Women, 2002; The Curse of the Appropriate Man, 2004. **Address:** c/o William Morris, 1325 Ave of Americas 15th Fl, New York, NY 10019, U.S.A. **Online address:** www.LynnFreed.com

FREEDLAND, Michael. British, b. 1934. **Genres:** Biography. **Career:** London Broadcasting Co., You Don't Have to Be Jewish, producer and editor. **Publications:** Al Jolson, 1972; Irving Berlin, 1974; James Cagney, 1975; Fred Astaire, 1976; Sophie: The Story of Sophie Tucker, 1978; Jerome Kern, 1978; Errol Flynn, 1979; Gregory Peck, 1980; (with Morecambe and Wise) There's No Answer to That, 1981; Maurice Chevalier, 1982; Peter O'Toole, 1982; The Warner Brothers, 1983; So Let's Hear the Applause: The Story of the Jewish Entertainer, 1983; Jack Lemmon, 1984; Dino: The Dean Martin Story, 1984; Katharine Hepburn, 1985; The Secret Life of Danny Kaye, 1985; Shirley MacLaine, 1986; Linda Evans, 1986; The Goldwyn Touch, 1986; Jane Fonda, 1987; Liza with a "Z," 1988, rev. ed., 2003; Leonard Bernstein, 1989; Dustin, 1989; Kenneth Williams, 1990; Andre Previn, 1991; Sean Connery, 1994, rev. ed., 2004; Music Man, 1994; All the Way: A Biography of Frank Sinatra, 1997; Michael Caine, 1999; Bing Crosby, 1999; Bob Hope, 1999; Doris Day, 2000; Some Like It Cool, 2002. **Address:** Bays Hill Lodge, Barnet Lane, Elstree, Herts., England. **Online address:** MichaelFreedland@boltblue.com

FREEDMAN, Anne (E.). American, b. 1938. **Genres:** Politics/Government, Literary criticism and history. **Career:** Bunting Institute, Cambridge, MA, research associate, 1964-66; Wheaton College, Norton, MA, instructor in political science, 1964-65; Saint Xavier College, Chicago, IL, instructor in political science, 1965-66; Roosevelt University, Chicago, became professor of political science and public administration, 1966-, chair of political science department, 1970-73, acting chair, 1983-84, head of graduate program, 1973-. Lecturer on public affairs issues. **Publications:** (with C. Smith) Voluntary Associations: Perceptions on Literature, 1972; The Planned Society, 1972; (with P.E. Freedman) The Psychology of Political Control, 1975; Patronage: An American Tradition, 1994. Contributor to books. Contributor of articles and reviews to professional journals. **Address:** Roosevelt University, 430 S. Michigan Ave., Chicago, IL 60605, U.S.A.

FREEDMAN, Eric. American, b. 1949. **Genres:** Business/Trade/Industry, Communications/Media, History, Law, Politics/Government, Recreation. **Career:** Aide to U.S. Representative Charles Rangel in Washington, DC, and NYC, 1971-76; Knickerbocker News, Albany, NY, reporter, 1976-84; Detroit News, Lansing, MI, reporter with Capitol Bureau, 1984-95. State Bar of Michigan, member. Michigan State University, faculty member, 1996-; Colorado State University, journalist in residence, 1983. Pulitzer Prize in Journalism, 1994. **Publications:** On the Water, Michigan: Your Comprehensive Guide to Water Recreation in the Great Lake State, 1992; Pioneering Michigan, 1992; Michigan Free: A Comprehensive Guide to Free Travel, Recreation, and Entertainment Opportunities, 1993; Great Lakes, Great National Forests, 1995; What to Study: 101 Fields in a Flash, 1997; How to Transfer to the College of Your Choice, 2002; John F. Kennedy in His Own Words, 2005. Contributor to periodicals. **Address:** 2698 Linden Dr, East Lansing, MI 48823, U.S.A. **Online address:** freedma5@msu.edu

FREEDMAN, James O. American, b. 1935. **Genres:** Politics/Government, Education. **Career:** U.S. Court of Appeals for the Second Circuit, law clerk to Judge Thurgood Marshall, 1962-63; Paul, Weiss, Rifkind, Wharton & Garrison (law firm), NYC, associate, 1963-64; University of Pennsylvania, Philadelphia, assistant professor, 1964-67, associate professor, 1967-69, professor of law, 1969-82, and political science, 1980-82, university ombudsman, 1973-76, associate dean of Law School, 1977-78, dean, 1979-82, associate provost of the university, 1978; University of Iowa, Iowa City, president, 1982-87; Dartmouth College, Hanover, NH, president, 1987-. Visiting professor at universities in the US and UK; Salzburg Seminar in American Studies, professor, 1979, 1983, member of board of directors, 1988-91, 1994-97; Georgetown University, visiting professor, 1981; Southern Methodist University, Roy R. Ray Lecturer, 1985; Washington University, St. Louis, MO, Tyrrell Williams Memorial Lecturer, 1994. **Publications:** Crisis and Legitimacy: The Administrative Process and American Government, 1978; Idealism and Liberal Education, 1996. Contributor to books. Contributor of articles and reviews to periodicals. **Address:** 207 Parkhurst Hall, Dartmouth College, Hanover, NH 03755, U.S.A.

FREEDMAN, Jeff. American, b. 1953. **Genres:** Children's fiction. **Career:** Intel, Hillsboro, OR, senior software engineer, 1988-90; Cypress Semiconductor, Beaverton, OR, senior software engineer, 1990-. **Publications:** The Magic Dishpan of Oz, 1995. **Address:** Cypress Semiconductor, 9125 SW Gemini Dr #200, Beaverton, OR 97008, U.S.A.

FREEDMAN, Jonathan (Borwick). American, b. 1950. **Genres:** Documentaries/Reportage, Essays, Adult non-fiction, Education. **Career:** Associated Press reporter in Sao Paulo and Rio de Janeiro, Brazil, 1974-75; The Tribune, San Diego, CA, editorial writer, 1981-90; Copley News Service, San Diego, syndicated columnist, 1987-89; free-lance opinion and editorial writer for both the Los Angeles Times and the New York Times, 1990-91; free-lance columnist and author of books; visiting lecturer at San Diego State University, 1990-. **Publications:** (and illustrator) The Man Who'd Bounce the World: A Story (juvenile fiction), 1979; The Editorials and Essays of Jonathan Freedman, 1988; The Pulitzer Prizes, Vol. 1, 1987, (anthology), 1988; From Cradle to Grave: The Human Face of Poverty in America (nonfiction), 1993; Wall of Fame: One Teacher, One Class & the Power to Save Schools & Transform Lives (nonfiction), 2000. Contributor of articles and editorials to periodicals. **Address:** 755 Genter St, La Jolla, CA 92037, U.S.A. **Online address:** jfreedman@att.net

FREEDMAN, Lawrence (David). British, b. 1948. **Genres:** Military/Defense/Arms control. **Career:** Political sciences educator. York University, teaching assistant, 1971-72; Nuffield College, Oxford, research fellow, 1974-75; International Institute for Strategic Studies, London, research associate, 1975-76; Royal Institute for International Affairs, London, research fellow, 1976-78, head of policy studies, 1978-82; King's College, London, Dept of War Studies, professor, 1982-, department head, 1992-97, chair of Board of War Studies, 1997-; Center for Defence Studies, London, honorary director, 1990-2001, vice-principal (research), 2003-. **Publications:** U.S. Intelligence and the Soviet Strategic Threat, 1977; The Price of Peace, 1978; The West and the Modernization of China, 1979; Britain and Nuclear Weapons, 1981; The Evolution of Nuclear Strategy, 1981; Atlas of Global Strategy, 1985; Arms Control: Management or Reform?, 1986; Terrorism and International Order, 1986; Strategic Defence in the Nuclear Age, 1987; Britain and the Falklands War, 1988; (with M. Navias and N. Wheeler) Independence in Concert, 1989; The South Atlantic Crisis of 1982, 1989; (with V. Gamba-Stonehouse) Signals of War: The Falklands Conflict of 1982, 1990; (with E. Karsh) The Gulf Conflict, 1990-1991: Diplomacy and War in the New World, 1993; Military Intervention in European Conflicts, 1994; The Revolution in Strategic Affairs, 1998; The Politics of British Defence, 1979-1998, 1999; Kennedy's Wars, 2000; Deterrence, 2004. EDITOR: The Troubled Alliance, 1983; (with P. Bobbitt and G. F. Treverton) U.S. Nuclear Strategy, 1989; Europe Transformed, 1990; Military Power in Europe: Essays in Memory of Jonathan Alford, 1990; (with J. Saunders) Population Change and European Security, 1991; (with M. Clarke) Britain in the World, 1991; (with P. Hayes and R. O'Neill) War, Strategy and International Politics: Essays in Honour of Sir Michael Howard, 1992; War, 1994; Strategic Coercion, 1998; Superterrorism, 2002. **Address:** Dept of War Studies, King's College, James Clerk Maxwell Bldg, 57 Waterloo Rd, London SE1 8WA, England. **Online address:** lawrence.freedman@kicl.ac.uk

FREEDMAN, Luba. Israeli (born Russia), b. 1953. **Genres:** Art/Art history. **Career:** Hebrew University of Jerusalem, Israel, instructor, 1985-86, teaching fellow, 1987-89, lecturer, 1992-95, senior lecturer in the history of art, 1995-; Cornell University, Ithaca, NY, visiting scholar in Society for the Humanities, 1990-92. **Publications:** The Classical Pastoral in the Visual Arts, 1989; Titian's Independent Self-Portraits, 1990; Titian's Portraits through Aretino's Lens, 1995; The Revival of the Olympian Gods in Renaissance Art, 2003. Contributor to periodicals in the United States and abroad. **Address:** Department of the History of Art, Faculty of the Humanities, Hebrew University of Jerusalem, Mount Scopus, 91905 Jerusalem, Israel. **Online address:** lubafre@mscc.huji.ac.il

FREEDMAN, Michael R. American, b. 1952. **Genres:** Psychology. **Career:** University of Colorado at Boulder, therapist at Raimy Psychology Clinic, 1982-83, and Wardenberg Student Health Center, 1983-84; Boulder County Mental Health Center, Boulder, primary therapist at Cedar House, 1984-85; University of Colorado at Boulder, clinical intern, 1985-86, instructor in psychology and assistant clinical professor of psychiatry at Health Sciences Center, both 1987-, clinical instructor, 1991-. National Register of Health Service Providers in Psychology, member; American Board of Forensic Examiners, diplomate. Private practice of psychotherapy; National Jewish Center for Immunology and Respiratory Medicine, staff psychologist, 1986-88, chief of adult clinical psychology, 1988-91. **Publications:** Living Well with Asthma, 1998. Contributor to professional journals and popular magazines. **Address:** 2027 11th St, Boulder, CO 80302, U.S.A.

FREEDMAN, Russell (Bruce). American, b. 1929. **Genres:** Children's non-fiction. **Career:** Associated Press, San Francisco, CA, reporter and editor, 1953-56; J. Walter Thompson Co., NYC, publicity writer for TV, 1956-60; Columbia Encyclopedia, Columbia University Press, NYC, associate

staff member, 1961-63; freelance writer, particularly for juveniles, 1961-; Crowell-Collier Educational Corp., NYC, editor, 1964-65; New School for Social Research, NYC, writing workshop instructor, 1969-86. **Publications:** NONFICTION FOR YOUNG READERS: Teenagers Who Made History, 1961; Two Thousand Years of Space Travel, 1963; Jules Verne, 1965; Thomas Alva Edison, 1966; Scouting with Baden-Powell, 1967; (with J.E. Morriss) How Animals Learn, 1969; (with J.E. Morriss) Animal Instincts, 1970; Animal Architects, 1971; (with J.E. Morriss) The Brains of Animals and Man, 1972; The First Days of Life, 1974; Growing Up Wild, 1975; Animal Fathers, 1976; Animal Games, 1976; Hanging On, 1977; How Birds Fly, 1977; Getting Born, 1978; How Animals Defend Their Young, 1978; Immigrant Kids, 1980; They Lived with the Dinosaurs, 1980; Tooth and Claw, 1980; Animal Superstars, 1981; Farm Babies, 1981; When Winter Comes, 1981; Can Bears Predict Earthquakes?, 1982; Killer Fish, 1982; Killer Snakes, 1982; Children of the Wild West, 1983; Dinosaurs and Their Young, 1983; Rattlesnakes, 1984; Cowboys of the Wild West, 1985; Sharks, 1985; Indian Chiefs, 1987; Lincoln: A Photobiography, 1987; Buffalo Hunt, 1988; Franklin Delano Roosevelt, 1990; The Wright Brothers, 1991; An Indian Winter, 1992; Eleanor Roosevelt, 1993; Kids at Work, 1994; The Life and Death of Crazy Horse, 1996; Out of Darkness: The Story of Louis Braille, 1997; Martha Graham, A Dancer's Life, 1998; Babe Didrickson Zaharias, 1999; Give Me Liberty, 2000; In the Days of the Vaqueros, 2001; Confucius: The Golden Rule, 2002; In Defense of Liberty, 2003; The Voice That Challenged a Nation, 2004. OTHER: Holiday House: The First Fifty Years (adult), 1985.

FREEDMAN, Sarah Warshauer. American, b. 1946. **Genres:** Education. **Career:** Philadelphia School District, Philadelphia, PA, English teacher, 1967-69; University of North Carolina at Wilmington, Wilmington, NC, instructor in English, 1970-71; Stanford University, Stanford, CA, instructor in English and linguistics, 1972-76; San Francisco State University, CA, English Department, assistant professor, 1977-79, associate professor, 1979-81; University of California, Berkeley, School of Education, assistant professor, 1981-83, associate professor, 1983-89, professor, 1989-. Served on the editorial board of journals. Has given papers and lectures in locations worldwide. **Publications:** NONFICTION: (ed.) The Acquisition of Written Language: Response and Revision, 1985; Response to Student Writing, 1987; Exchanging Writing, Exchanging Cultures: Lessons in School Reform from the United States and Great Britain, 1994; Inside City Schools, 1999. Contributor to books and periodicals. **Address:** School of Education, University of California, Berkeley, CA 94720, U.S.A. **Online address:** freedman@socrates.berkeley.edu

FREEDMAN, Stan. See COLLINSON, Alan S.

FREEHLING, William W(ilhartz). American, b. 1935. **Genres:** History. **Career:** University of California, Berkeley, Woodrow Wilson fellow, 1961-63; Harvard University, Cambridge, MA, instructor in history, 1963-64; University of Michigan, Ann Arbor, faculty member, from 1964, associate professor, 1967-70, professor of history, 1970-72; Johns Hopkins University, Baltimore, MD, professor of history, 1972-91; State University of New York, Buffalo, professor of history, 1991-94; University of Kentucky, Singletary Professor of the Humanities, 1994-. Bancroft History Prize, 1967; Owsley History Prize, 1990. National Humanities Fellow, 1968; Guggenheim Fellow, 1970; AAS/NEH Fellow, 1990. **Publications:** Prelude to the Civil War: The Nullification Controversy in South Carolina 1816-1836, 1965; The Nullification Era: A Documentary Record, 1967; Slavery and Freedom, 1982; The Road to Disunion, Volume I: Secessionists at Bay, 1776-1854, 1990; Secession Debated: Georgia's Showdown in 1860, 1992; The Reintegration of American History: Slavery and the Civil War, 1994; Place not Forgotten, 1999; South versus the South, 2001. **Address:** Dept of History, 1501 Patterson Office Tower 0027, University of Kentucky, Lexington, KY 40506, U.S.A. **Online address:** williamwfreehling@uky.edu

FREEHLING, William W(ilhartz). (born United States), b. 1935. **Genres:** Adult non-fiction. **Career:** Historian, educator, Civil War scholar. University of California-Berkeley, teaching fellow, 1961-63; Harvard University, Cambridge, MA, instructor, 1963-64; University of Michigan, assistant professor, 1964-67, associate professor, 1967-70, professor of history, 1970-72; Johns Hopkins University, Baltimore, MD, professor of history, 1972-91; State University of New York-Buffalo, Thomas B. Lockwood professor of history, 1991-94; University of Kentucky-Lexington, professor of history, Otis A. Singletary chair in humanities, 1994—. **Publications:** Prelude to Civil War: The Nullification Controversy in South Carolina, 1816-1836, 1966; (editor) The Nullification Era: A Documentary Record,1967; (editor) Willie Lee Rose, Slavery and Freedom, 1982; The Road to Disunion, Volume 1: Secessionists at Bay, 1776-1854, 1990; (editor, with Craig M. Simpson)

Secession Debated: Georgia's Showdown in 1860, 1992; The Reintegration of American History: Slavery and the Civil War, 1994; (with others) A Place Not Forgotten: Landscapes of the South from the Morris Museum of Art, 1999; The South vs. The South: How Anti-Confederate Southerners Shaped the Course of the Civil War, 2001. **Address:** 3500 Huntertown Rd., Versailles, KY 40383, U.S.A. **Online address:** wwfree0@uky.edu

FREEMAN, Anne Hobson. American, b. 1934. **Genres:** Novellas/Short stories, Biography. **Career:** Writer, 1956-. International News Service, Eastern Europe, reporter, 1957; Virginia Museum of Fine Arts, Richmond, editor of members' bulletin, 1958-63; University of Virginia, Charlottesville, lecturer in English, 1973-88; Bryn Mawr Bulletin, chair of advisory committee, Bryn Mawr, PA, 1978-81; Hunton & Williams (law firm), Richmond, VA, firm historian, 1984-88. **Publications:** The Style of a Law Firm: Eight Gentlemen from Virginia, 1989; A Hand Well Played: The Life of Jim Wheat, Jr., 1994. Contributor of articles and stories to anthologies and periodicals. **Address:** 314 Oyster Shell Ln, Callao, VA 22435-2016, U.S.A.

FREEMAN, Barbara M. Canadian, b. 1947. **Genres:** History, Women's studies and issues, Writing/Journalism. **Career:** Evening Telegram, St. John's, Newfoundland, general news reporter, summers, 1967-68; Canadian Broadcasting Corp., Ottawa, ON, TV current affairs researcher, reporter, and editor, 1969-70, radio and TV general news reporter and editor in St. John's and Goose Bay, Labrador, 1972-74, TV general news reporter and editor, and radio education and community affairs reporter and editor in Ottawa, 1974-78; British Broadcasting Corp., London, England, sub-editor for external radio services, 1970; Stratford and Newham Express, East London, police and municipal affairs reporter, 1971-72; KEY Radio, Ottawa, municipal affairs reporter, news reader, and editor, 1978-80; Carleton University, Ottawa, instructor, 1980-89, assistant professor of journalism, 1989-98, associate professor, 1998-, member of board of management, Institute of Women's Studies, School of Canadian Studies. Simone de Beauvoir Institute of Women's Studies, Concordia University, adjunct fellow 1990-92. **Publications:** Kit's Kingdom: The Journalism of Kathleen Blake Coleman, 1989; The Satellite Sex, 2001. **Address:** School of Journalism, 332 St. Patricks, Carleton University, Ottawa, ON, Canada K1S 5B6. **Online address:** barbara_freeman@carleton.ca

FREEMAN, Castle (William), Jr. American, b. 1944. **Genres:** Novels, Novellas/Short stories, Essays. **Career:** Franklin Institute, Philadelphia, PA, technical writer, 1970-72; Stephen Greene Press, Brattleboro, VT, editor, 1976-80; Old Farmer's Almanac, Dublin, NH, author of the column Farmer's Calendar, 1981-. Country Journal, copy editor, 1981-87. **Publications:** The Bride of Ambrose (stories), 1987; Spring Snow (essays), 1996; Judgment Hill (novel), 199; My Life and Adventures (novel), 2002. Contributor of articles and stories to periodicals. **Address:** c/o Christina Ward, Christina Ward Literary Agency, PO Box 505, North Scituate, MA 02060, U.S.A.

FREEMAN, Charles Wellman, Jr. Also writes as Limin Fu. American, b. 1943. **Genres:** Food and Wine, International relations/Current affairs. **Career:** U.S. Department of State. **Publications:** Cooking Western in China (bilingual cookbook), 1986; The Diplomat's Dictionary, 1994, rev. ed., 1997; Arts of Power, 1997. Contributor to books and periodicals. **Address:** Projects International Inc., 1800 K St NW Suite 1018, Washington, DC 20006, U.S.A.

FREEMAN, Daniel E(van). American, b. 1959. **Genres:** History, Humanities, Music. **Career:** University of Illinois, visiting assistant professor, 1987, 1995; University of Southern California, lecturer, 1988-91; University of Minnesota, Minneapolis, lecturer, 1991-; musicologist. **Publications:** The Opera Theater of Count Franz Anton von Sporck in Prague, 1992; Il Boemo, Josef Myslivecek, forthcoming; Mozart in Prague, forthcoming. Contributor to periodicals. **Address:** 6032 Sheridan Ave S, Minneapolis, MN 55410, U.S.A. **Online address:** freem005@tc.umn.edu

FREEMAN, Davis. See FRIEDMAN, David F.

FREEMAN, Gillian. Also writes as Eliot George, Elaine Jackson. British, b. 1929. **Genres:** Novels, Plays/Screenplays, Children's non-fiction, Literary criticism and history, Sociology. **Publications:** The Liberty Man, 1955; Fall of Innocence, 1956; Jack Would Be a Gentleman, 1959; The Story of Albert Einstein, 1960; (as Eliot George) The Leather Boys, 1961; The Campaign, 1963; The Leader, 1965; The Undergrowth of Literature, 1967; The Leather Boys (screenplay), 1967; Cold Day in the Park (screenplay), 1968; Pursuit (play), 1969; I Want What I Want (screenplay), 1970; The Alabaster Egg, 1970; Marriage Machine, 1975; The Schoolgirl Ethic, 1976; Nazi Lady (in U.S. as Confessions of Elisabeth von S.), 1978; An Easter Egg Hunt, 1981; (as Elaine Jackson) Lovechild, 1984; Day after the Fair (screenplay), 1986;

Mayerling (film; ballet scenarios), 1978; Isadora, 1981; (with E. Thorpe) Ballet Genius, 1988; Termination Rock, 1989; His Mistress's Voice, 1999. **Address:** c/o Rochelle Stevens and Co, 2 Terretts Pl, Upper St, London N1 1QZ, England.

FREEMAN, Harry M. American, b. 1943. **Genres:** Environmental sciences/Ecology. **Career:** U.S. Environmental Protection Agency, Cincinnati, OH, staff member, 1968-. University of New Orleans, director of Louisiana Environmental Leadership Program. **Publications:** Standard Handbook of Hazardous Waste Treatment and Disposal, 1989; Hazardous Waste Minimization, 1990; (ed.) Industrial Pollution Prevention Handbook, 1995. **Address:** 804 Engineering Bldg., University of New Orleans, New Orleans, LA 70148, U.S.A.

FREEMAN, Jo. American, b. 1945. **Genres:** History, Politics/Government, Sociology, Women's studies and issues, Autobiography/Memoirs. **Career:** Lawyer; political scientist; also lecturer, photographer and political consultant. **Publications:** The Politics of Women's Liberation, 1975; A Room at a Time: How Women Entered Party Politics, 2000; At Berkeley in the Sixties, 2004. EDITOR: Women: A Feminist Perspective, 1975, 5th ed., 1995; Social Movements of the Sixties and Seventies, 1983; (co) Waves of Protest: Social Movements since the Sixties, 1999. Contributor to publications. **Address:** 410 E 8th St, Brooklyn, NY 11218, U.S.A. **Online address:** Joreen@JoFreeman.com

FREEMAN, Joshua B. American, b. 1949. **Genres:** History, Organized labor. **Career:** State University of New York College at Old Westbury, instructor to assistant professor of history, 1980-83; Graduate Center of the City University of New York, senior research scholar, 1984-86; Columbia University, NYC, assistant professor, 1986-90, associate professor of history, 1990-97; Queen College and the Graduate Center, CUNY, associate professor, 1997-2000, professor, 2000-. **Publications:** In Transit: The Transport Workers Union in NYC, 1989; (coauthor) Who Built America? Working People and the Nation's Economy, Politics, Culture, and Society, Vol II, 1992; Working-Class New York: Life and Labor since World War II, 2000. **Address:** Department of History, Queens College, City University of New York, 65-30 Kissena Blvd, Flushing, NY 11367, U.S.A.

FREEMAN, Marcia S. American, b. 1937. **Genres:** Children's fiction, Children's non-fiction, Writing/Journalism. **Career:** High school science teacher in Moravia, NY, 1961-62; elementary school teacher in Caldwell, NJ, 1976-85; presenter of writing education in-service training to elementary and middle-school teachers throughout the U.S., 1987-2002. University of South Florida, member of board of directors and coordinator of Suncoast Young Author's Conference, 1988-94, adjunct member of faculty, 1994-95. **Publications:** FOR CHILDREN: Push and Pull, 1998; Catfish and Spaghetti, 1998; Wetlands, 1998; Giant Pandas, 1999; Polar Bears, 1999; Black Bears, 1999; Brown Bears, 1999; Pine Trees, 1999; Maple Trees, 1999; Palm Trees, 1999; Oak Trees, 1999; Fire Engines, 1999; Ambulances, 1999; Police Cars, 1999; Watching the Weather, 1999; A Bird's-Eye View, 1999; Where Do You Live?, 1999; Nature's Gift, 1999; Coast to Coast, 1999; Going to the City, 1999; Young Geographers, 1999; The Gift, 2002; Is It Alive?, 2002; Properties of Material, 2002; Predator and Prey, 2002; Living Color, 2004; What Can You Do with Water, 2004; Insects, 2004; Mammal Moms and Their Young, 2004; G Is for Grass, 2004; Plant Food, 2004; At the Pond, 2004; When It Rains, 2004; What Is Science, 2004; Let's Go Bird Watching, 2004; In All Directions, 2004; Making Things Move, 2004; Everything under the Sun, 2004; You Are a Scientist, 2004; What Plant Is This, 2004; Animal Lives, 2004. FOR ADULTS: Building a Writing Community, 1995; Listen to This, 1997; Teaching the Youngest Writers, 1998; Non-fiction Writing Strategies Using Science Books as Models, 2000; Craft Plus, 2003. Contributor to magazines for children and teachers. **Address:** 4668 Sweetmeadow Cir, Sarasota, FL 34238, U.S.A. **Online address:** mikeandmarcy@compuserve.com

FREEMAN, Martha. American, b. 1956. **Genres:** Children's fiction, Young adult fiction. **Career:** Writer. Freelance reporter/editor, Sonora, CA, 1980-95. **Publications:** Stink Bomb Mom, 1996; The Year My Parents Ruined My Life, 1997; The Polyester Grandpa, 1998; Fourth Grade Weirdo, 1999; The Trouble with Cats, 2000; The Spy Wore Shades, 2001; The Trouble with Babies, 2002; Who Is Stealing the 12 Days of Christmas?, 2003. **Address:** 454 E Prospect Ave, State College, PA 16801, U.S.A. **Online address:** mafreeman@home.com

FREEMAN, Sarah (Caroline). British, b. 1940. **Genres:** Food and Wine, History, Young adult non-fiction, Biography. **Career:** Penguin Books, London, England, member of editorial staff, c. 1961-63; Architectural Design, London, member of editorial staff, c. 1963-64; Harper's Bazaar, London, subeditor, c. 1964-67; Wine and Food, London, managing editor, c. 1968; Harpers and Queen, arts editor, until 1972; art director, Mary Somerville Art Trust. **Publications:** The Piccolo Picture Cook Book (juvenile), 1975; Isabella and Sam, 1977; Mutton and Oysters (self-illustrated), 1989; The Student Cook Book (self-illustrated), 1990; The Student Vegetarian Cookbook, 1992; The Student Pasta Cook Book (self-illustrated), 1993; The Student Oriental Cook Book (self-illustrated), 1994; The Best of Modern British Cookery, 1995, rev. ed., 2004; The Real Cheese Companion, 1998, rev. ed., 2003. **Address:** c/o Anthony Sheil Associates Ltd, 43 Doughty St, London WC1N 2LF, England. **Online address:** sarah@freeman9999.freeserve.co.uk

FREEMAN, Thomas. See **FEHRENBACH, T(heodore) R(eed).**

FREEMAN-GRENVILLE, Greville Stewart Parker. See Obituaries.

FREEMANTLE, Brian (Harry). Also writes as Harry Asher, Jonathan Evans, Richard Gant, Andre Hart, John Maxwell, Jack Winchester. British, b. 1936. **Genres:** Mystery/Crime/Suspense, Plays/Screenplays. **Career:** Reporter, New Milton Advertiser, 1953-58; Bristol Evening World, 1958, London Evening News, 1958-61, and Daily Express, London, 1961-63; Assistant Foreign Ed., Daily Express, 1963-69; Foreign Ed., Daily Sketch, London, 1969-71, and Daily Mail, London, 1971-75. **Publications:** The Touchables, 1968; Goodbye to an Old Friend, 1973; Face Me When You Walk Away, 1974; The Man Who Wanted Tomorrow, 1975; The November Man, 1976; Charlie Muffin, 1977; Clap Hands, Here Comes Charlie (in U.S. as Here Comes Charlie M), 1978; The Inscrutable Charlie Muffin, 1979; Charlie Muffin's Uncle Sam, 1980; Madrigal for Charlie Muffin, 1981; Deakin's War, 1982; KGB (non-fiction), 1982; CIA (non-fiction), 1983; Vietnam Legacy, 1984; The Lost American, 1984; The Fix (non-fiction), 1985; The Blind Run, 1986; Dirty White, 1986; The Steal (non-fiction), 1986; See Charlie Run, 1987; The Bearpit, 1988; Comrade Charlie, 1989; The Factory, 1990; Little Grey Mice, 1991; The Button Man, 1992; Charlie's Apprentice, 1993; No Time for Heros, 1994; The Octopus (non-fiction), 1995; Charlie's Chance, 1996; Charlie's Choice, 1997; Dead Men Living, 2000; Kings of Many Castles, 2002; Ice Age, 2002; Two Women, Triple Cross, 2003; The Holmes Inheritance: Dead End, 2004; The Holmes Factor, 2005. AS HARRY ASHER: The Profiler, 1997; The Predadots, 1998. AS JONATHAN EVANS: Misfire, 1980; The Midas Men, 1981; Chairman of the Board, 1982. AS RICHARD GANT: Sean Connery: Gilt-Edged Bond, 1967. AS ANDRE HART: A Mind to Kill, 1998; The Return, 1999. AS JOHN MAXWELL: H.M.S. Bounty, 1977; The Mary Celeste, 1979. AS JACK WINCHESTER: The Solitary Man, 1980. **Address:** c/o Jonathan Clowes, 10 Iron Bridge House, Bridge Approach, London NW1 8BD, England.

FREESE, Barbara. American, b. 1960. **Genres:** Adult non-fiction. **Career:** Attorney. State of Minnesota, assistant attorney general, served for twelve years. **Publications:** Coal: A Human History, 2003. **Address:** c/o Author Mail, Perseus Publishing, 11 Cambridge Center, Cambridge, MA 02142, U.S.A.

FREESE, Mathias B(alogh). American, b. 1940. **Genres:** Novels. **Career:** Junior high school teacher in Jamaica, NY, 1962-63; high school teacher in Elmont, NY, 1963-69, and Hauppauge, NY, 1972-74; Board of Cooperative Educational Services, Jericho, NY, curriculum writer, 1969-72; Half Hollow Hills High School East, Dix Hills, NY, teacher and administrator of alternative high school, 1974-79; Middle Country Center for Psychotherapy, clinical social worker, 1979-82; Center for Counseling Services, clinical social worker and senior therapist, 1987-. **Publications:** NOVELS: i, 1997; The i Tetralogy, 2005. Contributor of stories and articles to periodicals. **Address:** 13416 N Wide View Dr, Oro Valley, AZ 85737-1933, U.S.A. **Online address:** ifreese@hotmail.com

FREEZE, Gregory L. American, b. 1945. **Genres:** History. **Career:** Brandeis University, Waltham, MA, assistant professor, 1972-77, associate professor, 1977-83, professor of history, 1983-, head of department, 1990-96. Harvard University, research associate of Davis Center for Russian Studies, 1972-. Guest professor at institutions worldwide; lecturer at educational institutions. **Publications:** The Russian Levites: Parish Clergy in the Eighteenth Century, 1977; Parish Clergy in Nineteenth-Century Russia: Crisis, Reform, Counter-Reform, 1983; (trans. and author of notes) I.S. Belliustin, A Description of the Clergy in Rural Russia: The Memoir of a Nineteenth-Century Parish Priest, 1985; From Supplication to Revolution: A Documentary Social History of Imperial Russia, 1988. EDITOR: I. Smolitsch, Geschichte der Russischen Kirche, Vol II, 1991; Kratkii Putevoditel' (title means: Research Guide to the Central Party Archives), 1993; (and contrib.) Russia: A History, 1997; A.N. Nekrich, Pariahs, Partners, Predators:

German-Soviet Relations, 1922-1941, 1997. Contributor to books and scholarly journals. **Address:** Department of History, Brandeis University, Waltham, MA 02454, U.S.A. **Online address:** freeze@brandeis.edu

FREGA, Donnalee. American, b. 1956. **Genres:** Literary criticism and history, Biography. **Career:** University of North Carolina at Wilmington, assistant professor of English, 1990-96; Duke University, Durham, NC, visiting scholar in English, 1997-99. **Publications:** Speaking in Hunger: Gender, Discourse, and Consumption in Richardson's Clarissa, 1998; Walking the Wire: Telling a Circus Family's Story, in press. Contributor to periodicals. **Address:** 7020 Calais Dr, Durham, NC 27712-9624, U.S.A. **Online address:** fregad@wilmington.net

FREIREICH, Valerie J. American, b. 1952. **Genres:** Novels. **Career:** Lawyer at law firms, 1977-84; sole practitioner in small business and real estate law, 1984-. **Publications:** NOVELS: Becoming Human, 1995; Testament, 1995; Beacon, 1996. Contributor of short stories and novellas to periodicals. **Address:** 2 Paddock, Lemont, IL 60439, U.S.A.

FREKE, Timothy. British, b. 1959. **Genres:** Philosophy. **Career:** Author, philosopher, composer. **Publications:** Lao Tzu's Tao Te Ching, 1995; (with others) Exotic Massage for Lovers, 1996; Heaven: An Illustrated History of the Higher Realms, 1996; (with P. Gandy) The Hermetica: The Lost Wisdom of the Pharaohs, 1997; (Compiler) Children's Visions of Heaven and Hell: Innocent Observations on the Afterlife, 1997; Zen Wisdom: Daily Teachings from the Zen Masters, 1997; (with P. Gandy) The Complete Guide to World Mysticism, 1998; (with P. Gandy) The Wisdom of the Pagan Philosophers, 1998; The Wisdom of the Christian Mystics, 1998; The Wisdom of the Hindu Gurus, 1998; The Wisdom of the Sufi Sages, 1998; The Wisdom of the Tibetan Lamas, 1998; The Wisdom of the Zen Masters, 1998; The Illustrated Book of Sacred Scriptures, 1998; The Way of the Desert, 1998; The Way of the Sea, 1999; Zen Made Easy: An Introduction to the Basics of the Ancient Art of Zen, 1999; Shamanic Wisdomkeepers: Shamanism in the Modern World, 1999; Taoist Wisdom: Daily Teachings from the Taoist Sages, 1999; (with P. Gandy) The Jesus Mysteries: Was the Original Jesus a Pagan God?, 2000; The Encyclopedia of Spirituality: Information and Inspiration to Transform Your Life, 2000; (with P. Gandy) Jesus and the Lost Goddess: The Secret Teaching of the Original Christians, 2001. **Address:** c/o Susan Mears Literary Agency Crosswinds, Oaksey Park Farm, Oaksey nr Malmesbury, Wiltshire SN16 9SD, England. **Online address:** iam@timfrek.demon.co.uk

FREMGEN, James Morgan. American, b. 1933. **Genres:** Administration/ Management, Money/Finance. **Career:** Indiana University, Bloomington, Faculty Lecturer in Accounting, 1959-61; University of Notre Dame, IN, Assistant Professor, 1961-64, Associate Professor of Accounting, 1964-65; Naval Postgrad. School, Monterey, CA, Associate Professor, 1965-69, Professor of Accounting, 1969-2000. **Publications:** Accounting for Managerial Analysis, 1972, 3rd ed. 1976; (with S.S. Liao) The Allocation of Corporate Indirect Costs, 1981. **Address:** Code GB, Naval Postgrad. School, Monterey, CA 93943, U.S.A.

FREMLIN, Celia. British, b. 1914. **Genres:** Mystery/Crime/Suspense, Novellas/Short stories. **Publications:** The Seven Chars of Chelsea, 1940; The Hours Before Dawn, 1958; Uncle Paul, 1959; Seven Lean Years, 1961; The Trouble-Makers, 1963; The Jealous One, 1965; Prisoner's Base, 1967; Possession, 1969; Don't Go to Sleep in the Dark, 1970; Appointment with Yesterday, 1972; By Horror Haunted, 1974; The Long Shadow, 1975; The Spider Orchid, 1977; With No Crying, 1980; The Parasite Person, 1982; A Lovely Day to Die and Other Stories, 1984; Listening in the Dusk, 1990; Dangerous Thoughts, 1991; The Echoing Stones, 1993; King of the World, 1994; War Factory 1943. **Address:** c/o 82 Melbourne Rd, Bristol BS7 8LD, England.

FRENCH, Albert. American, b. 1943. **Genres:** Novels, Autobiography/ Memoirs. **Career:** Pittsburgh Post-Gazette, Pittsburgh, PA, photographer, c; 1971-83; Pittsburgh Preview Magazine, Pittsburgh, publisher, c; 1980-88; writer. **Publications:** NOVELS: Billy, 1993; Holly, 1995; I Can't Wait on God, 1998. OTHER: Patches of Fire: A Story of War and Redemption (autobiography), 1996. **Address:** c/o Anchor Books, Doubleday & Co. Inc., 1540 Broadway, New York, NY 10036-4094, U.S.A.

FRENCH, Fiona. British, b. 1944. **Genres:** Children's fiction, Illustrations. **Career:** Children's art therapy teacher, Long Grove Psychiatric Hospital, Epsom, Surrey, 1967-69; design teacher, Wimbledon School of Art, London, 1970-71, and Leicester and Brighton Polytechnics, 1973-74. **Publications:** Jack of Hearts, 1970; Huni, 1971; The Blue Bird, 1972; King Tree, 1973;

City of Gold, 1975; Aio the Rainmaker, 1975; Matteo, 1976; Hunt the Thimble, 1978; Oscar Wilde's Star Child, 1979; The Princess and the Musician, 1981; John Barley Corn, 1982; Future Story, 1983; Fat Cat, 1984; Going to Squintums, 1985; Maid of the Wood, 1985; Snow White in New York, 1986; Song of the Nightingale, 1986; Cinderella, 1987; Rise, Shine, 1989; The Magic Vase, 1991; Anancy and Mr. Dry-Bone, 1991; King Of Another Country, 1993; Little Incking, 1994; Pepi and the Secret Names, 1994; Miss Mouse Gets Married, 1996; Lord of the Animals, 1997; Jamil's Clever Cat, 1998; (ed.) Easter, 2002. Illustrator of books by: M. Mayo, R. Blythe, J. Westwood and others. **Address:** c/o Frances Lincoln Ltd, 4 Torriano Mews, Torriano Ave, London NW5 2RZ, England.

FRENCH, Linda. Also writes as Linda Mariz. American, b. 1948. **Genres:** Mystery/Crime/Suspense. **Career:** Whatcom Community College, Bellingham, WA, instructor in Western civilization, 1972-73; worked at Western Washington University, Bellingham, 1979-81. **Publications:** MYSTERIES: Talking Rain, 1998; Coffee to Die For, 1999; Steeped in Murder, 1999. MYSTERIES AS LINDA MARIZ: Body English, 1992; Snake Dance, 1992.

FRENCH, Marilyn. American, b. 1929. **Genres:** Novels, Literary criticism and history, Intellectual history. **Career:** Instructor in English, Hofstra University, Hempstead, New York, 1964-68; Teaching Assistant, Harvard University, Cambridge, Massachusetts, 1970-72; Assistant Professor of English, College of the Holy Cross, Worcester, Massachusetts, 1972-76; Mellon Fellow in English, Harvard University, Cambridge, Massachusetts, 1976-77. **Publications:** The Book as World: James Joyce's Ulysses, 1976; The Women's Room (novel), 1977; The Bleeding Heart (novel), 1980; Shakespeare's Division of Experience, 1981; Beyond Power: On Women, Men and Morals, 1985; Her Mother's Daughter, 1987; The War against Women, 1992; Our Father, 1994; My Summer with George, 1996; A Season in Hell, 1998; Women's History of the World; 2000; From Eve to Dawn: A History of Women, 2002. **Address:** c/o Charlotte Sheedy, Sheedy Literary Agency, 65 Bleecher St. Fl 12, New York, NY 10012-2420, U.S.A.

FRENCH, Nicci. See FRENCH, Sean.

FRENCH, Patrick. British, b. 1968?. **Genres:** History, Biography. **Career:** Writer. **Publications:** Younghusband: The Last Great Imperial Adventurer (biography), 1994; Liberty or Death: India's Journey to Independence and Division (history), 1997. **Address:** c/o Author Mail, Seventh Floor, HarperCollins Publishers, 10 East 53rd St., New York, NY 10022, U.S.A.

FRENCH, Philip (Neville). British, b. 1933. **Genres:** Film, Literary criticism and history. **Career:** BBC Radio, Sr. Talks and Documentary Producer, 1959-90; The Observer, London, Film Critic, 1978-. **Publications:** The Movie Moguls, 1969; Westerns: Aspects of a Movie Genre, 1974; Three Honest Men: Portraits of Edmund Wilson, F.R. Leavis, and Lionel Trilling, 1980; (with K. French) Wild Strawberries, 1995; (with K. French) Cult Movies, 1999. EDITOR/CO-EDITOR: The Age of Austerity 1945-51, 1963; The Novelist as Innovator, 1966; The Third Dimension: Voices from Radio 3, 1983; The Press: Observed and Projected 1991; Malle on Malle, 1992; The Faber Book of Movie Verse, 1993. **Address:** 62 Dartmouth Park Rd, London NW5 1SN, England.

FRENCH, Sean. Also writes as Nicci French. British, b. 1959. **Genres:** Novels, Trivia/Facts, Recreation, Film. **Career:** Sunday Times, London, literary editor, 1984-86; New Society, editor, 1986-87; New Statesman and Society (magazine), columnist, 1987-. **Publications:** (ed.) Fatherhood (essays), 1992; (with K. and P. French) The French Brothers' Wild and Crazy Film Quiz Book, 1992; The Imaginary Monkey (novel), 1993; Patrick Hamilton: A Life (biography), 1993; Bardot (biography), 1994; Dreamer of Dreams (novel), 1995; The Terminator (criticism), 1996; Jane Fonda (biography), 1997. AS NICCI FRENCH (with N. Gerrard): The Memory Game, 1997; The Safe House, 1998; Beneath the Skin, 2000; Land of the Living, 2003. **Address:** 54 Lady Somerset Rd., London NW5 1TU, England. **Online address:** seanicci@dircom.co.uk

FRENCH, Warren G. American, b. 1922. **Genres:** Film, Literary criticism and history. **Career:** Member of faculty, University of Mississippi, University, 1948-50, University of Kentucky, Lexington, 1954-56, Stetson University, Deland, FL, 1956-58, University of Florida, Gainesville, 1958-62, Kansas State University, Manhattan, 1962-65, and University of Missouri, Kansas City, 1965-70; University of Wales-Swansea, honorary professor; Indiana University, joined faculty, 1970, emeritus professor, 1986-. Editor, Twayne Film Series, and Twayne United States Authors Series, 1975-84. **Publications:** John Steinbeck, 1961; Frank Norris, 1962; J.D. Salinger, 1963; The Social Novel at the End of an Era, 1966; Season of Promise, 1968; Filmguide to The Grapes of Wrath, 1973; Jack Kerouac, 1986; J.D. Salinger Revisited, 1988; The San Francisco Poetry Renaissance, 1991; John Steinbeck's Fiction Revisited, 1994; John Steinbeck's Nonfiction Revisited, 1996. EDITOR: A Companion to The Grapes of Wrath, 1963; The Thirties: Fiction, Poetry, Drama, 1969; (with W. Kidd) American Winners of the Nobel Literary Prize, 1968; The Forties: Fiction, Poetry, Drama, 1969; The Twenties: Fiction, Poetry, Drama, 1975; The South and Film, 1981. **Address:** 1502 Jackson St, Tallahassee, FL 32303, U.S.A.

FREND, William (Hugh Clifford). British, b. 1916. **Genres:** Theology/Religion. **Career:** Asst Principal, War Office, 1940-41; Cabinet Offices, 1941-42; Intelligence Officer, Political Intelligence, 1942-46; Member, Board of Editors, Captured German Foreign Ministry Project, 1947-51; University Lecturer in Divinity, University of Cambridge, 1956-69; Fellow, 1956-69, Director of Studies in Archaeology and Anthropology, 1961-69, Bye Fellow, 1997-, Gonville and Caius College, Cambridge; Professor of Ecclesiastical History, 1969-84, and Dean of Divinity, University of Glasgow; Vicar of Barnwell, 1984-90. Ed., Modern Churchman, 1963-82; Visiting Professor, John Carroll University, Cleveland, Ohio, 1981; Fellow of the British Academy, 1983; Sr. Fellow, Dumbarton Oaks, Center for Byzantine Studies, Washington, DC, 1984. **Publications:** The Donatist Church, 1952; Martyrdom and Persecution in the Early Church, 1964; The Early Church, 1965; The Rise of the Monophysite Movement, 1972; Religion Popular and Unpopular in the Early Christian Centuries, 1976; Town and Countryside in the Early Christian Centuries, 1980; The Rise of Christianity, 1984; Saints and Sinners in the Early Church, 1985; History and Archaeology in the Study of Early Christianity, 1988; The Archaeology of Early Christianity: A History, 1996; Paganism, Orthodoxy and Dissent, 2002; From Dogma to History, 2003. **Address:** The Clerks Cottage, Little Wilbraham, Cambridge CB1 5LB, England.

FRERE, S(heppard) S(underland). British, b. 1916. **Genres:** Archaeology/Antiquities, History. **Career:** Taught at Epsom College, 1938-40, and Lancing College, 1945-54; Lecturer, Manchester University, 1954-55; Reader, Institute of Archaeology, 1955-62, and Professor, 1963-66, University of London; Professor of the Archaeology of the Roman Empire, Oxford University, 1966-83. Director, excavations at Canterbury, 1946-60, and at Verulamium, 1955-61; Member, Royal Commission on Historical Monuments (England), 1966-83, and Ancient Monuments Board (England), 1966-82; President, Royal Archaeological Institute, 1978-81; President, Society for the Promotion of Roman Studies, 1983-86. **Publications:** (ed.) Problems of the Iron Age in Southern Britain, 1961; Britannia: A History of Roman Britain, 1967, 4th ed. 1999; Verulamium Excavations, 3 vols., 1972-84; Excavations on the Roman and Medieval Defences of Canterbury, 1982; Excavations at Canterbury, vol. 7, 1987; (with J.K. St. Joseph) Roman Britain from the Air, 1983; (with F.A. Lepper) Trajan's Column, 1988; (with R.S. Tomlin) The Roman Inscriptions of Britain, II, fasc. 1, 1990, vol. 2, 1991; fasc. 3-4, 1992, fasc. 5, 1993, fasc. 6, 1994, fasc. 7, 8 and Epigraphic Indices, 1995. **Address:** Netherfield House, Marcham, Abingdon, Oxford, England.

FRETTER, T. W. See ANDRE, Michael.

FREUD, Esther. British, b. 1963. **Genres:** Novels. **Career:** Actress and writer; cofounder of Norfolk Broads (a women's theater company), England. **Publications:** Hideous Kinky, 1992; Peerless Flats, 1993; Summer at Gaglow, 1998; The Wild, 2000; The Sea House, 2004. Work represented in periodicals. **Address:** c/o A. P. Watt, 20 John St, London WC1N 2DR, England.

FREUD, Sophie. American (born Austria), b. 1924. **Genres:** Autobiography/Memoirs. **Career:** Simmons College, Boston, MA, professor of social work, 1978-92 writer. Harvard University Extension, lecturer. **Publications:** My Three Mothers and Other Passions, 1988. **Address:** 34 Laurel Drive, Lincoln, MA 01773, U.S.A.

FREUDENBERGER, Herman. American (born Germany), b. 1922. **Genres:** Economics. **Career:** Tulane University, New Orleans, Louisiana, Associate Professor, 1962-66, Chairman, Dept. of Economics, 1966-70, Professor of Economics, 1966-92, Professor Emeritus, 1992-. Business History Conference, President, 1978-79. **Publications:** The Waldstein Woolen Mill, 1963; (co-author) Von der Provinzstadt zur Industrieregion, 1975; The Industrialization of a Central European City, 1977; (co-author) A Redemptorist Missionary in Ireland 1851-1854: Memoirs by Joseph Prost. **Address:** 709 Ashlawn Dr, New Orleans, LA 70123, U.S.A.

FREUDENTHAL, Gad. Israeli (born Palestine), b. 1944. **Genres:** Physics. **Career:** Centre National de la Recherche Scientifique, Paris, France, director of research at Institute for the History of Science, 1982-. **Publications:** Aristotle's Theory of Material Substance: Heat and Pneuma, Form and Soul, 1995. EDITOR: Etudes sur Helene Metzger/Studies on Helene Metzger, 1990; Studies on Gersonides: A Fourteenth-Century Jewish Philosopher-Scientist, 1992. **Address:** Institut d'histoire des sciences, Centre National de la Recherche Scientifique, 13 rue du Four, 75006 Paris, France.

FREUND, Diane. American. **Genres:** Novels. **Career:** Writer, teacher. University of Arizona South, Sierra Vista, assistant professor of English. Worked as a waitress. **Publications:** Four Corners, 2001. **Address:** c/o Author Mail, MacAdam/Cage Publishing, 155 Sansome St Ste 550, San Francisco, CA 94104, U.S.A. **Online address:** dfreund@u.arizona.edu

FREUND, Thatcher. American, b. 1955. **Genres:** Antiques/Furnishings. **Career:** Substitute teacher at public schools in Cambridge, MA, 1979; Howard, Prim, San Francisco, CA, paralegal, 1979-82; New England Monthly, Northampton, MA, staff writer, 1986-89. Also worked as ice cream server and waiter. **Publications:** Objects of Desire: The Lives of Antiques and Those Who Pursue Them, 1994. **Address:** 704 E. Franklin St, Chapel Hill, NC 27514-3823, U.S.A.

FREWER, Glyn Mervyn Louis. Also writes as Mervyn Lewis. British, b. 1931. **Genres:** Mystery/Crime/Suspense, Children's fiction, Plays/Screenplays. **Career:** Student officer, British Council, Oxford, 1955; Copywriter for advertising agencies, 1955-74; Advertising agency Associate Director, 1974-85; Proprietor, antiquarian and secondhand bookshop, 1985-2001. **Publications:** The Hitch-Hikers (radio play), 1957; Adventure in Forgotten Valley, 1962; Adventure in the Barren Lands, 1964; The Last of the Wispies, 1965; The Token of Elkin, 1970; Crossroad, 1970; (as Mervyn Lewis) Death of Gold, 1970; The Square Peg, 1972; The Raid, 1976; The Trackers, 1976; Tyto: The Odyssey of an Owl, 1978; Bryn of Brockle Hanger, 1980; Fox, 1984; The Call of the Raven, 1987; also, scripts for industrial films and children's TV series. **Address:** Cottage Farm, Taston nr Charlbury, Oxon., England.

FREY, Julia (Bloch). American, b. 1943. **Genres:** Poetry, Art/Art history, Literary criticism and history, Biography. **Career:** Brown University, Providence, RI, instructor in French, 1972-73; University of Paris, chargee de cours, 1974-75; Yale University, New Haven, CT, lecturer in French, 1975-76; University of Colorado, Boulder, associate professor of French, 1976-98, professor of French, art history, 1999-2001, emerita, 2002-; University of San Diego Law School, Institute of International and Comparative Law, Paris, France, professor, 1979-89; Sarah Lawrence College, Bronxville, NY, guest professor, 1983. **Publications:** Toulouse-Lautrec: A Life (biography), 1994; (ed.) Toulouse-Lautrec, uno sguardo dentro la vita (exhibition catalog), 2003. Contributor of poetry and articles to periodicals and books. **Address:** 200 Rector Pl Apt 26-B, New York, NY 10280-1170, U.S.A. **Online address:** julia.frey@aya.yale.edu

FREY, Linda (Sue). American. **Genres:** History. **Career:** Denison University, Granville, OH, visiting lecturer in history, 1971; University of Montana, Missoula, assistant professor, 1971-76, associate professor, 1976-82, professor of history, 1982-. Visiting professor at Ohio State University, 1986, and U.S. Military Academy, West Point, NY, 1996-97; USMA, McDermott Chair, 2000-01. **Publications:** WITH M. FREY: (and J.C. Rule) Observations from The Hague and Utrecht: William Henry Harrison's Letters to Henry Watkins, 1711-1712, 1979; (trans., and R. Zylawy) Les Dieux Ont Soif, 1978; (and J. Schneider) Women in Western European History, 1982; A Question of Empire: Leopold I and the War of the Spanish Succession, 1701-1705, 1983; Frederick I: The Man and His Times, 1984; (and Schneider) Women in Western European History, 1984; (and Schneider) Women in Western European History, 1986; Societies in Upheaval: Insurrections in France, Hungary, and Spain in the Early 18th Century, 1987; (ed.) The Treaties of the War of the Spanish Succession, 1995; The History of Diplomatic Immunity, 1998; The French Revolution, 2004. Contributor to books. Contributor of articles and reviews to academic journals. **Address:** Dept of History, University of Montana, Missoula, MT 59812, U.S.A.

FREY, Marsha L. American. **Genres:** History. **Career:** Ohio State University, Columbus, lecturer, 1971-72; University of Oregon, Eugene, visiting assistant professor, 1972-73; Kansas State University, Manhattan, assistant professor, 1973-79, associate professor, 1980-84, professor of history, 1984-, MASUA honors lecturer, 1988-89. Indiana University-Bloomington, artist in residence at Living Learning Center, 1980; University of Montana, guest lecturer, 1994; lecturer at educational institutions. **Publications:** ALL WITH L. FREY: (trans. with R. Zylawy) A. France, Les Dieux Ont Soif, 1978; (ed. with J. Rule) Observations from the Hague and Utrecht: William

Henry Harrison's Letters to Henry Watkins, 1711-1712, 1979; A Question of Empire: Leopold I and the War of the Spanish Succession (monograph), 1983; Friedrich I: Preussens Erster Koenig, 1983, trans. as Frederick I: The Man and His Times (monograph), 1984; Societies in Upheaval: Insurrections in France, Hungary, and Spain in the Early Eighteenth Century, 1987; The Treaties of the War of the Spanish Succession: An Historical and Critical Dictionary, 1995; The History of Diplomatic Immunity, 1999. COMPILER WITH L. FREY & J. SCHNEIDER: Women in Western European History: A Select Chronological, Geographical, and Topical Bibliography from Antiquity to the French Revolution, 1982; Women in Western European History: A Select Chronological, Geographical, and Topical Bibliography: The Nineteenth and Twentieth Centuries, 1984; Women in Western European History: A Select Chronological, Geographical, and Topical Bibliography from Antiquity to the Present: Recent Research, 1986; Contributor to books. Contributor of articles and reviews to history journals. **Address:** Department of History, Kansas State University, Manhattan, KS 66506, U.S.A.

FREY, Stephen W. American. **Genres:** Money/Finance. **Career:** Westdeutsche Landesbank, NYC, vice-president of corporate finance. Worked previously in the mergers and acquisitions department, J.P. Morgan & Company. **Publications:** The Takeover, 1995; The Vulture Fund, 1996; Inner Sanctum, 1997; Legacy, 1998; Insider, 2000; Trust Fund, 2001; Silent Partner, 2002. **Address:** Westdeutsche Landesbank, 1211 Avenue of the Americas, 24th Floor, New York, NY 10036, U.S.A.

FREYD, Jennifer J. American, b. 1957. **Genres:** Psychology. **Career:** Cornell University, Ithaca, NY, assistant professor of psychology, 198387; University of Oregon, Eugene, OR, associate professor, 1987-92, member of executive committee, Center for the Study of Women in Society, 1991-92, member of executive committee, Institute for Cognitive and Decision Sciences, 1991-94, counselor at DeBusk Memorial Center, 1991-92, professor of psychology, 1992-; Aslan Counseling Center, Eugene, OR, counselor, 1992; Microsoft Corporation, Redmond, WA, psychology editorial advisor, 1995; contributor to many conferences and symposia. **Publications:** Betrayal Trauma: The Logic of Forgetting Childhood Abuse, 1996; (ed.) Trauma and Cognitive Science, 2001. Contributor to books. Contributor of articles and reviews to periodicals. **Address:** Department of Psychology, and Institute of Cognitive and Decision Sciences, University of Oregon, Eugene, OR 97403, U.S.A. **Online address:** jjf@dynamic.uoregon.edu

FREYDONT, Shelley. American, b. 1949. **Genres:** Mystery/Crime/Suspense. **Career:** Dancer and writer. California State University, Fresno, CA, professor, 1974-76; Louis Falco Dance Company, New York, NY, dancer, 1977-79; Twyla Tharp Dance, New York, NY, dancer 1979-85; American Ballroom Theater, New York, NY, 1986-90. Has also worked as a choreographer, rehearsal director, and dance teacher and consultant. **Publications:** LINDY HAGGERTY MYSTERY NOVELS: Backstage Murder, 1999; High Seas Murder, 2000; Midsummer Murder, 2001; Halloween Murder, 2002. **Address:** 370 Ponfield Pl., Ridgewood, NJ 07450, U.S.A. **Online address:** sfreydont@aol.com

FREYER, Tony (Allan). American, b. 1947. **Genres:** Law, Economics, History, Biography. **Career:** Indiana University-Bloomington, lecturer in law, 1974-75, Bicentennial of the Constitution Lecturer, 1984; University of Arkansas at Little Rock, assistant professor, 1976-80, associate professor of history, 1980-81; University of Alabama, Tuscaloosa, associate professor, 1983-86, professor of history and law, 1986-90, university research professor, 1990-. Harvard University, Harvard-Newcomen business history fellow at Harvard Business School, 1975-76, fellow of Charles Warren Center, 1981-82; University of California, Los Angeles, visiting professor, winter/spring, 1987. University of London, London School of Economics and Political Science, senior Fulbright scholar and visiting professor, 1986; Australian National University, senior Fulbright scholar, 1993; Burnum Distinguished Faculty Award, University of Alabama, 1992; Abe Fellowship, Japan, 1995-96; Fulbright Distinguished Chair in American Studies, University of Warsaw, Poland, 2000. **Publications:** Forums of Order, 1979; Harmony and Dissonance: The Swift and Erie Cases in American Federalism, 1981; The Little Rock Crisis, 1984; (ed.) Justice Hugo L. Black and Modern America, 1990; Hugo L. Black and the Dilemma of American Liberalism, 1990; Regulating Big Business: Antitrust in Great Britain and America, 1880-1990, 1992; Producers versus Capitalists, 1994; (with T. Dixon) Democracy and Judicial Independence, 1995; (ed.) Defending Constitutional Rights: Frank M. Johnson, 2001; Rights Defied, forthcoming; American Praxis, forthcoming. Work represented in books. Contributor of articles and reviews to history and law journals. **Address:** School of Law, University of Alabama, Box 870382, Tuscaloosa, AL 35487-0382, U.S.A. **Online address:** TFreyer@law.ua.edu

FREZZA, Robert (A.). American, b. 1956. **Genres:** Science fiction/Fantasy. **Career:** U.S. Army Claims Service, Fort Meade, MD, deputy chief of personnel in Claims and Recovery Division, 1985-93; writer, 1993-. **Publications:** A Small Colonial War (military science fiction), 1989; McLendon's Syndrome (humorous science fiction), 1993; Fire in a Faraway Place (military science fiction), 1994; Cain's Land (military science fiction), 1995; The VMR Theory (humorous science fiction), 1996. Contributor of short fiction to Amazing. **Address:** 8133 Turn Loop Rd., Glen Burnie, MD 21061, U.S.A.

FRICKER, Mary. American, b. 1940. **Genres:** Business/Trade/Industry. **Career:** Russian River News, reporter and news editor, 1982-83; high school English teacher, 1983-85; Press Democrat, Santa Rosa, CA, editorial assistant, 1985-86, editorial writer, 1986-90, business reporter and copy editor, 1990-92, assistant business editor, 1992-. Scholar in residence, Santa Rosa Junior College, 1990. Stringer and consultant, Arizona Republic, 1989. Assistant public relations director, College of William and Mary; owner, Serendip Carpet Co., Honolulu, HI. **Publications:** (With Stephen Pizzo and Paul Muolo) Inside Job: The Looting of America's Savings and Loans, McGraw, 1989. **Address:** Denise Marcil, Literary Agency, Inc, 685 West End Ave, New York, NY 10025, U.S.A.

FRIED, Dennis F. American, b. 1946. **Genres:** Humor/Satire. **Career:** Eiffel Press, Osprey, FL, publisher and president, 1999-. Formerly a professor of philosophy. **Publications:** Memoirs of a Papillon: The Canine Guide to Living with Humans without Going Mad, 2000. **Address:** Eiffel Press, PO Box 339, Osprey, FL 34229, U.S.A. **Online address:** eiffelpress@comcast.net

FRIEDAN, Betty. American, b. 1921. **Genres:** Women's studies and issues, Autobiography/Memoirs. **Career:** McCalls Magazine, contributing editor, 1971-. National Organization for Women, founding president, 1966-70. **Publications:** The Feminine Mystique, 1963; It Changed My Life: Writings on the Women's Movement, 1976; The Second Stage, 1982; The Fountain of Age, 1993; Beyond Gender: The New Politics of Work and Gender, 1997; Life So Far, 2000. **Address:** 2022 Columbia Rd NW Apt 414, Washington, DC 20009-1304, U.S.A.

FRIEDBERG, Maurice. American (born Poland), b. 1929. **Genres:** International relations/Current affairs, Literary criticism and history, Translations. **Career:** City University of New York, Hunter College, associate professor of Russian, chairman of Russian Division, 1955-65; Hebrew University, Jerusalem, Fulbright visiting professor of Russian literature, 1965-66; Indiana University, Bloomington, professor of Slavic languages and literatures, 1966-75, director of the Russian and East European Institute 1967-71; University of Illinois, Urbana, professor of Slavic languages and literatures, and dept. head, 1975-2000, Center for Advanced Study, professor emeritus of Slavic literature, 2000-. Ecole des Hautes Etudes en Sciences Sociales, Paris, director d'etudes associe, 1984-85. **Publications:** Russian Classics in Soviet Jackets, 1962; The Jew in Post Stalin Soviet Literature, 1970; A Decade of Euphoria: Western Literature in Post-Stalin Russia, 1977; Russian Culture in the 1980's, 1985; How Things Were Done in Odessa: Cultural and Intellectual Pursuits in a Soviet City, 1991; Literary Translation in Russia, 1997. EDITOR: A Bilingual Edition of Russian Short Stories, 1965, vol. II, and trans. with R.A. Maguire, 1965, 1966; (and co-author) Encyclopedia Judaica, 16 vols., 1971-72; The Young Lenin, by Leon Trotsky, 1972; Soviet Society Under Gorbachev, 1987; The Red Pencil: Artists, Scholars and Censors in the U.S.S.R., 1989. **Address:** 2406 N Nottingham Ct, Champaign, IL 61821, U.S.A. **Online address:** friedbrg@uiuc.edu

FRIEDEBERG-SEELEY, Frank (J. B.). Also writes as David Barraz. British, b. 1912. **Genres:** Literary criticism and history. **Career:** Oxford University, Oxford, England, part-time assistant lecturer, 1935-36; University of London, School of Slavonic and East European Studies, London, England, lecturer, 1943-57; University of Nottingham, Nottingham, England, senior lecturer and head of department of Slavonic studies, 1957-67; Columbia University, New York City, visiting professor of Russian literature, 1963-64; University of Pennsylvania, Philadelphia, professor of Russian literature, 1967-71; State University of New York, professor of Russian literature and chairman of department, 1971-76; professor of Comparative Literature, 1972-82; professor of Russian literature, 1979-82, emeritus professor of Russian and comparative literature, 1982-. **Publications:** (trans. with J. Barnes) Leone Ebreo: The Philosophy of Love, 1937; (with S. Konovalov) Russian Prose Reader: Nineteenth Century Authors, 1945; (with H. Rapp) The Gateway Russian Course, Book 1, 1963, Book 2, 1964; Turgenev: A Reading of His Fiction, 1991; From the Heyday of the Superfluous Man to Chekhov: Collected Papers I 1994. Contributor to Russian studies and literature journals in England, Scotland, Belgium, Italy, and the United States. **Address:** 404 Watters Crossing Court, Allen, TX 75013, U.S.A.

FRIEDEN, Bernard J. American, b. 1930. **Genres:** Regional/Urban planning. **Career:** Professor, Dept. of Urban Planning, 1969-, Ford Professor of Urban Development, 1989-, Associate Dean of Architecture and Planning, 1993-, Massachusetts Institute of Technology, Cambridge (Assistant Professor, 1961-65; Associate Professor, 1965-69; Research Director, MIT Centre for Real Estate Development, 1985-87; Chairman of MIT Faculty, 1987-89). Director, Massachusetts Institute of Technology-Harvard University Joint Center for Urban Studies, 1971-75. Ed., Journal of the American Institute of Planners, 1962-65. **Publications:** Future of Old Neighborhoods, 1964; (ed. with R. Morris) Urban Planning and Social Policy, 1968; (ed. with W. Nash) Shaping an Urban Future, 1969; (with M. Kaplan) The Politics of Neglect, 1975, 1977; (ed. with W. Anderson and M. Murphy) Managing Human Services, 1977; The Environmental Protection Hustle, 1979; (with L. Sagalyn) Downtown, Inc., 1989. **Address:** 7 Diamond Rd, Lexington, MA 02420, U.S.A.

FRIEDEN, Jeffry Alan. American, b. 1953. **Genres:** Money/Finance. **Career:** University of California-Los Angeles, member of department of political science, 1983-95; Centre for European Research Studies, Brussels, Belgium, member of Economic Policy Group, 1994-97; Harvard University, Cambridge, MA, member of department of government, 1995-, Weatherhead Center for International Affairs, acting director, 2000-01. **Publications:** Banking on the World: The Politics of American International Finance, 1987; (with D.G. Becker, S. Schatz, and R. Sklar) Postimperialism: International Capitalism and Development in the Late Twentieth Century, 1987; Debt, Development, and Democracy: Modern Political Economy and Latin America, 1965-1985, 1991; Studies in International Finance: Private Interest and Public Policy in the International Political Economy, 1993; (with B. Eichengreen) The Political Economy of European Monetary Unification, 1994. EDITOR: (with D.A. Lake) International Political Economy: Perspectives on Global Power and Wealth, 1987; (with N. Hamilton, L. Fuller, and M. Pastor) Crisis in Central America: Regional Dynamics and U.S. Policy in the 1980s, 1988; (with B. Eichengreen and J. von Hagen) Monetary and Fiscal Policy in an Integrated Europe, 1995; (with B. Eichengreen and J. von Hagen) Politics and Institutions in an Integrated Europe, 1995; (with D. Gros and E. Jones) The New Political Economy of European Monetary Unification, 1998; (with B. Eichengreen) Forging an Integrated Europe, 1998; (with E. Jones and F. Torres) Joining Europe's Monetary Club: The Challenge for Smaller Member States, 1998; (with M. Pastor and M. Tomz) Modern Political Economy and Latin America: Theory and Policy, 2000; (with E. Stein) The Currency Game: Exchange Rate Politics in Latin America, 2001. **Address:** Department of Government, Harvard University, 1737 Cambridge St. 406B, Cambridge, MA 02138, U.S.A. **Online address:** jfrieden@harvard.edu

FRIEDENBERG, Robert V. American, b. 1943. **Genres:** Communications/Media. **Career:** Miami University, Hamilton/Oxford, OH, professor of communication, 1970figures. **Publications:** Political Campaign Communication, 1983, 4th edition, 1999; Hear O' Israel: The History of American Jewish Preaching, 1654-1970, 1989 Theodore Roosevelt and the Rhetoric of Militant Decency, 1990; Communication Consultants in Political Campaigns: Ballot Box Warriors, 1997; Notable Speeches in Contemporary Political Campaigns, 2002. **Address:** Dept of Communication, Miami University, 1601 Peck Blvd, Hamilton, OH 45011, U.S.A.

FRIEDL, Erika (Loeffler). Austrian, b. 1940. **Genres:** Anthropology/Ethnology. **Career:** University of Chicago, Chicago, IL, research associate at Oriental Institute, 1964-65; Western Michigan University, Kalamazoo, instructor, 1968-69, assistant professor, 1971-78, associate professor, 1978-85, professor of anthropology, 1985-, director of Women's Studies Program, 1986-87. University of Heidelberg, guest lecturer at Southasia Institute, 1987. Conducted field research in Austria, 1976, 1978, 1984, and Turkey, 1991; conducted extensive field work in Iran, 1965-. Guest on television programs; lecturer at colleges and universities; public speaker on ethnography and on women in Iran. **Publications:** (ed. with M. Afkhami, and contrib.) In the Eye of the Storm: Women in Post-Revolutionary Iran, 1994. Contributor of articles and reviews to periodicals. **Address:** Department of Anthropology, Western Michigan University, Kalamazoo, MI 49008, U.S.A.

FRIEDLAND, Martin L(awrence). Canadian, b. 1932. **Genres:** Civil liberties/Human rights, Criminology/True Crime, Education, History, Law. **Career:** Osgoode Hall Law School, Toronto, ON, Canada, assistant professor, then associate professor of law, 1961-65; University of Toronto, associate professor, 1965-68, professor of law, 1968-98, dean of law faculty, 1972-79, University Professor, 1985-98, professor of law emeritus, 1998-; writer. Visiting professor at Hebrew University of Jerusalem and Tel Aviv University, both 1979; Cambridge University, visiting fellow of Clare Hall and Institute of Criminology, 1980; Centre of Criminology, member, 1984-; Massey College, senior fellow, 1985-; Canadian Institute for Advanced Research, fellow,

1986-98. **Publications:** Detention before Trial, 1965; Double Jeopardy, 1969; Courts and Trials: A Multidisciplinary Approach, 1975; Access to the Law, 1975; National Security: The Legal Dimensions, 1980; The Trials of Israel Lipski: A True Story of a Victorian Murder in the East End of London, 1984; A Century of Criminal Justice: Perspectives on the Development of Canadian Law, 1984; The Case of Valentine Shortis: A True Story of Crime and Politics in Canada, 1986; Sanctions and Rewards in the Legal System: A Multidisciplinary Approach, 1989; Securing Compliance: Seven Case Studies, 1990; (with M. Trebilcock and K. Roach) Regulating Traffic Safety, 1990; Rough Justice: Essays on Crime in Literature, 1991; (with Roach) Cases and Materials on Criminal Law and Procedure, 7th ed., 1994, 8th ed., 1997; The Death of Old Man Rice: A True Story of Criminal Justice in America, 1994; A Place Apart: Judicial Independence and Accountability in Canada, 1995; Controlling Misconduct in the Military, 1997; The University of Toronto: A History, 2002. **Address:** Faculty of Law, University of Toronto, 78 Queen's Park, Toronto, ON, Canada M5S 2C5.

FRIEDLAND, William H(erbert). American, b. 1923. **Genres:** Agriculture/Forestry, Food and Wine, Industrial relations. **Career:** Professor Emeritus of Community Studies and Sociology, University of California, Santa Cruz (Professor from 1969). Assistant Professor, and Associate Professor, Cornell University, Ithaca, NY, 1961-69. **Publications:** Unions and Industrial Relations in Underdeveloped Countries, 1963; Vuta Kamba: The Development of Trade Unions in Tanganyika, 1969; (with I.L. Horowitz) The Knowledge Factory, 1970; (with D. Nelkin) Migrant: Agriculture America's Northeast, 1971; (with A. Barton and R. Thomas) Manufacturing Green Gold: Capital, Labor, and Technology in the Lettuce Industry, 1981; Revolutionary Theory, 1982. EDITOR: (with C.G. Rosberg) African Socialism, 1964; (with F. Buttel, L. Busch, & A. Rudy) Toward a New Political Economy of Agriculture, 1991; (with A. Bonnano, L. Busch, L. Gouveia, and E. Mingione) From Columbus to Conagra: The Globalization of Agriculture and Food, 1994. **Address:** College Eight, University of California, Santa Cruz, CA 95064, U.S.A. **Online address:** friedla@ucsc.edu

FRIEDLANDER, Albert H(oschander). See Obituaries.

FRIEDLANDER, Henry (Egon). American (born Germany), b. 1930. **Genres:** History. **Career:** American History Association, staff member of war document project, 1957-58; Louisiana State University, New Orleans, instructor in history, 1958-64; McMaster University, assistant professor, 1964-67; University of Missouri, St. Louis, assistant professor, 1967-70; City College, NYC, assistant professor of history, 1970-72, assistant professor of Jewish studies, 1972-; Brooklyn College, City University of New York, professor of history in Judaic Studies Program. **Publications:** (ed. with G. Schwab) Detente in Historical Perspective: The First CUNY Conference on History and Politics, c. 1975; (ed. with S. Milton) The Holocaust: Ideology, Bureaucracy, and Genocide-The San Jose Papers, 1980; (ed. with Milton) Archives of the Holocaust: An International Collection of Selected Documents, 1989; The German Revolution of 1918, 1992; The Origins of Nazi Genocide: From Euthanasia to the Final Solution, 1995. Contributor of articles and reviews to periodicals. **Address:** Department of Judaic Studies, 3111 James Hall, Brooklyn College, City University of New York, 2900 Bedford Ave., Brooklyn, NY 11210, U.S.A.

FRIEDLANDER, Michael W. South African, b. 1928. **Genres:** Physics, Astronomy, Sciences. **Career:** University of Cape Town, Cape Town, South Africa, junior lecturer in physics, 1951 and 1952; University of Bristol, Bristol, England, research associate in physics, 1954-56; Washington University, St. Louis, MO, assistant professor, 1956-61, associate professor, 1961-67, professor of physics, 1967-. Imperial College of Science and Technology, London, visiting professor, 1962-63 and 1971. **Publications:** The Conduct of Science, 1972; Astronomy, 1985; Cosmic Rays, 1986; At the Fringes of Science, 1995; A Thin Cosmic Rain, 2000. **Address:** Department of Physics, Washington University, St. Louis, MO 63130, U.S.A.

FRIEDLANDER, Shems. American. **Genres:** Art/Art history. **Career:** Visual artist, educator, poet, filmmaker, and Islamic scholar. Parsons School of Design, New York, NY, professor of editorial communication, advertising, and design, 1987-88; American University, Cairo, Egypt, began in 1992, became senior lecturer in journalism and mass communication and founding director of the Apple Center for Graphic Communications, 1994-. Sony Gallery, chair of international advisory board; worked in New York, NY, as a designer and art director for various publications. Has had several photography and painting exhibitions, including ones in New York and Cairo. **Publications:** The Whirling Dervishes, Being an Account of the Sufi Order Known as the Mevlevis and Its Founder the Poet and Mystic Mevlana Jalalu'ddin Rumi, 1992, reprinted as Rumi and the Whirling Dervishes: Be-

ing an Account of the Sufi Order Known as the Mevlevis and Its Founder the Poet and Mystic Mevlana Jalalu'ddin Rumi, 2003; Submission: Sayings of the Prophet Muhammad, hadith notations by Al-Hajj Shaikh Muzaffereddin, 1977; Ninety-Nine Names of Allah: The Beautiful Names, calligraphy by Hamid al-Amidi, Arabic and Turkish translation by Tevfik Topuzoglu, 1978; When You Hear Hoofbeats, Think of a Zebra: Talks on Sufism, 1987; Sunlight, Poems, and Other Words, 1997; Rumi: The Hidden Treasure, 2001. Writer, producer, and director of documentary films. **Address:** c/o Author Mail, Parabola, 656 Broadway, New York, NY 10012, U.S.A. **Online address:** shem656 Broadways_f@aucegypt.edu

FRIEDMAN, Alan Warren. American, b. 1939. **Genres:** Literary criticism and history. **Career:** Professor of English, University of Texas, Austin, 1976- (Instructor, 1964-66; Assistant Professor, 1966-69; Associate Professor, 1969-76; Chair, Faculty Senate, 1987-89). **Publications:** Lawrence Durrell and The Alexandria Quartet: Art for Love's Sake, 1970; Multivalance: The Moral Quality of Form in the Modern Novel, 1978; William Faulkner, 1984; Fictional Death and the Modernist Enterprise, 1994. EDITOR: Forms of Modern British Fiction: A Symposium, 1975; (ed. with C. Rossman) Mario Vargas Llosa: A Collection of Critical Essays, 1978; (with C. Rossman and D. Sherzer) Beckett Translating/Translating Beckett, 1987; (with E. Carton) Situating College English: Lessons from an American University, 1996; Beckett in Black and Red: The Translations for Nancy Cunard's Negro Anthology, 2000. **Address:** Dept. of English, University of Texas, 1 University Station - B5000, Austin, TX 78712, U.S.A. **Online address:** friedman@uts.cc.utexas.edu

FRIEDMAN, B(ernard) H(arper). American, b. 1926. **Genres:** Novels, Novellas/Short stories, Plays/Screenplays, Art/Art history, Literary criticism and history, Biography. **Career:** Cornell University, Ithaca, New York, lecturer, 1966-67. **Publications:** Jackson Pollock: Energy Made Visible, 1972; Alfonso Ossorio, 1973; Gertrude Vanderbilt Whitney, 1978; Give My Regards to Eighth Street: Essays and Lectures of Morton Feldman, 2000; (ed.) School of New York, 1959. NOVELS: Circles, reprinted as I Need to Love, 1962; Yarborough, 1964; Whispers, 1972; Museum, 1974; Almost a Life, 1975; The Polygamist, 1981. SHORT STORIES: Coming Close, 1982; Between the Flags, 1990; Swimming Laps (and meditations), 1999. **Address:** 439 E 51st St, New York, NY 10022, U.S.A.

FRIEDMAN, Benjamin M. American, b. 1944. **Genres:** Economics. **Career:** Federal Reserve Bank of New York, NYC, research assistant, 1968; Federal Reserve Bank of Boston, Boston, MA, staff consultant, 1968-69, consultant to the president, 1969-71; Federal Reserve Board, assistant to the director of the division of research and statistics, 1969, staff member of the federal open market committee subcommittee on the directive, 1969-70; Morgan Stanley and Co., economist, 1971-72; Harvard University, Cambridge, MA, assistant professor, 1972-76, associate professor, 1976-80, professor of economics, 1980-89, William Joseph Maier Professor of Political Economy, 1989-, economics department chair, 1991-94; writer. **Publications:** Economic Stabilization Policy: Methods in Optimization, 1975; Monetary Policy in the United States: Design and Implementation, Association of Reserve City Bankers, 1981; Day of Reckoning: The Consequences of American Economic Policy under Reagan and After, 1988; (with J. Agell and M. Persson) Does Debt Management Policy Matter?, 1992. EDITOR & CONTRIBUTOR: New Challenges to the Role of Profit, 1978; The Changing Roles of Debt and Equity in Financing U.S. Capital Formation, 1982; Corporate Capital Structures in the United States, 1985; Financing Corporate Capital Formation, 1986; (with F.H. Hahn) Handbook of Monetary Economics, 1990. **Address:** Department of Economics, Littauer Center 127, Cambridge, MA 02138, U.S.A.

FRIEDMAN, Bonnie. American. **Genres:** Adult non-fiction. **Career:** Teacher and writer. Taught writing courses at Dartmouth College, New York University, University of Iowa, and Drew University. **Publications:** Writing Past Dark: Envy, Fear, Distraction, and Other Dilemmas in the Writer's Life, 1993; The Thief of Happiness: The Story of an Extraordinary Psychotherapy, 2002. Work represented in anthologies and textbooks. Contributor to newspapers and magazines. **Address:** c/o Beacon Press, 25 Beacon St, Boston, MA 02108, U.S.A.

FRIEDMAN, Bruce Jay. American, b. 1930. **Genres:** Novels, Novellas/Short stories, Plays/Screenplays. **Career:** Magazine Mgmt. Co., publrs., NYC, editorial director, 1953-64. **Publications:** Stern, 1962; Far from the City of Class and Other Stories, 1963; Mother's Kisses, 1964; (ed.) Black Humor, 1965; 23 Pat O'Brian Movies, 1966; Black Angels, 1966; Scuba Duba: A Tense Comedy, 1967; Steambath (play), 1970; The Dick, 1970; About Harry Towns, 1975; The Lonely Guy's Book of Life, 1979; Let's

Hear It for a Beautiful Guy, 1984; Tokyo Woes, 1985; The Current Climate, 1989; The Slightly Older Guy, 1995; Have You Spoken to Any Jews Lately? (play), 1995; Collected Short Fiction of Bruce Jay Friedman, 1996; A Father's Kisses, 1996; Even the Rhinos Were Nymphos (essays), 2000; Violencia, 2001. **Address:** 252 Seventh Ave (5-G), New York, NY 10001, U.S.A.

FRIEDMAN, C(elia) S. American, b. 1957. **Genres:** Science fiction/Fantasy. **Career:** Author. Taught university-level costume design; designs period dress patterns. **Publications:** In Conquest Born, 1986; The Madness Season, 1990; This Alien Shore, 1998. COLDFIRE TRILOGY: Black Sun Rising, 1991; When True Night Falls, 1993; Crown of Shadows, 1995. **Address:** c/o Author Mail, DAW Books, 375 Hudson St., New York, NY 10014, U.S.A. **Online address:** csfriedman@erols.com

FRIEDMAN, David F. Also writes as Davis Freeman. American, b. 1923. **Genres:** Film. **Career:** Worked as motion picture booker, carnival agent, and projectionist, 1940-44; Paramount Pictures Corp., press agent in Chicago, IL, New York City, Atlanta, GA, and Charlotte, NC, 1946-56; Friedman-Lewis Productions/Modern Film Distributors, Chicago partner, 1956-64; Entertainment Ventures, Inc., Los Angeles, CA, president, 1964-89; writer. Producer of 38 screenplays, under pseudonym Davis Freeman. **Publications:** (with D. DeNevi) A Youth in Babylon: Confessions of a Trash Film King, 1990; (with R. Arledge) Dynamic Fund Raising Projects, 1992. **Address:** PO Box 1910, Anniston, AL 36202, U.S.A.

FRIEDMAN, Debra. American, b. 1955. **Genres:** Children's non-fiction. **Career:** Art photographer, 1980-. **Publications:** Picture This: Fun Photography and Crafts, 2003. Creator of brochures and posters for corporate and civic clients. **Address:** 18 Langford Ave., Toronto, ON, Canada M4J 3E3.

FRIEDMAN, Kinky. American. **Genres:** Mystery/Crime/Suspense. **Career:** Singer and songwriter. **Publications:** Greenwich Killing Time, 1986; A Case of Lone Star, 1987; When the Cat's Away, 1988; Frequent Flyer, 1989; Musical Chairs, 1990; Elvis, Jesus and Coca-Cola, 1993; Armadillos and Old Lace, 1994; Spanking Watson, 1999; The Mile High Club, 2000; Stepping on a Rainbow, 2001; Kinky Friedman's Guide to Texas Etiquette, 2001; Meanwhile Back at the Ranch, 2002; Kill Two Birds and Get Stoned, 2003. **Address:** c/o Esther Newberg, International Creative Management, 8942 Wilshire Blvd, Beverly Hills, CA 90211, U.S.A. **Online address:** www.KinkyFriedman.com

FRIEDMAN, Lawrence M. American, b. 1930. **Genres:** Education, Law. **Career:** Stanford University, California, professor of law, 1968-, and Kirkwood Professor, 1976-. **Publications:** Contract Law in America, 1965; Government and Slum Housing: A Century of Frustration, 1968; A History of American Law, 1973, 2nd ed., 1985; The Legal System: A Social Science Perspective, 1975; Law and Society: An Introduction, 1977; (with R.V. Percival) The Roots of Justice: Crime and Punishment in Alameda County, California, 1870-1910, 1981; American Law, 1984, 2nd ed., 1998; Total Justice, 1985; Your Time Will Come, 1985; The Republic of Choice, 1990; Crime and Punishment in American History, 1993; The Horizontal Society, 1999; Law in America: A Short History, 2002; American Law in the Twentieth Century, 2002. EDITOR: (with S. Macaulay) Law and the Behavioral Sciences, 1969; (with H.N. Scheiber) American Law and Constitutional Order, 1978; (with J. Merryman and D. Clark) Law and Social Change in Mediterranean Europe and Latin America, 1980; (with S. Macauley and J. Stookey) Law and Society: Readings on the Social Study of Law, 1995; (with H.N. Scheiber) Legal Culture and the Legal Profession, 1996. **Address:** Stanford Law School, Stanford, CA 94305, U.S.A.

FRIEDMAN, Lawrence S(amuel). American, b. 1936. **Genres:** Literary criticism and history. **Career:** Stephens College, Columbia, MO, instructor in humanities, 1965; Indiana University-Purdue University, Fort Wayne, IN, assistant professor, then associate professor and later professor, 1965-. Fulbright lecturer in Ghent, Belgium, 1968-69; Timisoara, Romania, 1971-72; Yogyakarta, Indonesia, 1988-89; and Singapore, 1992-93 and 1993-94. Visiting professor, Warsaw University, Poland, 1979-81; Purdue University lecturer on Shakespeare, Oxford, England, 1995. **Publications:** Understanding Isaac Bashevis Singer, 1988; Understanding Cynthia Ozick, 1991; William Golding, 1993; The Cinema of Martin Scorsese, 1997. Contributor to books and periodicals. **Address:** Indiana University-Purdue University, Department of English and Linguistics, Fort Wayne, IN 46805, U.S.A.

FRIEDMAN, Matthew. Canadian. **Genres:** Writing/Journalism. **Career:** Journalist and educator. InternetWeek, became associate editor; Concordia University, Journalism Department, served as teacher of computer-assisted reporting. Speaker on hate propaganda and information freedom. **Publications:** Fuzzy Logic: Dispatches from the Information Revolution, 1997. Contributor of articles on computers and information technology to newspapers and periodicals. **Address:** c/o Vehicule Press, P.O.B. 125, Place du Parc Station, Montreal, QC, Canada H2W 2M9. **Online address:** mwf@total.net

FRIEDMAN, Milton. American, b. 1912. **Genres:** Economics. **Career:** Paul Snowden Russell Distinguished Service Professor Emeritus of Economics, University of Chicago, 1983- (Associate Professor, 1946-48; Professor, 1948-63; Paul Snowden Russell Distinguished Service Professor, 1963-83). Sr. Research Fellow, Hoover Institution, Stanford, CA, 1976-. Associate Economist, National Resources Committee, 1935-37; Member of Research Staff, National Bureau of Economic Research, 1937-45, 1948-81; Visiting Professor of Economics, University of Wisconsin, Madison, 1940-41; Principal Economist, Division of Tax Research, U.S. Treasury Dept., 1941-43; Associate Director, Statistical Research Group, Division of War Research, Columbia University, NYC, 1943-45; Associate Professor, University of Minnesota, Minneapolis, 1945-46; Columnist and Contributing Ed., Newsweek, NYC, 1966-84. **Publications:** (with S. Kuznets) Income from Independent Professional Practice, 1946; (with others) Sampling Inspection, 1948; Essays in Positive Economics, 1953; (ed.) Studies in the Quantity Theory of Money, 1956; A Theory of the Consumption Function, 1957; A Program for Monetary Stability, 1960; Capitalism and Freedom, 1962; Price Theory: A Provisional Text, 1962; (with A.J. Schwartz) A Monetary History of the United States, 1867-1960, 1963; (with R.V. Roosa) The Balance of Payments, 1967; Dollars and Deficits, 1968; The Optimum Quantity of Money and Other Essays, 1969; (with W.W. Heller) Monetary versus Fiscal Policy, 1969; (with A.J. Schwartz) Monetary Statistics of the United States, 1970; A Theoretical Framework for Monetary Analysis, 1971; (with W.J. Cohen) Social Security: Universal or Selective?, 1972; An Economist's Protest: Columns on Political Economy, 1972, 1975, 1983; Money and Economic Development, 1973; Tax Limitation, Inflation and the Role of Government, 1978; (with R. Friedman) Free to Choose, 1980; (with A.J. Schwartz) Monetary Trends in the United States and the United Kingdom, 1982; (with R.D. Friedman) Tyranny of the Status Quo, 1984; Money Mischief, 1992; (with T.S. Szasz) Friedman & Szasz on Liberty and Drugs, 1992; (with R.D. Friedman) Two Lucky People, 1998. **Address:** Hoover Institution, 434 Galvez Mall, Stanford, CA 94305-6010, U.S.A.

FRIEDMAN, Norman. American, b. 1925. **Genres:** Poetry, Literary criticism and history, Psychology. **Career:** University of Connecticut, Storrs, Dept. of English, Instructor to Associate Professor, 1952-63; New School for Social Research, NYC, 1964-66; Queens College, City University of New York, Flushing, Associate Professor to Professor, 1963-88, Professor Emeritus of English, 1988-. Gestalt Therapy Center of Queens, Flushing, Executive Director, 1984-; Gestalt Center for Psychotherapy & Training, NYC, Academic Director, 1996-2000, Executive Co-director, 2000-03, Academic Consultant, 2003-; also psychotherapist in private practice. Fulbright Lectureship, Nantes and Nice, France, 1966-67; E.E. Cummings Society, Co-ordinator, Spring (journal), Editor. **Publications:** E.E. Cummings: The Art of His Poetry, 1960; (with C.A. McLaughlin) Poetry: An Introduction to Its Form and Art, 1961; (with C.A. McLaughlin) Logic, Rhetoric, and Style, 1963; E.E. Cummings: The Growth of a Writer, 1964; (ed.) E.E. Cummings: A Collection of Critical Essays, 1972; Form and Meaning in Fiction, 1975; The Magic Badge: Poems 1953-1984, 1984; The Intrusions of Love: Poems, 1992; (Re)Valuing Cummings: Further Essays on the Poet, 1962-1993, 1996. **Address:** 33-54 164th St, Flushing, NY 11358-1442, U.S.A. **Online address:** eecspringnf@aol.com

FRIEDMAN, Paul (Alan). American, b. 1937. **Genres:** Novels, Novellas/Short stories. **Career:** Professor, University of Illinois, Urbana (member of the faculty, since 1968). Assistant Professor, University of Wisconsin, Stevens Point, 1964-68. **Publications:** STORIES: And If Defeated Allege Fraud, 1971; Serious Trouble, 1986. Author of articles. **Address:** 310 W. Illinois St, Urbana, IL 61801, U.S.A.

FRIEDMAN, Philip (J.). American. **Genres:** Novels, Plays/Screenplays. **Career:** Writer and lawyer. Called to the bar in New York. The High Frontier Co., general partner and chief executive officer, 1979-84; Sovereign International Inc., president and chief executive officer, 1988-89; Learning in Focus Inc., director, 1993-; MaxiVision Cinema Technology, senior vice president and general counsel, member of the board, 1998-2003. Photojournalist and portrait photographer, with work published in books and periodicals. **Publications:** NOVELS: Rage, 1972; Termination Order, 1979; Wall of Silence (Act of Love, Act of War), 1979; Reasonable Doubt, 1990; Inadmissible Evidence, 1992; Grand Jury, 1996; No Higher Law, 1999.

OTHER: (with D. Kleinman) Rage (screenplay), 1972; (with G. Eisen) The Pilates Method of Physical and Mental Conditioning, 1980; The Story of Billy Clay (television series), 1987. Also creator, with Kleinman, of the short film The Applicant. Contributor to periodicals. **Address:** c/o Michael Rudell, Franklin, Weinrib, Rudell & Vassallo, 488 Madison Ave, New York, NY 10022, U.S.A.

FRIEDMAN, Ron. American, b. 1943. **Genres:** Law. **Career:** Self-employed real estate attorney in State College, PA. **Publications:** Pennsylvania Guide to Real Estate Licensing Examinations, 1981; (with Henszey) Real Estate Law, 2nd ed., 1982; (with Henszey) Protecting Your Sales Commission, 1982; Pennsylvania Landlord-Tenant Law and Practice, 1988, 2nd ed., 1994; And Nothing But the Truth (novel), 1995. **Address:** P.O. Box 10362, State College, PA 16805, U.S.A.

FRIEDMAN, Ronald S(amuel). American, b. 1962. **Genres:** Chemistry. **Career:** Harvard-Smithsonian Center for Astrophysics, research assistant, 1984-89; University of Minnesota-Twin Cities, Minneapolis, postdoctoral research associate in chemistry, 1989-91; Indiana University Purdue University Fort Wayne, assistant professor, 1991-97, associate professor of chemistry, 1997-. University of Michigan, visiting assistant professor, 1996, visiting associate professor, 1997; Technion-Israel Institute of Technology, visiting associate professor, 1999. **Publications:** (with P.W. Atkins) Molecular Quantum Mechanics, with solutions manual, 3rd ed, 1997. Contributor to books and scientific journals. **Address:** Dept of Chemistry, Indiana University Purdue University, Fort Wayne, 2101 Coliseum Blvd E, Fort Wayne, IN 46805, U.S.A. **Online address:** friedmar@ipfw.edu

FRIEDMAN, Rosemary. Also writes as Robert Tibber, Rosemary Tibber. British, b. 1929. **Genres:** Novels, Inspirational/Motivational Literature. **Publications:** NOVELS: The Life Situation, 1977; The Long Hot Summer, 1980; Proofs of Affection, 1982; A Loving Mistress, 1983; Rose of Jericho, 1984; A Second Wife, 1986; To Live in Peace, 1987; An Eligible Man, 1989; Golden Boy, 1994; Vintage, 1996; Intensive Care, 2001. AS ROBERT TIBBER: No White Coat, 1957; Love on My List, 1959; We All Fall Down, 1960; Patients of a Saint, 1961; The Fraternity, 1963; The Commonplace Day, 1964; Aristide, 1966; The General Practice, 1967. AS ROSEMARY TIBBER: Practice Makes Perfect, 1969. OTHER: The Writing Game, 1999. **Address:** 3 Cambridge Gate Apt 5, Regent's Park NW1 4JX, England. **Online address:** RosemaryFriedman@hotmail.com

FRIEDMAN, Thomas L(oren). American, b. 1953. **Genres:** International relations/Current affairs. **Career:** United Press International, Staff Correspondent in London, 1978-79, Middle East Correspondent, Beirut, 1979-81; New York Times, Washington, D.C., Business Reporter, 1981-82, Beirut Bureau Chief, 1982-84, Jerusalem Bureau Chief, 1984-89, Chief Diplomatic Correspondent, 1989-95, Foreign Affairs Columnist, 1995-. Recipient of many awards including Overseas Press Club Award, 1980; Pulitzer Prize, 1983, 1988. **Publications:** From Beirut to Jerusalem, 1989; Israel: A Photography, 1998; The Lexus and the Olive Tree, 1999; Longitudes and Attitudes, 2002. **Address:** c/o New York Times, 1627 I St NW, Washington, DC 20006, U.S.A.

FRIEDMANN, Patty. American, b. 1946. **Genres:** Novels, Novellas/Short stories, Humor/Satire. **Career:** Writer. **Publications:** Too Smart to Be Rich (humor), 1988. NOVELS: The Exact Image of Mother, 1991; Eleanor Rushing, 1999; Odds, 2000; Secondhand Smoke, 2002 . Contributor of short stories and reviews to periodicals and newspapers. **Address:** 8330 Sycamore Pl, New Orleans, LA 70118, U.S.A. **Online address:** afreelunch@aol.com

FRIEDMANN, Yohanan. Israeli (born Czech Republic), b. 1936. **Genres:** History, Theology/Religion. **Career:** Associate Professor, then Professor, Institute of Asian and African Studies, Hebrew University, Jerusalem, 1966- (Dean, Faculty of Humanities, 1985-88). Israel Academy of Sciences and Humanities, member, 1999-. **Publications:** Shaykh Ahmad Sirhindi: An Outline of His Thought and a Study of His Image in the Eyes of Posterity, 1971; Prophecy Continuous: Aspects of Ahmadi Religious Thought and Its Medieval Background, 1989; (trans.) The History of Tabari: The Battle of al-Qadisiyya and the Conquest of Syria and Palestine, 1992; Tolerance and Coercion in Islam: Interfaith Relations in the Muslim Tradition, 2003. **Address:** Institute of Asian and African Studies, Hebrew University, Jerusalem, Israel. **Online address:** msyfried@mscc.huji.ac.il

FRIEDRICH, Paul. American, b. 1927. **Genres:** Poetry, Anthropology/Ethnology, Language/Linguistics. **Career:** Faculty member, University of Chicago, since 1962. Faculty member, Harvard University Cambridge, Massachusetts, 1957-58, and University of Pennsylvania, Philadelphia, 1959-62.

Publications: Proto-Indo-European Trees, 1970; Agrarian Revolt in a Mexican Village, 1970, 1978; The Tarascan Suffixes of Locative Space: Meaning and Morphotactics, 1971; Neighboring Leaves Ride This Wind, 1976; The Meaning of Aphrodite, 1978; Language, Context, and the Imagination, 1979; Bastard Moons, 1979; Redwing, 1982; The Language Parallax, 1986; The Princes of Naranja, 1987; (co-ed.) Russia and Eurasia/China, 1994; Music in Russian Poetry, 1997. **Address:** 1126 East 59th St, Chicago, IL 60637, U.S.A.

FRIEL, Brian. Irish, b. 1929. **Genres:** Novels, Novellas/Short stories, Plays/Screenplays. **Career:** Full-time writer, 1960-. Co-Founder of Field Day Theatre Co., Northern Ireland, 1980. **Publications:** A Saucer of Larks (short stories), 1962; The Enemy Within, 1962; Philadelphia, Here I Come!, 1964; The Gold in the Sea (short stories), 1966; The Loves of Cass McGuire, 1966; Lovers: Part I: Winners: Part II: Losers, 1967; Crystal and Fox, 1968; The Mundy Scheme, 1969; The Gentle Island, 1971; The Freedom of the City, 1973; Volunteers, 1975; Faith Healer, 1976; Living Quarters, 1977; Selected Stories, 1979; Aristocrats, 1979; Translations, 1981; The Diviner (short stories), 1982; The Communication Cord, 1983; Selected Plays of Brian Friel, 1986; Fathers and Sons (after Turgenev), 1987; (ed.) The Last of the Name, 1987; Making History, 1988; Dancing at Lughnasa, 1990; The London Vertigo, 1990; A Month in The Country, 1992; Wonderful Tennessee, 1993; Molly Sweeney, 1994; Give Me Your Answer, Do!, 1997; Plays Two, 1999; The Yalta Game, 2001; Afterplay, 2002; Performances, 2003. TRANSLATOR: Three Sisters, 1981; Uncle Vanya. **Address:** Drumaweir House, Greencastle, Donegal, Ireland.

FRIEND, Dorie. See **FRIEND, Theodore (Wood), (III).**

FRIEND, Theodore (Wood), (III). Also writes as Dorie Friend. American, b. 1931. **Genres:** Novels, History. **Career:** State University of New York at Buffalo, assistant professor to professor of history, 1959-73; Swarthmore College, Swarthmore, PA, president, 1973-82; Eisenhower Exchange Fellowships Inc., Philadelphia, PA, trustee, 1982-, president, 1984-96; Philadelphia Committee on Foreign Relations, member, 1973-, chairman, 1986-2000; Foreign Policy Research Institute, senior fellow, 1997-; U.S.-Indonesia Society, board of advisers, 1999-. **Publications:** Between Two Empires: The Ordeal of the Philippines, 1965; (as Dorie Friend) Family Laundry: A Novel, 1986; The Blue-Eyed Enemy: Japan against the West in Java and Luzon, 1942-1945, 1988; Indonesian Destinies, 2003. **Address:** 264 S Radnor-Chester Rd, Villanova, PA 19085, U.S.A.

FRIENDLY, Alfred, Jr. American, b. 1938. **Genres:** Documentaries/Reportage, Writing/Journalism. **Career:** New York Times, NYC, correspondent; Newsweek, NYC, worked as correspondent and bureau chief in Moscow. Writer on health and environmental issues for the U.S. Congress and the World Bank. **Publications:** (with R.L. Goldfarb) Crime and Publicity: The Impact of News on the Administration of Justice, 1967; (ed. with E. Yankelevich) Andrei D. Sakharov, Alarm and Hope, 1978; (with M. Feshbach) Ecocide in the USSR: Health and Nature under Siege, 1992; Editor, Gribkov, Anatoli I., and William Y. Smith, Operation ANADYR: U.S. and Soviet Generals Recount the Cuban Missile Crisis, 1994. **Address:** c/o Newsweek Inc., 251 W. 57th St., New York, NY 10019, U.S.A.

FRIESEL, Evyatar. Israeli (born Germany), b. 1930. **Genres:** History, Theology/Religion, Cultural/Ethnic topics, Autobiography/Memoirs. **Career:** Ben Gurion University of the Negev, Beer Sheva, Israel, professor, 1965-77; Hebrew University of Jerusalem, Jerusalem, Israel, professor of Jewish history, 1975-95; Hochschule fuer Juedische Studien, Heidelberg, Germany, professor, 1989-90; writer. **Publications:** The Zionist Movement in the United States, 1898-1914, 1970; Zionist Policy after the Balfour Declaration, 1917-1922, 1977; Atlas of Modern Jewish History, 1990; The Days and the Seasons (memoirs), 1996. **Address:** Klausner St. 7, Apt. 6, 93388 Jerusalem, Israel.

FRIESEN, Bernice (Sarah Anne). Canadian, b. 1966. **Genres:** Children's fiction, Novellas/Short stories, Poetry. **Career:** Department of Art, University of Saskatchewan, lab assistant, 1986-87; A.K.A. Gallery, Saskatoon, Saskatchewan, project coordinator of "26 and Under: Young Saskatoon Artists", 1987; Y.W.C.A., Saskatoon, art class instructor, 1988; Mendel Art Gallery, Saskatoon, instructor of "Clue Into Art", 1989, instructor of children's color class, 1993; Estevan National Exhibition Centre, art educator, 1990-91; Valley Action Industries, Rosthern, Saskatchewan, junior group home operator, 1992-93; freelance writer, 1995-. Art work has been shown in exhibitions. Illustrator for books and periodicals. **Publications:** The Seasons Are Horses, 1995; Sex, Death, and Naked Men, 1998. Contributor to anthologies. Writer for CBC Radio broadcasts. Contributor to periodicals. **Address:** c/o Thistledown Press, 633 Main St., Saskatoon, SK, Canada S7H 0J8.

FRIGSTAD, David B. American, b. 1954. **Genres:** Marketing. **Career:** Market Intelligence, founder, 1980-93; Frost & Sullivan, Mountain View, CA, chairperson, 1993-. **Publications:** Venture Capital Proposal Package, 1989; Know Your Market, 1991; Customer Engineering, 1993; Market Research in High Technology, 1993; Market Engineering in Health Care, 1996; Competitor Engineering, 1996; Market Research and Forecasting in Healthcare Industries, 1996. **Address:** Frost & Sullivan, 7550 IH 10 West, Ste. 400, San Antonio, TX 78229, U.S.A.

FRINDALL, Bill. (William Howard Frindall). British, b. 1939. **Genres:** Recreation, Sports/Fitness. **Career:** Lutterworth Press, London, England, assistant production manager, 1958-59; Legal and General Assurance Society, city branch, London, life assurance inspector trainee, 1965-66; free-lance cricket statistician, writer, editor, and broadcaster, 1966-. Founder and chairman of the Maltamaniacs (a cricket team). President of British Blind Sport, 1984-. The Playfair Cricket Annual, editor/compiler, 1986-. **Publications:** The Kaye Book of Cricket Records, 1968; Frindall's Score Book: England versus Australia, 1975, 1975; The Playfair Cricket Quiz Book, 1975; Frindall's Score Book: Australia versus the West Indies, 1975-76, 1976; Frindall's Score Book: England versus the West Indies, 1976, 1976; Frindall's Score Book: England versus Australia, 1977, 1977; The Wisden Book of Test Cricket, 1979, 5th ed., 3 vols., 2000; Frindall's Score Book: Australia versus England, 1978-79, 1979; Frindall's Score Book: Australia versus England and the West Indies, 1979-80, 1980; The Wisden Book of Cricket Records, 1982, 4th ed., 1998; The Guinness Book of Cricket Facts and Feats, 1983, 4th ed., 1995; (with M. Melford) Cricket, 1984; The Wisden Book of Limited-Overs Internationals, 1985; The Carphone Gallery of Cricketers, 1988; England Test Cricketers, 1989; Ten Tests for England, 1989; Gooch's Golden Summer, 1991; A Tale of Two Captains, 1992; Limited-overs International Cricket The Complete Record, 1997; Playfair Cricket World Cup, 1999. **Address:** The Beeches, Blackboard Lane, Urchfont, Devizes, Wilts. SN10 4RD, England. **Online address:** beardedwonder@btinternet. com

FRISBIE, Charlotte J(ohnson). (born United States), b. 1940. **Genres:** Anthropology/Ethnology. **Career:** Anna State Hospital, Anna, IL, social worker, 1968-70, coordinator of Aftercare Program, 1970; Southern Illinois University-Edwardsville, Edwardsville, IL, assistant professor, 1970-73, associate professor, 1973-77, professor of anthropology, 1977-98, professor emeritus, 1999-, chair of anthropology program, 1973-75, 1985-87, 1992-96. Indiana University, guest speaker, 1992; Laurentian University, distinguished lecturer, 1993; Colorado College, guest faculty, 1994; organizer and presenter of workshops and seminars; public speaker. Conducted extensive field research among the Navajos, beginning 1963. Wheelwright Museum, trustee, 1977-80, member of national advisory board, 1980-87; member of American Museum of Natural History and Museum of New Mexico; consultant to Smithsonian Institution, National Park Service, and U.S. Fish and Wildlife Service. Navajo Studies Conference, member of steering committee, 1984-2000, member of board of directors, 2000-; Music Research Institute, member of national academic advisory board, 1985-. Eden Village (retirement community), member of board of directors, 1986-; also works as church organist; volunteer with Senior Fit Program and Faith in Action. **Publications:** Kinaaldá: A Study of the Navaho Girl's Puberty Ceremony, 1967, reprinted with new preface, 1993; Music and Dance Research of Southwestern United States Indians: Past Trends, Present Activities, and Suggestions for Future Research, 1977; (editor, with David P. McAllester) Navajo Blessingway Singer: The Autobiography of Frank Mitchell (1881-1967), 1978, new edition (with introduction by Frisbie), 2003; (editor and contributor) Southwestern Indian Ritual Drama, 1980; (editor, with David M. Brugge, and contributor.) Navajo Religion and Culture: Selected Views; Papers in Honor of Leland C. Wyman, 1982; (editor and contributor) Explorations in Ethnomusicology: Essays in Honor of David P. McAllester, 1986; Navajo Medicine Bundles or Jish: Acquisition, Transmission, and Disposition in the Past and Present, 1987; (editor) Tall Woman: The Life Story of Rose Mitchell, a Navajo Woman, c. 1874-1977, 2001. Contributor to books, articles and reviews to periodicals. **Address:** 5923 Quercus Grove Rd, Edwardsville, IL 62025, U.S.A. **Online address:** cfrisbie@siue.edu

FRISBY, Terence. British, b. 1932. **Genres:** Plays/Screenplays, Autobiography/Memoirs. **Career:** Professional actor, director, and producer, 1957-. **Publications:** The Subtopians, 1964; There's a Girl in My Soup, 1966; The Bandwagon, 1970; It's All Right if I Do It, 1977; Seaside Postcard, 1978; Just Remember Two Things: It's Not Fair and Don't Be Late, 1989; Rough Justice, 1994; Outrageous Fortune (autobiography), 1998; Funny

about Love, 2003. Also films, radio, TV plays, series and comedy series. **Address:** 72 Bishops Mansions, Bishops Park Rd, London SW6 6DZ, England. **Online address:** Terence@tfrisby.wanadoo.co.uk

FRISCH, Walter. (born United States), b. 1951. **Genres:** Music. **Career:** Columbia University, professor, 1982-; writer. **Publications:** (editor) Schubert: Critical and Analytical Studies, 1986; (editor) Brahms and His World, 1990; Brahms and the Principle of Developing Variation, 1993; The Early Works of Arnold Schoenberg, 1893-1908, 1993; Brahms: The Four Symphonies, 1996; (editor) Schoenberg and His World, 1999. **Address:** Department of Music, 621 Dodge Hall, Columbia University, 2960 Broadway, New York, NY 10027, U.S.A.

FRIST, William H. American, b. 1952. **Genres:** Medicine/Health, Politics/Government. **Career:** Licensed to practice medicine in Tennessee and Washington DC; Massachusetts General Hospital, Boston, resident in surgery, 1978-83, research fellow in surgery, 1983, chief resident in cardiothoracic surgery, 1984; Southampton General Hospital, England, senior registrar in cardiothoracic surgery, 1983; Stanford University, Stanford, CA, senior fellow and chief resident in cardiovascular surgery at Cardiac Transplant Service, 1985-86; Vanderbilt University, Nashville, TN, assistant professor of cardiac and thoracic surgery, 1986-93, director of heart and heart-lung transplantation and surgical director of Vanderbilt Multi-Organ Transplant Center and chair of the center's executive committee, 1989-93; Nashville Veterans Administration Hospital, Nashville TN, staff surgeon, 1986-93. U.S. Senator, Tennessee, 1995-, member of Budget; Commerce, Science and Transportation; Foreign Relations; Health, Education, Labor and Pensions; and other committees. Congressional Heart and Stroke Coalition, founder and co-chairman; Senate Republican Medicare Working Group, chair, 1995-96; Alliance for Health Reform, vice chair, 1997-; National Bipartisan Commission for the Future of Medicare, member, 1998-99. **Publications:** Transplant: A Heart Surgeon's Account of the Life-and-Death Dramas of the New Medicine, 1989; Grand Rounds in Transplantation, 1995; Tennessee Senators, 1911-2001: Portraits of Leadership in a Century of Change, 1999. **Address:** U.S. Senate, 416 Russell Senate Office Building, Washington, DC 20510-4205, U.S.A. **Online address:** senator_frist@frist.senate.gov; www.senate.gov/~frist

FRITCHLEY, Alma. British, b. 1954. **Genres:** Mystery/Crime/Suspense. **Career:** Author. **Publications:** LETTY CAMPBELL MYSTERY SERIES: Chicken Run, 1997; Chicken Feed, 1998; Chicken Out, 1999; Chicken Shack, 2000. **Address:** c/o Author Mail, Women's Press, 34 Great Sutton Street, London EC1V 0LQ, England.

FRITH, David (Edward John). British, b. 1937. **Genres:** Autobiography/Memoirs, Sports/Fitness. **Career:** The Cricketer, Kent, England, editor, 1972-78; Wisden Cricket Monthly, Guildford, England, editor, 1979-96; writer. Producer of the videotapes Benson & Hedges Golden Greats: Batsmen and Benson & Hedges Golden Greats: Bowlers. **Publications:** (with John Edrich) Runs in the Family, Paul, 1969; My Dear Victorious Stod: A Biography of A. E. Stoddart, self-published, 1970; The Archie Jackson Story: A Biography, 1974; The Fast Men: A 200-year Cavalcade of Speed Bowlers, 1975; (ed.) Cricket Gallery: Fifty Profiles of Famous Players from "The Cricketer," 1976; England versus Australia: A Pictorial History of the Test Matches since 1877, 1977, 7th edition, 1990; (with Greg Chappell) The Ashes '77, 1977; The Golden Age of Cricket, 1890-1914, 1978; The Ashes '79, 1979; (ed. with Martin Tyler) The Illustrated History of Test Cricket, 1979; Thommo, 1980; (ed.) Ralph Dellor and Doug Ibbotson, A Hundred Years of the Ashes, 1982; The Slow Men, 1984; (with Gerry Wright) Cricket's Golden Summer, 1985; England versus Australia Test Match Records, 1877-1985, 1986; Pageant of Cricket, 1987; Guildford Jubilee, 1938-1988, 1988; By His Own Hand, Paul, 1990; Stoddy's Mission, 1994. **Address:** 6 Beech Lane, Guildown, Guildford, Surrey GU2 5ES, England.

FRITH, Katherine Toland. American, b. 1946. **Genres:** Communications/Media. **Career:** Iowa State University, Ames, teacher of journalism for five years; Pennsylvania State University, University Park, faculty member, c. 1988-, currently associate professor of advertising, past chairperson of advertising program. Fulbright professor in Malaysia, 1986-87, and Indonesia, 1993; Nanyang Technological University, visiting senior fellow, 1996-98; Asian Mass Communication and Information Center, Singapore, member. Worked as an advertising copywriter in NYC, for such firms as J. Walter Thompson, N. W. Ayer, and Grey Advertising. **Publications:** (ed.) Advertising in Asia: Communication, Culture, and Consumption, 1996; (ed.) Undressing the Ad: Reading Culture in Advertising, 1998. Contributor to periodicals. **Address:** 125 Carnegie Bldg., College of Communications, Pennsylvania State University, State College, PA 16801, U.S.A. **Online address:** Katherine@frith.com

FRITSCH, Albert J(oseph). American, b. 1933. **Genres:** Environmental sciences/Ecology, Ethics, Recreation, Theology/Religion, Self help. **Career:** Research Associate, Chemistry Dept., University of Texas, Austin, 1969-70, and Center for Study of Responsive Law, 1970-71; Director, Center for Science in the Public Interest, 1971-77; Director, Appalachia-Science in the Public Interest, 1977-2002. **Publications:** Theology of the Earth, 1972; The Contrasumers: A Citizen's Guide to Resource Conservation, 1974; 99 Ways to a Simple Lifestyle, 1976; Household Pollutants Guide, 1978; Environmental Ethics, 1980; Green Space, 1982; Appalachia: A Meditation, 1986; Renew the Face of the Earth, 1987; Earthen Vessels, 1990; Eco-Church, 1992; Down to Earth Spirituality, 1992; Out of the Waste Land, 1994; Religion in Ecology: Scientists Speak, 1998; Spirituality of Gardening, 2000; Ecotourism in Appalachia: Marketing the Mountains, 2003. **Address:** 719 Woodland Ave, Frankfort, KY 40601-3435, U.S.A.

FRITTS, Mary Bahr. Also writes as Mary Bahr. American, b. 1946. **Genres:** Children's fiction, Young adult fiction, Children's non-fiction, History, Literary criticism and history, Writing/Journalism, Young adult non-fiction, Humor/Satire. **Career:** Presbyterian Medical Center, Denver, medical librarian, 1969-70, registrar of Nursing School, 1971-74; church librarian, 1978-84; Pikes Peak Library District, Penrose Reference Library, information technician, 1990-97; speaker/workshop presenter/mentor, 1990-; New Writers Magazine, columnist, 1991-94; Five Owls, children's book reviewer, 1993-9. **Publications:** The Memory Box, 1992; If Nathan Were Here, 2000; My Brother, 2002. Author of articles, stories, columns, book reviews, poetry, and puzzles. **Address:** 807 Hercules Pl, Colorado Springs, CO 80906-1130, U.S.A.

FRITZ, Jean. American (born People's Republic of China), b. 1915. **Genres:** Children's fiction, Children's non-fiction. **Career:** Research assistant, Silver Burdett Co., NYC, 1938-41; children's librarian, Dobbs Ferry Library, NYC, 1955-57; teacher, Jean Fritz Writer's Workshop, Katonah, NY, 1962-70, and Board of Cooperative Educational Services, Westchester Co., NY, 1971-73; book reviewer, New York Times. **Publications:** Growing Up, 1956; The Animals of Dr. Schweitzer, 1958; San Francisco, 1962; Cast for a Revolution: Some American Friends and Enemies 1728-1814, 1972; And Then What Happened, Paul Revere?, 1973; Why Don't You Get a Horse, Sam Adams?, 1974; Where Was Patrick Henry on the 29th of May?, 1975; Who's That Stepping on Plymouth Rock?, 1975; Will You Sign Here, John Hancock?, 1976; What's the Big Idea, Ben Franklin?, 1976; Can't You Make Them Behave, King George?, 1977; Brendan the Navigator, 1979; Stonewall, 1979; Where Do You Think You're Going, Christopher Columbus?, 1980; Traitor: The Case of Benedict Arnold, 1981; The Double Life of Pocahontas, 1983; China Homecoming, 1985; Make Way for Sam Houston, 1986; Shh! We're Writing the Constitution, 1987; China's Long March, 1988; The Great Little Madison, 1989; Bully for You, Teddy Roosevelt!, 1991; George Washington's Mother, 1992; The Great Adventures of Christopher Columbus, 1992; Around the World in 100 Years, 1993; Harriet Beecher Stowe and the Beecher Preachers, 1994; You Want Women to Vote, Lizzie Stanton?, 1995; Leonardo's Horse, 2001; The Lost Colony, 2003. FICTION: Bunny Hopwell's First Spring, 1954; Help Mr. Willy Nilly, 1955; The Late Spring, 1957; The Cabin Faced West, 1958; (with T. Clute) Champion Dog, Prince Tom, 1958; How to Read a Rabbit, 1959; Brady, 1960; Tap, Tap, Lion-One, Two, Three, 1962; I, Adam, 1963; Magic to Burn, 1964; Early Thunder, 1967; George Washington's Breakfast, 1969; The Man Who Loved Books, 1981; The Good Giants and the Bad Pukwudgies, 1982; Homesick: My Own Story, 1982. READERS: Surprise, 1965; The Train (reader), 1965. **Address:** 50 Bellewood Ave, Dobbs Ferry, NY 10522, U.S.A.

FRITZE, Ronald H. American, b. 1951. **Genres:** Reference. **Career:** Louisiana State University, Baton Rouge, instructor in history, 1981-82; Rice University, Houston, TX, collection development librarian at Fondren Library, 1982-84; Lamar University, Beaumont, TX, assistant professor, 1984-89, associate professor, 1989-95, professor, 1995-96, university professor of history, 1996-. Louisiana State University, research assistant and research associate, between 1979 and 1992; Houston Community College, instructor, 1983-84. Sixteenth Century Studies Conference, secretary, 1997-. Lamar Journal of the Humanities, business manager, 1986-88. **Publications:** (with B. Coutts and L. Vyhnanek) Reference Sources in History: An Introductory Guide, 1990; (with R. Roberts and J. Olson) Reflections on Western Civilization: A Reader, 1990; (ed. in chief) Historical Dictionary of Tudor England, 1991; Legends and Lore of the Americas before 1492: An Encyclopedia of Visitors, Explorers, and Immigrants, 1993; (with Roberts and Olson) Reflections on World Civilization: A Reader, 1993; (ed. with W.B. Robison) Historical Dictionary of Stuart England, 1603-1689, 1996; Travel Legend and Lore: An Encyclopedia, American Bibliographical 1998. Contributor to books and periodicals. **Address:** Department of History, Lamar University, PO Box 10048, Beaumont, TX 77710, U.S.A. **Online address:** fritzerh@hal.lamar.edu

FRITZELL, Peter A(lgren). American, b. 1940. **Genres:** Poetry, Intellectual history, Literary criticism and history, Essays. **Career:** Lawrence University of Wisconsin, Appleton, assistant professor, 1966-73, associate professor, 1973-83, chair of department, 1973-77, 1987-90, professor of English, 1983-2003, Patricia Hamar Boldt Professor of Liberal Studies, 1989-2003, professor emeritus, 2003-; writer. London Study Center, director, 1977-78; Stanford University, visiting professor, 1968, 1974, 1977; Dartmouth College, visiting scholar in environmental studies, 1972-73; University of Wisconsin-Green Bay, lecturer, 1974. **Publications:** Nature Writing and America: Essays upon a Cultural Type, 1990. **Address:** PO Box 599, Appleton, WI 54912-0599, U.S.A. **Online address:** fritzelp@lawrence.edu

FRITZER, Penelope Joan. American, b. 1949. **Genres:** Education, Literary criticism and history. **Career:** State of Florida, Pompano Beach, social worker assigned to Aid to Families with Dependent Children, 1976-77; Broward Community College, Coconut Creek, FL, teacher of English, 1984-86; teacher of English and history at public schools in Broward County, FL, 1986-93; Florida Atlantic University, Davie, professor, 1993-. **Publications:** Jane Austen and Eighteenth-Century Courtesy Books, 1997; Ethnicity and Gender in the Barsetshire Novels of Angela Thirkell, 1999; Social Studies Content for Elementary and Middle School Teachers; Merry Wives: A History of Domestic Humor Writing. Contributor to professional journals. **Address:** Florida Atlantic University, ES221, 2912 College Ave, Davie, FL 33314, U.S.A. **Online address:** fritzer@fau.edu

FRITZSCHE, Peter. American, b. 1959. **Genres:** History. **Career:** University of Illinois at Urbana-Champaign, Urbana, professor of history, 1987-. **Publications:** Rehearsals for Fascism: Populism and Political Mobilization in Weimer Germany, 1990; A Nation of Fliers: German Aviation and the Popular Imagination, 1992; (with K. Hewitt) Berlinwalks, 1994; Reading Berlin 1900, 1996; (with C. Stewart) Imagining the Twentieth Century, 1997. **Address:** Department of History, University of Illinois at Urbana-Champaign, 810 South Wright St., Urbana, IL 61801, U.S.A.

FROHNEN, Bruce (P.). American, b. 1962. **Genres:** Law, Philosophy, Politics/Government. **Career:** National Federation of Independent Business, Sacramento, CA, legislative assistant, 1983-85; Reed College, Portland, OR, visiting assistant professor of political studies, 1988-89; Cornell College, Mount Vernon, IA, visiting assistant professor of political studies, 1989-90; Oglethorpe University, Atlanta, GA, instructor in political science, 1992-93. Cornell University, guest lecturer, 1987. Heritage Foundation, adjunct fellow of Henry Salvatori Center, 1991-93. U.S. Department of Justice, summer law clerk in Office of Policy Development, 1992. Guest on media programs. **Publications:** Virtue and the Promise of Conservatism: The Legacy of Burke and Tocqueville, 1993; New Communitarians and the Crisis of Modern Liberalism, 1996; The American Republic, 2002. Work represented in anthologies. Contributor of articles and reviews to political science journals. **Address:** Ave Maria School of Law, 3475 Plymouth Rd, Ann Arbor, MI 48105-2550, U.S.A.

FROME, Michael. American, b. 1920. **Genres:** Environmental sciences/Ecology, Natural history. **Career:** Washington Post, news reporter, 1945-46; American Forests, columnist, 1966-71; Field and Stream, conservation editor, and columnist, 1968-74; Defenders of Wildlife mag., columnist, 1975-94; Los Angeles Times, columnist, 1977-81. **Publications:** Whose Woods These Are, 1962; Strangers in High Places, 1966, 3rd ed., 1994; Virginia, 1966, 3rd ed., 1971; National Park Guide, annually 1968-; The Varmints, 1970; The Forest Service, 1972; Battle for the Wilderness, 1974, 3rd ed., 1997; (with D. Muench) The National Parks, 1977; Promised Land: Adventures and Encounters in Wild America, 1985, 2nd ed., 1994; Conscience of a Conservationist, 1989; (with D. Muench) Uncommon Places: A Celebration of Appalachian Trail Country, 1991; Regreening the National Parks, 1991; Chronicling the West, 1996; Green Ink, 1998; Greenspeak, 2002. **Address:** 638 N. Powers St, Port Washington, WI 53074-1633, U.S.A.

FROMM, Pete. American, b. 1958. **Genres:** Novels, Novellas/Short stories, Adult non-fiction. **Career:** Lake Mead National Recreation Area, Boulder City, NV, lifeguard supervisor, 1978-81; Idaho Department of Fish and Game, guarded salmon eggs, 1978-79; Grand Teton National Park, Moose, WY, supervisory river ranger, 1982-87; Big Bend National Park, river ranger, 1985; free-lance writer, 1987-. **Publications:** STORIES: The Tall Uncut, 1992; King of the Mountain, 1994; Dry Rain, 1997; Blood Knot, 1998; Night Swimming, 1999. NOVELS: Monkey Tag, 1994; How All This Started, 2000. OTHER: Indian Creek Chronicles: A Winter in the Wilderness (nonfiction), 1993. **Address:** c/o Amy Williams, ICM Agency, 40 W 57th St, New York, NY 10019, U.S.A.

FROMMEL, Christoph Lvitpold. German, b. 1933. **Genres:** Architecture. **Career:** Bibliotheca Hertziana, Rome, Italy, fellow and research assistant,

1959-67, director, 1980-2001; University of Bonn, Germany, professor, 1968-80; University La Sapienta, Rome, professor, 2002-. **Publications:** Die Farnesia und Peruzzis architektonisches Fruehwerk, 1961; Der roemische Palastbau der Hochrenaissance, 1973; Michelangelo und Tommaso de' Cavalieri, 1979; (with others) Raffaello architelto, 1984; The Architectural Drawings of Antonio de Sangallo the Younger and His Circle, Vol. 1, 1993, Vol. 2, 2000, Vol. 3, 2004; La Farnesina, 2003; Architeltura alla corte papale del Rinascimento, 2003; Renaissance Architecture, 2004. **Address:** Bibliotheca Hertziana, Via Gregoriana 28, I-00147 Rome, Italy. **Online address:** cfrommel@libero.it

FROST, Sir David (Paradine). British, b. 1939. **Genres:** Social commentary, Humor/Satire. **Career:** Television performer, producer and actor. Joint Founder, London Weekend Television; Chairman and Chief Executive, David Paradine Ltd., London, 1966-; Joint Deputy Chairman, Equity Enterprises, 1973-. **Publications:** That Was the Week That Was, 1963; How to Live under Labour, 1964; Talking with Frost, 1967; To England with Love, 1967; The Presidential Debate, 1968; The Americans, 1970; Whitlam and Frost, 1974; I Gave Them a Sword, 1978; I Could Have Kicked Myself, 1982; Who Wants to Be a Millionaire?, 1983; (with others) The Mid-Atlantic Companion, 1986; (with others) The Rich Tide, 1986; The World's Shortest Books, 1987; David Frost: An Autobiography - Part One from Congregation to Audiences, 1993. **Address:** David Paradine Ltd, 5 St Mary, Abbots Place, London W8 6LS, England.

FROST, Diane. British, b. 1962. **Genres:** History, Race relations, Sociology. **Career:** University of Central Lancashire, Preston, England, member of historical and critical studies dept. **Publications:** Work and Community among West African Migrant Workers since the Nineteenth Century, 1999. EDITOR: Ethnic Labour and British Imperial Trade: A History of Ethnic Seafarers in the U.K., 1995; (with T. Zack-Williams and A. Thomson) Africa in Crisis: New Challenges and Possibilities, 2001. **Address:** Department of Sociology, The University of Liverpool, Eleanor Rathbone Building, Bedford St. South, Liverpool L69 7ZA, England. **Online address:** dfrost@liv.ac.uk

FROST, Elizabeth. See **FROST-KNAPPMAN, L. Elizabeth.**

FROST, Mark. American, b. 1953. **Genres:** Plays/Screenplays, Novels. **Career:** Novelist and screenwriter. Producer and director for film and television series. **Publications:** SCREENPLAYS: Hill Street Blues (television series), 1981; The Believers, 1987; Twin Peaks (television series), 1990 Storyville, 1992; The Repair Shop, 1998. NOVELS: The List of 7, 1993; The Six Messiahs, 1995. **Address:** c/o William Morrow & Co. Inc., 1350 Avenue of the Americas, New York, NY 10019, U.S.A.

FROST, Shelley. American, b. 1960. **Genres:** Sports/Fitness. **Career:** Peninsula Humane Society, public relations officer, 1988-89; Pets in Need, Redwood City, CA, manager, 1989-94; Frosting on the Cake Productions, Belmont, CA, director and video producer, 1994-. HEN, judge of essay contest, 1990-; CAPE, founder, member of board of directors, 1993-2000, and volunteer. **Publications:** (with A. Troussieux) Throw like a Girl: Discovering the Body, Mind, and Spirit of the Athlete in You!, 2000. VIDEOS: Babymugs!, 1994; Kidstuff with Dick Clark, Real Girls, Real Sports, Old Friends, and Little Patriots. **Address:** 2404 Dekoven, Belmont, CA 94002, U.S.A.

FROST, Stanley Brice. Canadian (born England), b. 1913. **Genres:** Poetry, History, Theology/Religion. **Career:** Director, History of McGill Project, Montreal, 1974-. Professor of Old Testament, 1956-74, Dean of Graduate Studies and Research, 1963-69, and Vice-Principal of Administration and Professional Faculties, 1969-74, McGill University, Montreal. **Publications:** Old Testament Apocalyptic, Its Origin and Growth, 1952; The Beginning of the Promise, Eight Lectures on Genesis, 1960; Patriarchs and Prophets, 1963; Standing and Understanding: A Reappraisal of the Christian Faith, 1969; For the Advancement of Learning: McGill University, 2 vols., 1980-84; The Man in the Ivory Tower: F. Cyril James of McGill, 1991; James McGill of Montreal, 1995. POETRY: (privately published) Something for My Friends, 1993; Days of Grace and Favour, 1994; Drawn at a Venture, 1996; Memoranda: Moments for Recollection, 1999; A Tale of Two Books, 2000; Millennial Melange, 2001; Autumn Harvest, Selected Poems, 2003. **Address:** McGill University, 3459 McTavish St, Montreal, QC, Canada H3A 1Y1.

FROST-KNAPPMAN, L. Elizabeth. Also writes as Elizabeth Frost. American, b. 1943. **Genres:** Women's studies and issues, Trivia/Facts. **Career:** Natural History Press, NYC, editor specializing in anthropology and natural history books, 1970-71; William Collins and Sons, London, England,

editor specializing in natural history titles, 1967-69; Doubleday and Co. Inc., NYC, senior nonfiction editor, 1972-80; William Morrow and Co. Inc., NYC, senior nonfiction editor, 1980-82; New England Publishing Associates Inc. (literary agency), Chester, CT, founder and president, 1983-. Lecturer at New England colleges and universities. **Publications:** (ed. with D. Shrager) The Quotable Lawyer, 1986; (co-author) Women's Suffrage in America: An Eyewitness History, 1992, rev. ed., 2005; The World Almanac of Presidential Quotations, 1993; The ABC-CLIO Companion to Women's Progress in America, 1994; Women's Rights on Trial: 101 Historic Trials from Anne Hutchinson to the Virginia Military Institute Cadets, 1997; (ed.) American Journey: Women in America (CD-ROM). **Address:** New England Publishing Associates Inc., PO Box 5, Chester, CT 06412, U.S.A. **Online address:** nepa@nepa.com

FROUD, Brian. (born England), b. 1947. **Genres:** Young adult fiction. **Career:** Artist, illustrator, creative consultant to films. Work has been exhibited in England and America. **Publications:** The Land of Froud, 1977; (with Alan Lee) Faeries, 1978; The Faeries Pop-Up Book, 1980; Goblins, 1983; (with Terry Jones) The Goblins of Labyrinth: Invented and Illuminated by Brian Froud; Captured and Catalogued by Terry Jones, 1986; (with Charles de Lint) The Dreaming Place, 1990; (with Terry Jones) Lady Cottington's Pressed Fairy Book, 1994; (with Charles de Lint) The Wild Wood, 1994; (with Terry Jones) The Goblin Companion: Invented and Illustrated by Brian Froud; Captured and Catalogued by Terry Jones, 1996; (with Terry Jones) Strange Stains and Mysterious Smells: Quentin Cottington's Journal of Faery Research, 1996; Good Faeries/Bad Faeries, 1998; (with Jessica Macbeth) The Faeries' Oracle, 2000; (with Ari Berk) Brian Froud's the Runes of Elfland: Visions and Stories from the Faerie Alphabet, 2003; (with J. J. Llewellyn) The World of the Dark Crystal, 2003. ILLUSTRATOR: Charles Lamb, A Midsummer Night's Dream, 1972; Margaret Mahy, The Man Whose Mother Was a Pirate, 1972; Margaret Mahy, Ultra-Violet Catastrophe! Or, The Unexpected Walk with Great-Uncle Magnus Pringle, 1975; Mary Norton, Are All the Giants Dead?, 1975, 1997; Alexander Theroux, Master Snickup's Cloak, 1979; Charles De Lint, The Dreaming Place, 1990; Charles De Lint, Brian Froud's Faerielands: The Wild Wood, 1994; Patricia A. McKillip, Brian Froud's Faerielands: Something Rich and Strange, 1994; (Designer) Wendy Froud and Terri Windling, The Winter Child, 2001. **Address:** c/o Author Correspondence, Harry N. Abrams Inc., 110 E. 59th St., New York, NY 10022, U.S.A.

FROY, Harold. See **WATERHOUSE, Keith (Spencer).**

FRUIN, W. Mark. American, b. 1943. **Genres:** Business/Trade/Industry, Administration/Management. **Career:** European Institute of Business Administration, Fontainebleau, France, professor of strategy and management, 1988-92; University of British Columbia, Vancouver, Hong Kong Bank Professor of Asian Research and director of Institute of Asian Research, 1992-96. University of California, Los Angeles, visiting professor, 1991-92; University of Michigan, School of Business, visiting professor, 1996-. **Publications:** Kikkoman: Company, Clan, and Community, 1983; The Japanese Enterprise System: Competitive Strategies and Cooperative Structures, 1992; Knowledge Works, 1997; (ed.) Networks and Markets: Pacific Rim Strategies, 1997. **Address:** 4060 Amaranta Ave., Palo Alto, CA 94306, U.S.A.

FRUM, David. Canadian, b. 1960. **Genres:** Mystery/Crime/Suspense. **Career:** Saturday Night (magazine), Toronto, Ontario, Canada, associate editor, 1988-. Worked as weekly columnist for Toronto Sun, editor at Wall Street Journal, columnist for Forbes, and commentator for National Public Radio. Yale University, New Haven, CT, visiting lecturer, 1987; Speechwriter for George W. Bush. **Publications:** Dead Right, 1994; How We Got Here: The 70s, 2000; The Right Man, 2003. Contributor of articles to periodicals. **Address:** 3111 Foxhall Rd NW, Washington, DC 20016, U.S.A.

FRUTON, Joseph S(tewart). American/Polish, b. 1912. **Genres:** Biology, Chemistry, Autobiography/Memoirs, Bibliography. **Career:** Eugene Higgins Professor Emeritus of Biochemistry, Yale University, New Haven, CT, 1982- (Associate Professor of Physiological Chemistry, 1945-50; Professor of Biochemistry, 1950-57; Eugene Higgins Professor, 1957-82). Associate, Rockefeller Institute for Medical Research, 1934-45. **Publications:** (with S. Simmonds) General Biochemistry, 1953; Molecules and Life: Historical Essays on the Interplay of Chemistry and Biology, 1972; Selected Bibliography of Biographical Data for the History of Biochemistry since 1800, 1974, supplement 1985, 1994; Contrasts in Scientific Style: Research Groups in the Chemical and Biological Sciences, 1990; A Skeptical Biochemist, 1992; Eighty Years, 1994; Proteins, Enzymes, Genes: The Interplay of Chemistry and Biology, 1999; Methods and Styles in the Development of Chemistry, 2002. **Address:** 123 York St, New Haven, CT 06511, U.S.A.

FRY, Andrew C. American, b. 1956. **Genres:** Sports/Fitness. **Career:** Sweep Left Health Club, Lincoln, NE, owner and operator, 1979-85; National Strength and Conditioning Association, editorial assistant, 1986-88; University of Connecticut, Storrs, research coordinator at Human Performance Laboratory, 1988-89, research assistant at Osteoporosis Center, Medical Center, 1989; Ohio University, Athens, instructor in anatomy and physiology, 1992-94; University of Memphis, Memphis, TN, associate professor of human movement sciences and education, 1994-. National Strength and Conditioning Association, certified strength and conditioning specialist, 1985; U.S. Weightlifting Federation, weightlifting coach, 1988, research technician at U.S. Olympic Training Center, 1990; U.S.A.-Weightlifting, chairperson of Sports Science and Research Committee, 1994-. **Publications:** Overtraining in Sport, 1997. Contributor of articles and reviews to professional journals. **Address:** Department of Human Movement Sciences and Education, 135 Roane Field House, University of Memphis, Campus Box 526223, Memphis, TN 38152, U.S.A. **Online address:** fry.andrew@coe.memphis.edu

FRY, Christopher. British, b. 1907. **Genres:** Plays/Screenplays, Poetry, Songs/Lyrics and libretti, Autobiography/Memoirs, Translations. **Career:** Teacher, Bedford Froebel Kindergarten, 1926-27; schoolmaster, Hazelwood School, Limpsfield, Surrey, 1928-31; secretary to H. Rodney Bennett, 1931-32; founding director, Tunbridge Wells Repertory Players, 1932-35; lecturer, and ed. of schs. mag., Dr. Barnardo's Homes, 1934-39; director, 1940, and visiting director, 1945-46, Oxford Playhouse. **Publications:** Open Door, 1936; The Boy with a Cart: Cuthman, Saint of Sussex, 1938; Thursday's Child: A Pageant, 1939; Phoenix Too Frequent, 1946; The Firstborn, 1946; The Lady's Not for Burning, 1948; Thor, with Angels, 1948; Venus Observed, 1950; A Sleep of Prisoners, 1951; The Beggar's Opera (screenplay), 1953; The Queen Is Crowned (coronation film), 1953; The Dark Is Light Enough: A Winter Comedy, 1954; Ben Hur (screenplay), 1959; Curtmantle, 1961; Barabbas (screenplay), 1962; The Boat That Mooed, 1966; The Bible: Original Screenplay, 1966 (filmed as The Bible: In the Beginning); A Yard of Sun: A Summer Comedy, 1970; The Brontes of Haworth (TV plays), 1975; Sister Dora (TV play), 1977; The Best of Enemies (TV play), 1977; Can You Find Me: A Family History, 1978; Paradise Lost (opera), 1978; One Thing More, or Caedmon Construed, 1986; (ed.) A Sprinkle of Nutmeg, 1992; Early Days, 1997. TRANSLATOR: (and adapter) Ring round the Moon: A Charade with Music, 1950; The Lark, 1955; Tiger at the Gates, 1955; Duel of Angels, 1958; Judith, 1962; Colette, the Boy and the Magic, 1964; Peer Gynt, 1970; Edmond Rostand: Cyrano de Bergerac, 1975. **Address:** The Toft, East Dean, Chichester, W. Sussex PO18 0JA, England.

FRY, Edward B. American, b. 1925. **Genres:** Education. **Career:** Writer of curriculum materials 1963-. Associate Professor of Education, Loyola University, Los Angeles, California, 1955-63; Director of the Reading Center, Rutgers University, New Brunswick, New Jersey 1963-87; Visiting Professor, University of California at Riverside, 1988-89; Publisher, Laguna Beach Educational Books, 1991-98. **Publications:** Teaching Machine and Programmed Instruction, 1963; Teaching Faster Reading, 1963; Reading Faster: A Drill Book, 1963; The Emergency Reading Teachers Manual, 1969, 1980; Typing Course for Children, 1969; Reading for Classroom and Clinic, 1972; Elementary Reading Instruction, 1977; Skimming and Scanning, 1978; Dictionary Drills, 1980; Graphical Comprehension, 1981; The Reading Teachers Book of Lists, 1984, new ed, 1993; Spelling Book, 1992; How to Teach Reading 1992; Everyday Words, 1985; Vocabulary Drills, 1985; The New Reading Teachers Book of Lists, 1985; Fry's Instant Word Puzzles and Activities, 1987; (co-author) Jamestown Heritage Readers, 1991; Phonics Patterns, 1994; 1000 Instant Words, 1994; Beginning Writers Manual, 1993; Picture Nouns, 1996; Vocabulary Teachers Book of Lists, 2004. **Address:** 245 Grandview Ave, Laguna Beach, CA 92651, U.S.A.

FRY, Virginia Lynn. American, b. 1952. **Genres:** Medicine/Health, Psychology. **Career:** Hospice Council of Vermont, Montpelier, director, 1985-. Central Vermont Home Health and Hospice, bereavement coordinator. University of Vermont, adjunct faculty member; Woodbury College, teacher; national public speaker and workshop presenter; consultant. **Publications:** Arts-in-Hospice, 1990; Part of Me Died, Too: Stories of Creative Survival among Bereaved Children and Teenagers, 1995. **Address:** 23 Terrace St., Montpelier, VT 05602, U.S.A.

FRY, William Finley, Jr. Also writes as Will Finley. American, b. 1924. **Genres:** Poetry, Food and Wine, History, Literary criticism and history, Psychiatry, Sciences, Cartoons, Humor/Satire. **Career:** Stanford University, CA, Associate Clinical Professor, 1959-, now Emeritus. International Gelotology Institute, Nevada City, CA, Director; Mental Research Institute, Palo Alto, CA, Director of Education, 1962-67, Board of Directors, 1975-83; American Conservatory Theatre, San Francisco, Summer Institute, Comedy Consultant, 1969; Workshop Library of Humor, Washington, DC, Board of Directors, 1965-97; American Psychiatric Association, Life Fellow; International Society of Humor Studies; International Journal of Humor Research, Editorial Board; Humor in Life and Letters, publication series, Wayne State University Press, Detroit, MI, Advisory Editor; Spanish Academy of Humor; with artist Mark Briggs, author of series of weekly cartoon, 1977-80; Love of the Grape, weekly newspaper column, 1971-82. **Publications:** Sweet Madness: A Study of Humor, 1963; (with M. Allen) Make 'Em Laugh: Life Studies of Comedy Writers, 1976, as Life Studies of Comedy Writers: Creating Humor, 1998; (with W. Salameh) Handbook of Humor and Therapy, 1987; Advances in Humor and Psychotherapy, 1993; The Seasons (poems), 1999; (with W. Salameh) Humor and Wellness in Clinical Intervention, 2001. Author of chapters, articles, and reviews. **Address:** 156 Grove St, Nevada City, CA 95959, U.S.A. **Online address:** frywf@yahoo.com

FRYD, Vivien Green. American, b. 1952. **Genres:** Art/Art history. **Career:** Pittsburg State University, Pittsburg, KS, instructor, summer, 1978; Arizona State University, Tempe, visiting assistant professor, 1984-85; Vanderbilt University, Nashville, TN, assistant professor, 1985-92, associate professor of fine arts, 1992-2002, professor, 2003-, co-director of the fellows program "Transatlantic Voyages: Discovery of the New World and the Old" at Robert Penn Warren Center for the Humanities, 1991-, director of graduate studies in fine arts, 1992-2000. **Publications:** Art and Empire: The Politics of Ethnicity in the United States Capitol, 1815-1860, 1992; Art and the Crisis of Marriage: Georgia O'Keeffe and Edward Hopper, 2003. Work represented in anthologies. **Address:** Dept of Fine Arts, Vanderbilt University, Nashville, TN 37235, U.S.A. **Online address:** vivien.g.fryd@vanderbilt.edu

FRYE, Marilyn. American, b. 1941. **Genres:** Women's studies and issues. **Career:** Michigan State University, Lansing, currently professor of philosophy. **Publications:** The Politics of Reality: Essays in Feminist Theory, 1983; Willful Virgin: Essays in Feminism, 1976-1992, 1992. Contributor of essays to journals, anthologies, and periodicals. **Address:** Department of Philosophy, 503 South Kedzie Hall, Michigan State University, East Lansing, MI 48824, U.S.A.

FRYER, Jonathan. British, b. 1950. **Genres:** History, Theology/Religion, Third World, Biography. **Career:** Freelance writer and broadcaster, mainly for the BBC; Reuters correspondent, London and Brussels, 1973-74; School of Journalism, University of Nairobi, Kenya, visiting lecturer, 1976; World Council of Churches, Geneva, consultant, 1979-82; Earthscan Features, London, editor, 1986-87; member, Executive, English Pen, 1989-; Liberal International (British Group), chairman, 1989-92; Honorary Counsul, (in London) of Mauritania, 1990-; executive committee, Association of Foreign Affairs Journalists, 1993-. **Publications:** The Great Wall of China, 1975; Isherwood, 1977; (with R. Dobson) Brussels as Seen by Naif Artists, 1979; Food for Thought, 1981; George Fox and the Children of Light, 1991; Eye of the Camera, 1993; Dylan, 1993; (with S. Bradford and J. Pearson) The Silwells, 1994; Robbie Ross: Oscar Wilde's Devoted Friend, 2000. **Address:** 140 Bow Common Lane, London E3 4BH, England.

FRYKENBERG, Robert E(ric). American (born India), b. 1930. **Genres:** History. **Career:** University of Wisconsin, Madison, Assistant Professor, 1962-67, Associate Professor, 1967-71, Chairman, Dept. of South Asian Studies, 1970-73, Director, Center for South Asian Studies, 1970-73, Professor, Depts. of History and South Asian Studies, 1971-97, Emeritus Professor, 1997-. Trustee, American Institute of Indian Studies, 1970-81. **Publications:** Guntur District 1788-1848: A History of Local Influence and Central Authority in South India, 1965; Today's World in Focus: India, 1968; Land Control and Social Structure in Indian History, 1969; Land Tenure and Peasants in South Asia, 1979; History and Belief: The Foundations of Historical Understanding, 1996. EDITOR: (with P. Kolenda) Studies of South India, 1985; Delhi through the Ages: Essays on Urban Culture and Society, 1986, 1993.

FU, Limin. See FREEMAN, Charles Wellman, Jr.

FUCHS, Miriam. American, b. 1949. **Genres:** Literary criticism and history. **Career:** Elizabeth Seton College, Yonkers, NY, assistant professor, 1978-81, associate professor of English, 1981-87, department head, 1981-85; University of Hawaii at Manoa, Honolulu, visiting assistant professor, 1986-87, assistant professor, 1987-93, associate professor of English, 1993-, director of Honors Program in English, 1991-. York College of the City University of New York, adjunct lecturer, 1973-76; State University of New York, adjunct lecturer, 1974-79, adjunct assistant professor, 1979-86. **Publications:**

(ed. with E.G. Friedman, and coauthor of preface and intro) Breaking the Sequence: Women's Experimental Fiction, 1989; (ed.) Marguerite Young, Our Darling: Tributes and Essays, 1994. Work represented in anthologies. Contributor of articles and reviews to scholarly journals and popular magazines. **Address:** Department of English, University of Hawaii at Manoa, Honolulu, HI 96822, U.S.A.

FUCHS, Rachel G(innis). American, b. 1939. **Genres:** History, Social commentary. **Career:** Arizona State University, Tempe, professor of history. **Publications:** Abandoned Children: Foundlings and Child Welfare in Nineteenth-Century France, State University of New York Press, 1984; Poor and Pregnant in Paris: Strategies for Survival in the Nineteenth Century, Rutgers University Press, 1992; Gender and the Politics of Social Reform in France, 1870-1914, Johns Hopkins University Press, 1995. **Address:** Department of History, Arizona State University, Tempe, AZ 85287-2501, U.S.A.

FUEGI, John. American/Swiss (born England), b. 1936. **Genres:** Literary criticism and history, Biography, Documentaries/Reportage, Film, History. **Career:** Lecturer in American Literature, Freie Universitat, Berlin, 1965-67; Professor of Comparative Literature, University of Wisconsin, Milwaukee, 1974-76 (joined faculty as Assistant Professor, 1967); Professor and Director of Comparative Literature Program, 1976-86, 1994-, Director of Research Center for Arts and Humanities, 1986-88, and Academic Director of The Visual Press, 1988-90, University of Maryland, College Park. **Publications:** The Wall (documentary film), 1961; (prod) Beckett Directs Beckett (series of 5 documentary films); The Essential Brecht, 1972; (ed.) Brecht Today, 3 vols., 1972-74; (managing editor) The Brecht Yearbook, 14 vols., 1975-90; Brecht, 1986; Brecht: Chaos, According to Plan, Red Ruth (TV film), 1992; Brecht & Co.: Sex, Politics and the Making of the Modern Drama, 1994; The War Within (TV film), 1995; In the Symphony of the World (TV film), 1999.

FUGARD, Athol. South African, b. 1932. **Genres:** Novels, Plays/Screenplays, Autobiography/Memoirs. **Career:** Actor, dir., and playwright, 1959-; Director, Serpent Players, Port Elizabeth, 1965-. Co-founder, The Space experimental theatre, Cape Town, 1972. **Publications:** The Blood Knot, 1963; Hello and Goodbye, 1966; People Are Living There, 1969; Boesman and Lena, 1969; Three Plays, 1972, as Three Port Elizabeth Plays, 1974; Statements (3 plays), 1974; (with J. Kani and W. Ntshona) Two Plays: Sizwe Bansi Is Dead and The Island, 1976; Dimetos and Two Early Plays, 1977; The Guest (screenplay), 1977; Tsots (novel), 1980; A Lesson from Aloes, 1981; Master Harold and the Boys, 1982; Marigolds in August (screenplay), 1982; Notebooks 1960-1977, 1983; The Road to Mecca, 1985; Selected Plays, 1987; A Place with Pigs, 1988; My Children! My Africa!, 1990; Playland, 1991; Cousins: A Memoir, 1994; Valley Song, 1995; My Life, 1996; Plays One, 1998; The Captain's Tiger: A Memoir for the Stage, 1999; Sorrows & Rejoicings, 2001. **Address:** c/o Samuel Liff, William Morris Agency, 1325 Avenue of the Americas, New York, NY 10019, U.S.A. **Online address:** bl@wma.com

FUJIMURA, Joan H. American. **Genres:** Sociology. **Career:** Harvard University, Cambridge, MA, assistant professor of anthropology, 1988-93; Stanford University, Stanford, CA, associate professor of anthropology, 1993-. **Publications:** The Right Tools for the Job, 1992; Crafting Science, 1996. **Address:** Department of Sociology, 8103 Social Science, University of Wisconsin-Madison, 1180 Observatory Dr, Madison, WI 53706, U.S.A. **Online address:** fujimura@ssc.wisc.edu

FUKUDA, Haruko. British (born Japan), b. 1946. **Genres:** Economics, Third World. **Career:** Trade Policy Research Centre, research officer, 1968-70; Overseas Development Institute, research officer, 1970-71; Economics Dept., IBRD (World Bank), Washington, DC, 1971-72; Vickers da Costa & Co., Ltd., economist, 1972-74; James Capel and Co., London, member of staff, 1974-88, partner, 1980-88; Foreign and Colonial Investment Trust plc, director, 1988-; Nikko Europe, board director, 1988-94, vice chairman, 1994-98; Lazard Brothers & Co, Ltd, senior adviser, 1999-; World Gold Council, chief executive, 1999-. **Publications:** Britain in Europe: Impact on the Third World, 1973; Japan & World Trade: The Years Ahead, 1974; Britain and Japan, 1859-1991; Themes and Personalities, 1991. **Address:** Creems, Wissington, Nayland, Suffolk, England.

FUKUYAMA, Francis. American, b. 1952. **Genres:** Third World, Politics/Government, History. **Career:** Pan Heuristics Inc., Los Angeles, CA, consultant, 1978-79; RAND Corporation, Santa Monica, CA, associate social scientist, 1979-81, senior staff member of political science department, 1983-89; Policy Planning Staff, U.S. Department of State, Washington, DC, member of the U.S. Delegation to the Egyptian-Israeli talks on Palestinian

autonomy, 1981-82, deputy director, 1989-90. University of California, Los Angeles, visiting lecturer in political science, 1986, 1989; consultant. **Publications:** (ed. with A. Korbonski) The Soviet Union and the Third World: The Last Three Decades, 1987; A Look at "The End of History?," 1990; The End of History and the Last Man, 1992; United States-Japan Security Relationship after the Cold War, 1993; Trust, 1995; Virtual Corporation and Army Organization, 1997; Great Disruption, 1999; (with others) Information and Biological Revolutions, 2000. **Address:** Bernard Schwartz Professor of International Political Economy, The Paul H. Nitze School of Advanced International Studies, Johns Hopkins University, 1619 Massachusetts Ave. NW, Room 732, Washington, DC 20036-2213, U.S.A. **Online address:** fukuyama@jhu.edu; www.francisfukuyama.com

FULANI, Lenora (Branch). American, b. 1950. **Genres:** Politics/Government. **Career:** Political party leader, psychologist, and social therapist. Associated with Rockefeller Institute, NYC, 1970s; associated with New York Institute for Social Therapy and Research; East Side Center for Short Term Psychotherapy, NYC, psychotherapist; National Alliance Party, founder, presidential candidate, 1988 and 1992; "This Way for Black Empowerment" (newspaper column), columnist; All-Stars Talent Show Network, founder; Fulani! (television show), host. **Publications:** The Making of a Fringe Candidate, 1992. EDITOR: The Politics of Race and Gender in Therapy, 1988; The Psychopathology of Everyday Racism and Sexism, 1988. Contributor to books. **Address:** 225 Broadway RM 2010, New York, NY 10007-3001, U.S.A. **Online address:** lenora@fulani.org

FULCHER, James. British, b. 1942. **Genres:** Sociology. **Career:** University of Leicester, England, lecturer to senior lecturer in sociology, 1966-; writer. **Publications:** Labour Movements, Employers, and the State: Conflict and Cooperation in Britain and Sweden, 1991; (with J. Scott) Sociology, 1999, 2nd ed., 2003; Capitalism: A Very Short Introduction, 2004. Contributor to sociology journals. **Address:** Dept of Sociology, University of Leicester, Leicester LE1 7RH, England.

FULGHUM, Robert. American. **Genres:** Essays. **Publications:** All I Really Need to Know I Learned in Kindergarten, 1988; It Was on Fire When I Laid Down on It, 1989; Uh-Oh, 1991; Maybe (Maybe Not), 1993; From Beginning to End, 1995. **Address:** c/o Villard Books, 201 E. 50th St, New York, NY 10022, U.S.A.

FULLBROOK, Kate. *See* Obituaries.

FULLER, Charles. American, b. 1939. **Genres:** Plays/Screenplays. **Career:** Loan collector, counselor at Temple University, and city housing inspector, all in Philadelphia; co-founder dir., Afro-American Arts Theatre, Philadelphia, 1967-71; writer and dir., Black Experience program, WIP Radio, 1970-71. **Publications:** PLAYS AND SCREENPLAYS: The Village: A Party, 1968, rev. ed. The Perfect Party, 1969; The Rise, 1969; An Untitled Play, 1970; In My Many Names and Days, 1972; Candidate, 1974; In the Deepest Part of Sleep, 1974; First Love, 1974; The Lay Out Letter, 1975; The Brownsville Raid, 1976; Sparrow in Flight; 1978; Zooman and the Sign, 1982, screenplay, 1994; A Soldier's Play, 1982 (Pulitzer Prize, Drama Critics Award, Outer Circle Award); A Soldier's Story (screenplay), 1984; Sons of the Same Lion, 1991; Love Songs (screenplay), 1997. WE PLAY SERIES: Part I: Sally, 1988, Part II: Prince, 1988, Part III: Jonquil, 1989, Part IV: Burner's Frolic, 1990. TELEVISION PLAYS: Roots, 1967; Mitchell, 1968; Black America, 1970-71; The Sky Is Grey, 1987; A Gathering of Old Men, 1987; Zooman, 1995. **Address:** c/o Gwen Potiker, Creative Artist Agency, 9830 Wilshire Blvd, Beverly Hills, CA 90212, U.S.A.

FULLER, Jack (William). American, b. 1946. **Genres:** Novels. **Career:** Admitted to the bar of Illinois, 1974. Chicago Tribune, IL, reporter, 1973-75, Washington correspondent, 1977-78, editorial writer, 1978-79, deputy editorial page editor, 1979-82, editorial page editor, 1982-87, executive editor, 1987-89, editor, 1990-93, president, 1993-, publisher, 1994-97; U.S. Department of Justice, Washington, DC, special assistant to the attorney general, 1975-76; Tribune Publishing Co, president, 1997-. University of Chicago, trustee; Field Museum of Chicago, trustee; American Academy of Arts & Sciences, fellow; Inter American Press Association, president. **Publications:** NOVELS: Convergence, 1982; Fragments, 1984; Mass, 1985; Our Fathers' Shadows, 1987; Legend's End, 1990; The Best of Jackson Payne, 2000. NON-FICTION: News Values, 1996. **Address:** c/o Tribune Publishing Co, 435 N Michigan Ave, Chicago, IL 60611, U.S.A.

FULLER, Jean (Violet) Overton. British, b. 1915. **Genres:** Poetry, History, Biography, Translations. **Career:** Founding Director, Fuller d' Arch Smith Ltd., London, rare book sellers and publrs., 1969-. **Publications:** Madeleine,

1952, rev. ed. as Noor-un-Nisa Inayat Khan, 1971; The Starr Affair (in U.S. as No. 13 Bob), 1954; Double Webs, 1958; Horoscope for a Double Agent, 1960; Venus Protected, 1964; The Magical Dilemma of Victor Neuburg, 1965; Carthage and the Midnight Sun, 1966; Shelley: A Biography, 1968; Swinburne: A Biography, 1968; African Violets, 1968; Darun and Pitar, 1970; Tintagel, 1970; Conversations with a Captor, 1973; The German Penetration of SOE, 1975; Sir Francis Bacon, 1981; Blavastsky and Her Teachers, 1988; Dericourt, The Chequered Spy, 1989; The Comte de Saint-Germain, 1989; Sickert and the Ripper Crimes, 1990; Cats and Other Immortals, 1992; Joan Grant, Winged Pharaoh, 1992; The Bombed Years, 1995; Cyril Scott and a Hidden School, 1998; Krishnamurti: Der Geist Weht wo er will, 2000; Limehawk, Wevil and Frog, 2000; Of Time, Size and Space in Infinity, 2001; Two Poems Conceived in the Garden, 2002; Krishnamurti and the Wind, 2003; Driven to It (autobiography), 2005. TRANSLATIONS: Shiva's Dance, 1979; That the Gods May Remember, 1982; The Secret Garden, 1994; Espionage as a Fine Art, 2002. **Address:** 6 Church Lane, Wymington, Rushden, Northhants. NN10 9LW, England.

FULLER, John (Harold). British, b. 1916. **Genres:** Business/Trade/Industry, Food and Wine. **Career:** Editorial Board, Hospitality Management, 1974-. Ed., Journal of the Hotel and Catering Institute, 1949-54, and Food and Cookery Review, 1957-58; Professor of Hotel Mgmt., and Director, Scottish Hotel School, University of Strathclyde, 1959-70; Hon. Catering Adviser, R.A.F., 1971-91; Hon. Visiting Fellow, Oxford Brookes University, 1992. **Publications:** The Chef's Manual of Kitchen Management, 1962; (with E. Renold) The Chef's Compendium of Professional Recipes, 1963; The Caterer's Potato Manual, 1963; Gueridon and Lamp Cookery, 1965; (with A. Currie) The Waiter, 1965; Hotelkeeping and Catering as a Career, 1965; (with D. Gee) A Hotel and Catering Career, 1976; Professional Kitchen Management, 1981; Modern Restaurant Service, 1982; Pub Catering, 1985; (with J.B. Knight and L.A. Salter) The Professional Chef's Guide to Kitchen Management, 1985; Essential Table Service, 1986; (with D. Kirk) Kitchen Planning and Management, 1991; (with K. Waller) The Menu, Food and Profit, 1991; Advanced Food Service, 1992. EDITOR: Catering Management in the Technological Age, 1967; Pellaprat's Great Book of the Kitchen, 1968; (with J. Steel) Productivity and Profit in Catering, 1968; Catering and Hotelkeeping, 2 vols., 1975; Meat Dishes in International Cuisine, 1984.

FULLER, John (Leopold). British, b. 1937. **Genres:** Novels, Novellas/Short stories, Plays/Screenplays, Poetry, Literary criticism and history. **Career:** Magdalen College, Oxford, Fellow, 1966-2002, Emeritus Fellow, 2002-; Sycamore Press, Oxford, Publr. State University of New York, Buffalo, Visiting Lecturer, 1962-63; Manchester University, Assistant Lecturer, 1963-66. **Publications:** Fairground Music, 1961; The Tree That Walked, 1967; Herod Do Your Worst (play), 1967; The Art of Love, 1968; The Labours of Hercules: A Sonnet Sequence, 1969; Three London Songs, 1969; Annotations of Giant's Town, 1970; The Wreck, 1970; Half a Fortnight, 1970; A Reader's Guide to W. H. Auden, 1970; The Spider Monkey Uncle King (play), 1971; Cannibals and Missionaries, 1972; Boys in a Pie, 1972; Fox-Trot (libretto), 1972; The Sonnet, 1972; Hut Groups, 1973; (with A. Mitchell and P. Levi) Penguin Modern Poets 22, 1973; Epistles to Several Persons, 1973; Poems and Epistles, 1974; Squeaking Crust, 1974; The Queen in the Golden Tree (libretto), 1974; The Mountain in the Sea, 1975; The Last Bid, 1975; Carving Trifles, 1976; Bel and the Dragon, 1977; The Wilderness, 1977; Lies and Secrets, 1979; The Illusionists, 1980; The Extraordinary Wood Mill and Other Stories, 1980; The January Divan, 1980; The Ship of Sounds, 1981; Waiting for the Music, 1982; The Beautiful Inventions, 1983; Come Aboard and Sail Away (for children), 1983; The Adventures of Speedfall (stories), 1985; Selected Poems 1954-82, 1985; (with J. Fenton) Partingtime Hall, 1987; The Grey among the Green (poems), 1988; The Mechanical Body, 1991; The Worm and the Star (stories), 1993; Stones and Fires (poems), 1996; Collected Poems, 1996; W.H. Auden: A Commentary, 1998; W.H. Auden: A Selection by John Fuller, 2000; Now and for a Time (poems), 2002; Ghosts (poems), 2004. NOVELS: Flying to Nowhere, 1983; Tell It Me Again, 1988; The Burning Boys, 1989; Look Twice, 1991; A Skin Diary, 1997; The Memoirs of Laetitia Horsepole, 2001; Flawed Angel, 2005. EDITOR: Light Blue Dark Blue, 1960; Oxford Poetry, 1960, 1960; Poetry Supplement, 1962; (with H. Pinter and P. Redgrove) New Poems 1967, 1968; Poetry Supplement, 1970; Nemo's Almanac, 17 vols., 1971-87; The Dramatic Works by John Gay; Poets in Hand (for children), 1985; Chatto Book of Love Poetry, 1990; The Oxford Book of Sonnets, 2000. **Address:** 4 Benson Pl, Oxford OX2 6QH, England. **Online address:** john.fuller@magd.ox.ac.uk

FULLER, Mary Lou. American, b. 1929. **Genres:** Women's studies and issues, Autobiography/Memoirs, Humor/Satire. **Career:** Memoirist, small-press publisher, and former innkeeper; has also worked in banking. First

Pennsylvania Banking & Trust, assistant director of training, 1946-61; Guaranty Bank & Trust, Worcester, MA, assistant director of training, 1961-63; Fitzwilliam Inn, Fitzwilliam, NH, owner and innkeeper (with husband), 1963-73; National Grange Mutual, Keene, NH, assistant director of training, 1975-80; University of New Hampshire, Durham, NH, business manager for student dining, 1980-89; retired to become partner in KALM Publishing, 1989. **Publications:** A Horse in the Ladies' Room, 1997; (and illustrator) Where Lame Donkeys Lie, 1998; On the Wings of a Unicorn, 1999; How to Build a Book (pamphlet), 2001; Sisters by Heart-Partners in Aging, 2001. **Address:** 149 East Side Dr #135, Concord, NH 03301, U.S.A. **Online address:** uniqueyankee@aol.com

FULLER, Reginald Horace. American (born England), b. 1915. **Genres:** Theology/Religion. **Career:** Professor Emeritus of New Testament, Virginia Theological Seminary, Alexandria, 1985- (Professor, 1972-85). Professor of Theology, St. David's College, Lampeter, Wales, 1950-55; Professor of New Testament, Seabury-Western Theological Seminary, Evanston, IL, 1955-66; Baldwin Professor of Sacred Literature, Union Theological Seminary, NYC, 1966-72. **Publications:** (with R.P.C. Hanson) The Church of Rome, 1948; The Mission and Achievement of Jesus, 1954; What Is Liturgical Preaching?, 1957; (with G.E. Wright) The Book of the Acts of God, 1957; Luke's Witness to Jesus Christ, 1958; The New Testament in Current Study, 1962; Interpreting the Miracles, 1963; The Foundations of New Testament Christology, 1965; A Critical Introduction to the New Testament, 1966; (with B. Rice) Christianity and the Affluent Society, 1966; The Formation of the Resurrection Narratives, 1971; Preaching the New Lectionary, 1974; Proclamation 2: Advent and Christmas, 1979; The Use of the Bible in Preaching, 1980; (with P. Perkins) Who Is This Christ?, 1983; Preaching the Lectionary, 1984; He that Cometh, 1990; Christ and Christianity, 1994. TRANSLATOR: The Cost of Discipleship, by D. Bonhoeffer, 1948; Kerygma and Myth I, 1963; Bonhoeffer's Letters and Papers from Prison, 1954; Primitive Christianity, by R. Bultmann, 1956; Unknown Sayings of Jesus, by J. Jeremias, 1957; Modern Catholicism, by W. von Loewenich, 1959; Kerygma and Myth II, 1962; (with I. Fuller) Two Studies in the Theology of Bonhoeffer, 1967; Reverence for Life, by A. Schweitzer, 1971; (with I. Fuller) Church and Theology; (with I. Fuller) The New Testament: A Guide to Its Writings, by G. Bornkamm, 1973; (with I. Fuller) The Holy Spirit, by E. Schweizer, 1980; (with I. Fuller) The Johannine Episltes, by R. Schnackenburg, 1992. **Address:** Westminster Canterbury House, 1600 Westbrook Ave Apt 320, Richmond, VA 23227-3328, U.S.A.

FULLER, Steve William. American, b. 1959. **Genres:** Philosophy, Sciences, Sociology, Speech/Rhetoric. **Career:** University of Colorado, Boulder, assistant professor of philosophy, 1985-88; Virginia Polytechnic Institute and State University, Blacksburg, assistant professor, 1988-92, associate professor of science and technology studies, 1992-94. University of Pittsburgh, associate professor in the rhetoric of science, 1993-94; University of Durham (UK), Professorial Chair in sociology and social policy, 1994-99; University of Warwick, professorial chair in Sociology, 1999-. **Publications:** Social Epistemology, 1988; Philosophy of Science and Its Discontents, 1989, rev. ed., 1993; Philosophy, Rhetoric, and the End of Knowledge: The Coming of Science and Technology Studies, 1993; Science, 1997; The Governance of Science, 1999; Thomas Kuhn: A Philosophical History for our Times, 2000; Knowledge Management Foundation, 2002. Contributor to journals across the natural and human sciences. **Address:** Department of Sociology, University of Warwick, Coventry CV4 7AL, England. **Online address:** s.w.fuller@warwick.ac.uk

FULLERTON, Alexander (Fergus). Also writes as Anthony Fox. British, b. 1924. **Genres:** Novels. **Publications:** Surface!, 1953; Bury the Past, 1954; Old Moke, 1954; No Man's Mistress, 1955; A Wren Called Smith, 1957; The White Men Sang, 1958; The Yellow Ford, 1959; The Waiting Game, 1961; Soldier from the Sea, 1962; The Thunder and the Flame, 1964; Lionheart, 1965; Chief Executive, 1969; The Publisher, 1970; Store, 1971; The Escapists, 1972; Other Men's Wives, 1973; Piper's Leave, 1974; The Blooding of the Guns, 1976; Sixty Minutes for Saint George, 1977; Patrol to the Golden Horn, 1978; Storm Force to Narvik, 1979; Last Lift from Crete, 1980; All the Drowning Seas, 1981; A Share of Honour, 1982; Regenesis, 1983; The Torch Bearers, 1983; The Gatecrashers, 1984; The Aphrodite Cargo, 1985; Special Deliverance, 1986; Special Dynamic, 1987; Special Deception, 1989; Johnson's Bird, 1989; Bloody Sunset, 1991; Look to the Wolves, 1992; Love for an Enemy, 1993; Not Thinking of Death, 1994; Into the Fire, 1995; Band of Brothers, 1996; Return to the Field, 1997; Final Dive, 1998; In at the Kill, 1999; Wave Cry, 1999; The Floating Madhouse, 2000; Single to Paris, 2001; Flight to Mons, 2003; Westbound, Warbound, 2003. AS ANTHONY FOX: Threat Warning Red, 1979; Kingfisher Scream, 1980. **Address:** c/o John Johnson Ltd, 45-47 Clerkenwell Green, London EC1R 0HT, England. **Online address:** alex@fullerton.worldonline.co.uk

FULLERTON, Gail. Also writes as Gail J. Putney. American, b. 1927. **Genres:** Human relations/Parenting, Sociology. **Career:** Florida State University, Tallahassee, Assistant Professor of Sociology, 1957-60; San Jose State University, California, Assistant Professor, 1963-68, Associate Professor, 1968-72, Dean of Graduate Studies and Research, 1972-76, Professor of Sociology, 1972-91, Executive Vice-President, 1977-78, President, 1978-91. **Publications:** (as Gail J. Putney with Snell Putney) Normal Neurosis, 1964; The Adjusted American, 1966; Survival in Marriage, 1972, 1977. **Address:** 2030 N 13th Ct, Coos Bay, OR 97420, U.S.A.

FULTZ, Jay. American, b. 1936. **Genres:** Biography, Essays. **Career:** Northwest Missouri State College, Maryville, teacher of English composition and literature, 1965-66; Eastern College, Baltimore, MD, teacher of English composition and literature, 1966-67; South Dakota State University, Brookings, instructor in English, 1967-70; University of Nebraska-Lincoln, instructor in English, 1975-82; University of Nebraska Press, Lincoln, editorial associate, 1984-87, editor of Bison Books, 1987-98; freelance editor and writer, 1998-. Guest on television programs. **Publications:** In Search of Donna Reed, 1998. Contributor to periodicals. **Address:** 1024 S 28th St, Parsons, KS 67357, U.S.A. **Online address:** Jay@cpol.net

FUMENTO, Rocco. American, b. 1923. **Genres:** Novels, Film. **Career:** University of Illinois, Urbana, associate professor of English, 1964-, now retired (joined faculty, 1952); free-lance writer. **Publications:** Devil by the Tail, 1954; Tree of Dark Reflection, 1962; A Decent Girl Always Goes to Mass on Sunday, 2002. EDITOR: Introduction to the Short Story, 1962; 42nd Street, 1980; The Sea Wolf, 1997. **Address:** 1100 Main St, Dalton, MA 01226, U.S.A. **Online address:** RFumento@webtv.net

FUNAKAWA, Atsushi. Japanese, b. 1956. **Genres:** Administration/Management. **Career:** Toshiba, Tokyo, Japan, sales coordinator, 1980-82; American Life Insurance Co., Tokyo, section chief, 1983-90; Clarke Consulting Group, Redwood City, CA, intercultural business specialist, 1992-94; Globis Corp., Tokyo, program director for organizational learning, 1995-. Also worked for Geonexus Communications, Palo Alto, CA. **Publications:** Transcultural Management: A New Approach for Global Organizations, 1997. Author of magazine articles. **Address:** 2-14-10 Sazumachi, Chotu-shi, Tokyo, Japan. **Online address:** funakawa@globis.co.jp

FUNKHOUSER, Erica. American, b. 1949. **Genres:** Plays/Screenplays, Poetry. **Career:** Cambridge Historical Commission, Cambridge, MA, writer, 1974-77; part-time teacher in and around Boston, MA, 1976-87; Revels, Inc., Cambridge, scriptwriter, 1988-. Lesley College, adjunct lecturer in adult degree program, 1987-; Massachusetts Institute of Technology, Cambridge, MA, lecturer in poetry, 1998-. **Publications:** This Is Boston: A Walking Guide to Boston, 1974; Natural Affinities (poems), 1983; The Long Haul (play), 1991; Sure Shot and Other Poems, 1992; The Actual World (poetry), 1997; Pursuit (poetry), 2002.

FURDYNA, Anna M. Also writes as Alauda Arvensis, Aurelia Happenstance. American (born Poland), b. 1938. **Genres:** Translations. **Career:** Worked as a laboratory assistant in high-energy physics, 1959; Massachusetts Institute of Technology, Cambridge, staff physicist at National Magnet Laboratory, 1964-66; Purdue University, West Lafayette, IN, teaching assistant in physics, 1968-69; free-lance translator, 1972-78; Purdue University, research assistant at Center for Information and Numerical Analysis, 1978-79; freelance translator, 1979-. **Publications:** (trans.) K. Slomczynski and T. Krauze, editors, Class Structure and Social Mobility in Poland, M. E. Sharpe, 1978; (trans.) Iwo Birula-Bialynicki, M. Cieplak, and J. Kaminski, Theory of Quanta, Oxford University Press, 1992. Translator of Nativity Moderne, a play by Ireneusz Iredynski, and the libretto for Auschwitz Oratorio, by Alina Nowak, 1974; translator of poems by K. J. Galczynski and A. Warzecha; translator of songs by Bulat Okudzhava, Agnieszka Osiecka, Olearczyk, and Wozniak. Contributor of poems and translations to periodicals.

FURIA, Philip (G.). American, b. 1943. **Genres:** Biography. **Career:** University of Minnesota-Twin Cities, Minneapolis, assistant professor, 1970-76, associate professor, 1976-84, professor of English, 1984-96, director of undergraduate studies in English, 1977-80, chairman of individualized degree programs, 1980-82, assistant chairman of department, 1983-86, chair, 1991-94; University of East Anglia, visiting exchange professor, 1976-77; University of Graz, Fulbright professor, 1982-83; University of North Carolina at Wilmington, chair of Dept of English, 1996-99, director of Film Studies, 2000-02, chair of Dept of Creative Writing, 2004-. Minnesota State Arts Board, poetry judge, 1985-87. Guest on radio programs. **Publications:** Pound's Cantos Declassified, 1984; The Poets of Tin Pan Alley: A History of America's Great Lyricists, 1990; Ira Gershwin, 1996; Irving Berlin, 1998;

Johnny Mercer, 2003. **Address:** Creative Writing Dept, Morton Hall 126, University of North Carolina at Wilmington, 601 S College Rd, Wilmington, NC 28403-5938, U.S.A. **Online address:** furiap@uncw.edu

FURINO, Antonio. American (born Italy). **Genres:** Economics, Education, Information science/Computers, Medicine/Health, Politics/Government, Social sciences. **Career:** University of Texas Health Science Center, San Antonio, professor of economics, 1985-, director of Center for Health Economics and Policy, 1987-, director of Regional Center for Health Work-force Studies, Innovation Creativity, Capital Institute, 2001-. University of Texas at Austin, senior research fellow, 1986-. Development through Applied Science, director. **Publications:** Grassroots Entrepreneurship in the Health Arena: Technology for Communities at the Crossroads, 2003. EDITOR: Cooperation and Competition in the Global Economy, 1988; Mental Health Policy for Older Americans, 1990; Health Policy and the Hispanic, 1992. **Address:** 16114 Robinwood Ln, San Antonio, TX 78248-1744, U.S.A.

FURNISH, Victor Paul. American, b. 1931. **Genres:** Theology/Religion. **Career:** University Distinguished Professor of New Testament, Perkins School of Theology, Southern Methodist University, Dallas, since 1983 (Instructor, 1959-60; Assistant Professor, 1960-65; Associate Professor, 1965-71; Professor, 1971-83). Abingdon New Testament Commentaries, general editor, 1996-. **Publications:** Theology and Ethics in Paul, 1968; The Love Command in the New Testament, 1972; (with J. H. Snow) Easter, 1975; (ed. with K. Crim and L. Bailey) The Interpreter's Dictionary of the Bible, Supplementary vol., 1976; The Moral Teaching of Paul, 1979, 1985; (with R. L. Thulin) Pentecost, 1981; (with Leander E. Keck) The Pauline Letters, 1984; II Corinthians, 1984; Lent, 1986; Jesus According to Paul, 1993. **Address:** Southern Methodist University, Dallas, TX 75275, U.S.A.

FURNISS, Graham (Lytton). British (born India), b. 1949. **Genres:** Area studies, Language/Linguistics, Literary criticism and history. **Career:** Seminaire St. Louis, Ziguinchor, Casamance, Senegal, professor of English, 1967-68; Bayero University, Kano, Nigeria, part-time lecturer in Nigerian languages, 1973-74; University of Maiduguri, Nigeria, lecturer in languages and linguistics, 1977-79; University of London, School of Oriental and African Studies, England, lecturer, 1979-89, senior lecturer, 1990-96, reader in Hausa cultural studies, 1996-99, chairperson, Centre of African Studies, 1989-93, dean of languages, 1995-97, professor of African-language literature, 1999-, dean of the Faculty of Languages and Cultures, 2002-. Guest lecturer at universities worldwide; British Broadcasting Corp., occasional broadcaster for BBC Hausa Service. **Publications:** Second Level Hausa: Grammar in Action, 1991; Ideology in Practice: Hausa Poetry as Exposition of Values and Viewpoints, 1995; Poetry, Prose, and Popular Culture in Hausa, 1996. EDITOR: Writings on Hausa Grammar: The Collected Papers of F.W. Parsons, 1982; (with P.J. Jaggar, and contrib.) Studies in Hausa Language and Linguistics, 1988; African Languages and Cultures, 2 vols., 1988-89; (with R. Fardon, and contrib.) African Languages, Development, and the State, 1994; (with L. Gunner, and contrib.) Power, Marginality, and African Oral Literature, 1995; (with R. Fardon) African Broadcast Cultures: Radio in Transition, 2000. Contributor to books and periodicals. **Address:** Department of African Languages and Cultures, School of Oriental and African Studies, University of London, Thornhaugh St, Russell Sq, London WC1H 0XG, England.

FURSENKO, Aleksandr (A.). Russian. **Genres:** History, International relations/Current affairs. **Career:** Historian and writer specializing in American diplomatic history; Member of the Russian Academy of Sciences; former vice chair of the Leningrad Science Center presidium, USSR Academy of Sciences, Leningrad. **Publications:** NONFICTION: The American Bourgeois Revolution of the Eighteenth Century, 1960; The Oil Trusts and World Politics from the 1880s to 1918, 1965; The American Revolution and the Formation of the USA, 1978; The Oil Wars of the Late Nineteenth and Early Twentieth Centuries, 1985. U.S. Presidents and Politics in the 1970s, 1989; The Battle for Oil: The Economics and Politics of International Corporate Conflict over Petroleum, 1860-1930, trans. and edited by G.L. Freeze, 1990; (with T.J. Naftali) One Hell of a Gamble: Khrushchev, Castro, and Kennedy, 1958-64, 1997. Author of books published in Russian. **Address:** c/o W.W. Norton & Company, 500 Fifth Ave., New York, NY 10110, U.S.A.

FURST, Lilian R(enee). American (born Austria), b. 1931. **Genres:** Literary criticism and history, Medicine/Health, Autobiography/Memoirs. **Career:** Marcel Bataillon Professor of Comparative Literature, University of North Carolina, Chapel Hill, 1986-. Taught at the Queen's University of Belfast, 1955-66, University of Manchester, 1966-71, Dartmouth College, Hanover, NH, 1971-72, and the University of Oregon, Eugene, 1972-75; professor of comparative literature, University of Texas at Dallas, 1975-86. Flora Stone Mather Visiting Professor, Case Western Reserve University, Cleveland, OH, 1978-79; visiting professor at Stanford University, CA, 1981-82, and Harvard University, Cambridge, MA, 1983-84; Kenan Distinguished Professor in the Humanities, College of William and Mary, Williamsburg, VA, 1985-86. **Publications:** Romanticism in Perspective, 1969; Romanticism, 1969; (with P.N. Skrine) Naturalism, 1971; Counterparts: The Dynamics of Franco-German Literary Relations 1770-1895, 1977; The Contours of European Romanticism, 1979; European Romanticism, 1980; Fictions of Romantic Irony, 1984; L'Assommoir: A Working Woman's Life, 1990; Through the Lens of the Reader, 1991; (with P.W. Graham) Disorderly Eaters, 1992; Realism, 1992; Home Is Somewhere Else, 1994; All Is True: The Claims and Strategies of Realist Fiction, 1995; Women Healers and Physicians, 1997; Between Doctors and Patients: The Changing Balance of Power, 1998; Just Talk: Narratives of Psychotherapy, 1999; Medical Progress and Social Reality, 2001; Idioms of Distress: Psychosomatic Disorders in Medical and Imaginative Literature, 2003; Random Destinations: Escaping the Holocaust and Starting Life Anew, 2005. **Address:** 106 Arbutus Pl, Chapel Hill, NC 27514-8504, U.S.A.

FURTH, George. American, b. 1932. **Genres:** Plays/Screenplays. **Career:** Actor from 1956; taught in drama dept., University of Southern California, Los Angeles. **Publications:** Company, 1972; Twigs, 1972; The Act, 1977; The Supporting Cast, 1982; Merrily We Roll Along, 1982; Precious Sons, 1986; Getting Away with Murder, 1996. **Address:** c/o The Lantz Office, 200 W 57th St Ste 503, New York, NY 10019, U.S.A.

FURUBOTN, Eirik G. American, b. 1923. **Genres:** Economics. **Career:** Rice Institute (now Rice University), Houston, TX, instructor in economics, 1949-51; Wesleyan University, Middletown, CT, instructor in economics, 1953-55; Rensselaer Polytechnic Institute, Troy, NY, instructor in economics, 1955-58; Lafayette College, Easton, PA, assistant professor of economics, 1958-60; Emory University, Atlanta, GA, associate professor of economics, 1960-63; State University of New York at Binghamton, professor of economics, 1963-67, chair of department, 1966-67; Texas A&M University, College Station, professor of economics, 1967-82, Private Enterprise Research Center, research fellow, 1996-; University of Texas at Arlington, visiting professor, 1981-82, James L. West Professor of Economics, 1982-96; visiting professor at universities worldwide. **Publications:** (with R.B. Ekelund and W.P. Gramm) The Evolution of Modern Demand Theory (essays), 1972; (with R. Richter) Institutions and Economic Theory, 1997, 2nd ed., 2005. EDITOR & CONTRIBUTOR: (with S.A. Pejovich) The Economics of Property Rights, 1974; (with R. Richter) Some Views on Hospital Finance, 1988; (with R. Richter) The Economics and Law of Banking Regulation, 1990; (with R. Richter) The New Institutional Economics: A Collection of Articles from the Journal of Institutional and Theoretical Economics, 1991. Contributor to economic journals. **Address:** 750 N Rosemary Dr, Bryan, TX 77802, U.S.A.

FURUTANI, Dale. American, b. 1946. **Genres:** Mystery/Crime/Suspense. **Career:** Owner of a private consulting company for the automotive industry; president of a software company; Yamaha Motorcycles, parts marketing manager; Nissan Motor Corporation USA, director of information technology. **Publications:** MYSTERY NOVELS: Death in Little Tokyo, 1996; The Toyotomi Blades, 1997; Death at the Crossroads, 1998. Author of three nonfiction books; contributor to periodicals. **Address:** c/o St. Martin's Press, 175 Fifth Ave., New York, NY 10010, U.S.A.

FUSSELL, E. Robert. American (born Peru), b. 1942. **Genres:** Novels. **Career:** Secondary school teacher, Los Angeles, CA, 1966-68; E. Robert Fussell, P.C. (law office), LeRoy, NY, owner/president, 1972-; Ingham University Press, LeRoy, NY, owner/president, 1998-. Genesee County Chamber of Commerce, director, 1974-78, president, 1976; LeRoy Village trustee, 1992-, deputy-mayor, 1997-. **Publications:** Human-itis B: Family at War (fiction), 2000. **Address:** 46 Wolcott St Ste 1, LeRoy, NY 14482, U.S.A. **Online address:** gasholic@geneseeit.com

FUSSELL, Paul. American, b. 1924. **Genres:** Literary criticism and history, Social commentary. **Career:** Donald T. Regan Professor of English Literature, University of Pennsylvania, Philadelphia, 1983-. Instructor in English, Connecticut College, New London, 1951-54; Assistant Professor, 1955-59, Associate Professor, 1959-64, Professor of English, 1964-76, and John DeWitt Professor of English Literature, 1976-83, Rutgers University, New Brunswick, NJ; Fulbright Lecturer, University of Heidelberg, 1957-58; Regional Chairman, Woodrow Wilson National Fellowship Foundation, 1962-64; Consulting Ed., Random House, Inc., 1964-65; Visiting Prof, Univ. of London, 1990-92. **Publications:** Theory of Prosody in 18th-Century England, 1954; (co-author) The Presence of Walt Whitman, 1962; The Rhetorical World of Augustan Humanism, 1965; Poetic Meter and Poetic Form, 1965; Samuel Johnson and the Life of Writing, 1971; The Great War and Modern Memory, 1975 (National Book Award); Abroad: British Literary Traveling between the Wars, 1980; The Boy Scout Handbook and Other Observations, 1982; Class: A Guide through the American Status System, 1983 (in UK as Caste Marks: Style and Status in the USA, 1984); Thank God for the Atom Bomb and Other Essays, 1988; Wartime: Understanding and Behavior in the Second World War, 1990; BAD, or the Dumbing of America, 1991; The Anti-Egotist: Kingsley Amis, Man of Letters, 1994; Doing Battle: The Making of a Skeptic, 1996; Uniforms, 2002. EDITOR: The Ordeal of Alfred M. Hale, 1975; Siegfried Sassoon's Long Journey: Selections from the Sherston Memoirs, 1983; The Norton Book of Travel, 1987; The Norton Book of Modern War, 1990. **Address:** 2020 Walnut St, Philadelphia, PA 19103-5635, U.S.A.

FUSSNER, Frank Smith. American, b. 1920. **Genres:** History. **Career:** Professor Emeritus of History, Reed College, Portland, Oregon (joined faculty, 1950). Rancher, Circle-S Ranch, Spray, Oregon Ed., Wheeler County Historical Commission. **Publications:** The Historical Revolution, 1962; Tudor History and the Historians, 1970; (ed. and contrib.) Glimpses of Wheeler County's Past, 1975; Time's Silent Stealth... A Tribute to Jane, 1994. **Address:** Circle-S Ranch, 45534 Highway 207 South, Spray, OR 97874, U.S.A.

FUTCHER, Jane P. American, b. 1947. **Genres:** Novels, Adult non-fiction, Gay and lesbian issues, Medicine/Health. **Career:** Writer. Philadelphia Public School System, substitute teacher in junior high classrooms, 1972-73; Harper & Row Media, NYC, staff project editor, producer, and writer, 1973-77; Guidance Associates, NYC, scriptwriter, 1977-80; World College West, Petaluma, CA, adjunct faculty member and writing tutor, 1990-92; Marin Independent Journal, reporter, 1994-. **Publications:** NOVELS: Crush, 1981; Promise Not to Tell, 1991; Dream Lover, 1997. NONFICTION: (with R. Conover) Marin: The Place, the People, 1981. Author of educational filmstrips and teaching guides. Contributor to articles to periodicals. **Address:** 235 Shelvin Rd, Novato, CA 94947, U.S.A. **Online address:** jfutcher@aol.com

FUTTERMAN, Enid (Susan). American, b. 1943. **Genres:** Novels, Plays/Screenplays, Songs/Lyrics and libretti, Writing/Journalism. **Career:** Grey Advertising, Inc., NYC, copywriter and lyricist, 1964-76; lyricist and librettist, 1976-. Author and photographer, 1998-. Our Town magazine, 2004. **Publications:** (with H. Marren) Portrait of Jennie (musical), 1982; (with M.Cohen) Yours, Anne (musical), 1985; (with S. Ackerman) An Open Window (short musical), 1987; (with M. Cohen) I Remember (chamber piece), 1996; (with M. Cohen) I Am Anne Frank (song cycle), 1996; Bittersweet Journey: A Modestly Erotic Novel of Love, Longing, and Chocolate, 1998. **Address:** 661 Route 23, Craryville, NY 12521, U.S.A. **Online address:** EnidF@aol.com

FYFIELD, Frances. *See* **HEGARTY, Frances.**

G

GAARD, Greta. American, b. 1960. Genres: Environmental sciences/ Ecology, Gay and lesbian issues, Literary criticism and history, Women's studies and issues. Career: University of Minnesota, Twin Cities, instructor in English and women's studies, 1980-89; University of Minnesota, Duluth, assistant professor of writing and women's studies, 1989-94, associate professor writing and women's studies, 1994-. Inver Hills Community College, instructor in English, 1985; Hamline University, instructor in introductory composition, 1986; Augsburg College, instructor in English, 1986-87. Publications: EDITOR & CONTRIBUTOR: Ecofeminism: Women, Animals, Nature, 1993; Ecologica Politics: Ecofeminist and the Greens, forthcoming; Ecofeminist Literary Criticism, forthcoming. Author of essays and reviews. Address: University of Minnesota, 420 Humanities Bldg., Duluth, MN 55812, U.S.A.

GABEL, Gernot Uwe. German, b. 1941. Genres: Librarianship, Philosophy, Bibliography. Career: University of North Carolina at Chapel Hill, visiting assistant professor, 1972-73; University of Cologne, Germany, subject specialist at university library, 1976-, deputy chief librarian, 1987-. Publications: IN ENGLISH: Canadian Theses on German Philosophy, 1925-1980, 1985; Ludwig Wittgenstein: A Comprehensive Bibliography of International Theses and Dissertations, 1933-1985, 1988; Kant: An Index to Theses and Dissertations Accepted by Universities in Canada and the United States, 1879-1985, 1989; Sartre: A Comprehensive Bibliography of International Theses and Dissertations, 1950-1985, 1992; Catalogue of Austrian and Swiss Dissertations on English and American Literatures, 1997; Historic Libraries in Europe, 2001. OTHER: Drama und Theater des Deutschen Barock, 1976; Bibliographie Oesterreichischer und Schweizerischer Dissertationen zur Deutschen Philosophie, 1885-1975, 1982; Biblio et Franco: Beitraege zum Bibliotheks- und Verlagswesen Frankreichs, 1991; Verzeichnis Franzoesischer Dissertationen zur Deutschsprachigen Literatur vom Mittelalter bis zum 20. Jahrhundert, 1996; Europae Domus Editoriae: Beitraege zum Europaeischen Verlagswesen, 1998; Baugeschichtliche Perspektiven, 2002. Contributor to books and professional journals. Address: Juelichstrasse 7, D-50354 Huerth, Germany.

GABHART, Ann Houchin. American, b. 1947. Genres: Romance/ Historical, Children's fiction, Young adult fiction. Career: Writer, 1975-. Vice president, Academic Booster Club, 1989 and 1990; volunteer worker for Academic Booster Club and Library of the Blind and Physically Handicapped; teacher for Community Education. Publications: HISTORICAL ROMANCE NOVELS: A Forbidden Yearning, 1978; A Heart Divided, 1980. FOR YOUNG ADULTS: A Chance Hero, 1985; The Look of Eagles, 1986; The Gifting, 1987; A Kindred Spirit, 1987; Only in Sunshine, 1988; Wish Come True, 1988; For Sheila, 1991; Bridge to Courage, 1993; Secrets To Tell, 1994. FOR CHILDREN: Discovery at Coyote Point, 1989; Two of a Kind, 1992. Address: 1251 Bond Ln., Lawrenceburg, KY 40342, U.S.A.

GABLER, Hans Walter. German, b. 1938. Genres: Literary criticism and history. Career: University of Munich, Munich, Germany, Shakespeare librarian, 1965-68, assistant professor, 1970-81, professor of English, 1981-; University of Virginia, Charlottesville, VA, visiting professor, 1975. Publications: Zur Funktion Dramatischer und Literarischer Parodie im Elisabethanischen Drama: Beitraege zur Interpretation Ausgewaehlter Dramen aus dem Werk Lylys, Marlowes und Greenes und dem Fruehwerk Shakespeares, 1966; Geschmack und Gesellschaft: Rhetorische und Sozialgeschichtliche Aspekte der Fruehaufklaererischen Geschmackskategorie, 1982. EDITOR:

(author of intro and English index) English Renaissance Studies in German, 1971; (with W. Hettche and author of preface) J. Joyce, A Portrait of the Artist as a Young Man, 1977; (with W. Hettche; and author of preface) J. Joyce, Dubliners: A Facsimile of Drafts and Manuscripts, 1978; (with W. Steppe and C. Melchior) J. Joyce, Ulysses, 1984;(with W. Steppe) A Handlist to James Joyce's Ulysses: A Complete Alphabetical Index to the Critical Reading Text, 1985; (with W. Steppe and C. Melchior) J. Joyce, Ulysses: The Corrected Text, 1986; (with G. Bornstein and G. Borland Pierce) Contemporary German Editorial Theory, 1995. Address: University of Munich, Department of English, Schellingstrasse 3, D-80799 Munich, Germany. Online address: Hans_Walter.Gabler@anglistik.uni-muenchen.de

GABLIK, Suzi. American, b. 1934. Genres: Art/Art history. Publications: (with J. Russell) Pop Art Redefined, 1970; Magritte, 1970; Progress in Art, 1976; Has Modernism Failed?, 1984; The Reenchantment of Art, 1991; Conversations before the End of Time, 1995; Living the Magical Life, 2002. Address: 3271 Deer Run Rd, Blacksburg, VA 24060, U.S.A.

GABOR, Andrea (Anna Gisela). American. Genres: Intellectual history. Career: Writer and editor; Architectural Record, New York, NY, assistant editor, 1981-82; Business Week, New York, NY, staff editor, 1982-85; U.S. News and World Report, New York, NY, associate editor, 1985-. Publications: The Man Who Discovered Quality: How W. Edwards Deming Brought the Quality Revolution to America: The Stories of Ford, Xerox, and GM, 1990; Einstein's Wife: Work and Marriage in the Lives of Five Great Twentieth-Century Women, 1995; The Capitalist Philosophers: The Geniuses of Modern Business, Their Lives, Times, and Ideas, 1999. Address: 508 E 87th St, New York, NY 10128, U.S.A. Online address: AAGabor@aol.com

GABOR, Thomas. Hungarian/Canadian, b. 1952. Genres: Criminology/ True Crime, Sociology. Career: University of Ottawa, Ottawa, Ontario, lecturer, 1981-83, assistant professor, 1983-86, associate professor, 1986-90, professor of criminology, 1990-. Guest on television and radio programs. Publications: Prediction of Criminal Behaviour, 1986; Armed Robbery, 1987; "Everybody Does It": Crime by the Public, 1994. Contributor to books. Contributor to professional journals. Address: Department of Criminology, University of Ottawa, Ottawa, ON, Canada K1N 6N5. Online address: tgabor@cyberus.ca

GABRIEL, Adrianna. See ROJANY, Lisa.

GABRIEL, Jüri (Evald). British (born Estonia), b. 1940. Genres: Travel/ Exploration, Antiques/Furnishings, Communications/Media. Career: Freelance writer, photographer, trans. and ed., literary agent and lectr. Chmn., Dedalus, publrs., London and Sawtry, since 1984. Cameraman, Associated Rediffusion Television (programme contractors), London, 1963-65; Ed., Thames & Hudson Ltd., publr., London, 1965-67. Exec. Council member, Writers' Guild of Great Britain, London, 1982-85; Chairman, Copyright Licensing Agency, London, 1988-89; British Copyright Council, London, 1980-98. Publications: Victoriana, 1969; (with L. Hemmant) Europa: Gastronomic Guide to Europe, 3 vols., 1971; Thinking About Television, 1973; (ed.) Rand McNally/RAC Guide to British and Continental Camping and Caravanning Sites, 6 eds., 1974-81; Unqualified Success: Comprehensive Guide to Jobs for School Leavers, 1984, rev. ed. 1986. Address: 35 Camberwell Grove, London SE5 8JA, England.

GABRIEL (LOVING), Kathryn (Ann). American, b. 1955. Genres: Anthropology/Ethnology, Archaeology/Antiquities, History, Local history/

Rural topics, Mythology/Folklore, Travel/Exploration, Theology/Religion. **Career:** Guymon Daily Herald, Guymon, OK, agriculture and energy editor, 1980; Golden Star Pub and Brewery, Norwich, England, in public relations, 1981; State Bar of New Mexico, Albuquerque, assistant to editor of News and Views newsletter, 1983-84; Cystic Fibrosis Foundation, Albuquerque, assistant director, 1984-85; United Way of Greater Albuquerque, Albuquerque, communications specialist, 1985-86; University of New Mexico, Albuquerque, media relations specialist, 1986-90; writer. **Publications:** Death Comes to the Archdirector (play), 1989; Roads to Center Place: A Cultural Atlas to Chaco Canyon and the Anasazi, 1991; (ed) Marietta Wetherill: Reflections on Life with the Navajos in Chaco Canyon, 1992; Gambler Way: Indian Gaming in Mythology, History, and Archaeology in North America, 1996; Country Towns of New Mexico, 1997. FOR TELEVISION: Women Aware, 1986; Kids with Keys, 1986; Our Town, 1987; Pueblo on the Mesa, 1988; Second Century, 1989-90. **Address:** 2521 Wheeler Peak Dr. NE, Rio Rancho, NM 87124-6732, U.S.A. **Online address:** www.nmia.com~kgabriel

GABRIEL, Richard A(lan). American, b. 1942. **Genres:** Politics/Government, Psychology, History. **Career:** St. Anselm's College, Manchester, NH, professor of political science. **Publications:** Ethnic Voting in Primary Elections: The Irish and Italians of Providence, Rhode Island, 1969; Ethnic Attitudes and Political Behavior in City and Suburb: The Irish and Italians of Rhode Island, 1969, also published as The Irish and Italians: Ethnics in City and Suburb, 1980; (with P.L. Savage) The Ethnicity Attribute: Persistence and Change in an Urban and Suburban Environment, 1973; (with Savage) What Voters Think about Politics and Why: A Case Study of Political Ethos in a New England City, 1973; The Ethnic Factor in the Urban Polity, 1973; Program Evaluation: A Social Science Approach, 1975; (with Savage) Crisis in Command: Mismanagement in the Army, 1978; The New Red Legions, Vol 1: A Survey Data Source Book, Vol 2: An Attitudinal Portrait of the Soviet Soldier, 1980; To Serve with Honor: A Treatise on Military Ethics and the Way of the Soldier, 1982; The Antagonists: A Comparative Combat Assessment of the Soviet and American Soldier, 1984; (comp.) The Mind of the Soviet Fighting Man: A Quantitative Survey of Soviet Soldiers, Sailors, and Airmen, 1984; Operation Peace for Galilee: The Israeli-PLO War in Lebanon, 1984; Military Incompetence: Why the American Military Doesn't Win, 1985; Soviet Military Psychiatry: The Theory and Practice of Coping with Battle Stress, 1986; No More Heroes: Madness and Psychiatry in War, 1987; The Painful Field: The Psychiatric Dimension of Modern War, 1988; The Culture of War: Invention and Early Development, 1990; (with K.S. Metz) From Sumer to Rome: The Military Capabilities of Ancient Armies, 1991; (with Metz) A History of Military Medicine, Vol 1: From Ancient Times to the Middle Ages, Vol 2: From the Renaissance through Modern Times, 1992; (with Metz) A Short History of War: The Evolution of Warfare and Weapons, 1992; (with D.W. Boose, Jr.) The Great Battles of Antiquity: A Strategic and Tactical Guide to Great Battles That Shaped the Development of War, 1994. EDITOR: (with S.H. Cohen) The Environment: Critical Factors in Strategy Development, 1973; Antagonists in the Middle East: A Combat Assessment (part of "Fighting Armies" series), 1983; NATO and the Warsaw Pact: A Combat Assessment (part of "Fighting Armies" series), 1983; Nonaligned, Third World, and Other Ground Armies: A Combat Assessment (part of "Fighting Armies" series), 1983; Military Psychiatry: A Comparative Perspective, 1986. Contributor to periodicals. **Address:** 100 Allen St, Manchester, NH 03102, U.S.A.

GACKENBACH, Jayne. American, b. 1946. **Genres:** Psychology. **Career:** Writer and educator. Clarion State College, Clarion, PA, assistant professor of psychology, 1978-80; University of Northern Iowa, Cedar Falls, assistant professor to associate professor of psychology, 1980-89; part-time instructor in psychology and communication at Athabasca University, University of Alberta, and Grant MacEwan College, all Edmonton, Alberta, Canada, and at Northern Alberta Institute of Technology and Augustana University College, all 1989-. Also part-time instructor at Wartburg College, 1982; Virginia Commonwealth University, 1976-78, John Tyler Community College, 1977-78, Saybrook Institute, 1995-, Blue Quills Native College, and Maskwachees Cultural College, and for Yellowhead Tribal Council; also works as workshop facilitator, including workshops on the psychology of Internet use; host of television documentary programs; guest on media programs. Designer and manager of Internet Web sites. **Publications:** (with J. Bosveld) Control Your Dreams, 1989. EDITOR: Sleep and Dreams: A Sourcebook, 1987; (with S.P. LaBerge, and contrib) Conscious Mind, Sleeping Brain: Perspectives on Lucid Dreaming, 1988; (with A. Sheikh, and contrib) Dream Images: A Call to Mental Arms, 1991; (and contrib) Psychology and the Internet: Intrapersonal, Interpersonal, and Transpersonal Implications, 1998. Contributor to books and academic journals. **Address:** 4505 102nd Ave. No. 5, Edmonton, AB, Canada T6A 0M8. **Online address:** jayneg@athabascau.ca

GADDIS-ROSE, Marilyn. American, b. 1930. **Genres:** Biography, Translations. **Career:** Distinguished Service Prof. of Comparative Literature, and Dir., Translation Research and Instruction Prog., State Univ. of New York at Binghamton, 1968-. Managing Ed., Translation Perspectives, 1984-, and American Translators Assn. Series, 1987-98. Recipient, American Translators Assn. Gode Medal, 1988, Special Service Award, 1995. **Publications:** Julian Green, 1971; Jack B. Yeats, 1972; Katharine Tynan, 1973; (ed) Translation in the Humanities, 1977; Translation Spectrum, 1980; Translation and Literary Criticism, 1997. TRANSLATOR: V. de l'Isle-Adam, Axel, 1971; V. de l'Isle-Adam, Eve of the Future Eden, 1981; Louise Colet, Lui: A View of Him, 1986; (and reviser) J. Green, Adrienne Mesurat, 1991; C.A. Sainte-Beuve, Volupte, the Sensual Man, 1995.

GADNEY, Reg. British, b. 1941. **Genres:** Plays/Screenplays, Art/Art history, History, Mystery/Crime/Suspense. **Career:** Research Fellow and instr., School of Architecture and Planning, Massachusetts, Inst. of Technology, Cambridge, 1966-67; Deputy Controller, National Film Theatre, London, 1967-68; Sr. Tutor and Fellow, 1968-78, and Pro-Rector, 1978-83, Royal Coll. of Art, London. Regular Contributor, London Magazine, 1964-96. **Publications:** MYSTERY NOVELS: Drawn Blanc, 1970; Somewhere in England, 1972; Seduction of a Tall Man, 1972; Something Worth Fighting For, 1974; The Last Hours Before Dawn (in U.S. as Victoria), 1975; The Champagne Marxist (in U.S. as The Cage), 1976; Nightshade, 1987; Just When We Are Safets, 1995; Gone to Nagasaki, 1995; The Achilles Heel, 1996; Happy Christmas Lucy Smith, 1996. ART BOOKS: Constable and His World, 1976; A Catalogue of Drawings and Watercolours by John Constable, R.A., with a Selection of Mezzotints by David Lucas after Constable for "English Landscape Scenery" in the Fitzwilliam Museum, Cambridge, 1978. SCREENPLAYS: Forgive Our Foolish Ways, 1981; The Bell, 1982; Last Love, 1983; Kennedy, 1983; Drummonds, 1985, 2nd series, 1987; Goldeneye, 1989; A Woman at War, 1990; 444 Days, 1990; The Chronicles of Young Indiana Jones, 1991; The Sculptress, 1996. HISTORY: Kennedy, 1983; Cry Hungary!, 1986. **Address:** c/o ICM, Oxford House, 76 Oxford St., London W1R 1RB, England.

GADOL, Peter. American, b. 1964. **Genres:** Novels. **Career:** Writer. **Publications:** NOVELS: Coyote, 1990; The Mystery Roast, 1993; Closer to the Sun, 1996; The Long Rain, 1997; Light at Dusk, 2000. **Address:** c/o Sloan Harris, ICM, 40 W 57th St, New York, NY 10019, U.S.A.

GAETZ, Dayle Campbell. Canadian, b. 1947. **Genres:** Children's fiction, Young adult fiction, Children's non-fiction. **Career:** British Columbia Tel-Communications, Victoria, British Columbia, Canada, draftsperson; School District No. 64, Ganges, British Columbia, teacher on call; freelance writer and journalist, 1998-. **Publications:** FICTION. FOR CHILDREN: Grandfather Heron Finds a Friend, 1986; A Sea Lion Called Salena, 1994; The Mystery at Eagle Lake, 1995; Night of the Aliens, 1995; Alien Rescue, 1997; The Case of the Belly-up Fish, 1998; Mystery from History, 2001; Barkerville Gold, 2004; Alberta Alibi, 2005. FOR YOUNG ADULTS: Spoiled Rotten, 1991; Tell Me the Truth, 1992; Heather, Come Back, 1993; The Golden Rose, 1996; Living Freight, 1998; No Problem, 2003. NONFICTION: Birute Galdikas, Friend of the Orangutan; Catriona Le May Doan, Fastest Woman on Ice. **Address:** 3970 S Island Hwy, Campbell River, BC, Canada V9H 1L9. **Online address:** gdgaetz@oberon.ark.com

GAGE, S. R. Canadian, b. 1945. **Genres:** Architecture, History. **Career:** United Steelworkers of America, District 6, Ontario, Canada, staff member, 1975-79; McMaster University, Hamilton, Ontario, assistant director of Labour Studies Program, 1979-82; freelance writer and researcher, 1982-. Certified instructor, Canadian Association of Nordic Ski Instructors. **Publications:** (with L. Whiteson) The Liveable City: The Architecture and Neighbourhoods of Toronto, 1982; A Few Rustic Huts: Ranger Cabins and Logging Camp Buildings of Algonquin Park, 1985; A Walk on the Canol Road: Exploring the First Major Northern Pipeline, 1990. **Address:** Mosaic Press, PO Box 1032, Oakville, ON, Canada L6J 5E9.

GAGLIANO, Eugene M. (born United States), b. 1946. **Genres:** Children's fiction. **Career:** Elementary school teacher in Honeoye, NY, 1969-73; teacher in a K-5 country school, Buffalo, WY, 1973-77; elementary school teacher in Buffalo, WY, 1977-2003; full-time writer and lecturer, 2003-. **Publications:** Secret of the Black Widow, 2002; Inside the Clown, 2003; C Is for Cowboy: A Wyoming Alphabet, 2003. **Address:** 20 Hillside Dr., Buffalo, WY 82834, U.S.A. **Online address:** egagliano@wyoming.com

GAGLIANO, Frank. American, b. 1931. **Genres:** Novels, Plays/Screenplays. **Career:** Playwright-in-Residence, Royal Shakespeare Co., London, 1967-69; Asst. Prof. of Drama, Playwright-in-Residence, and Dir. of

Contemporary Playwright's Center, Florida State University, Tallahassee, 1969-73; Lectr. in Playwriting and Dir. of the Conkle Workshop for Playwrights, University of Texas, Austin, 1973-75; Distinguished Visiting Prof., University of Rhode Island, 1975; Benedum Prof. of Playwriting, West Virginia University, Morgantown, 1976-; Carnegie-Mellon University Theatre Co., Pittsburgh, Showcase of New Plays, Artistic Dir., 1987-98; University of Michigan, Ann Arbor, Festival of New Works, Artistic Director, 1999-. **Publications:** The City Scene (2 Plays), 1966; Night of the Dunce, 1967; Father Uxbridge Wants to Mary, 1968; The Hide-and-Seek Odyssey of Madeleine Gimple, 1970; Big Sur (TV play), 1970; The Prince of Peasantmania, 1970; The Private Eye of Hiram Bodini (TV play), 1971; Quasimodo (musical), 1971; Anywhere the Wind Blows (musical), 1972; In the Voodoo Parlour of Marie Laveau, 1974; The Commedia World of Lafcadio B., 1974; The Resurrection of Jackie Cramer (musical), 1974; Congo Square (musical), 1975; The Total Immersion of Madelaine Favorini, 1981; San Ysidro (dramatic cantata), 1985; From the Bodoni County Songbook Anthology, 1986, (musical version), 1987; Anton's Leap (novel), 1988; My Chekhov Light (play; monologue), 1987; Hanna: A Run on Odyssey, 1990-92; The Farewell Concert of Irene and Vernon Palazzo, 1995; And the Angels Sing (musical), 1996; Piano Bar (musical), 1998. **Address:** 49 Iroquois Dr, Pittsburgh, PA 15228, U.S.A. **Online address:** SandRico@aol.com

GAGLIARDO, John G. American, b. 1933. **Genres:** History. **Career:** Prof. of History, Boston University, since 1970 (Assoc. Prof., 1968-70). Instr. and Asst. Prof. of History, Amherst College, Massachusetts, 1960-65; Asst. Prof. and Assoc. Prof. of History, University of Illinois at Chicago Circle, 1965-68. **Publications:** Enlightened Despotism, 1967; From Pariah to Patriot: The Changing Image of the German Peasant, 1770-1840, 1969; Reich and Nation: The Holy Roman Empire as Idea and Reality 1763-1806, 1980; Germany under the Old Regime, 1600-1790, 1991. **Address:** 10 Emerson Pl Apt 7C, Boston, MA 02114, U.S.A. **Online address:** jgags@bu.edu

GAIDUK, Ilya V(alerievich). Russian, b. 1961. **Genres:** Military/Defense/Arms control, History. **Career:** High school teacher in Moscow, Russia, 1984-87; Russian Academy of Sciences, Institute of World History, Moscow, junior research fellow, 1990-93, research fellow, 1993-. **Publications:** The Soviet Union and the Vietnam War, 1996. Contributor to books in English and works published in Russian. Contributor to periodicals. **Address:** Institute of World History, Russian Academy of Sciences, 32a Leninskii Prospect, 117334 Moscow, Russia.

GAIL, Barbara. *See* KATZ, Bobbi.

GAILLARD, Frye. American, b. 1946. **Genres:** Novels, History, Music, Sports/Fitness, Writing/Journalism, Autobiography/Memoirs. **Career:** Race Relations Reporter, Nashville, TN, managing editor and staff writer, 1970-72; Charlotte Observer, Charlotte, NC, staff writer, editorial writer, and southern editor, 1972-90; Queens College, Charlotte, writer in residence, 1981, instructor in nonfiction writing, 1990-99; Novello Festival Press, founding editor, 2000-. Creative Loafing (alternative newspaper), columnist. **Publications:** Watermelon Wine: The Spirit of Country Music, 1978; Race, Rock, and Religion, 1982; (with D. Jackson and D. Sturkey) The Catawba River, 1983; The Unfinished Presidency: Essays on Jimmy Carter, 1986; The Dream Long Deferred, 1988; The Secret Diary of Mikhail Gorbachev (novel), 1990; (with N.B. Gaillard) Southern Voices, 1991; (with K. Petty) Kyle at 200 M.P.H., 1993; Lessons from the Big House: One Family's Passage through the History of the South, 1994; If I Were a Carpenter: 20 Years of Habitat for Humanity, 1996; The Heart of Dixie: Southern Rebels, Renegades and Heroes, 1996; (with R. Gaillard) The Way We See It, 1995; (with N. Gaillard and T. Gaillard) Mobile and the Eastern Shore, 1997; Voices from the Attic, 1997; As Long as the Waters Flow: Native Americans in the South and East, 1998; (with B. Baldwin) The 521 All-Stars: A Championship Story of Baseball and Community, 1999; The Greensboro Four: Civil Rights Pioneers, 2001; Cradle of Freedom: Alabama and the Movement That Changed America, 2004. **Address:** 7005 Providence Sq Dr, Charlotte, NC 28270, U.S.A.

GAIMAN, Neil (Richard). British, b. 1960. **Genres:** Science fiction/Fantasy. **Career:** Free-lance journalist, 1983-1987; writer, 1987-. **Publications:** (with K. Newman) Ghastly beyond Belief, 1985; Don't Panic-The Hitchhiker's Guide to the Galaxy Companion, 1987; Violent Cases, 1987; (with T. Pratchett) Good Omens: The Nice and Accurate Prophecies of Agnes Nutter, Witch, 1990; Sandman: The Doll's House, 1990; Black Orchid, 1991; Miracleman: The Golden Age, 1992; Signal to Noise, 1992; Angels and Visitations, 1993; Mr. Punch, 1994; Death: The High Cost of Living, 1994; Neverwhere, 1996; The Day I Swapped My Dad for Two Goldfish (for children), 1997; Smoke and Mirrors, 1998; Stardust, 1999; American Gods, 2001; The

Sandman: Endless Nights, 2003. EDITOR: (with S. Jones) Now We Are Sick, 1991; (with E. Kramer) The Sandman: Book of Dreams, 1996. **Address:** c/o Merrilee Heifetz, Writers House Inc., 21 West 26th St., New York, NY 10010, U.S.A.

GAINES, Jane (Marie). American, b. 1946. **Genres:** Plays/Screenplays, Art/Art history, Film. **Career:** Educator and author. Duke University, Durham, NC, assistant professor, 1982-91, associate professor, 1991-2001, professor of literature and English, 2001-, founder and director of program in film and video, 1985-, chair of Women Film Pioneers Project, 1994, and founder of Duke in Los Angeles program, School of Cinema-Television, University of Southern California, 1995, director of program, 2000. University of Iowa, visiting assistant professor, 1990; University of Washington, Seattle, Andrew A. Hilen Lecturer, 1990; Vassar College, Luce Distinguished Professor, 1993-94; guest speaker at other institutions. Consultant. **Publications:** Contested Culture: The Image, the Voice, and the Law, 1991; (with K. Mercer) Competing Glances: Reading Robert Mapplethorpe, 1992; Fire and Desire: Mixed-Race Movies in the Silent Era, 2000; The Fantasy of Creating Fantasies, in press. EDITOR: (with C. Herzog, and author of intro) Fabrications: Costume and the Female Body, 1990; (and contrib) Classical Hollywood Narrative: The Paradigm Wars, 1992; (with M. Renov, and author of intro) Collecting Visible Evidence, 1999; (with P. Bowser and C. Musser, and contrib) Oscar Micheaux and His Circle: African-American Filmmaking and Race Cinema of the Silent Era (exhibition catalogue), 2001. FILM SCRIPTS: Double Feature, 1978; Two Is Better, 1979; Project Discovery (or, Life, Learning, and the Pursuit of a College Degree), 1980. Contributor to books. Contributor of articles and reviews to periodicals. **Address:** 104 Crowell Hall, Box 90671, Duke University, Durham, NC 27708, U.S.A. **Online address:** jmgaines@duke.edu

GAINES, Thomas A. American, b. 1923. **Genres:** Architecture, Art/Art history, Cultural/Ethnic topics, Economics, History, Humanities. **Career:** New York Stock Exchange, NYC, member, 1949-50; Casas de Costa Rica, San Jose, president, 1950-77. President of Latin American Investment Council, 1952-55, House of Gaines Inc. (Stamford, CT), 1955-75, Proyecto SA (Panama City, Panama), 1961-76, and Modern Community Developers (NYC), 1965-70. Hampton Planning and Zoning Commission, chairman, 1977-78; member of Hampton Democratic Town Committee. White House Conference on International Cooperation, delegate, 1966; Guest Lecturer: Harvard University, University of Georgia, SUNY, Albany. **Publications:** Profits with Progress: Latin America's Bright Investment Future, 1954; The Campus as a Work of Art, 1991; 15 Pinnacles-History's Glorious Golden Ages, 2002. Contributor of columns and articles to magazines and newspapers. **Address:** 77 Edwards Rd, Hampton, CT 06247, U.S.A. **Online address:** kaytom77@earthlink.net

GAITHER, Carl C. American, b. 1944. **Genres:** Language/Linguistics. **Career:** Louisiana State Penitentiary, worked as hospital administrator for prison hospital; Texas Department of Corrections, worked as research assistant; University of Southwest Louisiana, Lafayette, teacher of remedial mathematics, 1983-85; McNeese State University, Lake Charles, LA, teacher of mathematics and statistics, 1985-86; Aviation Test Board, Dothan, AL, civilian mathematical statistician, 1987-88; Aviation Test Directorate, Fort Hood, TX, civilian engineering psychologist, 1988-90, civilian operations research analyst, 1990-95; free-lance writer, 1995-. **Publications:** WITH A.E. CAVAZOS-GAITHER: Statistically Speaking: A Dictionary of Quotations, 1996; Physically Speaking: A Dictionary of Quotations on Physics and Astronomy, 1997; Mathematically Speaking: A Dictionary of Quotations, 1998; Practically Speaking: A Dictionary of Quotations on Engineering, Technology and Architecture, 1998; Medically Speaking: A Dictionary of Quotations on Dentistry, Medicine and Nursing, 1999; Scientifically Speaking: A Dictionary of Quotations, 2000; Naturally Speaking: A Dictionary of Quotations on Biology, Botany, Nature and Zoology, 2001; Chemically Speaking: A Dictionary of Quotations, 2002; Astronomically Speaking: A Dictionary of Quotations on Astronomy and Physics, 2002. **Address:** 502 Weiss, Killeen, TX 76542, U.S.A. **Online address:** cgaither@n-link.com

GAL, Laszlo. Canadian (born Hungary), b. 1933. **Genres:** Children's fiction, Illustrations. **Career:** Teacher, freelance artist, graphic designer, illustrator, author. **Publications:** SELF-ILLUSTRATED FOR CHILDREN: Prince Ivan and the Firebird, 1991; East of the Sun and West of the Moon, 1993; Merlin's Castle, 1995; (with R. Gal) The Parrot, 1997. Illustrator of books by: M.L. Gefaell de Vivanco, H.C. Andersen, W. Toye, R. Melzack, S. Maas, N. Cleaver, M.A. Downie, M. Engel, M. Bertelli, B. Williams, J. Lunn, C. Ahearn, M. Maloney, E. Martin, M. Collins, R.D. San Souci, M. Mayer, P.K. Page, J. Robertson, D.B. Clenman, A. Erlich, M. Shaw-MacKinnon, L. Frost, M. Ralston, W. Shakespeare, E. Fowke, B. Stoker. **Address:** c/o Key Porter Books, 70 The Esplanade, Toronto, ON, Canada M5E 1R2.

GALA (Y VELASCO), Antonio (Ángel Custodio). Spanish, b. 1936. **Genres:** Plays/Screenplays, Poetry, Essays. **Career:** Poet, playwright, and novelist. Worked as a bricklayer's assistant, c. late 1950s; taught religion, art history, and philosophy in secondary schools in Madrid, Spain, c. 1959. Speaker at conferences. **Publications:** PLAYS: Los verdes campos del Edén (two-act), 1963 trans as The Green Fields of Eden in The Contemporary Spanish Theatre: The Social Comedies of the Sixties, 1983; (trans) P. Claudel, El zapato de raso, 1965; El sol en el hormiguero (two-act), 1966; Noviembre y un poco de yerba (title means: November and a Bit of Grass), 1967; Píldora nupcial; Corazones y diamantes; El "Weekend" de Andrómaca; Vieja se muere la alegría (television plays), 1968; Esa mujer (screenplay), 1968; (adaptor) E. Albee, Un delicado equilibrio, 1969; Spain's Strip-tease, 1970; Los buenos días perdidos (three-act), 1972, trans. as The Bells of Orleans, 1992; Anillos para una dama (title means: A Ring for a Lady), 1973; Suerte, campeón!, 1973; Canta, gallo acorralado (adaptation of a play by Sean O'Casey), 1973; Cantar de Santiago para todos (television play), 1974; Las cítaras colgadas de los árboles (title means: Zithers Hung in the Trees), 1974; Cuatro Conmemoraciones: Eterno Tuy; Auto del Santo Reino; Oratorio de Fuenterrabía; Retablo de Santa Teresa (television plays), 1976; Petra Regalada, 1980; La vieja señorita del Paraíso, 1981; El cemeterio de los pájaros (title means: The Bird Cemetery), 1982; Trilogía de la libertad, 1983; Obras escogidas, 1981; Paisaje Andaluz con figuras (title means: Andalusian Landscapes with Figures; television play), 2 vols., 1984; Samarkanda, 1985; El hotelito (title means: The Little Family Manor), 1985; (with E. Jiménez) El sombrero de tres picos, 1986; Seneca, o el beneficio de la duda, 1987; Carmen Carmen (musical), 1988; Cristóbal Colón (opera), 1989; La truhana (musical), 1992; Los bellos durmientes, 1994; Troneras, 1993-1996, 1996; Teatro musical, 2000. SCREENPLAYS: (with M. Rubio and M. Camús) Digan lo que digan, 1968; Esa mujer, 1968; (with L. Lucia) Pepa Doncel, 1969; (with Rubio) Los buenos días perdidos, 1975. NOVELS: El manuscrito carmesí (title means: The Crimson Manuscript), 1990; La pasión turca, 1993; Más allá del jardín, 1995; Si las piedras hablaran, 1995; La regla de tres, 1996; Café cantante, 1997; El corazón tardío, 1998; Las manzanas del viernes, 1999. POETRY: Enemigo íntimo, 1960; Testamento Andaluz, 1998; El águila bicéfala: textos de amor, 1993; Poemas de amor, 1997; Cuaderno de Amor (anthology), 2001. OTHER: Córdoba para vivir, 1965; Vicente Vela (criticism), 1975; Barrera-Wolff: enero 1976 (catalogue), 1975; Texto y pretexto, 1977; Teatro de hoy, teatro de mañana, 1978; Charlas con Troylo (essays; title means: Conversations with Troylo), 1981, enlarged ed. Charlas con Troylo y desde entonces, 1998; En propia mano (essays), 1983; Cuaderno de la dama de otoño (essays), 1985; Dedicado a Tobías (essays), 1988; Guía de los vinos españoles = Spanish Wines Guide (nonfiction), 1990; La soledad sonora (essays), 1991; La Granada de los nazaríes, 1992; Proas y troneras, 1993; Córdoba de Gala, 1993; Andaluz, 1994; Carta a los herederos, 1995; El don de la palabra, 1996; A quien va conmigo (essays), 1997; La casa sosegada, 1998; (text) Andalucía eterna, 1998; Ahora hablaré de mí (autobiography), 2000; Sobre la vida y el escenario (biography), 2001; Teatro de la historia, 2001; El imposible olvido, 2001, 2nd ed., 2001; Los invitados al jardín, 2002. **Address:** Calle Macarena No. 16, 28016 Madrid, Spain.

GALA, Candelas S. Also writes as Candelas Newton. American (born Spain), b. 1948. **Genres:** Literary criticism and history. **Career:** Teacher at a grammar school in London, England, 1972-73; Carlow College, Pittsburgh, PA, lecturer, 1973-74; Wake Forest University, Winston-Salem, NC, instructor, 1978-81, visiting assistant professor, 1981-82, assistant professor, 1982-85, associate professor, 1985-91, professor of Spanish, 1991-, chairperson, Department of Romance Languages, 1996-, director of Salamanca Semester Abroad Program, 1980, 1991, director of Wake Forest Universidad de Los Andes exchange scholarship, 1981-, member of university judicial council, 1990-95, professorship, 2000-; chairperson, Subcommittee on Technology and the Teaching of Foreign Languages, 1996-. Volunteer translator, Winston-Salem Police Department and Baptist Hospital. **Publications:** Lorca: Libro de poemas o las aventuras de una busqueda, 1986; Lorca: Una escritura en trance; Libro de poemas y Divan del Tamarit (monograph), 1992; Understanding Federico Garcia Lorca, 1995. Translator of English-language education books into Spanish. Contributor of articles and reviews to academic journals. **Address:** Department of Romance Languages, Wake Forest University, 7566 Reynolda Station, Winston-Salem, NC 27109, U.S.A. **Online address:** galascs@wfv.edu

GALANG, M. Evelina. American, b. 1961. **Genres:** Novellas/Short stories. **Career:** University of Wisconsin, Madison, University Theatre for Children and Young People, member of ensemble, 1982-86; WMTV Channel 15, Madison, WI, program creator, director, writer of promotions and public service announcements, production worker, program editor, 1982-86, creator, developer, and producer of 1986 children's special, "By Kids, For Kids"; Children's Theater of Madison, Madison, WI, ensemble member and teacher of creative dramatics for children, 1985-86; Sedelmaier Films, Chicago Story, GKO Productions, Finerty Films, Dix and Associates, Ebel Productions, and Genesis (all film production houses), and other New York and Los Angelesbased companies, Chicago, IL, script and continuity supervisor, 1986-; Women in the Director's Chair, Chicago, IL, public relations, 1987-88; Menomenee Boys and Girls Club, Chicago, IL, teacher of creative dramatics for children, 1988-90; Colorado Review, Fort Collins, CO, assistant manager, production coordinator, 1991-92; Guild Literary Complex, Chicago, IL, volunteer coordinator, supervisor, and planner of multicultural literary events and workshops in poetry, fiction, and music; Colorado State University, Fort Collins, instructor in composition and creative writing, 1992-94, graduate reader, 1993-94; Old Dominion University, Norfolk, VA, visiting assistant professor of creative writing in fiction, 1994-; writer. **Publications:** Her Wild American Self (short fiction), 1996. Contributor of essays and short fiction to periodicals. **Address:** Old Dominion University, Department of English, Norfolk, VA 23529, U.S.A.

GALANTE, Jane Hohfeld. American, b. 1924. **Genres:** Music, Translations. **Career:** University of California, Berkeley, instructor in music, 1948-51; Mills College, Oakland, CA, instructor in music, 1951-54; Berkeley, A Journal of Modern Culture, editor, 1949-52; concert pianist, touring Europe and the United States, 1952-89; writer, editor, and translator. Founder and director, Composers' Forum of San Francisco, 1947-56; trustee, Morrison Chamber Music Center, San Francisco State University, 1956-; honorary trustee, San Francisco Conservatory of Music, 1976-98; member of board of trustees, San Francisco Performances, 1987-91; co-founder, San Francisco Friends of Chamber Music, 1999-; Chevalier de l'ordre des arts et des lettres, 1983. **Publications:** (ed. and trans.) P. Collaer, Darius Milhaud, 1989; (trans.) D. Milhaud, Interviews with Claude Rostand, 2002. **Address:** 8 Sea Cliff Ave, San Francisco, CA 94121, U.S.A.

GALBRAITH, John Kenneth. American, b. 1908. **Genres:** Novels, Art/Art history, Economics, International relations/Current affairs. **Career:** Emeritus Prof., Harvard University, Cambridge, Mass., since 1975 (Instr. and Tutor, 1934-39; Prof. of Economics, 1949-59; Paul M. Warburg Prof. of Economic, 1959-60, 1963-75). Fellow, American Academy and Inst. of Arts and letters (Pres., 1984-87). Asst. Prof. of Economics, Princeton University, N.J., 1939-42; Economic Advisor, National Defense Advisory Commn., 1940-41; Member, Bd. of Eds., Fortune mag, 1943-48; U.S. Ambassador to India, 1961-63. **Publications:** American Capitalism: The Concept of Countervailing Power, 1951; A Theory of Price Control, 1952; The Great Crash 1929, 1955; The Affluent Society, 1958, 3rd ed. 1978; Journey to Poland and Yugoslavia, 1959; The Liberal Hour, 1960; (under pseudonym) The McLandress Dimension (satire), 1963; Made to Last, 1964; The Economic Discipline, 1967; The New Industrial State, 1967, 3rd ed. 1979; The Triumph (novel), 1968; Ambassador's Journal, 1969; (with M.S. Randawa) Indian Painting, 1969; Economics and the Public Purpose, 1973; A China Passage, 1973; Money: Whence It Came, Where It Went, 1975; The Age of Uncertainty, 1977; (with N. Salinger) Almost Everyone's Guide to Economics, 1978; The Nature of Mass Poverty, 1979; Annals of an Abiding Liberal, 1979; The Galbraith Reader, 1979; The Nature of Mass Poverty, 1979; A Life in Our Times, 1981; The Anatomy of Power, 1983; The Voice of the Poor: Essays in Economic and Political Persuasion, 1983; A View from the Stands: Of People, Politics, Military Power, and the Arts, 1986; Economics in Perspective: A Critical History, 1987; (co-author) Capitalism, Communism and Coexistence, 1988; A Tenured Professor (novel), 1990; The Culture of Contentment, 1992; A Journey Through Economic Time, 1994; Name-Dropping: From FDR On, 1999. **Address:** Harvard University, 206 Littauer Center, Cambridge, MA 02138, U.S.A.

GALBRAITH, Kathryn O(sebold). American, b. 1945. **Genres:** Novels, Children's fiction, Young adult fiction. **Career:** Seattle Public Library, Seattle, WA, children's librarian, 1970-71; Fordham University at Lincoln Center, NYC, business librarian, 1971-74; New City Rand Institute, NYC, librarian, 1974-75; Family Service Association of America, NYC, librarian, 1975-79; Tacoma Philharmonic, Tacoma, WA, director, 1982-. Frequent speaker at schools and writing conferences. **Publications:** PICTURE BOOKS: Spots Are Special!, 1976; Katie Did!, 1982; Waiting for Jennifer, 1987; Laura Charlotte, 1990; Look! Snow!, 1992. CHAPTER BOOKS: Roommates, 1990; Roommates and Rachel, 1991; Roommates Again, 1994; Holding onto Sunday, 1995. NOVELS: Come Spring, 1979; Something Suspicious, 1985. **Address:** Tacoma Philharmonic, 901 Broadway, Tacoma, WA 98402, U.S.A.

GALDORISI, George V(ictor). American. **Genres:** Law. **Career:** U.S. Navy, career officer, 1970-; assignments include executive officer of LAMPS MK III Squadron in San Diego, CA, 1985-86, commanding officer of the squadron, 1987-88, executive officer of U.S.S. New Orleans, 198890, commanding officer of LAMPS MK III Squadron, 1990-91, commanding officer of U.S.S. Cleveland, 1992-93, commander of Amphibious Squadron Seven, 1993-94, and chief of staff, Cruiser-Destroyer Group Three; present rank, captain. Naval War College, fellow at Center for Advanced Research. **Publications:** The United States and the 1982 Law of the Sea Convention: The Cases Pro and Con, 1995; (coauthor) Beyond the Law of the Sea: New Directions for United States Oceans Policy, 1997; Coronado Conspiracy (novel), 1998; Alert Seven (novel), 1999. Contributor to periodicals. **Address:** 1061 Pine St., Coronado, CA 92118, U.S.A. **Online address:** GALDORISI@aol.com; ggaldori@ccdg3.navy.mil

GALE, Fredric G. American, b. 1933. **Genres:** Writing/Journalism. **Career:** State University of New York at Binghamton, visiting lecturer, 1992; University of Arkansas, Little Rock, associate professor of rhetoric, 1992-. **Publications:** Writing the Winning Brief, 1992; Teaching Legal Writing, 1993; Political Literacy, 1994; Ethical Issues in Teaching Writing, 1996. **Address:** 39536 French Rd, Lady Lake, FL 32159-3501, U.S.A.

GALE, Monica R(achel). British, b. 1966. **Genres:** Classics. **Career:** University of Newcastle, Newcastle, England, Sir James Knott research fellow, 1992-93; University of London, Egham, Surrey, England, lecturer in classics, 1993-. **Publications:** Myth and Poetry in Lucretius, 1994. **Address:** Dept. of Classics, Royal Holloway, University of London, Egham, Surrey TW20 OEX, England.

GALEF, David. American, b. 1959. **Genres:** Novels, Novellas/Short stories, Children's fiction, Poetry, Language/Linguistics. **Career:** Freelance tutor in English and mathematics, 1977-80; Overseas Training Center, Osaka, Japan, English teacher, 1981-82; Stanley H. Kaplan Educational Centers, Boston, MA, teacher of English and mathematics in Boston and NYC, 1983-85; teacher of English at Japanese business seminars in and around NYC, 1985-86; Columbia University, NYC, teacher of logic and rhetoric, 1986-88, preceptor in literature and humanities, 1988-89; University of Mississippi, University, assistant professor of English, 1989-95, assistant director of graduate studies in English, 1993-95, associate professor, 1995-2002, MFA program administrator, 2001-, professor of English, 2002-. Gives fiction readings and lectures on creative writing. **Publications:** Even Monkeys Fall from Trees, and Other Japanese Proverbs, 1987; The Supporting Cast: A Study of Flat and Minor Characters, 1993; (ed.) Second Thoughts: A Focus on Rereading (anthology), 1998; Even a Stone Buddha Can Talk, and Other Japanese Proverbs, 2000; Laugh Track (short stories), 2000. NOVELS: Flesh, 1995; Turning Japanese, 1998. JUVENILE: The Little Red Bicycle, 1988; Tracks, 1996. Work represented in anthologies. Contributor of articles, stories, poems, and reviews to periodicals. **Address:** Dept of English, University of Mississippi, PO Box 1848, University, MS 38677-1848, U.S.A. **Online address:** dgalef@olemiss.edu

GALEOTTI, Mark. British, b. 1965. **Genres:** History. **Career:** University of Keele, England, lecturer in international history, 1991-96, Organised Russian & Eurasian Crime Research Unit, director, 1997-; Foreign & Commonwealth Office, senior research fellow, 1996-97. **Publications:** The Age of Anxiety, 1995; Afghanistan: The Soviet Union's Last War, 1995; The Kremlin's Agenda, 1995; Gorbachev and His Revolution, 1996; Unstable Russia, 1997; Criminal Russia, 1999; Putin's Russia, 2001; Soviet & Post-Soviet Organized Crime, 2002. **Address:** ORECRU, Department of History, University of Keele, Keele, Staffs ST5 5BG, England. **Online address:** hia15@keele.ac.uk

GALINSKY, Karl. American (born Germany), b. 1942. **Genres:** Classics. **Career:** Prof. of Classics, 1972-, Cailloux Centennial Prof., 1985-, and Distinguished Teaching Professor, 1999-, University of Texas at Austin (Asst. Prof. 1966-68; Assoc. Prof., 1968-72; Chmn., 1974-90). Member, Advisory Council to the Classical Sch. of the American Academy in Rome, 1968-. Member of Editorial Bd., Vergilius, 1973-, Classical Journal, 1990-98, Instr., Princeton University, NJ, 1965-66. **Publications:** Aeneas, Sicily and Rome, 1969, 1971; The Herakles Theme, 1972; Ovid's Metamorphoses, 1975; Classical and Modern Interactions, 1992; The Interpretation of Roman Poetry: Empiricism or Hermeneutics?, 1992; Augustan Culture, 1996. EDITOR: (with F.W. Lenz) Albii Tibulli aliorumque carminum libri tres, 1971; Perspectives of Roman Poetry, 1974; The Cambridge Companion to the Age of Augustus, 2005. **Address:** 4508 Edgemont Dr, Austin, TX 78731, U.S.A. **Online address:** galinsky@mail.utexas.edu

GALISON, Peter (Louis). American, b. 1955. **Genres:** Philosophy. **Career:** Stanford University, Stanford, CA, assistant professor, 1982-85, associate professor, 1985-90, professor of philosophy of physics and co-chair of history of science program, 1990-92; Harvard University, Cambridge, MA, chair of Department of History of Science, 1993-97, Mallinckrodt Professor of the History of Science and Physics, 1994-. Visiting assistant professor, Princeton University, 1985; Center for Advanced Study in Behavioral Science, fellow, 1989-90, co-chair of program in history of science, 1990-92; Center of the Philosophy and History of Science, Boston University, Boston, MA, member of board of directors, 1993-96. Recipient: MacArthur Grant. **Publications:** How Experiments End, 1987; Instruments, Culture, and Language in Modern Physics. EDITOR: (with B. Hevly) Big Science: The Growth of Large-scale Research, 1992; (with D.J. Stump) The Disunity of Science: Boundaries, Contexts, and Power, 1996; Image and Logic: A Material Culture of Microphysics, 1997; (with C.A. Jones) Picturing Science, Producing Art, 1998; (with E. Thompson) The Architecture of Science, 1999; (with A. Roland) Atmospheric Flight in the Twentieth Century, 2000; (and author of intro. with M. Gordin and D. Kaiser) Science and Society: The History of Modern Physical Science in the Twentieth Century, 2001; (with S.R. Graubard and E. Mendelsohn) Science in Culture, 2001. **Address:** Department of History of Science, 1 Oxford St., Science Center 235, Cambridge, MA 02138, U.S.A. **Online address:** galison@fas.harvard.edu

GALL, Lothar. German, b. 1936. **Genres:** History. **Career:** University of Giessen, Germany, professor of modern history, 1968-72; Free University of Berlin, Germany, 1972-75; Oxford University, England, guest professor, 1972-73; University of Frankfurt, Germany, 1975-. **Publications:** Bismarck: d. weisse Revolutionear, 1980, as Bismarck, the White Revolutionary, 1986. UNTRANSLATED WORKS: Fragen an die deutsche Geschichte, 1974, 20th ed., 2000; Europa auf dem Weg in die Moderne, 1850-1890, 1984, 4th ed., 2004; Buergertum in Deutschland, 1989; (with K.-H. Juergens) Bismarck: Lebensbilder, 1990; Von der staendischen zur buergerlichen Gesellschaft, 1993; Germania, eine deutsche Marianne?, 1993; (with and others) Die Deutsche Bank, 1870-1995, 1995; Buergertum, liberale Bewegung und Nation. Ausgewaehlte Aufsaetze, 1996; Otto von Bismarck und Wilhelm II, 2000; Krupp: Der Aufstieg eines Industrieimperiums, 2000. EDITOR: Liberalismus, 1976; O. von Bismarck, die grossen Reden, 1981; (with R. Koch) Der Europeaische Liberalismus im 19. Jahrhundert: Texte zu seiner Entwicklung, 1981; (with others) Enzyklopeadie deutscher Geschichte, 1988-96; Stadt und Buergertum im 19. Jahrhundert, 1990; Vom alten zum neuen Buergertum, 1991; Neuerscheinungen zur Geschichte des 20. Jahrhunderts, 1992; Stadt und Buergertum im Uebergang von der traditionalen zur modernen Gesellschaft, 1993; (with D. Langewiesche) Liberalismus und Region: Zur Geschichte des deutschen Liberalismus im 19. Jahrhundert, 1995; Frankfurter Gesellschaft fuer Handel, Industrie, und Wissenschaft, 1995; Die Grossen Deutschen unserer Epoche, 1995. **Address:** History Seminar, University of Frankfurt, Grueneburgplatz 1, Postfach 11 19 32, D-60629 Frankfurt am Main, Germany. **Online address:** L.Gall@em.uni-frankfurt.de

GALL, Sandy. (Henderson Alexander Gall). British (born Malaysia), b. 1927. **Genres:** Travel/Exploration, Writing/Journalism, Documentaries/Reportage. **Career:** Foreign correspondent for Reuters News Agency, 1953-63; Independent Television News, London, England, television journalist, 1963-92. Rector of University of Aberdeen, 1978-81; Free-lance writer, broadcaster, 1993-. CBE, 1988. **Publications:** Gold Scoop (novel), 1977; Chasing the Dragon (novel), 1981; Don't Worry about the Money Now, 1983; Behind Russian Lines: An Afghan Journal, 1983; Afghanistan: Agony of a Nation, 1988; Salang (novel), 1989; George Adamson, Lord of the Lions, 1991; News from the Front: A Television Reporter's Life, 1994; The Bushmen of Southern Africa: Slaughter of the Innocent, 2001. **Address:** Doubleton Oast House, Penshurst, Tonbridge, Kent TN11 8JA, England. **Online address:** sgaa@btinternet.com

GALLAGHER, Gary W(illiam). American, b. 1950. **Genres:** History. **Career:** National Archives and Records Administration, Washington, DC, archivist at Lyndon Baines Johnson Library, 1977-86; Pennsylvania State University, University Park, assistant professor, 1986-89, associate professor, 1989-91, professor of history, 1991-98, head of department, 1991-95; University of Virginia, professor of history, 1998-99, John L. Nau Professor of History, 1999-. University of Texas at Austin, visiting lecturer, spring, 1986. Penn State/Mont Alto Annual Conferences on the Civil War, academic coordinator, 1987-; American Battlefield Protection Foundation, member of board of trustees, 1991-. **Publications:** Stephen Dodson Ramseur: Lee's Gallant General, 1985; (ed.) Fighting for the Confederacy: The Personal Recollections of General Edward Porter Alexander, 1989; (ed. and contrib.) Lee the Soldier, 1996; The Confederate War, 1997; Lee and His Generals in War and Memory, 1998; Lee and His Army in Confederate History, 2001. **Address:** Dept of History, University of Virginia, Charlottesville, VA 22903, U.S.A.

GALLAGHER, Kathleen. Canadian, b. 1965. **Genres:** Plays/Screenplays, Education, Gay and lesbian issues, Popular Culture, Race relations, Theatre,

Urban studies, Women's studies and issues. **Career:** University of Toronto, ON, Dept of Curriculum, Teaching and Learning, associate professor, 1999-. **Publications:** Drama Education in the Lives of Girls: Imagining Possibilities, 2000; (ed. with K. Gallagher and D. Booth) How Theatre Educates: Convergences and Counterpoints with Artists, Scholars, and Advocates, 2003. Contributor to books. Contributor of articles and reviews to periodicals. **Address:** Dept of Curriculum Teaching and Learning, Ontario Institute for Studies in Education, University of Toronto, 252 Bloor St W, Toronto, ON, Canada M5S 1V6. **Online address:** kgallagher@oise.utoronto.ca

GALLAGHER, Patricia. American. **Genres:** Romance/Historical. **Publications:** The Sons and the Daughters, 1961; Answer to Heaven, 1964; The Fires of Brimstone, 1966; Shannon, 1967; Shadows of Passion, 1971; Summer of Sighs, 1971; The Thicket, 1974; Castles in the Air, 1976; Mystic Rose, 1977; No Greater Love, 1979; All for Love, 1981; Echoes and Embers, 1983; On Wings of Dreams, 1985; Love Springs Eternal, 1985; A Perfect Love, 1987. **Address:** 3111 Clearfield Dr., San Antonio, TX 78230, U.S.A.

GALLAGHER, Patricia C. American, b. 1951. **Genres:** Business/Trade/Industry, Crafts, Education, How-to books, Medicine/Health, Recreation. **Career:** Writer. Speaker for Book Publishing World and American Society of Journalists and Authors, 1991-92; leader of publishing workshops; publishing consultant. **Publications:** Child Care and You: A Comprehensive Guide to Organizing a Profitable Home Based Child Care Business, 1987; Robin's Play and Learn Book: Creative Activities for Preschoolers, 1988; How to Entertain Children at Home or in Preschool, 1988; Robin's Play and Learn Book: Creative Activites for Preschoolers, 1988; For All the Write Reasons, 1992; Raising Happy Kids on a Reasonable Budget, 1994; Start Your Own At-Home Child Care Business, 1996; So You Want to Open a Profitable Child Care Center, 1996. **Address:** 3111 Clearfield Dr, San Antonio, TX 78230, U.S.A.

GALLAGHER, Stephen. Also writes as Stephen Couper, John Lydecker. British, b. 1954. **Genres:** Mystery/Crime/Suspense, Horror, Plays/Screenplays, Art/Art history. **Career:** Yorkshire Television, Leeds, England, researcher for documentaries department, 1975; Granada Television, Manchester, England, transmission controller, 1975-80; Piccadilly Radio, Manchester, radio scriptwriter, 1977-80; British Broadcasting Corp., London, England, television scriptwriter for "Doctor Who" serial, 1978-80; full-time freelance writer, 1980-. **Publications:** FICTION: The Last Rose of Summer (adaptation of radio serial), 1978, reprinted, under pseudonym Stephen Couper, as Dying of Paradise, 1982; Warrior's Gate, 1982; (as John Lydecker) The Ice Belt, 1982; Chimera, 1982; Terminus (adaptation of a "Doctor Who" script), 1984; Follower, 1984; Valley of Lights, 1987; Oktober, 1988; Down River, 1990; Rain, 1990; Dark Visions (3-author collection), 1990; The Boat House, 1991; Nightmare, with Angel, 1992; Red, Red Robin, 1995; Journeyman-The Art of Chris Moore (nonfiction), 2000. Author of short stories and radio and television scripts. Contributor to criticism collections. **Address:** The Agency, 24 Pottery Lane, Holland Park, London W11 4LZ, England. **Online address:** www.stephengallagher.com

GALLAGHER, Susan VanZanten. American, b. 1955. **Genres:** Literary criticism and history. **Career:** Covenant College, Lookout Mountain, TN, assistant professor of English, 1982-86; Calvin College, Grand Rapids, MI, assistant professor, 1986-87, associate professor, 1987-91, professor of English, 1991-93; Seatte Pacific University, professor of English, 1993- writer. Baylor University, visiting assistant professor, summer, 1986. **Publications:** (with R. Lundin) Literature through the Eyes of Faith, 1989; A Story of South Africa: J. M. Coetzee's Fiction in Context, 1991; Postcolonial Literature and The Biblical Call to Justice, 1994. Work represented in anthologies. Contributor to periodicals. **Address:** Dept. of English, Seattle Pacific University, Seattle, WA 98119, U.S.A.

GALLAGHER, Tess. American, b. 1943. **Genres:** Novellas/Short stories, Poetry, Film, Travel/Exploration, Essays. **Career:** Taught at St. Lawrence University, Canton, NY, 1974-75, Kirkland College, Clinton, NY, 1975-77, University of Montana, Missoula, 1977-78, and University of Arizona, Tucson, 1979-80; Syracuse University, NY, professor, 1980-90; Whitman College, Visiting Arnold Professor, 1996-97; Stadler Poetry Center, Bucknell University, poet-in-residence. **Publications:** Stepping Outside, 1974; Instructions to the Double, 1976; Under Stars, 1978; Portable Kisses, 1978; Willingly, 1984; A Concert of Tenses: Essays on Poetry, 1986; The Lover of Horses, 1986; Amplitude: New and Selected Poems, 1987; Moon-Crossing Bridge, 1992; Portable Kisses, 1992; Portable Kisses Expanded, 1993; My Black Horse (new and selected poems), 1995; At the Owl Woman Saloon, 1997; Soul Barnacles, Ten More Years with Ray, 2000; Dear Ghosts, 2006. **Address:** c/o Amanda Urban, ICM, 40 W 57th St, New York, NY 10019, U.S.A.

GALLAHER, (William) Rhea, Jr. Also writes as Judith Gould. American, b. 1945. **Genres:** Novels. **Career:** English teacher at public schools in Harriman, TN, 1965-66; Biomedical Information Corp., NYC, editor and writer, 1975-76; free-lance editor in NYC, 1976-82; writer, 1979-. Also worked as waiter in a camp for wealthy boys, state road worker, elevator operator at U.S. Senate, library page, apartment complex manager, and off-off-Broadway stage manager. **Publications:** NOVELS AS JUDITH GOULD (with N.P. Bienes): Sins, 1982; Love-Makers, 1986; Dazzle, 1989; Never Too Rich, 1990; Texas Born, 1992; Forever, 1992; Too Damn Rich, 1995; Second Love, 1998; Till the End of Time, 1998; Rapsody, 1999; Time to Say Good-Bye, 2000.

GALLANT, Felicia. See DANO, Linda.

GALLANT, Jennie. See SMITH, Joan Gerarda.

GALLANT, Noelle. See BERMAN, Claire.

GALLANT, Roy Arthur. American, b. 1924. **Genres:** Astronomy, Biology, Chemistry, Children's non-fiction, Earth sciences, Environmental sciences/Ecology, Zoology, Biography. **Career:** Member of faculty, American Museum-Hayden Planetarium, 1972-80; Dir., Southworth Planetarium, and Adjunct Prof. of English, Univ. of Southern Maine, Portland, 1980-2000; Member of faculty, Maine College of Art, 1990-93. Managing Ed., Scholastic Teacher mag., 1954-57; Exec. Ed., Aldus Books Ltd., London, 1959-62; Ed.-in-Chief, The Natural Histotry Press, 1962-64. **Publications:** Exploring the Moon, 1955; Exploring Mars, 1956; Exploring the Universe, 1956; Exploring the Weather, 1957; Exploring the Sun, 1958; Exploring the Planets, 1958; Exploring Chemistry, 1958; Man's Reach into Space, 1959; Exploring under the Earth, 1960; Antartic, 1962; The ABC's of Astronomy, 1963; The ABC's of Chemistry, 1963; (with C.J. Schuberth) Discovering Rocks and Minerals, 1967; Man Must Speak, 1969; Man's Reach for the Stars, 1971; Man the Measurer, 1972; Charles Darwin, 1972; Explorers of the Atom, 1973; (with R.A. Suthers) Biology: The Behavioral View, 1973; Astrology: Sense or Nonsense?, 1974; How Life Began, 1975; Beyond Earth, 1977; Fires in the Sky, 1978; Earth's Changing Climate, 1979; The Constellations, 1979; You and Your Memory, 1980; The National Geographic Atlas of Our Universe, 1980; (with I. Asimov) Ginn Science Program (grades 4-8), 1981; The Planets, 1982; Once around the Galaxy, 1982; 101 Questions about the Universe, 1984; Lost Cities, 1985; Fossils, 1985; Ice Ages, 1985; Macmillan Book of Astronomy, 1986; Our Restless Earth, 1986; From Living Cells to Dinosaurs, 1986; The Rise of Mammals, 1986; Private Lives of the Stars, 1986; Rainbows, Mirages and Sundogs, 1987; When the Sun Dies, 1989; Ancients Indians, 1989; The Peopling of Planet Earth, 1990; Our Vanishing Forests, 1991; A Young Person's Guide to Science, 1993; The Day the Sky Split Apart, 1995; Sand Dunes, 1997; Geysers, 1997; Limestone Caves, 1997; Planet Earth, 1997; Glaciers, 1997; Early Humans, 2000; The Ever-Changing Atom, 2000; Earth's Place in Space, 2000; Dance of the Continents, 2000; The Origins of Life, 2000; The Life Stories of Stars, 2000; Inheritance, 2002; Biodiversity, 2002; Earth's Restless Crust, 2002; Earth's Natural Resources, 2002; Earth's Water, 2002; Earth's Atmosphere, 2002; Earth's Structure and Composition, 2002; Earth's History, 2002; Meteorite Hunter, 2002. EDITOR: (with Fisher & J. Huxley) Nature, 1960; (with F. Debenham) Discovery and Exploration, 1960; (with F. Manley) Geography, 1961; (with G.E.R. Deacon) Seas, Maps and Men, 1963; (with H. Garnott) Treasures of Yesterday, 1964; (with T.F. Gaskell) World beneath the Oceans, 1964; (with C.A. Ronan) Man Probes the Universe, 1964; (with R. Clark) Explorers of the World, 1964; (with McElroy) Foundations of Biology, 1968; (with C.E. Swartz) Measure and Find Out 1-3, 1969; Charting the Universe, 1969; The Universe in Motion, 1969; Gravitation, 1969; The Message of Starlight, 1969; The Life Story of a Star, 1969; Galaxies and the Universe, 1969. **Address:** PO Box 228, Rangeley, ME 04970, U.S.A.

GALLANT, Stephen I. American, b. 1946. **Genres:** Biology. **Career:** Northeastern University, Boston, MA, associate professor, 1983-90; HNC Inc., Cambridge, MA, senior scientist, 1990-93; Belmont Research Inc., Cambridge, senior scientist, 1993-. **Publications:** Neural Network Learning and Expert Systems, 1993. Contributor to scientific journals. **Address:** Belmont Research Inc., 84 Sherman St., Cambridge, MA 02140, U.S.A.

GALLARDO, Evelyn. American, b. 1948. **Genres:** Animals/Pets, Children's non-fiction, How-to books, Biography. **Career:** Writer and photographer, 1988-; Educational Travel Services, instructor, 1989-; actor, 2003-. **Publications:** Among the Orangutans: The Birute Galdikas Story, 1993; How to Promote Your Children's Book, 2000. Contributor to magazines. Gallardo's photographs have appeared in books, magazines and, newspapers internationally. **Address:** PO Box 3038, Manhattan Beach, CA 90266, U.S.A. **Online address:** evegal22@aol.com; evegallardo.com

GALLAS, John (Edward). New Zealander, b. 1950. **Genres:** Poetry. **Career:** University of Otago, Dunedin, New Zealand, assistant lecturer in English, 1975; Terry's Restaurant, York, England, assistant chef, 1976-77; University of Liverpool, England, archivist, 1977-78; Cizakca Lisesi, Bursa, Turkey, English teacher, 1980; Robert Smyth School, Market Harborough, England, English teacher, 1981-87; Akademi, Diyarbakir, Turkey, English teacher, 1988; Student Support Service, Leicester, England, teacher of students with special needs, 1989-. **Publications:** POETRY: Practical Anarchy, 1989; Flying Carpets over Filbert Street, 1993; Grrrrr, 1997; Resistance Is Futile, 1999; The Song Atlas, 2003; Two Ballad Books, 2003; Star City, 2004. **Address:** c/o Clare Pearson, Eddison Pearson Ltd, 3rd Floor, 22 Upper Grosvenor St, London W1X 9PB, England. **Online address:** john.gallas@ntlworld.com

GALLAS, Karen. American, b. 1949. **Genres:** Language/Linguistics. **Career:** Elementary schoolteacher in Beverly, MA, 1972-79; Bridgewater State College, Bridgewater, MA, demonstration teacher, 1979-80; University of Maine at Machias, assistant professor, 1981-85; teacher and director of gifted and talented education at public schools in Norwood, MA, 1985-87; Brookline Public Schools, Brookline, MA, elementary teacher, 1987-. Lesley College, faculty member, 1983-93. Consultant to Galef Institute. **Publications:** The Languages of Learning, 1994; Talking Their Way into Science, 1995. **Address:** Lawrence School, 27 Francis St., Brookline, MA 02446, U.S.A.

GALLENKAMP, Charles (Benton). American, b. 1930. **Genres:** Young adult fiction, Archaeology/Antiquities, Children's non-fiction, History. **Career:** University of New Mexico, Albuquerque, assistant director of Museum of Anthropology, 1948-51; Houston Museum of Natural History, research associate in anthropology, 1952-56; Interam Foundation, Inc., Denton, TX, director of Maya Research Fund, 1957-62; Janus Gallery, Santa Fe, NM, director, 1970-76. Writer and lecturer on archaeology, ethnology, and pre-Columbian art of the southwestern United States, Mexico, and Central America, 1959-. Conducted research at American Museum of Natural History, British Museum, and Museo Nacional de Antropologia, Mexico City; research associate of School of American Research, Santa Fe, 1976-98; exhibition coordinator for "Maya: Treasures of an Ancient Civilization," a traveling exhibition organized by the Albuquerque Museum, 1981-87. **Publications:** Maya: The Riddle and Rediscovery of a Lost Civilization 1959, 3rd ed., 1985; The Pueblo Indians in Story, Song, and Dance (juvenile), 1955; Finding Out about the Maya (juvenile), 1963; (with C. Meyer) The Mystery of the Ancient Maya, 1985; (gen. ed.) Maya: Treasures of an Ancient Civilization, 1985; Dragon Hunter: Roy Chapman Andrews and the Central Asiatic Expeditions, 2001. **Address:** PO Box 9275, Santa Fe, NM 87504, U.S.A.

GALLEYMORE, Frances. British, b. 1946. **Genres:** Novels, Novellas/Short stories. **Career:** Novelist and Screenwriter. **Publications:** The Orange Tree, 1970; Ground Wave Sailing, 1975; Dangerous Relations, 1994; Lifemask, 1995; Safe, 1996; Widow Maker, 1999.

GALLHOFER, Irmtraud N(ora). Dutch (born Austria), b. 1945. **Genres:** Politics/Government. **Career:** Free University of Amsterdam, Netherlands, research assistant in education, 1978-82; Sociometric Research Foundation, Amsterdam, managing director, 1984-. University of Essex, teacher at summer school of European Consortium for Political Research, 1985-90. Foundation for Psychonomics, member of Dutch research group, 1979-; National Science Foundation, researcher, 1997-. **Publications:** (with Saris) Foreign Policy Decision-Making: A Qualitative and Quantitative Analysis of Political Argumentation, 1996; (with Saris) Collective Choice Processes: A Qualitative and Quantitative Analysis of Foreign Policy Decision-Making, 1997. EDITOR AND CONTRIBUTOR: (with M. Melman and W.E. Saris) Different Text-Analysis Procedures for the Study of Decision-Making, 1986; (with Saris) Sociometric Research, 2 vol, 1988. Contributor to periodicals. **Address:** Meander 402, 1181 WN Amstelveen, Netherlands. **Online address:** gallhof@ibm.net

GALLO, Gina. American, b. 1954. **Genres:** Criminology/True Crime. **Career:** Chicago Department of Mental Health, Chicago, IL, clinical therapist, 1976-79; Chicago Police Department, Chicago, IL, police officer, 1982-98; writer; Columns, Street Beat and Crime Scenes, appear regularly in Blue Murder Magazine. She also writes for online magazines NYCOP Online and Backup. **Publications:** Crime Scenes, 2000; Armed and Dangerous: Memoirs of a Chicago Policewoman, 2001. **Address:** c/o Michael Congdon, Don Con-

gdon Associates, 156 Fifth Ave., Ste. 625, New York, NY 10010, U.S.A. **Online address:** swornsecrets@hotmail.com

GALLO, Patrick J. American, b. 1937. **Genres:** History, Cultural/Ethnic topics. **Career:** Teaneck High School, Teaneck, NJ, teacher of American history, 1968-. Member of Glen Rock Youth Guidance Council, 1983-88; New York University, adjunct professor, Political Science. Fulbright Scholar, 1984; NEH Fellow, 1986, 1993; American Academy-in-Rome, scholar in residence, 1994-95. **Publications:** Ethnic Alienation: The Italian Americans, 1974; The Urban Experience of Italian Americans, 1977; India's Image of the International System, 1980; Swords and Plowshares: The United States and Disarmament, 1898-1979, 1980; Old Bread, New Wine: A Portrait of the Italian-Americans, 1981; The American Paradox: Politics and Justice in America, 1995. Contributor to periodicals in the United States and abroad. **Address:** 100 Elizabeth Ave., Teaneck, NJ 07666, U.S.A.

GALLOWAY, Allan Douglas. British, b. 1920. **Genres:** Theology/Religion. **Career:** Prof. Emeritus of Divinity, Univ. of Glasgow, since 1982 (Sr. Lectr., 1960-66; Reader in Divinity, 1966-68; Prof. 1968-82; Gifford Lectr., 1984) Principal of Trinity Coll., Glasgow, 1972-82. Prof. of Religious Studies, Univ. of Ibadan, Nigeria, 1954-60. **Publications:** The Cosmic Christ, 1951; Basic Readings in Theology, 1964; Faith in a Changing Culture, 1966; Wolf-hart Pannenberg, 1973; History of Christian Theology, Vol. 1, Pt. III, 1986. **Address:** 5 Straid Bheag, Clynder, Hellensburgh, Dunbartonshire GQ4 0QX, Scotland.

GALLOWAY, Janice. British, b. 1956. **Genres:** Novels, Novellas/Short stories. **Career:** Writer; teacher of English, 1980-90; Glasgow University, tutor, 2002-03. American Academy of Arts and Letters, E.M. Forster Award, 1994; former classical music correspondent for Scotland on Sunday, Observer Scotland; Radios 3 and 4, music reviewer; British Library, research fellow, 1999. **Publications:** NOVELS: The Trick Is to Keep Breathing, 1990; Foreign Parts, 1994; Clara, 2002. STORIES: Blood, 1991; Where You Find It, 1996. OTHER: (with A. Bevan) Pipelines, 2000; Monster (libretto), 2002; boy, book, sea (poems & fragments), 2002. EDITOR: (with H. Whyte) New Writing Scotland 8 (fiction anthology), 1990; (with M. Sinclair) Meantime (fiction anthology), 1991; (with H. Whyte) New Writing Scotland 9, 1991; (with H. Whyte) New Writing Scotland 9, 1992. **Address:** c/o Derek Johns, A.P. Watt Ltd., 20 John St, London WC1N 2DR, England. **Online address:** webmaster@galloway1to1.org

GALLOWAY, Kara. *See* CAIL, Carol.

GALT, Anthony H(oward). American, b. 1944. **Genres:** Anthropology/Ethnology, Area studies, Local history/Rural topics. **Career:** University of Wisconsin-Green Bay, instructor to professor of social change and development and anthropology, 1971-, chair of Anthropology Disciplinary Program, 1975-76, 1979-84, and 1991-, chair of Concentration in Social Change and Development, 1976-79. Conducted field research in Sicily, 1968-70 and 1974, Locorotondo, Apulia, Italy, 1981-82, Tuscany, 1998, and California. **Publications:** (with L.J. Smith) Models and the Study of Social Change, 1976; Far from the Church Bells: Settlement and Society in an Apulian Town, 1991; Town and Country in Locorotondo, 1992. Work represented in anthologies. Contributor of articles and reviews to professional journals.

GALT, George. Canadian, b. 1948. **Genres:** Novels, Poetry, Essays. **Career:** Freelance writer, editor, and novelist. Associate editor and book reviews editor for Saturday Night for four years. **Publications:** Love Poems, 1974; Trailing Pythagoras, 1982; Whistlestop: A Journey across Canada, 1987; Scribes and Scoundrels (novel), 1997. EDITOR: The Purdy-Woodcock Letters: Selected Correspondence, 1964-1984, 1988; The Saturday Night Traveller (essays), 1990; The Thinking Heart: Best Canadian Essays, 1991. Contributor of essays to magazines. **Address:** 17 Fulton Ave, Toronto, ON, Canada M4K 1X6.

GALVIN, Brendan. American, b. 1938. **Genres:** Poetry. **Career:** Northeastern University, Boston, instructor in English, 1964-65; Slippery Rock State College, PA, assistant professor of English, 1968-69; Central Connecticut State University, New Britain, emeritus professor of English, 1997- (member of the faculty 1969-97). **Publications:** The Narrow Land, 1971; The Salt Farm, 1972; No Time for Good Reasons, 1974; The Minutes No One Owns, 1977; Atlantic Flyway, 1980; Winter Oysters 1983; A Birder's Dozen, 1984; Seals in the Inner Harbor, 1986; Raising Irish Walls, 1988; Wampanoag Traveler, 1989; Great Blue: New and Selected Poems, 1990; Outer Life: The Poetry of Brendan Galvin, 1991; Saints in Their Ox-Hide Boat, 1992; Early Returns, 1992; Sky and Island Light, 1997; Hotel Malabar, 1998; The Strength of a Named Thing, 1999; Place Keepers, 2003. **Address:** PO Box 383, Truro, MA 02666, U.S.A.

GALVIN, Matthew R(eppert). American, b. 1950. **Genres:** Medicine/Health, Children's non-fiction. **Career:** Indiana University Medical Center, Indianapolis, fellow in child psychiatry, 1982-84, assistant professor, 1984-89, clinical assistant professor, 1990-92, 1993-95, clinical associate professor of psychiatry, 1995-. Larue Carter Hospital, staff psychiatrist, 1984-88, acting director of Youth Service, 1988-90; Indiana University Hospitals, staff psychiatrist, 1984-, assistant director of Psychiatric Services for Children and Adolescents, 1991-98; Riley Child Psychiatric Services, staff child adolescent psychiatrist, 1990-, medical director of Child Adolescent Psychiatric Inpatient Program, 1991-98; St. Vincent's Hospital, staff psychiatrist, 1993-97; Methodist Hospital, staff psychiatrist, 1995-; Pleasant Run Inc, child psychiatrist, 1998-. Public speaker; guest on television and radio programs. **Publications:** Ignatius Finds Help: A Story about Psychotherapy for Children, 1988; Otto Learns about His Medicine: A Story about Stimulant Medication for Children, 1988, rev. ed., 1995; How Robby Really Transformed: A Story about Grownups Helping Children, 1988; Clouds and Clocks: A Story for Children Who Soil, 1989; (with R. Collins) Sometimes Y: A Story for Families with Gender Identity Issues, 1993; The Conscience Celebration, 1998. Contributor to medical books. Contributor to professional and medical journals.

GAMBETTA, Diego. Italian/British, b. 1952. **Genres:** Criminology/True Crime, Sociology. **Career:** University of Turin, Italy, Institute of Sociology, researcher, 1976-77; Regional Administration of the Piemonte, Italy, research officer, 1978-79, 1982-84; Cambridge University, England, junior research fellow of King's College, 1984-88, senior research fellow, 1988-91; Oxford University, England, lecturer, 1991-93, reader in sociology, 1993-95, fellow of St. Anne's College, 1991-, university reader in sociology, 1995-, fellow of All Souls College, 1995-2003, professor of sociology in recognition of distinction, 2002, official fellow of Nuffield College, 2003-. Lecturer at colleges and universities around the world; University of Chicago, visiting professor, 1994-95; Columbia University, NYC, Italian Academy for Advanced Studies, inaugural fellow, 1996-97; Stanford University, Center for Advanced Study in the Behavioral Sciences, fellow, 1998; British Academy, fellow, 2000, research reader, 2000-02. **Publications:** Were They Pushed or Did They Jump?, 1987; (ed. and contrib.) Trust: Making and Breaking Cooperative Relations, 1988; La mafia siciliana, 1992, trans. as The Sicilian Mafia, 1993; Crimes and Signs: Cracking the Codes of the Underworld, 2004. IN ITALIAN: (with L. Ricolfi) Il compromesso difficile, 1978; (with U. Colombino and F. Rondi) L'offerta di lavoro giovanile in Piemonte, 1980; (with S. Warner) La retorica della riforma, 1994; La Statua (screenplay). Work represented in anthologies. Contributor of articles, stories, and reviews to periodicals. **Address:** Nuffield College, Oxford OX1 1NF, England.

GAMBLE, Ed. American, b. 1943. **Genres:** Social commentary, Cartoons. **Career:** Worked as a reporter, sports editor, and sports cartoonist for several daily newspapers until 1972; Nashville Banner, Nashville, TN, editorial cartoonist, 1972-80; Florida Times-Union, Jacksonville, FL, editorial cartoonist, 1980-. Work syndicated by Register and Tribune Syndicate (later Cowles Syndicate), 1973-86, and King Features Syndicate, 1986-. **Publications:** A Peek at the Great Society, 1965; You Get Two for the Price of One, 1995. Contributor to magazines and cartoon anthologies. **Address:** Florida Times-Union, 1 Riverside Ave, Jacksonville, FL 32202, U.S.A.

GAMBLE, Terry. (born United States). **Genres:** Dance/Ballet. **Career:** University of Michigan, Ann Arbor, member of English advisory board. **Publications:** The Water Dancers (novel), 2003. Author of short stories, poetry, and essays for literary journals. **Address:** c/o Author Mail, HarperCollins Publishers, 10 East 53rd St., 7th Floor, New York, NY 10022, U.S.A. **Online address:** terry@terrygamble.com

GAMMEL, Irene. Canadian, b. 1959. **Genres:** Literary criticism and history. **Career:** University professor and writer. McMaster University, Toronto, Ontario, Canada, lecturer in English and comparative literature, 1992-93; University of Prince Edward Island, Charlottetown, Prince Edward Island, Canada, assistant professor, 1993-97, associate professor, 1997-2000, professor of English, 2000-. Visiting professor at Friedrich-Schiller-Universitat (Canadian studies) and Jena und Erfurt Universitat (spring term, 2001), both in Germany. **Publications:** Sexualizing Power in Naturalism: Theodore Dreiser and Frederick Philip Grove, 1994; Baroness Elsa: Gender, Dada, and Everyday Modernity: A Cultural Biography, 2002. EDITOR: (with E. Epperly), L.M. Montgomery and Canadian Culture, 1999; Confessional Politics: Women's Sexual Self-Representations in Life Writing and Popular Media, 1999. Contributor to literary journals and scholarly books. **Address:** Department of English, University of Prince Edward Island, 550 University Avenue, Charlottetown, PE, Canada C1A 4P3. **Online address:** lgammel@upei.ca

GAMMER, Moshe. Israeli (born Russia), b. 1950. **Genres:** Area studies, Human relations/Parenting, International relations/Current affairs. **Career:** Tel Aviv University, Tel Aviv, Israel, external teacher, 1989-93, postdoctoral fellow at Cummings Center for Russian and East European Studies, 1990-92, visiting lecturer, 1993, senior lecturer in Middle Eastern and African history, 1994-, Dayan fellow, Dayan Center for Middle Eastern and African Studies, 1990-91. Open University, Tel Aviv, tutor, 1989-90, 1991-93; Bar Ilan University, visiting lecturer, 1990-91. **Publications:** (ed.) The Political Negotiations between Israel and Egypt, September, 1978-March, 1979: Main Documents (in Hebrew), 1979; (ed.) The Normalization of Relations between Israel and Egypt, April, 1979-October, 1980: Main Documents (in Hebrew), 1981; (ed.) The Autonomy Negotiations, April, 1979-October, 1980: Main Documents (in Hebrew), 1981; Muslim Resistance to the Tsar: Shamil and the Conquest of Chechnia and Daghestan, 1993. Work represented in anthologies. Contributor of articles and reviews to scholarly journals. **Address:** Dept of Middle Eastern and African History, Tel Aviv University, 39040, 69978 Tel Aviv, Israel. **Online address:** gammer@post.tau.ac.il

GAMSON, Joshua (Paul). American, b. 1962. **Genres:** Sociology. **Career:** University of California, Berkeley, instructor and lecturer in sociology, 1992-93; Yale University, New Haven, CT, assistant professor, 1993-98, associate professor, 1998-. **Publications:** (with M. Burawoy, and others) Ethnography Unbound: Power and Resistance in the Modern Metropolis, 1991; Claims to Fame: Celebrity in Contemporary America, 1994; Freaks Talk Back: Tabloid Talk Shows and Sexual Nonconformity, 1998. Contributor to books. Contributor of articles and reviews to periodicals. **Address:** Department of Sociology, Yale University, PO Box 208265, New Haven, CT 06520, U.S.A.

GAMSON, William A(nthony). American, b. 1934. **Genres:** Politics/Government, Social sciences, Communications/Media. **Career:** Prof. of Sociology, Boston College, Chestnut Hill, Mass., since 1982. Research Assoc. in Social Psychology, Harvard University, Cambridge Mass., 1959-62; Research Sociologist, Center for Research on Conflict Resolution, 1962-71; Prof. of Sociology, University of Michigan, Ann Arbor, 1966-82 (Asst. Prof., 1962-64; Assoc. Prof., 1964-66; Chmn., 1974-78). **Publications:** Power and Discontent, 1968; SIMSOC: Simulated Society, 1969, 4th ed., 1991; (with A. Modigliani) Untangling the Cold War, 1971; (with A. Modigliani) Conceptions of Social Life: A Text-Reader for Psychology, 1974; The Strategy of Social Protest, 1975, 1990; (with B. Fireman and S. Rytina) Encounters with Unjust Authority, 1982; What's News: A Game Simulation of TV News, 1984; Talking Politics, 1992. **Address:** 5 Boston Hill Rd, Chilmark, MA 02535, U.S.A. **Online address:** gamson@bc.edu

GAMST, Frederick Charles. American, b. 1936. **Genres:** Anthropology/Ethnology. **Career:** Prof. of Anthropology, University of Massachusetts, Boston, since 1975 (Assoc. Provost for Graduate Studies, 1978-83). Instr., 1966-67, Asst. Prof., 1967-71, and Assoc. Prof., 1971-75, Rice University Houston. Acting Dir., Houston Inter-University African Studies Prog. 1968-71. **Publications:** Travel and Research in Northwestern Ethiopia, Notes for Anthropologists and Other Field Workers in Ethiopia No. 2, 1965; The Qemant: A Pagan-Hebraic Peasantry of Ethiopia, 1969; Peasants in Complex Society, 1974; Studies in Cultural Anthropology, 1975; (with E. Norbeck) Ideas of Culture, 1976; The Hoghead: An Industrial Ethnology of the Locomotive Engineer, 1980; (scriptwriter) T-Time: The History of Mass Transit in Boston, 1984; Highballing with Flimsies: Working under Train Orders on the Espee's Coast Line, 1990; (ed.) Letters from the United States of North America on Internal Improvements, Steam Navigation, Banking, Written by Francis Chevalier de Gerstner in 1839, 1990; (ed) Meanings of Work: Considerations for the 21st Century, 1995; Early American Railroads; Franz Anton Ritter Von Gerstners Die innern Communicationen (1842-1843), 2 vol, 1997. **Address:** Dept. of Anthropology, Univ. of Massachusetts, Harbor Campus, Boston, MA 02125-3393, U.S.A.

GANDER, Forrest. American, b. 1956. **Genres:** Poetry. **Career:** Providence College, 1990-98; Harvard University, 1999-2001; Brown University, 2001-. **Publications:** Rush to the Lake, 1988; Eggplants and Lotus Root, 1991; (ed.) Mouth to Mouth: Poems by 12 Contemporary Mexican Women, 1993; Deeds of Utmost Kindness, 1994; Science & Steepleflower, 1998; Torn Awake, 2001; No Shelter: Selected Poems of Pure Lopez-Colome, 2003; (with K. Johnson) Immanent Visitor: Selected Poems of Jaime Saenz, 2003. **Address:** Literary Arts, Box 1852, Brown University, Providence, RI 02912, U.S.A.

GANDEVIA, Bryan Harle. Australian, b. 1925. **Genres:** Medicine/Health, Bibliography. **Career:** Sr. Fellow, Occupational Health, University of Melbourne, 1958-62; Assoc. Prof. of Rspiratiory Medicine, University of New

South Wales, 1963-85. **Publications:** The Melbourne Medical Students, 1862-1942, 1948; Occupation & Disease in Australia since 1788, 1971. Tears Often Shed: Child Health and Welfare in Australia since 1788, 1978; (with A. Holster and S. Simpson) Annotated Bibliography of the History of Medicine and Health in Australia, 1984; Life in the First Settlement at Sydney Cove, 1985; Chairman, Editorial Board, Bibliography of Australian Medicine & Health Services to 1950, 4 vols., 1988. **Address:** Cregganduff, Mt. York Rd., Mount Victoria, NSW 2786, Australia.

GANESAN, Indira. American (born India). **Genres:** Novels. **Career:** Freelance writer, c. 1990-. **Publications:** NOVELS: The Journey, 1990; Inheritance, 1997. **Address:** c/o Knopf, 201 East 50th St., New York, NY 10022, U.S.A.

GANNETT, Ruth Stiles. American, b. 1923. **Genres:** Children's fiction. **Career:** Medical Technician, Boston City Hosp.; Radar Research Technician, Massachusetts Inst. of Technology, Cambridge,; Staff member, Children's Book Council, NYC. **Publications:** My Father's Dragon, 1948, 50th anniversary ed as Three Tales of My Father's Dragon, 1998; The Wonderful House-Boat-Train, 1949; Elmer and the Dragon, 1950; The Dragons of Blueland, 1951; Katie and the Sad Noise, 1961. **Address:** 8513 Rte. 277, Trumansburg, NY 14886, U.S.A.

GANNON, Martin John. American, b. 1934. **Genres:** Administration/Management. **Career:** University of Maryland at College Park, lecturer, 1968-69, assistant professor, 1969-71, associate professor, 1971-74, professor of management, 1981-, head of faculty of management and organizational behavior of the College of Business Management, 1977-81, acting associate dean for academic affairs, 1978-79; writer. Thammasat University, Fulbright visiting professor and scholar, 1988. Presenter of lectures and managerial training sessions. **Publications:** Management: An Integrated Framework, 1977, 2nd ed., 1982; Organizational Behavior, 1979; (with others) Strategic Management Skills, 1986; Management: Managing for Results, 1988; (with K.G. Smith and C.M. Grimm) The Dynamics of Competitive Strategy, 1992; (with others) Managing without Traditional Methods, 1996; (with S.J. Carroll Jr.) Ethical Dimensions of International Management, 1997; (with others) Understanding Global Cultures, 1997, 2nd ed., 2001; Working across Cultures, 2001; Cross-Cultural Paradoxes, forthcoming. EDITOR: (with C. Anderson) Readings in Management, 1977; (with K. Newman) Handbook of Cross-Cultural Management, 2002; Encyclopedia of Global Cultures, 2 vols., forthcoming. Contributor to booksn and periodicals. **Address:** Robert H. Smith School of Business, University of Maryland at College Park, College Park, MD 20742, U.S.A. **Online address:** mgannon@rhsmith.umd.edu

GANNON, Steve. American, b. 1944. **Genres:** Novels. **Career:** Engineer in the aerospace industry; doctor of dental surgery, Los Angeles (Brentwood), CA; building contractor, Malibu, CA; actor; writer, Sun Valley, ID. **Publications:** A Song for the Asking, 1997. **Address:** PO Box 722, Ketchum, ID 83340, U.S.A. **Online address:** sgannon@sunvalley.net

GANS, Chaim. Israeli, b. 1948. **Genres:** Law. **Career:** Tel Aviv University, Tel Aviv, Israel, professor of law and philosophy, 1981-. **Publications:** Philosophical Anarchism and Political Disobedience, 1992. Contributor to newspapers, literary and political. **Address:** Faculty of Law, Tel Aviv University, Ramat Aviv, Tel Aviv, Israel.

GANS, Eric L. American, b. 1941. **Genres:** Literary criticism and history, Humanities. **Career:** State University of New York at Fredonia, instr. in French, 1965-67; Indiana University, Bloomington, Dept. of French and Italian, asst. prof., 1967-69; University of California at Los Angeles, asst. prof., 1969-73, assoc. prof., 1973-76, chmn. of dept., 1974-77, 1981-86, prof. of French, 1976-. **Publications:** The Discovery of Illusion: Flaubert's Early Works 1835-1837, 1971; Un Pari Contre l'Histoire: Les Premieres Nouvelles de Merimee, 1972; Musset et le Drame Tragique, 1974; Le Paradoxe de Phedre, 1975; Essais d'esthetique paradoxale, 1977; The Origin of Language: A Formal Theory of Representation, 1981; The End of Culture: Toward a Generative Anthropology, 1985; Madame Bovary: The End of Romance, 1989; Science and Faith: The Anthropology of Revelation, 1990; Originary Thinking, 1993; Signs of Paradox, 1997. **Address:** Dept. of French, University of California at Los Angeles, Los Angeles, CA 90095-1550, U.S.A. **Online address:** gans@humnet.ucla.edu

GANS, Herbert J. American (born Germany), b. 1927. **Genres:** Sociology. **Career:** Advisory Ed., Ethnic and Racial Studies, Journal of Contemporary Ethnography, Critical Studies in Mass Communication, and Social Policy (Film Critic, 1971-78). Research Asst., American Soc. of Planning Officials, Chicago, 1950; Asst. Planner, Chicago Housing Authority, 1950-51; Chief Research Planner, P.A.C.E. Assocs., Chicago, 1951-52; Field Rep., Div. of Slum Clearance, U.S. Housing and Home Finance Agency, Washington, 1952-53; Research Assoc., Inst. for Urban Studies, 1953-57, Lectr., Dept. of City Planning, 1956-57, Asst. Prof. of City Planning, Inst. for Urban Studies and Dept. of City Planning, 1958-61, Lectr., Dept. of Sociology, 1958-59, and Research Assoc. Prof. of City Planning and Urban Studies, 1961-64, Univ. of Pennsylvania, Philadelphia; Assoc. Prof. of Sociology and Education, 1964-66, Research Assoc., Inst. of Urban Studies, 1964-65, and Adjunct Prof. of Sociology and Education, 1966-69, Teachers' Coll., Prof. of Sociology and Ford Foundn. Urban Chair, 1971-85, and Robert S. Lynd Prof. of Sociology, 1985-, Columbia University, NYC; Prof. of Sociology and Planning, Dept. of Urban Studies and Planning, Massachusetts Institute of Technology, and Faculty Assoc., MIT.-Harvard Joint Center for Urban Studies, Cambridge, 1969-71. **Publications:** The Urban Villagers, 1962, 2nd ed., 1982; The Levittowners, 1967, 2nd ed., 1982; People and Plans, 1968; More Equality, 1973; Popular Culture and High Culture, 1974, 2nd ed., 1999; Deciding What's News, 1979; Middle American Individualism, 1988; People, Plans and Policies, 1991; The War against the Poor, 1995; Making Sense of America, 1999; Democracy and the News, 2003. EDITOR: (co) On the Making of Americans, 1979; Sociology in America, 1990. **Address:** Dept of Sociology, 404 Fayerweather Hall, Columbia University, New York, NY 10027, U.S.A.

GANSKY, Alton. American, b. 1953. **Genres:** Mystery/Crime/Suspense. **Career:** High Desert Baptist Church, Phelan, CA, senior pastor, 1989-; Gansky Communications, Phelan, CA, founder, 1992-; author, 1996-. **Publications:** THRILLERS: By My Hands, 1996; Tarnished Image, 1998; Terminal Justice, 1998; Marked for Mercy, 1998; Though My Eyes: A Novel, 1998; A Ship Possessed, 1999; A Small Dose of Murder, 1999; Vanished, 2000; Distant Memory, 2000; The Prodigy: A Novel of Suspense, 2001; Dark Moon, 2002. OTHER: Uncovering the Bible's Greatest Mysteries, 2002. **Address:** Gansky Communications, 9983 Rose Dr., Oak Hills, CA 92345-0220, U.S.A. **Online address:** alton@ganskycom.com

GANSLER, Jacques Singleton. American, b. 1934. **Genres:** Military/Defense/Arms control. **Career:** Raytheon Corp., Bedford, MA, engineering manager, 1956-62; Singer Corp., Little Falls, NJ, program manager, 1962-70; International Telephone and Telegraph, Nutley, NJ, vicepresident, 1970-72; U.S. Department of Defense, Washington, DC, deputy assistant secretary, 1972-77; TASC, Arlington, VA, senior vice-president, 1977-; writer. Harvard University, John Fitzgerald Kennedy School of Government, visiting scholar, 1984-. **Publications:** The Defense Industry, 1980; Affording Defense, 1989; Defense Conversion, 1995. **Address:** TASC, 1101 Wilson Blvd Ste 1500, Arlington, VA 22209, U.S.A.

GANT, Richard. See FREEMANTLE, Brian (Harry).

GANTSCHEV, Ivan. Bulgarian, b. 1925. **Genres:** Children's fiction, Illustrations. **Career:** Writer. Freelance artist, Bulgaria, until 1966; J. Walter Thompson (advertising agency), Frankfurt, West Germany, illustrator, 1968-; freelance artist, 1989-. **Publications:** SELF-ILLUSTRATED FOR CHILDREN: The Volcano, 1981; The Christmas Train, 1984; Rumprump, 1984; Journey of the Storks, 1986; Otto the Bear, 1986; Walk under the Rainbow, 1986; The Train to Grandma's, 1987; Where Is Mr. Mole?, 1989; Good Morning, Good Night, 1991; The Christmas Story by Father Christmas, c. 1992; The Christmas Teddy Bear, 1994; Libby's Journey, c. 1995; The River; The Little Bird's Favorite Tree; The Cherrytree; When I Grow Up; The Story of the Rock; The Elephant; Old Woman and the Bear; Timmi and the Old Locomotive; Colors; Raindrop; The Tigers' Present; The Pear Tree; Hanibal; The Adventure of the Mouse. Illustrator of books by: H. Aoki, O. Gadsby, R. Saunders, L. Lattig-Ehlers, K. Baumann, A. Clements. OTHER: The Art of Ivan Gantschev. **Address:** Bettinastrasse 33, 6000 Frankfurt 1, Germany.

GÄNZL, Kurt (Friedrich). (originally Brian Roy Gallas). New Zealander, b. 1946. **Genres:** Plays/Screenplays, Songs/Lyrics and libretti, Music, Theatre, Reference. **Career:** New Zealand Opera Company, basso soloist, 1968; writer, 1976-; Talent Artists Ltd., theatrical agent and casting director, 1981-89. Lecturer and broadcaster. **Publications:** Elektra (play), 1966; The Women of Troy (play), 1967; British Musical Theatre, 2 vols., 1986; (with A. Lamb) Ganzl's Book of the Musical Theatre, 1988; The Complete "Aspects of Love," 1990; The Blackwell Guide to the Musical Theatre on Record, 1990; The Encyclopaedia of the Musical Theatre, 2 vols., 1994, rev. ed., 3 vols., 2001; Ganzl's Book of the Broadway Musical, 1995; Musicals (in US as Song & Dance), 1995, 2nd ed., 1997; The Musical: A Concise History, 1997; Lydia Thompson, Queen of Burlesque, 2002; William B Gill, from the Goldfields to Broadway, 2002. **Address:** Talent Artists Ltd, 59, Sydner Rd., London N16 7UF, England. **Online address:** ganzl@xtra.co.nz

GAO YUAN. Also writes as Hai Lan. Chinese, b. 1952. **Genres:** Cultural/Ethnic topics. **Career:** Writer. Shijiazhuang Diesel Engine Factory, Shijiazhuang, China, foundry workshop engineer, 1975-76; Hebei Provincial Foreign Trade Bureau, Shijiazhuang, agent for fruit exports, 1976-78; China Daily, Beijing, China, feature writer, 1981-82; Asia Cable, Lake Oswego, Oregon, political and legal correspondent, 1984-86. **Publications:** Born Red: A Chronicle of the Cultural Revolution, 1988; Lure the Tiger Out of the Mountains: the Thirty-six Stratagems of Ancient China, 1991. Contributor to periodicals. Has written under the pseudonym Hai Lan. **Address:** 6-B Escondido Village, Stanford, CA 94305, U.S.A.

GARAFOLA, Lynn. American, b. 1946. **Genres:** Dance/Ballet. **Career:** Berlitz Translation Service, New York City, translator and assistant director, 1970-72; Brooklyn College of the City University of New York, Brooklyn, part-time lecturer, 1975-77; Columbia University, New York City, lecturer, 1985, 1986, adjunct assistant professor, 1988-89; Dance Magazine, New York City, critic, feature writer, and contributing editor, 1985-; New York State Council on the Arts, New York City, dance department auditor, 1985-; Studies in Dance History, editor, 1991-98; The Nation, critic, 1994-; Barnard College, NYC, adjunct professor, 2000-; New York Historical Society, guest curator, 1998, 2000; writer. **Publications:** Diaghilev's Ballets Russes, 1989. EDITOR: (with J. Acocella) Andre Levinson on Dance: Writings from Paris in the Twenties, 1991; (trans. and author of intro.) The Diaries of Marius Petipa, 1993; Rethinking the Sylph: New Perspectives on the Romantic Ballet, 1997; Jose Limon: An Unfinished Memoir, 1998; (with N.V.N. Baer) The Ballet Russes and Its World; (with E. Foner) Dance for a City: Fifty Years of the New York City Ballet. **Address:** 606 W 116th St, New York, NY 10027, U.S.A. **Online address:** lg97@columbia.edu

GARAUDY, Roger. French, b. 1913. **Genres:** Philosophy. **Career:** Taught philosophy in Algeria and at lycee Buffon in Paris, France, 1958-59; director of the Centre d'Etudes et de Recherches Marxistes, 1960-70; Clermond-Ferrand, department of letters, master lecturer, 1962-65; professor in the department of literature in Poitiers, 1965-72; affiliated for many years with the Institut international pour le dialogue des civilizations in Geneva, Switzerland. **Publications:** NONFICTION: L'Eglise, le communisme et les chretiens, 1939; Le Communisme et la morale, 1945; Antee: Journal de Daniel Chenier, c. 1946; Les Sources francaises du socialisme scientifique, 1948; Grammaire de la liberte, 1950; La Theorie materialiste de la connaissance, 1953; La Liberte, 1955; (with others) Mesaventures de l'anti-marxisme: Les Malheurs de M. Merleau-Ponty, 1956; Humanisme marxiste: Cinq essais polemiques, 1957; Perspectives de l'homme: Existentialisme, pensee catholique, marxisme, 1959; Questions a Jean-Paul Sartre, precedees d'une lettre ouverte, 1960; L'Itineraire d'Aragon: Du Surrealisme au monde reel, 1961; Dieu est mort: Etude sur Hegel, 1962; Qu'est-ce que la morale marxiste?, 1963; D'Un Realisme sans rivages: Picasso, Saint-John Perse, Kafka, 1963; Karl Marx, 1964, trans by N. Apotheker as Karl Marx: The Evolution of His Thought, 1967; Femmes du XXe siecle, 1965; De L'Anatheme du dialogue: Un Marxiste s'adresse au Concile, 1965, trans by L. O'Neill as From Anathema to Dialogue: A Marxist Challenge to the Christian Churches, 1966; Marxisme du XXe siecle, 1966, trans by R. Hague as Marxism in the Twentieth Century, 1970; La Pensee de Hegel, 1966; Le Probleme chinois, 1967; (with G.M.-M. Cottier) Chretiens et marxistes, 1967; Lenine, 1968; (comp) La Liberte en sursis, 1968: Avec des textes traduits du tcheque, de Alexandre Dubcek, Ota Sik, Radovan Richta, Frantisek Chamalik, 1968; (with Q. Lauer) A Christian-Communist Dialogue, 1968; Peut-on etre communiste aujourd'hui!, 1968; Pour un realisme du xxe siecle: Dialogue posthume avec Fernand Leger, 1968; Pour un modele francais du socialisme (title means: For a French Model of Socialism), 1968; Le Grand Tournant du socialisme, 1969, trans by P. and B. Ross as The Turning-Point of Socialism, 1970; (comp) Toute la Verite, 1970, trans by P. and B. Ross as The Whole Truth, 1971; Esthetique et invention du futur, 1971; Reconquete de l'espoir, 1971; L'Alternative, 1972, trans by L. Mayhew as The Alternative Future: A Vision of Christian Marxism, 1974; Danser sa vie (essay; title means: Dancing Our Life), 1973; Soixante Oeuvres qui annoncerent le futur: Sept Siecles de peinture occidentale (title means: Sixty Paintings Which Announced the Future), 1974; Ludmila Tcherina: Erotisme et mystique, 1975; Parole d'homme (title means: Word of Honor), 1975; Le Projet esperance (title means: Project Hope), 1976; Le Marxisme, 1977; L'Islam habite notre avenir, c. 1981; Pour L'Avenement de la femme, c. 1981; Promesses de l'Islam, 1981; The Case of Israel, 1983; La Palestine, terre des messages divins, c. 1986; L'Islam en Occident: Cordoue, une capitale de l'esprit, c. 1987; An 2000 moins 10: Ou allons-nous?, c. 1990; Integrismes, c. 1990; Les Fossoyeurs: Un Nouvel Appel aux vivants, 1992. Garaudy's works have been translated into many languages, including Spanish and Arabic. **Address:** 69 rue de Sucy, 94430 Chennevieres-sur-Marne, Marne, France.

GARB, Tamar. German (born Israel), b. 1956. **Genres:** Art/Art history. **Career:** University College, London, England, professor, lecturer in art history. **Publications:** Women Impressionists, 1986; Berthe Morisot (monograph), 1987; Sisters of the Brush: Women's Artistic Culture in Late Nineteenth-Century Paris, 1994; (ed. with L. Nochlin) The Jew in the Text: Modernity and the Construction of Identity, 1995; Bodies of Modernity: Figure and Flesh in fin de siecle France, 1998. **Address:** Department of Art, University College, Gower St., London WC1E 6BT, England. **Online address:** t.garb@ucl.ac.uk

GARBER, Anne. Canadian, b. 1946. **Genres:** Food and Wine, Travel/Exploration. **Career:** Toronto Stock Exchange, ON, deputy supervisor, 1968-70; Recent Developments, CEO, 1972-; Dunsky Advertising Ltd., Vancouver, BC, account group supervisor, 1973-76; Asta Productions, Vancouver, head film writer, 1977-82; Canadian Broadcasting Corporation-TV, Vancouver, commentator on the program Consumers Report, 1983; BCTV-TV News, Vancouver, consumer commentator, 1984; CJOR-Radio, Vancouver, producer of the Dave Barrett Show and host of a talk show, 1984-89; CKVU-TV, consumer commentator, 1986-89; Commonwealth Summit Conference, media relations adviser, 1987; Vancouver film commissioner, 1987-88; Office of the Mayor of Vancouver, communications officer, 1987-88; Associated Producers Bureau, executive director, 1988-; The Province newspaper, Vancouver, featured columnist, 1988-, restaurant critic, 1990-; Serious Publishing, editor-in-chief, 1991-; Telus Multimedia, national food & book editor, 1998-2001; evalu8.org Media, Inc., managing director, 2002-. Canadian Food Museum Society, founding member and board secretary. **Publications:** Here Today (documentary film), 1977; The Vancouver Super Shopper, 1982, 4th ed., 1986; (with J. Crawford) Rise and Shine Vancouver, 1990; Vancouver Out to Lunch, 1990; Shopping the World, 1991; Cheap Eats, 1991, 2nd ed. (with J.T.D. Keyes), 1998; The Serious Shopper's Guide to Vancouver, 1992; (with J.T.D. Keyes) Victoria's Best Bargains, 1994; (with L. Gannon) Vancouver's Best Bargains, 1995; Exploring Ethnic Vancouver, 1996; (with J.T.D. Keyes) Vancouver's Cheap Eats, 1997; Vacation Planner, 2005. Contributor to magazines and newspapers. **Address:** 206 W 15th Ave, Vancouver, BC, Canada V5Y 1X9. **Online address:** anne@evalu8.org; www.evalu8.org; www.annegarber.com

GARBER, Joseph R(ene). Also writes as Edgar Still. American, b. 1943. **Genres:** Novels, Adult non-fiction, Literary criticism and history. **Career:** American Telephone and Telegraph Co., 1969-73; Booz, Allen & Hamilton, 1973-84; SRI International, Menlo Park, CA, 1984-85; A.T. Kearney, Redwood City, CA, 1985-93; Forbes magazine, 1993-2002. **Publications:** NOVELS: Rascal Money, 1989; Vertical Run, 1995; In a Perfect State, 1999; Whirlwind, 2004. Contributor of criticism and essays to periodicals. **Address:** c/o Trident Media, 41 Madison Ave, New York, NY 10010, U.S.A.

GARBER, Marjorie. American. **Genres:** Literary criticism and history. **Career:** Harvard University, Cambridge, MA, professor of English, beginning 1981, and director of the Center for Literary and Cultural Studies. Also taught at Yale University, New Haven, CT. **Publications:** Dream in Shakespeare: From Metaphor to Metamorphosis, 1974; Coming of Age in Shakespeare, 1981; Shakespeare's Ghost Writers: Literature as Uncanny Causality, 1987; Vested Interests: Cross-Dressing and Cultural Anxiety, 1992; Vice Versa: Bisexuality and the Eroticism of Everyday Life, 1995; Dog Love, 1996; Symptoms of Culture, 1998. EDITOR: Cannibals, Witches, and Divorce: Estranging the Renaissance, 1987; (with J. Matlock and R.L. Walkowitz) Media Spectacles, 1993; (with R.L. Walkowitz) Secret Agents, The Rosenberg Case, McCarthyism, and Fifties America, 1995; (with P.B. Franklin and R.L. Walkowitz) Field Work: Sites in Literary and Cultural Studies, 1996. **Address:** English Department, Harvard University, Cambridge, MA 02138, U.S.A.

GARBER, Zev. American, b. 1941. **Genres:** Education. **Career:** Los Angeles Valley College, Van Nuys, CA, professor of Jewish studies, 1970-; writer. University of California, Riverside, visiting professor of religious studies, 1983-94. Philadelphia Center for the Holocaust, educational consultant; Annual Scholars' Conference on the Holocaust, conference committee; Studies in Shoah, editor-in-chief; Shofar, editor. **Publications:** Shoah: The Paradigmatic Genocide: Essays in Exegesis and Eisegesis, 1994; (with J. Moore, S. Jacobs, and H. Knight) Post-Shoah Dialogues: Re-Thinking Our Texts Together, 2004; (with B. Zuckerman) Double Takes: Thinking and Rethinking Issues of Modern Judaism, 2004. EDITOR: Methodology in the Academic Teaching of Judaism, 1986; (with A. Berger and R. Libowitz) Methodology in the Academic Teaching of the Holocaust, 1988; Teaching Hebrew Language and Literature at the College Level, 1991; Perspectives on Zionism, 1994; What Kind of God, 1995; Peace, in Deed, 1998; Academic Approaches to Teaching Jewish Studies, 2000. Contributor to books and periodicals. **Address:** Los Angeles Valley College, 5800 Fulton, Van Nuys, CA 91401-4096, U.S.A. **Online address:** zevgarber@juno.com

GARBUS, Cassandra. American, b. 1966. **Genres:** Novels. **Career:** Musician and author. **Publications:** Solo Variations (novel), 1998. **Address:** 255 West 108th St., New York, NY 10025, U.S.A. **Online address:** CASS139207@aol.com

GARBUS, Martin. American, b. 1934. **Genres:** Law. **Career:** Admitted to the Bar of New York State, 1960, and the Bar of the U.S. Supreme Court, 1962. General counsel to Committee to Abolish Capital Punishment, 1964; Columbia University, New York City, director of Center on Social Welfare Policy and Law, 1968; associate director of American Civil Liberties Union, 1969; Yale University, New Haven, CT, lecturer in law, 1974; Frankfurt, Garbus, Klein & Selz, NYC, law partner, 1977-2003; Davis and Gilbert LLP, NYC, law partner, 2003-. General counsel to Viking Press and Grove Press. **Publications:** Ready for the Defense, 1970; Traitors and Heroes: A Lawyer's Memoir, 1987; Tough Talk 1998; Courting Disaster, 2002. **Address:** Davis and Gilbert LLP, 1740 Broadway, New York, NY 10019, U.S.A.

GARCEAU, Dee. American, b. 1955. **Genres:** Area studies. **Career:** Canyonlands Field Institute, Moab, UT, program coordinator and director of Desert Writer's Workshop, 1986-89; University of Montana, Missoula, visiting instructor in history, 1991-95; Rhodes College, Memphis, TN, assistant professor of history, 1995-. **Publications:** The Important Things of Life: Women, Work, and Family in Sweetwater County, Wyoming, 1880-1929, 1995. Contributor to books. **Address:** Department of History, Rhodes College, Memphis, TN 38122, U.S.A. **Online address:** garceau@rhodes.edu

GARCÍA, Cristina. Cuban, b. 1958. **Genres:** Novels. **Career:** Journalist and author. Time (magazine), reporter and researcher, 1983-85, correspondent, 1985-90, bureau chief in Miami, FL, 1987-88. **Publications:** NOVELS: Dreaming in Cuban, 1992; The Aguero Sisters, 1997; Monkey Hunting, 2003. OTHER: Cars of Cuba, 1995. **Address:** c/o Ellen Levine, Trident Media Group, 41 Madison Ave, Fl 36, New York, NY 10010-2257, U.S.A.

GARCIA, Diana. American, b. 1960. **Genres:** Novels. **Career:** Writer and computer analyst. **Publications:** NOVELS: Love Lessons/Lecciones amorosas, 1999; Help Wanted/Aviso oportuno, 2000; Stardust, 2001. **Address:** 2004 East Irvington Rd. #205, Tucson, AZ 85714, U.S.A. **Online address:** DianaGar1@aol.com

GARCIA-AGUILERA, Carolina. Cuban, b. 1949. **Genres:** Mystery/Crime/Suspense. **Career:** C & J Investigations (private investigative firm), Miami, FL, president, 1986-; novelist, 1995-. **Publications:** LUPE SOLANO MYSTERY NOVELS: Bloody Waters, 1996; Bloody Shame, 1997; Bloody Secrets, 1998; Miracle in Paradise, 1999; Havana Heat, 2000; Bitter Sugar, 2001; One Hot Summer, 2002; Luck of the Draw, 2003. Contributor to anthologies.

GARCÍA-CASTAÑÓN, Santiago. Spanish, b. 1959. **Genres:** Novels, Poetry, Language/Linguistics, Literary criticism and history, Translations. **Career:** Illinois Wesleyan University-Bloomington, assistant professor, 1989-92; University of Georgia-Athens, assistant professor, 1992-96; University of Oviedo, Spain, associate professor, 1996-98; Georgia College and State University-Milledgeville, associate professor, 1998-2003, professor of modern foreign languages, 2003-. **Publications:** Sangre, valor y fortuna (critical edition), 1990; Tiempos imperfectos (poetry), 1994; Entre las sombras (poetry), 1996; Por su rey y por su dama (critical edition), 1997; (co-trans.) Theories of Literary Realism, 1997; Diccionario de eponimos del espanol (Dictionary of Spanish Eponyms), 1997; Lo que queda (poetry), 2002; Verdadera relacion de la grandeza del reino de China (critical edition), 2002; El castillo de los halcones (novel), 2004; Poesia selecta de Francisco Bances Candamo (annotated), 2004. **Address:** Dept of Modern Foreign Languages, Georgia College and State University, Milledgeville, GA 31061, U.S.A. **Online address:** sgarcia@mail.gcsu.edu

GARCIA Y ROBERTSON, R(odrigo). American, b. 1949. **Genres:** Novels, Novellas/Short stories. **Career:** Writer. **Publications:** The Spiral Dance (novel), 1991; American Woman (novel), 1998; The Moon Maid and Other Fantastic Adventures (short stories), 1998. Contributor of short stories and essays to anthologies. Contributor of short stories to magazines. **Address:** c/o Forge, 175 Fifth Avenue, New York, NY 10010, U.S.A.

GARDAM, Jane. British, b. 1928. **Genres:** Novels, Novellas/Short stories, Children's fiction, Adult non-fiction. **Career:** Faculty Librarian, Red Cross Hospital Libraries, 1950-51; Sub-Ed., Weldons Ladies Journal, London, 1952-53; Asst. Literary Ed., Time and Tide, London, 1953-55. **Publications:** A Few Fair Days, 1971; A Long Way from Verona, 1971; The Summer after

the Funeral, 1973; Black Faces, White Faces, 1975; Bilgewater, 1977; God on the Rocks, 1978; The Sidmouth Letters (short stories), 1980; Bridget and William, 1981; The Hollow Land, 1981; Horse, 1982; The Pangs of Love and Other Stories, 1983; Kit, 1983; Crusoe's Daughter, 1985; Kit in Boots, 1986; Swan, 1987; Through the Doll's House Door 1987; Showing the Flag, 1989; The Queen of the Tambourine, 1991; The Iron Coast (non-fiction), 1994; Going into a Dark House (short stories), 1994; Faith Fox, 1996; Missing the Midnight (short stories), 1998; The Green Man, 1999; The Flight of the Maidens, 2000; Old Filth, 2004.

GARDAPHE, Fred L(ouis). American, b. 1952. **Genres:** Novellas/Short stories, Plays/Screenplays, Cultural/Ethnic topics, Literary criticism and history, Writing/Journalism. **Career:** High school English teacher in Sun Prairie, WI, 1976-77, and Mason City, IA, 1977-78; English teacher at Prologue alternative high school in Chicago, 1978-81; Columbia College, Chicago, IL, professor of English, 1979-99; State University of New York, Stony Brook, professor of Italian American Studies, 1999-. **Publications:** Arts and Culture in Italy (documentary film), 1987; Vinegar and Oil (one-act play), 1987; Imported from Italy (story adapted for the stage), 1991; Italian Signs, American Streets, 1996; Dagoes Read: Tradition and the Italian American Writer, 1996; Mustache Pete Is Dead, 1997; Leaving Little Italy: Essaying Italian American Culture, 2003. EDITOR & CONTRIBUTOR: Italian American Ways, 1989; (with A. Tamburri and P.A. Giordano) From the Margin: Writings in Italian Americana, 1991. EDITOR: (with D. Candeloro and P.A. Giordano) Italian Ethnics: Their Languages, Literature, and Lives, 1990; New Chicago Stories, 1991; (with D. Ashyk and A. Tamburri) Shades of Black & White, 1999. **Address:** Dept of European Studies, State University of New York, Stony Brook, Stony Brook, NY 11794-3359, U.S.A. **Online address:** fgardaphe@notes.cc.sunysb.edu

GARDELL, Mattias. American. **Genres:** Cultural/Ethnic topics. **Career:** University of Stockholm, Stockholm, Sweden, associate professor of religious history. **Publications:** In the Name of Elijah Muhammad: Louis Farrakhan and the Nation of Islam, 1996; Gods of the Blood: The Pagan Revival and White Separatism, 2003; Vad ar Rasism?, 2005; Globalisering och Politisk Islam, 2005. **Address:** CEIFO, Stockholm University, 106 91 Stockholm, Sweden. **Online address:** mattias.gardell@ceifo.su.se

GARDELLA, Robert (P.). American, b. 1943. **Genres:** History. **Career:** U.S. Merchant Marine Academy, Kings Point, NY, professor of humanities, 1977-. **Publications:** Harvesting Mountains: Fujian and the China Tea Trade, 1757-1937, 1994. Contributor to books. Contributor to Asian studies journals. **Address:** 13 Welwyn Rd #3-K, Great Neck, NY 11021, U.S.A.

GARDELLA, Tricia. American, b. 1944. **Genres:** Picture/board books. **Career:** Homemaker, rancher, and author. **Publications:** PICTURE BOOKS: Just Like My Dad, 1993; Casey's New Hat, 1997. **Address:** 8931 Montezuma, Jamestown, CA 95327, U.S.A. **Online address:** trigarmlode.com

GARDEN, Bruce. See MACKAY, James Alexander.

GARDEN, Edward (James Clarke). British, b. 1930. **Genres:** Music. **Career:** Member of Music Staff, Clifton Coll., Bristol, 1954-57; Dir. of Music, Loretto, nr. Edinburgh, 1957-66; Sr. Lectr. in Music, Univ. of Glasgow, 1966-75; Professor and Chairman of Music, 1975-93, and Dean of the Faculty of Arts, 1988-90, Univ. of Sheffield. **Publications:** Balakirev: A Critical Study of His Life and Music, 1967; Tchaikovsky, 1973, 2nd ed., 1993; Tschaikowsky: Leben und Werk, 1986; (ed.) Correspondence between Tchaikovsky and Nadezhda von Meck, 1876-1878, 1993. **Address:** Balchraggan Farm House, Kirkhill, Inverness IV5 7PJ, Scotland.

GARDEN, Nancy. American, b. 1938. **Genres:** Novels, Children's fiction, Children's non-fiction, Young adult fiction. **Career:** Teacher of writing for children. Contrib. ed., Junior Scholastic mag., NYC 1969-70; contrib. ed., American Observer mag., 1970-72; ed., Houghton Mifflin Co., Boston, 1971-76; contrib. ed., Lambda Book Report, 1991-. **Publications:** Berlin: City Split in Two, 1971; What Happened in Marston, 1971; The Loners, 1972; Vampires, 1973; Werewolves, 1973; Witches, 1975; Devils and Demons, 1976; Fours Crossing, 1980; The Kid's Code and Cipher Book, 1981; Annie on My Mind, 1982; Watersmeet, 1983; Prisoner of Vampires, 1984; Peace, O River, 1985; The Door Between, 1987; Mystery of the Night Raiders, 1987; Mystery of the Midnight Menace, 1988; Mystery of the Secret Marks, 1989; Lark in the Morning, 1991; My Sister, the Vampire, 1992; Mystery of the Kidnapped Kidnapped Kidnapper, 1994; Mystery of the Watchful Witches, 1995; My Brother, the Vampire, 1995; Dove and Sword: A Novel of Joan of Arc, 1995; Good Moon Rising, 1996; The Year They Burned the Books, 1999; Holly's Secret, 2000; The Secret of Smith's Hill (serial novel), 1999-

2003; Meeting Melanie, 2002; Nora and Liz, 2002. **Address:** c/o McIntosh & Otis, Inc., 353 Lexington Ave, New York, NY 10016, U.S.A.

GARDINER, Jeremy. German, b. 1957. **Genres:** Photography. **Career:** Ealing College of Arts, London, England, visiting professor, 1983-84; Massachusetts Institute of Technology, Cambridge, Harkness fellow, 1984-85; Pratt Institute, Brooklyn, NY, assistant professor of computer graphics, 1986-93; New World School of the Arts, Miami, FL, senior associate professor, 1993-. School of Visual Arts, visiting professor, 1988; Royal College of Art, visiting lecturer, 1992. CyberArts Productions, president; Charlex, paintbox artist, 1987-88. Gives lectures, workshops, and seminars; work represented at group and solo exhibitions. **Publications:** Digital Photo Illustration, 1994. Work represented in anthologies. Creator of CD-ROM "picturing history," 1994, and cyberarts gallery, 1995. **Address:** New World School of the Arts, 300 Northeast and Second Ave., Miami, FL 33129, U.S.A.

GARDINER, Judith Kegan. American, b. 1941. **Genres:** Literary criticism and history, Women's studies and issues. **Career:** Fisk University, Nashville, TN, assistant professor, 1968-69; University of Illinois at Chicago, assistant professor, 1969-76, associate professor, 1976-88, professor of English and women's studies, 1988-, acting director of Women's Studies Program, 1978-80, 1986, 1987, 1989, 1991, interim director of Center for Research on Women and Gender, 2002-; writer and editor. Radcliffe Institute, visiting research scholar, 1972-73; Stanford University Center for Research on Women, visiting scholar, 1983; Newberry Library, research associate, 1986-87; Rockefeller residency fellowship, Bellagio, Italy, 1996. **Publications:** Craftsmanship in Context: The Development of Ben Jonson's Poetry, 1975; Rhys, Stead, Lessing, and the Politics of Empathy, 1989. EDITOR: Provoking Agents, 1995; Masculinity Studies and Feminist Theory, 2002. Contributor to books and scholarly journals. **Address:** Department of English, m/c 162, University of Illinois at Chicago, 601 S Morgan St, Chicago, IL 60607-7120, U.S.A. **Online address:** Gardiner@uic.edu

GARDNER, (Robert) Brian. British, b. 1931. **Genres:** History, Biography. **Career:** Feature Writer, Western Mail, 1956-57; Reporter, Sunday Times, 1957; Feature Writer, Sunday Express, 1957-61; Television Critic, Daily Sketch, 1963-64. **Publications:** The Big Push, 1961; German East, 1963; The Wasted Hour, 1963; (anthologist) Up the Line to Death, 1964; Allenby, 1965; (anthologist) The Terrible Rain, 1966; Mafeking, 1966; The Quest for Timbuctoo, 1968; (anthologist) Churchill in His Time, 1968; The Lion's Cage, 1969; The African Dream, 1970; The East India Company, 1971; The Public Schools, 1973; East India Company, 1990. **Address:** c/o Marboro Books, 120 5th Ave., New York, NY 10011, U.S.A.

GARDNER, Craig Shaw. Also writes as Peter Garrison. American, b. 1949. **Genres:** Science fiction/Fantasy. **Career:** Science fiction and fantasy novelist. **Publications:** EBENEZUM SERIES: A Malady of Magicks, 1986; A Multitude of Monsters, 1986; A Night in the Netherhells, 1987; The Exploits of Ebenezum, 1987. WUNTVOR SERIES: A Difficulty with Dwarves, 1987; An Excess of Enchantment, 1988; A Disagreement with Death, 1989; The Wanderings of Wuntvor, 1989. CINEVERSE SERIES: Slaves of the Volcano God, 1989; Bride of the Slime Monster, 1990; Revenge of the Fluffy Bunnies, 1990; Cineverse Cycle, 1990. ARABIAN NIGHTS SERIES: The Other Sinbad, 1991; A Bad Day for Ali Baba, 1992; The Last Arabian Night, 1993. DRAGON CIRCLE SERIES: Dragon Sleeping, 1994; Dragon Waking, 1995; Dragon Burning, 1996. NOVELIZATIONS: The Lost Boys: A Novel, 1987; Wishbringer (novelization of a computer game), 1988; Back to the Future, Part II: A Novel, 1989; Batman, 1989; The Batman Murders, 1990; Back to the Future, Part III: A Novel, 1990; Batman Returns, 1992; (with M. Costello) The Seventh Guest, 1995; Buffy the Vampire Slayer: Return to Chaos, 1998; Spiderman-Wanted: Dead or Alive, 1998; Leprechauns, 1999. AS PETER GARRISON: The Changeling War, 1999; The Sorcerer's Gun, 1999; The Magic Dead, 2000. **Address:** PO Box 1281, East Arlington, MA 02474, U.S.A. **Online address:** csgcsgcsg@aol.com

GARDNER, Edward Clinton. American, b. 1920. **Genres:** Theology/Religion. **Career:** Prof. Emeritus of Christian Ethics, Candler Sch. of Theology, Emory Univ., Atlanta, GA., since 1990 (Prof., 1954-90). Pastor, South Meriden Methodist Church, Conn., 1948-49; Asst. Prof., of Philosophy and Religion, North Carolina State Coll., Raleigh, 1949-54. **Publications:** Biblical Faith and Social Ethics, 1960; The Church as a Prophetic Community, 1967; Christocentrism in Christian Social Ethics, 1983; Justice & Christian Ethics, 1995. **Address:** 2504 Tanglewood Rd., Decatur, GA 30033, U.S.A.

GARDNER, Jeremy. See GARDNER, Jerome.

GARDNER, Jerome. Also writes as Jeremy Gardner, John Gilchrist, Paul Sully. British, b. 1932. **Genres:** Novels, Westerns/Adventure. **Publications:**

WESTERNS: Trail Out of Leavenworth, 1970; Pistolero, 1971; Frenchman's Brand, 1972; Heist at Apache Pass, 1972; The Mossyhorns, 1972; Lucky Cowpoke, 1973; Wagon to Hangtown, 1973; Huntsville Break, 1973; Travelling Judge, 1974; The All-Show Sheriff, 1974; Wilderness Saloon, 1974; Gunman's Holiday, 1975; Dilemma at Dripspring, 1976; The Underhand Mail, 1976; Two-Bit Town, 1977; The Oldtimers, 1979; Confession at Dripspring, 1982; The Jayhawk Legacy, 1983; The Bounty Scalper, 1983; Medicine Show Doc, 1983; Judgment in the Territory, 1983; The Hangman and the Ladies' League, 1984; The Blood-Tie, 1984; The Hangman's Apprentice, 1985; The Pitchman Healer, 1985; The Rawhide Redeemer, 1986; The Tumbleweed Twosome, 1986; Get Maledon!, 1986; The Parker Ransom, 1987; The Hanging Week, 1987; Double on Death Row, 1988; The Owlhoot Convention, 1988; Wide Open Town, 1990; Date with a Noose, 1990; Maledon Calls the Shots, 1990; A Tale of Three Bullets, 1990; The Quick Hanging, 1991; The Wishbook Wife; The High-Toned Hellion, 1992; Hot Gun, 1992; The Saloonwoman, 1995; Fort Smith Posse, 1995. NOVELS AS JEREMY GARDNER: Summer Palace, 1960. NOVELS AS JOHN GILCHRIST: Birdbrain, 1975; Out North, 1975; Lifeline, 1975; The English Corridor, 1976; The Engendering, 1978. NOVELS AS PAUL TULLY: The Horsing Blackmsmith, 1985; The Bond Jumper, 1987; The Jehovahs' Jailbreak, 1987; The Strychnine Stand-Off, 1988; Night-Hawk, 1991. **Address:** c/o Robert Hale Ltd., Clerkenwell House, 45-47 Clerkenwell Green, London EC1R OHT, England.

GARDNER, Leonard. (born United States), b. 1934. **Genres:** Novels. **Career:** Writer; worked briefly as a boxer. **Publications:** Fat City (novel), 1969; Fat City, 1972. Contributor to journals. **Address:** c/o Author Mail, University of California Press, 2120 Berkeley Way, Berkeley, CA 94720, U.S.A.

GARDNER, Mark L(ee). American, b. 1960. **Genres:** History, Music. **Career:** Seasonal park ranger and living history interpreter, primarily at National Park Service historic sites, 1981-86; Colorado Historical Society, Trinidad, CO, historic site administrator, 1987-91; independent historian, writer, and consultant, 1991-. Member: Santa Fe National Historic Trail Advisory Council; editorial advisory board of Journal of the West. **Publications:** Santa Fe Trail: National Historic Trail, 1993; Elbert County: Window to the Past, 1993; Fort Bowie National Historic Site, 1994; Songs of the Santa Fe Trail and the Far West (compact disc), 1996; Little Bighorn Battlefield National Monument, 1996; Bent's Old Fort National Historic Site, 1998. EDITOR: (and contrib) The Mexican Road: Trade, Travel and Confrontation on the Santa Fe Trail, 1989; (annotator, and author of intro) Brothers on the Santa Fe and Chihuahua Trails: Edward James Glasgow and William Henry Glasgow, 1846-1848, 1993; (with M. Simmons) The Mexican War Correspondence of Richard Smith Elliott, 1997. Contributor to periodicals. Contributor of introductions and forewords to books. **Address:** PO Box 879, Cascade, CO 80809, U.S.A.

GARDNER, Michael R. (born United States), b. 1942. **Genres:** Biography. **Career:** Attorney and author. Bracewell and Patterson (law firm), partner, 1977-82; Akin, Gump, Strauss, Hauer, and Feld (law firm), Washington, DC, partner, 1982-89; The Law Offices of Michael R. Gardner, P.C., Washington, DC, communications policy lawyer, 1990-. College of Georgetown University, Washington, DC, adjunct professor, 1992-2000. United States Ambassador to the International Telecommunication Union (ITU) Plenipotentiary Conference, Nairobi, Kenya, 1982; United States Telecommunications Training Institute (USTTI), founder and pro bono chair, 1982-; served on Presidential Commissions of Presidents Richard Nixon, Gerald Ford, Ronald Reagan, and George H. W. Bush, including President's Committee for Mental Retardation, Council of the Administrative Conference of the United States, Board of Directors of the Pennsylvania Avenue Development Corporation of Washington, DC, and International Cultural Trace Center Commission. **Publications:** Harry Truman and Civil Rights: Moral Courage and Political Risks, 2002. **Address:** c/o Author Mail, Southern Illinois University Press, POB 3697, Carbondale, IL 62902, U.S.A.

GARDNER, Robert. American, b. 1929. **Genres:** Children's non-fiction, Criminology/True Crime, History, Sciences, Sports/Fitness, Technology, Young adult non-fiction. **Career:** American Cyanamid, worked in atomic energy division, 1951-52; Salisbury School, Salisbury, CT, science teacher, 1952-89, head of dept, 1959-89, director of admissions for Salisbury Summer School, 1976-87; writer and consultant on science education, 1989-. **Publications:** JUVENILE NONFICTION: (with D. Webster) Shadow Science, 1976; Magic through Science, 1978; (with Webster) Moving Right Along, 1978; (with H.E. Flanagan Jr.) Basic Lacrosse Strategy, 1979; This Is the Way It Works, 1980; Space: Frontier of the Future, 1980; Save That Energy, 1981; Kitchen Chemistry, 1982; Water, the Life Sustaining Resource,

1982; The Whale Watchers' Guide, 1984; (with C.S. Brockway and S.F. Howe) Allyn and Bacon General Science, 1985; Science around the House, 1985; The Young Athlete's Manual, 1985; Ideas for Science Projects, 1986, 2nd ed. (with R. Adams), 1997; (with Webster) Science in Your Backyard, 1987; Experiments with Balloons, 1987; Projects in Space Science, 1988; Science and Sports, 1988; Science Experiments, 1988; (with D. Shortelle) The Future and the Past, 1989; More Ideas for Science Projects, 1989, 2nd ed. (with Adams), 1998; Famous Experiments You Can Do, 1990; Experimenting with Illusions, 1990; Experimenting with Inventions, 1990; Light, 1991; Forces and Machines, 1991; Experimenting with Light, 1991; Experimenting with Sound, 1991; Experimenting with Energy Conservation, 1992; Celebrating Earth Day, 1992; Crime Lab 101, 1992; Robert Gardner's Favorite Science Experiments, 1992; (with Shortelle) The Forgotten Players, 1993; Robert Gardner's Challenging Science Experiments, 1993; (with E. Kemer) Making and Using Scientific Models, 1993; Experimenting with Water, 1993; Experimenting with Science in Sports, 1993; Electricity, 1993; (with Kemer) Temperature and Heat, 1993; Architecture, 1994; Communication, 1994; Electricity and Magnetism, 1994; Optics, 1994; Space, 1994; Transportation, 1994; (with E.A. Shore) Math in Science and Nature, 1994; Experimenting with Time, 1995; (with Shore) Math and Society, 1995; Make an Interactive Science Museum, 1995; (with E.A. Shore) Math You Really Need, 1996; Where on Earth Am I?, 1996; (with Shore) Middle School Math You Really Need, 1997; From Talking Drums to the Internet, 1997; What's So Super about the Supernatural?, 1998; Human Evolution, 1999; Science Fair Projects, 1999; (with Shortelle and B.G. Conklin) Encyclopedia of Forensic Science, 2002. GETTING STARTED IN SCIENCE: EXPERIMENTS WITH SERIES: ...Balloons, ...Bubbles, ...Mirrors, ...Motion, 1995; ...Speed, ...Weight, ...Time, ...Height & Depth, ...Volume, ...Temperature, 2003. HEALTH SCIENCE PROJECTS ABOUT SERIES: ...Anatomy and Physiology, ...Your Senses, ...Heredity and Family, 2001; ...Weight, Food, and Nutrition, (with B. Conklin) ...Psychology, (with B. Conklin) ...Sports Performance, 2002. SCIENCE PROJECT IDEAS ABOUT...SERIES: ...the Human Body, 1993; Chemistry, 1994; ...Electricity and Magnets, 1994; ...Light, 1994; (with Kemer) ...Temperature and Heat, 1994; (with Webster) ...Weather, 1994; ...the Sun, 1997; ...Rain, 1997; ...the Moon, 1997; ...Air, 1997; ...Trees, 1997; ...Animal Behavior, 1997; ...Plants, 1999; ...Physics in the Home, 1999; ...Kitchen Chemistry, 1999; ...the Environment and Ecology, 1999; ...Math, 1999; ...Magic, 2000; ...Toys, 2000; ...Solids, Liquids and Gases, 2000; ...Measuring, 2000; ...Sports, 2000; ...Sound, 2000, ...Space Science, ...Science in the House, 2002. Coauthor of textbooks and laboratory guides. Contributor to periodicals. **Address:** 535 Queen Anne Dr, PO Box 256, North Eastham, MA 02651-0256, U.S.A. **Online address:** gardnerbn@webtv.net

GARDNER, Robert W(ayne). American, b. 1940. **Genres:** Demography. **Career:** East-West Center, Honolulu, HI, research associate and assistant director of Population Institute, 1971-92; demographic consultant, 1992-. Military service: U.S. Army, 1963-66. **Publications:** (ed. with Gordon F. DeJong) Migration Decision Making, Pergamon (Elmsford, NY), 1983; (with James A. Palmore) Measuring Mortality, Fertility, and Natural Increase, East-West Center (Honolulu, HI), 1983; (with Herbert Barringer and Michael Levin) Asians and Pacific Islanders in the United States, Russell Sage Foundation (New York, NY), 1993. **Address:** 8 Noble St., Brunswick, ME 04011, U.S.A.

GARDNER, Sandra. American, b. 1940. **Genres:** Novels, Writing/Journalism, Young adult non-fiction. **Career:** Author of young adult books, 1981-. New Jersey weekly section of New York Times, columnist and social issues writer, 1981-86, 1991-93; public relations writer, 1986-96; health writer and editor, 1997-2000; writer/editor, 2002-. **Publications:** English Teacher's Companion, 1975; Southeast Asia, 1976; Mini-Mysteries, 2 vols, 1976; Six Who Dared, 1981; Street Gangs, 1983; Teenage Suicide, 1985, 2nd ed., 1990; Street Gangs in America, 1992. **Address:** 16 Cedar Way, Woodstock, NY 12498, U.S.A.

GARDNER, Theodore Roosevelt, II. American, b. 1934. **Genres:** Novels, Mystery/Crime/Suspense, Romance/Historical, Children's fiction, Environmental sciences/Ecology, Homes/Gardens, Humor/Satire. **Career:** Writer. **Publications:** Off the Wall (compilation of humorous newspaper columns), 1993; Something Nice to See (children's book), 1994; Lotusland: A Photographic Odyssey, 1995; The Real Sleeper: A Love Story 1995; Give Gravity a Chance: A Love Story 1998; Nature's Kaleidoscope, 1998; Wit's End (essays), 1999. NOVELS: The Paper Dynasty, 1990; Flipside: A Novel of Suspense, 1997; He's Back, 2000; All Lost Time: A Novel of Baby Fever, 2002. **Address:** c/o Allen A. Knoll Publishers, 200 W Victoria, Santa Barbara, CA 93101, U.S.A. **Online address:** bookinfo@knollpublishers.com

GARDNER, Tom. American, b. 1968. **Genres:** Economics, Money/Finance. **Career:** Investment advisor, creator of an investment website, newspaper columnist, and nationally syndicated radio show host. **Publications:** ALL WITH D. GARDNER: The Motley Fool Investment Guide: How the Fool Beats Wall Street's Wise Men and How You Can Too, 1996; The Motley Fool Investment Workbook, 1998; You Have More Than You Think: The Motley Fool Guide to Investing What You Have, 1998. **Address:** 123 North Pitt, Fourth Floor, Alexandria, VA 22314, U.S.A.

GARDON, Anne. Also writes as Justine Saint-Laurent. Canadian (born France), b. 1948. **Genres:** Novels, Food and Wine. **Career:** Photographer and writer. Also worked as a technician in a medical laboratory, a guide at the Palace of Monaco, a secretary, and a nanny. **Publications:** AND PHOTOGRAPHER: La cuisine des champs, 1994; La cuisine, naturellement, 1995; Délices en conserve, 1996; Le congelateur de gourmet, 1997; The Wild Food Gourmet, 1998; Preserving for All Seasons, 1999; Comfort Food Fast: Easy and Elegant Food That Soothes the Soul, 2001. EDITOR: Le gourmet au jardin, 2000. Contributor of photographs to Canadian travel books. Contributor of articles and short stories to magazines and newspapers. AS JUSTINE SAINT-LAURENT: Chantage No. 5 (novel), 2003. **Address:** 129 rang Duncan, Sainte-Chrysostome, QC, Canada. **Online address:** agardon@dsuper.net

GARDONS, S. S. See SNODGRASS, W. D.

GARETH-OWEN, John. See OWEN, (John) Gareth.

GARFIELD, Brian (F. W.). Also writes as Bennett Garland, Alex Hawk, John Ives, Drew Mallory, Frank O'Brian, Jonas Ward, Brian Wynne, Frank Wynne. American, b. 1939. **Genres:** Mystery/Crime/Suspense, Romance/Historical, Westerns/Adventure, Plays/Screenplays, Film, History. **Career:** Pres., Shan Productions Co. Inc. (motion picutre productions), 1974-96. Vice-Pres., 1965-66, Pres., 1966-67, and Dir., 1967-68, Western Writers of America Inc; Dir., 1974-84, and Pres., 1983, Mystery Writers of America, Inc. **Publications:** Range Justice, 1960; The Arizonans, 1961; The Lawbringers, 1962; Trail Drive, 1962; Vultures in the Sun, 1963; Apache Canyon, 1963; The Vanquished, 1964; The Last Bridge, 1966; The Thousand-Mile War, 1969, rev. ed., 1996; Valley of the Shadow, 1970; The Villiers Touch, 1970; Slip-hammer, 1970; The Hit, 1971; What of Terry Conniston?, 1971; Sweeny's Honour, 1971; Gun Down, 1971, as the Last Hard Men, 1976; Deep Cover, 1971; Relentless, 1972, screenplay, 1977; Line of Succession, 1972; Death Wish, 1972, screenplay, 1974; Tripwire, 1973, screenplay, 1976; (with D.W. Westlake) Gangway, 1973; Kolchak's Gold, 1974; The Threepersons Hunt, 1974; The Romanov Succession, 1974; Hopscotch (novel; and screenplay with B. Forbes), 1975; Death Sentence, 1976; Recoil, 1977; Wild Times, 1979; The Paladin, 1980; Checkpoint Charlie, 1981; Western Films: A Complete Guide, 1982; Suspended Sentences, 1983; Necessity, 1984; Manifest Destiny, 1989; Do or Die, 1997. EDITOR: War Whoop and Battle Cry, 1968; I Witness, 1978; The Crime of My Life, 1983. AS BENNETT GARLAND: Seven Brave Men, 1962, under own name, 1969; (with T.V. Olsen) High Storm, 1963, under own name, 1969; The Last Outlaw, 1964, under own name, 1969; Rio Chama, 1969. AS ALEX HAWK: Savage Guns, 1968. AS JOHN IVES: Fear in a Handful of Dust, 1977; The Marchand Woman, 1979. AS DREW MALLORY: Target Manhattan, 1975. AS FRANK O'BRIAN: The Rimfire Murders, 1962; Bugle and Spur, 1966; Act of Piracy, 1975. AS JONAS WARD: Buchanan's Gun, 1968. AS BRIAN WYNNE: Mr. Sixgun, 1964; The Night It Rained Bullets, 1965; The Bravos, 1966; The Proud Riders, 1967; Badge for a Badman, 1967; Brand of the Gun, 1968; Big Country, Big Men, 1969. AS FRANK WYNNE: Massacre Basin, 1961; The Big Snow, 1962; Arizona Rider, 1962; Dragoon Pass, 1963; Rio Concho, 1964; Rails West, 1964; Lynch Law Canyon, 1965; The Wolf Pack, 1966; Call Me Hazard, 1966; The Lusty Breed, 1966. **Address:** 11288 Ventura Blvd #603, Studio City, CA 91604, U.S.A.

GARFUNKEL, Trudy. American, b. 1944. **Genres:** Dance/Ballet, Food and Wine, Theology/Religion, Young adult non-fiction. **Career:** Dial Press, NYC, publicity-advertising manager, 1967-82; Garland Communications, NYC, director, 1982-. **Publications:** On Wings of Joy: The Story of Ballet from the 16th Century to Today, 1994, 2nd ed., 2002; Letter to the World: The Life and Dances of Martha Graham, 1995; Start Exploring: Ballet, 1996; The Kosher Companion: A Guide to Food, Cooking, Shopping, and Services, 1997; Kosher fro Everybody: The Complete Guide to Understanding, Shopping, Cooking, and Eating the Kosher Way, 2004. **Address:** 7003 Main St, Kew Gardens Hills, NY 11367-1704, U.S.A. **Online address:** wingsofjoy712@aol.com

GARGAN, Edward A. American, b. 1950. **Genres:** Area studies. **Career:** Journalist and author. New York Times, bureau chief, La Côte d'Ivoire, 1985-86, Beijing, China, 1986-89, New Delhi, India, 1991-94, Hong Kong,

1995-; Newsday, Asia bureau chief, 2000-. **Publications:** China's Fate: A People's Turbulent Struggle with Reform and Repression, 1980-1990, 1991; The River's Tale: A Year on the Mekong, 2002. **Address:** Newsday, 7.1.133, Jianguomenwai, Beijing 100600, People's Republic of China.

GARLAND, Alex. American, b. 1970. **Genres:** Novels. **Career:** Fiction writer. **Publications:** The Beach (novel), 1996. **Address:** c/o Putnam Publishing Group, 375 Hudson, New York, NY 10014, U.S.A.

GARLAND, Bennett. See GARFIELD, Brian (F. W.).

GARLAND, Mark (A.). American, b. 1953. **Genres:** Novels. **Career:** Automotive service manager for central New York dealerships including Ford, Chevrolet, Chrysler, and Lincoln-Mercury, c. 1978-; substitute school bus driver for North Syracuse, NY, school district; writer. **Publications:** NOVELS (with C. McGraw): Dorella, 1992; Demon Blade, 1994. Contributor of short fiction to publications. **Address:** 106 Cadillac St., Syracuse, NY 13208, U.S.A.

GARLAND, Max. American, b. 1950. **Genres:** Novels. **Career:** University of Iowa, Iowa City, creative writing instructor in Elderhostel Program, 1988-92; University of Wisconsin-Madison, visiting lecturer in creative writing, 1990-, poetry fellow, 1990-91. University of Iowa, instructor at Iowa Summer Writing Festival, 1990-; gives public lectures and readings from his works. Worked at a nursery and as a grounds keeper and janitor; spent ten years as a rural letter carrier. **Publications:** The Postal Confessions (poems), 1995. Work represented in anthologies. Contributor of poems, stories, and essays to periodicals. **Address:** Department of English, H.C. White Hall, University of Wisconsin-Madison, Madison, WI 53706, U.S.A.

GARLICK, Raymond. British, b. 1926. **Genres:** Poetry, Literary criticism and history. **Career:** Founding Ed., Dock Leaves, later the Anglo-Welsh Review, 1949-60; Head. English Dept., Intnl. Sch., Kasteel Eerde, Ommen, The Netherlands, 1961-67; Sr. Lectr. in English, 1967-72, and Dir. of Welsh Studies and Principal Lectr., 1972-86, Trinity Coll., Carmarthen. **Publications:** Poems from the Mountain-House, 1950; The Welsh-Speaking Sea, 1954; Blaenau Observed, 1957; Landscapes and Figures, 1964; A Sense of Europe: Collected Poems, 1954-1968, 1968; An Introduction to Anglo-Welsh Literature, 1970, rev. ed. 1972; Sense of Time: Poems and Anti-poems 1969-72, 1972; Incense: Poems 1972-1975, 1976, (ed. with Roland Mathias) Anglo-Welsh Poetry 1480-1980, 1984; The Hymn to the Virgin, 1985; Collected Poems, 1987; Travel Notes: New Poems, 1992; The Delphic Voyage & Other Poems, 2003. **Address:** 26 Glannant House, College Road, Carmarthen SA31 3EF, Wales.

GARMAISE, Freda. British, b. 1928. **Genres:** Novels, Writing/Journalism, Humor/Satire. **Career:** Commentator and writer for broadcast and print media, 1982-. **Publications:** Love Bites (comic novel), 1981; Tough Girls Don't Knit and Other Tales of Stylish Subversion, 1990. **Address:** 698 West End Ave, New York, NY 10025, U.S.A. **Online address:** GARM4@aol.com

GARNEAU, Michel. Canadian, b. 1939. **Genres:** Plays/Screenplays. **Career:** Poet, composer, singer, and playwright. Radio and television announcer and scriptwriter, Ontario and Quebec, mid-1950s; writer, 1958-; Canadian Broadcasting Corporation, television announcer and scriptwriter, 1960-68; singer in a band called Les Cailloux; freelance broadcaster from Paris, France, 1967-68. **Publications:** Eau de pluie, 1958; Langage, 1962; (with P. Chamberlain, G. Cote, N. Drassel and A. Major) Le Pays, 1963; Vous pouvez m'acheter pour 69 ct., 1972; Blues des elections, 1972; l'Animalhumain, 1972; Moments, 1973; J'aime la litterature, elle est utile, 1974; Politique, 1974; Sur le matelas, 1974; La Chanson d'amour de cul, 1974; Quatre a quatre, 1974, trans by C. Bedard and K. Turnbull as Four to Four, 1979; Strauss et Pesant (et Rosa), 1974, trans by A. Ravel as Strauss and Pesant (and Rosa); La plus belle ile, 1975; Les Petits Chevals amoureux (poetry), 1977, trans by R. McGee as Small Horses and Intimate Beasts, 1985; Abries, desabriees, suivi de L'Usage du coeur dans le domaine reel, 1979; Elegie au genocide des naspodes, 1979; Poesies completes, 1955-87 (poetry collection), 1988; Le phenix de neige (poetry), 1992. PLAYS: Sur le matelas, 1972; Quatre a quatre, 1973; Le Bonhomme Sept-Heures, 1974; La Chanson d'amour de cul, 1974; Strauss et Pesant (et Rosa), 1974; Abries,/desabriees, 1975; L'Usage du coeur dans le domaine reel, 1975; Les Voyagements, 1975; Les Celebrations, 1976; Rien que la memoire, 1976; Gilgamesh: Theatre, 1976; Adidou, Adidouce, 1977; Les Voyagements, suivi de Rien que la memoire, 1977; Les Celebrations, suivi de Adidou, Adidouce: Theatre, 1977; (trans. and adaptor) Macbeth, 1978; Emilie ne sera plus jamais cueillie par l'anemone, 1981, trans. by L. Gaboriau as Emilie Will Never Again Feel the Breath of the Delphinium; Petitpetant et le monde, suivi de Le Groupe,

1982; Les Neiges suivi de Le Bonhomme Sept-Heures, 1984; Les guerriers, 1989, trans. by L. Gaboriau as Warriors, 1990; Mademoiselle Rouge, 1989, trans. by L. Gaboriau as Miss Red and the Wolves; Heliotropes, 1994, trans. by L. Gaboriau as Morning Glories. **Address:** c/o VLB Editeur, 1010 La Gauchetiere E., Montreal, QC, Canada H2L 2N5.

GARNER, Alan. British, b. 1934. **Genres:** Novels, Science fiction/Fantasy, Children's fiction, Plays/Screenplays, Songs/Lyrics and libretti, Mythology/ Folklore, Documentaries/Reportage, Essays. **Career:** Author and filmmaker. **Publications:** The Weirdstone of Brisingamen, 1960; The Moon of Gomrath, 1963; Elidor, 1965; Holly from the Bongs, 1966; The Owl Service, 1967; (with R. Hill) The Old Man of Mow, 1967; Red Shift, 1973; (with A. Trowski) The Breadhorse, 1975; The Stone Book, 1976; Tom Fobble's Day, 1977; Granny Reardun, 1977; The Aimer Gate, 1978; Fairytales of Gold, 1979; The Lad of the Gad, 1980; A Book of British Fairy Tales, 1984; A Bag of Moonshine, 1986; Strandloper, 1996; The Voice That Thunders, 1997; Little Red Hen, 1997; Well of the Wind, 1998; Thursbitch, 2003. EDITOR: The Hamish Hamilton Book of Goblins: An Anthology of Folklore, 1969; The Guizer, 1975. **Address:** Toad Hall, Blackden, Cheshire CW4 8BY, England.

GARNER, Helen. Australian, b. 1942. **Genres:** Novels, Novellas/Short stories, Plays/Screenplays, Essays. **Career:** High school teacher, journalist, translator (French), film and theatre critic; New York University, Graduate Creative Writing Program, visiting professor, 1993. **Publications:** The Last Days of Chez Nous, 1993; The First Stone (non-fiction), 1995; True Stories (essays), 1996; The Feel of Steel (essays). NOVELS: Monkey Grip, 1977; The Children's Bach, 1984; Cosmo Cosmolino, 1992. STORIES: Honour, 1980; Postcards from Surfers, 1985; My Hard Heart, 1998. SCREENPLAYS: Two Friends, 1986; The Last Days of Chez Nous, 1991.

GARNER, John S. American, b. 1945. **Genres:** Architecture. **Career:** Texas A&M University, Denton, assistant professor, 1974-77, associate professor, 1977-81; University of Illinois at Urbana-Champaign, Urbana, associate professor, 1981-87, professor of architecture, 1987-. Consultant in architectural history and preservation. **Publications:** The Model Company Town, 1984; The Midwest in American Architecture, 1991; (ed.) The Company Town, 1992. **Address:** 502 East Sunnycrest Ct, Urbana, IL 61801, U.S.A.

GARNER, Wendell (Richard). American, b. 1921. **Genres:** Psychology. **Career:** James Rowland Angell Prof. Emeritus of Psychology, Yale Univ., New Haven, Conn. **Publications:** (co-author) Applied Experimental Psychology, 1949; Uncertainty and Structure as Psychological Concepts, 1962; The Processing of Information and Structure, 1974; (ed.) Ability Testing, 1982. **Address:** 1122 Meadow Ridge, Redding, CT 06896, U.S.A. **Online address:** wgarner0023@cs.com

GARNET, A. H. See SLOTE, Alfred.

GARNETT, Gale Zoë. Canadian (born New Zealand). **Genres:** Novels, Plays/Screenplays. **Career:** Actor, writer, and director. **Publications:** Visible Amazement (novel), 1999. ONE-WOMAN SHOWS: Gale Garnett & Company; and Life after Latex. Contributor of essays, columns, and book reviews to periodicals. Author of songs, 75 of which have been recorded and 5 of which have been used in feature films. **Address:** Box 367, Station P, 704, Spadina Ave, Toronto, ON, Canada M5S 2J9.

GARNETT, Isobel. See WADDINGTON, Patrick (Haynes).

GARNETT, Richard (Duncan Carey). British, b. 1923. **Genres:** Children's fiction, Biography, Translations. **Career:** Production Manager 1955-59, and Director 1957-66, Rupert Hart-Davis Ltd.; Director, Adlard Coles Ltd., 1963-66; Ed., 1966-82, and Director, 1972-82, Macmillan London; Director, Macmillan Publishers, 1982-87. **Publications:** The Silver Kingdom (in U.S. as The Undersea Treasure), 1956; The White Dragon, 1963; Jack of Dover, 1966; Constance Garnett: A Heroic Life, 1991. EDITOR: Goldsmith: Selected Works, 1950; (with R. Grenfell) Joyce, 1980; Sylvia and David: The Townsend Warner/Garnett Letters, 1994. TRANSLATOR: R. Gruss, The Art of the Aqualung, 1955; B. Heuvelmans, On the Track of the Unknown Animals, 1958; B. Heuvelmans, In the Wake of the Sea-Serpents, 1968. **Address:** Hilton Hall, Hilton, Huntingdon, Cambs. PE28 9NE, England.

GARNHAM, Trevor. British, b. 1947. **Genres:** Architecture. **Career:** University of Kingston, Kingston, England, senior lecturer in architecture, 1988-. **Publications:** The Oxford Museum, 1992; Melsetter House, 1993; St.

Andrew's Church, 1995. **Address:** School of Architecture, University of Kingston, Knights Park, Kingston, Surrey KT1 2QJ, England.

GARRARD, John (Gordon). American (born England), b. 1934. **Genres:** Literary criticism and history, Biography. **Career:** Carleton University, Ottawa, ON, Canada, lecturer in Russian language and literature, 1958-62; Dartmouth College, Hanover, NH, assistant professor, 1964-69, associate professor of Russian literature, 1969-71; University of Virginia, Charlottesville, professor of Russian literature, 1971-84, chair of the department of Slavic languages and literature, 1971-76, director of the Center for Russian and East European Studies, 1972-83; University of Arizona, Tucson, professor of Russian studies, 1984-, director of the Institute for the Study of the Soviet Union and Eastern Europe, 1985-87, head of the department of Russian and Slavic studies, 1985-88. Indiana University, Bloomington, visiting associate professor, 1970-71. **Publications:** Mixhail Chulkov: An Introduction to His Prose and Verse, 1970; Mikhail Lermontov, 1982; (with C. Garrard) Inside the Soviet Writers' Union, 1990; (with C. Garrard) The Bones of Berdichev: The Life and Fate of Vasily Grossman, 1996. EDITOR: (and contrib.) Vladimir Tendryakov; Three Novellas, 1967; The Eighteenth Century in Russia, 1973; The Russian Novel from Pushkin to Pasternak, 1983; (with C. Garrard) World War II and the Soviet People, 1993. Contributor to books. Contributor to professional journals. **Address:** Dept of Russian & Slavic Studies, Learning Services Bldg 305, University of Arizona, PO Box 210105, Tucson, AZ 85721-0105, U.S.A.

GARRARD, Timothy F(rancis). British, b. 1943. **Genres:** Art/Art history, History. **Career:** Called to the Bar at Lincoln's Inn, 1965; Central Criminal Court, London, England, clerk of arraigns, 1966-67; private practice of law in Accra, Ghana, 1968; Office of the Attorney General, Accra, state attorney, senior state attorney, 1969-76; solicitor and advocate of Supreme Court of Ghana, 1976; General Legal Council, Accra, senior lecturer in law, 1976-77; Supreme Court, Accra, senior legal draftsman, 1977-80; exhibition curator at Museum of Cultural History, 1983; archaeologist and writer. Legal draftsman for Ghana Law Reform Commission, 1969-73. Lecturer at University of Ghana, 1973-74; apprentice to an Asante brass caster in Krofufurom Village, near Kumasi, 1980; member of archaeological excavation teams Begho, Ghana, 1975-76 and 1979; Fort Ruychaver, Ghana, 1976; initiated into the Senufo Poro society, Ivory Coast, 1991. **Publications:** Akan Weights and the Gold Trade, 1980; (co-ed. with D.H. Ross, and contrib.) Akan Transformations: Problems in Ghanaian Art History, 1983; Gold of Africa, 1989; (co-author) Art of Cote d'Ivoire, 1993; (co-author) Africa: The Art of a Continent, 1995; La Sagesse d'un Peuple: 2000 Proverbes Senoufo, 2001. **Address:** 21 Richmond Rd, Malvern, Worcs WR14 1NE, England.

GARRATT, James E. Canadian, b. 1954. **Genres:** Environmental sciences/ Ecology, Natural history. **Career:** Scanlon Creek Outdoor Education Centre, Bradford, ON, Canada, environmental instructor for ten years; Kortright Center for Conservation, Woodbridge, ON, employed in operations for thirteen years. Save the Rouge Valley System, chair; Boyd North stewardship committee, member. **Publications:** The Rouge River Valley: An Urban Wilderness, 2000; Northen Euphoria: A Story about Northern Lands & Waters, & the People Who Fight to Save Them. Contributor to periodicals. **Address:** 4864 Major Mackenzie Dr, Woodbridge, ON, Canada L4L 1A6.

GARRETT, Charles C. *See* **WELLS, Angus.**

GARRETT, George (Palmer), (Jr.). American, b. 1929. **Genres:** Novels, Novellas/Short stories, Plays/Screenplays, Poetry, Literary criticism and history. **Career:** Wesleyan University, assistant professor, 1956-60; Rice University, visiting lecturer, 1961-62; University of Virginia, Charlottesville, associate professor, 1962-67, Henry Hoyns Professor of Creative Writing, 1984-; Princeton University, writer-in-residence, 1964-65, Council of the Humanities, sr. fellow, 1974-76; Hollins College, VA, professor of English, and director of writing program, 1967-71; University of South Carolina, Columbia, professor of English and writer-in-residence, 1971-73; Columbia University, School of the Arts, adjunct professor, 1976-77; University of Michigan, Ann Arbor, writer-in-residence, 1978-79, professor of English, 1982-84; Bennington College, professor of English, 1979-80; Virginia Military Institute, eminent scholar, 1981. Transatlantic Review, U.S. poetry ed., 1958-71; University of North Carolina Press, Chapel Hill, Contemporary Poetry Series ed., 1963-68; contributing ed., Contempora, Atlanta, GA, 1970-, and Film Journal, NYC, 1971-; Worksheet, Columbia, SC, co-ed., 1972-; University of Alabama, Coal Royalty Visiting Writer, 1989. **Publications:** POETRY: The Reverend Ghost, 1957; The Sleeping Gypsy and Other Poems, 1958; Abraham's Knife and Other Poems, 1961; For a Bitter Season, 1967; Welcome to the Medicine Show, 1978; Luck's Shining Child, 1981; The Collected Poems of George Garrett, 1984; Days of Our Lives Lie in

Fragments, 1998. SHORT STORIES: King of the Mountain, 1958; In the Briar Patch, 1961; A Wreath for Garibaldi, 1969; An Evening Performance, 1985; Bad Man Blues, 1998. PLAYS: Garden Spot U.S.A., 1962; Sir Slob and the Princess, 1962; Enchanted Ground, 1982. SCREENPLAYS: The Young Lovers, 1964; The Playground, 1965; Frankenstein Meets the Space Monster, 1966. OTHER: The Finished Man, 1959; Which Ones Are the Enemy?, 1961; Do, Lord, Remember Me, 1965; Death of the Fox, 1971; Magic Striptease, 1973; To Recollect a Cloud of Ghosts, 1979; The Succession (novel), 1983; James Jones (biography), 1984; Poison Pen, 1986; Understanding Mary Lee Settle, 1988; Entered from the Sun (novel), 1990; The Sorrows of Fat City, 1992; Whistling in the Dark, 1992; My Silk Purse and Yours, 1992; The Old Army Game, 1994; The King of Babylon Shall Not Come against You, 1996. EDITOR: New Writing from Virginia, 1963; The Girl in the Black Raincoat, 1966; (with W.R. Robinson) Man and the Movies, 1967; (with R.H.W. Dillard and J. Moore) The Sounder Few (essays), 1971; (with O.B. Hardison and J. Gelfman) Film Scripts One, Two, Three and Four, 1971-72; (with W. Peden) New Writing in South Carolina, 1971; (with J. Graham) Craft So Hard to Learn, 1972; (with J. Graham) The Writer's Voice, 1973; (with V. Walton) Intro 5, 1974; (with K.G. Biddle)The Botteghe Oscure Reader, 1974; Intro 6, 1974; Intro 7, 1975; (with S. Kendrick) Intro 8: The Liar's Craft, 1977; (with M. Mewshaw) Intro 8: Close to Home, 1978; (with S. McMillen) Eric Clapton's Lover and Other Stories from the Virginia Quarterly Review, 1990; (with P. Ruffin) Contemporary Southern Short Fiction, 1991; (with S. Stamberg) The Wedding Cake in the Middle of the Road, 1992; (with M. Flinn) Elvis in Oz, 1992; (with P. Ruffin) That's What I Like about the South, 1993; The Yellow Shoe Poets, 1999. **Address:** 1845 Wayside Pl, Charlottesville, VA 22903, U.S.A. **Online address:** gpg@virginia.edu

GARRETT, Laurie. American, b. 1951. **Genres:** Medicine/Health. **Career:** Worked at KPFA (radio station), Berkeley, CA, and for the California Department of Food and Agriculture; freelance journalist in Southern Europe and East Africa, 1979; freelance reporter for National Public Radio (NPR), British Broadcasting Corp. (BBC), American Broadcasting Co. (ABC), Canadian Broadcasting Corp. (CBC), Pacifica News Service, Pacifica Radio, and other media outlets, c. 1980-88; Newsday, science correspondent, 1988-. Visiting fellow, Harvard School of Public Health, 1992-93. Has made appearances on national television programs. **Publications:** The Coming Plague: Newly Emerging Diseases in a World Out of Balance, 1994; Microbes versus Mankind: The Coming Plague, 1996; Betrayal of Trust: The Collapse of Global Public Health, 2000. Contributor to periodicals and books. **Address:** Newsday, 2 Park Ave, New York, NY 10016, U.S.A.

GARRETT, Richard. British, b. 1920. **Genres:** History, Biography, Novellas/Short stories. **Career:** British Infantry Regiment, officer, 1939-46; Feature-writer for magazines; occasional broadcaster, 1946-. **Publications:** Fast and Furious, 1968; The Motor Racing Story, 1969; The Rally-Go-Round, 1970; Anatomy of a Grand Prix Driver, 1970; Motoring and the Mighty, 1971; Atlantic Jet, 1971; Great Sea Mysteries, 1971; Cross Channel, 1972; Hoaxes and Swindles, 1972; True Tales of Detection, 1972; The Search for Prosperity, 1973; Narrow Squeaks, 1973; Stories of Famous Ships, 1974; Heroines, 1974; General Gordon, 1974; Queen Victoria, 1974; Famous Characters of the Wild West, 1975; General Wolfe, 1975; The British Sailor, 1975; Stories of Famous Natural Disasters, 1976; Robert Clive, 1976; Clash of Arms, 1976; Famous Rescues at Sea, 1977; Submarines, 1977; Scharnhorst and Gneisenau: The Elusive Sisters, 1978; Mrs Simpson, 1979; The Raiders, 1980; P. O. W., 1981; File on Spies, 1981; File on Forgery, 1982; Royal Travel, 1982; Jailbrakers, 1983; The Story of Britain, 1983; Atlantic Disaster, 1986; Flight Into Mystery, 1986; Voyage Into Mystery, 1987; Great Escapes of World War II, 1989; The Final Betrayal, 1989; Sky High, 1991. **Address:** The White Cottage, 27A Broadwater Down, Tunbridge Wells, Kent TN2 5NL, England.

GARRETT, Susan. American, b. 1931. **Genres:** Medicine/Health. **Career:** York Hospital, York, ME, administrator, 1978-82; University of Michigan, Ann Arbor, associate administrator at Medical School, 1983-84; Martha Jefferson Hospital, Charlottesville, VA, vice-president, 1984-87; Hospice of the Piedmont, president, 1988-90. Coalition for Mentally Disabled Citizens of Virginia, co-chairperson, 1989-92. **Publications:** Taking Care of Our Own, 1994; Miles to Go: Aging in Rural Virginia, 1998. **Address:** 1845 Wayside Pl., Charlottesville, VA 22903, U.S.A.

GARRETTSON, Charles Lloyd, (III). American, b. 1953. **Genres:** Politics/ Government. **Career:** Muhlenberg College, Allentown, PA, visiting professor, 1990-93, assistant director of admissions, 1993-94. **Publications:** Hubert M. Humphrey and the Politics of Joy: A Case Study in Religious-Political Ethics, Transaction Books (New Brunswick), 1993. **Address:** 717 E. High Street, Pottstown, PA 19464, U.S.A.

GARRIS, Mick. American. **Genres:** Plays/Screenplays. **Career:** Screenwriter, director, and producer for feature films and television. Worked in a film production company; was hired as scriptwriter and story editor for Amazing Stories (NBC television series). Director of feature films, television series, episodes for television series, and television movies. Co-producer of films. **Publications:** SCREENPLAYS: Batteries Not Included, 1987; The Fly II, 1989; Hocus Pocus, 1993. TELEPLAYS. AMAZING STORIES EPISODES: Sitter, 1985; Amazing Falsworth, 1985; (with B. Bird) The Main Attraction, 1985; No Day at the Beach, 1985; The Greibble, 1986; (with T. McLoughlin) Go to the Head of the Class, 1986; (with T. McLoughlin and M. McDowell) Such Interesting Neighbors (adaptation), 1987; Without Diana, 1987. OTHER: She-Wolf of London (series); Quicksilver Highway (television movie), 1997; Michael Jackson's Ghosts, 1997. Author of unproduced screenplays and teleplays. Contributor of short stories and essays to magazines and anthologies. **Address:** c/o John Levan, Creative Artists Agency, 9830 Wilshire Blvd., Beverly Hills, CA 90212, U.S.A.

GARRISON, Bruce. American, b. 1950. **Genres:** Communications/Media, Writing/Journalism, Autobiography/Memoirs. **Career:** East Texas State University, Commerce, professor, 1975-77; Marquette University, Milwaukee, WI, professor, 1977-81; University of Miami, Coral Gables, FL, professor, 1981-. Editorial consultant for book authors and publishers; former daily newspaper reporter and copy editor. **Publications:** (with M. Sabljak) Sports Reporting, 1985, 2nd ed. 1993; Professional Feature Writing, 1989, 2nd ed. 1994; Professional News Writing, 1990; (with M. Salwen) Latin American Journalism, 1991; Advanced Reporting: Skills for the Professional, 1992; Professional News Reporting, 1992; Computer-Assisted Reporting, 1995; Successful Strategies for Computer-Assisted Reporting, 1996. **Address:** School of Communication, University of Miami, P.O. Box 248127, Coral Gables, FL 33124-2030, U.S.A.

GARRISON, Daniel H. American, b. 1937. **Genres:** Literary criticism and history, Intellectual history, Medicine/Health. **Career:** Latin teacher at private school in Exeter, NH, 1959-60; West Virginia University, Morgantown, instructor in classics and Spanish, 1962-63; University of California, Berkeley, acting instructor in comparative literature, 1963-66; Northwestern University, assistant professor, 1966-73, associate professor of classics, 1973-95, professor of classics, 1995-. **Publications:** Mild Frenzy: A Reading of the Hellenistic Love Epigram, 1978; The Language of Virgil: An Introduction to the Poetry of the Aeneid, 1984, user's guide, 1986, rev. ed., 1993; Who's Who in Wodehouse, 1987, rev. ed., 1989; How to Write an "A" Paper in an Emergency, rev. ed., 1987; The Student's Catullus, 1989, 3rd ed., 2004; Horace Epodes and Odes: A New Annotated Latin Edition, 1991; Sexual Culture in Ancient Greece, 2000. **Address:** Dept of Classics, Northwestern University, Evanston, IL 60208-2200, U.S.A. **Online address:** d_garrison@northwestern.edu

GARRISON, David Lee. American, b. 1945. **Genres:** Literary criticism and history, Translations. **Career:** Indiana University, Bloomington, visiting assistant professor, 1975-77; University of Kansas, Lawrence, visiting assistant professor, 1978-79; Wright State University, Dayton, OH, professor of Spanish and Portuguese and chair, Department of Modern Languages, 1979-. **Publications:** Gongora and the "Pyramus and Thisbe" Myth from Ovid to Shakespeare, 1994; Inside the Sound of Rain (poems), 1997; (ed. with T. Hermsen) O Taste and See: Food Poems, 2003. TRANSLATOR: A Bird of Paper: Poems of Vicente Aleixandre, 1982; Poems of Jose Bergamin (1895-1983): Echoes of a Distant Sea, 1991; Certain Chance: Poems of Pedro Salinas, 2000. Contributor to periodicals. **Address:** Department of Modern Languages, Wright State University, Dayton, OH 45435, U.S.A. **Online address:** david.garrison@wright.edu

GARRISON, Deborah (Gottlieb). American, b. 1965. **Genres:** Poetry. **Career:** Editor and poet. New Yorker, NYC, senior editor, 1986-98. **Publications:** A Working Girl Can't Win, and Other Poems, 1998. Contributor of poems to periodicals. **Address:** c/o Random House Publicity, 1540 Broadway, New York, NY 10036, U.S.A.

GARRISON, Dee. American, b. 1934. **Genres:** Librarianship, Biography, Women's studies and issues. **Career:** Professor of History, Rutgers University, New Brunswick, New Jersey (began as Assistant Professor, 1972). **Publications:** Apostles of Culture: The Public Librarian and American Society, 1979; (ed.) Rebel Pen: The Writings of Mary Heaton Vorse, 1986; Mary Heaton Vorse: The Life of an American Insurgent, 1989. **Address:** Dept. of History, Rutgers University, New Brunswick, NJ 08903, U.S.A.

GARRISON, J. Ritchie. American, b. 1951. **Genres:** History, Homes/Gardens. **Career:** Historic Deerfield, Inc., Deerfield, MA, director of education, 1976-85; University of Delaware, Newark, assistant professor, 1985-91, associate professor of museum studies, 1991-. **Publications:** (ed. with B.L. Herman and B.M. Ward) After Ratification: Material Life in Delaware, 1789-1820, 1988; Landscape and Material Life in Franklin County, Massachusetts, 1770-1860, 1991; (ed.) American Material Culture, 1997. **Address:** Department of Museum Studies, University of Delaware, 116 Old College, Newark, DE 19716, U.S.A. **Online address:** jrg@udel.edu

GARRISON, Peter. See **GARDNER, Craig Shaw.**

GARROW, David J. American, b. 1953. **Genres:** Civil liberties/Human rights, Politics/Government, Race relations. **Career:** Institute for Advanced Study, Princeton, NJ, visiting member, 1979-80; University of North Carolina, Chapel Hill, assistant professor of political science, 1980-84; Joint Center for Political Studies, Washington, DC, visiting fellow, 1984; City University of New York, College and the Graduate Center, associate professor, 1984-87, professor of political science, 1987-91; Cooper Union, visiting distinguished professor of history, 1992-93; College of William and Mary, James Pinckney Harrison Professor of History, 1994-95; American University, distinguished historian in residence, 1995-96; Emory University School of Law, presidential distinguished professor, 1997-. **Publications:** Protest at Selma: Martin Luther King, Jr., and the Voting Rights Act of 1965, 1978; The FBI and Martin Luther King, Jr.: From "Solo" to Memphis, 1981, rev. ed., 2002; Bearing the Cross: Martin Luther King, Jr., and the Southern Christian Leadership Conference, 1986; (ed.) The Montgomery Bus Boycott and the Women Who Started It: The Memoir of JoAnn Gibson Robinson, 1987; (co-ed.) Eyes on the Prize: Civil Rights Reader, 1987, rev. ed., 1991; Liberty and Sexuality: The Right to Privacy and the Making of Roe v. Wade, 1994, rev. ed., 1988; (coed.) The Forgotten Memoir of John Knox: A Year in the Life of a Supreme Court Clerk in FDR's Washington, 2002. **Address:** Emory University School of Law, 1301 Clifton Rd, Atlanta, GA 30322-2770, U.S.A. **Online address:** garrow@emory.edu

GARTEN, Helen A. American, b. 1953. **Genres:** Money/Finance. **Career:** Law clerk to judge of the Eastern District of New York, 1978-79; Sullivan & Cromwell, lawyer, 1979-83; Debevoise & Plimpton, lawyer, 1983-84; Rutgers University, Law School, Newark, NJ, faculty member, 1984-, professor of law, 1990-, and Professor Alan Schwartz Scholar. Speaker at educational institutions. **Publications:** Why Bank Regulation Failed: Designing a Bank Regulatory Strategy for the 1990s, 1991; U.S. Financial Regulation and the Level Playing Field, 2001. Contributor to books and law journals. **Address:** Law School, Rutgers University, 123 Washington St., Newark, NJ 07102, U.S.A. **Online address:** hgarten@kinoy.rutgers.edu

GARTEN, Jeffrey E. American, b. 1946. **Genres:** Business/Trade/Industry. **Career:** Wall Street, thirteen years, including time with Lehman Brothers, Kuhn Loeb, and the Blackstone Group; founded the Eliot Group (an investment bank). Served on the White House Council on International Policy during the Nixon administration and on the State Department Policy Planning Staff of Secretaries of State Henry Kissinger and Cyrus Vance. U.S. Government, Undersecretary of Commerce for International Trade, 1993-95; School of Management, Yale University, New Haven, CT, professor and dean, 1995-. **Publications:** A Cold Peace: America, Japan, Germany, and the Struggle for Supremacy, 1993; (with R.H. Brown) U.S. Industrial Outlook 1994: Forecasts for Selected Manufacturing and Service Industries, 1994; The Big Ten: The Big Emerging Markets and How They Will Change Our Lives, 1997; The Mind of the CEO, 2000. Author of articles for periodicals. **Address:** c/o Yale University, 56 Hillhouse Ave., Room 104, New Haven, CT 06511-3704, U.S.A. **Online address:** jeffrey.garten@yale.edu

GARTHOFF, Raymond L(eonard). American (born Egypt), b. 1929. **Genres:** History, International relations/Current affairs, Military/Defense/Arms control. **Career:** Employed by US Dept. of State, Washington, DC, 1961-79 (Special Assistant for Soviet Bloc Political-Military Affairs, 1961-67; Counselor, US Mission to NATO, 1968-70; Sr. State Dept. Adviser, US SALT Delegation, 1969-72; Deputy Director, Bureau of Political-Military Affairs, 1970-73; Sr. Foreign Service Inspector, 1974-77; US Ambassador to Bulgaria, 1977-79); Sr. Fellow, Brookings Institution, Washington, DC, 1980-94. Professorial Lecturer, Institute for Sino-Soviet Studies, George Washington University, 1963-64, and School for Advanced International Studies, Johns Hopkins University, 1964-67, both Washington, DC. **Publications:** Soviet Military Doctrine, 1953; How Russia Makes War, 1954; Soviet Strategy in the Nuclear Age, 1958, rev. ed., 1962; The Soviet Image of Future War, 1959; Soviet Military Policy: A Historical Analysis, 1966; Detente and Confrontation: American-Soviet Relations from Nixon to Reagan, 1985, rev. ed., 1994; Policy versus the Law: The Reinterpretation of the ABM Treaty, 1987; Reflections on the Cuban Missile Crisis, 1987, rev.

ed., 1989; Deterrence and the Revolution in Soviet Military Doctrine, 1990; The Great Transition: American-Soviet Relations and the End of the Cold War, 1994; A Journey through the Cold War: A Memoir of Containment and Coexistence, 2001. EDITOR: (and trans.) Maj. General G. Pokrovsky, Science and Technology in Contemporary War, 1959; (and trans.) Marshal V.D. Sokolovsky, Military Strategy, 1963; (and co-author) Sino-Soviet Military Relations, 1966. **Address:** 1901 Wyoming Ave, NW, No. 14, Washington, DC 20009, U.S.A.

GARTNER, Chloe Maria. American, b. 1916. **Genres:** Novels, Plays/ Screenplays. **Publications:** Perchance to Dream (play), 1983; The Infidels, 1960; Drums of Khartoum, 1967; Die Lange Sommer, 1970; Woman from the Glen, 1973; Mistress of the Highlands, 1976; Anne Bonny, 1977; The Image and the Dream, 1980; Still Falls the Rain, 1982; Greenleaf, 1987; Lower Than the Angels, 1989; three works in progress. **Address:** Kidde, Hoyt & Picard, 335 E. 51st St, New York, NY 10022, U.S.A.

GARTNER, Scott Sigmund. American, b. 1963. **Genres:** History. **Career:** Georgia Bureau of Investigation, Atlanta, intern, summer, 1985; Federal Bureau of Investigation, Washington, DC, honors intern, summer, 1986; National Institute of Justice, social science program specialist in drugs, alcohol, and crime section, summer, 1987; University of California, Davis, acting assistant professor, 1991-92, assistant professor, 1992-97, associate professor of political science, 1997-. Lecturer at educational institutions. **Publications:** Strategic Assessment in War, 1997; (with S. Carter, M. Haines, and others) U.S. Bureau of the Census, Historical Statistics of the United States: Colonial Times to 1970, electronic ed., 1997. Contributor of articles and reviews to periodicals. **Address:** Department of Political Science, University of California, 1 Shields Ave., Davis, CA 95616, U.S.A. **Online address:** ssgartner@ucdavis.edu

GARTON ASH, Timothy. British, b. 1955. **Genres:** History, International relations/Current affairs, Politics/Government, Autobiography/Memoirs, Essays. **Career:** Fellow, St. Antony's College, Oxford, and Hoover Institution, Stanford. **Publications:** The Polish Revolution: Solidarity, 1983; The Uses of Adversity: Essays on the Fate of Central Europe, 1989; The Magic Lantern: The Revolution of '89 Witnessed in Warsaw, Budapest, Berlin and Prague (in U.K. as We the People), 1990; In Europe's Name: Germany and the Divided Continent, 1993; The File: A Personal History, 1997; History of the Present: Essays, Sketches and Despatches from Europe in the 1990s, 1999; Free World: America, Europe and the Surprising Future of the West, 2004. **Address:** St. Antony's College, Oxford, England.

GARVER, Newton. American, b. 1928. **Genres:** Philosophy. **Career:** State University of New York at Buffalo, Buffalo, lecturer, 1961-66, associate professor, 1966-71, professor of philosophy, 1971-91, Distinguished Service Professor, 1991-. Oakwood School, member of board of managers, 1968-86, president, 1973-75, 1977-79; Alternatives to Violence Project, member of board of directors, 1992-94, vice-president, 1992-93. **Publications:** Jesus, Jefferson, and the Task of Friends, 1983; (ed. with P.H. Hare) Naturalism and Rationality, 1986; (ed. with J.B. Brady) Justice, Law, and Violence, 1991; (with S.C. Lee) Derrida and Wittgenstein, 1994; This Complicated Form of Life: Essays on Wittgenstein, 1994; (with E.H. Reitan) Nonviolence and Community, 1995. **Address:** 11253 Boston Rd, East Concord, NY 14055-9711, U.S.A. **Online address:** garver1928@aol.com

GARVEY, John H. American, b. 1948. **Genres:** Law. **Career:** Morrison & Foerster, San Francisco, CA, litigation associate, 1975-76; University of Kentucky, Lexington, Wendell Cherry Professor of Law, 1977-94, university research professor, 1989-90; University of Notre Dame, IN, professor of law, 1994-99; Boston College Law School, dean, 1999-. U.S. Department of Justice, assistant to the solicitor general, 1981-84; American Law Institute, member, 1982-. University of Michigan, visiting professor, 1985-86. **Publications:** Modern Constitutional Theory, 3rd ed., 1994, 4th ed., 1999; The First Amendment, 2nd ed., 1996; What Are Freedoms For?, 1996; Religion and the Constitution, 2002. **Address:** Boston College Law School, Stuart House, M305, 885 Centre St, Newton, MA 02459, U.S.A.

GARWOOD, Julie. Also writes as Emily Chase. American, b. 1946. **Genres:** Mystery/Crime/Suspense, Romance/Historical, Young adult fiction. **Career:** Writer. **Publications:** HISTORICAL ROMANCE NOVELS: Gentle Warrior, 1985; Rebellious Desire, 1986; Honor's Splendor, 1987; The Lion's Lady, 1988; The Bride, 1989; Guardian Angel, 1990; The Gift, 1990; The Prize, 1991; The Secret, 1992; Castles, 1993; Saving Grace, 1993; Prince Charming, 1994; For the Roses, 1995; The Wedding, 1996; Come the Spring, 1997; The Clayborne Brides, 1997; Ransom, 1998. CONTEMPORARY SUSPENSE NOVELS: Heartbreaker, 2000; Mercy, 2001; Killjoy, 2002; Murder List,

2004. FOR YOUNG ADULTS: A Girl Named Summer, 1985; (as Emily Chase) What's a Girl to Do, 1985. **Address:** PO Box 7574, Leawood, KS 66211, U.S.A.

GASAWAY, Laura N. American, b. 1945. **Genres:** Law, Librarianship. **Career:** University of Houston, Houston, TX, law librarian and assistant professor of law, 1973-75; University of Oklahoma, Tulsa, directory and professor of law, 1975-84; University of North Carolina at Chapel Hill, directory and professor of law, 1985-. **Publications:** (with J.L. Hoover and D.M. Warden) American Indian Legal Materials: A Union List, 1980; (with M. Murphy) Legal Protection for Computer Programs, 1980; (with B.S. Johnson and J.M. Murray) Law Library Management during Fiscal Austerity, 1992; (with S.K. Winant) Librarians and Copyright: A Guide to Copyright in the 1990s, 1994; (ed., with M.G. Chiorazzi) Law Librarianship: Historical Perspectives, 1996; Growing Pains: Adapting Copyright to Libraries, Education, and Society, 1997. **Address:** 905 Queensbury Cir., Durham, NC 27713, U.S.A.

GASCHNITZ, Michael K. Canadian. **Genres:** Sports/Fitness. **Career:** Works in the sports retail business. **Publications:** Professional Sports Statistics, 1997. **Address:** 59 Westview Cres., Spruce Grove, AB, Canada T7X 1K9.

GASCOIGNE, Bamber. British, b. 1935. **Genres:** Novels, History, Literary criticism and history, Theatre. **Career:** Drama Critic, Spectator, 1961-63, and Observer, 1963-64, both London; Chairman, University Challenge, Granada TV, Manchester, 1962-87; Presenter, Connoisseur, BBC2-TV, 1988-89. **Publications:** Twentieth Century Drama, 1962; World Theatre, 1968; The Great Moghuls, 1971; Murgatreud's Empire, 1972; Treasures and Dynasties of China, 1973; The Heyday, 1973; Ticker Khan, 1974; The Christians, 1977; Images of Richmond, 1978; Images of Twickenham, 1981; Why the Rope Went Tight, 1981; Fearless Freddie's Magic Wish (and Sunken Treasure), 1982; Quest for the Golden Hare, 1983; Cod Streuth, 1986; How to Identify Prints, 1986; Encyclopedia of Britain, 1993; Milestones in Colour Printing, 1997; World History: A Narrative Encyclopedia (e-book), 2001. **Address:** St. Helena Terr., Richmond TW9 1NR, England. **Online address:** bamber@ historyworld.net; www.historyworld.net

GASCOIGNE, John. Australian, b. 1951. **Genres:** Education, History. **Career:** University of Papua New Guinea, Port Moresby, lecturer in history, 1977-78; University of New South Wales, Kensington, Australia, tutor, 1980-84, lecturer, 1984-89, senior lecturer in history, 1989-96, associate professor, 1997-. **Publications:** Cambridge in the Age of the Enlightenment, 1989; Joseph Banks and the English Enlightenment: Useful Knowledge and Polite Cultural, 1994; Science in the Service of Empire: Joseph Banks, the British State and the Uses of Science in the Age of Revolution, 1998; Science, Politics and Universities of Europe, 1999. **Address:** School of History, University of New South Wales, Sydney, NSW 2052, Australia. **Online address:** j.gascoigne@unsw.edu.au

GASH, Jonathan. (John Grantt). Also writes as Graham Gaunt. British, b. 1933. **Genres:** Mystery/Crime/Suspense. **Career:** Physician: Private consultant on infectious diseases, since 1988. General practitioner, London, 1958-59; pathologist, London and Essex, 1959-62; Clinical Pathologist, Hannover and Berlin, 1962-65; Lecturer and Head of the Division of Clinical Pathology, University of Hong Kong, 1965-68; microbiologist, Hong Kong and London, 1968-71; Microbiologist, Faculty of Medicine, University of London, 1971-88. **Publications:** Terminus (play), 1976; The Judas Pair, 1977; Gold from Gemini, 1978, in U.S. as Gold by Gemini, 1979; The Grail Tree, 1979; Spend Game, 1980; The Vatican Rip, 1981; (as Graham Gaunt) The Incomer, 1981; Firefly Gadroon, 1982; The Sleepers of Erin, 1983; The Gondola Scam, 1983; Pearlhanger, 1985; Moonspender, 1986; Jade Woman, 1988; The Very Last Gambado, 1989; The Great California Game, 1990; The Lies of Fair Ladies, 1992; Paid and Loving Eyes, 1993; The Rich and the Profane, 1999; The Lies of Fair Ladies, 1991; Paid in Loving Eyes, 1992; The Sin Within Her Smile, 1993; The Grace in Older Women, 1994; The Possessions of a Lady, 1995; Different Women Dancing, 1996; The Rich and the Profane, 1997; Prey Dancing, 1997; A Rag, A Bone and A Hank of Hair, 1998. **Address:** Silver Willows, Chapel Lane, West Bergholt, Colchester, Essex CO6 3EF, England.

GASH, Norman. British (born India), b. 1912. **Genres:** History, Biography. **Career:** Lecturer in Modern History, University College, London, 1936-40; Lecturer in Modern History, University of St. Andrews, 1946-53; Professor of Modern History, University of Leeds, 1953-55; Professor of History, University of St. Andrews, 1955-80, professor emeritus, currently. **Publications:** Politics in the Age of Peel, 1953; Mr. Secretary Peel, 1961; Reaction and Reconstruction in English Politics 1832-1852, 1965; Age of Peel, 1968; Sir Robert Peel, 1973; (with others) The Conservative Leadership, 1974; Peel, 1976; (with others) The Conservatives, 1977; Aristocracy and People: Britain 1815-1865, 1979; Lord Liverpool, 1984; Pillars of Government, 1986; Robert Surtees and Early Victorian Society, 1993. **Address:** Old Gatehouse, Portway, Langport, Somerset, England.

GASKELL, Ivan. British, b. 1955. **Genres:** Art/Art history. **Career:** University of London, London, England, assistant curator of Photographic Collection, Warburg Institute, 1980-83; Cambridge University, Cambridge, England, fellow of Wolfson College, 1983-91; Harvard University, Cambridge, MA, curator of paintings and sculpture at Fogg Art Museum, 1991-. Cambridge Darkroom Gallery, chair of board of directors, 1989-91. **Publications:** The Thyssen-Bornemisza Collection: Seventeenth-Century Dutch and Flemish Painting, 1990; (with M. Jonker) Vermeer Studies, 1998; (with H. Lie) Sketches in Clay for Projects by Gian Lorenzo Bernini, 1999; Vermeer's Wager: Speculations on Art History, Theory, and Art Museums, 2000. Contributor to journals. Editor, "Cambridge Studies in Philosophy and the Arts" Series. **Address:** Fogg Art Museum, Harvard University, 32 Quincy St, Cambridge, MA 02138, U.S.A.

GASKELL, Jane. British, b. 1941. **Genres:** Novels. **Career:** Daily Express, former feature writer; London Daily Mail, London, roving correspondent. **Publications:** Strange Evil, 1957; King's Daughter, 1958; Attic Summer, 1958; The Serpent, 1963; The Shiny Narrow Grin, 1964; The Fabulous Heroine, 1965; Atlan, 1965; The City, 1966; All Neat in Black Stockings, 1966; A Sweet Sweet Summer, 1969; Summer Coming, 1974; Some Summer Lands, 1977; Sun Bubble, 1990. **Address:** c/o The Sharland Organisation Ltd, The Manor House, Manor St, Raunds, Northhants. NN9 6JW, England.

GASKIN, Catherine. Irish/Australian, b. 1929. **Genres:** Mystery/Crime/ Suspense, Romance/Historical. **Publications:** This Other Eden, 1947; With Every Year, 1949; Dust in Sunlight, 1950; All Else Is Folly, 1951; Daughter of the House, 1952; Sara Dane, 1955; Blake's Reach, 1958; Corporation Wife, 1960; I Know My Love, 1962; The Tilsit Inheritance, 1963; The File on Devlin, 1965; Edge of Glass, 1967; Fiona, 1970; A Falcon for a Queen, 1972; The Property of a Gentleman, 1974; The Lynmara Legacy, 1975; The Summer of the Spanish Woman, 1977; Family Affairs, 1980; Promises, 1982; The Ambassador's Women, 1985; The Charmed Circle, 1988. **Address:** Villa 139, The Manors, 15 Hale Rd, Mosman, NSW 2088, Australia.

GASKIN, J(ohn) C(harles) A(ddison). British, b. 1936. **Genres:** Novellas/ Short stories, Classics, Philosophy. **Career:** Royal Bank of Scotland, Edinburgh, accountant, 1960-62; University of Dublin, Trinity College, Ireland, lecturer, 1965-78, fellow, 1978-, professor of philosophy, 1982-97. **Publications:** Hume's Philosophy of Religion, 1978, rev. ed., 1988; The Quest for Eternity: An Outline of the Philosophy of Religion, 1984; Varieties of Unbelief from Epicurus to Sartre, 1989; The Epicurean Philosophers, 1994; The Dark Companion, Ghost Stories, 2001. **Address:** c/o Dept of Philosophy, Trinity College, University of Dublin, Dublin 2, Ireland.

GASKINS, Richard H. American, b. 1946. **Genres:** Environmental sciences/Ecology. **Career:** Bryn Mawr College, Bryn Mawr, PA, associate professor and dean of social work, 1975-87; University of Chicago, Chicago, IL, associate professor, 1987-91; New School for Social Research, NYC, associate dean of graduate faculty, 1992-94; Brandeis University, Waltham, MA, professor of legal studies, 1994-. **Publications:** Environmental Accidents, 1989; Burdens of Proof in Modern Discourse. **Address:** Brandeis University, Waltham, MA 02454, U.S.A.

GASS, William (Howard). American, b. 1924. **Genres:** Novels, Literary criticism and history, Novellas/Short stories. **Career:** Professor Emeritus, Washington University, St. Louis, Missouri, 1999- (David May Distinguished Professor in Humanities, Washington University, 1979-99; Professor of Philosophy, 1969-79). Director, International Writers Center, 1990. Instructor in Philosophy, College of Wooster, Ohio, 1950-54; Assistant Professor, 1955-58, Associate Professor, 1960-65, and Professor of Philosophy, 1966-69; Purdue University, Lafayette, Indiana; Visiting Lecturer in English and Philosophy, University of Illinois, Urbana, 1958-59. **Publications:** Omensetter's Luck, 1966; In the Heart of the Heart of the Country and Other Stories, 1968; Willie Masters' Lonesome Wife, 1968; Fiction and Figures of Life, 1971; On Being Blue, 1976; The World Within the Word, 1978; The First Winter of My Married Life, 1979; Habitations of the Word: Essays, 1985; Culp, 1985; The Tunnel, 1995; Finding A Form, 1996; Cartesian Sonata and Other Novellas, 1998; Reading Rilke, 1999; Tests of Time, 2002. EDITOR: The Writer in Politics, 1996; The Writer and Religion, 2000; Literary St. Louis, 2000. **Address:** 6304 Westminster Pl, St. Louis, MO 63130, U.S.A. **Online address:** iwl@artsci.wustl.edu

GASSENHEIMER, Linda. American, b. 1942. **Genres:** Food and Wine. **Career:** CuisinEase, London, England, founder and manager, 1977-86; Gardner's Markets, Miami, FL, executive director, Food and Public Relations, 1987-; author of Dinner in Minutes (syndicated column), 1988-; developer of Floribbean, a line of gourmet products based on tropical fruits grown in Florida. Lecturer and demonstrator on food trends and writing, food trend consultant and recipe developer; trainer of chefs guest teacher, Ariana's Cooking School; guest lecturer and cooking demonstrator on the Queen Elizabeth II. Creator of Dinner in Minutes episodes for the series Cooking with Professionals, 1988; and Cooking with Celebrities segments, Something on 17; guest on television programs. **Publications:** French Cuisine, 1984; Simply Sauces, 1984; Keys Cuisine: Flavors of the Florida Keys, 1992; Dinner in Minutes, 1993; Low-Carb Meals in Minutes; More Low-Carb Meals in Minutes; Mix 'n Match Meals in Minutes for People with Diabetes.

GASTIL, John (Webster). American, b. 1967. **Genres:** Politics/Government. **Career:** Institute for Public Policy, Albuquerque, NM, research manager, 1994-. **Publications:** Democracy in Small Groups: Participation, Decision Making, and Communication, 1993. **Address:** Institute for Public Policy, 1805 Sigma Chi, Albuquerque, NM 87131, U.S.A.

GASTON, Edwin Willmer, Jr. American, b. 1925. **Genres:** Literary criticism and history, Biography. **Career:** Professor Emeritus of English, Stephen F. Austin State University, Nacogdoches, Texas, 1986 (Professor of English, 1950-86; Graduate Dean, 1976-81; Vice President for Academic Affairs, 1981-86). Fulbright Lecturer in American Literature, University of Helsinki, 1964-65. President, Alpha Chi national Scholarship Society, 1967-79. Chairman, Editorial Board, Southwestern American Literature Journal, 1972-73. **Publications:** The Early Novel of the Southwest, 1961; A Manual of Style, 1961; Conrad Richter, 1965, 1989; Eugene Manlove Rhodes, 1967; Southwestern American Literature: A Bibliography, 1980. **Address:** 709 Bostwick, Nacogdoches, TX 75965-2416, U.S.A.

GASTON, Patricia S. American, b. 1946. **Genres:** Poetry, Literary criticism and history. **Career:** Jefferson State Junior College, Birmingham, AL, instructor in English department, 1972-75; Lawson State Community College, Birmingham, instructor, 1975-76; Jefferson County Community Schools, Birmingham, site coordinator, 1976-77; Stetson University, Deland, FL, instructor, 1984-86; University of Florida, Gainesville, instructor, 1986-87; Santa Fe Community College, adjunct, 1986-87; Auburn University, Auburn, AL, instructor in English department, 1987-92, editor of English department newsletter, 1989-92; West Virginia University, Parkersburg, WV, associate professor, 1992-. **Publications:** Prefacing the Waverly Prefaces: A Reading of Sir Walter Scott, 1992. Contributor of chapters to books and reviews and poetry to periodicals. **Address:** Route 9, Box 9-A, Parkersburg, WV 26101, U.S.A.

GAT, Azar. Israeli, b. 1959. **Genres:** Military/Defense/Arms control, Politics/ Government, History. **Career:** Tel Aviv University, Tel Aviv, Israel, lecturer, 1987-91, senior lecturer in political science, 1991-. Military service: Israel Defense Forces Reserve; present rank, major. **Publications:** The Origins of Military Thought from the Enlightenment to Clausewitz, Oxford University Press, 1989; The Development of Military Thought: The Nineteenth Century, Clarendon Press, 1992. **Address:** Department of Political Science, Tel Aviv University, Ramat Aviv, Tel Aviv, Israel.

GATCH, Milton McC., Jr. American, b. 1932. **Genres:** Librarianship, Literary criticism and history, Theology/Religion. **Career:** Shimer College, Mount Carroll, IL, Chaplain and Chairman of Humanities, 1964-67; Northern Illinois University, DeKalb, Associate Professor of English, 1967-68; University of Missouri, Columbia, Associate Professor, 1968-72, Chairman of Dept., 1971-74, Professor of English, 1972-78; Union Theological Seminary, NYC, Professor of Church History, 1978-98, Director of the Burke Library, 1991-98, Emeritus, 1998-. **Publications:** Death: Meaning and Mortality in Christian Thought and Contemporary Culture; 1969 Loyalties and Traditions: Man and His World in Old English Literature; Preaching and Theology in Anglo-Saxon England: Aelfric and Wulfstan, 1977; (ed. with C.T. Berkhout) Anglo-Saxon Scholarship: The First Three Centuries, 1982; So Precious a Foundation: The Library of Leander van Ess at the Burke Library of Union Theological Seminary, 1996; The Yeats Family and the Book, circa 1900, 2000; Eschatology and Christian Nurture: Themes on Anglo-Saxon and Medieval Religious Life, 2000. Author of articles. **Address:** 105 E 29th St, New York, NY 10016, U.S.A. **Online address:** mac@ miltongatch.us

GATENBY, Greg. Canadian, b. 1950. **Genres:** Poetry, Literary criticism and history. **Career:** Artistic dir., Harbourfront Reading Series, 1975-, and

Artistic dir., Harbourfront International Festival of Authors, Toronto, 1980-; League of Canadian Poets, Honourary Lifetime Member, 1991; Order of Canada, 2000. **Publications:** Rondeaus for Erica, 1976; Adrienne's Blessing, 1976; The Brown Stealer, 1977; The Salmon Country, 1978; Growing Still, 1981; The Wild Is Always There, 1993; The Very Richness of that Past, 1995; Toronto: A Literary Guide, 1999. EDITOR: 52 Pickup, 1976; Whale Sound: An Anthology of Poems About Whales and Dolphins, 1977; Whales: A Celebration, 1983. **Address:** c/o Harbourfront Reading Series, 235 Queen's Quay W, Toronto, ON, Canada M5J 2G8.

GATES, Barbara T(imm). American, b. 1936. **Genres:** History, Intellectual history, Literary criticism and history, Natural history, Illustrations. **Career:** Widener College, Chester, PA, lecturer in English, 1965-67; University of Delaware, Newark, DE, assistant professor, 1971-76, associate professor, 1976-88, professor of English, 1988-. Exchange professor, Monash University, Melbourne, Australia, 1983; visiting professor, University of California-Davis, 1986. **Publications:** Victorian Suicide: Mad Crimes and Sad Histories, 1988; Kindred Nature: Victorian and Edwardian Women Embrace the Living World, 1998. EDITOR: Critical Essays on Charlotte Bronte, 1989; Journal of Emily Shore, 1991; (with A.B. Shteir) Natural Eloquence: Women Reinscribe Science, 1997; In Nature's Name: An Anthology of Women's Writing and Art, 1780-1930, 2002. **Address:** Department of English, University of Delaware, Newark, DE 19716, U.S.A. **Online address:** bgates@udel.edu

GATES, David. American, b. 1947. **Genres:** Novels. **Career:** Worked as a cab driver and worked for wholesale book distributor and electronics company; taught at University of Virginia and Harvard University; Newsweek, NYC, 1979-, began in letters department, became senior writer. **Publications:** NOVELS: Jernigan, 1991; Preston Falls, 1998; The Wonders of the Invisible World, 1999. **Address:** Newsweek, 251 W 57th St, New York, NY 10019, U.S.A.

GATES, Henry Louis. American, b. 1950. **Genres:** Literary criticism and history, Bibliography, Race relations. **Career:** Lecturer and Director of Undergraduate Studies, 1976-79, Assistant Professor, 1979-84, and Associate Professor of English and Afro-American Studies, 1984-85, Yale University; Professor of English, Comparative Literature, and Africana Studies, 1985-88, and W.E.B. DuBois Professor of Literature, 1988-90, Cornell University; John Spencer Bassett Professor of English and Literature, Duke University, 1990-91; Harvard University, W.E.B. DuBois Professor of the Humanities, Chairman, Dept. of Afro-American studies, and Director, W.E.B. DuBois Institute for Afro-American Research, 1991-. Mellon Fellow, Cambridge University, 1973-75; Ford Foundation National Fellow, 1976-77; Rockefeller Foundation Minority Scholar Fellow, 1980-81; MacArthur Prize Fellow, 1981-86; Associate Fellow, W.E.B. DuBois Institute, Harvard University, 1987-88, 1988-89; Mellon Fellow, National Humanities Center, Research Triangle, North Carolina, 1989, 1989-90; Woodrow Wilson National Fellow, 1988-89, 1989-90. Recipient, Zora Neale Hurston Society Award, 1986. **Publications:** (ed.) Black Is the Color of the Cosmos: Charles T. Davis's Essays on Black Literature and Culture 1942-1981, 1982; (ed.) Our Nig, or, Sketches from the Life of a Free Black, by Harriet Wilson, 1983; (ed.) Black Literature and Literary Theory, 1984; (ed. with C.T. Davis) The Slave's Narrative: Texts and Contexts, 1985; (ed.) Race, Writing, and Difference, 1986; (co-ed.) Wole Soyinka: A Bibliography, 1986; Figures in Black: Words, Signs, and the Racial Self, 1987; (ed.) The Classic Slave Narratives, 1987; The Signifying Monkey: Towards a Theory of Afro-American Literary Criticism, 1988 (American Book Award, 1989; Anisfield-Wolf Book Award, 1989); (ed.) In the House of Osugbo: Critical Essays on Wole Soyinka, 1988; (series ed.) The Oxford-Schomburg Library of Nineteenth-Century Black Women Writers, 30 vols., 1988, 10 vol. supplement 1990; (ed.) The Souls of Black Folk, by W.E.B. DuBois, 1989; (ed.) The Autobiography of an Ex-Coloured Man, by James Weldon Johnson, 1989; (ed.) Their Eyes Were Watching God, 1990; (ed.) Jonah's Gourd Vine, 1990; (ed.) Tell My Horse, 1990; (ed.) Mules and Men, 1990; (ed.) Voodoo Gods of Haiti, 1990; (ed.) Reading Black, Reading Feminist, 1990; Loose Canons: Notes on the Culture Wars, 1992; Colored People: A Memoir, 1994; (with C. West) The Future of the Race, 1996; Thirteen Ways of Looking at a Black Man, 1997. **Address:** Dept. of Afro-American Studies, Harvard University, 1430 Massachusetts Ave., Cambridge, MA 02138-3810, U.S.A.

GATES, Marilyn. British/Canadian, b. 1944. **Genres:** Sociology, Anthropology/Ethnology. **Career:** Simon Fraser University, Burnaby, BC, associate professor of anthropology and associate faculty in Latin American studies, 1974-. **Publications:** In Default: Peasants, the Debt Crisis, and the Agricultural Challenge in Mexico, 1993. **Address:** Department of Sociology and Anthropology, Simon Fraser University, Burnaby, BC, Canada V5A 1S6. **Online address:** gates@sfu.ca

GATES, Norman T(immings). American, b. 1914. **Genres:** Literary criticism and history. **Career:** Professor Emeritus of English, Rider University, Lawrenceville, New Jersey, since 1985 (Assistant Professor, 1969-74; Associate Professor, 1974-77; Professor, 1977-85). **Publications:** The Poetry of Richard Aldington: Critical Evaluation and an Anthology of Uncollected Poems, 1974; A Checklist of the Letters of Richard Aldington, 1977; Richard Aldington: An Autobiography in Letters, 1992. Work appears in anthologies. **Address:** 520 Woodland Ave, Haddonfield, NJ 08033-2626, U.S.A. **Online address:** ntgates@worldnet.att.net

GATES, Ronda. American, b. 1940. **Genres:** Medicine/Health, Sports/Fitness. **Career:** LIFESTYLES by Ronda Gates, Lake Oswego, OR, president, founder, 1978-. Counseling certification; fellowships: American College of Sports Medicine, Association of Worksite Health Promotion, American and Council on Exercise; motivational speaker; spokesperson, PBS Speaking of Women's Health Foundation; television personality on health promotion; Fit or Fat System, associate producer; presentations on lifestyle-related subjects, including women's health, stress management/resiliency, weight control, exercise, and nutrition. Creator of LIFESTYLES Planner software package. **Publications:** The Lowfat Lifestyle, 1984; Nutrition Nuggets and More/Changes, 1990; (with C. Bailey) Smart Eating, 1996; (with F. and V. Katch) The Scale Companion, 1998; (with B. Whipple) Outwitting Osteoporosis: The Smart Woman's Guide to Bone Health, 2001. Contributor to health and fitness periodicals. **Address:** Lifestyles 4-Heart Press, PO Box 974, Lake Oswego, OR 97034, U.S.A. **Online address:** ronda@rondagates.com

GATES, Viola R. American, b. 1931. **Genres:** Children's fiction, Poetry. **Career:** Private piano teacher, 1961-85; Brico Studios, Denver, CO, piano teacher, 1970-82; Hamilton Middle School, Denver, piano teacher, 1983-85; Englewood Christian school, Englewood, CO, piano teacher, 1983-85. Church organist, pianist, and choral director; secretary, Brico Symphony Guild. **Publications:** Snow Storm, 1990; Journey to Center Place, 1996; Amanda's Gone (short story). Contributor to journals. **Address:** 2149-A Hartford Way, Montrose, CO 81401, U.S.A.

GATHORNE-HARDY, Jonathan. Also writes as Sylvia Thornton. British, b. 1933. **Genres:** Novels, Novellas/Short stories, Children's fiction, Plays/Screenplays, History, Social commentary, Autobiography/Memoirs, Biography. **Career:** Bookseller, tutor, hack reviewer, part-time advertising copy-writer, 1960-75; writer, 1975-. **Publications:** One Foot in the Clouds, 1961; Jane series, 3 vols., 1966-74; Chameleon, 1967; The Office, 1970; The Rise and Fall of the British Nanny (in US as The Unnatural History of the Nanny), 1972, plus reprints and new editions; The Public School Phenomenon (in US as The Old School Tie), 1977; Cyril Bonhamy series, 5 vols., 1978-87; Love, Sex, Marriage, and Divorce (in US as Sex, Love, Marriage, and Divorce), 1981; The Centre of the Universe Is 18 Baedekerstrasse (short stories), 1981; (as Sylvia Thornton) The Man from the Sea, 1982; Doctors, 1984; The City beneath the Skin, 1986; Gerald Brenan: The Interior Castle (biography), 1992; The Twin Detectives (children's fiction), 1995; Particle Theory (novel), 1996; Alfred C. Kinsey-Sex the Measure of All Things (biography), 1998; South from Granada (screenplay), 2001; (consultant) Kinsey (film and source book), 2004; Half an Arch (autobiography), 2004. **Address:** 31 Blacksmith's Yard, Binham, Fakenham, Norfolk NR21 0AL, England. **Online address:** jonnygathorne@freenet.co.uk

GATI, Charles. Hungarian, b. 1934. **Genres:** Politics/Government. **Career:** Union College, Schenectady, NY, instructor in political science, 1963-65, assistant professor, 1965-68, associate professor, 1969-74, professor, 1974-, founder and director of program in comparative communist studies, 1970-71 and 1972-74, chair of political science department, 1975-78; Columbia University, NYC, senior research scholar at Research Institute on International Change, 1971-72, 1977-78, and 1979-, visiting lecturer, 1972, visiting associate professor, 1972-74, visiting professor at Harriman Institute for Advanced Study of the Soviet Union, 1975-86, director of East Europe Project, Research Institute on International Change, 1984-85. Visiting professor, University of Kansas, 1968-69, and Yale University, 1975. **Publications:** (with T. Gati) The Debate over Detente, Foreign Policy Association 1977; Hungary and the Soviet Bloc, 1986; The Bloc That Failed: Soviet-East European Relations in Transition, 1990. EDITOR & CONTRIBUTOR: The Politics of Modernization in Eastern Europe: Testing the Soviet Model, 1974; Caging the Bear: Containment and the Cold War, 1974; The International Politics of Eastern Europe, 1976; (with J.F. Triska) Blue-Collar Workers in Eastern Europe, 1981. Contributor to books and periodicals. **Address:** Department of Political Science, Union College, Schenectady, NY 12308, U.S.A.

GATOS, Stephanie. *See* **KATZ, Steve.**

GATTEY, Charles Neilson. British, b. 1921. **Genres:** Novels, Romance/Historical, Plays/Screenplays, Social commentary, Biography. **Career:** Society of Civil Service Authors, London, president, 1981-. **Publications:** The Bloomer Girls, 1967; Gauguin's Astonishing Grandmother, 1970; A Bird of Curious Plumage, 1971; The Incredible Mrs. Van Der Elst, 1973; They Saw Tomorrow, 1977; Queens of Song, 1979; The Elephant That Swallowed a Nightingale, 1981; Peacocks on the Podium, 1982; Great Dining Disasters, 1984; Foie Gras and Trumpets, 1984; "Farmer" George's Black Sheep, 1986; Excess in Food, Drink and Sex, 1986; Visionaries and Seers, 1988; In Bed with an Elephant, 1989; Luisa Tetrazzini: A Tiger at the Tailor's, 1989; Prophecy and Prediction in the Twentieth Century, 1989; The Florentine Nightingale, 1995; Crowning Glory: Merits of the Monarchy, 2002. WITH J. LAWRENCE: The White Falcon, 1952; Queen's Night, 1953; The Birth of Elizabeth, 1954; Queen of a Thousand Dresses, 1955. WITH Z. BRAMLEY-MOORE: The Eleventh Hour, 1952; In the Maze, 1953; Tidings of Canute, 1954; A Spell of Virtue, 1955; The Birth of the Bloomer, 1955; Mightier than the Sword, 1955; Mrs. Adams and Eve, 1955; Treasure from France, 1956; Man in a Million, 1956; Farewell, Pots and Pans, 1956; True Love or The Bloomer, 1958; By a Hand Unknown, 1958; Life with Alfredo, 1958; The Cloak of Courage, 1959; The Landlady's Brother, 1959; The Colour of Anger, 1963; Fair Cops, 1965; The King Who Could not Stay the Tide, 1971. **Address:** 15 St Lawrence Dr, Pinner, Middlesex HA5 2RL, England.

GATTI, Anne. Irish, b. 1952. **Genres:** Young adult fiction, Young adult nonfiction. **Career:** Collins Harvill, London, England, editorial assistant, 1976-78; Reader's Digest, London, researcher, 1978-80; Eaglemoss Publications, London, editor, 1980-81; freelance writer and editor, 1984-. **Publications:** FOR YOUNG ADULTS. RETELLER: Aesop's Fables, 1992; Tales from the African Plains, 1994; The Magic Flute, 1997. NONFICTION: Isabella Bird Bishop (biography), 1988. OTHER: Stepping Out (youth information handbook), 1985. EDITOR: Edna O'Brien, Tales for the Telling: Irish Folk and Fairy Stories, 1986; Kiri Te Kanawa, Land of the Long White Cloud: Maori Myths, 1989. **Address:** 17 Boltons Ln., Pyrford, Woking Surrey, England. **Online address:** anniegatti@aol.com

GAUBATZ, Kathlyn Taylor. American, b. 1957. **Genres:** Criminology/True Crime. **Career:** Brandeis University, Waltham, MA, assistant director of National Institute for Sentencing Alternatives, 1980-81; New England Coalition Against Prisons, Boston, MA, coordinator, 1981-82; Compass Community Services, San Francisco, counselor, 1989-90, coordinator and case manager in Homeless Family Program, 1990-91; program director at CCR Family Center and Market Street Counseling Center, 1991-94, executive director, 1994-. **Publications:** Crime in the Public Mind, 1995. **Address:** Compass Community Services, 942 Market St. 6th Floor, San Francisco, CA 94102, U.S.A.

GAUBATZ, Kurt Taylor. American, b. 1957. **Genres:** Politics/Government. **Career:** Stanford University, Stanford, CA, assistant professor, 1990-99; Nuffield College, Oxford University, Oxford, England, visiting lecturer in American Foreign Policy, 1999-2000; Old Dominion University, Norfolk, VA, associate professor of international studies and political science, and director of graduate program, 2000-. **Publications:** Elections and War: The Electoral Incentive in the Democratic Politics of War and Peace, 1999. Contributor to books and periodicals. **Address:** Graduate Program in International Studies, Old Dominion University, Norfolk, VA 23529, U.S.A. **Online address:** kgaubatz@odu.edu

GAUCH, Patricia Lee. American, b. 1934. **Genres:** Children's fiction, Young adult fiction. **Career:** Writer and editor. Louisville Courier-Journal, reporter, 1957-59; Coward-McCann and Geoghegan/Putnam, NY, writer, 1969-; Gill-St. Berhards School, Gladstone, NJ, teacher, 1972-83; part-time professor, Drew University, Madison, NJ, Rutgers University, New Brunswick, NJ, Manhattanville College, Purchase, NY; Philomel Books, vice president and editorial director, New York, 1985-. **Publications:** FICTION FOR CHILDREN: My Old Tree, 1970; A Secret House, 1970; Christina Katerina and the Box, 1971; Aaron and the Green Mountain Boys, 1972; Grandpa and Me, 1972; Christina Katerina and the First Annual Grand Ballet, 1973; This Time, Tempe Wick?, 1974; Thunder at Gettysburg, 1975; The Impossible Major Rogers, 1977; Once upon a Dinkelsbuhl, 1977; On to Widecombe Fair, 1978; The Green of Me, 1979; Kate Alone, 1980; The Little Friar Who Flew, 1980; Morelli's Game, 1981; Night Talks, 1983; The Year the Summer Died, 1985; Christina Katerina and the Time She Quit the Family, 1987; Dance, Tanya, 1989; Christina Katerina and the Great Bear Train, 1990; Bravo, Tanya, 1992; Uncle Magic, 1992; Noah, 1994; Tanya and Emily in a Dance for Two, 1994; Christina Katerina and Fats Watson and the Great Neighborhood War, 1997; Tanya and the Magic Wardrobe, 1997; Tanya the Ugly Duckling, 1999; Poppy's Puppets, 1999. **Address:** 21 Curry Lane, Hyde Park, NY 12538, U.S.A.

GAULD, Alan (Ogilvie). British, b. 1932. **Genres:** Psychology, Paranormal. **Career:** Cambridge University, Cambridge, England, research fellow at Emmanuel College, 1958-62; University of Nottingham, Nottingham, England, lecturer to reader in psychology, 1962-96. **Publications:** The Founders of Psychical Research, 1968; (with J.D. Shotter) Human Action and Its Psychological Investigation, 1977; (with A.D. Cornell) Poltergeists, 1979; Mediumship and Survival, 1982; A History of Hypnotism, 1992. **Address:** School of Psychology, University of Nottingham, Nottingham NG7 2RD, England.

GAULDIE, Enid Elizabeth. British, b. 1928. **Genres:** Architecture, Business/Trade/Industry, Local history/Rural topics, History, Novellas/Short stories. **Career:** Department of Modern History, University of Dundee, 1966-71; writer. **Publications:** (ed.) The Dundee Textile Industry from the Papers of Peter Carmichael of Arthurstone, 1969; (co-author) Dundee and Its Textile Industry, 1850-1914, 1969; Cruel Habitations: A History of Working Class Housing, 1780-1918, 1974; The Scottish Country Miller: History of Water-powered Meal Milling in Scotland, 1980; The Quarries and the Feus, 1981; One Artful and Ambitious Individual: Alexander Riddoch, 1989; Flights of Angels: History Today, 1992; The Bonnets of Bonnie Dundee, 1993; Spinning and Weaving, 1995. **Address:** Waterside, Invergowrie, Dundee, Scotland.

GAULT, Peter. Canadian, b. 1958. **Genres:** Novels. **Career:** Writer. **Publications:** Goldenrod, 1988; Knucklehead: A Journey Out of the Mind, 1995. Contributor to periodicals. **Address:** 40 High Park Ave., No. 1912, Toronto, ON, Canada M6P 2S1.

GAUNT, Graham. See GASH, Jonathan.

GAVRONSKY, Serge. American (born France), b. 1932. **Genres:** Novels, Poetry, History, Translations. **Career:** Columbia University, Barnard College, NYC, associate professor, 1960-75; professor of French, 1975-. **Publications:** The French Liberal Opposition and the American Civil War, 1968;Culture/Ecriture, essais critiques, 1983; The German Friend (novel), 1984; Ecrire l'homme, essais critiques, 1986; The Name of the Father (novel), 1993; Louis Zukofsky, l'homme/poete, 1993; Toward a New Poetics: Contemporary Writing in France, 1994; Six Contemporary French Women Poets, 1997; Mallarme spectral, 1998. POETRY: Lectures et compte rendu, 1973; Meme-la suivi de Geste (poetry), 1992; L'interminable Discussion, 1996; L'obscur d'ici, 1998; France d'hier/Yesterday's France, 1999; Sixty Six for Starters, 2002; Temps mort, 2002; Une toute autre histoire, 2002. EDITOR: (and trans.) Poems and Texts, 1969; (with J-M. Blanchard) Le Moyen Age, 1974; (and trans. with P. Terry) Modern French Poetry, 1975; (and trans.) Francis Ponge: The Sun Placed in the Abyss and Other Texts, 1977; (and trans.) Francis Ponge: The Power of Language, 1979; (and trans.) Ten Poems, Dix Poemes de Francis Ponge, 1983; (and trans.) J. Mansour, Dechirures/Torn Apart, 1999; (and trans.) L. Zukofsky, "A"-8 a "A"-11, 2001. **Address:** 525 West End Ave, New York, NY 10024, U.S.A. **Online address:** sgavronsky@barnard.edu

GAY, John H. American, b. 1928. **Genres:** Young adult fiction, Anthropology/Ethnology, Area studies, Social sciences. **Career:** Cuttington University College, Liberia, dean of instruction, 1958-60, chair of social science division, 1958-68, 1970-73; UN Development Programme, Liberia, rural sociologist, 1973-74; UN Food and Agriculture Organization, Lesotho, rural sociologist, 1975-77; Ministry of Agriculture, Lesotho, social analyst, planning unit, 1977-79; National University of Lesotho, senior lecturer, 1979-80, Fulbright lecturer, 1979-82; Transformation Resource Centre, Lesotho, team member, 1986-92; Sechaba Consultants, Lesotho, consultant, 1992-2001; retired, 2001. **Publications:** (with M. Cole) The New Mathematics and an Old Culture, 1967; (with W. Welmers) Mathematics and Logic in the Kpelle Language, 1971; (with others) The Cultural Context of Learning and Thinking, 1971; Red Dust on the Green Leaves, 1973; (with B. Lloyd) Universals of Human Thought: Some African Evidence, 1981; The Brightening Shadow, 1981; (with A. Blair) Growing up in Lesotho, 1981; Lectures on Missiology, 1983; (with others) The Situation of Women and Children in Lesotho, 1991; (with others) Poverty in Lesotho, 1991, rev. ed., 2000; (with D. Gill) Health in Lesotho, 1993; (with D. Hall and D. Gill) Lesotho's Long Journey, 1995; Long Day's Anger, 2004; Africa: A Dream Deferred, 2004. **Address:** 59 Fenno St, Cambridge, MA 02138-6717, U.S.A. **Online address:** judyjohngay@comcast.net

GAY, Kathlyn R. American, b. 1930. **Genres:** Children's fiction, Plays/Screenplays, Communications/Media, Environmental sciences/Ecology, History, Social commentary, Sociology, Women's studies and issues, Young adult non-fiction, Biography, Reference. **Career:** Public relations; advertising; speech writing; editing; creative writing instructor; author. **Publications:** Girl Pilot, 1967; Money Isn't Everything, 1967; Meet Your Mayor, 1967; Meet Your Governor, 1968; Beth Donnis, 1968; Careers in Social Service, 1969; Where the People Are, 1969; The Germans Helped Build America, 1971; (with E. Wolk) Core English, 1972; (co) Young American Basic Reading series: Grades 1-3, 1972; A Family Is for Living, 1972; A Proud Heritage on Parade, 1972; (with L. Senesh) Our Working World, 1973; Body Talk, 1974; Be a Smart Shopper, 1974; (with B. Barnes) The River Flows Backward, 1975; Look Mom! No Words, 1977; Care and Share, 1977; (with M. and M. Gay) Get Hooked on Vegetables, 1978; English for a Changing World, 1979; (with B. Barnes) Your Fight Has Just Begun, 1980; (with B. Barnes) Beginner's Guide to Better Boxing, 1980; (with Martin Gay) Eating What Grows Naturally, 1980; (co) I Like English, 1981; Boxes and More Boxes, 1981; (co) Family Living, 1982; Junkyards, 1982; Acid Rain, 1983; Cities under Stress, 1985; Will the U.S. Be Ready for the Year 2000?, 1986; Ergonomics, 1986; The Greenhouse Effect, 1986; The Rainbow Effect, 1987; Changing Families, 1988; Science in Ancient Greece, 1988; Silent Killers, 1988; Bigotry, 1989; Ozone, 1989; Adoption and Foster Care, 1990; They Don't Wash Their Socks!, 1990; Water Pollution, 1990; Cleaning Nature Naturally, 1991; Garbage and Recycling, 1991; Air Pollution, 1991; (co) Indiana, 1991; Church and State, 1992; Day Care, 1992; Global Garbage, 1992; Caution: This May Be an Advertisement, 1992; Caretakers of the Earth, 1993; Breast Implants, 1993; The Right to Die, 1993; Pregnancy: Public and Private Dilemmas, 1993; Rainforests of the World, 1993; Getting Your Message Across, 1994; The New Power of Women in Politics, 1994; Pollution & the Powerless, 1994; "I Am Who I Am," 1995; Keep the Buttered Side Up, 1995; Rights and Respect, 1995; (with M. Gay) Voices from the Past (9-book series), 1995-; (with M. Gay) Emma Goldman, 1996; (with D. Gay) Not-So-Minor Leagues, 1996; (with M. Gay) Encyclopedia of North American Eating & Drinking Traditions Customs & Rituals, 1996; (with M. Gay) A Dictionary of 20th Century Heroes of Conscience, 1996; (with M. Gay) The Information Superhighway, 1996; Saving the Environment, Debating the Costs, 1996; Militias, 1997; Neo-Nazis, 1997; Communes & Cults, 1997; (with M. Gay) After the Shooting Stops, 1998; Who's Running the Nation?, 1998; Child Labor, 1998; (with M. Gay) The Encyclopedia of Political Anarchy, 1999; Fleeing Cuba, 2000; Silent Death, 2001; Eating Disorders, 2002; Encyclopedia of Women's Health Issues, 2002; (with C. Whittington) Body Marks, 2002; Epilepsy: The Ultimate Teen Guide, 2002; Cultural Diversity: Conflicts and Challenges, 2003; Volunteering: The Ultimate Teen Guide, 2004. **Address:** 11633 Bayonet Ln, New Port Richey, FL 34654, U.S.A. **Online address:** kgay@microd.com

GAY, Marie-Louise. Canadian, b. 1952. **Genres:** Children's fiction, Plays/Screenplays, Illustrations, Picture/board books. **Career:** Editorial illustrator of Canadian and American magazines, 1972-; Perspectives and Decormag, graphic designer, 1974-76; La Courte Echelle, Montreal, QC, art director, 1980; University of Quebec, Montreal, lecturer in illustration, 1981-89; illustrator and author. Host or speaker at workshops and conferences at schools and libraries, 1981-; Ahuntsic College,visiting lecturer in illustration, 1984-85. Designer of children's clothing, 1985-; author and set designer of plays and films, including the animated film La Boite, 1989. **Publications:** SELF-ILLUSTRATED FOR CHILDREN. IN ENGLISH: The Garden, 1985, in French as Mon Potager; Moonbeam on a Cat's Ear, 1986; Rainy Day Magic, 1987; Angel and the Polar Bear, 1988; Fat Charlie's Circus, 1989; Willy Nilly, 1990; Mademoiselle Moon, 1992; Rabbit Blue, 1993; Midnight Mimi, 1994; The Three Little Pigs, 1994; When Vegetables Go Bad, 1994; Rumpelstiltskin, 1997; The Fabulous Song, 1998; How to Take Your Grandmother to the Museum, 1998; The Christmas Orange, 1998; Stella, Star of the Sea, 1999; Stella, Queen of the Snow, 2000; Yuck, a Love Story, 2000; Didi and Daddy on the Promenade, 2000; Stella, Fairy of the Forest, 2002; Good Morning Sam, 2003; Good Night Sam, 2003. IN FRENCH: De Zero a minuit, 1981; La Soeur de Robert, 1983; Drole d'ecole (preschool series), 1984; Sophie series, 12 books, 1991-2003; Princesse Pistache, 1997; Sur mon ile, 1999. PLAYS: Bonne Fete Willy, 1989; Qui a Peur de Loulou?, 1994; Le Jardin de Babel, 1999. Illustrator of books by: B. Gauthier, D. Gillmor, D. Lee, M. Singer, A. Taylor, T. Wynne-Jones.

GAY, Peter. American (born Germany), b. 1923. **Genres:** History, Intellectual history. **Career:** Columbia University, NYC, Member of faculty, 1947-69; Yale University, New Haven, CT, Professor of Comparative European Intellectual History, 1969-93, Durfee Professor of History, 1970-84, Sterling Professor, 1984-93, Professor Emeritus, 1993-. Fellow, American Council of Learned Socs., 1959-60, and Center for Advanced Study in the Behavioral Sciences, 1963-64; Overseas Fellow, Churchill College, Cambridge, England, 1970-71. **Publications:** The Dilemma of Democratic Socialism: Edward Bernstein's Challenge to Marx, 1952; Voltaire's Politics: The Poet as Realist, 1959; The Party of Humanity: Essays in the French Enlightenment, 1964; A Loss of Mastery: Puritan Historians in Colonial

America, 1966; The Enlightenment, vol. I: The Rise of Modern Paganism, 1966, vol. II: The Science of Freedom, 1969; Deism: An Anthology, 1968; Weimar Culture: The Outsider as Insider, 1968; The Bridge of Criticism: Dialogues on the Enlightenment, 1970; (with R.K. Webb) Modern Europe, 1973; Art and Act: On Causes in History-Manet, Gropius, Mondrian, 1976; Style in History, 1976; Freud, Jews, and Other Germans, 1978; The Bourgeois Experience: Victoria to Freud, vol. I, Education of the Senses, 1984, vol. II, The Tender Passion, 1986, vol. III, The Cultivation of Hatred, 1993, vol. IV, the Naked Heart, 1995, vol. V, Pleasure Wars, 1998; Freud for Historians, 1985; A Godless Jew: Freud, Atheism, and the Making of Psychoanalysis, 1987; Freud: A Life in Our Time, 1988; A Freud Reader, 1989; Reading Freud: Explorations and Entertainments, 1990; My German Question: Growing up in Nazi Berlin, 1998; Mozart, 1999. **Address:** 760 West End Ave, Apt 15A, New York, NY 10025-5524, U.S.A.

GAY, Ruth. American, b. 1922. **Genres:** Cultural/Ethnic topics, History. **Career:** Amalgamated Clothing Workers of America, Education Department, 1943-46, Labor and Nation, staff writer and assistant editor, 1946-48; American Joint Distribution Committee, researcher and editor, 1948-50; freelance writer and editor, 1950-72, 1985-; Yale University, New Haven, CT, archivist and cataloger at university library, 1972-85. **Publications:** Jews in America: A Short History, 1965; The Jews of Germany: A Historical Portrait, 1992; Unfinished People: Eastern European Jews Encounter America, 1996; Safe among the Germans: Liberated Jews after World War II, 2002; The Jewish King Lear Comes to America, forthcoming. Contributor to periodicals. **Address:** 270 Riverside Dr, New York, NY 10025, U.S.A.

GAYLIN, Willard. American, b. 1925. **Genres:** Civil liberties/Human rights, Criminology/True Crime, Ethics, Law, Psychiatry, Psychology. **Career:** Clinical professor of psychiatry, Columbia Psychoanalytic School, NYC, 1972- (joined faculty, 1956); co-founder and president, Hastings Center (Institute of Society, Ethics and the Life Sciences), 1970-. Formerly adjunct professor of psychiatry, Union Theological Seminary, NYC; adjunct professor of psychiatry and law, Columbia University, School of Law, NYC, 1970; Planned Parenthood Federation of America, board of directors. **Publications:** (with H. Hendrin and A. Carr) Psychoanalysis and Social Research, 1965; The Meaning of Despair, 1968, 2nd ed. as Psychodynamic Understanding of Depression, 1984; In the Service of Their Country: War Resisters in Prison, 1970; (with R. Veatch and C. Morgan) The Teaching of Medical Ethics, 1973; Partial Justice, 1975; (with J. Meister and R. Neville) Operating on the Mind, 1975; Caring, 1976; (with I. Glasser, S. Marcus, and D. J. Rothman) Doing Good, 1978; Feelings: Our Vital Signs, 1979; The Killing of Bonnie Garland, 1982; The Rage Within, 1984; Rediscovering Love, 1986; Adam and Eve and Pinocchio, 1990; The Male Ego, 1992; (with B. Jennings) The Perversion of Autonomy, 1996; Talk Is not Enough: How Psychotherapy Works, 2000; Hatred: The Descent into Violence, 2002. EDITOR: (with others) Violence and the Politics of Research, 1981; (with R. Macklin) Who Speaks for the Child?, 1982; (with E. Person) Passionate Attachments, 1988. Contributor to periodicals. **Address:** 108 Circle Dr, Hastings on Hudson, NY 10706, U.S.A. **Online address:** willgaylin@aol.com

GAZE, R(aymond) Michael. British, b. 1927. **Genres:** Biology. **Career:** Head, Medical Research Council Neural Development and Regeneration Group, University of Edinburgh, 1984-92. Lecturer, 1955-62, and Reader, 1966-70, Dept. of Physiology, Edinburgh University, Head of the Division of Developmental Biology, 1970-83, and Deputy Director, 1977-83, National Institute for Medical Research, London. **Publications:** The Formation of Nerve Connections, 1970. Author of papers on neurobiology. **Address:** 37 Sciennes Rd, Edinburgh EH9 INS, Scotland. **Online address:** mikegaze@talk21.com

GAZETAS, Aristides. American, b. 1930. **Genres:** Art/Art history, Education, Film, Theatre. **Career:** National Theatre School, Montreal, Canada, chair of design program, 1968-72; University of Calgary, associate professor of drama and stage designer, 1972-76; Southern Alberta Institute of Technology, Calgary, Alberta, Canada, chair of art history program, 1976-80; Department of Theater, University of Lethbridge, Alberta, Canada, cinematic arts development officer, 1980-83; University of British Columbia, lecturer and associate professor of theater and film, 1988-93. Member of board of directors, Alberta Motion Picture Development Corporation, 1981-83; writer, host and tutor for educational courses associated with Knowledge Network, Open Learning Agency, and UBC Access, 1992-98. **Publications:** An Introduction to World Cinema, 2000; Imagining Selves: The Politics of Representation, Film Narratives and Adult Education, 2000. **Address:** 42-5840 Dover Crescent, Richmond, BC, Canada V7C 5P4. **Online address:** agazetas@shaw.ca; agm594@netscape.net

GEACH, Christine. Also writes as Elizabeth Dawson, Anne Lowing, Christine Wilson. British, b. 1930. **Genres:** Romance/Historical. **Career:**

Freelance writer. **Publications:** AS ELIZABETH DAWSON: Isle of Dreams; Wine in a Crystal Goblet; The Bending Reed, 1979. AS ANNE LOWING: Masked Ball, 1966; The Denbigh Affair, 1967; Yasmin, 1969; Shadow on the Wind, 1970; The Gossamer Thread; Melyonen; The Captain's Pawn; The Napoleon Ring; The Branch and the Briar, 1976; Copper Moon, 1979; Girl in the Shadows, 1984. AS CHRISTINE WILSON: Broken Vows; Trial of Love; A Husband for Charlotte; A Deeper Love; Love's True Face; The Doubting Heart; Nurse Emma in Love; Dr. Mary's Dilemma; Watch for Me by Moonlight; The Driven Clouds; Where Is Tomorrow; The Gift of Happy Rain; Is This My Island?; The Lonely Tower; This Nearly Was Mine; Some Other Spring; The Man Beyond Price; The Man in the Blue Car, 1978; Proud Swells the Tide, 1979; The Light in the Window, 1980.

GEAR, W. Michael. American, b. 1955. **Genres:** Westerns/Adventure. **Career:** Western Wyoming College, Rock Springs, archaeologist, 1979-81; Metcalf-Zier Archaeologists Inc., Eagle, CO, archaeologist, 1981; Pronghorn Anthropological Association, Casper, WY, owner and principal investigator, 1982-84; Wind River Archaeological Consultants, owner and principal investigator, 1988-2000. **Publications:** Long Ride Home, 1988; Big Horn Legacy, 1988; The Warriors of Spider, 1988; The Way of Spider, 1989; The Web of Spider, 1989; The Artifact, 1990; Starstrike, 1990; Requiem for the Conqueror, 1991; Relic of Empire, 1992; Countermeasures, 1993; The Morning River, 1996; Coyote Summer, 1997. WITH K.O.'N. GEAR: People of the Wolf, 1990; People of the Fire, 1991; People of the Earth, 1992; People of the River, 1992; People of the Sea, 1993; People of the Lakes, 1994; People of the Lightning, 1995; People of the Silence, 1996; People of the Mist, 1997; People of the Masks, 1998; The Visitant, 1999; The Summoning God, 2000; Dark Inheritance, 2001; Bone Walker, 2001; Raising Abel, 2002; People of the Owl, 2003; People of the Raven, 2004. **Address:** PO Box 1329, Thermopolis, WY 82443, U.S.A.

GEARY, Joseph. (born England). **Genres:** Art/Art history. **Career:** Author. **Publications:** Spiral (novel), 2003; Mirror, 2004. WITH PHILIP SINGTON; UNDER JOINT PSEUDONYM PATRICK LYNCH: The Annunciation, 1993; The Immaculate Conception, 1994; Carriers, 1995; Omega, 1997; The Policy, 1998; Figure of Eight, 2000. **Address:** c/o Author Mail, Pantheon Publicity, 1745 Broadway, New York, NY 10019, U.S.A.

GEARY, Patricia (Carol). American, b. 1951. **Genres:** Novels. **Career:** Orange Coast Community College, Costa Mesa, CA, instructor, 1976-81; Irvine Valley College, Irvine, CA, instructor, 197881; Louisiana State University, Baton Rouge, assistant professor, 1981-87; University of Redlands, Redlands, CA, assistant professor, beginning in 1987; writer. University of California, Irvine, visiting assistant professor, 1986-87. **Publications:** NOVELS: Living in Ether, 1982. Strange Toys, 1987. **Address:** Dept of English, University of Redlands, 1200 E. Colton Ave, Redlands, CA 92374-3720, U.S.A. **Online address:** geary@vor.edu

GEBHARDT, James F(rederick). American, b. 1948. **Genres:** Translations, Military/Defense/Arms control, History. **Career:** U.S. Army, career soldier and officer in Infantry and Armor, 1966-69, 1974-92, served in Vietnam, 1967-68, and Germany, later Soviet foreign area officer, 1983-92, retired as major; Cubic Applications Inc., computer simulation specialist, 1992-. **Publications:** Leavenworth Papers No. 17: The Petsamo-Kirkenes Operation: Soviet Breakthrough and Pursuit in the Arctic, October, 1944, 1990; (trans.) Blood on the Shores, 1993; (trans.) The Official Makarov 9mm Pistol Manual, 1995. **Address:** 1509 Jackson Ct., Leavenworth, KS 66048, U.S.A. **Online address:** kargeb@aol.com

GECAN, Michael. (born United States). **Genres:** Administration/Management. **Career:** Industrial Areas Foundation, Chicago, IL, organizer, became director for New York region. **Publications:** (editor) Charles A. Reich, Seen through Our Eyes, 1972; Going Public, 2002. **Address:** c/o Author Mail, Beacon Press, 25 Beacon St., Boston, MA 02108, U.S.A.

GEDDES, Gary. Canadian, b. 1940. **Genres:** Novellas/Short stories, Poetry, Archaeology/Antiquities, Travel/Exploration, Essays, Translations. **Career:** Concordia University, Montreal, visiting associate professor, 1978-79, professor of English, 1979-98; Western Washington University, Bellingham, distinguished professor of Canadian culture, 1998-2001. Douglas and McIntyre, Vancouver, Studies in Canadian Literature series, general editor. Trent University, Peterborough, ON, visiting assistant professor, 1968-69; lecturer: Carleton University, Ottawa, 1971-72, University of Victoria, BC, 1972-74; University of Alberta, Edmonton, writer-in-residence, 1976-77, visiting associate professor, 1977-78; University of Ottawa, writer-in-residence, 2004. **Publications:** POETRY: Poems, 1970; Rivers Inlet, 1972; Snakeroot, 1973; Letter of the Master of Horse, 1973; War and Other Measures, 1976; The

Acid Test, 1981; The Terracotta Army, 1984; Changes of State, 1986; Hong Kong, 1987; No Easy Exit/Salida dificil, 1989; Light of Burning Towers: Poems New and Selected, 1990; Girl by the Water, 1994; The Perfect Cold Warrior, 1995; Active Trading: Selected Poems 1970-1995, 1996; Flying Blind, 1998; Skaldance, 2004. OTHER: Conrad's Later Novels, 1980; (cotrans.) I Didn't Notice the Mountain Growing Dark, 1985; The Unsettling of the West (stories), 1986; Letters from Managua (essays), 1990; Sailing Home: A Journey through Time, Place & Memory, 2001; Kingdom of Ten Thousand Things, 2005. EDITOR: 20th Century Poetry and Poetics, 1969, 4th ed., 1996; (with P. Bruce) 15 Canadian Poets, 1970, 3rd 1988; Skookum Wawa: Writings of the Canadian Northwest, 1975; Divided We Stand, 1977; The Inner Ear: An Anthology of New Canadian Poets, 1983; Vancouver: Soul of a City, 1986; (with H. Hazelton) Companeros: An Anthology of Writings about Latin America, 1990; The Art of Short Fiction: An International Anthology, 1993. **Address:** 975 Seaside Dr, RR 2, Sooke, BC, Canada V0S 1N0. **Online address:** gedworks@islandnet.com

GEDGE, Pauline (Alice). New Zealander, b. 1945. **Genres:** Science fiction/Fantasy. **Career:** Taught briefly in New Zealand; returned to Canada to focus on writing. **Publications:** FICTION: Child of the Morning, 1977; The Eagle and the Raven, 1978; Stargate, 1982; The Twelfth Transforming, 1984; Mirage, 1990, in the US as Scroll of Saqqara; The Covenant, 1992; House of Dreams, 1994, in the US as Lady of the Reeds, 1995; House of Illusions, 1997; The Hippopotamus Marsh, 2000; The Oasis, 2001; The Horus Road, 2001. **Address:** c/o Soho Press, 853 Broadway, New York, NY 10003, U.S.A.

GEDIMAN, Helen K. American, b. 1931. **Genres:** Psychology. **Career:** Private practice of psychotherapy and psychoanalysis, NYC, 1961-. New York Freudian Society, faculty member and training and supervisory analyst, 1971-; New York University, clinical professor, 1973-. **Publications:** Fantasies of Love and Death in Life and Art, 1995; (with J.S. Lieberman) The Many Faces of Death, 1996. Contributor to psychology journals. **Address:** 55 E. 87th St. No. 1B, New York, NY 10128, U.S.A.

GEDMIN, Jeffrey (N.). American, b. 1958. **Genres:** Politics/Government. **Career:** High school teacher in Washington, DC, 1981-88, also head of modern foreign language department and director of foreign exchange programs for Germany, the Czech Republic, Austria, Greece, Turkey, Egypt, the former U.S.S.R., and Australia; American Enterprise Institute for Public Policy Research, Washington, DC, research fellow, Foreign Policy Program, 1988-, executive director, New Atlantic Initiative, 1996; Georgetown University, adjunct professor, 1985-97. Guest on radio and television programs. Editor of PBS documentary The Germans: Portrait of a New Nation, 1995. Georgetown University, adjunct professor, 1985-. Guest on radio and television programs. programs. **Publications:** The Hidden Hand: Gorbachev and the Collapse of East Germany, 1992; The Germans: Portrait of a New Nation. Contributor of articles and reviews to political science journals and magazines. **Address:** Aspen Institute Berlin, Inselstr 10, 14129 Berlin, Germany. **Online address:** jgedmin@aei.org

GEE, Maggie (Mary). British, b. 1948. **Genres:** Novels, Science fiction/Fantasy, Sciences, Art/Art history, Literary criticism and history, Writing/Journalism. **Career:** University of East Anglia, Norwich, Writing Fellow, 1982; Sussex University, visiting fellow, 1986-; Hawthornden fellow and Booker Prize judge, 1989; Royal Society of Literature, fellow, 1994, council member, 1999; Newcastle, Northern Arts writer in residence, 1996. **Publications:** Dying in Other Words, 1981; (ed) For Life on Earth, 1982; The Burning Book, 1983; Light Years, 1985; Grace, 1987; Where Are the Snows, 1991; Lost Children, 1994; The Ice People, 1998; The White Family, 2002; The Flood, 2004. **Address:** c/o Society of Authors, 84 Drayton Gardens, London SW10 9SB, England.

GEE, Maurice (Gough). New Zealander, b. 1931. **Genres:** Novels, Novellas/Short stories, Children's fiction. **Career:** Librarian and teacher, 1955-75; full-time writer, 1975-. **Publications:** The Big Season, 1962; A Special Flower, 1965; In My Father's Den, 1972; A Glorious Morning, Comrade: Stories, 1975; Games of Choice, 1976; Plumb, 1978; Under the Mountain, 1979; The World around the Corner, 1980; Meg, 1981; The Halfmen of O, 1982; Sole Survivor, 1983; The Priests of Ferris, 1984; Motherstone, 1985; Collected Stories, 1986; The Fireraiser, 1986; Prowlers, 1987; The Champion, 1989; The Burning Boy, 1990; Going West, 1993; Crime Story, 1994; The Fat Man, 1994; Loving Ways, 1996; Live Bodies, 1998; Orchard Street, 1998; Ellie and the Shadow Man, 2001; The Scornful Moon, 2003. **Address:** 41 Chelmsford St, Ngaio, Wellington, New Zealand.

GEE, Shirley. British, b. 1932. **Genres:** Plays/Screenplays. **Career:** Actress, 1952-66. **Publications:** Typhoid Mary (in Best Radio Plays of 1979), 1980;

Never in My Lifetime (in Best Radio Plays of 1983), 1984, as stage play, 1987; Ask for the Moon, 1988; Warrior 1989, 1991. **Address:** 28 Fernshaw Rd, London SW10 0TF, England.

GEEHR, Richard S. American, b. 1938. **Genres:** History. **Career:** Windham College, instructor in German and history, 1966-67; Keene State College, Keene, NH, instructor in history, 1967; Mark Hopkins College, instructor in history, 1967-68; Greenfield College, instructor, 1967-68; Lake Michigan College, Benton Harbor, MI, instructor in history, 1973-74; St. Mary's College, instructor in history, 1975-76; Bentley College, Waltham, MA, assistant professor, 1977-83, associate professor, 1983-88, professor of history, 1988-; writer. **Publications:** Adam Mueller-Guttenbrunn and the Aryan Theater of Vienna, 1898-1903: The Approach of Cultural Fascism, 1973; Karl Lueger: Mayor of Fin-de-Siecle Vienna, 1990. EDITOR: Soviet History and Film, 1980; (trans., and author of intro.) "I Decide Who Is a Jew!" The Papers of Karl Lueger, 1982; (trans., and author of intro.) Letters from the Doomed: Concentration Camp Correspondence, 1940-1945, 1992; The Aesthetics of Horror: The Career of Richard von Kralik, forthcoming. **Address:** Department of History, Bentley College, Beaver and Forest Sts, Waltham, MA 02454, U.S.A.

GEERING, R(onald) G(eorge). Australian (born England), b. 1918. **Genres:** Literary criticism and history. **Career:** Member, Executive Committee, since 1957, and Vice-President, since 1974, English Association, Sydney (President, 1968-74). Lecturer, 1952-57, Sr. Lecturer, 1957-68, and Associate Professor of English, 1969-78, University of New South Wales, Sydney; writer; Military service: Australian Imperial Forces, 1943-46; became lieutenant. **Publications:** Christina Stead, 1969, 1979; Recent Fiction, 1974; The Artist and the Tale: D.H. Lawrence and Sons and Lovers, 1976; Talking into the Typewriter, 1973-83, 1992; The War Poetry of Wilfred Owen, 1993; Reflections on Jonathan Swift's Gulliver's Travel, 1995. EDITOR: The Miner's Right by R. Boldrewood, 1973; Southern Lights and Shadows, by F. Fowler, 1975; Ocean of Story, by C. Stead, 1985; I'm Dying Laughing, by C. Stead, 1986; (and preface author) Selected Letters: A Web of Friendship, by C. Stead, 1928-73, 1990; (and introduction) Christina Stead, 1994. **Address:** 11 Burgoyne St, Gordon, Sydney, NSW 2072, Australia.

GEERTZ, Clifford (James). American, b. 1926. **Genres:** Anthropology/ Ethnology. **Career:** Professor of Social Science, Institute for Advanced Study, Princeton, NJ, 1970-. Research Associate, Center for International Studies, Massachusetts Institute of Technology, in Indonesia, 1957-58; Fellow, Center for Advanced Study in the Behavioral Sciences, Stanford, CA, 1958-59; Assistant Professor of Anthropology, University of California, Berkeley, 1959-60; Assistant Professor of Anthropology, 1960-61, Associate Professor, 1961-64, and Professor, 1964-70, University of Chicago; Eastman Professor, Oxford University, 1978-79. Chairman, Committee for the Comparative Study of New Nations, 1968-69. **Publications:** The Development of the Javanese Economy: A Socio-Cultural Approach, 1956; The Religion of Java, 1960; Agricultural Involution: The Process of Ecological Change in Indonesia, 1963; Peddlers and Princes: Social Change and Economic Modernization in Two Indonesian Towns, 1963; The Social History of an Indonesian Town, 1965; Person, Time and Conduct in Bali: An Essay in Cultural Analysis, 1966; Islam Observed: Religious Development in Morocco and Indonesia, 1968; The Interpretation of Cultures, 1973; (with H. Geertz) Kinship in Bali, 1975; (with L. Rosen and H. Geertz) Meaning and Order in Moroccan Society, 1979; Negara: The Theatre State in Nineteenth-Century Bali, 1980; Local Knowledge, 1983; Works and Lives: The Anthropologist as Author, 1988; After the Fact: Two Countries, Four Decades, One Anthropologist, 1995; Available Light, 2000. EDITOR: Old Societies and New States, 1963; Myth, Symbol and Culture, 1974. **Address:** School of Social Science, Institute for Advanced Study, Princeton, NJ 08540, U.S.A.

GEHMAN, Mary W. American, b. 1923. **Genres:** Children's fiction. **Career:** Gehmans Mennonite School, Denver, PA, elementary teacher, 1954-1957, 1976-79; elementary teacher and teacher of English as a second language with Eastern Mennonite Missions to Somalia, 1958-76; Cocalico School District, Denver, teacher of English as a second language, 1979-83; teacher of English as a second language in missions to Somalia, 1983-87, 1990. **Publications:** Abdi and the Elephants, 1995. Contributor to periodicals. **Address:** 111 Witmer Rd., Reinholds, PA 17569, U.S.A.

GEHRIG, Klaus. Canadian (born Germany), b. 1946. **Genres:** Novels, Travel/Exploration. **Publications:** Taking a Little Sailing Ship: A View of the World from a Thirty-Foot Schooner, 1991; The Eyes of the Roof, 2001. Contributor to periodicals. **Address:** 2270 Windsor Rd, RR #2, Chester, NS, Canada B0J 1J0. **Online address:** gehrig_k@hotmail.com

GEHRING, Wes D(avid). American, b. 1950. **Genres:** Film, Biography. **Career:** Ball State University, Muncie, IN, professor of film, 1978-; writer.

Publications: Leo McCarey and the Comic Anti-Hero in American Film, 1980; Charlie Chaplin's World of Comedy (monograph), 1980; Charlie Chaplin: A Bio-Bibliography, 1983; Screwball Comedy: Defining a Film Genre (monograph), 1983; W.C. Fields: A Bio-Bibliography, 1984; Screwball Comedy: A Genre of Madcap Romance, 1986; The Marx Brothers: A Bio-Bibliography, 1987; (ed. and contrib.) Handbook of American Film Genres, 1988; Laurel and Hardy: A Bio-Bibliography, 1990; "Mr. B" or Comforting Thoughts about the Bison: A Critical Biography of Robert Benchley, 1992; Groucho and W.C. Fields: Huckster Comedians, 1994; Populism and the Capra Legacy, 1995; Dark Humor: Beyond Satire, 1996; Personality Comedians: Selected Players, 1997; Parody as Genre: Never Give a Saga an Even Break, 1999; Seeing Red...The Skelton in Hollywood's Closet, 2001; Film Classics Reclassified, 2001; Romantic vs Screwball Comedy, 2002; Carole Lombard: The Hoosier Tornado, 2003; Irene Dunne: The First Lady of Hollywood, 2003; Mr. Deeds Goes to Yankee Stadium, 2004; Leo McCarey: From Marx to McCarthy, 2004. Works appear in anthologies and periodicals. **Address:** Dept of Telecommunications (BC201), Ball State University, Muncie, IN 47306, U.S.A.

GEISERT, Arthur (Frederick). American, b. 1941. **Genres:** Children's fiction. **Career:** Artist and writer. Former Art Teacher, Concordia College, River Forest, Illinois, and Concordia College, Seward, Nebraska. **Publications:** SELF-ILLUSTRATED FOR CHILDREN: Pa's Balloon and Other Pig Tales, 1984; Alphabet Book, 1985; Pigs from A to Z, 1986; The Ark, 1988; Oink, 1991; Aesop and Company, 1991; Pigs from 1 to 10, 1992; Oink Oink, 1993; After the Flood, 1994; Haystack, 1995; Roman Numerals I to MM, 1996; The Etcher's Studio, 1997; Prairie Town, 1998; River Town, 1999; Mountain Town, 2000; Desert Town, 2001; Nursery Crimes, 2001; The Giant Ball of String, 2002; Mystery, 2003; Pigaroons, 2004; Lights Out, 2005; Oops, 2006. **Address:** PO Box 3, Galena, IL 61036, U.S.A. **Online address:** geisert@galenalink.net

GEISMAR, Ludwig Leo. American (born Germany), b. 1921. **Genres:** Sociology. **Career:** Professor of Social Work and Sociology, and Director, Social Work Research Center, Graduate School of Social Work and Dept. of Sociology, Rutgers University, New Brunswick, New Jersey, since 1963, now Emeritus (Associate Professor, 1959-62). Coordinator of Social Research, Ministry of Social Welfare, Israel, 1954-56; Research Director, Family Centered Project, St. Paul, Minnesota, 1956-59. **Publications:** (with M. A. LaSorte) Understanding the Multi-Problem Family: A Conceptual Analysis and Exploration in Identification, 1964; (with J. Krisberg) The Forgotten Neighborhood: Site of an Early Skirmish in the War on Poverty, 1967; Preventive Intervention in Social Work, 1969; Family and Community Functioning, 1971, 1980; (with Lagay, Wolock, Gerhart and Fink) Early Supports for Family Life, 1972; 555 Families: A Social Psychological Study of Young Families in Transition, 1973; (with S. Geismar) Families in an Urban Mold, 1979; (ed. with M. Dinerman) A Quarter Century of Social Work Education, 1984; (with K. Wood) Family and Delinquency: Resocializing the Young Offender, 1986; (with K. Wood) Families at Risk: Treating the Multiproblem Family, 1989; (with M. Camasso) The Family Functioning Scale, 1993. **Address:** c/o Graduate School of Social Work, Rutgers University, New Brunswick, NJ 08903, U.S.A. **Online address:** geismar@rci.rutgers.edu

GEIST, Bill. (William E). American, b. 1945. **Genres:** Writing/Journalism, Essays, Essays. **Career:** Worked as photographer for U.S. Army in Vietnam; worked for Chicago Tribune, Chicago, IL, until 1980; New York Times, NYC, author of column "About New York," 1980-87; CBS News, NYC, commentator and feature reporter for shows such as CBS Evening News and Sunday Morning with Charles Kuralt, 1987-; writer. **Publications:** Toward a Safe and Sane Halloween, and Other Tales of Suburbia (essays), 1985, as The Zucchini Plague, and Other Tales of Suburbia, 1987; City Slickers (columns), 1987; About New York (columns), 1987; Little League Confidential: One Coach's Completely Unauthorized Tale of Survival (nonfiction), 1992; Monster Trucks and Hair-in-a-Can, 1994; Big Five-Oh!, 1997; Fore! Play, 2001. **Address:** CBS News, 51 W 52nd St, New York, NY 10019, U.S.A.

GELB, Michael J. American, b. 1952. **Genres:** Education, How-to books. **Career:** High Performance Learning, Great Falls, VA, founder, 1982, president, 1982-. International Brain Trust, vice president. **Publications:** Body Learning: An Introduction to the Alexander Technique, 1981; Present Yourself! Captivate Your Audience with Great Presentation Skills: Transforming Fear, Knowing Your Audience, Setting the Stage, Making Them Remember, 1988; (with T. Buzan) Lessons from the Art of Juggling: How to Achieve Your Full Potential in Business, Learning, and Life, 1994; Thinking for a Change, in press. Creator of the audiocassette series "Mind Mapping: How to Liberate Your Natural Genius". **Address:** 114 The Promenade, Edgewater, NJ 07020, U.S.A.

GELBART, Larry. American, b. 1928. **Genres:** Plays/Screenplays. **Career:** Writer and producer for radio, TV, film, and stage. Writer and producer, MASH, TV series, CBS, 1972-76. Recipient: Antoinette Perry Awards, 1962, 1990; Emmy Awards, 1960, 1974. **Publications:** My L.A. (play), 1950; The Conquering Hero (play), 1960; The Notorious Landlady (screenplay), 1960; A Funny Thing Happened on the Way to the Forum (musical comedy), 1961; The Wrong Box (screenplay), 1966; Not with My Wife You Don't (screenplay), 1966; Sly Fox (play), 1977; Oh, God! (screenplay), 1978; Movie, Movie (screenplay), 1979; Tootsie (screenplay), 1982; Blame It on Rio (screenplay), 1984; Mastergate (play), 1989; City of Angels (play), 1989; Power Failure (play), 1991; Barbarians at the Gate (screenplay), 1992; Weapons of Mass Distraction (screenplay), 1997; Laughing Matters (book), 1998; And Starring Pancho Villa as Himself (screenplay), 2002.

GELDARD, Richard G. American, b. 1935. **Genres:** Literary criticism and history, Travel/Exploration. **Career:** Collegiate School, New York, NY, head of school, 1979-88; Yeshiva University, New York, NY, teacher of philosophy, 1989-96; writer, 1996-. **Publications:** A Traveler's Key to Ancient Greece, 1989; Esoteric Emerson, 1993; Vision of Emerson, 1995; God in Concord, 1999; Heraclitus Remembered, 2000; Spiritual Teachings of Ralph Waldo Emerson, 2001. **Address:** 650 West End Ave, New York, NY 10025-7355, U.S.A. **Online address:** rgeldard@bestweb.net

GELDENHUYS, Deon. Also writes as Tom Barnard. South African, b. 1950. **Genres:** International relations/Current affairs, Politics/Government. **Career:** Rand Afrikaans University, Johannesburg, South Africa, professor of politics, 1981-; writer. **Publications:** The Diplomacy of Isolation: South African Foreign Policy Making, 1984; Isolated States: A Comparative Analysis, 1990; (as Tom Barnard) South Africa 1994-2004: A Popular History, 1991; Foreign Political Engagement: Remaking States in the Post-Cold War World, 1998; Deviant Conduct in World Politics, 2004. **Address:** Dept of Politics and Governance, University of Johannesburg, PO Box 524, Auckland Park 2006, Republic of South Africa. **Online address:** deong@ujhb.ac.za

GELDERMAN, Carol (Wettlaufer). American, b. 1939. **Genres:** Adult non-fiction, Theatre, Writing/Journalism, Biography, Essays. **Career:** Louisiana State University, New Orleans, assistant professor of English, 1972-77; University of New Orleans, Louisiana, associate professor, 1977-80, professor, 1980-88, research professor, 1988-93, distinguished professor of English, 1993-. **Publications:** George Fitzmaurice (literary criticism), 1979; Henry Ford: The Wayward Capitalist, 1981; Better Writing for Professionals, 1984; Mary McCarthy: A Life, 1988; Conversations with Mary McCarthy, 1991; Better Business Writing, 1992; Louis Auchincloss, A Writer's Life, 1993; All the Presidents' Words: The Bully Pulpit and the Creation of the Virtual Presidency, 1997. **Address:** Dept. of English, University of New Orleans, New Orleans, LA 70148, U.S.A. **Online address:** cgelderm@uno.edu

GELEK, Rimpoche Nawang. See RIMPOCHE, Nawang Gelek.

GELERNTER, David (Hillel). American, b. 1955. **Genres:** Information science/Computers. **Career:** Computer scientist and theorist, writer. Yale University, Department of Computer Science, professor; Mirros Worlds Technologies, chief scientist. **Publications:** (with N. Carriero) How to Write Parallel Programs: A First Course, 1990; (with S. Jagannathan) Programming Linguistics, 1990; (ed. with A. Nicolau and D. Padua) Languages and Compilers for Parallel Computing, 1990; Mirror Worlds, or, The Day Software Puts the Universe in a Shoebox: How It Will Happen and What It Will Mean, 1991; The Muse in the Machine: Computerizing the Poetry of Human Thought, 1994; 1939: The Lost World of the Fair, 1995; Drawing Life, 1997. Contributor to periodicals. **Address:** A.K. Watson Hall, Yale University, 51 Prospect St, New Haven, CT 06511, U.S.A.

GELLER, Jaclyn. American, b. 1963. **Genres:** Sociology. **Career:** New York University, New York, NY, instructor, 1997-; Barnard College, instructor, 2001-. **Publications:** Here Comes the Bride: Women, Weddings, and the Marriage Mystique, 2001. Contributor to books and periodicals. **Address:** 111 Hicks St. #14N, Brooklyn, NY 11201, U.S.A. **Online address:** jqg2039@nyu.edu

GELLIS, Roberta (Leah Jacobs). Also writes as Max Daniels, Priscilla Hamilton, Leah Jacobs. American, b. 1927. **Genres:** Novellas/Short stories, Mystery/Crime/Suspense, Romance/Historical, Science fiction/Fantasy. **Career:** Editor, Macmillan Co., NYC, 1956-58, and freelance, 1971-. Chemist, Foster D. Snell Inc., NYC, 1947-53; Ed., McGraw-Hill Book Co., NYC, 1953-56; freelance ed., Academic Press, NYC, 1956-70. **Publications:**

Knight's Honor, 1964; Bond of Blood, 1965; (as Leah Jacobs) The Psychiatrist's Wife, 1966; Sing Witch, Sing Death, 1975; The Dragon and the Rose, 1977; The Sword and the Swan, 1977; The Roselynde Chronicles: Roselynde, 1978, Alinor, 1978, Joanna, 1978, Gilliane, 1979, Rhiannon, 1982; Sybelle, 1983; (as Max Daniels) Space Guardian (science fiction), 1978; (as Max Daniels) Offworld! (science fiction), 1979; (as Priscilla Hamilton) Love Token, 1979; Heiress Series: The English Heiress, 1980, The Cornish Heiress, 1981; The Kent Heiress, 1982, Fortune's Bride, 1983, A Woman's Estate, 1984; Siren Song, 1981; Winter Song, 1982; Fire Song, 1984; A Tapestry of Dreams, 1985; The Rope Dancer, 1986; Fires of Winter, 1987; Masques of Gold, 1988; A Silver Mirror, 1989; A Delicate Balance, 1993; Dazzling Brightness, 1994; Shimmering Splendor, 1995; Enchanted Fire, 1996; A Mortal Bane, 1999; Bull God, 2000; A Personal Devil, 2001; Thrice Bound, 2001; Bone of Contention, 2002; Lucrezia Borgia and the Mother of Poisons, 2003; (with M. Lackey) This Scepter'd Isle, 2004; Desire, 2005. Contributor to books. **Address:** PO Box 67, Lafayette, IN 47902, U.S.A. **Online address:** robertagellis@juno.com

GELLMAN, Marc. American. **Genres:** Theology/Religion, Inspirational/Motivational Literature. **Career:** Reform rabbi and author of children's books. Beth Torah Synagogue, Melville, NY, rabbi; The God Squad (syndicated interfaith program), Faith & Values/VISN cable network, cohost, with Monsignor Thomas Hartman. Has made regular appearances on television and radio shows. Served on the faculty of Northwestern University and Hebrew Union College and as chair of the Medical Ethics Committee, UJA/Federation. **Publications:** FOR CHILDREN: Does God Have a Big Toe? Stories about Stories in the Bible, 1989; (with T. Hartman) Where Does God Live?, 1991; (with Hartman) How Do You Spell God? Answers to the Big Questions from Around the World, 1995; God's Mailbox: More Stories about Stories in the Bible, 1996; Always Wear Clean Underwear!: And Other Ways Parents Say I Love You, 1997. Contributor to books. Contributor of book reviews to periodicals. **Address:** Temple Beth Torah, 35 Bagatelle Rd., Melville, NY 11747, U.S.A.

GELL-MANN, Murray. American, b. 1929. **Genres:** Physics. **Career:** Professor, 1956-93, and Robert A. Millikan Professor of Physics Emeritus, 1993-, California Institute of Technology, Pasadena (Associate Professor, 1955-56; Robert A. Millikan Professor of Physics, 1967-93). Director, MacArthur Foundation, Chicago, 1979-. Founding Trustee, Santa Fe Institute, 1982-. Instructor, 1952-53, Assistant Professor, 1953-54, and Associate Professor, 1954-55, University of Chicago. Member, President's Science Advisory Committee, 1969-72; President's Committee of Advisers on Science and Technology, 1994-2001; Regent, Smithsonian Institution, Washington, D.C., 1974-88. Recipient, Nobel Prize in Physics, 1969. **Publications:** Lectures on Weak Interactions of Strongly Interacting Particles, 1961; (with Yuval Ne'eman) The Eightfold Way: A Review with a Collection of Reprints, 1964; The Quark and the Jaguar, 1994. **Address:** Santa Fe Institute, 1399 Hyde Park Rd, Santa Fe, NM 87501, U.S.A.

GELPI, Albert. American, b. 1931. **Genres:** Literary criticism and history. **Career:** Harvard University, Assistant Professor, 1962-68; Stanford University, CA, Associate Professor, 1968-74, Professor, 1974-78, Coe Professor of American Literature, 1978-. Ed., Cambridge Studies in American Literature and Culture. **Publications:** Emily Dickinson: The Mind of the Poet, 1965; The Poet in America: 1950 to Present, 1973; The Tenth Muse: The Psyche of the American Poet, 1975; A Coherent Splendor: The American Poetic Renaissance 1910-1950, 1988; Living in Time: The Poetry of C. Day Lewis, 1998; The Wild God of the World: An Anthology of Robinson Jeffers, 2003; Dark God of Eros: A William Everson Reader, 2003. EDITOR: (with B. Charlesworth Gelpi) Adrienne Rich's Poetry, 1975 as Adrienne Rich's Poetry and Prose, 1993; Wallace Stevens: The Poetics of Modernism, 1986; Denise Levertov: Selected Criticism, 1993; (with afterword) The Blood of the Poet: Selected Poems of William Everson, 1994; (with R.J. Bertholf) The Letters of Robert Duncan and Denise Levertov, 2003. **Address:** Dept of English, Stanford University, Stanford, CA 94305, U.S.A.

GELTMAKER, Ty. American, b. 1952. **Genres:** History, Psychology. **Career:** Peoria Journal Star, Peoria, IL, reporter and copy editor, summers, 1972-73; Rome Daily American, Rome, Italy, copy editor, feature writer, and page layout technician, 1976-77; International Daily News, Rome, Italy, editor, political writer, page layout technician, and typesetter, 1977-79; United Press International, New York, NY, editor at international and foreign desks, 1979-81; freelance writer and editor, 1981-. English teacher in Rome, 1976-78; Cerritos Community College, instructor, 1989; University of Southern California, instructor, 1994; visiting lecturer in Italian, 2001; California Institute of the Arts, Valencia, CA, instructor in history, 1993-95; Bronx Community College of the City University of New York, adjunct assistant professor, 1993-95. **Publications:** Tired of Living: Suicide in Italy from National Unification to World War I, 1860-1915, 2002. Contributor to books and periodicals. **Address:** c/o Author Mail, Peter Lang Publishing Inc., 275 Seventh Ave., 28th Floor, New York, NY 10001, U.S.A. **Online address:** echobamboo@sbcglobal.net

GEMMELL, David A(ndrew). Also writes as Ross Harding. British, b. 1948. **Genres:** Science fiction/Fantasy, Novels. **Career:** Worked for Pepsi Cola, London, 1965; Westminster Press, London, reporter and editor, 1966-72; Hastings Observer, editor, 1976; Folkestone Herald, editor, 1984; full-time writer, 1986-. **Publications:** FANTASY NOVELS. DRENAI SERIES: Legend, 1984, in the U.S. as Against the Horde, 1988; The King beyond the Gate, 1985; Waylander, 1986; Quest for Lost Heroes, 1990; Drenai Tales (omnibus), 1991; Waylander II: In the Realm of the Wolf, 1992. SIPSTRASSI SERIES: Wolf in Shadow, 1987, in the U.S. as The Jerusalem Man, 1988; Ghost King, 1988; Last Sword of Power, 1988; The Last Guardian, 1989; Stones of Power (omnibus), 1992; Bloodstone, 1994; The Complete Chronicles of the Jerusalem Man (omnibus), 1995. MACEDON SERIES: Lion of Macedon, 1990; The Dark Prince, 1991. THE HAWK QUEEN SERIES: Ironhand's Daughter, 1995; The Hawk Eternal, 1996. SHORT STORIES: The First Chronicles of Druss the Legend, 1993; The Second Chronicles of Druss the Legend: Druss the Axeman, 1995. OTHER: Knights of Dark Renown (novel), 1989; The Lost Crown (for children), 1989; Morningstar (novel), 1992; (As Ross Harding) White Knight, Black Swan (novel), 1993. **Address:** 180 Mill Lane, Hastings TN35 5EU, England.

GEMS, Pam. British, b. 1925. **Genres:** Novels, Plays/Screenplays. **Publications:** Dusa, Fish, Stas, and Vi, 1977; Piaf, 1979; Queen Christina, 1980; Camille, Piaf, Loving Woman, 1984; Mrs. Frampton (novel), 1989; Bon Voyage, Mrs. Frampton, 1990; Stanley, 1998; Marlene, 1999; The Snow Palace (play), 1998. ADAPTER: Chekhov, Uncle Vanya, 1979; Chekhov, The Seagull, 1996; Ibsen, A Doll's House; The Cherry Orchard; Ghosts; The Lady from the Sea, 2002; The Little Mermaid, 2004. **Address:** c/o Casarotto Ramsay & Associates Ltd, 60-66 Wardour St, London W1V 4ND, England.

GEMUNDEN, Gerd. German, b. 1959. **Genres:** Film. **Career:** Dartmouth College, Hanover, NH, associate professor of German and comparative literature. **Publications:** Wim Wenders: Einstellungen, 1993; The Cinema of Wim Wenders, 1996; Framed Visions, 1998. **Address:** 6084 Dartmouth Hall, Dartmouth College, Hanover, NH 03755, U.S.A. **Online address:** gerd@dartmouth.edu

GENASI, Chris. American, b. 1962. **Genres:** Business/Trade/Industry. **Career:** Author and public relations consultant. European Corporate Practice, chief executive; Weber Shandwick International, chief executive corporate division; Eloqui Public Relations, chief executive. Institute of Public Relations, director. **Publications:** Winning Reputations: How to Be Your Own Spin Doctor, 2002; (with Tim Bills) Creative Business: Achieving Your Goals through Creative Thinking and Action, 2003. **Address:** Institute of Public Relations, The Old Trading House, 15 Northburgh St., London EC1V 0PR, England.

GENIESSE, Jane Fletcher. American. **Genres:** Novels, Biography. **Career:** New York Times, reporter, 1978-82; freelance writer, 1982-; also worked as a reporter for the Boston Traveler. Environmental Defense Fund, trustee, 1979-. **Publications:** The Riches of Life (novel), 1976; Passionate Nomad: The Life of Freya Stark (biography), 1999. Contributor to magazines. **Address:** c/o Modern Library, Random House Inc, 1745 Broadway 18th Fl, New York, NY 10019, U.S.A.

GENINI, Ronald. American, b. 1946. **Genres:** Film. **Career:** Central Unified School District, Fresno, CA, history teacher, 1970-. **Publications:** (with R, Hutchinson) Romualdo Pacheco, 1985; (with T. Bond) Darn Right It's Butch, 1994; Theda Bara, 1996. Contributor of articles and reviews to periodicals. **Address:** Central High School, East Campus, 3535 North Cornelia, Fresno, CA 93722, U.S.A. **Online address:** rgenini@hotmail.com

GENTILE, John S(amuel). American, b. 1956. **Genres:** Theatre, Speech/Rhetoric. **Career:** University of Northern Iowa, Cedar Falls, IA, instructor in interpretation, 1984-85; Kennesaw State College, Marietta, GA, assistant professor, 1985-90, associate professor of communication and performance studies, 1990-, artistic director of the Performance Series, 1985-. Scholar and performer with the Wyoming Chautauqua, 1985, and Rocky Mountain Chautauqua, 1989-90. **Publications:** Cast of One: One-Person Shows from the Chautauqua Platform to the Broadway Stage, University of Illinois Press, 1989; contributor: Eighteenth Century British and American Rhetorical Theory; Text and Performance Quarterly; Literature in Performance; Studies

in Popular Culture; The American Institute for Discussion Review; On the Culture of the American South. **Address:** Kennesaw State University, 1000 Chastain Road, Kennesaw, GA 30144, U.S.A.

GENTLE, Mary. Also writes as Roxanne Morgan. British, b. 1956. **Genres:** Science fiction/Fantasy, Children's fiction. **Career:** Has worked as a movie projectionist, clerk, and civil servant. **Publications:** A Hawk in Silver (for children), 1977; Golden Witchbreed, 1983; Ancient Light, 1987; Scholars and Soldiers, 1989; Rats and Gargoyles, 1990; The Architecture of Desire, 1991; Grunts!, 1992; Left to His Own Devices, 1994; (ed) The Weerde (Books 1 & 2); (ed.) Villains!; Ash: A Secret History, 2001 (in U.S. as 4 vols.: A Secret History; Carthage Ascendant; The Wild Machines; Lost Burgundy, 1999). AS ROXANNE MORGAN: Who Dare Sins, 1995; Sinner Takes All, 1997; A Game of Masks, 1999; Degrees of Desire, 2001. **Address:** c/o Maggie Noach Literary Agency, 22 Dorville Crescent, London W6 0HJ, England. **Online address:** marygentle.org

GENTLEMAN, David. British, b. 1930. **Genres:** Children's fiction, Adult non-fiction, Architecture, Art/Art history, Design, Travel/Exploration, Documentaries/Reportage, Illustrations. **Career:** Painter and designer. **Publications:** Fenella in France, 1964; Fenella in Spain, 1964; Fenella in Greece, 1964; Fenella in Ireland, 1964; Design in Miniature, 1972; Everyday Architecture in Towns, 1975; Everyday Architecture in the Country, 1975; Everyday Architecture at the Seaside, 1975; Everyday Industrial Architecture, 1975; David Gentleman's Britain, 1982; David Gentleman's London, 1985; A Special Relationship, 1987; David Gentleman's Coastline, 1988; David Gentleman's Paris, 1991; (ed.) The Crooked Scythe, 1993; David Gentleman's India, 1994; David Gentleman's Italy, 1997; Artwork, 2002. **Address:** 25 Gloucester Crescent, London NW1 7DL, England. **Online address:** d@gentleman.demon.co.uk

GENTRY, Curt. American, b. 1931. **Genres:** Science fiction/Fantasy, History, Biography. **Career:** Freelance writer, 1961-. Head of Mail Order Dept., Paul Elder Books, San Francisco, 1954-57; Manager, Tro Harper Books, San Francisco, 1957-61. **Publications:** The Dolphin Guide to San Francisco and the Bay Area: Present and Past, 1962, rev. ed., 1982; (with R. Gump) Jade Stone of Heaven, 1962; The Madams of San Francisco: An Irreverent History of the City by the Golden Gate, 1964; (with J.M. Browning) John M. Browning, American Gunmaker, 1964, rev. ed., 1994; The Vulnerable Americans, 1966; Frame-Up: The Incredible Case of Tom Mooney and Warren Billings, 1967; The Killer Mountains: A Search for the Legendary Lost Dutchman Mine, 1968; The Last Days of the Late, Great State of California, 1968; (with F.G. Powers) Operation Overflight, 1970, rev. ed., 2004; (ed.) T.L. Scott, A Kind of Loving, 1970; (with E.R. Murphy Jr.) Second in Command, 1971; (with V. Bugliosi) Helter Skelter, 1974, 1994, in U.K. as The Manson Murders, 1975; J. Edgar Hoover: The Man and the Secrets, 1991; Vegas, 2005. **Address:** c/o Irving S. Feffer, 609 N Alta, Beverly Hills, CA 90210, U.S.A.

GENYA, Monica. Kenyan. **Genres:** Adult non-fiction. **Career:** Writer. **Publications:** Links of a Chain, 1996. **Address:** c/o East African Educational Publishers, PO Box 45314, Nairobi, Kenya.

GEOFFREY, Iqbal. See JAFREE, Mohammed Jawaid Iqbal.

GEORGE, Alice Rose. American, b. 1944. **Genres:** Poetry. **Career:** Photographic editor and consultant. Time Magazine, NYC, assistant photographic editor, 1968-79; GEO, photography editor, 1979-82; Fortune, photography editor, 1982-; photography editor for Granta and Double Take; Center for Documentary Studies, Duke University, Durham, NC, former member of staff; Details, NYC, currently director of photography. Curator and consultant for private and corporate photography collections; freelance consultant. Former director, Magnum Photos New York. **Publications:** Ceiling of the World (poetry), 1995. EDITOR: (with A. Heyman, and E. Hoffman) Flesh and Blood: Photographers' Images of Their Own Families, 1992; (with A. Harris) A New Life: Stories and Photographs from the Suburban South, 1997; Twenty-five and Under: Photographers, 1997; (with L. Marks) Hope Photographs (exhibition catalogue), 1998. **Address:** c/o Author Mail, W.W. Norton, 500 Fifth Avenue, New York, NY 10010, U.S.A.

GEORGE, David (John). Welsh, b. 1948. **Genres:** Literary criticism and history. **Career:** University of Wales, University College of Swansea, lecturer in Spanish, 1972-. Modern Language Review, Hispanic editor. **Publications:** The History of the Commedia dell'arte in Modern Hispanic Literature, 1995. EDITOR/COEDITOR: (with D. Gagen) La guerra civil espanola: Arte y violencia, 1990; (with C.J. Gossip, and contrib.) Studies in the Commedia Dell'arte, 1993; (and contrib.) Contemporary Catalan Drama, 1994; The

Theatre in Madrid and Barcelona, 1892-1936: Rivals or Colloraborators?, 2002. Work represented in anthologies. Contributor of articles and reviews to Hispanic studies journals. **Address:** Department of Hispanic Studies, University College of Swansea, Singleton Park, Swansea SA2 8PP, Wales. **Online address:** d.j.george@swansea.ac.uk

GEORGE, Eliot. *See* **FREEMAN, Gillian.**

GEORGE, Elizabeth. American, b. 1949. **Genres:** Mystery/Crime/Suspense. **Career:** English teacher, Mater Dei High School, Santa Ana, 1974-75, and El Toro High School, 1975-87, both California; Coastline College, Costa Mesa, CA, creative writing teacher, 1988-91; taught creative writing at Irvine College, 1989, and University of California, Irvine, 1990. Recipient: Anthony Award, 1989; Agatha Award, 1989; Le Grand Prix de Litterature Policiere, 1990; MIMI Award, 1992. **Publications:** A Great Deliverance, 1989; Payment in Blood, 1989; Well Schooled in Murder, 1990; A Suitable Vengeance, 1991; For the Sake of Elena, 1992; Missing Joseph, 1993; Playing for the Ashes, 1994; In the Presence of the Enemy, 1996; Deception on His Mind, 1997; A Traitor to Memory, 2001; A Place of Hiding, 2002; I, Richard, 2002; Write Away, 2004; A Moment on the Edge, 2004; With No One as Witness, 2005. **Address:** c/o Robert Gottlieb, Trident Media Group, 41 Madison Ave Fl 36, New York, NY 10010, U.S.A.

GEORGE, Emily. *See* **KATZ, Bobbi.**

GEORGE, Jean Craighead. American, b. 1919. **Genres:** Children's fiction, Young adult fiction, Children's non-fiction, Natural history. **Career:** Reporter, International News Service, 1942-44, and Washington Post, 1943-46, both Washington, DC; Artist Pageant Magazine, NYC, 1946-47; Staff Writer, 1969-74, and Roving Ed., 1974-81, Reader's Digest, Pleasantville, NY. **Publications:** (with J.L. George) Vulpes the Red Fox, 1948; (with J.L. George) Vison the Mink, 1949; (with J.L. George) Masked Prowler: The Story of a Raccoon, 1950; (with J.L. George) Meph, The Pet Skunk, 1952; (with J.L. George) Bubo the Great Horned Owl. 1954; (with J.L. George) Dipper of Copper Creek, 1956; Snow Tracks, 1958; My Side of the Mountain, 1959; The Summer of the Falcon, 1962; Red Robin Fly Up!, 1963; Gull Number 737, 1964; Hold Zero, 1966; Spring Comes to the Ocean, 1966; The Thirteen Moons (The Moon of the Owls, Bears, Salamander, Chicadee, Monarch, Butterfly, Fox Pups, Wild Pigs, Mountain Lion, Deer, Alligator, Wolves, Winter Bird, and Mole), 13 vols., 1967-69, new eds, 1991-93; The Hole in the Tree, 1967; Coyote in Manhattan, 1968; Beastly Inventions: A Surprising Investigation into How Smart Animals Really Are (in UK as Animals Can Do Anything), 1970; All upon a Stone, 1971; Who Really Killed Cock Robin?, 1971; Julie of the Wolves, 1972; Everglades Wildguide, 1972; All upon a Sidewalk, 1974; Hook a Fish, Catch a Mountain, 1975; Going to the Sun, 1976; The Wentletrap Trap, 1977; The American Walk Book, 1977; The Wounded Wolf, 1978; River Rats, 1979; Journey Inward (autobiography), 1982; The Wild Wild Cookbook, 1982; The Grizzly Bear with the Golden Ears, 1982; The Talking Earth, 1983; One Day in the Desert, Alpine Tundra, Prairie, Woods, Tropical Rain Forest, 5 vols., 1983-90; How to Talk to Your Animals, 1986; How to Talk to Your Dog, 1986; Water Sky, 1987; Shark Beneath the Reef, 1988; One Day in the Woods (children's musical), 1989; On the Far Side of the Mountain, 1990; The Missing Gator of Gimbo Limbo, 1992; The Firebay Connection, 1993; The First Thanksgiving, 1993; Dear Rebecca, Winter Is Here, 1993; The Everglades Fieldguide, 1994; Animals Who Have Won Our Hearts, 1994; Owl in the Shower, 1995; Julie, 1995; Everglades, 1995; To Climb a Waterfall, 1995; The Tarantula in My Purse, 1996; The Case of the Missing Cutthroats, 1996; Look to the North, 1997; Arctic Son, 1997; Julie's Wolf Pack, 1997; Giraffe Trouble, 1998; Gorilla Gang, 1998; Dear Katie, the Volcano Is a Girl, 1998; Elephant Walk, 1998; Rhino Romp, 1998; Morning, Noon, and Night, 1999; Frightful's Mountain, 1999; Snow Bear, 1999; Incredible Animal Adventures, 1999; How to Talk to Your Cat, 2000; Autumn Moon, 2001; Winter Moon, 2001; Lonesome George, 2001; Nutik, the Wolf Pup, 2001; Nutik & Amaroq Play Ball, 2001; Cliffhanger, 2002; Spring Moon, 2002; Summer Moon, 2002; Tree Castle Island, 2002; (with W. Minor) Firestorm, 2003. **Address:** 20 William St, Chappaqua, NY 10514-3114, U.S.A. **Online address:** jean@jeancraigheadgeorge.com

GEORGE, John. American, b. 1936. **Genres:** Politics/Government, Sociology. **Career:** Geologist in Colorado, Louisiana, California, and New Mexico for Conoco, 1960-65; Skelly, Oklahoma City, OK, geologist, 1965; University of Central Oklahoma (formerly Central State University), Edmond, OK, professor, 1968-, now professor emeritus of political science and sociology. **Publications:** (with H. Holloway) Public Opinion: Coalitions, Elites, and the Masses, 1979, 2nd ed., 1986; (with R. Hall) American National Government, 1988; (with P.F. Boller) They Never Said It: A Book of Fake

Quotes, Misquotes, and Misleading Attributions, 1989; (with L. Wilcox) Nazis, Communists, Klansmen, & Others on the Fringe, 1992; (with L. Wilcox) Be Reasonable, 1994; (with L. Wilcox) American Extremists, 1996. **Address:** Dept of Political Science, Box AE, University of Central Oklahoma, Edmond, OK 73034, U.S.A. **Online address:** jgeorge@ucok.edu

GEORGE, Judith W(ordsworth). British, b. 1940. **Genres:** Literary criticism and history, Education. **Career:** Open University, Edinburgh, Scotland, deputy Scottish director. Consultant in education in curriculum development and technologies in distance education. **Publications:** Venantius Fortunatus: A Latin Poet in Merovingian Gaul, 1992; Venantius Fortunatus: Personal & Political Poems, 1995; Distance Education in Norway & Scotland: Experiences & Reflections, 1996; (with J. Cowan) A Handbook of Techniques for Formative Evaluation: Mapping the Student's Learning Experience, 1999. **Address:** Open University, 10 Drumsheugh Gardens, Edinburgh EH3 7QJ, Scotland.

GEORGE, Kathleen Elizabeth. American, b. 1943. **Genres:** Novels, Theatre. **Career:** Theatre educator and writer; University of Pittsburgh, assistant instructor in theatre arts, 1964-66; Carlow College, assistant professor of speech and theatre arts, 1968-76; University of Pittsburgh, associate professor, 1976-2001, professor of theatre, 2001-; Semester-at-Sea, academic dean, 1987. **Publications:** Rhythm in Drama, 1980; Playwriting: The First Workshop, 1994; The Man in the Buick and Other Stories (short stories), 1999; Winter's Tales: Reflections on the Novelistic Stage, 2005. NOVELS: Taken, 2001; Fallen, 2003. Contributor of short stories to magazines. **Address:** University of Pittsburgh Theatre, 1617 Cathedral of Learning, Pittsburgh, PA 15260, U.S.A.

GEORGE, Lindsay Barrett. Dominican Republican, b. 1952. **Genres:** Children's fiction, Illustrations. **Career:** Fine art printer in Englewood, NJ, and NYC, 1978-81; mechanical artist working in the children's department of a publisher in NYC, 1981-84; children's book author and illustrator, 1985-. Also a lecturer and artist in residence at elementary schools, 1989-. **Publications:** SELF-ILLUSTRATED FOR CHILDREN: William and Boomer, 1987; (with W.T. George) Beaver at Long Pond, 1988; In the Snow: Who's Been Here?, 1995; In the Woods: Who's Been Here?, 1995; Around the Pond: Who's Been Here?, 1996; Around the World: Who's Been Here?, 1999; My Bunny and Me, 2001. Illustrator of books by W.T. George, C. Huck. **Address:** PO Box 190, White Mills, PA 18473, U.S.A. **Online address:** lindsybg@ptd.net

GEORGE, Margaret. American, b. 1943. **Genres:** Novels. **Career:** National Institutes of Health, science writer, 1966-70; Washington University, newswriter, 1970-72; freelance novelist, 1973-. **Publications:** The Autobiography of Henry VIII: With Notes by His Fool, Will Somers, 1986; Mary Queen of Scotland and the Isles, 1992; The Memoirs of Cleopatra, 1997; Mary, Called Magdalene, 2002. **Address:** c/o Jacques de Spoelberch, 9 Shagbark Rd, Wilson Pt, South Norwalk, CT 06854, U.S.A.

GEORGE, Sally. *See* **ORR, Wendy.**

GEORGE, Stephen (Alan). British, b. 1949. **Genres:** History, International relations/Current affairs, Politics/Government. **Career:** Huddersfield Polytechnic, England, research assistant, 1971-72; University of Sheffield, England, lecturer, 1973-90, senior lecturer, 1991-92, reader in politics, 1992-94, Jean Monnet professor in politics, 1994-2001, professor of politics, 2001-; writer. **Publications:** Politics and Policy in the European Community, 1985, 3rd ed., 1991; An Awkward Partner: Britain in the European Community, 1990, 3rd ed., 1998; Britain and European Integration since 1945, 1991; (ed.) Britain and the European Community: The Politics of Semi-Detachment, 1992; (ed. with S. Bulmer and A. Scott) The United Kingdom and European Community Membership Evaluated, 1992; (with I. Bache) Politics in the European Union, 2001. **Address:** Department of Politics, University of Sheffield, Elmfield, Northumberland Rd, Sheffield S10 2TU, England. **Online address:** s.a.george@shefield.ac.uk

GEORGE-BLOOMFIELD, Susanne K. American, b. 1947. **Genres:** Local history/Rural topics, Biography, Literary criticism and history, Women's studies and issues, Literary criticism and history, Women's studies and issues, Novellas/Short stories, Cultural/Ethnic topics, History. **Career:** Axtell Community Schools, Axtell, NE, teacher of English and French, 1968-73; Kearney State College, Kearney, NE, lecturer, 1979-87; University of Nebraska at Kearney, assistant professor, 1988-92, associate professor, 1992, member of academic committees. Elderhostel teacher, 1988-; public speaker for schools, libraries, and other organizations. **Publications:** The Adventures of the Woman Homesteader: The Life and Letters of Elinore Pruitt Stewart,

1992; (assoc. ed.) The Platte River: An Atlas of the Big Bend Region, 1993; Kate M. Cleary: A Literary Biography with Selected Works, 1997; (co-ed.) The Prairie Mosaic: An Atlas of Central Nebraska's Land, Culture, and Nature. Contributor of articles, stories, and poems to periodicals. **Address:** 204 Thomas Hall, University of Nebraska at Kearney, Kearney, NE 68849, U.S.A. **Online address:** georges@unk.edu

GEORGI-FINDLAY, Brigitte. German, b. 1956. **Genres:** Cultural/Ethnic topics. **Career:** Free University of Berlin, Berlin, Germany, assistant professor of American literature at John F. Kennedy Institute, 1988-95; University of Bremen, Bremen, Germany, associate professor of American studies, 1995-97; University of Dresden, Dresden, Germany, professor of North American studies, 1997-. University of Arizona, visiting scholar, 1991-93. **Publications:** The Frontiers of Women's Writing: Women's Narratives and the Rhetoric of Westward Expansion, 1996. **Address:** Institut fuer Anglistik/Amerikanistik, Technische Universitaet Dresden, D-01062 Dresden, Germany. **Online address:** gfindlay@rcs.urz.tu-dresden.de

GERAGHTY, Paul. British (born Republic of South Africa), b. 1959. **Genres:** Novels, Children's fiction, Young adult fiction, Picture/board books. **Career:** Illustrator and author. Taught art and English in Cape Town, South Africa; worked for an advertising agency. Musician, playing keyboard for several bands. **Publications:** Pig (young adult novel), 1988; Tina Come Home (novel). FOR CHILDREN, SELF-ILLUSTRATED: Over the Steamy Swamp, 1989; Look out, Patrick!, 1990; Slobcat, 1991; Stop That Noise!, 1992, in OK as The Great Green Forest, 1992; The Great Knitting Needle Hunt, 1992; Monty's Journey, 1993; The Hunter, 1994; Solo, 1996; The Wonderful Journey, 1999; Tortuga, 2001; The Hoppameleon, 2001; Dinosaur in Danger, 2004. Illustrator of books by P.A. Johnsgard, J. Bush, R. Lyttle, R. Klein. **Address:** 42 Dukes Ave, New Malden, Surrey KT3 4HN, England. **Online address:** www.paulgeraghty.net

GERARD, Charley. American, b. 1950. **Genres:** Cultural/Ethnic topics, Music, Race relations. **Career:** Gerard & Sarzin Publishing Co., Brooklyn, NY, editor, 1991-. Composer and saxophonist; appeared at festivals, libraries, museums, colleges, universities, concert halls, arts centers, and nightclubs, primarily in the eastern United States and New England. Cultural Arts Council of Houston, artist in residence. **Publications:** Jazz Riffs for Flute, Saxophone, Trumpet, and Other Treble Instruments, 1976; Improvising Jazz Sax, 1979; Sonny Rollins, 1981; (with M. Sheller) Salsa! The Rhythm of Latin Music, 1988, rev ed, 1998; Jazz in Black and White: Race, Culture, and Identity in the Jazz Community, 1998. EDITOR: T. Monk: Originals and Standards, 1991; Hard Bop Piano: Jazz Compositions of the Fifties and Sixties, 1992; Straight Ahead Jazz Fakebook, 1993. **Address:** 28 Old Fulton St T-K, Brooklyn, NY 11201, U.S.A. **Online address:** cgerard@pipeline.com

GERARD, Philip. American, b. 1955. **Genres:** Novels, Plays/Screenplays. **Career:** Arizona State University, Tempe, AZ, visiting assistant professor of English, 1981-82, writer in residence, 1983-86; Lake Forest College, Lake Forest, NY, assistant professor of English, 1986-89; University of North Carolina at Wilmington, associate professor of English, 1989-, acting director of professional and creative writing, 1990-91, director, 1991-98. **Publications:** NOVELS: Hatteras Light, 1986; Cape Fear Rising, 1994; Desert Kill, 1994. NONFICTION: Brilliant Passage, 1989; Creative Nonfiction: Researching and Crafting Stories of Real Life, 1996; Secret Soldiers: The Story of World War II's Heroic Army of Deception, 2002; Writing a Book That Makes a Difference, 2000; (ed. with C. Forche) Writing Creative Nonfiction, 2001. TELEVISION DOCUMENTARY SCRIPTS: River Run-Down the Cape Fear to the Sea; Hong Kong-A Little England in the Eastern Seas; Hong Kong-An Absolute Money Machine; Hong Kong-The Future of Freedom. Author and performer of radio essays for public radio. Contributor of stories and articles to periodicals. **Address:** Department of Creative Writing, University of North Carolina at Wilmington, Wilmington, NC 28403, U.S.A. **Online address:** gerardp@uncw.edu; philipgerard.com

GERAS, Adèle (Daphne Weston). British (born Israel), b. 1944. **Genres:** Novellas/Short stories, Children's fiction, Poetry. **Career:** Fairfield High School, Droylsden, Lancashire, French teacher, 1968-71. **Publications:** FOR CHILDREN: Tea at Mrs. Manderby's, 1976; Apricots at Midnight and Other Stories from a Patchwork Quilt, 1982; Beyond the Cross Stitch Mountains, 1977; The Girls in the Velvet Frame, 1979; The Painted Garden, 1979; A Thousand Yards of Sea, 1981; The Rug That Grew, 1981; The Green behind the Glass, 1982, in U.S. as Snapshots of Paradise: Love Stories, 1984; Other Echoes, 1982; The Christmas Cat, 1983; Voyage, 1983; Letters of Fire and Other Unsettling Stories, 1984; Happy Endings, 1986; Little Elephant's Moon, 1986; Ritchie's Rabbit, 1986; Finding Annabel, 1987; Fishpie for Flamingoes, 1987; The Fantora Family Files, 1988; The Strange Bird, 1988;

The Coronation Picnic, 1989; The Tower Room, 1990; My Grandmother's Stories, 1990; A Lane to the Land of the Dead, 1994; Beauty and the Beast and Other Stories, 1996; The Cats of Cuckoo Square series, 1997-98; The Little Swan series, 1997; From Lullaby to Lullaby, 1997. FOR ADULTS: (with P. Stainer) Up on the Roof (poetry), 1987; The Glittering River, 1990; Nina's Magic, 1990; A Magic Birthday, 1992; Yesterday, 1992; Watching the Roses, 1992; Pictures of the Night, 1993; Golden Windows, 1993; The Fantora Family Photographs, 1993; A Candle in the Dark, 1995; Silent Snow Secret Snow, 1998; Troy, 2001. **Address:** 10 Danesmoor Rd, Manchester M20 3JS, England.

GERAS, Norman (Myron). British, b. 1943. **Genres:** Politics/Government. **Career:** University of Manchester, lecturer, 1967-84; sr. lecturer, 1984-90, reader in government, 1990-94, professor, 1995-2003, professor emeritus, 2003-. Member, Editorial Committee, New Left Review, 1976-92. **Publications:** The Legacy of Rosa Luxemburg, 1976; Marx and Human Nature, 1983; Literature of Revolution, 1986; Discourses of Extremity, 1990; Solidarity in the Conversation of Humankind, 1995; Ashes '97: Two Views from the Boundary, 1997; The Contract of Mutual Indifference, 1998; Men of Waugh: Ashes 2001, 2002. **Address:** Dept. of Government, University of Manchester, Manchester M13 9PL, England. **Online address:** norman.geras@man.ac.uk

GERASSI, John. American/French, b. 1931. **Genres:** History, Politics/Government, Biography. **Career:** Professor of Political Science, Queens College, and The Graduate Center, City University of New York. Latin American Ed., Time mag., 1957-61; Correspondent, New York Times, 1961-62; freelance writer, 1962-63; Latin American Ed., Newsweek mag., 1963-66, and Ramparts, 1966-71. Former Instructor in International Relations, San Francisco State College, University of Paris, Free University of Berlin, University of California at Irvine, and Bard College. **Publications:** The Great Fear, 1963 (as The Great Fear in Latin America, 1965); Fidel Castro: A Biography, 1967; North Vietnam: A Documentary, 1968; The Boys of Boise: Furor, Vice and Folly in an American Society, 1969, rev. ed., 2002; The Coming of the New International, 1971; (with F. Browning) The American Way of Crime, 1980; The Premature Antifascists: North American Volunteers in the Spanish Civil War, 1936-1939, 1986; Jean-Paul Sartre: Hated Conscience of His Century, 1989. EDITOR: Venceremos: The Speeches and Writings of Ernesto Che Guevara, 1968; (with I.L. Horowitz and J. de Castro) Latin American Radicalism, 1969; Towards Revolution, 1971; Revolutionary Priest: The Complete Writings and Messages of Camilo Torres, 1973. **Address:** Dept. of Political Science, Queens College, Flushing, NY 11367, U.S.A. **Online address:** tgerassi@qcl.qc.edu

GERBER, Douglas E. Canadian, b. 1933. **Genres:** Classics, Literary criticism and history, Bibliography. **Career:** Professor in Classics, University of Western Ontario, London, 1969-99 (Lecturer, 1959-60; Assistant Professor, 1960-64; Associate Professor, 1964-69). Member, American Philological Association (Ed., Transactions of the American Philological Association, 1974-82), Classical Association of Canada (President, 1988-90), and Classical Association (Great Britain). Lecturer in Greek, University College, University of Toronto, ON, 1958-59. **Publications:** A Bibliography of Pindar, 1513-1966, 1969; Emendations in Pindar, 1513-1972, 1974; Pindar's Olympian One: A Commentary, 1982; Lexicon in Bacchylidem, 1984; Greek Iambic Poetry, 1999; Greek Elegiac Poetry, 1999; A Commentary on Pindar Olympian Nine, 2002. EDITOR: Euterpe: An Anthology of Early Greek Lyric, Elegiac and Iambic Poetry, 1970; A Companion to the Greek Lyric Poets, 1997. **Address:** 2 Grosvenor St, London, ON, Canada N6A 1Y4. **Online address:** degerber@uwo.ca

GERBER, Merrill Joan. American, b. 1938. **Genres:** Novels, Novellas/Short stories, Children's fiction, Autobiography/Memoirs, Essays. **Career:** Writer, lecturer, and teacher of creative writing. **Publications:** Stop Here, My Friend, 1965; An Antique Man, 1967; Now Molly Knows, 1974; The Lady with the Moving Parts, 1978; Please Don't Kiss Me Now, 1981; Name a Star for Me, 1983; Honeymoon: Stories, 1985; I'm Kissing as Fast as I Can, 1985; The Summer of My Indian Prince, 1986; Also Known as Sadzia! The Belly Dancer!, 1987; Marry Me Tomorrow, 1987; Even Pretty Girls Cry at Night, 1988; I'd Rather Think about Robby, 1988; King of the World, 1989; Handsome as Anything, 1990; The Kingdom of Brooklyn, 1992; This Old Heart of Mine, 1993; Old Mother, Little Cat (memoir), 1995; Anna in Chains, 1998; Anna in the Afterlife (novel), 2002; Botticelli Blue Skies: American in Florence (memoir), 2002; Gut Feelings: A Writer's Truths and Minute Inventions (essays), 2003.

GERBER, Michael E. American, b. 1936. **Genres:** Business/Trade/Industry. **Career:** E-Myth Worldwide, Santa Rosa, CA, founder and chief executive officer. **Publications:** The E-Myth, 1986; The Power Point, 1991; The E-Myth Revisited: Why Most Small Businesses Don't Work and What to Do about It, 1995; The E-Myth Manager: Why Management Doesn't Work and What to Do about It, 1998; The E-Myth Contractor: Why Most Contractors' Businesses Don't Work and What to Do about It, 2002; The E-Myth Physician: Why Most Medical Practices Don't Work and What to Do about It, 2003. **Address:** E-Myth Worldwide, 131-B Stony Circle Ste 2000, Santa Rosa, CA 95401, U.S.A. **Online address:** mgerber@e-myth.com

GERDES, Eckhard. American, b. 1959. **Genres:** Novels, Novellas/Short stories. **Career:** Bookcase, Wilmette, IL, sales clerk, 1978-80; assistant manager of bookstores in Evanston, IL, 1979-81; Waldenbooks, Iowa City, IA, assistant manager, 1981-82; Bob's News Emporium, Chicago, IL, manager, 1983-84; Bookcase, sales clerk, 1984; Barbara's Bookstore, sales clerk, 1984-86, 1990-91; Chicago-Main News, Evanston, book buyer and co-manager, 1985-87; University of Dubuque, Dubuque, IA, news assistant in university relations, 1987-88; Book Cache, Anchorage, AK, sales clerk, 1989-90; Bookworks, Chicago, trade book buyer, 1990-92; Barnes & Noble Books, Evanston, department supervisor, 1992-94; Roosevelt University, Chicago, instructor in English, 1994-; Hardy Freeman and Associates, executive assistant, 1994-. **Publications:** NOVELS: The Million-Year Centipede; or, Liquid Structures, 1976; Aspic Interregencies, 1978; Systems of Flux, 1980; The Intersection of Two Loops, 1985; Hugh Moore, 1987; Truly Fine Citizen, 1989; Citizen Reclaimed, 1990; Ring in a River, 1994. OTHER: Projections (novella), 1986. Contributor of articles, stories, plays, poems, art work, and reviews to periodicals. **Address:** Department of English, School of Liberal Studies, Roosevelt University, 435 South Michigan Ave., Chicago, IL 60605, U.S.A.

GERDY, John R. American, b. 1957. **Genres:** Education, Social commentary, Sports/Fitness. **Career:** National Collegiate Athletic Association, Overland Park, KS, legislative assistant, 198689; Southeastern Conference, Birmingham, AL, associate commissioner, 1989-95. Ohio University, visiting professor of sports administration. **Publications:** The Successful College Athletic Program: The New Standard, 1997; Sports in School: The Future of an Institution, 2000; Sports: The All-American Addiction, 2002. **Address:** 409 Sickman Mill Rd, Conestoga, PA 17516, U.S.A. **Online address:** jrg331234@aol.com

GERHARDT, Michael E. American, b. 1947. **Genres:** Novels. **Career:** Has written advertising for TV, radio, magazines, and newspapers. **Publications:** Presidential Powers, 1999; The Lincoln Affairs, 2003. **Address:** 3 N Line Rd, Newtown Square, PA 19073, U.S.A. **Online address:** Megerhardt@aol.com

GERLACH, Don R. American, b. 1932. **Genres:** History, Biography. **Career:** University of Nebraska, instructor, 1961-62; University of Akron, Ohio, assistant professor, 1962-65, associate professor, 1965-72, professor of history, 1972-94, emeritus, 1994-; Holyrood Seminary, instructor in history, 1983-94. **Publications:** Philip Schuyler and the American Revolution in New York 1733-1777, 1964; Twenty Years of the "Promotion of Literature": The Regents of the University of the State of New York 1784-1804, 1974; Proud Patriot: Philip Schuyler and the War of Independence 1775-1783, 1987. Contributor to history journals.

GERLACH, Douglas. American, b. 1963. **Genres:** Money/Finance. **Career:** Financial writer, Internet developer, and financial consultant. National Association of Investors Corporation, cocreator and senior editor of Web site, 1995, then consulting editor; Investorama.com (Web site), New York, NY, founder and editor-in-chief, 1995-2001; First Albany Corporation, New York, Internet business analyst, 1997-98; Armchair Millionaire.com (Web site), senior editor, 1998. Has appeared on television and radio programs, including CNN-FN's Digital Jam, Extra Help Channel's In the Money, and ZDTV's The Money Machine; host, Worth Online's Conference Call. **Publications:** Investor's Web Guide: Tools and Strategies for Building Your Portfolio (with CD-ROM), 1997; The Complete Idiot's Guide to Online Investing, 1998, 2nd ed, 2000; (with T. McFeat and J. Gravelle) The Complete Idiot's Guide to Online Investing for Canadians, 1999; (with L. Schiff) The Armchair Millionaire: Build and Protect an Extraordinary Portfolio, Even on an Ordinary Income, by Following One Commonsense Investing Strategy, 2001; (with A. McQuade) Investment Clubs for Dummies, 2002. Contributor to magazines and periodicals. **Address:** 615 Main St. No. 325, Stroudsburg, PA 18360-2005, U.S.A. **Online address:** gerlach@yahoo.com

GERLACH, Larry R(euben). American, b. 1941. **Genres:** Area studies, History, Sports/Fitness. **Career:** University of Utah, Salt Lake City, assistant professor, 1968-, professor of history, 1977-, associate dean of College of Humanities, 1982-83, chair of department of history, 1983-88; College of William and Mary, visiting assistant professor, 1970-71. Utah Humanities Center, director, 1988-90. **Publications:** Historical Studies and Documents Research Foundation (Salt Lake City), 1973; Prologue to Independence: New Jersey in the Coming of the American Revolution, 1976; Connecticut Congressman: Samuel Huntington, 1731-1796, 1977; The Men in Blue: Conversations with Umpires, 1980; Blazing Crosses in Zion: The Ku Klux Klan in Utah, 1982; (with C.B. von Schmidt) Dining in-Salt Lake City, 1985; The Olympic Games: Ancient to Modern, 2002. EDITOR: The American Revolution: New York as a Case Study, 1972; Documents Illustrative of the American Revolution, 1763-1788, New Jersey in the American Revolution, 1763-1783: A Documentary History, 1975; "We Hold These Truths": Fundamental Testaments of the American Revolution, 1976; Legacies of the American Revolution, 1978. **Address:** Department of History, University of Utah, 380 S 1400 East #211, Salt Lake City, UT 84112, U.S.A.

GERNET, Jacques. French (born Algeria), b. 1921. **Genres:** History. **Career:** Author and educator. Ecole Pratique des Hautes Etudes, then Ecole des Hautes Etudes en Sciences Sociales, Paris, professor of economic and social sciences, 1955-76; University of Paris, Sorbonne, professor of Chinese language and civilization, 1957-74; College de France, Paris, professor, 1975-. **Publications:** Daily Life in China on the Eve of the Mongol Invasion (1250-1276), 1962; Ancient China from the Beginnings to the Empire, trans by R. Rudorff, 1968; A History of Chinese Civilization, 1982; Chine et Christianisme: Action et Reaction, 1983, trans by J. Lloyd as China and the Christian Impact: A Conflict of Cultures, 1986; L'intelligence de la Chine: le social et le mental, 1994; Aspects economiques du Buddhism dans la societe chinoise du Ve au Xe siecle, trans by F. Verellen as Buddhism in Chinese Society: An Economic History from the Fifth to the Tenth Centuries, 1995; Monde chinois, trans by J.R. Foster and C. Hartman as A History of Chinese Civilization, 2nd ed., 1995. **Address:** College de France, 11 place Marcelin-Berthelot, 75005 Paris, France. **Online address:** gernet@ext.jussieu.fr

GERRARD, A. J. *See* GERRARD, John.

GERRARD, John. Also writes as A. J. Gerrard. British, b. 1944. **Genres:** Earth sciences. **Career:** University of Birmingham, Birmingham, England, lecturer, 1969-89, senior lecturer in geography, 1989-97, reader in geography, 1997-; writer. **Publications:** Soils and Landforms, 1981; The Book of Plymouth, 1982; Rocks and Landforms, 1988; Mountain Environments, 1990; Soil Geomorphology, 1992; Fundamentals of Soils, 2000; Encyclopedia of Geomorphology, forthcoming. EDITOR & CONTRIBUTOR: (as A.J. Gerrard) Alluvial Soils, 1987; Managing a Conurbation: Birmingham and Its Region, 1996. **Address:** Department of Geography, University of Birmingham, Edgbaston, Birmingham B15 2TT, England. **Online address:** A.J.W.Gerrard@bham.ac.uk

GERRARD, Michael B. American, b. 1951. **Genres:** Environmental sciences/Ecology, Law. **Career:** Berle, Kass & Case, NYC, environmental lawyer, 1978-94; Arnold & Porter, NYC, environmental lawyer, 1994-. Columbia University, adjunct faculty member, 1992-. New York Law Journal, monthly column on environmental law 1986-; Environmental Law in New York newsletter, editor, 1989-. **Publications:** (with D. Ruzow and P. Weinberg) Environmental Impact Review in New York, 1990; The Environmental Law Practice Guide, 8 vols, 1992; Whose Backyard, Whose Risk: Fear and Fairness in Toxic and Nuclear Waste Siting, 1994; The Law of Environmental Justice, 1999. **Address:** Arnold & Porter, 399 Park Ave 34th Fl, New York, NY 10022, U.S.A.

GERRIG, Richard J. American, b. 1959. **Genres:** Psychology. **Career:** Yale University, New Haven, CT, assistant professor, 1984-90, associate professor of psychology, 1990-94; State University of New York at Stony Brook, associate professor of psychology, 1994-. Stanford University, visiting assistant professor, 1989. **Publications:** Experiencing Narrative Worlds: On the Psychological Activities of Reading, 1993; (with P.G. Zimbardo) Psychology and Life, 14th ed, 1995. Contributor to books. Contributor of articles and reviews to psychology journals and other magazines. **Address:** Department of Psychology, State University of New York at Stony Brook, Stony Brook, NY 11794-2500, U.S.A.

GERRISH, Brian Albert. American/British (born United Kingdom), b. 1931. **Genres:** Theology/Religion. **Career:** McCormick Theological Seminary, Chicago, Instructor, 1958-59, Assistant Professor, 1959-63, Associate Professor of Church History, 1963-65; University of Chicago, Associate Professor 1965-68, Professor, 1968-85, John Nuveen Professor, 1985-96, John Nuveen Professor Emeritus, 1996-; Union Theological Seminary, VA, Distinguished Service Professor, 1996-2002. Journal of Religion, Co-ed.,

1972-85. American Society of Church History, President, 1979. **Publications:** Grace and Reason: a Study in the Theology of Luther, 1962; Tradition and the Modern World: Reformed Theology in the Nineteenth Century, 1978; The Old Protestantism and the New: Essays on the Reformation Heritage, 1982; A Prince of the Church: Schleiermacher and the Beginnings of Modern Theology, 1984; Grace and Gratitude: The Eucharistic Theology of John Calvin, 1993; Continuing the Reformation: Essays on Modern Religious Thought, 1993; Saving and Secular Faith: An Invitation to Systematic Theology, 1999; The Pilgrim Road: Sermons on Christian Life, 2000. EDITOR: The Faith of Christendom: A Source Book of Creeds and Confessions, 1963; Reformers in Profile, 1967; Reformatio Perennis: Essays on Calvin and the Reformation in Honor of Ford Lewis Battles, 1981; Reformed Theology for the Third Christian Millennium: The 2001 Sprunt Lectures, 2003. **Address:** 9142 Sycamore Hill Pl, Mechanicsville, VA 23116, U.S.A.

GERRITSEN, Tess. (Gerritsen). American, b. 1953. **Genres:** Mystery/Crime/Suspense, Romance/Historical, Plays/Screenplays. **Career:** Physician in Honolulu, HI, 1979-89; freelance writer, 1989-. **Publications:** NOVELS: Adventure's Mistress, 1985; Call after Midnight, 1987; Never Say Die, 1990; Under the Knife, 1990; Presumed Guilty, 1993; (as Terry Gerritsen) Peggy Sue Got Murdered, 1994; In Their Footsteps, 1994; Thief of Hearts, 1995; Keeper of the Bride, 1996. MEDICAL THRILLERS: Harvest, 1996; Life Support, 1997; Bloodstream, 1998; Gravity, 1999; The Surgeon, 2001; The Apprentice, 2002; The Sinner, 2003. TELEPLAYS: Adrift, 1993. **Address:** c/o Meg Ruley, Jane Rotrosen Agency, 318 E 51st St, New York, NY 10022, U.S.A.

GERSHONI, Israel. Israeli, b. 1946. **Genres:** History. **Career:** Tel Aviv University, Tel Aviv, Israel, department of Middle Eastern history, professor. **Publications:** (with J.P. Jankowski) Redefining the Egyptian Nation, 1930-1945, 1995. **Address:** School of History, Department of Middle Eastern & African History, Tel Aviv University, Ramat Aviv, 19104 Tel Aviv, Israel. **Online address:** gershon@post.tau.ac.il

GERSHTEN, Donna M. American, b. 1953. **Genres:** Novels. **Career:** Writer. **Publications:** Kissing the Virgin's Mouth, 2001. Contributor of short stories to literary journals. **Address:** c/o Author mail, HarperCollins, 10 E. 53rd St., 7th Floor, New York, NY 10023, U.S.A.

GERSHUNY, Grace. American, b. 1950. **Genres:** Agriculture/Forestry, Homes/Gardens. **Career:** Rural Education Center, Wilton, NH, horticultural director, 1982; organic certification field inspector and trainer, 1984-94; organic farmer and manager of a small certified organic market garden for perennial herbs and fruits and small livestock, 1985-93; GAIA Services, consultant, speaker, writer, and educator, 1985-; Institute for Social Ecology, Plainfield, VT, instructor, 1985-; Northeast Organic and Sustainable Farmers Network, in-service program developer, 1989-91; Organic Farmer: The Digest of Sustainable Agriculture, creator and editor, 1989-94; Goddard College, Plainfield, associate faculty member, 1991-2001; worked with U.S. Dept. of Agriculture to implement the National Organic Program, 1994-99. **Publications:** The Soul of Soil: A Guide to Ecological Soil Management, 1983, 4th ed. (with J. Smillie), 1999; (ed. with D. Martin) The Rodale Book of Composting, 1992; Start with the Soil: The Organic Gardener's Guide to Improving Soil for Higher Yields, More Beautiful Flowers, and a Healthy, Easy-Care Yard and Garden, 1993. Contributor to magazines. **Address:** 1417 Joe's Brook Rd, St. Johnsbury, VT 05819, U.S.A. **Online address:** graceg@kingcon.com

GERSON, Kathleen. American, b. 1947. **Genres:** Sociology. **Career:** New York University, NYC, assistant professor, 1980-87, associate professor, 1988-93, full professor of sociology, 1994 founding member of women's studies program. Russell Sage Foundation, visiting scholar, 1988; writer, public speaker, and consultant. **Publications:** (with C. Fisher and others) Networks and Places: Social Relations in the Urban Setting, 1977; Hard Choices: How Women Decide about Work, Career, and Motherhood, 1985; No Man's Land: Men's Changing Commitments to Family and Work, 1993. Contributor to journals. **Address:** Department of Sociology, New York University, 269 Mercer St., 4th Fl., New York, NY 10003, U.S.A.

GERSTENBERGER, Erhard S. German, b. 1932. **Genres:** Theology/Religion. **Career:** Pastor of a Protestant Reformed church in Duesseldorf, Germany, 1965-75; Yale University, New Haven, CT, instructor to assistant professor, 1962-64; Escola Superior de Teologia, Sao Leopoldo, Brazil, professor of Old Testament, 1975-81; University of Marburg, Marburg, Germany, professor of Old Testament, 1985-97. **Publications:** Psalms: A Form-Critical Commentary, vol. I, 1988, vol. II, 2001; Leviticus: A Commentary, 1996; Yahweh, 1996; Theologies in the Old Testament, 2002. Author

of books in German. **Address:** Fasanenweg 29, D-35394 Giessen, Germany. **Online address:** gersterh@staff.uni-marburg.de

GERSTLER, Amy. American, b. 1956. **Genres:** Poetry, Novels. **Career:** Poet, fiction writer, journalist. **Publications:** POETRY: Yonder, 1981; Christy's Alpine Inn, 1982; White Marriage/Recovery, 1984; Early Heaven, 1984; The True Bride, 1986; Bitter Angel, 1990; Nerve Storm, 1993. OTHER: Martine's Mouth (fiction), 1985; Primitive Man (fiction), 1987; (with A. Smith) Past Lives (artists book), 1989. Contributor to periodicals. **Address:** c/o Viking Penguin, 375 Hudson St., New York, NY 10014, U.S.A.

GERSTMANN, Evan. American. **Genres:** Gay and lesbian issues. **Career:** Loyola Marymount University, Los Angeles, CA, assistant professor of political science. **Publications:** The Constitutional Underclass: Gays, Lesbians, and the Failure of Class-Based Equal Protection, 1999. **Address:** Department of Political Science, Loyola Marymount University, Loyola Blvd. at West 80th St., Los Angeles, CA 90045, U.S.A. **Online address:** egerstma@lmumail.lmu.edu

GERTRIDGE, Allison. Canadian, b. 1967. **Genres:** Children's non-fiction. **Career:** Scholastic Canada Ltd., Markham, Canada, editor, 1989-93; writer, 1993-. **Publications:** Animals by Alphabet, 1991; Skating Superstars, 1994, rev. ed, 1996; Meet Canadian Authors and Illustrators, 1994; Skating Superstars II, 1997; Trim a Tree, 2000; Meet Canadian Authors and Illustrators II, 2001. **Address:** c/o Scholastic Canada Ltd., 175 Hillmount Rd., Markham, ON, Canada L6C 1Z7. **Online address:** allison.gertridge@rogers.com

GERVAIS, (George) Paul. American, b. 1946. **Genres:** Biography. **Career:** Worked in advertising and real estate sales. Full-time writer, 1984-. **Publications:** Extraordinary People, 1991; Gar-an-guli, 1999; A Garden in Lucca, 2000. **Address:** Villa Massei, Massa Macinaia, 55060 Lucca, Italy. **Online address:** vlmassei@lunet.it

GERZINA, Gretchen (Aletha) Holbrook. American, b. 1950. **Genres:** Biography. **Career:** Stanford University, Stanford, CA, assistant director of Center for Teaching and Learning, 1984-85; State University of New York at Albany, lecturer, 1985-86; Skidmore College, Saratoga Springs, NY, assistant professor of English, 1986-89; Princeton University, Princeton, NJ, humanities fellow, 1989-90; Vassar College, Poughkeepsie, NY, professor of English, 1989-, associate dean of the faculty. **Publications:** Carrington: A Life, published in England as Carrington: A Life of Dora Carrington, 1893-1932, 1989; Black London: Life before Emancipation, published in England as Black England: Life before Emancipation, 1996. **Address:** Department of English, Vassar College, Poughkeepsie, NY 12601, U.S.A.

GERZON, Robert. American, b. 1946. **Genres:** Self help. **Career:** Licensed psychotherapist, lecturer, and author; conducts a Mastering Anxiety program. **Publications:** Finding Serenity in an Age of Anxiety, 1997. **Address:** 77 Bolton St., Concord, MA 01742, U.S.A.

GESCH, Roy (George). American, b. 1920. **Genres:** Theology/Religion, Travel/Exploration. **Career:** Lutheran clergyman, 1944-. Messengers of Christ, Lutheran Bible Translators, Inc., Aurora, IL, executive director, 1976-86, associate director, 1986-. **Publications:** On Active Duty, 1967; A Husband Prays, 1968; A Wife Prays, 1968; Parent Pray, 1968; God's World through Young Eyes, 1969; Help! I'm in College, 1970; Man at Prayer, 1970; Lord of the Young Crowd, 1971; (with J. Nelesen) And Yet the Church Goes On, 1972; (with D. Gesch) Discover Europe, 1973; Service Prayer Book, 1981; Confirmed in Christ, 1984, rev. ed., 1997; To Love and to Cherish, 1985; Made for Each Other, 1987; Silver Reflections, 1989. **Address:** 72 LaMirage Circle, Aliso Viejo, CA 92656-4226, U.S.A. **Online address:** royndot@cox.net

GESLER, Wilbert M. American (born India), b. 1941. **Genres:** Geography, Medicine/Health. **Career:** Robert College for Girls, Istanbul, Turkey, instructor in mathematics, 1965-68; Pennsylvania State University, Behrend Campus, Erie, instructor in mathematics, 1968-69; University of Malawi, Bunda College of Agriculture, Lilongwe, lecturer in mathematics, 1969-71; Carolina Population Center, Chapel Hill, NC, research assistant on Noyes Fellowships, 1973-75; University of Lagos, Nigeria, research fellow at Institute of Child Health, 1976-77; University of North Carolina at Chapel Hill, instructor in geography, 1978, assistant professor, 1982-87, associate professor of geography, 1987-, director of graduate studies, 1988-; Rutgers University, New Brunswick, NJ, assistant professor of geography, 1978-81. **Publications:** Health Care Delivery in Developing Countries, 1984; (with M.S. Meade and J. Florin) Medical Geography, 1988; The Cultural

Geography of Health Care, 1991; (ed. with T. Ricketts) Health in Rural North America: The Geography of Health Care Services Delivery, 1992; Culture/Place/Health, 2001. Work represented in anthologies. Contributor to scholarly journals.

GESNER, Carol. American (born Panama), b. 1922. **Genres:** Poetry, Literary criticism and history. **Career:** Professor Emerita of English, Berea College, Kentucky, 1988- (Instructor, 1954-56; Assistant Professor, 1956-61; Associate Professor, 1961-67; Professor, 1967-88). **Publications:** The Crystal Spectrum (poetry), 1964-64; Shakespeare and the Greek Romance: A Study of Origins, 1970; Plymouth, 1977; Plymouth and the Palimpsest, 2002.

GESS, Denise. American, b. 1952. **Genres:** Novels, Adult non-fiction. **Career:** La Salle University, Philadelphia, PA, instructor in English composition, 1984; Rutgers, the State University, Camden Campus, Camden, NJ, instructor in English composition and creative writing, 1984-88, instructor in creative writing and literature, 1994, 1996, 1997; Temple University, Philadelphia, instructor in creative writing, 1987-; Camden County College, Blackwood, NJ, writer-in-residence, fall, 1992. Writer. Workshop instructor, Trenton State Writers Conference, 1985, and Stonecoast Writers Conference, 1989, 1990, 1991, 1993; University of North Carolina, Wilmington, visiting assistant professor of fiction writing, 2001-02. **Publications:** NOVELS: Good Deeds, 1984; Red Whiskey Blues, 1989. **Address:** c/o Jean V. Naggar, Jean V. Naggar Literary Agency, 216 E 75th St, New York, NY 10021, U.S.A. **Online address:** thegess@aol.com

GESSEL, Van C. American, b. 1950. **Genres:** Literary criticism and history, Biography, Translations. **Career:** Columbia University, NYC, assistant professor, 1979-80; University of Notre Dame, Notre Dame, IN, assistant professor of Japanese, 1980-82; University of California, Berkeley, assistant professor, 1982-89, associate professor of Japanese, 1989-90; Brigham Young University, associate professor, 1990-94, professor of Japanese, 1994-, College of Humanities, dean, 1997-. **Publications:** (ed. with T. Matsumoto) The Showa Anthology: Modern Japanese Short Stories, Vol 1: 1929-1961, Vol 2: 1961-1984, 1986; The Sting of Life: Four Contemporary Japanese Novelists, 1989; Three Modern Novelists: Soseki, Tanizaki, Kawabata, 1993. TRANSLATOR; ALL BY SHUSAKU ENDO: When I Whistle, 1979; The Samurai, 1982; Stained Glass Elegies, 1984; Scandal, c. 1988; The Final Martyrs, 1993; Deep River, 1994. **Address:** College of Humanities, Brigham Young University, Provo, UT 84602, U.S.A.

GESSNER, Lynne. Also writes as Merle Clark. American, b. 1919. **Genres:** Children's fiction, Novellas/Short stories. **Career:** The Encyclopaedia Britannica Reading Training Program, contributor. **Publications:** Trading Post Girl, 1968; Lightning Slinger, 1968; (as Merle Clark) Ramrod, 1969; Bonnie's Guatemala, 1970; Navajo Slave, 1976; Yamadan, 1976; Malcolm Yucca Seed, 1977, 1993; To See a Witch, 1978; Danny, 1978; Edge of Darkness, 1979; Brother to the Navajo, 1979. Author of articles, essays, short stories. **Address:** 6507 East Holly St, Scottsdale, AZ 85257, U.S.A.

GESTON, Mark S(ymington). American, b. 1946. **Genres:** Science fiction/Fantasy. **Career:** Eberle Berlin Kading, Turnbow and McKlveen, Boise, Idaho, attorney. **Publications:** Lords of the Starship, 1967; Out of the Mouth of the Dragon, 1969; The Day Star, 1972; The Siege of Wonder, 1976; Mirror to the Sky, 1992. Contributor of short fiction to anthologies and periodicals. **Address:** 1829 Edgecliff Terrace, Boise, ID 83702, U.S.A. **Online address:** mgeston@msn.com

GETIS, Victoria. American, b. 1966. **Genres:** History. **Career:** Mount Holyoke College, South Hadley, MA, visiting lecturer, 1997; University of Massachusetts at Amherst, senior research fellow at Center for Computer-Based Instructional Technology, 1999-. **Publications:** Muddy Boots and Ragged Aprons: Images of Working-Class Detroit, 1900-1930 (pictorial history), 1997; The Juvenile Court and the Progressives, 2000. **Address:** Center for Computer-Based Instructional Technology, 140 Governors Dr., University of Massachusetts at Amherst, Amherst, MA 01003, U.S.A. **Online address:** vgetis@cs.umass.edu

GETMAN, Julius (G.). American, b. 1931. **Genres:** Education, Organized labor. **Career:** National Labor Relations Board, Washington, DC, attorney, 1959-61; Indiana University-Bloomington, assistant professor, 1963-67, professor of law, 1967-76; Stanford University, Stanford, CA, professor of law, 1976-77; Yale University, New Haven, CT, William K. Townsend Professor of Law, 1978-86; University of Texas at Austin, Earl E. Sheffield Regents Professor of Law, 1986-. Visiting professor at Benares Hindu University and Indian Law Institute, 1967-68, and University of Chicago, 1970-71; Boston College, Richard Huber Distinguished Visiting Professor, 1991-92. **Publica-**

tions: (with S.B. Goldberg and J.B. Herman) Union Representation Elections: Law and Reality, 1976; Labor Relations: Law, Practice, and Policy, 1978, 2nd ed (with J.D. Blackburn), 1989; (with B.B. Pogrebin) Labor Relations: The Basic Processes, Law and Practice, 1988; (with W. Gould, C. Gramm, R. Marshall, and others) Employee Rights in a Changing Economy: The Issue of Replacement Workers, 1991; In the Company of Scholars: The Struggle for the Soul of Higher Education, 1992; (co-author) Casebook: Employment Discrimination BNA, 1979; The Betrayal of Local 14, 1998. **Address:** Law School, University of Texas at Austin, Austin, TX 78705, U.S.A.

GETZ, David. American, b. 1957. **Genres:** Novels, Adult non-fiction. **Career:** Author. NYC Board of Education, NYC, teacher, 1984-. **Publications:** FICTION: Thin Air, 1990; Almost Famous, 1992. NONFICTION: Frozen Man, 1994; Life on Mars, 1997; Frozen Girl, 1998. OTHER: Floating Home (picture book), 1997. **Address:** 375 Riverside Dr., Apt. 9D, New York, NY 10025, U.S.A.

GETZ, Marshall J(ay). (born United States), b. 1957. **Genres:** Biography. **Career:** Writer. **Publications:** Subhas Chandra Bose: A Biography, 2002. **Address:** POB 19159, Houston, TX 77224, U.S.A. **Online address:** marshallgetz@aol.com

GEWERTZ, Deborah B. American, b. 1948. **Genres:** Anthropology/Ethnology. **Career:** Queens College of the City University of New York, Flushing, NY, adjunct lecturer, 1972; Graduate Center of the CUNY, NYC, supervisor of Human Relations Area Files, 1972-73; Hunter College of the CUNY, NYC, adjunct instructor, 1976-77; Amherst College, MA, assistant professor, 1977-83, associate professor, 1983-88, professor of anthropology, 1988-94, G. Henry Whitcomb professor of anthology, 1994-, chairperson of Dept of Anthropology and Sociology, 1985-87, Elizabeth Bruss Reader in Anthropology and Women's Studies, 1985-87. Australian National University, research fellow, Research School for Pacific Studies, 1983-84. Conducted field research among the Chambri and their neighbors of the East Sepik Province, Papua New Guinea, 1974-75, 1979, 1983-84, 1987-88, 1994, in Rock Creek MT, summers, 1985-86, 1988-89, 1992, and among the Karavarans and their neighbors of the Duke of York Island Group, East New Britain Province, Papua New Guinea, 1991. **Publications:** Sepik River Societies, 1983; (with F. Errington) Cultural Alternatives and a Feminist Anthropology, 1989; (with F. Errington) Twisted Histories, Altered Contexts, 1991; (with F. Errington) Articulating Change in the "Last Unknown," 1995; Emerging Class in Papua New Guinea, 1999. EDITOR & CONTRIBUTOR: (with E. Schieffelin) History and Ethnography in New Guinea, 1985; Myths of Matriarchy Reconsidered, 1988. Work represented in anthologies. Contributor of articles and reviews to scholarly journals. **Address:** Dept of Anthropology-Sociology, Amherst College, Amherst, MA 01002-5000, U.S.A. **Online address:** dbgewertz@amherst.edu

GEYER, Georgie Anne. American, b. 1935. **Genres:** Area studies, Education, Geography, History, International relations/Current affairs, Autobiography/Memoirs, Biography. **Career:** Chicago Daily News, society desk reporter, 1959-60, general assignment reporter, 1960-64, foreign correspondent, 1964-75; Los Angeles Times Syndicate, syndicated columnist, 1975-80; Syracuse University, New York, Lyle M. Spencer Professor of Journalism, 1976; Universal Press Syndicate, syndicated columnist, 1980-; American University, Washington, DC, trustee, 1981-86; The Annenberg Washington Program, senior fellow, 1982-83, 1992-; radio and television news commentator. **Publications:** The New Latins: Fateful Change in South and Central America, 1970; The New 100 Years War, 1972; The Young Russians, 1976; Buying the Night Flight: The Autobiography of a Woman Foreign Correspondent, 1983; Guerrilla Prince: The Untold Story of Fidel Castro, 1991; Waiting for Winter to End: An Extraordinary Journey through Soviet Central Asia, 1994; Americans No More: The Death of Citizenship, 1996; Tunisia: A Journey through the Country That Works, 2003. **Address:** The Plaza, 800 25th St NW Ste 1006, Washington, DC 20037-2207, U.S.A. **Online address:** gigi_geyer@juno.com

GEYMAN, John P. American, b. 1931. **Genres:** Air/Space topics, Medicine/Health. **Career:** Associate Professor and Chairman, Division of Family Practice, University of Utah College of Medicine, Salt Lake City, 1971-72; Professor and Vice-Chairman, Dept. of Family Practice, School of Medicine, University of California at Davis, 1972-76; Professor and Chairman, Dept. of Family Medicine, School of Medicine, University of Washington, Seattle, 1976-90, Emeritus, 1993-. Ed., Journal of Family Practice, 1974-90; Ed., Journal of American Board of Family Practice, 1990-2003. **Publications:** The Modern Family Doctor and Changing Medical Practice, 1971; Content of Family Practice, 1976; Family Practice in the Medical School, 1977;

Research in Family Practice, 1978; Preventive Medicine in Family Practice, 1979; Profile of the Residency-Trained Family Physician, 1980; Family Practice: Foundation of Changing Health Care, 1980; Behavioral Science in Family Practice, 1980; Funding Patient Care, Education and Research in Family Practice, 1981; Family Practice: An International Perspective in Developed Countries, 1982; (with others) The Family Practice Drug Handbook, 1990; (ed. with others) Evidence-Based Clinical Practice: Concepts and Approaches, 2000; (with others) Textbook of Rural Medicine, 2000; Flight as a Lifetime Passion: Adventures, Misadventures, and Lessons, 2000; Health Care in America: Can Our Ailing System Be Healed?, 2001; Falling through the "Safety Net": Americans without Health Insurance, 2005; Corporate Transformation of Health Care; Can the Public Interest Still Be Served?, 2004. **Address:** 53 Avian Ridge Ln, Friday Harbor, WA 98250, U.S.A. **Online address:** jgeyman@u.washington.edu

GHAN, Linda (R.). Canadian, b. 1947. **Genres:** Children's fiction, Plays/Screenplays. **Career:** University of Regina, Regina, Saskatchewan, instructor in English, 1969-70; Ocho Rios Secondary School, Ocho Rios, St. Ann, Jamaica, instructor, 1971-72; St. Joseph's Teachers College, Kingston, Jamaica, instructor, 1973-76; Concordia University, Montreal, Quebec, instructor in TESL department, 1976-79, instructor in creative writing, 1979-93. Daily News, Kingston, feature writer, 1975-76; CINQ-FM Radio, Montreal, producer and host of "Art and Eggs" (weekly arts program), 1979-82. **Publications:** FOR CHILDREN: Anancy (script), 1974-75; Where's Zelda?, 1980; Beauty and the Beast (play), 1985; Muhla the Fair One, 1991. FOR ADULTS: Coldsnap (play), 1980; Toros' Daughter (play), 1985; O'Hara, A Coming of Age (play), 1986; A Gift of Sky (novel), 1988; A Touch of Nordic Madness. **Address:** Concordia University, 1455 de Raisonneuve Blvd. W., Montreal, QC, Canada H3G 1M8.

GHERMAN, Beverly. American, b. 1934. **Genres:** Biography. **Career:** University of California, San Francisco, medical researcher, 1956-58; San Francisco school system, teacher's aide, 1967-74; Kaiser Permanente, San Francisco, medical researcher, 1975; Jewish Community Library, San Francisco, library assistant, 1976-80; writer. **Publications:** Georgia O'Keeffe: The Wideness and Wonder of Her World, 1986; Agnes de Mille: Dancing off the Earth, 1990; Sandra Day O'Connor: Justice for All, 1991; E.B. White: Some Writer!, 1992; The Mysterious Rays of Dr. Roentgen, 1994; Robert Louis Stevenson: Teller of Tales, 1996; Norman Rockwell, Storyteller with a Brush, 2002; Ansel Adams: America's Photographer, 2002; Jimmy Carter, 2003. **Address:** 400 40th Ave, San Francisco, CA 94121, U.S.A.

GHILARDUCCI, Teresa. American, b. 1957. **Genres:** Economics, Organized labor, Women's studies and issues. **Career:** University of Notre Dame, IN, associate professor of economics, 1983-. Consultant to labor unions and law firms. Pension Benefit Guaranty Corp., Advisory Board, 1995-2002; Indiana Public Employees Retirement Fund, trustee, 1997-2002. **Publications:** Labor's Capital: The Economics and Politics of Private Pensions, 1992; Portable Pension Plans for Casual Labor Markets, 1995. Work represented in books. Contributor to economic and labor research journals. **Address:** Department of Economics, University of Notre Dame, Notre Dame, IN 46556, U.S.A. **Online address:** ghilarducci.1@nd.edu

GHOSE, Zulfikar. British/American (born Pakistan), b. 1935. **Genres:** Novels, Poetry, Literary criticism and history, Autobiography/Memoirs. **Career:** The Observer, London, cricket correspondent, 1960-65; teacher in London, 1963-69; University of Texas at Austin, professor of English, 1969-. **Publications:** (with B. S. Johnson) Statement Against Corpses, 1964; The Loss of India (verse) 1964; Confessions of a Native-Alien, 1965; The Contradictions (novel), 1966; The Murder of Aziz Khan (novel), 1967; Jets from Orange (verse), 1967; The Incredible Brazilian, Book I (novel) 1972; The Violent West (verse), 1972; (with Gavin Ewart and B. S. Johnson) Penguin Modern Poets 25, 1974; Crump's Terms (novel), 1975; The Beautiful Empire (novel), 1975; Hamlet, Prufrock, and Language, 1978; A Different World (novel), 1978; Hulme's Investigations into the Bogart Scipt (novel), 1981; A New History of Torments (novel), 1982; The Fiction of Reality (criticism), 1983; Don Bueno (novel), 1983; A Memory of Asia (poetry), 1984; Figures of Enchantment (novel), 1986; Selected Poems (poetry), 1991; The Triple Mirror of the Self (novel), 1992; Shakespeare's Mortal Knowledge (criticism), 1993; Veronica and the Gongora Passion (short fiction), 1998. **Address:** Dept of English, University of Texas, Austin, TX 78712, U.S.A. **Online address:** zulfji@mail.utexas.edu

GHOSH, Amitav. Indian, b. 1956. **Genres:** Sociology. **Career:** Indian Express, India, reporter and editor; Department of Sociology, Delhi University, Delhi, India, lecturer, 1983-. **Publications:** Bisvabidyara anandaprangane Rabindranatha, 1986; The Circle of Reason, 1986; The Shadow

Lines, 1988; In an Antique Land, 1992; Calcutta Chromosome (novel), 1995; Countdown, 1999; The Glass Palace, 2001. **Address:** Department of Sociology, Delhi School of Economics, Delhi University, Delhi 110007, India.

GHOSH, Arun Kumar. Indian, b. 1930. **Genres:** Economics, Money/Finance, Administration/Management. **Career:** Consultant in field, 1989-; Chairman, Examinations Committee, International Institute of Management Sciences, Calcutta, 1982-86; Institute of Cost and Works Accountants of India, and Ed. of the Institute's Bulletin, Tutor and Lecturer in Economics, 1965-70 and 1971-72; Assistant Director (Examinations), 1985-88, Assistant Director of Research, 1970-1985. Visiting Professor, Indian Institute of Management Calcutta, 1973-74; Assistant Teacher, Burdwan Town School, 1951; Postgraduate Research Fellow Dept. of Economics, University of Calcutta, 1952-55; Lect. in Economics and Commerce, Jaipuria College, University of Calcutta, 1955-56 and Research Assistant in Industrial Finance, Dept. of Economics, 1956-66, Calcutta University. **Publications:** Fiscal Problem of Growth with Stability, 1959; Fiscal Policy and Economic Growth: A Cross-Section Study, part I 1962, part II 1963; Monetary Policy of the Reserve Bank of India, 1964; Inflation and Price Control, 1975; Cost Accounting in Commercial Banking Industry, 1979; Management Accountants' Role in Monitoring Bank Financing, 1982; Introduction to Cost Accounting in Commercial Banking Industry, 1983; Fiscal Policy, Stability and Growth Experience and Problems of the Underdeveloped Economies, 1929-39 and 1945-65, 1990; Cost Accounting and Farm Product Costing, 1990. **Address:** 11500 Bucknell Dr., #3, Wheaton, MD 20902, U.S.A.

GIAMO, Benedict. American, b. 1954. **Genres:** Sociology. **Career:** University of Notre Dame, IN, assistant professor, 1990-97, associate professor of American studies, 1997-, department chair, 2000-. Doshisha University, Kyoto, Japan, visiting professor of American studies, 1993-95. **Publications:** On the Bowery: Confronting Homelessness in American Society, 1989; (with J. Grunberg) Beyond Homelessness: Frames of Reference, 1992; Kerouac, the Word and the Way: Prose Artist as Spiritual Quester, 2000; The Homeless of "Ironweed". **Address:** Dept of American Studies, University of Notre Dame, Notre Dame, IN 46556, U.S.A. **Online address:** giamo.1@nd.edu

GIAMPIERI-DEUTSCH, Patrizia. Italian. **Genres:** Ethics, Philosophy, Sciences. **Career:** University of Trieste, Italy, lecturer in ethics at Institute of Philosophy, 1986-93, visiting professor of theoretical philosophy, 1988-89, visiting professor of German literature at Institute of German Philology, 1989-90; University of Vienna, Austria, lecturer in ethics and contemporary philosophy, 1992-; Institute of Philosophy, assistant professor for ethics, 1997-98. **Publications:** (ed. with E. Brabant and E. Falzeder) The Correspondence of Sigmund Freud and Sandor Ferenczi, 3 vols., 1992-94; (ed. with A. Bokay and P.L. Rudnytsky) Ferenczi's Turn in Psychoanalysis, 1996; (ed.) Psychoanalyse im Dialog der Wissenschaften: Europaische Perspektiven, vol. 1, 2001; (ed.) Welche Forschung fur die Psychoanalyse?, 2001. Contributor to books and journals. **Address:** Univ-Doz, Olzeltgasse 1/3, A-1030 Vienna, Austria. **Online address:** Patrizia.Giampieri-Deutsch@univie.ac.at

GIANAKARIS, Constantine John. American, b. 1934. **Genres:** Literary criticism and history. **Career:** Illinois State University, Normal, Associate Professor of English, 1961-66; Western Michigan University, Kalamazoo, Associate Professor, 1966-72, Associate Dean, College of Arts and Sciences, 1979-82, Professor of English and Theatre, 1972. **Publications:** Plutarch, 1970; (and ed.) Foundations of Drama, 1974; Peter Shaffer, A Casebook, 1991; Peter Shaffer, 1992. EDITOR/CO-EDITOR: Antony and Cleopatra, 1969; Drama in the Middle Ages, 1984; Drama in the Twentieth Century, 1985; Drama in the Renaissance, 1985. **Address:** Dept of English, Western Michigan University, 1201 Oliver St, Kalamazoo, MI 49008-3805, U.S.A. **Online address:** gianakaris@wmich.edu

GIARDINELLI, Mempo. Argentine, b. 1947. **Genres:** Novels, Novellas/Short stories, Essays. **Career:** Fiction writer and essayist. Puro Cuento literary magazine, Buenos Aires, founder and editor; Premio Romulo Gallegos, 1993; Fundacion Mempo Giardinelli, Chaco Argentina, founder and director. **Publications:** NOVELS: La revolucion en bicicleta, 1980; El cielo con las manos, 1981; Luna caliente, 1983, trans. as Sultry Moon, 1998; Que solos se quedan los muertos, 1985; Santo Oficio de la Memoria, 1991; Imposible equilibrio, 1995; El Decimo Infierno, 1999, trans. as The Tenth Circle, 2001; Final de novela en Patagonia, 2000; Cuestiones interiores, 2003; Visitas despues de hora, 2003. SHORT STORIES: Vidas ejemplares, 1982; Antologia personal, 1987; El castigo de Dios, 1992; Cuentos Completos, 1999. ESSAYS: El genero Negro, 1984; Asi se escribe un cuento, 1992; El Pais de las maravillas, 1998; Los argentinos y sus intelectuales, 2005. Contributor to newspapers and magazines in Latin America and Europe. **Address:** Cacique

Nare 111, H3502BLC Resistencia, C1430 BEK Chaco, Argentina. **Online address:** mg47@fundamgiardinelli.org.ar; www.fundamgiardinelli.org.ar

GIBB, Lee. *See* **WATERHOUSE, Keith (Spencer).**

GIBB, Robert. American, b. 1946. **Genres:** Poetry. **Career:** Poet and creative writing and poetry instructor/professor. Cedar Crest College, 1978-87; Lehigh University, 1987; East Stroudsburg University, 1987-90; Mount Union College, 1990-93, Carnegie Mellon University, 1994-95; University of Pittsburgh, 1997-. **Publications:** Whale Songs, 1976; second ed. Whalesongs, 1979; The Margins, 1979; The Names of the Earth in Summer, 1983; The Winter House, 1984; Entering Time, 1986; A Geography of Common Names, 1987; Momentary Days, 1989; Fugue for a Late Snow, 1993; The Origins of Evening, 1998. Contributor to anthologies. Contributor of poems, short stories, essays, and reviews to periodicals. **Address:** 5036 Revenue Street, Homestead, PA 15120, U.S.A. **Online address:** gibb@gateway.net

GIBBONS, Anne R. American, b. 1947. **Genres:** Environmental sciences/Ecology. **Career:** ARG Editorial Services, Tuscaloosa, AL, proprietor, 1983-. **Publications:** (with W. Gibbons) Ecoviews: Snakes, Snails, and Environmental Tales, 1998. Contributor to Encyclopaedia Britannica. **Address:** 14 Hillcrest, Tuscaloosa, AL 35401-5922, U.S.A. **Online address:** argedit@comcast.net

GIBBONS, Gail (Gretchen). American, b. 1944. **Genres:** Children's fiction, Children's non-fiction. **Career:** WCIA-Television, Champaign, IL, artist, 1967-1969; WMAQ-TV, Chicago, promotions and animation artist, 1969; Bob Hower Agency, Chicago, staff artist, 1969-70; WNBC-Television, House of Animation, NYC, staff artist, 1970-76; freelance writer and illustrator of children's books, 1975-; United Press International, NYC, free-lance artist, 1977-. **Publications:** SELF-ILLUSTRATED FOR CHILDREN. NONFICTION: Things to Make and Do for Halloween, 1976; Things to Make and Do for Columbus Day, 1977; Things to Make and Do for Your Birthday, 1978; Clocks & How They Go, 1979; Lock and Keys, 1980; The Too-Great Bread Bake Book, 1980; Trucks, 1981; Christmas Time, 1982; The Post Office Book: Mail and How It Moves, 1982; Tool Book, 1982; Boat Book, 1983; New Road!, 1983; Sun Up, Sun Down, 1983; Thanksgiving Day, 1983; Department Store, 1984; Fire! Fire!, 1984; Halloween, 1984; The Seasons of Arnold's Apple Tree, 1984; Tunnels, 1984; Check It Out:, 1985; Fill It Up!, 1985; The Milk Makers, 1985; Playgrounds, 1985; Flying, 1986; From Path to Highway: The Story of the Boston Post Road, 1986; Happy Birthday!, 1986; Up Goes the Skyscraper!, 1986; Valentine's Day, 1986; Deadline!, 1987; Dinosaurs, 1987; Trains, 1987; Weather Forecasting, 1987; Zoo, 1987; Farming, 1988; Prehistoric Animals, 1988; Sunken Treasure, 1988; Catch the Wind!, 1989; Easter, 1989; Marge's Diner, 1989; Monarch Butterfly, 1989; Beacons of Light, 1990; How a House Is Built, 1990; Weather Words and What They Mean, 1990; From Seed to Plant, 1991; The Puffins Are Back!, 1991; Whales, 1991; The Great St. Lawrence Seaway, 1992; Recycle!, 1992; Sharks, 1992; Stargazers, 1992; Caves & Caverns, 1993; Frogs, 1993; Pirates: Robbers of the High Seas, 1993; The Planets, 1993; Puff-Flash-Bang!, 1993; Spiders, 1993; Christmas on an Island, 1994; Country Fair, 1994; Emergency!, 1994; Nature's Green Umbrella, 1994; St. Patrick's Day, 1994; Wolves, 1994; Bicycle Book, 1995; Knights in Shining Armor, 1995; Planet Earth/Inside Out, 1995; The Reasons for Seasons, 1995; Sea Turtles, 1995; Cats, 1996; Deserts, 1996; Dogs, 1996; Music Maker, 1996; Click!, 1997; Gulls...Gulls...Gulls..., 1997; The Honey Makers, 1997; The Moon Book, 1997; Paper, Paper Everywhere, 1997; Marshes & Swamps, 1998; Soaring with the Wind, 1998; Yippee-Yay!, 1998; Rabbits, Rabbits & More Rabbits, 2000; Apples, 2000; My Baseball Book, 2000; My Soccer Book, 2000; My Football Book, 2000; My Basketball Book, 2000; Ducks!, 2001; Polar Bears, 2001; Behold...the Unicorns!, 2001; The Berry Book, 2002; Halloween Is..., 2002; Giant Pandas, 2002; Tell Me Tree, 2002; Chicks & Chickens, 2003; Christmas Is..., 2003; Grizzly Bears, 2003; The Quilting Bee, 2004; Mummies, Pyramids & Pharaohs, 2004; Thanksgiving Is..., 2004. FICTION: Willie and His Wheel Wagon, 1975; Salvador and Mister Sam, 1976; The Missing Maple Syrup Sap Mystery, 1979; The Magnificent Morris Mouse Clubhouse, 1981. Illustrator of books by J. Yolen, J. Cole.

GIBBONS, Reginald. American, b. 1947. **Genres:** Novels, Novellas/Short stories, Poetry, Literary criticism and history. **Career:** Writer. Princeton University, Princeton, NJ, lecturer in creative writing, 1976-80; Northwestern University, Evanston, IL, professor of English, 1981-, member of core faculty for MFA Program for Writers at Warren Wilson College, 1989-. **Publications:** William Goyen: A Study of the Short Fiction, 1991; Five Pears or Peaches: Stories, 1991; Sweetbitter: A Novel, 1994. TRANSLATOR: Selected Poems of Luis Cernuda, 1978; (with A.L. Geist) Guillen on Guillen, 1979; (with C. Segal) Euripides, Bakkhai, 2001; (with C. Segal) Sophokles, Anti-

gone, 2003. POETRY: Roofs Voices Roads, 1979; The Ruined Motel, 1981; Saints, 1986; Maybe It Was So, 1991; Sparrow: New and Selected Poems, 1997; Homage to Longshot O'Leary: Poems, 1999; It's Time, 2003; In the Warhouse, 2004. EDITOR: The Poet's Work, 1979, reprinted, 1989; (with G. Graff) Criticism in the University, 1985; The Writer in Our World, 1986; W. Goyen, Had I a Hundred Mouths: New and Selected Stories, 1947-1983, 1986; New Writing from Mexico, 1992; (with T. Des Pres) Thomas McGrath: Life and the Poem, 1992; (author of afterword) W. Goyen, Half a Look of Cain: A Fantastical Narrative, 1994; W. Goyen, The House of Breath, 1999. Contributor to periodicals. **Address:** Dept of English, 215 University Hall, Northwestern University, Evanston, IL 60208, U.S.A.

GIBBS, Anthony Matthews. Australian, b. 1933. **Genres:** History, Humanities, Intellectual history, Literary criticism and history, Biography. **Career:** Rhodes Scholar, 1956; Fellow, 1982-, Ed. and Council Member, 1988-93, Australian Acad. of the Humanities (Vice-President, 1988-89). Lecturer in English, 1960-66, and Ed. with K.B. Magarey, Southern Review, 1963-64, University of Adelaide; Lecturer, University of Leeds, 1966-69; Professor of English and Head of Dept., University of Newcastle, NSW, 1969-75; Professor of English, 1975-98, and Emeritus Professor, 1998-, Macquarie University, NSW. **Publications:** Shaw, 1969; (ed.) Sir William Davenant: The Shorter Poems, and Songs from the Plays and Masques, 1972; The Art and Mind of Shaw, 1983; Shaw: Interviews and Recollections, 1990; Bernard Shaw: Man and Superman and Saint Joan: A Casebook, 1992; Heartbreak House: Preludes of Apocalypse, 1994; A Bernard Shaw Chronology, 2001; Bernard Shaw: A Life, 2005. **Address:** Department of English, Macquarie University, Sydney, NSW 2109, Australia. **Online address:** tony.gibbs@mq.edu.au

GIBBS, David N. American/German, b. 1958. **Genres:** Politics/Government. **Career:** U.S. Peace Corps, Washington, DC, volunteer English teacher at a high school in rural Niger, 1979-80; U.S. Department of Commerce, Washington, DC, foreign affairs assistant and head of Africa/Middle East desk at foreign fisheries analysis division, 1981-82; University of Wisconsin-Madison, MacArthur post doctoral fellow, 1989-90; University of Arizona, Tucson, assistant professor of political science, 1990-96, associate professor, 1996-2003, associate professor of history and political science, 2003-; Udall Center for Studies in Public Policy, research fellow, 1998, and member of center of Middle East studies. **Publications:** The Political Economy of Third World Intervention: Mines, Money, and U.S. Policy in the Congo Crisis, 1991. Work represented in anthologies. Contributor to political science journals, periodicals and newspapers. **Address:** Dept of History, 215 Social Sciences, University of Arizona, Tucson, AZ 85721, U.S.A. **Online address:** dgibbs@arizona.edu

GIBBS, Tyson. American. **Genres:** Anthropology/Ethnology. **Career:** Dartmouth College, Hanover, NH, assistant museum curator and computer programmer for School of Medicine, 1971-73; Baylor College of Medicine, Houston, TX, data clerk at Institute of Clinical Toxicology, 1974-75; North Central Florida Community Mental Health Center, Gainesville, research assistant, 1975-76, research coordinator, 1976-78; University of South Carolina at Columbia, instructor, 1980-81, assistant professor of preventive medicine and adjunct assistant professor of anthropology, 1981-83; Meharry Medical College, Nashville, TN, assistant professor of preventive dentistry and associate director of Center on Aging, 1983-87; Georgia State University, Atlanta, assistant professor of anthropology, 1991-92; West Georgia College, Carrollton, associate professor of sociology, 1992-93; Emory University, Atlanta, assistant professor of clinical medicine at Geriatric Center, 1993-94; University of North Texas, Denton, assistant professor, 1995-97, associate professor of anthropology, 1998-. **Publications:** (with P. Gibbs) Horsman Dolls, 1985, rev. ed., 1988; (with P. Gibbs) The Collector's Encyclopedia of Black Dolls, 1987, rev. ed., 1990; (with P. Gibbs) Black Collectibles Sold in America, 1987, rev. ed., 2000; Ethnic Health Collections in the United States: A Guide to Repositories, 1995; A Guide to Ethnic Health Collections in the United States, 1996; (with A. Frishkey) Guide to Resources in Ethnic Studies on Minority Populations, 2000. Contributor to books, professional journals, and popular magazines. **Address:** Dept of Anthropology, University of North Texas, PO Box 310409, Denton, TX 76203, U.S.A. **Online address:** Theone@up2me.com; TGibbs@scs.cmm.unt.edu

GIBLON, Shirley T(enhouse). Canadian, b. 1935. **Genres:** Education, Self help. **Career:** Children's Aid Society of Metropolitan Toronto, Toronto, Ontario, social worker, 1956-59; worked as business executive; writer. Volunteer worker for Art Gallery of Ontario, Jewish Welfare Board, Jewish Vocational Service, Jewish Home for the Aged, and local political candidates; husband's orthodontic practice, manager, currently. **Publications:** (with H. Narrol) The Fourth "R": Uncovering Hidden Learning Potential, 1984; (with B.

Schlesinger) Lasting Marriages, 1984, 2nd ed, 1985; (with B. Schlesinger) Postponed Parenthood, 1985. **Address:** 53 Montressor Dr, Toronto, ON, Canada M2P 1Z3.

GIBRAN, Daniel K. Guyanese, b. 1945. **Genres:** Military/Defense/Arms control. **Career:** Planning Institute of Jamaica, Kingston, senior political economist, 1987-90; Shaw University, Raleigh, NC, assistant professor to associate professor, 1991-96; Tennessee State University, Nashville, professor, 1996-. Raleigh Seventh-Day Adventist Church, religious liberty leader, 1992-95; Nashville First Seventh-Day Adventist Church, religious liberty leader, 1998-2000. **Publications:** The Exclusion of Black Soldiers from the Medal of Honor, 1997; The Falklands War: Britain versus the Past in the South Atlantic, 1998; Leadership and Courage: A Brief History of the All-Black 92nd Infantry Division in Italy during WWII, 2001. **Address:** Tennessee State University, 3500 John Merritt Blvd., Nashville, TN 37209, U.S.A. **Online address:** dgibran@tnstate.edu

GIBSON, A(lex) J. S. Chinese, b. 1958. **Genres:** History. **Career:** University of Exeter, Exeter, England, lecturer in historical geography, 1989-. **Publications:** (with T.C. Smout) Prices, Food, and Wages in Scotland, 1550-1780, 1995. **Address:** Department of Geography, Amory Bldg., University of Exeter, Exeter, Devon EX4 4RJ, England.

GIBSON, Ann Eden. American, b. 1944. **Genres:** Art/Art history. **Career:** Art teacher at public schools in Wooster, OH, 1966-69; Kent State University, Kent, OH, adjunct instructor in studio art, 1969-72; Akron State University, adjunct instructor, 1970-72; Art Institute of Pittsburgh, PA, studio instructor in design and drawing, 1972-75; Point Park College, Pittsburgh, assistant professor of art history and studio art, 1975-79; University of Pittsburgh, adjunct instructor in art history, 1979; University of Delaware, Newark, adjunct instructor in art history, 1980-81, professor of art history and chairperson of department, 1998-2003; Yale University, New Haven, CT, lecturer, 1982-84, assistant professor, 1984-87, associate professor of art history, 1987-90, Morse fellow, 1987-88, senior faculty fellow, 1990-91; State University of New York at Stony Brook, associate professor of art history, 1991-98, acting department head, 1993-94, associate director of Humanities Institute, 1995-98. Lecturer: University of Pittsburgh, 1994; Walker Art Center, 1996; Rhodes College, 1997; Tulane University, 1998; lecturer at educational institutions. **Publications:** Issues in Abstract Expressionism: The Artist-Run Periodicals, 1990; Abstract Expressionism: Other Politics, 1997; (with M. Scala) Judith Godwin: Style and Grace, 1997; (with D. Veneciano) Norman Lewis: The Black Paintings, 1946-1977, 1998. Contributor to exhibition catalogs. Contributor to books and periodicals. **Address:** Dept of Art History, University of Delaware, Newark, DE 19716, U.S.A. **Online address:** agibson@udel.edu

GIBSON, Charles E(dmund). See Obituaries.

GIBSON, Ian. Spanish/Irish, b. 1939. **Genres:** History, Biography. **Career:** Writer. **Publications:** The Assassination of Federico Garcia Lorca, 1973, 1979 (Prix Internationale de la Presse, 1971); The English Vice: Beating, Sex and Shame in Victorian England and After, 1978; Federico Garcia Lorca, 1989. **Address:** c/o Faber and Faber Ltd. Publishers, 3 Queen Sq, London WC1N 3AU, England.

GIBSON, Jo. See FLUKE, Joanne.

GIBSON, Margaret. American, b. 1944. **Genres:** Poetry. **Career:** Madison College, Harrisonburg, VA, 1967-68; Virginia Commonwealth University, 1968-70; George Mason University, 1970-75; Connecticut College, 1976-77; Phillips Academy, Andover, writer in residence, 1984-87; University of Connecticut, visiting professor, 1992-. **Publications:** POETRY COLLECTIONS: Signs, 1979; Long Walks in the Afternoon, 1982; Memories of the Future: The Daybooks of Tina Modotti, 1986; Out in the Open. 1989; The Vigil: A Poem in Four Voices, 1993; Earth Elegy: New and Selected Poems, 1997; Icon and Evidence, 2001; Autumn Grasses, 2003. OTHER: The Duel (chapbook), 1966; Lunes (chapbook), 1972; On the Cutting Edge (chapbook), 1975; (ed. with others) Landscape and Distance: Contemporary Poets from Virginia, 1975. **Address:** 154 Watson Rd, Preston, CT 06365, U.S.A.

GIBSON, Mary Ellis. American, b. 1952. **Genres:** Literary criticism and history. **Career:** Literary scholar and editor of fiction and nonfiction works; University of North Carolina, Greensboro, professor of English. **Publications:** History and the Prism of Art: Browning's Poetic Experiments, 1987; Epic Reinvented: Ezra Pound and the Victorians, 1995. EDITOR: New Stories by Southern Women, 1989; Homeplaces: Stories of the South by Women Writers, 1991; Critical Essays on Robert Browning, 1992. **Address:** c/o Cornell University Press, 512 East State St., Ithaca, NY 14850, U.S.A.

GIBSON, Miles. British, b. 1947. **Genres:** Novels, Poetry. **Publications:** The Guilty Bystander, 1970; Permanent Damage, 1973; The Sandman, 1984; Dancing with Mermaids, 1985; Vinegar Soup, 1987; Kingdom Swann, 1990; Fascinated, 1993; Say Hello to the Buffalo (poems for children), 1994; The Prisoner of Meadow Bank, 1995; Mr Romance, 2002; Little Archie (children's fiction), 2004; Einstein (novel), 2004. **Address:** c/o Jonathan Clowes, Iron Bridge House, Bridge Approach, London NW1 8BD, England.

GIBSON, Robert. British, b. 1927. **Genres:** Literary criticism and history, Biography. **Career:** Professor of French, University of Kent at Canterbury, 1965-94. Assistant Lecturer, University of St. Andrews, 1954-55; Lecturer, Queen's College, Dundee, 1955-58, and Aberdeen University, 1958-61; Professor of French, Queen's University, Belfast, 1961-65. **Publications:** The Quest of Alain-Fournier, 1953; Roger Martin du Gard; (comp.) Modern French Poets on Poetry, 1961; The Land without a Name, 1975; Annals of Ashdon, 1988; Best of Enemies, 1995, new ed., 2004; The End of Youth, 2005. EDITOR: C. Aveline: Brouart et Le Desordre, 1962; J. Giraudoux: Provinciales, 1965; Alain-Fournier: Le Grand Meaulnes, 1968; Studies in French Fiction, 1988. **Address:** Thalassa, Cliff Rd, Sidmouth, Devon, England.

GIBSON, Walter Samuel. American, b. 1932. **Genres:** Art/Art history, Bibliography. **Career:** Case Western Reserve University, Cleveland, assistant professor, 1966-71, acting chairman, 1970-71, associate professor, 1971-78, chairman, 1971-79, Mellon Professor of the Humanities, 1978-97; Williams College, Williamstown, MA, Clark Visiting Professor of Art History, 1989, 1992. **Publications:** Hieronymus Bosch, 1973; The Paintings of Cornelis Engebrechtsz, 1977; Bruegel, 1977; Hieronymus Bosch: An Annotated Bibliography, 1983; "Mirror of the Earth," The World Landscape in 16th Century Flemish Painting, 1989; Pieter Bruegel the Elder: Two Studies, 1991; Pleasant Places: The Rustic Landscape from Bruegel to Ruisdael, 2000. **Address:** 938 Mason Hill Rd N, Pownal, VT 05261-9767, U.S.A. **Online address:** wsgibson@together.net

GIDDENS, Anthony. British, b. 1938. **Genres:** Social work. **Career:** University of Leicester, Leicester, England, lecturer in sociology, 1961-70; Simon Fraser University, Vancouver, visiting assistant professor, 1967-68; University of California, Los Angeles, visiting assistant professor, 1968-69; King's College, Cambridge, lecturer in sociology, 1970-84, reader in sociology, 1984-86, professor of sociology, 1986-97; London School of Economics, director, 1997-. Polity Press Ltd., dhairman and director, 1985-; Blackwell-Polity Ltd., director, 1985-; Centre for Social Research, chairman and director, 1989-; Institute for Public Policy Research, trustee; University of Leicester, member of the court. Visiting professor or lecturer at universities worldwide. **Publications:** Positivism and Sociology, 1974; New Rules of Sociological Method: A Positive Critique of Interpretative Sociologies, 1976; Studies in Social and Political Theory, 1977; Durkheim, 1978; Emile Durkheim, 1979; Central Problems in Social Theory: Action, Structure, and Contradiction in Social Analysis, 1979; The Class Structure of the Advanced Societies, 1981; A Contemporary Critique of Historical Materialism, 1981; Sociology, a Brief but Critical Introduction, 1982; Profiles and Critiques in Social Theory, 1982; Social Class and the Division of Labour: Essays in Honour of Ilya Neustadt, 1982; Classes, Power, and Conflict: Classical and Contemporary Debates, 1982; The Constitution of Society: Outline of the Theory of Structuration, 1984; Durkheim on Politics and the State, 1986; Social Theory Today, 1987; Sociology, A Brief but Critical Introduction, 1987; Social Theory and Modern Sociology, 1987; The Consequences of Modernity, 1990; Modernity and Self-Identity: Self and Society in the Late Modern Age, 1991; Test-item File: Introduction of Sociology, 1991; Readings and Study Guide: Introduction of Sociology, 1991; Human Societies: An Introductory Reader in Sociology, 1992; The Transformation of Intimacy: Sexuality, Love and Eroticism in Modern Societies, 1992; New Rules of Sociological Method: A Positive Critique of Interpretative Sociologies, 1993; The Giddens Reader, 1993; Reflexive Modernization: Politics, Tradition and Aesthetics in the Modern Social Order, 1994; Beyond Left and Right: The Future of Radical Politics, 1994; Politics, Sociology and Social Theory: Encounters with Classical and Contemporary Social Thought, 1995; A Contemporary Critique of Historical Materialism, 1995; In Defence of Sociology: Essays, Interpertations, and Rejoinders, 1996. **Address:** London School of Economics, Houghton Street, London WC2A 2AE, England.

GIDDING, Nelson. See Obituaries.

GIENOW-HECHT, Jessica C. E. (born Germany), b. 1964. **Genres:** History. **Career:** University of Bielefeld, Bielefeld, Germany, postdoctoral fellow in history, 1995-96; Martin-Luther-University, Halle-Wittenberg, Germany, deputy director of Center for U.S. Studies, 1996-99; Harvard University, Cambridge, MA, John F. Kennedy fellow at Center for European Studies, 1999-2000, fellow at Charles Warren Center for Studies in American History, 2000-02, lecturer in History and Literature Program, 2002-. Worked as a trainee in journalism and advertising and as a clerk at a winery in Bordeaux, France. **Publications:** Transmission Impossible: American Journalism as Cultural Diplomacy in Postwar Germany, 1945-1955, 1999; (editor, with Frank Schumacher) Culture and International History, 2003. Contributor to periodicals. **Address:** Charles Warren Center for Studies in American History, Emerson Hall, Harvard University, Cambridge, MA 02138, U.S.A. **Online address:** gienow@fas.harvard.edu

GIER, Scott G. American. **Genres:** Science fiction/Fantasy. **Career:** Science fiction author. **Publications:** Genellan: Planetfall, 1995; Genellan: In the Shadow of the Moon, 1996; Genellan: First Victory, 1997. **Address:** c/o Ballantine, 201 E. 50 St., New York, NY 10022, U.S.A. **Online address:** scott@genellan.com

GIERSCH, Herbert. German, b. 1921. **Genres:** Economics. **Career:** OEEC Secretariat, Paris, France, administrator, 1950-51, counsellor, 1953-54; University of Muenster, Germany, lecturer, 1951-55; Saar University, Saarbruecken, Germany, professor of economics, 1955-69; University of Kiel, Germany, professor of economics and president of the Kiel Institut fuer Weltwirtschaft (Institute of World Economics), 1969-89, emeritus, 1989-. German Federal Ministry of Economics, member of advisory council, 1960-; German Council of Economic Advisors, founding member, 1964-70; author. **Publications:** Das Ausgleich der Kriegslasten vom Standpunkt sozialer Gerechtigkeit, 1948; Algemeuie Wirtschaftspolitik (title means: Economic Policy), 1967; Growth, Cycles, and Exchange Rates: The Experience of West Germany, 1970; Kontroverse Fragen der Wirtschaftspolitik (Controversial Issues in Economic Policymaking), 1971; Konjurktur-und Wachsturmspolitik in der offenen Wirtschaft (Business Cycle and Growth Policy in an Open Economy), 1977; The World Economy in Perspective: Essays on International Trade and European Integration, 1991; (with K.-H. Paque and H. Schmieding) The Fading Miracle: Four Decades of Market Economy in Germany, 1992; Openness for Prosperity: Essays in World Economics, 1993. EDITOR: (with K.H. Frank) Gegen Europessimismus: Kritische Beitrage 1977 bis 1985 (Countering Euro-Pessimism: Critical Essays from 1977 to 1985), 1977; (with Frank) Im Brennpunkt: Wirtschaftspolitik: Kritische Beitrage 1967 bis 1977 (Focus on Economic Policymaking: Critical Essays from 1967 to 1977), 1978; Wie es zu schaffen ist: Agenda fuer die deutsche Wirtschaftspolitik (New Directions in the Economy: An Agenda for German Economic Policymaking), 1983; The International Debt Problem: Lessons for the Future, 1987. Editor of collections of essays and papers on international and European economic issues. **Address:** Institut fur Weltwirtschaft, 24100 Kiel, Germany.

GIFALDI, David. American, b. 1950. **Genres:** Children's fiction, Young adult fiction. **Career:** Bellingham School District, Bellingham, WA, and Vancouver School District, Vancouver, WA, substitute teacher, 1980-83; Vancouver School District, teacher, 1985-. **Publications:** NOVELS: One Thing for Sure, 1986; Yours till Forever, 1989; Gregory, Maw, and the Mean One, 1992; Toby Scudder, Ultimate Warrior, 1993. OTHER: The Boy Who Spoke Colors (an original folktale), 1993; Rearranging and Other Stories (short stories), 1998; Ben, King of the River (picture book), 2001. Contributor to periodicals for children and young adults. **Address:** 4305 NE Skidmore St, Portland, OR 97218, U.S.A.

GIFFORD, Barry (Colby). American, b. 1946. **Genres:** Novels, Novellas/Short stories, Poetry, Autobiography/Memoirs, Biography, Essays, Graphic Novels. **Career:** Writer. **Publications:** POETRY: The Blood of the Parade, 1967; Coyote Tantras, 1973; Persimmons, 1976; The Boy You Have Always Loved, 1976; A Quinzaine in Return for a Portrait of Mary Sun, 1977; Horse Hauling Timber out of Hokkaido Forest, 1978; Lives of the French Impressionist Painters, 1978; Snail Hut, 1978; Beautiful Phantoms, 1981; Ghosts No Horse Can Carry, 1989; Flaubert at Key West, 1997; Replies to Wang Wei, 2001; Las cuatro reinas (& photos), 2001; Back in America, 2004. STORIES: A Boy's Novel, 1973; Francis Goes to the Seashore, 1982; The Wild Life of Sailor and Lula (novellas), 1996; American Falls, 2002; Do the Blind Dream?, 2004. NOVELS: Landscape with Traveler, 1980; Port Tropique, 1980; Wild at Heart: The Story of Sailor and Lula, 1990; Sailor's Holiday, 1991; Night People, 1992; Arise and Walk, 1994; Baby Cat-Face, 1995; Perdita Durango, 1996, as graphic novel, 1995; Wyoming, 2000. ESSAYS: Kerouac's Town, 1973; Out of the Past, 2001. MEMOIRS: The Neighborhood of Baseball, 1981; The Phantom Father, 1997. OTHER: (trans.) Selected Poems of Francis Jammes, 1976; (ed.) The Portable Curtis:

Selected Writings of Edward S. Curtis, 1976; Living in Advance, 1976; (ed.) As Ever: The Collected Correspondence of Allen Ginsberg and Neal Cassady, 1977; (co-author) Jack's Book: An Oral Biography of Jack Kerouac, 1978; (co-author) Saroyan: A Biography, 1984; A Day at the Races, 1988; The Devil Thumbs a Ride and Other Unforgettable Films, 1988; Giotto's Circle, 1988; Hotel Room Trilogy (plays), 1995; (with D. Lynch) Lost Highway (screenplay), 1997; (and photos) Bordertown, 1998; The Rooster Trapped in the Reptile Room, 2003; Brando Rides Alone, 2004. **Address:** c/o Curtis Brown Ltd, 10 Astor Place, New York, NY 10003, U.S.A. **Online address:** www.barrygifford.com

GIFFORD, James J. American, b. 1946. **Genres:** Film, Gay and lesbian issues, Literary criticism and history. **Career:** Mohawk Valley Community College, Utica, NY, professor of humanities, 1972-. **Publications:** Dayneford's Library: American Homosexual Writing, 1900-1913, 1995; (ed.) E. PrimeStevenson, Imre: A Memorandum, 2002. **Address:** Mohawk Valley Community College, Utica, NY 13501, U.S.A. **Online address:** jgifford@mvcc.edu

GIGLIO, James N. American, b. 1939. **Genres:** History, Bibliography, Biography. **Career:** U.S. Army Intelligence, officer, 1962-63; M. O'Neil Co., Akron, OH, assistant buyer, 1964-65; Southwest Missouri State University, Springfield, professor of history, 1968-, university distinguished scholar, 1988-98, university fellow in research, 1999-2001, university distinguished professor, 2000-. Missouri Conference on History, coordinator, 1972; Mid-America Conference on History, originator and coordinator, 1977-79, 1987; Missouri State Historical Records Board, member, 1985-87; Presidential Studies Quarterly, editorial board member, 1993-99. **Publications:** H.M. Daugherty and the Politics of Expediency, 1978; (with G.G. Thielen) Truman in Cartoon and Caricature, 1984; The Presidency of John F. Kennedy, 1991; John F. Kennedy: A Bibliography, 1995; Musial: From Stash to Stan the Man, 2001; (with S.G. Rabe) Debating the Kennedy Presidency, 2003. Work represented in anthologies. Contributor of articles and reviews to history journals. **Address:** Department of History, Southwest Missouri State University, 901 S National, Springfield, MO 65804-0089, U.S.A. **Online address:** jng89of@mail.smsu.edu

GIL, David Georg. American (born Austria), b. 1924. **Genres:** Social sciences, Social work. **Career:** Brandeis University, Waltham, MA, assistant professor, 1964-66, associate professor, 1966-69, professor of social policy, 1969-, director, Social Policy Study Program, 1969-73, director, Center for Social Change (Practice and Theory), 1983-2002, faculty senate, chair, 1989-92, board of trustees, faculty representative, 1990-94. **Publications:** Violence against Children: Physical Child Abuse in the United States, 1970-73; Unravelling Social Policy, Theory, Analysis, and Political Action toward Social Equality, 1973, 5th ed., 1992; The Challenge of Social Equality, 1976; Beyond the Jungle, 1979; Confronting Injustice and Oppression, 1998. EDITOR: Child Abuse and Violence, 1979; (with E.A. Gil) Toward Social and Economic Justice, 1985; (with E.A. Gil) The Future of Work, 1987. **Address:** Heller Graduate School, Brandeis University, Waltham, MA 02454-9110, U.S.A. **Online address:** gil@brandeis.edu

GIL, Moshe. Israeli (born Poland), b. 1921. **Genres:** History, Humanities. **Career:** Imprisoned in concentration camp during World War II and released in 1944; member of Kibbutz Reshafim, Bet Shean Valley, Palestine, 1945; Tel Aviv University, Israel, associate professor, 1974-80, professor, 1980-, dean of humanities, 1986-89. **Publications:** Documents of the Jewish Pious Foundations, 1976; The Tustaris (in Hebrew), 1981; Palestine during the First Muslim Period (in Hebrew), 1983; A History of Palestine, 634-1099, trans. by E. Broido, 1992; Jews in Islamic Countries in the Middle Ages (in Hebrew). **Address:** Carter Building, Tel Aviv University, PO Box 39040, 69978 Tel Aviv, Israel.

GILB, Dagoberto. American, b. 1950. **Genres:** Novels. **Career:** Los Angeles County, certified journeyman carpenter, 1976-91. University of Texas, Austin, Department of English, visiting fiction writer, 1988; University of Arizona, Tucson, Department of English, creative writing program, visiting writer, 1992; University of Wyoming, Laramie, Department of English, visiting writer, 1994. **Publications:** Winners on the Pass Line, 1985; The Magic of Blood, 1993; The Last Known Residence of Mickey Acuna, 1994; Woodcuts of Women, 2001; Gritos, 2003. Contributor of short stories and articles to magazines and anthologies. **Address:** Department of English, Southwest Texas State University, 601 University Dr, San Marcos, TX 78666-4685, U.S.A.

GILBERT, Alan (Graham). British, b. 1944. **Genres:** Area studies, Geography, Regional/Urban planning, Urban studies. **Career:** Professor of

Geography at University College London, 1970-. **Publications:** Latin American Development: A Geographical Perspective, 1974; (with J. Gugler) Cities, Poverty, and Development, 1982; (with P. Ward) Housing, the State, and the Poor, 1985; (with P. Healey) The Political Economy of Land, 1985; Latin America, 1990; (with A. Varley) Landlord and Tenant, 1991; In Search of a Home, 1993; The Latin American City, 1994. EDITOR: Development Planning and Spatial Structure, 1976; The Mega-city in Latin America, 1996. **Address:** Dept. of Geography, University College, 26 Bedford Way, London WC1H 0AP, England. **Online address:** agilbert@geog.ucl.ac.uk

GILBERT, Alma M. Mexican, b. 1937. **Genres:** Art/Art history. **Career:** Children's Asthma Research Center, Denver, CO, head of clinical laboratory, 1967-70; La Galeria (art gallery), San Mateo, CA, director, 1970-78; Maxfield Parrish Museum, Plainfield, NH, director, 197885; Alma Gilbert Galleries, Burlingame, CA, director, 1986-93; Cornish Colony Museum, Cornish, NH, director, 1998-. **Publications:** Maxfield Parrish: The Masterworks, 1992-96; The Make Believe World of Maxfield Parrish, 1994; A Treasury of Art in Children's Literature, 1995; Maxfield Parrish: The Landscapes, 1998; A Place of Beauty, 1999. **Address:** PO Box 63, Plainfield, NH 03781, U.S.A. **Online address:** agilbert@best.com

GILBERT, Anna. (Marguerite Lazarus). British, b. 1916. **Genres:** Romance/Historical. **Career:** Grammar sch. English teacher, 1938-73. **Publications:** Images of Rose, 1974; The Look of Innocence, 1975; A Family Likeness, 1977; Remembering Louise, 1978; The Leavetaking, 1979; Flowers for Lilian, 1980; Miss Bede Is Staying, 1982; The Long Shadow, 1984; A Walk in the Wood, 1989; The Wedding Guest, 1993; The Treachery of Time, 1995.

GILBERT, Barbara Snow. American, b. 1954. **Genres:** Novels, Young adult fiction. **Career:** Attorney, mediator, and writer. Lawyer in Oklahoma City, OK, 1980-; mediator, Oklahoma City, 1994-2001; law clerk to U.S. District Court Judge, 2001-. **Publications:** Stone Water, 1996; Broken Chords, 1998; Paper Trail, 2000. **Address:** 1121 Fenwick Pl, Oklahoma City, OK 73116, U.S.A. **Online address:** bsnowgilbert@cox.net

GILBERT, Bentley Brinkerhoff. American, b. 1924. **Genres:** History. **Career:** Professor of History, since 1967, and Chairman of the Dept., 1988-91, University of Illinois at Chicago (Associate Dean of Graduate College, 1971-72). Executive Secretary, National Conference on British Studies; Ed., Journal of British Studies. Associate Professor, Dept. of History, Colorado College, Colorado Springs, 1955-67; Midwest Conferemce on British Studies, president, 1989-91. **Publications:** The Evolution of National Insurance in Great Britain, 1966; Britain since 1918, 1967, 1995; British Social Policy, 1914-1939, 1971; The Heart of the Empire, 1973; David Lloyd George: A Political Life, vol. I, The Architect of Change, 1987, vol. II, The Organizer of Victory, 1992; Britain, 1914-1945, 1995. **Address:** 830-D Forest Ave, Evanston, IL 60202, U.S.A.

GILBERT, Bil. American, b. 1927. **Genres:** Natural history. **Career:** Journalist, historian, naturalist, and writer. **Publications:** Bears in the Ladies' Room, and Other Beastly Pursuits, 1966; How Animals Communicate (juvenile), 1966; The Weasels: A Sensible Look at a Family of Predators (juvenile), 1970; Chulo, 1973, as Chulo: A Year among the Coatimundis, 1984; (text) The Trailblazers, 1973; Westering Man: The Life of Joseph Walker, 1983; In God's Countries, 1984; Our Nature, 1986; God Gave Us This Country: Tekamthi and the First American Civil War, 1989; Natural Coincidence, 2004. **Address:** 700 Iron Springs Rd, Fairfield, PA 17320, U.S.A.

GILBERT, Creighton Eddy. American, b. 1924. **Genres:** Art/Art history, Translations. **Career:** Professor Emeritus, Yale University, New Haven, CT, 2000- (Professor of History of Art, 1981-2000). Associate Professor, 1961-65, and Sidney and Ellen Wien Professor of the History of Art, 1965-69, Brandeis University, Waltham, MA; Professor of the History of Art, Queens College of the City University of New York, 1969-77; Jacob Gould Schurman Professor of History of Art, Cornell University, Ithaca, NY, 1977-81. Ed., Art Bulletin, 1980-85. **Publications:** (trans.) Complete Poems and Selected Letters of Michelangelo, 1963; Michelangelo, 1967; Change in Piero della Francesca, 1968; History of Renaissance Art, 1972; (ed.) Italian Art 1400-1500: Sources and Documents, 1980; The Works of Girolamo Savoldo, 1986; Poets Seeing Artists' Work: Instances in the Italian Renaissance, 1991; Michelangelo on and off the Sistine Ceiling, 1994; Piero della Francesca et Giorgione; Problemes d'Interpretation, 1994; Caravaggio and His Two Cardinals, 1995; The Saints' Three Reasons for Paintings in Churches, 2001; How Fra Angelico and Signorelli Saw the End of the World, 2002. **Address:** Dept of History of Art, Box 208272, Yale University, New Haven, CT 06520, U.S.A.

GILBERT, Elizabeth. American, b. 1969. **Genres:** Novellas/Short stories. **Career:** Short story writer. **Publications:** Pilgrims, 1997. **Address:** c/o Houghton Mifflin, 222 Berkeley St., Boston, MA 02116, U.S.A.

GILBERT, Frances. See **COLLINGS, Gillian.**

GILBERT, Glenn G(ordon). American, b. 1936. **Genres:** Language/Linguistics. **Career:** University of Texas, Austin, Instructor to Assistant Professor in Germanic Languages, 1963-70; Southern Illinois University, Carbondale, Professor of Linguistics, German, and Anthropology, 1970-, Chair of the Linguistics Dept., 1987-89, 1999-2002. Journal of Pidgin and Creole Languages, Founder and Ed., 1986-2001. **Publications:** Linguistic Atlas of Texas German, 1972. EDITOR: Texas Studies in Bilingualism: Thirteen Studies of Romance, Germanic, and Slavic Immigrant Languages Spoken in Texas, Louisiana, and Oklahoma, 1970; The German Language in America, 1971; (co) Problems in Applied Educational Sociolinguistics: Readings on Language and Culture Problems of United States Ethnic Groups, 1974; (and trans.) Pidgin and Creole Languages: Selected Essays of Hugo Schuchardt, 1980; Pidgin and Creole Languages: Essays in Memory of John E. Reinecke, 1987; Pidgin and Creole Linguistics in the 21st Century, 2002. **Address:** 166 Union Grove Rd, Carbondale, IL 62903-7687, U.S.A. **Online address:** glennggilbert@msn.com; ggilbert@siu.edu

GILBERT, Harriett. British, b. 1948. **Genres:** Novels, Communications/Media. **Career:** New Statesman, London, literary editor, 1986-88; BBC World Service, Meridian Books, presenter, 1991-2003, The Word, presenter, 2003-; City University, London, lecturer in journalism, 1992-2004, director of MA programme in creative writing, 2004-. **Publications:** I Know Where I've Been, 1972; Hotels with Empty Rooms, 1973; An Offence against the Persons, 1974; Tide Race, 1977; Running Away, 1979; The Riding Mistress, 1983; A Women's History of Sex, 1987; (ed.) Fetishes, Florentine Girdles and Other Explorations into the Sexual Imagination, 1993; (co-author) Writing for Journalists, 1999. **Address:** Dept of Journalism and Publishing, City University, Northampton Sq, London EC1V 0HB, England. **Online address:** h.s.gilbert@city.ac.uk

GILBERT, John Raphael. British, b. 1926. **Genres:** Adult non-fiction, Art/Art history, Dance/Ballet, Film, Food and Wine, History, Homes/Gardens, Music, Natural history, Theatre, Travel/Exploration, Zoology, Biography, Translations. **Publications:** Modern World Book of Animals, 1947; Cats, Cats, Cats, 1961; Famous Jewish Lives, 1970; Myths of Ancient Rome, 1970; Pirates and Buccaneers, 1971; Highwaymen and Outlaws, 1971; Charting the Vast Pacific, 1971; National Costumes of the World, 1972; Miracles of Nature, 1975; Knights of the Crusades, 1978; Vikings, 1978; Prehistoric Man, 1978; Dinosaurs Discovered, 1980; Macdonald Encyclopedia of House Plants, 1986; Theory and Use of Colour, 1986; Macdonald Encyclopedia of Roses, 1987; Gardens of Britain, 1987; Trekking, USA, 1989; Trekking, Europe, 1990; Macdonald Encyclopedia of Herbs and Spices, 1990; Macdonald Encyclopedia of Bonsai, 1990; Macdonald Encyclopedia of Saltwater Fishes, 1994; Macdonald Encyclopedia of Climbing Plants, 1994; Prague Castle, 1994; Sevres Pottery, 1996; Caravaggio, 1998; Bosch, 1998; Leonardo da Vinci, 1999; Velasquez, 1999; Tortoises and Turtles, 2001; Sharks, 2001. TRANSLATOR: World of Wildlife, 1972-74; Leonardo da Vinci, 1978; La Scala, 1979; Macdonald Encyclopedia of Trees, 1983; Macdonald Encyclopedia of Butterflies and Moths, 1988; Decorating Chinese Porcelain, 1994. **Address:** 12 Decoy Ave, London NW11, England.

GILBERT, Sir Martin. British, b. 1936. **Genres:** History, Biography. **Career:** Merton College, Oxford, fellow, 1962-. Knighted, 1995. **Publications:** (with R. Gott) The Appeasers, 1963; Britain and Germany between the Wars, 1964; The European Powers 1900-1945; Plough My Own Furrow: The Life of Lord Allen of Hurtwood, 1965; Servant of India: A Study of Imperial Rule 1905-1910, 1966; The Roots of Appeasement, 1966; (ed.) A Century of Conflict: Essays Presented to A.J.P. Taylor, 1966; Recent History Atlas 1860-1960, 1966; Winston Churchill (for young people), 1966; Churchill, 1967; Lloyd George, 1968; British History Atlas, 1968; American History Atlas, 1968; Jewish History Atlas, 1969; First World War Atlas, 1970; Winston S. Churchill (biography), vols. 3-8, 1971-88; Russian History Atlas, 1972; Sir Horace Rumbold: Portrait of a Diplomat, 1973; The Coming of War in 1939, 1973; Churchill: Photographic Portrait, 1974; The Arab-Israel Conflict: Its History in Maps, 1974; Churchill and Zionism, 1974; The Jews in Arab Lands: Their History in Maps, 1975; Jerusalem Illustrated History Atlas, 1977; Exile and Return: The Struggle for a Jewish Homeland, 1978; Final Journey: The Fate of the Jews in Nazi Europe, 1979; Children's Illustrated Bible Atlas, 1979; Auschwitz and the Allies, 1981; Churchill's Political Philosophy, 1981; Churchill: The Wilderness Years, 1981; Atlas of the Holocaust, 1982; The Jews of Hope: The Plight of Soviet Jewry Today,

1984; Jerusalem: Rebirth of a City 1838-1898, 1985; Scharansky: Hero of Our Time, 1986; The Holocaust: The Jewish Tragedy, 1987; Second World War, 1989; Churchill: A Life, 1991; First World War, 1994; In Search of Churchill, 1994; The Day the War Ended, 1995; Israel: A History, 1998; A History of the 20th Century, vol. 1, 1997, vol. 2, 1998, vol. 3, 1999; Letters to Auntie Fori: 5,000 Years of Jewish History and Faith, 2002; The Righteous: The Unsung Heroes of the Holocaust, 2002. **Address:** Merton College, Oxford OX1 4JD, England.

GILBERT, Sister Mary. *See* **DEFREES, Madeline.**

GILBERT, Michael. British, b. 1912. **Genres:** Mystery/Crime/Suspense, Novellas/Short stories. **Career:** Solicitor, Trower Still & Keeling, since 1947 (Partner since 1952). Founder Member, Crime Writers Association, 1953. **Publications:** Close Quarters, 1947; They Never Looked Inside, 1948; The Doors Open, 1949; Smallbone Deceased, 1950; Death Has Deep Roots, 1951; Death in Captivity, 1952; Fear to Tread, 1953; Sky High, 1955; Be Shot for Sixpence, 1956; The Tichborne Claimant, 1957; Blood and Judgement, 1958; After the Fine Weather, 1963; The Crack in the Teacup, 1965; The Dust and the Heat, 1967; Game Without Rules (stories), 1967; The Etruscan Net, 1969; The Body of a Girl, 1972; The Ninety Second Tiger, 1973; Amateur in Violence (stories), 1973; Flash Point, 1975; The Night of the Twelfth, 1976; Petrella at Q (stories), 1977; The Empty House, 1978; Death of a Favourite Girl (in U.S. as The Killing of Katie Steelstock), 1980; Mr. Calder and Mr. Behrens (stories), 1982; The Final Throw (in U.S. as End-Game), 1982; The Black Seraphim, 1983; The Long Journey Home, 1985; (ed.) The Oxford Book of Legal Anecdotes, 1986; Trouble, 1987; Fraudsters, 1987; Young Petrella, 1988; Paint Gold or Blood, 1989; Anything for a Quiet Life, 1990; The Queen Against Karl Mullen, 1991; Roller-Coaster, 1993. **Address:** Luddesdown Old Rectory, Cobham, Kent DA13 0XE, England.

GILBERT, Ruth. New Zealander, b. 1917. **Genres:** Poetry. **Career:** Formerly physiotherapist in New Zealand, 1938-46. Past President, New Zealand P.E.N. **Publications:** Lazarus and Other Poems, 1949; The Sunlit Hour, 1955; The Luthier, 1966; Collected Poems, 1984; Breathings, 1992; Dream, Black Night's Child, 1993; Gongyla Remembers, 1994. **Address:** 23 Teece Dr, Motueka, New Zealand.

GILBERT, Sandra M(ortola). American, b. 1936. **Genres:** Novellas/Short stories, Poetry, Literary criticism and history, Women's studies and issues, Autobiography/Memoirs. **Career:** Lecturer in English, Queens College, City University of New York, Flushing, 1963-66, and Sacramento State College, CA, 1967-68; California State College, Hayward, assistant professor of English, 1968-71; St. Mary's College, Moraga, CA, lecturer in English, 1972; Indiana University, Bloomington, associate professor of English, 1973-75; University of California, Davis, professor of English, 1975-85, 1989-, distinguished professor, 1994-; Princeton University, NJ, professor of English, 1985-89. **Publications:** Shakespeare's Twelfth Night, 1964; Two Novels by E.M. Forster, 1965; D.H. Lawrence's Sons and Lovers, 1965; The Poetry of W.B. Yeats, 1965; Two Novels by Virginia Woolf, 1966; Acts of Attention: The Poems of D.H. Lawrence, 1973; (with S. Gubar) The Madwoman in the Attic: The Woman Writer and the 19th-Century Literary Imagination, 1979, 2nd ed., 2000; (with Gubar) No Man's Land: The Place of the Woman Writer in the 20th Century, 3 vols., 1988, 1989; Wrongful Death: A Medical Tragedy, 1995; (with Gubar) Masterpiece Theatre: An Academe Melodrama, 1995. POETRY: In the Fourth World, 1978; The Summer Kitchen, 1983; Emily's Bread, 1984; Blood Pressure, 1988; Ghost Volcano, 1995; Kissing the Bread: New & Selected Poems, 1969-1999, 2000; The Italian Collection, 2003; Belongings, 2004. EDITOR: (with Gubar) Shakespeare's Sisters, 1979; K. Chopin, The Awakening and Selected Stories, 1984; (with Gubar) The Norton Anthology of Literature by Women, 1985, 2nd ed., 1996; (with Gubar) The Female Imagination and the Modernist Aesthetic, 1986; V. Woolf, Orlando, 1993; (with Gubar and D. O'Hehir) Mothersongs, 1995; The House Is Made of Poetry, 1996. **Address:** Dept. of English, University of California, Davis, Davis, CT 95616, U.S.A.

GILBERT, Suzie. Also writes as Elizabeth T. Vulture. American, b. 1956. **Genres:** Environmental sciences/Ecology. **Career:** Writer. Hudson Valley Raptor Center (sanctuary for birds of prey), member of board of directors and volunteer. Has previously worked in a variety of occupations, including photographer, travel agent, dog trainer, chicken and turkey raiser, and for the National Hockey League. **Publications:** Hawk Hill, 1996. Author of an environmental column, under pseudonym Elizabeth T. Vulture, for Taconic Media Inc. Author of three screenplays. **Address:** 20 Cat Rock Rd., Garrison, NY 10524, U.S.A. **Online address:** Gilbert@highlands.com

GILBERT, Tom. American, b. 1955. **Genres:** Biography, Film, Business/Trade/Industry. **Career:** Variety, New York City, copy editor, 1984-85, as-

sistant managing editor, 1985-89, managing editor, 1989-91, slot editor, 1991-93; writer, 1993-. **Publications:** (with Coyne Steven Sanders) Desilu: The Story of Lucille Ball and Desi Arnaz, Morrow, 1993. **Address:** 5700 Wilshire Blvd., Suite 120, Los Angeles, CA 90036, U.S.A.

GILBERT, W(illiam) Stephen. British, b. 1947. **Genres:** Novels, Plays/Screenplays, Literary criticism and history. **Career:** Freelance writer. **Publications:** Circle Line (play), 1971; Private Means (play), 1986; Spiked (comic suspense novel), 1991; The Movie Superchallenge (quiz book), 1992; Fight and Kick and Bite: The Life and Work of Dennis Potter, 1995, in US as The Life and Work of Dennis Potter, 1998. Writer for television; playwright and scriptwriter. Contributor to magazines and newspapers. **Address:** Meadlands, Pickwick, Corsham, Wilts. SN13 OJD, England. **Online address:** WSteG@macunlimited.net

GILCHRIST, Ellen. American, b. 1935. **Genres:** Novels, Novellas/Short stories, Poetry. **Career:** Broadcaster on National Public Radio; also journalist. **Publications:** NOVELS: The Annunciation, 1983; The Anna Papers, 1988; Net of Jewels, 1992; Anabasis: A Journey to the Interior, 1994; Starcarbon: A Meditation on Love, 1994; Sarah Conley, 1997. POETRY: The Land Surveyor's Daughter, 1979; Riding Out the Tropical Depression, 1986. STORIES: In the Land of Dreamy Dreams, 1981; Victory over Japan, 1984; Drunk with Love, 1986; Two Stories, 1988; Light Can Be Both Wave and Particle, 1989; I Cannot Get You Close Enough (novellas), 1991; The Age of Miracles, 1995; Rhoda: A Life in Stories, 1995; The Courts of Love, 1996; Flights of Angels, 1998; The Cabal and Other Stories, 1999; Collected Stories, 2000; I, Rhoda Manning, Go Hunting with My Daddy, and Other Stories, 2002. OTHER: Muppets, No. 1-5, 1984-86; Falling through Space (journals), 1987; Muppets: Foggy Mountain Breakdown, 1988. **Address:** c/o Author Mail, Little, Brown & Co, 1271 Avenue of the Americas, New York, NY 10020, U.S.A.

GILCHRIST, John. *See* **GARDNER, Jerome.**

GILDEA, Robert. British, b. 1952. **Genres:** History. **Career:** Oxford University, Oxford, England, fellow and tutor in modern history at Merton College, 1979-, reader in modern history, 1996-. **Publications:** Education in Provincial France, 1800-1916, 1983; Barricades and Borders: Europe, 1800-1916, 1987, 2nd ed., 1996; France, 1870-1914, 1988, 2nd ed., 1996; The Past in French History, 1994; France since 1945, 1996, 2nd ed., 2002; Marianne in Chains: In Search of the German Occupation, 2002. **Address:** Merton College, Oxford University, Oxford OX1 4JD, England. **Online address:** Robert.Gildea@merton.ox.ac.uk

GILDEA, William. American, b. 1939. **Genres:** Sports/Fitness. **Career:** Washington Post, Washington, DC, journalist, 1965-. **Publications:** When the Colts Belonged to Baltimore: A Father and a Son, a Team and a Time, 1994; Where the Game Matters Most: A Last Championship Season in Indiana High School Basketball, 1997. **Address:** c/o Washington Post, 1150 15th St. NW, Washington, DC 20071, U.S.A.

GILDEN, Mel. American, b. 1947. **Genres:** Children's fiction, Young adult fiction. **Career:** Writer. **Publications:** The Return of Captain Conquer, 1986; Pokey to the Rescue, 1987; RV and the Haunted Garage, 1987; Harry Newberry and the Raiders of the Red Drink, 1989; Outer Space and All That Junk, 1989; Star Trek: The Next Generation: Boogeymen, 1991; The Planetoid of Amazement, 1991; Star Trek: The Starship Trap, 1993; The Pumpkins of Time (sequel to Outer Space and All That Junk), 1994; The Jungle Book: A Novelization, 1994; My Brother Blubb, 1994. FIFTH GRADE MONSTERS SERIES, JUVENILE FICTION: M Is for Monster, 1987; Born to Howl, 1987; The Pet of Frankenstein, 1988; Z Is for Zombie, 1988; Monster Mashers, 1989; Things That Go Bark in the Park, 1989; Yuckers!, 1989; The Monster in Creeps Head Bay, 1990; How to Be a Vampire in One Easy Lesson, 1990; Island of the Weird, 1990; Werewolf, Come Home, 1990; Monster Boy, 1991; Troll Patrol, 1991; The Secret of Dinosaur Bog, 1991. ZOOT MARLOWE SERIES: Surfing Samurai Robots, 1988; Hawaiian U.F.O. Aliens, 1991; Tubular Android Superheroes, 1991. BEVERLY HILLS 90210 SERIES (novelizations of teleplays): Beverly Hills 90210, 1991; More than Worlds, 1993; Graduation Day, 1994. CYBER-SURFERS SERIES (with Ted Pedersen): Pirates on the Internet, 1995; Cyberspace Cowboy, 1995; Ghost on the Net, 1996; Cybercops and Flame Wars, 1996. **Address:** c/o Pocket Books, Simon & Schuster Bldg., 1230 Ave. of the Americas, New York, NY 10020, U.S.A.

GILDNER, Gary. American, b. 1938. **Genres:** Novels, Autobiography/Memoirs, Novellas/Short stories, Poetry. **Career:** Drake University, Des Moines, IA, member of the faculty, 1966-91, emeritus professor of English,

1991-. Visiting professor and writer-in-residence, Reed College, Portland, OR, 1983-85, and Michigan State University, E. Lansing, 1987; University of Warsaw, senior Fulbright lecturer, 1987-88; Davidson College, McGee Professor of Writing, 1992; Safarik University, Slovakia, senior Fulbright lecturer, 1992-93; Seattle University, distinguished visiting writer-in-residence, 2002. **Publications:** POETRY: First Practice, 1969; Digging for Indians, 1971; Eight Poems, 1973; Nails, 1975; Letters from Vicksburg, 1976; The Runner, 1978; Jabon, 1981; Blue Like the Heavens: New and Selected Poems, 1984; Clackamas, 1991; The Swing, 1996; The Bunker in the Parsley Fields, 1997; The Birthday Party, 2000. OTHER: (ed. with J. Gildner) Out of This World: Poems from the Hawkeye State, 1975; Toads in the Greenhouse (film), 1978; The Crush (short stories), 1983; The Second Bridge (novel), 1987; A Week in South Dakota (short stories), 1987; The Warsaw Sparks (memoir), 1990; Pavol Hudak, The Poet, Is Talking (story), 1996; My Grandfather's Book (memoir), 2002. **Address:** R.R. 2, Box 219, Grangeville, ID 83530, U.S.A.

GILENS, Martin. American. **Genres:** Politics/Government. **Career:** Yale University, New Haven, CT, assistant professor, 1992-97, associate professor of political science, 1998-. Lecturer at educational institutions. **Publications:** Why Americans Hate Welfare: Race, Media, and the Politics of Anti-Poverty Policy, 1999. Contributor to books and professional journals. **Address:** Department of Political Science, Yale University, Box 208301, New Haven, CT 06520, U.S.A. **Online address:** martin.gilens@yale.edu

GILES, Frank (Thomas Robertson). British, b. 1919. **Genres:** Politics/Government, Writing/Journalism, Autobiography/Memoirs. **Career:** Times, London, England, assistant correspondent in Paris, France, 1947-50, chief correspondent in Rome, Italy, 1950-53, and Paris, 1953-60; Sunday Times, London, foreign editor, 1961-77, deputy editor, 1967-81, editor, 1981-83; Times Newspapers Ltd., London, director, 1981-85. Member of board of governors, Wellington College, and Sevenoaks School. **Publications:** A Prince of Journalists: The Life and Times of Henri S.O. de Blowitz, 1962; Sundry Times (autobiography), 1986; The Locust Years: The Story of the Fourth French Republic, 1946-1958, 1991; (ed.) Corfu, the Garden Isle, 1994; Napoleon Bonaparte, England's Prisoner, 2001. **Address:** 42 Blomfield Rd, London W9 2PF, England.

GILES, Gail. (born United States). **Genres:** Young adult fiction. **Career:** Writer. Taught high school in Angleton, TX. **Publications:** Breath of the Dragon, 1997; Shattering Glass, 2002; Dead Girls Don't Write Letters, 2003; Playing in Traffic, 2004. **Address:** c/o Scott Treimel, New York, NY 10003, U.S.A. **Online address:** 434 Lafayette St.gail@gailgiles.com

GILES, Paul. British, b. 1957. **Genres:** Literary criticism and history. **Career:** University of Staffordshire, Staffordshire, England, lecturer in English, 1985-87; Portland State University, Portland, OR, assistant professor, 1987-92, associate professor of English, 1992-. **Publications:** Hart Crane: The Contexts of "The Bridge," 1986; American Catholic Arts and Fictions: Culture, Ideology, Aesthetics, 1992. Contributor of articles and reviews to academic journals. **Address:** Department of English, Fitzwilliam College, Cambridge University, Cambridge CB3 0DG, England.

GILES, Robert Hartmann. American, b. 1933. **Genres:** Communications/Media. **Career:** Akron Beacon Journal, Akron, OH, reporter, 1958-63, editorial writer, 1963-65, city editor, 1966-68, metropolitan editor, 1968-69, managing editor, 1969-73, executive editor, 1973-76; University of Kansas School of Journalism, Lawrence, special lecturer, 1976-77; Gannett Newspapers, Rochester, NY, executive editor, 1977-81, editor, 1981-86; Detroit News, vice-president and executive editor, 1986-89, editor and publisher, 1989-. Newport News Daily Press, reporter, 1957-58. **Publications:** Editors and Stress: A Report to APME on Stress and How It Affects the Lives of Newspaper Editors, 1982; Newsroom Management: A Guide to Theory and Practice (textbook), 1987. **Address:** The New York Times, 229 W. 43rd St., New York, NY 10036, U.S.A.

GILKES, Cheryl Townsend. American, b. 1947. **Genres:** Race relations, Social sciences, Theology/Religion, Women's studies and issues. **Career:** Boston University, Boston, MA, assistant professor of sociology, 1978-87; Colby College, Waterville, ME, professor of African-American studies and sociology, 1987-. Ordained Baptist minister; Union Baptist Church, Cambridge, MA, assistant pastor for special projects, 1982-; United Baptist Convention of Massachusetts, Rhode Island, and New Hampshire, parliamentarian and member of board of directors. **Publications:** If It Wasn't for the Women...: Black Women's Experience and Womanist Culture in Church and Community, 2001. Contributor to books. Contributor of articles,

sermons, and reviews to periodicals. **Address:** Dept of Sociology, Colby College, Waterville, ME 04901, U.S.A.

GILL, Anton. Also writes as Ray Evans. British/German, b. 1948. **Genres:** Mystery/Crime/Suspense, History, Writing/Journalism, Biography. **Career:** Royal Court Theatre, London, England, assistant director, 1972-74; Arts Council of Great Britain, London, drama officer, 1976-78; British Broadcasting Corp., London, producer, 1976 and 1978-81; TV-AM Ltd., London, journalist/producer, 1982-84; writer, 1985-. **Publications:** Mad about the Boy: The Life and Times of Boy George and Culture Club, 1985; Martin Allen Is Missing, 1985; How to Be Oxbridge, 1986; Croquet, 1988; The Journey Back from Hell: An Oral History, Conversations with Concentration Camp Survivors, 1988; Berlin to Bucharest, 1990; A Dance between Flames: Berlin 1919-1939, 1993; A Honourable Defeat: The German Resistance to Hitler, 1994; The Devil's Mariner: A Life of William Dampier, 1997; Last Talons of the Eagle, 1998; Peggy Guggenheim, the Life, 2001; Il Gigante, 2002; Extinct, 2002; The Great Escape, 2002; Ancient Egyptians, 2003. EGYPTIAN MYSTERY TRILOGIES: City of the Horizon, City of Dreams, City of the Dead, 1991-93; City of Lies, City of Desire, City of the Sea, 1996-2000. **Address:** c/o Mark Lucas, Law Ltd, 14 Vernon St, London W14 0RJ, England.

GILL, Elizabeth. See HANKIN, Elizabeth Rosemary.

GILL, Gillian C(atherine). American/British, b. 1942. **Genres:** Women's studies and issues, Biography, Translations. **Career:** Assistant professor of French at Northeastern University, Boston, MA, Wellesley College, Wellesley, MA, and Yale University, New Haven, CT, 1970-81; real estate broker, 1982-86; lecturer in literature at Harvard University, Cambridge, MA; writer, Yale University, past resident fellow of Jonathan Edwards College and director of Women's Studies Program. **Publications:** Agatha Christie: The Woman and Her Mysteries, 1990; Mary Baker Eddy, 1998. TRANSLATOR: L. Irigaray, Speculum of the Other Woman, 1984; L. Irigaray, Marine Lover/of Friedrich Nietzsche, 1991; L. Irigaray, Sexes and Genealogies, 1993; (with C. Burke) L. Irigaray An Ethics of Sexual Difference, 1993; L. Frappier-Mazur, Sade Writes the Orgy, 1995. **Address:** 9 Arbella Rd, Bedford, MA 01730-1094, U.S.A.

GILL, Graeme. Australian, b. 1947. **Genres:** Politics/Government. **Career:** University of Tasmania, Hobart, Australia, tutor, 1976-77, lecturer, 1978-81; University of Sydney, Australia, lecturer to senior lecturer, 1981-88, associate professor, 1988-90, professor of government and public administration, 1990-. **Publications:** Peasants and Government in the Russian Revolution, 1979; Twentieth-Century Russia, 1987, 2nd ed. 1994; (ed.) The Rules of the Communist Party of the Soviet Union, 1988; Stalinism, 1990; The Origins of the Stalinist Political System, 1990; (coauthor) The Politics of Transition, 1993; The Collapse of a Single Party System, 1994; (co-author) Power in the Party, 1997; The Dynamics of Democratization, 2000; (co-author) Russia's Stillborn Democracy?, 2000; Democracy and Post-Communism, 2002; The Nature and Development of the Modern State, 2003. **Address:** School of Economics and Political Science, University of Sydney, Sydney, NSW 2006, Australia. **Online address:** g.gill@econ.usyd.edu.au

GILL, Lakshmi. Filipino. **Genres:** Poetry, Novels. **Career:** Educator and poet. Instructor at Notre Dame University of Nelson, Mount Allison University, and University of Victoria, Victoria, British Columbia, Canada; University of British Columbia, British Columbia, Canada, instructor at English Language Institute. **Publications:** POETRY: During Rain, I Plant Chrysanthemums, 1966; Mind Walls, 1970; Novena to St. Jude Thaddeus, 1979; Returning the Empties: Selected Poems, 1960s-1990s, 1998. OTHER: Rape of the Spirit, 1962; The Third Infinitive (novel), 1993; Contributor to anthologies. **Address:** c/o Author Mail, Tsar Press, PO Box 6996, Station A, Toronto, ON, Canada M5W 1X7.

GILL, LaVerne McCain. American, b. 1947. **Genres:** Cultural/Ethnic topics, Ethics, Politics/Government, Theology/Religion, Women's studies and issues. **Career:** Writer. **Publications:** African American Women in Congress, 1997; Daughters of Dignity: African Biblical Women & the Virtues of Black Womanhood, 2000; My Mother Prayed for Me: Faith Journaling for African American Women, 2000. **Address:** c/o Natasha Kern, A. Kern Agency, PO Box 2908, Portland, OR 97208-2908, U.S.A.

GILL, Peter. British, b. 1939. **Genres:** Plays/Screenplays. **Career:** Actor, 1957-65; Riverside Studios, London, 1976-80; National Theatre, London, associate director, 1980-. **Publications:** The Sleeper's Den, 1965; Over Gardens Out, 1970; Small Change, 1979; Small Change, and Kick for Touch, 1985; Mean Tears, 1987; The Cherry Orchard, 1995; The Look across the Eyes (short story), 1997; Cardiff East, 1997; Certain Young Men, 1999; The Seagull by Anton Chekhov, 2000; The York Realist, 2001; Peter Gill Plays: 1, 2001; Original Sin, 2002.

GILL, Ronald Crispin. British, b. 1916. **Genres:** History. **Career:** The Western Morning News, assistant editor, 1950-70; The Countryman, editor, 1971-81. **Publications:** The West Country, 1962; Plymouth: A New History, 1966, rev. ed., 1993; (with F. Booker and T. Soper) The Wreck of the Torrey Canyon, 1967; Plymouth in Pictures, 1968; Mayflower Remembered, 1970; Sutton Harbour, 1970, rev. ed., 1996; The Isles of Scilly, 1975; Dartmoor, 1976; The Countryman's Britain in Pictures, 1977, new ed., 1995; Plymouth: A New History, vol. II, 1979; Great Cornish Families, 1995; Plymouth River, 1996. EDITOR: Dartmoor: A New Study, 1970; The Countryman's Britain, 1976; The Duchy of Cornwall, 1987. Contributor to books. **Address:** 14 Harbourside Ct, Hawkers Ave, Plymouth PL4 0QT, England.

GILL, Sam D. American, b. 1943. **Genres:** Cultural/Ethnic topics, Theology/Religion, Humanities, Dance/Ballet. **Career:** Coleman Co., Wichita, Kan., research analyst, 1964-67; University of Chicago, Chicago, Ill., systems analyst, 196773; Oklahoma State University, Stillwater, visiting assistant professor of humanities and religion, 1974-75; Arizona State University, Tempe, assistant professor, 1975-80, associate professor of religious studies, 1980-83, administrator of Native American Religions Program, 1975-78; University of Colorado, Boulder, professor of religious studies, 1983-, director of graduate studies, 1984-87. Visiting instructor at Concordia College, Moorhead, Minn., fall, 1973; visiting professor at universities throughout the US. **Publications:** Songs of Life: An Introduction to Navajo Religious Culture, 1979; Sacred Words: A Study of Navajo Religion and Prayer, 1981; Beyond "The Primitive": The Religions of Nonliterate Peoples, 1982; Native American Religions: An Introduction, 1982; Native American Traditions: Sources and Interpretations, 1983; Mother Earth: An American Story, 1987; Native American Religious Action: A Performance Approach to Religion, 1987; (with I. Sullivan) Dictionary of Native American Mythology, 1992; Storytracking: Texts, Stories, and Histories in Central Australia, 1998. **Address:** Department of Religious Studies, University of Colorado, Campus Box 292, Boulder, CO 80309-0292, U.S.A. **Online address:** sam.gill@colorado.edu

GILL, Walter. Also writes as Brother Wali Hakeem. American, b. 1937. **Genres:** Education. **Career:** Junior high school art and social studies teacher, 1962-72; case worker, 1992-94; Millersville University, Millersville, PA, assistant professor of education, 1994-. Producer of educational films; actor in community theater productions; movie extra; newspaper columnist. **Publications:** Issues in African American Education, 1991. Contributor of more than 100 articles to periodicals, sometimes under the name Brother Wali Hakeem. **Address:** School of Education, Millersville University, Millersville, PA 17551-0302, U.S.A.

GILLESPIE, Angus Kress. American, b. 1942. **Genres:** Agriculture/Forestry, Architecture, History, Intellectual history, Mythology/Folklore. **Career:** Rutgers University, New Brunswick, NJ, instructor, 1973-75, assistant professor, 1975-81, associate professor, 1981-2000, professor of American studies, 2000-, American studies dept., acting chairman, 1997. Executive director, New Jersey Folk Festival; Fulbright Award, Philippines, 1985-86, Norway, 2002-03; guest on television and radio programs. Millstone Valley Fire Department, volunteer fireman, president, 1987. **Publications:** Folklorist of the Coal Fields: The Life and Work of George Korson, 1980; (ed. with J. Mechling, and contrib.) American Wildlife in Symbol and Story, 1987; (with M.A. Rockland) Looking for America on the New Jersey Turnpike, 1988; Twin Towers: The Life of New York City's World Trade Center, 1999; (ed. with D. Wilson) Rooted in American Soil: Foodlore of Popular Fruits and Vegetables, 1999. **Address:** Dept of American Studies, Rutgers University, 131 George St, New Brunswick, NJ 08901-1414, U.S.A. **Online address:** angusgi@rci.rutgers.edu

GILLESPIE, Diane Filby. American, b. 1943. **Genres:** Literary criticism and history, Essays. **Career:** University of Minnesota-Twin Cities, Minneapolis, instructor in English, 1966-67; Stephens College, Columbia, Mo., instructor in literature and writing, 1967-69; University of Alberta, Edmonton, lecturer in English, 1973-74; Washington State University, Pullman, assistant professor, 1975-80, associate professor, 1980-89, professor of English, 1989-2001, professor emeritus, 2001-. **Publications:** The Sisters' Arts: The Writing and Painting of Virginia Woolf and Vanessa Bell 1988. EDITOR: (with E. Steele) Julia Duckworth Stephen: Stories for Children, Essays for Adults, 1987; The Multiple Muses of Virginia Woolf, 1993; Roger Fry: A Biography by Virginia Woolf, 1995; (with L. Hankins) Virginia Woolf and the Arts: Selected Papers from the Sixth Annual Conference on Virginia Woolf, 1997; (with D. Birrer) C. Hamilton, Diana of Dobson's, 2003. **Address:** Department of English, Washington State University, Pullman, WA 99164-5020, U.S.A.

GILLESPIE, Gerald (Ernest Paul). American, b. 1933. **Genres:** Literary criticism and history, Translations. **Career:** University of Southern California, assistant professor of German and comparative literature, 1961-65; State University of New York at Binghamton, associate professor and professor of German and comparative literature, 1965-74; Stanford University, CA, professor of German studies and comparative literature, 1974-99, emeritus professor, 1999-. International Comparative Literature Association, secretary, vice president, president, 1979-88, 1994-97. **Publications:** Daniel Casper von Lohenstein's Historical Tragedies, 1965; College Level German Grammar, 1966; German Baroque Poetry, 1971; Ouzhou Xiaoshuo De Yanhua, 1987; Garden and Labyrinth of Time: Studies in Renaissance and Baroque Literature, 1988; Proust, Mann, Joyce in the Modernist Context, 2003; By Way of Comparison: Reflections on the Theory and Practice of Comparative Literature, 2004. EDITOR: (and trans.) Die Nachtwachen des Bonaventura, 1972; (and trans.) L. Tieck, Der gestiefelte Kater, 1974; (and trans. with A. Zahareas) R.M. del Valle-Inclan, Luces de Bohemia, 1976; (with E. Lohner) Herkommen und Erneuerung: Essays fur Oskar Seidlin, 1976; (with G. Spellerberg) Studien zum Werk D.C. von Lohenstein, 1983; Litterature comparee/litterature mondiale, 1990; German Theater before 1750, 1994; Romantic Drama, 1995; Visions in History, 1995; (with A. Lorant) Powers of Narration, 1995; (with R.A. Prier) Narrative Ironies, 1997; (with R.G. Cohn) Mallarme in the Twentieth Century, 1998. **Address:** Division of Literatures, Cultures, and Languages, Bldg. 260 Rm 205, Stanford University, Stanford, CA 94305-2030, U.S.A.

GILLESPIE, J(ohn) David. American, b. 1944. **Genres:** Politics/Government. **Career:** Samford University, Birmingham, AL, assistant professor, 1973-78, associate professor of political science, 1978-79; Presbyterian College, Clinton, SC, associate professor, 1979-88, professor of political science, 1988-, chairperson of department, 1985-88, 1990-91, vice president for academic affairs, 1997-, Charles A. Dana Professor, 1997-; commentator; cited in many newspapers and magazines. Carnegie Foundation South Carolina Professor of Year, 1993-94. Fulbright grant, Estonia, 1997. **Publications:** Politics at the Periphery: Third Parties in Two-Party America, 1993. Contributor of articles on third parties to periodicals, anthologies, and edited works. **Address:** Office of Academic Affairs, Presbyterian College, Clinton, SC 29325, U.S.A. **Online address:** dgillesp@presby.edu

GILLESPIE, Robert B. American. **Genres:** Mystery/Crime/Suspense. **Publications:** The Crossword Mystery, 1979; Little Sally Does It Again, 1982; Print-Out, 1983; Cryptopic Crosswords (puzzles), 1983; Heads You Lose, 1985; Empress of Coney Island, 1986; The Hell's Kitchen Connection, 1987; The Last of the Honeywells, 1988; Deathstorm, 1990. **Address:** 226 Bay St, Douglaston, NY 11363, U.S.A.

GILLETT, Charlie. British, b. 1942. **Genres:** Music. **Career:** Co-Director, Oval Records. Radio Presenter, 1972- (TV Presenter, The Late Shift, Channel 4, 1988). Lecturer in Social Studies, film making, and athletics, Kingsway College of Further Education, London, 1966-71; BBC-TV Production Assistant, 1971-72. **Publications:** The Sound of the City: The Rise of Rock and Roll, 1970, 1996; Making Tracks: The Story of Atlantic Records, 1974, 1986. EDITOR: All in the Game (sport), 1970; Rock File vols., 1972-78; The Beat Goes On, 1996. **Address:** 11 Liston Rd, London SW4 0DG, England. **Online address:** cgillett@oval.demon.co.uk

GILLETT, Grant (Randall). New Zealander, b. 1950. **Genres:** Philosophy. **Career:** Resident and lecturer in neurosurgery, Auckland, New Zealand, 1977-83; Oxford University, England, fellow in philosophy, 1986-88; University of Otago, Dunedin, New Zealand, associate professor of medical ethics and consultant neurosurgeon, 1988-, and honorary lecturer in philosophy. Oxford University, fellow of Magdalen College; consultant to New Zealand Department of Health. **Publications:** Reasonable Care, 1989; Representation, Meaning, and Thought, 1992; Practical Medical Ethics, 1992; The Mind and Its Discontents, 1994; (with J. McMillan) Consciousness and Intentionality, 2001. **Address:** Bioethics Research Centre, University of Otago, PO Box 913, Dunedin, New Zealand. **Online address:** grant.gillett@stonebow.otago.ac.nz

GILLETT, Margaret. Canadian (born Australia), b. 1930. **Genres:** Novels, Education, Women's studies and issues, Autobiography/Memoirs, Biography. **Career:** Commonwealth Office of Education, Australia, Education Officer, 1954-57; Dalhousie University, Halifax, NS, Canada, Assistant Professor, 1961-62; Haile Selassie I University, Ethiopia, Registrar, 1962-64; McGill

University, Montreal, Professor, 1964-82, Macdonald Professor of Education, 1982-95, William C. Macdonald Emeritus Professor, 1995-. McGill Journal of Education, Ed., 1966-77. **Publications:** A History of Education: Thought and Practice, 1966; (co-author) The Laurel and the Poppy (novel), 1968; Educational Technology: Toward Demystification, 1973; We Walked Very Warily: A History of Women at McGill, 1981; A Fair Shake: Autobiographical Essays by McGill Women, 1984; Dear Grace: A Romance of History, 1986; Our Own Agendas, 1995; A Fair Shake Revisited, 1996; Traf: A History of Trafalgar School for Girls, 2000. EDITOR/CO-EDITOR: Readings in the History of Education, 1969; Foundation Studies in Education: Justifications and New Directions, 1973; Aspects of Education, 1991. **Address:** 150 Berlioz, Apt. 320, Nuns' Island, Verdun, QC, Canada H3E 1K3. **Online address:** margaret.gillett@mcgill.ca

GILLETTE, J(an) Lynett. American, b. 1946. **Genres:** Natural history. **Career:** Department of Physical Anthropology, National Museum of History, Smithsonian Institution, Washington, DC, technician/research assistant, 1972-74; oil exploration geologist for small independent oil and gas companies, Dallas, TX, 1981-83; Ruth Hall Museum of Paleontology, Curator of Paleontology, Abiquiu, NM, 1986-97. Southwest Paleontology Foundation, president, 1987-92; served on National Ghost Ranch Foundation Board, 1987-91. **Publications:** Dinosaur Diary: My Triassic Homeland, 1988; The Search for Seismosaurus: The World's Longest Dinosaur, 1994; Dinosaur Ghosts: The Mystery of Coelophysis, 1997. **Address:** c/o Publicity Director, Dial, 375 Hudson St., New York, NY 10014, U.S.A.

GILLEY, Sheridan (Wayne). British (born Australia), b. 1945. **Genres:** History, Theology/Religion, Biography. **Career:** University of St. Andrews, Scotland, lecturer in ecclesiastical history, 1971-78; University of Durham, Durham, England, lecturer, 1978-82, senior lecturer in theology, 1982-94; reader, 1994-2002, emeritus reader, 2002-; writer. **Publications:** Newman and His Age (biography), 1990, new ed., 2003. EDITOR: (with R. Swift) The Irish in the Victorian City, 1985; (with R. Swift) The Irish in Britain, 1815-1939, 1989; (with W.J. Sheils) A History of Religion in Britain, 1994; (with R. Swift) The Irish in Victorian Britain: The Local Dimension, 1999. **Address:** Department of Theology, University of Durham, Abbey House, Palace Green, Durham DH1 3RS, England.

GILLIES, David. Canadian (born India), b. 1952. **Genres:** Politics/Government. **Career:** Northeast London Probation Service, London, England, probation officer, 1979-83; International Centre for Human Rights and Democratic Development, Montreal, Quebec, policy adviser, 1991-94; Aga Khan Foundation, Ottawa, Ontario, manager of policy and research, 1995-97; Canadian International Development Agency, Hull, Quebec, governance adviser, 1998-. **Publications:** Challenges of Democratic Development, 1992; Between Principle and Practice, 1997; (ed.) Strategies of Public Engagement: Shaping a Canadian Agenda for International Cooperation, 1997. **Address:** c/o Aga Khan Foundation Canada, 360 Albert St Ste 1220, Ottawa, ON, Canada K1R 7X7. **Online address:** marie.cocking@sympatico.ca

GILLIES, Valerie. Scottish (born Canada), b. 1948. **Genres:** Poetry, Songs/Lyrics and libretti, Adult non-fiction. **Career:** Writer-in-residence: Boroughmuir High School, Edinburgh, 1978, Edinburgh Academy, 1983, Duncan of Jordanstone College of Art, Dundee, 1988-90, Dundee District Libraries, 1988-90, Mid and East Lothian, 1991-93, University of Edinburgh, 1995-97; University of Edinburgh, fellow in creative writing, 2003-. **Publications:** Trio: New Poets from Edinburgh, 1971; Each Bright Eye: Selected Poems, 1976; Bed of Stone, 1984; Leopardi: A Scottis Quair, 1987; Tweed Journey, 1989; The Chanter's Tune, 1990; The Ringing Rock, 1995; Men and Beasts, 2000; The Lightning Tree, 2002. **Address:** 67 Braid Ave, Edinburgh EH10 6ED, Scotland.

GILLIGAN, Carol. American, b. 1936. **Genres:** Psychology, Women's studies and issues. **Career:** Psychologist, 1964-; Harvard University, Cambridge, MA, lecturer, beginning in 1968, assistant professor, 1971-78, associate professor, 1978-86, professor, 1986-. Rutgers University, Laurie Chair in Women's Studies, 1986-87; University of Cambridge, Pitt Professor, 1992-93. Bunting Institute, faculty fellow, 1982-83; Spencer Foundation, senior research fellow, 1989-93. **Publications:** In a Different Voice: Psychological Theory and Women's Development, 1982; (with N.P. Lyons and T.J. Hanmer) Making Connections: The Relational Worlds of Adolescent Girls at Emma Willard School, 1991; (with L.M. Brown) Meeting at the Crossroads: Women's Psychology and Girls' Development, 1992; (with J.M. Taylor and A. Sullivan) Between Voice and Silence: Women and Girls, Race and Relationship, 1995. EDITOR: (with J.V. Ward, J.M. Taylor, and B. Bardige) Mapping the Moral Domain: A Contribution of Women's Thinking to Psychological Theory and Education, 1989; (with A.G. Rogers and D. Tolman) Women, Girls, and Psychotherapy: Reframing Resistance. **Address:** Larsen Hall 503, Harvard University, Cambridge, MA 02138, U.S.A.

GILLIGAN, James F. American, b. 1935. **Genres:** Criminology/True Crime. **Career:** University of Chicago, Chicago, IL, intern at university hospitals and clinics, 1965-66; Harvard University, Cambridge, MA, resident in psychiatry at Massachusetts Mental Health Center, 1966-69, instructor, 1969-94, lecturer in psychiatry, 1994-, Erikson Lecturer, 1991, supervising psychiatrist for psychiatric residency training program, 196977, member of psychiatric residency and forensic psychiatry fellowship training programs of the Institute of Law and Psychiatry at McLean Hospital, 1977-89, member of forensic psychiatry fellowship training program at Massachusetts Mental Health Center, 1989-94, member of psychiatric residency training program at Cambridge Hospital, 1994-; Institute for Psychoanalysis, Chicago, IL, Esther Schour Zetland Lecturer, 1992; Cambridge University, visiting fellow of Clare Hall and visiting scholar at Institute of Criminology, both 1993-94; lecturer at colleges and universities. Private practice of clinical and forensic psychiatry, 1969-; McLean Hospital, director of Institute of Law and Psychiatry, 1977-80; Bridgewater State Hospital, deputy medical director, 1977, medical director, 1977-80, medical director of Bridgewater State Hospital and Center for the Study of Violence, 1991-92; Prison Mental Health Service, clinical director, 1981-91. **Publications:** Violence: Our Deadliest Epidemic and Its Causes, 1996, as Violence: Reflections on a National Epidemic, 1997; The Future of the Prison: Reform or Replacement?, 1998. Contributor to books. **Address:** PO Box 385, West Stockbridge, MA 01266, U.S.A. **Online address:** jgilliga@warren.med.harvard.edu

GILLILAND, Alexis A(rnaldus). American, b. 1931. **Genres:** Science fiction/Fantasy, Cartoons, Humor/Satire. **Career:** Thermochemist, National Bureau of Standards, Washington D.C., 1956-67; Chemist and Specification Writer, Federal Supply Service, Washington D.C., 1967-82; Freelance writer and cartoonist, 1982-. **Publications:** NOVELS: The Revolution from Rosinante, 1981; Long Shot for Rosinante, 1981; The Pirates of Rosinante, 1982; The End of the Empire, 1983; Wizenbeak, 1986; The Shadow Shaia, 1990; Lord of the Troll-Bats, 1992. CARTOONS: The Iron Law of Bureaucracy, 1979; Who Says Paranoia Isn't In Anymore, 1985; The Waltzing Wizard, 1990. **Address:** 4030 Eighth St. S, Arlington, VA 22204, U.S.A.

GILLIS, Chester. American, b. 1951. **Genres:** Theology/Religion. **Career:** Drew University, Madison, NJ, assistant professor of philosophy of religion, 1987-88; Georgetown University, Washington, DC, professor of theology, 1988-. **Publications:** A Question of Final Belief: John Hick's Pluralistic Theory of Salvation, 1989; Pluralism: A New Paradigm for Theology, 1993; Roman Catholicism in America, 1999; Catholic Faith in America, 2003. **Address:** Department of Theology, Box 571135, Georgetown University, Washington, DC 20057, U.S.A. **Online address:** gillisc@georgetown.edu

GILLMAN, Peter (Charles). British, b. 1942. **Genres:** Communications/Media, Writing/Journalism, Biography, Documentaries/Reportage, Sports/Fitness, History. **Career:** Town, London, England, assistant editor, 1964-65; Daily Telegraph, London, staff writer, 1965-66; free-lance writer, 1966-69; Radio Times, London, features editor, 1969-71; Sunday Times, staff writer, co-editor of "Insight," and correspondent, 1971-83; freelance writer and broadcaster, 1983-; writer for British newspapers and magazines, consultant and assistant producer to BBC TV documentaries; teaches journalism specialising in investigative and feature writing techniques. **Publications:** (with D. Haston) Direttissima, 1966 (in U.K. as Eiger Direct, 1966); (with E. Davenport and P. Eddy) The Plumbat Affair, 1978; Fitness on Foot: Climbing and Walking for Pleasure, 1978; (with P. Eddy and J. Connell) Siege!, 1980; (with L. Gillman) Collar the Lot!: How Britain Interned and Expelled Its Wartime Refugees, 1980; (with M. Linklater and P. Eddy) War in the Falklands, 1982 (in U.K. as The Falklands War, 1982); (with L. Gillman) Alias David Bowie, 1986; The Duty Men, 1987; In Balance: Twenty Years of Mountaineering Journalism, 1989; Everest: The Best Writing and Pictures, 1993; (with L. Gillman) The Wildest Dream: Biography of George Mallory, 2000; Everest: 80 Years of Triumph and Tragedy, 2001. **Address:** 21 Warminster Rd, London SE25 4DL, England. **Online address:** petergillman@clara.co.uk

GILLMEISTER, Heiner. German, b. 1939. **Genres:** Literary criticism and history. **Career:** Author and educator. University of Bonn, Germany, lecturer, 1968-71, senior lecturer, 1971-2004; Dusseldorf University, deputy chair of English-language history and medieval literature, 1980-81; German Sports University, Cologne, lecturer in sports history, 1980. Asian Games Scientific Congress, Hiroshima, Japan, 1994, sole European invited speaker. Kolnische

Rundschau, Cologne, Germany, theater critic, 1970-86. **Publications:** Chaucer und die Via Regia, 1972; Chaucer's Conversion: Allegorical Thought in Medieval Literature, 1984; Aufschlag fur Walter von der Vogelweide. Tennis seit dem Mittelalter, 1986; Kulturgeschichte des Tennis, 1990, rev. ed as Tennis: A Cultural History, 1997; (coauthor) Der Rheinische Merlin. Text, Ubersetzung der Merlin- und Luthild-Fragmente, 1991; Service. Kleine Geschichte der englischen Sprache, 1993, rev. ed. as Second Service, 2002; Olympisches Tennis. Die Geschichte der olympischen Tennisturniere (1896-1992), 1993; (ed.) In bester Gesellschaft: John Pius Boland-Reisetagebuch des Olympiasiegers aus dem Jahre 1896, trans. as In Good Company: John Pius Boland-The Diary of an Olympic Champion (Athens 1896), 2004. Contributor to books and periodicals. **Address:** University of Bonn, Dept of English, Regina-Pacis-Weg 5, D-53113 Bonn, Germany. **Online address:** h.gillmeister@uni-bonn.de; h.gillmeister@gmx.de

GILLON, Adam. American (born Poland), b. 1921. **Genres:** Novels, Plays/ Screenplays, Poetry, Film, Literary criticism and history, Translations. **Career:** Emeritus professor of English and comparative literature, State University of New York at New Paltz (joined faculty, 1962). Professor of English and head of Dept., Acadia University, Nova Scotia, 1957-62; emeritus professor of English, Haifa University, 1979-84. President, Joseph Conrad Society of America, and ed., Joseph Conrad Today, 1975-; member of Editorial Board, Institute for Textual Studies, Texas Technical University, Lubbock. Ed., Polish Series, Twayne Publishers Inc., 1963-72; regional ed., Conradiana, 1968-72. **Publications:** Joseph Conrad (radio play), 1959; The Bet (radio play), 1969; The Eternal Solitary: A Study of Joseph Conrad, 1960; A Cup of Fury (novel), 1962; Selected Poems and Translations, 1962; In the Manner of Haiku, 1967; (author and trans.) J. Tuwim, The Dancing Socrates and Other Poems, 1968; The Solitary (radio play), 1969; Daily New and Old: Poems in the Manner of Haiku, 1971; Strange Mutations, 1973; Summer Morn Winter Weather (poems), 1975; Conrad and Shakespeare and Other Essays, 1976; Joseph Conrad, 1982; The Withered Leaf: A Medley of Haiku and Senryu, 1982; Jared (novel), 1989; Joseph Conrad: Comparative Essays, 1994; (writer, director, producer) The Bet (film), 1994. SCREENPLAYS: (co-author) The Conspirators, 1985; Dark Country, 1989; Under Western Eyes, 1989; The Bet, 1990; From Russia with Hope, 1990. EDITOR: (trans. and contrib.) Introduction to Modern Polish Literature, 1964, 1982; (trans. and contrib.) Poems of the Ghetto: A Testament of Lost Men, 1969; Joseph Conrad: Commemorative Essays, 1975. **Address:** 490 Route 299 W, New Paltz, NY 12561, U.S.A. **Online address:** conradfilm@aol.com

GILMAN, Andrew D. American, b. 1951. **Genres:** Communications/Media. **Career:** Attorney in general practice, New York, 1980-; CommCore, Inc., New York City, president, 1985-. **Publications:** Get to the Point: How to Say What You Mean and Get What You Want, 1989. **Address:** CommCore Inc., 1133 21st St 3rd Fl, Washington, DC 20036, U.S.A. **Online address:** agilman@commcoreconsulting.com

GILMAN, George G. Also writes as Frank Chandler, David Ford, Terry Williams Harknett, Jane Harman, Joseph Hedges, William M. James, Charles R. Pike, William Pine, James Russell, Thomas H. Stone, William Terry. British, b. 1936. **Genres:** Mystery/Crime/Suspense, Westerns/Adventure, Travel/ Exploration, Ghost Writer. **Career:** Freelance writer, 1972-. Copyboy, Reuters, 1952; clerk, Newspaper Features Ltd., 1952-54; typist, Reuters Comtelburo, 1956-57; publicity asst. 20th-Century Fox, 1957-58; ed., Newspaper Features Ltd., 1958-61; reporter and features ed., National Newsagent, 1961-72, all London. **Publications:** WESTERNS. EDGE SERIES: The Loner, 1972; Ten Thousand Dollars, American (in U.S. as Ten Grand), 1972; Apache Death, 1972; Killer's Breed, 1972; Blood on Silver, 1972; The Blue, the Grey, and the Red (in U.S. as Red River), 1973; California Killing, 1973, in U.S. as California Kill, 1974; Seven Out of Hell (in U.S. as Hell's Seven), 1973; Bloody Summer, 1973; Vengeance Is Black, 1973, in U.S. as Black Vengeance, 1974; Sioux Uprising, 1974; The Biggest Bounty (in U.S. as Death's Bounty), 1974; A Town Called Hate, 1974, in U.S. as The Hated, 1975; The Big Gold, 1974, in U.S. as Tiger's Gold, 1975; Blood Run (in U.S. as Paradise Loses), 1975; The Final Shot, 1975; Vengeance Valley, 1975; Ten Tombstones to Texas, 1975, in U.S. as Ten Tombstones, 1976; Ashes and Dust, 1976; Sullivan's Law, 1976; Rhapsody in Red, 1976; Slaughter Road, 1977; Echoes of War, 1977; The Day Democracy Died, 1977, in U.S. as Slaughterday, 1978; Violence Trail, 1978; Savage Dawn, 1978; Eve of Evil, 1978; The Living, the Dying, and the Dead, 1978; Waiting for a Train (in U.S. as Towering Nightmare), 1979; The Guilty Ones, 1979; The Frightened Gun, 1979; The Hated, 1979, in U.S. as Red Fury, 1980; A Ride in the Sun, 1980; Death Deal, 1980; Two of a Kind: Edge Meets Steele, 1980; Town on Trial, 1981; Vengeance at Ventura, 1981; Massacre Mission, 1981; The Prisoners, 1981; Montana Melodrama, 1982; Matching Pair: Edge Meets Adam Steele, 1982; The Killing Claim, 1982;

Bloody Sunrise, 1982; Arapaho Revenge, 1983; The Blind Side, 1983; House on the Range, 1983; The Godforsaken, 1982; Edge Meets Steele No. 3 Double Action, 1984; The Moving Cage, 1984; School for Slaughter, 1985; Revenge Ride, 1985; Shadow of the Gallows, 1985; A Time for Killing, 1986; Brutal Border, 1986; Hitting Paydirt, 1986; Backshot, 1987; Uneasy Riders, 1987; Doom Town, 1987; Dying Is Forever, 1987; The Desperadoes, 1988; Terror Town, 1988; The Breed Woman, 1989; The Rifle, 1989. ADAM STEELE SERIES: The Violent Peace, 1974, in U.S. as Rebels and Assassins Die Hard, 1975; The Bounty Hunter, 1974; Hell's Junction, 1974; Valley of Blood, 1975; Gun Run, 1975; The Killing Art, 1975; Cross-Fire, 1975; Comanche Carnage, 1976; Badge in the Dust, 1976; The Losers, 1976; Lynch Town, 1976; Death Trail, 1977; Bloody Border, 1977; Delta Duel, 1977; River of Death, 1977; Nightmare at Noon, 1978; Satan's Daughters, 1978; The Hard Way, 1978; The Tarnished Star, 1979; Wanted for Murder, 1979; Wagons East, 1979; The Big Game, 1979; Fort Despair, 1979; Manhunt, 1980; Steele's War: The Woman, The Preacher, The Storekeeper, The Stranger, 4 vols., 1980-81; The Big Prize, 1981; The Killer Mountains, 1982; The Cheaters, 1982; The Wrong Man, 1982; The Valley of the Shadow, 1983; The Runaway, 1983; Stranger in a Strange Town, 1983; The Hellraisers, 1984; Canyon of Death, 1985; High Stakes, 1985; Rough Justice, 1985; The Sunset Ride, 1986; The Killing Strain, 1986; The Big Gunfight, 1987; The Hunted, 1987; Code of the West, 1987; The Outcasts, 1987; The Return, 1988; Trouble in Paradise, 1988; Going Back, 1989; The Long Shadow, 1989. THE UNDERTAKER SERIES: Black as Death, 1981; Destined to Die, 1981; Funeral by the Sea, 1982; Three Graves to a Showdown, 1982; Back from the Dead, 1982; Death in the Desert, 1982. AS WILLIAM TERRY, NOVELIZATIONS OF SCREENPLAYS: A Town Called Bastard, 1971; Hannie Caulder, 1971; Red Sun, 1972; (as Frank Chandler) A Fistful of Dollars, 1972. AS CHARLES R. PIKE: JUBAL CADE SERIES: The Killing Trail, 1974; Double Cross, 1974; The Hungry Gun, 1974. AS WILLIAM M. JAMES: APACHE SERIES: The First Death, 1974; Duel to the Death, 1974; Fort Treachery, 1975; Sonora Slaughter, 1976; Blood on the Tracks, 1977; All Blood Is Red, 1977; The Best Man, 1979. CRIME NOVELS AS TERRY HARKNETT: The Benevolent Blackmailer, 1962; The Scratch on the Surface, 1962; Invitation to a Funeral, 1963; Dead Little Rich Girl, 1963; The Evil Money, 1964; The Man Who Did Not Die, 1964; Death of an Aunt, 1967; The Two-Way Frame, 1967; The Softcover Kill, 1971; Promotion Tour, 1972; Crown series: The Sweet and Sour Kill, Macao Mayhem, Bamboo Shoot-Out, 3 vols, 1974-75. AS WILLIAM TERRY: Once a Copper, 1965; The Weekend Game, 1972. AS WILLIAM PINE: The Protectors, 1967. AS JANE HARMAN: W.I.T.C.H., 1971. AS THOMAS H. STONE: Dead Set, 1972; One Horse Race, 1972; Stopover Murder, 1973; Black Death, 1973; Squeeze Play, 1973. AS JOSEPH HEDGES: Funeral Rites, 1973; Arms for Oblivion, 1973; The Chinese Coffin, 1974; The Gold-Plated Hearse, 1974; Rainbow-Coloured Shroud, 1974; Corpse on Ice, 1975; The Mile-Deep Grave, 1975; Mexican Mourning, 1975; The Stainless Steel Wreath, 1975; The Chauffeur-Driven Pyre, 1976. NONFICTION: (as Terry Harknett) The Caribbean, 1972; (as James Russell) The Balearic Islands, 1972; (as David Ford) Cyprus, 1973. GHOSTWRITER: The Hero, by Peter Haining, 1973; The Savage, and Doomsday Island, both by Alex Peters, 1979. **Address:** Spring Acre, Springhead Rd, Uplyme, Lyme Regis, Dorset DT7 3RJ, England. **Online address:** terry.harknett@btinternet.com

GILMAN, Owen W(inslow), Jr. Also writes as M. Thrice. American, b. 1947. **Genres:** Novels, Film, Literary criticism and history, Humor/Satire. **Career:** University of Maine at Farmington, instructor, 1975-76; high school English teacher in Searsport, ME, 1976-77; St. Joseph's University, Philadelphia, PA, professor of English, 1979-. **Publications:** (ed. with L. Smith) America Rediscovered: Critical Essays on Literature and Film of the Vietnam War, 1990; Vietnam and the Southern Imagination, 1992. Contributor to professional journals and books dealing with Southern literature and culture. **Address:** Dept of English, St. Joseph's University, Philadelphia, PA 19131, U.S.A. **Online address:** ogilman@sju.edu

GILMAN, Richard. American, b. 1925. **Genres:** Literary criticism and history, Theatre, Autobiography/Memoirs. **Career:** Professor of Drama, Yale University, New Haven, CT, 1967-. President, 1981-83, and Vice President, 1983-85, P.E.N., New York. **Publications:** The Confusion of Realms, 1969; Common and Uncommon Masks, 1970; The Making of Modern Drama, 1974, 3rd ed., 2000; Decadence: The Strange Life of an Epithet, 1979; Faith, Sex, Mystery: A Memoir, 1987; Chekhov's Plays, 1995; The Making of Modern Drama, 2000. **Address:** Yale School of Drama, PO Box 208325, New Haven, CT 06520, U.S.A.

GILMAN, Robert Cham. See COPPEL, Alfred.

GILMORE, David D. American, b. 1943. **Genres:** Anthropology/Ethnology. **Career:** University of Pennsylvania, Philadelphia, lecturer in anthropology, summers, 1975-76; Rutgers University, New Brunswick, NJ, lecturer in anthropology, 1976; University of Iowa, Iowa City, assistant professor of anthropology, 1976-77; State University of New York at Stony Brook, assistant professor, 1977-80, associate professor, 1980-86, professor of anthropology and head of department, 1986-. Visiting scholar, Institute of Latin American and Iberian Studies, Columbia University, 1984-85. Conducted anthropological field work in Spain. **Publications:** The People of the Plain: Class and Community in Lower Andalusia, 1980; Aggression and the Community: Paradoxes of Andalusian Culture, 1987; (ed.) Honor and Shame and the Unity of the Mediterranean, 1987; Manhood in the Making: Cultural Concepts of Masculinity, 1990. Contributor to books. **Address:** Department of Anthropology, State University of New York at Stony Brook, Stony Brook, NY 11794-4364, U.S.A.

GILMORE, John. American, b. 1935. **Genres:** Criminology/True Crime, Novels, Autobiography/Memoirs, Plays/Screenplays. **Career:** Child actor in Hollywood became leading man, appeared in television, motion pictures and NY theatre; directed motion pictures; Antioch College, teacher of writing; London Express News & Feature Service, writer, 1972-78. **Publications:** Overpass Blues, 1967; The Tuscon Murders, 1970; The Garbage People, 1971; The Real James Dean, 1975; Night Shark, 1975; Severed: The True Story of the Black Dahlia Murder, 1994; Cold Blooded, 1996; Laid Bare, 1997; Live Fast-Die Young, 1997; Fetish Blond (novel), 1999; Manson, 2000; Hollywood Boulevard, 2003.

GILMORE, Kate. American, b. 1931. **Genres:** Horticulture. **Career:** Writer, 1983-. Temporary legal secretary, NYC, 1985-; Arboretal Artifacts, co-director and craftsman (making one-of-a-kind topiaries and wreaths from dried botanicals), 1989-. **Publications:** Of Griffins and Graffiti, 1986; Remembrance of the Sun, 1986; Enter Three Witches, 1991; Jason and the Bard, 1993. **Address:** 421 W 24th St #4C, New York, NY 10011, U.S.A.

GILMORE, Rachna. Also writes as Rachna Mara. Canadian (born India), b. 1953. **Genres:** Novellas/Short stories, Children's fiction, Young adult fiction. **Career:** Author. Has also worked as a paralegal and operated a pottery studio. **Publications:** FOR CHILDREN: My Mother Is Weird, 1988; Wheniwasalittlegirl, 1989; Jane's Loud Mouth, 1990; Aunt Fred Is a Witch, 1991; Lights for Gita, 1994; A Friend Like Zilla, 1995; Roses for Gita, 1996; Wild Rilla, 1997; A Gift for Gita, 1998; A Screaming Kind of Day, 1999; Fangs and Me, 1999; Ellen's Terrible TV Troubles, 1999; Mina's Spring of Colors, 2000; A Group of One, 2001. AS RACHNA MARA: Of Customs and Excise, 1991.

GILMOUR, David. Canadian, b. 1949. **Genres:** Novels. **Career:** Toronto Film Festival (annual film festival), Toronto, ON, managing editor, 1979-83; Canadian Broadcasting Corporation, ON, film critic for television program The Journal, 1986-; writer. Host of Show "On the Arts with David Gilmour," CBC Newsworld Network, 1994-. Speech writer for Ministry of Industry, Trade, and Technology and for Ministry of Citizenship and Culture. **Publications:** NOVELS: Back on Tuesday, 1986; How Boys See Girls, 1991; An Affair with the Moon, 1993; Lost between Houses, 1999; Sparrow Nights, 2001. OTHER: Glass Bottom Boat (nonfiction), 1986.

GILMOUR, David. British, b. 1952. **Genres:** Novels, Local history/Rural topics, Travel/Exploration. **Career:** Middle East International, London, deputy editor and contributing editor, 1978-85; St. Antony's College, Oxford, fellow, 1996-97; historian and author. **Publications:** Dispossessed: The Ordeal of the Palestinians, 1980; Lebanon: The Fractured Country, 1983; The Transformation of Spain: From Franco to the Constitutional Monarchy, 1985; The Hungry Generations (novel), 1991; Cities of Spain, 1992. BIOGRAPHIES: The Last Leopard: A Life of Giuseppe di Lampedusa, 1988; Curzon, 1994; The Long Recessional: The Imperial Life of Rudyard Kipling, 2002. EDITOR: R. Cobb, The French and Their Revolution, 1998; R. Cobb, Paris and Elsewhere, 1998. **Address:** c/o Aitken Stone and Wylie, 29 Fernshaw Rd, London SW10 OTG, England.

GILMOUR, John C. American, b. 1939. **Genres:** Philosophy. **Career:** Hofstra University, Hempstead, NY, instructor to assistant professor of philosophy, 1963-68; Norwich University, Northfield, VT, assistant professor of philosophy, 1968-70; Alfred University, Alfred, NY, assistant professor to associate professor, 1970-81, professor of philosophy, 1981-91, Margaret and Barbara Hagar Professor in the Humanities, 1991-96, Kruson Distinguished Professor, 1996-2001, professor emeritus, 2001-. **Publications:** Picturing the World, 1986; Fire on Earth: Anselm Kiefer and the Postmodern World, 1990. **Address:** 29 Glidden St, Newcastle, ME 04553, U.S.A. **Online address:** gilmourj@midcoast.com

GILROY, Frank D(aniel). American, b. 1925. **Genres:** Novels, Plays/Screenplays, Film. **Career:** Playwright; film dir., writer and producer. Member of Council, Dramatists Guild, NYC, 1964- (President, 1969-71). Formerly a scriptwriter for TV. **Publications:** About Those Roses: Or, How Not to Do a Play and Succeed, and the Text of The Subject Was Roses, 1965; That Summer-That Fall, 1967; The Only Game in Town, 1968: A Matter of Pride, 1970; (with R.C. Gilroy) Little Ego (for children), 1970; Present Tense, 1972; I Wake Up Screening: Everything You Need to Know about Making Independent Films Including a Thousand Reasons Not To (nonfiction), 1993. NOVELS: Private, 1970; From Noon till Three, 1973, in U.K. as For Want of a Horse, 1975. SCREENPLAYS: Desperate Characters, 1970; From Noon till Three, 1977; Once in Paris, 1978; The Gig, 1985; The Luckiest Man in the World, 1989. PLAYS: Who'll Save the Plowboy?, 1962; The Subject Was Roses, 1962; Last Licks, 1979; The Next Contestant, 1979; Dreams of Glory, 1980; Real to Reel, 1987; Match Point, 1990; A Way with Words, 1991; Give the Bishop My Faint Regards, 1992; Any Given Day, 1993; Fore, 1993; Getting In, 1997; The Golf Ball, 1999; Contact with the Enemy, 1999; Inspector Ohm, 2001. **Address:** c/o Dramatists Guild, 1501 Broadway, Ste. 701, New York, NY 10036, U.S.A.

GILSON, Christopher C. American. **Genres:** Business/Trade/Industry. **Career:** Writer. Worked as a television marketing executive and creative director. **Publications:** (with H.W. Berkman) Consumer Behavior: Concepts and Strategies, 1978, rev. ed, 1986; (with L.C. Cawley and W.R. Schmidt) How to Market Your Law Practice, 1979; (with H.W. Berkman) Advertising Concepts and Strategies, 1980; (with L. Cawley and R. Schmidt) Consumer Revenge, 1981; (as Chris Gilson) Dare to Be Square, 1988; (as Chris Gilson) Crazy for Cornelia (novel), 2000. **Address:** c/o Author Mail, Warner Books, 1271 Avenue of the Americas, New York, NY 10020, U.S.A. **Online address:** chris@chrisgilson.com

GILSTRAP, John. American, b. 1957?. **Genres:** Mystery/Crime/Suspense, Plays/Screenplays. **Career:** Worked as a journalist; also owner and founding president of an environmental compliance consulting company. Associated with Big Brothers and has worked with disadvantaged boys; also a volunteer fireman. **Publications:** NOVELS: Nathan's Run, 1996; Even Steven, 2000; At All Costs, 1998; Scott Free, 2003. **Address:** c/o Molly Friedrich, Aaron Priest Literary Agency, 708 3rd Ave 23rd Fl, New York, NY 10017, U.S.A. **Online address:** jtgilstrap@aol.com

GINAT, Joseph. Israeli. **Genres:** Area studies, Anthropology/Ethnology. **Career:** University of Haifa, Haifa, Israel, professor; deputy administrator for Arab affairs in Israel; lecturer. **Publications:** Women in Muslim Rural Society: Status and Role in Family and Community, 1982; Analysis of the Arab Vote in the 1984 Elections (monograph), 1987; Blood Disputes among Bedouin and Rural Arabs in Israel: Blood Revenge, Mediation, Outcasting, and Family Honor, 1987; (with I. Altman) Polygamous Families in Contemporary Society, 1996. EDITOR: (with E. Marx and A. Shmueli; and contrib.) The Changing Bedouin, 1984; (with B. Rubin and M. Ma'oz) From War to Peace: Arab-Israeli Relations, 1973-1993, 1994; (with A.M. Khazanov) Changing Nomads in a Changing World, 1997. **Address:** University of Haifa, Mount Carmel, 31905 Haifa, Israel. **Online address:** jginat@univ.haifa.ac.il

GINDORF, Rolf. German, b. 1939. **Genres:** Gay and lesbian issues, Psychology, Sex, Sociology. **Career:** Heinrich Schulte Industrieausruestungen Co., Duesseldorf, Germany, president and head of export sales, 1959-71; Deutsche Gesellschaft fuer Sozialwissenschaftliche Sexualforschung (German Society for Social Scientific Sex Research), Duesseldorf, founder, 1971, president, 1971-79, vice-president, 1979-2004, honorary president, 2004-, research and clinical sexologist and director of Institut fuer Lebens- und Sexualberatung (Sexual Therapy and Counseling Institute), 1978-. Duesseldorfer Arbeitskreis Homosexualitaet und Gesellschaft, founder, 1971. Shanghai Sex Research Center, scientific adviser. Also worked as a translator. **Publications:** IN ENGLISH TRANSLATION: (with E.J. Haeberle) Sexology Today, 1993; (ed. with Haeberle, and contrib) Bisexualitaeten, 1994, trans. as Bisexualities, 1998. Contributor to professional journals and other periodicals. CO-EDITOR, IN GERMAN: Beitraege zur Sozialwissenschaftlichen Sexualforschung series, 1979; Schriftenreihe Sozialwissenschaftliche Sexualforschung series, 1986; (with J.-Ch. Aigner, and contrib.) Von der Last der Lust, 1986; (with Haeberle, and contrib.) Sexualitaet als Sozialer Tatbestand, 1986; (with Haeberle, and contrib.) Sexualitaeten in unserer Gesellschaft, 1989; (with Haeberle, and contrib.) Sexualwissenschaft und Sexualpolitik, 1992; (with Haeberle) Sexualwissenschaft Heute, 1992. **Address:** c/o Deutsche Gesellschaft fur Sozialwissenschaftliche, Sexualforschung, Gerresheimer Strasse 20, D-40211 Duesseldorf, Germany. **Online address:** Rolf.Gindorf@sexologie.org

GINSBORG, Paul (Anthony). (born England), b. 1945. **Genres:** Politics/Government. **Career:** Historian and educator. Churchill College, Cambridge, England, member of faculty; University of Florence, Florence, Italy, professor of contemporary European history, 1992-. Visiting professor at University of Turin and University of Siena. **Publications:** The Politics of Lenin (pamphlet), 1974; Daniele Manin and the Venetian Revolution of 1848-49, 1979; Storia d'Italia dal dopoguerra a oggi: società e politica, 1943-1988, 1989, published as A History of Contemporary Italy: Society and Politics, 1943-1988, 1990; (editor, with John A. Davis) Society and Politics in the Age of the Risorgimento: Essays in Honour of Denis Mack Smith, 1991; (editor) Stato dell'Italia, 1994; L'Italia del tempo presente: famiglia, società civile, stato, 1980-1996, 1998, revised and translated as Italy and Its Discontents: Family, Civil Society, State, 1980-2001, 2001; (editor, with Francesco Ramella) Un'Italia minore: famiglia, istruzione e tradizioni civiche in Valdelsa, 1999; Silvio Berlusconi: Television, Power, and Patrimony, 2004. Contributor to periodicals. **Address:** Department of Geography, University of Florence, 10-50129 Florence, Italy. **Online address:** ginsborg@unifi.it

GINSBURG, Faye D(iana). American, b. 1952. **Genres:** Sex, Women's studies and issues, Film. **Career:** WCCO-TV, Minneapolis, MN, associate documentary producer, 1981-83; New York University, New York City, professor of anthropology and director of program in Culture & Media, 1986-, Center for Media, Culture & History, director, 1992-; writer. Jewish Museum, public education program, 1977-80; New School for Social Research, visiting assistant professor of anthropology, 1985-86; Margaret Mead Film Festival Advisory Board, 1990-; International Film Seminars, member of board of trustees, 1988-93; member of board of directors, 1987-89; National Archive of Jewish Broadcasting, member of advisory board, 1988-. **Publications:** Contested Lives: The Abortion Debate in an American Community, 1989; (ed with A. Tsing) Negotiating Gender in American Culture, 1990; Conceiving the New World Order: The Global Politics of Reproduction, 1995. **Address:** Department of Anthropology, New York University, 25 Waverly Place, New York, NY 10003, U.S.A.

GINSBURG, Mark B. American, b. 1949. **Genres:** Education. **Career:** University of Aston, Birmingham, England, lecturer, 1976-78; University of Houston, Houston, TX, assistant professor, 1979-82, associate professor, 1982-87; University of Pittsburgh, Pittsburgh, PA, associate professor, 1987-89, professor, 1989-, director of Institute for International Studies in Education, 1987-93, 1996-. Pittsburgh Peace Institute, member of board of directors, 1989-97, co-chairperson, 1991-93; Alliance for Progressive Action, member of board of directors and executive committee, 1992-. **Publications:** The Role of the Middle School Teacher, 1977; Contradictions in Teacher Education and Society, 1988; The Politics of Educators' Work and Lives, 1995; The Political Dimension in Teacher Education, 1995. EDITOR: Understanding Educational Reform in Global Context, 1991; Cuba in the Special Period: Cuban Perspectives, 1997. **Address:** Institute for International Studies in Education, School of Education, University of Pittsburgh, 5K01 Posvar Hall, Pittsburgh, PA 15260, U.S.A. **Online address:** mbg@pitt.edu

GINZBURG, Carlo. Italian, b. 1939. **Genres:** History. **Career:** University of Rome, Rome, Italy, assistant in modern Italian history, during the 1960s; University of Bologna, Bologna, Italy, professor of modern history, 1970-; University of California, Los Angeles, professor of Italian Renaissance studies. Visiting fellow at Harvard University Center for Italian Renaissance Studies in Florence; the Warburg Institute in London, 1964; the Princeton Institute for Advanced Study, 1975 and 1986; and Yale University, 1983. Visiting professor at Princeton University, 1973. **Publications:** I benandanti: Stregoneria e culti agrari tra cinquecento e seicento, 1966, trans by J. and A. Tedeschi as The Night Battles: Witchcraft and Agrarian Cults in the Sixteenth and Seventeenth Centuries, 1983; Il nicodemismo: Simulazione e dissimulazione religiosa nell'Europa del '500, 1970; (with A. Prosperi) Giochi di pazienza: Un seminario sul Beneficio di Cristo, 1975; Il formaggio e i vermi: Il cosmo di un mugnaio del '500, 1976, trans by J. and A. Tedeschi published as The Cheese and the Worms: The Cosmos of a Sixteenth-Century Miller, 1980; Indagini su Piero: Il Battesimo, il Ciclo di Arezzo, la Flagellazione di Urbino, 1982, trans by M. Ryle and K. Soper as The Enigma of Piero, Piero della Francesca: The Baptism, the Arezzo Cylce, the Flagellation, 1985; Miti, emblemi, spie: Morfologia e storia, 1986, trans by J. and A. Tedeschi as Clues, Myths, and the Historical Method, 1989, in UK as Myths, Emblems, Clues, 1990; Storia notturna: Una decifrazione del sabba, 1989, trans by R. Rosenthal as Ecstacies: Deciphering the Witches' Sabbath, 1991; Il giudice e lo storico: Considerazioni in margine al processo Sofri, 1991. **Address:** Dept of History, 6265 Bunche Hall Box 951473, University of California, Los Angeles, Los Angeles, CA 90095-1473, U.S.A.

GIOIA, (Michael) Dana. American, b. 1950. **Genres:** Novellas/Short stories, Poetry, Songs/Lyrics and libretti, Literary criticism and history, Translations. **Career:** General Foods Corp., White Plains, NY, manager of new business development, 1977-87, marketing manager, 1988-89, vice-president, 1990-92; writer, 1992-. Member of board of directors of Wesleyan University Writers Conference, 1985-2002; West Chester Poetry conference, co-director, 1995-2002; Teaching Poetry Conference, co-director, 2000-02; National Endowment for the Arts, chairman, 2003-. **Publications:** (author of intro.) W. Kees, Two Prose Sketches, 1984. POETRY: Summer, 1983; Daily Horoscope, 1986; The Gods of Winter, 1991; Interrogations at Noon, 2001. TRANSLATIONS: E. Montale, Mottetti: Poems of Love, 1990; Seneca, The Madness of Hercules, 1995. CRITICISM: Can Poetry Matter?: Essays on Poetry and American Culture, 1992; The Barrier of a Common Language: Essays on Contemporary British Poetry, 2002. EDITOR: W. Kees, The Ceremony and Other Stories, 1983; (with W.J. Smith) Poems from Italy, 1985; (with A. Reid) The Printed Poem: The Poem as Print, 1985; (with M. Palma) New Italian Poets, 1991; Formal Introductions, 1994; (with X.J. Kennedy) An Introduction to Poetry, 1994, 10th ed., 2002; (with X.J. Kennedy) An Introduction to Fiction, 1994, 9th ed., 2002; (with W. Logan) Certain Solitudes, 1997; (with X.J. Kennedy) Literature, 7th ed., 1999, 8th ed., 2002; (with R.S. Gwynn) The Longman Anthology of Short Fiction: Stories and Authors in Context, 2001; Nosferatu: An Opera Libretto, 2001; Selected Short Stories of Weldon Kees, 2002; (with S. Timberg) The Misread City, 2003. **Address:** The Nancy Hanks Center, 1100 Pennsylvania Ave NW, Washington, DC 20506, U.S.A.

GIOVAGNOLI, Melissa (E.). American, b. 1955. **Genres:** Business/Trade/Industry. **Career:** Networlding.com, Schaumburg, IL, president, 1986-. Closerlook.com, consultant; EnvisionaBetterWorld.org, co-founder; University of Chicago, Women's Business Graduate Advisory Board. **Publications:** The Chicago Entrepreneurs Sourcebook, 1992; Make Your Connections Count!, 1994; 50 Fabulous Places to Raise Your Family, 1996; Angels in the Workplace: Stories and Strategies to Create a New World of Work, 1997; 75 Cage Rattling Questions to Change the Way You Work, 1998; The Power of Two: Forming Alliance Networks That Work, 1998; Networlding: Building Relationships and Opportunities for Success, 2000. **Address:** 910 W. Madison St. #707, Chicago, IL 60607, U.S.A. **Online address:** megnetwork@aol.com

GIOVANNI, Nikki. (Yolande Cornelia , Jr). American, b. 1943. **Genres:** Children's fiction, Poetry, Race relations, Biography. **Career:** Rutgers University, Livingston College, New Brunswick, NJ, associate professor of English, 1968-70; Encore mag., Albuquerque, NM, former editorial consultant. **Publications:** Black Judgment, 1968; Black Feeling, Black Talk, 1968; Re: Creation, 1970; Poem of Angela Yvonne Davis, 1970; Spin a Soft Black Song: Poems for Children, 1971; Gemini: An Extended Autobiographical Statement on My First Twenty-Five Years of Being a Black Poet, 1971; My House, 1972; Ego Tripping and Other Poems for Young People, 1973; A Dialogue: James Baldwin and Nikki Giovanni, 1973; A Poetic Equation: Conversations between Nikki Giovanni and Margaret Walker, 1974; The Women and the Men, 1975; Cotton Candy on a Rainy Day, 1978; Vacation Time: Poems for Children, 1980; Those Who Ride the Night Winds, 1982; Sacred Cows (essays), 1988; Racism 101, 1994; The Genie in the Jar, 1996; The Selected Poems of Nikki Giovanni, 1968-1995, 1996; The Sun Is So Quiet, 1996; Love Poems, 1997; Blues: For All the Changes: New Poems, 1999; Quilting the Black-Eyed Pea: Poems and Not Quite Poems, 2002; Prosaic Soul, 2003; The Collected Poetry of Nikki Giovanni: 1968-1998, 2003; Girls in the Circle, 2004. EDITOR: Night Comes Softly, 1970; (with C. Dennison) Appalachian Elders, 1992; Grand Mothers: Poems, Reminiscences, and Short Stories about the Keepers of Our Traditions, 1994; Shimmy, Shimmy, Shimmy Like My Sister Kate, 1996; Grand Fathers: Reminiscences, Poems, Recipes and Photos of the Keepers of Our Traditions, 1999. **Address:** Virginia Polytechnic Institute and State University, Dept. of English, Shanks Hall, Blacksburg, VA 24061, U.S.A. **Online address:** ngiovann@vt.edu

GIPSON, Carolyn R. American, b. 1944. **Genres:** Economics, Biography. **Career:** University of Michigan, Ann Arbor, assistant professor of English, 1971-76; U.S. Senate, Washington, DC, legislative counsel, 1979-81; attorney with law firms in Washington, DC, 1983-89; Foreign Trading Services, High Point, NC, consultant, 1990-. **Publications:** The McGraw-Hill Dictionary of International Trade and Finance, 1993; Portraits of American Presidents: A Multimedia Adventure through American History, 1994. Contributor to periodicals. **Address:** C/O B.K. Nelson, 84 Woodland Road, Pleasantville, NY 10570, U.S.A.

GIRLING, John (Lawrence Scott). British/Australian, b. 1926. **Genres:** International relations/Current affairs, Politics/Government, Third World. **Career:** Member, Research Staff, Foreign Office, London, 1952-66; Sr. Fellow, Dept. of International Relations, Research School of Pacific Studies, Australian National University, Canberra, 1966-92; Fellow, Wilson Center, Washington, DC, 1987; Research Fellow, Institute of Southeast Asia Studies, Singapore, 1993. **Publications:** People's War: Conditions and Consequences in China and Southeast Asia, 1969; America and the Third World: Revolution and Intervention, 1980; The Bureaucratic Polity in Modernising Societies: Similarities, Differences and Prospects in the Asean Region, 1981; Thailand: Society and Politics, 1981; Capital and Power: Political Economy and Social Transformation, 1987; Myths and Politics in Western Societies: Evaluating the Crisis of Modernity in the United States, Germany, and Great Britain, 1993; Interpreting Development: Capitalism, Democracy, and The Middle Class in Thailand, 1996; Corruption, Capitalism and Democracy, 1997; France: Political and Social Change, 1998. **Address:** Appt. 33, 33 rue Achille Viadieu, 31400 Toulouse, France. **Online address:** john.nina.girling@wanadoo.fr

GIROUARD, Mark. British, b. 1931. **Genres:** Art/Art history, Architecture. **Career:** Architectural historian and author. Country Life, staff writer, 1958-66; Architectural Review, staff writer, 1971-75; Oxford University, Slade Professor of Fine Art, 1975-76; Columbia University, George Lurcy Visiting Professor, 1987; writer. Member of the advisory council of the Paul Mellon Centre for Studies in British Art, 1990-. **Publications:** Robert Smythson and the Architecture of the Elizabethan Era, 1967, 2nd ed published as Robert Smythson and the Elizabethan Country House, 1983; The Victorian Country House, 1971, rev and enlarged ed, 1985; Victorian Pubs, 1975; (with others) Spirit of the Age (based on the television series), 1975; Sweetness and Light: The "Queen Anne" Movement, 1860-1900, 1977; Life in the English Country House: A Social and Architectural History, 1978; Historic Houses of Britain, 1979; Alfred Waterhouse and the Natural History Museum, 1981; The Return to Camelot: Chivalry and the English Gentleman, 1982; John Piper's Stowe, 1983; Cities and People: A Social and Architectural History, 1985; A Country House Companion, 1987; Hardwick Hall, 1989; The English Town: A History of Urban Life, 1990; Town and Country, 1992; Windsor: The Most Romantic Castle, 1993; Life in the French Country House, 2000. **Address:** 35 Colville Rd., London W11 2BT, England.

GIROUX, E. X. See SHANNON, Doris.

GISH, Robert F. American, b. 1940. **Genres:** Novels, Novellas/Short stories, Literary criticism and history, Autobiography/Memoirs. **Career:** University of Northern Iowa, professor of English language and literature, 1967-91, emeritus university distinguished scholar, 2001-; California Polytechnic State University, ethnic studies, director, professor of English, 1992-2001. University of New Mexico, visiting New Mexico scholar/writer. Member of Cherokee Nation of Oklahoma. **Publications:** Hamlin Garland: The Far West, 1976; Paul Horgan, 1983; Frontier's End: The Life and Literature of Harvey Fergusson, 1988; William Carlos Williams: The Short Fiction, 1989; Songs of My Hunter Heart: A Western Kinship, 1992; First Horses: Stories of the New West, 1993; When Coyote Howls, 1994; Nueva Granada, 1995; Bad Boys and Black Sheep: Fateful Tales from the West, 1996; Beyond Bounds: Cross Cultural Essays on Anglo, American Indian, and Chicano Literature, 1996; Beautiful Swift Fox: Erna Fergusson and the Southwest, 1996; Dreams of Quivira: Stories in Search of the Golden West, 1997. **Address:** PO Box 12652, Albuquerque, NM 87195, U.S.A. **Online address:** rfg@robertfgish.com

GITLIN, Todd. American, b. 1943. **Genres:** Novels, Communications/ Media, Politics/Government, Sociology, Writing/Journalism. **Career:** San Francisco Express Times, California, writer, 1968-69; San Jose State College, California, lecturer, 1970-76; University of California, Santa Cruz, lecturer, 1974-77; University of California, Berkeley, assistant professor, 1978-83, associate professor, 1983-87, professor of sociology and director of Mass Communications Program, 1987-92; New York University, professor of culture, journalism and sociology, 1995-2002; Columbia University, professor of journalism and sociology, 2002-. **Publications:** (with N. Hollander) Uptown: Poor Whites in Chicago, 1970; Busy Being Born (poetry), 1974; The Whole World Is Watching: Mass Media and the Unmaking of the New Left, 1980; Inside Prime Time, 1983; The Sixties: Years of Hope, Days of Rage, 1987; The Murder of Albert Einstein, 1992; The Twilight of Common Dreams: Why America is Wracked by Culture Wars, 1995; Sacrifice, 1999; Media Unlimited: How the Torrent of Images and Sounds Overwhelms Our Lives, 2002; Letters to a Young Activist, 2003; The Intellectuals and the Flag, 2004. EDITOR: Campfires of Resistance: Poetry from the Movement, 1971; Watching Television, 1987. **Address:** Graduate School of Journalism, Columbia University, 2950 Broadway Rm 201F, New York, NY 10027, U.S.A. **Online address:** tg2058@columbia.edu

GITTER, Elisabeth. American, b. 1945. **Genres:** Biography. **Career:** John Jay College of Criminal Justice, New York, NY, professor of English.

Publications: The Imprisoned Guest: Samuel Howe and Laura Bridgman, the Original Deaf-Blind Girl, 2001. Contributor to periodicals. **Address:** Thematic Studies, John Jay College, 899 10th Ave Rm 432, New York, NY 10019, U.S.A. **Online address:** egitter@jjay.cuny.edu

GITTLER, Joseph B. American, b. 1912. **Genres:** Cultural/Ethnic topics, Philosophy, Race relations, Social commentary, Sociology, Civil liberties/ Human rights, Education, Ethics, Human relations/Parenting. **Career:** Co-Ed., International Journal of Group Tensions, 1985-. Instructor, Assistant Professor, and Associate Professor of Sociology, 1936-43, University of Georgia, Athens; Professor of Sociology and Head of Dept., Drake University, Des Moines, IA, 1943-45; Ed., Midwest Sociologist, 1945-48; Associate Professor and Professor of Sociology, 1945-54, and Director of Research Project, Intergroup Relations in Rural Areas, 1952-55, Iowa State University, Ames; Professor and Chairman, Dept. of Sociology and Anthropology, 1954-61, and Director, Center for the Study of Group Relations, 1954-60, University of Rochester, New York: Dean of Faculty, Queensborough College, CUNY, 1961-66; Dean, Ferkauf Graduate School of Humanities and Social Sciences, and University Professor of Sociology, Yeshiva University, NYC, 1966-78; George Mason University, Fairfax, VA, Distinguished Professor of Sociology, 1978-90, Director of the Center for the Study of Race and Ethnic Relations, 1987-90, Professor Emeritus, 1990-; Fulbright Scholar, Ben Gurion University, Israel, 1990-91; visiting professor and Fulbright Scholar, Hiroshima University, Japan, 1979-80; Professor of American Studies, Doshisha University, Kyoto, Japan, 1979; Duke University, Durham, NC, Distinguished Professor of Sociology, 1990-94, Scholar in Residence, 1994-99. **Publications:** Social Thought among the Early Greeks, 1940; Social Dynamics, 1952; (with L. Gittler) Your Neighbor Near and Far, 1955; (ed.) Understanding Minority Groups, 1956, 1964; (ed.) Review of Sociology, 1957; Ethnic Minorities in the U.S., 1977; Jewish Life in the U.S.: Perspectives from the Social Sciences, 1981; Problems of Racial and Ethnic Relations among High School Youth, 1983; Educational Curricula for Multi-Ethnic Societies, 1984; Integration in the Social Sciences, 1987; A Schematic Framework for Studying Human Social Conflict Resolution, 1988; American Society and Culture: Glossary of Terms and Concepts, 1979; Science and Morals, 1941; Social Effects of Inventions, 1941; How Social Change Comes About, 1951; Social Trends and Atomic Energy, 1953; Social Adjustment to Technological Innovation, 1957; Cultural Pluralism in Contemporary American Society, 1974; Educational Curricula for Multi-Ethnic Societies, 1984; Ethical Components in Conflict Resolution, 1987; Philosophical Questions in The Analysis of Conflict Knowledge and Conflict Resolution Practices, 1989; Towards a Definition of Human Social Conflict, 1990; Ethnic and Racial Conflict, 1995; Humanocentrism, 1995; Ideas of Concord and Discord in Religions of the World, 1999; (ed. and author) International Encyclopedia of Racial and Ethnic Relations, 2001. **Address:** 5 Glenmore Dr, Durham, NC 27707, U.S.A.

GIVEN, David R(oger). New Zealander, b. 1943. **Genres:** Environmental sciences/Ecology. **Career:** New Zealand Department of Scientific and Industrial Research, research scientist, 1965-92, herbarium keeper, 1974-87; National Museum of Natural Sciences, Ottawa, ON, postdoctoral research fellow, 1973-74; David Given & Associates, consultant, 1992-; Lincoln University, lecturer, 1993-95, honorary lecturer, 1996-, Isaac Centre for Nature Conservation, associate professor; Southern Heritage Expeditions, lecturer and tour guide, 1992-95; Christchurch City Council, botanical services curator, 2003-. University of Otago, Tennant Lecturer, 1991, Loder Cup, 1996; New Zealand Bible College, member of Canterbury regional board, 1994-2002. **Publications:** (with J.H. Soper) The Arctic-Alpine Element of the Vascular Flora of Lake Superior, 1981; (with G.A. Williams) New Zealand Red Data Book, 1981; Rare and Endangered Plants of New Zealand, 1981; (ed.) Conservation of Plant Species and Habitats, 1983; (with P.A. Williams) Conservation of Chatham Islands Flora and Vegetation, 1984; (with C. Wilson) Guide to Threatened Plants of New Zealand, 1990; (with W. Harris) Methods of Ethnobotany, 1994; Principles and Practice of Plant Conservation, 1994; (with I. Spellerberg) Going Native: A Future for NZ Plants, 2004 . Contributor of articles and photographs to scientific journals. **Address:** 101 Jeffreys Rd, Christchurch 5, New Zealand. **Online address:** givend@attglobal.net

GIZIOWSKI, Richard (John). American, b. 1946. **Genres:** History. **Career:** Auburn public schools, Auburn, MA, teacher, 1971-98. Teacher, writer, book reviewer for the Journal of Military History. **Publications:** The Enigma of General Blaskowitz, 1996.

GLADSTONE, Arthur M. Also writes as Maggie Gladstone, Lisabet Norcross, Margaret SeBastian, Cilla Whitmore. American, b. 1921. **Genres:** Romance/Historical. **Career:** Full-time writer since 1973. Retired Major,

U.S. Air Force, (enlisted, 1943); Research Chemist, American Cyanamid, Bridgeville, Pa., 1947-48; Research Supervisor, Pittsburgh Coke and Chemical, 1948-53; Product Manager, Nopco Chemical, Newark, New Jersey, 1953-59; Vice-President, Anchor Serum, St. Joseph, Missouri, 1959-61; Advanced Rocket Propulsion Marketer, Hercules, Rocket City, W. Virginia, 1962-68; Product Development Consultant, 1969-73. **Publications:** AS MARGARET SeBASTIAN: The Honorable Miss Clarendon, 1975; Meg Miller, 1976; Bow Street Gentleman, 1977; Bow Street Brangle, 1977; Miss Letty, 1977; My Lord Rakehell, 1977; Lord Orlando's Protegee, 1977; The Young Lady from Alton-St. Pancras, 1977; That Savage Yankee Squire!, 1978; The Poor Relation, 1978; Lord Dedringham's Divorce, 1978; The Courtship of Colonel Crowne, 1978; Her Knight on a Barge, 1979; The Awakening of Lord Dalby, 1979; Dilemma in Duet, 1979; Byway to Love, 1980; The Plight of Pamela Pollworth, 1980; Miss Keating's Temptation, 1981; A Keeper for Lord Linford, 1982. AS MAGGIE GLADSTONE: The Scandalous Lady, 1978; The Fortunate Belle, 1978; The Love Duel, 1978; The Reluctant Debutante, 1979; The Impudent Widow, 1979; The Love Tangle, 1980; The Lady's Masquerade, 1980; The Reluctant Protegee, 1980; A Lesson in Love, 1981. AS LISABET NORCROSS: Masquerade of Love, 1978; Heiress to Love, 1978; My Lady Scapegrace, 1979. AS CILLA WHITMORE: The Lady and the Rogue, 1978; Manner of a Lady, 1979; His Lordship's Landlady, 1979; Mansion for a Lady, 1980. **Address:** 323 Logtrac Rd, Stanardsville, VA 22973, U.S.A. **Online address:** amgladstone@hotmail.com

GLADSTONE, Maggie. *See* **GLADSTONE, Arthur M.**

GLAHE, Fred R. American, b. 1934. **Genres:** Economics. **Career:** Professor of Economics, University of Colorado, Boulder, since 1965. **Publications:** (with M. Dowling) Reading in Econometric Theory, 1970; Macroeconomics: Theory and Policy, 1973, 1985; (with D. Lee) Microeconomics: Theory and Applications, 1981, 1989; Keynes's The General Theory of Employment, Interest, and Money: A Concordance, 1991; Adam Smith's The Wealth of Nations: A Concordance, 1993; The Drama: The Keynes-Hayek Debate on the Nature & Causes of the Business Cycle, 1999. EDITOR: Collected Paper of Kenneth E. Boulding: Economics, 2 vols., 1971; Adam Smith and the Wealth of Nations, 1978; (with J. Peden) The American Family and the State, 1986. **Address:** Dept. of Economics, University of Colorado, Boulder, CO 80309, U.S.A.

GLAISTER, Lesley (G.). British, b. 1956. **Genres:** Novels. **Career:** Parsons Cross College, Sheffield, England, teacher of adult education courses, 1982-; writer. Tutor at Loxley College, University of Sheffield and The Arvan Foundation, 1992-93. Lecturer, Sheffield Hallam University, 1994-. **Publications:** NOVELS: Honour Thy Father, 1990; Trick or Treat, 1991; Digging to Australia, 1993; Limestone and Clay, 1993; Partial Eclipse, 1994; The Private Parts of Women, 1996; Easy Peasy, 1997; Sheer Blue Bliss, 1999; Now You See Me, 2001. **Address:** c/o Bill Hamilton, A. M. Heath and Co. Ltd, 79 St. Martin's Lane, London WC2N 4AA, England.

GLANCY, Diane. American, b. 1941. **Genres:** Novels, Novellas/Short stories, Plays/Screenplays, Poetry, Essays. **Career:** Macalester College, St. Paul, MN, professor of English, 1988-. **Publications:** POETRY: One Age in a Dream, 1986; Offering, 1988; Iron Woman, 1990; Lone Dog's Winter Count, 1991; The Relief of America, 2000; The Shadow's Horse, 2003; Primer of the Obsolete, 2004. STORIES: Trigger Dance, 1990; Firesticks; Monkey Secret, 1995; The Voice That Was in Travel, 1999. ESSAYS: Claiming Breath, 1992; The West Pole, 1997; The Cold-and-Hunger Dance, 1998. NOVELS: Pushing the Bear, 1996; The Only Piece of Furniture in the House, 1996; Flutie, 1998; Fuller Man, 1999; The Man Who Heard the Land, 2002; The Mask Maker, 2002; Designs of the Night Sky, 2002; Stone Heart: A Novel of Sacajawea, 2003; The Dance Partner, 2005. PLAYS: War Cries, 1996; American Gypsy, 2002. **Address:** Dept of English, Macalester College, 1600 Grand, St. Paul, MN 55105, U.S.A. **Online address:** glancy@macalester.edu

GLANCY, Diane. (born United States), b. 1941. **Genres:** Poetry. **Career:** Macalester College, St. Paul, MN, assistant professor of English, beginning 1988, became professor. Artist-in-residence of the Oklahoma State Arts Council, 1982-92; has traveled for the U.S. Information Agency to Syria and Jordan. **Publications:** Drystalks of the Moon, 1981; Traveling On, 1982; Brown Wolf Leaves the Res and Other Poems, 1984; (editor with C. W. Truesdale) Two Worlds Walking: Short Stories, Essays, and Poetry by Writers with Mixed Heritages, 1994; (editor, with Mark Nowak) Visit Teepee Town: Native Writings after the Detours, 1999; The Shadow's Horse, 2003. SHORT STORIES: Trigger Dance, 1990; Firesticks: A Collection of Stories, 1993; Monkey Secret (short stories), 1995; The Voice That Was in Travel:

Stories, 1999. NOVELS: The Only Piece of Furniture in the House: A Novel, 1996; Pushing the Bear: A Novel of the Trail of Tears, 1996; Flutie, 1998; The Closets of Heaven: A Novel of Dorcas, the New Testament Seamstress, 1999; Fuller Man, 1999; The Man Who Heard the Land, 2001; The Mask Maker, 2002; Designs of the Night Sky, 2002; Stone Heart: A Novel of Sacajawea, 2003. POETRY: One Age in a Dream, 1986; Offering: Aliscolidodi, 1988; Iron Woman, 1990; Lone Dog's Winter Count, 1991; Boom Town, 1995; Primer of the Obsolete, 1998; (Ado)ration, 1999; The Relief of America, 2000; The Stones for a Pillow, 2001. ESSAYS: Claiming Breath, 1992; The West Pole, 1997; The Cold-and-Hunger Dance, 1998; In-between Places, 2004. PLAYS: Segwohi, 1987; Testimony, 1987; Webjob, OK, 1987; Stick Horse, 1988; The Lesser Wars, 1989; Halfact, 1994; War Cries: A Collection of Plays, 1997; American Gypsy: Six Native American Plays, 2002. Author of plays. **Address:** 3508 W. 73rd Terr., Prairie Village, KS 66208, U.S.A.

GLANCY, Ruth F(ergusson). British/Canadian, b. 1948. **Genres:** Literary criticism and history, Bibliography. **Career:** University of Bristol, England, tutor in literature, 1976-80; University of Alberta, Edmonton, sessional lecturer, 1980-88; Concordia University College, Edmonton, associate professor in English, 1990-. **Publications:** Dickens's Christmas Books, Christmas Stories, and Other Short Fiction: An Annotated Bibliography, 1985; A Tale of Two Cities: Dickens's Revolutionary Novel, 1991; A Tale of Two Cities: An Annotated Bibliography, 1993; Student Companion to Dickens, 1999. EDITOR, AUTHOR OF INTRO. & NOTES: Dickens's Christmas Books, 1988; Dickens's Christmas Stories, 1996. Contributor of articles and reviews to literature journals. **Address:** Concordia University College, 7128 Ada Blvd, Edmonton, AB, Canada T5B 4E4. **Online address:** rglancy@concordia.ab.ca

GLANTZ, David M. American, b. 1942. **Genres:** History, Military/Defense/Arms control. **Career:** US Army, career officer, colonel (retired); battery commander in Germany, 1965-67; analyst with Fire Support Coordination Center in Vietnam, 1968-69; US Military Academy, West Point, NY, instructor to assistant professor of modern European history, 1969-73; US Army, Europe, Office of the Chief of Staff for Intelligence, intelligence analyst, 1977-79; US Army Command and General Staff College, Fort Leavenworth, KS, faculty member and deputy director of Combat Studies Institute; 1979-83; US Army War College, Carlisle Barracks, PA, faculty member and director of Soviet Studies and Center for Land Warfare, 1983-86; Combined Arms Center, Fort Leavenworth, director of research and deputy director of Soviet Army Studies Office, 1986-90, acting director, 1990, director of Foreign Military Studies Office, 1991-; writer. Lecturer at colleges and universities in US and UK. **Publications:** August Storm: The Soviet 1945 Strategic Offensive in Manchuria, 1983; August Storm: Soviet Tactical and Operational Combat in Manchuria, 1945, 1983; The Soviet Airborne Experience, 1984; Soviet Military Deception in the Second World War, 1989; The Role of Intelligence in Soviet Military Strategy in World War II, 1990; Soviet Military Intelligence in War, 1990; Soviet Military Operational Art, 1990; From the Don to the Dnepr, 1990; The Soviet Conduct of Tactical Maneuver, 1991; The Military Strategy of the Soviet Union, 1917-1990, 1991; Soviet Airborne Forces, 1993; A Clash of Titans, 1995; Stumbling Colossus, 1998; Kharkov, May 1942, 1998; Marshal Zhukov's Greatest Defeat, 1999; The Battle of Kursk, 1999; The Battle for Kursk, 1999; Barbarossa, 2001; Belorussia 1944, 2001; The Battle for L'vov, July 1944, 2002; The Battle for Leningrad 1941-1944, 2002; The Soviet Strategic Offensive in Manchuria, 1945, 2003; Soviet Operational and Tactical Combat in Manchuria, 2003. **Address:** 805 Forbes Rd, Carlisle, PA 17013, U.S.A. **Online address:** Rzhev@aol.com

GLANTZ, Kalman. American, b. 1937. **Genres:** Administration/Management, Psychology. **Career:** Psychotherapist in private practice, Cambridge, MA, 1977-. Campaign Research Associates (political and economic issues development firm), founder and director, 1975-80; Lesley College, Cambridge, professor of economics and social science, 1977-85; Massachusetts Institute of Technology, visiting scientist, 1996-99; Virtual Reality Therapies, Inc., clinical director, 1996-99. **Publications:** (with J.K. Pearce) Exiles from Eden: Psychotherapy from an Evolutionary Perspective, 1989; (with J.G. Bernhard) Staying Human in the Organization. **Address:** 12 Kinnaird St, Cambridge, MA 02139, U.S.A. **Online address:** kglantz@earthlink.net

GLANVILLE, Brian (Lester). British, b. 1931. **Genres:** Novels, Children's fiction, Plays/Screenplays, Sports/Fitness, Novellas/Short stories. **Career:** Bodley Head Ltd., publrs., London, literary adviser, 1958-62; Sunday Times Newspaper, London, sports columnist and chief football writer, 1958-92; football writer, 1998-; The People, sports columnist, 1992-96; The Times, sports columnist, 1996-98. **Publications:** (with C. Bastin) Cliff Bastin Remembers, 1950; The Reluctant Dictator, 1952; Henry Sows the Wind,

1954; Soccer Nemesis, 1955; Along the Arno, 1956; The Bankrupts, 1958; (with J. Weinstein) World Cup, 1958; After Rome, Africa, 1959; Soccer round the Globe, 1959; A Bad Streak and Other Stories, 1961; Diamond, 1962; (ed.) The Footballer's Companion, 1962; The Rise of Gerry Logan, 1963; The Director's Wife and Other Stories, 1963; Goalkeepers Are Crazy, 1964; The King of Hackney Marshes and Other Stories, 1965; Know about Football, 1965; A Second Home, 1965; A Roman Marriage, 1966; The Artist Type, 1967; People in Sport, 1967; Soccer, 1968; The Olympian, 1969; A Betting Man, 1969; A Cry of Crickets, 1970; Puffin Book of Football, 1970; Goalkeepers Are Different (children's fiction), 1971; The Financiers, 1972; Brian Glanville's Book of World Football, 1972; World Football Handbook, 1972; The Sunday Times History of the World Cup (in US as History of the Soccer World Cup), 1973; The Thing He Loves and Other Stories, 1973; The Comic, 1974; The Dying of the Light, 1976; Target Man (children's novel), 1978; A History of Soccer (in US as A Book of Soccer), 1979; Never Look Back, 1980; A Visit to the Villa (play), 1981; Underneath the Arches (musical play), 1981; (with K. Whitney) The British Challenge, 1984; Love Is Not Love and Other Stories, 1985; Kissing America, 1985; (ed.) The Joy of Football, 1986; The Catacomb, 1988; Football Memories, 1999; Dictators, 2001. **Address:** 160 Holland Park Ave, London W11 4UH, England.

GLASBERG, Davita Silfen. American (born Germany), b. 1951. **Genres:** Sociology. **Career:** Brooklyn College of the City University of New York, Brooklyn, NY, adjunct lecturer in sociology, 1975-76; State University of New York at Stony Brook, instructor in sociology, 1978-83; Southern Illinois University, Carbondale, assistant professor of sociology, 1983-88; University of Connecticut, Storrs, assistant professor, 1988-91, associate professor, 1991-97, professor of sociology, 1997-, member of departmental executive committee, 1989-, director of human rights minor. **Publications:** The Power of Collective Purse Strings: The Effect of Bank Hegemony on Corporations and the State, 1989; (with K. Neubeck) Sociology: A Critical Approach, 1996; (with D. Skidmore) Corporate Welfare Policy and the Welfare State: Bank Deregulation and the Savings and Loan Bailout, 1997. Contributor to books. Contributor of articles and reviews to scholarly journals. **Address:** Department of Sociology, Box U-68, University of Connecticut, Storrs Mansfield, CT 06269-2068, U.S.A. **Online address:** davita.glasberg@uconn.edu.

GLASCO, Michael. American, b. 1945. **Genres:** Novels. **Career:** Southern Methodist University, Dallas, TX, photography instructor, 196971; owner and operator of a commercial photography studio which did photography for national advertising campaigns and corporate annual reports, 1971-94; freelance writer, 1995-. Active in church outreach programs for the homeless and for poor neighborhoods in Dallas. **Publications:** Angels in Tesuque (novel), 1995. **Address:** 3244 Amherst, Dallas, TX 75225, U.S.A.

GLASER, James M. American, b. 1960. **Genres:** Politics/Government. **Career:** University of California, Berkeley, data consultant, 1986-90; Tufts University, Medford, MA, assistant professor, 1991-97, associate professor of political science, 1997-. **Publications:** Race, Campaign Politics, and the Realignment in the South, 1996. Contributor to journals. **Address:** Department of Political Science, Eaton Hall, Tufts University, Medford, MA 02155, U.S.A. **Online address:** jglaser@tufts.edu

GLASER, William Arnold. American, b. 1925. **Genres:** Social sciences. **Career:** Professor, Graduate School of Management, New School for Social Research, NYC, since 1982. Assistant Professor, Michigan State University, E. Lansing, 1952-56; Sr. Research Associate, Bureau of Applied Social Research, 1956-82, and Executive Director, Council of Social Sciences Data Archives, 1965-68, Columbia University, NYC. **Publications:** (co-ed.) Readings in Social Science, 1956; (co-author) Public Opinion and Congressional Elections, 1962; (co-ed.) The Government of Associations, 1966; Sheltered Employment of the Disabled, 1966; Pre-Trial Discovery and the Adversary System, 1968; Social Settings and Medical Organization 1970; The Brain Drain: Emigration and Return, 1978; Health Insurance Bargaining: Foreign Lessons for Americans, 1978; Paying the Hospital: The Organization, Dynamics, and Effects of Differing Financial Arrangements, 1987; Health Insurance in Practice, 1991; Teacher Unions and Policymaking, 1992. **Address:** 54 Morningside Dr., New York, NY 10025-1761, U.S.A.

GLASKIN, G(erald) M(arcus). Also writes as Neville Jackson. Australian, b. 1923. **Genres:** Novels, Novellas/Short stories, Science fiction/Fantasy, Children's fiction, Plays/Screenplays, Songs/Lyrics and libretti, Paranormal, Travel/Exploration, Autobiography/Memoirs. **Career:** Partner, Lyall & Evatt, Stockbrokers, Singapore, 1951-59. President, Fellowship of Australian Writers in Western Australia, 1968-69. **Publications:** A World of Our Own, 1955; A Minor Portrait, 1957; A Change of Mind, 1959; The Mistress, 1959; A Lion in the Sun, 1960; A Waltz through the Hills, 1961, musical play, 1976,

teleseries, 1988; The Land That Sleeps, 1961; The Beach of Passionate Love, 1962; A Small Selection (short stories), 1962; Flight to Landfall, 1963; O Love, O Loneliness, 1964; (as Neville Jackson) No End to the Way, 1965; The Man Who Didn't Count, 1965; Turn on the Heat (play), 1967; The Road to Nowhere (short stories), 1967; A Bird in My Hands, 1967; Sometimes It Wasn't So Nice (short stories), 1968; Windows of the Mind, 1974; Two Women: Turn on the Heat and The Eaves of Night, 1975; Worlds Within, 1976; Kabbarli (play), 1977; A Door to Eternity, 1979; Woman of the Dreaming (play), 1979; One Way to Wonderland, 1984; A Door to Infinity, 1989; A Many-Splendoured Woman: A Memoir of Han Suyin, 1995. **Address:** c/o David Bolt Associates, Cedar House, High St, Ripley, Surrey GU23 6AE, England. **Online address:** leovdpas@iinet.net.au

GLASMEIER, Amy (K.). American, b. 1955. **Genres:** Business/Trade/Industry, Economics. **Career:** Pennsylvania State University, University Park, assistant professor of community studies, 1985-86, associate professor, 1992-95, professor of geography and regional planning, 1995-, senior research associate at Institute for Policy Research and Evaluation, 1992-95, senior scientist, 1995-, director of Center for Trade, Technology, and Economic Growth, 1997-, director of Center for Regional Research and Industrial Studies, 1999-; University of Texas at Austin, assistant professor, 1986-90, associate professor of community and regional planning, 1990-91. University of Michigan, special lecturer, 1990; Aspen Institute, visiting scholar in rural economic policy program, 1991-92; Appalachian Regional Commission, John D. Whisman Appalachian regional scholar, 1996-98; Massachusetts Institute of Technology, visiting professor, 1998-99; University of Oslo, visiting professor, 2000; guest speaker at colleges and universities. **Publications:** Regional Planning and Economic Development: A Bibliography, 1983; (with A.R. Markusen and P. Hall) High-Tech America: The What, How, Where, and Why of the Sunrise Industries, 1986; (with G. Borchard) The Role of Services and Rural Economic Growth: A Bibliography, 1990; The High-Tech Potential: Economic Development in Rural America, 1991; (with M. Howland) From Combines to Computers: Rural Services and Development in the Age of Information Technology, 1995; (with A. Kays, J.W. Thompson, and R. Gurwitt) Branch Plants and Rural Development in the Age of Globalization, 1995; Global and Local Challenges to Theory, Practice, and Teaching in Economic Geography, 1998; (with L. Wood) On Hold: Telecommunications in Rural America, 2000; Manufacturing Time: Global Competition in the Watch Industry, 1795-2000, 2000. Contributor to books. Contributor of articles and reviews to professional journals. **Address:** Department of Geography, 308 Walker Bldg., Pennsylvania State University, University Park, PA 16802, U.S.A. **Online address:** akg1@ems.psu.edu

GLASS, Charles. American/British, b. 1951. **Genres:** Novellas/Short stories, Area studies, Civil liberties/Human rights, Film, Politics/Government, Theatre, Documentaries/Reportage, Essays. **Career:** Journalist, writer, and film maker. **Publications:** Tribes with Flags: A Dangerous Passage through the Chaos of the Middle East, 1990; Money for Old Rope, 1992. **Address:** PO Box 8308, London W11 2WX, England. **Online address:** charles.glass@abc.com

GLASS, Dee Dee. American, b. 1948. **Genres:** Human relations/Parenting. **Career:** Granada Television, researcher and script editor, 1976-78; Southern Television, producer and director, 1978-81; Reality Productions, producer and director, 1981-82; producer and director of documentary films, 1982-. Glass Pictures, producer for England's Channel 4 News, 1991. National Film and Television School, guest lecturer, 1987-89; guest tutor at Sheffield Hallam University, 1992, London College of Printing, 1992 and 1993-95, and Birkbeck College, London, 1993. Director of medical documentaries and films. **Publications:** "All My Fault": Why Women Don't Leave Abusive Men, 1995. **Address:** 21 Freegrove Rd., London N7 9JN, England.

GLASS, Leopold. See PASCOE, Bruce.

GLASS, Leslie. American. **Genres:** Novels, Mystery/Crime/Suspense. **Career:** Crime and mystery writer. **Publications:** NOVELS: Getting Away With It, 1976; Modern Love, 1983. MYSTERIES: Burning Time, 1993; Hanging Time, 1995; Loving Time, 1996; Judging Time, 1998; Stealing Time, 1999. OTHER: Strokes (play), 1984. Contributor to periodicals. **Address:** c/o Dutton, 375 Hudson St., New York, NY 10014, U.S.A.

GLASSBERG, David. American, b. 1954. **Genres:** History. **Career:** University of Massachusetts, Amherst, MA, professor of history; writer. **Publications:** American Historical Pageantry: The Uses of Tradition in the Early Twentieth Century, 1990; Sense of History: The Place of the Past in American Life, 2001. **Address:** Department of History, Herter Hall, University of Massachusetts, Amherst, MA 01003, U.S.A. **Online address:** glassberg@history.umass.edu

GLASSER, Ira. American, b. 1938. **Genres:** Civil liberties/Human rights. **Career:** Queens College of the City University of New York, Flushing, NY, lecturer in mathematics, 1960-62; Current, associate editor, 1962-64, editor, 1964-67; New York Civil Liberties Union, associate director, 1967-70, executive director, 1970-78; American Civil Liberties Union, New York City, executive director, 1978-2001, now retired. Sarah Lawrence College, member of science and mathematics faculty, 1962-65; St. Vincent's Hospital Community Advisory Board, chair, 1970-72; Asian-American Legal Defense and Education Fund, Board, 1975-. Worked at Vacation Camp for the Blind, 1954-63. Writer. **Publications:** (with W. Gaylin, S. Marcus, and D. Rothman) Doing Good: The Limits of Benevolence, 1978; Visions of Liberty: The Bill of Rights for All Americans, 1991. Work represented in anthologies. Contributor to magazines. **Address:** 290 9th Ave, New York, NY 10001-5704, U.S.A.

GLASSIE, Henry. American, b. 1941. **Genres:** Mythology/Folklore, Art/Art history, History. **Career:** Indiana University, Bloomington, professor (distinguished rank) of folklore, codirector of Turkish studies, member of the departments of folklore, American studies, Middle Eastern studies, and Central Eurasian studies. **Publications:** AND ILLUSTRATOR: Pattern in the Material Folk Culture of the Eastern United States, 1968; (with M. Leach) A Guide for Collectors of Oral Tradition and Folk Cultural Material in Pennsylvania, 1968; (with E.D. Ives and J.F. Szwed) Folksongs and Their Makers, 1970; All Silver and No Brass: An Irish Christmas Mumming, 1975; Folk Housing in Middle Virginia: A Structural Analysis of Historic Artifacts, 1975; (ed. with L. Degh and F.J. Oinas) Folklore Today: A Festschrift for Richard M. Dorson, 1976; Passing the Time in Ballymenone: Culture and History of an Ulster Community, 1982; Irish Folk History: Texts from the North, 1982; (ed.) Irish Folktales, 1985; The Spirit of Folk Art: The Girard Collection at the Museum of International Folk Art, 1989; (and designer) Turkish Traditional Art Today, 1993. Author of scholarly essays. **Address:** Folklore Institute, Indiana University, 504 North Fess Ave., Bloomington, IN 47405, U.S.A.

GLASSMAN, Bruce. American, b. 1961. **Genres:** Young adult fiction, Adult non-fiction, Biography. **Career:** Blackbirch Press Inc., San Diego, CA, publisher, 1985-. **Publications:** FOR YOUNG ADULTS. FICTION: The Marathon Race Mystery, 1985; Midnight Fridge, 1998. NONFICTION: The Crash of '29 and the New Deal, 1986; Everything You Need to Know about Step-Families, 1988; Everything You Need to Know about Growing up Male, 1991; New York: Gateway to the New World, 1991. BIOGRAPHY: J. Paul Getty: Oil Billionaire, 1989; Mikhail Baryshnikov, 1990; Arthur Miller, 1990; Wilma Mankiller: Chief of the Cherokee Nation, 1992; John Lennon & Paul McCartney, 1995. **Address:** c/o Blackbirch Press, 15822 Bernardo Center Dr Ste C, San Diego, CA 92127, U.S.A. **Online address:** bruce.glassman@ga6.com

GLASSMAN, Jonathon P. American, b. 1956. **Genres:** History. **Career:** Duke University, Durham, NC, visiting assistant professor of history, 1988-89; Northwestern University, Evanston, IL, associate professor of history, 1989-. **Publications:** Feasts and Riot: Revelry, Rebellion, and Popular Consciousness on the Swahili Coast, 1856-1888, 1995. **Address:** Department of History, Northwestern University, Evanston, IL 60208, U.S.A.

GLASSMAN, Ronald M. American, b. 1937. **Genres:** History, Sociology, Politics/Government. **Career:** Queens College of the City University of New York, Flushing, assistant professor of sociology, 1965-67; Connecticut College, New London, assistant professor of sociology, 1968-71; Herbert H. Lehman College of CUNY, Bronx, assistant professor of sociology, 1973-78; member of staff of William Paterson College, Wayne, NJ; writer, professor, 1980-; New York University, adjunct professor, 1995; New School for Social Research, visiting professor of sociology, 1976-78. **Publications:** The Political History of Latin America, 1969; Democracy and Despotism in Primitive Societies, 2 vols., 1986; Democracy and Equality, 1989; (with M. Green) A Democracy Agenda for the Year 2000, 1989; China in Transition, 1990; (with W. Swatos Jr. and P. Kivisto) For Democracy, 1993; The Middle Class and Democracy in Socio-Historical Perspective, 1995; The New Middle Class and Democracy in Global Perspective, 1996; Caring Capitalism; (with others) Social Problems in Global Perspective. EDITOR/CO-EDITOR: (with A.J. Vidich) Conflict and Control: The Challenge to Legitimacy of Modern Governments, 1979; (with V. Murvar) Max Weber's Political Sociology, 1984; (with R.J. Antonio) A Weber-Marx Dialogue, 1985; (with W.H. Swatus Jr., and contrib.) Charisma and Social Structure, 1985; Bureaucracy against Democracy and Socialism, 1987; (with H. Etzkowitz) The Renascence of Sociological Theory, 1989. **Address:** Dept of Sociology and Anthropology, William Paterson College, 300 Pompton Rd, Wayne, NJ 07470, U.S.A.

GLASSNER, Barry. American, b. 1952. **Genres:** Sociology, Social sciences. **Career:** Syracuse University, NY, assistant professor to professor of sociol-

ogy and department chair, 1978-88; University of Connecticut, Storrs, professor of sociology and department chair, 1988-91; University of Southern California, Los Angeles, professor of sociology and department chair, 1991-; writer. **Publications:** (with J. Freedman) Clinical Sociology, 1979; Essential Interactionism, 1980; (with J.D. Moreno) Discourse in the Social Sciences: Strategies for Translating Models of Mental Illness, 1982; (with D. Sylvan) A Rationalist Methodology for the Social Sciences, 1985; (with J. Loughlin) Drugs in Adolescent Worlds: Burnouts to Straights, 1987; Bodies, 1988; (with J. Moreno) Qualitative/Quantitative Distinction in the Social Sciences, 1989; Career Crash, 1994; The Culture of Fear, 1999. **Address:** Geri Thoma, Elaine Markson Literary Agency, Inc, 44 Greenwich Ave, New York, NY 10011, U.S.A.

GLATT, John. British, b. 1952. **Genres:** Biography. **Career:** Freelance journalist and writer. **Publications:** Rage and Roll: Bill Graham and the Selling of Rock, 1993; Lost in Hollywood: The Fast Times and Short Life of River Phoenix, 1995; The Chieftains: The Authorized Biography, 1997; The Royal House of Monaco, 1998; For I Have Sinned, 1998; Evil Twins, 1999; Cradle of Death, 2000; Blind Passion, 2001; Slave Master of the Internet, 2001. **Address:** c/o Peter Miller, PMA Literary and Film Management, Inc, PO Box 1817, New York, NY 10011, U.S.A. **Online address:** www.pmalitfilm.com

GLATTHAAR, Joseph T(homas). American, b. 1956. **Genres:** History, Military/Defense/Arms control. **Career:** Command and General Staff College, Combat Studies Institute, Fort Leavenworth, KS, visiting assistant professor of history, 1984-85; University of Houston, Houston, TX, assistant professor, 1985-89, associate professor, 1989-92, professor of history, 1992-, graduate program director, 1987-89, department chair, 1990-92, member of academic committees. U.S. Army Military History Institute, Harold K. Johnson Visiting Professor, 1991-92. Lecturer on the Civil War; participated in radio broadcasts; consultant for television programs on American history. **Publications:** The March to the Sea and Beyond: Sherman's Troops in the Savannah and Carolinas Campaigns, 1985; Forged in Battle: The Civil War Alliance of Black Soldiers and White Officers, 1990; Partners in Command: The Relationships between Leaders in the Civil War, 1994; Why the South Lost the Civil War. Contributor to books. Contributor of reviews to periodicals. **Address:** 4400 Jonathan, Bellaire, TX 77401, U.S.A.

GLAZEBROOK, Philip. British, b. 1937. **Genres:** Novels, Travel/Exploration. **Publications:** Try Pleasure, 1968; The Eye of the Beholder, 1974; The Burr Wood, 1977; Byzantine Honeymoon, 1979; Journey to Kars, 1984; Captain Vinegar's Commission, 1987; The Gate at the End of the World, 1989; Journey to Khiva, 1992; The Electric Rock Garden, 2001. **Address:** Mabledon Farmhouse, Vauxhall Ln, Tonbridge TN11 0NE, England.

GLAZER, Ellen Sarasohn. Also writes as Amy Schoenbrun, Ellen Jean Tepper. American, b. 1947. **Genres:** Young adult fiction, Environmental sciences/Ecology, Human relations/Parenting, Psychology, Social work, Women's studies and issues. **Career:** Mount Auburn Hospital, Cambridge, MA, clinical social worker, 1974-90; private practice of clinical social work, 1979-; Our Child Classes, Wellesley, MA, instructor, 1984-88; IVF-America, Waltham, MA, staff psychologist, 1990-91; New England Memorial Hospital, Stoneham, MA, program counselor at Fertility Center, 1991-98; New England Medical Center, Dept of Reproductive Medicine, 2000-; Act of Love Adoptions, consultant, 2000-; Boston Regional Center for Reproductive Medicine, staff social worker. Speaker at colleges and universities, medical and family centers, and public gatherings. **Publications:** (with S.S. Cooper) Without Child: Experiencing and Resolving Infertility, 1988; The Long Awaited Stork: A Guide for Parents after Infertility, 1990; When Is Enough, Enough?, 1991; (with Cooper) Beyond Infertility: New Paths to Parenthood, 1994; (with Cooper) Choosing Assisted Reproduction: Social, Emotional & Ethical Considerations, 1998; Experiencing Infertility: Stories to Inform and Inspire, 1998. Contributor to books and periodicals. **Address:** 55 Farlow Rd, Newton, MA 02458, U.S.A. **Online address:** eglazer@gis.net

GLAZER, Nathan. American, b. 1923. **Genres:** Race relations, Sociology, Urban studies. **Career:** Professor of Education and Social Structure, 1969-93, Professor Emeritus, 1993-, Harvard University, Cambridge Massachusetts, Co-Ed., The Public Interest, since 1973; Staff Member, Commentary Magazine, 1944-53; Ed. and Editorial Advisor, Doubleday Anchor Books, 1954-57; Editorial Adviser, Random House, publrs., 1958-62; Urban Sociologist, Housing and Home Finance Agency, Washington, D.C., 1962-63; Professor of Sociology, University of California at Berkeley, 1963-69. **Publications:** (with D. Riesman and R. Denney) The Lonely Crowd, 1950; (with D. Riesman) Faces in the Crowd, 1952; American Judaism, 1957, 1972; The Social Basis of American Communism, 1961; (with D.P. Moynihan) Beyond the Melting Pot, 1963, 1970; Remembering the Answers, 1970; Affirmative Discrimination: Ethnic Inequality and Public Policy, 1976; Ethnic Dilemmas 1964-1982, 1983; Clamor at the Gates: The New American Immigration, 1985; The Limits of Social Policy, 1988. EDITOR: (with D. McEntire) Studies in Housing and Minority Groups, 1960; (with D.P. Moynihan) Ethnicity: Theory and Experience, 1975; (with W. Gorham) The Urban Predicament, 1976; (with M. Lilla) The Public Face of Architecture, 1987; (with S.R. Glazer) Conflicting Images: India and the United States, 1990. **Address:** Graduate School of Education, Harvard University, Cambridge, MA 02138, U.S.A.

GLAZIER, Stephen D. American, b. 1949. **Genres:** Anthropology/Ethnology, Theology/Religion. **Career:** University of Connecticut, Storrs, lecturer, 1979-81; Trinity College, Hartford, CT, visiting assistant professor, 1981-82; Connecticut College, New London, visiting assistant professor, 1982-83; Wayland Baptist University, Plainview, TX, assistant professor, 1983-86; Westmont College, Santa Barbara, CA, associate professor, 1986-88; University of Nebraska, Kearney, associate professor, 1988-94, professor of sociology and anthropology, 1994-, head of department, 1988-91, research fellow, 1991-94. **Publications:** Marchin' the Pilgrims Home: Leadership and Decision-Making in an AfroCaribbean Faith, 1983, rev ed as Marchin' the Pilgrims Home: A Study of the Spiritual Baptists of Trinidad, 1991. EDITOR: (and contrib) Perspectives on Pentecostalism: Case Studies from the Caribbean and Latin America, 1980; (and author of intro) Caribbean Ethnicity Revisited, 1985; Anthropology of Religion: A Handbook, 1997; (with M. Leatham and C.G. Navarro) More Perspectives on Pentecostalism, 1999. Contributor to books and periodicals. **Address:** Department of Sociology and Anthropology, University of Nebraska, Kearney, NE 68849, U.S.A. **Online address:** glaziers@unk.edu

GLEASON, Katherine (A.). American, b. 1960. **Genres:** Children's nonfiction, Crafts, Self help, Theology/Religion. **Career:** Greenroom Enterprises (film production company), Astoria, NY, production associate, 1987-88; Michael Rowan Group (marketing and survey research firm), NYC, associate, 1988-90; Womanews, NYC, contributing editor, 1989-91; Lingua Franca, Mamaroneck, NY, managing editor, 1991-92; Lucas/Evans Books Inc., NYC, projects coordinator, 1992-94; freelance writer and editor, NYC, 1994-. **Publications:** Origami Ornaments, 1995; Flying Origami, 1996; Scary Origami, 1996; Native American Literature, 1996; Native American Art, 1996; Clay Pots: A Native American Craft Kit, 1997; Leap Frog Origami, 1997; Kirigami Christmas Tree, 1998; Paper Magic: The Art of Origami, 1998; (with D. Zimmermann) The Complete Idiot's Guide to Wicca and Witchcraft, 2000, 2nd ed., 2003; (with G.C. Feldman) Releasing the Goddess Within, 2003; Ancient World: A Chapter Book, 2003; The Intuitive Arts on Money: Using Astrology, Tarot, and Your Psychic Intuition to See Your Future, 2003. CRAFT KITS WITH INSTRUCTIONS: Egyptian Treasure Box, 1997; Frame Your Friends: Make Your Own Mini Photo Frames, 1998; Christmas Origami, 2003. **Address:** 199 E 7th St No 2D, New York, NY 10009, U.S.A. **Online address:** kag475@aol.com

GLEAVE, John T. British, b. 1917. **Genres:** Geography. **Career:** General Ed., Evans Bros., and Macmillan Ltd. Lecturer in Education, College of St. Mark and St. John, London, 1946-47; Assistant Education Officer, Ipswich, 1947-48; H. M. Overseas Civil Service, Uganda, 1949-62; Deputy Director of Education, 1958-62; Director of Extramural Classes and Courses, 1962-69, and Director of Special Courses, 1969-82, University of Leeds. **Publications:** Geography for Uganda Schools, Books I & II; Introducing Geography, Uganda, Books I & II: (adaptor) Civics for East African Schools; Visual Geography of East Africa: (co-author) Uganda Our Homeland. **Address:** Fulwith Close, Harrogate, N. Yorkshire, England.

GLECKNER, Robert F(rancis). *See* Obituaries.

GLEDHILL, John. British, b. 1949. **Genres:** Anthropology/Ethnology. **Career:** University of London, England, lecturer, 1976-88, senior lecturer, 1988-93, reader in anthropology, 1993-96, associate fellow of Institute of Latin American Studies, 1990-96; University of Manchester, England, professor of social anthropology, 1996-2000, Max Gluckman Professor of Social Anthropology, 2000-. **Publications:** (ed. with B. Bender and M.T. Larsen, and contrib.) State and Society: The Emergence and Development of Social Hierarchy and Political Centralization, 1988; Casi Nada: A Study of Agrarian Reform in the Homeland of Cardenismo, 1991, rev. ed. in Spanish, 1993; Power and Its Disguises: Anthropological Perspectives on Politics, 1994, 2nd ed., 2000; Neoliberalism, Transnationalization, and Rural Poverty, 1995; El Poder y Sus Distraces: perspectives antiopologicas de la politica, 2000; Cultura y Desafio en Ostula, 2004. Contributor to books and periodicals. **Address:** Social Anthropology, School of Social Sciences, Roscoe Bldg,

University of Manchester, Oxford Rd, Manchester M13 9PL, England. **Online address:** john.gledhill@manchester.ac.uk

GLEES, Anthony. British, b. 1948. **Genres:** History, International relations/Current affairs, Politics/Government. **Career:** University of Warwick, Coventry, England, lecturer in history, 1973-75; Brunel University, Uxbridge, England, lecturer in government, 1975-, reader and director of European studies, 1988-89, professor of contemporary history, 2003-; writer. Adviser to War Crimes Inquiry; contributor to British Broadcasting Corp; consultant to British television networks. **Publications:** Exile Politics during the Second World War: The German Social Democrats in Britain, 1983; The Secrets of the Service: British Intelligence and Communist Subversion, 1939-51, 1987; Reinventing Germany: German Political Development since 1945, 1996; The Stasi Files: East Germany's Secret Operations against Britain, 2003. Contributor to books and writer of scholarly articles on Anglo-German relations, German politics, war crimes, security service and intelligence issues. **Address:** Department of Government, Brunel University, Uxbridge, Middlesex UB8 3PH, England.

GLEESON, Libby. Australian, b. 1950. **Genres:** Children's fiction, Picture/board books, Reference. **Career:** Instructor in secondary school and university, 1974-86; visiting lecturer at universities, 1985-; full-time writer, 1989-. Has also been a consultant for teaching English as a second language, 1986-90. Authors' representative on Public Lending Right Committee of Australia; Australian Society of Authors, chair, 1999-2001. **Publications:** Eleanor, Elizabeth, 1984; I Am Susannah, 1987; One Sunday, 1988; The Great Big Scary Dog, 1991; Dodger, 1991; Uncle David, 1992; Hurry Up!, 1992; Where's Mum?, 1993; Mum Goes to Work, 1993; Love Me, Love Me Not, 1993; Sleeptime, 1993; Walking to School, 1994; Skating on Sand, 1994; The Princess and the Perfect Dish, 1995; Hannah Plus One, 1996; The Queen of the Universe, 1997; REFUGE, 1998; The Great Bear, 1999; Hannah and the Tomorrow Room, 1999; Writing Hannah: On Writing for Children, 1999; Dear Writer, 2000; Shutting the Chooks In, 2000; An Ordinary Day, 2001; The Rum Rebellion: The Diary of David Bellamy, 2001; Making Picture Books, 2003; Cuddle Time, 2004; Hannah the Famous, 2004. Author of short stories. **Address:** 11 Oxford St, Petersham, NSW 2049, Australia. **Online address:** libbygleeson@yahoo.com.au

GLEICK, Peter H. American, b. 1956. **Genres:** Marine sciences/Oceanography. **Career:** University of California, Lawrence Berkeley Laboratory, Berkeley, CA, research assistant, 1978-80; research and teaching associate, 1980-81; Office of the Governor of California, Sacramento, CA, deputy assistant for energy and environment, 1980-82; University of California-Berkeley, Energy and Resources Group, Berkeley, CA, research associate, 1983-86; post-doctoral position, 1986-88; Pacific Institute for Studies in Development, Environment, and Security, Oakland, CA, president and cofounder, 1987-. **Publications:** Water in Crisis: A Guide to the World's Fresh Water Resources, 1993; The World's Water 1998-1999, 1999; The World's Water 2000-2001, 2000; The World's Water 2002-2003, 2002. **Address:** Pacific Institute for Studies in Development, Environment, and Security, 654 13th St., Preservation Park, Oakland, CA 94612, U.S.A. **Online address:** pgleick@home.com

GLEITER, Jan. American, b. 1947. **Genres:** Children's fiction, Novels, Biography. **Career:** Novelist and author of children's books. **Publications:** NOVELS: Lie Down with Dogs, 1996; A House by the Side of the Road, 1998. FOR CHILDREN. FICTION: Color Rhymes: Teddies (poems), 1985; Seaside Adventure, 1987; Tell the Time, 1987. BIOGRAPHIES (with K. Thompson): Daniel Boone, 1985; Paul Bunyan and Babe the Blue Ox, 1985; Pocahontas, 1985; Annie Oakley, 1987; Casey Jones, 1987; Christopher Columbus, 1987; Johnny Appleseed, 1987; Kit Carson, 1987; Molly Pitcher, 1987; Paul Revere, 1987; Sacagawea, 1987; Booker T. Washington, 1988; David Farragut, 1988; Elizabeth Cady Stanton, 1988; Jack London, 1988; Jane Addams, 1988; John James Audobon, 1988; Matthew Henson, 1988; Sam Houston, 1988; Sequoya, 1988; Diego Rivera, 1989; Hernando de Soto, 1989; Jose Marti, 1989; Juniper Serra, 1989; Luis Munoz Marin, 1989; Miguel Hidalgo y Costilla, 1989; Simon Bolivar, 1989; Benito Juarez, 1990. ADAPTATIONS: W. Irving, The Legend of Sleepy Hollow, 1985; C. Dickens, Great Expectations, 1989; Sir W. Scott, Ivanhoe, 1989. **Address:** c/o St. Martin's Press, 175 Fifth Ave., Rm. 1715, New York, NY 10010, U.S.A.

GLEN, Frank Grenfell. New Zealander, b. 1933. **Genres:** History, Military/Defense/Arms control, Theology/Religion, Autobiography/Memoirs, Biography. **Career:** Ordained Minister of the Presbyterian Church of New Zealand, 1958. Chaplain to Industry at Manapouri, 1960-62; Chaplain to NZ Territorial Army, 1962-66; Supt., Far West Mission and Flying Padre, NSW, 1966-70; Chaplain, Royal Australian Air Force, 1970-76; with the New

Zealand Dept. of Justice, 1976-84; Police Chaplain, 1983-97; Chaplain, Presbyterian Support Services, 1985-86, and Thames Union Parish, 1986-91. Fellow, Australian Institute History & Arts, 1986. NZ Journal of Military History: "Volunteers," editor, 1998-2002. **Publications:** Methodism in Southland, 1956; Methodist in Auckland during Maori Wars, 1860-64, 1958; Methodism in the Coal Field of Southland, 1960; Journal of Rev. F. Glen 1960-62 in the Fiords of Southland; Rev. J.T. Luxford, Chaplain to the Forces, 1966; (ed.) Journal of Rev. J. Harris under Sail to New Zealand in 1874, 1966; Holy Joe's People, 1968, 3rd ed., 1975; Fly High Reach Far, 1971; Study of the Chaplain's Role and Religion in the R.A.A.F., 1973; Bush in Our Yard, 1981; For Glory and a Farm, 1984; Church Leaders and the First Taranaki War, 1860-61, 1992; New Zealand Army Chaplains at War, 1997; Bowler of Gallipoli Witness to the ANZAC Legend, 2003. **Address:** 32 Ti Rakau Dr, Woolston, Christchurch, New Zealand.

GLEN, Paul (Michael). (born United States), b. 1965. **Genres:** Administration/Management. **Career:** Management consultant and educator. SEI Information Technology, Chicago, IL, consultant, 1988-95, Los Angeles, CA, regional manager, 1995-99; C2 Consulting, Marina Del Rey, CA, founder, 1999-. Taught at the University of Southern California and Loyola Marymount University. **Publications:** Leading Geeks: How to Manage and Lead People Who Deliver Technology, 2003. Author of monthly column. **Address:** 3253 Malcolm Ave., Los Angeles, CA 90034, U.S.A. **Online address:** info@leadinggeeks.com

GLENDINNING, Miles. (Miles G. Horsey). Scottish, b. 1956. **Genres:** Architecture. **Career:** RCAHMS (National Monuments Record), Edinburgh, Scotland, manager of Threatened Buildings Survey, 1978-. University of Edinburgh, honorary fellow in social policy, 1993-. **Publications:** Preservation: Dawn of the Living Dead, 1986; Tenements and Towers, 1990; (Co-author) Tower Block: Modern Public Housing in England, Scotland, Wales, and Northern Ireland, 1994; (co-author) A History of Scottish Architecture from the Renaissance to the Present Day, 1996; (co-author) Rebuilding Scotland, 1997; (co-author) Building a Nation, 1999; (co-author) Clone City, 1999. **Address:** RCAHMS, 16 Bernard Terr., Edinburgh EH8 9NX, Scotland. **Online address:** milesh@reahms.gov.uk

GLENDOWER, Rose. *See* **HARRIS, Marion (Rose).**

GLENER, Doug. American. **Genres:** History. **Career:** Writer. **Publications:** (with Sarat Komagiri) Wisdom's Blossoms: Tales of the Saints of India, 2002. **Address:** Catalyst Creative Services, 283 Countryhaven Rd., Encinitas, CA 92024, U.S.A. **Online address:** doug.glener@sbcglobal.net

GLENN, Cheryl. American. **Genres:** Education. **Career:** High school English teacher, Marysville, OH, 1972-75; self-employed teacher and consultant, 1977-85; Oregon State University, Corvallis, assistant professor, 1989-94, associate professor of English, 1994-97, director of College of Liberal Arts Center for Teaching Excellence, 1996-97, Elizabeth P. Ritchie Distinguished Professor, 1996, faculty fellow, Center for the Humanities, 1993; Pennsylvania State University, University Park, associate professor of English, 1997-. Millikin University, visiting professor, 1997; speaker at colleges and universities. **Publications:** (with R.J. Connors) The St. Martin's Guide to Teaching Writing, 1989, 3rd ed., 1995; Rhetoric Retold: Regendering the Tradition from Antiquity through the Renaissance, 1997; Making Sense: A New Rhetorical Reader, 2002. Contributor to books. Contributor of articles and reviews to journals. **Address:** Department of English, 142 S Burrowes, Pennsylvania State University, University Park, PA 16802, U.S.A. **Online address:** cjg6@psu.edu

GLENN, Mel. American (born Switzerland), b. 1943. **Genres:** Children's fiction, Young adult fiction, Poetry. **Career:** Peace Corps volunteer, Sierra Leone, West Africa, 1964-66; Junior High School 240, Brooklyn, NY, teacher, 1967-70; Abraham Lincoln High School, Brooklyn, English teacher, 1970-2001; author, 1980-. **Publications:** YOUNG ADULT FICTION: One Order to Go, 1984. YOUNG ADULT POETRY: Class Dismissed!: High School Poems, 1982; Class Dismissed II: More High School Poems, 1986; Back to Class, 1988; My Friend's Got This Problem, Mr. Candler, 1991; Who Killed Mr. Chippendale?: A Mystery in Poems, 1996; The Taking of Room 114: A Hostage Drama in Poems, 1997; Jump Ball: A Basketball Season in Poems, 1997; Foreign Exchange, 1999; Split Image, 2000. CHILDREN'S FICTION: Play-by-Play, 1986; Squeeze Play: A Baseball Story, 1989. **Address:** 4288 Bedford Ave, Brooklyn, NY 11229, U.S.A. **Online address:** Author114@aol.com

GLENN, Patricia Brown. American, b. 1953. **Genres:** Architecture, Art/Art history. **Career:** Writer, researcher, and lecturer. Landmarks Commission,

Kansas City, MO, research historian, 1978-79; Historic Kansas City Foundation, Kansas City, survey coordinator and architectural historian, 1979-81, director of research and education, 1981-83, member of board of directors, 1992-94; Ottawa University, Kansas City, member of adjunct faculty, 1981-83; University of Missouri, Kansas City, member of adjunct faculty, 1983, 1985-90; consultant in art education and architectural history, 1983-. **Publications:** Under Every Roof: A Kid's Style and Field Guide to the Architecture of American Houses, 1993; From the Ground Up: Architects at Work in America, 1996. Contributor to periodicals. **Address:** 6336 Ensley Ln., Shawnee Mission, KS 66206-1930, U.S.A. **Online address:** closerlook@kc.rr.com

GLENNON, Karen M. American, b. 1946. **Genres:** Children's fiction, Poetry. **Career:** Writer. The Book Shop, Boise, ID, school liaison, 1991-93; West Junior High School, Nampa, ID, teacher, 1993-96; Nampa Senior High School, teacher, 1996-2000. Worked as a homemaker, waitress, clerk, artists' model, owner of a preschool, English and reading teacher, and children's book reviewer. **Publications:** Miss Eva and the Red Balloon, 1990. **Address:** Box 6177, Boise, ID 83707, U.S.A. **Online address:** ps6813@aol.com

GLICK, Bernard R. Canadian (born United States), b. 1945. **Genres:** Biology, Technology. **Career:** University of Toronto, Toronto, ON, postdoctoral fellow and research associate, 1974-78; National Research Council, research associate, 1978-79; BIO LOGICALS Inc., Toronto, group leader, Molecular Genetics and Biochemistry Group, 1979-82; University of Waterloo, Waterloo, ON, associate professor, 1982-89, professor of biology, 1989-, professor of chemical engineering, 1992-, and member of executive committee, Biotechnology Research Centre. Weizmann Institute of Science, Rehovot, Israel, visiting scientist, 1990; Technion, Haifa, Israel, Lady Davis Visiting Professor, 1992-93, 1994-95; lecturer at colleges and universities. **Publications:** (with J.J. Pasternak) Molecular Biotechnology, 1994, 3rd ed., 2003; (with C.L. Patten, G. Holguin, and D.M. Penrose) Biochemical and Genetic Mechanisms Used by Plant Growth-Promoting Bacteria, 1999. EDITOR: (with M. Moo-Young, J. Lamptey, and H.R. Bungay) Biomass Conversion Technologies, 1987; (with J.E. Thompson) Methods in Plant Molecular Biology and Biotechnology, 1993. Contributor to scientific books. Contributor of articles and reviews to scientific journals. **Address:** Dept of Biology, University of Waterloo, Waterloo, ON, Canada N2L 3G1. **Online address:** glick@sciborg.uwaterloo.ca

GLICK, William H. American, b. 1952. **Genres:** Administration/Management, Business/Trade/Industry. **Career:** University of Texas at Austin, assistant professor, 1981-87, associate professor of management, 1987-. **Publications:** (ed. with G.P. Huber and contrib.) Organizational Change and Redesign: Ideas and Insights for Improving Performance, 1993. Contributor to books. Contributor of articles and reviews to management journals. **Address:** Department of Management, University of Texas at Austin, Austin, TX 78712, U.S.A.

GLICKMAN, James (A.). American, b. 1948. **Genres:** Novels, Novellas/Short stories. **Career:** University of Arizona Law School, Tucson, instructor, 1972; Community College of Rhode Island, Lincoln, RI, English teacher, 1972-; Radcliffe Seminars, Cambridge, MA, 1985-88; writer. **Publications:** Sounding the Waters (novel), 1996. Contributor of short stories to periodicals. **Address:** 51 McGilpin Rd, Sturbridge, MA 01566, U.S.A. **Online address:** jaglickman@yahoo.com

GLICKMAN, Norman J. American, b. 1942. **Genres:** Economics, Social sciences, Urban studies. **Career:** National Industrial Conference Board, Inc., economist, 1963-65; City College of the City University of New York, New York City, research fellow, 1964-65, lecturer in economics, 1965; Hofstra University, Hempstead, NY, lecturer in economics, 1966; University of Pennsylvania, Philadelphia, lecturer, 1969-70, assistant professor, 1970-75, associate professor, 1975-82, professor of regional science, 1982-83, member of research council of Institute for Environmental Studies, 1970-72, director of urban studies program, 1970-74; University of Texas at Austin, Mike Hogg Professor of Urban Policy and professor of economics, Lyndon B. Johnson School of Public Affairs, 1983-89; Rutgers University, New Brunswick, NJ, State of New Jersey Professor of Planning and director of Center for Urban Policy Research, 1989-. Regional Science Research Institute, research associate, 1967 and 1969-71; visiting scholar, Japan Center for Area Development Research, 1971 and 1973, and Gakushuin University, 1974 and 1976; University of Haifa, senior Fulbright-Hays lecturer, 1972-73; International Institute for Applied Systems Analysis, senior research scholar, 1977, member of advisory board of Project on International Comparative Study of Regional Models, 1980-81; Netherlands Institute for Advanced Study in the Humanities and Social Sciences, fellow, 1981-82; University of

Iowa, Ida Beam Visiting Professor, 1984; Department of Land Economy, Cambridge University, Vivian Stewart visiting fellow, 1984; Instituto Tecnologico y de Estudios Superiores de Monterrey, Mexico, distinguished Fulbright professor, 1985-87; lecturer at colleges and universities in the United States, Europe, and Japan. **Publications:** Econometric Analysis of Regional Systems: Explorations in Model Building and Policy Analysis, 1977; The Growth and Management of the Japanese Urban System, 1979; (with S.S. Jacobs) HUD and the Cities: The Urban Impacts of HUD's Programs, 1979; (ed and contrib) The Urban Impacts of Federal Policies, 1980; (ed with F.G. Adams, and contrib) Modeling the Multiregion Economic System: Perspectives for the Eighties, 1980; (ed with D.A. Hicks, and contrib) Transition to the Twenty-first Century: Prospects and Policies for Economic and Urban-Regional Transformation, 1983; (with R. Marshall) Choices for American Industry, 1987; (with D.P. Woodward) The New Competitors: How Foreign Investors Are Changing the U.S. Economy, 1989. **Address:** Center for Urban Policy Research, Rutgers University, Civic Square Building, Ste. 400, New Brunswick, NJ 08901-1982, U.S.A.

GLIMM, James Y(ork). American, b. 1942. **Genres:** Mythology/Folklore. **Career:** Mansfield State College, Mansfield, PA, associate professor, 1968-76, professor of English, 1976-. **Publications:** Flatlanders and Ridgerunners: Folktales from the Mountains of Northern Pennsylvania, University of Pittsburgh Press, 1983. Snakebite: Lives and Legends from Central Pennsylvania, University of Pittsburgh Press, 1990. **Address:** Department of English, Mansfield State College, Mansfield, PA 16933, U.S.A.

GLISERMAN, Martin. American, b. 1945. **Genres:** Literary criticism and history. **Career:** Rutgers University, New Brunswick, NJ, associate professor of English, 1971-; psychoanalyst, Highland Park, NJ, 1987-. **Publications:** Psychoanalysis, Language, and the Body of the Text, 1997. **Address:** Dept of English, Rutgers University, 510 George St, New Brunswick, NJ 08901-1167, U.S.A. **Online address:** martin.gliserman@rutgers.edu

GLISSON, J(ake) T. American, b. 1927. **Genres:** Novels. **Career:** Artist and writer. Chief executive officer of Motivation Systems and Jaake' Creations. Steinmetz Studio, Sarasota, FL, photographer, 1950; Newman Lynde Advertising Agency, Miami, FL, artist and illustrator, 1951; Advertising Trade Services of New York, Miami, artist and illustrator, 1952; All Florida Magazine Ocala, art director, 1954; Cape Haze Marine Laboratory, Cape Haze, FL, artist, 1955; Social and Visitors Guides, Sarasota, chief executive officer and art director, 1964; Wild Wald Center, Menden, Germany, art director and conceptual artist, 1983. U.S. Army, Chemical Corps College, illustrator, 1956; National Mobile Home Dealers and Owners Association magazine, chief executive officer and art director, 1957; Florida State Museum, art director and designer of traveling museums, 1968. Creator of sets, story boards, and special effects for the film Where the River Flows North. Explored the Manso River in Argentina and Chile, funded by National Geographic Society. Florida Council for the Humanities, member; Southern Academy of Letters, Arts and Sciences, honorary member. **Publications:** The Creek, 1993; Sigsbee (play), 1996.

GLOAG, Julian. British, b. 1930. **Genres:** Novels, Plays/Screenplays. **Publications:** Our Mother's House, 1963; A Sentence of Life, 1966; Maundy, 1969; A Woman of Character, 1973; Sleeping Dogs Lie, 1980; Lost and Found, 1981; Blood for Blood, 1985; Only Yesterday, 1986; Love as a Foreign Language, 1991; Le passeur de la nuit, 1996; Chambre d'ombre, 1996. SCREENPLAYS: Only Yesterday, 1986; The Dark Room, 1987. **Address:** c/o Michelle Lapautre, 6 rue Jean Carries, 75007 Paris, France.

GLOCK, Allison. (born United States). **Genres:** Autobiography/Memoirs. **Career:** Writer. **Publications:** Beauty before Comfort: A Memoir, 2003. Contributor to periodicals. **Address:** c/o Author Mail, Alfred A. Knopf Publicity, 1745 Broadway, New York, NY 10019, U.S.A.

GLOSS, Molly. American, b. 1944. **Genres:** Novels, Science fiction/Fantasy, Young adult fiction. **Career:** Elementary schoolteacher in Portland, OR, 1966-67; Consolidated Freightways, Portland, correspondence clerk, 1967-70; free-lance writer, 1980-. **Publications:** NOVELS: Outside the Gates, 1986; The Jump-Off Creek, 1989; The Dazzle of Day, 1997; Wild Life, 2000. **Address:** c/o Wendy Weil Agency, 232 Madison Ave., Suite 1300, New York, NY 10016, U.S.A.

GLOSSOP, Ronald J. American, b. 1933. **Genres:** Philosophy, Politics/Government. **Career:** Boise Junior College (now Boise State University), Boise, ID, instructor in philosophy, 1960-61; Portland State University, Portland, OR, instructor, 1961-63, assistant professor of philosophy, 1963-65; Southern Illinois University at Edwardsville, assistant professor, 1965-68, as-

sociate professor, 1968-73, professor of philosophical studies, 1973-98, emeritus professor, 1998-. **Publications:** Philosophy: An Introduction to Its Problems and Vocabulary, 1974; Confronting War: An Examination of Humanity's Most Pressing Problem, 1983, 4th ed., 2001; World Federation? A Critical Analysis of Federal World Government, 1993;. Work represented in anthologies. Contributor to journals in philosophy, religion, gifted education, peace education, global issues, and Esperanto. **Address:** 8894 Berkay Ave, Jennings, MO 63136-5004, U.S.A. **Online address:** rglosso@siue.edu

GLOVER, Douglas. Canadian, b. 1948. **Genres:** Novels, Novellas/Short stories, Literary criticism and history. **Career:** University of New Brunswick, teacher, philosophy, 1971-72; reporter, and editor, daily newspapers in Saint John, Peterborough, Montreal, and Saskatoon, 1972-79; The Book Show, radio host, 1994-96; writer-in-residence: University of New Brunswick, 1987-88, University of Lethbridge, 1988, St. Thomas University, 1992, New York State Writers Institute, SUNY Albany, 1992-94; teacher, creative writing: Skidmore College, 1992-93, 1998-2000, Colgate University, 1995, University at Albany SUNY, 1996-2001, Vermont College, 1995-. **Publications:** STORIES: The Mad River, 1981; Dog Attempts to Drown Man in Saskatoon, 1985; A Guide to Animal Behaviour, 1991; 16 Categories of Desire, 2000. NOVELS: Precious, 1984; The South Will Rise at Noon, 1988; The Life and Times of Captain N., 1993; Elle, 2003. OTHER: (ed.) Best Canadian Stories, 1996-2002; Notes Home from a Prodigal Son (essays), 1999; The Enamoured Knight, 2004. **Address:** PO Box 2282, Wilton, NY 12831, U.S.A.

GLOVER, Judith. British, b. 1943. **Genres:** Romance/Historical, Food and Wine, History, Language/Linguistics, Local history/Rural topics. **Career:** Newspaper reporter; freelance journalist; author. **Publications:** The Place Names of Sussex, 1974; The Place Names of Kent, 1975; Colour Book of Sussex, 1975; Colour Book of Kent, 1976; (with Anthony Kersting) Sussex in Photographs, 1976; Drink Your Own Garden, 1979; The Stallion Man, 1982; Sisters and Brothers, 1984; To Everything a Season, 1986; Birds in a Gilded Cage, 1987; The Imagination of the Heart, 1989; Tiger Lilies, 1991; Mirabelle, 1992; Minerva Lane, 1993; Pride of Place, 1995; Sussex Place-Names, 1997. **Address:** Oaklands House, Llanteg, Narberth, Pembrokeshire, Wales. **Online address:** lanteague@aol.com

GLUCKMAN, Janet. See **BERLINER-GLUCKMAN, Janet.**

GLUT, Don(ald) F. American, b. 1944. **Genres:** Novels, Art/Art history, Film, Literary criticism and history. **Career:** Creator of many comic strip characters including Tragg, Simbar, Dagar, Durak, Dr. Spektor, and Baron Tibor. Associate Ed., Monsters of the Movies mag., Marvel comic Group, since 1974. Musician/singer, actor, book store clerk, asst. copyrwriter, 1965-71; Contributor Ed., Castle of Frankenstein, 1969-71. **Publications:** Frankenstein Lives Again (novels), 1971; Terror of Frankenstein, and sequels, 1971; (with Jim Harmon) The Great Movie Serials: Their Sound and Fury, 1972; True Vampires of History, 1972; The Dinosaur Dictionary, 1972, rev. ed. as The New Dinosaur Dictionary, 1982; The Frankenstein Legend: A Tribute to Mary Shelley and Boris Karloff, 1973; Bugged! (science fiction), 1974; The Dracula Book, 1974; Spawn (novel), 1976; Classic Movie Monsters, 1978; The Empire Strikes Back (novel), 1980; The Dinosaur Scrapbook, 1980; (with S. Massey) Dinosaurs, Mammoths, and Cavemen: The Art of Charles R. Knight, 1982; The Frankenstein Catalog, 1984; New Credits: Discover Dinosaurs, 1991; Amazing Dinosaurs, 1993; The Dinosaur Society Dinosaur Encyclopedia, 1993; (author and director) Dinosaur Movies, 1993; Dinosaur Tracks: Vol. 1, 1994; Hollywood Goes Ape!, 1995; Dinosaur Valley Girls, 1996; Before LaBrea, 1997; Dinosaurs: The Encyclopedia, 1997. Contributor to books.

GMELCH, George. American, b. 1944. **Genres:** Anthropology/Ethnology. **Career:** McGill University, Montreal, assistant professor, 1973-75; State University of New York, Albany, assistant professor, 1975-80; Union College, Schenectady, New York, professor and chairman of anthropology, 1981-. **Publications:** Irish Tinkers: The Urbanization of an Itinerant People, 1977, 1985; To Shorten the Road: Traveller Folk Tales from Ireland, 1978; (ed.) J.M. Synge: In Wicklow, West Kerry and Connemara, 1980; (with W.P. Zenner) Urban Life: Readings in Urban Anthropology, 1980; Double Passage: the Lives of Caribbean Migrants, 1992; The Parrish behind God's Back: The Changing Culture of Rural Barbados, 1996; In the Ballpark: The Working Lives of Baseball People, 1997; The Ballplayers: Inside the Life of Professional Baseball, 2000; Behind the Smile: The Working Lives of Caribbean Tourism, 2003. **Address:** Dept of Anthropology, Union College, Schenectady, NY 12308, U.S.A. **Online address:** gmelchg@union.edu

GMELCH, Sharon (Bohn). American (born Panama), b. 1947. **Genres:** Anthropology/Ethnology, Area studies, Cultural/Ethnic topics, Women's studies and issues, Biography. **Career:** Union College, Schenectady, NY, professor, 1981-. **Publications:** Tinkers and Travellers, 1975; (ed.) Irish Life and Traditions, 1979; Nan: The Life of an Irish Travelling Woman, 1986; (with G. Gmelch) The Parish behind God's Back: Life in Rural Barbados, 1997; Gender on Campus: Issues for College Women, 1998; (ed.) Tourists and Tourism, 2004. **Address:** Dept. of Anthropology, Union College, Schenectady, NY 12308, U.S.A.

GOBBELL, John J. American, b. 1937. **Genres:** Novels. **Career:** KPMG Peat Marwick (certified public accountants), Los Angeles, CA, consultant, 1967-70; Angeles Corp. (investors), Los Angeles, director of personnel, 1970-73; Boyden Associates Inc. (executive recruiters), NYC, vice-president of branch in Newport Beach, CA, 1973-83; Gobbell Co. (executive recruiters), Newport Beach, managing director, 1983-. USC Commerce Associates, president. Orange County Fictionaires (reading group), president, 1996. **Publications:** NOVELS: The Brutus Lie, 1991; The Last Lieutenant, 1995; A Code for Tomorrow, 1999; When Duty Whispers Low, 2002. **Address:** Gobbell Co., 1601 Dove St. Suite 145, Newport Beach, CA 92660-2410, U.S.A. **Online address:** jgobbell@johnjgobbell.com

GOBLE, Alan. British, b. 1938. **Genres:** Film. **Career:** Civil servant. Formerly assistant official receiver, Department of Trade and Industry, now retired. **Publications:** (ed.) The International Film Index: 1895-1990, Vol. 1: Film Titles, 1991, Vol. 2: Directors' Filmography and Indexes, 1996; The Complete Index to British Sound Films since 1928, 1999; The Complete Index to Literary Sources in Film, 1999; The Complete Index to World Film since 1895, 1996, rev. ed., 2002.

GOBLE, Paul. American/British, b. 1933. **Genres:** Children's fiction, Young adult fiction, Children's non-fiction, Mythology/Folklore, Young adult nonfiction, Illustrations. **Career:** Freelance industrial designer, 1960-68; Central School of Arts & Design, London, visiting lecturer, 1960-68; Ravensbourne College of Art and Design, London, England, senior lecturer, 1968-77; author and illustrator, 1969-. **Publications:** SELF-ILLUSTRATED FOR CHILDREN: (with D. Goble) Red Hawk's Account of Custer's Last Battle, 1969; (with D. Goble) Brave Eagle's Account of the Fetterman Fight, 21 December 1866, 1972, in UK as The Hundred in the Hands; (with D. Goble) Lone Bull's Horse Raid, 1973; (with D. Goble) The Friendly Wolf, 1974, rev. as Dream Wolf, 1990; The Girl Who Loved Wild Horses, 1978; The Gift of the Sacred Dog, 1980; Star Boy, 1982; Buffalo Woman, 1984; The Great Race of the Birds and Animals, 1985; Death of the Iron Horse, 1987; Her Seven Brothers, 1988; Iktomi and the Boulder: A Plains Indian Story, 1988; Beyond the Ridge, 1989; Iktomi and the Berries, 1989; Iktomi and the Ducks, 1990; I Sing for the Animals, 1991; Iktomi and the Buffalo Skull, 1991; Crow Chief, 1992; Love Flute, 1992; The Lost Children, 1993; Adopted by the Eagles, 1994; Iktomi and the Buzzard, 1994; Hau Kola-Hello Friend (autobiography for children), 1994; Remaking the Earth: A Creation Story from the Great Plains of North America, 1996; The Return of the Buffaloes, 1996; The Legend of the White Buffalo Woman, 1998; Iktomi and the Coyote, 1998; Iktomi Loses His Eyes, 1999; Paul Goble Gallery: 3 Native American Stories, 1999; Storm Maker's Tipi, 2001; Mystic Horse, 2003; Song of Creation, 2004; All Our Relatives, 2005. **Address:** 1803 9th St, Rapid City, SD 57701, U.S.A.

GOBODO-MADIKIZELA, Pumla. (born Republic of South Africa). **Genres:** Civil liberties/Human rights. **Career:** Human rights activist and educator. University of Transkei, South Africa, instructor; served with the Truth and Reconciliation Commission, 1996-; University of Cape Town, Cape Town, South Africa, associate professor of psychology; Unilever Ethics Centre, University of Natal, Pietermaritzburg, South Africa, adjunct professor. Brandeis Ethics Center, Coexistence Program, faculty affiliate; taught in the United States at Harvard University, Brandeis University, Wellesley College, and Tufts University. **Publications:** A Human Being Died That Night: A South African Story of Forgiveness, 2003, published as A Human Being Died That Night: A South African Woman Confronts the Legacy of Apartheid, 2004. Contributor to periodicals. **Address:** Dept. of Psychology, University of Cape Town, Rondebosch, Cape Town 7701, Republic of South Africa. **Online address:** pgobodo@humanities.uct.ac.za

GOCHFELD, Michael. American, b. 1940. **Genres:** Environmental sciences/Ecology, Medicine/Health. **Career:** Professor of environmental medicine. **Publications:** (with D. Sachsman, P. Sandman, and M. Greenberg) Environmental Risk and the Press, 1986; (with E.A. Favata) Hazardous Waste Workers, 1990; (with J. Burger) The Black Skimmers: Social Dynamics of a Colonial Species, 1990; (with J. Burger) The Common Tern: Breeding Ecology and Behavior, 1991; (with J. Burger) Butterflies of New Jersey, 1997. EDITOR: (with C. Witmer) The Chromium Problem, 1991; (with E.A.

Emmet, A.L. Frank, and S.M. Hessl) Yearbook of Occupational and Environmental Medicine, annually, 1994-; (with S. Brooks) Environmental Medicine, 1995; (with W.E. Martin) Protecting Hazardous Waste Workers, 1999. Contributor to scientific journals and natural history magazines journals and natural history magazines. **Address:** Division of Occupational Medicine, Robert Wood Johnson Medical School, Piscataway, NJ 08854, U.S.A. **Online address:** gochfeld@eohsi.rutgers.edu

GODBOLD, E(dward) Stanly, Jr. American, b. 1942. **Genres:** History, Biography. **Career:** Professor of History, Mississippi State University, 1977-. Assistant Professor, University of Tennessee at Chattanooga, 1969-70; Associate Professor, Valdosta State College, Georgia, 1970-77. **Publications:** Ellen Glasgow and the Woman Within, 1972; (co-ed.) Essays in Southern History in Honor of Robert H. Woody, 1974; (with R.H. Woody) Christopher Gadsden and the American Revolution, 1982; (with M.U. Russell) Confederate Colonel and Cherokee Chief: The Life of William Holand Thomas, 1990. **Address:** Dept. of History, Allen Hall Rm 214, PO Box H, Mississippi State University, Mississippi State, MS 39762, U.S.A. **Online address:** esg@ra.msstate.edu

GODBOUT, Jacques. Canadian, b. 1933. **Genres:** Poetry, Novels, Essays. **Career:** University of Addis Ababa, Ethiopia, assistant professor of French, 1954-57; National Film Board of Canada, filmmaker, 1957-. Liberte, cofounder, 1959; University of Montreal, lecturer, 1969; University of California, Berkeley, lecturer, 1985. **Publications:** Carton-pate (poetry), 1956; Les Paves secs, 1958; C'est la chaude loi des hommes (poetry), 1960; L'Aquarium (novel), 1962; (ed., with J.R. Colombo) Poesie/Poetry 64, 1963; Le Couteau sur la table (novel), 1965, trans. by P. Williams, as Knife on the Table, 1968; Salut Galarneau! (novel), 1967, trans. by A. Brown as Hail Galarneau!, 1970; (with Colombo) Le Grande Muraille de Chine (poem; title means: The Great Wall of China), 1969; D'Amour, P.Q. (novel), 1972; (with P. Turgeon) L'Interview: texteradiophonique, 1973; Le Reformiste: textes tranquilles (title means: The Reformer), 1975; L'Isle au dragon, 1976, trans. by D. Ellis as Dragon Island, 1978; Les Tetes a Papineau, 1981; Le Murmure marchand (essay), 1984; Souvenirs Shop: Poemes et prose 1956-1960, 1984; Une Histoire Americaine (novel), 1986, trans. by Y. Saint-Pierre as An American Story, 1988; (with L. Plamondon) Un Coeur de Rockeur (song lyrics; title means: Rocker's Heart), 1988; L'ecrivain de province (diary; title means: Writer from the Province), 1991; L'Ecran de bonheur (essay), 1990; Le Temps des Galarneau (novel), 1993; Une Lecon de chasse (short story), 1997; D'ile en ile (correspondence), 1997. Contributor to anthologies, reviews, magazines. Author of written material for films. **Address:** 815 Pratt, Outremont, Montreal, QC, Canada H2V 2T7.

GODDARD, Hugh (P.). British, b. 1953. **Genres:** Theology/Religion. **Career:** College of St. Paul and St. Mary, Cheltenham, Gloucestershire, England, lecturer in Islamic studies, 1981-84; University of Nottingham, Nottingham, England, lecturer in Islamic theology, 1984-. Nottingham Christian-Muslim Forum, secretary, 1990-94. **Publications:** Christians and Muslims: From Double Standard to Mutual Understanding, 1995; Muslim Perceptions of Christianity, 1996; History of Christian-Muslim Relations, c. 2000. **Address:** Department of Theology, University of Nottingham, Nottingham NG7 2RP, England. **Online address:** hugh.goddard@nottingham.ac.uk

GODDARD, Robert (William). British, b. 1954. **Genres:** Novels, Mystery/Crime/Suspense. **Career:** Devon County Council, Devon, England, educational administrator, 1978-87; full-time writer, 1987-. **Publications:** NOVELS: Past Caring, 1986; In Pale Battalions 1988; Painting the Darkness, 1989; Into the Blue, 1991; Hand in Glove, 1992; Closed Circle, 1993; Out of the Sun, 1996; Caught in the Light, 1999. **Address:** PFD, Drury House, 34-43 Russell St., London WC2B 5HA, England.

GODDARD, Tariq. (born England), b. 1975. **Genres:** Novels. **Career:** Writer. **Publications:** Homage to a Firing Squad, 2002; Dynamo, 2003. **Address:** c/o Author Mail, Sceptre, 338 Euston Road, London NW1 3B4, England.

GODDEN, Geoffrey Arthur. British, b. 1929. **Genres:** Antiques/Furnishings, Art/Art history. **Career:** Writer. **Publications:** Victorian Porcelain, 1961; Victorian Pottery, 1962; Encyclopaedia of British Poetry and Porcelain Marks, 1964; Antique China and Glass under Pounds, 1966; An Illustrated Encyclopaedia of British Pottery and Porcelain, 1966; The Handbook of British Pottery and Porcelain Marks, 1968; Minton Pottery and Porcelain of the First Period, 1793-1850, 1968; Caughley and Worcester Porcelains 1775-1800, 1969; Coalport and Coalbrookdale Porcelains, 1970; Stevengraphs and Other Victorian Silk Pictures, 1971; Jewitt's Ceramic Art of Great Britain 1800-1900, 1972; British Porcelain-An Illustrated Guide, 1973; British

Pottery-An Illustrated Guide, 1974; Godden's Guide to English Porcelain, 1978; Oriental Export Market Porcelain, 1979; Mason's China and the Ironstone Wares, 1980; Chamberlain-Worcester Porcelain, 1982; Staffordshire Porcelain, 1983; English China, 1985; Encyclopaedia of British Porcelain Manufacturers, 1988; Godden's Guide to European Porcelain, 1993; Collecting Picture Postcards, 1996; New Handbook of British Pottery & Porcelain Marks, 1999; Godden's New Guide to English Porcelain, 2004; Godden's Guide to English Blue and White Porcelain, 2004; New Hall Porcelains, 2004. **Address:** 3 The Square, Findon, W. Sussex, England.

GODFREY, Donald G. Canadian. **Genres:** Communications/Media, Writing/Journalism. **Career:** University of Washington, Seattle, faculty associate, 1969-72, lecturer, 1972-75, assistant professor of communication, 1976-81; University of Arizona, Tucson, associate professor of radio and television studies, 1981-83; Southern Utah University, Cedar City, associate professor of communication and coordinator of telecommunications, 1983-86; Arizona State University, Tempe, assistant professor, 1988-91, associate professor, 1991-95, professor of telecommunication, 1995-. KOET-Television, production director and local news anchor, 1966-68; KSVN-Radio, news director and news anchor, 1966-68; KEZI-Television, news reporter, 1968-69; KIRO-Television, production sound engineer, 1969-81; Philippine Imports, corporate communications director, 1986-87; media consultant to Corporate Communications. **Publications:** Reruns on File: A Guide to Electronic Media Archives, 1992; (with M.D. Murray) Television in America: Local Station History from Across the Nation, 1997; (with F. Leigh) Historical Dictionary of American Radio, 1998; Philo T. Farnsworth: The Father of Television, 2001. EDITOR: A Directory of Broadcast Archives, 1983; (with B.Y. Card) The Diaries of Charles Ora Card: The Canadian Years, 1886-1903, 1993. **Address:** Walter Cronkite School of Journalism & Mass Communication, Arizona State University, Tempe, AZ 85287, U.S.A.

GODFREY, Neale S. American, b. 1951. **Genres:** Money/Finance. **Career:** Chase Manhattan Bank, NYC, banker, 1972-85; First Women's Bank of New York, NYC, president, 1985-88; First Children's Bank, NYC, founder, 1988-; Children's Financial Network, founder, 1988-. **Publications:** The Kids' Money Book, 1991; (with C. Edwards) Money Doesn't Grow on Trees: A Parent's Guide to Raising Financially Responsible Children, 1994; A Penny Saved, 1995; From Cradle to College, 1996; (with T. Richards) Making Change, 1997; Ultimate Kids Money Book, 1998. **Address:** 31 Twin Brooks Trail, Chester, NJ 07930-2820, U.S.A.

GODFREY, William. See YOUD, Sam.

GODKIN, Celia (Marilyn). Canadian (born England), b. 1948. **Genres:** Children's non-fiction, Environmental sciences/Ecology, Illustrations, Picture/board books. **Career:** Worked as biologist and teacher, 1969-76; University of Toronto, ON, instructor in natural science illustration, 1981-82, assistant professor, 1987-99, associate professor of biomedical communications, 1999-, department program supervisor, 1988-89, instructor for school of continuing studies, 1988-; Wilfrid Laurier University, Waterloo, ON, presented weekend workshops in biological illustration, 1983-85. Arts and crafts instructor, Riverdale Community Action Centre, 1973-74; instructor, Network for Learning, 1985, and Royal Ontario Museum, 1985-90. Herpetologist, Reptile Breeding Foundation, 1974-76; fisheries biologist, Glenora Fisheries Station, Ontario Ministry of Natural Resources, summers, 1976-81; biological consultant, Ministry of the Environment, 1985-86. Illustrator, Assiniboine Park Zoo, 1983; work exhibited at galleries throughout the world. **Publications:** SELF-ILLUSTRATED FOR CHILDREN: Wolf Island, 1989; Ladybug Garden, 1995; Sea Otter Inlet, 1997; Flying Lessons, 1999; When the Giant Stirred, 2002. Illustrator of books by C. Roots, S. Woods. **Address:** Division of Biomedical Communications, Dept of Surgery, Medical Science Bldg, University of Toronto, Toronto, ON, Canada M5S 1A8. **Online address:** celia.godkin@utoronto.ca

GODLEY, John Raymond. See KILBRACKEN, Lord.

GODMAN, Arthur. See Obituaries.

GODSEY, John Drew. American, b. 1922. **Genres:** Theology/Religion. **Career:** Drew University, Madison, NJ, instructor, 1956-59, assistant professor, 1959-64, associate professor, 1964-66, professor of systematic theology, 1966-68; Wesley Theological Seminary, Washington, DC, associate dean and associate professor of systematic theology, 1968-71, professor, 1971-88, professor emeritus of systematic theology, 1988-. **Publications:** The Theology of Dietrich Bonhoeffer, 1960; Preface to Bonhoeffer: The Man and Two of His Shorter Writings, 1965; The Promise of H. Richard Niebuhr, 1970. EDITOR/CO-EDITOR: Karl Barth's Table Talk, 1963; K. Barth, How I Changed My Mind, 1966; Ethical Responsibility: Bonhoeffer's Legacy to the Churches, 1981; D. Bonhoeffer, Discipleship, 2001. **Address:** 8306 Bryant Dr, Bethesda, MD 20817, U.S.A.

GODSHALK, C. S. American. **Genres:** Novels. **Career:** Writer, freelance journalist. Formerly owned an import/export business in Southeast Asia, worked in a children's cancer hospital, and with inmates of a penitentiary. **Publications:** Kalimantaan, 1998. Contributor of short stories to anthologies. **Address:** c/o Henry Holt & Co., 115 West 18th St., 6th Floor, New York, NY 10011, U.S.A.

GODSON, Roy (S.). American, b. 1942. **Genres:** Organized labor, History, International relations/Current affairs. **Career:** Carnegie Mellon University, Pittsburgh, PA, instructor, 1967-69; World Affairs Councils of Pittsburgh, educational director, 1967-69; Georgetown University, Washington, DC, assistant professor and director of International Labor Program, 1969-. American Histadrut Cultural Exchange Institute, director, 1973-; FRONT-LASH, director, 1973-. **Publications:** American Labor and European Politics: The AFL as a Transnational Force, 1976; The Kremlin and Labor: A Study in National Security Policy, 1977; (with S. Haseler) Eurocommunism: Implications for East and West, 1978; (ed.) Intelligence Requirements for the 1980s, 7 vols, 1979-86; (with E.W. Lefever) The CIA and the American Ethic: An Unfinished Debate, 1979; (with R.H. Schultz) Dezinformatsia: Active Measures in Soviet Strategy, 1984; (ed.) Comparing Foreign Intelligence: The US and the USSR, the UK and the Third World, 1988; (ed.) Intelligence Requirements for the 1990s: Collection, Analysis, Counterintelligence, and Covert Action, 1989; (coeditor with Schultz and T. Greenwood) Security Studies for the 1990s, 1993. **Address:** Government Department, Georgetown University, 37th and O Sts. NW, Washington, DC 20057, U.S.A.

GODWIN, Gail (Kathleen). American, b. 1937. **Genres:** Novels, Novellas/Short stories, Literary criticism and history, Social sciences. **Career:** Miami Herald, reporter, 1959-60; U.S. Travel Service, London, consultant, 1962-65; Saturday Evening Post, NYC, research, 1966; University of Iowa, Iowa City, instructor, 1967-70; University of Illinois, Urbana, Center for Advanced Studies, instructor and fellow, 1971-72; University of Iowa, Writers' Workshop, lecturer, 1972-73; Vassar College, Poughkeepsie, NY, lecturer, 1975; Columbia University, NYC, lecturer, 1978, 1981. **Publications:** The Perfectionists, 1970; Glass People, 1972; The Odd Woman, 1974; Dream Children (short stories), 1976; Violet Clay, 1978; A Mother and Two Daughters, 1982; Mr. Bedford and the Muses, 1983; The Finishing School, 1985; A Southern Family, 1987; Father Melancholy's Daughter; The Good Husband, 1994; Evensong, 1999; Heart: A Personal Journey through Its Myths & Meanings, 2001; Evenings at Five, 2003. **Address:** PO Box 946, Woodstock, NY 12498, U.S.A.

GODWIN, Parke. American, b. 1929. **Genres:** Novels, Science fiction/Fantasy. **Career:** Writer. **Publications:** NOVELS: A Memory of Lions, 1983; A Truce with Time (A Love Story with Occasional Ghosts), 1988; Limbo Search, 1995; The Tower of Beowulf, 1995; Lord of Sunset (historical), 1998. SOLITUDE TRILOGY (with M. Kaye): The Masters of Solitude, 1978; Wintermind, 1982. ARTHURIAN SERIES: Firelord, 1980; Beloved Exile, 1984; The Last Rainbow, 1985. COLD BLUE LIGHT SERIES (with M. Kaye): A Cold Blue Light, 1983. SNAKE OIL WARS SERIES: Waiting for the Galactic Bus, 1988; The Snake Oil Wars, or, Scheherazade Ginsberg Strikes Again, 1989. ROBIN HOOD SERIES: Sherwood, 1991; Robin and the King, 1993. OTHER: The Fire When It Comes (novella and short stories), 1984; (ed.) Invitation to Camelot: An Arthurian Anthology of Short Stories (short stories), 1988.

GODWIN, Rebecca T. American, b. 1950. **Genres:** Novels, Novellas/Short stories, Essays. **Career:** Georgetown Steel Corp., Georgetown, SC, secretary, 1968-80; Bumpy Thompson Realty, Pawleys Island, SC, broker and partner, 1980-87; Higginbotham & Associates (advertising agency), Albany, NY, writer, 1988-92; Bennington College, Bennington, VT, writer, 1992-2002, MFA Writing Seminars, faculty member, 2002, faculty member, 2003-. National Endowment for the Arts, fellow, 1994-95; Bennington Writing Workshops, teacher, 1995; Wildacres Writing Workshop, teacher, 1996; MacDowell Colony, fellow, 2001. **Publications:** NOVELS: Private Parts, 1992; Keeper of the House, 1994. Contributor of short stories and essays to periodicals. **Address:** Bennington College, 1 College Dr, Bennington, VT 05201, U.S.A. **Online address:** rgodwin@bennington.edu

GOEDECKE, Christopher (John). American, b. 1951. **Genres:** Recreation, Sports/Fitness. **Career:** International School of Judo and Karate, Summit, NJ, senior staff instructor, 1972-75; Wind School, Chatham, NJ, self-employed karate instructor/director, 1975-. President, Wind Warrior Company

Inc., Chatham, 1975-; codirector, Reader's Rendezvous, 1989-91. Creator of Grand Master, a card game, 1980. **Publications:** A Guide to the Martial Arts of New Jersey, 1984; The Wind Warrior: The Training of a Karate Champion, 1992; Smart Moves: A Kid's Guide to Self-Defense, 1995. **Address:** 16 Braidburn Way, Convent Station, NJ 07961, U.S.A. **Online address:** windschool@earthlink.net

GOEDICKE, Patricia (McKenna). (Mrs. Leonard Robinson). American, b. 1931. **Genres:** Poetry. **Career:** Harcourt Brace & World publrs., NYC, editorial assistant, 1953-54; T. Y. Crowell publrs., NYC, editorial assistant, 1955-56; Page mag., Athens, OH, co-ed., 1961-66; taught at Ohio University, Athens, 1962-68; Hunter College, NYC, 1969-71; Instituto Allende, 1972-79, and Sarah Lawrence College, Bronxville, NY, 1980-81; University of Montana, Missoula, poet-in-residence, 1981-83, associate professor, 1983-90, professor of creative writing, 1990-2003, professor emerita, 2003-. **Publications:** Between Oceans, 1968; For the Four Corners, 1976; The Trail That Turns on Itself, 1978; The Dog That Was Barking Yesterday, 1980; Crossing the Same River, 1980; The King of Childhood, 1984; The Wind of Our Going, 1985; Listen Love, 1986; The Tongues We Speak, 1989; Paul Bunyan's Bearskin, 1992; Invisible Horses, 1996; As Earth Begins to End, 2000. **Address:** 310 McLeod Ave, Missoula, MT 59801, U.S.A. **Online address:** goedicke@earthlink.net

GOEHLERT, Robert. American, b. 1948. **Genres:** Bibliography, Reference. **Career:** Indiana University, Bloomington, Political Science Data Archive and Computing Library, archivist, 1971-72, College of Arts and Sciences, assistant instructor, 1973, Department of Political Science, research and editorial assistant, 1973-74, and instructor, 1975-; University Library, assistant to librarian for economics and political science, 1973-74, subject specialist for political science, economics, and criminal justice, 1974-, assistant head of subject and area librarians, 1974-, acting head for Interlibrary Services, 1985-86; Honor's Division, assistant instructor, 1974; School of Library and Information Science, adjunct faculty, 1985-. Guest lecturer for the School of Library and Information Science, Indiana University, 1975-; visiting librarian at the Commonwealth of Australia Parliamentary Library and Australian National University's Menzies Library, 1984; Chairman of library committees, 1978-96. **Publications:** NONFICTION (with F. Martin): The Parliament of Great Britain: A Bibliography, 1982; Policy Analysis and Management: A Bibliography, 1984; The Presidency: A Research Guide, 1984; The American Presidents: A Bibliography, 1988; The U.S. Supreme Court: A Bibliography, 1990; How to Research the Supreme Court, 1992; The United States Congress: An Annotated Bibliography 1980-93, 1995; (with J. Sayre) Members of Congress: A Bibliography, 1996; How to Research Congress, 1996; How to Research the Presidency, 1996; Political Science Journal of Information, 1997; American Government and Politics: A Guide to Books for Teachers, 1997. OTHER: (with T. Michalk) Reform of Local Government Structures in the United States 1945-1971: A Microfiche Library, 1976; Presidential Campaigns: A Cartoon History 1789-1976, 1977; Directory of Librarians and Information Specialists in Political Science, 1979; (with P. Baker and E. Ostrom) Metropolitan Reform: An Annotated Bibliography, 1979; (with J. Sayre) The United States Congress: A Bibliography, 1982; (with F. Musto) State Legislatures: A Bibliography, 1985; (with E. Hoffmeister) The Department of State and American Diplomacy: A Bibliography, 1986; (with N. Gunderson) Government Regulation of Business: An Information Sourcebook, 1987; The Parliament of Australia: A Bibliography, 1988; (with H. Reynolds) The Executive Branch of the U.S. Government: A Bibliography, 1988; Congress and Law-making: Researching the Legislative Process, 1989; (with M. Shaaban) The European Community: Basic Resources, 1991; (with M. Shaaban) UN Documentation: A Basic Guide, 1992; (with A.C. Stamatoples) The Chinese Economy: A Bibliography of Works in English, 1995. Contributor to anthologies. Contributor to periodicals. **Address:** 4519 East Deckard Drive, Bloomington, IN 47408, U.S.A.

GOEKLER, Susan. See WOOLEY, Susan Frelick.

GOEMANS, Hein E. Dutch, b. 1957. **Genres:** Politics/Government. **Career:** 36 op de schaal von Richter, Amsterdam, Netherlands, staff member, 1981-85; Harvard University, Cambridge, MA, postdoctoral fellow at Olin Institute, 1995-96; Duke University, Durham, NC, assistant professor of political science, 1996-. Hoover Institution on War, Revolution, and Peace, Stanford, CA, national fellow, 2000-01. **Publications:** War and Punishment: The Causes of War Termination and the First World War, 2000. Contributor to periodicals. **Address:** Department of Political Science, Box 90204, Duke University, Durham, NC 27708, U.S.A. **Online address:** hgoemans@duke.edu

GOERLER, Raimund E. American (born Germany), b. 1948. **Genres:** History. **Career:** Western Reserve Historical Society, Cleveland, OH,

manuscript specialist, 1976-78; Ohio State University, Columbus, university archivist, professor, and assistant director of libraries, 1978-. **Publications:** (with G.A. Fry and F.W. Hebbard) The Ohio State University and Its College of Optometry: A Photographic History, 1993. EDITOR: The Tom L. Johnson Papers in the Library of the Western Reserve Historical Society, 1976; From History to Pre-History--Archivists Face the Future: Essays in Honor of the 25th Anniversary of the Society of Ohio Archivists, 1994; To the Pole: The Diary and Notebook of Richard E. Byrd, 1925-1927, 1998. **Address:** University Archives, Ohio State University, 2700 Kenny Rd, Columbus, OH 43210, U.S.A. **Online address:** goerler.1@ohio-state.edu

GOERNER, Sally J. American, b. 1952. **Genres:** Environmental sciences/Ecology, Information science/Computers, Adult non-fiction, Intellectual history, Physics, Sciences. **Career:** NCR Corp., Ithaca, NY, systems programmer, 1975-79; Asyst Design Services, co-founder, 1976, business systems consultant, 1976-79; Adaptronics, McLean, VA, senior software engineer, 1979-81; private practice of psychotherapy, 1982-85; Bell Northern Research Laboratories, Research Triangle Park, NC, member of scientific staff, 1983-85; Data General Corp., senior technical communications specialist, 1986-92; Triangle Center for the Study of Complex Systems, Chapel Hill, NC, director and consultant, 1992-; Integral Science Institute, director, 1999-. **Publications:** Chaos and the Evolving Ecological Universe, 1994; Life after the Clockwork Universe, 1999. Contributor to books. Contributor of articles and reviews to scientific journals. Some writings appear under the name S. J. Goerner. **Address:** Integral Science Institute, 374 Wesley Ct., Chapel Hill, NC 27516, U.S.A. **Online address:** sgoerner@mindspring.com

GOETHE, Ann. American, b. 1945. **Genres:** Novels, Plays/Screenplays, Songs/Lyrics and libretti, Essays. **Career:** Writer. Worked as dancer and actress. Founded Blacksburg New School, 1971. **Publications:** Midnight Lemonade (novel), 1993; Coming of Age (play for young people); Something in the Air Feels Like Tomorrow (play for young people); (librettist) Travels (opera). Contributor, sometimes as Ann G. Distler or Ann Goette, to periodicals. **Address:** 911 Allendale Ct, Blacksburg, VA 24060, U.S.A.

GOFF, M(adison) Lee. American, b. 1944. **Genres:** Criminology/True Crime. **Career:** B.P. Bishop Museum, Honolulu, HI, research assistant, diptera section, 1964-66, acarology section, 1968-71, acarologist, 1977-83, research associate in entomology, 1994-97; Hawaii Volcanoes National Park, site manager for international biological program field station, 1971; California State University, Long Beach, CA, teaching assistant and research assistant, 1971-74; Kaiser Hospital, Harbor City, CA, clinical laboratory assistant, 1974; University of Hawaii at Manoa, Honolulu, HI, teaching assistant, 1974-77, professor of entomology, 1983-2001, curator, Entomology Museum, 1993-, chair of entomology graduate field, 1994-98; Chaminade University of Honolulu, Honolulu, HI, chair of forensic sciences program, 2001-. National Museum of Natural History/Smithsonian Institution, curatorial responsibility for national chigger collection, 1977-; Bulletin of the Society of Vector Ecologists, member of editorial board, 1986-92; city and county of Honolulu, Department of the Medical Examiner, consultant in forensic entomology. **Publications:** A Fly for the Prosecution: How Insect Evidence Helps Solve Crimes, 2000. Contributor to books. Contributor of papers to refereed journals. **Address:** Forensic Sciences Program, Chaminade University of Honolulu, 3140 Waialae Ave., Honolulu, HI 96816, U.S.A. **Online address:** lgoff@chaminade.edu

GOFF, Martyn. British, b. 1923. **Genres:** Novels, History, Music, Sociology. **Career:** Chairman, Henry Sotheran, booksellers, London. Director, National Book League, 1970-86; Vice President, Book Trust, 2000- (Chief Executive, 1986-88). Chairman, New Fiction Society, 1975-82; Honorary Treasurer, Intl. P.E.N.; Trustee, National Literacy Trust, 1993-; Chairman, National Life Story Collection, 1998-2003. OBE, 1977. **Publications:** The Plaster Fabric, 1956; A Short Guide to Long Play, 1956; A Season with Mammon, 1957; A Further Guide to Long Play, 1957; A Sort of Peace, 1959; Long Playing Collecting, 1959; The Youngest Director, 1961; Red on the Door, 1963; Flint Inheritance, 1965; Indecent Assault, 1967; Why Conform?, 1969; Victorian Surrey, 1972; Record Choice, 1974; The Royal Pavilion, 1976; The Liberation of Rupert Bannister, 1977; Tar and Cement (novel), 1988; Prize Writing, 1989. **Address:** 95 Sisters Ave, London SW11 5SW, England.

GOFORTH, Ellen. See FRANCIS, Dorothy Brenner.

GOGOL, Sara. See Obituaries.

GOINGBACK, Owl. American, b. 1959. **Genres:** Novels, Young adult fiction. **Career:** US Air Force, 1976-81; restaurant owner, c. 1981-86;

freelance writer, 1986-; lecturer on Native American folklore; speaker at science fiction conventions. **Publications:** NOVELS: Crota, 1996; Shaman Moon, 1997; Darker Than Night, 1999; Evil Whispers, 2001; Breed, 2002. OTHER: The Gift (juvenile), 1997; Eagle Feathers (juvenile), 1997. Contributor of stories to anthologies and books. **Address:** PO Box 5080, Winter Park, FL 32793, U.S.A.

GOLANT, Stephen M(yles). Canadian/American, b. 1945. **Genres:** Gerontology/Senior issues. **Career:** University of Chicago, Chicago, IL, postdoctoral research associate at Center for Urban Studies, 1972, assistant professor, 1974-77, associate professor of geography, 1979-80; University of Florida, Gainesville, associate professor, 1980-84, professor of geography and adjunct professor of urban and regional planning, 1984-, head of department of geography, 1982-88, faculty associate of Center for Gerontological Studies, 1980-. University of Guelph, Harshman Lecturer, 1974; University of Toronto, guest lecturer, 1974; speaker at U.S. colleges and universities. Responses to an Aging Florida magazine, editor-in-chief. **Publications:** The Residential Location and Spatial Behavior of the Elderly (monograph), 1972; Location and Environment of Elderly Population, 1979; A Place to Grow Old: The Meaning of Environment in Old Age, 1984; Housing America's Elderly: Many Possibilities, Few Choices, 1992; (assoc ed and contrib.) The Columbia Retirement Handbook, 1994; Smart Housing, 1994. Contributor to books. Contributor of articles and reviews to geography, gerontology, and community planning journals. **Address:** Department of Geography, 3142 Turlington Hall, University of Florida, Gainesville, FL 32611, U.S.A.

GOLAY, Michael. American, b. 1951. **Genres:** History. **Career:** Reporter and editor for daily newspapers in Connecticut and California, 1978-93; freelance writer and editor, 1993-. **Publications:** The Civil War, 1992; To Gettysburg and Beyond, 1994; The Spanish-American War, 1995; The Black Experience During Reconstruction, 1996; Where America Stands, 1996; Where America Stands 1997, 1997; A Ruined Land, 1999. **Address:** Box 1036, Exeter, NH 03833-2608, U.S.A.

GOLCZEWSKI, James A. American, b. 1945. **Genres:** Gerontology/Senior issues, Medicine/Health. **Career:** ITT Communications Division, electronics engineer, 1969-73; Litton Industries, Airtron Division, materials engineer, 1974-79; University of Alabama, Birmingham, postdoctoral research fellow, 1980-82; University of Pennsylvania, Philadelphia, postdoctoral fellow at Wistar Institute, 1982-83; Norwich University, Northfield, VT, assistant professor of physics, 1983-84; Passaic County Community College, Paterson, NJ, adjunct teacher of biology and nutrition, 1984-85; University of Medicine and Dentistry of New Jersey, Newark, NJ, research associate, 1985-86; Rutgers University, Newark Campus, research fellow, 1986-88; Medical Specialties and Devices, Nyack, NY, senior scientist, 1989-92; University of Medicine and Dentistry of New Jersey, research specialist, 1993-96; freelance medical writer, 1996-. **Publications:** Aging: Strategies for Maintaining Good Health and Extending Life, 1998. Contributor to scientific journals. **Address:** 45 Ridge Rd., Roseland, NJ 07068, U.S.A. **Online address:** jigo@erols.com

GOLD, Bernice. (born Canada). **Genres:** Children's fiction. **Career:** CBC Radio, Montreal, Quebec, Canada, freelance broadcaster; writer. Teacher of remedial subjects to children with learning disabilities, McGill-Montreal Children's Hospital Learning Centre, Montreal. **Publications:** My Four Lions, 1999; Strange School, Secret Wish, 2001. **Address:** POB 23, Victoria Station, Montreal, Quebec, Canada H3Z 2V4. **Online address:** agold@videotron.ca

GOLD, Hazel. American, b. 1953. **Genres:** Literary criticism and history. **Career:** University of Pennsylvania, Philadelphia, lecturer in Spanish, 1976-80; Columbia University, NYC, assistant professor of Spanish, 1980-85; Northwestern University, Evanston, IL, assistant professor of Spanish, 1985-92; Emory University, Atlanta, GA, associate professor of Spanish, 1992-, chair, dept of Spanish & Portuguese, 2000-. Consultant to International Orientation Resources Inc and Educational Testing Services; Anales Galdosianos, editor; Journal for Interdisciplinary Literary Studies, editorial board. **Publications:** The Reframing of Realism: Galdos and the Discourses of the Nineteenth-Century Spanish Novel, 1993. Work represented in books. Contributor of articles and reviews to academic journals. **Address:** Dept of Spanish, Emory University, Atlanta, GA 30322, U.S.A.

GOLD, Herbert. American, b. 1924. **Genres:** Novels, Novellas/Short stories, Autobiography/Memoirs, Essays. **Career:** Lecturer in philosophy and literature, Cornell University, University of California, Berkeley & Davis, Stanford University, Harvard University. **Publications:** Birth of a Hero, 1951; The Prospect before Us, 1954; The Man Who Was Not with It (in paperback as The Wildlife), 1956; (with R.V. Cassill and J.B. Hall) 15-3

(short stories), 1957; The Optimist, 1959; Therefore Be Bold, 1960; Love and Like (short stories), 1960; The Age of Happy Problems (essays), 1962; Salt, 1963; The Fathers: A Novel in the Form of a Memoir, 1967; The Great American Jackpot, 1970; The Magic Will: Stories and Essays of a Decade, 1971; My Last Two Thousand Years (autobiography), 1972; The Young Prince and the Magic Cone, 1973; Swiftie the Magician, 1974; Waiting for Cordelia, 1977; Slave Trade, 1979; He/She, 1980; A Walk on the West Side (essays), 1981; Family (novel), 1981; True Love, 1982; Mister White Eyes, 1984; Stories of Misbegotten Love, 1985; Lovers and Cohorts, 1986; A Girl of Forty, 1986; Dreaming, 1988; Best Nightmare on Earth: A Life in Haiti, (autobiography), 1991; Bohemia: Where Art, Angst, Love & Strong Coffee Meet, 1993; She Took My Arm as if She Loved Me (novel), 1997; Daughter Mine (novel), 2000. EDITOR: Fiction of the Fifties: A Decade of American Writing, 1959; (with D.L. Stevenson) Stories of Modern America, 1961, rev. ed., 1963; First Person Singular: Essays for the Sixties, 1963. **Address:** 1051-A Broadway, San Francisco, CA 94133, U.S.A.

GOLD, Janet N(owakowski). American, b. 1948. **Genres:** Literary criticism and history. **Career:** Teacher at an elementary school in Tegucigalpa, Honduras, 1971-72; Centro Internacional de Idiomas, Cuernavaca, Mexico, instructor in English as a second language, 1973; teacher in the Spanish-English bilingual program of elementary schools in Worcester, MA, 1974-82; University of Massachusetts, teaching assistant, 1984-88; Bates College, Lewiston, ME, instructor in Spanish language and literature, 1989-91; Louisiana State University, Baton Rouge, assistant professor of Spanish language and Latin American literature, 1991-95; University of New Hampshire, Durham, assistant professor of Spanish, 1995-. **Publications:** Clementina Suarez: Her Life and Poetry, 1995. Contributor to books. Contributor of articles and reviews to Hispanic studies journals. **Address:** Department of Spanish, Murkland 209, University of New Hampshire, Durham, NH 03824, U.S.A.

GOLD, Jerome. American, b. 1943. **Genres:** Novels, Novellas/Short stories, Poetry, Autobiography/Memoirs, Essays. **Career:** Juvenile rehabilitation counselor at a prison for children in the Pacific Northwest, 1991-. **Publications:** NOVELS: The Negligence of Death, 1984; The Inquisitor, 1991; The Prisoner's Son, 1996; Sergeant Dickinson, 1999. STORIES: (with L. Galloway) Of Great Spaces, 1987; War Stories, 1990; Life at the End of Time (and essays), 1992; Prisoners (and poems), 1999. OTHER: (ed.) Hurricanes, 1994; Publishing Lives: Interviews with Independent Book Publishers in the Pacific Northwest and British Columbia, 1996; Obscure in the Shade of the Giants: Publishing Lives, Vol. II, 2000; How I Learned That I Could Push the Button (memoirs/essays), 2003. Work represented in anthologies. Contributor of articles, essays, stories, poems, and reviews to periodicals. **Address:** c/o Black Heron Press, PO Box 95676, Seattle, WA 98145, U.S.A.

GOLD, Michael. American, b. 1950. **Genres:** Medicine/Health, Cultural/Ethnic topics, Theology/Religion. **Career:** Congregation Sons of Israel, Nyack, NY, rabbi, 1978-84; Beth El Congregation, Pittsburgh, PA, rabbi, 1984-90; Temple Beth Torah, Tamarac, FL, rabbi, 1990-. Writer, consultant, and lecturer on Jewish family issues. **Publications:** And Hannah Wept: Infertility, Adoption, and the Jewish Couple, 1988; Does God Belong in the Bedroom?, 1992; God, Love, Sex, and Family, 1998; The Ten Journeys of Life, 2001. **Address:** 9101-15 NW 57th St, Tamarac, FL 33351, U.S.A. **Online address:** rabbigold@aol.com

GOLD, Michael Evan. American, b. 1943. **Genres:** Law, Industrial relations. **Career:** Cornell University, Ithaca, NY, associate professor of industrial and labor relations; writer. **Publications:** Some Terms from Liberian Speech, rev ed, 1971; A Dialogue on Comparable Worth, 1983; An Introduction to Labor Law, 1989; An Introduction to the Law of Employment Discrimination, 1993. Work represented in anthologies. Contributor to law journals. **Address:** New York State School of Industrial and Labor Relations, 293 Ives Hall, Cornell University, Ithaca, NY 14853-3901, U.S.A. **Online address:** meg3@cornell.edu

GOLD, Nora. Canadian, b. 1953?. **Genres:** Sociology, Novellas/Short stories. **Career:** McMaster University, Hamilton, Ontario, Canada, associate professor of social work. **Publications:** Canadian Jewish Women and Their Experiences of Antisemitism and Sexism (nonfiction), 1997; Marrow and Other Stories (short stories), 1998. Contributor to books and periodicals. **Address:** School of Social Work, McMaster University, Kenneth Taylor Hall, Rm. 319, Hamilton, ON, Canada L8E 1A1. **Online address:** goldn@mcmaster.ca

GOLD, Steven J(ames). American, b. 1955. **Genres:** Sociology. **Career:** Off Track Betting Corporation, NYC, worked in market research department,

1977-78; Lawrence Berkeley Laboratory, research assistant in Applied Science Division, 1980-85; Center for Southeast Asian Refugee Resettlement, San Francisco, CA, program developer, 1982-84; Whittier College, CA, department of sociology, anthropology, and social work, assistant professor, 1985-91, associate professor of sociology, 1991-94, chair, 1993-94; Michigan State University, associate professor, 1994-. Wilstein Institute on Jewish Policy Studies, senior fellow, 1991-. Photographer, with work exhibited at shows and galleries in California. **Publications:** Refugee Communities: A Comparative Field Study, 1992; (with M. Tuan) Jews from the Former U.S. S.R. in the United States, 1993; From the Workers' State to the Golden State, 1995; Immigration Research for a New Century, 2000; Ethnic Economies, 2000. Contributor to books. Contributor of articles, reviews, and photographs to sociology journals. **Address:** Department of Sociology, 316 Berkley Hall, Michigan State University, East Lansing, MI 48824-1111, U.S.A. **Online address:** gold@msu.edu

GOLDBERG, Bruce (Edward). American, b. 1948. **Genres:** Medicine/Health. **Career:** Dental practice, Baltimore, MD, 1976-89; hypnotherapy practice, Baltimore, MD, 1976-89; hypnotherapy practice, Los Angeles, CA, 1989-; Los Angeles Academy of Clinical Hypnosis, Los Angeles, CA, president, 1990-. **Publications:** Past Lives, Future Lives: Accounts of Regression and Progression through Hypnosis, 1982, as Past Lives, Future Lives, 1988; The Search for Grace: A Documented Case of Murder and Reincarnation, 1994; Peaceful Transition, 1997; Soul Healing, 1997; Unleash Your Psychic Powers, 1997; Astral Voyages, 1998; Look Younger, Live Longer, 1998; New Age Hypnosis, 1998; Protected by the Light, 1998; Time Travelers from Our Future, 1998; Custom Design Your Own Destiny, 2000; Lose Weight Permanently and Naturally, 2000; Self Hypnosis, 2001; Dream Your Problems Away, 2003. Contributor to professional journals. **Address:** 4300 Natoma Ave, Woodland Hills, CA 91364, U.S.A. **Online address:** karma4u@webtv.net

GOLDBERG, Danny. American. **Genres:** Music. **Career:** Involved in politics, New York, NY, and worked for Billboard magazine; vice president of Swan Song Records and founder and co-owner of Modern Records; owner and president of Gold Mountain Entertainment (personal management firm), 1983-92; Atlantic Records, Los Angeles, CA, senior vice president, 1992, president, 1993-94; Warner Bros. Records, chair and chief executive officer, 1995; Mercury Records, president, 1996-97, chair and chief executive officer, 1998; Tikkun magazine, co-publisher, 1997-2001; Artemis Records, chair and chief executive officer, 1998-; president and chief executive officer of Sheridan Square Entertainment. Also worked as a television commercial and film producer in the 1980s, co-producing and directing No Nukes (documentary), 1980, co-producing voter registration commercials for MTV, 1984, and producing Rock against Drugs commercials, 1986. President, American Civil Liberties Union Foundation of Southern California; member of board of directors, New York Civil Liberties Union executive committee, Rock the Vote, Creative Coalition, Nation Institute, Jewish Television Network, and the Abraham Fund; served on the board for the Hollywood Policy Center and the Show Coalition. **Publications:** (editor, with father, Victor Goldberg, and Robert Greenwald) It's a Free Country: Personal Freedom in America after September 11, 2002; Dispatches from the Culture Wars: How the Left Lost Teen Spirit, 2003. **Address:** Artemis Records, 130 5th Ave, 7th Floor, New York, NY 10011, U.S.A. **Online address:** info@dannygoldberg.com

GOLDBERG, Jacob. American, b. 1943. **Genres:** Children's non-fiction, Young adult non-fiction. **Career:** Crown Publishers Inc., NYC, senior editor, 1970-90; Chelsea House Publishers, NYC, senior editor, 1990-96. **Publications:** FOR CHILDREN: Rachel Carson: Biologist and Author, 1993; Hawaii, 1997. FOR YOUNG ADULTS: Miguel Cervantes, 1994; Economics and the Environment, 1994; The Disappearing American Farm, 1995; Albert Einstein: The Rebel behind Relativity, 1995; Food, 1997. Has also written under the name Jake Goldberg. **Address:** c/o Author Mail, Watts Publishing Group, 96 Leonard St, London EC2A 4XD, England.

GOLDBERG, Jane G. American, b. 1946. **Genres:** Psychology, Medicine/Health, Human relations/Parenting. **Career:** Psychoanalyst in private practice, New York City, 1973-. Member of faculty, Center for Modern Psychoanalytic Studies (New York City), and Boston Center for Modern Psychoanalytic Studies (Boston, MA), both 1980-. Director of La Casa de Vida Natural and Holistic Health Spa (Puerto Rico), and La Casa de Vida Natural Day Spa (New York City). **Publications:** Psychotherapeutic Treatment of Cancer Patients, 1981; Deceits of the Mind and Their Effects on the Body, 1991; The Dark Side of Love: The Positive Role of Our Negative Feelings, 1993. **Address:** 41 E. 20th St., New York, NY 10003-1324, U.S.A.

GOLDBERG, Leonard S. American, b. 1936. **Genres:** Mystery/Crime/Suspense. **Career:** St. Louis City Hospital, MO, intern and resident in medicine, 1960-61; Medical College of Virginia, Richmond, resident in medicine, 1963-64; Jackson Memorial Hospital, Miami, FL, resident in medicine, 1964-65; University of California, Los Angeles, fellow in hematology, 1965-66, research fellow in immunology, 1966-67, assistant professor, 1968-71, associate professor, 1971-75, professor, 1975-79, clinical professor of medicine, 1979-, clinical investigator of the Veterans Administration, 1968-71; University of California, San Francisco, research fellow in immunology, 1967-68; Wadsworth Veterans Hospital, consultant in rheumatology, 1971-. American Board of Internal Medicine, diplomat in internal medicine, hematology, and rheumatology. **Publications:** MEDICAL SUSPENSE NOVELS: Transplant, 1980; Deadly Medicine, 1992; A Deadly Practice, 1994; Deadly Care, 1996; Deadly Harvest, 1997; Deadly Exposure, 1998; Lethal Measures, 2000; Fatal Care, 2001. Contributor of reviews to medical journals.

GOLDBERGER, Avriel H. American, b. 1928. **Genres:** History, Women's studies and issues, Autobiography/Memoirs, Biography, Essays. **Career:** Hofstra University, Hempstead, NY, professor of French, head of department, 1969-74, 1986-93. **Publications:** Visions of a New Hero: The Heroic Life According to Andre Malraux and Earlier Advocates of Human Grandeur, 1965; (ed.) Woman as Mediatrix: Essays on Nineteenth Century European Woman Writers, 1987; (ed.) The Stendhal Bicentennial Papers, 1987; (ed. with M. Gutwirth and K. Szmurlo) Germaine de Stael: Crossing the Borders, 1991. TRANSLATOR: (and author of intro. and notes) G. de Stael, Corinne or, Italy, 1987; (and author of intro. and afterword) E. Carles with R. Destarque, A Life of Her Own, 1991, in UK as A Wild Herb Soup, 1991; G. de Stael, Delphine, 1995; G. de Stael, Ten Years of Exile, 2000. **Address:** 1661 Crescent Pl NW, Washington, DC 20009, U.S.A.

GOLDEN, Arthur. American. **Genres:** Biography. **Career:** Writer. Has worked for an English-language magazine in Tokyo, 1980-82. **Publications:** Memoirs of a Geisha, 1997. **Address:** 43 Abbottsford Rd., Brookline, MA 02446, U.S.A.

GOLDEN, Mark. Canadian, b. 1948. **Genres:** Classics, History, Sports/Fitness. **Career:** University of Winnipeg, Winnipeg, Manitoba, professor of classics, 1982-; writer. **Publications:** Children and Childhood in Classical Athens, 1990; Sport and Society in Ancient Greece, 1998; Sport in Greece and Rome form A to Z, 2003. EDITOR: (with P. Toohey) Inventing Ancient Culture, 1997; (with P. Toohey) Sex and Difference in Ancient Greece and Rome, 2001. **Address:** Department of Classics, University of Winnipeg, Winnipeg, MB, Canada R3B 2E9. **Online address:** mgolden@uwinnipeg.ca

GOLDEN, Renny. American, b. 1937. **Genres:** Poetry, Civil liberties/Human rights, International relations/Current affairs, Politics/Government, Social sciences, Sociology. **Career:** Malcolm X College, Chicago, IL, dean and co-founder of St. Mary's Community Education, 1972-77; Harvard Divinity School, Cambridge, MA, research/faculty associate, 1977-78; Northeastern Illinois University, Chicago, professor, 1978-. Co-founded Chicago Religious Task Force on Central America, 1982. **Publications:** (with S. Collins and E. Kreutz) Half a Winter to Go: Poems, 1976; (with Collins) Struggle Is a Name for Hope, 1982; (with M. McConnell) Sanctuary: The New Underground Railroad, 1986; Dangerous Memories: Invasion and Resistance since 1492, 1991; The Hour of the Poor, the Hour of Women: Salvadoran Women Speak, 1991; Disposable Children: America's Child Welfare System, 1997; The Hour of the Furnaces, 2000; Branded: Imprisoned Mothers & Children They Left Behind, 2004. Contributor to books and periodicals. **Address:** Northeastern Illinois University, Dept of Justice Studies & Social Work, 5500 N St. Louis, Chicago, IL 60624, U.S.A.

GOLDENTYER, Debra. American, b. 1960. **Genres:** Young adult non-fiction. **Career:** Schaeffer and Goldentyer, Oakland, CA, partner in the production of videos and multimedia materials for education and training, 1989-. Assistant system operator, work-at-home forum, and section leader, video and multimedia section of Public Relations and Marketing Forum, for CompuServe. **Publications:** TEEN HOT LINE SERIES: Dropping out of School, 1994; Gangs, 1994; Family Violence, 1995; Parental Divorce, 1995. OTHER: You and the Law, 1992. **Address:** 933 Rose Ave., Oakland, CA 94611, U.S.A.

GOLDFARB, Ronald (Lawrence). American, b. 1933. **Genres:** Communications/Media, Law, Politics/Government. **Career:** Partner, Goldfarb & Associates and predecessor firms, Washington, DC, 1966-. Judge Advocate, General Corps. U.S. Air Force, 1957-60; Special Prosecutor, U.S. Dept. of Justice, 1961-64; admitted to NY bar, 1957, California bar, 1960, DC bar, 1965. **Publications:** The Contempt Power, 1963; Ransom: A Critique of the American Bail System, 1965; (with A. Friendly) Crime and Publicity:

The Impact of News on the Administration of Justice, 1967; (with L. Singer) After Conviction: A Review of the American Correction System, 1973; Jails: The Ultimate Ghetto, 1975; Migrant Farm Workers, A Caste of Despair, 1981; (with J. Raymond) Clear Understandings: Guide to Legal Writing, 1982; (with G. Ross) The Writer's Lawyer, 1989; Perfect Villains, Imperfect Heroes, RFK's War against Organized Crime, 1995; TV or Not TV, Television Justice and the Courts, 1998. **Address:** Goldfarb & Associates, 721 Gibbon Street, Alexandria, VA 22314, U.S.A. **Online address:** RGLawlit@ aol.com

GOLDHAMMER, Arthur. American, b. 1946. **Genres:** Translations. **Career:** Brandeis University, Waltham, MA, instructor in mathematics, 1973-75; free-lance writer and translator, 1975-. Boston University, visiting assistant professor, 1989. **Publications:** TRANSLATOR: M. Crozier, Actors and Systems, 1978; G. Duby, The Three Orders, 1980; J. LeGoff, Time, Work, and Culture in the Middle Ages, 1980; M. Rodinson, The Arabs, 1981; F. Bourricaud, The Sociology of Talcott Parsons, 1981; P. Dockes, Medieval Slavery and Liberation, 1982; F. Delaporte, Nature's Second Kingdom, 1982; R. Castel and others, The Psychiatric Society, 1982; C. Clement, The Lives and Legends of J. Lacan, 1983; S. Guilbaut, How New York Stole the Idea of Modern Art, 1983; P. Birnbaum, The Sociology of the State, 1983; D. Schnapper, Jewish Identities in France, 1983; P. Birnbaum, The Heights of Power, 1984; J. LeGoff, The Birth of Purgatory, 1984; M. Raeff, Understanding Imperial Russia, 1984; M. Mollat, The Poor in the Middle Ages, 1984; G. Bachelard, The New Scientific Spirit, 1984; R. Mousnier, The Institutions of France under the Absolute Monarchy, Vol. II, 1984; J. Starobinski, Montaigne in Motion, 1985; (co) C. Lemert, ed., French Sociology, 1985; M. Maurice and others, The Social Foundations of Industrial Power, 1986; K. Mattoso, To Be a Slave in Brazil, 1986; F. Delaporte, Disease and Civilization, 1986; M. Duras, Outside, 1986; R. Moulin, The French Art Market, 1986; J. Menetra, The Journal of My Life, 1986; B. Saint, Homosexuality in Greek Myth, 1986; A History of Private Life, Vol. I, 1987, Vol. II, 1988, Vol. III, 1989, Vol. IV, 1990, Vol. V, 1991; L. Boltanski, The Making of a Class, 1987; M. Yourcenar, With Open Eyes, 1987; J. Starobinski, J.-J. Rousseau: Transparency and Obstruction, 1988; J. Kristeva, In the Beginning was Faith, 1988; G. Canguilhem, Ideology and Rationality in the History of the Life Sciences, 1988; J. LeGoff, The Medieval Imagination, 1988; M. Tournier, The Wind Spirit, 1988; F. Furet and M. Ozouf, eds., A Critical Dictionary of the French Revolution, 1989; J.-C. Lamberti, Tocqueville and the Two Democracies, 1989; J. Starobinski, The Living Eye, 1989; M. Detienne, Dionysos at Large, 1989; B. Guenee, Between Church and State, 1990; G. Sissa, Greek Virginity, 1990; H. Rousso, The Vichy Syndrome, 1991; M. Olender, The Languages of Paradise, 1991; A. Corbin, The Village of Cannibals, 1991; F. Delaporte, Yellow Fever, 1991; A History of Women, 4 vols., 1992-93; J. Starobinski, The Blessings in Disguise, 1992; M. Lever, Sade: A Biography, 1993; D. Guedj, Measure of the World, 2001; E. LeRoy Ladurie, The Beggar and the Professor, 1997. Contributor of translations to periodicals. **Address:** c/o Minda de Gunzburg, Center for European Studies, Adolphus Busch Hall, 27 Kirkland St, Cambridge, MA 02138, U.S.A. **Online address:** agold1@attbi.com

GOLDIN, Barbara Diamond. American, b. 1946. **Genres:** Novellas/Short stories, Children's fiction, Young adult fiction, Theology/Religion. **Career:** Special education teacher at public schools in Gloucester and Ipswich, MA, 1970-72; preschool teacher in Missoula, MT, and Yellow Springs, OH, 1972-75; Children's Bookshop, Missoula, MT, co-owner and operator, 1975-76; Goldendale Public Library, Goldendale, WA, library assistant in children's section, 1976-78; preschool teacher in Bellingham, WA, 1980-82; free-lance writer, 1981-; Congregation B'nai Israel Preschool, Northampton, MA, head teacher, 1986-89; Heritage Academy, language arts teacher, 1990-. **Publications:** JUVENILE Just Enough Is Plenty, 1988; The World's Birthday, 1990; The Family Book of Midrash, 1990; Cakes and Miracles, 1991; Fire!, 1992; The Magician's Visit, 1993; The Passover Journey, 1994; Red Means Good Fortune, 1994; Night Lights, 1995; Bat Mitzvah, 1995; Creating Angels, 1996; Coyote and the Fire Stick, 1996; While the Candles Burn, 1996; The Girl Who Lived with the Bears, 1997; Journeys with Elijah, 1999; Ten Holiday Jewish Children's Stories, 2000; A Mountain of Blintzes, 2001. READERS: Honey Hunt, 2001; Osceola McCarty Woke up the World, 2001; Lilly in the Spotlight, 2001; Louis Armstrong, 2001; Berry Treats, 2001; Picture This!, 2001; River Wild, 2001. Contributor to children's magazines and newspapers. **Address:** PO Box 981, North Hampton, MA 01061-0981, U.S.A. **Online address:** barbaradiamond@rcn.com; www. barbaradiamondgoldin.com

GOLDIN, Owen. American, b. 1957. **Genres:** Philosophy. **Career:** Marquette University, Milwaukee, WI, assistant professor, 1987-94, associate professor of philosophy, 1994-. **Publications:** Explaining an Eclipse: Aristotle's Posterior Analytics 2.1-10, 1996; (ed. with P. Kilroe) Human Life and the Natural World: Readings in the History of Western Philosophy, 1997. Contributor to philosophy journals. **Address:** 2226 N Booth St, Milwaukee, WI 53212-3408, U.S.A. **Online address:** Owen.Goldin@marquette.edu

GOLDING, Alan. American (born England), b. 1952. **Genres:** Literary criticism and history. **Career:** Kishwaukee College, Malta, IL, lecturer, 1976; Roosevelt University, Chicago, IL, lecturer, 1977-79; University of California, Los Angeles, visiting lecturer in composition, 1980-84; University of Mississippi, Oxford, assistant professor of American literature, 1984-87; University of Louisville, KY, assistant professor, 1987-90, associate professor, 1990-96, professor of American literature, 1996-. **Publications:** From Outlaw to Classic: Canons in American Poetry, 1995. Contributor to books. Contributor of articles and reviews to periodicals. **Address:** Department of English, University of Louisville, Louisville, KY 40292, U.S.A. **Online address:** alan.golding@louisville.edu

GOLDING, Peter. British, b. 1947. **Genres:** Communications/Media, Sociology. **Career:** Leicester University, Centre for Mass Communication Research, sr. research fellow, 1970-89; Loughborough University, professor of sociology and head of social sciences, 1990-. **Publications:** The Mass Media, 1974; Making the News, 1979; Images of Welfare: Press and Public Attitudes to Poverty, 1982; Excluding the Poor, 1986; Communicating Politics: Mass Communication and the Political Process, 1986; The Politics of the Urban Crisis, 1988; Taxation and Representation: Political Communication, the Mass Media, and the Poll Tax, 1994; Political Economy of the Media, 1997; Beyond Cultural Imperialism, 1997; Cultural Studies in Question, 1997; Researching Communications, 1999; European Culture and the Media, 2004. **Address:** Dept. of Social Sciences, University of Loughborough, Leicestershire LE11 3TU, England. **Online address:** p.golding@ lboro.ac.uk

GOLDING, Raymund Marshall. Australian (born New Zealand), b. 1935. **Genres:** Chemistry, Mathematics/Statistics, Medicine/Health, Physics. **Career:** Dept. of Scientific and Industrial Research, Wellington, Staff member, 1957-68; University of New South Wales, Professor of Theoretical and Physical Chemistry, 1968-86, Pro-Vice-Chancellor, 1978-86; James Cook University, Townsville, Qld., Vice-Chancellor, 1986-96. Officer of the Order of Australia; Commonwealth Centenary Medal. **Publications:** Applied Wave Mechanics, 1969; (co-author) Multistrand Science of the Senior High School Students, 1975; The Goldings of Oakington, 1992. **Address:** 5 Tolson Rd, Mooloolah, QLD 4553, Australia. **Online address:** raygolding@m141.aone. net.au

GOLDING, Theresa Martin. (born United States), b. 1960. **Genres:** Children's fiction. **Career:** Writer. **Publications:** Kat's Surrender, 1999; The Secret Within, Boyds 2002; Memorial Day Surprise, 2004; The Truth about Twelve, 2004. **Address:** c/o Author Correspondence, Boyds Mills Press, 815 Church St., Honesdale, PA 18431, U.S.A. **Online address:** gjg874@aol.com

GOLDMAN, Ari L. American, b. 1949. **Genres:** Adult non-fiction, Theology/Religion. **Career:** New York Times, NYC, began as reporter, became religion correspondent in 1984. **Publications:** The Search for God at Harvard (nonfiction), 1991; Being Jewish (nonfiction), 2000. **Address:** Graduate School of Journalism, 807 Journalism 3818, Columbia University, 2950 Broadway, New York, NY 10027, U.S.A. **Online address:** alg18@columbia. edu

GOLDMAN, Arnold (Melvyn). American, b. 1936. **Genres:** Literary criticism and history, Education. **Career:** Faculty member, University of Manchester, 1961-65, and University of Sussex, 1966-74; Professor of American Studies, University of Keele, 1975-82; Deputy Chief Executive, Council for National Academic Awards, 1983-88; Director of Quality Enhancement, 1995-99, Hon. Professor of American Studies, 1985-99, University of Kent at Canterbury. **Publications:** The Joyce Paradox, 1966; James Joyce, 1968. EDITOR: Twentieth Century Interpretations of Absalom Absalom!, 1971; (co-) Charles Dickens' American Notes, 1972; Tender Is the Night, by F. Scott Fitzgerald, 1982; (gen.) American Literature in Context, 4 vols., 1982-83. **Address:** Beechcroft Farmhouse, Cowbeech, E. Sussex BN27 4JG, England. **Online address:** a.goldman@cowbeech.f9.co.uk

GOLDMAN, E(leanor) M(aureen). American, b. 1943. **Genres:** Young adult fiction. **Career:** Writer. Worked as a litigation secretary in San Francisco during the 1960s, and in British Columbia from 1981-92. **Publications:** FOR MIDDLE GRADE READERS: Money to Burn, 1994; Shrinking Pains, 1996. FOR YOUNG ADULT READERS: The Night Room, 1995;

Getting Lincoln's Goat: An Elliot Armbruster Mystery, 1995. **Address:** 295 Glassford RR8, Gibsons, BC, Canada V0N 1V8. **Online address:** inkslinger@sunshine.net

GOLDMAN, Elizabeth. American, b. 1949. **Genres:** Biography. **Career:** University of New Hampshire, Durham, lecturer, 1991-93; New England College, Dover, NH, lecturer, 1994-; McIntosh College, Dover, lecturer, 1994-; New Hampshire College, Portsmouth, NH, lecturer, 1994-; writer. Editor, 1974-78 and 1980-84. Has also worked as an abstractor/indexer and a secretary; volunteer educator and conductor of poetry workshops; vice president, Temple Israel (Dover, NH), 1995. **Publications:** Believers: Spiritual Leaders of the World, 1996. Contributor of articles and poems to periodicals.

GOLDMAN, Francisco. American, b. 1954. **Genres:** Novels. **Career:** Harper's Magazine,contributing editor, 1980s. **Publications:** The Long Night of White Chickens, 1994; The Ordinary Seaman, 1996. Also author of short stories. Contributor to periodicals. **Address:** c/o Amanda Urban, I.C.M., 40 West 57th Street, New York, NY 10019, U.S.A.

GOLDMAN, Karla. American, b. 1960. **Genres:** Theology/Religion. **Career:** Historian. Hebrew Union College, Cincinnati, OH, assistant professor to associate professor of American Jewish history, 1991-; Jewish Women's Archive, historian-in-residence, 2000-. **Publications:** Beyond the Synagogue Gallery: Finding a Place for Women in American Judaism, 2000. **Address:** Jewish Women's Archive, 68 Harvard St., Brookline, MA 02445, U.S.A. **Online address:** kgoldman@jwa.org

GOLDMAN, Katherine (Wyse). American, b. 1951. **Genres:** Essays, How-to books. **Career:** Cleveland Press, Cleveland, OH, intern, 1971; Taunton Daily Gazette, Taunton, MA, stringer, 1972-73; Random House Inc., NYC, copywriter, 1973-74; Wyse Advertising, NYC, senior copywriter, 1974-82; Shop, NYC, associate editor, 1979-80; Richardson, Myers and Donofrio, Philadelphia, PA, associate creative director, 1983-86; operator of a consulting business for advertising and promotion, 1986-. **Publications:** (Co-author) Disco Beauty, 1980; My Mother Worked and I Turned Out Okay, 1993; If You Can Raise Kids, You Can Get a Good Job, 1996. **Address:** c/o Jane Dystel, 1 Union Square West, New York, NY 10003, U.S.A.

GOLDMAN, Marshall I(rwin). American, b. 1930. **Genres:** Economics, Environmental sciences/Ecology, Politics/Government. **Career:** Harvard University, Davis Center for Russian Studies, Cambridge, MA, associate, 1957-75, associate director, 1975-; Wellesley College, MA, instructor, 1958-60, assistant professor, 1961-65, associate professor, 1966-68, professor of economics, 1968-98. **Publications:** Soviet Marketing: Distribution in a Controlled Economy, 1963; Soviet Foreign Aid, 1967; The Soviet Economy: Myth and Reality, 1968; The Spoils of Progress: Environmental Pollution in the Soviet Union, 1972; Detente and Dollars: Doing Business with the Soviets, 1975; The Enigma of Soviet Petroleum: Half Full or Half Empty, 1980; The Soviet Union in Crisis: The Failure of an Economic System, 1983; Gorbachev's Challenge: Economic Reform in the Age of High Technology, 1987; What Went Wrong with Perestroika, 1991; Lost Opportunity: Why Economic Reforms in Russia Have Not Worked, 1994; The Privatization of Russia: Russian Reform Goes Awry, 2003. EDITOR: Comparative Economic Systems: Reader, 1964; Controlling Pollution: The Economics of a Cleaner America, 1967; Ecology and Economics: Controlling Pollution in the 70s, 1972. **Address:** 17 Midland Rd, Wellesley, MA 02481, U.S.A. **Online address:** Goldman3@fas.harvard.edu

GOLDMAN, Minton F. American. **Genres:** Politics/Government, International relations/Current affairs. **Career:** Northeastern University, Boston, MA, professor of political science. **Publications:** Global Studies: The Soviet Union and Eastern Europe, 1986-90; Russia, the Eurasian Republics, and Central/Eastern Europe, 1994; Revolution and Change in Central and Eastern Europe: Political, Economic, and Social Challenges, 1997; Slovakia since Independence: A Struggle for Democracy, 1999. Contributor to anthologies and periodicals. **Address:** Department of Political Science, Northeastern University, 323 Meserve Hall, 360 Huntington Avenue, Boston, MA 02115, U.S.A. **Online address:** m.goldman@neu.edu; goldmanfacultypol@nunet.neu.edu

GOLDMAN, Roger L. American, b. 1941. **Genres:** Law. **Career:** Admitted to the Missouri Bar, 1966. St. Louis Legal Aid Society, St. Louis, MO, Reginald Heber Smith fellow, 1969-71; St. Louis University, St. Louis, assistant professor, 1971-74, associate professor, 1974-77; scholar in residence to selected Federal District Court judges in New York City, 1977-78; St. Louis University, professor of law, 1979-, associate dean, 1978-79. Gowen fellow at University of Pennsylvania, visiting scholar at Columbia University, and researcher for U.S. Department of Justice, all 1977-78; consultant to Coalition for Information on School Desegregation, 1982-84; lecturer at Maryville College, 1986. **Publications:** (with L. Riekes, S. Jenkins, and P. McKissack) The Bill of Rights and You, 1989; (with J. O'Brien) Federal Criminal Trial Evidence, 1989; (with S. Jenkins, L. Riekes, and S. Slane) Teacher's Resource Manual: The Bill of Rights and You, 1990; (with L. Riekes, C. Kelly, and C. Marske) Conflict, Courts and Trials, 3rd ed, 1991; (with L. Riekes, C. Kelly, and C. Marske) Teacher's Resource Guide: Conflicts, Courts and Trials, 1991; (with L. Riekes and S. Slane) Teaching about the Bill of Rights in Elementary and Middle School Classrooms, 1991; Individual Rights: The Universal Challenge, 1991; The Military and the Constitution, 1992; Alcohol, Drugs and the Bill of Rights, 1992; (with David Gallen) Thurgood Marshall: Justice for All, 1992; (with D. Gallen) Justice William J. Brennan, Jr.: Freedom First, 1994. Contributor to books and periodicals. **Address:** St. Louis University, School of Law, 3700 Lindell Blvd., St. Louis, MO 63108, U.S.A.

GOLDMAN, William. Also writes as Harry Longbaugh, S. Morgenstern. American, b. 1931. **Genres:** Novels, Children's fiction, Plays/Screenplays, Theatre. **Publications:** The Temple of Gold, 1957; Your Turn to Curtsy, My Turn to Bow, 1958; Soldier in the Rain, 1960; (with J Goldman) Blood, Sweat and Stanley Poole (play), 1961; (with J Goldman, J Kander) A Family Affair (play), 1962; Boys and Girls Together, 1964; (as Harry Longbaugh) No Way to Treat a Lady, 1964, (as William Goldman) 1968; The Thing of It Is, 1967; The Season: A Candid Look at Broadway, 1969; Father's Day, 1971; The Princess Bride: S. Morgenstern's Classic Tale of True Love and High Adventure, The "Good Parts" Version, Abridged, 1974; Marathon Man, 1974; Wigger (children's fiction), 1974; The Great Waldo Pepper, 1975; Magic, 1976; Tinsel, 1979; Control, 1982; Adventures in the Screen Trade (non-fiction), 1983; (as S. Morgenstern) The Silent Goldoliers, 1983; The Color of Light, 1984; Heat (in England as Edged Weapons), 1985; Brothers (novel), 1986; Heat (screenplay), 1987; The Princess Bride (screenplay), 1987; (with Mike Lupica) Wait Till Next Year (nonfiction), 1989; Misery (screenplay), 1990; Hype and Glory (nonfiction), 1990; The Year of the Comet, 1992; Memoirs of an Invisible Man (screenplay), 1992; Chaplin, 1992; Maverick, 1994; Four Screenplays, 1995; The Chamber (screenplay), 1996; The Ghost and the Darkness (screenplay), 1996; Absolute Power (screenplay), 1997; Five Screenplays, 1997; The General's Daughter (screenplay), 1999; Which Lie Did I Tell?: More Adventures of the Screen Trade, 2000; The Big Picture: Who Killed Hollywood and other Essays, 2001. **Address:** 50 E. 77th St, New York, NY 10021, U.S.A.

GOLDREIN, Iain S. British. **Genres:** Law. **Career:** Barrister, called to the bar in 1975. **Publications:** (with M. de Haas) Personal Injury Litigation, 1985; Ship Sale and Purchase: Law and Technique, 1985, 3rd ed., 1998; (with Kershaw and Wilkinson) Commercial Litigation: Pre-emptive Remedies, 1987, 3rd ed., 1996; (ed. with J. Jacob) Bullen and Leake and Jacob's Precedents of Pleadings, 1990; (with J. Jacob) Pleadings: Principles and Practice, 1990; (ed. with M. de Haas) Structured Settlements, 1993, 2nd ed., 1997; (with M. de Haas) Medical Negligence: Cost Effective Case Management, 1997; (co-ed. in chief) Insurance Disputes, 1999. **Address:** 7 Harrington St, Liverpool L2 9YH, England. **Online address:** harrington_street@bigfoot.com

GOLDSBOROUGH, Robert (Gerald). American, b. 1937. **Genres:** Mystery/Crime/Suspense. **Career:** Associated Press, Chicago, reporter, 1959; City News Bureau, Chicago, IL, 1959; Chicago Tribune, Chicago, IL, reporter, 1960-63, assistant editor of Sunday magazine and TV Week, 1963-66, editor of TV Week, 1966-67, assistant to features editor, 1967-71, assistant to editor, 1971-72, Sunday editor, 1972-75, editor of Sunday magazine, 1975-82; Advertising Age, Chicago, IL, executive editor, 1982-88, Corporate projects Editor, 1988-. **Publications:** (ed. and author of introduction) Great Railroad Paintings, 1976; The Crain Adventure, 1992. NERO WOLFE MYSTERIES: Murder in E minor, 1986; Death on Deadline, 1987; The Bloodied Ivy, 1988; The Last Coincidence, 1989; Fade to Black, 1990; Silver Spire, 1992; The Missing Chapter, 1994. **Address:** 360 N. Michigan Ave., Chicago, IL 60601, U.S.A.

GOLDSCHMIDT, Arthur (Eduard), Jr. American, b. 1938. **Genres:** Area studies, History. **Career:** Pennsylvania State University, University Park, assistant professor, 1965-73, associate professor, 1973-89, professor, 1989-2000, professor emeritus of Middle East history, 2000-. Haifa University, visiting associate professor, 1973-74; University of Cairo, visiting professor, 1981-82; New Jersey Scholars Program, academic dean, 1985; Semester at Sea Program, visiting lecturer, 1987, 2001. **Publications:** A Concise History of the Middle East, 1979, 7th ed, 2001; Modern Egypt: The Formation of a

Nation State, 1988, 2nd ed., 2004; (trans. and annotator) The Memoirs and Diaries of Muhammad Farid, 1992; Historical Dictionary of Egypt, 1994, 2nd ed., 2003; Biographical Dictionary of Modern Egypt, 2000. Contributor to periodicals. **Address:** 1173 Oneida St, State College, PA 16801, U.S.A. **Online address:** axg2@psu.edu

GOLDSCHMIDT, Tijs. Dutch. **Genres:** Botany. **Career:** Dutch evolutionary biologist specializing in the taxonomy of cichlids. **Publications:** Darwins hofvijver, 1994, trans by S. Marx-Macdonald as Darwin's Dreampond: Drama in Lake Victoria, 1996. **Address:** c/o The MIT Press, 5 Cambridge Center, Cambridge, MA 02142, U.S.A.

GOLDSCHNEIDER, Gary. (born United States), b. 1939. **Genres:** History. **Career:** Astrologer, writer, musician. Drexel University, Philadelphia, PA, teacher, 1964-70; Philadelphia City College, Philadelphia, PA, 1964-70, assistant professor and head of music department, 1968-70; Golden Chain Chorale, CA, conductor, 1978-85; formed and conducted the Sierra Philharmonic Orchestra; radio broadcaster, KVMR, CA; guest lecturer; astrologer for Mirabella, New York, NY, 1998-2000, and AvantGarde, Netherlands, 1989-. **Publications:** (with Joost Elffers) The Secret Language of Birthdays: Personology Profiles for Each Day of the Year, 1994; (with Joost Elffers) The Secret Language of Relationships: Your Complete Personology Guide to Any Relationship with Anyone, 1997; (with Joost Elffers) The Secret Language of Birthdays: Relationship Workbook and Birthday Keeper, 1998; (with Joost Elffers) The Secret Language of Destiny: A Personology Guide to Finding Your Life Purpose, 1999; The Astrology of Time, 2002. **Address:** c/o Author Mail, Atria Press, Simon & Schuster, 1230 Avenue of the Americas, New York, NY 10020, U.S.A. **Online address:** gary@goldschneider.com.

GOLDSMITH, Barbara. American. **Genres:** Novels, History, Social commentary, Biography, Essays. **Career:** Member, National Book Award Foundation, 1992, Guild, Author's League, 1983-. Trustee, New York Society Library, 1986-. Advisory Board, National Dance Institute, NYC, 1980-. Trustee, New York Public Library; Member, Executive Board, American P.E.N.; Director, New York State Council on the Arts, 1992; Commission for Preservational Access, 1984-94; Entertainment Ed., Woman's Home Companion, NYC, 1954-57; Founding Ed., New York Magazine, 1968-73; Sr. Ed., Harpers Bazaar, NYC, 1970-74. **Publications:** The Straw Man (novel), 1975; Little Gloria, Happy at Last, 1980; Johnson v. Johnson, 1987; Other Powers, 1998. Contributor of articles and essays to periodicals. **Address:** c/o Lynn Nesbit, Janklow & Nesbit Associates, 445 Park Ave Fl 13, New York, NY 10022, U.S.A.

GOLDSMITH, Lynn. American, b. 1948. **Genres:** Music, Photography. **Career:** Photographer and writer. Photography represented in the periodicals Harper's, Interview, Life, Newsweek, Rolling Stone, and Vogue as well as on record album covers and movie posters. As Will Powers, recording artist on Island Records: Dancing for Mental Health. **Publications:** The Police, 1983; Springsteen, 1984; New Kids on the Block, 1990; Circus Dreams, 1991; Marky Mark, 1992; Photodiary, 1995; Springsteen: Access All Areas, 2000; Flower, 2000. **Address:** 241 West 36th St., New York, NY 10018, U.S.A. **Online address:** Lynn@lynngoldsmith.com

GOLDSTEIN, Abraham S. American, b. 1925. **Genres:** Law. **Career:** Sterling Professor of Law, Yale University, New Haven, Conn. (Dean of Yale Law School, 1970-75). **Publications:** The Insanity Defense, 1967; (with J. Goldstein) Crime, Law and Society: Readings, 1971; (with Orland) Criminal Procedure, 1974; The Passive Judiciary: Prosecutorial Discretion and the Guilty Plea, 1981. **Address:** Yale Law School, PO Box 208215, New Haven, CT 06520-8215, U.S.A.

GOLDSTEIN, Carl. American, b. 1938. **Genres:** Art/Art history. **Career:** Wheaton College, Norton, Mass., visiting instructor in art history and acting director of art gallery, spring, 1966; Brown University, Providence, R.I., assistant professor of art history, 1966-71; University of North Carolina at Greensboro, associate professor, 1971-80, professor of art history, 1980-. **Publications:** Visual Fact Over Verbal Fiction: A Study of the Carracci and the Criticism, Theory, and Practice of Art in Renaissance and Baroque Italy (monograph), 1988; Teaching Art: Academies and Schools from Vasari to Albers (monograph), 1996. **Address:** Department of Art, University of North Carolina at Greensboro, Greensboro, NC 27412, U.S.A.

GOLDSTEIN, Harvey. British, b. 1939. **Genres:** Education, Mathematics/Statistics. **Career:** Professor of Statistics, University of London Institute of Education, 1977-. Jt. Ed., Statistics in Society, 1987-91. Lecturer in Statistics, Institute of Child Health, University of London, 1964-71; Head of the

Statistics Section, National Children's Bureau, 1971-77. Member of the Council, 1973-77, and Chairman of the Social Statistics Section, 1978-80, Royal Statistical Society. **Publications:** (with R. Davie and N.R. Butler) From Birth to Seven; (with others) Assessment of Skeletal Maturity and Prediction of Adult Height; The Design and Analysis of Longitudinal Studies; (with C. Gipps) Monitoring Children; Multilevel Models in Educational and Social Research, 1987; (co-author) Warnock's 18 Per Cent: Children with Special Needs in Primary Schools, 1987; Multilevel Statistical Models, 1995, rev. ed., 2003. EDITOR: (with L. Moss) The Recall Method in Social Surveys; (with P. Levy) Tests in Education. **Address:** Centre for Multilevel Modelling, Institute of Education, 20 Bedford Way, London WC1H OAL, England. **Online address:** h.goldstein@ioe.ac.uk

GOLDSTEIN, Imre. Israeli/American (born Hungary), b. 1938. **Genres:** Poetry, Translations. **Career:** Tel Aviv University, Israel, professor of theatre, 1974-2003; U.S. State Department, Washington, DC, escort and seminar interpreter (Hungarian and Hebrew), 1991-; director, translator, and writer. Hunter College, adjunct lecturer, 1972-74; University of North Carolina, visiting associate professor, 1990-91. **Publications:** Triple Jump (poems), 1984; Dream of the Last Moment (poems), 1998; November Spring (novel), 2000. TRANSLATOR: U. Oren, Loving Strangers, 1975; F. Karinthy, Three Short Plays, 1979; A. Artzi, Godly Forces Revealed, 1981; G. Ben Simhon, A Moroccan King (play), 1982; Y. Biro, Profane Mythology: The Savage Mind of the Cinema, 1982; D. Horowitz, Uncle Arthur (play), 1982; D. Horowitz, Yossele Golem (play), 1982; O. Strahl, Encounters in the Forest (play), 1984; M. Lerner, Kastner (play), 1993; T. Dery, The Giant Baby (play), 1986; The Dybbuk (play), 1991; G. Konrad, A Feast in the Garden, 1992; Oedipus Tyrannos (play), 1992; Ten Hungarian Plays, 1994; P. Salamon, The House of Sorel, 1994; (with I. Sanders) P. Nadas, A Book of Memories, 1997; P. Nadas, The End of a Family Story, 1998; P. Nadas, Burial (play), 1998; P. Nadas, A Lovely Tale of Photography, 1999; P. Nadas, Love (novel), 2000. Contributor of poems to periodicals. **Address:** 7 Kaplan St, 64734 Tel Aviv, Israel. **Online address:** dybbuk@post.tau.ac.il

GOLDSTEIN, Jonathan Amos. See Obituaries.

GOLDSTEIN, Joshua S. American, b. 1952. **Genres:** International relations/Current affairs, Politics/Government. **Career:** Professor of international relations. University of Southern California School of International Relations, assistant professor, 1986-89, associate professor, 1989-93; Harvard University, Cambridge, MA, associate, and Yale University, New Haven, CT, fellow, 1991-93; American University, Washington, DC, associate professor, 1993-95, professor of international relations, 1995-; Brown University, Providence, RI, adjunct professor, 2002-03; Center for Interdisciplinary Studies, Amherst, MA, director, 2002-. Guest expert on nationally syndicated radio and television programs and on radio programs. **Publications:** Long Cycles: Prosperity and War in the Modern Age, 1988; (with J.R. Freeman) Three-Way Street: Strategic Reciprocity in World Politics, 1990; International Relations (textbook), 1994, 5th ed, 2003; War and Gender: How Gender Shapes the War System and Vice Versa, 2001. Contributor to periodicals and books. **Address:** PO Box 3068, Amherst, MA 01004-3068, U.S.A. **Online address:** jg@joshuagoldstein.com

GOLDSTEIN, Larry Joel. American, b. 1944. **Genres:** Information science/Computers, Mathematics/Statistics. **Career:** Yale University, New Haven, CT, Josiah Willard Gibbs Instructor, 1967-69; University of Maryland at College Park, associate professor, 1969-72, professor, 1972-84, adjunct professor, 1985-; writer. Auerbach Corp., member of technical staff, 1960-66; Science Service Inc., judge for Westinghouse Science Talent Search, 1969-88; Robert J. Brady Co., founder of and adviser for Microcomputer Series, 1980-84; Larry Joel Goldstein Inc., president, 1980-; Goldstein Software Inc., president, 1985-; consultant to Analytics Inc. and CTEC Inc. U.S. Naval Academy, Secretary of the Navy Distinguished Professor, 1990-91; lecturer at colleges and universities. **Publications:** Lectures on Analytic Number Theory (monograph), 1968; Analytic Number Theory (monograph), 1971; Abstract Algebra: A First Course, 1973; (with W. Adams) An Introduction to Number Theory, 1976; The Theory of Numbers (monograph), 1976; (with D. Lay and D. Schneider) Calculus and Its Applications, 1977, abridged ed, 1980, 6th ed, 1993; (with D. Schneider) Introduction to Mathematics, 1976; (with David Schneider) Finite Mathematics and Its Applications, 1980, 4th ed (with Schneider and M. Siegel), 1991; (with D. Lay and D. Schneider) Modern Mathematics and Its Applications, 1980; TRS-80 Model III: Programming and Applications, 1982; IBM Personal Computer: Programming and Applications, 1982; BASIC for the Apple II, 1982; (with S. Campbell and S. Zimmerman) The Osborne Computer: Programming and Applications, 1982; (with G. Streitmatter) PET/CBM: Programming and Applications, 1983; (with S. Manetta) The Franklin ACE: Programming and Applications,

1983; (with L. Graff) AppleSoft BASIC for the Apple II and II/e, 1983; IBM PC: An Introduction to the Operating System (with software), 1983, 3rd ed as IBM PC: An Introduction to the Operating System, BASIC Language, and Applications, 1986; Advanced BASIC and Beyond (with software), 1983; IBM PCjr Buyer's Guide, 1983; The COMPAQ Computer: User's Guide, 1983; The Graphics Generator: A Business Graphics Package for the IBM PC, 1983; Mathematics for Management: Social and Biological Sciences, 2nd ed, 1984; IBM PCjr: An Introduction to the Operating System, BASIC Language, and Applications (with software), 1984; (with F. Mosher) An Introduction to the Commodore 64, 1984; (with J. Rensin) Basically Kaypro, 1984; TRS-80 Model III/4: An Introduction to the Operating System, BASIC Language, and Applications, 1984; (with J. Rensin) Hewlett-Packard 150: User's Guide, 1984; An Introduction to ADAM SmartBASIC, 1984; (with R. Ellis and M. Ellis) The Atari 600/800/1200, 1984; (with D. Schneider) Macintosh: An Introduction to Microsoft BASIC, 1984, 2nd ed (with Schneider and G. Helzer), 1986; (with L. Graff) Applesoft BASIC on the Apple IIc, 1984; Computers and Their Applications, 1986; TRUE BASIC: An Introduction to Structured Programming, 1986; Microcomputer Applications: A Hands-On Approach to Computer Literacy, 1987; PASCAL and Its Applications: An Introduction to Programming, 1988; Turbo Pascal and Its Applications, 1988; Hands-On QuickBASIC, 1988; Hands-On Turbo C, 1989; Hands-On Turbo BASIC, 1989; Hands-On Turbo Pascal, 1991; Algebra and Trigonometry and Their Applications, 1993; Algebra and Its Applications, 1993; Trigonometry and Its Applications, 1993; The Official Student Guide to QBASIC, 1993; IBM PC and Compatibles, 5th ed, 1993; Business Statistics and Its Applications, in press; College Algebra for Students of Business and the Social Sciences, in press; Precalculus and Its Applications, in press; Contributor to scientific periodicals. **Address:** 4 Bittersweet Dr, Doylestown, PA 18901, U.S.A. **Online address:** larrygoldstein@comcast.net

GOLDSTEIN, Michael S. American, b. 1944. **Genres:** Sports/Fitness, Sociology. **Career:** Brown University, Providence, RI, lecturer, 1970-71; University of California, Los Angeles, assistant professor, 1971-78, head of the division of Behavioral Sciences and Health Education, 1978-80, associate professor, 1978-88, vice chair of the department of Public Health, 1988-89, chair of department of Community Health and Sciences, 1989-91, professor of public health and sociology, 1988-; member of advisory committees, boards of directors, and steering committees. **Publications:** The Health Movement: Promoting Fitness in America, 1992. Contributor to periodicals. **Address:** Department of Community Health Sciences, School of Public Health, University of California, Box 951772, Los Angeles, CA 90095, U.S.A.

GOLDSTEIN, Rebecca. American, b. 1950. **Genres:** Novels, Novellas/Short stories. **Career:** Novelist. Barnard College, professor of philosophy, 1976-86. **Publications:** The Mind-Body Problem, 1983; The Late-Summer Passion of a Woman of Mind, 1989; The Dark Sister, 1991; Strange Attractors, 1993; Mazel, 1995; Properties of Light, 2000. **Address:** c/o Viking Penguin, 375 Hudson St., New York, NY 10014, U.S.A.

GOLDSTEIN, Robert Justin. American, b. 1947. **Genres:** Civil liberties/Human rights, History, Politics/Government. **Career:** University of Illinois at Urbana-Champaign, research and administrative assistant for Office of Instructional Research and Chancellor's Commission on Reform of Undergraduate Education and Living, 1972-73; San Diego State University, CA, lecturer in political science, 1974-76; Oakland University, Rochester, MI, assistant professor, 1976-81, associate professor, 1981-87, professor of political science, 1987-. **Publications:** Political Repression in Modern America: From 1870 to the Present, 1978, 2nd ed., 2000; Political Repression in Nineteenth Century Europe, 1983; Political Censorship of the Arts and the Press in Nineteenth-Century Europe, 1989; Censorship of Political Caricature in Nineteenth-Century France, 1989; Saving "Old Glory": The History of the American Flag Desecration Controversy, 1994; Burning the Flag: The Great 1989-90 American Flag Desecration Controversy, 1996; Desecrating the American Flag: Key Documents from the Controversy from the Civil War to 1995, 1996; The War for the Public Mind: Political Censorship in NineteenthCentury Europe, 2000; Flag Burning and Free Speech: The Case of Texas v. Johnson, 2000; Political Censorship: The New York Times 20th Century in Review, 2001. **Address:** Department of Political Science, Oakland University, Rochester, MI 48309, U.S.A. **Online address:** goldstei@oakland.edu

GOLDSTEIN, Sidney. American, b. 1927. **Genres:** Demography, Sociology. **Career:** Brown University, Providence, RI, assistant professor, 1955-57, associate professor, 1957-60, professor of sociology, 1960-93, chairman of dept., 1963-70, director, Population Studies and Training Center, 1966-89, George Hazard Crooker University Professor, 1977-93, professor emeritus,

1993-. UN Economic and Social Commission for Asia and the Pacific, consultant, 1977-82. **Publications:** Patterns of Mobility, 1910-1950, 1958; The Norristown Study, 1961; (with K.B. Mayer) The First Two Years: Problems of Small Business Growth and Survival, 1961; (with C. Goldscheider) Jewish-Americans: Three Generations in a Jewish Community, 1968; A Population Survey of the Greater Springfield Jewish Community, 1968; Urbanization in Thailand, 1970; The Demography of Bangkok, 1972; (with A. Speare and W. Frey) Residential Mobility, Migration and Metropolitan Change, 1975; Circulation in the Context of Total Mobility in Southeast Asia, 1978; (with A. Goldstein) A Test of the Potential Use of Multiplicity in Research on Population Movement, 1979; (with A. Goldstein) Surveys of Migration in Developing Countries, 1981; (with A. Goldstein) Migration and Fertility in Peninsular Malaysia, 1983; (with A. Goldstein) Urbanization in China; (with A. Goldstein) Migration in Thailand: A 25-Year Review, 1986; (with C. Goldscheider) The Jewish Community of Rhode Island, 1987; (with A. Goldstein) Permanent and Temporary Migration Differentials in China, 1990; Urbanization in China 1982-87: The Role of Migration and Reclassification, 1990; The Impact of Temporary Migration on Urban Places, 1993; (with A. Goldstein) Jews on the Move, 1996; (with A. Goldstein) Conservative Jewry in the United States, 1998; (with A. Goldstein and Y. Djamba) Permanent and Temporary Migration during Periods of Economic Change, 1999; (with A. Goldstein and Zai Liang) Migration, Gender, and Labor Force in Hubei Province, China, 1985-1990, 2000. EDITOR (with D. Sly): Basic Data Needed for the Study of Urbanization, 1975; Measurement of Urbanization and the Projection of Urban Population, 1975; Patterns of Urbanization, 1976. **Address:** Population Studies and Training Center, Brown University, Providence, RI 02912, U.S.A.

GOLDSTEIN-JACKSON, Kevin. British, b. 1946. **Genres:** Business/Trade/Industry, Children's non-fiction, Money/Finance, Recreation, Humor/Satire. **Career:** Worked on seven series of networked children's prog. for southern television in the UK; also on documentaries, religious series, political discussions, worked on television prog., HK-TVB, Hong Kong, 1973; Head of Film, Dhofar Region Television Service, Sultanate of Oman, 1975-76; Assistant to Head of Drama, Anglia Television, UK 1977-81; Director of Progs. and Chief Executive, Television South West Holdings PLC, Plymouth, 1981-85. Author of TV scripts and newspaper articles. **Publications:** The Right Joke for the Right Occasion, 1973; Ridiculous Facts, 1974; Encyclopaedia of Ridiculous Facts, 1975; Experiments with Everyday Objects, 1976; Joke After Joke After Joke, 1977; Things to Make with Everyday Objects, 1978; Magic with Everyday Objects, 1979; Activities with Everyday Objects, 1980; The Dictionary of Essential Quotations, 1983; Jokes for Telling, 1986; Share Millions, 1989; The Public Speaker's Joke Book, 1991; The Astute Private Investor, 1994; Quick Quips, 2002. **Address:** c/o Alcazar, 18 Martello Rd, Branksome Park, Poole, Dorset BH13 7DH, England.

GOLDSWORTHY, Peter. Australian, b. 1951. **Genres:** Novels, Novellas/Short stories, Plays/Screenplays, Poetry. **Career:** Medical practitioner in Adelaide, 1974-. Recipient: Commonwealth Poetry Prize, 1982; Anne Elder Prize, 1983; S. A. Biennial Literary Award, 1984, and Poetry Prize, 1988; Australia Council Fellowships, 1984, 1986, 1990-91; Fellowship of Australian Writers, Christina Stead Award, 2004. **Publications:** POETRY: Readings from Ecclesiastes, 1982; This Goes with This, 1988; This Goes with That, 1991; If, Then, 1996. STORIES: Archipelagoes, 1982; Zooing , 1986; Bleak Rooms, 1988; Little Deaths (and novella), 1993; Collected Stories, 2004. NOVELS: Maestro, 1989; Honk If You Are Jesus, 1992; Wish, 1995; Keep It Simple Stupid, 1996; Three Dog Night, 2003. OTHER: (with B. Matthews) Magpie, 1992. **Address:** c/o Fiona Inglis, Curtis Brown Pty. Ltd., PO Box 19, Paddington NSW 2021, Australia.

GOLDWASSER, Thomas. American, b. 1939. **Genres:** Business/Trade/Industry, Politics/Government, Ghost Writer. **Career:** Free-lance writer and consultant, 1970-; ghost writer. Montgomery College, adjunct professor in government, 1988-; Johns Hopkins University, instructor of American government; George Washington University, Graduate School of Political Management, adjunct professor, 2004-. Held positions in U.S. Senate and House of Representatives. **Publications:** Family Pride: Profiles of Five of America's Best-Run Family Businesses, 1986. Author of book reviews, articles, and opinion pieces in newspapers. **Address:** 5435 31st St NW, Washington, DC 20015, U.S.A. **Online address:** tombenton2@earthlink.net

GOLDWIN, Robert (Allen). American, b. 1922. **Genres:** International relations/Current affairs, Politics/Government. **Career:** Resident Scholar, American Enterprise Institute, Washington, DC, 1976-. Director, Public Affairs Conference Center, University of Chicago, 1960-66; Associate, Professor, Kenyon College, Gambier, OH, 1966-69; Dean, St. John's College, Annapolis, MD, 1969-73; Special Adviser to the Ambassador, US Mission to

NATO, Brussels, 1973-74; Special Consultant to the President of the U.S., 1974-76. **Publications:** Why Blacks, Women and Jews Are Not Mentioned in the Constitution, and Other Unorthodox Views, 1990; From Parchment to Power: How James Madison Used the Bill of Rights to Save the Constitution, 1997. EDITOR: Readings in World Politics, 1959; Readings in American Foreign Policy, 1959; Readings in Russian Foreign Policy, 1959; A Nation of States, 1963; America Armed, 1963; Why Foreign Aid?, 1963; Political Parties USA, 1964; Beyond the Cold War, 1964; 100 Years of Emancipation, 1965; Left, Right and Center, 1967; Higher Education and Modern Democracy, 1967; Representation and Misrepresentation, 1968; A Nation of Cities, 1968; On Civil Disobedience, 1969; How Democratic Is America?, 1971; Bureaucrats, Policy Analysts, Statesmen: Who Leads?, 1980; Political Parties in the Eighties, 1980; How Democratic Is the Constitution?, 1980; How Capitalistic Is the Constitution?, 1982; How Does the Constitution Secure Rights?, 1985; Separation of Powers-Does It Still Work?, 1986; How Does the Constitution Protect Religious Liberty?, 1987; How Federal Is the Constitution?, 1987; Slavery and Its Consequences, 1988; The Constitution, the Courts, and the Quest for Justice, 1989; Foreign Policy and the Constitution, 1990; The Spirit of the Constitution, 1990. **Address:** c/o American Enterprise Institute, 1150 17th St NW, Washington, DC 20036, U.S.A.

GOLINSKI, Jan. British, b. 1957. **Genres:** History, Sciences. **Career:** University of Lancaster, Lancaster, England, lecturer, 1983-86; Churchill College, Cambridge, Cambridge, England, junior research fellow, 1986-90; Huntington Library, San Marino, CA, V. M. Keck Foundation fellow, 1990-94. University of New Hampshire, Durham, NH, assistant professor of history and humanities, 1990-94, associate professor, 1994-2000, professor, 2000-. University of Wisconsin, Madison, Institute for Research in the Humanities, visiting post-doctoral fellow, 1989; University of California, Los Angeles, William Andrews Clark Memorial Library, visiting fellow, 1989; Princeton University, visiting assistant professor, 1992. **Publications:** Science as Public Culture: Chemistry and Enlightenment in Britain, 1760-1820, 1992; Making Natural Knowledge: Constructivism and the History of Science, 1998; (co-ed.) The Sciences in Enlightened Europe, 1999. Contributor to books. Contributor of articles and essay reviews to periodicals. **Address:** Dept of History, University of New Hampshire, Durham, NH 03824, U.S.A. **Online address:** jan.golinski@unh.edu

GOLLAHER, David L. American, b. 1949. **Genres:** Biography. **Career:** Young & Rubicam (advertising agency), New York City, account executive, 1981-82; Phillips Ramsey Advertising, San Diego, CA, vice president, 1982-85; Scripps Clinic and Research Foundation, La Jolla, CA, vice president, 1985-91; San Diego State University, San Diego, professor of public health, 1991-93; California Health Care Institute, La Jolla, president, 1993-. **Publications:** Voice for the Mad (biography), 1995; Circumcision: A History of the World's Most Controversial Surgery, 2000. **Address:** California Health Care Institute, 1020 Prospect St No 310, La Jolla, CA 92037, U.S.A.

GOLLIN, Rita K. American, b. 1928. **Genres:** Literary criticism and history, Bibliography, Biography. **Career:** University of Rochester, NY, lecturer to assistant professor of English, 1955-67; State University of New York at Geneseo, assistant professor, 1967-68, associate professor, 1968-75, professor of English, 1975-95, distinguished professor of English, 1995-, distinguished professor of English emerita, 2002-. **Publications:** Nathaniel Hawthorne and the Truth of Dreams, 1979; Portraits of Nathaniel Hawthorne: An Iconography, 1983; (with J.L. Idol Jr.) Prophetic Pictures: Hawthorne's Knowledge and Uses of the Visual Arts, 1991; Annie Adams Fields: Woman of Letters, 2001. EDITOR: C.D. Warner, A Little Journey in the World, 1970; S.J. Hale, Northwood, 1972; Thoreau Inter Alia: Essays in Honor of Walter Harding, 1985. Contributor of articles on 19th and 20th century American literature to scholarly periodicals and encyclopedias. **Address:** Department of English, State University of New York College at Geneseo, Geneseo, NY 14454, U.S.A. **Online address:** gollin@aol.com

GOLOMSTOCK, Igor (Naumovitch). Also writes as Fomin. British (born Russia), b. 1929. **Genres:** Art/Art history. **Career:** Oxford University, Oxford, England, lecturer, 1976-80; British Broadcasting Corp., London, England, scriptwriter, 1979-87. Visiting researcher, Stanford University, 1986-87, and Harvard University, 1988-89. **Publications:** (with A. Sinyarskii) Picasso, 1960; (as Fomin) Hieronymus Bosch, 1973; Cezanne, 1975; Unofficial Art from the Soviet Union, 1977; Totalitarian Art, 1990; The Camp Drawings of Boris Sveshnikov, 2000. **Address:** c/o Andrew Nurnberg, Andrew Nurnberg Associates Ltd, Clerkenwell House, 45-47 Clerkenwell Green, London EC1R 0HT, England. **Online address:** igor@golomstock.snet.co.uk

GOLUBITSKY, Martin. American, b. 1945. **Genres:** Mathematics/Statistics. **Career:** University of California, Los Angeles, instructor in

mathematics, 1970-71; Massachusetts Institute of Technology, instructor in mathematics, 1971-73; Queens College of City University of New York, assistant professor to associate professor of mathematics, 1973-79; Arizona State University, Tempe, professor of mathematics, 1979-83; University of Houston, TX, professor of mathematics, 1983-, Cullen Professor of Mathematics, 1989-, director of Institute for Theoretical and Engineering Science, 1988-. **Publications:** (with V. Guillemin) Stable Mappings and Their Singularities, 1974; (with D.G. Schaeffer) Singularities and Groups in Bifurcation Theory I, 1984; (with I. Stewart and D.G. Schaeffer) Singularities and Groups in Bifurcation Theory II, 1988; (with M. Field) Symmetry in Chaos, 1992; (with I. Stewart) Fearful Symmetry, 1992; (with M. Dellnitz) Linear Algebra and Differential Equations Using MATLAB, 1998; (with I. Stewart) The Symmetry Perspective, 2001. **Address:** Department of Mathematics, University of Houston, 4800 Calhoun, Houston, TX 77204-3476, U.S.A.

GOMBRICH, Richard Francis. British, b. 1937. **Genres:** Theology/Religion. **Career:** Oxford University, Oxford, England, lecturer in Sanskrit and Pali, 1965-76, Boden Professor of Sanskrit, 1976-2004. **Publications:** Precept and Practice: Traditional Buddhism in the Rural Highlands of Ceylon, 1971; (with M. Cone) The Perfect Generosity of Prince Vessantara, 1977; On Being Sanskritic, 1978; Theravada Buddhism: A Social History from Ancient Benares to Modern Colombo, 1988; (with G. Obeyesekere) Buddhism Transformed: Religious Change in Sri Lanka, 1988; How Buddhism Began: The Conditioned Genesis of the Early Teachings, 1996. EDITOR: (with H. Bechert, and contrib.) The World of Buddhism, 1984, in UK as The World of Buddhism: Buddhist Monks and Nuns in Society and Culture; (with J. Benson) M. Coulson, Sanskrit, 2nd rev. ed., 1992. Contributor of articles and book reviews to scholarly journals and newspapers. Works have been translated into German, French, Spanish, Italian, Japanese, and Korean. **Address:** Balliol College, Oxford OX1 3BJ, England.

GOMES, Peter J(ohn). American, b. 1942. **Genres:** History, Theology/Religion, Inspirational/Motivational Literature. **Career:** Minister, historian, church musician, and author. Ordained Baptist minister, 1968; Tuskegee Institute, Tuskegee, AL, instructor of history and director of freshman experimental program, 1968-70; Harvard University, The Memorial Church, assistant minister, then acting minister, 1970-74; minister, 1974-, Plummer Professor of Christian Morals, 1974-. **Publications:** (ed.) History of the Pilgrim Society, 1970; (with L.D. Geller) The Books of the Pilgrims, 1975; Proclamation Series Commentaries, 1985; (and ed) History of Harvard Divinity School, 1992; Proclamation Series, 1995; The Good Book: Reading the Bible with Mind and Heart, 1996. Author of 14 other books. Contributor to periodicals. **Address:** Memorial Church, Harvard University, Cambridge, MA 02138, U.S.A.

GOMEZ, Jewelle. American, b. 1948. **Genres:** Poetry, Essays, Novels, Plays/Screenplays, Novellas/Short stories. **Career:** Novelist, social activist, and teacher of creative writing. Worked as production assistant, WGBH-TV, Boston, MA, on Say Brother, 1968-71, and in New York City for Children's Television Workshop and WNET-TV during 1970s; stage manager for Off-Broadway theatres, 1975-80; New York State Council on the Arts, program associate, 1983-89, director of Literature Program, 1989-93; Hunter College, NYC, lecturer in women's studies and English, 1989-90; board member for organizations and task forces. **Publications:** The Lipstick Papers (poetry), 1980; Flamingoes and Bears (poetry), 1986; The Gilda Stories: A Novel, 1991; Forty-three Septembers (essays), 1993; Oral Tradition (poetry), 1995; Don't Explain (short stories); Bones and Ash (play), 1996. **Address:** c/o Frances Goldin Literary Agency, 57 # 11th St #5B, New York, NY 10003, U.S.A. **Online address:** www.jewellegomez.com

GOMEZ ROSA, Alexis. Dominican Republican, b. 1950. **Genres:** Poetry. **Career:** Colegio Onesimo Jimenez (high school), Dominican Republic, teacher, 1972-74; copywriter for Young & Rubicam advertising agency, 1974; teacher at Padre Billini High School, 1975-77; copywriter for RETHO advertising agency, 1975; Dominican Export Promotion Center, publicist, 1978-83; Noticias del Mundo, publicist, 1983-90; poetry instructor in the public schools of Boston and Dorchester, Massachusetts, 1984-85; Northern Manhattan Coalition for Immigrants Rights, NYC, community liaison, 1987-88; New York University, Spanish instructor. Journalist. Social worker with organizations and clubs of Washington Heights. **Publications:** POETRY: Oficio de post-muerte, 1973; High Quality, Ltd., 1985; Tiza & Tinta, 1990; Pluroscopo. Contributor to anthologies. **Address:** Spanish Dept., New York University, 19 University Place 4th floor, New York, NY 10003, U.S.A.

GOMI, Taro. Japanese, b. 1945. **Genres:** Children's fiction, Essays, Illustrations, Picture/board books. **Career:** Author and illustrator of children's books. **Publications:** SELF-ILLUSTRATED FOR CHILDREN: Michi, 1973; Himitsu no Gakki, 1975; Boku wa Zouda, 1976; Kingyo ga Nigeta, 1977, trans. as Where's the Fish?, 1986; Tabeta no Dare, 1977; Kakushita no Dare, 1977; Minna Unchi, 1977, trans. as Everyone Poops, 1993; Buta ga Bu Bu, 1977; Ojisan no Tsue, 1977; Yubikun, 1977; Chiisana Kisha, 1978; Kujirada!, 1978; Kakurenbo Kakurenbo, 1978, trans. as Hide and Seek, 1989; Kotoba, 1978; U(yu)shi to G(ji)shi, 1978; Umiwa Hiroine, Ojiichan, 1979; Kotoba no AIUEO, 1979; Sora Hadakanbo!, 1979; Hito ni Tsuite, 1979; Obasan no Gochisou, 1979; Rappa wo Narase, 1979, trans. as Toot!, 1986; Hayaku Aitaina, 1979, trans. as Coco Can't Wait, 1983; Minna ga Oshietekuremashita, 1979, trans. as My Friends, 1990; Kimi ha Shitteiru, 1979; Futari de Hanbun, 1979, trans. as Sharing, 1981; Aka no Hon, 1979; Kuro no Hon, 1979; Shiro no Hon, 1979; Omiseyasan, 1979; Tomodachi 15 nin, 1979; Ipponbashi Wataru, 1979; Saru-Rururu, 1979; Umi no Mukouwa, 1979; Ushiro ni Irunoha Daareda, 1980; Kanji no Ehon, 1980; Kurisumasu Niwa Okurimono, 1980; Norimono, 1980; Kimono, 1980; Koushi no Haru, 1980, trans. as Spring Is Here, 1989; Denwa de Ohanashi, 1980; Sakasu Sakasu, 1980; Itadakimasu Gochisousama, 1980; Kiiro no Hon, 1980; Midori no Hon, 1980; Chairo no Hon, 1980; Natsu, 1980; Takai Takai, 1980; Nagai Nagai, 1980; Midori no Boushi, 1980; Akachan, 1980; Okasan, 1980; Doubutsu Rando, 1980; Okusan To 9 Nin No Seirusuman, 1980; Kage, 1980, trans. as Shadows, 1981; Katakana Ehon AIUEO, 1980; Tenshisama ga Oritekuru, 1980; Fuyu, 1981; Aki, 1981; Haru, 1981; Nandaka Ureshikunattekita, 1981; Noharano Terebijyon, 1981; Toriaezu Ehon ni Tsuite (essay), 1981; Helikoputatachi, 1981; Hi, 1981; Mizu, 1981; Iro, 1981; Katachi, 1981; Baku-Kukuku, 1981, English version, 1993; Emono wa Dokoda, 1981; Akachan no enon, Vols 1-12, 1981; Mominoki Sono Mi Wo Kazarinasai, 1981; Ehon Kotoba Asobi, 1982; Gaikotsusan, 1982; Gu Gu Gu, 1982; Tokidoki no Shounen (essay), 1982; Ehon ABC, 1983; Kiiroino wa Choucho (trans. as Hi, Butterfly!), 1983; Geimu Bukku No. 1, 1983; Tamago wo Douzo, 1983; Kabusan Tonda, 1983; Geimu Bukku No. 2, 1983; Tosan Maigo, 1983; Geimu Bukku No. 3, 1983; Mado Kara no Okurimono, 1983, trans. as Santa through the Window, 1995; Nakushitamono Mitsuketa, 1983; Kotoba no Ehon AIUEO, 1983; Kazu No Ehon 1-2-3, 1983; Gomi Taro Catalogue-ehon, 1984; Wanisan Doki Haishasan Doki, 1984, trans. as The Crocodile and the Dentist, 1994; Kore wa Himo, 1984; Kore wa Hako, 1984; Tomodachi ga Kimashita, 1984; Tomodachi ga Imashita, 1984; Battakun, 1984; Kore wa Te, 1984; Kore wa Atama, 1984; Ichiban Hajimeni, 1984, trans. as First Comes Harry, 1987; Chibisuke Kirakira, 1985; Omen de Asobouyo, 1985; Doubutsu Sakasudan, 1985; Basu ga Kita, 1985, trans. as Bus Stops, 1988; Suji no Ehon, 1985; Sansansan, 1985; Omataseshimashita, 1985; Kyou Mo Genkisa, 1985; Kotoba Zukan 1 Ugokinokotoba (Doushi) (trans. as Seeing, Saying, Doing, Playing: A Big Book of Action Words), 1985; Ba Ba Zou Diu Le, Ying Wen Han Sheng Chu Ban Gong Si, 1985; Kotoba Zukan 2, 1985; Nihon Kotowaza Mongatari, 1985; Sanpo no Shirushi, 1986; Kotoba Zukan 3 Kazarukotoba (A)(Keiyoushi), 1986; Kotoba Zukan 4 Kazarukotoba (B)(Keiyoushi), 1986; Ne Ohanashi Shiteyo, 1986; Kotoba Zukan 5 Tsunaginokotoba (Joshi), 1986; Kotowaza Ehon 1, 1986; Gokigen Ikaga, 1986; Guruguru Doubutsuehon, 1986; Kotoba Zukan 6 Kurashinokotoba (Aisatsugo), 1986; Saru-rururu Karuta, 1986; Wo Shi Di Yi Ge, 1986; ABC Tu Hua Shu, 1986; Doubutsu Daisuki, 1987; Gomi Taro Poster Ehon, 1987; Kotoba Zukan 7 Tatoenokotoba (Hiyu), 1987; Kotowaza Ehon 2, 1988; What Does This Sign Say?, 1987; Kotoba Zukan 8, 1988; Boku ha Zouda, 1988; Aiue Obakedazo, 1988; Kumasan Home-Run, 1988; Kotoba Zukan 9 Shipponokotoba (Jodoushi), 1988; Otto Otoshimono, 1988; Gomi Taro Catalogue Ehon: Part II, 1988; Ehon wo Yondemiru, 1988; Hajimeteno Eigo 1, 1988; Hajimeteno Eigo 2, 1988; Kotoba Zukan 10 Namaenokotoba (Meishi), 1988; Jazz Song Book, 1988; Guru Guru Card (Doubutsu), 1988; Haiku Purasu Arufa Zou, 1988; Node node node, 1989; Hakigokochi no Yoi Kutsu, 1989; Uta ga Kikoetekuru, 1989; Popopopopo, 1989; Nihongo Gitaigo Jiten, 1990; Rakugaki Ehon, 1990; 12 Ko no E no Hako, 1990; Sekaijyu no Kodomotachiga, 1990; Boku no Uta, 1990; Parade, 1990; Boku Tooreruyo, 1990; Ya Minasan, 1990; Nanikashira, 1990; Jazz Song Book 2, 1991; Jyobuna Atama to Kashikoi Karada ni Narutameni, 1991; Kakakakaka, 1991; Rururururu, 1991; Hajimeteno Eigo 3, 1991; Hajimeteno Eigo 4, 1991; Shisumon Ehon, 1991; Iroirona Doubutsuni Nattemimashita, 1991; Iroirona Mononi Nattemimashita, 1991; Saru-rururu One More, 1991; Hajimeteno Piano Kyokushu, 1991; Hello!, 1991; Aisatsu Ehon, 1991; Guess Who?, 1991; Who Ate It?, 1991; Who Hid It?, 1991; Rakugaki Ehon Part 2, 1992; Ipponbashi Wataru One More, 1992; Ashita ga Suki, 1992; Doubutsu-hen, 1992; Dougu-hen, 1992; Kotoba-hen, 1992; Kanji Jyukugo-hen, 1992; Dododododo, 1992; Rakugaki Book Rakugaki Ehon, 1992; Kesshite Soudeha Arimasen, 1992; Kotobano Ehon AIUEO, 1992; Gomi Taro Design Work, 1992; Nanika Itteruyo, 1992; Kono Yubi Naani, 1992; Tsumande Goran, 1992; Rakugaki Hagaki, 1992; Guess What?, 1992; There's a Mouse in the House, 1992; Ouchi wo Tsukurimashou, 1993; Oshare wo Shimashou, 1993; Ki wo Uemashou, 1993; Saa Itadakimashou, 1993; Hajimenteno Piano Kyokushu 2, 1993; Kaimono Ehon, 1993; Tetetetete, 1993; Tonimokakunimo Sutekina Nakama, 1993; Ha-

hahahaha, 1993; Smile, 1993; Face Painting, 1993; Tadashii Kurashikata Dokuhon, 1993; Mouichido Sonokotowo, 1993; Sorezore no Jyoukyou, 1993; Matteimasu, 1994; Minnasorezore Kinoii Nakama, 1994; Gomi Taro Ehonsenshu Part 1, 1994; Darega Sunde Irunokana, 1994; Haiku wa Ikaga, 1994; Bibibibibi, 1994; Nunununununu, 1994; Pocket ni Uta wo Tsumete, 1994; Kotoba no Ehon Aiueo Karuta, 1994; Ah Iikimochi, 1995; Naniwatomoare Ganbaru Nakama, 1995; Ririririri, 1995; Kore wa Umi, 1995; Kore wa Yama, 1995; Nnnnn, 1995; 2, 1995; Sansansan Sono 2, 1995; Chikyu ha Utau, 1995; Tegami ga Kurukuru, 1995; Wakuwakusurune, 1996; Isshoni, 1996; Kochira to Sochira, 1996; Hidarinohon Miginohon, 1996; Waratteru Naiteiru, 1996; Anakara Nigeta, 1996; Dokoni Hairoukana, 1996; Tsukandegoran, 1996; Satori kun, 1996; Tanoshii Ookii Kotoba Ehon, 1996; Nuttari Kaitari Rakugaki Book, 1996; Otona Mondai, 1996; Rakugaki Ehon 1.2.3., 1996; Karada Shiata, 1997; Darekaga Imasu, 1997; Herikoputatachi, 1997. **Address:** 3-20-12 Uehara Shibuya-Ku, Tokyo 151-0064, Japan.

GOMMANS, Jos J. L. Dutch, b. 1963. **Genres:** History. **Career:** Netherlands Organization for Scientific Research, research student at Foundation for the Advancement of Tropical Research, 1989-93; University of Leiden, Leiden, Netherlands, member of Department of South and Central Asian Studies, 1993-. **Publications:** The Rise of the Indo-Afghan Empire, c. 1710-1780, 1995. Contributor of articles and reviews to scholarly journals. **Address:** Department of South and Central Asian Studies, Kern Institute, P.O. Box 9515, 2300 RA Leiden, Netherlands.

GONEN, Jay Y. Israeli, b. 1934. **Genres:** Psychology, History. **Career:** University of Cincinnati, Cincinnati, OH, professor of psychology; University of Rochester Medical Center, Rochester, NY, professor. **Publications:** A Psychohistory of Zionism, 1975; The Roots of Nazi Psychology: Hitler's Utopian Barbarism, 2000. Contributor to periodicals. **Address:** c/o Author Mail, University Press of Kentucky, 663 South Limestone St., Lexington, KY 40508, U.S.A.

GONZALES, Phillip B. American, b. 1946. **Genres:** Sociology. **Career:** Sociology professor. Academic research positions in sociology, 1978-87; University of Wisconsin-Madison, summer visiting professor in sociology and Chicano studies, 1990; University of New Mexico, Albuquerque, associate professor, 1987-, director, Southwest Hispanic Research Institute, 1996-. **Publications:** (with L. Lamphere and P. Zavella) Sunbelt Working Mothers: Reconciling Family and Factory, 1993; Forced Sacrifice as Ethnic Protest: The Hispano Cause in New Mexico and the Racial Attitude Confrontation of 1933, 2001. Contributor to periodicals. **Address:** University of New Mexico, Sociology Department, 1103 Social Science Building, Albuquerque, NM 87131, U.S.A. **Online address:** gonzales@unm.edu

GONZALEZ, Alexander G. American (born England), b. 1952. **Genres:** Literary criticism and history. **Career:** Queens College of the City University of New York, Flushing, team teacher of English composition, 1975-76; University of Oregon, Eugene, director of writing laboratory, 1978-79; University of California, Santa Barbara, visiting lecturer in English, 1980-81; University of Oregon, instructor in writing and composition, 1982-83; Ohio State University, Columbus, assistant professor of English, 1983-88; State University of New York College at Cortland, assistant professor, 1988-91, associate professor, 1991-94, professor of English, 1994-2003, distinguished teaching professor, 2003-. Pennsylvania State University, guest lecturer and distinguished scholar in residence, 1991. Central New York Conference on Language and Literature, director, 1995-2001. **Publications:** Darrell Figgis: A Study of His Novels, 1992; Short Stories from the Irish Renaissance: An Anthology, 1993; (ed.) Assessing the Achievement of J.M. Synge, 1996; Peadar O'Donnell: A Reader's Guide, 1997; Modern Irish Writers: A Bio-Critical Sourcebook, 1997; Contemporary Irish Women Poets: Some Male Perspectives, 1999. Contributor to books. Contributor of articles, poems, stories, and reviews to periodicals. **Address:** Department of English, State University of New York College at Cortland, PO Box 2000, Cortland, NY 13045, U.S.A.

GONZÁLEZ, Aníbal. American, b. 1956. **Genres:** Literary criticism and history. **Career:** University of Texas at Austin, assistant professor, 1982-87, associate professor of Spanish, 1987-90; Michigan State University, East Lansing, associate professor, 1990-93, professor of Spanish, 1993; Pennsylvania State University, University Park, Edwin Erle Sparks Professor of Spanish, 1994-. Vanderbilt University, visiting assistant professor, 1987; Michigan State University Press, member of editorial board, 1993-94; Cambridge University Press, Cambridge Studies in Latin American and Iberian Literature Series, general editor, 1995-97; Bucknell University Press, Bucknell Studies in Latin American Literature and Theory, general editor, 1998; Guggenheim Memorial Foundation Fellowship, 2001. **Publications:**

La cronica modernista hispanoamericana, 1983; La novela modernista hispanoamericana, 1987; Journalism and the Development of Spanish American Narrative, 1993; (trans. and author of prologue) J.L. Borges, Un ensayo autobiografico, 1999; Killer Books, 2001; Abusos y admoniciones, 2001. Contributor to books. Contributor of articles and reviews to scholarly journals. **Address:** Dept of Spanish, Italian, & Portuguese, 211 Burrowes Bldg, Pennsylvania State University, University Park, PA 16802, U.S.A.

GONZALEZ (MANDRI), Flora. Also writes as Flora Werner. American (born Cuba), b. 1948. **Genres:** Literary criticism and history. **Career:** Dartmouth College, Hanover, NH, lecturer, 1974-76, visiting assistant professor of Spanish and Portuguese, 1982-83; University of Chicago, assistant professor of Romance languages, 1983-86; Emerson College, Boston, MA, assistant professor, 1986-91, associate professor of writing, literature and publishing, 1991-, acting dean of graduate studies, 1994-95, director of Honors Program, 1995-99. Middlebury College, assistant professor, summers, 1984-89, associate professor, summer, 1993; lecturer at US colleges and universities; guest on television programs; consultant to Amigos de las Americas. **Publications:** Jose Donoso's House of Fiction: A Dramatic Construction of Time and Place, 1995; (ed. and trans. with R. Rosenmeier) E. Saldana, In the Vortex of the Cyclone: Selected Poems by Excilia Saldana, 2002. Contributor to books. Contributor of articles and reviews to periodicals. **Address:** Dept of Writing, Literature and Publishing, Emerson College, 120 Boylston St, Boston, MA 02116, U.S.A. **Online address:** flora_gonzalez@emerson.edu

GONZALEZ, Genaro. American, b. 1949. **Genres:** Novels, Novellas/Short stories. **Career:** Writer and educator. Pan American University, Edinburg, TX, instructor in psychology, 1979-82; University of the Americas, Puebla, Mexico, associate professor of psychology, 1983-85; Texas Governor's School, University of Texas, Austin, TX, instructor, 1986; Wichita State University, Wichita, KS, assistant professor of minority studies, 1986-88; University of Texas at Pan American, Edinburg, TX, associate professor in psychology, 1988-. **Publications:** Rainbow's End (novel), 1988; Only Sons (short story collection), 1991. Contributor of short stories to anthologies and periodicals. Contributor of scholarly articles to periodicals. **Address:** Psychology Department, University of Texas at Pan American, Edinburg, TX 78539, U.S.A.

GONZÁLEZ, Justo L(uis). American (born Cuba), b. 1937. **Genres:** Theology/Religion. **Career:** Ed., Apuntes. Professor of Historical Theology, 1966-69, and Dean, 1967-69, Evangelical Seminary of Puerto Rico; Assistant Professor, 1969-71, and Associate Professor, 1971-77, Emory University, Atlanta; Visiting Professor of Theology, Interdenominational Theological Center, 1977-87; Visiting Professor, Columbia Theological Seminary, 1987-91; Director, Hispanic Summer Program, Fund for Theological Education, 1988-. **Publications:** (in English): The Development of Christianity in the Latin Caribbean, 1969; A History of Christian Thought, 3 vols., 1970-79, 1987; (with C.G. Gonzalez) Their Souls Did Magnify the Lord, 1977; (with C.G. Gonzalez) Vision at Patmos, 1978; (with C.G. Gonzalez) Rejoice in Your Savior, 1979; (with C.G. Gonzalez) Liberation Preaching, 1980; (with C.G. Gonzalez) In Accord, 1981; The Story of Christianity, 2 vols., 1984-85; The Crusades: Piety Misguided, 1988; Monasticism: Patterns of Piety, 1988; Christian Thought Revisited, 1989; Faith and Wealth, 1990; Manana: Christian Theology from a Hispanic Perspective, 1990; Out of Every Tribe and Nation: Christian Theology at the Ethnic Roundtable, 1992; Santa Biblia, 1996; Church History, 1996; (with C.G. Gonzalez) Revelation, 1997; For the Healing of the Nations, 1999; Mark's Message for the New Millennium, 2000; Jonas, 2000. EDITOR: Proclaiming the Acceptable Years, 1982; Each in Our Own Tongue: A History of Hispanic United Methodism, 1991; Voices: Voices from the Hispanic Church, 1992. Author of books in Spanish. Author of articles and adult Bible lessons. **Address:** 336 S Columbia Dr, Decatur, GA 30030, U.S.A.

GONZALEZ, Ray. American, b. 1952. **Genres:** Poetry, Literary criticism and history. **Career:** Poet, editor and educator. Guadalupe Cultural Arts Center, San Antonio, TX, director, 1989-. Poet-in-residence, Woodinville, WA public schools, 1987. Also taught writing to juvenile offenders at the Emerson House Detention Center, Denver, CO. **Publications:** From the Restless Roots, 1986; Twilights and Chants: Poems, 1987; Memory Fever: A Journey Beyond El Paso del Norte, 1993; The Heat of Arrivals, 1996; Cabato Sentora, 1998. EDITOR: Without Discovery: A Native Response to Columbus, 1992; After Aztlan: Latino Poets of the Nineties, 1992; Mirrors Beneath the Earth: Short Fiction by Chicano Writers, 1992; Currents from the Dancing River: Contemporary Latino Fiction, Nonfiction, and Poetry, 1994; Under the Pomegranate Tree: The Best New Latino Erotica, 1996; Inheritance of Light, 1996; Muy Macho: Latino Men Confront Their Man-

hood, 1996; Touching the Fire: Fifteen Poets of Today's Latino Renaissance, 1998. **Address:** Dept of English, 310E Lind Hall, University of Minnesota, 207 Church St SE, Minneapolis, MN 55455, U.S.A. **Online address:** gonza049@umn.edu

GONZALEZ, Victor Hugo. Mexican, b. 1953. **Genres:** Novels, Autobiography/Memoirs. **Career:** Instituto Tecnologico Superior, Mexico, professor of English and French, summer, 1985; Kendall Industries, Mexico, documentation translator, 1986; Century 21 (real estate company), Whittier, CA, salesperson, 1986-88. **Publications:** Boundless Journey: The Stranger (novel), 1998; Who's the Stranger?, 2002. **Address:** 9622 Rex Rd, Pico Rivera, CA 90660, U.S.A.

GONZALEZ-BALADO, Jose Luis. Spanish, b. 1933. **Genres:** Biography, Theology/Religion. **Career:** Ediciones Paulinas, Madrid, Spain, editor; Rome-based correspondent of religious affairs for Spanish newspapers and magazines. **Publications:** Cristo en los arrables: Madre Teresa de Calcutta, 1974; Me llaman el obispo rojo: Dom Helder Camara, 1974; El desafio de Taize, 1976, trans. as The Story of Taize, 1980; Ernesto Cardenal poeta revolucionario monje, 1978; Always the Poor: Mother Teresa, Her Life and Message, 1980; Stories of Mother Teresa: Her Smile and Her Words, 1983; (with K. Spink) Spirit of Bethlehem: Brother Andrew and the Missionary Brothers of Charity, 1987; Ruiz-Gimenez, talante y figura: Trayectoria de un hombre discutido, 1989; Padre Llanos: Un jesuita en el suburbio, 1991; (Compiler) Mother Teresa, In My Own Words, 1996; Mother Teresa: Her Life, Her Work, Her Message: A Memoir, 1997. EDITOR: (with J.N. Playfoot) Mother Teresa, My Life for the Poor, 1985; Mother Teresa, One Heart Full of Love, 1988; Mother Teresa, Loving Jesus, 1991. **Address:** Parque Eugenia de Montijo 55, Madrid, Spain.

GONZÁLEZ-ECHEVARRIA, Roberto. American/Cuban, b. 1943. **Genres:** Literary criticism and history. **Career:** Cornell University, Ithaca, New York, Assistant Professor, 1971-75, Director of Graduate Studies, Dept. of Romance Studies, 1973-74, Associate Professor, 1975-77; Yale University, New Haven, Conn., Assistant Professor of Spanish, 1970-71, Associate Professor, 1977-80, Director of Undergraduate Studies in Latin American Studies, 1979-80, Professor, 1980-85; Chairman, Council on Latin American Studies, 1981-83, 1984-85, Chairman, Dept. of Spanish and Portuguese, 1983-89, 1990-93, R. Selden Rose Professor of Spanish, 1985-91, Bass Professor of Hispanic and Comparative Literatures, 1991-95, Sterling Professor of Hispanic and Comparative Literatures, 1995-. **Publications:** (with M. Duran) Calderon ante la Critica, 1976; Relecturas: Estudios de Literatura Cubana, 1976; Alejo Carpentier: The Pilgrim at Home, 1977; (with K. Muller-Bergh) Alejo Carpentier: Bibliographical Guide, 1983; Isla a su Vuelo Fugitiva: Ensayos Criticos sobre Literatura Hispanoamericana, 1983; Estatuas Sepultada y Otros Relatos, 1984; Historia y Ficcion en la Narrativa Hispanoamericana, 1985; Los Pasos Perididos, 1985; The Voice of the Masters: Writing and Authority in Modern Latin American Literature, 1985; La Ruta de Severa Sarduy, 1986; Myth and Archive: Toward a Theory of Latin American Narrative, 1990; Celestina's Brood, 1993; (co-ed with E. Pupo-Walker) The Cambridge History of Latin American Literature, 3 vols., 1996. **Address:** Dept. of Spanish and Portuguese, Yale University, 82-90 Wall St., New Haven, CT 06520, U.S.A.

GOOCH, Brad. American, b. 1952. **Genres:** Novels, Novellas/Short stories, Poetry, Gay and lesbian issues, Biography. **Career:** Free-lance writer. **Publications:** The Daily News, 1977; Jailbait and Other Stories, 1984; Scary Kisses, 1988; City Poet: The Life and Times of Frank O'Hara, 1993; The Golden Age of Promiscuity, 1996; Finding the Boyfriend Within, 1999; Zombie00, 2000. **Address:** c/o Joy Harris, Lantz Harris Literary Agency, 156 5th Ave Ste 617, New York, NY 10010, U.S.A. **Online address:** goochb@wpunj.edu; bradgooch.com

GOOCH, Paul W(illiam). Canadian, b. 1941. **Genres:** Philosophy. **Career:** University of Toronto, instructor, then professor of philosophy, 1967-, associate dean, vice dean, then acting dean of School of Graduate Studies, 1988-94, vice provost, 1994-2001, president of Victoria University, 2001-. **Publications:** Partial Knowledge: Philosophical Studies in Paul, 1987; Reflections on Jesus and Socrates: Word and Silence, 1996. Contributor of articles to periodicals on Greek philosophy, the philosophy of religion, and biblical studies. **Address:** Victoria University, 73 Queen's Park Crescent, Toronto, ON, Canada M5S 1K7. **Online address:** paul.gooch@utoronto.ca

GOOCH, Stanley (Alfred). British, b. 1932. **Genres:** Paranormal, Psychology, Anthropology/Ethnology, Archaeology/Antiquities. **Career:** Publisher's reader. Head of Modern Languages, Highbury County Boys School, London, 1958-61; Teacher, Colebrooke Row School for Maladjusted Children,

London, 1961-63; Sr. Research Psychologist, National Children's Bureau, London, 1964-68. **Publications:** Four Years On, 1966; Total Man, 1972; Personality and Evolution, 1973; The Neanderthal Question, 1977; The Paranormal, 1978; Guardians of the Ancient Wisdom, 1979; The Double Helix of the Mind, 1980; The Secret Life of Humans, 1981; Creatures from Inner Space, 1984; The Child with Asthma, 1986; Cities of Dreams, 1989, rev. ed., 1995. **Address:** Flat 7, 25 Bolsize Park, Hampstead, London NW3 4DU, England.

GOOCH, Steve. British, b. 1945. **Genres:** Plays/Screenplays, Translations, Writing/Journalism, Essays. **Career:** Assistant Ed., Plays and Players mag., London, 1972-73; Resident Dramatist, Half Moon Theatre, 1973-74, and Greenwich Theatre, 1974-75, both in London, Solent Peoples Theatre, Southampton, 1982, Theatre Venture, London, 1983-84, Warehouse Theatre, Croydon, 1986-87, and Gate Theatre, London, 1990-91. **Publications:** (trans.) Big Wolf, 1972; (trans.) The Mother, 1973; Female Transport, 1974, 2nd ed., 1983; (with P. Thompson) The Motor Show, 1974; Will Wat, If Not, What Will?, 1975; (trans.) Wolf Biermann's Poems and Ballads, 1977; The Women Pirates, 1978; (trans.) Wallraff: The Undesirable Journalist, 1978; Fast One, 1982; Landmark, 1982;(trans.) Gambit 39, 1982; All Together Now, 1984; Taking Liberties, 1984; Writing a Play, 1988, 3rd ed., 2001;(trans.) Lulu and the Marquis of Keith, 1990; Massa, 1990; Stages of Translation, 1996. Contributor to books. **Address:** M. Steinberg Playwrights, 409 Triumph House, 187-191 Regent St, London W1R 7WF, England.

GOOD, Howard. American, b. 1951. **Genres:** Documentaries/Reportage. **Career:** Ann Arbor News, Ann Arbor, MI, editor, 1977-78; Charlotte Observer, Charlotte, NC, editor, 1978-80; Grand Forks Herald, Grand Forks, ND, editor, 1980-83; University of North Dakota, Grand Forks, assistant professor of journalism, 1980-83; State University of New York, New Paltz, NY, associate professor of journalism, 1985-. **Publications:** Acquainted with the Night, 1986; Outcasts, 1989; The Journalist as Autobiographer, 1993; Diamonds in the Dark, 1997; Girl Reporter, 1998; The Drunken Journalist, 2000; (with M.J. Dillon) Media Ethics Goes to the Movies, 2002. **Address:** State University of New York, New Paltz, NY 12561, U.S.A. **Online address:** goodh@newpaltz.edu

GOODALL, Jane. British, b. 1934. **Genres:** Animals/Pets, Children's nonfiction, Zoology, Autobiography/Memoirs, Biology, Young adult non-fiction. **Career:** Researcher in Animal Behavior and Scientific Director, Gombe Stream Research Centre, Tanzania, 1960-. Hon. Visiting Professor, University of Dar Es Saalam, Tanzania, 1972-90. Visiting Professor of Psychiatry and Human Biology, Stanford, University, California, 1970-75. **Publications:** ADULT NON-FICTION: My Friends, the Wild Chimpanzees, 1967; The Behavior of Free-Living Chimpanzees in the Gombe Stream Reserve, 1968; (co-author) Innocent Killers, 1970; In the Shadow of Man, 1971; (co-author) Grub: The Bush Baby, 1972; The Chimpanzees of Gombe, 1986; Through a Window: My Thirty Years with the Chimpanzees of Gombe, 1990; (co-author) Visions of Caliban, 1994; With Love, 1994; Dr. White, 1999; Brutal Kinship, 1999; A Reason for Hope, 2000; Africa in My Blood: An Autobiography in Letters: The Early Years, 2000; Beyond Innocence: An Autobiography in Letters: The Later Years, 2001. JUVENILE NON-FICTION: My Life with the Chimpanzees, 1988; The Chimpanzee Family Book, 1989; Pandas, 1989; Lion Family, 1989; Hippos, 1989; Giraffe Family, 1990; Baboon Family, 1990; Elephant Family, 1990; Gorillas, 1990; Zebra Family, 1990; Sea Otters, 1990; Hyena Family, 1990; Wildebeast Family, 1990; Tigers, 1990; (reteller) The Eagle and the Wren, 2000; The Chimpanzees I Love: Saving Their World and Ours, 2001. **Address:** The Jane Goodall Institute, PO Box 14890, Silver Spring, MD 20911-4890, U.S.A. **Online address:** www.janegoodall.org

GOODAVAGE, Maria. American, b. 1962. **Genres:** Film. **Career:** Journalist and author. USA Today, former staff writer. **Publications:** The California Dog Lover's Companion, 1994, revised and published as The Dog Lover's Companion to California: The Inside Scoop on Where to Take Your Dog in the Golden State, 2002; The Dog Lover's Companion in the Bay Area, 2002; (with Jay Gordon) Good Nights: The Happy Parents' Guide to the Family Bed (and a Peaceful Night's Sleep!), 2002. **Address:** c/o Author Mail, St. Martin's Griffin, 175 Fifth Ave., New York, NY 10010, U.S.A.

GOODE, Erica. American. **Genres:** Adult non-fiction. **Career:** Staff writer, San Francisco Chronicle; associate editor, senior writer, assistant managing editor, U.S. News and World Report, 1987-. **Publications:** Letters for Our Children: Fifty Americans Share Lessons in Living, 1996. Contributor of essays to magazines. **Address:** U.S. News and World Report, 450 West 33rd Street, New York, NY 10001, U.S.A.

GOODENOUGH, Ward Hunt. American, b. 1919. **Genres:** Anthropology/Ethnology. **Career:** University of Pennsylvania, Philadelphia, assistant professor, 1949-54, associate professor, 1954-62, professor, 1962-80, university professor, 1980-89, university professor emeritus of anthropology, 1989-. **Publications:** Property, Kin, and Community on Truk, 1951; Cooperation in Change, 1963; Description and Comparison in Cultural Anthropology, 1970; Culture, Language, and Society, 1971; Trukese-English Dictionary, 1980; Under Heaven's Brow: Pre-Christian Religious Tradition in Chuuk, 2002. EDITOR: Explorations in Cultural Anthropology, 1964; Prehistoric Settlement of the Pacific, 1996. **Address:** Dept. of Anthropology, University of Pennsylvania, Philadelphia, PA 19104, U.S.A.

GOODERS, John. British, b. 1937. **Genres:** Natural history, Photography. **Career:** Ed., Birds of the World Encyclopedia, 1969-71; Consultant Ed., Encyclopedia of Birds, 1977-78; Writer, "Survival," television series; Presenter TVS, "Country Ways," television series, 1989-92; Director, Birding Travel Co. **Publications:** Where to Watch Birds, 1967; Where to Watch Birds in Europe, 1969; How and Why of Birds, 1971; How and Why of the Spoilt Earth, 1972; (with E. Hosking) Wildlife Photography, 1973; The Bird-Watcher's Book, 1974; Wildlife Paradises of the World, 1975; How to Watch Birds, 1976; Birds of Mountain and Moorlands Ocean and Estuary, Marsh and Shore, Hedgerow and Garden, 4 vols., 1978-79; (with P. Alden) Finding Birds around the World, 1979; A Day in the Country, 1979; (with S. Keith) Collins Bird Guide, 1980; Bird Seeker's Guide, 1980; Collins British Birds, 1982; The New Where to Watch Birds in Britain, 1986; (with T. Boyer) Ducks of North America and the Northern Hemisphere, 1986; The Complete Birdwatcher's Guide, 1988; Larousse Field Guide to the Birds of Britain and Ireland, 1986; Larousse Field Guide to the Birds of Britain and Europe, 1990; Outdoors Guide to Britain, 1990; The Practical Ornithologist, 1990; The Survival World of Birds, 1992; The Birdwatchers' Site Guide to Britain and Ireland, 1993; Larousse Pocket Guide to Birds of Britain and Ireland, 1995; Collins Guide to the Birds of Britain and Europe, 1998; Vogel Europas, 1999. **Address:** Finches House, Hiham Green, Winchelsea, E. Sussex TN36 4HB, England.

GOODFIELD, (Gwyneth) June. British, b. 1927. **Genres:** Novels, Sciences. **Career:** Clarence J. Robinson Professor, George Mason University, Fairfax, VA, 1990-. Assistant Director, Unit for the History of Ideas, Nuffield Foundation, England, 1961-64; Rebecca Bachrach Treves Professor, Wellesley College, MA, 1965-68; Professor of Philosophy and Medicine, College of Human Medicine, Michigan State University, East Lansing, 1968-77; Sr. Research Associate, Rockefeller University, NYC, 1976-83; Adjunct Professor, Cornell University Medical College, NY, 1977-89; President, International Health and Biomedicine Ltd., 1982-96. **Publications:** The Growth of Scientific Physiology, 1960; (co-author) The Fabric of the Heavens, 1961; (co-author) The Architect of Matter, 1962; (co-author) The Discovery of Time, 1965; Courier to Peking, 1973; The Siege of Cancer, 1974; Playing God, 1977; Reflections on Science and the Media, 1980; An Imagined World: A Story of Scientific Creativity, 1980; From the Face of the Earth, 1984; Quest for the Killers, 1985; The Planned Miracle, 1991; A Chance to Live, 1991; Rotten at the Core, 2001. **Address:** The Manor House, Alfriston, Polegate, E. Sussex, England.

GOODHEART, Eugene. American, b. 1931. **Genres:** Literary criticism and history. **Career:** Bard College, Annandale-on-Hudson, NY, instructor, then assistant professor, 1958-62; University of Chicago, assistant professor, 1962-66; Mount Holyoke College, South Hadley, MA, associate professor, 1966-67; Massachusetts Institute of Technology, Cambridge, associate professor, 1967-70, professor, 1970-74, co-director of Cambridge Humanities Seminar, 1973-82; Boston University, professor of English and chairman of dept., 1974-80; Brandeis University, Waltham, MA, Edytha Macy Gross Professor of Humanities, 1983-, now Emeritus, director of Brandeis Center for the Humanities, 1986-92, dept. chairman, 1989-94. **Publications:** The Utopian Vision of D.H. Lawrence, 1963; The Cult of the Ego: The Self in Modern Literature, 1968; Culture and the Radical Conscience, 1973; The Failure of Criticism, 1978; The Skeptic Disposition in Contemporary Criticism, 1985; Pieces of Resistance, 1987; Desire and Its Discontents, 1992; The Reign of Ideology, 1996; Does Literary Studies Have a Future, 1999; Confessions of a Secular Jew, 2001; Novel Practices: Classic Modern Fiction, 2003. **Address:** Dept of English, Brandeis University, Waltham, MA 02454, U.S.A. **Online address:** goodheart@brandeis.edu

GOODHUE, Thomas W. American, b. 1949. **Genres:** Children's nonfiction, Theology/Religion, Biography. **Career:** Youth minister in Palo Alto, CA, 1971-73; United Methodist Church, pastor in Hawaii, 1975-78, in Island Park, NY, 1985-92, in Bay Shore, NY, 1992-; Riverside Church Weekday School, Manhattan, NY, teacher, 1978-85; Long Island Council of Churches, executive director, 1999-. **Publications:** Kaahumanu, 1985; Stories for the Children of Light, 1986; Sharing the Good News with Children: Stories for the Common Lectionary, 1992; Curious Bones: Mary Anning and the Birth of Paleontology, 2002; Fossil Hunter: The Life and Times of Mary Anning, forthcoming. Contributor of film and television reviews to magazines. **Address:** Long Island Council of Churches, 1644 Denton Green, Hempstead, NY 11550, U.S.A. **Online address:** tgoodhue@suffolk.lib.ny.us

GOODING, Judson. American, b. 1926. **Genres:** Business/Trade/Industry, Communications/Media, Genealogy/Heraldry, International relations/Current affairs, Local history/Rural topics, Medicine/Health, Music, Travel/Exploration, Writing/Journalism. **Career:** Head, Trend Analysis Assocs., Walpole, N.H., since 1975. Reporter, Minneapolis Tribune, 1954-57; Reporter, Life mag., North and South America, Africa and Europe, 1957-62; Foreign Correspondent, Time mag., Paris Bureau, 1962-66; Bureau Chief, Time-Life News Service, San Francisco, 1966-68; Contributing Ed., Time mag., 1968-69; Associate Ed., Fortune mag., NYC, 1969-73; Ed., The Trend Report, Chicago, 1973-75; Executive Ed., Next mag., NYC, 1979-81; Member, U.S. Delegation to Unesco, Paris, 1982-84. **Publications:** The Job Revolution, 1972. Work appears in anthologies. Contributor to periodicals. **Address:** 21 Mountain View Dr, Keene, NH 03431, U.S.A.

GOODISON, Lorna (Gaye). Jamaican, b. 1947. **Genres:** Novels, Novellas/Short stories, Poetry. **Career:** Freelance writer and painter, 1977-. University of the West Indies, Kingston, writer-in-residence, 1973; CARIFESTA 76 mag., editor, 1976; Radcliffe College, Bunting Institute, Cambridge, MA, fellow, 1986-87. Recipient: Institute of Jamaica Centenary Medal, 1981, and Musgrave Medal, 1987; Commonwealth Poetry Prize, 1986; University of Michigan, Ann Arbor, visiting professor of English, 1992, 1993, 1995. **Publications:** POETRY: Tamarind Season, 1980; I Am Becoming My Mother, 1986; Heartease, 1988; Lorna Goodison, 1989; Selected Poems, 1992; To Us All Flowers Are Roses, 1995; The Book of Amber, 1995; Turn Thanks, 1999. STORIES: Baby Mother and the King of Swords, 1990; Traveling Mercies, 2001. **Address:** 8 Marley Close, Kingston 6, Jamaica.

GOODKIN, Richard E. American, b. 1953. **Genres:** Literary criticism and history, Classics, Language/Linguistics. **Career:** Yale University, New Haven, CT, assistant professor, 1980-86, associate professor, 1986-89; University of Wisconsin-Madison, associate professor, 1989-92, professor of French, 1992-. **Publications:** The Symbolist Home and the Tragic Home: Mallarme and Oedipus, 1984; Around Proust, 1991; The Tragic Middle: Racine, Aristotle, Euripides, 1991; (trans.) Antoine Campagnon, Proust between Two Centuries, 1992; Birth Marks: The Tragedy of Primogeniture in Pierre Corneille, Thomas Corneille, and Jean Racine, 2000. **Address:** Department of French and Italian, University of Wisconsin-Madison, 618 Van Hise Hall, 1220 Lincoln Drive, Madison, WI 53706, U.S.A.

GOODKIND, Terry. American, b. 1948. **Genres:** Science fiction/Fantasy. **Career:** Full-time novelist. **Publications:** NOVELS. THE SWORD OF TRUTH SERIES: Wizard's First Rule, 1994; Stone of Tears, 1995; Blood of the Fold, 1996; Temple of the Winds, 1997. **Address:** c/o Russell Galen, Scovil Chichak Galen Literary Agency Inc., 381 Park Avenue S., Ste 1020, New York, NY 10016, U.S.A.

GOODLAD, John I. American (born Canada), b. 1920. **Genres:** Education. **Career:** President, Institute for Educational Inquiry. Professor Emeritus of Education, University of Washington. Chairman, Editorial Advisory Board, New Standard Encyclopedia, 1953-. Professor of Education and Director of the University Elementary School, 1960-85, and Dean of the Graduate School of Education, 1967-83, University of California at Los Angeles. Member, Board of Editors: Child's World, 1952-75, School Review, 1956-58, and Journal of Teacher Education, 1958-60; Contributing Ed., Progressive Education, 1955-58, Educational Technology, 1970-72; Member, Editorial Board, American Educational Research Journal, 1964-66; Member, Board of Dirs., Encyclopaedia Britannica Educational Corp., 1966-93; Member, Editorial Advisory Board, Education Digest, 1968-70, and Editorial Board, Educational Forum, 1969-71. **Publications:** Planning and Organizing for Teaching, 1963; School Curriculum Reform in the United States, 1964; School, Curriculum, and the Individual, 1966; The Changing School Curriculum, 1966; The Development of a Conceptual System for Dealing with Problems of Curriculum and Instruction, 1966; The Dynamics of Educational Change, 1975; Facing the Future, 1976; What Schools Are For, 1979; A Place Called School, 1984, rev. ed., 2004; Teachers for Our Nations Schools, 1990; Educational Renewal: Better Teachers, Better Schools, 1994; In Praise of Education, 1997; Romances with Schools, 2004. CO-AUTHOR: The Elementary School, 1956; Educational Leadership and the Elementary School Principal, 1956; The Nongraded Elementary School, 1959, rev. ed., 1963; Computers and Information Systems in Education, 1966; Behind the Classroom Door, 1970, rev. ed. as Looking behind the Classroom Door, 1974; Early Schooling in England and Israel, 1973; Early Schooling in the United States, 1973; Toward a Mankind School, 1974; The Conventional and the Alternative in Education, 1975; Curriculum Inquiry, 1979; Education for Everyone, 2004. EDITOR: The Changing American School, 1966; Individual Differences and the Common Curriculum, 1983; The Ecology of School Renewal, 1987. CO-EDITOR: The Elementary School in the United States, 1973; School-University Partnerships in Action, 1988; Access to Knowledge, 1990; The Moral Dimensions of Teaching, 1990; Places Where Teachers Are Taught, 1990; Integrating General and Special Education, 1993; The Public Purpose of Education and Schooling, 1997; Developing Democratic Character in the Young, 2001; The Teaching Career, 2004. **Address:** Institute for Educational Inquiry, 124 E Edgar St, Seattle, WA 98102, U.S.A.

GOODMAN, Allegra. American. **Genres:** Novels, Novellas/Short stories. **Career:** Author. **Publications:** STORIES: Total Immersion, 1989; The Family Markowitz, 1996. NOVELS: Kaaterskill Falls, 1998; Paradise Park, 2001. Contributor to periodicals. **Address:** c/o Author Mail, Dial Press/Random House, 1745 Broadway, New York, NY 10019, U.S.A.

GOODMAN, Ellen (Holtz). American, b. 1941. **Genres:** Social commentary, Essays. **Career:** Associate Ed., Boston Globe, since 1986 (Feature Writer and Columnist, 1967-). Syndicated Columnist, Washington Post Writers Group, since 1976. Researcher and Reporter, Newsweek, NYC, 1963-65; Feature Writer, Detroit Free Press, 1965-67; Stanford University, Lorry I. Lokey Visiting Professor in Professional Journalism, 1996. Recipient of Pulitzer Prize for Commentary, 1980; Hubert H. Humphrey Civil Rights Award, 1988; National Women's Political Caucus President's Award, 1993. **Publications:** Close to Home, 1979; Turning Points, 1979; At Large, 1981; Keeping in Touch, 1985; Making Sense, 1989; Value Judgments, 1993; (with P. O'Brien) I Know Just What You Mean, 2000. **Address:** c/o Boston Globe, 135 Morrisey Blvd, Boston, MA 02107, U.S.A.

GOODMAN, Elliot R. American, b. 1923. **Genres:** Politics/Government. **Career:** Professor of Political Science, Brown University, Providence, Rhode Island, 1970- (joined faculty, 1955). Professor Emeritus. **Publications:** The Soviet Design for a World State, 1960; The Fate of the Atlantic Community, 1975. Author of scholarly journal articles. **Address:** 45 Amherst Rd, Cranston, RI 02920, U.S.A.

GOODMAN, Eric. American, b. 1953. **Genres:** Novels, Plays/Screenplays. **Career:** Associate professor of English, director of creative writing external programs, Miami University, Oxford, OH; writer. **Publications:** High on the Energy Bridge (novel), 1980; (with J.D. Snyder) Friend of the Court, 1947-1982; The Anti-Defamation League of B'nai B'rith: To Secure Justice and Fair Treatment for All (monograph), 1983; The First Time I Saw Jenny Hall (novel), 1983; In Days of Awe (novel), 1991. Contributor to periodicals. **Address:** Miami University, East High St., Oxford, OH 45056, U.S.A.

GOODMAN, James. American, b. 1956. **Genres:** History. **Career:** NYC Commission on Human Rights, NYC, assistant director of public relations, 1980-81; Daniel J. Edelman Public Relations Inc., NYC, account executive, 1981-82; Harvard University, Cambridge, MA, assistant professor of history and social studies, 1990-. Holy Roman Repertory Company, historical consultant. **Publications:** Stories of Scottsboro, 1994. Contributor of articles and reviews to periodicals. **Address:** Department of History, Rutgers University, 175 University Ave, Newark, NJ 07102, U.S.A.

GOODMAN, Jonathan. British, b. 1931. **Genres:** Novels, Plays/Screenplays, Poetry, Criminology/True Crime, History, Literary criticism and history. **Career:** Theatre dir. and television producer for companies in the UK, 1951-64; General Ed., Celebrated Trials Series, 1972-. **Publications:** Matinee Idylls (poetry), 1954; Instead of Murder (novel), 1961; Criminal Tendencies (novel), 1964; Hello Cruel World Goodbye (novel), 1964; The Killing of Julia Wallace, 1969; Bloody Versicles, 1971; Posts-Mortem, 1971; (ed.) Trial of Ian Brady and Myra Hindley, 1973; (ed.) Trial of Ruth Ellis, 1975; The Burning of Evelyn Foster, 1977; The Last Sentence (novel), 1978; The Stabbing of George Harry Storrs, 1982; The Pleasures of Murder, 1983; The Railway Murders, 1984; Who He?, 1984; The Seaside Murders, 1985; (ed.) The Crippen File, 1985; (with I. Will) Underworld, 1985; (ed.) The Christmas Murders, 1986; The Moors Murders, 1986; Acts of Murder, 1986; Murder in High Places, 1986; The Master Eccentric, 1986; The Slaying of Joseph Bowne Elwell, 1987; The Country House Murders, 1987; The Vintage Car Murders, 1988; Murder in Low Places, 1988; The Oscar Wilde File, 1988; The Lady Killers, 1989; The Art of Murder, 1990; The Passing of Starr Faithfull, 1990; The Medical Murders, 1991; The Supernatural Murders, 1992; Masterpieces of Murder, 1992; The Daily Telegraph Murder File, 1993; The Daily Telegraph Modern Murder File, 1995. **Address:** 43 Ealing Village, London W5 2LZ, England.

GOODMAN, Jordan E. American, b. 1954. **Genres:** Business/Trade/Industry, Money/Finance. **Career:** Money, NYC, Wall Street correspondent, 1979-97. Public speaker; guest on television and radio programs. **Publications:** Barron's Dictionary of Finance and Investment Terms, 1985, 6th ed., 2002; Barron's Finance and Investment Handbook, 1987, 6th ed., 2002; Barron's Dictionary of Business Terms, 1990, 2nd ed., 1995; (co-author) Everyone's Money Book, 1993, rev. ed., 6 vols., 2002; Reading between the Lies: How to Detect Fraud and Avoid Becoming a Victim of Wall Street's Next Scandal, 2003. **Address:** 84 Walworth Ave, Scarsdale, NY 10583, U.S.A. **Online address:** jordan.goodman@verizon.net

GOODMAN, Lizbeth (L.). American, b. 1964. **Genres:** Plays/Screenplays, Literary criticism and history, Women's studies and issues. **Career:** Open University, Milton Keynes, England, lecturer in literature, 1990-98; London Institute, College of Art and Design, SMARTlab Centre, director of Institute for New Media Performance Research, 1998-, director of Site Specific Media Arts, 2001-. Harvard University, visiting scholar at Radcliffe College, 1994-95; University of British Columbia, visiting fellow at Centre for Women's Studies and Gender Relations, 1995; Banff Centre for New Media and the Arts, visiting senior artist, 2000-02. **Publications:** Sexuality in Performance, 2000. EDITOR: (and author of intro.) Gender, Politics and Performance in South African Theatre Today, 3 vols., 1999; (and author of intro.) Feminist Stages, 1996; (and author of intro) Mythic Women/Real Women, 1999; The Routledge Reader in Gender and Performance, 1998; (with J. de Gay) The Routledge Reader in Politics and Performance, 2000; (with others) Voice of Theatre Shaped by Women, 2002. Work represented in anthologies. Contributor of articles and poems to journals. **Address:** SMARTlab Centre, Central Saint Martins, College of Art & Design, London Institute, Southampton Row, London WC1B 4AP, England. **Online address:** l.goodman@csm.linst.ac.uk

GOODMAN, Louis W. American, b. 1942. **Genres:** Sociology, International relations/Current affairs. **Career:** Assistant Professor of Sociology, Yale University, New Haven, Conn., 1969-74; Staff Associate, Social Science Research Council, NYC, 1974-78; Lecturer, Yale University, 1978-81; Director, Woodrow Wilson Center, 1981-86; Dean & Professor, American University, 1986-. **Publications:** The Structure of Human Society, 1975; The Alien Doctors, 1978; Small Nations and Giant Firms, 1987; The Military & Democracy, 1990; Political Parties & Democracy in Central America, 1992; Lessons from the Venezuelan Experience, 1995; International Relations Education at the Eve of the 21st Century, 1996. EDITOR: Selected Studies in Marriage and the Family, 1968; Workers and Managers in Latin America, 1973; (co-) Multi-National Corporations and Development, 1976. **Address:** The American University, School of International Service, 4400 Massachusetts Ave., NW, Washington, DC 20016-8071, U.S.A.

GOODMAN, Martin (David). British, b. 1953. **Genres:** History. **Career:** Birmingham University, lecturer in ancient history, 1977-86; Oxford University, St. Cross College, senior research fellow, 1986-91; Oxford Centre for Hebrew and Jewish Studies, fellow, 1986-; Oxford University, Wolfson College, fellow, 1991-, professor of Jewish studies, 1996-. **Publications:** State and Society in Roman Galilee, A.D. 132-212, 1983; The Ruling Class of Judaea: The Origins of the Jewish Revolt against Rome, A.D. 66-70, 1987; Mission and Conversion: Proselytizing in the Religious History of the Roman Empire, 1994; (with J. Sherwood) The Roman World, 44 B.C.-A.D. 180, 1997. EDITOR: (with G. Vermes) The Essenes according to the Classical Sources, 1989; Jews in a Graeco-Roman World, 1998; (with M.J. Edwards and S.R.F. Price) Apologetics in the Roman Empire: Pagans, Jews, and Christians, 1999; The Oxford Handbook of Jewish Studies, 2002. **Address:** Oriental Institute, Pusey Lane, Oxford OX1 2LE, England.

GOODMAN, Melvin A. American, b. 1938. **Genres:** International relations/Current affairs, Third World, Politics/Government. **Career:** Affiliated with Central Intelligence Agency (CIA), Washington, DC, 1966-86; National War College, Washington, DC, professor of national security, 1986-. **Publications:** Gorbachev's Retreat, 1991; The End of Superpower Competition in the Third World, 1992; Shevardnadze and the End of the Cold War, 1997; Lessons of the Cold War, 1999. Contributor to periodicals. **Address:** Department of National Security, National War College, Washington, DC 20319, U.S.A. **Online address:** goodmanm@ndu.edu

GOODMAN, Richard. American, b. 1945. **Genres:** Food and Wine, Horticulture, Travel/Exploration, Autobiography/Memoirs, Essays. **Career:** Writer. **Publications:** French Dirt: The Story of a Garden in the South of France, 1991, rev. ed., 2002. **Address:** c/o Darhansoff and Verrill Literary, 236 W 26th St Rm 802, New York, NY 10001-6736, U.S.A. **Online address:** RichGood711@earthlink.net

GOODMAN, Susan. American, b. 1951. **Genres:** History, Literary criticism and history, Women's studies and issues. **Career:** Public school teacher, 1972-83, including English teacher, high school reading specialist, and coordinator of English as a second language; California State University, Fresno, professor of English, 1990-94; University of Delaware, Newark, professor of English, 1994-. **Publications:** Edith Wharton's Women: Friends and Rivals, 1990; Edith Wharton's Inner Circle, 1994; Ellen Glasgow: A Biography, 1998; Civil Wars: American Novelists and Manners, 1880-1940, 2002. EDITOR: (with D. Ryot) Femmes de Conscience: Aspects du Feminisme Americain, 1848-1875, 1994; (with C. Colquitt and C. Ward) Edith Wharton: A Forward Glance, 1999.

GOODSON, Larry P. American. **Genres:** Area studies, Politics/Government. **Career:** Bentley College, Waltham, MA, associate professor of international studies, 2001-. Previously taught at University of the South, American University (Cairo, Egypt), Campbell University, University of North Carolina, Greensboro, and University of North Carolina, Chapel Hill. **Publications:** Afghanistan's Endless War: State Failure, Regional Politics, and the Rise of the Taliban, 2001. Contributor of articles and reviews to periodicals. **Address:** Bentley College, Department of International Studies, 175 Forest St., Waltham, MA 02452, U.S.A.

GOODSTEIN, Phil. American, b. 1952. **Genres:** Area studies. **Career:** History professor at a university in Denver, CO; Colorado Free University, Denver, tour guide; also affiliated with New Social Publications, Denver. Naysayer, monthly newsletter, editor. **Publications:** Exploring Jewish Colorado, 1992; The Seamy Side of Denver, 1993; Denver Streets, 1994; Murders in the Bank Vault (nonfiction), 1998; Ghosts of Denver, 1996; Denver in Our Time, 1999; DIA & Other Scams, 2000; Denver from the Bottom, Up, 2003. **Address:** 1330 Monroe St, Denver, CO 80206, U.S.A.

GOODWIN, Doris (Helen) Kearns. Also writes as Doris Helen Kearns. American, b. 1943. **Genres:** Novels, History, Autobiography/Memoirs. **Career:** History educator, writer. Harvard University, asst. professor, 1969-71; assoc. professor, 1972; spl. asst. to President Lyndon B. Johnson, 1968; spl. asst. to Willard Wirtz, U.S. Dept. Labor, DC, 1967; rsch. assoc., U.S. Dept. Health, Edn., and Welfare, DC, 1966; intern, Ho. of Reps., DC, 1965; intern, Dept. State, DC, 1963-. Career-Related: spl. cons. to President Johnson, 1969-73; asst. dir. Inst. Politics, 1971-; hostess "What's the Big Idea", WGBH-TV, Boston, 1972; polit. analyst news desk, WBZ-TV, Boston, 1972. **Publications:** (as Doris Kearns) Lyndon Johnson and the American Dream, 1976; The Fitzgeralds and the Kennedys: An American Saga, 1987; Mortal Friends: A Novel, 1992; No Ordinary Time: Franklin and Eleanor Roosevelt-The Homefront in World War II, 1994 (Pulitzer Prize for history 1995); Wait til Next Year: A Memoir, 1997. Contributor to books. **Address:** PO Box 477, Rockport, ME 04856-0477, U.S.A.

GOODWIN, Frederick K(ing). American, b. 1936. **Genres:** Medicine/Health, Psychology. **Career:** National Heart Institute, Laboratory of Clinical Biochemistry, research assistant, summers, 1960-62, special research fellow, 1967-68; State University of New York Upstate Medical Center, Syracuse, intern in medicine and psychiatry, 1963-64; University of North Carolina at Chapel Hill, resident in psychiatry, 1964-65; National Institute of Mental Health, clinical associate of Adult Psychiatry Branch, 1965-67, chief of clinical research unit at Laboratory of Clinical Science, 1968-73, chief of Section of Psychiatry, 1973-77, chief of Clinical Psychobiology Branch, 1977-81, director of Intramural Research Program, 1982-88, scientific director of National Depression Awareness, Recognition, and Treatment Program, 1985, director of the institute, 1992-94, senior scientific adviser to the director, 1994-; private practice of psychiatry and psychopharmacology, 1967-. Washington School of Psychiatry, fellow, 1969-71, faculty member, 1970-82; George Washington University, adjunct professor, 1972-82, professor of psychiatry and director of Center on Neuroscience, Behavior, and Society, 1994-; Uniformed Services University of the Health Sciences, adjunct professor, 1980-. U.S. Alcohol, Drug Abuse, and Mental Health Administration, coordinator of AIDS-related activities, 1986-90, administrator, 1988-92; visiting professor and lecturer at US colleges and universities. **Publications:** (with K.R. Jamison) Manic-Depressive Illness, 1990. Contributor to scientific and medical journals. **Address:** Department of Psychiatry, Center on Neuroscience, George Washington Medical Center, 2150 Pennsylvania Ave NW 8th Fl, Washington, DC 20037, U.S.A.

GOODWIN, Jan. British/American, b. 1944. **Genres:** Documentaries/Reportage. **Career:** Journalist. Women's Realm, London, England, diary and features editor; London News Service, England, news editor; Us, NYC, executive editor; Ladies' Home Journal, NYC, executive editor, 1978-88; Save the Children Federation, Pakistan/Afghanistan, program manager, 1988-

91; writer. Worked as a foreign correspondent for newspapers and as a reporter for BBC Radio in London. Participant in Public Broadcasting Service (PBS) documentary on Afghan war; guest on television and radio shows; guest lecturer on human rights issues; participant in president's Conflict Resolution Conference, 1991, and the Religion and Human Rights Conference, 1994. **Publications:** Caught in the Crossfire (nonfiction), 1987; Price of Honor: Muslim Women Lift the Veil of Silence on the Islamic World, 1994; Defending Our Daughters (documentary), 1998. Contributor to periodicals. **Address:** c/o Stedman, Mays, Clausen, 249 W 34th St Rm 605, New York, NY 10001-2815, U.S.A.

GOODWIN, Joanne L. American, b. 1949. **Genres:** History. **Career:** University of Nevada, Las Vegas, assistant professor of history, 1991-. **Publications:** Gender and the Politics of Welfare Reform: Mothers' Pensions in Chicago, 1911-1929, 1997. **Address:** University of Nevada, 4505 South Maryland Pkwy., Las Vegas, NV 89154-9900, U.S.A.

GOODWIN, Ken(neth Leslie). Australian, b. 1934. **Genres:** Literary criticism and history. **Career:** Teachers' College, Wagga Wagga, Australia, lecturer in English, 1958; University of Queensland, St. Lucia, lecturer, 1959-67, senior lecturer, 1967-69, reader, 1970-71, professor of English, 1971-92, head of department, 1974-79, 1992; University of Southern Queensland, deputy vice-chancellor, 1992-98; University of Sydney, honorary professor of English, 19992001; University of New England, adjunct professor, 2001-. University of California, Berkeley, visiting lecturer, 1967; Kelvin Grove College of Advanced Education, council member, 1971-82; Canada-Australia Literary Award, chairman of assessors, 1982; Queensland Board of Advanced Education, chairman of education committee, 1983-89; Queensland Art Gallery, trustee, 1983-95, deputy chair, 1990-95. Order of Australia, 1997. **Publications:** The Influence of Ezra Pound, 1966; An Approach to Modern Poetry, 1968; Understanding African Poetry: A Study of Ten Poets, 1982; Selected Poems of Bruce Dawe, 1984; A Preliminary Handlist of Manuscripts and Documents of William Morris, 1984; A History of Australian Literature, 1986; Adjacent Worlds: A Literary Life of Bruce Dawe, 1988. EDITOR: National Identity, 1970; Commonwealth Literature in the Curriculum, 1980; (with M. Freer) A Common Wealth of Words, 1982; (with A. Lawson) The Macmillan Anthology of Australian Literature, 1990; Bruce Dawe: Essays and Addresses, 1990; (with W. Zach) Nationalism vs. Internationalism, 1996. **Address:** 2 Stewart Crescent, Armidale, NSW 2350, Australia. **Online address:** ken_ness.goodwin@bigpond.com

GOODWIN, Michael. American, b. 1949. **Genres:** Biography. **Career:** New York Times, NYC, clerk, 1972-77, reporter, 1978-, later City Hall bureau chief; writer. **Publications:** (with Arthur Browne and Dan Collins) I, Koch: A Decidedly Unauthorized Biography of the Mayor of NYC, Edward I. Koch, Dodd, 1985; (with Naomi Wise) On the Edge: The Life and Times of Francis Coppola, Morrow, 1989. Affiliated with New York Times magazine. **Address:** c/o Betty Marks, 176 E. 77th St., New York, NY 10022, U.S.A.

GOODWIN, Neil. American, b. 1940. **Genres:** Adult non-fiction. **Career:** Architect, writer, and filmmaker. Stephenson, Gibney Architects, Dublin, Ireland, architect; F.A. Stahl and Associates, Boston, MA, architect, 1964-72; Peace River Films, Cambridge, MA, president and filmmaker/producer, 1972-. Has produced and directed films. **Publications:** The Apache Diaries, 1999. Has produced, directed, and written many films for PBS television series' The American Experience, NOVA, and Smithsonian World. Contributor to 3-2-1 Contact series and author of five short films for Children's Television Workshop. **Address:** 71 Washington Ave., Cambridge, MA 02140, U.S.A. **Online address:** neil@prfi.com

GOODWIN, Suzanne. Also writes as Suzanne Ebel, Cecily Shelbourne. British, b. 1916. **Genres:** Romance/Historical, Travel/Exploration. **Career:** Journalist; Advertising director; Novelist. **Publications:** NOVELS: The Winter Spring, 1978; The Winter Sisters, 1980; Emerald, 1980; Floodtide, 1983; Sisters, 1985; Cousins, 1986; Daughters, 1987; Lovers, 1988; Reflections in a Lake, 1989; To Love a Hero, 1989; A Change of Season, 1991; The Rising Storm, 1992; While the Music Lasts, 1993; The Difference, 1994; Sheer Chance, 1996; French Leave, 2001. AS SUZANNE EBEL: Love, the Magician, 1956; Journey from Yesterday, 1963; The Half-Enchanted, 1964; The Love Campaign, 1965; The Dangerous Winter, 1965; A Perfect Stranger, 1966; A Name in Lights, 1968; A Most Auspicious Star, 1968; Somersault, 1971; Portrait of Jill, 1972; Dear Kate, 1972; To Seek a Star, 1973; The Family Feeling, 1973; (with D. Impey) Explore the Cotswolds by Bicycle (non-fiction), 1973; Girl by the Sea, 1974; Music in Winter, 1975; (with D. Impey) London's Riverside, from Hampton Court in the West to Greenwich Palace in the East, 1975, as A Guide to London's Riverside, 1985; A Grove

of Olives, 1976; River Voices, 1976; The Double Rainbow, 1977; A Rose in Heather, 1978; Julia's Sister, 1982; The Provencal Summer, 1982; House of Nightingales, 1986; The Clover Field, 1987. AS CECILY SHELBOURNE: Stage of Love, 1978. **Address:** 52A Digby Mansions, Hammersmith Bridge Rd, London W6 9DF, England.

GOODWIN, Trevor W(alworth). British, b. 1916. **Genres:** Biology, Chemistry. **Career:** Johnston Professor Emeritus of Biochemistry, University of Liverpool, 1983- (Johnston Professor, 1966-83). Ed., Phytochemistry, Protoplasma, and Photosynthetica. Former Professor of Biochemistry, University College of Wales, Aberystwyth. **Publications:** Biochemistry of Carotenoids, 1954, 3rd ed., 1983; Recent Advances in Biochemistry, 1959; Biosynthesis of Vitamins, 1963; (co-author) Introduction to Plant Biochemistry, 1972, 2nd ed., 1982. EDITOR: Chemistry and Biochemistry of Plant Pigments, 1965, 3rd ed., 1987; Biochemistry of Chloroplasts, 2 vols.; Aspects of Insect Biochemistry; Instrumentation in Biochemistry; Metabolic Rates of Citrate; British Biochemistry Past and Present; (co-) Biological Structure and Function: History of the Biochemical Society 1911-1986, 1987; (subject) Oxford Dictionary of Biochemistry and Molecular Biology, 1997, 2nd ed., 2000. **Address:** Monzar, 9 Woodlands Close, Parkgate, Neston, Cheshire CH64 6RU, England. **Online address:** goodwinbiochemistry@bushinternet.com

GOODY, John R(ankine). British, b. 1919. **Genres:** Anthropology/Ethnology, History, Social sciences. **Career:** Fellow, St. John's College, Cambridge, 1960- (Assistant Lecturer, 1954-59, Lecturer, 1959-71, Director of the African Studies Centre, 1966-73, Smuts Reader in Commonwealth Studies, 1972, and William Wyse Professor of Social Anthropology, 1973-84, Cambridge University). **Publications:** The Social Organisation of the LoWiili, 1956; Death, Property, and the Ancestors, 1962; (with J.A. Braimah) Salaga: The Struggle for Power, 1967; Comparative Studies in Kinship, 1969; Technology, Tradition, and the State in Africa, 1971; The Myth of the Bagre, 1972; (with S.J. Tambiah) Bridewealth and Dowry, 1973; Production and Reproduction, 1977; The Domestication of the Savage Mind, 1977; (with J.W.D.K. Gandah) Une Recitation du Bagre, 1981; Cooking, Cuisine, and Class, 1982; The Development of the Family and Marriage in Europe, 1983; The Logic of Writing and the Organization of Society, 1986; The Interface between the Oral and the Written, 1987; The Oriental, the Ancient and the Primitive, 1989; The Culture of Flowers, 1993; The East in the West, 1996; The Expansive Moment, 1996; Jack Goody: L'Homme, l'ecriture et la mort, 1996; Representations and Contradictions, 1997; Food and Love, 1998; The European Family, 2000; The Power of the Written Word, 2000; A Myth Revisited, 2003; Ideas in Europe, 2003. EDITOR: The Developmental Cycle in Domestic Groups, 1958; Succession to High Office, 1966; Literacy in Traditional Societies, 1968; The Character of Kinship, 1973; Changing Social Structure in Ghana, 1975. **Address:** St. John's College, Cambridge CB2 1TP, England.

GOODY-JONES. *See* **JANKO, (Kathleen) Susan.**

GOONETILLEKE, D(evapriya) C(hitra) R(anjan) A(lwis). Sri Lankan, b. 1938. **Genres:** Literary criticism and history, Novellas/Short stories. **Career:** University of Ceylon, Peradeniya, temporary assistant lecturer in English, 1961-62; Vidyodaya University, Nugegoda, Ceylon (now Sri Lanka), assistant lecturer in English, 1962-70; University of Sri Lanka, Vidyodaya Campus (now University of Jayawardenapura), lecturer in English, 1970-73; University of Kelaniya, Sri Lanka, lecturer, 1973-74, senior lecturer, 1974-79, associate professor, 1979-80, professor of English, 1980-, head of department, 1978-87, 1989-95, 2001-. **Publications:** Introducing English Literature, Vol. I: First Steps to Literary Criticism, 1975, Vol. II: A Study of Fiction, 1976, Vol. III: A Study of Poetry, 1977; Developing Countries in British Fiction, 1977; (ed. and author of intro.) Modern Sri Lankan Stories: An Anthology, 1986; Between Cultures: Essays on Literature, Language, and Education, 1987; (ed. and author of intro.) Modern Sri Lankan Poetry: An Anthology, 1987; Images of the Raj: South Asia in the Literature of the Empire, 1988; (with M. Gooneratne and M. Jayawardena) Learning English: Book I, 1988; Joseph Conrad: Beyond Culture and Background, 1990; (ed. and author of intro.) The Penguin New Writing in Sri Lanka, 1992; (ed.) Joseph Conrad: Heart of Darkness, 1995, 2nd ed., 1999; (ed. and author of intro.) The Penguin Book of Modern Sri Lankan Stories, 1996; Salman Rushdie, 1998; (ed. and author of intro.) Sri Lankan Literature in English 1948-1998: A 50th Independence Anniversary Anthology, 1998; (ed. and author of intro.) Perspectives on PostColonial Literature, 2001. **Address:** Department of English, University of Kelaniya, Kelaniya, Sri Lanka. **Online address:** dcragoonetilleke@sdtnet.lk

GOOSSEN, Rachel Waltner. American, b. 1960. **Genres:** History. **Career:** Bethel College, North Newton, KS, instructor in history, 1984-85; freelance writer, 1985-87; Bethel College, instructor in history, 1987; University of Kansas, Lawrence, assistant instructor, 1988-92, instructor in history, 1992-94; Goshen College, Goshen, IN, assistant professor of history and head of department, 1995-. **Publications:** Brick and Mortar: A History of Newton, Kansas, 1984; (with R. Kreider) Hungry, Thirsty, a Stranger: The Mennonite Central Committee Story, 1988; (with Kreider) When Good People Quarrel: Studies of Conflict Resolution, 1989; (with W. Young) History of the United States through the Civil War: A Study Guide, revised edition, 1994; Women against the Good War: Conscientious Objection and Gender on the American Home Front, 1941-1947, 1997. **Address:** Department of History, Goshen College, Goshen, IN 46526, U.S.A. **Online address:** rachelwg@goshen.edu

GOOTENBERG, Paul. Also writes as Dr. Guano. American, b. 1954. **Genres:** History. **Career:** Brandeis University, Waltham, MA, assistant professor of history, 1987-90; State University of New York at Stony Brook, professor of Latin American and economic history, 1990-. **Publications:** Between Silver and Guano: Commercial Policy and the State in Postindependence Peru, 1989; Corazones y mentes: Tejidos y Harinas, 1989; Imagining Development: Economic Ideas in Peru's "Fictitious Prosperity" of Guano, 1840-1880, 1993; Cocaine: Global Histories, 1999. Some writings appear under the pseudonym Dr. Guano. **Address:** Department of History, State University of New York at Stony Brook, Stony Brook, NY 11794, U.S.A. **Online address:** gootenb@attglobal.net

GOPAL, Sarvepalli. *See* Obituaries.

GOPIAH. *See* **KEYS, Kerry Shawn.**

GORDIEVSKY, Oleg. British (born Russia), b. 1938. **Genres:** International relations/Current affairs, Politics/Government. **Career:** KGB, member of first chief directorate (KGB's foreign intelligence service), 1962-85, deputy head of station in Copenhagen, Denmark, 1975-78, deputy head of station in London, England, 1982-85; writer. Lecturer on Russian affairs. **Publications:** Next Stop Execution, 1995; (with I. Rogatchi) Blind Mirror, 1998; (with J. Andersen) De Rode Spioner, 2002. WITH CHRISTOPHER ANDREW: KGB: The Inside Story, 1990; Instructions from the Centre, 1991; More Instructions from the Centre, 1992. **Address:** c/o William Hamilton, 79 St. Martin's Lane, London WC2N 4AA, England. **Online address:** navole1@aol.com

GORDIMER, Nadine. South African, b. 1923. **Genres:** Novels, Novellas/Short stories, Literary criticism and history. **Career:** Recipient, Nobel Prize in Literature, 1991. **Publications:** NOVELS: The Lying Days, 1953; A World of Strangers, 1958; Occasion for Loving, 1963; The Late Bourgeois World, 1966; A Guest of Honour, 1970; The Conservationist, 1974; Burger's Daughter, 1979; July's People, 1981; A Sport of Nature, 1987; My Son's Story, 1990; None to Accompany Me, 1994; Harald, Claudia and their son, Duncan, 1996; The House Gun, 1998; The Pickup, 2001. SHORT STORIES: Face to Face: Short Stories, 1949; The Soft Voice of the Serpent and Other Stories, 1952; Six Feet of the Country, 1956, 1982; Friday's Footprint and Other Stories, 1960; Not for Publication and Other Stories, 1965; Livingstone's Companions: Stories, 1971; Selected Stories, 1975; Some Monday for Sure, 1976; A Soldier's Embrace, 1980; Town and Country Lovers, 1980; Something Out There, 1984; Reflections of South Africa: Short Stories, 1986; Crimes of Conscience: Selected Short Stories, 1991; Jump and Other Stories, 1991; Why Haven't You Written?: Selected Stories, 1950-1972, 1993; Loot, 2003. TELEVISION PLAYS AND DOCUMENTARIES: A Terrible Chemistry, 1981; (with H. Cassirer) Choosing for Justice: Allan Boesak, 1985; Country Lovers, A Chip of Glass Ruby, Praise, and Oral History, all part of The Gordimer Stories series adapted from stories of the same title, 1985. OTHER: (comp and ed. with L. Abrahams) South African Writing Today, 1967; African Literature: The Lectures Given on This Theme at the University of Cape Town's Public Summer School, February, 1972, 1972; The Black Interpreters: Notes on African Writing, 1973; On the Mines, 1973; (with others) What Happened to Burger's Daughter; or, How South African Censorship Works, 1980; Lifetimes under Apartheid, 1986; The Essential Gesture: Writing, Politics and Places, 1988; Three in a Bed: Fiction, Morals, and Politics, 1991; Writing and Being: The Charles Eliot Norton Lectures, 1995; Living in Hope & History: Notes from Our Century (essays), 1999. Contributor to periodicals.

GORDON, Andrew D. American, b. 1952. **Genres:** History, Area studies. **Career:** Harvard University, assistant professor, 1981-87, associate professor, 1987-91, professor of history, 1995-, director of Edwin O. Reischauer Institute of Japanese Studies, 1998-; Duke University, Durham, NC, professor of history, 1991-95. Member, Joint Committee on Japanese Studies of the Social Science Research Council. **Publications:** The Evolution of Labor

Relations in Japan: Heavy Industry, 1853-1955, 1985; Labor and Imperial Democracy in Prewar Japan, 1991; The Wages of Affluence: Labor and Management in Postwar Japan, 1998; A Modern History of Japan: From Tokugawa Times to Present, 2002. EDITOR: Postwar Japan as History, 1993; (and trans. with M. Hane) Kumazawa Makoto, Portraits of the Japanese Workplace, 1996; (and trans with T. Boardman) Nimura Kazuo, The Ashio Riot of 1907, 1997; (co-) Historical Perspectives on Contemporary East Asia, 2000; coeditor of a series of books on comparative and international labor history. Contributor to books about Japanese life, politics, and history. **Address:** Reischauer Institute, Coolidge Hall 319, 1737 Cambridge Street, Cambridge, MA 02138, U.S.A. **Online address:** agordon@fas.harvard.edu

GORDON, April A. American, b. 1947. **Genres:** Sociology. **Career:** Coker College, Hartsville, SC, assistant professor to associate professor of sociology, 1976-87; Winthrop University, Rock Hill, SC, assistant professor to professor of sociology, 1987-, coordinator of women's studies. University of Evansville, Igle Heart Public Affairs Lecturer, 1992. **Publications:** Soviet Family Policy: 1944 to the Present, 1979; Understanding Contemporary Africa, 1992; Transforming Capitalism and Patriarchy: Gender and Development in Africa, 1996. **Address:** Department of Sociology, Winthrop University, Rock Hill, SC 29733, U.S.A.

GORDON, Colin. Canadian, b. 1962. **Genres:** History. **Career:** University of British Columbia, Vancouver, assistant professor of history, 1990-94; University of Iowa, Iowa City, assistant professor of history, 1994-. **Publications:** New Deals, 1994. **Address:** Department of History, University of Iowa, Iowa City, IA 52242, U.S.A.

GORDON, Deborah Hannes. Also writes as Brooke Hastings. American, b. 1946. **Genres:** Mystery/Crime/Suspense, Romance/Historical, Education. **Career:** Research asst., Columbia University, NYC, 1968-70; Secretary, The Huron Institute and Working Papers magazine, Cambridge, MA, 1971-73; Researcher and Writer, CARD Consultants, Sacramento, CA, 1979. **Publications:** AS BROOKE HASTINGS: Desert Fire, 1980; Playing for Keeps, 1980; Rough Diamond, 1982; Innocent Fire, 1980; Island Conquest, 1981; Winner Take All, 1981; A Matter of Time, 1982; Intimate Strangers, 1982; An Act of Love, 1983; Interested Parties, 1984; Reasonable Doubts, 1984; Tell Me No Lies, 1984; Hard to Handle, 1985; As Time Goes By, 1986; Double Jeopardy, 1986; Forward Pass, 1986; Too Close for Comfort, 1987; Forbidden Fruit, 1987; Both Sides Now, 1988; Catch a Falling Star, 1988; So Sweet a Sin, 1989; Reluctant Mistress, 1990; Seduction, 1990. AS DEBORAH GORDON. FICTION: Beating the Odds, 1992; Runaway Bride, 1994; Runaway Time, 1995; Runaway Magic, 1996. NON-FICTION: (with L. Ramer) How to Help Students with AD/HD Succeed in School and in Life (non-fiction), 2001.

GORDON, Donald. *See* **PAYNE, Donald Gordon.**

GORDON, Eric A(rthur). American, b. 1945. **Genres:** Literary criticism and history, Music, Biography. **Career:** Manchester Community College, Manchester, CT, instructor in history, 1972-75; Hartford Advocate, Hartford, CT, writer, 1975-80; Sephardic Home for the Aged, Brooklyn, NY, editor, 1982-84; G. Schirmer (music publisher), New York City, publicity manager, 1984-86; Social and Public Art Resource Center, Venice, CA, director of public information, 1990-93; Workmen's Circle/Arbeter Ring, Southern California District, director, 1995-; writer. Founder and treasurer of the Peoples' Voice Cafe, New York City; secretary of Friends of Earl Robinson. **Publications:** Mark the Music: The Life and Work of Marc Blitzstein, 1989; (with E. Robinson) Ballad of an American: The Autobiography of Earl Robinson, 1998. **Address:** 9514 National Blvd, Los Angeles, CA 90034-2820, U.S.A. **Online address:** EricArthur@aol.com

GORDON, Frances. *See* **WOOD, Bridget.**

GORDON, Graeme. British, b. 1966. **Genres:** Plays/Screenplays. **Career:** Has as laundry assistant, bartender, door to door sales, market research interviewer, chat line monitor, library assistant, factory worker, photocopy clerk, message desk clerk, mailroom clerk, filing clerk, and data entry clerk. Actor, writer, and producer of video films and television pilots, c. 1988-. Cofounder of the Feline Partnership (video production company), 1990s; member of the London Film Makers Co-operative in 1990. Has appeared in plays and television pilots. **Publications:** Bayswater Bodycount, 1995; Traitors (stage play), 1996; In Too Deep (screenplay), 1996; Barking Mad (crime novel), 1997. Contributor of short stories to periodicals. **Address:** c/o Author Mail, Serpents Tail, 4 Blackstock Mew, London N4 2BT, England.

GORDON, Haim. Israeli, b. 1936. **Genres:** Literary criticism and history, Philosophy. **Career:** Ben-Gurion University of the Negev, Beer Sheva,

Israel, lecturer, 197581, senior lecturer, 1981-92, associate professor, 1992-98, professor of education, 1998-. Visiting professor at universities worldwide. **Publications:** (with J. Bloch) Martin Buber: A Centenary Volume, Hebrew ed., 1981, English trans., 1984; Dance, Dialogue, and Despair, 1986; The Other Martin Buber, 1988; Make Room for Dreams, 1989; Naguib Mahfouz's Egypt, 1990; (with R. Gordon) Sartre and Evil: Guidelines for a Struggle, 1995; Quicksand: Israel, the Intifada, and the Rise of Political Evil in Democracies, 1995; Fighting Evil: Unsung Heroes in the Novels of Graham Greene, 1997; Looking Back at the June, 1967 War, 1999; Dwelling Poetically, 2000; The Heidegger-Buber Controversy, 2001; (with R. Gordon) Sartre's Philosophy and the Challenge of Education, 2001; (with R. Gordon) Sophistry and 20th Century Art, 2002; (with R. Gordon and T. Shriteh) Beyond Intifada, 2003; Heroism and Friendship in the Novels of Erich Maria Remarque, 2003. FORTHCOMING: (with S. Tamari) Maurice Merleau Ponty's Phenomenology of Perception; (with R. Gordon) Heidegger on Truth and Myth. EDITOR: (with L. Grob, and contrib.) Education for Peace, 1987; (with Grob and R. Hassan, and contrib.) Women's and Men's Liberation: Testimonies of Spirit, 1991; (with R. Gordon, and contrib.) Israel/Palestine: The Quest for Dialogue, 1991; (and author of preface) Jochanan Bloch: Jews and Judaism-A Political Philosophy (in Hebrew), 1998; (ed. in chief and author of intro.) Dictionary of Existentialism, 1999. Contributor to books. Contributor of articles and reviews to scholarly journals. **Address:** Dept of Education, Ben-Gurion University of the Negev, PO Box 653, 94105 Beer-Sheva, Israel.

GORDON, Jacob U. American (born Nigeria), b. 1939. **Genres:** History, Cultural/Ethnic topics. **Career:** Albany State University, Albany, GA, associate professor of history and political science and department head, 1967-70; University of Kansas, Lawrence, professor of African and African American studies, 1970-, courtesy professor of American studies, executive director of Center for Black Leadership Development and Research, 1986-, research fellow of Schiefelbusch Institute for Life Span Studies, 1989-. Leavenworth Prison, lecturer, 1975-85; University of Missouri-Kansas City, visiting professor, 1984. **Publications:** (with J. Rosser) The Black Studies Debate, 1974; African Studies at Kansas, 1977; Multiculturalism in Alcohol and Other Drug Abuse Services, 1992; The Role of Higher Education in Alcohol and Other Drug Abuse Prevention, 1993; Narratives of African Americans in Kansas, 1870-1992: Beyond the Exodus Movement, 1993; Managing Multiculturalism in Substance Abuse Services, 1994; (with R. Majors) The American Black Male: His Present Status and His Future, 1994; (with E. Freeman and J. Lee) Supplemental Readings for Training in Multicultural Substance Abuse: Continuum of Care for the 21st Century, 1994; (with E.C. Jackson) A History of the National Bar Association, 1999; Black Leadership for Social Change, 2000. Contributor to books. Contributor to academic journals. **Address:** 1028 Dole Human Development Center, University of Kansas, Lawrence, KS 66045, U.S.A.

GORDON, Jaimy. American, b. 1944. **Genres:** Novels, Novellas/Short stories, Essays, Translations. **Career:** Rhode Island State Council on the Arts, writer in residence, 1975-77; Stephens College, Columbia, MO, director of creative writing program, 1980-81; Western Michigan University, Kalamazoo, assistant professor, 1981-87, associate professor, 1987-92, professor of English, 1992-; writer. **Publications:** NOVELS: Shamp of the City-Solo, 1974; She Drove without Stopping, 1990; Bogeywoman, 1999. OTHER: The Bend, the Lip, the Kid (narrative poem), 1978; Circumspections from an Equestrian Statue (novella), 1979; (trans. with P. Blickle) M. Beig, Lost Weddings (novel), 1990. **Address:** Department of English, Western Michigan University, Kalamazoo, MI 49008, U.S.A. **Online address:** gordonj@wmich.edu

GORDON, James S(amuel). American, b. 1941. **Genres:** Medicine/Health. **Career:** Albert Einstein College of Medicine, NYC, resident and chief resident psychiatrist, 1968-71; National Institutes for Mental Health, resident psychiatrist, 1971-82; Georgetown University, Washington, DC, clinical professor of psychiatry, 1980-; writer. Visiting professor at Catholic University of America, 1974-75; director of special studies and alternative services for President's Committee on Mental Health, 1978-79. **Publications:** Caring for Youth: Essays on Alternative Services, 1978; (ed. with A.C. Hastings and J. Fadiman) Health for the Whole Person: The Complete Guide to Holistic Medicine, 1980; (ed. with M. Beyer) Reaching Troubled Youth: Runaways and Community Mental Health, 1981; (ed. with D.T. Jaffe and D.E. Bresler) Mind, Body, and Health: Toward an Integral Medicine, 1984; The Golden Guru: The Strange Journey of Bhagwan Shree Rajneesh, 1987; Holistic Medicine, 1988; Stress Management, 1990; Manifesto for a New Medicine: Your Guide to Healing Partnerships and the Wise Use of Alternative Therapies, 1996. **Address:** 3733 Oliver St. NW, Washington, DC 20015, U.S.A.

GORDON, John (William). British, b. 1925. **Genres:** Horror, Science fiction/Fantasy, Children's fiction, Young adult fiction, Autobiography/Memoirs. **Publications:** The Giant under the Snow, 1968; The House on the Brink, 1970; The Ghost on the Hill, 1976; The Waterfall Box, 1978; The Spitfire Grave, 1979; The Edge of the World, 1983; Catch Your Death, 1984; The Quelling Eye, 1986; The Grasshopper, 1987; Ride the Wind, 1989; Secret Corridor, 1990; Ordinary Seaman (autobiography), 1992; Blood Brothers, 1991; The Burning Baby and Other Ghosts, 1992; Gilray's Ghost, 1995; The Flesh Eater, 1998; The Midwinter Watch, 1998; Skinners, 1999; The Ghosts of Blacklode, 2002. **Address:** 99 George Borrow Rd, Norwich, Norfolk NR4 7HU, England.

GORDON, Lewis Ricardo. Also writes as Nikki Del Rio. Jamaican, b. 1962. **Genres:** Philosophy. **Career:** Lehman High School, Bronx, NY, social studies teacher, 1985-89, Second Chance Program founder and coordinator, 1987-89; Yale University, New Haven, CT, teaching fellow in philosophy and classics, 1990-93; University of Hartford, West Hartford, CT, adjunct professor of philosophy, 1992; Lehman College, City University of New York, Bronx, adjunct assistant professor in Lehman Scholars Program, 1993; Purdue University, West Lafayette, IN, assistant professor of philosophy and African-American studies, 1993-95; Indiana University-Purdue University at Indianapolis, Indianapolis, IN, adjunct assistant professor of philosophy and American studies, summer, 1994; Purdue University, West Lafayette, associate professor of philosophy and African-American studies, 1996; Brown University, Providence, RI, visiting professor of Afro-American studies and religion, fall of 1996, became associate professor of Afro-American studies, contemporary religious thought, Latin-American studies, modern culture and media, and ethnic studies, 1997-. **Publications:** Bad Faith and Antiblack Racism, 1995; Fanon and the Crisis of European Man: An Essay on Philosophy and the Human Sciences, 1995; Her Majesty's Other Children: Sketches of Racism from a Neocolonial Age, 1997; What Fanon Really Said: An Introduction to His Life and Thought, 1998. EDITOR: (and trans. with T.D. Sharpley-Whiting and R.T. White) Fanon: A Critical Reader, 1996; Existence in Black: An Anthology of Black Existential Philosophy, 1997; (with R.T. White) Black Texts and Textuality: Constructing and De-Constructing Blackness, 1998; Key Figures in AfricanAmerican Thought, 1998; (contrib. ed) The Edinburgh Encyclopedia of Continental Philosophy: Philosophy of Existence, 1998. Contributor of chapters to books; author of articles and reviews in journals; wrote earlier essays under pseudonym Rikki Del Rio. **Address:** Department of Afro-American Studies, Brown University Box 1904, 155 Angell St., Providence, RI 02912, U.S.A. **Online address:** Lewis_Gordon@Brown.edu

GORDON, Lois G. American. **Genres:** History, Literary criticism and history, Biography, Reference. **Career:** City College of New York, NYC, lecturer, 1964-66; University of Missouri, Kansas City, assistant professor, 1966-68; Fairleigh Dickinson University, Teaneck, NJ, associate professor, 1971-75, professor of English and comparative literature, 1975-, chairman of dept., 1982-90; Rutgers University-New Brunswick, visiting professor, 1994. Consultant, Cambridge University Press, U. of Missouri Press, Doubleday, Prentice Hall, Rutgers University Press, Duke University Press, and Harper-Collins publrs; Literature and Psychology, assistant editor, 1968-70; book reviewer, professional journals and newspapers. **Publications:** Stratagems to Undercover Nakedness: The Dramas of Harold Pinter, 1969; Donald Barthelme, 1981: Robert Coover: The Universal Fiction-making Process, 1982; American Chronicle: Six Decades in American Life, 1920-1980, 1987 (rev. ed. as American Chronicle: Seven Decades in American Life, 1920-1989, 1990); Harold Pinter: A Casebook, 1990; Columbia Chronicles of American Life, 1910-1992, 1995; The World of Samuel Beckett, 1906-1946, 1996; (with A. Gordon) American Chronicle: Year by Year through the Twentieth Century, 1999; Pinter at 70, 2001; Reading Godot, 2002. **Address:** 300 Central Park W, New York, NY 10024, U.S.A. **Online address:** Loisgord@aol.com

GORDON, Lyndall (Felicity). South African, b. 1941. **Genres:** Literary criticism and history, Autobiography/Memoirs, Biography. **Career:** Columbia University, NYC, assistant professor of English, 1975-76; Jesus College, Oxford, England, lecturer in English, 1977-84; St. Hilda's College, Oxford, fellow and tutor in English, 1984-95; writer. Royal Society of Literature, fellow, 2002-. **Publications:** BIOGRAPHIES: Eliot's Early Years, 1977; Virginia Woolf: A Writer's Life, 1984; Eliot's New Life, 1988, rev. ed, as T.S. Eliot: An Imperfect Life, 1998; Charlotte Bronte: A Passionate Life, 1994; Henry James: A Private Life: Two Women and His Art, 1998; Vindication: A Life of Mary Wollstonecraft, 2005. OTHER: Shared Lives (memoir), 1992.

GORDON, Mary (Catherine). American, b. 1949. **Genres:** Novels, Novellas/Short stories. **Career:** English Teacher, Dutchess Community College, Poughkeepsie, New York, 1974-78; Amherst College, 1979; Barnard College, NY 1988-. **Publications:** Final Payments, 1978; The Company of Women, 1981; Men and Angels, 1985; Temporary Shelter (stories), 1987; The Other Side, 1989; Good Boys and Dead Girls, 1991; The Rest of Life (novellas), 1993; The Shadow Man, 1996; Spending, 1998; Seeing through Places, 2000; Joan of Arc, 2000; Pearl, 2005.

GORDON, Mike. British, b. 1948. **Genres:** Children's fiction, Children's non-fiction. **Career:** Illustrator and cartoonist, 1983-; greeting card designer; creator of promotional cartoons, 1989. Work represented in exhibitions. **Publications:** FOR CHILDREN. (with M. Gordon) Haunted House, 1989. LEARNING TOGETHER SERIES: Let's Write, 1997; Let's Read, 1997; Let's Count, 1997. FOR ADULTS. The Duffer's Guide to Coarse Fishing, 1985; The Duffer's Guide to Snooker, 1986; The Duffer's Guide to D.I.Y., 1986; The Duffer's Guide to Horse Racing, 1986; The Duffer's Guide to Squash, 1987; William Cooke, Howlers, 1988; The Duffer's Guide to Cycling, 1988; The Duffer's Guide to Boxing, 1989. Illustrator of adult books by C. Clarke, M. Stewart, J. Oram, M. Miller, S. Barlow and S. Skidmore. Illustrator of children's books by A. Pennycock, S. Lewis, A.J. Wood, W. Shepherd, W. Body and P. Edwards, V. Southgate, C. Fann, C. Gumbrell, E. McGee, I. Souter, D. Smith and S. Cassin, D. Hawcock and M. Gordon, L. Newson, J. Grant, J. Drinkwater, B. Girling, A. Ganeri, N. and T. Morris, M. Harvey, J.N. Hunter, P. Thompson, D. Dadey. Contributor of illustrations to magazines. **Address:** PO Box 91818, Santa Barbara, CA 93190, U.S.A.

GORDON, Richard. Also writes as Stuart Gordon, Alex R. Stuart. Scottish, b. 1947. **Genres:** Science fiction/Fantasy. **Career:** Writer. **Publications:** FANTASY AND SCIENCE FICTION NOVELS AS STUART GORDON: Time Story, 1972; Suaine and the Crow-God, 1975; Smile on the Void: The Mythhistory of Ralph M'Botu Kita, 1981; Fire in the Abyss, 1983. THE EYES SERIES AS STUART GORDON: One-Eye, 1973; Two-Eyes, 1974; Three-Eyes, 1975. THE BOOK OF THE WATCHERS SERIES AS STUART GORDON: Archon!, 1987; The Hidden World, 1988; The Mask, 1989; Eye in the Stone, 1990. NONFICTION AS STUART GORDON: The Paranormal: An Illustrated Encyclopedia, 1992; The Encyclopedia of Myths and Legends, 1993; The Book of Curses: True Tales of Voodoo, Hoodoo, and Hex, 1994, in US as The Book of Spells, Hexes, and Curses: True Tales from Around the World, 1995. FANTASY NOVELS AS ALEX R. STUART: The Outlaws, 1972; The Bike from Hell, 1973; The Devil's Rider, 1973. Contributor to periodicals. **Address:** c/o Maggie Noach, 22 Dorville Crescent, London W6 0HJ, England.

GORDON, Rivca. Israeli, b. 1945. **Genres:** International relations/Current affairs, Philosophy. **Career:** Teacher of special education at primary schools, 1973-83; Foundation for Democratic Education in Israel, general manager, 1989-. Gaza Team for Human Rights in the Gaza Strip, chairperson, 1988-. **Publications:** (ed. with H. Gordon, and coauthor of intro) Israel/Palestine: The Quest for Dialogue, 1991; (with H. Gordon) Sartre and Evil: Guidelines for a Struggle, 1995. Contributor to books and periodicals. **Address:** 258/7 Derech Metsada, Beer Sheva, Israel.

GORDON, Robert Ellis. American, b. 1954. **Genres:** Novels, Adult non-fiction. **Career:** Washington State Prison Writers Project, director. Novelist and short story writer. **Publications:** When Bobby Kennedy Was a Moving Man, 1993; The Funhouse Mirror: Reflections on Prison, 2000. Contributor of short stories to periodicals.

GORDON, Sheila. American (born Republic of South Africa), b. 1927. **Genres:** Young adult fiction, Autobiography/Memoirs, Novels, Literary criticism and history, Novellas/Short stories, Essays. **Career:** Writer. **Publications:** Unfinished Business: A Novel of South Africa, 1975; A Monster in the Mailbox (juvenile novel), 1978; A Modest Harmony: Seven Summers in a Scottish Glen (memoir), 1982; Waiting for the Rain: A Novel of South Africa (young adult novel), 1987; The Middle of Somewhere, 1990. Contributor to periodicals.

GORDON, Stuart. See GORDON, Richard.

GORDON, Stuart. American, b. 1947. **Genres:** Horror, Science fiction/Fantasy, Plays/Screenplays. **Career:** Director, writer, and producer. Co-founder and artistic director of the Organic Theater, 1969-85. **Publications:** SCREENPLAYS: Re-animator, 1985; From Beyond, 1986; Honey, I Shrunk the Kids, 1989; Robot Jox, 1990; Bodysnatchers, 1994; Castle Freak, 1995; The Dentist, 1996; Space Truckers, 1996; Progeny, 1999. TELEVISION SCRIPTS: Bleacher Bums, 1979; E/R (series), 1984; Kid Safe, 1988. PLAYS:

Warp, 1993; Bleacher Bums, 1979. **Address:** Red Hen Productions, 3607 W Magnolia Ste L, Burbank, CA 91505, U.S.A.

GORDON, W. Terrence. Also writes as Alan R. Lintrey. Canadian, b. 1942. **Genres:** Literary criticism and history. **Career:** University of Alberta, Edmonton, Canada, professor, 1970-72; Dalhousie University, Halifax, Nova Scotia, Canada, professor, 1972-, Alexander McLeod Chair in Modern Languages, 1999-. **Publications:** C.K. Ogden: A Bio-Bibliograpic Study, 1990; C.K. Ogden & Linguistics, 1994; Saussure for Beginners, 1996; Marshall McLuhan: Escape into Understanding, 1997; Linguistics for Beginners, 2001. Also writes under the pseudonym Alan R. Lintrey. **Address:** Department of French, Dalhousie University, Halifax, NS, Canada B3H 3J5.

GORDON, William A. American, b. 1950. **Genres:** History, Travel/ Exploration, Documentaries/Reportage, Humor/Satire. **Career:** Author, publisher and free-lance writer, 1973-. **Publications:** (ed.) "How Many Books Do You Sell in Ohio?" A Quote Book for Writers, 1986; The Fourth of May: Killings and Coverups at Kent State, 1990; The Ultimate Hollywood Tour Book, 1992; Shot on This Site, 1995; Four Dead in Ohio: Was There a Conspiracy at Kent State?, 1995; The Quotable Writer, 2000. **Address:** PO Box 1463, Lake Forest, CA 92609, U.S.A. **Online address:** BGordonLA@ aol.com

GORE, Ariel. American, b. 1971. **Genres:** Self help. **Career:** Journalist. Hip Mama (magazine), Oakland, CA, founder and editor, 1994-. **Publications:** The Hip Mama Survival Guide; Advice from the Trenches on Pregnancy, Childbirth, Cool Names, Clueless Doctors, Potty Training, Toddler Avengers, Domestic Mayhem, Support Groups, Right Wing Losers, Work, Day Care, Family Law, the Evil Patriarchy, Collection Agents, Nervous Breakdowns, 1998. **Address:** c/o Seal Press, PMB 375, 300 Queen Anne Ave N, Seattle, WA 98109-4512, U.S.A. **Online address:** hipmama@sirius. com

GOREHAM, Gary A. American, b. 1953. **Genres:** Local history/Rural topics, Agriculture/Forestry. **Career:** North Dakota State University, Fargo, assistant director of State Data Center for agricultural economics, 1985-87, assistant professor, 1987-94, associate professor of sociology and anthropology, 1994-. Maple Hills Orchards, Detroit Lakes, MN, owner. **Publications:** The Rural Church in America: A Century of Writings, 1990; The Socioeconomics of Sustainable Agriculture, 1993; Encyclopedia of Rural America: The Land and People, 1997. Author of educational materials about the rural church. **Address:** 408-B Minard Hall, Department of Sociology and Anthropology, North Dakota State University, Fargo, ND 58105, U.S.A. **Online address:** goreham@plains.nodak.edu

GORES, Joe. (Joseph N. Gores). American, b. 1931. **Genres:** Mystery/ Crime/Suspense, Novellas/Short stories, Plays/Screenplays. **Career:** Full-time writer. Private investigator, L.A. Walker Co., San Francisco, 1955-57, and David Kikkert and Assocs., San Francisco, 1959-62, 1965-67; English Teacher, Kakamega Boys Secondary School, Kenya, 1963-64; Manager, Automobile Auction Co., San Francisco, 1968-76; Story Ed., B.L. Stryker, TV series, 1988-89. President, Mystery Writers of America, 1986. Extensive film and TV writing. **Publications:** MYSTERY NOVELS: A Time of Predators, 1969; Dead Skip, 1972; Final Notice, 1973; Interface, 1974; Hammett: A Novel, 1975; Gone, No Forwarding, 1978; Come Morning, 1986; Wolf Time, 1989; 32 Cadillacs, 1992; Dead Man, 1993; Menaced Assassin, 1994; Contract Null & Void, 1996; Cases, 1999; Cons, Scams & Grifts, 2001. OTHER: Marine Salvage, 1971; (ed.) Honolulu: Port of Call, 1974; (ed. with B. Pronzini) Tricks or Treats, 1976, in U.K. as Mystery Writers' Choice, 1977; Mostly Murder: A Short Story Collection, 1992; Speak of the Devil: 14 Tales of Crimes and Their Punishments, 1999; Stakeout on Page Street and Other DKA Files, 2000. **Address:** PO Box 446, Fairfax, CA 94978-0446, U.S.A.

GORHAM, Deborah. American, b. 1937. **Genres:** Women's studies and issues. **Career:** Carleton University, Ottawa, Ontario, Canada, assistant professor, 1969-78, associate professor, 1978-88, professor of history, 1988-2002, professor emeritus, 2002-, member of management committee of Pauline Jewett Institute of Women's Studies, 1987-90, 2000-01, director of institute, 1994-97. Antioch College, Yellow Springs, OH, scholar-in-residence, 1979; Stanford University, affiliated scholar with Center for Research on Women and Gender, 1991-92; University of California-Berkeley, affiliated scholar with Beatrice M. Bain Research Group, 1991-92. Speaker at educational institutions and to community groups. **Publications:** The Victorian Girl and the Feminine Ideal, 1982; Women's Work in Historical Perspective: Parts 1 and 2 (videoscript), 1988; Vera Brittain: A Feminist Life, 1996. EDITOR: (with J. Williamson) Up and Doing: Canadian Women and

Peace, 1990; Women's Experience (series), 1990-91; (with D. Dodd, and contrib.) Caring and Curing: Historical Perspectives on Women and Healing in Canada, 1994. Contributor to books. Contributor of articles and reviews to periodicals. **Address:** 234 Daly Ave., Ottawa, ON, Canada K1N 6G2. **Online address:** dgorham@ccs.carleton.ca

GÖRLACH, Manfred. German, b. 1937. **Genres:** Mythology/Folklore, Cultural/Ethnic topics. **Career:** University of Heidelberg, Germany, lecturer in English, 1967-84; University of Cologne, Germany, professor of English language and medieval studies, 1984-. **Publications:** The South English Legendary, Gilte Legende and Golden Legend, 1972; The Textual Tradition of the South English Legendary, 1974; Englishes, 1991; Introduction to Early Modern English, 1991; Mac ond Mauris in Old English Rhymed an Alliterative Verse, 1992; (with B. Glauser and E.W. Schneider) A New Bibliography of Writings on Varieties of English, 1984-1992/93, 1993; More Englishes, 1995; A Linguistic History of English, 1997; Even More Englishes, 1998; An Annotated Bibliography of 19th-Century Grammars of English, 1998; English in Nineteenth-Century England, 1999. EDITOR: (with R.W. Bailey) English as a World Language, 1982; Focus on Scotland, 1985; Max and Moritz in English Dialects and Creoles, 1986; (with J. Holm) Focus on the Caribbean, 1987. Also writes in German. **Address:** English Seminar, University of Cologne, Albertus-Magnus-Platz, D-50923 Cologne (Koln), Germany.

GORMAN, Carol. (born United States). **Genres:** Children's fiction. **Career:** Middle school teacher in Cedar Rapids, IA, prior to 1984; writer, 1984-. Conducts writing workshops and makes presentations in elementary and middle schools; part-time instructor, Coe College. **Publications:** America's Farm Crisis, 1987; Chelsey and the Green-Haired Kid, 1987; Pornography, 1988; T. J. and the Pirate Who Wouldn't Go Home, 1990; The Biggest Bully in Brookdale, 1992; It's Not Fair, 1992; Die for Me, 1992; Graveyard Moon, 1993; The Great Director, 1993; Skin Deep, 1993; Nobody's Friend, 1993; The Richest Kid in the World, 1993; Brian's Footsteps, 1994; The Taming of Roberta Parsley, 1994; Million Dollar Winner, 1994; The Rumor, 1994; The Miraculous Makeover of Lizard Flanagan, 1994; Jennifer-the-Jerk Is Missing, 1994; Back from the Dead, 1995; Lizard Flanagan, Supermodel?, 1998; Dork in Disguise, 1999; (editor with husband, Ed Gorman) Felonious Felines, 2000; Dork on the Run, 2002; A Midsummer Night's Dork, 2004. Also author of adult books under pseudonym Jane Ballard; ghostwriter for mystery series books. **Address:** c/o Author Correspondence, HarperCollins Inc., 10 E. 53rd St., 7th Floor, New York, NY 10022, U.S.A.

GORMAN, James. American, b. 1949. **Genres:** Children's fiction, Children's non-fiction, Essays. **Career:** Journalist, columnist, and author. Associated with St. John Valley Times, Madawaska, ME; Discover magazine, columnist. **Publications:** NONFICTION, EXCEPT AS NOTED: First Aid for Hypochondriacs (humor), 1982; (with J.R. Horner) Maia: A Dinosaur Grows Up (juvenile fiction), 1985; (with Horner) Digging Dinosaurs, 1988; The Man with No Endorphins, and Other Reflections on Science (adapted from Gorman's column in Discover magazine), 1988; The Total Penguin, 1990; Ocean Enough and Time: Discovering the Waters around Antarctica, 1995. **Address:** c/o Discover Magazine, 114 Fifth Ave., New York, NY 10011, U.S.A.

GORMAN, Martha. American, b. 1953. **Genres:** Adult non-fiction. **Career:** Freelance writer and translator, 1979-92; Englewood-Colorado Chiropractic Association, Englewood, CO, director of public relations, 1992-. **Publications:** El Mercado del libro en Colombia, 1978; (with G. Campbell) Everybody for President, 1984; (with B. Pinsick) Ill, Not Insane, 1985; Environmental Hazards: Marine Pollution, 1993; Euthanasia: Death by Choice, in press. Contributor to magazines. **Address:** 4282 Eldorado Springs Dr., Boulder, CO 80303, U.S.A.

GORMAN, Michael E. American, b. 1952. **Genres:** Sciences. **Career:** Michigan Technological University, Houghton, assistant professor, 1981-87, associate professor of psychology and humanities, 1987-88; University of Virginia, Charlottesville, visiting associate professor, 1988-90, associate professor of technology, culture and communications, 1990-. **Publications:** Simulating Science: Heuristics, Mental Models, and Technoscientific Thinking, 1992; Transforming Nature, 1998; (co-ed.) Ethical and Environmental Challenges to Engineering, 2000. Work represented in anthologies. Contributor to academic journals. **Address:** Div of Tech Culture & Communications, Sch of Eng & Appl Sci, Box 400744 A 237 Thornton Hall, University of Virginia, 351 McCormick Rd, Charlottesville, VA 22904, U.S.A. **Online address:** meg3c@virginia.edu

GORN, Elliott (J.). American, b. 1951. **Genres:** History, Biography. **Career:** Taught at University of Alabama, Miami University, Oxford, OH, Purdue University, Brown University. **Publications:** The Manly Art: Bare-Knuckle Prize Fighting in America, 1986; (with W. Goldstein) A Brief History of American Sports, 1993; Mother Jones: The Most Dangerous Woman in America, 2001. EDITOR: (with R. Roberts and T. Bilhartz) Constructing the American Past: A Sourcebook of a Peoples' History, 1991, rev. ed., 2001; (with M.K. Cayton and P.W. Williams) The Encyclopedia of American Social History, 3 vols, 1993; Muhammad Ali: The People's Champ, 1996; The McGuffy Readers: Selections from the 1879 Edition, 1998. **Address:** Department of History, Box N, Brown University, Providence, RI 02912, U.S.A. **Online address:** elliott_gorn@brown.edu

GORN, Michael H. American, b. 1950. **Genres:** History, Sciences, Technology, Biography. **Career:** New England Historic Genealogical Society, Boston, MA, chief of archives, 1978-81; Headquarters Air Force Systems Command, Andrews Air Force Base, MD, staff historian, 1981-85; Office of Air Force History, Bolling Air Force Base, Washington, DC, staff historian, 1985-89; Headquarters Air Force Systems Command, chief historian, 1989-91; U.S. Environmental Protection Agency, Washington, DC, chief historian, 1991-93; Office of Air Force History, senior historian, 1993-95; National Air and Space Museum, research collaborator, 1994-; NASA, Dryden Flight Research Center, Aviation & Spaceflight History, author and researcher, 1996-; writer. **Publications:** Harnessing the Genie: Science and Technology Forecasting for the Air Force, 1944-1986, 1988; The Universal Man: Theodore von Karman's Life in Aeronautics, 1992; Hugh L. Dryden's Career in Aviation and Space, 1996. EDITOR: A Guide to the Massachusetts and Maine Direct Tax Census of 1798, 1979; Prophecy Fulfilled: Toward New Horizons and Its Legacy, 1994. Work represented in anthologies. **Address:** c/o Dryden Space Flight Research Center, PO Box 273, Edwards, CA 93523, U.S.A.

GORNICK, Vivian. American, b. 1935. **Genres:** Literary criticism and history, Women's studies and issues, Autobiography/Memoirs, Essays. **Publications:** In Search of Ali Mahmoud: An American Woman in Egypt, 1973; The Romance of American Communism, 1977; Essays in Feminism, 1978; Women in Science, 1983, 1990; Fierce Attachments, 1987; Approaching Eye Level, 1996; The End of the Novel of Love, 1997; The Situation and the Story: The Art of Personal Narrative, 2001.

GORRA, Michael (Edward). American, b. 1957. **Genres:** Literary criticism and history. **Career:** Smith College, Northampton, MA, professor of English, 1985-. Freelance book reviewer for periodicals. **Publications:** The English Novel at Mid-Century: From the Leaning Tower, 1990; After Empire: Scott, Naipaul, Rushdie, 1997; The Bells in Their Silence: Travels through Germany, 2004. **Address:** Smith College, Department of English, Seelye Hall 401, Northampton, MA 01063, U.S.A. **Online address:** mgorra@smith.edu

GORRELL, Lorraine. American. **Genres:** Music. **Career:** Winthrop University, Rock Hill, SC, professor of music, 1973-. Professional singer (mezzo soprano); performs recitals. **Publications:** The Nineteenth-Century German Lied, 1993; Discordant Melody: Alexander Zemlinsky, His Songs, and the Second Viennese School, 2002. Contributor to music journals. **Address:** Department of Music, Winthrop University, Rock Hill, SC 29733, U.S.A.

GORRELL, Robert (Mark). American, b. 1914. **Genres:** Mystery/Crime/Suspense, Language/Linguistics, Literary criticism and history. **Career:** Emeritus Professor of English and former Vice-President for Academic Affairs, University of Nevada, Reno (joined faculty, 1945). Instructor, Deep Springs College, California, 1939-42; Instructor, Indiana University, Bloomington, 1942-45; Fulbright Professor, University of Sydney, Aust., 1954-55; Consultant, Portland School District, Oregon, 1959-61; Fulbright Professor, University of Helsinki, Finland, 1961-62. **Publications:** (with C. Emery and K.N. Cameron) Practice in English Communication, 2 vols., 1944, rev. ed. in 1 vol., 1947; (with C. Laird) Modern English Handbook, 1953, 7th ed., 1988; (with C. Laird) Modern English Workbook, 1957, 1962; (with C. Laird) A Course in Modern English, 1960; (with C. Laird) English as Language, 1961; (with A. Kitzhaber and P. Roberts) Education for College, 1961; (with C. Laird and P. Pflug) A Basic Course in Modern English, 1963; (with C. Laird and W. Lutz) Modern English Reader, 1970; (with C. Laird) Reading about Language, 1971; (with M.M. Brown) Writing and Language: Books I and II, 1971; (with C. Laird) Writing Modern English, 1973; Watch Your Language: Mother Tongue and Her Wayward Children, 1994; Murder at the Rose, 2000; What's in a Word?, 2001. **Address:** 154 Greenridge Dr, Reno, NV 89509, U.S.A. **Online address:** RMGorrell@aol.com

GORUP, Radmila J(ovanovic). American (born Yugoslavia). **Genres:** Humanities, Language/Linguistics. **Career:** Columbia University, NYC, instructor in Slavic languages, 1980-86; University of California, Berkeley, lecturer in Slavic languages, 1986-93; Columbia University, lecturer to adjunct professor of Slavic languages, 1994-. **Publications:** The Prince of Fire, 1998; In a Foreign Harbor, 2000. Contributor of articles, reviews, and translations to periodicals.

GOSDEN, Roger. British, b. 1948. **Genres:** Medicine/Health. **Career:** Cambridge University, England, research scholar, 1970-74; Duke University, Durham, NC, Population Council research fellow, 1974-75; Cambridge University, research fellow, 1975-76; University of Edinburgh, Edinburgh, Scotland, lecturer to senior lecturer in physiology, 1970-94; University of Leeds, England, professor of reproductive biology, 1994-99; McGill University, professor, 1999-; lecturer and broadcaster. **Publications:** Biology of Menopause, 1985; Transplantation of Ovarian and Testicular Tissues, 1996; Cheating Time, 1996. Contributor to scientific journals. **Address:** Department of Obstetrics and Gynecology, McGill University, Montreal, QC, Canada H3A 1A1. **Online address:** roger.gosden@muhc.mcgill.ca

GOSE, Peter. Canadian, b. 1955. **Genres:** Anthropology/Ethnology. **Career:** University of Lethbridge, Lethbridge, Alberta, Canada, assistant professor, 1987-91, associate professor of anthropology, 1991-94; University of Regina, Regina, Saskatchewan, Canada, associate professor of anthropology and head of department, both 1994-. Lecturer at colleges and universities. Conducted field research in the Peruvian Andes, 1981-83, and in the Sierra Tarahumara of northern Mexico, 1989-90. **Publications:** Deathly Waters and Hungry Mountains: Agrarian Ritual and Class Formation in an Andean Town, 1994. Contributor to books. Contributor of articles and reviews to anthropology journals. **Address:** Department of Anthropology, University of Regina, Regina, SK, Canada S4S 0A2.

GOSHEN-GOTTSTEIN, Esther. Israeli/British (born Germany), b. 1928. **Genres:** Psychology, Humanities. **Career:** Clinical psychologist and freelance writer. Bar Ilan University, Israel, senior lecturer, 1975-85. **Publications:** Marriage and First Pregnancy, 1966; Coping Behavior of Mothers of Multiple Births, 1976; Recalled to Life: The Story of a Coma, 1990; Surviving Widowhood, 2002. Contributor to psychology journals. **Address:** 17 Jabotinsky St, 92141 Jerusalem, Israel. **Online address:** egoshen@netvision.net.il

GOSLING, J. C. B. British, b. 1930. **Genres:** Philosophy. **Career:** Principal, St. Edmund Hall, Oxford University, 1982-96 (Fellow and Tutor, 1960-82). **Publications:** Pleasure and Desire, 1969; Plato, 1973; Plato: Philebus, 1975; The Greeks on Pleasure, 1982; Weakness of the Will, 1990. **Address:** St. Edmund Hall, Oxford, England.

GOSLING, Paula. Also writes as Ainslie Skinner. American, b. 1939. **Genres:** Mystery/Crime/Suspense. **Career:** Full-time writer. Copywriter, Campbell Ewald Advertising, Detroit, 1962-64; Copywriter, Mitchell's Advertising, 1964-67, Pritchard-Wood Advertising, 1967-68, and David Williams Advertising, 1968-69, all London; Copy Consultant, Mitchell's Advertising, 1969-70, and ATA Advertising, Bristol, 1977-79; Chairman, Crime Writers Association, 1988-89. **Publications:** A Running Duck, in U.S. as Fair Game, 1978; The Zero Trap, 1979; Loser's Blues, 1980, in U.S. as Solo Blues, 1981; (as Ainslie Skinner) Mind's Eye, 1980, in U.S. as The Harrowing, 1981; The Woman in Red, 1983; Monkey Puzzle, 1985; The Wychford Murders, 1986; Hoodwink, 1988; Backlash, 1989; Death Penalties, 1991; The Body in Blackwater Bay, 1992; A Few Dying Words, 1993; The Dead of Winter, 1995; Death and Shadows, 1999; Underneath Every Stone, 2000; Ricochet, 2002; Tears of the Dragon, 2004. **Address:** c/o Greene and Heaton Ltd., 37 Goldhawk Rd, London W12 8QQ, England. **Online address:** paula.gosling@virgin.net

GOSS, Glenda Dawn. Also writes as Glenda Thompson. American, b. 1947. **Genres:** Music. **Career:** University of Georgia, Athens, lecturer, 1976-78, assistant professor, 1978-85, associate professor, 1985-93, professor of musicology, 1993-. University of the Philippines, visiting scholar, 1982; University of Delaware, visiting scholar, 1983; Sibelius Academy (Helsinki, Finland), visiting professor, 1995-96; guest on radio programs in the United States and Finland. Concert pianist. **Publications:** (ed. and author of introduction, as Glenda Thompson) Benedictus Appenzeller: Chansons, 1982; Music and the Moderns: The Life and Works of Carol Robinson, 1993; Jean Sibelius and Olin Downes: Music, Friendship, Criticism, 1995; (trans.) Kari Kilpelaainen, Sibelius: 1995; (ed.) The Sibelius Companion, 1996; (trans.) Werke Jean Sibelius, 1996. Editor of musical compositions. Contributor to books. Contributor of articles and reviews to musicology journals and other scholarly periodicals. **Address:** School of Music, University of Georgia, Athens, GA 30602, U.S.A.

GOTANDA, Philip Kan. American, b. 1951. **Genres:** Plays/Screenplays. **Career:** Playwright; filmmaker. **Publications:** The Avocado Kid, 1980; Bullet Headed Birds, 1981; A Song for a Nisei Fisherman, 1982; The Dream of Kitamura, 1984; The Wash, 1985; Yankee Dawg You Die, 1987; Fish Head Soup, and Other Plays, 1992; (and director) The Kiss (film), 1993; Day Standing on Its Head, 1994; Ballad of Yachiyo, 1996; Drinking Tea, 1996; Lafe Tastes Good, 1999; Sisters Matsumoto, 1998; The Wind Cries Mercy, 2000; Floating Weeds, 2001; Yohen, 2002; Fist of Roses, 2004; Under the Rainbow, 2004.

GOTFRYD, Bernard. Polish, b. 1924. **Genres:** Autobiography/Memoirs, Documentaries/Reportage. **Career:** Newsweek, New York City, photojournalist, 1957-88; writer. **Publications:** Anton the Dove Fancier and Other Tales of the Holocaust, 1990, rev. ed., 2000; Historier Fra Et Morkekammer (play; Stories from a Dark Chamber), 1996. Works have been produced as plays. **Address:** c/o IMG - Julian Bach Literary Agency Inc, 22 E 71st St, New York, NY 10021, U.S.A. **Online address:** gotfrydB@aol.com

GOTLIEB, Phyllis (Fay). Canadian, b. 1926. **Genres:** Novels, Novellas/Short stories, Science fiction/Fantasy, Poetry. **Publications:** Within the Zodiac, 1964; Ordinary, Moving, 1969; Doctor Umlaut's Earthly Kingdom, 1974; (co-ed.) Tesseracts 2, 1987. NOVELS: Sunburst, 1964; Why Should I Have All the Grief, 1969; O Master Caliban, 1976; Judgement of Dragons, 1980; Emperor, Swords, Pentacles, 1982; The Kingdom of the Cats, 1985; Heart of Red Iron, 1989; Flesh and Gold, 1998; Violent Stars, 1999; Mindworlds, 2002. POETRY: The Works, 1978; Red Blood Black Ink White Paper, 2002. STORIES: Son of the Morning and Other Stories, 1983; Blue Apes, 1996. **Address:** 19 Lower Village Gate #706, Toronto, ON, Canada M5P 3L9.

GOTO, Hiromi. Canadian (born Japan), b. 1966. **Genres:** Novels, Novellas/Short stories, Poetry. **Career:** Writer. Crownsnest Writers Retreat and Workshop, organizer and administrator, summers, 1993-94; Women of Colour Collective of Calgary Creative Writing Workshops for Aboriginal Women and Women of Colour, facilitator, 1998. Calgary Minquon Panchayat, member, 1993-95. Gives readings and performances from her work in Canada, the U.S., and England. **Publications:** Tea (poems and art work), 1992. NOVELS: Chorus of Mushrooms, 1994; The Water of Possibility, 2001; The Kappa Child, 2001. Work represented in anthologies. Contributor of short stories, articles, critical essays, and poems to periodicals. **Address:** c/o Author Mail, Red Deer Press, 2500 University Dr. NW, MLT 813, Calgary, AB, Canada T2N 1N4.

GOTO, Junichi. Japanese, b. 1951. **Genres:** Economics. **Career:** Affiliated with Japanese Ministry of Labor, 1975-86, deputy director of Labor Economy Division, 1990-91; World Bank, economist for International Economics Department, 1987-90; Kobe University, professor, 1991-; MIT, Visiting fellow, 1993-94; Yale University, visiting fellow, 1995; Inter-American Development Bank, consultant, 1998-2000. **Publications:** Kokusai Rodo no Keizaigaku (title means: International Labor Economics), 1988; Gaikokujin Rodo no Keizaigaku (title means: Economic Analysis of Migrant Workers and International Trade), 1990; Labor in International Trade Theory-A New Perspective on Japanese-American Issues, 1990; Gaikokujin Rodosha to Nihon Keizai (title means: Migrant Workers and the Japanese Economy), 1993; Economic Preconditions for Asian Regional Integration, 1994; Regional Economic Conditions and Article XXIV of the GATT, 2000. Contributor to periodicals. **Address:** Research Institute for Economics and Business, Kobe University, 2-1 Rokkodai-cho, Nada-Ku, Kobe 657, Japan. **Online address:** go4japan@aol.com

GOTSHALK, Richard. American, b. 1931. **Genres:** Philosophy. **Career:** Pennsylvania State University, University Park, member of philosophy faculty, 1957-77; University of Montana, Missoula, part-time member of philosophy faculty, 1982-95, Henry G. Bugbee Lecturer, 1999. University of Denver, visiting professor, 1975. City of Missoula, served as chair of Open Space Advisory Committee; founder of a neighborhood association and of a network of neighborhood associations. **Publications:** Bhagavad-Gita: A Translation and Commentary, 1985; The Beginnings of Philosophy in India, 1998; The Beginnings of Philosophy in China, 1999; Divination, Order, and the Zhouyi, 1999; The Beginnings of Philosophy in Greece, 2000; Homer and Hesiod, Myth and Philosophy, 2000; The Temporality of Human Excellence: A Reading of Five Dialogues of Plato, 2001; Loving and Dying: A Reading of Plato's Phaedo, Symposium, and Phaedrus, 2001. Contributor to philosophy journals. **Address:** c/o Author Mail University Press of America, 15200 NBN Way PO Box 191, Building B, Blue Ridge Summit, PA 17214, U.S.A.

GOTT, Richard (Willoughby). British, b. 1938. **Genres:** History, International relations/Current affairs, Third World. **Career:** Historian and journalist. Royal Institute of International Affairs, London, research assistant, 1962-65; Guardian newspaper, London, leader writer, 1964-66; Institute of International Studies, University of Chile, Santiago, research fellow, 1966-69; The Standard, Dar Es Salaam, Tanzania, foreign ed., 1970-72; Latin American Newsletters Ltd., director, 1976-80; The Guardian, features ed., 1978-89, literary ed., 1992-94. **Publications:** (co-ed.) Documents on International Affairs, 1960; (with M. Gilbert) The Appeasers, 1963; (with J. Gittings) NATO's Final Decade, 1964; (with J. Gittings) The End of the Alliance, 1965; Mobuto's Congo, 1968; Guerrilla Movements in Latin America, 1970; Close Your Frontiers: Development as the Ideology of Imperialism, 1983; Land without Evil: Utopian Journeys across the South American Watershed, 1993; In the Shadow of the Liberator: Hugo Chavez and the Transformation of Venezuela, 2001; Cuba: A New History, 2004. **Address:** 88 Ledbury Road, London W11 2AH, England.

GOTTFRIED, Robert R(ichard). American (born Mexico), b. 1948. **Genres:** Economics. **Career:** Universidad Rafael Landivar, Guatemala City, Guatemala, Fulbright lecturer in economics, 1979; University of the South, Sewanee, TN, MacArthur assistant professor, 1982-85, professor of economics, 1985-, head of Social Science Foreign Language Program, 1991-94, department head, 1994-. University of Puerto Rico, Center for Energy and Environment Research, Oak Ridge associated universities faculty research participant, 1983; Centro Agronomico Tropical de Investigacion y Ensenanza (Costa Rica), member of Regional Watershed Management Project, 1988-89; U.S. Man and the Biosphere Directorate for Temperate Ecosystems, member, 1989-92; Universidad Nacional (Heredia, Costa Rica), researcher for Central American Commission on Forests and the Environment, 1995-96. **Publications:** Economics, Ecology, and the Roots of Western Faith: Perspectives From the Garden, 1995. Contributor to books. Contributor to professional journals. **Address:** Department of Economics, University of the South, 735 University Ave., Sewanee, TN 37375, U.S.A.

GOTTLIEB, Alma. American, b. 1954. **Genres:** Anthropology/Ethnology, Autobiography/Memoirs. **Career:** Virginia Commonwealth University, Richmond, adjunct instructor in sociology and anthropology, 1977-79; Virginia Union University, adjunct instructor, 1978; University of Illinois at Urbana-Champaign, Urbana, visiting assistant professor, 1983-85, assistant professor, 1985-91, associate professor, 1991-98, professor of anthropology, 1998-. **Publications:** Under the Kapok Tree: Identity and Difference in Beng Thought, 1992; (with P. Graham) Parallel Worlds: An Anthropologist and a Writer Encounter Africa (memoir), 1993; (with M.L. Murphy) Beng-English Dictionary, 1995; The Afterlife Is Where We Come From: The Culture of Infancy in West Africa, 2004. EDITOR & CONTRIBUTOR: (with T. Buckley) Blood Magic: The Anthropology of Menstruation, 1988; (with J. DeLoache) A World of Babies: Imagined Infant and Childcare Guides for Seven Societies, 2000. Work represented in anthologies. Contributor of articles and reviews to periodicals. **Address:** Dept of Anthropology, University of Illinois at Urbana-Champaign, Urbana, IL 61801, U.S.A.

GOTTLIEB, Annie. American, b. 1946. **Genres:** Novels, Plays/Screenplays, Cultural/Ethnic topics, Literary criticism and history, Psychology, Theology/Religion. **Career:** Harcourt, Brace, Jovanovich, New York, NY, editorial assistant, 1967-70; writer. **Publications:** (with J. Sandulescu) The Carpathian Caper (novel), 1975; (author of intro. and captions) Women See Woman (photography), 1976; (with B. Sher) Wishcraft: How to Get What You Really Want, 1979; (with B. Stern) The Last Sitting, 1982; Do You Believe in Magic?: The Second Coming of the Sixties Generation, 1987, as Do You Believe in Magic?: Bringing the Sixties Back Home, 1988; (with B. Sher) Teamworks!: Building Support Groups That Guarantee Success, 1989; (author of intro.) Windows on Paradise, 1990; (author of text) T. McKnight, Voyage to Paradise: A Visual Odyssey, 1993; (with S.D. Pesic) The Cube: Keep the Secret, 1995; (with S.D. Pesic) Secrets of the Cube, 1998; (with J.M. Schwartz and P. Buckley) A Return to Innocence, 1998.

GOTTLIEB, Arthur. Also writes as Arthur Josephs. American, b. 1929. **Genres:** Medicine/Health, Plays/Screenplays. **Career:** Retired lawyer; writer. National Stroke Quality of Life Medical Education Institute, Columbia-Presbyterian Medical Center, co-chair. Author of column "You, Me, Them, and Us," Citizen News. **Publications:** Stroke: An Owner's Manual, 1992. PLAYS: Joseph; Maturity Manor; Choices; Journey to Canaan. **Address:** PO Box 13011, Long Beach, CA 90803, U.S.A. **Online address:** amadeuspr@earthlink.net

GOTTLIEB, Beatrice. American, b. 1925. **Genres:** History, Translations. **Career:** Time Inc., NYC, head of copy room for Sports Illustrated, 1954-67; Smith College, Northampton, MA, assistant professor, 1976-77; writer. **Publications:** (trans. and author of introduction) L. Febvre, The Problem of Unbelief in the Sixteenth Century, 1980; The Family in the Western World from the Black Death to the Industrial Age, 1993. **Address:** c/o William B. Goodman, 26 Pickman Dr., Bedford, MA 01730, U.S.A.

GOTTLIEB, Erika (Simon). Canadian (born Hungary), b. 1938. **Genres:** Literary criticism and history. **Career:** McGill University, Montreal, Canada, teaching assistant, 1969-72; Loyola College, Montreal, lecturer, 1973-74; Concordia University, part-time lecturer, 1969-74; Dawson College, Montreal, professor, 1974-78; Seneca College, Toronto, ON, professor, 1980-99; Ryerson University, Toronto, part-time professor, 2000-. Artist, with paintings exhibited in Montreal, Toronto, US, England, etc. **Publications:** Lost Angels of a Ruined Paradise: Themes of Cosmic Strife in Romantic Tragedy, 1981; The Orwell Conundrum 1992; Dystopian Fiction East and West: Universe of Terror and Trial, 2001. Work represented in anthologies. Contributor of articles and poems to literature journals and literary magazines. **Address:** 149 Lytton Blvd, Toronto, ON, Canada M4R 1L6. **Online address:** erikagottlieb@hotmail.com

GOTTLIEB, Freema (Peninah). British/American, b. 1946. **Genres:** Humanities, Mythology/Folklore, Biography, Essays. **Career:** Writer/Lecturer/Researcher. Speaker, New York Council of the Humanities, 1990. **Publications:** Jewish Folk Art, 1986; The Lamp of God: A Jewish Book of Light, 1989; Mystical Stonescapes: Symbols on Jewish Gravestones in Prague Old Jewish Cemetery and in Bohemia, 1997.

GOTTLIEB, Gilbert. American, b. 1929. **Genres:** Psychology. **Career:** Duke University Medical Center, Durham, NC, research associate in medical psychology, 1958-59; Dorothea Dix Hospital, Raleigh, NC, clinical psychologist, 1959-61; North Carolina Division of Mental Health, Raleigh, research scientist, 1961-82; University of North Carolina at Greensboro, Excellence Foundation Professor of Psychology, 1982-95, head of department, 1982-86; North Carolina State University, adjunct assistant professor to adjunct professor, 1961-72; University of North Carolina at Chapel Hill, adjunct research professor, 1974-82, research professor, Center for Developmental Science, 1995-; University of Colorado, Boulder, distinguished visiting professor, 1985. Consultant. **Publications:** Development of Species Identification in Birds: An Inquiry into the Prenatal Determinants of Perception, 1971; Individual Development and Evolution: The Genesis of Novel Behavior, 1992, repr., 2002; Synthesizing Nature-Nurture, 1997; Probabilistic Epigenesis and Evolution, 1999. EDITOR & CONTRIBUTOR: Behavioral Embryology, 1973; Aspects of Neurogenesis, 1974; Neural and Behavioral Specificity, 1976; Zing-Yang Kuo, The Dynamics of Behavior Development, rev. ed., 1976; Early Influences, 1978; (with N.A. Krasnegor) Measurement of Audition and Vision in the First Year of Postnatal Life: A Methodological Overview, 1985. Work represented in anthologies. Contributor of articles and reviews to scientific journals in the US and abroad. **Address:** Center for Developmental Science, CB #8115, University of North Carolina, Chapel Hill, NC 27599-8115, U.S.A.

GOTTLIEB, Sherry Gershon. American, b. 1948. **Genres:** Documentaries/Reportage. **Career:** Book doctor, editor, and writer; executive secretary, Budget Films, Los Angeles, CA, 1970-72; script reader, United Artists, Los Angeles, 1971-74; owner of Change of Hobbit Bookstore, Los Angeles and Santa Monica, CA, 1972-91; class coordinator, UCLA extension, 1982. **Publications:** Hell No, We Won't Go!: Resisting the Draft during the Vietnam War, 1991; Love Bite, 1994; Worse than Death, 2000. Contributor to anthologies. **Address:** c/o Author Mail, St. Martin's Press/Forge, 175 Fifth Ave., New York, NY 10010, U.S.A.

GOTTLIEB, Stephen E. American, b. 1941. **Genres:** Law. **Career:** U.S. Peace Corps, volunteer, instructor in law, history, and economics at Pahlavi University, Shiraz, Iran, 1966-67; Golenbock & Barell (law firm), New York City, associate, 1967-69; Legal Aid Society of St. Louis, MO, managing attorney and staff attorney, 1969-72; St. Louis University, adjunct instructor in research and writing, 1972; Community Action for Legal Services Inc., NYC, assistant general counsel and director of training, 1973-76; West Virginia University, Morgantown, associate professor of law, 1976-79; Albany Law School of Union University, NY, associate professor, 1979-82, professor of law, 1982-; Cleveland-Marshall College of Law, Joseph C. Hostetler-Baker & Hostetler Visiting Chair in Law, 1995-96; Marquette University Law School, Robert F. Boden Distinguished Visiting Chair, 1997; Suffolk University Law School, distinguished visiting professor, 2000; University of Akron Law School, John F. Seiberling Visiting Chair in Constitutional Law, 2002. **Publications:** Jurisprudence: Cases and Materials, 1993; Morality Imposed: The Rehnquist Court and Liberty in America, 2000. EDITOR: (with P. Finkelman) Toward a Usable Past: Liberty under State Constitutions, 1991; (and contrib.) Public Values in Constitutional Law, 1993. Contributor to law journals and legal periodicals. **Address:** Albany Law School, Union University, 80 New Scotland Ave, Albany, NY 12208, U.S.A.

GOTTSCHALL, Edward M(aurice). American, b. 1915. **Genres:** Advertising/Public relations, Art/Art history, Communications/Media, Technology, Illustrations. **Career:** Colton Press, New York City, managing editor of Graphic Arts Production Yearbook, 1937-51; Art Direction, New York City, editor, 1952-69; American Institute of Graphic Arts, New York City, executive director, 1969-75; International Typeface Corp., New York City, executive vice president, 1975-86, vice chairman, 1986-89, editorial consultant, 1990-98. Popular Merchandising Co., senior editor, 1964-67; co-publisher and editorial director, editor, U&lc, 1981-90, Advertising Trade Publications, Inc, 1967-69; Design Processing International, Inc., vice president, 1977-85. Lecturer, Pratt Institute, 1947-64, and New York University, 1955-64. **Publications:** (with F.C. Rodewald) Commercial Art as a Business, rev. ed., 1960, 2nd rev. ed., 1971; Graphic Communication '80s, 1981; Typographic Communications Today, 1989.

GÖTZ, Ignacio L. American (born Venezuela), b. 1933. **Genres:** Education, Philosophy, Theology/Religion. **Career:** Ordained Roman Catholic priest, 1962. Hofstra University, Hempstead, NY, adjunct assistant professor, 1966-68, assistant professor, 1968-72, associate professor, 1972-77, professor of philosophy of education, 1977-, and director Special Studies Program. **Publications:** (trans.) Pavitra Gulabmala, 1962; Joseph Fletcher's Situation Ethics and Education, 1968; (ed.) No Schools, 1971; The Psychedelic Teacher, 1972; Creativity, 1978; Zen and the Art of Teaching, 1988; Conceptions of Happiness, 1995; The Culture of Sexism, 1999; Manners and Violence, 2000; Technology and the Spirit, 2001; Faith, Humor, and Paradox, 2003. **Address:** PO Box 314, Point Harbor, NC 27964-0314, U.S.A. **Online address:** ignaciolleo@cs.com

GOUGEON, Len (G.). American, b. 1947. **Genres:** Literary criticism and history. **Career:** University of Massachusetts at Amherst, graduate instructor in rhetoric, 1970-74; University of Scranton, Scranton, PA, assistant professor, 1974-78, associate professor, 1978-82, professor of English, 1982-, chairman of university senate, 1979-80. University of Scranton Press, member of editorial board, 1987-93. **Publications:** Virtue's Hero: Emerson, Antislavery, and Reform, 1990; (ed. with J. Myerson) Emerson's Antislavery Writings, 1995. Contributor to books. **Address:** Department of English, University of Scranton, Scranton, PA 18510, U.S.A. **Online address:** gougeonl1@uofs.edu

GOUGH, Laurie. Canadian (born United States), b. 1964. **Genres:** Travel/Exploration. **Career:** Writer of articles, short stories, nonfiction, 1993-. Primary school and high school teacher; teacher of English as a second language. **Publications:** Island of the Human Heart: A Woman's Travel Odyssey (nonfiction), 1998, as Kite Strings of the Southern Cross: A Woman's Travel Odyssey, 1999. Author of a series of nature field guides. Contributor to anthologies and periodicals. **Address:** 19 Lewis St, Wakefield, QC, Canada J0X 3G0. **Online address:** lauriegough@sympatico.ca

GOUGH, Lawrence. Canadian. **Genres:** Mystery/Crime/Suspense. **Career:** Mystery novelist; scriptwriter for CBC. **Publications:** WILLOWS AND PARKER POLICE PROCEDURAL MYSTERY SERIES: The Goldfish Bowl, 1987; Death on a No. 8 Hook, 1988, in the U.S. as Silent Knives; Hot Shots, 1989; Serious Crimes, 1990; Accidental Deaths, 1991; Fall Down Easy, 1992; Killers, 1993; Heartbreaker, 1996; Memory Lane, 1996. OTHER: Sandstorm (thriller novel), 1990. Author of radio dramas for CBC. **Address:** c/o McClelland and Stewart Ltd, 481 University Ave Ste 900, Toronto, ON, Canada M5G 2E9.

GOUGH, Michael. American, b. 1939. **Genres:** Environmental sciences/Ecology. **Career:** Baylor College of Medicine, Houston, TX, assistant professor of microbiology, 1968-72; State University of New York, Stony Brook, assistant professor, 1972-75, associate professor, 1975-76; National Institute of Health, Bethesda, MD, health scientist administrator, 1976-78; United States Congressional Office of Technology Assessment, Washington, DC, director of special projects, 1978-85; Risk Science Institute, Washington, DC, director, 1985-86; Environ Corporation, Washington, DC, project manager, 1986-87; Center for Risk Management, Resources for the Future, Washington, DC, director, 1987-90; U.S. Congress Office of Technology Assessment, senior associate, 1990-. U.S. Veterans Administration Advisory Committee on Health-Related Effects of Herbicides, chair, 1987-90; U.S. Department of Health and Human Services Advisory Committee on the U.S. Air Force's Health Study of the Effects of Agent Orange ("Ranch Hand Advisory Committee"), chair, 1990-95. **Publications:** Dioxin, Agent Orange: The Facts, 1986; (with A.M. Ujihara) Managing Ash from Municipal Waste

Incinerators: A Report, 1989; (ed. with T.S. Glickman) Readings in Risk, 1990. Author of research papers on molecular biology, genetics, and environmental health. Contributor to books. **Address:** 6404 East Halbert Road, Bethesda, MD 20817, U.S.A.

GOUGH, Sue. British, b. 1940. **Genres:** Young adult fiction, Young adult non-fiction. **Career:** Canberra Times, Canberra, Australia, arts writer, 1963-68; freelance writer and editor, 1968-; Jacaranda Press, editor, Brisbane, Queensland, Australia, 1970-74. National Theatre Critic, 1984-98. **Publications:** YOUNG ADULT NOVELS: A Long Way to Tipperary, 1992; Wyrd, 1993; Here Comes the Night, 1997. OTHER: Queensland Colonial Years, 1984; (with D. Weedon) Tears in My Champagne (biography), 1984; The Book of Brisbane, 1985; Sugar, 1986; Hard Times and High Hopes, 1986; Issues of Today: Conservation, 1986; Issues of Today: AIDS, 1989; Unique Mammals of Australia, 1990; Creatures of the Antarctic, 1992; Big Beasts, Fact or Fiction, 1992; Keeping in Touch through Time, 1992; Thommo Makes His Mark, 1992; From Raw to Ready, 1992; Tell It in Print, 1992; The Daggs Meet the Bad Beasts, 1993; Punk Rocker from Hell, 1993; The Monster Manual, 1995; (ed.) J. Power, Setting the Stage: Queensland Performing Arts Complex: The First Ten Years, 1995. Author of storylines for the television series Barrier Reef, both 1970. **Address:** 344 Savages Rd., Brookfield, Brisbane, QLD 4069, Australia. **Online address:** Goughs. DandS@uq.net.au

GOULBOURNE, Harry. British/Jamaican, b. 1948. **Genres:** Politics/Government, Race relations, Sociology. **Career:** Assistant teacher, London, 1971-72; University of Dar es Salaam, Tanzania, senior lecturer, 1975-80; University of the West Indies, Jamaica, senior lecturer, 1980-86; University of Warwick, UK, principal research fellow, 1986-94; Cheltenham & Gloucester College of Higher Education, professor of political sociology, 1994-98; South Bank University, London, professor of sociology, 1998-. **Publications:** Teachers, Education, and Politics in Jamaica, 1892-1972, 1988; Ethnicity and Nationalism in Post-Imperial Britain, 1991; Race Relations in Britain since 1945, 1998; Caribbean Transnational Experience, 2002. EDITOR: Politics and State in the Third World, 1979; (with L. Sterling) Social Sciences and Caribbean Society, 2 vols, 1985; (and contrib.) Black Politics in Britain, 1990; (with R. Cohen, and contrib.) Taking Democracy Seriously: Socialists and Democracy in Africa, 1992; (with M. Chamberlain) Caribbean Families in the Atlantic World, 2000; Race & Ethnicity: Critical Concepts in Sociology, 2001. Work represented in anthologies. Contributor to professional journals. **Address:** Faculty of Humanities and Social Science, South Bank University, 103 Borough Rd, London SE1 0AA, England. **Online address:** goulbohd@sbu.ac.uk

GOULD, Bryan. New Zealander, b. 1939. **Genres:** Politics/Government. **Career:** Member of Her Majesty's Diplomatic Service, London, England, 1964-68; Oxford University, Oxford, England, tutor in law and fellow of Worcester College, 1968-74; British Parliament, London, Labour member of House of Commons for Southampton, 1974-79; Thames Television, England, reporter, 1979-83; British Parliament, Labour member of House of Commons for Dagenham, 1983-94; University of Waikato, vice-chancellor, 1994. **Publications:** Monetarism or Prosperity?, 1981; A Charter for the Disabled, 1981; Socialism and Freedom, 1986; A Future for Socialism, 1989; Goodbye to All That, 1995. **Address:** University of Waikato, Private Bag 3105, Hamilton W1R 5TA, New Zealand.

GOULD, James A. See Obituaries.

GOULD, James L. American, b. 1945. **Genres:** Biology. **Career:** Princeton University, NJ, assistant professor, 1975-80, associate professor, 1980-83, professor of biology, 1983-. **Publications:** Ethology: The Mechanisms and Evolution of Behavior, 1982. WITH C.G. GOULD: (and W.T. Keeton) Biological Science, 4th ed., 1986, 6th ed., 1996; The Honey Bee, 1988, 2nd ed., 1995; (ed.) Life at the Edge: Readings from Scientific American, 1989; Sexual Selection, 1989, 2nd ed., 1997; The Animal Mind, 1994, 2nd ed., 1999. WITH G.F. GOULD: BioStats Basics, 2002. Contributor to textbooks and professional and educational works. **Address:** Dept of Ecology & Evolutionary Biology, Princeton University, Princeton, NJ 08544-1003, U.S.A. **Online address:** gould@princeton.edu

GOULD, Janice. American, b. 1949. **Genres:** Poetry. **Career:** Writer and poet. **Publications:** Beneath My Heart: Poetry, 1990. Contributor of articles on Native American literature and issues to journals and periodicals. **Address:** 515 Fitzgerald Rd NW, Albuquerque, NM 87107, U.S.A.

GOULD, Judith. See BIENES, Nicholas Peter.

GOULD, Judith. *See* GALLAHER, (William) Rhea, Jr.

GOULD, K. Lance. American, b. 1938. **Genres:** Medicine/Health. **Career:** Physician, writer. Academic appointments: University of Hawaii School of Public Health, instructor, 1969; University of Washington School of Medicine, Seattle, instructor, 1970, assistant professor, 1972, associate professor, 1976; University of Texas Medical School, Houston, professor, 1979-; director, division of cardiology, 1979-85; vice chairman for clinical affairs, 1980-84; professor (Health Science Center), 1980-98; Positron Diagnostic and Research Center, director, 1979-87; Weatherhead PET Center for Preventing and Reversing Atherosclerosis, director, 1997-. Hospital appointments: VA Hospital, Seattle, WA, attending physician, 1970-79, education and research associate, 197174, clinical investigator, 1971-74; Hermann Hospital, Houston, TX, chief of cardiology, attending physician, 197985. Has served on national grant review panels and currently serves on the editorial boards of many professional journals. In addition to academic lectures, provides talks and presentations for the lay audience and for radio, television, and print media. **Publications:** Heal Your Heart: How You Can Prevent or Reverse Heart Disease, 1998; Coronary Artery Stenosis and Reversing Heart Disease, 1999. Contributor of articles to academic journals and to film productions. **Address:** University of Texas Medical School, Room 4.256 MSB, 6431 Fannin St., Houston, TX 77030, U.S.A. **Online address:** gould@heart.med.uth.tmc.edu

GOULD, Steven (Charles). American, b. 1955. **Genres:** Novels, Science fiction/Fantasy, Mystery/Crime/Suspense, Young adult fiction. **Career:** Brazos Valley Community Action Agency, Bryan, TX, data processing manager, 1987-90; free-lance writer and computer professional, 1990-. Texas A & M University, guest instructor. **Publications:** Jumper (novel), 1992; Wildside (science fiction novel), in press; (with L.J. Mixon) Greenwar (technical suspense novel), in press. **Address:** c/o Ralph M. Vicinanza Ltd., 303 W. 18th St., New York, NY 10011, U.S.A.

GOULD, William B(enjamin), (IV). American, b. 1936. **Genres:** Organized labor, Race relations. **Career:** United Auto Workers, Detroit, MI, assistant general counsel in labor law, 1961-62; National Labor Relations Board, Washington, DC, attorney, 1963-65, chairman, 1994; Battle, Fowler, Stokes, Kheel (law firm), New York City, associate, 1965-68; Wayne State University, Detroit, MI, professor of law, 1968-71; Harvard University, Cambridge, MA, visiting professor of law, 1971-72; Stanford University, CA, professor of law, 1972-94, on leave. Fulbright lecturer in Kyoto, Japan. Member of advisory council, New York State School of Industrial and Labor Relations, Cornell University. **Publications:** Black Workers in White Unions: Job Discrimination in the United States, 1977; A Primer on American Labor Law, 1982; Japan's Reshaping of American Labor Law, 1984; Strikes, Dispute Procedures, and Arbitration: Essays on Labor Law, 1985; (with others) Labor Relations in Professional Sports, 1986; Agenda for Reform, 1993; Labor Relations, 2000. **Address:** National Labor Relations Board, Crown Quadrangle, #310, Stanford University, Stanford, CA 94305-8610, U.S.A. **Online address:** wbgould@leland.stanford.edu

GOULDEN, Joseph C. Also writes as Henry S. A. Becket. American, b. 1934. **Genres:** History, Institutions/Organizations, Military/Defense/Arms control. **Publications:** The Curtis Caper, 1965; Monopoly: A Muckraking Study of AT & T, 1968; Truth Is the First Casualty: The Tonkin Gulf Incidents, 1969; The Money Givers: The Great American Foundations, 1971; The Superlawyers: The Small and Powerful World of the Great Washington Law Firms, 1972; Meany: The Unchallenged Strong Man of American Labor, 1972; The Benchwarmers: The Private World of the Federal Judiciary, 1974; The Best Years, 1976; (ed.) Mencken's Last Campaign, 1976; The Million Dollar Lawyers, 1978; Korea: The Untold Story, 1982; (with Paul A. Dickson) There Are Alligators in Our Sewers, 1983; The Death Merchant, 1984; (as Henry S.A. Becket) A Dictionary of Espionage, 1986; Fit to Print: A. M. Rosenthal and His Times, 1988; (with P.A. Dickson), Myth-Informed, 1993; (with R. Irvine and C. Kincaid), The News Manipulators, 1993. **Address:** 1534 29th St., NW, Washington, DC 20007-3060, U.S.A. **Online address:** JosephG894@AOL.com

GOULDING, Edwin (John). British, b. 1938. **Genres:** Horticulture. **Career:** Gouldings Fuchsias, Bentley, England, retired. **Publications:** Fuchsias: The Complete Guide, 1995. Contributor to plant magazines. **Address:** West View, Link Lane, Bentley, Suffolk 1P9 2DP, England.

GOULTER, Barbara. American. **Genres:** How-to books. **Career:** Freelance writer. Former teacher at University of San Francisco and Foothill College. Formerly Film Critic, San Francisco Chronicle. **Publications:** (with V. Goulter) How to Keep Your Car Mechanic Honest, 1990; (with J.

Minninger) The Perfect Presentation, 1992; (with Minninger) The Father-Daughter Dance, 1993. Contributor of articles and reviews to magazines and newspapers. **Address:** c/o Linda Allen Agency, 1949 Green St., San Francisco, CA 94123, U.S.A.

GOURGOURIS, Stathis. American, b. 1958. **Genres:** Poetry. **Career:** Princeton University, Department of Comparative Literature, assistant professor, 1992-. **Publications:** Dream Nation: Enlightenment, Colonization, and the Institution of Modern Greece, 1996; (trans) Y. Patilis, Camel of Darkness (Selected Poems 1970-1990), Vol 36, 1997. POETRY COLLECTIONS PUBLISHED IN GREEK: Ptoseis Falls, 1988; Autochthonies Indenticide, 1993. Contributor to books and journals. **Address:** Columbia University, Department of English, 602 Philosophy Hall MC4927, New York, NY 10027, U.S.A. **Online address:** ssg93@columbia.edu

GOVIER, Trudy. Canadian, b. 1944. **Genres:** Philosophy, Politics/Government. **Career:** Writer and philosopher. Trent University, Peterborough, ON, former philosophy professor. **Publications:** A Practical Study of Argument, 1985, rev. ed., 2005; Problems in Argument Analysis and Evaluation, 1987; (ed.) Selected Issues in Logic and Communication, 1988; God, the Devil, and the Perfect Pizza: Ten Philosophical Questions, 1989; Social Trust and Human Communities, 1997; Forgiveness and Revenge, 2002; A Delicate Balance, 2002. Contributor to periodicals. **Address:** 3207 Canmore Rd NW, Calgary, AB, Canada T2M 4J8. **Online address:** govier@shaw.com

GOW, Andrew Colin. Canadian, b. 1962. **Genres:** History, Cultural/Ethnic topics, Theology/Religion, Essays. **Career:** University of Alberta, Edmonton, assistant professor, 1993-99, associate professor, 1999-2003, professor of history, 2003-. **Publications:** (trans.) H.A. Oberman, The Reformation: Roots and Ramifications, 1994; The Red Jews: Anti-Semitism in an Apocalyptic Age, 1200-1600, 1995; (with L. Apps) Male Witches in Early Modern Europe, 2003. **Address:** Dept of History and Classics, 2-28 Tory Bldg, University of Alberta, Edmonton, AB, Canada T6G 2H4. **Online address:** Andrew.Gow@ualberta.ca

GOWAN, Lee. Canadian, b. 1961. **Genres:** Novellas/Short stories, Novels, Plays/Screenplays. **Career:** Freelance writer, 1980-91; University of Regina, Swift Current Extension, Swift Current, Saskatchewan, Canada, instructor in English and creative writing, 1991-96; University of Toronto, Toronto, Ontario, Canada, instructor and facilitator of writing program, Faculty of Landscape, Architecture, and Design, 1998-. Canadian Film Centre, member of resident program, 1996; workshop developer; script editor. **Publications:** Going to Cuba (short stories), 1990; Paris or Somewhere (television movie), 1995; Make Believe Love (novel), 2001; Sunbirds (screenplay). Work represented in anthologies. Contributor of fiction and poetry to magazines. **Address:** 195 Argyle St., Toronto, ON, Canada M6J 1P5. **Online address:** lee.gowan@utoronto.ca

GOWEN, Kenneth K. American, b. 1924. **Genres:** Romance/Historical, Autobiography/Memoirs. **Career:** International Harvester Co., Memphis, TN, day work analyst and design engineer for nearly 35 years. **Publications:** Granddaddy, Tell about the War, 1998. **Address:** 714 Manor Dr, Oxford, MS 38655, U.S.A. **Online address:** gowen@dixie-net.com

GOYER, David S. American, b. 1966. **Genres:** Cartoons. **Career:** Comics writer, novelist, short story writer, screenwriter, producer, and television series creator. **Publications:** COMICS: (with James Robinson) Justice Be Done: JSA, 2000; (with Geoff Johns) A Burning Hate, 2001; (with others) JSA: Darkness Falls, 2002; (with Geoff Johns) JLA, JSA: Virtue and Vice, 2002; (with Geoff Johns) JSA: The Return of Hawkman,, 2002; (with James Robinson) Starman: A Starry Knight, 2002; (with James Robinson and Chuck Dixon) The Justice Society Returns!, 2003; (with Leonard Kirk) JSA: Stealing Thunder, 2003; SCREENPLAYS: Death Warrant, 1990; (And associate producer) Kickboxer 2: The Road Back, 1991; Demonic Toys, 1992; Arcade, 1993; (with Ted Elliott and Terry Rossio) Robert A. Heinlein's The Puppet Masters, 1994; The Crow: City of Angels, 1996; Blade, 1998; Dark City, 1998; (And coproducer) Mission to Mars, 2000; (And executive producer) Blade 2, 2002; (And director) ZigZag, 2002; (And director and producer) Blade: Trinity, 2004. NOVELS: (with Frank Lauria, Lem Dobbs, and Alex Proyas) Dark City, 1998. TELEPLAYS: (And executive producer) Sleepwalkers, 1997. Author of television specials. **Address:** c/o Author Mail, DC Comics, 1700 Broadway, 7th floor, New York, NY 10019, U.S.A.

GRAAF, Peter. *See* YOUD, Sam.

GRABBE, Crockett L(ane). American, b. 1951. **Genres:** Inspirational/Motivational Literature, Physics, Politics/Government, Sciences, Technology,

Astronomy, Autobiography/Memoirs. **Career:** University of Tennessee, Knoxville, visiting assistant professor, 1978-79; Science Applications, Washington, DC, research scientist, 1979-81; University of Iowa, Iowa City, associate research scientist, 1981-88, research scientist, 1988-. Public speaker on science-related issues; scientific consultant. **Publications:** Plasma Waves and Instabilities, 1986; Space Weapons and the Strategic Defense Initiative, 1991; Duck Soup for the Diehard Soul, 2001; Power in Focus, 2004. Contributor to books. Contributor of articles and reviews to scientific journals and periodicals, newspapers, and magazines. **Address:** Department of Physics and Astronomy, VAN 203, University of Iowa, Iowa City, IA 52242, U.S.A.

GRABER, Julia A. American, b. 1961. **Genres:** Medicine/Health, Psychology, Human relations/Parenting. **Career:** Pennsylvania State University, University Park, research assistant in Adolescent Mental Health Study, 1987-90, data manager for the study and for Pennsylvania State Adolescence Study, 1990-91, instructor in psychology, 1990; Educational Testing Services, postdoctoral fellow in Adolescent Study Program, 1991-92; Columbia University, Teachers College, NYC, associate director of Adolescent Study Program, 1992-, senior research scientist, 1992-, director of graduate training at Center for Children and Families, 1993-, associate director of the center, 1994-, adjunct professor of developmental and educational psychology, 1992-94, adjunct associate professor of human development, 1997-. Consultant to NYC Health and Hospitals Corp. **Publications:** EDITOR & CONTIBUTOR: (with J. Brooks-Gunn and A.C. Petersen) Transitions through Adolescence: Interpersonal Domains and Context, 1996; (with J.S. Dubas) New Directions for Child Development, Vol 71: Leaving Home: Understanding the Transition to Adulthood, 1996. Contributor to books. Contributor of articles and reviews to psychology, health, and education journals. **Address:** Adolescent Study Program Box 39, Teachers College, Columbia University, 525 West 120th St., New York, NY 10027, U.S.A. **Online address:** JAG51@columbia.edu

GRABER MILLER, Keith Allen. Also writes as Keith G. Miller. American, b. 1959. **Genres:** Documentaries/Reportage. **Career:** Howard County News, Greentown, IN, editor and general manager, 1981-83; co-pastor of Mennonite church in Kokomo, IN, 1983-87; Goshen College, Goshen, IN, interim campus minister, 1987-88, assistant professor of communication, 1987-89, associate professor of Bible, religion, and philosophy, 1993-. Associated Mennonite Biblical Seminary, visiting faculty member, 1997-. Kokomo Tribune, bureau chief, 1981-83. **Publications:** (as Keith G. Miller) Wise as Serpents, Innocent as Doves: American Mennonites Engage Washington, 1996. Contributor to books. Contributor of articles and reviews to periodicals. **Address:** Goshen College, Goshen, IN 46526, U.S.A. **Online address:** keithgm@goshen.edu

GRACE, Alexander M. Also writes as Bruce Farcau. American, b. 1951. **Genres:** Novels, Adult non-fiction, History. **Career:** U.S. Department of State, Washington, DC, staff member, 1977-, political officer in Bolivia, 1979-81, Ecuador, 1981-84, France, 1985-87, the Dominican Republic, 1987-88, Spain, 1990-92, Mexico, 1995-97. **Publications:** NOVELS: Crisis, 1991; Coup!, 1992; Sky Blue, 1994; Holy War, 1997; Hegemon, 1995. AS BRUCE FARCAU: The Coup (political science), 1992; The Chaco War (history), 1994; The Ten Cents War (history), 2000; A Little Empire of Their Own (historical novel), 2000. Contributor to periodicals.

GRACE, C. L. See **DOHERTY, P(aul) C.**

GRACE, Nancy McCampbell. American, b. 1952. **Genres:** Literary criticism and history. **Career:** Women's Tribune, Columbus, OH, editor and publisher, 1978-80; Ohio State University, Columbus, director of Writing Skills Laboratory, 1983-84, editor for Department of Anesthesiology, 1985-86, lecturer in English, 1986-87; College of Wooster, Wooster, OH, associate professor of English, 1987-, department head, 1994-, director of writing, 1988-. Otterbein College, adjunct lecturer, 1986-87; Franklin University, adjunct lecturer, 1986-87. **Publications:** (with T.L. Milligan) The Waiting (poetry chapbook), 1980; (with G. DeLaVars) The Tutor Handbook, 1986; The Feminized Male Character in Twentieth-Century Literature, 1995. Contributor to books. Contributor of articles and reviews to periodicals. **Address:** Department of English, College of Wooster, Wooster, OH 44691, U.S.A.

GRACE, Patricia (Frances). New Zealander, b. 1937. **Genres:** Novels, Novellas/Short stories, Children's fiction. **Career:** Full-time writer. Formerly, Teacher in primary and secondary schools in King Country, Northland, and Porirua. **Publications:** FOR CHILDREN: The Kuia and the Spider, 1981; Watercress Tuna and the Children of Champion Street, 1984; He aha te mea

nui? Ma wai? Ko au tenei, and Ahakoa he iti (Maori readers), 4 vols., 1985; The Trolley, 1993; Areta and the Kahawai, 1994. FOR ADULTS. STORIES: Waiariki, 1975; The Dream Sleepers and Other Stories, 1980; Electric City, 1987; Selected Stories, 1991; Collected Stories, 1994. NOVELS: Mutuwhenua: The Moon Sleeps, 1978; Potiki, 1986; Cousins, 1992; Baby No-eyes, 1998; Dogside Story, 2001. OTHER: Wahine Toa: Women of Maori Myth (for adults), 1984; The Sky People, 1994. COntributor of stories to anthologies. **Address:** c/o Penguin Books, Provate Bag 102902, North Shore Mail Centre, Auckland, New Zealand.

GRAD, Laurie Burrows. American, b. 1944. **Genres:** Food and Wine. **Career:** AM-LA (television program), Los Angeles, CA, regular guest on cooking topics, 1978; Hour Magazine (nationally syndicated television show), regular guest, 1979-87; Los Angles Magazine, food editor, 1978-95; Buzz magazine, Los Angeles, CA, restaurant columnist, 1996-; cookbook author, 1982-; host of Laurie Cooks Light & Easy (television cooking program) on The Learning Channel (TLC), 1993-96, and on Travel and Living Channel, 1997-. **Publications:** Make It Easy in Your Kitchen, 1982; Make It Easy Entertaining, 1984; Make It Easy, Make It Light, 1987; Entertaining Light and Easy: Lower Fat Recipes for Festive Meals, 1998. Contributor to periodicals and Internet magazines. **Address:** 1250 Beverly Green Dr, Los Angeles, CA 90035, U.S.A. **Online address:** mkitezy@aol.com

GRAEBNER, Norman Arthur. American, b. 1915. **Genres:** International relations/Current affairs, Politics/Government. **Career:** Iowa State University, Ames, assistant professor to professor, 1948-56; University of Illinois, Urbana, professor of history, 1956-67, chairman, Dept. of History, 1961-63; University of Virginia, Charlottesville, professor of history, 1967-86; Oxford University, Harmsworth Professor of American History, 1978-79. Current History, contributing editor. **Publications:** Empire on the Pacific, 1955; The New Isolationism, 1956; Cold War Diplomacy, 1962; Ideas and Diplomacy, 1964; (with G.C. Fite and P.L. White) A History of the United States, 2 vols., 1970; (with G.C. Fite and P.L. White) A History of the American People, 1970; (with G.C. Fite) Recent United States History, 1972; The Age of Global Power, 1979; America as a World Power, 1984; Foundations of American Foreign Policy, 1985; A Twentieth-Century Odyssey, 2002. EDITOR: The Enduring Lincoln, 1959; An Uncertain Tradition: American Secretaries of State in the Twentieth Century, 1961; Politics and the Crisis of 1860, 1961; The Cold War: Conflict of Ideology and Power, 1963; Manifest Destiny, 1968; Nationalism and Communism in Asia: The American Response, 1977; Freedom in America: A 200-Year Perspective, 1977; American Diplomatic History before 1900, 1978; Traditions and Values: American Diplomacy 1790-1945, 2 vols., 1985; The National Security: Its Theory and Practice in the United States 1945-1960, 1986. **Address:** 205 Emerald Pond Ln #108, Durham, NC 27705-6052, U.S.A.

GRAEF, Roger (Arthur). American/British, b. 1936. **Genres:** Documentaries/Reportage. **Career:** Director, writer, and producer for film, opera, theatre, and TV. Observer/director, Actors Studio, NYC, 1958-62; has worked in England, 1962-. **Publications:** Talking Blues, 1989; Living Dangerously, 1992; Why Restorative Justice?, 2001. **Address:** Films of Record, 2 Elgin Ave, London W9 3QP, England. **Online address:** rogerg@filmsofrecord.com

GRAEME, Roderic. See **JEFFRIES, Roderic.**

GRAEUB, Ralph. Swiss, b. 1921. **Genres:** Environmental sciences/Ecology, Medicine/Health. **Career:** Faerberei AG, Zofingen, Switzerland, development engineer, 1950-72; Kammzugfaerberei AG, Zofingen, manager, 1972-87. Member of national and international environmental protection commissions. **Publications:** Die sanften Moerder: Atomkraftwerke demaskiert, 1972, trans as The Gentle Killers: Nuclear Power Stations, 1974; Der Petkau-Effekt und unsere strahlende Zukuft, 1985, 4th ed., 1990, rev. trans as The Petkau Effect: The Devastating Effect of Nuclear Radiation on Human Health and the Environment, 1992, 2nd ed., 1994; Four Walls Eight Windows. **Address:** Hoeflistrasse 102, PO Box, CH-8135 Langnau a/Albis, Switzerland.

GRAF, William L. American, b. 1947. **Genres:** Geography. **Career:** University of Iowa, Ames, assistant professor to associate professor of geography and research associate at Institute of Urban and Regional Research, 1974-78; Arizona State University, Tempe, associate professor to professor of geography, 1978-, Regents Professor 1994-, director of Center for Southwest Studies, 1981-83. Visiting lecturer and/or speaker at universities worldwide. Consultant to U.S. Army Corps of Engineers, Indian Claims Section of U.S. Department of Justice, U.S. Bureau of Reclamation, and law firms. **Publications:** The Colorado River: Instability and Basin Management,

1985; Fluvial Processes in Dryland Rivers, 1988; Wilderness Preservation and the Sagebrush Rebellions, 1990; Plutonium and the Rio Grande, 1994. EDITOR: (and contrib.) Geomorphic Systems of North America, 1987; The Salt and Gila Rivers in Central Arizona: A Geographic Field Trip Guide, 1988. Contributor to books. Contributor of articles and reviews to periodicals. **Address:** Department of Geography, Arizona State University, Tempe, AZ 85287, U.S.A.

GRAFF, Dale E(dward). American, b. 1934. **Genres:** Paranormal. **Career:** Bendix Systems Division, Ann Arbor, MI, aerospace engineer, 1959-61; Martin Marietta Corp., Baltimore, MD, aerospace engineer, 1961-64; U.S. Air Force, Foreign Technology Division, Dayton, OH, civilian aerospace engineer and physicist, 1964-81; Defense Intelligence Agency, Washington, DC, physicist, 1981-93; retired, 1993. **Publications:** Tracks in the Psychic Wilderness, 1998; River Dreams: Wilderness and Psychic Themes, 1998. **Address:** 168 Windcliff Rd., Prince Frederick, MD 20678, U.S.A. **Online address:** baygraff@chesapeake.net; www.chesapeake.net./~baygraff/

GRAFF, Henry Franklin. American, b. 1921. **Genres:** History, Biography. **Career:** Columbia University, NYC, joined faculty, 1946, chairman, Dept. of History, 1961-63, professor of history, 1961-91, professor emeritus, 1991-. **Publications:** Bluejackets with Perry in Japan, 1952; (with J. Barzun) The Modern Researcher, 1962, 6th ed., 2004; (with C. Lord) American Themes, 1963; Thomas Jefferson, 1968; The Free and the Brave, 1967, 5th ed., 1992; (ed.) American Imperialism and the Philippine Insurrection, 1969; The Tuesday Cabinet: Deliberation and Decision on Peace and War under Lyndon B. Johnson, 1970; (with J.A. Krout) The Adventure of the American People, 3rd ed., 1973; (with P. J. Bohannan) The Grand Experiment, vol. I: The Call of Freedom, vol. II: The Promise of Democracy, 1978; This Great Nation, 1983; The Presidents: A Reference History, 1984, 3rd ed., 2002; America: The Glorious Republic, 1985, 3rd ed., 1990; Grover Cleveland, 2002. **Address:** 47 Andrea Ln, Scarsdale, NY 10583, U.S.A.

GRAFTON, Anthony T(homas). American, b. 1950. **Genres:** History, Translations. **Career:** Historian, educator, and author, specializing in the history of classical scholarship, of Renaissance education, and of early astronomy; Cornell University, Ithaca, NY, instructor in history, 1974-1975; Princeton University, Department of History, assistant professor to associate professor, 1975-85, professor, 1985-, Andrew Mellon Professor of History, 1988-1993, Dodge Professor of History, 1993-; Exhibit curator, New York Public Library, NYC, 1992, and Library of Congress, Washington, DC, 1993; Meyer Schapiro lecturer, Columbia University, 1996-1997. **Publications:** Joseph Scaliger: A Study in the History of Classical Scholarship, Vol 1: Textual Criticism and Exegesis, 1983, Vol 2: Historical Chronology, 1993; (with L. Jardine) From Humanism to the Humanities: Education and the Liberal Arts in Fifteenth- and SixteenthCentury Europe, 1986; Forgers and Critics: Creativity and Duplicity in Western Scholarship, 1990; Defenders of the Text: The Traditions of Scholarship in an Age of Science, 1450-1800, 1991; (with A. Shelford and N. Siraisi) New Worlds, Ancient Texts: The Power of Tradition and the Shock of Discovery, 1992; (with E.F. Rice) The Foundations of Early Modern Europe, 1460-1559, 1994; The Footnote: A Curious History, 1997; Leon Battista Alberti, 2000. Contributor to periodicals. EDITOR: (comp, with H.J. de Jonge) Joseph Scaliger: A Bibliography, 1852-1982, 1982; (with A. Blair) The Transmission of Culture in Early Modern Europe, 1990; Rome Reborn: The Vatican Library and Renaissance Culture (catalogue of an exhibition held at the Library of Congress, Washington, DC, January 6April 30, 1993), 1993. TRANSLATOR: (with G.W. Most and J.E.G. Zetzel; also author of intro and notes with Most and Zetzel) Prolegomena to Homer, 1795, by F.A. Wolf, 1985. **Address:** Department of History, Dickinson Hall, Princeton University, Princeton, NJ 08544, U.S.A.

GRAFTON, Sue. American, b. 1940. **Genres:** Mystery/Crime/Suspense. **Career:** Full-time writer. Recipient: Private Eye Writers of America Shamus Award, 1986; Mystery Readers of America Macavity Award, 1986; Anthony Award, 1986, 1987, 1991; Doubleday Mystery Guild Award, 1989, 1990, 1991, 1992; and others. **Publications:** Keziah Dane, 1968; The Lolly-Madonna War, 1969; A Is for Alibi, 1982; B Is for Burglar, 1985; C Is for Corpse, 1986; D Is for Deadbeat, 1987; E Is for Evidence, 1988; F Is for Fugitive, 1989; G Is for Gumshoe, 1990, H Is for Homicide, 1991; I Is for Innocent, 1992; J Is for Judgment, 1993; K Is for Killer, 1994; L Is for Lawless, 1995; M Is for Malice, 1996; N Is for Noose, 1998; O Is for Outlaw, 1999; P Is for Peril, 2001; Q Is for Quarry, 2002; R is for Richochet, 2004. **Address:** PO Box 41447, Santa Barbara, CA 93140, U.S.A. **Online address:** www.suegrafton.com

GRAGG, Rod. American, b. 1950. **Genres:** History. **Career:** WBTW-TV, Florence, SC, reporter, editor; WWAY-TV, Wilmington, NC, news director,

1973-74; WBTV-TV, Charlotte, NC, news reporter, 1974-76; Montreat-Anderson College, Montreat, NC, administrator, 1977-78; University of South Carolina, Coastal Carolina College, Conway, SC, administrator and instructor, 1978-83; Southern Communications, Conway, president, 1983-. Board of directors, Conway Christian School; former member of South Carolina State Board of Education; ruling elder, Presbyterian Church in America. **Publications:** Bobby Bagley P.O.W., 1978; Pirates, Planters, and Patriots: Historical Tales from the South Carolina Grand Strand, 1985; The Civil War Quiz and Fact Book, 1985; The Old West Quiz and Fact Book, 1987; The Illustrated Confederate Reader, 1989; Confederate Goliath: The Battle of Fort Fisher, 1991; The Illustrated History of Horry County, 1994; Covered with Glory: The 26th North Carolina at Gettysburg, 2000. **Address:** Southern Communications, 311 Main St., Box 2006, Conway, SC 29526, U.S.A. **Online address:** southcom@sccoast.net

GRAHAM, Ada. American, b. 1931. **Genres:** Children's non-fiction. **Career:** Developer and Writer, Audubon Adventures (National Audubon Society), 1984-. Vice-Chairman, Maine State Commission on the Arts, 1975-80; Board Member, New England Foundation for the Arts, 1977-80; Member, Board of Dirs., Maine Family Planning Association, 1973-80. **Publications:** WITH FRANK GRAHAM: The Great American Shopping Cart, 1969; Wildlife Rescue, 1970; Puffing Island, 1971; The Milkweed and Its World of Animals, 1976; Audubon Readers, 6 vols., 1978-81; Alligators, 1979; Careers in Conservation, 1980; Birds of the Northern Seas, 1980; The Changing Desert, 1981; Jacob and Owl, 1981; Three Million Mice, 1981; Busy Bugs, 1983; The Big Stretch, 1985; We Watch Squirrels, 1985; Kate Furbish and the Flora of Maine, 1995. OTHER: The Mystery of the Everglades, 1972; Dooryard Garden, 1974; Let's Discover the Winter Woods, 1974; Let's Discover the Floor of the Forest, 1974; Let's Discover Changes Everywhere, 1974; Let's Discover Birds in Our World, 1974; The Careless Animal, 1974; Foxtails, Ferns and Fishscales: A Handbook of Art and Nature Projects, 1976; Whale Watch, 1978; Bug Hunters, 1978; Coyote Song, 1978; Falcon Flight, 1978; Bears, 1981; Six Little Chickadees, 1982. **Address:** c/o JCA Literary Agency, 27 W 20th St Ste 1103, New York, NY 10011, U.S.A.

GRAHAM, Alexander John. British, b. 1930. **Genres:** History. **Career:** Professor of Classical Studies, University of Pennsylvania, Philadelphia, 1977-95, emeritus, 1995-. Assistant Lecturer in Classics, Bedford College, University of London, 1955-57; Assistant Lecturer, Lecturer and Sr. Lecturer in History, University of Manchester, 1957-77. **Publications:** Colony and Mother City in Ancient Greece, 1964, 1983; (ed.) Polis und Imperium Beitrage zur alten Geschichte, by Victor Ehrenberg, 1965; An Attic Country House, Below the Cave of Pan at Vari, 1974. **Address:** Dept. of Classical Studies, 720 Logan Hall, University of Pennsylvania, Philadelphia, PA 19104-6304, U.S.A.

GRAHAM, Billy. (William F. Graham). American, b. 1918. **Genres:** Theology/Religion, Inspirational/Motivational Literature. **Career:** Evangelist; Billy Graham Evangelistic Association, founder, 1950-; Hour of Decision, leader of the weekly radio program, 1950-; My Answer, author of the syndicated newspaper column, 1952-; known for world evangelistic campaigns. Ordained Southern Baptist minister, 1939; First Baptist Church, Western Springs, IL, pastor, 1943-45; FirstYouth for Christ Intn., Chicago, vice-president, 1945-50; Northwestern College, Minneapolis, president, 1947-52. **Publications:** Peace with God, 1953; The Secret of Happiness, 1955; My Answer, 1960; World Aflame, 1965; The Challenge, 1969; The Jesus Generation, 1971; Angels: God's Secret Agents, 1975; Billy Graham Talks to Teenagers, 1976; How to Be Born Again, 1977; The Holy Spirit, 1978; Till Armageddon, 1981; Approaching Hoofbeats: The Four Horseman of the Apocalypse, 1983; A Biblical Standard for Evangelists, 1984; Unto the Hills, 1986; Facing Death and the Life After, 1987; Answers to Life's Problems, 1988; Hope for the Troubled Heart, 1991; Storm Warnings, 1992; Just as I Am, 1997. **Address:** 1300 Harmon Pl, Minneapolis, MN 55403, U.S.A.

GRAHAM, Bob. (Robert Graham). Australian, b. 1942. **Genres:** Children's fiction, Children's non-fiction, Illustrations. **Career:** Artist, New South Wales, Government Printers, Sydney, 1973-75; Dept. of Technical Education, Sydney, resource designer, 1975-82; Five Mile Press, Melbourne, illustrator, 1982-83. **Publications:** FOR CHILDREN. SELF-ILLUSTRATED FICTION: Pete and Roland, 1981; Here Comes John, 1983; Here Comes Theo, 1983; Pearl's Place, 1983; Libby, Oscar and Me, 1984; Bath Time for John, 1985; First There Was Frances, 1985; Where Is Sarah?, 1985; The Wild, 1986; The Adventures of Charlotte and Henry, 1987; Crusher Is Coming!, 1987; The Red Woollen Blanket, 1987; Has Anyone Seen William?, 1988; Grandad's Magic, 1989; Greetings from Sandy Beach, 1990; Rose Meets Mister Wintergarten, 1991; Brand New Baby, 1992; Spirit of Hope, 1993; Zoltan the

Magnificent, 1994; Queenie the Bantam, 1997; Buffy, 1999; Max, 2000; Let's Get a Pup, 2001; Jethro Byrde, 2002; Tales from the Waterhole, 2004; Oscar's Half Birthday, 2005. NON-FICTION (readers): I Can series: Actions 1, Actions 2, Babies, Bikes, Colour, Families, Helping, In the Water, My Senses, Pets, School, Shopping, 12 vols., 1984, in U.K. as Reading Is Fun series, 12 vols., 1986; Science Early Learners series: Heat, Moving, Push, Senses, Sound, Water, Wheels, 7 vols., 1985-86; Busy Day Board Books: Playing, Sleeping, Waking, 3 vols., 1988; (ed.) A First Australian Poetry Book, 1983. Illustrator of books by R. Harvey, K. Heinze, A.B. Ingram, I. Opie, M. Rosen, J. Ryles, E. Wignell.

GRAHAM, Caroline. British, b. 1931. **Genres:** Novels, Mystery/Crime/Suspense, Plays/Screenplays. **Career:** Has had a variety of jobs, including dancer, actress, stage manager, freelance radio journalist and radio dramatist. Recipient: Mystery Reader of America Macavity Award, 1989. **Publications:** NOVELS: Fire Dance, 1982; BMX Star Rider, 1985; BMX'ers Battle It Out, 1985. MYSTERIES: The Envy of the Stranger, 1984; The Killings at Badger's Drift, 1987; Death of a Hollow Man, 1989; Murder at Madingley Grange, 1990; Death in Disguise 1993; Written in Blood, 1994; Faithful unto Death, 1998; Killings at Badgers Drift, 1999; Place of Safety, 1999. PLAYS: Dummy Rum, 1994; Roma's Song, 1994. **Address:** c/o David Higham, 6-8 Lower John St, London WC1 4AR, England.

GRAHAM, Charles S. See TUBB, E(dwin) C(harles).

GRAHAM, Cosmo. British (born United States), b. 1956. **Genres:** Law. **Career:** Liverpool Polytechnic, England, lecturer in law, 1981-82; University of Sheffield, England, lecturer in law, 1982-92; University of Hull, England, professor of law, 1993-99; University of Leicester, professor of law, 1999-; writer. **Publications:** (ed. with T. Prosser) Waiving the Rules: The Constitution under Thatcherism, 1988; (with T. Prosser) Privatising Public Enterprises: Constitutions, the State, and Regulation in Comparative Perspective, 1991; Regulating Public Utilities, 2000. **Address:** Faculty of Law, University of Leicester, Leicester LE1 7RH, England.

GRAHAM, Daniel O., Jr. American, b. 1952. **Genres:** Writing/Journalism, Science fiction/Fantasy, Humor/Satire, Biography. **Career:** U.S. Army, career officer, 1974-83, leaving the service as captain; Kentec Corp., Arlington, VA, president, 1983-; Graham Associates, Fairfax, VA, principal, 1986-. **Publications:** (with J.H. Graham) The Writing System Workbook, 1994; The Gatekeepers (science fiction), 1995; The Politics of Meaning (humor), 1995; (ed.) Confessions of a Cold Warrior (biography), 1995. SCIENCE FICTION WITH R. DAWSON: Entering Tenebrea, 2000; Tenebrea's Hope, 2001; Tenebrea Rising, 2002.

GRAHAM, Desmond. British, b. 1940. **Genres:** Poetry, Literary criticism and history, Biography, Translations. **Career:** University of Newcastle upon Tyne, reader in modern English poetry, 1997-2000, professor of poetry, 2000-. Visiting lecturer, Munich University, Germany, 1968-70, Mannheim University, 1970-71, and Gdansk University, Poland, 1984. Opera News, NYC, correspondent, 1969-71. **Publications:** Introduction to Poetry, 1968; Keith Douglas 1920-1944: A Biography, 1974; The Truth of War: Owen, Blunden, and Rosenberg, 1984; Seren Poets 2, 1990; A Set of Signs for Chopin's 24 Preludes, 1990; A Rumtopt for Summer 1990; The Lie of Horizons, 1993; (trans. with T.P. Krzeszowski) A. Kamienska, Two Darknesses: Selected Poems, 1994; The Marching Bands, 1996; Not Falling, 1999; After Shakespeare, 2001; Milena Poems, 2004. EDITOR: The Complete Poems of Keith Douglas, 1978; K. Douglas, Alamein to Zem Zem, 1979; K. Douglas, A Prose Miscellany, 1985; Poetry of the Second World War: An International Anthology, 1995; Keith Douglas: The Letters, 2000. **Address:** 6 Greenfield Place, Newcastle upon Tyne NE4 6AX, England.

GRAHAM, Don(ald R.). Canadian, b. 1947. **Genres:** Intellectual history. **Career:** Economist, administrative analyst, and cultural conservation coordinator for Province of Saskatchewan, 1971-76; lighthouse keeper in British Columbia, 1977-. **Publications:** Red, White, and Black: An Interpretation of Ethnic and Racial Attitudes of Agrarian Radicals in Texas and Oklahoma, 1880-1920, 1971; Keepers of the Light: A History of British Columbia's Lighthouses and Their Keepers, 1985; Lights of the Inside Passage: A History of British Columbia's Lighthouses and Their Keepers, 1986. **Address:** Point Atkinson Lighthouse, P.O. Box 91338, West Vancouver, BC, Canada V7V 3N9.

GRAHAM, Edward M(ontgomery). American, b. 1944. **Genres:** Business/Trade/Industry, Economics. **Career:** Massachusetts Institute of Technology, Cambridge, assistant professor, 1974-79; U.S. Treasury Department, Washington, DC, international economist, 1979-82; University of North

Carolina at Chapel Hill, associate professor, 1982-88; Institute for International Economics, Washington, DC, senior fellow, 1990-. Member of advisory board, Korea Economic Institute of America. **Publications:** (with P. Krugman) Foreign Direct Investment in the United States: Effects on the U.S. Economy, Institute for International Economics, 1989, 3rd ed., 1995; (ed. with T.S. Arrison, C.F. Bergsten, and M.C. Harris, and contrib.) Japan's Growing Technological Capability: Implications for the U.S. Economy, 1992; Global Corporations and National Governments: Are Changes Needed in the International Economic and Political Order in Light of the Globalization of Business?, 1996; (with J.D. Richardson) Global Competition Policy; Fighting the Wrong Enemy: Antiglobalist Activists and Multinational Enterprises, 2000; Reforming Korea's Industrial Conglomerates, 2903. Work represented in anthologies. Contributor of articles and reviews to periodicals. **Address:** Institute for International Economics, 1750 Massachusetts Ave NW, Washington, DC 20036-1903, U.S.A. **Online address:** emgraham@iie.com

GRAHAM, Frank, Jr. American, b. 1925. **Genres:** Environmental sciences/Ecology, Natural history. **Career:** Field Ed., Audubon mag., since 1968. **Publications:** Disaster by Default, 1966; (with A. Graham) The Great American Shopping Cart, 1969; Since Silent Spring, 1970; (with A. Graham) Wildlife Rescue, 1970; (with A. Graham) Puffin Island, 1971; Man's Dominion, 1971; (with A. Graham) The Mystery of the Everglades, 1972; Where the Place Called Morning Lies, 1973; (with A. Graham) Aububon Primers, 4 vols., 1974; (with A. Graham) The Careless Animal, 1975; Gulls: A Social History, 1975; Potomac: The Nation's River, 1976; (with A. Graham) The Milkweed and Its World of Animals, 1976; The Adirondack Park: A Political History, 1978; (with A. Graham) Audubon Readers, 6 vols., 1978-81; (with A. Graham) Careers in Conservation, 1980; (with A. Graham) Birds of the Northern Seas, 1981; A Farewell to Heroes, 1981; (with A. Graham) The Changing Desert, 1981; (with A. Graham) Jacob and Owl, 1981; (with A. Graham) Three Million Mice, 1981; (with A. Graham) Busy Bugs, 1983; The Dragon Hunters, 1984; (with A. Graham) The Big Stretch, 1985; (with A. Graham) We Watch Squirrels, 1985; The Audubon Ark, 1990; (with A. Graham) Kate Furbish and the Flora of Maine, 1995. **Address:** c/o JCA Literary Agency, 27 W 20th St Ste 1103, New York, NY 10011, U.S.A.

GRAHAM, Henry. British, b. 1930. **Genres:** Poetry. **Career:** Lecturer in Art History, Liverpool Polytechnic, 1969-. Poetry Ed., Ambit mag., London. Atkinson Art Gallery, Merseyside, writer in residence, 1996. Former artist. **Publications:** (with J. Mangnall) Soup City Zoo: Poems, 1968; Good Luck to You Kafka/You'll Need It Boss, 1969; Passport to Earth, 1971; Poker in Paradise Lose, 1977; Bomb, 1985; Europe After Rain, 1982; The Very Fragrant Death of Paul Gauguin, 1987; Everywhere You Look, 1993; The Eye of the Beholder, 1997; Bar Room Ballads, 1999; Kafka in Liverpool, 2003. **Address:** c/o Ambit, 17 Priory Gardens, London N6 5QY, England.

GRAHAM, Jefferson. American, b. 1956. **Genres:** Communications/Media. **Career:** The Hollywood Reporter, columnist and reporter, 1981-84; USA Today, Los Angeles, CA, reporter, 1984-; Entertainment Tonight (television show), producer, 1984; Prodigy, columnist, 1992-. Has appeared on television programs. **Publications:** Come On Down: The TV Game Show Book, 1989; Vegas: Live and In Person, 1990; Fodor's Vegas '91, 1991; (with K. Kragen) Life Is a Contact Sport: Ten Great Career Strategies that Work, 1994; (with R. Popeil) As Seen on TV: Ron Popeil, His Incredible Inventions and How to Participate in the Home Shopping Revolution, 1995. Contributor to periodicals. **Address:** c/o Mel Berger, William Morris Agency, 1325 Avenue of the Americas, New York, NY 10019, U.S.A.

GRAHAM, John D. American, b. 1956. **Genres:** Medicine/Health. **Career:** Harvard University, Harvard School of Public Health, Boston, MA, assistant professor, 1985-87, associate professor, 1988-90, professor of policy and decision sciences, 1991-2001, founding director of Center for Risk Analysis, 1989-2001, director of Center for Injury Control, 1990-97; Office of Management and Budget, Office of Information and Regulatory Affairs, administrator, 2001-. **Publications:** (with L. Green and M.J. Roberts) In Search of Safety: Chemicals and Cancer Risk, 1988; Auto Safety: Assessing America's Performance, 1989. EDITOR: Preventing Automobile Injury: Recent Findings of Evaluation Research, 1988; Harnessing Science for Environmental Regulation, 1991; (with J.B. Wiener) Risk versus Risk: Tradeoffs in Protecting Health and the Environment, 1995; The Role of Epidemiology in Regulatory Risk Assessment, 1995; (with J.K. Hartwell) The Greening of Industry: A Risk Management Approach, 1997. Contributor to professional journals and national magazines. **Address:** 8607 Burdette Rd, Bethesda, MD 20817-2802, U.S.A.

GRAHAM, Jorie. American, b. 1951. **Genres:** Poetry. **Career:** University of Iowa, member of staff, 1983-. Formerly taught at California State

University, Humboldt, 1979-81, and Columbia University, NYC, 1981-83. **Publications:** Hybrids of Plants and of Ghosts, 1980; Erosion, 1983; The End of Beauty, 1987; The Dream of the Unified Field, 1995 (Pulitzer Prize, 1996); Errancy, 1997; Photographs and Poems, 1998; Swarm: Poems, 1999; Never, 2002. **Address:** Dept of English, Barker Center, Harvard University, 12 Quincy St, Cambridge, MA 02138, U.S.A. **Online address:** graham2@ fas.harvard.edu

GRAHAM, Robert. See **HALDEMAN, Joe (William).**

GRAHAM, Vanessa. See **FRASER, Anthea.**

GRAHAM, W(illiam) Fred. American, b. 1930. **Genres:** History, Theology/ Religion. **Career:** Emeritus Professor, Michigan State University, East Lansing, 1992- (Instructor, 1963-64; Assistant Professor, 1964-69; Associate Professor, 1969-73; Professor, 1973-92). Ordained Presbyterian Minister, 1955; Pastor, Bethel United Presbyterian Church, Waterloo, Iowa, 1955-61. President, Sixteenth-Century Studies Society, 1988-89. **Publications:** The Constructive Revolutionary: John Calvin and His Socio-Economic Impact, 1971; Picking Up the Pieces: A Christian Stance in a Godless Age, 1975; (editor) Later Calvinism: Internatonal Perspectives, 1994. **Address:** 332 Chesterfield Parkway, East Lansing, MI 48823, U.S.A. **Online address:** grahamw@msu.edu

GRAINGER, John D(ownie). British, b. 1939. **Genres:** Archaeology/ Antiquities, Classics, History, Biography. **Career:** Worked as a teacher, 1963-90; writer, 1990-. **Publications:** Seleukos Nikator (biography), 1990; The Royal Navy in the River Plate, 1996; A Seleukid Prosopography and Gazetter, 1997; Aitolian Prosopographical Studies, 2000; Nerva and the Roman Imperial Succession Crisis AD 96-99, 2002. HISTORY: The Cities of Seleukid Syria, 1990; Hellenistic Phoenicia, 1991; Cromwell against the Scots, 1997; The League of the Aitolains, 1999; The Maritime Blockade of Germany in the Great War, 2003; The Truce of Amiens 18011803, 2004. Contributor to periodicals and history journals. **Address:** 3 Tythe Barn View, School Lane, Middle Littleton, Evesham, Worcestershire WR11 8LN, England. **Online address:** john@grainger4737.freeserve.com

GRALLA, Cynthia. American. **Genres:** Adult non-fiction. **Career:** Writer and graduate student. Worked as a hostess in Tokyo, Japan. **Publications:** The Floating World, 2003. **Address:** c/o Author Mail, Ballantine Books, Random House, 1745 Broadway, New York, NY 10019, U.S.A.

GRAMBO, Rebecca L(ynn). American, b. 1963. **Genres:** Animals/Pets, Zoology, Children's non-fiction. **Career:** Grambo Photography and Design Inc., Warman, Saskatchewan, president, 1995-. **Publications:** The World of the Fox, 1995, as The Nature of Foxes, 1995; Eagles: Masters of the Sky, 1997; Mountain Lion, 1998; Weird Science (juvenile), 1998; Eagles, 1999; Dinosaurs (juvenile), 1999; Birds of Prey (juvenile), in press. AMAZING ANIMALS SERIES FOR CHILDREN: Amazing Animals: Eyes, 1997; Amazing Animals: Colors, 1997; Amazing Animals: Hunters, 1997; Amazing Animals: Defenses, 1997; Amazing Animals: Families, 1998; Amazing Animals: Claws and Jaws, 1998. **Address:** PO Box 910, Warman, SK, Canada S0K 4S0.

GRAMBS, David (Lawrence). American, b. 1938. **Genres:** Language/ Linguistics. **Career:** Stratemeyer Syndicate (publisher), juvenile fiction editor and author of "Hardy Boys" series mysteries, 1963-65; American Heritage Publishing Company, senior editor of American Heritage Dictionary, 1967-69; Funk & Wagnalls Inc., senior editor and writer of New Encyclopedia, 1969-71; Charles Scribner's Sons, associate editor of The Dictionary of Scientific Biography, 1971-73; Penthouse International Inc., copyeditor of Penthouse, 1976-83; Random House Inc., staff editor of Random House Dictionary of the English Language, 1983-1987; freelance editor and writer. **Publications:** (trans.) Cathedrals of Europe, 1976; Words about Words, 1984, published in U.K. as Literary Companion Dictionary, later revised as The Random House Dictionary for Writers and Readers, 1990; Dimboxes, Epopts, and Other Quidams: Words to Describe Life's Indescribable People, 1986; (ed.) Theodore Bernstein, Bernstein's Reverse Dictionary, 2nd ed, 1988; Death by Spelling, 1989, later published in hardcover as The Ultimate Spelling Quiz Book, 1992; The Describer's Dictionary, 1993; Did I Say Something Wrong?, 1993; The Endangered English Dictionary, 1994. Contributor to books and periodicals. **Address:** 22 West 90th St., New York, NY 10024, U.S.A.

GRAMER, Rod. American, b. 1953. **Genres:** Biography. **Career:** Idaho Statesman, Boise, reporter to city editor, political editor of editorial page, and editor, 1975-88; KTVB-TV, Boise, director of news and public affairs,

1988-. **Publications:** (with L. Ashby) Fighting the Odds: The Life of Senator Frank Church, 1994. **Address:** Station KTVG-TV, 5407 Fairview Ave, Boise, ID 83706, U.S.A.

GRAMLICH, Edward Martin. American, b. 1939. **Genres:** Money/ Finance, Economics. **Career:** Federal Reserve Board, Washington, DC, member of research and statistics division, 1965-70, governor, 1997-; U.S. Office of Economic Opportunity, Washington, DC, director of Policy Research Division, 1971-73, director, 1971-73; The Brookings Institute, senior fellow, 1973-76; University of Michigan, Ann Arbor, professor of economics and public policy, 1976-97, director of Institute of Public Policy Studies, 1973-83, 1991-95, chair of economics department, 1983-86, 1989-90, dean of School of Public Policy, 1995-97; Congressional Budget Office, deputy directory, 1986, acting director, 1987, member of Panel of Economics Advisors, 1988-92. Visiting lecturer at universities. **Publications:** Recent Controversies Concerning Monetary Policy, 1970; (ed., with D.M. Jaffee) Savings Deposits, Mortgages, and Housing in the FRB-MIT-Penn Econometric Model, 1972; (with P.P. Koshel) Educational Performance Contracting: An Evaluation of an Experiment, 1975; (with B.M. Blechman and R.W. Hartman) Setting National Priorities: The 1975 Budget, 1974; (with B.M. Blechman and R.W. Hartman) Setting National Priorities: The 1976 Budget, 1975; State and Local Budget Surpluses and the Effect of Federal Macroeconomic Policies: A Study, 1979; Benefit-Cost Analysis of Government Programs, 1981; (with P.N. Courant) Tax Reform: There Must Be a Better Way, 1981; (ed., with B-C Ysander) Control of Local Government, IUI Conference Reports Series 1985, 1985; (with P.N. Courant) Federal Budget Deficits: America's Great Consumption Binge, 1986; A Guide to Benefit-Cost Analysis, 1990; Financing Federal Systems: The Selected Essays of Edward M; Gramlich, 1997; Is it Time to Reform Social Security?, 1998; (with C.E. Steuerle, H. Hecho, and D.S. Nightengale) The Government We Deserve: Responsive Democracy and Changing Expectations, 1998. Contributor of chapters to books. Contributor to books and periodicals. **Address:** Board of Governors of the Federal Reserve System, 20th and Constitution Ave. N.W., Washington, DC 20551, U.S.A. **Online address:** edward. gramlich@frb.gov

GRAMPP, William D. American, b. 1914. **Genres:** Economics. **Career:** Akron Time-Press, Ohio, Member of Editorial Staff, 1937-38; Adelphi University, Garden City, New York, Instructor in Economics, 1942; Elmhurst College, Illinois, Assistant Professor of Economics, 1942-44; American Embassy, Rome, Italy, Vice-consul in Economics Section, 1944-45; De Paul University, Chicago, Associate Professor, 1945-47; University of Illinois, Chicago, Professor, 1940-44, 1947-80, Professor Emeritus of Economics, 1980-; University of Chicago, Visiting Professor of Social Sciences, 1980-94, Lecturer, Law School, 1994-2001. Rivista Internazionale di Scienze Economiche e Commerciali, Member, Editorial Board. **Publications:** (ed. with E.T. Weiler) Economic Policy, 1953, rev. ed., 1961; The Manchester School of Economics, 1960; Economic Liberalism, 1965; Pricing the Priceless: Art, Artists, and Economics, 1989. **Address:** 5426 Ridgewood Ct, Chicago, IL 60615, U.S.A.

GRAN, Peter. American, b. 1941. **Genres:** History. **Career:** Friends World College, member of core faculty, 1974-75; University of California, Los Angeles, visiting assistant professor of history, 1975-77; University of Texas, Austin, visiting assistant professor of history, 1977-79; Temple University, Philadelphia, PA, associate professor, 1979-97, professor of history, 1997-. Lecturer at universities. **Publications:** Islamic Roots of Capitalism: Egypt, 1760-1840, 1979, rev. ed. Al-Judhur al-Islamiyah li-l-ra'smaliya: Misr 1760-1840, 1992; Beyond Eurocentrism: A New View of Modern World History, 1996. Contributor to books. Contributor of articles and reviews to periodicals. **Address:** Department of History, Temple University, 951 Gladfelter Hall, Philadelphia, PA 19122, U.S.A. **Online address:** pgran@astro.ocis.temple. edu

GRAN, Sara. American, b. 1971. **Genres:** Novels. **Career:** Writer. **Publications:** NOVELS: Saturn's Return to New York, 2001; Come Closer, 2003. **Address:** c/o Sita White, Artists Agency, 230 West 55th St. Suite 29D, New York, NY 10019, U.S.A. **Online address:** saragran718@hotmail.com

GRANDIN, Temple. American, b. 1947. **Genres:** Animals/Pets, Autobiography/Memoirs. **Career:** Arizona Farmer Ranchman, Phoenix, livestock editor, 1973-78; Corral Industries, Phoenix, equipment designer, 1974-75; independent consultant, Grandin Livestock Systems in Tempe, AZ and Urbana, IL, 1975-90, and in Fort Collins, CO, 1990-; Colorado State University, Fort Collins, lecturer to assistant professor of animal science, 1990-. Chair of the handling committee, Livestock Conservation Institute, Madison, WI, 1976-95. Animal Welfare Committee of the American Meat

Institute, 1991-. **Publications:** (with M.M. Scariano) Emergence: Labeled Autistic (autobiography), 1986; Thinking in Pictures and Other Reports from My Life with Autism (autobiography), 1995; Recommended Animal Handling Guidelines for Meat Packers. EDITOR & CONTRIBUTOR: Livestock Handling and Transport, 1993, 2nd ed., 2000; Genetics and the Behavior of Domestic Animals, 1998. Contributor to periodicals and professional journals. **Address:** Animal Science Department, Colorado State University, Fort Collins, CO 80523, U.S.A.

GRANDOWER, Elissa. *See* **WAUGH, Hillary (Baldwin).**

GRANELLI, Roger. Welsh, b. 1950. **Genres:** Novels, Novellas/Short stories. **Career:** Professional musician, 1971-79; music teacher, 1984-. **Publications:** NOVELS: Crystal Spirit, 1992; Out of Nowhere, 1995; Dark Edge, 1997; Status Zero, 1999. OTHER: The Mark of Pain (stories), in press. Contributor of stories to periodicals. **Address:** 60 Hopkinstown Rd., Pontypridd, M. Glam CF37 2PS, Wales.

GRANGE, William M(arshall). American, b. 1947. **Genres:** Theatre. **Career:** Florida Southern College, Lakeland, assistant professor for six years; Marquette University, Milwaukee, WI, associate professor for nine years; University of Nebraska, Lincoln, professor. Professional actor. **Publications:** Partnership in the German Theatre, 1991; Comedy in the Weimar Republic, 1996. Contributor to books, scholarly journals, magazines, and encyclopedias. **Address:** 207 Temple, University of Nebraska, Lincoln, NE 68588, U.S.A.

GRANGER, (Patricia) Ann. Also writes as Ann Hulme. British, b. 1939. **Genres:** Mystery/Crime/Suspense. **Career:** Worked as English teacher in France, 1960-61; worked in visa section of British embassies in Europe, including Zagreb, Belgrade, Prague, and Vienna, 1962-66; writer. **Publications:** A Poor Relation, 1979; Interlaken Intrigue, 1986; The Garden of the Azure Dragon, 1986; No Place for a Lady, 1988. MITCHELL AND MARKBY SERIES, MYSTERY NOVELS: Say It with Poison, 1991; A Season for Murder, 1991; Cold in the Earth, 1992, Murder among Us, 1992; Where Old Bones Lie, 1993; A Fine Place for Death, 1994; Flowers for His Funeral, 1994; Candle for a Corpse, 1995; A Touch of Mortality, 1996; A Word after Dying, 1996; Call the Dead Again, 1998; Beneath These Stones, 1999; Shades of Murder, 2000; A Restless Evil, 2002. HISTORICAL ROMANCE NOVELS AS ANN HULME: Summer Heiress, 1981; The Gamester, 1982; The Emperor's Dragoon, 1983; Daughter of Spain, 1984; A Woman of the Regiment, 1985; The Hungarian Adventures, 1985; The Unexpected American, 1988; The Flying Man, 1988; A Scandalous Bargain, 1988; Captain Harland's Marriage, 1989; False Fortune, 1989; Whisper in the Wind, 1989. FRAN VARADY SERIES: Asking for Trouble, 1997; Keeping Bad Company, 1997; Running Scared, 1998; Risking It All, 2001. Contributor of serials to magazines.

GRANGER, Michele. American, b. 1949. **Genres:** Children's fiction. **Career:** Williamsburg Public Schools, Williamsburg, MA, first grade teacher 1971-73; DeKalb County Schools, Avondale and Decatur, GA, teacher, 1974-77, chairperson, Department of Early Childhood/Special Education, 1976-78; Fairfax County Adult Education, Fairfax County, VA, parent educator, 1980-83; Montclair State College, Upper Montclair, NJ, educational supervisor, 1984, member of adjunct faculty, 1985; Children's Hospital and University Hospital, Newark, NJ, teacher in early intervention and AIDS intervention program, 1985-98; Renaissance Middle School, Montclair, co-director of The Writers' Room, 1999-; educational consultant on issues related to early childhood/special education. **Publications:** The Summer House Cat, 1989; Eliza the Hypnotizer: And Other Eliza and Francie Stories, 1993; Fifth Grade Fever, 1995. **Address:** 25 Fairfield Street, Montclair, NJ 07042-4113, U.S.A.

GRANITE, Tony. *See* **POLITELLA, Dario.**

GRANT, Anne Underwood. American, b. 1946. **Genres:** Mystery/Crime/Suspense. **Career:** North Carolina Arts Council, Raleigh, worked as community associate in the early 1970s; Good Will Publishers, Gastonia, NC, worked as communications director in the early 1980s; Underwood Grant Advertising, Charlotte, NC, president from the mid-1980s to mid-1990s. **Publications:** MYSTERY NOVELS: Multiple Listing, 1998; Smoke Screen, 1998; Cuttings, 1999; Voices in the Sand, 2000. **Address:** 587 George Chastain Dr, Horse Shoe, NC 28742, U.S.A. **Online address:** annieug@sprynet.com; www.underwoodgrant.com

GRANT, Anthony. *See* **CAMPBELL, Judith.**

GRANT, Barbara L. *See* **LACHMAN, Barbara.**

GRANT, Barry Keith. American/Canadian, b. 1947. **Genres:** Film, Cultural/Ethnic topics. **Career:** Brock University, St. Catharines, ON, faculty member, 1975-91, professor of film studies, 1991-, chair of Dept of Fine Arts, 1982-85, and Dept of Film Studies, Drama, and Visual Arts, 1989-90, director of Film Studies Program, 1990-99, director, MA program in popular culture, 2000; writer. Media Study/Buffalo, assistant professor, 1974-75; York University, external faculty member, 1990. WBFO-FM Radio, cohost of Kino-Ear, 1974-75; CJQR-FM and CKTB-AM Radio, weekly film critic, 1981-84; CBC-AM Radio, monthly film columnist for Variety Tonight, 1984-85; St. Catharines Standard, weekly film columnist, 1997-; guest on television and radio programs. Cheetah Discotheque, codirector of mixed media light show, 1966-67. **Publications:** (ed.) Zoetrope, 1969; (ed.) Film Genre: Theory and Criticism, 1977; Saturday Night at the Movies (documentary film), TV Ontario, 1980; (ed.) Film Study in the Undergraduate Curriculum, 1983; (ed.) Planks of Reason: Essays on the Horror Film, 1984; (ed. and contrib.) Film Genre Reader, 1986; Voyages of Discovery: The Cinema of Frederick Wiseman, 1992; Film Genre Reader II, 1995; The Dread of Difference: Gender and the Horror Film, 1996; Documenting the Documentary: Close Readings of Documentary Film and Video, 1998; (series ed.) Genres in American Cinema, 1995; (series ed.) Contemporary Film and Television Series, 1999. Work represented in anthologies. **Address:** Dept of Communications, Popular Culture and Film, Brock University, Merrittville Highway, St. Catharines, ON, Canada L2S 3A1.

GRANT, Bruce (Alexander). Australian, b. 1925. **Genres:** Novels, International relations/Current affairs, Politics/Government. **Career:** The Age newspaper, Melbourne: Film Theatre Critic, 1949-53, Foreign Correspondent in Europe and Middle East (based in London), 1954-57, Washington Correspondent, 1964-65, Columnist on Public Affairs (Melbourne based), 1968-72; Foreign Correspondent in Asia for The Age and Sydney Morning Herald (based in Singapore), 1959-63; Fellow in Political Science, University of Melbourne, 1965-68; High Commissioner for Australia in India, and Ambassador to Nepal, 1973-76; Associate, International Institute for Strategic Studies, London, 1976-77; Writer-in-Residence, 1980, Professor of Graduate School of Government, 1994-97, Adjunct Professor of Dept of Management, 1997-2003, Monash University, Australia. Arts Adviser, Government of Victoria, 1982-86; President, Spoleto Melbourne Festival of Three Worlds, 1985-87; Consultant to the Australian Minister for Foreign Affairs and Trade, 1988-91; Chairman, Australia-Indonesia Institute, 1989-92. **Publications:** Indonesia, 1964; A Crisis of Loyalty, 1972; Arthur and Eric, 1977; The Security of South-East Asia, 1978; The Boat People, 1979; Cherry Bloom, 1980; Gods and Politicians, 1982; The Australian Dilemma, 1983; What Kind of Country?, 1988; (with G. Evans) Australia's Foreign Relations, 1991; The Budd Family, 1995; A Furious Hunger: America in the 21st Century, 1999. **Address:** c/o The Drummond Agency, PO Box 572, Woodend, VIC 3442, Australia. **Online address:** profbrucegrant@compuserve.com

GRANT, C. B. S. *See* **HAGA, Enoch John.**

GRANT, Cynthia D. American, b. 1950. **Genres:** Young adult fiction. **Career:** Writer, 1974-. **Publications:** YOUNG ADULT FICTION: Joshua Fortune, 1980; Summer Home, 1981; Big Time, 1982; Hard Love, 1983; Kumquat May, I'll Always Love You, 1986; Phoenix Rising, or, How to Survive Your Life, 1989; Keep Laughing, 1991; Shadow Man, 1992; Uncle Vampire, 1993; Mary Wolf, 1995; The White Horse, 1998; The Cannibals, 2002. **Address:** Box 95, Cloverdale, CA 95425, U.S.A.

GRANT, Daniel. American, b. 1954. **Genres:** Art/Art history. **Career:** Art and Artists, NYC, editor, 1976-84; Commercial Appeal, Memphis, TN, art critic, 1984-85; Boston Herald, Boston, MA, art critic, 1986-. Amherst Cultural Council, member, 1988-94, chair, 1992-94; Northampton Arts Lottery Council, member, 1988-90. **Publications:** The Business of Being an Artist, 1991; On Becoming an Artist, 1993; The Artist's Resource Handbook, 1994; The Writer's Resource Handbook, 1997; The Fine Artist's Career Guide, 1998; The Artist's Guide to Making It in New York, 2001. Contributor to magazines and newspapers. **Address:** 19 Summer St, Amherst, MA 01002, U.S.A. **Online address:** danhg@aol.com

GRANT, David. *See* **THOMAS, Craig.**

GRANT, Graeme. Also writes as Nick Leon, Tom McGregor. Scottish, b. 1961. **Genres:** Humor/Satire, Science fiction/Fantasy. **Career:** Writer, 1993-. Also worked as a copywriter. **Publications:** AS NICK LEON: The Christmas Pox: An Immoral Fable (satire), 1995. Contributor to magazines and newspapers. AS TOM McGREGOR: Between the Lines: The Chill Factor, 1993; Peak Practice 1, 1993; Between the Lines: Close Protection, 1994; The Knock 1, 1995; Roughnecks: The Official Guide to the BBC Drama Series,

1995; Kavanagh QC 1, 1995; Peak Practice 2, 1995; Kavanagh QC 2, 1996; The Knock 2, 1996. **Address:** c/o Laura Morris, Abner Stein, 10 Roland Gardens, London SW7 3PH, England.

GRANT, James Russell. Scottish, b. 1924. **Genres:** Poetry, Literary criticism and history, Medicine/Health, Psychiatry, Social sciences, Translations. **Career:** Medical practitioner, London, 1958-. Registrar, The Maudsley Hospital, Institute of Psychiatry, London, 1954-55; Psychiatrist, Provincial Guidance Clinic, Red Deer, Alberta, Canada, 1955-57. **Publications:** Hyphens, 1958; Poems, 1959; (trans.) Zone, by Apollinaire, 1962; The Excitement of Being Sam, 1977; Myths of My Age, 1985; In the 4 Cats, 1997; Essays on Anxiety, 2001; Jigsaw and the Art of Poetry, 2001. **Address:** 255 Creighton Ave, London N2 9BP, England. **Online address:** rusty@dircon.co.uk

GRANT, Jill. British/Canadian, b. 1951. **Genres:** Urban studies. **Career:** Nova Scotia College of Art and Design, Halifax, assistant professor, 1979-88, associate professor, 1988-95, professor of environmental planning, 1995, department head, 1980-81, 1985-87, 1992-95, vice president (academic dean) of the college, 1995-98; Dalhousie University, honorary research associate, 1991-, professor, 2001-. Japan Foundation Research Fellow, 1999; Chukyo University, Napoya, Japan, visiting researcher, 1999. Conducted anthropological field research in Canada's Northwest Territories, 1975, and in Papua New Guinea, 1977-78, 1981-82. **Publications:** The Drama of Democracy: Contention and Dispute in Community Planning, 1994. Contributor to books. Contributor of articles and reviews to planning and environmental studies journals. **Address:** School of Planning, Dalhousie University, Halifax, NS, Canada B3J 2X4. **Online address:** jill.grant@dal.ca

GRANT, John Webster. Canadian, b. 1919. **Genres:** Theology/Religion, History, Cultural/Ethnic topics. **Career:** Professor Emeritus of Church History, Emmanuel College of Victoria University, Toronto, since 1984 (Professor, 1963-84). Professor of Church History, Union College of British Columbia, Vancouver, 1949-59; Ed.-in-Chief, Ryerson Press, Toronto, 1960-63; Managing Ed., Studies in Religion/Science Religieuses, 1971-76. **Publications:** Free Churchmanship in England, 1955; God's People in India, 1959; The Ship Under the Cross, 1960; George Pidgeon, 1962; (compiler) God Speaks We Answer, 1965; The Canadian Experience of Church Union, 1967; The Church in the Canadian Era, 1972; Moon of Wintertime, 1984; A Profusion of Spires, 1988. EDITOR: The Churches and the Canadian Experience, 1965; Salvation! O the Joyful Sound: Selected Writings of John Carroll, 1967; Die Unierten Kirchen, 1973. **Address:** 86 Gloucester St., Apt. 1002, Toronto, ON, Canada M4Y 2S2.

GRANT, Maxwell. *See* **LYNDS, Dennis.**

GRANT, Michael. *See* Obituaries.

GRANT, Neil. Also writes as D. M. Field, David Mountfield, Gail Trenton. British, b. 1938. **Genres:** Novellas/Short stories, Art/Art history, Children's non-fiction, History, Travel/Exploration. **Publications:** Disraeli, 1969; Emperor Charles V, 1970; English Explorers of North America, 1970; Victoria, 1970; The Renaissance, 1971; Munich 1938, 1971; Kings and Queens of England, 1971; Cathedrals, 1972; Guilds, 1972; Easter Rising, 1972; World Leaders, 1972; Howards of Norfolk, 1972; Barbarossa, 1972; History Alive: Lives, 3 vols., 1972; The Industrial Revolution, 1973; Partition of Palestine, 1973; Basic Atlas (author of text), 1973; The New World Held Promise, 1974; David Livingstone, 1974; The Campbells of Argyll, 1975; Neil Grant's Book of Spies and Spying, 1975; The German-Soviet Pact, 1975; Buccaneers, 1976; Stagecoaches, 1977; Children's History of Britain, 1977; Smugglers, 1978; (with N. Viney) An Illustrated History of Ball Games, 1978; The Discoverers, 1979; Explorers, 1979; The Savage Trade, 1980; (with P. Womersley) Collecting Stamps, 1980; Conquerers, 1981; Great Palaces, 1982; Everyday Life in the 18th Century, 1983; Scottish Clans and Tartans, 1987; 500 Questions and Answers about the Bible, 1988; People and Places: The United Kingdom, 1988; Ireland, 1989; The World of Odysseus, 1990; How They Lived: The Egyptians, The Greeks, The Romans, 1990; Village London, 1990; Roman Conquests, 1991; (co-author) Royal Geographical Society History of World Exploration, 1991; Great Atlas of Discovery, 1992; Explorers and Discoverers, 1992; Chronicle of 20th Century Conflict, 1992; The Egyptians, 1993; Children's Concise History Encyclopedia, 1993; Ancient Greece, 1994; Record Breakers: People and Places, 1994; Kings and Queens, 1996; Eric the Red, 1997; The Vikings, 1998; Hamlyn History of Literature, 1998; Oxford Children's History of the World, 2000. AS D.M. FIELD: Great Masterpieces of World Art, 1979; The Nude in Art, 1981; The World's Greatest Architecture, 2001; Leonardo da Vinci, 2002; Rembrandt, 2003; Van Gogh, 2004. AS GAIL TRENTON: Whispers at Twilight, 1982;

The White Bear, 1983; Reflections in the Stream, 1983. AS DAVID MOUNTFIELD: A History of Polar Exploration, 1974; Antique Collectors Dictionary, 1974; A History of African Exploration, 1976; The Coaching Age, 1976; Brief Histories of Great Nations: England, 1978; Everyday Life in Elizabethan England, 1978; The Partisans, 1979; London, 1979; Britain, 1979; The Railway Barons, 1979; (with R. Markus) A Vulnerable Game, 1988; (co-author) Philip's Atlas of Exploration, 1996. **Address:** 2 Avenue Rd, Teddington, Middx TW11 0BT, England. **Online address:** neildgrant@aol.com.uk

GRANT, Patrick. Canadian (born Northern Ireland), b. 1941. **Genres:** Literary criticism and history, Theology/Religion. **Career:** University of Illinois at Urbana-Champaign, Urbana, visiting assistant professor of English, 1966-68; University of Victoria, British Columbia, assistant professor, 1968-77, associate professor, 1977-79, professor of English, 1979-. **Publications:** The Transformation of Sin: Studies in Donne, 1974; Images and Ideas in Literature of the English Renaissance, 1979; Six Modern Authors and Problems of Belief, 1979; The Literature of Mysticism in Western Tradition, 1983; Literature and the Discovery of Method in the English Renaissance, 1985; (ed.) A Dazzling Darkness: An Anthology of Western Mysticism, 1985; Reading the New Testament, 1989; Literature and Personal Values, 1991; Spiritual Discourse and the Meaning of Persons, 1994; Personalism and the Politics of Culture, 1996; Breaking Enmities: Religion, Literature and Culture in Northern Ireland, 1967-97, 1999. **Address:** Department of English, University of Victoria, Victoria, BC, Canada V8W 3W1.

GRANT, Pete. American. **Genres:** Law. **Career:** Surgeon and author. Chair of cancer commission for American College of Surgeons. **Publications:** (as Paul Kuehn) Breast Care Options: A Cancer Specialist Discusses Breast Care Options, Risk Factors, and How to Cope with Breast Cancer, 1986; (as Paul Kuehn) Breast Care Options for the 1990s, 1991; (as Jon Dijon) Who Is Robin? (novel), 1993. UNDER PSEUDONYM PETE GRANT: Night Flying Avenger, 1990; The Surgical Arena, 1993; Destination 2020 White House (novel), 1999; The Medical Supreme Court (novel), 2001. **Address:** c/o Author Mail, Newmark Publishing, POB 603, South Windsor, CT 06074, U.S.A.

GRANT, Stephanie. American. **Genres:** Novels. **Career:** Worked for a publishing company and as a fund-raiser for lesbian and gay nonprofit agencies; Lesbian and Gay Community Services Center, curator of reading series In Our Own Write. **Publications:** The Passion of Alice (novel), 1995. **Address:** c/o Sloan Harris, International Creative Management, 40 West 57th St., New York, NY 10019, U.S.A.

GRANT, Susan-Mary C. British, b. 1962. **Genres:** History. **Career:** University of Newcastle upon Tyne, Newcastle, England, member of history faculty. **Publications:** North over South: Northern Nationalism and American Identity in the Antebellum Era, 2000; (ed., with B.H. Reid) The American Civil War: Explorations and Reconsiderations, 2000; Legacy of Disunion: The Enduring Significance of the American Civil War, 2003. **Address:** School of Historical Studies, University of Newcastle upon Tyne, Newcastle NE1 7RU, England. **Online address:** susan.grant@ncl.ac.uk

GRANT, Vanessa. Canadian. **Genres:** Romance/Historical. **Career:** Accountant and college instructor; author and international lecturer. Family Life, volunteer counselor. **Publications:** Storm, 1988; Wild Passage, 1989; The Touch of Love, 1990; One Secret Too Many, 1990; So Much for Dreams, 1990; With Strings Attached, 1991; Angela's Affair, 1991; Yesterday's Vows, 1994; Writing Romance, 1997; After All This Time, 1998; Strangers by Day, 1998; If You Loved Me, 1999; The Colors of Love, 2000; Think about Love, 2001; Seeing Stars, 2001; Moon Lady's Lover; Dace of Seduction; Nothing Less than Love; Catalina's Lover; Shadows; Pacific Disturbance; Hidden Memories; When Love Returns; Taking Chances; Awakening Dreams; Takeover Man; Stray Lady; Jenny's Turn; The Chauvinist. Author of software including Dogwood Compendium of Names, for character naming; Story-Craft, for story development; and Templates and Macros. Author of Creativity Seminars: Writing Romance, an eight seminar audiotape album, and Creativity Seminars: A Writers Creativity, a four audiotape album. **Address:** c/o Writers Union of Canada, 40 Wellington St. E, 3rd Floor, Toronto, ON, Canada M5E 1C7. **Online address:** vanessa@vanessagrant.ca

GRANT, Verne. American, b. 1917. **Genres:** Biology, Botany, Zoology. **Career:** Professor Emeritus of Integrative Biology, University of Texas, Austin, 1987- (Professor, 1970-87). Geneticist and Experimental Taxonomist, Rancho Santa Ana Botanic Garden, Claremont, California, 1959-67; Assistant Professor, and subsequently Professor of Botany, Claremont Graduate School, 1952-67; Professor of Biology, Institute of Life Science, Texas A&M

University, College Station, 1967-68; Director, Boyce Thompson Southwestern Aboretum, and Professor of Biological Sciences, University of Arizona, Superior, 1968-70. **Publications:** Natural History of the Phlox Family, 1959; The Origin of Adaptations, 1963; The Architecture of the Germplasm, 1964; (with K. Grant) Flower Pollination in the Phlox Family, 1965; (with K. Grant) Hummingbirds and Their Flowers, 1968; Plant Speciation, 1971, 1981; Genetics of Flowering Plants, 1975; Organismic Evolution, 1977; The Evolutionary Process, 1985, 1991; The Edward Grant Family and Related Families in Massachusetts, Rhode Island, Pennsylvania, and California, 1997. **Address:** Dept. of Integrative Biology, University of Texas, Austin, TX 78712, U.S.A.

GRANT-ADAMSON, Lesley (Heycock). Also writes as Isobel Brown. British, b. 1942. **Genres:** Mystery/Crime/Suspense, Education, Travel/Exploration. **Career:** Leonard Hill Publishing, London, editorial assistant, 1960; Thomson Publications, London, sub-editor, 1961-63; reporter, Palmers Green and Southgate Gazette, London, 1963-66; The Citizen, Gloucester, 1966-68, and Rugby Advertiser, Warwickshire, 1969-71; Herts Advertiser, Hertfordshire, news ed., 1971-73; feature writer, The Guardian, London, 1973-80; freelance writer, 1980-. **Publications:** Patterns in the Dust (in US as Death on Widows Walk), 1985; The Face of Death, 1985; Guilty Knowledge, 1986; Wild Justice, 1987; Threatening Eye, 1988; Curse the Darkness, 1990; Flynn (in US as Too Many Questions), 1991; A Life of Adventure, 1992; The Dangerous Edge, 1992; Dangerous Games, 1994; (with A. Grant-Adamson) A Season in Spain, 1995; Wish You Were Here, 1995; Evil Acts, 1996; Writing Crime and Suspense Fiction, 1996, rev. ed., 2003; The Girl in the Case, 1997; Lipstick + Lies, 1998; Undertow, 1999; (as Isobel Brown) Domestic Crime, 2001; Music to Be Murdered By, 2000.

GRASS, Günter (Wilhelm). German (born Poland), b. 1927. **Genres:** Novels, Plays/Screenplays, Art/Art history, Literary criticism and history, Essays. **Career:** Novelist, poet, playwright, graphic artist, and sculptor. Former farm laborer in the Rhineland; worked in potash mine near Hildesheim, Germany; black marketeer; apprentice stonecutter during the late 1940s in Duesseldorf, Germany; worked with a jazz band. Speechwriter for Willy Brandt during his candidacy for the election of Bundeskanzler in West Germany. Visited the United States in 1964 and 1965, giving lectures and readings colleges, universities and art centers; writer in residence at Columbia University, 1966. Has exhibited his drawings, lithographs, and sculptures. Recipient of numerous prizes and awards including Nobel Prize for Literature, 1999. **Publications:** Die Vorzuege der Windhuehner (poems, prose, and drawings; title means: The Advantages of Windfowl), 1956, 3rd ed, 1967; O Susanna: Ein Jazzbilderbuch: Blues, Balladen, Spirituals, Jazz, 1959; Die Blechtrommel (novel),1959, trans. by R. Manheim as The Tin Drum, 1962; Gleisdreieck (poems and drawings; title means: Rail Triangle), 1960; Katz und Maus (novella), 1961, trans. by Manheim as Cat and Mouse, 1963; Hundejahre (novel), 1963, trans. by Manheim as Dog Years, 1965; Rede ueber das Selbstverstaendliche (speech), 1965; Dich singe ich, Demokratie, 1965; Fuenf Wahlreden (speeches), 1965; Selected Poems (in German and English), 1966, trans. by M. Hamburger and C. Middleton, as Poems of Gunter Grass, 1969; Ausgefragt (poems and drawings; title means: Questioned), 1967; Der Fall Axel C. Springer am Beispiel Arnold Zweig: Eine Rede, ihr Anlass, und die Folgen, 1967; New Poems, trans. by Hamburger, 1968; Ueber das Selbstverstaendliche: Reden, Aufsaetze, offene Briefe, Kommentare (title means: On the Self-Evident), 1968, rev ed as Ueber das Selbstverstaendliche: Politische Schriften, 1969; Briefe ueber die Grenze: Versuch eines Ost-West-Dialogs by Gunter Grass and Pavel Kohout (letters), 1968; Ueber meinen Lehrer Doeblin und andere Vortraege (title means: About My Teacher Doeblin and Other Lectures), 1968; Gunter Grass: Ausgewaehlte Texte, Abbildungen, Faksimiles, Bio-Bibliographie, 1968, also as Portraet und Poesie, 1968; Kunst oder Pornographie?, 1969; Speak Out: Speeches, Open Letters, Commentaries, trans. by Manheim, 1969; Oertlich betaeubt (novel), 1969, trans. by Manheim as Local Anaesthetic, 1970; Die Schweinekopfsuelze, 1969; Originalgraphik (poem with illustrations), 1970; Gesammelte Gedichte (poems), 1971; Dokumente zur politischen Wirkung, 1971; Aus dem Tagebuch einer Schnecke, 1972, trans. by Manheim as From the Diary of a Snail, 1973; Mariazuehren Hommageamarie Inmarypraise, 1973, bilingual ed. with trans. by Middleton as Inmarypraise, 1974; Liebe geprueft (poems), 1974; Der Buerger und seine Stimme (title means: The Citizen and His Voice), 1974; Gunter Grass Materialienbuch, 1976; Der Butt, 1977, trans. by Manheim as The Flounder, 1978; Denkzettel (title means: Note for Thought), 1978; In the Egg and Other Poems, trans. by Hamburger and Middleton, 1978; Das Treffen in Telgte, 1978, trans. by Manheim as The Meeting at Telgte, 1981; Werkverzeichnis der Radierungen (catalogue), 1979; (with V. Schlondorff) Die Blechtrommel als Film, 1979; Aufsaetze zur Literatur, 1957-1979 (title means: Essays on Literature, 1957-1979), 1980; Danziger Trilogie (title means: Danzig Trilogy), 1980; Kopfgeburten; oder Die Deutschen sterben aus, 1980, trans. by Manheim as Headbirths; or, The

Germans Are Dying Out, 1982; Zeichnen und Schreiben: Das bildnerische Werk des Schriftstellers Gunter Grass, 1982, trans. as Graphics and Writing, 1983; Kinderlied (poems and etchings), 1982; Zeichnungen und Texte, 1954-1977, 1982, trans. by Hamburger and W. Arndt as Drawings and Words, 1954-1977, 1983; Ach, Butt!: Dein Maerchen geht boese aus, 1983; Radierungen und Texte, 1972-1982, 1984, trans. by Hamburger and others as Etchings and Words, 1972-1982, 1985; Widerstand lernen: Politische Gegenreden, 1980-1983 (title means: Learning Resistance: Political Countertalk), 1984; On Writing and Politics: 1967-1983 (essays), trans. by Manheim, 1985; Geschenkt Freiheit, 1985; Die Raettin, 1986, trans. by Manheim as The Rat, 1987; Werkausgabe, 10 vols, 1987; Die Gedichte 1955-1986, 1988; Zunge Zeigen, 1988, trans. by J.E. Woods as Show Your Tongue, 1989; Deutscher Lastenausgleich: Wider das dumpfe Einheitsgebot; Reden und Gesprache, Texte zur Zeit, 1990; Ein Schnappchen namens DDR: Letzte Reden vorm Glockengelaut, 1990; Skizzenbuch, 1990; Schreiben nach Auschwitz, 1990; Totes Holz, illustrated by Grass, 1990; Two States-One Nation?, 1990; Ukenrufe: Eine Erzahlung, 1992; The Call of the Toad, trans. by R. Manheim, 1992; Unkenrufe (title means: Toad Croaks), 1992; In Kupfer, auf Stein: Das grafische Werk, edited by G.F. Margull, 1994; Cat and Mouse and Other Writings, 1994; Ein Weites Feld, 1995; (with K. Oe) Gestern, vor 50 Jahren: ein Deutsch-Japanischer Briefwechsel, 1995; Die Deutschen und Ihre Dichter, 1995; Novemberland: Selected Poems, 1956-1993, 1996; Aesthetik Des Engagements, 1996; Rede uber den Standort, 1997; My Century, trans. by M.H. Heim, 1999; Crabwalk (novel), 2003. PLAYS: Die boesen Koeche: Ein Drama in fuenf Akten, 1961, trans. by A.L. Willson as The Wicked Cooks on Broadway, 1967; Hochwasser: Ein Stueck in zwei Akten (two acts), 1963, 4th ed, 1968; Beritten hin und zurueck (title means: Rocking Back and Forth),1964; Onkel, Onkel (four acts; title means: Mister, Mister), 1965; Die Plebejer proben den Aufstand: Ein deutsches Trauerspiel, 1966, trans. by Manheim as The Plebeians Rehearse the Uprising: A German Tragedy, 1966; The World of Gunter Grass, adapted by D. Rosa, 1966; Noch zehn Minuten bis Buffalo (title means: Only Ten Minutes to Buffalo), 1967; The Flood, 1967; Davor: Ein Stuck in dreizehn Szenen, 1969, trans. by Wilson and Manheim produced as Uptight in Washington, DC, 1972, as Davor: Ein Stuck in dreizehn Szenen, 1973, trans. as Max: A Play, 1972; Theaterspiele, 1970; Zweiunddreizig Zaehne. OTHER: Collaborator with J-C Carriere, V. Schlondorff and F. Seitz on screenplay for film adaptation of Katz und Maus, 1967. Author of material for catalogues to accompany his art work. Work represented in anthologies. **Address:** Niedstrasse 13, 41 Berlin-Grunewald, Germany.

GRATUS, Jack. British (born Republic of South Africa), b. 1935. **Genres:** Writing/Journalism, Plays/Screenplays, Communications/Media, Novels, Novellas/Short stories. **Career:** Trained as a lawyer. Since 1970 writing fiction and non-fiction, journalism, radio and videos. Tutor of Creative Writing, journalism and communication skills. Executive training consultant, 1990-. Chairman, Writers Guild of Great Britain, 1982. **Publications:** A Man in His Position, 1968; The Victims, 1969; Mister Landlord Appel, 1971; (with T. Preston) Night Hair Child, 1971; The Great White Lie: History of the Anti-Slave Trade Campaign, 1973; The False Messiahs, 1976; The Joburgers, 1979; The Redneck Rebel, 1980; Successful Interviewing, 1988; Give and Take, 1990; Sharpen Up Your Interviewing, 1991; Facing Your Next Interview With Confidence, 1992. **Address:** 32 The Grove, Ealing, London W5 5LH, England.

GRAU, Shirley Ann. American, b. 1930. **Genres:** Novels, Novellas/Short stories. **Publications:** The Black Prince and Other Stories, 1955; The Hard Blue Sky, 1958; The House on Coliseum Street, 1961; The Keepers of the House, 1964; The Condor Passes, 1971; The Wind Shifting West (short stories), 1973; Evidence of Love, 1977; Nine Women, 1986; Roadwalkers, 1994; Selected Stories, 2003. **Address:** PO Box 9058, Metairie, LA 70005-9058, U.S.A. **Online address:** shirleygrau@bellsouth.net

GRAVELLE, Jane G(ibson). American, b. 1947. **Genres:** Economics. **Career:** Library of Congress, Congressional Research Service, Washington, DC, research assistant, 1969-72, economist, analyst, and senior specialist in economic policy, 1972-. Boston University, visiting professor, 1988. U.S. Department of Labor, visiting economist, 1977; U.S. Treasury Department, visiting economist, 1989-90; consultant to American Association of Retired Persons and National Science Foundation. **Publications:** The Economic Effects of Taxing Capital Income, 1994; (co-ed.) The Encyclopedia of Taxation & Tax Policy, 1999. Contributor to books. Contributor of articles and reviews to economic and tax journals and to newspapers. **Address:** Congressional Research Service, Library of Congress, 101 Independence Ave SE, Washington, DC 20540-7000, U.S.A.

GRAVER, Elizabeth. American, b. 1964. **Genres:** Novels, Novellas/Short stories, Essays. **Career:** Boston College, assistant professor, 1993-98, associate professor of English, 1998-. **Publications:** Have You Seen Me? (stories), 1991. NOVELS: Unravelling, 1997; The Honey Thief, 1999; Awake, 2004. Contributor to anthologies. **Address:** c/o Richard Parks, R. Parks Agency, 138 E 16th St No 5B, New York, NY 10003, U.S.A. **Online address:** Graver@bc.edu

GRAVER, Lawrence Stanley. American, b. 1931. **Genres:** Film, Literary criticism and history, Biography. **Career:** Williams College, Williamstown, MA, professor of English, 1964-. **Publications:** Conrad's Short Fiction, 1969; Carson McCullers, 1969; Mastering the Film, 1977; (with R. Federman) Samuel Beckett: The Critical Heritage, 1978; Beckett: Waiting for Godot, 1989; An Obsession with Anne Frank: Meyer Levin and the Diary, 1995. **Address:** Dept. of English, Williams College, Williamstown, MA 01267, U.S.A. **Online address:** lgraver@williams.edu

GRAVES, John. American, b. 1920. **Genres:** Novellas/Short stories, Environmental sciences/Ecology, Local history/Rural topics, Natural history, Autobiography/Memoirs. **Career:** Freelance writer, 1951-. Instructor in English, University of Texas, Austin, 1948-50; Adjunct Professor of English, Texas Christian University, Fort Worth, 1957-65; Consultant and writer, U.S. Dept. of the Interior, Washington, DC, 1965-68. Guggenheim Fellow, 1963. **Publications:** Home Place, 1958; Goodbye to a River: A Narrative, 1960; (co-author) The Water Hustlers, 1971; Hard Scrabble: Observations on a Patch of Land, 1974; The Last Running, 1974, 1990; Texas Heartland: A Hill Country Year, 1975; From a Limestone Ledge: Some Essays and Other Ruminations about Country Life in Texas, 1980; Blue and Some Other Dogs, 1981; Of Birds and Texas, 1986; Self-Portrait, with Birds, 1991; A John Graves Reader, 1996; John Graves and the Making of Goodbye to a River: Selected Letters, 1957-1960, 2000; Texas Rivers, 2002; Myself & Strangers (memoir), 2004.

GRAVES, Michael A(rthur) R(oy). British, b. 1933. **Genres:** History. **Career:** Teacher of history and English at a school in Nottinghamshire, England, 1957-59; Davies, Laing & Dick, London, England, history tutor, 1959-63; University of Otago, Dunedin, New Zealand, lecturer in history, 1963-67; University of Auckland, Auckland, New Zealand, senior lecturer, 1967-82, associate professor of history, 1982-99, honorary research fellow, 1999-. **Publications:** England under the Tudors and Stuarts, 1485-1689, 1965; The House of Lords in the Parliaments of Edward VI and Mary I, 1981; (with R.H. Silcock) Revolution, Reaction, and the Triumph of Conservatism, 1558-1700, 1984; The Tudor Parliaments: Crown, Lords, and Commons, 1485-1603, 1985; The Elizabethan Parliaments: Documents and Commentary, 1986, 2nd ed, 1996; (with R.H. Silcock) Studies in Early Modern English History, 1986; The Early Tudor Parliaments: 1485-1558, 1990; Thomas Norton: The Parliament Man, 1994; (with J. Frood) Change, Conflict and Crisis: England 1558-1660s, 1996; Burghley: William Cecil, Lord Burghley, 1998; The Parliaments of Early Modern Europe, 2001. **Address:** Department of History, University of Auckland, Prince's St, Auckland, New Zealand. **Online address:** m.graves@auckland.ac.nz

GRAVES, Ralph (Augustus). American, b. 1924. **Genres:** Novels, Autobiography/Memoirs. **Career:** Life magazine, New York City, reporter and writer, 1948-58, articles editor, 1958-61, assistant managing editor, 1961-67, managing editor, 1969-72; Time Inc., New York City, senior staff editor, 1968, associate publisher, 1975, corporate editor, 1976-78, editorial director, 1978-83; writer. Director of Book-of-the-Month Club; chair of Citizens' Crime Commission of New York. **Publications:** Thanks for the Ride, 1949; The Lost Eagles, 1955; August People, 1985; Share of Honor, 1989; Orion, 1993; (with E. Graves) Tables of Content, 1993; (with R. Ellis) Martha's Vineyard: An Affectionate Memoir, 1995. **Address:** c/o Julian Bach Literary Agency, 22 E 71st St, New York, NY 10021, U.S.A.

GRAVES, Russell A. (born United States), b. 1969. **Genres:** Environmental sciences/Ecology. **Career:** Childress Independent School District, Childress, TX, teacher, 1993-. Childress County Historical Museum, member of board of directors. **Publications:** Managing Wildlife as an Enterprise, 1997; The Prairie Dog: Sentinel of the Plains, 2001; The Hunting Dogs, 2002. **Address:** 706 Avenue I S.E., Childress, TX 79201, U.S.A. **Online address:** russell@russellgraves.com

GRAVITZ, Herbert L. American, b. 1942. **Genres:** Medicine/Health. **Career:** Larue D. Carter Memorial Hospital, Indianapolis, IN, clinical intern, 1967-68; University of Windsor, ON, assistant professor of psychology, 1969-72; University of California, Santa Barbara, assistant director of Counseling Center, 1972-79, counseling program director, 1979-80, coordinator of training for Counseling, Career Planning, and Placement Services, 1980-81; private practice of clinical psychology, Santa Barbara, CA, 1979-.

Academy of Experts in Traumatic Stress, diplomate; American Board of Forensic Examiners, diplomate and board certification; National Council of Health Service Providers in Psychology, certification. Affiliated with Cottage Hospital, Santa Barbara, 1974-96; Psychiatric Emergency Team, consulting psychologist, 1980-81; workshop presenter. **Publications:** (with J.D. Bowden) Guide to Recovery: A Book for Adult Children of Alcoholics, 1985; Children of Alcoholics Handbook: Who They Are, What They Experience, and How They Recover, 1985; Genesis: Spirituality in Recovery, 1988; Obsessive Compulsive Disorder: New Help for the Family, 1998; Words That Heal, 2004; Mental Illness and the Family, 2004. Contributor to books and periodicals. **Address:** 2020 Alameda Padre Serra Ste 217, Santa Barbara, CA 93103, U.S.A. **Online address:** gravitz@aol.com

GRAY, Alasdair (James). Scottish, b. 1934. **Genres:** Novels, Novellas/Short stories, Plays/Screenplays, Intellectual history. **Career:** Art teacher, Lanarkshire and Glasgow, 1958-62; Pavilion and Citizens' theatres, Glasgow, scene painter, 1962-63; freelance painter and writer, Glasgow, 1963-76; People's Palace Local History Museum, Glasgow, artist recorder, 1976-77; University of Glasgow, writer-in-residence, 1977-79, consulting professor of creative writing, 2001-03; freelance writer, painter, and book designer, 1979-2001; Oran Mor Arts and Leisure Centre, Hillhead, Glasgow, mural painter, 2003-. **Publications:** Five Scottish Artists (catalog), 1986; Saltire Self-Portrait 4 (autobiographical sketch), 1988; Old Negatives (4 verse sequences), 1989; Why Scots Should Rule Scotland, 1992, rev. ed., 1997; Working Legs (play), 1997; The Book of Prefaces, 2000; Sixteen Occasional Poems, 2000; A Short Survey of Classical Scottish Writing, 2001. NOVELS: Lanark: A Life in Four Books, 1981; 1982, Janine, 1984; The Fall of Kelvin Walker, 1985; Something Leather, 1990; McGrotty and Ludmilla; or, The Harbinger Report, 1990; Poor Things, 1992; A History Maker, 1994. STORIES: The Comedy of the White Dog, 1979; Unlikely Stories, Mostly, 1983; (with A. Owens and J. Kelman) Lean Tales, 1985; Ten Tales Tall and True, 1993; Mavis Belfrage: A Romantic Tale: With Five Shorter Tales, 1996; The End of Their Tethers, 2003. **Address:** 2 Marchmont Terrace, Glasgow G12 9LT, Scotland.

GRAY, Alfred Orren. American, b. 1914. **Genres:** Education, Genealogy/Heraldry, History, Military/Defense/Arms control, Theology/Religion, Writing/Journalism, Autobiography/Memoirs, Documentaries/Reportage. **Career:** Whitworth College, Spokane, WA, Professor, and Chairman of Dept., 1946-80, Emeritus Professor of Journalism, 1980-. Communications and historical research, 1980-. Editorial Advisory Board of Whitworth Today, 1988-90; reporting, free-lance feature writing, 1938-41; Historical Editor, Chief Writer, and Administrative Assistant for Public Relations, Office of the Chief Ordnance Officer, European Theater of Operations, Paris, France, and Frankfurt Am Main, Germany, 1944-46; Director of Whitworth College News Bureau, 1952-58; Ed. The Synod Story, 1953-55; Director, Inland Empire Publications Clinic, 1959-74; Board of Dirs., Presbyterian Historical Society, 1984-90, 1991-1994, chairman of Historical Sites Committee, 1986-90. Editorial reader, American Presbyterians: The Journal of Presbyterian History, 1991-95. **Publications:** History of U.S. Ordnance Service in the European Theater of Operations during World War II, 1946; Techniques of Communications for the Church, 1957; Not by Might: The Story of Whitworth College, 1965; The Whitworthian: A Crash Course in Leadership, 1980; Eight Generations from Gondelsheim: A Genealogical Study, 1980; (co-author) Many Lamps, One Light: A Centennial History, 1984; Of Time and Remembrance: A Memoir, 1996. **Address:** 101 E Hawthorne Rd Apt B8, Spokane, WA 99218-1557, U.S.A.

GRAY, Chris Hables. American, b. 1953. **Genres:** Ethics, History, Military/Defense/Arms control, Philosophy, Politics/Government. **Career:** Writer and professor. South Africa Catalyst Project, research director and traveling organizer, 1979-81; Zetetic Software Inc., Santa Cruz, CA, consultant, project developer, and technical writer, 1987-90; University of California at Santa Cruz, lecturer, 1989-91; Square One Software Inc., Aptos, CA, lead writer and consultant, 1991-93; Oregon State University, Corvallis, History Dept, courtesy graduate faculty and assistant professor, 1992-96; Goddard College, Plainfield, VT, BA/MA Off-Campus Program, associate faculty, 1994-; Hewlett-Packard, Corvallis, writer and consultant, 1994-95; University of Great Falls, South Great Falls, MT, Computer Science Dept, associate professor of computer science and cultural studies of science and technology, 1996-. Masaryk University, Brno, Czech Republic, guest professor and Eisenhower Fellow, 1995; Union Institute and University, core faculty, 1999-; has appeared on radio and TV programs. **Publications:** Postmodern War: The New Politics of Conflict, 1997; Cyborg Citizen, 2001. EDITOR: (with S. Mentor and L. Wagner) Lawrence Litvak and Kathleen McTigue, 1977; (with H. Figueroa-Sarriera and S. Mentor) The Cyborg Handbook, 1995; Technohistory: Using the History of American Technology in

Interdisciplinary Research, 1996. Contributor to books and periodicals. Author or editor of software manuals, guides for computer training programs, and other technical writing. **Address:** Dept of Computer Science, University of Great Falls, 1301 20th St S, Great Falls, MT 59405, U.S.A. **Online address:** cgray@ugf.edu; www.ugf.edu/compsci/gray/istpg.htm

GRAY, Christopher. American, b. 1950. **Genres:** Adult non-fiction. **Career:** Architectural historian, columnist, writer. Office for Metropolitan History, New York, NY, founder and director, 1975-. **Publications:** Blueprints: Twenty-Six Extraordinary Structures, 1981; Changing New York: The Architectural Scene, 1992; (editor) Fifth Avenue, 1911, from Start to Finish in Historic Block-by-Block Photographs, 1994; (with David Stravitz) The Chrysler Building: Creating a New York Icon Day by Day, 2002; New York Streetscapes: Tales of Manhattan's Significant Buildings and Landmarks, research by Suzanne Braley, 2003. **Address:** Office for Metropolitan History, 246 West 80th St., No. 8, New York, NY 10024, U.S.A. **Online address:** MetHistory@aol.com

GRAY, Clayton. Canadian, b. 1918. **Genres:** History, Travel/Exploration. **Career:** Historian, David M. Stewart Museum and Macdonald-Stewart Foundation, Que., since 1955. Ed., Canadian Press News Bureau, 1944-45; Lecturer, History of Canadian Literature, Concordia University, 1954-61; Vice-President, Lake St. Louis Historical Society, 1954-75; Member, National Liberal Club, London, 1982-83. Hon. Secretary, P.E.N. Canadian Centre, 1979-80. **Publications:** The Montreal Story, 1949; Montreal qui disparait, 1952; Conspiracy in Canada, 1959; Le Vieux Montreal, 1964; Montreal During the American Civil War, 1965; The Louisiana Affair, 1984; The Canadian Guide to Britain, vol. I, England, 1985; Le Castor Fait Tout, 1987. **Address:** 1495 Ste. Croix, Montreal, QC, Canada H4L 3Z5.

GRAY, Deborah D. (born United States), b. 1951. **Genres:** Social work. **Career:** Social Worker. North Slope Borough School District, Alaska, counselor, 1975-76; Regional Perinatal Center, Upstate Medical Center, Syracuse, NY, social worker, 1979-81; Catholic Community Services, Mt. Vernon, WA, therapist, 1982-84; New Hope Child and Family Services, Seattle, WA, casework supervisor, 1988-93; private practice as a clinical social worker, Kirkland, WA, 1993-. Antioch University's foster care and adoption therapy post-graduate certificate program, core faculty; Portland State University's foster care and adoption therapy post-graduate certificate program, faculty. **Publications:** Attaching in Adoption: Practical Tools for Today's Parents, 2002. Contributor to periodicals and various professional and parent newsletters. **Address:** 8011 118th Ave. NE, Kirkland, WA 98033, U.S.A. **Online address:** DeborahDGray@aol.com

GRAY, Dulcie. (Dulcie Denison). British (born Malaysia), b. 1920. **Genres:** Novels, Mystery/Crime/Suspense, Plays/Screenplays, Autobiography/Memoirs, Novellas/Short stories. **Career:** Actress, 1939-. **Publications:** Murder on the Stairs, 1957; Love Affair (play), 1957; Murder in Melbourne, 1958; Baby Face, 1959; Epitaph for a Dead Actor, 1960; Murder on a Saturday, 1961; Murder in Mind, 1963; The Devil Wore Scarlet, 1964; (with M. Denison) The Actor and His World, 1964; No Quarter for a Star, 1964; The Murder of Love, 1967; Died in the Red, 1968; Murder on Honeymoon, 1969; For Richer for Richer, 1970; Deadly Lampshade, 1971; Understudy to Murder, 1972; Dead Give Away, 1974; Ride on a Tiger, 1975; Stage-Door Fright (stories), 1977; Death in Denims, 1977; Butterflies on My Mind (non-fiction), 1978; Dark Calypso, 1979; The Glanville Women, 1982; Anna Starr, 1984; Mirror Image, 1987; Looking Forward, Looking Back (autobiography), 1991; J.B. Priestley, 2000. **Address:** c/o Barry Burrell Associates, Prince of Wales Theatre, 31 Coventry St, London W1V 8AS, England.

GRAY, Francine du Plessix. American (born Poland), b. 1930. **Genres:** Novels, History, Women's studies and issues. **Career:** Reporter, United Press International, NYC, 1952-54; Assistant Ed., Realities Magazine, Paris, 1954-55; Book Ed., Art in America, NYC, 1962-64; Visiting Professor, City University of New York, 1975, Yale University, New Haven, CT, 1981, and Columbia University, New York, 1983; Ferris Professor, Princeton University, NJ, 1986; Brown University, Annenberg Fellow, 1997; Distinguished Visiting Professor, Vassar College, 1999. **Publications:** Divine Disobedience: Profiles in Catholic Radicalism, 1970; Hawaii: The Sugar-Coated Fortress, 1972; Lovers and Tyrants, 1976; World without End, 1981; October Blood, 1985; Adam and Eve and the City, 1987; Soviet Women: Walking the Tightrope, 1989; Rage and Fire: A Life of Louise Colet, 1994; At Home with the Marquis de Sade, 1998; Simone Weil, 2001. **Address:** c/o Georges Borchardt Inc, 136 E 57th St, New York, NY 10022, U.S.A.

GRAY, Ian. Australian, b. 1951. **Genres:** Sociology. **Career:** Australian Government, research officer, 1979-88; Charles Sturt University, Wagga

Wagga, Australia, lecturer in sociology, 1989-99, associate professor, 1999-. **Publications:** Politics in Place, 1991; (with P. Dunn, B. Kelly, and C. Williams) Immigrant Settlement in Country Areas, 1991; (with G. Lawrence and T. Dunn) Coping with Change: Australian Farmers in the 1990s, 1993; (with G. Lawrence) A Future for Regional Australia, 2001. Contributor to journals. **Address:** Charles Sturt University, Locked Bag 678, Wagga Wagga, NSW 2678, Australia.

GRAY, John. American, b. 1951. **Genres:** Human relations/Parenting, Self help, Sex, Social commentary. **Career:** Writer. **Publications:** What You Feel, You Can Heal, 1989; Men, Women, and Relationships, 1990; Men Are from Mars, Women Are from Venus, 1992; Mars and Venus in the Bedroom, 1995; Mars and Venus in Love, 1996; Mars and Venus Together Forever, 1996; Mars and Venus on a Date, 1997; Mars and Venus Starting Over, 1998; Men Are from Mars, Women Are from Venus: Book of Days, 1998; How to Get What You Want and Want What You Have, 1999; Men Are from Mars, Women Are from Venus, Children Are from Heaven, 1999; Practical Miracles for Mars and Venus, 2000.

GRAY, Judith A(nne). New Zealander, b. 1949. **Genres:** Dance/Ballet, How-to books, Education. **Career:** Writer. University of Wisconsin-Madison, Assistant Professor, 1979-86; Abbott Middle School, San Mateo, CA, Assistant Principal, 1990-94; H.M. Jackson High School, Mill Creek, WA, Science Dept. Chair, 1994-. **Publications:** Dance Instruction: Science Applied to the Art of Movement, 1989; Dance Technology: Current Applications and Future Trends, 1989; Research in Dance IV: 1900-1990, 1992; (with S. Ellison) 365 Foods Kids Love to Eat: Nutritious and Kid-Tested, 1995; (with Ellison) 365 Afterschool Activities: TV-Free Fun for Kids Ages 7-12, 1995; (with Ellison) 365 Days of Creative Play: For Children 2 Years and Up, 3rd ed., 1995; (with Ellison) 365 Books Kids Will Love to Read, 1996; (with Ellison) 365 Puzzles and Tricks, 1996. **Address:** 1816 4th St., Kirkland, WA 98033, U.S.A. **Online address:** jgray803@aol.com

GRAY, Patience. British, b. 1917. **Genres:** Architecture, Design, Food and Wine, Homes/Gardens, Horticulture, Ghost Writer. **Career:** British Department of Information, Foreign Office, Whitehall, England, secretary, 1939; Art and Entertainment Emergency Council, London, England, secretary, 1940; Hurlingham Home Guard School, London, secretary, 1941; Frit Danmark: Journal of Free Danes, Aldwych, England, secretary to editor, 1942; Festival of Britain, South Bank, England, research assistant, 1950-51; cofounder of a free-lance research and writing firm, 1951-56. Royal College of Art, organizing secretary, 1951-55; Architectural Review, columnist, 1954; House & Garden, part-time editor, 1957; Observer, weekly column, "A Woman's Perspective," 1958-61. Designed gardens for architects in the 1950s. **Publications:** (ed. and ghostwriter) Indoor Plants and Gardens, 1952; (with P. Boyd) Plats du Jour, 1957; (co-trans.) Larousse Gastronomique (English-language ed.), 1961; Honey from a Weed: Fasting and Feasting in Tuscany, Catalonia, the Cyclades, and Apulia, 1986; Ring Doves and Snakes, 1989; (ed.) I. Davis, A Catalan Cookery book: A Collection of Impossible Recipes, 1999; Work, Adventures, Childhood, Dreams, 1999. Author of privately printed cookbook on Mediterranean food for Chinese cooks aboard Hong Kong-Australia route ships. Contributor of articles and book reviews to periodicals. **Address:** Masseria Spigolizzi, Presicce, 73054 Lecce, Italy.

GRAY, (John) Richard. British, b. 1929. **Genres:** History, Race relations, Theology/Religion. **Career:** Professor Emeritus of African History, School of Oriental and African Studies, University of London, since 1989 (Fellow, 1961-63; Reader, 1963-72; Professor, 1972-89; Chairman, Centre for African Studies, 1974-77; Chairman, Centre of Religion and Philosophy, 1986-89). Lecturer, University of Kartoum, 1959-61; Chairman, African Centre, Covent Garden, London, 1967-72; Ed., Journal of African History, 1968-71; Chairman, Britain-Zimbabwe Society, 1981-85. **Publications:** The Two Nations: Aspects of the Development of Race Relations in the Rhodesias and Nyasaland, 1960; A History of the Southern Sudan, 1839-1889, 1961; (with D. Chambers) Materials for West African History in Italian Archives, 1965; (ed. with D. Birmingham) Pre-Colonial African Trade, 1970; (ed.) Cambridge History of Africa, vol. IV, 1975; (ed., with E. Fashole-Luke and others) Christianity in Independent Africa, 1978; Black Christians and White Missionaries, 1990. **Address:** 39 Rotherwick Rd, London NW11 7DD, England. **Online address:** Jrichgray@aol.com

GRAY, Richard A. American, b. 1927. **Genres:** Bibliography, Bibliography. **Career:** Ohio State University, Columbus, senior reference librarian and associate professor, 1963-69; American Library Association, Chicago, IL, senior editor in Publishing Division, 1969-74; R.R. Bowker, NYC, acquisitions editor, 1974-75; Pierian Press, Ann Arbor, MI, senior editor, 1986-. **Publications:** Guide to Book Review Citations: A Bibliography of Sources,

1968; (Compiler with D. Villmow) Serial Bibliographies in the Humanities and Social Sciences, 1969; (with H.R. Malinowski and D.A. Gray) Science and Engineering Literature, 2nd ed., 1976; (with T.C. Weiskel) Environmental Decline and Public Policy: Pattern, Trend, and Prospect, 1992; (with C.M. Schmitz) The Gift of Life-Organ and Tissue Transplantation: An Introduction to Issues and Information Sources, 1993; (with Schmitz) Smoking-The Health Consequences of Tobacco Use: An Annotated Bibliography With an Analytical Introduction, 1995; (with C.M. Schultz) Alcoholism: The Health and Social Consequences of Alcohol Use, 1998. Contributor to periodicals. **Address:** 4307 Northwood Dr., Louisville, KY 40220, U.S.A. **Online address:** DGRAY4307@aol.com

GRAY, Robert (Archibald Speir). British, b. 1942. **Genres:** History, Biography. **Career:** Writer. Daily Telegraph, obituarist, 1990-. **Publications:** Rolls on the Rocks, 1971; The Man We Lost, 1972; A History of London, 1978; Cardinal Manning, 1985; The King's Wife: Five Queen Consorts, 1990. **Address:** 23 St. Luke's Rd, London W11 1DB, England.

GRAY, Simon (James Holliday). Also writes as Hamish Reade. British, b. 1936. **Genres:** Novels, Plays/Screenplays. **Career:** Lecturer in English, Queen Mary College, University of London, 1966-. Ed., Delta mag., Cambridge, 1964-. Lecturer, University of British Columbia, Vancouver, 1963-64; Supvr. in English, Trinity College, Cambridge, 1964-66. **Publications:** Colmain, 1963; Simple People, 1965; Little Portia, 1968; (as Hamish Reade) A Comeback for Stark, 1969; Dog Days, 1976; After Pilkington, 1987; Old Flames, 1990; Simply Disconnected, 1996; The Management of Government Debt, 1996; Life Support, 1997; Breaking Hearts, 1997; Just the Three of Us, 1999; The Late Middle Classes, 1999. PLAYS: Wise Child, 1968; Sleeping Dog, 1968; Dutch Uncle, 1969; The Idiot, 1970; Spoiled, 1971; Butley, 1971; Otherwise Engaged and Other Plays, 1975; Molly, 1977; The Rear Column and Other Plays, 1978, in U.S. as The Rear Column, Dog Days, and Other Plays, 1979; Stage Struck, 1979; Close of Play, and Pig in a Poke (plays), 1979; Quartermaine's Terms, 1981; The Common Pursuit, 1984; Plays One, 1986; Melon, 1987; Hidden Laughter, 1990; The Holy Terror, 1991; Cell Mates, 1995; Japes, 2000. TV FILMS: They Never Slept, 1990; Femme Fatale, 1992; Running Late, 1992; Unnatural Pursuits, 1992. NON-FICTION: An Unnatural Pursuit (journal), 1985; How's That for Telling 'Em, Fat Lady?, 1988; Fat Chance, 1995; Enter a Fox, 2001. EDITOR: (with K. Walker) Selected English Prose, 1967. **Address:** c/o Judy Daish Associates, 2 St. Charles Pl, London W10 6EG, England.

GRAY, Tony. (George Hugh Gray). Irish, b. 1922. **Genres:** Novels, History, Sociology, Biography. **Career:** Former Features Ed., Daily Mirror, London. **Publications:** Starting from Tomorrow, 1965; The Real Professionals, 1966; Gone the Time, 1967; The Irish Answer, 1967; (adaptor) Interlude, 1968; (with L. Villa) The Record Breakers, 1970; The Last Laugh, 1972; The Orange Order, 1972; Psalms and Slaughter, 1972; (with H. Ward) Buller, 1974; No Surrender, 1975; Champions of Peace, 1976; (with C. McBride) The White Lions of Timbavati, 1977; (with T. Murphy) Some of My Best Friends Are Animals, 1979; (with C. McBride) Operation White Lion, 1981; The Road to Success: Alfred McAlpine, 1935-85, 1987; Fleet Street Remembered, 1990; Mr. Smyllie, Sir, 1991; Europeople: The MacDonald Guide to the Nations of the European Community, 1992; Ireland This Century, 1994; A Peculiar Man: A New Light on George Moore, 1995; Saint Patrick's People, 1996; The Lost Years: The Emergency in Ireland 1939-1945, 1997. **Address:** 5 Crossways, Crookham Village, Hants. GU51 5TA, England. **Online address:** qhtonygray@onetel.net.uk

GRAY, Victor. See **CONQUEST, (George) Robert (Acworth).**

GRAYSON, Donald K. American, b. 1945. **Genres:** Bibliography, Earth sciences. **Career:** University of Oregon, Eugene, instructor in anthropology, 1969-71; Kirkland College, Clinton, NY, assistant professor of anthropology, 1971-74; Bureau of Land Management, Oregon State Office, Portland, state office archaeologist, 1974-75; University of Washington, Seattle, assistant professor, 1975-78, associate professor, 1978-83, professor of anthropology, 1983-, adjunct faculty at Quaternary Sciences Center, 1975-, adjunct assistant curator of environmental archaeology at Thomas Burke Memorial Museum, 1977-78, adjunct associate curator, 1978-83, adjunct curator, 1983-, acting curator of archaeology, 1988-89. New York University, visiting associate professor, 1981. American Museum of Natural History, research associate in anthropology, 1979-; National Science Foundation, member of Archaeology Panel, 1985-87; Desert Research Institute, member of National Scientific Advisory Board, 1989-90; conducted extensive archaeological and biological field work in the northwestern United States; also worked in France. **Publications:** A Bibliography of the Literature on North American Climates of the Past 13,000 Years, 1975; (ed. with P.D. Sheets, and contrib.) Volcanic Activ-

ity and Human Ecology, 1979; The Establishment of Human Antiquity, 1983; Quantitative Zooarchaeology: Topics in the Analysis of Archaeological Faunas, 1984; The Deserts' Past: A Natural Prehistory of the Great Basin, 1993. Work represented in anthologies. Contributor of about 100 articles and reviews to scholarly journals. **Address:** Department of Anthropology, University of Washington, Seattle, WA 98195, U.S.A.

GRAYSON, Paul. American, b. 1946. **Genres:** Psychology. **Career:** Clinical psychologist. New York University, University Counseling Service, director, 1989-. **Publications:** (ed. with K. Canley) College Psychology, 1989; (with P. Meilman) Beating the College Blues, 1992. **Address:** 726 Broadway Ste 471, New York, NY 10003, U.S.A.

GRAYSON, Richard. See **GRINDAL, Richard.**

GRAZER, Gigi Levangie. American. **Genres:** Film. **Career:** Novelist, screenwriter. **Publications:** (with others, and author of story) Stepmom (screenplay), 1998; Rescue Me: A Love Story (novel), 2000; Maneater: A Novel, 2003. **Address:** c/o Author Mail, Simon & Schuster, 1230 Avenue of the Americas, New York, NY 10020, U.S.A.

GREACEN, Lavinia. (born England). **Genres:** Biography. **Career:** Writer. **Publications:** Chink: A Biography, 1989; J. G. Farrell: The Making of a Writer, 1999. Contributor to periodicals. **Address:** c/o Author Mail, Bloomsbury Publishing PLC, 38 Soho Sq., London W1D 3HB, England.

GREAVES, Bettina Herbert Bien. American, b. 1917. **Genres:** Economics, Bibliography. **Career:** Secretarial positions, 1938-42; overseas assignments with the Foreign Economic Administration (U.S. government wartime agency), 1943-45; secretarial and editorial positions, 1946-50; Foundation for Economic Education Inc., Irvington-on-Hudson, NY, member of senior staff, 1951-92, resident scholar, 1993-. Liberty Fund series, The Library of the Works of Ludwig von Mises, consulting editor. **Publications:** Free Market Economics: A Syllabus, 1975; (comp.) Free Market Economics: A Basic Reader, 1975; (trans.) Ludwig von Mises, On the Manipulation of Money and Credit, 1978; (comp. with R.W. McGee) Mises: An Annotated Bibliography, 1993, rev. ed., 1997. EDITOR: L. von Mises, Economic Freedom and Interventionism, 1990; Austrian Economics: An Anthology, 1996; L. von Mises, Interventionism: An Economic Analysis, 1998; H. Hazlitt, Rules for Living: The Ethics of Social Cooperation, 1999. Contributor to periodicals. **Address:** Foundation for Economic Education Inc., 30 S Broadway, Irvington on Hudson, NY 10533, U.S.A.

GREAVES, Nick. British, b. 1955. **Genres:** Mythology/Folklore. **Career:** Anglo American Corp., Botswana, field geologist, 1976-80; Retreatments Group, East Transvaal, Zimbabwe, contracts manager, 1980-83; O. Connoly & Co., Bulawayo, Zimbabwe, sales manager, 1983-88; L&L Mining & Industrial Suppliers, Bulawayo, administrative manager, 1988-. **Publications:** When Hippo Was Hairy and Other Tales from Africa, 1988; When Lion Could Fly and More Tales from Africa, 1993. **Address:** c/o Ensign Agency, PO Box 66, Maun, Botswana.

GREBSTEIN, Sheldon Norman. American, b. 1928. **Genres:** Literary criticism and history. **Career:** Instructor, and Assistant Professor, University of Kentucky, Lexington, 1953-62; Assistant Professor, University of South Florida, Tampa, 1962-63; Associate Professor, 1963-68, Director of English Graduate Studies, 1966-72, Professor, 1968-81, and Dean of Arts and Science, 1975-81, State University of New York, Binghamton; President and Professor of Literature, 1981-93, University Professor of Literature, 1993-95, State University of New York at Purchase; Westchester Holocaust Commission, Director of Education, 1995-. **Publications:** Sinclair Lewis, 1962; John O'Hara, 1966; Hemingway's Craft, 1973. EDITOR: Monkey Trial, 1960; Perspectives in Contemporary Criticism, 1968; Studies in For Whom the Bell Tolls, 1971. **Address:** 31 Talcott Rd, Rye Brook, NY 10573-1420, U.S.A. **Online address:** whc@bestweb.net

GREELEY, Andrew (Moran). American, b. 1928. **Genres:** Novels, Education, Sociology, Theology/Religion, Mystery/Crime/Suspense, Inspirational/Motivational Literature. **Career:** Director, Center for the Study of American Pluralism, National Opinion Research Center, University of Chicago, 1971- (Sr. Study Director, 1962-68, and Program Director in Higher Education, 1968-70, National Opinion Research Center; Lecturer in Sociology, University of Chicago, 1963-72). Professor of Sociology, University of Arizona, Tucson, 1978-. Ed., Ethnicity; Syndicated columnist, "People and Values," Chicago Sun Times, 1985-. Past President, Catholic Sociological Society. **Publications:** RELIGION & THEOLOGY: The Church and the Suburbs, 1959; Strangers in the House, 1961, rev ed 1967; Religion and

Career, 1963; Letters to a Young Man, 1964; Letters to Nancy, from Andrew M. Greeley, 1964; Priests for Tomorrow, 1964; And Young Men Shall See Visions, 1964; (with P. Rossi) The Education of Catholic Americans, 1966; The Hesitant Pilgrim, 1966; The Catholic Experience, 1967; (with W. Van-Cleve and G.A. Carroll) The Changing Catholic College, 1967; The Crucible of Change, 1968; Uncertain Trumpet, 1968; Youth Asks, Does God Talk?, 1968 as Youth Asks, Does God Still Speak?, 1970; (with M. Marty and S. Rosenberg) What Do We Believe?, 1968; From Backwater to Mainstream, 1969; A Future to Hope In, 1969; Life for a Wanderer, 1969; Religion in the Year 2000, 1969; New Horizions fo the Priesthood, 1970; The Life of the Spirit, 1970; (with W.E. Brown) Can Catholic Schools Survive?, 1970; The Jesus Myth, 1971; The Touch of the Spirit, 1971; What a Modern Catholic Believes About God, 1971; Unsecular Man, 1972; Priests in the United States, 1972; The Sinai Myth, 1972; What a Modern Catholic Believes about the Church, 1972; The Devil, You Say, 1974; (with G. Baum) The Church as Institution, 1974; May the Wind Be at Your Back, 1975; (with W.C. Mc-Cready and K. McCourt) Catholic Schools in a Declining Church, 1976; The Communal Catholic, 1976; Death and Beyond, 1976; The American Catholic, 1977; The Mary Myth, 1977; An Ugly Little Secret, 1977; Everything You Wanted to Know About the Catholic Church but Were Too Pious to Ask, 1978; Crisis in the Church, 1979; The Making of the Popes, 1978; Catholic High School and Minority Students, 1983; The Bottom Line Catechism for Contemporary Catholics, 1982; Religion: A Secular Theory, 1982; The Catholic WHY? Book, 1983; How to Save the Catholic Church, 1984; (with M.G. Durka) Angry Catholic Women, 1984; American Catholics since the Council, 1985; Patience of a Saint, 1986; Catholic Contributions, 1987; When Life Hurts, 1988; 101 Irish-American Blessings, 1988; Religious Indicators, 1940-1985, 1989; God in Popular Culture, 1988; Myths of Religion, 1989; Religious Change in America, 1989; Complaints against God, 1989; Year of Grace, 1990; (with J. Neusner) The Bible and Us, 1990, rev.ed, Common Ground: A Priest and a Rabbi Read Scripture Together, 1996; Book of Irish American Prayers and Blessings, 1991; The Catholic Myth, 1990; Love Affair: A Prayer Journal, 1992; Religion as Poetry, 1994; Sociology and the Religion, 1994; Sacraments of Love: A Prayer Journal, 1994; Windows: A Prayer Journal, 1995; (with A.J. Bergesen) God in the Movies: A Sociological Investigation, 2000; Catholic Imagination, 2000; My Love: A Prayer Journal, 2001; Religion in Europe at the End of the Second Millennium, 2002; Priests: A Calling in Crisis, 2004. SOCIOLOGY: Why Can't They Be Like Us?, 1969; A Fresh Look At Vocations, 1969; (with J. Spaeth) Recent Alumni and Higher Education, 1970; Why Can't They Be Like Us?, 1971; The Denominational Society, 1972; That Most Distressing Nation, 1972; The New Agenda, 1973; Building Coalitions, 1974; Ethnicity in the United States, 1974; MEDIA, 1974; The Sociology of the Paranormal, 1975; Ethnicity, Denomination and Inequality, 1976; Great Mysteries: Essential Catechism, 1977; (with W.C. McCready) The Ultimate Values of the Americal Population, 1976; Neighborhood, 1977; No Bigger than Necessary, 1977; The Irish Americans, 1980; (with W. McCready) Ethnic Drinking Subcultures, 1980; The Sociology of Andrew M. Greeley, 1993; Forging a Common Future, 1997. RELATIONSHIPS: The Friendship Game, 1970; Sexual Intimacy, 1973; Ecstasy, 1974; Love and Play, 1977; Faithful Attraction, 1991; The Sense of Love (poems), 1992. OTHER: Come Blow Your Mind with Me (essays), 1971; (with J.N. Kotre) The Best of Times, the Worst of Times, 1978; Women I've Met (poetry), 1979; A Piece of My Mind, 1983; Confessions of a Parish Priest, 1986; An Andrew Greely Reader (essays), 1987; Andrew Greeley's Chicago, 1989; Andrew Greeley (autobiography), 1990; Furthermore, 1999; (with M.G. Durkin) An Epidemic of Joy: Stories in the Spirit of Jesus, 1999; (with J. Neusner and M.G. Durkin) Virtues and Vices: Stories of the Moral Life, 1999; (comp with M.G. Durkin) The Book of Love, 2002. NOVELS: Nora Maeve and Sebi, 1976; The Magic Cup, 1979; Death in April, 1980; The Cardinal Sins, 1981; Thy Brother's Wife, 1982; Ascent into Hell, 1984; Loed of the Dance, 1987; Love Song, 1988; All about Women (stories), 1990; The Cardinal Virtues, 1990; The Search for Maggie Ward, 1991; An Occasion of Sin, 1991; The Seven Sins, 1991; Wages of Sin, 1992; Fall from Grace, 1993; Angel Light, 1995; White Smoke, 1996; Summer at the Lake, 1997; Star Bright, 1997; Contract with an Angel, 1998; A Midwinter's Tale, 1998; Younger than Springtime, 1999; A Christmas Wedding, 2000; September Song, 2001; The Second Spring, 2003. SCIENCE FICTION NOVELS: Virgin and Martyr, 1985; Angels of September, 1986; The God Game, 1986; The Final Planet, 1987; Angel Fire, 1988; Rite of Spring, 1988; St. Valentine's Night, 1989. FATHER BLACKIE RYAN MYSTERIES: Happy are the Meek, 1986; Happy are the Clean of Heart, 1986; Happy Are Those Who Thirst for Justice, 1987; Happy Are the Merciful, 1992; Happy Are the Peace Makers, 1993; Happy Are the Poor in Spirit, 1994; Happy Are Those Who Mourn, 1995; Happy are the Oppressed, 1997; The Bishop at Sea, 1997; The Bishop and the Three Kings, 1998; The Bishop and the Missing L Train, 2000; The Bishop and the Beggar Girl of St. Germain, 2001; The Bishop in the West Wing, 2002. NUALA ANNE McGRAIL NOVELS: Irish Gold, 1994; Irish

Lace, 1996; Irish Whiskey, 1998; Irish Mist, 1999; Irish Eyes, 2000; Irish Love, 2001; Irish Stew, 2002. EDITOR: (with M.E. Schultz) Catholics in the Archdiocese of Chicago, 1962; (with G. Baum) The Persistence of Religion, 1973; (with G. Baum) Communication in the Church Concilium, 1978; The Family in Crisis or in Transition, 1979; (with M. Cassutt) Sacred Visions, 1991. **Address:** NORC, 1155 E. 60th St., Chicago, IL 60637, U.S.A. **Online address:** agreel@aol.com; www.agreeley.com

GREEN, Andrew M(alcolm). British, b. 1927. **Genres:** Paranormal. **Career:** Consultant and tutor in parapsychology and publishing, 1972-. Book reviewer, Prediction, 1973-. Development Chemist, Thermionic Products, London, 1948-52; Sales Executive, Thorn Electrical Industries, London, 1952-57; Sales Office Manager, Crypto, London, 1957-59; Publicity Manager, Stanley-Bridges, London, 1959-63; Press Relations Officer, Industrial and Trade Fairs, London, 1963-65; Ed., Trade and Technical Press, Morden, Surrey, 1965-68; Editorial Director, Perry Press Productions, London, 1968-72; Founder, Ealing Psychical Research Society, and Co-founder, National Federation of Psychical Research Societies, 1951. **Publications:** Mysteries of Surrey, 1972; Ghost Hunting, A Practical Guide, 1973; Our Haunted Kingdom, 1973, 3rd ed., 1975; Mysteries of Sussex, 1973; Mysteries of London, 1973; Haunted Houses, 1975, 5th ed., 1994; Ghosts of the South East, 1976; Phantom Ladies, 1977; Ghosts of Tunbridge Wells, 1978; The Ghostly Army, 1979; Ghosts of Today, 1980; Haunted Inns & Taverns, 1995; Haunted Sussex Today, 1997, rev. ed., 2001; Haunted Kent Today, 1999; A Caccia di Fantasmi, 1998; Presenze Invisibili, 2001. EDITOR: 500 British Ghosts and Hauntings, 1993; The World's Great Ghost and Poltergeist Stories, 1994; Enigma of Borley Rectory, 1996. **Address:** Scribes, 3 Church Cottages, Mountfield, Robertsbridge, E. Sussex TN32 5JS, England.

GREEN, Angela. American, b. 1949. **Genres:** Adult non-fiction. **Career:** Writer. Worked in marketing and as a public relations consultant. **Publications:** Cassandra's Disk, 2002; The Colour of Water, 2003. **Address:** c/o Author Mail, 73 Kenway Rd., London Owen Publishers, London SW5 0RE, England.

GREEN, Arthur. American, b. 1941. **Genres:** Theology/Religion. **Career:** University of Pennsylvania, Philadelphia, faculty member, 1973-84; Reconstructionist Rabbinical College, Wyncote, PA, dean, 1984-86, president, 1986-93; Brandeis University, Waltham, MA, Philip W. Lown Professor, 1994-. **Publications:** Tormented Master, 1979; (ed.) Jewish Spirituality, 1984; Seek My Face, Speak My Name, 1992; Your Word Is Fire, 1993; Keter: The Crown of God in Early Jewish Mysticism, 1997; The Language of Truth, 1998; These Are the Words, 1999. **Address:** Brandeis University, Waltham, MA 02454, U.S.A.

GREEN, Celia (Elizabeth). British, b. 1935. **Genres:** Psychology, Sciences. **Career:** Director, Institute of Psychophysical Research, Oxford, since 1961. **Publications:** Lucid Dreams, 1968; Out-of-the-Body Experiences, 1968; The Human Evasion, 1969; (with Charles McCreery) Apparitions, 1975; The Decline and Fall of Science, 1976; Advice to Clever Children, 1981; (with C. McCreery) Lucid Dreaming: The Paradox of Consciousness during Sleep, 1994. **Address:** Institute of Psychophysical Research, 118 Banbury Rd, Oxford OX2 6JU, England.

GREEN, Charles H. American, b. 1950. **Genres:** Administration/Management. **Career:** Author, business strategy consultant, and educator. Trusted Advisor Associates, founder, 1995-. Worked for more than twenty years in strategy consulting and planning for both MAC Group and Gemini Consulting. Taught executive education classes through Trusted Advisor Associates, as well as at Columbia Business School and Northwestern University's Kellogg School of Management. **Publications:** The Comprehensive Handbook for SBA Loans: An Easy Guide to Financing and Loan Guarantees from the U.S. Small Business Administration, 1996; The SBA Loan Book: How to Get a Small Business Loan, Even with Poor Credit, Weak Collateral, and No Experience, 1999; (with Robert M. Galford and David H. Maister) The Trusted Advisor, 2000; Financing the Small Business, 2003. Contributor to numerous periodicals. **Address:** c/o Adams Media Corporation, 57 Littlefield St., Avon, MA 02322, U.S.A.

GREEN, Chloe. See **FRANK, J. Suzanne.**

GREEN, Christine. British. **Genres:** Mystery/Crime/Suspense. **Career:** Mystery novelist. Worked as a nurse in Hampstead, England and the Royal National Throat, Nose, and Ear Hospital in London, England. Worked as a teacher and midwife. **Publications:** CHIEF INSPECTOR CONNOR O'NEILL AND DETECTIVE SGT. FRAN WILSON SERIES: Death in the Country, 1994; Die in My Dreams, 1995; Fatal Cut, 1996. KATE KIN-

SELLA SERIES: Deadly Errand, 1992; Deadly Admirer, 1993; Deadly Practice, 1995; Deadly Partners, 1996; Deadly Bond, 2002; Deadly Echo, 2003; Deadly Choice, 2003; Deadly Night, 2004. DETECTIVE INSPECTOR THOMAS RYDELL AND SERGEANT DENISE CALDECOTE SERIES: Fire Angels, 2001; Vain Hope, 2002. OTHER: Coronation Street: The Way to Victory, 2000; Coronation Street: The War Years, 2001. **Address:** c/o Author Mail, Severn House Publishers, 9-15 High St, Sutton, Surrey SM1 1DF, England. **Online address:** christine@christine-green.co.uk

GREEN, Cliff(ord). Australian, b. 1934. **Genres:** Novels, Children's fiction, Plays/Screenplays, Young adult fiction, Novellas/Short stories. **Career:** Apprentice in the printing trade in Melbourne, Victoria, Australia, 1951-56; Education Department of Victoria, head teacher in primary grades, 1960-69; Crawford Productions, Melbourne, staff writer, beginning in 1969; free-lance writer. Teacher of screenwriting at Victorian Council of Adult Education, Western Australian Institute of Technology, Australian Film and Television School, and Victorian College of the Arts; Royal Melbourne Institute of Technology, dramaturge at Australian National Playwrights' Conference. **Publications:** The Incredible Steam-Driven Adventures of Riverboat Bill (juvenile), 1975; Break of Day (novel), 1976; The Sun Is Up (stories), 1978; The Further Adventures of Riverboat Bill (juvenile), 1981; The Art of Dale Marsh, 1981; Evergreen: The Story of a Family, 1984; Riverboat Bill Steams Again (juvenile), 1985; Picnic at Hanging Rock: A Film, 1975; Marion, 1974; Four Scripts, 1978; Lawson's Mates, 1980; Cop Out!, 1983; Plays for Kids, 1984; Senior Drama, 1985; Boy Soldiers, 1990. **Address:** 23 Webb St, Warrandyte, VIC 3113, Australia.

GREEN, Connie Jordan. American, b. 1938. **Genres:** Young adult fiction. **Career:** Woodland Elementary, Oak Ridge, TN, teacher, 1960-61; Oak Ridge High School, Oak Ridge, TN, teacher, 1961; Robertson Junior High, Oak Ridge, TN, teacher, 1961-62; nursery school teacher, 1970-77; University of Tennessee, Knoxville, part-time instructor of composition and literature, 1986-. Conducts writing workshops. **Publications:** YOUNG ADULT NOVELS: The War at Home, 1989; Emmy, 1992. CONTRIBUTOR: An Encyclopedia of East Tennessee, ed by J. Stokely and J. Johnson, 1981; These Are Our Voices: The Story of Oak Ridge, ed by J. Overholt, 1987; several lessons in An Appalachian Studies Teacher's Manual, 1981. Contributor of articles and short fiction to periodicals. Contributor of poetry to journals and reviews. **Address:** Department of English, University of Tennessee, Knoxville, TN 37996, U.S.A.

GREEN, D(ennis) H(oward). British, b. 1922. **Genres:** Literary criticism and history. **Career:** Fellow, Trinity College, Cambridge University, 1949- (Assistant Lecturer, 1950-54; Teaching Fellow, 1952-66; Head of Dept. of Other Languages, 1956-79; Professor of Modern Languages, 1966-79; Schroeder Professor of German, 1979-89). Lecturer in German, St. Andrews University, 1949-50, FBA, 1992. **Publications:** The Carolingian Lord, 1965; The Millstaetter Exodus: A Crusading Epic, 1966; (with L. P. Johnson) Approaches to Wolfram von Eschenbach, 1978; Irony in the Medieval Romance, 1979; The Art of Recognition in Wolfram's Parzival, 1982; Medieval Listening and Reading, 1994; Language and History in the Early Germanic World, 1998; The Beginnings of Medieval Romance, 2002. **Address:** Trinity College, Cambridge, England.

GREEN, Daryl D. Also writes as Dewayne Green. American, b. 1966. **Genres:** Human relations/Parenting, Self help. **Career:** Tennessee Department of Energy, Oak Ridge, TN, program manager, 1994-97, account executive, 1997, technology-development manager, 1997-; writer; Performance Management and Logistics Associates (PMLA), Knoxville, TN, president, 1997-. **Publications:** My Cup Runneth Over: Setting Goals for Single Parents and Working Couples, 1998; Awakening the Talents Within, 2003; (co-author) Fruit of the Spirit, 2003. **Address:** PO Box 32733, Knoxville, TN 37930-2733, U.S.A. **Online address:** pmla@att.net

GREEN, December. American, b. 1961. **Genres:** Area studies, Politics/Government. **Career:** University of South Carolina, Columbia, SC, associate instructor, 1985-88; The Citadel, Charleston, SC, assistant professor, 1988-92, director of Non-Western Studies Program, 1989-92; Governor's School of South Carolina, Charleston, professor, 1989-98; Pacific Lutheran University, Tacoma, WA, assistant professor, 1992-94; Wright State University, Dayton, OH, assistant professor, 1994-98, associate professor, 1998-2001, director of International Studies Program, 2000-2001. Howard University, Washington, DC, faculty adviser, Model Organization of African Unity, 1988 and 1990-92; guest lecturer at libraries and for community organizations. **Publications:** (with M. DeLancey, et al.) Somalia, 1988; (with D. Sparks) Namibia: The Nation at Independence, 1992; Gender Violence in Africa/African Women's Responses, 1999. Contributor to encyclopedias.

Contributor of articles and book reviews to periodicals. **Address:** Department of Political Science, Wright State University, Dayton, OH 45435, U.S.A. **Online address:** december.green@wright.edu

GREEN, Dewayne. See **GREEN, Daryl D.**

GREEN, Donald Ross. American, b. 1924. **Genres:** Education, Psychology. **Career:** Associate in Education, University of California, Berkeley, 1956-57; Instructor to Associate Professor of Education, 1957-67, and Associate Professor of Psychology, 1963-67, Emory University, Atlanta; Sr. Research Psychologist, 1967, Director of Research, 1968-92, CTB/McGraw-Hill, Monterey, California, Chief Research Psychologist, 1992-. **Publications:** Educational Psychology, 1964; (with R. L. Henderson) Reading for Meaning in the Elementary School, 1969; (ed. with M. P. Ford and G. B. Flamer) Measurement and Piaget, 1971; (ed.) The Aptitude-Achievement Distinction, 1974; (ed. with M. J. Wargo) Achievement Testing of Disadvantaged and Minority Students for Educational Program Evalution, 1978. **Address:** CTB/McGraw-Hill, 20 Ryan Ranch Road, Monterey, CA 93940, U.S.A.

GREEN, Duncan. British, b. 1958. **Genres:** Area studies. **Career:** Greater London Council, London, England, policy researcher, 1985-86; freelance journalist on Latin America, 1986-88; Latin America Bureau, London, England, writer and editor, 1989-97; CAFOD, London, England, policy analyst, 1997-. **Publications:** NONFICTION: Faces of Latin America, 1991, 2nd ed., 1997; Guatemala: Burden of Paradise, 1992; Silent Revolution: The Rise of Market Economics in Latin America, 1995; Hidden Lives: Voices of Children in Latin America and the Caribbean, 1998. Contributor to periodicals. **Address:** CAFOD, 2 Romeo Close, Stockwell Rd, London SW9 9TY, England. **Online address:** dgreen@cafod.org.uk

GREEN, Elna C. American, b. 1959. **Genres:** History, Women's studies and issues. **Career:** Tulane University, New Orleans, LA, visiting assistant professor of history, 1992-93; Sweet Briar College, Sweet Briar, VA, assistant professor of history, 1993-98; Florida State University, Tallahassee, Allen Morris Associate Professor of History, 1998-. **Publications:** Southern Strategies: Southern Women and the Woman Suffrage Question, 1997; (ed.) Before the New Deal: Social Welfare in the South, 1830-1930, 1999. **Address:** Department of History, Florida State University, Tallahassee, FL 32306-2200, U.S.A.

GREEN, J. Paul. Canadian, b. 1929. **Genres:** Music. **Career:** Head of music department at a high school in Mississauga, Ontario, 1955-65; University of Western Ontario, London, professor emeritus, professor of music education, 1965-, head of department, 1969-79. Salvation Army, conductor of Dovercourt Citadel Band, 1963-65; Ontario Ministry of Education, chairperson of Instrumental Music Curriculum Revision Committee, 1963-65, teacher at Summer School of Music, 1964-66; Ontario Council on Graduate Studies, chairperson of Music Discipline Group, Committee on Academic Planning, 1978-80. Music adjudicator, arranger, and conductor. **Publications:** (Composer) Stephanos, 1978; (with K. Bray) Solos for Schools, twelve volumes, 1979-82; (with N.F. Vogan) Music Education in Canada: A Historical Account, 1991. Work represented in anthologies. Contributor to music journals. Member of editorial committee, CAUSM Journal, 1977-81. **Address:** 19B Fourth Ave., Ottawa, ON, Canada K1S 2K8.

GREEN, Jeffrey M. Israeli (born United States), b. 1944. **Genres:** Novels, Translations. **Career:** Writer and translator. **Publications:** (with T. Birger) A Daughter's Gift of Love, 1992; Half a Baker (novel), 1994; Back to Marcel Proust (memoir in Hebrew), 1996; American Weekend (novel in Hebrew), 1998. TRANSLATOR FROM HEBREW, EXCEPT WHERE INDICATED: (From French) Beatrice Leroy, The Jews of Navarre in the Late Middle Ages, 1985; Aharon Appelfeld, To the Land of the Cattails, 1986; Appelfeld, The Immortal Bartfuss, 1988; Appelfeld, For Every Sin, 1989; Gershon Shaked, Shmuel Yosef Agnon: A Revolutionary Traditionalist, 1989; Appelfeld, The Healer, 1990; Appelfeld, Katerina, 1992; Rachel Elior, The Paradoxical Ascent to God: The Kabbalistic Theosophy of Habad Hasidism, 1992; Appelfeld, Unto the Soul, 1994; Appelfeld, Beyond Despair, 1994; (from French) Lucien Lazare, Rescue as Resistance, 1996; Appelfeld, The Iron Traks, 1998; Appelfeld, The Conversion, 1999. **Address:** 3 Avigayil St., 93551 Jerusalem, Israel. **Online address:** msgreen@mscc.huji.ac.il

GREEN, Jesse. American, b. 1958. **Genres:** Novels, Novellas/Short stories, Writing/Journalism. **Career:** Writer and free-lance journalist; a regular contributor to the New York Times Magazine. Also worked as a music coordinator on Broadway shows, 1982-86. **Publications:** (with M. Wolitzer) Nutcrackers (puzzle collection), 1991; O Beautiful (novel), 1992; The

Velveteen Father, 1999. Contributor of short stories, articles, and puzzles to periodicals. **Address:** c/o Cynthia Cannell, Janklow and Nesbit Associates, 445 Park Ave., Fl 13, New York, NY 10022, U.S.A.

GREEN, Joseph (Lee). American, b. 1931. **Genres:** Science fiction/Fantasy, Novellas/Short stories, Novels. **Career:** Public Affairs Science Writer, Kennedy Space Center, Florida, 1965-97; Laboratory Technician, International Paper Co., Panama City, Florida, 1949-51; welder and shop worker, Panama City, 1952-54; millwright in Florida, Texas, and Alabama, 1955-58; Sr. Supvr., Boeing Co., Seattle, 1959-63. **Publications:** The Loafers of Refuge, 1965; An Affair with Genius (short stories), 1969; Gold the Man (in U.S. as The Mind Behind the Eye), 1971; Conscience Interplanetary, 1972; Star Probe, 1976; The Horde, 1976. **Address:** 1390 Holly Ave, Merritt Island, FL 32952-5883, U.S.A.

GREEN, Judith. *See* **RODRIGUEZ, Judith (Green).**

GREEN, Kenneth Hart. Canadian, b. 1953. **Genres:** Theology/Religion, Philosophy, Politics/Government. **Career:** University of Toronto, Toronto, Ontario, professor of religion, 1987-. **Publications:** NONFICTION: Jew and Philosopher: The Return to Maimonides in the Jewish Thought of Leo Strauss, 1993; (ed. and author of intro) Jewish Philosophy and the Crisis of Modernity: Essays and Lectures in Modern Jewish Thought, by L. Strauss, 1997. **Address:** Dept. of Religion, University College Room 318, University of Toronto, Toronto, ON, Canada M5S 3H7. **Online address:** kenneth. green@utoronto.ca

GREEN, Michael (Frederick). British, b. 1927. **Genres:** Novels, Autobiography/Memoirs, Humor/Satire. **Publications:** Art of Coarse Rugby, 1960; Art of Coarse Sailing, 1962; Even Coarser Rugby, 1963; Art of Coarse Acting, 1965; Don't Print My Name Upside Down (novel), 1965; Art of Coarse Sport, 1966; Art of Coarse Golf, 1967; Art of Coarse Moving, 1969; Rugby Alphabet, 1972; Art of Coarse Drinking, 1973; Squire Haggard's Journal (satire), 1975; Art of Coarse Cruising, 1976; Even Coarser Sport, 1978; Four Plays for Coarse Actors, 1978; The Coarse Acting Show 2, 1980; Art of Coarse Sex, 1981; Tonight Josephine, 1982; Don't Swing from the Balcony, Romeo, 1983; The Art of Coarse Office Life, 1985; The Third Great Coarse Acting Show, 1986; The Boy Who Shot Down an Airship, 1988; Nobody Hurt in Small Earthquake, 1990; Coarse Acting Strikes Back, 1999. **Address:** 31 Clive Rd, Twickenham TW1 4SQ, England.

GREEN, Miranda J(ane Aldhouse). British, b. 1947. **Genres:** Archaeology/ Antiquities, Mythology/Folklore. **Career:** Open University, Cardiff, Wales, administrator, assistant staff tutor, 1979-88; University of Wales, University College, Cardiff, part-time lecturer in Celtic studies, Gwent College of Higher Education, senior lecturer in archaeology, 1991-94, Caerleon Campus, Newport, professor of archaeology, 1998-. **Publications:** The Gods of the Celts, 1986; Symbol and Image in Celtic Religious Art, 1989; The Sun Gods of Ancient Europe, 1991; Dictionary of Celtic Myth and Legend, 1992; Animals in Celtic Life and Myth, 1992; Celtic Myths, 1993; Celtic Goddesses, 1995; Celtic Art, 1996; Exploring the World of the Druids, 1997; Celtic Wales, 2000; Dying for the Gods, 2001; An Archaeology of Images, 2004. **Address:** University of Wales, Newport, Caerleon Campus, Newport NP18 3YG, Wales. **Online address:** miranda.aldhouse-green@newport.ac.uk

GREEN, Norman. (born United States), b. 1954. **Genres:** Novels. **Career:** Author. **Publications:** NOVELS: Shooting Dr. Jack, 2001; The Angel of Montague Street, 2003; Way past Legal, 2004. **Address:** c/o Author Mail, HarperCollins Publishers, 10 East Fifty-third Street, 7th floor, New York, NY 10022, U.S.A.

GREEN, Peter (Morris). Also writes as Denis Delaney. British, b. 1924. **Genres:** Novels, Novellas/Short stories, Poetry, Children's non-fiction, Classics, History, Humanities, Biography, Essays, Translations. **Career:** Cambridge Review, ed., 1950-51; Selwyn College, Cambridge, director of Studies in Classics, 1952-53; Daily Telegraph, London, fiction critic, 1953-63; Bodley Head Ltd., London, literary adviser, 1957-58; Hodder & Stoughton Ltd., London, consultant ed., 1960-63; television critic, The Listener, London, and Film Critic, John o'London's, 1961-63; professor of Greek history and literature, College Year in Athens, 1966-71; University of Texas at Austin, professor, 1972-82, James R. Dougherty Centennial Professor of Classics, 1982-97, emeritus, 1997-. University of California, Los Angeles, visiting professor of classics, 1976; Tulane University, New Orleans, Mellon Chair of Humanities, 1986; University of Iowa, adjunct professor, 1998-; Princeton University, visiting research fellow and writer-in-residence, 2001. National Endowment for the Humanities, fellow, 1983-84. Syllecta Classica, editor, 1999-. **Publications:** The Expanding Eye, 1953; Achilles His Armour,

1955; (as Denis Delaney) Cat in Gloves, 1956; The Sword of Pleasure, 1957; Sir Thomas Browne, 1959; Kenneth Grahame, 1959; Essays in Antiquity, 1960; Habeas Corpus (short stories), 1962; Look at the Romans, 1963; The Laughter of Aphrodite, 1965; Alexander the Great, 1970; Armada from Athens, 1970; The Year of Salamis, 480-479 BC, 1970, as The Greco-Persian Wars, 1997; The Shadow of the Parthenon, 1972; The Parthenon, 1973; A Concise History of Ancient Greece (in US as Ancient Greece), 1973; Alexander of Macedon 356-323 BC, 1974, rev. ed., 1991; Beyond the Wild Wood: The World of Kenneth Grahame, 1983; Classical Bearings, 1989; Alexander to Actium, 1990, rev. ed., 1993; From Ikaria to the Stars, 2004. TRANSLATOR: Juvenal: The Sixteen Satires, 1967, 3rd ed., 1998; Ovid: The Erotic Poems, 1982; Y. Ritsos, The Fourth Dimension, 1993; Ovid: The Poems of Exile, 1994; (comm.) A. Rhodios, The Argonautika, 1998. EDITOR: Poetry from Cambridge, 1947-50, 1951; Appreciations: Essays by Clifton Fadiman, 1962; History and Culture, 1993. **Address:** c/o Dept of Classics, University of Iowa, 202A Schaeffer Hall, Iowa City, IA 52242, U.S.A. **Online address:** peter-green-1@uiowa.edu

GREEN, R. P. H. British, b. 1943. **Genres:** Literary criticism and history. **Career:** University of St. Andrews, St. Andrews, Scotland, senior lecturer in Latin and chair of department, 1992-95; University of Glasgow, professor of humanity, 1995-. **Publications:** The Poetry of Paulinus of Nola, 1971; Seven Versions of Carolingian Pastoral, 1980; The Works of Ausonius, 1991; Augustine, De Doctrina Christiana, 1995; Ausonii Opera, 1999. **Address:** Department of Classics, University of Glasgow, Glasgow G12 8QQ, Scotland.

GREEN, Richard. American/British, b. 1936. **Genres:** Law, Psychiatry, Sex. **Career:** Consultant Psychiatrist, Head, Director of Research, Gender Identity Clinic, Visiting Professor, Dept. of Psychiatry, Imperial College School of Medicine, Charing Cross Hospital, London, England. Emeritus Professor of Psychiatry, Neuropsychiatric Institute, University of California, Los Angeles; Formerly Professor of Law in Residence, UCLA Law School. Founder, International Academy of Sex Research. Affiliated Lecturer, University of Cambridge, Faculty of Law; Professor of Psychiatry and Psychology, State University of New York, Stony Brook. Ed., Archives of Sexual Behavior, 1971-2001. **Publications:** Sexual Identity Conflict in Children and Adults, 1974; Human Sexuality, 1979; (with G. Wagner) Impotence, 1981; The Sissy Boy Syndrome and the Development of Homosexuality, 1987; Sexual Science and the Law, 1992. EDITOR: (with J. Money) Transsexualism and Sex Reassignment, 1969; (with D. West) Sociolegal Control of Homosexuality, 1997. Contributor to books. **Address:** Claybrook Center, Psychiatry Dept, Gender Identity Clinic, London W6 8 LN, England. **Online address:** richard.green@ic.ac.uk

GREEN, Ricky K(enneth). American, b. 1958. **Genres:** Politics/ Government. **Career:** University of California-Santa Barbara, lecturer in political science, 1998; California State University-Sacramento, assistant professor of ethnic studies and government, 1998-. **Publications:** Democratic Virtue in the Trial and Death of Socrates: Resistance to Imperialism in Classical Athens, 2000. **Address:** Department of Ethnic Studies, California State University-Sacramento, 6000 J St., Sacramento, CA 95819, U.S.A. **Online address:** greenr@csus.edu

GREEN, Scott E. American, b. 1951. **Genres:** Science fiction/Fantasy, Business/Trade/Industry, History, Documentaries/Reportage. **Career:** Journalist; work has appeared in Antique Week Star Log, Snow Week, Ghost Town Quarterly, New Hampshire Sunday News, Independent Banker; Toy Trader, Antique Trader, correspondent; Atlantic Flyer (general aviation tabloid), correspondent; New England Entertainment Digest, Rising Star (newsletter), editor/publisher; Starline, contributor; New Hampshire House of Representatives, 8 years; Southern New Hampshire Services, board of directors; National Writers Union, Oversight Committee. **Publications:** Private Worlds (poems), 1983; Baby Sale at the 7-11 (poems), 1985; Science Fiction, Fantasy, and Horror Poetry: A Resource Guide and Biographical Directory, 1989; A Directory of Depositories of Family History in New Hampshire, 1995; Isaac Asimov: An Annotated Bibliography, 1996. **Address:** 47 Byledge Rd, Manchester, NH 03104, U.S.A.

GREEN, Sharony Andrews. American, b. 1967?. **Genres:** Biography. **Career:** Author and visual artist. Worked as a journalist for Miami Herald; Detroit Free Press, reporter and assistant national editor, until 1997. **Publications:** Cuttin' the Rug under the Moonlit Sky: Stories and Drawings about a Bunch of Women Named Mae, 1997; Grant Green: A Biography, with compact disc by Green, 1998. **Address:** Columbus Ledger-Enquirer, 17 W. 12th St., Columbus, GA 31901, U.S.A. **Online address:** sharonee@aol.com

GREEN, Simon R(ichard). British, b. 1955. **Genres:** Novels. **Career:** Writer. Has worked as a shop assistant, actor, and freelance writer. **Publica-**

tions: NOVELS. HAWK AND FISHER SERIES: Hawk and Fisher, 1990, in UK as No Haven for the Guilty, 1990; Winner Takes All, 1991, in UK as Devil Takes the Hindmost, 1991; The God Killer, 1991; Wolf in the Fold, 1991, in UK as Vengeance for a Lonely Man, 1992; Guard Against Dishonor, 1991; The Bones of Haven, 1992. FOREST KINGDOM SERIES: Blue Moon Rising, 1991; Blood and Honour, 1993; Down among the Dead Men, 1993. TWILIGHT OF THE EMPIRE SERIES: Mistworld, 1992; Ghostworld, 1993; Hellworld, 1995. DEATHSTALKER SERIES: Deathstalker, 1995; Deathstalker Rebellion, 1996; Deathstalker War, 1997. OTHER: Robin Hood: Prince of Thieves (novelization of screenplay), 1991; Shadows Fall, 1994. **Address:** 40 St. Laurence Rd., Bradford-on-Avon, Wiltshire BA15 1JQ, England.

GREEN, Stephen J(ohn). American, b. 1940. **Genres:** Education, Politics/Government, Military/Defense/Arms control. **Career:** U.S. Peace Corps, English teacher at secondary school in Niger, 1962-63; Gaffin & Weiss (law firm), NYC, clerk, 1964; American Friends of the Middle East, Washington, DC, assistant director of programs, 1965-67; UNICEF, asst program & supply officer, Manila, Philippines, 1967-69, planning & program officer at Area Office for Ethiopia and Somalia, 1973-74, assistant to the deputy director of Europe Office in Geneva, Switzerland, 1974-75; Vermont Office on Aging, Montpelier, director, 1970-71; Vermont Dept of Employment, Montpelier, chief of manpower support services, 1971-72; UN Association, NYC, National Policy Panel on International Disaster Relief, project director, 1976-77; UN Development Program, Office of Projects Execution in Chad, regional coordinator, 1978; writer, 1978-81; Basswood Associates, Montpelier, president, 1979-80; Oxford Committee for Famine Relief, UK, field director in Somalia, 1980-81; World Food Programme, senior relief officer, Rome, 1990-94, senior evaluation officer, 1997-99, coordinator for the Russia Federation, 2000; UN Dept. of Humanitarian Affairs, NYC, senior policy officer 1994-96, deputy head, civil affairs, UN Transitional Authority in Eastern Slavonia; elected to Vermont House of Representatives, 2004. **Publications:** Acts of Nature, Acts of Man, 1977; International Disaster Relief, 1977; (ed. with L.H. Stephens, and contrib.) Disaster Assistance, 1979; Taking Sides, 1984; Living by the Sword, 1988. **Address:** 242 Rowell Hill Rd, Berlin, VT 05602, U.S.A. **Online address:** sjgreen@sover.net

GREEN, Terence M(ichael). Canadian, b. 1947. **Genres:** Novels, Novellas/Short stories, Science fiction/Fantasy. **Career:** Science fiction and fantasy writer. English teacher at East York C.I., Toronto, Canada, 1968-99. Served as juror for the Philip K. Dick Award, 1995. **Publications:** FANTASY: The Woman Who Is the Midnight Wind (short stories), 1987. NOVELS: Barking Dogs, 1988; Children of the Rainbow, 1992; Shadow of Ashland, 1996; Blue Limbo, 1997; A Witness to Life, 1999; St. Patrick's Bed, 2001. Contributor of shorts stories, articles, interviews, reviews and poetry to periodicals. Contributor to anthologies.

GREEN, Timothy (S.). British, b. 1936. **Genres:** Money/Finance, Natural history, Travel/Exploration. **Career:** London Correspondent, Horizon, and American Heritage, 1959-62, and Life, 1962-64; Ed., Illustrated London News, 1964-66. **Publications:** The World of Gold, 1968, rev. ed., 1993; The Smugglers 1969; Restless Spirit (in U.K. as The Adventurers) 1970; The Universal Eye, 1972; World of Gold Today, 1973; How to Buy Gold, 1975; The Smuggling Business 1977; The World of Diamonds, 1981; The New World of Gold, 1982; (with M. Green) The Good Water Guide, 1985, rev. ed., 1994; The Prospect for Gold, 1987; The Gold Companion, 1991, rev. ed., 1997; (with D. Duval & R. Louthean) New Frontiers in Diamonds, 1996; The Millennium in Gold 1000-1999, 2000; The Millennium in Silver 1000-1999, 2000. **Address:** 8 Ponsonby Place, London SW1P 4PT, England.

GREEN, Timothy. American, b. 1953. **Genres:** Young adult fiction. **Career:** Bureau of Indian Affairs, junior high school English teacher on Navajo reservation in Arizona, 1989-. Has also taught art at Denver School for Gifted and Talented Students and for North Dakota Artist-in-Residence Program. **Publications:** (Self-illustrated) Mystery of Navajo Moon, 1991; (Self-illustrated) Mystery of Coyote Canyon (young adult novel), 1993; Twilight Boy (young adult novel), 1997. **Address:** c/o Northland Publishing, PO Box 1389, Flagstaff, AZ 86002-1389, U.S.A.

GREENBERG, Alvin. American, b. 1932. **Genres:** Songs/Lyrics and libretti, Novels, Poetry, Novellas/Short stories. **Career:** University of Kentucky, Lexington, instructor, 1963-65; Macalester College, St. Paul, Minnesota, professor of English, 1965-99; Minnesota Review, ed., 1967-71, fiction ed., 1971-73. **Publications:** NOVELS: The Small Waves, 1965; Going Nowhere, 1971; The Invention of the West, 1976. POETRY: The Metaphysical Giraffe, 1968; The House of the Would-Be Gardener, 1972; Dark Lands, 1973; Metaform, 1975; In Direction, 1978; And Yet, 1981; Heavy Wings, 1988;

Why We Live with Animals, 1990. OPERA LIBRETTI: Horspfal, 1969; The Jealous Cellist, 1979; Apollonia's Circus, 1994. STORIES: The Discovery of America, 1980; Delta Q, 1983; The Man in the Cardboard Mask, 1985; How the Dead Live, 1998. ESSAYS: The Dog of Memory, 2002. **Address:** 1304 N 26th St, Boise, ID 83702, U.S.A. **Online address:** alvindg@cs.com

GREENBERG, Cheryl Lynn. American, b. 1958. **Genres:** History. **Career:** Trinity College, Hartford, CT, assistant professor, 1986-92, associate professor, 1992-2000, professor of African American and twentieth-century American history, 2000-. **Publications:** "Or Does It Explode?" Black Harlem in the Great Depression, 1991. **Address:** Department of History, Trinity College, Hartford, CT 06106, U.S.A.

GREENBERG, Elinor Miller. American, b. 1932. **Genres:** Education, Human relations/Parenting, Institutions/Organizations, Psychology, Self help, Women's studies and issues, Autobiography/Memoirs, Essays. **Career:** Loretto Heights College, founding director of University without Walls, 1971-79, assistant academic dean, 1982-84, assistant to the president, 1984-85; Pathways to the Future, founding executive director, 1986-91; EMG and Associates, president/CEO, 1991-; University of Maryland at College Park, research associate at Institute for Research on Adults in Higher Education, 1991; Council for Adult and Experiential Learning, regional manager and executive officer for Mountains and Plains Region, 1979-91; Project Leadership, executive director, 1986-; National Center for Strategic Planning and Resource Development, senior consultant; University of Colorado Health Sciences Center, Area Health Education Center System, Mountain and Plains Partnership, founding regional coordinator, 1996-2002; Visible Human Undergraduate Edition Project, administrator, 2002-04; consultant, WICHE, NEON project, 2003-04, and University of Wisconsin-Madison, NEAT Project, 2003-04. **Publications:** (with W.H. Bergquist and R.A. Gould) Designing Undergraduate Education, 1981; (with others) Enhancing Leadership, 1989; Weaving: The Fabric of a Woman's Life, 1991; Journey for Justice, 1993; (with W.H. Bergquist and G.A. Klaum) In Our Fifties, 1993. EDITOR & CONTRIBUTOR: (with K.M. O'Donnell and W.H. Bergquist) Educating Learners of All Ages, 1980; New Partnerships: Higher Education and the Nonprofit Sector, 1982. Contributor to periodicals. **Address:** EMG and Associates, 6725 S Adams Way, Littleton, CO 80122, U.S.A. **Online address:** ellie.greenberg@uchsc.edu

GREENBERG, Gerald S. American, b. 1946. **Genres:** Writing/Journalism. **Career:** Teacher at public schools in NYC, 1969-71, and Columbus, OH, 1971-84; Ohio State University, Columbus, reference and bibliographic instruction librarian, 1987-, collection development officer for physical education and sports at Education, Human Ecology, Psychology, and Social Work Library, 1997-, and associate professor. **Publications:** Tabloid Journalism: An Annotated Bibliography of English-Language Sources, 1996; Historical Encyclopedia of U.S. Independent Counsel Investigations, 2000. Contributor to books and periodicals. **Address:** Education Human Ecology Psychology & Social Work Library, Ohio State University, 1813 N High St, Columbus, OH 43210, U.S.A. **Online address:** greenberg.3@osu.edu

GREENBERG, Joanne. American, b. 1932. **Genres:** Novels, Novellas/Short stories. **Career:** Assistant Professor of Anthropology and Creative Writing, Colorado School of Mines, Golden, since 1985. **Publications:** The King's Persons, 1963; I Never Promised You a Rose Garden, 1964; The Monday Voices, 1965; Summering, 1966; In This Sign, 1970; Rites of Passage, 1971; Founder's Praise, 1976; High Crimes and Misdemeanours, 1979; A Season of Delight, 1981; The Far Side of Victory, 1983; Simple Gifts, 1986; Age of Consent, 1987; Of Such Small Differences, 1988; With the Snow Queen (short stories), 1991; No Reck'ning Made, 1993; Where the Road Goes, 1998. **Address:** ZN101, Colorado School of Mines, 1500 Illinois St, Golden, CO 80401, U.S.A. **Online address:** jgreenbe@mines.edu

GREENBERG, Martin. American, b. 1918. **Genres:** Literary criticism and history, Translations. **Career:** Schocken Books, NYC, editor, 1946-49; Commentary (magazine), NYC, editor, 1953-60; The New School, NYC, lecturer, 1961-67; C.W. Post College, Greenvale, NY, assistant professor to professor of English literature, 1963-88. **Publications:** The Terror of Art; Kafka and Modern Literature, 1968; The Hamlet Vocation of Coleridge and Wordsworth, 1986. TRANSLATOR: The Diaries of Franz Kafka 1914-23, edited by Max Brod, 1948-49; Heinrich von Kleist, The Marquise of O- and Other Stories, 1960; Heinrich von Kleist, Five Plays, 1988; J.W. von Goethe, Faust, Part One, 1992; J.W. von Goethe, Faust, Part Two, 1998. **Address:** 306 Clinton St, Brooklyn, NY 11201, U.S.A.

GREENBERG, Roger P(aul). American, b. 1941. **Genres:** Psychology, Sciences. **Career:** Syracuse Veterans Administration Hospital, intern in clinical psychology, 1966-67; SUNY Health Science Center, assistant professor, 1968-72, associate professor, 1972-78, professor of psychiatry, director of psychology internship training, 1978-, professor, head, Division of Clinical Psychology, 1993-; private practice of clinical psychology, 1969-;. **Publications:** ALL WITH S. FISHER. The Scientific Credibility of Freud's Theories and Therapy, 1977, rev. ed., 1985; Freud Scientifically Reappraised: Testing the Theories and Therapy, 1996. EDITOR: The Scientific Evaluation of Freud's Theories and Therapy: A Book of Readings, 1978; The Limits of Biological Treatments for Psychological Distress: Comparisons with Psychotherapy and Placebo, 1989; From Placebo to Panacea: Putting Psychiatric Drugs to the Test, 1997. **Address:** 750 E Adams St, Syracuse, NY 13210, U.S.A. **Online address:** greenber@upstate.edu

GREENBERGER, Evelyn Barish. *See* BARISH, Evelyn.

GREENE, Bette. American, b. 1934. **Genres:** Children's fiction, Young adult fiction. **Publications:** Summer of My German Soldier, 1973; Philip Hall Likes Me, I Reckon Maybe, 1974; Morning Is a Long Time Coming, 1978; Bette Green's Survival Kit: 303 Tips from One Writer to Another, 1980; Get on Out of Here, Philip Hall, 1981; Them That Glitter and Them That Don't, 1983; I've Already Forgotten Your Name, Philip Hall, 1983; Drowning of Stephan Jones, 1991. **Address:** 338 Clinton Rd, Brookline, MA 02446, U.S.A. **Online address:** www.bettegreene.com

GREENE, Constance C(larke). American, b. 1924. **Genres:** Novels, Novellas/Short stories, Young adult fiction. **Publications:** A Girl Called Al, 1969; Leo the Lioness, 1970; Good Luck Bogie Hat, 1971; Unmaking of Rabbit, 1972; Isabelle the Itch, 1973; The Ears of Louis, 1974; I Know You, Al, 1975; Beat the Turtle Drum, 1976; Getting Nowhere, 1977; I and Sproggy, 1978; Your Old Pal, Al, 1979; Dotty's Suitcase, 1980; Double-Dare O'Toole, 1981; Al(exandra) the Great, 1982; Ask Anybody, 1983; Isabelle Shows Her Stuff, 1984; Star Shine, 1985.; Other Plans (for adults), 1985; Just Plain Al, 1986; The Love Letters of J. Timothy Owen, 1986; Monday I Love You, 1988; Isabelle and Little Orphan Frannie, 1988; Al's Blind Date, 1989; Funny You Should Ask (stories), 1992; Nora: Maybe a Ghost Story, 1993; Odds on Oliver, 1993; Within Reach (stories), 1993; Don't Give Up the Ghost, 1993. **Address:** c/o Marilyn Marlow, Curtis Brown Ltd., 10 Astor Pl, New York, NY 10003, U.S.A.

GREENE, Don. American. **Genres:** Medicine/Health. **Career:** U.S. Olympic Diving Team, sports psychologist; World Championship Swimming Team, sports psychologist; Golf Digest Schools, sports psychologist; Vail Ski School, Vail, CO, sports psychologist; Julliard School of Music, New York, NY, faculty member, 1998-; stress coach; author. **Publications:** Audition Success: An Olympic Sports Psychologist Teaches Performing Artists How to Win, 2001; Fight Your Fear and Win: Seven Skills for Performing Your Best Under Pressure-At Work, in Sports, on Stage, 2001; Performance Success: Performing Your Best Under Pressure, 2001. **Address:** Julliard School of Music, 60 Lincoln Center Plaza, New York, NY 10023, U.S.A. **Online address:** drdgreene@aol.com

GREENE, Douglas G. American, b. 1944. **Genres:** Mystery/Crime/Suspense, History, Bibliography, Biography. **Career:** University professor; writer. **Publications:** The Earl of Castlehaven's Memoirs of the Irish Wars, 1974; Bibliographia Oziana, A Concise Bibliography of the Oz Books by L. Frank Baum and His Successors, 1976, 2nd ed., 1988; W.W. Denslow, 1976; Diaries of the Popish Plot, 1977; The Meditations of Lady Elizabeth Delaval, 1978; The Door to Doom and Other Detections, 1980, rev. ed., 1991; The Dead Sleep Lightly, 1983; The Wizard of Way-Up and Other Wonders, 1985; Death Locked In: An Anthology of Locked Room Stories, 1987, 2nd ed., 1994; The Collected Short Fiction of Ngaio Marsh, 1989, 2nd ed., 1991; Merrivale, March and Murder, 1991; Fell and Foul Play, 1991; John Dickson Carr: The Man Who Explained Miracles, 1995; Detection by Gaslight, 1997; The Detections of Miss Cusack, 1998; The Dead Hand, 1999; Classic Mystery Stories, 1999; Grand Guignol (in Japanese), 1999; The Romance of the Secret Service Fund, 2003. **Address:** Dept of History, Old Dominion University, Norfolk, VA 23529-0091, U.S.A. **Online address:** DGreene@odu.edu

GREENE, Gayle. American, b. 1943. **Genres:** Literary criticism and history, Women's studies and issues. **Publications:** (ed. with C.R.S. Lenz and C. Neely, and coauthor of intro.) The Woman's Part: Feminist Criticism of Shakespeare, 1980; (ed. with C. Kahn, and contrib.) Making a Difference: Feminist Literary Criticism, 1985; Changing the Story: Feminist Fiction and the Tradition, 1991; Changing Subjects, 1993; Doris Lessing: The Poetics of Change, 1996; The Woman Who Knew Too Much: Alice Stewart and the Secrets of Radiation, 1999; Missing Persons, forthcoming. Work represented in anthologies. Contributor of articles and reviews to popular periodicals and literature journals. **Address:** Department of Language and Literature, Scripps College, Claremont, CA 91711, U.S.A. **Online address:** gaylegreene@earthlink.net

GREENE, Harlan. American, b. 1953. **Genres:** Local history/Rural topics. **Career:** Archivist, preservation educator, 1976-. **Publications:** Why We Never Danced the Charleston, St. Martin's, 1984; Charleston: City of Memory, with photographs by N. Jane Iseley, Legacy, 1987; What the Dead Remember, Dutton, 1991. **Address:** c/o University of Wisconsin Press, 1930 Monroe St 3rd Fl, Madison, WI 53711-2059, U.S.A.

GREENE, Jacqueline Dembar. American, b. 1946. **Genres:** Children's fiction, Children's non-fiction. **Career:** French teacher in and near Boston, MA, 1967-69; worked as reporter, columnist, and feature writer for newspapers in Massachusetts, 1971-80; writer, 1980-. **Publications:** A Classroom Hanukah, 1980; The Hanukah Tooth, 1981; Butchers and Bakers, Rabbis and Kings, 1984; The Leveller, 1984; Nathan's Hanukkah Bargain, 1984; Out of Many Waters, 1988; The Maya, 1992; What His Father Did, 1992; The Chippewa, 1993; One Foot Ashore, 1994; Manabozho's Gifts, 1994; Marie: Mystery at the Paris Ballet, 1997; Marie: Summer in the Country, 1997; The Tohono O'odham (Papago), 1998; Powwow: A Good Day to Dance, 1998; Slavery in Ancient Egypt and Mesopotamia, 2000; Slavery in Ancient Greece and Rome, 2000; The Emperor's Teacup, 2002. Contributor to periodicals and anthologies. **Address:** 21 Sunnyside Ave, Wellesley, MA 02482, U.S.A. **Online address:** jdgbooks.com

GREENE, James H. American, b. 1915. **Genres:** Business/Trade/Industry, Engineering, Technology. **Career:** Former Fulbright Lecturer, Finland Institute of Technology; professor of industrial engineering, Purdue University, West Lafayette, Indiana, since 1948. **Publications:** (ed.) Production and Inventory Control Handbook; Production Control Systems and Decisions, 1965, 1974; Operations Planning and Control, 1967; Operations Management for Productivity and Profit, 1984; Production and Inventory Control Handbook, 1987, 3rd ed. 1997. **Address:** 2252 Franciscan Dr, West Lafayette, IN 47906-4566, U.S.A.

GREENE, Jonathan (Edward). American, b. 1943. **Genres:** Poetry. **Career:** Gnomon Press, Frankfort, KY, founding editor and director, 1965-. Kentucky Renaissance, editor, 1976. **Publications:** The Reckoning, 1966; Instance, 1968; The Lapidary, 1969; A 17th Century Garner, 1969; An Unspoken Complaint, 1970; (trans.) A. Rimbaud, The Poor in Church, 1973; Scaling the Walls, 1974; Glossary of the Everyday, 1974; Peripatetics, 1978; (ed.) Jonathan Williams: A 50th Birthday Celebration, 1979; Once a Kingdom Again, 1979; Quiet Goods, 1980; Idylls, 1983, 1990; Small Change for the Long Haul, 1984; Trickster Tales, 1985. POETRY: Les Chambres des Poetes, 1990; The Man Came to Haul Stone, 1995; Of Moment, 1998; Inventions of Necessity: Selected Poems, 1998; Incidents of Travel in Japan, 1999; A Little Ink in the Paper Sea, 2001; Book of Correspondences, 2002; Watching Dewdrops Fall, 2003; Hummingbird's Water Trough, 2003. **Address:** PO Box 475, Frankfort, KY 40602-0475, U.S.A. **Online address:** jgnomon@aol.com

GREENE, Meg. *See* MALVASI, Meg Greene.

GREENE, Melissa Fay. American, b. 1952. **Genres:** Adult non-fiction. **Career:** Paralegal for General Assistance Legal Services Program, in Savannah, GA, 1975-79, and Rome, GA, 1980-81; writer. **Publications:** Praying for Sheetrock, 1991; Temple Bombing, 1996; Last Man Out, 2003. Work represented in anthologies. Contributor of articles and reviews to magazines and newspapers. **Address:** 1708 E Clifton Rd NE, Atlanta, GA 30307-1252, U.S.A. **Online address:** www.melissafaygreene.com

GREENE, Nathanael. American, b. 1935. **Genres:** History. **Career:** Wesleyan University, Middletown, CT, Instructor, 1963-64, Assistant Professor, 1964-68, Associate Professor, 1968-74, Professor of History, 1974-, Vice-President for Academic Affairs, 1977-90. **Publications:** (ed.) Fascism: An Anthology, 1968; Crisis and Decline: The French Socialist Party in the Popular Front Era, 1969; From Versailles to Vichy: The Third French Republic, 1919-1940, 1970; (ed.) European Socialism since World War I, 1971. **Address:** Dept. of History, Wesleyan University, Middletown, CT 06457, U.S.A.

GREENE, Pamela F. *See* FORMAN, Joan.

GREENE, Rhonda Gowler. American, b. 1955. **Genres:** Children's fiction. **Career:** Writer, 1985-. Goodridge Elementary School, Hebron, KY, learning disabilities teacher, 1977-79; Covenant Nursery School, West Bloomfield, MI, teacher, 1990-93. **Publications:** Barnyard Song, 1997; When a Line Bends...a Shape Begins, 1997; The Stable Where Jesus Was Born, 1999; Jamboree Day, 2001; Eek! Creak! Snicker, Sneak, 2002; The Beautiful World That God Made, 2002; The Very First Thanksgiving Day, 2002; At Grandma's, 2003; Firebears, the Rescue Team, forthcoming; This Is the Teacher, forthcoming. Contributor to magazines. **Address:** 5459 Claridge, West Bloomfield, MI 48322, U.S.A. **Online address:** rgowgreene@hotmail.com.

GREENE, Sheldon L. American, b. 1934. **Genres:** Novels. **Career:** Lawyer and writer. Worked as warden of insurance for State of Ohio, lawyer in private practice, and general counsel for California Rural Legal Assistance; partner in law firm of Greene & Allison, San Francisco, CA. **Publications:** NOVELS: Lost and Found, 1981; Burnt Umber, 2001. Contributor of law review articles.

GREENE, Victor. American, b. 1933. **Genres:** Cultural/Ethnic topics, Music, History. **Career:** Kansas State University, assistant professor, 1963-68, associate professor, 1968-71; University of Wisconsin, Milwaukee, History Dept., associate professor, 1971-77, professor, 1977-. **Publications:** Slavic Community on Strike, 1968; For God and Country: Polish and Lithuanian Ethnic Consciousness in America, 1975; American Immigrant Leaders, 1987; A Passion for Polka, 1992. **Address:** Dept. of History, University of Wisconsin, Milwaukee, WI 53201, U.S.A.

GREENER, Jack. See **BOUNDS, Sydney J(ames).**

GREENER, Michael John. British, b. 1931. **Genres:** Business/Trade/Industry, Law. **Career:** Sr. Audit Clerk, Deloitte Plender Griffiths, Cardiff, 1953-57; Associate, Institute Chartered Accountants, 1957, FCA 1967, Assistant to Secretary, Western Mail Echo Ltd., Cardiff, 1957-60; Lecturer in Accounting, College of Commerce, Wednesbury, 1960-63; Managing Dr., Greener & Sons Ltd., retail jewellers and booksellers, 1972-2001. **Publications:** Between the Lines of the Balance Sheet, 1968, rev. ed., 1980; Problems for Discussion in Mercantile Law, 1968; Penguin Dictionary of Commerce, 1970, rev. ed., 1980; Penguin Business Dictionary, 1987, rev. ed., 1994. **Address:** 33 Glan Hafren, Maes-Y-Coed, Barry, S. Glam CF62 6TA, Wales.

GREENFELD, Liah. American (born Russia), b. 1954. **Genres:** Social sciences, Sociology. **Career:** Harvard University, Cambridge, MA, assistant professor, 1985-89, associate professor of sociology and social studies, 1989, John L. Loeb Associate Professor of Social Sciences, 1989-92; writer. Institute for Advanced Study (Princeton, NJ), member, 1989-90; Massachusetts Institute of Technology, visiting associate professor, 1992-93; Boston University, fellow of the university professors, 1994-. **Publications:** (ed. with M. Martin) Center: Ideas and Institutions, 1988; Different Worlds: A Sociological Study of Taste, Choice, and Success in Art, 1989; Nationalism: Five Roads to Modernity, 1992; Nationalisme i Modernitat, 1999; The Spirit of Capitalism, Nationalism and Economic Growth, 2001. Contributor to professional journals. **Address:** Political Science Dept, Boston University, 232 Bay State Rd, Boston, MA 02215, U.S.A.

GREENFIELD, Jeanette. Australian. **Genres:** Area studies, Cultural/Ethnic topics, Environmental sciences/Ecology, Law. **Career:** Called to the Bar of the Supreme Court, Victoria, Australia, 1969; Monash University, Clayton, Australia, teaching fellow at law school, 1970-71; writer. Associate producer of film, Yani's Monkeys, commissioned by United Kingdom's Channel 4, 1987. **Publications:** China and the Law of the Sea, Air, and Environment, 1979; The Return of Cultural Treasures, 1989, 3rd ed., 2004; China's Practice in the Law of the Sea, 1991. **Address:** 59 River Ct, Upper Ground, London SE1 9PB, United Kingdom. **Online address:** greenf5@attglobal.net

GREENFIELD, Jerome. (Jerry). American (born Russia), b. 1923. **Genres:** Novels, History. **Career:** Associate Professor of English, State University of New York at New Paltz. **Publications:** The Chalk Line (novel), 1963; Wilhelm Reich vs. the USA, 1974. **Address:** 31 Beechwood Park, Poughkeepsie, NY 12601, U.S.A.

GREENHALGH, Paul. British, b. 1955. **Genres:** Art/Art history, Area studies. **Career:** Lecturer Cardiff, 1980-87; Tutor, Victoria and Albert Museum, and Royal College of Art, 1988-90; Camberwell College of Arts (London Institute), Head of Art History, 1992-94; Victoria and Albert Museum, Curator of Ceramics and Glass, 1990-92, Head of Research, 1994-. **Publications:** Ephemeral Vistas: Expositions Universelles, Great Exhibitions, and World's Fairs, 1851-1959, 1988; (ed.) Design and Modernism; Quotations and Sources from Design and the Decorative Arts, 1800-1990, 1993;

Art Nouveau 1890-1914, 2000; The Essential Art Nouveau, 2000. **Address:** Victoria and Albert Museum, South Kensington, London, England.

GREENHALL, Ken. Also writes as Jessica Hamilton. American, b. 1928. **Genres:** Novels. **Career:** Retired editor of reference books and journals. **Publications:** Childgrave, 1982; The Companion, 1988; Deathchain, 1991; Lenoir: A Novel, 1998. AS JESSICA HAMILTON: Elizabeth, 1976; Baxter, 1977. **Address:** 3840 Greystone Ave., Apt. 5M, Bronx, NY 10463, U.S.A.

GREENHILL, Pauline. Canadian, b. 1955. **Genres:** Anthropology/Ethnology, Cultural/Ethnic topics, Mythology/Folklore, Women's studies and issues. **Career:** University of Waterloo, ON, Canada, assistant professor, 1986-90, associate professor of Canadian studies, 1990-91, adjunct professor of anthropology, 1987-91, and English, 1989; University of Winnipeg, MB, associate professor of women's studies, 1991-96, and anthropology, 1995-97, coordinator of women's studies, 1992-94, professor of women's studies, 1996-. Canadian Women's Studies Association, president-elect, 1993-94, president, 1994-95, past president, 1995-96; Folklore Studies Association of Canada, secretary-treasury, 2000-. **Publications:** So We Can Remember: Showing Family Photographs, 1981; Lots of Stories: Maritime Narratives from the Creighton Collection, 1985; True Poetry: Traditional and Popular Verse in Ontario, 1989; Ethnicity in the Mainstream: Three Studies of English Canadian Culture, 1994; (ed. with D. Tye) Undisciplined Women: Tradition and Culture in Canada, 1997. Contributor to books. Contributor of articles and reviews to journals. **Address:** Women's Studies, University of Winnipeg, Winnipeg, MB, Canada R2B 2E9. **Online address:** p.greenhill@uwinnipeg.ca

GREENHOUSE, Carol J(ane). American, b. 1950. **Genres:** Anthropology/Ethnology. **Career:** Cornell University, Ithaca, NY, assistant professor to associate professor of anthropology, 1977-91; Indiana University-Bloomington, professor of anthropology, 1991-, holder of French-American Foundation Chair in American Civilization, 1998-99. **Publications:** Praying for Justice: Faith, Order, and Community in an American Town, 1986; (with B. Yugresson and D. Engel) Law and Community in Three American Towns, 1994; A Moment's Notice: Time Politics across Cultures, 1996; (ed.) Democracy and Ethnography: Constructing Identities in Multicultural States. **Address:** Department of Anthropology, Student Bldg. 130, Indiana University-Bloomington, Bloomington, IN 47405, U.S.A. **Online address:** cgreenho@indiana.edu

GREENING, John. American, b. 1954. **Genres:** Money/Finance. **Career:** Poet and teacher. **Publications:** COLLECTIONS OF POEMS: Westerners, 1984; The Tutankhamun Variations, 1991; Fotheringhay and Other Poems, 1995; The Bocase Stone, 1996; Nightflights: New and Selected Poems, 1999; Gascoigne's Egg, 2000; Omm Sety, 2001. Contributor of poems to literary magazines and anthologies. **Address:** c/o Cargo Press, The Sea House, Coverack, Helston, Cornwall TR12 6SA, England.

GREENLAW, Lavinia (Elaine). British, b. 1962. **Genres:** Novels, Poetry. **Career:** Imperial College of Science and Technology, London, England, publications editor, 1985-86; Allison and Busby, London, desk editor, 1986-87; Earthscan, London, managing editor, 1988-90; South Bank Centre, London, assistant literature officer, 1990-91; London Arts Board, principal literature officer, 1991-94; freelance writer and reviewer, 1994-. Writer-in-residence: Science Museum in London, 1994-95, Mishcon de Reya (law firm), 1997-98; Amherst College, British Council Fellow in Writing, 1995; National Endowment for Science, Technology and the Arts Fellowship, 2000; London University, Goldsmith's College, visiting lecturer in creative writing, 2002. **Publications:** POETRY: The Cost of Getting Lost in Space, 1991; Love from a Foreign City, 1992; Night Photograph, 1993; A World Where News Travelled Slowly, 1997; Minsk, 2003. NOVEL: Mary George of Allnorthover, 2001. **Address:** c/o Derek Johns, A.P. Watt Ltd., 20 John St, London WC1N 2DR, England.

GREENLEAF, Stephen (Howell). American, b. 1942. **Genres:** Mystery/Crime/Suspense. **Career:** Admitted to the Bar of California, 1968, and Iowa, 1977; Research, Multnomah County Legal Aid, Portland, OR, 1969-70; Associate Attorney, Thompson and Hubbard, Monterey, CA, 1970-71, and Sullivan Jones and Archer, San Francisco, 1972-76; Adjunct Professor of Trial Advocacy, University of Iowa, 1979-81. **Publications:** Grave Error, 1979; Death Bed, 1980; State's Evidence, 1982; Fatal Obsession, 1983; The Ditto List, 1985; Beyond Blame, 1986; Toll Call, 1987; Impact, 1989; Book Case, 1991; Blood Type, 1992; Southern Cross, 1993; False Conception, 1994; Flesh Wounds, 1996; Past Tense, 1997; Strawberry Sunday, 1999; Ellipsis, 2000. **Address:** 5726 N Commercial Ave, Portland, OR 97217, U.S.A.

GREENLEE, J(acob) Harold. American, b. 1918. **Genres:** Language/ Linguistics, Theology/Religion. **Career:** Christian Missionary, OMS International, 1969-. Adjunct Professor of Linguistics, University of Texas at Arlington, 1978-92. Trans. Consultant, Wycliffe Bible Translators. Professor of New Testament Greek, Asbury Theological Seminary, Wilmore, KY, 1947-65, and Oral Roberts University, 1965-69. **Publications:** The Gospel Text of Cyril of Jerusalem, 1955; Concise Exegetical Grammar of New Testament Greek, 1963, 5th ed., 1986; An Introduction to New Testament Textual Criticism, 1964, rev. ed., 1995; Nine Uncial Palimpsests of the Greek New Testament, 1969; A New Testament Greek Morpheme Lexicon, 1983; Scribes, Scrolls, and Scripture, 1985; An Exegetical Summary of Titus and Philemon, 1989; An Exegetical Summary of Philippians, 1992; An Exegetical Summary of James, 1993; What the New Testament Says about Holiness, 1994; (with R. Greenlee) With Two Suitcases and a Carry-On, 1994; An Exegetical Summary of Hebrews, 1998; An Exegetical Summary of Jude, 1999; Words from the Word, 2000. **Address:** Shell Point Retirement Community, 649 Coquina Ct, Ft. Myers, FL 33908-1621, U.S.A. **Online address:** haroldgreenlee@ compuserve.com

GREENLEE, Sharon. American, b. 1935. **Genres:** Self help. **Career:** University of Wyoming, Laramie, WY, instructor, 1985-. Freelance consultant and leader of workshops to develop self-esteem, communication and thinking skills, and creativity, 1983-; elementary school counselor, 1995-98; private counselor, 1997-. Taught elementary school for several years. **Publications:** When Someone Dies, 1992; Images of Me: A Guide for Those Who Work with Pre-School Age Children; Self Esteem, forthcoming; Ways to Help Yourself and Others When Someone Dies, forthcoming. **Address:** PO Box 104, Centennial, WY 82055, U.S.A.

GREENO, Gayle. American, b. 1949. **Genres:** Science fiction/Fantasy. **Career:** Sales and marketing positions, G.P. Putnam's Sons, NYC, 1973-75, Praeger Publishers, NYC, 1975-78, Fawcett Books, NYC, 1979-80, and New American Library, NYC, 1980-90. Author and publishing consultant, 1991-. **Publications:** The Ghatti's Tale: Book One: Finders-Seekers, 1993; Mindspeakers' Call: Book Two of The Ghatti's Tale, 1994; Exiles' Return: Book Three of The Ghatti's Tale, 1995. **Address:** c/o Susan Herner, Susan Herner Rights Agency, 10 Oxford Rd., Scarsdale, NY 10583, U.S.A.

GREENSIDE, Mark. American, b. 1944. **Genres:** Novellas/Short stories. **Career:** Peralta Community College District, Oakland and Berkeley, CA, teacher of history, political science, English, creative writing, and humanities, 1971-, staff development officer, 1992-94, 1996-98. Vista College, director of "older adult program," 1978-84. **Publications:** I Saw a Man Hit His Wife (short stories), 1997. Work represented in anthologies. Contributor of stories to periodicals.

GREENSPAN, Stanley I(ra). American, b. 1941. **Genres:** Psychology. **Career:** Clinical child/adult psychiatrist and psychoanalyst, 1970-. George Washington University Medical School, clinical professor of psychiatry, behavioral science, and pediatrics, 1982-. National Institutes of Mental Health, research psychiatrist, Laboratory of Psychology, 1970, research psychiatrist, 1972-74, assistant chief, 1974, acting chief, 1974-75, chief, 1975-82, Mental Health Study Center, chief, Clinical Infant Development Research Unit, Laboratory of Psychology and Psychopathology, 1982-84, chief, Clinical Infant/Child Development Research Center, 198486; Center for Clinical Infant Programs, founder and president, 1975-84. **Publications:** A Consideration of Some Learning Variables in the Context of Psychoanalytic Theory: Toward a Psychoanalytic Learning Perspective, 1975; Intelligence and Adaptation: An Integration of Psychoanalytic and Piagetian Developmental Psychology, 1979; (with N.T. Greenspan) The Clinical Interview of the Child, 1981; Psychopathology and Adaptation in Infancy and Early Childhood: Principles of Clinical Diagnosis and Preventive Intervention, 1981; (with N. Greenspan) First Feelings: Milestones in the Emotional Development of Your Baby and Child, 1985; The Development of the Ego: Implications for Personality Theory, Psychopathology, and the Psychotherapeutic Process, 1989; (with N. Greenspan) The Essential Partnership: How Parents and Children Can Meet the Emotional Challenges of Infancy and Childhood, 1989; Infancy and Early Childhood: The Practice of Clinical Assessments and Intervention with Emotional and Developmental Challenges, 1992; (with J. Salmon) Playground Politics: Understanding the Emotional Life of Your School-age Child, 1993; Developmentally Based Psychotherapy, 1995; (with Salmon) The Challenging Child: Understanding, Raising, and Enjoying the Five Difficult Types of Children, 1995; Developmentally Based Psychotherapy, 1996; (with B.L. Benderly) The Growth of the Mind and the Endangered Origins of Intelligence, 1996. EDITOR: Infants in Multirisk Families: Case Studies in Preventive Intervention, 1987; (with G.H. Pollock) The Course of Life, 4 vols, 1989-91. Contributor to scientific journals and popular magazines. **Address:** 7201 Glenbrook Rd., Bethesda, MD 20814, U.S.A.

GREENSTEIN, George. American, b. 1940. **Genres:** Astronomy. **Career:** Yeshiva University, New York, NY, research associate, 1968-70; Princeton University, Princeton, NJ, research associate at university observatory, 1970-71; Amherst College, Amherst, MA, assistant professor, 1971-77, associate professor, 1977-83, professor of astronomy, 1983-, chairman of Five-College Astronomy Department, 1981-84. **Publications:** Frozen Star: Of Pulsars, Black Holes, and the Fate of Stars, 1984; The Symbiotic Universe: Life and Mind in the Cosmos, 1988; The Quantem Challenge: Modern Research on the Foundations of Quantem Mechanics, 1997; Portraits of Discovery: Profiles in Scientific Genius, 1998. Author of technical and nontechnical articles. **Address:** Raines & Raines, 71 Park Ave, New York, NY 10016, U.S.A.

GREENWALD, G. Jonathan. American, b. 1943. **Genres:** International relations/Current affairs. **Career:** U.S. Department of State, Washington, D.C., foreign service officer, currently political minister-counselor to U.S. Mission to the European Union, Brussels. **Publications:** Berlin Witness, 1993. Contributor to periodicals. **Address:** U.S. Mission to the European Union, U.S. Department of State, 2201 C St. NW, Washington, DC 20520, U.S.A.

GREENWALD, Jeff. American, b. 1954. **Genres:** Cultural/Ethnic topics, Sciences, Travel/Exploration, Writing/Journalism, Essays. **Career:** World traveler, writer, photographer, videographer, and artist. Santa Barbara News & Review, Santa Barbara, CA, cultural and features editor, 1980; Art/Life, editor, 1981-83; Global Network, Navigator, CA, contributing travel editor, 1993-95; Wired magazine, San Francisco, CA, contributing editor, 1993-98; Yoga Journal magazine, Berkeley, CA, contributing editor, 2002-; Network of Ethical World Travelers (www.ethicaltraveler.org), founder and director, 2002. One-man show, Strange Travel Suggestions, 2003. Designed urban playgrounds for UNICEF and Nepal Children's Organization; prepared exhibits, lectures and educational programs for museums and exhibits. Engineer on the site of Khao-I-Dang, a Cambodian refugee camp. **Publications:** Mr. Raja's Neighborhood: Letters from Nepal, 1986; Shopping for Buddhas, 1990; (ed.) A. Clements, Burma: The Next Killing Fields?, 1992; The Size of the World: Once around without Leaving the Ground, 1995; Future Perfect: How Star Trek Conquered Planet Earth, 1998; Scratching the Surface: Impressions of Planet Earth (anthology), 2002. Contributor to magazines. Work represented in anthologies. **Address:** PO Box 5883, Berkeley, CA 94705, U.S.A. **Online address:** jeff@jeffgreenwald.com; www. jeffgreenwald.com

GREENWALD, Sheila. American, b. 1934. **Genres:** Young adult fiction, Illustrations. **Career:** Writer and illustrator. **Publications:** SELF-ILLUSTRATED YOUNG ADULT FICTION: A Metropolitan Love Story, 1962; Willie Bryant and the Flying Otis, 1971; The Hot Day, 1972; Miss Amanda Snap, 1972; Mat Pit and the Tunnel Tenants, 1972; The Secret Museum, 1974; The Secret in Miranda's Closet, 1977; The Mariah Delany Lending Library Disaster, 1977; The Atrocious Two, 1978; All the Way to Wits' End, 1979; It All Began with Jane Eyre, or, the Secret Life of Franny Dillman, 1980; Give Us a Great Big Smile, Rosy Cole, 1981; Blissful Joy and the SATs: A Multiple-Choice Romance, 1982; Will the Real Gertrude Hollings Please Stand Up?, 1983; Valentine Rosy, 1984; Rosy Cole's Great American Guilt Club, 1985; Alvin Webster's Sure Fire Plan for Success and How It Failed, 1987; Write on Rosy!, 1988; Rosy's Romance, 1989; The Mariah Delany Author of the Month Club, 1990; Here's Hermione, A Rosy Cole Production, 1991; Rosy Cole Discovers America!, 1992; My Fabulous New Life, 1993; Rosy Cole! She Walks in Beauty, 1994; Rosy Cole: She Grows and Graduates, 1997; Stucksville, 2000; Rosy Cole's Worst Ever, Best Yet Tour of New York City, 2003. Illustrator of books by M.L. Allen, J. Bothwell, C.R. Brink, H. Colman, M.J. Craig, G.V. Curl, M. Dreifus, L.H. Fisher, F. Laughlin, A. Mallet, B. Rinkoff, N.K. Robinson, M.J. Roth, J.P. Wood, E.V. Worstell, H. Youngman. **Address:** 175 Riverside Dr, New York, NY 10024, U.S.A. **Online address:** sheilagreenwald@usa.net

GREENWALT, Tibor J. American (born Hungary), b. 1914. **Genres:** Medicine/Health. **Career:** Professor Emeritus of Internal Medicine, University of Cincinnati College of Medicine. Director, Research Division, Hoxworth Blood Center, University of Cincinnati, 1987- (Director, 1979-87). Clinical Professor of Medicine, George Washington University School of Medicine, Washington, DC, and Director and Sr. Scientific Adviser, American Red Cross Blood Services, 1967-79; Sr. Member, Institute of Medicine, NAS, 1984. **Publications:** (with W. Dameshek and C. Dreyfus) Hemolytic Syndromes, 1942; (with S.A. Johnson) Coagulation and Transfusion in Clinical Medicine, 1965; (with G.A. Jamieson) Red Cell Membrane: Structure and Function, 1969; (with G.A. Jamieson) Formation and Destruction of Blood Cells, 1970; Transmissible Disease and Blood Transfusions, 1975;

Trace Components of Plasma, 1976; The Granulocyte: Function and Clinical Utilization, 1977; Blood Substitutes and Plasma Expanders, 1978; The Blood Platelet in Transfusion Therapy, 1978; (with C.T. Smit Sibinga and P.C. Das) Future Developments in Blood Banking, 1986; Blood Transfusion, 1988; History of the International Society of Blood Transfusion 1935-1995, 2000. EDITOR: (and contrib.) Immunogenetics, 1968; (with G.A. Jamieson) Glycoproteins of Blood Cells and Plasma, 1971; (with G.A. Jamieson) The Human Red Cell in Vitro, 1973, 1974; (with E.A. Steane) Handbook in Clinical Laboratory Science: Blood Banking, 3 vols., 1977-81.

GREENWOOD, Barbara. Canadian, b. 1940. **Genres:** Children's fiction, Young adult fiction, Children's non-fiction, Biography. **Career:** Teacher in elementary schools in and around Toronto, Ontario, 1961-66; free-lance creative writing teacher. Visiting lecturer at Ryerson University, 1984-2001; University of Toronto, 1990 & 1992, and University of New Brunswick, 1989 & 1991; conductor of writing workshops for teachers. Writer in residence, Markham Library System, 1989-90. **Publications:** A Question of Loyalty, 1984; (with A. McKim) Her Special Vision: A Biography of Jean Little, 1987; Jeanne Sauve, 1989; Spy in the Shadows, 1990; Klondike Challenge: Rachel Hanna, Frontier Nurse, 1990; (general ed.) Presenting...Children's Authors, Illustrators, and Performers, 1990; (with P. Hancock) The Other Side of the Story, 1990; A Pioneer Story: The Daily Life of a Canadian Family in 1840, 1994; (with B. Greenwood), Speak Up! Speak Out!, 1994; The Kids Book of Canada, 1997; Pioneer Crafts, 1997; The Last Safe House: A Story of the Underground Railroad, 1998; A Pioneer Thanksgiving: A Story of Harvest Celebrations in 1841, 1999; Gold Rush Fever: A Story of the Klondike, 1898, 2001; A Pioneer Thanksgiving: Celebrating in the Backwoods in 1841, 2003.

GREENWOOD, Leigh. (born United States), b. 1942. **Genres:** Romance/Historical. **Career:** Writer. Worked for more than thirty years as a music teacher; also worked as a church organist and choir director. Guest on television programs. **Address:** POB 470761, Charlotte, NC 28226, U.S.A. **Online address:** leighgwood@aol.com

GREENWOOD, Norman Neill. British (born Australia), b. 1925. **Genres:** Chemistry, Education, Biography. **Career:** Professor emeritus, University of Leeds, 1990-, professor, head, Dept of Inorganic & Structural Chemistry, 1971-90; resident tutor, lecturer, Chemistry, Trinity College, Melbourne, 1946-48; Sr Harwell Research Fellow, 1951-53; lecturer, sr lecturer, Inorganic Chemistry, University of Nottingham, 1953-61; professor, head, Dept of Inorganic Chemistry, University of Newcastle-upon-Tyne, 1961-71; fellow, Royal Society, 1987; Associe Etranger de l'Academie des Sciences, Institut de France, 1992. **Publications:** Principles of Atomic Orbitals, 1964, 4th ed., 1980; (ed. and co-author) Spectroscopic Properties of Inorganic and Organometallic Compounds, 9 vols., 1967-75; Ionic Crystals, Lattice Defects and Non-Stoichiometry, 1968; (with T.C. Gibb) Mossbauer Spectroscopy, 1971; (with W.A. Campbell) Contemporary British Chemists, 1971; Periodicity and Atomic Structure, 1971; (with E.J.F. Ross) Index of Vibrational Spectra of Inorganic and Organometallic Compounds, 3 vols., 1972, 1974, 1977; Boron, 1973; (with A. Earnshaw) Chemistry of the Elements, 1984, 2nd ed., 1997. Author of research articles and scholarly reviews. **Address:** School of Chemistry, University of Leeds, Leeds LS2 9JT, England. **Online address:** n.n.greenwood@chem.leeds.ac.uk

GREENWOOD, Ted. (Edward Alister Greenwood). Australian, b. 1930. **Genres:** Children's fiction, Young adult fiction. **Career:** Primary sch. teacher, Melbourne, 1948-56; Lecturer in art education, Melbourne Teachers' College, 1956-60, and Toorak Teachers' College, Melbourne, 1960-68. **Publications:** Obstreperous, 1969; Alfred, 1970; V.I.P.: Very Important Plant, 1971; Joseph and Lulu and the Prindiville House Pigeons, 1972; Terry's Brrrmmm GT, 1974; The Pochetto Coat, 1978; Ginnie, 1979; Curious Eddie, 1979; The Boy Who Saw God, 1980; Everlasting Circle, 1981; Flora's Treasures, 1982; Marley and Friends, 1983; (with S. Fennessy) Warts and All, 1984; Ship Rock, 1985; (with Fennessy) I Don't Want to Know, 1986; Windows, 1989; Uncle Theo Is a Number Nine, 1990; (with P. Jennings and T. Denton) Spooner Later, 1992; (with P Jennings and Denton) Duck For Cover, 1994; The Ventriloquist, 1994; (with P.Jennings and T. Denton), Freeze a Crowd, 1996; What do we do With Dawson, 1996; After Dusk, 1997. **Address:** 50 Hilton Rd, Ferny Creek, VIC 3786, Australia.

GREENWOOD-WALLER, Judith. American, b. 1941. **Genres:** Medicine/Health. **Career:** West Virginia University Medical Center, Charleston, research associate, 1977-79; West Virginia Department of Health, Charleston, director of human resource development, 1979-82; West Virginia Bureau of Employment Programs, Charleston, director of workers' compensation research, 1982-2000. West Virginia University Medical Center, Morgantown,

clinical associate professor, 1983-; Kanawha Valley Hospice, member of board of directors, 1983-88; Health Management Systems (Boston, MA), senior consultant, 1989. **Publications:** Physician Assistants in Primary Care, 1980; (ed. with A. Taricco) Workers' Compensation Health Care Cost Containment, 1992. Work represented in anthologies. Contributor to periodicals. **Address:** 9 Vail Dr, Ripley, WV 25271, U.S.A. **Online address:** jgreenwood@alpha.wvup.wvnet.edu

GREER, Germaine. Australian, b. 1939. **Genres:** Literary criticism and history, Women's studies and issues. **Career:** Sydney University, sr. tutor, 1963-64; University of Warwick, Coventry, assistant lecturer, then lecturer in English, 1967-72; Sunday Times newspaper, London, columnist, 1971-73; University of Tulsa, visiting professor, Graduate Faculty of Modern Letters, 1979, and professor of modern letters, 1980-83, Tulsa Centre for the Study of Women's Literature, Oklahoma director, 1980-82; Tulsa Studies in Women's Literature, founder-ed., 1981; Stump Cross Books, director, 1988-; Newnham College, Cambridge, special lecturer and unofficial fellow, 1989-98; University of Warwick, professor of English and comparative studies, 1998-2003. **Publications:** The Female Eunuch, 1969; The Obstacle Race, 1979; Sex and Destiny: The Politics of Human Fertility, 1984; Shakespeare, 1986; The Madwoman's Underclothes, 1986; Daddy We Hardly Knew You, 1989; The Change: Women, Ageing and Menopause, 1991; Slip-Shod Sybils: Recognition, Rejection and the Woman Poet, 1995; The Whole Woman, 1999; John Wilmot, Earl of Rochester, 1999; The Boy, 2003. EDITOR/CO-EDITOR: Kissing the Rod: An Anthology of Seventeenth-Century Women's Verse, 1989; The Uncollected Verse of Aphra Behn, 1989; (with S. Hastings) The Surviving Works of Anne Wharton, 1997; 101 Poems by 101 Women, 2001; Poems for Gardeners, 2003. **Address:** c/o Gillon Aitken and Associates, 29 Fernshaw Rd, London SW10 0TG, England.

GREER, Jane. American, b. 1951. **Genres:** Human relations/Parenting. **Career:** Therapist and author. Marriage and sex therapist in private practice, New York, NY. Formerly adjunct assistant professor, Adelphi University School of Social Work, Garden City, NY. Lecturer and guest on radio and television programs. **Publications:** (with E. Myers) Adult Sibling Rivalry: Understanding the Legacy of Childhood, 1992; (with M.D. Rosen) How Could You Do This to Me? Learning to Trust after Betrayal, 1997; (with M.D. Rosen) Gridlock: Finding the Courage to Move on in Love, Work, and Life, 2000. **Address:** c/o Author Mail, Doubleday Publicity, 1745 Broadway, New York, NY 10019, U.S.A.

GREER, Robert O. American. **Genres:** Mystery/Crime/Suspense. **Career:** Mystery novelist, surgical pathologist, and educator. University of Colorado Health Services Center, professor of pathology, medicine, surgery, and dentistry. **Publications:** C. J. FLOYD MYSTERY NOVELS: The Devil's Hatband, 1996; The Devil's Red Nickel, 1997; The Devil's Backbone, 1998. Contributor to periodicals. **Address:** 180 Adams St. Suite 250, Denver, CO 80206, U.S.A.

GREER, Steven (Crawford). Irish/British, b. 1956. **Genres:** Law. **Career:** University of Sussex, Brighton, England, lecturer in law, 1985-86; University of Bristol, England, lecturer in law, 1986-96, reader in law, 1996-. University of Hanover, visiting lecturer, summer 1988. Occasional consultant to the Council of Europe. **Publications:** (with A. White) Abolishing the Diplock Courts: The Case for Restoring Jury Trial to Scheduled Offences in Northern Ireland, 1986; (ed. with R. Morgan, and contrib.) The Right to Silence Debate, 1990; Supergrasses: A Study in Anti-Terrorist Law Enforcement in Northern Ireland, 1995. Contributor to books. Contributor of articles and reviews to academic and other journals. **Address:** School of Law, Wills Memorial Bldg, University of Bristol, Queens Rd, Bristol BS8 1RJ, England. **Online address:** Steven.Greer@bris.ac.uk

GREET, Kenneth Gerald. British, b. 1918. **Genres:** Theology/Religion. **Career:** With the Conference of the British Methodist Church, London: Secretary of Social Responsibility Division, 1954-71; Secretary of the Conference, 1971-84; President of the Conference, 1980-81. Religious Adviser, Thames Television, London, 1967-84. **Publications:** The Mutual Society, 1962; Man and Wife Together, 1962; Large Petitions, 1964; Guide to Loving, 1965; The Debate About Drink, 1969; The Sunday Question, 1970; The Art of Moral Judgment, 1970; When the Spirit Moves, 1975; A Lion from a Thicket, 1978; The Big Sin, 1982; Under the Rainbow Arch, 1984; What Shall I Cry?, 1986; Jabez Bunting, 1995; Fully Connected, 1997. **Address:** 89 Broadmark Lane, Rustington, Sussex BN16 2JA, England. **Online address:** greet@skynow.net

GREETHAM, D(avid) C. British, b. 1941. **Genres:** Writing/Journalism. **Career:** Procter and Gamble, Newcastle upon Tyne, England, public relations officer, 1963-65; International Schule, Hamburg, Germany, head of English department, 1965-67; City University of New York, NYC, instructor to Distinguished Professor, 1967-. **Publications:** (co-editor) Text: Transactions of the Society for Textual Scholarship, Vols 1-6, 1989-94, Vols 7-9, 1994-96; Textual Scholarship: An Introduction, 1992; (ed.) Scholarly Editing: A Guide to Research, 1995; (ed.) The Margins of the Text, 1997; Textual Transgressions: Essays toward the Construction of a Biobibliography, 1998; Theories of the Text, 1999. **Address:** Graduate Center, City University of New York, 365 5th Ave, New York, NY 10016-4309, U.S.A. **Online address:** dcgreetham@aol.com

GREGERSON, Linda. American, b. 1950. **Genres:** Poetry, Literary criticism and history. **Career:** Kraken (theater company), actress, 1972-75; Atlantic Monthly, Boston, MA, staff editor, 1982-87; University of Michigan, Ann Arbor, assistant professor, 1987-94, associate professor, 1994-2001, professor of English, 2001-03, Frederick G.L. Huetwell Professor of English, 2003-. Recipient: Academy of Arts and Letters, Award in Literature, 2002; Kingsley Tufts Poetry Prize, 2003. **Publications:** The Reformation of the Subject: Spenser, Milton, and the English Protestant Epic, 1995; Negative Capability: Contemporary American Poetry, 2001. POETRY: Fire in the Conservatory, 1982; The Woman Who Died in Her Sleep, 1996; Waterborne, 2002. Work represented in anthologies. Contributor to books. Contributor of poems to literary magazines. Contributor of articles and reviews to scholarly journals and newspapers. **Address:** Dept of English Language and Literature, 3187 Angell Hall, University of Michigan, Ann Arbor, MI 48109, U.S.A. **Online address:** gregerso@umich.edu

GREGG, Pauline. British. **Genres:** History, Biography. **Publications:** Social and Economic History of Britain from 1760 to the Present Day, 1950, 8th rev. ed. 1981; The Chain of History, 1958; Freeborn John: A Biography of John Lilburne, 1961; The Welfare State, 1963; Modern Britain, 1967; A Social and Economic History of England from the Black Death to the Industrial Revolution, 1975; King Charles the First, 1981; Oliver Cromwell, 1988. **Address:** c/o Weidenfeld and Nicolson, 91 Clapham High St, London SW4 7TA, England.

GREGOR, Arthur. American (born Austria), b. 1923. **Genres:** Children's fiction, Plays/Screenplays, Poetry, Autobiography/Memoirs. **Career:** Macmillan Co., publrs., NYC, sr. ed., 1962-70; Hofstra University, Hempstead, NY, professor, 1973-. **Publications:** Fire (play), 1952; Octavian Shooting Targets, 1954; 1 2 3 4 5, 1956; The Little Elephant, 1956; Declensions of a Refrain, 1957; Animal Babies, 1959; Basic Movements, 1966; Figure in the Door, 1968; Continued Departure (play), 1968; The Door Is Open (play), 1970; A Bed by the Sea, 1970; Selected Poems, 1971; The Past Now, 1975; Embodiment, 1982; A Longing in the Land, 1983; Secret Citizen, 1989; The River Serpent, 1994; That Other Side of Things, 2002; The Hand upon His Head, 2004. **Address:** 9 bis rue Gelee, 45360 Chatillon-sur-Loire, France. **Online address:** arthur.gregor@wanadoo.fr

GREGOR, Neil. British. **Genres:** History. **Career:** University of Southampton, Southampton, England, reader in modern German history. **Publications:** Daimler-Benz in the Third Reich, 1998; (ed.) Nazism: A Reader, 2000. **Address:** Department of History, University of Southampton, Highfield, Southampton, England. **Online address:** ng1@soton.ac.uk

GREGORY, Dick. American, b. 1932. **Genres:** Civil liberties/Human rights, Race relations, Social commentary. **Career:** Comedian and civil rights activist. President, Dick Gregory Enterprises, Chicago. **Publications:** From the Back of the Bus, 1964; Nigger, 1964; What's Happening, 1965; The Shadow That Scares Me, 1971; Write Me In, 1971; No More Lies, 1971; Dick Gregory's Political Primer, 1971; Natural Diet, 1973; Up from Nigger, 1976; (with M. Lane) Code Name Zorro: The Murder of Martin Luther King, 1971; Dick Gregory's Bible Tales, 1978; Murder in Memphis, 1992; Callus on My Soul, 2000.

GREGORY, Frederick. American, b. 1942. **Genres:** History. **Career:** Eisenhower College, Seneca Falls, NY, assistant professor of mathematics and history of science, 1973-78; University of Florida, Gainesville, associate professor, 1978-91, professor of history of science, 1992-. **Publications:** Scientific Materialism in Nineteenth-Century Germany, 1977; (ed.) J.F. Fries, Knowledge, Belief, and Aesthetic Sense, 1989; Nature Lost: Natural Science and the German Theological Traditions, 1992. Contributing editor of series Geschichte der Wissenschaftsphilosophie. **Address:** Department of History, PO Box 117320, University of Florida, Gainesville, FL 32611-7329, U.S.A.

GREGORY, Kristiana. American, b. 1951. **Genres:** Westerns/Adventure, Children's fiction, Young adult fiction. **Career:** Gardena Valley News, Gar-

dena, CA, free-lance feature writer, 1977-79, free-lance reporter, 1978; Southern California Business, Los Angeles, CA, associate editor, 1978; Los Angeles Times, book reviewer and columnist, 1978-91; San Luis Obispo County Telegram-Tribune, reporter, 1980-81; homemaker and writer, 1982-. **Publications:** HISTORICAL FICTION FOR YOUNG ADULTS: Jenny of the Tetons, 1989; The Legend of Jimmy Spoon, 1990; Earthquake at Dawn, 1992; Jimmy Spoon and the Pony Express, 1994; The Stowaway: A Tale of California Pirates, 1995; The Winter of Red Snow: The Revolutionary War Diary of Abigail Jane Stewart, 1996; Across the Wide and Lonesome Prairie: The Oregon Trail Diary of Hattie Campbell, 1997; Orphan Runaways, 1998; The Great Railroad Race: The Diary of Libby West, 1999; Cleopatra: Daughter of the Nile, 1999; Five Smooth Stones: The Revolutionary War Diary of Hope Penny Potter, in press; The Race to Miners Creek, California 1849, in press; Eleanor of Aquitane, in press. **Address:** PO Box 46021, Boise, ID 83711, U.S.A.

GREGORY, Philippa. (Kate Wedd). British (born Kenya), b. 1954. **Genres:** Novels, Novellas/Short stories. **Career:** Provincial journalist for newspapers in England, 1971-75; BBC-Radio, Southampton, England, radio journalist, 1978-80, 1984-. Writer. Founding member and vice-president of Hartlepool People, a community center for the unemployed and low-paid. **Publications:** Wideacre, 1987; The Favoured Child, 1989; Meridon, 1990; The Wise Woman, 1992; Mrs. Hartley and the Growth Centre, 1992; Fallen Skies, 1993; A Respectable Trade, 1995; Earthly Joys, 1998; Virgin Earth, 1999; Zelda's Cut, 2000; Bread and Chocolate, 2000; The Other Boleyn Girl, 2001. CHILDREN'S NOVELS: Princess Florizella, 1988; Florizella and the Wolves, 1991; Florizella and the Giant, 1992. **Address:** Rodgers, Coleridge & White, 20 Powis Mews, London W11 1JN, England.

GREGORY, Richard Langton. British, b. 1923. **Genres:** Biology, Psychology, Sciences. **Career:** Professor of Neuropsychology, University of Bristol, and Director, Brain and Perception Laboratory, Medical Research Council, 1970-, now Emeritus. Fellow, Corpus Christi College, Cambridge. Lecturer in Psychology, University of Cambridge, 1959-67; Professor of Bionics, Dept. of Machine Intelligence and Perception, University of Edinburgh, 1967-70. Perception, founder editor, 1972-. **Publications:** (with J. Wallace) Recovery from Early Blindness, 1963; Eye and Brain, 1966, 5th ed. 1997; The Intelligent Eye, 1970; (ed. with E.H. Gombrich) Illusions in Nature and Art, 1973; Concepts and Mechanisms of Perception, 1974; Mind in Science, 1981; Odd Perceptions, 1986; Oxford Companion to the Mind, 1987, 2nd ed., 2004; Mirrors in Mind, 1997. **Address:** 23 Royal York Crescent, Clifton, Bristol BS8 4JX, England. **Online address:** richard.gregory@bris.ac.uk

GREGORY, Steven. See **JONES, Stephen.**

GREGORY, Valiska. American, b. 1940. **Genres:** Children's fiction, Poetry. **Career:** White Oak Elementary School, Whiting, IN, music and drama teacher, 1962-64; Oak Lawn Memorial High School, Oak Lawn, IL, teacher, 1965-68; University of Wisconsin, Milwaukee, lecturer in English, 1968-74; University of Indianapolis, IN, adjunct professor of English, 1974-83; Butler University, Indianapolis, adjunct professor of English, 1983-85, fellow of Butler Writers' Studio and founding director of Butler University Midwinter Children's Literature Conference, 1989-92, writer-in-residence, 1993-. Speaker/workshop leader at schools, libraries, and conferences across the US, 1983-. **Publications:** FOR CHILDREN: Terribly Wonderful, 1986; Sunny Side Up, 1986; Riddle Soup, 1987; The Oatmeal Cookie Giant, 1987; Happy Burpday, Maggie McDougal!, 1992; Through the Mickle Woods, 1992; Babysitting for Benjamin, 1993; Looking for Angels, 1995; Stories from a Time Before, 1995; Kate's Giants, 1995; When Stories Fell Like Shooting Stars, 1996; A Valentine for Norman Noggs, 1999; Shirley's Wonderful Baby, 2002. Contributor of stories and poems for children to magazines. OTHER: The Words Like Angels Come (poetry for adults), 1987. Contributor of poetry and articles to periodicals. **Address:** Butler University, Writer-in-Residence, 4600 Sunset Ave, Indianapolis, IN 46208, U.S.A. **Online address:** vgregory@butler.edu

GREGORY, Vicki L. American, b. 1950. **Genres:** Librarianship, Bibliography. **Career:** Auburn University at Montgomery, Montgomery, AL, head of Department of Systems and Operations, University Library, 1976-88; University of South Florida-Tampa, professor of library and information science and head of School of Library and Information Science, 1988-. **Publications:** The State and the Academic Library, 1993; (with M. Stauffer and T. Keene) Multicultural Resources on the Internet: The United States and Canada, 1999; Selecting and Managing Electronic Resources, 2000. Contributor to books and periodicals. **Address:** School of Library and Information Science, University of South Florida, 4202 East Fowler Ave., Tampa, FL 33620, U.S.A. **Online address:** gregory@luna.cas.usf.edu

GREHAN, Ida. Irish, b. 1916. **Genres:** Area studies, History. **Career:** Freelance writer. Broadcaster for local radio programs in Nigeria. **Publications:** Irish Family Histories, 1992, revised ed, 1995; Waterford, an Irish Art: The History of Waterford Crystal; Dictionary of Irish Family Names, 1997. Contributor to periodicals in Malaysia, England, and Ireland.

GREIF, Geoffrey L. American, b. 1949. **Genres:** Social work, Human relations/Parenting. **Career:** School social worker in Camden, NJ, 1974-76; Drenk Memorial Guidance Center, Burlington, NJ, clinical social worker, 1976-79; University of Maryland at Baltimore, assistant professor, 1984-89, associate professor of social work, 1989-93, professor, 1993-, associate dean, 1996-. Adjunct instructor at Philadelphia College of the Performing Arts, 1974-76, Widener University, 1982-84, and Cabrini College, 1983-84. **Publications:** Single Fathers, 1985; (with M.S. Pabst) Mothers without Custody, 1988; The Daddy Track and the Single Father, 1990; (with R.L. Hegar) When Parents Kidnap: The Families behind the Headlines, 1993; (with Hegar) Understanding Abducted Children, 1993; (with Hegar) Parents Who Abduct (monograph), 1994; (ed. with P. Ephross) Group Work with Populations at Risk, 1997; Out of Touch, 1997; (with F. Hrabowksi and K. Maton) Beating the Odds: Raising Academically Successful African American Males, 1998; (with F. Hrabowski, K. Maton, and M. Greene) Overcoming the Odds: Raising Academically Successful African American Women, 2002. **Address:** School of Social Work, University of Maryland at Baltimore, 525 West Redwood St., Baltimore, MD 21201, U.S.A.

GREIFF, Barrie S(anford). American, b. 1935. **Genres:** Human relations/Parenting. **Career:** Jewish General Hospital, Montreal, Quebec, intern, 1960-61; Institute of Living, Hartford, CT, resident, 1961-64; Georgetown University, Washington, DC, clinical instructor in psychiatry, 1964-66; Harvard University, Cambridge, MA, fellow in psychiatry, 1964-66; psychiatrist at university health service, beginning in 1966, lecturer in occupational psychiatry at Harvard Business School, beginning in 1970. University of Hartford, adjunct assistant professor, 1963-64; Massachusetts General Hospital, clinical assistant psychiatrist, 1966-68. Consultant to Veterans Administration Hospital, Washington, DC, 1964-66. **Publications:** (with P.K. Munter) Tradeoffs: Executive, Family, and Organizational Life, 1980; Psychosocial Impact of Job Loss, 1990; Introduction of Occupational Psychiatry, 1993; Legacy, 1998. **Address:** 25 Montrose St, Newton, MA 02458-2717, U.S.A.

GREIL, Arthur L(awrence). American, b. 1949. **Genres:** Sociology. **Career:** Alfred University, Alfred, NY, instructor to professor of sociology, and health policy, 1977-, director of honors program, 1982-85, associate dean of liberal arts and sciences, 1985-92. Hillel at Alfred, counselor, 1979-. Member of boards of trustees. **Publications:** Georges Sorel and the Sociology of Virtue, 1981; Not Yet Pregnant: Infertile Couples in Contemporary America, 1991; (ed. with T. Robbins) Religion and Social Order, Vol. 4: Between Sacred and Secular: Theory and Research on Quasi-Religion, 1994. Work represented in anthologies. Contributor of articles and reviews to sociology journals and popular magazines. **Address:** Division of Social Sciences, Alfred University, 1 Saxon Dr., Alfred, NY 14802, U.S.A. **Online address:** fgreil@alfred.edu

GRENHAM, John. Irish, b. 1954. **Genres:** Area studies, History, Genealogy/Heraldry, Poetry. **Career:** National University of Ireland, University College, Dublin, tutor, 1981-85; professional genealogist, 1985-90; Irish Genealogical Project, Dublin, project manager, 1990-. **Publications:** Daedalus: Introductions, 1990; The Cloverdale Anthology of Irish Poetry, 1991; Tracing Your Irish Ancestors, 1992; Clans and Families of Ireland, 1993. **Address:** 2 Kildare St., Dublin 2, Ireland.

GRENNAN, Eamon. Irish, b. 1941. **Genres:** Poetry, Translations, Literary criticism and history. **Career:** Vassar College, Poughkeepsie, NY, member of English faculty, 1974-. **Publications:** Wildly for Days, 1983; What Light There Is, 1987; Twelve Poems, 1988; What Light There Is and Other Poems, 1989; As If It Matters, 1991; So It Goes, 1995; (trans.) Leopardi, Selected Poems, 1997; Relations: New and Selected Poems, 1998; Facing the Music: Irish Poetry in the Twentieth Century, 1999; Still Life with Waterfall, 2002. **Address:** Box 352, Vassar College, Poughkeepsie, NY 12604-0352, U.S.A.

GRENVILLE, John A. S. British, b. 1928. **Genres:** Plays/Screenplays, History, International relations/Current affairs. **Career:** University of Nottingham, Lecturer, 1953-66; Yale University, New Haven, CT, Fellow, 1960-64; University of Leeds, Professor in International History, 1966-69; University of Birmingham, Professor of Modern History, 1969-94, Institute for German Studies, Professorial Research Fellow, 1994-. Historical adviser, The World of the Thirties, 1985, and The World in Mid-Century, 1991 (TV series).

Publications: (with J. Fuller) The Coming of the Europeans, 1962; Lord Salisbury and Foreign Policy, 1964; (with G.B. Young) Politics Strategy and American Diplomacy 1873-1917, 1966; (with N. Pronay) The Munich Crisis 1938 (film), 1968; (with N. Pronay) The End of Illusions, from Munich to Dunkirk (film), 1970; The Major International Treaties, 1914-1973; A History and Guide with Texts, 1974, rev. ed. in 2 vols., 1987; Europe Reshaped 1848-1878, 1976, and subsequent eds.; Film as Evidence: Tomorrow the World (film), 1977; World History of the Twentieth Century, vol. I 1900-1945, 1980; Collins History of the World in the Twentieth Century, 1994, and subsequent eds. **Address:** Institute for German Studies, University of Birmingham, PO Box 363, Birmingham B15 2TT, England.

GRENZ, Stanley J. American, b. 1950. **Genres:** Theology/Religion, Inspirational/Motivational Literature. **Career:** University of Winnipeg, Manitoba, adjunct professor of theology, 1980-81; North American Baptist Seminary, Sioux Falls, SD, professor of systematic theology and Christian ethics, 1981-90; Regent College, Vancouver, BC, professor of theology and ethics, and Pioneer McDonald Professor of Baptist Heritage, Theology, and Ethics at Carey Theological College, 1990-2002; Baylor University and Truett Seminary, Waco TX, professor, 2002-. Winnipeg Theological Seminary (now Providence Seminary), adjunct professor, 1980-81; Northern Baptist Theological Seminary, Lombard, IL, affiliate professor, 1996-99; gives presentations and lectures worldwide. **Publications:** Isaac Backus: Puritan and Baptist, 1983; The Baptist Congregation, 1985; Prayer: The Cry for the Kingdom, 1988; Reason for Hope: The Systematic Theology of Wolfhart Pannenberg, 1990; (with W. Hoffman) AIDS: Ministry in the Midst of an Epidemic, 1990; Sexual Ethics: A Biblical Perspective, 1990, rev. ed. as Sexual Ethics: An Evangelical Perspective, 1997; (with R.E. Olson) Twentieth Century Theology, 1992; The Millennial Maze: Sorting out Evangelical Options, 1992; Revisioning Evangelical Theology, 1993; Theology for the Community of God, 1994; (with R.D. Bell) Betrayal of Trust: Sexual Misconduct in the Pastorate, 1995, 2nd ed as Betrayal of Trust: Confronting and Preventing Clergy Sexual Misconduct, 2001; (with D.M. Kjesbo) Women and the Church, 1995; A Primer on Postmodernism, 1996; Created for Community, 1996, 2nd ed, 1998; Korean ed, 2000; (with Olson) Who Needs Theology? An Invitation to the Study of God, 1996; The Moral Quest: Foundations for Christian Ethics, 1997; What Christians Really Believe...and Why, 1998; (with E.L. Miller) The Fortress Introduction to Contemporary Theologies, 1998; Welcoming but not Affirming: An Evangelical Response to Homosexuality, 1998; (with D. Guretzski and C.F. Nordling) Pocket Dictionary of Theological Terms, 1999, Portugese ed, 2000; Theology for the Community of God, 2000; Renewing the Center, 2000; Beyond Fundimentalism, 2001; The Social God and the Relational Self, 2001. EDITOR: (with K.W.M. Wozniak) Christian Freedom: Essays in Honor of Vernon Grounds, 1986; Perspectives on Theology in the Contemporary World: Essays in Honor of Bernard Ramm, 1990. Contributor of essays and book reviews to books, academic journals and other periodicals, and Baptist publications. Contributor of columns to newspapers. **Address:** Truett Seminary, 1100 S. 3rd St., PO Box 97126, Waco, TX 76798-7126, U.S.A. **Online address:** www.stanleyjgrenz.com

GRESCOE, Paul. Canadian, b. 1939. **Genres:** History, Travel/Exploration, Novels. **Career:** Writer and journalist. **Publications:** (with D. Cruise) The Money Rustlers: Self-Made Millionaires of the New West, 1985; Flesh Wound (novel), 1991; Blood Vessel (novel), 1993; (with A. Grescoe) Alaska: The Cruise-Lover's Guide, 1994; Fragments of Paradise: British Columbia's Wild and Wondrous Islands, 1995; The Merchants of Venus: Inside Harlequin and the Empire of Romance, 1996. **Address:** c/o Raincoast Books, 8680 Cambie St., Vancouver, BC, Canada V6P 6M9.

GRESHAKE, Gisbert. German, b. 1933. **Genres:** Theology/Religion. **Career:** Ordained a Roman Catholic priest, 1960; served at parishes in Dinslaken and Beckum, Germany, 1961-66; University of Munster and Tubingen, Germany, assistant professor, 1966-73; University of Vienna, Austria, professor, 1974-85, dean of theology faculty, 1979-83; University of Freiburg, Germany, professor, 1985-98, emeritus professor, 1998-; Rome, invited Professor Gregoriana, 1999-2003. Editor of several religious journals. **Publications:** Historie wird Geschichte, 1963; Auferstehung der Toten, 1969; Zum Thema: Busse und Bussfeier, 1971; Gnade als konkrete Freiheit, 1972; (with G. Lohfink) Naherwartung-Auferstehung-Untersterblichkeit, 1975; Staerker als der Tod, 1976; Geschenkte Freiheit, 1977; Der Preis der Liebe, 1978; (with G. Lohfink) Bittgebet: Testfal des Glaubens, 1978; Die Wueste bestehen, 1979; Signale des Glaubens, 1980; (with W. Geerlings and J. Weismayer) Quellen geistlichen Lebens, 4 vols, 1980-89; Priestersein, 1982, trans. as The Meaning of Christian Priesthood, 1989; Wer ist der Mensch?, 1983; Gottes Heil: Gluck des Menschen, 1983; Gottes Willen tun, 1984; Ungewisses Jenseits?, 1986; Gott in allen Dingen finden, 1986; (with J. Kremer) Resurrectio mortuorum, 1986; Erloest in einer unerloester Welt?, 1987; Tod-und dann?, 1988; Zur Frage der Bischofsernennung, 1990; Ruf Gottes: Anwort des Menschen, 1991; Wenn Leid mein Leben laehmt, 1992; Des dreieine Gott, 1997; Au den dreieinen Gott glauben, 1998; Priester sein in dienes Zeit, 2000; Spiritualitat der Wuste, 2002; Guade-Geschenk der Freiheit, 2004; Kleine Hinfuhrung zum Glauben an der drei-liven Gott, 2005. Contributor to journals and magazines. **Address:** Goethestr 40, D-79100 Freiburg, Germany. **Online address:** gisbert.greshake@theol.uni-freiburg.de

GRESKOVIC, Robert. American. **Genres:** Dance/Ballet. **Career:** Dance teacher and critic. Dance Magazine, reviewer. **Publications:** Ballet 101: A Complete Guide to Learning and Loving the Ballet, 1998. **Address:** c/o Hyperion, 114 5th Avenue, New York, NY 10011, U.S.A.

GRESSER, Seymour. American, b. 1926. **Genres:** Poetry. **Career:** Freelance sculptor, 1948-. Resident Sculptor, Mt. Rushmore, S. Dakota, 1980. **Publications:** Stone Elegies, 1955; Coming of the Atom, 1957; Poems from Mexico, 1964; Voyages, 1969; A Garland for Stephen, 1970; Departure for Sons, 1973; Fragments and Other Poems, 1982; Hagar and Her Elders, 1989. **Address:** 1015 Ruatan St, Silver Spring, MD 20903, U.S.A. **Online address:** sygr@erols.com

GREY, Amelia. *See* **SKINNER, Gloria Dale.**

GREY, Anthony. British, b. 1938. **Genres:** Novels, Autobiography/Memoirs, Novellas/Short stories, Plays/Screenplays, Romance/Historical, Politics/Government. **Career:** Journalist, Eastern Daily Press, 1960-64; Foreign Correspondent, East Berlin and Prague, 1965-67, and Peking, 1967-69, for Reuters, London; independent radio and television reporter and presenter. **Publications:** Hostage in Peking (autobiography), 1970; A Man Alone (short stories), 1972; Some Put Their Trust in Chariots, 1973; Crosswords from Peking, 1975; The Bulgarian Exclusive, 1976; The Chinese Assassin, 1978; Saigon, 1982; The Prime Minister Was a Spy (non-fiction), 1983; Peking, 1988; The Bangkok Secret (novel), 1990; The Naked Angels (novel), 1990; Tokyo Bay (novel) 1996; Hostage in Peking Plus, 2003; What Is the Universe In? (short stories), 2004. PLAYS: Himself, 1975. Radio Documentary Series: 1996 BBC World Service: "UFO's-Fact, Fiction or Fantasy?". **Address:** c/o PFD, Drury House, 34-43 Russell St, London WC2B 5HA, England. **Online address:** anthony.grey@virgin.net; editorial@tagman-press.com

GREY, Belinda. *See* **PETERS, Maureen.**

GREY, (Dame) Beryl (Elizabeth). British, b. 1927. **Genres:** Novellas/Short stories, Dance/Ballet, Travel/Exploration. **Career:** Royal Ballet (formerly Sadlers Wells Ballet), London, Prima Ballerina, 1941-57, Governor, 1983, Benevolent Fund, Chairman, 1992; Arts Education Trust, Artistic Director, 1966-68; London Festival Ballet (now English National Ballet), Artistic Director, 1968-79 (formerly guest prima ballerina and guest producer); Royal Academy of Dancing, Vice-President, 1980; Dance Council of Wales, President, 1981; Dance Teachers, Benevolent Fund, Vice Chairman, 1981; Imperial Society of Teachers of Dancing, Chairwoman, 1981-91, President, 1991-2001, Life President, 2001; Keep Fit Society, President, 1992; Birmingham Royal Ballet, Governor, 1995-99; Royal Opera House, Covent Garden, Director, 1999-2003. **Publications:** Red Curtain Up, 1958; Through the Bamboo Curtain, 1965; My Favourite Ballet Stories, 1981. **Address:** Fernhill, Priory Rd, Forest Row, E. Sussex RH18 5JE, England.

GREY, Charles. *See* **TUBB, E(dwin) C(harles).**

GREY, Jerry. American, b. 1926. **Genres:** Air/Space topics, Engineering, Sciences, Technology. **Career:** Director, Science and Technology Policy, American Institute of Aeronautics and Astronautics, 1987-. Instructor, Cornell University, Ithaca, NY, 1947-49; engineer, Fairchild Engine Division, 1949-50; hypersonic aerodynamicist, Galcit, 1950-51; sr. engineer, Marquardt Aircraft, 1951-52; Princeton University, NJ, professor, 1952-67, visiting professor, 1990-; president, Greyrad Corp., 1959-71; administrator, Public Policy, American Institute of Aeronautics and Astronautics, 1971-82; president, Calprobe Corp., 1972-83; adjunct professor, Long Island University, 1976-82; publr., Aerospace America, 1982-87. International Astronautical Federation, vice president, 1978-84, president, 1984-86; director, Applied Solar Energy Corp., 1979-92; deputy secretary general, UN Conference on the Exploration and Peaceful Uses of Outer Space, 1982; vice-president, International Academy of Astronautics, 1983-85. **Publications:** Nuclear Propulsion, 1970; The Race for Electric Power, 1972; The Facts of Flight, 1973; Noise, Noise, Noise!, 1975; Enterprise, 1979; Aeronautics in China, 1981; Space Tracking and Data Systems, 1981; Beachheads in Space, 1983; Issues in Strategic Planning for Commercial Space

Growth, 1989; Basis for R&D Planning for Civil Aviation in the 21st Century, 1989; Assessment of Strategic Defense Initiative Technologies, 1989; Highlights in Space Technology and Applications (annually), 1988-; The Role of Technology in Revitalizing Civil Aviation, 1990; Issues in Planning "Mission to Planet Earth," 1990; Assessment of New Technologies for the Space Exploration Initiative, 1990; Atmospheric Effects of Chemical Rocket Propulsion, 1991; Assessment of Technologies for Ballistic Missile Defense, 1993; Interactive Effects of Noise and Emission Reduction Technologies on Other Aviation System Technologies, 1993. EDITOR/COEDITOR: (with V. Grey) Space Flight Report to the Nation, 1962; Offshore Airport Center Planning, 1971; (with J.P. Layton) New Space Transportation Systems, 1973; (with A. Henderson) Solar System Exploration, 1974; Aircraft Fuel Conservation, 1974; Solar Energy for Earth, 1975; The Role of Technology in Civil Aviation Policy, 1976; Advanced Energy Conservation Technology, 1976; (with R. Downey and B. Davis) Space: A Resource for Earth, 1976; Space Manufacturing Facilities, 4 vols., 1977-81; (with M. Newman) Aerospace Technology Transfer to the Public Sector, 1978; (with R. Salkeld and D. Patterson) Space Transportation 1980-2000, 1978; Alternative Fuels for Transportation, 1979; (with C. Krop) Aerospace Technology and Marine Transport, 1979; International Aerospace Review, 1982; Working in Space, 1982; Global Implications of Space Activities, 1982; Aerospace Technology and Commercial Nuclear Power, 1983; Hybrid Rocket Propulsion, 1995; Space Launch Integration, 1998; Assessment of NASA Studies of Space Solar Power Concerts, 1998; Export Control Policy and the U.S. Satellite Industry, 1999; Defense Excellence, 2002. **Address:** 881 Ocean Dr, #22A, Key Biscayne, FL 33149, U.S.A.

GREY, Rudolph. (a pseudonym). American. **Genres:** Biography. **Career:** Has worked as a paste-up artist for publishers; rock guitarist, 1972-; freelance writer, c. 1992-. **Publications:** Nightmare of Ecstasy: The Life and Art of Edward D. Wood Jr. (biography), 1992. **Address:** c/o Feral House, PO Box 39910, Los Angeles, CA 90039, U.S.A.

GREYBEARD THE PIRATE. *See* **MACINTOSH, Brownie.**

GREY-WILSON, Christopher. British, b. 1944. **Genres:** Botany, Horticulture. **Career:** Ed, The Alpine Garden Society; freelance horticultural writer and botanist; formerly a Principal Scientific Officer (taxonomic botanist), Royal Botanic Gardens, 1968-90. **Publications:** Dionysia, 1970; Alpine Flowers of Britain and Europe, 1979; Impatiens of Africa, 1980; (with B. Mathew) Bulbs, 1981; (with V. Matthews) Gardening on Walls, 1983; Garden Flowers, 1986; The Genus Cyclamen, 1988; (ed.) A Manual of Alpine and Rock Garden Plants, 1988; (with M. Blamey) The Illustrated Flora of Britain and Northern Europe, 1988; (with M. Blamey) The Genus Dionysia, 1989; Mediterranean Wild Flowers, 1993; Poppies, 1993; (with V. Matthews) Gardening with Climbers, 1997; Cyclamen, 1997. **Address:** The Black House, Fenstead End nr Hawkedon, Bury St. Edmunds, Suffolk IP29 4LH, England. **Online address:** kit@agsbull.demon.co.uk

GRICE, Gordon. American, b. 1965. **Genres:** Zoology. **Career:** Writer. Part-time instructor at colleges and part-time teacher for state-funded literacy and advocacy programs, 1994-97; Panhandle Times, reporter and columnist, 1995-97; Oklahoma Today magazine, contributing editor, 1998-. **Publications:** The Red Hourglass: Lives of the Predators, 1998. Contributor of poems, short stories, and essays to periodicals. **Address:** c/o Elyse Cheney, Sanford J. Greenburger Associates, 55 Fifth Ave., New York, NY 10003, U.S.A.

GRIDBAN, Volsted. *See* **TUBB, E(dwin) C(harles).**

GRIDER, Jay. *See* **MILLER, John Grider.**

GRIEB, Kenneth J. American. **Genres:** History, International relations/Current affairs, Literary criticism and history, Politics/Government, Third World, Bibliography. **Career:** Indiana University, South Bend, resident lecturer in history, 1965-66; University of Wisconsin-Oshkosh, assistant professor, 1966-70, coordinator of Latin American studies, 1968-77, associate professor, 1970-74, professor of history and international studies, 1974-, coordinator of international studies, 1977-, director of the Interdisciplinary Center 1978-93, John McNaughton Rosebush University Professor, 1983-, SNC Corp. University Professor, 1993-. Member, board of editors, The Americas, 1976-92, and The Historian, 1981-; World of Latin America series, consulting editor, 1982-. **Publications:** The United States and Huerta, 1969; (co-author) Essays on Miguel Angel Asturias (literary criticism), 1972; The Latin American Policy of Warren G. Harding, 1976, rev. ed., 2000; Guatemalan Caudillo: The Regime of Jorge Ubico, 1979; Central America in the Nineteenth and Twentieth Centuries: An Annotated Bibliography, 1988.

EDITOR: (co) Latin American Government Leaders, 1970; Research Guide to Central America and the Caribbean, 1985. **Address:** International Studies Program, University of Wisconsin-Oshkosh, 800 Algoma Blvd, Oshkosh, WI 54901, U.S.A.

GRIERSON, Philip. British (born Ireland), b. 1910. **Genres:** History, Money/Finance. **Career:** Fellow, Gonville and Caius College, 1935-, Honorary Keeper of the Coins, Fitzwilliam Museum, 1949-, and Professor Emeritus of Numismatics, 1979-, University of Cambridge (Gonville and Caius College, Librarian, 1944-69, and President, 1966-76; Lecturer in History, 1945-59, Reader in Medieval Numismatics, 1959-71, and Professor of Numismatics, 1971-78). Adviser in Byzantine Numismatics to the Dumbarton Oaks Library and Collections, Harvard University, Washington, DC, 1955-98. Professor of Numismatics and the History of Coinage, University of Brussels, 1948-81. Literary Director, Royal Historical Society, 1945-55; President, Royal Numismatic Society, 1961-66. **Publications:** Les Annales de Saint-Pierre de Gand, 1937; Books on Soviet Russia 1917-42, 1943; Sylloge of Coins of the British Isles, vol. I, 1958; Bibliographie numismatique, 1966; English Linear Measures: A Study in Origins, 1973; (with A.R. Bellinger) Catalogue of the Byzantine Coins in the Dumbarton Oaks Collection and in the Whittemore Collections, 5 vols., 1966-99; Numismatics, 1975; Monnaies du Moyen Age, 1976; The Origins of Money, 1977; Dark Age Numismatics, 1979; Later Medieval Numismatics, 1979; Byzantine Coins, 1982; (with M. Blackburn) Medieval European Coinage, vol. 1, 1986, vol. 14 (with L. Travaini), 1999; The Coins of Medieval Europe, 1991; (with M. Mays) Catalogue of the Late Roman Coins in the Dumbarton Oaks Collection and in the Whittemore Collection, 1992; Scritti Storici e Numismatici, 2001. **Address:** Gonville and Caius College, Cambridge CB2 1TA, England.

GRIESEMER, John. American, b. 1947. **Genres:** Novels. **Career:** Fisherman, 1968; mental hospital orderly, 1972-73; newspaper journalist, 1973-76; actor and writer, 1973-. **Publications:** NOVELS: No One Thinks of Greenland, 2001; Signal and Noise, 2003. Contributor of short fiction to periodicals. **Address:** c/o Eastern Alliance Talent, 1501 Broadway Suite 404, New York, NY 10036, U.S.A.

GRIFFIN, Adele. American, b. 1970. **Genres:** Children's fiction, Young adult fiction. **Career:** Children's author. Clarion Books, New York, NY, assistant editor, 1996-98, freelance manuscript reader, 1996-. **Publications:** Rainy Season, 1996; Split Just Right, 1997; Sons of Liberty, 1997; The Other Shepards, 1998; Overnight, 2003. **Address:** c/o Charlotte Sheedy, Sheedy Literary Agency Inc, 65 Bleecker St Fl 12, New York, NY 10012, U.S.A. **Online address:** erichmauff@aol.com

GRIFFIN, Alice. American. **Genres:** Theatre. **Career:** Hunter College of the City University of New York, temporary tutor, 1948, faculty member, 1948-68; Herbert H. Lehman College of the City University of New York, Bronx, NY, professor of English and director of graduate studies, 1968-91. American National Theatre and Academy, member of board of directors; National Council on the Arts, member. Drama critic and interviewer for WBAI-Radio, WNYC-Radio, and WNCN-Radio, all NYC, 1957-61. **Publications:** Pageantry on the Shakespearean Stage, 1951; Living Theatre: A Study Guide to Great Plays, 1951; Living Theatre, 1953; The Sources of Ten Shakespearean Plays, 1966; Rebels and Lovers: Shakespeare's Young Heroes and Heroines, 1976; Understanding Tennessee Williams, 1995; Understanding Arthur Miller, 1996; Understanding Lillian Hellman, in press. Contributor of articles and reviews to periodicals. **Address:** 492 Southwest Pine Tree Lane, Palm City, FL 34991, U.S.A.

GRIFFIN, Farah Jasmine. American, b. 1963. **Genres:** Literary criticism and history. **Career:** University of Pennsylvania, Philadelphia, associate professor of English, 1993-. **Publications:** Who Set You Flowin'?, 1995; (with C. Fish) A Stranger in the Village: Two Centuries of African American Travel Writings, 1998; Beloved Sisters, Loving Friends: Letters between Addie Brown and Rebecca Primus, 1999. **Address:** Department of English, University of Pennsylvania, Philadelphia, PA 19104, U.S.A. **Online address:** fgriffin@dept.english.upenn.edu

GRIFFIN, Jasper. British, b. 1937. **Genres:** History, Classics. **Career:** Educator and writer. Balliol College, fellow and tutor in classics, 1963-, university reader, 1989-, professor of classical literature, 1992-, public orator, 1992-. Presented T.S. Eliot Memorial Lectures, University of Kent, 1984. **Publications:** Homer on Life and Death, 1980; Homer, 1980; Snobs, 1982; Latin Poets and Roman Life, 1985; The Mirror of Myth, 1986; Virgil, 1986; The Odyssey, 1987; The Iliad: Book Nine, 1995. EDITOR (with J. Boardman and O. Murray): The Oxford History of the Classical World, 1986; The

Oxford History of Greece and the Hellenistic World, 1991. Contributor to journals and periodicals. **Address:** Balliol College, Oxford OXI 3BJ, England.

GRIFFIN, Jill. American, b. 1955. **Genres:** Business/Trade/Industry. **Career:** AmeriSuite Hotels, Austin, TX, director of marketing and sales, 1985-87; R.J.R. Nabisco, brand manager, 1979-85; University of Texas, Austin, member of marketing faculty, 1988-90; Griffin Group, president, 1987-. **Publications:** NONFICTION: Power Packed Promotion, 1990; Selling the Sizzle, 1993; Customer Loyalty: How to Earn It, How to Keep It, 1995, 2nd ed.; Customer Winback: How to Recapture Lost Customers & Keep Them Loyal, 2001. **Address:** 2729 Exposition Blvd, Austin, TX 78703, U.S.A.

GRIFFIN, Keith B(roadwell). British (born Panama), b. 1938. **Genres:** Economics, Third World. **Career:** Magdalen College, Oxford, president, 1979-88; University of California at Riverside, Economics Dept., professor, 1988-2004. **Publications:** Underdevelopment in Spanish America, 1969; (with J. Enos) Planning Development, 1970; The Political Economy of Agrarian Change, 1974; Land Concentration and Rural Poverty, 1976; International Inequality and National Poverty, 1978; (with J. James) The Transition to Egalitarian Development, 1981; (with A. Saith) Growth and Equality in Rural China, 1981; World Hunger and the World Economy, 1987; Alternative Strategies for Economic Development, 1989; (with T. McKinley) Implementing a Human Development Strategy, 1994; Studies in Globalization and Economic Transitions, 1996; Studies in Development Strategy and Systemic Transformation, 2000. EDITOR: Financing Development in Latin America, 1971; (with A.R. Khan) Growth and Inequality in Pakistan, 1972; Institutional Reform and Economic Development in the Chinese Countryside, 1984; (with J. Knight) Human Development and the International Development Strategy for the 1990s, 1990; The Economy of Ethiopia, 1992; (with A.R. Khan) Globalisation and the Developing World, 1992; (with Z. Renwei) The Distribution of Income in China, 1993; Poverty and the Transition to a Market Economy in Mongolia, 1995; Social Policy and Economic Transformation in Uzbekistan, 1996; Economic Reform in Vietnam, 1998; Poverty Reduction in Mongolia, 2003.

GRIFFIN, P(auline) M. American, b. 1947. **Genres:** Novels, Novellas/Short stories, Science fiction/Fantasy. **Career:** Sweet's, McGraw-Hill, NYC, manager, directory services, 1966-; writer. **Publications:** Star Commandos, 1986; Star Commandos: Colony in Peril, 1987; Star Commandos: Mission Underground, 1988; Star Commandos: Death Planet, 1989; Star Commandos: Mind Slaver, 1990; Star Commandos: Return to War, 1990; Star Commandos: Fire Planet, 1990; Star Commandos: Jungle Assault, 1991; Star Commandos: Call to Arms, 1991; (with A. Norton) Storms of Victory, 1991; (with A. Norton and M.H. Schaub) Flight of Vengeance, 1992 (with A. Norton) Redline the Stars, 1993; (with A. Norton) Firehand, 1994; Watchdogs of Space, 2001. **Address:** 111 Prospect Park SW Apt 6, Brooklyn, NY 11218-1218, U.S.A.

GRIFFIN, Peni R(ae). American, b. 1961. **Genres:** Mystery/Crime/Suspense, Science fiction/Fantasy, Children's fiction. **Career:** City Public Service, San Antonio, TX, clerk, 1985-89; Manpower Temporary Services, San Antonio, temporary worker, 1990; writer; Masco/MSA Survey, production assistant, 1991-94; Renhill Temporaries, 1994-95; Eckmann, Groll, Runyan & Waters (appraisers), 1996-. **Publications:** Hobkin, 1992; The Switching Well (time travel fantasy), 1993; The Brick House Burglars (mystery), 1993; Vikki Vanishes (YA suspense), 1995. FOR CHILDREN: Otto from Otherwhere (science fiction), 1990; A Dig in Time (science fiction), 1991; Treasure Bird (mystery), 1992; The Maze (fantasy), 1994; Margo's House (fantasy), 1996; The Ghost Sitters (ghost story), 2001; The Music Thief, 2002. **Address:** 1123 W Magnolia Ave, San Antonio, TX 78201, U.S.A. **Online address:** griffin@txdirect.net

GRIFFIN, Steven A(rthur). American, b. 1953. **Genres:** Sports/Fitness, Children's non-fiction, Travel/Exploration. **Career:** Freelance writer and photographer, 1975-. Central Michigan University, Mt. Pleasant, MI, part-time instructor, 1987-. **Publications:** Ice Fishing: Methods and Magic, 1985; (with B. Tilton) First Aid for YOUths, 1994; The Fishing Sourcebook: Your One-Stop Resource for Everything to Feed Your Fishing Habit, 1996. OUTDOOR KIDS SERIES (with E.M. Griffin): Fishing for Kids: A Family Fishing Guide, 1993; Camping for Kids: A Family Camping Guide, 1994; Bird Watching for Kids: A Family Bird Watching Guide, 1995; Hiking for Kids: A Family Hiking Guide, 1996. Contributor to periodicals. Work represented in anthologies. **Address:** 1310 South Jefferson Ave., Midland, MI 48640, U.S.A.

GRIFFITH, Arthur Leonard. Canadian (born England), b. 1920. **Genres:** Theology/Religion. **Career:** Minister, Trinity United Church, Grimsby, 1947-

50, Chalmers United Church, Ottawa, 1950-60, City Temple, London, U.K., 1960-66, and Deer Park United Church, Toronto, 1966-75; Minister, St. Paul's Anglican Church, Bloor St., Toronto, 1975-85; Retired Minister. **Publications:** The Roman Letter Today, 1959; God and His People, 1960; Beneath the Cross of Jesus, 1961; What Is a Christian?, 1962; Barriers to Christian Belief, 1962; A Pilgrimage to the Holy Land, 1962; The Eternal Legacy, 1963; Pathways to Happiness, 1964; God's Time and Ours, 1964; The Crucial Encounter, 1965; This Is Living, 1966; God Is Man's Experience, 1968; Illusions of Our Culture, 1969; The Need to Preach, 1971; Hang on to the Lord's Prayer, 1973; We Have this Ministry, 1973; Ephesians: A Positive Affirmation, 1975; Gospel Characters, 1976; Reactions to God, 1979; Take Hold of the Treasure, 1981; From Sunday to Sunday, 1987. **Address:** 91 Old Mill Rd, Etobicoke, ON, Canada M8X 1G9. **Online address:** annemereli@aol.com

GRIFFITH, Helen V(irginia). American, b. 1934. **Genres:** Children's fiction. **Career:** Secretary and Treasurer, S. G. Williams and Bros., Wilmington, since 1976. **Publications:** Mine Will, Said John, 1980; Alex and the Cat, 1982; Alex Remembers, 1983; More Alex and the Cat, 1983; Foxy, 1985; Nata, 1985; Georgia Music, 1986; Grandaddy's Place, 1987; Journal of a Teenage Genius, 1987; Emily and the Enchanted Frog, 1989; Plunk's Dreams, 1990; Caitlin's Holiday, 1990; Grandaddy and Janetta, 1993; Doll Trouble, 1993; Dream Meadow, 1994; Grandaddy's Stars, 1995; Alex and the Cat (The 3 Alex books in one volume), 1997; Dinosaur Habitat, 1998; Cougar, 1999; How Many Candles?, 1999; Grandaddy and Janetta Together, 2000. **Address:** 410 Country Club Dr, Wilmington, DE 19803, U.S.A.

GRIFFITH, Ivelaw L(loyd). Guyanese, b. 1955. **Genres:** Politics/Government. **Career:** Florida International University, Miami, associate professor of political science. Woodrow Wilson International Center for Scholars, member of Peace and Security in the Americas Network; consultant to Ford Foundation, U.S. Department of State, Inter-American Defense Board, and Canadian Department of Foreign Affairs and International Trade. **Publications:** The Quest for Security in the Caribbean, 1993; Caribbean Security on the Eve of the Twenty-First Century, 1996; Drugs and Security in the Caribbean: Sovereignty under Siege, 1997. EDITOR & CONTRIBUTOR: Strategy and Security in the Caribbean, 1991; (with B. Sedoc-Dahlberg) Democracy and Human Rights in the Caribbean, 1997. Contributor to books. Contributor of articles and reviews to professional journals and newspapers. **Address:** Department of Political Science, Florida International University, University Park, Miami, FL 33199, U.S.A. **Online address:** Griffiti@servms.fiu.edu

GRIFFITH, Jim. American. **Genres:** Business/Trade/Industry. **Career:** eBay, customer relations, 1996-, Customer Support Training program, manager, 1999-; eBay University, traveling training program for using the Internet auction services, trainer, dean, 2000-. **Publications:** The Official eBay Bible: The Most Up-to-Date, Comprehensive How-to Manual for Everyone from First-Time Users to People Who Want to Run Their Own Business, 2003. **Address:** eBay Inc., 2145 Hamilton Avenue, San Jose, CA 95125, U.S.A.

GRIFFITH, Marlene. American (born Austria), b. 1928. **Genres:** Education. **Career:** San Francisco State College (now University), San Francisco, CA, English teacher, 1962-64; University of California, Berkeley, English professor, 1964-66; Laney College, Oakland, CA, English professor, 1966-87. **Publications:** (co-ed.) The Borzoi College Reader, 1966, 7th ed., 1992; Writing for the Inexperienced Write: Fluency, Shape, Correctness, 1979; (co-author) Democracy's Open Door, 1994. **Address:** 25 Stonewall Rd, Berkeley, CA 94705, U.S.A. **Online address:** mg01@sbcglobal.net

GRIFFITH, Nicola. British, b. 1960. **Genres:** Novels. **Career:** Singer and lyricist for music group Janes Plane, 1981-82; freelance writer, c. 1988-. **Publications:** NOVELS: Ammonite, 1993; Slow River, 1995. OTHER: (co-editor) Bending the Landscape (anthology), vol 1, 1997; Penny in My Mouth, 1998. Contributor of short fiction to books. Contributor to periodicals. **Address:** c/o Shawna McCarthy, Scovil Chichak Galen, 381 Park Ave. South Ste. 1020, New York, NY 10016, U.S.A.

GRIFFITH, Thomas Gwynfor. British, b. 1926. **Genres:** Language/Linguistics, Literary criticism and history. **Career:** Translations and literary studies. Professor Emeritus of Italian Language and Literature, University of Manchester, 1988- (Professor, 1971-88). University Lecturer in Italian, Oxford University, 1958-65; Fellow, St. Cross College, 1965; Professor of Italian, Hull University, 1966-71. **Publications:** (ed. and trans.) Boccaccio: Detholion o'r Decameron, 1951: Bandello's Fiction: An Examination of the Novelle, 1955; Avventure Linguistiche del Cinquecento, 1961; (with B.

Migliorini) The Italian Language, 1966, rev. ed., 1984; Italian Writers and the Italian Language, 1967; (ed. with P.R.J. Hainsworth) Petrarch: Selected Poems, 1971; Dau Ben y Daith, 1995; O Hendrefigillt i Livotno, 2000. **Address:** Dept. of Italian Studies, University of Manchester, Manchester M13 9PL, England.

GRIFFITHS, John Gwyn. Welsh, b. 1911. **Genres:** Poetry, Classics, Theology/Religion. **Career:** Y Fflam, Welsh literary journal, Co-ed., 1941-47; University of Wales, Lecturer, Sr. Lecturer, and Reader, 1946-72, Professor of Classics and Egyptology, 1973-79, now emeritus. University College, Oxford, Lady Wallis Budge Research Lecturer, 1957-58; The Welsh Nation, Ed., 1964-65; University of Cairo, Guest Professor in Classics and Egyptology, 1965-66; Journal of Egyptian Archaeology, Ed., 1970-78; All Souls College, Oxford, Visiting Fellow, 1976-77. **Publications:** The Conflict of Horus and Seth, 1960; Dragon's Nostrils, 1961; Songs of Cairo, 1970; Aristotle's Poetics, 1978; The Origins of Osiris and His Cult, 1980; The Divine Verdict, 1991; Atlantis and Egypt, 1991; Studies in Pharaonic Religion and Society, 1992; Triads and Trinity, 1996. EDITOR: Plutarch's de Iside et Osiride, 1970; The Isis-Book of Apuleius, 1975. **Address:** 3 Long Oaks Ave, Abertawe-Swansea, Wales.

GRIFFITHS, Linda. Canadian, b. 1956?. **Genres:** Plays/Screenplays, Film, Theatre. **Career:** Professional writer/actor; Opening Night, CBC Radio, host. **Publications:** PLAYS: Maggie and Pierre, 1980; The Darling Family, 1991, screenplay, 1994; Chronic, 2002. OTHER: (with M. Campbell) Jessica: A Theatrical Transformation, 1989; (with P. Brymer) Dangerous Traditions: O.D. On Paradise (anthology), 1993; The Duchess: a.k.a. Wallis Simpson, 1998; Sheer Nerve, 1999; Alien Creature, 2000. Works appear in anthologies. **Address:** c/o Patty Ney, Christopher Banks and Associates, 6 Adelaide St E Ste 610, Toronto, ON, Canada M5C 1H6. **Online address:** patricia@ chrisbanks.com

GRIFFITHS, Steve. Welsh, b. 1949. **Genres:** Poetry, Politics/Government, Public/Social administration. **Career:** Poet; freelance researcher, writer and consultant specializing in poverty and social security. Gives poetry readings. **Publications:** Poetry: Anglesey Material: Poems, 1975-1978, 1980; Civilised Airs: Poems, 1973-1982, 1984; Uncontrollable Fields, 1990; Selected Poems, 1993. Social Policy Research. Work represented in anthologies. Contributor to magazines. **Address:** 3 John Campbell Rd, Stoke Newington, London N16, England.

GRIFFITHS, Tom. Australian, b. 1957. **Genres:** History. **Career:** Writer. State Library of Victoria, Australia, field officer. **Publications:** Hunters and Collectors: The Antiquarian Imagination in Australia, 1996. EDITOR: (with A. Platt and author of intro) The Life and Adventures of Edward Snell: The Illustrated Diary of an Artist, Engineer, and Adventurer in the Australian Colonies 1849 to 1859, 1988; (with L. Robin) Ecology and Empire: The Environmental History of Settler Societies, 1997. **Address:** c/o Keele University Press, Keele University, Staffs ST5 5BG, England.

GRIFFITHS, Trevor. British, b. 1935. **Genres:** Plays/Screenplays. **Career:** BBC, London, education officer, 1965-72. **Publications:** Occupations, and The Big House, 1972; (with others) Lay By, 1972; Tip's Lot (children's fiction), 1972; The Party, 1974; Comedians, 1976, 1979; All Good Men, and Absolute Beginners, 1977; Through the Night, and Such Impossibilities, 1977; The Cherry Orchard (new English version), 1978; Apricots, and Thermidor, 1978; (with H. Brenton and others) Deeds, 1978; Country, 1981; Oi for England, 1982; Sons and Lovers (TV version), 1982; Judgement over the Dead, 1985; Real Dreams, 1987; Fatherland, 1987; Collected Plays for Television, 1988; Piano, 1990; The Gulf between US, 1992; Hope in the Year Two and Thatcher's Children, 1994; Plays I, 1996; Food for Ravens, 1998. **Address:** c/o PFD, Drury House, 34-43 Russell St, London WC2B 5HA, England.

GRIFFITHS, William G. (born United States). **Genres:** Autobiography/Memoirs. **Career:** Building contractor and writer. **Publications:** AS BILL GRIFFITHS: The Witness (novel), 2000; (with wife, Cindy Griffiths) The Road to Forgiveness (memoir), 2001; Malchus, 2002; Driven: A Novel (supernatural thriller), 2002; Takedown: A Gavin Pierce Novel, 2003; Stingers (novel), 2003. **Address:** c/o Author Mail, Warner Books, 1271 Avenue of the Americas, New York, NY 10020, U.S.A. **Online address:** wggriffiths@ juno.com

GRIGELY, Joseph Constantine, Jr. American, b. 1956. **Genres:** Art/Art history. **Career:** Stanford University, Stanford, CA, Mellon postdoctoral fellow, 1985-87; Gallaudet University, Washington, DC, associate professor of English, 1983-. Also exhibitor of art installations. **Publications:** Textualterity: Art, Theory, and Textual Criticism, 1995. **Address:** Department of History of Art, University of Michigan, 519 S. State St., Ann Arbor, MI 48109-1357, U.S.A.

GRIGG, Ray. Canadian, b. 1938. **Genres:** Philosophy. **Career:** Teacher of English, literary history, fine arts, cultural history, and comparative world religions at secondary schools in British Columbia; teacher at Omega Institute for Holistic Studies, in New York, and at Hollyhock Farm (experiential learning institute), Cortes Island, British Columbia; also worked as a sculptor, photographer, graphic artist, reporter, and columnist. Student and teacher of Zen, Taoism, and related Eastern philosophies. University of Victoria, Center for Studies in Religion and Society, advisory council. **Publications:** The Tao of Relationships: A Balancing of Man and Woman, 1988; The Tao of Being: A Think and Do Workbook, 1989; The Tao of Sailing: A Bamboo Way of Life, 1990; Zen Brushpoems, 1993; The Tao of Zen, 1994; The New Lao Tzu: A Contemporary Tao Te Ching, 1995. **Address:** Box 362, Quathiaski Cove, Quadra Island, BC, Canada V0P 1N0.

GRIGGS, Barbara. *See* **VAN DER ZEE, Barbara (Blanche).**

GRIGGS, Terry. Canadian, b. 1951. **Genres:** Novellas/Short stories, Novels, Young adult fiction. **Career:** Writer. **Publications:** Harrier, 1982; Quickening (short stories), 1990. YOUNG ADULT NOVELS: Cat's Eye Corner, 2000; The Silver Door, 2004. NOVELS: The Lusty Man, 1995; Rogues' Wedding, 2002. **Address:** 480 William St., Stratford, ON, Canada N5A 4Y8.

GRIHM, Amanda. American, b. 1952. **Genres:** e-Books. **Career:** JAG Enterprise, Stone Mountain, GA, consultant, 2000-02; Project Match, Chamblee, GA, executive director. Member of boards of directors. **Publications:** E-BOOKS: The Wolf, 2002; The Dark-skinned Sister, 2003; Dark Justice, 2003. Contributor of essays to www.yourpersonalstory.com. **Address:** Project Match Inc., 5502 Peachtree Rd. Ste. 207-A, Chamblee, GA 30341, U.S.A. **Online address:** agrihm34@attbi.com

GRIMALDI, Janette Pienkny. Also writes as Janette Habel. French, b. 1938. **Genres:** Social sciences, Third World. **Career:** Teacher in Paris, France, and at the University of Havana, Havana, Cuba, 1964-65; Societe d'Etudes de Mathematiques Appliquees (SEMA), Paris, director of studies; Mathe de Conférences à l'université de Marne-le-Vallée. **Publications:** (as Janette Habel) Cuba, 1989, trans. as Cuba: The Revolution in Peril, 1990, rev. ed., 1990. Contributor to periodicals. **Address:** 21 Blvd. Richard Lenoir, 75011 Paris, France. **Online address:** Janette.habel@wanadoo.fr

GRIMES, Alan P. American, b. 1919. **Genres:** History, Politics/Government. **Career:** Professor of Political Science, Michigan State University, East Lansing, since 1949, now Emeritus. **Publications:** The Political Liberalism of the New York Nation 1865-1932, 1953; American Political Thought, 1955; Equality in America, 1964; The Puritan Ethic and Woman Suffrage, 1967; Democracy and the Amendments to the Constitution, 1978. EDITOR: (with R. Horwitz) Modern Political Ideologies, 1959; Liberalism, by L. T. Hobhouse, 1964. **Address:** 728 Lantern Hill Dr., East Lansing, MI 48823, U.S.A.

GRIMES, Martha. American. **Genres:** Mystery/Crime/Suspense. **Career:** Formerly: English instructor, University of Iowa, Iowa City; assistant professor of English, Frostburg State College, Maryland; professor of English, Montgomery College, Takoma Park, Maryland. Recipient: Nero Wolfe Award, 1983. **Publications:** The Man with a Load of Mischief, 1981; The Old Fox Deceiv'd, 1982; The Anodyne Necklace, 1983; The Dirty Duck, 1984; Jerusalem Inn, 1984; Help the Poor Struggler, 1985; The Deer Leap, 1985; I Am the Only Running Footman, 1986; The Five Bells and Bladebone, 1987; The Old Silent, 1989; Send Bygraves, 1989; The Old Contemptibles, 1991; The End of the Pier, 1992; The Horse You Came In On, 1993; Rainbow's End, 1995; Hotel Paradise, 1996; The Case Has Altered, 1997; The Stargazer, 1998; Lamora Wink, 1999; Biting the Moon, 1999; The Train Now Departing, 2000; Cold Flat Junction, 2001; Blue Last, 2001; The Grave Maurice, 2002; Foul Matter, 2003. **Address:** c/o Viking, 375 Hudson St, New York, NY 10014, U.S.A.

GRIMES, Michael D. American, b. 1942. **Genres:** Sociology. **Career:** University of Houston, Houston, TX, assistant professor, 1970-73; Louisiana State University, Baton Rouge, associate professor to professor of sociology, 1973-. **Publications:** Class in Twentieth-Century American Sociology, 1991; (with J. Morris) Caught in the Middle: Contradictions in the Lives of Sociologists from Working-Class Backgrounds, 1997. Contributor to professional journals. **Address:** Department of Sociology, Louisiana State University, Baton Rouge, LA 70803, U.S.A. **Online address:** socgrm@lsu.edu

GRIMES, Tom. American, b. 1954. **Genres:** Novels, Plays/Screenplays. **Career:** Private Papers Inc., NYC, general manager, 1980-83; Wolfman-Gold & Good Co., NYC, general manager, 1983-86; Louie's Backyard, Key West, FL, waiter, 1986-89; University of Iowa, Writers Workshop, Iowa City, visiting professor, 1991-95; Southwest Texas State University, San Marcos, assistant professor of English/M.F.A. program, 1992-95, associate professor, 1995-, director, MFA Program in Creatie writing, 1996-. **Publications:** A Stone of the Heart (novel), Four Walls Eight Windows, 1990; Spec (play), 1991; Season's End (novel), 1992; City of God (novel), 1995. **Address:** M-25 Flowers Hall, Southwest Texas State University, 601 University Drive, San Marcos, TX 78666, U.S.A.

GRIMSLEY, Jim. American, b. 1955. **Genres:** Novels, Plays/Screenplays. **Career:** Writer. Seven Stages Theatre, Atlanta, GA, playwright in residence, 1986-. ACME Theatre Co., founding member 1983-87; Celeste Miller and Company, board of directors, 1988-89, president, 1989-94; Regional Organization of Theatres-South (ROOTS), chairman 1990-91. **Publications:** NOVELS: Comfort and Joy, 1993; Winter Birds, 1994; Dream Boy, 1995; My Drowning, 1997; Kirith Kirin, 2000. PLAYS: The Existentialists, 1983; The Earthlings, 1984; The Receptionist in Hell, 1985; Estelle and Otto, 1985; Dead of Winter, 1986; On the Appearance of a Fire in the West, 1987; Mr. Universe, 1987; Math and Aftermath, 1988; Man with a Gun, 1989; White People, 1989; The Lizard of Tarsus, 1990; The Fall of the House of Usher (adaption), 1991; Belle Ives, 1991; Aurora Be Mine, 1992; The Borderland, 1994; The Decline and Fall of the Rest, 1996; A Bird of Prey, 1996; The Non, 1996; In Berlin, 2001. PERFORMANCE PIECES: Stop and Think, 1987; 88; Anti-Gravity, 1988; Eating the Green Monkey, 1989; Shelter, 1991; Walk through Birdland, 1992; The Masturbator, 1992; Memo to the Assassin, 1992. Contributor to periodicals. **Address:** c/o Peter Hagen, The Gersh Agency, Inc., 41 Madison Ave, Fl 33, New York, NY 10010-2210, U.S.A.

GRINDAL, Richard. Also writes as Richard Grayson. British, b. 1922. **Genres:** Novels, Mystery/Crime/Suspense. **Career:** P.E. Management Consulting Group, London, England, consultant, 1961-63; Scotch Whisky Association, Edinburgh, Scotland, director, 1963-93. **Publications:** NOVELS: Over the Sea to Die, 1989; The Tartan Conspiracy, 1992. NONFICTION: Return to the Glen, 1989; The Spirit of Whisky, 1992. AS RICHARD GRAYSON: The Spiral Path, 1955; Death in Melting, 1957; Madman's Whisper, 1958; Dead So Soon, 1960; Murder Red-handed, 1965; Spy in Camera, 1968; Play the Roman Fool and Die, 1970; A Taste of Death, 1973; The Murders at Impasse Louvain, 1978; The Monterant Affair, 1980; The Death of Abbe Didier, 1981; The Montmartre Murders, 1982; Death Stalk, 1982; Crime Without Passion, 1983; The Whisky Murders, 1984; Death en Voyage, 1986; Death on the Cards, 1988; Death Off Stage, 1991; Death Au Gratin, 1994; And Death the Prize, 1996; Death in the Skies, 1998. **Address:** c/o A.M. Heath and Co., 79 St. Martin's Lane, London WC2N 4AA, England.

GRINDE, Donald A(ndrew), Jr. American, b. 1946. **Genres:** History, Race relations. **Career:** California Polytechnic State University, San Luis Obispo, professor of history, 1977-. University of California, Los Angeles, visiting associate professor, 1978-79; University of Utah, director of Native American studies, 1981-84; Gettysburg College, Distinguished Professor of Interdisciplinary Studies, 1987-88; University of California, Riverside, Rupert Costo Professor of American Indian Affairs, 1989-91. **Publications:** The Iroquois and the Founding of the American Nation, 1977; (with B.E. Johansen) Exemplar of Liberty: Native America and the Evolution of Democracy, 1991; (co-author) Exiles in the Land of the Free, 1992; (with B.E. Johansen) Ecocide of Native America, 1995; (with B.E. Johansen) Encyclopedia of Native American Biography, 1997. EDITOR: Unheard Voices, 1994; (co-) Apocalypse of Chiokoyhikoy, 1997. **Address:** Department of History, University of Vermont, Wheeler House, 442 Main St, Burlington, VT 05405, U.S.A. **Online address:** dgrinde@zoo.uvm.edu

GRISHAM, John. American, b. 1955. **Genres:** Mystery/Crime/Suspense. **Career:** Lawyer, 1981-91; State of Mississippi, member of house, 1984-90; writer. **Publications:** A Time to Kill, 1989; The Firm, 1991; The Pelican Brief, 1992; The Client, 1993; The Chamber, 1994; The Rainmaker, 1995; The Runaway Jury, 1996; The Partner, 1997; The Street Lawyer, 1998; The Testament, 1999; The Brethren, 2000; A Painted House, 2001; Skipping Christmas, 2001; The Summons, 2002; The King of Torts, 2003; Bleachers, 2003; The Last Juror, 2004; Broker, 2005. **Address:** c/o Random House, 1540 Broadway, New York, NY 10036, U.S.A.

GRISWOLD, Jerome. American, b. 1947. **Genres:** Literary criticism and history. **Career:** Northeastern University, Boston, MA., instructor in English,

1976-79; Houghton Mifflin Co., Boston, editor, 1979-80; San Diego State University, CA, assistant professor, 1980-83, associate professor, 1983-87, professor of English, 1987-; University of California, Los Angeles, visiting assistant professor autumn, 1983; University of California, San Diego, visiting associate professor, 1984-86, visiting professor, 1988-; University of Connecticut at Storrs, visiting professor of English 1989; National University of Ireland, Galway, Fulbright visiting professor, 1999-2000. **Publications:** The Children's Books of Randall Jarrell, 1988; Audacious Kids: The Classic American Children's Book, 1992; The Classic American Children's Story, 1996. **Address:** c/o Sandra Dijkstra, 1155 Camino del Mar, Suite 515C, Del Mar, CA 92014, U.S.A.

GRIZZLE, Ralph. American, b. 1957. **Genres:** Travel/Exploration. **Career:** Writer. Managing editor of ASTA Agency Management, 1990-95; cofounder of Cruise Week, 1995; columnist and contributing editor to Our State: Down-Home Living in North Carolina; editor and publisher of Cruiser Observer; president of Kenilworth Media, Asheville, NC. **Publications:** Remembering Charles Kuralt, 2000; Day Trips from Raleigh-Durham, 2002. **Address:** 28 Kenilworth Road, Asheville, NC 28803, U.S.A. **Online address:** ralph@kenilworthmedia.com

GROB, Gerald N. American, b. 1931. **Genres:** History, Psychiatry. **Career:** Henry E. Sigerist Professor of the History of Medicine, Rutgers University, New Brunswick, NJ, 1990- (Professor of History, 1969-90). Instructor to Professor of History, Clark University, Worcester, MA, 1957-69. **Publications:** Workers and Utopia: A Study of Ideological Conflict in the American Labor Movement 1865-1900, 1961; The State and the Mentally Ill, 1966 (compiler) American Social History Before 1860, 1970; Mental Institutions in America: Social Policy to 1875, 1973; Edward Jarvis and the Medical World of Nineteenth-Century America, 1978; Mental Illness and American Society 1875-1940, 1983; The Inner World of American Psychiatry 1890-1940, 1985; From Asylum to Community: Mental Health Policy in Modern America, 1991; The Mad among Us: A History of the Care of America's Mentally Ill, 1994; The Deadly Truth: A History of Disease in America, 2002. EDITOR: (with R.N. Beck) American Ideas, 2 vols., 1963, 1970; (with G.A. Billias) Interpretations of American History; Patterns and Perspectives, 2 vols., 1967, 6th ed., 1992; Statesmen and Statecraft of the Modern West, 1967; (with G.A. Billias) American History: Retrospect and Prospect, 1971; E. Jarvis, Insanity and Idiocy in Massachusetts: Report of the Commission on Lunacy, 1855, 1971. **Address:** Institute for Health, Health Care Policy, and Aging Research, Rutgers University, New Brunswick, NJ 08901-1293, U.S.A. **Online address:** GGROB@RCI.Rutgers.edu

GROBSMITH, Elizabeth S. (Liz). American, b. 1946. **Genres:** Anthropology/Ethnology. **Career:** University of Nebraska-Lincoln, instructor in anthropology, 1971-72, instructor, 1975-77, assistant professor, 1977-81, associate professor, 1981-91, professor of anthropology, 1991-, assistant dean, College of Arts and Sciences, 1989-91, assistant vice-chancellor for academic affairs, 1991-94, associate vice-chancellor, 1994-96, Center for Great Plains Studies, 1986-90; University of Arizona, Tucson, instructor in anthropology, 1973; Sinte Gleska College, Rosebud, SD, instructor in anthropology, 1973-74; University of Colorado at Colorado Springs, dean of College of Letters, Arts & Sciences, 1996-2001; Utah State University, dean of College of Humanities, Arts & Social Sciences, 2001-02; Northern Arizona University, professor of anthropology, 2002-, and provost and vice president for academic affairs, 2002-. Conducted extensive field research at Native American sites, including San Carlos Apache Reservation, Pine Ridge Reservation, and Rosebud Sioux Reservation; also worked among the Siouan and Caddoan tribes of Oklahoma, the Otoe-Missouria clans, and the Tlingit tribe of Yakutat, AK; expert witness and consultant in federal cases involving Native American claims against the Nebraska Department of Corrections. **Publications:** Lakota of the Rosebud: A Contemporary Ethnography, 1981; Indians in Prison: Incarcerated Native Americans in Nebraska, 1994. Contributor to books. Contributor of articles and reviews to anthropology journals. **Address:** Provost, Northern Arizona University, PO Box 4120, Flagstaff, AZ 86011, U.S.A. **Online address:** Liz.Grobsmith@nau.edu

GRODEN, Michael (Lewis). American/Canadian, b. 1947. **Genres:** Literary criticism and history. **Career:** University of Western Ontario, London, visiting assistant professor, 1975-77, assistant professor, 1977-78, associate professor, 1978-83, professor of English, 1983-. **Publications:** Ulysses in Progress, 1977. EDITOR: The James Joyce Archive, Vols. 5-6 and 12-27, 1977-79; James Joyce's Manuscripts: An Index, 1980; (co) The Johns Hopkins Guide to Literary Theory and Criticism, 1994. **Address:** Department of English, University of Western Ontario, London, ON, Canada N6A 3K7. **Online address:** mgroden@uwo.ca

GRODIN, Charles. American, b. 1935. **Genres:** Children's fiction, Plays/Screenplays, Autobiography/Memoirs, Humor/Satire. **Career:** Actor on stage,

screen and television; director of stage and television shows; film and television producer; writer. Host of the television talk show Charles Grodin, CNBC, 1995-. **Publications:** (with M. Teitelbaum) Hooray! It's a Glorious Day ... And All That (play), 1966; The Opening (play), 1972, rev. version as One of the All-Time Greats, 1992; (with J. Bloom) 11 Harrowhouse (screenplay; also released as Anything for Love) 1974; Movers and Shakers (screenplay), 1985; Price of Fame (play), 1990: It Would Be So Nice If You Weren't Here: My Journey Through Show Business (memoir), 1989; How I Get Through Life: A Wise and Witty Guide (book), 1992; Freddie the Fly (children's book), 1993; We're Ready for You, Mr. Grodin: Behind the Scenes at Talk Shows, Movies, and Elsewhere (memoir), 1994. Also wrote material for the television program Candid Camera, the 1977 NBC presentation The Paul Simon Special, and the 1983 ABC special Love, Sex ... and Marriage. **Address:** c/o United Talent Agency, 9560 Wilshire Blvd 5th Fl, Beverly Hills, CA 90210, U.S.A.

GROEMER, Gerald. American, b. 1957. **Genres:** Translations. **Career:** Ethnomusicologist, pianist, composer, and specialist on Japan. **Publications:** (trans. and ed.) The Autobiography of Takahashi Chikuzan: Adventures of a Tsugaru-Jamisen Musician, 1991; (trans.) Edo Culture, 1997; Spirit of Tsugaru, 1999. **Address:** 6820 E Rosewood Circle, Tucson, AZ 85710, U.S.A.

GROENEWEGEN, Peter. Dutch/Australian, b. 1939. **Genres:** Economics. **Career:** University of Sydney, Australia, professor of economics, 1980-2002, professor emeritus, 2002-, director of Centre for the Study of the History of Economic Thought, 1989-2002. **Publications:** The Economics of Turgot, 1977; Public Finance in Australia, 1979, 3rd ed., 1990; Everyone's Guide to Australian Taxation, 1985; (with B. McFarlane) A History of Australian Economic Thought, 1990; A Soaring Eagle: Alfred Marshall, 1842-1924, 1995; Eighteenth Century Economics: Turgot, Beccaria and Smith and Their Contemporaries, 2002; (with G. Vaggi) Il Pensiero economico: Dal Mercantilismo al monetarismo, 2002; Classics and Moderns in Economics: Essays in Nineteenth and Twentieth-Century Economic Thought, 2 vols., 2003. EDITOR & CONTRIBUTOR: Feminism and Political Economy in Victorian England, 1994; Physicians and Political Economy, 2001. Contributor to periodicals. **Address:** Department of Economics, University of Sydney, Sydney, NSW 2006, Australia.

GROENING, Matt. American, b. 1954. **Genres:** Humor/Satire. **Career:** The Simpsons animated tv series, Fox-TV, creator, producer, 1990-; Life in Hell cartoon strip, creator, cartoonist, currently; created Bongo Comics, 1993. **Publications:** Love Is Hell, 1985; Work Is Hell, 1986; School Is Hell, 1987; Childhood Is Hell, 1988; Greetings from Hell, 1989; Akbar and Jeff's Guide to Life, 1989; The Big Book of Hell, 1990; The Simpsons Christmas Book, 1990; Greetings from the Simpsons, 1990; With Love from Hell, 1991; How to Go to Hell, 1991; Simpsons Rainy Day Fun Book, 1991; Simpsons Family Album, 1991; Maggie Simpson's Alphabet Book, 1991; Maggie Simpson's Counting Book, 1991; Maggie Simpson's Book of Color & Shapes, 1991; Maggie Simpson's Book of Animals, 1991; The Road to Hell, 1992; Simpsons Fun in the Sun Book, 1992; Making Faces with the Simpsons, 1992; Simpsons Ultra Jumbo Rain or Shine Fun Book, 1993; Cartooning with the Simpsons, 1993; Bart Simpson's Guide to Life, 1993; Binky's Guide to Love, 1994; Love Is Still Hell, 1994; Simpsons Comics Extravaganza, 1994; Simpsons Comics Spectacular, 1995; Bartman: The Best of the Best, 1995; Simpsons Comics Simpsorama, 1996; Simpsons Comics Strike Back, 1996; Simpsons Comics Wingding, 1997; The Simpsons: A Complete Guide to Our Favorite Family, 1997; Huge Book of Hell, 1997; Are We There Yet? The Simpsons Guide to Springfield, 1998; Simpsons Comics on Parade, 1998; Simpsons Comics Big Bonanza, 1998; Bart Simpson's Treehouse of Horror Heebie-Jeebie Hullabaloo, 1999; The Simpsons Forever: A Complete Guide to Our Favorite Family Continued, 1999; Simpsons Comics A Go-Go, 2000; Simpsons Comics Royal, 2001; Bart Simpson's Treehouse of Horror Spine-Tingling Spooktacle, 2001; Simpsons Comics Unchained, 2002. **Address:** c/o Sondra Gatewood, ACME Features Syndicate, 147 NE Yamhill St., Sheridan, OR 97378, U.S.A. **Online address:** binky@acmefeatures.com

GROHSKOPF, Bernice. American. **Genres:** Novellas/Short stories, Young adult fiction, Literary criticism and history, Essays. **Career:** Banister Writer-in-Residence, Sweet Briar College, Virginia, 1980-82; Editorial staff member, William James Edition (Harvard University Press, Cambridge, MA), 1984-87; Editorial staff member, The Correspondence of William James (University Press of Virginia, Charlottesville), 1988-94; free-lance book reviewer, writer, editor. **Publications:** Seeds of Time, 1963; From Age to Age, 1968; The Treasure of Sutton Hoo (non-fiction), 1970; Shadow in the Sun, 1975; Notes on the Hauter Experiment, 1975; Children in the Wind, 1977; Blood and

Roses, 1979; Tell Me Your Dream, 1981; End of Summer, 1982; Saratoga (non-fiction), 1986. Contributor to professional journals. **Address:** 537 Riverdale Ave Apt 1117, Yonkers, NY 10705, U.S.A. **Online address:** Bergrow@aol.com

GRONEMAN, Carol. American, b. 1943. **Genres:** Women's studies and issues. **Career:** John Jay College of Criminal Justice, City University of New York (CUNY), New York, NY, assistant professor, 1973-76, associate professor, 1981-87, professor, 1987-; New York Council for the Humanities, New York, NY, research associate, 1976-78, executive director, 1978-81. New York University, New York, NY, adjunct associate professor, 1982-88; Smith College, co-chair, Berkshire Conference on the History of Woman, 1984; Institute for Research in History, chair of board of directors, 1986-89; American Social History Project, chair of board of directors, 1994-; member, Keen's womens sexuality study group, Columbia University Seminar on Women and Society, and Berkshire Conference of Women Historians. **Publications:** (with R.N. Lear) The Corporate Ph.D., 1987; (ed., with M.B. Norton) To Toil the Livelong Day: America's Women Workers 1780-1980, 1987; (Associate editor) Encyclopedia of NYC, 1995; Nymphomania: A History, 2000. Contributor to journals. **Address:** John Jay College, 899 Tenth Ave., New York, NY 10019, U.S.A. **Online address:** cgroneman@jjay.cuny.edu

GROOM, Gloria. American. **Genres:** Art/Art history. **Career:** Art Institute of Chicago, Chicago, IL, research assistant, 1984-85, assistant to the curator, 1986-89, assistant curator, 1989-94, associate curator, 1994-. **Publications:** Edouard Vuillard: Painter-Decorator, 1993. Contributor to art and museum journals. **Address:** Art Institute of Chicago, 111 S. Michigan Ave., Chicago, IL 60603, U.S.A.

GROOM, Winston (Francis), Jr. American. **Genres:** Novels, History. **Career:** Reporter and later columnist, Washington Star, Washington, D.C., 1967-76; full-time novelist, 1976-. **Publications:** NOVELS: Better Times Than These, 1978; As Summers Die, 1980; Only, 1984; Forrest Gump; 1986; Gone the Sun, 1988; Gump & Co., 1995; Such a Pretty, Pretty Girl, 1999. Other; Conversations with the Enemy: The Story of PFC Robert Garwood, 1983; Shrouds of Glory: From Atlanta to Nashville-The Last Great Campaign of the Civil War, 1994; Gumpisms: The Wit and Wisdom of Forrest Gump, 1994; The Bubba Gump Shrimp Co. Cookbook, 1994; Forrest Gump: My Favorite Chocolate Recipes: Mama's Fudge, Cookies, Cakes, and Candies, 1995; (author of forward) James Jones: A Friendship, 1999; The Crimson Tide: An Illustrated History of Football at the University of Alabama, 2000; A Storm in Flanders, 2002. **Address:** c/o Theron Raines, Raines & Raines, 103 Kenyon Rd, Medusa, NY 12120-1404, U.S.A.

GROSE, Peter (Bolton). American, b. 1934. **Genres:** International relations/Current affairs, History. **Career:** Associated Press, London correspondent, 1959-60, and from the Congo and West Africa, 1961-62; New York Times, New York City, correspondent in Paris, 1963, chief correspondent in Saigon, Vietnam, 1964-65, chief of Moscow bureau, 1965-67, diplomatic correspondent in Washington, DC, 1967-70, chief of Jerusalem bureau, 1970-72, member of editorial board, 1972-76, chief of United Nations bureau, 1976-77; United States Department of State, Policy Planning Staff, Washington, deputy director, 1977-78; Columbia University, New York City, research associate and international affairs fellow with the Rockefeller Foundation, 1978-80, research associate with the Middle East Institute, 1978-81; Seven Springs Center, Mt. Kisco, NY, director of studies, 1981-82; Council on Foreign Relations, New York City, senior fellow, 1982, and director of Middle East studies, 1982-84. **Publications:** The Next Steps toward Peace between Israel and Its Neighbors, 1980; The United States, NATO, and Israeli-Arab Peace, 1981; Israel in the Mind of America, 1983; A Changing Israel, 1985; Gentleman Spy: The Life of Allen Dulles, 1994; Operation Rollback: America's Secret War Behind the Iron Curtain, 2000. Contributor of articles and reviews to newspapers. **Address:** Foreign Affairs, 58 East 68th St., New York, NY 10021, U.S.A.

GROSECLOSE, Barbara. American, b. 1944. **Genres:** Art/Art history. **Career:** University of Wisconsin-Parkside, special lecturer in art history, 1972-74; Ohio State University, Columbus, assistant professor, 1974-80, associate professor, 1980-90, professor of art history, 1991-. U.S. Agency for International Development, lecturer in India and Sri Lanka, 1985; University of Utrecht, Fulbright professor and Walt Whitman Professor of American Studies, 1994; European University, Florence, Fulbright Distinguished Professor of History, 2002; lecturer at colleges and universities. Smithsonian Institution, guest curator at National Collection of Fine Arts, 1974-76, curator for Traveling Exhibition Service, 1988-89; public lecturer in art history; juror for fellowships and awards. **Publications:** Emanuel Leutze, 1816-1868:

Freedom Is the Only King, 1976; (co-editor and contrib.) Literature and the Visual Arts in Contemporary Society, 1985; British Sculpture and the Company Raj: Church Monuments and Public Statuary in Madras, Bombay, and Calcutta, 1995; Nineteenth-Century American Art, 2000. Contributor to exhibition catalogs and books. Contributor of articles and reviews to periodicals. **Address:** Department of Art History, Ohio State University, 108 North Oval Mall, Columbus, OH 43210, U.S.A.

GROSS, David. American, b. 1940. **Genres:** History. **Career:** University of Wisconsin-Madison, instructor in history, 1968-69; University of Colorado at Boulder, assistant professor, 1969-73, associate professor, 1973-81, professor of history, 1981-. University of California, Irvine, visiting associate professor, 1979. **Publications:** The Writer and Society: Heinrich Mann and Literary Politics in Germany, 1890-1940, 1980; The Past in Ruins: Tradition and the Critique of Modernity, 1992; Lost Time: On Remembering and Forgetting in Late Modern Culture, 2000. **Address:** Department of History, Box 234, University of Colorado at Boulder, Boulder, CO 80309, U.S.A.

GROSS, Ernie. Hungarian, b. 1913. **Genres:** History, Theology/Religion. **Career:** Writer. Lincoln Star, Lincoln, NE, reporter, 1937-41; Buffalo Evening News, Buffalo, NY, reporter, 1941-63; New York State Labor Department, Albany, NY, public relations director, 1963-64; US Office of Economic Opportunity, Washington, DC, public relations director of job corps, 1964-67; US Department of Housing and Urban Development, Washington DC, director of new services, 1967-75; writer. President, Hospice Care of Eastern Shore, 1982-90; town councilman, Accomac, VA, 1990-99. **Publications:** This Day in Religion, 1990; This Day in American History, 1990. **Address:** c/o Publicity Director, Neal-Schuman Publishers, Inc, 100 Varick St, New York, NY 10013, U.S.A.

GROSS, Jonathan David. American, b. 1962. **Genres:** Literary criticism and history. **Career:** DePaul University, Chicago, IL, assistant professor, 1992-98, associate professor of English, 1998-. University of Santa Clara, guest lecturer, 1995. **Publications:** (ed. and author of intro) Byron's Corbeau Blanc: The Life and Letters of Elizabeth Milbanke, Lady Melbourne (1751-1818), 1997. Contributor to books. Contributor of articles and reviews to scholarly journals. **Address:** Department of English, DePaul University, 802 West Belden Ave., Chicago, IL 60614, U.S.A. **Online address:** jgross@wppost.depaul.edu

GROSS, Philip (John). British, b. 1952. **Genres:** Poetry, Communications/Media, Children's fiction, Young adult fiction. **Career:** Collier Macmillan Ltd., London, England, editorial assistant, 1973-76; Croydon Public Libraries, Croydon, England, librarian, 1976-84; free-lance writer and tutor of creative writing, 1984-; lecturer (Creative Studies), Bath College of Higher Education, 1989-. **Publications:** Familiars (poems), 1983; The Ice Factory (poems), 1984; Cat's Whisker (poems), 1987; (with S. Kantaris) The Air Mines of Mistila (verse fable), 1988; Manifold Manor (poems for young people), 1989; The Song of Gail and Fludd (novel for young people), 1991; The Son of the Duke of Nowhere (poems), 1991; The All-Nite Cafe (poems for young people), 1994; Plex (novel for young people), 1994; I.D. (poems), 1994; The Wind Gate (novel for young people), 1995; Scratch City (poems for young people), 1995; Transformer (novel for young people), 1996; The Washing Game (poems), 1998. **Address:** 40 York Rd, Montpelier, Bristol BS6 5QF, England.

GROSS, Richard (Edmund). American, b. 1920. **Genres:** Education, History, Social sciences. **Career:** Professor, School of Education, Stanford University, California (joined faculty, 1955). **Publications:** (with M. Rodehaver and W. Axtell) The Sociology of the School, 1957; (with L. B. Zeleny) Educating Citizens for Democracy, 1958; (ed.) Report of the State Central Committee on Social Studies, 1959; (ed. and Contributor) The Heritage of American Education, 1962; United States History, 1964; (ed. and Contributor) British Secondary Education, 1965; (with V. Devereaux) Civics in Action, 1965, rev. ed. 1971; (with F. MacGraw) Man's World: A Physical Geography, 1966; (with W. McPhie and J. Fraenkel) Teaching the Social Studies: What, Why, and How, 1969; How to Handle controversial issues, 1969; (with J. Chapin and R. McHugh) Quest for Liberty, 1971, 3rd rev. ed. 1973; (ed. with R. Muessig) Problem-Centered Social Studies Instruction: Approaches to Reflective Teaching, 1971; (ed. with L. de la Cruz) Social Studies Dissertations, 1963-69, 1971; (with J. Chapin) Teaching Social Studies Skills, 1973; (with D. Weitzman) Man's World, 1973; The Human Experience, 1973; American Citizenship: The Way We Govern, 1978; Social Studies for Our Times, 1978; (with D. Duffy) Learning to Live in Society, 1980; (with T. Dynneson) What Should We Be Teaching in the Social Studies?, 1983; (with T. Dynneson) Social Science Perspectives on Citizenship Education, 1991; (with T. Dynneson) Designing Effective Instruction for Secondary Social Studies, 1995. **Address:** 26304 Esperanza Dr, Los Altos, CA 94022, U.S.A.

GROSSCUP, Beau. American. **Genres:** International relations/Current affairs. **Career:** Boston University/Europe, adjunct assistant professor of international relations, 1973-75; Ithaca College, Ithaca, NY, assistant professor of international relations, 1975-82; visiting faculty member at University of California, Irvine, and University of California, Santa Barbara, both 1983-86; California State University, Chico, lecturer, 1988-90, assistant professor, 1990-93, associate professor of international relations, 1993-, and vice-chairperson of Department of Political Science. University of Redlands, visiting associate professor, 1980-81. **Publications:** The Explosion of Terrorism, 1987, 4th ed. as The Newest Explosions of Terrorism, 2001. Contributor to books and periodicals. **Address:** Department of Political Science, California State University, Chico, CA 95929, U.S.A. **Online address:** bgrosscup@csuchico.edu

GROSSE, W. Jack. American, b. 1923. **Genres:** Law, Environmental sciences/Ecology, Photography. **Career:** Dun & Bradstreet, credit reporter, 1946-47; Fifth-Third Bank, credit manager, 1947-54; Chase College of Commerce, Cincinnati, OH, professor and associate dean, 1954-62; Northern Kentucky University, Highland Heights, professor of law and assistant dean of Chase College of Law, 1962-64; Clarkson College of Technology, Potsdam, NY, professor, 1964-66; Northern Kentucky University, professor of law, 1966-68; Xavier University, Cincinnati, professor and assistant dean, 1968-70; Northern Kentucky University, professor of law, 1970-91, professor emeritus, 1991-, dean of Chase College of Law, 1970-78, interim dean, 1992-93, member of board of trustees, university counsel, 1979-81. Private practice of law, 1962-. Underwriters Publishing Co., author of insurance summaries, 1962-82, editor, 1962-. **Publications:** (coauthor) Government Contract Law, 1970; School Law Handbook, 1981; The Protection and Management of Our Natural Resources: Wildlife and Habitat, 1992, 2nd ed., 1997; Natural Resource Law: Cases and Materials, 2 vols., 1993; (with C.M. Dieffenbach and S.E. Harper) A Centennial History of Chase College of Law, 1994. Contributor to law and education journals. **Address:** 3860 Vineyard Green Dr, Cincinnati, OH 45255, U.S.A. **Online address:** grosse@nku.edu

GROSSINGER, Harvey L. American, b. 1948. **Genres:** Novellas/Short stories. **Career:** R.R. Bowker Co., NYC, editorial associate, 1968-72; Indiana University-Bloomington, instructor in English, 1974-80; Globe Distributing Co., Alexandria, VA, supervisor and manager, 1980-82; American University, Washington, DC, writing instructor, 1990-95, adjunct professor in literature and creative writing, 1995-; University of Maryland Honors College, College Park, adjunct professor, 1995-97; Johns Hopkins University Part-Time Graduate Program in Writing, Washington, DC, adjunct professor, 2000-. Gives readings from his works. Houston Chronicle, book reviewer. **Publications:** The Quarry (stories), 1997. Contributor to periodicals.

GROSSINGER, Tania. American, b. 1937. **Genres:** Novels, Advertising/Public relations, Food and Wine, Human relations/Parenting, Psychology, Travel/Exploration, Writing/Journalism, Autobiography/Memoirs. **Career:** Public relations consultant. Director of Broadcast Promotion, Playboy Magazine, NYC, 1963-69; Director of Publicity, Stein & Day Inc., publrs., NYC, 1970-72; Israel Ministry of Tourism, Conn Communications, PR counsel, 1990-. **Publications:** The Book of Gadgets, 1974; Growing Up at Grossinger's, 1975; The Great Gadget Catalogue, 1978; (co-author) Weekend, 1980. Contributor of travel articles to magazines and newspapers. **Address:** 1 Christopher St Apt 7E, New York, NY 10014, U.S.A. **Online address:** tgrossinger@iopener.net

GROSSKURTH, Phyllis. Canadian, b. 1924. **Genres:** Literary criticism and history, Biography. **Career:** Carleton University, Ottawa, Ont., lecturer, 1964-65; University of Toronto, professor of English, 1965-. **Publications:** John Addington Symonds: A Biography, 1964, as The Woeful Victorian, 1965; Notes on Browning's Works, 1967; Leslie Stephen, 1968; Gabrielle Roy, 1969; Havelock Ellis: A Biography, 1980; (ed.) The Memoirs of John Addington Symonds: The Secret Homosexual Life of a Leading 19th Century Man of Letters, 1984; Melanie Klein: Her Work and Her World, 1986; Margaret Mead: A Life of Controversy, 1988; The Secret Ring: Freud's Inner Circle and the Politics of Psychoanalysis, 1991; Byron: The Flawed Angel, 1997; Elusive Subject: A Biographer's Life, 1999. **Address:** 147 Spruce St, Toronto, ON, Canada M5A 2J6.

GROSSMAN, David. Israeli, b. 1954. **Genres:** Novels, Novellas/Short stories, Adult non-fiction. **Career:** Writer. Has worked as a journalist for Kol Israel (Israeli Radio). **Publications:** FOR ADULTS: STORIES: Ratz (title means: Jogger), 1983. NOVELS: Hiyukh ha-gedi, 1983, trans. as The Smile of the Lamb, 1991; 'Ayen 'erekh-ahavah, 1986, trans. as See Under: Love, 1989; Sefer hadikduk hapnimi, 1992, trans. as The Book of Intimate Gram-

mar, 1994; The Zig-Zag Kid, 1996. NON-FICTION: Ha-Zeman ha-tsahov, 1987, trans. as The Yellow Wind, 1988; Nokhehim nifkadim, 1992, trans. as Sleeping on a Wire, 1992. PLAY: Gan Riki: mahazeh bi-shete ma'arakhot, 1988, trans. as Rikki's Kindergarten. OTHER: Ha-Safah ha-meyuhedet shel Uri, 1996; She-tihyi li ha-sakin, 1998; Mishelu la-ruts ito, 2000; Be My Knife, 2002. FOR CHILDREN: Du-krav (title means: Duel), 1984; Itamar metayel 'al kirot, 1986; Ach chadash l'gamrei, 1986; Itamar pogesh arnav, 1988; Itamar mikhtav, 1988; Itamar ye'koval ha'ksamim ha'shachor, 1992; Pajama Sam the Magic Hat Tree, 2000. Contributor to periodicals. **Address:** c/o Deborah Harris, The Harris/Elon Agency, PO Box 8528, 91083 Jerusalem, Israel.

GROSSMAN, Karl (H.). American, b. 1942. **Genres:** Writing/Journalism, Documentaries/Reportage. **Career:** Cleveland Press and News, Cleveland, OH, copyboy, 1960; New Voice, Suffolk County, NY, founder and first editor, 1961-62; Babylon Town Leader, Babylon, NY, reporter, 1962-64; Sunrise Press, reporter and associate editor, 1964; Long Island Press, Jamaica, NY, reporter, 1964-70, columnist, 1970-77; Island Closeup News Service, Sag Harbor, NY, founder and editor, 1977-. State University of New York College at Old Westbury, instructor, 1979-81, assistant professor, 1981-86, associate professor of American studies, 1986-92, professor, 1992-, supervisor of journalism internship program. EnviroVideo, Ft. Tilden, NY, program host, program director, 1992-. Host, television programs, guest on news and documentary programs, reporter for documentary series. Public lecturer on environmental and political issues and on investigative reporting. **Publications:** Cover Up: What You Are Not Supposed to Know about Nuclear Power, 1980, rev. ed., 1982; The Poison Conspiracy, 1983; Nicaragua: America's New Vietnam?, 1984, rev. ed., 1988; Power Crazy: Is Lilco Turning Shoreham into America's Chernobyl?, 1986; Wrong Stuff, 1997; Weapons in Space, 2000. **Address:** PO Box 1680, Sag Harbor, NY 11963, U.S.A. **Online address:** kgrossman@hamptons.com

GROSSMAN, Richard. American, b. 1943. **Genres:** Novels, Poetry. **Career:** Poet and novelist. **Publications:** POETRY: Tycoon Boy, 1977; The Animals, 1990. AMERICAN LETTERS TRILOGY: The Alphabet Man, 1993; The Book of Lazarus, 1997. **Address:** 2000 DeMille Dr., Los Angeles, CA 90027, U.S.A. **Online address:** RBGrossman@aol.com

GROSSMAN, Wendy. American. **Genres:** Poetry. **Career:** Writer. Folksinger, 1975-1983; The Skeptic (British periodical), founder and editor, 1987-; Internet Today, columnist, 1996-1997; Fleet Street Forum (online), site manager. **Publications:** (ed.) Remembering the Future, 1997; Net.Wars, 1997. RECORDINGS: Roseville Fair, 1980. Contributor to periodicals. **Address:** c/o The Skeptic, 10 Crescent View, Loughton, Essex 1G10 4PZ, England. **Online address:** wendyg@skeptic.demon.co.uk

GROSSMITH, Robert (Anthony). British, b. 1954. **Genres:** Novels, Novellas/Short stories. **Career:** Word and Action (community theater company), Weymouth, England, actor and organizer, 1976-77; British Institute, Stockholm, Sweden, English teacher, 1977-80; Swedish-English translator in New York and California, 1980-81; University of Keele, Keele, England, lecturer in American literature, 1987; Harper Collins Ltd., Glasgow, Scotland, bilingual dictionary editor, 1991-; writer. **Publications:** The Empire of Lights (novel), 1990. Contributor to journals and anthologies. **Address:** c/o Giles Gordon, Curtis Brown Group, 37 Queensferry St, Edinburgh EH2 4QS, Scotland. **Online address:** bgrossmith@aol.com

GROTE, David (G.). American, b. 1945. **Genres:** Theatre, Plays/Screenplays, Literary criticism and history. **Career:** Centre Theatre, Wichita Falls, Tex., director, 1964-65; Curtain Theater, Austin, Tex., director, 1965-67; high school English and theater teacher in Bakersfield, Calif., 1968-69 and 1971-80; Scripps College, Claremont, Calif., assistant professor of theater, 1980-81; Pomona College, Claremont, assistant professor of theater, 1981-82; writer, 1982-. Freelance stage director, 1984-, Artistic Director, Classic Theater Project of San Francisco, 1992-. **Publications:** The Undercover Lover, 1978; Rome Is Where the Heart Is; Widget's Worries, 1980; Help; The Medicine Man, 1980; The Women of Troy, 1981; Theater: Preparation and Performance, 1981, rev. ed., 1988; The End of Comedy, 1983; Script Analysis, 1984; Staging the Musical, 1986; Common Knowledge, 1987; Harlequin Holds the Bag, 1990; British English for American Readers, 1992; Play Directing in the School, 1997. **Address:** c/o Greenwood Publishing Group, Inc., 88 Post Rd. W., Box 5007, Westport, CT 06881, U.S.A.

GROTH, Janet. American, b. 1936. **Genres:** Literary criticism and history. **Career:** New Yorker, NYC, member of editorial staff, 1957-78; University of Cincinnati, OH, assistant professor of English, 1978-82; State University of New York College at Plattsburgh, associate professor, 1982-95, professor of English, 1995-. Queensborough Community College of the City University of New York, adjunct lecturer, 1970; Brooklyn College of the City University of New York, adjunct lecturer, 1970-74, instructor, 1971; Vassar College, visiting lecturer, 1976-77; University of Norway, Trondheim, Fulbright lecturer, 1996; Yale University, visiting fellow at Beineke Library, 1997. **Publications:** Edmund Wilson: A Critic for Our Time, 1989; (ed. with D. Castronovo and coauthor of intro) From the Uncollected Edmund Wilson, 1995. Contributor of articles and reviews to periodicals. **Address:** Department of English, CVH 205, State University of New York College at Plattsburgh, Plattsburgh, NY 12901, U.S.A.

GROULT, Benoite. French, b. 1920. **Genres:** Novels, Autobiography/Memoirs. **Career:** Worked as teacher of French and Latin, 1944-46, and as radio journalist, 1946-51; worked with Yvette Roudy, minister for women's rights, 1981-86; writer. **Publications:** (with F. Groult) Feminin pluriel (title means: Feminine Plural), 1965; Le Journal a 4 mains (novel; in English as: Double-Handed Diary), 1968; (with F. Groult) Il etait deux fois (novel), 1968; La part des choses, 1972; Les 3/4 du Temps (novel; title means: Most of the Time), 1975; Ainsi soit-elle, 1975, rev. ed., 2000; Le Feminisme au masculin, 1977; (with others) Des nouvelles de la famille, 1980; La moitie de la terre (essays), 1981; Les trois quarts du temps (novel), 1983; Les vaisseaux du coeur (novel), 1988, trans. as Salt on Our Skin, 1992; Pauline Roland, ou, Comment la liberte vint aux femmes (biography), 1991; (with J. Savigneau) Histoire d'une evasion (autobiography), 1997. **Address:** 54 rue de Bourgogne, 75007 Paris, France.

GROUNDS, Roger. British, b. 1938. **Genres:** Horticulture. **Career:** Garden designer. **Publications:** Gardening for Beginners, 1972; Simple Greenhouse Gardening, 1972; The Perfect Lawn, 1974; Shrubs and Decorative Evergreens, 1974; Trees for Smaller Gardens, 1974; Ferns, 1974; Bottle Gardens, 1974; Grow Your Own Vegetables, 1975; The Natural Garden, 1976; Growing Vegetables and Herbs, 1977; Everyday Gardening, 1977; Ornamental Grasses, 1979; The Private Life of Plants, 1980; The Multi-Coloured Garden, 1982; The White Garden, 1990; Small Garden, 1993; The Plantfinder's Guide to Ornamental Grasses, 1998; Grasses & Bamboos, 2002. EDITOR: Complete Handbook of Pruning, 1973; Making and Planning a Small Garden, 1973; Gardening in Colour, 1973. **Address:** c/o Laurence Pollinger Ltd, 9 Staple Inn, London WC1V 7QH, England.

GROVE, Richard H(ugh). British, b. 1955. **Genres:** Business/Trade/Industry, Agriculture/Forestry, Environmental sciences/Ecology. **Career:** Cambridge University, Cambridge, England, research fellow at Clare Hall, 1986-89, fellow and director of studies at Churchill College, 1989-94, now coordinator of Global Environmental History Unit. Woodrow Wilson Center for International Scholars (Washington, DC), fellow, 1992-93; Australian National University, senior fellow, Institute of Advanced Studies, 1993-; National Humanities Center (Research Triangle Park, NC), fellow, 1995-96; National Institute of Science, Technology, and Development Studies (New Delhi, India), research associate. **Publications:** The Cambridgeshire Coprolite Mining Rush, 1976; The Future for Forestry, 1983; The SSSI Handbook, 1985; Conservation in Africa: People, Policies, and Practice, 1987; Green Imperialism: Science, Colonial Expansion, and the Emergence of Global Environmentalism, 1660-1880, 1995. **Address:** Clare Hall, Herschel Rd., Cambridge University, Cambridge, England.

GROVER, Jan(ice) Zita. American. **Genres:** Adult non-fiction. **Career:** Writer. AIDS worker at San Francisco General Hospital. **Publications:** Silver Lining, 1983; North Enough: AIDS and Other Clear-Cuts, 1997. Contributor to periodicals. **Address:** 1400 Acroft Ct, Berkeley, CA 94702, U.S.A.

GROVER, Wayne. American. **Genres:** Children's fiction. **Career:** United States Air Force, 1954-76; News correspondent 1978-86; Senior International Correspondent, 1986-. **Publications:** Dolphin Adventure, 1990; Ali and the Golden Eagle, 1992; Dolphin Treasure, 1994; Dolphin Freedom, 1999. Contributor to newspapers, magazines, and tabloids.

GROVES, Seli. American. **Genres:** Adult non-fiction, Young adult non-fiction, Ghost Writer. **Career:** Developed prototype for first soap magazine later called Daytime TV; worked as a contributing editor for Soap Opera Digest, media editor for Youngperson, London editor for 16, and editor for VIBES, Movie Mirror, and America's Music; editor for Health Beat, Williams Publishing, London, England; creator and editor of Soap Beat, Weekday TV, Fun Fair, and Young Hollywood; King Features Weekly Service, columnist on entertainment, television, medical and nutrition news, working women, seniors, and veterans; columnist for Young Miss; WGCH, Greenwich, CT, producer and host of Seli on the Telly. Curator of "Summer

of Soaps-Sixty Years of Soap Operas," Chicago Museum of Broadcast Communications, 1991. Lecturer. Contributor to the creation of "Stage II," a trivia game for Hasbro. **Publications:** NONFICTION FOR YOUNG ADULTS: (with J.R. Rott) How in the World Do We Recycle Glass?, 1992; (with H.J. Fletcher) How in the World Do We Recycle Paper?, 1992. NONFICTION FOR ADULTS: (with the editors of the Associated Press) Soaps: A Pictorial History of America's Daytime Dramas, 1983; (with D.D. Buchman) The Writer's Digest Guide to Manuscript Formats, 1987; (coauthor) Fifty Blinks that Changed the World. Ghost writer of publications. Contributor to periodicals. Contributor of entries on international law, maritime law, the British legal system, and political science to Encyclopedia Britannica.

GROW, L(ynn) M(erle). American. **Genres:** Literary criticism and history. **Career:** Wichita State University, Wichita, KS, assistant professor, 1972-77; University of Maryland Far East Division, lecturer, 1977-81; College of the Bahamas, Nassau, lecturer in English, 1981-82, English language coordinator, 1982-83; Broward Community College, Davie, FL, senior professor of English, 1983-. **Publications:** The Prose Style of Samuel Taylor Coleridge, 1976; The Epistolary Criticism of Manuel A. Viray: In Memoriam, 1998; The Novels of Bienvenido N. Santos, 1999; World Enough and Time: Epistemologies and Ontologies in Modern Philippine Poetry, 2000; Distillation and Essence: World View in Modern Philippine Literature, 2002; And Quiet Flows the Dawn, 2003. Contributor to scholarly periodicals. Contributor of book reviews to periodicals. **Address:** Broward Community College, Central Campus, 3501 SW Davie Rd, Davie, FL 33314, U.S.A. **Online address:** lgrow@broward.edu

GROWE, Sarah Jane. Canadian (born United States), b. 1939. **Genres:** Medicine/Health. **Career:** High school teacher in Toronto, Ontario, 1961-64; Vancouver Sun, Vancouver, British Columbia, journalist, 1978; Richmond Review, Richmond, British Columbia, journalist, 1978-83; Toronto Star, reporter and feature writer, 1983-88, editor on foreign-national-city desk team, 1989-, columnist/feature writer, 1998-. Stringer, Kingston Whig Standard, 1981-82. Host of live radio show, CFRO-Radio, 1977, and of live current affairs television show in Vancouver and Richmond. **Publications:** Who Cares? The Crisis in Canadian Nursing, 1991. **Address:** c/o Toronto Star, 1 Yonge St, Toronto, ON, Canada M5E 1E6.

GRUBB, Michael (J.). British, b. 1960. **Genres:** Sciences. **Career:** Royal Institute of International Affairs, London, England, head of Energy and Environmental Programme; Imperial College, professor of climate change and energy policy. **Publications:** Energy Policies and the Greenhouse Effect, Dartmouth Publishing, Vol. 1: Policy Appraisal, 1990, Vol. 2: Country Studies and Technical Options, 1991; The Kyoto Protocol: A Guide and Assessment, 1999. **Address:** Dept of Environmental Science and Technology, Imperial College, RSM Bldg, Prince Consort Rd, London SW1Y 4LE, England. **Online address:** michael.grubb@ic.ac.uk

GRUBER, William E. American, b. 1943. **Genres:** Theatre. **Career:** Courier-Post, Camden, NJ, reporter, 1968-69; Age, Melbourne, Australia, reporter, 1969-70; Emory University, Atlanta, GA, professor of English, 1980-. **Publications:** Comic Theaters, 1986; Missing Persons, 1994; On All Sides Nowhere, 2002. **Address:** Department of English, Emory University, Atlanta, GA 30322, U.S.A.

GRUBERG, Martin. American, b. 1935. **Genres:** Politics/Government. **Career:** Professor, Political Science, University of Wisconsin, Oshkosh (Assistant Professor 1963-66; Associate Professor 1966-69). Instructor, Political Science, Hunter College NYC, 1961-62. **Publications:** Women in American Politics, 1968; (ed.) Encyclopedia of American Government, 3rd ed., 1985; A Case Study in U.S. Urban Leadership: The Incumbency of Milwaukee Mayor Henry Maier, 1996; A History of Winnebago County Government, 1998; Introduction to Law, 2003. Contributor to books and encyclopedias. **Address:** Department of Political Science, University of Wisconsin, Oshkosh, WI 54901, U.S.A. **Online address:** gruberg@uwosh.edu

GRUDIN, Robert. American, b. 1938. **Genres:** Novels, Novellas/Short stories, Poetry, Literary criticism and history, Essays. **Career:** University of Oregon, Eugene, assistant professor, 1971-78, associate professor, 1978-90, professor of English, 1990-. Bennington College, Bennington, VT, instructor in fiction workshop, summer, 1994. Philological Association of the Pacific Coast, Los Angeles, chair of comparative literature section, 1983; Globe Centre, member of regional council, 1983; University of Oregon Summer High School Principals' Institute, member, 1984; Pacific Northwest Renaissance Conference, member of program committee, 1988. Oregon Repertory

Theater, humanist in residence, 1982. Speaker and consultant. **Publications:** Mighty Opposites: Shakespeare and Renaissance Contrariety, 1979; Time and the Art of Living, 1982; The Grace of Great Things: Creativity and Innovation, 1990; Book: A Novel, 1992; On Dialogue, 1996: The Most Amazing Thing (novel), 2001. Contributor of articles, essays, short stories, and poems to periodicals. **Address:** Dept of English, University of Oregon, Eugene, OR 97403, U.S.A. **Online address:** rgrudin@yahoo.com

GRUESSER, John Cullen. American, b. 1959. **Genres:** Literary criticism and history. **Career:** Seton Hall University, South Orange, NJ, lecturer in English, 1982-84; Purdue University-Calumet, visiting assistant professor of English, 1989-90; Kean University, Union, NJ, professor of English, 1990-. **Publications:** White on Black: Contemporary Literature about Africa, 1992; The Unruly Voice: Rediscovering Pauline Elizabeth Hopkins, 1996; Black on Black: Twentieth-Century African American Literature about Africa, 2000; Confluences: Postcolonialism, African American Literary Studies, and the Black Atlantic, 2005. EDITOR: J.E. Bruce, The Black Sleuth, 2002. Work represented in anthologies. Contributor of articles and reviews to literature journals. **Address:** Dept of English, Kean University, Union, NJ 07083, U.S.A. **Online address:** jgruesse@kean.edu

GRUHN, George. American, b. 1945. **Genres:** Music. **Career:** Gruhn Guitars Inc., Nashville, TN, president, 1970-. Guild Guitars, executive vice president of research and development and artist relations, 1986-88. **Publications:** (with D. Green) Roy Acuff's Musical Collection at Opryland, 1982; (with W. Carter) Gruhn's Guide to Vintage Guitars, 1991, 2nd ed., 1999; (with Carter) Acoustic Guitars and Other Fretted Instruments, 1993; (with Carter) Electric Guitars and Basses, 1994. Contributor to periodicals. **Address:** Gruhn Guitars Inc., 400 Broadway, Nashville, TN 37203, U.S.A.

GRUMBACH, Doris. American, b. 1918. **Genres:** Novels, Literary criticism and history, Biography. **Career:** Title-writer, MGM, 1940; Associate Ed., Architectural Forum, 1941; Professor of English, College of St. Rose, Albany, NY, 1952-70; Literary Ed., New Republic, 1973-75; Columnist, Saturday Review, 1975-76, and New York Times Book Review, 1977-80; Professor of English, American University, Washington, D.C., 1976-85. **Publications:** The Spoil of the Flowers, 1962; The Short Throat, the Tender Mouth, 1964; The Company She Kept, 1967; Chamber Music, 1979; The Missing Person, 1981; The Ladies, 1984; The Magician's Girl, 1987; The Book of Knowledge, 1989; Coming into the End Zone, 1991; Extra Innings, 1993; 50 Days of Solitude, 1994; Life in a Day, 1996; The Presence of Absence, 1998; The Pleasure of Their Company, 2000. **Address:** c/o Tim Seldes, Russell and Volkening, 50 W. 29th St., New York, NY 10001, U.S.A.

GRUMBINE, R. Edward. American, b. 1953. **Genres:** Environmental sciences/Ecology. **Career:** Antioch College, Yellow Springs, OH, instructor in environmental studies, 1975 and 1977; Evergreen State College, Olympia, WA, instructor in environmental studies, 1979; University of Montana, Missoula, administrative assistant at Wilderness Institute, 1979-80, instructor, 1981; University of California Extension, Santa Cruz, instructor in environmental studies and director of Sierra Institute, 1982-. U.S. Forest Service, research intern in fire ecology at Sequoia National Forest, 1974, fire fighter at Mount Baker-Snoqualmie National Forest, 1977; National Park Service, interpretive naturalist at Sitka National Historical Park, 1976, backcountry ranger at Olympic National Park, 1978, and North Cascades National Park, 1982. **Publications:** Ghost Bears: Exploring the Biodiversity Crisis, Island Press (Washington, DC), 1992; Environmental Policy and Biodiversity, Island Press (Washington D.C.), 1994. **Address:** Sierra Institute, 1001 Smith Grade, Santa Cruz, CA 95060, U.S.A.

GRUMMAN, Bob. American, b. 1941. **Genres:** Plays/Screenplays, Poetry, Psychology. **Career:** Datagraphic Computer Services, North Hollywood, CA, delivery boy, then computer-operator, 1971-76; Charlotte County school board, Punta Gorda FL, substitute teacher, 1994-. **Publications:** Poemns (visual haiku), 1966; Preliminary Rough Draft of a Total Psychology (theoretical psychology), 1967; A Strayngebook (children's book), 1987; An April Poem (visual poetry), 1989; Spring Poem No. 3,719,242 (visual poetry), 1990; Of Manywhere-at-Once, Volume One (memoir/criticism), 1990; Mathemaku 1-5 (mathematical poetry), 1992; Barbaric Bart Meets Batperson and Her Indian Companion, Taco (play), 1992; Barbaric Bart Visits God (play), 1993. Rabbit Stew (play), 1994; Mathemaku 6-12 (mathematical poetry), 1994; Of Poem (solitextual poetry), 1994; Mathemaku 13-19 (mathematical poetry), 1996. EDITOR (with C. Hill): Vispo auf Deutsch, 1995; Writing to Be Seen, Vol. 1, 2001. **Address:** 1708 Hayworth Rd, Port Charlotte, FL 33952, U.S.A. **Online address:** BobGrumman@Nut-N-But.Net

GRÜNBAUM, Adolf. American (born Germany), b. 1923. **Genres:** Philosophy, Psychology. **Career:** Andrew Mellon Professor of Philosophy of Science, 1960-, Chairman of Center for Philosophy of Science, 1978-, Research Professor of Psychiatry, 1979-, University of Pittsburgh (director, Center for Philosophy of Science, 1960-78). Selfridge Professor of Philosophy, Lehigh University, 1956-60. Fellow, American Academy of Arts and Sciences, 1976-; governing bd, Philosophy of Science Assn, president, 1965-70; vice-president, American Assn for the Advancement of Science, 1963; president, American Philosophical Assn, 1982-83; president, International Union of History and Philosophy of Science, 2006-07. Gifford Lecturer, St. Andrews College, Scotland, 1985; Leibniz Lecturer, University of Hannover, Germany, 2003. **Publications:** Philosophical Problems of Space and Time, 1963, 2nd ed., 1973; Modern Science and Zeno's Paradoxes, 1967, rev. British ed., 1968; Geometry and Chronometry in Philosophical Perspective, 1968; The Foundations of Psychoanalysis: A Philosophical Critique, 1984; Psicoanalisi: Obiezioni E Risposte, 1988; (co-ed.) The Limitations of Deductivism, 1988; Kritische Betrachtungen zur Psychoanalyse, 1991; Freud e il Teismo, 1991; Validation in the Clinical Theory of Psychoanalysis, 1993. Contributor of articles to periodicals. **Address:** University of Pittsburgh, 2510 Cathedral of Learning, Pittsburgh, PA 15260-2510, U.S.A. **Online address:** grunbaum@pitt.edu

GRUNDY, Joan. British, b. 1920. **Genres:** Literary criticism and history. **Career:** Professor Emeritus of English Literature, Royal Holloway, College, University of London, since 1980 (Reader, 1965-79; Professor, 1979-80). Assistant Lecturer in English, University of Edinburgh, 1947-50; Lecturer in English, University of Liverpool, 1950-65. **Publications:** The Poems of Henry Constable, 1960; The Spenserian Poets, 1969; Hardy and the Sister Arts, 1979. **Address:** Rose Cottage, Lamb Park, Rosside, Ulverston, Cumbria LA12 7NR, England.

GRUNDY, Pamela C. American, b. 1962. **Genres:** Education, History, Local history/Rural topics, Race relations, Sports/Fitness, Women's studies and issues. **Career:** Star, Anniston, AL, reporter, 1986-87; Museum of the New South, Charlotte, NC, guest curator, 1992-; independent historian, 1998-. **Publications:** You Always Think of Home: A Portrait of Clay County, Alabama, 1991; Learning to Win: Sports, Education and Social Change in Twentieth-Century North Carolina, 2001. **Address:** 1713 Tippah Ave, Charlotte, NC 28205, U.S.A.

GRUNER, Charles R. American, b. 1931. **Genres:** Communications/Media, Speech/Rhetoric. **Career:** High school teacher of speech and drama, 1956-57; St. Lawrence University, Canton, NY, instructor, 1957-60, assistant professor of speech, 1960-64; University of Nebraska, Lincoln, assistant professor, 1964-66, associate professor of speech, 1966-69; University of Georgia, Athens, associate professor, 1969-74, professor of speech, 1974-97, General Sandy Beaver Teaching Professor, 1994-97, now retired. Guest lecturer, teacher or researcher for organizations and institutions. **Publications:** (with C.M. Logue, D.L. Freshley, and R.C. Huseman) Speech Communication in Society, with teacher's manual, 1972, 2nd ed., 1977; (with Logue, Freshley, and Huseman) Speaking: Back to Fundamentals, with teacher's manual, 1976, 4th ed. as Briefly Speaking, 1992; Understanding Laughter: The Workings of Wit and Humor, 1978; Plain Public Speaking, with teacher's manual, 1983; Essentials of Public Speaking, with teacher's manual, 1993; The Game of Humor: A Comprehensive Theory of Why We Laugh, 1997. **Address:** Dept of Speech Communication, University of Georgia, Athens, GA 30602, U.S.A. **Online address:** cgruner@bellsouth.net

GRUNEWALT, Pine. *See* KUNHARDT, Edith.

GRUSKY, Scott T. American, b. 1961. **Genres:** Novels. **Career:** Writer. **Publications:** Silicon Sunset (fiction), 1998. **Address:** c/o InfoNet Press, 23852 Pacific Coast Highway Suite 330, Malibu, CA 90265, U.S.A. **Online address:** scott@furthest.com

GRYLLS, Bear. (Edward Grylls). British, b. 1974. **Genres:** Travel/Exploration. **Career:** Writer. Led team from Halifax, NS, to John O'Groats across North Atlantic Arctic Ocean in small, open rigid inflatable boat, 2003. Works as a motivational speaker, television personality, mountaineer, and soldier. **Publications:** Facing Up: A Remarkable Journey to the Summit of Mount Everest (autobiography), 2000, in US as The Kid Who Climbed Everest: The Incredible Story of a Twenty-three Year Old's Summit of Mt. Everest, 2001; Facing the Frozen Ocean, 2003. Contributor to periodicals. **Address:** c/o Cunningham Management, London House, 271 Kings St, London W6 9LZ, England. **Online address:** bear@beargrylls.com

GUANO, Dr. *See* GOOTENBERG, Paul.

GUARE, John. American, b. 1938. **Genres:** Plays/Screenplays. **Publications:** The Loveliest Afternoon of the Year, and Something I'll Tell You

Tuesday, 1968; Muzeeka, and Other Plays, 1969; Kissing Sweet, and A Day for Surprises, 1970; Rich and Famous, 1977; The House of Blue Leaves, 1979; (with M. Shapiro) Two Gentlemen of Verona (adaptation), 1973; (with M. Forman) Taking Off (screenplay), 1971; Marco Polo Sings and Solo, 1977; The Landscape of the Body, 1978; Bosoms and Neglect, 1980; Atlantic City (screenplay), 1981; Three Exposures, 1982; Lydie Breeze, 1982; Gardenia, 1982; The Talking Dog, 1986; Women and Water, 1986; Moon over Miami, 1988; Six Degrees of Separation, 1990; Four Baboons Adoring the Sun and Other Plays, 1993; Moon under Miami, 1995; Chuck Close: Life and Work, 1988-1995, 1995; The War against the Kitchen Sink, 1996; A Few Stout Individuals, 2002. **Address:** c/o International Creative Management Inc, 40 W 57th St, New York, NY 10019, U.S.A.

GUARNIERI, Patrizia. Italian, b. 1954. **Genres:** Literary criticism and history, Psychiatry, History, How-to books. **Career:** University of Florence, Italy, teacher of Italian at Centro di Cultura per Stranieri, 1978-81, lecturer in moral philosophy, 1979-81, librarian at Architecture Library, 1980-81; Stanford University, Program in Italy, Florence, lecturer in Italian, 1982-93, lecturer in history of science, 1986-93; teacher of the history of psychiatry for psychiatric nurses, 1988-91; University of Trieste, professor of history of science, 1988-91; Istituto degli Innocenti, researcher, 1992-93; European University Institute, Jean Monnet Fellow, 1989-90, visiting professor, 2000. **Publications:** Luigi Credaro: Lo studioso e il politico, 1979; Filosofia e scuola nell'eta giolittiana, 1980; La Rivista Filosofica, 1899-1908: Conoscenza e valori nel neokantismo italiano, 1981; Introduzione a James, 1985; (ed.) Luigi Credaro nella scuola e nella storia, 1986; Individualita difformi: La psichiatria antropologica di Enrico Morselli, 1986; L'ammazzabambini: Legge e scienza in un processo toscano dell'Ottocento, 1988, trans. by C. Mieville as A Case of Child Murder: Law and Science in Nineteenth-Century Tuscany, 1993; La storia della psichiatria: Un secolo di studi in Italia, 1991; "Dangerous Girls": Family Secrets and Incest Law, 1998. Work represented in anthologies. Contributor to periodicals. **Address:** Via A. Baldesi 12, 50130 Florence, Italy. **Online address:** pguarn@tin.it

GUASPARI, John. American. **Genres:** Business/Trade/Industry. **Career:** Consultant. Worked thirteen years in automobile and aerospace industries; Rath & Strong, Lexington, MA, senior associate, became vice president; Guaspari & Salz Inc., Concord, MA, founder and president, 1986-. **Publications:** I Know It When I See It: A Modern Fable about Quality, 1985; Theory Why: In Which the Boss Solves the Riddle of Quality, 1986; The Customer Connection: Quality for the Rest of Us, 1988; It's about Time: A Fable about the Next Dimension of Quality, 1992; The Value Effect: A Murder Mystery about the Pursuit of "The Next Big Thing," 2000. Contributor to periodicals. **Address:** 2 Brook S, Walpole, MA 02081-2312, U.S.A. **Online address:** jguaspari@qualitydigest.com; contactus@guaspari-salz.com.

GUBAR, Susan (David). American, b. 1944. **Genres:** Literary criticism and history, Women's studies and issues. **Career:** Indiana University, Bloomington, professor of English. **Publications:** WITH S.M. GILBERT: The Madwoman in the Attic: The Woman Writer and the 19thCentury Literary Imagination, 1979, rev. ed., 2000; (ed.) Shakespeare's Sisters: Feminist Essays on Poets, 1979; (ed.) The Norton Anthology of Literature by Women, 1985, rev. ed., 1996; (ed.) The Female Imagination and the Modernist Aesthetic, 1986; No Man's Land: The Place of the Woman Writer in the 20th Century, 3 vols., 1989-94; Masterpiece Theatre: An Academic Melodrama, 1995; (ed., and with D. O'Hehir) Mothersongs: Poems For, By and About Mothers, 1995. OTHER: (ed. with J. Hoff) For Adult Users Only: The Dilemma of Violent Pornography, 1989; (ed with J. Kamholtz, and author of intro.) English Inside and Out: The Places of Literary Criticism, 1993; Racechanges: White Skin, Black Face in American Culture, 1997; Critical Condition: Feminism at the Turn of the Century, 2000; Poetry after Auschwitz: Remembering What One Never Knew, 2003. **Address:** Dept of English, Ballantine 442, Indiana University, 1020 E Kirkwood Ave, Bloomington, IN 47405-7103, U.S.A. **Online address:** gubar@indiana.edu

GUDORF, Christine E. American, b. 1949. **Genres:** Theology/Religion. **Career:** Xavier University, Cincinnati, OH, assistant professor to professor of religious studies, 1978-93; Florida International University, Miami, associate professor to professor of religious studies, 1993-. Visiting professor at colleges and universities. **Publications:** Catholic Social Teaching on Liberation Themes, 1980; (ed. with B. Andolsen and M. Pellauer, and contrib.) Women's Consciousness, Women's Conscience: A Reader in Feminist Ethics, 1985; (with R. Stivers, R. Evans, and A. Evans) Christian Ethics: A Case Method Approach, 1989, 2nd ed, 1994; Victimization: Examining Christian Complicity, 1992; Body, Sex, and Pleasure: Reconstructing Christian Sexual Ethics, 1994; (with R. Wolfe) Cross-Cultural Religious Ethics: A Casebook in World Religions, in press. Contributor to books. Contributor to academic

journals, religious magazines, and popular periodicals. **Address:** Department of Religious Studies, Florida International University, Miami, FL 33199, U.S.A.

GUELKE, Adrian. American. **Genres:** Business/Trade/Industry. **Career:** Educator and author. Queen's University, Belfast, Northern Ireland, professor of political science, director of the Center for Study of Ethnic Conflict. **Publications:** (with Stanley Siebert) The Control of Wages in South Africa, 1973; Northern Ireland: The International Perspective, 1989; Interdependence and Transition: The Cases of South Africa and Northern Ireland, 1993; (editor) New Perspectives on the Northern Ireland Conflict, 1994; The Age of Terrorism and the International Political System, 1995; South Africa in Transition: The Misunderstood Miracle, 1999; (editor, with Michael Cox and Fiona Stephen) A Farewell to Arms?: From 'Long War' to Long Peace in Northern Ireland, 2000; Contributor of articles to scholarly journals. **Address:** Center for Study of Ethnic Conflict, Queens University Belfast, Belfast BT7 1PA, Ireland. **Online address:** a.guelke@Queens-Belfast.ac.uk

GUENTHER, Charles (John). American, b. 1920. **Genres:** Poetry, Literary criticism and history, Translations. **Career:** Midwest Regional Vice-President, Poetry Society of America, 1977-91, Head, Archives Unit, 1943-45, Head, Research Unit, 1945-47, Assistant Chief and Chief of Library, 1945-57, and Chief of the Technical Library, 1957-75, Defense Mapping Agency Aerospace Center, St. Louis; Assistant Professor, St. Louis University, 1977-78. President, St. Louis Writers' Guild, 1959, 1976-77; Vice-President, 1971-73, and President, 1973-74, Missouri Writers' Guild; President, St. Louis Poetry Center, 1974-76. **Publications:** Phrase/Paraphrase, 1970; The Pluralism of Poetry, 1974; Jules Laforgue: Selected Poems, 1984; Moving the Seasons, Selected Poems, 1994. TRANSLATOR: (and ed.) Modern Italian Poets, 1961; (with Samuel Beckett et al.) Alain Bosquet: Selected Poems, 1963; Paul Valery in English, 1970; High Sundowns: Twelve Poems of Death and Resurrection from Juan Ramon Jimenez, 1974; (and ed.) Voices in the Dark (poetry and essay), 1974; The Hippopotamus: Selected Translations, 1986; Man of My Time: New & Selected Translations, 2003. **Address:** 9877 Allendale Dr, St. Louis, MO 63123-6450, U.S.A.

GUERIF, François. French, b. 1944. **Genres:** Film, Biography. **Career:** Editions Fayard, former editor; Editions Fleuve Noire, former editor; Editions PAC, former editor; Editions Rivages, Paris, editor. Editor of journal Polar. **Publications:** Paul Newman, 1975; Robert Redford, 1976; Marlon Brando, 1976; (with P. Merigeau) John Wayne: le Dernier Geant, 1979; Le Film Noir Americain, 1979; Le Cinema Policier Francais, 1981; (with R. Boyer) Brigitte Bardot: And God Created Woman, trans. by A. Collier, 1983; Clint Eastwood, 1983; Vincente Minnelli, 1984; Paul Newman, 1987; Francois Truffaut, 1988; Steve McQueen, 1988; Sans Espoir de Retour: Samuel Fuller, 1989; Le film Policier, 1989; James M. Cain: Biographie, 1992; Conversations with Claude Chabrol, 1997; Le film noir americain, 1999; (with C. Chabrol) Comment faire un film, 2003. **Address:** 12 Boulevard Saint Martin, 7510 Paris, France.

GUERNSEY, Thomas F. American, b. 1951. **Genres:** Law. **Career:** Admitted to the Bars of Virginia, New Hampshire, Supreme Court of the United States, United States Court of Appeals for the Fourth Circuit, United States District Courts, Eastern District of Virginia, Eastern District of Pennsylvania, and District of New Hampshire. Vermont Law School, South Royalton, instructor in law, 1976-78; Temple University, Philadelphia, PA, Abraham L. Freedman fellow and lecturer in law, and assistant general counsel for Temple Legal Aid Office, all 1978-80; University of Richmond, Richmond, VA, assistant professor, 1980-83, associate professor, 1983-86, professor of law, 1986-, associate dean for academic affairs, 1992-. Attorney specializing in disability law, 1985-. **Publications:** (with Bacigal) Admissibility of Evidence in Virginia, with supplements, 1990; Problems and Simulations in Evidence, with instructor's manual, 1991; (with L.A. Dubin) Trial Practice, 1991; Virginia Evidence, with supplements, 1992; (with K. Klare) Special Education Law, 1993; (with Klare) Negotiations for Health Care Materials Managers: A Systematic Approach, 1993; (with Harbaugh and Zwier) Negotiate for Success! (interactive computer program), 1994. Contributor of articles and reviews to law journals. **Address:** School of Law, Southern Illinois University, Carbondale, IL 62901, U.S.A.

GUEST, Barbara. American, b. 1920. **Genres:** Novels, Plays/Screenplays, Poetry, Biography. **Career:** Art News, NYC, editorial associate, 1951-54. **Publications:** The Ladies Choice (play), 1953; The Location of Things, 1960; Poems, 1962; (with B.H. Friedman) Robert Goodnough, Painter, 1962; The Office (play), 1963; Port (play), 1965; The Blue Stairs, 1968; (with S. Isham) I Ching: Poems and Lithographs, 1969; Moscow Mansions (poetry), 1973; The Countess from Minneapolis (poetry), 1977; Seeking Air (novel),

1978; The Turler Losses (poetry), 1979; Biography (poetry), 1981; Quilts (poetry), 1981; Herself Defined: The Poet H. D. and Her World, 1984; (with J. Felter) Musicality (poetry), 1989; Fair Realism (poetry), 1989; (with R. Tuttle) The Altos (poetry), 1991; Defensive Rapture (poetry) 1993; Selected Poems, 1995; Stripped Tales (poetry), 1996; Quill Solitary APPARITION (poetry), 1996; Rocks on a Platter (poetry), 1999; If So, Tell Me (poetry), 1999; (with L. Reid) Symbiosis (poetry), 2000; Miniatures and Other Poems (poetry), 2002; Forces of Imagination (essays), 2003; (with K. Killian) The Office (play), 2000. **Address:** 1301 Milvia St, Berkeley, CA 94709, U.S.A.

GUEST, Christopher. American, b. 1948. **Genres:** Plays/Screenplays, Songs/Lyrics and libretti. **Career:** Actor, writer, and director. Appeared in stage plays, films, television series, specials, pilots, and films; Director of television films, programs, pilots, series, and specials; appeared on radio comedy programs and comedy albums with the National Lampoon, with Spinal Tap, and with comedian Billy Crystal; went on concert tour as his This Is Spinal Tap character musician Nigel Tufnel. **Publications:** SCREEN AND TELEPLAYS: National Lampoon's Lemmings (lyrics), 1973; (with others) The Lily Tomlin Special, 1975; (with M. McKean and H. Shearer; and co-composer of music and lyrics, and actor) This is Spinal Tap, 1984; (with McKean and M. Varhol; and director, and composer of song) The Big Picture, 1989; (with others; and co-producer) A Spinal Tap Reunion, 1992; (with others; and director and actor) Waiting for Guffman, 1997. **Address:** c/o CU, 8383 Wilshire Blvd., Ste. 850, Beverly Hills, CA 90211-2420, U.S.A.

GUEST, Harry. (Henry Bayly Guest). British, b. 1932. **Genres:** Novels, Poetry, Literary criticism and history, Translations. **Career:** Assistant Master, Felsted School, Essex, 1955-61; Head of Modern Languages Dept., Lancing College, Sussex, 1961-66; Assistant Lecturer, Yokohama National University Japan, 1966-72; Head of Modern Languages, Exeter School, 1972-91; Honorary Res Fellow, Exeter University, 1994-. **Publications:** Private View, 1962; A Different Darkness, 1964; Arrangements, 1968; Another Island Country, 1970; The Cutting-Room, 1970; (with M. Mead and J. Beeching) Penguin Modern Poets 16, 1970; The Place, 1971; (trans. with L. Guest and Kajima S.) Post-War Japanese Poetry, 1972; The Inheritance (radio play), 1973; The Achievements of Memory, 1974; The Enchanted Acres, 1975; Mountain Journal, 1975; The Emperor of Outer Space (radio play), 1976; A House Against the Night, 1976; English Poems, 1976; Two Poems, 1977; Days (novel), 1978; The Hidden Change, 1978; Zeami in Exile, 1978; Elegies, 1980; The Distance, The Shadows, 1981; Lost and Found: Poems 1975-1982, 1983; The Emperor of Outer Space, 1983; Dealings with the Real World, 1987; Mastering Japanese, 1989; Lost Pictures (novel), 1991; Coming to Terms, 1994; Literary Companion to Japan, 1994; So Far, 1998; Versions, 1999; The Artist on the Artist, 2000; A Puzzling Harvest, Collected Poems 1955-2000, 2002. **Address:** 1 Alexandra Terr, Exeter, Devon EX4 6SY, England.

GUEST, Ivor (Forbes). British, b. 1920. **Genres:** Dance/Ballet. **Career:** Solicitor; Royal Academy of Dancing, chairman, 1969-93; British Theatre Museum, vice-chairman, 1966-77; Society of Dance Research, chairman, 1982-97; Radcliffe Trust, trustee, 1997-. Ordre des Arts et des Lettres, chevalier, 1998. **Publications:** Napoleon III in England, 1952; The Ballet of the Second Empire, 1858-70, 1953; The Romantic Ballet in England, 1954; The Ballet of the Second Empire, 1847-58, 1955; Fanny Cerrito, 1956; Victorian Ballet Girl, 1957; Adeline Genee, 1958; The Alhambra Ballet, 1959; The Dancer's Heritage, 1960; (ed. and co-author) La Fille mal Gardee, 1960; The Empire Ballet, 1962; A Gallery of Romantic Ballet, 1965; The Romantic Ballet in Paris, 1966; Dandies and Dancers, 1969; Carlotta Zambelli, 1969; Two Coppelias, 1970; Fanny Elssler, 1970; Pas de quatre, 1970; Le Ballet de l'Opera de Paris, 1976, rev. ed., 2001; The Divine Virginia, 1977; Adeline Genee: A Pictorial Record, 1978; Lettres d'un Maitre de Ballet, 1978; Adventures of a Ballet Historian, 1982; Jules Perrot, 1984; Gautier on Dance, 1986; Gautier on Spanish Dancing, 1987; Dr. John Radcliffe and His Trust, 1991; Ballet in Leicester Square, 1992; The Ballet of the Enlightenment, 1996; Ballet under Napoleon, 2002. **Address:** 17 Holland Park, London W11 3TD, England. **Online address:** ivorguest@lodc.org

GUEST, Jacqueline. Canadian, b. 1952. **Genres:** Children's fiction, Young adult fiction. **Career:** Author, Metis, Aboriginal culture and literacy presentations at schools and libraries. **Publications:** Hat Trick, 1997; Free Throw, 1999; Triple Threat, 1999; Rookie Season, 2000; Lightning Rider, 2000; Rink Rivals, 2001; A Goal in Sight, 2002; Soccer Star; Racing Fear; At Risk; Bell of Batoche; Wild Ride. **Address:** Box 522, Bragg Creek, AB, Canada T0L 0K0. **Online address:** writer@jacquelineguest.com

GUEST, Judith. American, b. 1936. **Genres:** Novels, Essays. **Publications:** Ordinary People, 1976; Second Heaven, 1982; (with R. Hill) Killing-Time in

St. Cloud, 1988; Mythic Family (essay), 1988; Rachel River (screenplay), 1989; Errands, 1996; Icewalk (essay), 2001; Tarnished Eye, 2004.

GUGGENBUHL, Allan. Swiss, b. 1952. **Genres:** Psychology. **Career:** Deputy director of an outpatient clinic for the group psychotherapy of children and adolescents; lecturer in psychology at a teacher training college in Zurich, Switzerland. **Publications:** Men, Power, and Myths, 1997; The Incredible Fascination of Violence, 1996. **Address:** Unter Zaunel, 8001 Zurich, Switzerland. **Online address:** algugg@swissonline.ch

GUGLER, Laurel Dee. Canadian/American. **Genres:** Children's fiction. **Career:** Children's author and storyteller. Has worked as a teacher and education coordinator at Hamilton Children's Museum, a volunteer with Canadian Crossroads International, and a coordinator for a multicultural storytelling group at SHAIR International Resource Centre in Hamilton, Ontario; storyteller/presenter at schools/libraries. **Publications:** Mashed Potato Mountain, 1988; Casey's Carousel, 1989; Little Wynne's Giggly Thing, 1995; Muddle Cuddle, 1997; Monkey Tales, 1998; Facing the Day, 1999; There's a Billy Goat in the Garden, 2003. Contributor to magazines.

GUIGNON, Charles B(urke). American, b. 1944. **Genres:** Literary criticism and history, Philosophy, Psychology. **Career:** Princeton University, Princeton, NJ, lecturer in philosophy, 1976-77; University of Texas at Austin, assistant professor of philosophy, 1977-84; University of Vermont, Burlington, professor of philosophy, 1985-99. **Publications:** Heidegger and the Problem of Knowledge, 1983; (with F. Richardson and B. Fowers) Re-envisioning Psychology, 1999. EDITOR: The Cambridge Companion to Heidegger, 1993; Dostoevsky's "The Grand Inquisitor," 1993; (with D. Pereboom) Existentialism: Basic Writings, 1995; The Good Life, 1999. **Address:** Department of Philosophy, University of Vermont, Burlington, VT 05405, U.S.A.

GUILE, Melanie. British, b. 1949. **Genres:** Children's fiction, Children's non-fiction. **Career:** Melbourne University and elsewhere, lecturer in English literature, 1972-88, lecturer in children's literature, 1988-94; Royal Melbourne Institute of Technology, Melbourne, Australia, instructional designer and educational editor, 1995-98; full-time writer. **Publications:** FOR CHILDREN: FICTION: Revenge of the Green Genie, 1996; Mr. Venus-Computer Wizard, 1997. NONFICTION: Australia's Neighbours series: Indonesia/Japan/New Zealand/China, 2000, Vietnam/Papua New Guinea, 2001; Culture in... series: New Zealand/Papua New Guinea/Japan/Indonesia, 2002, North and South Korea/China/Thailand/Singapore, 2003, India/Vietnam/Australia/Malaysia, 2005; Children in Australian History series: Little Felons/Bush Boys and Girls/Another Mouth to Feed/ Baby Boomers, 2005. **Address:** 47 Tongue St, Yarraville, VIC 3013, Australia. **Online address:** melanieguile@iinet.net.au

GUILLAUMIN, Colette. French, b. 1934. **Genres:** Social commentary. **Career:** Centre National de la Recherche Scientifique, University of Paris VII, Paris, researcher; lecturer on feminist social theory. **Publications:** L'ideologie raciste: Genese et langage actuel, 1972; Sexe, race et pratique du pouvoir. L'idee de nature, 1992, trans. as Racism, Sexism, Power, and Ideology, (London), 1995. Contributor of essays to anthologies. Contributor to journals. **Address:** Unite de Recherche Migrations et Societes, Centre National de la Recherche Scientifique, Universite de Paris VII Denis Diderot, 2 place Jussieu Tour Centrale, 75251 Paris Cedex 05, France.

GUILLEMIN, Jeanne (Harley). American, b. 1943. **Genres:** Anthropology/Ethnology. **Career:** Boston College, Chestnut Hill, MA, professor of sociology; Massachusetts Institute of Technology (MIT), Cambridge, Security Studies Program, senior fellow. **Publications:** Urban Renegades: The Cultural Strategy of American Indians, 1975; (ed.) Anthropological Realities: Readings in the Science of Culture, 1981; (with L.L. Holmstrom) Mixed Blessings: Intensive Care for Newborns, 1986, rev. ed., 1991; Anthrax: The Investigation of a Deadly Outbreak, 2000. **Address:** Boston College, Sociology Dept., McGuinn Hall, Chestnut Hill, MA 02467, U.S.A. **Online address:** jeanne.guillemin@bc.edu

GUILLEN, Michael (Arthur). American, b. 1940. **Genres:** Mathematics/Statistics, Sciences, Plays/Screenplays. **Career:** Harvard University, Cambridge, MA, teacher of physics and math in Core Curriculum Program, 1985-; WCVB-TV, Boston, MA, science editor, 1985-; ABC-TV, NYC, science editor for Good Morning, America, 1988-; ABC News, NYC, science correspondent for programs, 1990-; Writer and host of television specials; appeared in television specials; appeared as guest in television series; appears as "Dr. Universe" on Internet magazine, Kidzine, ABC-TV and America Online, 1996-; chief consultant to television special, "A Mathematical

Mystery Tour," Nova, PBS; science and technical contributor to CBS Morning News, CBS; technical advisor to Metro-Goldwyn-Mayer; participant in educational improvement programs. Conducted research on theoretical plasma physics, liquid physics, and astrophysics. **Publications:** NONFICTION: Bridges to Infinity: The Human Side of Mathematics, 1984; Five Equations that Changed the World: The Power and Poetry of Mathematics, 1995. TELEPLAYS: (and host) Heads or Tails: Predicting the Unpredictable, 1987; (and host) Greenland Polar Ice Cap, 1991; (and host) Monteverde Cloud Forest, 1991; (and host) War in the Gulf: Answering Children's Questions, 1991; (and host) What Are the Differences Between Men and Women?, 1991; (and host) Russian Space Program, 1992; (and host) U.S. Disabled Ski Team, 1992; Laetrile: The Last Chance; Time, Tides and Tuning Forks; To Be or Not to Be: Endangered Species of New England. Contributor to periodicals. **Address:** c/o Good Morning America, ABC-TV, 147 Columbus Avenue, New York, NY 10023, U.S.A.

GUILLÉN CUERVO, Fernando. Spanish. **Genres:** Plays/Screenplays. **Career:** Actor, director, and writer. **Publications:** SCREENPLAYS: Robo en el cine Capitol, 1996; (with K. Elejalde and J.B. Ulloa) Airbag, 1997; Año mariano (The Year of Maria), 2000. **Address:** c/o Hispano Foxfilm, S.A.E., Avenida de Burgos 8-A, Planta 11, 20836 Madrid, Spain.

GUILLERMOPRIETO, Alma. Mexican, b. 1949. **Genres:** Area studies. **Career:** Author and journalist. Worked as a professional dancer before becoming a reporter on Central America for the Guardian and the Washington Post; Newsweek, South American bureau chief; New York Review of Books, writer; New Yorker, contributing writer to staff correspondent, 1989-. **Publications:** Samba, 1990; The Heart That Bleeds: Latin America Now (essays), 1994; Los años en que no fuimos felices: Crónicas de la transición mexicana, 1999; Las guerras en Colombia: Tres ensayos, 2000; Looking for History: Dispatches from Central America (essays), 2001. **Address:** c/o Pantheon Publicity, 1945 Broadway #B1, New York, NY 10019-4305, U.S.A.

GUILLORY, Dan. American, b. 1944. **Genres:** Essays, Poetry, Novels. **Career:** Louisiana State University, New Orleans, instructor in English, 1967-70; Millikin University, Decatur, IL, assistant professor, 1972-78, associate professor, 1978-82, professor of English, 1982-. Senior Fulbright lecturer in Gabon, 1989. **Publications:** Living with Lincoln: Life and Art in the Heartland (essays), 1989; The Alligator Inventions (poems), 1991; Introduction to the Lemon Jelly Cake (novel), 1997; Introduction to Tramping across America (essays), 1999. Contributor of poetry to anthologies. Contributor of essays, poems, and reviews to periodicals. **Address:** Department of English, Millikin University, Decatur, IL 62522, U.S.A. **Online address:** dguillory@mail.millikin.edu

GUILLOU, Jan. Swedish, b. 1944. **Genres:** Politics/Government. **Career:** Worked as a reporter at a small radical magazine in Sweden during the early-1970s; convicted of espionage in 1973; author, c. 1976-. **Publications:** Journalistik 1967-1976, Oktober, 1976; (with Marina Stagh) Irak-det nya Arabien, 1977; (with J.H. Dahlstrom) Artister: Intervjuer och portratt, 1979; Reporter, Oktoberforl, 1979; Justitiemord: Fallet Keith Cederholm, foreword by Henning Sjostrom, 1983; (with Goran Skytte) Nya berattelser: Fran Geijer till Rainer, 1984; I nationen intresse: Coq Rouge, 1988; Fiendens fiende, 1989, trans. by T. Keeland as Enemy's Enemy, 1992; Vendetta: Coq Rouge VI, 1991; Ingen mans land: Coq Rouge VII, 1992; Den enda segern: Coq Rouge VIII, 1993; I hennes majestäts tjänst: Coq Rouge IX, 1994. **Address:** c/o Norstedt Publishers, Box 2052, S-103, 12 Stockholm, Sweden.

GUINIER, Lani. American, b. 1950. **Genres:** Law. **Career:** Damon J. Keith, U.S. Court of Appeals, Sixth Circuit, Detroit, MI, law clerk, 1974-76; Wayne County Juvenile Court, Detroit, juvenile court referee, 1976-77; Assistant Attorney General Drew S. Days, Civil Rights Division, U.S. Department of Justice, special assistant, 1977-81; National Association for the Advancement of Colored People (NAACP) Legal Defense and Educational Fund, assistant council, 1981-88; New York University School of Law, NYC, adjunct professor, 1985-89; University of Pennsylvania Law School, Philadelphia, PA, professor of law, 1988-. **Publications:** The Tyranny of the Majority: Fundamental Fairness in Representative Democracy, 1994; (with M. Fine and J. Balin) Becoming Gentleman: Women, Law School, and Institutional Change, 1997. Contributor to scholarly journals. **Address:** Griswold 503, Harvard Law School, 1563 Massachusetts Ave, Cambridge, MA 02138, U.S.A. **Online address:** lguinier@law.harvard.edu

GUINNESS, Desmond. British, b. 1931. **Genres:** Architecture. **Career:** Writer. Lecturer at universities in the United States and at museums in the United States and Canada. **Publications:** (with J. O'Brien) Great Irish Houses and Castles, 1992; Dublin-A Grand Tour, 1994; Georgian Dublin; Irish Houses and Castles; Palladio; (with W. Ryan) The White House: An Architectural History; (with J. Sadler) Newport Preserved and Mr. Jefferson, Architect. Contributor to periodicals. **Address:** Leixlip Castle, Leixlip, County Kildare, Ireland.

GUINNESS, Jonathan (Bryan). British, b. 1930. **Genres:** Biography. **Career:** Reuters, journalist, 1953-56; Erlangers Ltd., merchant banker trainee, 1956-59; Philip Hill, merchant banker trainee, 1959-62; Arthur Guinness Son & Co. Ltd., director, 1961-88; Leopold Joseph, executive director, 1962-64, non-executive director, 1964-91. **Publications:** (with C. Guinness) The House of Mitford (biography), 1984, reissued, 2004; Shoe: The Odyssey of a Sixties Survivor (biography), 1989; Requiem for a Family Business, 1997. **Address:** South Wing Rodmarton Manor, Cirencester GL7 6PF, England.

GUIVER, Patricia. British. **Genres:** Children's fiction. **Career:** Writer. Society for the Prevention of Cruelty to Animals (SPCA), Orange County Chapter, head. **Publications:** DELILAH DOOLITTLE PET DETECTIVE SERIES: Delilah Doolittle and the Purloined Pooch, 1997; Delilah Doolittle and the Motley Mutts, 1998; Delilah Doolittle and the Careless Coyote, 1998. **Address:** c/o Putnam & Berkley Group, 375 Hudson St, New York, NY 10014, U.S.A.

GULLOTTA, Thomas P. American, b. 1948. **Genres:** Medicine/Health. **Career:** Child and Family Services of Connecticut, Hartford, child care worker, 1971-73; Glastonbury Youth and Family Resource Center, Glastonbury, CT, assistant director, 1974-75, director of clinical services, 1975-81; United Social and Mental Health Services, Danielson, CT, director of consultation and education, 1981-84; Child and Family Agency of Southeast Connecticut, New London, CT, chief executive officer, 1985-. Central Connecticut State University, lecturer, 1974-81; University of Connecticut, West Hartford Campus, field instructor, 1976-80, 1989-92, lecturer, 1984; Manchester Community College, lecturer, 1978-79; Eastern Connecticut State University, lecturer, 1982-. **Publications:** (with G.R. Adams) Adolescent Life Experiences, 1983, 3rd ed (with Adams and C. Markstrom), 1994; (with G.R. Adams and S. Alexander) Today's Marriages and Families: A Wellness Approach, 1986; (with R. Hampton, E. Potter, and others) Issues in Children's and Families' Lives, Vol I: Family Violence: Prevention and Treatment, 1993. EDITOR (with G.R. Adams and R. Montemayor): The Biology of Adolescent Behavior and Development, 1989; From Childhood to Adolescence, 1990; Developing Social Competency in Adolescence, 1990; Adolescent Identity Formation, 1992; Adolescent Sexuality, 1993; (and contrib.) Adolescent Drug Misuse, in press. EDITOR & CONTRIBUTOR: (with G. Blau) Adolescent Dysfunctional Behavior: Causes, Interventions, and Prevention, in press; (with E. Newberger and R. Hampton) When Anger Governs: Stopping Violence in America, in press. Work represented in anthologies. Contributor of articles and reviews to periodicals. **Address:** Child and Family Agency, 255 Hempstead St., New London, CT 06320, U.S.A.

GUNDY, Jeff(rey Gene). American, b. 1952. **Genres:** Poetry, Adult nonfiction, Essays. **Career:** Indiana University-Bloomington, associate instructor in English, 197780; Goshen College, Goshen, IN, assistant professor of English, 1980; Hesston College, Hesston, KS, instructor in English, 1980-84; Bluffton College, Bluffton, OH, associate professor, 1984-89, professor of English, 1989-, C. Henry Smith Peace Lecturer, 1989, 1999. Gives lectures, workshops, and readings from his works at colleges and universities. **Publications:** POETRY: Inquiries, 1992; Flatlands, 1995; Rhapsody with Dark Matter, 2000; Greatest Hits 1986-2003, 2003. OTHER: A Community of Memory: My Days with George and Clara (nonfiction), 1996; Scattering Point: The World in a Mennonite Eye (nonfiction), 2003. Contributor of poems, articles, and reviews to periodicals. **Address:** Department of English, Bluffton College, 280 W College Ave, Bluffton, OH 45817-1196, U.S.A. **Online address:** gundyj@bluffton.edu

GUNETTI, Daniele. Italian, b. 1963. **Genres:** Information science/Computers. **Career:** Ministry of Communication, Turin, Italy, technician, 1983-87; University of Turin, Turin, technician, 1987-95, assistant professor of computer science, 1995-. **Publications:** (with F. Bergadano) Inductive Logic Programming: From Machine Learning to Software Engineering, 1995. **Address:** Department of Computer Science, University of Turin, S.C.O. Svizzera 185, 10149 Turin, Italy. **Online address:** gunetti@di.unito.it

GUNN, Brooke. See BROOKS-GUNN, Jeanne.

GUNN, James E(dwin). Also writes as Edwin James. American, b. 1923. **Genres:** Novels, Novellas/Short stories, Science fiction/Fantasy, Literary criticism and history. **Career:** University of Kansas, Lawrence, emeritus professor of English, 1993-, Center for the Study of Science Fiction, director, 1982- (managing ed., Alumni Publs., 1955-58; administrative assistant to chancellor for university relations, 1958-70; professor, 1970-93). Chairman, Campbell Award Jury, 1978-80, 1984-. Ed., Western Printing and Lithographing Co., Racine, WI, 1951-52. President, Science Fiction Writers of America. 1971-72; president, Science Fiction Research Association, 1980-82. **Publications:** This Fortress World, 1955; (with J. Williamson) Star Bridge, 1955; Station in Space, 1958; The Joy Makers, 1961; The Immortals, 1962; Future Imperfect (short stories), 1964; The Immortal (novelization of TV series), 1970; The Witching Hour (short stories), 1970; The Burning, 1972; Breaking Point (short stories), 1972; The Listeners, 1972; Some Dreams Are Nightmares (short stories), 1974; Alternate Worlds: The Illustrated History of Science Fiction, 1975; The End of the Dreams (3 short novels), 1975; The Magicians, 1976; Kampus, 1977; The Dreamers, 1981; Isaac Asimov: The Foundations of Science Fiction, 1982; Crisis!, 1986; Inside Science Fiction, 1992; The Unpublished Gunn, Part One, 1992, Part Two, 1996; The Joy Machine, 1996; Human Voices, 2002. EDITOR: Man and the Future, 1968; Nebula Award Stories 10, 1975; The Road to Science Fiction (short stories), 6 vols., 1977-99; The New Encyclopedia of Science Fiction, 1988; The Best of Astounding: Classic Short Novels from the Golden Age of Science Fiction, 1992; The Science of Science-Fiction Writing, 2000; The Millennium Blues, 2001. **Address:** 2215 Orchard Ln, Lawrence, KS 66049-2707, U.S.A. **Online address:** jgunn@ku.edu

GUNN, Kirsty. New Zealander, b. 1960. **Genres:** Novels. **Career:** Novelist and short story writer. **Publications:** NOVELS: Rain, 1995; The Keepsake, 1997. **Address:** c/o Heather Schroder, International Creative Management, 40 West 57th St., New York, NY 10019, U.S.A.

GUNN, Robin Jones. American, b. 1955. **Genres:** Children's fiction, Young adult fiction, Children's non-fiction, Theology/Religion, Young adult non-fiction. **Career:** Writer. Weekend announcer, interviewer on "His People Radio Magazine," and host of "Kids Korner" weekly program, KNIS Radio, Carson City, NV, and KCSP Radio, Casper, WY; speaker at women's group meetings, public and private schools, retreats, and writer's conferences. **Publications:** CHRISTY MILLER SERIES: Summer Promise, 1988; A Whisper and a Wish, 1989; Yours Forever, 1990; Surprise Endings, 1991; Island Dreamer, 1992; A Heart Full of Hope, 1992; True Friends, 1993; Starry Night, 1993; Seventeen Wishes, 1993; Sweet Dreams, 1994; A Promise Is Forever, 1994. MRS. ROSEY-POSEY SERIES: Mrs. Rosey-Posey and the Chocolate Cherry Treat, 1991; Mrs. Rosey-Posey and the Treasure Hunt, 1991; Mrs. Rosey-Posey and the Empty Nest, 1993. JESUS IS WITH ME SERIES: Jesus Is with Me When I Celebrate His Birthday, 1988; Jesus Is with Me When I Go to the Park, 1988; Jesus Is with Me When I Have a Babysitter, 1988; Jesus Is with Me When I Help My Mommy, 1988. PALISADES PURE ROMANCES SERIES: Secrets, 1995; Whispers, 1995. OTHER: God's Mountains, Meadows, and More, 1994; Only You, 1995; Sisterchicks on the Loose!, 2004; Sisterchicks Do the Hula!, 2004; Gardenias for Breakfast, 2004. Billy 'n' Bear series, six books for toddlers. Contributor to periodicals. **Address:** PO Box 56353, Portland, OR 97238, U.S.A. **Online address:** Robinsnest@robingunn.com

GUNNING, Sally (Carlson). American, b. 1951. **Genres:** Novels. **Career:** Writer. Worked as a museum tour guide, 1969-72, a cruise ship stewardess, 1973, and a bank accountant, 1974-79; office manager for a general practitioner, 1979-96. **Publications:** MYSTERY NOVELS. PETER BARTHOLOMEW SERIES: Hot Water, 1990; Under Water, 1992; Ice Water, 1993; Troubled Water, 1993; Rough Water, 1994; Still Water, 1995; Deep Water, 1996; Muddy Water, 1997; Dirty Water, 1998; Fire Water, 1999. **Address:** c/o Andrea Cirillo, Jane Rotrosen Agency, 318 E 51st St, New York, NY 10022, U.S.A.

GUNSTON, Bill. (William Tudor Gunston). British, b. 1927. **Genres:** Air/Space topics, Military/Defense/Arms control, Technology, Transportation, Biography. **Career:** Compiler, Jane's All the World's Aircraft, 1969-; European ed., Aircraft (Australia), 1973-; editor, Jane's Aero-Engines, 1996-; technical ed., Flight International, London, 1951-63; technology ed., Science Journal, London, 1964-70; director, So Few Ltd, 1990; fellow of the Royal Aeronautical Society, 1991; OBE, 1995. **Publications:** Your Book of Light, 1968; Hydrofoils and Hovercraft, 1969; The Jet Age, 1971; Transport Technology, 1972; Transport Problems and Prospects, 1972; (with F. Howard) Conquest of the Air, 1973; Bombers of the West, 1973; Shaping Metals, 1974; Attack Aircraft of the West, 1974; Philatelist's Companion, 1975; Supersonic Fighters, 1975; Submarines in Colour, 1975; F-4 Phantom, 1976; Night Fighters, 1976; Encyclopedia of Combat Aircraft, 1976; Modern Military Aircraft, 1977; Aircraft of World War II, 1978; (with B. Sweetman) Soviet Air Power, 1978; Spotting Planes, 1978; F-111, 1978; Bombers, 1978;

By Jupiter, 1978; Tornado, 1979; Encyclopedia of Missiles and Rockets, 1979; Find Out about Trains and Railways, 1979; Find Out about Aircraft, 1979; Water, 1980; Aircraft of World War 2, 1980; The Plane Makers, 1980; Jane's Aerospace Dictionary, 1980, 3rd ed., 1988; Harrier, 1980; Coal, 1981; Motor Cycles, 1981; Modern Warplanes, 1981; Airliners, 1981; Fighters of the Fifties, 1981; Bombers of World War II, 1981; Military Helicopters, 1981; Fighters 1914-1945, 1982; Record Breakers (Land), 1982; (with A. Wood) Hitler's Luftwaffe, 1982; St. Michael Airliners, 1982; Aeroplanes, Balloons and Rockets, 1982; The Israeli Air Force, 1982; Family Library of Aviation, 1982; St. Michael Modern Air Combat, 1982; F-16 Fighting Falcon, 1982; Air-Launched Missiles, 1982; Warships, 1982; (main contrib.) The Arms Yearbook, 1982; Fighter Aircraft in Colour, 1983; Aircraft of the Soviet Union, 1983; Spyplanes and RPVs, 1983; Fact File F-111, 1983; Missiles and Rockets of World War III, 1983; Encyclopedia of Modern Air Combat, 1983; Helicopters of the World, 1983; Naval and Maritime Aircraft, 1983; Falklands: The Aftermath, 1984; Fact File Harrier, 1984; Not Much of an Engineer (biography), 1984; Big Book of Fighter Planes, 1984; First Questions: Transport, 1984; Future Fighters and Combat Aircraft, 1984; Encyclopedia of Modern Fighting Aircraft, 1984; (with D. Taylor) The Guinness Book of Speed Facts and Feats, 1984; Aircraft of the RAF: Phantom, 1984; Air Superiority, 1985; F/A-18 Hornet, 1985; (with others) Advanced Technology Warfare, 1985; Commercial Aircraft, 1985; Military Aircraft, 1985; A Century of Flight, 1985; Warplanes of the Future, 1985; (co-author) Encyclopedia of Modern Weapons, 1985; Technology Series; Aircraft, 1985; Grumman X-29, 1985; World Encyclopedia of Aero Engines, 1986, 4th ed., 1999; Water Travel, 1986; EAP, 1986; Encyclopedia of Modern Fighting Helicopters, 1986, 2nd ed., 1997; Encyclopedia of American Warplanes, 1986, 2nd ed., 1997; MiG-21, 1986; British, German, Japanese, US Aircraft of World War II, 4 vols., 1986; Modern European Aircraft, 1986; Modern Soviet Aircraft, 1986; Modern US Aircraft, 1986; (with J. Golley) Whittle: The True Story, 1987, as Genesis of the Jet, 1996; MiG-23 Flogger, 1987; AH-64A Apache, 1987; Aircraft of the Vietnam War, 1987; Encyclopedia of Aircraft Armament, 1987; Diamond Flight: British Midland (airways), 1987; Topics: Railways, 1987; Stealth Warplanes, 1987; One of a Kind (history of Grumman aircraft), 1987; Airbus, 1988; Modern Combat Arms, 2 vols., 1988; American Military Aircraft, 1988; Guide to Modern Bombers, 1988; Flight without Formulae (update), 1988; Anatomy of Aircraft, 1988; (with L. Peacock) Encyclopedia of Fighter Missions, 1988; Rolls-Royce Aero Engines, 1989; Avionics, 1990; Stingers, F/A-18, 1990; Combat Arms: Helicopters, 1990; Classic Warplanes: P-51 Mustang, 1990; Combat Arms: Attack Aircraft, 1990; Flights of Fantasy, 1990; (co-author) So Few, 1990; Plane Speaking, 1991; Jet Bombers, 1991; Giants of the Sky, 1991; Passenger Airliners, 1991; Faster than Sound, 1992; Aircraft Piston Engines, 1992, 2nd ed., 1999; Visual Dictionary of Flight, 1992; How It Works: Flight, 1993; Encyclopedia of Piston Aero Engines, 1993, 2nd ed., 1999; World Encyclopedia of Aircraft Manufacturers, 1993; (co-author) Spirit in the Sky: F-4 Phantom, 1993; Thrust for Flight, 1994; The World Unfolds-Flight, 1995; Jet and Turbine Aero Engines, 1995, 2nd ed., 1997; Encyclopaedia of Russian Aircraft, 1995; World War II Aircraft Cutaways, 1995; (co-author) So Many, 1995; Back to the Drawing Board, 1996; (co-author) MiG-21, 1996; Hawker, Story of the 125, 1996; World Military Aircraft Forecast, 1997; Fighter!, 1997; Fedden (biography), 1998; Boeing Aircraft Cutaways, 1998; History of Fighter Planes, 1998; Lockheed Aircraft Cutaways, 1998; McDonnell Douglas Aircraft Cutaways, 1999; (co-author) Soviet X-Planes, 2000; History of Military Aviation, 2000; Aviation, the First 100 Years, 2002; Flight Path (biography), 2002; Night Fighters, 2003; Cambridge Dictionary of Aviation, 2004. PUTNAM AVIATION SERIES: Tupolev, 1995; (co-author) Yakovlev, 1996; (co-author) MiG Aircraft, 1997. EDITOR: Atlas of the Earth, 1972; St. Michael Encyclopedia of Aviation, 1979; The Flyer's Handbook (in U.S. as The Air Traveler's Handbook), 1979, 1989; Encyclopedia of World Air Power, 1980; The Colour Encyclopedia of Aviation, 1980; The Illustrated History of Propeller Airliners, Jet Airliners, Fighters, 3 vols., 1981; (in chief) Chronicle of Aviation, 1992. **Address:** High Beech, Kingsley Green, Haslemere, Surrey GU27 3LL, England.

GUNSTONE, Frank Denby. British, b. 1923. **Genres:** Chemistry. **Career:** University of Glasgow, Lecturer, 1946-54; St. Andrews University, Fife, Lecturer 1954-59, Sr. Lecturer 1959-65, Reader 1965-70, Professor, 1971-89, Professor Emeritus of Chemistry, 1989-. Scottish Crop Research Institute, Dundee, Scotland, Honorary Fellow, 1996. **Publications:** An Introduction to the Chemistry of Fats and Fatty Acids, 1958; (with J. Read) A Text-Book of Organic Chemistry, 1958; Programmes in Organic Chemistry, 6 vols., 1966-74; An Introduction to the Chemistry and Biochemistry of Fatty Acids and Their Glycerides, 1967; (with J.T. Sharp and D.M. Smith) An Introductory Course in Practical Organic Chemistry, 1970; Guidebook to Stereochemistry, 1975; (with F.A. Norris) Lipids in Foods, 1986; (with B.G. Herslof) A Lipid Glossary, 1992, rev. ed., 2000; Fatty Acid and Lipid Chemistry, 1996; Rapeseed and Canola Oil, 2004; The Chemistry of Oil and Fats, 2004. EDITOR:

Topics in Lipid Chemistry, 3 vols., 1970-72; (with J.T. Harwood and F.B. Padley) The Lipid Handbook, 1988, rev. ed., 1994; (with F.B. Padley) Lipid Technologies and Applications, 1997; Lipid Synthesis and Manufacture, 1999; Structured and Modified Lipids, 2001; Oleochemical Manufacture and Applications, 2001; Vegetable Oils in Food Technology, 2002; Lipids for Functional Foods and Nutraceticals, 2003. **Address:** 3 Dempster Ct, St Andrews, Fife KY16 9EU, Scotland. **Online address:** fdg1@st-and.ac.uk

GUNTER, Pete (Addison Yancey). American, b. 1936. **Genres:** Novels, Environmental sciences/Ecology, Philosophy, Bibliography. **Career:** Auburn University, Alabama, assistant professor, 1962-65; University of Tennessee, Knoxville, associate professor, 1965-69; University of North Texas, Denton, chairman, 1969-76, Regents' University Professor of Philosophy, 1969-. Southwestern Philosophical Society, president, 1978-79; Foundation for Philosophy of Creativity, executive director, 1982-92, chairman of the board, 1992-. **Publications:** The Big Thicket: A Challenge for Conservation, 1972; Henri Bergson: A Bibliography, 1974, 1986; (with J.R. Sibley) Process Philosophy: Basic Writings, 1978; River in Dry Grass (novel), 1985; (with A. Papanicolaou) Bergson and Modern Thought: Towards a Unification of the Sciences, 1987; (with D.R. Griffin, J.B. Cobb Jr., M.P. Ford, P. Ochs) Founders of Constructive Postmodern Philosophy, 1992; (with M.F. Oelschlaeger) Texas Land Ethics, 1997. EDITOR: (and trans.) Bergson and the Evolution of Physics, 1969; (with R. Calvert) The Memoirs of W.R. Strong; Creativity in George Herbert Mead, 1990. Contributor of book reviews to magazines and journals. **Address:** 225 Jagoe, Denton, TX 76201, U.S.A. **Online address:** gunter@unt.edu

GUP, Ted (S.). American, b. 1950. **Genres:** Documentaries/Reportage. **Career:** Admitted to the Bar of District of Columbia, 1978. Washington Post, Washington, DC, staff writer, 1978-86; Time, Washington, DC, correspondent, 1986-93; freelance writer/author, 1990-. Case Western Reserve University, Shirley Wormser Professor of Journalism, 1999-; also taught at universities and institutions worldwide; consultant; media interviews and public appearances. **Publications:** The Book of Honor: Covert Lives and Classified Deaths at the CIA, 2000. Contributor to anthologies and periodicals. **Address:** 31220 Shaker Blvd, Pepper Pike, OH 44124, U.S.A. **Online address:** tedgup@att.net

GUPPY, Stephen (Anthony). Canadian, b. 1951. **Genres:** Poetry, Novellas/Short stories. **Career:** School District #69, Qualicum, British Columbia, teacher, 1982-85; Malaspina University College, Nanaimo, British Columbia, instructor of English and creative writing, 1986-. **Publications:** POETRY: Ghostcatcher, 1979; Blind Date with the Angel, 1998. OTHER: (ed., with R. Smith) Rainshadow: Stories from Vancouver Island (anthology), 1982; Another Sad Day at the Edge of the Empire (short stories), 1985. Contributor of short stories to anthologies. **Address:** Department of Creative Writing and Journalism, Malaspina University College, 900 Fifth St., Nanaimo, BC, Canada V9R 5S5. **Online address:** guppy@mala.bc.ca

GUPTA, Anil K. American (born India), b. 1949. **Genres:** Philosophy. **Career:** McGill University, Montreal, Quebec, Canada, assistant professor of philosophy, 1975-79, associate professor of philosophy, 1980-82; University of Illinois at Chicago Circle, associate professor of philosophy, 1982-89, fellow of Institute for the Humanities, 1985-86; Indiana University-Bloomington, professor of philosophy, 1989-95, Rudy Professor of Philosophy, 1995-2000; University of Pittsburgh, PA, distinguished professor of philosophy, 2001-. National Endowment for the Humanities, Fellowship for University Teachers, 1988-89, 1995-96; Center for Advanced Study in the Behavioral Sciences, fellow, 1998-99. **Publications:** The Logic of Common Nouns, 1980; (ed. with J.M. Dunn, and contrib.) Truth or Consequences: Essays in Honor of Nuel Belnap, 1990; (with N. Belnap) The Revision Theory of Truth, 1993. Work represented in anthologies. Contributor of articles and reviews to scholarly journals. **Address:** Department of Philosophy, University of Pittsburgh, Pittsburgh, PA 15260, U.S.A.

GUPTA, Sunetra. Indian, b. 1965. **Genres:** Novels. **Career:** Scientist. **Publications:** Memories of Rain, 1992; The Glass Blower's Breath, 1993; Moonlight into Marzipan, 1995; A Sin of Colour, 1999. Contributor to scientific journals. **Address:** David Higham Associates Ltd, 5-8 Lower John St, London W1R 4HA, England.

GUPTA, U. S. Indian, b. 1940. **Genres:** Agriculture/Forestry. **Career:** Haryana Agricultural University, Hissar, Haryana, India, assistant professor, 1965-74, associate professor, 1975-76; University of Khartoum, Khartoum, Sudan, associate professor of crop production, 1976-78; Ahmadu Bello University, Zania, Nigeria, reader in crop physiology, 1978-90, professor of crop physiology, 1990-. **Publications:** Physiological Aspects of Dryland Farming, 1975; Physiological Aspects of Crop Nutrition and Resistance, 1977; Crop Physiology, 1978; Crop Physiology-Advancing Frontiers, 1984; Progress in Crop Physiology, 1988; Crop Improvement, Vol 1: Physiological Attributes, 1992; Production and Improvement of Crops for Dryland, 1994. Also editor of books. **Address:** Department of Plant Science, Faculty of Agriculture, PMB 1044 A.B.U., Zaria, Nigeria.

GURALNICK, Peter. American, b. 1943. **Genres:** Music, Biography. **Career:** Music journalist, non-fiction writer, short story writer, and novelist. Boston University, Boston, MA, classics instructor, 1967-73. **Publications:** Feel Like Going Home: Portraits in Blues and Rock n' Roll, 1971; Lost Highway: Journeys and Arrivals of American Musicians, 1979; Nighthawk Blues: A Novel, 1980; The Listener's Guide to the Blues, 1982; Sweet Soul Music: Rhythm and Blues and the Southern Dream of Freedom, 1986; Searching for Robert Johnson (originally published in Living Blues), 1989; Last Train to Memphis: The Rise of Elvis Presley, 1994; Careless Love: The Unmaking of Elvis, 1999; (with E. Jorgensen) Elvis Day by Day: The Definitive Record of His Life and Music, 1999. EDITOR: Da Capo Best Music Writing 2000, 2000; (co) Martin Scorsese Presents the Blues: A Musical Journey, 2003. Work represented in an anthology. Contributor to periodicals.

GUREVICH, Aaron. Russian, b. 1924. **Genres:** History. **Career:** Pedagogical Institute, Tver, USSR, lecturer, 1950-63, professor of history, 1963-66; Russian Academy of Sciences, Moscow, research professor at Institute of Philosophy, 1966-69, and Institute of General History, 1969-; Moscow University, professor, 1989-; lecturer at universities in Germany, the United States, France, Italy, England, the Netherlands, Norway, Denmark, Sweden, Poland, and Israel. **Publications:** IN ENGLISH TRANSLATION: Categories of Medieval Culture, 1972, 2nd ed., 1984, trans., 1985; Medieval Popular Culture: Problems of Belief and Perception, 1981, trans., 1988; Historical Anthropology of the Middle Ages, 1992; The Individual in Medieval Europe, 1995. IN RUSSIAN: Raids of the Vikings, 1966; Free Peasantry of Feudal Norway, 1967; Problemi genezisa feodalisma v Zapadnoi Evrope (title means On the Origins of Feudalism), 1970; History and Saga, 1972; Norwegian Society in the Early Middle Ages: Social Structure and Culture, 1977; Edda and Saga, 1978; The Culture and Society of Western Europe as Seen by Contemporaries: The Thirteenth-Century Exempla, 1989; The Medieval World: Culture of the Silent Majority, 1990; Historical Synthesis and the Annales School, 1993; A History of a Historian, 2004. OTHER: Historical Knowledge and Historical Anthropology (in Japanese), 1990; Antropologia e cultura medievale: Lezioni romane (in Italian), 1991. Contributor to periodicals worldwide.

GUREWITSCH, Edna P. American. **Genres:** Biography. **Career:** Art dealer. Vice president, E&A Silberman Galleries Inc, 1953-61; president, E.P. Gurewitsch Works of Art Inc., 1973-. **Publications:** Kindred Souls: The Friendship of David Gurewitsch and Eleanor Roosevelt, 2002. **Address:** c/o Georges Borchardt Inc., 136 East 57th St., New York, NY 10022, U.S.A.

GURGANUS, Allan. American, b. 1947. **Genres:** Novels, Novellas/Short stories, Essays. **Career:** Professor of fiction writing: University of Iowa, Iowa City, 1972-74, Stanford University, Stanford, CA, 1974-76, Duke University, Durham, NC, 1976-78, Sarah Lawrence College, Bronxville, 1978-86, and University of Iowa Writers' Workshop, 1989-90; writer. Artist, with paintings represented in many private and public collections. **Publications:** Breathing Lessons, 1981; Good Help, 1988; Oldest Living Confederate Widow Tells All (novel), 1989; Blessed Assurance: A Moral Tale (novella), 1990; White People: Stories and Novellas, 1991; Plays Well with Others (novel), 1997; The Practical Heart (novellas), 2001. **Address:** c/o Amanda Urban, International Creative Management, 40 West 57th St., 17th Fl., New York, NY 10019, U.S.A.

GURNEY, A(lbert) R(amsdell). American, b. 1930. **Genres:** Novels, Plays/Screenplays. **Career:** Massachusetts Institute of Technology, Cambridge, professor of literature, 1970-96 (member of the faculty beginning 1960). **Publications:** The Comeback, 1965; The Rape of Bunny Stuntz, 1966; The David Show, 1966; The Golden Fleece, 1968; The Problem, 1969; The Open Meeting, 1969; The Love Course, 1970; Scenes from American Life, 1970; The House of Mirth (screenplay), 1972; The Old One-Two, 1973; Children, 1974; The Gospel According to Joe (novel), 1974; Richard Cory, 1976; Entertaining Strangers (novel), 1976; The Wayside Motor Inn, 1977; The Middle Ages, 1977; The Dining Room, 1982; What I Did Last Summer, 1983; The Golden Age, 1984; The Snow Ball (novel), 1985; Sweet Sue, 1986; The Perfect Party, 1986; Another Antigone, 1987; The Cocktail Hour, 1988; Love Letters, 1989; The Snow Ball (play), 1991; The Old Boy, 1991; The Fourth Wall, 1992, rev. ed., 2002; Later Life, 1993; A Cheever Evening, 1994; Sylvia, 1995; Overtune, 1996; Labor Day; 1997; Far East, 1998;

Ancestral Voices, 1999; Strawberry Fields (opera), 1999; Human Events, 2000; Buffalo Gal, 2001; Strictly Academic, 2003. **Address:** 40 Wellers Bridge Rd, Roxbury, CT 06783, U.S.A. **Online address:** A.R.Gurney@charter.net

GURR, A(ndrew) J(ohn). New Zealander (born England), b. 1936. **Genres:** Literary criticism and history, Theatre. **Career:** Editor of Modern language Review and yearbook of English Studies, since 1988. Professor, Dept. of English Language and Literature, University of Reading, since 1976. Ed., Journal of Commonwealth Literature, 1979-84. Lecturer in English, University of Leeds, 1962-76; Professor and Head, Dept. of Literature, University of Nairobi, 1969-73. **Publications:** The Shakespearean Stage 1574-1642, 1970, 1980, 1992 Hamlet and the Distracted Globe, 1978; Writers in Exile, 1981; (with C. Hanson) Katherine Mansfield, 1981; Playgoing in Shakespeare's London, 1987; The Shakespearian Playing Companies, 1996. EDITOR: The Knight of the Burning Pestle, by Beaumont and Fletcher, 1968; The Maid's Tragedy, by Beaumont and Fletcher, 1969; Philaster, by Beaumont and Fletcher, 1969; (with P. Zirimu) Black Aesthetics, 1973; (with A. Calder) Writers in East Africa, 1974; Richard II, by Shakespeare, 1984; Henry V, by Shakespeare, 1992. **Address:** Dept. of English, University of Reading, Whiteknights Park, Reading RG6 2AA, England. **Online address:** ajgurr@reading.ac.uk

GURR, David. Also writes as William Breton, D. G. Courtney. Canadian (born England), b. 1936. **Genres:** Novels, Plays/Screenplays. **Career:** Royal Canadian Navy, 1954-1970, career officer, became lieutenant; Computer Devices of Canada, Ottawa, Ontario, systems analyst and project manager, 1970-71; house designer and builder, 1972-81; full-time writer, 1978-. **Publications:** NOVELS: Troika, 1979; A Woman Called Scylla, 1981; An American Spy Story, 1984; The Action of the Tiger, 1984; On the Endangered List, 1985; The Ring Master, 1987; The Voice of the Crane, 1989; Arcadia West, 1993; The Charlatan, 2000. SCREENPLAYS: (with G. Cosmatos) Cliffhanger; Second Sight. STAGE PLAYS: Leonora. AS WILLIAM BRETON: Ten Days to Zero Zero, 1989; Countdown, 1992. AS D.G. COURTNEY: Kings Cross, 1993. **Address:** 3914 Ansell Rd, Victoria, BC, Canada V8P 4W3. **Online address:** dgurr@shaw.ca; www.davidgarr.ca

GURTOV, Melvin. American, b. 1941. **Genres:** Area studies. **Career:** Educator and author. Rand Corporation, Santa Monica, CA, research associate, 1966-71; University of California, Riverside, associate professor, 1971-76, professor of political science, 1976-86; Portland State University, Portland, OR, professor of political science and director of International Studies, 1987-94, professor, 1987-, editor-in-chief, Asian Perspective, 1994-. **Publications:** NONFICTION: The First Vietnam Crisis: Chinese Communist Strategy and United States Involvement, 1953-1954, 1967; Problems and Prospects of United States Policy in Southeast Asia, 1969; Southeast Asia Tomorrow: Problems and Prospects for U.S; Policy, 1970; China and Southeast Asia, the Politics of Survival: A Study of Foreign Policy Interaction, 1971; The United States against the Third World: Antinationalism and Intervention, 1974; Making Changes: The Politics of Self Liberation, 1979; (with Byong-Moo Hwang) China under Threat: The Politics of Strategy and Diplomacy, 1980; (with R. Maghroori) The Roots of Failure: United States Policy in the Third World, 1984; (with D. Haghighat) Global Politics in the Human Interest, 1988, 4th ed, in press; (with Hwang) China's Security: The New Roles of the Military, 1998. EDITOR: (with S. Chawla and A-G Marsot) Southeast Asia under the New Balance of Power, 1974; (with J.K. Park) Southeast Asia in Transition: Regional and International Politics, 1977; The Transformation of Socialism: Perestroika and Reform in the Soviet Union and China, 1990; (with D. Lieberman) Revealing the World: An Interdisciplinary Reader for International Studies, 1992. **Address:** Dept of Political Science, Portland State University, PO Box 751, Portland, OR 97207, U.S.A. **Online address:** mgurtov@aol.com

GURVAL, Robert Alan. American, b. 1958. **Genres:** Classics. **Career:** University of Oregon, Eugene, assistant professor of classics, 1989-90; University of California, Los Angeles, assistant professor, 1990-96, associate professor of classics, 1996-. AIDS Project Los Angeles, volunteer; Gamble House (Pasadena, CA), docent. **Publications:** Actium and Augustus, 1995. **Address:** Department of Classics, 100 Dodd Hall, University of California, Los Angeles, CA 90095, U.S.A. **Online address:** GURVAL@HUMNET.UCLA.EDU

GURVIS, Sandra J. American, b. 1951. **Genres:** Novels, Medicine/Health, Popular Culture, Ghost Writer. **Career:** Defense Construction Supply Center, Columbus, OH, job classification analyst, 1973-78; Charles Merrill Publishing, Westerville, OH, textbook editor, 1983-84; freelance writer, 1978-; ghost writer. **Publications:** The Off-the-Beaten Path Job Book, 1995; America's

Strangest Museums: A Traveler's Guide to the Most Unusual and Eccentric Collections, 1996, rev. ed., 1998; Way Stations to Heaven: 50 Major Visionary Shrines in the United States, 1996; 30 Great Cities to Start out In, 1997; Careers for Nonconformists: A Practical Guide to Finding and Developing a Career Outside the Mainstream, 2000; The Well-Traveled Dog, 2001; The Pipe Dreamers, 2001; Day Trips from Columbus, 2002, rev. ed., 2004; Where Have All the Flower Children Gone?, forthcoming. Contributor to publications and anthologies. **Address:** 5204 Sabine Hall, New Albany, OH 43054-8711, U.S.A. **Online address:** sgurvis@sgurvis.com; www.sgurvis.com

GUSCHOV, Stephen D. American, b. 1965. **Genres:** Plays/Screenplays, Sports/Fitness. **Career:** Grenier & McCarron (law firm), Danvers, MA, attorney, 1990-. Massachusetts School of Law, adjunct professor, 1992-. WCCM-AM Radio, talk show host, 1998-. **Publications:** (adaptation) The Diary of Adam and Eve (play), 1997; The Prodigal (play), 1998; The Red Stockings of Cincinnati, 1998. **Address:** Grenier & McCarron, 435 Newbury St., Danvers, MA 01923-1065, U.S.A.

GUSTAFSON, Sid. (born United States), b. 1954. **Genres:** Novels. **Career:** Veterinarian and writer. U.S. Air Force. **Publications:** First Aid for the Active Dog: Canine Health and Prevention, 2003; Prisoners of Flight (novel), 2003. Author of the short fiction works. Contributor of short fiction, poetry, articles to journals, and anthologies. **Address:** Bozeman Veterinary Clinic, 918 South Church, Bozeman, MT 59715, U.S.A. **Online address:** sidgustafson@yahoo.com

GUSTE, Roy F(rancis), Jr. American, b. 1951. **Genres:** Food and Wine. **Career:** Restaurateur and author. Restaurant owner, New Orleans, LA; former manager of Antoine's (restaurant), New Orleans. **Publications:** COOKBOOKS: Antoine's Restaurant, since 1840, Cookbook: A Collection of the Original Recipes from New Orleans' Oldest and Most Famous Restaurant, 1978; The Restaurants of New Orleans Cookbook, 1982, rev ed, 1990; The One Hundred Greatest Dishes of Louisiana Cookery, 1988; (with the Ochsner Medical Institutions) Louisiana Light: Low-Fat, Low-Calorie, LowCholesterol, Low-Salt Cajun and Creole Cookery, 1990; The Fish of the Gulf Coast Cookbook, 1993; The Tomato Cookbook, 1995; Gulf Coast Fish: A Cookbook, 1996. OTHER: The Secret Gardens of the Vieux Carre: The Historic French Quarter of New Orleans, 1993. **Address:** c/o W.W. Norton & Co., 500 Fifth Ave., New York, NY 10110, U.S.A.

GUTERSON, David. American, b. 1956. **Genres:** Novels, Novellas/Short stories, Education. **Career:** Writer of Fiction and Non-Fiction; Journalist and Essayist. **Publications:** The Country Ahead of Us, the Country Behind (stories), 1989; Family Matters: Why Homeschooling Makes Sense (nonfiction), 1992; Snow Falling on Cedars (novel), 1994; East of the Mountains, 1999; Our Lady of the Forest, 2003. **Address:** c/o Georges Borchardt, Inc, 136 E. 57th St., New York, NY 10020, U.S.A.

GUTHRIE, Donna W. American, b. 1946. **Genres:** Children's fiction, Children's non-fiction. **Career:** Teacher in Paulsboro, NJ, Colorado Springs, CO, and Philadelphia, 1968-75; Colorado Springs Montessori School, Colorado Springs, vice president of education, 1976-77; scriptwriter of pilot video series about hospitalization, 1979; Kids Corner Ltd. (audio visual company), Colorado Springs, founder and president, 1980-1990. Writer, 1980-. **Publications:** PICTURE BOOKS: The Witch Who Lives Down the Hall, 1985; Grandpa Doesn't Know It's Me, 1986; This Little Pig Stayed Home, 1987; While I'm Waiting, 1988; A Rose for Abby, 1988; Mrs. Gigglebelly Is Coming for Tea, 1989; The Witch Has an Itch, 1990; Not for Babies, 1993; Nobiah's Well: A Modern African Folk Tale, 1993; One Hundred and Two Steps, 1995; The Secret Admirer, 1996. OTHER: (with Arnsteen) I Can't Believe It's History! Fun Facts from around the World, 1993; Frankie Murphy's Kiss List (chapter book), 1993; (with N. Bentley) The Young Author's Do-It-Yourself Book: How to Write, Illustrate, and Produce Your Own Book, 1994; The Better Letter Book, 1994; (with Bentley) The Young Producer's Video Book: How to Write, Direct, and Shoot Your Own Video, 1995; Donna Guthrie: An Author's Story, 1995; (with J.N. Hulme) How to Write, Recite, and Delight in All Kinds of Poetry, 1996; (with Bentley) Putting on a Play: The Young Playwright's Guide to Scripting, Directing, and Performing, 1996; (with J. Stiles) Real World Math: Money and Other Numbers in Your Life, 1998; (with Bentley) The Young Journalist's Book: How to Write and Produce Your Own Newspaper, 1998; Mysteries, Mats, and Monsters: A Kid's Guide to Writing Mysteries, Travel, Fantasy and Much, Much More, 1999; Supermarket Math, 1999. RADIO SCRIPTS: Mr. Vanatoli and the Magic Pumpkin Seeds, 1983. VIDEO SCRIPTS: Jasper Enters the Hospital; The Day of Jasper's Operation; Wellness: It's Not Magic!; I'm a Little Jealous of That Baby; My Brother Is Sick; Thea's Story:

A Young Woman's Life with Lupus. CLASSROOM PRESENTATIONS: Make Mine a Mystery!; Nine Nice Newberys and a Couple of Caldecotts; A Visit from History; A Time to Live and a Time to Die.Contributor of stories and articles to periodicals. **Address:** 7622 Eads Ave., La Jolla, CA 92037, U.S.A.

GUTHRIE, Randolph H. American, b. 1934. **Genres:** Medicine/Health. **Career:** New York Hospital, NYC, intern, 1961-62, resident, 1962-63 and 1969-71; St. Luke's Hospital, NYC, resident, 1963-66; Memorial Sloan-Kettering Cancer Center, chief of plastic surgery, 1971-77; New York Downtown Hospital, NYC, chief of plastic surgery, 1981-2000. New York Hospital, attending surgeon, 1988-2000; Cornell University, clinical professor of surgery, 1988-. Diplomate, American Board of Plastic and Reconstructive Surgery and American Board of Surgery; New York State Supreme Court, plastic surgery representative on Malpractice Panel, 1971-80. Guest on television and radio programs. **Publications:** (with G. Schwartz) Reconstructive and Aesthetic Mammoplasty, 1989; (with D. Podolsky) The Truth about Breast Implants, 1994. Contributor to medical journals. **Address:** 15 E 74th St, New York, NY 10021, U.S.A.

GUTMAN, Dan. American, b. 1955. **Genres:** Children's fiction, Children's non-fiction. **Career:** Video Review Publications, coeditor of Electronic Fun, 1982-83; Carnegie Publications, founder and editor in chief of Computer Games, 1983-84; free-lance writer, 1984-. **Publications:** The Greatest Games, 1985; I Didn't Know You Could Do THAT with a Computer!, 1986; It Ain't Cheatin' If You Don't Get Caught, 1990; Baseball Babylon, 1992; Baseball's Biggest Bloopers, 1993; Baseball's Greatest Games, 1994; World Series Classics, 1994; Banana Bats and Ding Dong Balls, 1995; They Came from Centerfield, 1995; Taking Flight, 1995; Ice Skating, 1995; Gymnastics, 1996; The Way Baseball Works, 1996; The Kid Who Ran for President, 1996; Honus & Me, 1997; The Shortstop Who Knew Too Much, 1997; The Green Monster in Left Field, 1997; The Catcher Who Shocked the World, 1997; The Pitcher Who Went Out of His Mind, 1997; The Million Dollar Shot, 1997; Virtually Perfect, 1998; Katy's Gift, 1998; Cal Ripken, Jr., 1999; Jackie & Me, 1999; Funny Boy #1, 1999, #2, #3, 2000; The Kid Who Became President, 1999; Babe & Me, 2000; Landslide! A Kids' Guide to US Elections, 2000; Johnny Hangtime, 2000; The Secret Life of Dr. Demented, 2001; The Million Dollar Kick, 2001; Qwerty Stevens Back in Time: The Edison Mystery, 2001; Qwerty Stevens Stuck in Time with Benjamin Franklin, 2002; Shoeless Joe & Me, 2002; Mickey & Me, 2003. **Address:** 224 Euclid Ave, Haddonfield, NJ 08033, U.S.A. **Online address:** dangut@aol.com; www.dangutman.com

GUTMAN, Judith Mara. American, b. 1928. **Genres:** Art/Art history, Intellectual history, Photography, Biography. **Career:** Freelance writer, lectr., and reviewer. Contributor to the International Herald Tribune, 1983-85, Connoisseur, NY Times, Vanity Fair, Washington Post. Former Lecturer, Hunter College, NYC; Director, Montefiore Nursery School, NYC; Instructor, University of Wisconsin, Madison; "Through Indian Eyes," international traveling exhibition, curator, 1982-86; New School for Social Research, NYC, adjunct professor, 1990-95, 1999-; New York University, adjunct professor, 1996; Parsons-New School, adjunct professor, 1999. **Publications:** The Colonial Venture, 1966; Lewis W. Hine and the American Social Conscience, 1967; (with E. Rozwenc) The Making of American Society, 1972; Is America Used Up?, 1973; Lewis W. Hine: Two Perspectives, 1974; Buying, 1975; Ethnic Heritage: Immigration, Migration and the Growth of Cities (film strip series), 1975; Through Indian Eyes, 1982; Alfred Stieglitz and Dorothy Norman, Passion and Power, forthcoming. Contributor to periodicals. **Address:** 15 W 72nd St 25F, New York, NY 10023, U.S.A. **Online address:** gutmanj@aol.com

GUTMAN, Robert W. American, b. 1925. **Genres:** Biography. **Career:** Founder and former Lecturer, Master Classes of Bayreuth Festival; Faculty member, 1957-88, Dean of Art and Design Division, 1974-80, and Dean of Graduate Studies, 1980-88, Fashion Institute of Technology, NYC; Visiting Professor, Bard College, Annandale-on-Hudson, New York, 1991. **Publications:** (ed.) Volsunga Saga, 1962; Richard Wagner: The Man, His Mind, and His Music, 1968, 3rd ed, 1990; Mozart, A Cultural Biography, 1999. **Address:** 37 W 12th St Apt 12G, New York, NY 10011, U.S.A.

GUTMANN, David L(eo). American, b. 1925. **Genres:** Gerontology/Senior issues, Psychology, Social commentary. **Career:** University of Illinois at Chicago Circle, intern, clinical psychology, Neuro-Psychiatric Institute, 1956-57, clinical instructor, psychology, 1959-60; private practice, psychotherapy, 1956-60, 1963-; Presbyterian-St Luke's Hospital, staff psychologist, 1959-60; Massachusetts Mental Health Center, staff psychologist, 1960-62; Harvard University, lecturer, social relations, 1960-62;

University of Michigan, senior staff psychologist, Psychological Clinic, 1962-66, assistant professor, 1962-67, associate professor, 1967-70, professor of psychology, 1970-78; Northwestern University Medical School, professor, psychiatry, education, 1976-, chief, division of psychology, 1976-81, director, older adult program, 1977-, associate faculty, human development, social policy, 1986-; University of Chicago, visiting professor, 1975, co-director, Research and Clinical Practice in the Mental Health of Later Life training program, 1977-79; Michael Reese Hospital, fellow in clinical psychology, Psychosomatic and Psychiatric Institute, 1958-59; Center for Psychosocial Studies, visiting fellow, 1974-75. advisory board, Buehler Center on Aging and Chicago School of Professional Psychology. **Publications:** Reclaimed Powers: Toward a New Psychology of Men and Women in Later Life, 1987, rev. ed. 1994; The Human Elder, 1997. **Address:** Division of Psychology, Northwestern University Medical School, 303 East Chicago Ave., Room 9-217, Chicago, IL 60611, U.S.A.

GUTTENPLAN, D. D. American, b. 1957. **Genres:** Documentaries/Reportage. **Career:** Journalist. Pantheon Books, New York, NY, member of staff; Village Voice, New York, NY, senior editor; member of staff at Vanity Fair and Newsweek, New York, NY; New York Newsday, New York, media columnist, 1988-91; Granta magazine, London, England; Nation, New York, NY, co-chief of London bureau, 1997-. **Publications:** The Holocaust on Trial: History, Justice, and the David Irving Libel Case, 2001. Contributor to periodicals. **Address:** c/o Author Mail, W.W. Norton, 500 Fifth Avenue, New York, NY 10110, U.S.A.

GUTTERIDGE, Don(ald George). Canadian, b. 1937. **Genres:** Novels, Poetry, Education. **Career:** University of Western Ontario, London, professor of English methods. **Publications:** Riel: A Poem for Voices, 1968; The Village Within, 1970; Language and Expression, 1970; Death at Quebec, 1971; Saying Grace, an Elegy, 1972; Coppermine: The Quest for North, 1973; Bus-Ride, 1974; Borderlands, 1975; Tecumseh, 1976; A True History of Lambton County, 1977; Mountain and Plain, 1978; The Country of the Young, 1978; Rites of Passage, 1979; All in Good Time, 1980; God's Geography, 1982; Brave Season, 1983; The Exiled Heart, 1986; Incredible Journeys, 1986; St. Vitus Dance, 1987; Shaman's Ground, 1988; The Dimension of Delight, 1988; Love in the Wintertime, 1990; How the World Began, 1991; Summer's Idyll, 1993; Stubborn Pilgrimage, 1994; Winter's Descent, 1996; Bewilderment (novel), 2000; Teaching English, 2000; Bloodlines (poetry), 2001; Turncoat, 2003; Solemn Vows, 2003; Something More Miraculous, 2004. **Address:** 114 Victoria St, London, ON, Canada N6A 2B5. **Online address:** dongutteridge@rogers.com

GUTTERIDGE, Thomas G. American, b. 1942. **Genres:** Business/Trade/Industry. **Career:** General Motors Corp., Buick Motor Division, assistant safety engineer and production supervisor, 1960-65; Industrial Nucleonics Corp., assistant to the vice president for marketing and corporate recruiter, 1966-67; Purdue University, West Lafayette, IN, instructor in personnel and industrial relations, 1967-69; State University of New York at Buffalo, assistant professor, beginning in 1970, associate professor of human resources and industrial relations, until 1983, director of Human Resources Institute, 1981-83, 1984, executive director of Regional Economic Assistance Center, 1978-83, director of Development Center for Business, 1982-83; Southern Illinois University at Carbondale, professor of management and dean of College of Business and Administration, 1983-92; University of Connecticut, Storrs, distinguished professor of management and dean of School of Business Administration, 1992-. Federal Mediation and Conciliation Service, member of arbitration panels, 1977-. New York State Public Employment Relations Board, labor mediator, fact-finder, and arbitrator, 1972-83. Erie County Manpower Planning Office, member of executive committee of Manpower Advisory Council, 1974-79; Erie County Economic Development Task Force, vice chairperson of Employment and Training Subcommittee, 1982. WEBR-Radio, labor commentator, 1976-77. **Publications:** Career Planning and Development: Perspectives of the Individual and the Organization, 1980; (with F. Otte) Organizational Career Development: State of the Practice, 1983; (with U. Sekaran) Career Planning and Development: A Multi-Dimensional Perspective, 1986; (with Z. Leibowitz and J. Shore) Organizational Career Development: On the Brink of the Twenty-First Century, 1994. Work represented in books. Contributor of articles and reviews to professional journals. **Address:** School of Business Administration, University of Connecticut, 368 Fairfield Rd., Storrs Mansfield, CT 06269, U.S.A.

GUTTERIDGE, William Frank. British, b. 1919. **Genres:** International relations/Current affairs. **Career:** Royal Military Academy Sandhurst, Camberley, Surrey, Lecturer and Sr. Lecturer of Commonwealth History and Government, 1949-63; Lanchester Polytechnic, Coventry, Head of Dept. of

Languages and Modern Studies, 1963-71; University of Aston in Birmingham, Director of Complementary Studies, 1971-80, Professor 1976-82, Professor Emeritus of International Studies, 1982-; Research Institute for the Study of Conflict and Terrorism, Executive and Editorial Director, 1989-94, Director, 1994-. Editorial Consultant, Institute for the Study of Conflict, 1982-89. **Publications:** Armed Forces in New States, 1962; Military Institutions and Power in the New States, 1965; The Military in African Politics, 1969; Military Regimes in Africa, 1975; (ed.) European Security, Nuclear Weapons and Public Confidence, 1982; Mineral Resources and National Security, 1984; South Africa: Evolution or Revolution?, 1985; The South African Crisis: Time for International Action, 1985; The New Terrorism, 1986; Contemporary Terrorism, 1987; South Africa: Apartheid's Endgame, 1990; Regional Security and Cooperation in Southern Africa, 1992; South Africa's Defence Forces in the Transitional Phase, 1993; The Military in South African Politics: Champions of National Unity, 1994; South Africa: From Apartheid to National Unity 1981-94, 1995; South Africa's Defence and Security into the 21st Century, 1996; South Africa's Future Defence and Security, 1997; South Africa: Potential of Mbaki's Presidency, 1999. **Address:** 26 St Mark's Rd, Leamington Spa CV32 6DL, England.

GUTTMANN, Allen. American, b. 1932. **Genres:** History, Literary criticism and history, Sports/Fitness. **Career:** Professor of English and American Studies, Amherst College, Massachusetts, since 1959. **Publications:** The Wound in the Heart: America and the Spanish Civil War, 1962; The Conservative Tradition in America, 1967; The Jewish Writer in America, 1971; From Ritual to Record: The Nature of Modern Sports, 1978; (co-ed.) Life of George Washington, by Washington Irving, 5 vols., 1981; The Games Must Go On: Avery Brundage and the Olympic Movement, 1984; Sports Spectators, 1986; A Whole New Ball Game: An Interpretation of American Sports, 1988; Women's Sports: A History, 1991; The Olympics: A History of the Modern Games, 1992; Games and Empires: Modern Sports and Cultural Imperialism, 1994; The Erotic in Sports, 1996; (co-ed.) International Encyclopedia of Women and Sport, 3 vols., 2000. **Address:** 6 Lead Mine Rd., Amherst, MA 01002, U.S.A. **Online address:** aguttmann@amherst.edu

GUTTMANN, Hadassah. American. **Genres:** Music. **Career:** Nassau Community College of the State University of New York, Garden City, adjunct and applied associate professor of music, 1984-. Lucy Moses Music School, Abraham Goodman House, Merkin Concert Hall, teacher, director, and coordinator, 1992-; Yshevda University High School for Girls, music director, 2000-. Guteri Trio, director. Pianist, performing at chamber music concerts in and around NYC and on radio and television programs. **Publications:** The Music of Paul Ben-Haim: A Performance Guide, 1992. Contributor to My Friend Lennie by O. Mintz. **Address:** Department of Music, Nassau Community College of the State University of New York, Garden City, NY 11530, U.S.A.

GUY, Mary E. American, b. 1947. **Genres:** Ethics, Institutions/Organizations, Public/Social administration. **Career:** Georgia Department of Human Resources, Augusta, counselor, 1970-73; South Carolina Department of Mental Health, Columbia, psychologist, 1973-82; University of Alabama in Birmingham, professor, 1982-97. Florida State University, 1997-. **Publications:** Professionals in Organizations: Debunking a Myth, 1985; From Organizational Decline to Organizational Renewal: The Phoenix Syndrome, 1989; Ethical Decision Making in Everyday Work Situations, 1990; (ed.) Women and Men of the States: Public Administrators at the State Level, 1992. Contributor to professional journals. **Address:** Askew School of Public Administration & Policy, Florida State University, Tallahassee, FL 32306-2250, U.S.A.

GUY, Ray. Canadian, b. 1939. **Genres:** Local history/Rural topics, Plays/Screenplays, Documentaries/Reportage, Humor/Satire. **Career:** Freelance journalist, short story writer, playwright, and actor. Evening Telegraph, St. John's, NL, Canada, general reporter to writer of commentary, 1963-75; Sunday Express, St. John's, reporter. **Publications:** You May Know Them As Sea Urchins, Ma'am (columns), 1975, rev ed., 1985; That Far Greater Bay (columns), 1976, rev ed., 1985; Outhouses of the East (local history), 1978; Beneficial Vapours (columns), 1981; An Heroine for Our Time (fiction), 1983; Newfoundland/Labrador, 1984; This Dear and Fine Country, 1985; Young Triffie's Been Made Away With (play), 1985. Author of plays for radio and television, including "Old Skipper's" monologues for CBC-TV program All around the Circle and episodes of CBC-TV's Up at Ours series. Contributor to magazines and newspapers. Work represented in several anthologies. **Address:** c/o Breakwater Books, 277 Duckworth St., P.O. Box 2188, St. John's, NL, Canada A1C 6E6.

GUY, Rosa (Cuthbert). American (born Trinidad and Tobago), b. 1928. **Genres:** Children's fiction, Plays/Screenplays. **Career:** Harlem Writer's Guild, founding president. **Publications:** Venetian Blinds (play), 1954; Bird at My Window, 1966; (ed.) Children of Longing, 1971; The Friends, 1973; Ruby, 1976; Edith Jackson, 1978; The Disappearance, 1979; Mirror of Her Own, 1981; (trans.) Mother Crocodile, by B. Diop, 1981; New Guys around the Block, 1983; A Measure of Time, 1983; Paris, Pee Wee and Big Dog, 1984; My Love, My Love, 1985; And I Heard a Bird Sing, 1987; The Ups and Downs of Carl Davis III, 1989; The Music of Summer, 1991; Billy the Great, 1992; The Sun, the Sea, a Touch of the Wind, 1995. **Address:** c/o Ellen Levine, Trident Media Group, 41 Madison Ave #36, New York, NY 10010-2257, U.S.A.

GUZZETTI, Alfred F. American, b. 1942. **Genres:** Film. **Career:** Harvard University, Cambridge, MA, assistant professor, beginning in 1971, associate professor, until 1975, professor of visual environmental studies, 1975-; filmmaker and writer; film credits include Air, 1971; Family Portrait Sittings, 1975; Scenes from Childhood, 1980; (with Susan Meiselas and Richard Rogers) Living at Risk: The Story of a Nicaraguan Family, 1985; Beginning Pieces, 1986; (with Susan Meiselas and Richard Rogers) Pictures from a Revolution, 1991. **Publications:** "Two or Three Things I Know About Her": Analysis of a Film by Godard, Harvard University Press, 1981. **Address:** Department of Visual Environmental Studies, Harvard University, Cambridge, MA 02138, U.S.A.

GUZZO, Lou(is Richard). American, b. 1919. **Genres:** Communications/Media, Environmental sciences/Ecology, Military/Defense/Arms control, Writing/Journalism. **Career:** Plain Dealer, Cleveland, OH, reporter, 1936-42; Seattle Times, Seattle, WA, reporter, editor, and copyreader, 1946-50, music, film, theater, and arts critic, 1947-65; Seattle Post-Intelligencer, Seattle, managing editor, executive editor, chief editorial writer, and columnist, 1965-75; freelance writer, 1976-; KIRO-TV, Seattle, commentator, 1984-95. Teacher at University of Washington and Seattle University, 1976. Appeared in feature film Waiting for the Light, 1990. Warehouse Container Systems, vice-president, 1981-89; Analytics Corp. and Grizzly Publishing Co., vice-president and director, 1981-89; Louis R. Guzzo and Associates, Inc., president, 1984-. Policy counselor to Washington Governor Dixy Lee Ray, state historic preservation officer, and state director of cultural affairs, 1977-81. **Publications:** (with D. Bodansky and F. Schmidt) The Fight over Nuclear Power, 1976; Artsplan of Washington State, 1979; Is It True What They Say about Dixy? 1980; (ed.) Partnership Power, 1984; Severo Antonelli, Photographer, 1988; (with T.C. Liberman) The Catalyst, 1989; (with D.L. Ray) Trashing the Planet, 1990; (with D.L. Ray) Environmental Overkill, 1993; A Soul Reclaimed, 1999; Memoirs of Virginia and Milton Katims, 2000; When Did I Die?: Biography of Artist Richard Lachman, 2001. **Address:** 4450 191st Pl SE, Issaquah, WA 98027-9709, U.S.A. **Online address:** louguzzo@msn.com; www.louguzzo.com

GWALTNEY, John Langston. See Obituaries.

GWYN, William Brent. American, b. 1927. **Genres:** Politics/Government. **Career:** Professor Emeritus of Political, Science Tulane University, New Orleans, 1993- (Associate Professor, 1963-69; Chairman of Dept., 1975-79; Professor, 1969-93). Assistant Professor, Bucknell University, Lewisburg, Pa., 1957-63. **Publications:** Democracy and the Cost of Politics in Britain, 1962; The Meaning of the Separation of Powers, 1965; Barriers to Establishing Urban Ombudsmen, 1974; (co-ed.) Perspectives on Public Policy, 1975; (co-ed.) Britain: Progress and Decline, 1980. **Address:** 123 Walnut St., Ste. 603, New Orleans, LA 70118-4845, U.S.A.

GWYNELLE (DISMUKES), Gwynelle. American. **Genres:** Cultural/Ethnic topics, Human relations/Parenting, Philosophy, Sociology. **Career:** Author, publisher. Brite Moments, monthly alternative paper, publisher/editor, 1995-97. **Publications:** Affirmations for a Year-Round Kwanzaa, 1993; Afrikan Alkhemy: Spiritual & Soul Transformation in America, 1994; The African Centered Family Unity Guide, 1998; Practicing Kwanzaa Year Round, 2000. Contributor to books. EDITOR & PUBLISHER: The Kwanzaa Resource Guide (annual), 1996-98; The Multicultural Resource Guide, 1997; The Millennial Resource Guide, 1999. **Address:** 20 The Farm, Summertown, TN 38483, U.S.A.

GWYNN, R(obert) S(amuel). American, b. 1948. **Genres:** Poetry, Literary criticism and history. **Career:** Southwest Texas State University, San Marcos, instructor in English, 1973-76; Lamar University, Beaumont, TX, University Professor of English, 1976-. Gives readings from his works throughout the United States. **Publications:** POETRY: Bearing and Distance, 1977; The Narcissiad, 1981; The Drive-In, 1986; The Area Code of God, 1994; No Word of Farewell: Selected Poems 1970-2000, 2001. EDITOR: Drama: A HarperCollins Pocket Anthology, 1993, rev. ed. as Drama: A

Pocket Anthology, 2002; Fiction: A HarperCollins Pocket Anthology, 1993, rev. ed. as Fiction: A Pocket Anthology, 2002; Poetry: A HarperCollins Pocket Anthology, 1993, rev. ed. as Poetry: A Pocket Anthology, 2002; The Advocates of Poetry: A Reader of American Poet-Critics of the Modern Era, 1996; Fiction: A Longman Pocket Anthology, 1997; Literature: A Pocket Anthology, 2002; (with D. Gioia) The Longman Anthology of Short Fiction, 2000. EDITOR & CONTRIBUTOR: Dictionary of Literary Biography, 2nd Series, Vol. 105: American Poets since World War II, 1991, 3rd Series, Vol. 120: American Poets since World War II, 1992; Poetry: A Longman Pocket Anthology, 1997. Work represented in books and anthologies. Contributor of articles, poems, and reviews to periodicals. **Address:** Department of English and Foreign Languages, Lamar University, Beaumont, TX 77710, U.S.A. **Online address:** rsgwynn1@cs.com

GYATSO, Palden. Tibetan, b. 1933. **Genres:** Autobiography/Memoirs. **Career:** Writer. Tibetan monk. **Publications:** (with Tsering Shakya) Fire Under the Snow: The Autobiography of a Tibetan Monk, trans. by Shakya, 1997. **Address:** c/o Grove/Atlantic Inc., 841 Broadway, 4th Floor, New York, NY 10003, U.S.A.

GYLFASON, Thorvaldur. Icelander, b. 1951. **Genres:** Economics, Politics/ Government. **Career:** International Monetary Fund, Washington, DC, economist, 1976-81; University of Iceland, Reykjavik, professor of economics, 1983-. University of Stockholm, Institute for International Economic Studies, senior research fellow, 1978-96; Princeton University, visiting professor, 1986-88; Centre for Economic Policy Research, London, research fellow, 1987-; New York University, Center for U.S.-Japan Business and Economic Studies, research associate, 1989-; SNS-Center for Business and Policy Studies, Stockholm, research associate, 1996-; University of Munich, Center for Economic Studies, research fellow, 1999-. **Publications:** (with A.J. Isachsen and C.B. Hamilton) Understanding the Market Economy, 1992; (with T. Andersen, S. Honkapohja, A.J. Isachsen, and J. Williamson) The Swedish Model under Stress: A View from the Stands, 1997; Understanding Economic Growth, 1998; To Build a Nation (in Icelandic), 1998; Principles of Economic Growth, 1999. ESSAY COLLECTIONS IN ICELANDIC: Public Interest, 1990; Political Economy and Culture, 1991; Efficiency and Fairness, 1993; High Time, 1995; Trade for Gain, 1999; The Future Is Another Country, 2001. **Address:** Dept of Economics, University of Iceland, 101 Reykjavik, Iceland. **Online address:** gylfason@hi.is

GYOHTEN, Toyoo. Japanese, b. 1931. **Genres:** Economics, International relations/Current affairs. **Career:** Ministry of Finance, Tokyo, Japan, 1955-; worked at International Monetary Fund, Washington, DC, Japan desk, 1964-66; Asian Development Bank, Manila, Philippines, special assistant to the president, 1966-69; director general of international finance bureau, 1984-86, vice minister of finance for international affairs, 1986-89, Joined the Bank of Tokyo, Tokyo, 1991-, chair of board of directors, 1992-. Senior Advisor, The Bank of Tokyo-Mitsubishi, Ltd., and President, Institute for International Monetary Affairs, 1996-. Visiting professor at universities; member of advisory groups, committees, and commissions. **Publications:** (with P. Volcker) Changing Fortunes: The World's Money and the Threat to American Leadership, 1992; (ed. with M. Kuroda) One Hundred Key Words to Understand U.S.-Japan Economic Relations, 1992; Nihon Keizai no Shiza, 1993; The Yen: Destination Unknown-Personal Perspective, 1996. **Address:** 3-2 Nihombashi Hongokucho 1-chome, Chuo-ku, Tokyo 103-0021, Japan.

H

HAAK, Bob. Dutch, b. 1926. **Genres:** Art/Art history. **Career:** D.A. Hoogendijk, Amsterdam, Holland, assistant to the art dealer, 1950-54; Rijksmuseum, Amsterdam, assistant in the department of paintings, 1954-63; Amsterdam Historical Museum, chief curator, 1963-75, director, 1975-86. **Publications:** The Art Treasures of the Rijksmuseum, 1966; Rembrandt: His Life, His Work, His Time, trans. by E. Willems-Treeman, 1968; Rembrandt Drawings, 1976; (co-author) A Corpus of Rembrandt Paintings, 3 vols., 1982-89; The Golden Age: Dutch Painters of the Seventeenth Century, 1984. **Address:** Nieuwe Keizersgracht 384, 1018 VC Amsterdam, Netherlands.

HAAR, Charles M(onroe). American, b. 1920. **Genres:** Regional/Urban planning. **Career:** Louis D. Brandeis Professor of Law, Harvard University, Cambridge, Massachusetts, since 1972 (Associate Professor, 1952-54; Professor, 1954-56 and 1966-72). Chairman, Joint Center for Urban Studies, Massachusetts Institute of Technology/Harvard University, Cambridge, since 1969. Admitted to New York Bar, 1949; in law practice, NYC, 1949-52; Assistant Secretary, Metropolitan Development, U.S. Dept. of Housing and Urban Development, Washington, 1966-69. Former Chairman, President's Task Force on Natural Beauty, and President's Commission on Suburban Problems. **Publications:** Land Planning Law in a Free Society, 1959; Land-Use Planning, 1959, 3rd ed. as Land Use Planning: A Casebook on the Use, Misuse and Reuse of Urban Land, 1977; Federal Credit and Private Housing, 1960; Law and Land, 1964, 2nd ed. as Property and Law, 1985; Golden Age of American Law, 1966; The End of Innocence, 1972; Housing the Poor in Suburbia, 1974; Between the Idea and the Reality, 1975; (with others) Transfer of Development Rights: A Primer, 1981; (with D.W. Fessler) Wrong Side of the Tracks, 1986; (with D.W. Fessler) Fairness and Justice: Law in the Service of Equality, 1987; (with J.S. Kayden) Landmark Justice: The Influence of William J. Brennan Jr. on America's Communities, 1988; Suburbs Under Siege, Race, Space, and Audacious Judges, 1996. EDITOR: Housing in the Eighties: Financial and Institutional Perspective, 1984; Cities, Law, and Social Policy: Learning from the British, 1984; Judges, Politics and Flounders: Perspectives on the Cleaning up of Boston Harbor, 1986; (with Kayden) Zoning at Sixty: Mediating Public and Private Rights, 1990. **Address:** 1121 Crandon Blvd. - F603, Key Biscayne, FL 33149, U.S.A.

HAAR, James. American, b. 1929. **Genres:** Music. **Career:** Professor of Music, University of North Carolina, Chapel Hill, since 1978. Member, Executive Board, Grove's Dictionary of Music and Musicians, 6th ed. Instructor, 1960-63, and Assistant Professor, 1963-67, Harvard University, Cambridge, Massachusetts; Associate Professor, University of Pennsylvania, Philadelphia, 1967-69; Professor of Music, New York University, NYC, 1969-78. **Publications:** (ed) Chanson and Madrigal 1480-1530, 1964; The Tugendsterne of Harsduorffer and Staden, 1965; (co-ed.) The Duos of Gero, 1980; (ed with L.F. Bernstein) Il Primo Libro de Madrigali Italiani e Canzone Francese a Due Voci: Masters and Monuments of the Renaissance, by Ihan Gero, 1980; Essays on Italian Poetry and Music in the Renaissance: 1350-1600, 1986; (with I.A. Fenlon) The Italian Madrigal in the Early 16th Century, 1988; The Science and Art of Renaissance Music, 1998. **Address:** 868 Shadylawn Rd, University of North Carolina, Chapel Hill, NC 27514, U.S.A.

HAARSAGER, Sandra (L.). Also writes as Sandra Watkinson. American, b. 1946. **Genres:** History, Women's studies and issues. **Career:** Times-News, Twin Falls, ID, general assignment reporter and special editions editor, summers, 1965-67, then 1968-69; Idaho Statesman, Boise, reporter and

editor, 1972-75; Idaho Department of Education, Boise, public information specialist and administrative assistant to the state superintendent, 1975-78; University of Idaho, Moscow, director of information services, 1979-83; Idahoan/Daily News, Moscow, reporter and editor, 1983-85; News-Review Publishing Co., Moscow, general manager, 1985-88; University of Idaho, instructor, 1988-89, assistant professor, 1989-94, associate professor of communication and coordinator of American studies program, 1994-. **Publications:** Student Rights and Responsibilities: A Handbook for Schools and Students (monograph), 1978; Bertha Knight Landes of Seattle: Big City Mayor, 1994; "Organized Womanhood": Women's Clubs and Cultural Politics in the Pacific Northwest, 1875-1915, 1995. Work represented in anthologies. Contributor of articles and reviews to periodicals, until 1977 under the name Sandra Watkinson. **Address:** School of Communication, University of Idaho, Moscow, ID 83843-1072, U.S.A.

HAAS, Dan. American, b. 1957. **Genres:** Education. **Career:** Writer and teacher. Millbrook Central Schools, Millbrook, NY, special education teacher, 1987-. **Publications:** You Can Call Me Worm, 1997. **Address:** Box 600, Copake, NY 12516, U.S.A. **Online address:** parkhaas@taconic.net

HAAS, Lawrence J. American, b. 1956. **Genres:** Politics/Government. **Career:** Daily Register, Shrewsbury, NJ, municipal reporter, 1980-82; Pittsburgh Post-Gazette, Harrisburg, PA, state house correspondent, 1982-83; United Press International, Harrisburg, state capital bureau chief, 1983-85; Bond Buyer, Washington, DC, reporter on budget and tax issues, 1985-87; National Journal, Washington, DC, correspondent on budget and tax issues, 1987-92; National Academy of Public Administration, Washington, DC, special assistant to the president, 1992-. **Publications:** Running on Empty: Bush, Congress, and the Politics of a Bankrupt Government, 1990; The Washington Almanac: A Guide to Federal Policy, 1992, rev ed, 1993; Thieves, Scoundrels, and Blowhards: Two Hundred Years on the Seamy Side of American Politics, in press. Contributor to periodicals. **Address:** National Academy of Public Administration, 1100 New York Ave NW Ste 1090 E, Washington, DC 20005, U.S.A.

HAASE, Donald. American, b. 1950. **Genres:** Literary criticism and history. **Career:** Miami University, Oxford, OH, visiting assistant professor of German, 1979-81; Wayne State University, Detroit, MI, assistant professor, 1981-86, associate professor, 1986-2004, professor of German, 2004-, head of Department of German and Slavic Studies, 1989-, director of Junior Year in Germany Programs, 1993-95. **Publications:** EDITOR: The Reception of Grimms' Fairy Tales, 1993; Marvels & Tales: Journal of Fairy-Tale Studies, 1997-; J. Jacobs, English Fairy Tales and More English Fairy Tales, 2002; Fairy Tales and Feminism: New Approaches, 2004; Fairy-Tale Studies series, 2004-. Work represented in anthologies. Contributor of articles and reviews to professional journals. **Address:** Dept of German and Slavic Studies, Wayne State University, Detroit, MI 48202, U.S.A. **Online address:** d.haase@wayne.edu

HAATAJA, Lance. See DRAKE, Timothy A.

HABEGGER, Alfred (Carl). American, b. 1941. **Genres:** Novellas/Short stories, Literary criticism and history, Biography. **Career:** University of Kansas, Lawrence, assistant professor, 1966-71, associate professor, 1971-82, professor of English, 1982-96; University of Bucharest, Fulbright lecturer, 1972-73; independent biographer, 1996-. **Publications:** (ed.) The Bostonians,

1976; Gender, Fantasy, and Realism in American Literature, 1982; Henry James and the "Woman Business," 1989; The Father: A Life of Henry James, Sr., 1994; My Wars Are Laid Away in Books: The Life of Emily Dickinson, 2001. Author of articles and short stories. **Address:** 85400 Lost Prairie Rd, Enterprise, OR 97828, U.S.A.

HABEL, Janette. *See* **GRIMALDI, Janette Pienkny.**

HABER, Karen. American, b. 1955. **Genres:** Science fiction/Fantasy, Young adult fiction, Art/Art history, Writing/Journalism. **Career:** Writer, editor, and journalist. **Publications:** (with R. Silverberg) The Mutant Season, 1990; Thieves' Carnival (novella), 1990; The Mutant Prime, 1991; Mutant Star, 1992; Mutant Legacy, 1993; Woman without a Shadow, 1995; The War Minstrels, 1996; Star Trek Voyager: Bless the Beasts, 1996; Sister Blood, 1997; (coauthor) Science of the X-Men; Crossing Infinity (YA science fiction), 2005. EDITOR: (with R.Silverberg) Universe (anthology); Meditations on Middle-Earth, 2001; Exploring the Matrix, 2003; (with J. Strahan) Year's Best Science Fiction, 2003, 2004; Year's Best Fantasy, 2004. Contributor of short stories and articles to journals and anthologies. **Address:** PO Box 13160, Station E, Oakland, CA 94661, U.S.A. **Online address:** karenhaber@yahoo.com

HABERMAN, Richard. American, b. 1945. **Genres:** Mathematics/Statistics. **Career:** Rutgers University, New Brunswick, NJ, assistant professor of mathematics, 1972-77; Ohio State University, Columbus, assistant professor of mathematics, 1977-78; Southern Methodist University, Dallas, associate professor, 1978-85, professor of mathematics, 1985-. **Publications:** Mathematical Models: Mechanical Vibrations, Population Dynamics, and Traffic Flow: An Introduction to Applied Mathematics, 1977, rev. ed., 1998; Applied Partial Differential Equations (with Fourier Series and Boundary Value Problems), 1983, rev. ed., 2003; (with S.L. Campbell) Introduction to Differential Equations with Boundary Value Problems, 1996. **Address:** Dept. of Mathematics, Southern Methodist University, Dallas, TX 75275, U.S.A.

HABERS, Walther A(drianus). Dutch, b. 1926. **Genres:** Novels. **Career:** Writer. Has worked as a police officer, bookkeeper, coffee dealer, and broker of cocoa, spices, tea, and peanuts. Dutch Ground Nut Association, chair. **Publications:** Involved (novel), 1994, as The Way Back, 1998; In Heaven It's Not All Roses Either (novel), 1996; The Penthouse People (novel), 2000. **Address:** Revius Rondeel 197, 2902 EE Capelle a/d IJssel, Netherlands. **Online address:** waltherh@hetnet.nl

HABGOOD, (The Rt. Rev.) Lord John Stapylton. British, b. 1927. **Genres:** Ethics, Sciences, Theology/Religion. **Career:** Life Peer, 1995. Anglican clergyman. Vice-Principal, Westcott House, Cambridge, 1956-62; Rector of St. John's Church, Jedburgh, 1962-67; Principal of The Queen's College, Birmingham, 1967-73; Bishop of Durham, 1973-83; Archbishop of York 1983-95. **Publications:** Religion and Science, 1964; The Proliferation of Nuclear Technology, 1977; A Working Faith, 1980; Church and Nation in a Secular Age, 1983; Confessions of a Conservative Liberal, 1988; Making Sense, 1993; Faith and Uncertainty, 1997; Being a Person, 1998; Varieties of Unbelief, 2000; The Concept of Nature, 2002. CO-AUTHOR: Soundings, 1962; The Bible Tells Me So, 1967; Christianity and Change, 1971; Queen's Sermons, 1973; Explorations in Ethics and International Relations, 1981; In Search of Christianity, 1986; Changing Britain, 1987; Liberating Life, 1990; The Divine Risk, 1990; Can Scientists Believe?, 1990; Tradition and Unity, 1991; The Weight of Glory, 1991; Using the Bible Today, 1991; Challenges in Medical Care, 1992; Treasure in the Field, 1993; Christian Values in Europe, 1993; Humanity Environment and God, 1993; Veritatis Splendor: A Response, 1994; The Sense of the Sacramental, 1995; The Christian Family, 1996; Seeing Ourselves, 1998; Community, Unity, Communion, 1998. **Address:** 18 The Mount, Malton, N. Yorkshire YO17 7ND, England.

HABILA, Helon. Nigerian, b. 1967. **Genres:** Novels. **Career:** Writer. University of East Anglia, writer-in-residence, 2002-; Federal Polytechnic, Bauchi, Nigeria, literature lecturer, 1997-99; Vanguard, (newspaper) Lagos, Nigeria, arts editor. **Publications:** Waiting for an Angel, 2002. **Address:** c/o Curtis Brown Literary Agency, Haymarket House, 28-29 Haymarket, London SW1Y 4SP, England. **Online address:** h.habila@uea.ac.uk

HABINEK, Thomas N. American, b. 1953. **Genres:** Literary criticism and history, Classics. **Career:** University of Southern California, Los Angeles, Department of Classics, professor. **Publications:** The Colometry of Latin Prose, 1985; (ed., with A. Schiesaro) The Roman Cultural Revolution, 1997; The Politics of Latin Literature: Writing, Identity, and Empire in Ancient Rome, 1998. **Address:** Department of Classics, University of Southern California, Los Angeles, CA 90089, U.S.A. **Online address:** habinek@usc.edu

HACKBARTH, Steven (L.). American, b. 1945. **Genres:** Education, Communications/Media. **Career:** NYC Board of Education, Primary Schools 6 and 116, Manhattan, computer specialist teacher, 1994-; University of Southern California, director of office of student services, adjunct faculty member in department of policy, planning, and administration, 1977-91. Consultant to UNICEF, 1992-93. Consulting editor: Tech Trends; Educational Technology Magazine; Journal of Confluent Education. **Publications:** The Educational Technology Handbook: A Comprehensive Guide: Process and Products for Learning, 1996. Contributor to books, periodicals, and professional journals on matters relating to discipline-based inquiry learning and use of the Internet in schooling. **Address:** Primary School 6, 45 E 81st St, New York, NY 10028, U.S.A. **Online address:** hackbarths@aol.com; www. educational-technology.com

HACKELSBERGER, Christoph. German, b. 1931. **Genres:** History. **Career:** Architect. Academie der Bildenden Kuenste, Munich, Germany, guest professor, 1990-92, honorary professor, 1992. **Publications:** Subway Architecture in Munich, 1997. IN GERMAN: Das k.k.oesterreichische Festungsviereck in Lombardo-Venetien, 1980; Ein Architekt sieht Muenchen, 1981; Muenchen und seine Isarbruecken, 1981; Plaedoyer fuer eine Befreiung des Wohnens aus den Zwaengen sinnloser Perfektion, 1983; Zeit im Aufriss, 1983; Die aufgeschobene Moderne, 1985; Lebensraum Stadt, 1985; Die Franzensfeste, 1986; Zweitausendzwoelf, 1986; BetonStein der Weisen, 1988; Hundert Jahre deutsche Wohnmisere und kein Ende?, 1990; Architektur eines labilen Jahrhunderts, 1991. **Address:** Hofmark 9, 84181 Neufraunhofen, Germany.

HACKER, Barton C(lyde). American, b. 1935. **Genres:** History, Bibliography. **Career:** University of Chicago, IL, lecturer in history of science, 1965-66; University of Houston, TX, research associate in history, 1966-69; National Aeronautics and Space Administration, historian at Manned Spacecraft Center, 1966-69; Iowa State University, Ames, assistant professor of history and mechanical engineering, 1970-75; Massachusetts Institute of Technology, Cambridge, research associate in Oral History Program and Archives for the History of 20th-Century Science and Technology, 1975-77; Reynolds Electrical and Engineering Co., Las Vegas, NV, historian for Dosimetry Research Project, 1978-86; Oregon State University, Corvallis, visiting professor to adjunct professor of history of technology, 1986-91; University of California, Lawrence Livermore National Laboratory, laboratory historian, 1992-98; Smithsonian Institution, National Museum of American History, Washington, DC, curator of military history, 1998-. **Publications:** (with J.M. Grimwood and P.J. Vorzimmer) Project Gemini Technology and Operations: A Chronology, 1969; An Annotated Index to Volumes 1 through 10 of "Technology and Culture," 1959-1969, 1976; (with Grimwood) On the Shoulders of Titans: A History of Project Gemini, 1977; The Dragon's Tail: Radiation Safety in the Manhattan Project, 1942-1946, 1987; An Annotated Index to Volumes 1 through 25 of "Technology and Culture," 1959-1984, 1991; Elements of Controversy: The Atomic Energy Commission and Radiation Safety in Nuclear Weapons Testing, 1947-1974, 1994. Contributor to books. Contributor of articles and reviews to a variety of scholarly journals. **Address:** 150 12th St NE, Washington, DC 20002-6471, U.S.A.

HACKER, Kenneth L. American, b. 1951. **Genres:** Communications/Media. **Career:** Marketing representative in telecommunications, Sacramento, CA, 1978-81; telecommunications system consultant, Sacramento, 1981-83; Michigan Technological University, Houghton, assistant professor of speech and communication, 1986-90; New Mexico State University, Las Cruces, visiting assistant professor, 1990-91, associate professor of communication studies, 1992-. San Juan College, lecturer, 1992; Dona Ana Community College, lecturer, 1997. **Publications:** Verbal and Nonverbal Communication for Technical Professionals, 1988; (ed. and contrib.) Candidate Images in Presidential Elections, 1995. Contributor to books. Contributor of articles and reviews to communication studies journals. **Address:** Department of Communication Studies, New Mexico State University, Las Cruces, NM 88003, U.S.A. **Online address:** khacker@zianet.com; comstudy@nmsu.edu

HACKER, Marilyn. American, b. 1942. **Genres:** Poetry, Translations. **Career:** Teacher, editor, critic, translator, former antiquarian bookseller. **Publications:** The Terrible Children, 1967; (with T.M. Disch and C. Platt) Highway Sandwiches, 1970; Presentation Piece, 1974; Separations, 1976; Taking Notice, 1980; Assumptions, 1985; Love, Death, and the Changing of the Seasons, 1986; Going Back to the River, 1990; The Hang-Glider's Daughter: Selected Poems, 1990; Selected Poems, 1994; Winter Numbers, 1994; Squares and Courtyards, 2000; Deses peranto, 2003; First Cities: Collected Early Poems, 2003. TRANSLATOR: Edge, 1996; A Long-Gone Sun, 2000; Here There Was Once a Country, 2001; She Says, 2003. **Address:** c/o W.W. Norton, 500 Fifth Ave, New York, NY 10110, U.S.A.

HACKETT, Robert A(nthony). British, b. 1952. **Genres:** Communications/Media. **Career:** Simon Fraser University, Burnaby, British Columbia, assistant professor, 1984-92, associate professor of communications, 1992-. NewsWatch Canada, codirector; Canadian Centre for Policy Alternatives, research associate. **Publications:** Pie in the Sky: A History of the Ontario Waffle, 1980; News and Dissent, 1991; Sustaining Democracy? Journalism and the Politics of Objectivity, 1998. Some writings appear under the name Bob Hackett. **Address:** School of Communication, Simon Fraser University, Burnaby, BC, Canada V5A 1S6. **Online address:** hackett@sfu.ca

HACKL, Erich. Austrian, b. 1954. **Genres:** Novels. **Publications:** Auroras Anlass, 1987, trans. as Aurora's Motive, 1989; Sidonie (television script adapted from Abschied von Sidonie), 1988; Abschied von Sidonie, 1989, trans. as Farewell Sidonia, 1991; Koenig Wamba (title means: King Wamba), 1991; Sara und Simon, 1995; In fester Umarmung (essays), 1996; Entwurf einer Liebe auf den ersten Blick (title means: Study of Love at First Sight), 1999; Materialien zu Abschied von Sidonie, 2000. EDITOR: (with P. Schultze-Kraft and others) Lesebuch Dritte Welt: Band 2, 1984; Hier ist niemand gestorben, 1985; Das Herz des Himmels, 1986; (with C.T. Solinis) Geschichten aus der Geschichte des Spanischen Buergerkriegs, 1986; Wien, Wien allein, 1987; Zugvoegel set jeher, 1987; (with M.L. Garcia) Spanien: Im Schatten der Sonne, 1989; (and trans.) I. Vilarino: An Liebe, 1994; (and trans.) A.M. Rodas: Gedichte der erotischen Linken, 1995; A. Bauer: Hexenprozess in Tucuman und andere Chroniken aus der neuen Welt, 1996; H. Haill, Strassenballade, 1996; Hochzeit von Auschwitz (title means: Wedding in Auschwitz) 2002; Anprobiesen eines Vaters (title means: If the Father Fits,), 2004. **Address:** c/o Diogenes Verlag, Sprecherstr 8, CH-8032 Zurich, Switzerland.

HACKLER, George. American, b. 1948. **Genres:** Administration/Management. **Career:** Alpine Avalanche, owner, editor, and publisher, 1972-76; Texas State Senate, press secretary for Senator Pete Snelson, 1976-78; El Paso Chamber of Commerce, El Paso, TX, business development officer, 1978; Independent Consultants, lobbyist in Washington, DC, 1978-81; Southwest Publications Inc., owner, editor, and publisher, 1981-95, and founder of Corporate Press. **Publications:** An Act of Faith: Twenty-five Golden Rules for Small Business Success, 2002. **Address:** PO Box 2445, Corrales, NM 87048, U.S.A. **Online address:** ghack73586@aol.com

HACKNEY, Rod(erick Peter). British, b. 1942. **Genres:** Architecture, Songs/Lyrics and libretti. **Career:** Expo 67, Montreal, Quebec, job architect for monorail stations, 1965-66; Government of Libya, Tripoli, housing architect, 1967-68; assistant to Arne Jacobsen, Copenhagen, Denmark, 1968-71; Rod Hackney, Architect, Macclesfield, England, principal, 1972-. Established architectural offices throughout England; founder, Castward Ltd., 1983; work exhibited in London, 1988. Visiting professor, University of Paris VI, 1984; special professor, University of Nottingham, 1987. Chairman, Times/RIBA Community Enterprise Scheme, 1985-89; president, Young Architect World Forum, Sofia, Bulgaria, 1985; president, Building Communities, International Community Architecture Conference, 1986. Member of award juries; patron, Llandudno Museum and Art Gallery; president of North Wales Centre, National Trust. Chairman of trustees, Inner City Trust, 1986. Honorary Librarian, Royal Institute of British Architects, 1998-. **Publications:** Highfield Hall, 1982; The Good, the Bad, and the Ugly, 1990; Good Golly, Miss Molly (musical), 1991. **Address:** St. Peter's House, Windmill St, Macclesfield, Cheshire SK11 7HS, England.

HADAS, Rachel. American, b. 1948. **Genres:** Humanities, Poetry, Literary criticism and history, Writing/Journalism, Essays, Translations. **Career:** Rutgers University, Newark, NJ, assistant professor, 1980-81, associate professor of English, 1981-92, professor, 1992-, Board of Governors Professor of English. **Publications:** POETRY: Starting from Troy, 1975; Slow Transparency, 1983; A Son from Sleep, 1987; Pass It On, 1989; Living in Time, 1990; Mirrors of Astonishment, 1992; Other Worlds Than This, 1994; The Empty Bed, 1995; The Double Legacy, 1995; Halfway down the Hall, 1998; Merrill, Cavafy, Poems, and Dreams, 2000; Indelible, 2001. OTHER: Trelles, by Stephanos Xenos, 1978; Form, Cycle, Infinity: Landscape Imagery in the Poetry of Robert Frost, 1985; Unending Dialogue: Voices from an AIDS Poetry Workshop, 1991. **Address:** Dept of English, 520 Hill Hall, Rutgers University, 360 Dr Martin Luther King Jr Blvd, Newark, NJ 07102-1801, U.S.A. **Online address:** rhadas@andromeda.rutgers.edu

HADDAD, Gladys. American, b. 1930. **Genres:** Area studies, Art/Art history, Film, History, Humanities, Literary criticism and history, Local history/Rural topics, Women's studies and issues, Autobiography/Memoirs, Biography, Documentaries/Reportage. **Career:** Schoolteacher in South Euclid-Lyndhurst, OH, 1952-60, and Cleveland Heights, OH, 1960-63; Lake Erie College, Painesville, OH, professor of American studies and administrator, academic dean and executive assistant to the president, 1963-89; Case Western Reserve University, Cleveland, OH, professor of American studies and director, Western Reserve studies symposia, 1990-. Writer and producer for films. **Publications:** Laukhuff's Book Store of Cleveland: An Epilogue, 1997. EDITOR: (with H.F. Lupold) Ohio's Western Reserve: A Regional Reader, 1988; (with D.R. Anderson) Anthology of Western Reserve Literature, 1992. **Address:** Interdisciplinary Centers and Programs, Clark Hall, Case Western Reserve University, Cleveland, OH 44106-7120, U.S.A. **Online address:** gmh3@po.cwru.edu

HADDEN, Sally E. American. **Genres:** History. **Career:** Writer, researcher, and professor. Assistant professor of history and law, Department of History, Florida State University, 1998-. **Publications:** Slave Patrols: Law and Violence in Virginia and the Carolinas, 2001. **Address:** Florida State University, Department of History, 255A William Johnston Building, Tallahassee, FL 32306, U.S.A. **Online address:** shadden@mailer.fsu.edu

HADDOCK, Lisa (Robyn). American, b. 1960. **Genres:** Novels. **Career:** University of Tulsa, Tulsa, OK, news editor and managing editor of Collegian, 1981-82, editor in chief, 1982-83; St. Louis Globe-Democrat, St. Louis, MO, clerk, 1984; substitute teacher at public schools in Tulsa, 1985; Tulsa World, Tulsa, copy editor, 1986-89; The Record, Hackensack, NJ, copy editor and layout editor, 1989-. Neighbor Newspapers, intern, 1982. **Publications:** NOVELS: Edited Out, 1994; Final Cut, 1995. **Address:** The Record, 150 River St., Hackensack, NJ 07601, U.S.A.

HADLEY, Joan. See HESS, Joan.

HADLEY, Leila (E. B.). American, b. 1925. **Genres:** Travel/Exploration. **Career:** Associate Ed., Diplomat Magazine, 1965-67, and Saturday Evening Post, 1967-68. **Publications:** Give Me the World, 1958; How to Travel with Children in Europe, 1964, 1984; (co-author) Manners for Young People, 1964; Fielding's Guide to Traveling with Children in Europe, 1972, 1974; Traveling with Children in the U.S.A.: A Guide to Pleasure, Adventure, Discovery, 1977; Tibet: 20 Years after the Chinese Takeover, 1979; Fielding's Europe with Children, 1984; A Journey with Elsa Cloud (travel memoir), 1997. **Address:** 4 Sutton Pl., New York, NY 10022, U.S.A.

HAEGER, John Denis. American, b. 1942. **Genres:** History, Biography. **Career:** Northern Arizona University, provost. Academic administrator. **Publications:** (ed. with M. Weber) The Bosses, 1974, rev. ed., 1979; The Investment Frontier: New York Businessmen and the Economic Development of the Old Northwest, 1981; John Jacob Astor and the Economic Growth of the Early Republic, 1991. Work represented in anthologies. Contributor of articles and reviews to history journals. **Address:** Provost, Northern Arizona University, PO Box 4120, Flagstaff, AZ 86011-4120, U.S.A. **Online address:** John.Haeger@nau.edu

HAENEL, Wolfram. German, b. 1956. **Genres:** Children's fiction, Plays/Screenplays. **Career:** Landestheater Hannover, Germany, photographer and graphic artist, 1983-85; Georg Buechner Gymnasium, Hannover, high school teacher, 1985-86; Atelier fuer Werbegestaltung, Hildesheim, Germany, public relations assistant, copywriter, photographer, and graphic artist, 1986-88; Theaterwerkstatt Hannover, drama producer and playwright, 1988-91; writer. Practiced social work with children in Hannover, 1977-78; public relations manager at a lawyers network in Hannover, 1993-94. **Publications:** FOR CHILDREN IN ENGLISH TRANSLATION: The Old Man and the Bear, 1994 (originally Der kleine Mann und der Baer, 1993); The Extraordinary Adventures of an Ordinary Hat (Waldemar und die weite Welt), 1994; Mia the Beach Cat (Mia, die Strandkatze), 1994; Lila's Little Dinosaur (Lila und der regenbogenbunte Dinosaurier), 1994; Jasmine and Rex (originally Romeo liebt Julia), 1995; The Other Side of the Bridge (Anders hat sich verlaufen), 1996; Abby (Angst um Abby), 1996; Old Mahony and the Bear Family (Eine falle fur familie bar), 1997; The Gold at the End of the Rainbow (Das gold am ende des regenbogens), 1997; Mary and the Mystery Dog (Willi, der strandhun), 1999; Rescue at Sea (Schiffshund in not), 1999; Little Elephant's Song (Oskar, der kleine elefant), 2000; Christmas with the Snowmen (Als die Schneemannes Weihnachten feiesten), 2004. FOR CHILDREN IN GERMAN: Willi Wolle, 1987; Mimmi an der Nordsee, 1990; Die Teddybaeren-Bande, 1994; Ein Huhn haut ab, 1995; Anna Nass, 1996; Ein Pferd fuer Runder Mond: Indianer-Geschichten, 1996; Der kleine Mann und Familie Bar, 1997; Lasses letzter Urlaub: Ferien-Geschichten, 1997; Der kleine Haewelmann, 1997; Anna Nass, die neue kommt, 1997; Die rauber vom Geistermoor, 1998; Anna Nass kusst Alexander, 1998; Das Weihnachtswunschtraumbett, 1999; Mein schwein, die drei rauber, dochen und ich, 1997; Giftiges gold oder grossvaters esel, 1997; Lola und Glatze, 1998; Lasse und das geheimnis der leuchtturmwarter, 1998; Die sache mit den weihnachts-mannern, 1999; Geheimpirat Herr Holtermann, 1999; Die wilden ponys von Dublin, 2000; Wie der Zauberlehrling die pommes frites erfand, 2000; Der tag, an dem lehrer roth verschwand, 2001; Oskar, der klein elefant, haut ab, 2001. PLAYS: Max laesst die Sau raus, 1986; Ohne Prinzessin laeuft gar nichts, 1987; (with P. Henze) Aidsfieber, 1988; (with I. Hentschel) Ca Ira! Es war einmal eine Revolution…, 1990; Der kleine Haewelmann, 1991; Mich aber schone, Tod, 1991; Die Eier des Kolumbus, 1992; Die Vier von der Tankstelle, 1992; Tod dem Mondschein oder Gelbe Ohrfiegen?, 1992; Das Meer im Bauch, Buehnen der Landeshauptstadt Kiel, 1995. OTHER: (with U. Gerold) Irland (guide book), 1991; (with U. Gerold) Irland (picture book), 1995; Irgendwo woandess (novel), 2002. **Address:** Weidkaempe 29, D-30659 Hannover, Germany.

HAERI, Shahla. (born Iran). **Genres:** Cultural/Ethnic topics. **Career:** Cultural anthropologist. Boston University, Boston, MA, assistant professor of anthropology and director of women's studies program, 1993-. Associated with University of Chicago's fundamentalism project. **Publications:** Law of Desire: Temporary Marriage in Shi'i Iran, 1989; No Shame for the Sun: Lives of Professional Pakistani Women, 2002. **Address:** Department of Anthropology, College of Arts and Sciences, Boston University, 704 Commonwealth Ave., Boston, MA 02215, U.S.A. **Online address:** shaeri@bu.edu

HAFERTEPE, Kenneth. American, b. 1955. **Genres:** Architecture. **Publications:** America's Castle: The Evolution of the Smithsonian Building and Its Institution, 1840-1878, 1984; (and photographer) A History of the French Legation in Texas: Alphonse Dubois de Saligny and His House, 1989; Ashton Villa: A Family and Its House in Victorian Galveston, Texas, 1991; Abner Cook: Master Builder on the Texas Frontier, 1991; (co-ed.) American Architects and Their Books to 1848, 2001. Work represented in anthologies. Contributor of articles and reviews to periodicals. **Address:** Dept of Museum Studies, Baylor University, PO Box 97154, Waco, TX 76798-7154, U.S.A.

HAFNER, Katie. American, b. 1957. **Genres:** Documentaries/Reportage. **Career:** Journalist and author. Computerworld, reporter, 1983; San Diego Union, reporter, 1984-85; Business Week, staff writer, 1986-89; freelance and book writer, 1990-94; Newsweek, contributing editor and technology correspondent, 1994-98; New York Times, computer technology reporter, 1998-. **Publications:** (with J. Markoff) Cyberpunk: Outlaws and Hackers on the Computer Frontier, 1991; The House at the Bridge: A Story of Modern Germany, 1995; (with M. Lyon) Where Wizards Stay up Late: The Origins of the Internet, 1996; The Well: A Story of Love, Death, and Real Life in the Seminal Online Community, 2001. Contributor to periodicals. **Address:** c/o Author Mail, Avalon Publishing Group, 245 W. 17th St. 11th Floor, New York, NY 10011, U.S.A. **Online address:** kmh@well.com

HAGA, Enoch John. Also writes as C. B. S. Grant. American, b. 1931. **Genres:** Education, Genealogy/Heraldry, Information science/Computers, Mathematics/Statistics. **Career:** Teacher and chairman, Business Education and Mathematics Depts., Pleasanton Unified School District (formerly Amador Valley High School District), Pleasanton, California, 1964-92; Sacramento State College, visiting asst. professor of business, 1967-69; coordinator of computer services, administration instruction, 1984-85; instructor, Chabot College, Hayward, California, 1970-89; Assistant Professor of Business, Stanislaus State College, Turlock, California, 1960-61; Engineering Writer, Sr. Publs. Engineer, Sr. Administration Analyst, and Procedures Analyst, Hughes Aircraft Co., Lockheed Missiles & Space Co., General Precision Inc., and Holmes & Narver Inc., 1961-64; Vice-President, California Institute of Asian Studies, 1972-75; Automedica, founder and co-editor, 1970-76. **Publications:** Understanding Automation: A Data Processing Curriculum Guide and Reference Text, 1965; Simplified Computer (Arithmetic, Logic, Input, Flowcharting) series, 4 vols., 1971-72; The 2000-Year History of the Haga-Helgoy and Krick-Keller Families, Ancestors and Descendants, 1994; Before the Apple Drops, 15 Essays on Dinosaur Education, 1994; Exploring Prime Numbers on Your PC, 1994; TARDsolution, A Complete Guide to Interpreting the Tarot, 1994; How to Prepare Your Genealogy for Publication on Your Home Computer, 2001; Exploring Prime Numbers on Your PC and the Internet, 2001. EDITOR: Total Systems, 1962; Automated Educational Systems, 1967; Computer Techniques in Biomedicine and Medicine, 1973. **Address:** 983 Venus Way, Livermore, CA 94550-6345, U.S.A. **Online address:** EnochHaga@msn.com

HAGAR, Judith. See POLLEY, Judith Anne.

HAGEDORN, Jessica Tarahata. American (born Philippines), b. 1949. **Genres:** Poetry, Novellas/Short stories, Novels. **Career:** Writer. Worked as performance artist in late 1970s. **Publications:** Dangerous Music (poems and prose), 1975; Pet Food and Tropical Apparitions (poems and prose), 1981; Dogeaters (novel), 1990; The Gangster of Love (novel), 1996. Work represented in anthologies. **Address:** c/o Harold Schmidt Literary Agency, 343 W. 12th St. #1B, New York, NY 10014, U.S.A.

HAGEDORN, John M. American, b. 1947. **Genres:** Urban studies, Social work. **Career:** Volunteers in Service to America (VISTA), community organizer with Southside Welfare Rights and Milwaukee Organizing Committee, 1968-73; industrial worker and editor of a rank-and-file newspaper in Chelsea, MA, 1974-78; Impact Press Service, Chicago, IL, journalist, 1978-80; Sherman Park Community Association, interim director, community organizer, and coordinator of anti-crime programs, 1982-83; Community Relations-Social Development Commission, Milwaukee, WI, director of Youth Diversion Project, 1983-85; University of Wisconsin-Milwaukee, project director at Urban Research Center, 1985-88; Milwaukee County Department of Health and Human Service, Milwaukee, youth program coordinator, 1988-91; University of Wisconsin-Milwaukee, principal investigator and project director, 199196; University of Illinois at Chicago Circle, Chicago, assistant professor of criminal justice, 1996-. Marquette University, instructor, 1988; Milwaukee Area Technical College, instructor, 1988; Beloit College, seminar speaker, 1990, 1992; Aurora University, instructor, 1992-96. **Publications:** (with P. Macon) People and Folks: Gangs, Crime, and the Underclass in a Rustbelt City, 1988; Forsaking Our Children: Bureaucracy and Reform in the Child Welfare System, 1995. Contributor to books. Contributor of articles and reviews to journals. **Address:** Urban Research Center, University of Wisconsin-Milwaukee, P.O. Box 413, Milwaukee, WI 53201, U.S.A.

HAGELIN, Aiban. Argentine (born Chile), b. 1934. **Genres:** Psychology. **Career:** Medical doctor and training analyst in Buenos Aires, Argentina, 1962-. Philosopher of science. **Publications:** Narcissism: Myth and Theory in Freud's Works, 1985; (coed.) On Freud's "Observations on Transference-Love"; Autism; Incest; Cannibalism. **Address:** Ayacucho 2030 7, 1112 Buenos Aires, Argentina.

HAGER, Alan. American, b. 1940. **Genres:** Literary criticism and history. **Career:** University of Oklahoma, Norman, instructor in English, 1977-79; Loyola University of Chicago, IL, assistant professor of English, 1979-88; University of Illinois, Chicago, visiting lecturer in English, 1989-93; State University of New York College at Cortland, assistant professor, 1993-96, associate professor, 1996-99, professor of English, 2000-. Visiting professor and lecturer at educational institutions; public speaker on literary topics; guest on media programs. **Publications:** Shakespeare's Political Animal: Schema and Schemata in the Canon, 1990; Dazzling Images: The Masks of Sir Philip Sidney, 1991. EDITOR: (and contrib.) Major Tudor Authors: A Bio-Bibliographical Critical Sourcebook, 1997; Understanding Romeo and Juliet: A Student Casebook to Issues, Sources, and Historic Documents, 1999; The Age of Milton: An Encyclopedia of Major 17th-Century British and American Authors, 2004. Contributor to books. Contributor of articles and reviews to academic journals and literary magazines. **Address:** Dept of English, State University of New York, Cortland, PO Box 2000, Cortland, NY 13045, U.S.A. **Online address:** hagera@cortland.edu

HAGER, Betty. American, b. 1923. **Genres:** Novellas/Short stories, Mythology/Folklore, Novels. **Career:** Writer. Participant in Ken Rotcop's Screenplay Workshop. **Publications:** TALES FROM THE BAYOU SERIES: Old Jake and the Pirate's Treasure, 1980, 1994; Miss Tilly and the Haunted Mansion, 1994; Marcie and the Shrimp Boat Adventure, 1994; Marcie and the Monster of the Bayou, 1994. OTHER: The Gift of the Dove (adult novel), 1991. Author of 11 musicals with composer F. Bock, 1977-94. **Address:** c/o Sandy Mackey, Quillco, 3104 Cumberland Ct., Westlake Village, CA 91362, U.S.A.

HAGERMAN, Edward. Canadian, b. 1939. **Genres:** History, International relations/Current affairs, Military/Defense/Arms control, Technology. **Career:** Ohio State University, Columbus, instructor in history, 1965-70; York University, Toronto, Ontario, assistant professor, 1970-76, associate professor, 1976-2002, professor of history, 2002-04, professor emeritus, 2004-. **Publications:** The American Civil War and the Origins of Modern Warfare: Ideas, Organization, and Field Command, 1988; The United States and Biological Warfare: Secrets from the Early Cold War and Korea, 1998. **Address:** Dept of History, Atkinson College, York University, Toronto, ON, Canada M3J 1P3. **Online address:** Hagerman@yorku.ca

HAGGER, Nicholas. British, b. 1939. **Genres:** Novellas/Short stories, Plays/Screenplays, Poetry, History, Philosophy, Autobiography/Memoirs. **Career:** Author, poet, philosopher, and historian. Gregory, Rowcliffe and Co.

(solicitors), London, England, articled clerk, 1957-58; British Council, London, lecturer in English at University of Baghdad, 1961-62, lecturer at Tokyo University of Education, Keio University, and Tokyo University, all 1963-67, lecturer at University of Libya, 1968-70; schoolteacher in London, 1971-73, senior English teacher and department head, 1973-85; Oaklands School, Loughton, England, principal, 1982-. Coopersale Hall School, principal, 1989-; Normanhurst School, principal, 1996-; Otley Hall historic house, proprietor, 1997-2004. Oak-Tree Books Ltd., editorial director, 1984-86. **Publications:** HISTORY: The Fire and the Stones: A Grand Unified Theory of World History and Religion; The Vision of God in Twenty-Five Civilisations, 1991. POEMS: Selected Poems: A Metaphysical's Way of Life, 1991; A White Radiance: The Collected Poems, 1958-1993, 1994; Overlord: The Triumph of Light, 1944-1945: An Epic Poem, 1995-97. PHILOSOPHY: The Universe and the Light: A New View of the Universe and Reality, 1993; The One and the Many (philosophy), 1999. MEMOIRS & DIARIES: A Mystic Way: A Spiritual Autobiography, 1994; Awakening to the Light: Diaries, Vol I: 1958-1967, 1994. STORIES: Collected Stories, Vol I: A Spade Fresh with Mud, Vol II: A Smell of Leaves and Summer, 1995, Vol III: Wheeling Bats and a Harvest Moon, 1999, Vol IV: The Warm Glow of the Monastery Courtyard, 1999. VERSE PLAYS: The Warlords: From D-Day to Berlin: A Verse Drama, 1995; The Tragedy of Prince Tudor, 1999. Author of short stories. Contributor to magazines.

HAGUE, Sir Douglas (Chalmers). British, b. 1926. **Genres:** Education, Economics, Business/Trade/Industry. **Career:** Chairman, Oxford Strategy Network, since 1984. Associate Fellow, Templeton College, Oxford (formerly Oxford Centre for Management Studies), since 1983 (Professorial Fellow, 1981-83). Assistant Lecturer, 1947-50, Lecturer, 1950-57, and Reader in Political Economy, 1957, University College, London; Newton Chambers Professor of Economics, 1957-63, and Head of Dept. of Business Studies, 1962-63, University of Sheffield; Professor of Managerial Economics 1965-81, and Deputy Director 1978-81, Manchester Business School, University of Manchester; British Chairman, Carnegie Corp's Anglo-American Project on Accountability, 1969-72; Chairman, Economic and Social Research Council, 1983-87. **Publications:** (with A. Stonier) A Textbook of Economic Theory, 1953; The Essentials of Economics, 1955; The Economics of Man-Man Fibres, 1957; Managerial Economics, 1969; (with B. Smith) The Dilemma of Accountability in Modern Government, 1971; Pricing in Business, 1971; (with W.J.M. Mackenzie and A. Barker) Public Policy and Private Interests: The Institutions of Compromise, 1975; (with G. Wilkinson) The IRC: An Experiment in Industrial Reorganization, 1983; (ed.) The Management of Science, 1991; Beyond Universities, 1991; Transforming the Dinosaurs, 1993.

HAGY, Alyson. American, b. 1960. **Genres:** Novellas/Short stories. **Career:** Teacher, University of Virginia and University of Southern Maine; University of Michigan, MFA program, teacher; University of Wyoming, teacher. **Publications:** STORIES: Madonna on Her Back, 1986; Hardware River, 1991; Graveyard of the Atlantic, 2000. NOVEL: Keeneland, 2000. Work represented in anthologies. Contributor to periodicals. **Address:** Dept 3353, English, University of Wyoming, 1000 E University Ave, Laramie, WY 82071, U.S.A.

HAGY, James William. American, b. 1936. **Genres:** Local history/Rural topics. **Career:** College of Charleston, Charleston, SC, member of history faculty, 1969-97. American Academy in Rome, Dr. Russell Scott Director of School of Classical Studies, 1976; University of South Carolina, fellow of Institute for Southern Studies, 1987, 1989. Conducted archaeological work in Sardinia, 1985, 1989. **Publications:** Castle's Woods: Frontier Virginia Settlement, 1769-1799, 1966; Castle's Woods and Early Russell County, 1769-1799, 1979; People and Professions in Charleston, S.C., 1782-1802, 1992; This Happy Land: The Jews of Colonial and Antebellum Charleston, 1993; To Take Charleston: The Civil War on Folly Island, 1993. Work represented in anthologies. Contributor to history and archaeology journals and literary journals. **Address:** Department of History, College of Charleston, Charleston, SC 29424, U.S.A.

HAHM, Sung Deuk. Korean, b. 1963. **Genres:** Politics/Government. **Career:** West Virginia University, Morgantown, assistant professor of public administration, 1992-94; Georgetown University, Washington, DC, assistant professor of public policy and business administration, 1994-97, director of Georgetown Center for Asian Public Policy, 1995-97; Korea University, Seoul, assistant professor of public administration and director of advanced program in policy studies, 1996-. Harvard University, researcher at John F. Kennedy School of Government, 1992-94; Ronald Reagan Center for Public Affairs, research associate, 1993-94; Stanford University, visiting scholar at Hoover Institution on War, Revolution, and Peace, 1996. Basil Blackwell (publisher), managing editor of Governance, 1995-97. **Publications:** After Development, 1997. **Address:** Dept of Public Administration, Korea University, S-1 Anamdong, Sungbuk-ku, Seoul 136-701, Republic of Korea. **Online address:** hahm33@hotmail.com

HAHN, Cynthia T. American, b. 1961. **Genres:** Translations. **Career:** University of Illinois at Chicago Circle, assistant professor of French, 1989-90; Lake Forest College, Lake Forest, IL, associate professor, 1990-2003, Hotchkiss fellow, 1993, associate dean of the faculty, 2002-05, professor of French, 2003-. Consultant to relocation firms. **Publications:** TRANSLATOR: E. Accad, Wounding Words: A Woman's Journal in Tunisia (novel), 1996; N. Aba, The Lost Song of a Rediscovered Country, 1999. Contributor to anthologies and academic journals. **Address:** Dept of Foreign Languages & Literatures, Lake Forest College, 555 N Sheridan Rd Box K1, Lake Forest, IL 60045, U.S.A. **Online address:** hahn@lakeforest.edu

HAHN, Frank H(orace). British (born Germany), b. 1925. **Genres:** Economics. **Career:** Universita di Siena, Italy, Professor of Economics, 1989-; Cambridge University, Professor Emeritus, 1992- (Lecturer, 1960-65; Fellow Churchill College, 1960-92; Professor of Economics, 1972-92). Lecturer, 1948-58, and Reader, 1958-60, University of Birmingham; Professor of Economics, London School of Economics, 1965-72. Managing Ed., Review of Economic Studies, 1963-66; President, Econometric Society, 1968-69; Member, Council for Scientific Policy, later Advisory Board, of Research Councils, 1972-75; President, Royal Econometric Society, 1986-89. **Publications:** (with K.J. Arrow) General Competitive Analysis, 1971; The Share of Wages in the National Income, 1972; Money and Inflation, 1982; Equilibrium and Macroeconomics, 1984; Money, Growth and Stability, 1985; (with R. Solow) A Critical Essay on Modern Macroeconomic Theory, 1995. EDITOR: (with F.P.R. Brechling) The Theory of Interest Rates, 1965; Readings in the Theory of Growth, 1971; The Economics of Missing Markets, Information and Games, 1989; (with B. Friedman) Handbook of Monetary Economics, 1990; The Market: Practice and Policy, 1992.

HAHN, Lewis E(dwin). American, b. 1908. **Genres:** Philosophy. **Career:** University of Missouri-Columbia, instructor, 1936-39, assistant professor, 1939-46, associate professor of philosophy, 1946-49; Washington University, St. Louis, MO, professor of philosophy, 194963, department head, 1949-63, associate dean of Graduate School of Arts and Sciences, 1953-54, dean, 1954-63; Southern Illinois University at Carbondale, research professor of philosophy, 1963-77, professor emeritus, 1977-, visiting professor, 1981-. Princeton University, visiting lecturer, 1947; Baylor University, distinguished visiting professor, 1977, 1979, 1980. Illinois Philosophy Conference, president, 1969-71. UNESCO, member of U.S. National Commission, 1965-67. **Publications:** A Contextualistic Theory of Perception, 1942; The Philosophy of Paul Weiss, 1995; The Philosophy of Hans-Georg Gadamer, 1997. EDITOR: (with P.A. Schilpp) The Philosophy of Gabriel Marcel, 1984; (with Schilpp) The Philosophy of W.V. Quine, 1986; (with Schilpp) The Philosophy of John Dewey, 1989; (with Schilpp) The Philosophy of G.H. von Wright, 1989; (with H.M. Kaplan and R.E. McCoy) Charles D. Tenney, The Discovery of Discovery, 1991; The Philosophy of Charles Hartshorne, 1991; The Philosophy of A.J. Ayer, 1992; The Philosophy of Paul Ricoeur, 1994. Contributor to books and philosophy journals. **Address:** Department of Philosophy, Southern Illinois University at Carbondale, Carbondale, IL 62901, U.S.A.

HAHN, Mary Downing. American, b. 1937. **Genres:** Children's fiction, Young adult fiction. **Career:** Prince George's County Memorial Library System, Laurel, Maryland, children's librarian assistant, 1975-91. **Publications:** The Sara Summer, 1979; The Time of the Witch, 1982; Daphne's Book, 1983; The Jellyfish Season, 1985; Wait till Helen Comes: A Ghost Story, 1986; Tallahassee Higgins, 1987; Following the Mystery Man, 1988; December Stillness, 1988; The Doll in the Garden, 1990; The Dead Man in Indian Creek, 1990; The Spanish Kidnapping Disaster, 1991; Stepping on the Cracks, 1991; The Wind Blows Backward, 1993; Time for Andrew, 1994; Look for Me by Moonlight, 1995; The Gentlemen Outlaw and Me, Eli, 1996; Following My Own Footsteps, 1996; As Ever Gordy, 1998; Anna All Year Round, 1999; Promises to the Dead, 2000; Anna on the Farm, 2001; Hear the Wind Blow, 2003.

HAHN, Michael T. American, b. 1953. **Genres:** Novels, Biography. **Career:** Performing musician; writer. Softball and basketball coach. Vermont Outdoors magazine, monthly columnist, feature writer, and photographer; Behind the Times, monthly columnist; Chronicle, journalist; Kingdom Historical, monthly columnist. **Publications:** Ethan Allen: A Life of Adventure, 1994; Ann Story: Vermont's Heroine of Independence, 1996; Alexander Twilight: Vermont's African-American Pioneer, 1998; Dad's Deer

Tactics: Tom Hahn's Hunting Secrets Revealed by His Son, 2003. Contributor to books. Contributor of short fiction to periodicals. **Address:** 869 Kittredge Rd, Orleans, VT 05860, U.S.A.

HAIG, Kathryn. Scottish, b. 1947. **Genres:** Romance/Historical. **Career:** Author of historical romance novels. Women's Royal Army Corps, officer, 1968-74; Civil service, Wiltshire, England, computer programmer, 1975-78; Computel Ltd., Berkshire, England, computer programmer, 1978-80; ICL Ltd., Berkshire, England, computer programmer, 1980-82. **Publications:** Shadows on the Sun, 1992; Secret Sins, 1993; Apple Blossom Time, 1997; a Time to Dance, 2000.

HAIGHT, Mary Ellen Jordan. American, b. 1927. **Genres:** Travel/Exploration. **Career:** Sierra Club, San Francisco, CA, development assistant, 1982-85; Bitburg American High School, Bitburg, Germany, teacher, 1985-86; writer, 1985-; Garden Sullivan Hospital, hospice counselor; San Francisco Volunteer Bureau, program coordinator; American Cancer Society, health educator; San Francisco Bar Association, member of arbitration panel; Sonoma State College, professor. **Publications:** Walks in Gertrude Stein's Paris, 1988; Paris Portraits: Renoir to Chanel, 1991; (with J.J. Haight) Walks in Picasso's Barcelona, 1992. Contributor of travel, biography and art articles to publications. **Address:** 2782 Bush St, San Francisco, CA 94115, U.S.A.

HAIKEN, Elizabeth. American. **Genres:** Medicine/Health. **Career:** University of Tennessee, assistant professor of history. **Publications:** Venus Envy: A History of Cosmetic Surgery, 1998. **Address:** c/o Johns Hopkins University Press, 2715 North Charles St., Baltimore, MD 21218, U.S.A.

HAI LAN. See **GAO YUAN.**

HAILES, Julia. British, b. 1961. **Genres:** Environmental sciences/Ecology, Food and Wine. **Career:** Sustainability Ltd. (environmental communications and consulting company), London, England, director and secretary, 1986-95; Creative Consumer Co-operative, director, 1994-2000; Jupiter Global Green Investment Trust, director, 2001-02; Haller Foundation, trustee, 2003-; writer. BBC Online, Planetfood, monthly column. **Publications:** (with J. Elkington) The Green Consumer Guide, 1988; Green Pages, 1987; The Green Consumer's Supermarket Shopping Guide, 1989; The Young Green Consumer Guide, 1990; The Green Business Guide, 1991; Holidays That Don't Cost the Earth, 1992; (with J. Elkington) Manual 2000, 1998; (with J. Elkington) The New Foods Guide, 1999. **Address:** Tintinhull House, Tintinhull, Somerset BA22 8PZ, England. **Online address:** julia@juliahailes.com; www.juliahailes.com

HAILEY, Arthur. See Obituaries.

HAILEY, Elizabeth Forsythe. American, b. 1938. **Genres:** Novels. **Publications:** A Woman of Independent Means, 1978; Life Sentences, 1982; Joanna's Husband and David's Wife, 1986; Home Free, 1991.

HAILEY, J. P. See **HALL, Parnell.**

HAILEY, (Elizabeth) Kendall. American, b. 1966. **Genres:** Novels, Plays/Screenplays. **Career:** Writer. **Publications:** (Co-author) The Bar Off Melrose (play), 1987; The Day I Became an Autodidact: And the Advice, Adventures, and Acrimonies That Befell Me Thereafter, 1988. **Address:** Molly Friedrich, Aaron M. Priest Literary Agency Inc, 708 Third Ave, 23rd Floor, New York, NY 10017, U.S.A.

HAIN, Peter. British (born Kenya), b. 1950. **Genres:** Mystery/Crime/Suspense, Civil liberties/Human rights, Politics/Government. **Career:** Leader of House of Commons and Secretary of State for Labour, currently; Labour Member of Parliament for Neath, currently. Union of Communication Workers, London, England, research officer, 1976-91; Privy Councillor, Welsh Office Minister, 1991-99, Foreign Minister, 1999-2001, Energy Minister, 2001, Europe Minister, 2001-02. Labour candidate for Parliament, running for Putney, 1983, 1987. **Publications:** Don't Play with Apartheid: The Background to the Stop the Seventy Tour Campaign, 1971; Radical Regeneration, 1975; Mistaken Identity: The Wrong Face of the Law, 1976; (ed.) Community Politics, 1976; (ed. with others) Policing the Police, Volume I, 1979, Volume II, 1980; Neighbourhood Participation, 1980; The Democratic Alternative: A Socialist Response to Britain's Crisis, 1983; Political Trials in Britain, Allen Lane, 1984, 1985; Political Strikes, 1986; Proportional Misrepresentation, 1986; A Putney Plot?, 1987; The Peking Connection, 1995; Ayes to the Left: A Future for Socialism, 1995; Sing the Beloved Country: The Struggle for the New South Africa, 1996 Africa, 1996 Africa, 1996. **Address:** House of Commons, Westminster, London SW1A 0AA, England.

HAINES, David W. American, b. 1947. **Genres:** Anthropology/Ethnology. **Career:** Republic of Vietnam, education adviser and civil affairs specialist, 1969-70; U.S. Office of Refugee Resettlement, research and policy analyst, 1980-84; Virginia Department of Information Technology, Richmond, management consultant, 1988-89; Virginia Workers' Compensation Commission, Richmond, senior manager, 1990-97; George Mason University, Fairfax, VA, associate professor of sociology and anthropology, 1997-. Lecturer at colleges and universities. **Publications:** EDITOR: (and contrib) Refugees in the United States: A Reference Handbook, 1985; Refugees as Immigrants: Cambodians, Laotians, and Vietnamese in America, 1989; (and contrib) Refugees in America in the 1990s: A Reference Handbook, 1996; (with K.E. Rosenblum, and contrib) Illegal Immigration in America: A Reference Handbook, 1999. Contributor to books. Contributor of articles and reviews to periodicals. **Address:** Department of Sociology and Anthropology, George Mason University, Fairfax, VA 22030, U.S.A. **Online address:** dhaines1@gmu.edu

HAINES, John (Meade). American, b. 1924. **Genres:** Poetry, Literary criticism and history, Autobiography/Memoirs, Essays, Translations. **Career:** Homesteader in Alaska, 1947-69; Guggenheim Fellowship, 1965-66, 1984-85; Poet-in-Residence: University of Alaska, Anchorage, 1972-73, Stadler Center for Poetry, Bucknell University, 2001; Visiting Professor: University of Washington, Seattle, 1974, Ohio University, Athens, 1989-90, George Washington University, 1991-92; Visiting Lecturer, University of Montana, Missoula, 1974-75; Distinguished Visiting Lecturer, University of California, Santa Cruz, 1986; Writer-in-Residence: Montalvo Center for the Arts, 1987-88, Djerassi Foundation, 1988; Elliston Fellow, Univ. of Cincinnati, 1993; Chair in Creative Arts, Austin Peay State University (TN), 1993; Resident Writer, Rockefeller Center for Intl Study, Belagio, Italy, 2000. **Publications:** Winter News: Poems, 1966; (trans.) M. Hernandez, El Amor Ascendia, 1967; Suite for the Pied Piper, 1967; The Legend of Paper Plates, 1970; The Mirror, 1971; The Stone Harp, 1971; Twenty Poems, 1971; Leaves and Ashes: Poems, 1974; In Five Years Time, 1976; The Sun on Your Shoulder, 1976; Cicada, 1977; In a Dusty Light, 1977; Living off the Country: Essays on Poetry and Place, 1981; Of Traps and Snares (essays), 1981; Other Days (essays), 1982; News from the Glacier: Selected Poems 1960-1980, 1982; Forest without Leaves, 1984; Stories We Listened To, 1986; The Stars, the Snow, the Fire, 1989; Meditation on a Skull Carved in Crystal, 1989; New Poems, 1980-88, 1990; Rain Country (poetry), 1990; The Owl in the Mask of the Dreamer, Collected Poems, 1993; Fables and Distances, New and Selected Essays, 1996; A Guide to the Four-Chambered Heart, 1997; At the End of This Summer, Poems 1948-54, 1997; For the Century's End, Poems 1990-99, 2001. **Address:** 717 Longstaff, Missoula, MT 59801, U.S.A. **Online address:** haines@mcn.net

HAINING, Peter Alexander. British, b. 1940. **Genres:** Novels, Novellas/Short stories, Criminology/True Crime, Paranormal, Biography. **Career:** New English Library, publrs., London, editorial director, 1970-73. **Publications:** The Clans of Darkness, 1971; The Warlock's Book, 1971; The Lucifer Society, 1972; Eurotunnel, 1973; The Hero (novel), 1974; The Witchcraft Papers, 1974; Ghosts: An Illustrated History, 1974; The Ancient Mysteries Reader, 1975; The Great English Earthquake, 1976; The Compleat Birdman, 1976; The Monster Trap, 1977; Spring Heeled Jack, 1977; The Restless Bones, 1978; Movable Books, 1979; Superstitions, 1979; The Leprechaun's Kingdom, 1979; The Man Who Was Frankenstein, 1980; Sweeney Todd, 1980; Buried Passions, 1980; Dictionary of Ghosts, 1982; The Traction Engine Companion, 1983; The Legend of Brigitte Bardot, 1983; Doctor Who: A Celebration, 1983; The Last Gentleman, 1984; Raquel Welch, 1984; Doctor Who: The Key to Time, 1984; Goldie Hawn, 1985; The Spitfire Log, 1985; Eyewitness to the Galaxy, 1985; For Mother, with Love, 1986; The Race for Mars, 1986; The Television Sherlock Holmes, 1986; The Doctor Who File, 1986; The Savage (novel), 1986; James Bond: A Celebration, 1987; Elvis in Private, 1987; Doctor Who: The Time Traveller's Guide, 1987; The Dracula Centenary Book, 1987; Doctor Who: 25 Glorious Years, 1988; The Scarecrow, 1988; The Day War Broke Out, 1989; Spitfire Summer, 1990; Agatha Christie: Murder in Four Acts-A Centenary Celebration, 1990; The English Highwayman, 1991; The Supernatural Coast, 1992; Sweeney Todd: The Real Story, 1993; The Flesh Eaters, 1993; The Complete Maigret, 1993; On Call with Dr. Finlay, 1993; Agatha Christie's Poirot, 1995; (with P. Tremayne) The Un-Dead, 1997; The Invasion Earth Companion, 1998; Nine Lives of Doctor Who, 1999; A Dictionary of Vampires, 2000; The Jail That Went to Sea, 2003; The Mystery of Rommel's Gold, 2004; Where the Eagle Landed, 2004; A Slip of the Pen, 2004. EDITOR: The Hell of Mirrors, 1966; Where Nightmares Are, 1966; Summoned from the Tomb, 1966; Beyond the Curtain of Dark, 1966; The Future Makers, 1968; The Gentlewomen of Evil, 1967; The Evil People, 1968; The Midnight People, 1968; The Unspeakable People, 1969; The Witchcraft Reader, 1969; A Circle of Witches, 1970; The Hollywood Nightmare, 1970; The Freak Show, 1970; The Wild Night Company, 1970; A Thousand Afternoons, 1970; The Necromancers, 1970; Witchcraft and Black Magic, 1970; The Ghouls, 1971; Tales of Terror, 2 vols., 1972; The Magicians, 1972; Anatomy of Witchcraft, 1972; Nightfrights, 1972; The Nightmare Reader, 1973; The Dream Machines, 1973; The Magic Valley Travellers, 1974; The Monster Makers, 1974; The Hashish Club, 1974; The Sherlock Holmes Scrapbook, 1974; The Fantastic Pulps, 1975; The Ghost's Companion, 1975; An Illustrated History of Witchcraft, 1975; Black Magic Omnibus, 1976; Weird Tales, 1976; First Book (and Second) of Unknown Tales of Horror, 1977-78; Deadly Nightshade, 1977; The Shilling Shockers, 1978; M. R. James Book of the Supernatural, 1979; The Edgar Allan Poe (and Gaston Leroux) Bedside Companion, 2 vols., 1980; The Final Adventures of Sherlock Holmes, 1981; The Best Short Stories of Rider Haggard, 1981; Dead of Night, 1981; Greasepaint and Ghosts, 1982; Lost Stories of W. S. Wilbert, 1982; The Legend of Charlie Chaplin, 1982; Shades of Dracula, 1982; The Complete Ghost Stories of Charles Dickens, 1982; Nightcaps and Nightmares, 1983; Paths to the River Bank, 1983; Christmas Spirits, 1983; Ghost Tour, 1984; Halloween Hauntings, 1984; Tune In for Fear, 1985; Zombie!, 1984; Vampire!, 1984; The Ghost Ship, 1985; Supernatural Sleuths, 1986; Tales of Dungeons and Dragons, 1986; Laughter Before Wicket, 1986; Book of Learned Nonsense, 1987; Supernatural Tales of Rudyard Kipling, 1987; Werewolf!, 1987; Supernatural Tales of Sir Arthur Conan Doyle, 1987; Poltergeist!, 1987; Movie Monsters, 1988; Hole in Fune, 1988; The Mummy!, 1988; The Supernatural Tales of Thomas Hardy, 1988; Charlie Chaplin: A Centenary Celebration, 1989; Hook, Line and Laughter, 1989; Bob Hope: Thanks for the Memory, 1989; W.H. Robinson: Meals on Wheels, 1989; The Legend of Garbo, 1990; Midnight Tales, 1990; The Best Supernatural Tales of Wilkie Collins, 1990; Laughter before Wicket, 1990; The Supernatural Stories of John Buchan, 1991; The Elvis Presley Scrapbooks, 1991; The Fantasy and Mystery Stories of F. Scott Fitzgerald, 1991; Murder on the Menu, 1991; Great Irish Stories of the Supernatural, 1992; Charles Dickens: Christmas Ghost Stories, 1992; The Television Detectives' Omnibus, 1992; Great Irish Detective Stories, 1993; The Television Late-Night Horror Omnibus, 1993; The Frankenstein Omnibus, 1994; Murder at the Races, 1995; London after Midnight, 1996; The Wizards of Odd, 1996; The Vampire Hunters' Casebook, 1996; The Flying Sorcerers, 1997; Timescapes, 1997; The Knights of Madness, 1998; Scary!, 1998; Twentieth Century Ghost Stories, 1998; Death on Wheels, 1999; Haunted House Stories, 2000; Classic Era of American Pulp Magazines, 2001; Classic Era of Crime Fiction, 2002; Scary 2!, 2002. **Address:** Peyton House, Boxford, Suffolk CO10 5DZ, England.

HAINSWORTH, D(avid) R(oger). Australian (born England), b. 1931. **Genres:** History. **Career:** Mitchell Library, Sydney, Australia, research fellow, 1960-62; James Cook University of North Queensland, Townsville, Australia, lecturer in history, 1963-65; University of Adelaide, Adelaide, Australia, lecturer, 1965-70, senior lecturer, 1970-78, associate professor of history, 1979-. **Publications:** Builders and Adventurers: The Traders and the Emergence of the Colony of New South Wales, 1788-1821, 1969; The Sydney Traders, 1788-1821: Simeon Lord and His Contemporaries, 1788-1821, 1972; Stewards, Lords, and People: The Estate Steward and His World in Later Stuart England, 1992; The Swordsmen in Power 1649-1660, 1996; (with C. Churches) The Anglo-Dutch Naval Wars 1652-1674, 1998. EDITOR: Commercial Papers of Sir Christopher Lowther of Whitehaven, 1611-1643, 1974; The Correspondence of Sir John Lowther of Whitehaven, 1693-1698: A Provincial Community in Wartime, 1983; The Correspondence of Lord Fitzwilliam of Milton and Francis Guybon His Steward, 1697-1709, 1990. Work represented in anthologies. Contributor to history journals. **Address:** Department of History, University of Adelaide, Adelaide, SA 5001, Australia. **Online address:** drogerh@mail.mdt.net.au

HAINSWORTH, Peter (R. J.). American. **Genres:** Essays. **Career:** Lady Margaret Hall, Oxford University, Oxford, England, professor. **Publications:** (editor and author of notes, with T. Gwynfor Griffith) Selected Poems of Petrarch, 1971; (editor, with Michael Caesar) Writers and Society in Contemporary Italy: A Collection of Essays, 1984; Petrarch the Poet: An Introduction to the Rerum Vulgarium Fragmenta, 1988; (editor and contributor, with V. Lucchesi, C. Roaf, David Robey, and J. R. Woodhouse) The Languages of Literature in Renaissance Italy, 1988; (editor, with David Robey) The Oxford Companion to Italian Literature, 2002. **Address:** Lady Margaret Hall, Oxford University, Oxford OX2 6QA, England.

HAIRSTON, William. American, b. 1928. **Genres:** Novels, Plays/Screenplays. **Career:** Playwright, author, poet, actor, director, producer, and business administrator. Scriptwriter for U.S. government presentations; professional actor, 1950-57; New York Shakespeare Festival, theater manager and administrator, 1963-66; director: Jericho-Jim Crow, 1964, Curtain Call Mr. Aldridge, Sir!, 1964; Democratic National Committee, radio news editor and correspondent, presidential campaign, 1968; District of Columbia, Executive Office of the Mayor, executive manager, 1970-90; DC Pipeline, Washington, DC, publisher and editor, 1973-79. Ford Foundation, Theatre Administration Grant, 1965-66; National Endowment for the Arts, Literary Study Grant, 1967. **Publications:** PLAYS: Walk in Darkness, 1963; Swan-Song of the 11th Dawn, 1962; Curtain Call Mr. Aldridge, Sir!, 1964; Black Antigone, 1965; Ira Aldridge, 1988; Double Dare, 1995. OTHER: The World of Carlos (novel), 1968; Sex and Conflict (short stories), 1993; Ira Aldridge (The London Conflict), 1998; Space Out: A Space Adventure, 1998; Showdown at Sundown, 1998; History of the National Capital Area Council/Boy Scouts of America, 1998; Passion and Politics (novel), 2001; Swan Song, 2003; Poetry and Prose of Passion & Compassion (poetry), 2002. SCRIPTS FOR US INFORMATION AGENCY: Apollo 11-Man on the Moon (TV program); Media Hora (TV series); Festival of Heritage (short film); Jules Verne vs. Real Flight to the Moon (short film); Operation Money-Wise; English Training-Teaching English as a Second Language; Chicago: Portrait of a City. Contributor of poems to anthologies, books, and magazines. **Address:** 5501 Seminary Rd No 511-S, Falls Church, VA 22041-3904, U.S.A.

HAIZLIP, Shirlee Taylor. American, b. 1937. **Genres:** Adult non-fiction. **Career:** WBNB-TV, St. Thomas, U.S. Virgin Islands, general manager, 1975-81; WNET-TV, NYC, director of corporate communications, 1981-86; National Center for Film and Video Preservation, Los Angeles, CA, executive director, 1989-93. Tufts University, teaching fellow; Allergy Center (Boston, MA), editorial director. **Publications:** The Sweeter the Juice, 1994; In the Garden of Our Dreams, 1998; Finding Grace, 2004. Work represented in anthologies. Contributor of articles, reviews, and editorials to periodicals and newspapers. **Address:** 1754 N Serrano Ave, Los Angeles, CA 90027, U.S.A. **Online address:** haizlip@earthlink.net

HAJDU, David. American, b. 1955. **Genres:** Film, Biography. **Career:** Author and editor of books on entertainment and the arts; Entertainment Weekly magazine, general editor. **Publications:** (with R. Hemming) Discovering Great Singers of Classic Pop: A New Listener's Guide to the Sounds and Lives of the Top Performers and their Recordings, Movies, and Videos, 1991; Lush Life: A Biography of Billy Strayhorn, 1996; Positively 4th Street, 2001. Contributor of articles to periodicals. EDITOR: Video Review's Best on Home Video, 1985. **Address:** c/o Chris Calhoun, Sterling Lord Literistic Inc., 65 Bleecker St., New York, NY 10012, U.S.A.

HAKALA, Dee. (born United States), b. 1958. **Genres:** Adult non-fiction. **Career:** Lake Charles Memorial Hospital, Lake Charles, LA, developer, instructor, and program director of exercise programs, 1991-93; MWR Sports, Governors Island, NY, program director, fitness instructor, and personal trainer, 1993-94; Advanced Health and Fitness Club, Detroit, MI, program director, fitness instructor, and personal trainer, 1998-99; Young Women's Christian Association, Aurora, IL, program director, 2001-. C.H.O.I.C.E.S. VVV with De, Inc., president and chief executive officer; New Face of Fitness (exercise and well-ness program), founder; Rush Copley Healthplex, personal trainer and fitness instructor; public speaker on fitness and exercise topics. American Council on Exercise, certified fitness instructor, 1991-, certified personal trainer, 1993-; certified by Aerobics and Fitness Association of America, 1995-; American College of Sports Medicine, certified health and fitness trainer, 1996-; American Red Cross, certified lifeguard, 2001. Laubach Literacy Volunteer Service, tutor, 1989-93; Women's Commission of Southwest Louisiana, member, 1992-93; P.L.A.Y., creator, facilitator, and volunteer teacher of activities courses, 1994-97. **Publications:** (with Micheal D'Orso) Thin Is Just a Four Letter Word: Living Fit for All Shapes and Sizes, 1997. **Address:** 3024 Long Grove Ln., Aurora, IL 60504, U.S.A. **Online address:** DeeVVV@aol.com

HAKEEM, Brother Wali. See GILL, Walter.

HAKIM, Catherine. British, b. 1948. **Genres:** Sociology, Women's studies and issues. **Career:** Conducted field research in Caracas, Venezuela, 1969-72; Tavistock Institute, London, research officer, 1972-74; British Office of Population Censuses and Surveys (now Office of National Statistics), London, senior research officer, 1974-78; British Dept of Employment, London, principal research officer, 1978-89; University of Essex, Colchester, England, professor of sociology and director of ESRC Data Archive, 1989-90; University of London, London School of Economics and Political Science, Morris Ginsberg fellow to senior research fellow in sociology, 1993-. **Publications:** (with W.R. Hawes) Labour Force Statistics, 1982; Secondary

Analysis in Social Research, 1982; Research Design: Strategies and Choices in the Design of Social Research, 1987; Key Issues in Women's Work, 1996; (ed. with H.-P. Blossfeld, and contrib.) Between Equalization and Marginalization: Women Working Part-Time in Europe and the USA, 1997; Social Change and Innovation in the Labour Market, 1998; Work-Lifestyle Choices in the 21st Century: Preference Theory, 2000; Models of the Family in Europe: Ideals and Realities, 2003; Key Issues in Women's Work, 2004. Contributor to books and professional journals. **Address:** Dept of Sociology, London School of Economics and Political Science, University of London, Houghton St, London WC2A 2AE, England. **Online address:** c.hakim@lse. ac.uk

HALAM, Ann. See JONES, Gwyneth A(nn).

HALBERSTAM, David. American, b. 1934. **Genres:** International relations/ Current affairs, Politics/Government, Biography. **Career:** Member of staff, Daily Times Leader, West Point, MS, 1955-56, and Nashville Tennessean, 1956-60; New York Times, NYC, foreign correspondent in Congo, Vietnam, and Eastern Europe, 1960-67; Harper's Magazine, NYC, contributing editor, 1967-71. Recipient, Pulitzer Prize for International Reporting, 1964. **Publications:** The Noblest Roman, 1961; The Making of a Quagmire, 1965, 2nd ed. as The Making of a Quagmire: America and Vietnam during the Kennedy Era, 1987; One Very Hot Day, 1968; The Unfinished Odyssey of Robert Kennedy, 1969; Ho, 1971; The Best and Brightest, 1972; The Powers That Be, 1979; The Breaks of the Game, 1981; The Amateurs, 1985; The Reckoning, 1986; The Summer of '49, 1989; The Next Century, 1991; The Fifties, 1993; October 1964, 1994; Kansas City: 100 Years of Championship Jayhawk Basketball, 1997; The Children, 1998; Playing for Keeps: Michael Jordan and the World That Made Him, 1999; (ed.) Best American Sports Writing of the Century, 1999; War in a Time of Peace, 2001; New York September 11, 2001; Firehouse, 2002; The Teammates, 2003. **Address:** c/o Hyperion, 77 W 66th St, New York, NY 10023, U.S.A.

HALDAR, Achintya. American (born India), b. 1945. **Genres:** Engineering. **Career:** Kuljian Corp., Calcutta, India, student engineer, 1967; Paharpur-Marley Cooling Tower Engineers, Calcutta, India, design engineer, 1968-70; Engineers India Ltd., New Delhi, India, junior engineer, 1970-72; Marco Steel Supply Co., Champaign, IL, designer, 1972; Bechtel Power Corp., Norwalk, CA, staff engineer, 1978; Illinois Institute of Technology-Chicago, assistant professor of civil engineering, 1978-79; Georgia Institute of Technology-Atlanta, assistant professor, 1979-85, associate professor of civil engineering, 1985-88; University of Arizona-Tucson, professor of civil engineering and engineering mechanics, 1988-. University of Trondheim, visiting scholar at Norwegian Institute of Technology, 1995; Academy of Sciences of the Czech Republic, visiting professor at Institute of Theoretical and Applied Mechanics, 2002; guest speaker throughout the world, including China; consultant. **Publications:** Probability Concepts in Engineering Planning and Design, Vol. 1: Basic Principles: Solution Manual, 1975; (ed., with B.M. Ayyub and A. Guran) Uncertainty Modeling in Vibration, Control, and Fuzzy Analysis of Systems, 1997; (ed., with B.M. Ayyub and A. Guran, and contrib) Uncertainty Modeling in Finite Element, Fatigue, and Stability of Systems, 1997; (with S. Mahadevan) Probability, Reliability, and Statistical Methods in Engineering Design, with solutions manual (with Mahadevan and J. Huh), 2000; (with S. Mahadevan) Reliability Assessment Using Stochastic Finite Element Analysis, 2000. Contributor to scientific books on engineering. Contributor to scientific and technical journals. **Address:** Department of Civil Engineering and Engineering Mechanics, University of Arizona, Tucson, AZ 85721, U.S.A. **Online address:** haldar@u.arizona.edu

HALDEMAN, Joe (William). Also writes as Robert Graham. American, b. 1943. **Genres:** Novels, Novellas/Short stories, Horror, Science fiction/ Fantasy, Plays/Screenplays, Poetry. **Career:** Freelance writer, 1970-; University of Iowa, Iowa City, teaching assistant, 1975; Astronomy mag., Milwaukee, editor, 1976; Massachusetts Institute of Technology, adjunct professor, 1983-. Science Fiction Writers of America, former treasurer. Science Fiction and Fantasy Writers of America, president, 1992-94. **Publications:** War Year, 1972; The Forever War, 1975; (as Robert Graham) Attar 1: Attar's Revenge, 1975; (as Robert Graham) Attar 2: War of Nerves, 1975; Mindbridge, 1976; Planet of Judgment, 1977; All My Sins Remembered, 1977; Infinite Dreams (short stories), 1978; World without End, 1979; Worlds, 1981; (with J.C. Haldeman) There Is No Darkness, 1983; Worlds Apart, 1983; The Forever War (stage play), 1984; Dealing in Futures (short stories), 1985; Tool of the Trade, 1987; Buying Time, 1989; The Hemingway Hoax, 1990; Robot Jox (screenplay), 1990; Worlds Enough and Time, 1992; Vietnam and Other Alien Worlds (essays, poetry, stories), 1993; "1968," 1995; None So Blind (short stories), 1996; Forever Peace, 1997; Saul's Death and Other Poems (poetry), 1997; Forever Free, 1999; The Coming,

2000; Guardian, 2002; Camouflage, 2004; Old Twentieth, 2005. EDITOR: Cosmic Laughter, 1974; Study War No More, 1977; Nebula Awards 17, 1984. **Address:** 5412 NW 14th Ave, Gainesville, FL 32605, U.S.A.

HALDON, John F. British. **Genres:** History, Military/Defense/Arms control. **Career:** Educator and author. University of Birmingham, Birmingham, England, reader in history. **Publications:** Recruitment and Conscription in the Byzantine Army c. 550-950: A Study on the Origins of the Stratiotika, 1979; Byzantine Praetorians: An Administrative, Institutional, and Social Survey of the Opsikion and Tagmata, c. 580-900, 1984; (trans. and author of intro. and commentary) Constantine VII Porphyrogenitus, Three Treatises on Imperial Military Expeditions, 1990; Byzantium in the Seventh Century: The Transformation of a Culture, 1990; The State and the Tributary Mode of Production, 1993; State, Army, and Society in Byzantium: Approaches to Military, Social, and Administrative History, 6th-12th Centuries, 1995; Warfare, State, and Society in the Byzantine World, 565-1204, 1999; Byzantium: A History, 2000; (with L. Brubaker) Byzantium in the Iconoclast Era (c. 680-850): The Sources: An Annotated Survey, 2001; The Byzantine Wars: Battles and Campaigns of the Byzantine Era, 2001; Byzantium at War, 2002. Contributor to books. **Address:** Centre for Byzantine Studies, Ottoman & Modern Greek Studies, University of Birmingham, Edgbaston, Birmingham B15 2TT, England. **Online address:** HaldonJF@hhs.bham.ac.uk

HALE, Antoinette. See STOCKENBERG, Antoinette.

HALE, Douglas. American, b. 1929. **Genres:** Genealogy/Heraldry, History, Military/Defense/Arms control. **Career:** University of North Carolina at Chapel Hill, assistant professor of history, 1961-63; Oklahoma State University, Stillwater, professor of history, 1963-82. **Publications:** The Germans from Russia in Oklahoma, 1980; The Third Texas Cavalry in the Civil War, 1993; Wanderers between Two Worlds: German Rebels in the American West, 1830-1860, 2004. **Address:** PO Box 1051, Stillwater, OK 74076, U.S.A.

HALE, Janice E(llen). American, b. 1948. **Genres:** Education. **Career:** Wayne State University, Detroit, MI, professor of education, 1991-. Educational consultant on the education of African-American children. **Publications:** Black Children: Their Roots, Culture, and Learning Styles, 1982; Unbank the Fire: Visions for the Education of African-American Children, 1994; Learning while Black: Creating Educational Excellence for African-American Children, 2001. **Address:** College of Education, Wayne State University, 5462 Gullen Mall Room 213, Detroit, MI 48231, U.S.A. **Online address:** JaniceEHale@cs.com

HALE, John. British, b. 1926. **Genres:** Novels, Plays/Screenplays. **Career:** Freelance writer and dir., 1964-. Founder and Artistic Director, Lincoln Theatre, 1955-58; Artistic Director, Arts Theatre, Ipswich, 1958-59, and Bristol Old Vic, 1959-61; Member, Board of Govs., and Associate Artistic Director, Greenwich Theatre, London, 1963-71. **Publications:** NOVELS: Kissed the Girls and Made Them Cry, 1963; The Grudge Fight, 1964; A Fool at the Feast, 1966; The Paradise Man, 1969; The Fort, 1973; The Love School, 1974; Lovers and Heretics, 1976; The Whistle Blower, 1984; PLAYS: The Black Swan Winter, 1968; It's All in the Mind, 1969; Spithead, 1969; Lorna and Ted, 1970; Love's Old Sweet Song, 1976; The Case of David Anderson, Q. C. 1980. SCRIPTS AND SCREENPLAYS: Nostromo (TV), 1996; Scum of the Earth (screenplay), 1999; Borrowed Time (TV), 1999; Children of the North (TV), 1998. **Address:** c/o Stephen Durbridge, Lemon, Unna and Durbridge Ltd, 24 Pottery Lane, London W11 4LZ, England.

HALE, Michael. See BULLOCK, Michael (Hale).

HALE, Nathan G., Jr. American, b. 1922. **Genres:** Psychology. **Career:** University of California, Berkeley, lecturer in history, 1965-69; University of California, Riverside, professor of history, 1970-79, professor emeritus, 1979-. Stanford University, visiting professor, 1982-83. **Publications:** (with K. Beutner) Emotional Illness: How Families Can Help, 1957; Freud and the Americans, Vol. I: The Beginnings of Psychoanalysis in the United States, 1876-1917, 1971, Vol. II: The Rise and Crisis of Psychoanalysis in America, 1917-1985, 1995. EDITOR & AUTHOR OF INTRO.: James Jackson Putnam and Psychoanalysis: Letters Between Putnam, Sigmund Freud, William James, Ernest Jones, Sandor Ferenczi, and Morton Prince, 1971; Psychotherapy and Multiple Personality: Selected Papers of Morton Prince, 1975. Contributor to books. **Address:** 309 Pala Ave., Piedmont, CA 94611, U.S.A.

HALE, Robert D(avid). American, b. 1928. **Genres:** Novels, Literary criticism and history, Photography, Autobiography/Memoirs, Essays. **Career:** Westwinds Bookshop, Duxbury, MA, manager, 1953-57; Curtiss Johnson

Publications, Deep River, CT, managing editor, 195761; Connecticut College Bookshop, New London, general manager, 1961-69; Hathaway House Bookshop, Wellesley, MA, president, 1969-77; American Booksellers Association, New York City, associate executive director, 1977-83; Westwinds Bookshop, owner, 1983-90; writer. Lecturer on books throughout New England and the southeastern United States. Member of founding committee and executive committee, Center for the Book, Library of Congress; member of White House Library Committee. Provided recreational reading for the White House and Camp David during Carter administration. **Publications:** (ed. and contrib.) Manual on Bookselling, 3rd ed., 1980, 4th ed., 1987; Massachusetts (photography and essays), 1992. NOVELS: The Elm at the Edge of the Earth, 1990; The Cloud Dweller, 2003. **Address:** 374 High St, Pembroke, MA 02359, U.S.A.

HALES, Steven D(ouglas). American, b. 1966. **Genres:** Philosophy. **Career:** Georgia State University, Atlanta, visiting assistant professor of philosophy, 1992-94; Bloomsburg University, Bloomsburg, PA, associate professor, 1994-2001, professor of philosophy, 2001-. **Publications:** (with R. Welshon) Nietzsche's Perspectivism, 2000. Contributor to periodicals. **Address:** Department of Philosophy, Bloomsburg University, Bloomsburg, PA 17815, U.S.A. **Online address:** hales@bloomu.edu

HALEVI, Zev ben Shimon. *See* KENTON, Warren.

HALEY, Gail E(inhart). American, b. 1939. **Genres:** Children's fiction, Novellas/Short stories, Illustrations. **Publications:** My Kingdom for a Dragon, 1962; The Wonderful Magical World of Marguerite, 1964; Round Stories about Things That Live on Land, 1966; Round Stories about Things That Live in Water, 1966; Round Stories about Things that Grow, 1966; Round Stories about Our World, 1966; A Story, a Story: An African Tale, Retold, 1970; Noah's Ark, 1971; Jack Jouett's Ride, 1973; The Abominable Swamp Man, 1975; The Post Office Cat, 1976; Go Away, Stay Away!, 1977; Costumes for Plays and Playing, 1978; Gail Haley's Costume Book, Volume I: Dress Up and Have Fun, 1979; A Story, a Day, 1979; Gail Haley's Costume Book, Volume II: Dress Up and Play, 1980; The Green Man, 1980; Birdsong, 1984; Jack and the Bean Tree, 1986; Play People: Pupperty in Education, 1988; Marguerite, 1988; (retold by and illus.) Jack and the Fire Dragon, 1988; Sea Tale, 1990; Puss in Boots, 1991; Mountain Jack Tales, 1992; (with D.M. Considine) Visual Messages: Integrating Imagery into Instruction (textbook), 1992; Dream Peddler, 1993; Imagine That: Developing Critical Thinking Skills through Children's Books, 1994; Two Bad Boys, 1996. Illustrator of books by B.K. Hunt, E.L. Konigsburg, R.P. Russell. **Address:** PO Box 1023, Blowing Rock, NC 28605, U.S.A.

HALFORD, Graeme S(ydney). Australian, b. 1937. **Genres:** Psychology, Education. **Career:** University of Newcastle, Australia, lecturer, 1965-70, senior lecturer in psychology, 1971-72; Queen's University, Kingston, Ontario, associate professor of psychology, 1972-75; University of Queensland, Brisbane, Australia, senior lecturer, 1975-79, reader, 1980-89, professor of psychology, 1989-. International Geosphere-Biosphere Programme, member of national committee. **Publications:** The Development of Thought, 1982; Children's Understanding: The Development of Mental Models, 1993; Developing Cognitive Competence: New Approaches to Process Modelling, 1995; (co-author) Mathematics Education. **Address:** School of Psychology, University of Queensland, Brisbane, QLD 4072, Australia. **Online address:** gsh@psy.uq.edu.au

HALKIN, Ariela. Israeli, b. 1942. **Genres:** Literary criticism and history. **Career:** Tel Aviv University, Tel Aviv, Israel, teacher of history. Director of family-owned businesses in Israel and Europe. **Publications:** The Enemy Reviewed: German Popular Literature through British Eyes between the Two World Wars, 1995. **Address:** 11 Hashikma St., 56518 Savyon, Israel. **Online address:** Halkin@netvision.net.il

HALL, Ann C. American, b. 1959. **Genres:** Literary criticism and history. **Career:** Marquette University, Milwaukee, WI, assistant professor of English, 1989-91; Ohio Dominican University, Columbus, associate professor of English, 1994-. Contemporary American Theatre Company, dramaturg and education director, 1991-94. **Publications:** "A Kind of Alaska": Women in the Plays of O'Neill, Pinter, and Shepard, 1993; (ed.) Delights, Desires, and Dilemmas: Essays on Women and the Media. Author of short plays. Contributor to theater journals. **Address:** Ohio Dominican University, Columbus, OH 43219, U.S.A. **Online address:** halla@ohiodominican.edu

HALL, Bert S(tewart). American, b. 1945. **Genres:** History. **Career:** State University of New York at Buffalo, assistant professor of history, 1972-77; University of Toronto, Toronto, Ontario, associate professor of history at

Institute for the History and Philosophy of Science and Technology, 1977-. **Publications:** Technological Illustrations, 1976; (ed.) Health, Disease, and Healing in Medieval Culture, 1991; Weapons and Warfare in Renaissance Europe: Gunpowder, Technology, and Tactics, 1997. **Address:** Room 316, Victoria College, University of Toronto, Toronto, ON, Canada M5S 1K7. **Online address:** bert.hall@utoronto.ca

HALL, Blaine H(ill). American, b. 1932. **Genres:** Librarianship, Literary criticism and history, Bibliography. **Career:** High school English teacher in Clearfield, UT, 1960-61; Brigham Young University, Provo, UT, instructor in English, 1963-72, senior English and American literature librarian at Harold B. Lee Library, 1972-96. **Publications:** (With C. Bradshaw and M. Wiggins) Using the Library: The Card Catalog, 1971; Collection Assessment Manual for College and University Libraries, 1985; (with G. Cronin) Saul Bellow: An Annotated Bibliography, 2nd ed., 1987; (with G. Cronin) Jerzy Kosinski: An Annotated Bibliography, 1991; (with G. Cronin and C. Lamb) Jewish American Fiction Writers: An Annotated Bibliography, 1991; (with G. Bach) Conversations with Grace Paley, 1997. **Address:** 230 E 1910 South, Orem, UT 84058, U.S.A. **Online address:** bhall11@att.net

HALL, Brian. American, b. 1959. **Genres:** Novels, Politics/Government, Travel/Exploration. **Career:** Freelance writer/author, 1984-. **Publications:** Stealing from a Deep Place: Travels in Southeastern Europe, 1988; The Dreamers (novel), 1989; The Impossible Country: A Journey through the Last Days of Yugoslavia, 1994; The Saskiad (novel), 1996; Madeleine's World: A Child's Journey from Birth to Age Three, 1988. Contributor to periodicals. **Address:** c/o David Chalfant, IMG Literary, 825 7th Ave, New York, NY 10019, U.S.A.

HALL, Carl W. American, b. 1924. **Genres:** Agriculture/Forestry, Engineering, Food and Wine, Technology. **Career:** U.S. Army, 1943-46; University of Delaware, Newark, instructor to assistant professor, 1948-51; Michigan State University, East Lansing, assistant professor to professor of agricultural engineering and chairman of dept, 1951-70; Washington State University, Pullman, professor of mechanical engineering and dean of College of Engineering, 1970-82; National Science Foundation, Washington, DC, deputy assistant director, Directorate for Engineering, 1982-90; Engineering Information Services, Arlington, VA, engineer, 1990-. President, ACA Engineering Consultants, 1960-70, and Washington State University Research Foundation, 1973-82; engineer, ESCOE, Inc., 1979; consultant; lecturer in Japan. **Publications:** Drying Farm Crops, 1957; (with C.B. Richey and P. Jacobson) Agricultural Engineers' Handbook, 1961; Agricultural Engineering Index, 1907-1960, 1961, (with G.E. Hall) 1961-1970, 1972, (with J. Basselman) 1971-1980, 1982, (with J. Basselman) 1981-1985, 1986; Processing Equipment for Agricultural Products, 1963, rev. ed. (with D.C. Davis), 1979; (with T. Hedrick) Drying of Milk and Milk Products, 1966; (with F. Salas) Equipo para Procesamiento de Productos Agricolas, 1968; (with A.W. Farrall and A.L. Rippen) Encyclopedia of Food Engineering, 1971, 2nd ed. (sr. ed.), 1986; (with M.L. Esmay) Agricultural Mechanization in Developing Countries, 1973; (with D.B. Brooker and F.W. Bakker) Drying Cereal Grains, 1974; (with W.J. Harper) Technology and Engineering of Dairy Manufacturing, 1976; Errors in Experimentation, 1977; Dictionary of Drying, 1979; Drying and Storage of Agricultural Crops, 1980; Biomass as an Alternative Fuel, 1981; (with G. Hinman) Dictionary of Energy, 1983; (with D. Pimentel) Food and Energy Resources, 1984; (with D. Pimentel) Food and Natural Resources, 1989; (with O. Kitani) Biomass Handbook, 1989; (with W. Vergara and N. Hay) Natural Gas, 1990; (with D. Brooker and F. Bakker-Arkema) Drying and Storage of Grains and Oil Seeds, 1992; The Age of Synthesis, 1995; Laws and Models, 1999. **Address:** 2454 N Rockingham St, Arlington, VA 22207-1033, U.S.A.

HALL, David C. American, b. 1943. **Genres:** Mystery/Crime/Suspense, Novels. **Career:** Self-employed English teacher in Barcelona, Spain, 1974-75; Summit School of English, Barcelona, teacher, 1975-79; English Three, Barcelona, teacher, 1980-; writer. Worked as a janitor, laborer in a frozen food plant, mail handler, forest service crew member, farm laborer, cook, bartender, library clerk, railroad clerk, and book warehouse clerk. **Publications:** CRIME NOVELS: Four Days, 1984; The Real Thing, 1988; Return Trip Ticket, 1992. Works have been translated into Spanish. **Address:** Avenida Virgen de Montserrat 18, Sant Cugat del Valles, 08190 Barcelona, Spain.

HALL, David Locke. American, b. 1955. **Genres:** Politics/Government, Military/Defense/Arms control. **Career:** Department of Justice, Philadelphia, PA, assistant U.S. attorney. **Publications:** The Reagan Wars: A Constitutional Perspective on War Powers and the Presidency, Westview, 1991. **Address:** c/o Westview Press Inc., 5500 Central Ave., Boulder, CO 80301, U.S.A.

HALL, Donald (Andrew), (Jr.). American, b. 1928. **Genres:** Children's fiction, Poetry, Art/Art history, Literary criticism and history. **Career:** Paris Review, Paris and NYC, poetry editor, 1953-62; Harvard University, Cambridge, MA, Society of Fellows, junior fellow, 1954-57; University of Michigan, Ann Arbor, assistant professor, 1957-61, associate professor, 1961-66, professor of English, 1966-76. **Publications:** Poems, 1952; Exile, 1952; To the Loud Wind and Other Poems, 1955; Exiles and Marriages, 1955; The Dark Houses, 1958; Andrew the Lion Farmer, 1959; String Too Short to Be Saved: Childhood Reminiscences, 1961; A Roof of Tiger Lilies: Poems, 1964; An Evening's Frost (play), 1965; Henry Moore: The Life and Work of Great Sculptor, 1966; The Alligator Bride, 1968; Marianne Moore: The Cage and the Animal, 1970; As the Eye Moves: A Sculpture by Henry Moore, 1970; The Yellow Room Love Poems, 1971; The Gentleman's Alphabet Book, 1972; Playing Around, 1974; A Blue Wing Tilts at the Edge of the Sea, 1975; Dock Ellis in the Country of Baseball, 1976; Remembering Poets, 1978; Goatfoot Milktongue Twinbird: Interviews, Essays, and Notes on Poetry 1970-76, 1978; Kicking the Leaves, 1978; Ox Cart Man, 1979; To Keep Moving, 1980; The Weather for Poetry, 1982; The Man Who Lived Alone, 1984; Fathers Playing Catch with Sons, 1985; The Happy Man, 1986; The Ideal Bakery, 1987; The Bone Ring, 1987; Seasons at Eagle Pond, 1987; Poetry and Ambition, 1988; The One Day, 1988; Anecdotes of Modern Art, 1990; Old and New Poems, 1990; Here at Eagle Pond, 1990; Their Ancient Glittering Eyes, 1991; The Museum of Clear Ideas, 1993; Life Work, 1993; When Willard Met Babe Ruth, 1996; Without, 1998; The Old Life, 1996; The Painted Bed, 2002; Willow Temple, 2003; Breakfast Served Any Time All Day (essays), 2003. EDITOR: The Harvard Advocate Anthology, 1950; (with R. Pack and L. Simpson) New Poets of England and America, 1957; Whittier, 1961; (with R. Pack) New Poets of England and America: Second Selection, 1962; Contemporary American Poetry, 1962; (with S. Spender) The Concise Encyclopedia of English and American Poets and Poetry, 1963; (with W. Taylor) Poetry in English, 1963; The Faber Book of Modern Verse, rev. ed., 1965; A Choice of Whitman's Verse, 1968; The Modern Stylists, 1968; Man and Boy: An Anthology, 1968; American Poetry: An Introductory Anthology, 1969; The Pleasures of Poetry, 1971; Writing Well, 1973, 5th ed., 1985; A Writer's Reader, 1976, 9th ed., 2002; To Read Literature, 1981; The Oxford Book of American Literary Anecdotes, 1981; Claims for Poetry, 1982; To Read Poetry, 1982; The Contemporary Essay, 1984, 3rd ed., 1995; The Oxford Book of Children's Verse in America, 1985; To Read Fiction, 1987; The Oxford Illustrated Book of American Children's Poems, 1999. **Address:** Eagle Pond Farm, 24 US Rte 4, Wilmot, NH 03287, U.S.A.

HALL, Gimone. Also writes as Shannon Willow. American, b. 1940. **Genres:** Novels. **Publications:** The Blue Taper, 1970; Witch's Suckling, 1970, 3rd ed., 1973; Devil's Walk, 1971; The Silver Strand, 1974; The Juliet Room, 1975; Hide My Savage Heart, 1976; Rapture's Mistress, 1978; Fury's Son, Passion's Moon, 1979; Ecstasy's Empire, 1980; The Jasmine Veil, 1982; Rules of the Heart, 1984; The Kiss Flower, 1985; (as Shannon Willow) Texas Jewel, 1993. **Address:** Million Wishes Farm, 55 Brennan Rd, Ottsville, PA 18942, U.S.A. **Online address:** romance@epix.net

HALL, H(ugh) Gaston. American, b. 1931. **Genres:** Poetry, Literary criticism and history. **Career:** Yale University, New Haven, CT, instructor in French, 1958-60; University of Glasgow, Scotland, lecturer in French, 1960-64; University of California, Berkeley, assistant professor, 1963; Monash University, Clayton, Australia, senior lecturer in French, 1965; University of Warwick, Coventry, England, senior lecturer, 1966-74, reader in French, 1974-89, chairman of School of Spanish, 1986-87, emeritus reader, 1989-. City University of New York, visiting professor, 1970-72. **Publications:** Moliere: Tartuffe, 1960; Quadruped Octaves, 1983; Comedy in Context: Essays on Moliere, 1984; Alphabet Aviary (poems), 1986; Moliere's Le Bourgeois Gentilhomme: Context and Stagecraft, 1990; Richelieu's Desmarets and the Century of Louis XIV, 1990; Sonnets, 2002; Reptile Rhymes (poems), 2002; Domestic Tales and Other Poems, 2002; Sketches (poems), 2003; Quatrains (poems), 2004. TRANSLATOR: (and author of notes) F. Simone, The French Renaissance, 1970; J. de La Fontaine, Forty Fables, 2002. EDITOR: Desmarets de Saint-Sorlin, les Visionnaires, 1963, rev. ed., 1995; Moliere: Les Femmes Savantes, 1974; Pierre Cerou, L'Amant auteur et valet: Comedie (title means: The Lover, Author, and Valet), 1978; Melanges a la memoire de F. Simone (title means: Miscellany in Memory of F. Simone), 4 vols., 1980-84; Critical Bibliography of French Literature, Vol. III A, 1983; W.E. Sly Jr., Poems, 2002. **Address:** 18 Abbey End, Kenilworth, Warwickshire CV8 1LS, England.

HALL, Ivan P(arker). American (born Bulgaria), b. 1932. **Genres:** Area studies. **Career:** Writer and historian. Worked in military intelligence, West Germany, 1954-56; worked for United States Information Service in Kabul, Afghanistan, and Dacca, East Pakistan, 1958-61; Philadelphia Bulletin, Japan correspondent, 1970-77; Washington Star, Japan correspondent, 1970-77; Japan-U.S. Friendship Commission, Japan Representative and Associate Executive Director, 1977-84; Tsukuba University, professor of international cultural relations and intellectual history, 1985-93; Keio University, professor of international cultural relations and intellectual history, 1985-93; Gakushuin University, professor of international cultural relations and intellectual history, 1985-93; Japan Policy Research Institute, Cardiff, CA, member of board of advisers, c. 1993-. Consultant to the Harvard-Yenching Institute for East Asia and for Harvard's Japan Fund Drive. **Publications:** Mori Arinori, 1973; Cartels of the Mind: Japan's Intellectual Closed Shop, 1997; Bamboozled! How America Loses the Intellectual Game with Japan and Its Implications for Our Future in Asia, 2002. **Address:** Liluokalani Gardens #803, 300 Y Nani Way, Honolulu, HI 96815, U.S.A. **Online address:** ivanphall@hotmail.com

HALL, J(ohn) C(live). British, b. 1920. **Genres:** Poetry, Literary criticism and history, Biography. **Career:** Former book and magazine publisher. **Publications:** (with K. Douglas and N. Nicholson) Selected Poems, 1943; The Summer Dance and Other Poems, 1951; (ed. with P. Dickinson and E. Marx) New Poems 1955, 1955; Edwin Muir, 1956; (ed. with W. Muir) Collected Poems of Edwin Muir, 1921-1958, 1960; The Burning Hare, 1966; (ed. with G.S. Fraser and J. Waller) The Collected Poems of Keith Douglas, rev. ed., 1966; A House of Voices, 1973; Selected and New Poems 1939-1984, 1985; Long Shadows: Poems 1938-2002, 2003. **Address:** 9 Warwick Rd, Mount Sion, Tunbridge Wells, Kent TN1 1YL, England.

HALL, James. British, b. 1918. **Genres:** Art/Art history, History, Travel/Exploration. **Publications:** Dictionary of Subjects and Symbols in Art, 1974; (ed.) Ehresmann's Pocket Dictionary of Art Terms, 1980; A History of Ideas and Images in Italian Art, 1983; Illustrated Dictionary of Symbols in Western and Eastern Art, 1994; (trans. & field research) Domenico Laffi's Viaggio in Ponente a San Giacomo...1681 (travel), 1996. **Address:** 19 Milton Rd, Harpenden, Herts. AL5 5LA, England. **Online address:** JamesHall@harpenden.swinternet.co.uk

HALL, Joan Wylie. American, b. 1947. **Genres:** Literary criticism and history, Women's studies and issues, Reference. **Career:** Franklin News-Herald, Franklin, PA, general reporter, summers 1966-69; University of Notre Dame, teaching assistant, 1971-72, part-time instructor, 1973-74; Saint Mary-of-the-Woods College, instructor, 1974-78; Harvard University, preceptor for junior English tutorials, 1983-84; University of Mississippi, part-time instructor, 1979-83, 1984-. **Publications:** Shirley Jackson: A Study of the Short Fiction, 1993; Conversations with Audre Lorde, 2004. Contributor of articles and book reviews to journals, reference books, and essay collections. **Address:** English Dept, University of Mississippi, University, MS 38677, U.S.A. **Online address:** egjwh@olemiss.edu

HALL, Kathleen (Mary). British, b. 1924. **Genres:** Literary criticism and history, Translations. **Career:** Queen's University, Belfast, assistant lecturer, 1953-55; University of Southampton, lecturer, 1955-69, sr. lecturer in French 1969-85. **Publications:** Pontus de Tyard and His Discours Philosophiques, 1963; (ed. with K. Cameron and F. Higman) Theodore de Beze: Abraham sacrifiant, 1967; (ed. with C. N. Smith) Jean de la Taille: Dramatic Works, 1972; (ed.) Estienne Jodelle: Cleopatre Captive, 1980; (with M. B. Wells) Du Bellay: Poems, 1985; Rabelais: Pantagruel and Gargantua, 1991; (trans. into Esperanto) R. Kipling: La Zodiakidoj kaj aliaj rakontoj, 1997. **Address:** 37 Granville Ct, Oxford OX3 OHS, England.

HALL, Kirsten Marie. American, b. 1974. **Genres:** Children's fiction. **Career:** Editorial assiatant at Random House. **Publications:** Bunny, Bunny, 1990; Who Says?, 1990; A Visit to France, 1991; Puppies, 1993; Kittens, 1993; Hot Summer Fun Friendship Bracelets, 1994; Ballerina Girl, 1995; The Tooth Fairy, 1995; I'm Not Scared, 1995; My Brother, the Brat, 1995; A Bad, Bad Day, 1995; I See a Bug, 1995; I'm a Princess, 1995; Boo!, 1995; Duck, Duck, Goose, 1995; My Trucks, 1995; Tea Party, 1996; At the Carnival, 1996; Madame Boskey's Fortune-Telling Kit, 1996; Noah's Ark, 1997; Princess Florella, 1997; Really Gross Stuff, 1998; Bad Jokes and Worse Riddles, 1998; Dinosaur Facts, 1998; Weird Animal Facts, 1998; My Best Friend, 1998; The Princess Who Never Smiled, 1999; We Are Different, 1999; A Practical Guide to Handwriting, 1999. **Address:** 435 E. 14th St, New York, NY 10009, U.S.A. **Online address:** Kirhall@aol.com

HALL, Lee. American, b. 1934. **Genres:** Art/Art history. **Career:** Artist, educator, and writer. New York State University College at Potsdam, NY, assistant professor of art, 1958-60; Keuka College, Keuka Park, NY, associate professor of art and chair of art department, 1960-62; Winthrop University, Rock Hill, SC, associate professor of art, 1962-65; Drew University,

Madison, NJ, assistant professor, 1965-67, associate professor, 1967-70, professor of art, 1970-74, chair of art department, 1965-74; National Endowment for Humanities, consultant, 1969-75, panelist 1972-80; State University of New York College at Purchase, NY, dean of visual arts, 1974-75; Rhode Island School of Design, Providence, president, 1975-83; Academy for Educational Development, NYC, senior vice president and director of arts and communications, 1984-92. Oil and watercolor works have been exhibited in group shows worldwide. **Publications:** Wallace Herndon Smith: Paintings, 1987; Abe Ajay, 1990; Betty Parsons: Artist, Dealer, Collector, 1991; Common Threads: A Parade of American Clothing, 1992; Elaine and Bill, Portrait of a Marriage: The Lives of Willem and Elaine de Kooning, 1993; Olmsted's America: An "Unpractical Man" and His Vision of Civilization, 1995; Athena, c. 1997. Contributor to professional journals. **Address:** 14 Silverwood Terrace, South Hadley, MA 01075, U.S.A.

HALL, Lesley A(nn). British, b. 1949. **Genres:** Adult non-fiction, Science fiction/Fantasy. **Career:** India Office Records, archives assistant, 1973-75, research assistant, 1975-79; Wellcome Institute for the History of Medicine, London, England, assistant archivist at Contemporary Medical Archives Centre, 1979-89, senior assistant archivist, 1989-. **Publications:** A Brief Guide to Sources for the Study of Afghanistan in the India Office Records, 1981; Hidden Anxieties: Male Sexuality, 1900-1950, 1991; (with J. Dixon and J. Sheppard) A Guide to the Contemporary Medical Archives Centre, 1995; (with R. Porter) The Facts of Life: The Creation of Sexual Knowledge in Britain, 1680-1950, 1995. Work represented in anthologies. Contributor of articles and reviews to periodicals. **Address:** Contemporary Medical Archives Centre, Wellcome Institute for the History of Medicine, 183 Euston Rd., London NW1 2BE, England.

HALL, Lynn. American, b. 1937. **Genres:** Novellas/Short stories, Children's fiction. **Career:** Children's writer, 1970-. **Publications:** The Shy Ones, 1967; The Secret of Stonehouse, 1968; Ride a Wild Dream, 1969; Too Near the Sun, 1970; Gently Touch the Milkweed, 1970; A Horse Called Dragon, 1971; Sticks and Stones, 1972; The Famous Battle of Bravery Creek, 1972; Dog Stories, 1972; The Siege of Silent Henry, 1972; Flash-Dog of Old Egypt, 1973; Barry The Bravest St. Bernard, 1973, 1979; Riff Remember, 1973; To Catch a Tartar, 1973; Troublemaker, 1974; Bob Watchdog of the River, 1974; Stray, 1974; Kids and Dog Shows, 1975; New Day for Dragon, 1975; Captain, Canada's Flying Pony, 1976; Flowers of Anger, 1976; Owney, The Traveling Dog, 1977; Dragon Defiant, 1977; Shadows, 1977, 1992; Careers for Dog Lovers, 1978; The Mystery of: Pony Hollow, the Lost and Found Hound, the Schoolhouse Dog, the Stubborn Old Man, the Plum Park Pony, 1978-80, the Caramel Cat, 1992, the Phantom Pony, 1993; Dog of the Bondi Castle, 1979; The Leaving, 1980; Dragon's Delight, 1980; The Horse Trader, 1980; The Haunting of the Green Bird, 1980; The Disappearing Grandad, 1980; The Mysterious Moortown Bridge, 1980; The Ghost of the Great River Inn, 1980; Danza!, 1981; Half the Battle, 1982; Tin Can Tucker, 1982; Denison's Daughter, 1983; Uphill All the Way, 1983; Megan's Mare, 1983; The Boy in the Off-White Hat, 1984; The Something-Special Horse, 1985; The Giver, 1985; Tazo and Me, 1985; Just One Friend, 1985; If Winter Comes, 1986; The Solitary, 1986; Letting Go, 1987; Flyaway, 1987; Ride a Dark Horse, 1987; In Trouble AGAIN, Zelda Hammersmith, 1987; Zelda Strikes Again, 1988; The Secret Life of Dagmar Schultz, 1988; Murder at the Spaniel Show, 1988; Where Have All the Tigers Gone, 1989; Dagmar Schultz and the Powers of Darkness, 1989; Here Comes Zelda Claus, 1989; Murder in a Pig's Eye, 1989; Fair Maiden, 1990; Halsey's Pride, 1990; The Tormentors, 1990; The Soul of the Silver Dog, 1992; Windsong, 1992; The More I See of Men, 1992; Decisions, 1992; Dog Showing for Beginners, 1994. **Address:** c/o Harcourt Brace Jovanovich, 6277 Sea Harbor Dr, Orlando, FL 32887, U.S.A.

HALL, Marie Boas. Also writes as Marie Boas. British (born United States), b. 1919. **Genres:** History. **Career:** Assistant Professor of History, University of Massachusetts, 1949-52; Assistant Professor of History, Brandeis University, Waltham, MA, 1952-57; Associate Professor of History of Science, University of California, Los Angeles, 1957-61; Professor of History and Logic of Science, Indiana University, Bloomington, 1961-63; Reader in History of Science and Technology, Imperial College, University of London, 1963-80, Reader Emeritus 1981-. Fellow of the British Academy, 1994. **Publications:** The Mechanical Philosophy, 1952; Robert Boyle and 17th Century Chemistry, 1958; The Scientific Renaissance, 1540-1630, 1962; (ed. with A.R. Hall) Unpublished Scientific Papers of Isaac Newton, 1962; (ed.) Robert Boyle's Experiments and Considerations Touching Colours, 1964; (with A.R. Hall) A Brief History of Science, 1964; Robert Boyle on Natural Philosophy, 1965; (ed. with A.R. Hall). The Correspondence of Henry Oldenburg, 13 vols., 1965-86; (ed.) Henry Power's Experimental Philosophy, 1966; Nature and Nature's Laws: Documents of the Scientific Revolution,

1970; (ed.) The Pneumatics of Hero of Alexandria, 1971; All Scientists Now: The Royal Society in the 19th Century, 1984; Promoting Experimental Learning: Experiment and the Royal Society 1660-1727, 1991; The Library and Archives of the Royal Society 1660-1990, 1992; Henry Oldenburg: Shaping the Royal Society, 2002. **Address:** 14 Ball Lane, Tackley via Kidlington, Oxon. OX5 3AG, England.

HALL, Marie-Beth. American, b. 1933. **Genres:** Military/Defense/Arms control, Women's studies and issues. **Career:** Pan American World Airways, flight purser, 1954-62; U.S. Department of Energy, Federal Energy Regulatory Commission, Washington, DC, writer and editor, 1978-2002. **Publications:** (with J. Ebbert) Crossed Currents: Navy Women in a Century of Change, 1993, 3rd. ed., 1998; The First, the Few, the Forgotten: Navy and Marine Women of World War I, 2002. **Address:** 5808 Hampton Forest Way, Fairfax, VA 22030-7253, U.S.A.

HALL, Martha Lacy. American, b. 1923. **Genres:** Novellas/Short stories. **Career:** Editor and short fiction writer. Louisiana State University Press, Baton Rouge, managing editor, 1968-84, fiction editor, 1984-94. **Publications:** Call It Living, 1981; Music Lesson, 1984; The Apple-Green Triumph and Other Stories, 1990. **Address:** 7665 Richards Dr, Baton Rouge, LA 70809, U.S.A. **Online address:** marthatheauthor@.com

HALL, Matthew. American, b. 1958. **Genres:** Mystery/Crime/Suspense. **Career:** Writer. Editor of medical textbooks; has worked as a temporary employee. **Publications:** Nightmare Logic, 1989; The Art of Breaking Glass: A Thriller, 1997. **Address:** c/o Laurie Liss, Harvey Klinger Inc., 301 West 53rd St., New York, NY 10019, U.S.A. **Online address:** petithall@dcdu.com

HALL, Oakley. Also writes as Jason Manor. American, b. 1920. **Genres:** Mystery/Crime/Suspense, Westerns/Adventure, Plays/Screenplays, Songs/Lyrics and libretti, Writing/Journalism. **Career:** University of California at Irvine, professor emeritus, 1990- (professor of English and director of Progs. in Writing, 1970-90). Squaw Valley Community of Writers, director, 1970-. **Publications:** (as O.M. Hall) Murder City, 1949; So Many Doors, 1950; Corpus of Joe Bailey, 1953; Mardios Beach, 1955; The Downhill Racers, 1963; The Pleasure Garden, 1966; A Game for Eagles, 1970; Report from Beau Harbor, 1971; Angle of Repose (opera), 1976; Lullaby, 1982; The Children of the Sun, 1983; The Art and Craft of Novel Writing, 1989; How Fiction Works, 2000. WESTERNS: Warlock, 1958; The Adelita, 1975; The Bad Lands, 1978; The Coming of the Kid, 1985; Apaches, 1986; Separations, 1997. MYSTERIES: Ambrose Bierce and the Queen of Spades, 1998; Ambrose Bierce and the Death of Kings, 2001; Ambrose Bierce and the OneEyed Jacks, 2003; Ambrose Bierce and the Trey of Pearls, 2004. AS JASON MANOR: Too Dead to Run, 1953; The Red Jaguar, 1954, as The Girl in the Red Jaguar, 1955; The Pawns of Fear, 1955, as No Halo for Me, 1956; The Tramplers, 1956.

HALL, Parnell. Also writes as J. P. Hailey. American, b. 1944. **Genres:** Mystery/Crime/Suspense. **Career:** Author of mystery novels featuring private investigator Stanley Hastings, and of other works under pseudonym J. P. Hailey. Actor, Marlboro Theatre Company, 1968, 1970-74; teacher, Windsor Mountain School, Lenox, MA, 1974-75, Berkshire Community College, Stockbridge, MA, 1975, and Stockbridge School, Stockbridge, MA, 1975-76; Claims Investigation Bureau, Mount Vernon, NY, private detective, 1985-87. **Publications:** STANLEY HASTINGS NOVELS: Detective, 1987; Murder, 1988; Favor, 1988; Strangler, 1989; Client, 1990; Juror, 1990; Shot, 1991; Actor, 1993; Blackmail, 1994; Movie, 1995; Trial, 1996; Scam, 1997; Suspense, 1998; Puzzled to Death, 2002. STEVE WINSLOW NOVELS AS J. P. HAILEY: The Baxter Trust, 1988; The Anonymous Client, 1989; The Underground Man, 1990; The Naked Typist, 1990; The Wrong Gun, 1992. **Address:** c/o Donald Maass, Donald Maass Literary Agency, 160 W. 95th St., Ste 1B, New York, NY 10025, U.S.A. **Online address:** parnellh@pipeline.com

HALL, Sir Peter (Geoffrey). British, b. 1932. **Genres:** Geography, Regional/Urban planning. **Career:** London School of Economics, reader in geography, 1965-67; University of Reading, professor of geography, 1968-89; University of California, Berkeley, professor, 1980-92, emeritus professor of city and regional planning, 1992-; University College London, Bartlett Professor of Planning, 1993-. **Publications:** The Industries of London, 1962; London 2000, 1963, rev. ed., 1969; The World Cities, 1966, 3rd ed., 1984; Theory and Practice of Regional Planning, 1970; Urban and Regional Planning: An Introduction, 1974; Europe 2000, 1977; Great Planning Disasters, 1980; Growth Centres in the European Urban System, 1980; London 2001, 1986; Cities of Tomorrow, 1988; Technopoles of the World, 1994; Cities in Civilization, 1998. CO-AUTHOR: An Advanced Geography of North-West Europe,

1967; Containment of Urban England: Urban and Metropolitan Growth Processes or Megalopolis Denied, 1973; Containment of Urban England: The Planning System: Objectives, Operations, Impacts, 1973; (with M. Clawson) Planning and Urban Growth: An Anglo-American Comparison, 1973; Can Rail Save the City, 1985; High-Tech America, 1986; Western Sunrise, 1987; Sociable Cities, 1999; Urban Future 21, 2000; Working Capital, 2002. EDITOR: Labour's New Frontiers, 1964; Land Values, 1965; Von Thunen's Isolated State, 1966; (with D. Banister) Transport and Public Policy Planning, 1980; The Inner City in Context, 1981; Silicon Landscapes, 1985; Cities of the 21st Century, 1991. **Address:** Institute of Community Studies, 18 Victoria Park Sq, London E2 9PF, England. **Online address:** phall@icstudies.ac.uk

HALL, Robert. *See* **WUBBELS, Lance.**

HALL, Rodney. Australian (born England), b. 1935. **Genres:** Novels, Poetry, Literary criticism and history, Race relations, Biography. **Career:** Advisory Ed., Overland mag., Melbourne, 1962-78. Poetry Ed., The Australian, newspaper, Sydney, 1967-78. Freelance Scriptwriter and Actor, 1957-67, and Film Critic, 1966-67, A. B. C., Brisbane; 1977-80; Tutor, New England University School of Music, Armidale, N. S. W., 1967-71, 1977-80; Youth Officer, Australian Council for the Arts, 1971-73; Lecturer in recorder, Canberra School of Music, 1979-83. Recipient: Commonwealth Literary Fund Fellowship, 1970; Literature Board Fellowship, 1973, 1976, 1982, 1986, 1990; Grace Leven Prize, 1974; Miles Franklin Award, Australian Natives Association Award, and Barbara Ramsden Award, all 1982; Victorian Premier's Literary Award, 1988. **Publications:** Penniless till Doomsday, 1962; Forty Beads on a Hangman's Rope: Fragments of Memory, 1963; (with S. Andrews) Social Services and the Aborigines, 1963; The Autobiography of a Gorgon, 1968; Focus on Andrew Sibley, 1968; J.S. Manifold (biography), 1978; (with D. Moore) Australia: Image of a Nation, 1983; Journey Through Australia, 1988. POETRY: Eyewitness: Poems, 1967; The Law of Karma: A Progression of Poems, 1968; Heaven, In a Way, 1970; The Soapbox Omnibus, 1973; Selected Poems, 1975; Black Bagatelles, 1978; The Most Beautiful World (verse), 1981. NOVELS: The Ship on the Coin, 1971; A Place among People, 1976; Just Relations, 1982; Captivity Captive, 1988; Kisses of the Enemy, 1988; The Second Bridegroom, 1991; The Grisly Wife, 1993; The Island of the Mind, 1996; The Day We Had Hitler Home, 2000. EDITOR: (with T. Shapcott) New Impulses in Australian Poetry, 1968; Australian Poetry 1970, 1970; Poems from Prison, 1973; The Collins Book of Australian Poetry, 1981. **Address:** Fran Bryson, C/O Bryson Agency, PO Box 226, Flinders Lane PO, Melbourne 8009, Australia.

HALL, Roger (Leighton). New Zealander (born England), b. 1939. **Genres:** Children's fiction, Plays/Screenplays. **Career:** Freelance writer and editor. Formerly worked in insurance, as a wine waiter, in factories, and as a teacher; Teaching Fellow, University of Otago, Dunedin, 1979-94. **Publications:** PLAYS: Glide Time, 1978; Middle-Age Spread, 1978; State of the Play, 1979; Cinderella, 1978; Prisoners of Mother England, 1981; Robinhood, 1980; Fifty-Fifty, 1981; The Rose, 1981; Hot Water, 1982; Footrot Flats (musical), 1983; Multiple Choice, 1984; Dream of Sussex Downs, 1986; Love off the Shelf (musical), 1986; The Hansard Show, 1986; The Share Club, 1987; After the Crash, 1988; Mr. Punch, 1989; Conjugal Rites, 1990; Making It Big (musical) 1991; By Degrees, 1993; Social Climbers, 1995; Market Forces, 1996; C'Mon Black, 1996; The Book Club, 1999; You Gotta Be Joking, 1999; Take a Chance on Me, 2001; A Way of Life, 2001. CHILDREN'S BOOKS: Sam, Max and Harold Meet Dracula, 1990; Penguin Trouble, 1991; My Aunt Went Shopping, 1991; Mum's Photo, 1993. TELEVISION SERIES: Gliding On; Neighbourhood Watch; Conjugal Rites; Market Forces; Spin Docotrs. **Address:** c/o Playmarket, PO Box 9767, Wellington, New Zealand. **Online address:** roger.h@xtra.co.nz

HALL, Sarah. (born England), b. 1974. **Genres:** Art/Art history. **Career:** Novelist and poet. Has taught at St. Andrews University in the undergraduate creative writing program. **Publications:** Haweswater (novel), 2002; The Electric Michelangelo (novel), 2004. Contributor of poems to various publications. **Address:** c/o Editorial Department, Faber and Faber Ltd., 3 Queen Sq., London WC1N 3AU, England.

HALL, Stacey A. American, b. 1957. **Genres:** Business/Trade/Industry. **Career:** Entrepreneur, business consultant, and writer. **Publications:** (with J. Brogniez) Attracting Perfect Customers: The Power of Strategic Synchronicity, 2001. **Address:** PerfectCustomers Unlimited, 2513 South Gessner Rd., Houston, TX 77098, U.S.A. **Online address:** info@perfectcustomer.com

HALL, Steffie. *See* **EVANOVICH, Janet.**

HALL, Susan Bard. American, b. 1954. **Genres:** Animals/Pets, Travel/Exploration. **Career:** Commodity News Services, Chicago, IL, reporter, copy editor, assistant bureau chief, 1977-79; Chicago Board of Trade, Chicago, staff writer in public relations department, 1979-80; Mid America Commodity Exchange, Chicago, local trader and broker, 1980-82; National Futures Association, Chicago, manager of public affairs department, 1982-83; Letters Etcetera, Chicago, owner and freelance writer, 1983-. **Publications:** Midway Airlines: The First Ten Years, 1979-1989, 1989; Purrfect Places to Stay: Beds and Breakfasts, Country Inns, and Hotels with Resident Cats, 1999. Contributor to books and periodicals.

HALL, Thor. American (born Norway), b. 1927. **Genres:** Theology/Religion, Translations. **Career:** LeRoy A. Martin Distinguished Professor of Religious Studies, University of Tennessee at Chattanooga, 1972-94, emeritus, 1994. Assistant Professor of Preaching and Theology, 1962-68, and Associate Professor, 1968-72, Duke University, Durham, North Carolina. **Publications:** (ed.) The Unfinished Pyramid, Ten Sermons by Charles P. Bowles, D.D., 1967; A Theology of Christian Devotion, 1969, 1972; A Framework for Faith, 1970; The Future Shape of Preaching, 1971, 1973; Whatever Happened to the Gospel?, 1973; Advent-Christmas, 1975; Directory of Systematic Theologians in North America, 1977; Anders Nygren, 1978, 1985, repr. 1991; Systematic Theology Today, 1978; The Evolution of Christology, 1982; Pentecost 1, 1991. Translator of 4 books. **Address:** 1102 Montvale Circle, Signal Mountain, TN 37377, U.S.A. **Online address:** thorhall1@msn.com

HALL, Timothy L. American, b. 1955. **Genres:** Law. **Career:** U.S. Court of Appeals for the Fifth Circuit, judicial clerk, 1983-84; Hughes & Luce, Austin, TX, litigation associate, 1984-89; University of Mississippi, University, assistant professor, 1989-93, associate professor, 1993-99, Mitchell, McNutt, Threadgill, Smith & Sams Lecturer in Law, 1997-99, professor, 1999-. University of Texas, visiting professor, 1994. Member of State Bar of Texas, U.S. Court of Appeals for the Fifth Circuit, and U.S. District Court for the Western District of Texas. **Publications:** (with M.L. Harrington) The University of Mississippi: In Principle and Practice, 3rd ed., 1997, 4th ed., 1998; Separating Church and State: Roger Williams in America, 1998; Entering the University, 2nd ed., 2001; Supreme Court Justices: A Biographical Dictionary, 2001; Biographical Dictionary of American Religious Leaders, 2003. EDITOR: U.S. Legal System, 2004; U.S. Laws, Acts, and Treaties, 2003; Magill's Legal Guide, 1999. EDITOR & CONTRIBUTOR: Ready Reference: American Justice, 1996; Ready Reference: Censorship, 3 vols., 1997; Civil Rights Encyclopedia, 3 vols., 1997; Ready Reference: Women's Issues, 3 vols, 1997; Ready Reference: Family Life, 3 vols., 1998. Contributor to law journals. **Address:** 311 Phillip Rd, Oxford, MS 38655, U.S.A. **Online address:** lwhall@olemiss.edu

HALL, Willis. British, b. 1929. **Genres:** Children's fiction, Young adult fiction, Plays/Screenplays, Sports/Fitness. **Publications:** Final at Furnell, 1954; Poet and Pheasant, 1955; The Gentle Knight, 1957; The Play of the Royal Astrologers, 1958; The Long and the Short and the Tall, 1958; (with I.O. Evans) They Found the World, 1959; A Glimpse of the Sea, and Last Days in Dreamland, 1959; Return to the Sea, 1960; The Royal Astrologers, 1960; The Days Beginning, 1963; Come Laughing Home, 1964; (with M. Parkinson) The A to Z of Soccer, 1970; (with B. Monkhouse) The A to Z of Television, 1971; The Railwayman's New Clothes, 1974; My Sporting Life, 1975; Walk on, Walk On, 1976; The Summer of the Dinosaur, 1977; The Last Vampire, 1982; The Inflatable Shop, 1984; Dragon Days, 1985; The Antelope Company Ashore, 1986; Spooky Rhymes, 1987; The Antelope Company at Large, 1987; Henry Hollins and the Dinosaur, 1988; Doctor Jekyll and Mr. Hollins, 1988; The Vampire's Holiday, 1991; The Vampire's Revenge, 1993; The Vampire's Christmas, 1994; The Vampire Vanishes, 1995; Vampire Park, 1996; Vampire Hunt, 1998; Vampire Island, 1999. ADAPTER: C. Bronte, Jane Eyre; (with D. King) Treasure Island, 1986; (with D. King) The Wind in the Willows, 1986; J. Austen, Mansfield Park, 1992. WITH K. WATERHOUSE: Billy Liar, 1960; England, Our England, 1962; Squat Betty, 1962; The Sponge Room, 1962; All Things Bright and Beautiful, 1962; Say Who You Are (in US as Help Stamp Out Marriage), 1965; (eds.) The Writers' Theatre, 1967; Whoops-a-Daisy, 1968; Children's Day, 1969; Who's Who, 1971. JUVENILE: The Incredible Kidnapping, 1975; Kidnapped at Christmas, Christmas Crackers, and A Right Christmas Caper (play trilogy), 1975-77. ADAPTER WITH K. WATERHOUSE: E. de Filippo, Saturday, Sunday, Monday, 1973; A. Bennett, The Card, 1973; Filumena, 1977; The Television Adventures of Worzel Gummidge, 2 vols., 1979; The Trials of Worzel Gummidge, 1980; Worzel Gummidge at the Fair, 1980; Worzel Gummidge, 1981. **Address:** c/o Nick Quinn, The Agency (London) Ltd, 24 Pottery Ln, Holland Park, London W11 4LZ, England.

HALLAHAN, William H(enry). American. **Genres:** Mystery/Crime/Suspense, History. **Publications:** MYSTERY: The Dead of Winter, 1972;

The Ross Forgery, 1973; The Search for Joseph Tully, 1974; Catch Me, Kill Me, 1977; Keeper of the Children, 1978; The Trade, 1981; The Monk, 1983; Foxcatcher, 1986; Tripletrap, 1989. OTHER: Misfire (history), 1994. **Address:** c/o Author Mail, John Wiley & Sons Inc, 111 River St, Hoboken, NJ 07030-5773, U.S.A.

HALLAM, Elizabeth. *See* **REASONER, Livia Jane Washburn.**

HALLAM, Elizabeth M. (Elizabeth Hallam-Smith). British, b. 1950. **Genres:** History. **Career:** Public Record Office, London, Assistant Keeper, 1976-93, Director of Public Services, 1993-. **Publications:** Capetian France 987-1328, 1980, 2nd ed., 2001; The Itinerary of Edward II and His Household 1307-28, 1984; The Domesday Project Book, 1986; Domesday Book through Nine Centuries, 1986; The Wars of the Roses: From Richard II to the Fall of Richard III at Bosworth Field, 1988; Gods and Goddesses, 1995; Domesday Souvenir Guide, 2000. EDITOR: The Plantagenet Chronicles, 1986; The Four Gothic Kings: The Turbulent History of Medieval England and the Plantagenet Kings 1216-1377, 1987; Chronicles of the Crusades, 1989; The Plantagenet Encyclopaedia, 1990; Saints, Who They Are and How They Help You, 1993; The British Inheritance, 2000; Domesday Book: New Perspectives, 2001. **Address:** c/o Public Record Office, Kew, Richmond, Surrey TW9 4DU, England. **Online address:** elizabeth.hallam-smith@ nationalarchives.gov.uk

HALLAS, James H(enry). American, b. 1952. **Genres:** Military/Defense/ Arms control. **Career:** Glastonbury Citizen, Glastonbury, CT, editor and publisher, 1979-. **Publications:** The Devil's Anvil, 1994; Squandered Victory, 1995; Killing Ground on Okinawa, 1996; Doughboy War: The American Expeditionary Force in World War I, 1999. **Address:** Glastonbury Citizen, PO Box 373, Glastonbury, CT 06033, U.S.A. **Online address:** DevAnuil@ aol.com

HALLENDY, Norman. Canadian, b. 1932. **Genres:** Anthropology/ Ethnology. **Career:** Ethnogeographer and writer. Smithsonian Institution, Washington, DC, research associate; Arctic Institute of North America, Calgary, Alberta, Canada, research associate; Canadian Museum of Civilization, Gatineau, Quebec, research fellow; Nunavut Research Institute, Iqaluit, Nunavut, research fellow. **Publications:** Inuksuit: Silent Messengers of the Arctic, 2001. Author of learned papers. **Address:** PO Box 1, Carp, ON, Canada K0A 1L0. **Online address:** tukilik@sympatico.ca

HALLER, Hermann W. American (born Switzerland), b. 1945. **Genres:** Language/Linguistics. **Career:** Educator and author. Queens College, City University of New York, assistant professor, 1974-79, associate professor, 1980-83, professor of Romance languages, 1984-96, professor of Italian, 1996-, chair of Department of European Languages and Literatures, 1999-2004; City University of New York, Graduate Center, PhD Program in Comparative Literature, head, doctoral specialization in Italian, 2003-. Visiting professor at US and European universities. **Publications:** Der deiktische Gebrauch des Demonstrativums im Altitalienisch, 1973; Il panfilo veneziano. Edizione critica con introduzione e glossario (bilingual Italian/Latin), 1982; (ed. and translator) The Hidden Italy: A Bilingual Edition of Italian Dialect Poetry, 1986; Una lingua perduta e ritrovata: l'italiano degli Italo-Americani, 1993; The Other Italy. The Literary Canon in Dialect, 1999; La festa delle lingue, 2002. Contributor of articles and reviews to periodicals. Contributor to books. **Address:** Dept of European Languages and Literatures, Queens College, City University of New York, 65-30 Kissena Blvd, Flushing, NY 11367, U.S.A. **Online address:** Hermann_Haller@gc.edu

HALLETT, Charles A(rthur). American, b. 1935. **Genres:** Plays/ Screenplays, Literary criticism and history, Theatre. **Career:** Brooklyn College of the City University of New York, Brooklyn, NY, lecturer in English, 1966-67; Fordham University, Bronx, NY, assistant professor, 1967-71, associate professor, 1971-81, professor of English, 1981-. University of Warwick, visiting fellow, 1978; Loyola University, New Orleans, visiting professor, 1994; Dartmouth College, visiting scholar, 2001-05. **Publications:** Middleton's Cynics: A Study of Middleton's Insight into the Moral Psychology of the Mediocre Mind, 1975; Aaron Burr (three-act play), 1976; (with E.S. Hallett) The Revenger's Madness: A Study of Revenge Tragedy Motifs, 1980; (with E.S. Hallett) Analyzing Shakespeare's Action: Scene vs. Sequence, 1991. Work represented in anthologies. Contributor to professional journals. **Address:** Department of English, Fordham University, Bronx, NY 10458, U.S.A.

HALLIBURTON, David (Garland). American, b. 1933. **Genres:** Literary criticism and history. **Career:** University of California-Riverside, Riverside, CA, assistant professor of English, 1966-72, associate professor of English,

comparative literature, and modern thought and literature, 1972-80; Stanford University, Stanford, CA, professor of English, 1980-. **Publications:** Edgar Allan Poe: A Phenomenological View, 1973; Poetic Thinking: An Approach to Heidegger, 1982; The Color of the Sky: A Study of Stephen Crane, 1989; The Fateful Discourse of Worldly Things, 1997. Contributor to periodicals. **Address:** Department of English, Stanford University, Stanford, CA 94305, U.S.A.

HALLIDAY, Nigel Vaux. British, b. 1956. **Genres:** Art/Art history, Theology/Religion. **Career:** Art historian and writer. **Publications:** More Than a Bookshop: Zwemmers and Art in the Twentieth Century, 1991. **Address:** Clarks, Huntsbottom Lane, Liss, Hants. GU33 7EU, England.

HALLIDAY, William R(oss). American, b. 1926. **Genres:** Earth sciences, Natural history, Recreation, Travel/Exploration. **Career:** Director, 1955-81, and Director of Research, 1981-96, Western Speleological Survey, Vancouver, WA. Thoracic surgeon, in private practice, Seattle, WA, 1957-65; Medical Consultant, 1965-71, and Chief Medical Consultant and Medical Director, Dept. of Labor and Industries, Olympia and Seattle, WA, 1971-76; Assistant Director, International Glaciaspeleological Survey, 1972-76; Medical Director, Washington State Division of Vocational Rehabilitation, 1976-82, N.W. Vocational Rehabilitation Group, Seattle, 1984, and Comprehensive Medical Rehabilitation Center, Brentwood, Tennessee, 1984-87; Staff Physician, N.W. Occupational Health Center, Seattle, 1983-84; National Speleological Society Board of Governors, intermittently 1950-2001; Chairman, Hawaii Speleological Survey, 1989-98; Chairman, International Union of Speleology Commission on Volcanic Caves, 1990-98. **Publications:** Adventure Is Underground, 1959; Depths of the Earth, 1966, 1976; American Caves and Caving, 1974, 1982; (with F.K. Walsh) Oregon Caves: Discovery and Exploration, 1971; Ape Cave, 1983; (with R. Nymeyer) Carlsbad Cavern: The Early Years, 1991; Floyd Collins of Sand Cave, 1998.

HALLIGAN, Marion (Mildred Crothall). Australian, b. 1940. **Genres:** Novels, Novellas/Short stories, Children's fiction, Plays/Screenplays, Essays. **Career:** Writer. Teacher in Canberra, Australia, 1963-65, 1974-86. Australian National Word Festival, chair, 1987-92; Charles Sturt University, Wagga Wagga, Riverina district, NSW, Australia, writer in residence, 1990; Literature Board of Australia Council, chair, 1992-95. Writer in residence at Monash University and La Trobe University, both in Australia. **Publications:** NOVELS: Self Possession, 1987; Spider Cup, 1990; Lovers' Knots: A Hundred-Year Novel, 1992; Wishbone, 1994; The Golden Dress, 1998; The Fog Garden, 2001; The Point, 2003. SHORT-STORY COLLECTIONS: The Living Hothouse, 1988; The Hanged Man in the Garden, 1989; The Worry Box, 1993; Collected Stories, 1997. ESSAYS: Eat My Words, 1990; Cockles of the Heart, 1996; The Taste of Memory, 2004. JUVENILE: The Midwife's Daughters, 1997. PLAYS: Kilcallow Catch (music theater piece for children), 1992; Gastronomica (five one-act plays), 1994. OTHER: Out of the Picture, 1996; (with L. Frost) Those Women Who Go to Hotels, 1997. Work represented in anthologies. Contributor to periodicals. **Address:** c/o Margaret Connolly, PO Box 945, Wahroonga, NSW 2076, Australia. **Online address:** wishbone@webone.com.au

HALLISSY, Margaret. American, b. 1945. **Genres:** Literary criticism and history, Women's studies and issues. **Career:** Teacher at a college preparatory school in Jamaica, NY, 1966-68; Long Island University, C.W. Post Campus, Brookville, NY, adjunct lecturer, 1974-75, adjunct assistant professor, 1975-77, assistant professor, 1977-82, associate professor, 1982-87, professor of English, 1987-, coordinator of Office of Life Experience Credit, 1979-81, director of Office of Interdisciplinary Studies, 1981-84, director of Writing Center, 1986-88. **Publications:** Venomous Woman: Fear of the Female in Literature, 1987; Clean Maids, True Wives, Steadfast Widows: Chaucer's Women and Medieval Codes of Conduct, 1993; A Companion to Chaucer's Canterbury Tales, 1995. Contributor to literature journals. **Address:** Department of English, C.W. Post Campus, Long Island University, 720 Northern Blvd., Brookville, NY 11548, U.S.A. **Online address:** profmarge@aol.com

HALLO, William W. American (born Germany), b. 1928. **Genres:** Archaeology/Antiquities, History, Literary criticism and history, Theology/ Religion. **Career:** Emeritus Laffan Professor of Assyriology and Babylonian Literature, Yale University, New Haven, CT, 2002- (associate professor of Assyriology, 1962-65; curator, Babylonian Collection, 1963-2001; professor of Assyriology, 1965-75; ed., Yale Near Eastern Researches, 1968-2002; Laffan Professor of Assyriology and Babylonian Literature, 1975-2002). Instructor, 1956-58, and assistant professor, 1958-62, Hebrew Union College-Jewish Institute of Religion, Cincinnati. **Publications:** Early Mesopotamian Royal Titles, 1957; (with J.J.A. van Dijk) The Exaltation of Inanna, 1968; (trans.)

F. Rosenzweig, The Star of Redemption, 1971; (with W.K. Simpson) The Ancient Near East, 1971; Sumerian Archival Texts, 1973; (with W.G. Plaut and B.T. Bamberger) The Torah, 1981; (with B. Buchanan) Early Near Eastern Seals in the Yale Babylonian Collection, 1981; (with S.G. Beld and P. Michalowski) The Tablets of Ebla, 1984; (with D.B. Ruderman and M. Stanislawski) Heritage: Civilization and the Jews, 2 vols., 1984; The Book of the People, 1991; Origins: The Ancient Near Eastern Background of Some Modern Western Institutions, 1996. EDITOR: Essays in Memory of E.A. Speiser, 1968; (with C.D. Evans and J.B. White) Scripture in Context, 1980; (with J.C. Moyer and L.G. Perdue) Scripture in Context II, 1983; (with B.W. Jones and G.L. Mattingly) The Bible in the Light of Cuneiform Literature: Scripture in Context III, 1990; (with K.L. Younger Jr. and B.F. Batto) The Biblical Canon in Comparative Perspective: Scripture in Context IV, 1991; (with K.L. Younger Jr.) The Context of Scripture, 3 vols., 1997-2002. Address: Babylonian Collection, Yale University, New Haven, CT 06520, U.S.A.

HALLOCK, John W(esley) M(atthew). American, b. 1959. **Genres:** Biography, Gay and lesbian issues, Literary criticism and history. **Career:** Teacher and counselor in Philadelphia, PA. **Publications:** The American Byron: Homosexuality and the Fall of Fitz-Green Halleck (biography), 2000. Contributor to books. **Address:** 1232 Waverly Walk, Philadelphia, PA 19147, U.S.A.

HALLOWELL, Edward McKey. American. **Genres:** Self help. **Career:** Psychiatrist specializing in Attention Deficit Disorder. Harvard Medical School, faculty member; private practice, Cambridge, MA. **Publications:** (with W.J. Grace, Jr.) What Are You Worth?, 1989; (with J.J. Ratey) Answers to Distraction, 1994;(with Ratey) Driven to Distraction: Attention Deficit Disorder in Children and Adults, 1994; When You Worry About the Children You Love, 1996; Worry: Controlling It and Using It Wisely, 1997. **Address:** 328 Broadway, Cambridge, MA 02139, U.S.A.

HALLOWELL, Tommy. See **HILL, Thomas.**

HALLWAS, John E. American, b. 1945. **Genres:** Plays/Screenplays, Area studies, History, Literary criticism and history, Autobiography/Memoirs. **Career:** University of Florida, Gainesville, member of English faculty, 1970; Western Illinois University, Macomb, assistant professor to associate professor, 1970-81, professor of American literature, 1981-, director of Regional Collections at university library, 1979-. **Publications:** The Western Illinois Poets (monograph), 1975; The Poems of H.: The Lost Poet of Lincoln's Springfield, 1982; Western Illinois Heritage, 1983; Thomas Gregg: Early Illinois Journalist and Author (monograph), 1983; McDonough County Heritage, 1984; Illinois Literature: The Nineteenth Century, 1986; Studies in Illinois Poetry, 1989; Macomb: A Pictorial History, 1990; The Legacy of the Mines: Memoirs of Coal Mining in Fulton County, Illinois, 1993; (with R.D. Launius) Cultures in Conflict, 1995; The Bootlegger: A Story of Small-Town America, 1998; First Century: A Pictorial History of Western Illinois University, 1999; Keokuk and the Great Dam, 2001; McDonough County Historic Sites, 2002. PLAYS: The Conflict, 1982; Four on the Frontier, 1982-83; (with G. Kozlowski) The Paper Town, 1985. EDITOR: (with D.J. Reader) The Vision of This Land: Studies of Vachel Lindsay, Edgar Lee Masters, and Carl Sandburg, 1976; Western Illinois University Libraries: A Handbook, 1980; (with J. Cain-Tyson and V. Hicken) Tales from Two Rivers, Vol. I, 1981, Vol. II, 1982, Vol. III, 1984, Vol. IV (with D.R. Pichaske), 1987, Vol. V (with A.J. Lindsey), 1990, Vol. VI (with Lindsey), 1996; (with others) Teaching the Middle Ages, Vol. II, 1985; (co) Prairie State Books series, 1987-; Spoon River Anthology, 1992; (with Launius) Kingdom on the Mississippi Revisited, 1996; Contributor to books. Contributor of articles and reviews to periodicals. **Address:** Dept of English, Western Illinois University, Macomb, IL 61455, U.S.A.

HALLWOOD, Jan. British. **Genres:** Autobiography/Memoirs. **Career:** Writer, music critic. **Publications:** (with S. Morris) Living with Eagles: Marcus Morris, Priest and Publisher, 1998. **Address:** c/o Lutterworth Press, PO Box 60, Cambridge CB1 2NT, England.

HALM, Ben B. Ghanaian, b. 1957. **Genres:** Theatre. **Career:** University of Ghana, Legon, senior research assistant in performing arts, 1980-82; Theatre Passe Muraille, Toronto, Ontario, playwright in residence, 1984-86; Webster University, St. Louis, MO, assistant professor of English, 1991-93; Fairfield University, Fairfield, CT, assistant professor of English, 1993-, and resident playwright at Theatre Fairfield. Union College, adjunct professor, 1996-. **Publications:** Theatre and Ideology, 1995. **Address:** Department of English, Fairfield University, 1073 N Benson Rd, Fairfield, CT 06824, U.S.A. **Online address:** bhalm@fair1.fairfield.edu

HALPERIN, James L(ewis). American, b. 1952. **Genres:** Novels, Antiques/Furnishings. **Career:** Heritage Galleries & Auctioneers, Dallas, TX, co-chairperson, 1982-. **Publications:** How to Grade U.S. Coins, 1990; The Truth Machine (novel), 1996; The First Immortal (novel), 1997. **Address:** Heritage Galleries & Auctioneers, 3500 Maple Ave 17th Fl, Dallas, TX 75219-3941, U.S.A. **Online address:** jim@heritagegalleries.com

HALPERIN, Joan Ungersma. American, b. 1932. **Genres:** Art/Art history, Humanities. **Career:** Sorbonne, lectrice d'americain, 1956-57; University of Chicago, instructor in French, 1964-65; Wesleyan University, CT, instructor in French, 1965-66; University of Maine, associate professor, 1967-70; St. Mary's College of California, professor of French, 1974-, chair of department of modern languages, 1985-90, 1993-94. **Publications:** (ed.) Felix Feneon, Oeuvres plus que completes, Vol 1: Chroniques d'art, Vol 2: Les Lettres, les moeurs, 1970; Studies in the Fine Arts, Vol 6: Felix Feneon and the Language of Art Criticism, 1980; Felix Feneon: Aesthete and Anarchist in Fin-de-Siecle Paris, 1988; (author of preface) Charles Angrand's Correspondence, 1989. Contributor to periodicals. **Address:** Dept of Modern Languages, St. Mary's College of California, Moraga, CA 94575, U.S.A. **Online address:** halperin@stmarys-ca.edu

HALPERIN, Jonathan L. American, b. 1949. **Genres:** Medicine/Health. **Career:** Boston City Hospital, Boston, MA; Boston University, University Hospital, Boston, intern in medicine, 1975-76, resident in internal medicine, 1976-77, clinical and research fellow in peripheral vascular diseases, 1977-78, fellow in cardiology, 1978-80; Mount Sinai School of Medicine of the City University of New York, NYC, assistant professor, 1980-85, associate professor of medicine, 1986-93, Professor of Medicine, 1993-. Diplomate of National Board of Medical Examiners, American Board of Internal Medicine, and Subspecialty Board in Cardiovascular Disease. Evans Medical Foundation, clinical and research fellow, 1977-78; American Heart Association, Howard B. Sprague research fellow, 1979-80; Mount Sinai Medical Center, director of clinical services of division of cardiology, 1983-; Mount Sinai Hospital, attending physician for cardiology, 1983-. **Publications:** (with R. Levine) Bypass: A Cardiologist Reveals What Every Patient Needs to Know, 1985. **Address:** Cardiovascular Institute, Mount Sinai Medical Center, Fifth Ave at 100th St, New York, NY 10029, U.S.A.

HALPERN, Cynthia Leone. American, b. 1952. **Genres:** History, Politics/Government, Theatre. **Career:** Cabrini College, Radnor, PA, associate professor, 1994-. **Publications:** The Political Theatre of Early Seventeenth-Century Spain, with Special Reference to Juan Ruiz de Alarcon, 1993. **Address:** Cabrini College, 610 King of Prussia Rd, Radnor, PA 19087, U.S.A.

HALPERN, Daniel. American, b. 1945. **Genres:** Novellas/Short stories, Poetry, Food and Wine. **Career:** Ed., Antaeus mag., NYC, since 1969. Ed.-in-Chief, Ecco Press, NYC, since 1971. Adjunct Professor of Writing, Columbia University, NYC, since 1975 (Chairman, Graduate Writing Division, 1982-84). Director, National Poetry Series, NYC, since 1978. Instructor, New School for Social Research, NYC, 1971-76; Visiting Professor, Princeton University, New Jersey, 1975-76, 1988. **Publications:** Traveling on Credit, 1972; (as Angela McCabe) The Keeper of Height, 1974; (trans.) Songs of Mririda, Courtesan of the High Atlas, by Mririda n'Ait Attik, 1974; The Lady Knife-Thrower, 1975; (with G. Mayer and F. Elon) Treble Poets 2, 1975; Street Fire, 1975; Life among Others, 1978; Seasonal Rights, 1982; (with J. Strand) The Good Food: Soups, Stews and Pastas, 1985; Tango, 1987; Writers on Artists, 1988; Halpern's Guide to the Essential Restaurants of Italy, 1990; Something Shining, 1999. EDITOR: (with N.T. di Giovanni and F. MacShane) Borges on Writing, 1973; The American Poetry Anthology, 1975; The Art of the Tale, 1986, in U.K. as The Penguin of International Short Stories 1945-85, 1989; The Antaeus Poetry Anthology, 1986; On Nature, 1987; On Reading, 1987; Literature as Pleasure, 1987; (with J.C. Oates) Reading the Fights, 1988; Our Private Lives: Journals, Notebooks and Diaries, 1989 in U.K. as Journals, Notebooks and Diaries. **Address:** Ecco Press Ltd., 10 E 53rd St, New York, NY 10022, U.S.A.

HALPERN, Paul. American, b. 1961. **Genres:** Physics. **Career:** Brookhaven National Laboratory, research assistant, 1983; Hamilton College, Clinton, NY, visiting assistant professor of physics, 1987-88; Philadelphia College of Pharmacy and Science, Philadelphia, PA, assistant professor, 1988-92, associate professor, 1992-99, professor of physics, 1999-. Guest on radio and television programs. **Publications:** Time Journeys: A Search for Cosmic Destiny and Meaning, 1990; Cosmic Wormholes: The Search for Interstellar Shortcuts, 1992; The Cyclical Serpent: Prospects for an Ever-Repeating Universe, 1995; The Structure of the Universe, 1996; The Quest for Alien Planets, 1997; Countdown to Apocalypse, 1998; The Pursuit of Destiny: A History of Prediction, 2000. Contributor to scientific journals. **Address:** Dept of Mathematics, Physics and Computer Science, University of the Sciences in Philadelphia, 600 S 43rd St, Philadelphia, PA 19104, U.S.A. **Online address:** p.halper@usip.edu

HALPERN, Sue. American. **Genres:** Sciences. **Career:** Columbia University, NYC, research associate, 1985-87; Bryn Mawr College, Bryn Mawr, PA, assistant professor, 1987-88; writer. **Publications:** Migrations to Solitude, 1992; Four Wings and a Prayer, 2001. Contributor to popular magazines and newspapers. **Address:** c/o Watkins Loomis Agency Inc., 133 E. 35th St., New York, NY 10016-3886, U.S.A.

HALPIN, Marlene. American, b. 1927. **Genres:** How-to books, Theology/Religion, Education, Inspirational/Motivational Literature, Inspirational/Motivational Literature. **Career:** Dominican nun, writer, photographer, educator. Molloy College, Rockville Centre, NY, academic dean & professor of philosophy, 1963-74; Aquinas Institute of Theology, Dubuque, IA, coordinator of continuing education & professor of philosophy, 1974-81; Notre Dame University, South Bend, IN, consultant, Clergy Institute of Retreat Instructors, 1981-82; Diocese of Kalamazoo, MI, director, Ministry Formation Program, 1982-. Keynote speaker, workshop and retreat director, 1979-; St. Augustine's School, grades K-8, director of prayer room, 1982-. **Publications:** (with P. Conway) Grammar-Logic-Rhetoric, rev. ed., 1964; (with M. Brill and W. Genne) Write Your Own Wedding, 1973, 3rd ed., 1985; Planned Continuing Education, 1979; Imagine That!, 1982; Puddles of Knowing, 1984; The Continuing Formation of Priests, 1984; Inside Out (photography and poetry), 1985; Forgiving: Present Perfect, 1987; Leading Prayer, 1990; Helping Children (and Anyone Else) to Pray (video and study guide), 1990; At Home with God: A Child's Book of Prayer, Vol 1, 1993, Vols 2-4, 1995; Imagine That, Too!: Imagination and SelfDiscovery, 1994; Following Jesus: A Way of the Cross for Children, 1995; Right Side Up: A Book of Reflections for People Living with Serious Illness, 1995; Grandparents!, 1996; Caregivers: Reflections on Coping with Caregiving, 1998; The Ball of Red String, 1998. Creator of calendars (photography and poetry) for Holy Cross Health Systems, 1983, 1984. Contributor to books. Has also published essays. Contributor of articles have appeared to religious periodicals. **Address:** 215 N Westnedge Ave, Kalamazoo, MI 49007, U.S.A. **Online address:** mhalpin@dioceseofkalamazoo.org

HALSEY, A(lbert) H(enry). British, b. 1923. **Genres:** Sociology, Autobiography/Memoirs. **Career:** Director, Dept. of Social and Administration Studies, University of Oxford, 1962-. Professorial Fellow, Nuffield College, Oxford. Lecturer and Sr. Lecturer, University of Birmingham, 1954-62; Fellow, Center for Advanced Study of the Behavioral Sciences, Palo Alto, CA, 1956-57; Visiting Professor, University of Chicago, 1959-60. **Publications:** (with J.E. Floud and F.M. Martin) Social Class and Educational Opportunity, 1956; (with J.E. Floud and C.A. Anderson) Education, Economy and Society, 1961; Ability and Educational Opportunity, 1962; (with G.N. Ostergaard) Power in Co-operatives, 1965; (with M. Trow) The British Academics, 1971; (with J. Karabel) Power and Ideology in Education, 1977; (with A.F. Heath and J.M. Ridge) Origins and Destinations, 1980; Change in British Society, 1981, 4th ed., 1995; (with N. Dennis) English Ethical Socialism, 1988; British Social Trends since 1900, 1988, rev. ed., 1999; The Decline of Donnish Dominion, 1992, rev. ed., 1995; No Discouragement: An Autobiography, 1996; Education, Culture, Economy and Society, 1997; Twentieth Century British Social Trends, 2000; A History of Sociology in Britain: Science, Literature and Society, 2004. EDITOR: Trends in British Society since 1900, 1972; Educational Priority, 1972; Heredity and Environment, 1977. **Address:** Nuffield College, Oxford, England. **Online address:** Chelly.Halsey@nuf.ox.ac.uk

HALSTEAD, Ted. American, b. 1968. **Genres:** Politics/Government. **Career:** Nonprofit leader, political analyst, and author. Redefining Progress, San Francisco, CA, founder, 1993, and executive director; New America Foundation, Washington, DC, founder, 1999, and C.E.O. Public speaker and media commentator. **Publications:** (with M. Lind) The Radical Center: The Politics of the Alienated Majority, 2001. Contributor to periodicals. **Address:** New America Foundation, 1630 Connecticut Ave. NW 7th Floor, Washington, DC 20009, U.S.A. **Online address:** president@newamerica.net

HALTER, Marek. Polish, b. 1936. **Genres:** Autobiography/Memoirs. **Career:** Artist, human rights activist, editor, and author. Worked as a mime for two years in Paris. **Publications:** Le fou et les rois (autobiography), c. 1976, trans. as The Jester and the Kings: A Political Autobiography, 1989; La vie incertaine de Marco Mahler (title means: The Uncertain Life of Marco Mahler), c. 1979; Le memoire d'Abraham, c. 1983, trans. by Bair as The Book of Abraham, 1986; The Children of Abraham, trans., 1990; Un homme, un cri (title means: One Man, One Cry), 1991; Memoire inquiete, 1993;

Messie, 1996; Stories of Deliverance, 1998; Mysteres de Jerusalem (novel), 1999; Judaisme raconte a mes filleuls, 1999; Vent des Khazars (novel), 2001. Illustrator of books by E. Morin. **Address:** 13 rue des Minimes, 75003 Paris, France.

HALVORSON, Marilyn. Canadian, b. 1948. **Genres:** Children's fiction, Young adult fiction, Local history/Rural topics. **Career:** Sundre High School, Alberta, teacher, until 1990; cattle ranching. **Publications:** Cowboys Don't Cry, 1984; Let It Go, 1985; Nobody Said It Would Be Easy, 1987; Hold on, Geronimo, 1988; Bull Rider, 1989; Brothers and Strangers, 1991; Stranger on the Run, 1992; To Everything Season, 1991; But Cows Can't Fly, 1993; Blue Moon, 1994; Cowboys Don't Quit, 1994; Dare, 1990; Stranger on the Line, 1997. **Address:** Box 9, Site 14, RR 2, Sundre, AB, Canada T0M 1X0.

HAM, Debra Newman. Also writes as Debra Lynn Newman. American, b. 1948. **Genres:** History. **Career:** National Archives, Washington, DC, summer intern, 1970-71, archivist working as assistant to the black history specialist, 1972-74, project archivist with Industrial and Social Branch, 1974-78, African American history specialist in Civil Archives Division, 1978-86; Library of Congress, Washington, DC, African American history and culture specialist, 1986-95; Morgan State University, Baltimore, MD, professor of African and archival history, 1995-. Syracuse University, member of Seminar in Kenya and Tanzania, 1973; University of Liberia, Liberian Women in Development Project, volunteer, 1981; Northern Virginia Community College, adjunct professor, 1986-88. **Publications:** AS DEBRA LYNN NEWMAN: List of Free Black Heads of Families in the 1790 Census, 1973; List of Black Servicemen Compiled from the War Department Collection of Revolutionary War Records, 1974; Preliminary Inventory of the Records of the Social Security Administration, 1976; Preliminary Inventory of the Records of the Office of Economic Opportunity, 1977; Selected Documents Pertaining to Black Workers among the Records of the Department of Labor and Its Component Bureaus, 1902-69, 1977; Black History: A Guide to Civilian Records in the National Archives, 1984. EDITOR AS DEBRA NEWMAN HAM: The African-American Mosaic: A Library of Congress Resource Guide for the Study of Black History and Culture, 1993; The African American Odyssey, 1998. Contributor to books and history journals. **Address:** Department of History, Morgan State University, 1700 E Cold Spring Lane, Baltimore, MD 21251, U.S.A. **Online address:** dham@moac.morgan.edu

HAMALAINEN, Pertti (Olavi). Also writes as Oskari Maskinen. Finnish, b. 1952. **Genres:** Travel/Exploration, Information science/Computers. **Career:** Worked in the computer business, 1974-; Kwayyis International Oy, Helsinki, Finland, owner, 1988-; writer. **Publications:** Yemen, 1988, 4th ed., 1999; Mikroverkot (title means: Microcomputer Networks), 1992; (co-author) Middle East on a Shoestring, 1994, 3rd ed., 2000; (co-author) Africa on a Shoestring, 7th ed., 1995. **Address:** Kwayyis International Oy, Tentaankatu 16B, FIN-00140 Helsinki, Finland. **Online address:** pertti.hamalainen@kwayyis.fi

HAMAMOTO, Darrell Y. American, b. 1953. **Genres:** Novels. **Career:** University of California, Davis, associate professor, 1995-. Yellow Entertainment Network, president. **Publications:** Nervous Laughter, 1989; Monitored Peril, 1994; (ed. with R.D. Torres) New American Destinies, 1996; (ed. with S. Liu) Countervisions: Asian American Film Criticism, 2000. **Address:** 3119 Hart Hall, University of California, Davis, CA 95616, U.S.A. **Online address:** dyhamamoto@ucdavis.edu

HAMBLIN, Robert W(ayne). American, b. 1938. **Genres:** Poetry, Documentaries/Reportage, Biography, Novellas/Short stories, Literary criticism and history, Bibliography. **Career:** High school English teacher, Sparrows Point, MD, 1960-62; Southeast Missouri State University, Cape Girardeau, instructor, 1965-66, assistant professor, 1967-70, associate professor, 1971-77, professor of English, 1978-; Missouri Committee for the Humanities programs, project director, 1983, 1986, 1989, 1996, 1999; Brodsky Collection, curator, 1983-89; National Endowment for the Humanities Summer Seminars for School Teachers, director, 1985-87; Center for Faulkner Studies, director, 1989-. **Publications:** (with L.D. Brodsky) Selections from the William Faulkner Collection of Louis Daniel Brodsky: A Descriptive Catalogue, 1979; (with L.D. Brodsky) Faulkner: A Comprehensive Guide to the Brodsky Collection, Vol I: The Biobibliography, 1982, Vol II: The Letters, 1984, Vol III: The De Gaulle Story, 1984, Vol IV: Battle Cry, 1985, Vol V: Manuscripts and Documents, 1988; (with L.D. Brodsky) Faulkner and Hollywood: A Retrospective from the Brodsky Collection, 1984; Perpendicular Rain (poems), 1986; (with L.D. Brodsky) Country Lawyer and Other Stories for the Screen by William Faulkner, 1987; (with L.D. Brodsky) Stallion Road: A Screenplay by William Faulkner, 1989; From the Ground Up (poems), 1992; Win or Win: A Season with Ron Shumate, 1993; (with C.A. Peek) A William Faulkner Encyclopedia, 1999; (with S. Hahn) Teaching Faulkner, 2000. Contributor of poetry, fiction, and essays to books and journals. **Address:** Department of English, Southeast Missouri State University, Cape Girardeau, MO 63701, U.S.A. **Online address:** rhamblin@ semo.edu

HAMBLY, Barbara. American, b. 1951. **Genres:** Science fiction/Fantasy. **Career:** Freelance writer. Has worked as a research assistant, high school teacher, and karate instructor. **Publications:** DARWATH SERIES: The Time of the Dark, 1982; The Walls of Air, 1983; The Armies of Daylight, 1983; Mothers of Winter, 1996; Icefalcon's Quest, 1998. SUN WOLF SERIES: The Ladies of Mandrigyn, 1984; The Witches of Wenshar, 1987; The Unschooled Wizard, 1987; The Dark Hand of Magic, 1990 SUN-CROSS SERIES: The Rainbow Abyss, 1991; Magicians of the Night, 1992; Sun-Cross, 1992. THE WINDROSE CHRONICLES: The Silent Tower, 1986; The Silicon Mage, 1988; Darkmage, 1988; Dog Wizard, 1993. STAR TREK BOOKS: Ishmael: A Star Trek Novel, 1985; Ghost Walker, 1991; Crossroad, 1994. OTHER NOVELS: The Quirinal Hill Affair, 1983, as Search for the Seven Hills, 1987; Dragonsbane, 1986; Those Who Hunt the Night, 1988, in UK as Immortal Blood; Beauty and the Beast (novelization of television script), 1989; Song of Orpheus (novelization of television script), 1990; Stranger at the Wedding, 1994, in UK as Sorcerer's Ward; Bride of the Rat God, 1994; Travelling with the Dead, 1995; Star Wars: Children of the Jedi, 1995; A Free Man of Color, 1997; Star Wars: Planet of Twilight, 1997; Fever Season, 1998; Die Upon a Kiss, 2001. EDITOR: Women of the Night, 1994; Sisters of the Night, 1995. Contributor of short fiction to anthologies and other publications. Author of scripts for animated cartoons. **Address:** c/o Del Rey Books, 1540 Broadway, New York, NY 10036, U.S.A.

HAMBOURG, Maria Morris. American, b. 1949. **Genres:** Art/Art history, Photography. **Career:** Museum of Modern Art, Department of Photography, NYC, curatorial intern, 1975-76, temporary exhibitions assistant, 1976, research assistant, 1978-79, consultant, 1980-83; Metropolitan Museum of Art, Department of Prints and Photography, associate curator 1985-91, Department of Photographs, associate curator, 1992, curator in charge, 1992-. Princeton University, visiting professor, 1984; New York University, Institute of Fine Arts, adjunct associate professor, 1989. **Publications:** (with J. Chambord) Charles Marville: Photographs of Paris at the Time of the 2nd Empire, 1981; (with J. Szarkowski) The Work of Atget, Vol 1: Old France, 1981, Vol 2: The Art of Old Paris, 1982, Vol 3: The Ancien Regime, 1983, Vol 4: Modern Times, 1985; Photographers and Authors: A Collection of Portraits of 20th-Century Writers, 1984; The New Vision: Photography between the Wars, 1989; (with S.S. Phillips) Helen Levitt, 1992; The Waking Dream, 1993; Nadar, 1995; (with P. Schimmel) Sigmar Polke Photoworks, 1995; Sugimoto, 1995; Georgia O'Keeffe: A Portrait by Alfred Stieglitz, 1997; Paul Strand circa 1916, 1998; (with others) Walker Evans, 2000; Earthly Bodies, 2002; (with R. Avedon and M. Fineman) Richard Avedon Portraits, 2002; Thomas Struth 1977-2002, 2002. **Address:** PO Box 753, Crugers, NY 10521, U.S.A.

HAMBREY, Michael (John). British, b. 1948. **Genres:** Earth sciences, Geography, Natural history. **Career:** Swiss Federal Institute of Technology, Zurich, postdoctoral research assistant, 1974-77; Cambridge University, Cambridge, England, research assistant and senior research associate, 1977-91, Fellow of St. Edmund's College, 1978-91; Chartered Geologist, 1991; Liverpool John Moores University, Liverpool, England, Professor of Quaternary Geology, 1991-. **Publications:** (ed. with W.B. Harland) Earth's Pre-Pleistocene Glacial Record, 1981; (with I.J. Fairchild, B.W. Glover, A.D. Stewart, and others) Late Precambrian Geology of the Scottish Highlands and Islands, 1991; (with J.C. Alean) Glaciers, 1992; Glacial Environments, 1994. Contributor of articles to scientific journals. **Address:** School of Biological and Earth Sciences, Liverpool John Moores University, Byrom St., Liverpool L3 3AF, England.

HAMBURGER, Michael (Peter Leopold). British (born Germany), b. 1924. **Genres:** Poetry, Literary criticism and history, Autobiography/ Memoirs, Translations. **Career:** Assistant Lecturer in German, University College, London, 1952-55; Lecturer, and Reader in German, University of Reading, Berks, 1955-64; and subsequent visiting professorships. **Publications:** Later Hogarth, 1945; Flowering Cactus: Poems 1942-49, 1950; Poems 1950-51, 1952; The Dual Site: Poems, 1957; Reason and Energy: Studies in German Literature, 1957, rev. ed. (in U.S. as Contraries: Studies in German Literature) 1971; Weather and Season: New Poems, 1963; Hugo von Hofmannsthal: Zwei Studien, 1964; In Flashlight: Poems, 1965; From Prophecy to Exorcism: The Premises of Modern German Literature, 1965; Zwischen den Sprachen: Essays und Gedichte, 1966; In Massachusetts, 1967; Feeding

the Chickadees, 1968; Travelling: Poems 1963-68, 1969; (with A. Brownjohn and C. Tomlinson) Penguin Modern Poets 14, 1969; Home, 1969; The Truth of Poetry, 1969; Travelling I-V, 1972; Ownerless Earth: New and Selected Poems 1950-72, 1973; Conversations with Charwomen, 1973; A Mug's Game: Intermittent Memoirs, 1973; Art as Second Nature: Occasional Pieces 1950-1974, 1975; Real Estate: Poems, 1977; Moralities: Poems, 1977; An Unofficial Rilke, 1981; Variations: Poems, 1981; In Suffolk: A Poem, 1982; Goethe: Poems and Epigrams, 1983, rev. ed., 1996; A Proliferation of Prophets: German Literature from Nietzsche to the Second World War, 1983; Collected Poems 1941-1983, 1984; After the Second Flood: Essays on Post-War German Literature, 1988; Trees (poetry) 1988; Selected Poems, 1988; Testimonies (essays), 1989; String of Beginnings: Intermittent Memoirs, 1924-54, 1991; Roots in the Air (poems), 1991; Collected Poems 1941-1994, 1995; Late (poem), 1997; The Take-Over (story), 2000; Intersections (poetry), 2000; From a Diary on Non-events (poem), 2002; Wild and Wounded (poetry), 2004. EDITOR & TRANSLATOR: Poems of Holderlin, 1943; Beethoven: Letters, Journals, and Conversations, 1951, rev. ed., 1992; Holderlin: Poems, 1952; Holderlin: Selected Poems, 1961; (with C. Middleton) Modern German Poetry, 1910-1960: An Anthology with Verse Translations, 1962; Holderlin: Poems and Fragments, 1966, rev. ed., 2004; East German Poetry (anthology in German & English), 1972; German Poetry 1910-75, 1977; W.G. Sebald, Unrecounted, 2004. TRANSLATOR: Paul Celan: Poems, 1980; Poems of Paul Celan, 1989, rev. ed., 2002; G. Eich, Pigeons and Moles: Selected Writings, 1991; W.G. Sebald, After Nature, 2002; (and author of intro.) P. Hochel, The Garden of Theophrastus, 2004; (and author of intro.) R.M. Rilke, Turning Point, 2003. EDITOR: J. Thoor, Das Werk: Sonette, Lieder, Erzahlungen, 1965; T. Good, Selected Poems, 1974. **Address:** c/o Johnson & Alcock, Clerkenwell House, 45/47 Clerkenwell Green, London EC1R 0HT, England.

HAMER, Forrest. American, b. 1956. **Genres:** Poetry. **Career:** Psychologist in Oakland, CA. **Publications:** POETRY: Call and Response, 1995; Middle Ear, 2000. **Address:** 3 Commodore Dr B155, Emeryville, CA 94608, U.S.A. **Online address:** fhamer8580@aol.com

HAMID, Ahmad A. Egyptian, b. 1948. **Genres:** Architecture. **Career:** University of Oklahoma, Norman, assistant professor, 1979-81; Drexel University, Philadelphia, PA, professor of civil engineering, 1982-. Consultant in structural engineering. **Publications:** (co-author) Masonry Structures, 1994. **Address:** Department of Civil and Architectural Engineering, Drexel University, Philadelphia, PA 19104, U.S.A.

HAMID, Mohsin. Pakistani, b. 1971. **Genres:** Novels. **Career:** McKinsey & Co., New York, NY, management consultant, 1997-; author. **Publications:** Moth Smoke, 2000. Contributor to periodicals. **Address:** c/o McKinsey & Co, 55 E 52nd St 21st Fl, New York, NY 10022, U.S.A.

HAMILL, Janet. American, b. 1945. **Genres:** Poetry, Novellas/Short stories. **Career:** Poet, painter, and performer. Performer as a poet with the musical group Moving Star, 1997-; gives readings from her work. **Publications:** POETRY: Troublante, 1975; The Temple, 1980; Nostalgia of the Infinite, 1992; Lost Ceilings, 1999. STORIES: (with P. Smith) The Eternal Café in press. Work represented in anthologies. Contributor to periodicals. **Address:** c/o Author Mail, W. W. Norton & Co. Inc., 500 Fifth Ave., New York, NY 10110, U.S.A. **Online address:** nightsky@warwick.net

HAMILL, Pete. American, b. 1935. **Genres:** Novels, Plays/Screenplays, Essays, Documentaries/Reportage. **Career:** Brooklyn Navy Yard, Brooklyn, NY, sheetmetal worker, 1951-52; advertisingdesigner, NYC, 1957-60; New York Post, NYC, reporter,1960-63, political columnist, 1965-67, 1969-74, columnist, 1988-93; Saturday Evening Post, Philadelphia, PA, contributing editor, 1964-65; war correspondent in South Vietnam, 1966; freelance writer, Brooklyn, 1968; former Washington columnist for Newsday; New York Daily News, NYC, columnist, 1977-79;Village Voice, NYC, columnist, 1974-; Mexico City News, editor,1986-87; Esquire, columnist, 1989-91. **Publications:** NOVELS : A Killing for Christ, 1968; The Gift, 1973; Flesh and Blood, 1977; Dirty Laundry, 1978; The Deadly Piece, 1979; The Guns of Heaven, 1983; Loving Women: A Novel of the Fifties, 1990; Snow in August, 1997; Diego Rivera, 1999. SHORT STORY COLLECTIONS: The Invisible City: A New York Sketchbook, 1980; Tokyo Sketches, 1993. NEWSPAPER COLUMN COLLECTIONS: Irrational Ravings, 1971; Piecework: Writings on Men and Women, Fools and Heroes, Lost Cities, Vanished Friends, Small Pleasures, Large Calamities, and How the Weather Was, 1996. SCREENPLAYS: Doc, 1971; Nightside, 1973; Liberty, 1986; Report from Engine Co. 82; Death at an Early Age; Neon Empire, 1987. RECORDINGS WITH MUSIC: AUTHOR OF SCRIPT: Massacre at My Lai, 1970; Murder at Kent State University, 1970; Snow in

August. OTHER: (preface) P. Sann, Kill the Dutchman!: The Story of Dutch Schultz, 1971; Fighters, 1978; (introduction) H. Wang, Harvey Wang's New York, 1990; (afterword) Tales from the Arabian Nights, 1991; A Drinking Life: A Memoir, 1994; (intro) The Brooklyn Reader: 30 Writers Celebrate America's Favorite Borough,, 1994; (intro) E.R. Ellis, A Diary of the Century: Tales from America's Greatest Diarist, 1995; Tools as Art: The Hechinger Collection, 1995; Times Square Gym, 1996; News is a Verb: Journalism at the End of the Twentieth Century, 1998; Why Sinatra Matters, 1998. Contributor to books, periodicals and newspapers. **Address:** c/o International Creative Management, 40 West 57th St., New York, NY 10019, U.S.A.

HAMILL, Sam. American, b. 1943. **Genres:** Poetry, Literary criticism and history, Translations. **Career:** Poet, publisher, editor, and translator. Co-founded Copper Canyon Press, 1972-. Port Townsend Leader, columnist, 1990-93; Reed College, University of Alaska, South Utah State University, South Oregon College, Austin College, Trinity College, writer-in-residence, 1974-; public schools, artist-in-residence, 1974-90; Department of Correction in Washington, Alaska, California, writer-in-residence, 1976-88. **Publications:** POETRY: Heroes of the Teton Mythos, 1973; Petroglyphs, 1975; Uintah Blue (chapbook), 1975; The Calling across Forever, 1976; The Book of Elegaic Geography, 1978; Triada (also known as Sam Hamill's Triada), 1978; animae, 1980; Fatal Pleasure, 1984; The Nootka Rose, 1987; Passport, 1988; A Dragon in the Clouds, 1989; Mandala, 1991; Destination Zero: Poems 1970-1995, 1995; Gratitude, 1999. ESSAYS: At Home in the World, 1980; Basho's Ghost (prose and poetry), 1989; A Poet's Work: The Other Side of Poetry, 1990. EDITOR: Selected Poems of Thomas McGrath, 1988; Collected Poems of Kay Boyle, 1991; T. McGrath, Death Song, 1991; The Erotic Spirit, 1996; The Gift of Tongues, 1996; Sacramental Acts: The Love Poems of Kenneth Rexroth, 1997. TRANSLATOR: Endless River: Li Po and Tu Fu, A Friendship in Poetry, 1993; Love Poems from the Japanese, 1994; The Lotus Lovers, 1985; Night Traveling, 1985; (with the author) J. Kaplinski, The Same Sea in Us All, 1985; Lu Chi, The Art of Writing, 1986, rev. ed., 1991; Catullus Redivivus, 1986; Li T'ai-po, Banished Immortal, 1987; (with the author) Kaplinski, The Wandering Border, 1987; Tu Fu, Facing the Snow, 1988; Basho, Narrow Road to the Interior, 1991; Only Companion: Japanese Poems of Love and Longing, 1991, rev. ed., 1996; The Infinite Moment, 1992; Midnight Flute, 1994; The Sound of Water: Haiku by Basho, Buson and Issa, 1997; (with K.M. Gibson) River of Stars: Selected Poems of Yosano Akiko, 1997; Spring of My Life, 1997; The Essential Basho, 1999; Crossing the Yellow River, 2000. Contributor of poetry, essays, and translations to anthologies and literary magazines. **Address:** c/o Copper Canyon Press, PO Box 271, Port Townsend, WA 98368, U.S.A.

HAMILTON, Alastair. British, b. 1941. **Genres:** Intellectual history, History. **Career:** University of Urbino, Italy, professor of English, 1977-88; University of Leiden, Louise Thijssen-Schouten Professor of the History of Ideas, 1986-; University of Amsterdam, Netherlands, professor of radical reformation history, 1987-2001. **Publications:** The Appeal of Fascism: A Study of Intellectuals and Fascism, 1919-1945, 1970; The Family of Love, 1981; William Bedwell, the Arabist, 1563-1632, 1985; Heresy and Mysticism in Sixteenth-Century Spain: The Alumbrados, 1992; Europe and the Arab World, 1994; The Apocryphal Apocalypse: The Reception of the Second Book of Esdras (4 Ezra) from the Renaissance to the Enlightenment, 1999; Arab Culture and Ottoman Magnificence in Antwerp's Golden Age, 2001; The Family of Love I: Hendrik Niclaes, 2003. **Address:** Opleiding Engels, University of Leiden, PO Box 9515, 2300 RA Leiden, Netherlands.

HAMILTON, Bernard. British, b. 1932. **Genres:** History. **Career:** University of Nottingham, professor emeritus of crusading history. **Publications:** Monastic Reform, Catharism, and the Crusades, 1979; The Latin Church in the Crusader States, 1980; The Medieval Inquisition, 1981; Religion in the Medieval West, 1986; (with J. Hamilton) Christian Dualist Heresies in the Byzantine World, 1998; The Crusades, 1998; Crusaders, Cathars and the Holy Places, 1999; The Leper King and His Heirs, 2000. EDITOR: (with B. Arbel and D. Jacoby) Latins and Greeks in the Eastern Mediterranean after 1204, 1989; (with C.F. Beckingham) Prester John, the Mongols and the Ten Lost Tribes, 1996. **Address:** Dept. of History, University of Nottingham, Nottingham, England.

HAMILTON, Carl. Swedish, b. 1956. **Genres:** Popular Culture. **Career:** Aftonbladet (newspaper), Stockholm, Sweden, columnist, and political commentator; Dilemma (Swedish television show), host. **Publications:** Absolut: Historien om Flasken, 1994, trans. as Absolut: Biography of a Bottle, 2000; Krönika II: fran Silicon Valley till adalen, 1998. **Address:** c/o Author Mail, Texere, 55 East 52nd St., New York, NY 10055, U.S.A. **Online address:** Hamilton@algonet.se

HAMILTON, Carol (Jean Barber). American, b. 1935. **Genres:** Young adult fiction, Poetry. **Career:** Elementary schoolteacher in North Haven, CT, 1957-60, Indianapolis, IN, 1970-71, and Tinker Air Force Base, OK, 1971-82; Academic Center for Enrichment, Midwest City/Del City, OK, teacher of elementary gifted education, 1982-93; Rose State College, Midwest City, OK, adjunct professor of English, 1988-96; University of Central Oklahoma, adjunct faculty, 19952002. Artist in residence at Contemporary Arts Foundation and Warehouse Theater. Interpreter at medical missions in Mexico, Bolivia, Dominican Republic, Panama, and Oklahoma City, OK. **Publications:** Daring the Wind, 1985; Once the Dust, 1992; Legends of Poland, 1992. JUVENILE NOVELS: The Dawn Seekers, 1987; Mystery of Black Mesa, 1995; I'm not from Neptune, 2003. NOVELS: POETRY: Deserts, Dry Places, and Other Aridities, 1999; Legerdemain, 2000; Gold: Greatest Hits, 2002; Breaking Bread, Breaking Silence, 2002; Vanishing Point, 2004. Contributor of articles, poems, and stories to periodicals. **Address:** 9608 Sonata Ct, Midwest City, OK 73130, U.S.A. **Online address:** hamiltoncj@earthlink.net; www.carolhamilton.org

HAMILTON, Hugo. Irish. **Genres:** Novels. **Career:** University of Bucharest, Romania, lecturer in Irish literature, 1994-96; University of York, writer in residence, 1998. **Publications:** NOVELS: Surrogate City, 1990; The Last Shot, 1991; The Love Test, 1995; Dublin Where the Palm Trees Grow, 1996; Headhanger, 1997; Sad Bastard, 1998. OTHER: The Speckled People (autobiography), 2003.

HAMILTON, J(ames) Scott. Canadian, b. 1956. **Genres:** Anthropology/Ethnology, Archaeology/Antiquities, History. **Career:** Archaeological consultant, 1979-88; Lakehead University, Thunder Bay, ON, Canada, professor of archaeology, 1988-. **Publications:** (with D.V. Burley and K.R. Fladmark) Prophecy of the Swan: The History and Archaeology of the Peace River Fur Trade, 1996. Contributor of chapters to books. Contributor to scholarly journals. **Address:** Department of Anthropology, Lakehead University, Thunder Bay, ON, Canada P7B 5E1. **Online address:** shamilto@lakeheadu.ca

HAMILTON, Jane. American, b. 1957. **Genres:** Novels. **Career:** Apple farmer, beginning c. 1979; freelance author, 1982-. **Publications:** NOVELS: The Book of Ruth, 1988, in UK as The Frogs Are Still Singing, 1989; A Map of the World, 1994; The Short History of a Prince, 1998; Disobedience, 2000. **Address:** c/o Doubleday Publishers, 1540 Broadway, New York, NY 10036, U.S.A.

HAMILTON, Jessica. *See* **GREENHALL, Ken.**

HAMILTON, John Maxwell. American, b. 1947. **Genres:** Communications/Media, Economics, International relations/Current affairs, Biography, Writing/Journalism, Essays. **Career:** Milwaukee Journal, WI, reporter, 1967-69; U.S. Marine Corps, officer, 1969-73; freelance journalist, 1973-78, 1986-88; Agency for International Development, Washington, DC, special assistant, 1979-81; U.S. House of Representatives Foreign Affairs Committee, Washington, DC, associate, 1981-82; World Bank, sr. counselor, 1983-86, 1988-92; Public Radio International, Marketplace, commentator, 1991-; Louisiana State University, Manship School of Mass Communication, director, 1992-94, dean, 1994-, Hopkins P. Braezeale Professor, 1998-. **Publications:** Main Street American and the Third World, 1986; Edgar Snow: A Biography, 1988; Entangling Alliances: How the Third World Shapes Our Lives, 1990; (with G.A. Krimsky) Hold the Press: The Inside Story on Newspapers, 1996; Casanova Was a Book Lover: And Other Naked Truths and Provocative Curiosities about the Writing, Selling, and Reading of Books, 2000. **Address:** 567 L.S.U. Ave, Baton Rouge, LA 70808, U.S.A. **Online address:** JHamilt@lsu.edu

HAMILTON, Kenneth (Morrison). Canadian (born England), b. 1917. **Genres:** Literary criticism and history, Theology/Religion. **Career:** Professor Emeritus of Theology and Literature, University of Winnipeg, 1982-(Assistant Professor, 1958-62; Associate Professor, 1962-68; Professor of Religious Studies, 1968-82). Minister of Religion, Nottingham, 1943-48, Wallington, Surrey, 1948-51, and Nova Scotia, 1951-58. **Publications:** The Protestant Way, 1956; The System and the Gospel: A Critique of Paul Tillich, 1963; Revolt against Heaven, 1965; God Is Dead, 1966; In Search of Contemporary Man, 1967; J. D. Salinger: A Critical Essay, 1967; (with A. Hamilton) John Updike: A Critical Essay, 1967; What's New in Religion, 1968; Life in One's Stride: A Short Study in Dietrich Bonhoffer, 1968; The Promise of Kierkegaard, 1969; (with A. Hamilton) The Elements of John Updike, 1970; Words and the Word, 1971; To Turn from Idols, 1973; (with A. Hamilton) To Be a Man-To Be a Woman, 1975; (with A. Hamilton) Condemned to Life: The World of Samuel Beckett, 1976;

Earthly Good, 1989. **Address:** 4-237 Thomas Berry St, Winnipeg, MB, Canada R2H 0P9. **Online address:** kmham@mts.net

HAMILTON, Neil (W.). American, b. 1945. **Genres:** Urban studies, Transportation. **Career:** Gray, Plant, Mooty, Mooty & Bennett, Minneapolis, MN, associate attorney, 1970-71; Krieg, Devault, Alexander & Capehart, Indianapolis, IN, associate attorney, 1971-72; Airlangga University, Surabaya, Indonesia, visiting professor of law and fellow at International Legal Center, 1972-74; Case Western Reserve University, Cleveland, OH, assistant professor of law, 1977-80; William Mitchell College of Law, St. Paul, MN, Trustees Professor of Regulatory Policy, 1980-. U.S. Army Finance School, instructor in accounting, 1971-72. Midwest Corporate Counsel Center, president and executive director, 1985-90. **Publications:** (with P. Hamilton) Governance of Public Enterprise: A Case Study of Urban Mass Transit, 1981; Zealotry and Academic Freedom: A Legal and Historical Perspective, 1995. Contributor to books. Contributor of about 30 articles to law journals. **Address:** William Mitchell College of Law, 875 Summit Ave., St. Paul, MN 55105, U.S.A. **Online address:** nhamilton@wmitchell.edu

HAMILTON, Peter F. British, b. 1960. **Genres:** Science fiction/Fantasy, Young adult fiction, Novellas/Short stories. **Career:** Writer. **Publications:** GREG MANDEL TRILOGY: Mindstar Rising, 1993; A Quantum Murder, 1994; The Nano Flower, 1995. NIGHTS DAWN TRILOGY: The Reality Dysfunction, 1996; The Neutronium Alchemist, 1997. SHORT STORIES: A Second Chance at Eden, 1998. JUVENILE FICTION: Lightstorm, 1998. Contributor to anthologies and science fiction magazines. **Address:** c/o Macmillan, 25 Eccleston Pl., London SW1W 9NF, England.

HAMILTON, Priscilla. See GELLIS, Roberta (Leah Jacobs).

HAMILTON, Saskia. American, b. 1967. **Genres:** Poetry. **Career:** Folger Shakespeare Library, Washington, DC, poetry coordinator, 1992-97; Lannan Foundation, Santa Fe, NM, director of literary programs, 1997-99; Kenyon College, Gambier, OH, visiting instructor, 2000-01; Stonehill College, Easton, MA, assistant professor of English, 2001-. **Publications:** As for Dream (poetry), 2001. **Address:** Department of English, Stonehill College, Easton, MA 02357, U.S.A.

HAMILTON, Sharon Jean. Canadian, b. 1944. **Genres:** Education, Adult non-fiction, Women's studies and issues, Autobiography/Memoirs. **Career:** Elementary school teacher, 1964-67; junior high school teacher, 1969-72; high school English teacher and department head, 1972-83; University of Manitoba, Winnipeg, assistant professor of English, 1986-87; Indiana University-Purdue University at Indianapolis, assistant professor, 1987-92, professor of English, 1992-, acting associate dean of external affairs, 1994-95, Chancellor's Professor, director of the Urban Universities Portfolio Project. **Publications:** (with E. Hansen) Sourcebook for Collaborative Learning in the Arts and Sciences, 1992; (ed. with K. Bosworth, and contrib.) Collaborative Learning in Higher Education: Underlying Processes and Effective Techniques, 1994; My Name's Not Susie: A Life Transformed by Literacy, 1995; My Mother Was My Brother's Only Child (play). Author of audiovisual materials. Contributor to books. Contributor of articles and reviews to professional journals. **Address:** University Library UL 1140C, Indiana University-Purdue University at Indianapolis, 755 W Michigan St, Indianapolis, IN 46202, U.S.A. **Online address:** shamilto@iupui.edu

HAMILTON-PATERSON, James. British, b. 1941. **Genres:** Marine sciences/Oceanography, Poetry, Novels, Novellas/Short stories. **Career:** Taught in Tripoli, Libya in early 1960s; Times Literary Supplement and New Stateman, writer, 1968-74; free-lance journalist; writer, poet. **Publications:** Flight Underground (juvenile), 1969; The House in the Waves (juvenile), 1970; A Very Personal War: The Story of Cornelius Hawkridge, 1971, published as The Greedy War, 1972; Option Three (poems), 1974; (with C. Andrews) Mummies: Death and Life in Ancient Egypt, 1978; Hostage! (juvenile), 1978; Dutch Alps (poems), 1984; The View from Mount Dog, 1986; Playing with Water: Passion and Solitude on a Philippine Island, 1987; Gerontius, 1989; That Time in Malomba (in UK as The Bell-Boy), 1990; The Great Deep (in UK as Seven-Tenths), 1992; Ghosts of Manila, 1994; The Music (short stories), 1996. **Address:** c/o John Johnson Ltd., Clerkenwell House, 45/47 Clerkenwell Green, London EC1R 0HT, England.

HAMLIN, Dallas. See SCHULZE, Dallas.

HAMLYN, D(avid) W(alter). British, b. 1924. **Genres:** Philosophy, Psychology. **Career:** Oxford University, research fellow at Corpus Christi College, 1950-53, lecturer in philosophy at Jesus College, 1953-54;

University of London, Birkbeck College, lecturer, 1954-63, reader, 1963-64, professor of philosophy, head of department, 1964-88, head of department of classics, 1981-86, vice-master of the college, 1983-88, chairman of board of governors of Heythrop College, 1971-78, member, 1984-95, university senate, 1981-87; bd of governors, City Literary Institute, London, 1982-90; editor, Mind, 1972-84, President of the Aristotelian Society, 1977-78. **Publications:** The Psychology of Perception, 1957, rev. ed., 1969; Sensation and Perception, 1961; Aristotle's "De Anima," Books II-III, 1968; The Theory of Knowledge, 1970, 1971; Experience and the Growth of Understanding, 1978; Schopenhauer, 1980; Perception, Learning, and the Self: Essays in the Philosophy of Psychology, 1983; Metaphysics, 1984; The Penguin History of Western Philosophy, 1987; In and Out of the Black Box, 1990; Being a Philosopher, 1992; Understanding Perception, 1996. **Address:** 38 Smithy Knoll Road, Calver, Derbyshire S32 3XW, England.

HAMM, Diane Johnston. American, b. 1949. **Genres:** Children's non-fiction, Young adult non-fiction. **Career:** Freelance writer, 1971-. Barranquilla, Colombia, teacher and community extension worker, 1973-75; Community School, Seattle, WA, workshop counselor, 1981-83; has also taught in Mexico and Spain. Health clinic, volunteer counselor, 1990-. **Publications:** FOR CHILDREN: Grandma Drives a Motor Bed, 1987; How Many Feet in the Bed, 1991; Laney's Lost Momma, 1991; Rockabye Farm, 1992. FOR YOUNG ADULTS: Bunkhouse Journal, 1990; Second Family, 1992. **Address:** 345 Luther St S, Salem, OR 97302-5218, U.S.A.

HAMMELL, Ian. See EMERY, Clayton.

HAMMER, Emanuel F. American, b. 1926. **Genres:** Psychology. **Career:** In private psychoanalytic practice, NYC, 1954-. Clinical Professor, Post-Doctoral Program in Psychoanalysis and Psychotherapy, Institute of Advanced Psychological Studies, Adelphi University, Garden City, Long Island, NY, 1980-; Professor, School of Visual Arts, NYC, 2002-. Sr. Research Scientist, New York State Psychiatric Institute, 1952-55; Chief Psychologist, Lincoln Institute for Psychotherapy, 1955-66; Research Consultant, Art Dept., 1958-61, and Adjunct Associate Professor of Psychology, Graduate School of Arts and Science, 1970-76, New York University; Director of Training, New York Center for Psychoanalytic Training, 1966-75; Adjunct Professor, Graduate Art Therapy Dept., Pratt Institute, Brooklyn, NY, 1977-81. **Publications:** The House-Tree-Person Clinical Research Manual, 1955; The Clinical Application of Projective Drawings, 1958; Creativity, 1961; Creativity, Talent, and Personality, 1984; Reaching the Affect: Style in the Psychodynamic Therapies, 1990; Advances in the Clinical Application of Projective Drawings, 1998. EDITOR: Personality Dimensions of Creativity, 1962; (with J.N. Buck) Advances in the House-Tree-Person Test: Variations and Applications, 1968; Use of Interpretation in Treatment: Its Role, Depth, Timing and Art, 1968; Anti-achievement: Perspectives on School Drop-outs, 1970. **Address:** 381 West End Ave, New York, NY 10024, U.S.A.

HAMMERSLOUGH, Jane. American. **Genres:** Young adult non-fiction, Children's fiction. **Career:** Writer, journalist. New York Post, New York, NY, columnist. **Publications:** JUVENILE BOARD BOOKS: Aladdin's Lamp, 1992; Firehouse Dogs, 1992; Hans Christian Andersen, The Little Mermaid, 1992; C. Collodi, Pinocchio, 1992. OTHER: Everything You Need to Know About Teen Motherhood, 1990, rev. ed, 2001; The Home Alone Survival Guide (juvenile), 1993; Everything You Need to Know About Skin Care, 1994; Dematerializing: Taming the Power of Possession, 2001. Contributor to periodicals. **Address:** 112 Easton Rd, Westport, CT 06880, U.S.A.

HAMMES, John A. American, b. 1924. **Genres:** Psychology, Theology/Religion. **Career:** University of Georgia, Athens, Assistant Professor, 1956-62, Associate Professor of Psychology and Director of Civil Defense Research, 1962-68, Professor of Psychology, 1968-90, Professor Emeritus of Psychology, 1990-. **Publications:** To Help You Say the Rosary Better, 1962; To Help You Follow the Way of the Cross, 1964; Humanistic Psychology: A Christian Interpretation, 1971; Human Destiny: Exploring Today's Value Systems, 1978; The Way of the Cross in Scriptural Meditation, 1979; In Praise of God, 1983; Ascend to Your Father, 1986; In Praise of God (vol. II), 1987; One Month Scriptural Rosary, 1999. **Address:** Dept. of Psychology, University of Georgia, Athens, GA 30602, U.S.A.

HAMMOND, Gerald (Arthur Douglas). Also writes as Arthur Douglas, Dalby Holden. British, b. 1926. **Genres:** Novels, Mystery/Crime/Suspense. **Career:** Full-time writer, 1983-. Assistant Resident Architect, St. Andrew University, Fife, 1959-69; Deputy Chief Architect and Planning Officer, Livingston Development Corp., Lothian, 1969-83. **Publications:** NOVELS AS

ARTHUR DOUGLAS: The Goods, 1985; Last Rights, 1986; A Very Wrong Number, 1987; A Worm Turns, 1988. CRIME NOVELS AS GERALD HAMMOND: Fred in Situ, 1965; The Loose Screw, 1966; Mud in His Eye, 1967; Dead Game, 1979; The Reward Game, 1980; The Revenge Game, 1981; Fair Game, 1982; The Game, 1982; Cousin Once Removed, 1984; Sauce for the Pigeon, 1984; Pursuit of Arms, 1985; Silver City Scandal, 1986; The Executor, 1986; The Worried Widow, 1987; Adverse Report, 1987; Stray Shot, 1988; Dog in the Dark, 1989; Doghouse, 1989; A Brace of Skeet, 1989; Whose Dog Are You?, 1990; Let Us Prey, 1990; Home to Roost, 1991; In Camera, 1992; Snatch Crop, 1992; Give a Dog a Name, 1992; Cash & Carry, 1993; The Curse of the Cockers, 1993; Thin Air, 1993; Hook or Crook, 1994; Sting in the Tail, 1994; Carriage of Justice, 1995; Mad Dogs and Scotsmen, 1995; Sink or Swim, 1996; Bloodlines, 1996; Follow that Gun, 1997; Twice Bitten, 1998; A Shocking Affair, 1998; Fine Tune, 1998; A Running Jump, 1998; Flamescape, 1999; Dogsbody, 1999; Dead Weight, 2000; Into the Blue, 2001; Illegal Tender, 2001; Grail for Sale, 2002; The Dirty Dollar, 2002; Into the Blue, 2000; The Snatch, 2003; Down the Garden Path, 2003. OTHER: (as Dalby Holden) Doldrum (crime novel), 1987. **Address:** CEILIDH, St. Eunan's Rd, Aboyne, Aberdeenshire AB34 5HH, Scotland. **Online address:** 100537.2445@compuserve.com

HAMMOND, Herb(ert L.). Canadian (born United States), b. 1945. **Genres:** Environmental sciences/Ecology. **Career:** University of Washington, Seattle, graduate research assistant in forest resources, 1972-73; Crown Zellerbach Corp., Courtenay Division, Courtenay, British Columbia, forester, 1973-74; Silva Ecosystem Consultants Ltd., Winlaw, British Columbia, president, 1976-. Registered Professional Forester, Province of British Columbia. Selkirk College, instructor in forest ecology and silviculture, 1974-82, chair, Department of Forest Resources, 1979-81, forestry extension coordinator, 1981-82. **Publications:** Reforestation Syllabus, 1982, rev. ed., 1984; British Columbia Watershed Protection Alliance Handbook, 1988; Seeing the Forest among the Trees: The Case for Wholistic Forest Use, 1991; (with S. Hammond) Community Guide to the Forest: Ecology, Planning, and Use, 1992. Contributor to books. **Address:** Silva Ecosystem Consultants Ltd., Box 9, Slocan Park, BC, Canada V0G 2E0. **Online address:** hhammond@ netidea.com

HAMMOND, Mac. *See* Obituaries.

HAMMOND, Wayne G(ordon). American, b. 1953. **Genres:** Bibliography. **Career:** Williams College, Williamstown, MA, assistant librarian at Chapin Library, 1976-. Book designer. **Publications:** The Graphic Art of C.B. Falls, 1982; J.R.R. Tolkien: A Descriptive Bibliography, 1993; (with C. Scull) J.R.R. Tolkien: Artist and Illustrator, 1995; (co-ed. with C. Scull) Roverandom, 1998; (co-ed. with C. Scull) Farmer Giles of Ham by J.R.R. Tolkien, 1999; Arthur Ransome: A Bibliography, 2000. Contributor to periodicals. **Address:** 30 Talcott Rd, Williamstown, MA 01267, U.S.A. **Online address:** Wayne.G.Hammond@williams.edu

HAMPSON, (Margaret) Daphne. British, b. 1944. **Genres:** Ethics, Intellectual history, Theology/Religion, Women's studies and issues. **Career:** University of North Carolina at Greensboro, instructor in British history, 1970-71; University of Stirling, Stirling, Scotland, lecturer in the history of religious thought, 1974-76; University of St. Andrews, St; Andrews, Scotland, lecturer in systematic theology, 1977-94, senior lecturer, 1994-99, reader, 1999-2001, professor, 2001-. Cambridge University, visiting academic at King's College, 1997. **Publications:** Theology and Feminism, 1990; After Christianity, 1996; (ed.) Swallowing a Fishbone? Feminist Theologians Debate Christianity, 1996; Christian Contradictions: The Structures of Lutheran and Catholic Thought, 2001. **Address:** St Mary's College, St. Andrews KY16 9JU, United Kingdom. **Online address:** dh1@st-and.ac.uk.

HAMPSON, Norman. British, b. 1922. **Genres:** History, Biography. **Career:** University of Newcastle upon Tyne, Professor of Modern History, 1967-74; University of York, Professor, 1974-89, Professor Emeritus of History, 1989-. **Publications:** La Marine de l'An II, 1959; A Social History of the French Revolution, 1963; Pelican History of European Thought: Volume IV, The Enlightenment, 1968; The First European Revolution, 1969; The Life and Opinions of Maxmilien Robespierre, 1974; A Concise History of the French Revolution, 1974; Danton, 1978; Will and Circumstance: Montesquieu, Rousseau, and the French Revolution, 1983; Prelude to Terror, 1988; St. Just, 1991; The Perfidy of Albion, 1998; Not Really What You'd Call a War, 2001. **Address:** 305 Hull Rd, York YO10 3LU, England.

HAMPSON, Robert (Gavin). British, b. 1948. **Genres:** Poetry, Literary criticism and history. **Career:** Royal Holloway, University of London, Egham, Surrey, England, professor of modern literature; writer. **Publica-**

tions: POETRY: Degrees of Addiction, 1975; How Nell Scored, 1976; A Necessary Displacement, 1978; A Feast of Friends, 1982; A City at War, 1985; A Human Measure, 1989; Unicorns, 1989; Seaport, 1995; A New Hampshire Sampler, 1996; Assembled Fugitives: Selected Poems 1973-1998, 2001; C for Security, 2002. LITERARY CRITICISM: Joseph Conrad: Betrayal and Identity, 1992; Cross-cultural Encounters in Conrad's Malay Fiction, 2000. EDITOR: J. Conrad, Lord Jim, 1986; R. Kipling, Something of Myself, 1987; J. Conrad, Victory, 1989; (with P. Barry) The Scope of the Possible: British Poetry since 1970, 1994; J. Conrad, Heart of Darkness, 1995; R. Kipling, Soldiers Three (In Black and White), 1998; J. Conrad, Nostromo, 2000; (with T. Davenport) Ford Madox Ford: A Reappraisal, 2002. **Address:** Department of English, Royal Holloway, University of London, Egham, Surrey TW20 0EX, England. **Online address:** r.hampson@ rhul.ac.uk

HAMPTON, Wilborn. American. **Genres:** Communications/Media, Environmental sciences/Ecology, History, Young adult non-fiction, Autobiography/Memoirs. **Career:** Worked as a reporter for UPI and as an editor for the New York Times. **Publications:** Kennedy Assassinated!: The World Mourns: A Reporter's Story, 1997; Meltdown: A Race against Nuclear Disaster at Three Mile Island: A Reporter's Story; September 11, 2001: Attack on New York City. **Address:** c/o Candlewick Press, 2067 Massachusetts Ave 5th Fl, Cambridge, MA 02140, U.S.A.

HAMPTON, William (Albert). British, b. 1929. **Genres:** Education, Politics/Government. **Career:** University of Sheffield, assistant lecturer 1963-64, lecturer 1964-70, sr. lecturer, 1970-77, reader, 1977-83, professor 1983-94, emeritus professor, 1994-. **Publications:** Democracy and Community, 1970; (co-author) Public Participation in Local Services, 1982; (ed.) Local Democracies, 1983; Local Government and Urban Politics, 1987, 1991. **Address:** 26 Meadow Bank Ave, Sheffield S7 1PB, England.

HAMPTON-JONES, Hollis. American. **Genres:** Dance/Ballet. **Career:** Writer, model. **Publications:** Vicious Spring (novel), 2003. **Address:** c/o Author Mail, Riverhead Books Publicity, 375 Hudson St., New York, NY 10014, U.S.A.

HAMRIN, Robert. American, b. 1946. **Genres:** Economics, Business/ Trade/Industry, Administration/Management, Essays, Human relations/ Parenting. **Career:** Joint Economic Committee of Congress, economist, 1974-78; Environmental Protection Agency, senior policy economist and director of benefits staff, 1979-82; economic advisor to Senator Gary Hart, 1982-83; independent economic consultant and author; National Association of Manufacturers, advisor. Member of staff of the President's Commission for a National Agenda for the Eighties, 1980. Lecturer and professor of economics at colleges and universities. **Publications:** (Compiler) The Political Economy of Federal Policy, 1973; Managing Growth in the 1980's: Toward a New Economics, 1980; Environmental Quality and Economic Growth, 1981; A Renewable Resource Economy, 1983; America's New Economy: The Basic Guide, 1988; Straight from a Dad's Heart: 12 Keys to Joy-Filled Fathering, 1993; (with J. Jasinowski) Making It in America: Proven Paths to Success from Fifty Top Companies, 1995. Contributor to books and journals. **Address:** 12211 Quinque Ln., Clifton, VA 20124, U.S.A.

HAN, Suzanne Crowder. American, b. 1953. **Genres:** Children's fiction, Novels, Translations, Mythology/Folklore, Travel/Exploration. **Career:** Freelance writer. U.S. Peace Corps, Chungju and Hongchon, Korea, volunteer, 1977-80; staff member, 1980-81; Korean Overseas Informational Service, Seoul, Korea, editorial consultant, 1981-88. Instructor at Yonsei, Chung-ang, and Hankuk Universities, Seoul, 1981; Franciscan Preschool and Kindergarten, Seoul, preschool and kindergarten teacher, 1991-92. **Publications:** CHILDREN'S FICTION: Let's Color Korea: Traditional Lifestyles, 1989; Korean Folk and Fairy Tales, 1991; Let's Learn about Korea: Customs, 1992; Let's Visit Seoul, 1993; Let's Visit Korea, 1993; The Rabbit's Judgment, 1994; The Rabbit's Escape, 1995; The Dried Persimmon, 1999. FOR ADULTS: Korea, 1986; Seoul, 1986; Kyongju, 1988; Chejudo, 1988; Notes on Things Korean, 1997. TRANSLATOR: Son So-hui, The Wind from the South, 1988 (originally Nampung, 1975); Han Mahlsook, Hymn of the Spirit, 1983 (originally Arumdaun yongga, 1981). **Address:** UN Village, D Apartment 302, Hannam-dong, Yongsan-gu, Seoul 140-210, Republic of Korea. **Online address:** hancrowd@nuri.net

HANBURY-TENISON, Robin. British, b. 1936. **Genres:** Children's fiction, Civil liberties/Human rights, Travel/Exploration. **Career:** Farmer, 1960-. Member of Council, Royal Geographical Society, 1968-86. President Survival International, 1969-. President, Rain Forest Club, 2002-. OBE, 1981. **Publications:** The Rough and the Smooth (exploration), 1969; A Question of

Survival for the Indians of Brazil, 1973; A Pattern of Peoples: A Journey among the Tribes of the Outer Indonesian Islands, 1975; Mulu: The Rain Forest, 1980; The Aborigines of the Amazon Rain Forest: The Yanomami, 1982; Worlds Apart, 1984; White Horses over France, 1985; A Ride along the Great Wall, 1987; Fragile Eden: A Ride through New Zealand, 1989; Spanish Pilgrimage: A Canter to St. James, 1990; (ed.) The Oxford Book of Exploration, 1993. CHILDREN'S BOOKS: Jake's Escape, 1996; Jake's Treasure, 1998; Jake's Safari, 1998. **Address:** Cabilla Manor, Bodmin, Cornwall PL30 4DW, England. **Online address:** Robin@cabilla.co.uk

HANCOCK, Herbie. (Herbert Jeffrey). American, b. 1940. **Genres:** Songs/ Lyrics and libretti. **Career:** Composer, musician, and actor. Keyboardist; Hancock Music Company, Los Angeles, founder, owner, and publisher, 1962-; Hancock and Joe Productions, Los Angeles, founder and owner, 1989-; Harlem Jazz Music Center, New York City, president; as a jazz performer, has appeared in concerts throughout the world. Contributor to film soundtracks. Contributor to recordings by other artists. **Publications:** LYRICIST: FILM AND TELEVISION MUSIC: Herbie (student film), 1966; Blow-Up, 1966; Hey, Hey, Hey, It's Fat Albert (TV series), 1969; The Spook Who Sat by the Door, 1973; Death Wish, 1974; A Soldier's Story, 1984; 'Round Midnight, 1986; Jo Jo Dancer, Your Life Is Calling, 1986; The George McKenna Story (made-for-television movie), 1986; (with M. Kamen) Action Jackson, 1988; Colors, 1988; Harlem Nights, 1989; "Koi and the Kola Nuts," (TV), 1992. **Address:** c/o Hancock Music, 1880 Century Park E Ste 1600, 1616 Butler Avenue, Los Angeles, CA 90067-1661, U.S.A.

HANCOCK, Ian (Robert). Australian, b. 1940. **Genres:** History. **Career:** Monash University, Clayton, Australia, lecturer in history, 1965-69; Australian National University, Canberra, senior lecturer, 1970-, reader in history, 1986-, head of department, 1986-91, member of university council, 1992-94. **Publications:** White Liberals, Moderates, and Radicals in Rhodesia, 1953-1980, 1984; (with P. Godwin) Rhodesians Never Die: The Impact of War and Political Change on White Rhodesia, c. 1970-1990, 1993; National and Permanent, 2000. **Address:** Research School of Social Sciences, HC Coombs Bldg, Australian National University, Canberra, ACT 0200, Australia. **Online address:** ian.hancock@anu.edu.au

HANCOCK, James (A.). British, b. 1921. **Genres:** Zoology. **Career:** Burmah Oil Co., Swindon, England, divisional director, 1947-75; Ethyl Corp., Richmond, VA, president of Cooper Division, 1975-79. Cox & Kings, guest lecturer for wildlife tours in Africa and India, and organizer of Jungle Odyssey Tours to India, Nepal, and Kenya; member of Mountfort Expedition to Pakistan; leader of colonial waterbird research expeditions to Argentina, 1980, China, 1981, and Australia, 1986; conducted field studies in India, Peru, Chile, Brazil, Indonesia, Thailand, Kenya, South Africa, the Seychelles, Singapore, Japan, Canada, Zimbabwe, and the United States. OBE for services to ornithology, 1991. **Publications:** (with H. Elliott) The Herons of the World, 1978; The Birds of the Wetlands, 1984, rev. ed., 1999; (with J.A. Kushlan) The Herons Handbook, 1984; (with J.A. Kushlan and M.P. Kahl) The Storks, Ibises, and Spoonbills of the World, 1992; Herons and Egrets of the World: Photographic Journey, 1999; Herons of North America: Their World in Focus, 1999. Contributor to ornithology journals and popular magazines. **Address:** Jollers, Sparsholt, Winchester SO21 2NS, England.

HAND, Geoffrey Joseph Philip. Irish, b. 1931. **Genres:** History, Law. **Career:** Emeritus Professor, 1992-, Barber Professor of Jurisprudence, 1980-92, University of Birmingham; Assistant Lecturer, University of Edinburgh, 1960-61; Lecturer, University of Southampton, 1961-65; Lecturer and Professor, University College, Dublin, 1965-76; Professor of Law, University Institute, Florence, 1976-80. Chairman, Arts Council of the Republic of Ireland, 1974-75; Chairman, Irish Manuscripts Commission, 1998-. **Publications:** English Law in Ireland, 1290-1324, 1967; (ed.) Report of the Irish Boundary Commission 1924, 1970; (ed. with Lord Cross of Chelsea) Radcliffe and Cross's English Legal System, 5th ed., 1971, 6th ed. (with D.J. Bentley), 1977; (with J. Georgel and C. Sasse) Handbook to the Electoral Systems of the Nine Member-States of the European Community, 1979; (co-author) The European Parliament: Towards a Uniform Procedure for Direct Elections, 1981; (with J. McBride) Droit sans Frontières, 1991.

HAND, Richard A(llen). American, b. 1941. **Genres:** Bibliography. **Career:** U.S. Air Force, marksmanship instructor, 1965-81; Bishop of Books Ltd., Wheeling, WV, antiquarian bookseller, 1983-86; writer in Ohio, 1986-92; antiquarian bookseller, 1992-2004. **Publications:** A Bookman's Guide to the Indians of the Americas: A Compilation of over 10,000 Catalogie Entries with Prices and Annotations, Both Bibliographical and Descriptive, 1989; A Bookman's Guide to Hunting, Shooting, Angling, and Related Subjects: A Compilation of over 13,450 Catalogue Entries with Prices and Annotations,

Both Bibliographical and Descriptive, 1991; The Indians of Ohio, Prehistoric and Historic: An Annotated Checklist of Articles That Have Appeared in the Ohio Archaeological and Historical Society Publications, 1887 to 1921, 1991; A Bookman's Guide to Archaeology: A Compilation of over 7,000 Books Pertaining to the Scientific Study of Prehistoric and Historic People, Their Artifacts, Inscriptions, and Monuments, with Prices and Annotations, Both Bibliographical and Descriptive, 1994. **Address:** 280 East Highland Dr., Zanesville, OH 43701, U.S.A.

HANDELMAN, Stephen. American, b. 1947. **Genres:** Area studies, International relations/Current affairs, Politics/Government. **Career:** New York Free Press, NYC, assistant editor, 1967-69; New York Times, NYC, news assistant, 1967-68; Penticton Herald/Prince George Citizen, reporter, 1969-71; Miami News, Miami, FL, and Jacksonville, MS, reporter, 1973-74; Toronto Star, ON, Canada, reporter, 1974-76, political writer, 1977-80, bureau chief in Middle East and Europe, 1981-87, bureau chief in Moscow, 1987-92; Time Canada, columnist, 1998-; writer. **Publications:** Uncommon Kingdom: The British in the 1980s, 1988; Comrade Criminal: Russia's New Mafiya, 1995, in UK as Comrade Criminal: The Theft of the Second Russian Revolution, 1995. Contributor to periodicals. **Address:** 102 W 85th St #8F, New York, NY 10024, U.S.A.

HANDLER, Daniel. *See* SNICKET, Lemony.

HANDLER, David. Also writes as Russell Andrews. American, b. 1952. **Genres:** Novels, Plays/Screenplays, Ghost Writer. **Career:** Writer, ghostwriter, screenwriter, and producer. Also worked as syndicated columnist and Broadway critic. **Publications:** NOVELS: Kiddo, 1987; Boss, 1988; The Man Who Died Laughing, 1988; The Man Who Lived by Night, 1989; The Man Who Would Be F. Scott Fitzgerald, 1990; The Woman Who Fell from Grace, 1991; The Boy Who Never Grew Up, 1992; The Man Who Canceled Himself, 1995; The Girl Who Ran off with Daddy, 1996; The Man Who Loved Women to Death, 1997; Cold Blue Blood, 2001. Author of screenplays, including scripts for television series. AS RUSSELL ANDREWS: Gideon, 1999; Icarus, 2000. **Address:** 7 Library Ln, Old Lyme, CT, U.S.A.

HANDLEY, Eric Walter. British, b. 1926. **Genres:** Classics. **Career:** Lecturer, 1946-61, Reader, 1961-67, and Professor of Greek, 1967-84, University College, London; Director of the Institute of Classical Studies, London, 1967-84; Regius Professor of Greek, Cambridge University, 1984-94; Fellow, Trinity College, Cambridge, 1984-; Professor of Ancient Literature, Royal Academy of Arts, 1990-. Foreign Secretary, British Academy, 1979-88. **Publications:** (with J. Rea) The Telephus of Euripides, 1957; The Dyskolos of Menander, 1965; (with A. Hurst) Relire Menandre, 1990; (with J.-M. Bremer) Aristophane, 1993; (with others) The Oxyrhynchus Papyri, vol. 59, 1992, vol. 64, 1997; (with R. Green) Images of the Greek Theatre, 1995. **Address:** Trinity College, Cambridge CB2 1TQ, England.

HANDS, D. Wade. American, b. 1951. **Genres:** Economics. **Career:** Indiana University-Bloomington, associate instructor in economics, 1976-79; University of Puget Sound, Tacoma, WA, assistant professor, 1980-86, associate professor, 1986-92, professor of economics, 1992-. University of Notre Dame, visiting associate professor, 1991. **Publications:** Introductory Mathematical Economics, 1991; Testing, Rationality, and Progress: Essays on the Popperian Tradition in Economic Methodology, 1993; (ed.) The Handbook of Economic Methodology, 1998. Work represented in anthologies. Contributor of articles and reviews to economic and philosophy journals. **Address:** Department of Economics, University of Puget Sound, Tacoma, WA 98416, U.S.A.

HANDY, Lowell K. American, b. 1949. **Genres:** Librarianship, Theology/ Religion, Bibliography. **Career:** American Theological Library Association, Evanston, IL, senior indexer/analyst, 1988-. Loyola University of Chicago, senior lecturer, 1987-2002. **Publications:** Among the Host of Heaven: The Syro-Palestinian Pantheon as Bureaucracy, 1994; The Educated Person's Thumbnail Introduction to the Bible, 1997; Entertaining Faith: Reading Short Stories in the Bible, 2000. EDITOR: Index to Book Reviews in Religion: An Author, Title, and Classification Index to Reviews of Books Published in and of Interest to the Field of Religion, 1969-1974, 1993; (with R.D. Hudgens) Index to Book Reviews in Religion: An Author, Title, and Classification Index to Reviews of Books Published in and of Interest to the Field of Religion, 1993. EDITOR AND CONTRIBUTOR: (with S.W. Holloway) The Pitcher Is Broken: Memorial Essays for Goesta W. Ahlstroem, 1995; The Age of Solomon: Scholarship at the Turn of the Millennium, 1997. Contributor to books. Contributor of articles and reviews to theology journals. **Address:** American Theological Library Association, 250 S Wackler Dr #1600, Chicago, IL 60606-5889, U.S.A.

HANDY, Rollo. American, b. 1927. **Genres:** Philosophy, Psychology. **Career:** American Institute for Economic Research, Great Barrington, Massachusetts, President, 1976-91, President Emeritus, 1991-; Assistant Professor to Professor and Head, Philosophy Dept., University of South Dakota, Vermillion, 1954-60; Associate Professor, Union College, 1960-61; Chairman and Professor, Philosophy Dept., 1962-67, and Provost, Faculty of Educational Studies, 1967-76, State University of New York at Buffalo. **Publications:** A Current Appraisal of the Behavioral Sciences, (with P. Kurtz) 1964, (with E.C. Harwood) 1973; Methodology of the Behavioral Sciences, 1964; (with E.C. Harwood) Useful Procedures of Inquiry, 1964; (co-ed.) Philosophical Perspectives on Punishment, 1968; (co-ed.) The Behavioral Sciences, 1968; (co-ed.) The Idea of God, 1968; Value Theory and the Behavioral Sciences, 1969; The Measurement of Values, 1970. **Address:** 750 Weaver Dairy Rd #159, Chapel Hill, NC 27514-1440, U.S.A. **Online address:** RHandy4728@aol.com

HANES, Frank Borden. American, b. 1920. **Genres:** Novels, Poetry. **Career:** Involved in real estate and farming. Chairman, Arts and Sciences Foundation, University of North Carolina, Chapel Hill. Past Chairman, North Carolina Writers' Conference; Past President, North Carolina Literary and Historical Association; Trustee, John M. Morehead Foundation and North Carolina Zoological Society; Director, Chatham Mfg. Co., and Hanes Dye & Finishing Co. **Publications:** Abel Anders, 1951; The Bat Brothers, 1953; Journey's Journal, 1956; The Fleet Rabble, 1961; Jackknife John, 1965; The Seeds of Ares, 1977; The Garden of Nonentities, 1983. **Address:** 1057 W. Kent Rd, Winston-Salem, NC 27104, U.S.A.

HANKIN, C(herry) A(nne). New Zealander, b. 1937. **Genres:** History, Novellas/Short stories, Literary criticism and history, Biography. **Career:** Teacher of English and Latin at secondary schools in Auckland, New Zealand, 1960-62, Croydon, England, 1962-63, and Montreal, Quebec, 1963-65; University of Canterbury, Christchurch, New Zealand, began as lecturer to reader in English, 1971-95. **Publications:** (ed.) Critical Essays on the New Zealand Novel, 1976; (ed.) Life in a Young Colony: Selections From Early New Zealand Writing, 1981; (ed.) Critical Essays on the New Zealand Short Story, 1982; Katherine Mansfield and Her Confessional Stories, 1983; (ed.) The Letters of John Middleton Murry to Katherine Mansfield, 1983; (ed.) Letters Between Katherine Mansfield and John Middleton Murry, 1988; New Amsterdam, 1991. **Address:** 22 West Tamaki Rd., St. Heliers, Auckland, New Zealand.

HANKIN, Elizabeth Rosemary. Also writes as Elizabeth Gill. British, b. 1950. **Genres:** Novels. **Career:** Journalist in Durham, England, 1970-75; writer. **Publications:** NOVELS: The Singing Winds, 1995; Far from My Father's House, 1995; Under a Cloud-Soft Sky, 1996; The Road to Berry Edge, 1997. Has also written under the name Elizabeth Gill. **Address:** 6 Watling Way, Lanchester, Durham DH7 OHN, England.

HANKINSON, Alan. British, b. 1926. **Genres:** History, Biography. **Career:** Bolton Evening News, Bolton, England, journalist, 1950-53; Nigerian Broadcasting Corp., Lagos, Nigeria, journalist, 1953-58; Independent Television News, London, England, journalist, 1958-75; free-lance journalist, 1975-. **Publications:** The First Tigers, 1972; Camera on the Crags, 1975; Changabang, 1975; The Mountain Men, 1977; Man of Wars: William Howard Russell of "The Times", 1982; The Blue Box, 1983; A Century on the Crags, 1988; The Regatta Men, 1988; First Bull Run 1861, 1991; Coleridge Walks the Fells, 1991; Vicksburg 1863, 1993; Geoffrey Winthrop Young, 1995; Twelve Miles from a Lemon, 1996. **Address:** 30 Skiddaw St, Keswick, Cumbria CA12 4BY, England.

HANLEY, William. American, b. 1931. **Genres:** Novels, Plays/Screenplays. **Publications:** Mrs. Dally Has a Lover, and Other Plays, 1963; Slow Dance on the Killing Ground, 1964; Flesh and Blood, 1968; No Answer, 1968; Blue Dreams; or, The End of Romance and the Continued Pursuit of Happiness (novel), 1971; Mixed Feelings (novel), 1972; Leaving Mount Venus (novel), 1977.

HANLON, Gregory. Canadian/French, b. 1953. **Genres:** History. **Career:** York University, Toronto, ON, Canada, part-time history teacher, 1983-88; University of California, Berkeley, visiting assistant professor of history, 1988-89; Dalhousie University, Halifax, NS, Canada, associate professor, 1989-97, professor of history, 1997-. Universite de Laval, adjunct professor, 1993; Universite de Paris-Sorbonne, visiting adjunct professor, 1996. **Publi-**

cations: L'Univers des gens de bien: Culture et comportements des elites urbaines en Aquitaine au 17e siecle, 1989; Community and Confession in Seventeenth-Century France: Catholic and Protestant Coexistence in Aquitaine, 1993; The Twilight of a Military Tradition: Italian Aristocrats and European Conflicts, 1560-1800, 1998; Early Modern Italy (1550-1800): Three Seasons in European History, 2000; Storia dell'Italia moderna (1550-1800), 2002. Contributor to periodicals. **Address:** Dept of History, Dalhousie University, Halifax, NS, Canada B3H 3J5. **Online address:** ghanlon@dal.ca

HANNA, Jack (Bushnell). American, b. 1947. **Genres:** Animals/Pets, Children's non-fiction. **Career:** Knoxville Zoological Park, Knoxville, TN, head curator, 1970-72; Central Florida Zoo, Sanford, FL, director, 1973-75; Stan Brock Wilderness Adventures, vice-president and associate producer, 1975-78; Columbus Zoological Park, Columbus, OH, executive director, 1978-93, director emeritus, 1993-. Speaker and wildlife conservator. Associate producer, The Forgotten Wilderness, 1975; co-host of television programs; regular guest on television and radio programs. Cofounder, Rhino Rescue Inc. **Publications:** (with J. Stravinsky) Monkeys on the Interstate, and Other Tales from America's Favorite Zookeeper, 1990; Let's Go to the Petting Zoo with Jungle Jack, 1992; (with K.A. Tate) The Lion's Share, 1992; (with H. Mundis) Jack Hanna's Ultimate Guide to Pets, 1996; Jungle Jack Hanna's Pocketful of Bugs, 1996; Jungle Jack Hanna's Safari Adventure, 1996; Friendship Tree, 1996; Jungle Jack Hanna's What Zookeepers Do, 1998. **Address:** c/o VT Entertainment, 1070 Commerce Dr, Perrysburg, OH 43551, U.S.A. **Online address:** www.jackhanna.com

HANNAFORD, Peter (Dor). American, b. 1932. **Genres:** Biography, Communications/Media. **Career:** Account executive for Helen A. Kennedy Advertising, 1956; Kennedy-Hannaford, Inc., San Francisco, Calif., vice-president, 1957-62; president, 1962-67; Kennedy, Hannaford & Dolman, Inc., Oakland, Calif.; Pettler & Hannaford, Inc., Oakland, president, 1967-69; vice-president of Wilton, Coombs & Colnett, Inc., 1969-72; Hannaford & Associates, Oakland, president, 1973; Office of the Governor of California, Sacramento, director of public affairs, 1974; Deaver & Hannaford, Inc., Los Angeles, Calif. and Washington, DC, chairman of board of directors, 1975-95; manager, director, The Franklin Firm director of the Carman Group, Inc., Washington, DC, 1996-; Instructor in advertising at Merritt College, 1964-67; national president of Mutual Advertising Agency Network, 1968-69. Republican nominee for U.S. Congress, 1972; vice-chairman of California Governor's Consumer Fraud Task Force, 1972-; member of Public Relations Advisory Commission of U.S. Information Agency, 1981-92; speech writer and adviser to former president Ronald Reagan. Member of Piedmont Park Commission, 1964-67; member of boards of Oakland Symphony Orchestra Association, 1963-69, Children's Hospital Medical Center of Northern California, 1967-70, Tahoe Regional Planning Agency, 1973-74; and White House Preservation Fund, 1981-89. **Publications:** The Reagans: A Political Portrait, 1983; Talking Back to the Media, 1986; (co-author) Remembering Reagan, 1994. **Address:** Bill Adler, 551 Fifth Ave., New York, NY 10017, U.S.A.

HANNAH, Barry. American, b. 1942. **Genres:** Novels, Novellas/Short stories. **Career:** Member of the English Dept., Clemson University, South Carolina, 1967-73; Writer-in-Residence, Middlebury College, Vermont, 1974-75; member of the English Dept., University of Alabama, 1975-80; writer for the director Robert Altman, Hollywood, 1980; Writer-in-Residence, University of Iowa, Iowa City, 1981, University of Mississippi, Oxford, 1982, 1984, 1985-93, and University of Montana, Missoula, 1982-83. **Publications:** NOVELS: Geronimo Rex, 1972; Nightwatchmen, 1973; Ray, 1981; The Tennis Handsome, 1983; Power and Light, 1983; Hey Jack!, 1987; Boomerang, 1989; Never Die, 1991; High Lonesome, 1996; Yonder Stands Your Orphan, 2001. STORIES: Airships, 1978; Black Butterfly, 1982; Captain Maximus, 1985; Bats out of Hell, 1994; Men without Ties, 1997. **Address:** Dept of English, Bondurant W205A, University of Mississippi, University, MS 38677-1848, U.S.A.

HANNAH, James. American, b. 1951. **Genres:** Novellas/Short stories, History, Literary criticism and history. **Career:** Texas A&M University, professor. **Publications:** Desperate Measures (stories), 1988; Sign Languages (stories), 1993; Tobias Wolff: A Study of the Short Fiction, 1994; The Great War Reader (anthology), 2000. **Address:** English Dept., Texas A & M University, College Station, TX 77843, U.S.A.

HANNAM, June. British, b. 1947. **Genres:** Biography, Bibliography. **Career:** Assistant lecturer at a technical secondary school, 1970-71; North East London Polytechnic, London, England, associate lecturer in history, 1971-73; University of the West of England, Bristol, lecturer to senior lecturer, 1973-86, principal lecturer in humanities, social science, and history, 1987-, department head, 1985-97, member of the university's board of governors, 1993-. **Publications:** Isabella Ford, 1855-1924, 1989; (Compiler with P. Stafford and A. Hughes) British Women's History: A Bibliographical Guide, 1996; (assoc ed) New Dictionary of National Biography. Contributor to works on womens history. Contributor of articles and reviews to periodicals. **Address:** University of the West of England, St. Matthias, Oldbury Court Rd., Fishponds, Bristol BS16 2JP, England. **Online address:** J2-hannam@uwe.ac.uk

HANNANT, Larry. Canadian. **Genres:** History. **Career:** University of Victoria, Victoria, British Columbia, Canada, professor, 1992-97; Camosun College, Victoria, British Columbia, professor, 1997-. **Publications:** The Infernal Machine: Investigating the Loyalty of Canada's Citizens, 1995; Politics of Passion: Norman Bethune's Writing and Art, 1998. **Address:** Camosun College, 3100 Foul Bay Rd, Victoria, BC, Canada V8P 5J2. **Online address:** hannant@camosun.bc.ca

HANNAY, Alastair. British, b. 1932. **Genres:** Philosophy, Translations. **Career:** Professor Emeritus of Philosophy, University of Oslo. Research Fellow, Norwegian Research Council, Oslo, 1968-71; Associate Professor, 1975-75, and Professor of Philosophy, 1975-86, University of Trondheim, Norway; Visiting Professor, University of California, Berkeley, 1982, and University of California, San Diego, 1985, 1988, 1991. **Publications:** (ed. with A. Naess) Invitation to Chinese Philosophy, 1972; Mental Images: A Defence, 1972; Kierkegaard, 1982, rev. ed., 1992; Human Consciousness, 1990; Kierkegaard: A Biography, 2001; On the Public, 2005. TRANSLATOR & INTRODUCTION: A. Naess, Four Modern Philosophies, 1968; S. Kierkegaard, Fear and Trembling: A Dialectical Lyric, 1984; The Sickness unto Death, by Kierkegaard, 1988; Kierkegaard, Either/Or, 1992; Kierkegaard, Papers and Journals, 1996; Kierkegaard, A Literary Review, 2001. Contributor to books. **Address:** Dept of Philosophy, University of Oslo, PO Box 1024 Blindern, 0315 Oslo 3, Norway.

HANNIBAL, Edward L. American, b. 1936. **Genres:** Novels, Advertising/Public relations. **Publications:** Chocolate Days, Popsicle Weeks, 1970; Dancing Man, 1973; Liberty Square Station, 1977, paperback as Better Days, 1979; (with R. Boris) Blood Feud, 1979; A Trace of Red, 1982. **Address:** c/o Grey Advt., 777 3rd Ave, New York, NY 10017, U.S.A. **Online address:** ehannibal@grey.com; ehanni2350@aol.com

HANNUM, Hurst. American, b. 1945. **Genres:** Food and Wine, Law. **Career:** Admitted to the Bar of California, 1974, and the Bar of Washington, DC, 1980; Northern Ireland Civil Rights Assn, Belfast, legal adviser, 1972-75; private law practice, California, 1975-77; Institute for International Law and Economic Development, Washington, DC, attorney, 1977-79; Procedural Aspects of International Law Institute, Washington, DC, executive director, 1979-89; Tufts University, Medford, MA, associate professor of international law, 1990-96, professor, 1996-, Center for Human Rights & Conflict Resolution, 1999-. University College Faculty of Law, Galway, Ireland, lecturer, 1982; University of Virginia, lecturer, 1986-87; American University, Washington, DC, adjunct professor of law, 1987-89; U.S. Institute for Peace, Washington, DC, Jennings Randolph Peace Fellow, 1989-90; Harvard Law School, visiting professor, 1991; University of Georgia School of Law, visiting senior scholar, 1997. **Publications:** (with R.S. Blumberg) The Fine Wines of California, 1971; (with R.S. Blumberg) Brandies and Liqueurs of the World, 1976; (with R.B. Lillich) Materials on International Human Rights and U.S. Constitutional Law, 1985; The Right to Leave and Return in International Law and Practice, 1987; Autonomy, Sovereignty, and Self-Determination, 1990, rev. ed., 1996; (with R.B. Lillich) International Human Rights: Problems of Law, Policy, and Practice, 1995. EDITOR: Guide to International Human Rights Practice, 1984, 3rd ed., 1999; (with E.L. Lutz and K.J. Burke) New Directions in Human Rights, 1989; Documents on Autonomy and Minority Rights, 1993; (with D.D. Fischer) U.S. Ratification of the International Covenants on Human Rights, 1993. **Address:** Fletcher School of Law and Diplomacy, Tufts University, Medford, MA 02155, U.S.A.

HANSCOMBE, Gillian E(ve). British/Australian, b. 1945. **Genres:** Novels, Poetry, Gay and lesbian issues, Literary criticism and history, Women's studies and issues. **Career:** Hitchin College of F.E. Herts, England, assistant lecturer, 1969-70; Queens College and Jews' College, London, assistant lecturer, 1970-74; Gay News, London, journalist, 1981-83; freelance writer in partnership with Marsaili Cameron, 1984-. Greater London Council, member of community arts subcommittee, 1982-84. Lecturer on feminist issues, literature, and sexual politics. **Publications:** Hecate's Charms, 1976; (with J. Forster) Rocking the Cradle: Lesbian Mothers: A Challenge in Family Living, 1981; Between Friends, 1982; The Art of Life: Dorothy Richardson and the Development of Feminist Consciousness, 1982; (with A.

Lumsden) Title Fight: The Battle for Gay News, 1983; William Golding: Lord of the Flies, 1986; (with S. Namjoshi) Flesh and Paper (poetry), c. 1987; (ed. with M. Humphries) Heterosexuality, 1987; (with V.L. Smyers) Writing for Their Lives: The Modernist Women, 1910-1940, 1987; Stan Barstow: Joby, 1988; Sybil: The Glide of Her Tongue (poetry), 1992; Figments of a Murder, 1995. Contributor of poetry to books. **Address:** Grindon Cottage, Combpyne Lane, Rousdon nr, Lyme Regis DT7 3XW, England. **Online address:** gillhans@freeuk.com

HANSEN, Ann Larkin. American, b. 1958. **Genres:** Animals/Pets. **Career:** Farmer and writer. **Publications:** THE FARM SERIES: All Kinds of Farms, 1996; Crops on the Farm, 1996; Farm Kids, 1996; Farm Machinery, 1996; Farmers, 1996; Seasons on the Farm, 1996. FARM ANIMALS SERIES: Cattle, 1996; Chickens, 1996; Goats, 1997; Pigs, 1997; Sheep, 1997; Uncommon Farm Animals, 1997. POPULAR PET CARE SERIES: Birds, 1997; Cats, 1997; Dogs, 1997; Fish, 1997; Hamsters and Gerbils, 1997; Turtles, 1997. Contributor to business magazines and art journals. **Address:** 19351 165th St., Bloomer, WI 54724, U.S.A. **Online address:** shansenwin.bright.ne

HANSEN, Ann Natalie. American, b. 1927. **Genres:** History. **Career:** Research Assistant and Ed., Martha Kinney Cooper Ohioana Library Association, 1951-54; on Editorial Staff, Columbus Dispatch, Ohio, 1954-58; Publr., At the Sign of the Cock, 1974-2004. **Publications:** (ed.) Ohio, 1954, 1955; Westward the Winds: Being Some of the Main Currents of Life in Ohio, 1788-1873, 1974; So You're Going Abroad: How to Do It, 1984; The English Origins of the Mary and John Passengers, 1985; The Dorchester Group: Puritanism and Revolution, 1987; Oxford Goldsmiths before 1800, 1996. **Address:** 2341 Brixton Rd, Columbus, OH 43221-3119, U.S.A.

HANSEN, Brooks. American, b. 1965. **Genres:** Novels, Young adult fiction. **Career:** Writer. **Publications:** NOVELS: (with N. Davis) Bonne, 1990; The Chess Garden, 1995; Caesar's Antlers (young adult), 1997; Perlman's Ordeal, 1998. **Address:** c/o Amanda Urban, International Creative Management, 40 West Fifty-seventh St, New York, NY 10019, U.S.A.

HANSEN, Chadwick. American, b. 1926. **Genres:** History, Literary criticism and history. **Career:** Professor of English, University of Illinois at Chicago, 1974-75, 1976-91, Professor Emeritus, 1991-. Instructor, Pennsylvania State University, 1955-71; Professor, University of Minnesota, Minneapolis, 1971-74; Professor of English, University of Iowa, Iowa City, 1975-76. **Publications:** (with D. Austin and R. W. Condee) Modern Fiction: Form and Idea in the Contemporary Novel and Short Story, 1959; (with others) The American Renaissance: The History and Literature of an Era, 1961; Witchcraft at Salem, 1969; (ed. with A. Hodes) Selections from the Gutter: Portraits from the Jazz Record, 1977; (with A. Hodes) Hot Man: The Life of Art Hodes, 1992. **Address:** 1325 N. State Parkway, Chicago, IL 60610-2170, U.S.A.

HANSEN, Debra Gold. American, b. 1953. **Genres:** Women's studies and issues, History. **Career:** Claremont Colleges, Claremont, CA, history bibliographer and reference librarian at Honnold Library, 1984-89; Anaheim Public Library, Anaheim, CA, archivist, 1989-90; San Jose State University, San Jose, CA, assistant professor of library and information science, 1989-. Pomona College, assistant coordinator of bibliographic instruction, 1988-89; California State University, Fullerton, instructor, 1990. California State Archives, editor of California State Legislature Oral History Project, 1991-93. **Publications:** Strained Sisterhood: Gender and Class in the Boston Female Anti-Slavery Society, 1993. Work represented in anthologies. Contributor of articles and reviews to history and library journals. **Address:** California State University, PO Box 1450, Fullerton, CA 92831, U.S.A.

HANSEN, Drew D. (born United States), b. 1964. **Genres:** Adult nonfiction. **Career:** Called to the bar of Washington State, 2000; teaching assistant to Professor Drew S. Days, III; law clerk to Honorable Pierre N. Leval, U.S. Court of Appeals for the Second Circuit, 1999-2000; Susman Godfrey Attorneys at Law, Seattle, WA, currently associate attorney. **Publications:** The Dream: Martin Luther King, Jr., and the Speech that Inspired a Nation, 2003. Contributor of articles to newspapers and professional journals. **Address:** Susman Godfrey Attorneys at Law, Suite 3100, 1201 Third Ave, Seattle, WA 98101, U.S.A. **Online address:** dhansen@susmangodfrey.com

HANSEN, G. Eric. (born United States), b. 1938. **Genres:** Cultural/Ethnic topics. **Career:** Wellesley College, Wellesley, MA, faculty member, 1963-64; Massachusetts Institute of Technology, Cambridge, faculty member, 1964-69; Haverford College, Haverford, PA, faculty member, 1969-73; San Francisco State University, San Francisco, CA, faculty member, 1973-77; Saint Mary's College of California, Moraga, professor of international political economy,

1977-, director of graduate business programs, 1979-89, and associate dean of School of Economics and Business Administration. **Publications:** The Culture of Strangers: Globalization, Localization, and the Phenomenon of Exchange, 2002. Contributor to books and periodicals. **Address:** 250 B Red Rock Way, San Francisco, CA 94131, U.S.A.

HANSEN, Karen V. American, b. 1955. **Genres:** Sociology, Women's studies and issues. **Career:** Foote, Cone & Belding/Honig, San Francisco, CA, project director, 1980-81; URSA Institute, San Francisco, research associate, 1981-84; University of California, Berkeley, acting instructor in sociology, 1988; Brandeis University, Waltham, MA, assistant professor, 1989-95, Marver and Sheva Bernstein faculty fellow, 1993-94, associate professor of sociology, 1995-. Radcliffe College, fellow at Bunting Institute, 1991-92, visiting scholar at Henry A. Murray Research Center, 1994-96; Harvard University, Andrew W. Mellon faculty fellow in women's studies, 1991-92; National Endowment for the Humanities, 1999. **Publications:** A Very Social Time: Crafting Community in Antebellum New England, 1994. EDITOR & CONTRIBUTOR: (with I. Philipson) Women, Class, and the Feminist Imagination: A Socialist-Feminist Reader, 1990; (with A. Garey) Families in the U.S.: Kinship and Domestic Politics, 1998; Not-So-Nuclear Families: Class, Gender, and Networks of Care, 2005. Contributor to books. Contributor of articles and reviews to a variety of academic journals. **Address:** Dept of Sociology, MS 071, Brandeis University, Waltham, MA 02454-9110, U.S.A. **Online address:** khansen@brandeis.edu

HANSEN, Maren Tonder. American, b. 1952. **Genres:** Adult non-fiction. **Career:** Writer. **Publications:** Increasing Organic Agriculture at the Local Level: A Manual for Consumers, Grocers, Farmers, and Policy Makers, 1992; Mother-Mysteries, 1997. **Address:** 904 Skyview Dr, Santa Barbara, CA 93108, U.S.A. **Online address:** maren@silcom.com

HANSEN, Mark Victor. American. **Genres:** Inspirational/Motivational Literature. **Career:** Motivational speaker and author of inspirational books. **Publications:** Future Diary, 1983; (with J. Canfield) Chicken Soup for the Soul: 101 Stories to Open the Heart & Rekindle the Spirit, 1993; (with Canfield) A 2nd Helping of Chicken Soup for the Soul: 101 More Stories to Open the Heart and Rekindle the Spirit, 1995; (with J.D. Batten) The Master Motivator: Secrets of Inspiring Leadership, 1995; (with Canfield and D.V. Wentworth) Chicken Soup for the Soul Cookbook: 101 Stories with Recipes from the Heart, 1995; (with Canfield) The Aladdin Factor, 1995; (with Canfield) A 3rd Helping of Chicken Soup for the Soul: 101 More Stories to Open the Heart and Rekindle the Spirit, 1996; (with B. Nichols and P. Hansen) Out of the Blue: Delight Comes into Our Lives, 1996; (with Canfield and P. Hansen) Condensed Chicken Soup for the Soul, 1996; (with Canfield and B. Spilchuk) A Cup of Chicken Soup for the Soul: Stories to Open the Heart and Rekindle the Spirit, 1996; (with Canfield and K. Kirberger) Chicken Soup for the Teenage Soul: 101 Stories of Life, Love, and Learning, 1997; (with Canfield) A Fifth Portion of Chicken Soup for the Soul: 101 More Stories to Open the Heart and Rekindle the Spirit, 1998; (with Canfield and R. Camacho) Chicken Soup for the Country Soul: Stories Served Up Country Style and Straight from the Heart, 1998; (with Canfield and Kirberger) Chicken Soup for the Teenage Soul II: 101 More Stories of Life, Love, and Learning, 1998; (with Canfield and Kirberger) Chicken Soup for the Teenage Soul: Journal, 1998; (with Canfield) The Best Night Out with Dad (children's book), 1998; (with R.G. Allen) The One Minute Millionaire, 2002. **Address:** c/o Health Communications Inc., 3201 SW 15th St., Deerfield Beach, FL 33442, U.S.A.

HANSEN, Matthew Scott. American, b. 1953. **Genres:** Business/Trade/Industry. **Career:** Writer. **Publications:** (with Bob Zmuda) Andy Kaufman Revealed! Best Friend Tells All, 1999; (with Lynn Brewer) House of Cards: Confessions of an Enron Executive, 2002; (with Bob Eubanks) That Would Be in the Book, Bob, forthcoming. **Address:** c/o Author Mail, Virtualbookworm.com Publishing Inc., POB 9949, College Station, TX 77842, U.S.A.

HANSEN, Poul Einer. Danish, b. 1939. **Genres:** Environmental sciences/Ecology, Mathematics/Statistics, Translations. **Career:** Royal Veterinary and Agricultural University, Frederiksberg, Denmark, associate professor of mathematics, 1963-2005. **Publications:** (ed. with S.E. Joergensen) Introduction to Environmental Management, 1991; (trans. into Danish)A. Dumas, The Count of Monte Cristo, 1991. Author of mathematics textbooks in Danish., and translator of children's books into Danish. **Address:** Dept of Natural Sciences, Royal Veterinary and Agricultural University, Thorvaldsensvej 40, DK-1871 Frederiksberg C, Denmark. **Online address:** peh@kvl.dk

HANSEN, Vern. See **HANSON, Vic(tor) J(oseph).**

HANSEN-HILL, N. D. American. **Genres:** Novels, e-Books. **Career:** Novelist and artist. Worked as a teacher, painter, in commercial irrigation, and as a graphic artist. Horticulture consultant. **Publications:** E-BOOK NOVELS. Grave Images, Books 1-3, 2000-02; Light Play, Books 1-3, 2000; Vision, 2001; Static, 2002. TREES SERIES: Trees, 1996; Crystals, 2000; Mud, 2000; Shades, 2001; Fire, 2002; Light, 2002. ELF CHRONICLES SERIES: Elf, 2002; Trolls, 2002. **Address:** c/o Author Mail Fictionwise, 407 Main St., Chatham, NJ 07928, U.S.A. **Online address:** hh1177@xtra.co.nz

HANSON, Neil. British, b. 1948. **Genres:** Novels, History, Autobiography/Memoirs, Biography. **Career:** Freelance writer, broadcaster, and speaker, 1977-. **Publications:** The Custom of the Sea, 2000; (with K. Jessop) Goldfinder, 2001; The Dreadful Judgment, 2001; The Great Fire of London, 2002; The Confident Hope of a Miracle, 2003.

HANSON, Paul R. American, b. 1952. **Genres:** History. **Career:** Arizona State University, visiting assistant professor of history, 1981-83; Butler University, Indianapolis, IN, 1984-, began as assistant professor, became associate professor of history, department chair, 1991-, professor, 1996-; writer. **Publications:** Revolutionary France (textbook), 1987; Provincial Politics in the French Revolution: Caen and Limoges, 1789-1794, 1989. **Address:** Department of History, Butler University, Indianapolis, IN 46208, U.S.A.

HANSON, Peter G. Canadian, b. 1947. **Genres:** Psychology. **Career:** University of Toronto, Toronto, Ontario, intern at Women's College Hospital, 1971-72; physician in Newmarket, Ontario, 1972-87; professional speaker, Toronto, 1987-92; acupuncturist in Denver, CO, 1992-. Toronto Argonauts football club, team doctor, 1972-74; worked as emergency room physician at York County Hospital and North York General Hospital; Porter Memorial Hospital, medical acupuncturist. Presenter of national syndicated radio feature; guest on television and radio programs in the United States and Canada. **Publications:** The Joy of Stress, 1985; Stress for Success, 1991; Counterattack!, 1994. **Address:** Hanson Peak Performance Clinic, 3300 E 1st Ave Ste 600, Denver, CO 80206, U.S.A. **Online address:** phansonmd@aol.com

HANSON, Philip. British, b. 1936. **Genres:** Economics. **Career:** H.M. Treasury, economic assistant, 1960-61; University of Exeter, lecturer in economics, 1961-67; University of Birmingham, lecturer, 1968-73, sr. lecturer, 1973-81, reader, 1981-87, professor of Soviet economics, then professor of the political economy of Russian and Eastern Europe, 1987-. Visiting professor, University of Michigan, 1967-68, 1977, Kyoto University, 2000; Foreign and Commonwealth Office, sr. research officer, 1971-72; Harvard University, Cambridge, MA, sr. Mellon fellow, 1986-87; United Nations, Geneva, senior economic affairs officer, 1991-92. Cambridge University Press, Soviet and East European Studies Monograph Series, member of the editorial board, 1973-77; Soviet Economy, contributing ed., 1985-. **Publications:** The Wage-Packet: How the Economy Works, 1968; The Consumer in the Soviet Economy, 1968; Advertising and Socialism, 1974; USSR: The Foreign Trade Implications of the 1976-80 Plan, 1976; Trade and Technology in Soviet-Western Relations, 1981; (with K. Pavitt) The Comparative Economics of Research, Development, and Innovation in East and West, 1987; Western Economic Statecraft in East-West Relations, 1988; The Baltic States: The Economic and Political Consequences of the Secession of Estonia, Latvia and Lithuania from the USSR, 1990; From Stagnation to Catastroika, 1992; The Rise and Fall of the Soviet Economy, 2003. EDITOR: (with K. Dawisha) Soviet-East European Dilemmas, 1981; (with M. Kirkwood) Alexander Zinoviev as Writer and Thinker, 1987; (with J. Gibson) Transformation from Below, 1996; (with M.J. Bradshaw) Regional Economic Change in Russia, 2000. **Address:** Centre for Russian and East European Studies, University of Birmingham, Birmingham B15 2TT, England. **Online address:** P.Hanson@bham.ac.uk

HANSON, Vern. See **HANSON, Vic(tor) J(oseph).**

HANSON, Vic(tor) J(oseph). (V. Joseph Hanson). Also writes as Vern Hansen, Jay Hill Potter, William Shand, Vern Hanson. British. **Genres:** Mystery/Crime/Suspense, Westerns/Adventure, Science fiction/Fantasy, Novellas/Short stories. **Career:** Worked for church magazine publishers, printers; former sales rep, ran junk shop, jazz club, book shop. **Publications:** WESTERN AND CRIME NOVELS: Black Heart Crowle, 1978; Savage Sunrise, 1979; Bells in an Empty Town, 1979; Muldare, 1980; Guns of Black Heart, 1980; The End of the Kill, 1980; Men on a Dusty Street, 1981; The Hands of Amos Crowle, 1981; Amos Crowle, Widow-maker, 1981; Black Heart's Bunch, 1982; Hardneck and Amos, 1982; Call Him Amos, 1982; One More Sundown, 1983; Black Amos, 1983; The Greenhorn Days, 1983; Black Amos, Law-bringer, 1984; Damnation Gap, 1984; The Plain

Rats, 1985; The Old-Time Years, 1985; The Law of Amos C., 1985; Assassin's Run, 1989; Amos Lives, 1990; Hannibal's Jump, 1990; A Shroud for Amos, 1990; Killer Alone, 1991; The Legend of Amos, 1991; A Grave for Gentle, 1992; Hell-Ride, 1992; Bloodstone, 1993; Death's Deputies, 1993; Wildwind, 1994; Silvo, 1994; Quest, 1995; Death-Drag, 1995; Killer's Harvest, 1996; Hardisty's Town, 1996; Nighthawks' Moon, 1997; A Loner's Revenge, 1997; Owlhoot Nights, 1998; Blacksnake Trail, 1998; StarPacker's Luck, 1999; Red Dawning, 1999; Retribution Guns, 2000; The Daybreak Siege, forthcoming. CRIME NOVELS AS WILLIAM SHAND: A Man Called Tempest, 1957; Tempest Weaves a Shroud, 1957; Tempest in a Tea-Cup, 1958; The Swinging Man (short), 1964; Crime and Western Novels as V. Joseph Hanson: Gunsmoke Saga, 1949; Lannigan's West, 1949; The Yellow Dust, 1949; The Creeper, 1950; The Morgue Has Guests: Diary of a Killer, 1950; Blue Lightnin', 1950; Bushwhacker!, 1951; Lead Bites Deep, 1950; Border Bullets, 1950; The Devil's Deputy, 1950; Fighting Gunman, 1950; Gun Wolf, 1950; Gun Toter, 1950; The Red Trail, 1950; Terror Town, 1950; Spawn of the Badlands, 1950; Lawless River, 1951; The Shotgun Kid, 1951; Red Silver, 1951; Savage Mesa!, 1951; Slick Lawman, 1951; Smoke in the Valley, 1951; Troubleshooter, 1951; The Bishop Riders, 1952; The Gunhawks, 1952; Shattering Guns, 1955; Guns of Hate, 1955; Death and Little Girl Blue, 1962. CRIME, HORROR, SCIENCE FICTION, WESTERN NOVELS AS VERN HANSEN: Angry Hooves, 1954; Greed of the Devil, 1960; Murder with Menaces, 1962; The Whisper of Death, 1963; The Twisters (short stories), 1963; Creatures of the Mist, 1963; Claws of the Night, 1963; The Grip of Fear (short stories), 1964; Savage Death (novelette), 1964; The Knocke-Man (short), 1965. WESTERNS AS VERN HANSON: Trail Wolves, 1951; Troubleshooting Johnny, 1951; The Sundown Riders, 1951; Colt Harvest, 1951; Guns of Lobo, 1954; Gunsmoke on the Border, 1959. WESTERNS AS JAY HILL POTTER: The Long Guns, 1979; Black Horse Moon, 1979; Killer's Journey, 1980; Harrigan's Dude, 1980; Call Me Pilgrim, 1981; The Bitter Trail, 1981; Jasper and Hack, 1981; Pilgrim's Trail, 1982; Pilgrim's Blood, 1982; Young Joe Pilgrim, 1982; Bounty for Pilgrim, 1983; Requiem for Pilgrim, 1983; The Pilgrim Raid, 1983; A Coffin for Pilgrim, 1984; Gunfighter's Pride, 1984; The Pilgrim Kill, 1985; Turkey Shoot, 1986; Pilgrim's Revenge, 1990; Restless Town, 1990; Hills of the Dead, 1991; Old Man's Gun, 1992; Murder Trail, 1993; Coyote Bait, 1994; Sodal Valley Shoot-out, 1994; Pilgrim's Return, 1996; The Big Hogleg, 1996; tiller's Watch, 1997; The Last Go-down, 1998.

HAN SUYIN. (Guanghu/Elizabeth Zhou). British/Chinese (born China), b. 1917. **Genres:** Novels, International relations/Current affairs, Travel/Exploration, Autobiography/Memoirs. **Career:** Medical practitioner, in London, Hong Kong, Singapore and Malaya, 1948-63; full-time writer since 1963. **Publications:** Destination Chungking, 1942; A Many-Splendoured Thing, 1952; And the Rain My Drink, 1956; The Mountain Is Young, 1958; Asia Today, 1969; Cast But One Shadow, 1962; Winter Love, 1963; Four Faces, 1964; The Crippled Tree, 1965; A Mortal Flower, 1967; China in 2001, 1967; Birdless Summer, 1969; The Morning Deluge, 1972; Wind in the Tower, 1975; Lhasa, The Open City, 1976; La Peinture Chinoise, 1977; La Chine au Mille Visages, 1978; Chine: Terre, Eau et Hommes, 1980; My House Has Two Doors, 1981; Phoenix Harvest, 1981; Till Morning Comes, 1982; The Enchantress, 1985; A Share of Loving, 1987; Han Suyin's China, 1988; Fleur de Soleil, 1988; Tigers and Butterflies, 1990; Les 100 Fleurs, 1978; La Peinture Chinoise, 1978; Les Yeux de Demain, 1992. **Address:** 37 Montoie, 1007 Lausanne, Switzerland.

HANZO, L(ajos). (born Hungary), b. 1952. **Genres:** Technology. **Career:** Telecommunications Research Institute, Budapest, Hungary, staff member, 1976-87; University of Southampton, Southampton, England, professor of communications. **Publications:** (with Raymond Steele) Mobile Radio Communications: Second and Third Generation Cellular and WATM Systems, 2nd edition, 1999; (with W. Webb and T. Keller) Single-and Multi-Carrier Quadrature Amplitude Modulation: Principles and Applications for Personal Communications, WLANs, and Broadcasting, 2000; (with Peter Cherriman and Jurgen Streit) Wireless Video Communications: Second to Third Generation Systems and Beyond, 2001; (with F. Clare, A. Somerville, and Jason P. Woodward) Voice Compression and Communications: Principles and Applications for Fixed and Wireless Channels, 2001; (with T. H. Liew and B. L. Yeap) Turbo Coding, Turbo Equalisation, and Space-Time Boding for Transmission over Fading Channels, 2002; (with C. H. Wong and M. S. Yee) Adaptive Wireless Transceivers: Turbo-Coded, Turbo-Equalised, and Space-Time Coded CDMA, TDMA, and OFDM Systems, 2002; (with J. S. Blogh) Third-Generation Systems and Intelligent Wireless Networking: Smart Antennas and Adaptive Modulation, 2002. (with M. Münster, B. J. Choi, and T. Keller) OFDM and MC-CDMA for Broadband Multi-user Communications, WLANs, and Broadcasting, 2003. **Address:** Department of Electronics and Computer Science, University of Southampton, Highfield, Southampton SO17 1BJ, England. **Online address:** lh@ecs.soton.ac.uk

HAPKE, Laura. American, b. 1946. **Genres:** Literary criticism and history. **Career:** Pace University, New York City, professor of English, 1990-. Formerly affiliated with several private colleges and universities in the New York City area, including the City University of New York. **Publications:** Girls Who Went Wrong: Prostitutes in American Fiction, 1885-1917, 1989; Tales of the Working Girl: Wage-Earning Women in American Literature, 1890-1925, 1992; Daughters of the Great Depression: Women, Work, and Fiction in the American 1930s, 1996. Contributor to women's studies encyclopedias. Contributor to women's studies and American studies journals. **Address:** Department of English, Pace University, Pace Plaza, New York, NY 10038-1598, U.S.A.

HAPPENSTANCE, Aurelia. See **FURDYNA, Anna M.**

HARADA, Masako. Also writes as Satoko Kizaki. Japanese (born China), b. 1939. **Genres:** Novels, Novellas/Short stories. **Career:** Short story writer and novelist. **Publications:** FICTION AS SATOKO KIZAKI: Rasoku (short stories; title means: Barefoot), 1982; Umi-to Rosoku (short stories), 1985; Aogiri (short stories), 1985, trans. by C.A. Flath as The Phoenix Tree and Other Stories, 1990; Shizumeru tera (novel), 1987, trans. by C.A. Flath as The Sunken Temple, 1993; Nami-Half-way (short stories), 1988; Sanzoku-no-Haka, 1989; Kagami-no-Tani, 1990; Toki-no-Shizuku, 1991; Atonaki-Niwa-ni, 1991; Shiawase no chiisana tobira, 1994. **Address:** 473-1-411 Iwase, Matsudo-Shi, Chiba-Ken 271, Japan.

HARAKAS, Stanley Samuel. Also writes as Exetastes. American, b. 1932. **Genres:** Theology/Religion. **Career:** Ordained priest of Greek Orthodox church, 1956; Holy Cross Greek Orthodox Theological School, Brookline, MA, instructor, 1966-67; Hellenic College-Holy Cross Orthodox School of Theology, Brookline, assistant professor, 1967-71, dean of Holy Cross Orthodox School of Theology, 1970-80, dean of Hellenic College, 1971-75, associate professor, 1971-72, professor, 1972-, Archbishop Iakovos Professor of Orthodox Theology, 1986-; writer. Visiting professor and lecturer at institutions. Awarded exomologos, 1958, economos, 1966, economos of the patriarchal throne, 1971, Gold Cross of Mount Athos, 1971, protopresbyter, 1971, and protopresbyter of the ecumenical throne, 1977, retired, 1995. **Publications:** Living the Liturgy, 1974; (trans.) George Stavropoulos, Partakers of Divine Nature, 1976; (as Exetastes) Contemporary Issues: Orthodox Christian Perspectives, 1976; Something Is Stirring in World Orthodoxy (booklet), 1978; Guidelines for Marriage in the Orthodox Church (booklet), 1979; The Melody of Prayer: How to Personally Experience the Divine Liturgy (booklet), 1979; For the Health of Body and Soul (booklet), 1980; Contemporary Moral Issues Facing the Orthodox Christian, 1982; Let Mercy Abound: A Chronicle of Greek Orthodox Social Concerns, 1983; Toward Transfigured Life, 1983; The Orthodox Church: 455 Questions and Answers, 1987; Proclaiming God's Word Today: Preaching Concerns in the Greek Orthodox Archdiocese of North and South America, 1989; Health and Medicine in the Eastern Orthodox Tradition, 1990; Living the Faith: The Praxis of Eastern Orthodox Ethics, 1992; Wholeness of Faith and Life: Orthodox Christian Ethics, 1999. **Address:** 12443 Little Farms Dr, Spring Hill, FL 34609, U.S.A. **Online address:** rharakas@aol.com

HARARI, Oren. Israeli, b. 1949. **Genres:** Administration/Management. **Career:** University of California at Berkeley, survey researcher in psychology and industrial engineering, 1975-76; St. Mary's College, Moraga, CA, program evaluator, 1976; U.S. Navy, personnel research psychologist; McLaren College of Business, University of San Francisco, San Francisco, CA, assistant professor of organizational psychology, 1977-82, associate professor, 1982, professor of management, Tom Peters Group, senior consultant, 1984-96; editorial board member for Tom Peters's "On Achieving Excellence" newsletter, 1993-96, and for Journal of Managerial Issues; Conservatree Paper Co., member of board of directors. **Publications:** (with D. Beaty) Lessons from South Africa: A New Perspective on Public Policy and Productivity, 1989; (with N. Imparato) Jumping the Curve: Innovation and Strategic Choice in an Age of Transition, 1994; Leapfrogging the Competition: Five Giant Steps to Becoming a Market Leader, 1997; (with C.R. Bell) Beep Beep! Competing in the Age of the Road Runner, 2000. Contributor to periodicals. **Address:** University of San Francisco, 2130 Fulton St., San Francisco, CA 94117, U.S.A. **Online address:** harario@usfca.edu

HARBERGER, Arnold C. American, b. 1924. **Genres:** Economics. **Career:** Johns Hopkins University, Baltimore, MD, assistant professor of political economy, 1949-53; University of Chicago, associate professor, 1953-59, professor, 1959-77, distinguished service professor, 1977-91, distinguished service professor emeritus, 1991-; University of California, Los Angeles, professor of economics, 1984-. **Publications:** Project Evaluation, 1972; Taxation and Welfare, 1974; World Economic Growth, 1985. EDITOR:

Demand for Durable Goods, 1960; (with M. J. Bailey) Taxation of Income from Capital, 1969. **Address:** 8283 Bunche Hall, University of California, Los Angeles, 405 Hilgard Ave, Los Angeles, CA 90095-1477, U.S.A.

HARBURG, Ernest. (Ernie). American, b. 1926. **Genres:** Songs/Lyrics and libretti, Film, Theatre. **Career:** Council for Rural Welfare, Caracas, Venezuela, research assistant in rural welfare, 1953; Wisconsin State Department of Public Welfare, research assistant, 1954-57; University of Michigan, Ann Arbor, study director at Institute for Social Research, 1957-64, associate professor of nursing, 1964-70, research scientist in psychology, 1965-82, and epidemiology, 1973-82, research scientist emeritus, 1982-; New York University, NYC, adjunct professor of psychology, 1982-. Harburg Foundation, president, 1981-. **Publications:** (as Ernie Harburg with H. Meyerson) Who Put the Rainbow in "The Wizard of Oz"? Yip Harburg, Lyricist, 1993; (with B. Rosenberg) The Broadway Musical: Collaboration in Commerce and Art, 1993. Contributor to scholarly journals. **Address:** 240 E 10th St #98, New York, NY 10003-7800, U.S.A.

HARCLERODE, Peter. British, b. 1947. **Genres:** Military/Defense/Arms control. **Career:** Writer. **Publications:** The Elite and Their Support, 1987; Go to It: The Illustrated History of the 6th Airborne, 1990; Para! Fifty Years of the Parachute Regiment, 1992; Arnhem: A Tragedy of Errors, 1994; (with B. Pittaway) The Lost Masters: The Looting of Europe's Treasurehouses, 1999; Fighting Dirty: The Inside Story of Covert Operations from Ho Chi Minh to Osama bin Laden, 2000; Equinox: Warfare, 2000; Secret Soldiers: Special Forces in the War against Terrorism, 2001. **Address:** c/o Natasha Galloway, PFD, 34-43 Russell St., Drury House, London WC2B 5HA, England. **Online address:** sirmoori@globalnet.co.uk

HARCOURT, Geoffrey Colin. Australian, b. 1931. **Genres:** Economics. **Career:** University of Cambridge, University Lecturer in Economics and Politics, 1964-66, 1982-90, Fellow, Trinity Hall, 1964-66, Reader in the History of Economic Theory, 1990-98, Emeritus Reader in the History of Economic Theory, 1998-;Jesus College, Cambridge, Fellow, 1982-98, President, 1988-89, 1990-92, Emeritus Fellow, 1998-; Professor Emeritus of Economics, University of Adelaide, 1988- (Lecturer to Professor, 1958-67). Joint Ed., Australian Economic Papers, 1967-82, and Cambridge Journal of Economics, 1983- (Associate Ed., 1976-82); Correspondent Ed., Manchester School of Economic and Social Studies, 1982-96; Academic Board, Journal of Post Keynesian Economics, 1978-; editorial board of many other journals and volume series. **Publications:** (with P.H. Karmel and R.H. Wallace) Economic Activity, 1967; Some Cambridge Controversies in the Theory of Capital, 1972; The Social Science Imperialists, 1982; Controversies in Political Economy, 1986; On Political Economists and Modern Political Economy, 1992; Post-Keynesian Essays in Biography, 1993; Capitalism, Socialism and Post-Keynesianism (essays), 1995; 50 Years a Keynesian and Other Essays, 2001; Selected Essays on Economic Policy, 2001. EDITOR: (with R.H. Parker) Readings in the Concept and Measurement of Income, 1969, 2nd ed. (with Parker and G. Whittington) 1986; (with N.F. Laing) Capital and Growth: Selected Readings, 1971; The Microeconomic Foundations of Macroeconomics, 1977; Keynes and His Contemporaries, 1985; (with J.S. Cohen) International Monetary Problems and Supply-Side Economics: Essays in Honour of Lorie Tarshis, 1986; (with M. Baranzini) The Dynamics of the Wealth of Nations: Growth, Distribution and Structural Change: Essays in Honour of Luigi Pasinetti; (with A. Roncaglia and R. Rowley) Income and Employment in Theory and Practice, 1994; (with P.A. Riach) A "Second Edition" of the General Theory, 1997; L' Economie Rebelle de Joan Robinson, 2001; (with H. Lim and U.K. Park) Editing Economics: Essays in Honour of Mark Perlman, 2002; (with P. Kerr) Joan Robinson: Critical Assessments of Leading Economists, 5 vols., 2002. **Address:** Jesus College, Cambridge CB5 8BL, England. **Online address:** fellows_secretary@jesus.cam.ac.uk

HARD, Charlotte (Ann). British, b. 1969. **Genres:** Children's fiction. **Career:** Children's book illustrator, 1990-. Volunteer at local primary school. **Publications:** One Green Island (self-illustrated), 1995, in UK as One Green Island: An Animal Counting Gamebook, 1996. Illustrator of books by H. Maisner, C. Watson, S. Allen, S. Ransford, M. Newman, K. Henderson, A. Shadwick. Contributor to periodicals. **Address:** 54 Chapel Lane, Headingley, Leeds LS6 3BW, England.

HARDCASTLE, Bob. (Robert B). American, b. 1940. **Genres:** Novels, Money/Finance. **Career:** Baltimore Orioles Baseball Team, professional baseball player; Southern Illinois University at Carbondale, teacher and coach; financial planner, 1964-; owner of a financial planning business, 1978-. Money Talk (nationally syndicated radio program), host. **Publications:** Hardcastle's Money Talk (novel), 1994. Contributor to magazines. **Address:** 16100 Chesterfield Parkway No. 150, Chesterfield, MO 63017, U.S.A. **Online address:** delta@moneytalk.org

HARDCASTLE, Michael. Also writes as David Clark. British, b. 1933. **Genres:** Children's fiction, Children's non-fiction. **Career:** Bristol Evening Post, Literary Ed., 1959-65; Liverpool Daily Post, Chief Feature Writer, 1965-67. **Publications:** Soccer Is Also a Game, 1966; Shoot on Sight, 1967; Redcap, 1967; Aim for the Flat, 1967; The Chasing Game, 1968; Goal, 1969; Dive to Danger, 1969; Shilling a Mile, 1969; Stop that Car!, 1970; Reds and Blues, 1970; Strike, 1970; Smashing, 1970; Don't Tell Me What To Do, 1970; The Hidden Enemy, 1970; Come and Get Me, 1971; Live in the Sky, 1971; Shelter, 1971; A Load of Trouble, 1971; Blood Money, 1971; It Wasn't Me, 1971; In the Net, 1971; Playing Ball, 1972; Goals in the Air, 1972; Island Magic, 1973; United!, 1973; Away from Home, 1974; Free Kick, 1974; The Demon Bowler, 1974; The Big One, 1974; The Chase, 1974; On the Run, 1974; Heading for Goal, 1974; Last Across, 1974; The Match, 1974; Dead of Night, 1974; Road Race, 1974; A Hard Man, 1974; Catch, 1974; Day in the Country, 1974; The Long Drop, 1974; Flare Up, 1975; Get Lost, 1975; Life Underground, 1975; Money for Sale, 1975; Where the Action Is, 1976; The First Goal, 1976; Breakaway, 1976; Go and Find Him, 1977; River of Danger, 1977; The Great Bed Race, 1977; Night Raid, 1977; On the Ball, 1977; Shooting Star, 1977; The Saturday Horse, 1977; Strong Arm, 1977; Fire on the Sea, 1977; Holiday House, 1977; Crash Car, 1977; Goal in Europe, 1978; Soccer Special, 1978; Top of the League, 1979; Top Soccer, 1979; The Switch Horse, 1980; Top Fishing, 1980; Go for Goal, 1980; Racing Bike, 1980; Snake Run, 1980; Hot Wheels, 1980; Half a Team, 1980; Behind the Goal, 1980; Kick Off, 1980; Top Speed, 1980; Gigantic Hit, 1982; Roar to Victory, 1982; Attack!, 1982; Fast from the Gate, 1983; Caught Out, 1983; The Team That Wouldn't Give In, 1984; Hooked!, 1984; Tiger of the Track, 1985; Double Holiday, 1985; Winning Rider, 1985; One Kick, 1986; James and the TV Star, 1986; No Defence, 1986; The Shooters, 1986; Snookered!, 1987; Quake, 1987; Mascot, 1987; The Rival Games, 1988; The Magic Party, 1988; The Green Machine, 1989; Kickback, 1989; Splashdown, 1989; Jump In, 1989; Lucky Break, 1990; Joanna's Goal, 1990; Mark England's Cap, 1990; Walking the Goldfish, 1990; Penalty, 1990; Second Chance, 1991; Soccer Star, 1991; James and the House of Fun, 1991; The Away Team, 1992; Own Goal; 1992; Dog Bites Goalie and Other Soccer Stories, 1993; Shooting Boots, 1993; Soccer Star, 1993; One Good Horse; 1994; You Won't Catch Me, 1994; Soccer Captain, 1994; Puzzle, 1995; Winning Goal, 1995; Please Come Home, 1995; Puzzle, 1995; The Fastest Bowler in the World, 1996; Matthew's Goals, 1997. AS DAVID CLARK: Goalie, 1972; Splash, 1972; Run, 1973; Top Spin, 1973; Grab, 1974; Winner, 1974; Volley, 1975; Roll Up, 1975. **Address:** 17 Molescroft Park, Beverley, North Humberside HU17 7EB, England.

HARDEN, Blaine. American, b. 1952. **Genres:** Environmental sciences/ Ecology, Geography, History. **Career:** Trenton Times, NJ, reporter, 1976-78; Washington Post, reporter, 1978-83, foreign correspondent, bureau chief in Nairobi, Kenya, 1984-89, bureau chief, Eastern Europe, 1989-93; political reporter, 1996-97, bureau chief, New York City, 1997-; Washingtonian, senior writer, 1983-84. **Publications:** Africa: Dispatches from a Fragile Continent, 1990; A River Lost: The Life and Death of the Columbia, 1996. **Address:** c/o Washington Post, 1150 15th St NW, Ste 675, Washington, DC 20071, U.S.A.

HARDER, Kelsie B(rown). American, b. 1922. **Genres:** Language/ Linguistics, Geography. **Career:** University of Florida, Gainesville, instructor in English, 1953-54; Youngstown University, Youngstown, OH, assistant professor, 1954-58, associate professor, 1958-60, professor of English, 1960-64; State University of New York College at Potsdam, professor of English, 1964-89, distinguished teaching professor, 1989-94. Fulbright professor in India, 1962, and Poland, 1971-72; consultant to Omnigraphics Inc. **Publications:** EDITOR: Illustrated Dictionary of Place Names: United States and Canada, 1976; Favorite Baby Names, 1985; Names and Their Varieties: A Collection of Essays in Onomastics, 1986; Unusual and Most Popular Baby Names: One Thousand Memorable Names, Survey-Selected for Popularity, 1988; (with S. Kingsbury and W. Mieder) Dictionary of American Proverbs, 1992; (with M.H. Smallman) Claims to Name: Toponyms of St. Lawrence County, 1992. Work represented in anthologies. Contributor of articles, poems, and reviews to magazines. **Address:** 5 Lawrence Ave, Potsdam, NY 13676, U.S.A. **Online address:** harderkb@northnet.org

HARDER, Leland. American, b. 1926. **Genres:** Theology/Religion. **Career:** Pastor of a Mennonite church in Chicago, IL, 1952-57; Mennonite Biblical Seminary, Elkhart, IN, professor, 1958-83; Great Plains Seminary Education Program, Newton, KS, director, 1983-86; Church Member Profile Research Project, associate director, 1988-92. A Family History, quarterly periodical, publisher. **Publications:** Anabaptists Four Centuries Later, 1975; The Pastor-People Partnership: The Call and Recall of Pastors from a Believer's Church Perspective, 1983; (ed.) Perspectives on the Nurturing of Faith, 1983; (ed.)

The Sources of Swiss Anabaptism, 1985; (ed. with L. Driedger) Anabaptist-Mennonite Identities in Ferment, 1990; Doors to Lock and Doors to Open: The Discerning People of God, 1993; The Blumstein Legacy: A Six Generation Family Saga. **Address:** PO Box 363, North Newton, KS 67117, U.S.A. **Online address:** ldharder@southwind.net

HARDESTY, Larry (Lynn). American, b. 1947. **Genres:** Education, Librarianship, Bibliography. **Career:** Kearney State College, Kearney, NE, assistant reference librarian and instructor in educational media, 1973-74, user services coordinator, 1974-75, director of Library Learning Program, 1975; DePauw University, Greencastle, IN, instructor, 1975-79, assistant professor, 1979-83, head of library reference department, 1975-83, project librarian, 1976-77, project director, 1977-82; Eckerd College, St. Petersburg, FL, associate professor, 1983-91, professor of library services, 1991-95, director of library services, 1983-95; Austin College, Sherman, TX, professor and college librarian, 1995-. **Publications:** The Use of Slide-Tape Presentations in Academic Libraries, 1978; Faculty and the Library: The Undergraduate Experience, 1991. EDITOR: (with Hastreiter and Henderson) Bibliographic Instruction in Practice: Dedicated to the Legacy of Evan Farber, 1993; Books Bytes and Bridges: Libraries and Computer Centers in Academic Institutions, 2000. COMPILER: (with J. Hastreiter and D. Henderson) Mission Statements for College Libraries, 1985; (with J.M. Tucker and J. Schmitt) User Instruction in Academic Libraries: A Century of Selected Readings, 1986; (with J. Hastreiter and D. Henderson) Periodicals in College Libraries, 1987. Contributor to books. Contributor of articles and reviews to library journals. **Address:** Abell College Library Center, Austin College, 900 N Grand Ave Ste 6L, Sherman, TX 75090-4402, U.S.A. **Online address:** lhardesty@austincollege.edu

HARDIE, David. See MCLEAN, (John David) Ruari.

HARDIE, Sean. Irish (born England), b. 1947. **Genres:** Novels, Plays/Screenplays. **Career:** BBC-TV, senior film producer for current affairs, 1969-79, senior producer for entertainment, 1979-81, head of entertainment for Scotland, 1981-84; writer. Radio and television broadcaster and producer. **Publications:** NOVELS: The Last Supper, 1990; Right Connections, 1991; Table for Five, 1991; Till the Fat Lady Sings, 1992; Son of a Preacher Man, 1997. **Address:** Toby Eady, 18 Park Walk, London SW10 0AQ, England. **Online address:** hardie@isl.ie

HARDIN, J. D. See RIEFE, Alan.

HARDIN, John A. American, b. 1948. **Genres:** History. **Career:** Kentucky State University, Frankfort, instructor, 1972-74, assistant professor of history, 1976-84; Eastern Washington University, Cheney, associate professor of black studies, 1984-91; Western Kentucky University, Bowling Green, associate professor of history, 1991-, assistant dean of Potter College of Arts, Humanities, and Social Sciences, 1997-2002, assistant to Provost for Diversity Enhancement, 2002-. Visiting faculty member at Kentucky Wesleyan College, Spokane Community College, University of Kentucky, and University of Louisville. **Publications:** Onward and Upward: A Centennial History of Kentucky State University, 1886-1986, 1987; Fifty Years of Segregation: Black Higher Education in Kentucky, 1904-1954, 1997; (coed.) Community Memories: A Glimpse of African American Life in Frankfort, Kentucky, 2003. Contributor of articles and reviews to periodicals. **Address:** Dept of History, Cherry Hall 200, Western Kentucky University, 1 Big Red Way, Bowling Green, KY 42101, U.S.A. **Online address:** john.hardin@wku.edu

HARDING, Duncan. See WHITING, Charles (Henry).

HARDING, Ian. See WHITING, Charles (Henry).

HARDING, James. British, b. 1929. **Genres:** Literary criticism and history, Music, Biography. **Career:** University of Greenwich, senior lecturer in French, 1966-94. **Publications:** Saint-Saens and His Circle, 1965; Sacha Guitry, The Last Boulevardier, 1968; The Duke of Wellington, 1968; Massenet, 1970; The Astonishing Adventure of General Boulanger, 1971; Rossini, 1971; The Ox on the Roof, 1972; Gounod, 1973; Lost Illusions: Paul Leautaud and His World, 1974; Erik Satie, 1975; (trans.) Poulenc: My Friends and Myself, 1978; Folies de Paris: The Rise and Fall of French Operetta, 1979; Offenbach, 1980; Maurice Chevalier, 1982; Jacques Tati: Frame by Frame, 1984; James Agate, 1986; Ivor Novello, 1987; The Rocky Horror Show Book, 1987; Cochran, 1988; Gerald du Maurier, 1989; George Robey and the Music Hall, 1991; Emlyn Williams: A Life, 1993; P. Ramlee, The Bright Star, 2002. EDITOR: The Maid of Sker, 1968; Lord Chesterfield's Letters to His Son, 1973. **Address:** 100 Ridgmount Gardens, Torrington Pl, London WC1E 7AZ, England.

HARDING, Les. Canadian, b. 1950. **Genres:** Children's non-fiction, History, Local history/Rural topics, Young adult non-fiction. **Career:** Statistics Canada, Ottawa, ON, reference librarian, 1977-78; Transport Canada, Cornwall, ON, librarian, 1980-82; Waterloo Regional Library, Elmira, ON, indexer, 1983-84; University of Waterloo, ON, reference librarian, 1985-90; Government of Newfoundland, St. John's, reference librarian, 1991-92; writer, 1993-. **Publications:** The Voyages of Lesser Men: Thumbnail Sketches in Canadian Exploration, 1991, rev. ed., 1999; Historic St. John's: City of Legends, 1992; A Book in Hand Is Worth Two in the Library, 1994; Journeys of Remarkable Women: Their Travels on the Canadian Frontier, 1994; (with G. Brannon) Carto-Quotes: An Inspirational Companion for the Map-Maker and the Map-User, 1996; Dead Countries of the 19th and 20th Centuries: Aden to Zululand, 1998; Exploring the Avalon, 1998; McCurdy and the Silver Dart, 1998; Elephant Story: Jumbo and P.T. Barnum under the Big Top, 1999; Damn the Mosquitoes! More Travellers on the Canadian Frontier, 2001. Contributor of articles and reviews to journals. **Address:** 18 Guzzwell Dr., St. John's, NL, Canada A1A 3X1. **Online address:** leslie_l_harding@yahoo.com

HARDING, Paul. See DOHERTY, P(aul) C.

HARDING, Ross. See GEMMELL, David A(ndrew).

HARDWICK, Elizabeth (Bruce). American, b. 1916. **Genres:** Novels, Literary criticism and history. **Career:** Adjunct Associate Professor, Barnard College, NYC. Founder and Ed., New York Review of Books. **Publications:** The Ghostly Lover, 1945; The Simple Truth, 1955; (ed.) The Selected Letters of William James, 1961; View of My Own (essays), 1962; Seduction and Betrayal: Women and Literature, 1974; (series) Rediscovered Fiction by American Women, 1977; Sleepless Nights, 1979; Bartleby in Manhattan and Other Essays, 1983; (ed. with R. Atwan) The Best American Essays 1986, 1986; Sight Readings, 1998; Herman Melville, 2000. **Address:** 15 W 67th St, New York, NY 10023-6226, U.S.A.

HARDWICK, Phil. (born United States), b. 1948. **Genres:** Mystery/Crime/Suspense. **Career:** Mississippi Valley Gas Co., Jackson, MS, vice president for ten years; also worked as a police officer and state investigator. Mississippi Economic Development Council, past president; member of Mississippi Sports Hall of Fame and Museum and Leadership Jackson. U.S. Army, 1968. **Publications:** MISSISSIPPI MYSTERIES SERIES: Found in Flora, Flora 1997; Captured in Canton, 1997; Justice in Jackson, 1997; Newcomer in New Albany, 1997; Vengeance in Vicksburg, 1998; Collision in Columbia, 1998; Conspiracy in Corinth, 1999; Cover-up in Columbus, 2001; Sixth Inning in Southaven, 2002; Mishap in Macon, 2003. **Address:** POB 55804, Jackson, MS 39296, U.S.A. **Online address:** phil@philhardwick.com

HARDY, Adam. See BULMER, (Henry) Kenneth.

HARDY, Antoinette. See STOCKENBERG, Antoinette.

HARDY, B. Carmon. American, b. 1934. **Genres:** History. **Career:** Brigham Young University, Provo, UT, assistant professor of history, 1961-66; California State University, Fullerton, assistant professor to professor of history, 1966-. **Publications:** Stalwarts South of the Border, 1985; Solemn Covenant: The Mormon Polygamous Passage, 1992; The World and the West: A Book of Readings, Vol. I, 1994, Vol. II, 1995. Author of articles. **Address:** Department of History, California State University, Fullerton, CA 92831, U.S.A.

HARDY, Barbara (Gladys). British (born Wales), b. 1924. **Genres:** Literary criticism and history, Autobiography/Memoirs, Novels, Poetry. **Career:** Professor Emeritus, University of London, 1989- (Professor of English, Birkbeck College, 1970-89, Professor, Royal Holloway College, 1965-70); Professor of English (Hon.), University College of Swansea; Hon. Member M.L.A., Fellow, Royal Society of Literature, Hon. Fellow, Birkbeck College, Royal Holloway College, University of Wales, Swansea. **Publications:** The Novels of George Eliot: A Study in Form, 1959; Twelfth Night, 1962; Wuthering Heights, 1963; The Appropriate Form: An Essay on the Novel, 1964; Jane Eyre, 1964; Charles Dickens: The Later Novels, 1968; The Moral Art of Dickens, 1970; The Exposure of Luxury: Radical Themes in Thackeray, 1972; Tellers and Listeners: The Narrative Imagination, 1975; A Reading of Jane Austen, 1976; The Advantage of Lyric: Essays on Feeling in Poetry, 1976; Particularities: Readings in George Eliot, 1983; Charles Dickens: The Writer and His Work, 1983; Forms of Feeling in Victorian Fiction, 1985; Narrators and Novelists: Collected Essays, Vol. 1, 1987; Swansea Girl, 1993; London Lovers, 1996; Henry James: The Later Writings, 1996; Shakespeare's Storytellers, 1997; Thomas Hardy: Imaging Imagination, 2000; Dy-

Ian Thomas: An Original Language, 2000; Severn Bridge: Collected and New Poems, 2001. EDITOR: Middlemarch: Critical Approaches to the Novel, 1967; Daniel Deronda, by G. Eliot, 1967; Critical Essays on George Eliot, 1970; The Trumpet Major, by T. Hardy, 1974; Laodicean, by Hardy, 1975; Not So Quiet, by H.Z. Smith, 1988. **Address:** Birkbeck College, Malet St, London WC1E 7HX, England.

HARDY, Gayle J. American, b. 1942. **Genres:** Civil liberties/Human rights, Librarianship, Politics/Government, Women's studies and issues, Bibliography, Reference. **Career:** Lockwood Library, State University of New York at Buffalo, Buffalo, head of the circulation department, 1974-85, senior assistant librarian, 1985-91, associate librarian-subject specialist for information and library studies, communication, and communicative disorders, 1992-2000. **Publications:** American Women Civil Rights Activists: Biobibliographies of 68 Leaders, 1825-1992, 1993; (with J.S. Robinson) Subject Guide to US Government Reference Sources, 2nd ed., 1996. Contributor to books and periodicals. **Address:** 10805 Boyd Dr, Clarence, NY 14031-2203, U.S.A.

HARDY, John Philips. Australian, b. 1933. **Genres:** Literary criticism and history, Novellas/Short stories. **Career:** Magdalen College, Oxford, jr. research fellow, 1962-65; University College, University of Toronto, visiting assistant professor, 1965-66; University of New England, Armidale, NSW, professor of English, 1966-72; Australian National University, ACT, professor of English, 1972-87; Bond University, foundation professor of humanities, 1988-93. **Publications:** Reinterpretations: Essays on Poems by Milton, Pope and Johnson, 1971; Samuel Johnson: A Critical Study, 1979; Jane Austen's Heroines: Intimacy in Human Relationships, 1984. EDITOR/CO-EDITOR: (with others) Johnson, Boswell and Their Circle: Essays Presented to Lawrence Fitzroy Powell, 1965; The Political Writings of Dr. Johnson: A Selection, 1968; The History of Rasselas, Prince of Abissinia, 1968; Johnson's Lives of the Poets: A Selection, 1971; The Classical Temper in Western Europe, 1983; Stories of Australian Migration, 1988; European Voyaging towards Australia, 1990. **Address:** 26 Rawson St, Deakin, Canberra, ACT 2600, Australia.

HARDY, Lyndon (Maurice). American, b. 1941. **Genres:** Science fiction/Fantasy. **Career:** Alodar Systems, Inc., president, 1992-; writer. **Publications:** FANTASY NOVELS: Master of the Five Magics, 1980; Secret of the Sixth Magic, 1984; Riddle of the Seven Realms, 1988. **Address:** 19616 Redbeam Ave, Torrance, CA 90503-1134, U.S.A.

HARDY, Richard Earl. American, b. 1938. **Genres:** Psychology, Sociology. **Career:** Medical College of Virginia/Virginia Commonwealth University, Richmond, Chairman, Dept. of Rehabilitation Counseling, 1969-96, Chairman and Professor Emeritus, 1996-. Ed., Social and Rehabilitation Psychology series, Charles C Thomas Publishing, Springfield, IL, 1972-. Rehabilitation Counselor, Richmond, VA, 1961-63; Rehabilitation Advisor, Dept. of Health, Education and Welfare, Washington, DC, 1963-66; Chief Psychologist, South Carolina Dept. of Rehabilitation, Columbia, 1966-68. former Member SC State Board of Psychology; former Certified Consultant in Clinical Hypnosis and Certified in Clinical Hypnosis, American Society of Clinical Hypnosis, 1994. Hypnosis, 1994. **Publications:** (with J. G. Cull) The Big Welfare Mess: Public Assistance & Rehabilitation Approaches; Introduction to Correctional Rehabilitation, 1972; Drug Dependence and Rehabilitation Approaches, 1972; Rehabilitation of the Drug Abuser with Delinquent Behavior; Climbing Ghetto Walls; (co-ed.) Vocational Rehabilitation: Profession and Process, 1972, 1996; Alcohol Dependence and Rehabilitation Approaches; Behavior Modification of the Mentally Ill; Drug Language and Lore; Counseling Strategies with Special Populations; (with Gandy and Martin) Rehab Counseling and Services, 1987; Hemingway: A Psychological Portrait, 1988; Gestalt Psychotherapy, 1991; Hispaniola Episode, 1992; (co-author) The Brass Chalice, A Book of Drug Prevention for Children, Youth and Parents, 1994; (with Gandy and Martin) Rehabilitation Counseling: Mental and Physical Disabilities, 1999; Woodpeckers Don't Get Headaches, 2001. Contributor to professional journals. **Address:** 9214 Groundhog Dr, Richmond, VA 23235, U.S.A. **Online address:** RichardEHardy@cs.com

HARE, Darrell T. American, b. 1930. **Genres:** Children's fiction. **Career:** Yeck Brothers Co., Dayton, OH, copywriter, creative director, vice president (creative), partner, 1955-93; Darrell T. Hare and the Wizards, owner. **Publications:** Ramar: The Rabbit with Rainbow Wings (inspirational book), 1996. Contributor of poems to periodicals. **Address:** 2175 Winters Rd., Dayton, OH 45459, U.S.A.

HARE, David. British, b. 1947. **Genres:** Plays/Screenplays, Songs/Lyrics and libretti. **Career:** Portable Theatre, London, director, 1968-71; Royal Court Theatre, London, literary manager, 1969-70, resident dramatist, 1970-71; Nottingham Playhouse, resident dramatist, 1973; Joint Stock Theatre Group, co-founder, 1975-80; Greenpoint Films, co-founder, 1983; National Theatre, London, associate director, 1984-97. **Publications:** (with others) Lay By, 1971; Acting Up, 1999. PLAYS: Slag, 1970; The Great Exhibition, 1972; (with H. Brenton) Brassneck, 1973; Knuckle, 1974; Fanshen, 1975; Teeth 'n' Smiles, 1975; Plenty, 1978; A Map of the World, 1983; The History Plays, 1984; (with H. Brenton) Pravda, 1985; The Asian Plays, 1986; The Bay at Nice and Wrecked Eggs, 1986; The Secret Rapture, 1988, screenplay, 1993; Racing Demon, 1990; Murmuring Judges, 1992; The Absence of War, 1993, teleplay, 1995; Skylight, 1995; David Hare: Plays, 1996; Amy's View, 1997; The Judas Kiss, 1998; Via Dolorosa, 1998; My Zinc Bed, 2000; The Breath of Life, 2002; The Permanent Way, 2003. TELEVISION FILMS: Licking Hitler; 1978; Dreams of Leaving, 1980; Saigon: Year of the Cat, 1983; Heading Home, 1991. SCREENPLAYS: Wetherby, 1985; Plenty, 1985; Paris by Night, 1989; Strapless, 1990; Damage, 1992; The Hours, 2001; Via Dolorosa, 2002; The Corrections, 2003. OPERA: The Knife, 1988. ESSAYS: Wrighting Lefthanded, 1991; Asking Around, 1993. ADAPTATIONS: The Rules of the Game, 1992; The Life of Galileo, 1994; Mother Courage and Her Children, 1995; Ivanov, 1996; The Blue Room, 1998; Platonov, 2001. **Address:** c/o Casarotto Ramsay & Associates Ltd, National House, 60-66 Wardour St, London W1V 4ND, England.

HARE DUKE, Michael (Geoffrey). Scottish (born India), b. 1925. **Genres:** Novellas/Short stories, Poetry, Psychology, Theology/Religion. **Career:** Ordained Deacon, 1952; Priest, 1953; Curate, St. Johns Wood Church, 1952-56; Vicar, St. Mark's Bury, 1956-62; Vicar, St. Paul's Daybrook, 1964-69; Officiating Chaplain to the Forces, E. Midlands Headquarters, 1968-69; Bishop of United Diocese of St. Andrews, Dunkeld and Dunblane, 1969-94. Pastoral Director, 1962-64, and Consultant, 1964-69, Clinical Theology Association; Chairman, Scottish Pastoral Association, 1972-76; Chairman, Scottish Association for Mental Health, 1978-85; Chairman, Age Concern Scotland, 1994-2000. Member, Scottish Institute of Human Relations, 1974-. **Publications:** (co-author) The Caring Church, 1963; (co-author) First Aid in Counselling, 1968; Understanding the Adolescent, 1969; The Break of Glory, 1970; Freud, 1972; Good News, 1978; Stories, Signs, and Sacraments in the Emerging Church, 1982; Praying for Peace: Reflections on the Gulf Crisis, 1991; Hearing the Stranger, Poems, Reflections and Hymns, 1994; Exits and Entrances, 1997; One Foot in Heaven: Growing Old and Living to the Full, 2001. **Address:** 2 Balhousie Ave, Perth PH1 5HN, Scotland. **Online address:** BishMick@aol.com

HARER, John B. American, b. 1948. **Genres:** Civil liberties/Human rights, Librarianship. **Career:** American International School, Duesseldorf, Germany, librarian, 1979-80; Radford University, Radford, VA, head of circulation at McConnell Library, 1980-83; Towson State University, Towson, MD, head of circulation at Cook Library, 1983-88; Texas A&M University, College Station, head of access services at Sterling C. Evans Library, 1988-. Literacy Volunteers of America, tutor, 1993-. **Publications:** Intellectual Freedom: A Reference Handbook, American Bibliographical Center-Clio Press, 1992; (with Steven Harris) Censorship of Expression in the 1980s: A Statistical Survey, Greenwood Press, 1994. Editor of "Information and Instruction Technologies," a column in Library Hi-Tech News, 1989-91. **Address:** Sterling C. Evans Library, Texas A&M University, College Station, TX 77843, U.S.A.

HARGARTEN, Stephen W. American, b. 1949. **Genres:** Documentaries/Reportage. **Career:** Medical College of Wisconsin, Milwaukee, chairperson, 1989-. **Publications:** Reducing Firearm Injury and Death. **Address:** 9200 West Wisconsin Ave., Milwaukee, WI 53226, U.S.A. **Online address:** hargart@mcw.edu

HARGRAVE, Leonie. See DISCH, Thomas M(ichael).

HARGREAVES, John D(esmond). British, b. 1924. **Genres:** History. **Career:** Lecturer, University of Manchester, 1948-52; Sr. Lecturer, Fourah Bay College, Sierra Leone, 1952-54; Visiting Professor, Union College, Schenectady, New York, 1960-61, and the University of Ibadan, 1970-71; Professor of History, University of Aberdeen, 1962-85. President, African Studies Association (U.K.) 1972-73. **Publications:** A Life of Sir Samuel Lewis, 1958; Prelude to the Partition of West Africa, 1963; West Africa: The Former French States, 1967; (ed.) France and West Africa, 1970; West Africa Partitioned, 2 vols., 1974-85; The End of Colonial Rule in West Africa: Essays in Contemporary History, 1979; Aberdeenshire to Africa, 1981; Decolonization in Africa, 1988, rev. ed. 1996; Academa and Empire, 1994. **Address:** 22 Raemoir Rd, Banchory, Aberdeen AB31 5UJ, Scotland.

HARGROVE, Erwin C. American, b. 1930. **Genres:** Politics/Government. **Career:** Professor of Political Science, Vanderbilt University, Nashville, Tennessee, now emeritus. Formerly, Sr. Fellow, The Urban Institute, Washington, D.C.; Professor of Political Science, Brown University, Providence, Rhode Island. **Publications:** Presidential Leadership: Personality and Political Style, 1966; The Power of the Modern Presidency, 1974; The Missing Link, 1975; TVA 50 Years of Grass-Roots Bureaucracy, 1983; (with M. Nelson) Presidents, Politics, and Policy, 1984; (co-ed.) The President and the Council of Economic Advisors, 1984; (co-ed.) Leadership and Innovation, 1987; Jimmy Carter as President, 1988; (co-ed.) Impossible Jobs in Public Management, 1990; Prisoners of Myth, The Leadership of the Tennessee Valley Authority, 1933-1990, 1994; The President as Leader: Appealing to the Better Angels of Our Nature, 1998. **Address:** Dept. of Political Science, Vanderbilt University, Nashville, TN 37235, U.S.A.

HARING, Lee. American, b. 1930. **Genres:** Area studies, Literary criticism and history, Mythology/Folklore, Third World. **Career:** Guilford College, Greensboro, NC, assistant professor of English, 1953-56; Brooklyn College of the City University of New York, Brooklyn, NY, lecturer, 1957-61, instructor, 1961-67, assistant professor, 1967-73, associate professor, 1973-81, professor, 1981-99, professor of English emeritus, 1999-. **Publications:** The Gypsy Laddie, 1962; Folk Songs for Guitar, 1964; Malagasy Tale Index, 1982; Verbal Arts in Madagascar, 1992; Ibonia, Epic of Madagascar, 1994; Ann Koleksyonn Folklor Moris, 2001; Indian Ocean Folktales, 2002. **Address:** 6 Cantine's Island Ln, Saugerties, NY 12477, U.S.A. **Online address:** lharing@hvc.rr.com

HARKNETT, Terry Williams. See GILMAN, George G.

HARLAN, Glen. See CEBULASH, Mel.

HARLAN, Judith. American, b. 1949. **Genres:** Adult non-fiction. **Career:** Freelance journalist and author. Harbor Times (a beach and harbor weekly), editor, 1980-81; Murphy Organization (advertising agency), news copywriter, 1982-83; Freebies (magazine), editor, 1984-85; Oxnard College, instructor, 1991-. Has also worked as a feature and news stringer for the Los Angeles Times, Los Angeles, CA. **Publications:** American Indians Today: Issues and Conflicts, 1987; Hispanic Voters: Gaining a Voice in American Politics, 1988; Sounding the Alarm: A Biography of Rachel Carson, 1989; Bilingualism in the United States: Conflict and Controversy, 1991; Puerto Rico: Deciding Its Future, 1996; Girl Talk: Staying Strong, Feeling Good, Sticking Together, 1997; Feminism: A Reference Handbook, 1998; Mamphela Ramphele: Ending Apartheid in South Africa, 2000. Contributor to periodicals. **Address:** c/o Author Mail, Feminist Press, 365 Fifth Ave., Ste. 5406, New York, NY 10016, U.S.A. **Online address:** judith_harlan@yahoo.com

HARLAN, Rex. See BUSLIK, Gary.

HARLAND, Christina. See PEMBERTON, Margaret.

HARLAND, Richard. (born England), b. 1947. **Genres:** Science fiction/Fantasy. **Career:** Writer, 1997-. University of New South Wales, Sydney, Australia, tutor; University of Wollongong, Wollongong, New South Wales, Australia, senior lecturer in English for ten years. Also worked as a singer and songwriter in Sydney, Australia. **Publications:** Testimony (poems and prose), 1981; Superstructuralism: The Philosophy of Structuralism and Post-Structuralism, 1987; Beyond Superstructuralism: The Syntagmatic Side of Language, 1993; Literary Theory from Plato to Barthes: An Introductory History, 1999; Walter Wants to Be a Werewolf (juvenile fiction), 2003. VICAR SERIES: The Vicar of Morbing Vyle, 1993; The Black Crusade, 2004. EDDON AND VAIL SERIES: The Dark Edge, 1997; Taken by Force, 1998; Hidden from View, 1999. HEAVEN AND EARTH TRILOGY: Ferren and the Angel, 2000; Ferren and the White Doctor, 2002; Ferren and the Invasion of Heaven, 2003. Contributor to anthologies and academic journals. **Address:** c/o Author Mail, Penguin Australia, 250 Camberwell Rd., Camberwell, Victoria 3124, Australia. **Online address:** richard@richardharland.net

HARLEMAN, Ann. American, b. 1945. **Genres:** Novellas/Short stories, Language/Linguistics, Literary criticism and history. **Career:** Rutgers University, New Brunswick, NJ, assistant professor of English, 1973-74; University of Washington, Seattle, assistant professor, 1974-79, associate professor of English, 1979-84; Massachusetts Institute of Technology, Cambridge, visiting associate professor of English, 1984-86; Brown University, Providence, RI, research associate in American civilization department, 1986-; Wheaton College, Wheaton, IL, Cole Distinguished Professor, 1992-93; visiting professor at Dartmouth College, Hanover, NH, 1981-82, Northeastern University, Boston, MA, Wheaton College, Wheaton, IL, Wes-

leyan University, Middletown, CT, and Rhode Island School of Design, Providence. **Publications:** FICTION: Happiness (short stories), 1994. Contributor of stories and poetry to periodicals. OTHER: Graphic Representation of Models in Linguistic Theory, 1976; (with B.A. Rosenberg) Ian Fleming: A Critical Biography, 1989; (trans. from Russian) Ruth Zernova, Mute Phone Calls, selected by Helen Reeve, 1991. Contributor to books. Contributor of articles on writing and linguistics to periodicals. **Address:** Brown University, American Civilization Dept., Providence, RI 02912, U.S.A.

HARLEY, Bill. American, b. 1954. **Genres:** Children's fiction, Songs/Lyrics and libretti. **Career:** American Friends Service Committee, Syracuse, NY, social worker, 1977-80; storyteller, author, songwriter, and musical performer with band, the Troublemakers, 1980-. Founder, Providence Learning Connection; co-founder, Stone Soup Coffeehouse, Providence, RI. Speaker at conferences and workshops; regular commentator, All Things Considered, National Public Radio, 1991-. **Publications:** FOR CHILDREN: Carna and the Boots of Seven Strides, 1994; Ready-to-Tell Tales, 1994; Nothing Happened, 1995; Sarah's Story, 1996; Sitting Down to Eat, 1996; Bear's All Night Party, 2001. RECORDINGS: Monsters in the Bathroom, 1984; 50 Ways to Fool Your Mother, 1986; Coyote, 1987; (with P. Alsop) Peter Alsop and Bill Harley: In the Hospital, 1989; Cool in School, 1990; Grownups Are Strange, 1990; Come on Out and Play, 1990; I'm Gonna Let It Shine, 1990; Who Made This Mess?, 1992; You're in Trouble, 1992; Dinosaurs Never Say Please, 1992; Big Big World, 1993; Already Someplace Warm, 1994; From the Back of the Bus, 1995; Wacka Wacka Woo and Other Stuff, 1995; Sitting on My Hands, 1995; Lunchroom Tales, 1996; There's a Pea on My Plate, 1997; Weezie and the Moonpies, 1998; The Battle of the Mad Scientists and Other Tales of Survival, 1999; Play It Again, 1999; Down in the Backpack, 2001. **Address:** 301 Jacob St, Seekonk, MA 02771, U.S.A. **Online address:** info@billharley.com

HARLEY, Willard F., Jr. American, b. 1941. **Genres:** Human relations/Parenting, Psychology, Self help. **Career:** Westmont College, Santa Barbara, CA, head of psychology department, 1968-71; Bethel College and Seminary, St. Paul, MN, professor of psychology, 1972-77; Harley Clinics of Minnesota, president, 1976-93; Marriage Builders, St. Paul, president, 1976-. **Publications:** His Needs, Her Needs, 1986; Marriage Insurance, 1988; Love Busters, 1992; Five Steps to Romantic Love, 1994; Give and Take, 1996; Your Love and Marriage, 1997; Four Gifts of Love, 1998; (with J.H. Chalmers) Surviving an Affair, 1998; Fall in Love, Stay in Love, 2000; Buyers, Renters, & Freeloaders, 2000; I Cherish You, 2002. **Address:** 12568 Ethan Ave N, White Bear Lake, MN 55110, U.S.A. **Online address:** bharley@marriagebuilders.com

HARLING, Robert. American, b. 1951. **Genres:** Plays/Screenplays. **Career:** Jubilation (a society orchestra), LA, singer; worked as a stage and television actor in NYC, 1979-87; playwright, 1987-; screenwriter, 1989-. **Publications:** Steel Magnolias, 1988. SCREENPLAYS: Steel Magnolias, 1989; (with A. Bergman) Soapdish, 1991; The First Wives Club, 1996; (and director) The Evening Star, 1996.

HARLOW, Michael. New Zealander (born United States), b. 1937. **Genres:** Poetry, Music, Psychology. **Career:** Writer; Jungian psychotherapist, private practice. **Publications:** The Book of Quiet, 1974; Edges, 1974; The Identikit, 1978; Texts, Identities, 1978; Nothing but Switzerland and Lemonade, 1980; Today Is the Piano's Birthday, 1981; Vlaminck's Tie, 1985; Giotto's Elephant, 1991. Author of texts and libretti in collaboration with composer K. Powell, for musical performance works. **Address:** 122 Earnscleugh Rd, Rapide 378, Alexandra, New Zealand. **Online address:** m.harlow@xtra.co.nz

HARLOW, Rosie. Scottish, b. 1961. **Genres:** Children's non-fiction. **Career:** South Oxfordshire Countryside Education Trust, Oxford, England, teacher, 1985-87; Hill End Residential Environment Centre, Oxford County Council, Oxford, England, teacher, 1987-88; Sutton Courtenay Field Study Centre, Oxford County Council, Oxford, England, head of centre, 1989-93. **Publications:** (with G. Morgan) 175 Amazing Nature Experiments, 1992. FUN WITH SCIENCE SERIES (with Morgan): Trees and Leaves, 1991; Energy and Growth, 1991; Observing Minibeasts, 1991; Cycles and Seasons, 1991; Nature: Experiments, Tricks, Things to Make, 1992. YOUNG DISCOVERER'S ENVIRONMENT SERIES: Energy and Power, 1995; Nature in Danger, 1995; Pollution and Waste, 1995; Rubbish and Recycling, 1995. **Address:** 12 Sunningwell Rd., Oxford OX1 45X, England.

HARMAN, Jane. See GILMAN, George G.

HARMETZ, Aljean. American. **Genres:** Film. **Career:** New York Times, New York, NY, culture and entertainment correspondent in California, 1978-1990, correspondent for Sunday arts and leisure section, 1990-; writer. **Publications:** The Making of "The Wizard of Oz": Movie Magic and Studio Power in the Prime of MGM-The Miracle of Production #1060, introduction by Margaret Hamilton, 1977; Rolling Breaks: And Other Movie Business (newspaper articles), 1983; Round Up the Usual Suspects: The Making of "Casablanca"-Bogart, Bergman, and World War II, 1992; On the Road To Tara: The Making of "Gone With the Wind", 1996. **Address:** c/o Candida Donadio, Donadio & Ashworth Inc., 121 West 27th St, Suite 704, New York, NY 10001, U.S.A.

HARMON, Louise. American. **Genres:** Law. **Career:** Lawyer in private practice in Chicago, IL; Touro College, Huntington, NY, professor of law at the Jacob D. Fuchsberg School of Law. **Publications:** (with D.W. Post) Cultivating Intelligence: Power, Law, and the Politics of Teaching, 1996; Fragments on the Deathwatch, 1998. **Address:** Touro College, Jacob D. Fuchsberg Law Center, 300 Nassau Rd., Huntington, NY 11743, U.S.A.

HARMON, Maurice. Irish, b. 1930. **Genres:** Songs/Lyrics and libretti, Literary criticism and history, Bibliography, Biography. **Career:** Professor Emeritus of Anglo-Irish Literature and Drama, University College, Dublin, 1990- (Lecturer in English, 1964-76; Associate Professor, 1976-90). Ed., Irish University Review, 1970- (Ed., University Review, 1964-68). Teaching Fellow and Research Assistant, Harvard University, Cambridge, MA, 1955-58; Instructor, Dept. of English, Lewis and Clark College, Portland, OR, 1958-61; Assistant Professor, Dept. of English, University of Notre Dame, IN, 1961-64. Chairman, International Association for the Study of Anglo-Irish Literature, 1979-82. **Publications:** Sean O'Faolain: A Critical Introduction, 1967; Modern Irish Literature, 1967; The Poetry of Thomas Kinsella, 1974; Select Bibliography for the Study of Anglo-Irish Literature and Its Background, 1976; (with R. McHugh) A Short History of Anglo-Irish Literature from Its Origins to the Present, 1982; Austin Clarke: A Critical Introduction, 1989; Sean O'Faolain: A Life, 1994; The Book of Precedence, 1994; A Stillness at Kiawah, 1996; No Author Better Served: The Correspondence of Samuel Beckett and Alan Schneider, 1998; The Last Regatta and Other Poems, 2000; The Colloquy of the Old Men, 2001; Tales of Death and Other Poems, 2001; The Dolman Poem: A Celebration, 2001. EDITOR: Fenians and Fenianism (essays), 1968; The Celtic Master (essays), 1969; W. Shakespeare, King Lear, 1970; W. Shakespeare, Romeo and Juliet, 1970; J. M. Synge Centenary Papers 1971, 1971; W. Shakespeare, King Richard II, 1971; W. Shakespeare, Coriolanus, 1972; (with P. Rafroidi) The Irish Novel in Our Times, 1976; Richard Murphy: Poet of Two Traditions, 1978; Irish Poetry after Yeats: Seven Poets, 1979; Image and Illusion: Anglo-Irish Literature and Its Contexts, 1979; The Irish Writer and the City, 1985. **Address:** 20 Sycamore Rd, Mount Merrion, Dublin, Ireland. **Online address:** morris.harmon@ucd.ie

HARMON, Sandra. American. **Genres:** Novels, Autobiography/Memoirs, How-to books. **Career:** Writer, Dick Cavett Show. **Publications:** A Girl Like Me (novel), 1975; (with P.B. Presley) Elvis and Me, 1985; (with P. Allen) Getting to I Do, 1994; (with Allen) Staying Married and Loving It!, 1998. **Address:** c/o Avon Books, 1350 Avenue of the Americas, New York, NY 10019, U.S.A.

HARNACK, Curtis. American, b. 1927. **Genres:** Novels, Novellas/Short stories, Poetry, History, Autobiography/Memoirs. **Career:** English Instructor, Grinnell College, 1952-56; Fulbright Professor of American Literature, University of Tabriz, Iran, 1958-59; Lecturer, University of Iowa Writers' Workshop, Iowa City, 1959-60; Member of Literature Faculty, Sarah Lawrence College, Bronxville, New York, 1960-71; Executive Director, Corp of Yaddo, Saratoga Springs, New York, 1971-87; School of American Ballet, Lincoln Center, president, 1992-97. **Publications:** (ed. with P. Engle) Prize Stories: The O. Henry Memorial Collection, 1958, and 1959; The Work of an Ancient Hand, 1960; Love and Be Silent, 1962; Persian Lions, Persian Lambs, 1965; We Have All Gone Away, 1973; Under My Wings Everything Prospers, 1977; Limits of the Land, 1979; Gentlemen on the Prairie, 1985; The Attic: A Memoir, 1993. **Address:** 205 W 57th St, New York, NY 10019, U.S.A. **Online address:** curharnack@aol.com

HARNER, Michael J(ames). American, b. 1929. **Genres:** Anthropology/Ethnology, Novels. **Career:** Arizona State University, Tempe, assistant professor of anthropology, 1958-61; University of California, Berkeley, senior museum anthropologist to associate research anthropologist and assistant director of Lowie Museum of Anthropology, 1961-66; Columbia University, NYC, visiting associate professor to associate professor of anthropology, 1966-70; Yale University, New Haven, CT, visiting associate professor of anthropology, 1970; New School for Social Research, New York City, 1970-87, began as associate professor, became professor of anthropology, chairman of department, 1973-87; writer. University of California, Berkeley, visiting associate professor, 1971, 1972, visiting professor, 1975. Foundation for Shamanic Studies, Mill Valley, CA, founding president and director, 1985-. Conducted anthropological research in Western North America, 1951-53, 1959, 1965, 1976, 1978, the Upper Amazon Basin, 1956-57, 1960-61, 1964, 1969, 1973, Lapland, 1983, 1984, and Canadian Arctic, 1987. **Publications:** (with A.L. Kroeber) Mohave Pottery, 1955; The Jivaro: People of the Sacred Waterfalls, 1972; (ed.) Hallucinogens and Shamanism, 1973; (with A. Meyer) Cannibal (novel), 1979; The Way of the Shaman, 1980. **Address:** Foundation for Shamanic Studies, PO Box 1939, Mill Valley, CA 94942, U.S.A.

HARNER, Stephen M. Also writes as Churchill East. American, b. 1949. **Genres:** Economics, Cultural/Ethnic topics. **Career:** U.S. Department of State, Washington, DC, foreign service officer, 1975-81; Citibank N.A., vice-president of offices in Japan and Taiwan, 1981-91; Deutsche Bank A.G., Shanghai Office, Shanghai, China, chief representative, 1995-. **Publications:** Living and Working in the People's Republic of China, 1980; Living and Working in Shanghai, privately printed, 1996; (trans.) China's New Political Economy. Some writings appear under the pseudonym Churchill East. **Address:** 5575 Allred Rd., Mariposa, CA 95338, U.S.A.

HARNESS, Charles L(eonard). American, b. 1915. **Genres:** Novellas/Short stories, Science fiction/Fantasy, Earth sciences, Marketing. **Career:** Mineral Economist, U.S. Bureau of Mines, Washington, DC, 1941-47; Patent Attorney, American Cyanamid Co., Stamford, CT, 1947-53, and W. R. Grace and Co., Columbia, MD, 1953-81. **Publications:** (with N.C. Jensen) Marketing Magnesite and Allied Products, 1943; (with F.M. Barsigian) Mining and Marketing of Barite, 1946; Flight into Yesterday, 1953, as The Paradox Men, 1955, in U.K. with Dome around America, 1964; The Rose (short stories), 1966; The Ring of Ritornel, 1968; Wolfhead, 1978; The Catalyst, 1980; Firebird, 1981; The Venetian Court, 1984; Redworld, 1986; Krono, 1988; Lurid Dreams, 1990; Lunar Justice, 1991; An Ornament to His Profession (short stories), 1998; Rings (novels), 2000; Cybele, with Bluebonnets, 2002.

HARNOIS, Albert J. American, b. 1945. **Genres:** Business/Trade/Industry, Money/Finance, Biography. **Career:** T.J.X. Companies Inc., Framingham, MA, manager of information systems audits, 1991-98; NEBS, Groton, MA, director of internal audit, 1998-. **Publications:** EDP Auditing: A Functional Approach, 1991; Accounting and Auditing in a New Environment, 1994; Growing Up with Guilt, 1996. **Address:** 122 Morris St., Cumberland, RI 02864, U.S.A.

HARNUM, Robert. American. **Genres:** Novels. **Career:** High school teacher in Brewer, ME. Also taught at University of Connecticut and at La Grande école de Commerce de Rouen, Rouen, France. **Publications:** Le festin des lions, 1998; La dernière sentinelle (novel), 1999, trans. as Exile in the Kingdom, 2001; Poursuite, 2001; Une rhapsodie Américaine, 2002. **Address:** c/o University Press of New England, PO Box 979, Hanover, NH 03755, U.S.A.

HAROIAN-GUERIN, Gil. American, b. 1957. **Genres:** Literary criticism and history. **Career:** Syracuse University, Syracuse, NY, instructor in writing program, 1995-. **Publications:** The Fatal Hero: Diana, Diety of the Moon, as an Archetype of the Modern Hero in English Literature, 1996, 2nd ed, 1998. **Address:** Writing Program, Syracuse University, Syracuse, NY 13244, U.S.A. **Online address:** gharoian@mailbox.syr.edu

HARPER, Jo. American, b. 1932. **Genres:** Children's fiction, Young adult fiction, Children's non-fiction, Young adult non-fiction. **Career:** Librarian at a junior high school in Plainview, TX, 1951-52; first-grade teacher for Spanish-speaking children, Plainview, 1959-60; high school teacher of English, Spanish, and humanities, Plainview, 1964-68; Texas A&I University, Kingsville, instructor in English, 1968-70; Rockingham Community College, Wentworth, NC, instructor in English and Spanish, 1971-77; Armstrong State College, Savannah, GA, assistant professor of English and Spanish, and foreign student adviser, 1977-80; Texas Southern University, Houston, director of intensive English for foreign students, 1980-84; University of Houston, Houston, lecturer in English, 1984-96; Spring Branch Education Center, Houston, teacher of English to at-risk high school students, 1996-99. **Publications:** PICTURE BOOKS: Pals, Potions, and Pixies: Family Songbook, 1988; Caves and Cowboys: Family Song Book, 1988; Jalapeno Hal, 1993; Outrageous, Bodacious Boliver Boggs!, 1996; Deaf Smith: Scout, Spy, Texas Hero, 1996; Bigfoot Wallace: Texas Ranger and Mier Survivor, 1997; The Legend of Mexicatl, 1998; Prairie Dog Pioneers, 1998; Ollie Jolly, Rodeo

Clown, 2002; Mayor Jalapeno Hal, 2003; Finding Daddy, 2004. OTHER: Delfino's Journey (young adult novel), 2001; Wilma Rudolph (middle grade biography), 2004. Contributor to magazines and newspapers. **Address:** 1605 Huge Oaks, Houston, TX 77055, U.S.A. **Online address:** joharper@juno.com

HARPER, Lila Marz. (born United States), b. 1955. **Genres:** Literary criticism and history. **Career:** Central Washington University, Ellensburg, instructor in English, 1989-. Field bibliographer for Modern Language Association of America and Modern Humanities Research Association, 1996-. **Publications:** Solitary Travelers: Nineteenth-Century Women's Travel Narratives and the Scientific Vocation, 2001; (editor) Edwin Abbott, Flatland (critical edition), 2003. Author of instructor's manuals and contributor to reference books and periodicals. **Address:** Department of English, Central Washington University, 400 East Eighth Ave., Ellensburg, WA 98926, U.S.A. **Online address:** harperl@cwu.edu

HARPER, Michael S(teven). (born United States), b. 1938. **Genres:** Poetry. **Career:** Contra Costa College, San Pablo, CA, instructor in English, 1964-68; Lewis and Clark College, Portland, OR, poet-in-residence, 1968-69; California State College (now University), Hayward, associate professor of English, 1970; Brown University, Providence, RI, associate professor, 1970-73; professor, 1973-, I. J. Kapstein Professor of English, 1983-, director of writing program. Visiting professor at Reed College, 1968-69, Harvard University, 1974, and Yale University, 1977; Benedict Distinguished Professor of English, Carleton College, 1979; Elliston Poet, University of Cincinnati, 1979; National Humanities Distinguished Professor, Colgate University, 1985. Bicentennial poet, Bicentennary Exchange: Britain/USA, 1976. American specialist, International Congress of Africanists (ICA) State Department tour of Africa, 1977; lecturer, German University ICA tour of nine universities, 1978. Council member, Massachusetts Council on the Arts and Humanities, 1977-80; board member, Yaddo Artists Colony, Sarasota Springs, NY; original founding member, African Continuum, St. Louis, MO; judge, National Book Awards in poetry, 1978, 1993, 2001, Pulitzer Prize for poetry, 1993, Poulin prize for BOA Editions, and Lenore Marshall Prize for the Academy of American Poets. **Publications:** POETRY: Dear John, Dear Coltrane, 1970; History Is Your Own Heartbeat, 1971; Photographs, Negatives: History as Apple Tree (also see below), 1972; Song: I Want a Witness 1972; Debridement, 1973; Nightmare Begins Responsibility, 1974, 1995; Images of Kin: New and Selected Poems, 1977; Rhode Island: Eight Poems, 1981; Healing Song for the Inner Ear, 1985; Songlines: Mosaics (limited edition), 1991; Honorable Amendments: Poems, 1995; Songlines in Michaeltree: New and Collected Poems, 2000; Selected Poems, 2002; Debridement/Song: I Want a Witness, 2002. OTHER: (Compiler) Ralph Dickey, Leaving Eden: Poems, 1974; (Compiler) Robert Hayden, 1978; (editor, with Robert B. Stepto; and contrib.) Chant of Saints: A Gathering of Afro-American Literature, Art, and Scholarship, 1979; (Compiler) Sterling Allen Brown, The Collected Poems, 1980; (editor, with Anthony Walton) Every Shut Eye Ain't Asleep: An Anthology of Poetry by African Americans since 1945, 1994; (editor, with Anthony Walton) The Vintage Book of African-American Poetry, 2000. Contributor to poetry anthologies and periodicals. **Address:** 116 Chestnut Street, Providence, RI 02903, U.S.A. **Online address:** Michael_Harper@brown.edu

HARPER, Piers. British, b. 1966. **Genres:** Children's fiction. **Career:** Author and illustrator of children's books, 1991-. Editor and advisor, Walker Books Ltd. **Publications:** AND ILLUSTRATOR: (Reteller) How the World Was Saved, 1994; Turtle Quest, 1997; 1997; Snakes and Ladders (and Hundreds of Mice): A Weird and Wonderful Tower Maze, 1997; If You Love a Bear, 1998; Checkmate at Chess City, in press. Illustrator of books by P. Borlenghi, T. Chadwick, N. Nelson, W. Body. **Address:** 40 Marne Ave., Ravenstown, Flookburgh, Grange-Over-Sands, Cumbria LA11 7LH, England.

HARPER, Susan (Rice). American, b. 1943. **Genres:** Local history/Rural topics. **Career:** San Francisco State University, San Francisco, CA, lecturer in creative writing, 1980-93; employed as director of the Commerce Public Library in Commerce, Georgia, 1986-93. **Publications:** The Oakland Paramount, Lancaster-Miller, 1981; The Year of the Buck, John Daniel, 1992. **Address:** BJE, 639 14th Ave, San Francisco, CA 94118, U.S.A.

HARPER, Tara K. American, b. 1961. **Genres:** Science fiction/Fantasy. **Career:** World, Coos Bay, OR, special reporter, 1983; Tektronix Inc., Beaverton, OR, senior technical writer and editor, 1984-90; Cascade Microtech Inc., Beaverton, technical documentation specialist, 1990-; Tigard School District, Tigard, OR, creative writing adviser at Fowler Middle School, 1992-, creative writing teacher for alternative education programs at Tigard High School, 1992-. Technical writer and editor for national committees of

National Institute of Standards and Technology, American National Standards Institute, and American Society for Quality Control, 1988-; Campfire, wilderness skills trainer, 1991-; Hillsboro School District, mentor in the TAG program, 1992-93. 1992-93. **Publications:** Wolfwalker, 1990; Shadow Leader, 1991; Lightwing, 1993; Storm Runner, 1993; Cat Scratch Fever, 1994; Cataract, 1995; Grayheart, 1996; Wolf's Bane, 1997; Silver Moons, Black Steel, 2001. **Address:** c/o James Allen, 180 Cranberry Ridge Dr, Milford, PA 18337, U.S.A. **Online address:** www.tarakharper.com

HARPHAM, Wendy S(chlessel). (born United States), b. 1954. **Genres:** Medicine/Health. **Career:** Writer, public speaker, and physician. Physician in private practice of internal medicine, beginning 1983. Host, ACS Cancer Survivors Network; speaker, consultant, and patient advocate. **Publications:** Diagnosis: Cancer. Your Guide through the First Few Months, 1992, published as Diagnosis Cancer: Your Guide to the First Months of Health Survivorship, 2003; After Cancer: A Guide to Your New Life, 1995; When a Parent Has Cancer: A Guide to Caring for Your Children, 1997; (with Laura Harpham) The Hope Tree: Kids Talk about Breast Cancer, 2001. Contributor to books, professional journals and periodicals. **Address:** POB 835574, Richardson, TX 75083, U.S.A. **Online address:** harpham@comcast.net

HARPUR, Tom. (Thomas William). Canadian, b. 1929. **Genres:** Ethics, Theology/Religion. **Career:** Syndicated journalist, TV host, and author. Life after Death, 10-part TV series, host, 1996, The Uncommon Touch, 12-part TV series, host, 1998; Toronto Sunday Star, columnist on spiritual issues. **Publications:** (with C. Templeton) Jesus, 1975; The Road to Bethlehem: Two Thousand Years Later, 1976; Harpur's Heaven and Hell (essays), 1983; For Christ's Sake, 1986; Communicating the Good News Today, 1987; Always on Sunday, 1988; Life after Death, 1991; God Help Us, 1992; The Uncommon Touch-An Investigation of Spiritual Healing, 1994; Harpur versus Hancock, 1994; The Divine Lover, 1994; Would You Believe?, 1996; The Thinking Person's Guide to God, 1996; Prayer The Hidden Fire, 1998; Finding the Still Point-A Spiritual Response to Stress, 2002. TELEVISION SCRIPTS: Man Alive; The Uncommon Touch, 1999. Contributor to periodicals.

HARRE, Rom. British, b. 1927. **Genres:** Psychology, Sciences. **Career:** University of Leicester, Lecturer, 1957-59; Linacre College, Oxford, University Lecturer in Philosophy of Science, 1960-97, Emeritus Fellow, 1997-; State University of New York, Binghamton, Adjunct Professor, 1973-98; Georgetown University, Washington, Professor of Psychology, DC, 1989-. **Publications:** An Introduction to the Logic of the Sciences, 1960; Theories and Things, 1961; Matter and Method, 1964; The Anticipation of Nature, 1965; The Method of Science, 1970; The Principles of Scientific Thinking, 1970; The Philosophies of Science, 1972; (with P.F. Second) The Explanation of Social Behaviour, 1972; (with E.H. Madden) Causal Powers, 1972; Social Being, 1979; Personal Being, 1983; Varieties of Realism, 1986; (with P. Muhlhausler) Pronouns and People, 1990; One Thousand Years of Philosophy, 2000. EDITOR: F. Waismann, The Principles of Linguistic Philosophy, 1965; The Sciences, 1967; Scientific Thought 1900-1960, 1969; Problems of Scientific Revolution, 1975. **Address:** Linacre College, Oxford OX1 3JA, England. **Online address:** harre@georgetown.edu

HARRELL, Beatrice Orcutt. American, b. 1943. **Genres:** Mythology/Folklore, Cultural/Ethnic topics. **Career:** Indian Health Care, Tulsa, OK, social service counselor, 1975-77; Green Bay Packaging, Tulsa, personnel assistant, 1987-91; Sapulpa Indian Education, Sapulpa, OK, tutor, 1995-. Adult Literacy Program, volunteer tutor, 1990-; Habitat for Humanity, volunteer coordinator, 1991-. **Publications:** (Reteller) How Thunder and Lightning Came to Be: A Choctaw Legend, 1995; Choctaw Mother (story), 1995. Contributor to magazines. **Address:** 13962 Hickory Pl., Glenpool, OK 74033, U.S.A.

HARRIES, Karsten. German, b. 1937. **Genres:** Architecture, Art/Art history, Philosophy. **Career:** Yale University, New Haven, CT, instructor in philosophy, 1961-63; University of Texas at Austin, assistant professor of philosophy, 1963-65; Yale University, assistant professor, 1965-66, associate professor, 1966-70, professor of philosophy, 1970-. University of Bonn, guest professor, 1965-66, 1968-69. **Publications:** The Meaning of Modern Art, 1967; The Bavarian Rococo Church, 1983; The Broken Frame, 1989; (ed. with C. Jamme) Martin Heidegger: Kunst, Politik, Technik, 1992, trans. as Martin Heidegger: Politics, Art, and Technology, 1994; The Ethical Function of Architecture, 1996; Infinity and Perspective, 2001. Contributor of articles and reviews to academic journals. **Address:** Dept of Philosophy, Yale University, PO Box 208306, New Haven, CT 06520-8306, U.S.A. **Online address:** karsten.harries@yale.edu

HARRIFORD, Daphne. See **HARRIS, Marion (Rose).**

HARRIGAN, Patrick J. American (born Canada), b. 1941. **Genres:** History. **Career:** University of Waterloo, Waterloo, Ontario, Canada, professor of history, 1969-. **Publications:** Lyceens et Collegiens sous le Second Empire: Etude statistique sur les fonctions sociales de l'enseignement secondaire public, d'apres l'anquete de Victor Duruy, 1864-1865, 1979; (with D. Baker) The Making of Frenchmen, 1980; Mobility, Elites, and Education in French Society of the Second Empire, 1980; (with R. Grew) School, State, and Society: The Growth of Elementary Schooling in Nineteenth-Century France, 1991; The Detroit Tigers: Club and Community 1945-1995, 1997. **Address:** Department of History, University of Waterloo, Waterloo, ON, Canada N2L 3G1. **Online address:** Harrigan@uwaterloo.ca

HARRIGER, Katy J(ean). American, b. 1957. **Genres:** Politics/Government. **Career:** University of Connecticut, Hartford Branch, instructor in political science, 1983, 1984; Wake Forest University, Winston-Salem, NC, instructor, 1985-86, assistant professor, 1986-91, associate professor, 1991-2002, Zachary T. Smith Professor, 2002-; resident scholar at Spice II Bicentennial Institute, 1987, 1988. **Publications:** Independent Justice: The Federal Special Prosecutor in American Politics, 1992; The Special Prosecutor in American Politics, 2000. EDITOR: Separation of Powers: Commentary & Documents, 2003. Work represented in anthologies. Contributor of articles and reviews to political science and history journals and newspapers. **Address:** Dept of Political Science, C-309 Tribble Hall, Wake Forest University, Box 7568, Winston-Salem, NC 27109, U.S.A. **Online address:** harriger@wfu.edu

HARRILL, Ronald. American, b. 1950. **Genres:** Biography. **Career:** Author, lecturer, and storyteller. First Union National Bank, Charlotte, NC, systems analyst to assistant vice president, 1978-. Member of committees; lecturer at schools, colleges, universities, churches, and other organizations. **Publications:** Makeda, Queen of Sheba, 1994. **Address:** 2311 Holly Ln., Shelby, NC 28150, U.S.A.

HARRINGTON, John P. American, b. 1952. **Genres:** Literary criticism and history. **Career:** Cooper Union, New York City, dean of humanities and social sciences, 1992-. **Publications:** The Irish Beckett, 1991; Modern Irish Drama, 1991; The English Traveller in Ireland, 1991; Irish Play on the New York Stage, 1997; (ed) Politics and Performance in Contemporary Northern Ireland, 1999. **Address:** Department of Humanities and Social Sciences, Cooper Union, Cooper Square, 51 Astor Place, New York, NY 10003-7120, U.S.A.

HARRINGTON, Kathleen. American. **Genres:** Romance/Historical. **Career:** Writer. **Publications:** HISTORICAL-ROMANCE NOVELS: Cherish the Dream, 1990; Warrior Dreams, 1992; Sunshine and Shadow, 1993; Promise Me, 1995; Dream Catcher, 1996; Fly with the Eagle, 1997; Enchanted by You, 1998; The MacLean Groom, 1999.

HARRINGTON, Philip S(tuart). American, b. 1956. **Genres:** Astronomy, Recreation. **Career:** Hayden Planetarium, NYC, planetarium professional, 1979-81; Vanderbilt Planetarium, instructor, 1982-98; Unisys Corp., Great Neck, NY, mechanical engineer, 1983-92; Brookhaven National Laboratory, Upton, NY, environmental engineer, 1992-. Suffolk County Community College, adjunct instructor, 1998-; Astronomy magazine, contributing editor. **Publications:** Touring the Universe through Binoculars, 1990; (with W. Harrington) Short Bike Rides in and around NYC, 1992; (with E. Pascuzzi) Astronomy for All Ages, 1994; Star Ware, 1994, 3rd ed., 2002; Eclipse!, 1997; The Deep Sky, 1998; The Space Shuttle: A Photographic History, 2003; Star Watch, 2003. **Address:** PO Box 732, Upton, NY 11973, U.S.A. **Online address:** pharrington@compuserve.com

HARRIOTT, Peter. American, b. 1927. **Genres:** Engineering. **Career:** E. I. duPont de Nemours, Wilmington, DE, engineer, 1949; General Electric Co., Schenectady, NY, research engineer, 1952-53; Cornell University, Ithaca, NY, assistant professor, 1953-54, associate professor, 1954-65, professor of chemical engineering, 1965-, F. H. Rhodes Professor, 1975-. Consultant to U.S. manufacturers. **Publications:** Process Control, 1964; (with W.L. McCabe and J.C. Smith) Unit Operations of Chemical Engineering, 4th ed., 1985, 7th ed., 2005; Chemical Reactor Design, 2002. **Address:** School of Chemical Engineering, Cornell University, Ithaca, NY 14853, U.S.A. **Online address:** ph@cheme.cornell.edu

HARRIS, Alan. American, b. 1944. **Genres:** Astronomy. **Career:** Jet Propulsion Lab, Pasadena, CA, member of technical staff, 1975-91, senior member of technical staff, 1991-97, senior research scientist, 1997-2002; Space Science Institute, Boulder, CO, senior research scientist, 2002-. **Publications:** (with P. Weissman) The Great Voyager Adventure, 1990. Author of technical papers and book chapters on astronomical subjects. **Address:** Space Science Institute, 4603 Orange Knoll Ave, La Canada, CA 91011, U.S.A. **Online address:** harrisaw@colorado.edu

HARRIS, Anne L. American, b. 1964. **Genres:** Science fiction/Fantasy. **Career:** Writer. **Publications:** The Nature of Smoke, 1996; Accidental Creatures, 1998. **Address:** c/o Tor Books, 175 Fifth Ave. 14th Fl., New York, NY 10010, U.S.A.

HARRIS, Archibald. *See* **FLEISSNER, Robert F.**

HARRIS, Brayton. American, b. 1932. **Genres:** Military/Defense/Arms control, Writing/Journalism. **Career:** U.S. Navy, career officer, 1953-78, retiring as captain; U.S. Selective Service System, Washington, DC, assistant director, 1980-81; Pratt & Whitney, West Palm Beach, FL, public relations representative, 1984-90; B. F. Goodrich Aerospace, Akron, OH, director of communications, 1990-98. **Publications:** Age of the Battleship, 1890-1922, 1965; Johann Gutenberg and the Invention of Printing, 1971; (with J. Kirschenbaum) Safe Boat, 1990; The Navy Times Book of Submarines, 1997; Blue & Gray in Black & White, 1999; (ed.) The Civil War: Ironweed American Newspapers and Periodicals Project, 2003. **Address:** 6521 Mission Rd, Mission Hills, KS 66208, U.S.A. **Online address:** brayton@harris.net

HARRIS, Charles Wesley. American, b. 1929. **Genres:** Politics/Government, Urban studies. **Career:** Coppin State College, Baltimore, MD, associate professor, 1961-66, chairperson, Division of Social Sciences, 1967-68, director of graduate studies, 1969-70; Howard University, Washington, DC, professor of political science, 1970-, department head, 1974-77, associate dean, College of Liberal Arts, 1988-92. U.S. Civil Service Commission, associate director of Executive Institutes, 1966-67; Library of Congress, Congressional Research Service, senior specialist and chief of Government Division, 1971-74. Brookings Institution, visiting scholar, 1987-88; Woodrow Wilson International Center for Scholars, fellow, 1992-93 and 1994. **Publications:** Regional Councils of Government and the Central City, 1970; Resolving the Legislative Veto Issue, 1979; (co-author) Perspectives of Political Power in the District of Columbia, 1981; Congress and the Governance of the Nation's Capital: The Conflict of Federal and Local Interests, 1995; Foreign Capital City Governance: Representation, Governmental Structure, Finances, and Intergovernmental Relations in Six Capital Cities, 1997. Contributor to books and professional journals. **Address:** Department of Political Science, Howard University, 2400 6th St NW, Washington, DC 20059, U.S.A.

HARRIS, Christine. Australian, b. 1955. **Genres:** Novellas/Short stories, Romance/Historical, Science fiction/Fantasy, Children's fiction, Young adult fiction, Plays/Screenplays, Picture/board books. **Career:** Writer, 1988-. Also works occasionally as a photographer, with work published in newspapers. **Publications:** SHORT STORY COLLECTIONS: Outer Face, 1992; Buried Secrets, 1993; Widdershins, 1995, as Party Animals, 1997; (with C. Carmichael and M. Clark) Deadly Friends, 1997; Fortune Cookies, 1998; Warped, 2000. NOVELS FOR YOUNG ADULTS: Strike!, 1994; Baptism of Fire, 1996; Pitt Man, 1996; Torture Chamber, 1997; Slime Time, 1997; Foreign Devil, 1999; Halfway round the World, 2001; Hairy Legs, 2001; Brain Drain, 2001; Windbag, 2001; Psycho Gran, 2001; Jamil's Shadow, 2002. SCIENCE-FICTION NOVELS: Suspicion, 1998; Masks, 1998; Jigsaw, 1998; Shadows, 1998; Omega, 2000; Headspace, 2004. FOR CHILDREN: Sleeping In (picture book), 1997; I Don't Want to Go to School (picture book), 1999; Spygirl, #1: Secrets, 2004, #2: Fugitive, 2004. EDITOR. NONFICTION: No Bed of Roses, 1993; Old Yanconian School Daze, 1995; What a Line!, 1995; In Looking-Glass Land, 1996. OTHER: Trees in My Ears: Children from around the World Talk to Christine Harris, 1992; Countdown (novel), 1995; A Real Corpse, 1997; Odd Balls: Jokes and Funny Stories, 1998; The Little Book of Elephants (humor and nonfiction), 1999; Break a Leg (plays), 2001. **Address:** PO Box 478, Mt. Barker, SA 5251, Australia. **Online address:** christine@christineharris.com

HARRIS, Claire (Kathleen Patricia). Canadian (born Trinidad and Tobago), b. 1937. **Genres:** Novellas/Short stories, Poetry, Essays. **Career:** Poet and editor. Poetry Goes Public, editor, 1976-79; Dandelion (magazine), poetry editor, 1981-89; Blue Buffalo, a Magazine of AB, co-founder, 1982, managing editor, 1982-84. Has worked as a secondary school teacher (English and drama) in Calgary, Alberta, Canada, c. 1966. **Publications:** Translation into Fiction, 1984; Fables from the Women's Quarters, 1984; Travelling to Find a Remedy, 1986; The Conception of Winter, 1989; Drawing down a Daughter, 1992; (ed. with E. Alford) Kitchen Talk: An Anthology of Writings by Canadian Women, 1992; (with D. Brand and M.N. Philip), Grammar of Dissent: Poetry and Prose, 1995; Dipped in Shadow, 1996; She (novella), 2000. Contributor to anthologies and magazines. **Address:** 300 Meredith Rd NE #701, Calgary, AB, Canada T2E 7A8.

HARRIS, Deborah Turner. American, b. 1951. **Genres:** Science fiction/ Fantasy. **Career:** Teacher of English literature and composition, 1974-83; part-time writer, 1983-87; full-time writer, 1987-. **Publications:** The Burning Stone, 1986; Gauntlet of Malice, 1987; Spiral of Fire, 1989; (with K. Kurtz) The Adept, 1991; (with K. Kurtz) The Lodge of the Lynx, 1992; (with K. Kurtz) The Templar Treasure, 1993; Caledon of the Mists, 1994; Queen of Ashes, 1995; Dagger Magic, 1995; Death of an Adept, 1996; City of Exile, 1997; (with K. Kurtz) The Temple and the Stone, 1998; (with K. Kurtz) The Temple and the Crown, 2000. **Address:** c/o Virginia Kidd Agency, 538 E Harford St, PO Box 278, Milford, PA 18337, U.S.A. **Online address:** www. harrisauthors.com

HARRIS, Dudley Arthur. South African, b. 1925. **Genres:** Chemistry, Horticulture. **Career:** With South African Council for Scientific and Industrial Research, 1948-51; Director and Analytical and Consulting Chemist, J. Muller Labs., Cape Town, 1953-81. **Publications:** Hydroponics: The Gardening without Soil, 1966, 4th ed., 1974; Hydroponics, 1975, 7th ed., 1987; The Illustrated Guide to Hydroponics, 1994. **Address:** A22 Larmenier Village, 1 Derry St, Vredehoek, Capetown 8001, Republic of South Africa.

HARRIS, E. Lynn. American, b. 1957. **Genres:** Novels. **Publications:** NOVELS: Invisible Life, 1991; Just as I am, 1994; And This Too Shall Pass, 1996; If the World Were Mine, 1997; Abide With Me, 1999; Not a Day Goes By, 2000; Any Way the Wind Blows, 2001; A Love of My Own, 2002. OTHER: What Becomes of the Brokenhearted (memoir), 2003. **Address:** c/o Doubleday, 1540 Broadway, New York, NY 10036, U.S.A.

HARRIS, Elizabeth. American, b. 1944. **Genres:** Novels, Novellas/Short stories. **Career:** University of Texas at Austin, Dept of English, assistant professor, 1976-83, associate professor, 1983-. **Publications:** The Ant Generator (stories), 1991. **Address:** Department of English, University of Texas at Austin, Austin, TX 78712, U.S.A.

HARRIS, Fred R(oy). American, b. 1930. **Genres:** Novels, Politics/ Government. **Career:** Professor of Political Science, University of New Mexico, Albuquerque, 1976-. Admitted to Oklahoma Bar, 1954; Sr. Partner in law firm of Harris, Newcombe, Redman and Doolin, Lawton, Oklahoma, 1954-64; Member, Oklahoma State Senate, 1956-64; Senator from Oklahoma (Democrat), U.S. Senate, 1964-72. **Publications:** NON-FICTION: Alarms and Hopes, 1968; Now Is the Time, 1971; The New Populism, 1973; Social Science and Public Policy, 1973; Potomac Fever, 1976; America's Democracy: The Ideal and Reality, 1980, rev. ed., 1986; America's Legislative Processes: Congress and the States, 1983; Readings on the Body Politic, 1987; Understanding American Government, 1988; Quiet Riots: Race and Poverty in the United States, 1988; America's Government, 1990; Deadlock or Decision: The U.S. Senate and the Rise of National Politics, 1993; In Defense of Congress, 1995; Locked in the Poorhouse: Cities, Race, and Poverty in the United States, 1999. NOVELS: Coyote Revenge, 1999; Easy Pickin's, 2000. **Address:** PO Box 1203, Corrales, NM 87048, U.S.A.

HARRIS, George A. American, b. 1950. **Genres:** Psychology. **Career:** Intern at Jackson County Department of Corrections, Mo.; Goodwill Industries, Kansas City, staff psychologist, 1975-76; Jackson County Department of Corrections, counselor, 1976-77; training coordinator, 1977-78; Washburn University of Topeka, Topeka, Kan., assistant professor of criminal justice, 1978-. Visiting scholar at University of Michigan's Inter-University Consortium for Political and Social Research, 1982. **Publications:** Broken Ears, Wounded Hearts, 1983; (with D. Watkins) Counseling the Involuntary and Resistant Client, 1987; (ed.) Tough Customers: Counseling Unwilling Clients, 1991; Overcoming Resistance: Success in Counseling Men, 1996. **Address:** c/o American Correctional Association, 4380 Forbes Blvd, Lanham, MD 20706-4322, U.S.A.

HARRIS, H(enry) S(ilton). Canadian (born England), b. 1926. **Genres:** Philosophy, Translations, Literary criticism and history. **Career:** University of Illinois, Urbana-Champaign, instructor, 1953-54, assistant professor, 1957-61, associate professor, 1961-62; Ohio State University, instructor, 1954-57; York University, Toronto, Glendon College, associate professor, 1962-65, professor of Philosophy and Humanities, 1965-84, chairman of Philosophy Dept., 1967-72, academic dean, 1967-69, distinguished research professor, 1984-. **Publications:** The Social Philosophy of G. Gentile, 1960; (trans.) Genesis and Structure of Society, by Giovanni Gentile, 1960; Hegel's Development, vol. 1: Toward the Sunlight, 1770-1801, 1972, Volume 2: Night Thoughts: Jena, 1801-1806, 1983; (ed. with L.M. Palmer) Thought, Action and Intuition: A Symposium on the Philosophy of Benedetto Croce, 1975; (trans. with W. Cerf) The Difference between Fichte's and Schelling's Systems of Philosophy, by G.W.F. Hegel, 1977; (trans. with Cerf) Faith and

Knowledge, by Hegel, 1977; (trans. with T.M. Knox) System of Ethical Life and First Philosophy of Spirit, by Hegel, 1979; (trans. and ed. with G. di Giovanni) From Kant to Hegel, 1985, rev. ed., 2000; (trans. with others) The Encyclopedia Logic, by Hegel, 1991; Hegel, Phenomenology and System, 1995; Hegel's Ladder, Vol 1: The Pilgrimage of Reason, 1997, Vol. 2: The Odyssey of Spirit, 1997. **Address:** 2527 Graham St., Victoria, BC, Canada V8T 3Y6.

HARRIS, Helen(a) (Barbara Mary). British, b. 1927. **Genres:** Agriculture/ Forestry, Archaeology/Antiquities, Area studies, Local history/Rural topics. **Career:** Dairy Adviser, Ministry of Agriculture, 1948-56. Hon. Ed., The Devon Historian, 1985-2005. **Publications:** The Industrial Archaeology of Dartmoor, 1968, rev. ed., 1992; The Industrial Archaeology of the Peak District, 1971, rev. ed., 1992; (with M. Ellis) The Bude Canal, 1972; The Grand Western Canal, 1973, rev. ed., 1996; The Haytor Granite Tramway and Stover Canal, 1994, rev. ed., 2002; The Church on the Hill (Buckfastleigh), 1996; Devon's Century of Change, 1998; A Handbook of Devon Parishes, 2004. **Address:** Hirondelles, 22 Churchill Rd, Whitchurch, Tavistock, Devon PL19 9BU, England.

HARRIS, James F. American, b. 1941. **Genres:** Philosophy. **Career:** Transylvania University, Lexington, KY, assistant professor of philosophy, 1966-67; University of Georgia, Athens, assistant professor of history, 1967-73; College of William and Mary, Williamsburg, VA, Haserot Professor of Philosophy, 1974-. **Publications:** Analyticity, 1970; Against Relativism, 1992; Single Malt Whiskies of Scotland, 1992; Philosophy at 33 1/3 RPM: Themes of Classic Rock Music, 1993; American Classic Whiskies, 1995; Analytic Philosophy of Religion, 2002. **Address:** Department of Philosophy, College of William and Mary, Williamsburg, VA 23187, U.S.A.

HARRIS, Jana. American, b. 1947. **Genres:** Novels, Poetry. **Career:** University of California, Berkeley, Lawrence Hall of Science, Project SEED Inc., educational mathematics consultant, 1970-76; Poetry in the Schools, San Francisco State University, instructor, 1972-78; Modesto Jr. College, CA, instructor in creative writing, 1975-78; Alameda County Neighborhood Arts, CA, poet-in-residence, 1977-78; New York University, instructor in creative writing, 1980; Manhattan Theatre Club, NYC, Writers in Performance Series, director, 1980-86; University of Washington, instructor, 1986-. Switched-on Gutenberg, founder and editor. **Publications:** This House That Rocks with Every Truck on the Road (poetry), 1976; Letters from the Promised Land: Alaska Poems, 1976; Pin Money (poetry), 1977; The Book of Common People: Poems in a Dime Store Sack, 1978; The Clackamas (poetry), 1980; Alaska (novel), 1980; Who's That Pushy Bitch? (poetry), 1981; Manhattan as a Second Language, and Other Poems, 1982; The Sourlands (poetry), 1989; Oh How Can I Keep on Singing? (poems); The Dust of Everyday Life (epic poem), 1997; The Pearl of Ruby City (novel). **Address:** 32814 120 St SE, Sultan, WA 98294, U.S.A. **Online address:** jnh@u. washington.edu

HARRIS, Jesse. See **STANDIFORD, Natalie.**

HARRIS, Jose. British. **Genres:** Politics/Government, Biography. **Career:** Oxford University, England, fellow of St. Catherine's College, 1977, reader in modern history, 1990-97, professor, 1997-. **Publications:** Unemployment and Politics, 1886-1914, 1972, 2nd ed., 1984; William Beveridge: A Biography, 1977; Private Lives, Public Spirit: A Social History of Britain, 1870-1914, 1993. **Address:** St. Catherine's College, Oxford University, Oxford, England.

HARRIS, Leonard. American, b. 1929. **Genres:** Novels, Plays/Screenplays, Communications/Media. **Career:** Freelance journalist and writer, critic, and host for network-and cable-television and radio; also actor. Reporter, Writer, and Ed., Hartford Courant, Connecticut, 1958-60; Reporter, and Critic, New York World Telegram & Sun, 1960-66; Critic, WCBS-TV News, NYC, 1966-74; Adjunct Associate Professor, Fordham University, Bronx, New York, 1969-74, and Hunter College, NYC, 1974-75; Broadway Theatre Critic, Soho News, NYC, 1977-78, and The Hollywood Reporter, 1982; Media Commentator, Entertainment Tonight, 1983-84; Writer, CBS Morning Program, 1986-87; Writer, CBS This Morning, 1987-91; Writer, Miss America Pageant, NBC, 1990, 1991, 1992; Writer, CBS Tournament of Roses and CBS Coming Up Roses, 1993-2001; Writer, CBS All-American Thanksgiving Parade, 1996-2000. **Publications:** The Masada Plan, 1976; Don't Be No Hero, 1978; The Hamptons, 1981. **Address:** 330 E. 71st St, #5A, New York, NY 10021, U.S.A.

HARRIS, Margaret. British, b. 1951. **Genres:** Psychology. **Career:** Psychologist and author. Royal Holloway, University of London, Surrey,

England, reader in developmental psychology. **Publications:** (with M. Coltheart) Language Processing in Children and Adults: An Introduction, 1986; Language Experience and Early Language Development: From Input to Uptake, 1992; (ed., with G. Hatano) Learning to Read and Write, 1999; (with G. Butterworth) Developmental Psychology: A Students Handbook, 2002. **Address:** Department of Psychology, Royal Holloway, University of London, Egham Hill, Egham, Surrey TW20 0EX, England.

HARRIS, Marilyn. American, b. 1931. **Genres:** Novels, Romance/ Historical, Children's fiction, Young adult fiction, Novellas/Short stories. **Publications:** King's Ex (short stories), 1967; In the Midst of Earth, 1969; The Peppersalt Land (juvenile), 1970; The Runaway's Diary (juvenile), 1971; Hatter Fox, 1973; The Conjurers, 1974; Bledding Sorrow (romance), 1976; Eden series (romance): This Other Eden, 1977, The Prince of Eden, 1978, The Eden Passion, 1979, The Women of Eden, 1980, Eden Rising, 1982; The Last Great Love, 1982; The Portent, 1982; The Diviner, 1984; Warrick, 1985; Night Games, 1987; American Eden, 1987; Eden and Honor, 1988; Lost and Found, 1991. **Address:** 1846 Rolling Hills, Norman, OK 73069, U.S.A.

HARRIS, Marion (Rose). Also writes as Henry Charles, Rose Glendower, Daphne Harriford, Rosie Harris, Keith Rogers, Rose Young. British, b. 1925. **Genres:** Novels, Adult non-fiction. **Career:** Ed. and Proprietor, Regional Feature Service, 1964-72; Editorial Controller, W. Foulsham & Co. Ltd., publishers, Slough, Bucks., 1974-83. **Publications:** Fresh Fruit Dishes, 1963; Making a House a Home, 1964; The Awful Slimmer, 1967; Flower Arranging, 1968; (as Daphne Harriford) Around the Home, 1974; (as Keith Rogers) Plumbing Repairs and Maintenance, 1974; Love Can Conquer, 1974; (as Henry Charles) Easy Guide to Growing Vegetables, 1975; When the Clouds Clear, 1975; Secret of Abbey Place, 1976; Captain of Her Heart, 1976; Just a Handsome Stranger, 1983; The Queen's Windsor, 1985; Soldiers' Wives, 1986; Officers' Ladies, 1987; Nesta, 1988; Amelda, 1989; (as Rose Glendower) Sighing for the Moon, 1991; To Love & Love Again, 1993. AS ROSIE HARRIS: The Turn of the Tide, 2002; Through Troubled Waters, 2002; Patsy of Paradise Place, 2003; One Step Forward, 2003; Looking for Love, 2003; Pins and Needles, 2004; Winnie of the Waterfront, 2004. **Address:** Walpole Cottage, Long Dr, Burnham Village, Slough, Bucks. SL1 8AJ, England. **Online address:** marionharris@btinternet.com

HARRIS, Mark. American, b. 1922. **Genres:** Novels, Plays/Screenplays, Autobiography/Memoirs, Biography. **Career:** Teacher, San Francisco State College, California, 1954-68, Purdue University, Lafayette Indiana, 1967-70, California Institute of the Arts, Valencia, 1970-73, Immaculate Heart College, Los Angeles, 1973-74, and University of Southern California, Los Angeles, 1973-75; Professor of English, University of Pittsburgh, 1975-80; Professor of English, Arizona State University, Tempe, 1980-97. **Publications:** NOVELS: Trumpet to the World, 1946; City of Discontent, 1952; The Southpaw, 1953; Bang the Drum Slowly, 1956; Something about a Soldier, 1957; A Ticket for a Seamstitch, 1957; Wake Up, Stupid, 1959; The Goy, 1970; Killing Everybody, 1973; It Looked Like for Ever, 1979; Lying in Bed, 1984; Speed, 1990; The Tale Maker, 1994. OTHER: Friedman & Son (play), 1963; Mark the Glove Boy, or The Last Days of Richard Nixon (autobiography), 1964; Twentyone Twice: A Journal, 1966; Best Father Ever Invented: An Autobiography, 1976; (co-ed.) The Design of Fiction (anthology), 1976; Short Work of It: Selected Writings, 1979; (ed.) The Heart of Boswell, 1980; Saul Bellow: Drumlin Woodchuck (non-fiction), 1980; How We Celebrated Christmas, 1993; The Diamond: Baseball Writings of ..., 1994; The Self-Made Brain Surgeon and Other Stories, 1999. **Address:** 300 Moreton Bay Ln #2, Goleta, CA 93117, U.S.A.

HARRIS, Mary Emma. American, b. 1943. **Genres:** Art/Art history. **Career:** Independent art historian and landscape designer; lecturer; Black Mountain College Project, Inc., project director. **Publications:** The Arts at Black Mountain College, 1987; Remembering Black Mountain College (exhibit catalogue), 1996. **Address:** 42 Grove St Apt 33, New York, NY 10014, U.S.A. **Online address:** harris@bmcproject.org

HARRIS, Neil. American, b. 1938. **Genres:** Art/Art history, History. **Career:** Harvard University, instructor to assistant professor of history, 1965-69; University of Chicago, IL, associate professor, 1969-72, professor of history, 1972-90, Preston and Sterling Morton Professor of History, 1990-, chair of history department, 1985-88. Yale University, visiting professor, 1974; Ecole des Hautes Etudes en Sciences Sociales, Paris, France, director d'etudes, 1985. National Humanities Institute, director, 1975-77. **Publications:** The Artist in American Society: The Formative Years, 1790-1860, 1966; Humbug: The Art of P.T. Barnum (nonfiction), 1973; Art, Design, and the Modern Corporation: The Collection of Container Corporation of America, a Gift to

the National Museum of American Art (art history/catalog), 1985; Cultural Excursions: Marketing Appetites and Cultural Tastes in Modern America, 1990; Planes, Trains and Automobiles, 1995; Building Lives, 1999. EDITOR: Readings in the History of the United States, 1969; The Land of Contrasts: 1880-1901 (history), 1970; The WPA Guide to Illinois, 1983. Contributor to books. **Address:** Department of History, University of Chicago, 1126 E 59th St, Chicago, IL 60637, U.S.A. **Online address:** nh16@ uchicago.edu

HARRIS, Paul. British, b. 1948. **Genres:** History, Biography, Reference. **Career:** Defense and intelligence analyst, publishing consultant, broadcaster on television programs in several countries. Freelance journalist in zones of conflict. Work has appeared in newspapers and on television and radio reports. Also photographer whose images have been exhibited in Slovenia and Scotland. **Publications:** The Garvie Trial, 1969; When Pirates Ruled the Waves, 1970; To Be a Pirate King, 1971; Oil, 1975; A Concise Dictionary of Scottish Painters, 1976; Broadcasting from the High Seas: 1858 to 1976, 1977; Investing in Scottish Pictures, 1977; Glasgow and the Clyde at War, 1986; Aberdeen and the North East at War, 1987; (with T. Miah) Tommy Miah Presents the Best of Bangladesh, 1987; Cooking with Beer, 1987; Edinburgh since 1900, 1987; Tyneside at War, 1987; Aberdeen since 1900, 1988; By Appointment: The Story in Pictures of Royal Deeside and Balmoral, 1988; Edinburgh: The Fabulous Fifties, 1988; A Little Scottish Cookbook, 1988; Disaster! One Hundred Years of Wreck, Rescue, and Tragedy in Scotland, 1989; Glasgow since 1900, 1989; Life in a Scottish Country House: The Story of AJ Balfour and Whittingehame House, 1989; (with J. Halsby) The Dictionary of Scottish Painters, 1600-1960, 1990; Somebody Else's War, 1992; (with Miah) Tommy Miah Presents the Secrets of the Indian Masterchefs, 1993; Cry Bosnia: Words and Photographs by Paul Harris, 1995; Glasgow: The People's Story, 1996; (with Miah) A True Taste of Asia, 1996; (with I. Elphick) TN Foulis: Bibliography and History of an Edinburgh Publisher; Scotland's Century 1900-2000: One Hundred Years of Photographs, 1999. SCREENPLAYS: (and presenter) Somebody Else's War (documentary), 1993. EDITOR: The DC Thomson Bumper Fun Book, 1977; The Rhythm of the Glass, 1977; Scotland: An Anthology, 1985; The Grizedale Experience, 1991. Contributor of articles and photographs to periodicals. **Address:** Whittingehame House, Haddington EH41 4QA, Scotland. **Online address:** journoharris@compuserve.com; www. conflictanalysis.com

HARRIS, Philip Robert. American, b. 1926. **Genres:** Novels, Administration/Management, Education. **Career:** President, Harris International Ltd., La Jolla, CA, 1972-. Editorial Board, European Business Review, 1990-. Vice president, St. Francis College, Brooklyn, NY, 1956-64; co-author, Challenge series, St. Paul Publs., Allahabad, India, 1963; visiting professor: Pennsylvania State University, University Park, 1965-66, Temple University, Philadelphia, 1967-69; Leadership Resources Inc., senior associate, 1966-69; Copley International Corp., vice president, 1970-71; California Space Institute, research associate, 1984-90; Netrologic, Inc., San Diego, sr. scientist, 1989-93; Lunar Power System Coalition, executive director/editor, 1990-93; United Societies in Space, executive vice president, founding executive editor of journal, Space Governance, 1993-98. **Publications:** Organizational Dynamics, 1973; Effective Management of Change, 1976; New Worlds, New Ways, New Management, 1983; Management in Transition, 1985; High Performance Leadership, 1989, 2nd ed., 1994; Living and Working in Space, 1992, 2nd ed., 1996; Launch Out (novel), 1996; New Work Culture Series, 3 vols., 1994-98: Twenty Reproducible Assessment Instruments, 1995; New York Culture, 1998; Managing the Knowledge Culture, 2005; Future Possibilities, 2006. EDITOR: Regents Study Guide to State Scholarships, 1949; Official Guide to Catholic Educational Institutions, 1959; Impact (textbook), 1965; (with G. Malin) Innovations in Global Consultation, 1980; Global Strategies for Human Resource Development, 1984; Innovations in Global Consultation, 1984. CO-AUTHOR: Insight Series, 4 vols., 1957-64; (with D. Harris) Improving Management Communication Skills, 1978; Managing Cultural Differences, 1979, 6th ed., 2004; (with R.T. Moran) Managing Cultural Synergy, 1982; Transcultural Leadership, 1993; Multicultural Management, 1992, 2nd ed., 2000; Developing Global Organizations, 1993; Multicultural Law Enforcement, 1995, 2nd ed., 2001. Contributor to publications. **Address:** c/o Harris International, 2702 Costebelle Dr, La Jolla, CA 92037-3524, U.S.A. **Online address:** Philharris@ aol.com

HARRIS, Randy Allen. Canadian, b. 1956. **Genres:** Language/Linguistics. **Career:** Bell-Northern Research, usability expert, 1988-90; University of Alberta, Edmonton, Killam fellow, 1990-92; University of Waterloo, Waterloo, Ontario, associate professor of English, 1992-. **Publications:** Functor Comprehension in Broca's Aphasia, 1985; The Linguistics Wars, 1993. EDI-

TOR: Technical Communication in Canada, 1994; Landmark Essays in the Rhetoric of Science, 1997; Rhetoric of Science in Canada, 2000. **Address:** Department of English, University of Waterloo, Waterloo, ON, Canada N2L 3G1. **Online address:** raha@watarts.uwaterloo.ca

HARRIS, Robert (Dennis). British, b. 1957. **Genres:** Military/Defense/ Arms control, Biography. **Career:** British Broadcasting Corporation (BBC-TV), England, researcher and film director for Tonight, Nationwide, and Panorama, 1978-81, reporter for Newsnight, 1981-85, and for Panorama, 1985-87; Observer, London, England, political editor, 1987-89; Thames TV, England, political reporter for This Week, 1988-89; Sunday Times, London, political columnist, 1989-92. **Publications:** (with J. Paxman) A Higher Form of Killing: The Secret Story of Gas and Germ Warfare, 1982, in the US as A Higher Form of Killing: The Secret Story of Chemical and Biological Warfare, 1982; Gotcha!: The Media, the Government, and the Falklands Crisis, 1983; The Making of Neil Kinnock, 1984; Selling Hitler, 1986; Good and Faithful Servant: The Unauthorized Biography of Bernard Ingham, 1990; Fatherland (novel), 1992; The Media Trilogy, 1994; Enigma, 1995; Archangel, 1998. **Address:** The Old Vicarage, Kintbury, Berkshire R915 OTR, England.

HARRIS, Robie H. American, b. 1940. **Genres:** Children's fiction, Children's non-fiction. **Career:** Freelance writer, 1975-. Taught at Bank Street College of Education's School for Children and in public schools for several years; has also worked in film and television, designed parks for children, and served as a consultant to the Children's Museum in Boston. **Publications:** NONFICTION: (with E. Levy) Before You Were Three: How You Began to Walk, Talk, Explore, and Have Feelings, 1977; It's Perfectly Normal: Changing Bodies, Growing Up, Sex, and Sexual Health, 1994; It's So Amazing, 1999. FICTION: Don't Forget to Come Back, 1978; Rosie's Double Dare, 1980; I Hate Kisses, 1981; Rosie's Razzle Dazzle Deal, 1982; Hot Henry, 1987; Messy Jessie, 1987; Rosie's Rock 'n' Roll Riot, 1990; Rosie's Secret Spell, 1991; Happy Birth Day!, 1996; Hi New Baby!, 1999; Goodbye Mousie, 2001; I Am not Going to School Today!, 2003; I'm So Mad, 2005; I'm not Sleepy, 2005; I Love Messes!, 2005; I'm All Dressed!, 2005. GROWING UP STORIES SERIES: Hello Benny! What It's Like to Be a Baby, 2002; Go! Go! Maria: What It's Like to Be 1, 2003 Maria: What It's Like to be 2, 2003; Sweet Jasmine, Nice Jackson, What It's Like to Be 2-And to Be Twins.

HARRIS, Rosemary (Jeanne). British, b. 1923. **Genres:** Mystery/Crime/ Suspense, Romance/Historical, Children's fiction, Young adult fiction, Mythology/Folklore, Novellas/Short stories. **Career:** Formerly, picture restorer; reader for Metro-Goldwyn-Mayer, 1951-52, and children's book reviewer, The Times, London, 1970-73. **Publications:** The Lotus and the Grail: Legends from East to West (abridged ed. in U.S. as Sea Magic and Other Stories of Enchantment), 1974; Beauty and the Beast (folklore), 1979; (ed.) Love and the Merry-Go-Round (poetry anthology), 1988. ROMANCE NOVELS: The Summer-House, 1956; Voyage to Cythera, 1958; Venus with Sparrows, 1961; The Moon in the Cloud, 1968; The Shadow on the Sun, 1970; The Seal-Singing, 1971; The Child in the Bamboo Grove, 1972; The Bright and Morning Star, 1972; The King's White Elephant, 1973; The Double Snare, 1974; The Flying Ship, 1975; The Little Dog of Fo, 1976; I Want to Be a Fish, 1977; A Quest for Orion, 1978; Green Finger House, 1980; Tower of the Stars, 1980; The Enchanted Horse, 1981; Janni's Stork, 1981; Zed, 1982; Summers of the Wild Rose, 1987; Colm of the Islands, 1989; Ticket to Freedom, 1991; The Wildcat Strike, 1995; The Haunting of Joey M'Basa, 1996. MYSTERY NOVELS: All My Enemies, 1967; The Nice Girl's Story, 1968, in U.S. as Nor Evil Dreams, 1974; A Wicked Pack of Cards, 1969; Three Candles for the Dark, 1976. **Address:** c/o A. P. Watt Ltd, 20 John St, London WC1N 2DR, England.

HARRIS, Rosie. See HARRIS, Marion (Rose).

HARRIS, Roy. British, b. 1931. **Genres:** Language/Linguistics. **Career:** Ecole Normale Superieure, Paris, lecturer, 1956-57; University of Leicester, assistant lecturer, 1957-58, lecturer, 1958-60; Oxford University, medieval and modern languages faculty, 1961-76, fellow and tutor, Keble College, 1967-76, professor of the Romance languages, 1976-77, professor of general linguistics and fellow, Worcester College, 1978-88, professor emeritus of general linguistics, 1988-. Language & Communication, editor, 1980-. Ecole Pratique des Hautes Etudes, Paris, directeur d'etudes associe, 1991-92. **Publications:** Synonymy and Linguistic Analysis, 1973; Communication and Language, 1978; The Language-Makers, 1980; The Language Myth, 1981; (trans.) Course in General Linguistics, by de Saussure, 1983; The Origin of Writing, 1986; Reading Saussure, 1987; Language, Saussure and Wittgenstein, 1988; (ed.) Linguistic Thought in England, 1914-1945, 1988; Signs of

Writing, 1996; The Language Connection, 1996; Introduction to Integrational Linguistics, 1998; Rethinking Writing, 2000; Saussure and His Interpreters, 2001; The Necessity of Artspeak, 2003; The Linguistics of History, 2004. **Address:** 2 Paddox Close, Oxford OX2 7LR, England.

HARRIS, Ruth Elwin. British, b. 1935. **Genres:** Novels. **Career:** Author. **Publications:** "QUANTOCKS QUARTET" NOVEL SERIES: The Silent Shore, 1986; The Beckoning Hills, 1987; The Dividing Sea, 1989; Beyond the Orchid House, 1994. OTHER: Billie: The Nevill Letters, 1914-1916, 1991. Author of articles and short stories; author of broadcasts for the British Broadcasting Corporation (BBC). **Address:** c/o Random House, 20 Vauxhall Bridge Rd., London SW1V 2SA, England.

HARRIS, Stacy. American, b. 1952. **Genres:** Music. **Career:** American Broadcasting Companies (ABC) Radio News, New York City, domestic stringer based in Nashville, TN, 1986-. Lecturer, guest commentator, music industry expert, music industry astrological consultant, radio and television talk show host. **Publications:** Comedians of Country Music, 1978; The Carter Family, 1978; The Best of Country: The Essential CD Guide, 1993. Scriptwriter for Nashville Network, SDX Gridiron Show, and MJI Broadcasting. Work represented in anthologies. Contributor to periodicals. **Address:** Windsor Tower, 4215 Harding Rd., Nashville, TN 37205, U.S.A. **Online address:** stacy@roughstock.com

HARRIS, Steve. British, b. 1954. **Genres:** Horror. **Career:** Author of horror fiction. **Publications:** Adventureland, 1990, in the U.S. as The Eyes of the Beast, 1993; Wulf, 1991; Hoodoo Man, 1992; Angels, 1993; Black Rock, 1996; The Devil on May Street, 1997; Challenging the Wolf (chapbook), 1998. **Address:** c/o Trafalgar Square, PO Box 257, North Pomfret, VT 05053, U.S.A.

HARRIS, Thomas (E.). American, b. 1944. **Genres:** Administration/ Management, Business/Trade/Industry, Communications/Media, Industrial relations. **Career:** George Washington University, Washington, DC, instructor, 1967-70; Rutgers University, New Brunswick, NJ, lecturer, 1970-78; University of Evansville, Evansville, IN, professor, 1980-89; University of Alabama, Tuscaloosa, professor, 1989-. **Publications:** Analysis of the Clash over Issues between Booker T. Washington and W.E.B. DuBois, 1993, rev. ed., 2005; Applied Organizational Communication: Perspectives, Principles, and Pragmatics, 1993; (with J. Sherblom) Small Group and Team Communication, 1999, 2nd ed., 2002; Conflict and Diversity, 1997; Applied Organizational Communication: Principles and Pragmatics for Future Success, 2002. Contributor to periodicals. **Address:** PO Box 20305, Tuscaloosa, AL 35487-0172, U.S.A. **Online address:** tharris@ccom.ua.edu

HARRIS, Thomas Walter. Also writes as T. H. Darling. American, b. 1930. **Genres:** Plays/Screenplays, Novels. **Career:** Affiliated with Appeal Printing Company, New York, 1948-49; affiliated with Bureau of Internal Revenue, Washington, DC, 1956-57; Los Angeles Public Library, Los Angeles, CA, librarian in literature and fiction department, 1961-; University of California, Los Angeles, teacher of playwriting, 1966-; teacher of mass communications at Inner City Cultural Center, 1968. Board member of Actors Studio West Playwrights Unit; director of Studio West; executive producer and director of Los Angeles Citizens Co. Actor, appearing in productions including Hometown U.S.A., a radio series For Voice Of America. Collector & Editor of Audrey Skirball-Kenis Theatre Collection, 1996-. **Publications:** PLAYS: Daddy Hugs and Kisses, 1960; The Relic, 1961; The Selma Maid, 1967; The Solution, 1970, rev. as Model City, 1991; Mary Queen of Crackers, 1971; Suds, 1973; A Streetcar Salad, 1979; Fall of an Iron Horse; All Tigers Are Tame; City Beneath the Skin; Who Killed Sweetie; Beverly Hills Olympics; At Wits End; The Man Handlers; Clothespins and Dreams (musical). OTHER: Always with Love, 1970; No Time to Play, 1977. TELEVISION SHOWS: I Spy; Rin Tin Tin; The Junkyard. FILMS: When I Grow Up; Man Made Angry; Desert Killing; The Ally; The Guardian; Street Heat; Then Came the Winter; The Brothers; The Voice. **Address:** 1786 S. Fairfax Ave., Los Angeles, CA 90019, U.S.A.

HARRIS, Walter A. American, b. 1929. **Genres:** Economics, Politics/ Government. **Career:** Midwood High School, NYC, teacher, social studies, 1957-65; Port Richmond High School, NYC, assistant principal, 1965-74; Sheepshead Bay High School, NYC, principal, 1974-90; Kolburne School, Inc., director of education, 1991-94; Stageworks on the Hudson, director of development, 1994-96; Upper Hudson Phi Beta Kappa Assn., president, 1994-96. **Publications:** Workbook: The Modern Economy in Action, 1968; Introductory Economics, 1970; Economics for Everybody, 1973, 3rd ed., 2003; Teacher's Manual for Economics for Everybody, 1973, 3rd ed., 2003; Current Issues in American Democracy, 1975, 2nd ed., 1992; Western

Civilization, 1982; Economics, Institutions and Analysis, 3rd ed., 1997, 4th ed., 2004; Teacher's Manual for Economics, Institutions and Analysis, 4th ed., 2004. **Address:** 50/16 Yehudah Hanassi, 42269 Netanya, Israel. **Online address:** barbarawalt@yahoo.com

HARRIS, William V. (born England), b. 1938. **Genres:** History. **Career:** Columbia University, New York, NY, Shepherd Professor of History. **Publications:** Rome in Etruria and Umbria, 1971; War and Imperialism in Republican Rome, 1979; Ancient Literacy, 1989; Restraining Rage: The Ideology of Anger Control in Classical Antiquity, 2002. **Address:** Department of History, Columbia University, 624 Fayerweather Hall, New York, NY 10027, U.S.A. **Online address:** wvh1@columbia.edu

HARRIS, (Theodore) Wilson. British (born Guyana), b. 1921. **Genres:** Novels, Poetry, Literary criticism and history. **Publications:** Fetish (poetry), 1951; Eternity to Season (poetry), 1954, 1978; Palace of the Peacock, 1960; The Far Journey of Oudin, 1961; The Whole Armour, 1962; The Secret Ladder, 1963; Heartland, 1964; The Eye of the Scarecrow, 1965; Tradition and the West Indian Novel, 1965; Tradition, The Writer and Society: Critical Essays, 1967; The Waiting Room, 1967; Tumatumari, 1968; Ascent to Omai, 1970; The Sleepers of Roraima, 1970; The Age of the Rainmakers, 1971; Black Marsden, 1972; Companions of the Day and Night, 1975; Da Silva da Silva's Cultivated Wilderness and Genesis of the Clowns, 1977; The Tree of the Sun, 1978; Explorations: A Selection of Talks and Articles, 1981; The Angel at the Gate, 1982; The Womb of Space: The Cross-Cultural Imagination, 1983; Carnival, 1985; The Infinite Rehearsal, 1987; The Four Banks of the River of Space, 1990; The Radical Imagination (essays), 1992; Resurrection At Sorrow Hill, 1993; Jonestown, 1996; Merlin and Parsifal: Adversarial Twins, 1997; Selected Essays of Wilson Harris, 1999; The Dark Jester, 2000. **Address:** c/o Faber & Faber Ltd, 3 Queen Sq, London WC1N 3AU, England.

HARRISON, Ann Tukey. American, b. 1938. **Genres:** History, Women's studies and issues. **Career:** University of Wisconsin-Madison, instructor, 1961-63, assistant professor, 1962-65; Michigan State University, East Lansing, professor, 1965-. Mount Holyoke College, Ruth Dean Lecturer, 1976. **Publications:** Charles d'Orleans and the Allegorical Mode, 1975; The Danse Macabre of Women, 1994. **Address:** 277 Maplewood Dr, East Lansing, MI 48823-4746, U.S.A. **Online address:** harris10@msu.edu

HARRISON, Antony H. American (born England), b. 1948. **Genres:** Poetry, Art/Art history. **Career:** North Carolina State University, Raleigh, assistant professor, 1974-80, associate professor, 1980-87, professor of English, 1987-. **Publications:** Christina Rossetti in Context, 1988; Swinburne's Medievalism, 1988; Victorian Poets and Romantic Poems, 1990; (ed. with B. Taylor) Gender and Sexuality in Victorian Literature and Art, 1991; The Letters of Christina Rossetti, vols. 1-3, 1997-2000; Victorian Poets and the Politics of Culture, 1998; (ed. with M. Arseneau and L.J. Kooistra) The Culture of Christina Rossetti, 1998. **Address:** Department of English, North Carolina State University, Box 8105, Raleigh, NC 27695-8105, U.S.A. **Online address:** engahh@unity.ncsu.edu

HARRISON, Brian (Howard). British, b. 1937. **Genres:** History. **Career:** Oxford University, England, senior scholar at St. Antony's College, 1961-64, junior research fellow at Nuffield College, 1964-67, fellow and tutor in modern history and politics at Corpus Christi College, 1967-99, reader in modern British history, 1990-99; Oxford Dictionary of National Biography, editor, 2000-. **Publications:** Drink and the Victorians: The Temperance Question in England, 1815-1872, Faber, 1971; Separate Spheres: The Opposition to Women's Suffrage in Britain, 1978; Peaceable Kingdom: Stability and Change in Modern Britain, 1982; Prudent Revolutionaries: Portraits of British Feminists between the Wars, 1987; (ed. and contrib.) The History of the University of Oxford, Volume VIII: Twentieth Century Oxford, 1994; The Transformation of British Politics 18601995, 1996; (joint ed. and contrib.) Civil Histories: Essays Presented to Sir Keith Thomas, 2000. **Address:** Corpus Christi College, Oxford University, Oxford OX1 4JF, England.

HARRISON, Chip. See BLOCK, Lawrence.

HARRISON, Colin. American, b. 1960. **Genres:** Novels. **Career:** Harper's (magazine), NYC, associate editor, 1988-93, senior editor, 1993-94, deputy editor, 1994-; writer. Member of Corporation of Haverford College. **Publications:** NOVELS: Break and Enter, 1990; Bodies Electric, 1993; Manhattan Nocturne, 1996; Afterburn, 2000; The Havana Room, 2004. **Address:** Harper's, 666 Broadway, New York, NY 10012, U.S.A.

HARRISON, David Lakin. British, b. 1926. **Genres:** Natural history, Travel/Exploration. **Career:** General medical practitioner, since 1956. Chairman of Trustees, Harrison Zoological Museum, Sevenoaks. House Physician, St. Thomas's Hospital, London, 1951-52. **Publications:** Footsteps in the Sand: The Mammals of Arabia, 3 vols.; Mammals of the Arabian Gulf; (with P.J.J. Bates) The Mammals of Arabia 2nd ed.; (with P.J.J. Bates) Bats of the Indian Subcontinent. **Address:** Bowerwood House, St. Botolph's Road, Sevenoaks, Kent, England.

HARRISON, Elizabeth Fancourt. British. **Genres:** Romance/Historical. **Publications:** Coffee at Dobree's, 1965; The Physicians, 1966; The Ravelston Affair, 1967; Emergency Call, 1970; Accident Call, 1971; Ambulance Call, 1972; Surgeon's Call, 1973; On Call, 1974; Hospital Call, 1975; Dangerous Call, 1976; To Mend a Heart, 1977; Young Doctor Goddard, 1978; A Doctor Called Caroline, 1979; A Surgeon Called Amanda, 1982; A Surgeon's Life, 1983; Marrying a Doctor, 1984; Surgeon's Affair, 1985; A Surgeon at St. Marks, 1986; The Surgeon She Married, 1988; The Faithful Type, 1993; The Senior Partner's Daughter, 1994; Made for Each Other, 1995. **Address:** c/o Mills and Boon Ltd, Eton House, 18-24 Paradise Rd, Richmond, Surrey TW9 1SR, England.

HARRISON, Gary. American, b. 1949. **Genres:** Literary criticism and history. **Career:** Freelance editor for publishing companies, 1978-; State University of New York College at Cortland, tutor at Writing Center, 1979-80; Western States Technical Assistance Resource, Seattle, WA, staff writer and editor, 1980, managing editor, 1980-81; University of Santa Clara, CA, adjunct lecturer in English, 1982-83; University of New Mexico, Albuquerque, assistant professor, 1987-93, associate professor of English, 1993-, director of graduate studies in English, 1995-. University of Colorado, Boulder, visiting scholar, Center for British Studies, 1990. Product Development Assistance Systems, staff writer and editor, 1980. **Publications:** Wordsworth's Vagrant Muse: Poetry, Poverty, and Power, 1994. EDITOR: (with D. Assael) Handicapped Children's Early Education Program: 1980-81 Overview and Directory, 1981; (with D. Mirkes) From Process to Product, 1981; (with P. Davis, D.M. Johnson, and others) Western Literature in a World Context, 2 vols., 1995; (with P. Davis, D.M. Johnson, and others) Bedford Anthology of World Literature, 6 vols., 2004. Contributor to books. Contributor of articles and reviews to literature journals. **Address:** Department of English, MSCO3 2170, University of New Mexico, Albuquerque, NM 87131-0001, U.S.A. **Online address:** garyh@unm.edu

HARRISON, Harry. (Henry Maxwell Dempsey). American, b. 1925. **Genres:** Novellas/Short stories, Science fiction/Fantasy, Children's fiction, Young adult fiction. **Career:** Science Fiction Writers of America, vice president, 1968-69. **Publications:** Deathworld, 3 vols. 1960-68; The Stainless Steel Rat series, 7 vols., 1961-87; Planet of the Damned, 1962; War with the Robots (short stories), 1962; Bill, the Gallactic Hero, 1965; Two Tales and 8 Tomorrows (short stories), 1965; Plague from Space, 1966; Make Room! Make Room!, 1966; The Technicolor Time Machine, 1967; (ed.) World of Wonder (juvenile), 1968; Captive Universe, 1969; In Our Hands the Stars, 1970; Prime Number (short stories), 1970; One Step from Earth (short stories), 1970; Spaceship Medic (children), 1970; A Transatlantic Tunnel, Hurrah!, 1972; Stonehenge, 1972; Montezuma's Revenge, 1972; Star Smashers of the Galaxy Rangers, 1973; The Men from P.I.G. and R.O.B.O.T. (for children), 1974; The California Iceberg (for children), 1974; Queen Victoria's Revenge, 1974; (ed. with B. Aldiss) Best SF: 1967 to 1975, 1975; (with G. Dickson) The Lifeship, 1976; The Best of Harry Harrison, 1976; Skyfall, 1977; Great Balls of Fire, 1977; Mechanismo, 1978; (with M. Edwards) Spacecraft in Fact and Fiction, 1979; Planet Story, 1979; The QE2 Is Missing, 1980; Wheelworld, 1980; Homeworld, 1980; Starworld, 1981; Planet of No Return, 1981; Invasion, Earth, 1982; Rebel in Time, 1983; West of Eden, 1984; Winter in Eden, 1986; Return to Eden, 1988; (with M. Minsky) The Turning Option, 1992; The Stainless Steel Rat Sings the Blues, 1993; The Hammer and the Cross, 1993; One King's Way, 1994; Galactic Dreams, 1994; King and Emperor, 1996; Stainless Steel Rat Goes to Hell, 1996; Stars and Stripes Forever, 1995; Stainless Steel Rat Joins the Circus, 1999; Stars and Stripes in Peril, 2000; 50 in 50, 2001. **Address:** c/o Sobel Weber Associates, 146 E 19th St, New York, NY 10003-2404, U.S.A. **Online address:** www.harryharrison.com

HARRISON, James (Ernest). British/Canadian (born Sri Lanka), b. 1927. **Genres:** Poetry. **Career:** Worcester College for the Blind, Worcester, England, teacher of English, 1952-56; Bournemouth Technical College, Bournemouth, England, lecturer in English, 1956-59; Shenstone College of Education, Bromsgrove, England, lecturer, 1959-62, senior lecturer, 1962-65, principal lecturer and department head, 1965-69; University of Guelph, Ontario, assistant professor, 1969-72, associate professor, 1972-82, professor of English, 1982-92, professor emeritus, 1993-95. **Publications:** Catchment Area (poems), 1958; (ed.) Scientists as Writers, 1965; Rudyard Kipling,

1982; Flying Dutchmen (poems), 1983; Salman Rushdie, 1992. **Address:** 18 Wolfrey Ave, Toronto, ON, Canada M4K 1K8.

HARRISON, Jim. (James Thomas Harrison). American, b. 1937. **Genres:** Novels, Poetry, Novellas/Short stories. **Career:** Former Assistant Professor of English, State University of New York, Stony Brook. **Publications:** Plain Song, 1965; Locations, 1968; Walking, 1969; Outlyers and Ghazals, 1971; Wolf (novel), 1971; A Good Day to Die (novel), 1973; Letters to Yesenin, 1973; Farmer (novel), 1976; Legends of the Fall (novella), 1979; Warlock (novel), 1981; New and Selected Poems, 1982; (with Diana Guest) Natural World, 1983; Sundog (novel), 1984; The Theory & Practice of Rivers (poetry), 1986; Dalva (novel), 1988; The Woman Lit by Fireflies (novella), 1990; Just Before Dark (non-fiction), 1991; Julip (novellas), 1994; After Ikkyu and Other Poems, 1996; The Road Home, 1998; The Shape of the Journey: New and Collected Poems, 1998; The Beast God Forgot to Invent, 2000; The Boy Who Ran to the Woods, 2000. **Address:** Box 135, Lake Leelanau, MI 49653, U.S.A.

HARRISON, John F(letcher) C(lews). British, b. 1921. **Genres:** History. **Career:** Professor Emeritus of History, University of Sussex, Brighton, since 1985 (Professor, 1970-85). Deputy Director, Extra Mural Dept., Leeds University, 1958-61; Professor, University of Wisconsin, Madison, 1961-70. **Publications:** History of the Working Men's College 1854-1954, 1954; Learning and Living 1790-1960, 1961; Society and Politics in England 1780-1960, 1965; Robert Owen and the Owenites, 1969; The Early Victorians 1832-1851, 1971; Birth and Growth of Industrial England 1714-1867, 1973; The Second Coming 1780-1850, 1979; The Common People, 1984; Late Victorian Britain, 1875-1901, 1990; Scholarship Boy, 1995. **Address:** Mill Cottage, Sandford Mill Close, Cheltenham GL53 7QZ, England.

HARRISON, Kathryn. American, b. 1961. **Genres:** Novels, Autobiography/Memoirs, Essays. **Career:** Writer. **Publications:** Thicker than Water, 1991; Exposure, 1993; Poison, 1995; The Kiss, 1997; The Binding Chair, 2000; The Seal Wife, 2002; Seeking Rapture, 2003. **Address:** c/o Amanda Urban, ICM Inc, 40 W 57th St, New York, NY 10019, U.S.A. **Online address:** thebindingchair@yahoo.com

HARRISON, Kenneth (Cecil). British, b. 1915. **Genres:** Librarianship, Autobiography/Memoirs, Essays. **Career:** Borough Librarian, Hyde, 1939-47, Hove, 1947-50, Eastbourne, 1950-58, Hendon, 1958-61; City Librarian, Westminster, 1961-80. Ed., Library World, 1961-71; President, Library Association, 1973. Commonwealth Library Association (President, 1972-75). **Publications:** First Steps in Librarianship, 1950, 5th ed., 1980; Libraries in Scandinavia, 1961; Public Libraries Today, 1963; The Library and the Community, 1963, 3rd ed., 1976; Facts at Your Fingertips: Everyman's Guide to Reference Books, 1964; British Public Library Buildings, 1966; Libraries in Britain, 1969; Public Relations for Librarians, 1973; International Librarianship, 1989; A Librarian's Odyssey: Episodes of Autobiography, 2000. EDITOR: Prospects for British Librarianship, 1976; Public Library Policy, 1981; Public Library Buildings, 1975-83, 1987; New Library Buildings, 1984-89, 1990. **Address:** 5 Tavistock, Devonshire Pl, Eastbourne, E. Sussex BN21 4AG, England. **Online address:** kcharrison88@hotmail.com

HARRISON, Lowell H. American, b. 1922. **Genres:** History, Biography. **Career:** Instructor, New York University, NYC, 1948-51; Faculty member, 1952-67, Head of Dept. 1957-67, and Chairman, Social Sciences Division, 1962-67, West Texas State University, Canyon; Professor of History, Western Kentucky University, Bowling Green, 1967-88. **Publications:** John Breckinridge, Jeffersonian Republican, 1969; The Civil War in Kentucky, 1975; George Rogers Clark and the War in the West, 1976; (co-ed.) A Kentucky Sampler, 1977; The Anti-Slavery Movement in Kentucky, 1978; (ed.) Kentucky's Governors, 1985, rev. ed., 2004; Western Kentucky University, 1987; Kentucky's Road to Statehood, 1992; (associate ed.) The Kentucky Encyclopedia, 1992; (co-author) A New History of Kentucky, 1997; Lincoln of Kentucky, 2000. **Address:** 1800 Westen St Apt 2306, Bowling Green, KY 42104-5851, U.S.A.

HARRISON, Michael. British, b. 1939. **Genres:** Children's fiction, Poetry. **Career:** Freelance author and editor. Teacher in North Queensland, Australia, and London and Oxford, England, 1961-94. **Publications:** FOR CHILDREN. FICTION: (reteller) The Doom of the Gods (mythology), 1985; (reteller) The Curse of the Ring (mythology), 1987; Bags of Trouble (comedy), 1988; Trouble Abroad (comedy), 1990; Trouble in Store (comedy), 1991; (reteller) Don Quixote, 1995; It's My Life (thriller), 1997; Facing the Dark (thriller), 1997; Junk Mail (poems), 1998; At the Deep End (thriller), 2001; Carried Away (thriller), 2003. OTHER: Scolding Tongues: The Persecution of Witches (history for children), 1987; (comp., with C. Stuart-Clark) The Oxford Treasury of Children's Stories, 1994; (reteller, with C. Stuart-Clark) The Oxford Treasury of World Stories, 1998. EDITOR. POETRY ANTHOLOGIES: Catch the Light, 1982; Upright Downfall, 1983; The Candy-Floss Tree, 1984; The Crystal Zoo, 1985; Bright Lights Blaze Out, 1986; Splinters: A Book of Very Short Poems, 1988. POETRY ANTHOLOGIES WITH C. STUART-CLARK: The New Dragon Book of Verse, 1977, as The Dragon Book of Verse, 1997; Poems 1, 1979; Poems 2, 1980; Narrative Poems, 1981; Noah's Ark, 1983; The Oxford Book of Christmas Poems, 1983; Writing Poems, 1985; The Oxford Treasury of Children's Poems, 1988; The Young Dragon Book of Verse, 1989; Peace and War: A Collection of Poems, 1989; The Oxford Book of Story Poems, 1990; A Year Full of Poems, 1991; The Oxford Book of Animal Poems, 1992; Writing Poems Plus, 1992; Bright Star Shining: Poems for Christmas, 1993; The Oxford Treasury of Classic Poems, 1996; The New Oxford Treasury of Children's Poems, 1997; The Oxford Treasury of Time Poems, 1998; 100 Years of Poetry, 1999; The Oxford Treasury of Christmas Poems, 1999. **Address:** 65 Bainton Rd, Oxford OX2 7A9, England.

HARRISON, Roy M(ichael). British, b. 1948. **Genres:** Chemistry, Environmental sciences/Ecology, Meteorology/Atmospheric sciences. **Career:** Imperial Chemical Industries Ltd., laboratory technician, 1966; University of Lancaster, England, lecturer in dept of environmental sciences, 1974-84; University of Essex, Colchester, England, reader in dept of chemistry and biological chemistry, 1984-91; Institute of Aerosol Science, director 1985-91; University of Birmingham, Edgbaston, England, Queen Elizabeth II Birmingham Centenary Professor of Environmental Health, 1991-93, director, 1993-2000, head, Division of Environmental Health and Risk Management, 2000-. **Publications:** (with D.P.H. Laxen) Lead Pollution, 1981; (with W.R. Johnston, S. Rapsomanikis, and S.J. de Mora) Introductory Chemistry for the Environmental Sciences, 1991, 2nd ed. (with S.J. de Mora), 1996; (with L. Butterwick and Q. Merritt) Handbook for Urban Air Improvement, 1992. EDITOR: Pollution, 1983, 4th ed., 2001; (with R. Perry) Handbook of Air Pollution Analysis, 2nd ed., 1986; (with J.N.B. Bell, J.N. Lester, and R. Perry, and contrib.) Acid Rain, 1987; (with S. Rapsomanikis, and contrib.) Environmental Analysis Using Chromatography Interfaced with Atomic Spectroscopy, 1989; (with R.S. Hamilton, and contrib.) Highway Pollution, 1991; Understanding Our Environment, 2nd ed., 1992, 3rd ed., 1999; (with M. Radojevic) Atmospheric Acidity, 1992; (with F.E. Warner) Radioecology after Chernobyl, 1993; (with R. van Grieken, and contrib.) Atmospheric Particles, 1998; (with R.E. Hester) Issues in Environmental Science and Technology, 20 vols., 1994-2004. **Address:** Division of Environmental Health and Risk Management, University of Birmingham, Edgbaston, Birmingham B15 2TT, England. **Online address:** r.m.harrison.ipe@bham.ac.uk

HARRISON, Russell (T.). American, b. 1944. **Genres:** Literary criticism and history. **Career:** Adjunct professor of English at colleges in Jersey City, NJ, including St. Peter's College and Hudson County Community College, 1984-87; Palacky University, Olomouc, Czechoslovakia, senior Fulbright lecturer in American literature, 1987-89; Hofstra University, Hempstead, NY, adjunct and associate of New College, 1989-90, assistant professor of English, 1990-94, adjunct assistant professor, 1998-; writer, 1994-; Minsk State Linguistic University, Minsk, Belarus, senior Fulbright lecturer in American literature, 1996-98. Guest on CNN Today. **Publications:** Against the American Dream: Essays on Charles Bukowski, 1994; Patricia Highsmith, 1997. Contributor of articles and reviews to periodicals. **Address:** 459 Seventh Ave., Brooklyn, NY 11215, U.S.A.

HARRISON, Sarah. British, b. 1946. **Genres:** Novels, Children's fiction, Writing/Journalism. **Career:** IPC Magazines, London, journalist, 1967-72. **Publications:** NOVELS: The Flowers of the Field, 1980; A Flower That's Free, 1984; Hot Breath, 1985; An Imperfect Lady, 1988; Cold Feet, 1989; The Forests of the Night, 1990; Foreign Parts, 1992; Be an Angel, 1993; Both Your Houses, 1995; Life after Lunch, 1996; Flowers Won't Fax, 1997; That Was Then, 1998; Heaven's on Hold, 2000; The Grass Memorial, 2000; The Dreaming Stones, 2003. CHILDREN'S BOOKS: In Granny's Garden, 1980; Laura from Lark Rise series, 4 vols., 1986. NONFICTION: How to Write a Blockbuster, 1995. **Address:** c/o Hodder and Stoughton, 338 Euston Rd, London NW1 3BH, England.

HARRISON, Sue. American, b. 1950. **Genres:** Novels. **Career:** Lake Superior State University, Sault Sainte Marie, MI, public relations writer, 1985-88, adjunct instructor in writing, 1988-90; writer. **Publications:** Mother Earth Father Sky, 1990; My Sister the Moon 1992; Brother Wind, 1994; Sisu (young adult novel), 1997; Song of the River, 1997; Cry of the Wind, 1998; Call down the Stars, 2001. **Address:** c/o Dunham Literary, 156 5th Ave Ste 625, New York, NY 10010-7002, U.S.A. **Online address:** sue@sueharrison.com

HARRISON, Suzan. American, b. 1956. **Genres:** Literary criticism and history. **Career:** Eckerd College, St. Petersburg, FL, assistant professor, 1989-95, associate professor in Writing Excellence Program, 1995-, director of program, 1992, 1993, director of Writing Center, 1995-96, chairperson of Letters Collegium, 1998-2000. National Conference on Undergraduate Research, member of national editorial board, 1993, 1995. **Publications:** A Sweet Devouring: Eudora Welty's Reading of Virginia Woolf, 1997. Contributor to books and journals. **Address:** Writing Excellence Program, Eckerd College, 4200 54th Ave. S., St. Petersburg, FL 33711, U.S.A. **Online address:** harrisms@eckerd.edu

HARRISON, Tony. British, b. 1937. **Genres:** Plays/Screenplays, Poetry, Translations. **Publications:** Earthworks, 1964; (with J. Simmons) Aikin Mata (play), 1965; Newcastle Is Peru, 1969; The Loiners, 1970; Voortrekker, 1972; The Misanthrope, 1973; (ed. and trans.) Poems of Palladas of Alexandria, 1973; Phaedra Britannica (play), 1975; Bow Down (music theatre), 1977; The Passion (play), 1977; The Bartered Bride (libretto), 1978; The School of Eloquence (poems), 1978; Oresteia (adaptation), 1981; Continuous, 1981; A Kumquat for John Keats, 1981; U.S. Martial, 1981; Selected Poems, 1984; The Fire Gap, 1985; Dramatic Verse 1973-1985, 1985; The Mysteries, 1985; V., 1985, 1990; Theatre Works, 1973-1985, 1986; Selected Poems, 1987; The Trackers of Oxyrhyncus, 1988; A Cold Coming: Gulf War Poems, 1991; The Common Chorus, 1992; Square Rounds, 1992; The Gaze of the Gorgon, 1992; Black Daisies for the Bride, 1993; Poetry or Bust, 1993; A Maybe Day in Kazakhstan, 1994; The Shadow of Hiroshima, 1995; Permanently Bard, 1995; Plays 3, 1996; (trans.) V. Hugo, The Prince's Play, 1996; Prometheus, 1998; Laureate's Block, 2000; (trans.) Plays 2, 2001; (trans.) Plays 4, 2001; Plays 5, 2004. **Address:** c/o Gordon Dickerson, 2 Crescent Grove, London SW4 7AH, England. **Online address:** gordondickerson@supanet.com

HARRISON, Trevor (W.). Canadian. **Genres:** Politics/Government, Public/Social administration, Sociology. **Career:** University of Lethbridge, AB, affiliated with sociology department. **Publications:** Of Passionate Intensity: Right-Wing Populism and the Reform Party of Canada, 1995; Requiem for a Lightweight: Stockwell Day and Image Politics, 2002; (with J. Friesen) Canadian Society in the Twenty-first Century: A Historical Sociological Approach, 2004. EDITOR: (with G. Laxer) The Trojan Horse: Alberta and the Future of Canada, 1995; (with J. Kachur) Contested Classrooms: Education, Globalization, and Democracy in Alberta, 1999. **Address:** Dept of Sociology, University of Lethbridge, Lethbridge, AB, Canada T1K 3M4. **Online address:** trevor.harrison@uleth.ca

HARROD-EAGLES, Cynthia. Also writes as Elizabeth Bennett, Emma Woodhouse. British, b. 1948. **Genres:** Novels, Mystery/Crime/Suspense, Romance/Historical, Science fiction/Fantasy. **Publications:** The Waiting Game, 1972; Shadows on the Mountain, 1973; Hollow Night, 1980; Deadfall, 1982; The Orange Tree Plot, 1989; The Horsemasters, 2001; The Longest Dance, 2001; Julia, 2002. BILL SLIDER SERIES (crime novels): Orchestrated Death, 1991; Death Watch, 1992; Necrochip, in U.S. Death to Go, 1993; Dead End, in U.S. as Grave Music, 1994; Blood Lines, 1996; Killing Time, 1998; Shallow Grave, 1999; Blood Sinister, 1999; Gone Tomorrow, 2001; Dear Departed, 2004. MORLAND DYNASTY SERIES: The Founding, 1980; The Dark Rose, 1981; The Princeling, 1981, in the U.S. as The Distant Wood, 1982; The Oak Apple, 1982, in U.S. as The Crystal Crown, 1982; The Black Pearl, 1982; The Long Shadow, 1983; The Chevalier, 1984; The Maiden, 1985; The Flood-Tide, 1986; The Tangled Thread, 1987; The Emperor, 1988; The Victory, 1989; The Regency, 1990; The Campaigners, 1991; The Reckoning, 1992; The Devil's Horse, 1993; The Poison Tree, 1994; The Abyss, 1995; The Hidden Shore, 1996; The Winter Journey, 1997; The Outcast, 1998; The Mirage, 1999; The Cause, 2000; The Homecoming, 2001; The Question, 2002; The Dream Kingdom, 2003; The Restless Sea, 2004. THE KIROV TRILOGY: Anna, 1990; Fleur, 1991; Emily, 1992. STORIES: Real Life, 1999. AS EMMA WOODHOUSE: A Rainbow Summer, 1976; A Well-Painted Passion, 1976; Romany Magic, 1977; Love's Perilous Passage, 1978; On Wings of Love, 1978; Never Love a Stranger, 1978. AS ELIZABETH BENNETT: Title Role, 1980; The Unfinished, 1983; Even Chance, 1984; Last Run, 1984; Historical Fiction: I, Victoria, 1994. **Address:** c/o Author Mail, Little Brown/Time Warner Books, Brettenham House, Lancaster Place, London WC2E 7EN, England. **Online address:** www.messages@cynthiaharrodeagles.com; www.cynthiaharrodeagles.com

HARROW, Kenneth W. American, b. 1943. **Genres:** Literary criticism and history. **Career:** Michigan State University, East Lansing, professor of English, 1966-. Has also been employed by the University of Yaounde, Cameroon, 1977-79; and the University of Dakar, Senegal, 1989-90. **Publications:** (ed.) Faces of Islam in African Literature, 1991; Thresholds of Change in African Literature, 1994; (ed.) The Marabout and the Muse: Aspects of Islam in African Literature, 1996; (ed.) African Cinema, 1999. **Address:** Department of English, Michigan State University, East Lansing, MI 48824, U.S.A.

HARROWER, Elizabeth. Australian, b. 1928. **Genres:** Novels. **Career:** Staff member, A. B. C., Sydney, 1959-60, and Macmillan & Co. Ltd., publrs., Sydney, 1961-67. **Publications:** Down in the City, 1957; The Long Prospect, 1958; The Catherine Wheel, 1960; The Watch Tower, 1966. **Address:** 21/26 Cranbrook Ave, Cremorne, NSW 2090, Australia.

HARSCH, Rich. Also writes as Blaise Cendrars, Carlos Oretti. American, b. 1949. **Genres:** Novels. **Career:** Writer. Also works as a taxicab driver. **Publications:** Driftless Zone, 1997; Billy Verite, 1998. Some writings appear under the pseudonyms Blaise Cendrars and Carlos Oretti. **Address:** c/o Warren Frazier, John Hawkins and Associates Inc., 71 West 23rd St. Suite 1600, New York, NY 10010, U.S.A.

HARSENT, David. British, b. 1942. **Genres:** Novels, Poetry. **Career:** Full-time writer. Times Literary Supplement, London, fiction critic, 1965-73; Spectator, London, poetry critic, 1970-73. Royal Society of Literature, fellow. **Publications:** Tonight's Lover, 1968; A Violent Country, 1969; Ashridge, 1970; After Dark, 1973; Truce, 1973; Dreams of the Dead, 1977; (ed.) New Poetry 7, 1981; Mister Punch, 1984; From an Inland Sea (novel), 1985; Playback, 1987; Selected Poems, 1989; Gawain (libretto), 1991; Storybook Hero, 1992; News from the Front, 1993; The Sorrow of Sarajevo (versions of poems by G. Simic), 1996; Sprinting from the Graveyard (versions of poems by G. Simic), 1997; The Potted Priest, 1997; A Bird's Idea of Flight, 1998; Marriage (poetry), 2002. **Address:** c/o Jonathan Clowes Agency, Iron Bridge House, Bridge Approach, London NW1 8BD, England.

HART, Andre. See **FREEMANTLE, Brian (Harry).**

HART, (Margaret Eleanor) Anne. Canadian. **Genres:** Novellas/Short stories, Plays/Screenplays, Poetry, Biography, Documentaries/Reportage. **Career:** Newfoundland Public Library Services, St. John's, part-time cataloger, 1969-72; Memorial University of Newfoundland, St. John's, librarian, 1973-74, assistant head of Centre for Newfoundland Studies, 1974-77, head of Centre for Newfoundland Studies, 1977-98, Memorial University Honourary Research Librarian, 1999-, member of arts and professional committees. **Publications:** Help Me Hepplewhite (play), 1975; The Life and Times of Miss Jane Marple, 1985; The Life and Times of Hercule Poirot, 1990; Cyberscribes 1: The New Journalists, 1997. EDITOR & COMPILER: (with W. Power, M. D'Entremont, and H.B. Neary) Newfoundland and Confederation, 1977; (with A. Mews, J. Tillotson, and A. Hiscock) My Inside Self: Writings and Pictures by Children of Newfoundland and Labrador, 1980; Work represented in books. **Address:** Library, Memorial University of Newfoundland, St. Johns, NL, Canada A1C 3X6. **Online address:** ahart@mun.ca

HART, Carolyn G(impel). American, b. 1936. **Genres:** Novels, Mystery/Crime/Suspense, Children's fiction, History. **Career:** Full-time writer, 1986-. Norman Transcript, Oklahoma, reporter, 1958-59; University of Oklahoma, Norman, Sooner Newsmakers, alumni newspaper, editor, 1959-60, and assistant professor of journalism, 1982-85; freelance writer, 1961-82. **Publications:** CRIME NOVELS: Flee from the Past, 1975; A Settling of Accounts, 1976; The Rich Die Young, 1983; Death by Surprise, 1983; Castle Rock, 1983; Skulduggery, 1984; Death on Demand, 1987; Design for Murder, 1988; Something Wicked, 1988; Honeymoon with Murder, 1989; A Little Class on Murder, 1989; Deadly Valentine, 1990; The Christie Caper, 1991; Southern Ghost, 1992; Dead Man's Island, 1993; Scandal in Fair Haven, 1994; Mint Julep Murder, 1995; Death in Lovers' Lane, 1997; Death in Paradise, 1998; Yankee Doodle Dead, 1998; Death on the River Walk, 1999; White Elephant Dead, 1999; Sugarplum Dead, 2000; Resort to Murder, 2001; April Fool Dead, 2002; Engaged to Die, 2003; Letter from Home, 2003. OTHER: The Secret of the Cellars (for children), 1964; Dangerous Summer (for children), 1968; No Easy Answers, 1970; Rendezvous in Veracruz, 1972; Danger, High Explosives!, 1972; (with C.F. Long) The Sooner Story, 1890-1980 (history), 1980; Escape from Paris (novel), 1982; The Devereaux Legacy (novel), 1986; Brave Hearts (novel), 1987; Crime on Her Mind (short stories), 1999. EDITOR: Crimes of the Heart (anthology), 1995; Love & Death (anthology), 2001.

HART, Catherine. American, b. 1948. **Genres:** Romance/Historical. **Career:** Dental assistant and receptionist in Ohio, 1965-66; dispensing optician and receptionist in Ohio, 1966-67; office manager and salesperson in Ohio, 1970 and 1977-83; writer, 1983-. **Publications:** ROMANCE FICTION: Fire and

Ice, 1984; Silken Savage, 1985; Ashes and Ecstasy, 1985; Satin and Steel, 1986; Summer Storm, 1987; Forever Gold, 1988; Night Flame, 1989; Fallen Angel, 1989; Sweet Fury, 1990; Tempest, 1991; Temptation, 1992; Splendor, 1993; Irresistible, 1994; Dazzled, 1994; Mischief, 1995; Charmed, 1996; Horizons, 1997; Impulsive, 1998. Work represented in anthologies. **Address:** c/o Maria Carvainis Agency, 1350 Ave of the Americas Ste 2905, New York, NY 10019, U.S.A.

HART, Charles (A.). American, b. 1940. **Genres:** Medicine/Health, Self help. **Career:** University of Washington Hospitals, Seattle, training administrator, 1972-78; homemaker, 1978-83; Writer and community advocate for people with developmental disabilities, 1984-. **Publications:** Without Reason: A Family Copes with Two Generations of Autism, Harper, 1989; A Parent's Guide to Autism, Pocketbooks, 1993. **Address:** Susan Ginsburg, Writers House, Inc, 21 West 26th St, New York, NY 10010, U.S.A.

HART, Christopher. American, b. 1957. **Genres:** Art/Art history, Children's non-fiction, How-to books, Cartoons. **Career:** Illustrator and writer. Writer for film and television studios, 1981-97. **Publications:** Cartooning for the Beginner: Everything You Ever Wanted to Know about Cartooning but Were Afraid to Draw; Christopher Hart's Cartoon Studio; Christopher Hart's Animation Studio; Drawing on the Funny Side of the Brain; Drawing Faeries; Merwin; Police Pups; Anime Mania; Mecha Mania. HOW TO DRAW SERIES: Cartoons for Comic Strips; Cartoon Animals; Comic Book Heroes and Villains; Animation; Comic Book Bad Guys and Gals; Cartoon Dogs, Puppies, and Wolves; Korean Comics; Mutants Aliens and Mysterious Creatures; Great Looking Comic Book Women; Fast Cars, Monster Trucks and Fighter Jets. KIDS DRAW SERIES: Manga; Funny and Spooky Holiday Characters; Angels, Elves, Fairies and More; Knights, Kings, Queens and Dragons; Dogs, Puppies and Wolves; Cats, Kittens, Lions and Tigers; Baby Animals. MANGA MANIA SERIES: Video Games; Shoujo; Villains; Fantasy Worlds; How to Draw Japanese Comics; Drawing Cutting Edge Comics. XTREME ART SERIES: Draw Manga; Draw Manga Villains. KIDS DRAW SERIES: Animals; Anime; Dinosaurs; Drawing Cutting Edge Comics; Human Anatomy Made Amazingly Easy. Contributor of copy and art to magazines.

HART, Ellen. American, b. 1949. **Genres:** Mystery/Crime/Suspense. **Career:** Chef. **Publications:** MYSTERIES: Hallowed Murder, 1989; Vital Lies, 1990; Stage Fright, 1992; A Killing Cure, 1993; A Small Sacrifice, 1994; This Little Piggy Went to Murder, 1994; For Every Evil, 1995; Faint Praise, 1995; Robber's Wine, 1996; The Oldest Sin, 1996; Murder in the Air, 1997. **Address:** c/o Seal Press, PMB 375, 300 Queen Anne Ave N, Seattle, WA 98109-4512, U.S.A.

HART, Jan Siegel. American, b. 1940. **Genres:** Children's fiction. **Career:** Writer, publisher, performer. Public speaker at schools and organizations with one-woman show, Hanna the Immigrant, and oral history workshops. **Publications:** Hanna, the Immigrant, 1991; The Many Adventures of Minnie, 1992; More Adventures of Minnie, 1994. **Address:** 1041 Clarence Rd, Temple, TX 76501, U.S.A. **Online address:** CBHart635@aol.com

HART, Jenifer. British, b. 1914. **Genres:** History, Autobiography/Memoirs. **Career:** Worked for British Home Office, 1936-47; Oxford University, Oxford, England, extra-mural delegacy, 1948-50, research fellow Nuffield College, Oxford, 1950-51, history and politics tutor at St. Anne's College, Oxford, 1952-81. Member of Oxford City Council, 1961-64. **Publications:** The British Police, 1951; Proportional Representation: Critics of the British Electoral System, 1820-1945, 1992; Ask Me No More (autobiography), 1998. Contributor to books and periodicals. **Address:** 11 Manor Pl., Oxford OX1 3UP, England.

HART, John Fraser. American, b. 1924. **Genres:** Geography. **Career:** Professor of Geography, University of Minnesota, Minneapolis, since 1967. Faculty member, University of Georgia, Athens, 1949-55 and Indiana University, 1955-67; Ed., Annals of the Association of American Geographers, 1970-75. **Publications:** The British Moorlands, 1955; The Southeastern United States, 1967; U.S. and Canada, 1967; (ed.) Regions of the United States, 1972; The Look of the Land, 1975; The South, 1977; (ed.) Our Changing Cities, 1991; The Land that Feeds Us, 1991. **Address:** Dept. of Geography, University of Minnesota, Minneapolis, MN 55455, U.S.A.

HART, John Mason. American, b. 1935. **Genres:** Area studies. **Career:** University of North Dakota, Grand Forks, assistant professor of history, 1969-73; University of Houston, Houston, TX, associate professor, 1973-78, professor of Mexican history, 1978-, chairman of history department, 1989-90. President, Southwestern Council on Latin American Studies, 1983; Rocky Mountain Council on Latin American Studies, director, 1983-2000. **Publications:** Los anarquistas Mexicanos, 1974; Anarchism and the Mexican Working Class, 1860-1931, 1978; Revolutionary Mexico, 1987; Empire and Revolution: The Americans in Mexico since the Civil War, 2002. Contributor to journals. **Address:** Department of History, University of Houston, Houston, TX 77204-3785, U.S.A.

HART, Jon. *See* **HARVEY, John B.**

HART, Jonathan (Locke). Canadian, b. 1956. **Genres:** Novellas/Short stories, Plays/Screenplays, Poetry, Theatre, Essays. **Career:** University of Alberta, Edmonton, lecturer in English, 1984-85, assistant professor, 1987-92, associate professor of English and adjunct professor of comparative literature, 1992-95, professor, 1995-; Trent University, Peterborough, ON, assistant professor of English, 1985-86; Harvard University, Cambridge, MA, visiting scholar and tutor at Kirkland House, 1986-87, associate at Kirkland House and visiting scholar, 1992-93, Fulbright faculty fellow of comparative literature, 1996-97; Cambridge University, visiting fellow, 1993-94; Princeton University, visiting professor of history and Canadian studies, 2000-02. **Publications:** More Than This Burning Ash (play), 1978-79; Hitler (play), 1988-89; Theater and World: The Problematics of Shakespeare's History, 1992; Northrop Frye: The Theoretical Imagination, 1994; Imagining Culture, 1996; Breath and Dust, 2000; Representing the New World, 2001; Columbus, Shakespeare and the Interpretation of the New World, 2002; Comparing Empires, forthcoming. Contributor of essays, stories, and poems to periodicals. **Address:** Dept of English, 3-35 Humanities Centre, University of Alberta, Edmonton, AB, Canada T6G 2E5. **Online address:** jonathan.hart@ualberta.ca

HART, Josephine. Irish, b. 1942. **Genres:** Novels. **Career:** Haymarket Publications, London, England, started in sales, became publishing director; theater producer; writer. **Publications:** NOVELS: Damage, 1991; Sin, 1992; Oblivion, 1995; Stillest Day, 1998; Reconstructionist, 2001. **Address:** c/o Ed Victor, Ed Victor Ltd., 6 Bayley St, Bedford Sq, London WC1B 3HB, England.

HART, Kevin. Australian (born England), b. 1954. **Genres:** Literary criticism and history, Poetry. **Career:** Geelong College, Victoria, Dept. of Philosophy and Religious Studies, co-ordinator, 1979-83; University of Melbourne, Dept. of Philosophy, part-time lecturer, 1985, Dept. of English, lecturer, 1986-87; Deakin University, lecturer then sr. lecturer in literary studies, 1987-91; Monash University, Vic., associate professor of critical theory, 1991-95, professor, 1995-. **Publications:** Nebuchadnezzar, 1976; The Departure, 1978; The Lines of the Hand: Poems 1976-79, 1981; Your Shadow, 1984; The Trespass of the Sign, 1989; The Buried Harbour: Selected Poems of Giuseppe Ungaretti, 1990; Peniel, 1991; A.D. Hope, 1992; The Oxford Book of Australian Religious Verse, 1994; New and Selected Poems, 1995; Dark Angel, 1996; Losing the Power to Say I, 1996; Wicked Heat (poetry), 1999; Samuel Johnson and the Culture of Property (criticism), 1999; Flame Tree: Selected Poems, 2002. **Address:** Dept. of English, Monash University, Victoria 3168, Australia. **Online address:** Kevin.Hart@arts.monash.edu.au

HART, Lynda. American, b. 1953. **Genres:** Theatre, Women's studies and issues. **Career:** Xavier University, Cincinnati, OH, assistant professor of English and director of women's studies, 1984-88; University of Pennsylvania, Philadelphia, PA, associate professor of English and theater, 1988-. **Publications:** Sam Shepard's Metaphorical Stages, 1987; Fatal Women: Lesbian Sexuality and the Mark of Aggression, 1994. EDITOR: Making a Spectacle: Feminist Essays on Contemporary Women's Theatre, 1989; (with P. Phelan) Acting Out: Feminist Performance, 1993. **Address:** 3440 Walnut, 119 Bennett Hall, University of Pennsylvania, Philadelphia, PA 19104, U.S.A.

HART, Veronica. See **KELLEHER, Victor (Michael Kitchener).**

HARTCUP, Guy. British, b. 1919. **Genres:** Military/Defense/Arms control, Sciences. **Career:** Historian, Air Ministry, 1948-60; English Ed., International Atomic Energy Agency, Vienna, 1961-62; Assistant Historian, Cabinet Office Historical Section, 1963-64; Historian, H. M. Treasury, London, 1965-77. **Publications:** Origins and Development of Operational Research in the Royal Air Force, 1963; The Challenge of War, 1970; The Achievement of the Airship, 1974; Code Name Mulberry, 1977; Camouflage, 1979; (with T.E. Allibone) Cockcroft and the Atom, 1984; The War of Invention, 1988; The Silent Revolution: Development of Conventional Weapons, 1945-1985, 1993; The Effect of Science on the Second World War, 2000. **Address:** 16 Temple Sheen, East Sheen, London SW14 7RP, England.

HART-DAVIS, Duff. British, b. 1936. **Genres:** Novels, History, Biography. **Career:** Feature writer 1972-76, Literary Ed., 1976-77 and Assistant Ed., 1977-78, Sunday Telegraph, London; The Independent, country columnist, 1986-. **Publications:** The Megacull, 1968; The Gold of St. Matthew (in U.S. as The Gold Trackers), 1968; Spider in the Morning, 1972; Ascension: The Story of a South Atlantic Island, 1972; Peter Fleming (biography), 1974; Monarchs of the Glen, 1978; The Heights of Rimring, 1980; (with C. Strong) Fighter Pilot, 1981; Level Five, 1982; Fire Falcon, 1984; The Man-Eater of Jassapur, 1985; Hitler's Games, 1986; Armada, 1988; Country Matters, 1988; The House the Berrys Built, 1990; Horses of War, 1991; Wildings: The Secret Garden of Eileen Soper, 1991; Further Country Matters, 1992; When the Country Went to Town, 1997; Raoul Millais, 1998; Fauna Britannica, 2002; Audubon's Elephant, 2003. EDITOR: End of an Era: Letters and Journals of Sir Alan Lascelles 1887-1920, 1987; In Royal Service: Letters and Journals of Sir Alan Lascelles, Vol. 2, 1920-36, 1989; Pavilions of Splendour, 2004. **Address:** Owlpen Farm, Uley, Dursley, Glos., England.

HARTE, Amanda. (born United States). **Genres:** Romance/Historical. **Career:** Writer. **Publications:** ROMANCE FICTION: Strings Attached, 2000; North Star, 2000; Moonlight Masquerade, 2001; Imperfect Together, 2001; Rainbows at Midnight, 2002; Carousel of Dreams, 2002. THE WAR BRIDES TRILOGY: Dancing in the Rain, 2003; Whistling in the Dark, 2004; Laughing at the Thunder, forthcoming. **Address:** POB 597, New Providence, NJ 07974, U.S.A. **Online address:** amanda.harte@sff.net

HARTE, Lara. Irish, b. 1975. **Genres:** Novels. **Career:** Author. **Publications:** First Time, 1996; Losing It, 1999; Wild Geese, 2003. **Address:** c/o Author Mail, Weidenfeld & Nicolson, Orion House, 5 Upper St. Martin's Ln, London WC2H 9EA, England. **Online address:** laraharte@eircom.net

HARTEIS, Richard. Bulgarian, b. 1946. **Genres:** Poetry, Adult non-fiction. **Career:** Teacher and writer. Poet-in-residence, American University, Bulgaria, 1995-96. Worked as physician's assistant, health-care consultant, and radio producer. **Publications:** POETRY: Fourteen Women, 1979; Morocco Journal: Love, Work, Play, 1981; Internal Geography, 1987; Keeping Heart, 1996. OTHER: Marathon: A Story of Endurance and Friendship (nonfiction), 1989; Sapphire Dawn (fiction), 1999; Provence, 2000. EDITOR: (and trans with others) Poets of Bulgaria, 1986; (with W. Meredith) Window on the Black Sea: Bulgarian Poetry in Translation, 1992. Contributor to periodicals. **Address:** 337 Kitemaug Rd., Uncasville, CT 06382, U.S.A. **Online address:** rfhar@concoll.edu

HARTER, Penny. Also writes as Penny Bihler. American, b. 1940. **Genres:** Poetry. **Career:** New Jersey State Council on Arts, Trenton, consultant in poets-in-schools program, 1973-79; Woodbridge Public Schools, NJ, teacher of writing, 1978-83; Madison Public Schools, Madison, NJ, teacher, 1983-91; Santa Fe Preparatory School, NM, teacher, 1991-2002; Oak Knoll School of the Holy Child, Summit, NJ, teacher, 2002-. **Publications:** POETRY: (as Penny Bihler) House by the Sea, 1975; (with W.J. Higginson) Used Poems, 1978; The Orange Balloon (haiku), 1980; Lovepoems, 1981; White Flowers in the Snow (poems and stories), 1981; From the Willow: Homage to Take-chi no Kurohito (haiku), 1983; Hiking the Crevasse: Poems on the Way to Divorce, 1983; In the Broken Curve (haiku), 1984; The Price of Admission, 1986; The Monkey's Face (haiku), 1987; At the Zendo (poems and journal), 1993; Stages and Views, 1994; Shadow Play, Night Haiku (children's haiku), 1994; Grandmother's Milk, 1995; Lizard Light: Poems from the Earth, 1998; Buried in the Sky, 2001. NONFICTION: (with Higginson) Met on the Road: A Transcontinental Haiku Journal, 1993; (with Higginson) The Haiku Handbook: How to Write, Share, and Teach Haiku, 1985. CO-EDITOR & CONTRIBUTOR: Advance Taken to Boardwalk: 28 New Jersey Poets, 1977; Between Two Rivers: Union County Literature Today, 1980; Between Two Rivers: Ten North Jersey Poets, 1981; (with C. van den Heuvel and others) An Anthology of Haiku by People of the United States and Canada, 1988; A Haiku Path: The Haiku Society of America 1968-1988, 1994. **Address:** PO Box 1402, Summit, NJ 07902, U.S.A.

HARTIG, John H. American, b. 1952. **Genres:** Environmental sciences/Ecology. **Career:** University of Michigan Great Lakes Research Division, Ann Arbor, research assistant, 1976-78; Michigan Department of Natural Resources, Lansing, water quality specialist, 1978-82; International Joint Commission, Windsor, Ontario, environmental scientist, 1985-; Wayne State University, Detroit, MI, adjunct professor of civil and environmental engineering, 1992-; writer. **Publications:** (ed. with M.A. Zarull) Under Raps: Toward Grassroots Ecological Democracy in the Great Lakes Basin, 1992. Contributor to books and periodicals. **Address:** Department of Civil and Environmental Engineering, Wayne State University, 5050 Anthony Wayne Dr., Detroit, MI 48202, U.S.A.

HARTJE, Tod D(ale). American, b. 1968. **Genres:** Sports/Fitness, Biography. **Career:** Professional hockey player: Soviet Elite League (Sokol Kiev), 1990-91, Winnipeg Jets Hockey Club (Moncton Hawks), 1990-92, Boston Bruins Hockey Club (Providence Bruins), 1993-96. Hartje Pro Edge Hockey Training, Anoka, MN, owner and director, 1991-; DaimlerChrysler Motors Corporation, sales & marketing and industrial relations, 1996-. **Publications:** (with L. Martin) From behind the Red Line: An American Hockey Player in the Soviet Union, 1992. **Address:** 1525 Threadneedle St, Bloomfield Hills, MI 48304-1020, U.S.A.

HARTLAND, Michael. Also writes as Ruth Carrington. British, b. 1941. **Genres:** Mystery/Crime/Suspense. **Career:** Full-time writer since 1983. In British Government service, 1963-78 (Private Secretary to Jennie Lee, Minister for the Arts, 1966-68; Planning Unit of Margaret Thatcher, Secretary of State for Education, 1970-73; then diplomatic duties overseas, intelligence and counter-terrorism); Director, U. N. Intl. Atomic Energy Agency, Vienna, 1978-83. FRSA 1982. Hon. Fellow, University of Exeter, 1985. Book reviewer for The Times, Sunday Times, Daily Telegraph (resident thriller critic since 1993), and Sunday Express. Travel and feature writer for The Times, Sunday Times, and Guardian. **Publications:** Down among the Dead Men, 1983; Seven Steps to Treason, 1985 (dramatised for BBC Radio-4 Saturday Night Theatre); The Third Betrayal, 1986; Frontier of Fear, 1989; The Year of the Scorpion, 1991; (as Ruth Carrington) Dead Fish, 1998. BROADCASTING: Sonja's Report (life of GRU Colonel Ruth Kuczynski, wartime controller of atom spy Klaus Fuchs), 1990; Masterspy: Interviews with KGB defector Oleg Gordievsky, 1991. **Address:** Cotte Barton, Branscombe, Devon EX12 3BH, England.

HARTLE, Anthony E. American, b. 1942. **Genres:** Ethics, Military/Defense/Arms control. **Career:** U.S. Army, infantry officer, 1964-94; Cambridge University, visiting fellow, 1991-92; U.S. Military Academy, instructor and assistant professor, 1971-74, associate professor, 1982-88, professor of philosophy, 1988-, deputy head, Department of English, 1994-. **Publications:** (ed. with John Kekes) Dimensions of Ethical Thought, Peter Lang, 1987; Moral Issues in Military Decision Making, University Press of Kansas, 1989. Contributor to Infantry in Vietnam, edited by Albert N. Garland, Battery Press, 1984. Contributor to periodicals. **Address:** Department of English, United States Military Academy, West Point, NY 10996, U.S.A.

HARTLEY, Aidan. (born Kenya), b. 1965. **Genres:** Autobiography/Memoirs. **Career:** Journalist. Foreign correspondent for the Reuters news agency, Financial Times, and the London Times. Cofounder, African Environment News Services (AENS; online African-wide environmental news and information service). **Publications:** The Zanzibar Chest: A Story of Life, Love, and Death in Foreign Lands, 2003. **Address:** c/o Author Mail, Grove/Atlantic, 841 Broadway, 4th Floor, New York, NY 10003, U.S.A. **Online address:** info@thezanzibarchest.com

HARTLEY, Hal. American, b. 1959. **Genres:** Plays/Screenplays. **Career:** Writer and director of motion pictures. **Publications:** SCREENPLAYS: The Unbelievable Truth, 1990; Trust, 1991; Simple Men and Trust, 1993; Surviving Desire (for television), 1992; Henry Fool, 1998. Contributor of short films to Alive from Off Center for PBS-TV.

HARTLEY, Jean. British, b. 1933. **Genres:** Autobiography/Memoirs, Biography, Literary criticism and history. **Career:** Marvell Press, Hull, England, joint proprietor, 1954-68; high school teacher in Hull, 1972-75; Hull College of Further Education, Hull, lecturer, 1976-89; writer. **Publications:** Philip Larkin, the Marvell Press, and Me, 1989; Philip Larkin's Hull and East Yorkshire, 1995. **Address:** c/o The Philip Larkin Society, c/o Dept of English, University of Hull, Hull HU6 7RX, England.

HARTLEY, Marie. British, b. 1905. **Genres:** History, Local history/Rural topics. **Career:** Author, artist, photographer. **Publications:** WITH ELLA PONTEFRACT: Swaledale, 1934; Wensleydale, 1936, Wharfedale, 1938; Yorkshire Tour, 1939; Yorkshire Cottage, 1942; Yorkshire Heritage, 1950. WITH JOAN INGILBY: Old Hand-Knitters of the Dales, 1951; Yorkshire Village, 1953; The Yorkshire Dales, 1956; The Wonders of Yorkshire, 1959; Yorkshire Portraits, 1961; Getting to Know Yorkshire, 1964; Life and Tradition in the Yorkshire Dales, 1968; Life in the Moorlands of North-East Yorkshire, 1972; Life and Tradition in West Yorkshire, 1976; A Dale's Heritage, 1982; Dales Memories, 1986; Yorkshire Album, 1988; A Dale's Album, 1991; Fifty Years in the Yorkshire Dales, 1995. MAKING series: Backran; Cartwheel; Stonewcyk; Boots and Shoes; Cheese and Butter; Oatrake. OTHER: The Yorkshire Dales: Wood-engravings, 1989, 1991; Forms and

Colours, 1992; Wood Engravings, 1996. **Address:** Coleshouse, Askrigg, Leyburn, N. Yorkshire DL8 3HA, England.

HARTLEY, Steven W. American, b. 1956. **Genres:** Marketing, Advertising/ Public relations, Business/Trade/Industry. **Career:** University of Denver, CO, assistant professor, 1983-87, associate professor, 1987-92, professor of marketing, 1992-. **Publications:** (with C.H. Patti and S.L. Kennedy) Business to Business Advertising, 1991; (with others) Marketing, 5th ed., 1997, 7th ed., 2003. **Address:** Department of Marketing, University of Denver, 2101 S University Blvd, Denver, CO 80208, U.S.A.

HARTMAN, Donald K. American, b. 1959. **Genres:** Bibliography, Reference. **Career:** Librarian and compiler of reference books on literature; on staff of Lockwood Library, State University of New York at Buffalo. Co-owner of Epoch Books Inc. (a small press). **Publications:** (with J. Drost) Themes and Settings in Fiction: A Bibliography of Bibliographies, 1988; (with G. Sapp) Historical Figures in Fiction, 1994; (with D.J. Beruca and S.M. Neumeister) World's Columbian Exposition: A Centennial Bibliographic Guide, 1996; Historical Figures in Nineteenth Century Fiction, 1999. EDITOR: Fairground Fiction: Detective Stories of the World's Columbian Exposition, 1992. Contributor to periodicals. **Address:** Lockwood Library, State University of New York at Buffalo, Buffalo, NY 14260, U.S.A.

HARTMAN, Geoffrey H. American (born Germany), b. 1929. **Genres:** Poetry, Literary criticism and history. **Career:** Yale University, New Haven, CT, Sterling Fellow, 1952-53, Instructor, 1955-60, Morse Faculty Fellow, 1958, Assistant Professor, 1961-62, Professor of English and Comparative Literature, 1967-97, Karl Young Professor, 1974-97, Sterling Professor, 1994-97, Emeritus Professor, 1997-; University of Chicago, Visiting Assistant Professor, 1960-61; University of Iowa, Iowa City, Associate Professor, 1962-64, Professor, 1964-65; Cornell University, Ithaca, NY, Professor, 1965-67; George Washington University, Distinguished Visiting Scholar, 19982000. Fulbright Fellow, University of Dijon, France, 1951-52. **Publications:** The Unmediated Vision: An Interpretation of Wordsworth, Hopkins, Rilke, and Valery, 1954; Andre Malraux, 1960; Wordsworth's Poetry 1787-1814, 1964; Beyond Formalism: Literary Essays 1958-1970, 1970; The Fate of Reading and Other Essays, 1975; Akiba's Children (poetry), 1978; Criticism in the Wilderness, 1980; Saving the Text, 1981; Easy Pieces, 1985; Psychoanalysis and the Question of the Text, 1985; The Unremarkable Wordsworth, 1987; Minor Prophecies, 1991; The Longest Shadow, 1996; The Fateful Question of Culture, 1997. EDITOR: Hopkins: A Collection of Critical Essays, 1966; Selected Poetry and Prose of William Wordsworth, 1970; New Perspectives on Coleridge and Wordsworth, 1972; Romanticism: Vistas, Instances, Continuities, 1973; Midrash and Literature, 1986; Bitburg in Moral and Political Perspective, 1986; Holocaust Remembrance: The Shapes of Memory, 1994. **Address:** 260 Everit St, New Haven, CT 06511, U.S.A.

HARTMAN, Victoria. American, b. 1942. **Genres:** Humor/Satire. **Career:** Lothrop, Lee & Shepard (publishing house), NYC, art director, 1967-74; freelance book designer, 1974-. **Publications:** The Silly Jokebook, 1987; Westward Ho Ho Ho!: Jokes from the Wild West, 1992; The Silliest Jokebook Ever, 1993; Too Cool: Jokes for School, 1996. **Address:** 164 Halsey St., Southampton, NY 11968, U.S.A.

HARTMAN, Virginia. American, b. 1959. **Genres:** Novels, Novellas/Short stories. **Career:** American University, Washington, DC, adjunct instructor in literature, 1993-97. **Publications:** (with B. Esstman) A More Perfect Union: Poems and Stories about the Modern Wedding, 1998. Contributor to periodicals. **Address:** 53 Old Post Rd N, Red Hook, NY 12571, U.S.A.

HARTMANN, Dennis L. American, b. 1949. **Genres:** Earth sciences, Environmental sciences/Ecology, Meteorology/Atmospheric sciences. **Career:** McGill University, Montreal, Quebec, Canada, research associate in meteorology, 1975-76; National Center for Atmospheric Research, Boulder, CO, visiting scientist, 1976-77; University of Washington, Seattle, assistant professor, 1977-83, associate professor, 1983-88, professor of atmospheric sciences, 1988-, adjunct faculty at Quaternary Research Center, 1978-. Lecturer at colleges and universities in the United States and abroad. **Publications:** Global Physical Climatology, 1994. Contributor to books. Contributor of articles and reviews to scientific journals and popular magazines. **Address:** Department of Atmospheric Sciences, University of Washington, Seattle, WA 98195, U.S.A.

HARTMANN, Ernest L. American (born Austria), b. 1934. **Genres:** Medicine/Health, Psychiatry, Psychology. **Career:** Director, Sleep Disorders Center, Newton-Wellesley Hospital, Newton MA. Director, Sleep and Dream Laboratory, Boston State Hospital, Massachusetts, 1964-85. Prof of Psychiatry, Tufts University School of Medicine, Boston, MA, 1975- (Associate Professor, 1969-75). Residency in Psychiatry, Massachusetts Mental Health Center, Boston, 1960-62; Clinical Associate, 1962-64, and Career Investigator, 1964-69, National Institute of Mental Health, Bethesda, MD. **Publications:** The Biology of Dreaming, 1967; (with B. Glasser, M. Greenblatt, M. Solomon, and D. Levinson) Adolescents in a Mental Hospital, 1968; (ed.) Sleep and Dreaming, 1970; The Functions of Sleep, 1973; The Sleeping Pill, 1978; The Nightmare, 1985; The Sleep Book, 1987; Boundaries in the Mind, 1992; Dreams and Nightmares: The New Theory, 1998; Dreams and Nightmares: The Origin and Meaning of Dreams. Contributor of scholarly papers to professional journals. **Address:** 27 Clark St, Newton, MA 02459, U.S.A.

HARTNETT, Sonya. Australian, b. 1968. **Genres:** Young adult fiction. **Career:** Bookseller. **Publications:** FOR YOUNG ADULTS: Trouble All the Way, 1984; Sparkle and Nightflower, 1986; The Glass House, 1990; Wilful Blue, 1994; Sleeping Dogs, 1995; The Devil Latch, 1996; Black Foxes, 1996; Princes, 1997; All My Dangerous Friends, 1998; Stripes of the Sidestep Wolf, 1999; Thursday's Child, 2000.

HARTOONIAN, Gevork. American (born Iran), b. 1947. **Genres:** Architecture. **Career:** Mirick, Pearson, Batcheler (architects), Philadelphia, PA, architect, 1984-87; Kling-Linquist Partnership Inc., Philadelphia, architect, 1988-96; freelance design consultant, NYC, 1996-; Spring Garden College, adjunct faculty member, 1988-90; Drury College, assistant professor, beginning in 1990, then lecturer at Hammons School of Architecture, 1991-92; University of Texas at San Antonio, visiting assistant professor, 1993-95; Rice University, Interstim Lecturer, 1995; Parsons School of Design, visiting associate professor, 1996; Pratt Institute, visiting associate professor, then adjunct associate professor, 1997-; Columbia University, visiting professor, then adjunct associate professor, 1997-; guest lecturer at colleges and universities. **Publications:** Ontology of Construction: On Nihilism of Technology in Theories of Modern Architecture, 1994; Modernity and Its Other: A Post-Script to Contemporary Architecture, 1997. **Address:** School of Design & Architecture, Canberra University, Canberra, ACT 2601, Australia. **Online address:** gevork@scredes.canberra.edu.au

HARTSHORNE, Thomas L. American, b. 1935. **Genres:** Cultural/Ethnic topics, History. **Career:** Kent State University, Ohio, instructor in history, 1962-65, assistant professor of history, 1965-66; Cleveland State University, Ohio, assistant professor, 1966-69, associate professor of history, 1969-2001, associate professor of history, emeritus, 2001-. **Publications:** The Distorted Image: Changing Conceptions of the American Character since Turner, 1968; (co-ed.) The Social Fabric, 6th ed., 1991, 9th ed., 2003. **Address:** Dept of History, Cleveland State University, Cleveland, OH 44115, U.S.A. **Online address:** thomas.hartshorne@att.net

HARTT, Julian N(orris). American, b. 1911. **Genres:** Philosophy, Theology/Religion. **Career:** Berea College, Berea, KY, instructor in philosophy and religion, 1940-43; Yale University, New Haven, CT, associate professor, 1943-53, Noah Porter Professor of Philosophy and Theology, 1953-72, chairman of department of religion, 1956-64, director of graduate religious studies, 1964-67, chairman of department of religious studies, 1967-72; University of Virginia, Charlottesville, William Kenan, Jr., Professor of Religious Studies, 1972-81, professor emeritus, 1981-. **Publications:** (with J.A.C. Fagginger Auer) Humanism versus Theism, 1951; Towards a Theology of Evangelism, 1955; Being Known and Being Revealed, 1957; The Lost Image of Man, 1963; A Christian Critique of American Culture: An Essay in Practical Theology, 1967; Theology and the Church in the University, 1969; The Restless Quest, 1975; Theological Method and Imagination, 1977; (with R.L. Hart and R.P. Scharlemann) The Critique of Modernity, 1988. Contributor to periodicals. **Address:** 500 Crestwood Dr #2303, Charlottesville, VA 22903-4881, U.S.A. **Online address:** jnh3c@ NTes.net

HARTWIG, Manfred. German, b. 1950. **Genres:** Animals/Pets. **Career:** Held positions in commercial businesses. Currently Vice President Supply management of Fossil Power Plants. **Publications:** (with P.H. Burgel) Gorillas, 1992 (originally published as Bei den Berggorillas, 1989). **Address:** Mecklenburger Str. 10, 91325 Adelsdorf, Germany.

HARTWIG, Michael J. American, b. 1953. **Genres:** Human relations/ Parenting. **Career:** Roman Catholic priest in Dallas, 1979-87; Immaculate Conception Parish, Tyler, middle school and high school teacher, coordinator of Hispanic ministries, and instructor in continuing education, 1980-83; John Paul I Catechetical Institute, lecturer, 1983-87; University of Dallas, adjunct instructor, 1983-85; University of New Haven, adjunct instructor, 1990-91;

St. Francis School of Nursing, Hartford, CT, member of adjunct faculty, 1991-97; Cambridge College, Cambridge, MA, member of adjunct faculty, 1998; Fisher College, Boston, member of adjunct faculty, 1998-2000; Charter Oak College, member of adjunct faulty, 1998-; University of Massachusetts, Boston, member of adjunct faculty at College of Public and Community Service, 1999-; workshop presenter and public speaker. Member of ethics committees at local hospitals and residential centers; consultant to Mental Health Center of Greater Manchester. **Publications:** The Poetics of Intimacy and the Problem of Sexual Abstinence, 2000. Contributor to periodicals. **Address:** 200 W Brookline St, Boston, MA 02118-1280, U.S.A. **Online address:** PortaMJH@aol.com

HARUF, Kent. American, b. 1943. **Genres:** Novels. **Career:** Worked odd jobs including farm laborer, construction worker, rural paper route carrier, hospital orderly, railroad worker, librarian, and orphanage house parent; taught high school English in Wisconsin and Colorado, 1976-86; served in the Peace Corps in Turkey, 1965-67; Nebraska Wesleyan University, Lincoln, assistant professor, 1986-91; Southern Illinois University, Carbondale, associate professor, 1991-. **Publications:** NOVELS: The Tie That Binds, 1984; Where You Once Belonged, 1991; Plainsong, 1999. Contributor of short stories to periodicals. **Address:** English Dept., Southern Illinois University, Carbondale, IL 62901, U.S.A.

HARVEY, Caroline. See TROLLOPE, Joanna.

HARVEY, Clay. American. **Genres:** Novels, Recreation. **Career:** Suspense novelist and author of books on arms and ammunition. **Publications:** NOVELS: A Flash of Red, 1996; A Whisper of Black, 1997. NONFICTION: Popular Sporting Rifle Cartridges, 1984; The Hunter's Rifle, 1988, rev ed, The Rifles, The Cartridges, and the Game, 1991. **Address:** c/o Putnam Berkley Group Inc., 375 Hudson, New York, NY 10014, U.S.A.

HARVEY, David. British, b. 1937. **Genres:** Classics. **Career:** University of Exeter, England, lecturer in classics, 1962-. Center for Hellenic Studies, Washington, DC, junior fellow, 1967-68. **Publications:** TRANSLATOR: (with H. Harvey) K. Reinhardt, Sophocles, 1979; (with H. Harvey and F. Robertson) R. Heinze, Virgil's Epic Technique, 1993. EDITOR: (with P. Cartledge) Crux: Essays Presented to G.E.M. de Ste. Croix on His 75th Birthday, 1985; (with J. Wilkins and M. Dobson) Food in Antiquity, 1994; (with J. Wilkins) The Rivals of Aristophanes, 2000; (with R. Parker) Greek Democratic Origins, 2003; (with F. McHardy and J. Robson) Lost Dramas of Classical Athens, 2005. Contributor of articles and reviews to classical journals. **Address:** 53 Thornton Hill, Exeter, Devon EX4 4NR, England. **Online address:** F.D.Harvey@exeter.ac.uk

HARVEY, Hazel (Mary). British, b. 1936. **Genres:** Translations, Local history/Rural topics. **Career:** Harrap (publisher), lexicographer, 1957-58; University of Exeter, Exeter, England, lecturer, 1961-64; University of London, National Extension College, tutor, 1975-. Devon Transport 2000, member. **Publications:** (trans. with D. Harvey) Karl Reinhardt, Sophocles, 1979; (trans. with D. Harvey and F. Robertson) Richard Heinze, Virgil's Epic Technique, 1993; Exeter: A Pictorial History, 1996; A Better Provision, Royal Devon & Exeter Hospital, 1948-1998, 1998. Author of booklets for the Exeter Civic Society. **Address:** 53 Thornton Hill, Exeter, Devon EX4 4NR, England.

HARVEY, Jack. See RANKIN, Ian (James).

HARVEY, John B. Also writes as James Barton, Jon Barton, William S. Brady, L. J. Coburn, J. B. Dancer, Jon Hart, William M. James, Terry Lennox, James Mann, John J. McLaglen, Thom Ryder, J. D. Sandon. British, b. 1938. **Genres:** Novels, Mystery/Crime/Suspense, Westerns/Adventure, Children's fiction, Young adult fiction, Poetry. **Career:** English and drama teacher in London, Heanor, Derbyshire, Andover, Hants., and Stevenage, Herts., 1963-74; part-time film and literature teacher, Nottingham University, 1979-86; film reviewer, Nottingham News and Trader, 1981-86. **Publications:** NOVELS: Amphetamines and Pearls, 1976; The Geranium Kiss, 1976; Junkyard Angel, 1977; Neon Madman, 1977; Frame, 1979; Blind, 1980; (as James Mann) Endgame, 1985; (as Terry Lennox) Daniel Draws a Wild Card, 1985; Lonely Hearts, 1989; Rough Treatment, 1990; Cutting Edge, 1991; Off Minor, 1992; Wasted Years, 1993; Cold Light, 1994; Living Proof, 1995; Easy Meat, 1996; Still Water, 1997; Last Rites, 1998; Now's the Time (stories), 1999; In a True Light, 2001; Flesh and Blood, 2004. POETRY: Provence, 1978; The Old Postcard Trick, 1984; Neil Sedaka Lied, 1987; Taking the Long Road Home, 1988; (with S. Dymoke) Sometime Other Than Now, 1989; The Downeast Poems, 1989; Territory, 1991; Ghosts of a Chance, 1992; Bluer Than This, 1998. EDITOR: Blue Lightning, 1998;

Men from Boys, 2003. NOVELIZATION OF SCREENPLAYS: One of Our Dinosaurs Is Missing, 1976; Herbie Rides Again, 1977; Herbie Goes to Monte Carlo, 1978; The Eagle's Way, 1978; Duty Free, 1985; More Duty Free, 1986; Hard Cases, 1988. FOR JUVENILES: What about It, Sharon, 1979; Reel Love, 1982; Don't Forget Our Sundae Date, 1983; What Game Are You Playing?, 1983; Footwork, 1984; Wild Love, 1986; Last Summer, First Love, 1986; Kidnap!, 1987; Daylight Robbery!, 1987; Hot Property!, 1987; Terror Trap!, 1988; Downeast to Danger, 1988; Runner!, 1988. WESTERNS. HART THE REGULATOR SERIES: Cherokee Outlet, 1980; Blood Trail, 1980; Tago, 1980; The Silver Lie, 1980; Blood on the Border, 1981; Ride the Wide Country, 1981; Arkansas Breakout, 1982; John Wesley Hardin, 1982; California Bloodlines, 1982, The Skinning Place, 1982. AS JOHN J. McLAGLEN: HERNE THE HUNTER SERIES: River of Blood, 1976; Shadow of the Vulture, 1977; Death in Gold, 1977; Criss-Draw, 1978; Vigilante!, 1979; Sun Dance, 1980; Billy the Kid, 1980; Till Death, 1980; Dying Ways, 1982; Hearts of Gold, 1982; Wild Blood, 1983. WESTERNS AS J.B. DANCER. LAWMEN SERIES: Evil Breed, 1977; Judgement Day, 1978; The Hanged Man, 1979. WESTERNS AS L.J. COBURN. CALEB THORN SERIES: The Raiders, 1977; Bloody Shiloh, 1978. WESTERNS AS WILLIAM S. BRADY. HAWK SERIES: Blood Money, 1979; Killing Time, 1980; Blood Kin, 1980; Desperadoes, 1981; Dead Man's Hand, 1981; Sierra Gold, 1981; Death and Jack Shade, 1982; Border War, 1982; Killer, 1983. PEACEMAKER SERIES: Whiplash, 1981; War Party, 1983. WESTERNS AS WILLIAM M. JAMES: APACHE SERIES: Blood Rising, 1979; Blood Brother, 1980; Death Dragon, 1981; Death Ride, 1983; The Hanging, 1983. WESTERNS AS J.D. SANDON. GRINGOS SERIES: Cannons in the Rain, 1979; Border Affair, 1979; Mazatlan, 1980; Wheels of Thunder, 1981; Durango, 1982. OTHER FICTION: AS THOM RYDER: Avenging Angel, 1975; Angel Alone, 1975. AS JON HART: Black Blood, 1977; High Slaughter, 1977; Triangle of Death, 1977; Guerilla Attack, 1977; Death Raid, 1978. AS JON BARTON: Kill Hitler!, 1976; Forest of Death, 1977; Lightning Strikes, 1977. **Address:** c/o Sarah Lutyens, Lutyens & Rubinstein, 231 Westbourne Park Rd, London W11 1EB, England. **Online address:** john@mellotone.co.uk

HARVEY, John F(rederick). American, b. 1921. **Genres:** Librarianship, Information science/Computers. **Career:** International Library Consultant, since 1967. Dean of Students, Intercollege, Nicosia, Cyprus, 1984-91. Professor and administrator in library science, Drexel University, Philadelphia, 1958-67, University of Tehran, 1967-71, University of New Mexico, Albuquerque, 1972-74, Hofstra University, Hempstead, New York, 1974-76; Consultant in Library and Information Science, 1964-. **Publications:** (with others) The Library Periodical Directory, 1955, 1967; (with L. Shores and R. Jordan) The Library College, 1964; Data Processing in College and Public Libraries, 1966; Comparative and International Library Science, 1977; Church and Synagogue Libraries, 1980; (with E. M. Dickinson) Affirmative Action in Libraries, 1982; (with P. Spyers-Duran) Austerity Management in Academic Libraries, 1984; (with F. L. Carroll) Internationalizing Library and Information Science Education, 1987; Scholarly Religious Libraries in North America: a Statistical Examination, 1998; Popular Religious Libraries in North America: a Statistical Examination, 1998. **Address:** 82 Wall Street, Ste. 1105, New York, NY 10005-3682, U.S.A. **Online address:** john.f.harvey@usa.net

HARVEY, Karen D. American, b. 1935. **Genres:** Education, Cultural/Ethnic topics, Anthropology/Ethnology. **Career:** Classroom teacher, 1956-74; University of Denver, Denver, CO, professor, 1978-84, director of Teacher Education, 1978-84; Cherry Creek Schools, Denver, CO, director of staff development, 1984-91; University of Denver, Denver, CO, associate dean of academic affairs, 1991-. University of Denver American Indian Studies Program, advisory board member, 1994-. **Publications:** (with L.D. Harjo and J.K. Jackson) Teaching about Native Americans, 1990; Indians of the Great Plains, 1993; (with L.D. Harjo) Indian Country: A History of Native People in America, 1994; (with L.D. Harjo) Indian Country Teachers' Guide, 1994; (with L.D. Harjo and L. Welborn) How to Teach about American Indians: A Guide for the School Library Media Specialist, 1995; (ed. and author of introduction and notes) American Indian Voices, 1995. Author of articles and reviews. Contributor of articles on Native Americans and Hispanic Americans to Education Resources Information Center (ERIC). **Address:** 2211 South Josephine, Denver, CO 80208, U.S.A.

HARVEY, P(aul) D(ean) A(dshead). British, b. 1930. **Genres:** Geography, History. **Career:** Assistant Archivist, Warwick County Record Office, 1954-56; Assistant Keeper, Dept. of Manuscripts, British Museum, London, 1957-66; University of Southampton, Lecturer, 1966-70, Sr. Lecturer, in Medieval Economic and Social History, 1970-78; University of Durham, Professor 1978-85, Professor Emeritus of Medieval History, 1985-. General Ed.,

Portsmouth Record Series, 1969-2002. **Publications:** (with H. Thorpe) Printed Maps of Warwickshire 1576-1900, 1959; A Medieval Oxfordshire Village: Cuxham 1240-1400, 1965; (with W. Albert) Portsmouth and Sheet Turnpike Commissioners' Minute Book 1711-1754, 1973; Manorial Records of Cuxham, Oxfordshire, circa 1200-1359, 1976; The History of Topographical Maps: Symbols, Pictures and Surveys, 1980; Manorial Records, 1984; Medieval Maps, 1991; Maps in Tudor England, 1993; (with A. McGuinness) Guide to British Medieval Seals, 1996; Mappa Mundi, 1996; Editing Historical Records, 2001. EDITOR: The Peasant Land Market in Medieval England, 1984; (with R.A. Skelton) Local Maps and Plans from Medieval England, 1986. **Address:** Lyndhurst, Farnley Hey Rd, Durham, Durham DH1 4EA, England.

HARVEY, (Brian) Peter. British, b. 1951. **Genres:** Theology/Religion. **Career:** University of Sunderland (formerly Sunderland Polytechnic), Sunderland, England, 1976-, lecturer, then senior lecturer in religious studies and philosophy, reader in Buddhist studies, 1992, professor of Buddhist studies, 1996-. Samatha Trust, meditation teacher, 1977-; adviser on Theravada Buddhism to International Sacred Literature Trust, 1994-; participant in Project on Religion and Reconciliation, Gresham College, London, 1994-; co-founder and secretary of UK Association for Buddhist Studies, 1996-. **Publications:** An Introduction to Buddhism: Teachings, History, and Practices, 1990; The Selfless Mind: Personality, Consciousness and Nirvana in Early Buddhism, 1995; An Introduction to Buddhist Ethics: Foundations, Values and Issues, 2001; (ed.) Buddhism, 2001. **Address:** University of Sunderland, Ryhope Rd, Sunderland SR2 7EE, England.

HARVEY, Robert C. American, b. 1937. **Genres:** Art/Art history, Biography, Cartoons, Humor/Satire. **Career:** Wyandotte High School, Kansas City, KS, English teacher, 1964-69; National Council of Teachers of English, Urbana, IL, assistant director of Educational Resources Information Center Clearinghouse, 1969-70, convention director, 1971-98. Freelance writer and cartoonist; conducts online bi-weekly magazine, www.RCHarvey.com. **Publications:** The Art of the Funnies: An Aesthetic History, 1994; The Art of the Comic Book: An Aesthetic History, 1996; The Genius of Winsor McCay, 1998; Children of the Yellow Kid: The Evolution of the American Comic Strip, 1998; A Gallery of Rogues: Cartoonists' Self-Caricatures, 1999; (with G. Arriola) Accidental Ambassador Gordo: The Comic Strip Art of Gus Arriola, 2000. EDITOR & COMPILER: Cartoons of the Roaring Twenties, Vol. I: 1920-22, 1991, Vol. II, 1923-25, 1992; Milton Caniff Conversations, 2002. Author of the unpublished authorized biography Meanwhile: The Life and Art of Milton Caniff, on file at Ohio State University's Cartoon and Graphic Arts Research Library; contributor of columns, articles, and cartoons to magazines and periodicals. **Address:** 2701 Maplewood Dr, Champaign, IL 61821, U.S.A. **Online address:** RCHarvey@worldnet.att.net; RCHarvey.com

HARVEY, Steven. American, b. 1949. **Genres:** Poetry, Adult non-fiction. **Career:** English teacher at a day school in Charlotte, NC, 1974-76; Young Harris College, Young Harris, GA, professor of English, 1976-. John C; Campbell Folk School, writing instructor, 1995-; Butternut Creek and Friend (folk music group), performer. **Publications:** Powerlines (poems), 1976; A Geometry of Lilies (nonfiction), 1993; Lost in Translation (nonfiction), 1997; (ed.) In a Dark Wood: Personal Essays by Men on Middle Age, 1997. Work represented in anthologies. Contributor of essays, poems, and reviews to periodicals. **Address:** Humanities Division, Young Harris College, Young Harris, GA 30582, U.S.A. **Online address:** sharvey@yhc.edu

HARVEY, Thomas. American, b. 1956. **Genres:** Politics/Government. **Career:** Missionary and educator. Fuxin Mining Institute, Fuxin, China, English instructor; Guangzhou Foreign Language Institute, Guangzhou, China, instructor in American cultural studies; Trinity Avenue Presbyterian Church, Durham, NC, director of Christian education; Trinity Theological College, Singapore, lecturer of systematic theology and ethics, 1997-. **Publications:** Acquainted with Grief: Wang Mingdao's Stand for the Persecuted Church in China, 2002. **Address:** Trinity Theological College, 490 Upper Bukit, Timah 678093, Singapore. **Online address:** Tharvey@ttc.edu.sg

HARVEY-JONES, John (Henry). British, b. 1924. **Genres:** Business/Trade/Industry, Autobiography/Memoirs. **Career:** Imperial Chemical Industries (ICI), London, England, work study officer, 1956, executive in Heavy Organic Chemicals Division, 1956-67, deputy chair of Heavy Organic Chemical Division, 1968, chair of Petrochemicals Division, 1970-73, member of main board, 1973, director of ICI Americas, 1975-76, deputy chair, 1978-82, chair, 1982-87; writer. **Publications:** Making It Happen: Reflections on Leadership, 1988; (with A. Masey) Troubleshooter, 1990; Getting It Together: Memoirs of a Troubleshooter, 1991; Troubleshooter Two, 1992; Managing to Survive: A Guide to Management through the Nineties, 1993; All Together

Now, 1994; Troubleshooter Returns, 1995. **Address:** PO Box 18, Ross-on-Wye, Ross-on-Wye, Herefordshire HR9 7PH, England.

HARVIE, Christopher (Thomas). Scottish, b. 1944. **Genres:** History. **Career:** Open University, Milton Keynes, England, lecturer in history, 1969-80; University of Tuebingen, Germany, professor of British studies, 1980-. Held Labour Party posts, 1962-80; Scottish Centre for Social and Economic Research, vice-president 1990-99; Scottish Association for Public Transport, hon. president, 2002-. **Publications:** War and Society in the Nineteenth Century, 1973; The Lights of Liberalism: University Liberals and the Challenge of Democracy, 1860-1886, 1976; Scotland and Nationalism: Scottish Society and Politics, 1977, rev. ed., 2000; No Gods and Precious Few Heroes: Scotland, 1914-1980, 1981, rev. ed. as No Gods and Precious Few Heroes: Scotland since 1914, 2000; Against Metropolis, 1982; The Centre of Things: Political Fiction in Britain from Disraeli to the Present, 1991; Cultural Weapons: Scotland and Survival in a New Europe, 1992; Fool's Gold: The Story of North Sea Oil, 1994; The Rise of Regional Europe, 1994; Travelling Scot, 1999; Deep-Fried Hillman Imp, 2001; (with P. James) The Road to Home Rule, 2000; Scotland: A Short History, 2002. EDITOR: (with G. Martin and A. Scharf) Industrialisation and Culture, 1830-1914, 1970; (with A. Marwick, C. Knightly, and K. Wrightson) The Illustrated Dictionary of British History, 1981; (with I. Donnachie and I.S. Wood) Forward: Labour Politics in Scotland, 1888-1988, 1989; (and author of intro) J. Buchan, The Thirty Nine Steps, 1993. Contributor to books. **Address:** University of Tuebingen, Wilhelmstrasse 50, 72074 Tuebingen, Germany. **Online address:** christopher.harvie@uni-tuebingen.de

HARVOR, Elisabeth. ((Erica) Elisabeth (Arendt Deichmann) Harvor). Canadian, b. 1936. **Genres:** Novels, Novellas/Short stories, Poetry. **Career:** Concordia University, Montreal, PQ, sessional lecturer, 1986-87, 1995-97, writer-in-residence, 1996-97; York University, Downsview, ON, sessional lecturer in writing program, 1987-93; Ottawa Public Library and Carleton University, writer-in-residence, 1993-94; University of New Brunswick, writer-in-residence, 1994-95, instructor, 1995; Humber School for Writers, Toronto, instructor, 1996-98, 2000-03; Saskatoon Public Library, writer-in-residence, 1998-99; writer. **Publications:** STORIES: Women and Children, 1973, rev. ed. as Our Lady of All the Distances, 1991; If Only We Could Drive Like This Forever, 1988, rev. ed., 2004; Let Me Be the One, 1996. POEMS: Fortress of Chairs, 1992; (ed.) The Long Cold Green Evenings of Spring, 1997; A Room at the Heart of Things (anthology), 1997. NOVELS: Excessive Joy Injures the Heart, 2000; All Times Have Been Modern, 2004. Work represented in anthologies. Contributor of articles, stories, and reviews to periodicals and newspapers. **Address:** c/o Writers' Union of Canada, 40 Wellington St E 3rd Fl, Toronto, ON, Canada M5E 1C7. **Online address:** elisabeth.harvor@sympatico.ca; www.elisabeth-harvor.com

HARWOOD, (Henry) David. British, b. 1938. **Genres:** Children's fiction, Children's non-fiction, Demography, Gerontology/Senior issues. **Career:** Administrative officer, Medical Research Council, London, 1960-66; freelance writer and photographer, 1966-70; Youth and Community Service Officer, Wiltshire County Council, 1970-74; Lecturer/Marketing Officer, Filton College, Bristol, 1974-96; Chief officer, Age Concern South Gloucestershire, 1996-. **Publications:** Scouts in Action, 1963; Scouts on Safari, 1965; The Scout Handbook, 1967; Scouts Indeed!, 1967; Alert to Danger!, 1969; Cub Scouts, 1970; How to Read Maps, 1970; Discover Your Neighbourhood, 1970; Scouts, 1971; The Extension Activities Handbook, 1972; Camping, 1977; Car Games, 1978; Butterflies, 1990; Alumni Relations, 1995; Survey of People Aged 50+ in South Gloucestershire, 1997. EDITOR: (with V. Peters) The Bronze Arrow, 1973; (with V. Peters) The Silver Arrow, 1973; (with V. Peters) The Gold Arrow, 1973; The Cub Scout Annual, 1977-89; The International Cub Scout Book, 1980; Older & Bolder Extending Learning Opportunities for Older People, 1999. **Address:** 4 Prospect Close, Frampton Cotterell, Bristol BS36 2DQ, England.

HARWOOD, Melanie. *See* MURPHEY, Cecil B(laine).

HARWOOD, Ronald. British (born Republic of South Africa), b. 1934. **Genres:** Novels, Plays/Screenplays, Biography, Novellas/Short stories. **Career:** Balliol College, Oxford, visitor in theatre, 1986; English P.E.N., president, 1989-93; International P.E.N., president, 1993. **Publications:** All the Same Shadows (in U.S. as George Washington September Sir!), 1961; The Guilt Merchants, 1963; The Girl in Melanie Klein, 1969; Sir Donald Wolfit: His Life and Work in the Unfashionable Theatre, 1971; One Day in the Life of Ivan Denisovich (screenplay), 1971; Articles of Faith, 1973; The Genoa Ferry, 1976; Cesar and Augusta, 1978; One. Interior. Day. Adventures in the Film Trade, 1978; A Family, 1978; The Dresser, 1980; A Night at the Theatre, 1982; After the Lions, 1982; The Ordeal of Gilbert Pinfold, 1983;

All the World's a Stage, 1984; Tramway Road, 1984; The Deliberate Death of a Polish Priest, 1985; Interpreters, 1985; J.J. Farr, 1987; Ivanov (from Chekhov), 1989; Another Time, 1989; Reflected Glory, 1992; Poison Pen, 1993; Home, 1993; The Faber Book of Theatre, 1993; Taking Sides, 1995; The Handyman, 1996; Quartet, 1999. EDITOR: (co-) New Stories 3, 1978; The Ages of Gielgud, 1984; Dear Alec: Guinness at 75, 1989. **Address:** c/o Judy Daish Assocs, 2 St. Charles Place, London W10 6EG, England.

HASELEY, Dennis. American, b. 1950. **Genres:** Children's fiction, Young adult fiction. **Career:** Teacher and author. Worked as a professional fund raiser and a community organizer. Jewish Board of Family and Children's Services, NYC, therapist, 1982-86; author of books for children, 1982-; private practice in psychotherapy, 1984-. **Publications:** The Scared One, 1983; The Old Banjo, 1983; The Pirate Who Tried to Capture the Moon, 1983; The Soap Bandit, 1984; The Kite Flier, 1986; The Cave of Snores, 1987; The Counterfeiter (young adult novel), 1987; My Father Doesn't Know about the Woods and Me, 1988; Ghost Catcher, 1989; Shadows, 1991; The Thieves' Market, 1991; Ghost Catcher, 1991; Dr. Gravity (young adult novel), 1992; Horses with Wings, 1993; Getting Him (middle-grade novel), 1994; Crosby, 1996. **Address:** c/o Jennifer Flannery, Flannery Literary, 1140 Wickfield Ct., Naperville, IL 60563, U.S.A.

HASHMI, (Aurangzeb) Alamgir. Pakistani, b. 1951. **Genres:** Literary criticism and history, Poetry, Novellas/Short stories. **Career:** Professor and Head of Dept. of English, University of Azad Jammu and Kashmir, Muzaffarabad, Pakistan, 1986-. Literary Ed. and Chief of Publs. Division, PIDE, Islamabad, 1988-. Course Director, Foreign Service Training Institute, Pakistan Ministry of Foreign Affairs, Islamabad, 1988-; Townsend Poetry Prize, founder, 1986-; Standing International Conference Committee on English in South Asia, chairman, 1989-. **Publications:** POETRY: The Oath and Amen, 1976; America Is a Punjabi Word, 1979; An Old Chair, 1979; My Second in Kentucky, 1981; This Time in Lahore, 1983; Neither This Time/Nor That Place, 1984; Inland and Other Poems, 1988; The Poems of Alamgir Hashmi (Collected Poems), 1992; Sun and Moon and Other Poems, 1992; A Choice of Hashmi's Verse, 1997; The Ramaxan Libation, 2003. OTHER: Commonwealth Literature: An Essay Towards the Re-Definition of a Popular/ Counter Culture, 1983; The Commonwealth, Comparative Literature and the World, 1988; Ezra Pound, 1983. EDITOR: Pakistani Literature: The Contemporary English Writers, 2 vols., 1978, rev. ed. as 1 vol., 1987; The Worlds of Muslim Imagination, 1986; Pakistani Short Stories in English, 1997; Postindependence Voices in South Asian Writings, 2001. **Address:** 1542 Service Rd. West, Islamabad G-11/2, Pakistan.

HASKELL, Guy H. American, b. 1956. **Genres:** Area studies, Medicine/ Health. **Career:** Indiana University-Bloomington, associate instructor in Near Eastern languages and culture and in folklore, 1978-80, interim director of B'nai B'rith Hillel Foundation, 1981-82, associate instructor, 1982-85; Oberlin College, Oberlin, OH, lecturer, 1985-88, assistant professor of Judaic and Near Eastern studies, 1988-94, director of Judaic and Near Eastern Studies, 1991-94; Emory University, Atlanta, GA, visiting assistant professor of Judaic and Near Eastern languages and literatures, 1994-; Quinsigamond CC, Dept of EMS, 1999-. Lecturer at colleges and universities. **Publications:** From Sofia to Jaffa: The Jews of Bulgaria and Israel, 1994; Emergency Medical Technician-Basic Pearls of Wisdom, 1999; EMT-Intermediate P.O. W., 1999; Paramedic P.O.W., 2000. Contributor to books. Contributor of articles and reviews to scholarly journals. **Address:** Dept. of EMS, Quinsigamond CC, 670 W Boylston, Worcester, MA 01606, U.S.A. **Online address:** guyh@qcc.mass.edu

HASKELL, Molly. American, b. 1939. **Genres:** Film, Women's studies and issues. **Career:** Sperry Rand, public relations associate; French Film Office, NYC, writer and editor; film critic for Village Voice, Viva, New York Magazine, and Vogue; regular film reviewer for Special Edition, Public Television, and All Things Considered, National Public Radio; Barnard College, NYC, associate professor, 1989; writer. Guest on television shows; lecturer. **Publications:** From Reverence to Rape: The Treatment of Women in the Movies, 1973, rev. ed. 1987; Love and Other Infectious Diseases: A Memoir, 1990; The Last Anniversary (one-act play), 1990; Holding My Own In No Man's Land: Women and Men and Film and Feminists, 1997. **Address:** 19 East 88th St, New York, NY 10128, U.S.A.

HASKINS, Jim. (James S). American, b. 1941. **Genres:** Children's non-fiction, Social commentary, Biography. **Career:** City University of New York, Staten Island Community College, Experimental College, assistant professor, 1970-77; University of Florida, professor of English, 1977-. **Publications:** Diary of a Harlem Schoolteacher, 1969; Resistance, 1970; The War and the Protest: Vietnam, 1971; Revolutionaries, 1971; Profiles in Black

Power, 1972; From Lew Alcindor to Kareem Abdul Jabbar, 1972; (with H.F. Butts) The Psychology of Black Language, 1973; Religions, 1973; Deep Like the Rivers: Biography of Langston Hughes, 1973; Pinckney Benton Stewart Pinchback, 1973; Jobs in Business and Office, 1974; Witchcraft, Mysticism and Magic in the Black World, 1974; Adam Clayton Powell, 1974; Street Gangs, 1974; Ralph Bunche, 1974; Babe Ruth and Hank Aaron, 1974; Snow Sculpture and Ice Carving, 1974; The Creoles of Color of New Orleans, 1975; Fighting Shirley Chisholm, 1975; The Consumer Movement, 1975; The Picture Life of Malcolm X, 1975; Dr. J, 1975; Your Rights, 1975; New Kind of Joy: The Story of the Special Olympics, 1976; Teenage Alcoholism, 1976; The Story of Stevie Wonder, 1976; The Long Struggle, 1976; Pele, 1976; Scott Joplin, 1976; The Life and Death of Martin Luther King, Jr., 1977; Barbara Jordan, 1977; The Cotton Club, 1977; Who Are the Handicapped?, 1978; Voodoo and Hoodoo, 1978; George McGinnis, 1978; The Stevie Wonder Scrapbook, 1978; Bob McAdoo, Superstar, 1978; James Van Der Zee, 1979; Andrew Young, 1979; Gambling, 1979; The New Americans: Vietnamese Boat People, 1980; I'm Gonna Make You Love Me: The Story of Diana Ross, 1980; Werewolves, 1981; Magic, 1982; The Child Abuse Help Book, 1982; The New Americans: Cuban Boat People, 1982; Sugar Ray Leonard, 1982; Black Theater in America, 1982; Katherine Dunham, 1982; Lena, 1983; Bricktop, 1983; Richard Pryor, 1984; Space Challenger: The Story of Guion Bluford, 1984; Nat King Cole, 1984; About Michael Jackson, 1985; Leaders of the Middle East, 1985; Breakdancing, 1985; Diana Ross, 1985; The Statue of Liberty, 1986; Black Music in America, 1987; Queen of the Blues: A Biography of Dinah Washington, 1987; Count Your Way through the Arab World/China/Japan/Russia (4 vols.), 1987; Mabel Mercer, 1988; Corazon Aquino, 1988; Winnie Mandela, 1988; Bill Cosby, 1988; Shirley Temple Black, 1988; (with N.R. Mitgang) Mr. Bojangles: The Biography of Bill Robinson, 1988; (with K. Benson) The Sixties Reader, 1988; India under Indira and Rajiv Gandhi, 1989; Count Your Way through Africa/Canada/Korea/Mexico, 1989; (with L. Hampton) Hamp: An Autobiography, 1989; Count Your Way through Germany/Italy, 1990; Black Dance in America, 1990; Count Your Way through India/Israel, 1991; (with H. Crothers) Scatman, 1991; Outward Dreams, 1991; Christopher Columbus, 1991; Ella Fitzgerald, 1991; (with R. Parks) My Story, 1992; The Day Martin Luther King, Jr., Was Shot, 1992; One More River to Cross, 1992; Amazing Grace, 1992; Against All Opposition: Black Explorers in America, 1992; Colin Powell, 1992; Thurgood Marshall, 1992; Get on Board: The Story of the Underground Railroad, 1992; I Have a Dream, 1992; The Methodist Church, 1992; The March on Washington, 1993; The Headless Haunt and Other African-American Ghost Stories, 1994; The Scottsboro Boys, 1994; The Harlem Renaissance, 1996; The First Black Governor, Pinckney Bentan Stewart, 1996; Count Your Way through Brazil/Greece/ France/Ireland (4 vols.), 1996; Louis Farrakhan and the Nation of Islam, 1996; Power to the People, 1997; Spike Lee, 1997; Separate, but Not Equal, 1997; I Am Rosa Parks, 1997; Bayard Rustin, 1997; Black, Blue and Gray, 1998; African American Entrepreneurs, 1998; Moaning Bones, 1998; African American Military Heroes, 1998; African Beginnings, 1998; Bound for America, 1999; (with K. Benson) Carter G. Woodson, 1999; Distinguished African American Political and Governmental Leaders, 1999; Jesse Jackson, 2000; One Nation under Groove, 2000; (with K. Benson) Out of the Darkness, 2000; Toni Morrison: The Magic of Words, 2000; One Love, One Heart, 2001; (with K. Benson) Following Freedom's Star, 2001; (with K. Benson) Conjure Times, 2001; Champion, 2002; Toni Morrison: Telling a Tale Untold, 2002; Black Stars of the Harlem Renaissance, 2002; Black Stars of Colonial and Revolutionary Times, 2002; Cecil Poole: A Life in the Law, 2000; Black Stars of Civil Rights, 2003; Black Stars of the Civil War Times, 2003. EDITOR: (and contrib.) Black Manifesto for Education, 1973; Jokes from Black Folks, 1973; The Filipino Nation, 3 vols., 1982; Keeping the Faith, 2001. **Address:** 325 West End Ave Apt 7D, New York, NY 10023, U.S.A.

HASKINS, Scott (M.). American, b. 1953. **Genres:** Antiques/Furnishings. **Career:** Private practice as a conservator of fine arts, 1976-77; Ex Monastero della Trinita Museum, intern, 1977-78; Brigham Young University, Provo, UT, director of conservation, 1978-84; Fine Art Conservation Laboratories, Santa Barbara, CA, chief conservator, 1984-, director, 1986-. Shroud of Turin Research Project, participant and consultant. **Publications:** The Emergency Care Book for Your Possessions, 1994; How to Save Your Stuff from a Disaster, 1996. **Address:** Fine Art Conservation Laboratories, P.O. Box 23557, Santa Barbara, CA 93121, U.S.A.

HASLAM, Gerald William. American, b. 1937. **Genres:** Novels, Novellas/ Short stories, Literary criticism and history, Autobiography/Memoirs, Essays, Humor/Satire. **Career:** California State University, Sonoma, professor of English, 1967-97; Sonoma State University, professor emeritus, 1997-. ETC.: A Review of General Semantics, production ed., 1968-70; ECOLIT, Environmental Awareness in the English Class, ed., 1972-80; Everett/

Edwards Inc., Western Writers Series, ed.-in-chief, 1973-80; Literary History of the American West, Editorial Board, member, 1978-87. **Publications:** William Eastlake, 1970; The Language of the Oil Fields, 1972; OKIES: Selected Stories, 1973; Afro-American Oral Literature, 1974; Jack Schaefer, 1976; Masks: A Novel, 1976; The Wages of Sin, 1980; Hawk Flights: Visions of the West, 1983; Snapshots: Glimpses of the Other California, 1985; Voices of a Place, 1987; The Man Who Cultivated Fire, 1987; Coming of Age in California, 1990; That Constant Coyote, 1990; The Other California, 1990; The Great Central Valley: California's Heartland, 1993; Condor Dreams and Other Fictions, 1994; The Great Tejon Club Jubilee, 1996; Workin' Man Blues: Country Music in California, 1999; Manuel and the Madman, 2000; Straight White Male, 2000. EDITOR: Forgotten Pages of American Literature, 1970; Western Writing, 1974; California Heartland, 1978; Many California's, 1992; Jack London's Golden State, 1999. **Address:** PO Box 969, Penngrove, CA 94951, U.S.A. **Online address:** ghaslam@sonic.net

HASLER, Julie. British, b. 1963. **Genres:** Crafts. **Career:** Review (newspaper), St. Albans, England, pasteup artist, 1978-80; freelance designer, writer, model, and film "extra," 1985-. Welwyn Hatfield Line, bus driver, 1986-87. Lecturer on cross-stitch and needlepoint topics; guest on television and radio programs. **Publications:** Cats and Kittens Charted Designs, 1986; Kate Greenaway Alphabet Charted Designs, 1986; Peter Rabbit Iron-On Transfer Patterns, 1987; Wild Flowers in Cross Stitch, 1988; Dogs and Puppies in Cross Stitch, 1988; Kate Greenaway Cross Stitch Designs, 1989; Kate Greenaway Iron-On Transfer Patterns, 1990; The Little Tale of Benjamin Bunny, 1990; The Little Tale of Tom Kitten, 1991; Needlepoint Designs, 1991; Egyptian Charted Designs, 1992; Cats and Kittens in Cross Stitch, 1992; Decorative Charted Designs for Children's Clothing and Accessories, 1993; Wild Animals in Cross Stitch, 1993; The Crafty Cat Workbasket, 1993; (with V. Janitch) Five Hundred Cross Stitch Charted Designs, 1993; Cuddly Cats and Kittens in Cross Stitch, 1993; Silhouettes in Cross Stitch, 1993; Cats: A Cross Stitch Alphabet, 1993; Teddy Bears in Cross Stitch, 1994; Christmas in Cross Stitch, 1994; Julie Hasler's Cross Stitch Designs, 1994; Nursery Cross Stitch, 1995; Clowns in Cross Stitch, 1996; Cross Stitch Gifts for Special Occasions, 1996; (with Janitch) Five Hundred Flower and Animal Charted Designs, 1996; Julie Hasler's Cross Stitch Projects, 1996; Julie Hasler's Fantasy Cross Stitch, Zodiac Signs, Mythical Beasts, and Mystical Characters, 1997; (with Janitch) Five Hundred Alphabets in Cross Stitch, 1998; Needlepoint Cats, 1998; Native American Cross Stitch, 1999. Contributor to needlecraft books and periodicals. **Address:** 561 Howlands, Welwyn Garden City, Herts. AL7 4HT, England.

HASLETT, Adam. American, b. 1970. **Genres:** Novellas/Short stories. **Career:** Writer and attorney. **Publications:** You Are Not a Stranger Here (stories), 2002. Contributor to periodicals. **Address:** c/o Author Mail, Nan A. Talese, Doubleday, 1540 Broadway, New York, NY 10036, U.S.A.

HASLUCK, Nicholas. Australian, b. 1942. **Genres:** Novels, Novellas/Short stories, Poetry. **Career:** Lawyer: admitted to the Supreme Court of Western Australia as barrister and solicitor, 1968. Australia Council, deputy chairman, 1978-82, chairman of Literature Board, 1998-2001. **Publications:** POETRY: Anchor and Other Poems, 1976; (with W. Grono) On the Edge, 1980; (with C. J. Koch) Chinese Journey, 1985. STORIES: The Hat on the Letter O and Other Stories, 1978. NOVELS: Quarantine, 1978; The Blue Guitar, 1980; The Hand That Feeds You, 1982; The Bellarmine Jug, 1984; Truant State, 1987; The Country without Music, 1990; The Blosseville File, 1992; A Grain of Truth, 1994; Our Man K, 1999. ESSAYS: Collage, 1988; Offcuts from a Legal Literary Life, 1993; The Legal Labyrinth, 2003. **Address:** 14 Reserve St, Claremont, WA 6010, Australia. **Online address:** hasluck@iinet.net.au

HASPIEL, Dean. American, b. 1968?. **Genres:** Cartoons. **Career:** Began working as an assistant to comics illustrators Bill Sienkiewicz, Howard Chaykin, and Walter Simonson, c. 1985; Upstart Studios, New York, NY, assistant illustrator; cofounder of Keyhole (mini-comic series), 1995; file clerk at an investment company, New York, NY, c. 1997. **Publications:** Daydream Lullabies: A Billy Dogma Experience, 1999. Creator of the Billy Dogma comic book series, and Opposable Thumbs. **Address:** 335 Court St. Suite #131, Brooklyn, NY 11231, U.S.A. **Online address:** dino@cobite.com

HASSAM, Nick. See CROWTHER, Nick.

HASSAN, Aftab Syed. Pakistani, b. 1952. **Genres:** Education, Information science/Computers. **Career:** Georgetown University, Washington, DC, program coordinator for health careers programs, Department of Community and Academic Family Medicine, 1983-87; Betz Publishing Co. Inc., Rockville, MD, technical editor and coordinating author for Medical College Admission Test and Dental Admission Test books, 1984-90, director of Divi-

sion of Scientific and Educational Research, 1991-94; Williams & Wilkins Educational Services, Rockville, vice-president for academic development and strategic planning, 1994-. Emerson Preparatory Institute, head of mathematics and science department, 1979-89; Charles R. Drew University of Medicine and Science, consulting professor, 1985-86. **Publications:** (with A. Braestrup) Skills Development in Reading, Writing, and Quantitative on the MCAT, 4th ed, 1984; (with Braestrup) The MCAT Primer, 1985; (Co-author) A Complete Preparation for the MCAT, 4th ed, 1989, 6th ed, 1991; (with L. Anderson, R. Gordon, and J.D. Zubkowski) Preparing for the DAT, 1992; Establishing Nonparametric Discrimination Variables with Frequency Analysis for Two Pseudo-Identical Manuscripts, 1992; Design of Biological Sciences Software: Using Immersion Approach with Enhanced Problem Solving, 1992; (with Anderson, Gordon, and Zubkowski) Dental Admission Test: The Betz Guide, 1993; A Personal MCAT Prep Planner, 1993; Preparing for the Optometry Admission Test: The Betz Guide, 2nd ed, 1993; Allied Health Professions Admission Test: The Betz Guide, 1994; Pharmacy College Admission Test: The Betz Guide, 1994; Veterinary Entrance Tests (V.E. T.): The Betz Guide, 1995. Some writings appear under the name Richard Hassan. **Address:** American Soc. Landscape Assoc., 636 Eye St. N.W., Washington, DC 20001-3736, U.S.A.

HASSAN, Ihab (Habib). American (born Egypt), b. 1925. **Genres:** Literary criticism and history, Autobiography/Memoirs. **Career:** Vilas Research Professor of English and Comparative Literature, University of Wisconsin at Milwaukee, 1970-. Instructor of English, Rensselaer Polytechnic Institute, Troy, NY, 1952-54; assistant professor, 1954-58, associate professor, 1958-62, professor, 1962-63, Benjamin L. Waite Professor of English, 1963-70, chairman of the Dept. of English, 1963-64, 1968-69, director of the College of Letters, 1964-66, and director of the Center for the Humanities, 1969-70, Wesleyan University, Middletown, CT; Guggenheim fellow, 1958-59, 1962-63; Fulbright lecturer, Grenoble, France, 1966-67, Nice, 1974-75; visiting fellow, Woodrow Wilson International Center, 1972; Fulbright distinguished lecturer, Kyoto American Studies Seminars, 1975; resident scholar, Rockefeller Bellagio Study Center, 1978; director, NEH Summer Seminars, 1982, 1984, 1989; fellow, Research Humanities Institute, University of California, Irvine, 1990; fellow, Humanities Research Center, National Australian University, Canberra, 1990, 2003; visiting professor, Seijo University, Tokyo, 1991; lecturer, Scandinavian Summer School of Literature & Theory, 2000, 2001, 2004. **Publications:** Radical Innocence: Studies in the Contemporary American Novel, 1961; Crise du Heros dans le Roman Americain Contemporain 1963; The Literature of Silence: Henry Miller and Samuel Beckett, 1967; The Dismemberment of Orpheus, 1971; Contemporary American Literature: An Introduction, 1973; Paracriticisms: Seven Speculations of the Times, 1975; The Right Promethean Fire: Imagination, Science, and Cultural Change, 1980; Out of Egypt: Scenes and Fragments of an Autobiography, 1986; The Postmodern Turn (essays), 1987; Selves at Risk: Patterns of Quest in Contemporary American Letters, 1990; Rumors of Change (essays), 1995; Between the Eagle and the Sun: Traces of Japan, 1996. EDITOR: Liberations: New Essays on the Humanities in Revolution, 1971; (with S. Hassan) Innovation/Renovation: New Perspectives on the Humanities, 1983. **Address:** 2137 N Terrace Ave, Milwaukee, WI 53202-1338, U.S.A.

HASSELSTROM, Linda (Michele). American, b. 1943. **Genres:** Poetry, Adult non-fiction, Environmental sciences/Ecology, Autobiography/Memoirs. **Career:** Writer, rancher, and educator. Cattle rancher, SD, 1953-; Sioux City Journal, IA, reporter, night staff, 1965-66; Christian College (now Columbia College), Columbia, MO, teacher of journalism, and director of student publications, 1966-69; University of Missouri-Columbia, instructor in English, 1969-71; Lame Johnny Press, Hermosa, SD, owner and publisher, 1971-85; Sunday Clothes, editor, 1971-82; National College, Rapid City, SD, instructor in English, 1987-88; Black Hills State College, Ellsworth AFB branch, SD, instructor in English, 1987-88; Oglala Lakota College, Rapid City, SD, teacher, 1989; South Dakota School of Mines, Rapid City, professor of English, 1989-90. **Publications:** NONFICTION AND POETRY: Windbreak: A Woman Rancher on the Northern Plains, 1987; Going over East: Reflections of a Woman Rancher, 1987; Land Circle: Writings Collected from the Land (poems and essays), 1991; Dakota Bones: The Collected Poems of Linda Hasselstrom, 1992; A Roadside History of South Dakota, 1994; Bison: Monarch of the Plains, 1998; Feels Like Far, 1999; Bitter Creek Junction, 2000. EDITOR: Journal of a Mountain Man: James Clyman, 1984; (with N. Curtis and G. Collier) Leaning into the Wind (anthology), 1997; (with G. Collier and N. Curtis) Woven on the Wind, 2001; Between Grass and Sky, 2002; Crazy Woman Creek, 2004. Contributor to books and periodicals. **Address:** Windbreak House Retreats for Women, PO Box 169, Hermosa, SD 57744, U.S.A. **Online address:** info@windbreakhouse.com; www.windbreakhouse.com

HASSEN, Philip Charles. American, b. 1943. **Genres:** Medicine/Health. **Career:** Washtenaw County Community Mental Health Center, Ann Arbor,

MI, mental health specialist, 1971-73; Metro-Calgary and Rural General Hospital District No. 93, Calgary, Alberta, Canada, assistant administrator at Rockyview General Hospital, 1974-76, assistant administrator at Holy Cross Hospital, 1976-78; Foothills Provincial General Hospital, Calgary, assistant executive director of services, 1978-81, executive vice president, 1981-87; The Toronto Hospital, Toronto Western Division, Toronto, Ontario, Canada, chief operating officer and senior vice president, 1987-88; St. Joseph's Health Centre, London, Ontario, president, 1988-. School of Public Health, University of Michigan, guest lecturer, 1972-76; Faculty of Medicine, University of Calgary, assistant professor, 1978-87; University of Toronto, Department of Health Administration, lecturer, 1988-; University of Western Ontario, Department of Medicine, guest lecturer, 1989. **Publications:** (with S. Lindenburger) Rx for Hospitals: New Hope for Medicare in the Nineties, 1993. Contributor to professional journals. **Address:** Ministry of Health & Long-Term Care, 80 Grosveneur St., 10th Floor, Hepburn Block, Toronto, ON, Canada M7A 1R9.

HASSLER, Donald M(ackey). American, b. 1937. **Genres:** Science fiction/ Fantasy, Poetry, Literary criticism and history. **Career:** Crowell-Collier Encyclopedia, NYC, writer, 1960; University of Montreal, instructor of English, 1961-65; Kent State University, Kent, OH, instructor through associate professor of English, 1965-77, director of experimental progs., 1973-83, professor of English, 1977-, coordinator of Writing Certificate Program, 1986-. Extrapolation, co-editor, 1986-89, editor, 1990-2002, executive editor, 2002-; Hellas, advisory editor, 1990-. **Publications:** The Comedian as Letter D: Erasmus Darwin's Comic Materialism, 1973; (co-author) On Weighing a Pound of Flesh (verse), 1973; Erasmus Darwin, 1974; Comic Tones in Science Fiction, 1982; Hal Clement, 1982; Patterns of the Fantastic, 1983; Patterns of the Fantastic II, 1984; (co-ed.) Death and the Serpent! Immortality in Science Fiction and Fantasy, 1985; Isaac Asimov, 1991; (co-ed.) The Letters of Arthur Machen to Montgomery Evans, 1994; (co-ed.) Political Science Fiction, 1997. **Address:** 1226 Woodhill Dr, Kent, OH 44240, U.S.A. **Online address:** extrap@kent.edu

HASSLER, Jon (Francis). American, b. 1933. **Genres:** Novels, Children's fiction, Young adult fiction. **Career:** High sch. English teacher in Minnesota, 1955-65; Instructor in English, Bemidji State University, Bemidji, MN, 1965-68, and Brainerd Community College, Brainerd, MN, 1968-80; St. John's University, Collegeville, MN, Writer-in-Residence, 1980-97, Regent's Professor Emeritus, 1997-. **Publications:** NOVELS: Staggerford, 1977; Simon's Night, 1979; The Love Hunter, 1981; A Green Journey, 1985; Grand Opening, 1987; North of Hope, 1990; Dear James, 1993; Rookery Blues, 1995; The Dean's List, 1997; Keepsakes and Other Stories, 1999; Underground Christmas, 1999; My Staggerford Journal, 1999; Rufus at the Door and Other Stories, 2000; Good People, 2001; The Staggerford Flood, 2002. FOR CHILDREN: Four Miles to Pinecone, 1977; Jemmy, 1980. **Address:** Dept. of English, St. John's University, Collegeville, MN 56321, U.S.A.

HASSMANN, Rhoda E. See **HOWARD-HASSMANN, Rhoda E.**

HASTINGS, Brooke. See **GORDON, Deborah Hannes.**

HASTINGS, Graham. See **JEFFRIES, Roderic.**

HASTINGS, Max M(acdonald). British, b. 1945. **Genres:** History, Military/ Defense/Arms control, Biography, Documentaries/Reportage. **Career:** Freelance writer, broadcaster and journalist, London, 1973-. Sunday Times, London, contributor; BBC-TV, researcher, 1963-64, roving correspondent, 1970-73; The Evening Standard newspaper, London, reporter, 1965-67, 1968-70, editor, 1996-2001; World Press Institute, St. Paul, Minnesota, fellow, 1967-68; The Daily Telegraph, London, editor, 1986-95. Somerset Maugham Prize, 1979; Journalist of the Year, 1982; Granada TV Reporter of the Year, 1982; What the Paper Say, Granada TV: Editor of the Year, 1988. **Publications:** America 1968: The Fire This Time, 1968; Ulster 1969: The Struggle for Civil Rights in Northern Ireland, 1970; Montrose, The King's Champion, 1977; Yoni, Hero of Entebbe, 1979; Bomber Command, 1979; (with others) The Battle of Britain, 1980; Das Reich, 1981; (with S. Jenkins) The Battle for the Falklands, 1983; Overlord, 1984; (ed.) The Oxford Book of Military Anecdotes, 1985; The Korean War, 1987; Outside Days, 1989; Scattered Shots, 1999; Going to the Wars, 2000; Editor: A Memoir, 2002. **Address:** Northcliffe House, 2 Derry St, London W8 5EE, England.

HASTINGS, Michael. British, b. 1938. **Genres:** Novels, Plays/Screenplays, Poetry, Biography. **Publications:** NOVELS: The Game, 1957; The Frauds, 1960; Tussy Is Me, 1970; The Nightcomers, 1972; And In the Forest the Indians, 1975. OTHER: Love Me, Lambeth (poems), 1961; Three Plays,

1966; Rupert Brooke: The Handsomest Young Man in England, 1967; Bart's Mornings and Other Tales of Modern Brazil, 1975; Sir Richard Burton, 1978; Three Plays, 1980; Two Plays, 1981; Stars of the Roller State Disco, 1984; Tom and Viv (play), 1985, 1994; (with J. Miller) The Emperor, 1987; Three Political Plays, 1988; (trans) Roberto Cossa, La Nona, 1989; A Dream of People, 1990; (trans) Ariel Dorfman, Death and the Maiden, 1991; Unfinished Business, 1994; Unfinished Business and Other Plays, 1994. **Address:** 2 Helix Gardens, London SW2, England.

HASTORF, Christine Ann. American, b. 1950. **Genres:** Archaeology/ Antiquities, Anthropology/Ethnology. **Career:** US Geological Survey, Division of Western Regional Geology, Menlo Park, CA, archaeologist, 1977-79, 1980-82; University of Minnesota-Twin Cities, Minneapolis, assistant professor, 1983-90, associate professor of anthropology, 1990-93, director of Archaeobotany Laboratory, 1983-93; University of California, Berkeley, associate professor of anthropology, 1994-. Guest lecturer at universities. Conducted extensive field work in the Peruvian Andes; adviser to field teams in Bolivia and Denmark. **Publications:** (ed. with V. Popper, and contrib.) Current Paleoethnobotany: Analytical Methods and Cultural Interpretation of Archaeological Plant Remains, 1988; (ed. with M.W. Conkey, and contrib.) The Uses of Style in Archaeology, 1990, 2nd ed, 1993; Agriculture and the Onset of Political Inequality before the Inka, 1993; (ed. with S. Johannessen, and contrib.) Corn and Culture in the Prehistoric New World, 1994. Work represented in anthologies. Contributor of articles and reviews to professional journals. **Address:** Department of Anthropology, University of California, Berkeley, CA 94720, U.S.A.

HASTY, Will. American. **Genres:** Literary criticism and history. **Career:** Educator. Illinois Wesleyan University, Department of Foreign Languages, assistant professor, 1987-88; Yale University, Department of Germanic Languages and Literatures, assistant professor, 1988-93, director of undergraduate studies, 1992-93; University of Florida, Department of Germanic and Slavic Studies, associate professor, coordinator of undergraduate studies, 1993-99, professor, 1999-. University of Birmingham, England, Department of German Studies, visiting professor, 1999-2000. **Publications:** Adventures as Social Performance: A Study of the German Court Epic, 1990; Adventures in Interpretation: The Works of Hartmann von Aue and Their Critical Reception, 1996. EDITOR: (with J. Hardin; and contrib.) Dictionary of Literary Biography, Vol 138: German Writers and Works of the High Middle Ages, 1170-1280, 1994; (with J. Hardin; and contrib) Dictionary of Literary Biography, Vol 148: German Writers and Works of the Early Middle Ages, 800-1170, 1995; (with C. Merkes-Frei) Werkheft Literatur: Sinasi Dikmen und Zehra Cirak, 1996; A Companion to Wolfram's Parzival, 1999. Contributor of articles and reviews to publications. **Address:** Department of Germanic and Slavic Studies, 263 Dauer Hall, University of Florida, Gainesville, FL 32611, U.S.A.

HASWELL, Janis Tedesco. American, b. 1950. **Genres:** Literary criticism and history, Young adult non-fiction. **Career:** University of the Incarnate Word, San Antonio, TX, assistant professor of English, 199394; Washington State University, Pullman, visiting assistant professor of English, 1994-96; Texas A&M University-Corpus Christi, associate professor of English, 1996-. **Publications:** (with J. Popham) Introduction to the Raj Quartet, 1985; Pressed against Divinity: W.B. Yeats and the Feminine Mask, 1997; Paul Scott's Philosophy of Place(s): The Fiction of Relationality, 2002. **Address:** Dept of English, Texas A&M University-Corpus Christi, 6300 Ocean Dr, Corpus Christi, TX 78412-5813, U.S.A. **Online address:** jhaswell@falcon. tamucc.edu

HASWELL, Richard H(enry). American, b. 1940. **Genres:** Education. **Career:** Washington State University, Pullman, professor of English, 1962-96; Texas A & M University-Corpus Christi, Haas Professor of English, 1996-. **Publications:** Gaining Ground in College Writing: Tales of Development and Interpretation, 1991; (with M.-Z. Lu) Comp Tales: An Introduction to College Composition through Its Stories, 2000. EDITOR: (with J. Ehrstine) A Baker's Dozen, 1979, 3rd ed., 1992; (with Ehrstine and R. Wilkinson) The HBJ Reader, 1987; Beyond Outcomes: Assessment and Instruction within a University Writing Program, 2001. Contributor of scholarly articles to professional journals. Translator from Spanish and French. **Address:** Department of English, Texas A & M University-Corpus Christi, Corpus Christi, TX 78412, U.S.A.

HATAB, Lawrence J. American, b. 1946. **Genres:** Philosophy. **Career:** Old Dominion University, Norfolk, VA, teacher of philosophy, 1976-, Faculty Senate, 1980-88, department head, 1994-00. **Publications:** Nietzsche and Eternal Recurrence: The Redemption of Time and Becoming, 1978; Myth and Philosophy: A Contest of Truths, 1990; A Nietzschean Defense of

Democracy: An Experiment in Postmodern Politics, 1995; Ethics and Finitude: Heideggerian Contributions to Moral Philosophy, 2000. Contributor to books. Contributor of articles and reviews to academic journals. **Address:** Department of Philosophy, Old Dominion University, Norfolk, VA 23529, U.S.A. **Online address:** lhatab@odu.edu

HATCH, Lynda S. American, b. 1950. **Genres:** Travel/Exploration, Local history/Rural topics, Education. **Career:** Clover Park School District, Tacoma, WA, teacher, 1971-72; Hillsboro Elementary District, Hillsboro, OR, teacher, 1972-78; Bend-La Pine Public Schools, Bend, OR, teacher and elementary curriculum specialist, 1978-90; Northern Arizona University, Flagstaff, associate professor and coordinator of elementary education, chair of Instructional Leadership, 1990-99; Washington State University, Pullman, Boeing Distinguished Professor of Science Education, 1999-. Adjunct professor at Oregon State University, Portland State University, and the University of Oregon; consultant in science, math, and language arts to schools around the world. Selected as a Great Explorations in Math and Science Associate II, Lawrence Hall of Science, University of California, Berkeley, 1994, and for international workshop presentations, National Science Teachers Association, 1991-95; presents workshops and lectures on education, the Oregon Trail, bookbinding, informal education, Russian culture, and other topics. **Publications:** PATHWAYS OF AMERICA SERIES: The Oregon Trail, 1994; Lewis and Clark, 1994; The California Gold Rush Trail, 1994; The Santa Fe Trail, 1995. OTHER: Tools for Teachers: Teaching Curriculum for Home and the Classroom (18 guides), 1994-; Fifty States, 1996; U.S. Presidents, 1996; U.S. Map Skills, 1996; National Parks and Other Park Service Sites, 1999; Our National Parks, 1999; the California Mission Trail, 2000; Festivals and Celebrations, 2000; Endangered Species, 2001. Contributor to professional periodicals. **Address:** Dept of Teaching and Learning, Washington State University, PO Box 642132, Cleveland 333, Pullman, WA 99164-2132, U.S.A. **Online address:** lhatch@wsu.edu

HATCH, Michael F. (Hatch). American, b. 1947. **Genres:** Novels, Administration/Management. **Career:** Has worked as a farm hand, fruit picker, mechanic, machinist, race car driver, industrial engineer, computer programmer, business executive, and management consultant; University of Wisconsin-Oshkosh, Oshkosh, WI, adjunct instructor, 1993-. **Publications:** (as Mike Hatch) Horseshoes and Nuclear Weapons (novel), 1997; Production and Inventory Control Handbook-Manufacturing Resource Planning, 1997; Take It to the Limit, 1998. **Address:** University of Wisconsin-Oshkosh, 800 Algoma Blvd., COBA, Oshkosh, WI 54901, U.S.A. **Online address:** hatch@uwosh.edu

HATCHER, Robin Lee. American, b. 1951. **Genres:** Novels, Romance/Historical. **Career:** Novelist. Public speaker. **Publications:** ROMANCE NOVELS: Stormy Surrender, 1984; Heart's Landing, 1984; Thorn of Love, 1985; Heart Storm, 1986; Passion's Gamble, 1986; Pirate's Lady, 1987; Gemfire, 1988; The Wager, 1989; Dream Tide, 1990; Promised Sunrise, 1990; Rugged Splendor, 1991; Promise Me Spring, 1991; The Hawk and the Heather, 1992; Devlin's Promise, 1992; A Frontier Christmas (novella collection), 1992; Midnight Rose, 1992; The Magic, 1993; Where the Heart Is, 1993; Forever, Rose, 1994; Remember When, 1994; A Purrfect Romance (novella collection), 1995; Liberty Blue, 1995; Chances Are, 1996; Kiss Me, Katie!, 1996; Dear Lady, 1997; Patterns of Love, 1998; In His Arms, 1998; Hometown Girl, 1999; Taking Care of the Twins, 1999; Daddy Claus, 1999. CHRISTIAN FICTION: The Forgiving Hour, 1999; Whispers from Yesterday, 1999; The Shepherd's Voice, 2000; The Story Jar, 2001; Ribbon of Years, 2001; Firstborn, 2002; Promised to Me, 2003. Contributor to periodicals. **Address:** PO Box 4722, Boise, ID 83711, U.S.A. **Online address:** robinlee@robinleehatcher.com

HATFIELD, Kate. See WRIGHT, Daphne.

HATFIELD, Phyllis. American, b. 1944. **Genres:** Biography. **Career:** Freelance book editor and writer. **Publications:** Pencil Me In: A Memoir of Stanley Olson, 1994.

HATHORN, Libby. Australian, b. 1943. **Genres:** Novels, Novellas/Short stories, Children's fiction, Plays/Screenplays, Songs/Lyrics and libretti, Education. **Career:** Teacher and librarian in schools in Sydney, 1965-81, deputy principal, 1977; consultant and senior education officer for government adult education programs, 1981-86; full-time writer, 1987-. Sydney University, occasional lecturer in English and children's literature, 1982-; writer in residence, University of Technology, Sydney, 1990, Woollahra Library, 1992; and Edith Cowan University, 1992. Speaker for student, teacher, and parent groups. **Publications:** FOR CHILDREN. FICTION: Stephen's Tree, 1979; Lachlan's Walk, 1980; The Tram to Bondi Beach,

1981; Paolo's Secret, 1985; All about Anna, 1986; Looking Out for Sampson, 1987, screenplay, 1988; Freya's Fantastic Surprise, 1988; The Extraordinary Magics of Emma McDade, 1989; Stuntumble Monday, 1989; The Garden of the World, 1989; Thunderwith, 1989; Jezza Says, 1990; So Who Needs Lotto?, 1990; Love Me Tender, 1992; The Lenski Kids and Dracula, 1992; Valley under the Rock, 1993; Way Home, 1993; Feral Kid, 1994; Grandma's Shoes, 1994; The Wonder Thing, 1995; What a Star, 1994; The Climb, 1996; Chrysalis, 1997; Rift, 1998; Sky Sash So Blue, 1998; Magical Ride, 1999; The Gift, 2000; Wattle Pattern Plate, 2001; The River, 2001; The Wishing Cupboard, 2002; Over the Moon, 2003. POETRY: Talks with My Skateboard, 1991. OTHER: (ed) The Blue Dress (stories), 1991; Help for Young Writers, 1991; Good to Read (textbook), 1991; Who? (stories), 1992. FOR YOUNG ADULTS. FICTION: Ghostop, 1999; (with G. Crew) Dear Venny, Dear Saffron, 1999; The Painter, 2001. POETRY: Volcano Boy, 2001. FOR ADULTS: (with G. Bates) Half-Time, 1987; Better Strangers (stories), 1989; Damascus, a Rooming House (libretto), 1990; The Maroubra Cycle: A Journey around Childhood (performance poetry), 1990; The Blue Dress Suite (music theater), 1991; Grandma's Shoes (libretto); The Echo of Thunder (screenplay), 1999. **Address:** c/o Joel Gotler, Artists Management Group, 9465 Wiltshire Blvd, Beverly Hills, CA 90212, U.S.A. **Online address:** www.libbyhathorn.com

HATKOFF, Amy. American. **Genres:** Film, Social work, Writing/Journalism. **Career:** Children's Aid Society, Homeless Families Service Program, NYC, volunteer director and special events coordinator, 1987-89; Women's Group (support group), NYC, founder, 1988, director, 1988-; The Hadar Foundation, executive director, 1993-96; ParentWise, founder; Jewish Book of Family and Children's Services, 2001-. Producer of films: Neglect Not the Children, for public television, 1989-92; also worked in films and for television networks, including CBS-TV; consultant. **Publications:** (with K.K. Klopp) How to Save the Children, 1992. Contributor to periodicals. **Address:** 136 E. 76th St. Apt 6E, New York, NY 10021, U.S.A. **Online address:** alhatkoff@aol.com

HATLEY, Allen G., Jr. American, b. 1930. **Genres:** Earth sciences, History. **Career:** Standard Oil Co., NJ and Philippines, geologist, 1955-61; Cabeen Exploration, Philippines and Peru, general manager, 1961-67; Cities Service Company, Singapore and Houston, TX, vice president, eastern hemisphere, 1972-82; Murexco Petroleum Co., Dallas, TX, president and CEO, 1985-87; law enforcement jobs, 1988-92, 1998-2001. Elected Constable, Precinct 4, Bandera Co., 1992-98; consultant. **Publications:** The Oil Finders, A Collection of Stories about Exploration, 1995; Texas Constables, A Frontier Heritage, 1999; The Indian Wars in Stephen F. Austin's Texas Colony, 2001; Bringing the Law to Texas, 2002; The First Texas Legion during the American Civil War, 2004. Contributor to publications. **Address:** PO Box 506, Eagle Lake, TX 77434, U.S.A. **Online address:** allen@elc.net

HATOUM, Milton. Brazilian, b. 1952. **Genres:** Poetry, Novels. **Career:** University of Amazonas Manaus, Brazil, professor of French Literature, 1983-; journalist and writer. **Publications:** Um rio entre ruinas (poetry), 1978; Relato de um Certo Oriente (novel), 1989, English trans. as The Tree of the Seventh Heaven, 1994. Contributor of short stories and articles to periodicals. Translator for Brazilian edition of Salman Rushdie's Haroun and the Sea of Stories. **Address:** Rua Recife, 1128 casa 14-B, 69057-002 Manaus, Amazonas, Brazil.

HATTENDORF, John B(rewster). American, b. 1941. **Genres:** History, Local history/Rural topics, Marine sciences/Oceanography, Military/Defense/Arms control, Transportation, Travel/Exploration. **Career:** U.S. Naval War College, Newport, RI, instructor and research associate, 1972-73, from assistant professor to associate professor of strategy, 1977-81, professor of naval history, 1983-84, Ernest J. King professor of maritime history, 1984-, director of department of advanced research, 1988-2003, chairman, Maritime History Dept, 2003-. Visiting professor, National University of Singapore, 1981-83, and University of Freiburg, 1991; member of faculty, Salve Regina College, 1988-92, and Frank Munson Institute of American Maritime History, 1990-, director, 1995-2001; St. Antony's College, Oxford, senior associate member, 1986; Pembroke College, Oxford, visiting fellow, 2000-02. Assistant head of ships' histories section and research section, Office of the Chief of Naval Operations, naval history division, 1967-69; exchange researcher at German Armed Forces Military History Research Office, U.S. Department of Defense, 1990-91. **Publications:** A Dusty Path, 1964; (with J.D. Hayes) The Writings of Stephen B. Luce, 1975; On His Majesty's Service, 1983; (with B.M. Simpson III and J.R. Wadleigh) Sailors and Scholars, 1984; Two Beginnings, 1984; England in the War of the Spanish Succession, 1987; The Evolution of the U.S. Navy's Maritime Strategy, 1977-1987, 1989; (with D.H. King and W. Estes) A Sea of Words, 1995;

(with D.H. King) Harbors and High Seas, 1996; (with D.H. King) Every Man Will Do His Duty, 1997; (with others) America and the Sea, 1998; John Robinson's Account of Sweden, 1688, 1998; Naval History and Maritime Strategy (essays), 2000; Semper Endem, 2001; The Boundless Deep, 2003; The Evolution of the U.S. Navy's Maritime Strategy, 2004; Newport, the French Navy, and the American Independence, 2004. EDITOR: (with R.S. Jordan) Maritime Strategy and the Balance of Power, 1989; (with M.H. Murfett) The Limitations of Military Power, 1990; Mahan on Naval Strategy, 1991; The Influence of History on Mahan, 1991; (with others) British Naval Documents, 1704-1960, 1993; (with T. Goldrick) Mahan Is Not Enough, 1993; Ubi Sumus?, 1994; Maritime History, 1995, vol. 2: The 18th Century and the Classic Age of Sail, 1997; St. Barthelemy and the Swedish West Indies Company, 1995; Josiah Burchert's Transaction, 1995; Doing Naval History (essays), 1995; Naval Policy and Strategy in the Mediterranean, 1999; (with R.W. Unger) War at Sea in the Middle Ages and the Renaissance, 2002. **Address:** Maritime History Dept (Code 37), U.S. Naval War College, 686 Cushing Rd, Newport, RI 02841-1207, U.S.A. **Online address:** hattendj@nwc.navy.mil

HATTERSLEY, Roy (Sydney George). British, b. 1932. **Genres:** Autobiography/Memoirs, Biography, Novels, Politics/Government. **Career:** Parliamentary Private Secretary, Minister of Pensions and National Insurance, 1964-67; Labour Member of Parliament (U.K.) for Sparkbrook div. of Birmingham, 1964-97; Parliamentary Secretary, Ministry of Labour, 1967-68, and Dept. of Employment and Productivity, 1968-69; Minister of Defence for Administration, 1969-70; Labour Party Spokesman on Defence, 1972, and on Education, 1972-74; Minister of State, Foreign and Commonwealth Office, 1974-76; Secretary of State for Prices and Consumer Protection, 1976-79; Opposition Spokesman on Home Affairs, 1980-83, and on Treasury Affairs, 1983-87; Deputy Leader of the Labour Party, 1983-92; Opposition Spokesman on Home Affairs, 1987-92. Columnist for the Guardian, 1981-; Columnist, Lustie, 1980-81, 1988-. Journalist and Health Service Executive, 1956-64; Member of City Council, Sheffield, 1957-65; Director, Campaign for a European Political Community, 1966-67; Columnist, Punch, 1982-88. **Publications:** Nelson: A Biography, 1974; Goodbye to Yorkshire, 1976; Politics Apart, 1982; A Yorkshire Boyhood, 1983; Press Gang, 1983; Endpiece Revisited, 1984; Choose Freedom, 1987; The Maker's Mark, 1990; In That Quiet Earth, 1991; Skylark's Song, 1993; Between Ourselves, 1994; Who Goes Home?, 1995; Fifty Years On: A Prejudiced History of Britain since the War, 1997; Buster's Diaries As Told to Roy Hattersley, 1998; Blood and Fire: The Story of William and Catherine Booth and Their Salvation Army, 1999. **Address:** 59 St Martin's Lane, London WC2N 4JS, England.

HAUG, James. American, b. 1954. **Genres:** Poetry. **Career:** Poet. **Publications:** POETRY: The Stolen Car, 1989; Walking Liberty, 1999; Fox Luck, 1998. Contributor to publications. **Address:** 15 Washington Ave, Northampton, MA 01060, U.S.A. **Online address:** alix1@comcast.net

HAUGAARD, Erik (Christian). Danish, b. 1923. **Genres:** Children's fiction, Novellas/Short stories. **Publications:** Hakon of Rogen's Saga, 1963; A Slave's Tale, 1965; Orphans of the Wind, 1966; The Little Fishes, 1967; The Rider and His Horse, 1968; The Untold Tale, 1971; (trans.) The Complete Fairy Tales and Stories of Hans Andersen, 1974; A Messenger for Parliament, 1976; Cromwell's Boy, 1978; Chase Me, Catch Nobody, 1980; Leif the Unlucky, 1982; A Boy's Will, 1983; The Samurai's Tale, 1984; Prince Boghole, 1987; Princess Horrid, 1990; The Boy and the Samurai, 1991; The Story of Yuriwaka, 1991; The Death of Mr. Angel, 1992; Under the Black Flag, 1994; The Revenge of the Forty-seven Samurai, 1995; (trans.) Thumbelina, 1997. **Address:** Toad Hall, Ballydehob, Cork, Ireland.

HAUGHT, James A(lbert), (Jr.). American, b. 1932. **Genres:** Theology/Religion, Children's non-fiction, Sex. **Career:** Daily Mail, Charleston, WV, apprentice printer, 1951-53; Gazette, Charleston, reporter, 1953-, full-time investigator, 1970-82, associate editor, 1983-92, editor, 1993-. Press aide to Senator Robert C. Byrd of West Virginia, 1959; Free Inquiry magazine, senior editor (part-time), 1996-. **Publications:** Holy Horrors: An Illustrated History of Religious Murder and Madness, 1990; Science in a Nanosecond: Illustrated Answers to 100 Basic Science Questions (for children), 1990; The Art of Lovemaking: An Illustrated Tribute, 1992; Holy Hatred: Religious Conflicts of the '90s, 1994; 2000 Years of Disbelief: Famous People with the Courage to Doubt, 1996. Contributor to magazines. **Address:** The Charleston Gazette, 1001 Virginia St E, Charleston, WV 25301, U.S.A. **Online address:** haught@wvinter.net; haught@wvgazette.com

HAUGHTON, Rosemary Luling. British/American, b. 1927. **Genres:** Novels, Children's non-fiction, Mythology/Folklore, Theology/Religion,

Philosophy. **Career:** Writer, lecturer. Wellspring House, Inc, associate director. **Publications:** Jesus With Me, 1950; Therese Martin: The Story of St. Therese of Lisieux, 1957; The Family Book, 1959; The Children: Heirs to the Kingdom, 1961; Six Saints for Parents, 1962; The Family God Chose, 1964; The Young St. Mark, 1964; A Home for God's Family, 1965; The Carpenter's Son, 1965; The Boy from the Lake, 1965; Beginning Life in Christ: The Gospel in Christian Education, 1966; On Trying to be Human, 1966; The Young Moses, 1966; The Young Thomas More, 1966; (with A. M. Cocagnac) Bible for Young Christians: The Old Testament, 1966; The Transformation of Man, 1967; (with Cardinal Heenan) Dialogue: The State of the Church Today, 1968; Why Be a Christian?, 1968; Elizabeth's Greeting, 1968; Matthew's Good News of Jesus, 1968; John's Good News of Jesus, 1968; Act of Love, 1969; Holiness of Sex, 1969; Why the Epistles Were Written, 1972; The Theology of Experience (in U.K. as The Knife-Edge of Experience), 1972; Love, 1973; In Search of Tomorrow, 1973; Tales From Eternity, 1974; The Liberated Heart, 1975; The Gospel Where It Hits Us, 1975; The Drama of Salvation, 1976; Feminine Spirituality, 1977; The Catholic Thing, 1980; The Passionate God, 1980; The Re-Creation of Eve, 1985; Song in a Strange Land: The Wellspring Story and the Homelessness of Women, 1990; The Tower that Fell, 1997; Images for Change, 1997. **Address:** c/o Templegate Publs, 302 E. Adam St, P. O. Box 5152, Springfield, IL 62705, U.S.A.

HAUPTMAN, Don. American, b. 1947. **Genres:** Language/Linguistics, Marketing, Humor/Satire. **Career:** Independent advertising copywriter and consultant, 1974-. **Publications:** Cruel and Unusual Puns: A Celebration of Spoonerisms, 1991; Acronymania, 1993. Contributor to marketing and publishing journals and popular magazines. **Address:** 61 W 62nd St, New York, NY 10023, U.S.A.

HAUPTMAN, Laurence Marc. American, b. 1945. **Genres:** Cultural/Ethnic topics, History. **Career:** State University of New York at New Paltz, professor of history, 1971-99, faculty exchange scholar, 1988-, distinguished professor of history, 1999-. Member of summer faculty at New York University, 1974, 1981, University of New Mexico, 1987, and St. Bonaventure University, 1992; Nelson A. Rockefeller Institute of Government, senior fellow, 1986. Expert witness. **Publications:** The Iroquois and the New Deal, 1981; The Iroquois Struggle for Survival: World War II to Red Power, 1986; Formulating American Indian Policy in New York State, 1970-1986, 1988; The Iroquois and the Civil War Year: From Battlefield to Reservation, 1993; Tribes & Tribulations: Misconceptions about American Indians and Their Histories, 1995; Between Two Fires: American Indians in the Civil War, 1995; Conspiracy of Interests, 1999; (with L.G. McLester) Chief Daniel Bread and the Oneida Indians of Wisconsin, 2002. EDITOR: (with J. Campisi) Neighbors and Intruders: An Ethnohistorical Exploration of the Indians of Hudson's River, 1978; (with J. Campisi) The Oneida Indian Experience: Two Perspectives, 1988; (with J. Campisi and J. Wherry) The Pequots in Southern New England: The Fall and Rise of an American Indian Nation, 1990; A Seneca Indian in the Union Army, 1995; (with L.G. McLester) The Oneida Indian Journey, 1999. **Address:** Dept of History, State University of New York at New Paltz, New Paltz, NY 12561, U.S.A.

HAUPTMAN, Robert. American, b. 1941. **Genres:** Ethics, Librarianship, Literary criticism and history, Travel/Exploration, Reference. **Career:** University of Oklahoma, Norman, humanities librarian and assistant professor of bibliography, 1980-84; St. Cloud State University, St. Cloud, MN, reference librarian and professor of library science, 1984-. Special editor, Library Trends, 1991, and Reference Librarian, 1992; Journal of Information Ethics, founding editor, 1992-. **Publications:** Twenty Poems Adjuring Death, 1973; The Pathological Vision: Jean Genet, Louis-Ferdinand Celine, and Tennessee Williams, 1984; Ethical Challenges in Librarianship, 1988; (with C. Anderson) Technology and Information Services, 1993; Ethics & Librarianship, 2002; (with F. Hartemann) The Mountain Encyclopedia, 2005; The Desert Encyclopedia, 2007. EDITOR: (with R. Stichler) Ethics, Information and Technology: Readings, 1998; (with S. Motin) The Holocaust: Memories, Research, Reference, 1998. Work represented in anthologies. Contributor of articles and reviews to academic and commercial periodicals. **Address:** LR&TS, James W. Miller Learning Resources Center, St. Cloud State University, 720 Fourth Ave S, St. Cloud, MN 56301-4498, U.S.A. **Online address:** hauptman@stcloudstate.edu

HAUPTMAN, William (Thornton). American, b. 1942. **Genres:** Plays/Screenplays, Novels, Novellas/Short stories. **Publications:** Heat, 1977; Domino Courts, and Comanche Cafe, 1977; Gillette, 1985; Big River, 1986; Good Rockin' Tonight and Other Stories, 1988; The Storm Season (novel), 1992. **Address:** c/o Watkins Loomis Agency Inc., 133 E. 35th St., New York, NY 10016-3886, U.S.A.

HAUSER, Marianne. American (born France), b. 1910. **Genres:** Novels, Novellas/Short stories. **Career:** Lecturer, Queens College, City University of New York, NYC, 1965-79, New York University, New School. **Publications:** Monique, 1935; Indian Phantom Play, 1937. NOVELS: Dark Dominion, 1947; The Living Shall Praise Thee, 1957; The Choir Invisible, 1958; Prince Ishmael, 1963; The Talking Room, 1976; The Memoirs of the Late Mr. Ashley; 1986; Me & My Mom, 1993; Shootout with Father: A Fiction, 2002. SHORT STORIES: A Lesson in Music, 1964; Too Old to Know Better: A Collection of Latest Stories, 2003. **Address:** 2 Washington Sq Village Apt 13-M, New York, NY 10012, U.S.A.

HAUSER, Susan Carol. American, b. 1942. **Genres:** Adult non-fiction. **Career:** Freelance writer, Bemidji, MN, 1976-; Bemidji State University, Bemidji, MN, writer/editor, 1980-98, professor, 1998-. Minnesota Public radio, former commentator; National Public Radio, commentator on "Living on Earth" and "The Cultivated Gardener.". **Publications:** Meant to Be Read Out Loud, 1988; Girl to Woman: A Gathering of Images, 1992; Redpoll on a Broken Branch, 1992; What the Animals Know, 1992; Which Way to Look, 1992; Full Moon: Reflections on Turning Fifty, 1996; Nature's Revenge: The Secrets of Poison Ivy, Poison Oak, Poison Sumac, and Their Remedies, 1996; Sugartime: The Hidden Pleasures of Making Maple Syrup with a Primer for the Nove Sugarer, 1997; Wild Rice Cooking: Harvesting, History, Natural History, Lore & Recipes, 2000; You Can Write a Memoir, 2001. Contributor to periodicals. **Address:** c/o Author Mail, Writer's Digest Books, 1507 Dana Ave., Cincinnati, OH 45207, U.S.A. **Online address:** schauser@paulbunyan.net

HAUSMANN, Winifred Wilkinson. Also writes as Winifred Wilkinson. American, b. 1922. **Genres:** Self help, Theology/Religion. **Career:** Minister Emeritus, Unity Center of Cleveland, 1988- (Ministry, 1958-87). Ministry, Unity Church, Little Rock, Arkansas, 1957-58. Member, Board of Dirs., Association of Unity Churches, 1964-66. **Publications:** Focus on Living, 1967; Miracle Power for Today, 1969; Your God-Given Potential, 1978, new ed. 1999; How to Live Life Victoriously, 1982; Dealing with Stress through Spiritual Methods, 1985; A Guide to Love-Powered Living, 1986. **Address:** 327 Katey Rose Lane, Euclid, OH 44143-2429, U.S.A.

HAUTH, Katherine B. American, b. 1940. **Genres:** Children's fiction. **Career:** South Milwaukee High School, Milwaukee, WI, teacher, 1962-65; University of Washington and King County, Seattle, WA, personnel analyst, 1966-76; writer, Rio Rancho, NM, 1976-. Mentor, counselor, sponsor, and facilitator for New Mexico mentorship program Celebrate Youth! Conducts neighborhood reading program. **Publications:** Night Life of the Yucca, 1996. **Address:** c/o Roberts Rinehart Publishers, PO Box 666, Niwot, CO 80544-0666, U.S.A.

HAUTZIG, Esther Rudomin. Also writes as Esther Rudomin. American (born Poland), b. 1930. **Genres:** Novellas/Short stories, Children's fiction, Children's non-fiction, Autobiography/Memoirs. **Career:** Writer. **Publications:** (as Esther Rudomin) Let's Cook without Cooking, 1955; Let's Make Presents, 1961; Redecorating Your Room for Practically Nothing, 1967; The Endless Steppe, 1968; In the Park, 1968; At Home, 1969; In School, 1971; Let's Make More Presents, 1973; Cool Cooking, 1974; (trans. and adaptor) I. L. Peretz: The Case against the Wind and Other Stories, 1975; Life with Working Parents, 1976; A Gift for Mama, 1981; Holiday Treats, 1983; (trans. and adaptor) I. L. Peretz: The Seven Good Years and Other Stories, 1984; Make It Special, 1986; Remember Who You Are: Stories about Being Jewish, 1990; On the Air: People behind a TV Newscast, 1991; Riches, 1992; A Picture of Grandmother, 2002. **Address:** PO Box 101, Spencertown, NY 12165, U.S.A.

HAVARD, Cyril (William Holmes). British, b. 1925. **Genres:** Medicine/Health. **Career:** Consultant Physician, Royal Free Hospital, and Royal Northern Hospital, London. Casualty Physician, St. Bartholomews Hospital, London., 1964-66. **Publications:** (ed. and Contributor) Frontiers in Medicine, 1973; (ed. and Contributor) Current Medical Treatment, 5th ed., 1983; The Laboratory Investigations of Endocrine Diseases, 1979, 1983. **Address:** 8 Upper Wimpole St, London W1M 7TD, England.

HAVAZELET, Ehud. American (born Israel), b. 1955. **Genres:** Novellas/Short stories. **Career:** Writer. Associate professor, Oregon State University, 1995-99; University of Oregon, Eugene, OR, department of creative writing, associate professor, 1999-. Faculty member, Warren Wilson MFA Program for Writers, 1995; Jones Lecturer, Stanford University, 1985-89; Wallace Stegner Fellow, Stanford University. **Publications:** What Is It Then between Us? (short stories), 1988; Like Never Before, 1998. **Address:** 34232 Colorado Lake Drive, Corvallis, OR 97333, U.S.A. **Online address:** havazele@oregon.uoregon.edu

HAVEL, Geoff. American, b. 1955. **Genres:** Children's fiction. **Publications:** Ca-a-r Ca-a-a-a-r (picture book), 1996; Punzie, ICQ! (picture book), 1999; The Real Facts of Life (chapter book), 2001; Grave of the Roti Men (young adult novel), 2003. **Address:** 25 Bergalia Mews, Perth, Western Australia 6028, Australia. **Online address:** ghavel@smartchat.net.au

HAVEL, Harvey. American (born Pakistan), b. 1971. **Genres:** Novels. **Career:** CBS-TV, NYC, production assistant for CBS Evening News with Dan Rather, 1991-92 and 1996, page for CBS Democratic National Convention, 1996-97; CBS-Radio, NYC, assistant for CBS News Radio, 1996-98; freelance writer. **Publications:** NOVELS: Noble McCloud, 1999; The Imam, in press. **Address:** c/o First Amendment Press International Co., 38 East Ridgewood Ave. Suite 217, Ridgewood, NJ 07450, U.S.A. **Online address:** fapic@msn.com

HAVEMAN, Robert Henry. American, b. 1936. **Genres:** Economics. **Career:** John Bascom Professor of Economics and Public Affairs, University of Wisconsin, Madison, since 1970. Sr. Economist, Subcttee. on Economy in Government, U.S. Congress, 1968-69; Research Associate, Resources for the Future Inc., 1969-70; Director, Institute for Research on Poverty, 1971-76; Director, La Follette Institute of Public Affairs, 1987-91, Chair, Department of Economies, 1993-96. **Publications:** Water Resource Investment and the Public Interest, 1965; (with K. Knopf) The Market System, 1966, 4th 1981; (with J.V. Krutilla) Unemployment, Idle Capacity and the Evaluation of Public Expenditures, 1968; The Economics of the Public Sector, 1970, 1977; The Economic Performance of Public Investments, 1972; (with A.M. Freeman and A.V. Kneese) The Economics of Environmental Policy, 1973; (with F. Golladay) The Economic Impacts of Tax-Transfer Policy: Regional and Distributional Effects, 1977; A Decade of Federal Anti-Poverty Programs: Achievements, Failures, and Lessons, 1977; (with I. Garfinkel) Earnings Capacity, Poverty, and Inequality, 1978; (with R. Burkhauser) Disability Policy in the United States, 1982; (with R. Burkhauser and V. Halberstadt) Public Policy Toward Disabled Workers, 1985; Poverty Policy and Poverty Research, 1987; Starting Even: An Equal Opportunity Program to Combat the Nation's New Poverty, 1988; (with B. Wolfe), Succeeding Generations: On the Effects of Investments in Children, 1994. EDITOR: (with J. Margolis) Public Expenditures and Policy Analysis, 1970, 3rd 1982; (co-) Benefit-Cost Annual-1971, 1972; (with R. Hamrin) The Political Economy of Federal Policy, 1973; (co-) Benefit-Cost and Policy Analysis-1972, 1973, and 1974, 3 vols., 1973-75; (with B. Zellner) Policy Studies Review Annual, 1979; (with J. Palmer) Jobs for Disadvantaged Workers, 1982; (with K. Hollenbeck) Microeconomic Simulation Models for Public Policy Analysis, 2 vols., 1982; Public Finance and Public Employment, 1982;. **Address:** Dept. of Economics, University of Wisconsin, 1180 Observatory Dr, Madison, WI 53706, U.S.A.

HAVERTY, Anne. Irish. **Genres:** Novels, Poetry. **Career:** Novelist. **Publications:** Constance Markievicz: Irish Revolutionary (biography), 1993; One Day as a Tiger (novel), 1997; The Beauty of the Moon (poems), 1999; The Far Side of a Kiss (novel), 2000. **Address:** c/o Chatto & Windus, Random House UK, 20 Vauxhall Bridge Rd, London SW1V 2SA, England. **Online address:** annehaverty@ireland.com

HAVET, Jose (L.). Canadian (born Belgium), b. 1937. **Genres:** Sociology. **Career:** School teacher, Belgium, 1960-63; Universidad S. Francisco Xavier, Sucre, Bolivia, professor, 1970-72; Universidad Interamericana de Puerto Rico, professor, 1976-80; University of Ottawa, professor, 1980-2003. **Publications:** The Diffusion of Power: Rural Elites in a Bolivian Province, 1985. EDITOR: (and author of intro) Le village et le bidonville: Retention et migration des populations rurales d'Afrique, 1986; (and contrib.) L'etude du developpement international au Canada: Evolution, recherche et enseignement, 1987; (and author of intro.) Staying On: Retention and Migration in Peasant Societies, 1988; (with L. Dignard) Women in Micro- and Small-Scale Enterprise Development, 1995; (author of intro., and contrib.) Identities, State, Markets: Looking at Social Change in Latin America, 1999. Contributor of articles and reviews to academic journals. **Address:** 346 Mountbatten Ave, Ottawa, ON, Canada K1H 5W3. **Online address:** jhavet@uottawa.cA

HAVIARAS, Stratis. American (born Greece), b. 1935. **Genres:** Novels, Poetry, Art/Art history, Translations. **Career:** Harvard University Library, Cambridge, MA, Acquisitions Specialist, and Head of the Gifts and Exchange Division, 1968-74, Curator of the Poetry Collection, Woodberry Poetry Room, 1974-2000. Arion's Dolphin poetry quarterly, editor, 1971-76; Harvard Review, editor, 1992-. **Publications:** POETRY IN GREEK: Lady with a Compass, 1963; Berlin, 1965; Night of the Stiltwalker, 1967; Apparent Death, 1972. IN ENGLISH: (trans.) 35 Post-War Greek Poets, 1972; (with P.

Hannigan and J. Batki) Kiss: A Collaboration (art), 1976; Crossing the River Twice (verse), 1976; When the Tree Sings (novel), 1979; The Heroic Age (novel), 1985; Millennial Afterlives: A Retrospective (short fiction), 2000. **Address:** 19 Clinton St, Cambridge, MA 02139, U.S.A.

HAVIL, Anthony. See **PHILIPP, Elliot Elias.**

HAVRAN, Martin Joseph. Canadian, b. 1929. **Genres:** History, Biography. **Career:** Kent State University, Ohio, Assistant Professor, then Associate Professor, 1957-67; University of Virginia, Charlottesville, Associate Professor of History, 1968-72, Chairman, 1974-79, Director, University Self-Study Program, 1984-86, Professor, 1972-99, Professor of History Emeritus, 1999-; Royal Historical Society, Fellow, 1974-. Visiting Professor, University of Alberta, Edmonton, 1965, and Northwestern University, Evanston, Illinois, 1967-68; Case Western Reserve University, Cleveland, Member, Board of Overseers, 1976-79; North American Conference on British Studies, Vice-President, 1978-79, and President, 1979-81; American Catholic Historical Association, President, 1982. **Publications:** Catholics in Caroline England, 1962; (ed. with A.B. Erickson) Readings in English History, 1967; (with A.B. Erickson) England: Prehistory to the Present, 1968; Caroline Courtier: The Life of Lord Cottington, 1973; The British Isles, in Catholicism in Early Modern History: A Guide to Research, 1988. **Address:** Corcoran Dept of History, Randall Hall, University of Virginia, Charlottesville, VA 22903, U.S.A. **Online address:** mjhbf@virginia.edu

HAWES, Judy. American, b. 1913. **Genres:** Children's fiction, Children's non-fiction. **Career:** Retired teacher of the handicapped. **Publications:** Fire Flies in the Night, 1963, rev. ed., 1992; Bees and Beelines, 1964; Watch Honey Bees with Me, 1964; Shrimps, 1966; Ladybug, Ladybug Fly away Home, 1967; Why Frogs Are Wet, 1968, rev. ed., 2000; What I Like about Toads, 1969; The Goats Who Killed the Leopard (A Story of Ethiopia), 1970; My Daddylonglegs, 1972; Spring Peepers, 1975. **Address:** 79 Abbington Terr, Glen Rock, NJ 07452, U.S.A. **Online address:** hawesglenrocknew@juno.com

HAWK, Alex. See **GARFIELD, Brian (F. W.).**

HAWK, Alex. See **KELTON, Elmer.**

HAWKE, Ethan. American, b. 1970. **Genres:** Novels. **Career:** Screen and stage actor; novelist. Co-founder and artistic director, Malaparte Theater Company, NYC, 1993-; director of music video Stay, by Lisa Loeb, 1994. **Publications:** NOVELS: The Hottest State, 1996. **Address:** c/o Creative Artists Agency, 9830 Wilshire Blvd., Beverly Hills, CA 90212, U.S.A.

HAWKE, Gary Richard. New Zealander, b. 1942. **Genres:** Economics, History. **Career:** Victoria University of Wellington, lecturer, 1968-70, reader 1971-73, professor of economic history, 1974-, head, School of Government, 2003-. New Zealand Economic Papers, editor, 1973-77; Institute of Policy Studies, director, 1987-98. **Publications:** Railways and Economic Growth in England and Wales, 1840-1870, 1970; The Development of the British Economy, 1870-1914, 1970; Between Governments and Banks: A History of the Reserve Bank of New Zealand, 1973; The Evolution of the New Zealand Economy, 1977; Economics for Historians, 1980; The Making of New Zealand, 1985; (ed.) Changing Politics? The Electoral Referendum, 1993; Improving Policy Advice, 1993; The Thoroughbred among Yanks in New Zealand, vol. 1: 1872-1947, The Early Years, 1997; (ed.) Free Trade in the New Millennium, 1999. **Address:** School of Government, Victoria University of Wellington, PO Box 600, Wellington, New Zealand. **Online address:** Gary.Hawke@vuw.ac.nz

HAWKE, Simon. Also writes as Nicholas Yermakov, J. D. Masters. American, b. 1951. **Genres:** Novels, Science fiction/Fantasy, Mystery/Crime/Suspense. **Career:** Has worked as a musician, broadcaster, journalist, salesman, bartender, and factory worker. **Publications:** NOVELS: The Ivanhoe Gambit, 1984; The Timekeeper Conspiracy, 1984; The Pimpernel Plot, 1984; The Zenda Vendetta, 1985; The Nautilus Sanction, 1985; The Khyber Connection, 1986; Psychodrome, 1987; The Wizard of 4th Street, 1987; The Argonaut Affair, 1987; The Wizard of Whitechapel, 1988; The Dracula Caper, 1988; The Shapechanger Sceanario, 1988; The Lilliput Legion, 1989; The Wizard of Sunset Strip, 1989; The Wizard of Rue Morgue, 1990; The Hellfire Rebellion, 1990; The Cleopatra Crisis, 1990; Predator 2, 1990; Batman: To Stalk a Spector, 1991; The Samurai Wizard, 1991; The Six-Gun Solution, 1991; The Wizard of Santa Fe, 1991; Sons of Glory, 1992; The Reluctant Scorcerer, 1992; The Nine Lives of Catseye Gomez, 1992; Call to Battle, 1993; The Inadequate Adept, 1993; Dark Sun: The Outcast, 1993; The Romulan Prize, 1993; The Wizard of Camelot, 1993; Dark Sun: The

Seeker, 1994; Dark Sun: The Nomad, 1994; The Patrician Transgression, 1994; The Whims of Creation, 1995; Blaze of Glory, 1995; Dark Sun: The Broken Blade, 1995; Birthright: War, 1996; Birthright: The Iron Throne, 1995; The Ivanhoe Gambit, 1999; The Pimpernel Plot, 1999; The Zenda Vendetta, 1999; The Nautilus Sanction, 1999; The Timekeeper Conspiracy, 1999; Mystery of Errors, 2000; Slaying of the Shrew, 2001; Much Ado about Murder, 2002; Merchant of Vengeance, 2003. NOVELS AS J.D. MASTERS: Steele, 1989; Cold Steele, 1989; Killer Steele, 1990; Jagged Steele, 1990; Renegade Steele, 1990; Target Steele, 1990. NOVELS AS NICHOLAS YERMAKOV: Journey from Flesh, 1981; Last Communion, 1981; Fall into Darkness, 1982; Clique, 1982; Epiphany, 1982; (with G.A. Larson) Battlestar Galactica 6: The Living Legend, 1982; (with G.A. Larson) Battlestar Galactica 7: War of the Gods, 1982; Jehad, 1984.

HAWKES, G(ary) W(arren). American, b. 1953. **Genres:** Novellas/Short stories, Novels. **Career:** Writer. Worked as a truck driver, pipelayer, and construction worker. Lycoming College, Williamsport, PA, professor of English, 1989-. **Publications:** Spies in the Blue Smoke: 13 Stories, 1992; Playing Out of the Deep Woods: 13 Stories, 1995; Surveyor, a Novel, 1998; Semaphore, a Novel, 1998; Gambler's Rose, 2000. **Address:** Department of English, Lycoming College, Williamsport, PA 17701, U.S.A.

HAWKES, J(ohn) G(regory). British, b. 1915. **Genres:** Biology, Botany, Bibliography. **Career:** Commonwealth Agricultural Bureau, Cambridge, England, taxonomist, 1940-48; Colombian Ministry of Agriculture, Bogota, director of potato research program, 1948-51; Agricultural Research Council, Cambridge, taxonomist, 1951-52; University of Birmingham, England, lecturer, 1952-61, professor of plant taxonomy to Mason Professor of Botany, 1961-82, head of department of plant biology, 1967-82, honorary senior research fellow, School of Continuing Studies, professor emeritus, 1982-. Conducted plant collecting expeditions in Colombia, Ecuador, Peru, Bolivia, Argentina, Venezuela, Mexico, Uruguay, Brazil, Guatemala, Honduras, Nicaragua, and the United States, 1939-81. Station of Wisconsin, adviser, 1965-82; Royal Botanic Gardens, member of scientific advisory panel, 1975-84; consultant to International Potato Center, 1972-82. Conducted plant collecting expeditions in Colombia, Ecuador, Peru, Bolivia, Argentina, Venezuela, Mexico, Uruguay, Brazil, Guatemala, Honduras, Nicaragua, and the United States, 1939-81. **Publications:** (with J.P. Hjerting) The Potatoes of Argentina, Brazil, Paraguay, and Uruguay: A Biosystematic Study, 1969; (with Cadbury and Readett) A Computer-Mapped Flora, 1971; The Diversity of Crop Plants, 1983; (with Williams and Croston) A Bibliography of Crop Genetic Resources, 1984; Plant Genetic Resources: The Impact of the International Research Centers, 1985; (with J.P. Hjerting) The Potatoes of Bolivia, 1989; The Potato, 1990; Collecta Clusiana, 1994; (with N. Maxted and B.V. Ford-Lloyd) Plant Genetic Conservation: The in situ Approach, 1997. EDITOR: Reproductive Biology and Taxonomy of Vascular Plants, 1966; Chemotaxonomy and Serotaxonomy, 1968; (with W. Lange) European and Regional Gene Banks, 1974; (with O.H. Frankel) Crop Genetic Resources for Today and Tomorrow, 1975; Conservation and Agriculture, 1978; (with Lester and Skelding) The Biology and Taxonomy of the Solanaceae, 1979; (with Harris) The N.I. Vavilov Centenary Symposium, 1990; (with Engels and Woreda) Crop Genetic Resources of Ethiopia, 1991; (with Lester, Nee, and Estrada) Solanaceae III, 1991; Genetic Conservation of World Crop Plants, 1991; Vavilov Lectures, 1994. **Address:** Winterbourne Botanical Gardens, School for Professional and Continuing Education, 58 Edgbaston Park Rd, Edgbaston, Birmingham B15 2RT, England. **Online address:** J.G.Hawkes@bham.ac.uk

HAWKES, Judith. American, b. 1949. **Genres:** Novels. **Career:** Saint Ann's School, Brooklyn, NY, computer programmer, 1974-91, martial arts instructor, 1990-; writer. **Publications:** Julian's House (novel), 1989; My Soul to Keep (novel), 1996. **Address:** John Farquharson Ltd, 250 West 57th St, New York, NY 10019, U.S.A.

HAWKES, Kevin. American, b. 1959. **Genres:** Children's fiction, Illustrations. **Career:** Book store clerk in Boston, MA, 1986-87; free-lance illustrator, 1987-90; children's illustrator and writer, 1990-. **Publications:** Then the Troll Heard the Squeak (self-illustrated), 1991; His Royal Buckliness, 1992. Illustrator of books by J. Aiken, M. D. Bauen, C. Cowan, W. de la Mare, M. Dionetti, P. Fleischman, B.H. Grossman, M.A. Hoberman, E. Ibbotson, K. Lasky, E. Loredo, J. Maxner, M.L. Miller, J. Prelutsky, P. Pullman, R. Schotter, C. Stutson. **Address:** 5 Robie St, Gorham, ME 04038, U.S.A.

HAWKES, Zachary. See **RIEFE, Alan.**

HAWKING, Stephen W(illiam). British, b. 1942. **Genres:** Physics. **Career:** Fellow, Gonville and Caius College, Cambridge, 1965-, and Lucasian Professor of Mathematics, Cambridge University, 1979- (Member, Institute of Theoretical Astronomy, 1968-72; Research Assistant, Institute of Astronomy, 1972-73; Research Assistant, Dept. of Applied Mathematics and Theoretical Physics, 1973-75; Reader, 1975-77; Professor of Gravitational Physics, 1977-79). **Publications:** (with G. Ellis) The Large Scale Structure of Space-Time, 1973; (ed. with W. Israel) General Relativity: An Einstein Centenary Survey, 1979; (ed. with M. Rocek) Superspace and Supergravity, 1981; A Brief History of Time, 1988; Black Holes and Baby Universes, 1993; (with R. Penrose) Nature of Space and Time, 1996; Universe in a Nut-Shell, 2001. **Address:** University of Cambridge, Centre for Mathematical Sciences, DAMTP, Wilberforce Rd, Cambridge CB3 0WA, England.

HAWKINS, Anne Hunsaker. American, b. 1944. **Genres:** Humanities. **Career:** Pennsylvania State University, Hershey, PA, associate professor of humanities at the College of Medicine, 1990-. **Publications:** Archetypes of Conversion, Bucknell University Press, 1985; Reconstructing Illness, Purdue University Press, 1992. **Address:** Department of Humanities, College of Medicine, Pennsylvania State University, Box 850, Hershey, PA 17033, U.S.A.

HAWKINS, Bradford A(lan). American, b. 1952. **Genres:** Biology, Environmental sciences/Ecology. **Career:** Texas A&M University, College Station, postdoctoral fellow in entomology, 1984; University of Puerto Rico, Rio Piedras, assistant professor of biology, 1985-86; University of York, Heslington, England, postdoctoral fellow in biology, 1986-88; University of Texas at Austin, lecturer in zoology, 1988-89; Imperial College, Silwood Park, England, staff research scientist at Centre for Population Biology, 1990-94; University of California, Irvine, assistant professor, 1994-97, associate professor of ecology and evolutionary biology, 1997-. Lecturer at colleges and universities. **Publications:** EDITOR: (with W. Sheehan) Parasitoid Community Ecology, 1994; Pattern and Process in Host-Parasitoid Interactions, 1994; (with W.V. Cornell) Theoretical Approaches to Biological Control, 1999. Contributor to scientific journals. **Address:** Department of Ecology and Evolutionary Biology, 321 Steinhaus Hall, University of California, Irvine, CA 92697, U.S.A.

HAWKINS, Harrison. See HOOKS, William H.

HAWKINS, Hunt. American, b. 1943. **Genres:** Poetry. **Career:** Kurasini College, Dar Es Salaam, Tanzania, teacher, 1966-67; Texas Southern University, Houston, instructor, 1968-70; University of Minnesota, Minneapolis, assistant professor of English, 1977-78; Florida State University, Tallahassee, assistant professor, 1978-83, associate professor, 1983-94, professor of English, 1994-; writer. **Publications:** The Domestic Life (poetry), 1994. Work represented in anthologies. Contributor to periodicals. **Address:** Department of English, Florida State University, Tallahassee, FL 32306, U.S.A.

HAWKINS, Regina Trice. American, b. 1938. **Genres:** Biography. **Career:** Buckhead Brokers, Atlanta, GA, referral agent. Georgia Women of Achievement, member of board of directors. **Publications:** Hazel Jane Raines, Pioneer Lady of Flight, 1996. **Address:** 7 Bohler Mews, Atlanta, GA 30327, U.S.A. **Online address:** reghawk@mediaone.net

HAWLEY, Ellen. American, b. 1947. **Genres:** Novels. **Career:** Editor and teacher of writing. Has worked as cab driver, radio talk show host, assembler, janitor, and file clerk. **Publications:** Trip Sheets (fiction), 1998. **Address:** 3223 36th Ave S, Minneapolis, MN 55406, U.S.A. **Online address:** ellenhawley@yahoo.com

HAWLEY, John C(harles). American, b. 1947. **Genres:** Literary criticism and history, Theology/Religion. **Career:** High school English teacher in Kansas City, MO, 1972-74; Santa Clara University, CA, assistant professor, 1986-92, associate professor of English, 1992-. South Asian Review, associate editor. Lecturer at educational institutions worldwide. Former member of Society of Jesus; Georgetown University Hospital, assistant chaplain, 1977; Mercy Hospital, Denver, CO, assistant chaplain, 1978; University of Pennsylvania, assistant chaplain at Newman Center, 1979-82; assistant pastor of Roman Catholic congregations in Golden, CO, 1977, St. John's, Belize, 1978, Copiague, NY, 1982-84, Nanakuli, HI, 1986, and Honaunau, HI, 1989; performer as choral singer; work recorded on albums; performed in concerts in the United States, Canada, and England. **Publications:** EDITOR & CONTRIBUTOR: Reform and Counterreform, 1994; Writing the Nation, 1996; Through a Glass Darkly: Essays in the Religious Imagination, 1996; Cross-Addressing, 1996; The Postcolonial Crescent, 1998; Christian Encounters with the Other (in UK as Historicizing Christian Encounters with the Other), 1998; Postcolonial and Queer Theories, 2001; Postcolonial,

Queer, 2001; Divine Aporia, 2001; Encyclopedia of Postcolonial Studies, 2001. Contributor to books. Contributor of articles and reviews to periodicals. **Address:** Dept of English, Santa Clara University, Santa Clara, CA 95053, U.S.A. **Online address:** jhawley@scu.edu

HAWLEY, Richard A. American, b. 1945. **Genres:** Novels, Poetry, Education, Social commentary, Autobiography/Memoirs, Essays. **Career:** University School, Chagrin Falls, OH, teacher, 1968-86, dean of students, 1973-79, director, Upper School, 1980-87, headmaster, 1988-. **Publications:** Aspects of Vision, 1976; With Love to My Survivors, 1982; (ed.) Coming through School, 1982; Purposes of Pleasure, 1983; The Headmaster's Papers, 1983; A School Answers Back, 1984; (with R. Peterson and M. Mason) Building Drug-Free Schools, 1987; St. Julian, 1987; Seeing Things: A Chronicle of Surprises, 1987; The Big Issues in the Passage to Adulthood, 1988; Drugs and Society: Responding to an Epidemic, 1988; In Praise of the Teaching Life, 1988; Hail, University!, 1990; Boys Will Be Men, 1993; Papers from the Headmaster (essays), 1996; The Headmaster's Wife (novel), 2000; Hard Lessons, 2002; The Headmaster's Poems, 2002; Paul and Juliana, 2003. **Address:** c/o University School, Chagrin Falls, OH 44022, U.S.A.

HAWTHORNE, Douglas B(ruce). American, b. 1948. **Genres:** Air/Space topics, History, Military/Defense/Arms control, Writing/Journalism, Biography, Reference. **Career:** Tombstone Epitaph, Tombstone, AZ, city editor and reporter, 1985; Territorial Publishers Inc., Tucson, AZ, copy editor and reporter, 1986-87; free-lance journalist and writer, 1987-; Hawthorne's Militaria, co-owner, 1999-. Arizona Department of Economic Security, new and continued claims deputy, 1982. **Publications:** Men and Women of Space, 1992, 2nd ed. forthcoming. **Address:** 5946 N Camino Del Conde, Tucson, AZ 85718-4312, U.S.A.

HAXTON, Brooks. American, b. 1950. **Genres:** Poetry. **Career:** Associate Professor of English, Syracuse University, 1993-. Resident Poet, Warren Wilson College, Swannanoa, North Carolina, 1990-. Adjunct Professor, Syracuse University, New York, 1981-82, George Washington University, Washington, D.C., 1982-84, American University, Washington, D.C., 1983-84, George Mason University, Fairfax, Virginia, 1984-85, and University of Maryland, College Park, 1984-85. Visiting Poet, Sarah Lawrence College, Bronxville, New York, 1985. **Publications:** POETRY: The Lay of Eleanor and Irene, 1985; Dominion, 1986; Dead Reckoning, 1989; Traveling Companion, 1989; The Sun at Night, 1995; V. Hugo, Selected Poems, 2002; Nakedness Death & the Number Zero, 2001; Uproar: Antiphones to the Psalms, 2004. TRANSLATIONS: Dances for Flute & Thunder, 1999; Fragments, the Collected Wisdom of Heraclitus, 2001. OTHER: Tennessee Williams, 1994. Contributor of poetry to periodicals. **Address:** English Department, 401 Hall of Languages, Syracuse University, Syracuse, NY 13244, U.S.A. **Online address:** bhaxton@syr.edu

HAY, Elizabeth (Jean). British (born India), b. 1936. **Genres:** Biography. **Career:** Broadcasting executive. **Publications:** Sambo Sahib: The Story of Little Black Sambo and Helen Bannerman, 1981; Sayonara Sambo, 1994. **Address:** 12 Highbury Ter, London N5 1UP, England. **Online address:** elizabeth@cba.org.uk

HAY, Samuel A. American, b. 1937. **Genres:** Literary criticism and history, Plays/Screenplays, Theatre. **Career:** Playwright. Drama teacher in West Palm Beach, FL, and Baltimore, MD, early 1960s; University of Maryland, Baltimore, assistant professor of English, 1971-72, assistant professor of African American studies, 1972-73; Purdue University, West Lafayette, IN, director of Africana Studies and Research Center, 1974-78; Washington University, St. Louis, MO, director of Black Studies program and professor of theater, 1978-79; Morgan State University, Baltimore, MD, professor of theater and chair of department of communication and theater arts, 1979-84; founder of the Black Theater Project in Ithaca, NY, and of the National Conference on African American Theater. **Publications:** African American Theatre: An Historical and Critical Analysis, 1994; Ed Bullins: A Literary Biography, 1997. PLAYS: Yes in a Pleasant Country (includes Parting Shocks and Getting Some), 1970; The Robeson Place Singers, 1976; An American Passport, 1981; Sistah Rachel, 1982; A Woman against Apartheid, 1985. Contributor to professional journals. **Address:** c/o Wayne State University Press, Leonard N. Simons Bldg., 4809 Woodward Ave., Detroit, MI 48201, U.S.A.

HAYASHI, Nancy. American, b. 1939. **Genres:** Young adult fiction, Illustrations. **Career:** Worked as a layout artist at Higbee's Department Store, 1964-66; art director at Bowes Advertising, 1966-75, and Baxter, Gurian and Mazzei Advertising, 1975-77; writer. **Publications:** SELF-ILLUSTRATED FOR MIDDLE-GRADE READERS: Cosmic Cousin (mystery), 1988; The Fantastic Stay-Home-from-School Day, 1992; Superbird to the Rescue, 1995. Illustrator of books by C. Rylant. **Address:** 3507 Landa St., Los Angeles, CA 90039, U.S.A.

HAYCOCK, Kate. British, b. 1962. **Genres:** Sports/Fitness, Theatre, Food and Wine, Film. **Career:** Freelance computing PR and lecturer/trainer. **Publications:** Fitness, 1990; Plays, 1990; Pasta, 1991; Skiing, 1991; Gymnastics, 1991; Science Fiction Films, 1992. **Address:** Derwen, Pentir, Bangor LLS7 4EG, Wales. **Online address:** kate@rpmguiding.com

HAYCRAFT, Anna Margaret. See ELLIS, Alice Thomas.

HAYDEN, Brian (Douglas). American/Canadian, b. 1946. **Genres:** Anthropology/Ethnology, Archaeology/Antiquities. **Career:** American Stock Exchange, NYC, research worker, 1964; Virginia Commonwealth University, Richmond, instructor in sociology and anthropology, 1973-74; Simon Fraser University, Burnaby, BC, instructor, 1974-76, assistant professor, 1976-78, associate professor, 1978-84, professor of archaeology, 1984-. Dinosaur National Monument, field assistant, 1965-66; field assistant for archaeological excavations in Tunisia, 1967, Guatemala, 1970, Lebanon, 1970, and in the US and Canada; principal investigator and field director of Coxoh ethnoarchaeological project in Mexico and Guatemala, 1977-85; Villatoro Mastodon Site, Guatemala, principal investigator, 1978; conducted archaeological field research in France and Keatley Creek, British Columbia, 1986-2003; ethnoarchaeological field research on feasting in SE Asia, 1994-2003. **Publications:** Paleolithic Reflections: Lithic Technology of the Western Desert Aborigines, 1979; (with A. Cannon) The Structure of Material Systems: Ethnoarchaeology in the Maya Highlands, 1984; Archaeology: The Science of Once and Future Things, 1993; The Pithouses of Keatley Creek, 1997; Shamans, Sorcerers, and Saints: The Prehistory of Religion, 2003. EDITOR & CONTRIBUTOR: Lithic Use-Wear Analysis, 1979; Lithic Studies among the Contemporary Highland Maya, 1987; A Complex Culture of the British Columbia Plateau: Traditional Stl'atl'imx Resource Use, 1992; The Ancient Part of Keatley Creek, 3 vols.; Feasts, 2001. Work represented in anthologies. Contributor of articles and reviews to archaeology and anthropology journals. **Address:** Department of Archaeology, Simon Fraser University, Burnaby, BC, Canada V5A 1S6. **Online address:** bhayden@sfu.ca

HAYDEN, C. J. American, b. 1956. **Genres:** Business/Trade/Industry. **Career:** Hayden Consulting, San Francisco, CA, training consultant, 1983-85; Telelearning Inc., San Francisco, manager of collegiate administration, 1986-87; Morrison & Foerster, San Francisco, human resources database administrator, 1987-90; Winston Human Resource Solutions, San Francisco, principal and senior consultant, 1990-92; Wings Business Coaching, San Francisco, business coach and workshop leader, 1992-. Marketing and management instructor, Mills College, 1994-97; marketing instructor, John F. Kennedy University, 2000-. Entrepreneurship instructor of alumnae resources, 1993-99. Member of boards of directors. **Publications:** Get Clients Now! A Twenty-eight-Day Program for Professionals and Consultants, 1999. Contributor to print and online periodicals. **Address:** Wings Business Coaching, PO Box 2838, San Francisco, CA 94126, U.S.A. **Online address:** CoachCJ@getclientsnow.com

HAYDEN, Eric William. British, b. 1919. **Genres:** Children's fiction, Theology/Religion, Novellas/Short stories. **Career:** Baptist Minister. **Publications:** Church Publicity, 1952; Faith's Glorious Achievement, 1958; Spurgeon on Revival, 1962; History of Spurgeons Tabernacle, 1962, rev. ed., 1992; Preaching through the Bible, 2 vols., 1964, 1966; Everyday Yoga for Christians, 1966; Bible Object Lessons, 3 vols., 1968; When God Takes Over, 1969; Miracle of Time, 1970; Searchlight on Spurgeon, 1973; Jimmy in Space, 1973; Jimmy Plays Cricket, 1974; Traveller's Guide to Spurgeon Country, 1974; Sermon Outlines series, 6 vols., 1974-80; Joshua Thomas, 1976; Just the Girl You Want and Other Stories, 1977; Meditation, 1978; Praying for Revival, 1978; The Adventures of Bobby Wildgoose, 1980; Learning to Cope with Agoraphobia, 1983; Letting the Lion Loose, 1984; God's Answer for Fear, 1985; God's Answer for Pressure, 1987; People Like Us, 1989; Highlights in the Life of C.H. Spurgeon, 1990; The Spurgeon Family, 1993; The Light of the World, 1993; He Won Them for Christ, 1993; (with P. Hayden) Lectures on C.H. Spurgeon, 1994; Poems and Letters of C.H. Spurgeon, 1994; The Unforgettable Spurgeon, 1996; My Spurgeon Souvenirs, 1996. **Address:** 7 Nanfan and Dobyn Place, Newent, Glos. GL18 1TF, England.

HAYDON, Elizabeth. American. **Genres:** Science fiction/Fantasy. **Career:** Writer. Educational book editor. **Publications:** RAPSODY TRILOGY: Rhapsody: Child of Blood, 1999; Prophecy: Child of the Earth, 2000; Destiny: Child of the Sky, 2001. **Address:** c/o Richard Curtis, 171 East 74th St., New York, NY 10021, U.S.A. **Online address:** elizabethhaydon@hotmail.com

HAYES, Charles Langley. See HOLMES, B(ryan) J(ohn).

HAYES, Christopher L. American, b. 1958. **Genres:** Gerontology/Senior issues. **Career:** Project T.L.C., Santa Ana, CA, director of social service and personnel, 1978-79; Coastline Community College, Fountain Valley, CA, faculty member, 1980-82; Santa Ana College, faculty member, 1981-83; Catholic University of America, Washington, DC, director of education and training, and acting director of Center for the Study of Pre-Retirement and Aging, 1984-85, director of the center, 1985-86; Long Island University, Southampton College, Southampton, NY, assistant professor, 1986-89, associate professor of psychology, 1989-, director of National Center for Women and Retirement Research, 1988-, director of Master's Program in Gerontology, 1988-. Project PACE, Inc., executive director, 1979-83. **Publications:** (with D. Guttmann, T. Ooms, and P. Mahon-Stetson) The European-American Elderly in the United States, 1986; (ed. with D. Kalish and D. Guttmann, and contrib.) The European-American Elderly, 1986; (with J. Deren) Employment and Retirement Issues for Mid-Life Women, 1988; (with J. Deren) Looking Ahead to Your Financial Future, 1988; (with J. Deren) Pre-Retirement Planning for Women, 1990; (with D. Anderson and M. Blau) Our Turn: The Good News about Divorce, 1993; (with D. Anderson) Gender Identity and Self-Esteem, 1996; (with K. Kelly) Money Makeovers, 1998. Work represented in books. Contributor to periodicals. **Address:** Professional Studies Division, Long Island University, Southampton College, 8-4196, 239 Montauk Hwy, Southampton, NY 11968, U.S.A. **Online address:** chayes@southampton.liu.edu

HAYES, Daniel. American, b. 1952. **Genres:** Novels. **Career:** Waterford Central Catholic School, Waterford, NY, English teacher, 1975-84; Troy High School, Troy, NY, English teacher, 1984-; freelance writer. **Publications:** The Trouble with Lemons, 1991; Eye of the Beholder, 1992; No Effect, 1993; Flyers, 1996. **Address:** RD #1 Rte 40, Schaghticoke, NY 12154, U.S.A. **Online address:** hayesdm@aol.com

HAYES, Joe. American, b. 1945. **Genres:** Children's fiction. **Career:** Writer. **Publications:** The Day It Snowed Tortillas, 1982; Coyote &, 1983; The Checker Playing Hound Dog, 1986; No Way, Jose!/De Ninguna Manera, Jose!, 1986; La Llorona/The Weeping Woman, 1987; Monday, Tuesday, Wednesday, Oh!/Lunes, Martes, Miercoles, O!, 1987; A Heart Full of Turquoise, 1988; Mariposa, Mariposa, 1988; The Wise Little Burro, 1990; That's Not Fair! Earth Friendly Tales, 1991; Everyone Knows Gato Pinto: More Tales from Spanish New Mexico, 1992; Soft Child: How Rattlesnake Got Its Fangs, 1993; Antonio's Lucky Day, 1993; The Butterflies Trick Coyote, 1993; Watch out for Clever Women/Cuidado con las mujeres astutas, 1994; Where There's a Will, There's a Way/Donde hay ganas hay manas, 1995; A Spoon for Every Bite, 1996. Contributor of essays to anthologies. Several of Hayes's works are available on audiotape. **Address:** 1602 Sunset Gardens SW, Albuquerque, NM 87105, U.S.A.

HAYES, John (Trevor). British, b. 1929. **Genres:** Art/Art history. **Career:** Assistant Keeper, 1954-70, and Director, 1970-74, London Museum; Director, National Portrait Gallery, London, 1974-94. **Publications:** London: A Pictorial History, 1969; The Drawings of Thomas Gainsborough, 1970; Catalogue of Oil Paintings in the London Museum, 1970; Gainsborough as Printmaker, 1971; Rowlandson: Watercolours and Drawings, 1972; Gainsborough: Paintings and Drawings, 1975; The Art of Graham Sutherland, 1980; The Landscape Paintings of Thomas Gainsborough, 1982; The Art of Thomas Rowlandson, 1990; The Portrait in British Art, 1991; Catalogue of the British Paintings in the National Gallery of Art, Washington, 1992; (with M. Galinou) London in Paint, 1996; Gainsborough and Rowlandson: A New York Private Collection, 1998; (ed.) The Letters of Thomas Gainsborough, 2001. **Address:** 61 Grantham Rd, Chiswick, London W4 2RT, England.

HAYFLICK, Leonard. American, b. 1928. **Genres:** Biology, Medicine/Health. **Career:** University of Texas Medical Branch, Galveston, Dept of Microbiology, McLaughlin research fellow in infection and immunity, 1956-58; Wistar Institute of Anatomy and Biology, Philadelphia, PA, associate member, 1958-68; University of Pennsylvania, Philadelphia, assistant professor of research medicine, 1966-68; Stanford University, Stanford, CA, School of Medicine, professor of medical microbiology, 1968-76, senator-at-large for basic medical sciences, 1970-73, chair of general research support grant committee, 1972-74; Children's Hospital, Oakland, CA, senior research cell biologist, 1976-81; University of Florida, Gainesville, professor of zoology and professor of microbiology and immunology, 1981-87, director of the

Center for Gerontology Studies of the College of Liberal Arts and Sciences, 1981-87; University of California, San Francisco, School of Medicine, professor of anatomy, cell biology, and aging, 1988-. Visiting professor/scientist to institutions worldwide; consultant to committees of the US Congress. **Publications:** How and Why We Age, 1994. EDITOR: (with others) Biology of the Mycoplasma, 1967; The Mycoplasmatales and the L-Phase of Bacteria, 1969; (with others) Handbook of the Biology of Aging, 1977. Contributor to professional journals. **Address:** University of California-San Francisco, PO Box 89, The Sea Ranch, CA 95497, U.S.A.

HAYFORD, Charles W. American, b. 1941. **Genres:** Cultural/Ethnic topics, History, Bibliography. **Career:** Oberlin College, OH, instructor to assistant professor, 1971-77; International Asian Studies Program, Hong Kong, associate director, 1978-81; University of Chicago, IL, coordinator of outreach for Center for East Asian Studies, 1981-87; Northwestern University, Evanston, IL, visiting assistant professor to visiting professor, 1981-. Chinese University of Hong Kong, visiting lecturer, 1978-81; Yale-China Association, Hong Kong representative, 1978-81; Stanford University, visiting professor, 1995-96. Consultant. Journal of Asian Studies, book review editor, 1990-94. **Publications:** To the People: James Yen and Village China, 1990; China, 1997; Bibliography of American-East Asian Relations, 2002. **Address:** 1401 Lake St, Evanston, IL 60201, U.S.A. **Online address:** chayford@aol.com

HAYGOOD, Wil. American, b. 1954. **Genres:** Biography, Documentaries/Reportage. **Career:** Call and Post, Columbus, OH, reporter, 1977-78; Community Information and Referral, hotline operator, 1978-79; R. H. Macy's, New York City, retail manager, 1980-82; Charleston Gazette, Charleston, WV, copy editor, 1982-84; Pittsburgh Post-Gazette, Pittsburgh, PA, reporter, 1984-85; Boston Globe, Boston, MA, writer, 1985-. **Publications:** Two on the River, 1986; King of the Cats: The Life and Times of Adam Clayton Powell, Jr. (biography), 1993; The Haygoods of Columbus, 1997; In Black & White: The Life of Sammy Davis, Jr., 2003. Contributor to periodicals. **Address:** c/o Boston Globe, 135 Morrissey Blvd, Dorchester, MA 02125, U.S.A.

HAYLOCK, John (Mervyn). British, b. 1918. **Genres:** Novels, Literary criticism and history. **Career:** Ministry of Education, Baghdad, Iraq, English teacher, 1948-56; Waseda University, Tokyo, Japan, English teacher, 1958-60 and 1962-65; Rikkyo University, Tokyo, visiting professor of English literature, 1975-84; writer. **Publications:** (with D. Stewart) New Babylon: Portrait of Iraq, 1956; See You Again (novel), 1963; It's All Your Fault (novel), 1964; (trans. with F. King) R. de Montesquiou, a Fin-de-Siecle Prince, 1967; (trans.) P. Jullian, Flight into Egypt, 1970; One Hot Summer in Kyoto, 1981; A Touch of the Orient, 1990; Uneasy Relations, 1993; Eastern Exchange, 1997; Doubtful Partners, 1998; Body of Contention, 1999. **Address:** Flat 28, 15 Grand Avenue, Hove BN3 2NG, England.

HAYMAN, Carol Bessent. American, b. 1927. **Genres:** Poetry, Communications/Media, Gerontology/Senior issues, Inspirational/Motivational Literature, Local history/Rural topics, Self help, Autobiography/Memoirs. **Career:** Carteret County Community College, instructor in creative writing, 1985-. Poet Laureate of Beaufort, North Carolina, 1989-, and Carteret County, North Carolina, 1993-. **Publications:** Keepsake, 1962; These Lovely Days, 1971; A Collection of Writings, 1972; What Is Christmas?, 1974; (ed.) The Bessent Story, 1978; Images & Echoes of Beaufort-by-the-Sea, 1993. Contributor of articles to periodicals. **Address:** 618 Ann St, Beaufort, NC 28516, U.S.A.

HAYMAN, David. American, b. 1927. **Genres:** Literary criticism and history. **Career:** Professor of English, University of Texas, Austin, 1955-65, and University of Iowa, Iowa City, 1965-73; Professor of English and American Literature, University de Paris, 1972-73; University of Wisconsin, Madison, Professor of Comparative Literature, 1973-89, Evjue-Bascom Professor in the Humanities, 1989-96, Emeritus, 1996-. Prof of English and Am. Literature, Goethe University, Frankfurt, Germany, 1984-85; Professor of English, Coimbra University, Coimbra, Portugal, 1994. **Publications:** Joyce et Mallarmae, 1956; A First-Draft Version of Finnegan's Wake, 1963; Louis Ferdinand Celine, 1965; Ulysses: The Mechanics of Meaning, 1970, 1982; (with E. Rabkin) Form in Fiction, 1973; (with C. Hart) Ulysses: Critical Essays, 1974; (ed.) The James Joyce Archive, 1978; (ed.) In the Wake of the Wake, 1978; (ed.) Philippe Sollers, Writing and the Experience of Limits, 1983; Re-Forming the Narrative: Toward a Mechanics of Modernist Fiction, 1987; The Wake in Transit, 1990; (with S. Slate) Probes: Genetic Studies in Joyce, 1995. **Address:** 2913 Columbia Rd., Madison, WI 53705, U.S.A. **Online address:** hayjube@aol.com

HAYMAN, Richard. British, b. 1959. **Genres:** Archaeology/Antiquities. **Career:** National Trust, Neath, South Wales, archaeologist, 1983-85; Mer-

thyr Tydfil Heritage Trust, Merthyr Tydfil, South Wales, archaeologist, 1985-88; Ironbridge Gorge Museum, Telford, England, archaeologist, 1994-. **Publications:** Riddles in Stone, 1997. **Address:** Ironbridge Gorge Museum Trust, Ironbridge, Telford, Shropshire, England.

HAYMAN, Ronald. British, b. 1932. **Genres:** Plays/Screenplays, Literary criticism and history, Theatre, Autobiography/Memoirs, Biography. **Career:** Northampton Repertory Co., assistant producer, 1962-63. **Publications:** Harold Pinter, 1968; Samuel Beckett, 1968; John Osborne, 1968; John Arden, 1968; Robert Bolt, 1969; John Whiting, 1969; Techniques of Acting, 1969; Arthur Miller, 1970; Tolstoy, 1970; Arnold Wesker, 1970; John Gielgud, 1971; Edward Albee, 1971; Eugene Ionesco, 1972; Playback, 1973; The Set-Up, 1974; Playback 2, 1974; The First Thrust, 1975; The Novel Today 1967-1975, 1976; Leavis, 1976; Tom Stoppard, 1977; How to Read a Play, 1977; Artaud and After, 1977; De Sade, 1978; Theatre and Anti-Theatre, 1979; British Theatre since 1955: A Reassessment, 1979; Nietzsche: A Critical Life, 1980; K: A Biography of Kafka, 1981; Brecht: A Biography, 1983; Fassbinder, Film Maker, 1984; Brecht: The Plays, 1984; Gunter Grass, 1985; Secrets: Boyhood in a Jewish Hotel, 1985; Writing Against: A Biography of Sartre, 1986; Proust: A Biography, 1990; The Death and Life of Sylvia Plath, 1991; Tennessee Williams: Everyone Else Is an Audience, 1993; Playing the Wife, 1995; Thomas Mann, 1996; Hitler and Geli, 1997; A Life of Jung, 1999. EDITOR: Collected Plays of John Whiting, 2 vols., 1969; J. Whiting, The Art of the Dramatist and Other Pieces, 1970; The German Theatre, 1975; My Cambridge, 1977. **Address:** c/o Gillon Aitken Associates, 18-21 Cavaye Pl, London SW10 9PT, England.

HAYMAN, Walter Kurt. British (born Germany), b. 1926. **Genres:** Mathematics/Statistics. **Career:** University of Exeter, lecturer 1947-53, reader, 1953-56; University of London, Imperial College London, professor of pure mathematics, 1956-85, professor emeritus, 1985-, senior research fellow, 1995-; University of York, professor of mathematics, 1985-93, professor emeritus, 1993-. **Publications:** Multivalent Functions, 1958; 2nd ed., 1994; Meromorphic Functions, 1964; Research Problems in Function Theory, 1967; Subharmonic Functions, vol. 1 (with P. B. Kennedy), 1976, vol. 2, 1989. **Address:** Dept. of Mathematics, Imperial College London, Huxley Bldg, 180 Queen's Gate, London SW7 2AZ, England.

HAYNES, C. Rayfield. American, b. 1943. **Genres:** Sociology, Race relations. **Career:** U.S. Government, schoolteacher and principal in Alaska, 1966-71; University of Miami, Coral Gables, FL, assistant professor, 1975-76; University of Wisconsin-Madison, assistant professor, 1976-79; clinical psychologist in Phoenix, AZ, 1979-. **Publications:** Growing Up Colored in Mississippi, 1992. **Address:** 222 W. Brown Road, Mesa, AZ 85201-3422, U.S.A.

HAYNES, David. American, b. 1955. **Genres:** Novels, Young adult fiction. **Career:** C.V. Mosby Publishing Co., St. Louis, MO, associate editor, 1978-81; schoolteacher in St. Paul, MN, 1981-93; writer, 1993-. Morehead State University, visiting scholar, 1994; Mankato State University, visiting writer, 1994; teacher at Writer's Center, Bethesda, MD, 1994-95, and Hamline University, 1995; Warren Wilson College M.F.A. Program for Writers, faculty member, spring, 1996, and 1997. National Board for Professional Teaching Standards, member of adolescent generalist standards committee, 1990-, teacher in residence, 1994-; Minnesota Humanities Commission, member of advisory committee, Teacher Institute, 1993-94. **Publications:** ADULT NOVELS: Somebody Else's Mama, 1995; Heathens, 1996; Live at Five, 1996; All American Dream Dolls, 1997. JUVENILE FICTION: Right by My Side (young adult novel), 1993; Business as Usual (West 7th Wildcats 1), 1997; The Gumma Wars (West 7th Wildcats 2), 1997. Contributor to anthologies. Contributor of short stories to periodicals. **Address:** c/o Milkweed Editions, 1011 Washington Ave. S. #300, Minneapolis, MN 55415, U.S.A.

HAYNES, Duncan H(arold). Also writes as Dirk Wyle. American, b. 1945. **Genres:** Mystery/Crime/Suspense. **Career:** University of Miami, Coral Gables, FL, assistant professor, 1973-77, associate professor, 1977-82, professor of pharmacology, 1982-2001; retired, 2001. Pharma-Logic Inc. (inventors and developers of medical technology), founder and principal, 1983-. Inventor of phospholipid-coated micro-droplets and micro-crystals as an injectable delivery system for water-insoluble drugs; holder of patents. **Publications:** MYSTERY NOVELS AS DIRK WYLE: Pharmacology Is Murder, 1998; Biotechnology Is Murder, 2000; Medical School Is Murder, 2001; Amazon Gold, 2003. Contributor to scientific journals. **Address:** 4051 Barbarossa Ave., Miami, FL 33133, U.S.A. **Online address:** dirk@dirk-wyle.com

HAYNES, Gary (Anthony). American, b. 1948. **Genres:** Anthropology/Ethnology. **Career:** Smithsonian Institution, Washington, DC, research associate, 1981-85; George Washington University, Washington, DC, associate professor, 1982; University of Nevada, Reno, assistant professor, 1985-88, associate professor, 1988-95, professor, 1995-; Catholic University of America, visiting assistant professor, 1981; Hwange Research Trust, Reno, and Bulawayo, Zimbabwe, Africa, chairperson, 1987-. **Publications:** Mammoths, Mastodons, and Elephants, Cambridge University Press, 1991. **Address:** Anthropology Department, University of Nevada, Reno, NV 89557, U.S.A.

HAYNES, Jim. (James Almand). American, b. 1933. **Genres:** Philosophy, Theatre, Travel/Exploration, Autobiography/Memoirs, Essays. **Career:** Paperback Bookshop and Gallery, Edinburgh, Scotland, founder and proprietor, 1959-64; Traverse Theatre, Edinburgh, founder and artistic director, 1962-66; Traverse Theatre, London, England, founder and co-artistic director, 1966-67; Arts Laboratory, London, co-founder and co-artistic director, 1967-69; University of Paris VIII, Paris, France, associate professor of media studies, 1969-99. Co-founder and co-director of Videoheads (video research foundation, with branches in London, Amsterdam, and Paris), 1968-; founder and director of Handshake Editions, Paris, 1979-; director of Wet Dream Film Festival, Amsterdam 1970-71. **Publications:** Workers of the World, Unite and Stop Working! A Reply to Marxism, 1978; Everything Is!, 1980; More Romance, Less Romanticism, 1981; Thanks for Coming! An Autobiography, 1984; Round the World in 33 Days, 1998. EDITOR: Traverse Plays, 1965; (with J. Pasle-Green) Hello, I Love You! Voices from within the Sexual Revolution, 1971; Homage to Henry (tribute to Henry Miller), 1982. TRAVEL GUIDE SERIES (ed.): People to People...: Poland; Romania; Czech Republic, Slovakia, Hungary, Bulgaria; Baltic Republics; Russia. **Address:** Atelier A-2, 83 rue de la Tombe Issoire, 75014 Paris, France. **Online address:** jim_haynes@wanadoo.fr

HAYNES, John Earl. American, b. 1944. **Genres:** History. **Career:** Library of Congress, Washington, DC, 20th-century political historian in Manuscript Division, 1987-. Historians of American Communism (newsletter), editor, 1982-. **Publications:** Dubious Alliance: The Making of Minnesota's DFL Party, 1984; Communism and Anti-Communism in the United States: An Annotated Guide to Historical Writings, 1987; (with H. Klehr) The American Communist Movement, 1992; (with H. Klehr and F. Firsov) The Secret World of American Communism, 1995; Red Scare or Red Menace? American Communism and Anticommunism in the Cold War Era, 1996; (with H. Klehr and K. Anderson) The Soviet World of American Communism, 1998; (ed.) Calvin Coolidge and the Coolidge Era, 1998; (with H. Klehr) Verona: Decoding Soviet Espionage in America, 1999; (with H. Klehr) In Denial: Historians, Communism and Espionage, 2002. **Address:** Manuscript Division, Library of Congress, Washington, DC 20540, U.S.A. **Online address:** jhay@loc.gov

HAYNES, Jonathan. American, b. 1952. **Genres:** Film. **Career:** American University in Cairo, Cairo, Egypt, visiting assistant professor of English and director of freshman writing program, 1980-82; Tufts University, Medford, MA, visiting assistant professor of English, 1982-83; Albion College, Albion, MI, assistant professor of English, 1983-85; Bennington College, Bennington, VT, professor of English, 1985-94; New York University, English Department, visiting scholar, 1994-. **Publications:** The Humanist as Traveler: George Sandys's "Relation of a Journey Begun An. Dom. 1610", 1986; The Social Relations of Jonson's Theater, 1992. EDITOR: Nigerina Video Films, 2000. Work represented in anthologies. Contributor of articles and reviews to periodicals. **Address:** Humanities Division, Southampton College, Southampton, NY 11968, U.S.A. **Online address:** jhaynes50@yahoo.com

HAYNES, Melinda. American, b. 1955. **Genres:** Novels. **Career:** Painter and writer. Archdiocese of Mobile, Catholic Week, typesetter, 1987-95. **Publications:** Mother of Pearl, 1999; Chalktown, 2001. Contributor to periodicals. **Address:** c/o Author Mail, Hyperion Books, 77 West 66th St., 11th Fl., New York, NY 10023, U.S.A.

HAYNES, Sybille (Edith). British (born Germany), b. 1926. **Genres:** Romance/Historical, Archaeology/Antiquities, Travel/Exploration. **Career:** British Museum, London, Greek and Roman Dept., voluntary assistant, 1951-76. **Publications:** Land of the Chimaera, 1974; Etruscan Sculpture, 1971; Etruscan Bronze Utensils, 1974; Zwischen Maander and Taurus, 1977; Die Tochter der Augurs, 1981; Etruscan Bronzes, 1985; The Augur's Daughter, 1987; Etruscan Civilization: A Cultural History, 2000; Kulturgeschichte der Etrusker, 2005. **Address:** Flat 17, Murray Ct, 80 Banbury Rd, Oxford OX2 6LQ, England.

HAYNIE, Barbara. (born United States), b. 1947. **Genres:** Air/Space topics. **Career:** Writer, landscape designer, businesswoman, and artist. **Publica-**

tions: The Terrain of Paradise, 2002. **Address:** 1224 N. Shields, Fort Collins, CO 80524, U.S.A. **Online address:** tbhaynie@msn.com

HAYS, Kelley Ann. See **HAYS-GILPIN, Kelley.**

HAYS, Peter L. American (born Germany), b. 1938. **Genres:** Literary criticism and history. **Career:** University of California, Davis, joined faculty, 1966, coordinator of undergrad. studies, 1973-74, chairman, dept. of English, 1974-77, professor of English, 1977-, chair, dept. of German, 1997-98. **Publications:** The Limping Hero, 1971; Ernest Hemingway, 1990; A Concordance to Hemingway's In Our Time, 1990; Teaching Hemingway's The Sun Also Rises, 2003. Contributor to professional journals. **Address:** English Dept, University of California-Davis, Davis, CA 95616, U.S.A. **Online address:** plhays@ucdavis.edu

HAYS, Tommy. American. **Genres:** Fashion/Costume. **Career:** University of North Carolina at Asheville, faculty member; teacher at South Carolina Governor's School for the Arts; director of Great Smokies Writing Program. **Publications:** Sam's Crossing (novel), 1992; In the Family Way (novel), 1999. **Address:** Literature and Language Department, 233 Karpen Hall, CPO #2130, One University Heights, Asheville, NC 28804, U.S.A.

HAYS, Tony. (Thomas Anthony). American, b. 1957. **Genres:** Novels, Mystery/Crime/Suspense, Archaeology/Antiquities, History, Politics/Government. **Career:** YMCA of Sendai, Sendai, Japan, English instructor, 1992; Motlow State Community College, Tullahoma, TN, English instructor, 1992-94; freelance writer, 1994-. Part-time English instructor; lecturer at conferences and festivals; investigative journalist. **Publications:** FICTION: Murder on the Twelfth Night, 1993; Murder in the Latin Quarter, 1993; The Trouble with Patriots, 2002. OTHER: Hardin County, Tennessee, Records, 1820-1860, 1985. Contributor of articles and short fiction to periodicals. **Address:** 951 Airways Blvd, Savannah, TN 38372, U.S.A. **Online address:** haye7434@bellsouth.net

HAYS-GILPIN, Kelley. Also writes as Kelley Ann Hays. American, b. 1960. **Genres:** Archaeology/Antiquities. **Career:** Arizona State Museum, Tucson, research associate, 1984-90; SWCA Environmental Consultants, archaeologist in Tucson and Flagstaff, AZ, 1990-92; Navajo Nation Archaeology Department, Flagstaff, ceramic specialist and editor, 1992-97; Northern Arizona University, assistant professor, 1997-2003, associate professor, 2003-. **Publications:** AS KELLEY HAYS: (ed. with E.C. Adams) Homol'ovi II: Archaeology of an Ancestral Hopi Village, 1991. EDITOR, AS KELLEY HAYS-GILPIN: (with A.C. Deegan and E.A. Morris) Prehistoric Sandals from Northeastern Arizona: The Earl H. Morris and Ann Axtell Morris Research, 1998; (with D.S. Whitley) Reader in Gender Archaeology, 1998; (with E. van Hartesveldt) Prehistoric Ceramics of the Puerco Valley, Arizona, 1998; Ambiguous Images: Gender and Rock Art, 2003. Work represented in anthologies. **Address:** Dept of Anthropology, Northern Arizona University, Box 15200, Flagstaff, AZ 86011-5200, U.S.A. **Online address:** kelley.haysgilpin@nau.edu

HAYSLIP, Le Ly. Vietnamese, b. 1949. **Genres:** Autobiography/Memoirs. **Career:** Writer. In South Vietnam, worked as a maid, black-market vendor, waitress, and hospital attendant; in United States worked as a housekeeper, factory assembly line worker, and in a restaurant. **Publications:** (with J. Wurts) When Heaven and Earth Changed Places: A Vietnamese Woman's Journey from War to Peace, 1989; (with J. Hayslip) Child of War, Woman of Peace, 1993; (author of intro. with J. Wurts) Heaven and Earth (film), 1993. **Address:** c/o Tuttle Publishing, 153 Milk St, Boston, MA 02109, U.S.A.

HAYTER, Alethea (Catharine). British (born Egypt), b. 1911. **Genres:** Literary criticism and history, Biography. **Career:** On editorial staff, Country Life, 1933-38; with British Council, London, Athens, Paris, Brussels, 1945-71. **Publications:** Mrs. Browning: A Poet's Work and Its Setting, 1962; A Sultry Month: Scenes of London Literary Life in 1846, 1965; Elizabeth Barrett Browning, 1965; Opium and the Romantic Imagination, 1968; Horatio's Version (fiction), 1972; A Voyage in Vain: Coleridge's Journey to Malta in 1804, 1973; Portrait of a Friendship: Drawn from New Letters of James Russell Lowell to Sybella Lady Lyttelton, 1881-1891, 1990; Charlotte Yonge, 1996; A Wise Woman: A Memoir of Lavinia Mynors from Her Diaries and Letters, 1996; The Wreck of the Abergavenny, 2002. EDITOR: Confessions of an English Opium Eater, by T. de Quincey, 1971; Melmoth the Wanderer, 1977; FitzGerald to His Friends: Selected Letters of Edward FitzGerald, 1979; The Backbone: Diaries of a Military Family in the Napoleonic Wars, 1993. **Address:** 22 Aldebert Terr, London SW8 1BJ, England.

HAYTER, Teresa. British (born People's Republic of China), b. 1940. **Genres:** Business/Trade/Industry, Civil liberties/Human rights, Economics,

Environmental sciences/Ecology, Geography, Industrial relations, International relations/Current affairs, Organized labor, Politics/Government, Race relations, Social sciences, Third World, Urban studies, Autobiography/Memoirs. **Career:** Researcher, writer, political activist. **Publications:** (with A. Moyes) World III, 1964; French Aid, 1966; Aid as Imperialism, 1971; Hayter of the Bourgeoisie, 1972; The Creation of World Poverty, 1981, 2nd ed., 1990; (with C. Watson) Aid: Rhetoric and Reality, 1985; Exploited Earth: Britain's Aid and the Environment, 1989; (ed. with D. Harvey) The Factory and the City: The Story of the Cowley Automobile Workers in Oxford, 1993; Urban Politics: Accommodation or Resistance?, 1997; Open Borders: The Case against Immigration Controls, 2000, 2nd ed., 2004. **Address:** c/o Pluto Publishing, 345a Archway Rd, London N6 5AA, England. **Online address:** teresahayter@onetel.com

HAYTHORNTHWAITE, Philip John. British, b. 1951. **Genres:** History, Military/Defense/Arms control. **Career:** H. Gerrard Ltd., company director, 1970-. **Publications:** Uniforms of the Napoleonic Wars, 1973; Uniforms of Waterloo, 1974; Uniforms of the American Civil War, 1975; World Uniforms and Battles 1815-50, 1976; Uniforms of the Retreat from Moscow 1812, 1976; Uniforms of the Peninsular War 1807-14, 1978; Weapons and Equipment of the Napoleonic Wars, 1979; Uniforms of the French Revolutionary Wars 1789-1802, 1981; The English Civil War, 1982; Napoleon's Line Infantry, 1983; Uniforms of 1812, 1982; Napoleon's Light Infantry, 1983; Napoleon's Guard Infantry, 2 vols., 1984-85; Civil War Soldiers, 1985; The Alamo and War of Texan Independence, 1986; Austrian Army of the Napoleonic Wars, 2 vols., 1986; Russian Army of the Napoleonic Wars, 2 vols., 1987; Uniforms Illustrated: The Boer War, 1987; British Infantry of the Napoleonic Wars, 1987; Uniforms Illustrated: The Victorian Colonial Wars, 1988; Napoleon's Military Machine, 1988; Napoleon's Specialist Troops, 1988; Wellington's Military Machine, 1989; Wellington's Specialist Troops, 1989; Fotofax: 1914, 1989; Fotofax: 1915, 1989; Fotofax: 1916, 1990; Austrian Specialist Troops of the Napoleonic Wars, 1990; Napoleonic Source Book, 1990; Fotofax: 1917, 1990; Fotofax: 1918, 1990; Gallipoli 1915, 1991; Frederick the Great's Cavalry, 1991; Frederick the Great's Infantry, 1991; Frederick the Great's Specialist Troops, 1992; World War I Source Book, 1992; Invincible Generals, 1991; Poster Book of the Civil War, 1987; Napoleon's Campaigns in Italy, 1993; Nelson's Navy, 1993; A Photohistory of World War I, 1993; The British Cavalryman 1792-1815, 1994; Armies of Wellington, 1994; Austrian Cavalry 1740-80, 1994; Austrian Infantry 1740-80, 1994; Austrian Specialist Troops 1740-80, 1995; Colonial Wars Sourcebook, 1995; Die Hard!: Dramatic Actions from the Napoleonic Wars, 1996; Imperial Guardsman, 1997; Who Was Who in the Napoleonic Wars, 1998; Waterloo Men, 1999; Corunna 1809, 2001; Napoleon's Commanders 1792-1809, 2001; Weapons & Warfare: Napoleonic Infantry, 2001, Napoleonic Cavalry, 2001; British Rifleman 1797-1815, 2002; Napoleon's Commanders 1809-1815, 2002; Wellington's Army, 2002; Peninsular War Almanac, 2004; Military Profile: Wellington, 2005. **Address:** Park Hill, Parrock Rd, Barrowford, Nelson, Lancs. BB9 6QF, England.

HAYWARD, Jennifer (Poole). American, b. 1961. **Genres:** Literary criticism and history. **Career:** High school teacher and developer of creative writing program, 1983-86; College of Wooster, Wooster, OH, associate professor of English, 1992-. Great Lakes College Association, judge of New Writers Awards, 1994-96. **Publications:** Consuming Pleasures: Active Audiences and Serial Fictions from Dickens to Soaps, 1997. Contributor to periodicals. **Address:** Department of English, College of Wooster, Wooster, OH 44691, U.S.A. **Online address:** jhayward@acs.wooster.edu

HAYWARD, Philip. British, b. 1956. **Genres:** Art/Art history. **Career:** West Surrey College of Art, Farnham, England, lecturer in media studies, 1988-90; Macquarie University, Sydney, Australia, senior lecturer in mass communications, 1991-. University of London, new technologies projects officer, 1989-90. **Publications:** (with R. Coyle) 3-D Images: Australian Holography. EDITOR: Picture This: Media Representations of Modern Art, 1988; Culture, Technology, and Creativity, 1991; From Pop to Punk to Postmodernism, 1992; (with T. Wollen) Future Visions: New Technologies of the Screen, 1993. **Address:** School of English and Linguistics, Macquarie University, Sydney, NSW 2109, Australia.

HAYWOOD, C. Robert. American, b. 1921. **Genres:** History. **Career:** Southwestern College, instructor to professor, 1948-66; Millikin University, professor of history and dean of college, 1966-69; Washburn University, professor of history and vice-president for academic affairs, 1969-82, professor of history, 1982-88, professor emeritus, 1988-; writer. **Publications:** The Doing of History, 1978; Preacher's Kid, 1985; Trails South, 1986; Cowtown Lawyers, 1988; Victorian West, 1991; Funnie Place, No Fences, 1992; Tough Daisies, 1995; Merchant Prince of Dodge City: Robert M. Wright, 1998. **Address:** 2001 Southwest Oakley Ave., Topeka, KS 66604, U.S.A.

HAYWOOD, Gar Anthony. American, b. 1954. **Genres:** Mystery/Crime/Suspense, Bibliography, Theology/Religion. **Career:** Novelist. Bell Atlantic, field engineer, 1976-88; freelance novelist, 1988-. **Publications:** Fear of the Night, 1988; Not Long for This World, 1990; You Can Die Trying, 1993; Going Nowhere Fast, 1994; Bad News Travels Fast, 1995; It's Not a Pretty Sight, 1996; When Last Seen Alive, Putnam 1997; All the Lucky Ones are Dead, 1999. **Address:** 2296 W Earl Street, Los Angeles, CA 90039, U.S.A. **Online address:** PurpleMoon@Prodigy.net

HAYWOOD, Kathleen M. American, b. 1950. **Genres:** Medicine/Health, Sports/Fitness. **Career:** University of Missouri-St. Louis, professor and associate dean, 1976-. **Publications:** (with C.F. Lewis) Teaching Archery: Steps to Success, 1989, 2nd ed, 1997; (with N. Getchell) Life Span Motor Development, 1986, 3rd ed, Learning Activities for Life Span Motor Development, 2001. **Address:** University of Missouri-St. Louis, 8001 Natural Bridge Rd., St. Louis, MO 63121, U.S.A. **Online address:** kathleen_haywood@umsl.edu

HAYWOOD, Steve. (Stephen Patrick). British, b. 1949. **Genres:** Novels. **Career:** Journalist and television producer. Worked as a journalist for Westminster Press Group and Time Out; cofounder of the magazine City Limits; worked as a producer for Thames Television; British Broadcasting Corp., producer of the investigative program Rough Justice, 1989-92, then editor of the documentary series Taking Liberties; owner and producer of Just TV (television production company). **Publications:** Murderous Justice (novel), 1991; Fruit Flies Like a Banana (travel), 2004. Contributor to magazines and newspapers. **Address:** 18 Quentin Rd, Blackheath, London SE13 5DF, England. **Online address:** sphaywood@aol.com

HAZARD, Ann. American, b. 1952. **Genres:** Novels, Food and Wine, Self help. **Career:** R.E. Hazard, Jr. Inc. (general building contractors), new project administrator, 1974-76, marketing and administration manager, 1982-85, corporate communications manager, 1988-92; Robert G. Fisher Construction Co. Inc., project administrator, 1976-79; WESTEC Services Inc., personnel administrator, 1979-80; TRW Colorado Electronics, technical writer, 1980-82; Child Protective Services for the County of San Diego, case analyst with Voices for Children, 1987-88; Childcare Connection Inc. (nanny placement agency), owner, 1986-88; freelance writer, 1992-; coordinator of divorce recovery programs; freelance writer. **Publications:** Cooking with Baja Magic (cookbook), 1997; Cartwheels in the Sand (novel), 1999; Agave Sunsets (travel stories), 2002; Rise Up & Walk (self-help), 2001. **Address:** PMB 734, PO Box 439022, San Ysidro, CA 92143-9022, U.S.A. **Online address:** cookbaja@aol.com

HAZELWOOD, Robert R. American. **Genres:** Law. **Career:** Federal Bureau of Investigation, agent beginning 1971, supervisory agent with Behavioral Science Unit, FBI Academy, beginning 1978; retired; Academy Group, Inc., Manassas, VA, forensics consultant. Writer and speaker. U.S. Military Police Corps; served as major. **Publications:** (with Park Elliott Dietz and Ann Wolbert Burgess) Autoerotic Fatalities, 1983; (with Ann Wolbert Burgess) Practical Aspects of Rape Investigation: A Multidisciplinary Approach, 1987, third edition, 2001; (As Roy Hazelwood; with Stephen G. Michaud) The Evil That Men Do: FBI Profiler Roy Hazelwood's Journey into the Minds of Sexual Predators, 1998; (As Roy Hazelwood; with Stephen G. Michaud) Dark Dreams: Sexual Violence, Homicide, and the Criminal Mind, 2001. Contributor to over forty professional journals. **Address:** c/o Author Mail, St. Martin's Press, 175 Fifth Ave, New York, NY 10010, U.S.A.

HAZLEHURST, Cameron. Australian (born United Kingdom), b. 1941. **Genres:** Criminology/True Crime, History, Politics/Government, Biography. **Career:** Oxford University, research fellow, Nuffield College, 1968-70, and Queen's College, 1970-72, and lecturer in politics, University College, 1969-72; Jonathan Cape Ltd., London, historical adviser, 1968-72; BBC television British Empire Series, series research consultant, 1969-72; Times Higher Education Supplement, London, contributing ed., 1971-72; Australian National University, Canberra, Institute of Advanced Studies, fellow, 1972-88, sr. fellow, 1988-92; Australian Dept. of Urban and Regional Development, assistant secretary, 1974-75; ABC-TV Mastermind Series, research consultant, 1977-82; Queensland University of Technology, School of Humanities, foundation professor and head, 1992-97; Flaxton Mill House, managing director, 1997-; University of South Australia, Hawke Institute, adjunct professor of government, 2002-. **Publications:** Politicians at War, July 1914 to May 1915, 1971; (with C. Woodland) A Guide to the Papers of British Cabinet Ministers 1900-1951, 1974; Menzies Observed, 1979; Gordon Chalk: A Political Life, 1987; (with C. Forster) Australian Statisticians and the Development of Official Statistics, 1988; (with G. Terrill and S.

Mendra) Government Communication, 1993; (with C. Woodland) A Liberal Chronicle: The Political Journal and Papers of J.A. Pease, 1st Lord Gainford 1908-1910, 1994; (with S. Whitehead and C. Woodland) A Guide to the Papers of British Cabinet Ministers, 1900-1964, 1995. EDITOR: W.S. Churchill, The People's Rights, 1970; The Lloyd George Liberal Magazine, 1974; The History of the Ministry of Munitions, 1974; (with J.R. Nethercote) Reforming Australian Government, 1977; Australian Conservatism, 1979; The Mastermind Book, 1979; The Mastermind General Knowledge Book, 1982; (with K.M. Hazlehurst) Gangs and Youth Subcultures, 1998. **Address:** PO Box 60, Mapleton, QLD 4560, Australia. **Online address:** flaxmill@ozconnect.net

HAZO, Samuel (John). American, b. 1928. **Genres:** Autobiography/Memoirs, Novels, Poetry, Literary criticism and history. **Career:** Professor of English, Duquesne University, Pittsburgh, 1965- (joined faculty, 1955; Dean, College of Arts and Sciences, 1961-66). Director, International Poetry Forum, Pittsburgh, 1966-. **Publications:** Discovery and Other Poems, 1959; The Quiet Wars (verse), 1962; Hart Crane: An Introduction and Interpretation, 1963, as Smithereened Apart: A Critique of Hart Crane, 1978; (ed.) The Christian Intellectual: Studies in the Relation of Catholicism to the Human Sciences, 1963; (ed.) A Selection of Contemporary Religious Poetry, 1963; Listen with the Eye (verse), 1964; My Sons in God: Selected and New Poems, 1965; Blood Rights (verse), 1968; (with A.A. Said) The Blood of Adonis (verse), 1971; (with G. Nama) Twelve Poems, 1972; Seascript: A Mediterranean Logbook (fiction), 1972; Once for the Last Bandit: New and Previous Poems, 1972; Quartered (verse), 1974; Inscripts (fiction), 1975; The Very Fall of the Sun (novel), 1978; To Paris (verse), 1981; The Wanton Summer Air (novel), 1982; Thank a Bored Angel (verse), 1983; The Feast of Icarus (essays), 1984; The Color of Reluctance (verse), 1986; The Pittsburgh that Starts within You (memoir), 1986; Nightwords (verse), 1987; Silence Spoken Here (verse), 1988; Stills (fiction), 1989; The Rest is Prose (essays), 1989; The Past Won't Stay behind You (poetry), 1993; The Pages of Day and Night (verse), 1995; The Holy Surprise of Right Now (verse), 1996; Latching the Fist (verse), 1996; As They Sail (poetry), 1999; Spying for God (essays), 1999. **Address:** 785 Somerville Dr, Pittsburgh, PA 15243, U.S.A.

HAZZARD, Shirley. American (born Australia), b. 1931. **Genres:** Novels, International relations/Current affairs. **Career:** U.N. Headquarters, NYC, member of staff, General Service Category, 1952-60; writer. **Publications:** Cliffs of Fall, 1963; The Evening of the Holiday, 1966; People in Glass Houses, 1967; The Bay of Noon, 1970; Defeat of an Ideal (intl. affairs), 1973; The Transit of Venus, 1980; Countenance of Truth (intl. affairs), 1990; Greene on Capri: A Memoir, 2000; The Great Fire (novel), 2003. **Address:** 200 E 66th St Apt C-1705, New York, NY 10021-9175, U.S.A.

HEACOX, Kim. American, b. 1951. **Genres:** Travel/Exploration, Photography, Autobiography/Memoirs, Biography. **Career:** Writer and photographer. **Publications:** California State Parks, 1987; Bush Pilots of Alaska, 1989; Alaska's National Parks, 1990; (and photographer) Iditarod Spirit, 1991; In Denali, 1992; Visions of a Wild America, 1996; (and photographer) Alaska's Inside Passage, 1997; Antarctica: The Last Continent, 1998; (and photographer) Alaska Light, 1998; Shackleton: The Antarctic Challenge, 1999; Caribou Crossing, 2001; Making the National Parks: An American Idea, 2001; The Only Kayak, 2005. Contributor to periodicals.

HEAD, David M. American, b. 1951. **Genres:** Biography. **Career:** Middle Georgia College, Cochran, GA, assistant professor of history, 198290; University System of Georgia, London, UK, assistant professor in charge of studies abroad program, 1984; South Georgia College, Douglas, GA, associate professor of history, 1990-93; John Tyler Community College, professor of history, 1993-. **Publications:** The Ebbs and Flows of Fortune: The Life of Thomas Howard, Third Duke of Norfolk, 1995. Contributor to periodicals and journals. **Address:** John Tyler Community College, 13101 Jefferson Davis Hwy, Chester, VA 23831, U.S.A. **Online address:** dhead@jt.cc.va.us

HEAD, Dominic. British, b. 1962. **Genres:** Literary criticism and history. **Career:** University of Warwick, Coventry, England, tutor in department of English and comparative literary studies, 1988-89, tutor in department of arts education, spring, 1990; University of Keele, Keele, Staffordshire, England, lecturer in English department, autumn, 1989; Open University, West Midlands, tutor, 1990; University of Central England, Perry Barr, Birmingham, England, lecturer in school of English, 1990-97; senior lecturer, 1997-98, reader, 1998-. **Publications:** The Modernist Short Story: A Study in Theory and Practice, 1992; Nadine Gordimer, 1994; J.M. Coztzee, 1997; Modern British Fiction, 1950-2000, forthcoming. Author of essays and papers presented as lectures. **Address:** School of English, University of Central England, Perry Barr, Birmingham B42 2SU, England.

HEADLEY, John M. American, b. 1929. **Genres:** History, Theology/Religion. **Career:** University of Massachusetts, instructor in history, 1959-61; Yale University, research associate, 1961-62; University of British Columbia, instructor in history, 1962-64; Southeastern Institute for Medieval and Renaissance Studies, chairman, 1967; University of North Carolina, assistant professor, 1964-66, associate professor, 1966-70, professor of early modern European history, 1970-. **Publications:** Luther's View of Church History, 1963; Responsio ad Lutherum, 1969; The Emperor and His Chancellor: A Study of the Imperial Chancellery under Gattinara, 1983; (ed. with J.B. Tomaro) San Carlo Borromeo: Catholic Reform and Ecclesiastical Politics in the Second Half of the Sixteenth Century, 1988; Tommaso Campanella and the Transformation of the World, 1997; Church, Empire and World, 1997. **Address:** Dept. of History, University of North Carolina, Chapel Hill, NC 27599-3915, U.S.A.

HEADLEY, Victor. Jamaican, b. 1960. **Genres:** Novels. **Career:** Writer. **Publications:** Yardie, 1992; Excess, 1993; Yush!, 1994. **Address:** c/o X Press, 55 Broadway Marker, London E8 4PH, England.

HEADRICK, Daniel R. American, b. 1941. **Genres:** History. **Career:** Tuskegee Institute, Tuskegee, AL, instructor, 1968-71, assistant professor, 1971-73, associate professor of history, 1973-75; Roosevelt University, Chicago, IL, associate professor, 1975-82, professor of social sciences and history, 1982-. **Publications:** Ejercito y politica en Espana, 1866-1898 (title means: The Army and Politics in Spain, 1866-1898), 1981; The Tools of Empire: Technology and European Imperialism in the Nineteenth Century, 1981; The Tentacles of Progress: Technology Transfer in the Age of Imperialism, 1851-1945, 1988; The Invisible Weapon: Telecommunications and International Politics, 1851-1945, 1991; When Information Came of Age: Technologies of Knowledge in the Age of Reason and Revolution, 1700-1850, 2000. Work represented in anthologies. Contributor of articles and reviews to scholarly journals. **Address:** University College, Roosevelt University, 430 S Michigan Ave, Chicago, IL 60605, U.S.A.

HEADY, Harold F(ranklin). American, b. 1916. **Genres:** Environmental sciences/Ecology. **Career:** Professor Emeritus of Range Mgmt. and Plant Ecology, and Assistant Vice-President, Agriculture and University Services, University of California, Berkeley (Associate Dean, College of Natural Resources, 1974-77; Associate Director, Agricultural Experiment Station, 1977-80). Assistant Professor Montana State University, Bozeman, 1942-47; Associate Professor, Texas University, College Station, 1947-51. **Publications:** (with E.B. Heady) High Meadow, 1970; Range Management, 1975; Rangeland Ecology and Management, 1994, rev. ed., 2001. **Address:** 1864 Capistrano Ave, Berkeley, CA 94707, U.S.A.

HEAL, Gillian. (Gillian Ferguson). British, b. 1934. **Genres:** Children's fiction, Illustrations. **Career:** Halfpenny Houses (toy designers and manufacturers), Bideford, England, co-founder, 1972, toy design, 1972-2000. Graphic designer; painter with solo exhibitions and group shows. **Publications:** SELF-ILLUSTRATED FOR CHILDREN: The Halfpennys Find a Home, 1994; Jack and the Beanstalk, 1995; Tom Thumb, 1995; Rapunzel, 1996; Grandpa Bear's Fantastic Scarf, 1996; Thumbelina & Rumpelstiltskin, 1997; Hansel & Gretel, 1998; Opa Bar und Sein Langer, Bunter Schal, 1998; Cinderella, 1999; Aunt Lily's Great Adventure, 2000. **Address:** Overskern, Churchill Way, Appledore, Bideford EX39 1PA, England.

HEALD, Suzette. Scottish, b. 1943. **Genres:** Anthropology/Ethnology. **Career:** Makerere University, Kampala, Uganda, research fellow, 1965-69; University of Lancaster, Lancaster, England, lecturer and senior lecturer, 1971-99; Smithsonian Institution, research fellow, 1987-88; University of Botswana, associate professor, 1997-99; Brunel University, professor of social anthropology, 2000-. **Publications:** Controlling Anger: The Sociology of Gisu Violence, 1989; (co-ed.) Anthropology and Psychoanalysis: An Encounter through Culture, 1994; Praise Poems of the Kuria, 1997; Manhood and Morality: Sex, Violence and Ritual in Gisa Society, 1999. **Address:** Dept of Human Sciences, Brunel University, Uxbridge UB3 3PH, England. **Online address:** Suzette.Heald@brunel.ac.uk

HEALD, Tim(othy Villiers). Also writes as David Lancaster. British, b. 1944. **Genres:** Novels, Novellas/Short stories, Mystery/Crime/Suspense, Biography. **Career:** Sunday Times, London, Atticus column, reporter, 1965-67; Town mag., London, feature editor, 1967; Daily Express, London, feature writer, 1967-72; freelance journalist, London, 1972-77; Weekend Magazine, Toronto, associate editor, 1977-78; freelance journalist, 1978-; The Observer, London, author of Pendennis column, 1990; University of Tasmania, writer-in-residence, 1997-99; University of S Australia, writer-in-residence, 2001. FRSL, 2000. **Publications:** MYSTERY NOVELS: Unbecoming Habits,

1973; Blue Blood Will Out, 1974; Deadline, 1975; Let Sleeping Dogs Lie, 1976; Just Desserts, 1977; Murder at Moose Jaw, 1981; Masterstroke, 1982; Red Herrings, 1985; Brought to Book, 1988; Business Unusual, 1989; Death and the Visiting Fellow, 2004. NOVELS: It's a Dog's Life, 1971; (as David Lancaster in U.K.) Caroline R., 1981; Class Distinctions, 1984; Stop Press, 1998. BIOGRAPHY: John Steed: An Authorized Biography, 1977; (with M. Mohs) H.R.H.: The Man Who Will Be King, 1979; The Duke: A Portrait of Prince Philip, 1991; Barbara Cartland: A Life of Love, 1994; Denis: The Authorised Biography of the Incomparable Compton, 1994; Brian Johnston, The Authorised Biography, 1995. OTHER: The Making of Space 1999, 1976; Networks, 1983; The Character of Cricket, 1986; Honourable Estates, 1992; By Appointment: 150 Years of the Royal Warrant, 1989; Beating Retreat: Hong Kong under the Last Governor, 1997; A Peerage for Trade, 2001; Village Cricket, 2004. EDITOR: The Newest London Spy, 1988; A Classic English Crime, 1990; My Lord's, 1990; A Classic Christmas Crime, 1995. **Address:** 66 The Esplanade, Fowey, Cornwall PL23 1JA, England. **Online address:** tim@timheald.com

HEALEY, Denis (Winston). (Lord Healey of Riddlesden). British, b. 1917. **Genres:** Economics, International relations/Current affairs, Politics/Government. **Career:** Lord Healey of Riddlesden, 1992. Labour M.P. for Leeds East 1955-82 (M.P. for S.E. Leeds, 1952-55; Secretary of State for Defence, 1964-70; Chancellor of the Exchequer, 1974-79). Member, Labour Party National Executive Committee Secretary, Labour Party International Dept., 1946-52. Member of Council, Royal Institute of International Affairs, London, 1948-60; Member of the Executive, Fabian Society, 1954-61; Member of the Council, Institute of Strategic Studies, London, 1958-61. **Publications:** The Curtain Falls, 1951; New Fabian Essays, 1952; Neutralism, 1955; Fabian International Essays, 1956; A Neutral Belt in Europe, 1958; NATO and American Security, 1959; The Race Against the H Bomb, 1960; Labour Britain and the World, 1963; Managing the Economy, 1979; Healey's Eye, 1980; Labour and World Society, 1985; Beyond Nuclear Deterrence, 1986; The Time of My Life, 1989; When Shrimps Learn to Whistle, 1990; My Secret Planet, 1992; Denis Healey's Yorkshire Dales, 1995; Healey's World, 2002. **Address:** House of Lords, London SW1, England.

HEALEY, Dorothy (Ray). American, b. 1914. **Genres:** Autobiography/Memoirs, Politics/Government, Documentaries/Reportage. **Career:** United Cannery, Agricultural & Packing-House Workers' Union, vice president, 1937-40; State of California, deputy labor commissioner, 1940-43; Mine, Mill & Smelter Workers' Union, international representative, 1944-46; Communist Party of Southern California, chair, 1949-69; writer. **Publications:** (with Maurice Isserman) Dorothy Healey Remembers a Life in the American Communist Party, Oxford University Press, 1990.

HEALY, Jeremiah. Also writes as Terry Devane. American, b. 1948. **Genres:** Mystery/Crime/Suspense. **Career:** Lawyer. New England School of Law, Boston, professor, 1978-96; full-time novelist, 1996-. Recipient: Private Eye Writers of America Shamus Award, 1986. **Publications:** Blunt Darts, 1984; The Staked Goat (in U.K. as The Tethered Goat), 1986; So Like Sleep, 1987; Swan Dive, 1988; Yesterday's News, 1989; Right to Die, 1991; Shallow Graves, 1992; Foursome, 1993; Act of God, 1994; Rescue, 1995; Invasion of Privacy, 1996; The Only Good Lawyer, 1998; The Stalking of Sheilah Quinn, 1998; The Concise Cuddy, 1998; Spiral, 1999; Turnabout, 2000; Cuddy Plus One, 2002; Off-Season and Other Stories, 2003. AS TERRY DEVANE: Uncommon Justice, 2001; Juror #11, 2002; A Skin upon the Robe, 2003. **Address:** 186 Commonwealth Ave Ste 31, Boston, MA 02116, U.S.A. **Online address:** jeremiahhealy@earthlink.net; www.jeremiahhealy.com

HEALY, Sophia (Warner). American, b. 1938. **Genres:** Novels. **Career:** Artist and Novelist. Teacher of drawing and papermaking at Bennington College, 1968-82; director of Trout Paper (workshop), 1980-. **Publications:** Lone Stars (novel), 1989. **Address:** P.O. Box 528, North Bennington, VT 05257-0528, U.S.A.

HEANEY, Seamus. Irish, b. 1939. **Genres:** Poetry, Literary criticism and history. **Career:** Harvard University, Cambridge, MA, visiting professor, 1982-85, Boylston Professor of Rhetoric and Oratory, 1985-96, Ralph Waldo Emerson Poet-in-Residence, 1996-. Secondary sch. teacher, 1962-63; lecturer, St. Joseph's College of Education, Belfast, 1963-66; lecturer in English, Queen's University, Belfast, 1966-72, and Carysfort Training College, Dublin, 1975-81; professor of poetry, Oxford University, 1989-94. **Publications:** Eleven Poems, 1965; Death of a Naturalist, 1966; (with D. Hammond and M. Longley) Room to Rhyme, 1968; A Lough Neagh Sequence, 1969; Door into the Dark, 1969; Night Drive: Poems, 1970; Boy Driving His Father to Confession, 1970; Land, 1971; (ed. with Alan Brownjohn and Jon

Stallworthy) New Poems 1970-71, 1971; Wintering Out, 1972; (ed.) Soundings 2, 1974; North, 1975; The Fire i' the Flint: Reflections on the Poetry of Gerard Manley Hopkins, 1975; Bog Poems, 1975; Stations, 1975; Robert Lowell: A Memorial Lecture and an Eulogy, 1978; Field Work, 1979; Selected Poems, 1980; Preoccupations: Selected Prose, 1980; An Open Letter, 1983; Sweeney Astray: A Version from the Irish, 1983; Station Island, 1984; The Haw Lantern, 1987; The Government of the Tongue, 1988; (ed.) The Essential Wordsworth, 1988; The Place of Writing, 1990; New Selected Poems 1966-1987, 1990; Seeing Things, 1991; The Cure at Troy, 1991; Sweeney's Flight, 1992; The Midnight Verdict, 1993; The Spirit Level (poetry), 1996; Crediting Poetry: The Nobel Lecture, 1996; Opened Ground: Poems, 1966-1996, 1998; Beowulf: A New Verse Translation, 1999 (Whitbread Award); L. Janacek of poems by O. Kalda, Diary of One Who Vanished: A Song Cycle, 2000; Electric Light, 2001; Finders Keepers: Selected Prose 1971-2001, 2002; Burial at Thebes, 2004. **Address:** Department of English & American Literature & Language, Harvard University, Barker Center, 12 Quincy St, Cambridge, MA 02138, U.S.A.

HEARD, Anthony Hazlitt. South African, b. 1937. **Genres:** History. **Career:** Cape Times, Cape Town, South Africa, reporter, 1955-64, assistant editor, 1967-71, editor, 1971-87; Financial Mail, Cape Town, Cape editor, 1964-65; South African Morning Newspapers Bureau, London, England, senior correspondent, 1965-66; free-lance writer, 1987-94; Special Adviser to Minister Kader Asmal in S. Africa Government, 1994-; Visiting fellow, Harvard University, 1987-88; Visiting associate professor, and fellow, Fulbright Institute, University of Arkansas, 1989, 1992. World Assn. of Newspapers, Golden Pen of Freedom, 1986; Pringle Award for South African journalism, 1986. **Publications:** The Cape of Storms: A Personal History of the Crisis in South Africa, 1990, rev. ed., 1991. **Address:** P.O. Box 12189, Mill St, Cape Town 8010, Republic of South Africa.

HEARDEN, Patrick J. American, b. 1942. **Genres:** History. **Career:** Case Western Reserve University, Cleveland, OH, assistant professor, 1971-72; University of South Dakota, Vermillion, assistant professor, 1972-75; University of Missouri-Columbia, assistant professor, 1975-76 and 1977-79; University of Wisconsin-Madison, assistant professor, 1976-77 and 1981-82; University of Arizona, Tucson, assistant professor, 1979-80; Purdue University, West Lafayette, IN, professor, 1983-; writer. **Publications:** Independence and Empire, 1982; Roosevelt Confronts Hitler, 1987; (ed.) Vietnam: Four American Perspectives, 1990; The Tragedy of Vietnam, 1991, 2nd ed., 2005; Architects of Globalism, 2002. **Address:** Dept of History, Purdue University, West Lafayette, IN 47907, U.S.A.

HEARN, Chester G. American, b. 1932. **Genres:** History, Humanities, Inspirational/Motivational Literature, Marine sciences/Oceanography, Meteorology/Atmospheric sciences, Military/Defense/Arms control, Theology/Religion, Biography. **Career:** Combustion Engineering, Muncy, PA, vice-president for manufacturing, 1973-90; Philip A. Crosby Associates Inc., consultant, 1990-93; CJ Quality Associates, vice president, 1997-98. **Publications:** Gray Raiders of the Sea, 1992; Mobile Bay and the Mobile Campaign, 1993; George Washington's Schooners, 1995; The Capture of New Orleans, 1862, 1995; Admiral David Dixon Porter, 1996; Six Years of Hell, 1996; Companions in Conspiracy, 1996; Admiral David Glasgow Farragut, 1998; When the Devil Came Down to Dixie, 1997; (with S.A. Hearn) Safe in the Arms of Jesus: The Story of Fanny Crosby, 1998; Ellet's Brigade, 2000; The Impeachment of Andrew Johnson, 2000; Naval Battles of the Civil War, 2000; The American Soldier in World War II, 2001; An Illustrated History of the U.S. Navy; An Illustrated History of the U.S. Marines; Tracks in the Sea: Matthew Fontaine Maury and the Mapping of the Oceans; Sorties into Hell, 2003; Circuits in the Sea, 2004; The Maccabees, 2004; Herod the Great, 2004. Contributor to magazines. **Address:** 5266 Wolf Run Village Ln, Erie, PA 16505, U.S.A.

HEARN, Julie. American. **Genres:** Children's fiction. **Career:** Writer, editor, and educator. Worked as a journalist in Australia, Spain, and England. Presenter at workshops for children. **Publications:** Follow Me Down, 2003. **Address:** c/o Author Mail, Oxford University Press, Great Clarendon St., Oxford OX2 6DP, England.

HEARN, Otis. See **TRENERRY, Walter N.**

HEARNE, Reginald. British, b. 1929. **Genres:** Plays/Screenplays, Songs/Lyrics and libretti. **Career:** Freelance actor, writer, 1948-; film producer, Columbia Films, 1961-; involved in production administration, Play Fare Productions Ltd, currently. **Publications:** Serena: Echo of Diana; The Little Crime; The Sicians; The Colonel's Ride; Bank Raid; Tangle; The Web; Over

My Shoulder; The Practice; A Strange Place to Meet. **Address:** Lion Cottage, 14 Greys Rd, Henley-on-Thames, Oxon., England.

HEARON, Shelby. American, b. 1931. **Genres:** Novels. **Career:** Novelist, 1968-. Guggenheim Fiction Fellowship, 1982; National Endowment Fiction Fellowship, 1983; Ingram-Merrill Grant, 1986; American Academy and Institute of Letters Literature Award, 1990. Visiting professor, University of California, Irvine, 1987, University of Illinois, Chicago, 1983, University of Miami, Coral Gables, 1994, University of Massachusetts, Amherst, 1994-96, Middlebury College, 1996-98. **Publications:** NOVELS: Armadillo in the Grass, 1968; The Second Dune, 1973; Hannah's House, 1975; Now and Another Time, 1976; A Prince of a Fellow, 1978; Painted Dresses, 1981; Afternoon of a Faun, 1983; Group Therapy, 1984; A Small Town, 1985; Five Hundred Scorpions, 1987; Owning Jolene, 1989; Hug Dancing, 1991; Life Estates, 1994; Footprints, 1996; Ella in Bloom, 2001. Works appear in periodicals. **Address:** 246 S Union St, Burlington, VT 05401-5414, U.S.A.

HEATER, Derek Benjamin. British, b. 1931. **Genres:** Education, History, International relations/Current affairs, Politics/Government. **Career:** Education Officer, RAF, 1954-57; Assistant Master in secondary schs., 1957-62; Lecturer in History, 1962-66, and Head of the Dept. of History, 1966-76, Brighton College of Education; Dean of the Faculty of Social and Cultural Studies, 1976-79, and Head of the Humanities Dept., 1976-83, Brighton Polytechnic. Chairman, Politics Association, 1969-73; Ed., Teaching Politics, 1973-79. **Publications:** Political Ideas in the Modern World, 1960; Order and Rebellion, 1964; The Cold War, 1964; (with G. Owen) World Affairs, 1972; Contemporary Political Ideas, 1974; Britain and the Outside World, 1976; (with B. Crick) Essays on Political Education, 1977; Peace and War, 1978; Essays on Contemporary Studies, 1979; World Studies: Education for International Understanding in Britain, 1980; Our World This Century, 1982; Peace through Education, 1984; Our World Today, 1985; Reform and Revolution, 1987; Refugees, 1988; Case Studies in Twentieth-Century World History, 1989; Citizenship, 1990, 3rd ed., 2004; The Idea of European Unity, 1992; (with G.R. Berridge) Introduction to International Politics, 1993; The Remarkable History of Rottingdean, 1993; (with D. Oliver) The Foundations of Citizenship, 1994; National Self-Determination: Woodrow Wilson and His Legacy, 1994; World Citizenship and Government, 1996; The Theory of Nationhood, 1998; Keeping Faith: A History of Sutton Grammar School, 1998; What Is Citizenship?, 1999; World Citizenship: Cosmopolitan Thinking and Its Opponents, 2002; A History of Education for Citizenship, 2004; A Short History of Citizenship, 2004. EDITOR: The Teaching of Politics, 1969; (with J. Gillespie) Political Education in Flux, 1981. **Address:** 3 The Rotyngs, Rottingdean, Brighton BN2 7DX, England.

HEATH, Dwight B. American, b. 1930. **Genres:** Anthropology/Ethnology, History, Sociology. **Career:** Brown University, Providence, RI, professor of anthropology, 1959-. World Health Organization, consultant in mental health, 1973-. **Publications:** A Journal of the Pilgrims at Plymouth: Mourt's Relation, 1963, rev. ed., 1986; (with C.J Erasmus and H.C. Buechler) Land Reform and Social Revolution in Bolivia, 1969; Historical Dictionary of Bolivia, 1972; (with A.M. Cooper) Alcohol Use in World Cultures, 1981; Drinking Occasions, 2000. EDITOR: (with R.N. Adams) Contemporary Cultures and Societies of Latin America: A Reader in the Social Anthropology of Middle and South America, 1965, (sole ed.) 1974, 2001; (with M.W. Everett and J.O. Waddell) Cross-Cultural Approaches in the Study of Alcohol, 1976; (with J.O. Waddell and M.D. Topper) Cultural Factors in Alcohol Research and Treatment of Drinking Problems, 1981; International Handbook on Alcohol and Culture, 1995. Articles in journals, chapters in books, and entries in encyclopedias. **Address:** Dept of Anthropology, Box 1921, Brown University, Providence, RI 02912, U.S.A.

HEATH, (Sir) Edward (Richard George). British, b. 1916. **Genres:** Music, Politics/Government, Sports/Fitness, Autobiography/Memoirs, International relations/Current affairs. **Career:** Conservative Member of Parliament (U.K.) for Old Bexley and Sidcup, since 1983 (M.P. for Bexley, 1950-74, for Bexley-Sidcup, 1974-83); Assistant Conservative Whip, 1951; Lord Commissioner of the Treasury, 1951; Joint Deputy Government Chief Whip, 1952, and Deputy Government Chief Whip, 1953-55; Parliamentary Secretary to the Treasury and Government Chief Whip, 1955-59; Minister of Labour, 1959-60; Lord Privy Seal, 1960-63; Secretary of State for Industry, Trade, and Regional Development, and President of the Board of Trade, 1963-64; Leader of the Opposition, 1965-70; Prime Minister, Minister for the Civil Service, and First Lord of the Treasury, 1970-74; Leader of the Opposition, 1974-75. President, Federation of University Conservative and Unionist Assns., since 1959. Chairman, of Commonwealth Parliamentary Association, since 1970. Vice President, Bach Choir, since 1970. Member, Brandt Independent Commission on International Development Issues, from 1977. President, Oxford

University Conservative Association, 1937; Chairman, Federation of University Conservative Assns., 1938; President, Oxford Union, 1939; served in the Administration Civil Service, 1946-47. Member of Council, Royal College of Music, London, 1961-70; Chairman, London Symphony Orchestra Trust, 1963-70; Knight of the Garter, 1992. **Publications:** (with others) One Nation: A Tory Approach to Social Problems, 1950; One World, New Horizons (Godkin Lectures), 1970; Sailing: A Course of My Life, 1975; Music, A Joy for Life, 1976, rev. ed. 1997; Travels: Peoples and Places in My Life, 1977; Carols: The Joy of Christmas, 1977. **Address:** House of Commons, London SW1A 0AA, England.

HEATH, Jennifer. Australian. **Genres:** Novels, Art/Art history, Literary criticism and history. **Career:** Writer. **Publications:** Black Velvet: The Art We Love to Hate, 1994; On the Edge of Dream: Celtic Tales for Grown Women, 1995; A House White with Sorrow (novel), 1996; (with N. Berry) Cerridwen and the Cauldron of Knowledge (juvenile fiction), 1997; On the Edge of Dream: The Women in Celtic Myth and Legend, 1998; Super ColCn: A Historical Comic Book; El Repelente (or the Anti-Nuke Antics of Anabela). Contributor to newspapers. **Address:** 4125 Nassau Pl, Boulder, CO 80301-6029, U.S.A.

HEATH, Lorraine. American (born England), b. 1954. **Genres:** Romance/Historical, Young adult fiction. **Career:** Romance novelist, 1993-. **Publications:** HISTORICAL ROMANCE NOVELS: Sweet Lullaby, 1994; Parting Gifts, 1994; The Ladies' Man, 1995; Always to Remember, 1996; Texas Destiny, 1997; Texas Glory, 1998; Texas Splendor, 1999; To Tame a Texan Anthology, 1999; A Rogue in Texas, 1999; Never Love a Cowboy, 2000; Never Marry a Cowboy, 2001; The Outlaw & the Lady, 2001; Samantha and the Cowboy, 2002; To Marry an Heiress, 2002; Amelia and the Outlaw, 2003; Love with a Scandalous Lord, 2003; Hard Lovin' Man, 2003; Smooth Talkin' Stranger, 2004; An Invitation to Seduction, 2004; As an Earl Desires, 2005; A Matter of Temptation, 2005. **Address:** PO Box 250034, Plano, TX 75025-0034, U.S.A. **Online address:** lorraine-heath@comcast.net

HEATH, Malcolm (Frederick). British, b. 1957. **Genres:** Classics. **Career:** Hertford College, Oxford, research fellow, 1984-87; University of St. Andrews, Scotland, lecturer in Greek, 1987-88; University of Leeds, lecturer, 1988-92, reader, 1992-2000, professor of Greek, 2000-. **Publications:** The Poetics of Greek Tragedy, 1987; Political Comedy in Aristophanes, 1987; Unity in Greek Poetics, 1989; Hermogenes on Issues: Strategies of Argument in Later Greek Rhetoric, 1995; Aristotle: Poetics, 1996; Interpreting Classical Texts, 2002; Menander: A Rhetor in Context, 2004. **Address:** School of Classics, University of Leeds, Leeds LS2 9JT, England.

HEATH, Sandra. *See* WILSON, Sandra.

HEATH, Sebastian E. American, b. 1955. **Genres:** Animals/Pets. **Career:** Oleoducto Nor Peruano, Peru, industrial radiographer, 197576; University of Maryland, Overseas Branch, instructor in biology, 1984-85; junior assistant for a large-animal veterinary practice in Carmarthen, Wales, 1985-86, and for a companion-animal and equine practice in Epping, England, 1986-87; Marquis Downs, Saskatoon, Saskatchewan, Thoroughbred Race Track Commission veterinarian, 1987-88; Montclair Veterinary Hospital, Oakland, CA, associate, 198889; University of Florida, Rural Animal Medicine Service, clinical instructor, 1989-90, assistant professor of largeanimal clinical sciences, 1990-91; Purdue University, West Lafayette, IN, section chief for large animal medicine, 1991-94; Federal Emergency Management Agency, project coordinator for Animals in Disaster, an independent study course, 1996-98; Purdue University, assistant professor of veterinary clinical services, 1998-. Diplomate of American College of Internal Medicine and American College of Veterinary Preventive Medicine; Tripler Army Medical Center, Hawaii, adjunct faculty member, 1996 and 1997. **Publications:** Rescuing Rover: A First Aid & Disaster Guide for Dog Owners, 1998; Animal Management in Disasters, 1999. **Address:** 1650 Harvard St NW #718, Washington, DC 20009-3737, U.S.A.

HEATH, Veronica. (Veronica Heath Blackett). British, b. 1927. **Genres:** Animals/Pets, Food and Wine, Natural history. **Career:** Freelance journalist and Northumberland Country Diarist for The Guardian newspaper, London; regular freelance contributor to many publications. **Publications:** Susan's Riding School, 1956; Ponies in the Heather, 1959; Come Riding with Me, 1964; Come Show Jumping with Me, 1966; Ponies and Pony Management, 1966; Come Pony Trekking with Me, 1966; Ponies, 1969; Beginner's Guide to Riding, 1971; The Family Dog, 1972; So You Want to Be a Showjumper, 1974; So You Want to Own a Pony, 1974; Riding for Beginners, 1978; Perfect Cooking with Game, 1983; A Dog at Heel, 1987, rev. ed., 1999; Geordie Cook Book, 1995; A Gundog Handler's Guide to Picking Up, 1999;

Taste of Northumberland, 2001. **Address:** Seven Stars House, Whalton, Morpeth, Northd. NE61 3XA, England.

HEATH-STUBBS, John (Francis Alexander). British, b. 1918. **Genres:** Plays/Screenplays, Poetry, Literary criticism and history, Translations. **Career:** English teacher, Hall School, Hampstead, London, 1944-45; Editorial Assistant, Hutchinson & Co., publrs., London, 1945-46; Gregory Fellow in Poetry, Leeds University, 1952-55; Visiting Professor of English, University of Alexandria, Egypt, 1955-58, and University of Michigan, Ann Arbor, 1960-61; Lecturer in English, College of St. Mark and St. John, London, 1963-72; Tutor, Merton College, Oxford, 1975-91. **Publications:** Wounded Thammuz, 1942; Beauty and the Beast, 1943; The Divided Ways, 1947; The Charity of the Stars, 1949; The Swarming of the Bees, 1950; The Darkling Plain, 1950; The Talking Ass (play), 1953; A Charm against the Toothache, 1954; Charles Williams, 1955; The Triumph of the Muse and Other Poems, 1958; Helen in Egypt and Other Plays, 1958; The Blue-Fly in His Head: Poems, 1962; Selected Poems, 1965; Satires and Epigrams, 1968; The Verse Satire, 1969; The Ode, 1969; The Pastoral, 1969; Artorius, 1970; Indifferent Weather (poetry), 1975; A Parliament of Birds, 1975; The Watchman's Flute, 1978; The Mouse, the Bird and the Sausage, 1978; Birds Reconvened, 1980; Buzz Buzz, 1981; Naming the Beasts, 1982; The Immolation of Aleph, 1986; Cats Parnassus, 1988; Time Pieces, 1988; A Partridge in a Pear Tree, 1988; Collected Poems, 1988; A Ninefold of Charms, 1989; Selected Poems, 1990; Game of Love and Death, 1990; The Parson's Cat, 1991; Sweetapple Earth, 1993; Chimeras, 1994; Galileo's Salad, 1996; Torriano Sequenius, 1999; Sound of Light, 1999; Eight Poems of Sulpicia, 2000; The Return of the Cranes, 2003. TRANSLATOR: Poems from Giocomo Leopardi, 1946; Aphrodite's Garland, 1952; (with P. Avery) Thirty Poems of Hafiz of Shiraz, 1955; (with I. Origo) G. Leopardi, Selected Poetry and Prose, 1966; A. de Vigny, The Horn/Le Cor, 1969; (with P. Avery) The Ruba'iyat of Omar Khayyam, 1979; (with C. Whiteside) Anyte, 1979. EDITOR: Selected Poems of Shelley, 1947; Selected Poems of Tennyson, 1947; Selected Poems of Swift, 1947; (with D. Wright) The Forsaken Garden: An Anthology of Poetry 1824-1909, 1950; Images of Tomorrow (poetry anthology), 1953; (with D. Wright) The Faber Book of Twentieth Century Verse, 1953; Selected Poems of Alexander Pope, 1964; (with F.T. Prince and S. Spender) Penguin Modern Poets 20, 1971; (with M. Green) Homage to George Barker on His 60th Birthday, 1973; (with D. Wright) The Faber Book of Twentieth Century Verse, 1975; (with P. Salman) Poems of Science, 1984. **Address:** 22 Artesian Rd, London W2, England.

HEATON, Tom. (Thomas Peter Starke). British (born Germany), b. 1928. **Genres:** Area studies, Third World. **Career:** BBC Monitoring Service, Caversham, England, Persian monitor, 1955-56; British Overseas Civil Service, Aden, South Arabia, education officer, 1957-61, vice-principal of government secondary school, 1961-64, chief inspector of schools, 1964-66, deputy permanent secretary of Ministry of Supreme Council Affairs, 1966-68; Ministry of Education, Nairobi, Kenya, high school English teacher and department head, 1968-70; BBC Monitoring Service, Arabic monitor, 1970-73, editor of Middle East/Africa Summary of World Broadcasts, 1973-76, senior assistant in East African Unit, 1976-81; conducted field work in East Africa, 1981-83; BBC Monitoring Service, Arabic monitor and editor in East African Unit, 1983-. **Publications:** In Teleki's Footsteps: A Walk across East Africa, 1990. **Address:** East African Unit, BBC Monitoring Service, P.O. Box 24945, Nairobi, Kenya.

HEBER, R. See COX, Richard (Hubert Francis).

HECHT, Anthony (Evan). See Obituaries.

HECHT, Jeff(rey Charles). American, b. 1947. **Genres:** Natural history, Sciences, Technology, Young adult non-fiction. **Career:** Laser Focus, Newton, Mass., managing editor, 1974-81; freelance science and technology writer and consultant, 1981-, Boston correspondent, New Scientist (part-time), 1985-. **Publications:** (with D. Teresi) Laser: Super Tool of the 1980s, 1982; Beam Weapons: The Next Arms Race, 1984; The Laser Guidebook, 1986, 2nd ed., 1991; Understanding Fiber Optics, 1987, 4th ed., 2002; Understanding Lasers, 1988, 2nd ed., 1993; Optics: Light for a New Age (juvenile), 1988; Shifting Shores: Rising Seas, Retreating Coastlines (juvenile), 1990; Laser Pioneers, 1992; Vanishing Life (juvenile), 1993; City of Light: The Story of Fiber Optics, 1999; (with B. Hitz and J.J. Ewing) Introduction to Laser Technology, 2001. **Address:** 525 Auburn St, Auburndale, MA 02466, U.S.A. **Online address:** jeff@jeffhecht.com

HECHT, Jennifer Michael. American, b. 1965. **Genres:** Anthropology/Ethnology. **Career:** Educator, writer, poet. Nassau Community College, Garden City, NY, assistant professor of history. **Publications:** The Next

Ancient World (poetry), 2001; The End of the Soul: Scientific Modernity, Atheism, and Anthropology in France, 2003; Doubt: A History: The Great Doubters and Their Legacy of Innovation from Socrates and Jesus to Thomas Jefferson and Emily Dickinson, 2003. Contributor of poems to anthologies and of poems to periodicals and Web sites. **Address:** Nassau Community College, Education Dr., Garden City, NY 11530, U.S.A. **Online address:** hechtjm@aol.com

HECHT, Michael L. American, b. 1949. **Genres:** Communications/Media, Cultural/Ethnic topics, Speech/Rhetoric. **Career:** University of Illinois at Urbana-Champaign, Urbana, instructor in communication, 1975-76; University of Montana, Missoula, assistant professor of communication, 1976-78; California State University, Northridge, assistant professor of communication, 1978-79; Xerox Corp., Systemix Division, data analyst and project manager, 1979-81; University of Southern California, Los Angeles, assistant professor of communication, 1979-83; Arizona State University, Tempe, assistant professor, 1983-85, associate professor, 1985-89, professor of communication, 1989-98; Penn State University, professor, 1998-, department head, 1999-. Executive producer of the drug prevention videotape Killing Time, 1990; producer and writer of the videotape Homelessness: Everybody's Problem, 1993; producer of the public access cable production Kids Broadcasting System News. **Publications:** (with M.J. Collier and S. Ribeau) African American Communication, 1993, 2nd ed. (with R.L. Jackson and S. Ribeau), 2003; (with others) Adolescent Relationships; and Drug Abuse, 2000; (with R.R. Baldwin, S.L. Faulkner, and S.L. Lindsley) Conceptualizing Culture, forthcoming. EDITOR: (with J.A. DeVito) The Nonverbal Communication Reader, 1989, 2nd ed. (with L. Guerrero and J.A. DeVito), 1999; Communicating Prejudice, 1998. **Address:** Department of Communication Arts and Sciences, Penn State University, 234 Sparks Bldg, University Park, PA 16802, U.S.A. **Online address:** mhecht@psu.edu

HECKERT, Connie K(aye Delp). American, b. 1948. **Genres:** Children's fiction, Human relations/Parenting, Local history/Rural topics. **Career:** Iowa State University Veterinary Clinics, Ames, IA, medical records librarian, 1968-1973; freelance writer, 1972-; Peoria Engineering, East Moline, IL, proofreader, 1975; Illowa Health Systems Agency, Davenport, IA, assistant health planner, 1977-1978; Black Hawk College, Moline, IL, instructor, 1985; St. Ambrose University, Davenport, adjunct assistant professor of English, 1985-1993; Augustana College, Rock Island, IL, Dept of English, 2002-. Society of Children's Book Writers and Illustrators-Iowa, regional adviser, 2000-. Keynote speaker and teacher of conferences and workshops. **Publications:** FOR CHILDREN: Miss Rochelle and the Lost Bell, 1985; Dribbles, 1993. FOR ADULTS: Lyons: 150 Years North of the Big Tree, 1985; The Swedish Connections, 1986; The First 100 Years: A Pictorial History of Lindsay Park Yacht Club, 1987; (with K.M. Becker) To Keera with Love: Abortion, Adoption or Keeping the Baby, 1987; (with V. Berry) Roots & Recipes: Six Generations of Heartland Cookery, 1995. Contributor to periodicals. Frequently writes for Des Moines Register. **Address:** 1462 Old Freeport Pl, Bettendorf, IA 52722-7001, U.S.A.

HECKSCHER, Charles. American, b. 1949. **Genres:** Organized labor. **Career:** Harvard University, Cambridge, MA, Harman fellow at John F. Kennedy School of Government, 1979-81; Communications Workers of America, Washington, DC, research economist, 1981-84; Harvard University, assistant professor at Harvard Business School, 1986-91, associate professor of human resource management, 1991-92, codirector of Project on Employment Relations, Program on Negotiation, Harvard Law School, 1988-; Rutgers University, New Brunswick, NJ, associate professor of labor studies and employment relations and head of department, 1992-. **Publications:** The New Unionism: Employee Involvement in the Changing Corporation, 1988; (ed. with A. Donnellon and contrib) The Post-Bureaucratic Organization: New Perspectives on Organizational Change, 1994; White-Collar Blues: Management Loyalties in an Age of Corporate Restructuring, 1995. Contributor to books. Contributor to professional journals. **Address:** School of Management and Labor Relations, Rutgers University, Ryders Lane, New Brunswick, NJ 08903, U.S.A.

HEDDERWICK, Mairi. British (born Scotland), b. 1939. **Genres:** Children's fiction, Travel/Exploration, Illustrations. **Publications:** FOR CHILDREN: Katie Morag Delivers the Mail, 1984; Katie Morag and the Two Grandmothers, 1985; Katie Morag and the Tiresome Ted, 1986; Katie Morag and the Big Boy Cousins, 1987; Peedie Peebles' Summer or Winter Book in U.S. as P.D. Peebles' Summer or Winter Book, 1989; Katie Morag and the New Pier, 1993; Peedie Peebles Colour Book, 1994; The Tale of Carpenter MacPheigh, 1994; Katie Morag and the Wedding, 1995; The Big Katie Morag Storybook, 1996; Katie Morag and the Grand Concert, 1997; The Second Katie Morag Storybook, 1998; Katie Morag's Rainy Day Book,

1999; Katie Morag and the Riddles, 2001; Katie Morag's Island Stories, 2003; A Walk with Grannie, 2003; Katie Morag, of Course, 2003; Katie Morag and the Birthdays, 2005. ADULT NON-FICTION: An Eye on the Hebrides: Illustrated Travel, 1989; A Highland Journey: Illustrated Travel, 1992; Sea-Change: Illustrated Travel, 1999. Illustrator of books by others. **Address:** c/o Curtis Brown Ltd, Haymarket House, 28/29 Haymarket 4th Fl, London SWIY 4SP, England.

HEDGECOE, John. British, b. 1937. **Genres:** Photography. **Career:** Queen Magazine, London, staff photographer, 1957-72; freelance photographer for international magazines, 1958-; freelance photographer for the London Sunday Times and Observer, 1960-70; Royal College of Art, Kensington Gore, London, reader in photography and head of photography department, 1965-74, chair of photography department, 1975, professor of photography, 1975-94, professor emeritus, 1994-, fellow, 1973, managing trustee, 1983, senior fellow, 1992. John Hedgecoe Ltd., director, 1965-95; Perennial Pictures Ltd., director 1980, 1991; Lion & Unicorn Press Ltd., director 1986-94. Works have been exhibited worldwide; photographs are also featured in a number of permanent collections. **Publications:** Kevin Crossley-Holland Book of Norfolk Poems, 1970; Sculptures of Picasso, 1970; (with others) Photography, Material and Methods (annual publication), 1971-74; Henry Moore, Energy in Space, 1973; The Book of Photography, 1976, rev. and updated ed., as The Book of Photography: How to See and Take Better Pictures, 1984; Handbook of Photographic Techniques, 1977; Possessions, 1978; John Hedgecoe's Pocket Guide to Practical Photography, 1979, rev. and expanded as The Photographer's Workbook, 1983; Introductory Photography Course, 1979; Master Classes in Photography: Children and Child Portraiture, 1980; What a Picture!, 1983, in US as John Hedgecoe's Taking Great Photographs, 1984; (with J. Tresidder and R. Platt) The Art of Colour Photography, 1978, rev. and updated ed. as The Art of Color Photography, 1989; The Book of Advanced Photography, 1982; Aesthetics of Nude Photography, 1984; The Workbook of Photo Techniques, 1984; The Workbook of Darkroom Techniques, 1984; John Hedgecoe's Nude Photography, 1984; John Hedgecoe's Darkroom Techniques, 1985, in UK as The Workbook of Darkroom Techniques, 1990; John Hedgecoe's Photographer's Workbook, 1985; John Hedgecoe's Photographic Techniques, 1985; John Hedgecoe's Nude and Portrait Photography, 1985; John Hedgecoe's New Manual of Photography, 1986; John Hedgecoe's Pocket Guide to Vacation Photography, 1986; (with R. van der Meer) The Working Camera: The World's First Three-Dimensional Guide to Photography Made Easy, 1986; Pocket Book of Travel and Holiday Photography, 1986; Henry Moore: His Ideas, Inspirations and Life as an Artist, 1986; The Three Dimensional Pop-up Photography Book, 1986; Photographer's Manual of Creative Ideas, 1986; John Hedgecoe's Practical Portrait Photography, 1987; The Photographer's Sourcebook, 1987; John Hedgecoe's Practical Landscape Photography, 1988, as John Hedgecoe's Landscape Photography, 1994; Hedgecoe on Photography, 1988; Hedgecoe on Video: A Complete Creative and Technical Guide to Making Videos, 1989; John Hedgecoe's Complete Video Course: A Step-by-Step, SelfInstruction Guide to Making Great Videos, 1989; The Workbook of Photographic Techniques, 1990; Complete Photography Guide, 1990; John Hedgecoe's Practical Portrait Photography, 1991, in US as John Hedgecoe's Complete Guide to Photographing People, 1992; The Workbook of Nudes and Glamour, 1991; The Photographer's Handbook, 3rd rev. ed., 1992; John Hedgecoe's Complete Guide to Video, 1992; (with S.S. Damluji) Zillij: The Art of Moroccan Ceramics, 1992; Video Photographer's Handbook, 1992; John Hedgecoe's Photography Basics, 1993; John Hedgecoe's Compete Guide to Black and White Photography: And Darkroom Techniques, 1994; John Hedgecoe's New Book of Photography, 1994; The Spirit of the Garden, 1994; Black and White Photography, 1994; John Hedgecoe's Camcorder Basics, 1995; John Hedgecoe-A Complete Introductory Guide-Video, 1995; Breakfast with Dolly (novel), 1996; Figure and Form, 1996; John Hedgecoe's New Introductory Photography Course, 1996. Contributor of photographs to books. **Address:** 47 Riverside Court, Nine Elms Lane, London SW8 5BY, England.

HEDGES, Joseph. See GILMAN, George G.

HEDIN, Robert (Alexander). American, b. 1949. **Genres:** Poetry. **Career:** Sheldon Jackson College, Sitka, AK, instructor in English, 1973-76; University of Alaska, Anchorage, visiting instructor in creative writing, 1976-77; Ecole Nationale d'Administration, Paris, France, teacher of English as a second language, 1978; University of Alaska, Fairbanks, visiting assistant professor of English, 1979-80; Wake Forest University, Winston-Salem, NC, poet-in-residence, 1980-92, 1995-96; Loft Literacy Center, Minneapolis, MN, instructor, 1993-94, 1996-97; Associated Colleges of the Twin Cities, visiting writer-in-residence, 1995-96; University of Minnesota, lecturer, 1995-96, Edelstein-Keller Minnesota Writer of Distinction, 2001-02;

Anderson Center for Interdisciplinary Studies, executive director, 1997-; Great River Review, editor, 1997-; St. Olaf College, visiting poet-in-residence, 2000-01. **Publications:** POETRY: Snow Country, 1975; At the Home-Altar, 1979; County O, 1984; Tornadoes, 1990; The Old Liberators, 1998. EDITOR OF ANTHOLOGIES: (with D. Stark) In the Dreamlight, 1984; (with G. Holthaus) Alaska, 1989; (with Holthaus) The Great Land, 1994; The Great Machines, 1996; The Zeppelin Reader, 1998; Perfect in Their Art, 2003. TRANSLATOR: In Lands Where Light Has Another Color: Poems of Rolf Jacobsen, 1990; Night Music: Poems of Rolf Jacobsen, 1994; B. Sortland, The Dream Factory, 2001; O.H. Hauge, The Bullfinch Rising from the Cherry Tree, 2001; R. Jacobsen, (with R. Bly and R. Greenwald) The Roads Have Come to an End Now, 2001; (with R. Bly) O.H. Hauge, Passing the Arctic Circle, 2003. Work represented in anthologies. Contributor of articles, poems, translations from Swedish and Norwegian poetry, and reviews to periodicals. **Address:** PO Box 59, Frontenac, MN 55026, U.S.A.

HEEFNER, Wilson A. American, b. 1931. **Genres:** Military/Defense/Arms control. **Career:** University of Maryland School of Medicine, Baltimore, assistant professor, 1966-68; Dameron Hospital, Stockton, CA, pathologist, 1968-88; military historian and writer, 1988-. **Publications:** Twentieth Century Warrior, 1995; Patton's Bulldog: The Life and Service of General Walton H. Walker, 2001. Contributor to periodicals. **Address:** 7205 Park Woods Dr, Stockton, CA 95207-1409, U.S.A. **Online address:** w.heefner@comcast.net

HEER, David M(acAlpine). American, b. 1930. **Genres:** Demography. **Career:** U.S. Bureau of the Census, statistician in Social Statistics Branch, Population Division, 1957-61; University of California, Berkeley, lecturer in sociology and assistant research sociologist, 1961-64; Harvard University, Cambridge, MA, assistant professor, 1964-68, associate professor of demography, 1968-72; University of Southern California, Los Angeles, professor of sociology and director of Population Research Laboratory, 1972-2000; University of California, San Diego, Center for Comparative Immigration Studies, senior scholar, 2000-. **Publications:** After Nuclear Attack: A Demographic Inquiry, 1965; Society and Population, 1968, 3rd ed. (with J. Grigsby), 1992; (with P. Herman) A Human Mosaic: An Atlas of Ethnicity in Los Angeles County, 1980-1986, 1990; Undocumented Mexicans in the United States, 1990; Immigration in America's Future: Social Science Findings and the Policy Debate, 1996; Kingsley Davis: A Biography and Selections from His Writings, 2005. EDITOR: Social Statistics and the City, 1968; Readings on Population, 1968. **Address:** Center for Comparative Immigration Studies, University of California, San Diego, La Jolla, CA 92093-0548, U.S.A. **Online address:** dheer@ucsd.edu

HEERBOTH, Sharon. See LEON, Sharon.

HEERTJE, Arnold. Dutch, b. 1934. **Genres:** Economics, Marketing, Money/Finance. **Career:** University of Amsterdam, Netherlands, professor of economics, 1964-99, professor of history of economic thought, 1997-. Adviser to government and private companies. **Publications:** Economics and Technical Change, 1977; Basic Economics, 1980; The Black Economy, 1982. EDITOR: Schumpeter's Vision: Capitalism, Socialism, and Democracy after Forty Years, 1982; Investing in Europe's Future, 1983; Innovation, Technical and Financial, 1988; The Economics of the State, 1989; (with M. Perlman) Studies in Schumpeterian Economics, (with J. Van Daal) History of Economic Thought in the Netherlands, 1650-1950, 1992; World Savings, 1993; The Makers of Modern Economics, Vol. 1, 1993, Vol. 2, 1995, Vol. 3, 1997, Vol. 4, 1999; (with J. Polak) European Transport Economics, 1993; (with J. Polak) Analytical Transport Economics, 2001. Contributor to periodicals periodicals. **Address:** 17 Laegieskampweg, 1412ER Naarden, Netherlands. **Online address:** joab@heertje.nl

HEFER, Hayim (Baruch). (born Poland), b. 1925. **Genres:** Adult non-fiction. **Career:** Writer, translator. Former columnist for Yediot Ahronot. El-Hamam Satirical Theater, cofounder, 1960. Worked for the Consul for Cultural Affairs for the West Coast. **Publications:** Milim la-manginot, 1961; The Megilla of Itzik Manger (play), 1969; To Live Another Summer, to Pass Another Winter (play), 1971; (with Dan Ben-Amotz) Tel-Aviv ha-ketanah: hizayon, 1980; Af milah ra ah, 1998. Author of screenplays and over a thousand song lyrics. **Address:** 53 Arlozoroff St., Tel Aviv, Israel.

HEFFER, Simon (James). British, b. 1960. **Genres:** History. **Career:** Medical journalist, 1983-85; freelance journalist, 1985-86; Daily Telegraph, London, England, leader writer, 1986-91, deputy correspondent, 1987-88, political sketch writer, 1988-91, political columnist 1990-91, deputy editor and political columnist, 1994-95; Spectator, deputy editor, 1991-94; Evening Standard, columnist, 1991-93; Daily Mail, columnist, 1993- 94, 1995-.

Publications: (ed., with C. Moore) A Tory Seer: The Selected Journalism of T.E. Utley, 1989; Moral Desperado: A Life of Thomas Carlyle, 1995; Power and Place: The Political Consequences of King Edward VII, 1998; Like the Roman: The Life of Enoch Powell, 1998; The End of the Peer Show?, 1998; Nor Shall My Sword: The Reinvention of England, 1999. **Address:** c/o Daily Mail, 2 Derry St., London W8 5TT, England.

HEFFERNAN, Nancy Coffey. American, b. 1936. **Genres:** History, Area studies. **Career:** Writer. **Publications:** WITH ANN PAGE STECKER: New Hampshire: Crosscurrents in Its Development, 1986; Sisters of Fortune: Being the True Story of How Three Motherless Sisters Saved Their Home in New England and Raised Their Younger Brother While Their Father Went Fortune Hunting in the California Gold Rush, 1993. OTHER: (with L. Judson) What's In a Name?: The Heroes and Heroines Baby Name Book, 1990. **Address:** c/o University Press of New England, 23 South Main St., Hanover, NH 03755, U.S.A.

HEFFRON, Dorris. Canadian, b. 1944. **Genres:** Novels, Young adult fiction, Essays. **Career:** Oxford University, tutor in literature, 1970-79; Wainfleet Public Library, writer-in-residence, 1989-90. **Publications:** NOVEL: A Shark in the House, 1996. ESSAYS: More than Words Can Say, 1990. YOUNG ADULT NOVELS: A Nice Fire and Some Moonpennies, 1971; Crusty Crossed, 1976; Rain and I, 1982. **Address:** Little Creek Wolf Range, RR#1, Clarksburg, ON, Canada N0H 1J0.

HEGARTY, Frances. Also writes as Frances Fyfield. British, b. 1948. **Genres:** Mystery/Crime/Suspense. **Career:** Crown Prosecution Service, London, England, solicitor, 1975-. **Publications:** MYSTERY NOVELS AS FRANCES FYFIELD: A Question of Guilt, 1989; Deep Sleep, 1992; Shadowplay, 1993; Perfectly Pure and Good, 1994; A Clear Conscience, 1994; without Consent, 1997; Blind Date, 1998; Staring at the Light, 2000; Undercurrents, 2001. MYSTERY NOVELS AS FRANCES HEGARTY: Trial by Fire, 1990; Shadows on the Mirror, 1991; The Playroom, 1991; Half Light, 1993; Deep Sleep, 1992; Let's Dance, 1994.

HEGEMAN, (Sister) Mary Theodore. (Sister Mary Theodore). American, b. 1907. **Genres:** Education, History, Biography. **Career:** Principal, 1947-64, Supt., 1964-70, and Director of Public Relations, 1970-87, St. Coletta School, Jefferson, Wisconsin. **Publications:** The Challenge of the Retarded Child, 1959, 3rd ed. 1969; Developmental Disability-A Family Challenge, 1984; A Short Life of Saint Coletta, 1987; History of St. Coletta School, 1989. **Address:** St. Coletta School, Jefferson, WI 53549, U.S.A.

HEGENBERGER, John. American, b. 1947. **Genres:** How-to books. **Career:** Writer of software documentation, film scripts, and advertising copy; arts and entertainment editor of This Week. Military service: U.S. Navy. **Publications:** Collector's Guide to Comic Books, Chilton, 1990. Collector's Guide to Treasures of the Silver Screen, Chilton, 1991. **Address:** William Morris Agency, 6487 Ethen Dr., Reynoldsburg, OH 43068, U.S.A.

HEIDAR, Knut (Martin). Norwegian, b. 1949. **Genres:** Politics/Government. **Career:** Institute for Social Research, research assistant to senior research assistant, 1972-74; University of Oslo, Oslo, Norway, faculty member, 1975-, professor of political science, 1992-. University of Warwick, visiting researcher, 1986-87; University of Denver, visiting researcher, 1998. **Publications:** Norske politiske fakta 1884-1982, 1983; Partidemokrati på prøve: Norske partieliter i demokratisk perspektiv, 1988; (with L. Svåsand) Partiene i en brytningstid, 1994; (with L. Svåsand) Partier uten grenser?, 1997; (with E. Berntzen) Vesteuropeisk politikk, 3rd ed, 1998. EDITOR: (with P. Esaiasson) Beyond Westminster and Congress: The Nordic Experience, 2000; (with R. Koole) Parliamentary Party Groups in European Democracies: Political Parties behind Closed Doors, 2000. **Address:** Institut for statsvitenskap, University of Oslo, Postboks 1097-Blindern, 0317 Oslo, Norway. **Online address:** k.m.heidar@stv.uio.no

HEIDBREDER, Robert K. Canadian/American (born United States), b. 1947. **Genres:** Poetry. **Career:** Vancouver School Board, Vancouver, Canada, primary school teacher, 1975-; gives readings, lectures, workshops, and conferences on poetry and language development. **Publications:** Don't Eat Spiders (poems), 1985; (comp. and contrib.) I Hate Dinosaurs, 1992; Eenie Meenie Manitoba: Playful Poems from Coast to Coast, 1996; Python Play and Other Recipes for Fun (poems), 2000; I Wished for a Unicorn, 2000; SeeSaw Saskatchewan, 2002; Drumheller Dinosaur Dance, 2004. Poems collected in anthologies. **Address:** 1124 Cloverley St, North Vancouver, BC, Canada V7L 1N6.

HEIDE, Florence Parry. Also writes as Alex B. Allen, Jamie McDonald. American, b. 1919. **Genres:** Children's fiction. **Career:** Full-time writer.

Formerly worked for RKO and in public relations and advertising, New York; former public relations dir., Pittsburgh Playhouse. **Publications:** Benjamin Budge and Barnaby Ball, 1967; (with S.W. Van Clief) Maximilian, 1967; (with S.W. Van Clief) The Day It Snowed in Summer, 1968; (with S.W. Van Clief) How Big Am I?, 1968; (with S.W. Van Clief) It Never Is Dark, 1968; (with S.W. Van Clief) Sebastian, 1968; (with S.W. Van Clief) That's What Friends Are For, 1968; (as Jamie McDonald; with A. and W. Theiss) Hannibal, 1968; Maximilian Becomes Famous, 1969; (with S.W. Van Clief) The New Neighbor, 1970; Alphabet Zoop, 1970; Giants Are Very Brave People, 1970; The Little One, 1970; Sound of Sunshine, Sound of Rain, 1970; Look! Look! A Story Book, 1971; The Key, 1971; The Shrinking of Treehorn, 1971; Some Things Are Scary, 1971; Who Needs Me?, 1971; Songs to Sing about Things You Think About (songs), 1971; Christmas Bells and Snowflakes (songs), 1971; Holidays! Holidays! (songs), 1971; My Castle, 1972; (with S.W. Van Clief) The Mystery of the Missing Suitcase, 1972; (with S.W. Van Clief) The Mystery of the Silver Tag, 1972; (as Alex B. Allen; with S.W. Van Clief) Basketball Toss Up, 1972; (as Alex B. Allen; with S.W. Van Clief) No Place for Baseball, 1973; (with S.W. Van Clief) The Hidden Box Mystery, 1973; (with S.W. Van Clief) Mystery at MacAdoo Zoo, 1973; (with R. Heide) Lost! (textbook), 1973; (with R. Heide) I See America Smiling (textbook), 1973; (with S.W. Van Clief) Mystery of the Whispering Voice, 1974; (with R. Heide) Mystery of the Melting Snowman, 1974; (with D.F. Parry) No Roads for the Wind (textbook), 1974; (with S.W. Van Clief) Who Can? (reader), 1974; (with S.W. Van Clief) Lost and Found (reader), 1974; (with S.W. Van Clief) Hats and Bears (reader), 1974; (with R. Heide) Tell about Someone You Love (textbook), 1974; (as Alex B. Allen; with S.W. Van Clief) Danger on Broken Arrow Trail, 1974 (as Alex B. Allen; with S.W. Van Clief) Fifth Down, 1974; (as Alex B. Allen; with S.W. Van Clief and D. Heide) The Tennis Menace, 1975; God and Me (non-fiction), 1975; You and Me (non-fiction), 1975; (with R. Heide) Mystery of the Vanishing Visitor, 1975; (with R. Heide) Mystery of the Bewitched Bookmobile, 1975; When the Sad One Comes to Stay, 1975; Growing Anyway Up, 1976; (with R. Heide) Mystery of the Lonely Lantern, 1976; (with R. Heide) Mystery at Keyhole Carnival, 1977; (with R. Heide) Brillstone Break-In, 1977; (with R. Heide) Mystery of the Midnight Message, 1977 (with S.W. Van Clief) Fables You Shouldn't Pay Any Attention To, 1978; Banana Twist, 1978; Secret Dreamer, Secret Dreams, 1978; (with R. Heide) Fear at Brillstone, 1978; (with R. Heide) Mystery at Southport Cinema, 1978; (with R. Heide) I Love Every-People, 1978; Changes (non-fiction), 1978; Who Taught Me? Was It You, God? (non-fiction), 1978; By the Time You Count to Ten (non-fiction), 1979; (with R. Heide) Face at the Brillstone Window, 1979; (with R. Heide) Mystery of the Mummy's Mask, 1979; (with R. Heide) Body in the Brillstone Garage, 1980; (with R. Heide) Mystery of the Forgotten Island, 1980; (with R. Heide) A Monster Is Coming! A Monster Is Coming!, 1980; (with R. Heide) Black Magic at Brillstone, 1981; Treehorn's Treasure, 1981; Time's Up!, 1982; The Problem with Pulcifer, 1982; The Wendy Puzzle, 1982; (with R. Heide) Time Bomb at Brillstone, 1982; (with R. Heide) Mystery On Danger Road, 1983; Banana Blitz, 1983; Treehorn's Wish, 1984; Time Flies, 1984; Tales for the Perfect Child, 1985; (with J.H. Gilliland) The Day of Ahmed's Secret, 1990; (with J.H. Gilliland) Sami and the Time of the Troubles, 1992; Grim and Ghastly Goings On (songs), 1992; The Bigness Contest, 1993; (with R. Heide Pierce) Timothy Twinge, 1993; (with R. Heide Pierce) Oh, Grow Up, 1996; (with R. Heide Pierce) Tio Armando, 1998; The House of Wisdom, 1998; It's about Time: Poems, 1999; Some Things Are Scary, 2000. **Address:** c/o Marilyn Marlow, Curtis Brown, 10 Astor Place, New York, NY 10003, U.S.A.

HEIDE, Kathleen M. American, b. 1954. **Genres:** Criminology/True Crime. **Career:** University of South Florida, Tampa, assistant professor, 1981-87, associate professor, 1987-94, professor of criminology, 1994-. Center for Mental Health Education, Assessment, and Therapy, licensed psychotherapist; Hillsborough County Sexual Abuse Treatment Center, member of board of directors, 1983-87; Hillsborough County Crisis Center, member of board of directors, 1983-87; Hillsborough County Constituency for Children, member of board of directors, 1992-; court-appointed expert for Florida's circuit courts; guest on television programs. **Publications:** Why Kids Kill Parents: Child Abuse and Adolescent Homicide, 1992; Young Killers: The Challenge of Juvenile Homicide, 1999. Work represented in anthologies. Contributor of articles and reviews to periodicals. **Address:** Department of Criminology SOC 107, University of South Florida, 4202 E Fowler Ave, Tampa, FL 33620-8100, U.S.A. **Online address:** kheide@chuma1.cas.usf.edu

HEIDEL, R. Andrew. American, b. 1969. **Genres:** Poetry. **Career:** Writer. Avon Books, NYC, publicist to senior publicist, 1996-. Worked on Wall Street, for a cleaning company, and as a dancer, disc jockey, zine editor, milliner, wire sculptor, and puppeteer. **Publications:** Beyond the Wall of Sleep:

A Collection of Prose and Poetry, 1988-1997, 1997, 2nd ed, 1998. **Address:** c/o Avon Books, HarperCollins Publishers, 10 E 53rd St, New York, NY 10022, U.S.A.

HEIDENRY, John. American, b. 1939. **Genres:** Communications/Media, Sex, Sports/Fitness. **Career:** Social Justice Review, St. Louis, MO, assistant editor, c. 1957-61; St. Louis Review, St. Louis reporter, c. 1961-63; Herder & Herder, NYC, managing editor, 1963-72; St. Louis, editor, 1977-82; Penthouse Forum, NYC, executive editor to editor, 1982-89; freelance writer, 1989-. St. Louis Literary Supplement, co-founder, 1977; Continuum Publishing Group, consultant editor; The Week, executive editor, 2000-. **Publications:** Test Your Sex I.Q., 1988; Theirs Was the Kingdom, 1993; What Wild Ecstasy, 1997; Leftover Heroes, 2005. EDITOR: The Penthouse Letters, 1989; Erotica from Penthouse, 1990.

HEIDLER, David S(tephen). American, b. 1955. **Genres:** History. **Career:** Salisbury State University, Salisbury, MD, assistant professor of history, 1984-93; University of Southern Colorado, Pueblo, visiting professor of history, 1994-2002. **Publications:** Pulling the Temple Down: The Fire-Eaters and the Destruction of the Union, 1994; (with J.T. Heidler) Old Hickory's War: Andrew Jackson and the Quest for Empire, 1996; The War of 1812, 2002; Manifest Destiny, 2003; Daily Life in the Early Republic: Creating a New Nation, 1790-1820, 2004. EDITOR WITH J.T. HEIDLER: Encyclopedia of the War of 1812, 1997; Encyclopedia of the American Civil War, 2000.

HEIDLER, Jeanne T(wiggs). American, b. 1956. **Genres:** History. **Career:** Salisbury State University, Salisbury, MD, assistant professor of history, 1985-93; U.S. Air Force Academy, Colorado Springs, CO, associate professor of history, 1993-. **Publications:** (with D.S. Heidler) Old Hickory's War: Andrew Jackson and the Quest for Empire, 1996; (ed. with D.S. Heidler) Encyclopedia of the War of 1812, 1997. **Address:** 187 Dolomite Dr, Colorado Springs, CO 80919, U.S.A. **Online address:** jtheidler@aol.com

HEILBRONER, Robert L. *See* Obituaries.

HEILMAN, Robert B. American, b. 1906. **Genres:** Literary criticism and history, Education, Adult non-fiction. **Career:** Professor Emeritus of English, University of Washington, Seattle, since 1977 (Professor, 1948-76; Chairman of Dept., 1948-71). Staff member, Ohio University, Athens, 1928-30, University of Maine, 1931-35, and Louisiana State University, Baton Rouge, 1935-48; Arnold Professor, Whitman College, Walla Walla, Wash., 1977. President, Philological Association of Pacific Coast, 1959; Member, Executive Council, American Association of University Profs., 1963-65, and Modern Language Association of America, 1966-70. Senator, Phi Beta Kappa, 1967-85. **Publications:** America in English Fiction 1760-1800, 1937; This Great Stage: Image and Structure in King Lear, 1948; Magic in the Web: Action and Language in Othello, 1956; Tragedy and Melodrama: Versions of Experience, 1968; The Iceman, the Arsonist, and the Troubled Agent: Tragedy and Melodrama on the Modern Stage, 1973; The Charliad, 1973; The Ghost on the Ramparts, and Other Essays in the Humanities, 1974; The Ways of the World: Comedy and Society, 1978; The Southern Connection: Selected Essays, 1991; The Workings of Fiction: Essays, 1991; The Professor and the Profession (essays), 1999. EDITOR: (with C. Brooks) Understanding Drama, 1948; Modern Short Stories, 1950; Conrad's Lord Jim, 1957; English Drama before Shakespeare, 1962; Hardy's Mayor of Casterbridge, 1962; Eliot's Silas Marner, 1962; Shakespeare's Cymbeline, 1964; Euripides' Alcestis, 1965; Hardy's Jude the Obscure, 1966; Shakespeare's The Taming of the Shrew, 1966; Hardy's Tess of the d'Urbervilles, 1971; Shakespeare: The Tragedies, 1984. **Address:** c/o Dept. of English, Box 354330, University of Washington, Seattle, WA 98195, U.S.A.

HEIM, Michael Henry. American, b. 1943. **Genres:** Politics/Government, Translations. **Career:** Czech Commission for Cooperation with UNESCO, Prague, Czechoslovakia, translator, summers of 1965, 1966, and 1968; Czechoslovak Academy of Sciences, Prague, lexicographer, summers of 1966 and 1968; Harvard University, Cambridge, MA, teaching fellow, 1966-69, visiting associate professor, 1985-86; University of Wisconsin, Madison, assistant professor, 1970-72; University of California, Los Angeles, assistant professor, 1972-79, associate professor, 1979-86, professor, 1986-; University of California, Berkeley, visiting assistant professor, 1977-78. **Publications:** NONFICTION: Contemporary Czech, 1976; The Russian Journey of Karel Havlicek Borovsky, 1979. TRANSLATOR: The Letters of Anton Chekhov, 1973, as Anton Chekhov's Life and Thought: Selected Letters and Commentary, 1996; The Death of Mr. Baltisberger by B. Hrabal, 1975; Three Sisters (play) by A. Chekhov, 1976; Uncle Vanya (play) by A. Chekhov, 1976; The Seagull (play) by A. Chekhov, 1979; The Cherry Orchard (play) by A. Chekhov, 1980; The Book of Laughter and Forgetting by M. Kundera,

1980; The Joke by M. Kundera, 1982; The Island of Crimea by V. Aksyonov, 1983; Novel With Cocaine by M. Ageyev, 1984; The Unbearable Lightness of Being by M. Kundera, 1984; Jacques and His Master: An Homage to Diderot in Three Acts (play) by M. Kundera, 1985; Crime and Punishment (play), 1986; Chekhov by H. Troyat, 1986; Master and Margarita (play), 1987; (with A.W. Bouis) In Search of Melancholy Baby by V. Aksyonov, 1987; The White Plague (play) by K. Capek, 1988; The Encyclopedia of the Dead (short stories) by D. Kis, 1989; Astrophobia by S. Sokolov, 1990; Too Loud a Solitude by B. Hrabal, 1990; Helping Verbs of the Heart by P. Esterhazy, 1991; A Certain Finkelmeyer by F. Roziner, 1991; Fording the Stream of Consciousness (short stories) by D. Ugresic, 1991; (with C. Hawkesworth) In the Jaws of Life (short stories) by D. Ugresic, 1992; Uncle Fedya, His Dog, and His Cat (children's book) by E. Uspensky, 1993; Prague Tales (short stories) by J. Neruda, 1993; Migrations, Vol 1, by M. Tsernianski, 1994; (and selector and author of afterword) The Melancholy of Rebirth: Essays from Post-Communist Central Europe, 1989-1994 (nonfiction) by G. Konrad, 1995; Dancing Lessons for the Advanced in Age by B. Hrabal, 1995. EDITOR: (with O. Matich) The Third Wave: Russian Literature in Emigration, 1984; (with Z. Meyerstein and D. Worth) Readings in Czech, 1985; Maria and the Angels (play) by P. Kohout, 1989; Magic Prague, by A.M. Ripellino, trans by D.N. Marinelli, 1993; Talks With T.G. Masaryk (nonfiction), by K. Capek, trans by D. Round, 1995. Contributor of scholarly articles and reviews to journals; contributor of reviews of contemporary East European literature to periodicals. **Address:** Department of Slavic Languages and Literatures, 115 Kinsey Hall, University of California, 405 Hilgard Ave., Los Angeles, CA 90095, U.S.A. **Online address:** heim@humnet.ucla.edu

HEIM, Scott. American, b. 1966. **Genres:** Novels, Poetry. **Career:** Novelist and poet. **Publications:** Saved from Drowning: Poems, 1993. NOVELS: Mysterious Skin, 1995; In Awe, 1997. **Address:** c/o Louise Quayle, Trident Media Group, 41 Madison Ave, Fl 38, New York, NY 10010-2257, U.S.A. **Online address:** scottheim@aol.com

HEIMANN, Judith M(oscow). American, b. 1936. **Genres:** Biography. **Career:** Foreign Area Studies Program, American University, Washington, DC, researcher, 196872; U.S. Embassy, Brussels, Belgium, vice consul, 1972-75, assistant attache, 1975-78; U.S. Embassy, Kinshasa, Zaire, second secretary, 1978-80; U.S. Mission to the European Economic Community (EEC), Brussels, Belgium, first secretary, 1980-84; EEC political affairs, U.S. Department of State, Washington, DC, officer-in-charge, 1984-86; U.S. Consulate, Bordeaux, France, consul general, 1987-91; Indochinese refugee program, U.S. Embassy, Manila, coordinator, 1991-92. **Publications:** The Most Offending Soul Alive: Tom Harrisson and His Remarkable Life, 1999. **Address:** PO Box 578, Oxford, MD 21654, U.S.A.

HEIMS, Steve J(oshua). American (born Germany), b. 1926. **Genres:** Environmental sciences/Ecology, History, Intellectual history, Physics, Sciences, Biography. **Career:** Friends' Service Committee, volunteer worker in Mexico, 1951-52; National Advisory Commission for Aeronautics, Mountain View, CA, research scientist, 1955-58; Brandeis University, Waltham, MA, research fellow and assistant professor of physics, 1960-65; Wayne State University, Detroit, MI, associate professor of physics, 1966-69; Boston University, MA, visiting professor of history and philosophy of science, 1970-71. Visiting member of faculty at University of New Hampshire, Brandeis University, University of Massachusetts at Boston, Lesley College, and Worcester Polytechnic Institute, 1975-84. **Publications:** John von Neumann and Norbert Wiener: From Mathematics to the Technologies of Life and Death, 1980; (ed. and contrib.) Passages from Berlin, 1987; The Cybernetics Group, 1991 (as Constructing a Social Science for Postwar America: The Cybernetics Group 1946-1953, 1993). **Address:** 14 Babson St, Gloucester, MA 01930-3604, U.S.A.

HEIN, Christoph. German (born Poland), b. 1944. **Genres:** Novels, Plays/Screenplays, Translations. **Career:** German playwright, novelist, political essayist and speaker. Volksbuhne (People's Stage), East Berlin, dramaturge and director's assistant, 19711974, house author, 1974-1979. Visiting dramatist at universities and theaters. Has also worked as book dealer, waiter, and factory worker. **Publications:** NOVELS: Einladung zum Lever bourgeois, 1980 as Nachfahrt und fruher Morgen, 1982; Cromwell, under andere Stucke (title means: Cromwell and Other Plays), 1981; Der fremde Freund (title means: The Distant Lover), 1982 as Drachenblut (Dragonblood), 1983 trans. by K. Winston as The Distant Lover, 1989; Nachtfahrt und fruher Morgen, 1982; Das Wildpferd unterm Kachelofen: Ein schones dickes Buch von Jakob Borg und seinen Freunden, 1984; Die wahre Geschichte des Ah Q (title means: The True Story of Ah Q, based on a novel by Lu Hsun), 1984 as The True Story of Ah Q, 1990; Horns Ende (Horn's End), 1985; Schlotel oder Was solls: Stucke und Essays, 1986; Offentlich arbeiten: Essais und Gesprache, 1987; Die Ritter der Tafelrunde: Komodie, 1989; Der Tangospieler (title means: The Tango Player), 1989; trans. by P. Boehm as The Tango Player, 1991; Als Kind habe ich stalin gesehen: Essais und Reden, 1990; Die funfte Grundrechenart: Aufsatze und Reden, 1990; Bridge Freezes before Roadway, 1990; Das Napoleon-Spiel, 1993. PLAYS: Schlotel, oder Was solls, 1974; Vom hungrigen Hennicke, 1974; Cromwell, 1980; Lassalle fragt Herrn Herbert nach Sonja: Die Szene ein Salon, 1980; Der Neue Menoza oder Geschichte des kumbanischen Prinzen Tandi: Komodie nach Jakob Michael Reinhold Lenz, 1981; Die wahre Geschichte des Ah Q, 1983; Passage, 1987; Die Ritter der Tafelrunde (The Knights of the Round Table), 1989; Ma … Ma … Marlene: Szenen aus Horns Ende, 1990. OTHER: (trans. of play) Britannicus, by J. Racine, 1980; Das Wildpferd unterm Kachelofen (children's book), 1984 trans. as Jamie and His Friends, 1988; Der Bund proletarischrevolutionarer Schriftsteller Deutschland: Biography eines Kulturpolitischen Experiments in der Weimarer Republik (nonfiction), 1991; Exekution eines Kalbes und andere Erzahlungern, 1994; (contrib of introductory essay) Nachdenken uber Deutschland: Herausgegeben von Dietmar Keller (speeches by Gunther Grass and others), 1990-1991. **Address:** c/o Aufblau-Verlag, Postfach 1217, 1086 Berlin, Germany.

HEINBUCH, Jean (M.). American, b. 1953. **Genres:** Art/Art history. **Career:** Artist, working with traditional Native American art forms, such as porcupine quill embroidery, beadwork, and painting on leather and rawhide for museums and collectors. Instructor and consultant on Native American art forms. **Publications:** A Quillwork Companion (self-illustrated), Eagle's View, 1990; A Beadwork Companion (self-illustrated), Eagle's View, 1992. **Address:** P.O. Box 444, Clark Fork, ID 83811, U.S.A.

HEINE, Arthur J. American, b. 1940. **Genres:** Administration/Management, Business/Trade/Industry, Self help, Young adult non-fiction. **Career:** Instructor at a vocational technical school in Jefferson Parish, LA, 1963-67; U.S. Navy, instructor at supply corps school in Athens, GA, 1968-84, instructor and curriculum writer in Chesapeake, VA, 1984-; writer. King's Point Civic League, officer, 1987-91, president, 1991-92. **Publications:** Surviving after High School: Overcoming Life's Hurdles, 1991; Book Selling 101, 1995. Author of works on automated information systems, management, instructor training, and employee relations. **Address:** J-MART Enterprises, 787 Biltmore Dr, Virginia Beach, VA 23454, U.S.A. **Online address:** jmartpress@ aol.com

HEINEMAN, Kenneth J. American, b. 1962. **Genres:** History. **Career:** U.S. Department of the Interior, National Park Service, Johnstown, PA, historian, 1987; Historical Society of Western Pennsylvania, Pittsburgh, historian, 1988-89; Pennsylvania State University, New Kensington, visiting instructor in history, 1989; University of Toledo, OH, visiting assistant professor of history, 1989-90; Iowa State University, Ames, visiting assistant professor of history, 1990-91; Ohio University, Lancaster Campus, assistant professor of history, 1991-. **Publications:** Campus Wars: The Peace Movement at American State Universities in the Vietnam Era, 1993; God Is a Conservative, 1998; Catholic New Deal, 1999; Put Your Bodies upon the Wheels, 2001. Work represented in books. Contributor of articles and reviews to periodicals. **Address:** Dept of History, Lancaster Campus, Ohio University, 1570 Granville Pike, Lancaster, OH 43130, U.S.A. **Online address:** heineman@ohio.edu

HEINRICH, Will. (born United States), b. 1978. **Genres:** Communications/Media. **Career:** Writer. Harper's magazine, intern, 2001. **Publications:** The King's Evil (novel), 2003. **Address:** c/o Author Mail, Charles Scribner's Sons, 1230 Avenue of the Americas, New York, NY 10020, U.S.A.

HEINZ, Brian J(ames). American, b. 1946. **Genres:** Children's non-fiction, Children's fiction. **Career:** Middle Country School District, elementary teacher, 1974-78; William Floyd School District, elementary science teacher, 1978-. State University of New York at Stony Brook, adjunct instructor at Center for Science, Math, and Technology Education, 1987-92. New York State Department of Education, regional elementary science mentor for eastern Long Island, 198595; workshop leader. **Publications:** Beachcraft Bonanza, 1986; Beachcrafts, Too!, 1988; The Alley Cat, 1993; Introduction to Space, 1994; The Wolves, 1996; Kayuktuk: An Arctic Quest, 1996; The Monsters' Test, 1996; Nanuk: Lord of the Ice, 1999; Butternut Hollow Pond, 2000, The Barnyard Cat, 2000. Contributor to magazines. **Address:** 1 Sylvan Dr., Wading River, NY 11792, U.S.A.

HEISEL, Sharon E(laine). American, b. 1941. **Genres:** Young adult fiction. **Career:** Sacred Heart Junior High School, Medford, OR, science teacher, 1978-87; Providence Hospital, Medford, OR, health educator, 1988-93; McLoughlin Middle School, Medford, OR, science teacher. Also active in

children's advocacy and literacy (Laubach teacher). **Publications:** A Little Magic, 1991; Wrapped in a Riddle, 1993; Eyes of a Stranger, 1996; Precious Gold, Precious Jade, 2000. **Address:** 3775 Roads End Blvd., Central Point, OR 97502, U.S.A.

HEISER, Charles B(ixler), Jr. American, b. 1920. **Genres:** Botany. **Career:** Indiana University, Bloomington, Assistant Professor to Professor, 1947-79, Distinguished Professor Emeritus of Botany, 1979-. President, American Society of Plant Taxonomists, 1967, Society for the Study of Evolution, 1975, Society for Economic Botany, 1978, Botanical Society of America, 1980; elected to the National Academy of Sciences, 1987. **Publications:** Nightshades, The Paradoxical Plants, 1969; Seed to Civilization: The Story of Food, 1973, 3rd ed. 1990; The Sunflower, 1976; The Gourd Book, 1979; Of Plants and People, 1985; Weeds in My Garden: Observations on Some Misunderstood Plants, 2003. **Address:** Dept of Biology, Indiana University, Bloomington, IN 47405, U.S.A. **Online address:** cbheiser@bio.indiana.edu

HEISING, Willetta L. American, b. 1947. **Genres:** Bibliography. **Career:** Wayne State University, Detroit, MI, instructor in geography, 1970-71; Model Cities Program, City of Detroit, city planner, 1971-73; Chatham Supermarkets, site location analyst, 1973-74; Marketing Research and Private Banking, National Bank of Detroit, facilities planning, 1974-92; The Writing Company, owner, 1992-94; Purple Moon Press, publisher, 1994-. **Publications:** Detecting Women: A Reader's Guide and Checklist for Mystery Series Written by Women, 1994, 3rd ed., 1999; Detecting Women Pocket Guide: A Checklist for Mystery Series Written by Women, 1995, 3rd. ed, 1998; Detecting Men Pocket Guide: A Checklist for Mystery Series Written by Men, 1997; Detecting Men: A Reader's Guide and Checklist for Mystery Series Written by Men, 1998. **Address:** Purple Moon Press, 3319 Greenfield Rd., # 317, Dearborn, MI 48120-1212, U.S.A. **Online address:** willetta@ purplemoonpress.com

HEITMILLER, David A. American, b. 1945. **Genres:** Documentaries/Reportage. **Career:** Sunbeam Appliance Co., Oakland, CA, branch manager, 1969-76; US West Communications, Seattle, WA, product manager, 1977-94. **Publications:** (with J. Blix) Getting a Life: Real Lives Transformed by "Your Money or Your Life," 1997. **Address:** 1745 NW 59th St, Seattle, WA 98107, U.S.A. **Online address:** david@gettingalife.org; www.gettingalife.org

HEITSCHMIDT, Rodney K. American, b. 1944. **Genres:** Environmental sciences/Ecology, Agriculture/Forestry. **Career:** Texas Agricultural Experiment Station, Vernon, professor, 1977-90; U.S. Department of Agriculture, Agricultural Research Service, Miles City, MT, research leader, 1990-. **Publications:** (ed. with J.W. Stuth) Grazing Management: An Ecological Perspective, 1991. **Address:** R.R.1, Box 2021, Miles City, MT 59301, U.S.A. **Online address:** rod@larrl.ars.usda.gov

HEJINIAN, Lyn. American, b. 1941. **Genres:** Poetry, Translations. **Career:** Editor, Tuumba Press and Poetics Journal, both Berkeley, CA. **Publications:** My Life, 1980, rev. ed., 1988; The Cell, 1990; Oxota: A Short Russian Novel, 1993; Happily, 2000; Language of Inquiry, 2000; Border Comedy, 2001; Lake, 2002. POETRY: A Thought Is the Bride of What Thinking, 1976; A Mask of Motion, 1977; Writing Is an Aid to Memory, 1978; Individuals, 1988; The Cold of Poetry, 1994; Fatalist, 2003. TRANSLATOR: A. Dragomoshchenko, Description, 1990; A. Dragomoshchenko, Xenia, 1994. **Address:** 2639 Russell St, Berkeley, CA 94705-2131, U.S.A.

HELD, Peter. See VANCE, Jack.

HELD, Virginia. American, b. 1929. **Genres:** Economics, Philosophy, Politics/Government, Ethics, Women's studies and issues. **Career:** Distinguished Professor of Philosophy, Graduate School, and Hunter College, City University of New York, 1996- (Assistant Professor, 1969-72; Associate Professor, 1973-76; Professor, 1977-95). **Publications:** The Public Interest and Individual Interests, 1970; (co-author) Women's Realities, Women's Choices, 1983, 2nd ed. 1995; Rights and Goods: Justifying Social Action, 1984, 1989; Feminist Morality: Transforming Culture, Society, and Politics, 1993. EDITOR: (with K. Nielsen and C. Parsons, and contrib.) Philosophy and Political Action, 1972; (with S. Morgenbesser and T. Nagel) Philosophy, Morality, and International Affairs, 1974; Property, Profits, and Economic Justice, 1980; Justice and Care: Essential Readings in Feminist Ethics, 1995. Author of articles and chapters in books. **Address:** Dept. of Philosophy, City University of New York, Graduate School, 365 Fifth Ave, New York, NY 10016, U.S.A.

HELFGOTT, Gillian. Australian. **Genres:** Autobiography/Memoirs. **Career:** Astrologer, lecturer in astrology, and writer. **Publications:** (with A.

Tanskaya) Love You to Bits and Pieces: Life with David Helfgott, 1997. Contributor to periodicals and books. **Address:** PO Box 264, PO Box 257, Bellingen, NSW 2454, Australia. **Online address:** helfgott@bigpond.com

HELLEINER, Gerald K(arl). Canadian (born Austria), b. 1936. **Genres:** Economics, International relations/Current affairs, Third World. **Career:** Yale University, New Haven, CT, instructor to assistant professor, 1961-65; University of Toronto, ON, Canada, associate professor, 1965-71, professor, 1971-98, emeritus, 1998-; Munk Centre for International Studies, distinguished research fellow, 1998-. University College, Dar es Salaam, Tanzania, director of the Economic Research Bureau, 1966-68; North-South Institute, Board of Directors and Chairman, 1976-92; Royal Society of Canada, fellow, 1979; International Development Research Center, member of board of governors and executive committee, 1985-91; International Food Policy Research Institute, board of directors and chairman, 1988-94; Group of 24, researcher and consultant, 1979-, research coordinator, 1991-99; International Lawyers and Economists against Poverty, chairman, 2003-; Order of Canada, officer, 2002. **Publications:** Peasant Agriculture, Government, and Economic Growth in Nigeria, 1966; International Trade and Economic Development, 1972; International Economic Disorder (essays), 1980; Intra-firm Trade and the Developing Countries, 1981; The New Global Economy and the Developing Countries (essays), 1990. EDITOR: Agricultural Planning in East Africa, 1968; A World Divided: The Less Developed Countries in the International Economy, 1976; For Good or Evil: Economic Theory and North-South Negotiations, 1982; The IMF and Africa, 1986; The Other Side of International Development Policy, 1990; Trade Policy, Industrialization and Development, 1992; Trade Policy and Industrialization in Turbulent Times, 1994; (co) From Adjustment to Development in Africa, 1994; Manufacturing for Export in the Developing World, 1995; (co) Poverty, Prosperity and the World Economy, 1995; The International Monetary and Financial System: Developing Country Perspectives, 1996; Capital Account Regimes and the Developing Countries, 1998; Non-Traditional Export Promotion in Africa, 2002. **Address:** Dept of Economics, University of Toronto, 150 St George St, Toronto, ON, Canada M5S 3G7. **Online address:** ghellein@chass. utoronto.ca

HELLENGA, Robert. American, b. 1941. **Genres:** Adult non-fiction. **Career:** Professor of English and writer. Knox College, Galesburg, IL, assistant professor, 1968-76, associate professor, 1976-; Newberry Library Seminar in Humanities, faculty fellow, 1973-74; ACM Florence Programs, director, 1981-82. **Publications:** The Sixteen Pleasures, 1994; The Fall of a Sparrow, 1998; Blues Lessons, 2002; Philosophy Made Simple, 2005. Contributor of scholarly articles and fiction to periodicals. **Address:** English Dept. K-38, Knox College, Galesburg, IL 61401, U.S.A. **Online address:** rhelleng@ knox.edu

HELLER, Agnes. Hungarian, b. 1929. **Genres:** Sociology, Philosophy. **Career:** Writer. La Trobe University, Bundoora, Victoria, Australia, reader in sociology; New School for Social Research, NYC, professor of philosophy, c. 1985-. **Publications:** The Theory of Need in Marx, trans. by A. Booth, 1976; Renaissance Man, 1978; A Theory of Feelings, 1979; On Instincts, trans. by M. Fenyeo, 1979; A Theory of History, 1981; (with F. Feher) Hungary 1956 Revisited: The Message of a Revolution-A Quarter-Century After, 1982; (with Feher and G. Markus) Dictatorship Over Needs, 1983; Everyday Life, trans. by G.L. Campbell, 1984; The Power of Shame: A Rational Perspective, 1985; (with Feher) Doomsday or Deterrence? On the Antinuclear Issue, 1986; (with Feher) Eastern Left, Western Left: Totalitarianism, Freedom, and Democracy, 1987; Beyond Justice, 1987; (with Feher) The Postmodern Political Condition, 1988; General Ethics, 1988; A Philosophy of Morals, 1990; Can Modernity Survive?, 1990; (with Feher) From Yalta to Glasnost: The Dismantling of Stalin's Empire, 1991; (with Feher) The Grandeur and Twilight of Radical Universalism, 1991; A Philosophy of History in Fragments, 1993; The Limits to Natural Law and the Paradox of Evil, 1993; An Ethics of Personality, 1995. EDITOR: Lukacs Reappraised, 1983, in UK as Lukacs Revalued; A Radical Philosophy, trans. by J. Wickham, 1984; (with Feher) Reconstructing Aesthetics: Writings of the Budapest School, 1986. Author of titles in Hungarian; contributor to academic journals and newspapers; many of Heller's books have been translated. **Address:** Eugene Lang College, New School for Social Research, 66 W 12th St., New York, NY 10011, U.S.A.

HELLER, Jane. American. **Genres:** Novels. **Career:** Writer. Coward, McCann & Geoghegan, New York, NY, publicity assistant; New American Library, NYC, publicity manager; Dell/Delacorte, NYC, publicity director; Jove, NYC, vice president of advertising, promotion, and publicity. **Publications:** Cha Cha Cha, 1994; The Club, 1995; Infernal Affairs, 1996; Prince Charming, 1997; Crystal Clear, 1998; Sis Boom Bah, 1999; Name Dropping,

2000; Female Intelligence, 2001; The Secret Ingredient, 2002; Lucky Stars, 2003; Best Enemies, 2004; An Ex to Grind, 2005. **Address:** c/o Ellen Levine, c/o Trident Media Group., 41 Madison Ave Fl 36, New York, NY 10010-2257, U.S.A. **Online address:** jane@janeheller.com

HELLER, Marvin J. American, b. 1940. **Genres:** Theology/Religion, Bibliography. **Career:** Writer. **Publications:** Printing the Talmud: A History of the Earliest Printed Editions of the Talmud, 1992; Printing the Talmud: A History of the Individual Treatises Printed from 1700 to 1750, 1999. Contributor to periodicals. **Address:** 1028 E 28th St, Brooklyn, NY 11210, U.S.A. **Online address:** mjh1mjh@juno.com

HELLER, Michael D. American, b. 1937. **Genres:** Poetry, Songs/Lyrics and libretti, Literary criticism and history, Autobiography/Memoirs, Essays. **Career:** Writer and independent scholar. New York University, American Language Institute, member of the faculty, 1967-98. Member, Advisory Board, 1970-: Poets House; PEN, MLA and American Academy of Poets. **Publications:** Two Poems, 1970; Accidental Center, 1972; Figures of Speaking, 1977; Knowledge, 1979; Conviction's Net of Branches: Essays on the Objectivist Poets and Poetry, 1985; In the Builded Place (poetry), 1989; (ed.) Carl Rakosi: Man and Poet, 1991; Wordflow: New & Selected Poems, 1970-1995, 1997; Living Root: A Memoir, 2000; Exigent Futures: New and Selected Poems, 2003. **Address:** 346 E 18th St Apt 3C, New York, NY 10003-2811, U.S.A. **Online address:** mh7@nyu.edu

HELLER, Steven. American, b. 1950. **Genres:** Art/Art history, Design. **Career:** Pushpin Editions, NYC, co-director, 1983-; New York Times, senior art director, 1986-, Book Review, art director, 1986-; School of Visual Arts, New York, instructor, 1985-99, MFA/design program, chairperson, 1998-2000, co-chair, 1997-. **Publications:** Artists Christmas Cards, 1978; The Book of Waters, 1979; The Empire State Building Book, 1979; Sin City Fables, 1980; War Heads, 1982; The Art of New York, 1983; Art against War, 1984; The Art of Satire, 1984; The Fifties Revisited, 1985; The Little Theatre, 1985; (with L. Talarico) Design Career, 1987; (with Chwast) Graphic Style, 1987; (with K. Pomeroy) Designing with Illustration, 1988; (with Cohen and Chwast) Trylon and Perisphere: The 1939 New York World's Fair, 1988; (with A. Fink) Low-Budget, High-Quality Design, 1988; Communications, 1988; (with G. Anderson) Graphic Wit, 1989; (with K. Jacobs) Angry Graphics: Protest Posters of the Reagan/Bush Era, 1990; (with V.G. Levi and Chwast) You Must Have Been a Beautiful Baby, 1990; (with S. Guarnaccia) School Days, 1991; (with J. Lasky) Borrowed Design, 1991; (with Anderson) The Savage Mirror, 1992; (with L. Fili) Italian Art Deco, 1993; (with Fili) Dutch Moderne, 1994; (with Guarnaccia) Designing for Children, 1994; Carta Italiana, 1995; Looking Closer, 1996, II, 1999, III, 1999, 4, 2002; (with Anderson) American Typeplay, 1996; (with Fili) Streamline, 1996; (with Chwast) Jackets Required, 1920-1950, 1996; (with T. Fernandes) The Business of Illustration, 1997; 101 Best Posters of Europe and America, 1997; (with J. Fraser and Chwast) Japanese Modern, 1996; (with E. Pettit) Newsletters Now!, 1997; (with Fink) That's Entertainment, 1997; (with Fili) Cover Story, 1998; French Modern, 1998; (with Fernandes) Magazines Inside & Out, 1998; Food Wrap, 1998; Deco Type, 1998; Faces on the Edge, 1998; Papier Francias, 1999; The Italian Art Deco Address Book, 1999; Deco Espana, 1999; The Digital Designer, 1999; Teenage Confidential, 1999; Design Literacy, 1999; Design Culture, 1999; British Art Deco, 1999; Belle Lettres, 1998; Design Dialogues, 1998; German Modern, 1998; The Education of a Graphic Designer, 1998; Typology, 1999; On Becoming a Graphic Designer, 1999; Paul Rand, 1999; Less Is More, 1999; The Swastika, 2000; Wedding Bell Blues, 2000; Sex Appeal, 2000; Letterforms, 2000; Design Connoisseur, 2000; Graphic Design Timeline, 2000; The Education of an Illustrator, 2000; Genius Rules, 2001; Texts on Type, 2001; Graphic Style, 2001; Graphic Design History, 2001; Red Scared, 2001; The Education of an E-Designer, 2001; Counter Culture, 2001; The Graphic Design Reader, 2002; The Education of a Design Entrepreneur, 2002; Design Humor, 2002; Cuba Style, 2002; From Merz to Emigre and Beyond, 2003; Citizen Designer, 2003; Teaching Design, 2003. EDITOR: Man Bites Man, 1980; Jules Feiffer's America, 1982; Seymour Chwast: The Left-Handed Designer, 1985; Innovators of American Illustration, 1986; (with Chwast) The Sourcebook of Visual Ideas, 1989. COMPILER: (with B. Cohen and S. Chwast) New York Observed: Artists and Writers Look at the City, 1650 to the Present, 1987; (with Fink) Covers & Jackets!, 1993.

HELLIE, Richard. American, b. 1937. **Genres:** History. **Career:** Rutgers University, NJ, visiting assistant professor, 1965-66; University of Chicago, assistant professor, 1966-71, associate professor, 1971-80, professor of Russian history, 1980-2001, Thomas E. Donnelley Professor, 2001-. Russian History, editor, 1988-. **Publications:** Enserfment and Military Change in Muscovy, 1971; Slavery in Russia, 1450-1725, 1982, 2nd ed., 1984; (trans.)

Ulozhenie: The Law Code of 1649, 1988; Khololpstvo v Rossii 1450-1725, 1998; The Economy and Material Culture of Russia 1600-1725, 1999. EDITOR: (author, and trans.) Muscovite Society, 1967; A. Kahan, The Plow, the Hammer, and the Knout: Essays in 18th-Century Russian Economic History, 1985; Ivan the Terrible, 1987; The Frontier in Russian History, 1995; The Soviet Global Impact: 1945-1991, 2002. Contributor of scholarly articles to books, encyclopedias, and journals. **Address:** 1126 E 59th St Box 78, Chicago, IL 60637-1587, U.S.A. **Online address:** hell@midway.uchicago.edu

HELLMAN, Hal. American, b. 1927. **Genres:** History, Physics, Sciences, Technology, Biography. **Career:** Freelance writer, 1966-. Technical Information Manager, General Precision Inc., Little Falls, New Jersey, 1956-66. **Publications:** Navigation-Land, Sea and Sky, 1966; The Art and Science of Color, 1967; Controlled Guidance Systems, 1967; Light and Electricity in the Atmosphere, 1968; The Right Size, 1968; Transportation in the World of the Future, 1968, 1974; High Energy Physics, 1968; Communications in the World of the Future, 1969, 1975; Defense Mechanisms, from Virus to Man, 1969; The City in the World of the Future, 1970; Helicopters and Other VTOLs, 1970; Energy and Inertia, 1970; Biology in the World of the Future, 1971; (co-author) The Kinds of Mankind: An Introduction to Race and Racism, 1971; The Lever and the Pulley, 1971; Feeding the World of the Future, 1972; Population, 1972; Energy in the World of the Future, 1973; (ed.) Epidemiological Aspects of Carcinogenesis, 1973; Technophobia: Getting Out of the Technology Trap, 1976; (co-author) Understanding Physics, 1978; Deadly Bugs and Killer Insects, 1978; Computer Basics, 1983; Industrial Sensors-A Report on Leading Edge Technology, 1985; Intelligent Sensors-The Merging of Electronics and Sensing, 1988; The Story of Gold, 1996; Beyond Your Senses: The New World of Sensors, 1997; Great Feuds in Science; Ten of the Liveliest Disputes Ever, 1998; Great Feuds in Medicine, 2001; Great Feuds in Technology, 2004. **Address:** 100 High St, Leonia, NJ 07605, U.S.A. **Online address:** hal.hellman@earthlink.net

HELLMAN, Stephen. American/Canadian, b. 1943. **Genres:** Politics/Government. **Career:** York University, North York, Ontario, Canada, assistant professor, 1971-76, associate professor, 1976-89, professor of political science, 1990-. **Publications:** (trans.) Maria Antonietta Macciocchi, Letters from Inside the Italian Communist Party, 1974; (with M. Kesselman, J. Krieger, and others) European Politics in Transition, 1987, second edition, 1992, 3rd ed. 1997; Italian Communism in Transition, 1988; (ed. with G. Pasquino) Italian Politics: A Review, Frances Pinter, Volume 7, 1992, Volume 8, 1993. **Address:** Department of Political Science, York University, North York, ON, Canada M3J 1P3.

HELLSTROM, Ward. American, b. 1930. **Genres:** Literary criticism and history. **Career:** Professor of English, Formerly, Dean of Arts, Humanities and Social Sciences, 1981-92, Western Kentucky University, Bowling Green. Formerly Assistant Professor to Professor of English, University of Florida, Gainesville, from 1961; Victorian Newsletter, Editor, 1978-. **Publications:** On the Poems of Tennyson, 1972; Children and Childhood in the Nineteenth Century in England and America, 1985. **Address:** CH 106, Western Kentucky University, Bowling Green, KY 42101, U.S.A. **Online address:** wardhellstrom@wku.edu

HELLYER, Jill. Australian, b. 1925. **Genres:** Novels, Poetry. **Career:** Executive Secretary, Australian Society of Authors, 1963-71; writer. **Publications:** The Exile (verse) 1969; Not Enough Savages (novel), 1975; Song of the Humpback Whales (verse), 1981. **Address:** 25 Berowra Rd, Mount Colah, NSW 2079, Australia.

HELLYER, Paul T. Canadian, b. 1923. **Genres:** Economics, Politics/Government. **Career:** Member of Parliament (Canada), 1949-57, 1958-74: Parliamentary Assistant to Minister of National Defence, 1956-57; Associate Minister, 1957; Minister of National Defence, 1963-67; Minister of Transport, 1967-69; Acting Prime Minister, 1968-69; Syndicated columnist, Toronto Sun, 1974-84. **Publications:** Agenda: A Plan for Action, 1971; Exit Inflation, 1981; Jobs for All: Capitalism on Trial, 1984; Canada at the Crossroads, 1990; Damn the Torpedoes, 1990; Funny Money: A Common Sense Alternative to Mainline Economics, 1994; Surviving the Global Financial Crisis: The Economics of Hope for Generation X, 1996; Arundel Lodge: A Little Bit of Old Muskoka, 1996; The Evil Empire: Globalization's Darker Side, 1997; Stop: Think, 1999; Goodbye Canada, 2001; One Big Party: To Keep Canada Independent, 2003. **Address:** 506, 65 Harbour Sq, Toronto, ON, Canada M5J 2L4. **Online address:** cap-pac@istar.ca

HELMER, Diana Star. American, b. 1962. **Genres:** Children's fiction, Plays/Screenplays, Children's non-fiction, Sports/Fitness. **Career:** Writer.

Early journalism career emphasized arts reviews and features in newspapers and magazines. Later work focuses on children's books. **Publications:** Belles of the Ballpark, 1993; American Woman Suffragists, 1998; The Believers, 2000; Give Me Liberty, 2000; We're behind You, George Washington, 2000; Half Free, 2000; The Secret Soldier, 2000; Once upon a War, 2001; Diary of a War Child, 2001; The War between Bosses and Workers, 2003. BEARS SERIES, 1997: Black Bears; Brown Bears; The Koala (The Bear That's Not a Bear); Pandas; Polar Bears; Famous Bears. LET'S TALK ABOUT... SERIES, 1999: Adoption; Feeling Sad; Having a New Brother or Sister; Moving to a New Place; When Your Mom or Dad Is Feeling Sad; When Someone You Love Is in a Nursing Home. WITH T.S. OWENS: Inside Collectible Card Games, 1996. GAME PLAN SERIES: Football, 1998; Baseball, 1999; Basketball, 1999; Hockey, 1999; Soccer, 2000; Stock Car Racing, 2001. TEAMWORK...IN ACTION SERIES, 1999: The Charlotte Sting; The Cleveland Rockers; The Houston Comets; The Los Angeles Sparks; The New York Liberty; The Phoenix Mercury; The Sacramento Monarchs; The Utah Starzz. **Address:** 1001 W Boone St, Marshalltown, IA 50158, U.S.A.

HELMER, Marilyn. Canadian. **Genres:** Children's fiction. **Career:** Author of books for children and young adults. **Publications:** The Boy, the Dollar and the Wonderful Hat, 1992; Boathouse Treasure, 1998; Fog Cat, 1998; Mr. McGratt and the Ornery Cat, 1999; Dinosaurs on the Beach (novel), 2003. ONCEUPON-A-TIME RETOLD FAIRY TALES SERIES: 3 Tales of 3, 2000; 3 Prince Charming Tales, 2000; 3 Tales of Enchantment, 2001; 3 Teeny Tiny Tales, 2001; 3 Barnyard Tales, 2002; 3 Tales of Trickery, 2002; 3 Tuneful Tales, 2003; 3 Royal Tales, 2003. RIDDLE BOOKS-KIDS CAN READ SERIES: Critter Riddles, 2003; Yummy Riddles, 2003; Spooky Riddles, 2003; Yucky Riddles, 2003. Contributor of articles, stories and poems to juvenile periodicals and anthologies. **Address:** 3191 Heathfield Dr, Burlington, ON, Canada L7M 1E1. **Online address:** helmerg@mail.mohawkc.on.ca

HELMS, Mary W. American, b. 1938. **Genres:** Anthropology/Ethnology. **Career:** Wayne State University, Detroit, MI, instructor in anthropology, 1965-67; Syracuse University, Syracuse, NY, assistant professor of anthropology, 1967-68; Northwestern University, Evanston, IL, lecturer in anthropology, 1969-79; University of North Carolina at Greensboro, professor of anthropology, 1979-2004, department head, 1979-85. **Publications:** Asang: Adaptations to Culture Contact in a Miskito Community, 1971; Middle America: A Culture History of Heartland and Frontiers, 1975; Ancient Panama: Chiefs in Search of Power, 1979; Cuna Molas and Cocle Art Forms: Reflections on Panamanian Design Styles and Symbolism (monograph), 1981; Ulysses' Sail: An Ethnographic Odyssey of Power, Knowledge, and Geographical Distance, 1988; Craft and the Kingly Ideal: Art, Trade, Power, 1993; Creations of the Rainbow Serpent: Polychrome Ceramic Designs from Ancient Panama, 1995; Access to Origins: Affines, Ancestors, and Aristocrats, 1998; The Curassow's Crest, 2000. EDITOR: (with F.O. Loveland) Frontier Adaptations in Lower Central America, 1976; (with J.R. Bort) Panama in Transition: Local Reactions to Development Policies (monograph), 1983. Contributor to books. Contributor of articles and reviews to anthropology journals. **Address:** Department of Anthropology, University of North Carolina at Greensboro, PO Box 26170, Greensboro, NC 27402, U.S.A.

HELMS, Robert B(rake). American, b. 1940. **Genres:** Medicine/Health, Economics. **Career:** Loyola College, Baltimore, MD, assistant professor of economics, 1971-74; American Enterprise Institute for Public Policy Research, Washington, DC, director of health policy studies, 1974-90; U.S. Department of Health and Human Services, Washington, DC, deputy assistant secretary for planning and evaluation/health, 1981-84, assistant secretary for planning and evaluation, 1984-89; American Pharmaceutical Institute, Washington, DC, executive director, 1989-90; American Enterprise Institute for Public Policy Research, director of health policy studies, 1990-. **Publications:** Natural Gas Regulation: An Evaluation of FPC Price Controls, 1974. EDITOR: Drug Development and Marketing, 1975; The International Supply of Medicines, 1980; Drugs and Health: Economic Issues and Policy Objectives, 1981; American Health Policy: Critical Issues for Reform, 1993; Health Care Policy and Politics: Lessons from Four Countries, 1993; Health Policy Reform: Competition and Controls, 1993; Competitive Strategies in the Pharmaceutical Industry, 1995. Contributor to books and professional journals. **Address:** American Enterprise Institute for Public Policy Research, 1150 17th St. N.W., Washington, DC 20036, U.S.A. **Online address:** RHelms@AEI.org

HELPRIN, Mark. American, b. 1947. **Genres:** Novels, Novellas/Short stories. **Publications:** A Dove of the East and Other Stories, 1975; Refiner's Fire, 1977; Ellis Island and Other Stories, 1980; Winter's Tale, 1983; (ed. with S. Ravenel) Best American Short Stories 1988, 1988; (adapter) Swan

Lake, 1989; A Soldier of the Great War, 1992; Memoir from Antproof Case (novel), 1995; A City in Winter, 1996; The Veil of Snows, 1997. **Address:** Claremont Institute, 937 W Foothill Blvd Ste E, Claremont, CA 91711, U.S.A.

HELVARG, David. American, b. 1951. **Genres:** History. **Career:** Reporter in Northern Ireland, 1973; print reporter in San Diego, CA, 1974-79; print, radio, and television reporter in Central America, 1979-83; television news and documentary producer, 1983-93; writer and television producer, 1993-. **Publications:** The War Against the Greens, 1994. Contributor to magazines and newspapers. **Address:** c/o Joe Spigler, 154 West 57th St., Room 135, New York, NY 10019, U.S.A.

HELWIG, Maggie. British/Canadian, b. 1961. **Genres:** Novels, Novellas/ Short stories, Poetry, Essays. **Career:** Founder, editor, and production manager of Lowlife Publishing; British Coalition for East Timor, national organizer, 1994-96; Canadian Action for Indonesia and East Timor, researcher, 1998-2001; has also worked as a bookstore clerk, typesetter and page designer, book reviewer and freelance journalist. **Publications:** POETRY: Walking through Fire, 1981; Tongues of Men and Angels, 1985; Eden, 1987; Because the Gunman, 1988; Talking Prophet Blues, 1989; Graffiti for J.J. Harper, 1991; Eating Glass, 1994; One Building in the Earth, 2002. ESSAYS: Apocalypse Jazz, 1993; Real Bodies, 2002. SHORT STORIES: Gravity Lets You Down, 1997. NOVEL: Where She Was Standing, 2001; Between Mountains, 2004. **Address:** PO Box 562, Station P, Toronto, ON, Canada M5S 2T1. **Online address:** maggie@web.net

HELY, Sara. (born England). **Genres:** Novels. **Career:** Writer. Has also managed a farm and a fast-food restaurant. **Publications:** The Legend of the Green Man, 1972; The Sign of the Serpent, 1984; War Story, 2002, 2003. **Address:** c/o Author Mail, St. Martin's Press, 175 Fifth Ave., New York, NY 10010, U.S.A.

HEMINGS, T. J. *See* **REITER, Victoria (Kelrich).**

HEMINGWAY, Hilary. (born United States), b. 1961. **Genres:** Novels. **Career:** Writer, television producer, and documentary filmmaker. **Publications:** (with Jeffry P. Lindsay) Dreamland: A Novel of the UFO Cover-Up, 1995; (with Jeffry P. Lindsay) Dreamchild, 1998; (with Jeffry P. Lindsay) Hunting with Hemingway: Based on the Stories of Leicester Hemingway, 2000; (with Carlene Brennen) Hemingway in Cuba, 2003. **Address:** c/o Author Mail, Rugged Land, LLC, 276, Canal St., Fifth Floor, New York, NY 10013, U.S.A.

HEMINGWAY, Lorian. American, b. 1951. **Genres:** Novels, Novellas/ Short stories. **Career:** Writer, 1965-. Hemingway Short Story Competition, coordinator and judge, 1980-; also worked as copyeditor and swimming pool cleaner. **Publications:** Walking into the River (novel), 1992; Walk on Water (memoir), 1998; World Turned Over, 2002. Work represented in anthologies. **Address:** c/o Susan Crawford, Box 198, 94 Evans Rd, Barnstead, NH 03218, U.S.A.

HEMINWAY, John Hylan, Jr. American, b. 1944. **Genres:** Sciences, Travel/Exploration, Biography. **Career:** ABC Sports' The American Sportsman, field producer/writer, 1970-73; Survival Anglia in London, writer/ producer, 1973-76; writer/director/producer, The Brain series, 1982-84, The Mind series, 1985-87, The Search for Mind; PBS Travels, executive producer/ host, 1988-92; Travel Channel, John Heminway's Travels on Native Soil, host/writer/producer; Evolution series: The Mind's Big Bang, writer/co-producer, 2001; writer/presenter/producer for TV presentations. Conde Nast Traveler Magazine, contributing editor. **Publications:** The Imminent Rains: A Visit among the Last Pioneers of Africa, 1968; No Man's Land: The Last of White Africa, 1983; African Journeys: A Personal Guidebook, 1990; Yonder: A Place in Montana, 2000; Flight: Based on a True Story (screenplay), 2003. **Address:** Wind's Eye, 289 S Cross Rd, Chatham, NY 12037, U.S.A. **Online address:** bar20@aol.com

HEMMING, John Henry. Canadian, b. 1935. **Genres:** Anthropology/ Ethnology, History. **Career:** Joint chairman, Hemming Group Ltd., London; chairman, Newman Books Ltd., Brintex Ltd., London. Director and secretary, Royal Geographical Society, 1975-96. **Publications:** The Conquest of the Incas, 1970; (with E. Brooks, R. Fuerst, and F. Huxley) Tribes of the Amazon Basin, Brazil, 1973; Red Gold: The Conquest of the Brazilian Indians, 1978; The Search for El Dorado, 1978; Machu Picchu, 1981; Monuments of the Incas, 1982; (ed.) Change in the Amazon Basin, 2 vols., 1985; Amazon Frontier: The Defeat of the Brazilian Indians, 1987; (with J. Ratter and A. dos Santos) Maracá, 1988; Roraima, Brazil's Northernmost Frontier, 1991;

(with J. Ratter) Maracá Rainforest Island, 1993; (ed.) The Forest Frontier, 1995; The Golden Age of Discovery, 1998; Die if You Must: Brazilian Indians in the Twentieth Century, 2003. **Address:** Hemming Group Ltd, 32 Vauxhall Bridge Rd, London SW1V 2SS, England. **Online address:** j.hemming@hgluk.com

HEMPHILL, Kenneth S. American, b. 1948. **Genres:** Theology/Religion. **Career:** Ordained Baptist minister, 1970. Calvary Baptist Church, Winston-Salem, NC, youth pastor, 1968-70; Wolf Creek Baptist Church, Battletown, KY, pastor, 1970-72; Meadow Hill Baptist Church, Louisville, KY, youth and education worker, 1973; Temple Southern Baptist Church, Little Stukeley, England, interim pastor, 1975; Wingate College, Wingate, NC, instructor in religion, 1976-77; First Baptist Church, Galax, VA, pastor, 1977-81; First Baptist Church of Norfolk, VA, pastor, 1981-92; Southern Baptist Center for Church Growth, Atlanta, GA, director, 1992-94; Southwestern Baptist Theological Seminary, Fort Worth, TX, President, 1994; writer. Member of executive committees and boards of directors; Bible teacher on WTKR-Radio, Norfolk, 1984-85. Leader of Bible conferences in the United States and England. **Publications:** Spiritual Gifts: Empowering the New Testament Church, 1988; (with R.W. Jones) Growing an Evangelistic Sunday School, 1989; The Official Rule Book for the New Church Game, 1990; The Bonsai Theory of Church Growth, 1991; Mirror, Mirror on the Wall: Discovering Your True Self through Spiritual Gifts, 1992; The Antioch Effect, 1994; Revitalizing the Sunday Morning Dinosaur, 1996. **Address:** c/o Casa Bautista de Publicaciones, PO Box 4255, 7000 Alabama St., El Paso, TX 79914, U.S.A.

HEMPHILL, Paul (James). American, b. 1936. **Genres:** Social commentary, Autobiography/Memoirs, Novels, Essays, Race relations. **Career:** Sports writer and gen. columnist for newspapers in the American South, 1958-69. **Publications:** The Nashville Sound, 1970; (with Ivan Allen) Mayor: Notes on the Sixties, 1970; The Good Old Boys, 1974; Long Gone, 1979; Too Old to Cry, 1981; The Six Killer Chronicles, 1985; Me and the Boy, 1986; King of the Road, 1989; The Heart of the Game: The Education of a Minor League Ballplayer, 1996; Wheels, 1997.

HEN, Yitzhak. Israeli, b. 1963. **Genres:** History. **Career:** Historian; University of Haifa, Haifa, Israel, Department of History, lecturer, 1994-. **Publications:** Culture and Religion in Merovingian Gaul, A.D. 481-751, 1995; The Sacramentary of Echternach, 1997. **Address:** Department of History, University of Haifa, 31905 Haifa, Israel.

HENBEST, Nigel. British, b. 1951. **Genres:** Astronomy, Children's non-fiction, Air/Space topics, Reference. **Career:** Broadcaster for BBC World Service and British Radio. Producer and scriptwriter for British and American television. Ed., British Astronomical Association Journal, 1985-87. **Publications:** (with L. Mots) The Night Sky, 1979; (with M. Marten) The New Astronomy, 1983; (ed.) The Planets, 1985; The Universe: A Computer-Generated Voyage through Time and Space, 1992; The Planets: A Guided Tour of Our Solar System through the Eyes of America's Space Probes, 1992. TELEVISION SCRIPTS: Space Shuttle Discovery, 1993; Body Atlas, 1994; Universe 2001, 2000; Edge of the Universe, 2002; The Day the Earth was Born, 2002. WITH H. COUPER: Space Frontiers, 1978; The Restless Universe, 1982; Astronomy, 1983; Physics, 1983; The Sun, 1986; New Worlds: In Search of Planets, 1986; The Moon, 1987; Spaceprobes and Satellites, 1987; Telescopes and Observatories, 1987; The Space Atlas, 1992; The Guide to the Galaxy, 1994; How the Universe Works, 1994; Black Holes, 1996; Big Bang, 1997; Is Anybody Out There?, 1998; To the Ends of the Universe, 1998; Universe, 2000; Extreme Universe, 2001; Mars: The Inside Story of the Red Planet, 2001; Philip's Stargazing 2005, 2004.

HENDERSON, Dan Fenno. *See* Obituaries.

HENDERSON, F(rancis) M(artin). New Zealander, b. 1921. **Genres:** Engineering, Technology. **Career:** Professor Emeritus of Civil Engineering, University of Newcastle, N.S.W., since 1982 (Professor, 1968-82). Sr. Lecturer, 1952-63, and Professor, 1964-68, University of Canterbury, Christchurch. **Publications:** Elliptic Functions with Complex Arguments, 1960; Open Channel Flow, 1966. **Address:** 3 Ashby St., Dudley, NSW 2290, Australia.

HENDERSON, Harold. American, b. 1948. **Genres:** Adult non-fiction. **Career:** Illinois Times, staff writer, 1980-85; Chicago Reader, staff writer, 1985-. **Publications:** Seizing the Day, 1983; Catalyst for Controversy: Paul Carus of Open Court, 1993. **Address:** 11 East Illinois, Chicago, IL 60611, U.S.A.

HENDERSON, Meg. Scottish, b. 1948. **Genres:** Novels. **Career:** Journalist and author. **Publications:** Finding Peggy, 1995; The Holy City, 1997; Bloody Mary, 1999; Chasing Angels, 2001. **Address:** c/o Author Mail, HarperCollins Canada Ltd., 55 Avenue Rd. Suite 2900, Toronto, ON, Canada M5R 3L2.

HENDERSON, Richard (Jud). American, b. 1924. **Genres:** Recreation, Travel/Exploration. **Career:** Freelance writer and illustrator. Member, Seaworthiness Project Technical Committee, American Boat and Yacht Council, 1973-. Former member, Board of Advisors, The Telltale Compass, yachtsman's newsletter. **Publications:** First Sail for Skipper, 1960; Hand, Reef and Steer, 1965, 1991; (ed. and contrib.) Dangerous Voyages of Captain Andrews, 1966; Single-Handed Sailing: The Experiences and Techniques of the Lone Voyager, 1967, 2nd ed., 1988; The Racing-Cruiser, 1970; Sea Sense, 1972, 3rd ed., 1991; The Cruiser's Compendium, 1973; Better Sailing, 1977; East to the Azores, 1978; Choice Yacht Designs, 1979; Philip L. Rhodes and His Yacht Designs, 1981; (with R.W. Carrick) John G. Alden and His Yacht Designs, 1983; (with W.J. Kotsch) Heavy Weather Guide, 2nd ed., 1984; 53 Boats You Can Build, 1985; Understanding Rigs and Rigging, 1985, 1991; Sailing at Night, 1987; Sailing in Windy Weather, 1987; Sail and Power, 4th ed., 1991; First Sail, 1993; Essential Seamanship, 1994; Chesapeake Sails: A History of Yachting on the Bay, 1999. **Address:** c/o Cornell Maritime Press, 101 Water Way, PO Box 456, Centreville, MD 21617, U.S.A. **Online address:** judsalhen@toad.net

HENDERSON, William Darryl. American (born Canada), b. 1938. **Genres:** Military/Defense/Arms control. **Career:** U.S. Army, career officer, serving in Korea and Vietnam as infantry commander, 1961-88, retiring as colonel. U.S. Military Academy, assistant professor, 1970-74; other military assignments include deputy commander of Joint Security Area for Panmunjom, Korea, staff assistant in Office of the Deputy Secretary of Defense, executive assistant to the assistant secretary of defense legislative affairs, battalion commander, senior adviser to a major Army Reserve command, senior arms control planner on International Military Staff, Headquarters, North Atlantic Treaty Organization (NATO), and commander of U.S. Army Research Institute for the Behavioral and Social Sciences; Member, Presidential Commission on Women in Combat. **Publications:** (associate ed.) Handbook of World Conflicts, 1970; Why the Viet Cong Fought: A Study of Motivation and Control in a Modern Army in Combat, 1979; Cohesion: The Human Element in Combat, 1985; The Hollow Army: How the U.S. Army Is Oversold and Undermanned, 1990.

HENDERSON SMITH, Stephen Lane. British (born People's Republic of China), b. 1919. **Genres:** Poetry, Autobiography/Memoirs. **Career:** General medical practice, Huddersfield, 1956-89; medical missionary, China and Congo, 1943-55. **Publications:** Four Minutes and Other Verses, 1967; Snow Children, 1968; Beyond the City, 1971; Intimations, 1972; Celebrations, 1973; Glimmerings, 1975; Filterings, 1977; Transparencies, 1980; Soundings, 1982; Foundlings, 1984; What Purpose Burns (autobiography). **Address:** 2 Crosland Ct, Oakes, Huddersfield, Yorks HD3 4AL, England.

HENDRICKS, Obery M(ack), Jr. American, b. 1953. **Genres:** Novels. **Career:** Theologian, minister, educator. Investment advisor, New York, NY, 1977-86; Payne Theological Seminary, Wilberforce, OH, former president; New York Theological Seminary, currently professor of biblical studies; Princeton Theological Seminary, visiting scholar. **Publications:** Living Water (novel), 2003. **Address:** c/o Author Mail, HarperCollins Publishing, 10 East 53rd St., 7th Fl., New York, NY 10022, U.S.A.

HENDRICKS, Vicki (Due). American, b. 1951. **Genres:** Novels, Novellas/Short stories, Mystery/Crime/Suspense. **Career:** Broward Community College, Pembroke Pines, FL, professor, 1981-; writer. **Publications:** NOVELS: Miami Purity, 1995; Iguana Love, 1998; Voluntary Madness, 1999; Sky Blues, 2001. Work represented in anthologies. Contributor to periodicals and websites. **Address:** Broward Community College, 7200 Pines Blvd, Pembroke Pines, FL 33024, U.S.A. **Online address:** www.vickihendricks.com

HENDRICKSON, R. J. See JENSEN, Ruby Jean.

HENDRY, Diana. British, b. 1941. **Genres:** Novellas/Short stories, Children's fiction, Young adult fiction, Poetry. **Career:** Sunday Times, London, England, assistant to literary editor, 1958-60; Western Mail, Cardiff, Wales, reporter and feature writer, 1960-65; free-lance journalist for newspapers in Liverpool and Bristol, England, 1965-80; Clifton College, Bristol, instructor in English, 1987-90; Bristol Polytechnic, part-time lecturer, 1987-; Open University, tutor, 1991-92; University of Bristol, Department of Continuing Education, instructor, 1987-92; University of the West of England, part-time lecturer. **Publications:** Midnight Pirate, 1984; Fiona Finds Her Tongue, 1985; Hetty's First Fling, 1985; The Not Anywhere House, 1989; The Rainbow Watchers, 1989; The Carey Street Cat, 1989; Christmas on Exeter Street, 1989; Sam Sticks and Delilah, 1990; A Camel Called April, 1990; Double Vision (young adult novel), 1990; Harvey Angell, 1991; The Thing-in-a-Box, 1992; Wonderful Robert and Sweetie-Pie Nell, 1992; Kid Kibble, 1993; Why Father Christmas Was Late for Hartlepool, 1994; Strange Goings-On (children's poetry), 1995; The Awesome Bird, 1995; Happy Old Birthday Owl, 1995; Flower Street Friends, 1995; Dog Dottington, 1995; The Thing-on-Two Legs, 1995; Harvey Angell and the Ghost Child, 1997; Fiona Says..., 1998; Minders, 1998; The Very Noisy Night, 1999; Harvey Angell Beats Time, 2000; The Very Busy Day, 2001; You Can't Kiss It Better, 2003; Swan Boy, 2004. POETRY FOR ADULTS: Making Blue, 1995; Borderers, 2001; Twelve Lilts: Psalms & Responses, 2003. **Address:** 23 Dunrobin Pl, Edinburgh EH3 5HZ, Scotland. **Online address:** d.hendry@tiscali.co.uk

HENDRY, Joy (McLaggan). Scottish, b. 1953. **Genres:** Poetry, Communications/Media, Intellectual history, Literary criticism and history, Philosophy, Theatre, Women's studies and issues, Writing/Journalism. **Career:** Register House, Edinburgh, Scotland, civil servant, 1974-75; Knox Academy, Haddington, Scotland, teacher of English, 1977-84; writer, 1984-. Chapman: Scotland's Quality Literary Magazine, editor, 1972-; Scottish Poetry Library, deputy convener; Scottish Actors Studio, chair, 1993-2000; The Scotsman, radio critic, 1988-97; broadcaster and presenter of radio programs. Teaches drama at Queen Margaret University College and periodical journalism at Napier University, both Edinburgh. **Publications:** Scots: The Way Forward, 1981; Gang Doun wi' a Sang (play), 1995. EDITOR: Poems and Pictures of Wendy Wood, 1985; (with I. Evans) The Land for the People, 1985; (with R. Ross) Sorley MacLean: Critical Essays, 1987; (with Ross) Norman MacCaig: Critical Essays, 1991. **Address:** 4 Broughton Place, Edinburgh EH1 3RX, Scotland. **Online address:** JoyHendry@aol.com

HENG, Liu. Chinese, b. 1954. **Genres:** Novels, Plays/Screenplays. **Career:** Novelist and screenwriter. Former laborer for Beijing Motor Factory; editor, Beijing Literature, 1979-. **Publications:** (trans. D. Kwan) The Obsessed, 1991; (trans H. Goldblatt) Black Snow, 1993. SCREENPLAYS: Red Sorghum, 1987; Ju Dou, 1990; The Story of Qiu Ju, 1991. **Address:** c/o Grove Atlantic, 841 Broadway, 4th Floor, New York, NY 10003, U.S.A.

HENGGELER, Paul R. American, b. 1955. **Genres:** Politics/Government. **Career:** Western Ohio Youth Center, Troy, OH, social studies teacher, 1980-83; Bowling Green State University, OH, assistant professor of history, 1989-91; University of Texas-Pan American, Edinburg, TX, assistant professor, 1992-95, associate professor of history, 1995-. Governor's Summer Institute for Talented and Gifted Students, program director, 1992-95. **Publications:** In His Steps: Lyndon Johnson and the Kennedy Mystique, 1991; (asst. ed.) The Cambridge History and Geography of Human Disease, 1993; The Kennedy Persuasion: The Politics of Style since JFK, 1995; After the Harvest: The Decline and Fall of Cesar Chavez, forthcoming. Contributor to books. **Address:** Department of History, University of Texas-Pan American, Edinburg, TX 78539, U.S.A. **Online address:** henggeler@panam.edu

HENGGELER, Scott Walter. American, b. 1950. **Genres:** Psychology. **Career:** University of Virginia, Charlottesville, pediatric clinical psychology intern at Children and Youth Center, 1974-76; Memphis State University, Memphis, TN, assistant professor, 1976-81, associate professor, 1981-86, professor of psychology, 1986-88, clinical director of psychology at Psychological Services Center, 1976-84, and member of its governing board; U.S. International University, San Diego, CA, professor of human behavior, 1988-92; Medical University of South Carolina, Charleston, professor of psychiatry and behavioral sciences, 1992-. University of Virginia, visiting assistant professor, 1977; University of Nebraska, affiliate of Law and Psychology Program, 1989-; San Diego State University, adjunct professor, 1990-92; University of South Carolina, clinical professor, 1992-. Family and Health Institute of Memphis, director, 1981-88; Human Affairs International, director of Memphis Office, 1983-88; consultant to Tall Trees Residential Program for Violent Offenders, South Carolina Department of Mental Health, and Memphis Federal Corrections Institute. **Publications:** (ed. and contrib.) Delinquency and Adolescent Psychopathology: A Family-Ecological Systems Approach, 1982; Developmental Clinical Psychology and Psychiatry, 1989; (with C.M. Borduin) Family Therapy and Beyond: A Multisystemic Approach to Treating the Behavior Problems of Children and Adolescents, 1990; (with G.B. Melton and J.R. Rodrigue) Pediatric and Adolescent AIDS: Research Findings From the Social Sciences, 1992; (ed. with A.B. Santos, and contrib.) Innovative Services for Difficult to Treat Populations, 1994. Work represented in anthologies. Contributor to psychology journals. **Address:** Department of Psychiatry and Behavioral Sciences, Medical University of South Carolina, 171 Ashley Ave., Charleston, SC 29425, U.S.A.

HENKE, Shirl. American. **Genres:** Romance/Historical. **Career:** Romance novelist. Former teacher at the university level. **Publications:** ROMANCE NOVELS. Golden Lady, 1986; Love Unwilling, 1987; Capture the Sun, 1988; Summer Has No Name, 1991; Bouquet, 1994; A Fire in the Blood, 1994; Love a Rebel, Love a Rogue, 1994; Broken Vows, 1995; McCrory's Lady, 1995; Bride of Fortune, 1996; The Endless Sky, 1998; Sundancer, 1999. GONE TO TEXAS TRILOGY: Cactus Flower, 1988; Moon Flower, 1989; Night Flower, 1990. DISCOVERY DUET: Paradise and More, 1991; Return to Paradise, 1992. NIGHT WIND SERIES: Night Wind's Women, 1991; White Apache's Woman, 1993; Deep as the Rivers, 1997. ROCKY MOUNTAIN SERIES: Terms of Love, 1992; Terms of Surrender, 1993. Contributor to anthologies. **Address:** c/o St. Martin's Press, 175 5th Ave, New York, NY 10010, U.S.A. **Online address:** shenke@c4systm.com; shirl@shirlhenke.com

HENKIN, Joshua. American. **Genres:** Novels. **Career:** Fiction reader for a magazine in San Francisco, California during the late 1980s; teacher of independent creative writing classes; freelance writer, c. 1993-; University of Michigan, Ann Arbor, instructor in creative writing, 1997-. **Publications:** Swimming across the Hudson (novel), 1997. Contributor of fiction and articles to periodicals. **Address:** c/o Sarah Lawrence College, 1 Mead Way, Bronxville, NY 10708, U.S.A. **Online address:** Josherb@umich.edu

HENKIN, Louis. American (born Russia), b. 1917. **Genres:** Civil liberties/Human rights, Law, International relations/Current affairs, Politics/Government. **Career:** University professor emeritus and special service professor, Columbia University, NYC, 1988- (professor of international law and diplomacy, 1962; Hamilton Fish Professor of International Law and Diplomacy, 1963-78; Harlan Fiske Stone Professor of Constitutional Law, 1978-79; university professor, 1979-88). Chairman of directorate, Center for Study of Human Rights, 1986- (co-director, 1976-86); Immigration and Refugee Services of America, emeritus, 1998- (vice president, 1995-98); professor of law, University of Pennsylvania Law School, Philadelphia, 1957-62. Chief reporter, Restatement of the Law (Third), Foreign Relations Law of the United States, 1980-87. **Publications:** Arms Control and Inspection in American Law, 1958; The Berlin Crisis and the United Nations, 1959; Law for the Sea's Mineral Resources, 1968; How Nations Behave, 1968; Foreign Affairs and the Constitution, 1972; The Rights of Man Today, 1978; (co-author) Human Rights: France and the United States of America, 1984; (co-author) Human Rights in Contemporary China, 1986; (co-author) Right v. Might: International Law and the Use of Force, 1989; The Age of Rights, 1990; Constitutionalism, Democracy, and Foreign Affairs, 1990; International Law: Politics and Values, 1995. EDITOR/CO-EDITOR: Arms Control, 1961; World Politics and the Jewish Condition, 1973; (with W. Friedman and O. Lissitzyn) Transnational Law in a Changing Society, 1974; International Law: Cases and Materials, 1980, rev. ed., 1993; The International Bill of Rights, 1981; Constitutionalism and Rights, 1989; Foreign Affairs and the U.S. Constitution, 1990. **Address:** Columbia Law School, 435 W 116th St, New York, NY 10027, U.S.A.

HENLEY, Arthur. Also writes as Webb Jones. American. **Genres:** Plays/Screenplays, Medicine/Health, Psychology, Sociology, Travel/Exploration, Humor/Satire. **Career:** Former Keynote Speaker, National Association of Mental Health, and Creative Writing teacher, New York University. **Publications:** Demon in My View, 1966; Make Up Your Mind, 1967; (with R. L. Wolk) Yes Power, 1969; (with R. L. Wolk) The Right to Lie, 1970; (with A. J. Montanari) The Montanari Book, 1971; Schizophrenia, 1971, 1987; (with M. Weisinger) The Complete Alibi Handbook, 1972; (with A. J. Montanari) What Other Child Care Books Won't Tell You, 1973; (with A. J. Montanari) The Difficult Child, 1973; Human Resources and Population Policies, 1974; (with D. Brooks) Don't Be Afraid of Cataracts, 1978, rev. ed. 1983; Phobias: The Crippling Fears, 1987, rev. ed., 1988; Lily & Joel: A Novel of Life, Love and AudioTapes, 1992. **Address:** 73-37 Austin St, Forest Hills, NY 11375-6219, U.S.A. **Online address:** ah55@webtv.net

HENLEY, Beth. (Elizabeth Becker Henley). American, b. 1952. **Genres:** Novellas/Short stories, Plays/Screenplays. **Career:** Recipient: Pulitzer Prize for Drama, 1981, New York Drama Critics Circle Award for Best Play, 1981, and George Oppenheimer/Newsday Playwriting Award, 1980-81, all for Crimes of the Heart. **Publications:** Crimes of the Heart, 1982, screenplay 1986; Am I Blue?, 1982; The Wake of Jamey Foster, 1983; The Miss Firecracker Contest, 1985, screenplay 1988; (co-author) True Stories (screenplay), 1986; Nobody's Fool (screenplay), 1988; The Lucky Spot, 1987; Abundance, 1989; Signature, 1990: The Debutante Ball, 1991; Monologues for Women, 1992; Control Freaks, 1992; Revelers, 1994; L-Play, 1995; Impossible Marriage, 1999; Exposed, 2001; Ridiculous Fraud, 2003. **Address:** c/o Peter Hagan, Gersh Agency, 130 W 42nd St, New York, NY 10036, U.S.A.

HENLEY, Patricia. American, b. 1947. **Genres:** Novels, Novellas/Short stories, Poetry. **Career:** Purdue University, West Lafayette, IN, professor of English, 1987-; writer. Volunteer, St. Thomas Aquinas Center. **Publications:** Learning to Die: Poems, 1979; STORIES: Friday Night at Silver Star: Stories, 1986; The Secret of Cartwheels: Short Stories, 1992; Back Roads, 1996; Worship of the Common Heart: New and Selected Stories, 2000. NOVELS: Hummingbird House, 1999; In the River Sweet, 2002. **Address:** Purdue University, Department of English, Heavilon Hall, West Lafayette, IN 47906, U.S.A. **Online address:** phenley@hotmail.com

HENNESSY, John J(oseph). American, b. 1958. **Genres:** History, Military/Defense/Arms control. **Career:** Manassas National Battlefield, Manassas, VA, staff historian, 1981-85; New York State Office of Historic Preservation, historian, 1987-91; National Park Service, Harpers Ferry, VA, exhibit planner, 1991-95. Save Historic Antietam Foundation, director, 1992-; Fredericksburg and Spotsylvania NMP, assistant superintendent, 1995-. **Publications:** An End to Innocence: The First Battle of Manassas, 1989; Return to Bull Run: The Campaign and Battle of Second Manassas, 1992. **Address:** 13102 Beckman St., Fredericksburg, VA 22408-0274, U.S.A.

HENNESSY, Peter. British, b. 1947. **Genres:** History, Politics/Government. **Career:** Whitehall, Watch, Columnist, The Independent, London, 1987-91. Visiting Professor of Government, University of Strathclyde, since 1989. Reporter, 1974-76, Whitehall Correspondent, 1976-82, and Leader Writer, 1982-84, The Times, London. Visiting Fellow, Policies Studies Institute, London, 1985-91; Presenter of Granada Television Series "Under Fire," 1985-87; Author and Presenter of Brook Prod. Television "All the Prime Minister's Men," 1986; Author and Presenter, BBC Radio 3's prog., A Canal Too Far, 170, 1987; BBC Radio 4's Analysis, Presenter, 1986-92; University of London, director magazine, columnist, 1989; Queen Mary and Westfield College, professor of contemporary history, 1992. **Publications:** (with C. Bennett) A Consumer's Guide to Open Government, 1980; (with K. Jeffery) States of Emergency: British Governments and Strikebreaking since 1919, 1983; (with A. Arends) Mr. Attlee's Engine Room, 1983; (with M. Cockerell and D. Walker) Sources Close to the Prime Minister: Inside the Hidden World of the News Manipulators, 1984; (with S. Morrison and R. Townsend) Routine Punctuated by Orgies: The Central Policy Review Staff, 1970-83, 1985; (with Sir D. Hague) How Adolph Hitler Reformed Whitehall, 1985; What the Papers Never Said, 1985; Cabinet, 1986; The Great and the Good: An Inquiry Into the British Establishment, 1986; (ed. with A. Seldon) Ruling Performance: British Governments from Attlee to Thatcher, 1987; Whitehall, 1989; Never Again: Britain 1945-51, 1992; The Hidden Wiring: Unearthing the British Constitution, 1995; Muddling Through: Power, Politics and the Quality of Government in Postwar Britain, 1996. **Address:** Department of History, Queen Mary University of London, Mile End Road, London E1 4NS, England.

HENNEY, Carolee Wells. American, b. 1928. **Genres:** Novels, Children's fiction. **Career:** Hampton School System, Hampton, VA, elementary teacher, 1968-88; writer and speaker. Interpreter, Virginia Living Museum, 1993-. **Publications:** Calbert and His Adventures, 1990; Tac and Tuk, 1992; The B & O Engineer (poem). **Address:** 407 Wormley Creek Dr, Yorktown, VA 23692, U.S.A. **Online address:** chenney@earthlink.net

HENNING, Ann. Also writes as Ann Henning Jocelyn. Swedish, b. 1948. **Genres:** Children's fiction, Plays/Screenplays, Poetry, Adult non-fiction, Translations. **Career:** Author, playwright, and translator. Artistic Director, 4th International Women Playwrights Conference; Artistic Director, Connemara Theatre Co. **Publications:** Modern Astrology, 1983; The Connemara Whirlwind, 1990; The Connemara Stallion, 1991; The Connemara Champion, 1994; The Cosmos and You (nonfiction), 1995; Honeylove the Bear Cub, 1995; Keylines (poetry), 2000. STAGE PLAYS: Smile, 1972; Baptism of Fire, 1997; The Alternative, 1999. **Address:** 4 The Boltons, London SW10 9TB, England.

HENRICKSSON, John. American, b. 1926. **Genres:** Environmental sciences/Ecology. **Career:** Writer. **Publications:** Rachel Carson: The Environmental Movement, 1991; North Writers, Vol I: A Strong Woods Collection, 1991, Vol II: Our Place in the Woods, 1997; A Wild Neighborhood, 1997; Gunflint: The Trail, the People, the Stories, 2003. **Address:** 79 Neptune St, Mahtomedi, MN 55115, U.S.A. **Online address:** henricksson@aol.com

HENRIKSEN, Margot A. American. **Genres:** History. **Career:** University of Hawaii-Manoa, Hawaii, became professor of history. **Publications:** Dr. Strangelove's America: Society and Culture in the Atomic Age, 1997. **Address:** Department of History, Sakamaki Hall, B-403, University of Hawaii Manoa, 2444 Dole Street, Honolulu, HI 96822, U.S.A. **Online address:** henrikm@hawaii.edu

HENRIOT, Christian. American. **Genres:** Air/Space topics. **Career:** Institute of East Asian Studies, Lumière-Lyon II University, Lyon, France, director. **Publications:** (Compiler) La Femme en Asie orientale: Politique, société, littérature, Université Jean Moulin-Lyon III, 1988; Shanghai, 1927-1937: Élites locales et modernisation dans la Chine nationaliste, 1991, translation by Noël Castelino published as Shanghai, 1927-1937: Municipal Power, Locality, and Modernization, 1993; (with Shi Lu) La Réforme des entreprises en Chine: Les Industries shanghaiennes entre état et marché, 1996; Belles de Shanghai: Prostitution et sexualité en Chine aux XIXe-XXe siècle, 1997, translation by Noël Castelino published as Prostitution and Sexuality in Shanghai: A Social History, 1849-1949, 2001; (with Zheng Zu'an and others) Atlas de Shanghai: Espaces et représentations de 1849 à nos jours, 1999; (editor, with Robert Bickers) New Frontiers: Imperialism's New Communities in East Asia, 1842-1953, 2000; (editor, with Geneviève Dubois-Taine) Cities of the Pacific Rim: Diversity and Sustainability, 2001; (editor, with Wen-hsin Yeh) In the Shadow of the Rising Sun: Shanghai under Japanese Occupation, 2003. **Address:** c/o Author Mail, Cambridge University Press, 40 West Twentieth St., Seventh Floor, New York, NY 10011, U.S.A.

HENRY, Chad. (born United States), b. 1946. **Genres:** Plays/Screenplays. **Career:** Professional actor, director, composer, playwright, and author. Affiliate of Denver Center Theater Company, Denver, CO. U.S. Army, 1965-68. **Publications:** (Librettist and composer) A. M. Collins, Angry Housewives, 1983; (Librettist and composer) Stevie Kallos, adaptor, Pinocchio (children's musical play), 1996; DogBreath Victorious (novel), 1999; (Adaptor, librettist, and composer) The Magic Mrs. Piggle-Wiggle (musical play), 2001. Author of more than twenty musical plays. **Address:** 1681 South Perry St., Denver, CO 80219, U.S.A. **Online address:** gregcat@msn.com

HENRY, DeWitt (Pawling), (II). American, b. 1941. **Genres:** Novels, Autobiography/Memoirs. **Career:** Ploughshares, Inc., Boston, Mass., editor and director, 1971-89; Emerson College, prose writer in residence, 1973-74, adjunct professor, 1982-83, assistant professor 1983-89, associate professor of creative writing and literature, 1989-, acting chair, 1987-88, chair of writing, publishing, and literature division, 1989-93, executive director of Ploughshares (journal currently owned by Emerson College), 1990-95. Instructor in English at Simmons College, 1971-72. Director of Book Affairs, Inc., 1975-82. Member of advisory panels, boards, and councils. **Publications:** EDITOR: The Ploughshares Reader: New Fiction for the Eighties, 1985; Other Sides of Silence: New Fiction from Ploughshares, 1992; (with J.A. McPherson) Fathering Daughters: Reflections by Men, 1998; Breaking into Print, 2000; Sorrow's Company, 2001; The Marriage of Anna Maye Potts, 2001. **Address:** Writing Literature, Publishing Div, Emerson College, 120 Boylston St, Boston, MA 02116-4624, U.S.A. **Online address:** dewitt_henry@emerson.edu

HENRY, Gordon D., Jr. American, b. 1955. **Genres:** Novels. **Career:** Ferris State University, Big Rapids, MI, assistant professor, 1988-92; Michigan State University, East Lansing, MI, assistant professor of English, 1993-. Lecturer, storyteller. **Publications:** The Light People (novel), 1994. **Address:** Department of English, 201 Morrill, Michigan State University, East Lansing, MI 48824, U.S.A.

HENRY, Jay C(harles). American, b. 1939. **Genres:** Architecture. **Career:** University of Texas at Arlington, 1972-, became professor of architecture. **Publications:** Architecture in Texas 1895-1945, 1993. **Address:** School of Architecture, Box 19108, 601 West Nedderman Dr., University of Texas at Arlington, Arlington, TX 76019, U.S.A.

HENRY, Maeve. Irish, b. 1960. **Genres:** Novels. **Career:** Oxford Intensive School of English, Oxford, England, English and foreign language teacher, 1987-. **Publications:** The Witch King, 1987; A Gift for a Gift, 1990; Listen to the Dark, 1993; A Summer Dance, 1994; Midwinter, 1997; Just a Boy, 2001. **Address:** c/o Felicity Bryan, 2A North Parade, Banbury Rd, Oxford OX2 6LX, England.

HENRY, Patrick. American, b. 1940. **Genres:** Literary criticism and history. **Career:** Rice University, Houston, TX, instructor in French, 1968-69; Whitman College, Walla Walla, WA, instructor in French, 1969-70; University of Strasbourg, Strasbourg, France, Fulbright lecturer in American literature, 1971-72; Willamette University, Salem, OR, assistant professor of French, 1973-76; Whitman College, assistant professor, 1976-79, associate professor, 1979-88, professor of French, 1988-, head of department of foreign languages and literatures, 1979-82. Has taught three National Endowment for the Humanities (NEH) seminars on Montaigne to high school teachers, 1990, 1993, 1994. **Publications:** Voltaire and Camus: The Limits of Reason and the Awareness of Absurdity, 1975; Montaigne in Dialogue: Censorship and

Defensive Writing, Architecture and Friendship, the Self and the Other, 1987. EDITOR: (and contrib.) An Inimitable Example: The Case for the Princesse de Cleves, 1992; Approaches to Teaching Montaigne's "Essays," 1993. Contributor of articles, stories, and reviews to language and literature journals and newspapers. **Address:** Department of Foreign Languages and Literatures, Whitman College, Walla Walla, WA 99362, U.S.A. **Online address:** henrypg@whitman.edu

HENRY, Stuart (Dennis). British, b. 1949. **Genres:** Criminology/True Crime, Economics, Sociology. **Career:** University of London, Institute of Psychiatry, England, research sociologist at Addiction Research Unit, 1975-78; University of Middlesex, Enfield, England, research fellow at Centre for Occupational and Community Research, 1978-79; Nottingham Polytechnic, England, senior lecturer, 1979-83; Old Dominion University, Norfolk, VA, assistant professor of sociology and criminal justice, 1984-87; Eastern Michigan University, Ypsilanti, associate professor, 1987-92, professor of sociology and criminology, 1992-98; Valparaiso University, IN, chair of sociology, 1998-99; Wayne State University, Detroit, College of Lifelong Learning, director and associate dean, 1999-2002, Interdisciplinary Studies, chair, 2002-. Guest on radio and TV programs. **Publications:** (with D. Robinson) Self-Help and Health, 1977; The Hidden Economy, 1978; Private Justice, 1983; (with R. Cantor and S. Rayner) Making Markets, 1992; (with E.H. Pfuhl) The Deviance Process, 3rd ed., 1993; (with W. Einstadter) Criminological Theory, 1995; (with D. Milovanovic) Constitutive Criminology, 1996; (with M. Lanier) Essential Criminology, 1998, 2nd ed., 2004. EDITOR: Informal Institutions, in UK as Can I Have It in Cash?, 1981; Degrees of Deviance, 1989; (with L.A. Ferman and L.E. Berndt) Work beyond Employment in Advanced Capitalist Countries, Vol. I: Concepts, Evidence, and Measurement, Vol. II: Revisions and Criticism, 1993; Social Control, 1994; Inside Jobs, 1994; (with W. Einstadter) The Criminology Theory Reader, 1998; (with D. Milovarovic) Constitutive Criminology at Work, 1999; (with W.G. Hinkle) School Violence, 2000; (with M. Lanier) What Is Crime?, 2001. Work represented in anthologies. Contributor of articles and reviews to periodicals. **Address:** Dept of Interdisciplinary Studies, College of Urban Labor and Metropolitan Affairs, Wayne State University, 5700 Cass Ave, Detroit, MI 48202, U.S.A. **Online address:** Stuart.Henry@wayne.edu

HENRY, Sue. American, b. 1940. **Genres:** Mystery/Crime/Suspense. **Career:** Writer. Education administrator and grant writer; former instructor at University of Alaska. **Publications:** Murder on the Iditarod Trail, 1991; Termination Dust, 1995; Sleeping Lady, 1996; Death Takes Passage: An Alex Jansen Alaska Mystery, 1997; Deadfall, 1998; Murder on the Yukon Quest, 1999; Beneath the Ashes, 2000; Dead North, 2001; Cold Company, 2002. **Address:** c/o Author Mail, Avon Books, 10 East 53rd St., New York, NY 10022, U.S.A.

HENSLEY, Christopher. American, b. 1972. **Genres:** Sex. **Career:** Northeastern State University, Tahlequah, OK, assistant professor of sociology, 1997-99; Morehead State University, Morehead, KY, assistant professor of sociology and director of Institute for Correctional Research and Training, 1999-. Guest on media programs. **Publications:** (editor and contrib.) Prison Sex: Practice and Policy, 2002. (editor, with Richard Tewksbury) Sexual Deviance: A Reader, 2002. Contributor to professional journals and other periodicals. **Address:** 292 Woodland Lane, Mount Sterling, KY 40353, U.S.A. **Online address:** ch.hensley@moreheadstate.edu

HENSLEY, Dennis. Also writes as Craig Clybourn. American, b. 1964. **Genres:** Novels, Film, Gay and lesbian issues. **Career:** Writer, journalist, and performer. Has also worked as a page on sitcom sets, 1986-87, and as an entertainer and assistant cruise director for Princess Cruises, 1987-. Columnist, as Craig Clybourn, for Detour Magazine. **Publications:** Misadventures in the (213), 1998; Screening Party, 2002; (co-writer) Testosterone (screenplay), 2004. Contributor to periodicals. **Address:** c/o Bonnie Nadell, Frederick Hill and Associates, 1842 Union St, San Francisco, CA 94123, U.S.A. **Online address:** dhensley@aol.com

HENSLEY, Joe L. American, b. 1926. **Genres:** Novellas/Short stories, Mystery/Crime/Suspense, Science fiction/Fantasy, Novels. **Career:** Partner, Hensley, Walro, Collins and Hensley, now retired. Freelance writer, mainly of suspense novels. Partner, Metford and Hensley, 1955-72, and Hensley, Todd and Castor, 1972-75, Madison; Judge Pro-Tempore, 80th Judicial Circuit, Versailles, Indiana, 1975-76. Judge, 5th Judicial Circuit, Madison, Indiana, 1977-88. **Publications:** The Color of Hate, 1960; Deliver Us to Evil, 1971; Legislative Body, 1972; The Poison Summer, 1974; Song of Corpus Juris, 1974; The Black Roads (SF novel), 1976; Rivertown Risk, 1977; A Killing in Gold, 1978; Minor Murders, 1979; Outcasts, 1981; Final

Doors (short stories), 1981; Robak's Cross, 1985; Robak's Fire, 1987; Robak's Firm (short stories), 1987; Color Him Guilty, 1987; Fort's Law, 1987; Robak's Run, 1990; Grim City, 1994; Robak's Witch, 1997; (with G. Townsend) Loose Coins, 1998; Deadly Hunger & Other Tales, 2001; Robak in Black, 2001. **Address:** 2315 Blackmore, Madison, IN 47250-2303, U.S.A.

HENTOFF, Nat(han Irving). American, b. 1925. **Genres:** Novels, Young adult fiction, Civil liberties/Human rights, Music, Social commentary. **Career:** Down Beat Magazine, NYC, associate ed., 1953-57; Village Voice, NYC, columnist, 1957-; Jazz Review, co-founder and co-ed., 1958-60; New Yorker, staff writer, 1960-97; Washington Post, columnist, 1984-99; Washington Times, columnist, 2000-. **Publications:** The Jazz Life, 1961; The Peace Agitator, 1963; The New Equality, 1964; Jazz Country, 1965; Call the Keeper, 1966; Our Children Are Dying, 1966; Onwards, 1967; A Doctor among the Addicts, 1967; I'm Really Dragged but Nothing Gets Me Down, 1967; Journey into Jazz, 1968; A Political Life: The Education of John V. Lindsay, 1969; In the Country of Ourselves, 1971; (with others) State Secrets: Police Surveillance in America, 1973; This School Is Driving Me Crazy, 1976; Jazz Is, 1976; Does Anybody Give a Damn, 1977; The First Freedom, 1979; Does This School Have Capital Punishment?, 1981; Blues for Charlie Darwin, 1982; The Day They Came to Arrest the Book, 1982; The Man from Internal Affairs, 1983; Boston Boy: A Memoir, 1986; American Heroes: In and Out of School, 1987; John Cardinal O'Connor: At the Storm Center of a Changing American Catholic Church, 1988; Free Speech for Me-But Not for Thee, 1992; Listen to the Stories, 1995; Speaking Freely: A Memoir, 1997; Living the Bill of Rights: How to Be an Authentic American, 1998; The Nat Hentoff Reader, 2001; The War on the Bill of Rights and the Gathering Resistance, 2003; American Music!, 2004. EDITOR: (with N. Shapiro) Hear Me Talkin' to Ya, 1955; The Jazz Makers, 1957; (with A. McCarthy) Jazz, 1959; The Collected Essays of A.J. Muste, 1966. **Address:** c/o The Village Voice, 37 W 12th St, New York, NY 10011, U.S.A.

HEPBURN, Ronald William. British, b. 1927. **Genres:** Philosophy. **Career:** University of Nottingham, professor, 1960-64; University of Edinburgh, professor of philosophy, 1964-75, professor of moral philosophy, 1975-96. **Publications:** Christianity and Paradox: Critical Studies in Twentieth-Century Theology, 1958; Wonder and Other Essays in Aesthetics and Neighbouring Fields, 1984; The Reach of the Aesthetic: Collected Essays on Art and Nature, 2001. Contributor to books and academic journals. **Address:** 8 Albert Terrace, Edinburgh EH10 5EA, Scotland. **Online address:** ronaldhepburn@aol.com

HEPER, Metin. Turkish, b. 1940. **Genres:** History, Politics/Government. **Career:** Middle East Technical University, Ankara, Turkey, assistant professor, 1970-74; Bogazici University, Istanbul, assistant professor, 1974-76, associate professor, 1976-81, professor of public administration, 1981-88, department head, 1985-88; Bilkent University, Ankara, professor of political science and public administration and chairperson of department, both 1988-, dean of Faculty of Economics, Administrative, and Social Sciences, 1996-98, 2004-. Visiting professor/research fellow at universities worldwide, including Harvard and Princeton. **Publications:** Decision-Making in the Middle East Technical University, 1973; Gecekondu Policy in Turkey, 1978; (with A. Umit Berkman) Development Administration in Turkey, 1980; The State Tradition in Turkey, 1985; Historical Dictionary of Turkey, 1994, rev. ed., 2002; Ismet Inonu: The Making of a Turkish Statesman, 1998. EDITOR & CONTRIBUTOR: Turkey: Past Achievement & Future Prospects, 1983; (with I. Raphaeli) Islam and Politics in the Modern Middle East, 1984; Dilemmas of Decentralization, 1986; Democracy and Local Government, 1987; The State and Public Bureaucracies, 1987; (with A. Evin) The State, Military, and Democracy, 1988; Local Government in Turkey, 1989; (with J. Landau) Political Parties and Democracy in Turkey, 1991; Strong State and Economic Interest Groups, 1991; (with A. Oncu and H. Kramer) Turkey and the West, 1993; (with Evin) Politics in the Third Turkish Republic, 1994; (with B. Rockman and A. Kazancigil) Institutions and Democratic Statecraft, 1997; (with S. Sayari) Political Leaders and Democracy in Turkey, 2002; (with B. Rubin) Political Parties in Turkey. UNTRANSLATED WORKS: Kisa Amme Idaresi Bibliografyasi, 1958-1966 (title means: A Concise Bibliography of Public Administration, 1958-1966), 1966; Modernlesme ve Burokrasin (Modernization and Bureaucracy), 1973; Burokratik Yonetim Gelenegi (Bureaucratic Ruling Tradition), 1974; Turk Kamu Burokrasisinde Gelenekcilik ve Modernlesme: Siyaset Sosyolojisi Acisindan Bir Inceleme (Bureaucracy: A Political Sociology Perspective), 1978; Turkiye'de Kent Gocmeni ve Burokratik Orgutler (Urban Migrant and Bureaucratic Organizations in Turkey), 1983. Contributor to books and professional journals in English and Turkish. **Address:** Dept of Political Science & Public Administration, Bilkent University, 06533 Bilkent, Ankara, Turkey. **Online address:** heper@bilkent.edu.tr

HEPPENHEIMER, Thomas A. American, b. 1947. **Genres:** Air/Space topics, Physics, Technology. **Career:** Science Applications Inc., Schiller Park, IL, scientist, 1972-73; Rockwell International Corp., Downey, CA, member, technical staff, 1973-74; California Institute of Technology, Pasadena, research fellow in planetary science, 1974-75; Max-Planck-Institut, Heidelberg, Alexander von Humboldt Fellow, 1976-78; University of California, Irvine, instructor, 1988-90. Journal of the Astronautical Sciences, book review ed., 1979-86. **Publications:** Colonies in Space, 1977; Toward Distant Suns, 1979; The Real Future, 1983; The Man-Made Sun, 1984; The Coming Quake, 1988; Anti Submarine Warfare, 1989; Hypersonic Technologies and the National Aerospace Plane, 1990; Air Traffic Control, 1995; Turbulent Skies, 1995; Countdown, 1997; The Space Shuttle Decision, 1999; A Brief History of Flight, 2000; Development of the Space Shuttle, 2002; First Flight, 2003; Flight, 2003. **Address:** 11040 Blue Allium Ave, Fountain Valley, CA 92708, U.S.A. **Online address:** taheppenheimer@yahoo.com

HEPPNER, Cheryl M. American, b. 1951. **Genres:** Autobiography/Memoirs. **Career:** Handley Library, Winchester, VA, affiliated with technical services and reference, 1977-85; Virginia Department for the Deaf and Hard of Hearing, Richmond, outreach specialist, 1986-91; Northern Virginia Resource Center for Deaf and Hard of Hearing Persons, Fairfax, executive director, 1991-. Cheryl A. Heppner Public Relations, public relations consultant, 1979-91; Telecommunications for the Deaf, Inc., vice-president, 1993; Shenandoah Valley Independent Living Center, cofounder. White House Conference on Libraries and Information Services, delegate, 1991. **Publications:** Seeds of Disquiet: One Deaf Woman's Experience, 1992. **Address:** 10121 Glenmere Rd, Fairfax, VA 22030, U.S.A.

HEPPNER, Ernest G. American (born Germany), b. 1921. **Genres:** Autobiography/Memoirs. **Career:** Worked various jobs during internment in a ghetto in Shanghai, China, 1939-45; affiliated with U.S. Advisory Group to the Chinese Armed Forces, 1945-47; REX Business Machines, manager, 1953-60; Monroe division of Litton Industries, systems manager, 1960-; RANAC Computer Corporation, vice president and general manager, 1975-87; independent management consultant, 1987-. **Publications:** Shanghai Refuge: A Memoir of the World War II Jewish Ghetto, 1993-95. **Address:** Management Advisory Services, 6930 North Delaware St, Indianapolis, IN 46220-1032, U.S.A. **Online address:** ernsth@iquest.net

HEPPNER, P(uncky) Paul. American, b. 1951. **Genres:** Psychology. **Career:** University of Minnesota-Morris, counselor, 1976; Tomah Veterans Administration Hospital, Tomah, WA, psychology trainee, 1977; University of Nebraska-Lincoln, counselor, 1977-78; Colorado State University, Fort Collins, doctoral intern, 1979; University of Missouri-Columbia, assistant professor, 1979-84, associate professor, 1984-88, professor of psychology, 1988-, Frederick A. Middlebush Professor of Social Sciences, 1990-95, senior staff psychologist in Counseling Services, 1979-88, adjunct psychologist at Counseling Center, 1991-, associate chair of department, 1990-98. University of London, visiting fellow in psychology at Goldsmith's College, 1987. Fulbright Scholar, Sweden, 1985, Ireland, 1994, Taiwan, 2002. Counseling Psychologist, editor, 1997-2002. **Publications:** (ed.) Pioneers in Counseling and Human Development: Personal and Professional Perspectives, 1990; (with D. Kivlighan and B.E. Wampold) Research Methods in Counseling, 1992, 1999. Work represented in anthologies. Contributor of chapters to books. Contributor to psychology journals. **Address:** Department of Educational, School and Counseling Psychology, 16 Hill Hall, University of Missouri-Columbia, Columbia, MO 65211, U.S.A. **Online address:** HeppnerP@Missouri.edu

HEPWORTH, Noel P. British, b. 1934. **Genres:** Money/Finance, Politics/Government. **Career:** Chairman, Institute of Public Finance, 1996-; Director, Chartered Institute of Public Finance and Accountancy, 1980-96. Assistant City Treasurer, Manchester, 1968-72; Director of Finance, London Borough of Croydon, 1972-80. **Publications:** Local Government Finance, 1970, 7th ed., 1983; (with J. Odling-Smee and A. Grey) Housing Rents, Costs, and Subsidies, 1978; The Reform of Local Government, 1985; What Future for Local Government, 1988. **Address:** NLA Town, Addisombe Rd, Croyden CR0 0XT, England.

HERALD, Kathleen. *See* **PEYTON, K. M.**

HERBERT, Brian. American, b. 1947. **Genres:** Mystery/Crime/Suspense, Science fiction/Fantasy, Humor/Satire. **Career:** Crowell Collier Macmillan, San Rafael and Stockton, CA, field manager, 1966; Fireman's Fund America, San Francisco, CA, and Seattle, WA, underwriter, 1968-73; Insurance Co. of North America, Seattle, underwriter, 1973-77; Stanley Scott & Co., Seattle, broker, 1977-84; writer. Has worked as inventor, job printer, import shop owner, and catalog company owner. **Publications:** HUMOR: Classic Comebacks, 1981; Incredible Insurance Claims, 1982. SCIENCE FICTION/ FANTASY NOVELS: Sidney's Comet, 1983; The Garbage Chronicles, 1985; Sudanna, Sudanna, 1985; (with F. Herbert) Man of Two Worlds, 1986; Prisoners of Arionn, 1987; The Race for God, 1990; (with M. Landis) Memorymakers, 1991; (with M. Landis) Blood on the Sun, 1996. SCIENCE FICTION/FANTASY NOVELS WITH K.J. ANDERSON: Dune: House Atreides, 1999; Dune: House Harkonnen, 2000; Dune: House Corrino, 2001; Dune: The Butlerian Jihad, 2002; Dune: The Machine Crusade, 2003; Dune: The Battle of Corrin, 2004; forthcoming: Hunters of Dune; The Road to Dune; Sandworms of Dune. OTHER: Dreamer of Dune (biography), 2003; The Forgotten Heroes (history), 2004. EDITOR: The Notebooks of Frank Herbert's Dune, 1988; The Songs of Muad'Dib (collection of F. Herbert's poetry), 1992; B. Brubaker, Never as It Seems, 1992; O. Lang, A Bird of Passage, 1995. Contributor of articles and short stories to periodicals. **Address:** PO Box 10164, Bainbridge Island, WA 98110, U.S.A. **Online address:** www.dunenovels.com

HERBERT, Gilbert. Israeli (born Republic of South Africa), b. 1924. **Genres:** Architecture. **Career:** Lecturer in Architecture, University of the Witwatersrand, Johannesburg, 1947-61; Reader in Architecture and Town Planning, University of Adelaide, 1961-68; Part-time Professor, Bezalel Academy of Art and Design, Jerusalem, 1970-72, 1976-78; Associate Ed., South African Architectural Record, Johannesburg, 1949-60; Technion, Haifa, Associate Professor, 1968-72, Professor, 1972-92, Dean of the Faculty of Architecture and Town Planning, 1973-74, Mary Hill Swope Professor of Architecture, 1974-92, Professor Emeritus, 1992-. **Publications:** The Synthetic Vision of Walter Gropius, 1959; Martienssen and the International Style, 1975; Pioneers of Prefabrication, 1978; The Dream of the Factory-Made House: Walter Gropius and Konrad Wachsmann, 1984; (with S. Sosnovsky) Bauhaus-on-the-Carmel and the Crossroads of the Empire, 1993; (with I. Heinze-Greenberg) The Beginnings of Modern Architecture in Israel: The First Power Stations, 1921-1932, 1996; The Search for Synthesis: Selected Writings on Architecture and Planning, 1997; (with I. Heinze-Greenberg and S. Sosnovsky) In Search of Excellence: The Architecture and Building Projects of the Electric Industry in the Land of Israel 1921-1942. **Address:** Faculty of Architecture and Town Planning, Technion: Israel Institute of Technology, Haifa, Israel. **Online address:** herbert@tx.technion. ac.il

HERBERT, Ivor. British (born Republic of South Africa), b. 1925. **Genres:** Novels, Plays/Screenplays, Sports/Fitness, Biography. **Career:** Racehorse trainer, 1953-60, 1964-68; Feature Writer, and Columnist, London Evening News, 1954-70, and Sunday Express, London, 1970-80; Chief Travel Writer and Racing Ed., Mail on Sunday, London, 1980-2002. **Publications:** Eastern Windows, 1953; Point to Point, 1964; Arkle: The Story of a Champion, 1966, 1975; The Great St. Trinian's Train Robbery (screenplay), 1966; The Queen Mother's Horses, 1967; (with P. Smyly) The Winter Kings, 1968; The Way to the Top, 1969; (co-author) Night of the Blue Demands (play), 1971; Over Our Dead Bodies, 1972; The Diamond Diggers, 1972; (with J. Cusack) Scarlet Fever, 1972; Winter's Tale, 1974; Red Rum: Story of a Horse of Courage, 1974; The Filly (novel), 1977; Six at the Top, 1977; Spot the Winner, 1978; Longacre, 1978; (ed.) Horse Racing, 1980; (with J. O'Brien) Vincent O'Brien's Great Horses, 1984; Revolting Behaviour, 1987; Herbert's Travels, 1987; (with M. Rimell) Reflections on Racing, 1989; Spot the Winner, 1990; (with The Princess Royal) Riding through My Life, 1991; also TV scripts. **Address:** The Old Rectory, Bradenham, nr High Wycombe, Bucks. HP14 4HD, England.

HERBERT, James. British, b. 1943. **Genres:** Novels, Horror, Science fiction/Fantasy, Biography, Graphic Novels. **Career:** Art director in advertising, 1962-77. **Publications:** The Rats, 1974; The Fog, 1975; The Survivor, 1976; Fluke, 1977; The Spear, 1978; Lair, 1979; The Dark, 1980; The Jonah, 1981; Shrine, 1983; Domain, 1984; Moon, 1985; The Magic Cottage, 1986; Sepulchre, 1987; Haunted, 1988; Creed, 1990; Portent, 1992; Dark Places (non-fiction), 1993; The City (graphic novel), 1994; The Ghosts of Sleath, 1994; '48, 1996; Others, 2000; Once..., 2001; Nobody True, 2003. BIOGRAPHIES: Devil in the Dark; By Horror Haunted. **Address:** c/o Bruce Hunter, David Higham Assocs, 5-8 Lower John St, London W1R 4HA, England.

HERBERT, Sandra (Swanson). American, b. 1942. **Genres:** Sciences, Biography. **Career:** Smithsonian Institution, Washington, DC, visiting curator, 1967-68; University of Maryland at College Park, lecturer in history, 1969-72; University of Maryland, Baltimore County, Baltimore, assistant professor, 1973-78, associate professor, 1978-86, professor of history, 1986-, director, program in Human Context of Science and Technology. **Publica-**

tions: EDITOR: (and author of intro. and notes) The Red Notebook of Charles Darwin, 1980; (co) Charles Darwin's Notebooks, 1836-1844, 1987. FORTHCOMING: Charles Darwin, Geologist. **Address:** Department of History, University of Maryland Baltimore County, 1000 Hilltop Circle, Baltimore, MD 21250, U.S.A.

HERBST, Jurgen. American (born Germany), b. 1928. **Genres:** Education, History, Autobiography/Memoirs. **Career:** Wesleyan University, Middletown, CT, Associate Professor, 1958-66; University of Wisconsin, Madison, Professor of Educational Policy Studies and of History, 1966-94, Professor Emeritus, 1994-. **Publications:** The German Historical School in American Scholarship, 1965, 1972; The History of American Education, 1973; From Crisis to Crisis: American College Government, 1639-1819, 1982; And Sadly Teach: Teacher Education and Professionalization in American Culture, 1989; The Once and Future School: Three Hundred and Fifty Years of American Secondary Education, 1996; Requiem for a German Past: A Boyhood among the Nazis, 1999. EDITOR: Josiah Strong, Our Country, 1963; (with G. Genovesi, B.B. Gundem, M. Heinemann, T. Harbo, and T. Sirevag), History of Elementary School Teaching and Curriculum, International Series for the History of Education, vol. 1, 1990; (with F-P Hager, M. Depaepe, M. Heinemann, and R. Lowe) Aspects of Antiquity in the History of Education, International Series for History of Education, vol. 3, 1992; (with H. Geitz and J. Heideking) German Influences on Education in the United States to 1917, 1995; (with J. Heideking and M. Depaepe) Mutual Influences on Education: Germany and the United States in the Twentieth Century, 1997. **Address:** 321 Pine Ridge Loop, Durango, CO 81301-7510, U.S.A. **Online address:** jherbst22@compuserve.com

HERBST, Phil(ip H.). American, b. 1944. **Genres:** Language/Linguistics, Reference, Social sciences. **Career:** National Institutes of Health, conducted anthropological field work in Suva, Fiji, 1969-70; State University of New York College, Potsdam, instructor in anthropology, 1971-74; Follett Corp., American Publishers Co., Chicago, IL, educational sales representative in New England, 1974-75; Chicago Daily News/Sun Times, Chicago, educational consultant, 1975-79; free-lance editor, 1979-81; American Society of Clinical Pathologists Press, Chicago, product development editor, 1981-85; Scott, Foresman/Little, Brown (publishing companies), Glenview, IL, project editor, 1985-90; New Trier Extension, Wilmette, IL, instructor in anthropology, 1990; Northwestern University, Evanston, IL, visiting scholar in anthropology, 1990-92, visiting scholar in gender studies, 1998-2000; Harold Washington College, Chicago, lecturer in English as a second language, 1995-96; Evanston Township High School, Evanston, instructor in English as a second language, 1996-97. **Publications:** The Multicultural Dictionary: A Usage Guide to Ethnic and Racial Words, 1993; The Color of Words: An Encyclopaedic Dictionary of Ethnic Bias in the United States, 1997; Wimmin, Wimps & Wallflowers: An Encyclopaedic Dictionary of Gender and Sexual Orientation Bias in the United States, 2001; Color of Words, Teaching Tolerance, 2001. Contributor of articles and reviews to periodicals; co-writer of college textbooks. **Address:** 2415 Central St. Suite D, Evanston, IL 60201, U.S.A. **Online address:** tkherbst@earthlink.net

HERDAN, Innes. Also writes as Innes Jackson. British, b. 1911. **Genres:** Literary criticism and history, Biography, Translations. **Career:** Writer and translator. **Publications:** AS INNES JACKSON: China Only Yesterday, 1938; (trans.) Give Back My Rivers and Hills, 1945. AS INNES HERDAN: (trans. with G. Herdan) Lichtenberg's Commentaries on Hogarth's Engravings, 1966; The Three Hundred Tang Poems, 1973; Introduction to China, 1976; The Pen and the Sword: Literature and Revolution in Modern China, 1992; Liao Hongying - Fragments of a Life, 1996. **Address:** 2 Octagon Ct, Calvert St, Norwich NR3 1AN, England.

HERDING, Klaus. German, b. 1939. **Genres:** Art/Art history. **Career:** National Gallery, Berlin, Germany, assistant to the director, 1968-70; Technische and Free University of Berlin, assistant professor of art history, 1971-74; University of Hamburg, Germany, professor of art history, 1975-92, head of faculty of cultural sciences, 1987-88; University of Frankfurt, Germany, professor of art history, 1993-, head of faculty of cultural sciences, 1994-95. L'Ecole des Hautes Etudes, Paris, director of studies and guest professor, 1988-90; scholar in the Getty Center, 1992-93; Siemens Foundation, Munich, research fellow, 1996-93. **Publications:** Pierre Puget: Das bildnerische Werk, 1970; Propylaen Kunstgeschichte (title means: The History of Art), 1970; (with H.E. Mittig) Kunst und Alltag im NS-System (title means: Art and Everyday Life during the National Socialist Era), 1975; Egalitaet und Autoritaet in Courbets Landschaftsmalerei (title means: Courbet's Landscape Painting), 1975; (with G. Otto) Karikaturen (title means: Caricatures), 1980; La Revolution Francaise et l'Europe (title means: Europe and the French Revolution), 1989; (with R. Reichardt) Die Bildpublizistik der Franzoesischen Revolution (title means: Broadsheets and Graphics of the French Revolution), 1989; Im Zeichen der Aufklarung (title means: Under the Sign of Enlightenment), 1989; Courbet: To Venture Independence, 1991; Picasso, Les Demoiselles d'Avignon, 1992; Freud's Leonardo, 1998. EDITOR/CO-EDITOR: (with W. Hofmann) Courbet und Deutschland (title means: Courbet and Germany), 1978; Realismus als Widerspruch (title means: Contradictions in Realism), 1978; Malerei und Theorie (title means: Painting and Theory), 1980; Courbet, Gustave, 1819-1877: Les Voyages Secrets de Monsieur Courbet (title means: The Secret Travels of Gustave Courbet), 1984; (and trans. and author of intro.) Proudhon's Art Theory, 1988; Aufklaerung anstelle von Andacht Kulturwissen-schafteishe Dimensionan bildender Kunst, 1997; Die Kunstgeschichte au Goethe-Universifurt, 2002. **Address:** c/o Kunstgeschichtliches Institut, Hausener Weg 120, D-60489 Frankfurt, Germany. **Online address:** herding@kunst.uni-frankfurt.de

HERF, Jeffrey. American, b. 1947. **Genres:** History. **Career:** Ohio University, Athens, OH, associate professor of history; writer. **Publications:** Reactionary Modernism: Technology, Culture, and Politics in Weimar and the Third Reich, 1984; War By Other Means: Soviet Power, West German Resistance, and the Battle of the Euromissiles, 1991; East German Communists and the Jewish Question: The Case of Paul Merker, 1994; Divided Memory: The Nazi Past in the Two Germanys, 1997. **Address:** Department of History, Bentley Hall, Room 56, Ohio University, Athens, OH 45701, U.S.A. **Online address:** herf@oak.cats.ohiou.edu

HERIVEL, Tara. (born United States). **Genres:** Adult non-fiction. **Career:** Lawyer and prison rights activist. Washington Protection and Advocacy System, attorney, 2002-; has also worked as an actor and waitress. **Publications:** (editor, with Paul Wright) Prison Nation: The Warehousing of America's Poor, 2003. Contributor of articles to periodicals. **Address:** c/o Author Mail, Routledge, 29 W. Thirty-fifth St., New York, NY 10001, U.S.A.

HERMAN, Barbara. American, b. 1945. **Genres:** Philosophy, Ethics. **Career:** Massachusetts Institute of Technology, Cambridge, assistant professor of philosophy, 1973-80; University of Southern California, Los Angeles, visiting assistant professor, 1980-81, assistant professor, 1981-84, associate professor, 1984-92, professor of philosophy and law, 1992-94; University of California, Los Angeles, Griffin Professor of Philosophy, 1994-. Princeton University, visiting associate professor, 1987. **Publications:** Morality and Rationality: A Study of Kant's Ethics, 1990; The Practice of Moral Judgment, 1993. Contributor to books and philosophy journals. **Address:** Department of Philosophy, University of California, Los Angeles, Los Angeles, CA 90024, U.S.A.

HERMAN, Bernard L. American, b. 1951. **Genres:** Architecture, Local history/Rural topics. **Career:** Worked as professor of history at University of Delaware, Newark; writer. **Publications:** Architectural and Rural Life in Delaware, 1700-1900, 1987; (with S.E. Holsoe) A Land and Life Remembered: Americo-Liberian Folk Architecture, 1988; The Stolen House: Material Culture, History, and Metaphor in the Early Republic, 1992; Everyday Architecture of the Mid-Atlantic, 1997. **Address:** Department of Art History, University of Delaware, 323 Old College, Newark, DE 19716, U.S.A. **Online address:** bherman@udel.edu

HERMAN, Didi. Canadian/British, b. 1961. **Genres:** Gay and lesbian issues, Law. **Career:** University of Kent, England, professor in law. **Publications:** Rights of Passage, 1994; Legal Inversions: Lesbians, Gay Men, and the Politics of Law, 1995; The Antigay Agenda: Orthodox Vision and the Christian Right, 1997; Sexuality in the Legal Arena, 2000; (with D. Buss) Globalizing Family Values, 2003. **Address:** Department of Law, University of Kent, Canterbury, Kent CT2 7NZ, England. **Online address:** d.herman@kent.ac.uk

HERMAN, Ellen. American, b. 1957. **Genres:** Psychology, Gay and lesbian issues. **Career:** Harvard University, Cambridge, MA, member of social studies faculty. **Publications:** The Romance of American Psychology: Political Culture in the Age of Experts, 1995; Psychiatry, Psychology, and Homosexuality, 1995. **Address:** Department of History, University of Oregon, 321 Grayson Hall, Eugene, OR 97403-1288, U.S.A. **Online address:** eherman@darkwing.uoregon.edu

HERMAN, Michael. British, b. 1929. **Genres:** Military/Defense/Arms control. **Career:** Government Communications Headquarters, Cheltenham, England, intelligence practitioner for Great Britain, 1952-87; also served as secretary of Joint Intelligence Committee, Cabinet Office, and a member of Defence Intelligence Staff. Nuffield College, Oxford, Gwilym Gibbon Research Fellow, 1987-88, associate member, 1988-94; former honorary

research fellow at King's College, London, and Keele University; Aberystwyth, departmental fellow, 2001-; University of Oxford, St. Antony's College, senior associate member, 2000-03, director of Oxford Intelligence Group; has presented seminars and papers at universities. **Publications:** Intelligence Power in Peace and War, 1996; Intelligence Services in the Information Age, 2001. Contributor to books. Contributor of papers and articles to periodicals. **Address:** 24 Albert Rd, Cheltenham GL52 2QX, England. **Online address:** MHE24@aol.com

HERMAN, Michelle. American, b. 1955. **Genres:** Novels, Novellas/Short stories. **Career:** Associated Press, freelance book editor and reporter, 1976-88; Ohio State University, Columbus, associate professor of English, 1988-. **Publications:** Missing (novel), 1990; New and Glorious Life, 1998. Short stories. **Address:** Dept of English, Ohio State University, 164 W 17th Ave, Columbus, OH 43210, U.S.A. **Online address:** herman.2@osu.edu

HERMAN, Richard, Jr. American, b. 1939. **Genres:** Mystery/Crime/Suspense. **Publications:** MILITARY AND POLITICAL THRILLERS: The Warbirds, 1989; Force of Eagles, 1990; Firebreak, 1991; Call to Duty, 1993; Dark Wing, 1994; Iron Gate, 1996; Power Curve, 1997; Against All Enemies, 1998; Edge of Honor, 1999. **Address:** c/o John Hawkins & Associates Inc., 71 West 23rd St., New York, NY 10010, U.S.A.

HERMAN, Stephen L. (born United States), b. 1946. **Genres:** Education. **Career:** Teacher of electrical technology for thirty years, including positions at Lee College, Baytown, TX, and Randolph Technical College, Asheboro, NC. U.S. Army; served in Vietnam. **Publications:** (with Walter N. Alerich) Industrial Motor Control, 1985; Electronics for Industrial Electricians, 1985; (with Bennie L. Sparkman) Electricity and Controls for Heating, Ventilating, and Air Conditioning, 1986, 4th edition published as Electricity and Controls for HVAC/R, 2000; (with John R. Duff) Alternating Current Fundamentals, 1986; (with Robert L. Smith) Electrical Wiring: Industrial, 1987; (with Crawford G. Garrard) Practical Problems in Mathematics for Electricians, 1987; Delmar's Standard Textbook of Electricity, 1993; Electrical Studies for Trades, 1997, (with Donald E. Singleton) Delmar's Standard Guide to Transformers, 1997; Electrician's Technical Reference: Theory and Calculations, 1998; (with Walter N. Alerich) Electric Motor Control, 1998; Electrician's Technical Reference: Transformers, 1999; Electrician's Technical Reference: Industrial Electronics, 1999; Electrical Transformers and Rotating Machines, 1999; The Complete Lab Manual for Industrial Electricity, 2001; Electronics for Electricians, 2002; Practical Problems in Mathematics for Electronic Technicians, 2003; Residential Construction Academy: Electrical Principles, 2003. **Address:** 135 PR 52336, Pittsburg, TX 75686, U.S.A.

HERMANN, L. William. *See* LICHT, H. William (Bill).

HERMANS, Hubert J. M. Dutch, b. 1937. **Genres:** Psychology. **Career:** Asthma Center, Groesbeek, Netherlands, assistant psychologist and diagnostician, 1963-65; Catholic University of Nijmegen, Netherlands, staff member at Psychology Laboratory, 1965-72, lecturer, 1972-80, professor of psychology, 1980-. Guest lecturer at Catholic University of Lublin and University of Ghent; guest professor at University of Louvain and Duquesne University. **Publications:** (with H. Kempen) The Dialogical Self: Meaning as Movement, 1993; (with E. Hermans-Jansen) Self-Narratives: The Construction of Meaning in Psychotherapy, 1995. Contributor to periodicals. **Address:** Department of Clinical Psychology and Personality, Catholic University of Nijmegen, PO Box 9104, 6500 HE Nymegen, Netherlands. **Online address:** HHermans@psych.kun.nl

HERMES, Jules. American, b. 1962. **Genres:** Documentaries/Reportage. **Career:** International Commentary Service, NYC, senior writer, 1989-90; FLIP Writers and Photographers, Manitou Springs, CO, writer/photographer, 1990-93; Carolrhoda Books Inc., Minneapolis, MN, contract writer/photographer, 1991-97; American Refugee Committee, public relations director, 1997-. **Publications:** Children of India, 1993; Children of Micronesia, 1994; Children of Morocco, 1995; The Dalai Lama: A Biography, 1995; Children of Bolivia, 1996; Children of Guatemala, 1997. **Address:** c/o Carolrhoda Books, Learner Publishing Group, 241 1st Ave N, Minneapolis, MN 55401, U.S.A. **Online address:** pr@archq.org

HERMES, Patricia. American, b. 1936. **Genres:** Young adult fiction. **Career:** Rollingcrest Junior High School, Takoma Park, MD, teacher of English and social studies, 1957-58; Delcastle Technical High School, DE, teacher of home-bound children, 1972-73; writer, 1977-; Norfolk Public School System, VA, writer in residence, 1981-; Scared Heart University, Fairfield, CT, teacher of English and writing, 1986-87. **Publications:** YOUNG ADULT FICTION:

What If They Knew, 1980; Nobody's Fault, 1981; You Shouldn't Have to Say Goodbye, 1982; Who Will Take Care of Me?, 1983; Friends Are Like That, 1984; A Solitary Secret, 1985; Kevin Corbett Eats Flies, 1986; A Place for Jeremy, 1987; A Time to Listen: Preventing Youth Suicide, 1987; Heads, I Win, 1988; Be Still My Heart, 1989; I Hate Being Gifted, 1990; Mama, Let's Dance, 1991; My Girl, 1991; Take Care of My Girl, 1992; Someone to Count On, 1993; I'll Pulverize You, William, 1994; Nothing but Trouble, Trouble, Trouble, 1994; Everything Stinks, 1995; On Winter's Wind, 1995; Christmas Magic, 1996; Fly Away Home (novel based on the autobiography of B. Lishman), 1996; When Snow Lay Soft on the Mountain, 1996; Boys Are Even Worse than I Thought, 1997; Zeuss and Roxanne, 1997; Calling Me Home, 1998; Cheat the Moon, 1998. **Address:** 1414 Melville Avenue, Fairfield, CT 06824, U.S.A.

HERNANDEZ, Jaime. American, b. 1959. **Genres:** Cartoons. **Career:** Graphic artist, writer, and comix creator. **Publications:** (with Gilbert Hernandez and Mario Hernandez; as Los Bros Hernandez) Love and Rockets 1982; The Lost Women: And Other Stories, 1988; Whoa Nellie! (collection), 2000. **Address:** c/o Author Mail, Fantagraphics Books, 7563 Lake City Way NE, Seattle, WA 98115, U.S.A.

HERNANDEZ, Jo(anne) Farb. American, b. 1952. **Genres:** Art/Art history, Cultural/Ethnic topics, Mythology/Folklore. **Career:** Museum of Cultural History, University of California, Los Angeles, curatorial assistant, 1974-75; Dallas Museum of Fine Arts, TX, curator and educational assistant, 1976-77; East Texas State University, Commerce, adjunct professor, 1977; Triton Museum of Art, Santa Clara, CA, assistant to the director, 1977-78; director, 1978-85; John F. Kennedy University, San Francisco, CA, adjunct professor of museum studies, 1979; Monterey Peninsula Museum of Art, CA, director, 1985-93, consulting curator, 1994-; Curatorial and Museum Management Services, Watsonville, CA, director, 1993-; San Diego Museum of Art, CA, guest curator, 1995-; University of California, Santa Cruz, lecturer, 1999-2000; San Jose State University, professor and gallery director, 2000-. Visiting lecturer at institutions worldwide. **Publications:** (with S.R. Hernandez) The Day of the Dead: Tradition and Change in Contemporary Mexico, 1979; Crime and Punishment: Reflections of Violence in Contemporary Art, 1984; Three from the Northern Island: Contemporary Sculpture from Hokkaido, 1984; Anders Aldrin, 1990; (with C. Shere) The Expressive Sculpture of Alvin Light, 1990; Lorser Feitelson: Exploration of the Figure, 1919-1929, 1990; Two Sides of the Same Reality: The World and I, 1990; (with M. Levy) Alan Shepp: The Language of Stone, 1991; The Quiet Eye: Poetry of Shoji Hamada and Bernard Leach, 1991; (with C. Berney and A. White) Armin Hansen: The Jane and Justin Dart Collection, 1993; (with N. Boas) Wonderful Colors: The Paintings of August Francois Gay, 1993; Jeanette Maxfield Lewis: A Centennial Celebration, 1994; Jeremy Anderson: The Critical Link/A Quiet Revolution, 1995; (with J. Beardsley and R. Cardinal) A.G. Rizzoli: Architect of Magnificent Visions, 1997; Misch Kohn: Beyond the Tradition, 1998; (with P. Karlstrom) Fire and Flux/An Undaunted Vision: The Art of Charles Strong, 1998; Mel Ramos: The Galatea Series, 2000; Holly Lane: Small Miracles, 2001; (with F. Gualdoni and E. Mascelloni) Mel Ramos, 2001; (with others) Irvin Tepper: When Cops Speak/Life with the Cop, 2002; (with P. Sanders) Sam Richardson, 2002; (with P. Linhares and M. Tromble) Marc D'Estout: Domestic Objects, 2003. Contributor to books and periodicals. **Address:** Curatorial and Museum Management Services, 345 White Rd, Watsonville, CA 95076, U.S.A.

HERNDON, Ernest. American, b. 1955. **Genres:** Novels, Children's fiction, Travel/Exploration, Essays. **Career:** Enterprise-Journal, McComb, MS, reporter, 1979-; freelance writer. **Publications:** FOR CHILDREN: The Secret of Lizard Island, 1994; Double-Crossed in Gator Country, 1994; Night of the Jungle Cat, 1994; Smugglers on Grizzly Mountain, 1994; Sisters of the Wolf, 1996; Trouble at Bamboo Bay, 1996; Death Bird of Paradise, 1997; Little People of the Lost Coast, 1997. OTHER: In the Hearts of Wild Men, 1987; (with T. Seabourne) Self-Defense: A Body-Mind Approach (textbook), 1987; Morning Morning True: A Novel of Intrigue in New Guinea, 1988; Island Quarry: A Novel of Suspense, 1990; Backwater Blues: A Novel of Faith and Fury, 1991; Canoeing Mississippi, 2001; Canoeing Louisiana, 2003; Nature Trails and Gospel Tales, 2004. Contributor to anthologies and periodicals. **Address:** c/o Enterprise-Journal, PO Box 2009, McComb, MS 39649, U.S.A.

HERNDON, Nancy. Also writes as Elizabeth Chadwick, Nancy Fairbanks. American, b. 1934. **Genres:** Novels, Mystery/Crime/Suspense. **Career:** Novelist. Foley's Department Store, Houston, TX, advertising writer and proofreader, 1957; Darcy Advertising Company, NYC, advertising proofreader, 1958; Howland's Department Store, Bridgeport, CT, advertising copywriter, 1959; lecturer in English at New York University, NYC, 1959-61, University of Mississippi/Oxford, 1962-63, Florida Atlantic University,

Boca Raton, 1965-66, and University of Texas, El Paso, 1976-81; freelance writer, 1989-. **Publications:** MYSTERY NOVELS. AS NANCY HERNDON: Acid Bath, 1995; Widow's Watch, 1995; Lethal Statues, 1996; Hunting Game, 1996; Time Bombs, 1997; C.O.P. Out, 1998; Casanova Crimes, 1999. AS ELIZABETH CHADWICK: Wanton Angel, 1989; Widows' Fire, 1990; Virgin Fire, 1991; Bride Fire, 1992; Reluctant Lovers, 1993; Elusive Lovers, 1994. AS NANCY FAIRBANKS: Crime Brulee, 2001; Truffled Feathers, 2001; Death a l'Orange, 2002; Chocolate Quake, 2003; Perils of Paella, 2004. **Address:** 6504 Pino Real Dr, El Paso, TX 79912, U.S.A. **Online address:** nrherndon@elp.rr.com

HERNDON, Terry (Eugene). American, b. 1939. **Genres:** Education. **Career:** Teacher at public schools in Warren, Mich., 1962-67; National Education Association, Washington, D.C., urban representative, 1967-68, specialist in negotiations, 1968, executive director, 1973-83; Michigan Education Association, Lansing, Mich., executive director, 1969-73; WEA Insurance Group, Madison, Wis., president, 1985-. Chair of Integrated Teaching Corp., 1984; president of National Foundation for the Improvement of Education and Center for Education on Nuclear War. **Publications:** We, the Teachers: Terry Herndon on Education and Democracy, 1983. **Address:** Herndon, Mays & Skomicka, 5712 Odana Rd., Madison, WI 53719, U.S.A.

HERON, Ann. American, b. 1954. **Genres:** Young adult non-fiction, Gay and lesbian issues. **Career:** Affiliated with Alyson Publications, Boston, MA, 1980-84, and Nolo Press, Berkeley, CA, 1985-. **Publications:** One Teenager in Ten, 1983; (with M. Maran) How Would You Feel If Your Dad Was Gay?, 1990; (ed.) Two Teenagers in Twenty: Writings by Lesbian and Gay Youth, 1994. **Address:** c/o Nolo Press, 950 Parker St., Berkeley, CA 94710, U.S.A.

HERR, Michael. American, b. 1940. **Genres:** Novels, Plays/Screenplays, Autobiography/Memoirs, Biography. **Career:** Writer. **Publications:** Dispatches (memoir), 1977; (co-author) Apocalypse Now (screenplay), 1979; The Big Room (biographies), 1984; (co-author) Full Metal Jacket (screenplay), 1988; Walter Winchell: A Novel, 1990; Kubrick, 2000. **Address:** c/o Alfred A. Knopf, Inc Publicity, 1745 Broadway #B1, New York, NY 10019-4305, U.S.A.

HERRERA, (C.) Andrea O'Reilly. American, b. 1959. **Genres:** Novels. **Career:** University of Colorado, Colorado Springs, professor of English, 1999-, director of Ethnic Studies Program, 1999-, assistant vice chancellor of academic diversity and development, 2002-. Guest speaker at institutions in the United States and abroad; gives readings from her works. **Publications:** The Pearl of the Antilles (novel), 2001. EDITOR: (with S. Foor and E. Nollen, and contrib) Family Matters in the British and American Novel, 1997; (and author of intro.) A Secret Weavers Anthology, 1998; ReMembering Cuba: Legacy of a Diaspora, 2001. Contributor to books. Contributor of articles, poetry, and fiction to periodicals. **Address:** Ethnic Studies Program, Department of English, University of Colorado, 1420 Austin Bluffs Pkwy, Colorado Springs, CO 80933, U.S.A.

HERRICK, James A. American, b. 1954. **Genres:** Adult non-fiction. **Career:** Hope College, Holland, MI, instructor, 1984-90, associate professor, 1990-93, professor, 1997-, Guy Vander Jagt Professor of Communication, 2001-, department chair, 1993-2002. **Publications:** Critical Thinking: The Analysis of Arguments, 1991; Argumentation: Understanding and Shaping Arguments, 1995; The History and Theory of Rhetoric: An Introduction, 1997; The Radical Rhetoric of the English Deists: The Discourse of Skepticism, 1680-1750, 1997; The Making of the New Spirituality: The Eclipse of the Western Religious Tradition, 2003. Contributor to academic journals and periodicals. Manuscript reviewer, referee, and editorial board member for various academic publications and journals. **Address:** 35 East 28th St., Holland, MI 49423, U.S.A. **Online address:** herrick@hope.edu

HERRICK, Steven. Australian, b. 1958. **Genres:** Poetry. **Career:** Poet, 1988-. **Publications:** FOR CHILDREN. POETRY: My Life, My Love, My Lasagne, 1997; Poetry to the Rescue, 1998; The Spangled Drongo (verse-novel), 1999; Love Poems and Leg-Spinners, 2001. PICTURE BOOKS: The Place Where the Planes Take Off, 1995. FOR YOUNG ADULTS. POETRY: Caboolture, 1990; Water Bombs: A Book of Poems for Teenagers, 1992. NOVELS IN VERSE: Love, Ghosts, & Nose Hair, 1996; A Place Like This, 1998; The Simple Gift, 2000. FOR ADULTS. POETRY: The Esoteric Herrick: Poems & Things, 1982; The Sound of Chopping, 1994. **Address:** PO Box 116, Hazelbrook, NSW 2780, Australia. **Online address:** sherrick@acay.com.au

HERRIN, Lamar. American, b. 1940. **Genres:** History, Novels. **Career:** Writer. Affiliated with Cornell University, Ithaca, NY, 1977-, currently professor of English. **Publications:** The Rio Loja Ringmaster, 1977; American Baroque, 1981; The Unwritten Chronicles of Robert E. Lee, 1989; The Lies Boys Tell, 1991. Contributor of short stories to periodicals. **Address:** English Department, Cornell University, Ithaca, NY 14853, U.S.A.

HERRING, Phillip F. American, b. 1936. **Genres:** Literary criticism and history. **Career:** University of Texas, instructor in English, 1964-65; University of Virginia, assistant professor of English, 1965-70; University of Wisconsin, Madison, associate professor of English, 1970-74, professor of English, 1974-1996; University of Texas at Austin, Humanities Research Center, special assistant to director, 1996-. **Publications:** Joyce's Uncertainty Principle, 1987; Djuna: The Life and Work of Djuna Barnes, 1995. EDITOR: Joyce's Ulysses Notesheets in the British Museum, 1972; Joyce's Notes and Early Drafts for Ulysses: Selections from the Buffalo Collection, 1977. Contributor to books and professional journals. **Address:** HRHRC, University of Texas at Austin, PO Box 7219, Austin, TX 78713, U.S.A. **Online address:** pherring@mail.utexas.edu

HERRINGTON, Anne J. American, b. 1948. **Genres:** Education, Writing/Journalism. **Career:** Johnson State College, Johnson, VT, director of Developmental Skills, 1972-80; Pennsylvania State University, State College, PA, assistant professor, 1983-86; University of Massachusetts, Amherst, MA, professor and director of undergraduate writing program, 1986-. **Publications:** (ed. with C. Moran) Writing, Teaching, and Learning in the Disciplines, 1992. **Address:** University of Massachusetts, Bartlett Hall 305, Amherst, MA 01003, U.S.A.

HERRINGTON, Terri. See BLACKSTOCK, Terri.

HERRMANN, Luke John. British, b. 1932. **Genres:** Art/Art history. **Career:** Professor Emeritus of the History of Art, University of Leicester, 1988- (Paul Mellon Foundation Lecturer, 1967-70; Sr. Lecturer and Head of Dept., 1970-73; Professor, 1973-88). Assistant Ed., The Illustrated London News, 1955-58; Assistant Keeper and Sr. Assistant Keeper, Dept. of Western Art, Ashmolean Museum, Oxford, 1958-67. Walpole Society, Honorary Editor, 1993-2000. **Publications:** J.M.W. Turner, 1963; Ruskin and Turner, 1968; British Landscape Painting of the 18th Century, 1973; Turner: Paintings, Watercolours, Drawings and Prints, 1975, 1986; Paul and Thomas Sandby, 1986; Turner Prints: The Engraved Work of J.M.W. Turner, 1990; Katalog der Albertina, Band VII, Die Englische Schule, 1992; (with T. Cubberley) Catalogue of the Drawings by James Hakewill in the British School at Rome Library, 1992; Nineteenth Century British Painting, 2000; (ed. with E. Joll and M. Bublin) The Oxford Companion to J.M.W. Turner, 2001. **Address:** The Old Vicarage, Penrhos, Raglan, Usk, Monmouthshire NP15 2LE, England.

HERRMANNS, Ralph. Swedish, b. 1933. **Genres:** Novels, Children's fiction, Plays/Screenplays, Art/Art history, Biography. **Career:** Former Foreign Correspondent, Bonnier Group, Stockholm, and Travelling Correspondent, Time-Life Inc., NYC. Art commentator, Dagens Industri, Stockholm, 1991-2001. **Publications:** Picasso and His Friends (screenplay); Lee Lan Flies the Dragon Kite, 1961; Our Car Julia, 1963; Children of the North Pole, 1964; River Boy, 1965; Flickan som hade brattom, 1967; Den fortrollade ladan, 1968; The Abominable Snowman, 1969; The World's Most Beautiful Painting, 1970; Natten och drommen, 1972; Joan Miro, 1972; Sweden 1850 (screenplay), 1973; Posters by Miro, 1974; Goya's Witches (TV) 1974; The Enchanted Forest (screenplay), 1974; Carl Gustaf von Rosen: A Biography, 1975; Stockholm's Royal Palace, 1978; A World of Islands, 1980; En fest for ogat, 1980; Och solen gick ned over profeterna, 1981; Gosta Werner, A Biography, 1981; Den enes brod, 1982; Jenny Nystrom's Art, 1982; Desprez and the Swedish Theatre (TV), 1982; Why New York?, 1982; Israel talar, 1982; Tank pa de dagar, 1984; Slott och herremanshus, 1985; Lognens triumf, 1985; Blott doden, blott doden, 1986; Hunden i Konsten, 1987; Tapies (TV), 1988; Hasten hos manniskan, 1990; Tapies, 1993; 1900-talets maleri, 1994; Haberlands, 1996; Detjudiska Prag, 1998; Portratten pa Gripsholm, 1998; Miro, 2001; Karl-Axel Pehrson, 2001; Botero, 2001; Calatrava, 2001. **Address:** Brannkyrkagatan 77, 118 23 Stockholm, Sweden. **Online address:** rh@moviemakers.se

HERRNSTEIN, Barbara. See SMITH, Barbara Herrnstein.

HERROLD, Tracey. See DILS, Tracey E.

HERRON, Carolivia. American, b. 1947. **Genres:** Novels, Literary criticism and history, Children's fiction. **Career:** Harvard University, Cambridge, MA, assistant professor of Afro-American studies and comparative literature, 1986-90; Mount Holyoke College, South Hadley, MA, director of Epicenter

Literary Software, 1988-, associate professor of English, 1990-92; Hebrew College, Brookline, MA, Visiting scholar, 1994-95; Harvard University Divinity School & Graduate School of Education, visiting scholar, 1995-97. National Endowment for the Humanities, member of board of directors of curriculum development program, 1988-90; Carleton College, visiting professor, 1989. **Publications:** Thereafter Johnnie (novel), 1991; (ed.) Selected Works of Angelina Weld Grimke, 1991; Nappy Hair (children's fiction), 1997. Contributor to professional journals. **Address:** 6514 7th St., NW, Washington, DC 20012, U.S.A.

HERRON, Nancy L. American, b. 1942. **Genres:** Librarianship. **Career:** Wilkinsburg Public Library, Pittsburgh, PA, director, 1979-84; Pennsylvania State University, McKeesport, professor of library science and head librarian, 1984-90, director of academic affairs, 1991-. **Publications:** The Social Sciences, 1989, 2nd ed, 1996; The Leisure Literature, 1992; (ed. with D. Zabel) Bridging the Gap, 1995. **Address:** Pennsylvania State University, University Dr., McKeesport, PA 15132, U.S.A.

HERRON, William G. American, b. 1933. **Genres:** Novels, Psychology. **Career:** Practicing psychotherapist and psychoanalyst, 1962-; St. Bonaventure University, New York, Dept. of Psychology, associate professor and chairman, 1959-65; St. John's University, Jamaica, NY, professor, 1965-2000; Fairleigh Dickinson University, Contemporary Center for Advanced Psychoanalytic Studies, dean of training, 2000-04. **Publications:** (with R.E. Kantor) Reactive and Process Schizophrenia, 1966; (with M. Green, M. Guild, A. Smith, and R.E. Kantor) Contemporary School Psychology, 1970; F. Quantmeyer Hose No. 7 (novel), 1972; (with M. Herron and J. Handron) School Psychology: A Challenge for Change, 1980; (with S. Rouslin) Issues in Psychotherapy, 1982; (with S.R. Welt) Narcissism and the Psychotherapist, 1990; (with S.R. Welt) Money Matters: The Fee in Psychotherapy & Psychoanalysis, 1992; (with R. Javier and A. Bergman) Domestic Violence: Assessment and Treatment, 1996; (with R. Javier) Personality Development and Psychotherapy in Our Diverse Society, 1998; Narcissism and the Relational World, 1999. **Address:** 5 Pascack Rd, Woodcliff Lake, NJ 07677-8317, U.S.A.

HERSCHLER, Mildred Barger. American. **Genres:** Children's fiction, Young adult fiction. **Career:** Research Institute of America, New York, NY, editor, 1973-75; Sales Executives Clubs of New York, editor and advertising manager, 1976-81; freelance writer, 1982-. Worked as a civil rights and anti-war activist; headed a task force to add black history into school curricula in Huntington, NY, 1964-65. **Publications:** Frederick Douglass (juvenile biography), 1969; The Walk into Morning (historical novel), 1993; The Darkest Corner (young adult novel), 2000. Author of short fiction. **Address:** 305 Hearthstone Ridge Rd., Landrum, SC 29356, U.S.A. **Online address:** mbhersch@aol.com

HERSHENHORN, Esther. (born United States), b. 1945. **Genres:** Children's fiction. **Career:** Writer and educator. Previously worked as an elementary school teacher in Illinois. **Publications:** There Goes Lowell's Party, 1998; Illinois: Fun Facts and Games, 2000; The Confe$$ion$ and $ecret$ of Howard J. Fingerhut, 2002; Chicken Soup by Heart, 2002; Fancy That, 2003. **Address:** c/o Author Mail, Holiday House, 425 Madison Ave. #12, New York, NY 10017, U.S.A. **Online address:** esthers@aol.com

HERSHEY, Kathleen M. American, b. 1934. **Genres:** Mystery/Crime/Suspense. **Career:** Writer. Worked in a pre-school, as a library page, as an elementary school librarian, and as a children's bookstore manager. **Publications:** Cotton Mill Town, 1993. Also author of stories in magazines for children; contributor to adult mystery anthologies; also contributor of stories to magazines. **Address:** 23011 La Granja Dr., Valencia, CA 91355, U.S.A.

HERSHEY, Olive. American, b. 1941. **Genres:** Novels, Poetry, Plays/Screenplays. **Career:** St. Stephens Episcopal School, Austin, Tex., teacher of English, 1973-1978; Wall Street Transcript, New York, N.Y., editor, 1980; University of Houston, Houston, Tex., lecturer in English, 1983-88; Rice University, Houston, visiting assistant professor of fiction writing and English as a second language, 1988-. **Publications:** Floating Face Up (poems), 1984; Truck Dance (novel), 1988. **Address:** c/o Darhansoff and Verrill Literary, 236 W. 26th St, Rm 802, New York, NY 10001-6736, U.S.A.

HERSHMAN, Marcie. American, b. 1951. **Genres:** Novels, Autobiography/Memoirs, Essays. **Career:** Boston Globe, Boston, book reviewer/arts correspondent, 1975-82; Tufts University, Medford, MA, lecturer in English, 1981-. Emerson College, Boston, instructor in MFA writing program, 1982-98; Bunting Institute/Radcliffe College, Cambridge, fellow in fiction, 1992-93; PEN/New England, Boston, Executive Board, 1997-2003; Warren Wilson

College, MFA writing program, 1998; Fine Arts Work Center, Provincetown, MA, faculty, 1998-; Brandeis University, Waltham, MA, Fannie Hurst Writer-in-Residence, 1999-2001; University of Minnesota/Split Rock Arts, on-line mentor, 2003-. Residencies at Yaddow and MacDowell; judge for writing awards and contests. **Publications:** Tales of the Master Race (novel), 1991; Safe in America (novel), 1995; Speak to Me (memoir), 2001. Work represented in anthologies. Contributor to periodicals. **Address:** c/o English Dept, Tufts University, Medford, MA 02155, U.S.A. **Online address:** marcie.hershman@tufts.edu

HERSPRING, Dale R. American, b. 1940. **Genres:** Politics/Government. **Career:** U.S. Department of State, Washington, DC, foreign service officer, 1971-91, including assignments as arms control specialist for Bureau of Politico-Military Affairs, consular officer at U.S. embassy in Warsaw, Poland, political-military affairs officer at U.S. embassy in Moscow, USSR, deputy director of Office of East European Affairs, director of Office of Security Analysis, senior staff member of Policy Planning Council of the Secretary of State, and senior adviser for Soviet and academic affairs to the chief of naval operations; National War College, professor, 1991-2000; Kansas State University, Manhattan, professor of political science, 1993-, head of Dept of Political Science, 1993-2000. Adjunct professor: Georgetown University, 1982-93; University of Maryland at College Park, 1988-89; Columbia University, Harriman Institute for the Advanced Study of the Soviet Union, 1990-91; George Washington University, 1992-93. **Publications:** East German Civil-Military Relations: The Impact of Technology, 1949-1972, 1973; (ed. with I. Volgyes) Civil-Military Relations in Communist Systems, 1978; (with R. Laird) The Soviet Union and Strategic Arms, 1984; The Soviet High Command, 1964-1969, 1990; Russian Civil-Military Relations, 1996; Requiem for an Army: The Case of the East German Military, 1998; Soldiers, Commissars and Chaplains: Civil-Military Relations since Cromwell, 2001; Putin's Russia, 2003, 2nd ed., 2004; The Pentagon and the Presidency, 2005. Contributor to books. Contributor of articles and reviews to periodicals. **Address:** Department of Political Science, Kansas State University, Manhattan, KS 66506, U.S.A. **Online address:** Falka@ksu.edu

HERTZBERG, Arthur. American (born Poland), b. 1921. **Genres:** Theology/Religion. **Career:** Dartmouth College, Hanover, NH, professor of religion, 1984-91, professor emeritus, 1992-. Visiting professor of the humanities, NYU, currently. Hillel Director, Smith College, Northampton, MA, 1943-44; Rabbi, Congregation Ahavath Israel of Oak Park, Philadelphia, Pa., 1944-47, West End Synagogue, Nashville, TN, 1947-56, and Temple Emanuel, Englewood, NJ, 1956-85. Lecturer, 1959-68, and adjunct professor of history, Columbia University, 1968-90; visiting associate professor of Jewish studies, Rutgers University, New Brunswick, NJ, 1966-68; lecturer in religion, Princeton University, NJ, 1968-69; visiting professor of history, Hebrew University, Jerusalem, 1970-72. **Publications:** The Zionist Idea, 1959; (with M. Marty and J. Moody) The Outbursts that Await Us, 1963; The French Enlightenment and the Jews, 1968; Being Jewish in America, 1979; The Jews in America: Four Centuries of an Uneasy Encounter, 1989; Jewish Polemics, 1992; At Home Only with God, 1993; Jews: The Essence and Character of a People, 1998; A Jew in America, 2002; The Fate of Zionism, 2003. EDITOR: (with J.L. Blau) Essays in Jewish Life and Thought, 1959; Judaism, 1961, rev, 1992; (sr. ed.) Encyclopedia Judaica, 1972. **Address:** 726 Broadway Rm 603, New York, NY 10003, U.S.A. **Online address:** arthur.hertzberg@nyu.edu

HERTZKE, Allen D. American, b. 1950. **Genres:** Politics/Government. **Career:** University of Oklahoma, Norman, professor of political science. **Publications:** Representing God in Washington: The Role of Religious Lobbies in the American Polity, 1988; (ed. with Ron Peters) The Atomistic Congress: An Interpretation of Congressional Change, 1992; Echoes of Discontent: Jesse Jackson, Pat Robertson, and the Resurgence of Populism, 1993: (with R. Booth Fowler) Religion and Politics in America: Faith, Culture, and Strategic Choices, 1995. Work represented in anthologies. Contributor to periodicals. **Address:** Carl Albert Congressional Research Center, University of Oklahoma, 660 Parrington Oval, Norman, OK 73019, U.S.A.

HERZBERG, Nancy K. American, b. 1951. **Genres:** Biography, Anthropology/Ethnology. **Career:** East Tennessee Research Corporation, Jacksboro, grant writer and paralegal, 1973-74; Inter-Cooperative Council, University of Michigan, Ann Arbor, membership coordinator, 1974-76; Consumers Cooperative Association of Eau Claire, Eau Claire, WI, director of membership education, 1977-78; National Cooperative Bank, Upper Midwest Regional Office, Minneapolis, MN, technical assistance officer, 1980-83; Passamaquoddy Tribe, Perry, ME, coordinator of Passamaquoddy Women's Project and grant writer, 1985-87; University of New England,

Biddeford, ME, grant writer-social and global awareness, curriculum reform, and coordinator, rural health project, 1987-92; American Indian Science and Engineering Society, Boulder, CO, grant writer and project development coordinator, 1992-94; Winds of Change magazine, American Indian Education and Opportunity, Boulder, CO, editorial associate, 1993-95; The Wheetley Company, Wilmette, IL, associate editor, 1994-95. Little Bear Trading Company, Roots and Fruits Cooperative Produce, Sundance Natural Foods, West Bank Cooperative Grocery, Agway Inc., and Ontario Midland-Ontario Central Railroad, Sodus, NY, consultant for market research, marketing plans, long-range planning, and inventory management, 1979-84. Cofounder, International Alliance for Sustainable Agriculture, 1983. **Publications:** (ed. and Transcriber) From Roots to Roses: The Autobiography of Tilda Kemplen, 1992. Also author of reports, including "Perspectives on Economic Development in Indian Country: A Report on the National Symposium on Native American Enterprise Zone Development," published as a deliverable under an Administration for Native Americans grant, Washington, DC, 1990; and "A Journey of a Thousand Miles Begins with a Single Step: The Story of the Passamaquoddy Women's Project," published as a deliverable under a Women's Bureau/U.S. Department of Labor grant, Perry, ME, 1986. **Address:** c/o Dr. S. Boldrey, 4048 Rose Ave., Western Springs, IL 60558, U.S.A.

HERZFELD, Michael (F.). American, b. 1947. **Genres:** Anthropology/Ethnology. **Career:** Social anthropologist and educator. Has taught at Indiana University; Harvard University, Cambridge, MA, professor of anthropology, 1991-. Harvard University Greek Study Group, co-chair. **Publications:** Ours Once More: Folklore, Ideology, and the Making of Modern Greece, 1982; The Poetics of Manhood: Contest and Identity in a Cretan Mountain Village, 1985; Anthropology through the Looking-Glass: Critical Ethnography in the Margins of Europe, 1987; A Place in History: Social and Monumental Time in a Cretan Town, 1991; The Social Production of Indifference: Exploring the Symbolic Roots of Western Bureaucracy, 1992; Cultural Intimacy: Social Poetics in the Nation-State, 1997; Portrait of a Greek Imagination: An Ethnographic Biography of Andreas Nenedakis, 1997. EDITOR: (with P. Bouissac and R. Posner) Iconicity: Essays on the Nature of Culture: Festschrift for Thomas A. Sebeokon, 1986; (with L. Melazzo) Semiotic Theory and Practice: Proceedings of the Third International Congress of the IASS, 1984; Mouton de Gruyter 1988; Property, Production, and Family in Neckarhausen, 1700-1870, 1994. Contributor to journals. **Address:** Harvard University, Department of Anthropology, William James Hall Rm. 380, 33 Kirkland St., Cambridge, MA 02138, U.S.A. **Online address:** herzfeld@wjh.harvard.edu

HERZIG, Alison Cragin. American, b. 1935. **Genres:** Children's fiction, Young adult fiction. **Career:** Writer and founding partner of Editors Ink; worked for a number of years as an art dealer and briefly as a fiction editor and writer for a national magazine. **Publications:** (with J.L. Mali) A Word to the Wise, 1978; (with Mali) Oh, Boy! Babies!, 1980; (with Mali) A Season of Secrets, 1982; (with Mali) Thaddeus, 1984; Shadows on the Pond, 1985; (with Mali) The Ten-Speed Babysitter, 1987; (with Mali) Sam and the Moon Queen, 1992; The Big Deal, 1992; The Boonsville Bombers, 1993; (with Mali) Mystery on October Road, 1993; (with Mali) The Wimp of the World, 1994; Bronco Busters, 1998. Herzig's works have been translated into German, Swedish, French, Norwegian, Danish, and Japanese. ADAPTATIONS: Oh, Boy! Babies was made into an ABC primetime television special. **Address:** 15 West 81st St., New York, NY 10024, U.S.A.

HERZOG, Arthur. American, b. 1927. **Genres:** Novels, International relations/Current affairs, Politics/Government, Theology/Religion. **Career:** Writer. **Publications:** NOVELS: The Swarm, 1974; Earthsound, 1975; Orca, 1976; Heat, 1977, 1989; I.Q. 83, 1978; Make Us Happy, 1978; Glad to Be Here, 1979; Aries Rising, 1980; The Craving, 1982; L*S*I*T*T* (reissued as Takeover), 1984. OTHER: Smoking and the Public Interest, 1963; The War-Peace Establishment, 1965; The Church Trap, 1968; McCarthy for President, 1969; The B.S. Factor (social satire), 1973; Vesco, 1987; How to Write Almost Anything Better, 1987, rev. ed., 1994; The Woodchipper Murder, 1989; Seventeen Days: The Katie Beers Story, 1993; Body Parts, 2000; The Voice, 2001; Imortalon, 2002; The Town Buyers, 2003. **Address:** 4 E 81st St, Penthouse, New York, NY 10028, U.S.A. **Online address:** ArthurHerzog@aol.com

HERZOG, Brad. American, b. 1968. **Genres:** Children's fiction, Children's non-fiction, Sports/Fitness. **Career:** Ithaca Journal, Ithaca, NY, journalist, 1990-92. Freelance writer, 1992-. **Publications:** States of Mind: A Search for Faith, Hope, Inspiration, Harmony, Unity, Friendship, Love, Pride, Wisdom, Honor, Comfort, Joy, Bliss, Freedom, Justice, Glory, Triumph, and Truth or Consequences in America, 1999; Small World: A Microcosmic Journey,

2004. FOR CHILDREN. NOVELS: Freddy in the Fridge, 2000; The Hero in the Mirror, 2000; The Monster's New Friend, 2000; The Runaway Ball, 2000; Shake, Rattle and Roll, 2002; Having a Ball, 2002; K is for Kick: A Soccer Alphabet, 2003; H is for Home Run: A Baseball Alphabet, 2004; T is for Touchdown: A Football Alphabet, 2004; P is for Putt: A Golf Alphabet, 2005. NONFICTION: The Everything You Want to Know about Sports Encyclopedia, 1994; Heads Up!, 1994; Seventh-Inning Stretch: Time-out for Baseball Trivia, 1994; MVP Sports Puzzles, 1995; Hoopmania!: The Jam-Packed Book of Basketball Trivia, 1995; The Sports One Hundred: The One Hundred Most Important People in American Sports History, 1995; Soccer, 1996; Hot Summer Stars, 1997; The Fifty Greatest Athletes of Today, 1998; 2000: A Celebration of Sports, 1999; Olympics 2000: Stars and Stats, 2000; The Twenty Greatest Athletes of the Twentieth Century, 2000; Laugh Locker, 2000; Dare to Be Different: Athletes Who Changed Sports, 2003. OTHER: Spin Art (screenplay). Contributor of articles to magazines. **Address:** c/o Mariah Cherem, Sleeping Bear Press, 310 N Main St Ste 300, Chelsea, MI 48118, U.S.A. **Online address:** brad@bradherzog.com

HERZOG, Tobey C. American, b. 1946. **Genres:** Literary criticism and history. **Career:** Wabash College, Crawfordsville, IN, professor of English, 1976-, faculty marshal, 1985-, chair of English department, 1992-95, chair of Humanities division, 1998-2002. Writing consultant, 1980-. **Publications:** Vietnam War Stories: Innocence Lost, 1992; Tim O'Brien, 1997. Contributor to books and periodicals. **Address:** English Department, Wabash College, PO Box 352, Crawfordsville, IN 47933, U.S.A. **Online address:** herzogt@wabash.edu

HESKETH, Phoebe. See Obituaries.

HESLAM, Peter S. British (born Netherlands), b. 1963. **Genres:** Business/Trade/Industry, Economics, Ethics, Theology/Religion, Third World. **Career:** University of Hull, England, tutor, 1988-89; Commonwealth House, Oxford, deputy warden, 1990-92; Church of England, curate, 1996-99; Cambridge Theological Federation, England, tutor, 1997-99, director of studies, 1999-2000; Ridley Hall, tutor, 2000-; London Institute for Contemporary Christianity, lecturer in social and economic ethics, 2000-. **Publications:** Creating a Christian Worldview: Abraham Kuyper's Lectures on Calvinism, 1998; Globalization: Unravelling the New Capitalism, 2002; Globalization and the Good, 2004. Contributor to scholarly journals. **Address:** London Institute for Contemporary Christianity, St Peter's, Vere St, London W1G 0DQ, England. **Online address:** peter.heslam@licc.org.uk

HESLEP, Robert Durham. American, b. 1930. **Genres:** Education, Philosophy. **Career:** Professor of Philosophy of Education, University of Georgia, College of Education, Athens, since 1972 (Assistant Professor, 1965-67; Associate Professor, 1967-72). Instructor of Philosophy of Education, Pestalozzi-Froebel Teachers College, Chicago, 1959-61; Associate Professor of Educational Foundns. and Philosophy, Edinboro State College, Pa., 1963-65. President, Philosophy of Education Society, 1976-77. **Publications:** Thomas Jefferson and Education, 1969; (ed.) Philosophy of Education, 1971; (ed. with W. Blackstone) Social Justice and Preferential Treatment, 1977; The Mental in Education: A Philosophical Study, 1981; Professional Ethics and the Georgia Public School Administrator, 1988; Education in Democracy: The Moral Role of Education in the Democratic State, 1989; La Educacion en Democracia: La Funcion Moral de la en Educacion en el Estrado Democratico, 1993; Moral Education for Americans, 1995. **Address:** College of Education, University of Georgia, Athens, GA 30602, U.S.A.

HESLEWOOD, Juliet. British, b. 1951. **Genres:** Art/Art history, Mythology/Folklore. **Career:** Writer, playwright, and art historian. **Publications:** JUVENILE: Tales of Sea and Shore (legends and folktales), 1983; Earth, Air, Fire and Water (legends and folktales), 1985; Introducing Picasso, 1993; The History of Western Painting, 1993; The History of Western Sculpture, 1994; Tales of Two Rivers, the Dordogne and the Lot, 1994; The Magic Sandals of Hualachi (Inca myth), 1995. TRANSLATOR: The Valleys of the Lot and Cele, 1993; The Segala, 1994; The Causse, 1995; OTHER: Maui Plays with Death (radio play; adapted from a Polynesian myth); A Travelling Actress (radio play).

HESS, David J. American, b. 1956. **Genres:** Sciences. **Career:** Rensselaer Polytechnic Institute, Troy, NY, professor of science and technology studies, 1989-. **Publications:** Spirits and Scientists, 1991; Science in the New Age, 1993; Samba in the Night: Spiritism in Brazil, 1994; Science and Technology in a Multicultural World, 1995; (with R. Da Matta) The Brazilian Puzzle, 1995; Can Bacteria Cause Cancer?, 1997; Science Studies: An Advanced Introduction, 1997; (with M. Wooddell) Women Confront Cancer, 1998; Evaluating Alternative Cancer Therapies, 1999. **Address:** Department of Sci-

ence and Technology Studies, Sage Building, Rensselaer Polytechnic Institute, Troy, NY 12180, U.S.A. **Online address:** hessd@rpi.edu

HESS, Edward. See BUNGERT, D. Edward.

HESS, Elizabeth. American. **Genres:** Adult non-fiction. **Career:** Journalist and writer. Also worked as an art critic. **Publications:** Lost and Found: Dogs, Cats and Everyday Heroes at a Country Animal Shelter, 1998. Contributor to periodicals. **Address:** c/o Harcourt Brace & Co., 15 East 26th St., New York, NY 10010, U.S.A.

HESS, Gary R. American, b. 1937. **Genres:** International relations/Current affairs, Biography. **Career:** Bowling Green State University, OH, Professor of History, 1964-, Chairman, History Dept., 1973-81, 1985-92, Acting Dean of College of Arts and Sciences, 1981-82. Society for Historians of American Foreign Relations, Executive Secretary-Treasurer, 1979-82; Society of Historians of American Foreign Relations, President, 1991. **Publications:** Sam Higginbottom of Allahabad: Pioneer of Point IV to India, 1967; America Encounters India, 1941-47, 1971; (ed.) America and Russia: Cold War Confrontation to Coexistence, 1973; The United States at War 1941-45, 1985; The United States' Emergence as a Southeast Asian Power 1940-1950, 1987; Vietnam and the United States: Origins and Legacy of War, 1990; Presidential Decisions of rWar: Korea, Vietnam, Persian Gulf, 2001. **Address:** Dept. of History, Bowling Green State University, Bowling Green, OH 43403, U.S.A.

HESS, Joan. Also writes as Joan Hadley. American, b. 1949. **Genres:** Mystery/Crime/Suspense, Romance/Historical. **Career:** Has had a variety of jobs including in real estate, insurance, and teaching. **Publications:** ROMANCE NOVELS: Future Tense, 1987; Red Rover, Red Rover, 1988. MYSTERY NOVELS: Strangled Prose, 1986; The Night-Blooming Cereus, 1986; The Murder at the Murder at the Mimosa Inn, 1986; Malice in Maggody, 1987; Dear Miss Demeanor, 1987; Mischief in Maggody, 1988; A Really Cute Corpse, 1988; (as Joan Hadley) The Deadly Ackee, 1988; Much Ado in Maggody, 1989; A Diet to Die For, 1989; Madness in Maggody, 1990; Mortal Remains in Maggody, 1991; Death by the Light of the Moon, 1992; Maggody in Manhattan, 1992; Poisoned Pins, 1993; O Little Town of Maggody, 1993; Tickled to Death, 1994; Martians in Maggody, 1994; Busy Bodies, 1995; Miracles in Maggody, 1995; Closely Akin to Murder, 1996; The Maggody Militia, 1997; A Holly, Jolly Murder, 1997; Misery Loves Maggody, 1999; A Conventional Corpse, 2000; murder@maggody.com, 2001; Out on a Limb, 2002; Maggody and the Moonbeams, 2002; Mule Train to Maggody, 2004.

HESSE, Karen. American, b. 1952. **Genres:** Children's fiction, Young adult fiction, Picture/board books. **Career:** Writer, 1969-. Leave benefit coordinator for the University of Maryland, 1975-76; worked as a teacher, a librarian, an advertising secretary, a typesetter, and a proofreader. **Publications:** Wish on a Unicorn, 1991; Letters form Rifka, 1992; Lavender (chapter book), 1993; Phoenix Rising, 1994; A Time of Angels, 1995; The Music of Dolphins, 1996; Out of the Dust, 1997; Just Juice (chapter book), 1998; A Light in the Storm, 1999; Stowaway, 2000; Witness; 2001; Aleutian Sparrow, 2003; The Stone Lamp, 2003. PICTURE BOOKS: Poppy's Chair, 1993; Lester's Dog, 1993; Sable, 1994; Come on, Rain, 1999; The Cats in Krasinski Square, 2004. **Address:** c/o Scholastic Books, 557 Broadway, New York, NY 10012-3919, U.S.A.

HESSE, Mary Brenda. British, b. 1924. **Genres:** Archaeology/Antiquities, Philosophy, Sciences. **Career:** Fellow, Wolfson College, Cambridge, 1965-. Reader, 1968-75, and Professor of Philosophy of Science, 1975-85, University of Cambridge. **Publications:** Science and the Human Imagination, 1954; Forces and Fields, 1961; Models and Analogies in Science, 1963; The Structure of Scientific Inference, 1974; Revolutions and Reconstructions in the Philosophy of Science, 1980; (with M.A. Arbib) The Construction of Reality, 1987.

HESTER, Katherine L. American, b. 1964. **Genres:** Novellas/Short stories. **Career:** Fiction writer. **Publications:** Eggs for Young America (short stories), 1997. Contributor of short stories to periodicals. **Address:** c/o Nina Ryan, 42 Barrow St., New York, NY 10014, U.S.A.

HESTER, M(arvin) Thomas. American, b. 1941. **Genres:** Literary criticism and history, Translations. **Career:** University of Florida, Gainesville, lecturer, 1966-69; North Carolina State University, Raleigh, assistant professor, 1972-76, associate professor, 1977-82, professor of English, 1983-, Alumni Distinguished Professor, 1989-, director of university honors council, 1985-87. Member of executive committee of Folger Library Institute, 1989-.

Member of board of directors of Montessori School, 1983-86, and of New Wave Swim Team, 1989-91; member of executive council of Hidden Valley Association, 1987-92. **Publications:** (ed. with J. Durant) A Fair Day in the Affections: Literary Essays, 1980; Kinde Pitty and Brave Scorn: John Donne's Satyres, 1982; (with R.V. Young) Justus Lipsius: Epistolica institutio, 1995; (ed. with R.V. Young) John Donne: Selected Prose, 1995. **Address:** Department of English, 269 Thompkins Hall Box 8105, North Carolina State University, Raleigh, NC 27695, U.S.A. **Online address:** hester@unity.ncsu.edu

HETHERINGTON, Stephen Cade. Australian, b. 1959. **Genres:** Philosophy. **Career:** West Virginia University, Morgantown, WV, assistant professor of philosophy, 1987-90; University of New South Wales, Sydney, lecturer in philosophy, 1990-94, senior lecturer in philosophy, 1994-2000, associate professor of philosophy, 2001-. **Publications:** Epistemology's Paradox: Is a Theory of Knowledge Possible?, 1992; Knowledge Puzzles: An Introduction to Epistemology, 1996; Good Knowledge, Bad Knowledge: On Two Dogmas of Epistemology, 2001; Reality? Knowledge? Philosophy!, 2003. Contributed articles to philosophy journals. **Address:** School of Philosophy, University of New South Wales, Sydney 2052, Australia. **Online address:** s.hetherington@unsw.edu.au

HEUSER, Beatrice. British/German (born Thailand), b. 1961. **Genres:** History, International relations/Current affairs, Military/Defense/Arms control. **Career:** University of Reims, France, lecturer, 1991; University of London, King's College, England, Dept of War Studies, professor of international and strategic studies, 1991-2003; Military History Research Institute of the Bundeswehr, director of research, 2003-. **Publications:** Western Containment Policies in the Cold War: The Yugoslav Case, 1948-1953, 1989; (ed.) Securing Peace in Europe, 1945-62: Thoughts for the Post-Cold War Era, 1992; Transatlantic Relations: Sharing Ideals and Costs, 1996; NATO, Britain, France and the FRG: Nuclear Strategies and Fares for Europe 1949-2000, 1997; Nuclear Mentalities?, 1998; The Bomb: Nuclear Weapons in Their Historical, Strategic and Ethical Context, 1999; Reading Clausewitz, 2002. **Address:** MGFA, Zeppelinstrasse 127/128, D-14471 Potsdam, Germany.

HEVIA, James L. American, b. 1947. **Genres:** History. **Career:** Service representative for a computer maintenance firm, 1969-72; University of Chicago, Chicago, IL, lecturer in social science, 1983; Purdue University-Calumet, Hammond, IN, visiting assistant professor of history, 1988; Indiana State University, assistant professor of history, 1988-92; North Carolina Agricultural and Technical State University, Greensboro, assistant professor of history, 1992-. Shandong University, visiting professor, 1991; University of North Carolina, visiting professor, 1991-92. **Publications:** Cherishing Men from Afar: Qing Guest Ritual and the Macartney Embassy of 1793, 1995; Making China Perfectly Equal, in press. Contributor to books. Contributor of articles and reviews to academic journals. **Address:** 335 Gibbs Hall, Department of History, North Carolina Agricultural and Technical State University, Greensboro, NC 27411, U.S.A.

HEWETT, Joan. American, b. 1930. **Genres:** Children's non-fiction. **Career:** Writer. **Publications:** NONFICTION (PHOTOS BY R. HEWETT): The Mouse and the Elephant, 1977; Watching Them Grow: Inside a Zoo Nursery, 1979; Fly Away Free, 1980; When You Fight the Tiger, 1984; Motorcycle on Patrol: The Story of a Highway Officer, 1986; On Camera: The Story of a Child Actor, 1987; Getting Elected: The Diary of a Campaign, 1989; Laura Loves Horses, 1990; Hector Lives in the United States Now, 1990; Public Defender: Lawyer for the People, 1991; Tiger, Tiger, Growing Up, 1993; Tunnels, Tracks and Trains: Building a Subway, 1995. OTHER: Rosalie, 1987. **Address:** c/o Author Mail, Carolrhoda, 241 First Ave N, Minneapolis, MN 55401, U.S.A.

HEWITT, Geof. American, b. 1943. **Genres:** Poetry, Education. **Career:** Founding Ed., The Kumquat Press, Montclair, New Jersey, later Enosburg, Vermont, since 1966. Assistant Ed., Epoch Magazine, Ithaca, New York, 1964-66; Ed.-in-Chief, The Trojan Horse mag., Ithaca, New York, 1965-66; Gilman Teaching Fellow, Johns Hopkins University, Baltimore, Maryland, 1966-67; Teaching Assistant, University of Iowa, Iowa City, 1967-69; Instructor, University of Hawaii, Honolulu, 1969-70. Contributor Ed., Cornell Alumni News, Ithaca, New York, 1970-75, and New Letters, Kansas City, Missouri, 1971-75. **Publications:** Poem and Other Poems, 1966; Waking Up Still Pickled, 1967; Stone Soup, 1974; I Think They'll Lay My Egg Tomorrow, 1976; Working for Yourself, 1977; Just Worlds, 1989; A Portolio Primer: Teaching, Collecting, and Assessing Student Writing. EDITOR: Quickly Aging Here: Some Poets of the 1970s, 1969; Selected Poems of Alfred Starr Hamilton, 1969; Living in Whales: Stories and Poems from Vermont Public Schools, 1972. **Address:** Calais, VT 05648, U.S.A.

HEWITT, W(arren) E(dward). Canadian, b. 1954. **Genres:** Area studies, International relations/Current affairs, Politics/Government, Sociology, Urban studies. **Career:** University of Lethbridge, Lethbridge, Alberta, assistant professor of sociology, 1986-89; University of Western Ontario, London, assistant professor, 1989-93, associate professor, 1993-2001, professor of sociology, 2001-, associate dean of faculty of social sciences, 1998-2001, associate vice-president (research), 2001-. **Publications:** Base Christian Communities and Social Change in Brazil, 1991. EDITOR/CO-EDITOR: The Sociology of Religion: A Canadian Focus, 1993; Introduction to Sociology: A Canadian Focus, 1994, rev. ed., 2000; The Church at the Grassroots in Latin America: Perplexities on Thirty Years of Activism, 2000. Work represented in anthologies. Contributor to sociology, political science, development, and Latin American studies journals. **Address:** President's Office, University of Western Ontario, London, ON, Canada N6A 5C2. **Online address:** hewitt@uwo.ca

HEWSON, John. Canadian (born England), b. 1930. **Genres:** Language/Linguistics. **Career:** Memorial University of Newfoundland, Assistant Professor of French, 1960-64, Associate Professor of French, 1964-68, Professor of Linguistics, 1968-, University Research Professor, 1985-90, Henrietta Harvey Professor, 1997-. **Publications:** Oral French Pattern Practice, 1963; La Pratique du francais, 1965; Article and Noun in English, 1972; Beothuk Vocabularies, 1978; (with B. Francis) The Micmac Grammar of Father Pacifique, 1990; A Computer Generated Dictionary of Proto-Algonquian, 1993; The Cognitive System of the French Verb, 1997; (with V. Bubenik) Tense and Aspect in Indo-European Languages: Theory, Typology, Diachrony, 1997; Workbook for Historical Romance Linguistics, 1998; The French Language in Canada, 2000. **Address:** Dept. of Linguistics, Memorial University of Newfoundland, St. John's, NL, Canada A1B 3X9. **Online address:** jhewson@mun.ca

HEY, Jeanne A. K. Italian, b. 1963. **Genres:** International relations/Current affairs. **Career:** Miami University, Oxford, OH, assistant professor of political science and international studies, 1992-97. **Publications:** Theories of Dependent Foreign Policy and the Case of Ecuador in the 1980s, 1995. **Address:** 218 Harrison Hall, Miami University, Oxford, OH 45056, U.S.A.

HEYEN, William. American, b. 1940. **Genres:** Novellas/Short stories, Poetry, Essays. **Career:** Springville High School, New York, English teacher, 1961-62; State University of New York at Cortland, instructor in English, 1963-65; State University of New York at Brockport, member of the English Dept., 1967-, professor; University of Hawaii, English Dept., visiting professor, 1985. **Publications:** Depth of Field, 1970; Noise in the Trees: Poems and a Memoir, 1974; The Swastika Poems, 1977; Long Island Light: Poems and a Memoir, 1979; The City Parables, 1979; Lord Dragonfly: Five Sequences, 1981; Erika: Poems of the Holocaust, 1984; Vic Holyfield and the Class of 1957: A Romance, 1986; The Chestnut Rain, 1987; Brockport, New York: Beginning with "And," 1988; (with L.D. Brodsky) Falling from Heaven, 1991; Pterodactyl Rose, 1991; The Host: Selected Poems, 1965-1990, 1994; With Me Far Away: A Memoir, 1994; Crazy Horse in Stillness: Poems, 1996; Pig Notes & Dumb Music: Prose on Poetry, 1997; Diana, Charles, and the Queen: Poems, 1998; Shoah Train: Poems, 2003; The Rope: Poems, 2003; The Hummingbird Corporation: Stories, 2003. EDITOR: Profile of Theodore Roethke, 1971; American Poets in 1976, 1976; The Generation of 2000: Contemporary American Poets, 1984; September 11, 2001: American Writers Respond, 2002. **Address:** 142 Frazier St, Brockport, NY 14420, U.S.A. **Online address:** wheyenl@aol.com; wheyen@rochester.rr.com

HEYER, Carol. American, b. 1950. **Genres:** Science fiction/Fantasy, Children's fiction, Plays/Screenplays, Art/Art history, Illustrations. **Career:** Lynn-Davis Productions, Westlake Village, Calif., staff artist and writer, 1982-86; Lynn-Wenger Productions, Westlake Village, staff writer and artist, 1986-88; Touchmark, Thousand Oaks, Calif., writer and illustrator, 1988-. Artist at Hollywood Film School, 1986-88. **Publications:** (with C. Davis) Thunder Run (film), 1986; May Day (screenplay), 2002. FOR CHILDREN (author and illustrator): Beauty and the Beast, 1989; The Easter Story, 1989; Excalibur, 1990; Robin Hood; The Christmas Story; The Sleeping Beauty in the Wood; The First Easter, 2003; The First Christmas, 2003. Illustrator of books by: Stephen Cosgrove, L. Pringle, H. Winkler and L. Oliver, K. Zwers and J. Tobin, and others. **Address:** Touchmark, 925 E. Avenida de los Arboles, Thousand Oaks, CA 91360, U.S.A. **Online address:** carol@carolheyer.com; www.carolheyer.com

HEYES, (Nancy) Eileen. American, b. 1956. **Genres:** History, Biography. **Career:** Los Angeles Times, Costa Mesa, CA, copy editor, 1979-81; The Aptos Post, Aptos, CA, news editor, 1981-82; The Desert Sun, Palm Springs,

CA, staff writer, 1982; Orange County Register, Santa Ana, CA, copy editor, 1982-84; Los Angeles Times, Los Angeles, CA, electronic publishing copy editor, 1984-86, features section copy editor, 1986-90, business section copy editor, 1993-94; Los Angeles Times, Chatsworth, CA, copy editor of San Fernando Valley and Ventura County editions, 1991-93. Freelance writer, 1990-. **Publications:** Children of the Swastika: The Hitler Youth, 1993; Adolf Hitler, 1994. Contributor to newspapers and periodicals. **Address:** c/o Publicity Director, Millbrook Press, 2 Old New Milford Rd., P.O. Box 335, Brookfield, CT 06804-0335, U.S.A.

HEYMAN, Abigail. American, b. 1942. **Genres:** Human relations/Parenting, Women's studies and issues, Autobiography/Memoirs. **Career:** Freelance photo-journalist. Partner, Archive Pictures (photography agency), 1981-87; Director of Documentary and Photojournalism Full-Time Studies Program, International Center for Photography, NYC, 1986-88. Recipient: Mexican-American Legal Defense and Education Fund Grant, 1977-79, and New York Foundation for the Arts Fellowship, 1985. **Publications:** Growing Up Female: A Personal Photo-Journal, 1974; Butcher, Baker, Cabinet-Maker: Photographs of Women at Work, 1978; Dreams and Schemes: Love and Marriage in Modern Times, 1987; (co-editor) Flesh & Blood: Photographers' Images of Their Own Families, 1992. **Address:** 40 W. 12th St., New York, NY 10011, U.S.A.

HEYMAN, Jacques. British, b. 1925. **Genres:** Architecture, Engineering. **Career:** Fellow, Peterhouse, Cambridge, 1949-51, 1955-92, Emeritus Fellow, 1992-; Cambridge University, Sr. Bursar, Peterhouse, 1962-64, Demonstrator, 1951, Lecturer, 1954, Reader, 1968, Professor of Engineering, 1971-92, Head of Dept., 1983-92, Emeritus Professor, 1992-. Consultant Engineer, Ely Cathedral, 1972-, St. Albans Cathedral, 1978-, and Lichfield and Worcester Cathedrals, 1986-; Member, Architectural Advisory Panel, Westminster Abbey, 197398, and Cathedrals Fabric Commission for England, 1981-. Member of the Council, Institution of Civil Engineers, 1960-63, 1975-78. **Publications:** (with Lord Baker and M.R. Horne) The Steel Skeleton, vol. 2, 1956; Plastic Design of Portal Frames, 1957; Beams and Framed Structures, 1964, 1974; Plastic Design of Frames, 2 vols., 1969-71; Coulomb's Memoir on Statics, 1972; Equilibrium of Shell Structures, 1977; Elements of Stress Analysis, 1982; The Masonry Arch, 1982; The Stone Skeleton, 1995; Estructuras de fabrica, 1995; Elements of the Theory of Structures, 1996; Arches, Vaults and Buttresses, 1996; Structural Analysis: A Historical Approach, 1998; The Science of Structural Engineering, 1999. **Address:** 3 Banhams Close, Cambridge, England.

HEYMAN, Josiah McC(onnell). American, b. 1958. **Genres:** Anthropology/Ethnology. **Career:** Michigan Technological University, Houghton, associate professor of anthropology, 1989-. **Publications:** Life and Labor on the Border, University of Arizona Press, 1991. **Address:** Department of Social Sciences, Michigan Technological University, Houghton, MI 49931, U.S.A.

HEYWARD, Vivian H. American, b. 1947. **Genres:** Sports/Fitness. **Career:** High school physical education teacher in Centereach, NY, 1968-71; University of New Mexico, Albuquerque, Regents Professor of Exercise Science, 1974-. Certified health and fitness instructor by American College of Sports Medicine, 1985-. **Publications:** Designs for Fitness, 1984; Advanced Fitness Assessment and Exercise Prescription, 1991, 3rd ed (including software for instructor's guide), 1998; (with L.M. Stolarczyk) Applied Body Composition Assessment, 1996. **Address:** Johnson Center, University of New Mexico, Albuquerque, NM 87131, U.S.A. **Online address:** vheyward@unm.edu

HEYWOOD, Andrew. British, b. 1952. **Genres:** Philosophy, Politics/Government. **Career:** Farnborough College, Farnborough, Hampshire, head of political studies department, 1981-86; Orpington College, Orpington, Kent, course director for political studies, history, and law, 1986-. Chief examiner, "A" Level Government and Political Studies, at the University of London. **Publications:** Political Ideologies: An Introduction, 1992, 3rd ed., 2003; Political Ideas and Concepts: An Introduction, 1994; Politics, 1997; Political Theory: An Introduction, 1999; Key Political Concepts, 2001. Contributor to books and periodicals. **Address:** Orpington College, The Walnuts, Orpington, Kent BR6 OTE, England. **Online address:** aheywood@orpington.ac.uk

HEYWOOD, Colin. British, b. 1947. **Genres:** History. **Career:** University of Loughborough, England, lecturer in economic history, 1973-88; University of Nottingham, England, senior lecturer in economic and social history, 1988-2004, reader in modern French history, 2004-. **Publications:** Childhood in Nineteenth-Century France: Work, Health, and Education among the "Classes populaires," 1988; The Development of the French Economy, 1750-

1914, 1992; A History of Childhood: Children and Childhood in the West from Medieval to Modern Times, 2001. **Address:** Dept of History, University of Nottingham, Nottingham NG7 2RD, England. **Online address:** colin.heywood@nottingham.ac.uk

HEYWOOD THOMAS, John. British, b. 1926. **Genres:** Philosophy, Theology/Religion. **Career:** Lecturer in Philosophy of Religion, University of Manchester, 1957-65; Reader in Divinity, 1965-74, Dean of Divinity, 1970-72, University of Durham; Professor of Theology, University of Nottingham, 1974-92 (Pro-Vice-Chancellor, 1979-84; Dean of Arts, 1985-88). Honorary Professor, University of Bangor, 1993-. **Publications:** Subjectivity and Paradox, 1957, rev. ed., 1993; Paul Tillich: An Appraisal, 1963; Paul Tillich, 1965; Tillich, 2000; Models in Theology, 2003. **Address:** 1 Village Farm, Vale of Glamorgan CF5 6TY, Wales.

HEZLEP, William (Earl). American, b. 1936. **Genres:** Mystery/Crime/Suspense, Children's fiction, Young adult fiction, Plays/Screenplays. **Career:** Wayne State University, Detroit, MI, instructor, 1965-68; Southwest State University, Marshall, MN, assistant professor, 1968-72, associate professor and department chairman, 1973-76, professor of theatre arts, 1976-. Director, Southwest Summer Theatre, Marshall, 1968-77. Stage actor with the Hilberry repertory company in Detroit, summer stock productions in Pennsylvania, Illinois and Minnesota, and with Pittsburgh touring children's theatre company; actor in films and television commercials. **Publications:** "TRAVELERS" PLAY SERIES (FOR CHILDREN): Nessie, 1978, adapted as Nessie: The Musical, 1986; Ghost Town, 1981; Pharaoh's Dagger, 1982; Cayman Duppy, 1984; Treasure of the Mayans, 1988; Tower of London, 1990; Red Cloud's Revenge, 1990; How Come Christmas?, 1991; Merlin's Cave, 1993; Shipwrecked, 1998; Kokopelli's Cave, 2001; Trouble in the Mountains, 2003; Bog Bodies, 2004; Big Foot, 2004; Plays of the Past, 2004; Plays of the Present, 2004. OTHER: Pipestone Cafe, 1977; Winterkill, 1978; It's a Living, 1979; Time Pockets, 1979; Computer Bait, 1983; Obit for a Polar Bear, 1985. **Address:** 104 E Marshall, Marshall, MN 56258, U.S.A. **Online address:** hezlep@southwest.msus.edu; hezlep@chartermi.net

HIAASEN, Carl. American, b. 1953. **Genres:** Mystery/Crime/Suspense, Humor/Satire. **Career:** Miami Herald, Florida, reporter, 1976-. **Publications:** (with W.D. Montalbano) Powder Burn, 1981; (with W.D. Montalbano) Trap Line, 1982; (with W.D. Montalbano) A Death in China, 1984; Tourist Season, 1986; Double Whammy, 1988; Skin Tight, 1989; Native Tongue, 1991; Strip Tease, 1993; Stormy Weather, 1995; (with others) Naked Came the Manatee, 1997; Lucky You, 1997; Team Rodent: How Disney Devours the World (essay), 1998; Kick Ass (selected columns, vol. 1), 1999; Sick Puppy, 2000; Basket Case, 2002; Skinny Dip, 2004. FOR YOUNG ADULTS: Hoot, 2002 (Newbery Honor, 2003). **Address:** c/o Esther Newberg, International Creative Management, 40 W 57th St, New York, NY 10019, U.S.A.

HIAM, Alexander. American, b. 1957. **Genres:** Administration/Management, Business/Trade/Industry. **Career:** Worked in management positions at companies in the Silicon Valley of California, 1980-88; Alexander Hiam and Associates (consulting and training firm), Amherst, MA, director, 1988-. **Publications:** The Vest-Pocket CEO: Decision-Making Tools for Executives, 1990; The Vest-Pocket Marketer, 1991; (with S. Angle) Adventure Careers, 1992; (with members of Conference Board) Closing the Quality Gap: Lessons from America's Leading Companies, 1992; (with K. Blanchard, C. Schewe, and B. Nelson) Exploring the World of Business, 1996; (with R.J. Lewicki) Think before You Speak, 1996; The Entrepreneur's Complete Sourcebook, 1996; The Portable Conference on Change Management, 1997; Marketing for Dummies, 1997; The Manager's Pocket Guide to Creativity, 1998; (with Schewe) The Portable MBA in Marketing, 2nd ed, 1998; (with Lewicki) The Fast-Forward MBA in Negotiation and Deal-Making, 1999; Streetwise Motivating and Rewarding Employees: New and Better Ways to Inspire Your People, 1999. **Address:** Alexander Hiam and Associates, 295 Amity St., Amherst, MA 01002-3810, U.S.A.

HIATT, Howard H(aym). American, b. 1925. **Genres:** Medicine/Health. **Career:** Harvard University, Cambridge, MA, instructor, 1955-57, assistant professor, 1957-63, professor of medicine, 1963-, Herrman L. Blumgart Professor, 1963-72, dean of School of Public Health, 1972-84. Medical College, Cornell University and New York Hospital, research fellow, 1951-53; National Institute for Arthritis and Metabolic Disorders, investigator, 1953-55; Beth Israel Hospital, associate in medicine, 1955-63, physician-in-chief, 1963-72; Brigham and Women's Hospital, senior physician, 1985-; Imperial Cancer Research Fund Laboratory, London, visiting scientist, 1969-70; American Academy of Arts & Sciences, director, initiatives for children, 1992-. **Publications:** America's Health in the Balance: Choice or Chance?, 1987, as Medical Lifeboat: Will There Be Room for You in the Health Care

System?, 1989; A Measure of Malpractice, 1993. **Address:** Brigham and Women's Hospital, 75 Francis St, Boston, MA 02115, U.S.A. **Online address:** HHIATT@BICS.BWH.HARVARD.EDU

HIBBERT, Christopher. British, b. 1924. **Genres:** History, Biography. **Career:** Freelance writer. **Publications:** The Road to Tyburn, 1957; King Mob, 1958; Wolfe at Quebec, 1959; The Destruction of Lord Raglan, 1961; Corunna, 1961; Benito Mussolini, 1962; The Battle of Arnhem, 1962; The Roots of Evil, 1963; The Court at Windsor, 1964; Agincourt, 1964; Garibaldi and His Enemies, 1965; The Making of Charles Dickens, 1967; Charles I, 1968; The Grand Tour, 1969; London: Biography of a City, 1969; The Dragon Wakes, 1970; The Personal History of Samuel Johnson, 1971; George IV: Prince of Wales, 1972; George IV: Regent and King, 1973; The Rise and Fall of the House of Medici, 1974; The Illustrated London News: Social History of Victorian Britain, 1975; Daily Life in Victorian England, 1975; Edward VII, 1976; The Great Mutiny: India 1857, 1978; Disraeli and His World, 1979; The Court of St. James's, 1979; The French Revolution, 1980; Africa Explored, 1982; Queen Victoria in Her Letters and Journals, 1984; Rome: Biography of a City, 1985; Cities and Civilizations, 1986; The English: A Social History, 1066-1945, 1987; Venice: The Biography of a City, 1988; Redcoats and Rebels: The War for America, 1762-1783, 1990; The Virgin Queen: The Personal History of Elizabeth I, 1990; The Story of England, 1992; Cavaliers and Roundheads, the English at War 1642-1649, 1993; Florence: Biography of a City, 1993; Nelson: A Personal History, 1994; Wellington: A Personal History, 1997; George III: A Personal History, 1998; Queen Victoria, 2000; The Marlboroughs: John and Sarah Churchill, 2001; Napoleon: His Wives and Women, 2002. EDITOR: A Soldier of the Seventy First, 1975; (with B. Weinreb) The London Encyclopaedia, 1983; The Encyclopaedia of Oxford, 1988; Gronow: Reminiscences of Regency and Victorian England, 1991. **Address:** 6 Albion Pl, West St, Henley-on-Thames RG9 2DT, England.

HIBBING, John R. American, b. 1953. **Genres:** Politics/Government. **Career:** Oakland University, Rochester, MI, visiting instructor in political science, 1980-81; University of Nebraska-Lincoln, assistant professor, 1981-85, associate professor, 1985-90, professor of political science, 1990-, chair of department, 1991-. University of Essex, fellow in science and government, 1984-85; Institute of Regional Studies in Budapest, Hungary, visiting professor, 1990. **Publications:** Choosing to Leave, 1982; Congressional Careers: Contours of Life in the US House of Representatives, 1991; (with E. Theiss-Morse) Congress as Public Enemy, 1995. EDITOR: (with J.G. Peters) The Changing World of the US Senate, 1990; (with E. Theiss-Morse) What Is It about Government that Americans Dislike, 2001. **Address:** Department of Political Science, University of Nebraska-Lincoln, 511 Oldfather Hall, Lincoln, NE 68588-0328, U.S.A. **Online address:** jhibbing1@unl.edu

HIBBS, Euthymia D. American (born Greece), b. 1937. **Genres:** Psychology. **Career:** Catholic University of St. Louis, Brussels, Belgium, instructor, 1963-65; Titeca Mental Health Hospital, Brussels, intern in clinical psychology and psychotherapy, 1964-67; North Atlantic Treaty Organization, International Staff, Brussels, staff psychologist, 1967-71; Tufts University Medical School, Boston, MA, director of community mental health and social works departments at Tufts-Columbia Point Health Center, 1971-74, and lecturer in psychiatry, 1972-74; American Oil Companies School, Tripoli, Libya, school psychologist, 1974-76; private practice of psychotherapy, 1974-76, 1983-; National Institute of Mental Health, clinical research psychologist at mental health study center, 1977-83, research psychologist in division of intramural research programs, 1982-83, and division's biological psychiatry branch, 1983-85, clinical research psychologist in child psychiatry branch, 1985-91, head of psychosocial treatment research program in clinical research division, 1991-2002; George Washington University, adjunct associate professor of psychiatry and behavioral sciences 1994-; speaker at international psychiatry conferences; consultant. **Publications:** Psychosocial Treatment Research of Child and Adolescent Disorders, 1996, 2nd ed., 2004. EDITOR & CONTRIBUTOR: Children and Families: Studies in Prevention and Intervention, 1988; Adoption: International Perspectives, 1991. Contributor to books. Author of articles in Greek. Contributor to scientific journals. **Address:** 7302 Durbin Terrace, Bethesda, MD 20817, U.S.A. **Online address:** euthymiah@aol.com

HIBBS, John. Also writes as John Blyth. British, b. 1925. **Genres:** Poetry, Economics, Marketing, Transportation. **Career:** University of Central England, principal lecturer, 1973-82, director of transport studies, 1982-90, professor, 1987-90, professor emeritus of transport management, 1990-. Premier Travel Ltd., personal assistant to managing director, 1950-52; Corona Coaches Ltd., joint managing director, 1956-60; British Railways Eastern Region, traffic survey officer and market research officer, 1961-67; City of

London Polytechnic, sr. lecturer and principal lecturer in transport, 1967-73; Proceedings of the Chartered Institute of Transport, editor, 1991-. **Publications:** Transport for Passengers, 1963; (as John Blyth) New Found Land, 1965; (as John Blyth) Being a Patient, 1967; The History of British Bus Services, 1968; Transport Studies: An Introduction, 1970, 3rd ed., 1999; (ed.) The Omnibus, 1971; How to Run the Buses, 1972; People and Transport, 1973; The Bus and Coach Industry: Its Economics and Organization, 1975; Transport without Politics?, 1982; Bus and Coach Management, 1985; Regulation: An International Study of Bus and Coach Licensing, 1985; The Country Bus, 1986; The Country Chapel, 1987; The Bus and Coach Operator's Handbook, 1987; Marketing Management in the Bus and Coach Industry, 1989; (with G. Roth) Tomorrow's Way, 1992; On the Move: A Market for Mobility on the Roads, 1993; Glossary of Economic and Related Terms for the Use of Students on Transport Courses, 1993; Transport Policy: The Myth of Integrated Planning, 2000; Transport Economics & Policy, 2003; A Country Busman, 2003. **Address:** 134 Wood End Rd, Erdington, Birmingham B24 8BN, England.

HICHWA, John S. American, b. 1938. **Genres:** Sports/Fitness, Education. **Career:** Physical education teacher at elementary school in Redding, CT, 1960-65; John Read Middle School, Redding, physical education teacher, 1965-95, Project Adventure teacher, 1982-95. Teaching tennis professional at Old Lyme Country Club, 1960-65, and Country Club of Fairfield, 1966-80; American School in Japan Summer Day Camp, physical education teacher, 1997; consultant to Sportime International. **Publications:** Right Fielders Are People Too: An Inclusive Approach to Teaching Middle School Physical Education, 1998. **Address:** 10 Beauiles Lane, West Redding, CT 06896, U.S.A. **Online address:** toy1993@mindspring.com

HICK, John (Harwood). British, b. 1922. **Genres:** Theology/Religion. **Career:** Assistant Professor of Philosophy, Cornell University, Ithaca, NY, 1956-59; Stuart Professor of Christian Philosophy, Princeton Theological Seminary, NJ, 1959-64; Lecturer in Divinity, Cambridge University, 1964-67; University of Birmingham, H.G. Wood Professor of Theology, 1967-82, Emeritus, 1982-, Fellow of Institute for Advanced Research in Arts and Social Sciences, 1992-; Claremont Graduate University, CA, Danforth Professor of Religion, 1980-92, Emeritus, 1992-. **Publications:** Faith and Knowledge, 1957, 2nd ed., 1967; Philosophy of Religion, 1963, 4th ed., 1990; Evil and the God of Love, 1966, 2nd ed., 1977; Christianity at the Centre, 1968; Arguments for the Existence of God, 1971; God and the Universe of Faiths, 1973; Death and Eternal Life, 1976; God Has Many Names, 1980; (with M. Goulder) Why Believe in God?, 1983; The Second Christianity, 1983; Problems of Religious Pluralism, 1985; An Interpretation of Religion, 1989; Disputed Questions in Theology and the Philosophy of Religion, 1993; The Metaphor of God Incarnate, 1993; A Christian Theology of Religions (in UK as The Rainbow of Faiths), 1995; The Fifth Dimension: An Exploration of the Spiritual Realm, 1999; Dialogues in the Philosophy of Religion, 2000; John Hick: An Autobiography, 1993. EDITOR: The Existence of God, 1964; Faith and the Philosophers, 1964; Classical and Contemporary Readings in the Philosophy of Religion, 1964, 3rd ed., 1990; Truth and Dialogue, 1974; The Myth of God Incarnate, 1977; (with B. Hebblethwaite) Christianity and Other Religions, 1980, 2nd ed., 2000; (with H. Askari) The Experience of Religious Diversity, 1985; (with E. Meltzer) Three Faiths-One God, 1989; (with L. Hempel) Gandhi's Significance for Today, 1989. **Address:** 144 Oak Tree Ln, Selly Oak, Birmingham B29 6HU, England. **Online address:** j.h.hick@bham.ac.uk; www.johnhick.org.uk

HICKEN, Mandy. (Marilyn E. Hicken). British, b. 1938. **Genres:** Adult non-fiction. **Career:** Chesterfield Borough Library, chief cataloger, 1962-74; Derbyshire Library Service, special services librarian, 1974-80, group librarian, 1980-97; writer; independent researcher. **Publications:** (comp.) Fiction Index, 1974-; (comp.) Sequels, 1978-; Now Read on, Gower, 1990, 1997; A History of Brimington, 1990; Filmed Books and Plays, 1991. **Address:** Manor House Farm, 76 Manor Road, Brimington, Chesterfield, Derbyshire S43 1NN, England. **Online address:** mhicken@talk21.com

HICKEN, Victor. American, b. 1921. **Genres:** History, Military/Defense/Arms control. **Career:** Distinguished Professor of History, Western Illinois University, Macomb, 1976-81 (Instructor, 1947-50, Professor, 1950-76, Chairman of Dept., 1967-69). Chief Researcher, Carnegie Foundation Grant, American Association for the Advancement of Science. **Publications:** Illinois in the Civil War, 1966; The Settlement of Western Illinois, 1966, 2nd ed., 1991; Western Illinois Factbook, 1968; Illinois at War, 1968; The American Fighting Man, 1969; The Purple and the Gold, 1971; The World Is Coming to an End, 1975; Gallery of American Heroes, 3 vols., 1976; Between the Rivers, Vols. I-III, 1981-83; Illinois: Its History and Legacy, 1983; (co-ed.) Episodes of a Farm Boy, by Carl C. Lewis, 1986. **Address:** 615 Lincoln Dr, Macomb, IL 61455, U.S.A.

HICKMAN, Bert G(eorge). American, b. 1924. **Genres:** Economics. **Career:** Professor Emeritus of Economics, Stanford University, California. Sr. Staff, Council of Economic Advisors, Washington, D.C., 1954-56; Sr. Staff, Brookings Institution, Washington, D.C., 1956-66. **Publications:** Growth and Stability of Post War Economy, 1960; Investment Demand and U.S. Economic Growth, 1965; (with R.M. Coen) Annual Growth Model of the United States Economy, 1976. EDITOR: Quantitative Planning of Economic Policy, 1965; Econometric Models of Cyclical Behavior, 1972; Global International Economic Models, 1983; Global Econometrics, 1983; International Monetary Stabilization and the Foreign Debt Problem, 1984; Macroeconomic Impacts of Energy Shocks, 1987; Macroeconomic Impacts of Energy Shocks: Contributions from Participating Modelers, 1987; International Productivity and Competitiveness, 1992; LINK Proceedings, 1991-1992, Studies in Applied International Economics, Vol. 1, 1998. **Address:** Dept. of Economics, Stanford University, Stanford, CA 94305, U.S.A.

HICKOK, Ralph. American, b. 1938. **Genres:** Sports/Fitness. **Career:** Green Bay Press-Gazette, Green Bay, WI, general assignment reporter, 1954-57; Gloucester Daily Times, Gloucester, MA, general assignment reporter, 1960-61; Celina Daily Standard, Celina, OH, sports editor, 1961-63; New Bedford Standard-Times, New Bedford, MA, feature writer and editor of Sunday magazine, 1963-73; Southeastern Advertising Agency Inc., New Bedford, chief copywriter, 1973-92; SEA Tourism/Travel Research, New Bedford, director of data processing, 1992-. **Publications:** Who Was Who in American Sports, 1971; The New Encyclopedia of Sports, 1977; The Encyclopedia of North American Sports History, 1992, 2nd ed., 2002; The Pro Football Fan's Companion, 1995; Who's Who of Sports Champions, 1995. Contributor to magazines. **Address:** 60 Orchard St, New Bedford, MA 02740, U.S.A. **Online address:** www.hickocksports.com

HICKS, Carola. British, b. 1941. **Genres:** Art/Art history, History. **Career:** Scholar, educator, and author. Institute of Continuing Education, University of Cambridge, England, staff tutor in art history; fellow of Newnham College. **Publications:** (ed.) England in the Eleventh Century, 1992; Animals in Early Medieval Art, 1993; Cambridgeshire Churches, 1997; Discovering Stained Glass, 1996; Improper Pursuits: The Scandalous Life of Lady Di Beauclerk, 2001 in US as Improper Pursuits: The Scandalous Life of an Earlier Lady Diana Spencer, 2002. **Address:** Newnham College, Cambridge CB3 9DF, England. **Online address:** cmh19@cus.cam.ac.uk

HICKS, Eleanor. See COERR, Eleanor Beatrice.

HICKS, L. Edward. American, b. 1946. **Genres:** Biography. **Career:** High school teacher and coach in Fullerton, CA, 1968-70, and Buena Park, CA, 1970-76; Fullerton Junior College, adjunct instructor, 1970-76; B.D. Hicks Enterprises Inc., vice-president to president, 1976-90; University of Memphis, instructor, 1987-91; Christian Brothers University, Memphis, TN, instructor in European history, 1990-91; Faulkner University, Montgomery, AL, professor of history, 1991-, head of Humanities and Fine Arts Division, 1991-93, and Department of Behavioral and Social Science, 1991-2002. **Publications:** Sometimes in the Wrong, But Never in Doubt: George S. Benson and the Education of the New Religious Right, 1995. Contributor to history and religious studies journals. **Address:** Department of Social and Behavioral Science, Faulkner University, 5345 Atlanta Highway, Montgomery, AL 36109, U.S.A.

HICOK, Bob. American, b. 1960. **Genres:** Poetry. **Career:** Poet. Western Michigan University, Kalamazoo, visiting instructor in English, 2002-. Automotive die designer and computer systems administrator in Ann Arbor, MI. **Publications:** POETRY: Bearing Witness, 1991; The Legend of Light, 1995; Plus Shipping, 1998; Animal Soul, 2001; Insomnia Diary, 2004. Contributor of poems to periodicals. Work represented in anthologies. **Address:** 5100 Clinton Rd, Jackson, MI 49201-8287, U.S.A. **Online address:** bob.hicok@wmich.edu

HICYILMAZ, Gay. British. **Genres:** Children's fiction, Young adult fiction. **Publications:** Against the Storm (children's novel), 1990; The Frozen Waterfall; Watching the Watcher; And the Stars Were Gold, 1997. **Address:** c/o Rosemary Bromley, Juvenalia, Avington, Winchester, Hants. SO21 1DB, England.

HIDDEN, Norman (Frederick). British, b. 1913. **Genres:** Poetry, Literary criticism and history, Autobiography/Memoirs. **Career:** Founding Ed., Workshop New Poetry, London, 1967-81. Chairman, The Poetry Society, London, 1968-71. Member, Executive Committee, The English Association, 1967-81. **Publications:** These Images Claw, 1966; Dr. Kink and His Old Style Boarding School: Fragments of Autobiography, 1973; A Study Guide to "Under Milk Wood," 1973; A Study Guide to Twelfth Night, 1978; How to Be Your Own Publisher, 1979; How to Get Your Poems Accepted, 1981; For My Friends, 1981; Liaison Officer: Anglo-US Occupation of Germany 1946-47 (memoirs/autobiography), 1994; Caravan Summer & Other Stories (short stories), 1999. EDITOR: A National Anthology of Student Poetry, 1968; Say It Aloud, 1972; Over to You (verse anthology), 1975; (with A. Hollins) Many People, Many Voices, 1978. **Address:** 99 Pole Barn Lane, Frinton on Sea, Essex CO13 9NQ, England.

HIEATT, Constance B(artlett). American/Canadian, b. 1928. **Genres:** Children's fiction, Food and Wine, Literary criticism and history, Translations. **Career:** Member of faculty, City College, 1959-60, and Queensborough Community College, 1960-65, City University of New York; St. John's University, Jamaica, NY, professor of English, 1965-69; University of Western Ontario, London, professor of English, 1968-93, emeritus, 1993-. **Publications:** The Realism of Dream Visions: The Poetic Exploitation of the Dream Experience in Chaucer and His Contemporaries, 1967; (trans.) Beowulf and Other Old English Poems, 1967; Essentials of Old English: Readings with Keyed Grammar, 1970; (ed.) The Miller's Tale of Geoffrey Chaucer, 1970; (trans.) Karlamagnus Saga: the Saga of Charlemagne and His Heroes, I, parts 1-3, II, part 4, 1975, and III, part 5-10, 1980; (co-author) Pleyn Delit: Medieval Cookery for Modern Cooks, 1976, 2nd ed., 1996; An Ordinance of Pottage, 1988. ADAPTER: Sir Gawain and the Green Knight, 1967; The Knight of the Lion, 1968; The Knight of the Cart, 1969; The Joy of the Court, 1971; The Sword and the Grail, 1972; The Castle of Ladies, 1973; The Minstrel Knight, 1974. CO-EDITOR: (trans. and adapter) The Canterbury Tales of Geoffrey Chaucer, 1961; (and trans.) The Canterbury Tales of Geoffrey Chaucer, 1964; Edmund Spenser: Selected Poetry, 1970; Curye on Inglysch, 1985; La Novele Cirurgerie, 1990; Beginning Old English, 1994; (and trans.) Guillaume de Machaut's Tale of the Alerion, 1994; Libellus de arte coquinaria: An Early Northern Cookery Book, 2001. **Address:** 335 Essex Meadows, Essex, CT 06426, U.S.A. **Online address:** constance.hieatt@yale.edu

HIESTAND, Emily (L.). American, b. 1947. **Genres:** Poetry, Social commentary, Travel/Exploration. **Career:** Curriculum designer, 1971-73; Hiestand Design Associates, principal and senior designer, 1973-88; Artemis Ensemble, Cambridge, creative director, 1988-; Boston University, visiting poet, 1991-92; Orion Magazine, literary and poetry editor, 1991-2001; Elements Communications, creative director, 2000-. **Publications:** Green the Witch-Hazel Wood (poems), 1989; The Very Rich Hours (travel literature), 1992; Angela the Upside-Down Girl: And Other Domestic Travels (essays), 1998.

HIGDON, Hal. American, b. 1931. **Genres:** Children's fiction, Children's non-fiction, Sports/Fitness. **Career:** The Kiwanis mag., assistant ed., 1957-59; Runner's World, contributing editor. **Publications:** The Union vs. Dr. Mudd, 1964; Heroes of the Olympics, 1965; Pro Football U.S.A., 1967; The Horse That Played Center Field, 1967; The Business Healers, 1968; Stars of the Tennis Courts, 1969; 30 Days in May, 1969; The Electronic Olympics, 1969; On the Run from Dogs and People, 1969; Finding the Groove, 1973; Find the Key Man, 1974; The Last Series, 1974; Six Seconds to Glory, 1974; The Crime of the Century, 1975; Summer of Triumph, 1977; Fitness after Forty, 1977; Complete Diet Guide: For Runners and Other Athletes, 1978; Beginner's Running Guide, 1978; Runner's Cookbook, 1979; Johnny Rutherford, 1980; The Marathoners, 1980; The Team That Played in the Space Bowl, 1981; The Masters Running Guide, 1990; Run Fast, 1992; Marathon, 1993; Falconara, 1993; Boston: A Century of Running, 1995; Hal Higdon's How to Train, 1997; Hal Higdon's Smart Running, 1998; Run, Dogs, Run,!, 2000; Marathoning A to Z, 2002; Masters Running, 2005. **Address:** Hal Higdon Communications, 2815 Lake Shore Dr, Long Beach, IN 46360-1619, U.S.A. **Online address:** www.halhigdon.com

HIGGINBOTHAM, Elizabeth. American, b. 1948. **Genres:** Women's studies and issues, Race relations. **Career:** University of Pittsburgh, assistant professor, 1979-81; Columbia University, assistant professor, 1981-83; University of Memphis, assistant professor, 1985-88, associate professor 1988-95, professor of sociology and social work, 1995-98; University of Delaware, Newark, professor of sociology, 1998-. **Publications:** Too Much to Ask: Black Women in the Era of Integration, 2001. EDITOR: (with M. Romero) Women and Work: Exploring Race, Ethnicity, and Class, 1997. Author of articles in academic journals. **Address:** Dept of Sociology, 322 Smith Hall, University of Delaware, Newark, DE 19716, U.S.A. **Online address:** ehiggin@udel.edu

HIGGINBOTHAM, Jay. American, b. 1937. **Genres:** Novels, Plays/Screenplays, History, Social commentary, Travel/Exploration, Autobiography/

Memoirs. **Career:** Director, Mobile Municipal Archives, 1983-, and Research Consultant, 1980-, Mobile Public Library, Alabama (Head, Dept. of Local History, 1973-78; Acting Head, Special Collections Dept., 1979-80). Assistant Clerk, Mississippi House of Reps., 1955-60; Teacher, Mobile County Public Schools, 1962-72. **Publications:** The Mobile Indians, 1966; The World Around (travel), 1966; Family Biographies, 1967; The Pascagoula Indians, 1967; Pascagoula: Singing River City, 1968; Mobile: City by the Bay, 1968; (trans.) The Journal of Sauvole, 1969; The Birth of Louisiana, 1969; (with F. Escoffier) A Voyage to Dauphin Island, 1974; Old Mobile: Fort Louis de la Louisiane 1702-1711, 1977; Fast Train Russia (reminiscences), 1981; Autumn in Petrischevo (travel), 1985; The Vital Alliance (speeches and essays), 1988; Discovering Russia (travel), 1989; Kazula (play), 1993; Man, Nature & the Infinite (social commentary), 1998. NOVELS: Brother Holyfield, 1972; Mauvila, 1990; Alma, 2002. **Address:** 60 N Monterey, Mobile, AL 36604, U.S.A.

HIGGINS, Aidan. Irish, b. 1927. **Genres:** Novels, Novellas/Short stories, Autobiography/Memoirs. **Career:** Puppet-operator, John Wright's Marionettes in Europe, South Africa and Rhodesia, 1958-60; Scriptwriter, Filmlets, advertising films, Johannesburg, 1960-61. **Publications:** Felo de Se (in U.S. as Killachter Meadow), 1960; Langrishe, Go Down, 1966; Images of Africa, 1971; Balcony of Europe, 1972; (ed.) A Century of Short Stories, 1977; Scenes from a Receding Past, 1977; (ed.) Colossal Gongorr and the Turkes of Mars, 1979; Bornholm Night Ferry, 1983; Helsingor Station and Other Departures, 1987; Ronda Gorge and Other Precipices, 1987; Lions of the Grunewald, 1993; Donkey's Years, 1995; Flotsam & Jetsam, 1997; Dog Days, 1998; The Whole Hog, 2000; A Bestiary, 2004. **Address:** c/o Secker and Warburg, 20 Vauxhall Bridge Rd, London SW1V 2SA, England.

HIGGINS, Gina O'Connell. American, b. 1950. **Genres:** Psychology. **Career:** Lesley College, Cambridge, MA, lecturer, 1974-76, assistant professor of special education, 1976-81, clinical placement supervisor in special education, 1974-76; North Shore Children's Hospital, Salem, MA, psychology intern, 1981-82, diagnostician at Medical Educational Evaluation Clinic, 1982-87, psychotherapist and intake diagnostician at Mental Health Center, 1982-86; private practice of psychotherapy and psychodiagnostics, 1986-. Middlesex Community College, lecturer, 1974-75; Tufts University, lecturer, 1974-75; Harvard University, clinical instructor at Harvard Medical School, 1993-94, clinical associate, 1994-2000, faculty member at Clinical Developmental Institute, 1986, 1990. Clinical Developmental Institute (Belmont, MA), associate fellow, 1985-86, fellow, 1990-; Massachusetts General Hospital, staff psychologist, 1993-2000. **Publications:** Resilient Adults: Overcoming a Cruel Past, 1994. Contributor to books. **Address:** 1 Salem Green Ste 555, Salem, MA 01970, U.S.A.

HIGGINS, Ian (Kevin). Australian, b. 1959. **Genres:** Literary criticism and history. **Career:** La Trobe University, Melbourne, Australia, senior tutor in English literature, 1985-91; Australian National University, Canberra, lecturer in English, 1991-97, senior lecturer, 1997-. **Publications:** Swift's Politics: A Study in Disaffection, 1994; Jonathan Swift, 2004. Contributor to academic journals. **Address:** Dept of English, Australian National University, Canberra, ACT 0200, Australia.

HIGGINS, Joanna. American, b. 1945. **Genres:** Novellas/Short stories, Children's fiction. **Career:** Grand Rapids Junior College, Grand Rapids, MI, instructor in English, 1968-69; University of Maryland Overseas program, England, instructor in English, 1970-71; Keystone Junior College, La Plume, PA, instructor in English, 1974-77; Hilo College (now University of Hawaii at Hilo), assistant professor of English, 1977-78; University of Hawaii, West Oahu College, Pearl City, assistant professor of English, 1978-79; State University of New York at Binghamton, adjunct member of creative writing faculty, 1982; writer, 1982-. **Publications:** The Magic Crystal (juvenile), 1987; Quest for the Golden Flower (juvenile), 1988; In the Treasure House of the Ten Masters (juvenile), 1990; The Importance of High Places, 1993; A Soldier's Book, 1998. PLAYS: Grant, 1983; Dreamers, 1985. Work represented in anthologies. Contributor of stories and articles to periodicals. **Address:** 21 Gardner Rd, Vestal, NY 13850, U.S.A.

HIGGINS, Kathleen M(arie). American, b. 1954. **Genres:** Philosophy. **Career:** University of Texas at Austin, instructor, 1982-83, assistant professor, 1983-89, associate professor, 1989-95, professor of philosophy, 1995-. University of California, Riverside, visiting assistant professor, 1986-87; University of Auckland, New Zealand, visiting senior lecturer and visiting professor, summers, 1989-. **Publications:** Nietzsche's Zarathustra, 1987; The Music of Our Lives, 1991; (with R.C. Solomon) A Short History of Philosophy, 1996; (with R.C. Solomon) A Passion for Wisdom: A Very Brief History of Philosophy, 1997; Comic Relief, 2000; (with R.C. Solomon) What

Nietzsche Really Said, 2000. EDITOR: (with R.C. Solomon) Reading Nietzsche, 1988; (with R.C. Solomon) The Philosophy of (Erotic) Love, 1992; (with L. Bowie and M. Michaels) Thirteen Questions: An Introduction to Ethics, 1992, 2nd ed. as Thirteen Questions in Ethics and Social Philosophy, 1998; (with R.C. Solomon) From Africa to Zen: An Invitation to World Philosophy, 1993; (with R.C. Solomon) Routledge History of Philosophy, Vol. VI: The Age of German Idealism, 1993; (with R.C. Solomon) World Philosophy: A Text with Readings, 1995; (with B. Magnus) The Cambridge Companion to Nietzsche, 1996; Aesthetics in Perspective, 1996. **Address:** Department of Philosophy, University of Texas at Austin, 1 University Station C3500, Austin, TX 78712, U.S.A.

HIGGINS, Michael James. American, b. 1946. **Genres:** Anthropology/Ethnology. **Career:** Anthropologist. University of Northern Colorado, Greeley, professor, 1974-2000, now retired. **Publications:** Oigame! Oigame!, 1992; (with T. COen) Streets, Bedrooms and Patios: The Ordinariness of Diversity in Urban Oaxaca, 2000. Author of two books in Spanish. **Address:** Apt. Postal 742, Oaxaca, 68000 Oaxaca, Mexico. **Online address:** mjhiggi55@hotmail.com

HIGGINS, Dame Rosalyn. British, b. 1937. **Genres:** International relations/Current affairs, Law. **Career:** Royal Institute of International Affairs, Research Specialist in International Law and U.N. Affairs, 1963-74; London School of Economics, Visiting Fellow, 1974-78, Professor of International Law, 1981-95; University of Kent, Canterbury, Professor, 1978-81; International Court of Justice, Judge, 1995. **Publications:** The Development of International Law through the Political Organs of the United Nations, 1963; Conflict of Interests: International law in a Divided World, 1965; The Administration of United Kingdom Foreign Policy through the United Nations, 1966; United Nations Peacekeeping: Documents and Commentary, vol. I, The Middle East, 1969, vol. II, Asia, 1971, vol. III, Africa, 1980, vol. IV, Europe, 1981; Problems and Process: International Law and How We Use It, 1994. EDITOR: (with J. Fawcett) Law in Movement: Essays in Honour of John McMahon, 1974; (with M. Flory) Libertae de Circulation des Personnes en Droit International, 1989; (with M. Flory) Terrorism and International Law, 1997.

HIGGINS, Simon (Richard). Australian (born England), b. 1958. **Genres:** Young adult fiction. **Career:** Police officer, Adelaide, Australia, 1986-94, leaving service as senior constable; private investigator, Adelaide, 1994-96; novelist, 1996-. **Publications:** FOR YOUNG ADULTS: Doctor Id, 1998; Thunderfish, 1999; Cybercage, 2000; Beyond the Shaking Time, 2000; Under No Flag, 2001; The Stalking Zone, 2002; In the Jaws of the Sea, 2003; The Dream Web Files, 2003. Contributor to books and magazines. **Address:** PO Box 140, Murwillumbah, NSW 2484, Australia. **Online address:** www.homepages.better.net.au/doctorid

HIGGINSEN, Vy. American. **Genres:** Plays/Screenplays, Young adult fiction. **Career:** Writer. Ebony magazine, NYC, worked in advertising and sales, 1970-71; WBLS-FM, NYC, on-air personality, 1971-75; Unique, NY, NYC, publisher, 1974-78; associated with WRVR-FM. Produced a Broadway version of August Wilson's play, Joe Turner's Come and Gone, 1988. **Publications:** Mama I Want to Sing (play), 1983; Let the Music Play Gospel, 1988; (with T. Bolden) Mama I Want to Sing (young adult novel based on play), 1992. **Address:** 149 W 126th St, New York, NY 10027, U.S.A. **Online address:** mamaofc@aol.com

HIGH, Linda Oatman. American, b. 1958. **Genres:** Novels, Children's fiction, Young adult fiction, Poetry, Songs/Lyrics and libretti. **Career:** Songwriter; teacher at writing workshops; news reporter and feature writer; contributor of a weekly column, "Jake's View," to local newspapers. **Publications:** YOUNG ADULT NOVELS: Maizie, 1995; Hound Heaven, 1995; The Summer of the Great Divide, 1996. NOVEL: A Stone's Throw from Paradise, 1997. FOR CHILDREN: A Christmas Star, 1997; Bee Keepers, 1998; Barn Savers, 1999; Under New York, 2001; Winter Shoes for Shadow Horse, 2001; Last Chimney of Christmas Eve, 2001; A Humble Life, 2001; The Girl on the High-Diving Horse, 2003; Sister Slam and the Poetic Motormouth Road Trip, 2004. **Address:** 1209 Reading Rd, Narvon, PA 17555, U.S.A. **Online address:** lohigh@desupernet.net; www.lindaoatmanhigh.com

HIGHAM, Robin. American (born England), b. 1925. **Genres:** Administration/Management, Air/Space topics, Archaeology/Antiquities, History, Military/Defense/Arms control, Bibliography. **Career:** Kansas State University, Manhattan, professor of history, 1963-98. Editor emeritus, Military Affairs (ed., 1968-88), and Aerospace Historian (ed., 1970-88); Journal of the West, ed., 1977-; Sunflower University Press, founder and president, 1977-; Greenwood Press, advisory editor, 1993-. **Publications:**

Britain's Imperial Air Routes, 1960; The British Rigid Airship, 1908-1931, 1961; Armed Forces in Peacetime, 1963; The Military Intellectuals, 1966; (with D. Zook) A Short History of Warfare, 1966; Air Power, 1972, 3rd ed., 1988; The Compleat Academic, 1975, rev. ed., 1993; Diary of a Disaster: British Aid to Greece, 1940-1941, 1986; The Bases of Air Strategy, 1998; Research on World War I: A Handbook, 2003; 100 Years of Air Power and Aviation, 2004. EDITOR: Bayonets in the Street, 1969, rev. ed., 1989; Civil Wars in the Twentieth Century, 1972; A Guide to the Sources of British Military History, 1972; Intervention or Abstention, 1975; Guide to the Sources of U.S. Military History, 1975, (with D.J. Mrozek) Supplement I, 1981, Supplement II, 1985, Supplement III, 1993; Supplement IV, 1997; (with A.T. Siddall) Flying Combat Aircraft I, 1978, (with C. Williams) II, 1978, III, 1981, IV, 1998; (with J.W. Kipp) Soviet Aviation and Air Power, 1978; (with J.W. Kipp) The Garland Military History Bibliographies, 1978-92; (with D.J. Mrozek and J.L.A. Newell) The Martin Marauder and the Franklin Allens: A Wartime Love Story, 1980; (with J.T. Greenwood and V. Hardesty) Russian Aviation and Air Power, 1998; A Handbook on Air Ministry Organization, 1998; Writing Official Military History, 1999; Official Military History I & II, 2000; (with F. Kagan) The Military History of Tsarist Russia, 2002; (with F. Kagan) The Military History of the Soviet Union 1917-1991, 2002; (with D.A. Graff) A Military of History of China, 2002; (with S.J. Harris) The Defense of Air Forces, 2004. **Address:** 2961 Nevada St, Manhattan, KS 66502, U.S.A.

HIGHFIELD, (John) Roger (Loxdale). British, b. 1922. **Genres:** History. **Career:** Oxford University, Oxford, England, fellow of Merton College, 1949-89, lecturer in history, 1951-89, emeritus fellow, 1989-. **Publications:** (with C. Brooke and W. Swann) Oxford and Cambridge, 1988; (with G. Martin) History of Merton College, Oxford, 1997. EDITOR: The Early Rolls of Merton College, 1964; (with B. Smalley and J. Hale) Europe in the Late Middle Ages, 1965; Spain in the Fifteenth Century, 1972; (with R. Jeffs) The Crown and Local Communities in England and France in the Fifteenth Century, 1983. **Address:** Merton College, Oxford University, Oxford OX1 4TD, England.

HIGHLAND, Monica. See **SEE, Carolyn.**

HIGHTOWER, Lynn S. American. **Genres:** Novels, Mystery/Crime/Suspense. **Career:** Full-time fiction writer. **Publications:** Alien Blues, 1991; Satan's Lambs, 1992; Alien Eyes, 1993; Alien Heat, 1994; Alien Rites, 1995; Flashpoint, 1995; Eyeshot, 1996. **Address:** c/o Delacorte Press Publicity, 1540 Broadway, New York, NY 10036, U.S.A.

HIGHTOWER, Scott. (born United States), b. 1952. **Genres:** Poetry. **Career:** Fordham University, New York, NY, poet in residence at Lincoln Center Campus. Worked as junior high school and high school teacher; also taught at Gallatin School of Individualized Study, New York University, and at Gay Men's Health Crisis. **Publications:** Tin Can Tourist (poetry), 2001; Contributor of poetry to periodicals. **Address:** Lincoln Center Campus, Fordham University, New York, NY 10023, U.S.A.

HIGHWAY, Tomson. Canadian, b. 1951. **Genres:** Plays/Screenplays. **Career:** Worked with Canadian writer James Reaney on plays; associated with Native support groups; Deba-jeh-mu-jig Theatre Group, formerly located in West Bay, ON; Native Earth Performing Arts Inc., Toronto, artistic director, until 1992. **Publications:** The Rez Sisters (two-act play) 1986; Aria (monologues), 1987; Dry Lips Oughta Move to Kapuskasing (also known as The Red Brothers), 1989; (with R. Highway and B. Merasty) The Sage, the Dancer, and the Fool (play), 1989. Collaborated with R. Highway on the multimedia dance-production New Song … New Dance, 1987-88. **Address:** 4 Sackville Place, Toronto, ON, Canada M4X 1A4.

HILBERRY, Conrad Arthur. American, b. 1928. **Genres:** Poetry. **Career:** Kalamazoo College, Michigan, English teacher, 1962-. **Publications:** POETRY: Encounter on Burrows Hill and Other Poems, 1968; Rust, 1974; Man in the Attic, 1980; Housemarks, 1980; The Moon Seen as a Slice of Pineapple, 1984; Sorting the Smoke: New and Selected Poems, 1990; Player Piano, 1999; Taking Notes on Nature's Wild Inventions, 1999. OTHER: Luke Karamazov (case study), 1987. EDITOR: The Poems of John Collop, 1962; (with M. Keeton) Struggle and Promise: A Future for Colleges, 1968; (with H. Scott and J. Tipton) The Third Coast: Contemporary Michigan Poets, 1976; (with M. Delp and H. Scott) Contemporary Michigan Poetry: Poems from the Third Coast, 1988; (with M. Delp and J. Kearns) New Poems from the Third Coast, 2000. **Address:** Kalamazoo College, Kalamazoo, MI 49006, U.S.A. **Online address:** hilberry@core.com

HILBERT, Richard A. American, b. 1947. **Genres:** Anthropology/Ethnology, Sociology. **Career:** University of California, Santa Barbara,

member of sociology faculty, 1978; Gustavus Adolphus College, St. Peter, MN, teacher of sociology, 1978-81, 1983-, full professor and head of Department of Sociology and Anthropology, 1991-. University of Wisconsin-Madison, guest lecturer, 1980. **Publications:** The Classical Roots of Ethnomethodology: Durkheim, Weber, and Garfinkel, 1992; Duck King, 1998. Work represented in anthologies. Contributor of articles and reviews to sociology journals. **Address:** Dept of Sociology and Anthropology, Gustavus Adolphus College, 800 W College Ave, St. Peter, MN 56082, U.S.A. **Online address:** rhilbert@gustavus.edu

HILBORN, Robert C. American, b. 1943. **Genres:** Physics. **Career:** State University of New York at Stony Brook, research associate and lecturer, 1971-73; Oberlin College, Oberlin, OH, assistant professor to professor, 1973-86; Amherst College, Amherst, MA, professor of physics, 1986-94, Lisa and Amanda Cross Professor, 1994-. **Publications:** Chaos and Nonlinear Dynamics, 1994, 2nd ed., 2000; Spin-Statistic Connection and Commutation Relations, 2000. **Address:** Department of Physics, Amherst College, Amherst, MA 01002, U.S.A. **Online address:** rchilborn@amherst.edu

HILDEBRAND, Ann Meinzen. American (born Canada), b. 1933. **Genres:** Children's non-fiction, Literary criticism and history, Biography. **Career:** High school English teacher in Euclid, OH, 1955-58; Kent State University, Kent, OH, part-time instructor, 1965-76, visiting assistant professor, 1976-86, visiting associate professor, 1986-93, visiting professor of children's and adolescent literature, 1993-, visiting professor of English, 1993-98, emeritus professor of English, 1998-. **Publications:** Jean and Laurent de Brunhoff: The Legacy of Babar, 1992; (with W.H. Hildebrand) Anne Chamberlain: A Writer's Story (monograph), 2001. Work represented in anthologies. Contributor of articles and reviews to scholarly journals. **Address:** 11 Glenside Dr, Munroe Falls, OH 44262, U.S.A. **Online address:** ahildeb0@kent.edu

HILDEBRAND, John. American, b. 1949. **Genres:** Literary criticism and history. **Career:** University of Alaska, Fairbanks, instructor in English, 1974-76; University of Wisconsin-Eau Claire, assistant professor of English, 1977-. **Publications:** Reading the River: A Voyage Down the Yukon, Houghton, 1988; Mapping the Farm: Chronical of an American Family, 1995. **Address:** c/o Beth Vesel, Sanford J. Greenburger Associates, Inc, 55 Fifth Ave, New York, NY 10003, U.S.A.

HILDEBRAND, Klaus. German, b. 1941. **Genres:** History. **Career:** University of Mannheim, Mannheim, Germany, research assistant, 1967-72; University of Bielefeld, Bielfeld, Germany, professor of modern history, 1972-74; University of Frankfurt, Frankfurt, Germany, professor, 1974-77; University of Muenster, Muenster, Germany, professor, 1977-82; University of Bonn, Bonn, Germany, professor, 1982-; writer. **Publications:** IN ENGLISH TRANSLATION: Deutsche Aussenpolitik, 1933-45, 1973; Das Dritte Reich, 1979 trans. by P.S. Falla as The Third Reich, 1984; Staatskunst oder Systemzwang, trans. by L. Willmot as German Foreign Policy from Bismarck to Adenauaer: The Limits of Statecraft, 1989. IN GERMAN: Bundesrepublik Deuhcchlarest, 1963-67; Vom Reich zum Weltreich, 1967; Bethmann Hollweg, 1970; Das Deutsche Reich und die Sowjetunion im Internationalen System: 1918-1932: Legitimiteat Oder Revolution?, 1977; (with others) Wem gehoert die deutsche Geschichte?: Deutschlands Weg vom alten Europa in die europaeische Moderne Hanns Martin Schleyer-Stiftung, 1987; (with J. Schmaedeke and K. Zernack) 1939, an der Schwelle zum Weltkrieg: Die Entfesselung des Zweiten Weltkrieges und das internationale System, 1990; Das Vergangene Reich: Deutsche Aussenpolitik von Bismarck bis Hitler, 1871-1945, 1995; Das Deutsche Reich im Urteil der grossen Maechte und europaeischen Nachbarn (1871-1945), 1995. EDITOR: (with J. Becker) Internationale Beziehungen (1929-1933), 1980; (with K.F. Werner) Deutschland und Frankscich (1936-1939), 1981; (with R. Pommerin) Deutsche Frage und europaeisches Gleichgewicht, 1985; Integration und Souvereaniteat: die Aussenpolitik der Bundesrepublik Deutschland, 19491982, 1991. **Address:** 11 Konviktstrasse, 5300 Bonn, Germany.

HILDEBRAND, Verna. American, b. 1924. **Genres:** Education. **Career:** Kansas State University, Manhattan, instructor, 1953-54, 1959; Oklahoma State University, Stillwater, instructor, 1955-56; Texas Tech University, Lubbock, assistant professor of home and family life, 1962-67; Michigan State University, East Lansing, Dept. of Family and Child Ecology, professor, 1967-96, professor emeritus, 1996-. **Publications:** Introduction to Early Childhood Education, 1971, 6th ed., 1997; A Laboratory Workbook for Introduction to Early Childhood Education, 1971, 5th ed., 1991; Guiding Young Children, 1975, 6th ed., 1998; Parenting and Teaching Young Children, 1981, 3rd ed., 1990; (with J.R. Hildebrand) China's Families: Experiment in Societal Change, 1981; Management of Child Development

Centers, 1984, 4th ed., 1997; Fundamentos de Educacion Infantil: Jardin de ninos y preprimariam, 1987; Parenting: Rewards and Responsibilities, 1993, 7th ed., 2003; Knowing and Serving Diverse Families, 1996, 2nd ed., 1999. **Address:** 4570 E Yale Ave #904, Denver, CO 80222-6543, U.S.A.

HILDEBRANDT, Erik A(lan). American, b. 1966. **Genres:** Military/Defense/Arms control. **Career:** Writer. **Publications:** Blue Water Ops: On the Front Line of Naval Aviation, 1998. **Address:** 3331 Buchanan St NE, Minneapolis, MN 55418, U.S.A. **Online address:** erik@avsnaps.com

HILDT, Elisabeth. German, b. 1966. **Genres:** Medicine/Health. **Career:** European Network for Biomedical Ethics, scientific coordinator, 1996-98; Institut Technik-Theologie-Naturwissenschaften, Munich, Germany, researcher in biomedical ethics, 1998-. **Publications:** Hirngewebetransplantation und Personale Identitat, 1996; (ed. with D. Meth) In Vitro Fertilisation in the 1990s, 1998; (ed. with S. Graumann) Genetics in Human Reproduction, 1999. Contributor to books and scientific journals. **Address:** Institut Technik-Theologie-Naturwissenschaften, Marsstrasse 19, 80335 Munich, Germany. **Online address:** E.Hildt@lrz.uni-muenchen.de

HILL, Anthony (Robert). Australian, b. 1942. **Genres:** Novellas/Short stories, Children's fiction, Young adult fiction, Antiques/Furnishings. **Career:** Melbourne Herald, Australia, journalist, 1960-75; Australian Financial Review, Canberra, journalist, 1976-77; self-employed antiques dealer in New South Wales, Australia, 1977-82; free-lance journalist in Canberra, 1982-89; Office of the Governor-General of Australia, Canberra, speechwriter, 1989-99; full-time writer, 1999-. **Publications:** JUVENILE FICTION: Birdsong, 1988; The Burnt Stick, 1994; Spindrift, 1996; The Grandfather Clock, 1996. OTHER: Antique Furniture in Australia, 1985; The Bunburyists (nonfiction), 1985; Growing Up & Other Stories, 1999; Soldier Boy, 2001; Forbidden, 2002; Young Digger, 2002; The Shadow Dog, 2003; Animal Heroes, 2005. **Address:** c/o Penguin Books Australia Ltd., PO Box 701, Hawthorn, VIC 3122, Australia.

HILL, Brian W. British, b. 1932. **Genres:** Biography, History. **Career:** University of East Anglia, Norwich, England, reader in history, 1963-. **Publications:** Edmund Burke, 1975; The Growth of Parliamentary Parties, 1976; British Parliamentary Parties, 1985; Robert Harley, 1988; Sir Robert Walpole, 1989; The Early Parties and Politics in Britain 1688-1832, 1996. **Address:** Department of History, University of East Anglia, Norwich, England.

HILL, Carol. American, b. 1942. **Genres:** Novels, Plays/Screenplays, Social commentary. **Career:** Former actress; Publicist, Crown Publishers, NYC, 1965-67; Publicity Manager, Random House Inc., publishers, NYC, 1973-74; Sr. Ed., William Morrow & Co., 1974-75; Harcourt Brace, NYC, vice president & publisher, 1976-79, senior editor, 1995-96. **Publications:** Mother Loves (play), 1967; Jeremiah 8:20, 1970; Subsistence US, 1973; Let's Fall in Love, 1974; An Unmarried Woman (novelization of screenplay), 1978; The Eleven Million Mile High Dancer, 1985; Henry James' Midnight Song, 1993.

HILL, David. New Zealander, b. 1942. **Genres:** Children's fiction, Young adult fiction, Plays/Screenplays, Novels. **Career:** High school teacher, Tanaki College, Takapuna Grammar School, and schools in England, 1965-82; full-time writer, 1982-. **Publications:** FOR CHILDREN: The Games of Nanny Miro, 1990; See Ya Simon, 1992; Kick Back, 1995; The Winning Touch, 1995; Take It Easy, 1995; Help Yourself, 1995; Old Bones, 1995; Hats Off!, 1995; Seconds Best, 1996; Cold Comfort, 1996; Fat, Four-eyed and Useless, 1997; Treasure Deep, 1997; Good Move, 1997; Ganging Up, 1997; Give It Hoops, 1998; Boots 'n All, 1998; Comes Naturally, 1998; Time Out, 1999; Just Looking, Thanks, 1999; Impact, 2000; The High Wind Blows, 2000; Afterwards, 2000; The Sleeper Wakes, 2000; The Name of the Game, 2001; Where All Things End, 2002; Right Where It Hurts, 2002; No Safe Harbour, 2003; Journey to Tangiwai, 2003. PLAYS FOR YOUNG ADULTS: The Big Drip, 1983; Down Broad Street, 1985; Get in the Act, 1985; Ours But to Do, 1986; Been There, 1990; A Time to Laugh, 1990; Branches, 1993; A Day at a Time, 1994; Takes Two, 1996; Be All Right, 1998. FOR ADULTS: The Seventies Connection, 1980; Moaville Magic, 1985; Taranaki, 1987; The Boy, 1988; More from Moaville, 1988; The Year in Moaville, 1991. **Address:** 21 Timandra Street, New Plymouth, New Zealand. **Online address:** david.hill@clear.net.nz

HILL, Douglas. Canadian, b. 1935. **Genres:** Science fiction/Fantasy, Children's fiction, Children's non-fiction, History, Literary criticism and history, Paranormal. **Career:** Ed., Aldus Books, London, 1962-64; Literary Ed., Tribune, London, 1971-84. **Publications:** (with P. Williams) The Supernatu-

ral, 1965; The Opening of the Canadian West, 1967; John Keats, 1968; Regency London, 1969; Magic and Superstition, 1969; Georgian London, 1970; Fortune Telling, 1970; Return from the Dead, 1970, in US as the History of Ghosts, Vampires, and Werewolves, 1973; The Scots to Canada, 1972; The Comet, 1973; The English to New England, 1974; (with G. Robinson) Coyote the Trickster, 1975; Tribune 40, 1977; The Exploits of Hercules, 1978; Galactic Warlord, 1979; Deathwing over Veynaa, 1980; Day of the Starwind, 1981; Planet of the Warlord, 1981; The Huntsman, 1982; Young Legionary, 1982; Warriors of the Wasteland, 1983; Alien Citadel, 1984; Exiles of ColSec, 1984; The Caves of Klydor, 1984; The Moon Monsters, 1984; ColSec Rebellion, 1985; How Jennifer (and Speckle) Saved the Earth, 1986; Blade of the Poisoner, 1987; Master of Fiends, 1988; Goblin Party, 1988; The Fraxilly Fracas, 1989; Penelope's Pendant, 1990; The Colloghi Conspiracy, 1990; Trellie the Troog, 1991; The Unicorn Dream, 1992; The Voyage of Mudjack, 1993; The Lightless Dome, 1993; The World of the Stiks, 1994; The Leafless Forest, 1994; Fireball and the Hero, 1995; The Magical Tree-castle, 1995; Malcolm and the Cloud-stealer, 1995; The Moons of Lannamur, 1995; Galaxy's Edge, 1996; The Dragon Charmer, 1997; Witch and Wizard, 1997; Space Girls Don't Cry, 1998; Melleron's Monsters, 1999; Alien Deeps, 2000; Monster Maze, 2001; Star Dragon, 2002; Space Boots, 2003. EDITOR: Window on the Future, 1967; Warlocks and Warriors, 1971; The Shape of Sex to Come, 1978; Planetfall, 1986. **Address:** 138 Maryland Rd, London N22 5AP, England.

HILL, Edmund. British (born Spain), b. 1923. **Genres:** Theology/Religion. **Career:** Joined Order of Preachers (Dominicans; O.P.), 1948; Blackfriars, Oxford, England, teacher, 1956-66; teacher in Stellenbosch, South Africa, 1966-69; St. Peter's Seminary for Africans, Hammanskraal, South Africa, 1969-72; teacher in Swaziland, 1973-74; St. Augustine's Seminary, in Lesotho, teacher, 1974-90; Holy Spirit Seminary, Port Moresby, Papua New Guinea, teacher, 1991; St. Augustine's Seminary, teacher, 1992-94. **Publications:** Nine Sermons of St. Augustine on the Psalms, 1958; Prayer, Praise, and Politics, Relections on Psalms, 1973; Being Human, 1984; The Mystery of the Trinity, 1985; Ministry and Authority in the Catholic Church, 1988. TRANSLATOR AND AUTHOR OF INTRO./NOTES: Summa Theologiae, vol. XIII of St. Thomas, 1964; The Sermons of St. Augustine, Volumes I-XI, 1990-97; The Trinity of St. Augustine, 1991; Teaching Christianity (De Doctrina Christiana of St Augustine). **Address:** Blackfriars, Buckingham Rd, Cambridge CB3 0DD, England.

HILL, Elizabeth Starr. American, b. 1925. **Genres:** Children's fiction. **Career:** Freelance writer. **Publications:** The Wonderful Visit to Miss Liberty, 1961; The Window Tulip, 1964; Evan's Corner, 1967, (with new illustrations) 1991; Master Mike and the Miracle Maid, 1967; Pardon My Fangs, 1969; Bells: A Book to Begin On, 1970; Ever-After Island, 1977; Fangs Aren't Everything, 1985; When Christmas Comes, 1989; The Street Dancers, 1991; Broadway Chances, 1992; The Banjo Player, 1993; Curtain Going Up!, 1995; Bird Boy, 1999; Chang and the Bamboo Flute, 2002; Wildfire!, 2004. **Address:** The Studio, 503 N Interlachen Ave, Winter Park, FL 32789, U.S.A.

HILL, Eric. British, b. 1927. **Genres:** Novellas/Short stories, Children's fiction, Illustrations. **Career:** Graphic designer, author and illustrator of books for children. Cooper Studio (art studio), London, England, messenger and sweeper, 1943-45; free-lance cartoonist, 1948; Erwin Wasey (advertising agency), London, art director, 1955-58; free-lance artist, 1958-80; author, 1980-. **Publications:** SELF-ILLUSTRATED FOR CHILDREN. SPOT SERIES: Where's Spot?, 1980; Spot's First Walk, 1981; Spot's Birthday Party, 1982; Puppy Love, 1982; Spot's Busy Year, 1983; Spot's First Christmas, 1983; Spot Learns to Count, 1983; Spot Tells the Time, 1983; Spot's Alphabet, 1983; Sweet Dreams, Spot!, 1984; Spot's Friends, 1984; Spot's Toys, 1984; Here's Spot, 1984; Spot Goes Splash!, 1984; Spot Goes to School, 1984; Spot on the Farm, 1985; Spot Goes to the Beach, 1985; Spot at Play, 1985; Spot at the Fair, 1985; Spot Goes to the Circus, 1986; Spot's First Words, 1986; Spot's Doghouse, 1986; Spot Looks at Colors, 1986; Spot Looks at Shapes, 1986; Spot Goes to the Farm, 1987; Spot's First Picnic, 1987; Spot Visits the Hospital, 1987; Spot's Big Book of Words, 1988; Spot's First Easter, 1988; Spot Counts from One to Ten, 1989; Spot Looks at Opposites, 1989; Spot Looks at the Weather, 1989; Spot's Baby Sister, 1989; Spot Sleeps Over, 1990; Spot Goes to the Park, 1991; Spot in the Garden, 1991; Spot's Toy Box, 1991; Spot at Home, 1991; Spot Goes to a Party, 1992; Spot's Toy Box, 1991; My Very Own Spot Book, 1993; Spot's Walk in the Woods, 1993; Spot's Big Book of Colors, Shapes, and Numbers, 1994; Spot's First 1, 2, 3 Frieze, 1994; Spot's Magical Christmas, 1995; Spot Bakes a Cake, 1999; Spot Visits His Grandparents, 1996; Spot and Friends Dress Up, 1996; Spot and Friends Play, 1996; Spot's Touch and Feel Book, 1997; Spot's Touch and Feel Day, 1997; Spot's Favorite Baby Animals, 1997; Spot's Favorite Colors, 1997; Spot's Favorite Numbers,

1997; Spot's Favorite Words, 1997; Spot's Noisy Walk, 1998; Spot and His Grandparents Go to the Carnival, 1998; Spot Joins the Parade, 1998; Spot's Bedtime Storybook, 1998; Spot Helps Out, 1999; Good Night, Spot, 1999; Spot Can Count, 1999; Spot's Windy Day and Other Stories, 2000. PEEK-A-BOOK SERIES: Nursery Rhymes, 1982; Opposites, 1982; Animals, 1982; Who Does What?, 1982; Baby Animals, 1984; More Opposites, 1985; Fairy Tales, 1985; What's Inside?, 1985. BABY BEAR STORYBOOK SERIES: At Home, 1983; My Pets, 1983; The Park, 1983; Up There, 1983; Baby Bear's Bedtime, 1984; Good Morning, Baby Bear, 1984. OTHER: S.S. Happiness Crew Book of Numbers, 1983; Book of Colors, 1984; Book of Shapes, 1984; Eric Hill's Crazy Mix or Match: Funny Picture Stories for Preschoolers, 1984; Eric Hill's Crazy Crazy Wheels Mix or Match, 1984. Illustrator of books by: A. Ahlberg, J. Dutton, H. Hoke. **Address:** c/o Putnam Publishing, 375 Hudson, New York, NY 10014, U.S.A.

HILL, Geoffrey. British, b. 1932. **Genres:** Poetry, Literary criticism and history. **Career:** English Dept, 1954-80, professor of English, 1976-80, University of Leeds; fellow, Emmanuel College, and university lecturer in English, University of Cambridge, 1981-88; Boston University, university professor, professor of literature and religion, 1988-. **Publications:** Poems, 1952; For the Unfallen: Poems, 1952-58, 1959; Preghiere, 1964; (with E. Brock and S. Smith) Penguin Modern Poets 8, 1966; King Log, 1968; Mercian Hymns, 1971; Somewhere Is Such a Kingdom: Poems 1952-1971, 1975; Tenebrae, 1978; (adaptor) Brand, 1978; The Mystery of the Charity of Charles Peguy, 1983; The Lords of Limit: Essays on Literature and Ideas, 1984; Collected Poems, 1985; The Enemy's Country: Words, Contexture, and Other Circumstances of Language, 1991; New and Collected Poems, 1952-1992, 1994; Canaan, 1997; The Triumph of Love, 1998; Speech! Speech!, 2000; The Orchids of Syon, 2002; Style and Faith, 2003.

HILL, Gerald N. American, b. 1929. **Genres:** History, Politics/Government, Law. **Career:** Attorney in San Francisco, CA, 1958-76, and Sonoma, CA, 1976-. Golden Gate University, instructor in law, 1970-71; University of California, visiting scholar at Institute for Governmental Studies, 1993-95. **Publications:** (ed. and contrib.) Housing in California, 1963; (with K.T. Hill) The Aquino Assassination, 1984; (with Hill) Real Life Dictionary of American Politics: What They're Saying and What It Really Means, 1994; (with Hill) Real Life Dictionary of the Law, 1995. **Address:** P.O. Box 258, Sonoma, CA 95476, U.S.A.

HILL, Janet Muirhead. American, b. 1942. **Genres:** Children's fiction. **Career:** MJH Enterprises Business (manufacturing business), Bozeman, MT, co-owner, 1984-89; home care provider, Bozeman, MT, 1990-92; Raven Publishing, Norris, MT, publisher, editor, and writer, 1997-; Alone Together, bi-monthly newsletter, publisher, writer, and editor, 1997-; book publisher, 2002-. Madison Manor, licensed practical nurse, 1999-2001;. **Publications:** Miranda and Starlight (juvenile fiction), 2002; Starlight's Courage, 2002; Starlight, Star Bright, 2003; Starlight's Shooting Star, 2003; Starlight Shines for Miranda, 2004; Starlight Comes Home, 2004. Contributor of short stories to children's magazines. **Address:** Raven Publishing, 10 Cherry Creek Rd, PO Box 2885, Norris, MT 59745, U.S.A. **Online address:** cherycrk@3rivers.net

HILL, John. *See* KOONTZ, Dean R(ay).

HILL, Johnson. *See* KUNHARDT, Edith.

HILL, Jonathan D. American, b. 1954. **Genres:** Anthropology/Ethnology. **Career:** Indiana University-Bloomington, instructor in anthropology, 1982-83; University of Georgia, Athens, visiting assistant professor of anthropology, 1983-86; Southern Illinois University at Carbondale, assistant professor, 1986-89, associate professor of anthropology, 1990-95, professor, 1996-, chair, 1999-. University of California, Los Angeles, visiting associate professor, 1993-94. Conducted extensive anthropological research in Venezuela and Colombia. **Publications:** Keepers of the Sacred Chants: The Poetics of Ritual Power in an Amazonian Society, 1993. EDITOR: Rethinking History and Myth: Indigenous South American Perspectives on the Past, 1988; Anthropological Discourses and the Expression of Personhood in South American Inter-Ethnic Relations, 1993; History, Power, and Identity: Ethnogenesis in the Americas, 1492-1992, 1996. Contributor to books and anthropology and music journals. Contributing editor, Handbook of Latin American Studies, 1986-94. **Address:** Department of Anthropology, Mail Code 4502, Southern Illinois University, Carbondale, IL 62901-4502, U.S.A.

HILL, Justin. Bahamian, b. 1971. **Genres:** Novels. **Career:** Author. **Publications:** A Bend in the Yellow River, 1997; The Drink and Dream Teahouse,

2001; Ciao Asmara, 2002. **Address:** c/o Author Mail, Warner Books, 1271 Avenue of the Americas, New York, NY 10020, U.S.A.

HILL, Kathleen Thompson. American, b. 1941. **Genres:** History, Law, Politics/Government, Travel/Exploration. **Career:** Writer and lecturer. University of California, Berkeley, visiting scholar at Institute of Governmental Studies, 1993-94; lecturer on political science: University of British Columbia, 2000-, Sonoma State University, 2000-; Coro Foundation, fellow in public affairs. Guest on television and radio news and talk shows. **Publications:** Festivals U.S.A.: Western States, 1982; (with G.N. Hill) The Aquino Assassination, 1983; (ed.) Sonoma Poets: A Collection, 1986, 2nd ed., 1995; Festivals U.S.A., 1988; Santa Barbara and Central Coast, 1991, rev. ed., 2001; (with G.N. Hill) Real Life Dictionary of American Politics, 1994, rev. ed. as Facts on File Dictionary of American Politics, 2001; (with G.N. Hill) Real Life Dictionary of the Law, 1995, rev. ed. as People's Law Dictionary, 2002; Victoria & Vancouver Island, 1997, rev. ed., 2000; (with G.N. Hill) Hill Guides to Sonoma Valley, 1998, rev. ed., 2002; Northwest Wine Country, 1998, rev. ed., 2000; Napa Valley, 1999, rev. ed., 2003; Monterey and Carmel, 1999, rev. ed., 2001. Contributor to magazines and newspapers. **Address:** PO Box 654, Sonoma, CA 95476, U.S.A. **Online address:** hilltopub@aol.com

HILL, Pamela. Also writes as Sharon Fiske. British (born Kenya), b. 1920. **Genres:** Mystery/Crime/Suspense, Romance/Historical. **Publications:** Flaming Janet (in U.S. as King's Vixen), 1954; Shadow of Palaces (in U.S. as Crown and the Shadow), 1955; Marjory of Scotland, 1956; Here Lies Margot, 1957; Maddalena, 1963; Forget Not Ariadne, 1965; Julia, 1967; The Devil of Aske, 1972; The Malvie Inheritance, 1973; The Incumbent, 1974, in U.S. as The Heatherton Heritage, 1976; Whitton's Folly, 1975; Norah Stroyan, 1976; The Green Salamander, 1977; Tsar's Woman, 1978; Strangers' Forest, 1978; Daneclere, 1978; Homage to a Rose, 1979; Daughter of Midnight, 1979; Fire Opal, 1980; A Place of Ravens, 1980; (as Sharon Fiske) Summer Cypress, 1981; The House of Cray, 1982; The Fairest One of All, 1982; Duchess Cain, 1983; The Copper-Haired Marshal, 1983; Bride of Ae, 1983; Children of Lucifer, 1984; Still Blooms the Rose, 1984; The Governess, 1985; Sable for the Count, 1985; My Lady Glamis, 1985; Digby, 1987; Fenfallow, 1987; The Sutburys, 1988; Jeannie Urquahart, 1988; The Woman in the Cloak, 1988; Artemia, 1989; Trevithick, 1989; The Loves of Ginevra, 1990; Vollands, 1990; A Dark Star Passing, 1990; The Brocken, 1990; The Sword and the Flame, 1991; The Silver Runaways, 1991; Angell and Sons, 1992; Mercer, 1992; Aunt Lucy, 1993; O Madcap Duchess, 1993; The Parson's Children, 1994; The Man from the North, 1994; Journey beyond Innocence, 1994; The Charmed Descent, 1995; The Inadvisable Marriages, 1995; Curtmantle, 1996; Murder in Store, 1996; Alice the Palace, 1996; The Supplanter, 1997; Countess Isabel, 1998; The Small Black Knife, 1998; The Lion's Daughter, 1999; Bailie's Wake, 2000; The Gods Return, 2000. **Address:** c/o Hale, 45-47 Clerkenwell Green, London EC1R 0HT, England.

HILL, Reginald (Charles). Also writes as Dick Morland, Patrick Ruell, Charles Underhill. British, b. 1936. **Genres:** Novels, Novellas/Short stories, Mystery/Crime/Suspense, Plays/Screenplays. **Career:** Teacher/lecturer, 1960-80; full-time writer, 1980-. **Publications:** A Clubbable Woman, 1970; Fell of Dark, 1971; An Advancement of Learning, 1972; A Fairly Dangerous Thing, 1972; An Affair of Honour (play), 1972; Ruling Passion, 1973; A Very Good Hater, 1974; An April Shroud, 1975; Another Death in Venice, 1976; A Pinch of Snuff, 1978; Pascoe's Ghost (stories), 1979; A Killing Kindness, 1980; The Spy's Wife, 1980; Who Guards a Prince, 1981; Ordinary Levels (radio play), 1982; Traitor's Blood, 1983; Deadheads, 1983; Exit Lines, 1984; No Man's Land, 1985; Child's Play, 1987; The Collaborators, 1987; There Are No Ghosts in the Soviet Union (stories), 1987; Underworld, 1988; Bones and Silence, 1990; One Small Step (novella), 1990; Recalled to Life, 1992; Blood Sympathy, 1993; Pictures of Perfection, 1994; Asking for the Moon (stories), 1994; Born Guilty, 1995; The Wood Beyond, 1996; Killing the Lawyers, 1997; On Beulah Height, 1998; Singing the Sadness, 1999; Arms and the Women, 2000; Dialogues of the Dead, 2001; Death's Jest-Book, 2002. AS DICK MORLAND: Heart Clock, 1973; Albion! Albion!, 1974. AS PATRICK RUELL: The Castle of the Demon, 1971; Red Christmas, 1972; Death Takes the Low Road, 1974; Urn Burial, 1976; The Long Kill, 1986; Death of a Dormouse, 1987; Dream of Darkness, 1989; The Only Game, 1991. AS CHARLES UNDERHILL: Captain Fantom, 1978; The Forging of Fantom, 1979. **Address:** c/o A.P. Watt, 20 John St, London WC1N 2DR, England.

HILL, Robert S. Australian, b. 1954. **Genres:** Botany. **Career:** University of Tasmania, Hobart, professor of plant science, 1980-99; University of Adelaide, senior research fellow, 1999-. **Publications:** History of the Australian Vegetation: Cretaceous to Recent, 1994; Ecology of the Southern Conifers,

1995. CO-EDITOR: The Ecology and Biogeography of Nothofagus Forests, 1996; The Vegetation of Tasmania, 1999. **Address:** Department of Environmental Biology, University of Adelaide, Adelaide, SA 5005, Australia. **Online address:** Bob.Hill@adelaide.edu.au

HILL, Ronald C. American, b. 1937. **Genres:** Transportation. **Career:** Anstine & Hill (after 1996 Anstine, Hill, Richards & Simpson), Denver, CO, attorney, 1969-. **Publications:** (with J.T. Brouws) Railroading West, 1975, 2nd ed., 1979; Rio Grande in the Rockies, 1977, 2nd ed, 1979; (with D. Stanley) Rails in the Northwest, 1978; (with R.H. Kindig) Union Pacific 8444, 1978; (ed., with R.H. Kindig) Locomotive 346: The First One Hundred Years, 1981; Rio Grande West, 1982; (with W.E. Botkin and R.H. Kindig) Union Pacific 3985, 1985; (with W.E. Botkin and V. Hand) Union Pacific-Mainline West, 1986; Mountain Mainlines of the West, 1988; Colorful Colorado Railroads in the 1960s, 1992; (with A. Chione) The Railroad Artistry of Howard Fogg, 1999; Those Magnificent Planes (annual calendar), 1985-. Contributor to books; contributor of articles and photographs to periodicals. **Address:** Anstine Hill Richards & Simpson, 899 Logan St. Suite 406, Denver, CO 80203, U.S.A.

HILL, Russell. American, b. 1935. **Genres:** Novels, Natural history. **Career:** English teacher for 35 years; writer. **Publications:** Cold Creek Cash Store, c. 1986, as Edge of the Earth, 1986; Lucy Boomer, 1992; the Search for Sheepheaven Trout, 2003. **Address:** Frederick Hill/Bonnie Nadell Inc. Literary Agency, 1842 Union St, San Francisco, CA 94123, U.S.A.

HILL, Sarah H. American. **Genres:** History. **Career:** Emory University, Atlanta, GA, adjunct assistant professor, 1996-. DeKalb College, honors lecturer, 1995, 1997; Oglethorpe University, lecturer, 1995. Guest curator, Atlanta Historical Society, 1995-2001, and Asheville Museum of Art, 2004; member of board of trustees, Coosawattee Foundation, 1996-, Georgia Trail of Tears, and Chieftains Museum/Major Ridge Home Museum; consultant to McKissick Museum, National Park Service, The Hermitage, and Qualla Arts and Crafts Cooperative. **Publications:** Weaving New Worlds: Southeastern Cherokee Women and Their Basketry, 1997. Contributor to books and periodicals.

HILL, Selima (Wood). British, b. 1945. **Genres:** Poetry. **Career:** University of East Anglia, writing fellow, 1991; Royal Festival Hall Dance Festival, writer-in-residence, 1992; South Bank Centre, reader-in-residence, 1998. Recipient: Whitbread Prize for Poetry, 2001. **Publications:** Saying Hello at the Station, 1984; My Darling Camel, 1988; The Accumulation of Small Acts of Kindness, 1989; A Little Book of Meat, 1993; Trembling Hearts in the Bodies of Dogs, 1994; Violet, 1997; Bunny, 1999; Portrait of My Lover as a Horse, 2002; Mr. Silver-Shoes, 2003. **Address:** Bloodaxe Books, PO Box 15N, New Castle upon Tyme NE99 15N, England.

HILL, Susan (Elizabeth). British, b. 1942. **Genres:** Novels, Novellas/Short stories, Children's fiction, Plays/Screenplays. **Career:** Novelist, playwright and critic, 1960-. **Publications:** The Enclosure, 1961; Do Me a Favour, 1963; Gentleman & Ladies, 1969; A Change for the Better, 1969; I'm the King of the Castle, 1970; Strange Meeting, 1971; The Albatross (short stories; in US as The Albatross and Other Stories), 1971; The Bird of Night, 1972; A Bit of Singing and Dancing (short stories), 1973; In the Springtime of the Year, 1974; The Cold Country and Other Plays for Radio, 1975; The Magic Apple Tree, 1982; The Woman in Black, 1983; Through the Kitchen Window, 1984; One Night at a Time (for children), 1984; Go Away Bad Dreams, 1984; Through the Garden Gate, 1986; Mother's Magic (for children), 1986; Shakespeare Country, 1987; The Lighting of the Lamps, 1987; Lanterns across the Snow (novella), 1988; The Spirit of the Cotswolds, 1988; Can It Be True (for children), 1988; Family (autobiography), 1989; Suzie's Shoes (for children), 1989; (with T. Hill) The Collaborative Classroom, 1990; Stories from Codling Village, 1990; I've Forgotten Edward, 1990; I Won't Go There Again, 1990; Pirate Poll, 1991; (trans. with J. Tittler) Juyungo: The First Black Ecuadorian Novel, 1991; The Glass Angels, 1992; Mrs. de Winter, 1993; Beware, Beware, 1993; King of Kings, 1993; The Christmas Collection, 1994; (with R. Stuart) Reflections from a Garden, 1995; Listening to the Orchestra (stories), 1996; Simba's A-Z, 1998; Service of Clouds, 1999; Stuart Sets Sail, 2001; Stuart Hides Out, 2001; Stuart at the Library, 2001; Stuart at the Fun House, 2001; Backyard Bedtime, 2001; The Boy Who Taught the Beekeeper to Read, 2003; Ruby Bakes a Cake, 2004. EDITOR: Hardy, The Distracted Preacher and Other Stories, 1979; Ghost Stories, 1984; (with J. Hancock) Literature-Based Reading Programs at Work, 1988; The Random House Book of Ghost Stories, 1991; Spirit of Britain, 1994; Contemporary Women's Short Stories, 1995; (with S. Topley) Counting My Chickens, 2002. **Address:** c/o Vivien Green, Sheil Land, 43 Doughty St, London WC1N 2LF, England. **Online address:** susan@susan-hill.com

HILL, Thomas. Also writes as Tommy Hallowell. American, b. 1960. **Genres:** Young adult fiction, Humor/Satire. **Career:** Free-lance writer, 1984-89; Nick at Nite/TV Land, New York City, copywriter and creative director, 1989-. **Publications:** (with S. Slavkin) Salute Your Shorts: Life at Summer Camp, 1986; (with A. Hill) Otherwise Engaged; or, How to Survive the Happiest Time of Your Life, 1988; What to Expect When Your Wife Is Expanding, 1993; (with D. Friedman) Pat the Stimpy, 1993; Nick at Nites' Classic TV Companion, 1996. AS TOMMY HALLOWELL: Varsity Coach: Fourth and Goal (young adult), 1986; Varsity Coach: Out of Bounds (young adult), 1987; The Alden All Stars: Duel on the Diamond, 1990; The Alden All Stars: Jester in the Backcourt, 1990; The Alden All Stars: Shot from Midfield, 1990; The Alden All Stars: Last Chance Quarterback, 1990. **Address:** Nick at Nite/TV Land, 1515 Broadway, New York, NY 10036, U.S.A.

HILL, Thomas E(nglish), Jr. American, b. 1937. **Genres:** Philosophy. **Career:** UCLA, professor, 1968-84; University of North Carolina, professor, 1984-. **Publications:** Autonomy and Self-Respect, 1991; Dignity and Practical Reason in Kant's Moral Theory, 1992; Respect, Pluralism, and Justice: Kantian Perspectives, 2000. Contributor of articles and reviews to philosophy journals. **Address:** Department of Philosophy, University of North Carolina at Chapel Hill, Chapel Hill, NC 27599, U.S.A. **Online address:** thill@email.unc.edu

HILL, Tobias. British, b. 1970. **Genres:** Poetry, Novels, Novellas/Short stories. **Career:** Apex School, Anjo, Aichi, Japan, teacher, 1993-94; writer; editor; music critic. **Publications:** Year of the Dog (poetry), 1995; Midnight in the City of Clocks, 1996; Skin (short stories), 1997; Zoo (poetry), 1998; Underground, (novel) 1999. **Address:** Flat 4, 1 Minster Rd., London NW2 3SD, England.

HILL, William. American, b. 1959. **Genres:** Science fiction/Fantasy. **Career:** Nortel Telecommunications, Richardson, TX, employee relations, 1983-86; Vistawall/Butler Manufacturing, Terrell, TX, human resources manager, 1987-89; Tahoe Seasons Resort, South Lake Tahoe, CA, head bartender, 1990-92; Diamond Peak Ski Resort, Indian Village, NV, ski patroller, 1994-; author, 1994-. **Publications:** Dawn of the Vampire, 1991; Vampire's Kiss, 1994; The Magic Bicycle, 1997; California Ghosting, 1998; The Vampire Hunters, 1998; Chasing Time-The Magic Bicycle Two, 1999; The Wizard Sword, 2000. **Address:** c/o Otter Creek Press, 3154 Nautilus, Middleburg, FL 32068, U.S.A. **Online address:** Otterpress@aol.com

HILLARD, Darla. American, b. 1946. **Genres:** Environmental sciences/Ecology, Natural history, Travel/Exploration, Natural history. **Career:** Snow Leopard Conservancy, Los Gatos, CA, program coordinator. **Publications:** Vanishing Tracks: Four Years among the Snow Leopards of Nepal, 1989. **Address:** Carl D. Brandt, Brandt & Brandt Literary Agents, Inc, 1501 Broadway, No. 2310, New York, NY 10036, U.S.A.

HILLERMAN, Tony. American, b. 1925. **Genres:** Novels, Mystery/Crime/Suspense, Children's fiction, Young adult fiction, Literary criticism and history. **Career:** News Herald, Borger, TX, reporter, 1948; Morning Press, Lawton, OK, news editor, 1949; Constitution, Lawton, city editor, 1950; United Press, Oklahoma City, political reporter, 1952, Santa Fe, NM, bureau manager, 1953; The New Mexican, Santa Fe, executive editor, 1954; University of New Mexico, Albuquerque, associate professor, 1965-66, professor and chairman, 1966-85, assistant to the president, 1975-80, professor emeritus of journalism, 1985-. **Publications:** The Great Taos Bank Robbery and Other Affairs of Indian Country (essays), 1970; The Boy Who Made Dragonfly (juvenile), 1972; New Mexico, 1975; Rio Grande, 1976; (ed.) The Spell of New Mexico, 1977; Hillerman Country, 1991; The Best of the West (anthology), 1992; Seldom Disappointed (memoir), 2002. MYSTERIES: The Blessing Way, 1970; The Fly on the Wall, 1971; Dance Hall of the Dead, 1973; The Listening Woman, 1978; People of Darkness, 1980; The Dark Wind, 1982; The Ghostway, 1985; Skinwalkers, 1986; A Thief of Time, 1988; Talking God, 1989; Coyote Waits, 1990; Sacred Clown, 1993; Finding Moon, 1994; The Fallen Man, 1996; (with R. Herbert) The Oxford Book of American Detective Stories, 1996; Hunting Badger, 1999; The Wailing Wind, 2002; The Sinister Pig, 2003; Skeleton Man, 2004; Kilroy Was There, 2004. **Address:** 1632 Francisca Rd NW, Albuquerque, NM 87107-7118, U.S.A. **Online address:** tonyhillerman@msn.com

HILLES, Robert. Canadian. **Genres:** Poetry, Novellas/Short stories. **Career:** Poet and writer; DeVry Institute of Technology, Calgary, Alberta, Canada, faculty member. **Publications:** POETRY: Look the Lovely Animal Speaks, 1980; The Surprise Element, 1982; An Angel in the Works, 1983; Outlasting the Landscape, 1989; Finding the Lights On, 1991; A Breath at a Time, 1992; Cantos From a Small Room, 1993; Nothing Vanishes, 1997; Breathing

Distance, 1997. OTHER: Raising of Voices (prose), 1993; Near Morning (short fiction collection), 1995; Kissing the Smoke (nonfiction), 1996. Contributor of poetry and fiction to anthologies. Contributor of poetry to periodicals. **Address:** 438 19 Ave NW, Calgary, AB, Canada T2M 0Y4. **Online address:** rhilles@shaw.wave.ca; rhilles@smaug.devry.ca

HILLGARTH, J(ocelyn) N(igel). British, b. 1929. **Genres:** History. **Career:** Sr. Research Fellow, Warburg Institute, London, 1959-62; Fellow, Institute for Advanced Studies, Princeton, NJ, 1963-64; Assistant Professor of History, Harvard University, Cambridge, MA, 1965-70; Associate Professor, 1970-73, and Professor of History, 1973-77, Boston College; Professor of History, University of Toronto and Pontifical Institute of Mediaeval Studies, Toronto, 1977-95. **Publications:** (ed.) The Conversion of Western Europe 350-750, 1969; Ramon Lull and Lullism in 14th Century France, 1971; The Spanish Kingdoms, 2 vols., 1976-78; (with Mary Hillgarth) Pere III of Catalonia, Chronicle, 2 vols., 1980; Visigothic Spain, Byzantium and the Irish, 1985; (ed.) Christianity and Paganism 350-750: The Conversion of Western Europe, 1985; Readers and Books in Majorca, 1229-1550, 1991; The Mirror of Spain 1500-1700, 2000.

HILLIARD, Asa G(rant), III. American, b. 1933. **Genres:** Education, Race relations. **Career:** Denver Public Schools, Denver, CO, teacher, 1955-60; University of Denver, teaching fellow, 1960-63; San Francisco State University, San Francisco, CA, professor and dean of education, 1963-83; Georgia State University, Atlanta, distinguished professor of education, 1980-. Automated Services Inc., director of research, 1970-72. **Publications:** An Exploratory Study of Relationships between Student Teachers' Personality, Ability, Lower Division Grades, and the Student Teachers' Evaluation of Pupils, 1963; Strengths: African American Children and Families, 1982; (with B.M. Caldwell) What Is Quality Child Care?, 1985; (ed. with L. Williams and N. Damali) The Teachings of Ptahhotep: The Oldest Book in the World, 1987; The Maroon within Us: Selected Essays on African American Community Socialization, 1995. **Address:** Georgia State University, P.O. Box 243, Atlanta, GA 30303, U.S.A.

HILLIER, Jim. British, b. 1941. **Genres:** Film. **Career:** British Film Institute, London, teacher/adviser, 1969-73, Educational Advisory Service, deputy head, 1974-78; University of Reading (formerly Bulmershe College of Higher Education), senior lecturer in film studies, 1979-. Movie, member of editorial board, 1971-. **Publications:** (with A. Lovell) Studies in Documentary, 1972; (with A. Lipstadt) Roger Corman's New World, 1981; The New Hollywood, 1993; (with S. Blandford and B.K. Grant) The Film Studies Dictionary, 2001. EDITOR: New Cinema Finland, 1972; Cinema in Finland, 1975; Cahiers du Cinema, vol. I: The 1950's, 1985, vol. 2, The 1960s, 1986; (with P. Wollen) Howard Hawks: American Artist, 1996; American Independent Cinema, 2001. **Address:** 19 Marlborough Rd, Grand-Pont, Oxford, Oxon. OX1 4LW, England. **Online address:** j.m.hillier@reading.ac.uk

HILLIS, Bryan V. Canadian, b. 1956. **Genres:** Theology/Religion. **Career:** Saskatchewan Government Insurance, corporate business analyst, 1981-82; Memorial University, St. John's, NL, Canada, lecturer, 1988; York University, Toronto, ON, Canada, lecturer, 1989-; Luther College, University of Regina, Regina, SK, Canada, assistant professor, 1989-95, associate professor, 1995-2002, professor, 2002-, academic dean, 1995-. **Publications:** Can Two Walk Together Unless They Be Agreed? American Religious Schisms in the 1970s, 1991. Contributor to periodicals. **Address:** Luther College, University of Regina, Regina, SK, Canada S4S 0A2.

HILLMAN, Barry (Leslie). British, b. 1945. **Genres:** Plays/Screenplays, Poetry. **Career:** Northamptonshire County Council, local government officer, 1974-. **Publications:** Endymion Rampant (poetry), 1964; Happy Returns, 1970; Partly Furnished, 1971; Roly-Poly, 1973; Two Can Play at That Game, 1975; The Dispossessed, 1975; Face the Music, 1975; (with R. Newton) Bibs and Bobs, 1975; Six for the Charleston, 1976; (with R. Newton) Odds and Sods, 1977; The Queen and the Axe, 1978; The Guests, 1978; (with R. Newton) A Few Minor Dischords, 1978; These Little Songs (poetry), 1979; Castle on the Rocks, 1979; Never the Blushing Bride, 1981; The Establishment at Arles, 1982; Beyond Necessity, 1981; Three's a Crowd, 1982; The Amazing Dancing Bear (play), 1985; Iron Magnolias, 1994; Housewarming, 1999; Till the Devil Be Up, 2000; At the End of the Day, 2000; An Enemy of the People (adaptation), 2000; A Night at the Moulin Rouge, 2001; A Simple Ceremony, 2002. **Address:** Lynry, 48 Louise Rd, Northampton, England.

HILLMAN, Elizabeth. British, b. 1942. **Genres:** Poetry. **Career:** San Diego State University Library, San Diego, CA, clerk, 1970-74; National Steel and Shipbuilding Co., CA, engineering aide, 1975-80; writer. **Publications:** Tudo Bem! (Haiku chapbook), 1989; Apitos Da Brisa (Haiku chapbook), 1989; Min-Yo and the Moon Dragon, 1992. **Address:** 41 Love Lane, Oldswinford, Stourbridge, West Midlands DY8 2DH, England.

HILLMAN, Richard S. American, b. 1943. **Genres:** Novels, Politics/Government. **Career:** St. John Fisher College, Rochester, NY, professor of political science, 1971-, Director, Institute for the Study of Democracy and Human Rights. **Publications:** (with T.J. D'Agostino) Distant Neighbors in the Caribbean: The Dominican Republic and Jamaica in Comparative Perspective, 1992; Democracy for the Privileged: Crisis and Transition in Venezuela, 1994; Understanding Contemporary Latin America, 1996, 2nd ed., 2000; (with J. Peeler and E. Cardozo) Democracy and Human Rights in Latin America, 2002. **Address:** Institute for the Study of Democracy and Human Rights, St. John Fisher College, Rochester, NY 14618, U.S.A.

HILL-MILLER, Katherine C(ecelia). American, b. 1949. **Genres:** Writing/Journalism, Language/Linguistics. **Career:** Kingsborough Community College of the City University of New York, Brooklyn, NY, adjunct lecturer in English, 1972-73; College of William and Mary, Williamsburg, VA, assistant professor of English, 1978-80; Long Island University, C.W. Post Center, Greenvale, NY, assistant professor, 1980-84, associate professor, 1984-89, professor of English, 1989-. University of Bonn, guest lecturer, spring, 1986. **Publications:** (with S. Weidenborner) Writing Effective Paragraphs, 1974; The Bantam Book of Spelling, 1986; My Hideous Progeny: Mary Shelley, William Godwin, and the Father-Daughter Relationship, 1995; From the Lighthouse to Monk's House: A Guide to Virginia Woolf's Literary Landscapes. Work represented in anthologies. **Address:** Department of English, C.W. Post Campus, Long Island University, 720 Northern Blvd, Brookville, NY 11548-1300, U.S.A. **Online address:** Katherine.Hill-Miller@liu.edu

HILLS, Philip James. British, b. 1933. **Genres:** Education, Information science/Computers, Sciences. **Career:** Head, Center for Research into Human Communication and Learning, Cambridge, 1986-; Lecturer in Educational Technology, Institute for Educational Technology, University of Surrey, Guildford, 1972- (Leverhulme Research Fellow, 1969-72). Sr. Science Master and Head of the Chemistry Dept., Netherthorpe Grammar School, Staveley, 1959-64; Lecturer in Education and Science, Institute of Education, University of Sheffield, 1964-69. International Journal of Information Management, Editor. **Publications:** Small Scale Physical Chemistry, 1966; Chemical Equilibria, 1969; (with J. Leisten) Studies in Atomic Structure, 1969; The Self-Teaching Process in Higher Education, 1976; Study Courses and Counselling, 1979; The Future of the Printed Word: Teaching and Learning as a Communications Process, 1979; (with H. Barlow) Effective Study Skills, 1980; Teaching, Learning, and Communication, 1986; Educating for a Computer Age, 1986; (with M. McLaren) Communication Skills, 1986; (with McLaren) Teaching Communication Skills, 1986; (with McLaren) Communication Skills: A International Review, 2 vols., 1987; Educational Futures, 1987; Publish or Perish, 1989, 2nd ed., 1999; Management Information Systems: The Human/Computer Interface, 1990; (with H. Lewis) Time Management for Academics, 1999; Aspects of Human Communication, Vol. 1: As Others See Us, 2004. EDITOR: (with L.J. Hayness, C.R. Palmer and D.S. Trickey) Alternatives to the Lecture, 1974; (with J. Gilbert) Aspects of Educational Technology, vol. II, 1977; Trends in Information Transfer, 1981; Dictionary of Education, 1984. **Address:** c/o Frances Kelly, Authors Agent, 111 Clifton Rd, Kingston-upon-Thames, Surrey KT2 6PL, England.

HILLYER, Barbara. American, b. 1934. **Genres:** Human relations/Parenting, Women's studies and issues. **Career:** University of Oklahoma, Norman, assistant professor, 1976-82, associate professor of women's studies and human relations, 1982-, director of women's studies, 1976-88. **Publications:** Feminism and Disability, 1993. **Address:** Department of Human Relations, University of Oklahoma, Norman, OK 73019, U.S.A.

HILMES, Michele. American, b. 1953. **Genres:** Communications/Media. **Career:** University of Wisconsin-Madison, associate professor of communication arts. **Publications:** Hollywood and Broadcasting: From Radio to Cable, 1990; Radio Voices, 1997; Only Connect, 2002; (ed.) The Radio Reader, 2002. **Address:** Department of Communication Arts, 6156 Vilas Hall, University of Wisconsin-Madison, 821 University Ave, Madison, WI 53706-1412, U.S.A. **Online address:** mhilmes@wisc.edu

HILSMAN, Roger. American, b. 1919. **Genres:** International relations/Current affairs, Politics/Government. **Career:** Professor Emeritus of Government, Columbia University, New York City. Research Associate, Center of

International Studies, Princeton, New Jersey, 1953-56; Chief, Foreign Affairs Division, 1956-58, Deputy Director for Research, Legislative Reference Service, 1958-61, Library of Congress, Washington, D.C.; Director of Intelligence and Research, U.S. Dept. of State, Washington, 1961-63; Assistant Secretary of State for Far Eastern Affairs, 1963-64. **Publications:** Strategic Intelligence and National Decisions, 1956; (co-author) Military Policy and National Security, 1956; (co-author) NATO and American Security, 1958; (co-author) Alliance Policy in the Cold War, 1958; (co-author) The Guerrilla and How to Fight Him, 1960; (with Good) Foreign Policy in the Sixties, 1965; To Move a Nation, 1967; The Politics of Policy Making in Defense and Foreign Affairs, 1971; The Crouching Future, 1975; To Govern America, 1979; The Politics of Governing America, 1985; Politics of Policy Making: Conceptual Models, 1987, 1990, 1993; American Guerilla: My War Behind Japanese Lines, 1990; George Bush vs. Saddam Hussein: Military Success! Political Failure?, 1992; The Cuban Missile Crisis, the Struggle over Policy, 1996; From Nuclear Military Strategy to a World without War; A History and a Proposal, 1999. **Address:** 317 W Main St #2105, Chester, CT 06412-1057, U.S.A.

HILTON, (Andrew John) Boyd. British, b. 1944. **Genres:** History. **Career:** Christ Church, Oxford, Research Lecturer, 1969-74; Trinity College, Cambridge, Fellow and Lecturer in History, 1974-, Sr. Tutor, 1983-88; University of Cambridge, Reader in Modern British History, 1996-. **Publications:** Corn, Cash and Commerce: The Economic Policies of the Tory Government, 1815-1830, 1980; The Age of Atonement: The Influence of Evangelicalism on Social and Economic Thought, ca. 1785-1865, 1988. **Address:** Trinity College, Cambridge CB2 1TQ, England.

HILTON, George Woodman. American, b. 1925. **Genres:** Sports/Fitness, Theatre, Transportation. **Career:** University of Maryland, College Park, instructor, 1949-51, 1954-55; Stanford University, California, assistant professor, 1955-60; University of California, Berkeley, lecturer, 1961-62; University of California, Los Angeles, lecturer, 1962-63, associate professor, 1963-66, professor of economics, 1966-92, professor emeritus, 1993-. **Publications:** (with J. F. Due) The Electric Interurban Railways in America, 1960; The Truck System, 1960; The Great Lakes Car Ferries, 1962; The Ma & Pa, 1963; The Night Boat, 1968; The Transportation Act of 1958, 1969; The Cable Car in America, 1971; Monon Route, 1978; American Narrow Gauge Railroads, 1990; The Baseball Stories of Ring W. Lardner, 1990; Eastland, 1994; The Front Page, 2002; Lake Michigan Passenger Steamers, 2002. **Address:** 6498 Summer Cloud Way, Columbia, MD 21045, U.S.A.

HILTON, Joni. American, b. 1956. **Genres:** Inspirational/Motivational Literature, Novels. **Career:** Journalist and broadcaster. Hour Family (syndicated television specials), cohost; host of daily television program in Los Angeles, CA, for four years; guest on radio programs; national spokesperson for corporations. **Publications:** Braces, Gym Suits, and Early-Morning Seminary: A Youthquake Survival Manual, 1985; Five-Minute Miracles: 373 Quick Daily Projects for You and Your Kids to Share, 1992; Guilt-free Motherhood: How to Raise Great Kids and Have Fun Doing It, 1996; Honey on Hot Bread and Other Heartfelt Wishes, 1997; Family Fun Book: More than 400 Amazing, Amusing, and All-around Awesome Activities for the Entire Family!, 1998; The Once-a-Week Cooking Plan: The Incredible Cooking Program That Will Save You Twenty Hours a Week (and Have Your Family Begging for More!), 1999; Housekeeping Secrets My Mother Never Taught Me, 2001; Cooking Secrets My Mother Never Taught Me, 2001. NOVELS: Dating: No Guts, No Glory (for teens), 1989; As the Ward Turns, 1991; Around the Ward in Eighty Days, 1993; Scrambled Home Evenings, 1994; That's What Friends Are For (for teens), 1997; Stop the Ward: I Want to Get Off!, 1999. Author of screenplays, television episodes, film treatments, adaptations, and stage plays. Contributor to periodicals. **Address:** c/o Author Mail, Random House Inc, 1745 Broadway, New York, NY 10019, U.S.A. **Online address:** jonihilton@mstar2.net

HILTON, Margery. Also writes as Rebecca Caine. British. **Genres:** Romance/Historical. **Publications:** The Dutch Uncle, 1966; Young Ellis, 1966; Darling Rhadamanthus!, 1966; The Grotto of Jade, 1968; Girl Crusoe, 1969; The Flower of Eternity, 1970; Interlude in Arcady, 1970; Bitter Masquerade, 1970; The Whispering Grove, 1971; A Man Without Mercy, 1971; Trust in Tomorrow, 1971; Dear Conquistador, 1972; The House of the Amulet, 1972; The Spell of the Enchanter, 1972; Frail Sanctuary, 1973; The Inshine Girl, 1973; Miranda's Marriage, 1974; The Beach of Sweet Returns, 1976; The Dark Side of Marriage, 1978; The House of Strange Music, 1978; Snow Bride, 1979; The Velvet Touch, 1979; Way of a Man, 1981. As Rebecca Caine: Pagan Heart, 1971; That Summer of Surrender, 1974; Child of Tahiti, 1976. **Address:** c/o Harlequin, Mills & Boon Ltd, Eton House, 18-24 Paradise Rd., Richmond, Surrey, England.

HILTON, Peter (John). American (born England), b. 1923. **Genres:** Mathematics/Statistics. **Career:** Assistant Lecturer, 1948-51, Lecturer, 1951-52, and Sr. Lecturer, 1956-58, Manchester University; Lecturer, Cambridge University, 1952-55; Mason Professor of Pure Mathematics, University of Birmingham, 1958-62; Professor of Mathematics, Cornell University, Ithaca, NY, 1962-71, and University of Washington, Seattle, 1971-73; Beaumont University Professor, Case Western Reserve University, Cleveland, 1972-82. Chairman, U.S. Commission on Mathematical Instruction, 1971-74; State University of New York at Binghamton, Distinguished Professor of Mathematics, 1982-93, Distinguished Professor Emeritus, 1993-; University of Central Florida, Distinguished Professor of Mathematics, 1994-. **Publications:** Introduction to Homotopy Theory, 1953; Differential Calculus, 1958; (with S. Wylie) Homology Theory, 1960; Partial Derivatives, 1960; Homotopy Theory and Duality, 1965; (with H.B. Griffiths) Classical Mathematics, 1970; General Cohomology Theory and K-Theory, 1971; (with U. Stammbach) Course in Homological Algebra, 1971, 2nd ed., 1997; (with Y.-C. Wu) Course in Modern Algebra, 1974; (with G. Mislin and J. Roitberg) Localization of Nilpotent Groups and Spaces, 1975; (with J. Pedersen) Fear No More, 1982; Nilpotente Gruppen und nilpotente Raume, 1984; (with J. Pedersen) Build Your Own Polyhedra, 1987; (with J. Benson and J. Pedersen) College Preparatory Mathematics, 1992; (with D. Holton and J. Pedersen) Mathematical Reflections, 1997; (with D. Holton and J. Pedersen) Mathematical Vistas, 2002. **Address:** Dept of Mathematics, State University of New York, Binghamton, NY 13902-6000, U.S.A. **Online address:** marge@math.binghamton.edu

HILTON, Suzanne. American, b. 1922. **Genres:** Children's non-fiction, Genealogy/Heraldry, History. **Career:** Writer. **Publications:** How Do They Get Rid of It?, 1970; How Do They Cope With It?, 1970; It's Smart to Use a Dummy, 1971; It's A Model World, 1972; Beat It, Burn It, and Drown It, 1973; The Way It Was-1876, 1975; Who Do You Think You Are?: Digging for Your Family Roots, 1976; Here Today and Gone Tomorrow: The Story of America's World's Fairs, 1978; Getting There: Frontier Travel Without Power, 1980; We the People: The Way We Were 1783 to 1793, 1981; Faster Than a Horse: Moving West with Engine Power, 1983; (ed. and contrib.) Montgomery County, The Second Hundred Years 1880-1980, 1983; The World of Young Tom Jefferson, George Washington, Herbert Hoover, Andrew Jackson, 4 vols., 1986-88; A Capital Capital City: The First Years of Washington, D.C., 1992; Miners, Merchants, and Maids (Settlers of the West Series), 1995.

HILTY, James W. American, b. 1939. **Genres:** History. **Career:** History teacher at public schools in Columbus, OH, 1965; Ohio State University, Columbus, assistant track coach, 1965-66; Temple University, Philadelphia, PA, instructor to professor of history, 1970-, department head, 1988-94, associate dean and acting dean of graduate school, 1979-81, director of university planning, 1982-84, and assistant vice-president for academic affairs. University of Pennsylvania, adjunct professor, 1976. **Publications:** John F. Kennedy: An Idealist without Illusions (monograph), 1976; Robert Kennedy, Brother Protector, 1997. Contributor to history journals. **Address:** 1670 Miller Circle, Blue Bell, PA 19422, U.S.A. **Online address:** hilty@vm.temple.edu

HIM, Chanrithy. American (born Cambodia), b. 1965. **Genres:** Autobiography/Memoirs. **Career:** Writer and public speaker. Khmer Adolescent Project, Eugene, OR; Oregon Health Sciences University, medical interpreter. **Publications:** When Broken Glass Floats: Growing up under the Khmer Rouge, 2000. **Address:** c/o Author Mail, W. W. Norton & Co. Inc., 500 5th Ave, New York, NY 10110, U.S.A. **Online address:** chanrithy@chanrithyhim.com

HIME, James. (born United States), b. 1954. **Genres:** Novels. **Career:** Tax attorney and author. Baker & Botts (law firm), Houston, TX, associate, beginning 1976, became partner, established Washington, DC office, 1985-90, and New York, NY office, 1992-95; Gerald Hines, Houston, fund manager, beginning 1995; venture capitalist. **Publications:** The Night of the Dance, 2003. **Address:** c/o Author Mail, 175 Fifth Ave., New York, NY 10010, U.S.A. **Online address:** Jim_hime@hines.com

HIMELFARB, Richard. American, b. 1963. **Genres:** Politics/Government. **Career:** Hofstra University, Hempstead, NY, assistant professor of political science, 1993-. **Publications:** Catastrophic Politics: The Rise and Fall of the Medicare Catastrophic Coverage Act of 1988, 1995. **Address:** Department of Political Science, Hofstra University, Hempstead, NY 11550, U.S.A.

HIMELSTEIN, Morgan Y. American, b. 1926. **Genres:** Literary criticism and history, Music, Theatre, Translations. **Career:** University of Rochester,

NY, instructor in English, 1948-50; Adelphi University, Garden City, NY, instructor, 1957-60, assistant professor, 1960-64, associate professor, 1964-68, Dir of Graduate Studies in English, 1965-74, professor, 1968-93, emeritus professor of English, 1993-; consultant for opera theatres, 1980-. **Publications:** Drama Was a Weapon: The Left-Wing Theatre in New York, 1929-1941, 1963, 1976. OPERA TRANSLATIONS: Offenbach: La Grande Duchesse de Gerolstein, 1977; Offenbach: La Perichole, 1982; Offenbach: Orphee aux Enfers, 1985; J. Strauss: Die Fledermaus, 1990. **Address:** 2401 Pennsylvania Ave #12B35, Philadelphia, PA 19130, U.S.A.

HIMELSTEIN, Shmuel. South African, b. 1940. **Genres:** Theology/Religion, Humor/Satire. **Career:** Jewish Day School, NYC, teacher, 1964-68, assistant principal, 1968-70; Jewish Day School, Los Angeles, CA, principal, 1970-73; Jewish Day School, Winnipeg, Canada, principal, 1973-75. Currently working as a translator, writer, and editor in Israel. **Publications:** The Jewish Primer: Questions and Answers on Jewish Faith and Culture, 1990; A Touch of Wisdom, A Touch of Wit, 1991; (ed.) Zvi Elpeleg, The Grand Mufti: Haj Amin al-Hussaini, Founder of the Palestinian National Movement, trans by D. Harvey, 1992; (trans.) Aharon Yaakov Greenberg (compiler), Torah Gems, 1992; Words of Wisdom, Words of Wit, 1993. **Address:** 22 Shear Yashuv St., 97280 Jerusalem, Israel.

HIMMEL, Richard L. American, b. 1950. **Genres:** History. **Career:** University of North Texas, Denton, university archivist, 1975-, assistant director for special collections, 1989-. **Publications:** (with R.S. La Forte) "Down the Corridor of Years": A Centennial History of the University of North Texas in Photographs, 1890-1990, 1989; (ed. with La Forte and R.E. Marcello) With Only the Will to Live: Accounts of Americans in Japanese Prison Camps, 1941-1945, 1994. Contributor to history journals. **Address:** University Library, University of North Texas, Box 5188 NT Station, Denton, TX 76203, U.S.A.

HIMMELFARB, Gertrude. American, b. 1922. **Genres:** History, Intellectual history, Social commentary. **Career:** Professor Emeritus of History, Graduate School of the City University of New York, 1988- (Distinguished Professor, 1965-88). Trustee, Woodrow Wilson Center, 1985-96; Member, Council of Scholars, Library of Congress, 1984-. Council of Scholars, American Council of Trustees and Alumni, 1995-; Council of Academic Advisors, American Enterprise Institute, 1987-; Council of Scholars, American Academy for Liberal Education, 1993-; Board of Advisors, Library of America, 1992-; Jefferson Lecturer, National Endowment for the Humanities, 1991. **Publications:** Lord Acton: A Study in Conscience and Politics, 1952; Darwin and the Darwinian Revolution, 1959; Victorian Minds, 1968; On Liberty and Liberalism: The Case of John Stuart Mill, 1974; The Idea of Poverty, 1984; Marriage and Morals among the Victorians, 1986; The New History and the Old, 1987; Poverty and Compassion, 1991; On Looking into the Abyss, 1994; The De-Moralization of Society: From Victorian Virtues to Modern Values, 1995; One Nation, Two Cultures, 1999; The Roads to Modernity: The British, French, and American Enlightenments, 2004. EDITOR: Acton, Essays on Freedom and Power, 1948; Malthus, On Population, 1960; J.S. Mill, Essays on Politics and Culture, 1962; J.S. Mill, On Liberty, 1974; de Tocqueville, Memoir on Pauperism, 1997. **Address:** Graduate School of the City University of New York, 365 5th Ave, New York, NY 10016, U.S.A.

HIMRICH, Brenda L. American, b. 1954. **Genres:** Children's non-fiction. **Career:** Certified Industrial Hygenist. **Publications:** (with S. Thornley) Electrifying Medicine: How Electricity Sparked a Medical Revolution, 1995. **Address:** 1082 Lovell, Roseville, MN 55113, U.S.A.

HINCHMAN, Lewis P(atrick). American, b. 1946. **Genres:** Humanities. **Career:** State University of New York College at Potsdam, adjunct assistant professor of philosophy, 1979-82; St. Lawrence University, adjunct assistant professor, 1980-82; Clarkson University, Potsdam, NY, adjunct assistant professor, 1981-82, assistant professor, 1982-87, associate professor, 1987-94, professor of government, 1994-. **Publications:** Hegel's Critique of the Enlightenment, 1984; (ed. with S.K. Hinchman) Hannah Arendt: Critical Essays, 1994; (ed. with Hinchman) Memory, Identity, Community: The Idea of Narrative in the Human Sciences, 1996; Hiking Tropical Australia: Queensland and Northern New South Wales, 1999. Contributor to books. Contributor of articles and reviews to political science and philosophy journals. **Address:** School of Liberal Arts, Clarkson University, Box 5750, Potsdam, NY 13699-5750, U.S.A. **Online address:** hinchman@clarkson.edu

HINCHMAN, Sandra K(uracina). American, b. 1950. **Genres:** Literary criticism and history, Travel/Exploration. **Career:** St. Lawrence University, Canton, NY, professor of government, 1975-. **Publications:** Hiking the Southwest's Canyon Country, 1990, 3rd ed., 2004. EDITOR (with L.P. Hinchman): Hannah Arendt: Critical Essays, 1994; Memory, Identity, Community: The Idea of Narrative in the Human Sciences, 1996. **Address:** Dept of Government, St. Lawrence University, Canton, NY 13617, U.S.A.

HINDE, Thomas. (Sir Thomas Willes Chitty). British, b. 1926. **Genres:** Novels, History, Travel/Exploration, Autobiography/Memoirs. **Career:** With Inland Revenue, London, 1951-53, and Shell Petroleum Co., in England, 1953-58, and Nairobi, 1958-60. **Publications:** Mr. Nicholas, 1952; Happy as Larry, 1957; For the Good of the Company, 1961; A Place Like Home, 1962; The Cage, 1962; Spain: A Personal Anthology, 1963; Ninety Double Martinis, 1963; The Day the Call Came, 1964; Games of Chance: The Interviewer and the Investigator, 1965; The Village, 1966; High, 1968; Bird, 1970; Generally a Virgin, 1972; Agent, 1974; Our Father, 1975; (with S. Hinde) On Next to Nothing, 1975; (with S.N. Chitty) The Great Donkey Walk, 1977; The Cottage Book, 1979; Sir Henry and Sons: A Memoir, 1981; Daymare, 1981; Field Guide to the Country Parson, 1982; Stately Gardens of Britain, 1983; Forests of Britain, 1985; Courtiers, 1986; Tales from the Pumproom: An Informal History of Bath, 1988; Imps of Promise: A History of the King's School, Canterbury, 1990; Looking-Glass Letters, 1991; Paths of Progress: A History of Marlborough College, 1993; Highgate School: A History, 1993; King's College School, A History, 1995; Carpenter's Children, A History of the City of London School, 1995; University of Greenwich, 1996; The Martlet and the Griffen: A History of Abingdon School, 1997. **Address:** Bow Cottage, North Lane, West Hoathly, Near East Grinstead, Sussex RH19 4QF, England. **Online address:** thomas.chitty@ukgateway.net

HINDESS, Barry. British, b. 1939. **Genres:** Politics/Government, Social sciences. **Career:** University of Liverpool, England, lecturer to professor of sociology, 1968-87; Australian National University, Canberra, professor of political science, 1987-. **Publications:** The Decline of Working Class Politics, 1971; The Use of Official Statistics in Sociology: A Critique of Positivism and Ethnomethodology, 1973; (with P. Hirst) Pre-Capitalist Modes of Production, 1975; Philosophy and Methodology in the Social Sciences, 1977; (with Hirst) Mode of Production and Social Formation, 1977; (with Hirst, T. Cutler, and A. Hussain) Marx's Capital and Capitalism Today, Vol. I, 1977, Vol. II, 1978; Parliamentary Democracy and Socialist Politics, 1983; Freedom, Equality, and the Market: Arguments in Social Policy, 1986; Politics and Class Analysis, 1987; Choice, Rationality, and Social Theory, 1988; Political Choice and Social Structure, 1989; Discourses of Power: From Hobbes to Foucault, 1996; Democracy, in press. EDITOR: (and contrib.) Sociological Theories of the Economy, 1977; (and contrib.) Reactions to the Right, 1990; (with M. Dean) Governing Australia, 1998. **Address:** Research School of Social Sciences, Australian National University, Canberra 0200, Australia. **Online address:** B.Hindess@anu.edu.au

HINDS, P(atricia) Mignon. American. **Genres:** Children's fiction, Children's non-fiction. **Career:** Writer. Mignon Communications, owner; Essence Books, director. **Publications:** Kittens Need Someone to Love, 1981; Puppies Need Someone to Love, 1981; Baby Pig, 1988; Baby Calf, 1990; A Day in the Life of Morgan Freeman, 1994; (ed.) A. Edwards, Essence: Twenty-Five Years Celebrating Black Women, 1995; What I Want to Be, 1995, as Essence: What I Want to Be, 1997; My Best Friend, 1996, as Essence: My Best Friend, 1997; Best Friends, 1997; The King's Daughters, 1997. **Address:** 333 East 55th St., New York, NY 10022, U.S.A.

HINE, Darlene Clark. American, b. 1947. **Genres:** Cultural/Ethnic topics, History. **Career:** South Carolina State College, asst professor of history and coordinator of black studies, 1972-74; Purdue University, asst professor, 1974-79, associate professor, 1979-85, professor of history, 1985-87, interim director of Africana Studies and Research Center, 1978-79, vice-provost, 1981-86; Michigan State University, John A. Hannah Professor of History, 1987-2004; Northwestern University, Board of Trustees Professor of African American Studies and professor of history, 2004-. Arizona State University, distinguished visiting professor, 1985; University of Delaware, distinguished visiting professor of women's studies, 1989-90; lecturer at colleges and universities; consultant. **Publications:** Black Victory, 1979, rev. ed., 2003; When the Truth Is Told, 1981; Black Women in White, 1989; Hine Sight, 1994; Speak Truth to Power: Black Professional Class in United States History, 1996; (with K. Thompson) A Shining Thread of Hope, 1998; (with S. Harrold and W. Hine) The African-American Odyssey (textbook), 2 vols., 2000, 2nd ed., 2002. EDITOR: Black Women in the Nursing Profession: An Anthology of Historical Sources, 1985; Black Women in the Middle West Project, 1985; (and contrib.) The State of Afro-American History, 1986; Black Women in the United States, 1619-1989, 16 vols., 1990; (with C. Carson, D. Garrow, and V. Harding) Eyes on the Prize, a History of the Civil Rights Era, 1991; (with E.B. Brown and R. Terborg-Penn) Black Women in

America, 2 vols., 1993; (with Carson) Milestones in African American History, 16 vols., 1994; (with L. Reed and W. King) "We Specialize in the Wholly Impossible": A Reader in Black Women's History, 1995; (with D.B. Gaspar) More Than Chattel: Black Women and Slavery in the Americas, 1996; (with E. Jenkins) A Question of Manhood, vol. 1, 1999, vol. 2, 2001; (with J. McLeod) Crossing Boundaries, 1999; (with E.B. Higginbotham and L. Litwack) The Harvard Guide to African-American History, 2001. Work represented in books. Contributor of articles and reviews to history, black studies, and women's studies journals. **Address:** Dept of African American Studies, 2-320 Kresge Hall, Northwestern University, Evanston, IL 60208, U.S.A. **Online address:** d-hine@northwestern.edu

HINE, Robert V. American, b. 1921. **Genres:** History. **Career:** University of California, Riverside, faculty member, 1954-90, professor emeritus of history, 1990; University of California, Irvine, recalled professor, 1990-. **Publications:** California's Utopian Colonies, 1953; Edward Kern and American Expansion, 1962, rev. ed. as In the Shadow of Fremont, 1982; (reviser) The Irvine Ranch, by Robert Glass Cleland, 1962; Bartlett's West: Drawing the Mexican Boundary, 1968; The American West: An Interpretive History, 1973, 2nd ed., 1984; Community on the American Frontier: Separate but Not Alone, 1980; California Utopianism: Contemplations of Eden, 1981; Josiah Royce: From Grass Valley to Harvard, 1992; Second Sight, 1993; (with J.M. Faragher) The American West: A New Interpretive History, 2000. EDITOR: William Andrew Spalding, Los Angeles Newspaperman: An Autobiographical Account, 1961; (with E.R. Bingham) The Frontier Experience, 1963, rev. ed. as The American Frontier: Readings and Documents, 1972; (with S. Lottinville) Soldier in the West: Letters of Theodore Talbot during His Services in California, Mexico, and Oregon, 1845-53, 1972. **Address:** 19191 Harvard Ave No. 233, Irvine, CA 92612-4671, U.S.A. **Online address:** rvhine@uci.edu

HINES, (Melvin) Barry. British, b. 1939. **Genres:** Novels, Plays/Screenplays, Novels. **Career:** Teacher with L.C.C., 1960-62, and Barnsley Education Authority, Yorks., 1963-68; Yorkshire Arts Association Fellow, University of Sheffield, 1972-74; East Midlands Arts Fellow in Creative Writing, Matlock College of Education, 1975-77; Fellow in Creative Writing, University of Wollongong, Australia, 1979. **Publications:** Billy's Last Stand, 1965; The Blinder, 1966; Continental Size Six, 1966; A Kestrel for a Knave, 1968; (with T. Garnett and Ken Loach) Kes (screenplay), 1968; First Signs, 1972; Speech Day, 1973; Gamekeeper, 1975; Two Men from Derby, 1976; The Price of Coal (two films), 1977; The Price of Coal (novel), 1979; Looks and Smiles (novel), 1981; Looks and Smiles (screenplay), 1981; Unfinished Business (novel), 1983; Threads (TV film), 1984; Shooting Stars (TV film), 1990; Born Kicking (TV film), 1992; The Heart of It (novel), 1994; Elvis Over England (novel), 1998.

HINES, Jeanne. Also writes as Rosamond Royal, Valerie Sherwood. American, b. 1922. **Genres:** Romance/Historical, Novels, Literary criticism and history, Children's fiction, Mystery/Crime/Suspense. **Career:** Writer. Taught at National Art Academy in Washington, DC; worked as magazine illustrator for ten years; worked as fashion artist, art director and free-lance commercial artist; reporter for the Judge Advocate General of the Air Force the Pentagon for six years; conference reporter for national organizations and learned societies; columnist (book critic) for the Washington Star, the Georgetowner. **Publications:** The Slashed Portrait, 1973; Tidehawks, 1974; Talons of the Hawk, 1975; Brides of Terror, 1976; Scarecrow House, 1976; The Keys to Queenscourt, 1976; The Legend of Witchwynd, 1976; The Third Wife, 1977. AS VALERIE SHERWOOD: This Loving Torment, 1977; These Golden Pleasures, 1977; This Towering Passion, 1978; Her Shining Splendor, 1980; Bold Breathless Love, 1981; Rash Reckless Love, 1981; Wild Willful Love, 1982; Rich Radiant Love, 1983; Lovely Lying Lips, 1983; Born to Love, 1984; Lovesong, 1985; Windsong, 1986; Nightsong, 1986; To Love a Rogue, 1987; Lisbon, 1988. AS ROSAMOND ROYAL: Rapture, 1979. Contributor of short stories and children's stories to magazines and anthologies, as Jeanne Hines. **Address:** c/o Severn House Publishers, Mercedes Distribution Center, Building #3 Brooklyn Navy Yard, Brooklyn, NY 11205, U.S.A.

HINES, Joanna. British, b. 1949. **Genres:** Novels, Mystery/Crime/Suspense. **Career:** Writer. **Publications:** NOVELS: Dora's Room, 1993; The Cornish Girl, 1994; The Fifth Secret, 1995; The Puritan's Wife, 1996; Autumn of Strangers, 1997; The Lost Daughter, 1999; Improvising Carla, 2001; Surface Tension, 2002; Angels of the Flood, 2004. **Address:** c/o Jennifer Kavanagh, 44 Langham St, London, England.

HINES, Robert S. American, b. 1926. **Genres:** Music. **Career:** Assistant Professor, Southern Illinois University, 1957-61; Professor, Wichita State

University, Kansas, 1961-71; Visiting Professor, University of Miami, Florida, 1971-72; University of Hawaii, Honolulu, Professor of Music, 1972-94, Chairman of Dept., 1980-84, Dean, College of Arts and Humanities, 1984-94, Emeritus Professor of Music, 1994. **Publications:** (ed.) The Composer's Point of View: Essays on 20th Century Choral Music, 1963; (ed.) The Orchestral Composer's Point of View: Essays on 20th Century Music, 1970; Singer's Manual of Latin Diction and Phonetics, 1975; (with A.R. Trubitt) Ear Training and Sight Singing: An Integrated Approach, vol. I 1979, vol. II 1980; Choral Composition: A Handbook for Composers, Arrangers, Conductors and Singers, 2001; Singer's Liturgical Latin, 2003. **Address:** 555 University Ave Apt 3500, Honolulu, HI 96826-5046, U.S.A. **Online address:** hines@hawaii.edu

HINES, Thomas S(pight). American, b. 1936. **Genres:** Architecture, Biography, History. **Career:** Professor, Dept. of History and School of the Arts and Architecture, University of California, Los Angeles, since 1968. National Endowment for the Humanities Fellow, 1978-79; Fulbright Fellow, University of Exeter, 1984-85; Guggenheim Fellow, 1987-88; American Academy of Arts and Sciences, 1994; Getty Scholar, 1996-97. **Publications:** Burnham of Chicago: Architect and Planner, 1974, 1979; (with A. Drexler) The Architecture of Richard Neutra: From International Style to California Modern, 1982; Richard Neutra and the Search for Modern Architecture: A Biography and History, 1982; (with R.J. Clark) Los Angeles Transfer: Architecture in Southern California, 1983; William Faulkner and the Tangible Past: The Architecture of Yoknapatawpha, 1996; Irving Gill and the Architecture of Reform, 2000. **Address:** Department of Architecture, University of California, Los Angeles, Perloff Hall B237A, 405 Hilgard Ave, Los Angeles, CA 90095, U.S.A. **Online address:** hines@history.ucla.edu

HINN, Benny. Israeli, b. 1952. **Genres:** Theology/Religion. **Career:** Evangelist. Preached in Toronto, ON, Canada, 1975-83; Orlando Christian Center, Orlando, FL, founder and pastor, 1983-. Host of a weekly religious television program for Trinity Broadcasting Network. **Publications:** Good Morning, Holy Spirit, 1990; The Anointing, 1992; Blood, 1993; Lord, I Need a Miracle, 1993; Welcome, Holy Spirit, 1995; Power of the Blood Study Guide, 1996; This Is Your Day for a Miracle, 1996; Biblical Road to Blessing, 1997; Promises of Healing from Every Book in the Bible, 1998; He Touched Me (autobiography), 1999; Kathryn Kuhlman, 1999. **Address:** Benny Hinn Ministries, PO Box 162000, Irving, TX 75016-2000, U.S.A.

HINNEFELD, Joyce. American, b. 1961. **Genres:** Medicine/Health, Novellas/Short stories. **Career:** Author and educator. Moravian College, Bethlehem, PA, assistant professor of English. Held teaching positions at the College of New Rochelle, Siena College, State University of New York (Albany), and Dutchess Community College. **Publications:** Everything You Need to Know When Someone You Love Has Alzheimer's Disease, 1994; Tell Me Everything, and Other Stories, 1998. Contributor to periodicals. Work included in anthologies. **Address:** English Department, Moravian College, 1200 Main St., Bethlehem, PA 18018, U.S.A.

HINOJOSA, Gilberto Miguel. American, b. 1942. **Genres:** History. **Career:** Lowell Junior High School, San Antonio, TX, history teacher, 1969-70; Laredo Junior College, TX, instructor, 1970-71; Pan American University, Edinburg, TX, assistant instructor, 1974; University of Texas at Austin, assistant instructor, 1975-76, adjunct faculty member at Mexican American Cultural Center, 1980-; University of Texas at San Antonio, instructor, 1976-79, assistant professor, 1979-84, associate professor of history, 1984-93, assistant vice-president for academic affairs, 1988-90, discipline coordinator for history in Division of Behavioral and Cultural Sciences, 1992-93; University of the Incarnate Word, San Antonio, associate professor, 1993-95, professor of history, 1995-, dean of arts and sciences, 1993-99, dean of graduate studies and research, 1999-. Juarez-Lincoln University, adjunct faculty member, 1976-79; Institute of Texan Cultures, lecturer, 1979-; Universidad Autonoma de Nuevo Leon, Fulbright professor, 1981-82. Bexar County Archives, assistant archivist, 1968-69; Yturria Papers Collection, archivist, 1986-. **Publications:** A Borderlands Town in Transition: Laredo, 1755-1870, 1983; (with M.A. Bruni) Viva la Virgen de Guadalupe! A History of Our Lady of Guadalupe Parish, 1988. EDITOR & CONTRIBUTOR: (with G.E. Poyo) Tejano Origins in Eighteenth-Century San Antonio, 1991; (co) Mexican Americans and the Catholic Church, 1900-1965, 1994. Contributor to books. Contributor of articles and reviews to periodicals. **Address:** School of Graduate Studies and Research, University of the Incarnate Word, 4301 Broadway, San Antonio, TX 78209, U.S.A. **Online address:** hinojosa@universe.uiwtx.edu

HINOJOSA, Maria (de Lourdes). American (born Mexico), b. 1961. **Genres:** Documentaries/Reportage, Criminology/True Crime. **Career:** Radio and television journalist. WKCR-FM, NYC, producer and host of radio program Nueva cancion y demas, 1980-, program director, 1983; National Public Radio, Washington, DC, production assistant, 1985-86, free-lance reporter/producer, 1988-89, New York Bureau staff reporter, 1990-96, host of weekly radio program Latino USA, 1993-96; Enfoque Nacional, KPBS, San Diego, CA, associate producer, 1986-87; CBS News, NYC, producer, 1987, researcher/producer, 1988; WNYC Radio, NYC, staff reporter, 1990; WNYC Public Television, NYC, host of talk show New York Hotline, 1990-91; WNET Channel 13, NYC, host and guest of talk show Informed Sources, 1992-; WNBC-TV, NYC, host of talk show Visiones, 1993-; CNN, NY Bureau, correspondent, 1997-. Lecturer at colleges and universities; public speaker on Latino, women's, and multicultural issues. **Publications:** Crews: Gang Members Talk to Maria Hinojosa, 1995; Raising Raul: Adventures Raising Myself and My Son, 1999. **Address:** c/o CNN, 5 Penn Plaza, 20th Fl, New York, NY 10001-1878, U.S.A.

HINRICHS, Ernest H(enry). American, b. 1922. **Genres:** Military/Defense/Arms control. **Career:** Private practice of dentistry; now retired. **Publications:** Listening In, 1996. Author of article on Eagles Mere and Sones Lumber Railroads. Contributor to dental journals. **Address:** 270 Ridgecrest Circle #311, Lewisburg, PA 17837, U.S.A.

HINSON, E. Glenn. American, b. 1931. **Genres:** Theology/Religion. **Career:** Baptist Theological Seminary at Richmond, professor of spirituality and John Loftis Professor of church history; Professor of Church History, Southern Baptist Theological Seminary, Louisville, Kentucky, 1962-92 (Instructor in New Testament, 1959-60, and in Church History, 1960-62). Professor of Religion, Wake Forest University, Winston-Salem, North Carolina, 1982-84. Pastor, First Baptist Church, Eminence, Indiana, 1957-59. **Publications:** The Church: Design for Survival, 1967; (co-author) Glossolalia, 1967; Seekers After Mature Faith, 1968; I and II Timothy and Titus, 1971; A Serious Call to a Contemplative Life Style, 1974, rev. 1993; Soul Liberty, 1975; Jesus Christ, 1977; The Integrity of the Church, 1978; The Reaffirmation of Prayer, 1979; A History of Baptists in Arkansas, 1980; The Evangelization of the Roman Empire, 1981; The Priesthood of Believers, 1982; Are Southern Baptists Evangelicals?, 1983; Understandings of the Church, 1986; Religious Liberty, 1991; Vozes do Christiano Primitivo, 1993; The Church Triumphant: A History of Christianity up to 1300, 1995; The Early Church, 1996; Love at the Heart of Things: A Biography of Douglas V. Steele, 1998; The Spiritual Formation of Pastors, 1999. EDITOR: The Early Church Fathers, 1975; Doubleday Devotional Classics, 3 vols., 1978; Spirituality in Ecumenical Perceptive, 1993. **Address:** Baptist Theological Seminary, 651 Upland Dr., Louisville, KY 40206, U.S.A.

HINTON, Michael. British, b. 1927. **Genres:** Self help, Ethics, Philosophy, Education, Theology/Religion, History. **Career:** Ordained minister of Church of England, 1983; assistant teacher at schools in Reading and Lancaster, England, 1949-59; headmaster at Dover Grammar School for Boys in Dover, England, 1960-68, at Sevenoaks School, 1968-70, and at Broadoak School in Weston-super-Mare, England, 1971-84; Parish of Shepherdswell, Kent, England, minister, 1985-95. **Publications:** A History of the Town of Reading, 1954; Ethics, 1974; Authority, 1974; Comprehensive Schools: A Christian's View, 1979; The Anglican Parochial Clergy: A Celebration, 1994. **Address:** 212 The Gateway, Dover, Kent CT16 1LL, England. **Online address:** michael@hintonm.demon.co.uk

HINTON, S(usan) E(loise). American, b. 1948. **Genres:** Children's fiction. **Publications:** The Outsiders, 1967; That Was Then, This Is Now, 1971; Rumble Fish, 1975, screenplay, 1983; Tex, 1979; Taming the Star Runner, 1988; Big David, Little David, 1994; The Puppy Sister, 1995; Hawkes Harbor (for adults), 2004. **Address:** c/o Delacorte Press, 1540 Broadway, New York, NY 10036-4039, U.S.A. **Online address:** sehinton@sehinton.com; www.sehinton.com

HIRABAYASHI, Lane Ryo. American, b. 1952. **Genres:** Cultural/Ethnic topics, Anthropology/Ethnology. **Career:** University of California, Los Angeles, lecturer in Asian American studies, 1981-82; University of California, Santa Barbara, lecturer in Asian American studies, 1982; California State University, Long Beach, lecturer in Asian American studies, 1982; San Francisco State University, San Francisco, CA, lecturer, 1983, associate professor, 1984-88, professor of Asian American studies, 1988-91; University of Colorado, Boulder, associate professor of Asian American studies and anthropology, 1991-, ethnic studies, 1996-, coordinator of Asian American studies, 1992-. Center for Japanese American Studies, San Francisco, CA, member, 1975-; Japanese Community Youth Council, San Francisco, member of board of directors, 1984-91; performed as a musician with Asian American Theater Company, San Francisco, and East-West Play-

ers, Los Angeles; consultant to Japanese American National Museum and National Japanese American Historical Society. **Publications:** (with G. Tanaka) The Early Gardena Valley and the Issei (monograph), 1986; The Delectable Berry: Japanese American Contributions to the Development of the Strawberry Industry on the West Coast (monograph), 1989; Cultural Capital: Mountain Zapotec Regional Associations in Mexico City, 1993. EDITOR: (and author of introduction) Inside an American Concentration Camp: Japanese American Resistance in Poston, 1995; (with T. Altamirano and contrib.) Migrants, Regional Identities, and Latin American Cities, 1996. Contributor to books and academic journals. **Address:** Department of Ethnic Studies, Ketchum 30, University of Colorado, Campus Box 339, Boulder, CO 80309, U.S.A.

HIRO, Dilip. Indian. **Genres:** Novels, Plays/Screenplays, Poetry, History, International relations/Current affairs, Race relations. **Career:** Writer. **Publications:** A Triangular View (novel), 1969; Black British, White British, 1971; To Anchor a Cloud (play), 1972; The Untouchables of India, 1975; Inside India Today, 1976; Apply, Apply, No Reply, and A Clean Break (plays), 1978; Interior, Exchange, Exterior (poetry), 1980; Inside the Middle East, 1982; Iran under the Ayatollahs, 1985; Three Plays, 1987; Iran: The Revolution Within, 1988; Islamic Fundamentalism, 1988; The Longest War: The Iran-Iraq Military Conflict, 1989; Islamic Fundamentalism/Holy Wars: The Rise of Islamic Fundamentalism, 1988; Black British, White British, 1991; Desert Shield to Desert Storm, 1992; Lebanon, Fire and Embers, 1993; Between Marx and Muhammad, 1994; Dictionary of the Middle East, 1996; The Middle East, 1996; Sharing the Promised Land, 1996; Neighbors, not Friends: Iraq and Iran after the Gulf Wars, 2001; War without End, 2002; India: The Rough Guide Chronicle, 2020; Iraq: In the Eye of the Storm, 2002; The Essential Middle East, 2003; Secrets and Lies: Operation "Iraqi Freedom": and After, 2003. **Address:** 31 Waldegrave Rd, Ealing, London W5 3HT, England.

HIRONS, Montague (John David). British, b. 1916. **Genres:** Biology, Botany, Natural history, Zoology. **Career:** Sr. Lecturer in Biology and Environmental Studies, Berkshire College of Education, Woodley, Reading, since 1968. **Publications:** (with G. A. Perry) Flowers of Common Trees, 1965; (with G. A. Perry) Fruits of Common Trees, 1965; (with G. A. Perry) Spring Flowers of Wood and Copses, 1965; (with G. A. Perry) Spring Flowers of Hedgerow and Roadside, 1965; (with G. A. Perry) Common Wild Flowers and Fruits, 1965; Insect Life of Farm and Garden, 1966; Progressive Biology: Books 1-3, 1967-70; (with A. Darlington) Pocket Encyclopedia of Plant Galls, 1968; (with G. J. M. Hirons) Farne Islands: The Problems of Soil Erosion, vol. 4, 1972; Biological Teaching Aids for National Curriculum Key Stage Level 4, Set KS4A: The Plant Kingdom, Set KS4B: The Animal Kingdom, 1994; The Flora of the Farne Islands, 1994. **Address:** Betula House, Barford Rd., Bloxham, Banbury, Oxon. OX15 4EZ, England.

HIRSCH, E(ric) D(onald), Jr. American, b. 1928. **Genres:** Education, Literary criticism and history. **Career:** University Professor of Education and Humanities, University of Virginia, Charlottesville, 1994- (Professor, 1966-73, Kenan Professor of English, 1973-94, Chairman of Dept., 1968-71, 1981-83). Served in the U.S. Navy, 1950-52; Instructor in English, 1956-60, Assistant Professor, 1960-63, and Associate Professor, 1963-66, Yale University, New Haven, Conn. President, Core Knowledge Foundation, since 1986. **Publications:** Wordsworth and Schelling: A Typological Study of Romanticism, 1960, 1971; Innocence and Experience; an Introduction to Blake, 1964; Validity in Interpretation, 1966; The Aims of Interpretation, 1976; The Philosophy of Composition, 1977; Cultural Literacy: What Every American Needs to Know, 1987; Dictionary of Cultural Literacy, 1988; A First Dictionary of Cultural Literacy, 1989, 2nd ed., 1996; The Core Knowledge Series, 7 book series, 1991-96; The Schools We Need and Why We Don't Have Them, 1996; Books to Build On: A Grade by Grade Resource for Parents and Teachers, 1996. **Address:** 2006 Pine Top Rd, Charlottesville, VA 22903, U.S.A.

HIRSCH, Edward. American, b. 1950. **Genres:** Poetry. **Career:** Wayne State University, Detroit, MI, assistant professor, 1979-82, associate professor of English, 1982-85; University of Houston, TX, professor of English, 1985-2002; John Simon Guggenheim Memorial Foundation, president, 2003-. Watson fellow, 1972-73; American Council of Learned Socs., fellow, 1981; National Endowment for the Arts fellow, 1982; Guggenheim fellow, 1985-86; MacArthur fellow, 1998. Recipient: Ingrim Merrill Award, 1978-79; Lavan Younger Poets Award, 1983; National Book Critics Circle Award, 1987; Rome Fellowship in Literature, 1988; Lyndhurst Prize, 1994-96; American Academy of Arts and Letters, Award in Literature, 1998. **Publications:** For the Sleepwalkers, 1981; Wild Gratitude, 1986; The Night Parade, 1989; Earthly Measures, 1994; On Love, 1998; How to Read a Poem and Fall in

Love with Poetry, 1999; Responsive Reading, 1999; The Demon and the Angel, 2002; Lay Back the Darkness, 2003. **Address:** John Simon Guggenheim Memorial Foundation, 90 Park Ave, New York, NY 10016, U.S.A. **Online address:** eh@gf.org

HIRSCH, James (S.). American, b. 1962. **Genres:** Documentaries/Reportage. **Career:** New York Times, news staff/reporter, 1986-89; Wall Street Journal, reporter, 1989-98. **Publications:** Hurricane: The Miraculous Journey of Rubin Carter, 2000; Riot and Remembrance: The Tulsa Race War and Its Legacy, 2002. **Address:** 17 Hollow Ridge Rd., Needham, MA 02494, U.S.A. **Online address:** jshirsch@mediaone.net

HIRSCH, Pam. British, b. 1947. **Genres:** Literary criticism and history, Biography. **Career:** Literature and history teacher in Cumbria state schools, 1972-78; Cambridgeshire College of Arts and Technology, lecturer, 1982-89; nursery school principal, 1992; Homerton College, lecturer, senior research associate, and research mentor, 1992; University of Cambridge, lecturer in the Education Faculty, 2002, graduate tutor and fellow of Newnham College. **Publications:** Barbara Leigh Smith Bodichon: Feminist, Artist and Rebel, 1998. CO-EDITOR: Practical Visionaries: Women, Education and Social Progress, 1790-1930, 2000; Teacher Training at Cambridge: The Initiatives of Oscar Browning and Elizabeth Hughes, 2003. Contributor of articles on women and their role in literature to periodicals. Contributor to books. **Address:** Newnham College, Cambridge CB3 9DF, England. **Online address:** ph211@cam.ac.uk

HIRSCH, Seev. Israeli (born Germany), b. 1931. **Genres:** Business/Trade/Industry, Economics. **Career:** Tel-Aviv University, joined faculty, 1965, Head, Dept. of Accounting, 1966-68, Dean, Leon Recanati Graduate School of Business Administration, 1970-73, Associate Professor, 1971-78, Sr. Lecturer, 1976-71, Professor, 1978-81, Jaffee Professor, 1981-95, Professor Emeritus, 1995, College of Management, MBA program, director, 1995-. **Publications:** Location of Industry and International Competitiveness, 1967; Identification and Exploitation of the Export Potential of Industrial Firms in Israel, 1969; The Export Performance of Six Manufacturing Industries: A Comparative Study of Denmark, Holland and Israel, 1971; (with R.L. Ankum, H.C.C. Dekker, M.F. Koster and O. Wiberg) Profiles of Six Export Oriented Industries A & B, 1973; Rich Man's, Poor Man's, and Every Man's Goods, 1977; (with R. Arad and A. Tovias) The Economics of Peacemaking: Focus on the Egyptian-Israeli Situation, 1983; (co-ed.) Economic Cooperation and Middle East Peace, 1989; (co-ed.) Outsiders Response to European Integration, 1996. **Address:** Leon Recanati Graduate School of Business Admin, Tel Aviv University, Tel Aviv, Israel. **Online address:** hirsch@post.tau.ac.il

HIRSCH, Werner Z. American (born Germany), b. 1920. **Genres:** Economics, Law, Regional/Urban planning. **Career:** University of California, Los Angeles, Professor of Economics, 1963-, Director, Institute of Government and Public Affairs, 1963-73. Consultant, Rand Corp., 1958-. Member, Board of Dirs., California Council for Environmental and Economic Balance, 1973-. Fiscal Affairs Officer, U.N., 1951-52; Economist, Brookings Institution, Washington, DC, 1952-53; Assistant Research Director, St. Louis Metropolitan Survey, 1956-57; Economist, Resources for the Future Inc., Washington, DC, 1958-59. **Publications:** Introduction to Modern Statistics, 1957; (with J.L. Kunen, L.J. Duhl and R. Park) Universities and Foundations Search for Relevance, 1968; (with E.W. Segelhorst and M.J. Marcus) Spillover on Public Education Costs and Benefits, 2nd ed., 1969; The Economics of State and Local Government, 1970; (with S. Sonenblum) Selecting Regional Information for Government Planning and Decision Making, 1970; (with others) Fiscal Pressures on the Central City, 1971; (with M.J. Marcus and R.M. Gay) Program Budgeting for Primary and Secondary Public Education, 1972; Financing Public First-Level and Second-Level Education in the U.S., 1973; Urban Economic Analysis, 1973; (with S. Sonenblum and R. Teeples) Local Government Program Budgeting: Theory and Practice, 1974; Recent Experience with National Planning in the United Kingdom, 1977; (with R. Ferber) Social Experimentation and Economic Policy, 1982; Urban Economics, 1984; (with A.M. Rufolo) Public Finance and Expenditures under Federalism, 1990; Privatizing Government Services, 1991; (with L. Weber) Challenges Facing Higher Education at the Millennium, 1999; Governance in Higher Education, 2001; As the Walls of Academia Are Tumbling Down, 2002. EDITOR: (and contrib.) Urban Life and Form, 1963; Elements of Regional Accounts, 1964; (with R. Baisden, and contrib.) California's Future Economic Growth, 1965; (and contrib.) Regional Accounts for Policy Decisions, 1966; (and contrib.) Inventing Education for the Future, 1967; (with S. Hale) Agenda for the Los Angeles Area in 1970, 1969; (and contrib.) Los Angeles: Viability and Prospects for Metropolitan Leadership, 1971; (with S. Sonenblum, and contrib.) Governing Urban America in the 1970s, 1973.

HIRSCHFELD, Fritz. American (born Germany), b. 1924. **Genres:** History, Education. **Career:** Lago Oil and Transport Co., junior engineer for oil refineries in Aruba, the Netherlands, West Indies, 1948-50; Consulting Engineer, St. Joseph, MI, associate editor and European editor, 1951-54; European Engineering News Report, Zurich, Switzerland, publisher and editor, 1955-57; independent consulting engineer in London, Paris, Zurich, and Frankfurt, 1958-86; John Hancock Papers, Williamsburg, VA, editor. **Publications:** George Washington and Slavery: A Documentary Portrayal, 1997; George Washington and the Jews, 1999; The John Hancock Papers, series I, vol. 1: The Early Years (1736/7-1764), 2000; George Washington and the Native Americans, 2002. **Address:** John Hancock Papers, PO Box 1816, Williamsburg, VA 23187-1816, U.S.A.

HIRSCHFELD, Lawrence A. American, b. 1947. **Genres:** Anthropology/Ethnology, Psychology. **Career:** College de France, Paris, Laboratoire d'Anthropologie Sociale, associate member, 1979-83; University of Wisconsin, Madison, assistant scientist in anthropology, 1983-89, research associate in psychology, 1984-85, fellow of Eugene Havens Center for the Study of Social Structure and Social Change, 1985-86; University of Michigan, Ann Arbor, assistant professor, 1989-96, associate professor of anthropology and psychology, 1996-, faculty associate at Research Center for Group Dynamics, Institute for Social Research, 1992-, co-director of Graduate Program in Culture and Cognition, 1993-. Centre Nationale de la Recherche Scientifique, researcher at Laboratoire de Psycho-Biologie de l'Enfant, 1987-88, head of research at Centre de Recherche en Epistemologie Appliquee, Groupe de Recherche sur la Cognition, Ecole Polytechnique, 1988-89. U.S. Census Bureau, member of expert panel for Census 2000. Presenter, panel member, discussion group member, and organizer of symposia, meetings, conferences, and other academic gatherings. **Publications:** (ed. with S. Gelman and contrib) Mapping the Mind: Domain Specificity in Cognition and Culture, 1994; Race in the Making: Cognition, Culture, and the Child's Construction of Human Kinds, 1996. Contributor to books. Contributor of articles and reviews to professional journals. **Address:** Departments of Anthropology and Psychology, 1020 LS&A, University of Michigan, Ann Arbor, MI 48109, U.S.A. **Online address:** lhirsch@umich.edu

HIRSCHFELD, Yizhar. Israeli, b. 1950. **Genres:** Archaeology/Antiquities. **Career:** Hebrew University of Jerusalem, Lecturer at Institute of Archaeology; director of excavations for the Roman Bath of Hammat Gader, 1978-82, the site of Ramat Hanadiv, 1984-94, and the site of Tiberias, 1989-. **Publications:** The Survey of Israel: Herodium Map, 1985; The Judean Desert Monasteries in the Byzantine Period, 1992; Palestinian Dwelling Houses, 1994. **Address:** Institute of Archaeology, Hebrew University, Mt. Scopus, Jerusalem, Israel.

HIRSCHFELDER, Arlene B. American, b. 1943. **Genres:** Children's non-fiction, Cultural/Ethnic topics, Young adult non-fiction, Bibliography. **Career:** Association on American Indian Affairs, NYC, scholarship director and education consultant, 1969-91; New School for Social Research, NYC, faculty member, 1984-96. **Publications:** American Indian and Eskimo Authors: A Comprehensive Bibliography, 1973; This Land Is Ours: A Native American Anthology and Teacher's Guide, 1978; Annotated Bibliography of the Literature on American Indians Published in State Historical Society Publications: New England and Middle Atlantic States, 1982; American Indian Stereotypes in the World of Children: A Reader and Bibliography, 1982, rev. ed. (with P.F. Molin and Y. Wakim), 1999; (with M.G. Byler and M. Dorris) Guide to Research on North American Indians, 1983; American Indian Desk Calendar, 1985; Happily May I Walk: American Indians and Alaska Natives Today, 1986; (with P.F. Molin) Encyclopedia of Native American Religions, 1992, rev. ed., 1999; (ed. with B.R. Singer) Rising Voices: Writings of Young Native Americans, 1992; (with M.K. de Montano) Native American Almanac, 1993; Arts and Craftspeople, 1994; Native Heritage, 1995; Native Americans: A History in Photographs, 2000; Photo Odyssey: Solomon Carvalho's Remarkable Western Adventure, 2000; Native Americans Today: Resources and Activities for Educators, Grades 4-8, 2000; (with Y. Dennis) Children of Native America Today, 2003. Contributor to journals and periodicals. **Address:** 170 Copley Ave, Teaneck, NJ 07666-4100, U.S.A. **Online address:** arlene0417@aol.com

HIRSCHHORN, Clive. South African, b. 1940. **Genres:** Film, Biography. **Career:** Applause Magazine, editor; LBC Radio, theatre critic, ABC-TV, story editor, 1963-64; Daily Mail, London, pop columnist, 1964-65; Sunday Express London, drama critic, 1966-96, film critic, 1966-69. **Publications:** Gene Kelly, 1974, 1984; The Films of James Mason, 1975; The Warner Bros. Story, 1979; The Hollywood Musical, 1981; The Universal Story, 1983, rev. ed., 2000; The Columbia Story, 1989, rev. ed., 1999. **Address:** 42D South Audley St, Mayfair, London W1, England. **Online address:** cliveh@cwcom.net

HIRSCHMAN, Jack. American, b. 1933. **Genres:** Poetry, Translations. **Career:** Painter and collage-maker. Instructor, Dartmouth College, Hanover, New Hampshire, 1959-61; Assistant Professor, University of California, Los Angeles, 1961-66. **Publications:** Fragments, 1952; A Correspondence of Americans, 1960; Two, 1963; Interchange, 1964; Kline Sky, 1965; (ed.) Artaud Anthology, 1965; Yod, 1966; London Seen Directly, 1967; Wasn't It Like This in the Woodcut, 1967; William Blake, 1967; (with A. Benveniste) A Word in Your Season, 1967; Ltd. Interchangeable in Eternity: Poems of Jackruthdavidcelia Hirschman, 1967; Jerusalem: A Three Part Poem, 1968; Aleph, Benoni and Zaddik, 1968; Jerusalem, Ltd., 1968; Shekinah, 1969; Broadside Golem, 1969; Black Alephs: Poems 1960-68, 1969; NHR, 1970; Scintilla, 1970; Soledeth, 1971; DT, 1971; The Burning of Los Angeles, 1971; HNYC, 1971; Les Vidanges, 1972; The R of the Ari's Raziel, 1972; Adamnan, 1972; Aur Sea, 1973; Cantillations, 1973; Djackson, 1974; Cockroach Street, 1975; The Cool Boyetz Cycle, 1975; Kashtaninyah Segodnyah, 1976; Lyripol, 1976; The Arcanes of Le Comte de St. Germain, 1977; The Jonestown Arcane, 1979; The Cagliostro Arcane, 1981; The David Arcane, 1982; Kallatumba, 1984; The Necessary Is, 1984; The Bottom Line, 1988; The Satin Arcane, 1991; Endless Threshold, 1992; The Back of a Spoon, 1992; The Xibalba Arcane, 1994. TRANSLATOR: (with V. Erlich) Electric Iron, by V. Mayakovsky, 1970; Love Is a Tree, by A. Artaud, 1972; A Rainbow for the Christian West, by R. Depestre, 1972; The Exiled Angel, by L. Pasamanik, 1973; Igitur, by S. Mallarme, 1973; Wail for the Arab Beggars of the Casbah, by A Djafer, 1973; Yossiph Shyryn, by S. Calí, 1980; Jabixshak, 1982; Clandestine Poems, by Roque Dalton, 1985; Slingshot by P. Laraque, 1989; In Memory of the Children, by D. Lefteria, 1994; Seven Poems by R. Scotellaro, 1994; (with A. Beske) Light-Force, by P. Celan, 1996. **Address:** P. O. Box 26517, San Francisco, CA 94126, U.S.A.

HIRSHFELD, Alan. American, b. 1951. **Genres:** Astronomy. **Career:** University of Massachusetts at Dartmouth, North Dartmouth, professor of physics, 1978-. **Publications:** (ed. with R.W. Sinnott) Sky Catalogue 2000.0, Vol. I: Stars to Magnitude 8.0, 1982, 2nd ed., 1991, Vol. II: Double Stars, Variable Stars and Nonstellar Objects, 1985; Parallax, 2001. **Address:** Department of Physics, University of Massachusetts at Dartmouth, 285 Old Westport Rd, North Dartmouth, MA 02747-2300, U.S.A. **Online address:** ahirshfeld@umassd.edu

HIRSHFIELD, Jane. American, b. 1953. **Genres:** Poetry, Literary criticism and history. **Career:** Bennington College MFA Writing Seminars, core faculty, 1999-. University of San Francisco, lecturer in creative writing, 1991-98; University of California, Berkeley, visiting associate professor, 1995. Member of the faculties of writers conferences and in-school programs. Freelance editor, 1983-; translator. **Publications:** POETRY: Alaya, 1982; Of Gravity & Angels, 1988; The October Palace, 1994; The Lives of the Heart, 1997; Given Sugar, Given Salt, 2001. OTHER: (trans with M. Aratani) The Ink Dark Moon: Poems by Ono no Komachi and Izumi Shikibu, 1988, rev. ed, 1990; (ed. and trans) Women in Praise of the Sacred: 43 Centuries of Spiritual Poetry by Women, 1994; Nine Gates: Essays on Poetry, 1997; (trans. with R. Bly) Mirabai: Ecstatic Poems, 2004. Contributor of poems and translations to anthologies. Contributor to periodicals. **Address:** c/o Michael Katz, 367 Molino Ave, Mill Valley, CA 94941, U.S.A.

HIRSHMAN, Linda R. American, b. 1944. **Genres:** Women's studies and issues. **Career:** Brandeis University, Waltham, MA, member of national board for women's studies, 1995-, Allen/Berenson Distinguished Visiting Professor of Philosophy and Women's Studies, 1998-. Quinnipiac College, distinguished professional scholar at law school, 1998-; University of Iowa, Mason Ladd Distinguished Visitor at law school, 1999. Arizona Foundation for Women, member of board of directors, 1995-. **Publications:** (with J. Larson) Hard Bargains: The Politics of Sex, 1998; The Woman's Guide to Law School, 1999. **Address:** 5813 E Ocutillo, Cave Creek, AZ 85331, U.S.A. **Online address:** LRHirshman@cs.com

HIRSH-PASEK, Kathy. American, b. 1953. **Genres:** Language/Linguistics. **Career:** Sperry Univac Inc., Blue Bell, PA, consultant research psychologist on software ease of use, 1980-84; Rutgers University, Medical College of New Jersey, Piscataway (now University of Medicine and Dentistry of New Jersey, Newark), assistant professor of psychiatry, 1981-85; Haverford College, Haverford, PA, assistant professor of psychology and director of Infant Langnuage and Perception Laboratory, 1984-87; Temple University, Philadelphia, PA, assistant professor, 1987-90, associate professor, 1990-97, professor of psychology, 1997-, director of Infant Language and Perception Laboratory, 1987-. Swarthmore College, assistant professor and director of Infant Speech Perception Laboratory, 1982-84; speaker at colleges and universities. **Publications:** (ed. with L. Rescorla and M. Hyson, and contrib) Academic Instruction in Early Childhood: Challenge or Pressure?, 1991;

(with Golinkoff) The Origins of Grammar: Evidence from Comprehension, 1996. MUSIC ALBUMS FOR CHILDREN: Jumpin' in a Puddle, 1987; Staying Up, 1988; Hugs and Kisses, 1990; Around the World, 1991; Making a Difference for K.I.D.S., 1993; creator (and co-producer) of television series Captain Tikkun. Contributor of articles and reviews to books and periodicals. **Address:** Department of Psychology, Temple University, Philadelphia, PA 19122, U.S.A. **Online address:** khirshpa@nimbus.ocis.temple.edu

HISCHAK, Thomas S. American, b. 1951. **Genres:** Plays/Screenplays, Theatre. **Career:** Point Park College, Pittsburgh, PA, instructor, 1978-82; Delaware Theatre Company, Wilmington, worked in audience development, 1982-83; State University of New York College at Cortland, professor of performing arts, 1983-. **Publications:** Word Crazy: Broadway Lyricists from Cohan to Sondheim, 1991; Stage It with Music: An Encyclopedic Guide to the American Musical Theatre, 1993; The American Musical Theatre Song Encyclopedia, 1995; The Theatregoer's Almanac: A Collection of Lists, People, History, and Commentary on the American Theatre, 1997; The American Musical Film Song Encyclopedia, 1999; The Tin Pan Alley Song Encyclopedia, 2002; Boy Loses Girl: Broadway's Librettists, 2002; Enter the Players, 2003; Oxford Companion to American Theatre, 2004. Contributor to books. PLAYS: The Dolls of Poplar House, 1979; Murder by Membership Only, 1980; A Christmas Carol, 1981; The Gift of the Magi, 1984; Murder in Bloom, 1985; A New Style for Murder, 1992; Murder on Reserve, 1994; Murder by the Book, 1995; Little Women, 1995; Cold War Comedy, 1996; Tiny Tim's Christmas, 1997; Rutherford Wolf, 1997; The Phony Physician, 1997; Willabella Witch's Last Spell, 1999; five one-act plays. **Address:** Performing Arts Department, State University of New York College at Cortland, Cortland, NY 13045, U.S.A. **Online address:** hischakt@cortland.edu

HISCOE, Helen B. American, b. 1919. **Genres:** Sociology, Natural history. **Career:** Professor, Department of Natural Science, Michigan State University 1968. **Publications:** Appalachian Passage, 1992. Contributor to scientific journals and professional magazines. **Address:** 1817 Walnut Heights Dr., East Lansing, MI 48823-2945, U.S.A.

HISE, Greg. American, b. 1953. **Genres:** Urban studies. **Career:** University of California-Berkeley, instructor, 1988-90; University of Southern California, assistant professor, 1992-98, associate professor, 1998-. University of California-Los Angeles, visiting scholar, 1996-97; Caltech, visiting associate professor, 1997-98. Rutgers Center for Historical Analysis, senior fellow, 2001-02. **Publications:** (ed., with M.J. Dear and H.E. Schockman) Rethinking Los Angeles, 1996; Magnetic Los Angeles: Planning the Twentieth-Century Metropolis, 1999; (with W. Deverell) Eden by Design: The 1930 Olmsted-Bartholomew Plan for the Los Angeles Region, 2000. **Address:** University of Southern California, School of Policy Planning and Development, 315 Lewis Hall, Los Angeles, CA 90089, U.S.A. **Online address:** hise@usc.edu

HITCHINS, Keith. American, b. 1931. **Genres:** History. **Career:** Wake Forest University, Winston-Salem, NC, instructor in history, 1958-60, 1962-64, assistant professor, 1964-65; Rice University, Houston, TX, assistant professor, 1966-67; University of Illinois at Urbana-Champaign, Urbana, associate professor, 1967-69, professor of history, 1969-. Journal of Kurdish Studies, editor, 1995-. **Publications:** The Rumanian National Movement in Transylvania, 1780-1849, 1969; Rumanian Studies, 1970, Vol II, 1971-72, Vol III, 1973-75, Vol IV, 1976-79, Vol V, 1980-86; The Nationality Problem in Austria-Hungary, 1974; Orthodoxy and Nationality: Andreiu Saguna and the Rumanians of Transylvania, 1846-1873, 1977; Hungarica 1961-1974, 1981; Studies on Romanian National Consciousness, 1983; The Idea of Nation: The Romanians of Transylvania, 1691-1849, 1985; (assoc. ed.) Great Historians from Antiquity to 1800, 1989; (assoc. ed.) Great Historians of the Modern Age, 1991; Biserica Ortodoxa Romana in secolul XVIII, 1991; Constiinta nationala si actiune politica la Romanii din Transilvania, Vol I (1700-1868), 1987, Vol II (1868-1918), 1992; Rumania: 1866-1947, 1994; The Romanians 1774-1866, 1996; Mit si realitate in istoriografia romaneasca, 1997; A Nation Discovered: Romanian Intellectuals in Transylvania and the Idea of Nation, 1700-1848, 1999, 1999; A Nation Affirmed: The Romanian National Movement in Transylvania, 1860-1914, 1999; Romanian-American Relations: Diplomatic and Consular Documents, 1859-1901, 2001; The Identity of Romania, 2003. Contributor to periodicals. **Address:** Dept of History, 309 Gregory Hall, University of Illinois at Urbana-Champaign, 810 S Wright St, Urbana, IL 61801, U.S.A.

HITTINGER, (F.) Russell. American, b. 1949. **Genres:** Philosophy. **Career:** Fordham University, Bronx, NY, assistant professor of philosophy, 1987-91; Catholic University of America, Washington, DC, associate professor of philosophy, 1991-96; University of Tulsa, research professor of law, 1996-,

Warren Professor of Catholic Studies, 1996-, chair of Dept of Philosophy and Religion, 2002-. Pace University, adjunct professor, 1988-89; American Enterprise Institute for Public Policy Research, research fellow, 1991-96, adjunct scholar, 1996-; University of Notre Dame, senior research fellow, 2000-01; visiting professor at universities in the US and Italy; lecturer at colleges and universities. **Publications:** (ed.) Linking the Human Life Issues, 1986; A Critique of the New Natural Law Theory, 1987; The First Grace, 1993. Work represented in anthologies. Contributor to scholarly journals. **Address:** Dept of Philosophy and Religion, University of Tulsa, 600 S College Ave, Tulsa, OK 74104-3189, U.S.A.

HJORTSBERG, William. American, b. 1941. **Genres:** Novels, Novellas/Short stories, Plays/Screenplays. **Career:** Writer. **Publications:** Alp, 1969; Gray Matters, 1971; Symbiography (novella), 1973; Toro! Toro! Toro!, 1974; Thunder & Lightning (screenplay) 1977; Falling Angel, 1978; Tales & Fables (short stories), 1985; Legend (screenplay), 1986; Nevermore, 1994; Odd Corners, 2004. **Address:** c/o The Harold Matson Co, 276 Fifth Ave Ste 713, New York, NY 10001, U.S.A.

HO, Minfong. Singaporean (born Myanmar), b. 1951. **Genres:** Young adult fiction, Children's fiction, Novellas/Short stories. **Career:** Starlight Plywood Factory, Singapore, manual worker, 1973; Straits Times, Singapore, journalist, 1973-75; Chiengmai University, Thailand, lecturer in English, 1975-76; trade union representative, 1973-75; Cornell University, teaching assistant in English literature, 1978-80; Catholic Relief Services, nutritionist and relief worker, Thai-Cambodian border, 1980; Singapore University, writer-in-residence, 1983; presenter of writing workshops in Switzerland, Indonesia, Thailand, Malaysia, and New York, 1990-96;. **Publications:** FOR YOUNG ADULTS. FICTION: Sing to the Dawn, 1975; Rice without Rain, 1986; The Clay Marble, 1991. OTHER: (with S. Clark) Sing to the Dawn (libretto), 1996. FOR CHILDREN: (trans. and comp.) Maples in the Mist: Children's Poems from the Tang Dynasty, 1995; (reteller with S. Ros) Two Brothers, 1995; Hush!: A Thai Lullaby (poetry), 1996; (reteller with S. Ros) Brother Rabbit: A Cambodian Tale, 1997. FOR ADULTS: Tanjong Rhu and Other Stories, 1986. **Address:** 893 Cayuga Heights Road, Ithaca, NY 14850, U.S.A. **Online address:** minfong@aol.com

HOAG, Tami. American, b. 1959. **Genres:** Mystery/Crime/Suspense. **Career:** Writer, 1987-. **Publications:** ROMANCE NOVELS: McKnight in Shining Armor, 1988; The Trouble with J.J., 1988; Straight from the Heart, 1989; Mismatch, 1989; Man of Her Dreams, 1989; Rumor Has It, 1989; Magic, 1990; Tempestuous, 1990; The Rainbow Chasers: Heart of Gold, 1990; The Rainbow Chasers: Keeping Company, 1990; The Rainbow Chasers: Reilly's Return, 1990; Heart of Dixie, 1991; Sarah's Sin, 1991; Magic, 1991; The Restless Heart, 1991; Still Waters, 1992; The Last White Knight, 1992; Taken by Storm, 1992; Lucky's Lady, 1992; Still Waters, 1992; Lucky's Lady, 1992; Cry Wolf, 1993; Dark Paradise, 1994. MYSTERY NOVELS: Night Sins, 1995; Guilty as Sin, 1996; A Thin Dark Line, 1997; Ashes to Ashes, 1999; Dark Horse, 2002. **Address:** Andrea Cirillo, Jane Rotrosen Agency, 318 East 51st St., New York, NY 10022, U.S.A.

HOAGLAND, Edward. American, b. 1932. **Genres:** Novels, Novellas/Short stories, Travel/Exploration, Autobiography/Memoirs, Essays. **Career:** Faculty member: New School for Social Research, NYC, 1963-64; Rutgers University, New Brunswick, NJ, 1966; Sarah Lawrence College, Bronxville, NY, 1967, 1971; City University of New York, 1967-68; University of Iowa, Iowa City, 1978, 1982; Columbia University, NYC, 1980, 1981; Bennington College, VT, 1987-; Brown University, Providence, RI, 1988; University of California, Davis, 1990, 1992; Beloit College, WI, 1995. **Publications:** NOVELS: Cat Man, 1956; The Circle Home, 1960; The Peacock's Tail, 1965; Seven Rivers West, 1986. TRAVEL: Notes from the Century Before: A Journal from British Columbia, 1969; African Calliope: A Journey to the Sudan, 1979. ESSAYS: The Courage of Turtles, 1971; Walking the Dead Diamond River, 1973; The Moose on the Wall: Field Notes from the Vermont Wilderness, 1974; Red Wolves and Black Bears, 1976; The Tugman's Passage, 1982; Hearts Desire, 1988; Balancing Acts, 1992; Tigers & Ice, 1999; Compass Points: How I Lived, 2001. OTHER: The Edward Hoagland Reader, 1979; Hoagland on Nature, 2003. STORIES: City Tales, 1986; The Final Fate of the Alligators, 1992. **Address:** PO Box 51, Barton, VT 05822, U.S.A.

HOAR, Jere (Richmond). American, b. 1929. **Genres:** Novels, Novellas/Short stories, Communications/Media, Writing/Journalism. **Career:** University of Mississippi, University, professor of journalism, 1956-92; lawyer in private practice, 1971-. Also worked as reporter and news editor for community newspapers. **Publications:** SHORT STORIES: Body Parts, 1997. NOVELS: The Hit, 2003. Author of television scripts. Work represented in anthologies. Contributor of short stories and articles to magazines. **Address:** 71 CR 215, Oxford, MS 38655, U.S.A.

HOARE, Philip. British, b. 1958. **Genres:** Art/Art history, History, Literary criticism and history, Biography. **Career:** Writer, broadcaster, lecturer, and curator. **Publications:** Serious Pleasures: The Life of Stephen Tennant, 1990; Noel Coward: A Biography, 1995; Wilde's Last Stand: Decadence, Conspiracy & the First World War, 1997; (ed.) The Sayings of Noel Coward, 1997; Icons of Pop, 1999; Spike Island: The Memory of a Military Hospital, 2001. **Address:** c/o Gillon Aitken Associates Ltd, 29 Fernshaw Rd, London SW10 0TG, England.

HOBAN, Russell. American, b. 1925. **Genres:** Novels, Science fiction/Fantasy, Children's fiction, Songs/Lyrics and libretti. **Career:** Freelance writer and illustrator. **Publications:** What Does It Do and How Does It Work, 1959; The Atomic Submarine, 1960; Bedtime for Frances, 1960; Herman the Loser, 1961; London Men and English Men, 1962; The Song in My Drum, 1962; Some Snow Said Hello, 1963; The Sorely Trying Day, 1964; A Baby Sister for Frances, 1964; Nothing to Do, 1964; Bread and Jam for Frances, 1964; Tom and the Two Handles, 1965; The Story of Hester Mouse, 1965; What Happened When Jack and Daisy Tried to Fool the Tooth Fairies, 1966; Goodnight, 1966; Henry and the Monstrous Din, 1966; The Little Brute Family, 1966; Save My Place, 1967; Charlie the Tramp, 1967; The Mouse and His Child, 1967; Birthday for Frances, 1968; The Pedaling Man and Other Poems, 1968; The Stone Doll of Sister Brute, 1968; Harvey's Hideout, 1969; (with S. Selig) Ten What? 1974; How to Beat Captain Najork and His Hired Sportsmen, 1974; Kleinzeit (adult novel), 1974; Turtle Diary (adult novel), 1975; Dinner at Alberta's, 1975; A Near Thing for Captain Najork, 1975; (with S. Selig) Crocodile and Pierrot, 1975; The Dancing Tigers, 1978; Arthur's New Power, 1978; The Twenty-Elephant Restaurant, 1978; La Corona and the Tin Frog, 1979; Riddley Walker (adult novel), 1980; Flat Cat, 1980; Ace Dragon Ltd., 1980; The Serpent Tower, 1981; The Great Fruit Gum Robbery, 1981; They Came from Aargh!, 1981; The Battle of Zormla, 1982; The Flight of Bembel Rudzuk, 1982; Pilgermann (adult novel), 1983; Ponders, 4 vols., 1983-84; The Rain Door, 1986; The Marzipan Pig, 1986; The Medusa Frequency (adult novel), 1987; Ponders, 1988; Monsters, 1989; Jim Hedgehog's Supernatural Christmas, 1989; Jim Hedgehog and the Lonesome Tower, 1990; Monsters, 1990; Emmet Otter's Jug Band Christmas, 1992; The Moment under the Moment (adult novel), 1992; A Bargain for Frances, 1992; I Thought I'd Take My Rat to School: Poems from September to June, 1993; M.O.L.E., 1993; Egg Thoughts and Other Frances Songs, 1994; The Court of the Winged Serpent, 1994; The Second Mrs. Kong (libretto), 1994; Best Friends for Frances, 1994; Fremder, 1996; The Trokeville Way, 1996; The Sea-Thing Child, 1999; Trouble on Thunder Mountain, 2000; Jim's Lion, 2001; Angelica's Grotto (novel), 2001; Her Name Was Lola, 2003. **Address:** c/o David Higham Associates, Ltd., 5-8 Lower John St, Golden Sq, London W1F 9HA, England.

HOBBS, Anne Stevenson. British, b. 1942. **Genres:** Art/Art history, Adult non-fiction, Natural history. **Career:** British Museum, London, England, curator, 1964-66; Victoria and Albert Museum's National Art Library, London, curator, 1966-90, (Curator of special collections), 1990-; Frederick Warne Curator of Children's Literature, 1991-; writer. Founder member of the Mantegazza String Quartet; violinist and pianist. **Publications:** (ed. with J.I. Whalley) Beatrix Potter, the V & A Collection: The Leslie Linder Bequest of Beatrix Potter Material, 1985; Fables: Five Hundred Years of Illustration and Text, 1986; (with J. Taylor, Whalley, and E. Battrick) Beatrix Potter, 1866-1943: The Artist and Her World, 1987; Beatrix Potter's Art, 1990; (trans.) Naissance de Pierre Lapin, 1992; (with E. Jay and M. Noble) A Victorian Naturalist: Beatrix Potter's Drawings from the Armitt Collection, 1992; The Linder Collection of the Works and Drawings of Beatrix Potter, 1996; (intro.) Les Champignons, 1996. **Address:** Archive of Art and Design, 23 Blythe Rd, London WI4 0QF, England.

HOBBS, Valerie. American, b. 1941. **Genres:** Children's fiction, Young adult fiction. **Career:** High school English teacher, Oahu, HI, 1971-74; University of California, Santa Barbara, lecturer in writing, 1981-. **Publications:** YOUNG ADULT FICTION: How Far Would You Have Gotten If I Hadn't Called You Back?, 1995; Get It While It's Hot. Or Not, 1996; Tender, 2001; Sonny's War, 2002. CHILDREN'S FICTION: Carolina Crow Girl, 1999; Charlie's Run, 2000. Work represented in anthologies. Contributor of stories to magazines. **Address:** 69 Skyline Cir, Santa Barbara, CA 93109, U.S.A. **Online address:** hobbs@humanitas.ucsb.edu

HOBBY, Elaine (Ann). British, b. 1956. **Genres:** Literary criticism and history, Medicine/Health, Women's studies and issues, Autobiography/Memoirs. **Career:** Workers' Education Association, W. Midlands, part-time tutor in women's studies, 1980-81; Cambridgeshire College of Arts and Technology, Cambridge, lecturer in English and General Studies, 1985-87; Cambridge Women's Resources Centre, part-time tutor in English and women's studies,

1987-88; Lougborough University, Leics., professor of seventeenth-century studies, 1988-. **Publications:** Virtue of Necessity: English Women's Writing, 1649-1688, 1988. EDITOR: (co-) Her Own Life: Autobiographical Writings by Seventeenth-Century Women, 1989; (co-) What Lesbians Do in Books, 1991; J. Sharp, The Midwives Book, 1999. **Address:** Dept. of English and Drama, Loughborough University, Loughborough, Leics. LE11 3TU, England. **Online address:** e.a.hobby@lboro.ac.uk

HOBDAY, Charles (Henry). British, b. 1917. **Genres:** Poetry, Literary criticism and history, Politics/Government, Biography. **Career:** Hutchinson Publishing Group Ltd., London, England, subeditor, 1946-48; Keesing's Publications, Bath, England, subeditor, 1949-82; writer. **Publications:** The Return of Cain (poems), 1974; A Wreath for Inez (poems), 1976; Talking of Michelangelo (poems), 1978; Communist and Marxist Parties of the World, 1986; Edgell Rickword: A Poet at War (biography), 1989; (ed.) The Collected Poems of Edgell Rickword, 1991; A Golden Ring: English Poets in Florence from 1373 to the Present Day (biography and literary criticism), 1998; How Goes the Enemy? Selected Poems 1960-2000, 2000; Elegy for a Sergeant (poem), 2003. **Address:** 28 Ingelow House, Holland St, London W8 4NF, England.

HOBERMAN, Mary Ann. American, b. 1930. **Genres:** Children's fiction, Poetry. **Career:** Writer, poet, speaker, consultant, and artist-in-the-schools, from 1955; The Pocket People (children's theater group), founder and member, 1968-75; Fairfield University, Fairfield, CT, adjunct professor, 1980-83; C.G. Jung Center, NYC, program coordinator, 1981. **Publications:** CHILDREN'S BOOKS: All My Shoes Come in Two's, 1957; How Do I Go?, 1958; Hello and Good-by, 1959; What Jim Knew, 1963; Not Enough Beds for the Babies, 1965; A Little Book of Little Beasts, 1973; The Looking Book, 1973, rev. ed., 2001; The Raucous Auk, 1973; Nuts to You and Nuts to Me, 1974; I Like Old Clothes, 1976; Bugs, 1976; A House Is a House for Me, 1978; Yellow Butter, Purple Jelly, Red Jam, Black Bread: Poems, 1981; The Cozy Book, 1982, rev. ed., 1995; Mr. and Mrs. Muddle, 1988; A Fine Fat Pig, and Other Animal Poems, 1991; Fathers, Mothers, Sisters, Brothers: A Collection of Family Poems, 1991; One of Each, 1997; The Seven Silly Eaters, 1997; The Llama Who Had No Pajama, 1998; Miss Mary Mack: A Hand-Clapping Rhyme, 1998; The Eensy Weensy Spider, 2000; The Two Sillies, 2000; And to Think That I Thought We Would Never Be Friends, 1999; Michael Finnegan, 2001; It's Simple, Said Simon, 2001; You Read to Me, I'll Read to You: Very Short Stories to Read Together, 2001; Bill Grogan's Goat, 2002; The Marvelous Mouse Man, 2002; Right outside My Window, 2002; Mary Had a Little Lamb, 2003; You Read to Me, I'll Read to You: Very Short Fairy Tales to Read Together, 2004; Whose Garden Is It?, 2004; Yankee Doodle, 2004. OTHER: (ed.) My Song Is Beautiful: Poems and Pictures in Many Voices, 1994. **Address:** 98 Hunting Ridge Rd, Greenwich, CT 06831, U.S.A. **Online address:** mahoberm@optonline.net; Maryannhoberman.com

HOBHOUSE, Hermione. British, b. 1934. **Genres:** Architecture, Biography. **Career:** Freelance journalist, reviewer and lectr. General Ed., Survey of London, 1983-94. Researcher and Scriptwriter, Associated-Rediffusion Television, 1956-58, and Granada Television, 1958-63; Part-time Tutor, Architectural Association School, London, 1973-79. **Publications:** The Ward of Cheap in the City of London: A Short History, 1963; Thomas Cubitt: Master Builder, 1971, 2nd ed., 1995; Lost London, 1971; History of Regent Street, 1975; Oxford and Cambridge, 1980; Prince Albert: His Life and Work, 1983; (ed.) Survey of London, Volume XLII: Southern Kensington, 1986; Survey of London Monograph 17, 1991; (ed.) Survey of London vols. XLIII & XlIV Poplar, Blackwater & The Isle of Dogs, 1994; London Survey'd: The Work of the Survey of London 1894-1994, 1995; The Crystal Palace and Great Exhibition: A History of the Royal Commission for the Exhibition of 1851, 2002. **Address:** Westcombe Stables, Westcombe, Evercreech, Shepton Mallet, Somerset BA4 6ES, England.

HOBSBAUM, Philip (Dennis). British, b. 1932. **Genres:** Poetry, Literary criticism and history. **Career:** Queen's University, Belfast, lecturer in English, 1962-66; University of Glasgow, lecturer, 1966-72, Sr. lecturer, 1972-79, Reader, 1985-97, professor, 1985-97, Emeritus professor of English Literature, 1997-. **Publications:** The Place's Fault and Other Poems, 1964; Snapshots, 1965; In Retreat and Other Poems, 1966; Coming Out Fighting, 1969; Some Lovely Glorious Nothing, 1969; A Theory of Communication: A Study of Value in Literature (in U.S. as Theory of Criticism), 1970; Women and Animals, 1972; A Reader's Guide to Charles Dickens, 1973; Tradition and Experiment in English Poetry, 1979; A Reader's Guide to D.H. Lawrence, 1981; Essentials of Literary Criticism, 1983; A Reader's Guide to Robert Lowell, 1988; Metre, Rhythm and Verse Form, 1996. EDITOR: (with E. Lucie-Smith) A Group Anthology, 1963; Ten Elizabethan Poets, 1969; Word-

sworth: Selected Poetry and Prose, 1989; (with P. Lyons and J. McGhee) Channels of Communication, 1993. **Address:** Dept of English, University of Glasgow, Glasgow G12 8QQ, Scotland. **Online address:** P.Hobsbaum@englit.arts.gla.ac.uk

HOBSBAWM, Eric (John Ernest). Also writes as Francis Newton. British, b. 1917. **Genres:** History, Music. **Career:** Emeritus Professor of Economic and Social History, Birkbeck College, University of London. Fellow, King's College, Cambridge, 1949-55. **Publications:** Labour's Turning Point, 1948; Primitive Rebels, 1959; (as Francis Newton) The Jazz Scene, 1959; The Age of Revolution, 1962; Labouring Men, 1964; (ed.) Karl Marx, Precapitalist Economic Formations, 1964; Industry and Empire, 1968; Bandits, 1969; (with G. Rude) Captain Swing: A Social History of the Great English Uprising, 1969; Revolutionaries, 1973; The Age of Capital, 1975; Worlds of Labour, 1984; The Age of Empire, 1987; Echoes of the Marseillaise, 1990; Nations and Nationalism, 1990; The Age of Extremes, 1994; On History, 1997; Uncommon People, 1998; The New Century, 1999; Interesting Times, 2002. **Address:** Birkbeck College, University of London, Malet St, London WC1, England.

HOBSON, Anthony Robert Alwyn. British, b. 1921. **Genres:** History, Librarianship. **Career:** Director, 1949-71, and Associate, 1971-77, Sotheby and Co., London; Sandars Reader in Bibliography, University of Cambridge, 1973-74; Franklin Jasper Walls Lecturer, Pierpont Morgan Library, New York, 1979; Rosenbach Fellow, University of Pennsylvania, 1990; Lyell Reader in Bibliography, University of Oxford, 1990-91; Fellow of the British Academy, 1992-. **Publications:** French and Italian Collectors and Their Bindings, 1953; Great Libraries, 1970; Apollo and Pegasus, 1975; Humanists and Bookbinders, 1989; Renaissance Book Collecting: Jean Grolier and Diego Hurtado, Their Books and Bindings, 1999; (ed.) Ronald Firbank, Letters to His Mother 1920-1924, 2001. **Address:** The Glebe House, Whitsbury, Fordingbridge, Hants., England.

HOBSON, Fred Colby, (Jr.). American, b. 1943. **Genres:** Literary criticism and history. **Career:** University of Alabama, Tuscaloosa, assistant professor to professor of English, 1972-86; Louisiana State University, Baton Rouge, professor of English and co-ed. of Southern Review, 1986-89; University of North Carolina, Chapel Hill, Lineberger Professor of English, and co-ed. of Southern Literary Journal, 1989-. Former editorial writer, Journal and Sentinel, Winston-Salem, NC. Co-recipient, Pulitzer Prize, 1970. **Publications:** Serpent in Eden: H.L. Mencken and the South, 1974; Southern Mythmaking: The Savage and the Ideal, 1978; Tell about the South: The Southern Rage to Explain, 1983; The Southern Writer in the Post-Modern World, 1990; Mencken: A Life, 1994; But Now I See: The White Southern Racial Conversion Narrative, 1999. EDITOR/CO-EDITOR: Literature at the Barricades: The American Writer in the 1930's, 1982; South-Watching: Selected Essays of Gerald W. Johnson, 1982; H.L. Mencken's Thirty-Five Years of Newspaper Work, 1994; The Literature of the American South: A Norton Anthology, 1998; South to the Future: An American Region in the Twenty-First Century, 2001. **Address:** Dept of English, University of North Carolina, Chapel Hill, NC 27599-3520, U.S.A. **Online address:** fhobson@email.unc.edu

HOBSON, J(ohn) Allan. American, b. 1933. **Genres:** Psychiatry, Bibliography. **Career:** Certification as diplomate by American Board of Psychiatry and Neurology, 1968; physician licensed in Massachusetts. Bellevue Hospital, NYC, intern in medicine, 1959-60; Massachusetts Mental Health Center, Boston, resident in psychiatry, 1960-61, 1964-66, senior psychiatrist, 1965-67, director of laboratory of neurophysiology, 1967, principal psychiatrist, 1967-, director of group psychotherapy training program, 1972-80; National Institute of Mental Health, Bethesda, MD, clinical associate, 1961-63; Harvard Medical School, Boston, research associate in physiology dept, 1964-67, instructor in psychiatry, 1966-67, associate in psychiatry, 1967-69, assistant professor, 1969-74, associate professor, 1974, professor of psychiatry, 1978-, professor of psychiatry (neuroscience), 1983-, director of behavioral science teaching program, 1980-86. University of Lyon, special fellow of the National Institute of Mental Health, 1963-64; University of Bordeaux, visiting scientist and lecturer, 1973; Istituto di Psicologia, Universita degli Studi, Rome, visiting professor, 1983; Rockefeller Foundation, scholar in residence, Bellagio Conference and Study Center, 1987; MacArthur Foundation, health programs consultant, 1989-91, member of Mind-Body Interaction Network, 1992-; University of Messina, visiting professor, 1992-. **Publications:** (with R.W. McCarley) Neuronal Activity in Sleep: An Annotated Bibliography, 1971, 2nd ed., 1977; (ed. with M.A. Brazier) The Reticular Formation Revisited, 1979; (selector and author of intro.) States of Brain and Mind and Abnormal States of Brain and Mind, c. 1988; The Dreaming Brain, 1988; Sleep, 1989; The Chemistry of Conscious

States, 1994; Consciousness, 1999; Out of Its Mind, 2001; The Dream Drug Store, 2001. **Address:** Harvard Medical School, 74 Fenwood Rd., Boston, MA 02115, U.S.A.

HOCH, Edward D. American, b. 1930. **Genres:** Novellas/Short stories, Mystery/Crime/Suspense. **Career:** With Pocket Books Inc., NYC, 1952-54; Hutchins Advertising Co., Rochester, New York, copy writer, 1954-68. Mystery Writers of America, president, 1982; Rochester Public Library, trustee, 1981-98. **Publications:** The Shattered Raven, 1969; The Transvection Machine, 1971; The Fellowship of the Hand, 1973; The Frankenstein Factory, 1975. STORIES: The Judges of Hades, 1971; City of Brass, 1972; The Spy and the Thief, 1972; The Thefts of Nick Velvet, 1978; The Quests of Simon Ark, 1984; Leopold's Way, 1985; The Night My Friend, 1991; Diagnosis: Impossible, 1996; The Ripper of Storyville, 1997; The Velvet Touch, 2000; The Old Spies Club, 2001; The Night People, 2001; The Ironangel, 2003. EDITOR: Dear Dead Days, 1972; Best Detective Stories of the Year, 6 vols., 1976-81; Year's Best Mystery and Suspense Stories, 14 vols., 1982-95; All But Impossible, 1981; Murder Most Sacred, 1989; Twelve American Detective Stories, 1997. **Address:** 2941 Lake Ave, Rochester, NY 14612, U.S.A. **Online address:** ehoch-rochester@worldnet.att.net

HOCHMAN, Elaine S(chwartz). American. **Genres:** Architecture. **Career:** Metropolitan Museum of Art, NYC, staff member, 1957-58; New School for Social Research, NYC, faculty member, 1969-; New York City Real Estate Developers, architectural consultant, 1970-; Art Ventures International Inc., New York, president, 1985-. **Publications:** Architects of Fortune: Mies van der Rohe and the Third Reich, 1989; Bauhaus: Crucible of Modernism, 1997. Contributor of essays to journals. **Address:** c/o Fromm International, 1919 Stanley St, Northbrook, IL 60062, U.S.A.

HOCHMAN, Gloria. American, b. 1943. **Genres:** Adult non-fiction. **Career:** National Adoption Center, director of communications and marketing, 1977-. Public speaker, with appearances on radio and television programs. **Publications:** Heart Bypass: What Every Patient Must Know, 1982; (with E. Beal) Adult Children of Divorce, 1991; (with P. Duke) A Brilliant Madness: Living with Manic-Depressive Illness, 1992. Contributor to periodicals. **Address:** 1500 Walnut St Ste 701, Philadelphia, PA 19102, U.S.A. **Online address:** glorhoch@aol.com

HOCHMAN, Jiri. Czech, b. 1926. **Genres:** Novels, History, Politics/Government. **Career:** Writer and editor. Ohio State University, professor emeritus. **Publications:** European Crossroads, 1957; Spain Twenty Years Later, 1959; Cuban Diary, 1961; Algerian Report, 1964; Deer Creek (novel), 1970, 3rd ed., 1992; Chronicle of Regentship in Bohemia, 1972, 2nd ed., 1991; Letters from Prison, 1973; Boehmisches Happening, 1977; The Other Way Round, 1980; The Soviet Union and the Failure of Collective Security, 1934-38, 1985; (with A. Dubcek) Hope Dies Last: Dubcek by Dubcek, 1993; Historical Dictionary of the Czech State, 1998. Author of short stories. **Address:** 103 Putter Dr, Palm Coast, FL 32164, U.S.A. **Online address:** jirhoch@pcfl.net

HOCKE, Martin. German, b. 1938. **Genres:** Science fiction/Fantasy. **Career:** English teacher, Berlitz School and others, in Germany, Italy and Britain; briefly location manager for Paramount Pictures; actor and broadcaster, Italian radio; translator from Italian into English; freelance writer, 1988-. **Publications:** FANTASY NOVELS: The Ancient Solitary Reign, 1989; The Lost Domain, 1993. **Address:** c/o Dialogue Business Services, 5 Hillcrest, Broadway Road, Evesham, Worcestershire CV32 5HR, England.

HOCKENBERRY, John. American, b. 1956. **Genres:** Documentaries/Reportage. **Career:** Journalist and author. National Public Radio, stringer, 1980-81, correspondent from Seattle, 1981, newscaster on All Things Considered, Washington, DC, until 1984, correspondent from Chicago, 1984-88, Middle East correspondent, 1988-90, host of Heat, NYC, 1990-91, correspondent during the Persian Gulf War, 1991, host of Talk of the Nation, Washington, DC, 1991-92; Day One, ABC-TV News, NYC, correspondent, 1992-. **Publications:** Moving Violations: War Zones, Wheelchairs, and Declarations of Independence, 1995; A River Out of Eden (novel), 2001. Contributor to periodicals. **Address:** c/o Watkins Loomis Agency, 133 E 35th St Ste 1, New York, NY 10016, U.S.A.

HOCKENSMITH, Sean M. American, b. 1972. **Genres:** Self help. **Career:** Dynamic Life Publishing, Johnstown, PA, owner. **Publications:** Smashing the Wall of Fear: Dynamic Strategies to Overcome the Obstacles in Your Life, 1997. **Address:** 3310 Graham Ave, Windber, PA 15963, U.S.A. **Online address:** Sean@seanhockensmith.com

HOCKING, Mary (Eunice). British, b. 1921. **Genres:** Novels. **Career:** Local Government Officer, 1946-70. **Publications:** The Winter City, 1961; Visitors to the Crescent, 1962; The Sparrow, 1964; The Young Spaniard, 1965; Ask No Question, 1967; A Time of War, 1968; Checkmate, 1969; The Hopeful Traveller, 1970; The Climbing Frame, 1971; Family Circle, 1972; Daniel Come to Judgement, 1974; The Bright Day, 1975; The Mind Has Mountains, 1976; Look Stranger, 1979; He Who Plays the King, 1980; March House, 1981; Good Daughters, 1984; Indifferent Heroes, 1985; Welcome Strangers, 1986; An Irrelevant Woman, 1987; A Particular Place, 1989; Letters from Constance, 1991; The Very Dead of Winter, 1993; The Meeting Place, 1996.

HOCKNEY, David. British, b. 1937. **Genres:** Design, Photography, Art/Art history, Illustrations. **Career:** Artist. Maidstone College of Art, England, instructor, 1962; University of Iowa, Iowa City, lecturer, 1964; University of Colorado, Boulder, lecturer, 1965; University of California at Los Angeles, lecturer, 1966, honorary chair of drawing, 1980; University of California at Berkeley, lecturer, 1967. Exhibitions: (One-person shows) in London, NYC, Amsterdam, Manchester, England, Berlin, Paris, Mexico City, Tokyo, Los Angeles. Designer for stage productions. **Publications:** David Hockney by David Hockney, 1976, 2nd ed, 1977; Paper Pools, 1980; David Hockney: Looking at Pictures in a Book, 1981; Cameraworks, 1984; Martha's Vineyard: My Third Sketchbook from the Summer of 1982, 1985; Hockney on Photography: Conversations with Paul Joyce, 1988; Picasso, 1990; Hockney's Alphabet, 1991; That's the Way I See It, 1993. AUTHOR OF INTRODUCTIONS: Draw: How to Master the Art, by J. Camp, 1994; Making It New: Collected Essays and Writings of Henry Geldzahler, 1994. ILLUSTRATOR of books by: D. Posner, the Brothers Grimm, W. Hogarth, W. Stephens, T. Seidler, S. Spender, H. Bienek. COLLECTIONS: 72 Drawings Chosen by the Artist, 1971; 18 Portraits by David Hockney, 1977; David Hockney Prints, 1954-77, 1979; Pictures by David Hockney, 1979, 2nd ed, 1979; David Hockney, 23 Lithographs, 1980; David Hockney Photographs, 1982; Hockney's Photographs, 1983; Kasmin's Hockneys: 45 Drawings, 1983; David Hockney fotografo, 1983; David Hockney in America, 1983; Hockney Posters, 1983; Photographs by David Hockney, 1986; David Hockney: Etchings and Lithographs, 1988; David Hockney: Graphics, 1992; Off the Wall, 1994, in the US as David Hockney: Poster Art, 1994. EXHIBIT CATALOGS: Paintings, Prints, and Drawings, 1960-1970, 1970; David Hockney: tableau et dessins: Musee des arts decoratifs, Palais du Louvre, Pavillon de Marsan, 11 Octobre-9 Decembre 1974, 1974; David Hockney: dessins et gravures, Galerie Claude Bernard, Paris, Avril 1975, 1975; David Hockney: Prints and Drawings Circulated by the International Exhibits Foundation, Washington, DC, 1978-1980, 1978; Travels with Pen, Pencil, and Ink, 1978; David Hockney: Sources and Experiments: An Exhibition Held at the Sewall Gallery, Rice University, September 7 to October 15, 1982, 1982; David Hockney: Frankfurter Kunstverein, Steinernes Haus am Romerberg, Frankfurt am Main, 15.3.-24.4. 1983, 1983; Hockney Paints the Stage, 1983; Photographs by David Hockney: Organized and Circulated by the International Exhibitions Foundation, Washington, DC, 1986-88, 1986; David Hockney: A Retrospective, Organized by Maurice Tuchman and Stephanie Barron, 1988; David Hockney: Fax Cuadros, 1990. **Address:** 7508 Santa Monica Blvd., West Hollywood, CA 90046, U.S.A.

HODDINOTT, R(alph) F(ield). British, b. 1913. **Genres:** Archaeology/Antiquities, Architecture, Art/Art history, History, Anthropology/Ethnology. **Career:** Worked for the British Council, Athens, 1939-41, UNRRA, 1945-47; International Refugee Organization, 1947-52, and in government, 1955-67; now retired. Fellow, Society of Antiquaries. **Publications:** Early Byzantine Churches in Macedonia and Southern Serbia, 1963; Bulgaria in Antiquity, 1975; The Thracians, 1981; (co-author) The New Thracian Treasure from Rogozen, Bulgaria, 1986; (co-author) The Rogozen Treasure, 1989; (co-author) APMOE (Thessalonica), 1992. **Address:** 11 Sydney House, Woodstock Rd, Chiswick, London W4 1DP, England.

HODGE, Francis. American, b. 1915. **Genres:** Theatre. **Career:** Professor Emeritus, Dept. of Drama, University of Texas, Austin, since 1979 (Assistant Professor, 1949-55; Associate Professor, 1955-62; Professor, 1962-79). Instructor, Carroll College, Waukesha, Wisconsin, 1940-42; Instructor, Cornell University, Ithaca, New York, 1946-48; Assistant Professor, University of Iowa, Iowa City, 1948-49; Summer Instructor, University of Colorado, 1961, Banff School of Fine Art, 1962-68, University of British Columbia, 1963. Ed., Educational Theatre Journal, Washington, D.C. 1966-68. **Publications:** Yankee Theatre, 1964; Play Directing, 1971, 5th ed, 2000; (ed.) Innovations in Stage and Theatre Design, 1972. Contributor to books, reference books. Contributor of articles and book reviews about theatre to periodical journals. **Address:** 1109 Bluebonnet Lane, Austin, TX 78704, U.S.A.

HODGE, Jane Aiken. British (born United States), b. 1917. **Genres:** Mystery/Crime/Suspense, Romance/Historical, Biography. **Career:** Member,

British Board of Trade, British Supply Council, North America, 1942-44; with Time Inc., NYC, 1944-47, and Life mag., London, 1947-48. **Publications:** Maulever Hall, 1964; The Adventures, 1965; Watch the Wall, My Darling, 1966; Here Comes a Candle, 1967, in U.S. as The Master of Penrose, 1968; The Winding Stair, 1968; Marry in Haste, 1969; Greek Wedding, 1970; Savannah Purchase, 1971; Only a Novel: The Double Life of Jane Austen, 1972; Strangers in Company, 1973; Shadow of a Lady, 1973; One Way to Venice, 1974; Runaway Bride, 1975; Rebel Heiress, 1975; Judas Flowering, 1976; Red Sky at Night, 1977; Last Act, 1979; Wide Is the Water, 1981; The Lost Garden, 1982; The Private World of Georgette Heyer, 1984; Secret Island, 1985; Polonaise, 1987; First Night, 1989; Leading Lady, 1990; Windover, 1992; Escapade, 1993; Whispering, 1995; Passion and Principle, 1996; Bride of Dreams, 1996; Unsafe Hands, 1997; Susan in America, 1998; Caterina, 1999; A Death in Two Parts, 2000; Deathline, 2003. **Address:** 23 Eastport Lane, Lewes, E. Sussex BN7 1TL, England.

HODGE, Paul William. American, b. 1934. **Genres:** Astronomy, Physics. **Career:** Harvard University, Cambridge, MA, lecturer, 1960-61; University of California, Berkeley, assistant professor, 1961-65; University of Washington, Seattle, Dept. of Astronomy, professor, 1965-. **Publications:** (with J.C. Brandt) Solar System Astrophysics, 1963; Galaxies and Cosmology, 1965; (with F.W. Wright) The Large Magellanic Cloud, 1966; An Atlas and Catalog of HII Regions in Galaxies, 1966; Concepts of the Universe, 1967; The Revolution in Astronomy, 1969; Slides for Astronomy, 1971; Concepts of Contemporary Astronomy, 1974; (with F.W. Wright) The Small Magellanic Cloud, 1978; An Atlas of the Andromeda Galaxy, 1981; Interplanetary Dust, 1981; (with R.C. Kennicutt) HII Regions in Galaxies, 1982; (ed.) Galaxies and the Universe, 1984; Galaxies, 1986; The Andromeda Galaxy, 1992; Meteoritic Craters and Impact Structures of the World, 1993; Higher than Everest, 2001. **Address:** Dept. of Astronomy, University of Washington, Seattle, WA 98195, U.S.A.

HODGES, Donald Clark. American, b. 1923. **Genres:** History, Politics/Government, Sociology. **Career:** University of Missouri, associate professor of philosophy, 1957-63; University of South Florida, Tampa, professor of philosophy, 1963-64; Florida State University, Tallahassee, professor of philosophy, 1964-69, chairman, Dept of Philosophy, 1964-69, director of Center for Graduate and Postgraduate Studies in Social Philosophy, 1967-71, director of Latin American and Caribbean Studies, 1987-95, affiliate professor of political science, 1988-, professor emeritus of philosophy, 2003-. Visiting professor of philosophy at U.S. universities; University of Buenos Aires, professor of sociology, 1974-75; Autonomous National University of Mexico, professor of political science, 1982. **Publications:** Socialist Humanism, 1974; The Latin American Revolution, 1974; Argentina, 1943-1976, 1976; (with R. Gandy) El destino de la Revolucion Mexicana, 1977; (with A. Guillen) Revaloracion de la guerrilla urbana, 1977; Marxismo y Revolucion en el Siglo XX, 1978; (with R. Gandy) Mexico 1910-1976, 1979; The Bureaucratization of Socialism, 1981; (with R. Gandy) Mexico 1910-82, 1983; (with R. Gandy) Todos los Revolucionarios van al Infierno!, 1984; Intellectual Foundations of the Nicaraguan Revolution, 1987; Argentina 1943-1987, 1988; Argentina's "Dirty War," 1991; Sandino's Communism, 1992; Mexican Anarchism after the Revolution, 1995; America's New Economic Order, 1996; The Literate Communist, 1999; Class Politics in the Information Age, 2000; (with R. Gandy) Mexico, the End of the Revolution, 2001; (with R. Gandy) Mexico under Siege, 2002; Deep Republicanism: Prelude to Professionalism, 2003. EDITOR: (with K.T. Fann) Readings in U.S. Imperialism, 1971; (with A. Shanab) National Liberation Fronts 1960-1970; 1972; (and trans.) Philosophy of the Urban Guerrilla, 1973; The Legacy of Che Guevara, 1977. **Address:** Dept of Philosophy, Florida State University, Tallahassee, FL 32306-1500, U.S.A. **Online address:** kfoulke@mailer.fsu.edu

HODGES, Margaret. American, b. 1911. **Genres:** Novellas/Short stories, Children's fiction, Children's non-fiction, Mythology/Folklore, Biography. **Career:** Professor Emeritus, School of Library and Information Science, University of Pittsburgh, PA, 1977- (Lecturer, 1964-68; Assistant Professor, 1968-72; Associate Professor, 1972-75; Professor, 1975-77). Storyteller, WQED-TV Schools Services Dept. series, Tell Me a Story, 1965-. Radio and Television Storyteller, 1953-64, and Children's Librarian, 1958-64, Carnegie Library of Pittsburgh, PA; Story Specialist, Pittsburgh Public Schools, PA, 1964-68. **Publications:** One Little Drum, 1958; (co-ed.) Stories to Tell to Children, 1960; What's for Lunch, Charley?, 1961; A Club against Keats, 1962; (ed.) Tell It Again, Great Tales from around the World, 1963; Secret in the Woods, 1963; The Wave, 1964; Tell Me a Story (teacher's manual), 1966; Hatching of Joshua Cobb, 1967; (ed.) Constellation, a Shakespearean Anthology, 1968; Sing Out, Charley!, 1968; Lady Queen Anne, a Biography of Queen Anne of England, 1969; Making of Joshua Cobb, 1971; Gorgon's

Head, 1972; Hopkins of the Mayflower, Portrait of a Dissenter, 1972; Fire Bringer, 1972; Persephone and the Springtime, 1973; Other World, Myths of the Celts, 1973; Baldur and the Mistletoe, 1974; Freewheeling of Joshua Cobb, 1974; Knight Prisoner, 1976; The High Riders, 1980; The Little Humpbacked Horse, 1980; (co-ed.) Elva Smith's History of Children's Literature, 1980; The Avenger, 1982; Saint George and the Dragon, 1984; Making a Difference, 1989; The Voice of the Great Bell, 1989; The Kitchen Knight, 1990; Buried Moon, 1990; Brother Francis and the Friendly Beasts, 1991; St. Jerome and the Lion, 1991; Hauntings, Ghosts and Ghouls from around the World, 1991; The Golden Deer, 1992; Don Quixote and Sancho Panza, 1992; Of Swords and Sorcerers, 1993; Saint Patrick and the Peddler, 1993; The Hero of Bremen, 1993; Hidden in Sand, 1994; Gulliver in Lilliput, 1995; Comus, 1996; Molly Limbo, 1996; True Tale of Johnny Appleseed, 1997; Silent Night: The Song and Its Story, 1997; Up the Chimney, 1998; Joan of Arc: The Lily Maid, 1999; (adapter) The Boy Who Drew Cats, 2002; The Legend of Saint Christopher, 2002; Merlin and the Making of a King, 2004. **Address:** Information Science Bldg Rm 600, University of Pittsburgh, Pittsburgh, PA 15260, U.S.A.

HODGETTS, Richard M(ichael). *See* Obituaries.

HODGINS, Jack. (John Stanley Hodgins). Canadian, b. 1938. **Genres:** Novels, Novellas/Short stories, Children's fiction, Travel/Exploration, Writing/Journalism. **Career:** Nanaimo District Sr. Secondary School, BC, teacher, 1961-80; University of Ottawa, visiting professor, 1981-83; writer-in-residence, Simon Fraser University, Burnaby, BC, 1977, and University of Ottawa, 1979; University of Victoria, BC, visiting professor, 1983-85, professor of creative writing, 1985-2002. **Publications:** NOVELS: The Invention of the World, 1977; The Resurrection of Joseph Bourne, 1979; The Honorary Patron, 1987; Left Behind in Squabble Bay (for children), 1988; Innocent Cities, 1990; The Mackin Charm, 1995; Broken Ground, 1998; Distance, 2003. STORIES: Spit Delaney's Island: Selected Stories, 1976; The Barclay Family Theatre, 1981; Beginnings, 1983. OTHER: (with B. Nesbitt) Teachers' Resource Book to Transition II: Short Fiction, 1978; (with Nesbitt) Teaching Short Fiction, 1981; Over Forty in Broken Hill (travel), 1992; A Passion for Narrative (non-fiction), 1993. EDITOR: (with W.H. New) Voice and Vision, 1972; The Frontier Experience, 1975; The West Coast Experience, 1976. **Address:** 2640 MacDonald Dr E, Victoria, BC, Canada V8N 1X9. **Online address:** hodginsj@shaw.ca

HODGKISS, Alan Geoffrey. British, b. 1921. **Genres:** Geography. **Career:** Experimental Officer, University of Liverpool, 1946-83. Ed., Society of University Cartographers Bulletin, 1964-73. Contributing Ed., Canadian Cartographer, 1965-75. **Publications:** Maps for Books and Theses, 1970; (ed. with J. A. Patmore) Merseyside in Maps, 1970; Discovering Antique Maps, 1970; Understanding Maps, 1981; (ed. with W. T. S. Gould) Resources of Merseyside, 1982; (with J. J. Bagley) Lancashire: A History of the County Palatine in Early Maps, 1985; (with A. F. Tatham) Keyguide to Information Sources: Cartography, 1986. **Address:** 25 Burnham Rd, Allerton, Liverpool L18 6JU, England.

HODGSON, Geoffrey M. British, b. 1946. **Genres:** Business/Trade/Industry, Economics, Politics/Government, Social sciences. **Career:** University of Northumbria, Newcastle upon Tyne, England, professor of economics, 1990-92; Cambridge University, England, lecturer in economics, 1992-98; University of Hertfordshire, research professor, 1999-. **Publications:** Socialism and Parliamentary Democracy, 1977; Labour at the Crossroads, 1981; Capitalism, Value, and Exploitation, 1982; The Democratic Economy, 1984; Economics and Institutions, 1988; After Marx and Sraffa: Essays in Political Economy, 1991; Economics and Evolution: Bringing Life Back Into Economics, 1993; Economics & Utopia, 1999; Evolution & Institutions, 1999; How Economics Forgot History, 2001. EDITOR: (with E. Screpanti) Rethinking Economics, 1991; The Economics of Institutions, 1993; (with W. Samuels and M. Tool) The Elgar Companion to Institutional and Evolutionary Economics, 1994; Economics and Biology, 1994. Contributor to economic and future studies journals. **Address:** Malting House, 1 Burton End, West Wickham, Cambridge CB1 6SD, England. **Online address:** g.m.hodgson@herts.ac.uk

HODGSON, Harriet. American, b. 1935. **Genres:** How-to books, Human relations/Parenting, Medicine/Health. **Career:** Freelance writer and editor; teacher. Rochester Post-Bulletin, freelance special features writer; KSMQ, Austin, MN, producer and host of "Parenting Today"; writer and narrator of "Parent Talk," a weekly radio commentary program; guest on radio and TV talk shows. **Publications:** Just for You, 1978; "I Made It Myself!", 1979; E Is for Energy, M Is for Me; 1980; Artworks, 1986; Gameworks, 1986; A Parent's Survival Guide, 1986; Toyworks, 1986; Contraptions, 1987; My

First Fourth of July Book (poetry), 1987; Parents Recover Too, 1988; Rochester: City of the Prairie, 1989; When You Love a Child, 1992; Powerplays Leader's Guide, 1993; Powerplays: How Teens Can Pull the Plug on Sexual Harassment, 1993; Heart Surgery and You: A Guide for Teens, 1994; Heart Surgery and You: An Activity Book for Gradeschoolers, 1994; Heart Surgery and You: An Activity Book for Preschoolers, 1994; Alzheimer's: Finding the Words, 1995; The Alzheimer's Caregiver, 1998; Smart Aging, 1999; Food Label Detective, 2002; Grieving Too Soon, 2002; Why Do I Feel This Way?, 2002; Good Samaritan Dental Clinic, 2003; Cracking the Health Words Code, 2003; Catching the Exercise Thief, 2003. Contributor to anthologies, books, and periodicals. **Address:** 1107 Foxcroft Ln SW, Rochester, MN 55902-3411, U.S.A.

HODGSON, Peter C. American, b. 1934. **Genres:** Theology/Religion. **Career:** Trinity University, San Antonio, TX, Assistant Professor of Religion, 1963-65; Vanderbilt University, Nashville, TN, Assistant Professor, 1965-69, Associate Professor, 1969-73, Chairman of the Graduate Dept. of Religion, 1975-80, Professor of Theology, 1973-97, Chairman of the Graduate Dept. of Religion, 1990-97, Charles G. Finney Professor of Theology, 1997-2003. **Publications:** The Formation of Historical Theology: A Study of F.C. Baur, 1966; Jesus Word and Presence: An Essay in Christology, 1971; Children of Freedom: Black Liberation in Christian Perspective, 1974; New Birth of Freedom: A Theology of Bondage and Liberation, 1976; Revisioning the Church: Ecclesial Freedom in the New Paradigm, 1988; God in History: Shapes of Freedom, 1989; Winds of the Spirit: A Constructive Christian Theology, 1994; God's Wisdom: Toward a Theology of Education, 1999; Theology in the Fiction of George Eliot, 2001; Christian Faith: A Brief Introduction, 2001; Hegel and Christian Theology, 2005. EDITOR: (and trans.) Ferdinand Christian Baur on the Writing of Church History, 1968; The Life of Jesus Critically Examined, by D. F. Strauss, 1972; (co-) Christian Theology, 1985; (co-) Readings in Christian Theology, 1985; (and trans.) Lectures on the Philosophy of Religion, by G.W.F. Hegel, vol. 1, 1984, vol. 2, 1987, vol. 3, 1985 (1-vol. as The Lectures of 1827, 1988); (and trans.) G.W.F. Hegel: Theologian of the Spirit, 1997. **Address:** 1742 Kingsbury Dr, Nashville, TN 37215, U.S.A.

HODGSON, Peter Edward. British, b. 1928. **Genres:** Physics. **Career:** Oxford University, lecturer in nuclear physics, 1967-95; Corpus Christi College, Oxford, sr. research fellow, now emeritus fellow. **Publications:** Optical Model of Elastic Scattering, 1963; Nuclear Reactions and Nuclear Structure, 1971; Nuclear Heavy-Ion Reactions, 1978; Growth Points in Nuclear Physics, 3 vols., 1980-81; Our Nuclear Future, 1983; The Nucleon Optical Model, 1994; Energy and Environment, 1997; Nuclear Power, Energy and the Environment, 1999; The Roots of Science and Its Fruits, 2003. **Address:** Dept of Physics, University of Oxford, Denys Wilkinson Bldg, Keble Rd, Oxford OX1 3RH, England. **Online address:** p.hodgson1@physics.ox.ac.uk

HØECK, Klaus. Danish, b. 1938. **Genres:** Poetry. **Career:** Poet; University of Copenhagen, Denmark, member of faculty; City of Copenhagen, mail carrier. **Publications:** POETRY: Yggdrasil: Indvendig rejse udvendig, 1966; Mitr-enf-snee: Indvendig rejse udvendig, 1967; Rejse (title means: Journey), Vol. I: Yggdrasil, Vol. II: Lejre, Vol. III: Alpha, Vol. IV: Omega, Vol. V: Hymne, 1971-73; Transformations, 1974; Pentagram, 1976; Projekt Perseus: Data og science fiction digte, 1977; Ulrike Marie Meinhof: Et digt; Firdobbelt sonetkreds: 1. bind af en trilogi, 1977; Topia eller Che Guevara: digte et epos, 1978; Skygger at efterårsdigt, 1978; Dylan Forever, 1979; Winterreisse: Dobbelte sonetkredse, 1979; (with A. Schnack) Bowie, Bowie, 1980; (with Schnack and F.P. Jac) Nul, 1980; (with Schnack) Eno one, 1980; (with Schnack) Renaldo and Clara, 1980; Canzone: Digte fra Norrebro, 1981; Sorte sonetter et digt, 1981; (with Schnack) Eno zebra, 1982; Metamorphoses, 1983; (with Schnack) Eno high, 1983; (with Schnack) Blåvand Revisited: Et topografisk digt i 4 moduler, 1984; Marienbad, 1984; International Klein Bleu, 1984; (with Schnack) Javngogn, 1985; Hjem (title means: Home), 1985; Blackberry Winter, 1987; Udvalgte digte, 1988; Lukas O'Kech: En digtroman, 1988; Heptameron, 1989; Salme, 1991; Eventyr (title means: Fairy Tales), 1992, selections published as The Woods, 1998; Hommage, 1995; 1001 digt: Med 18 ordsnit, 1995; Honeymoon, 1997; In Nomine, 2001; www.triptychon.com, 2003; Hsieh, 2004. Contributor to periodicals. **Address:** Hedebovej 84, 5474 Veflinge, Denmark.

HOEDEMAKER, Bert. Dutch, b. 1935. **Genres:** Theology/Religion. **Career:** Teacher at a theological seminary in Jakarta, Indonesia, 1967-71; professor at the state university in Groningen, Netherlands, 1981-. **Publications:** The Theology of H. Richard Niebuhr, 1970; (ed. and contrib) Missiology: An Ecumenical Introduction, 1995; Secularization and Mission, 1998. **Address:** van Ewsumweg 4, 9955 VL Rasquert, Netherlands. **Online address:** L.A.Hoedemaker@theol.rug.nl

HOEG, Peter. Danish, b. 1957. **Genres:** Novels. **Career:** Actor; dancer; drama teacher; sailor; writer, 1983-. **Publications:** Forestilling om det tyvende arhundrede, 1988, trans. as The History of Danish Dreams, 1995; Fortaellinger om natten, 1990, trans. by B. Haveland as Borderliners, 1994; Froken Smillas fornemmelse for sne, 1992, trans. by T. Nunnally as Smilla's Sense of Snow, 1993. **Address:** c/o Author Mail, Random House, 1745 Broadway #B1, New York, NY 10019-4305, U.S.A.

HOEHNE, Marcia. American, b. 1951. **Genres:** Children's fiction, Young adult fiction. **Career:** Kaukauna Public Schools, paraprofessional, summers 1970-73; affiliated with Kaukauna Public Library, Kaukauna, WI, 1975-79; La Leche League International, leader, 1980-86, district adviser, 1983-86; writer, 1988-, freelance editor, 2000-; Institute of Children's Literature, instructor, 2000-. **Publications:** The Journey of Emilie, 1999. THE ADVENTURES OF JENNA V. SERIES: A Place of My Own, 1993; A Pocket in My Heart, 1994; The Fairy Tale Friend, 1994; Sunflower Girl, 1995. CAROLINE GRADE MYSTERIES SERIES: The Music Box Test, 1994; The Paper Route Treasure, 1994. **Address:** 609 Walter St, Kaukauna, WI 54130, U.S.A.

HOEHNER, Harold W. American/Swiss, b. 1935. **Genres:** Theology/Religion. **Career:** Dallas Theological Seminary, instructor, 1968, assistant professor, 1968-73, associate professor, 1973-77, director of Ph.D. studies, 1975-2002, chairman, 1977-2001, distinguished professor of New Testament studies, 1977-. Bibliotheca Sacra, associate editor, 1969-74. **Publications:** Herod Antipas, 1972; Chronological Aspects of the Life of Christ, 1977; Ephesians: An Exegetical Commentary, 2002. **Address:** Dallas Theological Seminary, 3909 Swiss Ave, Dallas, TX 75204, U.S.A.

HOEPFFNER, Bernard. French, b. 1946. **Genres:** Translations. **Career:** Writer. La Main de Singe (literary magazine), co-founder, 1991. **Publications:** (trans.) Jacques Roubaud, The Princess Hoppy; or, The Tale of Labrador, 1993. Contributor of stories and articles to magazines. **Address:** Dieugrace, Les Bas-Hubacs, 26220 Dieulefit, France. **Online address:** bhoepf@vallee-drome.com

HOEPPNER, Edward Haworth. American, b. 1951. **Genres:** Poetry, Literary criticism and history. **Career:** Writer. **Publications:** Echoes and Moving Fields (critical study), 1994; Rain through High Windows (poetry), 2000. **Address:** 168 Krause St, Rockford, MI 49341-1214, U.S.A. **Online address:** hoeppner@oakland.edu

HOERDER, Dirk. German, b. 1943. **Genres:** History. **Career:** Free University of Berlin, Germany, assistant at John F. Kennedy Institute for North American Studies, 1969-75, part-time teacher, 1975-77; University of Bremen, Germany, part-time teacher, 1975-77, professor of the social history of North America, 1977-, director of Labor Migration Project, 1978-93. Visiting fellow, professor, and lecturer at universities and institutions worldwide. **Publications:** Protest, Direct Action, Repression: Dissent in American Society from Colonial Times to the Present, 1977; Creating Societies: Immigrant Lives in Canada, 1999; Cultures in Contact, 2002. EDITOR: Plutokraten und Sozialisten (title means: Plutocrats and Socialists), 1981; American Labor and Immigration History, 1877-1920s, 1982; (with C. Harzig) The Press of Labor Migrants in Europe and North America, 1880s-1930s, 1985; (and author of intro.) Struggle a Hard Battle (essays), 1986; (assoc. with others) The Settling of North America, 1995; J.N. Jodlbauer, Dreizehn Jahre in Amerika, 1910-1923, 1996. EDITOR & CONTRIBUTOR: Labor Migration in the Atlantic Economies, 1985; (with C. Harzig) The Immigrant Labor Press in North America, 1840s-1970s: An Annotated Bibliography, Vol. 1: Migrants from Northern Europe, Vol. 2: Migrants from Eastern and Southeastern Europe, Vol. 3: Migrants from Southern and Western Europe, 1987; (with D. Knauf) Fame, Fortune, and Sweet Liberty, 1992; (with H. Rossler) Distant Magnets, 1993; (with I. Blank and H. Rossler) Roots of the Transplanted, Vol. 1: Late 19th-Century East Central and Southeastern Europe, Vol. 2: Plebeian Culture, Class, and Politics in the Life of Labor Migrants, 1994; (with J. Nagler) People in Transit, 1995; (with L.P. Moch) European Migrants, 1996; (with R.-O. Schultze) Socio-Cultural Developments in the Metropolis, 2000; (with C. Harzig and A. Shubert) The Historical Practice of Diversity, 2003. Contributor to books. Contributor of articles and reviews to scholarly journals. **Address:** Dept of History, FB8, University of Bremen, Postfach 330440, D-28334 Bremen, Germany. **Online address:** hoerder@univ-bremen.de

HOERR, John P. American, b. 1930. **Genres:** Business/Trade/Industry, Industrial relations, History, Organized labor. **Career:** United Press International, wire service reporter in Newark and Trenton, NJ, 1956-57, Chicago, IL, 1958-60; Daily Tribune, Royal Oak, MI, reporter, 1957-58;

Business Week, New York City, correspondent from Detroit, MI, 1960-63, correspondent from Pittsburgh, PA, 1965-69, labor editor, 1975-79, associate editor, 1979-85, senior writer, 1985-91; freelance writer in Detroit, 1963-64; WQED-TV, Pittsburgh, labor reporter, commentator, and producer, 1969-74; freelance writer in Teaneck, NJ, 1991-. **Publications:** And the Wolf Finally Came: The Decline of the American Steel Industry, 1988; We Can't Eat Pestige: The Women Who Organized Harvard, 1997. **Address:** 12 Parker Lane, Teaneck, NJ 07666, U.S.A.

HOESTLANDT, Jo(celyne). French, b. 1948. **Genres:** Children's fiction. **Career:** Teacher in Paris, France, 1969-72; writer. Organizer of reading and writing animations for children in art centers and schools. **Publications:** La rentree de mamans, 1990, trans. as Back to School with Mom: A Story, 1992; La grande peur sous les etoiles, trans. by M. Polizzotti as Star of Fear, Star of Hope, 1995; Les passants de Noel, 1996; Les amoureux de Leonie, 1996. IN FRENCH: Emile bille de clown; Peurs. **Address:** 5 rue Felix Faure, 92500 Rueil Malmaison, France. **Online address:** js.hoestlandt@caramail.com

HOEZEE, Scott E. American, b. 1964. **Genres:** Theology/Religion. **Career:** Pastor of Christian Reformed church in Fremont, MI, 1990-93; Calvin Christian Reformed Church, Grand Rapids, MI, minister of preaching and administration, 1993-. Christian Reformed Ministers Institute, corresponding secretary, 1993-96; Princeton Theological Seminary, member of Pastor Theologian Program, 1998-2001. Newaygo County Habitat for Humanity, founding member and president, 1991-93. **Publications:** The Riddle of Grace: Applying Grace to the Christian Life, 1996; Flourishing in the Land: A Hundred Year History of Christian Reformed Home Missions in North America, 1996; Speaking as One: A Look at the Ecumenical Creeds, 1997; Remember Creation: God's World of Wonder and Delight, 1998; Speaking of Comfort: A Look at the Heidelberg Catechism, 1998: Proclaim the Wonder: Engaging Science on Sunday, 2003. Contributor of articles and reviews to periodicals. **Address:** 1634 Fisk Rd SE, Grand Rapids, MI 49506, U.S.A. **Online address:** shoezee@iserv.net

HOFF, Al. American, b. 1964. **Genres:** Humor/Satire. **Career:** Writer. **Publications:** Thrift Score (nonfiction), 1997; Funny Personal Ads, in press. **Address:** PO Box 90282, Pittsburgh, PA 15224, U.S.A. **Online address:** al@girlreporter.com

HOFF, B. J. American. **Genres:** Novels, Romance/Historical, Inspirational/Motivational Literature. **Career:** Writer. Former church music director. **Publications:** The Penny Whistle (novel), 1996; Cloth of Heaven (historical novel), 1997; Ashes and Lace (historical novel), 1999. EMERALD BALLAD SERIES: Song of the Silent Harp; Heart of the Lonely Exile; Land of a Thousand Dreams; Sons of an Ancient Glory; Dawn of the Golden Promise. OTHER NOVELS: Masquerade (originally published as Mists of Danger); Winds of Graystone Manor. **Address:** c/o Tyndale House Publishers, 351 Executive Dr, Carol Stream, IL 60188, U.S.A.

HOFF, Joan. American, b. 1937. **Genres:** Biography, History, Women's studies and issues, Law, Politics/Government. **Career:** California State University, Sacramento, assistant professor of U.S. diplomatic history, 1967-70; Arizona State University, Tempe, associate professor, 1970-76, professor of U.S. foreign relations, beginning in 1976; editor and writer. Harvard Law School, visiting scholar, 1976-77. **Publications:** American Business and Foreign Policy, 1920-1933, 1971; (ed.) The Twenties: The Critical Issues, 1971; Ideology and Economics: U.S. Relations with the Soviet Union, 1918-1933, 1974; (ed.) Report on the West Coast Women's Studies Conference, 1974; Herbert Hoover: Forgotten Progressive, 1975; (with A. Sachs) Sexism and the Law: A Study of Male Beliefs and Legal Bias in Britain and the United States, 1979; (ed. with E.W. Hawley and R. Zieger) Herbert Hoover as Secretary of Commerce, 1921-1928: Studies in New Era Thought and Practice, 1981; (ed., as Joan Hoff-Wilson with M. Lightman) Without Precedent: The Life and Career of Eleanor Roosevelt, 1984; (ed. as Joan Hoff-Wilson) Rights of Passage: The Past and Future of the ERA, 1986; Wellington's Marriage: A Soldier's Wife, 1987; (ed., with Susan Gubar) For Adult Users Only: The Dilemma of Violent Pornography, 1989; Law, Gender, and Injustice: A Legal History of U.S. Women, 1991, rev. ed. 1994; Nixon Reconsidered, 1994; (co-ed. with D. Ink) The Nixon Presidency, 1996; (with M. Yeates) The Cooper's Wife is Missing, 2000. **Address:** PO Box 160806, Big Sky, MT 59716, U.S.A.

HOFFER, Peter T(homas). American, b. 1942. **Genres:** Psychology, History, Translations. **Career:** Lincoln University, Lincoln University, PA, instructor, 1971-75, assistant professor of German, 1975-82; Philadelphia College of Pharmacy and Science, Philadelphia, PA, assistant professor,

1982-87, associate professor of German, 1988-93; University of the Sciences in Philadelphia, professor of German, 1993-. Library of Congress, official translator of Sigmund Freud Archives. **Publications:** Klaus Mann, 1978. TRANSLATOR: (with A. Hoffer) Sigmund Freud, A Phylogenetic Fantasy: Overview of the Transference Neuroses, 1987; The Correspondence of Sigmund Freud and Sandor Ferenczi, Vol. 1: 1908-1914, 1993, Vol. 2: 1914-1920, 1996, Vol. 3: 1920-1933, 2000. Contributor of articles and reviews to scholarly journals. **Address:** University of the Sciences in Philadelphia, 600 S 43rd St, Philadelphia, PA 19104, U.S.A. **Online address:** p.hoffer@usip.edu

HOFFMAN, Alice. American, b. 1952. **Genres:** Novels, Plays/Screenplays. **Career:** Freelance writer. **Publications:** Property Of, 1977; The Drowning Season, 1979; Angel Landing, 1980; White Horses, 1982; Independence Day (screenplay), 1983; Fortune's Daughter, 1985; Illumination Night, 1987; At Risk, 1988; Seventh Heaven, 1990; Turtle Moon, 1992; Second Nature, 1994; Practical Magic, 1995; Fireflies, 1997; Scribner's Best of Fiction Workshops, 1997; Here on Earth, 1998; Local Girls, 1999; River King, 2000; Horsefly, 2000; Aquamarine, 2001; Blue Diary, 2001; Indigo, 2002; Green Angel, 2003; The Probable Future, 2003; Blackbird House, 2004; The Ice Queen, 2005. **Address:** c/o Elaine Markson, 44 Greenwich Ave, New York, NY 10011, U.S.A. **Online address:** www.alicehoffman.com

HOFFMAN, Allan M. American, b. 1948. **Genres:** Medicine/Health. **Career:** California State University, dean; University of Southern California, director of medical education at St. Francis Medical Center and clinical professor; Des Moines University, IA, professor and dean of College of Health Sciences, 1998-, director of Center for the Prevention of Community Violence, 1999. **Publications:** History of an Idea, 1981. EDITOR & CONTRIBUTOR: (with D. Julius) Managing Colleges: Perspectives for the Next Century, 1994; (with Julius) Total Quality Management: Implications for Higher Education, 1995; Schools: Violence, and Society, 1996; (with R. Fenske and J. Schuh) Violence on the College Campus, 1998; (with R. Summers) Managing Colleges and Universities: Issues for Leadership, 1999; Teen Violence: A Global Perspective, 2002. Contributor of articles and reviews to professional journals. **Address:** College of Health Sciences, Des Moines University, 3200 Grand Ave, Des Moines, IA 50312, U.S.A. **Online address:** Allan.Hoffman@dmu.edu

HOFFMAN, Andrew. American, b. 1956. **Genres:** Literary criticism and history, Novels. **Career:** Brown University, Providence, RI, visiting scholar in English, 1992-, and American civilization, 1994-. **Publications:** Twain's Heroes, Twain's Worlds, 1988; Beehive (novel), 1992; Inventing Mark Twain, 1997. Contributor to periodicals. **Address:** 76 Wilcox Ave., Pawtucket, RI 02860, U.S.A.

HOFFMAN, Andy. (Andrew Jay). American, b. 1956. **Genres:** Novels, Literary criticism and history, Biography. **Career:** Running Press, Philadelphia, PA, editor, 1976-77; Headlands Press, San Francisco, CA, editor, 1977-79; University of Oregon, Eugene, instructor in writing, 1979-81; Us Magazine, New York City, copy chief, 1981-82; Brown University, Providence, RI, special assistant to the dean of the graduate school, 1986-90, visiting scholar, 1993; Central Connecticut State University, New Britain, assistant professor of English, 1990-91; freelance writer and editor, 1991-; Goosewing, founder and CEO, 1999-2003; Bristol Community College, Fall River, MA, director of teaching American history projects, 2003-. **Publications:** Twain's Heroes, Twain's Worlds, 1988; Beehive (novel), 1992; Inventing Mark Twain: A Biography of Samuel Langhorne Clemens, 1997. Contributor of short stories to magazines and journals. **Address:** 76 Wilcox Ave, Pawtucket, RI 02860, U.S.A. **Online address:** jamall@juno.com

HOFFMAN, Bruce. American, b. 1954. **Genres:** International relations/Current affairs, Military/Defense/Arms control, Politics/Government. **Career:** Rand Corporation Washington, DC, member of the senior research staff in the International Policy Department, 1981-94, director of strategy and doctrine program for the Army Research Division, 1993-94, director, 1998-; St. Andrews University, St. Andrews, Fife, Scotland, chair of the department of international relations, 1994-98, director of the Centre for the Study of Terrorism and Political Violence, 1994-98, and reader in international relations; served on the advisory board of the International Group for Research and Information on Security, Brussels, Belgium; instructor at the University of Buckingham. Editor in chief of Studies in Conflict and Terrorism; member of the advisory board of Terrorism and Political Violence. **Publications:** The PLO and Israel in Central America: The Geopolitical Dimension, 1988; The Potential Terrorist Threat to Commercial Nuclear Facilities, 1988; British Air Power in Peripheral Conflict, 1919-1976, 1989; Insider Crime: The Threat to Nuclear Facilities and Programs, 1990; (with K. Gardela) The Rand Chronology of International Terrorism for 1986, 1990; Recent Trends and Future Prospects of Iranian Sponsored International Terrorism, 1990; (with J.M. Taw) Defense Policy and Low-Intensity Conflict: The Development of Britain's "Small Wars" Doctrine during the 1950s, 1991; (with J.M. Taw and D. Arnold) Lessons for Contemporary Counterinsurgencies: The Rhodesian Experience, 1991; (with K. Gardela) The Rand Chronology of International Terrorism for 1987, 1991; (with S. Sayari) Urbanization and Insurgency: The Turkish Case, 1976-1980, 1991; (with K. Gardela) The Rand Chronology of International Terrorism for 1988, 1992; (with J.M. Taw) A Strategic Framework for Countering Terrorism and Insurgency, 1992; (with C. Meyer and J. Duncan) Force-on-Force Attacks: Their Implications for the Defense of U.S. Nuclear Facilities, 1993; (with T. Downes-Le Guin) The Impact of Terrorism on Public Opinion, 1988 to 1989, 1993; Holy Terror: The Implications of Terrorism Motivated by a Religious Imperative, 1993; Responding to Terrorism across the Technological Spectrum, 1994; (with J.M. Taw) The Urbanization of Insurgency: The Potential Challenge to U.S. Army Operations, 1994; (with K.J. Riley) Domestic Terrorism: A National Assessment of State and Local Preparedness, 1995; Inside Terrorism, 1998. Contributor to periodicals. **Address:** Rand Corporation, 1200 S Hayes St, Arlington, VA 22202-5050, U.S.A. **Online address:** hoffman@rand.org

HOFFMAN, Carl. American, b. 1960. **Genres:** Documentaries/Reportage. **Career:** Freelance writer, 1984-. **Publications:** Hunting Warbirds: The Obsessive Quest for Lost Aircraft of World War II, 2001. Contributor to periodicals. **Address:** 5239 Sherier Place NW, Washington, DC 20016, U.S.A.

HOFFMAN, Daniel. American, b. 1923. **Genres:** Poetry, Literary criticism and history, Mythology/Folklore. **Career:** Schelling Professor of English, 1983-93, and Poet-in-Residence, 1978-93, Emeritus, 1993-; University of Pennsylvania, Philadelphia (Professor of English, 1966-83). Chancellor, Academy of American Poets, 1974-98. Faculty member, Columbia University, NYC, 1952-56, Faculte des Lettres, Dijon, France, 1956-57, and Swarthmore College, Pa., 1957-66. Consultant in Poetry, Library of Congress, 1973-74; Kings's College London, 1991-92. **Publications:** Paul Bunyan, Last of the Frontier Demigods, 1952; An Armada of Thirty Whales, 1954; The Poetry of Stephen Crane, 1957; A Little Geste, 1960; Form and Fable in American Fiction, 1961; The City of Satisfactions, 1963; Barbarous Knowledge, 1967; Striking the Stones, 1968; Broken Laws, 1970; Poe Poe Poe Poe Poe Poe Poe, 1972; The Center of Attention, 1974; Able Was I Ere I Saw Elba: Selected Poems, 1977; Brotherly Love, 1981; Hang-Gliding from Helicon: New and Selected Poems 1948-1988, 1988; Faulkner's Country Matters: Folklore and Fable in Yoknapatawpha, 1989; Words to Create a World, 1993; Middens of the Tribe, 1995; Zone of the Interior: A Memoir 1942-1947, 2000; Darkening Water: Poems, 2002; (trans.) A Play of Mirrors: Poems by Ruth Domino, 2002; Beyond Silence: Selected Shorter Poems 1948-2003, 2003. EDITOR: The Red Badge of Courage and Other Stories, 1957; American Poetry and Poetics, 1962; (with S. Hynes) English Literary Criticism: Romantic and Victorian, 1963; The Harvard Guide to Contemporary American Writing, 1979; Ezra Pound and William Carlos Williams, 1983;. **Address:** 502 Cedar Ln, Swarthmore, PA 19081, U.S.A.

HOFFMAN, Eva. American (born Poland), b. 1945. **Genres:** Autobiography/Memoirs, Travel/Exploration, History. **Career:** University of New Hampshire, Durham, assistant professor of literature, 1975-76; Tufts University, Medford, MA, assistant professor of literature, 1976-77; New York Times, New York City, "Week in Review" editor, 1980-82, "Arts and Leisure" deputy editor, 1982-85; New York Times Book Review, New York City, editor, 1987-89. **Publications:** Lost in Translation: A Life in a New Language (autobiography), 1989; Exit into History: A Journey through the New Eastern Europe, 1993; Shtetl: A History of a Small Town and the Life and Death of Polish Jews; The Sevret, 2002. **Address:** Georges Borchardt, 136 E 57th St, New York, NY 10022, U.S.A.

HOFFMAN, Mary (Margaret). Also writes as Mary Lassiter. British, b. 1945. **Genres:** Children's fiction, Education, Writing/Journalism. **Career:** Writer, 1970-; Open University, Milton Keynes, England, lecturer in education, 1975-80; reading consultant to BBC-TV, 1977-95; University of Exeter, research associate, 1993-94. **Publications:** FOR ADULTS: Reading, Writing, and Relevance, 1976; (as Mary Lassiter) Our Names, Ourselves, 1983. FOR CHILDREN: White Magic, 1975; (with C. Callery) Buttercup Buskers' Rainy Day, 1982; Tiger, 1983; Monkey, 1983; Elephant, 1983; Panda, 1983; Lion, 1985; Zebra, 1985; Hippo, 1985; Gorilla, 1985; (with W. Hall) The Return of the Antelope, 1985; Whales and Sharks, 1986; (with T. Weston) Dangerous Animals, 1986; Beware, Princess!, 1986; The Second-hand Ghost, 1986; King of the Castle, 1986; A Fine Picnic, 1986, 1994; Animal Hide and Seek, 1986; The Perfect Pet, 1986; Clothes for Sale, 1986; Wild Cat, 1986;

Giraffe, 1986; Snake, 1986; Bear, 1986; Wild Dog, 1987; Seal, 1987; Antelope, 1987; Bird of Prey, 1987; Nancy No-Size, 1987; Specially Sarah, 1987; My Grandma Has Black Hair, 1988; Dracula's Daughter, 1988; All about Lucy, 1989; Min's First Jump, 1989; Mermaid and Chips, 1989; Dog Powder, 1989; Catwalk, 1989; Just Jack, 1990; Leon's Lucky Lunchbreak, 1991; The Babies' Hotel, 1991; Amazing Grace, 1991; Max in the Jungle, 1991; The Ghost Menagerie, 1992; Henry's Baby, 1993; Cyril MC, 1993; Bump in the Night, 1993; Amazing Mammals, 1993; Boundless, Grace, 1995; Earth, Fire, Water, Air, 1995; Trace in Space, 1996; A Vanishing Tail, 1996; Quantum Squeak, 1996; Special Powers, 1997; A First Bible Storybook, 1997; An Angel Just Like Me, 1997; Comet, 1997; Sun, Moon and Stars, 1998; A Twist in the Tail, 1998; Virtual Friend, 1998; Clever Katya, 1998; A First Book of Myths, 1999; Three Wise Women, 1999; Starring Grace, 2000; Women of Camelot, 2000; Brother & Sister Tales, 2000; Parables, 2000; A Treasury of Nursery Stories, 2000; Miracles, 2001; The Colour of Home, 2002; Animals of the Bible, 2002; Stravaganza series, City of Masks, 2002, City of Stars, 2003, City of Plovers, 2005; Bravo, Grace!, 2005. EDITOR: Ip, Dip, Sky Blue, 1990; Stacks of Stories, 1997. **Address:** c/o Rogers, Coleridge & White, 20 Powis Mews, London W11 1JN, England. **Online address:** maryhoffman@maryhoffman.co.uk

HOFFMAN, Mat. American, b. 1972. **Genres:** Young adult fiction. **Career:** Amateur freestyle BMX stunt bicyclist, 1984-88; professional freestyle BMX vert-ramp bicyclist, 1988-. Ten-time vert world champion; high air world record holder. Founder and president, Hoffman Promotions and Hoffman Bikes; producer, director, and host of bicycle competitions and television shows. **Publications:** (with Mark Lewman) The Ride of My Life (autobiography), 2003. **Address:** Hoffman Enterprises, POB 18931, Oklahoma City, OK 73154, U.S.A.

HOFFMAN, Michael J. American, b. 1939. **Genres:** Novels, Literary criticism and history. **Career:** Washington College, Chestertown, MD, instructor of English, 1962-64; University of Pennsylvania, Philadelphia, assistant professor of English, 1964-67; University of California, Davis, assistant professor, 1967-71, graduate chairman, 1971-72, 1995-98, associate professor, 1971-75, assistant vice chancellor of academic affairs, 1974-83, professor of English, 1975-2001, dept. chairman, 1984-89, director of Humanities Institute, 1986-91, coordinator of writing programs, 1991-94, master undergraduate adviser, 1994-95. **Publications:** The Development of Abstractionism in the Writings of Gertrude Stein, 1965; The Buddy System (novel), 1973; The Subversive Vision: American Romanticism in Literature, 1973; Gertrude Stein, 1976. EDITOR: Critical Essays on Gertrude Stein, 1986; Essentials of the Theory of Fiction, 1988, 3rd ed., 2005; Critical Essays on American Modernism, 1992. **Address:** Dept of English, University of California, Davis, CA 95616, U.S.A. **Online address:** mjhoffman@ucdavis.edu

HOFFMAN, Ronald. American, b. 1941. **Genres:** History. **Career:** University of Maryland, College Park, assistant professor, 1969-73, associate professor of history, 1973-92, professor of history, 1992-; Institute of Early American History and Culture, director, 1992-; College of William and Mary, professor of history, 1993-. **Publications:** A Spirit of Dissension, 1973; Sovereign States in an Age of Uncertainty, 1982; (with others) The Pursuit of Liberty, 1983; (with S.D. Mason) Princes of Ireland, Planters of Maryland, 2000. EDITOR: (with I. Berlin) Slavery and Freedom in the Age of American Revolution, 1983; (co) An Uncivil War, 1985; (co) The Economy of Early America, 1988; (with M. Sobel and F.J. Teute) Through a Glass Darkly, 1997; (with S.D. Mason and E.S. Darcy) Dear Papa, Dear Charley, 3 vols., 2001. EDITOR WITH P.J. ALBERT: Diplomacy and Revolution, 1981; Arms and Independence, 1984; Peace and the Peacemakers, 1986; Women in the Age of the American Revolution, 1989; We Shall Overcome: Martin Luther King, Jr, and the Book Freedom Struggle, 1990; To Form a More Perfect Union, 1992; (and C. Carson) Of Consuming Interests: The Style of Life in the Eighteenth Century, 1994; Religion in a Revolutionary Age, 1994; The Transforming Hand of Revolution, 1996; Launching the "Extended Republic," 1996; The Bill of Rights, 1997; (and F.E. Hoxie) Native Americans and the Early Republic, 1999. **Address:** Omohundro Institute of Early American History & Culture, PO Box 8781, Williamsburg, VA 23187-8781, U.S.A. **Online address:** ieahe1@wm.edu

HOFFMAN, Valerie J. American, b. 1954. **Genres:** Theology/Religion. **Career:** University of Illinois at Chicago Circle, Chicago, instructor in Arabic at Spertus College of Judaica, 1978; University of Illinois at Urbana-Champaign, associate professor of religion, 1983-. Dialogue Mission III (cultural mission), member, 1979; Fulbright scholar, Egypt, 1987-88, Oman, 2000-01; Ecole des Hautes Etudes en Sciences Sociales, Paris, France, lecturer, 1993. **Publications:** Sufism, Mystics, and Saints in Modern Egypt,

1995. Author of videotape Celebrating the Prophet in the Remembrance of God: Sufi "Dhikr" in Egypt, 1997. Contributor of articles and reviews to scholarly journals. **Address:** Program for the Study of Religion, University of Illinois at Urbana-Champaign, 707 South Mathews Ave., Urbana, IL 61801, U.S.A. **Online address:** vhoffman@uiuc.edu

HOFFMAN, William M(oses). American, b. 1939. **Genres:** Plays/Screenplays, Songs/Lyrics and libretti, Gay and lesbian issues. **Career:** Ed., New American Play series, Hill & Wang publrs., NYC, 1968- (Drama Ed., 1961-68). Playwright-in-Residence, La Mama Theatre, NYC, 1978-79. Star Professor, Hofstra University, Hempstead, New York, 1980. One Life to Live, staff writer, 1991-92. **Publications:** PLAYS: Thank You, Miss Victoria, 1965; Saturday Night at the Movies, 1966; Good Night, I Love You, 1966; Spring Play, 1967; Three Masked Dances, 1967; Incantation, 1967; Uptight!, 1968; XXX, 1969, in London as Nativity Play, 1970; Luna, 1970; A Quick Nut Bread to Make Your Mouth Water, 1970; From Fool to Hanged Man, 1972; The Children's Crusade, 1972; I Love Ya, Ya Big Ape, 1973; Gilles de Rais, 1975; (with R. Englender) Notes from the New World, 1976; (with A. Holland) Cornbury, 1977; The Last Days of Stephen Foster, 1978; A Book of Etiquette, 1978; Gulliver's Travels, 1978; (with A. Holland) Shoe Palace Murray, 1978; Whistler: 5 Portraits, 1978; (with A. Holland) The Cherry Orchard: Part II, 1983; As Is, 1985. LIBRETTI: The Cloisters, 1968; Wedding Song, 1984; The Ghost of Versailles, 1991; Jack and Jill, 1994; Of Rage and Remembrance, 1996. EDITOR: New American Plays 2, 3, 4, 3 vols., 1968-71; Gay Plays: The First Collection, 1979. OTHER: Fine Frenzy (poems), 1972. **Address:** c/o Mitch Douglas, ICM, 40 W 57th St 16th Fl, New York, NY 10019-4098, U.S.A.

HOFFMANN, Donald. American, b. 1933. **Genres:** Architecture. **Career:** General assignment reporter, 1956-65, and Art Critic, 1965-90, Kansas City Star, Missouri; Assistant Ed., Journal of the Society of Architectural Historians, 1970-71. **Publications:** (ed.) The Meanings of Architecture: Buildings and Writings by John Wellborn Root, 1967; The Architecture of John Wellborn Root, 1973; Frank Lloyd Wright's Fallingwater, 1978; Frank Lloyd Wright's Robie House, 1984; Frank Lloyd Wright: Architecture and Nature, 1986; Frank Lloyd Wright's Hollyhock House, 1992; Understanding Frank Lloyd Wright's Architecture, 1995; Frank Lloyd Wright's Dana House, 1996; Frank Lloyd Wright, Louis Sullivan and the Skyscraper, 1998; Frank Lloyd Wright's House on Kentuck Knob, 2000. **Address:** 6441 Holmes, Kansas City, MO 64131, U.S.A.

HOFFMANN, Peter (Conrad Werner). Canadian (born Germany), b. 1930. **Genres:** History. **Career:** University of Northern Iowa, Cedar Falls, assistant professor, 1965-68, associate professor, 1968-70; McGill University, Montreal, William Kingsford Professor of History, 1970/1988-. **Publications:** Die diplomatischen Beziehungen zwischen Württemberg und Bayern im Krimkrieg und bis zum Beginn der Italienischen Krise 1853-1858, 1963; (trans.) John J. McCloy II: Die Verschwörung gegen Hitler: Ein Geschenk an die deutsche Zukunft, 1963; Widerstand, Staatsstreich, Attentat: Der Kampf der Opposition gegen Hitler, 1969; Die Sicherheit des Diktators: Hitlers Leibwachen, Schutzmassnahmen, Residenzen, Hauptquartiere, 1975; The History of the German Resistance 1933-1945, 1977; Hitler's Personal Security, 1979; Widerstand gegen Hitler, 1979; German Resistance to Hitler, 1988; Claus Schenk Graf von Stauffenberg und seine Brüder, 1992; Stauffenberg: A Family History, 1905-1944, 1995; Stauffenberg und der 20. Juli 1944, 1998. **Address:** Dept of History, McGill University, 855 Sherbrooke St W, Montreal, QC, Canada H3A 2T7.

HOFFMANN, Roald. American (born Poland), b. 1937. **Genres:** Plays/Screenplays, Poetry, Sciences. **Career:** Harvard University, junior fellow of Society of Fellows, 1962-65; Cornell University, Ithaca, NY, faculty member, 1965-, currently Frank H.T. Rhodes Professor of Humane Letters. **Publications:** (with R.B. Woodward) Conservation of Orbital Symmetry, 1970; The Metamict State (poems), 1987; Solids and Surfaces, 1988; Gaps and Verges (poems), 1990; (with V. Torrence) Chemistry Imagined, 1993; The Same and Not the Same, 1995; (with S.L. Schmidt) Old Wine, New Flasks, 1997; Memory Effects (poems), 1999; (with C. Djerassi) Oxygen (play), 2001; Soliton (poems) 2002; Catalista (poems, Spanish), 2002. Work represented in anthologies. Contributor of articles to scientific journals and poems to literary magazines. **Address:** Dept of Chemistry, Cornell University, Ithaca, NY 14853, U.S.A. **Online address:** rh34@cornell.edu

HOFFMANN, Stanley. American/French (born Austria), b. 1928. **Genres:** International relations/Current affairs, Politics/Government. **Career:** Harvard University, Cambridge, MA, member of faculty, 1955-, professor of government, 1963-80, chairman, Center for European Studies, 1969-95, Douglas Dillon Professor of the Civilization of France, 1980-96, Paul and Catherine Buttenwieser University Professor, 1997-. **Publications:** Organisations internationales et pouvoirs politiques des Etats, 1954; Le Mouvement Poujade, 1956; Contemporary Theory in International Relations, 1963; The State of War, 1963; (ed.) Conditions of World Order, 1968; Gulliver's Troubles, 1968; Decline or Renewal?, 1974; Primacy or World Order, 1978; Duties beyond Borders, 1981; Dead Ends, 1983; Janus and Minerva, 1986; The European Sisyphus, 1995; The Ethics and Politics of Humanitarian Intervention, 1996; World Disorders, 1998. CO-AUTHOR: In Search of France, 1963; The Relevance of International Law, 1968; La Politique des Sciences Sociales en France, 1975; The Fifth Republic at Twenty, 1981; Living with Nuclear Weapons, 1983; The Mitterrand Experiment, 1987; Rousseau and International Relations, 1991; The New European Community, 1992; After the Cold War, 1993; The Tanner Lecture on Human Values, vol. 15, 1994. **Address:** 61 Brewster St, Cambridge, MA 02138, U.S.A. **Online address:** shhoffm@fas.harvard.edu

HOFFMEISTER, Donald Frederick. American, b. 1916. **Genres:** Natural history, Zoology. **Career:** Associate Curator, Museum of Natural History; Assistant Professor, University of Kansas, Lawrence, 1944-46; Director, Museum of Natural History, 1946-84; Professor of Zoology, 1959-84, University of Illinois, Urbana, Professor Emeritus, 1984-. **Publications:** (With Zim) Mammals, 1955; (with Mohr) Fieldbook of Illinois Mammals, 1957; Mammals, 1963; Zoo Animals, 1967; Mammals of Grand Canyon, 1971; Mammals of Arizona, 1986; Mammals of Illinois, 1989. **Address:** Museum of Natural History, University of Illinois, Urbana, IL 61801, U.S.A.

HOFMANN, Michael. German, b. 1957. **Genres:** Poetry, Literary criticism and history, Translations. **Career:** Writer, poet, and translator, 1983-. University of Florida, Gainesville, distinguished lecturer, 1993-. University of Michigan, Ann Arbor, visiting associate professor, 1994; Rutgers University, NJ, Craig-Kade, visiting writer, 2003. **Publications:** POETRY: Nights in the Iron Hotel, 1983; Acrimony, 1986; K.S. in Lakeland: New and Selected Poems, 1990; Corona, Corona, 1993; Approximately Nowhere, 1999. TRANSLATOR: (and author of intro.) K. Tucholsky, Castle Gripsholm, 1985; B. Sterchi, Bloesch, 1988, in US as Cow, 1990; (with C. Middleton) G. Hofmann, Balzac's Horse and Other Stories, 1989; J. Roth, The Legend of the Holy Drinker, 1989; (with S. Whiteside) W. Wenders, Emotion Pictures: Reflections on the Cinema, 1990; W. Wenders, The Logic of Images, 1991; P. Suskind, The Story of Mr. Sommer, 1992; J. Roth, Right and Left, 1992; (and author of intro) W. Koeppen, Death in Rome, 1993; H. von Hofmannsthal, The Lord Chandos Letter, 1995; G. Hofmann, The Film Explainer, 1995; H. Mueller, The Land of the Green Plums, 1996; (and author of intro.) F. Kafka, The Man Who Disappeared, 1997; W. Wenders, The Act of Seeing, 1997; Z. Jenny, The Pollen Room, 1998; J. Roth, The String of Peaks, 1998; J. Roth, Rebellion, 1999; P. Stamm, Agnes, 2000; W. Werder, My Time with Antonioni, 2000; J. Roth, The Collected Stories, 2001; J. Roth, The Wandering Jews, 2001; W. Wenders, On Film, 2001; S. Hofmann, Luck, 2002; W. Koeppen, The Hothouse, 2002; (and author of intro.) J. Roth, The Radetzky March, 2002; P. Junge, The Snowflake Constant, 2002; W. Koeppen, A Sad Affair, 2003; (and author of intro.) E. Junger, Storm of Steel, 2003; (and author of intro.) J. Roth, Report from a Parisian Paradise, 2003. PLAYS: The Double-Bass, 1987; The Good Person of Sichuan, 1989. CRITICISM: Behind the Lines, 2001; (and author of intro.) Robert Lowell, 2001; (and author of intro.) John Berryman, 2004. OTHER: (with J. Lasdun) After Ovid: New Metamorphoses, 1994. Contributor of poetry to anthologies. Contributor to periodicals. **Address:** Dept of English, University of Florida, 4008 Turlington Hall, PO Box 117310, Gainesville, FL 32611-7310, U.S.A.

HOFSTADTER, Douglas (Richard). American, b. 1945. **Genres:** Information science/Computers, Language/Linguistics, Philosophy, Translations. **Career:** Indiana University, Bloomington, computer science, asst professor, associate professor, 1977-84, professor, cognitive science and computer science, director, Center for Research on Concepts and Cognition, 1988-; University of Michigan, Ann Arbor, psychology, professor, 1984-88. Former columnist, Scientific American. **Publications:** Goedel, Escher, Bach, an Eternal Golden Braid, 1979; (with D. Dennett) The Mind's I, 1981; Metamagical Themas, 1985; Ambigrammi, 1987; Fluid Concepts and Creative Analogies, 1995; Le Ton beau de Marot: In Praise of the Music of Language, 1997; Eugene Onegin: A Novel in Verse by Alexander Pushkin (novel versification), 1999. **Address:** Indiana University, Center for Research on Concepts and Cognition, 510-512 N Fess St, Bloomington, IN 47408-3822, U.S.A. **Online address:** dughof@cogsci.indiana.edu

HOGAN, David Gerard. American, b. 1959. **Genres:** Adult non-fiction. **Career:** Rogers State College, Claremont, OK, instructor, 1988-89; Heidelberg College, Tiffin, OH, associate professor, 1989-. **Publications:** Selling 'em by the Sack, 1997. **Address:** Heidelberg College, Tiffin, OH 44883, U.S.A. **Online address:** hogan@acc-net.com and dhogan@mail.heidelberg.edu

HOGAN, J. Michael. American, b. 1953. **Genres:** Communications/Media, Politics/Government, Speech/Rhetoric. **Career:** University of Virginia, Charlottesville, assistant professor of rhetoric and communication studies, 1981-86; Indiana University-Bloomington, associate professor, 1986-95, professor of speech communication, 1995-97; Penn State University, professor of communication arts and sciences, 1997-. **Publications:** The Panama Canal in American Politics: Domestic Advocacy and the Evolution of Policy, 1986; The Nuclear Freeze Campaign: Rhetoric and Foreign Policy in the Telepolitical Age, 1994; EDITOR: Rhetoric and Community: Case Studies in Unity and Fragmentation, 1998; Rhetoric and Reform in the Progressive Era, 2003. Contributor to books. Contributor of articles and reviews to communication journals. **Address:** Dept of Communication Arts and Sciences, Penn State University, 234 Sparks Bldg, University Park, PA 16802, U.S.A. **Online address:** jmh32@psu.edu

HOGAN, James P(atrick). British, b. 1941. **Genres:** Novellas/Short stories, Science fiction/Fantasy, Information science/Computers. **Career:** Full-time writer, 1979-. Engineer, Solarton Electronics, Farnborough, 1961-62, and Racal Electronics, Bracknell, Berks., 1962-64; Sales Engineer, 1964-66, and Sales Manager, 1966-68, International Telephone and Telegraph Co., Harlow, Herts.; Computer Sales Executive, Honeywell, London, 1968-70, and Leeds, 1970-72; Insurance Salesman, 1974-75; Sales Executive, Digital Equipment Corp., Leeds, 1975-77; Sales Training Consultant in Maynard, MA, 1977-79. **Publications:** Inherit the Stars, 1977; The Genesis Machine, 1977; The Gentle Giants of Ganymede, 1978; The Two Faces of Tomorrow, 1979; Thrice upon a Time, 1980; Giants' Star, 1981; Voyage From Yesteryear, 1982; Code of the Lifemaker, 1983; The Proteus Operation, 1985; Minds, Machines and Evolution (short stories), 1986; Endgame Enigma, 1987; The Mirror Maze, 1989; The Infinity Gambit, 1991; Entoverse, 1991; The Multiplex Man, 1992; Out of Time, 1993; Realtime Interrupt, 1995; The Immortality Option, 1995; Paths to Otherwhere, 1996; Bug Park, 1997; Outward Bound, 1999; Cradle of Saturn, 1999; Rockets, Redheads & Revolution (short stories), 1999; Mind Matters (nonfiction), 1998; The Legend that Was Earth, 2000; Martian Knightlife, 2001. **Address:** c/o Eleanor Wood, Spectrum Literary Agency, 320 Central Park W Ste 1-D, New York, NY 10025, U.S.A. **Online address:** jim@jamesphogan.com

HOGAN, Linda. American, b. 1947. **Genres:** Novels, Novellas/Short stories, Plays/Screenplays, Poetry, Animals/Pets, Environmental sciences/Ecology. **Career:** University of Colorado, Boulder, instructor in creative writing, fiction, and Native American literature, 1977-79, professor of English/creative writing, 1989-98; University of Minnesota, Minneapolis, associate professor of American studies/American Indian studies, 1984-89. **Publications:** POETRY: Calling Myself Home, 1979; Daughters, I Love You, 1981; Eclipse, 1984; Seeing through the Sun, 1985; Savings, 1988; The Book of Medicines, 1995. PLAYS/SCREENPLAYS: A Piece of Moon, 1981; Mean Spirit, 1986; Aunt Moon, 1986. NOVELS: Mean Spirit, 1990; Red Claw, 1994; Solar Storms, 1995, Power, 1997. OTHER: That Horse (stories), 1985; Dwellings (essays), 1995; Sightings: The Mysterious Journey of the Gray Whale; Woman Who Watches over the World: A Native Memoir, 2001. EDITOR: (with C. Buechal and J. McDaniel) The Stories We Hold Secret, 1985; (with B. Peterson and D. Metzger) Intimate Nature: The Bond between Women and Animals, 1997; (with B. Peterson) The Sweet Breathing of Plants, 2001; Face to Face, 2004. **Address:** PO Box 141, Idledale, CO 80453, U.S.A.

HOGAN, Patrick Colm. American, b. 1957. **Genres:** Literary criticism and history. **Career:** University of Kentucky, Lexington, assistant professor of English, 1983-87; University of Connecticut, Storrs, assistant professor, 1987-90, associate professor, 1990-96, acting department head, 1994-95, professor of English and Comparative literature, 1996-, cognitive science faculty, 2003-. **Publications:** The Politics of Interpretation: Ideology, Professionalism, and the Study of Literature, 1990; Joyce Milton, the Theory of Influence, 1995; On Interpretation: Meaning and Inference in Law, Psychoanalysis, and Literature, 1996; Colonialism and Cultural Identity: Crises of Tradition in the Anglophone Literatures of India, Africa, and the Caribbean, 2000; Philosophical Approaches to the Study of Literature, 2000; The Culture of Conformism, 2001; Cognitive Science, Literature, and the Arts: A Guide for Humanists, 2003; The Mind and Its Stories: Narrative Universals and Human Emotion, 2003; Empire and Poetic Voice, 2004. EDITOR: (with L. Pandit) Criticism and Lacan: Essays and Dialogue on Language, Structure, and the Unconscious, 1990; (with L. Pandit) Literary India: Comparative Studies in Aesthetics, Colonialism, and Culture, 1995. **Address:** Dept of English, University of Connecticut, Storrs Mansfield, CT 06269, U.S.A. **Online address:** hogan@uconnvm.uconn.edu

HOGAN, Robert (Goode). See Obituaries.

HOGENDORN, Jan Stafford. American, b. 1937. **Genres:** Economics. **Career:** Boston University, Massachusetts, Instructor of Economics, 1963-64; Colby College, Waterville, Maine, Assistant Professor, 1966-69, Associate Professor, 1969-76, Professor, 1976-77, Grossman Professor of Economics, 1977-. **Publications:** Managing the Modern Economy, 1972, 1975; Markets in the Modern Economy, 1974; Modern Economics, 1975, new ed., 1995; Nigerian Groundnut Exports, 1978; The Uncommon Market, 1979; The New International Economics, 1979; The Grossman Lectures at Colby College 1977-1983, 1984-1992; The Shell Money of the Slave Trade, 1986; Economic Development, 1987, rev. ed., 1996; Slow Death for Slavery, 1993; International Economics in the Age of Globalization, 2000. **Address:** Dept. of Economics, Colby College, Waterville, ME 04901, U.S.A.

HOGG, James (Dalby). British, b. 1937. **Genres:** Biography, Humor/Satire. **Career:** BBC television, reporter and documentary presenter. **Publications:** Lord Emsworth's Annotated Whiffle: "The Care of the Pig" by Augustus Whiffle, 1991; The Queen Mother Remembered, 2002. **Address:** Noon's Folly Cottage, Noon's Folly, Melbourn, Cambs. SG8 7NG, England. **Online address:** jmshogg@aol.com

HOGG, Patrick Scott. Scottish, b. 1961?. **Genres:** Literary criticism and history. **Career:** Scholar, poet, and songwriter. **Publications:** EDITOR: Robert Burns: The Lost Poems, 1997; (with A. Noble) The Canongate Burns: The Complete Poems and Songs of Robert Burns, 2001. **Address:** c/o Canongate Books, 14 High St., Edinburgh EH1 1TE, Scotland.

HOGGARD, James. American, b. 1941. **Genres:** Novels, Novellas/Short stories, Plays/Screenplays, Poetry, Essays, Translations. **Career:** Midwestern State University, Wichita Falls, TX, instructor, 1966-68, assistant professor, 1968-72, associate professor, 1972-77, professor, 1977-, McMurtry Distinguished Professor of English, 1997-2001, Parkins-Prothro Distinguished Professor of English, 2001-. **Publications:** Isometrics and the Towel; Property; Sunrise; Swinger; Conspiracy; Morganatic Marriage; Elevator Man (non-fiction), 1983. POETRY: (with B. Voss) Beau-Bo; Eyesigns, 1977; The Shaper Poems, 1983; Two Gulls, One Hawk, 1983; Breaking an Indelicate Statue, 1986; Medea in Taos, 2000; Rain in a Sunlit Sky, 2000. NOVELS: Trotter Ross, 1981. STORIES: Riding the Wind and Other Tales, 1997; Patterns of Illusion: Stories & a Novella, 2002. TRANSLATOR: The Art of Dying, 1988; Love Breaks, 1991; Chronicle of My Worst Years, 1994; Alone against the Sea: Poems from Cuba, 1998; Stolen Verses & Other Poems, 2000; Splintered Silences, 2000. **Address:** 111 Pembroke Lane, Wichita Falls, TX 76301-3941, U.S.A. **Online address:** james.hoggard@mwsu.edu

HOGGART, Richard. British, b. 1918. **Genres:** Communications/Media, Cultural/Ethnic topics, Education, Literary criticism and history. **Career:** University of Hull, staff tutor, 1946-57, sr. staff tutor, 1957-59; University of Leicester, sr. lecturer, 1959-62; University of Birmingham, professor of English, 1962-73, director of Centre for Contemporary Cultural Studies, 1964-73; UNESCO, assistant director-general, 1970-75; Goldsmith's College, University of London, warden, 1976-84. National Advisory Council for Adult and Continuing Education, chairman; Broadcasting Research Unit, chairman; European Museum of the Year Award, chairman; Book Trust, chairman, 1995. **Publications:** Auden, 1951; The Uses of Literacy, 1957; W.H. Auden, 1957; (ed.) W.H. Auden: A Selection, 1961; Teaching Literature, 1963; Speaking to Each Other, 2 vols., 1970; Only Connect (Reith Lectures), 1972; An Idea and Its Servants, 1978; An English Temper, 1982; (with D. Johnson) An Idea of Europe, 1987; A Local Habitation, 1988; A Sort of Clowning, 1990; An Imagined Life, 1992; Townscape with Figures, 1994; The Way We Live Now, 1995; First and Last Things, 1999; Between Two Worlds, 2001; Everyday Language and Everyday Life, 2003; Mass Media in Mass Society: Myths and Reality, 2004. **Address:** 19 Mount Pleasant, Norwich, Norfolk NR2 2DH, England. **Online address:** richardhoggart@onetel.net.uk

HOILE, David. British (born Zambia), b. 1960. **Genres:** Politics/Government. **Career:** House of Commons, London, private secretary and research assistant, 1986-90; National Center for Public Policy Research, Washington, DC, visiting research fellow, 1988-; Westminster Associates, political consultant, 1988-; Mozambique Institute, executive director, 1991-95. **Publications:** Understanding Sanctions, 1988; Mozambique: A Nation in Crisis, 1989; Mozambique, Resistance and Freedom: A Case for Reassessment, 1994; (ed.) Mozambique 1962-93: A Political Chronology. **Address:** Westminster Associates, 31 Bedford Square, London WC1B 3EG, England.

HOKANSON, (Anthony) Drake. American, b. 1951. **Genres:** Travel/Exploration, Air/Space topics, Transportation, Area studies, Essays,

Photography, Writing/Journalism. **Career:** Johnson County Regional Planning Commission, photographer and producer, 1973; University of Iowa, Iowa City, photojournalist and manager of Photography Unit at Office of Public Information, 1974-82, instructor, 1982-84, lecturer in journalism and mass communication, 1984-88; Lakeland College, Sheboygan, WI, assistant professor of writing, 1991-97, Tokyo branch, 1995, instructor at Summer Writing Festival, 1987-; Winona State University, Winona, MN, assistant professor of mass communication, 1997-. City University, London, England, lecturer, 1989; University of Nebraska, associate fellow of Center for Great Plains Studies, 1985-; guest lecturer at universities. Photographer, with solo exhibitions throughout the U.S., group exhibitions, and commissioned work. Also worked as mechanic, recreation assistant for handicapped children, ranch hand, and truck driver; qualified steam locomotive fireman for Mid-Continent Railway and Chicago & Northwestern Railroad; licensed aircraft pilot. **Publications:** Lincoln Highway: Main Street across America, 1988; Reflecting a Prairie Town: A Year in Peterson, 1994; (author of foreword) A Complete Official Road Guide of the Lincoln Highway, 1924, 1993. Contributor of articles, photographs, and reviews to periodicals. **Address:** Department of Mass Communication, Winona State University, PO Box 5838, Winona, MN 55987, U.S.A. **Online address:** rivercityairlines@fflax.net

HOLAHAN, Susan. American, b. 1940. **Genres:** Poetry. **Career:** Writer. Has taught writing at the University of Rochester and Yale University; former editor for Newsday, Yale University Press, and other newspapers; practiced law in Connecticut. **Publications:** Sister Betty Reads the Whole You (poetry), 1998. Contributor to literary journals, magazines, newspapers, and scholarly journals. **Address:** PO Box 155, East Middlebury, VT 05740-0155, U.S.A.

HOLBIK, Karel. American (born Czech Republic), b. 1920. **Genres:** Economics. **Career:** Professor of Economics Emeritus, Boston University, Massachusetts, 1986- (joined faculty 1958). Visiting Professor, University of Brussels, 1969-70; Visiting Faculty, Harvard University, Cambridge, MA, 1973-98. International financial consultant, 1986-. Chief, Section for Development of Financial Instns., United Nations, NYC, 1975-79; Fulbright Scholar, University of Tunis, 1983-84. **Publications:** Italy in International Cooperation, 1959; (co-author) Postwar Trade in Divided Germany, 1964; (co-author) West German Foreign Aid 1956-66, 1968; The United States, The Soviet Union and the Third World, 1968; (co-author) American-East European Trade, 1969; (co-author) Trade and Industrialization in the Central American Common Market, 1971; (ed.) Monetary Policy in Twelve Industrial Countries, 1973; (co-author) Industrialization and Employment in Puerto Rico, 1974. **Address:** 313 Country Club Rd, Newton, MA 02459, U.S.A.

HOLBROOK, David (Kenneth). British, b. 1923. **Genres:** Novels, Poetry, Songs/Lyrics and libretti, Education, Literary criticism and history, Philosophy. **Career:** Emeritus Fellow, Downing College, University of Cambridge, 1988- (Fellow, King's College, 1961-65; part-time Lecturer in English, Jesus College, 1968-70; Assistant Director of English Studies, 1973-74, and Director, 1981-88, Downing College; Leverhulme Emeritus Research Fellow, 1988-90). Assistant Ed., Our Time mag., 1947-48, and Bureau of Current Affairs, 1948-51, both London; Tutor in Adult Education, 1951-61, and at Bassingbourn Village College, Cambs., 1954-61; Writer-in-Residence, Dartington Hall, Devon, 1970-72. **Publications:** Children's Games, 1957; The Borderline, 1959; Imaginings, 1961; English for Maturity, 1961; Llareggub Revisited, 1962; Lights in the Sky Country, 1962; Against the Cruel Frost, 1963; (co-author) Penguin Modern Poets, 4, 1963; The Secret Places, 1964; English for the Rejected, 1964; The Quest for Love, 1964; I've Got to Use Words, 1966; The Flowers Shake Themselves Free, 1966; The Exploring Word, 1967; Children's Writing, 1967; Object Relations, 1967; Old World, New World, 1969; Human Hope and the Death Instinct, 1971; The Masks of Hate: The Problem of False Solutions in the Culture of an Acquisitive Society, 1972; Sex and Dehumanisation in Art, Thought and Life in Our Time, 1972; Dylan Thomas and the Code of Night, 1972; The Pseudo-Revolution, 1972; English in Australia Now, 1972; Gustav Mahler and the Courage to Be, 1975; Sylvia Plath: Poetry and Existence, 1976; Lost Bearings in English Poetry, 1977; Education, Nihilism and Survival, 1977; Chance of a Lifetime, 1978; Moments in Italy, 1978; English for Meaning, 1980; Selected Poems, 1980; Evolution and the Humanities, 1987; The Novel and Authenticity, 1987; Education and Philosophical Anthropology, 1987; Further Studies in Philosophical Anthropology, 1988; Images of Woman in Literature, 1990; Edith Wharton and the Unsatisfactory Man, 1991; The Skeleton in the Wardrobe: The Fantasies of C.S. Lewis, 1991; Where D.H. Lawrence Was Wrong about Woman, 1992; Charles Dickens and the Image of Woman, 1993; Creativity and Popular Culture, 1994; Bringing Everything Home (poems), 1999; George MacDonald and the Phantom Woman, 2000; Nonsense against Sorrow: Lewis Carroll's "Alice" Books, 2001. NOVELS:

Flesh Wounds, 1966; A Play of Passion, 1978; Nothing Larger Than Life, 1987; Worlds Apart, 1988; A Little Athens, 1990; Jennifer, 1991; The Gold in Father's Heart, 1992; Even If They Fail, 1993; Getting It Wrong with Uncle Tom, 1998; Going off the Rails, 2003. EDITOR: Iron Honey Gold, 1961; People and Diamonds, 1962; Thieves and Angels, 1963; Visions of Life, 1964; (with E. Poston) The Cambridge Hymnal, 1967; Plucking the Rushes, 1968; The Case against Pornography, 1972; What Is It to Be Human?, 1990. **Address:** 1 Tennis Court Terrace, Cambridge, England. **Online address:** Dkh1000@cam.ac.uk

HOLBROOK, Sara. American. **Genres:** Novels, Children's non-fiction. **Career:** Writer and performance poet. Worked as part-time teacher; worked in public relations, for law, public housing, and drug prevention fields. Presents poetry and writing workshops at schools and teacher meetings. **Publications:** FOR CHILDREN. POETRY: The Dog Ate My Home Work, 1990, rev. ed, 1996; Kid Poems for the Not-So-Bad, 1992, as I Never Said I Wasn't Difficult, 1997; Nothing's the End of the World, 1995; Am I Naturally This Crazy?, 1996; Which Way to the Dragon! Poems for the Coming-on-Strong, 1996; Walking on the Boundaries of Change: Poems of Transition, 1998. OTHER: Feelings Make Me Real, 1990; Some Families, 1990; What's So Big about Cleveland, Ohio? (picture book), 1997; Wham! It's a Poetry Jam: Discovering Performance Poetry, 2002; Isn't She Ladylike, 2002. FOR ADULTS: Chicks up Front (poetry), 1998. Contributor to periodicals. **Address:** 7326 Presley Ave., Mentor, OH 44060, U.S.A.

HOLBROOK, Teri. American. **Genres:** Mystery/Crime/Suspense. **Career:** Mystery novelist. Former journalist. Has spoken or made appearances at the University of Georgia, Emory University, Cluefest, Malice Domestic, Bouchercon, Sleuthfest, Southeastern Booksellers Association, and the Houston SinC conference. **Publications:** A Far and Deadly Cry, 1995; The Grass Widow, 1996. Contributor of short stories to anthologies. **Address:** c/o Bantam Books, 1540 Broadway Suite 9E, New York, NY 10036, U.S.A. **Online address:** BTHolbrook@compuserve.com

HOLCOMB, Brent H. American, b. 1950. **Genres:** History, Genealogy/Heraldry. **Career:** South Carolina Magazine of Ancestral Research, editor. Also serves as church organist and choirmaster. **Publications:** Petitions for Land from the South Carolina Council Journals, Volumes I-VII, 1996-98. Author of more than 100 volumes. **Address:** PO Box 21766, Columbia, SC 29221, U.S.A. **Online address:** scmar@juno.com

HOLCOMB, Nan. See MCPHEE, Norma H.

HOLDEFER, Charles. American, b. 1959. **Genres:** Novels. **Career:** Universite de Poitiers, Poitiers, France, instructor in language, 1989-. **Publications:** NOVELS: Apology for Big Rod, 1997; Nice, 2001. **Address:** c/o Permanent Press, 4170 Noyac Rd., Sag Harbor, NY 11963, U.S.A.

HOLDEN, Anthony (Ivan). British, b. 1947. **Genres:** Biography, Translations. **Career:** General Reporter, 1973-77, and Columnist, 1977-79, Sunday Times newspaper, London; Washington Correspondent, The Observer newspaper, London, and Columnist, Punch mag., London, 1979-81; Features Ed., The Times newspaper, London, 1981-82. Presenter, In the Air, BBC Radio 4, 1982-84; Columnist, Sunday Express Magazine, 1982-85; Executive Ed., Sunday Today, 1985-86; freelance journalist. **Publications:** (ed. and trans.) Agamemnon, 1969; (ed. and trans.) Greek Pastoral Poetry, 1974; The St. Albans Poisoner, 1974; Charles, Prince of Wales, 1979; Their Royal Highnesses, 1981; Royal Quiz, 1983; Of Presidents, Prime Ministers, and Princes, 1984; The Queen Mother, 1985; (trans. with A. Holden) Don Giovanni, 1987; Olivier, 1988; Charles, 1988; Big Deal, 1989; (ed.) The Last Paragraph, 1990; A Princely Marriage, 1991; The Oscars, 1993; The Tarnished Crown, 1993; Tchaikovsky: A Biography, 1995; Diana: Her Life & Legacy, 1997; Charles at Fifty, 1998; William Shakespeare, 2000. Contributor to magazines. **Address:** c/o Rogers Coleridge White, 20 Powis Mews, London W1I 1JN, England.

HOLDEN, Dalby. See HAMMOND, Gerald (Arthur Douglas).

HOLDEN, Peter. British, b. 1948. **Genres:** Adult non-fiction, Animals/Pets, Children's non-fiction, Natural history, Zoology, Reference. **Career:** Freelance genealogist, London, England, 1968-69; Royal Society for the Protection of Birds (RSPB), Sandy, England, assistant education officer, 1969-74, national organizer of Young Ornithologists Club, 1974-92, head of RSPB Youth and Volunteer Department, 1992-. **Publications:** The RSPB Book of British Birds, 1982; (co-author) Bird in the Nest, 1995; Collins Wild Guide to Birds, 1996; (co-author) RSPB Handbook of British Birds, 2002. FOR CHILDREN: Spotter's Guide to Birds, 1978; Spotter's Guide to Birds of

Prey, 1981; First Book Birds, 1984; Migrants and Migration, 1994. **Address:** 3 Grange Rd, Blunham, Bedford MK44 3NS, England.

HOLDEN, Philip (Joseph). British, b. 1962. **Genres:** Literary criticism and history. **Career:** Hunan Normal University, Changsha, China, foreign expert, 1986-87; Nanyang Technological University, National Institute of Education, Singapore, lecturer, 1994-97, assistant professor of literature and cultural studies, 1998-. University of Hong Kong, visiting scholar at Centre for Asian Studies, 1991; Open University, Singapore, tutor and counselor, 1996-97, 1999-; visiting fellow at Institute of Commonwealth Studies, University of London, 1996, and at Centre for British and Comparative Cultural Studies, University of Warwick, 1997-98. **Publications:** Orienting Masculinity, Orienting Nation: W. Somerset Maugham's Exotic Fiction, 1996; Modern Subjects/Colonial Texts: Hugh Clifford and the Discipline of English Literature in the Straits Settlements, 1895-1907, 1999. Contributor to books. Contributor of articles and reviews to periodicals. **Address:** Division of Literature and Drama School of Arts, National Institute of Education, Nanyang Technological University, 469 Bukit Timah Rd., Singapore 259756, Singapore. **Online address:** philiph@cyberway.com.sg; pjholden@nie.edu.sg

HOLDER, Nancy L. Also writes as Laurel Chandler, Wendi Davis, Nancy L. Jones. American, b. 1953. **Genres:** Horror, Romance/Historical. **Career:** Writer. **Publications:** ROMANCE NOVELS: The Greatest Show on Earth, 1984; Winner Take All, 1984; Finders Keepers, 1985; His Fair Lady, 1985; Out of This World, 1985; Emerald Fire, 1986; Once in Love With Amy, 1986. HORROR NOVELS: Rough Cut, 1990; The Ghosts of Tivoli, 1992; (with M. Tem) Making Love, 1993; Dead in the Water, 1994; (with M.Tem) Witch-Light, 1996; Measure of a Man (Highlander), 1997. BUFFY THE VAMPIRE SLAYER SERIES: (with C. Golden) Halloween Rain, 1997; The Angel Chronicles, 1998. ROMANCE NOVELS AS LAUREL CHANDLER: Treasure of Love, 1983; Heart's Victory, 1983; Shades of Moonlight, 1984; Boundless Love, 1984. ROMANCE NOVELS AS WENDI DAVIS: Teach Me to Love, 1982; Sealed with a Kiss, 1984. ROMANCE NOVELS AS NANCY L. JONES: Jessie's Song, 1983. Author of more than 100 horror short stories. **Address:** 11365 Lakerim Rd, San Diego, CA 92131-2314, U.S.A.

HOLDGATE, Sir Martin W. British, b. 1931. **Genres:** Biology, Environmental sciences/Ecology, History. **Career:** University Lecturer, Durham University, 1957-60; Assistant Director of Research, Scott Polar Research Institute, Cambridge, 1960-63; Chief Biologist, British Antarctic Survey, 1963-66; Deputy Director (Research), Nature Conservancy, London, 1966-70; Director, Central Unit of Environmental Pollution, Dept. of the Environment, London, 1970-74; Director, Institute of Terrestrial Ecology, Natural Environment Research Council, 1974-76; Chief Scientist, Depts. of the Environment and Transport, London, 1976-88; Director-General, International Union for Conservation of Nature and Natural Resources, 1988-94. **Publications:** History of Appleby, County Town of Westmorland, 1956, rev. ed., 1971; Mountains in the Sea-The Story of the Gough Island Expedition, 1958; From Care to Action: Making a Sustainable World, 1996; The Green Web: A Union for World Conservation, 1999; Penguins and Mandarins, 2003. EDITOR: Antarctic Ecology, 1970; The Restoration of Damaged Ecosystems, 1976; Environmental Issues, 1977; A Perspective of Environmental Pollution, 1979; The World Environment 1972-82, 1982; The World Environment, 1972-92, 1992. **Address:** Fell Beck, Hartley, Kirkby Stephen, Cumbria CA17 4JH, England. **Online address:** martin@fellbeck.fsnet.co.uk

HOLDHEIM, W(illiam) Wolfgang. American (born Germany), b. 1926. **Genres:** Literary criticism and history, Philosophy, Translations. **Career:** Professor Emeritus, Cornell University, Ithaca, NY, 1990- (Professor of Comparative Literature, 1969-90; Frederic J. Whiton Professor of Liberal Studies, 1974-90). Instructor of French, Ohio State University, 1955-57; Instructor of European Languages and Literature, 1957-58, Assistant Professor, 1958-61, and Associate Professor, 1961-64, Brandeis University, Waltham, MA; Professor of French and Comparative Literature, Washington University, 1964-69. **Publications:** Benjamin Constant, 1961; (trans.) Ressentiment, by Max Scheler, 1961; Theory and Practice of the Novel, 1968; Der Justizirrtum als literarische Problematik, 1969; Die Suche nach dem Epos, 1978; The Hermeneutic Mode, 1984. **Address:** 600 S Ocean Blvd Apt 1204, Boca Raton, FL 33432, U.S.A. **Online address:** csspeast@sgi.net

HOLDSTOCK, Robert. Also writes as Robert Black, Chris Carlsen, Robert Faulcon. British, b. 1948. **Genres:** Novels, Novellas/Short stories, Science fiction/Fantasy, Mythology/Folklore. **Career:** Medical Research Council, London, England, medical researcher, 1971-74; free-lance writer, 1976-. **Publications:** NOVELS: Eye among the Blind, 1976; Earthwind, 1977; Necromancer, 1978; Where Time Winds Blow (novel), 1981; Mythago Wood (novel), 1984; Bulman (novel), 1984; John Boorman's "The Emerald Forest" (novelization), 1985; One of Our Pigeons Is Missing (novel), 1985; Lavondyss: Journey to an Unknown Region (novel), 1989; The Fetch (novel), 1991; The Hollowing (novel), 1993. EDITOR: Encyclopedia of Science Fiction, 1978; (with C. Priest) Stars of Albion (anthology), 1979; (with C. Evans) Other Edens (anthology), 1987; (with C. Evans) Other Edens 2 (anthology), 1988; (with C. Evans) Other Edens 3 (anthology), 1989. OTHER: (with M. Edwards) Alien Landscapes (nonfiction), 1979; (with M. Edwards) Tour of the Universe, 1980; In the Valley of the Statues (short stories), 1982; (with M. Edwards) Magician: The Lost Journals of the Magus Geoffrey Carlyle, 1982; (with M. Edwards) Realms of Fantasy, 1983; (with M. Edwards) Lost Realms, 1984; The Bone Forest (stories), 1991. AS ROBERT BLACK: Legend of the Werewolf, 1976; The Satanists, 1978. BERSERKER NOVELS AS CHRIS CARLSEN: Shadow of the Wolf, 1977; The Bull Chief, 1979; The Horned Warrior, 1979. NIGHT HUNTER NOVELS AS ROBERT FAULCON: The Stalking, 1983; The Talisman, 1983; The Ghost Dance, 1983; The Shrine, 1984; The Hexing, 1984; The Labyrinth, 1986; Merlin's Wood, 1994; Ancient Echoes, 1996; Gate of Ivory, Gate of Horn, 1998; Celtika, 2001; The Iron Grail, 2002. **Address:** 54 Raleigh Rd, London N8 0HY, England.

HOLEMAN, Linda. Canadian, b. 1949. **Genres:** Novellas/Short stories, Children's fiction, Young adult fiction. **Career:** Frontier School Division, South Indian Lake, Manitoba, classroom and resource teacher, 1974-76; Ryerson School, Fort Garry School Division, Winnipeg, classroom and resource teacher, 1977-84; Continuing Education Division, University of Winnipeg, creative writing instructor, 1996-; Winnipeg Public Library, writer-in-residence, 1999-2000. **Publications:** FOR YOUNG ADULTS. STORIES: Saying Good-bye, 1995, as Toxic Love, 2003; NOVELS: Promise Song, 1997; Mercy's Birds, 1998; Raspberry House Blues, 2000; Search of the Moon King's Daughter, 2002. FOR CHILDREN: Frankie on the Run, 1995. FOR ADULTS: Flying to Yellow (short stories), 1996; Devil's Darning Needle (short stories), 1999. **Address:** 728 South Dr, Winnipeg, MB, Canada R3T 0C3. **Online address:** lholeman@shaw.ca

HOLLAND, James R. Also writes as J. H. Rand. American, b. 1944. **Genres:** Music, Travel/Exploration, Biography. **Career:** National Geographic Magazine, Washington, DC, photographer trainee, 1966, contract photographer, 1967-68; Christian Science Center, Boston, film producer, 1969-75; real estate developer, 1976-. **Publications:** The Amazon, 1971; Mr. Pops, 1972; Tanglewood, 1973. **Address:** 5 Brimmer St, Boston, MA 02108, U.S.A.

HOLLAND, Max (Mendel). American, b. 1950. **Genres:** Business/Trade/Industry, History, Politics/Government, Biography. **Career:** Lincoln Star, Lincoln, NE, copy editor, 1975-76; Voice of America, Washington, DC, newswriter, 1976; Center for International Policy, Washington, DC, fellow, 1977-80; aide to U.S. Representative Toby Moffett, Washington, DC, 1980; American Friends Service Committee, Philadelphia, PA, Washington representative, 1980-82; Nation, New York City, columnist in Washington bureau, 1982-86, contributing editor, 1986-; Wilson Quarterly, Washington, DC, contributing editor, 1991-; writer. **Publications:** When the Machine Stopped: A Cautionary Tale from Industrial America (nonfiction), 1989; The CEO Goes to Washington: Negotiating the Halls of Power, 1994; A Need to Know: Inside the Warren Commission, 2002. **Address:** c/o Elaine Markson, Elaine Markson Literary Agency, Inc, 44 Greenwich Ave, New York, NY 10011, U.S.A.

HOLLAND, Norman N. American, b. 1927. **Genres:** Literary criticism and history, Psychology. **Career:** Marston-Milbauer Professor, University of Florida, Gainesville, since 1983. Instructor to Associate Professor, Massachusetts Institute of Technology, Cambridge, 1955-66; Professor, 1966-79; McNulty Professor, 1979-83, and Chairman of the English Dept., 1966-68, State University of New York at Buffalo. **Publications:** The First Modern Comedies, 1959; The Shakespearean Imagination, 1964; Psychoanalysis and Shakespeare, 1966, 1975; The Dynamics of Literary Response, 1968; Poems in Persons, 1973, rev. ed., 2000; 5 Readers Reading, 1975; Laughing, 1982; The I, 1985; The Brain of Robert Frost, 1988; Holland's Guide to Psychoanalytic Psychology and Literature-and-Psychology, 1990; The Critical I, 1992; Death in a Delphi Seminar, 1995. **Address:** Dept. of English, University of Florida, Gainesville, FL 32611-7310, U.S.A. **Online address:** nholland@ufl.edu

HOLLAND, Noy. American, b. 1960. **Genres:** Novels. **Career:** Hotchkiss School, Lakeville, CT, instructor, 1983; Esquire, NYC, editorial assistant, 1984-85; Charles Scribner's Sons, NYC, assistant to the senior editor, 1986-87; New York Association for New Americans, NYC, instructor, 1990; University of Florida, Gainesville, instructor, 1992-94; Phillips Academy,

Andover, MA, writer-in-residence, 1994-96; University of Massachusetts, associate professor, MFA program, 1997-. **Publications:** The Spectacle of the Body, 1994. Contributor to periodicals. **Address:** PO Box 85, Heath, MA 01346-0085, U.S.A.

HOLLANDER, David. American. **Genres:** Novels. **Career:** Purchase College, State University of New York, Purchase, NY, writing instructor; Sarah Lawrence College, Bronxville, NY, writing instructor. Teachers & Writers Collaborative, New York, NY, instructor in the public school writing program. **Publications:** L.I.E. (novel), 2000. Contributor to publications. **Address:** Sarah Lawrence College, Slonim Annex, Rm. 1, Bronxville, NY 10708, U.S.A. **Online address:** dholland98@hotmail.com

HOLLANDER, John. American, b. 1929. **Genres:** Children's fiction, Poetry, Literary criticism and history. **Career:** Harvard University, Society of Fellows, Junior Fellow, 1954-57; Connecticut College, New London, Lecturer, 1957-59; Yale University, New Haven, CT, Instructor, 1959-61, Assistant Professor, 1961-63, Associate Professor, 1963-66, Professor of English, 1977-, A. Bartlett Giamatti Professor of English, 1986-95, Sterling Professor of English, 1995-; City University of New York, Hunter College, Professor of English, 1966-77. Princeton University, Christian Gauss Seminarian, 1962; Indiana University, Visiting Professor, Linguistic Institute and School of Letters, 1964, Fellow, Institute for Advanced Study, 1986; University of Cincinnati, Elliston Poetry Professor, 1969. American Academy of Arts and Sciences, Fellow; Partisan Review, New Brunswick, NJ, Poetry Editor, 1959-65; Churchill College, Cambridge, Overseas Fellow, 1967-68; Harper's mag., NYC, Contributor Ed., 1969-71. **Publications:** POETRY: A Crackling of Thorns, 1958; Movie-Going and Other Poems, 1962; A Beach Vision, 1962; A Book of Various Owls (children's), 1962; Visions from the Ramble, 1965; The Quest of the Gole (children's), 1966; Philomel, 1968; Types of Shape, 1969; Images of Voice, 1969; The Night Mirror, 1971; Town and Country Matters: Erotica and Satirica, 1972; Selected Poems, 1972; The Head of the Bed, 1974; Tales Told of the Fathers, 1975; Reflections on Espionage, 1976, 2nd ed., 1999; Spectral Emanations: New and Selected Poems, 1978; Blue Wine and Other Poems, 1979; Powers of Thirteen, 1983; In Time and Place, 1986; Harp Lake, 1988; Tesserae, 1993; Selected Poetry, 1993; Figurehead and Other Poems, 1999. CRITICISM: Vision and Resonance: Two Senses of Poetic Form, 1975, rev. ed., 2000; William Bailey, 1990; The Work of Poetry, 1997; The Poetry of Everyday Life, 1998. OTHER: An Entertainment for Elizabeth, Being a Masque of the Seven Motions: or, Terpischore Unchained (play), 1969; The Immense Parade on Supererogation Day (children's fiction), 1972; In Place, 1978; Rhyme's Reason, 1981; The Figure of Echo, 1981; Melodious Guile, 1988; The Gazer's Spirit, 1995. EDITOR: B. Jonson, Selected Poems, 1961; (with H. Bloom) The Wind and the Rain: An Anthology of Poems for Young People, 1961; (with A. Hecht) Jiggery-Pokery: A Compendium of Double Dactyls, 1967; Poems of Our Moment, 1968; Modern Poetry, 1968; American Short Stories since 1945, 1968; (co-ed.) The Oxford Anthology of English Literature, 2 vols., 1973; (with R. Brower and H. Vendler) I.A. Richards: Essays in His Honor, 1973; (with D. Bromwich) Literature as Experience, 1979; The Poetics of Influence, 1988; The Essential Rossetti, 1990; E.L. Masters, Spoon River Anthology, 1992; Garden Poems, 1996; Animal Poems, 1996; Marriage Poems, 1997; Nineteenth Century American Poetry, 1996; Committed to Memory, 1996; Poems of Robert Frost, 1997; The Best American Poetry, 1998; War Poems, 1999; (with J.D. McClatchy) Christmas Poems, 1999; Sonnets, 2000. **Address:** Dept. of English, Yale University, PO Box 208302, New Haven, CT 06520-8302, U.S.A.

HOLLANDER, Nicole. American, b. 1940?. **Genres:** Cartoons. **Career:** Worked as a graphic designer during the 1970s; cartoonist, 1979-; creator of syndicated cartoon Sylvia. Head of Sylvia products, including dolls and calendars. **Publications:** COLLECTED CARTOONS: I'm in Training to Be Tall and Blonde, 1979; Ma, Can I Be a Feminist and Still Like Men?: Lyrics from Life, 1980; That Woman Must Be on Drugs: A Collection of Sylvia, 1981; Mercy, It's the Revolution and I'm in My Bathrobe: More Sylvia, 1982; My Weight Is Always Perfect for My Height-Which Varies: More Sylvia, 1982; Sylvia on Sundays, 1983; (ed, with S. Morrow and R. Wolin) Drawn Together: Relationships Lampooned, Harpooned, and Cartooned, 1983; Hi, This Is Sylvia: I Can't Come to the Phone Right Now, So When You Hear the Beep, Please Hang Up, 1983; Okay, Thinner Thighs for Everyone, 1984; Never Tell Your Mother This Dream, 1985; The Whole Enchilada: A Spicy Collection of Sylvia's Best, 1986; Never Take Your Cat to a Salad Bar: New Sylvia Cartoons, 1987; You Can't Take It with You, So Eat It Now: Everyday Strategies from Sylvia, 1989; Tales from the Planet Sylvia, 1990; (with others) Sylvia's Real Good Advice (musical stage play), 1991; Everything Here Is Mine: An Unhelpful Guide to Cat Behavior, 1992; Female Problems: An Unhelpful Guide, 1995. Contributor to feminist

periodicals. Illustrator of works by: R.H. Harris, A. Zobel. **Address:** c/o Adams Media Corp, 57 Littlefield St #2, Avon, MA 02322-1914, U.S.A.

HOLLANDER, Samuel. Canadian/British, b. 1937. **Genres:** Economics. **Career:** Professor of Economics, since 1970, and University Professor, since 1984, University of Toronto (Assistant Professor, 1963-67; Associate Professor, 1967-70). Assistant, Princeton University, New Jersey, 1962-63. **Publications:** The Sources of Increased Efficiency: A Study of DuPont Rayon Plants, 1965; The Economics of Adam Smith, 1973; The Economics of David Ricardo, 1979; The Economics of John Stuart Mill, 1985; Classical Economics, 1987; Ricardo, The New View: Collected Essays I, 1995; The Economics of Thomas Robert Malthus, 1997; Collected Essay II, 1997. **Address:** Dept. of Economics, University of Toronto, 150 St. George St, Toronto, ON, Canada M5S 1A1.

HOLLANDER, Stanley C(harles). See Obituaries.

HOLLANDSWORTH, James G., Jr. American, b. 1944. **Genres:** History, Psychology. **Career:** Duke University Medical Center, Highland Hospital, Asheville, NC, psychiatric social worker, 1972-73; Community Mental Health Center of Palm Beach County, West Palm Beach, FL, clinical and community psychology intern, 1975-76; University of Southern Mississippi, Hattiesburg, assistant professor, 1976, associate professor, 1979, professor of psychology, 1984-, director of training, 1987-89, assistant vice-president for academic affairs, 1989-98, associate provost, 1998-; writer. American Board of Professional Psychology, diplomate, 1985-95. Member of Mississippi State Board of Psychological Examiners, 1986-89. America Board of Professional Psychology, diplomate, 1985-95. **Publications:** Physiology and Behavior Therapy: Conceptual Guidelines for the Clinician, 1986; The Physiology of Psychological Disorders: Schizophrenia, Depression, Anxiety, and Substance Abuse, 1990; The Louisiana Native Guards: The Black Military Experience during the Civil War, 1995; Pretense of Glory: The Life of General Nathaniel P. Banks, 1998; Absolute Massacre: The New Orleans Race Riot of July 30, 1866, 2001. **Address:** 44 Eastbrooke St, Jackson, MS 39216-4714, U.S.A. **Online address:** jgh@netdoor.com

HOLLAR, David W(ason), (Jr.). American, b. 1960. **Genres:** Medicine/Health, Natural history. **Career:** Roanoke-Chowan Community College, Ahoskie, NC, instructor in science, 1986-89; Rockingham Community College, Wentworth, NC, instructor in biology, 1989-2001; Wright State University School of Medicine, Dayton, OH, postdoctoral research scientist, 2001-. Volunteer emergency medical technician, Ahoskie Rescue Squad, 1986-89, Reidsville Rescue Squad, 1989-90, and Eden Rescue Squad, 1990-93. **Publications:** The Origin and Evolution of Life on Earth, 1992. Work represented in anthologies. **Address:** PO Box 6524, Maryville, TN 37802-6524, U.S.A. **Online address:** david.hollar@wright.edu

HOLLDOBLER, Bert(hold Karl). German, b. 1936. **Genres:** Biology, Zoology. **Career:** Professor of Zoology, University of Würzburg, Germany, 1989; Adjunct Professor, University of Arizona, Tucson, 1989-; Alexander Agassiz Professor of Zoology, Harvard University, Cambridge, Massachusetts, 1982-90 (Professor of Biology, 1973-). Professor of Zoology, University of Frankfurt, 1971-72. Recipient: John Simon Guggenheim Fellowship, 1980, and Sr. Scientist Award, Alexander von Humboldt Foundation, 1986-87. **Publications:** (ed. with M. Lindauer) Experimental Behavioral Ecology and Sociobiology, 1985; (with E.O. Wilson) The Ants, 1990 (Pulitzer Prize for general non-fiction, 1991); (with E.O. Wilson) Journey to the Ants, 1994. **Address:** Dept. of Organic and Evolutionary Biology, Harvard University, 26 Oxford St, Cambridge, MA 02138, U.S.A.

HOLLENBERG, Donna Krolik. American (born Canada), b. 1942. **Genres:** Literary criticism and history. **Career:** Simmons College, Boston, MA, instructor in English, 1986-91; University of Connecticut, assistant professor, 1991-97, associate professor of English, 1997-. **Publications:** H.D.: The Poetics of Childbirth and Creativity, 1991; Between History and Poetry: The Letters of H.D. and Norman Holmes Pearson, 1997; H.D. and Poets After, 2000. **Address:** Department of English, University of Connecticut, Storrs Mansfield, CT 06269, U.S.A.

HOLLERAN, Andrew. American, b. 1944. **Genres:** Novels, Novellas/Short stories. **Career:** Writer. **Publications:** Dancer from the Dance (novel), 1978; Nights in Aruba (novel), 1983; (author of intro) The Normal Heart, by L. Kramer, 1985; Ground Zero (essays), 1988; (author of afterword) Men on Men 4, 1992; In September the Light Changes: Stories, 1999. Short stories represented anthologies. Contributor to periodicals. **Address:** c/o Ron Bernstein Agency, 200 West 58th St., New York, NY 10019, U.S.A.

HOLLEY, Edward Gailon. American, b. 1927. **Genres:** Librarianship, Biography. **Career:** William Rand Kenan, Jr., Professor, School of Info. and Library Science, University of North Carolina, Chapel Hill, 1989-95 (Dean, 1972-85). Trustee, OCLC, Inc., 1985-94. Chairman 1989-92; UNC Press Bog 1975-95; Chairman, Board of Governors, UNC Press, 1989-94. Education, Philosophy and Psychology Librarian, University of Illinois, Urbana, 1957-62; Director of Libraries, University of Houston, Texas, 1962-71. President, American Library Association, 1974-75. **Publications:** Charles Evans: American Bibliographer, 1963; (compiler) Raking the Historic Coals: The ALA Scrapbook of 1876, 1967; (with D.D. Hendricks) Resources of Texas Libraries, 1968; (with others) Resources of South Carolina Libraries, 1976; (with R.F. Shremser) Library Services and Construction Act, 1983; Other articles. **Address:** 2600 Croasdaile Farm Pkwy Apt D106, Durham, NC 27705-1331, U.S.A.

HOLLEY, Margaret. American, b. 1944. **Genres:** Poetry, Literary criticism and history. **Career:** Franklin College, Lugano, Switzerland, professor of literature, 1972-80; Bryn Mawr College, Bryn Mawr, PA, instructor in English, director of creative writing program, and assistant to the president, 1981-2000. **Publications:** The Poetry of Marianne Moore: A Study in Voice and Value, 1988. POETRY: The Dark Horses (chapbook), 1980; The Mayflower (chapbook), 1989; The Smoke Tree, 1991; Morning Star, 1992; Beyond Me, 1993; Kyrie for One Voice (chapbook), 1993; Kore in Bloom, 1998; Walking through the Horizon (chapbook), 1999. Contributor to books. Contributor of essays to periodicals. **Address:** Creative Writing Program, Bryn Mawr College, 101 N Merion Ave, Bryn Mawr, PA 19010, U.S.A. **Online address:** Margaret.Holley@att.net

HOLLI, Betsy B. American, b. 1933. **Genres:** Communications/Media. **Career:** Rush Presbyterian-St. Luke's Medical Center, Chicago, health center nutritionist, 1965-69; University of Illinois at the Medical Center, Chicago, professor, 1969-70; Dominican University, River Forest, IL, professor of nutrition sciences, 1970-2004. **Publications:** Communication and Education Skills: The Dietitian's Guide, 1986, 2nd ed., 1992; (with R.J. Calabrese) Communication and Education Skills for Dietetics Professionals, 3rd ed., 1998, 4th ed., 2003. Contributor to professional journals. **Address:** Dominican University, 7900 W Division St, River Forest, IL 60305, U.S.A. **Online address:** holli@dom.edu

HOLLI, Melvin George. American, b. 1933. **Genres:** Cultural/Ethnic topics, History, Biography. **Career:** Associate Professor to Professor of History, 1965-, chairman, Dept. of History, 1991-94, University of Illinois, Chicago, 1965-. Research Assistant and Curator of Manuscripts, Historical Collection, and Research and Teaching Fellow, University of Michigan, Ann Arbor, 1961-64. Society of Midland book prize, 1982. **Publications:** Reform in Detroit, 1969; Detroit: Fur Trading Post to Industrial Metropolis, 1975; (ed. with P. Jones) The Ethnic Frontiers, 1977; (with P. Jones) Ethnic Chicago, 1981; (ed.) Biographical Dictionary of American Mayors 1820-1980, 1981; The Making of the Mayor, Chicago 1983, 1984; (with P.M. Green) The Mayors: The Chicago Political Tradition, 1987; (with P.M. Green) Bashing Chicago Traditions: Harold Washington's Last Campaign, 1989; Restoration: Chicago Elects a New Daley, 1992; Ethnic Chicago: A Multi-Cultural Portrait, 1995; The American Mayor: The Best and Worst Big City Leaders, 1999; (with P.M. Green) A View from Chicago's City Hall: Mid-Century to Millennium, 1999; The Wizard of Washington: Emil Hurja, Franklin Roosevelt and the Birth of Public Opinion Polling, 2002. **Address:** 1311 Ashland Ave, River Forest, IL 60305, U.S.A. **Online address:** mholli@uic.edu

HOLLIFIELD, James F. American, b. 1954. **Genres:** Politics/Government. **Career:** Duke University, Durham, NC, instructor in political science, 1982-84; Brandeis University, Waltham, MA, assistant professor of political science, 1985-92; Auburn University, Auburn, AL, Alumni associate professor of political science, 1992-. Harvard University, research associate, 1986-; Centre National de la Recherche Scientifique (Paris), director of research at Centre d'Etudes et de Recherches Internationales, 1992-93; consultant to: U.S. Department of State, U.S. Department of Labor, UN High Commissioner for Refugees, and Organization for Economic Cooperation and Development. **Publications:** Searching for the New France, 1991; Immigrants, Markets, and States, 1992; State and Public Policy, 1995; Controlling Immigration, 1995. **Address:** Political Science Department, 222 Carv Collins, Southern Methodist University, PO Box 750117, Dallas, TX 75205, U.S.A. **Online address:** jhollifi@mail.smu.edu

HOLLINDALE, Peter. British, b. 1936. **Genres:** Literary criticism and history. **Career:** Clifton College, Bristol, Assistant Master in English, 1962-65; University of York, Lecturer, then Reader in English and Educational Studies, 1965-99. **Publications:** A Critical Commentary on Shakespeare's King Henry IV, Part Two, 1971; Choosing Books for Children, 1974; Ideology and the Children's Book, 1988; William Shakespeare: A Midsummer Night's Dream, 1992; Signs of Childness in Children's Books, 1997; (with A. Fine) An Interview with A. Fine, 1999. EDITOR: Shakespeare: As You Like It, 1974; Shakespeare: King Henry IV, Part One, 1975; Lord Jim, by Conrad, 1982; Volpone, by Jonson, 1985; Peter Pan in Kensington Gardens, and Peter and Wendy, by J.M. Barrie, 1991; A. Sewell, Black Beauty, 1992; J.M. Barrie, Peter Pan and Other Plays, 1995. **Address:** 6 Grange Garth, York, England.

HOLLINGDALE, Reginald John. *See* Obituaries.

HOLLINGS, Robert L. American, b. 1953. **Genres:** Bibliography. **Career:** Screen Tech Inc., shipping and receiving supervisor, 1978-82; State of Utah, Department of Health, Division of Healthcare Financing, Bureau of Provider and Client Services, Salt Lake City, UT, health program representative, 1984; Pennsylvania Legislative Budget and Finance Committee, Harrisburg, PA, analyst, 1984-96; independent public policy analyst, 1996-98; Arizona Department of Economic Security, Office of Audit and Management Services, Phoenix, AZ, program compliance auditor, 1998-. Glendale Community College, adjunct instructor in sociology, 1998-. **Publications:** The General Accounting Office: An Annotated Bibliography, 1991; Nonprofit Public Policy Research Organization: A Sourcebook on Think Tanks in Government, 1993; Reinventing Government: An Analysis and Annotated Bibliography, 1996; (with C. Pike-Nase) Professional and Occupational Licensure in the United States: An Annotated Bibliography and Professional Resource, 1997. **Address:** Office of Audit and Management Services, Arizona Department of Economic Security, 1140 East Washington Suite 203, Phoenix, AZ 85034, U.S.A. **Online address:** hollingsr@juno.com

HOLLINGSHEAD, Greg. Canadian, b. 1947. **Genres:** Novels, Novellas/Short stories. **Career:** Educator, novelist, and short story writer. University of Alberta, Edmonton, AB, Canada, professor of English, 1975-; Banff Centre, Banff, AB, director of writing programs, 1999-. **Publications:** NOVELS: Spin Dry, 1992; The Healer, 1998; Bedlam, 2004. STORIES: Famous Players, 1982; White Buick, 1992; The Roaring Girl, 1995. Work represented in anthologies and publications. **Address:** Department of English, University of Alberta, Edmonton, AB, Canada T6G 2E5. **Online address:** greg.hollingshead@ualberta.ca; www.greghollingshead.com

HOLLINGSWORTH, Brian. *See* Obituaries.

HOLLINGSWORTH, Margaret. Canadian (born England), b. 1940. **Genres:** Novels, Plays/Screenplays, Novellas/Short stories. **Career:** Freelance writer since 1972. Journalist, librarian, and teacher in England, 1960-68; librarian, Fort William Public Library, Ont., 1968-72; Assistant Professor, David Thompson University Centre, Nelson, B.C., 1981-83; University of Victoria, associate professor, 1991-. **Publications:** PLAYS: Dance for My Father, 1976; Alli Alli Oh, 1979; Mother Country, 1980; Bushed, and Operators, 1981; Ever Loving, 1981; Islands, 1983; Willful Acts (collection), 1985; Endangered Species (collection), 1988; In Confidence, 1994; Numbrains, 1995. SHORT STORIES: Smiling Under Water, 1989. **Address:** Department of Writing, University of Victoria, Victoria, BC, Canada V8W 2Y2.

HOLLINGSWORTH, Mary. Also writes as Professor Scribbler, Mary Shrode. American, b. 1947. **Genres:** Children's fiction, Plays/Screenplays, Poetry, Songs/Lyrics and libretti, Adult non-fiction, Children's non-fiction, Inspirational/Motivational Literature, Picture/board books. **Career:** Sweet Publishing, Fort Worth, TX, managing editor, 1984-95; Shady Oaks Studio, Bedford, TX, owner, author, editor, and consultant, 1988-; A Capella Junction, online distributor of a capella music, owner, 1991-. **Publications:** JUVENILES: International Children's Story Bible, 1991; (reteller) My Little Bible, 1991; The Captain, the Countess, and Cobby the Swabby, 1992; Parrots, Pirates, and Walking the Plank, 1992; A Girl's Diary of Prayers, 1992; A Boy's Book of Prayers, 1992; (as Mary Shrode) Just Imagine! with Barney, 1992; Journey to Jesus, 1993; The Kids-Life Bible Storybook, 1994; The Children's Topical Bible, 1994; Bumper and Noah, 1994; Songs and Rhymes for Wiggle Worms, 1995; Who Is Jesus?, 1995; What Does Jesus Say?, 1995; The Story of Jesus, 1995; Bumper the Dinosaur, 1996; Into My Heart, 1996; The Preschooler's Picture-Reading Bible, 1998; The Amazing Expedition Bible, 1998; Hugs for Kids, 2000; Tall Body, Short Body, 2000; The Upside-Down, Inside-Out, Backwards, Oopsie Daisy Book, 2000; Little Taps on the Shoulder from God, 2002; My Bible Journey, 2002; Love Notes from God, 2003. CHILDREN OF THE KING SERIES: The King's Alphabet, 1988; The King's Numbers, 1988; The King's Workers, 1990; The King's Manners, 1990; The King's Animals, 1991; The King's Children, 1991.

GOD'S HAPPY FOREST SERIES: Polka Dots, Stripes, Humps, 'n' Hatracks: How God Created Happy Forest, 1990; Twizzler, the Unlikely Hero, 1990; Christmas in Happy Forest, 1990. MY VERY FIRST BOOK ... SERIES: My Very First Book of Bible Heroes, 1993; ...of Bible Lessons, 1993; ...of Bible Words, 1993; ...of Prayers, 1993; ...on God, 1994; ...of God's Animals-and Other Creatures, 1994; ...of Bible Questions, 1994; ...of Bible Fun Facts, 1994. AS PROFESSOR SCRIBBLER: Charlie and the Shabby Tabby, 1989; Charlie and the Missing Music, 1989; Charlie and the Jinglemouse, 1989; Charlie and the Gold Mine, 1989. OTHER: Help! I Need a Bulletin Board, 1975; For Mom with Love, 1987; A Few Hallelujas for Your Ho-Hums, 1988; Just between Friends, 1988; It's a One-derful Life!, 1989; Rainbows, 1989; Apple Blossoms, 1990; (with C.A. Greeson and M. Washburn) The Grief Adjustment Guide, 1990; (with C.A. Greeson and M. Washburn) The Divorce Recovery Guide, 1991; (comp.) Together Forever, 1993; (comp.) On Raising Children, 1993; (with F. and A. Kendall) Speaking of Love, 1995; Reborn! (play), 1995; The Last Journey (musical), 1997; Suddenly One Morning (musical adaptation), 1998; Hugs for Women, 1998; Arise!, 1999; Fireside Stories, 2 vols., 2000. Contributor to periodicals. **Address:** Shady Oaks Studio, 1507 Shirley Way, Bedford, TX 76022-6737, U.S.A.

HOLLINS, Etta R(uth). American. **Genres:** Education. **Career:** Elementary schoolteacher in Parsons, KS, 1964-65; California State Department of Youth Authority, Paso Robles, classroom teacher, 1966-69; social studies teacher and dept head at middle schools in Seattle, WA, 1969-72; primary resource teacher at public schools in Sacramento, CA, 1972-73; consultant in multicultural education for public schools in San Mateo, CA, 1973-75; administrator of public schools in Palo Alto, CA, 1975-79; Education Service Center, Region XIII, Austin, TX, consultant in social studies and multicultural education, 1979-82; coordinator of teacher training program for public schools in Austin, 1982-84; University of Utah, Salt Lake City, assistant professor of educational studies, 1984-86; Weber State College, Ogden, UT, asst professor of teacher education, 1986-87; Delaware State University, Dover, associate professor of education and head of dept, 1987-88; California State University, Hayward, professor of teacher education, 1988-95; Washington State University, Pullman, professor of teaching and learning and dept head, 1995-98; Wright State University, Dayton, OH, College of Education and Human Services, professor of education and associate dean, 1998-2000. **Publications:** (with K. Spencer) A Conceptual Framework for Selecting Instructional Approaches and Materials for Inner City Black Youngsters, 1989; Schooling in a Context of Cultural Isolation (monograph), 1991; Culture in School Learning, 1996. EDITOR: (with J.E. King and W.A. Hayman, and contrib.) Teaching Diverse Populations, 1994; Transforming Curriculum for a Culturally Diverse Society, 1996; (with King and Hayman, and contrib.) Preparing Teachers for Cultural Diversity, 1997; (with E.I. Oliver, and contrib.) Reflective Teaching in a Culturally Diverse Society: Finding Pathways to Success, 1998. Contributor to books. Contributor of articles and reviews to academic journals. **Address:** University of Southern California, Los Angeles, CA 90089-0031, U.S.A.

HOLLIS, Stephanie. British, b. 1946. **Genres:** Literary criticism and history, Bibliography. **Career:** University of Auckland, Auckland, New Zealand, lecturer, 1972-76, senior lecturer in Old and Middle English and Old Icelandic, 1977-94; associate professor, 1995-. **Publications:** Anglo-Saxon Women and the Church, 1992; (with M. Wright) Annotated Bibliographies of Old and Middle English IV: Old English Prose of Secular Learning, 1992. Contributor to scholarly journals. **Address:** Department of English, University of Auckland, P.O. Box 92019, Auckland, New Zealand.

HOLLIS, Tim. American, b. 1963. **Genres:** Popular Culture. **Career:** Writer. Campbell's Publishing, Birmingham, AL, editor-in-chief, 1986-. **Publications:** Cousin Cliff: 40 Magical Years, 1991; Dixie before Disney: 100 Years of Roadside Fun, 1999; Hi There Boys and Girls! America's Local Children's Shows, 2001; Florida's Miracle Strip: From Redneck Riviera to Emerald Coast, 2004. **Address:** PO Box 310727, Birmingham, AL 35231, U.S.A. **Online address:** CampHoll@aol.com

HOLLO, Anselm (Paul Alexis). Finnish, b. 1934. **Genres:** Poetry, Autobiography/Memoirs, Essays, Translations. **Career:** Program Assistant and Coordinator, BBC, London, 1958-66; Visiting Professor, Dept. of English, State University of New York, Buffalo, 1967; Lecturer, Creative Writing Program, 1968-73, and Lecturer in English and Music, Center for New Performing Arts, University of Iowa, Iowa City; Visiting Professor, Bowling Green State University, OH, 1972-73, and Hobart and William Smith Colls., Geneva, NY, 1973-75; Distinguished Visiting Poet, Michigan State University, 1974; Associate Professor, of Literature and Creative Writing, University of Maryland, Catonsville, 1975-77; Visiting Lecturer in

Creative Writing, Southwest Minnesota State College, Marshall, 1977-78; Margaret Bannister Distinguished Writer-in-Residence, Sweet Briar College, Amherst, VA, 1978-81; Poet in Residence, 1981, Associate Lecturer in Poetry and Poetics, Kerouac School of Poetics, Boulder, CO, 1986-89; Visiting Lecturer in Poetics, New College of California, San Francisco, 1981-82; Visiting Lecturer and Participant in Black Mountain College Symposium, Maryland Institute of Art, Baltimore, 1983-84; Visiting Professor of Poetry, Creative Writing Dept., University of Colorado, Boulder, 1985; Professor in Poetry, Poetics and Translation, Kerouac School of Poetics at Naropa Institute, 1989. **Publications:** Sateiden Valilla, 1956; St. Texts and Finnpoems, 1961; Loverman, 1961; We Just Wanted to Tell You, 1963; And What Else Is New, 1963; History, 1964; Trobar: Loytaa (poetry), 1964; Here We Go, 1965; The Claim, 1966; The Going-On Poem, 1966; Poems/Runoja, 1967; Isadora and Other Poems, 1967; Leaf Times, 1967; The Man in the Tree-Top Hat, 1968; The Coherences, 1968; Tumbleweed: Poems, 1968; (with J. Esam and T. Raworth) Haiku, 1968; Waiting for a Beautiful Bather: Ten Poems, 1969; Maya: Works, 1959-69, 1970; America del Norte and Other Peace Herb Poems, 1970; Message, 1970; (with J. Marshall and S. Hamod) Surviving in America, 1972; Sensation 27, 1972; Some Worlds, 1974; Lingering Tangos, 1976; Sojourner Microcosms: New and Selected Poems 1959-1977, 1977; Heavy Jars, 1977; Curious Data, 1978; With Ruth in Mind, 1979; Finite Continued, 1980; No Complaints, 1983; Pick Up the House, 1986; Outlying Districts, 1987; Near Miss Haiku (poetry), 1990; Space Baltic: The Science Fiction Poems, 1962-1987, 1991; High Beam: 12 Poems, 1993; West Is Left on the Map, 1993; Survival Dancing, 1995; Corvus: New Poems, 1995; Caws & Causeries, 1998; Rue Wilson Monday, 2000; Notes on the Possibilities and Attractions of Existence: Selected Poems 1965-2000, 2001; So the Ants Made It to the Cat Food, 2002; The Guy in the Little Room, 2002. EDITOR: Jazz Poems, 1963; Negro Verse, 1964. TRANSLATOR: L. Malle, Au Revoir les Enfants, 1988; Egon Schiele: The Poems, 1988; P.S. Jungk, Frans Werfel: The Story of a Life, 1990; Paavo Haavikko: Selected Poems, 1949-1989, 1991; J. Kross, The Czar's Madman, 1991; R. Liksom, One Night Stands, 1993; Z. Dizdarevic, Sarajevo: A War Journal, 1993; J. Kross, Professor Martens' Departure, 1994; The Poems of Hipponax of Ephesus, 1996. EDITOR & TRANSLATOR: A. Ginsberg, Kaddish, 1962; Red Cats: Selection from Three Russian Poets, 1962; G. Corso, In der Fluchtigen Hand der Zeit, 1963; A. Ginsberg, Huuto ja Muita Runoja, 1963; A. Ginsberg, Kuolema van Goghin Korvalle, 1963; (with M. Lahtela) Idan ja Lannen Runot, 1963; Selected Poems by Andrei Voznesensky, 1964; Nain Ihminen Vastaa, 1964; R.-G. Dienst, Five Feet Two, 1965; Word from the North: New Poetry from Finland, 1965; P. Saarikoski, Helsinki: Selected Poems, 1967; P. Haavikko, Selected Poems, 1968; A. Blok, The Twelve and Other Poems, 1971; (with G. Harding) Recent Swedish Poetry in Translation, 1979; Pentti Saarikoski: Poems 1958-80, 1984; Pentti Saarikoski; Trilogy, 2003. **Address:** c/o Writing & Poetics, Naropa Institute, 2130 Arapaho Ave, Boulder, CO 80302, U.S.A.

HOLLOS, Marida. Hungarian, b. 1940. **Genres:** Geography, Local history/Rural topics, Autobiography/Memoirs. **Career:** Brown University, Providence, RI, associate professor, 1974-; writer. **Publications:** Growing Up in Flathill, 1974; New Hungarian Peasants: An East Central European Experience with Collectivization, 1983; Becoming Nigerian in Ijo Society, 1989; Scandal in a Small Town, 2001. **Address:** Dept of Anthropology, Box 1921, Brown University, Providence, RI 02912, U.S.A. **Online address:** Marida_Hollos@brown.edu

HOLLOWAY, Harry (Albert). American, b. 1925. **Genres:** Politics/Government. **Career:** Professor of Political Science, University of Oklahoma, Norman, 1962-91; with Dept. of Government, University of Texas, Austin, 1957-62. **Publications:** (co-author) Party and Factional Division in Texas, 1964; The Politics of the Southern Negro, 1969; (co-author) Public Opinion: Coalitions, Elites, and Masses, 1979; Bad Times for Good Ol' Boys: The Oklahoma County Commissioner Scandal, 1993. **Address:** 1029 W Imhoff Rd, Norman, OK 73072, U.S.A. **Online address:** hholloway@cox.net

HOLLOWAY, John. British, b. 1920. **Genres:** Poetry, Literary criticism and history, Autobiography/Memoirs. **Career:** Fellow, All Souls College, 1946-60, and John Locke Scholar, 1947, Oxford; Lecturer in English, Aberdeen University, 1949-54; University Lecturer in English, 1954-66, Fellow of Queens College, 1955-82, Reader in Modern English, 1966-72, and Professor of Modern English, 1972-82, Cambridge University; Byron Professor, University of Athens, 1961-63; Alexander White Professor, University of Chicago, 1965; Hinkley Professor, Johns Hopkins University, Baltimore, 1972; Berg Professor, New York University, NYC, 1977. **Publications:** Language and Intelligence, 1951; The Victorian Sage: Studies in Argument, 1953; The Minute and Longer Poems, 1956; The Fugue and Shorter Pieces (poetry), 1960; The Charted Mirror: Literary and Critical Essays, 1960; The

Story of the Night: Studies in Shakespeare's Major Tragedies, 1961; The Landfallers: A Poem in Twelve Parts, 1962; The Colours of Clarity: Essays on Contemporary Literature and Education, 1964; The Lion Hunt: A Pursuit of Poetry and Reality, 1964; Wood and Windfall (poetry), 1965; Widening Horizons in English Verse, 1966; A London Childhood (autobiography), 1966; Blake: The Lyric Poetry, 1968; New Poems, 1970; The Proud Knowledge: Poetry, Insight, and the Self 1620-1920, 1977; Planet of Winds (poetry), 1977; Narrative and Structure: Exploratory Essays, 1979; The Slumber of Apollo: Reflections on Recent Art, Literature, Language, and the Individual Consciousness, 1983; Oxford Book of Local Verses, 1987; Civitatula: Cambridge, the Little City (long poem), 1993. EDITOR: Poems of the Mid-Century, 1957; Selected Poems, by Percy Bysshe Shelley, 1959; Little Dorrit, by Charles Dickens, 1967; (with J. Black) Later English Broadside Ballads, 2 vols., 1974-79. **Address:** Queens' College, Cambridge CB3 9ET, England.

HOLLOWAY, Karla F. C. American, b. 1949. **Genres:** Literary criticism and history. **Career:** Old Dominion University, Norfolk, VA, instructor in English, 1972-74; Western Michigan University, Kalamazoo, assistant professor, 1978-82, associate professor of English, 1982-86; North Carolina State University, Raleigh, professor of English, 1988-93; Duke University, Durham, NC, professor of English and African-American literature, 1993-. **Publications:** The Character of the Word, 1987; (with S. Demetrakopoulos) New Dimensions of Spirituality, 1987; Moorings and Metaphors, 1992; Codes of Conduct: Race, Ethics, and the Color of Our Character, 1994. Contributor of periodicals. **Address:** Department of English, 304 Allen Building, Duke University, Durham, NC 27708-0015, U.S.A.

HOLLOWAY, Richard (Frederick). Scottish, b. 1933. **Genres:** Theology/Religion. **Career:** St. Ninian's, Glasgow, curate, 1959-63; St. Margaret and St. Mungo's Church, Glasgow, Scotland, priest in charge, 1963-68; Old St. Paul's Church, Edinburgh, Scotland, rector, 1968-80; Church of the Advent, Boston, MA, rector, 1980-84; St. Mary Magdalen Church, Oxford, England, vicar, 1984-86; Scottish Episcopal Church, Edinburgh, Scotland, bishop of Edinburgh, 1986-2000, primus, 1992-2000. Gresham College, London, England, professor of divinity, 1997-2001. **Publications:** Let God Arise, 1972; New Vision of Glory, 1974; A New Heaven, 1979; Beyond Belief: The Christian Encounter with God, 1981; Signs of Glory, 1983; Paradoxes of Christian Faith and Life, 1984, in US as Suffering, Sex, and Other Paradoxes, 1985; The Killing: Meditations on the Death of Christ, 1985; The Way of the Cross, 1986, in US as A Death in Jerusalem, 1986; Seven to Flee, Seven to Follow, 1986; The Sidelong Glance: Politics, Conflict, and the Church, 1986; Crossfire: Faith and Doubt in an Age of Certainty, 1988; When I Get to Heaven, 1988; Another Country, Another King, 1988; Anger, Sex, Doubt, and Death, 1992; The Stranger in the Wings, 1994; (with B. Avery) Churches and How to Survive Them, 1994; Behold Your King, 1995; Limping towards the Sunrise, 1995; Dancing on the Edge, 1997; Godless Morality: Keeping Religion out of Ethics, 1999; Doubts and Loves: What Is Left of Christianity, 2001; On Forgiveness, 2002. EDITOR: The Anglican Tradition, 1984; Who Needs Feminism: Male Responses to Sexism in the Church, 1991. **Address:** 6 Blantyre Terrace, Edinburgh EH10 5AE, Scotland. **Online address:** doc.holloway@virgin.net

HOLLOWAY, Sue (A.). American, b. 1944. **Genres:** Poetry. **Career:** Southern Connecticut State University, New Haven, CT, adjunct professor, Foundations of Education/Women's Studies Departments, 1991-2000. Teachers' Creative Workshop, founder/facilitator, 1993-95; Branford Land Trust, advisory board member, 1996-2000; Branford River Raptor, board of directors member, 1998-2000; InterCity Cultural Development Project, mentor, 1999-2000; TWR Associates, qualitative researcher; Southern Connecticut Library Council, lecturer and workshop facilitator; gives poetry performances and lectures. **Publications:** (coed) A Community of Young Poets (poetry), 1995; Artemis' Arrow (poetry; audiotape), 1999; Swan in the Grail (nonfiction), 1999; Chronicles of Healing Self with Nature (poetry), in press. Contributor to anthologies. Contributor of essays, reviews, and poetry to journals. Contributor of articles, poetry, and photos to newsletters. Contributor of feature articles, photo features, and op-editorials to newspapers. **Address:** 168 Thimble Islands Rd, Branford, CT 06405, U.S.A.

HOLM, Jeanne M(arjorie). American, b. 1921. **Genres:** Women's studies and issues, Military/Defense/Arms control. **Career:** U.S. Air Force, career officer, 1942-45, commander of a Women's Army Corps basic training company, commander of a training regiment at Fort Oglethorpe, Ga., wing war plans officer at Erding Air Depot in Germany, personnel staff officer at Air Force Headquarters in the Pentagon, chief of manpower at North Atlantic Treaty Organization (NATO) Air Headquarters in Naples, Italy, 1957-61, manpower staff officer in Directorate of Manpower and Organization at the Pentagon, 1961-65, director of Women in the Air Force, 1965-73, director of Air Force Personnel Council, 1973-75, retired as major general; special assistant to President Gerald Ford, 1976-77; writer and public speaker, 1977-. Trustees Air Force Aid Society, 1988-96; member of boards of United Service Organizations International and National Defense University Foundation, 1982-89; member of advisory committees of Veterans Administration, Coast Guard Academy, and United Services Life Insurance Co. Director of Pentagon Federal Credit Union, 1973-75; consultant to Defense Manpower Commission and Under Secretary of the Air Force. Director of national boards of Camp Fire Girls, Inc., 1969-75. **Publications:** Women in the Military: An Unfinished Revolution, 1982, rev. ed., 1992; In Defense of a Nation: Servicewomen in World War II, 1998. **Address:** 2707 Thyme Rd, Edgewater, MD 21037, U.S.A.

HOLMAN, J. Alan. American, b. 1931. **Genres:** Zoology. **Career:** Michigan State University, East Lansing, professor of zoological and geological sciences, and Michigan State University Museum curator (emeritus) of vertebrate paleontology. **Publications:** (with D. Gringhuis) Mystery Mammals of the Ice Age: Great Lakes Region (juvenile), 1975; Ancient Life of the Great Lakes Basin, 1995; Pleistocene Amphibians and Reptiles in North America, 1995; Pleistocene Amphibians and Reptiles in Britain and Europe, 1998; Fossil Snakes of North America, 2000; In Quest of Great Lakes Ice-Age Vertebrates, 2001. **Address:** 540 Linden St., East Lansing, MI 48823, U.S.A. **Online address:** holman@msu.edu

HOLMAN, Sheri. American. **Genres:** Novels. **Career:** Worked as an aide at the Aaron M. Priest Literary Agency, c. 1996. **Publications:** A Stolen Tongue, 1997; The Mammoth Cheese, 2003. **Address:** c/o Atlantic Monthly Press, 841 Broadway, New York, NY 10003, U.S.A.

HOLMES, Arthur F(rank). American (born England), b. 1924. **Genres:** Philosophy, Theology/Religion. **Career:** Wheaton College, Illinois, professor of philosophy, 1951-94, emeritus professor, 1994-. **Publications:** Christianity and Philosophy, 1960; Christian Philosophy in the Twentieth Century, 1969; Faith Seeks Understanding, 1971; The Idea of a Christian College, 1975, 1987; All Truth Is God's Truth, 1977; Contours of a World View, 1983; Ethics: Approaching Moral Decisions, 1985; Shaping Character, 1990; Fact, Value and God, 1997; Building the Christian Academy, 2001. EDITOR: War and Christian Ethics, 1975, 1992; The Making of a Christian Mind, 1984. **Address:** 841 Pinegrove Court, Wheaton, IL 60187, U.S.A.

HOLMES, B(ryan) J(ohn). Also writes as Charles Langley Hayes, Ethan Wall. British, b. 1939. **Genres:** Novellas/Short stories, Westerns/Adventure, Reference. **Career:** Retired after careers in industrial advertising and lecturing, North Staffordshire Polytechnic, Stafford, and University of Derby. **Publications:** The Avenging Four, 1978; Hazard, 1979; Blood, Sweat and Gold, 1980; Gunfall, 1980; A Noose for Yanqui, 1981; Shard, 1982; Bad Times at Backwheel, 1982; On the Spin of a Dollar, 1983; Guns of the Reaper, 1983; Another Day, Another Dollar, 1984; Dark Rider, 1987; I Rode with Wyatt, 1989; A Legend Called Shatterhand, 1990; Dollars for the Reaper, 1990; Shatterhand and the People, 1992; The Last Days of Billy Patch, 1992; Blood on the Reaper, 1992; A Coffin for the Reaper, 1994; Comes the Reaper, 1995; Viva Reaper!, 1996; The Shard Brand, 1996; Smoking Star, 1997; Crowfeeders, 1999; Jake's Women, 2002. REFERENCE: Pocket Crossword Dictionary, 2001; The Guide to Solving Crosswords, 2002; Solving Cryptic Crosswords, 2003. Author of scholarly papers and short stories. AS CHARLES LANGLEY HAYES: Montana Hit, 1993; Dakota Hit, 1995; Utah Hit, 1995. AS ETHAN WALL: Loco, 1991; All Trails Lead to Dodge, 1993; High Plains Death, 1997; North of the Bravo, 2001. **Address:** c/o Robert Hale Ltd, 45-47 Clerkenwell Green, London EC1R 0HT, England.

HOLMES, Diana. British, b. 1949. **Genres:** Literary criticism and history. **Career:** Wolverhampton Polytechnic (now University of Wolverhampton), England, lecturer in French, 1975-80, senior lecturer, 1984-90, principal lecturer in French, 1990; North London Polytechnic, part-time lecturer in French, 1981-84; Keele University, England, lecturer, 1992-94, senior lecturer, 1994-95, professor of French and head of French studies, 1995-99; University of Leeds, professor of French, 1999-. Speaker at educational institutions. Modern & Contemporary France, co-editor; French Film Directors, co-editor. **Publications:** Colette, 1991; Women in Context: French Women Writers, 1848-1994, 1996; Francois Truffaut, 1998; Rachilde: Decadence, Gender and the Woman Writer, 2001. Contributor to books on French literature and film. Contributor to periodicals. **Address:** Department of French, University of Leeds, Leeds LS2 9JT, England. **Online address:** d.holmes@leeds.ac.uk

HOLMES, John. See SOUSTER, Raymond.

HOLMES, Katie. Australian. **Genres:** Literary criticism and history. **Career:** Freelance writer, c. 1996-. **Publications:** Spaces in Her Day: Australian Women's Diaries of the 1920s and 1930s, 1996. **Address:** c/o Allen & Unwin Pty. Ltd., 9 Atchinson St., PO Box 8500, St. Leonards, Sydney, NSW 2065, Australia.

HOLMES, Leslie (Templeman). Australian (born England), b. 1948. **Genres:** Politics/Government. **Career:** University of Wales, Aberystwyth, lecturer in political science, 1976-78; University of Kent at Canterbury, England, lecturer to senior lecturer in political science, 1978-83; University of Melbourne, Parkville, Australia, lecturer to senior lecturer, 1983-88, professor of political science, 1988-, department head, 1988-93, director, Contemporary Europe Research Centre, 1997-2000. Oxford University, senior associate member of St. Antony's College, 1987, 1993, 1996; Harvard University, visiting fellow at Russian Research Center, 1993. International Council for Central and East European Studies, president, 2000-05; consultant to Australian radio and television networks and the World Bank. **Publications:** The Policy Process in Communist States: Industrial Administration and Politics, 1981; (ed.) The Withering Away of the State? 1981; Politics in the Communist World, 1986; The End of Communist Power: Anti-Corruption Campaigns and Legitimation Crisis, 1993; Post-Communism, 1997; (ed. with P. Murray) Europe: Rethinking the Boundaries, 1998; (ed. with P. Murray) Citizenship and Identity in Europe, 1999; (with J. Dryzek) Post-Communist Democratization, 2002. Work represented in anthologies. Contributor to political studies journals. **Address:** Department of Political Science, University of Melbourne, Melbourne, VIC 3010, Australia. **Online address:** lesliech@unimelb.edu.au

HOLMES, Lowell D. American, b. 1925. **Genres:** Anthropology/Ethnology, Music, Bibliography, Biography. **Career:** Distinguished Professor Emeritus of Anthropology, Wichita State University, Kansas, 1990- (Professor, 1959-90). Assistant Professor of Anthropology, Missouri Valley College, Marshall, 1956-58. **Publications:** Ta'u, Stability and Change in a Samoan Village, 1958; Anthropology: An Introduction, 1965, 4th ed., 1987; The Story of Samoa, 1967; Samoan Village, 1974; Other Cultures, Elder Years, 1983, 2nd ed. (with E.R. Holmes), 1995; Samoan Islands Bibliography, 1984; (with J.W. Thomson) Jazz Greats, Getting Better with Age, 1986; Quest for the Real Samoa: The Mead-Freeman Controversy and Beyond, 1987; (with E.R. Holmes) Samoan Village, Then and Now, 1991; Treasured Islands: Cruising the South Seas with Robert Louis Stevenson, 2001. EDITOR: Readings in General Anthropology, 1971; (with D.O. Cowgill) Aging and Modernization, 1972; The Anthropology of Modern Life, 1975; The American Tribe, 1978. **Address:** Dept of Anthropology, Wichita State University, Wichita, KS 67208, U.S.A.

HOLMES, Mary Tavener. American, b. 1954. **Genres:** Art/Art history, Biography. **Career:** College of the City University of New York, NYC, assistant professor, 1985-92; Cooper Hewitt Masters Program, instructor, 1992-93. Special curator at Houston Museum of Fine Art, 1986, and Frick Museum, 1992. **Publications:** (with George T. M. Shackelford) The Magic Mirror: The Portrait in France, 1700-1900, 1986; Nicolas Lancret, 1690-1743, 1992; (with D. Posner) French Drawings in the Robert Lehman Collection; (with Perrin Stein) French Drawings in New York Collections (catalogue). **Address:** 7 West 81st St., New York, NY 10024, U.S.A.

HOLMES, Mary Z(astrow). American, b. 1943. **Genres:** Romance/Historical. **Career:** Raintree Publishers, Milwaukee, WI, general manager and publisher, 1981-85; Agridata Resources, Milwaukee, executive vice president, 1982-87; freelance writer and consultant specializing in commodity market textbooks, software, training, marketing, and promotion, 1987-. Founding partner, Stone Bank Books, a book development company specializing in historical fiction for middle-school-aged children. Has also worked for educational publishers. **Publications:** Cross of Gold, 1992; Two Chimneys, 1992; Thunder Foot, 1992; Year of the Sevens, 1992; See You in Heaven, 1992; For Bread, 1992; Dear Dad, 1992; Dust of Life, 1992. **Address:** 6910 Reynolds Dr., Oconomowoc, WI 53066, U.S.A.

HOLMES, Raymond. See SOUSTER, Raymond.

HOLMES, Richard. British, b. 1945. **Genres:** Poetry, Literary criticism and history, Biography. **Career:** Writer. **Publications:** One for Sorrow, Two for Joy (poems), 1970; Shelley: The Pursuit, 1974; (trans.) My Fantoms, by Theophile Gaurier, 1976; (ed.) Shelley on Love: An Anthology, 1980; Coleridge, 1982; Footsteps: Adventures of a Romantic Biographer, 1985; Coleridge: Early Visions, 1989; Dr. Johnson and Mr. Savage, 1993; Coleridge: Darker Reflections, 1804-1834, 1999; Sidetracks: Explorations of a Romantic Biographer, 2000. **Address:** c/o David Godwin Associates, 55 Monmouth St, London WC2H 90G, England.

HOLROYD, Michael. British, b. 1935. **Genres:** Literary criticism and history, Biography. **Career:** Society of Authors, chairman, London, 1973-74; National Book League, chairman, 1976-78; BBC Archives Committee, member, 1976-79; English PEN, president, 1985-88; Strachey Trust, chairman, 1990-95; Arts Council of Great Britain, chairman of literature panel 1992-95; Public Lending Right, Advisory Committee, chairman, 1997-2000; Royal Society of Literature, chairman, 1998-2001, president, 2003-. **Publications:** Hugh Kingsmill: A Biography, 1964; Lytton Strachey, 2 vols., 1967-68, rev. ed., 1994; A Dog's Life, 1969; Unreceived Opinions, 1973; Augustus John, 2 vols., 1974-75, 1976, rev. ed., 1996; (with M. Easton) The Art of Augustus John, 1974; Themes and Variations: The Drawings of Augustus John 1901-1931, 1996; Bernard Shaw, 4 vols., 1988-93, rev. ed. in 1 vol., 1997; Basil Street Blues, 1999; Works on Paper, 2002; Mosaic, 2004. EDITOR: The Best of Hugh Kingsmill, 1970; Lytton Strachey by Himself, 1971; The Genius of Shaw, 1979; (with P. Levy) The Shorter Strachey, 1980; (with R. Skidelsky) W. Gerhardie, God's Fifth Column, 1981; Essays by Divers Hands, XLII, 1982. **Address:** c/o A. P. Watt Ltd, 20 John St, London WC1N 2DR, England.

HOLSTAD, Scott Cameron. American, b. 1966. **Genres:** Poetry. **Career:** Big Head Press, editor, 1990-; APIPA, Phoenix, AZ, document control technician, 1991; California State University, Long Beach, CA, lecturer, 1993-94; TSI Pubus., editorial coordinator, 1994-. **Publications:** Street Poems, 1991; Industrial Madness, 1991; Dancing with the Lights Out, 1992; Grungy Ass Swaying, 1993; Junction City, 1993; Distant Visions, Again and Again, 1994; Places, 1995. Contributor to periodicals. **Address:** 733 Villa Crest Dr., Knoxville, TN 37923-6313, U.S.A.

HOLSTI, Kalevi J. Canadian (born Switzerland), b. 1935. **Genres:** International relations/Current affairs. **Career:** Professor of Political Science, University of British Columbia, Vancouver, 1970- (Acting Director, Institute of International Relations, 1970-71). Co-Ed., Canadian Journal of Political Science, 1978-82. President, International Studies Association, 1986-87. **Publications:** Suomen Ulkopolitiikka Suuntaansa Etsimassa, 1963; International Politics: A Framework for Analysis, 1967, 7th ed., 1995; Why Nations Realign: Foreign Policy Restructuring, 1982; The Dividing Discipline: Hegemony and Pluralism in International Theory, 1985; Peace & War: Armed Conflicts and International Order, 1648-1989, 1991; Change in the International System: Essays on the Theory and Practice of International Politics, 1991; The State, War, and the State of War, 1996; Taming the Sovereigns: Institutional Change in International Politics, 2004. **Address:** Dept of Political Science, University of British Columbia, Vancouver, BC, Canada V6T 1W5. **Online address:** holsti@interchange.ubc.ca

HOLSTI, Ole Rudolf. American (born Switzerland), b. 1933. **Genres:** International relations/Current affairs, Politics/Government, Sports/Fitness. **Career:** Duke University, Durham, NC, George V. Allen Professor of Political Science, 1974-, Chairman, Dept. of Political Science, 1978-83. Associate Ed., International Studies Quarterly, 1980-; Western Political Quarterly, 1970-; Correspondent and Contributing Ed., Racing South, and Running Journal mags; American Review of Politics, 1992-; Editorial Board, Duke University Press, 1984-92, University Press of America, 1980-, and International Interaction, 1984-. Instructor, 1962-65, Assistant Professor, 1965-67, and Research Coordinator and Associate Director, Studies in International Conflict and Integration, 1962-67, Stanford University, California; Associate Ed., Journal of Conflict Resolution, 1967-72; Associate Professor, 1967-71, and Professor, 1971-74, University of British Columbia, Vancouver. President, International Studies Association, 1979-80. **Publications:** AUTHOR/CO-AUTHOR: Content Analysis: A Handbook with Application for the Study of International Crisis, 1963; Enemies in Politics, 1967; Content Analysis for the Social Sciences and Humanities, 1969; (and co-ed.) The Analysis of Communication Content: Developments in Scientific Theories and Computer Techniques, 1969; Crisis Escalation War, 1972; Unity and Disintegration in International Alliances: Comparative Studies, 1973; (and co-ed.) Change in the International System, 1980; American Leadership in World Affairs: Vietnam and the Breakdown of Consensus, 1984; Public Opinion and American Foreign Policy, 1996, 2nd ed., 2004; (co) On the Cutting Edge of Globalization, 2005. CO-EDITOR: Encyclopedia of U.S. Foreign Relation, 1997. **Address:** 608 Croom Ct, Chapel Hill, NC 27514-6706, U.S.A. **Online address:** holsti@duke.edu

HOLST-WARHAFT, Gail. Australian, b. 1941. **Genres:** Literary criticism and history, Music. **Career:** Educator, writer, translator, musician, and poet. Journalist and musician in Greece, 1970s; Cornell University, Ithaca, NY, adjunct associate professor, acting director of Institute for European Studies. **Publications:** Road to Rembetika: Music of a Greek Sub-Culture: Songs of Love, Sorrow, and Hashish, 1975, 3rd ed., 1983; Theodorakis: Myth and

Politics in Modern Greek Music, 1980; Dangerous Voices: Women's Laments and Greek Literature, 1992; (ed. with D.R. McCann) The Classical Moment: Views from Seven Literatures, 1999; The Cue for Passion: Grief and Its Political Uses, 2000. Contributor to books and periodicals. Poetry published in journals. Translator of poetry and prose from modern and ancient Greek by N. Kavadias, A. Zei, I. Kambanellis, Aeschylus, and M. Theodorakis. **Address:** 113 East Upland Rd., Ithaca, NY 14850, U.S.A. **Online address:** glh3@cornell.edu

HOLT, (Wilma) Geraldene. British. **Genres:** Food and Wine, Homes/Gardens, Horticulture, Food and Wine. **Career:** Freelance food and cookery writer. **Publications:** Geraldene Holt's Cake Stall, 1980; Geraldene Holt's Travelling Food, 1982; (Compiler) Devon Air Cookbook, 1982; Budget Gourmet, 1984; French Country Kitchen, 1987; Tuckbox Treats, 1987; Recipes from a French Herb Garden, 1989; The Gourmet Garden, 1990; Geraldene Holt's Book of Herbs, 1991; A Cup of Tea, 1991; Geraldene Holt's Country House Cooking, 1996.

HOLT, James Clarke. British, b. 1922. **Genres:** History. **Career:** Hon. Fellow, Emmanuel College Cambridge, 1985- (Professorial Fellow, Emmanuel College, 1978-81; Professor of Medieval History, Cambridge University, 1978-88; Master of Fitzwilliam College, Cambridge, 1981-88); Queen's College, Oxford, Hon. Fellow, 1998-. Assistant Lecturer, 1949-51, Lecturer, 1951-61, Sr. Lecturer, 1961-62, and Professor of Medieval History, 1962, University of Nottingham; Professor of History, 1966-78, and Dean, Faculty of Letters and Social Sciences, 1972-76, University of Reading. Member, Advisory Council on Public Records, 1974-81; President, Royal Historical Society, 1980-84. **Publications:** The Northerners: A Study in the Reign of King John, 1961, 1992; Praestita Roll 14-18 John, 1964; Magna Carta, 1965, 1992; The Making of Magna Carta, 1966; Magna Carta and the Idea of Liberty, 1972; The University of Reading: The First Fifty Years, 1977; Robin Hood, 1982, 1989; (ed. with J. Gillingham) War and Government in the Middle Ages, 1984; Magna Carta and Medieval Government 1985; (with R. Mortimer) Handlist of the Acta of Henry II and Richard I, 1986; Colonial England 1066-1215, 1997. **Address:** Fitzwilliam College, Cambridge, Cambs. CB3 0DG, England.

HOLT, Marilyn Irvin. American, b. 1949. **Genres:** History, Local history/Rural topics. **Career:** Teacher at public schools in Illinois, 1970-79; Illinois State Historical Library, Springfield, editor, 1983-86; Kansas State Historical Society, Topeka, director of publications, 1986-90; University of Kansas, Lawrence, adjunct faculty member, 1988-98. Kansas Humanities Council, member of Speakers Bureau, 1993-; consultant for Public Broadcasting System documentaries on orphan trains and western settlement. **Publications:** The Orphan Trains: Placing Out in America, 1992; Model T's, Pep Chapels, and a Wolf at the Door: Kansas Teenagers of the Early Twentieth Century, 1900-1941, 1994; Linoleum, Better Babies & the Modern Farm Woman, 1890-1930, 1995; Indian Orphanages, 2001; Children of the Western Plains: The 19th Century Experience, 2003. Work represented in books. Contributor to history journals.

HOLT, Michael (Paul). British, b. 1929. **Genres:** Children's fiction, Recreation, Mathematics/Statistics, Sciences. **Career:** Sr. Science and Mathematics Ed., Ginn and Co. Ltd., London, 1965-67; Sr. Lecturer in Mathematics, Goldsmiths College, University of London, 1967-70; Chairman, Educational Writers Group, Society of Authors, London, 1971-73. **Publications:** (with D.T.E. Marjoram) Mathematics Through Experience, 7 books, 1966-75; Exercises, 4 books, 1972; What Is the New Maths?, 1968; Science Happenings, 6 books, 1969; Mathematics in Art, 1971; (with R. Ridout) Joe's Trip to the Moon, 1971; (with R. Ridout) The Train Thief, 1971; (with Z.P. Dienes) Zoo, 1972; (with R. Ridout) The Big Book of Puzzles, 3 vols., 1972-79; (with Z. P. Dienes) Let's Play Maths, 1973; (with D.T.E. Marjoram) Mathematics in a Changing World, 1973; Inner Ring Maths, 1973; Maths, 6 books, 1973-74; (with R. Ridout) All Round English, 1974; (with R. Ridout) Life Cycle Books, 4 books, 1974; Monkey Puzzle Books, 6 books, 1974; Ready for Science, 6 books, 1974; Maps, Tracks, and the Bridges of Konigsberg, 1975; Fun with Numbers, 1976; Math Puzzles and Games, 1977; More Math Puzzles and Games, 1978; Figure It Out Books, 4 vols., 1978-81; (with A. Rothery) Mathsworks, books, 1979; The Puma Puzzle Book, 1980; Basic Skills in Maths, 1981; Answer Me This, 1981; Holt Counting Board, 1981; The Bumper Quiz Book, 1981; (with A. Rothery) Maths Alive, 1982; The Amazing Invisible Ink Puzzle Books, 1982; (with A. Ward) Wide Range Science Story Books 1-2, 1982; The Amazing Invisible Ink Puzzle Books, 1983; Basic Arithmetic Puzzles: Adding and Subtracting, Multiplying and Dividing, 1983; The Dr. Who Quiz Book of Dinosaurs Magic, Science, 3 vols., 1983; (with A. Ward) Wide Range Science Story Books 3-4, 1984; The Dr. Who Book of Space, 1984; Now I Can

Count to 3 Count to 5, 1984; Basic Arithmetic Puzzles: Fractions, Decimals, 1984; Now I Can Count to 10, 1985; Dr. Who Book of Puzzles, 1985; The Pan Pocket Puzzler, 1985; Crisis in Space, 1986; Getting on with Maths, 6 vols., 1986; The Great Spy Race, 1987; The Riddle of the Sphinx, 1987; Match and Sort, 6 vols., 1989; Getting Ahead in Maths, 1990; Inventions, 1990. **Address:** Highley, Whitbourne, Worcester, England. **Online address:** WR6 5RZ

HOLT, Stephen. Australian, b. 1949. **Genres:** Biography. **Career:** Writer and biographer. **Publications:** Manning Clark and Australian History 1915-1963, 1982; A Veritable Dynamo: Lloyd Ross and Australian Labor, 1901-1987, 1996; A Short History of Manning Clark, 1999. **Address:** 75 Blackman Crescent, MacQuarie, ACT 2614, Australia. **Online address:** stephenholt34@dewr.gov.au

HOLTE, James Craig. American, b. 1949. **Genres:** Theology/Religion, Cultural/Ethnic topics, Literary criticism and history. **Career:** University of Cincinnati, Cincinnati, OH, instructor in English, 1976; University of New Orleans, New Orleans, LA, instructor in English, 1976-81; East Carolina University, Greenville, associate professor of English, 1981-. WWNO-Radio, film critic. **Publications:** The Ethnic I, 1988; The Conversion Experience in America, 1992; Dracula in the Dark, 1997. **Address:** Department of English, East Carolina University, Greenville, NC 27858, U.S.A.

HOLTER, Knut. (born Norway), b. 1958. **Genres:** Theology/Religion. **Career:** School of Mission and Theology, Stavanger, Norway, associate professor, 1993-2002, professor, 2003-. Norwegian Army, 1986-87; became captain. **Publications:** Second Isaiah's Idol-Fabrication Passages, 1995; Yahweh in Africa, 2000; (with Mary Getui and Victor Zinkuratire) Interpreting the Old Testament in Africa, 2001; Old Testament Research for Africa, 2002; Deuteronomy 4 and the Second Commandment, 2003. **Address:** School of Mission and Theology, N 4024 Stavanger, Norway.

HOLTHE, Tess Uriza. American, b. 1966. **Genres:** Novels. **Career:** Author; previously employed as an accountant. **Publications:** When the Elephants Dance (novel), 2002. **Address:** c/o Author Mail, Crown Books, 1745 Broadway, New York, NY 10019, U.S.A.

HOLTZMAN, Abraham. American, b. 1921. **Genres:** Politics/Government. **Career:** Professor of Political Science, North Carolina State University, Raleigh, 1962-95, now emeritus (Assistant Professor, 1955-57; Associate Professor, 1957-62). Teaching Assistant, University of California, Los Angeles, 1945-47; Election Examiner, National Labor Relations Board, 1950; Teaching Fellow and Tutor, Harvard University, Cambridge, Massachusetts, 1950-52; Instructor, Dartmouth College, Hanover, New Hampshire, 1952-53; Congressional Fellow, 1953-54; Staff Assistant to Chairman, Democratic National Committee, 1954; Advisor to Rules Committee, Democratic National Convention, 1960. **Publications:** Los Angeles County Chief Administrative Officer: Ten Years Experience, 1948; The Loyalty Pledge Controversy in the Democratic Party, 1960; Interest Groups and Lobbying, 1966; Legislative Liaison: Executive Leadership in Congress, 1970; The Townsend Movement, A Political Study, 1970; American Government: Ideals and Reality, 1980, 1984. **Address:** 3606 Alamance Dr, Raleigh, NC 27609, U.S.A.

HOLTZMAN, Wayne Harold. American, b. 1923. **Genres:** Education, Psychology. **Career:** President, Hogg Foundation for Mental Health, 1970-93, and Professor of Psychology, 1959-, University of Texas, Austin (Assistant Professor, 1949-53; Associate Professor, 1953-59; Associate Director, Hogg Foundation, 1955-64; Dean, College of Education, 1964-70). **Publications:** (with W. F. Brown) Survey of Study Habits and Attitudes, 1953; (with J. S. Thorpe, J. D. Swartz and E. W. Herron) Inkblot Perception and Personality, 1961; (with B. M. Moore) Tomorrow's Parents, 1965; (with J. F. Santos, S. Bouquet and P. Barth) The Peace Corps in Brazil, 1966; Computer-Assisted Instruction, Testing and Guidance, 1971; (with W. F. Brown) A Guide to College Survival, 1972, 1987; (with R. Diaz-Guerrero and J. D. Swartz) Personality Development in Two Cultures, 1975; Introduction to Psychology, 1978; (with I. Reyes) Impact of Educational Television on Young Children, 1981; (with K. A. Heller and S. Messick) Placing Children in Special Education, 1982; American Families and Social Policies for Services to Children, 1983; Texas Universities and Mexico, 1984; Beyond the Rorschach, 1988; School of the Future, 1992; Holtzman Inkblot Technique Research Guide, 1999; History of the International Union of Psychology and Science, 2000. **Address:** 3300 Foothill Dr, Austin, TX 78731, U.S.A.

HOLUB, Joan. American, b. 1956. **Genres:** Children's fiction. **Career:** Communications Plus, TX, art director, 1980-89; Scholastic Inc., NYC, associate art director, children's trade books, 1989-91; author and illustrator, 1991-. **Publications:** SELF-ILLUSTRATED FOR CHILDREN: Pen Pals, 1997; Boo Who? A Spooky Lift-the-Flap Book, 1997; Ivy Green, Cootie Queen, 1998; Red, Yellow, Green: What Do Signs Mean?, 1998; Pajama Party, 1998; Space Dogs from Planet K-9, 1998. Illustrator of books by E. Levy, J. Gire, K. Hall, W. Lewison, A. Medearis, C. Holtzman, I.H. Arno, J. Nobisso. Contributor to periodicals. **Address:** c/o Scholastic Inc., 555 Broadway, New York, NY 10012, U.S.A. **Online address:** joanholub@aol.com

HOLYER, Erna. Also writes as Ernie (M.) Holyer. American (born Germany), b. 1925. **Genres:** Novels, Novellas/Short stories, Children's fiction, Young adult fiction, Animals/Pets, Children's non-fiction, History, Marine sciences/Oceanography, Natural history, Writing/Journalism, Young adult non-fiction, Biography. **Career:** San Jose Metropolitan Adult Education Program, creative writing teacher, 1968-. **Publications:** Rescue at Sunrise and Other Stories, 1965; Steve's Night of Silence and Other Stories, 1966; A Cow for Hansel, 1967; At the Forest's Edge, 1969; Song of Courage (biography), 1970; Lone Brown Gull and Other Stories, 1971; Shoes for Daniel, 1974; Sigis's Fire Helmet, 1975; The Southern Sea Otter, 1975; Reservoir Road Adventure, 1982; Wilderness Journey, Golden Journey, California Journey (trilogy), 1997; Self-Help for Writers: Winners Show You How, 200w; Dangerous Secrets: A Young Girl's Travails under the Nazis, 2003. Stories and articles included in anthologies. **Address:** 1314 Rimrock Dr, San Jose, CA 95120-5611, U.S.A. **Online address:** HolyerE@aol.com

HOLYER, Ernie (M.). *See* HOLYER, Erna.

HOLZ, Cynthia. (born United States), b. 1950. **Genres:** Novels. **Career:** Writer and educator. Business Week, Toronto, Ontario, Canada, correspondent, beginning in 1976; Ryerson Polytechnic University, Toronto, Ontario, Canada, teacher of creative writing, 1990-; Toronto Public Library, Toronto, Ontario, Canada, writer-in-residence, 1999. **Publications:** Home Again (short stories), 1989; Onlyville (novel), 1994; The Other Side, 1994; Semi-Detached, 1999; A Good Man, 2003. Contributor to periodicals. **Address:** c/o Author Mail, Thomas Allen Publishers, 145 Front St. East Suite 209, Toronto, ON, Canada M5A 1E3.

HOMAN, Sidney. American, b. 1938. **Genres:** Literary criticism and history, Theatre. **Career:** University of Illinois at Urbana-Champaign, assistant professor of English, 1965-69; Boston University, MA, associate professor of English, 1969-72; University of Florida, Gainesville, professor of English and theater, 1977-. Jilin University, People's Republic of China, visiting professor, 1986-. Theatrical director and actor; member of Theatre Strike Force improv company; Acrosstown Repertory Theatre, artistic director. **Publications:** Shakespeare's "More Than Words Can Witness," 1981; When the Theatre Turns to Itself, 1982; Beckett's Theatres, 1983; Shakespeare and the Triple Play, 1986; Shakespeare's Theatre of Presence, 1987; The Audience As Actor and Character, 1989; (coed) Shakespeare's Personality, 1989; Beckett's Television Plays, 1992; Pinter's Odd Man Out: Staging and Filming "Old Times," 1993; Directing Shakespeare: A Scholar Onstage, 2004; Staging Modern Playwrights: From Director's Concept to Performance, 2004. **Address:** Dept of English, 4008 Turlington Hall, University of Florida, PO Box 117310, Gainesville, FL 32611-7310, U.S.A. **Online address:** shakes@ufl.edu

HOMANS, Peter. American, b. 1930. **Genres:** Theology/Religion, Social sciences, Psychology. **Career:** Professor of psychology and religious studies, University of Chicago, since 1978 (Assistant Professor, 1965-68; Associate Professor, 1968-78). Lecturer, University of Toronto, 1962-64; Assistant Professor, Hartford Seminary Foundation, 1964-65. **Publications:** (ed. and contrib.) The Dialogue Between Psychology and Theology, 1968; Theology After Freud: An Interpretive Inquiry, 1970; (ed. and contrib.) Childhood and Selfhood: Essays on Tradition, Religion and Modernity in the Psychology of Erik H. Erikson; Jung in Context: Modernity and the Making of a Psychology, 1979, Italian translation, 1982, Japanese translation, 1986; The Ability to Mourn: Disillusionment and the Social Origins of Psychoanalysis, 1989. **Address:** 1025 E. 58th St, University of Chicago, Chicago, IL 60637, U.S.A.

HOMBERGER, Eric. American, b. 1942. **Genres:** History, Literary criticism and history, Photography, Urban studies. **Career:** University of East Anglia, Norwich, professor of American studies. **Publications:** The Art of the Real: Poetry in England and America since 1939, 1977; American Writers and Radical Politics 1900-1939: Equivocal Commitments, 1986; John le Carre, 1986; John Reed, 1990; The Historical Atlas of New York City 1994; Scenes from the Life of a City: Corruption and Conscience in Old New York, 1994; The Penguin Historical Atlas of North America, 1995; Mrs As-

tor's New York: Money and Social Power in a Gilded Age, 2002; New York City: A Cultural and Literary Companion, 2002. EDITOR: (with W. Janeway and S. Schama) The Cambridge Mind: Ninety Years of the "Cambridge Review" 1879-1969, 1970; Ezra Pound: The Critical Heritage; (with H. Klein and J. Flower) The Second World War in Fiction, 1984; (with J. Charmley) The Troubled Face of Biography, 1987; (with J. Biggart) John Reed and the Russian Revolution: Uncollected Articles, Letters and Speeches on Russia, 1917-1920, 1991. **Address:** School of American Studies, University of East Anglia, Norwich NR4 7TJ, England. **Online address:** e.homberger@uea.ac.uk

HOMEL, David. Canadian/American, b. 1952. **Genres:** Novels, Plays/Screenplays, Essays, Translations. **Career:** Novelist. Also freelance journalist, translator, screenwriter, and editor, 1977-. Concordia University, Montreal, Canada, part-time teacher, 1983-. Features and columns on arts and politics in daily papers across Canada; regular contributor to Radio-Canada; radio documentaries for Canadian Broadcasting Corporation. **Publications:** NOVELS: Electrical Storms, 1988; Rat Palms, 1992; Sonya & Jack, 1995; Get on Top, 1999; The Speaking Cure, 2003. NONFICTION: Mapping Literature: The Art and Politics of Translation (essays), 1988. Contributor of fiction and nonfiction to periodicals and anthologies. FILM PRODUCTIONS: Salut, Montreal, Bon Appetit!, 1980; Supervising for Results, 1980-81; Great North, 2000. TELEVISION PRODUCTIONS: Visions (documentary series), 1981-83; Realities, 1982-83; Todo Incluiclo, 2003. TRANSLATOR: L. Caron, The Draft Dodger, 1980; S. Martel, The King's Daughter, 1980; M. Corriveau, A Perfect Day for Kites, 1981; G. Bureau, Mona: A Mother's Story, 1981; R. Lalonde, Sweet Madness, 1982; Archambault Prison Theatre Collective, No Big Deal!, 1982; R. Marteau, Mount Royal, 1983; C. Brouillet, Dear Neighbor, 1984; J. Renaud, Broke City, 1984; M. Raboy, Media and Messages, 1984; R. Marteau, Pig-Skinning Day, 1984; R. Ducharme, Ha! Ha!, 1986; C. Couture and J-Y Rousseau, The Life of a Document: A Global Approach to Archives and Records Management, 1987; F. Simard, Talking It Out: The October Crisis from Inside, 1987; R. Marteau, River without End, 1987; D. Laferriere, How to Make Love to a Negro, 1988; R. Marteau, Voyage to Vendee, 1988; R. Simard and M. Vastel, The Nephew: Making of a Mafia Hitman, 1988; M. Begin, Canada's Right to Health, 1988; M. Corriveau, Seasons of the Sea, 1989; D. Sernine, Those Who Watch over the Earth, 1990; D. Cote, The Invisible Empire, 1990; W. Grady and M. Henrie, The Mandarine Syndrome, 1990; D. Laferriere, Eroshima, 1991; P. Bourgault, Now or Never!, 1991; C. Marchand, Vanishing Villages, 1992; D. Laferriere, An Aroma of Coffee, 1993; L. Caron and F. Poche, Montreal: A Scent of the Islands, 1994; D. Laferriere, Dining with the Dictator, 1994; D. Laferriere, Why Must a Black Writer Write about Sex?, 1994; D. Pennac, Better than Life, 1994; D. Laferriere, Down among the Dead Men, 1997; D. Laferriere, A Drifting Year, 1997; Y. Beauchemin, Second Fiddle, 1998; P. Poloni, Olivo Oliva, 1999; (with F. Reed) S. Kokis, Funhouse, 1999; (with F. Reed) M. Desjardins, Fairy Ring, 2000. Contributor of translated material to periodicals and anthologies.

HOMER, William Innes. American, b. 1929. **Genres:** Art/Art history, Photography, Biography. **Career:** Professor, Dept. of Art History, 1966-99, and Chairman of Dept., 1966-81, 1986-93, University of Delaware, Newark. Member, Editorial Board, American Art Journal, 1970-; Member, Editorial Board, Winterthur Portfolio, 1978-80; Member, Advisory Board, CASVA, National Gallery of Art, 1995-98. **Publications:** Seurat and the Science of Painting, 1964; Robert Henri and His Circle, 1969; (ed.) Avant-Garde Painting and Sculpture in America 1910-1925, 1975; Alfred Stieglitz and the American Avant-Garde, 1977; The Photographs of Gertrude Kasebier, 1979; Alfred Stieglitz and the Photo-Secession, 1983; (with L. Goodrich) Albert Pinkham Ryder: Painter of Dreams, 1989; Thomas Eakins: His Life and Art, 1992; The Language of Contemporary Criticism Clarified, 1999. **Address:** 200 Jackson Blvd, Wilmington, DE 19803, U.S.A.

HOMES, A. M. American. **Genres:** Novels, Novellas/Short stories. **Career:** Writer. **Publications:** NOVELS: Jack, 1989; In a Country of Mothers, 1993; The End of Alice, 1996; Music for Torching, 1999. STORIES: The Safety of Objects, 1990; Things You Should Know, 2002. NONFICTION: Los Angeles: People, Places and the Castle on the Hill, 2002.

HOMSHER, Deborah. American, b. 1952. **Genres:** Criminology/True Crime. **Career:** Ithaca College, instructor in English department, 1988-94; Cornell University, Ithaca, NY, Southeast Asia Program, managing editor of publications, 1995-. **Publications:** From Blood to Verdict: Three Women on Trial, 1993; Women and Guns: Politics and the Culture of Firearms, 2001. **Address:** The Kahin Center, Cornell University, 640 Stewart Ave., Ithaca, NY 14850, U.S.A.

HONAN, Park. American, b. 1928. **Genres:** Literary criticism and history, Biography. **Career:** Reader in English, University of Birmingham, since

1976 (Lecturer, 1968-72; Sr. Lecturer, 1968-76). Professor of English and American Literature, University of Leeds, 1984-93. **Publications:** Browning's Characters: A Study in Poetic Technique, 1961; (co-author) The Book, The Ring, and The Poet: A Biography of Robert Browning, 1975; Matthew Arnold: A Life, 1981; Jane Austen: Her Life, 1988; Authors' Lives: On Literary Biography and the Arts of Language, 1990; Shakespeare: A Life, 1998. Contributor to books. **Address:** 11 Vinery Rd., Burley, Leeds LS4 2LB, England.

HOND, Paul. American. **Genres:** Novels. **Career:** Writer. **Publications:** The Baker (novel), 1997. **Address:** c/o Barbara J. Zitwer Agency, 525 West End Ave. Suite 7H, New York, NY 10024, U.S.A.

HONDERICH, Ted. British (born Canada), b. 1933. **Genres:** Philosophy, Politics/Government. **Career:** University of Sussex, Lecturer in Philosophy, 1962-64; University College, University of London, Lecturer, 1964-72, Reader, 1972-83, Professor of Philosophy, 1983-88, Grote Professor of the Philosophy of Mind and Logic, 1988-98, Grote Professor of the Philosophy of Mind and Logic Emeritus, 1998-. Visiting Professor, Yale University and City University of New York, 1970-71. **Publications:** Punishment: The Supposed Justifications, 1969, 3rd ed., 2004; Violence for Equality: Inquiries in Political Philosophy, 1979, rev. ed. as Terrorism for Humanity, 2003; A Theory of Determinism: The Mind, Neuroscience, and Life-Hopes, 1988; Conservatism, 1990, rev. ed., 2004; How Free Are You?, 1993, rev. ed., 2002; Philosopher: A Kind of Life, 2000; After the Terror, 2002, rev. ed., 2003; On Political Means and Social Ends, 2003; On Consciousness, 2004; On Freedom and Determinism, 2004. EDITOR: International Library of Philosophy and Scientific Method series; The Arguments of Philosophers series; Essays on Freedom of Action, 1973; Social Ends and Political Means, 1975; Philosophy as It Is, 1979; Philosophy through Its Past, 1984; Morality and Objectivity, 1985; Oxford Companion to Philosophy, 1995, rev. ed., 2004. **Address:** Fountain House, Gould's Grounds, Frome BA11 3DW, England.

HONE, Joseph. Irish, b. 1937. **Genres:** Mystery/Crime/Suspense, Travel/Exploration, Romance/Historical. **Career:** Freelance writer and broadcaster since 1968. Part-time Ed. for Hamish Hamilton, publrs., London. Radio Producer, BBC, 1963-67; Information Officer, Radio and Television, U. N. Secretariat, NYC, 1967-68. **Publications:** The Private Sector, 1971; The Sixth Directorate, 1975; The Dancing Waiters: Collected Travels, 1975; The Paris Trap, 1977; The Flowers of the Forest (in U.S. as The Oxford Gambit), 1980; Gone Tomorrow: Some More Collected Travels, 1981; The Valley of the Fox, 1982; Children of the Country: Coast to Coast Across Africa, 1986; Duck Soup in the Black Sea: Further Collected Travels, 1988; Summer Hill (novel), 1990; Return to Summer Hill (novel), 1992; Firesong (novel), 1997. **Address:** Manor Cottage, Shutford, Banbury, Oxon., England.

HONERKAMP, Nicholas. American, b. 1950. **Genres:** Archaeology/Antiquities, Business/Trade/Industry, History. **Career:** Jeffrey L. Brown Institute of Archaeology, director, 1980-; University of Tennessee at Chattanooga, Dept of Sociology, Anthropology and Geography, assistant professor, 1981-86, associate professor, 1986-89, UC Foundation associate professor, 1989-93, professor, 1993-, acting head of Dept of Sociology, Anthropology and Geography, 2003-. Bass guitarist and vocalist for bands. **Publications:** (with R.B. Council and M.E. Will) Industry and Technology in Antebellum Tennessee: The Archaeology of Bluff Furnace, 1992. Contributor to professional journals. **Address:** Dept of Sociology, Anthropology and Geography, University of Tennessee at Chattanooga, 615 McCallie Ave, Chattanooga, TN 37403, U.S.A. **Online address:** Nick-Honerkamp@utc.edu

HONEYCUTT, Natalie. American, b. 1945. **Genres:** Young adult fiction. **Career:** Writer. **Publications:** Invisible Lissa, 1985; The All New Jonah Twist, 1986; Josie's Beau, 1987; The BestLaid Plans of Jonah Twist, 1988; Ask Me Something Easy, 1991; Juliet Fisher and the Foolproof Plan, 1992; Whistle Home, 1993; Lydia Jane and the Babysitter Exchange, 1993; Twilight in Grace Falls, 1997; Granville Jones: Commando, Farrar, Straus, 1998. **Address:** PO Box 1078, McCloud, CA 96057, U.S.A.

HONEYGOSKY, Stephen R(aymond). American, b. 1948. **Genres:** Theology/Religion, Literary criticism and history. **Career:** St. Vincent Archabbey, Latrobe, PA, member of monastic community, 1969-; St. Vincent College, Latrobe, director of campus ministry, 1980-86, assistant professor, 1986-90; St. Vincent Seminary, Latrobe, dean of students, 1988-89; University of Pittsburgh, Pittsburgh, PA, lecturer, 1991-; St. Bruno Church, Greensburg, PA, associate pastor, 1992-96; St. Benedict Church, Greensburg, PA, pastor, 1996-. **Publications:** Milton's House of God: The Invisible and

Visible Church, University of Missouri Press, 1993. **Address:** 526 Cathedral of Learning, Department of English, University of Pittsburgh, Pittsburgh, PA 15260, U.S.A.

HONEYMAN, Brenda. *See* **CLARKE, Brenda.**

HONG, Howard V. American, b. 1912. **Genres:** Philosophy, Theology/Religion, Translations, Education. **Career:** Professor of Philosophy, St. Olaf College, Northfield, Minnesota, 1938-. Associate Curator, Kierkegaard Library, St. Olaf College, and General Ed., Kierkegaard's Writings (Princeton University Pr., NJ); Field Secretary, US and Germany, War Prisoners Aid, World YMCA, 1943-46; Sr. Representative, Service to Refugees, Lutheran World Federation, Germany, 1947-49. **Publications:** (trans. with E.H. Hong) For Self-Examination, by Kierkegaard, 1940; (with E.H. Hong) Muskego Boy, 1944; (with E.H. Hong) The Boy Who Fought with Kings, 1946; This World and the Church, 1955; (ed.) Integration and the Christian Liberal Arts College, 1956; (co-ed.) Christian Faith and the Liberal Arts, 1960; (re-trans.) Philosophical Fragments, by Kierkegaard, 1962. EDITOR & TRANSLATOR WITH E.H. HONG (by S. Kierkegaard unless noted): Works of Love, 1962; Soren Kierkegaard's Journals and Papers, vol. I, 1967, vol. II, 1970, vols. III-IV, 1975, vols. V-VII, 1978; Armed Neutrality and An Open Letter, 1968; Kierkegaard's Thought, by G. Malantschuk, 1971; Two Ages, 1978; The Sickness unto Death, 1980; The Corsair Affair, 1982; Fear and Trembling and Repetition, 1983; Philosophical Fragments and Johannes Climacus, or De omnibus dubitandum est, 1985; Either/Or, 1987; Stages on Life's Way, 1988; The Concept of Irony, 1989; Eighteen Discourses, 1990; For Self-Examination and Judge for Yourself, 1990; Concluding Unscientific Postscript, 1992; Practice in Christianity, 1991; Three Discourses on Imagined Occasions, 1993; Upbuilding Discourses in Various Spirits, 1993; Works of Love, 1995; Christian Discourses, 1997; Without Authority, 1997; The Moment, 1998; The Book on Adler, 1998; The Point of View, 1998; The Essential Kierkegaard, 2000. **Address:** 5174 E. 90 Old Dutch Rd, Northfield, MN 55057, U.S.A.

HONG, Lily Toy. American, b. 1958. **Genres:** Mythology/Folklore. **Career:** Hallmark Cards Inc., artist-designer and production artist, 1983-86; freelance author and illustrator, 1988-. **Publications:** SELF-ILLUSTRATED: How the Ox Star Fell from Heaven, 1991; The Moon in the Well, 1992; (with K. Hatch) Marco Polo and Kublai Khan: A Great Friendship, 1993; Two of Everything, 1993; The Empress and the Silkworm, 1995; Jungle Spots, 1997. Illustrator of books by others.

HONIG, Edwin. American, b. 1919. **Genres:** Poetry, Literary criticism and history, Translations. **Career:** Library of Congress, Washington, DC, library assistant, 1941-42; instructor, Purdue University, Lafayette, IN, 1942-43, New York University and Illinois Institute of Technology, Chicago, 1946-47, and University of New Mexico, Albuquerque, 1947-49; Harvard University, Cambridge, MA, instructor, 1949-52, Briggs Copeland Assistant Professor of English, 1952-57; Brown University, Providence, RI, associate professor, 1957-60, professor of English, 1960-82, professor of comparative literature, 1962-82, chairman of English, 1968-69, professor emeritus of English, 1982-. **Publications:** Garcia Lorca, 1944; The Moral Circus: Poems, 1955; The Gazabos: Forty-One Poems, 1959, rev. ed. as The Gazabos: Forty-One Poems, and The Widow, 1961; Dark Conceit: The Making of Allegory, 1959, 3rd ed., 1973; Poems for Charlotte, 1963; Survivals: Poems, 1965; Spring Journal: Poems, 1968; Calisto and Melibea, 1972; Calderon and the Seizures of Honor, 1972; Four Springs (poems), 1972; Shake a Spear with Me, John Berryman: New Poems, 1974; At Sixes, 1974; The Affinities of Orpheus, 1977; The Selected Poems of Edwin Honig 1955-1976, 1979; The Foibles and Fables of an Abstract Man, 1979; Interrupted Praise (poems), 1983; Ends of the World and Other Plays, 1982; Gifts of Light: A Poem, 1983; The Poet's Other Voice, 1985; The Imminence of Love (Poems 1962-1992), 1993; Time and Again (Poems 1940-1997), 2000. TRANSLATOR: Cervantes, The Cave of Salamanca, 1960; Calderon: Four Plays, 1961; Cervantes: Eight Interludes, 1964; Calderon: Life Is a Dream 1970; Selected Poems of Fernando Pessoa, 1971; Garcia Lorca, Divan and Other Writings, 1974;(with A. Trueblood) Lope de Vega: La Dorotea, 1985; (with S.M. Brown) Poems of Fernando Pessoa, 1986; (with S.M. Brown) F. Pessoa, The Keeper of Sheep, 1986; Fernando Pessoa: Always Astonished (prose), 1988; M. Hernandez, The Unending Lightning, 1990; F. Garcia Lorca, Divan, and the Four Puppet Plays, 1990; Calderon de la Barca: Six Plays, 1993. EDITOR: (with O. Williams) The Mentor Book of Major American Poets, 1961; (with O. Williams) The Major Metaphysical Poets, 1968; Spenser, 1968. **Address:** 229 Medway St Apt 305, Providence, RI 02906, U.S.A.

HONIGSBAUM, Mark. British. **Genres:** Documentaries/Reportage. **Career:** Observer, London, England, former chief reporter; writer. **Publica-**

tions: The Fever Trail: In Search of the Cure for Malaria, 2002. Contributor to newspapers and periodicals. **Address:** c/o Author Mail, Farrar Straus & Giroux, 19 Union Square West, New York, NY 10003, U.S.A.

HONNEF, Klaus. German, b. 1939. **Genres:** Photography. **Career:** Aachener Nachrichten (newspaper), Aachen, Germany, editor, 1965-70; Westfaelischer Kunstverein (arts organization), Muenster, Germany, director, 1970-74; Rheinisches Landesmuseum Bonn (museum), Bonn, Germany, chief exhibition officer, 1974-94, curator of photography, 1994-99. **Publications:** Concept Art, 1971; Gerhard Richter, 1977; Kunst der Gegenwart, 1988; Andy Warhol, 1989; (ed. with P. Pachnicke) John Heartfield, 1991; Pantheon der Photography, 1992; Art of the 20th Century (section photography), 1998; (with G. Honnef-Harling) Von Korpen und anderen Dingen, 2003; Pop Art, 2004. **Address:** Baumschulallee 3, D-53115 Bonn, Germany.

HONORÉ, Tony. (Antony Maurice Honoré). British, b. 1921. **Genres:** Law. **Career:** Fellow Emeritus, All Souls College, Oxford, 1989- (Fellow, Queen's College, 1949-64, and New College, 1964-71; Rhodes Reader in Roman-Dutch Law, 1957-71; Regius Professor of Civil Law, Oxford University and Fellow, All Souls College, 1971-88; Acting Warden, All Souls College, 1987-89). Lecturer, Nottingham University, 1948. **Publications:** (with H.L.A. Hart) Causation in the Law, 1959, 1985; Gaius, 1962; The South African Law of Trusts, 1966, 5th ed. (by E. Cameron and others), 2002; Tribonian, 1978; Sex Law, 1978; (with J. Menner) Concordance to the Digest Jurists, 1980; Emperors and Lawyers, 1981, 1994; The Quest for Security, 1982; Ulpian, 1982, rev. ed., 2002; Making Law Bind, 1987; About Law, 1996; Responsibility and Fault, 1999; Law in the Crisis of Empire, 1998. **Address:** 94c Banbury Rd, Oxford OX2 6JT, England. **Online address:** tony.honore@all-souls.ox.ac.uk

HONRI, Peter. British, b. 1929. **Genres:** Film, Industrial relations, Music, Organized labor, Theatre. **Career:** Actor, 1948-. **Publications:** Working the Halls, 1973; John Wilton's Music Hall, 1985; Music Hall Warriors, 1997. **Address:** c/o Pollinger Ltd, 9 Staple Inn, London WC1V 7QH, England.

HOOD, Ann. American, b. 1956. **Genres:** Novels. **Career:** Trans World Airlines (TWA), New York City, flight attendant, 1979-86; writer. **Publications:** NOVELS Somewhere off the Coast of Maine, 1987; Waiting to Vanish, 1988; Three-Legged Horse, 1989; Something Blue, 1991; Places to Stay the Night, 1992; Properties of Water, 1996. NON-FICTION: Do Not Go Gentle, 2000. **Address:** Gail Hochman, Brandt & Brandt Literary Agents, Inc, 1501 Broadway, New York, NY 10036, U.S.A.

HOOD, Daniel. American, b. 1967. **Genres:** Science fiction/Fantasy. **Career:** IMP (publisher), NYC, art director, 1989-94; Wall Street Journal Europe, Brussels, Belgium, desktop manager, 1994-96; Faulkner & Gray (publisher), NYC, managing editor, 1996-2000. **Publications:** FANTASY NOVELS: Fanuilh, 1994; Wizard's Heir, 1996; Beggar's Banquet, 1997; Scales of Justice, 1998; King's cure, 2000. **Address:** 315 E 92nd St No. 2E, New York, NY 10128, U.S.A. **Online address:** DanHood@earthlink.net

HOOD, Lynley (Jane). New Zealander, b. 1942. **Genres:** Law, Social sciences, Biography. **Career:** University of Otago, Dunedin, New Zealand, research physiologist at medical school, 1965-68, Robert Burns fellow, 1991; homemaker, 1969-; free-lance writer, 1973-. **Publications:** Sylvia! The Biography of Sylvia Ashton-Warner, 1988; Who Is Sylvia? The Diary of a Biography, 1990; Minnie Dean-Her Life and Crimes, 1994; A City Possessed & the Christchurch Civic Creche Case, 2001. **Address:** PO Box 2041, South Dunedin, New Zealand. **Online address:** enquiries@lynleyhood.org

HOOD, Mary. American, b. 1946. **Genres:** Novels. **Career:** Writer, 1967-. **Publications:** How Far She Went, 1984; And Venus Is Blue, 1986; Familiar Heat, 1995. **Address:** c/o Candida Donadio & Associates, 231 West 22nd St., New York, NY 10011, U.S.A.

HOOD, Stuart (Clink). Scottish, b. 1915. **Genres:** Communications/Media, Novels, Translations. **Career:** Worked in executive capacities for British television stations including BBC and Rediffusion; Royal College of Art, England, professor of film. **Publications:** NONFICTION: Pebbles from My Skull (memoirs), 1963, as Carlino, 1985; A Survey of Television, 1967; The Mass Media, 1972; Radio and Television, 1975; On Television, 1980, 2nd ed., 1983; (with G. O'Leary) Questions of Broadcasting, 1990; Fascism for Beginners (juvenile), 1993, in North America as Introducing Fascism, 1994; (with H. Bresheeth and L. Jansz) Introducing the Holocaust (juvenile), 1994. FICTION: The Circle of the Minotaur; and, The Fisherman's Daughter, 1950; Since the Fall, 1955; In and Out the Windows, 1974; A Storm from

Paradise, 1985; The Upper Hand, 1987; The Brutal Heart, 1989; A Den of Foxes, 1991; Book of Judith, 1995. TRANSLATOR: On the Marble Cliffs, by E. Juenger, 1970; Moscow, by T. Plievier, 1976; Raids and Reconstructions: Essays on Politics, Crime, and Culture, by H.M. Enzensberger, 1976; One Hundred Poems without a Country, by E. Fried, 1978; Love Poems, by Fried, 1991; (and author of introduction) Theorem, by P.P. Pasolini, 1992; The Letters of Pier Paolo Pasolini, 1992; Appearances, by G. Celati, 1992; Sodomies in Eleven-Point, by A. Busi, 1993; The Way Back, by E. Palandri, 1994. EDITOR: (and author of intro.) Elizabeth: Almost by Chance a Woman (play), by D. Fo, trans. by G. Hanna, 1987; (Author of intro.) Archangels Don't Play Pinball (play), by Fo, trans. by R.C. McAvoy and A.M. Giugni, 1987; (and author of intro.) Mistero buffo: Comic Mysteries (play), by Fo, trans. by E. Emery, 1988; (and author of notes) The Tricks of the Trade (play), by Fo, trans. by J. Farrell, 1991; Behind the Screens: The Structure of British Broadcasting in the 1990s, 1994. Author of television scripts and translator of plays. **Address:** c/o Carcanet Press Ltd., 4th Floor, Conavon Court, 12-16 Blackfriars St., Manchester M3 5BQ, England.

HOODBHOY, Pervez. Pakistani, b. 1950. **Genres:** Sciences, Plays/Screenplays. **Career:** Quaid-e-Azam University, Islamabad, Pakistan, physicist, 1973-. Director and producer of a television series on popular science; Mashal, chairman. Writer for 13 educational programs for Pakistan Television. **Publications:** Islam and Science, 1991; M.A. Beg Memorial Volume, 1991. **Address:** Department of Physics, Quaid-e-Azam University, Islamabad, Pakistan. **Online address:** hoodbhoy@isb.pol.com.pk

HOOFT, Hendrik (G. A.). Dutch, b. 1939. **Genres:** History. **Career:** Attorney in Amsterdam, Netherlands, 1966-71; Pierson Heldring and Pierson Bank, Amsterdam, Netherlands, executive vice president, 1971-75; Oryx Investments, Dubai, United Arab Emirates, president and CEO, 1975-80; Woodmont Head Management Ltd., president and CEO, 1980-. Member of boards of directors. **Publications:** De burgher en de burgemeester, 1994, trans. as Patriot and Patrician: To Holland and Ceylon in the Steps of Henrik Hooft and Pieter Ondaatje, Champions of Dutch Democracy, 1999. Contributor of articles to newspapers and periodicals. **Address:** 9 High Point Rd., Don Mills, ON, Canada M3B 2A3.

HOOK, Brendan. Australian, b. 1963. **Genres:** Children's fiction. **Career:** Moonee Valley Instrumental Music Program, primary and junior high music teacher, 1991-. Saxophonist. **Publications:** Harry the Honkerzoid, 1997; Planet of the Honkerzoids, 1998. **Address:** 5 McLean Ave, Bentleigh 3204, Australia.

HOOK, Brian. British. **Genres:** Area studies. **Career:** Hong Kong Government, Hong Kong, worked as assistant secretary for Chinese affairs; University of Leeds, Leeds, England, staff member; University of Hull, Hull, England, visiting professor at Centre for Southeast Asian Studies; Middlesex University, London, England, visiting professor at Business School. Cambridge University, senior member of Wolfson College; University of Hong Kong, honorary research fellow at Centre of Asian Studies. **Publications:** The Cambridge Encyclopedia of China, 1983, 2nd ed, 1991; Guangdong: China's Promised Land, 1996; Fujian: Gateway to Taiwan, 1996; Shanghai and the Yangtze Delta: A City Reborn, 1998; The Individual and the State in China; Beijing and Tianjin: Towards a Millennial Megalopolis. **Address:** China Studies Program, Business School, Middlesex University, Burroughs Hendon, London, England.

HOOK, Geoffrey R(aynor). (Jeff Hook). Australian, b. 1928. **Genres:** Cartoons. **Career:** Davies Brothers Ltd., Hobart, Australia, press artist, 1951-64; Herald and Weekly Times, Melbourne, Australia, editorial cartoonist, 1964-93, editorial cartoonist for Sunday Herald-Sun, 1993-. Work represented in international cartoon collections, corporate collections in Australia, and in the collection of political cartoons at the National Museum of Australia, Canberra. **Publications:** AUTHOR AND ILLUSTRATOR AS JEFF HOOK: Jamie the Jumbo Jet, 1971; Hook Book: Cartoons by Jeff of the Sun, 1978; The Hook Book No. 2, 1979; The Penguin Hook, 1984; The Laugh's on Us: Cricket's Finest Tell Their Funniest, 1989; Ashes: Battles and Bellylaughs, 1990; More Laughs on Us, 1991; Just for Kicks, 1992; Look Who's Laughing Now, 1995. AUTHOR AND ILLUSTRATOR AS GEOFFREY HOOK: (with D. Rankine) Kangapossum and Crocoroo, 1969; Boom, Bust, and Polka Dots, 1992. Illustrator (as Jeff Hook) of books by H.E. Ward, S. Marks, O. White, D. Burnard, K. Dunstan, L. Richards and T. Prior, J.C. White and W.K. Halliwell, J. Weaver and F. Weaver, L. Wilson, D. Zwar, D. Walters, M. Stewart, J. Fraser, J. Factor, A. Veitch, R. Marsh, K. Piesse, B. Hook. **Address:** 2 Montana St., Glen Iris, VIC 3146, Australia.

HOOK, Jonathan B(yron). American, b. 1953. **Genres:** History, Anthropology/Ethnology. **Career:** Teacher of mathematics and English and football coach at preparatory high school in San Antonio, TX, 1978-79; teacher of television production and coach of football and wrestling at American high school in Bonn, Germany, 1980-81; University of Texas at San Antonio, instructor, 1982-85; Houston Community College, Houston, TX, instructor, 1988-90; Lee College, Baytown, TX, instructor, 1990-91; Houston Community College, instructor, 1993-94; University of Houston Downtown, Houston, instructor, summer, 1995; Angelina College, Livingston, TX, instructor at Chief Kina Alabama-Coushatta Indian Reservation, summer, 1996. Cherokee Nation of Oklahoma, enrolled member. Ordained Baptist minister; pastor of Methodist and Presbyterian congregations; leader of American Indian religious ceremonies in Texas prisons, 1998; guest lecturer at colleges and universities. Worked as freelance industrial and wildlife photographer, 1983-86, and computer hardware and software consultant, 1988-96. Project Nicaragua (medical relief organization), founding member of board of directors, 1993-97; Alabama-Coushatta Presbyterian Self-Determination of Peoples Committee, cochairperson, 1995. **Publications:** The Alabama-Coushatta Indians, 1997. Contributor to periodicals. **Address:** 4914 Nuthatch St., San Antonio, TX 78217, U.S.A. **Online address:** jonhook@wt.net

HOOKER, Jeremy. British, b. 1941. **Genres:** Poetry, Literary criticism and history, Autobiography/Memoirs. **Career:** University College of Wales, Aberystwyth, Lecturer in English, 1965-84; Bath Spa University College (formerly Bath College of Higher Education), MA course director, creative writing, 1988-96, professor, 1994-. LeMoyne College, Syracuse, NY, Visiting professor, 1994-95. **Publications:** The Elements, 1972; John Cowper Powys, 1973; Soliloquies of a Chalk Giant, 1974; David Jones: An Exploratory Study, 1975; Solent Shore, 1978; Landscape of the Daylight Moon, 1978; John Cowper Powys and David Jones, 1979; Englishman's Road, 1980; (ed. with Gweno Lewis) Selected Poems of Alun Lewis, 1981; Poetry of Place: Essays and Reviews 1970-1981, 1982; A View from the Source: Selected Poems, 1982; Itchen Water, 1982; (ed.) Selected Stories, by Francis Bellerby, 1986; The Presence of the Past, 1987; Master of the Leaping Figures, 1987; In Praise of Windmills, 1990; (with L. Grandjean) Their Silence a Language, 1993; Writers in a Landscape, 1996; Our Lady of Europe, 1997; (with L. Grandjean) Groundwork, 1998. **Address:** Department of English, University of Glamorgan, Pontypridd CF37 1DL, Wales. **Online address:** jhooker@glam.ac.uk

HOOKER, John (Williamson). Australian, b. 1932. **Genres:** History, Novels, Poetry. **Career:** Full-time writer, 1983-. Publisher, Penguin Books Australia, Melbourne, 1969-79, and William Collins Australia, Melbourne, 1979-83. **Publications:** Jacob's Season, 1973; The Bush Soldiers, 1984; Standing Orders, 1986; Captain James Cook, 1988; Australians at War-Korea, 1989; Rubicon, 1991; The Life and Times of Jack Lamberton, 1995; Beyond the Pale, 1998. **Address:** c/o Allen and Unwin, PO Box 8500, St. Leonards, NSW 1590, Australia.

HOOKER, Morna Dorothy. British, b. 1931. **Genres:** Theology/Religion. **Career:** Lady Margaret's Professor of Divinity, Cambridge University, 1976-98. Fellow, Robinson College, Cambridge. Co-Ed., Journal of Theological Studies, 1985-. Lecturer, King's College, London, 1961-70; Lecturer, Oxford University, and Fellow, Linacre College, Oxford, 1970-76, Lecturer, Keble College, Oxford, 1972-76. **Publications:** Jesus and the Servant, 1959; The Son of Man in Mark, 1967; Pauline Pieces, 1979; Studying the New Testament, 1979; The Message of Mark, 1983; Continuity and Discontinuity, 1986; From Adam to Christ, 1990; A Commentary on the Gospel of St. Mark, 1991; Not Ashamed of the Gospel, 1994; The Signs of a Prophet, 1997; Beginnings, 1997; Paul: A Short Introduction, 2003; Endings, 2003. EDITOR?CO-EDITOR: What about the New Testament?, 1975; Paul and Paulinism, 1982; Not in Word Alone, 2003. **Address:** Robinson College, Cambridge CB3 9AN, England.

HOOKS, Bell. (Gloria Watkins). American, b. 1955. **Genres:** Philosophy, Race relations, Women's studies and issues, Essays, Adult non-fiction. **Career:** Social critic, educator, and writer. Yale University, New Haven, CT, assistant professor of Afro-American studies and English, beginning in the middle-1980s. **Publications:** Ain't I a Woman: Black Women and Feminism, 1981; Feminist Theory: From Margin to Center, 1984, 2nd ed., 2000; Talking Back: Thinking Feminist, Thinking Black, Between-the-Lines, 1988; Yearning: Race, Gender, and Cultural Politics, Between-the-Lines, 1990; (with C. West) Breaking Bread: Insurgent Black Intellectual Life, 1991; A Woman's Mourning Song, Writers and Readers, 1992; Black Looks: Race and Representation, 1992; Sisters of the Yam: Black Women and Self Recovery, 1993; Outlaw Culture, 1994; Teaching to Transgress, 1994; Art on My Mind: Visual Politics, 1995; Killing Rage: Ending Racism, 1995; Bone Black: Memories of Girlhood, 1996; Reel to Reel: Race, Sex, and Class at the Mov-

ies, 1996; Wounds of Passion, 1997; Remembered Rapture, 1999; Happy to Be Nappy (for children), 1999; All about Love: New Visions, 2000; Feminism Is for Everybody, 2000; Where We Stand, 2000; Homemade Love, 2001; Salvation, 2001. **Address:** 749 Westmoreland Ave, Syracuse, NY 13210-2662, U.S.A.

HOOKS, Gregory M. American, b. 1953. **Genres:** Sociology, Politics/Government, Regional/Urban planning, Military/Defense/Arms control. **Career:** Indiana University-Bloomington, assistant professor, 1985-90; Washington State University, Pullman, assistant professor, 1990-93, associate professor in department of sociology, 1993-. **Publications:** Forging the Military-Industrial Complex: World War II's Battle of the Potomac, 1991. Contributor to journals. **Address:** Department of Sociology, Washington State University, PO Box 644020, Pullman, WA 99164-4020, U.S.A.

HOOKS, William H. Also writes as Harrison Hawkins. American, b. 1921. **Genres:** Children's fiction, Young adult fiction, Education. **Career:** High school history and social studies teacher, Chapel Hill, North Carolina, 1949; Hampton Institute, VA, history and dance instructor, 1950; Brooklyn College of the City University of New York, choreographer at opera workshop, 1955-64; owned dance studio, NYC, 1965-70; Bank Street College, NYC, publications division staff member, 1970-72, chairperson of division, 1972-91, managing editor, "Bank Street Readers"; educational consultant, ABC-TV children's programs, 1973-86; reviewer; script writer, Captain Kangaroo television program. **Publications:** FOR CHILDREN: The Seventeen Gerbils of Class 4A, 1976; Maria's Cave, 1977; Doug Meets the Nutcracker, 1977; The Mystery on Bleecker Street, 1980; Mean Jake and the Devils, 1981; The Mystery on Liberty Street, 1982; Three Rounds With Rabbit, 1984; (with S.V. Reit and B.D. Boegehold) When Small Is Tall, and Other Read-Together Tales, 1985; (with B.D. Boegehold and J. Openheim) Read-a-Rebus: Tales and Rhymes in Words and Pictures, 1986; Moss Gown, 1987; The Legend of the White Doe, 1988; Pioneer Cat, 1988; (with B. Brenner) Lion and Lamb, 1989; Mr. Bubble Gum, 1989; The Three Little Pigs and the Fox, 1989; The Ballad of Belle Dorcas, 1990; Mr. Monster, 1990; A Dozen Dizzy Dogs, 1990; The Gruff Brothers, 1990; (with B. Brenner) Lion & Lamb Step Out, 1990; Lo-Jack & Pirates, 1991; Where's Lulu?, 1991; (with B. Brenner) Ups and Downs With Lion and Lamb, 1991; Mr. Baseball, 1991; (with B. Beogehold) The Rainbow Ribbon: A Bank Street Book About Values, 1991; Peach Boy, 1992; (with B. Brenner and J. Openheim) How Do You Make a Bubble?, 1992; Monster from the Sea, 1992; Little Poss & Horrible Hound, 1992; Rough, Tough, and Rowdy: A Bank Street Book About Values, 1992; The Monster From the Sea, 1992; Feed Me!: An Aesop Fable, 1992; The Mighty Santa Fe, 1993; Mr. Dinosaur, 1994; The Rainbow Ribbon, 1994; Snowbear Whittington: An Appalachian Beauty & the Beast, 1994; The Girl Who Could Fly, 1995; Freedom's Fruit, 1996; Mr. Garbage, 1996; The Mystery of Missing Tooth, 1997; Mr. Big Brother, 1998; The Legend of the Christmas Rose, 1999. OTHER: (co-author) Barron's Book of Fun and Learning: Preschool Learning Activities, 1987; (with B. Brenner and J. Openheim) No Way, Slippery Slick! A Child's First Book About Drugs, 1991. FOR YOUNG ADULTS: Crossing the Line, 1978; Circle of Fire, 1982; A Flight of Dazzle Angels, 1988. OTHER: (with E. Galinsky) The New Extended Family: Day Care That Works, 1977. **Address:** 718 E. Franklin St., Chapel Hill, NC 27514, U.S.A.

HOOLEY, D(aniel) M. American, b. 1950. **Genres:** Classics. **Career:** Carleton College, Northfield, MN, lecturer in classics, 1985-88; Princeton University, Princeton, NJ, Perkins Lecturer in Classics and Humanities, 1988-89; Allegheny College, Meadville, PA, assistant professor of classics, 1989-92; University of MissouriColumbia, assistant professor, 1992-96, associate professor of classics, 1996-. Guest lecturer at colleges and universities. **Publications:** The Classics in Paraphrase: Ezra Pound and Modern Translators of Latin Poetry, 1988; The Knotted Thong: Structures of Mimesis in Persius, 1997. Contributor of articles and reviews to periodicals. **Address:** Department of Classical Studies, 420 GCB, University of Missouri-Columbia, Columbia, MO 65211, U.S.A. **Online address:** clstuddh@showme.missouri.edu; www.missouri.edu/~classwww

HOOPER, Chloe. Australian, b. 1973. **Genres:** Children's non-fiction. **Career:** Writer. Melbourne Grammar, Shelford Girls School, and Lauriston Girls School, Melbourne, Australia, writer-in-residence. **Publications:** A Child's Book of True Crime, 2002. Contributor of short stories to anthologies and journals. **Address:** c/o Author Mail, Scribner, 1230 Avenue of the Americas, New York, NY 10020, U.S.A.

HOOPER, Kay. Also writes as Kay Robbins. American. **Genres:** Novels, Novellas/Short stories, Mystery/Crime/Suspense, Romance/Historical. **Publications:** Lady Thief, 1981; Breathless Surrender, 1982; Mask of Passion,

1982; On the Wings of Magic, 1983; C.J.'s Fate, 1984; If There Be Dragons, 1984; Pepper's Way, 1984; Something Different, 1984; Illegal Possession, 1985; Rafe, The Maverick, 1986; Rebel Waltz, 1986; Time after Time, 1986; Larger than Life, 1986; Adelaide, The Enchantress, 1987; In Serena's Web, 1987; Rafferty's Wife, 1987; Zach's Law, 1987; Raven on the Wing, 1987; Velvet Lightning, 1988; Captain's Paradise, 1988; Out-law Derek, 1988; Summer of the Unicorn, 1988; Shades of Grey, 1988; The Fall of Lucas Kendrick, 1988; Unmasking Kelsey, 1988; Golden Flames 1988; It Takes a Thief, 1989; Aces High, 1989; Golden Threads, 1989; The Glass Shoe, 1989; What Dreams May Come, 1990; Star Crossed Lovers, 1990; Through the Looking Glass, 1990; The Lady and the Lion, 1990, Crime of Passion, 1991; The Matchmaker, 1991; The Haviland Touch, 1991; House of Cards, 1991; The Delaney Christmas Carol: Christmas Future, 1992; The Touch of Max, 1993; Hunting the Wolfe, 1993; The Trouble with Jared, 1993; The Wizard of Seattle, 1993; All for Quinn, 1993; The Haunting of Josie, 1994; Amanda, 1995; After Caroline, 1996; Finding Laura, 1997; Haunting Rachel, 1998; Stealing Shadows, 2000; Hiding in the Shadows, 2000; Out of the Shadows, 2000; Touching Evil, 2001; Whisper of Evil, 2003; Sense of Evil, 2003; Once a Thief, 2003; Always a Thief, 2003; Hunting Fear, 2004; Chill fo Fear, 2005. NOVELLAS: Holiday Spirit, 1991; Masquerade, 1994; Almost an Angel, 1995; Arts Magica, 1999. AS KAY ROBBINS: Return Engagement, 1982; Elusive Dawn, 1983; Kissed by Magic, 1983; Taken by Storm, 1983; Moonlight Rhapsody, 1984; Eye of the Beholder, 1985; Belonging to Taylor, 1986; On Her Doorstep, 1986. **Address:** PO Box 370, Bostic, NC 28018, U.S.A. **Online address:** kay@kayhooper.com

HOOPER, Maureen Brett. American, b. 1927. **Genres:** Children's fiction, Young adult fiction. **Career:** Los Angeles Unified School District, Los Angeles, CA, music teacher, 1949-62; University of California, Los Angeles, senior lecturer of music education, 1962-91, emeritus lecturer, 1991-. Curriculum consultant and music textbook consultant; speaker and clinician for gifted and talented programs; director of the American Suzuki Institute West. **Publications:** The Violin Man (middle grade novel), 1991; The Christmas Drum (picture book), 1994; Silent Night: A Christmas Carol Is Born, 2001. Author of professional articles and curriculum guides. **Address:** c/o University of California Los Angeles, Department of Music, 405 Hilgard Ave, Los Angeles, CA 90024, U.S.A.

HOOPER, Meredith Jean. Australian, b. 1939. **Genres:** Science fiction/ Fantasy, Children's fiction, Air/Space topics, Art/Art history, Children's nonfiction, Engineering, History, Mythology/Folklore, Natural history, Sciences, Technology, Travel/Exploration, Picture/board books. **Career:** Commonwealth Journal of International Affairs, editorial board, 1988-; Royal Institution and History of Science and Technology, visiting research fellow, 1988-; Australian National Antarctic Research Expedition, visiting writer, 1994. NJF Artists & Writers Program, grantee, 1998-99, 2002. **Publications:** NONFICTION: Land of the Free, 1968; The Gold Rush in Australia, 1969; Everyday Inventions, 1972; The Story of Australia, 1974; More Everyday Inventions, 1976; Doctor Hunger and Captain Thirst, 1982; Kangaroo Route, 1985; God 'Elp All of Us, 1986; Cleared for Take-Off, 1986; History of Australia, 1988; How High Is the Sky?, 1990; A for Antarctica, 1991; I for Invention, 1992; Balls, Bangs & Flashes, 1994; Germs, Jabs & Laughing Gas, 1994; The Feast, 1994; The Planets, 1994; Looking after the Egg, 1994; Count Down to Take Off, 1995; The Pebble in My Pocket, 1996; January, 1996; Entering the Ark, 1996; Hunting in the Marshes, 1996; Dinosaur, 1996; Osprey, 1996; Seal, 1996; The Bridge, 1996; The Forest, 1996; The Harbour, 1996; Coral Reef, 1997; Desert, 1997; Rainforest, 1997; The Tomb of Nebamma, 1997; A Book of Hours, 1997; Noah's Ark, 1997; Journey to Antarctica, 1997; The Colour of Light, 1997; Honey Biscuits, 1997; The Drop in My Drink, 1998; The Pear Tree, 1998; Tigers, 1999; River Story, 2000; Ice Trap!, 2000; Gandali the Whale, 2000; Antarctic Adventure, 2000; A Song for Planet Earth, 2000; Animals in the Ark, 2000; Who Built the Pyramid?, 2001; Race to the Pole, 2002; Gold: A Treasure Hunt through Time, 2002; Sticky Jam, 2003; Woolly Jumper, 2003. FICTION: Seven Eggs, 1985; The Journal of Watkin Stench, 1988; Evie's Magic Lamp, 1990; The Great Stone Circle, 1992; The Lost Purse, 1994; Monkeys, 1994; The Pole-Seekers, 2000; Dog's Night, 2000; Thank You for My Yukky Present, 2001; Tom's Rabbit, 1998; Ponko and the South Pole, 2002. **Address:** c/o David Higham Associates Ltd., 5-8 Lower John St, Golden Square, London W1R 4HA, England.

HOOPES, John W. American, b. 1958. **Genres:** Anthropology/Ethnology. **Career:** University of Kansas, Lawrence, associate professor of anthropology, 1989-, and associate curator, Museum of Anthropology. **Publications:** The Emergence of Pottery, 1995. **Address:** Department of Anthropology, University of Kansas, Lawrence, KS 66045, U.S.A. **Online address:** hoopes@ukans.edu

HOOSE, Phillip M. American, b. 1947. **Genres:** Adult non-fiction, Children's non-fiction. **Career:** Author, musician, and conservationist. Nature Conservancy, Portland, ME, staff member, 1977-; songwriter and performing musician, 1984-. Cofounder and member of board of directors, Children's Music Network, 1986-. **Publications:** Building an Ark: Tools for the Preservation of Natural Diversity through Land Protection, 1981; Hoosiers: The Fabulous Basketball Life of Indiana, 1986, rev, ed, 1995; Necessities: Racial Barriers in American Sports, 1989. FOR CHILDREN: It's Our World Too!: Stories of Young People Who Are Making a Difference, 1993, as It's Our World Too!: Stories of Young People Who Are Making a Difference: How They Do It-How YOU Can, Too!, 2002; (with H. Hoose) Hey, Little Ant, 1998; We Were There, Too!: Young People in U.S. History, 2001. **Address:** 8 Arlington St, Portland, ME 04101, U.S.A. **Online address:** Hoose@gwi.net

HOOVER, Dwight Wesley. American, b. 1926. **Genres:** History, Bibliography. **Career:** Professor of History, 1967-91, and Director, Center for Middletown Studies, Ball State University, Muncie, IN (Assistant Professor, 1959-63; Associate Professor, 1964-67); Professor of Historical Sociology, University of Virginia, Charlottesville, 1977-79. Consultant, Middletown Film Project, 1976-81. Senior Fulbright Lecturer in American History, Budapest, 1988; Fulbright Lecturer in American Studies, Jozsef Attila University, Hungary, 1991-92; Visiting Professor, Doshisha University, Japan, 1992; Visiting Professor, Kansai Gaidai, Japan, 1996-97. **Publications:** Henry James, Sr., and the Religion of Community, 1969; The Red and the Black, 1976; Cities, 1976; A Pictorial History of Indiana, 1980; Magic Middletown, 1986; Middletown: An Annotated Bibliography, 1988; Middletown: The Making of a Documentary Film Series, 1992. EDITOR/CO-EDITOR: Understanding Negro History, 1968; American Society in the 20th Century, 1972; Conspectus of History: Focus on Biography (Issues in World Diplomacy, Revolution, Cities, Family History, Science and History), 6 vols., 1975-81. **Address:** 11 Sunset Dr. #203, Sarasota, FL 34236, U.S.A. **Online address:** jmhdwh@aol.com

HOOVER, H(elen) M(ary). American, b. 1935. **Genres:** Science fiction/ Fantasy. **Career:** Natl Gallery of Art, manuscript concerning myths, illustrated by the collection of the Gallery; working on fiction manuscript. **Publications:** SCIENCE FICTION FOR CHILDREN: Children of Morrow, 1973; The Lion's Cub (historical fiction), 1974; Treasures of Morrow, 1976; The Delikon, 1977; The Rains of Eridan, 1977; The Lost Star, 1979; Return to Earth, 1980; This Time of Darkness, 1980; Another Heaven, Another Earth, 1981; The Bell Tree, 1982; The Shepherd Moon, 1984; Orvis, 1987; The Dawn Palace: The Story of Medea, 1988; Away Is a Strange Place to Be, 1990; Only Child, 1991; The Winds of Mars, 1995; The Whole Truth and Other Myths: Retelling Ancient Tales, 1996. **Address:** 120 Appleview Ct, Locust Grove, VA 22508, U.S.A.

HOOVER, Kenneth R(ay). American, b. 1940. **Genres:** Politics/ Government. **Career:** Assistant to president of Johnson Foundation, 1962-64; University of Wisconsin-Whitewater, instructor, 1964-65, assistant professor of political science, 1965-69; College of Wooster, Wooster, OH, assistant professor, 1970-76, associate professor of political science, 1976-78; University of Wisconsin-Parkside, Kenosha, associate professor, 1978-85, professor of political science, 1985-88; Western Washington University, Bellingham, WA, professor of political science, 1988-2004, professor emeritus, 2004-. **Publications:** A Politics of Identity: Liberation and the Natural Community, 1975; (with R. Plant) Conservative Capitalism in Britain and the United States: A Critical Appraisal, 1986; The Elements of Social Scientific Thinking, 1976, 8th ed., 2004; Ideology and Political Life, 2nd ed., 1992, 3rd ed., 2001; The Power of Identity: Politics in a New Key, 1997; Economics as Ideology: Keynes, Laski, Hayek and the Creation of Contemporary Politics, 2003; (ed.) The Future of Identity, 2004.

HOOVER, Paul. American, b. 1946. **Genres:** Plays/Screenplays, Poetry, Literary criticism and history. **Career:** University of Illinois Press, Champaign, IL, assistant editor, 1973-74; Columbia College, Chicago, IL, poet-in-residence and professor of English, 1974-2003; San Francisco State University, visiting professor, 2003-. **Publications:** POETRY: Letter to Einstein Beginning Dear Albert, 1979; Somebody Talks a Lot, 1983; Nervous Songs, 1986; Idea, 1987; The Novel: A Poem, 1990; Viridian, 1997; Totem and Shadow: New & Selected Poems, 1999; Rehearsal in Black, 2001; Winter (Mirror), 2002. OTHER: Saigon, Illinois (novel), 1988; (ed.) Postmodern American Poetry: A Norton Anthology, 1994; Viridian (screenplay) 1994; Fables of Representation (essays), 2004. Contributor to periodicals. **Address:** Creative Writing Department, San Francisco State University, 1600 Holloway, San Francisco, CA 94132, U.S.A. **Online address:** viridian@hotmail.com

HOPCKE, Robert H(enry). American, b. 1958. **Genres:** Psychology. **Career:** Unitas Personal Counseling, Berkeley, CA, senior intern, 1981-86, staff clinical supervisor, 1986-89; Operation Concern, San Francisco, CA, coordinator of AIDS Prevention Program, 1989-95; private practice of psychotherapy and couples counseling, 1995-. Pastoral Psychotherapy Group of Berkeley, member, 1986-88; Center of Symbolic Studies, cofounder, director, 1990-. **Publications:** A Guided Tour of the "Collected Works" of C.G. Jung, 1989; Jung, Jungians, and Homosexuality, 1989; Men's Dreams, Men's Healing, 1990; (trans. with P.A. Schwartz) M. Brusatin, The History of Colors, 1991; (ed. with K. Carrington and S. Wirth, and contrib) Same-Sex Love: A Path to Wholeness, 1993; The Persona: Where Sacred Meets Profane, 1995; There Are No Accidents: Synchronicity and the Stories of Our Lives, 1997. Contributor to books. Contributor of articles and reviews to periodicals. **Address:** 2920 Domingo Ave, Berkeley, CA 94705, U.S.A.

HOPCRAFT, Arthur. See Obituaries.

HOPE, Christopher (David Tully). South African, b. 1944. **Genres:** Novels, Novellas/Short stories, Children's fiction, Poetry, Travel/Exploration. **Career:** South British Insurance, Johannesburg, underwriter, 1966; Nasionale Pers, publishers, Cape Town, ed., 1966-67; Durban Sunday Tribune, reviewer, 1968-69; Lintas, copywriter, Durban, 1967-69, and Durban and Johannesburg, 1973-75; Halesowen Secondary Modern School, English teacher, 1972; Bolt, Durban, editor, 1972-73; Gordonstoun School, Elgin, Scotland, writer-in-residence, 1978; Royal Society of Literature, fellow, 1990. **Publications:** NOVELS: A Separate Development, 1980; Kruger's Alp, 1984; The Hottentot Room, 1986 My Chocolate Redeemer, 1989; Serenity House, 1992; Darkest England, 1996; Me, the Moon and Elvis Presley, 1997; Heaven Forbid, 2002; Brothers under the Skin, 2003. STORIES: Learning to Fly and Other Tales, 1981; Black Swan (novella), 1987; The Love Songs of Nathan J. Swirsky, 1993. FOR CHILDREN: (with Y. Menuhin) The King, The Cat, and the Fiddle, 1983; The Dragon Wore Pink, 1985. TRAVEL: Moscow! Moscow!, 1990; Signs of the Heart: Love and Death in Languedoc, 1999. POETRY: (with M. Kirkwood) Whitewashes, 1971; Cape Drives, 1974; In the Country of the Black Pig and Other Poems, 1981; Englishmen, 1985. OTHER: White Boy Running (memoir), 1988. **Address:** c/o Rogers, Coleridge and White, 20 Powis Mews, London W11 1JN, England. **Online address:** christopher1hope@aol.com

HOPE, Margaret. See KNIGHT, Alanna (Cleet).

HOPE, Marjorie (Cecelia). American, b. 1923. **Genres:** Civil liberties/Human rights, Environmental sciences/Ecology, International relations/Current affairs, Politics/Government, Sociology. **Career:** Professor of Sociology, Wilmington College, Ohio, since 1975. Professor of Sociology, East Stroudsburg State College, Pennsylvania, 1973-75. Social Worker, International Rescue Committee, 1960-63, and East Orange Head Start, New Jersey, 1970-72. **Publications:** Youth against the World, 1971. WITH J. YOUNG: The Struggle for Humanity, 1977; The South African Churches in a Revolutionary Situation, 1981; The Faces of Homelessness, 1986; Voices of Hope in the Struggle to Save the Planet, 2000. Author of articles. **Address:** 1941 Ogden Rd, Wilmington, OH 45177, U.S.A.

HOPE, Ronald. British, b. 1921. **Genres:** Geography, History, Travel/Exploration. **Career:** Fellow, Brasenose College, Oxford, 1945-47; Director, Seafarers Education Service, London, 1947-76; Director, The Marine Society, 1976-86. **Publications:** Spare Time at Sea, 1954, rev. ed., 1974; Economic Geography, 1956, 5th ed., 1969; Dick Small in the Half-Deck (novel), 1958; Ships, 1958; The British Shipping Industry, 1959; The Shoregoer's Guide to World Ports, 1963; Introduction to the Merchant Navy, 1965, 4th ed., 1973; In Cabined Ships at Sea, 1969; The Merchant Navy, 1980; A New History of British Shipping, 1990; Poor Jack, 2001. EDITOR: The Harrap Book of Sea Verse, 1960; Seamen and the Sea, 1965; Retirement from the Sea, 1967; Voices from the Sea, 1977; John Masefield: The Sea Poems, 1978; Twenty Singing Seamen, 1979; The Seaman's World, 1982; Sea Pie, 1984. **Address:** 2 Park Place, Dollar FK14 7AA, Scotland.

HOPKINS, Antony. British, b. 1921. **Genres:** Music, Autobiography/Memoirs, Children's fiction. **Career:** Composer and Presenter, Talking about Music, BBC. Former Professor, Royal College of Music, London. **Publications:** Talking about Symphonies, 1961; Talking about Concertos, 1964; Music All around Me, 1967; Lucy and Peterkin, 1968; (with A. Previn) Music Face to Face, 1971; Talking about Sonatas, 1971; Downbeat Guide, 1977; Understanding Music, 1979; The Nine Symphonies of Beethoven, 1980; Songs for Swinging Golfers, 1981; Sounds of Music, 1982; Beating Time (autobiography), 1982; Musicamusings, 1983; Pathway to Music, 1983; The Concertgoer's Companion, vol. I, 1984, vol. II, 1985, as single vol., 1993; The Seven Concertos of Beethoven, 1996. **Address:** Woodyard, Ashridge, Berkhamsted, Herts., England.

HOPKINS, Bruce R. American, b. 1941. **Genres:** Law, Money/Finance. **Career:** Private practice of law in Washington, DC, 1969-; Powers, Pyles, Sutter, & Verville, Washington, DC, lawyer, 1992-. **Publications:** The Law of Tax-Exempt Organizations, 1975, 6th ed, 1992; Charity Under Siege: Government Regulation of Fund-Raising, 1980, rev ed as The Law of Fund-Raising, 2nd ed, 1996; Charity, Advocacy, and the Law, 1992; The Tax Law of Charitable Giving, 1993; A Legal Guide to Starting and Managing a Nonprofit Organization, 2nd ed, 1993; (with T.K. Hyatt) The Law of Tax-Exempt Healthcare Organizations, 1995; The Legal Answer Book for Nonprofit Organizations, 1996; Nonprofit Law Dictionary. **Address:** Powers Pyles Sutter & Verville P.C., 1875 Eye St. N.W., 12th Fl., Washington, DC 20006, U.S.A.

HOPKINS, Dwight N. American, b. 1953. **Genres:** Theology/Religion. **Career:** University of Chicago, IL, professor of theology, 1996-. **Publications:** Black Theology USA and South Africa, 1989; Shoes That Feel Our Feet: Sources for a Constructive Black Theology, 1993; Down, Up, and Over: Slave Religion and Black Theology, 1999; Introducing Black Theology of Liberation, 1999; Heart and Head: Black Theology Past, Present, and Future, 2002; (ed.) Black Faith and Public Talk: Critical Essay on James H. Cone's Black Theology and Black Power, 1999. CO-EDITOR: We Are One Voice: Black Theology in South Africa and the USA, 1989; Cut Loose Your Stammering Tongue: Black Theology in the Slave Narratives, 1991; Changing Conversations: Religious Reflection and Cultural Analysis, 1996; Liberation Theologies: Post-Modernity and the Americas, 1997; Global Voices for Gender Justice, 2003. **Address:** Swift Hall, University of Chicago, 1025 E 58th St, Chicago, IL 60637, U.S.A. **Online address:** dhopkins@uchicago.edu

HOPKINS, George Emil. American, b. 1937. **Genres:** Air/Space topics, History, Industrial relations, Organized labor, Politics/Government, Transportation. **Career:** Western Illinois University, Macomb, professor of history, 1968-. **Publications:** The Airline Pilots: A Study in Elite Unionization, 1971; Flying the Line, 1982, vol. 2, 2000; PanAm Pioneer, 1995. **Address:** 1825 E Maple Ridge, Peoria, IL 61614, U.S.A. **Online address:** ehopkins7@prodigy.net

HOPKINS, Jackie (Mims). American, b. 1952. **Genres:** Young adult fiction. **Career:** Eastdale Academy, Memphis, TN, elementary school teacher, 1976-78; Lamkin Elementary, Houston, TX, elementary school teacher, 1978-81; Building Rainbows, Houston, kindergarten teacher, 1985-88; Matzke Elementary, Houston, elementary school teacher, 1988-91, librarian/media specialist, 1994-; Horne Elementary, Houston, librarian/media specialist, 1991-93. **Publications:** Tumbleweed Tom on the Texas Trail, 1994. **Address:** 13223 Golden Valley, Cypress, TX 77429, U.S.A.

HOPKINS, Jasper. American, b. 1936. **Genres:** Philosophy, Theology/Religion, Translations. **Career:** Case Western Reserve University, Cleveland, OH, assistant professor, 1963-68; University of Massachusetts, Boston, associate professor, 1969-70; University of Minnesota, Minneapolis, associate professor, 1970-74, professor of philosophy, 1974-. Visiting professor of philosophy at universities worldwide consulting ed., Mitteilungen und Forschungsbeitraege der Cusanus-Gesellschaft, Trier, Germany. **Publications:** A Companion to the Study of St. Anselm, 1972; Hermeneutical and Textual Problems in the Complete Treatises of St. Anselm, 1976; A Concise Introduction to the Philosophy of Nicholas of Cusa, 1978; Nicholas of Cusa on God as Not-other, 1979; Nicholas of Cusa on Learned Ignorance: A Translation and an Appraisal of De Docta Ignorantia, 1981; Nicholas of Cusa's Debate with John Wenck: A Translation and an Appraisal of De Ignota Litteratura and Apologia Doctae Ignorantiae, 1981; Nicholas of Cusa's Metaphysic of Contraction, 1983; Nicholas of Cusa's Dialectical Mysticism: Text, Translation, and Interpretive Study of De Visione Dei, 1985, 3rd ed., 2001; A New, Interpretive Translation of St. Anselm's Monologion and Proslogion, 1986; Nicholas of Cusa's De Pace Fidei and Cribratio Alkorani: Translation and Analysis, 1990; A Miscellany on Nicholas of Cusa, 1994; Philosophical Criticism: Essays and Reviews, 1994; Nicholas of Cusa on Wisdom and Knowledge, 1996; Glaube und Vernunft im Denken des Nikolaus von Kues, 1996; Hugh of Balma on Mystical Theology: A Translation and an Overview of His De Theologia Mystica, 2002. EDITOR & TRANSLATOR: Truth, Freedom, and Evil: Three Philosophical Dialogues by Anselm of Canterbury, 1967; Trinity, Incarnation, and Redemption: Theological Treatises by Anselm of Canterbury, 1970; (with H. Richardson) Anselm of Canterbury, 3 vols., 1974-76. TRANSLATOR: Nicholas of Cusa: Metaphysical Speculations, 1998, vol. 2, 2000; (with H. Richardson) Complete Philosophical and

Theological Treatises of Anselm of Canterbury, 2000; Complete Philosophical and Theological Treatises of Nicholas of Cusa, 2 vols., 2001. **Address:** Philosophy Dept, University of Minnesota, Minneapolis, MN 55455, U.S.A. **Online address:** hopki001@umn.edu; www.cla.umn.edu/jhopkins/

HOPKINS, John. American, b. 1938. **Genres:** Novels, Novellas/Short stories. **Career:** Writer. **Publications:** NOVELS: The Attempt, 1967; Tangier Buzzless Flies, 1972; The Flight of the Pelican, 1983; In the Chinese Mountains, 1990; All I Wanted Was Company, 1999. OTHER: Rendez-vous ultimes (stories), 1991; The Tangier Diaries, 1962-1979, 1998; The South American Diaries, 2004. **Address:** The Old Parsonage, Buscot, Oxon. SN7 8DQ, England. **Online address:** theoldparsonage@hotmail.com

HOPKINS, Judy. American, b. 1941. **Genres:** Crafts. **Career:** Oil company secretary in Anchorage, AK, 1962-78; Legislative Affairs Agency, Anchorage, information officer and operations director, 1979-85; craftsperson and writer, 1985-. Creator of Class-in-a-Box, mailorder mystery classes for groups and craft shops; Mystery Quilt Singles, mystery patterns for individual quilters; and ScrapMaster (also known as ScrapSaver), a cutting tool for quilters. Quilter, with work exhibited throughout the United States. **Publications:** One-of-a-Kind Quilts, 1989, rev. ed., Design Your Own Quilts, 1998; Fit to Be Tied, 1990; (with N.J. Martin) Rotary Riot, 1992; Blocks and Quilts for the ScrapSaver, 3 vols, 1992; (with Martin) Rotary Roundup, 1993; Around the Block with Judy Hopkins, 1994; Down the Rotary Road with Judy Hopkins, 1996; (with Martin) 101 Fabulous Rotary-Cut Quilts, 1998. Contributor to periodicals. **Address:** 3231 Douglas Hwy, Juneau, AK 99801, U.S.A.

HOPKINS, Lee Bennett. American, b. 1938. **Genres:** Novels, Children's fiction, Poetry, Children's non-fiction. **Career:** Freelance writer and educational consultant. **Publications:** (with A.F. Shapiro) Creative Activities for the Gifted Child, 1968; Books Are by People, 1969; Let Them Be Themselves, 1969, rev. ed., 1992; Important Dates in Afro-American History, 1969; This Street's for Me!, 1970; (with M. Arenstein) Partners in Learning, 1971; Pass the Poetry, Please!, 1972; Charlie's World: A Book of Poems, 1972; Pick a Peck o' Poems, 1972; Kim's Place and Other Poems, 1974; (with S. Rasch) I Really Want to Feel Good about Myself, 1974; More Books by More People, 1974; Meet Madeleine L'Engle, 1974; (with M. Arenstein) Do You Know What Day Tomorrow Is?: A Teacher's Almanac, 1975, 1990; I Loved Rose Ann, 1976; Mama (novel), 1977; Poetry to Hear, Read, Write and Love, 1978; Wonder Wheels (novel), 1979; The Best of Book Bonanza, 1980; Mama and Her Boys (novel), 1981; Side by Side: Poems to Read Together, 1988; Still as a Star: Nighttime Poems, 1989; People from Mother Goose, 1989; Animals from Mother Goose, 1989; Mother Goose and Her Children, 1989. EDITOR: Don't You Turn Back: Poems by Langston Hughes, 1969; I Think I Saw a Snail, 1969; City Spreads Its Wings, 1970; City Talk, 1970; Me!: A Book of Poems, 1970; (with M. Arenstein) Faces and Places, 1971; Zoo!, 1971; Girls Can Too!, 1972; (with M. Arenstein) Time to Shout, 1973; On Our Way: Poems of Pride and Love, 1974; Hey-How for Halloween, 1974; Poetry on Wheels, 1974; Take Hold!, 1974; Sing Hey for Christmas Day, 1975; (with M. Arenstein) Potato Chips and a Slice of Moon, 1976; (with M. Arenstein) Thread One to a Star, 1976; Good Morning to You, Valentine, 1976; Beat the Drum! Independence Day Has Come, 1977; A-Haunting We Will Go, 1977; Monsters, Ghoulies and Creepy Creatures, 1977; Witching Time, 1977; To Look at Any Thing, 1978; Merrily Comes Our Harvest In, 1978; Kits, Cats, Lions and Tigers, 1978; Go to Bed, 1979; Merely Players, 1979; Easter Buds Are Springing, 1979; My Mane Catches the Wind: Poems about Horses, 1979; Pups, Dogs, Foxes and Wolves, 1979; Elves, Fairies and Gnomes, 1980; Moments: Poems about the Seasons, 1980; By Myself, 1980; Morning, Noon and Nightime, Too!, 1980; And God Bless Me, 1982; Circus! Circus!, 1982; Rainbows Are Made: Poems by Carl Sandburg, 1982; The Sky Is Full of Song, 1983; A Song in Stone, 1983; A Dog's Life, 1983; Crickets and Bullfrogs and Whispers of Thunder: Poems by Harry Behn, 1984; Surprises, 1984; Creatures, 1985; Munching: Poems about Food and Eating, 1985; Love and Kisses, 1984; Best Friends, 1986; The Sea Is Calling Me, 1986; Dinosaurs, 1987; Click, Rumble, Roar: Poems about Machines, 1987; More Surprises, 1987; Voyages: Poems by Walt Whitman, 1988; Good Books, Good Times, 1990; On the Farm: Poems, 1991; Questions, 1992; Flit, Flutter, Fly!, 1992; It's About Time, 1992; Extra Innings: Baseball Poems, 1993; April, Bubbles, Chocolate, 1993; Weather, 1994; Hand in Hand: An American History through Poetry, 1994; Pauses, 1995; Good Rhymes, Good Times, 1995; Been to Yesterdays, 1995; Blast Off!: Space Poems, 1995; Opening Days: Sports Poems, 1996; School Supplies: A Book of Poems, 1996; Marvelous Math, 1997; Song and Dance, 1997; All God's Children, 1998; Sports, Sports, Sports, 1999; Spectacular Science, 1999; Climb into My Lap, 1999; Dino-roars, 1999; Lives, 1999; Yummy, 2000; My America, 2000; Home to Me: Poems, 2002; Hoofbeats, Claws & Rippled Fins, 2002; Alphathoughts, 2003.

HOPKINS, Mary R(ice). American, b. 1956. **Genres:** Children's fiction. **Career:** Sparrow Records, Brentwood, TX, recording artist; Maranatha! Music, San Juan Capistrano, CA, recording artist; Big Steps Records, Montrose, CA, founder. Presenter of family concerts, under auspices of Big Steps Ministries; works recorded on audio cassettes and videotapes. **Publications:** HipHipHip Hippopotamus, 1996; Animal Alphabet, 1997. **Address:** Big Steps 4 U, PO Box 362, Montrose, CA 91021, U.S.A. **Online address:** BigSteps@aol.com.; http://maryricehopkins.com

HOPKINSON, Amanda. British, b. 1948. **Genres:** Photography, Women's studies and issues, Translations. **Career:** Writer. **Publications:** Julia Margaret Cameron, 1986; Desires and Disguises: 5 Latin American Photographers, 1992; The Forbidden Rainbow, 1992; Mexico (children's nonfiction), 1992; (ed.) Contemporary Photographers, 1995; Chicano/Latino Writings, 1996; Diary of an Unofficial War Artist, 2000; (ed. and contrib.) Encyclopaedia of Latin American Culture, 2000. PHOTOGRAPHY BOOKS: A Hidden View: Photography from Bahia, Brazil, 1994; History through Photography: Images from the Hulton Deutsch Collection, 1995; Sixties London, 1996; Adults in Wonderland, 1997; Lund Humphries Gallery Guide, 1997; Between Ourselves, 1998; Rehearsal, 1998; Martin Chambi, 2001; Manuel Alvarez Bravo, 2002. TRANSLATIONS: C. Alegria, They Won't Take Me Alive, 1987; (and ed.) Lovers and Comrades: Women's Resistance Poetry from Central America, 1988; C. Alegria, Family Album, 1989; C. Boullosa, The Miracle Worker, 1994; D. Eltir, Sacred Cow, 1995; J. Saramago, Journey to Portugal, 1999; P. Coelho: The Devil & Miss Prym, 2001; R. Piglia, Money to Burn, 2003. **Address:** BCLT School of Literature, University of East Anglia, Norwich NR4 7PD, England. **Online address:** A.Hopkinson@uea.ac.uk

HOPPER, Kim. American. **Genres:** Social sciences. **Career:** Nathan S. Kline Institute for Psychiatric Research, Orangeburg, NY, research scientist; Columbia University School of Public Health and Law, New York, NY, lecturer. **Publications:** (with Ellen Baxter) Private Lives/Public Spaces: Homeless Adults on the Streets of New York City, Community Service Society, 1981; (with others) One Year Later: The Homeless Poor in NYC, 1982; Community Service Society, 1982; (with Jill Hamberg) The Making of America's Homeless: From Skid Row to New Poor, Community Service Society, 1984; (with Baxter and Dan Salerno) Hardship in the Heartland: Homelessness in Eight U.S. Cities, Community Service Society, 1984; (with Mervyn Susser and William Watson) Sociology in Medicine, 1985; (editor with others) Recovery from Schizophrenia: An International Perspective, 2003.; Reckoning with Homelessness, 2003; (with Ernest Cook) Conservation Finance Handbook, 2004. **Address:** Nathan S. Kline Institute for Psychiatric Research, 40 Old Orangeburg Rd., Orangeburg, NY 10962, U.S.A.

HORADAM, Alwyn Francis. Australian, b. 1923. **Genres:** Mathematics/Statistics. **Career:** Lecturer, 1947-58, Sr. Lecturer, 1958-63, Associate Professor of Mathematics, 1963-87, Dean of the Faculty of Science, 1966-68, University Ombudsman, 1984, and Head, Dept of Mathematics, 1985-87, University of New England, Armidale, NSW (Retired 1987); Co-chairman, International Committee for Conferences on Fibonacci Numbers and Their Applications, 1986-. **Publications:** Outline Course of Pure Mathematics, 1969; Guide to Undergraduate Projective Geometry, 1970; (with M.E. Dunkley and I.W. Stewart) New Horizons in Mathematics, Book I, 1970, Book II, 1972; (with M.E. Dunkley and I.W. Stewart) Teacher's Manual to New Horizons in Mathematics, Book I, 1970, Book II, 1972. EDITOR: (with W.D. Wallis) Combinatorial Mathematics VI: Proceedings, Armidale, 1979; (with A.N. Philippou and G.E. Bergum) Fibonacci Numbers and Their Applications: Proceedings, 1986; (with G.E. Bergum and A.N. Philippou) Applications of Fibonacci Numbers: Proceedings, vol. 2, 1988, vol. 3, 1990, vol. 4, 1991, vol. 5, 1993, vol. 6, 1996; vol. 7, 1998.

HORAK, Jan-Christopher. American (born Germany), b. 1951. **Genres:** Film. **Career:** George Eastman House, Rochester, NY, senior curator, 1984-94; Munich Filmmuseum, Germany, director, 1994-98. University of Rochester, professor of English, 1985-94; Hochschule Fernsehen/Film, lecturer in film, 1995-98; Universal Studios, director, Archives & Collections, 1998-2000; University of California, Los Angeles, professor of critical studies, 1999-; Hollywood Entertainment Museum, curator, 2000-. Consultant to International Design Center, Edgar Reitz Films, and U.S. Information Agency. **Publications:** IN ENGLISH: (trans. from German) U. Eskildsen, Helmar Lerski: Metamorphosis through Light, 1983; The Dream Merchants: Making and Selling Films in Hollywood's Golden Age, 1989; Lovers of Cinema: The First American Film Avant-Garde, 1919-1945, 1995; Making Images Move: Photographers and Avant-Garde Cinema, 1996. EDITOR: (with H.-J. Wulff and K.-D. Moeller) Bibliography of Film Bibliographies/ Bibliographie der Filmbibliographien, 1987. IN GERMAN: (ed. with U.

Eskildsen) Film und Foto der zwanziger Jahre, 1979; (with U. Eskildsen) Helmar Lerski: Lichtbildner, Fotographien und Filme, 1910-1947, 1982; Fluchtpunkt Hollywood: Eine Dokumentation zur Filmemigration nach 1933, 1984, rev. ed., 1986; Anti Nazi Filme der deutschsprachigen Emigration von Hollywood, 1984; Berge, Licht und Traum Dr. Arnold Fanck und der deutsche Bergfilm, 1998. Contributor of articles and reviews to periodicals and anthologies. **Address:** 545 Sierra Vista Ave, Pasadena, CA 91107, U.S.A. **Online address:** c.horak@hollywoodmuseum.com

HORAN, Elizabeth (Rosa). American, b. 1956. **Genres:** Literary criticism and history. **Career:** Cabrillo Community College, Aptos, CA, instructor in English, 1984; Tufts University, Medford, MA, lecturer, 1987-88, visiting assistant professor of English, 1989; Arizona State University, Tempe, assistant professor of English and women's studies and director of Comparative Literature Program, 1989-. Wheelock College, lecturer, 1987-88. **Publications:** (trans. and author of intro) Happiness: Stories by Marjorie Agosin, 1993; Gabriela Mistral: An Artist and Her People, 1994; Imagining the Audience: Gabriela Mistral among Latin American Women, in press. Work represented in anthologies. Contributor of articles, poems, translations, and reviews to periodicals. **Address:** Department of English, Arizona State University, Tempe, AZ 85287-0302, U.S.A.

HORD, Frederick (Lee). Also writes as Mzee Lasana Okpara. American, b. 1941. **Genres:** Poetry, Literary criticism and history, Essays. **Career:** Wabash College, Crawfordsville, IN, professor of black studies, 1972-76; Indiana University, guest lecturer in black studies, 1976; Community Service Administration, research director, 1977-80; Frostburg State University, Frostburg, MD, assistant director of minority affairs, 1980-84; Howard University, Washington, DC, professor of Afro-American studies, 1984-87; West Virginia University, Morgantown, WV, Center for Black Culture, director, 1987-88; Knox College, Galesburg, IL, director of black studies, 1988-. Performer/lecturer with PANFRE, 1981-; regional consultant for NAMSE; consultant on black studies for Aframeric Enterprises. **Publications:** POEMS: After(h)ours, 1974; Into Africa, the Color Black, 1987; Life Sentences, 1994; Africa to Me, 1999; The Rhythm of Home: Selected Poems, forthcoming. OTHER: Reconstructing Memory: Black Literary Criticism (essays), 1991; Straight Wobblings of My Father, 2000. Contributor of poems and articles to journals. **Address:** Director of Black Studies, Knox College, 2 E. South St, Galesburg, IL 61401-4999, U.S.A. **Online address:** fhord@knox.edu

HORGAN, John. American, b. 1953. **Genres:** Sciences. **Career:** IEEE Spectrum, NYC, associate editor, 1983-86; Scientific American, NYC, senior writer, 1986-97; free-lance writer, 1997-. **Publications:** The End of Science, 1996; The Undiscovered Mind, 1999; Rational Mysticism, 2003. **Address:** 241 Rt 403, Garrison, NY 10524, U.S.A. **Online address:** jhorgan@highlands.com

HORLICK, Allan S. American, b. 1941. **Genres:** History, Intellectual history. **Career:** New York University, NYC, assistant professor to associate professor of educational history, 1969-76; Trinity School, NYC, history teacher and department head, 1988-. **Publications:** Country Boys and Merchant Princes, 1975; Patricians, Professors, and Public Schools, 1994. **Address:** Trinity School, 139 W 91st St, New York, NY 10024, U.S.A.

HORLOCK, Sir John Harold. British, b. 1928. **Genres:** Engineering. **Career:** Fellow, Open University, 1991- (Vice-Chancellor, 1981-90). Treasurer and Vice-President, Royal Society, 1992-97; Harrison Professor of Mechanical Engineering, University of Liverpool, 1958-66; Professor of Engineering, University of Cambridge, 1967-74; Vice-Chancellor, University of Salford, 1974-80. **Publications:** Axial-Flow Compressors, 1958; Axial-Flow Turbines, 1966; Actuator Disk Theory, 1978; Cogeneration: Combined Heat and Power, 1987; Combined Power Plants, 1992; Advanced Gas Turbine Cycles, 2003. EDITOR: Thermodynamics and Gas Dynamics of I.C. Engines, 2 vols., 1982-86; Energy for the Future, 1995. **Address:** 2 The Avenue, Ampthill, Bedford MK45 2NR, England. **Online address:** john.horlock1@btinternet.com

HORN, Michiel. Canadian (born Netherlands), b. 1939. **Genres:** History, Translations. **Career:** Canadian historian and educator. Bank of Montreal, Victoria, BC, Canada, bank officer, 1956-58; Glendon College, York University, Toronto, ON, lecturer in history, 1968-69, assistant professor, 1969-73, associate professor, 1973-82, professor, 1982-, department chair, 1982-93, associate principal of the college, 1978-81, director of Canadian Studies, 1986-89. **Publications:** (and ed.) The Dirty Thirties: Canadians in the Great Depression, 1972; The League for Social Reconstruction: Intellectual Origins of the Democratic Left in Canada, 1930-1942, 1980; A Liberation Album: Canadians in the Netherlands, 1944-45, 1980; (with E.

McInnis) Canada, a Political and Social History, 1982; The Great Depression of the 1930s in Canada (booklet), 1984; Years of Despair, 1986; Becoming Canadian: Memoirs of an Invisible Immigrant, 1997; Academic Freedom in Canada: A History, 1999. EDITOR: (with R. Sabourin) Studies in Canadian Social History, 1974; (and author of intro.) F.R. Scott, A New Endeavour: Selected Political Essays, Letters, and Addresses, 1986; Academic Freedom: The Harry Crowe Memorial Lectures, 1987; The Depression in Canada: Responses to Economic Crisis, 1988. ANTHOLOGIES: Dutch Immigration to North America, 1983; Building the Co-operative Commonwealth: Essays on the Democratic Socialist Tradition in Canada, 1984; and other volumes. TRANSLATOR: M. 't Hart, The Sundial, 2004. Contributor to periodicals and journals. **Address:** 18 Walder Ave, Toronto, ON, Canada M4P 2R5. **Online address:** mhorn@glendon.yorku.ca

HORN, Stacy. American, b. 1956. **Genres:** Sociology. **Career:** Founder, Echo Communications Group, New York, NY, 1989-. **Publications:** Cyberville: Clicks, Culture and the Creation of an Online Town, 1998. **Address:** Echo Communications Group, 97 Perry St. Apt 13, New York, NY 10014-7107, U.S.A. **Online address:** horn@echonyc.com

HORN, (John) Stephen. American, b. 1931. **Genres:** Politics/Government. **Career:** U.S. Representative, 38th District, California, 1992-. Trustee Professor of Political Science, California State University, Long Beach, since 1988 (President, 1970-88). Administrative Assistant, Secretary of Labor James P. Mitchell, Washington, D.C., 1959-60; Legislative Assistant to U.S. Sen. Thomas H. Kuchel, Washington, D.C., 1960-66; Sr. Fellow, The Brookings Institution, Washington, D.C., 1966-69; Dean, Graduate Studies and Research, American University, Washington, D.C., 1969-70. **Publications:** The Cabinet and the Congress, 1960; Unused Power: The Work of the Senate Committee on Appropriations, 1970; (co-author) Congressional Ethics: The View from the House, 1975. **Address:** 3944 Pine Ave, Long Beach, CA 90807, U.S.A.

HORNBOSTEL, Lloyd. American, b. 1934. **Genres:** Romance/Historical, Science fiction/Fantasy. **Career:** Business Technology Services, partner. Worked in manufacturing operations and research and in corporate executive positions; holder of more than 20 U.S. patents. **Publications:** An Act of God (science fiction), 1996; War Kids, 1941-1945 (historical fiction), 1996. **Address:** 7062 Kinnikimmick Dr., Roscoe, IL 61073, U.S.A. **Online address:** clockhse@inwave.com

HORNBY, Nick. British, b. 1957. **Genres:** Novels, Literary criticism and history, Autobiography/Memoirs. **Career:** Freelance journalist, novelist, and teacher. **Publications:** Contemporary American Fiction (essays), 1992; Fever Pitch (memoir), 1992. NOVELS: High Fidelity, 1995; About a Boy, 1998; How to Be Good, 2001. EDITOR: My Favourite Year: A Collection of New Football Writing, 1993; (with N. Coleman) The Picado Book of Sportswriting, 1996; Speaking with the Angel, 2000. **Address:** c/o Penguin Books Ltd, 80 Strand, London WC2R 0RL, England.

HORNE, Sir Alistair (Allan). British, b. 1925. **Genres:** History, Politics/Government, Social commentary, Biography. **Career:** Hon. Fellow, St. Antony's College, Oxford; Hon. Fellow, Jesus College, Cambridge. Foreign Correspondent, Daily Telegraph, London, 1952-55. Member of Committee of Mgmt., Royal Literary Fund, 1969-90; author, lecturer, journalist. CBE. **Publications:** Back into Power, 1955; Return to Power, 1956; The Land Is Bright, 1958; Canada and the Canadians, 1961; The Price of Glory, Verdun 1916, 1962; The Fall of Paris, The Siege and the Commune 1870-71, 1976; To Lose a Battle, France 1940, 1969; Death of a Generation, 1970; The Terrible Year, 1971; Small Earthquake in Chile, 1972; A Savage War of Peace: Algeria 1954-62, 1977; Napoleon, Master of Europe 1805-07, 1979; The French Army and Politics, 1870-1970, 1984; Macmillan: The Official Biography, 2 vols., 1988-89; A Bundle from Britain, 1993; (with D. Montgomery) The Lonely Leader: Monty 1944-65, 1994; How Far from Austerlitz? Napoleon 1805-1815, 1996; (ed.) Telling Lives, 2000; Seven Ages of Paris, 2002. Contributor to books and periodicals. **Address:** The Old Vicarage, Turville, Oxon. RG9 6QU, England.

HORNE, Donald Richmond. Australian, b. 1921. **Genres:** Novels, History, Social commentary, Autobiography/Memoirs. **Career:** Professor Emeritus, University of New South Wales; University of Canberra, Chancellor, 1992-. Ed., The Observer, Sydney, 1958-61, and The Bulletin, Sydney, 1960-62 and 1967-72; Co-Ed., Quadrant, 1964-66; Contributor Ed., Newsweek International, 1973-76; President, Australian Society of Authors, 1984-85; Chairman, The Australia Council, 1985-90. **Publications:** The Lucky Country, 1964; The Permit (novel), 1965; The Education of Young Donald (autobiography), 1967; (with Beal) Southern Exposure, 1967; God Is an

Englishman, 1969; The Next Australia, 1970; But What if There Are No Pelicans? (novel), 1971; The Australian People (history), 1972; Death of the Lucky Country, 1976; Money Made Us, 1976; His Excellency's Pleasure (novel), 1977; Right Way, Don't Go Back, 1977; In Search of Billy Hughes (history), 1978; Time of Hope, 1980; Winner Take All, 1981; The Great Museum, 1984; The Story of the Australian People (history), 1985; Confessions of a New Boy (autobiography), 1985; The Public Culture, 1986; The Lucky Country Revisited, 1987; Portrait of an Optimist (autobiography), 1988; Ideas for a Nation, 1989; The Coming Republic, 1992; The Intelligent Tourist, 1993; The Avenue of the Fair Go, 1997; An Interrupted Life (autobiography), 1998; Into the Open (autobiography), 2000; Looking for Leadership, 2001. **Address:** 53 Grosvenor St, Woollahra, NSW 2025, Australia.

HORNE, Gerald. American, b. 1949. **Genres:** Cultural/Ethnic topics, Literary criticism and history. **Career:** Writer, lawyer, journalist. **Publications:** Black and Red: W.E.B. Du Bois and the Afro-American Response to the Cold War, 1944-1963, 1985; Communist Front? The Civil Rights Congress, 1946-1956, 1988; Studies in Black: Progressive Views and Reviews of the African American Experience, 1992; Reversing Discrimination: The Case for Affirmative Action, 1992; Black Liberation/Red Scare: Ben Davis & the Communist Party, 1994; Fire This Time: The Watts Uprising & the 1960s, 1995. **Address:** Communication Studies, CB #3285, University of North Carolina at Chapel Hill, Chapel Hill, NC 27599-3195, U.S.A.

HORNE, R(alph) A(lbert). Also writes as Blaise Bulot. American, b. 1929. **Genres:** Novels, Novellas/Short stories, Poetry, Antiques/Furnishings, Civil liberties/Human rights, Chemistry, Environmental sciences/Ecology, Marine sciences/Oceanography, Race relations, Autobiography/Memoirs. **Career:** Senior Scientist, Radio Corp. of America, Needham, Massachusetts, 1957-58, and Joseph Kaye & Co., Cambridge, Massachusetts, 1958-60; Scientific Staff, Arthur D. Little Inc., Cambridge, Massachusetts, 1960-69, 1972-78; Associate Scientist, Woods Hole Oceanographic Institute, 1970-71; Principal Scientist, JBF Scientific Corp., Lexington, Massachusetts, 1971-72; Senior Scientist, GCA/Technology Division, Burlington, Massachusetts, 1978-80; Energy & Environmental Engineering, Inc., 1980-85. **Publications:** Marine Chemistry, 1969; Water and Aqueous Solutions, 1972; The Chemistry of Our Environment, 1978; Dark Waters, 1993; Starr Lyte, 1996. Author of poetry, reviews, short stories, articles. **Address:** 39 Currier Rd, Candia, NH 03034-2002, U.S.A.

HORNE, T. G. See **RIEFE, Alan.**

HORNER, John R(obert). American, b. 1946. **Genres:** Adult non-fiction, Children's non-fiction. **Career:** Managed sand-and-gravel business in Shelby, MT, 1973-75; Princeton University Museum of Natural History, Princeton, NJ, preparator, 1975-; Montana State University, Bozeman, MT, adjunct professor of paleontology and curator of paleontology at Museum of the Rockies, 1982-; writer. **Publications:** (with J. Gorman) Maia: A Dinosaur Grows Up (children's book), c. 1985; (with Gorman) Digging Dinosaurs, 1988 as Digging Dinosaurs: The Search That Unraveled the Mystery of Baby Dinosaurs, 1990; Cranial Morphology of Prosaurolophus (Ornithischia: Hadrosauridae): With Descriptions of Two New Hadrosaurid Species and an Evolution of Hadrosaurid Phyolgenetic Relationships, c. 1992; (with D. Lessem) Digging Up Tyrannosaurus Rex (children's book), 1992; (with Lessem) The Complete T. Rex: How Stunning New Discoveries Are Changing Our Understanding of the World's Most Famous Dinosaur, 1993; (ed., with K. Carpenter and K.F. Hirsch) Dinosaur Eggs and Babies, 1994; (with E. Dobb) Dinosaur Lives: Unearthing an Evolutionary Saga, 1997. Contributor to periodicals. **Address:** Department of Geology, Montana State University, Bozeman, MT 59717, U.S.A.

HORNIMAN, Joanne. Australian, b. 1951. **Genres:** Novels, Children's fiction, Young adult fiction. **Career:** New South Wales Department of Education's School Magazine, Sydney, New South Wales, Australia, assistant editor, 1973-77; writer. Part-time lecturer in children's literature at Southern Cross University; adult literacy teacher at New South Wales department of technical and further education. **Publications:** The End of the World Girl, 1988; The Ghost Lasagne, 1992; Sand Monkeys, 1992; The Serpentine Belt, 1994; Furry-Back and the Lizard-Thing, 1995; Jasmine, 1995; (with J. Kent) Bad Behaviour (stories), 1996; Billygoat Goes Wild, 1996; Loving Athena, 1997; Sunflower!, 1999; Mahalia, 2001; A Charm of Powerful Trouble, 2002. **Address:** 602 Cawongla Rd., Via Lismore, NSW 2480, Australia.

HORNING, Alice S. American, b. 1950. **Genres:** Language/Linguistics, Writing/Journalism. **Career:** Oakland University, professor. **Publications:** Readings in Contemporary Culture, 1979; Teaching Writing as a Second Language, 1987; The Psycholinguistics of Readable Writing: A Multidisciplinary Exploration, 1993; Revision Revisited, 2002. Work represented in anthologies. Contributor of articles and reviews to academic journals. **Address:** Dept of Rhetoric, Communication and Journalism, Oakland University, Rochester, MI 48309, U.S.A. **Online address:** horning@oakland.edu

HORNSBY, Alton, Jr. American, b. 1940. **Genres:** History, Race relations. **Career:** Tuskegee Institute, AL, instructor, 1962-65; Morehouse College, Atlanta, Dept. of History, professor, 1968-, Fuller E. Calloway Professor of History, and Chairman, 1988. Journal of Negro History, editor, 1976-. **Publications:** (ed.) In The Cage: Eyewitness Accounts of the Freed Negro in Southern Society, 1877-1929, 1971; The Black Almanac, 1972, 1973, 1975, 1977; The Negro in Revolutionary Georgia, 1977; Chronology of African-American History, 1991, 2nd ed., 1997; Milestones in 20th Century African-American History, 1993. **Address:** Dept. of History, Box 20, Morehouse College, Atlanta, GA 30314, U.S.A. **Online address:** ahornsby@morehouse.edu

HORNSTEIN, Gail A. American, b. 1951. **Genres:** Psychology, Biography. **Career:** Mount Holyoke College, South Hadley, MA, professor of psychology. **Publications:** To Redeem One Person Is to Redeem the World: The Life of Frieda Fromm-Reichmann, 2000. Contributor to books and journals. **Address:** Dept of Psychology, Mount Holyoke College, 207A Reese Psych-Ed Bldg, South Hadley, MA 01075, U.S.A. **Online address:** ghornste@mtholyoke.edu

HOROVITZ, Michael. British, b. 1935. **Genres:** Poetry, Art/Art history, Literary criticism and history, Music, Translations. **Career:** Ed. and Publr., New Departures intnl. review, 1959-. Director, Live New Departures road show, 1959-, World's Best Jam arts circuses, 1966-, and International Poetry Olympics festivals, 1980-. Painter, singer, musician, songwriter, poet, and critic. OBE. **Publications:** (trans.) Europa, 1961; Alan Davie, 1963; Declaration, 1965; Strangers: Fauve Poems, 1965; Poetry for the People: A Verse Essay in Bop Prose, 1966; Bank Holiday: A New Testament for the Love Generation, 1967; The Wolverhampton Wanderer: An Epic of Football, Fate and Fun, 1970; Love Poems, 1971; A Contemplation, 1978; Growing Up: Selected Poems and Pictures 1951-1979, 1979; (trans.) The Egghead Republic, 1979; Midsummer Morning Jog Log, 1986; Michael Horovitz Goes Visual, 1987; Bop Paintings, Collages, Drawings and Picture Poems, 1989; Wordsounds & Sightlines: New & Selected Poems, 1994; A New Waste Land, 2005. EDITOR: Children of Albion, 1969; Poetry Olympics Anthology, 3 vols., 1980-83; A Celebration of and for Francis Horovitz (1938-1983), 1984; Grandchildren of Albion, 1992; The POW! Anthology, 1996; The POP! Anthology, 2000; The POM! Anthology, 2001; Jeff Nuttall's Wake, 2004. **Address:** PO Box 9819, London W11 2G6, England.

HOROWITZ, Daniel. American, b. 1938. **Genres:** Urban studies, History. **Career:** Wellesley College, Wellesley, MA, instructor in history, 1966-67; Harvard University, Cambridge, MA, instructor, 1967-69, lecturer in history, 1969-70; Skidmore College, Saratoga Springs, NY, assistant professor of history, 1970-72; Scripps College, Claremont, CA, assistant professor, 1972-78, associate professor, 1978-86, Nathaniel Wright Stephenson Professor of History and Biography, 1986-88; Smith College, Northampton, MA, professor of American studies and history, 1989-, and director of American Studies Program. Carleton College, visiting professor, 1980; University of Michigan, visiting associate professor, 1983-84. **Publications:** The Morality of Spending: Attitudes toward the Consumer Society in America, 1875-1940, 1985; Vance Packard and American Social Criticism, 1994; (ed. and author of intro) Suburban Life in the 1950s: Selections from Vance Packard's "Status Seekers," 1995; Betty Friedan and the Making of "The Feminine Mystique," 1998. Contributor of articles and reviews to history and social science journals. **Address:** American Studies Program, Smith College, Northampton, MA 01063, U.S.A.

HOROWITZ, Irving Louis. American, b. 1929. **Genres:** Education, Politics/Government, Social sciences, Sociology. **Career:** Hobart and William Smith Colls., Dept of Sociology, chairman, 1960-63; Washington University, St. Louis, associate professor to professor of sociology, 1963-69; Rutgers University, New Brunswick, NJ, university professor of sociology, 1969-, chairman, Dept of Sociology, Livingston College at Rutgers, 1969-73, Hannah Arendt Distinguished Professor of Sociology and Political Science, 1979-. Transaction Pubs, New Brunswick, president and ed.-in-chief. **Publications:** Idea of War and Peace in Contemporary Philosophy, 1957, 2nd ed. as War and Peace in Contemporary Social and Philosophy Theory, 1973; Philosophy, Science, and the Sociology of Knowledge, 1961; Radicalism and the Revolt against Reason, 1961; The War Game, 1963; Revolution in Brazil, 1964; Three Worlds of Development, 1966, 1972; Professing Sociology,

1968; Sociological Self-Images, 1969; The Struggle Is the Message, 1970; (with W.H. Friedland) The Knowledge Factory, 1970; Foundations of Political Sociology, 1972; Israeli Ecstasies/Jewish Agonies, 1974; (with J.E. Katz) Social Science and Public Policy in the United States, 1975; Genocide, 1976, 5th ed. as Taking Lives, 2001; Ideology and Utopia in the United States 1956-1976, 1977; (with S.M. Lipset) Dialogues on American Politics, 1978; El Comunismo Cubano 1959-1979, 1979; Beyond Empire and Revolution, 1982; C. Wright Mills: An American Utopian, 1983; Winners and Losers, 1984; Communicating Ideas, 1986; Persuasions and Prejudices, 1989; Daydreams and Nightmares, 1990; The Decomposition of Sociology, 1993; Behemoth, 1999; Veblen's Century, 2002. TRANSLATOR: Gumplowicz, Outlines of Sociology, 1963. EDITOR: Power, Politics and People, 1963; Historia y Elementos de la Sociologia del Conocimiento, 2 vols., 1964; The New Sociology, 1964; Sociology and Pragmatism, 1964; The Rise and Fall of Project Camelot, 1967; (with J. de Castro and J. Gerassi) Latin American Radicalism, 1969; Cuban Communism, 1970, 11th ed., 2003; Masses in Latin America, 1970; The Use and Abuse of Social Science, 1971; (with M.S. Strong) Sociological Realities, 1971; The Troubled Conscience, 1971; (with C. Nanry) Sociological Realities II, 1975; Equity, Income, and Policy, 1977; Science, Sin and Scholarship, 1978; Constructing Policy, 1979; (with J.C. Leggett and M. Oppenheimer) The American Working Class, 1979; Policy Studies Review Annual: Vol. 5, 1981. **Address:** 1247 State Rd (Rte 206), Blawenburg Rd/Rocky Hill Intersection, Princeton, NJ 08540-1619, U.S.A. **Online address:** ihorowitz@transactionpub.com

HOROWITZ, Renee B(arbara). American, b. 1932. **Genres:** Mystery/Crime/Suspense. **Career:** U.S. Department of Commerce, Institute for Telecommunication Sciences, writer and editor, 1974-80; Sperry Flight Systems, editor in publications engineering, 1980-81; AlliedSignal Companies, Documentation and Data Management Group, senior documentation engineer, 1981-86; Arizona State University, Tempe, associate professor, 1986-91, professor of information and management technology, 1991-, course coordinator, 1989-. University of Colorado, Boulder, visiting lecturer and instructor, 1974-80; Metropolitan State College, Denver, CO, instructor, 1977-79. Volunteer computer Braille transcriber and teacher for Foundation for Blind Children, Desert Volunteer Braille Guild, and Library of Congress; public speaker. **Publications:** MYSTERY NOVELS: Rx for Murder, 1997; Deadly Rx, 1997. Contributor to books and professional journals. **Address:** 6257 E. Calle Camelia, Scottsdale, AZ 85251, U.S.A. **Online address:** rbhorow@asu.edu

HORRIE, Chris(topher). British, b. 1956. **Genres:** Communications/Media, Documentaries/Reportage. **Career:** Journalist. Staff member on newspaper News on Sunday, 1987; author. University lecturer in journalism; television researcher and producer. **Publications:** (with P. Chippindale) Disaster! The Rise and Fall of "News on Sunday," 1987; (with Chippindale) Stick It up Your Punter: The Rise and Fall of "The Sun," 1990; What Is Islam?, 1991; Sick As a Parrot, 1993; (with S. Clark) Fuzzy Monsters: Fear and Loathing at the BBC, 1994; Live TV, 1999. **Address:** c/o PFD, Drury House, 34-43 Russell Street, London WC2B 5HA, England. **Online address:** Chris28@CHORRIE.FREESERVE.CO.UK

HORSEY, David. (born United States), b. 1951. **Genres:** Politics/Government. **Career:** Political cartoonist and journalist. Worked as a political reporter at Washington State capitol; Daily Journal-American, Bellevue, WA, political reporter, columnist, and editorial cartoonist, 1976-79; Seattle Post-Intelligencer, Seattle, WA, editorial cartoonist, columnist, and member of editorial board, beginning 1979; syndicated by Tribune Media Services, 1986-89, King Features, 1988-2000, and Los Angeles Times Syndicate, 2000-. Horsey-Words and Pictures, Seattle, owner, 1993-; Academy of Realist Art, Seattle, instructor, 1998; active in local educational and youth athletic organizations; member of advisory board, University of Washington College of Arts and Sciences. Cartoons exhibited at Art Institute of Seattle, 1992, Michael Pierce Gallery, Seattle, 1997, Shoreline Country Club, 1999, and Frye Art Museum, Seattle, 2004. **Publications:** Politics and Other Perversions, 1974; Horsey's Rude Awakenings, 1981; Horsey's Greatest Hits of the '80s, 1989. (Coeditor with Maury Forman) Cartooning AIDS around the World, 1992; (Cartoonist) Mary Waterhouse, Farewell Warfare, 1992; The Fall of Man, 1994; One-Man Show, 1999. Some writings appear under the name Dave Horsey. **Address:** Seattle Post-Intelligencer, POB 19099, 101 Elliott Ave. W. Suite 200, Seattle, WA 98119, U.S.A. **Online address:** davidhorsey@seattle-pi.com

HORSLEY, Richard A. American. **Genres:** History. **Career:** New Testament author and scholar. University of Massachusetts, Boston, professor of religious studies. **Publications:** (with J.S. Hanson) Bandits, Prophets, and Messiahs, 1986; Jesus and the Spiral of Violence: Popular Jewish Resistance

in Roman Palestine, 1987; The Liberation of Christmas: The Infancy Narratives in Social Context, 1989; Sociology and the Jesus Movement, 1989; Galilee: History, Politics, People, 1995; Archaeology, History and Society in Galilee: The Social Context of Jesus and the Rabbis, 1996; (with N.A. Silberman) The Message and the Kingdom: How Jesus and Paul Ignited a Revolution and Transformed the Ancient World, 1997; (ed) Paul and Empire: Religion and Power in Roman Imperial Society, 1997; First Corinthians, 1998; (with J.A. Draper) Whoever Hears You, Hears Me, 1999; Saul and Politics, 2000; (ed with J. Tracy) Christmas Unwrapped, 2001. **Address:** University of Massachusetts, 100 Morrissey Blvd., Boston, MA 02125, U.S.A. **Online address:** rhorsley@umbsky.cc.umb.edu

HORSMAN, Reginald. American (born England), b. 1931. **Genres:** History. **Career:** University of Wisconsin at Milwaukee, instructor, 1958-59, assistant professor, 1959-62, associate professor, 1962-64, professor, 1964-73, distinguished professor of history, 1973-99, distinguished professor emeritus, 1999-. **Publications:** The Causes of the War of 1812, 1962; Matthew Elliott: British Indian Agent, 1964; Expansion and American Indian Policy 1783-1812, 1967; The War of 1812, 1969; Napoleon's Europe, 1970; The Frontier in the Formative Years 1783-1815, 1970; Race and Manifest Destiny: The Origins of American Racial Anglo-Saxonism, 1981; The Diplomacy of the New Republic 1776-1815, 1985; Dr. Nott of Mobile: Southerner, Physician, and Racial Theorist, 1987; Frontier Doctor: William Beaumont, America's First Great Medical Scientist, 1996; The New Republic: The United States of America, 1789-1815, 2000. **Address:** Dept of History, University of Wisconsin, Milwaukee, WI 53201, U.S.A. **Online address:** Horsman@csd.uwm.edu

HORTON, David (Edward). American, b. 1931. **Genres:** Young adult fiction. **Career:** Minister. Cardiff Baptist Church, NJ, pastor, 1960-64; First Baptist Church, Saginaw, MI, pastor, 1964-72; American Baptists of Michigan, Lansing, MI, area director, 1972-. **Publications:** A Legion of Honor (young adult), 1995. **Address:** c/o Cygnet Publishing Group, 4821 54th St, Red Deer, AB, Canada T4N 2G5.

HORTON, Frank E. American, b. 1939. **Genres:** Transportation, Urban studies. **Career:** University of Iowa, Iowa City, assistant professor, 1966-68, associate professor, 1968-70, director of the Institute of Urban and Regional Research, 1968-71, professor of geography, 1970-75, dean for Advanced Studies, 1971-75; Southern Illinois University, Carbondale, vice-president for academic affairs and research, 1975-80; University of Wisconsin, Milwaukee, chancellor and professor of geography and urban affairs, 1980-85; University of Oklahoma, Norman, president and professor of geography, 1985-88; University of Toledo, Ohio, president, and professor of geography and higher education, 1989-2000; Horton & Associates, principal, 2000-. **Publications:** (with B.J.L. Berry) Geographic Perspectives on Urban Studies, 1970; (with B.J.L. Berry) Urban Environmental Management: Planning for Pollution Control, 1974. EDITOR: Geographic Research in Urban Transportation and Network Analysis, 1968; Geographic Perspectives on Contemporary Urban Problems, 1973. **Address:** 288 River Ranch Circle, Bayfield, CO 81122, U.S.A.

HORTON, J(ames) Wright, (Jr.). American, b. 1950. **Genres:** Earth sciences. **Career:** University of Southern Maine, assistant professor of geology at Portland and Gorham campuses, 1977-78; U.S. Geological Survey, Reston, VA, research geologist, 1978-. **Publications:** EDITOR: (with J.R. Butler and D.J. Milton) Geological Investigations of the Kings Mountain Belt and Adjacent Areas in the Carolinas, 1981; (with N. Rast) Melanges and Olistostromes of the U.S. Appalachians, 1989; (with V.A. Zullo) The Geology of the Carolinas, 1991; (with E.T. Cleaves) Forum on Geologic Mapping Applications in the Washington-Baltimore Urban Area, 1997. Contributor to scientific journals.

HORTON, Madelyn (Stacey). American, b. 1962. **Genres:** Air/Space topics, Children's non-fiction, Documentaries/Reportage, Biography. **Career:** University of Louisville, Louisville, KY, writing instructor, 1984-87; children's book writer. **Publications:** The Lockerbie Airline Crash, 1991; The Importance of Mother Jones, 1996. **Address:** 3331 Vivienda Circle, Carlsbad, CA 92009, U.S.A.

HORTON, Michael Scott. American, b. 1964. **Genres:** Adult non-fiction, Theology/Religion. **Career:** Ordained reformed minister, writer. Christians United for Reformation, Inc. (CURE), Anaheim CA, founder and president. **Publications:** Mission Accomplished, 1985; Made in America, 1991; Putting "Amazing" Back into "Grace," 1991; The Law of Perfect Freedom, 1993; Beyond Culture Wars, 1994; Where in the World Is the Church, 1995; In the Face of God, 1996; We Believe, 1998. EDITOR: Agony of Deceit, 1990;

Power Religion, 1992; Christ the Lords, 1993; Confessing Theology for Post-Modern Times, 1998. **Address:** c/o Alliance of Confessing Evangelicals, 1716 Spruce St, Philadelphia, PA 19103, U.S.A.

HORTON, Thomas R. American, b. 1926. **Genres:** Administration/Management, Business/Trade/Industry. **Career:** Assistant headmaster at a private school in Jacksonville, FL, 1950-52; International Business Machines (IBM) Corp., Armonk, NY, vice-president of marketing and director of university relations, 1954-82; American Management Association, NYC, chairperson and chief executive officer, 1982-92; Stetson University, DeLand, FL, adviser, 1991-96. Member of numerous boards of directors. **Publications:** (ed.) Traffic Control, 1965; What Works for Me, 1986; (with P. C. Reid) Beyond the Trust Gap, 1991; The CEO Paradox, 1992. **Address:** 825 Pine Tree Ct, DeLand, FL 32724, U.S.A. **Online address:** thorton@stetson.edu

HORVATH, Betty. American, b. 1927. **Genres:** Children's fiction. **Publications:** Hooray for Jasper, 1966; Jasper Makes Music, 1967; Will the Real Tommy Wilson Please Stand Up, 1969; The Cheerful Quiet, 1969; Be Nice to Josephine, 1970; Not Enough Indians, 1971; Small Paul and the Bully of Morgan Court, 1971; Jasper and the Hero Business, 1977; Sir Galahad, Mr. Longfellow, and Me, 1998. **Address:** 2340 Waite Ave, Kalamazoo, MI 49008, U.S.A. **Online address:** gmabbh@chartermi.net

HORVÁTH, John, Jr. American, b. 1948. **Genres:** Poetry, Literary criticism and history. **Career:** Poet, editor, and author. Formerly worked as a steel-mill mechanic. Tougaloo College, Tougaloo, MS, professor of literature and criticism and chair, department of English, 1992-97. **Publications:** Cain' Country: A Volume of Oral Poetry, 1977; Illiana Region Poems: Harboring the Enemy, c. 2000; Conus: The First Tour (chapbook), 2001; (with others) Reverend Terrebonne (poetry performance; CD), 2002. Contributor of poetry to print and online periodicals. **Address:** c/o Author Mail, EBookstand, 1170 Mukilteo Speedway Suite 201, Mukilteo, WA 98275, U.S.A. **Online address:** john@horvath.zzm.com

HORWITZ, Tony. American, b. 1958. **Genres:** Travel/Exploration. **Career:** United Woodcutters Association, labor organizer, 1982-83; News-Sentinel, Fort Wayne, IN, reporter, 1983-84; Sydney Morning Herald, reporter, 1985-87; Wall Street Journal, NYC, reporter, 1989-; writer. **Publications:** One for the Road: Hitchhiking through the Australian Outback, 1987; Baghdad without a Map, and Other Misadventures in Arabia, 1991; Confederates in the Attic, 1998; Blue Latitudes, 2002. **Address:** PO Box 359, Waterford, VA 20197-0359, U.S.A.

HORWOOD, William. British, b. 1944. **Genres:** Novels, Sports/Fitness. **Career:** London Preparatory School, London, England, teacher, 1966-68; Campaign, London, news reporter and feature writer, 1968-69; management, marketing, and business free-lance journalist for Financial Times, Guardian, Marketing, and Reader's Digest, 1970-71; Daily Mail, feature editor, 1972-77; writer. Managing director of Steppenmole Enterprises, Ltd. **Publications:** (with J. Horwood) Superhealth: A Challenge for All the Family, 1979; Duncton Wood (novel), 1979; The Stonor Eagles, 1982; Lands of Never, 1982; Callanish, 1984; Skallagrigg, 1987; Duncton Quest, 1988; Duncton Found, 1989; Duncton Tales, 1991; Duncton Rising, 1992; Duncton Stone, 1993; The Willows in Winter, 1994; Journeys to the Heartland, 1995; Toad Triumphant, 1996; The Willows and Beyond, 1997; Seekers at the WulfRock, 1997; The Willows at Christmas, 1999. **Address:** 30 Hamilton Rd, Oxford OX2 7P2, England. **Online address:** fevra@geocities.com

HOSKYNS, Tam. British, b. 1961. **Genres:** Mystery/Crime/Suspense. **Career:** Actress on stage and television. **Publications:** CRIME NOVELS: The Talking Cure, 1997; Peculiar Things. 1998. **Address:** c/o Gill Coleridge, Rogers Coleridge & White, 20 Powis Mews, London W11 1JN, England.

HOSOZAWA-NAGANO, Elaine. American, b. 1954. **Genres:** Children's fiction. **Publications:** FOR CHILDREN: Chopsticks from America, 1995. **Address:** c/o Polychrome Publishing Corp., 4509 North Francisco Ave., Chicago, IL 60625, U.S.A.

HOSSACK, Joei Carlton. Canadian, b. 1944. **Genres:** Travel/Exploration. **Career:** Kraft Foods, office worker and sales representative in Montreal, QC, 1974-78, and Toronto, ON, 1978-80; Joei's Place (wool and craft store), Toronto, owner, 1980-89. **Publications:** Restless from the Start (travel essays), 1997; Everyone's Dream Everyone's Nightmare, 1998; Kiss This Florida, I'm Outta Here, 2000; A Million Miles from Home, 2001; Alaska Bound and Gagged, 2002; Free Spirit: Born to Wander, 2004. Contributor to magazines and newspapers. **Address:** PMB 9385, PO Box 2428, Pensacola, FL 32513-2428, U.S.A. **Online address:** JoeiCarlton@hotmail.com

HOSSEINI, Khaled. (born Algeria), b. 1965. **Genres:** Young adult fiction. **Career:** Practicing physician specializing in internal medicine, 1996-; The Permanente Medical Group, Mountain View, CA, physician, 1999-. **Publications:** The Kite Runner, 2003. **Address:** The Permanente Medical Group, 555 Castro St.i.com, 3rd Fl., Mountain View, CA 94041, U.S.A. **Online address:** khaled@khaledhossein.com

HOSTROP, Richard W. American, b. 1925. **Genres:** Education, Librarianship, Travel/Exploration. **Career:** Prairie State College, Chicago Heights, IL, president, 1967-70; Linnet Books, Hamden, CT, editor, 1970-72; ETC Publications, president/publisher, 1972-. **Publications:** Teaching and the Community College Library, 1968; Orientation to the Two-Year College, 1970; Handbook for Achieving Academic Success, 1970; Learning inside the Library Media Center, 1972; Managing Education for Results, 1983; United States History Simulations, 1787-1868, 1988; United States History Simulations, 1925-1964, 1990; Prairie State - The Civil Rights of Administrators, 1995; Profiles in Courage Simulations, 1995; (with L.S. Hostrop) Australia and New Zealand by Campervan and/or Car-with Stopovers in the Cook Islands, Fiji, Hawaii, and Tahiti, 1998. EDITOR/CO-EDITOR: Learning C.O.D.-Can the Schools Buy Success?, 1972; Accountability for Educational Results, 1972; (with J. Mecklenburger) Education Vouchers: From Theory to Alum Rock, 1972; Foundations of Futurology in Education, 1973; Education beyond Tomorrow, 1975; Outstanding Public and Private Elementary Schools in the United States, 1989; The Effective School Administrator, 1990.

HOTCHNER, A(aron) E(dward). American, b. 1920. **Genres:** Novels, Plays/Screenplays, Biography. **Career:** Admitted to the Missouri Bar, 1941; practiced law in St. Louis, 1941-42; Major, US Air Force, 1942-46; Articles Ed., Cosmopolitan mag., 1948-50. **Publications:** The Dangerous American, 1958; (adaptor) E. Hemingway, For Whom the Bell Tolls, (television play), 1958; (adaptor) E. Hemingway, The Killers (television play), 1959; E. Hemingway, Adventures of a Young Man (screenplay), 1961; The White House (play), 1964; Papa Hemingway: A Personal Memoir, 1966; The Hemingway Hero (play), 1967; Treasure, 1970; Do You Take This Man? (play), 1970; King of the Hill, 1972; Looking for Miracles, 1974; Doris Day: Her Own Story, 1976; Sophia: Living and Loving, 1979; Sweet Prince (play), 1980; The Man Who Lived at the Ritz, 1982; Choice People, 1984; Welcome to the Club (musical comedy), 1988; Hemingway and His World, 1989; Blown Away, 1990; Exactly Like You (musical comedy), 1995; Louisiana Purchase, 1996; After the Storm, 2000, (screenplay), 2001; The Day I Fired Alan Ladd, 2002; (with P. Newman) Shameful Exploitation, 2003; The World of Nick Adams (play), 2003; Everyone Comes to Elaine's, 2004. **Address:** 14 Hillandale Rd, Westport, CT 06880, U.S.A.

HOUGAN, Carolyn. Also writes as Malcolm Bell, John Case. American, b. 1943. **Genres:** Novels, Mystery/Crime/Suspense. **Career:** Writer, 1980-. Worked as cocktail waitress, school bus driver, legal secretary, and staffer in Wisconsin governor's office. Speaker in high school and university writing classes. **Publications:** Shooting in the Dark, 1984; The Romeo Flag, 1989; Blood Relative, 1992; (as Malcolm Bell) The Last Goodbye, 1999. AS JOHN CASE, WITH J. HOUGAN: The Genesis Code, 1997; The First Horseman, 1998; The Syndrome, 2001. **Address:** c/o Elaine Markson Agency, 44 Greenwich Ave, New York, NY 10011, U.S.A.

HOUGH, Charlotte. British, b. 1924. **Genres:** Mystery/Crime/Suspense, Children's fiction. **Career:** Artist and writer. **Publications:** Jim Tiger, 1956; Morton's Pony, 1957; The Home-makers, 1957; The Hampshire Pig, 1958; The Story of Mr. Pinks, 1958; The Animal Game, 1959; The Trackers, 1960; Algernon, 1961; 3 Little Funny Ones, 1962; Anna and Minnie, 1962; The Owl in the Barn, 1964; More Funny Ones, 1965; Red Biddy, 1966; Sir Frog, 1968; Educating Flora, 1968; My Aunt's Alphabet, 1969; Queer Customer, 1972; Wonky Donkey, 1974; Bad Cat, 1975; Pink Pig, 1975; Charlotte Hough's Holiday Book, 1975; The Mixture as Before, 1976; Verse and Various (miscellany), 1979; The Bassington Murder (adult fiction), 1980. **Address:** 1A Ivor St, London NW1 9PL, England.

HOUGH, Michael. Canadian/British (born France), b. 1928. **Genres:** Regional/Urban planning. **Career:** Basil Spence and Partners, Edinburgh, Scotland, assistant architect, 1955-56; landscape architect in the United States, 1958-59; Hough, Stansbury & Associates Ltd., principal and director of design, 1964-79; Hough, Stansbury & Michalski Ltd., founder and partner, 1979-83; Hough, Stansbury & Woodland Ltd., Rexdale, Ontario, partner, 1984-91;ENVision The Hough Group, Ltd., partner, 1992-. University of Toronto, architect for Planning Office, 1962-70, associate professor of landscape architecture, 1963-70; professor of environment studies at York University, 1970-. **Publications:** City Form and Natural Process, 1984, (with S. Barrett) People and City Landscapes, 1987; Out of Place: Restoring Identity to the Regional Landscape, 1990; Cities and Natural Process, 1995; Cities and Natural Process: A Basis for Sustainability, 2004. **Address:** ENVision The Hough Group, 916 The East Mall Ste B, Etobicoke, ON, Canada M9B 6K1. **Online address:** mh@yorku.ca

HOUGH, Peter A. British, b. 1954. **Genres:** Paranormal, Novellas/Short stories, Science fiction/Fantasy. **Career:** Writer. Wigan & Leigh Liberal Democrats, Chairman; Northern Auomalies Research Organization (NARO) chair. **Publications:** Witchcraft: A Strange Conflict, 1991; Supernatural Britain, 1995; One in a Million, 1996; WITH JENNY RANDLES: Death by Supernatural Causes?, 1988, 1989; Scary Stories, 1991; Looking for the Aliens, 1992; Spontaneous Human Combustion, 1992; Mysteries of the Mersey Valley, 1993; The Afterlife: An Investigation into the Mysteries of Life after Death, 1993; The Complete Book of UFOs, 1994; Strange But True?, 1994. The Encyclopedia of the Unexplained, 1995; Life After Death and The World Beyond, 1996; World's Best "True" UFO Stories, 1994; (with Moyshe Kalman) The Truth About Alien Abductions, 1997. **Address:** 6 Silsden Ave., Lowton, Warrington WA3 1EN, England.

HOUGHTON, Eric. British, b. 1930. **Genres:** Children's fiction. **Career:** Full-time writer, 1985-. History teacher, Newham Co. Borough, 1953-64; teacher, Hastings, Sussex, 1965-85. **Publications:** The White Wall, 1961; They Marched with Spartacus, 1963; Summer Silver, 1963; The Mouse and the Magician, 1970; A Giant Can Do Anything, 1975; (as Hugo Rice) The Remarkable Feat of King Caboodle, 1978; Steps out of Time, 1979; Time-Piece, 1981; Gates of Glass, 1987; Walter's Wand, 1989 (in U.S. as Walter's Magic Wand, 1990); The Backwards Watch, 1991; The Magic Cheese, 1991; Vincent the Invisible, 1993; Rosie and the Robbers, 1996; The Crooked Apple Tree, 1999. **Address:** 42 Collier Rd, Hastings, Sussex TN34 3JR, England.

HOUGHTON, Gordon. British, b. 1965. **Genres:** Novels. **Career:** Writer. Founded his own freelance writing and editing company. **Publications:** The Dinner Party, 1998; The Apprentice, 1999, in US as Damned If You Do, 2000. **Address:** c/o St. Martin's Press, 175 Fifth Ave., New York, NY 10010, U.S.A. **Online address:** gordon@the-burrow.freeserve.co.uk

HOUGHTON, John T(heodore). Welsh, b. 1931. **Genres:** Meteorology/ Atmospheric sciences, Theology/Religion. **Career:** Physicist. Royal Aircraft Establishment, Farnborough, England, research fellow, 1954-57; Oxford University, lecturer in physics, 1958-62, reader 1962-76, professor, 1976-83, Jesus College, fellow, 1960-83. Meteorological Office, director-general, 1983-90, chief executive 1990-91. **Publications:** (with S.D. Smith) Infra-red Physics, 1966; The Physics of Atmospheres, 1977, 3rd ed., 2002; (with F.W. Taylor and C.D. Rodgers) Remote Sounding of Atmospheres, 1984; Does God Play Dice? A Look at the Story of the Universe, 1988; Global Warming: The Complete Briefing, 1994, 2nd ed., 1997; The Search for God: Can Science Help, 1995; Climate Change 2001: The Scientific Basis, 2001. EDITOR: (with A.H. Cook and H. Charnock) The Study of the Ocean and the Land Surface from Satellites, 1983; The Global Climate, 1984; (with G.J. Jenkins and J.J. Ephraums) Climate Change: The IPCC Scientific Assessment, 1990; (with B.A. Callander and S.K. Varney) Climate Change 1992: The Supplementary Report to the IPCC Scientific Assessment, 1992; (with others) Climate Change 1994: Radiative Forcing of Climate Change and an Evaluation of the IPCC IS92 Emission Scenarios, 1995; (with others) Climate Change 1995: The Science of Climate Change, 1996. **Address:** Hadley Centre for Climate Prediction and Research, Fitzroy Rd, Exeter, Devon EX1 3PB, England.

HOUGHTON, Katharine. American, b. 1945. **Genres:** Plays/Screenplays, Songs/Lyrics and libretti, Autobiography/Memoirs, Biography. **Career:** Professional actress on stage, screen, and television, 1965-. Founding member of Pilgrim Repertory Co. **Publications:** PLAYS: To Heaven in a Swing, 1984; Merlin (children's play), 1985; Buddha (one-act), 1987; On the Shady Side (one-act), 1987; The Right Number (one-act), 1987; The Hooded Eye, 1987; Phone Play (one-act), 1988; Marry Month of May (lyrics), 1988; Mortal Friends (one-act), 1988; Best Kept Secret, 1998. SCREENPLAYS: The Heart of the Matter, 1989; Journey to Glasnost, 1990; Motherman, 1993; Acting in Concert, 1994; Spot, 1996. OTHER: (with J.B. Grant) Two Beastly Tales, 1975; MHG: A Biography, 1989; My Grandmother's House near the River and The Three Katharines (memoirs, now titled Katharine Time 3), 1999-2000; The Secret Life of Louisa May Alcott, 2002. **Address:** c/o Grada Fischer, Fischer Ross Group, Inc, 249 E 48th St, New York, NY 10017, U.S.A.

HOUK, Randy. Also writes as Joey Elliott. American, b. 1944. **Genres:** Children's fiction. **Career:** Soundworks, Arlington, VA, president; National Public Radio, Washington, DC, director of publishing; Soundprints, Norwalk, CT, founder, president, and chief executive officer; Benefactory Inc., Fairfield, CT, president, writer, and illustrator. **Publications:** CHILDREN'S BOOKS: Ruffle, Coo, and Hoo Doo, 1993; Bentley and Blueberry, 1993; Jasmine, 1993; Hope, 1995; Wolves in Yellowstone, 1995; Chessie, the Travelin' Man, 1997; Rico's Hawk, 1998. CHILDREN'S BOOKS AS JOEY ELLIOTT: Beezle's Bravery, 1989; Scout's New Home, 1989. **Address:** 573 Jerusalem Rd., Cohasset, MA 02025-1014, U.S.A.

HOULBROOKE, Ralph (A.). British, b. 1944. **Genres:** History, Theology/ Religion. **Career:** University of Reading, Reading, England, lecturer, 1971-88, reader, 1988-. **Publications:** Church Courts and the People during the English Reformation, 1979; The English Family, 1450-1700, 1984; (ed.) English Family Life, 1576-1716, 1988; (ed.) Death, Ritual, and Bereavement, 1989. **Address:** University of Reading, Whiteknights, School of History, PO Box 217, Reading, Berks. RG6 6AH, England. **Online address:** r.a. houlbrooke@reading.ac.uk

HOUSE, James S. American, b. 1944. **Genres:** Gerontology/Senior issues, Medicine/Health, Sociology. **Career:** Duke University, Durham, NC, instructor to associate professor of sociology, 1970-78; University of Michigan, Ann Arbor, associate professor of sociology, 1978-82, professor of sociology, Dept of Sociology, chairperson, 1986-90; Institute for Social Research, Survey Research Center, associate research scientist, 1978-82, senior research scientist/research professor, 1982-, director, 1991-2001. Associate editor, Work and Stress, 1985-88, and Social Psychology Quarterly, 1988-91. **Publications:** Work, Stress, and Social Support, 1981. EDITOR & CONTRIBUTOR: (with K.W. Schaie and D. Blazer) Aging, Health Behaviors, and Health Outcomes, 1992; (with K. Cook and G. Fine) Sociological Perspectives on Social Psychology, 1995. Contributor to sociology journals and other periodicals. **Address:** Institute for Social Research, University of Michigan, Box 1248, Ann Arbor, MI 48106, U.S.A.

HOUSE, Silas D. American, b. 1971. **Genres:** Novels, Novellas/Short stories. **Career:** United States Post Office, Lily, KY, substitute rural carrier, 1996-2001; author. **Publications:** Clay's Quilt: A Novel, 2001; A Parchment of Leaves, 2002; The Coal Tattoo, 2004. **Address:** c/o Author Mail, Algonquin Books of Chapel Hill, PO Box 2225, Chapel Hill, NC 27515, U.S.A. **Online address:** tgmedia@bellsouth.net

HOUSE, Tom. (born United States), b. 1962. **Genres:** Novels. **Career:** Writer. Formerly worked as a bartender on Long Island, NY; State University of New York at Stony Brook, professor of English. **Publications:** The Beginning of Calamities: A Novel, 2003. Contributor to anthologies and periodicals. **Address:** POB 856, Wainscott, NY 11975, U.S.A. **Online address:** tomhouse1@aol.com

HOUSEWRIGHT, David. American, b. 1955. **Genres:** Mystery/Crime/ Suspense. **Career:** Freelance writer. Worked as a newspaper reporter at the Minneapolis Star Tribune, and the Grand Forks Herald. Worked in advertising for fourteen years. **Publications:** Penance, 1995; Practice to Deceive, 1997. **Address:** 2014 Cleveland Ave N, Saint Paul, MN 55113, U.S.A.

HOUSTON, Cecil J(ames). Canadian (born Ireland), b. 1943. **Genres:** Area studies, Cultural/Ethnic topics, Geography, History. **Career:** University of Toronto, Ontario, lecturer, 1972-75, assistant professor, 1975-77, associate professor, 1977-91, professor of geography, 1991-; University of Windsor, professor and dean, Faculty of Arts and Social Sciences. **Publications:** (with W.J. Smyth) The Sash Canada Wore, 1980; (with Smyth) Irish Emigration and Canadian Settlement, 1990; (with J. Leydon) Ireland: The Haunted Ark, 1996. **Address:** Room 101 A Chrysler Hall Tower, University of Windsor, Windsor, ON, Canada N9B 3P4. **Online address:** chouston@uwindsor.ca

HOUSTON, Gloria. American. **Genres:** Children's fiction, Young adult fiction, Education. **Career:** Junior high and high school teacher in Winston-Salem, NC, 1963-64, Irving, TX, 1967-72, Riverview, FL, 1972-73, Brandon, FL, 1974-79, 1983, and Plant City, FL, 1981-82; University of South Florida, instructor, 1982-, author in residence, 1989-94, assistant professor and director of Center for the Study of Child-Writing, 1992-; Western Carolina University, Cullowhee, NC, author in residence, 1994-2002. Gives lectures and conducts workshops on teaching and writing; consultant in educational curricula. **Publications:** My Brother Joey Died, 1982; The Year of the Perfect Christmas Tree, 1988; Littlejim, 1990; My Great-Aunt Arizona, 1992; But No Candy, 1992; Mountain Valor, 1994; Littlejim's Gift, 1994; Littlejim's Dreams, 1998; Bright Freedom's Song, 1998; Miss Dorothy and

Her Bookmobile, 2001. Contributor of chapters to scholarly books, and author of instructional materials, textbooks, academic papers, and articles. **Address:** c/o McIntosh & Otis, 353 Lexington Ave, New York, NY 10016, U.S.A. **Online address:** ghinc@ioa.com; houston@wcu.edu

HOUSTON, James A(rchibald). Canadian/American, b. 1921. **Genres:** Novels, Children's fiction, Anthropology/Ethnology. **Career:** Artist: Consultative Designer, since 1972, and Master Designer, since 1988, Steuben Glass, NYC, (Associate Director, 1962-72). Government administrator, West Baffin, 1953-62. **Publications:** Tikta-liktak, 1965; Eagle Mask, 1966; The White Archer, 1967; Eskimo Prints, 1967; Akavak, 1968; Wolf Run, 1971; The White Dawn (for adults), 1971; Ghost Paddle, 1972; Ojibwa Summer, 1972; Kiviok's Magic Journey, 1973; Frozen Fire, 1977; Ghost Fox (for adults), 1977; River Runners, 1979; Spirit Wrestler (for adults), 1980; Long Claws, 1981; Black Diamonds, 1982; Eagle Song, 1983; Ice Swords, 1985; The Falcon Bow, 1986; Whiteout, 1988; Running West, 1990; Drifting Snow, 1992; Confessions of an Igloo Dweller, 1995. **Address:** 24 Main St, Stonington, CT 06378, U.S.A.

HOUSTON, James D. American, b. 1933. **Genres:** Novels, Plays/Screenplays, Adult non-fiction, Biography, Film, Travel/Exploration. **Career:** Cabrillo College, Aptos, CA, instructor in English, 1962-64; guitar instructor in Santa Cruz, CA, 1964-66; Stanford University, Stanford, CA, lecturer in English, 1967-68; University of California, Santa Cruz, lecturer in writing, 1969-88, visiting professor in literature, 1989-93. Writer-in-residence and visiting writer at US universities. Consultant. **Publications:** NOVELS: Between Battles, 1968; Gig, 1969; A Native Son of the Golden West, 1971; Continental Drift, 1978; Love Life, 1985; The Last Paradise, 1998; Snow Mountain Passage, 2001. NONFICTION: (with B. Finney) Surfing: The Sport of Hawaiian Kings, 1996, rev. ed, Surfing: A History of the Ancient Hawaiian Sport, 1996; (with J.W. Houston) Farewell to Manzanar: A True Story of Japanese American Experience during and after the World War II Internment, 1973, new ed, 2002; Writing from the Inside (textbook), 1973; (with J.R. Brodie) Open Field (biography), 1974; Three Songs for My Father (essays), 1974; (with J.W. Houston and J. Korty) Farewell to Manzanar (screenplay), 1976; Californians: Searching for the Golden State, 1982; One Can Think about Life after the Fish Is in the Canoe and Other Coastal Sketches, 1985; The Men in My Life, and Other More or Less True Recollections of Kinship (personal stories), 1987; In the Ring of Fire: A Pacific Basin Journey, 1997. SCREENPLAYS, HAWAIIAN LEGACY FOUNDATION FILM SERIES (cultural documentaries): Li'a: The Legacy of the Hawaiian Man, 1988; Listen to the Forest, 1991; The Hawaiian Way: The Art and Family Tradition of Slack-Key Music, 1993; Words, Earth, and Aloha: The Sources of Hawaiian Music, 1995; Luther Makekau: One Kine Hawaiian Man, 1997; Hawaiian Voices: Bridging Past to Present, 1998; The Sons of Hawai'i: A Sound, a Band, a Legend, 2000. EDITOR: (with G. Haslam) California Heartland: Writings from the Great Central Valley, 1978; West Coast Fiction: Modern Writing from California, Oregon, and Washington, 1979; (with J. Hicks, M.H. Kingston, and A. Young) The Literature of California: Writings from the Golden State, Vol. 1: Native American Beginnings to 1945, 2000. OTHER: The Adventures of Charlie Bates (short stories), 1973, enlarged ed. as Gasoline: The Automotive Adventures of Charlie Bates, 1980; (with J.W. Houston) Barrio (teleplay). Contributor to books. Contributor of short stories and articles periodicals. **Address:** 2-1130 East Cliff Dr., Santa Cruz, CA 95062, U.S.A. **Online address:** jhouston@cruzio.com

HOUSTON, R. B. See RAE, Hugh C(rawford).

HOUSTON, Velina Hasu. American, b. 1958. **Genres:** Plays/Screenplays, Poetry, Children's fiction, Novels, Cultural/Ethnic topics, Essays. **Career:** Playwright, screenwriter, essayist, and poet, 1979-; University of Southern California, Los Angeles, School of Theater, visiting professor, 1990-91, associate professor and director of playwriting program, 1991-. Visiting professor at University of California at Los Angeles School of Theater, Film, and Television, 1993. Guest lecturer and poet at several universities and conferences. **Publications:** PLAYS: Asa Ga Kimashita, 1981; American Dreams, 1984; Tea 1987; Thirst, 1986; The Legend of Bobbi Chicago, 1987; Amerasian Girls, 1987; My Life a Loaded Gun, 1988; Albatross, 1988; Necessities, 1991; Broken English, 1991; The Confusion of Tongues, 1991; Christmas Cake, 1992; Tokyo Valentine, 1992; The Matsuyama Mirror, 1993; Rain, 1993; Kumo Kumo, 1993; Kapi'olani's Faith, 1994; Kokoro, 1994; As Sometimes in a Dead Man's Face, 1994; Cultivated Lives, 1994; Zyanya; The Revenant; There Ought to Be Magnolias. SCREENPLAYS: War Brides, 1984; Journey Home, 1984; Kalito, 1991; Hishoku (title means: Not Color; adapted from Sawako Ariyoshi's novel of the same name), 1992; Golden Opportunity, 1993; The Rest Test, 1993; Pretty Perfect, 1993; Leon for

President, 1993; Hothouse Flowers, 1994; Summer Knowledge. OTHER: Green Tea Girl in Orange Pekoe Country (poetry), 1993; (contrib. and ed.) The Politics of Life, 1993; But Still, Like Air, I'll Rise, 1997; No Passing Zone, 1997. Contributor to anthologies and periodicals. **Address:** University of Southern California, DRC-0791, University Park, Los Angeles, CA 90089-0791, U.S.A.

HOUSTON, W. Robert. American, b. 1928. **Genres:** Education, Mathematics/Statistics. **Career:** Michigan State University, East Lansing, Texas professor of education, 1961-70, project director, Model Elementary Teacher Education Program, 1968-70; University of Houston, professor of education, 1970-, associate dean 1973-92; Texas Center for University School Partnerships, executive director, 1990-95; Institute for Urban Education, executive director. **Publications:** Strategies and Resources for Developing Competency-Based Teacher Education Program, 1972; Resources for Performance-Based Education, 1973; Competency Assessment, Research, and Evaluation, 1975; Modern Elementary Education Teaching and Learning, 1976; Exploring World Regions, 1977; Assessing School/College/Community Needs, 1978; Emerging Professional Roles in Teacher Education, 1978; Focus on the Future Implications for Education, 1978; Designing Short-Term Instructional Programs, 1979; Staff Development and Educational Change, 1980; Mirrors of Excellence, 1986. CO-AUTHOR: Sir Isaac Newton, 1960; Extending Mathematics Understanding, 1961; Professional Growth through Student Teaching, 1965; Teaching in the Modern Elementary School, 1967; Exploring Regions of Latin America and Canada, 1968; Extending Understandings of Mathematics, 1969; Understanding the Number System, 1969; The Elementary School Curriculum, 1970; Elementary Education in the Seventies, 1970; Acquiring Competencies to Teach Mathematics in Elementary Schools, 1973; Competency-Based Instructional Design, 1973; Adult Learners, 1981; Touch the Future: Teach!, 1988; Encouraging Reflective Practice in Education, 1990. EDITOR: (co) Competency-Based Teacher Education, 1972; Exploring Competency-Based Education, 1974; Handbook of Research on Teacher Education, 1990. **Address:** College of Education, University of Houston, Houston, TX 77204-5031, U.S.A. **Online address:** rhouston@uh.edu

HOVANNISIAN, Richard G. American, b. 1932. **Genres:** History. **Career:** Professor of Armenian and Near Eastern History, 1969-, Holder, Armenian Educational Foundation Chair in Modern Armenian History, 1987-, University of California, Los Angeles (Lecturer in Armenian Studies, 1962-69; Associate Director of Near Eastern Center, 1979-95). Member of Editorial Board, Armenian Review, International Journal of Middle East Studies, Ararat, and Haigazian Armenological Review, Beirut. Professor of History, Mount Saint Mary College, Los Angeles, CA, 1965-69. **Publications:** Armenia on the Road to Independence, 1967, 4th ed., 1984; The Republic of Armenia, vol. I, 1971, 4th ed., 1996, vol. II, 1982, vols. III-IV, 1996; The Armenian Holocaust, 1978; The Armenian Image in History and Literature, 1982; (ed. with S. Vryonis Jr.) Islam's Understanding of Itself, 1983; Ethics in Islam, 1985; The Armenian Genocide in Perspective, 1986; The Armenian Genocide: History, Politics, Ethics, 1991; Poetry and Mysticism in Islam: The Heritage of Rumi, 1994; The "Thousand and One Nights" in Arabic Literature and Society, 1997; The Armenian People from Ancient to Modern Times, 2 vols., 1997; The Persian Presence in Islam, 1998; Remembrance and Denial: The Case of the Armenian Genocide, 1998; Religion and Culture in Medieval Islam, 1999; Enlightenment and Diaspora, 1999; Armenian Van/Vaspurakan, 2000; Armenian Baghesh/Bitlis and Taron/Mush, 2001; Armenian Tsopk/Kharpert, 2002; Armenian Karin Erzetum, 2003; Looking Backward, Moving Forward: Confronting the Armenian Genocide, 2003. **Address:** Dept. of History, University of California, 405 Hilgard Ave, Los Angeles, CA 90095, U.S.A.

HOWARD, A(rthur) E(llsworth) Dick. American, b. 1933. **Genres:** History, Law, Politics/Government. **Career:** White Burkett Miller Professor of Law and Public Affairs, University of Virginia, Charlottesville, since 1976. Fellow, Woodrow Wilson International Center for Scholars, 1974-75, 1976-77. **Publications:** Magna Carta: Text and Commentary, 1965, rev. ed., 1998; The Road from Runnymede, 1968; (with Barnes, Mashaw and Grosnick) Virginia's Urban Corridor, 1970; Commentaries on the Constitution of Virginia, 1974; State Aid to Private Higher Eduction, 1977; (with Baker and Derr) Church, State, and Politics, 1982; Democracy's Dawn: America's Initiatives in Central and Eastern Europe, 1990; Constitution Making in Eastern Europe, 1993; Toward the Open Society in Central and Eastern Europe, 1994. **Address:** School of Law, University of Virginia, 580 Massie Rd., Charlottesville, VA 22903, U.S.A.

HOWARD, Audrey. British, b. 1929. **Genres:** Romance/Historical. **Career:** Writer. Worked as a model, shop assistant, hairstylist, and civil servant.

Publications: ROMANCE NOVELS: The Skylark's Song, 1984; The Morning Tide, 1985; Ambitions, 1987; The Juniper Bush, 1987; Between Friends, Century, 1988; The Mallow Years, 1989; Shining Threads, 1990; A Day Will Come, 1992; All the Dear Faces, 1992; There Is No Parting, 1993; Promises Lost, 1997.

HOWARD, Clark. Also writes as Rich Howard. American, b. 1934. **Genres:** Novels, Novellas/Short stories, Mystery/Crime/Suspense, Criminology/True Crime, Sports/Fitness. **Career:** The Ring magazine, boxing column, On the Strip, 1968-70. Recipient: Edgar Allan Poe Award, 1981, and Ellery Queen Award, 1985, 1986, 1988, and 1990. **Publications:** NOVELS: The Arm, 1967. MYSTERY NOVELS: A Movement Toward Eden, 1969; The Doomsday Squad, 1970; Siberia 10, 1973; The Killings, 1973; Last Contract, 1973; Summit Kill, 1975; Mark the Sparrow, 1975; The Hunters, 1976; The Last Great Death Stunt, 1977; Traces of Mercury, 1979; Hard City, 1990; City Blood, 1994. SHORT STORIES: Crowded Lives, 1999; Challenge the Widow-Maker, 2000; Derringer Award (novelette), 2003. OTHER: Six against the Rock, 1977; The Wardens, 1979; Zebra: The True Account of the 179 Days of Terror in San Francisco, 1979, in U.K. as The Zebra Killings, 1980; American Saturday, 1981; Brothers in Blood, 1983; Dirt Rich, 1986; Quick Silver, 1988; Love's Blood, 1993. **Address:** PO Box 1527, Palm Springs, FL 92263, U.S.A. **Online address:** RCHoward440@cs.com

HOWARD, David A. American, b. 1942. **Genres:** History. **Career:** Houghton College, Houghton, NY, professor of history, 1969-. **Publications:** The Royal Indian Hospital of Mexico City, 1980; Conquistador in Chains: Cabeza de Vaca and the Indians of the Americas, 1997. **Address:** Department of History, Houghton College, Houghton, NY 14744, U.S.A.

HOWARD, David M. American, b. 1928. **Genres:** Theology/Religion. **Career:** Latin America Mission, Assistant General Director, serving in Costa Rica, 1953-57, and Colombia, 1958-68, President, 1995-99; Inter-Varsity Christian Fellowship, Campus staff member, 1949-51, Missions Director, 1969-76, Assistant to the President, 1977; International Director, World Evangelical Fellowship, 1982-92; David C. Cook Foundation, Senior Vice President, 1992-95. **Publications:** Hammered as Gold, 1969, as The Costly Harvest, 1975; Student Power in World Evangelism, 1970, as Student Power in World Missions, 1979; How Come, God?, 1972; By the Power of the Holy Spirit, 1973; Words of Fire, Rivers of Tears, 1975; The Great Commission for Today, 1976; The Dream That Would Not Die, 1986; What Makes a Missionary, 1987; From Wheaton to the Nations, 2001. EDITOR: Jesus Christ: Lord of the Universe, Hope of the World, 1974; Declare His Glory, 1977. **Address:** 14571 Daffodil Dr Apt 2007, Fort Myers, FL 33919-7480, U.S.A.

HOWARD, Elizabeth Jane. British, b. 1923. **Genres:** Novels, Plays/Screenplays, Novellas/Short stories. **Career:** Secretary, Inland Waterways Association, London, 1947-50; Ed., Chatto & Windus Ltd., publrs., 1953-56, and Weidenfeld & Nicolson Ltd., publrs., 1957, both London; Book Critic, Queen Magazine, London, 1957-60. Has written 14 plays for TV and two film scripts. **Publications:** The Beautiful Visit, 1950; (with R. Aickman) We Are for the Dark: Six Ghost Stories, 1951; The Long View, 1956; (with A. Helps) Bettina: A Portrait, 1957; The Sea Change, 1959; After Julius, 1965; Something in Disguise, 1969; Odd Girl Out, 1972; Mr. Wrong: Short stories, 1975; (ed.) The Lover's Companion, 1978; Getting It Right, 1982; (with F. Maschler) Howard and Maschler on Food, 1987; The Light Years, 1990; Green Shades, 1991; Marking Time, 1991; Confusion, 1992; Casting Off, 1995; Falling, 1999. **Address:** c/o Jonathan Clowes Ltd, Iron Bridge House, Bridge Approach, London NW1 8BD, England.

HOWARD, Ellen. American, b. 1943. **Genres:** Children's fiction. **Career:** Writer, 1983-. Office and library worker, 1963-77; Secretary, The Collins Foundation, Portland, Oregon, 1980-88. **Publications:** Circle of Giving, 1984; When Daylight Comes, 1985; Gillyflower, 1986; Edith Herself, 1987; Her Own Song, 1988; Sister, 1990; The Cellar, 1992; The Chickenhouse House , 1991; The Big Seed, 1993; The Tower Room, 1993; Murphy and Kate, 1995; Different Kind of Courage, 1996; The Log Cabin Quilt, 1996; The Gate in the Wall, 1999; The Log Cabin Christmas, 2000; The Log Cabin Church, 2002. **Address:** 980 Holiday Ct S, Salem, OR 97302-5927, U.S.A.

HOWARD, J. Woodford, Jr. American, b. 1931. **Genres:** Law, Politics/Government, Biography. **Career:** Thomas P. Stran Professor, Johns Hopkins University, Baltimore, 1975-, now emeritus (Associate Professor, 1967-69; Professor, 1969-75). Instructor, Lafayette College, Easton, Pa., 1958-59; Assistant Professor, 1962-66 and Associate Professor, 1966-67, Duke University, Durham. North Carolina. **Publications:** Mr. Justice Murphy: A Political Biography, 1968; Courts of Appeals in the Federal Judicial System: A Study

of the Second, Fifth, and District of Columbia Circuits, 1981. **Address:** Dept. of Political Science, Johns Hopkins University, Baltimore, MD 21218-2686, U.S.A.

HOWARD, Jane R(uble). American, b. 1924. **Genres:** Children's fiction, Plays/Screenplays. **Career:** Children's book writer, playwright, and occasional poet; also teacher, editor, and theatrical director. Cole Marionettes, Chicago, IL, puppeteer, 1946-47; Hingham High School, Hingham, MA, English teacher and drama coach, 1948-51; Scott Foresman & Co., editorial assistant, 1951-52, part-time editor, 1967-69; Apple Tree Theatre, Highland Park, IL, public relations worker, manager of children's theater, and assistant director, 1986-90; The Standard Club, Chicago, editor of newsletter, 1990-95. Speaker and lecturer at schools and writers' workshops; writer in residence, Acts Institute, Lake Ozark, MO, 1984, 1985; member of writing workshops. **Publications:** FOR CHILDREN: When I'm Sleepy, 1985; When I'm Hungry, 1992. PLAYS: The Porch Swing (one-act), 1974; Maria's Loom (play with music), 1976; Frank + Marianne, 1982; Marquee (musical comedy), 1983; Dreamzzz (musical comedy). Contributor to books. Contributor of short stories to magazines. **Address:** 370 Satinwood Ct N, Buffalo Grove, IL 60089, U.S.A.

HOWARD, Joan E. American, b. 1951. **Genres:** Literary criticism and history, Biography, Reference, Translations. **Career:** University of New Hampshire, Durham, instructor, 1981-87, assistant professor of French, 1987-89; Word Works Editing and Translating, director, 1991-; Petite Plaisance, director, 2000-. **Publications:** From Violence to Vision: Sacrifice in the Works of Marguerite Yourcenar, 1992. TRANSLATOR: J. Savigneau, Marguerite Yourcenar: Inventing a Life, 1993; J. Savigneau, Carson McCullers: A Life, 2001. EDITOR: Actes: Marguerite Yourcenar et la mort, 1993; (assoc.) Encyclopedia of New England Culture, forthcoming. **Address:** 51 Congress St, Augusta, ME 04330-6603, U.S.A. **Online address:** vze265vd@verizon.net

HOWARD, Kathleen L. American, b. 1942. **Genres:** History. **Career:** Motorola, Phoenix and Scottsdale, AZ, and Schamburg, IL, purchasing agent, 1965-87; Newberry Library, Chicago, IL, researcher, 1986-87; Heard Museum, Phoenix, AZ, research associate, 1988-. **Publications:** (with D.F. Pardue) Inventing the Southwest: The Fred Harvey Company and Native American Art, 1996. Contributor to exhibition catalogs and scholarly periodicals. **Address:** 10642 E San Salvador Dr, Scottsdale, AZ 85258, U.S.A. **Online address:** Kathy.Howard@att.net

HOWARD, M(ichael) C. British/Canadian, b. 1945. **Genres:** Economics. **Career:** University of Lancaster, Bailrigg, England, lecturer in economics, 1970-72; University of Leicester, Leicester, England, lecturer in economics, 1972-79; University of Waterloo, Waterloo, Ontario, assistant professor, 1979-83, associate professor, 1983-89, professor of economics, 1989-; University of California, Riverside, professor of economics, 1991-93. University of British Columbia, visiting professor, 1976-77; LaTrobe University, distinguished visiting fellow, 1991; Universidad Autonoma Metropolitana, Mexico City, visiting professor, 1992. **Publications:** (with J.E. King) The Political Economy of Marx, 1975, 2nd ed., 1985, 1988; Modern Theories of Income Distribution, 1979; Profits in Economic Theory, 1983; (with J.E. King) A History of Marxian Economics, Vol. I: 1883-1929, 1989, Vol. II: 1929-1990, 1992. EDITOR & CONTRIBUTOR: (with J.E. King) The Economics of Marx: Selected Readings of Exposition and Criticism, 1976; (with I.G. Bradley) Classical and Marxian Political Economy: Essays in Honour of Ronald Meek, 1982. Work represented in anthologies. Contributor of articles and reviews to economics, politics, and history journals. **Address:** Department of Economics, University of Waterloo, Waterloo, ON, Canada N2L 3G1. **Online address:** mchoward@watarts.uwaterloo.ca

HOWARD, Maureen. American, b. 1930. **Genres:** Novels, Autobiography/Memoirs. **Career:** Yale University, New Haven, CT, member of the English Dept., 1991-. Lecturer in English, New School for Social Research, NYC, 1967-68, 1970-71, 1974-. Lecturer, University of California at Santa Barbara, 1968-69, Amherst College, MA, Brooklyn College, and Columbia University, School of the Arts, 1995-; member of English Dept., Princeton University, NJ, 1989, and Columbia University, 1990. **Publications:** NOVELS: Not a Word about Nightingales, 1960; Bridgeport Bus, 1965; Before My Time, 1975; Grace Abounding, 1982; Expensive Habits, 1986; Natural History, 1992; A Lover's Almanac, 1998. OTHER: Facts of Life (autobiography), 1978; (ed) The Penguin Book of Contemporary Essays, 1985; Big as Life: Three Tales for Spring (novellas), 2001. **Address:** c/o Watkins Loomis, 133 E 35th St, New York, NY 10016, U.S.A.

HOWARD, (Sir) Michael (Eliot). British, b. 1922. **Genres:** History, Military/Defense/Arms control. **Career:** University of London, King's College, lecturer in history, 1947-53, lecturer in war studies, 1953-63, professor of war studies, 1963-68, faculty of arts, dean, 1964-68, member of senate, 1966-68; Oxford University, All Souls College, fellow, 1968-80, Regius Professor of Modern History, 1980-89, professor emeritus of modern history, 1993-; Yale University, Robert A. Lovett Professor of Naval and Military History, 1989-93. Intl. Institute for Strategic Studies, president. **Publications:** (with J. Sparrow) The Coldstream Guards 1920-1946, 1951; Disengagement in Europe, 1958; The Franco-Prussian War, 1961; The Mediterranean Strategy in the Second World War, 1967; Studies in War and Peace, 1970; The Continental Commitment, 1972; Grand Strategy Volume IV: 1942-43 (U.K. Official History of Second World War, Military Series) 1972; (with P. Paret) Clausewitz on War; War in European History, 1976; War and the Liberal Conscience, 1978; Causes of Wars, 1983; British Intelligence in the Second World War: Strategic Deception, 1990; Lessons of History, 1991; The Invention of Peace, 2000; The First World War, 2002. EDITOR: Wellingtonian Studies, 1959; The Theory and Practice of War, 1965; (with W.R. Louis) The Oxford History of the Twentieth Century, 1998. **Address:** The Old Farm, Eastbury, Hungerford, Berks. RG17 7JN, England.

HOWARD, Patricia. British, b. 1937. **Genres:** Music. **Career:** Lecturer in Music, Open University. **Publications:** Gluck and the Birth of Modern Opera, 1963; The Operas of Benjamin Britten: An Introduction, 1969; Haydn in London, 1980; Mozart's Marriage of Figaro, 1980; C.W. Gluck: Orfeo, 1981; Haydn's String Quartets, 1984; Beethoven's Eroica Symphony, 1984; Benjamin Britten: "The Turn of the Screw," 1985; Christoph Willibald Gluck: A Guide to Research, 1987; Music in Vienna 1790-1800, 1988; Beethoven's "Fidelio," 1988; Music and the Enlightenment, 1992; Gluck: An Eighteenth-Century Portrait in Letters and Documents, 1995. **Address:** Stepping Stones, Gomshall, Surrey GU5 9NL, England.

HOWARD, Philip (Nicholas Charles). British, b. 1933. **Genres:** Language/Linguistics, Military/Defense/Arms control, Travel/Exploration. **Career:** Senior Leader Writer, Literary Ed., The Times, London, 1978-92; Columnist, 1964-. Parliamentary Correspondent, Glasgow Herald, 1960-64. **Publications:** The Black Watch, 1968; The Royal Palaces, 1970; London's River, 1975; The British Monarchy, 1977; New Words for Old, 1977; Weasel Words, 1978; U and Non-U Revisited, 1978; Words Fail Me, 1980; A Word in Your Ear, 1983; The State of the Language: English Observed, 1984; We Thundered Out: 200 Years of The Times 1785-1985, 1985; Winged Words, 1988; Word-Watching, 1988; A Word in Time, 1990; (ed.) The Times Bedside Book, 1991, 1992. **Address:** Flat 1, 47 Ladbroke Grove, London W11, England. **Online address:** philip.howard@the-times.co.uk

HOWARD, Philip K. American, b. 1948. **Genres:** Law. **Career:** Writer and attorney. Covington & Burling (law firm); special adviser to SEC Task Force of Simplification, 1996; consultant to other government officials and agencies. **Publications:** The Death of Common Sense: How Law Is Suffocating America, 1995; (author of intro.) A. Gore, Common Sense Government; The Collapse of the Common Good: How America's Lawsuit Culture Undermines Our Freedom, 2001. Contributor to periodicals. **Address:** Covington & Burling, 1330 Ave of Americas, New York, NY 10019, U.S.A. **Online address:** phoward@cov.com

HOWARD, Rich. See HOWARD, Clark.

HOWARD, Roger. British, b. 1938. **Genres:** Novels, Plays/Screenplays, Poetry, Literary criticism and history, Politics/Government, Theatre. **Career:** Lecturer, 1979-93, Founding Director, Theatre Underground, 1979-, and Senior Lecturer, 1993, and Ed., New Plays series, 1980-, University of Essex. Teacher, Nankai University, Tientsin, China, 1965-67; Lecturer, University of Peking, 1972-74; Fellow in Creative Writing, University of York, 1976-78; Writing Fellow, University of East Anglia, 1979. **Publications:** A Phantastic Satire (novel), 1960; From the Life of a Patient (novel), 1961; To the People (poetry), 1966; Praise Songs (poetry), 1966; The Technique of the Struggle Meeting, 1968; The Use of Wall Newspapers, 1968; New Plays 1, 1968; Fin's Doubts, 1968; The Hooligan's Handbook, 1971; Method for Revolutionary Writing, 1972; (ed.) Culture and Agitation: Theatre Documents, 1972; Episodes from the Fighting in the East, 1971; Slaughter Night and Other Plays, 1971; Contemporary Chinese Theatre, 1977; Mao Tse-tung and the Chinese People, 1978; The Society of Poets, 1979; A Break in Berlin, 1980; The Siege, 1981; Partisans, 1983; Ancient Rivers, 1984; The Speechifier, 1984; Contradictory Theatres, 1985; (trans.) Sappa, 1985; Senile Poems, 1988; The Tragedy of Mao and Other Plays, 1989; Britannia and Other Plays, 1990; Selected Poems 1966-1996, 1997; Three War Plays, 2004. **Address:** Dept of Literature, Wivenhoe Park, University of Essex, Colchester, Essex CO4 3SQ, England.

HOWARD, Todd. American, b. 1964. **Genres:** Novels, Literary criticism and history. **Career:** Freelance writer and editor, 1994-. English instructor,

California State University-Long Beach and California State University-Dominguez Hills, 1995-2000. Story analyst for the motion picture industry. **Publications:** Ether (novel), 1999; (ed.) William J. Clinton (nonfiction), 2001; Understanding The Outsiders (nonfiction), 2001; (ed.) Mark Twain (nonfiction), 2002; Heroin (nonfiction), 2002. Contributor of poetry to journals. **Address:** c/o Author Mail, Lucent Books, 15822 Bernardo Center Dr., San Diego, CA 92127-2320, U.S.A.

HOWARD, Walter T. American, b. 1951. **Genres:** Law, History. **Career:** University of South Florida, Tampa, adjunct instructor in history, 1981-90; Bloomsburg University, Bloomsburg, PA, assistant professor, 1990-95, associate professor of history, 1995-. St. Leo College, adjunct instructor, 1987-90; Hillsborough Community College, adjunct instructor, 1988-90. **Publications:** Lynchings: Extralegal Violence in Florida during the 1930s, 1995. Contributor of articles and reviews to magazines. **Address:** Department of History, Bloomsburg University, 400 East Second St., Bloomsburg, PA 17815, U.S.A. **Online address:** whoward@bloomv.edu

HOWARD-HASSMANN, Rhoda E. Also writes as Rhoda E. Hassmann. Canadian (born Scotland), b. 1948. **Genres:** Politics/Government, Sociology. **Career:** McMaster University, Hamilton, ON, professor of sociology, 1976-2003; Wilfrid Laurier University, Waterloo, ON, Canada Research Chair in Global Studies and Political Science, Global Studies Program, 2003-. **Publications:** Colonialism and Underdevelopment in Ghana, 1978; Human Rights in Commonwealth Africa, 1986; (ed. with J. Donnelly) International Handbook of Human Rights, 1987; Human Rights and the Search for Community, 1995; Compassionate Canadians: Civic Leaders Discuss Human Rights, 2003. **Address:** Global Studies Program, Wilfrid Laurier University, Waterloo, ON, Canada N2L 3C5. **Online address:** hassmann@wlu.ca

HOWARTH, Lesley. British, b. 1952. **Genres:** Children's fiction, Children's non-fiction. **Career:** Writer. Worked at market gardens, a pottery, and a home for the elderly. **Publications:** CHILDREN'S BOOKS: The Flower King, 1993; MapHead, 1994; Weather Eye, 1995; The Pits, 1996; Fort Biscuit, 1996; Maphead Z, 1997; Mister Spaceman, 1999; Paulina, 1999. **Address:** The Agency, 24 Pottery Lane, Holland Park, London W11 4LZ, England.

HOWARTH, Patrick (John Fielding). See Obituaries.

HOWARTH, William (Louis). American, b. 1940. **Genres:** Environmental sciences/Ecology, Literary criticism and history, Natural history. **Career:** Professor of English, Princeton University, NJ, 1981- (Instructor 1966-68; Assistant Professor 1968-73; Associate Professor, 1973-81). Ed.-in-Chief, the Writings of Henry D. Thoreau, 1972-80; President, Thoreau Society, 1974-75. **Publications:** The Literary Manuscripts of Henry David Thoreau, 1974; The Book of Concord: Thoreau's Life as a Writer, 1982; Thoreau in the Mountains, 1982; Traveling the Trans-Canada, 1987; Walking with Thoreau, 2001. EDITOR: A Thoreau Gazetteer, 1970; Twentieth-Century Interpretations of Poe's Tales, 1971; The John McPhee Reader, 1977; A Week on the Concord and Merrimack Rivers, 1980; Walden and Other Writings, 1980; C. King, Mountaineering in the Sierra Nevada, 1989. **Address:** Dept. of English, McCosh 22, Princeton University, Princeton, NJ 08544, U.S.A.

HOWAT, Gerald (Malcolm David). British, b. 1928. **Genres:** Education, History, Sports/Fitness, Biography. **Career:** Principal Lecturer-Emeritus, Culham College, Oxon, 1984- (Head, Dept. of History, 1960-73). Visiting Professor of History, University of Western Kentucky, 1990-96; Royal Air Force, 1950-52; Staff Texaco (Trinidad), 1952-55; Head, Dept. of History, Kelly College, Tavistock, 1955-60, and Radley College, Oxon, 1973-77; Sr. Tutor, Lord Williams's School, Thame, Oxon., 1977-86; Chief Examiner in History, Oxford and Cambridge Schools Examination Board, 1962-88; cricket journalist, 1975-. Schools' and England Under 19 Cricket Correspondent, Daily Telegraph, 1996-2002, and Cricketer International, 1990-2002. **Publications:** From Chatham to Churchill, 1966; (with A. Howat) The Story of Health, 1967; The Teaching of Empire and Commonwealth History, 1967; Stuart and Cromwellian Foreign Policy, 1974; The Oxford and Cambridge Schools Examination Board 1873-1973, 1974; Learie Constantine, 1975; Village Cricket, 1980; Cricketer Militant, 1980; (with L.G.R. Naylor) Culham College: A History, 1982; Walter Hammond, 1984; Plum Warner, 1987; Len Hutton, 1988; Cricket's Second Golden Age, 1989; Cricket Medley, 1993; A History of North Moreton, 2000; A History of the School of St Helen and St Katharine, 2003. EDITOR: Essays to a Young Teacher, 1966; Dictionary of World History, 1973; Documents in European History 1789-1970, 1974; Who Did What, 1975; Bud Finch Remembers, 1989; (associate and contrib.) Oxford Dictionary of National Biography, 2003. **Address:** Old School House, North Moreton, Didcot, Oxon. OX11 9BA, England.

HOWATCH, Susan. British, b. 1940. **Genres:** Novels, Mystery/Crime/Suspense, Theology/Religion. **Career:** Writer. **Publications:** The Dark Shore, 1965; The Waiting Sands, 1966; Call in the Night, 1967; The Shrouded Walls, 1968; April's Grave, 1969; The Devil on Lammas Night, 1970; Penmarric, 1971; Cashelmara, 1974; The Rich Are Different, 1977; Sins of the Fathers, 1980; The Wheel of Fortune, 1984; Glittering Images, 1987; Glamorous Powers, 1988; Ultimate Prizes, 1989; Scandalous Risks, 1991; Mystical Paths, 1992; Absolute Truths, 1994; The Wonder Worker, 1997; The High Flyer, 2000; The Heartbreaker, 2003. **Address:** c/o Gillon Aitken Associates, 29 Fernshaw Rd, London SW10 OTG, England.

HOWE, Christine J. British, b. 1948. **Genres:** Education, Language/Linguistics, Psychology. **Career:** Sussex University, Brighton, England, lecturer, 1974-76; Strathclyde University, Glasgow, Scotland, lecturer, 1976-90, senior lecturer, 1990-95, reader, 1995-98, professor, 1998-. Consultant to Craig Corporate Managements. **Publications:** Acquiring Language in a Conversational Context, 1981; Language Learning: A Special Case for Developmental Psychology, 1993; Group and Interactive Learning, 1994; Gender and Classroom Interaction, 1997; Conceptual Structures in Childhood and Adolescence: The Case of Everyday Physics, 1998. **Address:** Dept of Psychology, Strathclyde University, 40 George St, Glasgow G1 1QE, Scotland. **Online address:** c.j.howe@strath.ac.uk

HOWE, Fanny. American, b. 1940. **Genres:** Novels, Children's fiction, Poetry. **Career:** Visiting writer, Massachusetts Institute of Technology, Cambridge, 1978-87. Lecturer in Creative Writing, Tufts University, Medford, Massachusetts, 1968-72, Emerson College, Boston, 1973-74, and Columbia University, NYC, 1974-77; University of California, San Diego, professor, 1988-. **Publications:** Forty Whacks, 1969; Eggs, 1970; First Marriage, 1974; Bronte Wilde, 1976; The Amerindian Coastline Poem, 1976; Holy Smoke, 1979; Poems From a Single Pallet, 1980; The White Slave, 1980; The Blue Hills, 1981; Alsace-Lorraine, 1982; Yeah, But, 1982; In the Middle of Nowhere, 1984; Radio City, 1984; For Erato: The Meaning of Life, 1984; Taking Care, 1985; The Race of the Radical, 1985; Robeson Street, 1985; Introduction to the World, 1986; The Lives of a Spirit, 1986; The Vineyard, 1988; Deep North, 1988; Saving History, 1993; The End, 1993. **Address:** Literature Department, 0410 UCSD, La Jolla, CA 92093, U.S.A.

HOWE, (Richard Edward) Geoffrey. (Lord Howe of Aberavon). Welsh, b. 1926. **Genres:** Politics/Government. **Career:** Called to the bar of the Middle Temple, 1952; in private practice as a member of Wales and Chester circuit from chambers in London, 1952-70; created Queen's Counsel, 1965, bencher, 1969, privy councillor, 1972. Member of Parliament for Bebington on Merseyside, 1964-66, Reigate, 1970-74, and East Surrey, 1974-92; solicitor-general, 1970-72; minister for trade and consumer affairs, 1972-74; member of Conservative shadow cabinet, 1974-79; chief front bench spokesman on treasury and economic affairs, 1975-79; chancellor of exchequer, 1979-83; secretary of state for foreign and commonwealth affairs, 1983-89; deputy prime minister, 1989-90; leader of House of Commons and lord president of Council, 1989-90; member, House of Lords, 2001-. John F. Kennedy School of Government, Harvard University, visiting fellow, 1991-92. **Publications:** (with C. Jones) Houses to Let, 1956; (with T. Hooson) Work for Wales, 1959; (with T. Raison and others) Principles in Practice, 1961; Conservative Opportunity, 1965; (with H. Street and G. Bindman) Anti-discrimination Legislation: The Street Report, 1967; (with M. Thatcher and K. Joseph) The Right Angle: Three Studies in Conservatism, 1978; Europe Tomorrow, 1985; East-West Relations, 1987; Down to Earth Diplomacy, 1988; Conflict of Loyalty (memoir), 1994. **Address:** House of Lords, London SW1A 0PW, England.

HOWE, James. American, b. 1946. **Genres:** Children's fiction, Children's non-fiction. **Career:** Freelance actor and director, 1971-75; Literary agent, Lucy Kroll Agency, NYC, 1976-81. **Publications:** (with D. Howe) Bunnicula: A Rabbit Tale of Mystery, 1979; (with D. Howe) Teddy Bear's Scrapbook, 1980; The Hospital Book, 1981, new ed, 1994; Annie Joins the Circus, 1982; Howliday Inn, 1982; The Case of the Missing Mother, 1983; The Celery Stalks at Midnight, 1983; A Night without Stars, 1983; The Day the Teacher Went Bananas, 1984; The Muppet Guide to Magnificent Manners, 1984; How the Ewoks Saved the Trees, 1984; Morgan's Zoo, 1984; Mister Tinker in Oz, 1985; What Eric Knew, 1985; Eat Your Poison, Dear, 1986; When You Go to Kindergarten, 1986, rev. ed., 1994; Babes in Toyland (retelling), 1986; A Love Note for Baby Piggy, 1986; Stage Fright, 1986; There's a Monster under My Bed, 1986; I Wish I Were a Butterfly, 1987; Carol Burnett: The Sound of Laughter, 1987; The Secret Garden (retelling), 1987; Nighty-Nightmare, 1987; Harold & Chester in the Fright before Christmas, 1988; Harold & Chester in Scared Silly, 1989; Dew Drop Dead,

1990; Pinky and Rex, 1990; Pinky and Rex Get Married, 1990; Harold & Chester in Hot Fudge, 1990; Harold & Chester in Creepy-Crawly Birthday, 1991; Pinky and Rex and the Spelling Bee, 1991; Pinky and Rex and the Mean Old Witch, 1991; Pinky and Rex Go to Camp, 1992; Pinky and Rex and the New Baby, 1993; Return to Howliday Inn, 1992; Dances with Wolves (retelling of film for children), 1991; Rabbit-Cadabra!, 1993; Bunnicula Fun Book, 1993; Playing with Words, 1994; There's a Dragon in My Sleeping Bag, 1994; Bunnicula Escapes!, 1994; Pinky and Rex and the Double-Dad Weekend, 1995; New Nick Kramer, or My Life as a Babysitter, 1995; Pinky and Rex and the Bully, 1996; Pinky and Rex and the New Neighbors, 1997; The Watcher, 1997; Horace and Morris but Mostly Dolores, 1997; Pinky and Rex and the School Play, 1998; Pinky and Rex and the Perfect Pumpkin, 1998; Bunnicula's Wickedly Wacky Word Games, 1998; Bunnicula Strikes Again, 1999; Bunnicula's Frightfully Fabulous Factoids, 1999; Bunnicula's Long-Lasting LaughAlouds, 1999; Horace and Morris Join the Chorus, 2001; Pinky and Rex and the Just-Right Pet, 2001; (ed.) Color of Absence, 2001; Misfits, 2001; Invasion of the Mind Swappers from Asteroid 6, 2002; It Came from beneath the Bed!, 2002. **Address:** c/o Amy Berkower, Writers House Inc, 21 W. 26th St, New York, NY 10010, U.S.A.

HOWE, Marie. American, b. 1950. **Genres:** Poetry. **Career:** Poet. Columbia University School of the Arts, NYC, adjunct assistant professor of writing; has taught for the graduate writing programs at Sarah Lawrence College and New York University. **Publications:** POETRY: The Good Thief, 1988; What the Living Do: Poems, 1997. OTHER: (ed. with M. Klein) In the Company of My Solitude: American Writing from the AIDS Pandemic, 1994. Contributor of poems to periodicals. **Address:** c/o Columbia University School of the Arts, 116th St. and Broadway, New York, NY 10027, U.S.A.

HOWE, Melodie Johnson. American. **Genres:** Mystery/Crime/Suspense. **Career:** Has worked as an actor in television, movies, and commercials. **Publications:** MYSTERY NOVELS: The Mother Shadow, 1989; Beauty Dies, 1994. **Address:** c/o Viking Penguin USA, 375 Hudson St., New York, NY 10014, U.S.A.

HOWE, Muriel. Also writes as Barbara Redmayne, Newlyn Nash. British. **Genres:** Romance/Historical. **Career:** Writer and artist (painter). **Publications:** House of Character; Affair at Falconers; Still They Come, Winter Tariff; Master of Skelgale; Stairs of Sand; Pendragon; Private Road to Beyond First Affections; Heatherling; Until the Day. AS NEWLYN NASH, with D. Howe, 9 novels. AS BARBARA REDMAYNE: Ambitious Angel; Lovely Day. **Address:** Skelwith Bridge, Ambleside, Cumbria LA22 9NW, England.

HOWE, Neil. American, b. 1951. **Genres:** Economics, Politics/Government, History. **Career:** American Spectator, Bloomington, IN, managing editor, 1972-74; Smith Richardson Foundation, New York City, program officer, 1979-80; free-lance writer and consultant on economics and public policy in Washington, DC, and New Haven, CT, 1980-. **Publications:** (with P.G. Peterson) On Borrowed Time, 1988; (with W. Strauss) Generations, 1991; (with W. Strauss) 13th-Gen, 1993; (with W. Strauss) Millennials Rising: The Next Generation, 2000. **Address:** c/o Raphael Sagalyn Agency, 7201 Wisconsin Ave, Ste 675, Bethesda, MD 20814-7213, U.S.A.

HOWE, Stephen. American, b. 1958. **Genres:** Politics/Government. **Career:** Writer. **Publications:** (ed.) Lines of Dissent: Writing from the New Statesman, 1913-1988, 1988; Anticolonialism in British Politics: The Left and the End of the Empire, 1918-1964, 1993; Afrocentrism: Mythical Pasts and Imagined Homes, 1998. **Address:** c/o Reed Reference Publishing, 121 Chanlon Rd., New Providence, NJ 07974, U.S.A.

HOWE, Susan. (Susan von Schlegell). American, b. 1937. **Genres:** Poetry. **Career:** Butler Fellow in English, 1988, and Professor of English, 1989, State University of New York, Buffalo; Visiting Scholar and Professor of English, Temple University, Philadelphia, 1990; Leo Block Chair, visiting artist, University of Denver, 1992-93; Stanford Humanities Center, Distinguished Fellow, spring 1998; John Simon Guggenheim Fellowship, 1996; Stanford Universtiy, Dept. of English, visiting professor, spring, 1998. **Publications:** POETRY: Hinge Picture, 1974; The Western Borders, 1976; Secret History of the Dividing Line, 1978; Cabbage Gardens, 1979; The Liberties, 1980; Pythagorean Silence, 1982; Defenestration of Prague, 1983; Articulation of Sound Forms in Time, 1987; A Bibliography of the King's Book, or Eikon Basilike, 1989; The Europe of Trusts: Selected Poems, 1990; Singularities, 1990; The Nonconformist's Memorial: Poems by Susan Howe, 1993; Frame Structures: Early Poems 1974-1979, 1996; Pierce-Arrow, 1999. OTHER: My Emily Dickinson, 1985; The Birth-Mark: Unsettling the Wilderness in American Literary History (criticism), 1990. **Address:** 115 New Quarry Road, Guilford, CT 06437, U.S.A.

HOWELL, Anthony. British, b. 1945. **Genres:** Novels, Poetry. **Career:** Ed., Softly Loudly Books, London. Lecturer, Cardiff School of Art, 1990-. Dancer with the Royal Ballet, London, 1966; Lecturer in Creative Writing, Grenoble University, 1969-70, Editor, Wallpaper Magazine 1974-76 Director, Theatre of Mistakes, 1972-84; Currently, Editor Grey Suit, quarterly magazine for art and literature on VHS cassette. **Publications:** Sergei de Diaghileff (1929) (poetry), 1968; Inside the Castle: Poems, 1969; Imruil: A Naturalized Version of His First Ode-Book (pre-Islamic Arabic) 1970; (ed.) Erotic Lyrics, 1970; Femina Deserta, 1971; Anchovy, 1973; The Mekon, 1976; (ed. with F. Templeton) Elements of Performance Art, 1977; Notions of a Mirror: Poems Previously Uncollected 1964-1982, 1983; Why I May Never See the Walls of China (poems), 1986; In the Company of Others (novel), 1986; Howell's Law (poems); 1990, Near Calvary (selected poems of Nick Lafitte), 1992; First Time in Japan (poems), 1995; Sonnets, 1999; The Analysis of Performance Art: A Guide to Its Theory and Practice, 1999, rev. ed., 2000; Selected Poems, 2000. **Address:** 80 Sparkford House, Battersea Church Rd, London SW11 3NQ, England. **Online address:** howell@fut.net; www.anthonyhowell.org

HOWELL, David. *See* **WYNNE, John (Stewart).**

HOWELL, Dorothy J(ulia). American, b. 1940. **Genres:** Environmental sciences/Ecology, History, Law. **Career:** Metropolitan Sanitary District of Greater Chicago, IL, microbiologist, 1969-75; Office of the Illinois Attorney General, assistant attorney general in Environmental Control Division, 1975-76; Borg-Warner Corp., attorney, 1976-85; Chemical Waste Management, environmental counsel, 1985-87; Boston University, MA, Bell & Howell research fellow at Center for Technology and Policy, 1987-88; Vermont Law School, South Royalton, visiting professor, 1988-92, assistant professor, 1992-96, academic counselor and director of internships at Environmental Law Center, 1993-96. Franklin Pierce Law Center, adjunct professor, 1989-90. **Publications:** Federal Environmental Release Reporting: Memorandum of Case Law, 1982; (ed. and contrib.) The Compleat Library for the Environmental Practitioner, 1984; Intellectual Properties and the Legal Protection of Fictional Characters: Copyright, Trademark, or Unfair Competition? 1990; Scientific Literacy and Environmental Policy, 1992; Ecology for Environmental Professionals, 1993; Environmental Stewardship, 1997. Work represented in anthologies. Contributor of articles and reviews to scientific and law journals. **Address:** 506 Leetes Island Rd #3, Branford, CT 06405-3373, U.S.A.

HOWELL, F(rancis) Clark. American, b. 1925. **Genres:** Anthropology/Ethnology. **Career:** Washington University, St. Louis, MO, instructor, 1953-55; University of Chicago, assistant professor, 1955-59, associate professor, 1959-62, professor of anthropology, 1962-70; University of California, Berkeley, professor of anthropology, 1970-92, professor emeritus, 1992-. **Publications:** (ed.) Early Man and Pleistocene Stratigraphy in the Circum-Mediterranean Regions, 1960; (ed.) African Ecology and Human Evolution, 1963; Early Man, 1965; (ed.) Earliest Man and Environments in the Rudolf Basin, East Africa, 1976.

HOWELL, John Christian. American, b. 1924. **Genres:** Human relations/Parenting, Sex, Theology/Religion. **Career:** First Baptist Church, Crowley, TX, Pastor, 1950-56; Southwestern Baptist Theological Seminary, Fort Worth, TX, Fellow, 1954-56; Volunteers of America Maternity Home, Fort Worth, Chaplain-Counselor, 1954-56; West Bradenton Baptist Church, Florida, Pastor, 1956-60; Midwestern Baptist Theological Seminary, Kansas City, MO, Professor of Christian Ethics, 1960-99, Academic Dean, 1975-82, Interim Vice-President of Academic Affairs and Academic Dean, 1994-95, Academic Dean Emeritus, 2003-. **Publications:** Teaching about Sex-A Christian Approach, 1966; Growing in Oneness, 1972; Teaching Your Children about Sex, 1973; Equality and Submission in Christian Marriage, 1979; Senior Adult Family Life, 1979; Christian Marriage: Growing in Oneness, 1983; Church and Family Growing Together, 1984; Transitions in Mature Marriage, 1989. **Address:** 5001 N Oak St Trafficway, Kansas City, MO 64118, U.S.A.

HOWELLS, John Gwilym. British, b. 1918. **Genres:** Horticulture, Psychiatry, Psychology, Sociology. **Career:** Formerly, Director, Institute of Family Psychiatry. **Publications:** Family Psychiatry, 1963; (co-author) Family Relations Indicator, 1967; Theory and Practice of Family Psychiatry, 1968; Remember Maria, 1974; Principles of Family Psychiatry, 1975; Integral Clinical Investigation, 1982; (with Osborne) A Reference Companion to the History of Abnormal Psychology, 2 vols., 1984; (co-author) The Family and

Schizophrenia, 1985; (co-author) Family Diagnosis, 1986; Plantsman's Guide to Clematis, 1990; Growing Clematis, 1994; Roses & Clematis, 1995; The Viticellas, 1999; Choosing Your Clematis, 2000. EDITOR: Modern Perspectives in Psychiatry Series, 1965-; World History of Psychiatry, 1974; Advances in Family Psychiatry, 2 vols., 1979-80. **Address:** c/o Hill House, Higham, Colchester CO7 6LD, England.

HOWELLS, William White. American, b. 1908. **Genres:** Anthropology/Ethnology, Biology. **Career:** Professor of Anthropology Emeritus, Harvard University, Cambridge, Massachusetts, since 1974 (Professor, 1954-74). Professor of Anthropology, University of Wisconsin, Madison, 1939-54. **Publications:** Mankind So Far, 1944; The Heathens, 1948; Back of History (in U.K. as Man in the Beginning), 1954; Mankind in the Making, 1959, rev. ed. 1967; (ed.) Ideas of Human Evolution, 1962; The Pacific Islanders, 1973; Evolution of the Genus Homo, 1973; Cranial Variation in Man, 1973; Skull Shapes and the Map, 1989; Getting Here: The Story of Human Evolution, 1993, rev. ed. 1997; Who's Who in Skulls, 1995. **Address:** 11 Lawrence Lane, Kittery Point, ME 03905, U.S.A.

HOWES, Craig. Canadian, b. 1955. **Genres:** Documentaries/Reportage. **Career:** University of Hawaii at Manoa, Honolulu, assistant professor, 1980-87, associate professor, 1987-94, professor of English, 1994-, overseas director of Study Abroad Program in London, 1995. **Publications:** Voices of the Vietnam POWs: Witnesses to Their Fight, 1993. Work represented in anthologies. Contributor of stories, articles, and reviews to periodicals. **Address:** Department of English, University of Hawaii at Manoa, 1733 Donaghho Rd., Honolulu, HI 96822, U.S.A.

HOWES, Laura L(ouise). American (born Germany), b. 1956. **Genres:** Literary criticism and history. **Career:** University of Tennessee, Knoxville, associate professor of English, 1990-. **Publications:** Chaucer's Gardens and the Language of Convention, 1997. Contributor to books. Contributor of articles and reviews to academic journals. **Address:** Department of English, McClung Tower, University of Tennessee, Knoxville, TN 37996, U.S.A. **Online address:** lhowes@utk.edu

HOWEY, John. American, b. 1933. **Genres:** Architecture. **Career:** Architect with firms in Atlanta, GA, San Francisco, CA, and Tampa, FL, 1958-65; architect in Tampa, 1965-73; John Howey and Associates, Tampa, architect, 1973-. Baypark Inc., president. **Publications:** The Sarasota School of Architecture, 1941-1966, 1995; Florida Architecture-A Celebration, 2000. Contributor to periodicals. **Address:** John Howey and Associates, 121 W Whiting St, Tampa, FL 33602, U.S.A.

HOWKER, Janni. British (born Cyprus), b. 1957. **Genres:** Young adult fiction. **Career:** Writer; creator of writing workshops. Worked as hospital aide to mentally ill patients, research assistant in sociology department at Lancaster University, examiner at Open University, census officer, park attendant, tutor, and assistant on an archeological site. **Publications:** For young adults: Badger on the Barge and Other Stories, 1984; The Nature of the Beast (novel), 1985; Isaac Campion (novel), 1986; The Topiary Garden, 1994; Martin Farrell, 1994; Walk with a Wolf, 1997. **Address:** c/o Walker Books, 87 Vauschall Walk, London SE11 5HJ, England.

HOWLAND, Ethan. American, b. 1963. **Genres:** Young adult fiction. **Career:** U.S. Peace Corps, high school English teacher in Morocco, 1987-89; U.S. Embassy Press Office, Rabat, Morocco, reporter, 1989; Central New Jersey Home News, New Brunswick, NJ, Washington correspondent, 1991; National Wildlife Federation, Washington, DC, assistant editor, 1992; Inside EPA's Environmental Policy Alert, Arlington, VA, associate editor, 1992-94, managing editor, 1994-95; Children's Hospital, Boston, MA, publications editor at Brazelton Institute, 1996-97; Maine Hospital Association, Augusta, ME, communications manager, 1997-2000; freelance reporter, 2000-. **Publications:** The Lobster War, 2001. **Address:** 28 Mayland St, Portland, ME 04103, U.S.A. **Online address:** ehowland@maine.rr.com

HOY, Claire. Canadian, b. 1940. **Genres:** Biography, Politics/Government. **Career:** Toronto Telegram, Toronto, ON, Canada, political columnist, 1966-70; Toronto Star, political columnist, 1970-74; Toronto Sun, political columnist and bureau chief, 1975-87; Global Television Network, Toronto, political columnist, 1980; Southern News, free-lance columnist, 1988-. Frequent panelist and commentator on Canadian television and radio; lecturer. **Publications:** Bill Davis: A Biography, 1985; Friends in High Places: Politics and Patronage in the Mulroney Government, 1987; Margin of Error: Pollsters and the Manipulation of Canadian Politics, 1989; (with V. Ostrovsky) By Way of Deception, 1990; Clyde Wells: A Political Biography, 1992; The Truth about Breast Cancer, 1995; Nice Work, 1999; Stockwell Day, 2000.

Address: c/o The Hill Times, 69 Sparks St, Ottawa, ON, Canada K1P 5A5. **Online address:** sallyclaire@sympatico.ca

HOY, David Couzens. American, b. 1944. **Genres:** Philosophy. **Career:** Professor of Philosophy, University of California, Santa Cruz, since 1981. Instructor, Yale University, New Haven, Conn., 1969-70; Assistant Professor, Princeton University, New Jersey, 1970-76; Assistant Professor in Residence, University of California, Los Angeles, 1976-77; Associate Professor, Barnard College, Columbia University, New York, 1977-81; Sr. Mellon Fellow in Humanities and Sr. Lecturer in Philosophy, Columbia University, New York, 1981-82. **Publications:** The Critical Circle: Literature, History, and Philosophical Hermeneutics, 1978, 1982; (ed.) Foucault: A Critical Reader, 1986; (with T. McCarthy), Critical Theory, 1994. **Address:** Dept. of Philosophy, University of California, Santa Cruz, CA 95064, U.S.A.

HOY, Linda. British, b. 1946. **Genres:** Children's fiction, Plays/Screenplays. **Career:** Worked as shop assistant, barmaid, and civil servant; Gosforth Comprehensive School, near Sheffield, England, English teacher, 1974-83; Sheffield City Polytechnic, lecturer, 1986-89. **Publications:** The Alternative Assembly Book (for teachers), 1985; Emily (television play), 1985; (ed.) Poems for Peace, 1986. FOR YOUNG PEOPLE: Your Friend Rebecca (novel), 1981; The Damned (novel), 1983; Emmeline Pankhurst (biography), 1985; Kiss File JC 110 (novel), 1988; Nightmare Park, 1989; Ring of Death, 1990; Haddock 'N' Chips, 1993; United on Vacation, 1994; Nightmare Express, 1995; Dear Poltergeist, 1996. **Address:** c/o David Higham Associates, Ltd., 5-8 Lower John St, Golden Sq, London W1R 4HA, England.

HOYEM, Andrew. American, b. 1935. **Genres:** Poetry, Translations. **Career:** President, The Arion Press, San Francisco, since 1979 (Owner, 1973-79). President, M & H Type, since 1989. Partner, Auerhahn Press, San Francisco, 1961-64, and Grabhorn-Hoyem, Printers, San Francisco, 1966-73. **Publications:** The Wake, 1963; The Music Room, 1965; (trans. and author) Chimeras, by Nerval, 1966; (trans. and author with John Crawford) The Pearl, 1967; Articles, Poems 1960-67, 1969; Picture/Poems, 1975; The First Poet Travels to the Moon, 1975; What If, 1987. **Address:** Arion Press, 1802 Hays St, The Presidio, San Francisco, CA 94129, U.S.A.

HOYLE, Geoffrey. British, b. 1942. **Genres:** Science fiction/Fantasy, Children's fiction, Children's non-fiction. **Career:** Worked in documentary films, 1963-67. **Publications:** 2010, 1972; Disasters, 1975; Flight, 1984. WITH F. HOYLE: Fifth Planet, 1963; Rockets in Ursa Major, 1969; Seven Steps to the Sun, 1970; Molecule Men, 1971; The Inferno, 1973; Into Deepest Space, 1976; The Incandescent Ones, 1977: The Westminster Disaster, 1978; Commonsense in Nuclear Energy, 1979; The Energy Pirate (for children), 1982; The Giants of Universal Park (for children), 1982; The Frozen Planet of Azuron (for children), 1982; The Planet of Death (for children), 1982.

HOYLE, Trevor. Also writes as Larry Milne, Joseph Rance. British, b. 1940. **Genres:** Novels, Mystery/Crime/Suspense, Science fiction/Fantasy, Plays/Screenplays. **Career:** Actor, 1960-62; advertising copywriter, 1963-69; lecturer in creative writing, 1975-. **Publications:** NOVELS: The Relatively Constant Copywriter, 1972; The Adulterer, 1972; Rule of Night, 1975, new ed., 2003; The Sexless Spy, 1977; The Svengali Plot, 1978; The Man Who Travelled on Motorways, 1979; Earth Cult (in U.S. as This Sentient Earth), 1979; The Stigma, 1980; (as Joseph Rance) Bullet Train, 1980; Ultraworld, 1980; The Last Gasp, 1983; Vail, 1984; (as Larry Milne) Ghostbusters, 1985; (as Larry Milne) Biggles, 1986; (as Larry Milne) Hearts of Fire, 1987; K.I.D.S., 1987; Blind Needle, 1994. SCIENCE-FICTION. THE Q SERIES: Seeking the Mythical Future, 1977; Through the Eye of Time, 1977; The Gods Look Down, 1978; Mirrorman, 1999. THE BLAKE'S SEVEN SERIES: Blake's Seven, 1977; Blake's Seven: Project Avalon, 1979; Blake's Seven: Scorpio Attack, 1981. TELEVISION PLAYS: Whatever Happened to the Heroes?, 1982; Blake's Seven, 1981. RADIO PLAYS: Conflagration, 1991; Gigo, 1991; Randle's Scandals, 1992. MYSTERIES: Prime Suspect 2, 1992; Prime Suspect 3, 1993; The Governor, 1995. **Address:** c/o Tanja Howarth, 19 New Row, London WC2N 4LA, England.

HOYNINGEN-HUENE, Paul. German, b. 1946. **Genres:** Philosophy. **Career:** University of Zurich, Switzerland, lecturer in philosophy of science, 1976-87, 1990-95; University of Bern, lecturer, 1980-98; Massachusetts Institute of Technology, Cambridge, visiting scholar in linguistics and philosophy, 1984-85; University of Pittsburgh, PA, senior visiting fellow at Center for the Philosophy of Science, 1987-88; Swiss Federal Institute of Technology, Zurich, senior research fellow for environmental sciences, 1989-90; University of Konstanz, professor of foundational theory and history of the sciences, 1990-97; University of Hannover, Center for Philosophy and Ethics of Science, Germany, professor and director. **Publications:** (ed. with F.M. Wuketits, and contrib.) Reductionism and Systems Theory in the Life Sciences, 1989; Die Wissenschaftsphilosophie Thomas S. Kuhns: Rekonstruktion und Grundlagenprobleme, 1989, trans. as Reconstructing Scientific Revolutions: Thomas S. Kuhn's Philosophy of Science, 1993. IN GERMAN: (ed. and author of intro) Die Mathematisierung der Wissenschaften (title means: The Mathematization of the Sciences), 1983; (ed. with G. Hirsch, and contrib.) Wozu Wissenschaftsphilosophie? (title means: Why Philosophy of Science?), 1988; (ed. with M. Fischer, and contrib.) Paradigmen (title means: Paradigms), 1997; Formale Logik, 1998, trans. as Formal Logic: A Philosophical Approach, 2004. Work represented in anthologies. Contributor of articles and reviews to scientific and philosophy journals. **Address:** Winzerstrasse 104, CH-8049 Zurich, Switzerland. **Online address:** hoyningen@ww.uni-hannover.de

HRIBAL, C. J. American, b. 1956. **Genres:** Novellas/Short stories, Novels. **Career:** Writer. Marquette University, Milwaukee, WI, professor of English. **Publications:** Matty's Heart (short stories), 1984; American Beauty (novel), 1987; (ed. and author of intro.) The Boundaries of Twilight: Czecho-Slovak Writing from the New World, 1991; The Clouds in Memphis (novellas and short stories), 2000; The Company Car (novel), 2005. Contributor to periodicals. **Address:** PO Box 1881, Dept of English, Marquette University, Milwaukee, WI 53201, U.S.A. **Online address:** cj.hribal@marquette.edu

HRYCEJ, Tomas. German (born Czech Republic), b. 1954. **Genres:** Information science/Computers. **Career:** Institute for Financial and Insurance Mathematics, Munich, Germany, mathematician, 1981-85; PCS Computer Systems, Munich, software developer, 1985-90; DaimlerChrysler AG, Ulm, Germany, senior researcher, 1991-. **Publications:** Modular Learning in Neural Networks, 1992; Neurocontrol, 1997. **Address:** Research Center Ulm, DaimlerChrysler AG, Wilhelm-Runge-Strasse 11, D-89013 Ulm, Germany. **Online address:** Tomas.Hrycej@DaimlerChrysler.com

HSU, Madeleine (DeMory). American, b. 1938. **Genres:** Music. **Career:** Teacher at a private studio in Paris, France, 1955-64; Ecole Magda Tagliaferro, Paris, private instructor, 1960-63; teacher at private studios in Rio de Janeiro, Brazil, 1965-66, and NYC, 1966-71; Boise State University, Boise, ID, professor of piano, 1971-. Yale University, visiting Hendon fellow, 1996. Professional pianist, 1952-; performed in solo, with orchestras, and on radio and television broadcasts in the United States, Europe, Africa, and South America. **Publications:** Olivier Messiaen, the Musical Mediator: A Study of the Influence of Liszt, Debussy, and Bartok, 1996. Contributor to periodicals. **Address:** Department of Music, Morrison Center for the Performing Arts, Boise State University, 1910 University Dr., Boise, ID 83725, U.S.A.

HSUEH, Tien-tung. Taiwanese, b. 1939. **Genres:** Economics. **Career:** Council for U.S. Aid, Taipei, Taiwan, member of research staff at Economic Research Center, 1962-63; National Taiwan University, Taipei, instructor, 1965-67, associate professor of economics, 1969-71; Chinese University of Hong Kong, lecturer, 1971-80, senior lecturer, 1980-90, reader in economics, 1990-99, head of department at United College, 1972-77, director of China's Reform and Development Programme at Hong Kong Institute of Asia-Pacific Studies, 1990-99; National Cheng Kung University, Tainan, professor of economics & Graduate Institute of Political Economy, 2000-03, dean of College of Social Sciences, 2000-03, director of Taiwan Center of Asian Pacific Studies, 2000-03. Harvard University, research fellow at Harvard-Yenching Institute, 1977-78; Peking University, educational expert in economics, 1985-86; Nagoya University, visiting research fellow in economics, 1993; lecturer at institutions of higher learning. **Publications:** An Econometric Model for Taiwan Economic Development, 1971; (with T.-O. Woo) The Economics of Industrial Development in the People's Republic of China, 1991; (with T.-O. Woo) The Comparative Development Study of Taiwan, Japan and Mainland China, 2002. IN CHINESE: (trans., and author of notes) P.A. Samuelson, Foundations of Economic Analysis, 2 vols., 1974; Modern Western Public Finance, 1983; National Economic Management, 1983; (with T.-O. Woo) Trade between Hong Kong and China, 1984; Quantitative Economics, 1986; The Church Governance, 2004. EDITOR & CONTRIBUTOR: (with Sung Y.-W. and Yu J.) Studies on Economic Reforms and Development in the People's Republic of China, 1993; (with Li Q. and Liu S.) China's Provincial Statistics, 1949-1989, 1993; (with K.-Y. Tsui and T.G. Rawski) Productivity, Efficiency, and Reform in China's Economy, 1995; (with R.C.K. Chan and C.-M. Luk) China's Regional Economic Development, 1996; (with Li Q.) China's National Income, 1952-1995, 1999. EDITOR & CONTRIBUTOR (in Chinese): (with Yu J. and Shi R.) Studies on Economic Reforms and Development in the People's Republic of China, 1990; (with Li J. and Zheng Y.) Studies on China's Productivity Trend, 1993; (with Liu S. and Li Q.) Studies on China's Regional Economic Development, 1994; (with Li Q.)

China's Economic Development in Sectoral Analysis, 1998; The Future of Taiwan, 2002; (with C.-F. Wang) International Comparisons of Taiwan and Japan, 2003. Work represented in anthologies. Contributor of articles and reviews to economic journals. **Address:** 7A Bl 2, Ravana, Garden, Shatin, New Territory, Hong Kong.

HU, Xu-wei. Chinese, b. 1928. **Genres:** Economics, Geography, Regional/Urban planning. **Career:** Institute of Geography, Chinese Academy of Sciences, Beijing, China, assistant professor, 1954-78, associate professor, 1978-86, professor of geography, 1986-, director of branch economic geography, 1986-94, deputy director of academic committee and deputy director of experts committee for regional development research, 1991-95. International Engineering Consulting Corp., member of experts committee, 1988-94; vice president of association for China's regional sciences, 1992-; vice president of association for China's urban planning, 1999-. Journal of Economic Geography, editor in chief, 1991-96. **Publications:** (with others) East China Economic Geography, 1959; (with others) Northwest China Economic Geography, 1963; Regional and Urban Study, 1998; (with others) Studies on the Spatial Agglomeration and Dispersion in China's Coastal City-and-Town Concentrated Areas, 2000. EDITOR: The Distribution of Cities and Industries in Regional Study, 1986; (with Yue-man Yeung) China's Coastal Cities, 1990; China's Coastal Zone: Social and Economic Survey, 1992. **Address:** Institute of Geography, Chinese Academy of Sciences, Beijing 100101, People's Republic of China.

HUA, Gu. Chinese, b. 1942. **Genres:** Novels, Novellas/Short stories. **Career:** Chengzhou Regional Agricultural Institute, Chengzhou, Hunan, China, farmer, 1962-75; Chengzhou Regional Song and Dance Ensemble, Chengzhou, writer, 1975-79; Chengzhou Regional Writers' and Artists' Association, Chengzhou, Hunan, cadre member, 1979-82; Hunan Provincial Writers' Association, Changsha, Hunan, professional writer, 1983-. **Publications:** Furongzhen, 1981, trans. by G. Yang as A Small Town Called Hibiscus, 1983; Paman Qingteng Oe Muwu, 1982, trans. as Pagoda Ridge and Other Stories, 1986; Gu Hua Zhongpian Xiaoshuoji, 1984, trans. as Collected Novellas of Gu Hua; Jiejie Zhai, 1984, trans. as Sisters' Village; Gu Hua Xiaoshud Xuan, 1985, trans. as Selected Novels of Gu Hua; Chen Neu, 1985, translation by Howard Goldblatt published as Virgin Widows, 1997. Author of books published in Chinese; author of screenplays of own novels. **Address:** 302 Bayi Lu, Changsha, Hunan, People's Republic of China.

HUA, Li Min. See CREW, Louie.

HUANG, Chun-chieh. Taiwanese, b. 1946. **Genres:** History, Area studies. **Career:** National Taiwan University, Taipei, lecturer, 1975-80, associate professor, 1980-84, professor of history, 1984-97, distinguished professor of history, 1997-, director of Center for General Education, 1995-. National Tsing Hua University, professor, 1985-86; University of Washington, Seattle, visiting professor, 1986-87; University of Leiden, visiting scholar, 1989; National Chung-cheng University, professor, 1991-92; Free University of Berlin, visiting scholar, 1992; Chinese University of Hong Kong, visiting scholar, 1993; Rutgers University, visiting professor, 1994; Academia Sinica, research fellow, 1998-. **Publications:** Mencian Hermeneutics: A History of Praxis-Reflections in China, 2000. EDITOR: (with S. Harrell) Cultural Change in Postwar Taiwan, 1993; (with E. Zuercher) Norms and the State in China, 1993; (with F.P. Brandauer) Imperial Rulership and Cultural Change in Traditional China, 1994; (with Zuercher) Time and Space in Chinese Culture, 1995; (with F.F. Taso) Postwar Taiwan Experience in Historical Perspectives, 1998. IN CHINESE: Lih-shih te T'an-suo (Enquiries Into History), 1981; (ed. and trans.) Shih-Hsueh Fang-fa Lun-ts'ung (Essays on Historical Methodology), 1981; Ku-tai Hsi-la Ch'eng-pang yu Min-chu Cheng-chih (The Ancient Greek City-States and Democracy), 1981; (ed.) Shen Tsung-han Hsien-sheng Nien-p'u (Dr. Shen Tsung-han: Chronological Biography), 1981; Li-shih yu Hsien-shih (History and Reality), 1982; (ed.) T'ien Tao yu Jen Tao (The Way of Nature and the Way of Man), 1982; (ed.) Li-hsiang yu Hsien-shih (Ideals and Reality), 1982; (co-author) Wuo-kuo Nung-yeh Chien-she ti Hui-ku yu Chang-wang (Agricultural Construction in Mainland China and Taiwan: Retrospect and Prospect), 1983; Ju-chia Ch'uan-t'ung yu Wen-hua Ch'uang-hsin (The Confucian Tradition and Cultural Innovation), 1983; (ed.) Mien-tui Lih-shih ti T'iao-chan: Shen Tsung-han yu Wuo-kuo Nung-yeh Hsien-tai Hua (Meeting the Challenge of History: Dr. Shen Tsung-han and the Modernization of Agriculture in China), 1984; (co-author) Kuang-fu Hou T'ai-wan Nung-yeh Cheng-ts'e ti Yen-pien: Lih-shih yu She-hui ti Fen-hsi (Development of Agricultural Policies in Postwar Taiwan: A Socio-Historical Analysis), 1986; (ed.) Chung-kuo Wen-hua Shih, I (The Cultural History of China, Vol I), 1986; (ed.) Chung-kuo Wen-hua Shih Shang Ts'e, Chiao-shih Shou-ts'e, I, II (teacher's manual; The Cultural History of China, Vol I, Parts 1 and 2), 1987; T'ai-wan Nung-ts'un ti Huang-

hun (The Dusk in Rural Taiwan), 1988; Nung-fu-hui yu T'ai-wan Ching-yen, 1949-79 (The Sino-American Commission Reconstruction and Taiwan Experience, 1949-79), 1991; Meng Hsueh Ssuhsiang Shih Lun (Treatise on the History of Thoughts on the Mencius), Vol. I, 1991, Vol. II, 1997; (co-editor) Kuang-fu Huo T'ai-wan Ti-ch'u Fa-chan Ching-yen (The Development of Taiwan After World War II), 1991; (co-author) Chan-huo T'ai-wan Nung-min Chia-chih Ch'u-hsiang ti Chuan-pien (Transformation of Farmers' Value Orientation in Postwar Taiwan), 1992; Chan-huo T'ai-wan te Chiao-yu yu Ssu-hsiang (Education and Thought in Postwar Taiwan), 1992; (ed.) Chung-kuo Nung-ts'un Fu-hsing Lien-ho Wei-yuan Hui K'uo-shu Li-shih Fang-wen Chi-lu (Reminiscences of the Staffs of the Sino-American Joint Commission on Rural Reconstruction), 1992; Meng Tzu (Mencius), 1993; Chan-huo Tai-wan ti chuan-hsing chi-ch'i chan-wan (The Postwar Taiwan Transformation and Its Prospect), 1995; (ed.) Meng-tzu ssu-hsiang ti li-shih fa-chan (The Historical Development of Mencius's Thought), 1995; (ed.) Kaohsiung Li-shih yu Wenhua lun-chi (Essay on the History and Culture of Kaohsiung), Vol. I, 1994, Vol. II, 1995, Vol. III, 1996, Vol. IV, 1997; (ed.) Chung-kuo Nung-ts'un Fu-hsing Lien-ho Wei-yuan Hui Shihliao Hui-pien (Selected Historical Materials of the Sino-American Joint Commission on Rural Reconstruction); (co-ed) Tung-ya Wen-hua ti t'an-shou (Inquiries into East Asian Culture), 2 vols, 1997. Contributor to books and scholarly journals. **Address:** Commission for General Education, National Taiwan University, 1, Sec. 4, Roosevelt Rd., Taipei 107, Taiwan. **Online address:** chun_chieh_huang@hotmail.com

HUANG, Ch'un-ming. Taiwanese, b. 1939. **Genres:** Novellas/Short stories. **Career:** Short-story writer, folklorist, and author of children's books. **Publications:** IN ENGLISH TRANSLATION: The Drowning of an Old Cat and Other Stories, 1980, as The Taste of Apples: Taiwanese Stories, 2001; Lo (short stories) 1974, 1981, trans by M. Chu as Town Crier, 1984. UNTRANSLATED WORKS: Er zi di da wan ou, 1969; Shayu-na-la, tsai-chien, 1974; Hsiao kua fu (short stories), 1975; Wo ai Ma Li (short stories), 1975; Hsiang t'u tsu ch'u: T'ai-wan min yao ching hsu an chi (Chinese folk songs), 1977; Erh tzu ti ta wan ou (short stories; title means: The Sandwich Man), 1978; Hsiao shuo tsi, c. 1980; Lo han shih pa shou (on martial arts), 1980; Shang yeh hsin li hsu, 1980; Luo, 1984; Hu shan tzu men Shao lin lo han ch'uan, 1984; Ch'ing-fan Kung ti ku-shih, 1985; K'an hai ti jih tzu (short stories), 1985; Huang Ch'un-ming hsiao shuo chi (collected stories), 1985; (with Chun-cheng Liu), Ai tu ti ti jen (biographical fiction), 1985; Teng tai i to hua ti ming tzu, 1989; Wang Shan-shou yu niu chin, 1990; Hsiao t'o pei (juvenile fiction), 1993; Tuan pi hsiang (juvenile fiction), 1993; Wo shih mao yeh (juvenile fiction), 1993; Ai ch'ih t'ang ti huang ti (juvenile fiction), 1993; Hsiao ma ch'ueh, tao ts'ao jen (juvenile fiction), 1993; Mao-mao yu hua (juvenile fiction), 1993; Fang sheng, 1999. **Address:** c/o Columbia University Press, Attn: Author Mail, 61 West 62nd St., New York, NY 10023, U.S.A.

HUBBARD, Bill. (William M. Hubbard). American, b. 1954. **Genres:** Documentaries/Reportage. **Career:** Lubbock Police Department, TX, homicide sergeant, 1979-95; Red River Marshal's Office, NM, deputy marshal, 1995-2000; New Mexico Office of the Medical Investigator, deputy medical investigator, 1996-2000; State of New Mexico, 8th District, chief investigator, 2000-. Texas Commission on Law Enforcement, certified master peace officer, 1995; New Mexico Department of Public Safety, certified executive peace officer, 1998. Women's Protective Services, Lubbock, vice-president, 1984-88. **Publications:** Substantial Evidence (nonfiction), 1998. **Address:** PO Box 593, Red River, NM 87558, U.S.A. **Online address:** rr4marsh@yahoo.com

HUBBARD, Charles M. American, b. 1939. **Genres:** History. **Career:** Middle Tennessee State University, Murfreesboro, adjunct instructor in history, 1991-94; Lincoln Memorial University, Harrogate, TN, associate professor of history, director of Abraham Lincoln Library and Museum, and managing editor of Lincoln Herald, all 1995Community College, adjunct assistant professor, 1995; University of Tennessee, Knoxville, lecturer, 1995. Lincoln Forum, director. Worked as owner and operator of an insurance agency for more than thirty years. **Publications:** (coed) The Many Faces of Lincoln, 1997; The Burden of Confederate Diplomacy, 1998; (ed.) Lincoln and His Contemporaries, 1999. Contributor of articles and reviews to periodicals. **Address:** Abraham Lincoln Library and Museum, Lincoln Memorial University, Cumberland Gap Parkway, Harrogate, TN 37752, U.S.A. **Online address:** chubbard@inetlmu.lmunet.edu

HUBBARD, Dolan. American, b. 1949. **Genres:** Literary criticism and history. **Career:** Frederick County Board of Education, Frederick County, MD, teacher, 1971-72, 1974-76; Catawba College, Salisbury, NC, minority counselor and admissions counselor, 1976-77; Winston-Salem State University, NC, instructor, 1977-82; University of Cincinnati, OH, assistant professor, 1988-89; University of Tennessee, Knoxville, assistant professor, 1989-94; University of Georgia, Athens, associate professor of English, 1994-98; Morgan State University, Baltimore, MD, professor of English and chairperson of Dept of English and Language Arts, 1998-. College Language Association, president, 1994-96; Langston Hughes Review, editor, 1994-98; Langston Hughes Society, president, 2000-; South Atlantic Association of Departments of English, president, 2001-02. **Publications:** The Sermon and the African American Literary Imagination, 1994. EDITOR: Recovered Writers/Recovered Texts: Race, Class, and Gender in Black Women's Literature, 1997; (gen. ed. with A. Rampersad, L. Sanders and S. Tracy) The Collected Works of Langston Hughes, 13 vols., 2001-; The Souls of Black Folk: 100 Years Later, 2003. Contributor to books. Contributor of articles and reviews to academic journals. **Address:** Dept of English and Language Arts, Morgan State University, 1700 E Cold Spring Ln, Baltimore, MD 21251-0001, U.S.A. **Online address:** dhubbard@morgan.edu

HUBBARD, Steve (Albert). American, b. 1957. **Genres:** Sports/Fitness. **Career:** Plain Dealer, Cleveland, OH, intern, 1978; Springfield Daily News, Springfield, OH, sports writer, 1979; Sun, Springfield, sports editor, 1979-81; Delaware County Times, Primos, PA, sports writer, 1981-86; Pittsburgh Press, Pittsburgh, PA, sports writer, 1986-92; X-Press Publishing, Pittsburgh, freelance writer, 1992-. **Publications:** The 1993 Fantasy Football Insider, 1993; Great Running Backs: Football's Fearless Foot Soldiers, 1996; How to Raise an MVP: Most Valuable Person, 1996; David Robinson, 1996; Shark among Dolphins: Inside Jimmy Johnson's Transformation of the Miami Dolphins, 1997; Faith in Sports: Athletes and Their Religion on and off the Field, 1998. Contributor to magazines and newspapers. **Address:** 960 Lakemont Dr., Pittsburgh, PA 15243-1816, U.S.A. **Online address:** sportwriter@aol.com

HUBBARD, Susan (S.). American, b. 1951. **Genres:** Novellas/Short stories. **Career:** Instructor magazine, Dansville, NY, editorial intern, 1973; Evening Press, Binghamton, NY, reporter, 1974-76, business columnist, 1974-75, general columnist, 1975-76; Evening Sentinel, Ansonia, CT, reporter and columnist, 1976-78; Journal-Courier, New Haven, CT, investigative reporter, 1978; Herald-Journal, Syracuse, NY, reporter, 1979-80; Syracuse University, Syracuse, instructor in English, 1984-88, project editor at Educational Resources Information Center, 1986-87; State University of New York College of Environmental Science and Forestry, Syracuse, instructor in English, 1988; Pitzer College, Claremont, CA, writer in residence, 1995; Cornell University, Ithaca, NY, senior lecturer in creative writing and engineering communications, 1988-, faculty adviser, Cornell Engineer, 1991-. Quadrant Research Associates, co-founder and partner, 1980-. **Publications:** STORIES: Walking on Ice, 1990; Blue Money, 1999. Contributor of articles and stories to periodicals. **Address:** English Department, University of Central Florida, PO Box 161346, Orlando, FL 32816-1346, U.S.A. **Online address:** shubbard@pegasus.cc.ucf.edu

HUBBARD, Thomas K. American, b. 1956. **Genres:** Literary criticism and history. **Career:** Bard College, Annandale-on-Hudson, NY, assistant professor of classics, 1980-81; Skidmore College, Saratoga Springs, NY, assistant professor of classics, 1982-84; University of Minnesota-Twin Cities, Minneapolis, assistant professor of classics, 1984-85; University of Texas at Austin, lecturer in classics, 1985-86; Cornell University, Ithaca, NY, James Hutton Assistant Professor, 1986-88; University of Texas at Austin, assistant professor of classics, 1988-93, associate professor, 1993-98, professor, 1998-. **Publications:** The Pindaric Mind, 1985; The Mask of Comedy, 1991; The Pipes of Pan, 1998. **Address:** Department of Classics, University of Texas at Austin, Austin, TX 78712-1181, U.S.A. **Online address:** tkh@mail.utexas.edu

HUBBARD, Woodleigh Marx. American. **Genres:** Children's fiction. **Career:** Writer and illustrator. **Publications:** SELF-ILLUSTRATED: C Is for Curious: An ABC of Feelings, 1990; Two Is for Dancing: A 1, 2, 3 of Actions, 1991; The Friendship Book, 1993; C Is for Curious: An Emotional Address Book, 1993; Visual Feast Recipe Journal, 1995; Woodleigh Marx Hubbard's Twelve Days of Christmas, 1996. Illustrator of books by H.H. Kwon, J. London, M.W. Brown, E. Jackson, L. Longfellow. **Address:** PO Box 10645, Bainbridge Island, WA 98110-0645, U.S.A. **Online address:** wmh@aol.com

HUBER, Evelyne. See STEPHENS, Evelyne Huber.

HUBER, Jack T. American. **Genres:** Psychology. **Career:** Professeor Emeritus, Hunter College, City University of New York (joined faculty, 1967). Professor of Clinical Psychology, Adelphi University, Garden City, New York, 1955-67. **Publications:** Report Writing in Psychology and

Psychiatry, 1958; Through an Eastern Window (in U.K. as Psychotherapy and Meditation), 1963; (co-ed.) Goals and Behavior in Psychotherapy and Counseling, 1972; (co-author) The Human Personality, 1977; (co-ed.) Therapies for Adults, 1982; (co-author) Interviewing America's Top Interviewers, 1991. **Address:** 22 Trafton Lane, Kittery, ME 03904-5401, U.S.A.

HUBER, Jeffrey T(odd). American, b. 1960. **Genres:** Medicine/Health. **Career:** Huber Electric Co. Inc., administrative assistant, 1983-86; New York Public Library, NYC, serials cataloger in Research Division, 1987-88; Brookdale Hospital Medical Center, assistant librarian at Marie Smith Schwartz Medical Library, 1988-89; Whitman-Walker Clinic, AIDS information specialist intern, 1990; Pennsylvania AIDS Education and Training Center, AIDS information specialist intern, 1990; University of Pittsburgh, Pittsburgh, PA, library specialist on Pneumonia Patient Outcomes Research Team, 1991-92, fellow of Section of Medical Informatics, Department of Medicine, 1992-93, visiting lecturer in library science, 1992-93; Texas Woman's University, Denton, assistant professor of library and information studies, 1993-95; Vauderbilt University Medical Center, Nashville, research information scientist in the Active Digital Library, Eskind Biomedical Library, 1995-. Co-chairperson of Task Force on HIV/AIDS, 1993-95. National Clearinghouse for Mental Health Pamphlets, member of advisory committee, 1992-93. Member of National Lesbian and Gay Health Foundation, 1990-, and Global AIDS Information Network, 1993-. **Publications:** EDITOR: How to Find Information About AIDS, 2nd ed, 1992; Dictionary of AIDS Related Terminology, 1993. Work represented in books. Contributor of articles and reviews to periodicals. **Address:** Texas Woman's University, School of Library and Information Studies, PO Box 425438, Denton, TX 76204-5438, U.S.A. **Online address:** jhuber@mail.twu.edu

HUBER, Richard Miller. American, b. 1922. **Genres:** Education, Intellectual history, Race relations, Biography. **Career:** Faculty, dept. of history, 1946-47; Princeton University, New Jersey, depts. of history, politics, English, and American civilization program, 1950-54; trustee, Historical Society of Princeton, 1955; assistant secretary, Society of American Historians, 1956-58; president, Princeton Manor Construction Co., 1958-62; co-ed., New Jersey Historical Series, 1963-67; producer and moderator, WHWH public affairs radio prog., Princeton, NJ, 1965-67; moderator, channel 13 television, NYC, 1967-68; Oral History Project, Princeton, NJ, 1969-71; dean, School of General Studies, 1971-77, and executive director, Division of Continuing Education, Hunter College, City University of New York, 1977-82; assistant director for TV and radio, 1983-84, and special assistant to the chairman, 1984-85, National Endowment for the Humanities; president, Huber Assocs., Washington, DC, 1985-; president, Productions-in-Progress, Inc., 1986-89; consultant on American Studies to the U.S. State Department, 1989-. **Publications:** Big All the Way Through: The Life of Van Santvoord Merle-Smith, 1952; (ed. with W.J. Lane) The New Jersey Historical Series, 31 vols., 1964-65; The American Idea of Success, 1971, 1987; How Professors Play the Cat Guarding the Cream: Why We're Paying More and Getting Less in Higher Education, 1992. **Address:** 2950 Van Ness St NW Ste 926, Washington, DC 20008-1120, U.S.A. **Online address:** www.richardmhuber.com

HUBY, Pamela Margaret. British, b. 1922. **Genres:** Classics, Philosophy. **Career:** Assistant Lecturer, 1949-52, Lecturer, 1952-71, Sr. Lecturer, 1971-83, and Reader in Philosophy, 1983-87, University of Liverpool. Assistant Lecturer, Dept. of Classics, University of Reading, 1944-45; Lecturer in Philosophy, St. Anne's Society, Oxford, 1947-49. **Publications:** Greek Ethics, 1967; Plato and Modern Morality, 1972; Priscian on Theophrastus on Sense-Perception, 1997; Commentary on Theophrastus-Psychology, 1999. CO-AUTHOR: Critical History of Western Philosophy, 1964; Philosophy and Psychical Research, 1976; Stoic and Peripatetic Ethics, 1983; Aristotle on Nature and Living Things, 1986; The Criterion of Truth, 1989; Cicero's Knowledge of the Peripatos, 1989; The Human Embryo, 1990; Logical Foundations, 1991; The Pursuit of Mind, 1991; Aristotle and the Later Tradition, 1991; Theophrastus of Eresus, 1991; The Divine Iamblichus, 1993; Infinity, 1993; Peripatetic Rhetoric after Aristotle, 1994; Historical Foundations of Informal Logic, 1997; Dicaearchus of Messana, 2001; Eudemus of Rhodes, 2002. **Address:** 33a Barton Rd, Harlington, Beds. LU5 6LG, England. **Online address:** pamela-huby@lineone.net

HUCHTHAUSEN, Peter. American, b. 1939. **Genres:** Autobiography/Memoirs. **Career:** U.S. Navy, retired 1990; commanded River Patrol Section in Vietnam War; served as U.S. Naval Attaché in Yugoslavia, Romania, and Soviet Union. **Publications:** (with Nguyen Thi Lung) Echoes of the Mekong, 1996; (with Igor Kurdin and R. Alan White) Hostile Waters, 1997; Frye Island: Maine's Newest Town, a History, 1748-1998, 1998; K-19: The Widowmaker: The Secret Story of the Soviet Nuclear Submarine, 2002; October

Fury, 2002; America's Splendid Little Wars: A Short History of U.S. Military Engagements, 1975-2000, 2003. **Address:** c/o Author Mail, Viking Press, 375 Hudson Street, New York, NY 10014, U.S.A.

HUCK, Arthur. Australian, b. 1926. **Genres:** International relations/Current affairs, Politics/Government. **Career:** Sr. Associate in Political Science, University of Melbourne, since 1989 (joined faculty, 1958; Dean, Faculty of Arts, 1976-81). **Publications:** The Chinese in Australia, 1968; The Security of China, 1970. **Address:** Dept. of Political Science, University of Melbourne, Parkville, VIC 3052, Australia.

HUCKER, Hazel. British, b. 1937. **Genres:** Novels. **Career:** Winchester City Council, Winchester, England, organization and methods officer, 1969-71; teacher of history and economics at county schools in Hampshire, England, 1972-78. Justice of the Peace, 1982-98. **Publications:** NOVELS: The Aftermath of Oliver, 1993; A Dangerous Happiness, 1994; Cousin Susannah, 1995; Trials of Friendship, 1996; The Real Claudia Charles, 1998; Changing Status, 2000. **Address:** c/o MBA Literary Agents, 62 Grafton Way, London W1P 5LD, England.

HUDAK, Michal. Slovak, b. 1956. **Genres:** Children's fiction, Illustrations. **Career:** Lundquist & Carrier, Stockholm, Sweden, architect, 1985-88; Glimakra FHS, Glimakra, Sweden, teacher, 1994-97; artist and illustrator. Works included in exhibitions throughout Scandinavia. Work represented in private collections. **Publications:** AND ILLUSTRATOR: Vem spelar i natten?, 1981; Skeppet över Gamla Stan, 1988; Skeppet och eldstenen, 1990; Herden och den 100 faren, 1998, trans. as The Shepherd and the 100 Sheep, 1999; Kalabaliken i Betlehem, 2001, trans. as The Uproar in Bethlehem, 2001. Illustrator of books published in Swedish, illustrations also represented in anthologies and textbooks. **Address:** c/o Author Mail, Liturgical Press, St. John's Abbey, PO Box 7500, Collegeville, MN 56321, U.S.A. **Online address:** samhudak@spray.se

HUDDLE, David. American, b. 1942. **Genres:** Novels, Novellas/Short stories, Poetry, Writing/Journalism. **Career:** University of Vermont, Burlington, instructor to associate professor, 1971-81, professor of English, 1982-. Virginia Center for the Creative Arts, Sweet Briar, fellow, 1976, 1982; Bread Loaf Writers' Conference, William Raney Fellow in Prose, 1977, faculty member, 1989-; National Endowment for the Arts Fellow in Creative Writing, 1978, 1987; Bread Loaf School of English, Middlebury, VT, faculty member, 1979, 1985-; Middlebury College, Vermont, visiting professor, 1981-82. Recipient: James Wright Prize for Poetry, Mid-American Review, 1982. **Publications:** STORY COLLECTIONS: A Dream with No Stump Roots in It, 1975; Only the Little Bone, 1986; The High Spirits: Stories of Men and Women, 1989; Intimates, 1993; Not: A Trio-A Novella and Two Stories, 2000. POETRY: Paper Boy, 1979; Stopping by Home, 1988; The Nature of Yearning, 1992; Summer Lake: New & Selected Poems, 1999; Grayscale, 2004. NOVELS: The Story of 2 Million Years, 1999; La Tour Dreams of the Wolf Girl, 2002. OTHER: The Writing Habit: Essays on Writing, 1992; A David Huddle Reader (poetry, fiction, and essays), 1994. **Address:** 34 N Williams St, Burlington, VT 05401, U.S.A. **Online address:** dhuddle@zoo.uvm.edu

HUDDLESTON, Mark W. American, b. 1950. **Genres:** Public/Social administration. **Career:** State University of New York at Buffalo, assistant professor of political science, 1977-80; University of Delaware, Newark, assistant professor, 1980-83, associate professor, 1983-94, professor of political science, 1994-. Consultant to U.S. Office of Personnel Management, U.S. General Accounting Office, and U.S. Agency for International Development. **Publications:** Comparative Public Administration, 1984; The Government's Managers, 1987; The Public Administration Workbook, 1987, 3rd ed., 1996; (with W.W. Boyer) The Higher Civil Service in the United States, 1996. Contributor to journals. **Address:** Department of Political Science, University of Delaware, Newark, DE 19716, U.S.A.

HUDLER, Ad. American, b. 1965?. **Genres:** Novels. **Career:** Writer. Fort Myers News-Press, Fort Myers, FL, journalist. **Publications:** Househusband, 2002. **Address:** c/o Author Mail, Random House, 1540 Broadway, New York, NY 10036, U.S.A. **Online address:** ad@adhudler.com

HUDNUT, Robert K. American, b. 1934. **Genres:** Theology/Religion. **Career:** Trustee, Asheville School, North Carolina, 1978-. Pastor, St. Luke Presbyterian Church, Wayzata, Minnesota, 1962-73; Trustee, Princeton University, 1972-76; Executive Director, Minnesota Public Interest Research Group, 1973-75; Pastor, Winnetka Presbyterian Church, Illinois, 1975-94. **Publications:** Surprised by God: What It Means to Be a Minister in Middle-Class America Today, 1967; A Sensitive Man and the Christ, 1969; An Ac-

tive Man and the Christ, 1971; A Thinking Man and the Christ, 1971; The Sleeping Giant: Arousing Church Power in America, 1971; Arousing the Sleeping Giant: How to Organize Your Church for Action, 1973; Church Growth Is Not the Point, 1975; The Bootstrap Fallacy: What the Self-Help Books Don't Tell You, 1978; This People, This Parish, 1986; Meeting God in the Darkness, 1989; Emerson's Aesthetic, 1996; Call Waiting: How to Hear God Speak, 1999. **Address:** 7145 65th St., Cottage Grove, MN 55016, U.S.A.

HUDSON, Charles. American, b. 1932. **Genres:** Anthropology/Ethnology, History. **Career:** University of Georgia, Athens, assistant professor, 1964-68, associate professor, 1968-77, professor of anthropology, 1977-. **Publications:** The Catawba Nation, 1970; The Southeastern Indians, 1976; Elements of Southeastern Indian Religion, 1984; The Juan Pardo Expeditions, 1990; (with J. Milanich) Hernando de Soto and the Indians of Florida, 1993; Knights of Spain, Warriors of the Sun: Hernando deSoto and the South's Ancient Chiefdoms, 1997; Conversations with the High Priest of Coosa, 2003. EDITOR: Red, White, and Black: Symposium on Indians in the Old South, 1971; Four Centuries of Southern Indians, 1974; Black Drink: A Native American Tea, 1978; Ethnology of the Southeastern Indians: A Sourcebook, 1985; (with C. Tesser) The Forgotten Centuries, 1994. **Address:** Dept of Anthropology, University of Georgia, Athens, GA 30602, U.S.A. **Online address:** chudson@arches.uga.edu

HUDSON, Jeffrey. See **CRICHTON, (John) Michael.**

HUDSON, John B. American, b. 1934. **Genres:** Sciences. **Career:** Rensselaer Polytechnic Institute, Troy, NY, research associate, 1963-65, assistant professor, 1965-67, associate professor, 1967-72, professor of materials engineering, 1972-. Technical consultant to business and industry. **Publications:** Surface Science: An Introduction, 1992; Thermodynamics of Materials, 1996. **Address:** Department of Materials Engineering, Rensselaer Polytechnic Institute, Troy, NY 12180, U.S.A.

HUDSON, Liam. See Obituaries.

HUDSON, Maggie. See **PEMBERTON, Margaret.**

HUDSON, Miles (Matthew Lee). British, b. 1925. **Genres:** History, Politics/Government, Third World. **Career:** British Army, career officer, 1943-64, retiring as lieutenant colonel; Conservative Research Department, 1964-70, head of overseas affairs, 1968-70; political adviser to the British foreign secretary, 1970-74; farmer near Basingstoke, England, 1974-. Secretary of Hansard Commission for Electoral Reform, 1976; director of Conservative Group for Europe, 1977; member of Boyd Commission, Rhodesia, 1979. **Publications:** Triumph of Tragedy?: Rhodesia to Zimbabwe, 1981; (with J. Stanier) War and the Media: A Random Searchlight, 1997; Assassination, 2000; Intervention in Russia, 1918-20, 2004. **Address:** Priors Farm, Mattingley, Hook, Hants., England.

HUDSON, Wade. American, b. 1946. **Genres:** Children's non-fiction. **Career:** Just Us Books, Orange, NJ, co-owner, 1987-; writer. **Publications:** (with V.W. Wesley) Afro-Bets Book of Black Heroes from A to Z: An Introduction to Important Black Achievers, 1988; Afro-Bets Alphabet Rap Song, 1990; Jamal's Busy Day, 1991; Afro-Bets Kids: I'm Gonna Be!, 1993; I Love My Family, 1993; (ed.) Pass It On: African-American Poetry for Children, 1993; Beebe's Lonely Saturday; (with C.W. Hudson) How Sweet the Sound: African American Songs for Children, 1995; Great Black Heroes: Five Brave Explorers, 1995; (with C.W. Hudson) Kids Book of Wisdom, 1995; Great Black Heroes: Five Notable Inventors, 1997; (with C.W. Hudson) In Praise of Our Fathers and Our Mothers, 1997; NEATE: Anthony's Big Surprise, 1998; Robo's Favorite Places, 1999; Great Black Heroes: Five Famous Freedom Fighters, 2001; Book of Black Heroes, vol. 3: Scientists, Healers & Inventors, 2002; God Smiles When, 2003; God Gave Me, 2003; Poetry from the Masters: The Pioneers, 2003; Powerful Words, 2004. STAGE PLAYS: Freedom Star; Sam Carter Belongs Here; The Return; A House Divided...; Black Love Story; Dead End. **Address:** Just Us Books, 356 Glenwood Ave 3rd Fl, East Orange, NJ 07017, U.S.A. **Online address:** wadehudson@justusbooks.com

HUFF, Brent. American, b. 1961. **Genres:** Film. **Career:** Actor, director, and screenwriter. **Publications:** SCREENPLAYS: (with Douglas L. Walton) The Bad Pack, 1998. **Address:** 2203 Ridgemont Dr, Los Angeles, CA 90046, U.S.A.

HUFF, Toby E. American, b. 1942. **Genres:** Sciences, Social sciences. **Career:** University of Massachusetts at Dartmouth, North Dartmouth, chancellor professor of sociology, 1971-. Institute for Advanced Study, Princeton, NJ, member, 1978-79. **Publications:** Max Weber and the Methodology of the Social Sciences, 1984; The Rise of Early Modern Science, 1993. EDITOR: On the Roads to Modernity, 1981; Max Weber and Islam, 1999. **Address:** Center for Policy Analysis, University of Massachusetts at Dartmouth, 285 Old Westport Rd, North Dartmouth, MA 02747, U.S.A. **Online address:** THuff@umassd.edu

HUFFER, Lynne. American, b. 1960. **Genres:** Women's studies and issues. **Career:** Yale University, New Haven, CT, assistant professor, then associate professor of French literature and women's studies, 1989-98; Rice University, Houston, TX, professor of French studies and women and gender studies, 1998-. **Publications:** Another Colette, 1992; Maternal Pasts, Feminist Futures, 1998. **Address:** Department of French Studies, Rice University, PO Box 1892, Houston, TX 77251-1892, U.S.A. **Online address:** huffer@rice.edu

HUFFINGTON, Arianna. Also writes as Arianna Stassinopoulos. Greek, b. 1950. **Genres:** Social commentary, Women's studies and issues, Biography. **Career:** Syndicated columnist. **Publications:** The Female Woman, 1973; The Other Revolution, 1978; Maria: Beyond the Callas Legend, 1980; The Gods of Greece, 1983; Picasso, Creator and Destroyer, 1988; The Fourth Instinct: The Call of the Soul, 1995; How to Overthrow the Government, 2000. **Address:** c/o Harriet Sternberg Management, 3667 Valley Meadow Rd., Sherman Oaks, CA 91403, U.S.A.

HUFFMAN, Jennifer Lee. American, b. 1950. **Genres:** Adult non-fiction. **Career:** High school French teacher, Albion, MI, 1973-75; City of Lansing, MI, clerk and receptionist for mayor's office, 1975-76; manager of an apartment complex in Lansing, 1976-78; GMI Engineering and Management Institute, Flint, MI, assistant director of financial aid, 1983-85; Rehabitat Systems of Michigan (adult foster care homes), director of administration and finance, 1986-96; Jennifer Lee Huffman Family Limited Partnership, general partner, 1989-. Torch Lake Publishing, owner. Bas de Laine Investment Club, president. **Publications:** (with others) What Fits You? (career planning manual), 1980; Money and Marriage: Choices, Rights, and Responsibilities, 1999. Contributor to newspapers. **Address:** Torch Lake Publishing, PO Box R, Petoskey, MI 49770, U.S.A. **Online address:** torchlake@racc2000.com

HUGDAHL, Kenneth. Swedish, b. 1948. **Genres:** Psychology. **Career:** Uppsala University, Uppsala, Sweden, senior lecturer in psychology, 1980-84; University of Bergen, Bergen, Norway, professor of biological and medical psychology, 1984-. **Publications:** Psychophysiology, 1995. EDITOR: Handbook of Dichotic Listening, 1988; Brain Asymmetry, 1995. **Address:** Department of Biological and Medical Psychology, University of Bergen, Bergen, Norway. **Online address:** hugdahl@psych.uib.no

HUGGETT, Frank Edward. British, b. 1924. **Genres:** Plays/Screenplays, History, Local history/Rural topics, Travel/Exploration. **Career:** Sub-Ed., Daily Telegraph, 1951-53; Ed., Look and Listen, 1956-57; Visiting Lecturer, Polytechnic of Central London, 1957-65, and Ministry of Defence, 1965-72. **Publications:** South of Lisbon, 1960; Farming, 1963, 3rd ed., 1975; The Newspapers, 1969; Modern Belgium, 1969; A Short History of Farming, 1970; Nineteenth Century Reformers, 1971; How It Happened, 1971; Nineteenth Century Statesmen, 1972; Travel and Communications, 1972; A Day in the Life of a Victorian Farm Worker, 1972; The Modern Netherlands, 1972; The Battle for Reform 1815-32, 1973; A Day in the Life of a Victorian Factory Worker, 1973; Factory Life and Work, 1973; The Dutch Today, 2nd ed., 1974; History Not So Long Ago (radio drama), 1974-75; A Dictionary of British History 1815-1973, 1975; The Land Question and European Society, 1975; Life and Work at Sea, 1975; Slavery and the Slave Trade, 1975; Life below Stairs, 1977; Victorian England as Seen by Punch, 1978; Goodnight Sweetheart, 1979; Carriages at Eight, 1979; Cartoonists at War, 1981; The Dutch Connection, 1982; Teachers, 1986. **Address:** c/o Dufour Editions, Inc., PO Box 7, Chester Springs, PA 19425-0007, U.S.A. **Online address:** frankhuggett@aol.com

HUGHART, Barry. American, b. 1934. **Genres:** Novels, Plays/Screenplays. **Career:** Affiliated with TechTop (military surplus weapons supplier) in the Near East, 1960-63, and in the Far East, 1963-65; Lenox Hill Book Shop, New York City, manager, 1965-70; writer, 1970. Worked as dialogue writer for films. Occasional lecturer at the University of Arizona. **Publications:** Bridge of Birds: A Novel of an Ancient China that Never Was, 1984; The Story of the Stone (novel), 1988; Eight Skilled Gentlemen (novel), 1991; Bridge of Birds (screenplay). Contributor to periodicals. **Address:** 2928 N Beverly Ave, Tucson, AZ 85712, U.S.A. **Online address:** yrrab@spearnet.net

HUGHES, Colin Anfield. Australian (born Bahamas), b. 1930. **Genres:** Politics/Government. **Career:** Professor of Political Science, University of Queensland, St. Lucia, 1965-75, 1989-95; Professorial Fellow in Political Science, Australian National University, Canberra, 1975-84; Electoral Commissioner, 1984-89. **Publications:** (with J.S. Western) The Prime Minister's Policy Speech: A Case Study in Televised Politics, 1966; Images and Issues: The Queensland State Elections of 1963 and 1966, 1969; (with J.S. Western) The Mass Media in Australia, 1972; Mr. Prime Minister: Australian Prime Ministers 1901-1972, 1976; The Government of Queensland, 1980; Race and Politics in the Bahamas, 1981. EDITOR: (with D.G. Bettison and P.W. van der Veur) The Papua New Guinea Elections 1964, 1965; Readings in Australian Government, 1968; (with B.D. Graham) A Handbook of Australian Government and Politics 1890-1964, 1968; (with D.J. Murphy and R.B. Joyce) Prelude to Power, 1970; (with I.F. Nicolson) Pacific Polities, 1972; (with B.D. Graham) Voting for the Australian House of Representatives 1901-1964, 1974; (with B.D. Graham) Voting for the Queensland Legislative Assembly 1890-1964, 1974; (with B.D. Graham) Voting for the New South Wales Legislative Assembly 1890-1964, 1975; (with B.D. Graham) Voting for the Victoria Legislative Assembly 1890-1964, 1975; (with B.D. Graham) Voting for the South Australian, Western Australian and Tasmanian Lower Houses 1890-1964, 1976; A Handbook of Australian Government and Politics, 1965-74, 1977, 1975-84, 1987, 1985-99, 2002; (with D.J. Murphy and R.B. Joyce) Labor in Power: The Labor Party in Queensland 1915-1957, 1980; Voting for the Australian State Lower Houses, 2 vols., 1981-87; (with B.J. Costar) Labor to Office: The Victorian State Election 1982, 1983; (with D. Aitkin) Voting for the Australian State Upper Houses 1890-1984, 1986; (with R. Whip) Political Crossroads: The 1989 Queensland Election, 1991; Voting for the Australian House of Representatives 1965-84, 1995. **Address:** School of Political Science, University of Queensland, St. Lucia, QLD 4072, Australia.

HUGHES, Dean. American, b. 1943. **Genres:** Novels, Romance/Historical, Children's fiction, Young adult fiction, Children's non-fiction. **Career:** Central Missouri State University, Warrensburg, associate professor of English, 1972-80; Brigham Young University, Provo, UT, part-time visiting professor, 1980-82, guest professor, 1997-98, associate professor, 1998-2002; writer, part-time editor, and consultant, 1980-89, 2002-. **Publications:** FOR YOUNG ADULTS. FICTION: Nutty for President, 1981; Hooper Haller, 1981; Honestly, Myron, 1982; Switching Tracks, 1982; Jenny Haller, 1983; Millie Willenheimer and the Chestnut Corporation, 1983; Nutty and the Case of the Mastermind Thief, 1985; Nutty and the Case of the Ski-Slope Spy, 1985; Brothers, 1986; Nutty Can't Miss, 1987; Theo Zephyr, 1987; Nutty Knows All, 1988; Family Pose, 1989 as Family Picture, 1990; Jelly's Circus, 1989; Nutty the Movie Star, 1989; End of the Race, 1993; Nutty's Ghost, 1993; Re-Elect Nutty!, 1994; The Trophy, 1994; Backup Soccer Star, 1995; Brad and Butter: Play Ball!, 1998; Search and Destroy, 2005. ANGEL PARK ALL-STARS SERIES: Making the Team, 1990; Big Base Hit, 1990; Winning Streak, 1990; What a Catch!, 1990; Rookie Star, 1990; Pressure Play, 1990; Line Drive, 1990; Championship Game, 1990; Superstar Team, 1991; Stroke of Luck, 1991; Safe at First, 1991; Up to Bat, 1991; Play-Off, 1991; All Together Now, 1991. ANGEL PARK SOCCER STARS SERIES: Kickoff Time, 1991; Defense!, 1991; Victory Goal, 1992; Psyched!, 1992; Backup Goalie, 1992; Total Soccer, 1992; Shake Up, 1993; Quick Moves, 1993. ANGEL PARK HOOP STARS SERIES: Nothing but Net, 1992; Point Guard, 1992; Go to the Hoop!, 1993; On the Line, 1993. ANGEL PARK KARATE STARS SERIES: Find the Power, 1994. ANGEL PARK FOOTBALL STARS SERIES: Quarterback Hero, 1994. LUCKY SERIES: Lucky Breaks Loose, 1990; Lucky's Crash Landing, 1990; Lucky's Gold Mine, 1990; Lucky Fights Back, 1991; Lucky's Mud Festival, 1991; Lucky the Detective, 1992; Lucky's Tricks, 1992; Lucky's Cool Club, 1993; Lucky in Love, 1993; Lucky Comes Home, 1994. SCRAPPERS SERIES: Play Ball!, 1999; Home Run Hero, 1999; Team Player, 1999; Now We're Talking, 1999; Bases Loaded, 1999; No Easy Out, 1999; Take Your Base, 1999; No Fear, 1999; Grand Slam, 1999; Soldier Boys, 2001. MORMON HISTORICAL FICTION SERIES: Under the Same Stars, 1979; As Wide as the River, 1980; Facing the Enemy, 1982; Cornbread and Prayer, 1988. OTHER: Romance and Psychological Realism in William Godwin's Novels, 1981; The Mormon Church: A Basic History, 1986; (with T. Hughes) Baseball Tips (nonfiction), 1993; (with T. Hughes) Great Stories from Mormon History (nonfiction), 1995; (with T. Hughes) We'll Bring the World His Truth (nonfiction), 1995. FOR ADULTS. FICTION: Lullaby and Goodnight, 1992. CHILDREN OF THE PROMISE SERIES: Rumors of War, 1997; Since You Went Away, 1997; Far from Home, 1998; I'll Be Seeing You, 1999; As Long as I Have You, 2000; Midway to Heaven, 2004. HEARTS OF THE CHILDREN SERIES: The Writing on the Wall, 2001; Troubled Waters, 2002; How Many Roads?, 2003. NONFICTION: Lullaby and Goodnight, 1992. **Address:** PO Box 307, Midway, UT 84049, U.S.A. **Online address:** DTHughes@qwest.net

HUGHES, Gerard J. (born Scotland). **Genres:** Philosophy, Theology/Religion. **Career:** Ordained Roman Catholic priest, 1967. Heythorp College, University of London, London, England, lecturer, 1970-, vice-principal, 1984-; British Province, Vice-Provincial, 1982-88; Oxford University, Oxford, England, master of Campion Hall, 1998-. **Publications:** Authority in Morals: An Essay in Christian Ethics, 1978, 1978; Moral Decisions, 1980; (editor) The Philosophical Assessment of Theology: Essays in Honour of Frederick C. Copleston, 1987; The Nature of God, 1995; Routledge Philosophy Guidebook to Aristotle on Ethics, 2001. **Address:** Campion Hall, Oxford University, Oxford OXI 1QS, England. **Online address:** gerard.hughes@campion-hall.oxford.ac.uk

HUGHES, Glenn. American, b. 1951. **Genres:** Poetry, Philosophy. **Career:** Simmons College, Boston, MA, assistant professor of philosophy, 1988-90; St. Mary's University, San Antonio, TX, associate professor of philosophy, 1990-. **Publications:** Mystery and Myth in the Philosophy of Eric Voegelin, 1993. EDITOR: The Politics of the Soul: Eric Voegelin on Religious Experience, 1999; (co-) Politics, Order and History: Themes in the Work of Eric Voegelin, 2001. Contributor of poems to magazines. **Address:** Department of Philosophy, St. Mary's University, 1 Camino Santa Maria, San Antonio, TX 78228, U.S.A. **Online address:** ghughes@stmarytx.edu

HUGHES, Glyn. British. **Genres:** Novels, Plays/Screenplays, Poetry, Autobiography/Memoirs. **Career:** Arts Council Writer-in-Residence, Lincoln, 1979-81, Hampshire, 1982-84, and Eastwood, Notts., 1985. **Publications:** POETRY: The Stanedge Bull, 1966; Almost-Love Poems, 1968; Love on the Moor: Poems 1965-1968, 1969; Neighbours: Poems 1965-1969, 1970; Presence, 1971; Toward the Sun: Poems and Photographs, 1971; Rest the Poor Struggler: Poems 1969-1971, 1972; Alibis and Convictions, 1978; Best of Neighbours: New and Selected Poems, 1979; (ed.) Selected Poems of Samuel Laycock, 1981. NOVELS: Where I Used to Play on the Green, 1981; The Hawthorn Goddess, 1984; The Rape of the Rose, 1987; The Antique Collector, 1990; Roth, 1992; Bronte, 1996. RADIO PLAYS: The Yorkshire Women (in verse), 1978; Dreamers, 1979; Pursuit, 2000; Mr Lowry's Loves, 2001; Glorious John, 2002. OTHER: Millstone Grit (autobiography), 1975; Fair Prospects: Journeys in Greece, 1976; Glyn Hughes's Yorkshire, 1985. **Address:** 1 Mill Bank Rd, Sowerby Bridge, Yorks HX6 3DY, England. **Online address:** Glyn.millbank@virgin.net

HUGHES, Judith M. American, b. 1941. **Genres:** Intellectual history. **Career:** Harvard University, Cambridge, MA, assistant professor of social studies, 1970-75; University of California at San Diego, associate professor, 1975-84, professor of history, 1984-. **Publications:** To the Maginot Line: The Politics of French Military Preparation in the 1920s, 1971; Emotion and High Politics: Personal Relations at the Summit in Late Nineteenth-Century Britain and Germany, 1983; Reshaping the Psychoanalytic Domain: The Work of Melanie Klein, W.R.D. Fairbairn and D.W. Winnicott, 1989; From Freud's Consulting Room: The Unconscious in a Scientific Age, 1994; Freudian Analysts/Feminist Issues, 1999; From Obstacle to Ally: The Evolution of Psychoanalytic Practice, 2004. **Address:** 8531 Avenida de las Ondas, La Jolla, CA 92037, U.S.A. **Online address:** jhughes@ucsd.edu

HUGHES, Matilda. See MACLEOD, Charlotte (Matilda) in the Obituaries.

HUGHES, Matt. See MATTHEWS, Jack.

HUGHES, Phillip William. Australian, b. 1926. **Genres:** Education, Mathematics/Statistics, Social commentary. **Career:** Principal, Hobart Teachers College, Tasmania, 1963-65; Deputy Director General, Education Dept., Tas., 1965-69; Head, School of Education, Canberra College of Advanced Education, ACT, 1970-80; Professor of Education, University of Tasmania, 1981-91; CEO, Australian Prins Ctr, Melbourne, 1995-97. Consultant. **Publications:** Academic Achievement at the University, 1960; Statistics of Academic Progress 1950-59, 1960; (with J.A. Pitman) An Introduction to Calculus, 1963; Mathematics for 20th Century Schools, 1964; (with K.A. Wilson) Explorations in Mathematics, 1965; An Introduction to Sets, 1966; (with K.A. Wilson) The World of Mathematics 1-4, 1966-67; The Teacher's Role in Curriculum Design, 1973; A Design for the Governance and Organisation of Education in the Australian Capital Territory, 1973; (with W. Mulford) The Development of an Independent Education Authority, 1978; (with C. Collins) Where Junior Secondary Schools Are Heading, 1988; Quality in Education, 1988; Identification and Development of Intellectual Ability, 1990; Teachers' Professional Development, 1991; Assessment of the Value of Hospital Training for APs, 1993; Issues in Education in Asia and the Pacific, 1994; The Curriculum Redefined: Schooling for the 21st Century, 1994; Education for the 21st Century for Asia and the Pacific, 1998; Teach-

ers Make a Difference, 2000; Monitoring Curriculum Reform, 2002; Reforming Secondary Education, 2003; How Do Teachers Influence People, 2004. **Address:** 20 Kookaburra Ridge, Bruce, ACT 2617, Australia. **Online address:** Phillip.Hughes@anu.edu.au

HUGHES, (James) Quentin. British, b. 1920. **Genres:** Architecture, History, Military/Defense/Arms control, Travel/Exploration. **Career:** Hon. Research Fellow, University of Liverpool, 1989- (University Reader, 1967-89). Ed., Fort mag. Dean of the Faculty of Engineering and Architecture, and Professor of Architecture, Royal University of Malta, 1968-72; Hon. Professor, J.M. University, 1999; OBE. **Publications:** The Building of Malta, 1956; (with N. Lynton) Renaissance Architecture, 1962; Seaport: Architecture and Townscape in Liverpool, 1964, 2nd ed., 1994; Fortress, 1966; (ed.) Le Fabbriche e i Desegni di Andrea Palladio, by Ottavio Bertotti Scamozzi, 1968; Liverpool, 1970; Malta, 1972; Military Architecture, 1974, 1991; Britain in the Mediterranean and the Defence of Her Naval Stations, 1981; Military Architecture, 1991; Malta, a Guide to the Fortifications, 1993; (with A. Migos) Strong as the Rock of Gibraltar, 1995; Who Cares Who Wins, 1998; Liverpool: A City of Architecture, 1999: (with C. Thake) Malta: The Baroque Island, 2003. **Address:** 10A Fulwood Park, Liverpool L17 5AH, England. **Online address:** jqh@quentinhugh.u-net.com

HUGHES, Rhys H(enry). Welsh, b. 1966. **Genres:** Novellas/Short stories. **Publications:** SHORT STORIES/NOVELLAS: Worming the Harpy and Other Bitter Pills, 1995; Eyelidiad, 1997; Rawhead and Bloody Bones, 1998; The Smell of Telescopes, 1999; Stories from a Lost Anthology, 2002; Journeys beyond Advice, 2002; A New Universal History of Infamy, 2003. CHAPBOOKS: Romance with Capsicum and Other Piquant Assignations, 1995; In Praise of Ridicule (poetry), 2003. NOVELS: Nowhere near Milk Wood, 2002; The Percolated Stars, 2003; Engelbrecht Again, 2003. Contributor of short stories to journals of fiction and anthologies. **Address:** 133 Rhondda St, Swansea SA1 6EU, Wales. **Online address:** rhysaurus@yahoo.co.uk

HUGHES, Richard (Edward). American, b. 1950. **Genres:** Novels. **Career:** Played semi-professional baseball; American Samoa Community College, Pago Pago, professor of English as a second language, 1984-86; Cambria English Language Institute, Los Angeles, CA, instructor in English, 1986-88; freelance writer, 1988-. **Publications:** NOVELS: Isla Grande, 1994; Legends of the Heart, 1997. Contributor of poems to magazines and anthologies. **Address:** Casilla 6572, Torres Sofer, Cochabamba, Bolivia.

HUGHES, Richard T(homas). American, b. 1943. **Genres:** Theology/Religion. **Career:** Pepperdine University, Malibu, CA, assistant professor, 1971-76, professor of religion, 1988-94, acting chairperson of division, 1992-93, Distinguished Professor, 1994-; Southwest Missouri State University, Springfield, associate professor to professor of religious studies, 1977-82; Abilene Christian University, Abilene, TX, scholar in residence, 1982-84, 1986-88, professor of history, 1983-88, department head, 1984-86. University of Iowa, visiting associate professor, 1977; lecturer at educational institutions. **Publications:** (with L. Allen and M. Weed) The Worldly Church: A Call for Biblical Renewal, 1988; (with Allen) Discovering Our Roots: The Ancestry of Churches of Christ, 1988; (with Allen) Illusions of Innocence: Protestant Primitivism in America, 1630-1875, 1988; Reviving the Ancient Faith: The Story of Churches of Christ in America, 1996; How Christian Faith Can Sustain the Life of the Mind, 2001; Myths America Lives By, 2003; The Vocation of the Christian Scholar, 2005. EDITOR: The American Quest for the Primitive Church, 1988; The Primitive Church in the Modern World, 1995; (with T.F. Schlabach) Proclaim Peace: Christian Pacifism from Unexpected Quarters, 1997; (with W.B. Adrian) Models for Christian Higher Education: Strategies for Survival and Success in the 21st Century, 1997. Contributor to books and periodicals. **Address:** Religion Division, Pepperdine University, Malibu, CA 90263, U.S.A.

HUGHES, Shirley. British, b. 1927. **Genres:** Children's fiction, Autobiography/Memoirs. **Career:** Author and illustrator. **Publications:** Lucy and Tom series, 6 vols., 1960-87; The Trouble with Jack, 1970; Sally's Secret, 1973; Helpers, 1975; It's Too Frightening for Me, 1977; Dogger, 1977; Moving Molly, 1978; Up and Up, 1979; Here Comes Charlie Moon, 1980; Alfie Gets in First, 1981; Alfie's Feet, 1982; Charlie Moon and the Big Bonanza Bust-Up, 1982; Alfie Gives a Hand, 1983; An Evening at Alfie's, 1984; The Nursery Collection, 6 vols., 1985-86; Another Helping of Chips, 1986; Out and About, 1988; The Big Alfie and Annie Rose Story Book, 1988; Tales of Trotter Street, 4 vols., 1988-91; The Big Alfie Out of Doors Story Book, 1992; Giving, 1993; Bouncing, 1993; Stories by Firelight, 1993; Chatting Hiding, 1994; Rhymes for Annie Rose, 1995; Enchantment in the Garden, 1996; Being Together, 1997; Playing, 1997; All about Alfie, 1997;

Alfie and the Birthday Surprise, 1998; Alfie's Alphabet, 1998; The Lion and the Unicorn, 1998; Let's Join In: Four Stories, 1999; Abel's Moon, 1999; Alfie's 1 2 3, 2000; The Shirley Hughes Collection, 2000; Alfie Weather, 2001; Annie Rose Is My Little Sister, 2002; A Life Drawing: Recollections of an Illustrator, 2002; Ollie and Me, 2003; Ella's Big Chance, 2003; Alfie Wins a Prize, 2004.

HUGHES, Tracy. *See* **BLACKSTOCK, Terri.**

HUGHES-HALLETT, Lucy. British, b. 1951. **Genres:** Biography, History. **Career:** Writer. Vogue magazine, writer, 1974-79; London Evening Standard, television critic, 1983-87; Sunday Times, Books Section, reviewer, 1987-. **Publications:** Cleopatra: Histories, Dreams, and Distortions, 1990. **Address:** c/o Felicity Rubinstein, Lutyers and Rubinstein, 231 Westbourne Park Road, London W11 1EB, England.

HUGON, Anne. French, b. 1965. **Genres:** History, Third World. **Career:** University of Lyon, Lyon, France, assistant lecturer in history, 1990-. Translator from English into French. **Publications:** L'Afrique des Explorateurs, 1991, trans as The Exploration of Africa, 1993; (trans. from English) Mary Kingsley, Une odyssee Africaine (title means: Travels in West Africa), 1992; Towards Timbuctoo (in French), 1994. **Address:** 23 rue Berthollet, 75005 Paris, France.

HUHNE, Christopher. British, b. 1954. **Genres:** Economics, Politics/Government, Money/Finance. **Career:** Freelance journalist in India, 1975-76; Liverpool Daily Post and Echo, Liverpool, England, graduate trainee, 1976-77; Economist, London, England, Brussels correspondent, 1977-80; Guardian, London, economic leader writer, 1980-85, economic editor and weekly columnist, 1985-90; The Independent, and The Independent on Sunday, London, business and economics editor and department head, 1990-94; IBCA Ltd, economics director, 1994-97, group managing director, 1997-99; European Parliament, member, 1999-. Occasional broadcaster and lecturer. SDP Liberal Alliance candidate for Parliament for Reading East, 1983, and Oxford West and Abingdon, 1987. **Publications:** Issues in the 1984 European Parliamentary Elections, 1984; (with H. Lever) Debt and Danger: The World Financial Crisis, 1985, rev. ed., 1987; The Forces Shaping British Attitudes towards the European Community, 1985; Real World Economics, 1990; (with M. Emerson) The ECU Report, 1991; (with J. Kordor) Both Sides of the Coin, 1999. **Address:** European Parliament, Rue Wiertz, B-1047 Brussels, Belgium. **Online address:** chuhne@eruoparl.eu.int

HUIZENGA, John R(obert). American, b. 1921. **Genres:** Physics, Chemistry. **Career:** Manhattan Wartime Project, Oak Ridge, TN, laboratory supervisor, 1944-46; Calvin College, Grand Rapids, MI, instructor in chemistry, 1946-47; Argonne National Laboratory, associate scientist, 1949-57, senior scientist, 1958-67; University of Chicago, Chicago, IL, professorial lecturer, 1963-67; University of Rochester, Rochester, NY, professor of chemistry and physics, 1967-78, Tracy H. Harris Professor of Chemistry and Physics, 1978-91, chair of chemistry department, 1983-88, Tracy H. Harris Professor Emeritus of Chemistry and Physics, 1991-. Visiting professor at US institutions. Participant in congressional hearings on atomic energy, 1958; U.S. delegation scientific advisor to the Second International Conference on the Peaceful Uses of Atomic Energy, 1958; chair of Gordon Research Conference on Nuclear Chemistry, 1958; member of U.S. delegation visiting Soviet laboratories, 1966; organizer of Third International Symposium on the Physics and Chemistry of Fission, (Rochester, NY), 1973; chair of National Academy of Science-National Research Council Committee on Nuclear Science, 1974-77; chair of the subcommittee on University Research and Education in Nuclear Science for the Department of Energy/National Science Foundation Nuclear Science Advisory Committee, 1980-83; member of the U.S. Energy Research Advisory Board, 1984-90. Member of government, academic, and national laboratory advisory committees. **Publications:** (with R. Vandenbosch) Nuclear Fission, 1973; Cold Fusion: The Scientific Fiasco of the Century, 1992, updated ed., 1993; (with W.U. Schroeder) Damped Nuclear Reactions, 1994. **Address:** 43 McMichael Drive, Pinehurst, NC 28374, U.S.A.

HULL, David Stewart. *See* Obituaries.

HULL, Isabel V. American, b. 1949. **Genres:** History. **Career:** Cornell University, Ithaca, NY, assistant professor to professor of history, 1977-. **Publications:** The Entourage of Kaiser Wilhelm III, 1888-1918, 1982; Sexuality, State, and Civil Society in Germany, 1700-1815, 1996. **Address:** Department of History, Cornell University, McGraw Hall, Ithaca, NY 14853, U.S.A.

HULL, John M. Australian/British, b. 1935. **Genres:** Education, Theology/Religion. **Career:** Schoolteacher, Melbourne, Australia, 1957-59, and London, England, 1962-66; Westhill College, Birmingham, England, lecturer, 1966-68; University of Birmingham, lecturer in religious education, 1968-78, senior lecturer, 1978-86, reader, 1986-89, professor of religious education, 1989-2002, dean of faculty of education and continuing studies, 1990-93, emeritus professor, 2002-. British Journal of Religious Education, editor, 1971-96. **Publications:** Sense and Nonsense about God, 1974, 2nd ed., 1999; Hellenistic Magic and the Synoptic Tradition, 1974; School Worship: An Obituary, 1975; Studies in Religion and Education, 1984; What Prevents Christian Adults from Learning?, 1985; Touching the Rock: An Experience of Blindness, 1990; God-Talk with Young Children: Notes for Parents and Teachers, 1991; (with M.H. Grimmitt, J. Grove, and L. Spencer) A Gift to the Child: Religious Education in the Primary School, 1991; Mish-Mash: Religious Education in Multi-Cultural Britain: A Study of Metaphor, 1991; On Sight & Insight: A Journey into the World of Blindness, 1997; Utopian Whispers: Moral, Religious & Spiritual Values in Schools, 1998; In the Beginning There Was Darkness: A Blind Person's Conversations with the Bible, 2001. EDITOR: The Child in the Church, 1976; (with M. Keys) Religion in Education and Learning for Living: Index 1934-1978, 1979; Understanding Christian Nurture, 1981; (and author of intro. and commentary) New Directions in Religious Education, 1982. Work represented in anthologies. Contributor to books, religious and education journals. **Address:** School of Education, University of Birmingham, Edgbaston, Birmingham B15 2TT, England. **Online address:** j.m.hull@bham.ac.uk; www.johnmhull.biz

HULL, William E(dward). American, b. 1930. **Genres:** Theology/Religion. **Career:** Provost and University Professor, Samford University, Birmingham, AL, 1987-, now retired as Research Professor. Fellow, 1954-55, Instructor, 1955-58, Assistant Professor, 1958-61, Associate Professor, 1961-67, Professor, 1967-75, Director of Graduate Studies, 1968-70, Dean of the School of Theology, 1969-75, and Provost, 1972-75; Southern Baptist Theological Seminary, Louisville, KY; Pastor, First Baptist Church, Shreveport, LA, 1975-87. President, Association of Baptist Profs. of Religion, 1967-68. **Publications:** The Gospel of John, 1964; The Broadman Bible, 1970; Beyond the Barriers, 1981; Love in Four Dimensions, 1982; The Christian Experience of Salvation, 1987; Southern Baptist Higher Education: Retrospect and Prospect, 2001; The Quest for Spiritual Maturity, 2004. Contributor to periodicals. **Address:** Samford University, Birmingham, AL 35229, U.S.A. **Online address:** wehull@samford.edu

HULME, Ann. *See* **GRANGER, (Patricia) Ann.**

HULSE, James Warren. American, b. 1930. **Genres:** History. **Career:** Professor of History, Univ of Nevada, Reno, 1962-97 (retired). Journalist, Nevada State Journal, 1954-59; Assistant Professor, Central Washington State College, Ellensburg, 1961-62. **Publications:** The Forming of the Communist International, 1964; The Nevada Adventure: A History, 1965, 6th ed., 1990; Revolutionists in London: A Study of Five Unorthodox Socialists, 1970; The University of Nevada: A Centennial History, 1974; Forty Years in the Wilderness, 1986; The Silver State: Nevada's History Reinterpreted, 1991, 3rd ed., 2004; The Reputations of Socrates, 1995. **Address:** Dept of History, University of Nevada, Reno, NV 89557, U.S.A.

HULSE, Michael (William). British, b. 1955. **Genres:** Poetry, Literary criticism and history, Translations. **Career:** University of Erlangen/Nuremberg, W. Germany, lecturer, 1977-79; Catholic University of Eichstatt, W. Germany, lecturer, 1981-83; University of Cologne, Germany, part-time lecturer, 1985-95; Deutsche Welle TV, Cologne, translator, 1986-2000; Arc International Poets, editor, 1993-98; University of Zurich, Switzerland, lecturer, 1994; Konemann Clothbound Classics Series and Travel Classics, general editor, 1994-; Stand magazine, co-editor, 1999-freelance writer. **Publications:** POETRY: Monochrome Blood, 1980; Dole Queue, 1981; Knowing and Forgetting, 1981; Propaganda, 1985; Eating Strawberries in the Necropolis, 1991; Mother of Battles, 1991; (ed with D. Kennedy and D. Morley) The New Poetry, 1993. TRANSLATIONS: Tumult, by B. Strauss, 1987; Essays in Honor of Elias Canetti, 1987; Prison Journal, by L. Rinser, 1987, in U.S. as A Woman's Prison Journal, 1988; The Sorrows of Young Werther, by J.W. Goethe, 1989; The Complete Paintings of van Gogh, by I.F. Walther and R. Metzger, 2 vols., 1990; Wonderful, Wonderful Times, by E. Jelinek, 1990; Jan Lobel from Warsaw, by L. Rinser, 1991; Picasso, by I.F. Walther, 2 vols., 1992; Gauguin in Tahiti, by G. Metken, 1992; Caspar Hauser, by J. Wassermann, 1992; Lust, by E. Jelinek, 1992; Impressionism, by P.H. Feist, 2 vols., 1993; Written in the West, by W. Wenders, 1993; Salvador Dalí: The Paintings, by G. Néret, 2 vols., 1994; The Emigrants, by W.G. Sebald, 1996; The Rings of Saturn, by W.G. Sebald, 1998; Vertigo, by W.G. Sebald, 1999. **Address:** Author Mail, c/o Salt Publishing, PO Box 937, Great Wilbraham, Cambridge CB1 5JX, England.

HULSKER, Jan. *See* Obituaries.

HULT, Karen M(arie). American, b. 1956. **Genres:** Institutions/Organizations, Politics/Government, Public/Social administration. **Career:** US Department of Health and Human Services, Washington, DC, analyst in Office of Adolescent Pregnancy Programs, 1982; Pomona College, Claremont, CA, assistant professor, 1984-89, associate professor of government, 1990, director of Program in Public Policy Analysis, 1988-90; Virginia Polytechnic Institute and State University, Blacksburg, associate professor, 1990-98, professor of political science, 1998-. Claremont Graduate School, faculty member, 1986-90; Orange County Grand Jury, consultant. Presidential Studies Quarterly, book review editor. **Publications:** Agency Merger and Bureaucratic Redesign, 1987; (with C. Walcott) Governing Public Organizations: Politics, Structures, and Institutional Design, 1990; (with C. Walcott) Governing the White House: From Hoover through LBJ, 1995; (with C. Walcott) Empowering the White House: Governance under Nixon, Ford, & Carter, 2004. Contributor to books. Contributor of articles and reviews to academic journals. **Address:** Dept of Political Science, Virginia Polytechnic Institute and State University, Blacksburg, VA 24061, U.S.A. **Online address:** KHult@vt.edu

HULTKRANTZ, Åke G. B. Swedish, b. 1920. **Genres:** Anthropology/Ethnology, History, Theology/Religion. **Career:** University of Stockholm, Sweden, docent, 1954-58, professor of comparative religion and chairman of Institute of Comparative Religion, 1958-86, professor emeritus, 1986-. Visiting professor at universities in the United States, Canada, Western Europe, and Hungary. Conducted field research among the Shoshoni Indians, and the Arapaho, Flathead, Stoney, and Chumash tribes, 1948-. Shaman (journal), honorary chief editor. **Publications:** Conceptions of the Soul among North American Indians (monograph), 1953; The North American Indian Orpheus Tradition (monograph), 1957; International Dictionary of Regional European Ethnology and Folklore, Vol. I: General Ethnological Concepts, 1960; The Supernatural Owners of Nature, 1961; (with I. Paulson and K. Lettmar) Die Religionen Nordeurasiens und der amerikanischen Arktis (title means: Religions of Northern Eurasia and the American Arctic), 1962; Type of Religion in the Arctic Hunting Cultures, 1963; Les Religions des indiens primitifs de l'Amerique (title means: Religions of the Primitive Indians in America), 1963; De amerikanska indianernas religioner (title means: Religions of American Indians), 1967; (with E. Arbman, E. Ehnmark, and O. Pettersson) Primitiv religion och magi, 1968; Prairie and Plains Indians, 1973; Metodvaegar inom den jaemfoerande religionsforskningen (title means: Research Methods in Comparative Religion), 1973; The Shoshones in the Rocky Mountain Area, 1974; Seeing with a Native Eye: Essays on Native American Religion, 1976; (with L. Baeckman) Studies in Lapp Shamanism, 1978; The Religions of the American Indians, 1979; Belief and Worship in Native North America, 1981; (with O. Vorren) The Hunters, 1982; The Study of American Indian Religions, 1983; (with Baeckman) Saami Pre-Christian Religion, 1985; Native Religions of North America, 1987; The Drum in Shamanism, 1991; Vew är vem i nordisk mylologi, 1991; Shamanic Healing and Ritual Drama, 1992; Religion and Environment among the Saami, 1994; Soul and Native Americans, 1997; The Attraction of Peyote, 1997; Das Buch Der Schamanen: Nord-und Sudamerika, 2002. **Address:** Seglarvagen 7, 181 62 Lidingo, Sweden.

HUME, John Robert. Scottish, b. 1939. **Genres:** Archaeology/Antiquities, Business/Trade/Industry. **Career:** University of Strathclyde, Glasgow, lecturer, 1964-82, senior lecturer in history, 1982-91; Historic Scotland, on assignment to Historic Buildings and Monuments Commission, 1984-91, principal inspector of historic buildings, 1991-93, chief inspector of historic buildings, 1993. Member, Inland Waterways Amenity Advisory Council, 1974-. Chairman, Scottish Railway Preservation Society, 1966-75; treasurer, 1968-71, and ed., 1971-79, Scottish Society for Industrial Archaeology, 1968-71; director, Scottish Industrial Archaeology Survey, 1978-85. **Publications:** (with J. Butt & I.L. Donnachie) Industrial History in Pictures: Scotland, 1968; The Industrial Archaeology of Glasgow, 1974; (with M. Moss) Glasgow as It Was, 3 vols., 1975-76; (with M. Moss) A Plumber's Pastime (photographs), 1975; The Industrial Archaeology of Scotland: The Lowlands and the Borders, 1976; (with M. Moss) The Workshop of the British Empire, 1977; The Industrial Archaeology of Scotland: The Highlands and Islands, 1977; (with M. Moss) Beardmore: History of a Scottish Industrial Giant, 1979; (with M. Moss) The Making of Scotch Whisky, 1981; (with M. Moss) A Bed of Nails, 1983; (with G. Douglas & M. Oglethorpe) Scottish Windmills, 1984; (with others) Scottish Brickmarks, 1985; (with M. Moss) Shipbuilders to the World: A History of Harland Wolff, Belfast, 1986; Scotland's Industrial Past, 1990; Dumfries and Galloway, 2000. **Address:** c/o Historic Scotland, Longmore House, Salisbury Place, Edinburgh EH9 1SH, Scotland.

HUME, Robert D. American, b. 1944. **Genres:** Literary criticism and history, Theatre. **Career:** Cornell University, assistant, then associate professor of English, 1969-77; Pennsylvania State University, University Park, professor of English, 1977-90, distinguished professor, 1990-91, Edwin Erle Sparks Professor, 1991-98, Evan Pugh Professor of English Literature, 1998-. **Publications:** Dryden's Criticism, 1970; The Development of English Drama in the Late Seventeenth Century, 1976; The London Theatre World 1660-1800, 1980; Vice Chamberlain Coke's Theatrical Papers 1706-1715, 1982; The Rakish Stage, 1983; Producible Interpretation, 1985; Henry Fielding and the London Theatre, 1988; A Register of English Theatrical Documents, 1660-1737, 2 vols., 1991; Italian Opera in Late Eighteenth-Century London, Vol. 1: The King's Theater Haymarket, 1778-1791, 1995, Vol. 2: The Pantheon Opera and Its Aftermath, 17891795, 2001; Reconstructing Contexts: The Aims and Principles of Archaeo-Historicism, 1999. **Address:** Dept of English, Pennsylvania State University, University Park, PA 16802, U.S.A. **Online address:** Rob-Hume@psu.edu

HUMEZ, Nicholas (David). (Nicks Speakwellontis). Also writes as Hippoclides Aphrontis, Guillard Desguin, Justus Speakwell. American, b. 1948. **Genres:** Adult non-fiction. **Career:** Silversmith in Cambridge, MA, 1970-84, and Portland, ME, 1984-. Composer of classical music, 1959-; cartoonist, 1967-; indexer. **Publications:** (with A. Humez, E. Goldfrank, and J. Goldfrank) The Boston Basin Bicycle Book, 1975; (with A. Humez) Latin for People/Latina pro Populo, 1976; Silversmithing: A Basic Manual, 1976; (with A. Humez) Alpha to Omega: The Life and Times of the Greek Alphabet, 1981; (with A. Humez) ABC et cetera: The Life and Times of the Roman Alphabet, 1985; (with A. Humez and J. Maguire) Zero to Lazy Eight: The Romance of Numbers, 1993. Also writes under the name Nick Humez and under the pseudonyms Hippoclides Aphrontis, Guillard Desguin, and Justus Speakwell. **Address:** Features Department, Portland Newspapers, 390 Congress St., Portland, ME 04101, U.S.A.

HUMMEL, Jeffrey Rogers. American, b. 1949. **Genres:** Economics, History. **Career:** University of Texas at Austin, assistant instructor in history, 1978-79; Libertarian Party of California, research director, 1982; Independent Institute, publications director, 1988-93; Golden Gate University, San Francisco, CA, adjunct associate professor of economics and history, 1989-; Hoover Institution, William C. Bork National Fellow, 2001-02. **Publications:** Emancipating Slaves, Enslaving Free Men: A History of the American Civil War, 1996. Scriptwriter for audio cassette series on the U.S. Constitution and the Civil War. Contributor to books. Contributor of articles and reviews to periodicals. **Address:** William C. Bork National Fellow, Hoover Institution, Stanford University, Stanford, CA 94305, U.S.A.

HUMMEL, Monte. Canadian, b. 1946. **Genres:** Environmental sciences/Ecology. **Career:** Pollution Probe, Ontario, Canada, executive director and chairman, 1969-81; World Wildlife Fund Canada, Toronto, Ontario, president, 1978-. Coordinator of Environmental Studies Program, Innis College, University of Toronto, 1974-81, and associate, Institute of Environmental Studies; director of Outdoor Canada Sportsmen's Shows and Canadian Coalition on Acid Rain. **Publications:** Arctic Wildlife, 1984; (ed. and contrib.) Endangered Spaces, 1989; (with S. Pettigrew) Wild Hunters: Predators in Peril, 1991; Protecting Canada's Endangered Spaces, 1995. **Address:** World Wildlife Fund Canada, 90 Eglinton Ave. N., Suite 504, Toronto, ON, Canada M4P 2Z7.

HUMMER, T(errence) R(andolph). American, b. 1950. **Genres:** Poetry. **Career:** Oklahoma State University, Stillwater, assistant professor of English, 1980-84; Kenyon College, Gambier, OH, and Middlebury College, VT, assistant professor of English; Exeter College, England, visiting professor; University of California, Irvine, writer-in-residence; University of Oregon, Eugene, professor and director of creative writing. **Publications:** POETRY: Translation of Light, 1976; The Angelic Orders, 1982; The Passion of the Right-Angled Man, 1984; Lower-Class Heresy, 1987; The 18,000-Ton Olympic Dream, 1990; Walt Whitman in Hell, 1996. EDITOR: (with B. Weigl) The Imagination as Glory: Essays on the Poetry of James Dickey, 1984; (with D. Jersild) The Unfeigned Word: Fifteen Years of New England Review, 1993. **Address:** Department of English, Virginia Commonwealth University, PO Box 842005, Richmond, VA 23284-2005, U.S.A.

HUMPHREY, Carol Sue. American, b. 1956. **Genres:** History. **Career:** Oklahoma Baptist University, Shawnee, assistant professor, 1985-92, associate professor, 1992-98, professor of history, 1998-. **Publications:** "This Popular Engine": The Role of New England Newspapers during the American Revolution, 1992; The Press of the Young Republic, 1783-1833, 1996. Work represented in books. Contributor of articles and reviews to history and journalism magazines. **Address:** Department of History, Oklahoma Baptist University, Shawnee, OK 74804, U.S.A. **Online address:** carol.humphrey@okbu.edu

HUMPHREY, James. American, b. 1939. **Genres:** Poetry, Literary criticism and history. **Career:** Poetry writing teacher, National Endowment for the Arts, 1969-, and for Poets Who Teach, 1974-. **Publications:** Argument for Love, 1970; The Visitor, 1972; An Homage: The End of Some More Land, 1972; Looking at Love: Poem for the Experimental Theatre, 1975; Concepts in Imagery, 1975; The Relearning, 1976; After I'm Dead, Will My Life Begin?, 1986; The Athlete, 1988; Ice, 1990; The Freak, 1995; Lief, 1997; Siz, 1997; Mize and Kathy, 1998; Paying the Price, 1998. **Address:** c/o Poets Alive Press, 13 Neperhan Ave, Hastings on Hudson, NY 10706, U.S.A.

HUMPHREY, Kate. See **FORSYTH, Kate.**

HUMPHREY, Sandra McLeod. American, b. 1936. **Genres:** Children's fiction, Children's non-fiction. **Career:** Anoka Metro Regional Treatment Center, Anoka, MN, clinical psychologist, 1961-92; writer of children's books, 1992-. Public speaker. Volunteer. **Publications:** FOR CHILDREN: A Dog Named Sleet, 1984; If You Had to Choose, What Would You Do?, 1995; It's Up to You...What Do You Do?, 1999; Keepin' It Real: A Young Teen Talks with God, 2003; More-If You Had to Choose, What Would You Do?, 2003. **Address:** 19 Westwood Rd, Minnetonka, MN 55305, U.S.A. **Online address:** Sandra305@aol.com

HUMPHREY-KEEVER, Mary Ann. American, b. 1943. **Genres:** Civil liberties/Human rights, Gay and lesbian issues, History, Military/Defense/Arms control, Psychiatry, Psychology, Recreation, Sports/Fitness. **Career:** Portland Community College, Portland, OR, coordinator of physical education, 1973-. **Publications:** My Country, My Right to Serve: Experiences of Gay Men and Women in the Military, World War II to the Present, 1990; Waterplay, 1990. **Address:** Portland Community College, 12000 SW 49th Ave, Portland, OR 97219, U.S.A. **Online address:** MHumphre@pcc.edu; drhumphreykeever@attbi.com

HUMPHREYS, Emyr (Owen). Welsh, b. 1919. **Genres:** Novels, Novellas/Short stories, Plays/Screenplays, Poetry, Literary criticism and history. **Career:** Teacher, Wimbledon Technical College, London, 1948-50, and Pwllheli Grammar School, N. Wales, 1951-54; producer, BBC Radio, Cardiff, 1955-58; drama producer, BBC Television, 1958-62; freelance writer and dir., 1962-65; first lecturer in drama, University College of North Wales, Bangor, 1965-72; hon fellow University of Wales, 1987; hon prof. English, Bangor, 1988; fellow of the Royal Society of Literature, 1994. **Publications:** The Little Kingdom, 1947; The Voice of a Stranger, 1949; A Change of Heart, 1951; Hear and Forgive, 1952; A Man's Estate, 1955; The Italian Wife, 1957; Y Tri Llais, 1958; A Toy Epic, 1959; King's Daughter, 1959, televised as Siwan, 1960; The Gift, 1962; Outside the House of Baal, 1965; Natives, 1968; Roman Dream, 1968; An Apple Tree and a Pig, 1969; (with W.S. Jones) Dinas, 1970; Ancestor Worship: A Cycle of 18 Poems, 1970; Flesh and Blood, 1974; Landscapes, 1976; The Best of Friends, 1978; Penguin Modern Poets 27, 1978; The Anchor Tree, 1980; Miscellany Two, 1981; The Taliesin Tradition, 1983; Jones: A Novel, 1984; Salt of the Earth, 1985; An Absolute Hero, 1986; Open Secrets, 1988; The Triple Net, 1988; The Crucible of Myth, 1991; Bonds of Attachment, 1991; Outside Time, 1991; Brodyr A Chwiorydd, 1994; Dwylo, 1994; Unconditional Surrender, 1996; The Gift of a Daughter, 1998; Collected Poems, 1999; Dal Pen Rheswm, 1999; Land of the Living, 2000; Ghosts and Strangers, 2001; Conversations and Reflections, 2002; Old People Are a Problem, 2003.

HUMPHREYS, George G(ary). American, b. 1949. **Genres:** Politics/Government, History. **Career:** Oklahoma House of Representatives, Oklahoma City, fiscal director, 1981-83; Oklahoma Department of Economic and Community Affairs, Oklahoma City, director of information services, 1983-85; Oklahoma House of Representatives, research director, 1985-. **Publications:** Taylorism in France, 1904-1920: The Impact of Scientific Management on Factory Relations and Society, Garland Publishing, 1986; (co-author) Oklahoma Politics and Policies: Governing the Sooner State, University of Nebraska Press, 1991. **Address:** Oklahoma House of Representatives, 305 State Capitol Building, Oklahoma City, OK 73105, U.S.A.

HUMPHREYS, Helen (Caroline). Also writes as Catherine Brett. Canadian (born England), b. 1961. **Genres:** Poetry, Novels, Young adult fiction. **Career:** Writer. **Publications:** POETRY: Gods and Other Mortals, 1986; Nuns Looking Anxious, Listening to Radios, 1990; The Perils of Geography, 1995; Anthem, 1999. NOVELS: Ethel on Fire, 1991; Leaving Earth, 1997; Afterimage, 2000. OTHER: What Wants to Be Spoken, What Remains to Be Said (screenplay), 1992. YA NOVELS AS CATHERINE BRETT: Things

Just Aren't the Same, 1987; S.P. Likes A.D., 1989. Contributor of poetry, short stories, and articles to periodicals. **Address:** 56 Chestnut St., Kingston, ON, Canada K7K 3X5.

HUMPHREYS, Margaret. Also writes as Margaret Warner. American, b. 1955. **Genres:** History. **Career:** Harvard University, Cambridge, MA, instructor, 1983-84, lecturer, 1986-93, Fae Kass Lecturer, 1987; Duke University, Durham, NC, assistant professor of history and medicine, and physician (internal medicine) at university medical center, both 1993-. Francis Wood Institute, editorial consultant, 1993-. **Publications:** Yellow Fever and the South, 1992. Contributor to history journals, sometimes under the name Margaret Warner. **Address:** Department of History, Box 90719, Duke University, Durham, NC 27710, U.S.A.

HUMPHRYS, Geoffrey. See **HUMPHRYS, Leslie George.**

HUMPHRYS, Leslie George. Also writes as Geoffrey Humphrys. British, b. 1921. **Genres:** Children's non-fiction, Writing/Journalism. **Career:** Freelance journalist. Headmaster, North Walsham County Primary School, Norfolk, 1959-81, now retired. **Publications:** (as Geoffrey Humphrys) Time to Live, 1959; Wonders of Life (Books 1-4), 1959; Weather in Britain, 1963; Your Body at Work, 1963; Men Learn to Fly, 1966; Life is Exciting, 1966; Science Through Experience (Books 1-3), 1967; Fruit and Fruit Growing, 1969; Drinks, 1970; Men Travel in Space, 1971; Glass and Glass Making, 1971; Tools, 1974; Motion and Power, 1974; Machines, 1976. **Address:** 27 Litester Close, North Walsham, Norfolk, England.

HUNDERT, E(dward) J. American/Canadian, b. 1940. **Genres:** History. **Career:** University of British Columbia, Vancouver, Canada, historian. **Publications:** The Enlightenment's Fable, 1994. **Address:** Department of History, University of British Columbia, Vancouver, BC, Canada V6T 1Z1. **Online address:** hundert@home.com

HUNDERT, Edward M. American, b. 1956. **Genres:** Medicine/Health. **Career:** Harvard University, Harvard Medical School, Boston, MA, associate professor of psychiatry and associate dean for student affairs, 1990-. McLean Hospital (Belmont, MA), psychiatrist, 1984-. **Publications:** Philosophy, Psychiatry, and Neuroscience: Three Approaches to the Mind, 1989; Lessons from an Optical Illusion: On Nature and Nurture, Knowledge and Values, 1995. **Address:** Harvard Medical School, 260 Longwood Ave., Boston, MA 02115, U.S.A.

HUNDLEY, Norris C., Jr. American, b. 1935. **Genres:** History. **Career:** Emeritus Professor of History, University of California, Los Angeles, 1994- (Assistant Professor, 1964-69; Associate Professor, 1969-73; Professor of History, 1973-94; Chairman of University Program on Mexico, 1981-94; Acting Director of Latin American Center, 1989-90); Director of Latin American Center, 1990-94; Managing Ed., Pacific Historical Review, 1968-97; Guggenheim Fellow, 1978-79; Instructor, University of Houston, Texas, 1963-64. **Publications:** John Walton Caughey, Historian, 1961; Dividing the Waters: A Century of Controversy between the United States and Mexico, 1966; California History: A Teacher's Manual, 1970; Water and the West: The Colorado River Compact and the Politics of Water in the American West, 1975; (with others) The California Water Atlas, 1979; (with J. Caughey) California: History of a Remarkable State, 1982; The Great Thirst: Californians and Water, 1770s-1990s, 1992, rev. ed. as The Great Thirst: Californians and Water: A History, 2001; Las aguas divididas: Un siglo de controversia entre Mexico y Estados Unidos, 2000. EDITOR: (with J. Schutz) The American West: Frontier and Region, 1969; The American Indian, 1974; The Chicano, 1975; The Asian American, 1976. **Address:** Dept of History, University of California, Los Angeles, CA 90095-1473, U.S.A. **Online address:** hundley@history.ucla.edu

HUNG, Chang-tai. American (born People's Republic of China), b. 1949. **Genres:** History, Politics/Government, Popular Culture. **Career:** Carleton College, Northfield, MN, assistant professor, 1981-87, associate professor, 1987-92, professor of history, 1992-98, Jane and Raphael Bernstein Professor of Asian Studies, 1993-98; Hong Kong University of Science and Technology, Clearwater Bay, Hong Kong, visiting professor of humanities, 1994, professor of humanities, 1995-, associate dean, School of Humanities and Social Science, 1999-2000. **Publications:** Going to the People: Chinese Intellectuals and Folk Literature, 1918-1937, 1985; War and Popular Culture: Resistance in Modern China, 1937-1945, 1994; The New Cultural History and Chinese Politics (in Chinese), 2003. **Address:** Division of Humanities, Hong Kong University of Science & Technology, Clearwater Bay, Kowloon, Hong Kong.

HUNGERFORD, Rachael A. American. **Genres:** Education. **Career:** Lycoming College, Williamsport, PA, assistant professor, 1989-. Children's Literature Jubilee, director. **Publications:** (Co-ed, and contrib.) Journeying: Children Responding to Literature, 1993. **Address:** Lycoming College, Williamsport, PA 17701, U.S.A.

HUNKER, Henry L. American, b. 1924. **Genres:** Urban studies, Geography. **Career:** Professor Emeritus, Geography and Public Policy and Management, 1994-,Ohio State University, Columbus (faculty member since 1949; Assistant Dean, College of Commerce and Administration, 1966-68; Director, Center for Community Analysis, 1968-70; Acting Director, School of Public Policy and Management, 1989-91). Fulbright Lecturer, Australia, 1957; Battelle Fellow, Battelle Memorial Institute, Columbus, Ohio, 1972-73. **Publications:** Industrial Evolution of Columbus, Ohio, 1958; Ohio, 1960; (with A. J. Wright) Factors of Industrial Location in Ohio, 1963; (ed.) Introduction to World Resources, 1964; Industrial Development: Concepts and Principles, 1974; Ohio and Its Resources (18 filmstrips/cassettes), 1975; Community Attitudes and Perceptions of Selected Manufacturers in Ohio, 1979; The Teaching and Study of Geography, 1980; Columbus, Ohio: A Personal Geogrpahy, 2000. Contributor of articles and chapters in books. **Address:** Dept. of Geography, Ohio State University, 154 N Oval Mall, Columbus, OH 43214, U.S.A. **Online address:** Hunker.1@osu.edu

HUNKIN, Tim(othy) Mark Trelawney. British, b. 1950. **Genres:** Children's fiction, Children's non-fiction. **Career:** Exhibit designer, Science Museum, London. Cartoonist, The Observer, London, 1973-87; Secret Life of Machines, tv series, writer, presenter, 1987-93. **Publications:** Mrs Gronkwonk and the Post Office Tower; Rudiments of Wisdom, 1974; Almost Everything There Is to Know, 1988. **Address:** Bulcamp House, Blythburgh, Suffolk IP19 9LG, England. **Online address:** tim@hunkin.u-net.com

HUNNICUTT, Benjamin Kline. American, b. 1943. **Genres:** Recreation, History, Organized labor, Sociology. **Career:** Council for Senior Citizens, Durham, N.C., day-care director for senior citizens, 1973-75; University of Iowa, Iowa City, professor of leisure studies, 1975-, chairman of department, 1985-. Member of board of directors of Children's Museum of Iowa City. **Publications:** Work without End: Abandoning Shorter Hours for the Right to Work, 1988; Kellogg's Six-Hour Day, 1996. **Address:** Department of Leisure Studies, University of Iowa, Iowa City, IA 52242, U.S.A.

HUNT, Angela Elwell. American, b. 1957. **Genres:** Novels, Romance/Historical, Children's fiction, Young adult fiction, Human relations/Parenting, Autobiography/Memoirs, Picture/board books. **Career:** Worked as an English teacher; writer, 1983-. **Publications:** YOUNG ADULT NOVELS. CASSIE PERKINS SERIES: No More Broken Promises, 1991; A Forever Friend, 1991; A Basket of Roses, 1991; A Dream to Cherish, 1992; The Much-Adored Sandy Shore, 1992; Love Burning Bright, 1992; Star Light, Star Bright, 1993; The Chance of a Lifetime, 1993; The Glory of Love, 1993. YOUNG ADULT MYSTERIES. NICKI HOLLAND SERIES: The Case of the Mystery Mark, 1991; The Case of the Phantom Friend, 1991; The Case of the Teenage Terminator, 1991; The Case of the Terrified Track Star, 1992; The Case of the Counterfeit Cash, 1992; The Case of the Haunting of Lowell Lanes, 1992; The Case of the Birthday Bracelet, 1993; The Secret of Cravenhill Castle, 1993; The Riddle of Baby Rosalind, 1993. HISTORICAL FICTION. THEYN CHRONICLES SERIES: Afton of Margate Castle, 1993; The Troubadour's Quest, 1994; Ingram of the Irish, 1995. LEGACIES OF THE ANCIENT RIVER SERIES: Dreamers, 1996; Brothers, 1997; Journey, 1997. JUVENILE HISTORICAL FICTION. THE COLONIAL CAPTIVES SERIES: Books 1 and 2: Kimberly and the Captives, 1996; Books 3 and 4: The Deadly Chase, 1996. HISTORICAL FICTION. THE KEEPERS OF THE RING SERIES: Roanoke: The Lost Colony, 1996; Jamestown, 1996; Hartford, 1996; Rehoboth, 1997; Charleston, 1998. YOUNG BELIEVERS SERIES (2004; with S. Arterburn): Josiah; Liane; Noah; Paige; Shane; Taz. HEAVENLY DAZE SERIES (with L. Coopeland): The Island of Heavenly Daze, 2000; Grace in Autumn, 2001; Warmth in Winter, 2002; A Perfect Love, 2002; Hearts at Home, 2003. HEIRS OF CAHIRA O'CONNOR SERIES: The Silver Sword, 1998; The Golden Cross, 1998; The Velvet Shadow, 1999; The Emerald Isle, 1999. OTHER: (with G. Hunt) Surviving the Teenage Years, 1988, as Too Young to Drive, Too Old to Ride, 1993; If I Had Long, Long Hair, 1988; (with G. Hunt) Mom and Dad Don't Live Together Anymore, 1989; The Tale of Three Trees, 1989; The Adoption Option, 1989; (with G. Hunt) Now That You've Asked Her Out, 1989; (with G. Hunt) Now That He's Asked You Out, 1989; Calico Bear (picture book), 1991; A Gift for Grandpa, 1991; If God Is Real, Where on Earth Is He?, 1991; (with C. Dyer) The Rise of Babylon: Sign of the End Times, 1991; Loving Someone Else's Child, 1992; The Singing Shepherd, 1992; The True Princess, 1992; (with L.K. Calenberg) Beauty from the Inside Out: Becom-

ing the Best You Can Be, 1993; Howie Hugemouth, 1993; When Your Parents Pull Apart, 1995; Where Dragons Dance, 1995; The Proposal, 1996; (with H. Whitestone) Listening with My Heart, 1997; Gentle Touch, 1997; (with G. Jeffrey) Flee the Darkness, 1998; (with G. Jeffrey) By Dawn's Early Light, 1999; (with G. Jeffrey) The Spear of Tyranny, 2000; The Truth Teller, 1999; The Immortal, 2000; The Note, 2001; (with B. Myers) Then Comes Marriage, 2001; The Justice, 2002; The Shadow Women, 2002; The Pearl, 2003; The Canopy, 2003; The Awakening, 2004; The Debt, 2004; The Third Adam, 2005; Unspoken, 2005. Contributor to magazines.

HUNT, Bruce J. American, b. 1956. **Genres:** History, Physics. **Career:** University of Texas at Austin, assistant professor of history, 1985-92, associate professor of history, 1992-. **Publications:** The Maxwellians, 1991. **Address:** Department of History, University of Texas at Austin, Austin, TX 78712, U.S.A. **Online address:** bjhunt@mail.utexas.edu

HUNT, David. See **BAYER, William.**

HUNT, Edward H. British, b. 1939. **Genres:** History, Industrial relations. **Career:** Sr. Lecturer in Economic History, London School of Economics, since 1969. Assistant Lecturer in Economic History, Queen's University of Belfast, 1966-69. Book Review Ed., Economic History Review, 1981-86. **Publications:** Regional Wage Variations in Britain 1850-1914, 1973; British Labour History 1815-1914, 1981. **Address:** London School of Economics, Houghton St, London WC2A 2AE, England. **Online address:** E.H.Hunt@lse.ac.uk

HUNT, Gil. See **TUBB, E(dwin) C(harles).**

HUNT, Gladys M. American, b. 1926. **Genres:** Human relations/Parenting, Inspirational/Motivational Literature, Theology/Religion. **Career:** Journalist/writer. **Publications:** Does Anyone Here Know God?, 1967; Honey for a Child's Heart, 1969, 4th ed., 2002; Listen to Me, 1969; Focus on Family Life, 1970, as Family Secrets, 1985; The Christian Way of Death, 1971, as Living and Dying, 1981, 3rd ed. as Close to Home, 1990; John: Eyewitness, 1971; The God Who Understands Me: The Sermon on the Mount, 1971; It's Alive, 1971; Ms Means Myself, 1972, 2nd ed. as A Persuaded Heart, 1990; Revelation: The Lamb Who Is the Lion, 1972; Hebrews: From Shadows to Reality, 1979; Romans: Made Righteous by Faith, 1980; Relationships, 1983; Stories Jesus Told, 1985; (with K.L. Hunt) Not Alone: The Necessity of Relationships, 1985, 2nd ed. as We Need Each Other: The Miracle of Relationships, 1990; Luke: A Daily Dialogue with God, 1986; Women of the Old Testament, 1990; (with B. Hampton) Read for Your Life: Turning Teens into Readers, 1992; (with K. Hunt) For Christ and the University, 1991; Building Character, 1992; Now You Can Start a Bible Study Group, 1994; Genesis II, 1998; Honey for a Woman's Heart: Growing Your World through Reading Great Books, 2002; (with B. Hampton) Honey for a Teen's Heart: Using Books to Communicate with Teens, 2002. **Address:** 6348 Tahoe Ln SE, Grand Rapids, MI 49546, U.S.A. **Online address:** gladyshunt@cs.com

HUNT, Janie Louise. Kenyan, b. 1963. **Genres:** Children's fiction. **Career:** Templar Publishing Co., Dorking, England, illustrator, 1986-, currently senior designer. **Publications:** SELF-ILLUSTRATED FOR CHILDREN: Big and Small: A Book of Opposites, 1997; Red and Yellow, 1997; One, Two, Three: A Through the Window Book of Counting, 1998; Round and Square: A Through the Window Book of Shapes, 1998. **Address:** 15-C Cotmandene, Dorking, Surrey RH4 2BT, England.

HUNT, Lynn (Avery). American (born Panama), b. 1945. **Genres:** Politics/Government. **Career:** University of California, Berkeley, assistant professor, 1974-79, associate professor, 1979-84, professor of history, 1984-87; University of Pennsylvania, Philadelphia, professor of history, 1987-98; University of California, Los Angeles, professor of history, 1999-. **Publications:** Revolution and Urban Politics in France, 1978; Politics, Culture, and Class in the French Revolution, 1984; (ed.) The New Cultural History, 1989; (ed.) Eroticism and the Body Politic, 1990; The Family Romance of the French Revolution, 1992; (ed.) Invention of Pornography, 1993; (with J. Appleby and M. Jacob) Telling the Truth about History, 1994; (with others) Challenge of the West, 1995; (ed. with J. Revel) Histories, 1995;(ed. and trans.) French Revolution and Human Rights, 1996; (ed. with V.E. Bonnell) Beyond the Cultural Turn, 1999; (ed. with J.N. Wasserstrom and M.B. Young) Human Rights and Revolutions, 2000; (with J.R. Censer) Liberty, Equality, Fraternity, 2001. **Address:** Department of History, University California, Los Angeles, 6265 Bunche Hall, Box 951473, Los Angeles, CA 90095-1473, U.S.A.

HUNT, Marjorie. American, b. 1954. **Genres:** Art/Art history, Architecture. **Career:** Smithsonian Institution, Center for Folklife and Cultural Heritage,

Washington, DC, education specialist and curator of the building arts program. **Publications:** (with M. Hufford and S. Zeitlin) The Grand Generation: Memory, Mastery, Legacy (originally produced as a documentary film), 1987; The Stone Carvers: Master Craftsmen of Washington National Cathedral (originally produced as a documentary film), 1999. **Address:** Smithsonian Institution, Center for Folklife and Cultural Heritage, 750 9th Street NW, 4th Floor, Washington, DC 20560, U.S.A. **Online address:** marjorie@folklife.si.edu

HUNT, Peter (Leonard). British, b. 1945. **Genres:** Children's fiction, Literary criticism and history. **Career:** University of Wales Institute of Science and Technology, Cardiff, lecturer in English, 1968-87; University of Michigan, Ann Arbor, visiting professor, 1977; Massachusetts Institute of Technology, Cambridge, visiting lecturer, 1982; University of Wales, Cardiff, sr. lecturer, 1988-95, reader, 1995, professor of English, 1996-2004; San Diego State University, adjunct professor, 1990; University of Wollongong, Australia, visiting fellow, 1991. **Publications:** Children's Book Research in Britain, 1977, rev. ed., 1982; The Maps of Time, 1983; A Step Off the Path, 1985; Backtrack, 1986; Sue and the Honey Machine, 1989; Fay Cow and the Mystery of the Missing Milk, 1989; Going Up, 1989; Criticism, Theory and Children's Literature, 1991; Approaching Arthur Ransome, 1992; An Introduction to Children's Literature, 1994; The Wind in the Willows: A Fragmented Arcadia, 1994. EDITOR: Further Approaches to Research in Children's Literature, 1982; Bevis, 1989; Critical Approaches to Children's Literature, 1989; Children's Literature, the Development of Criticism, 1990; Literature for Children (contemporary criticism), 1992; An Illustrated History of Children's Literature, 1995; International Companion Encyclopedia of Children's Literature, 1996, 2nd ed., 2001; Understanding Children's Literature, 1999, 2nd ed., 2005; Children's Literature: A Guide, 2001; Children's Literature: An Anthology 801-1902, 2001; Alternative Worlds in Fantasy Fiction, 2003. **Address:** W Sundial Cottage, Downend, Horsley, Stroud, Glos. GL6 0PF, England.

HUNT, Richard (Patrick). British, b. 1938. **Genres:** Mystery/Crime/Suspense. **Career:** Writer. **Publications:** Murder in Ruins, 1991; Death Sounds Grand, 1991; The Death of a Merry Widow, 1992; Deadlocked, 1994; Murder Benign, 1995; Cure for Killers, 1996; The Mantrap, 1997; A Ring of Vultures, 1998; Dead Man's Shoes, 1999. **Address:** Garden Bungalow, The Driftway, Wootton Rd., King's Lynn, England.

HUNT, Robert (William Gainer). British, b. 1923. **Genres:** Photography. **Career:** Served in the U.K. Ministry of Supply, 1943-46; Kodak Ltd., Harrow, Assistant Director of Research, 1947-82; City University, London, Visiting Professor of Physiological Optics, 1968-98; University of Derby, Colour Science, Visiting Professor, 1993-. **Publications:** The Reproduction of Colour, 1957, 5th ed., 1995; (trans.) Light, Colour, and Vision, 1957, 1968; Measuring Colour, 1987, 3rd ed., 1998. **Address:** Barrowpoint, 18 Millennium Close, Odstock Rd, Salisbury SP2 8TB, England.

HUNT, Tony. British, b. 1944. **Genres:** History. **Career:** University of St. Andrews, Scotland, lecturer, 1968-79, reader, 1979-90; University of London, Westfield College, visiting professor of medieval studies, 1986-88; St. Peter's College, Oxford, England, lecturer and tutorial fellow, 1990-. **Publications:** (ed.) Kalender, 1983; Chretien de Troyes: Yvain (Le Chevalier au Lion), 1986; (ed.) Les Gius Partiz des Eschez: Two Anglo-Norman Chess Treatises, 1986; Plant Names of Medieval England, 1989; Popular Medicine in Thirteenth-Century England, 1990; Teaching and Learning Latin in Thirteenth-Century England, 1991; The Medieval Surgery, 1992; (ed.) AngloNorman Medicine, 1994; Villon's Last Will: Language and Authority in the Testament, 1996. **Address:** St. Peter's College, Oxford, England.

HUNT, Tristram. American, b. 1974. **Genres:** Administration/Management. **Career:** Historian, writer, and television host. Queen Mary College, London, London, England, lecturer in history; Institute for Public Policy Research, London, fellow. Worked for Demos (think tank); London; worked for U.K. Labour Party during Tony Blair's campaign for prime minister, 1996-97; presenter of BBC television documentaries on the English Civil War, and on Sir Isaac Newton, both 2002. **Publications:** The English Civil War at First Hand, 2002. Contributor to periodicals. **Address:** Queen Mary College, University of London, Mile End Road, London E1 4NS, England. **Online address:** tristramhunt@hotmail.com

HUNT, Walter H. American, b. 1959. **Genres:** Science fiction/Fantasy. **Career:** Technical writer. Worked as a software developer. Has done extensive work for the gaming industry, including work on Mechwarrior/Battletech system, Middle Earth role-playing game, and DC heroes RPG.

Publications: The Dark Wing, 2001. **Address:** c/o Author Mail, Tor Books., 175 Fifth Avenue, New York, NY 10010, U.S.A.

HUNTER, Alan (James Herbert). British, b. 1922. **Genres:** Mystery/Crime/Suspense. **Career:** Eastern Daily Press, Norwich, Fiction Critic, 1955-75. **Publications:** The Norwich Poems, 1945; Gently Does It, 1955; Gently by the Shore, 1956; Gently down the Stream, 1957; Landed Gently, 1957; Gently Through the Mill, 1958; Gently in the Sun, 1959; Gently with the Painters, 1960; Gently to the Summit, 1961; Gently Go Man, 1961; Gently Where the Roads Go, 1962; Gently Floating, 1963; Gently Sahib, 1964; Gently with the Ladies, 1965; Gently North-West, 1967 (in U.S. as Gently in the Highlands, 1975); Gently Continental, 1967; Gently Coloured, 1969; Gently with the Innocents, 1970; Gently at a Gallop, 1971; Vivienne: Gently Where She Lay, 1972; Gently French, 1973; Gently in Trees, 1974 (in U.S. as Gently through the Woods, 1975); Gently with Love, 1975; Gently Where the Birds Are, 1976; Gently Instrumental, 1977; Gently to Sleep, 1978; The Honfleur Decision, 1980; Gabrielle's Way (in U.S. as The Scottish Decision), 1981; Fields of Heather (in U.S. as Death on the Heath), 1981; Gently between Tides, 1982; Amorous Leander, 1983 (in U.S. as Death on the Broadlands), 1984; The Unhung Man, 1983; Once a Prostitute, 1984; The Chelsea Ghost, 1985; Goodnight, Sweet Prince, 1986; Strangling Man, 1987; Traitor's End, 1988; Gently with the Millions, 1989; Gently Scandalous, 1990; Gently to a Kill, 1992; Gently Tragic, 1992; Gently in the Glens, 1993; Bomber's Moon, 1994; Jackpot!, 1995; The Love of Gods, 1997; Over Here, 1998; Gently Mistaken, 1999. **Address:** 3 St. Laurence Ave, Brundall, Norwich NR13 5QH, England.

HUNTER, Chris. See **FLUKE, Joanne.**

HUNTER, Eric J. British, b. 1930. **Genres:** Novels, Information science/Computers, Librarianship. **Career:** Liverpool John Moores University (formerly Liverpool Polytechnic), lecturer 1969-76, senior lecturer, 1976-89, reader, 1989-92, head of information and library studies, 1992-94, professor of information management, Liverpool Business School, 1994-95, emeritus professor of information management, 1995-. Previous appointments in libraries: Bootle, 1948-65, Warrington, 1965-68, and Liverpool, 1968-69. Also visiting professor/lecturer in USA, Norway, Italy and Japan. **Publications:** John J. Ogle, 1966; Anglo-American Cataloguing Rules 1967: An Introduction, 1972; Examples Illustrating Anglo-American Cataloguing Rules, 1973, 3rd ed., 1989; Cataloguing: A Guidebook, 1974; Display for Librarians, 1975; AACR 2: An Introduction, 1979, 1989; Cataloguing, 1979, 3rd ed., 1991; The ABC of BASIC: An Introduction to Programming for Librarians, 1982; Computerized Cataloguing, 1985; Classification Made Simple, 1988, rev. ed., 2002; A Guide to the Concise AACR 2, 1994; For Those in Peril (novel), forthcoming. Contributor to monographs, periodicals, conference proceedings. **Address:** 44 Cornwall Way, Ainsdale, Southport, Merseyside PR8 3SH, England. **Online address:** e.j.hunter@livjm.ac.uk; Eric@ejhunter.freeserve.co.uk

HUNTER, Fred (W.). American, b. 1954. **Genres:** Design. **Career:** Writer. **Publications:** MYSTERY NOVELS; JEREMY RANSOM/EMILY CHARTERS SERIES: Presence of Mind, 1994; Ransom for an Angel, 1995; Ransom for Our Sins, 1996; Ransom for a Holiday, 1997; Ransom for a Killing, 1998; Ransom Unpaid, 1999; Ransom at the Opera, 2000; The Mummy's Ransom, 2002; Ransom at Sea, 2003. MYSTERY NOVELS; ALEX REYNOLDS SERIES: Government Gay, 1997; Federal Fag, 1998; Capital Queers, 1999; National Nancys, 2000; The Chicken Asylum, 2001. OTHER: (with Jane Rubino and Kathleen Anne Barnett) Homicide for the Holidays, 2000. **Address:** c/o Author Mail, St. Martin's Press, Publicity Department, 175 Fifth Ave., New York, NY 10010, U.S.A. **Online address:** fhunter@earthlink.net

HUNTER, Gary. See **HUNTER, Gwen.**

HUNTER, Gwen. Also writes as Gary Hunter. American, b. 1956. **Genres:** Mystery/Crime/Suspense, Westerns/Adventure. **Career:** ASCP, medical laboratory technician, 1976; U.S. Department of Health, Education, and Welfare, medical technologist, 1977-; writer, 1989-. **Publications:** SUSPENSE NOVELS: Betrayal, 1994; False Truths, 1995; Ashes to Ashes, 1996; Law of the Wild, 1997. ADVENTURE NOVELS with G. Leveille AS GARY HUNTER: Death Warrant, 1990; Death Sentence, 1992. **Address:** P.O. Box 4251, Rock Hill, SC 29731, U.S.A. **Online address:** Thrilwrtr@aol.com

HUNTER, J(ames) Paul. American, b. 1934. **Genres:** Literary criticism and history. **Career:** University of Florida, instructor, 1957-59; Williams College, Williamstown, MA, instructor, 1962-64; University of California, Riverside, assistant professor, 1964-66; Emory University, Atlanta, associate professor, 1966-68, professor of English, 1968-80, chairman of English, 1973-79; University of Rochester, New York, College of Arts and Science, dean, 1981-86; University of Chicago, professor of English, 1987-90, Chester D. Tripp Professor, 1990-96, Barbara E. and Richard J. Franke Professor in the Humanities, 1996-2001, Franke Professor Emeritus, 2001-; University of Virginia, professor of English, 2001-. **Publications:** The Reluctant Pilgrim, 1966; Norton Introduction to Poetry, 1973, 8th ed., 2001; (co-author) Norton Introduction to Literature, 1973, 8th ed., 1999; Occasional Form, 1975; Before Novels, 1990. EDITOR: Moll Flanders: A Critical Edition, 1970; The Plays of Edward Moore, 1982; (co) Rhetorics of Order/Ordering Rhetorics in English Neoclassical Literature, 1989; Frankenstein: A Norton Critical Edition, 1996. **Address:** 1218 E Madison Park, Chicago, IL 60615-2963, U.S.A.

HUNTER, Jessie Prichard. American, b. 1957?. **Genres:** Mystery/Crime/Suspense. **Career:** Writer. Formerly worked at Diversion magazine, NYC, receptionist; Lear's magazine, NYC, copy chief; and Success magazine, NYC, copy editor. **Publications:** Blood Music, 1993; One, Two, Buckle My Shoe, 1997. **Address:** c/o Jane Cushman, JCA Literary Agency, 27 West Twentieth St. Suite 1103, New York, NY 10011, U.S.A.

HUNTER, Kristin. See LATTANY, Kristin.

HUNTER, Matthew. See STONE, Rodney.

HUNTER, Michael (Cyril William). British, b. 1949. **Genres:** Intellectual history, Biography, Archaeology/Antiquities. **Career:** Birkbeck College, University of London, lecturer, 1976-84, reader, 1984-92, professor of History, 1992-; Research Fellow, Worcester College, Oxford, 1972-75, and University of Reading, 1975-76. **Publications:** John Aubrey and the Realm of Learning, 1975; Science and Society in Restoration England, 1981; The Royal Society and Its Fellows 1660-1700, 1982, rev. ed., 1994; (with A. Gregory) An Astrological Diary of the 17th Century, 1988; Establishing the New Science: The Experience of the Early Royal Society, 1989; (with S. Schaffer) Robert Hooke: New Studies, 1989; (with R. Thorne) Change at King's Cross, 1990; (co-author) Avebury Reconsidered: From the 1600s to the 1990s, 1991; Letters and Papers of Robert Boyle, 1992; (with D. Wootton) Atheism from the Reformation to the Enlightenment, 1992; Robert Boyle Reconsidered, 1994; Robert Boyle by Himself and His Friends, 1994; Science and the Shape of Orthodoxy, 1995; Preserving the Past: The Rise of Heritage in Modern Britain, 1996; (with E.B. Davis) R. Boyle, ed.: A Free Enquiry into the Vulgarly Received Notion of Nature, 1996; Archives of the Scientific Revolution, 1998; (co-author) A Radical's Books, 1999; (with E.B. Davis) The Works of Robert Boyle, 14 vols., 1999-2000; Robert Boyle (1627-91): Scrupulosity and Science, 2000; (coauthor) The Correspondence of Robert Boyle, 6 vols., 2001; The Occult Laboratory: Magic Science and Second Sight in Late 17th-Century Scotland, 2001; (co-author) London's Leonardo: The Life and Work of Robert Hooke, 2003. **Address:** Birkbeck College, School of History, Classics & Archaeology, University of London, Malet St, London WC1E 7HX, England. **Online address:** m.hunter@bbk.ac.uk

HUNTER, Mollie. Scottish, b. 1922. **Genres:** Novels, Children's fiction, Plays/Screenplays, History. **Career:** Poet, journalist, lecturer. **Publications:** A Love-Song for My Lady (play), 1961; Stay for an Answer (play), 1961; Patrick Kentigern Keenan (in U.S. as The Smartest Man in Ireland), 1963; Hi Johnny, 1963; The Kelpie's Pearls, 1964; The Spanish Letters, 1964; A Pistol in Greenyards, 1965; The Ghosts of Glencoe, 1966; Thomas and the Warlock, 1967; The Ferlie, 1968, as The Enchanted Whistle, 1986; The Bodach (in U.S. as The Walking Stones), 1970; The Lothian Run, 1970; The 13th Member, 1971; The Haunted Mountain, 1972; A Sound of Chariots, 1972; The Stronghold, 1974 (Carnegie Medal Winner, 1975); A Stranger Came Ashore, 1975; Talent Is Not Enough: Writing for Children (nonfiction) 1976; The Wicked One, 1977; A Furl of Fairy Wind, 1977; The Third Eye, 1979; You Never Knew Her as I Did, 1981; The Dragonfly Years (in U.S. as Hold on to Love), 1983; The Knight of the Golden Plain, 1983; I'll Go My Own Way (in U.S. as Cat, Herself), 1985; The Three-Day Enchantment, 1985; The Mermaid Summer, 1988; Flora MacDonald & Bonny Prince Charlie, 1988; Day of the Unicorn, 1992; The Pied-Piper Syndrome (nonfiction), 1992; Gilly Martin the Fox, 1994; The King's Swift Rider: A Novel on Robert the Bruce, 1998. **Address:** Rose Cottage, 7 Mary Ann Court, Inverness IV3 5BZ, Scotland.

HUNTER, R(ichard) L(awrence). Australian, b. 1953. **Genres:** Classics. **Career:** Cambridge University, England, Pembroke College, fellow, 1977-2001, director of studies in classics, 1979-99, university lecturer in classics, 1987-97, reader in Greek and Latin literature, 1997-2001, Regius Professor of Greek, 2001-; Trinity College, fellow, 2001-. **Publications:** A Study of

Daphnis and Chloe, 1983; The New Comedy of Greece and Rome, 1985; The Argonautica of Apollonius: Literary Studies, 1993; Jason and the Golden Fleece: The Argonautica, 1993; Theocritus and the Archaeology of Greek Poetry, 1996; (with M. Fantuzzi) Muse e modelli, 2001; Theocritus, The Encomium for Ptolemy Philadelphus, 2003; Plato's Symposium, 2004. EDITOR: Eubulus: The Fragments, 1983; Book III/Apollonius of Rhodes, 1989; Theocritus, A Selection, 1999. Contributor of articles and reviews in learned journals. **Address:** Trinity College, Cambridge CB2 1TQ, England. **Online address:** rlh10@cam.ac.uk

HUNTER, Sara Hoagland. American, b. 1954. **Genres:** Children's fiction, Songs/Lyrics and libretti. **Career:** Christian Science Monitor, writer and radio producer, 1976-80; Massachusetts Public School system, teacher of English, drama, and public speaking, 1982-94; Sara Hunter Productions Inc. (producer of children's videos, books, and music), South Natick, MA, founder and president, 1994-. **Publications:** Miss Piggy's Night Out, 1995; Rondo's Stuff, 1996; The Good, the Bad, and the Tweety, 1996; Beauty and the Feast, 1996; The Unbreakable Code, 1996; Chocolate Yak-A-Lot, 1997. Lyricist for Born to Sing, Vols 1 and 2. **Address:** 8C Pleasant St., South Natick, MA 01760, U.S.A. **Online address:** sarahunter@aol.com

HUNTER, T. Willard. American, b. 1915. **Genres:** Air/Space topics, Autobiography/Memoirs, Biography. **Career:** Moral Re-Armament, Washington, DC, staff executive, 1938-56; Macalester College, St. Paul, MN, development, 1957-59; Guest Scholar, Brookings Institution, 1966-67. Claremont Colleges, Claremont, CA, development, 1959-66; Independent Colleges of Southern California, Los Angeles, executive vice-president, 1967-70; pastor of Congregational churches in New England, California, and Hawaii, 1970-80. School of Theology, Claremont, assistant to the president. Newspaper columnist, California and Illinois, 1983-99. **Publications:** The Tax Climate for Philanthropy, 1968; We Mutually Pledge (Fourth of July oratory), privately printed, 1982; The Spirit of Charles Lindbergh: Another Dimension, 1993; Bus Drivers Never Get Anywhere, 2002. Work represented in anthologies. Contributor to periodicals. **Address:** 525 W Sixth St, Claremont, CA 91711, U.S.A.

HUNTINGTON, Samuel Phillips. American, b. 1927. **Genres:** Military/Defense/Arms control, Politics/Government. **Career:** Albert J. Weatherhead III University Professor, Eaton Professor of Science of Government, Harvard University, Cambridge., Massachusetts, since 1982 (joined faculty, 1950; Director, Center for International Affairs, 1978-89; Dillon Professor of International Affairs, 1981-82). Director, John M. Olin Institute for Strategic Studies, since 1989. Vice-President, 1984-85, and President, 1986-87, American Political Science Associate Assistant Director, 1958-59, Associate Director, 1959-62, Institute of War and Peace Studies, and Associate Professor of Government, 1959-62, Columbia University, NYC. Member of Council, American Political Science Association, 1969-71; Member, Presidential Task Force on International Development, 1969-70; Member, Commission on U.S./Latin American Relations, 1974-75; Coord. of Security Planning, Natl. Security Council, 1977-78; Member, Commission on Integrated Long Term Strategy, 1986-88. Co-ed., Foreign Policy journal, 1970-77. **Publications:** The Soldier and the State: The Theory and Politics of Civil-Military Relations, 1957; The Common Defense: Strategic Programs in National Politics, 1961; (ed.) Changing Patterns of Military Politics, 1962; (co-author) Political Power: USA/USSR, 1964; Political order in Changing Societies, 1968; (co-ed.) Authoritarian Politics in Modern Society: The Dynamics of Established One-Party Systems, 1970 (co-author) The Crisis of Democracy, 1975; (with J. M. Nelson) No Easy Choice: Political Participation in Developing Countries, 1976; American Politics: The Promise of Disharmony, 1981; (ed.) The Strategic Imperative: New Policies for American Security, 1982; (co-author) Living with Nuclear Weapons, 1983; (co-ed.) Global Dilemmas, 1985; (co-ed.) Reorganizing America's Defense, 1985; (co-ed.) Understanding Political Development, 1987; The Third War: Democratization in the Late Twentieth Century, 1991; The Clash of Civilizations and the Remaking of World Order, 1996. **Address:** 1737 Cambridge St, Cambridge, MA 02138, U.S.A.

HUNTLEY, James Robert. American, b. 1923. **Genres:** International relations/Current affairs. **Career:** Government official, consultant on international affairs, and author, Sequim, WA. With Government of State of Washington, 1949-51, and U.S. Foreign Service, 1952-60; Atlantic Institute, Paris, founder and executive officer, 1960-65; Ford Foundation, NYC, International Affairs Division, program associate, 1965-67; Council of Atlantic Colleges, London, secretary-general, 1967-68; freelance writer and lectr., England, 1968-74; Battelle Memorial Institute, Seattle, research fellow, 1974-83; Atlantic Council of the U.S., president, 1983-85. **Publications:** The NATO Story, 1965, 1969; (with W.R. Burgess) Europe and America-The

Next Ten Years, 1970; Toward New Transatlantic Education Relationships, 1970; Man's Environment and the Atlantic Alliance, 1971; Uniting the Democracies: Institutions of the Atlantic-Pacific System, 1980; Pax Democratica: A Strategy for the 21st Century, 1998, 2001. EDITOR/CO-EDITOR: The Atlantic Community, A Force for Peace, 1963; Teaching about the American Impact on Europe, 1970; Teaching about Collective Security and Conflict, 1972. **Address:** 1213 Towne Rd, Sequim, WA 98382, U.S.A.

HUNTLEY, Paula (Bowlin). (born United States), b. 1944. **Genres:** Adult non-fiction. **Career:** English teacher and marketing consultant. **Publications:** The Hemingway Book Club of Kosovo (memoir), 2003. **Address:** POB 318, Bolinas, CA 94924, U.S.A. **Online address:** paula@bookclubofkosovo.com

HUNTON, Richard Edwin. American, b. 1924. **Genres:** Medicine/Health. **Career:** Clinical Assistant Professor of Family Medicine, Medical University of South Carolina. Resident Physician, Spartanburg General Hospital, South Carolina, 1953-54; Physician, Scurry Clinic, Greenwood, South Carolina, 1954-89; Staff Physician, Carolina Health Centers, 1990-; Book reviewer, Broadman Press, 1973-75. **Publications:** Formula for Fitness, 1966. **Address:** 112 Wendover Rd, Forest Hills, Greenwood, SC 29649-8923, U.S.A. **Online address:** drhunton@greenwood.net

HUPCHICK, Dennis P(aul). American, b. 1948. **Genres:** Area studies, History. **Career:** Wilkes University, Wilkes-Barre, PA, professor of history, 1990-. **Publications:** (ed. and author of intro.) The Pen and the Sword: Studies in Bulgarian History by J.F. Clarke, 1988; The Bulgarians in the Seventeenth Century: Slavic Orthodox Society and Culture under Ottoman Rule, 1993; Culture and History in Eastern Europe, 1994; Conflict and Chaos in Eastern Europe, 1995; (with H.E. Cox) A Concise Historical Atlas of Eastern Europe, 1996, rev. ed. as The Palgrave Concise Historical Atlas of Eastern Europe, 2001; (ed. with R.W. Weisberger) Hungary's Historical Legacies, 2000; (with H.E. Cox) The Palgrave Concise Historical Atlas of the Balkans, 2001; The Balkans: From Constantinople to Communism, 2002. Contributor to books and academic journals. **Address:** Department of Humanities/History, Wilkes University, PO Box 111, Wilkes Barre, PA 18766, U.S.A. **Online address:** dhupchi@wilkes.edu

HURD, Michael John. British, b. 1928. **Genres:** Songs/Lyrics and libretti, Music, Biography. **Career:** Freelance composer, writer, and lectr. on music. Professor of Theory, Royal Marines School of Music, 1953-59. **Publications:** Immortal Hour: The Life and Period of Rutland Boughton, 1962; Young Person's Guide to Concerts, 1962; Young Person's Guide to Opera, 1963; Young Person's Guide to English Music, 1965; Sailors' Songs and Shanties, 1965; Soldiers' Songs and Marches, 1966; Benjamin Britten, 1966; The Composer, 1968; An Outline History of European Music, 1969; Elgar, 1969; Vaughan Williams, 1970; Mendelssohn, 1970; The Ordeal of Ivor Gurney, 1978; Tippett, 1978; The Oxford Junior Companion to Music, 1979; The Orchestra, 1980; Vincent Novello-and Company, 1981; Rutland Boughton and the Glastonbury Festivals, 1993; Letters of Gerald Finzi and Howard Ferguson, 2001. LIBRETTIST AND COMPOSER: Little Billy, 1966; Jonah-Man Jazz, 1966; Mr. Punch, 1970; (with D. Hughes) The Widow of Ephesus, 1972; Swingin' Samson, 1974; Rooster Rag, 1976; Pilgrim, 1978; Adam-in-Eden, 1982; Mrs. Beeton's Book, 1983; A New Nowell, 1987; Captain Coram's Kids, 1988; Prodigal, 1989; The Liberty Tree, 1990; King and Conscience, 1990; Mr. Owen's Great Endeavour, 1991; The Aspern Papers, 1993; The Night of the Wedding, 1998. **Address:** 4 Church St, West Liss, Hants., England.

HURKA, Thomas. Canadian, b. 1952. **Genres:** Ethics, Philosophy. **Career:** University of Calgary, Alberta, Canada, assistant professor of philosophy, 1979-84, associate professor, 1984-92, professor, 1992-2002; University of Toronto, ON, Canada, professor of philosophy, 2002-, Jackman Distinguished Professor of Philosophical Studies, 2003-. **Publications:** Perfectionism, 1993; (ed. with H.G. Coward) Ethics and Climate Change: The Greenhouse Effect, 1993; Principles: Short Essays on Ethics, 1993; Virtue, Vice, and Value, 2001. **Address:** Department of Philosophy, University of Toronto, 215 Huron St., Toronto, ON, Canada M5S 1A1. **Online address:** tom.hurka@utoronto.ca

HURLBUT, Cornelius Searle, Jr. American, b. 1906. **Genres:** Earth sciences. **Career:** Professor of Mineralogy, Harvard University, Cambridge, Massachusetts, 1940-72; Visiting Professor, Boston College, 1972-78. **Publications:** (ed.) Minerals and How to Study Them, by E. S. Dana, 1949; (with H. E. Wenden) The Changing Science of Mineralogy, 1964; Minerals and Man, 1968; (with C. Klein) Manual of Mineralogy, 1993; (ed.) The Planet We Live On: An Illustrated Encyclopedia of the Earth Sciences, 1978; (with

R. C. Kammerling) Gemology, 1991. **Address:** c/o Dept. of Earth and Planetary Sciences, Harvard University, 24 Oxford St, Cambridge, MA 02138, U.S.A.

HURLEY, Andrew. American, b. 1944. **Genres:** Translations. **Career:** Translator. University of Puerto Rico, Department of English, professor of English, has worked as director of Graduate Program in Translation, College of Humanities. **Publications:** TRANSLATOR: Legacies: Selected Poems by Heberto Padilla, 1982; H. Padilla, Heroes Are Grazing in My Garden, 1984; R. Arenas, Farewell to the Sea, 1985; Against All Hope: The Prison Memoirs of Armando Valladares, 1986; R. Arenas, The Ill-Fated Peregrinations of Fray Servando, 1987; F. Arrabal, The Compass-Stone, 1987; G. Sainz, The Princess of the Iron Palace, 1987; R. Arenas, Singing from the Well, 1987; R. Arenas, The Brightest Star (novella), 1989; R. Arenas, The Palace of the White Skunks, 1990; E. Sabato, The Angel of Darkness, 1991; F. Arrabal, El Greco and Fernando Arrabal, 1991; L. Lopez-Baralt, Islam and Spanish Literature, 1992; F. Arrabal, The Red Virgin, 1993; G.A. Baralt, Tradition into the Future: The First Hundred Years of the Banco Popular de Puerto Rico, 1993; J. Edwards, Persona Non Grata, 1993; R. Arenas, The Assault, 1994; A. Lydia Vega, True and False Romances, 1994; E. Rodriguez-Julia, The Renunciation, 1997; S. Puledda, On Being Human: Interpretations of Humanism from the Renaissance to the Present, 1997; Collected Fictions of Jorge Luis Borges, 1998; R. Arenas, The Color of Summer, 2000; Z. Valdes, Dear First Love, 2002. Translator of short fiction, poetry, criticism, and articles appearing in books and periodicals. **Address:** Department of English, College of Humanities, University of Puerto Rico, Rio Piedras, PR 00931, U.S.A. **Online address:** memail@yunque.com

HURST, Frances. *See* MAYHAR, Ardath (Hurst).

HURT, Harry, III. American, b. 1951. **Genres:** Adult non-fiction, Biography. **Career:** Texas Monthly, Austin, TX, senior editor, 1975-86; Newsweek, NYC, correspondent based in Los Angeles, CA, 1988-90. **Publications:** Texas Rich: The Hunt Dynasty from the Early Oil Days through the Silver Crash, 1981; For All Mankind, 1988; Lost Tycoon: The Many Lives of Donald J. Trump, 1993; Chasing the Dream, 1997; How to Learn Golf, 2002. **Address:** 4600 Post Oak Pl., Suite 306, Houston, TX 77027, U.S.A.

HURTADO, Albert L. American, b. 1946. **Genres:** History. **Career:** California Department of Parks and Recreation, Sacramento, park interpretive specialist in Office of Historic Preservation, 1977-78; Theodoratus Cultural Research, Fair Oaks, Calif., senior staff historian, 1978-80; Sierra College, Rocklin, Calif., instructor in social science, 1981-82; University of Maryland at College Park, lecturer in history, spring, 1983; Indiana University-Purdue University at Indianapolis, assistant professor of history, 1983-86; Arizona State University, Tempe, assistant professor of history, 1986-89, Associate Professor, 1990-; Chairman of California Committee for the Promotion of History, 1981-82; member of board of directors of National Council on Public History, 1982-85; consultant with Public History Services Associates, 1980-83; expert witness in Superior Court of the State of California, 1982. Military service: U.S. Army, special agent in Military Intelligence, 1969-71; Literary Prizes: Herbert E. Bolton Prize, 1982; Ray A. Billingham Prize, 1989; Vivian Palladin Award, 1991; Louis Knott Koontz Prize, 1994; Bolton-Kinnaird Prize, 1994. **Publications:** Indian Survival on the California Frontier, 1988. EDITOR: (with T.J. Karamanski and C. Davis) Public History Education in America: A Guide, 1986; (with P. Iverson) Major Problems in American Indian History, 1994. Contributor to books. **Address:** Department of History, University of Oklahoma, West Lindsey, Room 403A, Norman, OK 73019, U.S.A. **Online address:** ahurtado@ou.edu

HURTADO, Larry W. American/Canadian, b. 1943. **Genres:** Literary criticism and history, Theology/Religion. **Career:** Educator and author. Regent College, Vancouver, BC, Canada, assistant professor of New Testament, 1975-78; University of Manitoba, Winnipeg, professor of religion, 1978-96; University of Edinburgh, Scotland, professor of New Testament language, literature & theology, 1996-. **Publications:** Text-Critical Methodology and the Pre-Caesarean Text: Codex W in the Gospel of Mark, 1981; One God, One Lord: Early Christian Devotion and Ancient Jewish Monotheism, 1988, 2nd ed., 1998; Mark: New International Biblical Commentary, 1989; At the Origins of Christian Worship: The Content and Character of Earliest Christian Devotion, 1999; Lord Jesus Christ: Devotion to Jesus in Earliest Christianity, 2003. EDITOR: Goddess in Religions and Modern Debate, 1990; (with K. Klostermaier) Religious Studies: Issues, Prospects and Proposals, 1991; (with D.L. Jeffrey) A Dictionary of Biblical Tradition in English Literature, 1992. Contributor to books, dictionaries and encyclopedias, and professional periodicals. **Address:** New College, University of Edinburgh, Mound Place, Edinburgh EH1 2LX, Scotland. **Online address:** L.Hurtado@ed.ac.uk

HURTIG, Mel. Canadian. **Genres:** Politics/Government. **Career:** Owner and operator of book stores throughout Canada, 1956-72; Hurtig Publishers Ltd., owner and president, 1972-1991. **Publications:** The Betrayal of Canada, 1991; A New and Better Canada, 1993; At Twilight in the Country, 1996. **Address:** 9905 115th St., Edmonton, AB, Canada T5K 1S4.

HURWITZ, Johanna (Frank). American, b. 1937. **Genres:** Children's fiction, Children's non-fiction. **Career:** New York Public Library, children's librarian, 1959-64; Queen's College, lecturer in children's literature, 1965-68; librarian, Calhoun School, NY, 1968-75; and New Hyde Park school district, NY, 1975-77; Great Neck Public Library, NY, children's librarian, 1978-92. **Publications:** Busybody Nora, 1976; Nora and Mrs. Mind-Your-Own-Business, 1977; The Law of Gravity, 1978; Much Ado about Nothing, 1978; Aldo Applesauce, 1979; New Neighbors for Nora, 1979; Once I Was a Plum Tree, 1980; Superduper Teddy, 1980; Aldo Ice Cream, 1981; Baseball Fever, 1981; The Rabbi's Girls, 1982; Tough-Luck Karen, 1982; Rip-Roaring Russell, 1983; DeDe Takes Charge!, 1984; The Hot and Cold Summer, 1984; The Adventures of Ali Baba Berstein, 1985; Russell Rides Again, 1985; Hurricane Elaine, 1986; Yellow Blue Jay, 1986; Class Clown, 1987; Russell Sprouts, 1987; The Cold and Hot Winter, 1988; Teacher's Pet, 1988; Anne Frank: Life in Hiding, 1988; Hurray for Ali Baba Bernstein, 1989; Russell and Elisa, 1989; Astrid Lindgren: Storyteller to the World, 1989; Class President, 1990; Aldo Peanut Butter, 1990; School's Out, 1991; Roz and Ozzie, 1992; Ali Baba Bernstein, Lost and Found, 1992; The Up and Down Spring, 1993; Make Room for Elisa, 1993; New Shoes for Silvia, 1993; Leonard Bernstein, A Passion for Music, 1993; School Spirit, 1994; A Llama in the Family, 1994; Even Stephen, 1995; The Down and Up Fall, 1995; Spring Break, 1997; Ever-Clever Elisa, 1997; Helen Keller: Courage in the Dark 1997; Elisa in the Middle, 1998; Faraway Summer, 1998; Starting School, 1998; A Dream Come True, 1998; Llama in the Library, 1999; The Just Desserts Club, 1999; Summer with Elisa, 2000; One Small Dog, 2000; PeeWee's Tale, 2000; Russell's Secret, 2001; Lexi's Tale, 2001; Oh No, Noah, 2002; PeeWee & Plush, 2002; Dear Emma, 2002; Elisa Michaels, Bigger and Better, 2003. **Address:** 10 Spruce Pl, Great Neck, NY 11021, U.S.A.

HUSAIN, Shahrukh. Pakistani, b. 1950. **Genres:** Autobiography/Memoirs. **Career:** Writer. **Publications:** Journeys to the Promised Land, 1998. **Address:** 29 Winchester Ave., London NW6 7TT, England.

HUSER, Glen. (born Canada), b. 1943. **Genres:** Children's fiction. **Career:** Teacher, educational consultant, and writer. Teacher at Rosslyn and Highlands Schools, 1962-65; McArthur School, 1967-69; and librarian, Holyrood, Lendrum, Homestead, Kirkness, and Overlanders Schools, 1970-88. Learning Resources, Edmonton Public Schools, consultant, 1988-96; Concordia College, student teaching advisor, 1997-98; University of Alberta, sessional instructor, 1997-98, 1999-2000, and 2003-2004; Oz New Media/Education-on-line, language arts resource writer, 2000-01. Writer-in-residence, Mee-Yah-Noh Elementary School, 2001-02, and Virginia Park Elementary School, 2003-04. Leader of workshops and conference sessions at various schools and education conventions. **Publications:** Grace Lake (for adults), 1990; Touch of the Clown, 1999; Jeremy's Christmas Wish, 2000; Stitches, 2003. Contributor of short stories to anthologies and periodicals. **Address:** 6012 Ada Blvd., Edmonton, Alberta, Canada T5W 4N9. **Online address:** glenh@planet.eon.net

HUSKEY, Eugene. American, b. 1952. **Genres:** International relations/Current affairs, Politics/Government. **Career:** Colgate University, Hamilton, NY, visiting instructor, 1981-83; Bowdoin College, Brunswick, ME, assistant professor, 1983-89; Stetson University, DeLand, FL, associate professor, 1989-96, professor, 1996-99, William R. Kenan Jr. Professor of Political Science and Russian Studies, 1999-. **Publications:** Russian Lawyers and the Soviet State, 1986; (ed.) Executive Power and Soviet Politics: The Rise and Decline of the Soviet State, 1992; Presidential Power in Russia, 1999. Contributor to academic journals. **Address:** Stetson University, Box 8313, DeLand, FL 32720, U.S.A.

HUSS, Sandy. American, b. 1953. **Genres:** Novellas/Short stories. **Career:** Washington University, St. Louis, MO, lecturer in fiction writing and exposition, 1987-88; University of Alabama, Tuscaloosa, assistant professor of English, 1988-95, associate professor, 1995-. Gives readings of her works. **Publications:** Labor for Love: Stories, 1992. Contributor to anthologies. **Address:** Department of English, University of Alabama, PO Box 870244, Tuscaloosa, AL 35487, U.S.A. **Online address:** www.bama.ua.edu/~shuss

HUSSEY, Mark. American (born England), b. 1956. **Genres:** Humanities, Literary criticism and history, Women's studies and issues, Autobiography/Memoirs. **Career:** Sussex Publications, Wiltshire, England, editor of English

Tapes Program and Sussex Tapes, 1976-82; Association of American Publishers, New York City, assistant to the director, International Division and Professional and Scholarly Publishing Division, 1982-84; Pace University, NYC, adjunct assistant professor, 1984-88, professor of English, 1988-, assistant to the director, Thinking and Learning Center, 1985-88, coordinator, Feminist Research Group, 1990-91; writer. Sander Gallery, assistant to the directors, 1985-86; Northern Business Information, writing consultant, 1985-86; New School for Social Research, member of faculty, 1987-90. Pace University Press, chairperson of editorial committee, 1987-. **Publications:** The Singing of the Real World: The Philosophy of Virginia Woolf's Fiction, 1986; Virginia Woolf A to Z, 1995. EDITOR/CO-EDITOR & AUTHOR OF INTRO.: Virginia Woolf and War: Fiction, Reality, and Myth, 1991; Virginia Woolf Miscellanies, Proceedings of the First Annual Conference on Virginia Woolf, 1992; Virginia Woolf: Themes and Variations, Selected Papers from the 2nd Annual Conference on Virginia Woolf, 1993; Virginia Woolf: Emerging Perspectives, Selected Papers from the 3rd Annual Conference on Virginia Woolf, 1994; (gen. ed.) Harcourt Annotated Edition of Virginia Woolf, 2005. **Address:** Dept of English, Pace University, 1 Pace Plaza, New York, NY 10038, U.S.A. **Online address:** mhussey@pace.edu

HUSSEY, Patricia (Ann). American, b. 1949. **Genres:** Theology/Religion. **Career:** Entered the Order of the Sisters of Notre Dame de Namur (a Roman Catholic religious order for women) in 1967, took final vows, 1980, left the order, 1988; co-director of Covenant House (a shelter and counseling center for the homeless), Charleston, WV, 1981-. St. Teresa's School, Providence, RI, teacher, 1972-73; Long Lane School, Middletown, CT, youth service worker, 1973-76, recreation worker, 1977; United States Representative for the Sisters in Initial Formation, Rome, Italy, 1978; Stringer and Racker, Providence, RI, jewelry factory worker, 1979-81; Advent House (a shelter for the homeless and battered women), volunteer, 1979-81. **Publications:** (with Barbara Ferraro and Jane O'Reilly) No Turning Back: Two Nuns' Battle with the Vatican Over Women's Right to Choose, Poseidon Press, 1990. **Address:** Covenant House, 600 Shrewsbury St, Charleston, WV 25301-1211, U.S.A. **Online address:** phussey@wvcovenanthouse.org

HUSTON, James E(dward). American, b. 1930. **Genres:** Medicine/Health. **Career:** Family physician in San Leandro, CA, 1959-69; Kaiser Foundation Hospital, San Francisco, CA, resident in obstetrics and gynecology, 1969-72; practiced obstetrics and gynecology in Castro Valley, CA, 1972-91, and Medford, OR, 1991-94; retired, 1994. **Publications:** (with L.D. Lanka) Perimenopause: Changes in Women's Health after Thirty-Five, 1997; Menopause: A Guide to Health and Happiness, 1998; PMDD: A Guide to Coping with Premenstrual Dysphoric Disorder, 2002. Contributor to medical journals and newsletters. **Address:** 2424 London Circle, Medford, OR 97504, U.S.A. **Online address:** jhuston@mind.net

HUSTON, James W(ebb). American, b. 1953. **Genres:** Novels. **Career:** Attorney and writer. Admitted to the California Bar, 1984; Gray, Cary, Ames & Frye (now Gray, Cary, Ware & Freidenrich LLP), San Diego, CA, attorney, 1984-90, partner, 1990-. **Publications:** NOVELS: Balance of Power, 1998; Price of Power, 1999; Flash Point, 2000; Fallout, 2001; The Shadows of Power, 2002; Secret Justice, 2003. **Address:** Gray Cary Ware & Freidenrich LLP, 401 B St. Suite 1700, San Diego, CA 92101, U.S.A.

HUSTON, Nancy. Canadian/French, b. 1953. **Genres:** Novels, Human relations/Parenting. **Career:** Columbia University, Paris, France, instructor, 1976-92. Visiting professor, University of Massachusetts at Amherst, 1990; and Harvard University, 1994. Guest lecturer at universities. **Publications:** Jouer au papa et a l'amant: De l'amour des petites filles, 1979; Dire et interdire: Elements de jurologie, 1980; Les Variations Goldberg, 1981; Mosaique de la pornographie: Marie-Therese et les autres, 1982; (with S. Kinser) A l'amour comme a la guerre, 1984; Histoire d'Omaya, 1985, as The Story of Omaya, 1987; (ed. with P. Magli) Le Donne e i segni: Scrittura, linguaggio, identita nel segno della differenza femminile, 1985; (with L. Sebbar) Lettres parisiennes: Autopsie de l'exil, 1986; Trois fois septembre, 1989; Journal de la creation, 1990; Plainsong, in France as Cantique des plaines, 1993; La Virevolte, 1994, as Slow Emergencies, 1996; Tombeau de Romain Gary, 1995; Desirs et realites, 1995; Instruments des tenebres, 1996, as Instruments of Darkness, 1997; Desirs et realites, 1997; L'Empreinte de l'ange, 1998, as The Mark of the Angel, 1999; Prodige, 1999, as Prodigy, 2000; Nord perdu, 1999; Limbes/Limbo: un homage a Samuel Beckett, 2000; Dolce Agonia, 2001.

HUSTVEDT, Siri. American, b. 1955. **Genres:** Novels, Poetry, Essays, Translations. **Career:** Writer. **Publications:** Reading to You (poems), 1983; (trans. from Norwegian, with D. McDuff) Geir Kjetsaa, Fyodor Dostoyevsky: A Writer's Life, 1987; (translation ed.) Fragments for a History of the Human Body, edited by Michel Feher, Parts I-III, 1989; The Blindfold (novel), 1992; The Enchantment of Lily Dahl (novel), 1996; Yonder (essays), 1998; What I Loved (novel), 2003. Work represented in anthologies. **Address:** c/o Amanda Urban, International Creative Management Inc, 40 W 57th St, New York, NY 10019, U.S.A.

HUTCHEON, Linda. Canadian, b. 1947. **Genres:** Humanities, Literary criticism and history, Music. **Career:** McMaster University, Hamilton, ON, assistant professor, 1976-82, associate professor, 1982-85, professor of English, 1985-88; University of Toronto, ON, adjunct professor at Center for Comparative Literature, beginning in 1980, professor of English and comparative literature, 1988-96, university professor, 1996-. Robarts Chair of Canadian Studies at York University, 1988-89. **Publications:** Narcissistic Narrative: The Metafictional Paradox, 1980; Formalism and the Freudian Aesthetic, 1984; A Theory of Parody: The Teachings of Twentieth-Century Art Forms, 1985; A Poetics of Postmodernism: History, Theory, Fiction, 1988; The Canadian Postmodern: A Study of Contemporary English-Canadian Fiction, 1989; The Politics of Postmodernism, 1989; Splitting Images: Contemporary Canadian Ironies, 1991; Irony's Edge: The Theory and Politics of Irony, 1995; (with M. Hutcheon) Opera: Desire, Disease and Death, 1996; (with M. Hutcheon) Bodily Charm: Living Opera, 2000. TRANSLATOR: F. Leclerc, Allegro, 1974. EDITOR: Other Solitudes: Canadian Multicultural Fiction and Interviews, 1990; Double-Talking: Essays on Verbal and Visual Ironies in Contemporary Canadian Art and Literature, 1992; Likely Stories: A Postmodern Sampler, 1992; A Postmodern Reader, 1993. **Address:** Department of English, University of Toronto, Toronto, ON, Canada M5S 3K1.

HUTCHEON, Michael. Canadian, b. 1945. **Genres:** Music. **Career:** Department of medicine, University of Toronto, Toronto, Ontario, Canada, medical director, lung transplantation, 1996-. **Publications:** (with L. Hutcheon) Opera: Desire, Disease, Death, 1996; (with L. Hutcheon) Bodily Charm: Living Opera, 2000. **Address:** 10EN-236, University of Toronto, 200 Elizabeth St, Toronto, ON, Canada M5G 2C4.

HUTCHERSON, Hilda. American, b. 1955. **Genres:** Medicine/Health. **Career:** Physician. Columbia University, New York, NY, associate dean, assistant professor of clinical obstetrics and gynecology, and co-director of New York Center for Women's Sexual Health. Affiliated with Pelham Family Service, 1996-2000. **Publications:** (with M. Williams) Having Your Baby: A Guide for African-American Women, 1997; What Your Mother Never Told You about S.E.X., 2002. **Address:** 225 Eastland Ave., Pelham, NY 10803, U.S.A. **Online address:** Drhilhut@aol.com

HUTCHINS, Hazel J. Canadian, b. 1952. **Genres:** Novels, Children's fiction. **Career:** Author of children's novels and picture books. **Publications:** The Three and Many Wishes of Jason Reid, 1983; Anastasia Morningstar and the Crystal Butterfly, 1984; Leanna Builds a Genie Trap, 1986; Ben's Snow Song: A Winter Picnic, 1987; Casey Webber, the Great, 1988; Norman's Snowball, 1989; Nicholas at the Library, 1990; Katie's Babbling Brother, 1991; A Cat of Artimus Pride, 1991; And You Can Be a Cat, 1992; The Best of Arlie Zack, 1993; The Catfish Palace, 1993; Within a Painted Post, 1994; Believing Sophie, 1995; Tess, 1995; Yancy and Bear, 1996; The Prince of Tarn, 1997; Reach for the Moon Robyn, 1997; It's Raining Yancy and Bear, 1998; Robyn's Want Ad, 1998; One Duck, 1999; Two So Small, 2000; Robyn Looks for Bears, 2000; The Wide World of Suzie Mallard, 2000; Robyn's Best Idea, 2001; One Dark Night, 2001; Robyn's Art Attack, 2002; TJ and the Cats, 2002; I'd Know You Anywhere, 2002; TJ and the Haunted House, 2003; Robyn Makes the News, 3003; TJ and the Rockets, 2004; Skate, Robyn, Skate, 2004; A Second Is a Hiccup, 2004; The Sidewalk Rescue, 2004; Beneath the Bridge, 2004. **Address:** c/o Annick Press, 15 Patricia Ave, Willowdale, ON, Canada M2M 1H9. **Online address:** hjhutch@telusplanet.net

HUTCHINS, Pat. British, b. 1942. **Genres:** Children's fiction, Poetry. **Career:** Freelance writer and illustrator. J. Walter Thompson Ltd., advertising agency, London, art director, 1963-66. **Publications:** Rosie's Walk, 1968; Tom and Sam, 1968; The Surprise Party, 1969; Clocks and More Clocks, 1970; Changes, Changes, 1971; Titch, 1971; Good-Night, Owl, 1972; The Wind Blew (poetry), 1974; The Silver Christmas Tree, 1974; Don't Forget the Bacon (poetry), 1975; The House That Sailed Away, 1976; Follow That Bus, 1977; Happy Birthday Sam, 1978; The Best Train Set Ever, 1978; One Eyed Jake, 1979; The Tale of Thomas Mead (poetry), 1979; The Mona Lisa Mystery, 1980; One Hunter, 1981; You'll Soon Grow into Them, Titch!, 1983; The Curse of the Egyptian Mummy, 1983; King Henry's Palace, 1983; The Very Worst Monster, 1985; The Doorbell Rang, 1986; Where's the Baby?, 1987; Which Witch Is Which?, 1989; Rats! 1989; What Game Shall We Play?, 1990; Tidy Titch, 1991; Silly Billy, 1992; My Best

Friend, 1993; Three-Star Billy, 1994; Little Pink Pig, 1994; Titch and Daisy, 1996; Shrinking Mouse, 1998; It's My Birthday!, 1999; Ten Red Apples, 2000; We're Going on a Picnic!, 2001; Sticky Titch, 2000; Titch out and About, 2000; It's Bathtime, Titch, 2000; Titch's Windy Day, 2000; Only One of Me, 2003.

HUTCHINSON, Allan C. British, b. 1951. **Genres:** Law, Education. **Career:** Called to the Bar at Gray's Inn, 1975; York University, North York, Ontario, sessional lecturer in law, 1978-80; University of Newcastleupon-Tyne, Newcastle-upon-Tyne, England, lecturer in law, 1980-82; York University, assistant professor, 1982-84, associate professor, 1984-88, professor of law, 1988-, associate dean of Osgoode Hall Law School, 1994-96. Cambridge University, Cambridge Lecturer at Queen's College, 1985, 1987; visiting professor at Monash University, 1986, University of Toronto, 1989-90, and University of Western Australia, 1991; University of Sydney, Parsons Professor, 1995; University of London, Inns of Court fellow at Institute of Advanced Legal Studies, 1997; guest lecturer at colleges and universities throughout the English-speaking world. **Publications:** (ed. with P. Monahan) The Rule of Law: Ideal or Ideology, 1986; Dwelling on the Threshold: Critical Essays on Modern Legal Thought, 1987; (ed. with G. Watson, R. Sharpe, and W. Bogart) Canadian Civil Procedure, 3rd ed., 1988; (ed.) Critical Legal Studies, 1988; (ed. with L. Green) Law and Community: The End of Individualism? 1989; (ed.) Access to Justice: Barriers and Bridges, 1990; (ed. with Watson, Bogart, K. Roach, and J. Mosher) Civil Litigation: Cases and Materials, 4th ed., 1991; Waiting for Coraf: A Critique of Law and Rights, 1995; The Law School Book: Succeeding at Law School, 1996; (ed. with K. Peterson) Censorship in Canada, 1997; Professional Responsibilities, 1997. Contributor to books. Contributor of articles and reviews to scholarly journals and newspapers. **Address:** Osgoode Hall Law School, York University, 4700 Keele St., North York, ON, Canada M3J 1P3.

HUTCHINSON, Bill. American, b. 1947. **Genres:** Area studies. **Career:** Minister of United Church of Christ; United Way of the Bay Area, San Francisco, CA, associate campaign director, 1974-81; Marin Interfaith Task Force on Central America, Mill Valley, CA, director, 1985-95; Hew Hope Church, Sonoma, CA, founding minister, 1990-94; Hutchinson Personnel Consulting, Sonoma, co-owner, 1996-. Christians for Peace in El Salvador, president of board of directors, 1999-2000; United Way of Sonoma, Mendocino, and Lake Counties, member of board of directors, 1996-2002. **Publications:** When the Dogs Ate Candles: A Time in El Salvador, 1998. **Address:** 20735 Fifth St. E., Sonoma, CA 95476, U.S.A. **Online address:** hutchpc@aol.com

HUTCHINSON, Earl Ofari. American, b. 1945. **Genres:** Race relations, Human relations/Parenting, Social commentary. **Career:** Writer and public speaker; lecturer at colleges and universities; guest on radio stations. Paul Robeson Community Center, member of board of directors. **Publications:** The Myth of Black Capitalism, 1970; Let Your Motto Be Resistance, 1974; Crime: Why It Exists, What Can Be Done, 1986; Crime, Drugs, and African Americans, 1987; The Mugging of Black America, 1990; Black Fatherhood: Guide to Male Parenting, 1992; The Assassination of the Black Male Image, 1994; Blacks and Reds: Race and Class Conflict, 1919-1990, 1994; Black Fatherhood II: Black Women Talk about Their Men, 1994; Betrayed: A History of Presidential Failure to Protect Black Lives, 1996; Beyond O.J.: Race Sex amd Class Lessons for America, 1996; The Crisis in Black and Black, 1998; The Disappearance of Black Leadership, 2000. Contributor to periodicals. **Address:** 5517 Secrest Dr., Los Angeles, CA 90043, U.S.A.

HUTCHINSON, G(regory) O(wen). British, b. 1957. **Genres:** Classics, Literary criticism and history. **Career:** Oxford University, Oxford, England, research lecturer at Christ Church, 1981-84, fellow and tutor in classics at Exeter College, 1984-, professor of Greek and Latin languages and literature, 1998-. **Publications:** (ed. and author of commentary) Aeschylus, Septem contra Thebas, 1984, published as Seven Against Thebes, 1994; Hellenistic Poetry, 1988; Latin Literature from Seneca to Juvenal: A Critical Study, 1993; Cicero's Correspondence: A Literary Study, 1998; Greek Lyric Poetry: A Commentary on Selected Larger Pieces, 2001. **Address:** Exeter College, Oxford OX1 3DP, England.

HUTCHINSON, John F(ranklin). Canadian, b. 1938. **Genres:** History, Medicine/Health. **Career:** Simon Fraser University, Burnaby, British Columbia, faculty member, 1966-, currently professor of history. **Publications:** Politics and Public Health in Revolutionary Russia, 1890-1918, 1990; (coed) Health and Society in Revolutionary Russia, 1990; Champions of Charity, 1996; Late Imperial Russia, 1890-1917, 1997.

HUTCHINSON, Timothy A. (born United States), b. 1960. **Genres:** Adult non-fiction. **Career:** Writer. Also works as emergency medical technician.

Publications: Battlescars (autobiography), 2003. Author of articles on the prevention of teen violence. **Address:** c/o Author Mail, Riverstone Publishing, POB 270852, St. Paul, MN 55127, U.S.A. **Online address:** contact@ americanyouth.net

HUTCHISON, Linda. (born Canada), b. 1942. **Genres:** Children's nonfiction. **Career:** Worked as technical writer in Los Angeles and San Diego, CA, a journalist in Los Angeles, CA, and a copywriter for advertising agencies in San Diego; freelance writer and poet. **Publications:** Lebanon, 2003; Finland, 2004. Contributor of poetry to national journals. **Address:** 841 Loring St., San Diego, CA 92109, U.S.A.

HUTCHISSON, James M. American, b. 1961. **Genres:** Literary criticism and history, Biography. **Career:** Washington & Jefferson College, Washington, PA, assistant professor of English, 1987-89; The Citadel, Charleston, SC, professor, 1989-. **Publications:** (ed.) S. Lewis, Babbit, 1995; The Rise of Sinclair Lewis 1920-1930 (literary criticism/biography), 1996; Sinclair Lewis: New Essays in Criticism (essays), 1997; DuBose Heyward: A Charleston Gentleman and the World of Porgy and Bess (biography), 2000; Perspectives on the Charleston Renaissance (essays); A DuBose Heyward Reader (collection). Author of articles on American literature. **Address:** Department of English, The Citadel, 171 Moultrie St, Charleston, SC 29409, U.S.A.

HUTSON, Lorna. German, b. 1958. **Genres:** Literary criticism and history. **Career:** University of London, Queen Mary and Westfield College, London, England, lecturer in English, 1986-. **Publications:** Thomas Nashe in Context, 1989; The Usurer's Daughter: Male Friendship and Fictions of Women in Sixteenth-Century England, 1994. **Address:** Department of English, University of St. Andrews, St. Andrews, Fife KY16 9AJ, Scotland.

HUTTNER, Harry J. M. Dutch, b. 1938. **Genres:** Social sciences. **Career:** Catholic University of Nijmegen, Nijmegen, Netherlands, lecturer in research methodology, 1965-. **Publications:** (with P. Van Den Eeden) Multi-Level Research, 1982; Multilevel Onderzoek: De Operationalisatie van Omgevingskenmerken (title means: Multilevel Research: The Operationalization of Collective Properties), 1985; (with Van Den Eeden) The Multilevel Design: A Guide with an Annotated Bibliography, 1980-1993, 1995. EDITOR: (with H. Kleijer) Gezin en Onderwijs (title means: Family and Education), 1990; (with Van Den Eeden) Onderzoeken op Niveau: Toepassingen van Multilevel Analyse (title means: Investigations on a High Level: Applications of Multilevel Analysis), 1995; (with K. Renckstorf and F. Wester) Onderzoekstypen in de Communicatiewetenschap (title means: Designs in Communication Research), 1995. Contributor to books and journals. **Address:** Research Methodology Division, Department of Social Sciences, Catholic University of Nijmegen, Thomas Van Aquinostraat 4 Postbus 9104, 6500 HE Nijmegen, Netherlands.

HUTTON, Barbara (Audrey). British, b. 1920. **Genres:** Architecture, Homes/Gardens. **Career:** Part-time schoolteacher in Hertfordshire, England, 1959-60; University of Leeds, England, part-time teacher for Workers' Educational Association, 1975-84; writer, 1984-. Member of Royal National Lifeboat Institution and Hertfordshire Local History Council, 1961-66; member of council of York Civic Trust, 1967-86; member of board of trustees of York Archaeological Trust, 1972-86; President, Vernacular Architecture Group, 1986-90; co-ordinator, Derby Buildings Record for Derbyshire Archaeological Society, 1987-. **Publications:** The Works in Architecture of John Carr, Sessions of York, 1973; (with B. Harrison) Vernacular Houses in North Yorkshire and Cleveland, 1983; (co-author) Horton-in-Ribblesdale: The Story of an Upland Parish, 1984; Historic Farmhouses Around Derby, 1991; Houses and Everyday Life in Weston on Trent, 1994. **Address:** 50 Daventry Close, Mickleover, Derbyshire DE3 5QT, England.

HUTTON, Drew. Australian, b. 1947. **Genres:** Area studies, Environmental sciences/Ecology. **Career:** Queensland University of Technology, Brisbane, Australia, department of applied ethics, lecturer. Australian Greens, founding member, National Council and National Conference delegate; Queensland Greens, founding member and spokesperson; member, Brisbane City Council Clean Air Task Force and Queensland Conservation Council advisory group; author. **Publications:** (ed.) Green Politics in Australia: A Collection of Essays, 1987; (with L. Connors) A History of the Australian Environment Movement, 1999. **Address:** c/o Queensland Greens, PO Box 5763, West End, QLD 4101, Australia. **Online address:** d.hutton@qut.edu.au

HUTTON, Frankie. American. **Genres:** History, Communications/Media, Writing/Journalism. **Career:** Mitre Corporation, Bedford, MA, senior technical editor, 1980-82; Lehigh University, Bethlehem, PA, assistant professor of journalism, 1988-94; Hampton University, Hampton, VA, associate professor of mass media studies, 1996-. Member, commission on Sex Discrimination in the New Jersey Statutes, 1988-89; Pennsylvania Historical and Museum Committee, member of black history advisory committee, 1989-91. University of Virginia, visiting lecturer, 1978, 1980-81; Howard University, visiting professor of history, 1998-2000; Montclair State University, adjunct professor of history, 2001-. **Publications:** NONFICTION: The Early Black Press in America, 1827-1860, 1993; (with B.S. Reed) Outsiders in Nineteenth-Century Press History: Multicultural Perspectives, 1995. Contributor of articles and reviews to scholarly periodicals. Contributor of chapters to books. **Address:** PO Box 649, Little Silver, NJ 07739, U.S.A. **Online address:** FHutton@aol.com

HUTTON, John (Harwood). British, b. 1928. **Genres:** Novels. **Career:** Sr. Lecturer in English, Cartrefle College, North East Wales Institute, Wrexham, 1967-85; now retired. Supply teacher, West Bromwich Education Authority, 1953; Assistant Lecturer in English, University College, Bangor, 1953-54; Lecturer, Wigan and District Mining and Technical College, 1954-58; Head of the English Dept., Ruabon Girls' Grammar School, 1959-67. **Publications:** 29 Herriott Street, 1979; Accidental Crimes, 1983. **Address:** Ty Mawr, Penmynydd, Llanfairpwll, Anglesey LL61 5BX, Wales.

HUTTON, Paul Andrew. American (born Germany), b. 1949. **Genres:** Plays/Screenplays, History, Biography, Military/Defense/Arms control. **Career:** Utah State University, Logan, visiting instructor, 1977-80, assistant professor of American history, 1980-84; University of New Mexico, Albuquerque, assistant professor, 1984-86, associate professor of American history, 1986-96, professor of American history, 1996-; writer. **Publications:** Phil Sheridan and His Army, 1985; Soldiers West: Biographies from the Military Frontier, 1987. EDITOR: Custer and His Times, 1981; Henry Eugene Davies, Ten Days on the Plains, 1985; The Custer Reader, 1992; Eyewitness to the Civil War, 10 vol. series, 1992-93; (co-ed.) Frontier and Region, 1997. **Address:** Department of History, University of New Mexico, Albuquerque, NM 87131, U.S.A. **Online address:** wha@umn.edu

HUTTON, Ronald. British, b. 1953. **Genres:** History. **Career:** Home Civil Service, London, England, clerical officer, 1972-73; Guardian, London, editorial junior, 1974; Oxford University, England, fellow of Magdalen College, 1979-81, lecturer, 1981-89; Cornwall College, reader, 1985-93; University of Bristol, England, reader in British history, 1989-96, professor of history, 1996-. **Publications:** The Royalist War Effort, 1642-1646, 1982; The Restoration: A Political and Religious History of England and Wales, 1658-1667, 1985; Charles II: King of England, Scotland, and Ireland, 1989; The British Republic, 1649-1660, 1990; The Pagan Religions of the Ancient British Isles, 1991; The Rise and Fall of Merry England, 1994; The Stations of the Sun, 1996; The Triumph of the Moon, 1999; Shamans, 2001; Witches, Druids and King Arthur, 2003. **Address:** History Dept, University of Bristol, Bristol BS8 1TH, England.

HUXLEY, George Leonard. British, b. 1932. **Genres:** Classics, History, Literary criticism and history. **Career:** Director, Gennadius Library, American School of Classical Studies at Athens, 1986-89; Hon. Professor, Trinity College, Dublin, 1989- (Hon. Research Associate, 1983-89). Hon. Librarian, 1990-94, Special Envoy, 1994-97 Royal Irish Academy. Member, Managing Committee, American School of Classical Studies at Athens, 1991-. Fellow, All Souls College, Oxford, 1955-61; Professor of Greek, Queen's University of Belfast, 1962-83. **Publications:** Achaeans and Hittites, 1960; Early Sparta, 1962; The Early Ionians, 1966; Greek Epic Poetry from Eumelos to Panyassis, 1969; (ed. with J. N. Coldstream) Excavations and Studies in Kythera, 1972; Pindar's Vision of the Past, 1975; On Aristotle and Greek Society, 1979; Homer and the Travellers, 1988. **Address:** School of Classics, Trinity College, Dublin 2, Ireland.

HUYGHE, Patrick. American, b. 1952. **Genres:** History, Medicine/Health, Paranormal, Psychiatry, Psychology, Sciences, Biography. **Career:** University of Virginia, Dept of Psychology, researcher, 1974; teacher at public high schools in Charlottesville, VA, 1975; US magazine, columnist and staff editor, 1977-78; free-lance writer, 1978-79; Newsweek, NYC, staff writer for "Newsweek Focus," 1980; WLSA-Radio, disc jockey, 1980; Hearst Magazines, NYC, contributing editor of Science Digest, 1981-84; science reporter and producer, All Things Considered and Morning Edition, National Public Radio and WGBH-FM Radio, 1985; staff producer, Ten O'Clock News and New England Science Gazette, WGBH-TV, 1985; Virginia Polytechnic Institute and State University, Blacksburg, Center for the Study of Science in Society, science writer in residence, 1986; WNET-TV, NYC, Innovation, associate producer, 1987, producer, 1988-90; Reeves Corporate Services, senior project writer, "Space Quest: 2090," 1988; Liberty Science

Center, Jersey City, NJ, label writer, environment, 1991-92; Petronas Project, DMCD, senior exhibit writer, 1996-97; Omni magazine online, Edge science editor, 1996-98; Biotechnology Exhibit at EPCOT, Thinc, 1999; Paraview Publishing, editor in chief, 2000-2003. **Publications:** Glowing Birds, 1985; (with L.A. Frank) The Big Splash, 1990; Columbus Was Last, 1992; The Field Guide to Extraterrestrials, 1996; (with L. Coleman) The Field Guide to Bigfoot, Yeti and Other Mystery Primates Worldwide, 1999; (with H. Evans) The Field Guide to Ghosts and Other Apparitions, 2000; (with D.Stacy) The Field Guide to UFOs, 2000; Swamp Gas Times, 2001; (with L. Coleman) The Field Guide to Lake Monsters and Sea Serpents, 2003. Contributor to books. **Address:** c/o Harvey Klinger, 301 W 53rd St, New York, NY 10019, U.S.A. **Online address:** huyghe@anomalist.com

HWANG, David Henry. American, b. 1957. **Genres:** Plays/Screenplays. **Publications:** Broken Promises: Four Plays, 1983; The Sound of a Voice (acting edition), 1984; The Dance and the Railroad and Family Devotions (acting ed.), 1989; FOB and the House of Sleeping Beauties (acting ed.), 1989; M. Butterfly, 1989; FOB and Other Plays, 1989; Golden Child, 1998; Trying to Find Chinatown, 2000. **Address:** c/o William Craver, Writers and Artists Agency, 19 W 44th St, New York, NY 10036, U.S.A.

HYAM, Ronald. British, b. 1936. **Genres:** History. **Career:** Cambridge University, Magdalene College, Lecturer in History, 1960-2002, Fellow, 1962-, President, 1996-98; University Reader in British Imperial History, 1996-99. **Publications:** Elgin and Churchill at the Colonial Office 1905-1908, 1968; A History of Isleworth Grammar School, 1969; The Failure of South African Expansion 1908-1948, 1972; (with G.W. Martin) Reappraisals in British Imperial History, 1975; Britain's Imperial Century 1815-1914: A Study of Empire and Expansion, 1976, 3rd ed., 2002; Empire and Sexuality: The British Experience, 1990; (with P.J. Henshaw) The Lion and the Springbok: Britain and South Africa since the Boer War, 2003. EDITOR: The Labour Government and the End of Empire, 4 vols, 1945-1951; A History of Magdalene College, Cambridge, 1428-1988, 1994; (joint) The Conservative Government and the End of Empire, 1957-64, 2 vols., 2000. **Address:** Magdalene College, Cambridge CB3 0AG, England.

HYAMS, Joe. American, b. 1923. **Genres:** Plays/Screenplays, Recreation, Sports/Fitness, Biography, Novels. **Career:** Ed., reporter, and columnist. **Publications:** (with W. Wagner) My Life with Cleopatra, 1963; (with M. Riddle) A Weekend Gambler's Handbook, 1963; (with E. Head) How to Dress for Success, 1966; (with P. Sellers) Seller's Market, 1966; Bogie, 1966; A Field of Buttercups, 1968; (with T. Murton) Accomplices to the Crime, 1969; (with T. Trabert) Winning Tactics for Weekend Tennis, 1972; Mislaid in Hollywood, 1973; (with P. Gonzales) Winning Tactics for Singles, 1973; (with B.J. King) Billie Jean King's Secrets of Winning Tennis, 1974; Bogart and Bacall; A Love Story, 1975; The Pool (novel), 1978; Zen in the Martial Arts, 1978; The Last Award, 1981; Murder at the Academy Awards, 1981; Playboy Guide to Self-Defense, 1981; (with C. Norris) Secrets of Inner Strength, 1987; (with M. Reagan) On the Outside Looking In, 1987; Flight of the Avenger, 1991; (with J. Hyams) James Dean, Little Boy Lost, 1992. **Address:** c/o Warner Books, 1271 Ave of the Americas, Rm 964B, New York, NY 10020, U.S.A. **Online address:** JHyams@aol.com

HYDE, Anthony. Also writes as Nicholas Chase. Canadian, b. 1946. **Genres:** Novels, Mystery/Crime/Suspense. **Career:** Free-lance writer, 1968-. **Publications:** (with C. Hyde as Nicholas Chase) Locksley (novel), 1983; The Red Fox (thriller), 1985; China Lake (thriller), 1992; Formosa Straits, 1995; Promises, Promises, 1997; Double Helix, 1999. **Address:** c/o Douglas & McIntyre, 2323 Quebec St Ste 201, Vancouver, BC, Canada V5T 4S7.

HYDE, Christopher. Also writes as Nicholas Chase. Canadian, b. 1949. **Genres:** Novels. **Career:** Writer. Freelance broadcaster for Canadian Broadcasting Corporation (CBC), Ottawa, Ottawa, Ontario, Canada, 1966-68, CBC Vancouver, Vancouver, British Columbia, Canada, 1969, 1973-75, CJOH-TV Ottawa, 1970-71, and CBC, Canadian Television (CTV), and Ontario Educational Communications Authority (OECA), 1971-72; full-time writer, 1977-. Ripping Yarns Inc., president; Nicholas Chase Productions, partner; Plain Brown Wrapper Puzzles, owner. **Publications:** Temple of the Winds, 1965; The Wave, 1979; The Icarus Seal, 1982; Styx, 1982; The Tenth Crusade, 1983; (with A. Hyde as Nicholas Chase) Locksley, 1983; Echo Drive, 1983; Maxwell's Train, 1985; Jericho Falls, 1986; Whisperland: A Chilling Tale of Dynastic Evil, 1987; Holy Ghost, 1987; Crestwood Heights, 1988; Egypt Green, 1989; White Lies, 1990, as Hard Target, 1991; Abuse of Trust: The Career of Dr. James Tyhurst, 1991; Black Dragon, 1992; The Paranoid's Handbook, 1993; A Gathering of Saints, 1996; The Second Assassin, 2002; Wisdom of the Bones, 2003. **Address:** c/o Penguin Publicity, 375 Hudson Street, New York, NY 10014, U.S.A.

HYDE, Eleanor (M.). American. **Genres:** Novels, Mystery/Crime/Suspense, Plays/Screenplays. **Publications:** Those Who Stayed Behind (novel), 1981; In Murder We Trust (mystery novel), 1995; Animal Instincts (mystery novel), 1996; Home Permanent (one-act play), 1996. Contributor to literary quarterlies and national magazines. **Address:** c/o Agnes Birnbaum, Bleecker Street Associates, 532 LaGuardia Pl #617, New York, NY 10012, U.S.A.

HYDE, (W.) Lewis. American, b. 1945. **Genres:** Poetry, Cultural/Ethnic topics, Literary criticism and history, Translations. **Career:** University of Iowa, Iowa City, instructor in literature, 1969-71; Cambridge Hospital, Cambridge, MA, alcoholism counselor, 1974-76; Harvard University, Cambridge, researcher in the study of adult development, 1976, lecturer in expository writing, 1983-85; Briggs-Copeland assistant professor of English, 1985-89; Tufts University, Medford, MA, Experimental College, visiting lecturer, 1977; poet in residence for public schools in Cohasset, Hopkinton, Lexington, and Nantucket, MA, 1981-83; Kenyon College, Gambier, OH, Luce Professor of Art and Politics, 1989-. MacArthur Fellow, 1991-96. **Publications:** (trans. with D. Unger) Vicente Aleixandre, World Alone (poems), 1982; The Gift: Imagination and the Erotic Life of Property, 1983; Trickster Makes This World, 1997. EDITOR: (and trans. with R. Bly) Twenty Poems of Vicente Aleixandre, 1977; (and trans. with others) A Longing for the Light: Selected Poems of Vicente Aleixandre, 1979; The Essays of Henry D. Thoreau, 2002. Contributor of poetry to periodicals. **Address:** Thomas Professor of Creative Writing, Kenyon College, Gambier, OH 43022, U.S.A. **Online address:** hydel@kenyon.edu

HYDE, Samuel C., Jr. American, b. 1958. **Genres:** History. **Career:** Southeastern Louisiana University, Hammond, associate professor of history, 1992-, director of Center for Regional Studies, 1997-. **Publications:** (coeditor) Two Hundred Years a Nation: Aspects of the American Experience, 1994; An Unforgotten Silence: Camp Moore, the Confederate Base (documentary television script), 1994; Pistols and Politics: The Dilemma of Democracy in Louisiana's Florida Parishes, 1810-99, 1996; (ed. and contrib.) Plain Folk of the South Revisited, 1997; (coeditor) An American Retrospective: People and Places from Our Nation's Past, 1997. Contributor of articles and reviews to scholarly journals. **Address:** 26541 Debra Dr., Denham Springs, LA 70726, U.S.A. **Online address:** shyde@selu.edu

HYDE-PRICE, Adrian. British, b. 1957. **Genres:** International relations/Current affairs, Politics/Government. **Career:** University of Birmingham, England, senior lecturer in international politics; writer. **Publications:** European Security beyond the Cold War, 1991; The New International Politics of East Central Europe, 1996. **Address:** Institute for German Studies, University of Birmingham, Edgbaston, Birmingham B17 2TT, England.

HYLAND, William G. American, b. 1929. **Genres:** History, Politics/Government, Music. **Career:** Employed by the U.S. Government, 1954-77, served as deputy assistant to the President, 1975-77. **Publications:** The Fall of Khrushchev, 1967; Mortal Rivals: Superpower Relations from Nixon to Reagan, 1986; The Cold War Is Over, 1990; The Song Is Ended: Songwriters and American Music, 1900-1950, 1994. EDITOR: America and the World, 1987-88, 1988; The Foreign Affairs Chronology of World Events: 1978-1991, 2nd ed, 1992. **Address:** 501 Wolftrap Rd., Vienna, VA 22180, U.S.A.

HYMAN, Harold M(elvin). American, b. 1924. **Genres:** History. **Career:** Emeritus William P. Hobby Professor of History, 1997-, Rice University, Houston, TX, (Chairman of Dept., 1968-70; William P. Hobby Professor of History, 1968-96). Assistant Professor of History, Earlham College, Richmond, IN, 1952-55; Visiting Asst Professor, 1955-56, and Professor of History, 1957-63, University of California, Los Angeles; Associate Professor, Arizona State University, Tempe, 1956-57; Professor, University of Illinois, 1963-68. Member, Board of Eds., Reviews in American History, 1964, Ulysses S. Grant Association, 1968; Member, Permanent Committee of the Oliver Wendell Holmes Trust, 1993-2001. **Publications:** Era of the Oath, 1954; To Try Men's Souls, 1959; (with B.P. Thomas) Stanton: The Life and Times of Lincoln's Secretary of War, 1962; Soldiers and Spruce, 1963; The Handbook of Politics, 6 vols., 1972-73; A More Perfect Union, 1973; Union and Confidence, 1976; (with W. Wiecek) Equal Justice under Law: Constitutional History, 1833-1880, 1982; Quiet Past and Stormy Present, 1986; American Singularity, 1987; Oleander Odyssey, 1990; The Reconstruction Justice of Salmon P. Chase, 1997; Craftsmanship and Character: A History of Houston's Vinson & Elkins Law Firm, 1917-1990s, 1998. EDITOR: The Radical Republicans and Reconstruction, 1861-1870, 1966; New Frontiers of the American Reconstruction, 1967; (with L.W. Levy) Freedom and Reform: Essays in Honor of Henry Steele Commager, 1967; Carleton Parker: The Casual Laborer and Other Essays, 1972; Heard 'Round the World: The Impact Aboard of the Civil War and Reconstruction, 1968; (with

F.B. Hyman) The Circuit Court Opinions of Salmon Portland Chase, 1972; Sidney George Fisher: The Trial of the Constitution, 1972; (with H.L. Trefousse) The Political History of the United States of America during the Great Rebellion, 1860-1865, The Political History of the United States of America during the Period of Reconstruction, April 15, 1867-July 15, 1870. **Address:** Dept of History - MS 42, Rice University, 6100 S Main St, Houston, TX 77005-1892, U.S.A. **Online address:** hyman@rice.edu

HYMAN, Meryl. American, b. 1950. **Genres:** Anthropology/Ethnology. **Career:** Gannett Newspapers, White Plains, NY, member of staff, 1981-. **Publications:** Who Is a Jew? Conversations, Not Conclusions, 1998. **Address:** c/o Jewish Lights Publishing, Sunset Farm Offices, Route 4, PO Box 237, Woodstock, VT 05091, U.S.A.

HYMAN, Ronald T(erry). American, b. 1933. **Genres:** Education, Law. **Career:** Columbia University, NYC, research assistant, 1962-64; Queens College, City University of New York, assistant professor, 1964-66; Rutgers University, New Brunswick, NJ, associate professor, 1966-74, professor of education, 1974-. Lawyer, practicing in New Jersey, 1986-. **Publications:** The Principles of Contemporary Education, 1966; (with A.A. Bellack, H.M. Kliebard and F.L. Smith) The Language of the Classroom, 1966; Ways of Teaching, 1970, rev. ed., 1974; School Administrator's Handbook of Teacher Supervision and Evaluation Methods, 1975; (with A. Teplitsky) Walk in My Shoes, 1976; Paper, Pencils, and Pennies, 1977; (with A. Pessin) The Securities Industry, 1977; (with K. Goldstein-Jackson and N. Rudnick) Experiments with Everyday Objects, 1978; Simulation Gaming for Values Education, 1978; Strategic Questioning, 1979; Improving Discussion Leadership, 1980; Administrator's Faculty Supervision Handbook, 1986; Administrator's Staff Development Activities Manual, 1986; Corporal Punishment in the Schools, 1993; The Principal's Decision on Corporal Punishment, 1993; Mandatory Community Service in High School, 1999. EDITOR: Teaching: Vantage Points for Study, 1968, rev. ed., 1974; Contemporary Thought on Teaching, 1971; (with M. Hillson) Change and Innovation in Elementary and Secondary Organization, 2nd ed., 1971; Approaches in Curriculum, 1973; (with S.L. Baily and contrib.) Perspectives on Latin America, 1974. Contributor to periodicals. **Address:** Graduate School of Education, Rutgers University, New Brunswick, NJ 08901-1183, U.S.A. **Online address:** rhyman@rci.rutgers.edu

HYMAN, Steven E(dward). American, b. 1952. **Genres:** Psychiatry, Medicine/Health. **Career:** Massachusetts General Hospital, Boston, intern in medicine, 1980-81; McLean Hospital, Belmont, MA, resident in psychiatry, 1981-84, chief resident, 1982; Massachusetts General Hospital, clinical and research fellow in endocrinology and neurology, 1983-84, research fellow in molecular biology, 1984-88, supervisor of psychiatric residents, 1984-, assistant in psychiatry, 1989, member of executive committee of Neuroscience Center, 1989-, assistant psychiatrist, 1990-, director of research in psychiatry, 1990-. Harvard University, Medical School, clinical fellow in medicine, 1980-81, and psychiatry, 1981-84, research fellow in genetics, 1984-87, instructor, 1987-89, assistant professor, 1989-92, associate professor, 1993-, director of Division on Addictions, 1992-. **Publications:** (ed.) Manual of

Psychiatric Emergencies, 1984, 3rd ed (with G.T. Tesar), 1994; (with G.W. Arana) Handbook of Psychiatric Drug Therapy, 1987, 2nd ed, 1991; (ed. with M. Jenike) Manual of Clinical Problems in Psychiatry, 1990; (with E. Nestler) The Molecular Foundations of Psychiatry, 1993. Work represented in anthologies. Contributor of more than 40 articles and reviews to medical journals. **Address:** Massachusetts General Hospital, CNY-2 Building 149, 13th St., Charlestown, MA 02129, U.S.A.

HYMAN, Timothy. British, b. 1946. **Genres:** Art/Art history. **Career:** Artist (painter) and writer. **Publications:** Bonnard, 1998; Bhupen Khakhar, 1998; Carnivalesque, 2000; Stanley Spencer, 2001. Contributor to magazines and newspapers. **Address:** 62 Myddelton Sq, London EC1R 1XX, England.

HYNES, Pat. Irish. **Genres:** Children's fiction. **Career:** Secondary school teacher. **Publications:** FOR CHILDREN: Land of Deep Shadow, 1993; Dawn Flight, 1994; Chase the Wind, 1996. **Address:** Castle Jordan, Tullamore, Offlay, Ireland.

HYNES, Samuel. American, b. 1924. **Genres:** Literary criticism and history. **Career:** Professor Emeritus, Princeton University, New Jersey, since 1990 (Professor of English, 1976-90; Woodrow Wilson Professor of Literature, 1978-90). Member of Faculty, 1949-68, and Professor of English Literature, 1965-68, Swarthmore College; Professor of English, Northwestern University, Evanston, Illinois, 1968-76. **Publications:** (ed) Further Speculations, by T.E. Hulme, 1955; The Pattern of Hardy's Poetry, 1961; (ed) English Literary Criticism: Restoration and Eighteenth Century, 1963; William Golding, 1964; (ed) The Author's Craft and Other Critical Writings of Arnold Bennett, 1968; The Edwardian Turn of Mind, 1968; (ed) Romance and Realism, 1970; Edwardian Occasions, 1972; The Auden Generation: Literature and Politics in England in the 1930's, 1976; (ed) Complete Poetical Works of Thomas Hardy, Vol I, 1982, Vol II, 1984, Vol III, 1985, Vols IV & I, 1995; (ed) Thomas Hardy, 1984; Flights of Passage: Reflections of a World War II Aviator, 1988; A War Imagined: The First World War and English Culture, 1990; Complete Short Fiction of Joseph Conrad, Vols I-III, 1992, Vol IV, 1993; The Soldiers Tale, 1997. **Address:** 130 Moore St., Princeton, NJ 08540-3359, U.S.A.

HYSON, Marion C. American, b. 1942. **Genres:** Education. **Career:** Teacher and director of programs for infants and preschool-age children, 1975-82; University of Delaware, Newark, assistant professor, 1983-88, associate professor, 1988-95, professor of individual and family studies, 1995-, head of department, 1995-, head of Commission on the Status of Women, 1993-95. **Publications:** (with S. Hatoff and C. Byram) Teachers' Practical Guide to Educating Young Children: A Growing Program, 1981; (ed. with L. Rescorla and K. Hirsh-Pasek, and contrib.) Academic Instruction in Early Childhood: Challenge or Pressure? New Directions for Child Development, 1991; The Emotional Development of Young Children: Building an Emotion-Centered Curriculum, 1994. Contributor to books. Contributor to education and psychology journals. **Address:** Department of Individual and Family Studies, University of Delaware, Newark, DE 19716, U.S.A.

I

IACCINO, James F(rancis). American, b. 1955. **Genres:** Psychology, Film. **Career:** DePaul University, Chicago, IL, instructor in psychology, 1978-80; Rosary College, River Forest, IL, instructor in psychology, 1980; Benedictine University (formerly Illinois Benedictine College), Lisle, assistant professor, 1981-84, associate professor, 1984-91, professor of psychology, 1991-, director of academic advising, 1987-95, and experimental psychologist. Guest on local television programs. **Publications:** Left Brain-Right Brain Differences: Inquiries, Evidence, and New Approaches, 1993; Psychological Reflections on Cinematic Terror: Jungian Archetypes in Horror Films, 1994; More Jungian Reflections in the Cinema: A Psychological Analysis of Science Fiction and Fantasy Archetypes, 1998. Some writing appears under the name Jim Iaccino. Contributor of articles and reviews to psychology and education journals. **Address:** Department of Psychology, Benedictine University, 5700 College Rd., Lisle, IL 60532, U.S.A. **Online address:** jiaccino@ben.edu

IAGNEMMA, Karl. (born United States), b. 1972. **Genres:** Novellas/Short stories. **Career:** Massachusetts Institute of Technology, Cambridge, MA, research scientist. **Publications:** On the Nature of Human Romantic Interaction (short stories), 2003. **Address:** Department of Mechanical Engineering, Massachusetts Institute of Technology, 77 Massachusetts Ave., Cambridge, MA 02139, U.S.A. **Online address:** kdi@mit.edu

IAKOBSON, Mikhail. *See* JAKOBSON, Michael.

IAKOVOU, Judy. (born United States). **Genres:** Mystery/Crime/Suspense. **Career:** Restaurant owner in Georgia, currently co-proprietor of Silver Screen Grill, Crawford, GA, and Checkered Cloth Café, Arnoldsville, GA. Writer. **Publications:** (with husband, Takis Iakovou) So Dear to Wicked Men, 1996; (with Takis Iakovou) Go Close against the Enemy, 1998; (with Takis Iakovou) There Lies a Hidden Scorpion, 1999. **Address:** c/o Author Mail, St. Martin's Press, 175 Fifth Ave., New York, NY 10010, U.S.A. **Online address:** iakovou@ibm.net

IAKOVOU, Takis. (born Greece). **Genres:** Mystery/Crime/Suspense. **Career:** Restaurant owner in Georgia, currently co-proprietor of Silver Screen Grill, Crawford, GA, and Checkered Cloth Café, Arnoldsville, GA. Writer. **Publications:** (with wife, Judy Iakovou) So Dear to Wicked Men, 1996; (with Judy Iakovou) Go Close against the Enemy, 1998; (with Judy Iakovou) There Lies a Hidden Scorpion, 1999. **Address:** c/o Author Mail, St. Martin's Press, 175 Fifth Ave., New York, NY 10010, U.S.A. **Online address:** iakovou@ibm.net

IANNUZZI, John Nicholas. American, b. 1935. **Genres:** Mystery/Crime/Suspense, Law. **Career:** Lawyer in New York City. Adjunct Professor of Law, Fordham University School of Law. **Publications:** What's Happening?, 1963; Part 35, 1970; Sicilian Defense, 1972; Courthouse, 1975; J. T., 1982; Cross Examination: The Mosaic Art, 1983; Trial: Strategy and Psychology, 1992; Handbook of Cross Examination, 1999; Handbook of Trial Strategy, 2000. **Address:** Iannuzzi and Iannuzzi, 74 Trinity Place, Rm 1800, New York, NY 10006, U.S.A. **Online address:** iannuzzi@aol.com

IBBITSON, John Perrie. Canadian, b. 1955. **Genres:** Young adult fiction, Plays/Screenplays, Politics/Government. **Career:** Writer/journalist, 1979-. Collier Macmillan, Toronto, Ontario, editorial secretary, 1984-1986, junior editor, 1986-1987; Ottawa Citizen, Ottawa, Ontario, reporter, columnist, and feature writer, 1988-1995, Toronto, Queen's Park correspondent, 1995-1996; Southam News, Toronto, Ontario correspondent, 1996-. Worked as a box office clerk in London, England, and Toronto from the late 1970s through the mid-1980s to subsidize his early writing career. **Publications:** YOUNG ADULT FICTION: The Wimp, 1985; The Wimp and the Jock, 1986; The Wimp and Easy Money, 1987; Starcrosser, 1990; The Big Story, 1990; 1812: Jeremy and the General, 1991; The Night Hazel Came to Town, 1993. ADULT NONFICTION: (ed. and contrib) Fair Play and Daylight: The Ottawa Citizen Essays, 1995; Promised Land: Inside the Mike Harris Revolution, 1997. PLAYS AND TELEPLAYS: I Pagliacci (later renamed The Clown), 1973; The Ritual (one-act play), 1974; Catalyst (one-act play), 1974; First Taste (three-act drama), 1976; Shadows (two-act historical drama), 1977; Hardy's Belief (two-act drama), 1978; Mayonnaise (two-act comedy), 1980; (with E. Heeley) Mayonnaise (adapted from his play as a three-part sitcom), 1983; Country Matters (two-act farce), 1982. **Address:** 298 5th Ave, Ottawa, ON, Canada K1S 2N5.

IBBOTSON, Eva (Maria Charlotte Michele Wiesner). British (born Austria), b. 1925. **Genres:** Romance/Historical, Children's fiction, Plays/Screenplays. **Publications:** The Great Ghost Rescue, 1975; Which Witch, 1979; A Countess Below Stairs, 1981; Magic Flutes, 1982; The Worm and the Toffee Nosed Princess, 1983; A Glove Shop in Vienna, 1984; A Company of Swans, 1985; The Haunting of Hiram, 1987; Madensky Square, 1988; Not Just a Witch, 1989; The Morning Gift, 1993; The Secret of Platform Thirteen, 1994; Dial a Ghost, 1996; A Song for Summer, 1997; Monster Mission, 1999; Journey to the River Sea, 2001; The Star of Kazan, 2004. **Address:** 2 Collingwood Terr, Jesmond, Newcastle upon Tyne NE2 2JP, England.

IBBOTSON, Roger G. American, b. 1943. **Genres:** Economics, Money/Finance. **Career:** First National City Bank of New York, security analyst, 1966; Nevada Garvey Ranches, Winnemucca, NV, administrative coordinator, 1967; Pfizer International, NYC, assistant to vice-president, 1967-68; Bank of Japan, Tokyo, economist, 1969; Tau Investments, Botswana, developer, 1970; Ibbotson Associates (financial and investment advisers), Chicago, IL, president and chairperson, 1977-. University of Chicago, lecturer, 1971-75, assistant professor, 1975-79, senior lecturer, 1979-84, executive director of Center for Research in Security Prices, 1979-84, bond portfolio manager for Office of the Treasurer, 1972-75, manager of securities trading department, 1974-75; Yale University, professor, 1984-. Williams and Associates, general partner, 1979-. **Publications:** (with R.A. Sinquefield) Stocks, Bonds, Bills, and Inflation: The Past (1926-1976) and the Future (1977-2000), 1977, 3rd ed, 1989; (with Sinquefield) Stocks, Bonds, Bills, and Inflation: Historical Returns, 1926-1978, 1979; (with G.P. Brinson) Investment Markets: Gaining the Performance Advantage, 1987; (with Y. Hamao) Stocks, Bonds, and Inflation Japan, 1989; (with T.S. Coleman and L. Fisher) U.S. Treasury Yield Curves, 1926-1988, 1989, 2nd ed, 1993; (with Brinson) Global Investing: A Professional's Guide to the World's Capital Markets, 1993. Work represented in anthologies. Contributor to business and finance journals. **Address:** Ibbotson Associates, 225 North Michigan Ave. Suite 700, Chicago, IL 60601, U.S.A.

IBER, Jorge. American (born Cuba), b. 1961. **Genres:** History. **Career:** Salt Lake Community College, adjunct instructor, 1992-96; Texas Tech University-Lubbock, assistant professor of history, 1997-, member of Teaching Academy, 2001, and director of Ethnic Studies Program. **Publications:** Hispanics in the Land of Zion, 1912-1999, 2000. Contributor to books.

Contributor of articles and reviews to periodicals. **Address:** Department of History, Box 41013, Texas Tech University, Lubbock, TX 79409, U.S.A. **Online address:** jiber@ettses.ttu.edu

IBRAHIM, Sami. *See* **MOREH, Shmuel.**

IDINOPULOS, Thomas A. American, b. 1935. **Genres:** Theology/Religion. **Career:** Miami University, Oxford, OH, began as assistant professor, became associate professor, and currently professor of religious studies. University of Notre Dame, resident scholar at Ecumenical Institute for Advanced Theological Studies in Israel, 1973; Jerusalem Foundation, guest scholar at Mishkenot Sha'nanim, 1975 and 1977; guest speaker at colleges and universities throughout the world; consultant to Center on Holocaust, Genocide, and Human Rights (Philadelphia). **Publications:** The Erosion of Faith: An Inquiry into the Origins of the Contemporary Crisis in Religious Thought, 1971; Jerusalem Blessed, Jerusalem Cursed: Jews, Christians, and Muslims in the Holy City from David's Time to Our Own, 1991; Jerusalem: A History of the Holiest City, 1994; (with M.J. Berger) Jerusalem's Holy Places and the Peace Process, 1998; Weathered by Miracles, 1998. CO-EDITOR: Mysticism, Nihilism, Feminism: New Critical Essays in the Theology of Simone Weil, 1984; Religion and Reductionism, 1994; The Sacred and Its Scholars, 1996; What Is Religion?, 1998. Contributor to scholarly journals and popular magazines. **Address:** Dept of Comparative Religion, 103 Old Manse, Miami University, Oxford, OH 45056, U.S.A. **Online address:** idinopta@muohio.edu

IDOL, John L(ane), Jr. American, b. 1932. **Genres:** Biography. **Career:** English teacher, 1958; Clemson University, Clemson, SC, English teacher, 1964-. **Publications:** A Thomas Wolfe Companion, 1987; (with R.K. Gollin and S. Eisiminger) Prophetic Pictures: Nathaniel Hawthorne's Knowledge and Uses of the Visual Arts, 1991. EDITOR: (with S. Eisiminger) Why Can't They Write? A Symposium on the State of Written Communication, 1979; T. Wolfe, K-19: Salvaged Pieces, 1983; (with L.D. Rubin Jr.) T. Wolfe, Mannerhouse, 1985; T. Wolfe, The Hound of Darkness, 1986; (with B. Jones) Nathaniel Hawthorne: Contemporary Reviews, 1994; Party at Jack's, 1995; (with M.M. Ponder) Hawthorne and Women, 1999; Thomas Wolfe, 2001. **Address:** PO Box 413, Hillsborough, NC 27278-0413, U.S.A. **Online address:** balder@mindspring.com

IGGERS, Georg G(erson). American (born Germany), b. 1926. **Genres:** History. **Career:** State University of New York, Buffalo, Professor of History, 1965-97, Distinguished Professor, 1978-97, Emeritus Professor, 1997-. Member of faculty, University of Akron, OH, 1948-50, Philander Smith College, Little Rock, AR, 1950-56, University of Arkansas, Fayetteville, 1956-57, Dillard University, New Orleans, Louisiana, 1957-63, Tulane University, New Orleans, 1958-60, 1963, and Roosevelt University, Chicago, 1963-65. **Publications:** The Cult of Authority: The Political Philosophy of the Saint-Simonians, 1958; The German Conception of History, 1968; New Directions in European Historiography: Four Essays, 1975; The Social History of Politics, 1986; Geschichtswissenschaft im 20. Jahrhundert, 1993; Historiography in the Twentieth Century, 1997; (with W. Iggers) Zwei Seiten der Geschichte, 2002. EDITOR: (and trans.) The Doctrine of Saint-Simon: An Exposition, 1972; (with K. von Moltke) Leopold von Ranke: The Theory and Practice of History, 1973; (with H.T. Parker) International Handbook of Historical Studies, 1979; (with J. Powell) Leopold von Ranke and the Shaping of Historical Discipline, 1990; Marxist Historiography in Transition, 1991; (with Q.E. Wang) Turning Points in Historiography, 2002. **Address:** 100 Ivyhurst Rd, Buffalo, NY 14226, U.S.A. **Online address:** iggers@buffalo.edu

IGGULDEN, John Manners. Australian, b. 1917. **Genres:** Novels, Money/Finance. **Career:** Planet Lighting, Dukesea Pty Ltd., chairman. **Publications:** Breakthrough, 1960; The Storms of Summer, 1960; The Clouded Sky, 1963; Dark Stranger, 1965; (ed.) Summer's Tales 3, 1966; The Promised Land Papers, vol. 1: The Revolution of the Good, 1986, vol. 2: How Things Are Wrong and How to Fix Them, 1989; The Modification of Freedom, 1993; Silent Lies, 1996; Good World (novel), 1999; The Good World Reader, 2004. **Address:** Evandale, Promised Land, Bellingen, NSW 2454, Australia.

IGNATIEFF, Michael. Canadian, b. 1947. **Genres:** Novels, Civil liberties/Human rights, Ethics, History. **Career:** Globe and Mail, Toronto, ON, reporter, 1966-67; Harvard University, Cambridge, MA, teaching fellow, 1971-74, John F. Kennedy School of Government, professor of human rights, and director of Carr Center for Human Rights Policy; University of British Columbia, Vancouver, assistant professor of history, 1976-78; King's College, Cambridge University, senior research fellow, 1978-84; Ecole des Hautes Etudes, Paris, visiting professor, 1985; BBC Television, Thinking

Aloud, host, 1986-; Channel Four, Voices, host, 1986; BBC-2, Late Show, host, 1989-; Observer, London, editorial columnist, 1990-93. Member of campaign staff for P.E. Trudeau, former prime minister of Canada, 1968. prime minister of Canada, 1968. **Publications:** A Just Measure of Pain: The Penitentiary in the Industrial Revolution, 1978; (ed. with I. Hont) Wealth and Virtue: The Shaping of Classical Political Economy in the Scottish Enlightenment, 1983; The Needs of Strangers, 1984; (with H. Brody) Nineteen Nineteen (filmscript), 1985; The Russian Album, 1987; Blood and Belonging: Journeys into the New Nationalism, 1994; Isiah Berlin: A Life, 1998; Warrior's Honor: Ethnic War and the Modern Conscience, 1998; Virtual War: Kosovo and Beyond, 2000; Rights Revolution, 2000; Human Rights as Politics and Idolatry, 2001; Empire Lite: Nationbuilding in Bosnia, Kosovo and Afghanistan (essays), 2003. NOVELS: Asya, 1991; Scar Tissue, 1993; Charlie Johnson in the Flames, 2003. **Address:** John F. Kennedy School of Government, Harvard University, 79 John F. Kennedy St, Cambridge, MA 02138, U.S.A. **Online address:** michael_ignatieff@harvard.edu

IGNATIEV, Noel. American, b. 1940. **Genres:** History, Race relations. **Career:** Laborer, machinist, maintenance worker, and college instructor. Writer. **Publications:** How the Irish Became White, 1995; (with J. Garvey) Race Traitor, 1996; The Lesson of the Hour, 2001. Author of articles and pamphlets. **Address:** Department of Critical Studies, Massachusetts College of Art, 621 Huntington Ave, Boston, MA 02115, U.S.A. **Online address:** Ignatiev@massart.edu

IGO, John (N.), (Jr.). American, b. 1927. **Genres:** Poetry, Literary criticism and history, Mythology/Folklore. **Career:** Trinity University, San Antonio, TX, member of English faculty, and acquisitions librarian, 1952-53; San Antonio College, Texas, professor of English, 1953-99; Choice mag., staff reviewer, 1964-2002. **Publications:** God of Gardens, 1962; (comp. and ed.) Yanaguana: A Chapbook of College Poetry, 1963; A Chamber Faust, 1964; Igo on Poetry, 1965; The Tempted Monk, 1967; (author and compiler) Los Pastores: A Triple Tradition, 1967; No Harbor, Else, 1972; Golgotha, 1973; Day of Elegies, 1974; Alien, 1977; Tropic of Gemini, 1981; Coven, 1984; The Mitotes, 1989; The Third Temptation of St. John, 1992; Charco Martinez (poems), 1997; Oenone (drama), 1999; The Bozzetti (poems), 2001; On Poetry and Poetics (textbook), 2001; Lost Landscape, 2004. **Address:** 12505 Woller Rd, San Antonio, TX 78249, U.S.A.

IHDE, Don. American, b. 1934. **Genres:** Philosophy. **Career:** State University of New York at Stony Brook, Distinguished Professor of Philosophy, 1969-. **Publications:** Hermeneutic Phenomenology, 1971; (co-ed.) Phenomenology and Existentialism, 1973; Sense and Significance, 1973; Listening and Voice, 1976; Experimental Phenomenology, 1977; Technics and Praxis, 1979; Existential Technics, 1983; Consequences of Phenomenology, 1986; Technology and the Lifeworld, 1990; Instrumental Realism, 1991; Philosophy of Technology, 1993; Postphenomenology, 1993; Expanding Hermeneutics, 1998; Bodies in Technology, 2001. **Address:** Dept. of Philosophy, State University of New York, Stony Brook, NY 11794-3750, U.S.A. **Online address:** dihde@notes.CC.sunysb.edu

IHIMAERA, Witi. New Zealander, b. 1944. **Genres:** Novels, Novellas/Short stories. **Career:** Post Office Headquarters, Wellington, journalist, 1968-72; Ministry of Foreign Affairs, Wellington, information officer, 1973-74; Otago University, Robert Burns Fellow, 1975; Ministry of Foreign Affairs, Wellington, third secretary, 1976-77; New Zealand High Commissioner, Canberra, second secretary, 1978; Ministry of Foreign Affairs, first secretary, 1979-85; New Zealand consul, NYC, 1986-88; New Zealand Embassy, Washington, DC, Public Affairs, counsellor, 1989; University of Auckland, lecturer, 1990-95, professor, 1996-. Member, Te Whanau A Kai, Maori tribe. **Publications:** NOVELS: Tangi, 1973; Whanau, 1974; The Matriarch, 1986; The Whale Rider, 1987; Bulibasha, 1994; Nights in the Gardens of Spain, 1995; The Dream Swimmer, 1997; The Uncle's Story, 2000; Sky Dancer, 2002; Whanau II, 2004. SHORT STORIES: Pounamu, Pounamu, 1972; The New Net Goes Fishing, 1977; Dear Miss Mansfield, 1989; Kingfisher Come Home, 1996; Ihimaera: His Best Stories, 2003. OTHER: Maori, 1975; (with T. Woollaston and A. Curnow) New Zealand through the Arts, 1982. EDITOR: (with D.S. Long) Into the World of Light, 1982; Te Ao Marama: Maori Writing since the 1980s, vols. 1-4, 1992-94; Growing Up Maori, 1998; Where's Waari?, 2000; Te Ata: Maori Art, 2002. **Address:** 2 Bella Vista Rd, Herne Bay, Auckland, New Zealand. **Online address:** w.ihimaera@auckland.ac.nz

IIDA, Deborah. American, b. 1956. **Genres:** Novels. **Career:** Writer. **Publications:** Middle Son, 1996. **Address:** 291 Mohalu St., Kahului, HI 96732, U.S.A.

IKE, Vincent Chukwuemeka. Nigerian, b. 1931. **Genres:** Novels, Area studies, Education, How-to books, Writing/Journalism. **Career:** Novelist, short-story writer, educator, and administrator. Teacher in Nigeria, 1950-51, girls' secondary school, Nkwerre, 1955-56; University College, Ibadan, Nigeria, administrative assistant and assistant registrar, 1957-60; University of Nigeria, Nsukka, deputy registrar, 1960-63, registrar, 1963-71, chairman of planning & management committee and interim CEO, 1970; provincial refugee officer, Umuahia Province, 1968-69; headquarters scout commissioner in charge of Nsukka Province, 1970-71; West African Examinations Council, Accra, Ghana, registrar and CEO, 1971-79; Daily Times of Nigeria, director, 1971-87; University Press, director, 1978-2002; Emekike and Co., executive chair, 1979-81; University of Benin, pro-chancellor, 1990-91; Nigerian Book Foundation, president/CEO, 1993-; Anambra State University of Science & Technology, pro-chancellor, 2001-. Okike literary journal, founding editorial committee. **Publications:** FICTION: Toads for Supper, 1965; The Naked Gods, 1970; The Potter's Wheel, 1973; Sunset at Dawn, 1976; The Chicken Chasers, 1980; Expo '77, 1980; The Bottled Leopard, 1985; Our Children Are Coming!, 1990; The Search, 1991; To My Husband, from Iowa, 1996; Anu Ebu Nwa, 1999; Conspiracy of Silence, 2001; The Accra Riviera (short stories), 2001. NONFICTION: University Development in Africa: The Nigerian Experience, 1976; How to Become a Published Writer, 1991. EDITOR: (with E. Obiechina and J.A. Umeh) The University of Nigeria, 1960-1985, 1986; Creating a Conducive Environment for Book Publishing, 1996; Meeting the Books Needs of the Rural Family, 1998; Directory of Nigerian Book Development, 1998; Ndikelionwu and the Spread of Christianity, 2000; The Book in 21st Century Nigeria and Universal Basic Education, 2000; Creating and Sustaining a Reading Culture, 2000. Contributor to books and periodicals. **Address:** Chinwuba House, Ndikelionwu Postal Agency, Orumba North L.G.A., Via Awka, Anambra, Nigeria.

ILES, Jane. British, b. 1954. **Genres:** Crafts. **Career:** Free-lance writer and designer, 1976-81; teacher of art and textiles at a girls' secondary school in London, England, 1982-86; designer and writer, 1985-; freelance commissions for craft and specialist magazines, part works, etc. Designer of Hallmark greeting cards; designer of embroidery kits for National Trust. Work exhibited at Royal School of Needlework, Commonwealth Institute, and Royal Festival Halls; contributor to special interest magazines; gives talks and workshops. **Publications:** (coauthor) Machine Embroidery, 1979; Old English Roses in Needlework, 1986; Learn Embroidery, 1987; The Needlework Garden, 1989; Wildflowers in Cross Stitch, 1990; (ed.) Embroidery Projects Book, 1990; Needlework Magic, 1992; Old English Roses in Embroidery, 1993; Cross Stitch Country Garden, 1996. **Address:** c/o Jane Judd, 18 Belitha Villas, Barnsbury, London N1 1PD, England. **Online address:** D.Moynihan1@talk21.com

ILIE, Paul. American, b. 1932. **Genres:** Literary criticism and history, Art/Art history, Intellectual history. **Career:** Professor of Spanish and Comparative Literature, University of Southern California, Los Angeles, since 1982. Instructor, 1959-62, Assistant Professor, 1962-65; Associate Professor, 1965-68, and Professor, 1968-82, Dept. of Romance Languages, University of Michigan, Ann Arbor. **Publications:** La novelistica de Camilo Jose Cela, 1963; 3rd ed. 1978; Unamuno: An Existential View of Self and Society, 1967; The Surrealistic Mode in Spanish Literature, 1968; (ed.) Documents of the Spanish Vanguard, 1969; Los surrealistas espanoles, 1974; Literature and Inner Exile, 1981; The Age of Minerva, 2 vols., 1995. **Address:** Dept. of Spanish, University of Southern California, Los Angeles, CA 90087, U.S.A. **Online address:** PILIE@USC.EDU

IMES, Birney. American, b. 1951. **Genres:** Photography. **Career:** Columbus Commercial Dispatch, photographer, Columbus, MS, 1973-; independent photographer and author. Exhibits throughout the United States. **Publications:** Juke Joint: Photographs, 1990; Partial to Home (photographs), 1994; Whispering Pines (photographs), 1994. **Address:** 802 Third Ave., Columbus, MS 39701, U.S.A.

IMMELL, Myra H. American, b. 1941. **Genres:** Children's non-fiction, Young adult non-fiction. **Career:** Merrill Publishing Co., Westerville, OH, foreign languages and social studies editorial department, 1969-90; project manager/author/editor, 1990-93; Quest International, Newark, OH, director of high school programs, 1993-96; Meeks Heit Publishing Co., Columbus, OH, managing editor, 1996-97; L3Comm, Hilliard, OH, director of projects, 1997-2000; USi, Columbus, proposal writer, 2000-04; Redemtech, Inc, business communications specialist, 2004-. **Publications:** Automobiles: Connecting People and Places, 1994; (with W.H. Immell) Tecumseh, 1996; Eating Disorders, 1999; Ethnic Violence, 2000; Teen Pregnancy, 2000; America's Decades: The 1900s, 2000; Turning Points: World War II, 2001; Teens and Sex, 2002; The World Wars, 2002; Han Dynasty, 2002. EDITOR: (with M. Sader) The Young Adult Reader's Adviser, 1992; Readings on the Diary of a Young Girl, 1998.

IMPOLA, Richard A(arre). American, b. 1923. **Genres:** Translations, Literary criticism and history. **Career:** Michigan Technological University, Houghton, instructor to assistant professor, 1950-62; State University of New York College at New Paltz, assistant professor to associate professor, 1963-83. **Publications:** TRANSLATOR: K. Paatalo, Our Daily Bread (novel), 1990; A. Kivi, Seven Brothers (novel), 1991; T. Yliruusi, Hand in Hand (novel), 1992; K. Paatalo, Storm over the Land (novel), 1993; A. Tervasmaa, The Life and Times of an Ordinary Captain (autobiography), 1994; Words of Wisdom and Magic from the Kalevala (poetry), 1998; H. Nast, In Wartime Finland (memoirs); J. Mattinen, The History of Thomson Township (local history), 2000; K. Paatalo, Before the Storm (novel), 2000; V. Linna, Under the North Star (novel), 2001; J. Rislakki, No Home for Us Here (history), 2002; L. Wilson, Sisu Mother (memoirs), 2002; K. Paatalo, After the Storm (novel), 2002; K. Paatalo, The Winter of the Black Snow (novel), 2002; V. Linna, Under the North Star: The Uprising (novel), 2002; V. Linna, Under the North Star: The Reconciliation (novel), 2003. EDITOR: (with S. Stone) Texts in Translation: Kielikannas, 1992; E. Joenpelto, The Bride of Life (novel), 1995; E. Komulainen, A Grave in Karelia (novel), 1995. Translator of poetry and short stories in anthologies; translator of articles in periodicals. Contributor of articles to periodicals. **Address:** 20 Du Bois Rd, New Paltz, NY 12561, U.S.A. **Online address:** impolar@newpaltz.edu

INCH, Morris Alton. American, b. 1925. **Genres:** Theology/Religion. **Career:** Gordon College, Wenham, MA, Associate Professor of Christian Education, 1955-62, Academic Dean, 1959-60, 1961-62, Dean of Students, 1960-61; Wheaton College, IL, Professor of Theology, 1962-86, Chairman, Dept. of Religious Studies, 1969-84, Professor Emeritus, 1986; Institute of Holy Land Studies, Jerusalem, President, 1986-90; Institutul Biblique din OradeaRomania, Visiting Professor, 1991-93. **Publications:** Psychology in the Psalms, 1969; Christianity without Walls, 1972; Paced by God, 1973; Celebrating Jesus as Lord, 1974; (ed. with S.J. Schultz) Interpreting the Word of God, 1976; Understanding Bible Prophecy, 1977; The Evangelical Challenge, 1978; My Servant Job, 1979; (gen. ed.) The Literature and Meaning of Scripture, 1981; Doing Theology across Cultures, 1982; Saga of the Spirit: A Biblical, Systematic and Historical Theology of the Holy Spirit, 1985; Making the Gospel Relevant, 1986; Revelation across Cultures, 1995; Charting a Good Church Trip, 1995; Exhortations of Jesus according to Matthew, 1997; Up from the Depths: Mark as Tragedy, 1997; A Case for Christianity, 1997; Sage Sayings, 1997; Chaos Paradigm: A Theological Exploration, 1998; In Tune with God: A User-Friendly Theology, 1998; Man: The Perennial Question, 1999; Devotions with David, 2000; Demetrius the Disciple, 2000; Casey and Tonka, 2000; Scripture as Story, 2000; Two Gospel Motifs, 2001; The High God, 2001; Why Take the Bible Seriously?, 2001; Whispers of Heaven, 2002; 12 Who Changed the World, 2003; Why Take Jesus Seriously?, 2003; Two Mosaic Motifs, 2003. **Address:** 349 Cagle Rock Circle, Russellville, AR 72802, U.S.A. **Online address:** minch@centurytel.net

INDIANA, Gary a pseudonym. American, b. 1950. **Genres:** Novels, Novellas/Short stories, Essays, Plays/Screenplays. **Career:** Novelist. Worked in an insurance firm, a plastic surgery clinic, a psychiatric hospital, and selling popcorn in a theater. Legal Aid, Los Angeles, volunteer, c. 1970s; actor and playwright; Village Voice, NYC, senior art critic, 1985-88. **Publications:** FICTION: Scar Tissue (stories) 1987; White Trash Boulevard (stories), 1988; Horse Crazy (novel), 1988; Gone Tomorrow (novel), 1993; Rent Boy (novel), 1994; Resentment: A Comedy, 1997. OTHER: Roberto Juarez (nonfiction), 1986; (ed.) Living with the Animals, 1994; Let It Bleed: Essays, 1985-1995, 1996. PLAYS: Alligator Girls Go to College, 1979; The Roman Polanski Story, 1982. Contributor of essays to books. Contributor of art criticism to periodicals. **Address:** c/o Doubleday, 1540 Broadway, New York, NY 10036, U.S.A.

INEZ, Colette. American (born Belgium), b. 1931. **Genres:** Poetry. **Career:** New York University, adult education, instructor, 1962-63; Federal Title III Anti-Poverty Progs., NYC, teacher, 1964-70; New School for Social Research, NYC, poetry workshop, instructor, 1974-83; Columbia University, NYC, associate professor, 1983-. Denison University, Granville, OH, Beck Lecturer, 1974; State University of New York at Stony Brook, lecturer, poetry workshop, 1975-76; poet-in-residence and visiting professor at US colleges and universities. Fellowships: National Endowment for the Arts, 1974, 1988, Rockefeller Foundation, 1980, Guggenheim Foundation, 1985-86, New York Foundation for the Arts, 1995. Poetry reviewer for magazines. **Publications:** The Woman Who Loved Worms, 1972; Alive and Taking Names, 1977; Eight Minutes from the Sun, 1983; Family Life, 1988; Getting Underway: New and Selected Poetry, 1992; Naming the Moons, 1994; For Reasons for Music, 1994; Clemency, 1998. **Address:** 5 W 86th St, New York, NY 10024-3603, U.S.A.

ING, Dean. American, b. 1931. **Genres:** Novellas/Short stories, Mystery/Crime/Suspense, Science fiction/Fantasy, Air/Space topics, Military/Defense/Arms control. **Career:** Freelance writer, 1977-. Engineer, Aerojet-General, Sacramento, CA, 1957-62, and Lockheed, San Jose, CA, 1962, 1965-70; Missouri State University, assistant professor of speech, 1974-77. **Publications:** NOVELS: Soft Targets, 1979; Systemic Shock, 1981; Pulling Through, 1983; Single Combat, 1983; Wild Country, 1985; Blood of Eagles, 1987; The Big Lifters, 1988; The Ransom of Black Stealth One, 1989; Cathouse, 1989; The Nemesis Mission, 1991; Butcher Bird, 1993; Spooker, 1995; Flying to Pieces, 1997; The Skins of Dead Men, 1998; Loose Cannon, 2000. NONFICTION: (with J. Pournelle) Mutual Assured Survival, 1984; (with L. Myrabo) The Future of Flight, 1985. STORIES: Anasazi, 1980; High Tension, 1982; Firefight 2000 (collection), 1987; The Chernobyl Syndrome (collection), 1987; The Rackham Files (collection), 2004. EDITOR (all by Mack Reynolds): The Lagrangists, 1983; Home Sweet Home 2010 A.D., 1984; Eternity, 1984; The Other Time, 1984; Trojan Orbit, 1985; Deathwish World, 1986. **Address:** 1105 Ivy Ln, Ashland, OR 97520, U.S.A.

INGE, M. Thomas. American, b. 1936. **Genres:** Cultural/Ethnic topics, Bibliography, Cartoons, Humor/Satire. **Career:** Blackwell Professor of Humanities, Randolph-Macon College, Ashland, VA, 1984-; general ed., Greenwood Pr. reference series on American popular culture, 1976-; Cambridge University Press, American Critical Archives series, 1987-; University Press of Mississippi, Studies in Popular Culture series, 1987-; instructor of English, Vanderbilt University, Nashville, 1962-64; assistant professor to associate professor of American thought and language, Michigan State University, East Lansing, 1964-69; associate professor to professor of English and chair, Virginia Commonwealth University, Richmond, 1969-80; professor of English and head of dept., Clemson University, SC, 1980-82; resident scholar in American studies, U.S. Information Agency, Washington, DC, 1982-84. **Publications:** (with T.D. Young) Donald Davidson: An Essay and a Bibliography, 1965; (with T.D. Young) Donald Davidson, 1971; The American Comic Book, 1985; Comics in the Classroom, 1989; Comics as Culture; 1990; Great American Comics, 1990; Faulkner, Sut, and Other Southerners, 1992; Perspectives on American Culture: Essays on Humor, Literature, and the Popular Arts, 1994; Anything Can Happen in a Comic Strip, 1995; William Faulkner: An Illustrated Life, 2005. EDITOR: Publications of the Faculty of the University College: A Bibliography, 1966; G.W. Harris, Sut Lovingood's Yarns, 1966; G.W. Harris, High Times and Hard Times: Sketches and Tales, 1967; Agrarianism in American Literature, 1969; J.D. Wade, Augustus Baldwin Longstreet: A Study of the Development of Culture in the South, 1969; Honors College Essays 1967-1968, 1969; Faulkner: A Rose for Emily, 1970; R.C. Beatty, William Byrd of Westover, 1970; Studies in Light in August, 1971; Virginia Commonwealth University Self-Study, 1972; The Frontier Humorists, 1975; Ellen Glasgow: Centennial Essays, 1976; (with M. Duke and J.R. Bryer) Black American Writers: Bibliographical Essays, 2 vols., 1978; Bartleby the Inscrutable (collection of commentary on Melville story), 1979; Concise Histories of American Popular Culture, 1982; (with E.E. MacDonald) James Branch Cabell: Centennial Essays, 1983; (with M. Duke and J.R. Bryer) American Women Writers: Bibliographic Essays, 1983; Huck Finn among the Critics: A Centennial Selection, 1984; Truman Capote: Conversations, 1987; Handbook of American Popular Literature, 1988; Naming the Rose, 1988; A Nineteenth-Century American Reader, 1988; Handbook of American Popular Culture, 3 vols., 1978-81, 1989; C. Waugh, The Comics, 1991; Dark Laughter: The Satiric Art of Oliver W. Harrington, 1993; O.W. Harrington, Why I Left America and Other Essays, 1993; William Faulkner: The Contemporary Reviews, 1994; (with J.E. Caron) Sut Lovingood's Natural Born Yarnspinner: Essays on George Washington Harris, 1996; A Connecticut Yankee in King Arthur's Court, 1997; The Achievement of William Falukner, 1998; Conversations with William Faulkner, 1999; Company Aytch: or, A Sideshow of the Big Show, 1999; Charles M. Schulz: Conversations, 2000. EDITOR: (with others) The Black Experience, 1969; (with S. Chakovsky) Russian Eyes on American Literature, 1993; (with E. Piacentino) Humor of the Old South, 2001; (with D. Hall) Greenwood Guide to American Popular Culture, 4 vols., 2002. **Address:** Blackwell Chair in the Humanities, Randolph-Macon College, Ashland, VA 23005, U.S.A. **Online address:** tinge@rmc.edu

INGERSOLL, Earl G(eorge). American, b. 1938. **Genres:** Literary criticism and history. **Career:** State University of New York College at Brockport, instructor, 1964-71, assistant professor, 1971-87, associate professor, 1987-91, professor, 1991-96, distinguished teaching professor of English, 1996-, distinguished professor, 2002-. **Publications:** Margaret Atwood: Conversations, 1990; Conversations with May Sarton, 1991; Representations of Science and Technology in British Literature since 1880, 1992; Doris Lessing: Conversations, 1994, in UK as Putting the Question Differently, 1996; Engendered Trope in Joyce's Dubliners, 1996; Lawrence Durrell: Conversations, 1998; D.H. Lawrence, Desire, and Narrative, 2001; Conversa-

tions with Rita Dove, 2003. EDITOR: (with J. Kitchen and S.S. Rubin) The Post-Confessionals: Conversations with American Poets of the Eighties, 1989; (with K. Cushman) D.H. Lawrence: New Worlds, 2003. Contributor to language and literature journals. **Address:** State University of New York College at Brockport, Brockport, NY 14420, U.S.A. **Online address:** eingerso@po.brockport.edu

INGHAM, John N. American, b. 1939. **Genres:** Biography, Business/Trade/Industry, Race relations, Urban studies. **Career:** Carnegie-Mellon University, Pittsburgh, PA, lecturer in history, 1966-68; University of Bridgeport, Bridgeport, CT, instructor in history, 1968-70; State University of New York, State University College at Brockport assistant professor to associate professor of history, 1970-77; University of Toronto, ON, associate professor to professor of history, 1977-; writer. **Publications:** The Iron Barons: A Social Analysis of an American Urban Elite, 1978; Biographical Dictionary of American Business Leaders, 4 vols., 1983; The Rise of Popular Culture, 1985; Assault on Victorianism, 1987; (ed.) Sex 'n' Drugs 'n' Rock 'n' Roll: American Popular Culture since 1945, c. 1988; (with L.B. Feldman) Contemporary American Business Leaders, 1990; Making Iron and Steel, 1991; (with L.B. Feldman) African American Business Leaders: A Biographical History, 1993. **Address:** Department of History, University of Toronto, 100 St. George St., Toronto, ON, Canada M5S 1A1. **Online address:** jningham@interlog.com

INGHAM, Kenneth. British, b. 1921. **Genres:** History. **Career:** Emeritus Professor of History, University of Bristol, since 1986 (Professor, 1967-86). Lecturer, 1950-56, and Professor of History, 1956-62, Makerere University, Uganda; Director of Studies, Royal Military Academy, Sandhurst, 1962-67. **Publications:** Europe and Africa, 1953; Reformers in India 1793-1833, 1956, 1973; The Making of Modern Uganda, 1958, 1983; A History of East Africa, 1962; (ed.) Foreign Relations of African States, 1974; The Kingdom of Toro in Uganda, 1975; Jan Smuts: The Conscience of a South African, 1986; Politics in Modern Africa: The Uneven Tribal Dimension, 1990; Obote: A Political Biography, 1994. **Address:** The Woodlands, 94 West Town Lane, Bristol BS4 5DZ, England.

INGHAM, R(ichard) A(rnison). British, b. 1935. **Genres:** Plays/Screenplays, Poetry, Education, Speech/Rhetoric. **Career:** Writer; Education Consultant. Adult Education/Lifelong Learning Quarterly, Individual Learning News, editor and writer. **Publications:** Yoris, 1974; (with J.M. Buffton) Making Contact, 2 vols., 1980-81; Fifteen from Twenty-Two (verse), 1979; Ski Whizz (play), 1990. **Address:** 26 Devonshire Buildings, Bath, England.

INGLIS, Janet. Canadian, b. 1946. **Genres:** Novels. **Career:** Writer. **Publications:** NOVELS: Daddy's Girl, 1994; Father of Lies, 1995. **Address:** c/o David Higham Associates Ltd., 5-8 Lower John St., Golden Sq., London W1R 4HA, England.

INGMAN, Nicholas. British, b. 1948. **Genres:** Children's non-fiction, Music. **Career:** Freelance musical arranger; composer and conductor for television, films, and radio; recording artist. Arranger and producer. **Publications:** The Story of Music, 1972; What Instrument Shall I Play?, 1975; Gifted Children of Music: The Young Lives of the Great Musicians, 1978. **Address:** 10 The Gardens, E. Dulwich, London SE22 9QD, England.

INGRAM, Derek Thynne. British, b. 1925. **Genres:** Politics/Government. **Career:** Ed., Gemini News Service, London, 1967-93. Vice-President, Royal Commonwealth Society, Member, Editorial Board, Round Table; Deputy Ed., Daily Mail, London, 1963-66; President, Diplomatic and Commonwealth Writers Association of Britain, 1972-74; Governor, Commonwealth Institute, 1972-88; President, Commonwealth Journalists Association, 1983-90; Ed., Commonwealth Journal, 1983-86; Commonwealth Observer for elections in Pakistan, 1993; and Malawi, 1994. Media adviser to European Union Election Unit in South Africa, 1994. **Publications:** Partners in Adventure, 1960; The Commonwealth Challenge, 1962; Commonwealth for a Colour-Blind World, 1965; The Commonwealth at Work, 1969; The Imperfect Commonwealth, 1977; Review of Commonwealth Secretariat's Information Programme, 1997. **Address:** 5 Wyndham Mews, London W1H 2PN, England. **Online address:** derekingram@gn.apc.org

INGRAM, Heather E(lizabeth). (born Canada), b. 1969. **Genres:** Administration/Management. **Career:** Educator, office administrator, and author. Chatelech High School, Sechelt, British Columbia, Canada, math, business, and accounting teacher, 1994-99; worked as a math tutor and an office administrator for a British Columbia environmental consulting firm. Has appeared on radio and television shows. **Publications:** Risking It All: My

Student, My Lover, My Story, 2003. **Address:** c/o Author Mail, Greystone Books, Douglas & McIntyre Publishing Group, Ste 201, 2323 Quebec St., Vancouver, BC, Canada V5T 4S7.

INGRAM, Paul O. American, b. 1939. **Genres:** Theology/Religion. **Career:** Pacific Lutheran University, Tacoma, WA, professor of religion, c. 1975-. **Publications:** The Dharma of Faith, 1977; The Modern Buddhist-Christian Dialogue, 1987; Wrestling with the Ox, 1997. **Address:** Department of Religion, Pacific Lutheran University, Tacoma, WA 98447, U.S.A. **Online address:** ingrampo@plu.edu

INGVES, Gunilla (Anna Maria Folkesdotter). Swedish, b. 1939. **Genres:** Children's fiction, Animals/Pets, Illustrations. **Career:** Author and illustrator. Oestgoeta Correspondenten (daily newspaper), Linkoeping, Sweden, illustrator, 1962-74. **Publications:** (and illustrator) To Pluto and Back: A Voyage in the Milky Way, trans by S.T. Murray, 1992. ANIMALS ON THE FARM SERIES (children's books): titles include Cows, Hens, and Pigs. Ingves is also the author and illustrator of books for children in Swedish; some, including The Ant, The Spider, The Worm, The Grasshopper, The Potato, and The Mushroom, have been translated into English and were published in the First Nature Books series during the 1980s. **Address:** Uttersbo, 59052 NYKIL SW, Sweden.

INIGO, Martin. *See* **MILES, Keith.**

INKPEN, Mick. British, b. 1952. **Genres:** Children's fiction. **Career:** Graphic designer, 1970-86. Greeting card designer; TV AM (England), writer for Rub-a-Dub-Tub. Freelance writer and illustrator of children's books, 1986-. **Publications:** WRITTEN AND ILLUSTRATED WITH N. BUTTERWORTH: The Nativity Play, 1985; The House on the Rock, 1986; The Precious Pearl, 1986; The Lost Sheep, 1986; The Two Sons, 1986; Nice and Nasty: A Book of Opposites, in the US as Nice or Nasty: A Book of Opposites, 1987; I Wonder at the Zoo, 1987; I Wonder in the Garden, 1987; I Wonder in the Country, 1987; I Wonder at the Farm, 1987, in the US as I Wonder on the Farm, 1994; Who Made...In the Country, 1987; Who Made...On the Farm, 1987; Who Made...At the Zoo, 1987; Who Made...In the Garden, 1987; Sports Day, 1988; The Magpie's Story: Jesus and Bacchaeus, 1988; The Mouse's Story: Jesus and the Storm, 1988; The Cat's Story: Jesus at the Wedding, 1988; The Fox's Story: Jesus Is Born, 1988; The Good Stranger, 1989; Just Like Jasper!, 1989; The Little Gate, 1989; The Rich Farmer, 1989; Ten Silver Coins, 1989; The School Trip, 1990; The Wonderful Earth, 1990; Field Day, 1991; Jasper's Beanstalk, 1992; Opposites, 1997. SELF-ILLUSTRATED: One Bear at Bedtime: A Counting Book, 1987; If I Had a Pig, 1988; If I Had a Sheep, 1988; Jojo's Revenge, 1989; The Blue Balloon, 1989; Gumboot's Chocolatey Day, 1989; Threadbear, 1990; Billy's Beetle, 1991; Penguin Small, 1992; Anything Cuddly Will Do!, 1993; Crocodile!, 1993; The Very Good Dinosaur, 1993; This Troll, That Troll, 1993; Lullaby-hullaballoo!, 1993; Nothing, 1995; Don't Do That, 1996; Bear, 1997; Little Spotty Thing, 1997; Say "Aaah"!, 1997; Silly Billies, 1997; Arnold, 1998; Honk, 1998; Sandcastle, 1998; Splosh!, 1998. KIPPER SERIES: Kipper, 1991; Kipper's Toybox, 1992; Kipper's Birthday, 1993; Kipper's Book of Colours, 1994; Kipper's Book of Counting, 1994, in the US as Kipper's Book of Numbers, 1995; Kipper's Book of Opposites, 1994; Kipper's Book of Weather, 1994; Where, Oh Where, Is Kipper's Bear: A Pop-Up Book with Light!, 1994; Kipper's Snowy Day, 1996. WIBBLY PIG SERIES: Wibbly Pig Is Upset, 1995; Wibbly Pig Can Dance!, 1995; Wibbly Pig Can Make a Tent, 1995; Wibbly Pig Likes Bananas, 1995; Wibbly Pig Makes Pictures, 1995; Wibbly Pig Opens His Presents, 1995; Everyone Hide from Wibbly Pig, 1997. Illustrator of books by M. and M. Doney, E. Lawrence and N. Werron. **Address:** c/o Hodder & Stoughton Ltd., 338 Euston Road, London NW1 3BH, England.

INMAN, Robert (Anthony). American, b. 1931. **Genres:** Novels. **Career:** Freelance book consultant and ed., since 1990. Instructor in Germanics, 1957-59, and Ed. and Administrative Assistant, 1960-62, University of Washington, Seattle; Head Librarian, Denver Post, Colorado, 1964-71; Managing Ed., Journals, AIAA, New York, 1983-87. **Publications:** The Torturer's Horse, 1965; The Blood Endures, 1981. **Address:** 720 Gough St., San Francisco, CA 94102, U.S.A.

INNES, Jean. *See* **SAUNDERS, Jean.**

INNESS, Sherrie A. American, b. 1965. **Genres:** Women's studies and issues. **Career:** University of California, San Diego, La Jolla, instructor in writing and in dimensions of culture, 1989-91, 1992, 1993; Miami University, Hamilton, OH, assistant professor, 1993-94, associate professor of English, 1994-. **Publications:** Intimate Communities: Representation and Social

Transformation in Women's College Fiction, 1895-1910, 1995; The Lesbian Menace: Ideology, Identity, and the Representation of Lesbian Life, 1997; Tough Girls: Women, Popular Culture, and the Gendering of Toughness, 1999. EDITOR & CONTRIBUTOR: (with D. Royer) Breaking Boundaries: New Perspectives on Women's Regional Writing, 1997; Nancy Drew and Company: Culture, Gender, and Girls' Series, 1997; Delinquents and Debutantes: Twentieth-Century American Girls' Cultures, 1998. Contributor to books on popular culture and women's studies. Contributor of articles and reviews to academic journals. **Address:** Department of English, Miami University, 1601 Peck Blvd., Hamilton, OH 45011, U.S.A. **Online address:** inness@muohio.edu

INNESS-BROWN, Elizabeth (Ann). American, b. 1954. **Genres:** Novels, Novellas/Short stories. **Career:** University of Southern Mississippi, Hattiesburg, MS, assistant professor of English, 1979-84, acting director, Center for Writers graduate program in creative writing, 1983, associate professor of English, 1985-86; St. Lawrence University, Canton, NY, visiting writer, 1984-85; Purdue University, West Lafayette, IN, visiting writer, 1987; University of Hartford, Hartford, CT, visiting writer, 1987-88; St. Michael's College, Colchester, VT, English lecturer, 1988-90, director of the Writing Center, 1988-, assistant professor of English, 1990-94, associate professor of English, 1994-. Vermont College, adjunct and field faculty member, 1988-90. **Publications:** STORIES: Satin Palms, 1981; Here, 1994. OTHER: Burning Marguerite (novel), 2002. Work represented in anthologies. Contributor to periodicals. **Address:** St. Michael's College, Colchester, VT 05439, U.S.A.

INNIS, Robert E(dward). American, b. 1941. **Genres:** Language/Linguistics, Philosophy, Humanities. **Career:** Fordham University, instructor in philosophy, 1968-69; University of Massachusetts (Lowell), instructor, 1969-70, assistant professor, 1970-73, associate professor, 1973-77, University professor, 1981-84, professor of philosophy, 1977-. University of Copenhagen, Fulbright Professor, 1990-91. **Publications:** (trans.) The Central Texts of Ludwig Wittgenstein, by Gerd Brand, 1979; Karl Buehler: Semiotic Foundations of Language Theory, 1982; Semiotics: An Introductory Anthology, 1985; (ed.) Meaning and Context: An Introduction to the Psychology of Language, by Hans Hoerman, 1986; (trans. and author of intro.) Tentamina Semiologica, by Johann Christoph Hoffbauer, 1991; Consciousness and the Play of Signs, 1994. **Address:** Dept. of Philosophy, University of Massachusetts, 1 University Ave, Lowell, MA 01854, U.S.A. **Online address:** Robert_Innis@uml.edu

IOFFE, Grigory. American (born Russia), b. 1951. **Genres:** Area studies, Demography, Geography. **Career:** Institute for Rural Construction Planning, Moscow, USSR, junior research associate, 1974-77, senior research associate, 1977-80; USSR Academy of Sciences, Moscow, junior research associate at Institute of Geography, 1980-86, senior research associate, 1986-88, department head, 1988-89; Radford University, Radford, VA, assistant professor, 1990-94, associate professor, 1994-2000, professor of geography, 2000-. **Publications:** (with T. Nefedova) Continuity and Change in Rural Russia, 1997; (with T. Nefedova) Environs of Russian Cities, 2000. Contributor to professional journals. ENGLISH TITLES OF BOOKS PUBLISHED IN RUSSIAN: (with A. Igudina) Applications of the Factor Analysis in Physical Planning: Guidelines for Planners, 1980; Non-Chernozem Zone: Social Geography and Agriculture, 1986; Agriculture in the Non-Chernozem Zone: Regional Problems, 1990; (with O. Gritsai and A. Treivisch) Center and Periphery in Regional Development, 1991; (with Treivisch, G. Privalovskaya, S. Tarkhov, and others) Territorial Structure of the Economy in the Regions of Old Colonization, 1995. EDITOR & CONTRIBUTOR: Territorial Organization of the Economy as a Development Factor, 1987; Population under Duress: The Geodemography of Post-Soviet Russia, 1999. **Address:** 2113 Charlton Ln, Radford, VA 24141, U.S.A. **Online address:** gioffe@radford.edu

IONAZZI, Daniel A. American. **Genres:** Theatre. **Career:** Worked as production manager and technical manager for a variety of companies, including NBC Studios, Sander Gossard and Associates, Crawford Studios, Macy's Parade Studio, Colorado Music Hall, Lincoln Center Institute, Continental Theater Company, and Detroit Institute of Arts, 1973-77; Juilliard School, NYC, assistant technical director, 1977-80; Denver Center Theater Company, Denver, CO, technical director, 1980-81, production manager, 1981-84; Colorado Stage Company, Denver, executive director, 1984-86; Denver Partnership, Denver, director of festivals and events, 1987-88; University of California, Los Angeles, director of productions, 1988-. Santa Fe Festival Theater, production manager, 1981-82. **Publications:** The Stage Management Handbook, 1992. **Address:** Department of Theater, University of California, 405 Hilgard Ave., Los Angeles, CA 90024, U.S.A.

IONE, Carole. Also writes as Bovoso Carole. American, b. 1937. **Genres:** Poetry, Theatre, Plays/Screenplays. **Career:** Author. Letters (now Live

Letters), founder, 1974, and editor; Essence, contributing editor, 1981-83; Village Voice, poetry editor. Manhattan Theatre Club, director of Writers in Performance; producer of plays and performances. Pauline Oliveros Foundation, coartistic director; Renaissance House, Inc., artistic director; Unison Learning Center, poetry curator; Live Letters (literary program), artistic director. Poet in residence, Jazzmobile, Inc. and Teachers and Writers Collaborative; gives readings and presentations on television and radio programs and at colleges and universities. **Publications:** The Coffee Table Lover, 1973; Private Pages, 1987; Unsealedlips, 1990; Piramida Negro: Selected Poetry, 1973-1991, 1991; Pride of Family: Four Generations of American Women of Color, 1991. Scripts include Evidence, a work for five voices; A Friend, a multimedia performance work, Cycle Arts Foundation; Mirage (with Hugues Lavergne); and A Diary of Reconstruction, South Carolina Commission for the Humanities. Work represented in anthologies. Contributor to periodicals. **Address:** 156 Hunter St., Kingston, NY 12401, U.S.A.

IPSEN, D. C. American, b. 1921. **Genres:** Children's non-fiction, Engineering, Young adult non-fiction. **Publications:** Units, Dimensions, and Dimensionless Numbers (engineering), 1960; The Riddle of the Stegosaurus, 1969; Rattlesnakes and Scientists, 1970; What Does a Bee See?, 1971; The Elusive Zebra, 1971; Eye of the Whirlwind: The Story of John Scopes, 1973; Isaac Newton: Reluctant Genius, 1985; Archimedes: Greatest Scientist of the Ancient World, 1989; Endeavour: Quest for the Distance of the Sun, 2004; Edmond Halley: More Than a Man with a Comet, 2004. **Address:** 655 Vistamont Ave, Berkeley, CA 94708, U.S.A. **Online address:** dcipsen@juno.com

IRELAND, David. Australian, b. 1927. **Genres:** Novels, Plays/Screenplays. **Career:** Freelance writer. **Publications:** Image in the Clay (play), 1962; The Chantic Bird, 1968; The Unknown Industrial Prisoner, 1971; The Flesheaters, 1972; Burn, 1975; The Glass Canoe, 1976; A Woman of the Future, 1979; City of Woman, 1981; Archimedes and the Seagle, 1984; Bloodfather, 1988; The Chosen, 1997. **Address:** c/o Curtis Brown Pty, PO Box 19, Paddington, NSW 2021, Australia.

IRELAND, Kevin (Mark). New Zealander, b. 1933. **Genres:** Novels, Poetry, Autobiography/Memoirs. **Career:** Mate mag., Auckland, founding editor; Quote Unquote mag., Auckland, assistant editor; PEN, New Zealand, national president, until 1992. Canterbury University, writer-in-residence, 1986; Sargeson Fellow, Auckland, 1987; Auckland University, Literary Fellow, 1988; Commemoration Medal, 1990; OBE, 1993. **Publications:** A Grammar of Dreams, 1975; Literary Cartoons, 1978; Practice Night in the Drill Hall, 1985; The Year of the Comet, 1986; Tiberius at the Beehive, 1990; Skinning a Fish, 1994; Sleeping with the Angels (stories), 1994; Under the Bridge & over the Moon: A Memoir, 1999; Backwards to Forwards: A Memoir, 2002. POETRY: Face to Face, 1963; Educating the Body, 1968; A Letter from Amsterdam, 1972; Orchids, Hummingbirds, and Other Poems, 1974; The Dangers of Art: Poems 1975-1980, 1981; Selected Poems, 1987; Anzac Day: Selected Poems, 1997; Fourteen Reasons for Writing, 2001; Walking the Land, 2003. NOVELS: Blowing My Top, 1996; The Man Who Never Lived, 1997; The Craymore Affair, 2000. **Address:** 8 Domain St, Devonport, New Zealand. **Online address:** kireland@xtra.co.nz

IRELAND, Patrick R(ichard). American, b. 1961. **Genres:** Politics/Government. **Career:** Commonwealth of Massachusetts, Boston, researcher for Commission on Indian Affairs, 1984; Massachusetts Urban Reinvestment Advisory Group, Boston, researcher, 1984-85; Connecticut College, New London, assistant professor of government, 1989-92; University of Denver, CO, associate professor of comparative public policy and comparative and European politics, 1992-. University of Bremen, visiting fellow at Center for Social Policy Research, 1992; Berlin Institute for Comparative Social Policy Research, visiting fellow, 1993, 1996; visiting faculty, Tubingen, Germany, 1994, and Legon, Ghana, 1997; speaker at colleges and universities. **Publications:** The Policy Challenge of Ethnic Diversity: Immigrant Politics in France and Switzerland, 1994. Contributor to books. Contributor to political science and European studies journals. **Address:** Graduate School of International Studies, University of Denver, Denver, CO 80208, U.S.A.

IRION, Mary Jean. American, b. 1922. **Genres:** Poetry, Theology/Religion. **Career:** Lancaster Country Day School, teacher of English literature, 1968-74, 1980-81; Countermeasure poets workshop, Lancaster, PA, founder and coordinator, 1974-94; Chautauqua Institution, Chautauqua Writers' Center, NY, founder, teacher of modern poetry, 1983-97, director, 1987-97; Lancaster Theological Seminary, PA, visiting lecturer in theology and literature, 1983-90; Society for the Arts and Religion in Contemporary Culture, fellow, 1990-. **Publications:** From the Ashes of Christianity, 1968; Yes, World, 1970; Holding On, 1984 (poetry); WORK IN PROGRESS: She-fire: A Safari into the Religious Animal (creative non-fiction). **Address:** 32 Meadow Ln, Grove City, PA 16127-6452, U.S.A.

IRMSCHER, Christoph. German, b. 1962. **Genres:** Literary criticism and history. **Career:** University of Bonn, Germany, lecturer in English, 1992-96; University of Tennessee, Knoxville, visiting assistant professor of English, 1993-94; Harvard University, Cambridge, MA, lecturer in English and literature and history, 1998-2000; University of Maryland, Baltimore, assistant professor, 2000-03, professor of English, 2003-. **Publications:** Masken der Moderne, 1992; The Poetics of Natural History: From John Bartram to William James, 1999; (ed.) J.J. Audubon, Writings and Drawings, 1999. Contributor to periodicals. **Address:** English Department, University of Maryland Baltimore County, Baltimore, MD 21250, U.S.A. **Online address:** irmscher@umbc.edu

IRVINE, William. American, b. 1958. **Genres:** Adult non-fiction. **Career:** The Drawing Center, assistant to the director, 1982-84; Avenue, assistant editor, 1984-86; freelance writer and editor, 1986-91; House Beautiful, copy chief and staff writer, 1992-. **Publications:** Madam I'm Adam and Other Palindromes, 1987; If I Had a Hi-Fi and Other Palindromes, 1992. Contributor to periodicals. **Address:** 96 Schermerhorn St. Apt 106, Brooklyn, NY 11201-5037, U.S.A.

IRVING, John (Winslow). American, b. 1942. **Genres:** Novels. **Career:** University of Iowa, writer-in-residence, 1972-75; Mount Holyoke College, Dept. of English, associate professor, 1975-78; Brandeis University, writer-in-residence, 1979-80; Northfield Mt. Hermon School, assistant wrestling coach, 1981-83; Fessenden School, assistant wrestling coach, 1984-86; Vermont Academy, head wrestling coach, 1987-89. **Publications:** Setting Free the Bears, 1968; The Water-Method Man, 1972; The 158-Pound Marriage, 1974; The World according to Garp, 1978; The Hotel New Hampshire, 1981; The Cider House Rules (novel), 1985, (screenplay), 1999; A Prayer for Owen Meany, 1989; A Son of the Circus, 1994; Trying to Save Piggy Sneed, 1996; A Widow for One Year, 1998; My Movie Business: A Memoir, 1999; The Fourth Hand, 2001; Until I Find You, 2005.

IRVING, Shae (Lyn). American, b. 1966. **Genres:** Money/Finance. **Career:** Nolo Press, Berkeley, CA, legal editor, 1994-. **Publications:** The Financial Power of Attorney Workbook: Who Will Handle Your Finances if You Can't, 1997; (with R. Leonard) Take Control of Your Student Loans, 1997; (with B.K. Repa, R. Warner, and S. Elias) Willmaker, 1998; Nolo's Everyday Law Book, 1996, 2nd ed, 1999. **Address:** Nolo Press, 950 Parker St., Berkeley, CA 94710, U.S.A. **Online address:** shae@california.com

IRVING, Stephanie (Jean). American, b. 1962. **Genres:** Travel/Exploration. **Career:** University of Washington, Seattle, technical writer at Academic Computer Center, 1985-86; St. Martin's Press Inc., NYC, editorial assistant, 1986; Sasquatch Books, Seattle, editorial assistant to senior acquisitions editor, 1987-96; Irving Ink, owner, 1996-; editor and writer. **Publications:** Restaurants, Lodgings, and Touring in Washington, Oregon, and British Columbia, 1991, 1995. EDITOR: (with D. Brewster) Seattle Best Places: The Most Discriminating Guide to Seattle's Restaurants, Shops, Hotels, Nightlife, Sights, Outings, and Annual Events, 1990, 7th ed., 1996; (with K. Carlson) Portland Best Places: A Discriminating Guide to Portland's Restaurants, Lodgings, Shopping, Nightlife, Arts, Sights, and Outings, 1990, 3rd ed., 1995; (with K. Robinson) Seattle Cheap Eats: Three Hundred Terrific Bargain Eateries, 1990; Northwest Best Places, 1992, 1998; Northwest Cheap Sleeps: Mountain Motels, Island Cabins, Ski Bunks, Beach Cottages, and Hundreds of Penny-Pinching Travel Ideas for the Adventurous Road Tripper, 1992, 1994; (with L. Hagar) Northern California Best Places, 1993-1994, 1995-1996: Restaurants, Lodgings, Touring, 1992, 1994. Work represented in anthologies. **Address:** PO Box 200, Trout Lake, WA 98650-0200, U.S.A.

IRWIN, Peter George. Australian, b. 1925. **Genres:** Geography. **Career:** Member of Staff, Newcastle Teachers College, 1959-65; Sr. Lecturer, 1966-74, and Associate Professor, 1974-85, Dept. of Geography, University of Newcastle NSW. **Publications:** (with D.A.M. Lea) New Guinea: The Territory and Its People, 1967; Equatorial and Tropical Rainforest, 1968; The Monsoon Asia, 1968; The Tropical Savanna, 1969; Human Geography, 1970; Cotton Systems of the Namoi Valley, 1972; Systems in Human Geography, 1973; (with J.C.R. Camm) Space, People, Place, 1979; (with J.C.R. Camm) Land, Man, Region, 1982; (with E. and J.C.R. Camm) Skills for Senior School Geography, 1985; (with E. and J.C.R. Camm) Australians in Their Environment, 1987; (with E. and J.C.R. Camm) Resources, Settlement, Livelihood: Perspectives on a Changing World, 1989; (with R.E. Bernard and P.P. Courtenay) Australia's Neighbours, 1990. **Address:** 16/16 Myall Rd, Waratah, NSW 2298, Australia.

IRWIN, Robert (Graham). British, b. 1946. **Genres:** Novels, History, Literary criticism and history. **Career:** Writer and part-time teacher.

University of St. Andrews, Scotland, lecturer in medieval history, 1972-77; London University, School of Oriental and African Studies, senior research associate. Fellow: Royal Asiatic Society; Society of Antiquaries; Royal Society of Literature. Times Literary Supplement, consulting editor. **Publications:** NOVELS: The Arabian Nightmare, 1983; The Limits of Vision, 1986; The Mysteries of Algiers, 1988; Exquisite Corpse, 1995; Prayer-Cushions of the Flesh, 1997; Satan Wants Me, 1999. OTHER: The Middle East in the Middle Ages: The Early Mamluk Sultanate, 1250-1382, 1986; The Arabian Nights: A Companion, 1994; Islamic Art, 1997; Night and Horses and the Desert: An Anthology of Classical Arabic Literature, 1999. **Address:** 39 Harleyford Rd, London SE11 5AX, England.

ISAACS, Anne. American, b. 1949. **Genres:** Children's fiction, Young adult fiction, Poetry. **Career:** Writer of children's books and poetry, 1983-. **Publications:** Swamp Angel, 1994; Treehouse Tales, 1997; Cat up a Tree, 1998; Torn Thread, 2000. **Address:** c/o Gail Hochman, Brandt & Hochman, 1501 Broadway Ste 2310, New York, NY 10036, U.S.A.

ISAACS, Arnold R. American, b. 1941. **Genres:** History, Military/Defense/Arms control. **Career:** Sun, Baltimore, MD, reporter, 1962-66, chief of Rio de Janeiro bureau and chief Latin America correspondent, 1966-69, correspondent in Washington, DC, bureau, 1969-72, chief of the Saigon bureau, Vietnam, 1972-73, chief of the Hong Kong bureau and chief Asia correspondent, 1973-78, Sunday features editor, 1978-81; free-lance writer, 1981-. Towson State University, Baltimore, MD, visiting scholar, 1983, lecturer, 1984-2001; Johns Hopkins University, Baltimore, MD, visiting professor of communications, 1983-88; Visiting lectureships: Northwest University, Xi'an, China, 1990-91; Odessa State Pedagogic Institute, Ukraine, USSR, 1991; Warsaw Journalism Center and Marie Curie-Sklodowska University, Lublin, Poland, 1994. **Publications:** Without Honor: Defeat in Vietnam and Cambodia, 1983; (with editors of Boston Publishing Company) Pawns of War: Cambodia and Laos, 1987; Vietnam Shadows: Reflections on the War, Its Ghosts, and Its Legacy, 1997. Contributor to periodicals. **Address:** 1788 Chesapeake Pl, Pasadena, MD 21122, U.S.A. **Online address:** aisaacs@mindspring.com

ISAACS, Ronald (Howard). American (born Canada), b. 1947. **Genres:** Theology/Religion, Inspirational/Motivational Literature. **Career:** Temple Sholom, Bridgewater, NJ, rabbi, 1975-. Jewish Theological Seminary of America, member of publications committee. **Publications:** Shabbat Delight: A Celebration in Stories, Songs, and Games; Jewish Expressions: My Holiday Activity Book; The Jewish Family Game Book for the Sabbath and Festivals; The Jewish Instructional Games Book; The Bride and Groom Handbook; Loving Companions: Our Jewish Wedding Album; Jewish Mourner's Handbook; Reaching for Sinai How-to Handbook for Celebrating a Meaningful Bar/Bat Mitzvah; Vesheenantam Levanekha: A Jewish Parents Handbook; Rites of Passage: Guide to the Jewish Life Cycle; How to Handbook for Jewish Living, 2 vols; Sacred Moments: Tales of the Jewish Life Cycle; Becoming Jewish: A Handbook for Conversion; The Discovery Haggada; Reflections: A Jewish Grandparents Gift of Memories; The Jewish Information Source Book: A Dictionary and Almanac; Glossary of Jewish Life; Doing Mitzvot: Mitzvah Projects for Bar/Bat Mitzvah; Sacred Celebrations: A Jewish Holiday Handbook; Jewish Family Matters: A Leader's Guide; Chain of Life: A Curricular Guide; Shma Kolaynu: A High Holy Day Youth Machtzor; Shir Chadash; Gleanings: Four Shavuot Scripts; Critical Documents of Jewish History: A Sourcebook; Lively Student Prayer Services: A Handbook of Teaching Strategies; Critical Issues: A Book for Teenagers; The Jewish Book of Numbers; Words for the Soul: Jewish Wisdom for Life's Journey; Mitzvot: A Sourcebook for the 613 Commandments; Madrich LeGabbai: A Gabbai's How-to Manual; Close Encounters: Jewish Views of God; Jewish Music: Its History, People, and Song; Sacred Seasons; Derech Eretz: Pathways to an Ethical Life; Sidra Reflections: Guide to Sidrot and Haftarot; Rediscovering Judaism: Bar and Bat Mitzvah for Adults; A Course of Study; Jewish Bible Almanac; and Every Person's Guide to Jewish Prayer.

ISAACS, Susan. American, b. 1943. **Genres:** Novels, Mystery/Crime/Suspense, Plays/Screenplays, Film, Writing/Journalism. **Career:** Seventeen Magazine, editor, 1966-70; freelance writer, 1970-76. **Publications:** Compromising Positions, 1978, screenplay, 1985; Close Relations, 1980; Almost Paradise, 1984; Hello Again (screenplay), 1987; Shining Through, 1988; Magic Hour, 1991; After All These Years, 1993; Lily White, 1996; Red, White and Blue, 1998; Brave Dames and Wimpettes: What Women Are Really Doing on Page and Screen (non-fiction), 1999; Long Time No See, 2001; Any Place I Hang My Hat, 2004.

ISADORA, Rachel. American. **Genres:** Children's fiction, Illustrations. **Career:** Boston Ballet Company, MA, dancer; author and illustrator of

children's books. **Publications:** SELF-ILLUSTRATED FOR CHILDREN: Max, 1976; The Potter's Kitchen, 1977; Willaby, 1977; Ben's Trumpet, 1979; My Ballet Class, 1980; No, Agatha!, 1980; Jesse and Abe, 1981; City Seen from A to Z, 1983; Opening Night, 1984; I Hear, 1985; I See, 1985; I Touch, 1985; The Pirates of Bedford Street, 1988; Babies, 1990; Friends, 1990; At the Crossroads, 1991; Over the Green Hills, 1992; Lili at the Ballet, 1993; Lili On Stage, 1995; My Ballet Diary, 1995; Newsboy, 1995; A South African Night, 1998. ADAPTATIONS & RETELLINGS: The Nutcracker, 1981; The Little Match Girl, 1987; The Princess and the Frog, 1989; Swan Lake: A Ballet Story, 1989; Firebird, 1994; The Steadfast Tin Soldier, 1996. BIOGRAPHY: Young Mozart, 1997; Isadora Dances, 1998. Illustrator of books by R. Maiorano, E. Schub, P.C. McKissack, S. Stoddard, R. Lindberg. **Address:** c/o William Morrow and Co., 1325 Avenue of the Americas, New York, NY 10019, U.S.A.

ISBISTER, John. American (born Canada), b. 1942. **Genres:** Economics, Philosophy, Third World. **Career:** Merrill College, University of California, Santa Cruz, CA, assistant professor, 1968-72, associate professor, 1972-78, professor of economics, 1978-, provost, 1984-99. **Publications:** Promises not Kept: The Betrayal of Social Change in the Third World, 1991, 5th ed., 2001; Thin Cats: The Community Development Credit Union Movement in the United States, 1994; The Immigration Debate: Remaking America, 1996; Capitalism and Justice: Envisioning Social and Economic Fairness. **Address:** Social Sciences I, University of California, Santa Cruz, CA 95064, U.S.A. **Online address:** isbister@cats.ucsc.edu

ISENBERG, Barbara. American. **Genres:** Art/Art history, Theatre. **Career:** Business Week, assistant editor, 1964-67; McGraw-Hill World News, correspondent from Mexico City, 1967-69; Wall Street Journal, Los Angeles, CA, staff reporter, 1969-73; California Business, Los Angeles, senior editor, 1973-75; Los Angeles Times, Los Angeles, staff writer, 1976-95, coordinator of arts and feature coverage of 1984 Olympic games, and editor of Festival, 1984; freelance writer, 1995-. KUSC-FM Radio, host of Live from Trumps, 1987, host of Getty Center Art Matters series, 2000-; guest on television and radio programs. University of California, Los Angeles, instructor in arts journalism, 1979-81, coordinator and moderator of Evenings Out with the Critics, 1985-87; British Theatre Backstage (tour group), theater expert and host, 1983-. **Publications:** (ed.) California Theater Annual, 1981-83; Making It Big: The Diary of a Broadway Musical, 1996; State of the Arts: California Artists Talk About Their Work, 2000. **Address:** c/o Susan Ramer, Don Congdon Associates, 156 5th Ave #625, New York, NY 10010, U.S.A.

ISENBERG, Joan P. American, b. 1941. **Genres:** Education. **Career:** Kindergarten teacher, 1963-68; Beth-El Pre-School, director and teacher, 1968-69; preschool teacher, 1970-71; substitute elementary teacher at public schools in Princeton, NJ, 1971-79; Rutgers College, New Brunswick, NJ, instructor in education at Douglass College, 1978; George Mason University, Fairfax, VA, assistant professor, 1978-84, associate professor, 1984-92, professor of education, 1992-97, coordinator of early childhood undergraduate and graduate programs, 1978-97, director, advanced studies in teaching & learning, 1997-. National Board for Professional Teaching Standards, visiting scholar, 2002-03. **Publications:** (with J. Jacobs) Playthings as Learning Tools: A Parents' Guide, 1982; (with S. Snover) MAZE-0 (computer games for teaching spelling), 1985; (with L. Hoffman) About the Preschool Years: Book I, 1986; (with M.R. Jalongo) Teachers' Stories: From Personal Narrative to Professional Insight, 1995; (with Jalongo) Creative Expression and Play in Early Childhood, 2nd ed., 1997, 3rd ed., 2001; (ed. with Jalongo, and contrib.) Major Trends and Issues in Early Childhood Education, 1997, 2nd ed., 2003; (with Jalongo) Exploring Your Role: A Practitioner's Introduction to Early Childhood Education, 2nd ed., 2003. Contributor to books on education. Contributor to periodicals. **Address:** Graduate School of Education, MSN3B3, George Mason University, Fairfax, VA 22030, U.S.A. **Online address:** jisenber@gmu.edu

ISENBERG, Sheila. American, b. 1943. **Genres:** Human relations/Parenting, Biography. **Career:** Journalist and author. Investigative staff reporter, The Daily Freeman, Kingston, NY, 1983-88. Principal media coordinator, New York State Assembly Task Force on Women's Issues, 1988-92; writer. **Publications:** Women Who Love Men Who Kill, 1991; (with W.M. Kunstler) My Life As a Radical Lawyer, 1994. Contributor to periodicals. **Address:** c/o Elizabeth Kaplan, Trident Media Group, 41 Madison Ave. Fl 36, New York, NY 10010-2257, U.S.A.

ISERSON, Kenneth Victor. American, b. 1949. **Genres:** Criminology/True Crime, Education, Ethics, History, Medicine/Health, Biography, Reference. **Career:** Cincinnati General Hospital, OH, emergency medicine residency, 1976-78, chief resident, 1977-78; Community Mercy Hospital, Onamia, MN, general practice, 1976; Texas A&M University College of Medicine, Division of Emergency Medicine, clinical associate professor and chairman, 1980-81; University of Arizona College of Medicine, section of emergency medicine, department of surgery, emergency physician, 1981-, assistant professor, 1981-85, associate professor, 1985-92, professor, 1992-. University of Chicago, senior fellow in bioethics, 1990-91. Medical Society US & Mexico, vice president, 2002-04. Journal of Emergency Medicine, ethics section editor, 1990-; Cambridge Quarterly of Healthcare Ethics, abstract editor, 1991-. **Publications:** (ed. with A.B. Sanders and D.R. Mathieu) Ethics in Emergency Medicine, 1986, 2nd ed., 1995; Getting into a Residency, 1988, 6th ed., 2003; Death to Dust: What Happens to Dead Bodies?, 1994, 2nd ed., 2000; Get into Medical School!, 1997, 2nd ed., 2004; Non-standard Medical Electives in the U.S. and Canada, 1997, 2nd ed., 1998; Grave Words, 1999; Pocket Protocols, 1999; Demon Doctors, 2002. Author of professional journal articles, textbook chapters, and other publications. Reviewer for medical journals. **Address:** Dept of Emergency Medicine, University of Arizona, College of Medicine Box 245057, 1501 N Campbell Ave, Tucson, AZ 85724, U.S.A.

ISHERWOOD, Charles. American, b. 1964. **Genres:** Biography. **Career:** L.A. Style, Los Angeles, CA, articles editor, 1989-93; Variety, Los Angeles, senior editor and theater critic, 1993-. **Publications:** Wonder Bread and Ecstasy (biography), 1996. Contributor to periodicals. **Address:** c/o Variety Magazine, 5700 Wilshire Blve, Ste 120, Los Angeles, CA 90036, U.S.A.

ISHIGURO, Kazuo. British (born Japan), b. 1954. **Genres:** Novels, Novellas/Short stories. **Career:** Full-time writer, 1982-. Grouse-Beater for the Queen Mother, Balmoral, Scotland, 1973-76; community worker, Glasgow, 1976-79; residential social worker, London, 1979-81. **Publications:** (with others) Introduction 7: Stories by New Writers, 1981; A Pale View of Hills, 1982; An Artist of the Floating World, 1986; The Remains of the Day, 1989 (Booker Prize); The Unconsoled, 1995; When We Were Orphans, 2000. **Address:** c/o Rogers, Coleridge & White, 20 Powis Mews, London W11 1JN, England.

ISRAEL, Betsy. American, b. 1958. **Genres:** Writing/Journalism. **Career:** Journalist; Mademoiselle, editor. **Publications:** Grown-up Fast: A True Story of Teenage Life in Suburban America, 1988; Bachelor Girl: The Secret History of the Single Woman in the Twentieth Century, 2002. Contributor to periodicals. **Address:** c/o Author Mail, William Morrow/HarperCollins, 10 E. 53rd Street, 7th Floor, New York, NY 10022, U.S.A.

ISRAEL, Lee. American, b. 1939. **Genres:** Biography, Humor/Satire. **Career:** WRVR-FM Radio, New York, NY, producer and broadcaster; Eros magazine, associate editor; Virginia Kirkus Service (now Kirkus Reviews), New York, NY, book reviewer. **Publications:** Miss Tallulah Bankhead, 1971; Kilgallen, 1979; Estee Lauder: Beyond the Magic, 1985. Contributor to newspapers and magazines. **Address:** 98 Riverside Drive, New York, NY 10024, U.S.A.

ISSAKSON, C. Ben. *See* **BORDOWITZ, Hank.**

ITZKOFF, Seymour William. American. **Genres:** Education, Biography, Philosophy. **Career:** Professor, Smith College, Northampton, Massachusetts, since 1965 (Director of Campus School, 1968-71). Faculty member, Herbert Lehman College, NYC, 1960-65. **Publications:** Cultural Pluralism and American Education, 1969; Ernst Cassirer: Scientific Knowledge and the Concept of Man, 1971, 2nd ed., 1997; A New Public Education, 1976; Ernst Cassirer, Philosopher of Culture, 1977; Emanuel Feuermann: Virtuoso, 1979, 2nd ed. 1995; The Form of Man, 1983; Triumph of the Intelligent, 1985; How We Learn to Read, 1986; Why Humans Vary in Intelligence, 1987; The Making of the Civilized Mind, 1990; Human Intelligence and National Power, 1991; The Road To Equality, 1992; The Decline of Intelligence in America, 1994; Children Learning to Read, 1996. **Address:** Smith College, Mason Hall 12, Dept. of Education and Child Study, Northampton, MA 01063, U.S.A.

IVERSEN, Leslie. British, b. 1937. **Genres:** Medicine/Health. **Career:** UK Medical Research Council, Cambridge, England, director, 1970-83; Merck Sharp & Dohme Ltd., Harlow, England, research director, 1983-95; King's College, London, England, 1999-, director, Wolfson Centre for Age-Related Diseases. Military service: Royal Navy Education Branch, 1956-58. **Publications:** The Uptake Storage of Noradraline, 1967; (with S. Iversen) Behavioural Pharmacology, 1970; The Science of Marijuana, 2000. **Address:** The Doctor's House, Little Milton OX 44 7PU, England. **Online address:** les.iversen@pharm.ox.ac.uk

IVERSON, Eric. *See* **TURTLEDOVE, Harry (Norman).**

IVES, John. *See* **GARFIELD, Brian (F. W.).**

IVINS, Molly. American, b. 1944. **Genres:** Politics/Government. **Career:** Worked as a reporter for the Chronicle, Houston, TX, and the Star Tribune, Minneapolis, MN; Texas Observer, Austin, reporter, 1970-76; New York Times, New York City, reporter, 1976-77, Rocky Mountain bureau chief in Denver, CO, 1977-82; Dallas Times Herald, Dallas, TX, columnist, 1982-91; Fort Worth Star-Telegram, columnist, 1992-. **Publications:** Molly Ivins Can't Say That, Can She?, 1991; Nothin' But Good Times Ahead, 1993; You've Got to Dance With Them What Brung You, 1998; (with L. Dubose) Shrub: THe Short but Happy Life Political Life of George W. Bush, 2000. Contributor to periodicals. **Address:** c/o Creators Syndicate, 5777 W. Century Blvd., Suite 700, Los Angeles, CA 90045, U.S.A.

IVORY, James (Francis). American, b. 1928. **Genres:** Plays/Screenplays, Film. **Career:** Film director and screenwriter, 1957-. Partner in Merchant Ivory Productions, NYC, 1963-. **Publications:** FILM SCREENPLAYS: (with R.P. Jhabvala) Shakespeare Wallah, 1965; (with Jhabvala) The Guru, 1969; (with Jhabvala) Bombay Talkie, 1970; (with Jhabvala) Quartet, 1981; (with K. Hesketh-Harvey) Maurice, 1987; (with others) A Soldier's Daughter Never Cries, 1998. DOCUMENTARIES: Venice: Theme and Variations, 1957; The Sword and the Flute, 1959; Helen, Queen of the Nautch Girls, 1973. TELEVISION SCREENPLAYS: Adventures of a Brown Man in Search of Civilization, 1971. BOOKS: Savages and Shakespeare Wallah, 1973; (comp.) Autobiography of a Princess: Also Being the Adventures of an American Film Director in the Land of the Maharajas, 1975. **Address:** Merchant Ivory Productions, 250 W 57th St #1825, New York, NY 10107, U.S.A.

IVORY, Judith. Also writes as Judy Cuevas. American. **Genres:** Romance/Historical. **Career:** Dade County public schools, Dade County, FL, teacher; University of Miami, FL, instructor; Miami Writes program, Young Men's Christian Association (YMCA), Miami, writing instructor; The Writers' Workshop public television program, writing instructor based on Ivory's workshop The Writer's Toolbox; Miami Book Fair International, Miami, featured speaker; also a writing instructor for other organizations and a speaker at other book fairs. **Publications:** AS JUDY CUEVAS: Starlit Surrender, 1988; Black Silk, 1991; Bliss, 1995; Dance, 1996. AS JUDITH IVORY: Beast, 1997; Sleeping Beauty, 1998; The Proposition, 1999; The Indiscretion, 2001; Untie My Heart, 2002. **Address:** c/o Avon Books, 1350 Avenue of the Americas, New York, NY 10019, U.S.A.

IWAJIN, Antony. *See* **STEINER, Evgeny.**

IWAO, Sumiko. Japanese, b. 1935. **Genres:** Women's studies and issues. **Career:** Harvard University, Cambridge, MA, instructor in psychology, 1962-63; Keio University, Tokyo, Japan, assistant professor, 1963-67, associate professor, 196775, professor of psychology, 1975-. National Public Safety Commission, member, 1992-. International Group for the Study of Women, founder, 1977. **Publications:** The Japanese Woman: Traditional Image and Changing Reality, Free Press, 1993. Work represented in anthologies. **Address:** Institute for Communication Research, Keio University, 2-15-45 Mita, Minato-ku, Tokyo 108, Japan.

IYER, Pico. British, b. 1957. **Genres:** Novels, Travel/Exploration, Essays. **Career:** Time magazine, NYC, writer, 1982-; author of fiction and nonfiction, 1988-. **Publications:** TRAVEL: Video Night in Kathmandu: And Other Reports from the Not-So-Far East, 1988; The Lady and the Monk: Four Seasons in Kyoto, 1991; Falling off the Map: Some Lonely Places of the World, 1993; Sun after Dark: Flights into the Foreign, 2004. FICTION: Cuba and the Night, 1995. ESSAY: Tropical Classical: Essays from Several Directions, 1997; The Global Soul: Jet Lag, Shopping Malls, and the Search for Home, 2000; Abandon, 2003.

IZZI DIEN, Mawil. British, b. 1948. **Genres:** Law, Theology/Religion. **Career:** University of Wales, Lampeter, senior lecturer in Islamic studies. **Publications:** The Environmental Dimensions of Islam, 2001; The Theory and Practice of Market Law in Medieval Islam, 1997; Islamic Law from Historical Foundations to Contemporary Practice, 2004. Contributor to encyclopedias. **Address:** Islamic Studies Program, University of Wales, Lampeter SA48 7ED, Wales. **Online address:** izzidien@hotmail.com

J

JABINE, Thomas B(oyd). American, b. 1925. **Genres:** Mathematics/ Statistics. **Career:** US Bureau of the Census, mathematical statistician in Population and Housing Division, 1949-52, in Transportation Division, 1952-55, in Statistical Research Division, 1960-63, and at Center for Research in Measurement Methods, 1965-66, special assistant to the deputy director, 1966-68, mathematical statistician in Office of the Associate Director for Research & Development, 1968-69, chief of Statistical Research Division, 1969-73; International Cooperation Administration, adviser in vital and health statistics to Brazil's Special Public Health Service, 1955-57, sampling adviser to Brazilian Institute of Geography and Statistics, 1957-60; Agency for International Development, sampling adviser to National Statistical Office of Thailand, 1963-65, acting principal statistical adviser, 1963-64; Social Security Administration, Washington, DC, chief mathematical statistician in Office of Research and Statistics, 1973-79; Energy Information Administration, Washington, DC, statistical policy expert in Office of the Administrator, 1979-80; independent statistical consultant, 1980-. George Washington University, professorial lecturer, 1982-83. Organization of American States, adviser to Direccion General de Estadisticas y Censos, Montevideo, Uruguay, 1962; sampling adviser in Nepal; consultant in Iran, Turkey, Afghanistan, Sri Lanka, Bangladesh, and Papua New Guinea. **Publications:** EDITOR: (with others) Cognitive Aspects of Survey Methodology, 1984; (with R.P. Claude) Human Rights and Statistics, 1992; (with T.A. Louis and A.L. Schirm) Choosing the Right Formula, 2001; (with T.A. Louis and M.A. Gerstein) Statistical Issues in Allocating Funds by Formula, 2003. Work represented in anthologies. Contributor to periodicals. **Address:** 3231 Worthington St NW, Washington, DC 20015-2362, U.S.A. **Online address:** tbjabine@starpower. net

JACK, Dana Crowley. American, b. 1945. **Genres:** Women's studies and issues, Psychology. **Career:** Department of Social and Health Services, Seattle, WA, caseworker, 1968-70; Western Washington University, Bellingham, WA, counselor at University Counseling Center, 1972-79, instructor, 1984-92, and professor, both at Fairhaven College, 1992-. Whatcom Counseling and Psychiatric Counseling Clinic, Bellingham, therapist, 1973-74; Groton School, Groton, MA, counselor and member of faculty, 1975-76; University of Washington, Seattle, WA, field supervisor, 1977-78; Northwest Women's Services, Bellingham, supervisor of staff counselors, 1985-87; Womencare Shelter, Bellingham, trainer for volunteers, 1987-90. Speaker at conferences and workshops. **Publications:** (with R. Jack) Moral Vision and Professional Decisions: The Changing Values of Women and Men Lawyers, 1989; Silencing the Self: Women and Depression, 1991; Behind the Mask: Destruction & Creativity in Women's Aggression, 1999. Contributor to books. Contributor of articles to professional journals. **Address:** Fairhaven College, Western Washington University, Bellingham, WA 98225, U.S.A. **Online address:** jack@cc.wwu.edu

JACK, Ian (Robert James). British, b. 1923. **Genres:** Literary criticism and history. **Career:** Lecturer, then Fellow, Brasenose College, Oxford, 1950-61; Pembroke College, Cambridge, fellow, 1961-89, emeritus, 1989-; Cambridge University, lecturer in English, 1961-73, reader in English Poetry, 1973-76, professor of English Literature, 1976-89, FBA, 1986, emeritus professor, 1989-. Visiting Professor, University of Alexandria, 1960; de Carle Lecturer, University of Otago, N.Z., 1964; Warton Lecturer, British Academy, 1967; Visiting Professor, University of Chicago, 1968-69, University of California, Berkeley, 1968-69, University of BC, 1975, University of Virginia, 1980-81, Tsuda College, Tokyo, 1981, and New York University, 1989. **Publications:** Augustan Satire, 1952; English Literature 1815-1832 (Oxford History of English Literature, Vol. 12), 1963; Keats and the Mirror of Art, 1967; Browning's Major Poetry, 1973; (gen. ed.) The Novels of the Brontes; (ed. with H. Marsden) E. Bronte's Wuthering Heights, 1976; (ed.) Oxford English Texts Ed. of Brownings Poetical Works, 5 vols., 1983-; The Poet and His Audience, 1984. **Address:** Highfield House, High St, Fen Ditton, Cambs. CB5 8ST, England.

JACK, Malcolm Roy. (born England), b. 1946. **Genres:** Biography. **Career:** House of Commons, London, England, clerk, 1967-; House of Commons, Ways and Means Committee, private secretary to chairman, 1977-80; Agriculture Select Committee, clerk, 1980-88; House of Commons, clerk of supply, 1989-91, clerk of standing committees, 1991-95, secretary to House of Commons Commission, 1995-2001, clerk of the journals, 2001-02, clerk of legislation, 2003. **Publications:** The Social and Political Thought of Bernard Mandeville, 1987; Corruption and Progress: The Eighteenth-Century Debate, 1989; (editor, with Anita Desai) The Turkish Embassy Letters of Lady Mary Wortley Montagu, 1993; (editor) Vathek and Other Stories: A William Beckford Reader, 1993; (editor) Episodes of Vathek, 1994; William Beckford: An English Fidalgo, 1996; Sintra: A Glorious Eden, 2001. **Address:** Public Bill Office, House of Common, London SW1A 0AA, England. **Online address:** malcolm.jack@btinternest.com

JACKALL, Robert. American. **Genres:** Business/Trade/Industry. **Career:** Part-time teacher, 1966-75; Williams College, Williamstown, MA, visiting lecturer, 1976-77, assistant professor, 1977-84, associate professor, 1984-87, professor of sociology, 1987-, chairman of department of anthropology and sociology, 1984-91, 1993. Adjunct professor, Columbia University, 1989-90; visiting professor, New York University, 1990-94. Research associate, Center for Economic Studies, Palo Alto, CA, 1976-80. Director of Georgetown University Community Action Program, 1966-67. Guest on radio programs. **Publications:** Workers in a Labyrinth: Jobs and Survival in a Bank Bureaucracy, 1978; Moral Mazes: The World of Corporate Managers, 1988; (with J. M. Hirota) Exputi with Symbols: Advertising, Public Relations, and the Ethos of Advocacy, 2000. EDITOR & CONTRIBUTOR: (with H.M. Levin) Worker Cooperatives in America, 1984; Propaganda; Wild Cowboys: Urban Marauders & the Forces of Order, 1997. **Address:** Department of Anthropology and Sociology, Stetson Hall, Williams College, Williamstown, MA 01267, U.S.A. **Online address:** Robert.Jackall@williams.edu

JACKER, Corinne. American, b. 1933. **Genres:** Plays/Screenplays, Children's non-fiction, Information science/Computers, Physics, Politics/Government. **Career:** Freelance writer. **Publications:** Man, Memory, and Machines: An Introduction to Cybernetics, 1964; Window on the Unknown: A History of the Microscope, 1966; The Black Flag of Anarchy: Antistatism in America, 1968; A Little History of Cocoa, 1968; 1868, 1968; The Biological Revolution, 1971. PLAYS: Bits and Pieces, 1975; Harry Outside, 1975; Night Thoughts, and Terminal, 1977; Later, 1979; Domestic Issues, 1981; In Place, 1982; Let's Dance, 1985; Hedda Gabler (adaptation), 1986; Three Sisters (adaption), 1988; After the Season, 1994; Parties (adaptation), 1999.

JACKMAN, Stuart (Brooke). British, b. 1922. **Genres:** Mystery/Crime/ Suspense, Plays/Screenplays, Theology/Religion, Young adult fiction, Novellas/Short stories. **Career:** Congregational minister, serving in Barnstaple, Devon, 1948-52, Pretoria, South Africa, 1952-55, Caterham, Surrey, 1955-61, Auckland, 1961-65, Upminster, Essex, 1965-67, Oxted, Surrey, 1969-81, and Melbourne, Cambs., 1981-87; retired, 1987. Ed., Council for

World Mission, London, 1967-71. **Publications:** MYSTERY NOVELS: Portrait in Two Colours, 1948; The Daybreak Boys, 1961; The Davidson Affair, 1966; The Golden Orphans, 1968; Guns Covered with Flowers, 1973; Slingshot, 1975; The Burning Men, 1976; Operation Catcher, 1980; A Game of Soldiers, 1981; Death Wish, 1998. OTHER: But They Won't Lie Down: Three Plays, 1954; The Numbered Days, 1954; Angels Unawares (play), 1956; One Finger for God, 1957; My Friend, My Brother (play), 1958; The Waters of Dinyanti, 1959; The Lazy T.V. and Other Stories (juvenile), 1961; This Desirable Property, 1966; Post Mortem (play), 1979; The Davidson File, 1981; A Word in Season, 1995. **Address:** c/o Curtis Brown, 4th Floor, Haymarket House, 28/29 Haymarket, London SW1Y 45P, England.

JACKMAN, Sydney Wayne. Canadian, b. 1925. **Genres:** History, Politics/Government, Travel/Exploration, Biography. **Career:** Professor of History, University of Victoria, B. C., since 1964. **Publications:** Galloping Head, 1958; Man of Mercury, 1965; Portraits of the Premiers, 1969; The Men at Cary Castle, 1971; Vancouver Island, 1972; Tasmania, 1974; Nicholas Cardinal Wiseman, 1977; A People's Princess, 1984; (with H. Haase) Een Freemdelinge in den Haag, 1984; Romerov Relatie, 1987; Chere Annette, 1990. EDITOR: Frederick Marryat: A Diary in America, 1962; With Burgoyne from Quebec, 1963; The English Reform Tradition, 1965; The Idea of a Patriot King, 1965; (co-) American Voyageur, 1969; Romanov Relations, 1969; A Middle Passage, 1970; The Journal of William Sturgis, 1978; Acton in America, 1979; A Curious Cage, 1981; At Sea and By Land, 1984.

JACKONT, Amnon. Israeli, b. 1948. **Genres:** Novels. **Career:** Member of editorial staff of Keter publishing company; host of a regular radio program; editor of a literary magazine. **Publications:** NOVELS: Pesek-Zman, 1982, trans. as Borrowed Time, 1986; Ish-Hasagrir (title means: Rainy-Day Man), 1987; Achron Hameahim Hachachamim (title means: Last of the Wise Lovers), 1991; Malkodet Dvash (title means: Honey Trap), 1994; Mavo Le-Ahava (title means: Introduction to Love), 2001. **Address:** 15 King David Blvd, 64953 Tel Aviv, Israel. **Online address:** amjack@netvision.net.il

JACKS, Oliver. See ROYCE, Kenneth.

JACKSON, Angela. American, b. 1951. **Genres:** Poetry, Plays/Screenplays. **Career:** Poet. Organization of Black American Culture (OBAC) Workshop, Chicago, IL, coordinator, 1976-. Active in the Poets-in-the-Schools Program in the state of Illinois throughout the 1970s. **Publications:** POETRY: Voo Doo/Love Magic, 1974; The Greenville Club (chapbook), 1977; Solo in the Boxcar Third Floor E, 1985; The Man with the White Liver, 1987; Dark Legs and Silk Kisses: The Beatitudes of the Spinners, 1993; And All These Roads Be Luminous: Poems Selected and New, 1997. PLAYS: Witness!, 1978; Shango Diaspora: An African-American Myth of Womanhood and Love, 1980; When the Wind Blows, 1984. Contributor of poetry and short stories to periodicals. **Address:** c/o Northwestern University Press, 625 Colfax St., Evanston, IL 60208, U.S.A.

JACKSON, Anthony. Canadian (born United Kingdom), b. 1926. **Genres:** Architecture. **Career:** Professor Emeritus, Technical University of Nova Scotia, Halifax, 1991-, (Associate Professor, 1963-73; Professor, 1973-91). Designer, Design Research Unit, London, 1950-51; Assistant Lecturer, School of Architecture, Southend-on-Sea, Essex, 1951-56; Designer, Canadian Government Exhibition Commission, Ottawa, 1957-59; Technical Ed., 1959-61, and Managing Ed., 1961-62, The Canadian Architect, Toronto. **Publications:** The Politics of Architecture: A History of Modern Architecture in Britain, 1970; A Place Called Home: A History of Low-Cost Housing in Manhattan, 1976; The Democratization of Canadian Architecture, 1978; The Future of Canadian Architecture, 1979; Space in Canadian Architecture, 1981; (with Ramuna Macdonald), Built in Canada/Du Construction Canadienne (film), 1985; Reconstructing Architecture for the 21st Century: An Inquiry into the Architect's World, 1995. **Address:** 6095 Coburg Rd #601, Halifax, NS, Canada B3H 4K1. **Online address:** anthonyjackson@ns.sympatico.ca

JACKSON, Belle. See CARR, Margaret.

JACKSON, David Cooper. British, b. 1931. **Genres:** Law. **Career:** Sir John Latham Professor of Law, Monash University, Clayton, VIC, Australia, 1965-70; University of Southampton, professor of law, 1971-98, director, Institute of Maritime Law, 1987-90, emeritus professor of law, 1998-. **Publications:** Principles of Property Law, 1967; The Conflicts Process, 1975; Enforcement of Maritime Claims, 1985, 3rd ed., 2000; Maritime Claims: Jurisdiction and Judgements, 1987; Immigration Law and Practice, 1996, 2nd ed., 1999; loose-leaf, 2001. **Address:** Dept of Law, University of Southampton, Southampton, England.

JACKSON, E. F. See TUBB, E(dwin) C(harles).

JACKSON, Edwardo. American, b. 1975. **Genres:** Novels, Plays/Screenplays. **Career:** Writer, actor. JCM Entertainment, LLC, co-president. **Publications:** NOVELS: Ever After, 2001; Neva Hafta, 2002. SCREENPLAYS: Road to Freaknik; Boys Club. **Address:** c/o Janell Walden Agyeman, Marie Brown Associates, 990 Northeast 82nd Terrace, Miami, FL 33138, U.S.A. **Online address:** EverAfterANovel@aol.com

JACKSON, Elaine. See FREEMAN, Gillian.

JACKSON, Eve. Welsh, b. 1943. **Genres:** Psychology. **Career:** Teacher of English as a foreign language; practicing astrologer; Jungian analyst; writer; teacher of T'ai Chi Ch'uan. **Publications:** Jupiter, 1986; Astrology, 1987; Food and Transformation, 1996. **Address:** 54 Eade Rd., London N4 1DH, England. **Online address:** unus.mundus@btinternet.com

JACKSON, Everatt. See MUGGESON, Margaret Elizabeth.

JACKSON, G. Mark. (Kano Shinichi). American, b. 1952. **Genres:** Novels, Criminology/True Crime. **Career:** Jefferson Advertiser, Birmingham, AL, writer, 1978-79; Southside News and Sentinel Star (now Orlando Sentinel), Orlando, FL, writer, 1979-81; free-lance writer, 1981-. **Publications:** Ninja: Men of Iga, 1989.

JACKSON, Gina. See FLUKE, Joanne.

JACKSON, Innes. See HERDAN, Innes.

JACKSON, J(ames) R(obert) de J(ager). Canadian (born Scotland), b. 1935. **Genres:** Literary criticism and history, Bibliography. **Career:** McMaster University, Hamilton, ON, Canada, assistant professor, 1963-64; University of Toronto, ON, assistant professor, 1964-, professor, 1974-94, university professor, 1994-2001, university professor emeritus, 2001-. **Publications:** Method and Imagination in Coleridge's Criticism, 1969; Poetry of the Romantic Period, 1980; Annals of English Verse, 1770-1835, 1985; Historical Criticism and the Meaning of Texts, 1989; Romantic Poetry by Women: A Bibliography 1770-1835, 1993. EDITOR: Coleridge: The Critical Heritage, 2 vols., 1970-1991; S.T. Coleridge, Logic, 1981; (with H.J. Jackson) S.T. Coleridge, Shorter Works and Fragments, 2 vols., 1995; S.T. Coleridge, Lectures 1818-1819 on the History of Philosophy, 2 vols., 2000. **Address:** Department of English, University of Toronto, 7 King's College Circle, Toronto, ON, Canada M5S 3K1.

JACKSON, Jesse, Jr. American, b. 1965. **Genres:** Money/Finance. **Career:** Politician and author. Field director for the Rainbow Coalition/Operation PUSH, 1993-95; U.S. House of Representatives, 1995-. **Publications:** (with J. Jackson Sr., and B. Shapiro) Legal Lynching: Racism, Injustice, and the Death Penalty, 1996; (with J. Jackson Sr.) It's about the Money! The Fourth Movement of the Freedom Symphony: How to Build Wealth, Get Access to Capital, and Achieve Your Financial Dreams, 2000; (with F.E. Watkins) A More Perfect Union: Advancing New American Rights, 2001. **Address:** 17926 S Halsted, Homewood, IL 60430, U.S.A.

JACKSON, John A. American, b. 1943. **Genres:** Music. **Career:** Farmingdale Public Schools, Farmingdale, NY, physical education teacher, 1966-98. Columnist for Rockin' 50s, 1986-87. **Publications:** Big Beat Legends: Rock and Roll's Evolution on Television, 1988; Big Beat Heat: Alan Freed and the Early Years of Rock and Roll, 1991; American Bandstand: Dick Clark and the Making of a Rock and Roll Empire, 1997; A House on Fire: The Rise and Fall of Philadelphia Soul, 2004. Contributor to periodicals.

JACKSON, John N. Canadian/British (born England), b. 1925. **Genres:** Geography, Regional/Urban planning, Urban studies. **Career:** Manchester University, England, lecturer in town and country planning, 1956-65; Brock University, St. Catharines, ON, professor of applied geography, 1965-91, professor emeritus, 1991-. **Publications:** Surveys for Town and Country Planning, 1963; Recreational Development and the Lake Erie Shore, 1967; The Industrial Structure of the Niagara Peninsula, 1971; The Urban Future, 1972; The Canadian City: Space, Form, Quality, 1973; Practical Geography: Strategies for Study, 1974; Welland and the Welland Canal: The Welland Canal By-Pass, 1975; (co-author) Railways in the Niagara Peninsula, 1978; (co-author) The Welland Canals: A Comprehensive Guide, 1982; (co-author) The Welland Canals: The Growth of Mr. Merritt's Ditch, 1988; The Four Welland Canals, 1988; Names across Niagara, 1990; (co-author) St. Catharines: Canada's Canal City, 1992; The Welland Canals and Their Communities: Engineering, Industrial, and Urban Transformation, 1997; The Mighty Niagara: One River-Two Frontiers, 2002. **Address:** 80 Marsdale Dr, St. Catharines, ON, Canada L2T 3S3.

JACKSON, Kathy Merlock. American, b. 1955. **Genres:** Film, Bibliography. **Career:** QPA Personnel Consultants, Boston, MA, employment counselor, 1979; Tufts University, Medford, MA, researcher and writer in Office of Research and Development, 1979-81; Smithsonian Institution, National Museum of American History, Washington, DC, researcher for Division of Transportation, 1982; Virginia Wesleyan College, Norfolk, professor and coordinator of communications, 1984-. Research Communications Ltd., research consultant, 1986-89. **Publications:** Images of Children in American Film: A Socio-Cultural Analysis, 1986; Walt Disney: A Bio-Bibliography, 1993. Work represented in anthologies. Contributor of articles and reviews to periodicals. **Address:** Department of Communications, Virginia Wesleyan College, 1584 Wesleyan Dr, Norfolk, VA 23502, U.S.A. **Online address:** kmjackson@vwc.edu

JACKSON, Kenneth T(erry). American, b. 1939. **Genres:** History, Regional/Urban planning, Urban studies. **Career:** Columbia University, NYC, assistant professor of history, 1968-71, director of urban studies, 1970-77, associate professor, 1971-76, professor of history, 1976-, Barzun Professor, 1990-, chairman, dept. of history, 1994-97; General Ed., Columbia History of Urban Life series, 1980-. **Publications:** The Ku Klux Klan in the City, 1915-1930, 1967; (ed. with L. Dinnerstein) American Vistas, 2 vols., 1971, 7th ed. 1995; (ed. with S.K. Schultz) Cities in American History, 1972; Atlas of American History, 1978; Crabgrass Frontier: The Suburbanization of the United States, 1985 (Bancroft Prize, Francis Parkman Prize); (with C. Vergara) Silent Cities: The Evolution of American Cemeteries, 1989; (ed.-in-chief) The Encyclopedia of New York City, 1995. **Address:** Dept. of History, Columbia University, New York, NY 10027, U.S.A. **Online address:** ktj1@columbia.edu

JACKSON, Kevin. British, b. 1955. **Genres:** Film, Plays/Screenplays. **Career:** Vanderbilt University, Nashville, TN, teaching fellow in English, 1980-82; British Broadcasting Corp. (BBC), London, England, producer and director for radio and television, 1983-87; Independent, London, associate arts editor, 1987-. Alces Press, managing director; writer and presenter of documentary films; lecturer at institutions, including Royal College of Art. **Publications:** Cinema: A Book of Words, in press. EDITOR: Schrader on Schrader, 1990; The Humphrey Jennings Film Reader, 1993; The Oxford Book of Money, 1995; Selected Writings of Dylan Francis, 1995. DOCUMENTARIES: Middlemarch: A User's Guide; Dennis Potter: A Tribute; Who Framed Charles Dickens?; Thinker, Painter,...Scholar, Spy. Contributor to periodicals in England and abroad. **Address:** Independent, 1 Canada Sq., Canary Wharf, London, England.

JACKSON, Maggie. American. **Genres:** Adult non-fiction. **Career:** Associated Press, reporter in London and Tokyo, editor on foreign and business desks, and national workplace columnist, 1995-2001. **Publications:** What's Happening to Home?: Balancing Work, Life, and Refuge in the Information Age, 2002. Contributor to newspapers. **Address:** c/o Author Mail, Sorin Books, PO Box 1006, Notre Dame, IN 46556, U.S.A.

JACKSON, Marian J. A. (Marian H. Rogers). American, b. 1932. **Genres:** Mystery/Crime/Suspense. **Career:** Institute of Electrical and Electronics Engineers, NYC, manager of technical services department, 1970-78; freelance writer, 1985-. **Publications:** The Punjat's Ruby, 1990; The Arabian Pearl, 1991; The Cat's Eye, 1991; Diamond Head, 1992; Sunken Treasure (tentative title), in press. **Address:** c/o Elizabeth Backman, Box 536, Johnnycake Hollow Rd., Pine Plains, NY 12567, U.S.A.

JACKSON, Marni. Canadian, b. 1946. **Genres:** Cultural/Ethnic topics, Medicine/Health, Women's studies and issues. **Career:** Canadian journalist, columnist, and nonfiction writer. Former host of the literary program Imprint, TVO network; Ryerson University, Toronto, writing instructor. **Publications:** The Mother Zone, 1993. Contributor to anthologies. **Address:** c/o Anne MacDermid & Associates, 92 Willcocks St, Toronto, ON, Canada M5S 1C8. **Online address:** marnijackson@rogers.com; www.marnijackson.com

JACKSON, Neville. See GLASKIN, G(erald) M(arcus).

JACKSON, Richard D(ean) W(ells). New Zealander (born Zambia), b. 1967. **Genres:** International relations/Current affairs. **Career:** University of Otago, Dunedin, New Zealand, teaching fellow, 1996-2001, chairperson of Foreign Policy School, 1997-98; University of Canterbury, Christchurch, New Zealand, senior teaching fellow, 2002-. **Publications:** (with J.

Bercovitch) International Conflict: A Chronological Encyclopedia of Conflicts and Their Management, 1945-1995, 1997. Contributor to journals. **Address:** Department of Political Science, University of Canterbury, Private Bag 4800, Christchurch, New Zealand. **Online address:** r.jackson@pols.canterbury.ac.nz

JACKSON, Robert H. American, b. 1955. **Genres:** History. **Career:** Gettysburg College, Gettysburg, PA, instructor in history, 1988; University of Minnesota-Twin Cities, Minneapolis, lecturer in history, 1989; University of Miami, Coral Gables, FL, visiting assistant professor of history, 1989-90; Texas Southern University, Houston, assistant professor of history, 1990-. **Publications:** (ed. with E. Langer) The New Latin American Mission History, 1985; Indian Population Decline, 1994; Regional Markets and Agrarian Transformation, 1994; (with E. Castillo) Indians, Franciscans, and Spanish Colonization, 1995. **Address:** 22830 Thadds Trl, Spring, TX 77373-7248, U.S.A.

JACKSON, Robert J. Canadian. **Genres:** International relations/Current affairs, Politics/Government. **Career:** McGill University, Montreal, associate professor, 1968-70; Office of the President of the Privy Council, Ottawa, legislative adviser and director of research, 1971-73; House of Commons, sr. policy adviser, leader of the opposition, 1987-89; Carleton University, Ottawa, department of political science, assistant professor, 1965-68, associate professor and supvr. of graduate studies, 1970-71, professor and chair, 1974-97; University of Redlands, Fletcher Jones Professor of Government and director of International Relations, 1997-. **Publications:** Rebels and Whips: Dissensions, Discipline, and Cohesion in British Parties, 1968; (with M. Stein) Issues in Comparative Politics, 1971; Canadian Legislative System: Politicians and Policy-Making, 1974, 1980; Continuity and Discord: Crises and Responses in the Altantic Community, 1985; Politics in Canada, 1985, 6th ed., 2004; The Politicization of Business in Western Europe, 1987; Contemporary Canadian Politics, 1987; Stand Up for Canada, 1992; Europe in Transition, 1992; Contemporary Government and Politics, 1993; Canadian Government in Transition, 1996; Politics in Canada, 1997; Comparative Government, 1997; Introduction to Political Science, 2003; North American Politics, 2004. **Address:** Fletcher Jones Professor of Government, University of Redlands, Hall of Letters, Room 324, Redlands, CA 92373, U.S.A. **Online address:** robert-jackson@redlands.edu

JACKSON, Sheneska. American, b. 1970?. **Genres:** Novels. **Career:** Novelist. UCLA Extension Program, writing instructor; worked as a medical secretary, 1992-95. **Publications:** Caught up in the Rapture, 1996; Li'l Mama's Rules, 1997. **Address:** c/o Simon & Schuster, 1230 Ave. of the Americas, New York, NY 10020, U.S.A.

JACKSON, William J(oseph). American, b. 1943. **Genres:** Novels, History, Humanities. **Career:** Indiana University, Indianapolis, assistant professor, 1985-92, associate professor of religious studies, 1992-. **Publications:** Walk through a Hill Town, 1977; SaiKrishnaLila, 1980; Tyagaraja-Life and Lyrics, 1991; Tyagaraja and the Renewal of Tradition, 1995; Songs of Three Great South Indian Saints, 1998; Heaven's Fractal Net: Retrieving Lost Visions in the Humanities, 2004; Diving for Carlos, or, Heroes' Welcome Blues, 2004; Soul Images in Hindu Traditions: Patterns East and West, 2004. EDITOR: J.L. Mehta on Heidegger, Hermeneutics and Indian Tradition, 1992; The Power of the Sacred Name, 1994. **Address:** Department of Religious Studies, Indiana University, 425 University Blvd, Indianapolis, IN 46202, U.S.A. **Online address:** wijackso@iupui.edu

JACKSON, William Keith. New Zealander (born England), b. 1928. **Genres:** Politics/Government. **Career:** University of Canterbury, Christchurch, Professor of Political Science, 1968-94, Emeritus Professor, 1994-. **Publications:** (with A. Mitchell and R. Chapman) New Zealand Politics in Action, 1963; (with J. Harre) New Zealand, 1969; The New Zealand Legislative Council, 1972; New Zealand: Politics of Change, 1973; The Dilemma of Parliament, 1987; (with A. McRobie) Historical Dictionary of New Zealand, 1996; (with A. McRobie) New Zealand Adopts Proportional Representation. EDITOR: Fight for Life: New Zealand, Britain and the European Economic Community, 1972; (co-) Beyond New Zealand: The Foreign Policy of a Small State, 1980. **Address:** 92A, Hinau St, Christchurch 4, New Zealand. **Online address:** keith.jackson@canterbury.ac.nz

JACKSON, William M. American, b. 1936. **Genres:** Chemistry. **Career:** National Bureau of Standards, Washington, DC, chemist, 1960-61; Martin-Marietta Aerospace Co., Baltimore, MD, aerospace scientist, 1961-63; National Bureau of Standards, chemist, 1963-64; Godard Space Flight Center, Greenbelt, MD, scientist, 1964-74; Howard University, Washington, DC, professor of chemistry, 1974-85; University of California, Davis, professor of chemistry, 1985-. **Publications:** (ed. with A. Harvey) Lasers as Reactants and Probes, 1985; (ed. with B.J. Evans) Henry C. McBay, 1994. Contributor to conference proceedings. **Address:** Department of Chemistry, University of California, Davis, CA 95616, U.S.A.

JACOB, James R. American, b. 1940. **Genres:** History. **Career:** Affiliated with John Jay College of Criminal Justice of the City University of New York, New York City. **Publications:** Robert Boyle and the English Revolution, 1978; Henry Stubbe: Radical Protestantism and the Early Enlightenment, 1983, rev. ed., 2002; (ed. with M.C. Jacob) The Origins of Anglo-American Radicalism, 1984; Scientific Revolution, 1998. **Address:** History Dept, 4315 North Hall, John Jay College of Criminal Justice, CUNY, 899 10th Ave, New York, NY 10019, U.S.A. **Online address:** jjacob1067@aol.com

JACOB, Joseph M. British, b. 1943. **Genres:** Politics/Government. **Career:** Called to the Bar at Gray's Inn; University of London, London School of Economics and Political Science, London, England, faculty member. **Publications:** Doctrine and Rules, 1988, 2nd ed, 1998; The Republican Crown, 1996. **Address:** London School of Economics and Political Science, University of London, Houghton St., Aldwych, London WC2A 2AE, England. **Online address:** j.jacob@lse.ac.uk

JACOB, Merle (Lynn). American, b. 1945. **Genres:** Literary criticism and history, Bibliography. **Career:** Chicago Historical Society Library, Chicago, IL, manuscript librarian, 1967; Academy of the Sacred Heart, Chicago, head of history department, 1969-75; Park Ridge Public Library, Park Ridge, IL, reference librarian, 1976-78; Skokie Public Library, Skokie, IL, young adult librarian, 1978-80, head of Readers Advisory, 1980-86, coordinator of collection development, 1986-91; Chicago Public Library, Chicago, adult materials selection specialist, 1991-. **Publications:** (with H. Apple) To Be Continued: Fiction in Sequels, 1995; Collection Development Plan: Skokie Public Library. Contributor to books and periodicals. **Address:** Chicago Public Library, 400 South State St., Chicago, IL 60605, U.S.A.

JACOBS, Anna. Also writes as Sherry-Anne Jacobs, Shannah Jay. British, b. 1941. **Genres:** Young adult fiction. **Career:** Writer. Formerly a teacher, a lecturer in adult technical college, and a human resources officer. **Publications:** GIBSON FAMILY SERIES: Salem Street, 1994; High Street, 1995; Ridge Hill, 1996; Hallam Square, 1996; Spinner's Lake, 1997. KERSHAW SISTERS SERIES: Our Lizzie, 1999; Our Polly, 2001; Our Eva, 2003; Our Mary Ann, 2003. OTHER HISTORICAL SAGAS; Jessie, 1998; Like No Other, 1999; Lancashire Lass, 2000; Seasons of Love, 2000; A Forbidden Embrace, 2001; Lancashire Legacy, 2001; Replenish the Earth, 2001; Down Weavers Lane, 2002; Mistress of Marymoor, 2002; A Pennyworth of Sunshine, 2003; Change of Season, 2003. AS SHERRY-ANNE JACOBS: Persons of Rank, 1992, as A Proper Match, 2000; An Introduction to Romance Writing, 1998; Plotting and Editing, 1998. FANTASY FICTION AS SHANNAH JAY; Quest, 1993; Envoy, 1994; Lands of Nowhere, 1995; Shadow of the Serpent, 1995; The Price of Wisdom, 1996. E-BOOKS: Sword of Azaray (fantasy for young adults), 1999; Worlds Beyond (short-story collection), 1999. **Address:** c/o International Scripts, 1 Norland Square, London W11 4PX, England. **Online address:** anna@annajacobs.com

JACOBS, Barbara. Mexican, b. 1947. **Genres:** Novels, Novellas/Short stories, Essays. **Career:** Writer. Lecturer at institutions throughout the world, including Stanford University and New York University. College of Mexico, investigator and professor, 1974-77. **Publications:** Un justo acuerdo (stories; title means: A Just Agreement), 1979; Doce cuentos en contra (stories; title means: Twelve Stories Against), 1982; Escrito en el tiempo (essays; title means: Written on Time), 1985; Las hojas muertas (novel), 1987, trans. as The Dead Leaves, 1993; Las siete fugas de Saab, alias el Rizos (novel; title means: The Seven Flights of Saab, alias Curly Hair), 1992; Vida con mi amigo (novel; title means: Life with My Friend), 1994; Juego limpio (essays; title means: Fair Play), 1997; Adios humanidad (novel; title means: Goodbye to Mankind), 2000. Contributor of essays and stories to periodicals. **Address:** Rafael Checa 53, 01070 Chimalistac, DF, Mexico. **Online address:** barjaco@nidr.com

JACOB, Clyde (Edward). American, b. 1925. **Genres:** Politics/Government. **Career:** University of California, Davis, faculty member, 1952-84, associate professor, 1960-63, professor, 1963-84, professor emeritus of political science, 1984-. **Publications:** Law Writers and the Courts, 1954, 3rd ed., 2001; Justice Frankfurter, 1960; (co-author) California Government, 1965; (co-author) The Selective Service Act, 1967; The Eleventh Amendment, 1972. **Address:** 2708 Cadiz St, Davis, CA 95616, U.S.A.

JACOBS, Dan(iel) N(orman). American, b. 1924. **Genres:** Politics/Government. **Career:** Miami University, Oxford, Ohio, assistant professor of political science, 1959-62, associate professor, 1962-65, professor, 1965-98, emeritus, 1998-. **Publications:** (ed.) The New Communist Manifesto, 1961, 3rd. ed., 1965; The Masks of Communism, 1963; (ed. with H.H. Baerwald) Chinese Communism, 1963; The New Communisms, 1969; (co-author) Ideologies and Modern Politics, 1972; From Marx to Mao and Marchais, 1979; Borodin: Stalin's Man in China, 1981; (co-author) Studies of the Third Wave: Recent Migration of Soviet Jews to the United States, 1981; Comparative Politics, 1983. Contributor to reference works. **Address:** 2444 Madison Rd Apt 508, Cincinnati, OH 45208, U.S.A. **Online address:** jacobsdn@muohio.edu

JACOBS, Francis G(eoffrey). British, b. 1939. **Genres:** Law. **Career:** Lecturer in Jurisprudence, University of Glasgow, 1963-65; Lecturer in Law, London School of Economics and Political Science, 1965-69; Member of the Secretariat, European Commission of Human Rights, and of the Legal Directorate, Council of Europe, Strasbourg, 1969-72; Law Clerk, Court of Justice of the European Communities, Luxembourg, 1972-74; Professor of European Law, University of London, 1974-88; Advocate-General, Court of Justice of the European Communities, 1988-. Ed., Yearbook of European Law, 1981-88. **Publications:** Criminal Responsibility, 1971; (with A. Durand) References to the European Court: Practice and Procedure, 1975; The European Convention on Human Rights, 1975, 2nd ed. (with R.C.A. White), 1996; (with L.N. Brown) The Court of Justice of the European Communities, 1977, 3rd ed., 1989; The European Union Treaty, 1986. EDITOR/CO-EDITOR: European Law and the Individual, 1976; The European Community and GATT, 1986; The Effect of Treaties in Domestic Law, 1987; Liber Amicorum Pierre Pescatore, 1987. **Address:** Court of Justice of the European Communities, L2925 Luxembourg, Luxembourg.

JACOBS, Jack L. American, b. 1953. **Genres:** Politics/Government. **Career:** Queens College of the City University of New York, Flushing, NY, adjunct lecturer, 1978; Marymount College, Tarrytown, NY, adjunct lecturer, 1979; Columbia University, New York City, preceptor, 1979-83, assistant professor, 1983-86, adjunct assistant professor, 1990; John Jay College of Criminal Justice of the City University of New York, NYC, assistant professor, 1986-90, associate professor of government, 1991-. Member of consulting faculty of Max Weinreich Center for Advanced Jewish Studies, YIVO Institute for Jewish Research, 1986-; Hunter College of the City University of New York, visiting associate professor, 1992; Leo Baeck Institute, member of academic council, 1993-; consultant to U.S. Holocaust Memorial Museum. **Publications:** On Socialists and the Jewish Question after Marx, 1992; (ed.) Jewish Politics in Eastern Europe, 2001. Work represented in anthologies. Contributor of articles and reviews to periodicals. **Address:** Dept of Government, 3255 North Hall, John Jay College of Criminal Justice, 445 W 59th St, New York, NY 10019, U.S.A.

JACOBS, Jane. Canadian (born United States), b. 1916. **Genres:** Adult non-fiction, Economics, Ethics, Urban studies. **Publications:** The Death and Life of Great American Cities, 1961; The Economy of Cities, 1969; The Question of Separatism, 1980; Cities and the Wealth of Nations, 1984; The Girl on the Hat (children's book), 1989; Systems of Survival, 1993; (ed. and author of commentary) A School Teacher in Old Alaska: The Story of Hannah Breece, 1995; The Nature of Economies, 2000. **Address:** c/o Random House, 201 E 50th St, New York, NY 10022, U.S.A.

JACOBS, Jonnie. American. **Genres:** Mystery/Crime/Suspense. **Career:** Mystery writer. Has worked as a high school English teacher, a high school counselor, and an attorney for a San Francisco, CA, law firm. **Publications:** MYSTERY NOVELS: Murder among Neighbors, 1994; Murder among Friends, 1995; Shadow of Doubt, 1996; Evidence of Guilt, 1997; Murder among Us, 1998. **Address:** c/o Deborah Schneider, Gelfman Schneider Literary Agency, 250 West 57th St., New York, NY 10017, U.S.A. **Online address:** Jonnie@netcom.com

JACOBS, Leah. See GELLIS, Roberta (Leah Jacobs).

JACOBS, Louis. British, b. 1920. **Genres:** Theology/Religion, Autobiography/Memoirs. **Career:** New London Synagogue, London, Rabbi, 1963-. **Publications:** Jewish Values, 1960; Studies in Talmudic Logic, 1961; Jewish Prayer, 3rd ed., 1962; Principles of the Jewish Faith, 1964; We Have Reason to Believe, 3rd ed., 1965; Chain of Tradition, 4 vols., 1968-73; Hasidic Prayer, 1972; A Jewish Theology, 1973; What Does Judaism Say About?, 1974; Jewish Mystical Testimonies, 1977; A Tree of Life, 1984; The Talmudic Argument, 1984; The Book of Jewish Belief, 1984; Helping with Inquiries: An Autobiography, 1989; Holy Living, 1990; God, Torah and

Israel, 1990; Religion and the Individual, 1991; Structure and Form in the Babylonian Talmud, 1991; The Jewish Religion: A Companion, 1995; Beyond Reasonable Doubt, 1999; Ask the Rabbi, 1999; Concise Companion to the Jewish Religion, 1999. **Address:** 27 Clifton Hill, London NW8, England.

JACOBS, Margaret (D.). American, b. 1963. **Genres:** History, Women's studies and issues. **Career:** Historian. New Mexico State University, Las Cruces, assistant professor, 1997-2002, associate professor of history, 2002-. **Publications:** Engendered Encounters: Feminism and Pueblo Cultures, 1879-1934, 1999. **Address:** Department of History, MSC 3H, New Mexico State University, PO Box 30001, Las Cruces, NM 88003, U.S.A. **Online address:** marjacob@nmsu.edu

JACOBS, Shannon K. American. **Genres:** Plays/Screenplays, Children's fiction, Animals/Pets, Children's non-fiction. **Career:** Freelance writer. **Publications:** BOOKS FOR YOUNG PEOPLE: Song of the Giraffe, 1991; The Boy Who Loved Morning, 1993; Healers of the World, 1999. Contributor of articles and poetry to periodicals. **Address:** c/o Coyote Moon Press, PO Box 6867, Denver, CO 80206, U.S.A.

JACOBS, Sherry-Anne. *See* **JACOBS, Anna.**

JACOBS, Steve. American, b. 1955. **Genres:** Novels. **Career:** Writer. Worked as a lawyer. **Publications:** NOVELS: Under the Lion, 1993; The Enemy Within, 1996. **Address:** c/o Heinemann Publishers, 88 Post Rd. W., PO Box 5007, Westport, CT 06881, U.S.A.

JACOBS, Walter Darnell. American, b. 1922. **Genres:** International relations/Current affairs, Politics/Government. **Career:** Professor of Government and Politics, University of Maryland, College Park, 1961-78; President, Free Ukraine, 1965; Co-Chairman, American-African Affairs Association, 1967-80. Director, Defense Orientation Conference Association, 1971-74. **Publications:** (co-author) Modern Governments, 3rd ed. 1966; Frunze, 1969; South Africa Looks Outward, 1970; Rhodesia Going on Eight, 1973; (co-author) Terrorism in Southern Africa, 1973; (co-author) At the Sharp Edge in Africa, 1975; Rhodesia to Zimbabwe, 1980; Peccavi, 1993; The Flaw in the CAD, 1998. **Address:** 662 Harbor Creek Pl, Charleston, SC 29412-3203, U.S.A. **Online address:** darnell62@msn.com

JACOBSEN, Douglas G. American, b. 1951. **Genres:** History, Theology/Religion. **Career:** University of Illinois at Urbana-Champaign, visiting lecturer in religious studies, 1981-82; College of St. Francis, Joliet, IL, adjunct professor of religion, 1983; Messiah College, Grantham, PA, professor of church history and theology, 1984-. **Publications:** An Unprov'd Experiment: Religious Pluralism in Colonial New Jersey, 1991; (ed. with W.V. Trollinger Jr.) Re-forming the Center: American Protestantism, 1900 to the Present, 1998. **Address:** Messiah College, Grantham, PA 17027, U.S.A.

JACOBSON, Dan. British (born Republic of South Africa), b. 1929. **Genres:** Novels, Novellas/Short stories, Poetry, Literary criticism and history, Travel/Exploration. **Career:** Stanford University, CA, Fellow in Creative Writing, 1956-57; University College, London, Lecturer, 1976-80, Reader, 1980-88, Professor, 1988-95; Emeritus Professor of English, 1995. Visiting Professor at US and Australian universities. **Publications:** The Trap, 1955; A Dance in the Sun, 1956; The Price of Diamonds, 1957; A Long Way from London, 1958; The Zulu and the Zeide, 1959; No Further West, 1959; Evidence of Love, 1960; Time of Arrival, 1962; Beggar My Neighbour, 1964; The Beginners, 1966; Through the Wilderness, 1968; The Rape of Tamar, 1970; Inklings, 1973; The Wonder Worker, 1973; The Confessions of Josef Baisz, 1977; The Story of the Stories, 1982; Time and Time Again, 1985; Her Story, 1987; Adult Pleasures, 1988; Hidden in the Heart, 1991; The God-Fearer, 1992; The Electronic Elephant, 1994; Heshel's Kingdom, 1998; (trans.) H. van Woerden, The Assassin: A Story of Race and Rage in the Land of Apartheid, 2001. **Address:** c/o A.M. Heath & Co Ltd, 79 St. Martin's Ln, London WC2N 4RE, England.

JACOBSON, Joanne. American, b. 1952. **Genres:** Literary criticism and history, Area studies, Autobiography/Memoirs. **Career:** University of Angers, France, Fulbright Jr. Lecturer, American Literature and Civilization, 1979-80; Middlebury College, Middlebury, VT, visiting instructor, 1981-82, assistant professor of American literature and civilization, 1982-90, director of American Civilization Program, 1983-89; Yeshiva University, NYC, associate professor of English, 1990-. **Publications:** Authority and Alliance in the Letters of Henry Adams, 1992. Contributor of articles and reviews to periodicals. **Address:** Department of English, Yeshiva University, 500 West 185th St., New York, NY 10033, U.S.A.

JACOBSON, Judy. (born United States), b. 1947. **Genres:** Adult non-fiction. **Career:** Worked for public schools in Livonia, MI, and at Starkville Public Library, Starkville, MS; Mississippi State University, Mississippi State, worked at library; Oktibbeha County Heritage, Starkville, worked as museum curator. **Publications:** Southold Connections, 1991; Massachusetts Bay Connections, 1992; Detroit River Connections, 1994; A Genealogist's Refresher Course, 1995; Alabama and Mississippi Connections, 1999; A Field Guide for Genealogists, 2001. **Address:** c/o Author Mail, Clearfield Co., 200 East Eager St., Baltimore, MD 21202, U.S.A.

JACOBSON, Matthew Frye. American, b. 1958. **Genres:** History. **Career:** State University of New York at Stony Brook, assistant professor of history, 1992-95; Yale University, New Haven, CT, assistant professor of history, 1995-, associate professor of American studies, history, and African American Studies, currently. **Publications:** Special Sorrows: The Diasporic Imagination of Irish, Polish, and Jewish Immigrants in the United States, 1995; Whiteness of a Different Color: European Immigrants and the Alchemy of Race, 1998. **Address:** American Studies Program, H6S 230, Yale University, New Haven, CT 06520, U.S.A.

JACOBUS, Mary. British, b. 1944. **Genres:** Literary criticism and history. **Career:** Manchester University, Dept. of English, lecturer, 1970-71; Oxford University, fellow and tutor in English, Lady Margaret Hall, and lecturer in English, 1971-80; Cornell University, Ithaca, NY, Dept. of English, associate professor, 1980-82, professor, 1982-90, John Wendell Anderson Professor, 1990-2000; University of Cambridge, professor of English, Grace University, 2000-, fellow of Churchill College, 2000-. **Publications:** Tradition and Experiment in Wordsworth's Lyrical Ballads (1798), 1976; Reading Woman, 1986; Romanticism, Writing and Sexual Difference: Essays on The Prelude, 1989; First Things: The Maternal Imaginary, Psychoanalysis and the Scene of Reading, 1999. EDITOR: Woman Writing and Writing about Women, 1979; (co-) Body/Politics: Women and the Discourses of Science, 1989. **Address:** Churchill College, Cambridge CB3 0AS, England. **Online address:** mlj25@cam.ac.uk

JACOBY, Tamar. American, b. 1954. **Genres:** Race relations, Sociology. **Career:** Hudson Research, Paris, France, writer and editor, 1976-77; New York Review of Books, NYC, editorial staff, 1977-81; New York Times, NYC, department editor for Op-Ed page, 1981-87; Newsweek, senior editor, 1987-89, justice editor, 1988-89; Yale University, New Haven, CT, lecturer, 1986-90; New School for Social Research, NYC, instructor, 1991-. **Publications:** Someone Else's House: America's Unfinished Struggle for Integration, 1998. Contributor of articles to periodicals. **Address:** 78 Hawthorne Pl., Montclair, NJ 07042, U.S.A.

JACQ, Christian. Also writes as J. B. Livingstone. French, b. 1947. **Genres:** Novels, Mystery/Crime/Suspense, Archaeology/Antiquities, History. **Career:** Writer, 1974-. French Radio, producer, 1979-83; Groupe de la Cite, literary director, 1983-88; Ramses Institute, cofounder and head, 1986. **Publications:** L'astrologie relativiste, 1970; Le message spirituel de Saint Just de Valcabrere, 1972; Le message des batisseurs de cathedrales, 1974; La Franc-Maconnerie, histoire et initiation, 1975; Akhenaton et Nefertiti: le couple solaire, 1976; De sable et d'or: symbolique heraldique, l'honneur du nom, 1976; Le livre des deux chemins: symbolique du Puy-en-Velay, 1976; Le message des constructeurs de cathedrales, 1980; La confrerie des sages du nord, 1980; Les trente-trois degres de la sagesse; ou, comment vivre l'initiation en occident: dialogues avec Pierre Deloeuvre, 1981, as Le voyage initiatique, ou, les trente-trois degres de la sagesse: dialogues avec Pierre Deloeuvre, 1986; (with P. de La Perriere) Les origines sacrees de la royaute francaise, 1981; L'Egypte des grands pharaons, 1981; La prodigieuse aventure du lama Dancing, 1982; Le monde magique de l'Egypte ancienne, 1983, trans. as Egyptian Magic, 1985; Les grands monuments de l'Egypte ancienne, 1984; Le moine et le venerable: roman, 1985; L'Egypte ancienne au jour le jour, 1985; L'Empire du pape blanc, 1986; Le voyage dans l'autre monde selon l'Egypte ancienne, 1986; Champollion l'Egyptien, 1987; Le voyage sur le Nil, 1987; La reine soleil: l'aimee de Toutankhamon, 1988; La fiancee du Nil, 1988; Sur les pas de Champollion: l'Egypte des hieroglyphes, 1988; Le voyage aux pyramides, 1989; Maitre Hiram et le roi Salomon, 1989; Pour l'amour de Philae, 1990; Nefertiti et Akhenaton, le couple solaire, 1990; Un espion pour l'eternite, 1990; Karnak et Louxor, 1990; L'affaire Toutankhamon, 1992; La vallee des rois, 1992; Le juge d' Egypte, Vol. 1: La pyramide assassinee, 1993, Vol. 2: La loi du desert, 1993, Vol. 3: La justice du vizir, 1994; La vallee des rois, images et mysteres, 1993; Recherches sur les paradis de l'autre monde d'apres les Textes des Pyramides et les Textes des Sarcophages, 1993; L'enseignement du sage egyptien Ptahhotep, le plus ancien livre du monde, 1993; Barrage sur le Nil, 1994; Initiation a l'egyptologie, 1994; Le petit Champollion illustre, 1994, trans. as Fascinating Hieroglyphs, 1996; Le message initiatique des cathedrales, 1995; Ramses, Vol. 1: Le fils de la lumiere, 1995, trans. as The Son of Light, 1997, Vol. 2: Le temple des millions d'annees, 1996, trans. as The Temple of a Million Years, 1997, Vol. 3: la Bataille de Kadesh, 1996, trans. as The Battle of Kadesh, 1998, Vol. 4: La Dame d'Abou Simbel, 1996, trans. as The Lady of Abu Simbel, 1998, Vol. 5: Sous l'acacia d'Occident, 1997, trans. as Under the Western Acacia, 1999; Contes et Legendes du temps des pyramides, 1996; Les Egyptiennes: portraits des femmes de l'Egypte pharaonique, 1996; Les pharoans racontes, 1996; La sagesse vivante de l'Egypte ancienne, 1998, trans. as The Living Wisdom of Ancient Egypt, 1999; La Tradition primordiale de l'Egypte ancienne selon les Textes des pyramides, 1998; La Pierre de lumiere, Vol. 1: Nefer le silencieux (trans. as Nefer the Silent), 2000, Vol. 2: La femme sage (trans. as The Wise Woman), 2000, Vol. 3: Paneb l'ardent, 2000, trans. as Paneb the Ardent, 2001, Vol. 4: la Place de verite, 2000, trans. as The Place of Truth, 2001; La Reine Liberte, Vol. 1: L'Empire des tenebres, 2001, trans. as The Empire of Darkness, 2002, Vol. 2: La Guerre des couronnes (trans. as The War of the Crowns), 2002, Vol. 3: L'Epee flamboyante, 2002, trans. as The Flaming Sword, 2003; Voyage dans l'Egypte des pharaons, 2002; Les Mysteres d'Osiris, Vol. 1: L'arbre de vie, 2003, Vol. 2: La conspiration du Mal, 2003. AS J. B. LIVINGSTONE, DOSSIERS DE SCOTLAND YARD SERIES: Higgins mene l'enquete, 1989; Meurtre au British Museum, 1989; Le secret des Mac Gordon, 1989; Crime a Lindenbourne, 1989; L'assassin de la Tour de Londres, 1990; Les trois crimes de Noel, 1990; Meurtre a Cambridge, 1990; Meurtre chez les Druides, 1990; Meurtre a quatre mains, 1990; Le mystere de Kensington, 1991; Qui a tue Sir Charles, 1991; Meutres au Touquet, 1991; Le retour de Jack l'Eventreur, 1991; Meurtre chez un editeur, 1992; Meurtre dans le vieux Nice, 1992; Quatre femmes pur un meurtre, 1992; Le secret de la chambre noire, 1992; Meurtre sur invitation, 1993; Noces mortelles a Aix-en-Provence, 1993; Les disparus du Loch Ness, 1993; L'assissination du roi Arthur, 1993; L'horloger de Buckingham, 1994; Qui a tue l'astrologue?, 1994; La jeune fille et la mort, 1994; La malediction du templier, 1994; Crime printanier, 1995; Timbre mortel, 1995; Crime au festival de Cannes, 1995; Balle mortelle a Wimbledon, 1995; Higgins contre Scotland Yard, 1995; Meurtre dans la City, 1996; Un parfait temoin, 1996; Meurtre sur canape, 1996; Le crime d'Ivanhoe, 1996; L'assassin du golf, 1997; Mourir pour la couronne, 1997; Un cadavre sans importance, 1997; Meurtre a Canterbury, 1997; Le cercle des assassins, 1998; Fenetre sur crime, 1998; Meurtre a l'indienne, 1998; Crime souterrains, 1998; L'affaire Julius Fogg, 1999; Crime a Oxford, 1999. **Address:** 80 Avenue C.F. Ramuz, 1009 Pully-Lausanne CH, Switzerland.

JACQUES, Brian. British. **Genres:** Science fiction/Fantasy. **Career:** Worked as seaman, 1954-57, railway fireman, 1957-60, longshoreman, 1960-65, long-distance truck driver, 1965-75, docks representative, 1975-80, as well as logger, bus driver, boxer, policeman, postmaster, stand-up comic, and member of folk singer group; freelance radio broadcaster, 1980-. **Publications:** REDWALL SERIES: Redwall, 1986; Mossflower, 1988; Mattimeo, 1989; The Redwall Trilogy, 3 vols, 1991; Mariel of Redwall, 1991; Salamandastron, 1992; Martin the Warrior, 1993; The Bellmaker, 1994; The Outcast of Redwall, 1995; The Great Redwall Feast, 1995; Pearls of Lutra, 1996; The Long Patrol, 1997; Marlfox, 1998; The Legend of Luke, 1999; Lord Brocktree: A Tale of Redwall, 2000; A Redwall Winter's Tale, 2001; Castaways of the Flying Dutchman, 2001; Taggerung, 2001; Triss, 2002. OTHER: Seven Strange and Ghostly Tales, 1991; The Angel's Command, 2003. PLAYS: Brown Bitter; Wet Nellies; Scouse. **Address:** c/o Redwall Readers Club, PO Box 57, Mossley Hill L18 3NZ, England.

JAECK, Lois Marie. Canadian, b. 1946. **Genres:** Literary criticism and history. **Career:** Teacher of French, Spanish, and home economics in British Columbia public high schools, 1970-77, 1985-86; St. Francis Xavier University, Antigonish, Nova Scotia, assistant professor of modern languages (French and Spanish), 1986-88; University of Saskatchewan, Saskatoon, associate professor of Spanish and comparative literature, 1988-. **Publications:** Marcel Proust and the Text as Macrometaphor, 1990. Contributor to academic journals. **Address:** Department of Languages and Linguistics, 9 Campus Dr, University of Saskatchewan, Saskatoon, SK, Canada S7N 5A5. **Online address:** jaecklm@duke.usask.ca

JAFFE, Betsy. (Elizabeth Latimer Jaffe). American, b. 1935. **Genres:** Business/Trade/Industry. **Career:** Buyer for department stores in NYC, 1963-76; Catalyst, NYC, director of corporate board resource and operations, 1977-82; Career Continuum (consultants), NYC, owner and president, 1982-98. **Publications:** Altered Ambitions: What's Next in Your Life?, 1991, rev. ed., 2000. Contributor to professional journals. **Address:** c/o Anne Edelstein, 404 Riverside Dr, New York, NY 10025, U.S.A.

JAFFE, Rona. American. **Genres:** Novels, Children's fiction. **Career:** Freelance writer, and television personality. **Publications:** The Best of Everything, 1958; Away from Home, 1960; The Last of the Wizards, 1961; Mr. Right Is Dead, 1965; The Cherry in the Martini, 1966; The Fame Game, 1969; The Other Woman, 1972; Family Secrets, 1974; The Last Chance, 1976; Class Reunion, 1979; Mazes and Monsters, 1981; After the Reunion, 1985; An American Love Story, 1990; Cousins, 1995; Road Taken, 2000; The Room Mating Season, 2003. **Address:** c/o Janklow and Nesbit Associates, 445 Park Ave Fl 13, New York, NY 10022, U.S.A.

JAFFEE, Al(lan). American, b. 1921. **Genres:** Humor/Satire, Cartoons. **Career:** Quality Comics, writer and artist for Inferior Man, 1941; Marvel Comics, humor feature writer, 1942-55; Trump and Humbug (magazines), writer and artist, 1955-58; Mad (magazine), writer and artist, 1955 and 1958-; free-lance advertising illustrator, 1958-; illustrator of children's books, 1960-. Author and illustrator of syndicated comic strips "Tall Tales," 1958-65, and "Debbie Deere," 1966; Playboy (magazine), contributing artist and writer for "Little Annie Fanny" (comic strip), 1964-66. **Publications:** SELF-ILLUSTRATED: Tall Tales, 1960; Mad's Al Jaffee Spews Out Snappy Answers to Stupid Questions, 1968; Funny Jokes and Foxy Riddles, 1968; Witty Jokes and Wild Riddles, 1968; Al Jaffee's Mad (Yecch!) Monstrosities, 1974; Al Jaffee Gags, 1974; Al Jaffee Gags Again, 1975; Al Jaffee Blows His Mind, 1975; Mad's Al Jaffee Spews Out Still More Snappy Answers to Stupid Questions, 1976; Ghastly Jokes, 1976; (with F. Jacobs) Sing Along with Mad, 1977; Al Jaffee Draws a Crowd, 1978; (with N. Meglin) Rotten Rhymes and Other Crimes, 1978; Al Jaffee Bombs Again, 1978; Al Jaffee Sinks to a New Low, 1978; Al Jaffee's Mad Inventions, 1978; Al Jaffee Meets His End, 1979; The Ghoulish Book of Weird Records, 1979; More Snappy Answers to Stupid Questions, 1979; Good Lord! Not Another Book of Snappy Answers to Stupid Questions, 1980; Al Jaffee Gets His Just Desserts, 1980; Al Jaffee: Dead or Alive, 1980; Al Jaffee Fowls His Nest, 1981; Al Jaffee Meets Willie Weirdie, 1981; Al Jaffee Hogs the Show, 1981; Al Jaffee Goes Bananas, 1982; Al Jaffee Shoots His Mouth Off, 1982; Mad's Al Jaffee Freaks Out, 1982; Willie Weirdie Zaps Al Jaffee, 1983; Mad's Vastly Overrated Al Jaffee, 1983; Snappy Answers to Stupid Questions, No. 5, 1984; A Pretentious Compendium of "Mad"'s Very Best Snappy Answers to Stupid Questions, 1986; Mad Book of Puzzles, Games, and Lousy Jokes, 1986; Once Again Mad's Al Jaffee Spews Out Snappy Answers to Stupid Questions, 1987; Al Jaffee's Mad Book of Magic and Other Dirty Tricks, 1988; Snappy Answers to Stupid Questions, No. 7, 1989; Al Jaffee's Mad Rejects, 1990; An Overblown Collection: MORE Mad Snappy Answers to Stupid Questions, 1990; Fold This Book, 1997. ILLUSTRATOR: Editors of Mad magazine, Clods' Letters to Mad, 1981; Daniel Goleman and Jonathan Freedman, What Psychology Knows That Everyone Should, 1981. **Address:** c/o Mad, E.C. Publications, Inc, 1700 Broadway, New York, NY 10019, U.S.A.

JAFFEE, Annette Williams. American, b. 1945. **Genres:** Novels. **Career:** Little, Brown & Co., Boston, Mass., editorial assistant, 1966-67; writer. **Publications:** NOVELS: Adult Education, 1981; Recent History, 1988; The Dangerous Age, 1999. **Address:** PO Box 26, River Rd, Lumberville, PA 18933, U.S.A.

JAFFIN, David. American, b. 1937. **Genres:** Novellas/Short stories, Poetry, Art/Art history, History, Theology/Religion, Humor/Satire. **Career:** Minister, Lutheran Church of Wurttemberg, Germany, 1974-. Lecturer in European History, University of Maryland, European Division, 1966-70. **Publications:** 18th and 19th Century Historical Interpretations of the Reign of James I of England, 1966; Conformed to Stone, 1968; Emptied Spaces, 1972; In the Glass of Winter, 1975; As One, 1975; The Half of a Circle, 1977; Space Of, 1978; Preceptions, 1979; INRI, 1980; The Density for Color, 1982; For the Finger's Want of Sound, 1982; Selected Poems, 1982; 74 New Poems, 1994; The Telling of Time, 2000; That Sense for Meaning, 2001; Into the Timeless Deep, 2002; A Birth in Seeing, 2003; Through Lost Silences, 2003; A Voiced Awakening, 2004; These Time-Shifting Thoughts, 2004. Author of books in German. **Address:** 88636 Ilmensee, 9 Sonnenhalde, Germany.

JAFREE, Mohammed Jawaid Iqbal. Also writes as Iqbal Geoffrey. Indian, b. 1939. **Genres:** Law. **Career:** Geoffrey & Khitran (international law firm), Lahore, Pakistan, partner and chairperson, 1960-. Pakistan Institute for Human Rights, general counsel, 1960-; United Nations, human rights officer, 1966-67; Embassy of Kuwait, London, England, chief accountant, 1974-75. British Lion Films, chief accountant, 1968-69. State of Illinois, assistant attorney general, 1972-73. Shahzadi Mumtaz Jehan Trust, general counsel, 1972-. St; Mary's College, professor, 1967-68; CWS University, professor, 1970-71; Cleveland State University, professor, 1971-72; Hunerkada College of Art, distinguished visiting professor, member of board of governors, 1991-; University of Reading, professor at Law Center; distinguished visiting professor at Lahore Law College and Silver Jubilee University. Professional artist, with solo and group shows throughout the world; work represented in permanent collections. **Publications:** Qose-Qizah, 1957; Justice Is the Absence of Dictatorial Prerogative, 1965; Human Rights in Pakistan, 1966; A Critical Study of Moral Dilemmas, Iconographical Confusions, and Complicated Politics of Twentieth-Century Art, 1967; The Concept of Human Rights in Islam, 1980; (co-author) ABA: BLI Recognition and Enforcement of Money Judgments, 1994; (co-author) International Agency and Distribution Law, 1996. Some writings appear under the name variation Iqbal Geoffrey. **Address:** 66 Hall Tower, Hall Place, London W2 1LW, England.

JAHODA, Gustav. British (born Austria), b. 1920. **Genres:** Anthropology/ Ethnology, Psychology, Race relations. **Career:** University of Manchester, Manchester, England, lecturer in psychology, 1949-52; University College of Gold Coast (now University of Ghana), lecturer in psychology, 1952-56; University of Glasgow, Glasgow, Scotland, senior lecturer in social psychology, 1956-64; University of Strathclyde, Glasgow, professor of psychology, 1964-86, professor emeritus, 1986-. **Publications:** White Man: A Study of the Attitudes of Africans to Europeans in Ghana before Independence, 1961; The Psychology of Superstition, 1969, rev. ed., 1974; (with J. Cramond) Children and Alcohol: A Developmental Study in Glasgow, 1972; Psychology and Anthropology: A Psychological Perspective, 1982; (with I.M. Lewis) Acquiring Culture, 1989; Crossroads between Culture and Mind, 1993; Images of Savages, 1999. **Address:** Department of Psychology, University of Strathclyde, Glasgow G1 1RD, Scotland. **Online address:** G.Jahoda@strath.ac.uk

JAIMES-GUERRERO, M(aja) A(nnette). American, b. 1946. **Genres:** Cultural/Ethnic topics, International relations/Current affairs, Race relations, Third World, Women's studies and issues. **Career:** University of Colorado at Boulder, Center for Studies of Ethnicity and Race in America, lecturer, 1988-94; San Francisco State University, College of Humanities, professor, 1995-. Cornell University, visiting professor, 1991-92; Arizona State University, Tempe, School of Justice Studies, visiting professor, 1994-95. **Publications:** EDITOR: The State of Native America, 1992; Historical Reflections: Cross-Cultural Contact for Interdisciplinary Anti-Colonial Discourse, 1995. Work represented in anthologies. Contributor to academic and activist journals in women's studies and ethnic studies. **Address:** College of Humanities, San Francisco State University, San Francisco, CA 94132, U.S.A. **Online address:** guerrero@sfsu.edu

JAIN, Raj. American (born India), b. 1951. **Genres:** Information science/ Computers. **Career:** Digital Equipment Corp., Littleton, MA, senior consulting engineer, 1978-94; Ohio State University, Columbus, OH, professor, 1994-2002; Nayna Networks, Inc., Milpitas, CA, co-founder and CTO, 2000-. Conductor of technological seminars and tutorials; writer. Massachusetts Institute of Technology, visiting scholar, 1983-84, honorary lecturer, 1987; IEEE Communications Society, distinguished lecturer. Member of U.S. computer communications delegation to China, 1987. Holder of patents for Congestion Avoidance Scheme for Computer Networks and Token Ring Network Having Token Request Mechanism. On board of advisers of several networking start-ups. Jain Center of Greater Boston, secretary, 1979-83. **Publications:** Control-Theoretic Formulation of Operating Systems Resource Management Policies, 1979; The Art of Computer Systems Performance Analysis: Techniques for Experimental Design, Measurement, Simulation, and Modeling, 1991; FDDI Handbook: High-Speed Networking Using Fiber and Other Media, 1994; High Performance TCP/IP Networking, 2003. **Address:** 19886 Bonnie Ridge Way, Saratoga, CA 95070, U.S.A. **Online address:** jain@acm.org

JAKES, John. Also writes as Alan Payne, Jay Scotland. American, b. 1932. **Genres:** Novels, Mystery/Crime/Suspense, Romance/Historical, Science fiction/Fantasy, Westerns/Adventure, Young adult fiction, Novellas/Short stories. **Career:** Worked in advertising, 1954-70; freelance writer, 1971-. **Publications:** The Texans Ride North (juvenile), 1952; Wear a Fast Gun, 1956; A Night for Treason, 1956; The Devil Has Four Faces, 1958; The Imposter, 1959; Johnny Havoc, 1960; Johnny Havoc Meets Zelda, 1962; Johnny Havoc and the Doll Who Had "It," 1963; G.I. Girls, 1963; Tiros: Weather Eye in Space (nonfiction), 1966; Famous Firsts in Sports (nonfiction), 1967; When the Star Kings Die, 1967; Making It Big, 1968; Great War Correspondents (nonfiction), 1968; Brak the Barbarian (short stories), 1968; Great Women Reporters (nonfiction), 1969; The Asylum World, 1969; Brak versus the Mark of the Demons, 1969, in U.K. as Brak the Barbarian: The Mark of the Demons, 1970; Brak the Barbarian versus the Sorceress, 1969, in U.K. as Brak the Barbarian: The Sorceress, 1970; The Hybrid, 1969; The Last Magicians, 1969; The Planet Wizard, 1969; Secrets of Stardeep (juvenile), 1969; Tonight We Steal the Stars, 1969; Black

in Time, 1970; Mask of Chaos, 1970; Master of the Dark Gate, 1970; Monte Cristo 99, 1970; Six-Gun Planet, 1970; Mention My Name in Atlantis, 1972; Time Gate (juvenile), 1972; Witch of the Dark Gate, 1972; Conquest of the Planet of the Apes (novelization of screenplay), 1972; On Wheels, 1973; Kent Family Chronicles: The Bastard, 1974, The Rebels, 1975, The Seekers, 1975, The Furies, 1976, The Titans, 1976, The Warriors, 1977, The Lawless, 1978, and The Americans, 1980; The Best of John Jakes (short stories/ science fiction), 1977; King's Crusader (reprint of Sir Scoundrel), 1977; When The Idols Walked, 1978; Excalibur, 1980; The Bastard Photostory (nonfiction), 1980; North and South, 1982; Love and War, 1984; Heaven and Hell, 1987; California Gold, 1989; In the Big Country, the Best Western Stories of John Jakes, 1993, rev. ed. as The Bold Frontier, 2001; Homeland, 1993; (ed. with M.H. Greenberg) New Trails, 23 Original Stories of the West, 1994; American Dreams, 1998; On Secret Service, 2000; (ed.) A Century of Great Western Stories, 2000; Charleston, 2002. AS ALAN PAYNE: This'll Slay You, 1958; Murder He Says, 1958. AS JAY SCOTLAND: The Seventh Man, 1958; I, Barbarian, 1959; Strike the Black Flag, 1961; Sir Scoundrel, 1962; Veils of Salome, 1962; Arena, 1963; Traitors' Legion, 1963, as The Man from Cannae, 1977. **Address:** c/o Rembar and Curtis, 19 W 44th St, New York, NY 10036, U.S.A. **Online address:** jjfiction@aol.com

JAKOBSON, Michael. Also writes as Mikhail Iakobson. American (born Russia), b. 1939. **Genres:** Novels, History. **Career:** West Virginia University, Morgantown, assistant professor of history, 1989-91; University of Toledo, OH, associate professor, 1991-98, professor of history, 1999-. **Publications:** Guide to the Boris I. Nicolaevsky Collection, 1989; Origins of the GULAG: The Soviet Prison-Camp System, 1917-1934, 1992; Musical Folklore of the Gulag as Historical Source 1917-1939, 1998; Musical Folklore of the Gulag as Historical Source 1940-1990, 2001. **Address:** Department of History, University of Toledo, Toledo, OH 43606, U.S.A.

JAKSIC, Ivan (Andrades). American (born Chile), b. 1954. **Genres:** Area studies, History, International relations/Current affairs, Politics/Government. **Career:** Philosophy teacher at a school in Santiago, Chile, 1975-76; University of California, Berkeley, postdoctoral research associate at Center for Latin American Studies, 1982-83, vice-chairperson of the center, 1984-89, visiting lecturer, autumn, 1986, 1987; State University of New York College at Buffalo, assistant professor, summer, 1983; Stanford University, consulting assistant professor, winter, 1988; University of Wisconsin-Milwaukee, associate professor of history, 1989-94, director of Center for Latin America, 1989-94; University of Notre Dame, Helen Kellogg Institute for International Studies, associate professor of history and faculty fellow, 1994-. **Publications:** (ed. with J.J.E. Gracia) Filosofia e identidad cultural en America Latina, 1988; Academic Rebels in Chile: The Role of Philosophy in Higher Education and Politics, 1989; (ed. with P.W. Drake, and contrib.) The Struggle for Democracy in Chile, 1982-1990, 1991; (ed. with T. Halperin-Donghi, G. Kirkpatrick, and F. Masiello, and contrib.) Sarmiento: Author of a Nation, 1994; Andres Bello and the Problem of Order in Post-Independence Spanish America, 1997; Andres Bello, 2001. Work represented in anthologies. Contributor of articles, translations, and reviews to scholarly journals. **Address:** Department of History, 219 O'Shaughnessy Hall, University of Notre Dame, Notre Dame, IN 46556, U.S.A. **Online address:** Ivan.Jasic.1@nd.edu

JALATA, Asafa. American (born Ethiopia), b. 1954. **Genres:** Area studies, Cultural/Ethnic topics, International relations/Current affairs, Politics/ Government, Race relations, Sociology, Third World. **Career:** Teacher of history, English, and geography at a religious high school in Oromia (Ethiopia), 1976-77; Arssi Rural Development Project, Ethiopia, regional development officer and instructor in rural sociology, 1978-79; State University of New York at Binghamton, lecturer in sociology and African studies, 1989; Ithaca College, NY, visiting assistant professor of sociology and African-American studies, 1989-90; Clinton Community College, Plattsburgh, NY, assistant professor of sociology, 1990-91; State University of New York College at Plattsburgh, adjunct professor, 1990-91; University of Tennessee, Knoxville, assistant professor, 1991-96, associate professor, 1997-2004, professor of sociology and African and African-American studies, 2004-. **Publications:** Oromia and Ethiopia: State Formation and Ethnonational Conflict, 1868-1992, 1993; Oromo Nationalism and the Ethiopian Discourse: The Search for Freedom and Democracy, 1998; Fighting against the Injustice of the State and Globalization: Comparing the African American and Oromo Movements, 2001; (ed.) State Crises, Globalisation, and National Movements in NorthEast Africa, 2004. Contributor to books and journals. **Address:** Dept of Sociology, 901 McClung Tower, University of Tennessee, Knoxville, TN 37996, U.S.A. **Online address:** Ajalata@utk.edu

JALLAND, Pat(ricia). British/Australian. **Genres:** History, Women's studies and issues. **Career:** Lucy Cavendish College, Cambridge University, research fellow, 1973-76; University of London, England, special lecturer in history at University College London, 1974-75; Curtin University, Perth, Australia, lecturer, 1976-81, senior lecturer in history, 1981-83; Australian National University, Canberra, senior research fellow in history at research school of social sciences, 1983-86, 1991-92; Murdoch University, Murdoch, Australia, senior lecturer, 1986-88, associate professor of history, 1988-96; Australian National University, Research School of Social Sciences, professor of history, 1997-. Academy of Social Sciences in Australia, fellow; Royal Historical Society, London, fellow. **Publications:** The Liberals and Ireland: The Ulster Question in British Politics to 1914, 1980; Women, Marriage, and Politics, 1860-1914, 1986; (ed. with J.P. Hooper) Women from Birth to Death, 1830-1914, 1986; Octavia Wilberforce: The Autobiography of a Pioneer Woman Doctor, 1989; Death in the Victorian Family, 1996; Australian Ways of Death: A Social and Cultural History, 1840-1918, 2002. **Address:** History Program, Research School of Social Sciences, Australian National University, Canberra, ACT 0200, Australia.

JALONGO, Mary Renck. American, b. 1950. **Genres:** Education. **Career:** Elementary teacher at public school in Capac, MI, 1971-72, and in Ohio, 1972-75; University of Toledo, OH, instructor, 1977-78; Indiana University of Pennsylvania, assistant professor, 1978-82, associate professor, 1982-85, professor of education, 1985-, coordinator of Doctoral Program, 2002-. **Publications:** Young Children and Picture Books, 1988, 2nd ed., 2004; Early Childhood Language Arts, 1992, 3rd ed., 2003; (with Isenberg) Creative Expression and Play in Early Childhood, 1995, 4th ed., 2005; (with L.N. Stamp) The Arts in Young Children's Lives, 1997; (with M.M. Twiest and G. Gerlach) The College Learner, 1997, 2nd ed., 1999; Writing for Professional Publication, 2002; (with Isenberg) Exploring Your Role, 2nd ed., 2004. EDITOR/CO-EDITOR: (with Isenberg, and contrib.) Major Trends and Issues in Early Childhood, 1997, 2nd ed., 2003; Resisting the Pendulum Swing, 1999; (with G. Gerlach and W. Yan) Research Methods (annual), 2000; The World's Children and Their Companion Animals, 2004. Contributor to professional journals. **Address:** Professional Studies in Education Dept, 122 Davis Hall, Indiana University of Pennsylvania, 570 S 11th St, Indiana, PA 15705-1087, U.S.A. **Online address:** mjalongo@iup.edu

JAMES, Bill. See TUCKER, (Allan) James.

JAMES, Brian. American, b. 1976. **Genres:** Children's fiction, Young adult fiction. **Career:** Writer. **Publications:** Pure Sunshine (young adult novel), 2002; The Shark Who Was Afraid of Everything, 2002; The Spooky Hayride, 2003; Tomorrow, Maybe (young adult novel), 2003. SUPERTWINS SERIES: The Supertwins: Bad Dogs from Space, 2003; The Supertwins: The Terrible Tooth Snatcher, 2003; The Supertwins: Meet the Dangerous Dinobots, 2003; The Supertwins: Meet the Sneaky, Slimy Bookworms, 2004. **Address:** 1380 Riverside Dr. Apt. 6B, New York, NY 10033, U.S.A. **Online address:** brianjamespush@hotmail.com

JAMES, Caryn. American. **Genres:** Novels. **Career:** New York Times, New York, NY, chief television critic. Has also worked as a New York Times film critic and cultural reporter, and as an editor for the New York Times Book Review. **Publications:** Glorie, 1998. Contributor to periodicals. **Address:** New York Times, 229 West 43rd St., New York, NY 10036, U.S.A.

JAMES, Clive (Vivian Leopold). Australian, b. 1939. **Genres:** Novels, Poetry, Literary criticism and history, Autobiography/Memoirs, Humor/Satire. **Career:** The Observer newspaper, London, feature writer, 1972- (TV critic, 1972-82). **Publications:** The Metropolitan Critic, 1974; The Fate of Felicity Fark in the Land of the Media, 1975; Peregrine Prykke's Pilgrimage through the London World, 1976; Britannia Bright's Bewilderment in the Wilderness of Westminster, 1976; Visions before Midnight, 1977; Fan-Mail, 1977; At the Pillars of Hercules, 1979; Unreliable Memoirs, 1980; The Crystal Bucket, 1981; Charles Charming's Challenges on the Pathway to the Throne, 1981; From the Land of Shadows, 1982; Glued to the Box, 1982; Brilliant Creatures, 1983; Poem of the Year, 1983; Flying Visits: Postcards from the Observer, 1976-1983, 1984; Falling towards England: Unreliable Memoirs II, 1985; Other Passports: Poems, 1958-1985, 1986; The Remake, 1987; Snakecharmers in Texas, 1988; May Week Was in June, 1991; Brrm! Brrm!, 1991, as The Man from Japan, 1993; The Dreaming Swimmer: Nonfiction, 1987-1992, 1992; Clive James on Television, 1993; Fame in the 20th Century, 1993; The Silver Castle (novel), 1996; Reliable Essays: The Best of Clive James, 2001; Even as We Speak: New Essays, 1993-2000, 2001; As of This Writing: The Essential Essays, 1968-2002, 2003. **Address:** c/o PFD, Drury House, 34-43 Russell St, London WC2B 5HA, England. **Online address:** www.clivejames.com

JAMES, David Edward. British, b. 1937. **Genres:** Education, Psychology. **Career:** University of Surrey, Guildford, lecturer in Human Biology, 1965-

69, professor of Educational Studies, 1969-96, Dean of Associated Institutions, 1996-. Head of Biology Section, City of Bath Technical College, 1961-63; Head of Educational Psychology, St. Mary's College of Education, Newcastle upon Tyne, 1963-65. **Publications:** A Students Guide to Efficient Study, 1966; Introduction to Psychology, 1968, 1969. **Address:** Dean of Associated Institutions, University of Surrey, Guildford, Surrey GU2 5XH, England.

JAMES, David Geraint. Also writes as Aerynog. British, b. 1922. **Genres:** Medicine/Health. **Career:** Consultant Physician, 1959-, and Dean, 1968-, Royal Northern Hospital, London. Professor of Medicine, Royal Free Hospital, University of London. Ed.-in-Chief, Sarcoidosis Journal. Professor of Medicine, University of Miami, Florida; Consulting Ophthalmic Physician, St. Thomas Hospital, London; Consulting Physician, Royal Navy; Hon. Consultant Physician, Sydney Hospital. **Publications:** The Diagnosis and Treatment of Infections, 1957; Circulation of the Blood, 1978; A Colour Atlas of Respiratory Diseases, 1981, 2nd ed., 1992; Sarcoidosis and Other Granulomatous Disorders, 1985, 2nd ed., 1993; (ed.) The Granulomatous Disorders, 1999. **Address:** 41 York Terrace E, London NW1 4PT, England.

JAMES, (Darryl) Dean. (born United States). **Genres:** Mystery/Crime/Suspense. **Career:** Writer. Houston Academy of Medicine-Texas Medical Center Library, Houston, TX, worked as librarian and director of cataloging; Murder by the Book (mystery book store), Houston, general manager, 1996-. **Publications:** SIMON KIRBY-JONES MYSTERY SERIES: Posted to Death, 2002; Faked to Death, 2003; Decorated to Death, 2004. WITH JEAN SWANSON: By a Woman's Hand: A Guide to Mystery Fiction by Women, 1991; Killer Books: A Reader's Guide to Exploring the Popular World of Mystery and Suspense, 1998; The Dick Francis Companion, 2003. OTHER: (editor, with Jan Grape and Ellen Nehr) Deadly Women, 1998; Cruel as the Grave, 2000; Closer than the Bones, 2001; Death by Dissertation, 2004; (editor, with Claudia Bishop) Death Dines In (anthology), 2004. Work represented in anthologies. **Address:** Murder by the Book, 2342 Bissonnet St., Houston, TX 77005, U.S.A.

JAMES, Deana. (Mona Young Sizer). American, b. 1934. **Genres:** Romance/Historical. **Career:** Novelist. Worked for thirty-five years as a high school English teacher; Brookhaven College, creative writing teacher. **Publications:** ROMANCE NOVELS: Lovestone, 1983; Lovespell, 1984; Lovefire, 1985; Texas Storm, 1986; Texas Tempest, 1986; Texas Star, 1987; Crimson Obsession, 1988; Hot December, Bantam, 1988; Captive Angel, 1988; Angel's Caress, 1989; Masque of Sapphire, 1990; Texas Heart, 1990; Speak Only Love, 1991; Acts of Passion, 1992; Acts of Love, 1992; Seek Only Passion, 1993; Beloved Rogue, 1994. **Address:** 13229 Meandering Way, Dallas, TX 75240, U.S.A.

JAMES, Dynely. See MAYNE, William.

JAMES, Edwin. See GUNN, James E(dwin).

JAMES, Emily. See STANDIFORD, Natalie.

JAMES, Frederick. See MARTIN, William.

JAMES, Jamie. American. **Genres:** Sciences. **Career:** Former staff member, Discover magazine; music critic, London Times; contributor, Connoisseur magazine. **Publications:** (with D. Soren) Kourion: The Search for a Lost Roman City, 1988; (with R. Ciochon and J. Olsen) Other Origins: The Search for the Giant Ape in Human Prehistory, 1990; The Music of the Spheres: Music, Sciences, and the Natural Order of the Universe, 1993; (with D. Weeks) Eccentrics: A Study of Sanity and Strangeness, 1995. **Address:** 10497 Wolfanger Rd, Wayland, NY 14572, U.S.A.

JAMES, Kelvin Christopher. Trinidadian/American. **Genres:** Novels, Novellas/Short stories, Mystery/Crime/Suspense, Horror, Science fiction/Fantasy, Young adult fiction, Poetry. **Career:** Trinidad, scientific research assistant, 1960-64; high school science teacher in Trinidad, 1968; Harlem Hospital, New York City, clinical technologist, 1973-79; freelance writer, 1980-. **Publications:** Jumping Ship and Other Stories, 1992. NOVELS: Secrets, 1993; A Fling with a Demon Lover, 1996.

JAMES, Laurie. American, b. 1930. **Genres:** History, Literary criticism and history, Plays/Screenplays, Women's studies and issues. **Career:** Actor and writer. "Margaret Fuller Day," Harvard University, Cambridge, MA, actor portraying Margaret Fuller, 1979; New York State Convention, Delta Kappa Gamma keynote address speaker, 1988; Edinburgh Fringe Festival, Edinburgh, Scotland, performer, 1988, performances later aired on BBC; American-Italian Historical Association Conference, presenter of "Italian Letters of Margaret Fuller Ossoli," 1991; Great Plains Chautauqua Society, touring performer in American Renaissance programs and facilitator of children's workshops, 1991-93; Hofstra University, Long Island, NY, presenter of "How I Got to Harvard," 1997; performances also broadcast on PBS. **Publications:** NONFICTION: Outrageous Questions, Legacy of Bronson Alcott and America's One-Room Schools, 1993; (ed.) M.F. Ossoli, The Wit and Wisdom of Margaret Fuller Ossoli, 1988; Why Margaret Fuller Ossoli Is Forgotten, 1988. BIOGRAPHIES: Men, Women, and Margaret Fuller, 1990; How I Got to Harvard, Off and On Stage with Margaret Fuller, 1998. PLAYS: Men, Women, and Margaret Fuller (also known as Still Beat Noble Hearts), 1974; O Excellent Friend!, 1988; Stones Turned, 1997. RADIO PLAYS: Roots of Rebellion, 1984. JUVENILE LITERATURE: Author of Adventure, Discovery, and Horizon, national "New Day" books for girls ages seven through seventeen, 1970-73. PROGRAMS: Famous American Women Poets, 1970; Edna St. Vincent Millay Reading Edna St. Vincent Millay, 1989-97; Skimming the Cream of Herself. Contributor to periodicals.

JAMES, Livia. *See* **REASONER, Livia Jane Washburn.**

JAMES, (William) Louis (Gabriel). British, b. 1933. **Genres:** History, Literary criticism and history. **Career:** Professor in English and American Studies, University of Kent, Canterbury, since 1966. Associate Ed. Victorian Periodicals Review. Member of faculty, University of Hull, 1958-63, and University of the West Indies, 1963-66. **Publications:** Fiction for the Working Man, 1830-50, 1963; (ed.) The Islands in Between, 1968; (ed.) Print and the People 1815-1851, 1976; Jean Rhys, 1979; (ed.) Performance and Politics in Popular Theatre, 1980; Caribbean Literature in English, 1999. **Address:** Rutherford College, The University, Canterbury, Kent, England.

JAMES, Mary. *See* **MEAKER, Marijane (Agnes).**

JAMES, P(hyllis) D(orothy). (Baroness James of Holland Park). British, b. 1920. **Genres:** Mystery/Crime/Suspense. **Career:** Principal Administrative Assistant, NW Metropolitan Regional Hospital Board, London, 1949-68; Civil Service appt. Principal, Home Office, 1968-79; Principal, Police Dept, 1968-72; Criminal Policy Dept., 1972-79. Associate Fellow, 1986, Hon. Fellow, 2000, Downing College, Cambridge; Hon. Fellow St. Hilda's College, Oxford, 1996; Hon. Fellow, Girton College, Cambridge, 2000; Governor, BBC, 1988-93; Board Member, British Council, 1988-93; Member of the Arts Council, and Chmn. of Literature Panel, 1988-92; Society of Authors, Chairman, 1985-87, President, 1997; Fellow of the Royal Society of Literature, Fellow of the Royal Society of the Arts. Order of the British Empire, 1983, created life peer (Baroness) 1991. **Publications:** Cover Her Face, 1962; A Mind to Murder, 1963; Unnatural Causes, 1967; Shroud for a Nightingale, 1971; (with T.A. Critchley) The Maul and the Pear Tree (nonfiction), 1971; An Unsuitable Job for a Woman, 1972; The Black Tower, 1975; Death of an Expert Witness, 1977; Innocent Blood, 1980; The Skull beneath the Skin, 1982; A Taste for Death, 1986; Devices and Desires, 1989; The Children of Men, 1992; Original Sin, 1994; A Certain Justice, 1997; Time to Be in Earnest: A Fragment of Autobiography, 1999; Death in Holy Orders, 2001; The Murder Room, 2003. **Address:** c/o Greene & Heaton Ltd, 37 Goldhawk Rd, London W12 8QQ, England.

JAMES, Peter. British, b. 1948. **Genres:** Novels, Mystery/Crime/Suspense. **Career:** Writer. Worked as an assistant on the Brighton Evening Argus, and as cleaning person for the home of Orson Welles. Polka Dot Door, writer, 1970; Quadrant Films, film producer, 1971-78; Novelist, 1980-. Founder, Pavilion Internet plc (an early British internet and e-mail service providers). **Publications:** SPY THRILLER NOVELS: Dead Letter Drop, 1980; Atom Bomb Angel, 1981. FINANCIAL THRILLER NOVELS: Billionaire, 1982. SUPERNATURAL THRILLER NOVELS: Possession, 1988; Dreamer, 1989; Sweet Heart, 1990; Twilight, 1991; Prophecy, 1992; Host, 1993. MEDICAL THRILLER NOVELS: Alchemist, 1996. OTHER NOVELS: Travelling Man, 1984; TechnoTerrors (juvenile fiction), 1996; Horror Hospital CD, 1997. **Address:** c/o Michael Siegel, Creative Artists Agency, 9830 Wilshire Blvd., Beverly Hills, CA 90212, U.S.A.

JAMES, Russell. British, b. 1942. **Genres:** Mystery/Crime/Suspense. **Career:** Broadcaster and actor, 1960-67; worked for International Business Machines (IBM) in England, 1967-70; held managerial position, 1970-79; Business Aid, owner and business consultant, 1979-2000. **Publications:** Underground, 1989; Daylight, 1990; Payback, 1991; Slaughter Music, 1993; Count Me Out, 1995; Oh No, Not My Baby, 1998; Painting in the Dark, 2000; Pick Any Title, 2002; The Annex, 2002; No One Gets Hurt, 2004.

Contributor of stories, articles, scripts, and theater sketches. **Address:** c/o Jane Conway-Gordon, 1 Old Compton St, London W1D 5JA, England. **Online address:** findrj@lineone.net

JAMES, Sibyl. American, b. 1946. **Genres:** Novellas/Short stories, Poetry, Essays. **Career:** Teacher at colleges and universities in the United States, Mexico, Tunisia, Cote d'Ivoire and China. **Publications:** The White Junk of Love, Again (poetry), 1986; Vallarta Street (poetry), 1988; In China with Harpo and Karl (essays), 1990; The Adventures of Stout Mama (stories), 1993; The Bakery of the Three Whores (poetry), 1994. Work represented in anthologies. Contributor to periodicals.

JAMES, Susan. *See* **SCHIFFER, James (M.).**

JAMES, Thurston. American, b. 1933. **Genres:** Theatre. **Career:** University of California, Los Angeles, scenic artist, then stage carpenter, 1960-68; Immaculate Heart College, Hollywood, CA, technical director and instructor in theater arts, 1968-78; University of California, Los Angeles, property master, 1978-91; mask-maker, specializing in leather masks of the Commedia dell'Arte, 1991-. Free-lance properties builder for motion picture and television studios; gives workshops and demonstrations. **Publications:** The Theater Props Handbook, 1987; The Prop Builder's Molding and Casting Handbook, 1989; The Prop Builder's Mask-Making Handbook, 1990; The What, Where, and When of Theater Props, 1992. **Address:** 15136 Hartsook St., Sherman Oaks, CA 91403, U.S.A. **Online address:** ThurstonJms@cs.com

JAMES, Vanessa. *See* **BEAUMAN, Sally.**

JAMES, W(illiam) Martin, (III). American, b. 1952. **Genres:** Politics/Government. **Career:** Foreign affairs research assistant to U.S. Senator Henry Bellmon, 1977-78; legislative and research assistant to U.S. Representative Bill Alexander, 1978-83; research director for Arkansas's auditor of state, 1983-88; Henderson State University, Arkadelphia, AR, assistant professor, 1988-91, associate professor of political science, 1991-. Accredited observer of elections in Angola, 1992; testified before the U.S. Senate Foreign Relations Committee. **Publications:** (with J.P. Vanneman) Soviet Foreign Policy in Southern Africa: Problems and Prospects, 1983; A Political History of the Civil War in Angola, 1974-1990, Vol I, 1991. Contributor to scholarly journals and newspapers. **Address:** Department of Political Science, Henderson State University, P.O. Box 7511, Arkadelphia, AR 71999, U.S.A.

JAMES, Warren A. American (born Puerto Rico), b. 1959. **Genres:** Architecture, Art/Art history, Design, Essays, Translations. **Career:** Catalan Art and Architecture Archives, research asst, 1982-84; Robert A.M. Stern Architects, NYC, designer and junior project architect, 1984-88; Ricardo Bofill/Taller de Arquitectura, Barcelona, Spain, and Paris, France, designer and junior project architect, 1985-86; Warren A. James & Associates, Architects, NYC, designer and principal, 1988-. Consultant to museums; instructor, New Jersey Institute of Technology, 1987-89, and Universidad Complutense, Madrid, architecture program, 1990; Arquitectura (magazine), U.S. correspondent, 1987-91. Participant in architecture exhibitions, 1983-; guest juror for universities; guest speaker in lectures, symposia, television programs and documentaries, 1988-. **Publications:** Ricardo Bofill/Taller de Arquitectura: Buildings and Projects 1960-1985, 1988; (trans.) J. Larrea and Q. Capella, Designed by Architects in the '80s, 1989; (trans.) The Catalan Spirit: Gaudi and His Contemporaries (exhibition catalog), 1991; (trans. of essay) Barragan: Armando Salas Portugal Photographs of the Architecture of Luis Barragan, 1992; (ed. and contrib.) Kohn Pedersen Fox: Architecture and Urbanism 1986-1992, 1993; (trans. with H. Salichs) A. Rossi: Architecture (Spanish ed.), 1994; Dream Houses: Three Latino Constructions (exhibition catalog), 1998. **Address:** c/o David A. Morton, Rizzoli International Publications Inc, 300 Park Ave S, New York, NY 10010, U.S.A. **Online address:** warrenjames@juno.com

JAMES, William M. *See* **GILMAN, George G.**

JAMES, William M. *See* **HARVEY, John B.**

JAMES, Wilmot G. South African, b. 1953. **Genres:** Sociology. **Career:** University of the Western Cape, Bellville, South Africa, lecturer in politics, 1983-84; University of Cape Town, Rondebosch, South Africa, lecturer to professor of sociology, 1992. Institute For Democracy in South Africa (IDASA), executive director. **Publications:** Our Precious Metal, 1992. EDITOR: The State of Apartheid, 1987; (with M. Simons) The Angry Divide, 1989; (with J. Crush) Crossing Boundaries: Mine Migrancy in a Democratic

South Africa, 1995; (with D. Caliguire and K. Cullinan) Now That We Are Free: Coloured Communities in a Democratic South Africa, 1996. **Address:** IDASA, PO Box 1739, Cape Town 8000, Republic of South Africa.

JAMESON, W. C. American, b. 1942. **Genres:** Poetry, Area studies, History, Travel/Exploration. **Career:** University of Central Arkansas, Conway, professor of geography, 1974-. **Publications:** Concepts in Biometeorology, 1970; (with B.M. Barker) Platt National Park, 1975; Buried Treasures of the American Southwest, 1989; Buried Treasures of the Ozarks, 1990; Buried Treasures of the Appalachians, 1991; Buried Treasures of Texas, 1991; A Sense of Place: Essays on the Ozarks, 1992; Buried Treasures of the South, 1992; Buried Treasures from America's Heartland, 1993; Buried Treasures of the Ozarks and Appalachians, 1993; I Missed the Train to Little Rock (poems), 1993; Buried Treasures of the Rocky Mountain West, 1993; The Guadalupe Mountains: Island in the Desert, 1994; (ed.) J. Hamilton, River of Used to Be, 1994; Buried Treasures of California, 1995; Buried Treasures of the Pacific Northwest, 1995; Tales of the Guadalupe Mountains, 1995; America's Buried Treasures, 1996; Buried Treasures of the Atlantic Coast, 1997; Buried Treasures of the New England States, 1997; Buried Treasures of the Great Plains, 1997. Contributor to books. Author of newspaper columns. Contributor of articles and reviews to newspapers and periodicals. **Address:** 386 Hwy 124 West, Damascus, AR 72039, U.S.A. **Online address:** carlj@ccl.uca.edu

JAMIESON, Kathleen Hall. American, b. 1946. **Genres:** Communications/Media. **Career:** University of Maryland, professor of communications, 1971-86; University of Texas at Austin, professor of communications, 1986-89; University of Pennsylvania, Philadelphia, professor of communications, 1989-, director of Annenberg School of Communications, 1993-. Has appeared on television news programs as a political analyst. **Publications:** NONFICTION: (with H. Hellman and W. Semlak) Debating Crime Control, 1967; (Compiler) A Critical Anthology of Public Speeches, 1978; (with K.K. Campbell) The Interplay of Influence: Mass Media and Their Publics in News, Advertising, and Politics, 1982; Packaging the Presidency: A History and Criticism of Presidential Campaign Advertising, 1984; Eloquence in an Electronic Age: The Transformation of Political Speechmaking, 1988; (with D.S. Birdsell) Presidential Debates: The Challenge of Creating an Informed Electorate, 1988; (with Campbell) Deeds Done in Words: Presidential Rhetoric and the Genres of Governance, 1990; Dirty Politics: Deception, Distraction, and Democracy, 1992; (with K. Auletta and T.E. Patterson) 1800-President: The Report of the Twentieth Century Fund Task Force on Television and the Campaign of 1992, 1993; Beyond the Double Bind: Women and Leadership, 1995; (with J. Cappella) Spiral of Cynicism: The Press and the Public Good, 1996. Contributor to periodicals and professional journals. EDITOR: (with K.K. Campbell) Form and Genre: Shaping Rhetorical Action, 1978; Age Stereotyping and Television, 1978; Televised Advertising and the Elderly, 1978. **Address:** Annenberg School of Communications, University of Pennsylvania, 3620 Walnut St., Philadelphia, PA 19104, U.S.A.

JAMIOLKOWSKI, Raymond M. American, b. 1953. **Genres:** Education, Young adult non-fiction. **Career:** Schaumburg School District #54, Schaumburg, IL, elementary teacher, 1975-80; Marion County schools, Ocala, FL, guidance counselor and research specialist, 1980-84; Naperville School District #203, Naperville, IL, guidance counselor, 1984-98; Naperville Central High School, Dist #203, director of guidance, 1998-. **Publications:** (with T. Dewing) I Get It! Critical Thinking for Kids, 1986; (with T. Dewing and D. Andre) The Inquiry Method of Teaching Science, 1988; Coping with an Emotionally Distant Father, 1994, rev. ed., 1998; Drugs & Domestic Violence, 1996; A Baby Doesn't Make the Man, 1997. **Address:** Naperville Central High School, 440 Aurora Ave, Naperville, IL 60540, U.S.A. **Online address:** rjamiolkowski@ncusd203.org

JAMISON, Bill. American, b. 1942. **Genres:** Food and Wine. **Career:** Writer. **Publications:** WITH C.A. JAMISON: The Rancho de Chimayo Cookbook: The Traditional Cooking of New Mexico, 1991; Texas Home Cooking, 1993; Smoke and Spice, 1994; The Border Cookbook: Authentic Home Cooking from the American Southwest and Northern Mexico, 1995; Best Places to Stay in Mexico, 3rd ed., 1995; Best Places to Stay in Hawaii, 3rd ed., 1995; Sublime Smoke: Bold New Flavors Inspired by the Old Art of Barbecue, 1996; The Insider's Guide to Santa Fe, Taos, and Albuquerque, 4th ed., 1996; Best Places to Stay in the Caribbean, 4th ed., 1996; Born to Grill, 1998; American Home Cooking, 1999; A Real American Breakfast, 2002. **Address:** PO Box 1804, Santa Fe, NM 87504, U.S.A.

JAMISON, Cheryl Alters. American, b. 1953. **Genres:** Food and Wine. **Career:** Writer. **Publications:** WITH B. JAMISON: The Rancho de Chimayo Cookbook: The Traditional Cooking of New Mexico, 1991; Texas

Home Cooking, 1993; Smoke and Spice, 1994, rev. ed., 2003; The Border Cookbook: Authentic Home Cooking from the American Southwest and Northern Mexico, 1995; Best Places to Stay in Mexico, 3rd ed., 1995; Best Places to Stay in Hawaii, 3rd ed., 1995; Sublime Smoke: Bold New Flavors Inspired by the Old Art of Barbecue, 1996; The Insider's Guide to Santa Fe, Taos, and Albuquerque, 4th ed., 1996; Best Places to Stay in the Caribbean, 4th ed., 1996; American Home Cooking, 1999; A Real American Breakfast, 2002. **Address:** PO Box 1804, Santa Fe, NM 87504, U.S.A.

JAMISON, Janelle. *See* **PETERSON, Tracie.**

JAMISON, Kay Redfield. American. **Genres:** Medicine/Health, Psychology. **Career:** Taught at University of California, Los Angeles; Johns Hopkins University, Baltimore, MD, professor of psychiatry; writer. **Publications:** (with B.L. Baker and M.J. Goldstein) Abnormal Psychology: Experiences, Origins, and Interventions, 1980; (with F.K. Goodwin) Manic-Depressive Illness, 1990; Touched with Fire: Manic-Depressive Illness and the Creative Temperament, 1993; An Unquiet Mind (memoir), 1995; Night Falls Fast, 1999. **Address:** Dept of Psychiatry and Behavioral Sciences, 3-181 Meyer Hospital, Johns Hopkins University School of Medicine, Baltimore, MD 21287, U.S.A.

JANCE, J(udith) A(nn). American. **Genres:** Mystery/Crime/Suspense, Children's fiction. **Career:** Pueblo High School, Tucson, AZ, teacher, 1966-68; Indian Oasis Schools, Sells, AZ, librarian, 1968-73; Equitable Life Assurance Society, New York, NY, life insurance salesperson and district manager, 1974-84. Writer, 1985-. **Publications:** MYSTERY NOVELS. J.P. BEAUMONT SERIES: Until Proven Guilty, 1985; Injustice for All, 1986; Trial by Fury, 1987; Improbable Cause, 1987; A More Perfect Union, 1988; Dismissed with Prejudice, 1989; Minor in Possession, 1990; Payment in Kind, 1991; Without Due Process, 1992; Failure to Appear, 1993; Lying in Wait, 1994; Name Withheld, 1995; Breach of Duty, 1999; Birds of Prey, 2001. JOANNA BRADY SERIES: Desert Heat, 1993; Tombstone Courage, 1994; Shoot/Don't Shoot, 1995; Dead to Rights, 1997; Skeleton Canyon, 1997; Rattlesnake Crossing, 1998; Outlaw Mountain, 1999; Devil's Claw, 2000; Paradise Lost, 2001; Partner in Crime, 2002; Exit Wounds, 2003. FOR CHILDREN: It's Not Your Fault, 1985; Dial Zero for Help: A Story of Parental Kidnapping, 1985; Welcome Home, Stranger: A Child's View of Family Alcoholism, 1986. OTHER: After the Fire (poetry), 1984; Hour of the Hunter (novel), 1991; Kiss of the Bees (novel), 2000.

JANCOVICH, Mark. British, b. 1960. **Genres:** Film, Literary criticism and history. **Career:** Victoria University of Manchester, England, lecturer, 1990-93; University of Keele, Stoke on Trent, England, lecturer, 1993-95; University of Nottingham, England, lecturer, to professor in American studies, 1995-. **Publications:** Horror, 1992; The Cultural Politics of the New Criticism, 1993; Rational Fears, 1996. COEDITOR: Approaches to Popular Film, 1995; Quality Popular Television, 2003; The Place of the Audience, 2003. **Address:** Department of American Studies, University of Nottingham, Nottingham NG7 2RD, England. **Online address:** m.jancovich@nottingham.ac.uk

JANECZKO, Paul B(ryan). Also writes as P. Wolny. American, b. 1945. **Genres:** Young adult fiction, Poetry. **Career:** Poet and anthologist. High school English teacher in Parma, OH, 1968-72, and Topsfield, MA, 1972-77; Gray-New Gloucester High School, ME, teacher of language arts, 1977-90, visiting writer, 1990-. **Publications:** FOR YOUNG ADULTS. POETRY: Brickyard Summer, 1989; Stardust Hotel, 1993; That Sweet Diamond: Baseball Poems, 1998. EDITOR & COMPILER: The Crystal Image, 1977; Postcard Poems, 1979; It's Elementary, 1981; Don't Forget to Fly: A Cycle of Modern Poems, 1981; Poetspeak: In Their Work, about Their Work, 1983; Strings: A Gathering of Family Poems, 1984; Pocket Poems: Selected for a Journey, 1985; This Delicious Day: 65 Poems, 1987; Going over to Your Place: Poems for Each Other, 1987; The Music of What Happens: Poems That Tell Stories, 1988; The Place My Words Are Looking For: What Poets Say about and through Their Work, 1990; Preposterous: Poems of Youth, 1991; Looking for Your Name, 1993; Poetry from A to Z: A Guide for Young Writers, 1994; Wherever Home Begins: 100 Contemporary Poems, 1995; (with N.S. Nye) I Feel a Little Jumpy Around You: A Book of Her Poems & His Poems Collected in Pairs, 1996; Home on the Range: Cowboy Poetry, 1997. FICTION: Bridges to Cross, 1986. NONFICTION: Loads of Codes and Secret Ciphers, 1981. Contributor to books. Contributor of articles, stories, poems (as P. Wolny), and reviews to newspapers, professional and popular magazines. **Address:** c/o Author Mail, Candlewick Press Inc, 2067 Massachusetts Ave, Cambridge, MA 02140, U.S.A.

JANELLO, Amy (Elizabeth). American, b. 1962. **Genres:** Writing/Journalism. **Career:** New York Foundation for the Arts, program assistant,

1985-86; American Showcase, executive assistant, 1986; Collins Publishers, Inc., New York City, assistant managing editor of A Day in the Life of America, associate managing editor of A Day in the Life of Spain, and editor, 1986-87; Jones & Janello, New York City, partner and editor, 1987-. American Showcase, executive assistant. **Publications:** (co-ed.) The Wall: Images and Offerings from the Vietnam Veterans Memorial, 1987; The American Magazine, 1991; USSR: The Collapse of an Empire, 1992; Essential Liberty: First Amendment Battles for a Free Press, 1992; I Dream of Peace: Images of War by Children of Former Yugoslavia, 1994; Golf-The Greatest Game, 1994. **Address:** 7 Homestead Ln, Bedford, NY 10506, U.S.A.

JANES, J(oseph) Robert. Canadian, b. 1935. **Genres:** Novels, Novellas/Short stories, Mystery/Crime/Suspense, Children's fiction, Young adult fiction, Children's non-fiction, Earth sciences, Natural history. **Career:** Mobil Oil of Canada, petroleum engineer in Alberta and Saskatchewan, 1958-59; Ontario Research Foundation, Toronto, research engineer in minerals benefication, 1959-64, field researcher in geology, 1966; high school geology, geography, and mathematics teacher in Toronto, 1964-66; Brock University, St. Catharines, ON, lecturer in geology and consulting field geologist, 1966-70; Ontario Science Centre, Toronto, earth scientist, 1967-68; full-time writer, 1970-. **Publications:** NONFICTION: Geology and the New Global Tectonics, 1976; The Great Canadian Outback, 1978; (with J.D. Mollard) Airphoto Interpretation and the Canadian Landscape, 1984. NOVELS: The Toy Shop, 1981; The Watcher, 1982; The Third Story, 1983; The Hiding Place, 1984; The Alice Factor, 1991; Mayhem (in US as Mirage), 1992; Carousel, 1992; Kaleidoscope, 1993; Salamander, 1994; Mannequin, 1994; Dollmaker, 1995; Stonekiller, 1995; Sandman, 1996; Gypsy, 1997; Madrigal, 1999; Beekeeper, 2001; Flykiller, 2002. FOR CHILDREN: Rocks, Minerals, and Fossils, 1973; Earth Science, 1974; The Odd-Lot Boys and Tree-Fort War, 1976; (with C. Hopkins and J.D. Hoyes) Searching for Structure, vols. I and II, 1977; Theft of Gold, 1980; Danger on the River, 1982; Spies for Dinner, 1984; Murder in the Market, 1985. Contributor of articles and stories to magazines and newspapers. **Address:** c/o Acacia House Publishing Services Ltd., 51 Acacia Rd, Toronto, ON, Canada M4S 2K6.

JANKEN, Kenneth Robert. (born United States), b. 1956. **Genres:** Biography. **Career:** Educator and writer. University of North Carolina-Chapel Hill, assistant professor, 1991-97, associate professor of African and Afro-American studies, 1997-, adjunct professor of history, member of faculty advisory board, Office of Undergraduate Research. **Publications:** Rayford W. Logan and the Dilemma of the African-American Intellectual, 1993; White: The Biography of Walter White, Mr. NAACP, 2003. Contributor of articles to professional journals. **Address:** Department of African and Afro-American Studies, University of North Carolina Chapel Hill, Chapel Hill, NC 27599, U.S.A. **Online address:** krjanken@email.unc.edu

JANKO, (Kathleen) Susan. Also writes as Goody-Jones. American, b. 1951. **Genres:** Human relations/Parenting. **Career:** Teacher of children with severe disabilities in Orange County, CA, 1982; University of Oregon, Eugene, head teacher in Early Intervention Program, Center on Human Development, 1984-85, assistant coordinator of Early Intervention Program, 1985-87; Oregon State Children's Services Division, Lane County Relief Nursery, Eugene, program director for Therapeutic Daycare and Family Intervention Programs, 1987-89; University of Oregon, Center on Human Development, outreach trainer, 1988-91; University of Washington, Seattle, coordinator of High Priority Infant Tracking Program at Child Development and Mental Retardation Center, 1989-91, coordinator of evaluation and community outreach, 1991-93, associate director of University Affiliated Program, 1993-94; Washington State University, Vancouver, research coordinator for Early Childhood Research Institute on Inclusion, 1994-95; University of Washington, Seattle, assistant professor of early childhood special education, 1995-. **Publications:** Vulnerable Children, Vulnerable Families: The Social Construction of Child Maltreatment, 1994. Contributor to books. Also uses the joint pseudonym Goody-Jones. **Address:** College of Education, University of Washington, Seattle, WA 98195, U.S.A.

JANKOWSKI, James P. American, b. 1937. **Genres:** History. **Career:** University of Colorado, Boulder, instructor, 1966-67, assistant professor, 1967-72, associate professor, 1972-77, professor of history, 1977-, department head, 1985-89, 1995. **Publications:** Egypt's Young Rebels, 1975; Egypt, Islam, and the Arabs, 1986; (with I. Gershoni) Redefining the Egyptian Nation, 1930-1945, 1995. **Address:** Department of History, CB 234, University of Colorado, Boulder, CO 80309, U.S.A.

JANOV, Jill E. American, b. 1942. **Genres:** Administration/Management, Business/Trade/Industry. **Career:** Jill Janov Associates, principal; Block Petrella Weisbord, senior associate; Wallingford Consulting Group, principal;

Federal National Mortgage Association, director of human resources; Levi Strauss and Co., manager of human resource development; Federal Home Loan Bank of San Francisco, assistant vice president for human resources; Automobile Club of Southern California, management development specialist. Worked as publications manager, editor, and copywriter, 1966-70. Visiting faculty member at Stanford University, John F. Kennedy University (Orinda, CA), Gestalt Academy of Sweden, and Gestalt Institute of Cleveland. **Publications:** The Inventive Organization: Hope and Daring at Work, 1994. Contributor to periodicals. **Address:** Jill Janov Associates, 343 Adams St, Denver, CO 80206, U.S.A. **Online address:** JJ343@aol.com

JANOVER, Caroline (Davis). American, b. 1943. **Genres:** Children's fiction, Young adult fiction. **Career:** Dalton School, NYC, first, second, and third grade teacher, 1968-77; Ridge School, Ridgewood, NJ, learning disabilities teacher/consultant, 1979-2003. Speaker on increasing the skills and self-esteem of people with ADHD and learning differences. **Publications:** Josh: A Boy with Dyslexia, 1988; The Worst Speller in Junior High, 1995; Zipper: The Kid with ADHD, 1997; How Many Days until Tomorrow?, 2000; The Worst Speller: A One Act Comedic Drama, 2004. Author of articles about dyslexia. **Address:** PO Box 1300, Damariscotta, ME 04543, U.S.A.

JANOWITZ, Henry D. American, b. 1918. **Genres:** Medicine/Health. **Career:** Mount Sinai Hospital, NYC, professor of medicine, 1958-83. **Publications:** Inflammatory Bowel Disease: A Personal View, 1985; Your Gut Feelings: A Complete Guide to Living Better with Intestinal Problems, 1989, 2nd ed., 1994; Indigestion: Living Better with Upper Intestinal Problems from Heartburn to Ulcers and Gallstones, 1993; Good Food for Bad Stomachs, 1998. **Address:** 180 East End Ave, New York, NY 10128-7763, U.S.A.

JANOWITZ, Tama. American, b. 1957. **Genres:** Novels, Cultural/Ethnic topics, Food and Wine, Travel/Exploration, Humor/Satire. **Career:** Freelance journalist, 1985-. **Publications:** American Dad, 1981; Slaves of New York, 1986; A Cannibal in Manhattan, 1987; The Male Cross-Dresser Support Group, 1992; By the Shores of Gitchi Gumee, 1996; A Certain Age, 1999. FOR CHILDREN: Hear That?, 2001; Area Code 212, 2002; Peyton Amberg, 2003. Contributor of non-fiction to popular periodicals and newspapers. **Address:** c/o Betsy Lerner, The Gernert Co, 136 E 57th St, New York, NY 10022, U.S.A.

JANOWSKI, Thaddeus-Marian. American (born Poland), b. 1923. **Genres:** Architecture, Art/Art history. **Career:** Professor of Architecture, Syracuse University, New York, since 1971. President, Institute for 3-Dimensional Perception, Inc., since 1985. Former Chief Consultant, Committee for Urban Affairs and Architecture, Warsaw, Poland; Associate Professor, University of Manitoba, Winnipeg, 1962-65, and Iowa State University, Ames, 1965-71; Consulting architect. **Publications:** Sacred Art in Poland, 1956; The Urban Scale, 1969; Architectural Graphics and Three Dimensional Communications, 1976. **Address:** 575 Reynolds Bend Rd, Rome, GA 30161, U.S.A.

JANSEN, Jared. See CEBULASH, Mel.

JANSEN, Michael E(lin). American, b. 1940. **Genres:** Novels, International relations/Current affairs. **Career:** Free-lance writer and journalist since 1967. Ed., American University of Beirut, 1964-67; Assistant Ed., Middle East Forum, 1965-67. **Publications:** The United States and the Palestinian People, 1970; (with Godfrey H. Jansen) The Battle of Beirut: Why Israel Invaded Lebanon, 1982; The Aphrodite Plot (novel), 1983; Dissonance in Zion, 1987. **Address:** Jansen Partners, P.O. Box 7621, Nicosia, Cyprus.

JANSEN, Sharon L. American, b. 1951. **Genres:** Literary criticism and history. **Career:** Pacific Lutheran University, Tacoma, assistant professor, 1980-86, associate professor of English, 1986-94, professor of English, 1994-. **Publications:** Political Protest and Prophecy under Henry VIII, 1991; (with K. Jordan) The Welles Anthology (Ms. Rawlinson C.813): A Critical Edition, 1991; Dangerous Talk and Strange Behavior, 1996. **Address:** Department of English, Pacific Lutheran University, Tacoma, WA 98447, U.S.A. **Online address:** jansensl@plu.edu

JANSSEN, Marian (L. M.). Dutch, b. 1953. **Genres:** Literary criticism and history, Biography. **Career:** Radboud University Nijmegen, Netherlands, research assistant, 1977-80, research fellow, 1980-84, instructor in American literature, 1985-86, coordinator of American studies program, 1986-95, postdoctoral research fellow, 1988-92, External Relations, director, 1995-. **Publications:** The Kenyon Review: 1939-1970: A Critical History, 1990. **Ad-**

dress: External Relations, Radboud University Nijmegen, PO Box 9102, 6500 HC Nijmegen, Netherlands. **Online address:** m.janssen@er.ru.nl

JANSSON, Bruce S. American. **Genres:** Social commentary, Social work. **Career:** University of Southern California, professor of social work to Driscoll/Clevenger Professor of social policy and administration, 1973-; City University of New York Graduate Center, New York, NY, Moses Professor, 1990; community organizer/planner. **Publications:** Theory and Practice of Social Welfare Policy: Analysis, Processes, and Current Issues, 1984, rev. ed. as Becoming an Effective Policy Advocate: From Policy Practice to Social Justice, 1999; The Reluctant Welfare State: A History of American Social Welfare Policies, 1988; Social Welfare Policy: From Theory to Practice, 1990, 2nd ed. as Social Policy: From Theory to Policy Practice, 1994; The Reluctant Welfare State: American Social Welfare Policies-Past, Present, and Future, 3rd ed, 1997, 4th ed, 2000; The Sixteen-Trillion-Dollar Mistake: How the U.S. Bungled Its National Priorities from the New Deal to the Present, 2001. **Address:** University of Southern California, Department of Social Work, Montgomery Ross Fisher Building 214, Los Angeles, CA 90089, U.S.A. **Online address:** jansson@usc.edu

JARAMILLO, Stephan. American, b. 1970?. **Genres:** Novels. **Career:** Writer. Employed as a chef in the San Francisco Bay area, CA. **Publications:** Going Postal, 1997; Chocolate Jesus, 1998; The Scoundrel, 1999. **Address:** c/o Berkley Publicity, 375 Hudson St., New York, NY 10014, U.S.A.

JARAUSCH, Konrad H(ugo). American (born Germany), b. 1941. **Genres:** Area studies, History, International relations/Current affairs. **Career:** University of Wisconsin-Madison, instructor in history, 1965-68; University of Missouri-Columbia, assistant professor, 1968-71, associate professor, 1971-78, professor of history, 1978-83; University of North Carolina at Chapel Hill, Lurcy Professor of European Civilization, 1983-. Visiting professor: University of Saarbruecken, 1975-76, University of Goettingen; visiting fellow: Shelby Cullom Davis Center for Historical Studies, Princeton University, 1970-71, Woodrow Wilson Center for International Scholars, 1979-80; fellow: Netherlands Institute for Advanced studies, 1986, Swedish Center for Advanced Studies, 1988. **Publications:** The Four Power Pact, 1933, 1965; The Enigmatic Chancellor: Bethmann Hollweg and the Hubris of Imperial Germany, 1973; Students, Society, and Politics in Imperial Germany: The Rise of Academic Illiberalism, 1982; Deutsche Studenten, 1800-1970 (title means: German Students, 1800-1970), 1984; (with G. Arminger and M. Thaller) Quantitative Methoden in der Geschichtswissenschaft: Eine Einfuerung (title means: Quantitative Methods in History: An Introduction), 1985; The Unfree Professions: German Lawyers, Teachers, and Engineers, 1900-1950, 1990; (with K. Hardy) Quantitative Methods for Historians: An Introduction to Research, Data, and Statistics, 1991; (with V. Gransow) Unititng Germany: Documents and Debates, 1994-1993, 1994. EDITOR: Quantifizierung in der Geschichtswissenschaft: Probleme und Moeglichkeiten (title means: Quantification in Historical Research: Problems and Possibilities), 1976; The Transformation of Higher Learning, 1860-1930, 1982; (with W.H. Schroeder) Quantitative History of Society and Economy: Some International Studies, 1987; (with G. Cocks) German Professions, 1800-1950, 1990; (with L.E. Jones) In Search of a Liberal Germany: Essays on German Liberalism, 1990; (with V. Gransow) Die Deutsche Vereinigung, 1991; The Rush to German Unity, 1994; (with M. Middell) Nach dem Erdbeben, 1994; After Unity: Reconfiguring German Identities, 1997. Contributor to books. **Address:** Department of History, University of North Carolina at Chapel Hill, Chapel Hill, NC 27514, U.S.A.

JARES, Joe. American, b. 1937. **Genres:** Sports/Fitness. **Career:** Staff Writer, U.P.I., Los Angeles, 1959; Sports Writer, Los Angeles Herald-Express, 1959-60; Staff Writer, Los Angeles Times, 1961-65, and Sports Illustrated mag., NYC, 1965-80; Sports Ed., Los Angeles Daily News, 1982-85; Sports Staff, Los Angeles Daily News, 1985-2002. **Publications:** (co-author) White House Sportsmen, 1964; (co-author) Clyde, 1970; Basketball, The American Game, 1971; Whatever Happened to Gorgeous George? The Blood and Ballyhoo of Professional Wrestling, 1974; (co-author) Conquest: A Cavalcade of USC Football, 1981; (co-author) The Athlete's Body, 1981; (ed.) A Marmac Guide to Los Angeles, 1996. **Address:** 9701 Cresta Dr, Los Angeles, CA 90035, U.S.A. **Online address:** JFJares@aol.com

JARMAN, Julia. British, b. 1946. **Genres:** Children's fiction, Picture/board books. **Career:** Author, 1983-. Worked previously as a teacher of English and drama. **Publications:** FOR CHILDREN: When Poppy Ran Away, 1985; Ollie and the Bogle, 1987; Poppy and the Vicarage Ghost, 1988; Squonk, 1989; The Ghost of Tantony Pig, 1990; Pippa and the Witch, 1990; Toby and the Space Cats, 1990; Not-So-Silly Billy, 1990; The Magic Carrot, 1990; Emily the Spy, 1990; Aunt Horrible and the Very Good Idea, 1990; James

and the Dragon, 1990; The Rabbit Said Miaow, 1990; The Goat Is Eating Debbie!, 1990; Naughty Norman, 1990; Fat Cat, 1990; Lucy Calls the Fire Brigade, 1990; Babies Are Yuck!, 1990; There's a Monster, 1990; Upstarts series; Paul and the Robber, 1990; Look at My Spots, 1990; Lucy the Tiger, 1990; (with D. Burnard) Georgie and the Dragon, 1991; Topher and the Time-Travelling Cat, 1992, as The Time-Travelling Cat and the Egyptian Goddess, 2001; (with D. Burnard) Georgie and the Planet Raider, 1993; Will There Be Polar Bears?, 1993; The Jessame Stories, 1994; (with D. Burnard) Georgie and the Computer Bugs, 1995; Return of Squonk, 1995; (with J. Anderson) Gertie and the Bloop, 1996; The Crow Haunting, 1996; A Test for the Time-Travelling Cat, 1997, as The Time-Travelling Cat and the Tudor Treasure, 2001; More Jessame Stories, 1997; Little Mouse Grandma, 1997; Convict: A Tale of Criminals Sent to Australia, 1997; The Sewer Sleuth, 1997; Chillers: The Haunting of Nadia, 1998; Hangman, 1999; The Revenge of Tommy Bones, 2001; The Time-Travelling Cat and the Roman Eagle, 2001; The Magic Backpack; Bully Bear; Rabbit's Birthday Surprise; Terrible Tiger; Flying Friends, 2002; Mole's Useful Day, 2002; Owl's Big Mistake, 2003; Rabbit Helps Out, 2003; Ghost Writer, 2003; Peace Weavers, 2004; Big Red Bath, 2004; Kangaroo's Cancan Cafe, 2004; Jack in a Box, 2004. ALL ABOARD SERIES: Sam and the Tadpoles, 1994; You Can't Scare Me, 1994; Detective Tilak, 1994; Mountain Rescue, 1994; The Great Lorenzo, 1994; Speedy's Day Out, 1994; Hiccups!, 1994; Big Sister Rosie, 1994; Clumsy Clara, 1994; Little Monster, 1994; Clouds, 1994; No, Sam!, 1994; The Terrible Fright, 1994; Computer Kate, 1994; Bobby's Bad Day, 1994; The Magic Smell, 1994; Rosie and the Dinosaurs, 1994; Nog's Dinner, 1994; Jabeen and the New Moon, 1994; Pancakes, 1994; Grandad's Balloon, 1994; Pandora and the Pirates, 1994; The Hot Pepper Queen and the Mango Babies, 1994; Fussy Frieda, 1994; (reteller) The Ghost Next Door, 1994; Swan Rescue, 1994; The Parrot, 1994; (with M. Simon) All Aboard: Extended Stories for Reading Aloud, 1994; Something in the Fridge, 1994; The Giant Sandwich, 1994; The Ghost in the Castle, 1994; The Greedy Guinea-Pig, 1994; Lizzie and the Car Wash, 1994; Scat Cat!, 1994; A Guinea-Pig for Rosie, 1994; (with M. Simon) Sam and Rosie's ABC, 1994; The Wizard, 1995; Dognapped? and Other Stories from Mulberry Green, 1995; Rosie's Photo Album, 1996; Naughty Nog; It's Not Fair; The Fun Run; Jessame to the Rescue and Other Stories;. **Address:** c/o Scholastic Children's Books, 1-19 New Oxford St, London WC1A 1NU, England. **Online address:** juliajarman@btopenworld.com

JARMAN, Mark (F.). American, b. 1952. **Genres:** Poetry, Literary criticism and history. **Career:** Indiana State University, Evansville, instructor in English, 1976-78; University of California, Irvine, visiting lecturer, 1979-80; Murray State University, Murray, KY, assistant professor, 1980-83; Vanderbilt University, Nashville, TN, assistant professor, 1983-86, associate professor, 1986-92, professor of English, 1992-. Cofounder and editor, The Reaper (poetry journal), until 1989; Story Line Press, Brownsville, OR, cofounder. **Publications:** POETRY: Tonight is the Night of the Prom (chapbook), 1974; North Sea, 1978; The Rote Walker, 1981; Far and Away, 1985; The Black Riviera, 1990; Iris, 1992; (ed., with D. Mason) Rebel Angels: 25 Poets of the New Formalism, 1996; Questions for Ecclesiastes, 1997; Unholy Sonnets, 2000. Contributor of poems to periodicals. OTHER: (with R. McDowell) The Reaper Essays, 1996; The Secret of Poetry, 2001. **Address:** Department of English, Vanderbilt University, Nashville, TN 37235, U.S.A. **Online address:** mark.jarman@vanderbilt.edu

JARMAN, Rosemary (Josephine) Hawley (Smith). British, b. 1935. **Genres:** Romance/Historical. **Career:** Winner, Authors Club Silver Quill First Novel Award, 1971. **Publications:** We Speak No Treason, 1971; The King's Grey Mare, 1973, in U.S.A. as Crown of Glory, 1987; Crown in Candlelight, 1978; Crispin's Day, The Courts of Illusion, 1983.

JAROFF, Leon Morton. American, b. 1927. **Genres:** Air/Space topics, Astronomy, Biology, Communications/Media, Medicine/Health, Physics, Sciences, Technology. **Career:** Life, NYC, reporter and correspondent from Detroit, MI, and Chicago, IL, 1951-58; Time, NYC, correspondent from Chicago and Detroit, and senior editor, 1959-79; Discover, NYC, founder and managing editor, 1979-84; Time, sciences editor, 1985-87, contributor, 1987-. Member of boards and committees. **Publications:** The New Genetics, 1991. **Address:** Time, Time and Life Building, 1271 Avenue of the Americas, New York, NY 10020, U.S.A. **Online address:** neonleo@aol.com

JARROW, Gail. American, b. 1952. **Genres:** Children's fiction, Children's non-fiction. **Career:** Children's book author and teacher. Taught elementary and middle school math and science in Cambridge, MA, and Hanover, NH, 1974-79; freelance writer, 1983-; Institute of Children's Literature, Redding Ridge, CT, instructor, 1991-. **Publications:** FICTION: That Special Someone, 1985; If Phyllis Were Here, 1987; The Two-Ton Secret, 1989; Beyond the

Magic Sphere, 1994. NONFICTION: The Naked Mole-Rat: Solving the Mystery (with P. Sherman), 1996; Naked Mole-Rats, 1996; Animal Babysitters, 2001; Animals Attack: Bears, 2003; Animals Attack: Rhinos, 2003; Parasites: Hookworms, 2004; Parasites: Chiggers, 2004. Author of stories and articles in periodicals.

JARVIK, Laurence. American, b. 1956. **Genres:** Communications/Media. **Career:** Writer, and director of motion pictures. University of California, Los Angeles, Department of Film and Television, teaching assistant and teaching associate, 1986-88, teaching fellow, 1990-91; California State University, Department of Communication Studies, assistant professor, 1989-90; The Heritage Foundation, Washington, DC, Bradley Resident Scholar, 1991-92, adjunct scholar, 1992-96, 1996-97; Comint: A Journal about Public Media, Washington editor, 1992-96; Center for the Study of Popular Culture, Washington, DC, Director, 1992-96; Capital Research Center, Washington, DC, Cultural Studies fellow, editor of Culture Watch and Foundation Watch, 1996-97; Also producer, director, and writer of documentary films. **Publications:** PBS: Behind the Screen, 1997; Masterpiece Theatre and the Politics of Quality, 1998. SCREENPLAYS: Who Shall Live and Who Shall Die? (documentary), 1981. EDITOR: (with D. Horowitz) Public Broadcasting and the Public Trust, 1995; (with H.I. London and J.F. Cooper) The National Endowments: A Critical Symposium, 1995. Contributor to periodicals. **Address:** c/o Carol Mann, Carol Mann Agency, 55 Fifth Ave., 15th Floor, New York, NY 10003, U.S.A. **Online address:** E-mail-lajarvik@erols.com

JASON, Sonya. American, b. 1927. **Genres:** Novels, Plays/Screenplays, Adult non-fiction, Young adult non-fiction, Essays. **Career:** Medical receptionist, 1955-63; Los Angeles Welfare Department, Los Angeles, CA, social worker, 1963-66; deputy probation officer in Los Angeles, 1966-76; writer, 1976-. **Publications:** Concomitant Soldier, 1974; Helper, 1994; Icon of Spring, 1994; Professional Angel, 2001. Contributor to periodicals. **Address:** 21165 Escondido St, Woodland Hills, CA 91364, U.S.A. **Online address:** JohnJJason@aol.com

JASPER, James M(acdonald). American, b. 1957. **Genres:** Politics/Government, Social commentary, Sociology. **Career:** New York University, New York City, faculty member, 1986-96; Princeton University, visiting professor, 1997, 1999-2000, 2003-04; writer. **Publications:** Nuclear Politics: Energy and the State in the United States, Sweden, and France, 1990; (with D. Nelkin) The Animal Rights Crusade: The Growth of a Moral Protest, 1992; The Art of Moral Protest, 1997; Restless Nation: Starting over in America, 2000; (with J. Goodwin and F. Polletta) Passionate Politics: Emotions and Social Movements, 2001; (with J. Goodwin) The Social Movements Reader, 2003; (with J. Goodwin) Rethinking Social Movements, 2003. Contributor to periodicals. **Address:** 346 W 15th St, New York, NY 10011, U.S.A. **Online address:** jmjasper@juno.com

JASTROW, Robert. American, b. 1925. **Genres:** Air/Space topics, Astronomy, Earth sciences. **Career:** Columbia University, NYC, adjunct professor of astronomy and geology, 1961-81; Goddard Institute for Space Studies, NASA, director, 1961-81; Dartmouth College, Hanover, NH, adjunct professor of earth sciences, 1973-93; Mount Wilson Institute, Pasadena, CA, director. **Publications:** Red Giants and White Dwarfs: The Evolution of Stars, Planets and Life, 1967, 1969; (with M. Thompson) Astronomy: Fundamentals and Frontiers, 1972; Until the Sun Dies, 1977; God and the Astronomers, 1978; The Enchanted Loom: Mind in the Universe, 1981; How to Make Nuclear Weapons Obsolete, 1985; Journey to the Stars, 1989. EDITOR: Exploration of Space, 1960; (with A.G.W. Cameron) Origin of the Solar System, 1963; (with S.I. Rasool) The Venus Atmosphere, 1969. **Address:** 106 Central Park S #24-C, New York, NY 10019, U.S.A. **Online address:** jastrow@marshall.org

JAUNCEY, James. Scottish, b. 1949. **Genres:** Novels. **Career:** Writer. Radio Heartland, governor. **Publications:** NOVELS: The Albatross Conspiracy, 1990; The Mapmaker, 1994; The Crystal Keeper, 1996. **Address:** c/o Society of Authors, 8 Briar Rd, Kirkin-Hilloch, Glasgow G66 3SA, Scotland.

JAUSS, David. American, b. 1951. **Genres:** Novellas/Short stories, Poetry. **Career:** Southwest State University, Marshall, MN, instructor in English, 1974-77; University of Arkansas at Little Rock, assistant professor, 1980-83, associate professor, 1983-88, professor of English and creative writing, 1988-, director of creative writing, 1980-; Vermont College MFA in Writing Program, faculty member, 1998-; fiction editor, Crazyhorse, 1981-91. **Publications:** SHORT STORY COLLECTIONS: Crimes of Passion, 1984; Black Maps, 1996. POETRY COLLECTIONS: Improvising Rivers, 1995; You Are Not Here, 2002. EDITOR: Strong Measures: Contemporary American Poetry

in Traditional Forms, 1986; The Best of Crazyhorse, 1990. Contributor of short stories, poems and essays to periodicals and anthologies. **Address:** Department of English, University of Arkansas at Little Rock, 2801 S University, Little Rock, AR 72204, U.S.A.

JAVERNICK, Ellen. American, b. 1938. **Genres:** Education, Children's fiction, Young adult fiction. **Career:** Elementary school teacher, Loveland, CO, 1976-. Writer. Serves on local boards. **Publications:** Christmas Bulletin Boards, Walls, Windows, Doors & More, 1986; Celebrate the Christian Family, 1987; Celebrate Me Made in God's Image, 1988; What If Everybody Did That?, 1990; Where's Brooke?, 1992; Double the Trouble, 1994; Time for Bed!, 1994; Ms. Pollywog's Problem-Solving Service, 1995; Patient Papas, 1996; Show and Tell, 1996; Crash, Flash, 1998; Allie's Plan, 1998; God's House, 1999. Contributor of articles and stories to magazines and journals. **Address:** 815 West 5th St., Loveland, CO 80537, U.S.A.

JAVOR, Frank A. (Francis Anthony Jaworski). American, b. 1916. **Genres:** Science fiction/Fantasy, Novellas/Short stories, Mystery/Crime/Suspense, Plays/Screenplays, Photography. **Career:** Writer. **Publications:** NOVELS: The Rim-World Legacy, 1967; Scor-Sting, 1990; The Ice Beast, 1990; The Rim-World Legacy and Beyond, 1991. **Address:** c/o DAW Books, 375 Hudson St., New York, NY 10014-3658, U.S.A.

JAY, Sir Antony (Rupert). British, b. 1930. **Genres:** Administration/Management, Business/Trade/Industry, Politics/Government, Speech/Rhetoric. **Career:** Ed., Tonight prog., 1962-63, and Head of Talks Features, 1963-64, BBC, London; Chairman, Video Arts Ltd., 1972-89. Member, Annan Committee on Future Broadcasting, 1974-77. **Publications:** (ed.) The Pick of the Rhubarb, 1965; (with D. Frost) To England with Love, 1967; Management and Machiavelli, 1967; Effective Presentation, 1970; Corporation Man, 1972; The Householder's Guide to Community Defence against Bureaucratic Aggression, 1972; (with J. Lynn) Yes, Minister (television series), 1980-82, (book versions), 3 vols., 1981-83; The Complete Yes, Minister, 1984; Yes, Prime Minister (television series), 1986, (book version), vol. 1, 1986, vol. 2, 1989; Elizabeth R., 1992; (ed.) Oxford Dictionary of Political Quotations, 1996, 3rd ed., 2006; How to Beat Sir Humphrey, 1997; Not in Our Back Yard, 2005. **Address:** c/o Alan Brodie Representation Ltd, 211 Piccadilly, London W1V 9LD, England. **Online address:** antony.jay@virgin.net

JAY, Marion. See SPALDING, Ruth.

JAY, Mel. See FANTHORPE, R(obert) Lionel.

JAY, Peter. British, b. 1937. **Genres:** Economics, International relations/Current affairs. **Career:** Principal, Treasury, London, 1964-67; Economics Ed., The Times, London, 1967-77, and Associate Ed., Times Business News, 1969-77; Presenter, Weekend World, TV programme, 1972-77; British Ambassador to the United States, 1977-79; Director, Economist Intelligence Unit, London, 1979-83; Chairman, National Council for Voluntary Organisations, 1981-86; Sr. Editorial Consultant, 1983-84, and Ed., 1984-86, Banking World, London; Chief of Staff to Robert Maxwell, Publisher of Mirror Group Newspapers and Chairman of Maxwell; Communication Corp. and Pergamon, 1986-90; Economics Ed., BBC, London, 1990-2001; Director, Bank of England, 2003-. **Publications:** The Budget, 1972; (with others) America and the World 1979, 1980; The Crisis for Western Political Economy and Other Essays, 1984; (with M. Stewart) Apocalypse 2000, 1987; The Road to Riches, or the Wealth of Man, 2000. **Address:** Hensington Farmhouse, Woodstock, Oxon. OX20 1LH, England. **Online address:** peter@jay.prestel.co.uk

JAY, Ricky. American, b. 1949?. **Genres:** Social work, History, Trivia/Facts. **Career:** Illusionist, performer, magic historian, consultant, actor, and writer. Worked as a sideshow barker, sideshow magician, accountant, and encyclopedia salesman; lecturer in the United States and abroad. Actor. **Publications:** Learned Pigs and Fireproof Women: Unique, Eccentric, and Amazing Entertainers: Stone Eaters, Mind Readers, Poison Resisters, Daredevils, Singing Mice, etc., etc., etc., etc., 1986; Cards as Weapons, 1977; Many Mysteries Unraveled, or, Conjuring Literature in America, 1786-1874, 1990; Ricky Jay and His Fifty-two Assistants (show), 1994; The Magic Magic Book: An Inquiry into the Venerable History and Operation of the Oldest Trick-Conjuring Volumes, 1998; Jay's Journal of Anomalies: Conjurers, Cheats, Hustlers, Hoaxsters, Pranksters, Jokesters, Imposters, Pretenders, Sideshow Showmen, Armless Calligraphers, Mechanical Marvels, Popular Entertainments (originally published in Jay's Journal of Anomalies), 2001; Ricky Jay: On the Stem, (show), 2002. Contributor to books. **Address:** Dailey Booksellers, 8216 Melrose Ave., Los Angeles, CA 90046, U.S.A.

JAY, Shannah. *See* **JACOBS, Anna.**

JEAL, (John Julian) Tim(othy). British, b. 1945. **Genres:** Novels, Biography. **Career:** Novelist and Biographer. **Publications:** For Love or Money, 1967; Somewhere beyond Reproach, 1968; Livingstone, 1973; Cushings Crusade, 1974; Until the Colours Fade, 1976; A Marriage of Convenience, 1979; Carnforth's Creation 1983; Baden-Powell, 1989 (in U.S. as The Boy-Man, 1990); The Missionary's Wife, in U.S. as For God and Glory, 1997; Deep Water, 2000. **Address:** 29 Willow Rd, London NW3, England.

JEANS, Peter D(ouglas). Australian, b. 1936. **Genres:** Language/Linguistics. **Career:** Department of Education of Western Australia, secondary schoolteacher, 1958-, including English teacher and department head, 1972-87. **Publications:** My Word, 1993; Ship to Shore: A Dictionary of Everyday Words and Phrases Derived from the Sea, 1993; The Long Road to London, 1995. **Address:** 36 Acanthus Rd., Willetton, Perth, WA 6155, Australia.

JECKS, Michael. British, b. 1960. **Genres:** Mystery/Crime/Suspense. **Career:** Novelist. Worked as computer salesperson for Wordplex, Wang, and Xerox. **Publications:** The Last Templar, 1995; The Merchant's Partner, 1995; A Moorland Hanging, 1996; The Crediton Killings, 1997; The Abbot's Gibbet, 1998; The Leper's Return, 1998; Squire Throwleigh's Heir, 1999; Belladonna at Belstone, 1999; The Traitor of St. Giles, 1999; The Boy-Bishop's Glovemaker, 2000; The Tournament of Blood, 2001; The Sticklepath Strangler, 2001; The Devil's Acolyte, 2002; The Mad Monk of Gidleigh, 2002. **Address:** c/o Jane Conway-Gordon, 1 Old Compton Street, London W1D 5JA, England. **Online address:** mail@michaeljecks.co.uk

JEEVES, Malcolm. British, b. 1926. **Genres:** Psychology, Sciences, Theology/Religion. **Career:** University of St. Andrews, Fife, Vice-Principal, 1981-85, Professor of Psychology, 1969-. Professor and Head, Dept. of Psychology, University of Adelaide, S.A. 1959-69. Royal Society of Edinburgh, President, 1996-99. **Publications:** (co-author) Where Science and Faith Meet, 1955; Scientific Psychology and Christian Belief, 1965; (with Z.P. Dienes) Thinking in Structures, 1965; (with Z.P. Dienes) The Effects of Structural Relations on Transfer, 1968; The Scientific Enterprise and Christian Faith, 1968; Experimental Psychology: An Introduction for Biologists, 1974; Psychology and Christianity: The View Both Ways, 1976; Psychology Survey No. 3, 1980; (co-author) Analysis of Structural Learning, 1983; Behavioral Sciences: A Christian Perspective, 1983; (co-author) Psychology: Through the Eyes of Faith, 1987, rev. ed., 2002; Mind Fields, 1993; Human Nature at the Millennium, 1997; (with R.J. Berry) Science, Life and Christian Belief, 1998; From Cells to Souls-and Beyond, 2004; (ed. and contrib.) Human Nature, 2005. **Address:** School of Psychology, University of St. Andrews, St. Andrews, Fife, Scotland.

JEFFARES, A(lexander) Norman. British (born Ireland), b. 1920. **Genres:** Literary criticism and history, Biography. **Career:** Lecturer in classics, University of Dublin, 1943-44; lector in English, University of Groningen, 1946-48; lecturer in English, University of Edinburgh, 1949-51; jury professor of English, University of Adelaide, 1951-56; professor of English, University of Leeds, 1957-74; professor of English studies, University of Stirling, 1974-86. **Publications:** W.B. Yeats: Man and Poet, 1949; Seven Centuries of Poetry, 1955; Oliver Goldsmith, 1959; Language, Literature and Science, 1959; The Poetry of W.B. Yeats, 1961; Selected Plays of W.B. Yeats, 1964; Selected Prose of W.B. Yeats, 1964; Selected Poetry and Prose of Whitman, 1965; Fair Liberty Was All His Cry, 1967; A Commentary on the Collected Poems of W.B. Yeats, 1969; The Circus Animals, 1970; Farquhar's The Beaux Stratagem, 1972; Farquhar's The Recruiting Officer, 1973; (with A.S. Knowland) A Commentary on the Collected Plays of W.B. Yeats, 1975; Anglo-Irish Literature, 1982; A New Commentary on the Poems of Yeats, 1984; The Poems of Yeats, 1984; Brought Up in Dublin, 1986; Brought Up to Leave, 1986; W.B. Yeats: A New Biography, 1988; Yeats's Poems, 1989; W.B. Yeats: The Love Poems, 1990; W.B. Yeats: A Vision and Related Writings, 1990; Yeats's Poems of Place, 1991; Images of Invention (essays), 1995; Victorian Love Poetry, 1996; A Pocket History of Irish Literature, 1997; Irish Love Poems, 1997; The Irish Literary Movement, 1998; The Secret Rose, 1998; Ireland's Love Poems, 2000; The Poems and Plays of Oliver St. John Gogarty, 2001. EDITOR: (with G.F. Cross) In Excited Reverie, 1965; Restoration Comedy, 1974; Yeats: The Critical Reception, 1977; (with A. Kamm) An Irish Childhood, 1986, rev. ed., 1992; (with A. Kamm) A Jewish Childhood, 1988; (with A.M. White) The Gonne-Yeats Letters, 1893-1938, 1992; Jonathan Swift: The Selected Poems, 1992; (with B. Kennelly) Joycechoyce, 1992; (with K. Donovan and B. Kennelly) Ireland's Women, 1994; (with M. Gray) The Collins Dictionary of Quotations, 1995; (with C.

Bridgwater and A. M. White) Letters to W.B. Yeats and Ezra Pound from Iseult Gonne, a Girl That Knew All Dante Once, 2003. **Address:** Craighead Cottage, Fife Ness, Crail, Scotland.

JEFFERIES, Matthew (Martin). British, b. 1962. **Genres:** History. **Career:** University of Warwick, Coventry, England, lecturer in history, 1990-91; Victoria University of Manchester, England, lecturer in German history, 1991-. Sovereign Education, lecturer and consultant. **Publications:** Politics and Culture in Wilhelmine Germany, 1995; Imperial Culture in Germany, 18711918, 2003. Contributor to books. Contributor to periodicals. **Address:** Department of German, Victoria University of Manchester, Manchester M13 9PL, England. **Online address:** matt.jefferies@man.ac.uk

JEFFERIES, William. *See* **DEAVER, Jeffery Wilds.**

JEFFERSON, Alan. British, b. 1921. **Genres:** Military/Defense/Arms control, Music. **Career:** Stage Manager & Producer in West End Theatre, 1947-54; Administrator, London Symphony Orchestra, 1967-68; Visiting Professor of Vocal Interpretation, Guildhall School of Music and Drama. London, 1967-74; Manager, BBC Concert Orchestra, London, 1968-73; Critic, Vocal CDs, Classic, 1985-98. **Publications:** The Operas of Richard Strauss in Great Britain 1910-1963; The Lieder of Richard Strauss, 1971; Delius, 1972; The Life of Richard Strauss, 1973; Inside the Orchestra, 1974; Strauss, The Musicians, 1975; The Glory of Opera, 1976; Sir Thomas Beecham, 1979; The Complete Gilbert and Sullivan Opera Guide, 1984; Richard Strauss: Der Rosenkavalier, 1986; Assault on the Guns of Merville, 1987; Lotte Lehmann, 1988; Elisabeth Schwarzkopf, 1995. **Address:** c/o The Society of Authors, 84, Drayton Gardens, London SW10 9SB, England.

JEFFREY, Francis. American, b. 1950. **Genres:** Sciences, Biography. **Career:** University of California, San Diego, research associate, 1972-73; Institute for Advanced Computation, Sunnyvale, CA, consultant, 1973-75; Scientific Applications Inc., La Jolla, CA, consultant, 1973-75; Alive Systems Informational Sciences, consultant, 1978-87; Human-Dolphin Foundation, Redwood City, CA, consultant, 1980-82, 1987-89; Esalen Institute, Big Sur, CA, consultant, 1982-83; Alive Systems Inc. and Elfnet Inc., both Malibu, CA, founder, president, and chief executive officer, 1987-; Arthur C. Clarke Communicators, cofounder, 2000-; software developer; writer. New Forum, cofounder, 1984; Great Whales Foundation, cofounder and director, 1986-; Instigator of City of Malibu Human-Dolphin Shared Environment resolution, 1992. **Publications:** Handbook of States of Consciousness (collection) 1986; John Lilly, So Far... (biography), 1990; (with others) Voices from the Edge (collection), 1995. **Address:** 3020 Bridgeway #222, Sausalito, CA 94965, U.S.A. **Online address:** francis@elfi.com

JEFFREY, Thomas E. American, b. 1947. **Genres:** Politics/Government. **Career:** Benjamin Henry Latrobe Papers, Baltimore, MD, microfiche editor, 1972-77; Vanderbilt University, Nashville, TN, visiting assistant professor of history, 1977-79; Rutgers University, New Brunswick, NJ, associate director and microfilm editor of Thomas A. Edison Papers, 1979-. **Publications:** State Parties and National Politics: North Carolina, 1815-1861, 1989; Thomas Lanier Clingman, 1998. **Address:** Thomas A. Edison Papers, Rutgers University, 16 Seminary Pl, New Brunswick, NJ 08901, U.S.A. **Online address:** tjeffrey@rci.rutgers.edu

JEFFREY, William. *See* **PRONZINI, Bill.**

JEFFRIES, Don. American, b. 1940. **Genres:** Biography. **Career:** Cargill, Wilson & Acree Advertising, copywriter, 1965-69; Garner & Associates Advertising, creative director, 1969-74; Ullman, Fowler & Jeffries Advertising, creative director, 1974-76; William Cook Advertising, copywriter, 1976-77; Newman, Saylor & Gregory, creative director, 1977-79; Wray Ward Advertising, Charlotte, NC, vice-president and creative director, 1979-95; freelance writer, 1995-. **Publications:** Balm in Gilead: A Baptist Minister's Personal Journey through Drug Addiction, 1992, in paperback as No Fall Too Far, 1995. **Address:** 2001 Dugan Drive, Charlotte, NC 28270, U.S.A.

JEFFRIES, Ian. Welsh, b. 1942. **Genres:** Economics. **Career:** University of Wales, Swansea (formerly National University of Wales, University College of Swansea), lecturer in economics and member of Centre of Russian and East European Studies, 1966-. **Publications:** A Guide to the Socialist Economies, 1990; Socialist Economies and the Transition to the Market, 1993; A Guide to the Economies in Transition, 1996; (with R. Bideleux) A History of Eastern Europe: Crisis and Change, 1998; Economies in Transition: A Guide to China, Cuba, Mongolia, North Korea and Vietnam at the Turn of the 21st Century, 2001; The New Russia: A Handbook of Economic and Political Development, 2002; Eastern Europe at the Turn of the 21st

Century: A Guide to Economies in Transition, 2002; The Former Yugoslavia at the Turn of the 21st Century: A Guide to Economies in Transition, 2002; The Caucasus and Central Asian Republics at the Turn of the 21st Century: A Guide to Economies in Transition, 2003; The Former Soviet Union at the Turn of the 21st Century: The Baltic and European States in Transition, 2004. EDITOR: The Industrial Enterprise in Eastern Europe, 1981; (with M. Melzer) The East German Economy, 1987; Industrial Reform in Socialist Countries, 1992; Problems of Economic and Political Transformation in the Balkans, 1996. **Address:** Department of Economics, University of Wales, Swansea, Singleton Park, Swansea SA2 8PP, Wales. **Online address:** I.Jeffries@swansea.ac.uk

JEFFRIES, John C., Jr. American, b. 1948. **Genres:** Law. **Career:** University of Virginia, Charlottesville, professor of law, 1973-86, Emerson Spies Professor, 1986-, Horace W. Goldsmith Research Professor, 1992-, academic associate Dean, 1994-. **Publications:** Federal Courts and the Law of Federal-State Relations, 1987, 3rd ed, 1994; Civil Rights Actions: Section 1983 and Related Statutes, 1988, 2nd ed, 1994; Justice Lewis Powell, Jr., 1994. **Address:** Law School, University of Virginia, Charlottesville, VA 22903, U.S.A.

JEFFRIES, Roderic. Also writes as Peter Alding, Jeffrey Ashford, Hastings Draper, Roderic Graeme, Graham Hastings. British, b. 1926. **Genres:** Novels, Mystery/Crime/Suspense, Children's fiction. **Career:** Full-time writer. Formerly, barrister in London. **Publications:** Evidence of the Accused, 1961; Exhibit No. Thirteen, 1962; The Benefits of Death, 1963; An Embarrassing Death, 1964; Dead against the Lawyers, 1965; Death in the Coverts, 1966; A Traitor's Crime, 1968; Dead Man's Bluff, 1970; Mistakenly in Mallorca, 1974; Two-Faced Death, 1976; Troubled Deaths, 1977; Murder Begets Murder, 1979; Just Deserts, 1980; Unseemly End, 1981; Deadly Petard, 1983; Three and One Make Five, 1984; Layers of Deceit, 1985; Almost Murder, 1986; Relatively Dangerous, 1987; Death Trick, 1988; Dead Clever, 1989; Too Clever by Half, 1990; Murder's Long Memory, 1991; A Fatal Fleece, 1992; Murder Confounded, 1993; Death Takes Time, 1994; An Arcadian Death, 1995; An Artistic Way to Go, 1996; A Maze of Murders, 1997; An Enigmatic Disappearance, 1998; The Ambiguity of Murder, 1999; Definitely Deceased, 2000; Seeing Is Deceiving, 2002; An Artful Death, 2003. FOR CHILDREN: Police and Detection, 1962 (in US as Against Time!, 1964); Police Car (in US as Patrol Car), 1967; Police Dog, 1965; River Patrol, 1969; Police Patrol Boat, 1971; Trapped, 1972; The Riddle of the Parchment, 1976; The Boy Who Knew Too Much, 1977; Eighteen Desperate Hours, 1979; The Missing Man, 1980; Voyage into Danger, 1981; Peril at Sea, 1983; Sunken Danger, 1985; Meeting Trouble, 1986; The Man Who Couldn't, 1987. AS PETER ALDING: The C.I.D. Room (in US as All Leads Negative), 1967; Circle of Danger, 1968; Murder among Thieves, 1969; Guilt without Proof, 1970; Despite the Evidence, 1971; Call Back to Crime, 1972; Field of Fire, 1973; The Murder Line, 1974; Six Days to Death, 1975; Murder Is Suspected, 1977; Ransom Town, 1979; A Man Condemned, 1981; Betrayed by Death, 1982. AS JEFFERY ASHFORD: Counsel for the Defence, 1960; Investigations Are Proceeding, 1961 (in US as The D.I., 1962); The Burden of Proof, 1962; Will Anyone Who Saw the Accident, 1963 (as UK as Hit and Run, 1966); Enquiries Are Continuing, 1964 (in US as The Superintendent's Room, 1965); The Hands of Innocence, 1965; Forget What You Saw, 1967; Grand Prix Monaco (children), 1968; Prisoner at the Bar, 1969; To Protect the Guilty, 1970; Grand Prix Germany (children), 1970; Grand Prix United States (children), 1971; Bent Copper, 1971; A Man Will Be Kidnapped Tomorrow, 1972; The Double Run, 1973; Grand Prix Britain (children), 1973; Dick Knox at Le Mans (children), 1974; The Colour of Violence, 1974; Three Layers of Guilt, 1975; Slow Down the World, 1976; Hostage to Death, 1977; The Anger of Fear, 1978; A Recipe for Murder, 1980; The Loss of the Culion, 1981; Guilt with Honour, 1982; A Sense of Loyalty, 1983; Presumption of Guilt, 1984; An Ideal Crime, 1985; A Question of Principle, 1986; A Crime Remembered, 1987; The Honourable Detective, 1988; A Conflict of Interests, 1989; An Illegal Solution, 1990; Deadly Reunion, 1991; Twisted Justice, 1992; Judgement Deferred, 1993; The Bitter Bite, 1994; The Price of Failure, 1995; Loyal Disloyalty, 1996; A Web of Circumstances, 1997; The Cost of Innocence, 1998; An Honest Betrayal, 1999; Murder Will Out, 2000; Looking-Glass Justice, 2001; A Truthful Injustice, 2002. AS HASTING DRAPER: Wiggery Pokery (novel), 1956; Wigged and Gowned (novel), 1958; Brief Help, 1961. AS RODERIC GRAEME: Blackshirt series, 20 vols., 1952-69; Brandy Ahoy!, 1951; Where's Brandy?, 1953; Brandy Goes a Cruising, 1954. AS GRAHAM HASTINGS: Twice Checked, 1959; Deadly Game, 1961. **Address:** Ca Na Paiaia, 07460 Pollenca, Mallorca, Spain.

JEFFS, Julian. British, b. 1931. **Genres:** Food and Wine, Law. **Career:** Barrister. Wine and Food, London, ed., 1965-67; Faber's Wine Series, general ed., 1966-2002. Recipient: Glenfiddich Awards, 1976, 1978; Office International de la Vigne et du Vin, Paris, awards, 1962, 2001. **Publications:** Sherry, 1961, 4th ed., 1992; (ed. with R. Harling) Wine, 1966; (contrib. ed.) Clerk and Lindsell on Torts, 13th ed., 1969, 16th ed., 1989; The Wines of Europe, 1971; Little Dictionary of Drink, 1973; (with others) Encyclopedia of United Kingdom and European Patent Law, 1977; The Wines of Spain, 1999. **Address:** Church Farm House, East Ilsley, Newbury, Berks. RG20 7LP, England.

JEFFS, Rae. (Frances Rae Sebley). British, b. 1921. **Genres:** Biography. **Career:** Publisher's Reader, Hutchinson and Co., London, 1964- (Publicity Manager for the Hutchinson Group, 1957-64). Copy Writer, Heron Books, London, 1966-69; Four Oaks Foundation film on Brendan Behan, consultant, participant. **Publications:** (with B. Behan) Confessions of An Irish Rebel, 1965; Brendan Behan: Man and Showman, 1966. EDITOR: Brendan Behan's Island, 1962; Hold Your Hour and Have Another, 1963; Brendan Behan's New York, 1964; The Scarperer, 1966. **Address:** Rotherfield Farmhouse, Newick, Lewes, Sussex BN8 4JJ, England.

JELEN, Ted G. American, b. 1950. **Genres:** Politics/Government, Bibliography. **Career:** Ohio State University, Columbus, instructor in political science, 1976-77; Lamar University, Beaumont, TX, instructor of political science, 1978-79; Illinois State University, Normal, assistant professor of political science, 1979-80; University of Kentucky, Lexington, assistant professor of political science, 1980-81; Illinois Benedictine College, Lisle, assistant professor to professor of political science, 1981-90, department head, 1989-90; Georgetown University, Washington, DC, visiting professor of political science, 1990-91; Illinois Benedictine College, professor of political science and head of department, 1991-93. **Publications:** (ed.) Religion and Political Behavior in the United States, 1989; The Political Mobilization of Religious Beliefs, 1991; (with E.A. Cook and C. Wilcox) Between the Absolutes: American Public Opinion and the Politics of Abortion, 1992; The Political World of the Clergy, 1993; (ed. with M.A. Chandler, and contrib.) Abortion Politics in the United States and Canada: Studies in Public Opinion, 1994; The Religious Dimension of Political Behavior: A Critical Assessment and Annotated Bibliography, 1994; (with Wilcox) Public Attitudes Toward Church-States Issues, 1995. Work represented in anthologies. Contributor of articles and reviews to political science, religious studies, psychology, and social science journals. **Address:** Department of Political Science, University of Nevada at Las Vegas, Box 455029, 4505 Maryland Parkway, Las Vegas, NV 89154-5029, U.S.A. **Online address:** jelent@unlv.nevada.edu

JELLICOE, Ann. British, b. 1927. **Genres:** Plays/Screenplays, Travel/Exploration, Songs/Lyrics and libretti. **Career:** Founding Director, Colway Theatre Trust, since 1979. Actress, stage mgr., dir., in London and the provinces, 1947-51; Founding Director, Cockpit Theatre Club, London, 1950-53; Lecturer and Director, Central School of Speech and Drama, London, 1953-55. Literary Manager, Royal Court Theatre, London, 1973-75. **Publications:** Rosmersholm, 1960; The Knack, 1962; Two Plays: The Knack, and The Sport of My Mad Mother, 1964; Shelley: or, The Idealist, 1966; Some Unconscious Influences in the Theatre, 1967; The Giveaway, 1970; (with Roger Mayne) Shell Guide to Devon, 1975; 3 Jelliplays, 1975; Community Plays: How to Put Them On, 1987. **Address:** c/o Cassarotto Ramsay Ltd, National House, 60-66 Wardour St, London W1V 3HP, England.

JELLISON, Katherine. American, b. 1960. **Genres:** History. **Career:** University of Iowa, Iowa City, visiting instructor in history, 1990; Memphis State University, Memphis, TN, assistant professor of history, 1991-93; Ohio University, Athens, assistant professor, 1993-96, associate professor of history, 1996-. **Publications:** Entitled to Power: Farm Women and Technology, 1913-1963, 1993; (intro.) Years of Struggle: The Farm Diary of Elmer G. Powers, 1931-1936. Contributor to history journals. **Address:** Department of History, Ohio University, Athens, OH 45701, U.S.A. **Online address:** jellison@ohio.edu

JEN, Gish. (Lillian Jen). American, b. 1955. **Genres:** Novels. **Career:** Writer. Tufts University, lecturer in fiction writing, 1986; University of Massachusetts, visiting writer, 1990-91. **Publications:** NOVELS: Typical American, 1991; Mona in the Promised Land, 1996. STORIES: Who's Irish, 1999. **Address:** 18 Bates St #2, Cambridge, MA 02140, U.S.A.

JENCKS, Charles (Alexander). American, b. 1939. **Genres:** Architecture. **Publications:** Architecture 2000, 1971; (with N. Silver) Adhocism, 1972; Modern Movements in Architecture, 1973; Le Corbusier and the Tragic View of Architecture, 1974, 2nd ed., 1987; The Language of Post-Modern Architecture, 1977, 7th ed. as The New Paradigm in Architecture, 2002; The

Daydream Houses of Los Angeles, 1978; Bizarre Architecture, 1979; Late-Modern Architecture: Selected Essays, 1980; Skyscrapers-Skycities, 1980; Post-Modern Classicism, 1981; Free-Style Classicism, 1980; Current Architecture, (in U.S. as Architecture Today), 1982; Abstract Representation, 1983; Kings of Infinite Space, 1983; Towards a Symbolic Architecture, 1985; What Is Post-Modernism?, 1986, 4th ed., 1996; Post-Modernism: The New Classicism in Art and Architecture, 1987; The Prince, the Architects and New Wave Monarchy, 1988; The New Moderns, 1990; Heteropolis: Los Angeles, the Riots and Hetero-Architecture, 1993; The Architecture of the Jumping Universe, 1995, 2nd ed., 1997; Ecstatic Architecture, 1999; Architecture 2000 and Beyond, 2000; Le Corbusier and the Continual Revolution in Architecture, 2000; The Garden of Cosmic Speculation, 2003; Scottish Parliament, 2005; The Iconic Building, 2005. EDITOR: (with G. Baird) Meaning in Architecture, 1969; (with R. Bunt and G. Broadbent) Signs, Symbols and Architecture, 1980; The Architecture of Democracy, 1987; The Post-Modern Reader, 1992; (with K. Kropf) Theories & Manifestos of Contemporary Architecture, 1997; (guest ed. with M. Toy) Millennium Architecture, 2000.

JENKINS, Amy. British, b. 1963. **Genres:** Mystery/Crime/Suspense. **Career:** Writer and film producer. Worked as a paralegal in a law office. **Publications:** Honeymoon: A Romantic Rampage, 2000. **Address:** c/o Little Brown & Company, 1271 Avenue of the Americas, New York, NY 10020, U.S.A.

JENKINS, Beverly. American, b. 1951. **Genres:** Novels. **Career:** Writer. Associated with Michigan State University graduate library, 1974-80; started student-theater company, Michigan State University; read poetry in library shows, East Lansing, MI; worked as a librarian in Ann Arbor, MI. **Publications:** Night Song, 1994; Vivid, 1995; Indigo, 1996; Topaz, 1997; Through the Storm, 1998; The Taming of Jessi Rose, 1999; Always and Forever, 2000. **Address:** c/o Avon Books, 10 E 53rd St, New York, NY 10022-5299, U.S.A.

JENKINS, Catherine. Canadian, b. 1962. **Genres:** Novels, Poetry. **Career:** Sam the Record Man, Peterborough, Ontario, Canada, manager, 1984-93; freelance writer and editor, 1993-99; Solidus Communications, Toronto, Ontario, Canada, owner, 1999-. **Publications:** POETRY: Submerge (chapbook), 1997; Blood, Love, and Boomerangs, 1999. NOVEL: Swimming in the Ocean, 2002. Work represented in anthologies. Contributor of poems, stories, and reviews to periodicals. **Address:** 604-35 Walmer Rd., Toronto, ON, Canada M5R 2X3. **Online address:** scripted@hotmail.com

JENKINS, Dafydd. British, b. 1911. **Genres:** History. **Career:** Called to the Bar at Gray's Inn, 1934; barrister, 1934-38; Welsh Language Petition, organizing secretary, 1938-39; agricultural worker and organizer, 1940-69; University of Wales, Aberystwyth, law teacher, 1962-75, professor of history and Welsh law, 1975-78. **Publications:** Tan yn Llyn, 1937, 2nd ed, 1975; Thomas Johnes o'r Hafod, 1948; Llyfr Colan, 1963; Gyfraith Hywel, 1970, 2nd ed, 1976; Damisciniau Colan, Cymdeithas Lyfrau Cereligion, 1973; (ed.) Hywel Dda: The Law, 1986, 2nd ed published as The Law of Hywel the Good, 1990. **Address:** 17 Min y Bryn, Aberystwyth SY23 1LZ, Wales.

JENKINS, David L. American, b. 1931. **Genres:** Theology/Religion. **Career:** Baptist minister and writer. **Publications:** Find Yourself in Genesis, Convention Press, 1976. God's People: United for Conquest, Convention Press, 1977. Planning a Family Budget, Morningstar Books, 1981. Windows on the Gospel of John, Broadman, 1988. Great Prayers of the Bible, Broadman, 1990. **Address:** First Baptist Church, 217 West Cass, Gilmer, TX 75644, U.S.A.

JENKINS, Edith A(rnstein). American, b. 1913. **Genres:** Novellas/Short stories, Poetry, Autobiography/Memoirs. **Career:** Laney College, Oakland, CA, member of English faculty, 1959-62; Merritt College, Oakland, member of English faculty, 1962-79, writer. **Publications:** Divisions on a Ground, 1986; The Width of a Vibrato, 1990; Against a Field Sinister, 1991; Selected Poems, 2001.

JENKINS, Fred W(illiam). American, b. 1957. **Genres:** Bibliography, Classics. **Career:** College of Physicians of Philadelphia, PA, historical collections cataloger, 1986-87; University of Dayton, OH, catalog specialist, 1987-96, assistant professor, 1987-96, rare book librarian, 1993-96, associate professor, 1996-2001, coordinator and head of collection management, 1996-, professor, 2001-. **Publications:** Classical Studies: A Guide to the Reference Literature, 1996. Contributor of articles and reviews to library and papyrology journals. **Address:** 105-F Roesch Library, University of Dayton, 300 College Park, Dayton, OH 45469, U.S.A. **Online address:** fred.jenkins@udayton.edu

JENKINS, Jean. Also writes as Jean Loewer. American. **Genres:** Children's fiction, Botany, Children's non-fiction, Natural history, Picture/board books. **Career:** Freelance book illustrator, c. 1972-. Works at Graphos Studio; Asheville-Buncombe Library System, part-time employee at children's library; art teacher in public schools; teacher of adult education classes in art; mural in children's library, Pack Memorial Library, Asheville, NC. **Publications:** NONFICTION PICTURE BOOKS WITH PETER LOEWER, SELF-ILLUSTRATED: The Moonflower, 1998; Inside-Out Stomach; Pond Water Zoo. Illustrator of books by D.A. Adler, S. Campbell, P.S. Catling, P. Loewer, A.V. Lord, A. Norton and D. Madlee. Illustrator for trade and textbook publishers, newspapers, and magazines. **Address:** 185 Lakewood Dr, Asheville, NC 28803, U.S.A.

JENKINS, John Geraint. Welsh, b. 1929. **Genres:** Area studies, Business/Trade/Industry, Crafts, History. **Career:** Freelance lecturer and writer, 1991-; Curator, Welsh Folk Museum, 1987-91. Assistant, Leicester City Museums, 1952-53; Assistant Keeper, University of Reading Museum of English Rural Life, 1953-60; Keeper for Material Collections, Welsh Folk Museum, Cardiff, 1960-79; Curator, Welsh Industrial and Maritime Museum, Cardiff, 1979-87. **Publications:** Agricultural Transport in Wales, 1962; Traditional Country Craftsmen, 1965; Studies in Folk Life, 1969; The Welsh Woollen Industry, 1969; The Wool Textile Industry in Great Britain, 1971; Crefftwyr Gwledig, 1971; The English Farm Wagon, 1972; The Craft Industries, 1972; Nets and Coracles, 1974; Life and Traditions in Rural Wales, 1976; Exploring Country Crafts, 1977; Maritime Heritage, 1983; Cockles and Mussels, 1984; The Flannel Makers, 1985; From Fleece to Fabric, 1987; The Coracle, 1987; In-Shore Fisherman, 1991; Getting Yesterday Right, 1992; Museum of the Welsh Woolen Industry (guide), 1993; Llanfrannoc (bilingual), 2001; Wales and the Sea (in Welsh), 2003. **Address:** Cihaul, Sarnau, Llandysul, Credigion SA44 6QT, Wales.

JENKINS, Mark. American, b. 1958. **Genres:** Travel/Exploration. **Career:** Cross Country Skier Magazine, Emmaus, PA, managing editor, 1988-89; Backpacker Magazine, Emmaus, PA, Rocky Mountain editor, 1989-96; Men's Health Magazine, Emmaus, PA, investigative editor, 1997-; freelance writer, 1983-. **Publications:** Off the Map: Bicycling across Siberia, 1992; To Timbuktu: A Journey Down the Niger, 1997. **Address:** 1102 Grand, Laramie, WY 82070, U.S.A.

JENKINS, (Sir) Michael (Romilly Heald). British, b. 1936. **Genres:** Autobiography/Memoirs, Biography. **Career:** Entered U.K. Diplomatic Service, 1959; Deputy Secretary-General, Commission of the European Communities, Brussels, 1981-83; Assistant Under-Secretary of State, Foreign and Commonwealth Office, London, 1983-85; Minister, British Embassy, Washington, 1985-87; British Ambassador to The Netherlands, 1988-93; Vice-Chairman, Dresdner Kleinwort Wasserstein, 1993-; Chairman, we-Comm Ltd; Adviser, The Prince's Trust. **Publications:** Arakcheev, Grand Vizir of the Russian Empire, 1969; A House in Flanders, 1992. **Address:** c/o Dresdner Kleinwort Wasserstein, 20 Fenchurch St, London EC3, England.

JENKINS, Philip. American, b. 1952. **Genres:** Theology/Religion, History. **Career:** Pennsylvania State University, University Park, PA, assistant professor of criminal justice, 1980-1993, professor of history and religious studies, 1993-, became Distinguished Professor of History and Religious Studies, Religious Studies Program, director, 1992-. **Publications:** The Making of a Ruling Class: The Glamorgan Gentry, 1640-1790, 1983; Crime and Justice: Issues and Ideas, 1984; (with G.W. Potter) The City and the Syndicate: Organizing Crime in Philadelphia, 1985; Intimate Enemies: Moral Panics in Contemporary Great Britain, 1992; A History of Modern Wales, 1536-1990, 1992; Using Murder: The Social Construction of Serial Homicide, 1994; Pedophiles and Priests: Anatomy of a Contemporary Crisis, 1996; Hoods and Shirts: The Extreme Right in Pennsylvania, 1925-1950, 1997; A History of the United States, 1997; Moral Panic: Changing Concepts of the Child Molester in Modern America, 1998; The Cold War at Home: The Red Scare in Pennsylvania, 1945-1960, 1999; Synthetic Panics: The Symbolic Politics of Designer Drugs, 1999; Mystics and Messiahs: Cults and New Religions in American History, 2000; Beyond Tolerance: Child Pornography on the Internet, 2001; Hidden Gospels: How the Search for Jesus Lost Its Way, 2001; The Next Christendom: The Rise of Global Christianity, 2002. EDITOR: (with E. Schuerer) B. Traven: Life and Work, 1987; (with E. Schuerer and M. Keune) The Berlin Wall: Representations and Perspectives, 1996. **Address:** 407 Weaver Building, Pennsylvania State University, University Park, PA 16802, U.S.A. **Online address:** jpj1@psu.edu

JENKINS, (John) Robin. British, b. 1912. **Genres:** Novels. **Career:** Teacher, Ghazi College, Khabul, 1957-59; British Institute, Barcelona, 1959-61, Gaya School, Sabah, 1963-68. **Publications:** Go Gaily Sings the Lark,

1951; Happy for the Child, 1953; The Thistle and the Grail, 1954; The Cone-Gatherers, 1955; Guests of War, 1956; The Missionaries, 1957; The Changeling, 1958; Love is a Fervent Fire, 1959; Some Kind of Grace, 1960; Dust on the Paw, 1961; The Tiger of Gold, 1962; A Love of Innocence, 1963; The Sardana Dancers, 1964; A Very Scotch Affair, 1968; The Holy Tree, 1969; The Expatriates, 1971; A Toast to the Lord, 1972; A Figure of Fun, 1974; A Would-Be-Saint, 1978; Fergus Lamont, 1979; The Awakening of George Darroch, 1985; Poverty Castle, 1986; Just Duffy, 1988; Willie Hogg, 1993; Leila, 1995; Lunderston Tales, 1996. **Address:** Fairhaven, Toward, by Dunoon, Argyll, Scotland.

JENKINS, Simon. British, b. 1943. **Genres:** Environmental sciences/ Ecology, Urban studies, Writing/Journalism. **Career:** Times Educational Supplement, news ed., 1966-68; joined Evening Standard, 1968, and ed., 1976-78; Sunday Times, Insight ed., 1974-75; The Economist, London, political ed., 1979-86; Sunday Times, London, columnist, 1986-90; Historic Bldgs. and Monuments Commission, deputy chairman, 1988-90 (millennium commissioner 1994-); The Times, editor, 1990-92; columnist, The Times, and Evening Standard, 1992-. **Publications:** City at Risk, 1971; Landlord to London, 1974; (ed.) Insight on Portugal, 1975; Newspapers: The Power and the Money, 1979; Companion Guide to Outer London, 1981; The Battle for the Falklands, 1983; Images of Hampstead, 1983; With Respect, Ambassador, 1985; The Market for Glory, 1986; The Times Guide to English Style and Usage, 1992; The Selling of Mary Davies, 1993; Against the Grain, 1994; England's 1,000 Best Churches, 2000; England's 1,000 Best Houses, 2003; Big Bang Localism, 2004. **Address:** The Times, 1 Virginia St, London E.1, England.

JENKINS, Steven. American, b. 1950. **Genres:** Food and Wine. **Career:** Dean & Deluca, NYC, general manager, 1977-79; Fairway Market, NYC, general manager, 1980-88; consultant, 1988-96; Fairway Markets, NYC, partner, 1996-. **Publications:** Cheese Primer. **Address:** 545 West 111th St., Apt. 9-A, New York, NY 10025, U.S.A.

JENKINS, T(erence) A(ndrew). British, b. 1958. **Genres:** History, Politics/ Government. **Career:** Cambridge University, Cambridge, England, British Academy postdoctoral fellow, 1987-90; University of East Anglia, Norwich, England, lecturer, 1990-91; University of Exeter, Exeter, England, lecturer, 1991-92; University of East Anglia, lecturer, 1992-94, 1995-96; University of Bristol, Bristol, England, lecturer, 1996-97; History of Parliament, London, England, researcher, 1998-. **Publications:** Gladstone, Whiggery, and the Liberal party, 1874-1886, 1988; The Liberal Ascendancy, 1830-1886, 1994; Disraeli and Victorian Conservatism, 1996; Parliament, Party, and Politics in Victorian Britain, 1996; Sir Robert Peel, 1999; Britain: A Short History, 2001. EDITOR: The Parliamentary Diaries of Sir John Trelawny, 1858-1865, 1990; The Parliamentary Diaries of Sir John Trelawny, 1868-1873, 1994. Contributor to periodicals. **Address:** History of Parliament, Wedgwood House, 15 Woburn Sq., London WC1H 0NS, England.

JENKINS, Virginia Scott. American, b. 1948. **Genres:** Horticulture, Advertising/Public relations, Cultural/Ethnic topics, Environmental sciences/ Ecology, Food and Wine, History, Technology. **Career:** Harvard University Graduate School of Design, Cambridge, MA, staff assistant to the registrar, 1973-75; Mount Auburn Hospital, Cambridge, planning assistant, staff assistant, and assistant director of development, 1975-83; George Washington University, Washington, DC, teaching assistant, 1986-89; US Department of Agriculture Graduate School, instructor in history, 1993; Catholic University of America, Washington, DC, lecturer in history, 1994; University of Maryland at College Park, visiting assistant professor, 1996-99; Chesapeake Bay Maritime Museum, St. Michaels, MD, scholar in residence, 1999-. Consultant to companies and organizations, 1984-. **Publications:** The Lawn: A History of an American Obsession, 1994; Bananas: An American History, 2000. Contributor to books and periodicals. **Address:** 315 Oakley St, Cambridge, MD 21613, U.S.A. **Online address:** virginiajenkins@earthlink. net

JENNINGS, Charles. British. **Genres:** Documentaries/Reportage. **Career:** Writer and journalist for the Daily Telegraph, Guardian, Independent, and Observer, all London, England. **Publications:** The Confidence Trick: The City's Progress from Big Bang to Great Crash, 1988; Up North: Travels beyond the Watford Gap, 1995; People Like Us: A Season among the Upper Classes, 1997. Contributor to periodicals. **Address:** c/o Abacus/Little Brown, Brettenham House, Lancaster Place, London WC2E 7EN, England.

JENNINGS, Dana Andrew. American, b. 1957. **Genres:** Novels, Children's fiction. **Career:** Wall Street Journal, NYC, editor and writer, 1983-91; New York Times, NYC, editor and writer, 1993-. **Publications:** Mosquito Games,

1989; Women of Granite, 1992; Lonesome Standard Time, 1996; Me, Dad, and No. 6 (children's fiction), 1997. **Address:** 34 Godfrey Rd., Upper Montclair, NJ 07043, U.S.A.

JENNINGS, Kate. Australian/American, b. 1948. **Genres:** Novels, Novellas/ Short stories, Poetry, Essays. **Career:** Writer. **Publications:** Come to Me My Melancholy Baby (poetry), 1975; (ed.) Mother, I'm Rooted: An Anthology of Australian Women Poets, 1975; Women Falling Down in the Street (short fiction), 1990; Snake (novel), 1997; Save Me, Joe Louis (essays), 1988; Bad Manners (essays) 1993; Cats, Dogs and Pitchforks (poems), 1993; Moral Hazard, 2002. **Address:** c/o Author mail, 7th Floor, HarperCollins Publishers, 10 E 53rd St, New York, NY 10022, U.S.A. **Online address:** kjennings@ att.net

JENNINGS, Maureen. Canadian (born England). **Genres:** Novels. **Publications:** NOVELS: Except the Dying, 1997; Under the Dragon's Tail, 1998. **Address:** c/o St. Martin's Press, 175 Fifth Ave., New York, NY 10010, U.S.A.

JENNINGS, Patrick. American, b. 1962. **Genres:** Children's fiction. **Career:** Educator in San Francisco, CA, San Cristobal de las Casas, Chiapas, Mexico, and Bisbee, AZ, 1991-96; writer, Bisbee, AZ, 1991-.. **Publications:** Faith and the Electric Dogs, 1996; Faith and the Rocket Cat, 1998; Putnam and Pennyroyal, 1999; The Beastly Arms, 2001; The Bird Shadow, 2001. **Address:** c/o Copper Queen Library, PO Box 1857, 6 Main St, Bisbee, AZ 85603, U.S.A.

JENNINGS, Paul. Australian (born England), b. 1943. **Genres:** Young adult fiction, Young adult non-fiction. **Career:** Writer, speech pathologist, and special education teacher, 1963-68; Ministry of Education, Australia, speech pathologist, 1972-75; Burwood State College, lecturer in special education, 1976-78; Language and Literature, Warrnambool Institute of Adult Education, senior lecturer, 1979-88; full-time writer, 1989-. **Publications:** JUVENILE: Unreal! Eight Surprising Stories, 1985; Unbelievable! More Surprising Stories, 1986; Quirky Tails! More Oddball Stories, 1987; The Cabbage Patch Fib, 1988; Uncanny! Even More Surprising Stories, 1988; The Paw Thing, 1989; Round the Twist, 1990; Unbearable! More Bizarre Stories, 1990; The Naked Ghost, Burp! and Blue Jam, 1991; Unmentionable! More Amazing Stories, 1991; Round the Twist 1, 1993; Undone! More Mad Endings, 1993; The Gizmo, 1994; The Gizmo Again, 1995; Uncovered! Weird, Weird Stories, 1995; Come Back Gizmo, 1996; Thirteen! Unpredictable Tales from Paul Jennings, 1996; Sink the Gizmo, 1997; Wicked, 1998; Singenpoo Strikes Again, 1998. PICTURE BOOKS: Teacher Eater, 1991; Grandad's Gifts, 1991; (with T. Greenwood and T. Denton) Spooner or Later, 1992; The Fisherman and the Theefyspray, 1994; (with T. Greenwood and T. Denton) Duck for Cover, 1994. Contributor to anthologies. **Address:** PO Box 1459, Warrnambool, VIC 3280, Australia.

JENSEN, Arthur Robert. American, b. 1923. **Genres:** Education, Psychology. **Career:** University of London, Institute of Psychiatry, Research Fellow, 1956-58; University of California, Berkeley, Professor of Educational Psychology, 1958-94, and Research Psychologist, Institute of Human Learning, 1962-, Professor Emeritus, 1994-. **Publications:** (with P.M. Symonds) From Adolescent to Adult, 1961; (ed. with M. Deutsch and I. Katz) Social Class, Race, and Psychological Development, 1968; Genetics and Education, 1973; Educability and Group Differences, 1973; Educational Differences, 1973; Bias in Mental Testing, 1980; Straight Talk about Mental Tests, 1981; The g Factor, 1998. Contributor to scientific and professional journals. **Address:** School of Education, University of California, Berkeley, CA 94720, U.S.A.

JENSEN, Clayne. American, b. 1930. **Genres:** Administration/Management, Recreation, Sports/Fitness. **Career:** Brigham Young University, Provo, UT, professor and associate dean, 1968-74, dean, College of Physical Education/ Athletics, 1974-92, associate vice president and director of athletics, 1992-95. **Publications:** (with K. Tucker) Skiing, 1968, 4th ed., 1982; (co-author) To Improve Body Form and Function, 1968, 3rd ed., 1977; (co-author) Applied Kinesiology, 1970, 3rd ed., 1982; Outdoor Recreation in America, 1970, 6th ed., 2004; (co-author) Scientific Basis of Athletic Conditioning, 1972, 3rd ed., 1991; (co-author) Measurement and Statistics in Physical Education, 1972, 3rd ed., 1989; (with C. Thorstenson) Issues in Outdoor Recreation, 1972; (with M.B. Jensen) Square Dance, 1973; (with M.B. Jensen) Folk Dance, 1973; (with C. Robison) Modern Track and Field Coaching Technique, 1974; Administrative Management of Physical Education and Athletics, 1982, 4th ed., 2002. **Address:** College of Physical Education, Brigham Young University, 212 Richards Bldg, Provo, UT 84602, U.S.A.

JENSEN, Ejner J. American, b. 1937. **Genres:** Literary criticism and history. **Career:** University of Michigan, Ann Arbor, instructor to professor of English, 1964-. **Publications:** John Marston, Dramatist, 1979; (ed.) The Future of "1984," 1984; Ben Jonson's Comedies on the Modern Stage, 1985; Shakespeare and the Ends of Comedy, 1991. **Address:** Department of English, 3127 Angell Hall, University of Michigan, Ann Arbor, MI 48109, U.S.A. **Online address:** ejjensen@umich.edu

JENSEN, Emma. American. **Genres:** Romance/Historical. **Publications:** Choice Deceptions, 1996; Coup de Grace, 1996; Vivid Notions, 1996; What Chloe Wants, 1996; Entwined, 1997; Best Laid Schemes, 1998; His Grace Endures, 1998; The Irish Rogue, 1999; A Grand Design, 2000; Fallen, 2001; Moonlit, 2002. **Address:** c/o Author Mail, Ballantine Publishing Group, 1540 Broadway, New York, NY 10036, U.S.A.

JENSEN, Kathryn. Also writes as Nicole Davidson. American, b. 1949. **Genres:** Young adult fiction, Novels. **Career:** Writer, 1975-. The Publishing Institute, University of Pennsylvania, Philadelphia, PA, instructor, 1988-89; Johns Hopkins University, Baltimore, MD, lecturer and seminar leader, 1990-; Institute of Children's Literature, West Redding, CT, instructor, 1992-; Columbia Literary Associates Inc., Ellicott City, MD, part-time literary agent, 1992-. Speaker at schools, libraries, and conferences. **Publications:** FICTION FOR YOUNG ADULTS. CHRISMA Inc. SERIES: Breathless, 1988; Risky Venture, 1989; The Big Score, 1989; Nightstalker, 1989. Served as coordinating editor for the thirteen-book Charisma Inc. series. FICTION FOR YOUNG ADULTS: Pocket Change, 1989. AS NICOLE DAVIDSON: Crash Course, 1990; Winterkill, 1991; Demon's Beach, 1992; The Stalker, 1992; Fan Mail, 1993; Surprise Party, 1993; Night Terrors, 1994. FICTION FOR ADULTS: Select Circles, 1987; Sing to Me, Saigon, 1994; Couples, 1995. **Address:** Columbia Literary Association, 7902 Nottingham Way, Ellicott City, MD 21043, U.S.A.

JENSEN, Muriel. American, b. 1945. **Genres:** Romance/Historical. **Career:** Writer. **Publications:** ROMANCE NOVELS: Lovers Never Lose, 1985; Fantasies and Memories, 1987; Love and Lavender, 1987; The Mallory Touch, 1987; The Duck Shack Agreement, 1988; Carol Christmas, 1989; Side by Side, 1989; A Wild Iris, 1990; Everything, 1990; Trust a Hero, 1990; Bridge to Yesterday, 1991; Fantasies and Memories, Silhouette, 1991; The Miracle, 1991; Racing With the Moon, 1991; In Good Time, 1992; Middle of the Rainbow, 1992; Milky Way, 1992; Strings, 1992; Valentine Hearts and Flowers, 1992; The Unexpected Groom, 1993; Candy Kisses, 1994; Make-Believe Mom, 1994; Trust Historicals, 1994; Night Prince, 1994; The Wedding Gamble, 1994; A Bride for Adam Historicals, 1995; The Courtship of Dusty's Daddy, 1995; Make Way for Mommy, 1995; Merry Christmas, Mommy, 1995; Mommy on Board, 1995; The Comeback Mom, 1996; Husband in a Hurry, 1996; Christmas in the Country, 1997; The Fraudulent Fiancee, 1997; The Heart of the Matter Yours Truly, 1997; Kids & Co., 1997; Hot Pursuit (Hometown Reunion), 1997; The Little Matchmaker, 1997; The Prince, the Lady & the Tower, 1997; Undercover Mom, 1997; One and One Makes Three, 1998. Contributor to the volumes Just Married, 1993; Little Matchmakers, 1994; My Valentine, 1994; This Time ... Marriage, 1996; How to Marry a Millionaire, 1997; Love by Chocolate, 1997. **Address:** 659 15th St., Astoria, OR 97103, U.S.A.

JENSEN, Ruby Jean. Also writes as R. J. Hendrickson. American. **Genres:** Horror. **Career:** Writer. **Publications:** NOVELS: The House That Samael Built, 1974; Seventh All Hallows' Eve, 1974; The Girl Who Didn't Die, 1975; House at River's Bend, 1975; Satan's Sister, 1978; Child of Satan House, 1978; Dark Angel, 1978; (as R.J. Hendrickson) Hear the Children Cry, 1981; Such a Good Baby, 1982; The Lake, 1983; Mama, 1983; Home Sweet Home, 1985; Best Friends, 1985; Wait and See, 1986; Annabelle, 1987; Chain Letter, 1987; Smoke, 1988; House of Illusions, 1988; Jump Rope, 1988; Pendulum, 1989; Death Stone, 1989; Vampire Child, 1990; Lost and Found, 1990; Victoria, 1990; Celia, 1991; Baby Dolly, 1991; The Reckoning, 1992; Living Doll, 1993; The Haunting, 1994; Night Thunder, 1995. Contributor of articles and stories to periodicals. **Address:** c/o Publicity Director, Zebra Books, 850 Third Ave., New York, NY 10022, U.S.A.

JENSEN, Vickie (Dee). American/Canadian, b. 1946. **Genres:** Children's non-fiction, Language/Linguistics. **Career:** English Valleys School District, English teacher, 1971-72; Sioux Falls Continuing Education Centre, instructor, 1971-72; Sioux Falls Public School System, English teacher, 1972; Vancouver Image Exploration Workshops, photography instructor, 1974-78; author, photographer, and curriculum designer for native language education projects, 1975-86; U'mista Cultural Centre and North Island Community College, instructor, 1983-85; Westcoast Mariner, editor, 1987-91; Simon Fraser University, native education program, Prince Rupert, BC, instructor,

1993. B.C. Photographer, contributing editor, 1974-76. **Publications:** (with C. McLaren) Musqueam for Kids: Books 1-3, 1975; (with McLaren) Quileute for Kids: Books 1-3, 1975-76; (with J. Powell) Quileute: An Introduction to the Indians of La Push, 1976; (with Powell) Gitksan for Kids: Books 1-7, 1977-80; (with Powell) Let's Study Shuswap: Books 1-2, 1979; (with Powell) Learning Shuswap: Books 1-2, 1980; (with Powell) Learning Gitksan: Books 1-4, 1980; (with Powell) Learning Kwa'kwala: Books 1-12, 1980-82; (with Powell) Gitksan Teachers Manual, 1981; (with Powell and J. Wild) Shuswap Teachers Manual, 1983; Where the People Gather, 1992; Carving a Totem Pole (children's book), 1994; Saltwater Women at Work, 1995; Working These Waters, 1996; (with H. Bohm) Build Your Own Underwater Robot and Other Wet Projects, 1997; Totem Pole Carving, 1999; (with A. McLaren) Ships of Steel, 2000; (with H. Bohm) Introduction to Underwater Technology and Vehicle Design, 2002. **Address:** 3036 Waterloo St, Vancouver, BC, Canada V6R 3J6.

JENSON-ELLIOTT, Cynthia L(ouise). American, b. 1962. **Genres:** Children's non-fiction. **Career:** Writer and teacher. Cuyamaca Outdoor School, outdoor educator; Girl Scouts, USA, education program coordinator. Affiliated with International Center for Children and Families. Volunteer for local non-profits. **Publications:** (with L.C. Wood) Cheetahs, 1991; East Africa, 2001; Southern Africa, 2002. **Address:** c/o Author Mail, Lucent Books, 15822 Bernardo Center Dr., San Diego, CA 92127-2320, U.S.A. **Online address:** cjensonelliott@aol.com

JEPSON, Jill. American, b. 1950. **Genres:** Novels, Anthropology/Ethnology, Cultural/Ethnic topics, Environmental sciences/Ecology, Food and Wine, History, Local history/Rural topics, Essays. **Career:** University of Minnesota, Minneapolis, research fellow at Center for Research in Human Learning, 1986-87; American Institute of Indian Studies, New Delhi, India, senior fellow, 1987-88; University of California, San Francisco, research fellow in Program in Medical Anthropology, 1989-93; College of St. Catherine, St. Paul, MN, assistant professor English, 2001-. **Publications:** No Walls of Stone: An Anthology of Literature by Deaf and Hard of Hearing Writers, 1992. Contributor to magazines, newspapers, anthologies, and literary journals.

JERAM, Anita. British, b. 1965. **Genres:** Children's fiction. **Career:** Factory worker in Portsmouth, England, 1983; shop assistant in Portsmouth, 1984; kennel assistant in Hampshire, England, 1985-86; writer and illustrator of children's books. St. Tiggywinkles Hospital for Sick and Injured Wildlife, supporting member. **Publications:** CHILDREN'S BOOKS: Bill's Belly Button, 1991; It Was Jake!, 1991; The Most Obedient Dog in the World, 1993; Contrary Mary, 1995; Daisy Dare, 1995. Illustrator of books by: Dick King-Smith, Karen Wallace, Sam McBratney. **Address:** c/o Author Mail, Candlewick Press Inc, 2067 Massachusetts Ave, Cambridge, MA 02140, U.S.A.

JERMAN, Jerry. American. **Genres:** Young adult fiction. **Career:** Oklahoma City University, instructor, 1974-77; The Economy Company, Oklahoma City, writer/editor, 1978-81; Blue Cross and Blue Shield, Tulsa, OK, technical writer, 1981-82; University of Oklahoma, Norman, promotion and information specialist, 1982-83, assistant to the vice provost, 1983-90, director of marketing, 1990-2002, director of development, 2002-. Freelance writer and editor for textbook publishers, 1981-89. **Publications:** THE JOURNEYS OF JESSIE LAND SERIES: The Long Way Home, 1995; My Father the Horse Thief, 1995; Phantom of the Pueblo, 1995; Danger at Outlaw Creek, 1995; Calamity at the Circus, 1996; The Secret of Whispering Woods, 1996. **Address:** University of Oklahoma, 1700 Asp Ave, Norman, OK 73072, U.S.A. **Online address:** jjerman@ou.edu

JERNIGAN, Brenda K. American, b. 1950. **Genres:** Romance/Historical. **Career:** Novelist. **Publications:** HISTORICAL FICTION: The Duke's Lady, 1999; The Wicked Lady, 2000; Love Only Once, 2001; Christmas in Camelot, 2002; Dance on the Wind, 2002; Until September, 2003; Whispers on the Wind, 2004. **Address:** 80 Pine St. W., Lillington, NC 27546, U.S.A. **Online address:** bkj1608@juno.com

JERNIGAN, Gisela (Evelyn). American, b. 1948. **Genres:** Botany. **Career:** Freelance writer, 1986-. Harbinger House Publishers, Tucson, freelance editor, 1989-91; University of Arizona, Tucson, instructor in language, reading, and culture, 1993-. **Publications:** One Green Mesquite Tree, 1988; Agave Blooms Just Once, 1989; Sonoran Seasons: A Year in the Desert, 1994. **Address:** 2532 N Columbus, Tucson, AZ 85712, U.S.A.

JERSILD, Devon. American, b. 1958. **Genres:** Novellas/Short stories. **Career:** Freelance journalist. New England Review, Middlebury, VT, associate editor, 1990-94; Middlebury College, Middlebury, VT, administrative director, 1994-; Bread Loaf Writer's Conference, Middlebury, VT, administrative director. **Publications:** Happy Hours: Alcohol in a Woman's Life, 2001. EDITOR: The Unfeigned Word: Fifteen Years of New England Review, 1993. Work represented in anthologies. Contributor of book reviews, articles, and short stories to periodicals. **Address:** 1641 Horse Farm Rd., Weybridge, VT 05753, U.S.A. **Online address:** jersild@middlebury.edu

JERVEY, Edward D(rewry). American, b. 1929. **Genres:** History. **Career:** Lambuth College, Jackson, TN, associate professor of history, 1958-61; Radford University, Radford, VA, associate professor, 1961-63, professor of history, 1963-91; writer. Member of Radford City Council, 1980-84; volunteer at Radford Community Hospital. **Publications:** History of Methodism in Southern California and Arizona, 1960; (ed.) Prison Life among the Rebels: Recollections of a Union Chaplain, 1990. **Address:** 135 Greenbrier Dr, Radford, VA 24141-3809, U.S.A. **Online address:** TJED1234@aol.com

JERVIS, Robert. American, b. 1940. **Genres:** International relations/Current affairs, Military/Defense/Arms control, Politics/Government. **Career:** Professor of Political Science, Columbia University, NYC, since 1980. Assistant Professor, 1968-73, and Associate Professor of Government, 1973-75, Harvard University, Cambridge, Massachusetts; Visiting Associate Professor of Political Science, Yale University, New Haven, Conn., 1974-75; Professor of Political Science, University of California, Los Angeles, 1975-80. **Publications:** Perception and Misperception in International Politics, 1976; Deterrence Theory Revisited, 1978; Deterrence and Perception, 1982; The Illogic of American Nuclear Strategy, 1984; Psychology and Deterrence, 1985; (co-author) International Politics: Anarchy, Force, Political Economy, and Decision-Making, 2nd ed., 1985; The Logic of Images in International Relations, 1989; The Meaning of Nuclear Revolution: Statecraft and the Prospect of Armageddon, 1989; (co-ed.) Soviet-American Relations after the Cold War, 1990; (co-ed.) Dominoes and Bandwagons: Strategic Beliefs and Great Power, 1991; (co-ed.) Coping with Complexity in the International System, 1993; System Effects: Complexity in Social and Political Life, 1997. **Address:** Dept. of Political Science, Columbia University, New York, NY 10027, U.S.A.

JESCHKE, Wolfgang. Czech, b. 1936. **Genres:** Science fiction/Fantasy. **Career:** Writer, editor, and publisher of science fiction. Kindler Verlag, editor, 1960-69; Kindlers Literaturlexikon, editor, 1969-73; Wilhelm Heyne Verlag, editor, 1973-. **Publications:** Der Zeiter (short stories), 1970; Der letzte Tag der Schopfung (novel), 1981, as The Last Day of Creation, trans. by G. Mander, 1982; Midas (novel), 1987, trans. by Jeschke, 1990; Schlechte Nachrichten aus dem Vatikan (short stories and radio dramas), 1993. Author of science fiction stories; author of on-line essays. **Address:** Kurfuertenstrasse 47, D-8000 Munich 40, Germany.

JETT, Stephen Clinton. American, b. 1938. **Genres:** Anthropology/Ethnology, Geography, History. **Career:** Ohio State University, Columbus, instructor, 1963-64; University of California, Davis, assistant professor of geography, 1964-72, associate professor, 1972-79, chairperson, 1978-82, 1987-89, professor of geography, 1979-2000, professor of textiles and clothing, 1996-2000, professor of geography and of textiles and clothing emeritus, 2000-. **Publications:** Tourism in the Navajo Country: Resources and Planning, 1966; Navajo Wildlands: As Long as the Rivers Shall Run, 1967; House of Three Turkeys: Anasazi Redoubt, 1977; Navajo Architecture: Forms, History, Distributions, 1981; Navajo Placenames and Trails of the Canyon de Chelly System, Arizona, 2001; France, 2004. **Address:** 333 Court St NE, Abingdon, VA 24210-2921, U.S.A.

JHABVALA, Ruth Prawer. American, b. 1927. **Genres:** Novels, Plays/Screenplays. **Publications:** FICTION: To Whom She Will (in U.S. as Amrita), 1955; The Nature of Passion, 1956; Esmond in India, 1957; The Householder, 1960; Get Ready for Battle, 1962; Like Birds, Like Fishes and Other Stories, 1963; A Backward Place, 1965 (Booker Award); A Stronger Climate: 9 Stories, 1968; An Experience of India, 1971; Heat and Dust, 1975; How I Became a Holy Mother and Other Stories, 1976; In Search of Love and Beauty, 1983; Out of India: Selected Stories, 1986; Three Continents, 1987; Poet and Dancer, 1993; Shards of Memory, 1995; East into Upper East (stories), 1999. SCREENPLAYS: The Householder, 1963; Shakespeare Wallah, 1965; The Guru, 1969; Bombay Talkie, 1971; Autobiography of a Princess, 1975; Roseland, 1977; Hulabaloo over Georgie and Bonnie's Pictures, 1978; The Europeans, 1979; Jane Austen in Manhattan, 1980; Quartet, 1981; Heat and Dust, 1983; The Bostonians, 1984; A Room with a View, 1986 (Academy Award); Mr. and Mrs. Bridge, 1990; Howards End, 1992 (Academy Award); Remains of the Day, 1993; Jefferson in Paris, 1995; Surviving Picasso, 1996; The Golden Bowl, 2000. **Address:** 400 E 52nd St, New York, NY 10022, U.S.A.

JIANG, Ji-li. Chinese, b. 1954. **Genres:** Autobiography/Memoirs. **Career:** Aston Hotels and Resorts, Honolulu, HI, corporate operations analyst, 1987-92; University Health System, Chicago, IL, budgeting director, 1995-96; East West Exchange Inc., Emeryville, CA, founder and president. **Publications:** Red Scarf Girl: A Memoir of the Cultural Revolution, 1997. **Address:** c/o Kathleen Anderson, Scovil Chichak Galen Literary Agency, 381 Park Ave. S, New York, NY 10016, U.S.A. **Online address:** jjiang8888@aol.com

JIN, Ha. American (born People's Republic of China), b. 1956. **Genres:** Novels, Poetry. **Career:** Emory University, Atlanta, GA, associate professor of creative writing, 1993-96; Boston University, MA, professor of English, 2002-. **Publications:** POETRY: Between Silences, 1990; Facing Shadows, 1996; Wreckage, 2001. FICTION: Ocean of Words: Army Stories, 1996; Under the Red Flag, 1997; In the Pond, 1998; Waiting (National Book Award), 1999; The Bridegroom: Stories, 2000; The Crazed, 2002. **Address:** Department of English, Boston University, 236 Bay State Rd, Boston, MA 02215, U.S.A.

JINKS, Catherine. Australian, b. 1963. **Genres:** Children's fiction, Novels. **Career:** Westpac Banking Corp., Sydney, Australia, journalist, 1986-93. **Publications:** This Way Out, 1991; Pagan's Crusade, 1992; The Future Trap, 1993; Pagan in Exile, 1994; Witch Bank, 1995; Pagan's Vows, 1995; Pagan's Scribe, 1996; An Evening with the Messiah (adult novel), 1996; Eye to Eye, 1997; Little White Secrets (adult novel), 1997; The Secret of Hermitage Isle (cartoon book), 1997. **Address:** c/o Margaret Connolly, 16 Winton St., Warrawee, Sydney, NSW 2074, Australia.

JINPA, Thupten. Tibetan, b. 1958. **Genres:** Theology/Religion, Poetry. **Career:** Office of the Dalai Lama, India, translator, 1986-. Gaden Shartse, lecturer, 1985-89, and project supervisor. **Publications:** (trans.) The Path to Bliss, 1989; (ed. and translator) The World of Tibetan Buddhism, 1995; Echoes of Mystical Songs: An Anthology of Tibetan Religious Poems, in press. Contributor to books. **Address:** Tashi Gephel House, Gaden Shartse, P.O. Tibetan Colony 581411 N.K., Karnataka, India.

JIRGENS, Karl (Edward). Canadian, b. 1952. **Genres:** Novels, Novellas/Short stories. **Career:** York University, Downsview, Canada, instructor of English, 1982-; Algoma University College, Sault Ste. Marie, Canada, teacher; writer. **Publications:** Strappado: Elemental Tales: A Novel Collection of Short Stories, 1984; Measure of Time (novel), 1996. Contributor to periodicals. **Address:** 95 Rivercrest Rd., Toronto, ON, Canada M6S 4H7.

JOAS, Hans. German, b. 1948. **Genres:** Philosophy, Sociology. **Career:** University of Erlangen, Germany, associate professor, 1987-90; Free University of Berlin, West Berlin, Germany, professor, 1990-2002; University of Erfurt, Max Weber Center, professor, 2002-. Visiting professor: University of Chicago, IL, 1985, 2000-04, University of Toronto, ON, 1986; University of Wisconsin-Madison, 1996, 1998, New School for Social Research, NY, 1997, Duke University, 1998, University of Uppsala, Sweden, 1992, 1999-2000. **Publications:** Die gegenwaertige Lage der soziologischen Rollentheorie, 1975; Praktische Intersubjektivitaet, 1980, trans. as G.H. Mead: A Contemporary Re-examination of His Thought, 1985; (with A. Honneth) Soziales Handeln und menschliche Natur, 1980, trans. as Social Action and Human Nature, 1988; (with M. Bochow) Wissenschaft und Karriere, 1987; Die Kreativiteat des Handelns, 1992, trans. as The Creativity of Action, 1996; Pragmatism and Social Theory, 1993; Die Entstehung der Werte, 1996, trans. as The Genesis of Values, 2000; Kriege und Werte, 2000, trans. as War and Modernity, 2002. EDITOR: Das Problem der Intersubjektivitaet: Neuere Beitraege zum Werk George Herbert Mead, 1985; Kommunikatives Handeln: Beitraege zu Juergen Habermas' Theorie des kommunikativen Handelns, 1986, trans. as Communicative Action: Essays on Juergen Habermas's The Theory of Communicative Action, 1991; (with H. Steiner) Machtpolitischer Realismus und pazifistische Utopie, 1989; (with M. Kohli) Der Zusammenbruch der DDR: Soziologische Analysen, 1993; (with W. Knoebl) Gewalt in den USA, 1994; Philosophie der Demokratie, 2000; Lehrbuch der Soziologie, 2001. **Address:** Max Weber Center, University of Erfurt, Am Huegel 1, 99084 Erfurt, Germany.

JOBLING, Curtis. British. **Genres:** Children's fiction. **Career:** Author. HOT Animation, model maker and animator for "Bob the Builder." Worked on animated shows and movies. **Publications:** Frankenstein's Cat, 2001. Illustrator of books by J. Emmett. **Address:** c/o Rod Hall Agency Ltd., 3 Charlotte Mews, London W1T 4DZ, England.

JOCELYN, Ann Henning. *See* HENNING, Ann.

JOHANSEN, Iris. American. **Genres:** Mystery/Crime/Suspense, Romance/Historical. **Career:** Romance and romantic suspense, and mystery and suspense novelist. Previously worked for a major airline. **Publications:** DELANEYS OF KILLAROO SERIES: Wild Silver, 1988; Satin Ice, 1988; Matilda the Adventuress, 1997. WILD DANCER TRILOGY (1991): The Wind Dancer; Storm Winds; Reap the Wind. OTHER NOVELS: Stormy Vows, 1983; Tempest at Sea, 1983; The Reluctant Lark, 1983; The Bronzed Hawk, 1983; The Lady and the Unicorn, 1984; The Golden Valkyrie, 1984; The Trustworthy Redhead, 1984; Return to Santa Flores, 1984; No Red Roses, 1984; Capture the Rainbow, 1984; Touch the Horizon, 1984; The Forever Dream, 1985; White Satin, 1985; Blue Velvet, 1985; A Summer Smile, 1985; York the Renegade, 1986; And the Desert Blooms, 1986; Always, 1986; Everlasting, 1986; 'Til the End of Time, 1987; Last Bridge Home, 1987; Across the River of Yesterday, 1987; The Spellbinder, 1987; Magnificent Folly, 1987; One Touch of Topaz, 1988; Star Light, Star Bright, 1988; This Fierce Splendor, 1988; Man from Half Moon Bay, 1988; Blue Skies and Shining Promises, 1988; Strong, Hot Winds, 1988; Notorious, 1990; Wicked Jake Darcy, 1990; Tender Savage, 1991; The Golden Barbarian, 1990; The Tiger Prince, 1993; Star Spangled Bride, 1993; The Magnificent Rogue, 1993; The Beloved Scoundrel, 1994; Midnight Warrior, 1994; Dark Rider, 1995; Lion's Bride, 1995; The Ugly Duckling, 1996; Long After Midnight, 1996; The Face of Deception, 1998; And Then You Die, 1998; Killing Game, 1999; The Search, 2000; Final Target, 2001; Body of Lies, 2002; No One to Trust, 2002; Fatal Tide, 2003; Firestorm, 2003; Dead Aim, 2003; Blind Alley, 2004; Countdown, 2005. Contributor to anthologies. **Address:** c/o Bantam Books, 1540 Broadway, New York, NY 10036, U.S.A.

JOHN, Juliet. British, b. 1967. **Genres:** Literary criticism and history. **Career:** Academic. Lecturer in English, University of Manchester, Manchester, England; senior lecturer in English, University of Salford, Salford, Greater Manchester, England, 1997-. Has also taught at the University of Liverpool, Liverpool, England, and Edge Hill University College, Lancashire, England. **Publications:** Dickens's Villains: Melodrama, Character, Popular Culture, 2001. EDITOR: (and author of introd) Cult Criminals: The Newgate Novels, 1830-1947, 1997; (with A. Jenkins) Rereading Victorian Fiction, 1999; (with A. Jenkins) Rethinking Victorian Culture, 2000. **Address:** c/o University of Salford, Salford, Greater Manchester M5 4WT, England. **Online address:** jjohn@salford.ac.uk.

JOHN, Robert. American (born France). **Genres:** Anthropology/Ethnology, International relations/Current affairs, Philosophy. **Career:** Director-General, Commission for Human Ecology. Natural scientist and diplomatic historian. **Publications:** (with S. Hadawi) The Palestine Diary, 2 vols., 1970, 3rd ed. 1972; Behind the Balfour Declaration: The Hidden Origins of Today's Mid-East Crisis, 1988; Washington or Wilson, 2000; Our War and Terrorism, 2001. **Address:** 1080 Park Ave, New York, NY 10128-1167, U.S.A.

JOHNS, Linda. Canadian, b. 1945. **Genres:** Poetry, Animals/Pets, Natural history. **Career:** Professional artist, 1975-, with exhibitions of acrylics, linoprints, wood engravings, clay sculptures, carvings in wood and stone, pastels, pen and ink drawings, and brush and ink drawings throughout eastern Canada. **Publications:** Sharing a Robin's Life, 1993; In the Company of Birds, 1995. SELF-ILLUSTRATED: Touching Water, Touching Light (poems), privately printed, 1990; Spiritus (poems), privately printed, 1992; The Eyes of the Elders (poem), 1995; For the Birds, 1999, in US as A Feathered Family, 2000; Wild and Woolly, 2000; Touchstone (poems), privately printed, 2004; Birds of a Feather, 2005. Contributor of art work to periodicals. **Address:** R.R. 1, James River, Antigonish, NS, Canada B2G 2K8.

JOHNS, Marston. See FANTHORPE, R(obert) Lionel.

JOHNS, Richard A. American, b. 1929. **Genres:** Novels, Novellas/Short stories, Plays/Screenplays, Poetry, Advertising/Public relations, History, Theology/Religion. **Career:** Commercial artist and freelance writer. **Publications:** The Legacy (teleplay), 1965; Thirteenth Apostle, 1966; Garden of the Okapi, 1968; Return to Heroism, 1969; (co-author) Everyday, Five Minutes with God, 1969; History of the Mental Health Mental Retardation Center, 1991; History of Jarvis Christian College, 1993. **Address:** 3324 Teakwood, Tyler, TX 75701, U.S.A.

JOHNSGARD, Paul A. American, b. 1931. **Genres:** Biology, Environmental sciences/Ecology, Zoology. **Career:** University of Bristol, England, postdoctoral fellow, 1959-61; University of Nebraska, Lincoln, instructor, 1961-62, assistant professor, 1962-63, associate professor, 1964-68, foundation professor of life sciences, 1968-2001, foundation professor emeritus, 2001-. **Publications:** Handbook of Waterfowl Behavior, 1965; Animal Behavior, 1967; Waterfowl, 1968; Grouse and Quails of North America, 1973; Song of the

North Wind, 1974; Waterfowl of North America, 1975; North American Game Birds of Upland Shoreline, 1975; The Bird Decoy, 1976; Ducks, Geese and Swans of the World, 1978; A Guide to North American Waterfowl, 1979; Birds of the Great Plains, 1979; The Plovers, Sandpipers and Snipes of the World, 1981; Those of the Gray Wind, 1981; Teton Wildlife, 1982; (with K.L. Johnsgard) The Natural History of Dragons and Unicorns, 1982; Grouse of the World, 1983; Cranes of the World, 1983; The Platte, 1984; Prairie Children, Mountain Dreams, 1985; The Pheasants of the World, 1986, rev. ed., 1999; Quails, Partridges and Francolins of the World, 1987; North American Owls, 1988; Hawks, Eagles and Falcons of North America, 1990; Bustards, Hemipodes and Sandgrouse, 1991; Ducks in the Wild, 1992; Cormorants, Darters and Pelicans of the World, 1993; Arena Birds, 1994; This Fragile Land, 1995; Ruddy Ducks and Other Stifftails, 1996; The Avian Brood Parasites, 1998; Earth, Water and Sky, 1999; Trogons and Quetzals of the World, 2001; Prairie Birds, 2001; The Nature of Nebraska, 2001; Grassland Grows, 2002; Lewis & Clark on the Great Plains, 2003; Great Wildlife of the Great Plains, 2003; Faces of the Great Plains, 2003. **Address:** School of Biological Sciences, University of Nebraska, Lincoln, NE 68588-0118, U.S.A. **Online address:** pjohnsga@unlserve.unl.edu

JOHNSON, A. E. See JOHNSON, Annabel (Jones).

JOHNSON, A. Ross. American, b. 1939. **Genres:** International relations/Current affairs, Politics/Government. **Career:** Rand Corp., Santa Monica, CA, sr. social scientist, 1969-88. Radio Free Europe, policy assistant, Munich, 1966-69, director, 1988-91; Radio Free Europe/Radio Liberty Research Institute, director, 1991-94; Radio Free Europe/Radio Liberty Inc, counselor, 1994-2000; Hoover Institution, research fellow, 2002-. **Publications:** The Transformation of Communist Ideology: The Yugoslav Case 1945-53, 1972; Yugoslavia: In the Twilight of Tito, 1974; (with A.L. Horelick and J.D. Steinbruner) The Study of Soviet Foreign Policy: Decision-Theory-Related Approaches, 1975; (with R. Dean and A. Alexieo) East European Military Establishments: The Warsaw Pact Northern Tier, 1982. **Address:** Radio Free Europe, Radio Liberty, 1201 Connecticut Ave NW, Washington, DC 20036, U.S.A. **Online address:** johnsonr@rferl.org

JOHNSON, Alexandra. American, b. 1949. **Genres:** Literary criticism and history. **Career:** Christian Science Monitor, Boston, MA, writer and assistant literary editor, 1976-82; free-lance writer, 1982-. Harvard University, instructor in creative writing at university extension, 1990-98; Wellesley College, creative writing teacher. WGBH-TV, writer, 1986, member of televised book group. **Publications:** The Hidden Writer: Diaries and the Creative Life, 1997. Contributor of articles and reviews to magazines and newspapers. **Address:** 11 Chestnut St., Medford, MA 02155, U.S.A.

JOHNSON, Allan G. American, b. 1946. **Genres:** Sociology, Mathematics/Statistics. **Career:** Sociologist, writer, public speaker. Wesleyan University, Middletown, CT, assistant professor, 1972-80; Hartford College for Women, Hartford, CT, professor, 1984-. **Publications:** Social Statistics Without Tears, 1977; Statistics, 1988; The Forest for the Trees: An Introduction to Sociological Thinking, 1991; The Blackwell Dictionary of Sociology: A User's Guide to Sociological Language, 4th ed, 1996; Human Arrangements: An Introduction to Sociology, 4th ed., 1996; The Forest and the Trees: Sociology as Life, Practice, and Promise, 1997; The Gender Knot: Unraveling Our Patriarchal Legacy, 1997. **Address:** c/o Hartford College for Women, 1265 Asylum Ave., Hartford, CT 06105, U.S.A. **Online address:** agjohnson@mail.hartford.edu

JOHNSON, Andrew. British, b. 1949. **Genres:** Adult non-fiction. **Career:** Schoolteacher, 1973-77; hotelier, 1978-90; publisher, 1990-. **Publications:** Factory Farming, 1991. Contributor to periodicals.

JOHNSON, Angela. American, b. 1961. **Genres:** Children's fiction. **Career:** Volunteers in Service to America (VISTA), Ravenna, OH, child development worker, 1981-82; free-lance writer of children's books, 1989-. **Publications:** FOR CHILDREN: Tell Me a Story, Mama, 1989; Do Like Kyla, 1990; When I Am Old with You, 1990; One of Three, 1991; The Leaving Morning, 1992; One of Three, 1992; Julius, 1993; The Girl Who Wore Snakes, 1993; Shoes Like Miss Alice, 1995; The Aunt in Our House, 1996; The Rolling Store, 1997; Daddy Calls Me Man, 1997; Wedding, 1998; Those Building Men, 1999; Maniac Monkeys on Magnolia Street, 1999; When mules Flew on Magnolia Street, 2000; Casey Jones, 2000; Down the Winding Road, 2000; Running Back to Ludie, 2001. BOARD BOOKS: Joshua by the Sea, 1994; Mama Bird, Baby Birds, 1994; Joshua's Night Whispers, 1994; Rain Feet, 1994. NOVELS: Toning the Sweep, 1993; Humming Whispers, 1995; Songs of Faith, 1998; Heaven, 1998; Gone from Home, 1998. POETRY: The Other Side, 1998. **Address:** c/o Orchard Books, 557 Broadway, #95G, New York, NY 10012-3958, U.S.A.

JOHNSON, Annabel (Jones). Also writes as A. E. Johnson. American, b. 1921. **Genres:** Novels, Children's fiction, Young adult fiction. **Publications:** As a Speckled Bird, 1956; I Am Leaper, 1990. WITH E. JOHNSON: The Big Rock Candy, 1957; The Black Symbol, 1959; Torrie, 1960; The Bearcat, 1960; The Rescued Heart, 1961; Pickpocket Run, 1961; Wilderness Bride, 1962; A Golden Touch, 1963; The Grizzly, 1964; A Peculiar Magic, 1965; The Burning Glass, 1966; Count Me Gone, 1968; The Last Knife, 1971; Finders Keepers, 1981; An Alien Music, 1982; The Danger Quotient, 1984; Prisoner of PSI, 1985; A Memory of Dragons, 1986; Gamebuster, 1990; Last Days of a Toyshop, 2003; The Craft So Long to Lerne, 2004. WITH E. JOHNSON AS A.E. JOHNSON: The Secret Gift, 1961; A Blues Can Whistle, 1969. **Address:** 21 Leisure World, Mesa, AZ 85206, U.S.A. **Online address:** annjite@cs.com

JOHNSON, Barbara. American, b. 1947. **Genres:** Literary criticism and history. **Career:** Professor and author. Harvard University, professor in departments of English and Comparative Literature, chair of women's studies program, Frederic Wertham Professor of Law and Psychiatry in Society. **Publications:** Defigurations du langage poetique: La seconde revolution baudelairienne, 1979; The Critical Difference: Essays in the Contemporary Rhetoric of Reading, 1981; (ed.) The Pedagogical Imperative: Teaching as a Literary Genre, 1982; A World of Difference, 1987; (ed. with J. Arac) Consequences of Theory, 1991; (ed.) Freedom and Interpretation: The Oxford Amnesty Lectures, 1992; The Wake of Deconstruction, 1994; The Feminist Difference: Literature, Psychoanalysis, Race, and Gender, 1998. **Address:** Boylston Hall, Ground Floor, Harvard University, Cambridge, MA 02138, U.S.A. **Online address:** johnson@fas.harvard.edu

JOHNSON, Barbara E. American. **Genres:** Information science/Computers. **Career:** Writer. **Publications:** Where Does a Mother Go to Resign?, 1979; Fresh Elastic for Stretched Out Moms, 1986; Pain Is Inevitable but Misery Is Optional, 1990; Splashes of Joy in the Cesspools of Life, 1992; Pack Up Your Gloomees in a Great Big Box, Then Sit on Them, 1993; Stick a Geranium in Your Hat and Be Happy, 1993; Mama, Get the Hammer, 1994; Motherhood, 1994; I'm So Glad You Told Me What I Didn't Wanna Hear, 1996; Living Somewhere between Estrogen and Death, 1997; (with P. Clairmont, M. Meberg, and L. Swindoll) The Joyful Journey, 1997; The Upside-down Frown and Splashes of Joy, 1998; Boomerang Joy, 1998; Superscrumptious Jelly Donuts Sprinkled with Hugs, 1998; He's Gonna Toot and I'm Gonna Scoot: Waiting for Gabriel's Horn, 1999. **Address:** c/o Tommy Nelson, PO Box 141000, Nashville, TN 37214, U.S.A.

JOHNSON, Bettye. See ROGERS, Bettye.

JOHNSON, Cait. American, b. 1952. **Genres:** Food and Wine, Inspirational/Motivational Literature, Paranormal. **Career:** Intuitive counselor, teacher, workshop, and ritual facilitator at healing and spiritual centers, 1981-. **Publications:** Tarot for Every Day: Ideas and Activities for Bringing Tarot Wisdom into Your Daily Life, 1994; (with M.D. Shaw) Tarot Games: Forty-Five Playful Ways to Explore Tarot Cards Together; a New Vision for the Circle of Community, 1994; (with Shaw) Celebrating the Great Mother: A Handbook of Earth-Honoring Activities for Parents and Children, 1995; Cooking like a Goddess: Bringing Seasonal Magic into the Kitchen, 1997; (with E. Cunningham) Naked Masks, 1998; Witch in the Kitchen: Magical Cooking for All Seasons, 2001; Earth, Water, Fire, and Air: Essential Ways of Connecting to Spirit, 2003.

JOHNSON, Cathy Marie. American, b. 1956. **Genres:** Politics/Government. **Career:** University of Wisconsin-Madison, assistant professor of political science and public policy, 1986-90; State of Wisconsin, program and planning analyst in Department of Health and Social Services, 1990-91; Williams College, Williamstown, MA, assistant professor of political science, 1991-. **Publications:** The Dynamics of Conflict between Bureaucrats and Legislators, 1992. **Address:** Stetson Hall, Williams College, Williamstown, MA 01267, U.S.A.

JOHNSON, Charles R(ichard). American, b. 1948. **Genres:** Novels, Plays/Screenplays, Literary criticism and history, Humor/Satire, Novellas/Short stories. **Career:** Chicago Tribune, cartoonist and reporter, 1969-70; St. Louis Proud, St. Louis, MO, member of art staff, 1971-72; University of Washington, Seattle, assistant professor, 1976-79, associate professor, 1979-82, professor of English, 1982-. **Publications:** Black Humor (cartoon collection), 1970; Half-Past Nation Time (cartoon collection), 1972; Faith and the Good Thing (novel), 1974; Oxherding Tale (novel), 1982; The Sorcerer's Apprentice (short stories), 1986; Olly Olly Oxen Free: A Farce in Three Acts, 1988; Being and Race: Black Writing since 1970, 1988; Middle Passage (novel), 1990 (National Book Award); All This and Moonlight,

1990; (with R. Chernow) In Search of a Voice, 1991; (ed.) Black Men Speaking, 1997; Dreamer (novel), 1998; (with others) Africans in America, 1998; (with others) King, 2000; Soul Catcher and Other Stories, 2001. Contributor to books, journals, and periodicals. **Address:** Dept. of English, PO Box 354330, University of Washington, Seattle, WA 98195-4330, U.S.A. **Online address:** chasjohn@u.washington.edu

JOHNSON, Cherry L(urae) F(lake). American, b. 1968. **Genres:** Novels. **Career:** Business owner. Wake Technical Community College, English instructor. **Publications:** Half Moon Pocosin, 1996. **Address:** 500 Penwood Road, Willow Spring, NC 27592, U.S.A.

JOHNSON, Chester L. American, b. 1951. **Genres:** Novels, Poetry. **Career:** Entrepreneur, broadcaster, and writer. CEO and founder, C. Johnson Enterprises Ltd.com (business consultants), Richmond, CA, 1995-; Naval Aviation Depot, Alameda, CA, security supervisor, 1985-95; KCMO/KC95 FM Radio, Fairway, KS, master control operator, announcer, and writer, 1983-85; KACE FM Radio, Los Angeles, CA, announcer/operator, 1977-82; KCMJ Radio (CBS 1010), Palm Springs, CA, announcer/operator and music director, 1974-77. **Publications:** Wisdom (poetry), 1998; White Man Brown, a Failure of the American Dream (noir fiction), 2001. Author of television script for Banachek series, produced 1973. **Address:** C. Johnson Enterprises Ltd.com, 3043 Hyde St, Oakland, CA 94601-1918, U.S.A. **Online address:** CBebee510@aol.com

JOHNSON, Colin. British, b. 1939. **Genres:** Medicine/Health, Philosophy. **Career:** Writer. Odd jobs include work as automotive mechanic, kitchen porter, toolmaker, draftsman, design engineer, factory manager for a cooperative, designer of plastic structures, and magazine distributor; farmer and philosopher. **Publications:** WITH ARABELLA MELVILLE: Cured to Death: The Effects of Prescription Drugs, 1982; Hayfever: No Need to Suffer, 1985; The Long-Life Heart: How to Avoid Heart Disease and Live a Longer Life, 1985; Persistent Fat and How to Lose It, 1986 (in U.S. as Fat Free Forever, 1987); Alternatives to Drugs: A Handbook to Health without Hazards, 1987 (in U.S. as Health without Hazards, 1990); Immunity Plus: How to Be Healthy in an Age of New Infections, 1988; The Complete Diet Book, 1989; Eat Yourself Thin, 1990. SOLE AUTHOR: Green Dictionary, 1991. **Address:** David Grossman Literary Agency Ltd., 118B Holland Park Ave., London W11 4UA, England. **Online address:** colcon@enterprise.net

JOHNSON, Diane. American, b. 1934. **Genres:** Novels, Biography. **Publications:** Fair Game, 1965; Loving Hands at Home, 1965; Burning, 1970; Lesser Lives (biography), 1972; The Shadow Knows, 1974; Lying Low, 1978; Terrorists and Novelists, 1983; Dashiell Hammett (biography), 1985; Persian Nights, 1987; Health and Happiness, 1990; Natural Opium, 1993; Le Divorce, 1997; Le Mariage, 2000; L'Affaire, 2003. **Address:** c/o Hasse Molesley Law Offices, 530 Jackson St 3rd Fl, San Francisco, CA 94102, U.S.A.

JOHNSON, Dianne. Also writes as Dinah Johnson. American, b. 1960. **Genres:** Literary criticism and history, Children's non-fiction. **Career:** Author and educator. University of South Carolina, Columbia, SC, associate professor of English, 1990-, interim director, African-American studies program, 1998-2000. **Publications:** Telling Tales: The Pedagogy and Promise of African American Literature for Youth, 1990; Presenting Laurence Yep, 1995; (ed.) The Best of The Brownies' Book, 1996. JUVENILE. AS DINAH JOHNSON: All around Town: The Photographs of Richard Samuel Roberts, 1998; Sunday Week, 1999; Quinnie Blue, 2000; Sitting Pretty: A Celebration of Black Dolls (poetry), 2000. Contributor of essays to books and anthologies. Some of the author's work appears under the name Dianne Johnson-Feelings. **Address:** Department of English, University of South Carolina, Columbia, SC 29208, U.S.A. **Online address:** dianne@sc.edu

JOHNSON, Dick. (Richard A. Johnson). American, b. 1955. **Genres:** Sports/Fitness. **Career:** Sports Museum, Boston, MA, associate director and curator, 1982-. Founder and director, U.S.A./Norway Soccer Committee; consultant to Florentine Films and Museum of Science. **Publications:** The Baseball Almanac, 1991; (ed. with G. Stout) Ted Williams: A Portrait in Words and Pictures, 1991; Twentieth Century Baseball Chronicle, 1991; Players of Cooperstown, 1992; (with F. Lewis) Young at Heart: The Story of Johnny Kelley, 1992; Soccer Zones, 1994; Treasury of Baseball, 1994; (contrib. ed.) Boston Garden: Banner Years, 1994; (with G. Stout) DiMaggio: An Illustrated Life, 1995; (with G. Stout) Jackie Robinson: Between the Baselines, 1997; (with G. Stout) Red Sox Century, 2000. **Address:** Sports Museum, 1175 Soldiers Field Rd, Boston, MA 02134, U.S.A. **Online address:** DJcurator@aol.com

JOHNSON, Dinah. See JOHNSON, Dianne.

JOHNSON, Dolores. American, b. 1949. **Genres:** Children's non-fiction. **Career:** Author and illustrator. Worked in advertising, Los Angeles, CA, 1974-88. Tutor, Library Adult Reading Project. Works included in exhibitions and group exhibits. **Publications:** FOR CHILDREN: Bessie Coleman, 1996. FOR CHILDREN, SELF-ILLUSTRATED: What Will Mommy Do When I'm at School?, 1990; What Kind of Baby-Sitter Is This?, 1991; The Best Bug to Be, 1992; Your Dad Was Just Like You, 1992; Now Let Me Fly: The Story of a Slave Family, 1993; Papa's Stories, 1994; The Children's Book of Kwanzaa, 1996; Grandma's Hands, 1998; My Mom Is My Show-and-Tell, 1999. Illustrator of books by: B.P. Wilson, E. Jenkins, C. Miles. **Address:** 127 North Eucalyptus Ave., No. 10, Inglewood, CA 90301, U.S.A.

JOHNSON, Donald Leslie. American, b. 1930. **Genres:** Architecture, Humanities, Regional/Urban planning. **Career:** C.V. Rueger and Associates (architects), Tacoma, WA, drafter, 1956, 1958; Bassetti & Morse (architects), Seattle, designer and drafter, 1957, 1961; Harbeson, Hough, Livingston & Larson (architects), Philadelphia, designer and drafter, 1958-60; Grant, Copeland & Chervenak (architects), Seattle, designer and drafter, 1960-61; Cain, Nelson & Wares (architects), Tucson, AZ, design associate, 1965-67; architect in Tucson, 1962-65; teacher of architecture courses at Universities of Pennsylvania, Arizona, and Adelaide, and Washington State University, 1965-72; Flinders University of South Australia, Bedford Park, teacher of architectural history, 1972-88, founder & founding director of Australia Studies Program. University of Arizona, founder of Architecture Library; University of South Australia, founder & director of Architecture Archives, adjunct associate professor, currently; curator of architectural exhibitions. Appeared in documentary films; guest on Australian radio programs. Also works as vocal coach and musical director of choruses. **Publications:** The Architecture of Walter Burley Griffin, 1977; Canberra and Walter Burley Griffin, 1979; Assessment of 20th-Century Architecture, 1980; Australian Architecture, 1901-51, 1980, rev. ed., 2002; Canberra and Walter Burley Griffin: A Bibliography of 1876 to 1976, 1980; (with M.S. Fallon) 18th- and 19th-Century Architecture Books and Serials in South Australia, 1981; (with D. Langmead) The Adelaide City Plan, 1986; Frank Lloyd Wright versus America, 1990; (with Langmead) Makers of 20th-Century Modern Architecture, 1997; (with Langmead) Architectural Excursions: Frank Lloyd Wright, Holland, and Europe, 2000; The Fountainheads, Wright, Rand, the FBI, Hollywood, 2005. Contributor to books and professional journals. **Address:** Box 75, Kangarilla, SA 5157, Australia.

JOHNSON, Doug(las A.). (born United States), b. 1952. **Genres:** Librarianship. **Career:** Stuart-Menlo Schools, Stuart, IA, English teacher, 1976-78; West Branch Schools, West Branch, IA, English teacher and librarian, 1979-84; Aramco Schools, Dhahran, Saudi Arabia, library media specialist, 1984-89; St. Peter Schools, St. Peter, MN, library media specialist, 1989-91; Mankato Area Public Schools, Mankato, MN, director of media and technology, 1991-. Minnesota State University-Mankato, adjunct faculty member. Mankato Downtown Kiwanis, member. **Publications:** The Indispensable Librarian: Surviving (and Thriving) in School Media Centers in the Information Age, 1997; The Indispensable Teacher's Guide to Computer Skills, 2002; Teaching Right from Wrong in the Digital Age, 2003. **Address:** 46813 Cape Horn Rd., Cleveland, MN 56017, U.S.A. **Online address:** dougj@doug-johnson.com

JOHNSON, Elizabeth A. American, b. 1941. **Genres:** Theology/Religion. **Career:** Catholic University of America, Washington, DC, professor of theology, 1981-91; Fordham University, Bronx, NY, distinguished professor of theology, 1991-. **Publications:** Consider Jesus: Waves of Renewal in Christology, 1990; She Who Is: The Mystery of God in Feminist Theological Discourse, 1992; Women, Earth, and Creator Spirit, 1993; Friends of God and Prophets: A Feminist Theological Reading of the Communion of Saints, 1998; Truly Our Sister: A Theology of Mary in the Communion of Saints, 2003. Contributor to books, scholarly journals and religious magazines. **Address:** Department of Theology, Fordham University, Bronx, NY 10458, U.S.A.

JOHNSON, Elmer Hubert. American, b. 1917. **Genres:** Criminology/True Crime, Sociology. **Career:** Distinguished Professor of Sociology and Criminal Justice, Center for Study of Crime, Delinquency and Corrections, Southern Illinois University, Carbondale, 1966-. Assistant Professor, then Professor, Dept. of Sociology and Anthropology, North Carolina State University, Raleigh, 1949-66; Assistant Director, North Carolina Prison Dept., Raleigh, 1958-60. **Publications:** Crime, Correction and Society, 1964, 4th ed., 1978; Social Problems of Urban Man, 1973; International Handbook on Contemporary Development in Criminology, 2 vols., 1984; Handbook on Crime and Delinquency Prevention, 1987; Japanese Corrections: Managing Convicted Offenders in an Orderly Society, 1996; Criminalization and Prison-

ers in Japan: Six Contrary Cohorts, 1997; Linking Community and Corrections in Japan, 2000. **Address:** Center for Study of Crime, Delinquency and Corrections, Southern Illinois University, Carbondale, IL 62901, U.S.A. **Online address:** j194197@siu.edu

JOHNSON, Fenton. American, b. 1953. **Genres:** Novels, Gay and lesbian issues, Intellectual history, Theology/Religion, Autobiography/Memoirs. **Career:** Novelist, essayist, journalist, and writer of short fiction; University of Arizona, associate professor of creative writing (nonfiction). Contributor to National Public Radio, Harper's, and New York Times Magazine. **Publications:** Crossing the River: A Novel, 1989; Scissors, Paper, Rock, 1993; Geography of the Heart: A Memoir, 1996; Keeping Faith: A Skeptic's Journey among Christian and Buddhist Monks, 2003. **Address:** c/o Trident Media Group, 41 Madison Ave Fl 36, New York, NY 10010-2257, U.S.A. **Online address:** johnfenton@aol.com

JOHNSON, Freddie Lee, III. American. **Genres:** Novels. **Career:** Malone College, Canton, OH, professor of history; Walsh University, North Canton, OH, professor of history; Hope College, Holland, MI, professor of history. **Publications:** Bittersweet, 2002. **Address:** Hope College, Lubbers 337, 126 East 10th Street, Holland, MI 49423, U.S.A. **Online address:** johnson@hope.edu

JOHNSON, George (Laclede). American, b. 1952. **Genres:** Information science/Computers, Politics/Government, Sciences, Social commentary. **Career:** Albuquerque Journal, New Mexico, staff writer and copy editor, 1976-78; Minneapolis Star, staff writer, 1979-82; New York Times, editor, The Week in Review, 1986-94, science writer, 1994-. **Publications:** Architects of Fear: Conspiracy Theories and Paranoia in American Politics, 1984; Machinery of the Mind: Inside the New Science of Artificial Intelligence, 1986; In the Palaces of Memory: How We Build the Worlds inside Our Heads, 1991; Fire in the Mind: Science, Faith, and the Search for Order, 1995; Strange Beauty: Murray Gell-Mann and the Revolution in 20thCentury Physics, 2000; A Shortcut through Time: The Path to the Quantum Computer, 2003. **Address:** c/o Esther Newberg, International Creative Management, 40 W 57th St, New York, NY 10019, U.S.A. **Online address:** johnson@nytimes.com

JOHNSON, George Lloyd. American, b. 1955. **Genres:** History. **Career:** University of South Carolina at Columbia, instructor in history, 1990-91; Campbell University, Buies Creek, NC, assistant professor, 1991-97, associate professor of history, 1997-, director of Historical Studies, 2003-. **Publications:** The Frontier in the Colonial South, 1997. Contributor to books, encyclopedias and professional journals. **Address:** Dept of Government and History, Campbell University, PO Box 356, Buies Creek, NC 27506, U.S.A. **Online address:** johnson@campbell.edu

JOHNSON, Greg. American, b. 1953. **Genres:** Novels, Novellas/Short stories, Poetry, Literary criticism and history, Biography. **Career:** Kennesaw State University, Marietta, GA, associate professor, 1989-95, professor of English, 1995-; writer. Has also taught at Emory University and the University of Mississippi. **Publications:** CRITICISM: Emily Dickinson: Perception and the Poet's Quest 1985; Understanding Joyce Carol Oates, 1987; Joyce Carol Oates: A Study of the Short Fiction, 1994; Invisible Writer: A Biography of Joyce Carol Oates, 1998. STORIES: Distant Friends, 1990; A Friendly Deceit, 1992; I Am Dangerous, 1996; Last Encounter with the Enemy, 2004. NOVELS: Pagan Babies, 1993; Sticky Kisses, 2001. POEMS: Aid and Comfort, 1993. **Address:** Kennesaw State University, English Department, 1000 Chastain Rd, Kennesaw, GA 30144, U.S.A. **Online address:** RJohn713@aol.com

JOHNSON, Jesse J. American, b. 1914. **Genres:** Military/Defense/Arms control, Race relations. **Career:** Writer, U.S. Army Aviation. Served in the U.S. Army, 1942-62 (retiring as Lt. Col.). **Publications:** Ebony Brass; The Black Soldier; A Pictorial History of the Black Soldier in the United States (1619-1969) in Peace and War; A Pictorial History of Black Servicemen (Air Force, Army, Navy, Marines); Black Armed Forces Officers (1736-1971): A Documented Pictorial History; Black Women in the Armed Forces: A Pictorial History; Roots of Two Black Marine Sergeants Major; Jesse J. Johnson, Prose for One's Self. **Address:** 3 Hillside Dr, Hampton, VA 23666, U.S.A.

JOHNSON, John L. American, b. 1945. **Genres:** Theology/Religion. **Career:** Former U.S. Postal Service worker. **Publications:** Black Biblical Heritage, 1994; God's Kinship with Dark Colors. **Address:** 8312 Pepperidge Dr., Berkeley, MO 63134, U.S.A.

JOHNSON, Jory (F.). American, b. 1950. **Genres:** Architecture. **Career:** New York Shakespeare Festival, New York City, dramaturge, 1973-79; Hunter

Reynolds Jewell, Raleigh, NC, landscape architect, 1985-87; University of North Carolina at Charlotte, assistant professor of architecture, 1987-91; University of Illinois at Urbana-Champaign, Urbana, assistant professor of landscape architecture, 1991-. **Publications:** Modern Landscape Architecture: Redefining the Garden, 1991. **Address:** 2202 S Cottage Grove, Urbana, IL 61801, U.S.A. **Online address:** johnson5100@insightbb.com

JOHNSON, Leland R(oss). Also writes as J. Cleo Lee. American, b. 1937. **Genres:** Local history/Rural topics. **Career:** Rock Island Railroad, Chicago, IL, construction manager, c. 1955-57; Trunkline Gas Co., Houston, TX, construction manager, c. 1955-57; teacher and coach at public schools in Illinois, 1957-61; history teacher at public schools in St. Louis, MO, 1961-63; Western Kentucky University, Bowling Green, instructor in history, 1964-67; Clio Research Co., Westmoreland, TN, founder, 1967, owner, 1967-. Vanderbilt University, George Peabody College, instructor, 1967-70. U.S. Army, historian and technical writer for Corps of Engineers, 1978-79, senior historian, 1980-81; Sandia National Laboratories, corporate historian, 1994-96. **Publications:** The Building of Nashville, 1968; From Memphis to Bristol: A Half-Century of Highway Construction in Tennessee, 1978; The Tennessee Limestone Industry: A History of Its Association, 1982; Boys Will Be Men: Middle Tennessee Scouting Since 1910, 1983; The First Presbyterian Church of Nashville: A Documentary History, 1986; The Parthenon of Nashville, 1991; Oak Ridge National Laboratory: The First Fifty Years, 1994. Fiction writer, under the pseudonym J. Cleo Lee. Contributor to history and engineering journals. **Address:** 301 Lake Westmoreland, Westmoreland, TN 37186, U.S.A.

JOHNSON, LouAnne. American, b. 1953. **Genres:** Documentaries/Reportage, Adult non-fiction. **Career:** Copley News Service, San Diego, CA, special sections editor, 1982-84; Xerox PARC, Palo Alto, CA, personal assistant to the corporate director of systems technology, 1984-87; Del Mar Publishing, Del Mar, CA, assistant editor, editorial supervisor, and staff writer, 1988-89; Carlmont High School, Belmont, CA, English teacher and department head, 1989-. **Publications:** Making Waves: A Woman in This Man's Navy, 1986; My Posse Don't Do Homework, 1992; (with others) Dangerous Minds, 1995; Girls in the Back of the Class, 1995; School is not a Four Letter Word, 1997; Two Parts Text Book, One Part Love, 1998. Contributor to periodicals. **Address:** Carlmont High School, 1400 Alameda, Belmont, CA 94002, U.S.A.

JOHNSON, Lynn Staley. See STALEY, Lynn.

JOHNSON, Marilynn S. American, b. 1957. **Genres:** History. **Career:** Boston College, Chestnut Hill, MA, professor of history, 1995-. **Publications:** The Second Gold Rush: Oakland and the East Bay in World War II, 1993; Street Justice: A History of Police Violence in New York City, 2003.

JOHNSON, Michael P(aul). American, b. 1941. **Genres:** History. **Career:** LeMoyne College, Memphis, TN, assistant professor of history, 1967-68; San Jose State College (now University), San Jose, CA, instructor in history, 1970-71; University of California, Irvine, lecturer, 1971-73, assistant professor, 1973-76, associate professor, 1976-84, professor of history, 1984-94; Johns Hopkins University, professor of history, 1994-. **Publications:** Toward a Patriarchal Republic: The Secession of Georgia, 1977; (with J.L. Roark) Black Masters: A Free Family of Color in the Old South, 1984; (with J.L. Roark) No Chariot Let Down: Charleston's Free People of Color on the Eve of the Civil War, 1984; (co-author) The American Promise: A History of the United States, 1998; (ed.) Reading the American Past: Selected Historical Documents to 1877 (vol. I) and since 1865 (vol. II), 1998; Abraham Lincoln, Slavery, and the Civil War: Selected Writings and Speeches, 2001; The Making of a Slave Conspiracy, 2002. **Address:** Department of History, Johns Hopkins University, Baltimore, MD 21218, U.S.A.

JOHNSON, Neil. American, b. 1954. **Genres:** Children's non-fiction. **Career:** Photo lab technician, Shreveport, LA, 1976-80; photographer and writer, 1980-; Centenary College of Louisiana, Shreveport, photography instructor, 1981-2004. Marjorie Lyons Playhouse, official photographer, 1987-; Red River Rally (hot air balloon festival), founder and co-chair, 1991, 1992. Created Portrait 2000, a community public art project to celebrate the millennium. **Publications:** PHOTO-ILLUSTRATOR AND AUTHOR: Step into China, 1988; Born to Run: A Racehorse Grows Up, 1988; The Battle of Gettysburg, 1989; All in a Day's Work, 1989; Batter Up!, 1990; Fire and Silk: Flying in a Hot Air Balloon, 1991; The Battle of Lexington and Concord, 1992; Jack Creek Cowboy, 1993; Big-Top Circus, 1995; Shreveport and Bossier City, 1995; Ghost Night: An Adventure in 3-D, 1996; Louisiana Journey, 1997; National Geographic Photography Guide for Kids, 2001.

Contributor of photos to periodicals. **Address:** 1301 Louisiana, Shreveport, LA 71101, U.S.A. **Online address:** njohnson@njphoto.com

JOHNSON, Paul (Bede). British, b. 1928. **Genres:** Architecture, History, Travel/Exploration. **Career:** Realities mag., assistant executive editor, 1952-55; New Statesman, London, member of editorial staff, 1955-, editor, 1965-70. **Publications:** The Suez War, 1957; Journey into Chaos, 1958; Left of Centre, 1960; Merrie England, 1964; Statesmen and Nations, 1971; The Offshore Islanders, 1972; (with G. Gale) The Highland Jaunt, 1973; A Place in History, 1974; The Life and Times of Edward III, 1974; Elizabeth I, 1974; Pope John XXIII, 1975; A History of Christianity, 1976; Enemies of Society, 1977; The National Trust Book of British Castles, 1978; The Recovery of Freedom, 1980; British Cathedrals, 1980; Ireland, 1980; Pope John Paul II and the Catholic Restoration, 1982; A History of the Modern World from 1917 to the 1980's, 1983; The Pick of Paul Johnson, 1985; Oxford Book of Political Anecdotes, 1986; A History of the Jews, 1987; Intellectuals, 1988; The Birth of the Modern: World Society, 1815-1830, 1991; Wakes Up Britain!, 1994; Paul Johnson: A Topical Compilation of His Wit, Wisdom and Satire, 1994; The Renaissance: A Short History, 2001. **Address:** 29 Newton Rd, London W2 5JR, England.

JOHNSON, R(odney) M(arcus). American, b. 1968. **Genres:** Novels. **Career:** Writer. Has worked as a radiation therapist, Little Company of Mary Hospital, Evergreen Park, IL. **Publications:** The Harris Men, 1999; Father Found, 2000; The Harris Family, 2001; Love Frustration, 2002. Work represented in anthologies. **Address:** c/o Warren Frazier, John Hawkins & Associates, 71 West 23rd St., Ste. 1600, New York, NY 10010, U.S.A.

JOHNSON, Rebecca L. American, b. 1956. **Genres:** Natural history, Children's non-fiction, Sciences, Illustrations, Young adult non-fiction. **Career:** Free-lance science writer and illustrator, 1987-. **Publications:** FOR YOUNG ADULTS: The Secret Language: Pheromones in the Animal World, 1989; Diving into Darkness: A Submersible Explores the Sea, 1989; The Greenhouse Effect: Life on a Warmer Planet, Lerner, 1990; The Great Barrier Reef: A Living Laboratory, 1991; Investigating the Ozone Hole, 1993; Science on Ice: An Antarctic Journal, 1995; Braving the Frozen Frontier: Women Working in Antarctica, 1997. OTHER: (with L.G. Johnson) Essentials of Biology (college text), 1986. Contributing author and feature writer for grade school, middle school, and highschool science and health texts. **Address:** c/o Publicity Director, Lerner Publications Company, 241 First Ave. North, Minneapolis, MN 55401, U.S.A.

JOHNSON, Rick L. American, b. 1954. **Genres:** Children's non-fiction, Biography. **Career:** Concordia Blade-Empire, Concordia, KS, part-time reporter and photographer, 1972-75, sports editor, 1976-78, copy editor and Associated Press wire editor, 1978-81; freelance writer, 1981-; studentprofileservices.com, founder/owner, 2002-. Cloud County Community College, Concordia, part-time assistant in Travel/Tourism and Management department, 1981-82. **Publications:** Jim Abbott: Beating the Odds, 1991; Bo Jackson: Baseball/Football Superstar, 1991; Magic Johnson: Basketball's Smiling Superstar, 1992. Contributor to children's periodicals. **Address:** 328 W 15th St, Concordia, KS 66901, U.S.A.

JOHNSON, Rob. (Robert Vincent). Australian (born England), b. 1927. **Genres:** Poetry, Literary criticism and history. **Career:** Lecturer in English, University of New England, Armidale, 1954-58; Lecturer, 1958-63, Sr. Lecturer, 1963-70, and Reader, 1971-88, University of Adelaide, S.A. **Publications:** Walter Pater: A Study of His Critical Outlook and Achievement, 1961; Aestheticism, 1969; Caught on the Hop (poetry), 1984. **Address:** 3/63 Hackney Rd, Hackney, SA 5069, Australia. **Online address:** rhjohn@picknow1.com.au

JOHNSON, Robert E(rwin). American, b. 1923. **Genres:** History, Biography. **Career:** Professor of History, University of Alabama, Tuscaloosa, 1967-93 (Assistant Professor, 1956-63; Associate Professor, 1963-67). **Publications:** Thence Round Cape Horn: The Story of U.S. Naval Forces on Pacific Station 1818-1923, 1963; Rear Admiral John Rodgers, 1812-1882, 1967; Far China Station: The U.S. Navy in Asian Waters 1800-1898, 1979; Guardians of the Sea: History of the U.S. Coast Guard 1915 to the Present, 1987; Bering Sea Escort: Life Aboard a Coast Guard Cutter in World War II, 1992. **Address:** 61 The Downs, Tuscaloosa, AL 35401, U.S.A.

JOHNSON, Roger. American, b. 1942. **Genres:** Literary criticism and history. **Career:** Lewis-Clark State College, Lewiston, ID, member of Division of Literature and Languages. **Publications:** (Coeditor) Moliere and the Commonwealth of Letters (essays), 1975; (Cotrans) Fifty Years of a Life in Music. **Address:** Division of Literature and Languages, Lewis-Clark State College, Lewiston, ID 83501, U.S.A.

JOHNSON, Sandy. American. **Genres:** Information science/Computers. **Career:** Writer. **Publications:** The CUPPI (novel), 1979; Walk a Winter Beach, 1982; Against the Law (nonfiction), 1986; The Book of Elders: The Life Stories of Great American Indians (nonfiction), 1994; The Book of Tibetan Elders: Life Stories and Spiritual Wisdom from the Great Spiritual Masters of Tibet (nonfiction), 1996. **Address:** c/o Publicity, Riverhead Books, 375 Hudson St, New York, NY 10014, U.S.A.

JOHNSON, Sherrie. American, b. 1948. **Genres:** Theology/Religion, Children's fiction. **Career:** Writer. Brigham Young University, instructor. **Publications:** PICTURE BOOKS FOR CHILDREN: The Broken Bow, 1994; The Gadianton Robbers, 1994; Nephi and Lehi in Prison, 1994; Abinadi, 1994; Ammon and the King, 1994; Captain Moroni's Title of Liberty, 1994; Alma at the Waters of Mormon, 1994; Jesus Is Born, 1994; Enos Prays, 1995; Jesus Visits the Nephites, 1995; Jared and His Brother, 1995; Abish, 1995; Bible Treasury for LDS Children, 1999. OTHER: Spiritually Centered Motherhood, 1983; Man, Woman and Deity, 1991; A House with Wings (historical fiction), 1995. Has published over 100 articles and short stories. **Address:** 1167 E 140 N, Orem, UT 84097, U.S.A.

JOHNSON, Steven F(orrest). American, b. 1954. **Genres:** Local history/Rural topics. **Career:** Lawrence Academy, Groton, MA, adult education lecturer, 1981; Lowell University, Lowell, MA, teacher of history, 1980-82; high school teacher of geography, world civilization, law, and government in Lowell, 1982-84; DC Heath Publishing Co., Lexington, MA, college textbook salesperson, 1984-85; eighth-grade social studies teacher in Acton, MA, 1985-86; Marlborough High School, Marlborough, MA, instructor in history, 1986-. **Publications:** Ninnuock (the People): The Algonkian People of New England, 1995, 2nd ed., 1997. **Address:** 155 County Rd., Ashby, MA 01431, U.S.A. **Online address:** VHSJohnson@hotmail.com

JOHNSON, Susan (M.). Also writes as Jill Barkin. American, b. 1939. **Genres:** Romance/Historical. **Publications:** Seized by Love, 1979; Lovestorm, 1981; Sweet Love, Survive, 1985; Blaze, 1986; The Play, 1987; Silver Flame, 1988; (as Jill Barkin) Hot Streak, 1990; Golden Paradise, 1990; Forbidden, 1991; Sinful, 1992; Outlaw, 1993; Pure Sin, 1994; Brazen, 1995; Wicked, 1996; Taboo, 1997; A Touch of Sin, 1999; To Please a Lady, 1999; Legendary Lover, 2000; Temporary Mistress, 2000; Tempting, 2001; Seduction in Mind, 2001; Again and Again, 2002; Blond Heat, 2002; Delighted, 2002. Works appear in anthologies.

JOHNSON, Susan (Ruth). Australian, b. 1956. **Genres:** Novels. **Career:** Courier-Mail, Brisbane, Australia, cadet journalist, 1975-77; Australian Women's Weekly, Sydney, Australia, journalist, 1977-78; Sun-Herald, Sydney, journalist, 1980; Sydney Morning Herald, Sydney, feature writer, 1980-82; National Times, correspondent from Queensland, Australia, 1982-84; novelist, 1984-. **Publications:** FICTION: Messages from Chaos, 1987; Flying Lessons, 1990; A Big Life, 1993; Hungry Ghosts, 1996. NONFICTION: A Better Woman, 1999. EDITOR: (co) Latitudes: New Writing from the North, 1986; Women Love Sex, 1996. Contributor of short stories to literary magazines. **Address:** c/o Margaret Connolly and Associates, PO Box 945, Wahroonga NSW 2076, Australia. **Online address:** sjreaders@hotmail.com; www.abetterwoman.net

JOHNSON, Victoria. (born United States), b. 1958. **Genres:** Dance/Ballet. **Career:** Fitness trainer and educator, entrepreneur, consultant, lecturer, and author. Owner and president, Victoria Johnson International, a marketing, management, and consulting company; owner of a distribution and sales company marketing health and fitness products. Star and producer of more than twenty-four dance fitness video programs; executive producer and host of Celebrity Health and Fitness television program. **Publications:** (with Megan V. Davis) Victoria Johnson's Attitude: An Inspirational Guide to Redefining Your Body, Your Health, and Your Outlook, 1993; Body Revival: Lose Weight, Feel Great, and Pump Up Your Faith, 2002. Contributor to periodical. **Address:** Victoria Johnson International, POB 1744, Lake Oswego, OR 97035, U.S.A. **Online address:** info@victoriajohnson.com

JOHNSON, Whittington B. American, b. 1931. **Genres:** History. **Career:** Edward Waters College, Jacksonville, FL, instructor in social science, 1957-62; Savannah State College (now University), Savannah, GA, assistant professor of social science, 1962-67; University of Miami, Coral Gables, FL, associate professor, 1970-95, professor of history, 1995-, department head, 1976-77, director of Afro-American Studies Center, 1972-73. Wisconsin State University (now University of Wisconsin-Superior), guest lecturer, 1972. **Publications:** The Promising Years, 1750-1830: The Emergence of Black Labor and Business, 1993; Black Savannah, 1788-1864, 1996; Race Relations in the Bahamas, 1784-1834: The Nonviolent Transformation from a Slave to a Free Society, 2000. Contributor of articles and reviews to periodicals. **Address:** Department of History, University of Miami, Coral Gables, FL 33124, U.S.A.

JOHNSON, William Stacy. American, b. 1956. **Genres:** Theology/Religion. **Career:** Austin Presbyterian Theological Seminary, Austin, TX, associate professor of theology, 1992-. Attorney at law. **Publications:** (ed.) H.R. Niebuhr, Theology, History, and Culture, 1996; The Mystery of God: Karl Barth and the Postmodern Foundations of Theology, 1997. **Address:** Princeton Theological Seminary, 64 Mercer St, PO Box 821, Princeton, NJ 08542-0821, U.S.A.

JOHNSTON, Alan (William). British, b. 1942. **Genres:** Archaeology/Antiquities. **Career:** Reader, Dept. of Greek and Roman Archaeology, University College London. Assistant Lecturer, Dept. of Classics, University College, Dublin, Ireland, 1969-72. Member of Council, Society for the Promotion of Hellenic Studies, 1976-79, 1983-86, and 1989-92. **Publications:** The Emergence of Greece, 1976; Trademarks on Greek Vases, 1980. **Address:** Dept. of Greek and Roman Archaeology, University College, Gower St, London WC1E 6BT, England.

JOHNSTON, Barbara Rose. American, b. 1957. **Genres:** Environmental sciences/Ecology. **Career:** County of Santa Clara, CA, environmental planner, 1978-80; Territorial Government of the U.S. Virgin Islands, Charlotte Amalie, environmental planner and consultant on community development and the environment, 1980-87; California State University, Sacramento, lecturer in environmental studies, 1988-90; Simon Fraser University, Burnaby, British Columbia, adjunct professor and visiting lecturer in anthropology, 1990-91; Center for Political Ecology, Santa Cruz, CA, research associate, 1991-. Archaeologist; conducted field research in the Caribbean, British Columbia, and western United States; consultant on cultural resource management. **Publications:** (ed. and contrib.) Who Pays the Price? The Sociocultural Context of Environmental Crisis, 1994. Contributor of articles and reviews to anthropology and environmental studies journals. **Address:** Center for Political Ecology, P.O. Box 84647, Santa Cruz, CA 95061, U.S.A.

JOHNSTON, George (Benson). Canadian, b. 1913. **Genres:** Poetry, Translations. **Career:** Professor Emeritus of English, Carleton University, Ottawa (joined faculty, 1950). Assistant Professor of English, Mount Allison University, Sackville, New Brunswick, 1946-48. **Publications:** The Cruising Auk, 1959; (trans.) The Saga of Gisli, 1963; Home Free, 1966; Happy Enough, 1972; (trans.) The Faroe Islander's Saga, 1975; (trans.) The Greenlander's Saga, 1976; Between, 1977; Taking a Grip, 1978; (trans.) Rocky Shores, 1981; Auk Redivivus, 1981; (trans.) Wind Over Romsdal, 1982; Ask Again, 1984; (trans.) Pastor Bodvar's Letter, 1985; Carl: Portrait of a Painter, 1986; (trans.) Seeing and Remembering, 1988; (trans.) Bee-Buzz, Salmon-Leap, 1988; Endeared by Dark: The Collected Poems, 1990; (trans.) Barbara; (trans.) Thrand of Gotu; What Is To Come (poems). **Address:** 27 Henderson, PO Box 1706, Huntingdon, QC, Canada J0S 1H0.

JOHNSTON, Jennifer. Irish, b. 1930. **Genres:** Novels, Plays/Screenplays. **Publications:** The Captains and the Kings, 1972; The Gates, 1973; How Many Miles to Babylon?, 1974; Shadows on Our Skin, 1977; The Old Jest, 1979; The Christmas Tree, 1981; The Nightingale and Not the Lark (play), 1981; The Railway Station Man, 1984; Fool's Sanctuary, 1987; The Invisible Man (play) 1987; Tryptich (play), 1988; O, Ananias, Azarias and Mivael (play), 1989; The Invisible Worm 1991; The Illusionist (monologues), 1995; The Desert Lullaby (play), 1996. **Address:** Brook Hall, Culmore Rd, Derry BT48 8JE, Northern Ireland.

JOHNSTON, Joan. American, b. 1948. **Genres:** Westerns/Adventure, Romance/Historical. **Career:** Weekly Herald, San Antonio, TX, news editor and drama critic, 1971-73; Southwest Texas Junior College, Uvalde, director of theater, 1973-77; Hunton & Williams, Richmond, VA, attorney, 1980-83; Squire, Sanders & Dempsey, Miami, FL, attorney, 1983-85; Barry University, Miami Shores, FL, instructor, 1985-88; University of Miami, Coral Gables, FL, assistant professor, 1988-91; writer, 1991-. Florida Bar, member; Virginia Bar, associate. **Publications:** NOVELS: The Cowboy, 2000; The Texan, 2001; The Loner, 2002; Sisters Found, 2002. ROMANCE NOVELS: A Loving Defiance, 1985; Colter's Wife, 1986; Frontier Woman, 1988; Fit to Be Tied, 1988; Comanche Woman, 1989; Texas Woman, 1989; Marriage by the Book, 1989; Sweetwater Seduction, 1991; Never Tease a Wolf, 1991; A Wolf in Sheep's Clothing, 1991; The Barefoot Bride, 1992; A Little Time in Texas, 1992; Honey and the Hired Hand, 1992; Kid Calhoun, 1992; Outlaw's Bride, 1993; The Rancher and the Runaway Bride, 1993; The Cowboy and the Princess, 1993; The Wrangler and the Rich Girl, 1993; The Cowboy

Takes a Wife, 1994; The Unforgiving Bride, 1994; The Headstrong Bride, 1994; The Inheritance, 1995; The Disobedient Bride, 1995; Maverick Heart, 1995; Captive, 1996; After the Kiss, 1997; The Bodyguard, 1998; The Bridegroom, 1999. Work represented in anthologies. **Address:** c/o Robert Gottlieb, Trident Media Group, LLC, 41 Madison Ave., New York, NY 10010-2202, U.S.A.

JOHNSTON, Joni E. American, b. 1960. **Genres:** Psychology, How-to books. **Career:** West Side Veterans Administration Medical Center, Chicago, IL, intern in clinical psychology and neuropsychology, 1984-85; Dallas Child Guidance Clinic, Dallas, TX, staff psychologist, 1985-87; clinical psychologist in private practice, 1987-. Growth Co., Dallas, founder, 1991, professional speaker and consultant, 1991-. Hawthorne College, associate professor, 1984; University of Texas at Dallas, adjunct professor, 1992-; guest on television and radio shows; sexual harassment expert witness. **Publications:** Appearance Obsession: Learning to Love the Way You Look, 1994; How Hearts Heal: Lessons of Hope and Courage Therapists Have Learned from Their Clients, in press. Contributor to magazines. **Address:** 1940 Seaview Ave., Del Mar, CA 92014-2228, U.S.A.

JOHNSTON, Julie. Canadian, b. 1941. **Genres:** Young adult fiction, Plays/Screenplays, Young adult non-fiction. **Career:** Occupational therapist at a school for mentally handicapped children, Smith's Falls, ON, 1963-65; Rehabilitation Centre, Kingston, ON, occupational therapist, 1965-69. Peterborough Board of Education, Continuing Education Department, creative writing instructor, 1988-89. **Publications:** PLAYS: There's Going to Be a Frost, 1980; Lucid Intervals, 1984. FOR YOUNG ADULT NOVELS: Hero of Lesser Causes, 1992; Adam and Eve and Pinch-Me, 1994; The Only Outcast, 1998; In Spite of Killer Bees, 2001. NONFICTION: (ed.) Love Ya Like a Sister, 1999. Contributor to periodicals. **Address:** 463 Hunter St W, Peterborough, ON, Canada K9H 2M7. **Online address:** julie.johnston@ sympatico.ca

JOHNSTON, Marguerite. American, b. 1917. **Genres:** History. **Career:** Birmingham News, Birmingham, AL, reporter, 1939-44, Washington correspondent, 1945-46; Houston Post, Houston, TX, columnist, 1947-69, foreign news editor and member of editorial board, 1969-, associate editor of editorial page, 1972-77, assistant editor of editorial page, 1977-85. Washington correspondent for Birmingham Age-Herald and London Daily Mirror, both 1945-46. University of Houston, instructor in creative writing, 1946-47, lecturer in feature writing, 1965-66; lecturer at Baker College and Rice University, 1977-78; public speaker. **Publications:** A Happy Worldly Abode: Christ Church Cathedral, 1839-1964, 1964; Houston: The Unknown City, 1991. **Address:** 2929 Buffalo Speedway, Houston, TX 77098, U.S.A.

JOHNSTON, Marilyn. American, b. 1942. **Genres:** Education. **Career:** Ohio State University, Columbus, faculty member. **Publications:** Contradictions in Collaboration: New Thinking on School/University Partnerships, 1997; (ed. with P. Brosnan, D. Cramer, and T. Dove, and contrib) Collaborative Reform and Other Improbable Dreams: Professional Development Schools at the Ohio State University, in press. Contributor to books. Contributor of articles and reviews to academic journals. **Address:** 40 Smith Pl., Columbus, OH 43201, U.S.A.

JOHNSTON, Michael. American, b. 1974. **Genres:** Autobiography/Memoirs. **Career:** Author and educator. **Publications:** The Deep Heart's Core, 2002. **Address:** c/o Sterling Lord, Sterling Lord Literistic, 65 Bleeker St., New York, NY 10012, U.S.A. **Online address:** deepheartscore@hotmail.com

JOHNSTON, R(onald) J(ohn). British, b. 1941. **Genres:** Geography. **Career:** Monash University, Australia, teaching fellow, 1964, sr. teaching fellow, 1965, lecturer, 1966; University of Canterbury, New Zealand, lecturer, 1967-69, sr. lecturer, 1969-72, reader, 1972-74; University of Sheffield, professor of geography, 1974-92; University of Essex, vice-chancellor, 1992-95; University of Bristol, professor of geography, 1995-. Institute of British Geographers, secretary, 1982-85, president, 1990; editor: Environment and Planning A, and Progress in Human Geography. **Publications:** (co) Retailing in Melbourne, 1969; Urban Residential Patterns, 1971; (ed.) Urbanization in New Zealand, 1973; Spatial Structures, 1973; (ed.) Society and Environment in New Zealand, 1974; The World Trade System, 1976; The New Zealanders, 1976; (co-ed.) Social Areas in Cities, 3 vols., 1976-78; (co) Geography and Inequality, 1977; Multivariate Statistical Analysis in Geography, 1978; (co-ed.) Geography and the Urban Environment (annual), 1978; (with P.J. Taylor) Geography of Elections, 1979; Political, Electoral and Spatial Systems, 1979; Geography and Geographers, 1979, 5th ed., 1997; City and Society, 1980; The American Urban System, 1982; Geography and the State, 1982;

Philosophy and Human Geography, 1983; Residential Segregation: The State and Constitutional Conflict in American Urban Areas, 1984; The Geography of English Politics, 1985; On Human Geography, 1986; Bellringing, 1986; A Nation Dividing?, 1988; Environmental Problems, 1989; An Atlas of Bells, 1990; A Question of Place, 1991; Nature, State and Economy, 1996; The Boundary Commissions, 1999; From Votes to Seats, 2001. **Address:** School of Geographical Sciences, University of Bristol, Bristol BS8 1SS, England. **Online address:** R.Johnston@bristol.ac.uk

JOHNSTON, Richard. Canadian, b. 1948. **Genres:** Politics/Government. **Career:** University of Toronto, ON, assistant professor of political science, 1975-77; University of British Columbia, Vancouver, assistant professor to professor of political science, 1977-86; Harvard University, Mackenzie King Professor of Canadian Studies, 1994-95. **Publications:** Public Opinion and Public Policy in Canada, 1986; (with A. Blais, H.E. Brady, and J. Crete) Letting the People Decide, 1992; (with Blais, E. Gidengil, and N. Nevitte) The Challenge of Direct Democracy, 1996. **Address:** Department of Political Science, University of British Columbia, C472-1866 Main Mall, Vancouver, BC, Canada V6T 1Z1. **Online address:** rjohnstn@interchange.ubc.ca

JOHNSTON, Ronald. Also writes as Mark Nelson. British (born Scotland), b. 1926. **Genres:** Novels. **Career:** Master Mariner, Merchant Marine, 1942-47, 1951-59, 1975-80; Associate, Chartered Insurance Institute; with Manufacturers Life Insurance of Canada, 1947-51; Salesman, General Manager then Director, Anglo-Dutch Cigar Co. Ltd., 1959-68; Boston University, Mugar Memorial Library Special Collections, archival material, 1964-; Managing Partner, Dunswood Products, 1982-. Member, Mgmt. Committee, Society of Authors, 1970-75; Council Member, Scottish Arts Council, 1973-75. **Publications:** Disaster at Dungeness (in U.S. as Collision Ahead), 1964; Red Sky in the Morning (in U.S. as Danger at Bravo Key), 1965; The Stowaway, 1966; The Wrecking of Offshore Five, 1967; The Angry Ocean, 1968; The Black Camels of Qahran (in U.S. as The Black Camels), 1969; Paradise Smith, 1972; The Eye of the Needle, 1975; (as Mark Nelson) The Crusoe Test, 1976; Sea Story, 1980; Flying Dutchman, 1983. **Address:** Manderston Mill, Duns, Berwickshire TD11 3PP, Scotland.

JOHNSTON, Stanley H(oward), Jr. American, b. 1946. **Genres:** History, Horticulture, Bibliography. **Career:** University of Western Ontario, London, assistant to the editor of Spenser Newsletter, 1972-73; Holden Arboretum, Mentor, OH, bibliographer for Cleveland Herbals Project, a joint effort of the Arboretum, Cleveland Medical Library Association, and Garden Center of Greater Cleveland, 1984-90, curator of rare books, 1989-. **Publications:** The Cleveland Herbal, Botanical, and Horticultural Collections, 1992; Cleveland's Treasures from the World of Botanical Literature, 1998. **Address:** The Holden Arboretum, 9500 Sperry Rd, Kirtland, OH 44094, U.S.A. **Online address:** stanley177@aol.com

JOHNSTON, William Murray. American, b. 1936. **Genres:** History, Theology/Religion. **Career:** University of Massachusetts, Amherst, assistant professor, 1965-70, associate professor, 1970-75, professor of history, 1975-99. **Publications:** The Formative Years of R.G. Collingwood, 1967; The Austrian Mind: An Intellectual and Social History 1848-1938, 1972; Vienna, Vienna, 1981; In Search of Italy: Foreign Writers in Northern Italy since 1800, 1987; Celebrations: The Cult of Anniversaries in Europe and the United States Today, 1991; Recent Reference Books in Religion, 1996; (ed.) The Encyclopedia of Monasticism, 2000. **Address:** 369 Rae St, Fitzroy North, VIC 3068, Australia.

JOHNSTONE, Nick. American, b. 1970. **Genres:** Autobiography/Memoirs. **Career:** Journalist and author. Writer for the Guardian and Observer newspapers, London, England. **Publications:** Radiohead: An Illustrated Biography, 1997; Patti Smith: A Biography, 1997; Melody Maker History of Twentieth-Century Popular Music, 1999; Abel Ferrara: The King of New York, 1999; Sean Penn: A Biography, 2000; A Head Full of Blue (autobiography), 2002. **Address:** Guardian/Observer, 119 Farringdon Rd., London EC1R 3ER, England.

JOLAOSO. See SEGUN, Mabel D(orothy Aig-Imoukhuede).

JOLLES, Michael Adam. British, b. 1951. **Genres:** History, Biography. **Career:** Medical Practitioner in London; Jewish Historical Society of England, Council Member. **Publications:** The Northampton Jewish Cemetery, 1994; A Short History of the Jews of Northampton, 1159-1996, 1996; Samuel Isaac, Saul Isaac and Nathaniel Isaacs, 1998; Report of the Discovery of a Medieval Decorated Stone Capital at Lochstadt, 1999; The Chatham Hebrew Society Synagogue Ledger, 1839-1865, 2000; Jews and the Carlton Club, 2002; A Directory of Distinguished British Jews, 1830-1930 with selected Compilations Extending from 1830 to 2000, 2002. **Address:** 78 Greenfield Gardens, London NW2 1HY, England.

JOLLEY, (Monica) Elizabeth. Australian (born England), b. 1923. **Genres:** Novels, Novellas/Short stories. **Career:** Part-time Tutor in English, Fremantle Arts Centre, Western Australia, since 1974. Writer-in-Residence, The Curtin University of Technology Perth (formerly Western Australian Institute of Technology), Bentley, since 1982. **Publications:** NOVELS: Palomino, 1980; The Newspaper of Claremont Street, 1981; Mr. Scobie's Riddle, 1983; Miss Peabody's Inheritance, 1983; Milk and Honey, 1984; Foxybaby, 1985; The Well, 1986; The Sugar Mother, 1988; My Father's Moon, 1989; Cabin Fever, 1990; The Georges' Wife, 1993; The Orchard Thieves, 1995. STORIES: Five Acre Virgin and Other Stories, 1976; The Travelling Entertainer and Other Stories, 1979; Woman in a Lampshade (short story), 1983; Stories, 1984. OTHER: Central Mischief (autobiographical essays), 1992; Diary of a Weekend Farmer (diary and poems), 1993; Off the Air: 9 Radio Plays, 1995. **Address:** 28 Agett Rd, Claremont, WA 6010, Australia.

JOLLY, Roslyn. Australian, b. 1963. **Genres:** Literary criticism and history. **Career:** University of Newcastle, NSW, Australia, lecturer in English, 1990-94; University of New South Wales, Sydney, Australia, lecturer, 1994-96, senior lecturer in English, 1997-. **Publications:** Henry James: History, Narrative, Fiction, 1993. EDITOR: R.L. Stevenson, South Sea Tales, 1996; F. Van de Grift Stevenson, The Cruise of the "Janet Nichol" among the South Sea Islands, 2003. **Address:** School of English, University of New South Wales, Sydney, NSW 2052, Australia. **Online address:** r.jolly@unsw.edu.au

JOLOWICZ, J(ohn) A(nthony). British, b. 1926. **Genres:** Law. **Career:** Fellow, Trinity College, Cambridge University, 1952- (Assistant Lecturer, 1955-59, Lecturer, 1959-72, Reader, 1972-76, and Professor of Comparative Law, 1976-93). Ed., Journal of Society of Public Teachers of Law, 1962-80. Queen's Counsel, 1990; Chevalier de la Legion d'honneur. **Publications:** (ed.) H. F. Jolowicz's Lectures on Jurisprudence, 1963; Winfield and Jolowicz on Tort, 1971, 16th ed. (by W.V.H. Rogers), 2002; (with M. Cappelletti) Public Interest Parties and the Active Role of the Judge, 1975; (with others) Droit Anglais, 1986, 2nd ed., 1992; (with others) Recourse against Judgments in the European Union, 1999; On Civil Procedure, 2000. Contributor to legal journals, English and foreign. **Address:** Trinity College, Cambridge CB2 1TQ, England.

JONAITIS, Aldona. American, b. 1948. **Genres:** Natural history, Art/Art history, Anthropology/Ethnology. **Career:** State University of New York at Stony Brook, assistant professor to professor, 1976-89, associate provost of the university, 1984-86, vice-provost for undergraduate studies, 1986-89; American Museum of Natural History, NYC, vice-president for public programs, 1989-93; University of Alaska Museum, director, 1993-. **Publications:** Art of the Northern Tlingit, 1986; From the Land of the Totem Poles, 1988; (ed.) Chiefly Feasts: The Enduring Kwakiutl Potlatch, 1991; A Wealth of Thought: Franz Boas and Native American Art, 1993. **Address:** University of Alaska Museum, 907 Yukon Drive, Fairbanks, AK 99775, U.S.A.

JONAS, Ann. American, b. 1932. **Genres:** Children's fiction. **Career:** Rudolph de Harak, Inc. (design company), New York City, designer, 1959-62; Advertis, Inc. (advertising agency), Frankfurt, Germany, designer, 1962-63; Donald & Ann Crews (design company), New York City, designer, 1964-; author and illustrator of children's books, 1981-. **Publications:** SELF-ILLUSTRATED FOR CHILDREN: When You Were a Baby, 1982; Two Bear Cubs, 1982; Round Trip, 1983; Holes and Peeks, 1984; The Quilt, 1984; The Trek, 1985; Now We Can Go, 1986; Where Can It Be?, 1986; Reflections, 1987; Color Dance, 1989; Aardvarks, Disembark, 1990; The 13th Clue, 1992; Splash!, 1995; Watch William Walk, 1997; Bird Talk, 1999. **Address:** c/o Greenwillow Books, 1350 Avenue of the Americas, New York, NY 10019, U.S.A.

JONAS, Manfred. American (born Germany), b. 1927. **Genres:** History, International relations/Current affairs. **Career:** John Bigelow Professor of History, Union College, Schenectady, NY, 1986-, now emeritus (Assistant to Associate Professor, 1963-67; Professor, 1967-81; Washington Irving Professor in Modern Literary and Historical Studies, 1981-86). Visiting Professor in American History, Freie University, Berlin, 1959-62; Associate Professor of History, Widener College, Chester, PA, 1962-63; Dr. Otto Salgo Visiting Professor of American Studies, Eotvos Lorand University, Budapest, 1983-84. **Publications:** Isolationism in America, 1935-1941, 1966, rev. ed., 1990; The United States and Germany: A Diplomatic History, 1984. EDITOR: Die Unabhangigkeitserklarung der Vereinigten Staaten, 1965; American Foreign Relations in the Twentieth Century, 1967; (with F.L. Loewenheim and H.D. Langley) Roosevelt and Churchill: Their Secret Wartime Correspondence,

1975, rev. ed., 1990; (with R.V. Wells) New Opportunities in a New Nation: The Development of New York after the Revolution, 1982. **Address:** Dept. of History, Union College, Schenectady, NY 12308, U.S.A.

JONAS, Susan. American, b. 1938. **Genres:** Antiques/Furnishings. **Career:** Time Inc., NYC, secretary for Time magazine, deputy picture editor of Time, picture editor of Discover, 1961-87; freelance writer. **Publications:** WITH M. NISSENSON: Cuff Links, 1991; The Ubiquitous Pig, 1992; Going, Going, Gone: Vanishing Americana, 1994; Snake-Charm, 1995; Friends for Life, 19976; Jewelled Bugs and Butterflies, 2000. **Address:** 450 West End Ave, New York, NY 10024-5343, U.S.A.

JONASDOTTIR, Anna G(udrun). Icelander, b. 1942. **Genres:** Politics/Government, Sociology, Women's studies and issues. **Career:** Taught courses and lectured in sociology, politics, and women's studies, beginning in 1973; Orebro University, Sweden, senior lecturer in politics, 1986-2000, professor of women's studies, 2000-; University of Gothenburg, Sweden, affiliated with women's studies and political science departments. **Publications:** Why Women Are Oppressed, 1994. EDITOR: (with K.B. Jones), The Political Interests of Gender, 1988; (with D. von der Fehr and B. Rosenbeck) Is There a Nordic Feminism?, 1998. **Address:** Department of Social and Political Sciences, Orebro University, SE-701 82 Orebro, Sweden.

JONELL, Lynne. American. **Genres:** Children's fiction. **Career:** Writer. **Publications:** JUVENILE FICTION: Mommy Go Away!, 1997; I Need a Snake, 1998; It's My Birthday, Too!, Putnam, 1999. **Address:** c/o Putnam, 375 Hudson St., New York, NY 10014, U.S.A.

JONES, Alan Griffith. British, b. 1943. **Genres:** Language/Linguistics, Travel/Exploration. **Career:** Adviser, Parbeck Citizens' Advice Bureau, 1999-. Principal Lecturer, University of Hertfordshire, 1985-97 (Lecturer, 1968-72; Sr. Lecturer, 1973-82; Head of German Centre, 1973-89). Hon. Ed., Treffpunkt, 1977-86; Hon. Ed., German Teaching, 1991-94. **Publications:** The Germans: An Englishman's Notebook, 1968; This Is Germany, 1980; (co-author) Practice in German Grammar, 1992, 2nd ed., 2001; Chapters in Open University German courses, 1998, 1999. EDITOR/CO-EDITOR: Anglo-German Songbook, 1968; Deutsche Schuler in England, 1972; British Teenagers on the Rhine, 1975; A Handbook of Information for Teachers of German, 1979; German in the Classroom, 1984; Wende 89, 1992; Aspekte deutscher Gegenwart, 1999. **Address:** 17 Bay Crescent, Swsanage, Dorset BH19 1RB, England.

JONES, Alex S. American, b. 1946. **Genres:** Writing/Journalism, Biography. **Career:** Daily Post-Athenian, Athens, TN, managing editor, 1974-78; Greeneville Sun, Greeneville, TN, editor, 1978-83; New York Times, media reporter, 1983-92; WNYC-AM, New York City Public Radio, On the Media radio programming, host, 1993; PBS, Media Matters, host & exec. ed., 1996-; Duke University, Eugene Patterson professor of journalism, 1998-2000; Harvard University, Shorenstein Center on the Press, Politics & Public Policy, director, 2000-. Pulitzer Prize, 1987. **Publications:** (with S.E. Tifft) The Patriarch: The Rise and Fall of the Bingham Dynasty, 1991; (with Tifft) The Trust: The Private and Powerful Family behind the New York Times, 1999. **Address:** c/o Kathy Robbins, Robbins Office Inc, 405 Park Ave 9th Fl, New York, NY 10022, U.S.A. **Online address:** jonesalex@aol.com

JONES, Allan Frewin. Also writes as Steven Saunders, Fiona Kelly, Michael Coleman. British, b. 1954. **Genres:** Young adult fiction. **Publications:** FOR YOUNG ADULTS. FICTION: The Mole and Beverley Miller, 1987; The Cost of Going Free, 1988; Rabbit Back and Doubled, 1989; Bad Penny, 1990; Millions of Lisa, 1990; The Half-Good Samaritan, 1991; Tommy and the Sloth, 1992; Wishing Bird & Co, 1993; Burning Issues, 1994. STACEY & FRIENDS SERIES: The Great Sister War, 1998; Pippa's Problem Page, 1998; My Sister, My Slave, 1998; My Real Best Friend, 1998; Stacy the Matchmaker, 1998; The New Guy, 1998; Copycat, 1998; Party Time, 1998; Sneaking Out, 1998; Scary Sleepover, 1998; Sister Switch, 1999; Fern Flips, 1999; Full House, 1999; You Look Great!, 1999; Bad Boy, 1999; The New Stacy!, 1999; Pippa on Air, 1999; Dream Sister, 1999. THE HUNTER & MOON MYSTERIES: The Weird Eyes File, 1997; The Alien Fire File, 1997; The Skull Stone File, 1997; The Time Traveller File, 1988; The Thunderbolt File, 1998; The Star Ship File, 1998. DARK PATH SERIES: The Wicker Man, 1998; The Plague Pit, 1998; Unquiet Graves, 1999; The Phantom Pilot, 1999; The Wreckers, 1999; Blood Stone, 1999; The Monk's Curse, 1999; Ghostlight, 1999. FOR CHILDREN: Anna's Birthday Adventure, 1997; Meerkat in Trouble, 1998. OTHER: (with L. Pollinger) Teach Yourself Writing Children's Books, 1997. AS FIONA KELLY. THE MYSTERY CLUB SERIES: Secret Clues, 1993; Dangerous Tricks, 1993; Hide & Seek, 1994; Secret Treasure, 1994; Crossed Line, 1994; Crash Landing, 1995; Poison!, 1995; Out of Control, 1995; The Secret Room, 1995. THE MYSTERY KIDS SERIES: Spy-catchers, 1995; The Empty House, 1995; Blackmail!, 1996; Hostage!, 1996. AS MICHAEL COLEMAN: Virus Attack, 1997; Access Denied, 1997. AS STEVEN SAUNDERS: Dark Secrets, Red Ink, 1988; Kisschase, 1989; Blind Ally, 1989. **Address:** c/o Laurence Pollinger Ltd., 9 Staple Inn, London WC1V 7QH, England. **Online address:** AllanFrewin@tesco.net

JONES, Amelia. American, b. 1961. **Genres:** Art/Art history. **Career:** Art Center College of Design, Pasadena, CA, instructor and adviser, 1990-91; University of Southern California, Los Angeles, instructor in art history, 1992; Frame-Work, executive editor, 1995-98; University of California, Riverside, assistant professor 1991-96, associate professor of 20th-century art and theory, 1996-99, professor, 1999-. Curator of exhibitions at California Museum of Photography and Armand Hammer Museum of Art. **Publications:** Postmodernism and the En-Gendering of Marcel Duchamp, 1994; Body Art/Performing the Subject, 1998; (co-ed.) Performing the Body, Performing the Text, 1999. Work represented in anthologies. Contributor of articles and reviews to art and history journals. **Address:** 339 S Orange Dr, Los Angeles, CA 90036-3008, U.S.A. **Online address:** jonessher@aol.com

JONES, Ann (Maret). American, b. 1937. **Genres:** Criminology/True Crime, Travel/Exploration, Women's studies and issues. **Career:** City College of New York, assistant professor of English, 1970-73; University of Massachusetts, Amherst, assistant professor of English and coordinator of women's studies, 1973-75; free-lance writer, NYC, 1975-; Mount Holyoke College, South Hadley, MA, member of writing faculty, 1986-97. **Publications:** Uncle Tom's Campus, 1973; Women Who Kill, 1980, rev. ed., 1981; Everyday Death: The Case of Bernadette Powell, 1985; (with S. Schechter) When Love Goes Wrong: What to Do When You Can't Do Anything Right, 1992; Next Time, She'll Be Dead: Battering and How to Stop It, 1994, rev. ed., 2000; Looking for Lovedu, 2001. Contributor of articles and reviews to periodicals.

JONES, Brennon. American, b. 1945. **Genres:** Writing/Journalism. **Career:** Free-lance journalist, 1968-79; CBS-TV, New York City, researcher and reporter, 1971-72; Interlink Press Service, executive editor, 1979-86; William Collins Publishers, Inc., NYC, managing editor, 1986-87; Jones & Janello, NYC, partner and editor, 1987-. **Publications:** EDITOR WITH A. JANELLO: (and contrib.) The American Magazine, 1991; Essential Liberty: First Amendment Battles for a Free Press, 1992; USSR: The Collapse of an Empire, 1992; I Dream of Peace, 1994; Golf-The Greatest Game, 1994.

JONES, Bridget. Welsh, b. 1955. **Genres:** Food and Wine. **Career:** Hamlyn Test Kitchen, assistant home economist, 1978-80, home economist, 1980-81; Hamlyn Publishing, staff member in cookery editorial department, associate editor, 1981-84, deputy editor, 1984-85, cookery editor, 1985-88; free-lance writer and editor, 1988-. Guest on radio and television programs. **Publications:** Fred's Pastry Book, 1981; Contact Grill, 1982; Jams, Pickles, and Chutneys, 1983; Gale's Honey Book, 1983; Cooking with a Wok, 1984; Meals in Minutes, 1984; Complete Mince Cookbook, 1985; Making the Most of Your Microwave, 1985; Seasonal Cookery, 1986; Combination Microwave Cookbook, 1987; High Speed Food (juvenile), 1987; Microwave Tips and Timings, 1989; Barbecue Tips and Timings, 1990; Recipes from a Polish Kitchen, 1990; Kid's Cookbook, 1990; Does It Freeze?, 1991; Cooking and Kitchen Skills, 1991; Stir Fry Cooking, 1992; Diabetic Cookbook, 1992; The Quilting and Patchwork Project Book, 1992; Fresh Pasta Cookbook, 1993; Encyclopedia of Pasta, 1994; Book of Claypot Cooking, 1996; Mrs. Beeton's Christmas Menus, 1997; Le Cordon Bleu Dessert Techniques, 1999; Farmer's Market Guide to Vegetables, 2001. EDITOR: Mrs. Beeton's Complete Book of Fish and Seafood Cookery, 1992; The Book of Cookery and Household Management, 1992. Author of volumes in Checkpoint Books cookbook series. Contributor to magazines. **Address:** 88 High View Rd, Guildford, Surrey GU2 5RY, England.

JONES, Bryan D(avidson). American, b. 1944. **Genres:** Politics/Government. **Career:** University of Houston, Houston, TX, assistant professor of political science, 1970-71; Wayne State University, Detroit, MI, 1972-85, assistant professor to professor of political science and chair of department; Texas A&M University, College Station, professor of political science and head of department, 1985-96, Puryear Professor of Liberal Arts, 1991; University of Washington, professor, 1996-; writer. **Publications:** Service Delivery in the City, 1980; Governing Urban America, 1983; Governing Buildings and Building Government: A New Perspective on the Old Party, 1985; (with L.W. Bachelor and C. Wilson) The Sustaining Hand: Community Leadership and Corporate Power, 1986, 2nd ed, 1993; (with F. Baumgartner) Agendas and Instability in American Politics, 1993; Reconceiv-

ing Decision-Making in Democratic Politics, 1994. EDITOR: Leadership and Politics: New Perspectives in Political Science, 1989; The New American Politics, 1995. **Address:** 2361 West Briargate, Bryan, TX 77802, U.S.A.

JONES, Caroly. American, b. 1941. **Genres:** Travel/Exploration. **Career:** Writer. **Publications:** The Frugal Traveler. Contributor to periodicals. **Address:** HC 61, Box 5040, Ramah, NM 87321, U.S.A.

JONES, Charlotte Foltz. American, b. 1945. **Genres:** Young adult nonfiction, Children's non-fiction, Technology, Food and Wine, History. **Career:** Boulder Valley Public Schools, Boulder, CO, secretary, 1966-75; free-lance writer, 1976-. Writing instructor, Boulder Valley Schools Lifelong Learning, 1990-, and Boulder Senior Center, 1991. **Publications:** Only Child: Clues for Coping, 1984; Mistakes That Worked: 40 Familiar Inventions and How They Came to Be, 1991; Colorado Wildflowers: A Beginner's Field Guide to the State's Most Common Flowers, 1994; Accidents May Happen: Fifty Inventions Discovered by Mistake, 1996; Fingerprints and Talking Bones: How Real-Life Crimes Are Solved, 1997; Yukon Gold: The Story of the Klondike Gold Rush, 1999; Eat Your Words: A Fascinating Look at the Language of Food, 1999. Contributor to magazines.

JONES, Constance. American, b. 1961. **Genres:** History. **Career:** Writer. **Publications:** (with D.L. Raper and J.J. Sbrega) The American Experience: Documents and Notes, 1985; Karen Horney, 1989; Pasta, 1990, enlarged as Pasta: Sauces and Fillings for All Shapes and Sizes, 1993; (with D.L. Rapper) A Goodly Heritage: The Episcopal Diocese of Southern Virginia, 1992; Africa, 15001900, 1993; The European Conquest of North America, 1995; Trailblazers: The Men and Women Who Forged the West, 1995; Sexual Harassment, 1996. **Address:** c/o Author Mail, 7th Fl, HarperCollins Publishers, 10 E 53rd St, New York, NY 10022, U.S.A.

JONES, D(ouglas) G(ordon). Canadian, b. 1929. **Genres:** Poetry, Literary criticism and history, Translations. **Career:** University of Sherbrooke, QC, English Dept., Professor Titulaire, now retired. (joined faculty, 1963). **Publications:** POETRY: Frost on the Sun, 1957; Sun Is Axeman, 1961; Phrases from Orpheus, 1967; Under the Thunder, the Flowers Light Up the Earth, 1977; A Throw of Particles, 1983; Balthazar and Other Poems, 1988; The Floating Garden, 1995; Wild Asterisks in Cloud, 1997; Grounding Sight, 1999. TRANSLATOR: P.M. Lapointe, The Terror of the Snows, 1976; Categorics, 1992; E. Martel, For Orchestra & Solo Poet, 1996. OTHER: Butterfly on Rock: A Study of Themes and Images in Canadian Literature, 1970. **Address:** 120 Houghton St, North Hatley, QC, Canada J0B 2C0.

JONES, D. S. British, b. 1922. **Genres:** Information science/Computers, Physics. **Career:** Massachusetts Institute of Technology, fellow, 1947-48; Victoria University of Manchester, England, assistant lecturer to senior lecturer, 1948-57; New York University, research professor, 1955, 1962-63; University of Keele, England, professor, 1957-64; University of Dundee, Scotland, Ivory Professor of mathematics and computer science, 1965-92, professor emeritus, 1992-, member of grants committee, 1976-86. Associate editor, Journal of the Institute of Mathematics and Its Applications, 1964-, Proceedings of the Royal Society of Edinburgh, 1969-82, SIAM Journal of Applied Mathematics, 1975-92, Applicable Analysis, 1976-92, Mathematical Methods in the Applied Sciences, 1977-2002, Proceedings of the Royal Society, 1978-83, Methods and Applications of Analysis, 1992-, Journal of Engineering Mathematics, 1992-, and Communications in Applied Analysis, 1997-; trustee, Quarterly Journal of Mechanics and Applied Mathematics, 1980-92. **Publications:** Electrical and Mechanical Oscillations, 1961; Theory of Electromagnetism, 1964; Generalised Functions, 1966; (with D.W. Jordan) Introductory Analysis, Vol. I, 1969, Vol. II, 1970; Methods in Electromagnetic Wave Propagation, 1979, 2nd ed., 1994; Elementary Information Theory, 1979; The Theory of Generalised Functions, 1982; (with B.D. Sleeman) Differential Equations and Mathematical Biology, 1983; Acoustic and Electromagnetic Waves, 1986; Assembly Programming and the 8086 Microprocessor, 1988; 80x86 Assembly Programming, 1991; Introduction to Asymptotics, 1997. **Address:** 1 The Nurseries, St. Madoes, Glencarse, Perth PH2 7NX, Scotland.

JONES, Daryl (Emrys). American, b. 1946. **Genres:** Literary criticism and history, Poetry. **Career:** Texas Tech University, Lubbock, assistant professor, 1973-79, associate professor, 1979-82, professor of English and chairman of department, 1982-86; Boise State University, Boise, ID, professor of English and dean, College of Arts and Sciences, 1986-91, provost and vice president for Academic Affairs, 1991-. Member of board of directors, Idaho Humanities Council, 1989-1993; Member of the Texas Institute of Letters; Writer-in-Residence, State of Idaho, 1992-93. **Publications:** The Dime Novel Western,

1978; Someone Going Home Late (poems), 1990. **Address:** Office of the Provost, Boise State University, 1910 University Dr, Boise, ID 83725, U.S.A.

JONES, David (Erik) Hay. British, b. 1959. **Genres:** Travel/Exploration, Business/Trade/Industry, Politics/Government. **Career:** Go For It, London, England, editor, 1982-83; Big Sur, London, editor, 1984-85; Architectural Press, London, sub-editor, 1985-86; Surveyor, Surrey, England, chief sub-editor, 1986-87; Athens News, Athens, Greece, sub-editor, 1987; free-lance writer, 1987-; construction and forestry worker; lumberjack; True North Adventure Holidays, director; Lapland Picture Library, managing director; Survival and Outdoor Techniques Magazine, Scandinavian correspondent, 1991-; Wilderness News, editorial director. The Public Ledger, London, Scandinavian correspondent, 1994-; Chairman, Swedish Conservative Party, Jorrmokk county. **Publications:** Sunday Times Travel Book 1985, 1985; Night Times and Light Times: A Journey through Lapland, 1990; Göra upp eld-berättelser om ett annat Sverige, 1996. **Address:** Box 65, Porjus, 982 60 Lapland, Sweden.

JONES, David Lee. American, b. 1948. **Genres:** Science fiction/Fantasy. **Career:** Applied Magnetics, Goleta, CA, quality engineer, 1973-78; General Dynamics, Goleta, senior quality engineer, 1978-. **Publications:** FANTASY NOVELS: Unicorn Highway, 1992; Zeus and Company, 1993; Montezuma's Pearl, 1995.

JONES, David Martin. Also writes as Jonah M. David. Welsh, b. 1951. **Genres:** Politics/Government. **Career:** Teacher at secondary schools in Brent borough, London, England, 1975-77; Brent Educational Workshop, London, coordinator of truancy project, 1981-88; history teacher and department head at a girls' school in Bushey, England, 1988-90; National University of Singapore, Singapore, lecturer in political science, 1990-95; University of Tasmania, Hobart, Australia, senior lecturer in political theory, 1995-. University of London, teacher at London School of Economics and Political Science, 1984-90, and researcher at Centre for Urban Education, King's College, 1987-90, and visiting fellow in war studies; North East London Polytechnic, teacher fellow, 1986-87. **Publications:** (with D.A. Bell, D. Brown, and K. Jayasuriya) Towards Illiberal Democracy in Pacific Asia, 1995; Political Development in Pacific Asia, 1997; Conscience and Allegiance: The Political Significance of Oaths and Engagements, 1999; The Image of China in Western Social and Political Thought, 2000. Contributor to books. Contributor of articles and reviews to professional journals, popular magazines, and newspapers. **Address:** c/o Author Mail, St. Martin's Press, 175 5th Ave, New York, NY 10010, U.S.A. **Online address:** d.m.jones@utas.edu.au

JONES, David W(yn). Welsh, b. 1950. **Genres:** Music. **Career:** University of Wales, University College Cardiff, Wales, lecturer in music, 1974-95, senior lecturer in music, 1995-2002, reader in music, 2002-. **Publications:** (with H.C. Robbins-Landon) Haydn: His Life and Music, 1988; Beethoven Pastoral Symphony, 1995; (ed.) Music in Eighteenth-Century Austria, 1996; (co-ed. with O. Biba) Studies in Music History Presented to H.C. Robbins Landon on His 70th Birthday, 1996; Life of Beethoven, 1998; Haydn: Oxford Composer Companions, 2002. **Address:** School of Music, Cardiff University, Cardiff CF10 3EB, Wales. **Online address:** jonesdw@cardiff.ac.uk

JONES, Denice. American, b. 1965. **Genres:** Adult non-fiction. **Career:** Crestfield Convalescent Home, Manchester, CT, certified aide, 1981-85; Visiting Nurses of Manchester, Manchester, certified health aide, 1990-93. Author. Founder of Living in Fear Ends Foundation (LIFE Foundation). **Publications:** The Other Side, 2000. **Address:** LIFE Foundation, PO Box 1112, Manchester, CT 06040, U.S.A. **Online address:** dajones1315@aol.com

JONES, (R.) Dennis. Canadian, b. 1945. **Genres:** Novels. **Career:** London Board of Education, London, Ontario, office manager, 1971-85; writer. **Publications:** (as R.D. Jones) Fenris Option, 1981; Rubicon One, 1983; Russian Spring, 1984; Barbarossa Red, 1985; Winter Palace, 1988; Concerto, 1989; The Minstral Boy, 1991; The Stone and the Maiden, 1999; The Mask and the Sorceress, 2001. **Address:** c/o Writers Union of Canada, 40 Wellington St E 3rd Fl, Toronto, ON, Canada M5E 1C7.

JONES, Diana Wynne. British, b. 1934. **Genres:** Novels, Novellas/Short stories, Science fiction/Fantasy, Children's fiction, Young adult fiction, Plays/Screenplays, Animals/Pets, Mythology/Folklore, Humor/Satire. **Career:** Writer. **Publications:** FICTION: Changeover, 1970; Wilkins' Tooth (in US as Witch's Business), 1973; The Ogre Downstairs, 1974; Eight Days of Luke, 1975; Cart and Cwidder, 1975; Dogsbody, 1975; Power of Three, 1976; Charmed Life, 1977; Drowned Ammet, 1977; Who Got Rid of Angus Flint?, 1978; The Spellcoats, 1979; The Magicians of Caprona, 1980; The Four Grannies, 1980; The Homeward Bounders, 1981; The Time of the Ghost, 1981; Witch Week, 1982; The Skiver's Guide, 1984; Archer's Goon, 1984; Warlock at the Wheel, 1984; Fire and Hemlock, 1985; Howl's Moving Castle, 1986; A Tale of Time City, 1987; The Lives of Christopher Chant, 1988; Chair Person, 1989; Castle in the Air, 1990; Black Maria, 1991; Yes Dear, 1992; A Sudden Wild Magic, 1992; Stopping for a Spell, 1993; The Crown of Dalemark, 1993; Hexwood, 1993; Everard's Ride, 1995; The Tough Guide to Fantasyland, 1996; Minor Arcana, 1996; Deep Secret, 1997; The Dark Lord of Derkholm, 1998; Puss in Boots, 1999; Mixed Magics, 2000; Year of the Griffin, 2000; The Marlin Conspiracy, 2003; Conrad's Fate, 2005. PLAYS: The Batterpool Business, 1965; The King's Things, 1968; The Terrible Fisk Machine, 1969. EDITOR: Hidden Turnings, 1989; Fantasy Stories, 1994. **Address:** c/o Laura Cecil, 17 Alwyne Villas, London N1 2HG, England. **Online address:** www.leemac.freeserve.co.uk; www.dianawynnejones.com

JONES, Eileen. British, b. 1952. **Genres:** Biography, Travel/Exploration. **Career:** Worked as staff reporter for Yorkshire Post, England, and Holland Herald, Amsterdam, Netherlands; freelance journalist and writer. **Publications:** Neil Kinnock, 1994; (with others) The Yorkshire Guide, 1994. **Address:** Oakcrest, Heben Bridge, Yorkshire, England.

JONES, Emrys. British (born Wales), b. 1920. **Genres:** Geography, Regional/Urban planning, Social sciences. **Career:** Queen's University, Belfast, lecturer in geography, 1950-59; University of London, professor of geography, 1960-84. **Publications:** Social Geography of Belfast, 1960; Introduction to Human Geography, 1964; Towns and Cities, 1965; (with D.J. Sinclair) Atlas of London and the London Region, 1970; (with E. van Zandt) Cities, 1974; (with J. Eyles) Introduction to Social Geography, 1977; Metropolis, 1990. EDITOR: Belfast in its Regional Setting, 1952; (with R. Buchanan and D. McCourt) Man and His Habitat, 1971; Readings in Social Geography, 1974; Encyclopedia of the World and Its People, 1978; The Welsh in London 1500-2000, 2001. **Address:** 51 Lower Kings Rd, Berkhamsted HP4 2AA, England.

JONES, Evan (Lloyd). Australian, b. 1931. **Genres:** Poetry, Literary criticism and history, Biography. **Career:** Associate of English, University of Melbourne, since 1989 (Tutor, and Sr. Tutor in History, 1955-58; Lecturer in English, 1964; Sr. Lecturer, 1965-89). Lecturer in English, Australian National University, Canberra, 1960-63. **Publications:** Inside the Whale: Poems, 1960; Understandings: Poems, 1967; Kenneth Mackenzie, 1969; (ed. with G. Little) The Poems of Kenneth Mackenzie, 1972; Recognitions: Poems, 1978; Left at the Post, 1984; Alone at Last!, forthcoming. **Address:** PO Box 122, North Carleton, VIC 3054, Australia.

JONES, Frank Lancaster. Australian, b. 1937. **Genres:** Race relations, Sociology. **Career:** Professor and Head Dept. of Sociology, Australian National University, Canberra, since 1972 (Research Assistant in Demography, 1958; Research Scholar in Demography, 1959-62; Research Fellow in Sociology, 1963-66; Fellow in Sociology, 1966-69; Sr. Fellow in Sociology, 1969-72; Acting Head, Dept. of Sociology, 1970-72). Research Officer, Australian Institute of Aboriginal Studies, Canberra, 1962; Executive Member, Sociological Association of Australia and New Zealand, 1965, 1970-73; Ed., Australian and New Zealand Journal of Sociology, 1970-72, 1990-92. **Publications:** A Demographic Survey of the Aboriginal Population of the Northern Territory, with Special Reference to Bathurst Island Mission, 1963; Dimensions of Urban Social Structure: The Social Areas of Melbourne, 1969; (with L. Broom) A Blanket a Year, 1973; (with Broom) Opportunity and Attainment in Australia, 1976; (co-author) Investigating Social Mobility, 1977; (co-author) The Inheritance of Inequality, 1980; (with P. Davis) Models of Society, 1986; Sex and Ethnicity in the Australian Labour Market: The Immigrant Experience, 1992. **Address:** Sociology Program, Australian National University, P. O. Box 4, Canberra, ACT 2600, Australia.

JONES, Frederic J. British, b. 1925. **Genres:** Literary criticism and history, Language/Linguistics, Poetry, Economics, Money/Finance, Sciences. **Career:** British Council, England, courses officer, 1947-49; University of Wales, University College, Cardiff, professor of Italian, 1953-88. **Publications:** (ed. and author of introduction and notes) Andre Gide, Les caves du Vatican, 2nd ed, 1952; A Modern Italian Grammar, 1960, 6th ed, 1975; La poesia italiana contemporanea, 1975; Giuseppe Ungaretti, Poet and Critic, 1977; The Modern Italian Lyric, 1986; The Structure of Petrarch's "Canzoniere", 1995. Contributor to academic journals. **Address:** 63 Black Oak Rd., Cyn Coed, Cardiff CF2 6QU, Wales.

JONES, Gayl. American, b. 1949. **Genres:** Novels, Novellas/Short stories, Plays/Screenplays, Poetry. **Career:** University of Michigan, Ann Arbor, member of the English Dept., 1975-83. **Publications:** Corregidora (novel), 1975; Chile Woman (play), 1975; Eva's Man (novel), 1976; White Rat (short stories), 1977; Song for Anninho (poetry), 1981; The Hermit-Woman (poetry), 1983; Xarque (poetry), 1985; Die Uogel fangerin: novel (German translation of The Birdcatcher), 1986; Liberating Voices: Oral Tradition in African American Literature, 1991; The Healing, 1998; Mosquito, 1999. **Address:** c/o Beacon Press, 25 Beacon St., Boston, MA 02108, U.S.A.

JONES, Gerard. American. **Genres:** Popular Culture. **Career:** Media critic, comic and screenplay writer, and cultural analyst. Lemon Custard Comics, cofounder; Art & Story Workshops, founder. Guest appearances radio and television programs; screenplay writer; worked with Nintendo and Shodakukan. **Publications:** (with W. Jacobs) The Beaver Papers: The Story of the "Lost Season," 1983; (with W. Jacobs) The Comic Book Heroes: From the Silver Age to the Present, 1985; Green Lantern: The Road Back, 1992; Honey, I'm Home!: Sitcoms, Selling the American Dream, 1992; (with L. Strazewski) Prime Time, 1994; The Comic Book Heroes, 1997; Batman: Fortunate Son, 1999; Killing Monsters: Why Children Need Fantasy and Make-believe Violence, 2002. Contributor to print and on-line magazines and comic strips. National Lampoon, contributing editor. Writer of screenplays for Warner Bros, Twentieth Century-Fox, Silver Pictures, and Savoy Films; author of teleplays for HBO. **Address:** c/o Author Mail, HarperCollins, 10 East 53rd St., 7th Floor, New York, NY 10016, U.S.A. **Online address:** gerardjones@earthlink.net

JONES, Gwyneth A(nn). Also writes as Ann Halam. British, b. 1952. **Genres:** Novels, Science fiction/Fantasy, Children's fiction. **Career:** Writer, 1984-. **Publications:** NOVELS AS GWYNETH A. JONES: Escape Plans, 1986; Divine Endurance, 1987; Kairos, 1988; White Queen, 1991; Flowerdust, 1993; North Wind, 1994; Seven Tales and a Fable, 1995; Phoenix Cafe, 1997; Deconstructing the Starships, 1999; Bold as Love, 2001; Castles Made of Sand, 2002. CHILDREN'S FICTION AS GWYNETH A. JONES: Water in the Air, 1977; The Influence of Ironwood, 1978; The Exchange, 1979; Dear Hill, 1980; The Hidden Ones, 1988. CHILDREN'S FICTION AS ANN HALAM: Ally Ally, Aster, 1981; The Alder Tree, 1982; King Death's Garden, 1986; The Daymaker, 1987; Transformations, 1988; The Sky Breaker, 1990; Dinosaur Junction, 1992; The Haunting Ravin, 1994; The Fear Man, 1995. **Address:** c/o David Higham Associates, Ltd., 5-8 Lower John St, Golden Sq, London W1R 4HA, England. **Online address:** gwyneth.jones@ntlworld.com

JONES, J. Barrie. British, b. 1946. **Genres:** Music. **Career:** Cambridge University, England, music supervisor at Downing College, 1970-72; Open University, Milton Keynes, England, research assistant, 1972-75, research fellow, 1975-83, lecturer in music, 1983-; Trinity College, Cambridge, lector in music, 1983-84. **Publications:** Gabriel Faure: A Life in Letters, 1989; (gen. ed.) The Hutchinson Concise Dictionary of Music, 1998. Contributor of articles and reviews to periodicals. **Address:** Department of Music, Open University, Milton Keynes MK7 6AA, England. **Online address:** B.Jones@open.ac.uk

JONES, J. Gwynfor. Welsh, b. 1936. **Genres:** History, Politics/Government. **Career:** University of Wales, University College, Cardiff, senior lecturer in Welsh history, 1975-95, reader, 1995-97, Personal Chair, 1997. **Publications:** Wales and the Tudor State, 1534-1605, 1989; (ed.) The Memoirs of Sir John Wynn, 1990; Concepts of Order and Gentility in Wales, 1540-1640, 1992; Early Modern Wales, 1526-1640, 1994; The Welsh Gentry 1536-1640, 1998. **Address:** School of History and Archaeology, University College, University of Wales, Cardiff, Wales.

JONES, J(on) Sydney. American, b. 1948. **Genres:** Children's fiction, Novels, Travel/Exploration, History. **Career:** Writer. Journalist, 1971-76; instructor, English as a Second Language and writing, 1977-. **Publications:** FOR YOUNG PEOPLE: Frankie, 1997. FOR ADULTS. FICTION: Time of the Wolf, 1990; The Hero Game, 1992. NONFICTION: Bike and Hike: Sixty Tours Around Great Britain and Ireland, 1977; Vienna Inside-Out: Sixteen Walking Tours, 1979; Hitler in Vienna, 1983; Tramping in Europe: A Walking Guide, 1984; (and photographer) Viennawalks, 1985, rev. ed, 1994. Contributor to newspapers in the U.S. and in Europe. **Address:** 210 Martin Dr., Aptos, CA 95003, U.S.A. **Online address:** sjones@cats.ucsc.edu

JONES, Jacqueline. American, b. 1948. **Genres:** Cultural/Ethnic topics, History, Race relations. **Career:** Brandeis University, MA, Truman Professor of American History. **Publications:** Soldiers of Light and Love: Northern Teachers and Georgia Blacks 1865-1873, 1980; Labor of Love, Labor of Sorrow: Black Women, Work and the Family from Slavery to the Present, 1985; The Dispossessed: America's Underclasses from the Civil War to the Present, 1993; American Work, 1998; A Social History of the Laboring Classes, 1999. **Address:** Dept. of History, Brandeis University, Olin Sang 215, MS 036, PO Box 9110, Waltham, MA 02454, U.S.A. **Online address:** jones@brandeis.edu

JONES, Jenny. British, b. 1954. **Genres:** Science fiction/Fantasy, Novels. **Career:** Writer. **Publications:** FANTASY NOVELS: The Webbed Hand, 1994; The Blue Manor, 1995; Firefly Dreams, 1995; The House of Birds, 1996. "FLIGHT OVER FIRE" SERIES: Fly by Night, 1990; The Edge of Vengeance, 1991; Lies and Flames, 1992. **Address:** c/o Gollancz, Wellington House, 125 Strand, London WC2R 0BB, England.

JONES, Jerry W. American, b. 1964. **Genres:** Military/Defense/Arms control. **Career:** University of Central Texas, Killeen, assistant professor of history, 1996-99; Tarleton State University, Killeen, assistant professor of history, 1999-. **Publications:** U.S. Battleship Operations in World War I, 1998. **Address:** Department of History, Tarleton University Center, 1901 South Clear Creek Rd., Killeen, TX 76549, U.S.A. **Online address:** jjones@tarleton.edu

JONES, Jill. American, b. 1945. **Genres:** Romance/Historical. **Career:** Worked as advertising copywriter and in public relations, 1972-87; writer. **Publications:** ROMANCE NOVELS: Emily's Secret, 1995; My Lady Caroline, 1996; The Scottish Rose, 1997; Essence of My Desire, 1998; Circle of the Lily, 1998. Contributor to anthologies. **Address:** P. O. Box 696, Montreat, NC 28757, U.S.A.

JONES, (Henry) John (Franklin). British (born Myanmar), b. 1924. **Genres:** Novels, Literary criticism and history. **Career:** Fellow and Tutor in Jurisprudence, 1949-62, and Fellow and Tutor in English Literature, from 1962, Merton College, Oxford; Professor of Poetry, Oxford University, 1979-84; Football Correspondent, The Observer, London, 1956-59. **Publications:** The Egotistical Sublime, 1954; On Aristotle and Greek Tragedy, 1962; (ed.) The Study of Good Letters, by H. W. Garrod, 1963; John Keats's Dream of Truth, 1969; The Same God, 1971; Dostoevsky, 1983, 1985; Shakespeare at Work, 1995. **Address:** Garden Flat, 41 Buckland Crescent, London NW3 5DJ, England.

JONES, John Henry. British, b. 1942. **Genres:** Chemistry, History, Local history/Rural topics. **Career:** Oxford University, Oxford, England, official fellow and tutor in organic chemistry, 1968-, university lecturer in organic chemistry, 1970-, Balliol College, junior research fellow in biological sciences at 1966-68, dean, 1972-2002, archivist, 1981-, vice-master, 2002-. Journal of Peptide Science, editor-in-chief, 1999-. **Publications:** Balliol College: A History, 1263-1939, 1988, 2nd ed., 1997; The Chemical Synthesis of Peptides, 1990; Amino Acid and Peptide Synthesis, 1992; The Records of Balliol College, Oxford, 1992; Core Carbonyl Chemistry, 1997, 2nd ed., 2002. **Address:** Balliol College, Oxford University, Oxford OX1 3BJ, England. **Online address:** john.jones@balliol.ox.ac.uk

JONES, John Philip. American (born United Kingdom), b. 1930. **Genres:** Advertising/Public relations, Marketing. **Career:** British Market Research Bureau, London, England, research officer, 1953-55; Colman, Prentis & Varley (advertising company), London, account executive, 1955-57; J. Walter Thompson Co. (advertising company), account executive in London, 1957-65, account director in Amsterdam, Netherlands, 1965-67, in Copenhagen, Denmark, 1967-72, and in London, 1972-80; Syracuse University, Syracuse, NY, professor of advertising, 1981-, chair of advertising, Newhouse School of Public Communications, 1983-91. RGC Consulting Corp., Syracuse, president, 1986-. **Publications:** The Great Gray Spire, 1985; What's in a Name? Advertising and the Concept of Brands, 1986; Does It Pay to Advertise? Cases Illustrating Successful Brand Advertising, 1989; How Much Is Enough? Getting the Most from Your Advertising Dollar, 1992; When Ads Work: New Proof that Advertising Triggers Sales, 1995. Editor and part-author of handbooks on advertising practices, 1998-2000. **Address:** Newhouse School of Public Communications, Syracuse University, Syracuse, NY 13244, U.S.A. **Online address:** jpjones@syr.edu

JONES, Judith. See TUCKER, (Allan) James.

JONES, Julia. British, b. 1923. **Genres:** Novels, Plays/Screenplays. **Career:** Writer. **Publications:** Take Three Girls, 1970; Still Waters; Back of Beyond, 1974; Duchess of Duke Street, 1977; Country Ways (theatre), 1985; Ladies in Charge, 1986; Echoes, 1987; The Navigators (novel), 1987; The Snow Spider, 1988; Bowling Ladies (radio). DRAMATIZATIONS: Quiet as a Nun, 1985; Tom's Midnight Garden, 1989; The Cuckoo Sister; Emlyn's Moon, 1990; The Chestnut Soldier, 1991; A Likely Lad, 1991; The Cycle of Death,

1992; E. Blyton, Famous Five series, 1996; A Child in the Forest; C. Dickens, Our Mutual Friend; E. Raymonds, We the Accused. **Address:** c/o Jill Foster Ltd, 9 Barb Mews, Brook Green, London W6 7PA, England.

JONES, Kaylie (Ann). American/French, b. 1960. **Genres:** Novels. **Career:** Grants coordinator, 1983-84, Free-lance Worker, 1984-85, and Assistant to Development Director, 1985-86, Poets and Writers, Inc., NYC; instructor of creative writing at the writer's voice, west side YMCA NYC, writer in residence in NYC schools through Teachers and Writers Collaborative; Book of The Month Club Reader. **Publications:** As Soon as It Rains, 1986; Quite the Other Way, 1988; A Soldier's Daughter Never Cries, 1990; Celeste Ascending, 2000. **Address:** Southampton College, Long Island University, 239 Montauk Highway, Southampton, NY 11968, U.S.A.

JONES, Laurie Beth. American, b. 1952. **Genres:** Theology/Religion. **Career:** Jones Group (marketing, business, and leadership development firm), founder and president. Motivational speaker at places of business, educational institutions, and places of worship. **Publications:** Jesus, CEO: Using Ancient Wisdom for Visionary Leadership, 1996; The Path: Creating Your Mission Statement for Work and for Life, 1996; Grow Something Besides Old, 1998; The Power of Positive Prophecy, 1999; Jesus, Inc., 2000. **Address:** 609 Blacker Ave, El Paso, TX 79902, U.S.A.

JONES, Lawrence K. American, b. 1940. **Genres:** Education. **Career:** High school teacher in Tarsus, Turkey, 1963-66; Philadelphia Child Study Center, Philadelphia, PA, teacher, 1967; counselor at a junior high school in Greece, NY, 1967-68; Fort Roots Veterans Administration Hospital, Little Rock, AR, counseling psychology intern, 1970; Stephens College, Columbia, MO, instructor in psychology, 1970-71; North Carolina State University, Raleigh, assistant professor, 1971-76, associate professor, 1976-84, professor of counseling psychology, 1985-2002, acting head of department, 1976, 1984, professor emeritus, 2002-. Vanderbilt University, visiting associate professor with Overseas Program in England and West Berlin, 1979-80. **Publications:** (ed.) The Encyclopedia of Career Change and Work Issues, 1993; Job Skills for the 21st Century, 1995. Contributor to books and education and counseling journals. **Address:** Dept of Educational Research, Leadership & Counselor Ed, Box 7801, North Carolina State University, Raleigh, NC 27695, U.S.A. **Online address:** larryjeanine@earthlink.net

JONES, (Everett) LeRoi. See BARAKA, Imamu Amiri.

JONES, Louis B. American, b. 1953. **Genres:** Novels. **Career:** Writer. **Publications:** Ordinary Money (novel), 1990; Particles and Luck (novel), 1993; California's Over (novel), 1997. Contributor to periodicals. **Address:** c/o Joy Harris, Joy Harris Literary Agency, 156 5th Ave #156, New York, NY 10010, U.S.A.

JONES, Madison (Percy), (Jr.). American, b. 1925. **Genres:** Novels. **Career:** Miami Univ, Oxford, OH, instructor in English, 1953-54; University of Tennessee, Knoxville, instructor in English, 1955-56; Auburn University, AL, joined faculty 1956, writer-in-residence, 1967-87, professor of English, 1968-87, university writer-in-residence emeritus, 1987-. **Publications:** The Innocent, 1957; Forest of the Night, 1960; A Buried Land, 1963; An Exile, 1967; A Cry of Absence, 1971; Passage through Gehenna, 1978; Season of the Strangler, 1982; Last Things, 1989; To the Winds, 1996; Nashville 1864: The Dying of the Light, 1997; Herod's Wife, 2003. **Address:** 800 Kuderna Acres, Auburn, AL 36832-6539, U.S.A. **Online address:** m.p.jones@att.net

JONES, Malcolm V(ince). British, b. 1940. **Genres:** Intellectual history, Literary criticism and history. **Career:** University of Nottingham, lecturer, 1967-73, sr lecturer, 1973-80, Faculty of Arts, vice dean, 1976-79, dean, 1982-85, Slavonic studies, professor, 1980-97, pro vice chancellor, 1987-91, emeritus professor, 1997-. Intl Dostoevsky Society, honorary vice president, 1983-86, honorary president, 1995-98; Birmingham Slavonic Monographs, ed bd; Cambridge Studies in Russian Literature, general editor, 1985-96; University of Sussex, School of European Studies, asst lecturer, Russian, 1965-67; British Universities Assn of Slavists, president, 1986-88; British Assn for Soviet, Slavonic and East European Studies, vice president, 1988-91. **Publications:** Dostoevsky: The Novel of Discord, 1976; (ed.) New Essays on Tolstoy, 1978; (ed.) New Essays on Dostoevsky, 1983; Dostoevsky after Bakhtin, 1990; (ed.) The Cambridge Companion to the Classic Russian Novel, 1998; Dostoevsky posle Bakhtina, 1998. **Address:** Dept. of Russian and Slavonic Studies, University of Nottingham, Nottingham NG7 2RD, England. **Online address:** Malcolm.Jones@nottingham.ac.uk

JONES, Margaret C. American, b. 1949. **Genres:** Literary criticism and history. **Career:** University of Alexandria, Alexandria, Egypt, teacher, 1972-

76; Goucher College, Towson, MD, instructor, 1987-88; Central Washington University, Ellensburg, assistant professor, 1990-92; University of the West of England, Bristol, senior lecturer in humanities and coordinator of American studies, 1992-94. **Publications:** In Shadow (play), 1982; Prophets in Babylon: Five California Novelists in the 1930s, 1992; Heretics and Hellraisers: Women Contributors to "The Masses", 1911-1917, 1993; (ed.) Elsie Clews Parsons, The Journal of a Feminist, 1994. **Address:** Department of Humanities, University of the West of England, Bristol BS16 2JP, England.

JONES, Mary Voell. American, b. 1933. **Genres:** Children's fiction, Songs/Lyrics and libretti. **Publications:** Captain Kangaroo's Picnic, 1959; Huckleberry Hound Helps a Pal, 1960; Tick Tock Trouble, 1961; Yogi Bear's Secret, 1963; (with N.R. Knoche) What Do Mothers Do?, 1966; First Songs, 1976; Let's Make Music Today, 1977. **Address:** 2167 Mohawk Trail, Maitland, FL 32751, U.S.A.

JONES, Matthew F. American. **Genres:** Novels. **Career:** Author. Lynchburg College, Lynchburg, VA, writer in residence, 1995; University of Virginia, Charlottesville, VA, workshop leader, 1996; Randolph-Macon Woman's College, Lynchburg, VA, writer in residence, 1997-98. **Publications:** NOVELS: The Cooter Farm, 1991; The Elements of Hitting, 1994; A Single Shot, 1996; Blind Pursuit, 1997. **Address:** c/o Suzanne Gluck, International Creative Management, 40 West 57th St., New York, NY 10019, U.S.A.

JONES, Merry Bloch. Also writes as Robert Llewellyn Jones. American, b. 1948. **Genres:** Adult non-fiction, Humor/Satire. **Career:** Writer, 1989-. Video producer, scriptwriter, and consultant, 1975-; operator of a video production company, 1980-89. Worked as producer and director for WKBS-TV; staff communication consultant for Sun Co.; instructor at Temple University; assistant producer for WCAU-TV and KYW-TV; seminar leader; guest on television and radio talk shows. **Publications:** (with J.A. Schiller) Stepmothers: Keeping It Together with Your Husband and His Kids, 1992; Birthmothers, 1993; I Love Him, But..., 1995; (as Robert Llewellyn Jones) I Love Her, But..., 1996; Please Don't Kiss Me at the Bus Stop, 1997; If She Weren't My Best Friend, I'd Kill Her, 1997; America's Dumbest Dates, 1998.

JONES, Mervyn. British, b. 1922. **Genres:** Novels, Social commentary, Biography. **Career:** Assistant Ed., 1955-60, and Drama Critic, 1958-66, Tribune, London; Assistant Ed., New Statesman, London, 1966-68. **Publications:** No Time to Be Young, 1952; The New Town, 1953; The Last Barricade, 1953; Helen Blake, 1955; (with M. Foot) Guilty Men, 1957; On the Last Day, 1958; Potbank, 1961; Big Two (in U.S. as The Antagonists), 1962; Two Ears of Corn: Oxfam in Action (in U.S. as In Famine's Shadow: A Private War on Hunger), 1965; A Set of Wives, 1965; John and Mary, 1966; A Survivor, 1968; (editor) Kingsley Martin: Portrait and Self-Portrait, 1969; Joseph, 1970; Mr. Armitage Isn't Back Yet, 1971; Life on the Dole, 1972; Holding On (in U.S. as Twilight of the Day), 1973; The Revolving Door, 1973; Lord Richard's Passion, 1974; Strangers, 1974; (ed) Privacy, 1974; (trans.) K. S. Karol: The Second Chinese Revolution, 1974; The Pursuit of Happiness, 1975; (with F. Godwin) The Oil Rush, 1976; Scenes from Bourgeois Life, 1976; Nobody's Fault, 1977; Today the Struggle, 1978; The Beautiful Words, 1979; A Short Time to Live, 1980; Two Women and Their Man, 1982; The Sami of Lapland, 1982; Joanna's Luck, 1985; Coming Home, 1986; Chances, 1987; That Year in Paris, 1988; (with P. Wall) Defeating Pain, 1991; A Radical Life, 1991; Michael Foot (biography), 1994; The Amazing Victorian (biography), 1999. **Address:** Flat 1, 20 Brunswick Terrace, Hove, E. Sussex BN3 1HJ, England.

JONES, Nancy L. See HOLDER, Nancy L.

JONES, Naomi Brooks. American, b. 1941. **Genres:** Poetry, Young adult fiction, Theology/Religion. **Career:** Writer. Former meat wrapper for Safeway, Brownwood, TX, and Concord, CA. **Publications:** Turn Back, Teenager, Turn Back (poem), 1959; Jessie's Table, 1993; The Prodigal's Christmas (play). **Address:** 12136 S. Broadway, Los Angeles, CA 90061-1319, U.S.A.

JONES, Norman (Leslie). American, b. 1951. **Genres:** History, Law. **Career:** Utah State University, Logan, instructor, 1977, assistant professor, 1978-81, associate professor, 1981-87, professor of history, 1987-, head of department, 1994-, head of Oxford University Exchange Program, 1989-, acting director of Liberal Arts and Sciences Program, 1993-94. Harvard University, Mellon faculty fellow, 1982-83; Cambridge University, visiting fellow of Clare College, 1992; guest speaker at colleges and universities; gives workshops and public lectures. **Publications:** Faith by Statute: Parliament and the Settlement of Religion, 1559, 1982; God and the Moneylenders: Usury and Law in Early Modern England, 1989; (ed. with D. Dean, and contrib.) The Parliaments of Elizabethan England, 1993; The Birth of the Elizabethan Age: England in the 1560s, 1993. Work represented in anthologies. Contributor to scholarly journals. **Address:** Department of History, Utah State University, Logan, UT 84322-0710, U.S.A.

JONES, Owen Rogers. Welsh, b. 1922. **Genres:** Philosophy, Theology/Religion. **Career:** Guest Lecturer, St. Olaf College, Northfield, MN, 1964-65; Assistant Lecturer to Sr. Lecturer, 1957-76, and Reader in Philosophy, 1976-83, University College of Wales, Aberystwyth. **Publications:** The Concept of Holiness, 1961; (ed.) The Private Language Argument, 1971; (with P. Smith) The Philosophy of Mind, 1986. **Address:** Cilan, Cae Melyn, Aberystwyth SY23 2HA, Wales.

JONES, Pamela M. American, b. 1953. **Genres:** Art/Art history. **Career:** National Museum of American Art, intern, 1977-78, cataloger of twentieth-century painting and sculpture, 1978-79; Franklin and Marshall College, Lancaster, PA, visiting assistant professor of art history, 1985-86; University of Maine at Orono, visiting assistant professor of art history, 1987-88; University of Massachusetts at Boston, assistant professor, 1988-94, associate professor of art history, 1994-, chair of Art Dept., 1998-; McMullen Museum of Art, Boston College, co-curator of exhibition "Saints and Sinners", 1999. **Publications:** Federico Borromeo and the Ambrosiana: Art, Patronage, and Reform in Seventeenth-Century Milan, 1993. Work represented in anthologies. Contributor of articles and reviews to art and history journals. **Address:** Department of Art, University of Massachusetts at Boston, 100 Morrissey Blvd., Boston, MA 02125-3393, U.S.A.

JONES, R(obert) M(aynard). (Bobi Jones). Welsh, b. 1929. **Genres:** Novellas/Short stories, Poetry, Literary criticism and history. **Career:** Trinity College, Carmarthen, Wales, lecturer, 1956-58; University of Wales, University College of Wales, Aberystwyth, lecturer in education, 1959-66, lecturer in Welsh, 1966-80, professor, 1980-89. **Publications:** Highlights in Welsh Literature, 1969; System in Child Language, 1970; The Dragon's Pen (criticism), 1986; The Christian Heritage of Welsh Education, 1986; (as Bobi Jones) Selected Poems, 1987; (as Bobi Jones) Language Regained, 1993. IN WELSH. CRITICISM: I'r Arch, 1959; Y Tair Rhamant, 1960; Llenyddiaeth Gymraeg yn Addysg Cymru, 1961; Guto'r Glyn a'i Gyfnod, 1963; Angau Ellis Wynne, 1968; (ed.) Kate Roberts, 1969; Pedwar Emynydd, 1970; Tafod y Llenor, 1974; Llenyddiaeth Gymraeg, 1936-1972, 1975; (ed.) Ym Marn Alwyn D. Rees, 1976; Llen Cymru a Chrefydd, 1977; Ann Griffiths, 1977; Llenyddiaeth Gymraeg, 1902-1936, 1987; Seiliau Beirniadaeth, Vol I, 1984, Vol II, 1986, Vol III, 1987, Vol IV, 1988; (ed.) Yr Hen Ganrif, 1991; (ed.) Detholiad o Gerddi W.J. Gruffydd, 1991; Cyfriniaeth Gymraeg, 1994; Crist a Chenedlaetholdeb, 1994; Ysbryd y Cwlwm, 1998; Mawl a'i Gyfeillion, 2000; Mawl a Gelynion ei Elynion, 2002; Bairniadaeth Gyfansawdd, 2003. LINGUISTICS: Graddio Geirfa, 1962; Cymraeg i Oedolion, 1963; Cyflwyno'r Gymraeg, 1964; Cymraeg i Oedolion: I Nodiadau'r Dysgwyr, 1965, 2nd ed., 1966; Cymraeg i Oedolion: I Llyfr yr Athro, 1965, 2nd ed., 1966; Beirniadu Gwersi Ail Iaith, 1966; Cyfeiriadur i'r Athro, Vols I-II, 1974, Vol III, 1979; Cymraeg Drwy Ddamhegion, 1982; Gloywi Iaith, 3 vols., 1988; (ed.) Iaith Ifanc, 1994; Dysgu Cyfanswdd, 2002. POEMS: (ed.) Camre Cymru, 1952; Y Gan Gyntaf, 1957; Rhwng Taf a Thaf, 1960; Tyred Allan, 1965; Man Gwyn, 1965; Yr Wyl Ifori, 1967; Allor Wydn, 1971; Gwlad Llun, 1976; Hunllef Arthur, 1986; Bwyta'n Te, 1988; Casgliad o Gerddi, 1989; Canu Arnaf I, 1995; Canu Arnaf II, 1995. NOVELS: Nid yw Dwr yn Plygu, 1958; Bod yn Wraig, 1960; Epistol Serch ae Selsig, 1997. STORIES: Y Dyn na Ddaeth adref, 1966; Ci wrth y Drws, 1968; Daw'r Pasg i Bawb, 1969; Traed Prydferth, 1973; (ed.) Storiau Tramor, 1975; (ed.) Storiau Tramor III, 1976; Pwy Laddodd Miss Wales?, 1977; Crio Chwerthin, 1990; Dawn Gweddwon, 1992; Rhy Iach, 2004. JUVENILE: Ysgol yr Anifeiliaid, 1966; Gwiffred, 1966; Y Tri Mochyn Bach, 1966; Hugan Goch Fach, 1966; Tanwen, 1966. OTHER: Crwydro Mon (travel), 1957; Geiriadur Lluniau (dictionary), 1969; Sioc o'r Gofod (essays), 1971; Beth yw Pwrpas Llenydda? (lecture), 1974; Llenyddiaeth Gymraeg a Phrifysgol Cymru (lecture), 1993; O'r Bedd i'r Crud (autobiography), 2000. **Address:** Tandderwen, Ffordd Llanbadarn, Aberystwyth SY23 1HB, Wales.

JONES, Richard Allan. Canadian (born United States), b. 1943. **Genres:** History. **Career:** Professor of History, Universite Laval. Quebec, since 1970. **Publications:** Community in Crisis: French-Canadian Nationalism in Perspective, 1967, 1972; L'Idéologie de "L'Action catholique," 1974; Histoire du Quebec, 1976; Vers une hegemonie liberale: Apercu de la politique canadienne de Laurier a King, 1980; Duplessis and the Union Nationale Administration, 1983; Origins, 1988, 1996; Destinies, 1988, 1996. **Address:** St. Cyrille-de-L'Islet, Quebec, QC, Canada G0R 2W0.

JONES, Richard Granville. British, b. 1926. **Genres:** Theology/Religion. **Career:** Lecturer, Faculty of Theology, University of Manchester, 1969-82;

Former Methodist Minister in Sheffield and Birkenhead; Principal, Hartley Victoria College, Manchester, 1973-82; Chairman, East Anglia District of the Methodist Church, 1983-93; President, The Methodist Conference, 1988-89. **Publications:** (ed.) Worship for Today, 1968; (co-author) Towards a Radical Church, 1969; How Goes Christian Marriage?, 1978; Groundwork of Worship and Preaching, 1980; Groundwork of Christian Ethics, 1984; What to Do?: Christians and Ethics, 1999. **Address:** 35 Davies Rd., West Ridgford, Nottingham N6L 5JE, England.

JONES, Robert Llewellyn. See **JONES, Merry Bloch.**

JONES, Rodney. American, b. 1950. **Genres:** Poetry. **Career:** Professor, Dept. of English, Southern Illinois University, Carbondale; Virginia Intermont College, Bristol, writer in residence, 1978-84. **Publications:** Going Ahead, Looking Back, 1977; The Story They Told Us of Light, 1980; The Unborn, 1985; Transparent Gestures, 1989 (National Book Critics Circle Award for Poetry); Apocalyptic Narrative and Other Poems, 1993; Things that Happen Once, 1996; Elegy for the Southern Drawl, 1999. **Address:** Dept. of English, Southern Illinois University, Carbondale, IL 62901, U.S.A. **Online address:** rodjones@siu.edu

JONES, Sally Roberts. Also writes as Sally Roberts. British, b. 1935. **Genres:** Novellas/Short stories, Poetry, History, Bibliography. **Career:** Reference Library, London Borough of Havering, sr. assistant, 1964, 1967; Borough of Port Talbot, reference librarian, 1967-70; Alun Books, publisher, 1977-; Port Talbot Historical Society, general secretary, 1982-; Swansea Writers and Artists Group, chairman, 1999-. **Publications:** (as Sally Roberts) Turning Away, 1969; (as Sally Roberts) Romford in the Nineteenth Century, 1969; (compiler) About Welsh Literature, 1970; Elen and the Goblin, 1977; Strangers and Brothers, 1977; The Forgotten Country, 1977; Books of Welsh Interest: A Bibliography, 1977; Allen Raine, 1979; (ed.) Margam through the Ages, 1979; Welcome to Town, 1980; Relative Values, 1985; The History of Port Talbot, 1991; Pendaruis, 1992; Dic Penderyn: The Man and the Martyr, 1993. **Address:** 3 Crown St, Port Talbot, Wales.

JONES, Simmons. American, b. 1920. **Genres:** Novels, Poetry. **Career:** Fashion photographer, New York City, and Charlotte News, Charlotte, NC; Military service: U.S. Army, 1941-45, served in 771st Tank Destroyer Battalion; became corporal. **Publications:** Show Me the Way to Go Home, 1991. **Address:** 301 West 10th St., No. 305, Charlotte, NC 28202, U.S.A.

JONES, Solomon. (born United States), b. 1969. **Genres:** Law. **Career:** Philadelphia Weekly, Philadelphia, PA, senior contributing editor; Salvation Army of Eastern Pennsylvania and Delaware, former regional director of public relations; Philadelphia Committee to End Homelessness, former director of development and outreach; Calvary Baptist Church of Philadelphia, volunteer public relations director. **Publications:** Pipe Dream, 2001; The Bridge, 2003. **Address:** c/o Author Mail, St. Martin's Press, 175 Fifth Ave., New York, NY 10010, U.S.A. **Online address:** info@solomonjones.com

JONES, Star(let Marie). American, b. 1962. **Genres:** Essays. **Career:** Kings County District Attorney's Office, Brooklyn, NY, member of prosecution staff, 1986-91, senior assistant district attorney, 1991-92; Court TV, correspondent, 1991; NBC-TV, NYC, legal correspondent, 1992-93; Jones & Jury (syndicated television program produced by Group W Productions), Los Angeles, host and co-owner, 1994-; The View (NBC-TV), co-host, 1997-. **Publications:** (with D. Paisner) You Have to Stand for Something, or You'll Fall for Anything, 1998. **Address:** c/o Group W Television, 6500 Wilshire Blvd., Los Angeles, CA 90048, U.S.A.

JONES, Stephen. Also writes as Steven Gregory. British, b. 1953. **Genres:** Novellas/Short stories, Horror, Science fiction/Fantasy, Film, Reference. **Career:** Stephen Jones Media, Wembley, England, owner, 1987-. Television producer and director, horror/science fiction film publicist and consultant. **Publications:** The Illustrated Vampire Movie Guide, 1993; The Illustrated Dinosaur Movie Guide, 1993; The Illustrated Frankenstein Movie Guide, 1994; The Illustrated Werewolf Movie Guide, 1996; The Essential Monster Movie Guide, 1999; Creepshows, 2001. EDITOR: (with K. Newman) Horror: 100 Best Books, 1988; (with J. Fletcher) Gaslight and Ghosts, 1988; (with C. Paget) Dark Voices: The Best from the Pan Book of Horror Stories, 1990; (with R. Campbell) Best New Horror, Vols 1-7, 1990-96; Clive Barker's The Nightbreed Chronicles, 1990; The Mammoth Book of Terror, 1991; Clive Barker's Shadows in Eden, 1991; James Herbert: By Horror Haunted, 1991; (with N. Gaiman) Now We Are Sick, 1991; (with Campbell) The Hellraiser Chronicles, 1992; The Mammoth Book of Vampire Stories, 1992, new ed., 2004; (with Campbell) The Giant Book of Best New Horror, 1993; The Mammoth Book of Zombies, 1993; (with D. Carson) H.P. Lovecraft's Book of Horror, 1993; The Mammoth Book of Werewolves, 1994; (with Campbell) The Giant Book of Terror, 1994; The Mammoth Book of Frankenstein, 1994; Shadows over Innsmouth, 1994; Clive Barker's A-Z of Horror, 1997; The Mammoth Book of Dracula, 1997; Dancing with the Dark, 1997; The Mammoth Book of Best New Horror, Vols. 8-15, 1997-2004; K.E. Wagner, Exorcisms and Ecstasies, 1997; The Vampire Stories of R. Chetwynd-Hayes, 1997; (with Fletcher) Secret City, 1997; Dark of the Night, 1997; White of the Moon, 1999; Dark Detectives, 1999; R.E. Howard, The Conan Chronicles, Vol. 1: The People of the Black Circle, 2000, Vol. 2: The Hour of the Dragon, 2001; R. Chetwynd-Hayes, Phantoms and Fiends, 2000; The Mammoth Book of Vampire Stories by Women, 2001; C.A. Smith, The Emperor of Dreams, 2002; Keep out the Night, 2002; R. Chetwynd-Hayes, Frights and Fancies, 2002; By Moonlight Only, 2003; Great Ghost Stories, 2004; The Mammoth Book of New Terror, 2004. EDITOR WITH DAVID SUTTON: Fantasy Tales 1-7, 1988-91; The Best Horror from Fantasy Tales, 1988; Dark Voices, Vols. 2-6, 1990-94; The Anthology of Fantasy & the Supernatural, 1994; Dark Terrors, Vols. 1-6, 1995-2002; The Giant Book of Fantasy Tales, 1996. **Address:** 130 Park View, Wembley, Middlesex HA9 6JU, England. **Online address:** www.herebedragons.co.uk/Jones

JONES, Ted. (Theodor Edward). American, b. 1937. **Genres:** History. **Career:** Superintendent of schools in Valley Falls, KS, 1968-71, Phillipsburg, KS, 1971-81, Derby, KS, 1981-83, and Atwood, KS, 1985-91; Boeing Military Aircraft Co., Wichita, KS, project administrator for development, 1984-85; Unified School District 434, Carbondale, KS, superintendent of schools, 1991-94. **Publications:** NOVELS: Grant's War, 1992; Hard Road to Gettysburg, 1993; Fifth Conspiracy, 1995; While God Slept, 1996. **Address:** 2105 Hageman Ave, Salina, KS 67401, U.S.A.

JONES, Thom. American, b. 1945?. **Genres:** Novellas/Short stories. **Career:** Writer. Worked as a boxer, an ad copywriter, and a janitor. **Publications:** SHORT STORIES: The Pugilist at Rest, 1993; Cold Snap: Stories, 1995; Sonny Liston Was a Friend of Mine, 1999. Contributor to periodicals. **Address:** Little Brown, 3 Center Plaza, Floor 3, Boston, MA 02108, U.S.A.

JONES, Tobias. (born England), b. 1972. **Genres:** Air/Space topics. **Career:** London Review of Books, London, England, member of editorial department; Independent on Sunday, staff writer; freelance journalist, 1999-; Worked as a framer and seller of antiquarian maps at a bookshop in Bloomsbury, England. **Publications:** The Dark Heart of Italy: Travels through Time and Space across Italy, published as The Dark Heart of Italy: An Incisive Portrait of Europe's Most Beautiful, Most Disconcerting Country, 2004. Contributor of essays and articles to periodicals. **Address:** c/o Editorial Department, Faber and Faber Ltd., Three Queen Square, London WC1N 3AU, England.

JONES, Webb. *See* **HENLEY, Arthur.**

JONES, William B(ryan), Jr. (Bill). American, b. 1950. **Genres:** Plays/Screenplays, Humanities, Intellectual history, Literary criticism and history. **Career:** Catholic High School for Boys, Little Rock, AR, English teacher, 1975-78; Office of the Arkansas Attorney General, Little Rock, legal intern, 1980-81; Roman Catholic High School, Little Rock, English teacher, 1982-83; Arkansas Court of Appeals, Little Rock, attorney law clerk, 1984-88; Arkansas Supreme Court, Little Rock, attorney law clerk, 1989-95, reporter of decisions,1995-. Friends of the Central Arkansas Library System, member of board of directors, 1984-92; Butler Center for Arkansas Studies, member of board of advisers, 2003-. Compiler and coproducer of compact disc The Little Rock Sound, 1965-69, 1999. **Publications:** PLAYS: Home from Sea: An Inland Voyage through the Writings of Robert Louis Stevenson, 2000; Arkansas Alive, 2003; Lost in Darkness and Distance: A Readers' Theatre Adaptation of Mary Shelley's Frankenstein. AS WILLIAM B. JONES JR.: Classics Illustrated: A Cultural History, 2002; author biographies and introductions for Classics Illustrated Junior series, 2003-. EDITOR & CONTRIBUTOR: (as Bill Jones with P. Martin and S. Buel) A Spectrum Reader: Five Years of Iconoclastic Reporting, Criticism, and Essays, 1991; Robert Louis Stevenson Reconsidered: New Critical Perspectives, 2003. Contributor to periodicals. **Address:** 420 N McAdoo St, Little Rock, AR 72205, U.S.A. **Online address:** bottleimp2000@yahoo.com

JONG, Erica (Mann). American, b. 1942. **Genres:** Novels, Poetry, Children's non-fiction, Essays, Adult non-fiction, Plays/Screenplays. **Career:** Lecturer in English, City College of New York, 1964-66, and University of Maryland European Extension, Heidelberg, W. Germany, 1967-68; Instructor in English, Manhattan Community College, NYC, 1969-70; Instructor in Poetry, YM-YWHA Poetry Center, NYC, 1971-73. **Publications:** Fruits & Vegetables (poems), 1971; Half-Lives (poems), 1973; Fear of Flying (novel), 1973; Loveroot (poems), 1975; How to Save Your Own Life (novel), 1977; Megan's Book of Divorce (children's non-fiction), 1977, as Megan's Two Houses, 1996; At the Edge of the Body (poems), 1979; Fanny (novel), 1980; Witches (poetry/fiction), 1981; Ordinary Miracles (poems), 1983; Parachutes & Kisses, 1984; Serenissima (novel), 1987, as Shylock's Daughter, 1995; Any Woman's Blues (novel), 1990; Becoming Light: Poems New and Selected, 1991; The Devil at Large: Erica Jong on Henry Miller (non-fiction), 1993; Fear of Fifty (memoir), 1994; Inventing Memory: A Novel of Mothers and Daughters, 1997; What Do Women Want? Bread. Roses. Sex. Power (non-fiction), 1998; Sappho's Leap (novel), 2003. **Address:** Erica Jong Productions, PO Box 1434, New York, NY 10021, U.S.A. **Online address:** queryjongleur@rcn.com; www.ericajong.com

JOOSSE, Barbara M(onnot). American, b. 1949. **Genres:** Children's fiction, Biography, Essays, Picture/board books. **Publications:** The Thinking Place, 1982; Spiders in the Fruit Cellars, 1983; Fourth of July, 1985; Jam Day, 1987; Anna, The One and Only, 1988; Pieces of the Picture, 1988; Better with Two, 1988; Dinah's Mad, Bad Wishes, 1989; Mama, Do You Love Me?, 1991; The Pitiful Life of Simon Schultz, 1991; Anna and the Cat Lady, 1992; Nobody's Cat, 1992; Wild Willie and King Kyle, Detectives, 1993; The Losers Fight Back, 1994; The Morning Chair, 1994; I Love You the Purplest, 1996; Snow Day!, 1996; Nugget and Darling, 1997; Ghost Trap, 1998; Lewis and Papa, 1998; Alien Brain Tryout;, 2000; Ghost Wings, 2001; A Houseful of Christmas, 2001; Stars in the Darkness, 2002. **Address:** W61 N764 Riveredge Dr, Cedarburg, WI 53012, U.S.A. **Online address:** stjoan1@execpc.com

JOOSTE, Pamela. South African, b. 1946?. **Genres:** Adult non-fiction. **Publications:** Dance with a Poor Man's Daughter, 1998; Frieda and Min, 1999; Like Water in Wild Places, 2000. **Address:** c/o Author Mail, Doubleday, 1540 Broadway, New York, NY 10036-4094, U.S.A.

JOPPKE, Christian. German, b. 1959. **Genres:** Military/Defense/Arms control. **Career:** University of Southern California, Los Angeles, assistant professor of sociology, 1990-94; Zumberge fellow, 1992; European University Institute, Florence, Italy, associate professor of sociology and political science, 1995-. University of California, Berkeley, John L. Simpson fellow at Institute of International Studies, 1989; Georgetown University, research associate at Center for German and European Studies, 1993-94. **Publications:** Mobilizing against Nuclear Energy: A Comparison of Germany and the United States, 1993; East German Dissidents and the Revolution of 1989: Social Movement in a Leninist Regime, 1995; Immigration and the Nation-State: The United States, Germany, and Great Britain, 1999. Contributor of articles and reviews to sociology and political science journals. **Address:** School of Humanities and Social Sciences, International University Breman, PO Box 750 561, Breman, Germany.

JORDAN, Alma Theodora. Trinidadian, b. 1929. **Genres:** Librarianship, Bibliography. **Career:** Campus Librarian, 1960-89, and University Librarian, 1982-89, University of West Indies, Trinidad and Tobago. **Publications:** The Development of Library Service in the West Indies Through Inter-Library Cooperation, 1970; (ed.) Research Library Cooperation in the Caribbean, 1973; The English-speaking Caribbean: A Bibliography of Bibliographies, 1984. **Address:** 28 Gilwell Rd, Valsayn Park, Trinidad and Tobago.

JORDAN, Anne Devereaux. American, b. 1943. **Genres:** Novels, Novellas/Short stories, Science fiction/Fantasy, Children's fiction, History, Literary criticism and history, Ghost Writer. **Career:** Western Michigan University, Kalamazoo, instructor in English, 1970-73; University of Connecticut, Storrs, instructor in English, 1973-74; Parousia Press, Storrs, graphic and layout artist and camera person, 1977-79; Magazine of Fantasy and Science Fiction, Cornwall, CT, assistant editor, 1979-83, associate editor, 1984-85, managing editor, 1985-89; ghostwriter, 1986-; free-lance writer and editor, 1989-; Teaching & Learning Literature & Young Adults, senior editor, 1994-98. Literary consultant, Cowan, Liebowitz & Latman, 1986-, Weiss, David, Fross, Zelnick, & Lehrman, NY, 1990-, and David, Wright, Tremaine, 1994-. Wesleyan University, artist in residence, 1977, visiting lecturer in graduate studies, 1990-; member of adjunct faculty, University of Hartford, 1980-87, and Eastern Connecticut State University, 1993; Children's Literature Association, founder; contributor of "Seminar & Workshop" & Senior Editor, Teaching and Learning Literature with Children and Young Adult, 1993-. **Publications:** The Seventh-Day Adventists: A History, 1988; (with J.M. Stifle) The Baptists, 1990; Following the Gleam: Teaching & Learning Genre with Children & Young Adults, vols. 1 & 2, 1997; Romancing the Book: Teaching & Learning Literary Elements with Children & Young Adults, 1997; Literature? Why Bother?, 1997. EDITOR: (with F. Butler and R. Rotert) The Wide World All Around: A Creative Anthology of Children's

Literature, 1986; (with E.L. Ferman) The Best Horror Stories from the Magazine of Fantasy and Science Fiction, 1988; Fires of the Past: 13 Contemporary Fantasies about Hometowns, 1991. **Address:** 117 Mansfield Hollow Rd., A4, Mansfield Center, CT 06250, U.S.A.

JORDAN, Constance. American. **Genres:** Literary criticism and history, History. **Career:** Yale University, New Haven, CT, visiting lecturer in English, 1974 and 1977; Bryn Mawr College, Bryn Mawr, PA, lecturer in comparative literature, 1977-78; Columbia University, NYC, assistant professor of English and comparative literature, 1978-87; Northwestern University, Evanston, IL, visiting associate professor of English, 1987-88; Claremont Graduate School, Claremont, CA, associate professor, 1988-92, professor of English, 1993-. University of California, Los Angeles, associate of Center for Medieval and Renaissance Studies, 1992-; lecturer at colleges and universities. **Publications:** Pulci's Morgante: Poetry and History in Fifteenth-Century Florence, 1986; Renaissance Feminism: Literary Texts and Political Models, 1990; Shakespeare's Monarchies: Ruler and Subject in Shakespeare's Romances, 1997; (assoc ed) Longman Anthology of British Literature, Vol. I: Middle Ages, Early Modern, Restoration, and Eighteenth Century, 1998. Contributor of articles and reviews to periodicals. **Address:** Department of English, Claremont Graduate School, Claremont, CA 91711, U.S.A.

JORDAN, Daniel P(orter), Jr. American, b. 1938. **Genres:** History. **Career:** University of Maryland Overseas Division in Europe and Korea, instructor in history, 1963-65; University of Richmond, Richmond, VA, instructor in history, 1968-69; Virginia Commonwealth University, Richmond, instructor, 1969-70, assistant professor, 1970-73, associate professor, 1973-80, professor of American history, 1980-84; Thomas Jefferson Foundation, Monticello, Charlottesville, VA, director, 1985-, president, 1994-. Director of Monticello-Stratford Hall Summer Seminar for teachers, 1981-; University of Virginia, scholar in residence, 1985-; member of advisory committee for papers of Thomas Jefferson at Princeton University, 1989-; Secretary of the Interior's Advisory Board for the National Park System, member, 1984-88, chairman, 1987-88; board member of Virginia Advisory Council on Libraries and Edgar Allan Poe Foundation; consultant to National Endowment for the Humanities, National Park Service, and Museum of the Confederacy; Virginia Historical Society, Eastern National, National Parks and Conservation Association, state review board, chairman; Virginia Department of Historic Resources; President of Richmond Civil Round Table, 1983. **Publications:** Political Leadership in Jefferson's Virginia, 1983; (ed. with M. Duke) A Richmond Reader, 1733-1983, 1983; (with M. Duke) Tobacco Merchant: The Story of Universal Leaf Tabacco Company, 1995. Contributor to books. **Address:** Monticello, P.O. Box 316, Charlottesville, VA 22902, U.S.A.

JORDAN, David C. American, b. 1935. **Genres:** Politics/Government. **Career:** University of Virginia, Charlottesville, professor of government and foreign affairs, 1965-, department head, 1969-77. U.S. ambassador to Peru, 1984-86; New World Institute, president, 1993-. **Publications:** (with A.P. Whitaker) Nationalism in Contemporary Latin America, 1966; World Politics in Our Time, 1970; Spain, the Monarchy, and the Atlantic Community (monograph), 1979; Revolutionary Cuba and the End of the Cold War, 1993. EDITOR & CONTRIBUTOR: A Strategy for Latin America in the Nineties (monograph), 1988; U.S. Latin American Policy for the Nineties (monograph), 1994. **Address:** Department of Government, Cabell 232, University of Virginia, Charlottesville, VA 22903, U.S.A.

JORDAN, Laura. See **BROWN, Sandra.**

JORDAN, Lee. See **SCHOLEFIELD, Alan (A. T.).**

JORDAN, Michele Anna. American, b. 1949. **Genres:** Food and Wine, Travel/Exploration, Documentaries/Reportage, Essays. **Career:** Writer, chef, and radio host/producer. KRCB-FM Radio, Santa Rosa, CA, host of Mouthful and Red Shoes Rodeo, 1995-; Sonoma-Provence Exchange, Sonoma, CA, founder, 1995-; Santa Rosa Press Democrat, columnist; teaches cooking and lectures on a variety of foodand wine-related topics. **Publications:** A Cook's Tour of Sonoma, 1990; The Good Cook's Book of Oil & Vinegar, 1992; The Good Cook's Book of Mustard, 1994; The Good Cook's Book of Tomatoes, 1995; The Good Cook's Book of Days, 1995; Ravioli & Lasagne, 1996; Pasta with Sauces, 1996; Polenta: 100 Innovative Recipes from Appetizers to Desserts, 1997; California Home Cooking, 1997; Salt & Pepper: 135 Perfectly Seasoned Recipes for the Cook's Best Friends, 1999; Williams-Sonoma Complete Pasta Cookbook, 1999; Complete Pasta Cookbook, 1999; San Francisco Seafood, 2000; Pasta Classics, 2000; The New Cook's Tour of Sonoma, 2000; Veg Out!, 2004; (and narrator) Sonoma County Appellations (14-part series of short documentaries). Work represented in anthologies.

Contributor to periodicals. **Address:** PO Box 1552, Sebastopol, CA 95473, U.S.A. **Online address:** michele@micheleannajordan.com

JORDAN, Penny. British, b. 1946. **Genres:** Romance/Historical. **Career:** Novelist. **Publications:** NOVELS: Falcon's Prey, 1981; Marriage without Love, 1981; Tiger Man, 1982; Northern Sunset, 1982; Blackmail, 1982; Bought with His Name, 1982; The Caged Tiger, 1982; Daughter of Hassan, 1982; Island of the Dawn, 1982; Long Cold Winter, 1982; Escape from Desire, 1982; Desire's Captive, 1982; An Unbroken Marriage, 1982; Passionate Protection, 1983; Forgotten Passion, 1983; Phantom Marriage, 1983; The Flawed Marriage, 1983; Rescue Operation, 1983; Man-Hater, 1983; A Sudden Engagement, 1983; Savage Atonement, 1983; Response, 1984; Shadow Marriage, 1984; Darker Side of Desire, 1984; The Inward Storm, 1984; The Friendship Barrier, 1984; Rules of the Game, 1984; Campaign for Loving, 1984; Wanting, 1985; Injured Innocent, 1985; The Hard Man, 1985; Permission to Love, 1985; Desire for Revenge, 1985; Exorcism, 1985; Fire with Fire, 1985; Time Fuse, 1985; The Six-Month Marriage, 1985; Taken Over, 1985; What You Made Me, 1985; You Owe Me, 1985; A Man Possessed, 1986; Stronger than Yearning, 1986; Capable of Feeling, 1986; Desire Never Changes, 1986; Return Match, 1986; A Reason for Marriage, 1986; Loving, 1986; Research into Marriage, 1987; Passionate Relations, 1987; For One Night, 1987; A Savage Adoration, 1987; Substitute Lover, 1987; Too Short a Blessing, 1987; Fight for Fight, 1988; Levelling the Score, 1988; Potential Danger, 1988; Without Trust, 1988; Special Treatment, 1988; Power Play, 1988; Love's Choices, 1988; Stronger than Yearning, 1988; Lovers' Touch, 1988; So Close & No Closer, 1989; Valentine's Night, 1989; Power Play Sampler, 1989; Force of Feeling, 1989; Equal Opportunities, 1989; A Reason for Being, 1989; A Rekindled Passion, 1989; Beyond Compare, 1989; Bitter Betrayal, 1989; Free Spirit, 1989; Silver, 1989; An Expert Teacher, 1989; Payment in Kind, 1990; Unspoken Desire, 1990; Rival Attractions, 1990; Breaking Away, 1990; Time for Trust, 1990; Out of the Night, 1990; The Hidden Years, 1990; Game of Love, 1990; Second Time Loving, 1990; A Kind of Madness, 1990; A Time to Dream, 1991; A Cure for Love, 1991; Second-best Husband, 1991; Dangerous Interloper, 1991; A Forbidden Leaving, 1991; Payment Due, 1991; Stranger from the Past, 1992; Tug of Love, 1992; Lingering Shadows, 1992; Laws of Attraction, 1992; Lesson to Learn, 1992; A Matter of Trust, 1992; Mistaken Adversary, 1992; Past Passion, 1992; Yesterday's Echoes, 1993; Lingering Shadows, 1993; For Better, For Worse, 1993; French Leave, 1994; Cruel Legacy, 1995; Unwanted Wedding, 1995; An Unforgettable Man, 1996; Her Christmas Fantasy, 1996; Love's Choices, 1996; Power Games, 1996; Valentine's Night, 1996; The Trusting Game, 1996; Too Wise to Wed?, 1997; Woman to Wed?, 1997; Yours, Mine & Ours, 1997; Best Man to Wed?, 1997; A Perfect Family, 1998; Perfect Marriage Material, 1998; The Perfect Seduction, 1998; Nine Months. **Address:** c/o Harlequin Mills & Boon Ltd., Eton House, 18-24 Paradise Rd., Richmond, Surrey TW9 1SR, England.

JORDAN, Richard Tyler. American, b. 1960. **Genres:** Novels. **Career:** Walt Disney Studios, Burbank, CA, senior publicist and writer, 1984-. **Publications:** But Darling, I'm Your Auntie Mame! (biography), 1998; Suffer Fools (novel), in press; Goodbye to the Buttermilk Sky (screenplay). **Address:** Walt Disney Studios, 500 South Buena Vista St., Burbank, CA 91521, U.S.A. **Online address:** richard.jordan@disney.com

JORDAN, Robert. See **RIGNEY, James Oliver, Jr.**

JORDAN, Robert B. Canadian, b. 1939. **Genres:** Chemistry. **Career:** University of Alberta, Edmonton, member of chemistry faculty. **Publications:** Reaction Mechanisms of Inorganic and Organometallic Systems, 1991. **Address:** Department of Chemistry, University of Alberta, Edmonton, AB, Canada T6G 2G2.

JORDAN, Robert Smith. American, b. 1929. **Genres:** Institutions/Organizations, International relations/Current affairs, Military/Defense/Arms control, Politics/Government, Biography. **Career:** Assistant director, Army War College Center, 1960-61, director, Air University Center, 1961-62, associate professor of political science and international affairs, 1962-70, assistant to the president, 1962-64, associate director, International Organization and International Security Studies, Program of Policy Studies, 1964-65, and director, Foreign Affairs Intern Program, School of Public and International Affairs, 1968-70, George Washington University, Washington, DC; dean, Faculty of Economics and Social Studies, and head, Dept. of Political Science, University of Sierra Leone, 1965-67; professor of political science, 1970-76, and dept. Chairman, 1970-74, State University of New York at Binghamton; sr. research specialist and director of research, UN Institute for Training and Research, NYC, 1974-80; adjunct professor of political science, Columbia University, NYC, 1978-80; professor of political science, university research professor of public and international affairs, College of Urban and Public Affairs, University of New Orleans, 1980-2004. Fulbright professor, Centre for the Study of Arms Control and International Security, University of Lancaster, UK, 1988; visiting professor at universities and colleges. **Publications:** The NATO International Staff/Secretariat, 1952-57, 1967; Government and Power in West Africa, 1969; (with T. Weiss) The World Food Conference and Global Problem-Solving, 1975; Political Leadership in NATO, 1979; (with N. Graham) The International Civil Service, 1980; (with W. Feld) International Organizations, 1983; (with W. Feld) Europe in the Balance, 1987; Alliance Strategy and Navies, 1990; Norstad, Cold War NATO Supreme Commander, Airman, Strategist, Diplomat, 2000; International Organizations: A Comparative Approach to the Management of Cooperation, 2001. EDITOR: (with H. Gibbs and A. Gyorgy) Problems in International Relations, 3rd ed., 1970; Multinational Cooperation, 1972; (with P. Toma and A. Gyorgy) Basic Issues in International Relations, 2nd ed., 1974; The U.S. and Multilateral Resource Management, 1985; Generals in International Politics, 1987; (with J. Hattendorf) Maritime Strategy and the Balance of Power, 1989. EDITOR & CONTRIBUTOR: Europe and the Superpowers, 1971; International Administration, 1971; Dag Hammarskjold Revisited, 1982; Europe and the Super Powers (essays), 1991. **Address:** 132 Belle Terre Blvd, Covington, LA 70433-4327, U.S.A. **Online address:** rjordan@uno.edu

JORDAN, Sherryl. New Zealander, b. 1949. **Genres:** Children's fiction, Young adult fiction. **Career:** Part-time work as a teacher's aide in primary schools, working with profoundly deaf children, 1979-87; illustrator, 1980-85; full-time writer, 1988-; University of Iowa, writer-in-residence, 1993. Margaret Mahy Lecture Award (New Zealand), 2001. **Publications:** CHILDREN'S FICTION: The Firewind and the Song, 1984; Matthew's Monsters, 1986; No Problem Pomperoy, 1988; Kittens (school reader), 1989; The Wobbly Tooth, 1989; Babysitter Bear, 1990; Rocco, 1990 in US as A Time of Darkness; The Juniper Game, 1991; The Wednesday Wizard, 1991; Denzil's Dilemma, 1992; Winter of Fire, 1993; Other Side of Midnight, 1993; Tanith, 1994 in US as Wolf-woman; Sign of the Lion, 1995; Secret Sacrament, 1996; Denzil's Great Bear Burglary, 1997; The Raging Quiet, 1999; The Hunting of the Last Dragon, 2002. Illustrator of books by J. Cowley. **Address:** 1496 Kings Ave, Matua, Tauranga, New Zealand.

JORDAN, Wendy A(dler). American. **Genres:** Homes/Gardens, Architecture. **Career:** Writer, editor, and editorial consultant. Washington Daily News, Washington, DC, assistant in Women's Department, 1969-72; National Trust for Historic Preservation, Washington, DC, editor of Historic Preservation magazine, 1972-77, director of programs for Preservation Press, 1977-79; Hanley-Wood Co., Washington, DC, managing editor of Builder magazine, 1979-82, executive editor of Builder, 1982-85, editor for Remodeling magazine, 1985-96, vice president, 1990-96; Washington Lawyer, Washington, DC, editor, 1996-98; Rails to Trails, editor and editorial consultant, 1998-; Wendy A. Jordan Co., Washington, DC, owner, 1996-. **Publications:** By the Light of the Qulliq: Eskimo Life in the Canadian Arctic (for children), 1979; Lead Carpenter System: A Guide for Remodelers and Their Employees, 1999; (with E. Whitaker and C. Mahoney) Great Kitchens: At Home with America's Top Chefs, 2000, paperback ed. as Great Kitchens: Design Ideas from America's Top Chefs, 2001; (with L. Case and V. Downing) Mastering the Business of Design/Build Remodeling, 2001; The Kidspace Idea Book, 2001. Contributor to magazines and trade journals. **Address:** c/o Professional Remodeler Magazine, 2000 Clearwater Dr., Oak Brook, IL 60523, U.S.A. **Online address:** jordanm@erols.com

JORDEN, William John. American, b. 1923. **Genres:** Politics/Government, History, Writing/Journalism. **Career:** Vineyard Gazette, Edgartown, MA, reporter, 1947; New York Herald Tribune, NYC, member of news staff, 1948; Associated Press, foreign correspondent in the Far East, 1948-52; New York Times, foreign correspondent in Japan and Korea, 1952-55, Moscow bureau chief, 1956-58, diplomatic correspondent in Washington, DC, 1958-61; US Department of State, Washington, DC, member of Policy Planning Council, 1961-62, special assistant to under secretary of state, 1962-65, deputy assistant secretary of state for public affairs, 1965-66, member and spokesperson of US delegation to the Vietnam Peace Talks in Paris, France, 1968-69, US Ambassador to Panama, 1974-78; US National Security Council, Washington, DC, member of senior staff, 1966-68 and 1972-74; assistant to President Lyndon B. Johnson, 1969-72; Lyndon B. Johnson Library, Austin, TX, scholar in residence, 1978-80; US chairman, US-Panama Consultative Committe, 1991-95; writer. **Publications:** (with H. Borton and others) Japan between East and West, 1957; Panama Odyssey, 1984. **Address:** 5934 Frazier Lane, Mc Lean, VA 22101, U.S.A.

JORGENSEN, Ivar. See **SILVERBERG, Robert.**

JORGENSEN-EARP, Cheryl R(uth). American, b. 1952. **Genres:** Women's studies and issues. **Career:** Virginia Intermont College, Bristol, instructor in speech and theater, 1980-81; John Umstead Psychiatric Hospital, Butner, NC, instructor in speech and theater, 1982; Fort Steilacoom Community College, Tacoma, WA, instructor in speech communication, 1983; Tacoma Community College, Tacoma, instructor in speech and theater, 1982-83; University of Puget Sound, Tacoma, instructor in communication and theater arts, 198590; Lynchburg College, Lynchburg, VA, associate professor of communication studies, 1993-. Visiting artist at Haywood Technical College and Halifax Community College, Weldon, NC. **Publications:** The Transfiguring Sword: Reformist Terrorism and the Just War of the Women's Social and Political Union, 1997; Speeches and Trials of the Militant Suffragettes, 1998. Contributor to academic journals. **Address:** 351 Polar Lane, Salem, VA 24153, U.S.A.

JOSEPH, Henry. American, b. 1948. **Genres:** Novels. **Career:** Professional wanderer, 1970-90; writer. **Publications:** Bloodwork: The New Rugged Cross (novel), 1994; Dinosaur Heaven, 1997; The Well Spent Death of Eightball Barnett, 2000. **Address:** PO Box 734, Bowdon, GA 30108, U.S.A.

JOSEPH, Lawrence. American, b. 1948. **Genres:** Poetry, Law. **Career:** Poet, prose writer, critic, law professor. Office of Michigan Supreme Court Justice G. Mennen Williams, law clerk; Shearman & Sterling, NYC, litigator; Princeton University, Princeton, NJ, creative writing professor; St. John's University School of Law, Jamaica, NY, professor of law, 1987-. **Publications:** POETRY: Shouting at No One, 1983; Curriculum Vitae, 1988; Before Our Eyes, 1993. NONFICTION: Lawyerland: What Lawyers Talk about When They Talk about the Law, 1997. **Address:** St. John's University Law School, Jamaica, NY 11439, U.S.A.

JOSEPHS, Arthur. See **GOTTLIEB, Arthur.**

JOSEPHS, Ray. American, b. 1912. **Genres:** Business/Trade/Industry, International relations/Current affairs, Advertising/Public relations, Communications/Media, Education, How-to books, Self help. **Career:** Writer & Consultant on personal time management; Consultant, Business Council for International Understanding, NYC. Public relations writer. Former journalist, corresp., and consultant on Latin American affairs, and Japanese-U.S. economic developments; Chairman, Ray Josephs & David E. Levy Inc., and International Public Relations Co., 1961-86; Lecturer on inter-American affairs and international public relations; broadcasts on CBS-TV, NBC-TV, BBC-TV, and public service stations. **Publications:** Spies and Saboteurs in Argentina, 1943; Argentine Diary, 1944; Latin America: Continent in Crisis, 1948; (with J. Bruce) Those Perplexing Argentines, 1952; How to Make Money from Your Ideas, 1954; How to Gain an Extra Hour Every Day, 1955, 1992; (with D. Kemp) Memoirs of a Live Wire, 1956; Streamlining Your Executive Workload, 1958; (with O. Steiner) Our Housing Jungle and Your Pocketbook, 1960; (with S. Arnold) The Magic Power of Putting Yourself Over with People, 1962. Contributor to magazines. **Address:** 860 United Nations Plaza, New York, NY 10017-1815, U.S.A.

JOSEPHY, Alvin M., Jr. American, b. 1915. **Genres:** Politics/Government, Business/Trade/Industry, Cultural/Ethnic topics, History. **Career:** Director, and Sr. Ed., American Heritage Publishing Co. Inc., NYC, 1960-79. **Publications:** The Long and the Short and the Tall, 1946; The Patriot Chiefs, 1961; Chief Joseph's People and Their War, 1964; The Nez Perce Indians and the Opening of the Northwest, 1965; The Indian Heritage of America, 1968; The Artist was a Young Man, 1970; Red Power, 1971; (reviser) The Pictorial History of the American Indians, by Oliver La Farge, 1974; History of the U.S. Congress, 1975; Black Hills, White Sky, 1978; On the Hill: A History of the American Congress, 1979; Now That the Buffalo's Gone, 1982; War on the Frontier, 1986; The Civil War in the American West, 1991; 500 Nations, 1994; A Walk Toward Oregon: A Memoir, 2000. EDITOR: The American Heritage Book of Indians, 1961; The American Heritage Book of Natural Wonders, 1963; The American Heritage History of the Great West, 1965; RFK: His Life and Death, 1968; The Horizon History of Africa, 1971; American Heritage History of Business and Industry, 1972; The Law in America, 1974; America in 1492, 1992. **Address:** 4 Kinsman Lane, Greenwich, CT 06830, U.S.A. **Online address:** ajosephy@discovernet.net

JOSHI, S(unand) T(ryambak). American (born India), b. 1958. **Genres:** Romance/Historical, Poetry, Literary criticism and history, Bibliography. **Career:** Chelsea House Publishers, NYC, associate editor, 1984-85, managing editor, literary criticism division, 1985-89, senior editor, literary criticism division, 1989-. **Publications:** An Index to the Selected Letters of H.P. Lovecraft, 1980; (with M.A. Michaud) Lovecraft's Library: A Catalogue, 1980; H.P. Lovecraft and Lovecraft Criticism: An Annotated Bibliography, 1981, supplement, 1981-84, 1985; Reader's Guide to H.P. Lovecraft, 1982; (trans.) M. Levy, Lovecraft: A Study in the Fantastic (monograph), 1988; Selected Papers on Lovecraft, 1989; The Weird Tale, 1990; John Dickson Carr: A Critical Study, 1990; H.P. Lovecraft: The Decline of the West, 1990; An Index to the Fiction and Poetry of H.P. Lovecraft, 1992; (with D. Schweitzer) Lord Dunsany: A Bibliography, 1993; Lord Dunsany: Master of the Anglo-Irish Imagination, 1995; A Subtler Magick, 1996; H.P. Lovecraft: A Life, 1996. EDITOR: (with M.A. Michaud) H.P. Lovecraft, Uncollected Prose and Poetry, 3 vols., 1978-82; (with M.A. Michaud) H.P. Lovecraft in The Eyrie, 1979; (with S. Connors) H.P. Lovecraft, Science versus Charlatanry: Essays on Astrology, 1979; H.P. Lovecraft: Four Decades of Criticism, 1980; H.P. Lovecraft, Saturnalia and Other Poems, 1984; H.P. Lovecraft, Juvenilia, 1897-1905, 1984; H.P. Lovecraft, The Dunwich Horror and Others, 1984; H.P. Lovecraft, In Defence of Dagon, 1985; H.P. Lovecraft, At the Mountains of Madness and Other Novels, 1985; H.P. Lovecraft, Dagon and Other Macabre Tales, 1986; H.P. Lovecraft, Uncollected Letters, 1986; D. Wandrei, Collected Poems, 1988; H.P. Lovecraft, The Horror in the Museum and Other Revisions, 1989; H.P. Lovecraft, The Conservative, 1990; (with D.E. Schultz) An Epicure in the Terrible, 1991; H.P. Lovecraft Centennial Conference Proceedings, 1991; R.H. Barlow, On Lovecraft and Life, 1992; The Count of Thirty: A Tribute to Ramsey Campbell, 1993; H.P. Lovecraft, Autobiographical Writings, 1992; (with D.E. Schultz) H.P. Lovecraft, Letters to Richard F. Searight, 1992; H.P. Lovecraft, The Fantastic Poetry, 1990, rev. ed., 1993; (with D.E. Schultz) H.P. Lovecraft, Letters to Robert Bloch, 1993; H.P. Lovecraft in The Argosy, 1994; (with D.E. Schultz and W. Murray) H.P. Lovecraft, The H.P. Lovecraft Dreambook, 1994; (with D.E. Schultz) H.P. Lovecraft, The Shadow over Innsmouth, 1994; (with D.E. Schultz) H.P. Lovecraft, Letters to Samuel Loveman and Vincent Starrett, 1994; H.P. Lovecraft, Miscellaneous Writings, 1995; (with R. Dalby and S. Dziemianowicz) B. Stoker, Best Ghost and Horror Stories, 1997; H.P. Lovecraft, The Call of Cthulhu and Other Weird Stories, 1999; Documents of American Prejudice, 1999; Sixty Years of Arkham House, 1999; (with D.E. Schultz) Ambrose Bierce: An Annotated Bibliography of Sources, 1999; (with P.H. Cannon) More Annotated H.P. Lovecraft, 2999; Lord of a Visible World, 200; Atheism, 2000; Civil War Memories, 2000; The Collected Fables of Ambrose Bierce, 2000; (with D.E. Schultz) The Unabridged Devil's Dictionary, 2000; A. Bierce, the Fall of the Republic and Other Political Satires, 2000. **Address:** Chelsea House Publishers, 1974 Sproul Rd Ste 400, Broomall, PA 19008, U.S.A.

JOSIPOVICI, Gabriel (David). British (born France), b. 1940. **Genres:** Novels, Novellas/Short stories, Plays/Screenplays, Literary criticism and history. **Career:** University of Sussex, lecturer, 1963-74, reader, 1974-84, part-time professor, 1984-. **Publications:** The Inventory, 1968; Words, 1971; The World and the Book: A Study of Modern Fiction, 1971; Mobius the Stripper (plays and short stories), 1974; The Present, 1975; (ed.) The Modern English Novel: The Reader, The Writer, and the Book, 1976; Migrations, 1977; The Lessons of Modernism and Other Essays, 1977; Four Stories, 1977; The Echo Chamber, 1980; The Air We Breathe, 1981; Vergil Dying (play), 1981; Writing and the Body, 1982; Conversations in Another Room, 1984; Contre-Jour, 1986; In the Fertile Land (stories), 1987; The Book of God: A Response to the Bible, 1988; Steps: Selected Fiction and Drama, 1990; The Big Glass, 1991; Text and Voice, 1992; In a Hotel Garden, 1993; Moo Pak, 1994; Touch, 1996; Now, 1998; On Trust, 1999; A Life, 2001; Goldberg: Variations. **Address:** 60 Prince Edward's Rd, Lewes, Sussex BN7 1BH, England.

JOSSELSON, Ruthellen (Lefkowitz). American, b. 1946. **Genres:** Psychology. **Career:** University of Toledo, Toledo, OH, assistant professor of psychology, 1972-73; Towson State University, Baltimore, MD, assistant professor, 1975-82, associate professor, 1982-89, professor of psychology, 1989-, director of Clinical Concentration Program, 1975-; writer. Johns Hopkins University, associate research scientist, 1973-75; University of Paris, researcher at School of Medicine, 1982-83; Hebrew University of Jerusalem, Fulbright professor, 1989-90; Harvard University, visiting professor, 1992-93. Psychological Clinic (Ann Arbor, MI), clinical psychology intern, 1968-70; Massachusetts Mental Health Center, clinical fellow in psychiatry, 1970-71, staff psychologist, 1971-72; private practice of psychotherapy in Ann Arbor, 1972-73, and Baltimore, 1974-. A. K. Rice Institute, associate of Washington-Baltimore Center. **Publications:** Finding Herself: Pathways to Identity Development in Women, 1987; The Space between Us: Exploring the Dimensions of Human Relationships, 1992; (ed. with A. Lieblich) The Narrative Study of Lives: An Annual Review, 1993-96; Revising Herself: The Story of Women's Identity from College to Midlife, 1996. Work represented in anthologies. Contributor to psychology periodicals. **Address:** Department of Psychology, Towson State University, Baltimore, MD 21204, U.S.A.

JOURDAIN, Robert. American, b. 1950. **Genres:** Information science/Computers, Music. **Career:** Writer. **Publications:** Programmer's Problem 1985, 2nd ed, 1992; Turbo Pascal Express: 250 Ready-to-Run Assembly Language Routines (computer file), 1987, rev. 2nd ed, 1988; C Express: 250 Ready-to-Run Assembly Language Routines (computer file), 1989; (with P. Norton and the Peter Norton Computing Group) The Hard Disk Companion, 1988, 2nd ed, 1991; Music, the Brain, and Ecstasy: How Music Captures Our Imagination, 1997. **Address:** c/o William Morrow & Co. Inc., 1350 Avenue of the Americas, New York, NY 10019, U.S.A.

JOUVE, Nicole Ward. American. **Genres:** Literary criticism and history. **Career:** Literary critic and writer. **Publications:** Spectre du Gris, 1977, in English as Shades of Grey, 1981; L'Entremise, 1980; Baudelaire: A Fire to Conquer Darkness, 1979; Un Homme Nommae Zopolski, 1983; The Streetcleaner: The Yorkshire Ripper Case on Trial, 1987; Colette, 1987; White Woman Speaks with Forked Tongue: Criticism as Autobiography, 1991; (with M. Roberts) The Semi-Transparent Envelope: Women Writing-Feminism and Fiction, 1994; Female Genesis: Creativity, Self and Gender, 1997. Author of a collection of short stories. **Address:** c/o Routledge, 29 West 35th St., New York, NY 10001, U.S.A.

JOVANOVSKI, Meto. Macedonian, b. 1928. **Genres:** Novels, Novellas/Short stories, Children's fiction, Mythology/Folklore, Travel/Exploration, Translations. **Career:** Pirin Macedonia, Bulgaria, teacher of Macedonian language and history; Makedonska kniga (publishing house), Skopje, Macedonia, editor, 1954-63; TV Skopje, Skopje, head of foreign programming department, 1963-88; writer and translator. Macedonian PEN Centre, secretary and president, 1972-84, honorary vice-president, 1984-; Forum for Human Rights of Macedonia, vice-president, 1989-; Committee for Macedono-Greek Dialogue and Understanding, founding president, 1991-; Helsinki Committee for Human Rights of Macedonia, founding president, 1994-. **Publications:** NOVELS: Slana vo cutot na bademite (title means: Frost in the Blossom of the Almondtree), 1967; Zemja i tegoba (Earth and Toil), 1968; Svedoci (Witnesses), 1972; Budaletinki, 1976, trans. as Cousins, 1987; Secho Sekula (novella), 1977; Orlovata dolina (Valley of the Eagles), 1979; Krlezi (Ticks), 1984; Balkan Book of the Death, 1992; Prodavnica za ljubopitnite (Shop for the Curious), 2003. SHORT STORIES: Jadres: Raskazi (Bloom), 1952; Meni na mojata mesecina (Changes on My Moon), 1956; Nateznati dzvezdi, 1969; Prvite covekovi umiranja, 1971; Patot do osamata (Road to Loneliness), 1979; Krstopatot kon osamata (The Crossroad to Serenity). NOVELS FOR CHILDREN: Ljuman aramijata (Ljuman the Robber), 1954; Krstot, kambanata, znameto (The Cross, the Bell, the Banner), 1990. OTHER: (with K. Kamilov and S. Janevski) Temni khzuvanjh (oral stories), 1962; Koj e koj, sto e sto: kratok literaturno-jazicen leksikon, 1963; (ed. and trans.) Edna druga Amerika (Another America; anthology of contemporary American poetry), 1978; Klucevite na Manhatan: zapisi od za-padnite predeli (The Keys to Manhattan; travelogue), 1983; Zborovnik po brajcinski (Talking in a Brajcino Way), 1998. Translator of works into Macedonian. **Address:** St. Partenij Zografski 51, 1000 Skopje, Macedonia. **Online address:** metoj@mhc.org.mk

JOY, Camden. American, b. 1963. **Genres:** Art/Art history. **Career:** Author. Has worked as a receptionist, word processor, and legal secretary; worked for fourteen years as a musician, singer, and song writer. **Publications:** The Greatest Record Album Ever Told (also see below), 1995; The Greatest Record Album Singer That Ever Was (also see below), 1996; The Last Rock Star Book; or, Liz Phair: A Rant (novel), 1998; Boy Island (novel), 2000; Hubcap Diamondstar Halo (novella), 2001; Camden Joy, 2002; Pan (novella), 2002; Lost Joy, 2002; Palm Tree 13 (novella), 2003. Author of numerous tracts and manifestos about music and contributor to periodicals. **Address:** c/o Author Mail, Highwater Books, 5944 Rue Waverly, Montreal, Quebec, Canada H2T 2Y3.

JOY, David (Anthony Welton). British, b. 1942. **Genres:** History, Transportation, Local history/Rural topics. **Career:** Ed., Dalesman Publishing Co. Ltd., since 1988 (Editorial Assistant, 1965-70; Books Ed., 1970-88). General Reporter, Yorkshire Post Newspapers, 1962-65. **Publications:** (with W.R. Mitchell) Settle-Carlisle Railway, 1966; Main Line Over Shap, 1967; Cumbrian Coast Railways, 1968; Whitby-Pickering Railway, 1969; Railways in the North, 1970; Traction Engines in the North, 1970; (with A.J. Peacock) George Hudson of York, 1971; Railways of the Lake Counties, 1973; Regional History of the Railways of Great Britain: South and West Yorkshire, 1975; Railways in Lancashire, 1975; Settle-Carlisle Centenary, 1975; Railways of Yorkshire: The West Riding, 1976; (with P. Williams) North Yorkshire Moors Railway, 1977; Steam on the North York Moors, 1978; (with A. Haigh) Yorkshire Railways, 1979; Steam on the Settle and Carlisle, 1981; Yorkshire Dales Railway, 1983; Settle-Carlisle in Colour, 1983;

Regional History of the Railways of Great Britain: The Lake Counties, 1984; Portrait of the Settle-Carlisle, 1985; The Dalesman: A Celebration of 50 Years, 1989; Life in the Yorkshire Coalfield, 1989; Settle-Carlisle Celebration, 1990; Uphill to Paradise, 1991; Yorkshire's Christmas, 1992; Best Yorkshire Tales, 1993; Thr Dalesman Bedside Books, 1993; Yorkshire's Farm Life, 1994; (with D. Pratt) Railways in Your Garden, 1994. **Address:** Hole Bottom, Hebden, Skipton, N. Yorkshire BD23 5DI, England.

JOY, Donald Marvin. American, b. 1928. **Genres:** Education, Human relations/Parenting, Psychology, Recreation, Theology/Religion, Women's studies and issues. **Career:** Asbury Theological Seminary, Wilmore, KY, professor of human development and Christian education, 1971-98, professor emeritus, 1998-. Free Methodist Publishing House, Winona Lake, IN, executive editor, 1958-72. **Publications:** The Holy Spirit and You, 1965; Meaningful Learning in the Church, 1969; (ed.) Moral Development Foundations: Theological Alternatives to Piaget and Kohlberg, 1983; Bonding: Relationships in the Image of God, 1985; Re-Bonding: Preventing and Restoring Broken Relationships, 1986; (with R. Joy) Lovers: Whatever Happened to Eden?, 1987; Parent, Kids, and Sexual Integrity, 1988; Walk On!, 1988; Unfinished Business: How a Man Can Make Peace with His Past, 1989; Becoming a Man, 1991; (with D. Hager) Women at Risk, 1993; Celebrating the New Woman, 1993; Men under Construction, 1993; Risk-Proofing Your Family, 1995; (with S.F. Venable) How to Use Christian Camping Experiences in Religious Education, 1998; Empower Your Kids to Be Adults, 2000; (with R. Joy) Two Became One, 2002. **Address:** Asbury Theological Seminary, Wilmore, KY 40390, U.S.A. **Online address:** Don_Joy@asburyseminary.edu; www.donaldjoy.com

JOYAUX, Julia. *See* **KRISTEVA, Julia.**

JOYCE, Brenda. American. **Genres:** Romance/Historical. **Career:** Writer. Worked as a landscaper, truck driver, bartender, and waitress. **Publications:** BRAGG SAGA SERIES: Innocent Fire, 1988; Firestorm, 1988; Violet Fire, 1989; The Darkest Heart, 1990; Dark Fires, 1991; Fire of Paradise, 1992; Scandalous Love, 1992; Secrets, 1993. DEADLY/CAHILL-BRAGG SERIES: Deadly Love, 2001; Deadly Pleasure, 2002; Deadly Affairs, 2002; Deadly Desire, 2002; Deadly Love, 2002; Deadly Caress, 2003. OTHER: Lovers and Liars, 1989; The Conqueror, 1990; Promise of the Rose, 1993; After the Innocence, 1994; The Game, 1994; Beyond Scandal, 1995; A Gift of Joy, 1995; Captive, 1996; The Finer Things, 1997; Splendor, 1997; The Rival, 1998; The Third Heiress, 1999; House of Dreams, 2000; The Chase, 2002. Contributor of novellas to collections. **Address:** St. Martin's Press, Attn: Publicity Dept., 175 Fifth Avenue, New York, NY 10010, U.S.A.

JOYCE, Davis D. American, b. 1940. **Genres:** History. **Career:** University of Tulsa, OK, assistant professor to associate professor of history, 1966-83; East Central University, Ada, OK, associate professor to professor of history, 1987-. University of Keele, visiting professor, 1981; L. Kossuth University, Soros Professor of American Studies, 1994-96. **Publications:** Edward Channing and the Great Work, 1974; History and Historians, 1983; (with M. Kraus) The Writing of American History, rev. ed., 1985; (with T. Glant) United States History: A Brief Introduction for Hungarian Students, 1996; (with P. Boeger) East Central University: The Wagner Years, 1969-1989. EDITOR: E. Channing, A History of the United States, 1993; An Oklahoma I Had Never Seen Before: Alternative Views of Oklahoma History, 1994. Contributor to history and social science journals. **Address:** Department of History, East Central University, Ada, OK 74820, U.S.A.

JOYCE, Graham. British, b. 1954. **Genres:** Novels, Horror, Science fiction/Fantasy. **Career:** National Association of Youth Clubs, Leicester, England, youth officer, 1980-88; writer, 1988-. **Publications:** NOVELS: Dreamside (fantasy), 1991; Dark Sister (horror), 1992; House of Lost Dreams (horror/fantasy), 1993; Requiem (fantasy), 1995; The Tooth Fairy, 1996; The Stormwatcher, 1998; Indigo, 2000; Smoking Poppy, 2001; The Facts of Life, 2002. **Address:** 66 Shanklin Dr, Leicester LE2 3QA, England. **Online address:** grafire@aol.com

JOYCE, Joyce Ann. American, b. 1949. **Genres:** Literary criticism and history. **Career:** Valdosta State College, Valdosta, GA, instructor in English, 1972-74; University of Georgia, Athens, instructor in English, 1978-79; University of Maryland at College Park, assistant professor, 1979-86, associate professor of English, 1986-89; University of Nebraska, Lincoln, professor of English, 1989-. Black Books Bulletin, contributing editor. **Publications:** Native Son: Richard Wright's Art of Tragedy, 1986; (ed. with A.P. Davis and S. Redding) Cavalcade: An Anthology of Afro-American Literature, 1991; (ed. with Davis and Redding) The New Cavalcade: An Anthology of Afro-American Literature, 1992; Warriors, Conjurers and Priests, 1994; Ijala,

1996. Work represented in anthologies. Contributor to periodicals. **Address:** Dept of African American Studies, 809 Gladfelter Hall, Temple University, 1115 W Berks St, Philadelphia, PA 19122, U.S.A. **Online address:** joyce.joyce@temple.edu

JOYCE, Michael. American, b. 1945. **Genres:** Novels, Essays. **Career:** Jackson Community College, MI, associate professor of language and literature and coordinator of Center for Narrative and Technology, 1975-95; Vassar College, Poughkeepsie, NY, visiting professor in hypertext media, technology, and culture, 1992-93, Randolph Visiting Distinguished Professor of English and the Library, 1993-, associate professor, 1994-2003, faculty director of media cloisters, 1994-, professor of English and media studies, 2003-; writer. Consultant on computers and hypertext programs. **Publications:** (trans. with M. Cain) A. Chekhov, The Cherry Orchard (play), 1980; Of Two Minds: Hypertext Pedagogy and Poetics (essays), 1995; Othermindedness: The Emergence of Network Culture (essays), 2000; Moral Tales and Meditations: Technological Parables and Refractions, 2001. NOVELS: The War outside Ireland, 1982; afternoon, a story (interactive), 1987, rev. ed., 1993; Liam's Going, 2002. Contributor to books and periodicals. **Address:** English Dept, Box 360, Vassar College, Poughkeepsie, NY 12604, U.S.A.

JOYCE, Rosemary A. American, b. 1956. **Genres:** Anthropology/Ethnology, Archaeology/Antiquities. **Career:** Jackson Community College, Jackson, MI, instructor in social sciences department, 1983-84; University of Illinois at Urbana-Champaign, Urbana, lecturer in anthropology department, 1984-85; Harvard University, Cambridge, MA, assistant curator of pre-Columbian archaeology at Peabody Museum of Archaeology and Ethnology, 1985-94, assistant director of the museum, 1985-89, lecturer at the university, 1986-89, assistant professor, 1989-91, associate professor of anthropology, 1991-94; University of California, Berkeley, associate professor, 1994-2001, professor of anthropology, 2001-, and director, 1994-99, Hearst Museum of Anthropology, 1994-99. Museum of San Pedro Sula (Honduras), member of technical advisory committee for development of the museum, 1993-94. **Publications:** Cerro Palenque: Power and Identity on the Maya Periphery, 1991; (ed.) T. Proskouriakoff, Maya History, 1993; (with S.A.M. Shumaker) Encounters with the Americas, 1995; (with C. Claassen) Women in Prehistory: North America and Meso America, 1997; (with D. Grove) Social Patterns in Pre-Classic Mesoamerica, 1999; (with S. Gillespie) Beyond Kinship, 2000; Gender and Power in Prehispanic Mesoamerica, 2001; The Languages of Archaeology, 2002; (with L. Meskell) Embodied Lives, 2003; (with J. Hendon) Mesoamerican Archaeology, 2004. **Address:** Dept of Anthropology, 232 Kroeber Hall #3710, University of California-Berkeley, Berkeley, CA 94720-3710, U.S.A. **Online address:** rajoyce@uclink.berkeley.edu

JOYCE, William. American, b. 1957. **Genres:** Children's fiction, Illustrations. **Career:** Screenwriter, author, and illustrator; contributor of illustrations to periodicals. **Publications:** SELF-ILLUSTRATED FOR CHILDREN: George Shrinks, 1985; Dinosaur Bob and His Adventures with the Family Lazardo, 1988; A Day with Wilbur Robinson, 1990; Bently & Egg, 1992; Santa Calls, 1993; The Leaf Men and the Brave Good Bugs, 1996; Buddy, 1997; Rolie, Polie, Olie, 1999. Illustrator of books by C. and J. Gray, M. Mayer, B. Roberts, E. Winthrop, J. Wahl, J. Maxner, S. Manes. **Address:** 2911 Centenary Blvd 2nd Fl Sam Peters Bldg, Shreveport, LA 71104, U.S.A. **Online address:** wjoyce@williamjoyce.com

JOYNER, Tim(othy). American, b. 1922. **Genres:** Marine sciences/Oceanography. **Career:** Texas Co., geophysicist, 1945-48; University of Washington, Seattle, geochemist in Laboratory of Radiation Biology, 1957-62; National Marine Fisheries Service, oceanographer, 1962-75; United Nations Food and Agriculture Organization, director of marine aquaculture, 1975. **Publications:** Magellan, 1992. Contributor to scientific and fishing industry journals. **Address:** 3284 Rickey Rd. NE Apt D101, Bremerton, WA 98310-6633, U.S.A.

JUAREZ, Tina. American, b. 1942. **Genres:** Education. **Career:** Austin Independent School District, Stephen F. Austin High School, Austin, TX, high school principal. University of Texas at Austin, Department of Educational Administration, Austin, TX, adjunct professor. Novelist. **Publications:** (ed. with J.A. Laska), Grading and Marking in American Schools: Two Centuries of Debate, 1992; Call No Man Master, 1995; South Wind Come, 1998. Contributor of articles on grading and assessment to educational journals. **Address:** 3208 Glenview, Austin, TX 78703, U.S.A.

JUDAH, Aaron. British, b. 1923. **Genres:** Novels, Children's fiction. **Publications:** Tommy with Hole in His Shoe, 1957; Tales of Teddy Bear, 1958; The Adventures of Henrietta Hen, 1958; Miss Hare and Mr. Tortoise, 1959; The Pot of Gold and Two Other Tales, 1959; God and Mr. Sourpuss, 1959;

Basil Chimpy Isn't Bright, 1959; Henrietta in the Snow, 1960; Basil Chimpy's Comic Light, 1960; Anna Anaconda: The Swallowing Wonder, 1960; Henrietta In Love, 1961; The Proud Duck, 1961; The Elf's New House, 1962; Ex-King Max Forever!, 1963; The Careless Cuckoos, 1963; Clown of Bombay, 1963; The Fabulous Haircut, 1964; Clown on Fire, 1965; On the Feast of Stephen, 1965; Cobweb Pennant, 1968; Lillian's Dam, 1970. **Address:** 6 Lower Denmark Rd, Ashford, Kent TN23 7SU, England.

JUDD, Alan. Also writes as Holly Budd. British, b. 1946. **Genres:** Novels, History, Biography, Humor/Satire. **Career:** Royal Society of Literature, fellow, 1990. **Publications:** NOVELS: A Breed of Heroes, 1981; Short of Glory, 1984; The Noonday Devil, 1987; Tango, 1989; The Devil's Own Work, 1991; Legacy, 2001; The Kaiser's Last Kiss, 2003. OTHER: Ford Maddox Ford (biography), 1990; (with D. Crane) First World War Poets (biography), 1997; (as Holly Budd) The Office Life Little Instruction Book, 1996; The Quest for "C": Mansfield Cumming and the Founding of the Secret Service (biography), 1999. **Address:** c/o David Higham Associates, Ltd., 5-8 Lower John St, Golden Sq, London W1R 4HA, England.

JUDD, Denis. British, b. 1938. **Genres:** Novels, Children's fiction, History, Biography. **Career:** Principal Lecturer, since 1972, and Professor of History, since 1990, University of North London (Lecturer, 1964-68; Sr. Lecturer, 1968-72). Fellow, Royal Historical Society. **Publications:** Balfour and The British Empire, 1968; The Victorian Empire, 1970; Posters of World War Two, 1972; The British Raj, 1972; Livingstone in Africa, 1973; George V, 1973, new ed., 1994; Someone Has Blundered, 1973; The House of Windsor, 1973; Edward VII, 1975; Palmerston, 1957; The Crimean War, 1975; Eclipse of Kings, 1976; The Adventures of Long John Silver, 1977; Radical Joe: A Life of Joseph Chamberlain, 1977, new ed., 1993; The Boer War, 1977; Return to Treasure Island, 1978; Prince Philip, 1980, new ed., 1991; Lord Reading: A Biography of Rufus Isaacs, 1982; (with P. Slinn) The Evolution of the Modern Commonwealth, 1982; George VI, 1982; Alison Uttley: The Life of a Country Child, 1986; Further Tales of Little Grey Rabbit, 1989; Jawaharlal Nehru, 1993; Empire: The British Imperial Experience from 1765 to the Present, 1996. **Address:** 20 Mount Pleasant Rd, London NW10 3EL, England.

JUDD, Lord Frank (Ashcroft). (Lord Judd of Porrsea). British, b. 1935. **Genres:** International relations/Current affairs, Politics/Government. **Career:** Created Life Peer, 1991. Intl Voluntary Service, secretary general, 1960-66; Portsmouth West, Member of Parliament, 1966-74; Portsmouth North, Member of Parliament, 1974-79; Parliamentary Under Secretary of State for Defence for the Royal Navy, 1974-76; Minister of State for Overseas Development, 1976-77; Minister of State, Foreign and Commonwealth Office, 1977-79; Intl Defence and Aid Fund for Southern Africa, associate director, 1979-80; Voluntary Service Overseas, director, 1980-85; Centre for World Development Education, chairman, 1980-85; Oxfam, director, 1985-91; Intl Council of Voluntary Agencies, chairman, 1985-90; London School of Economics, member of court of governors, 1986-; World Economic Forum Conference on South Africa, chairman, 1990, 1991; Oxford Diocesan Board for Social Responsibility, chairman, 1992-94; Natl Tenants Resource Centre, director, 1992-95; Westminster College, Oxford, governor, 1992-98; Intl Commission on Global Governance, 1992-2001; Selly Oak Colleges, chair, 1996-98; Lancaster University, member of council, 1996-2002, and member of court, 2002-; Ruskin Foundation, trustee, 2002-; Saterworld, trustee, 2002-; University of Newcastle, member of court, 2004-. **Publications:** CO-AUTHOR: Radical Future, 1967; Fabian International Essays, 1970; Purpose in Socialism, 1973; Imagining Tomorrow, 2000. Author of papers and articles. **Address:** House of Lords, London SW1A 0PW, England.

JUDGE, Edward H. American, b. 1945. **Genres:** History. **Career:** General Motors Corp., Detroit, MI, materials coordinator, summers, 1965-68; substitute teacher at public schools in Ann Arbor, MI, 1968-69; Ford Motor Co., Ypsilanti, MI, quality control inspector, 1969-70; General Motors Corp., materials coordinator, 1970; University of Michigan, Residential College, Ann Arbor, lecturer in history, 1976; State University of New York College at Plattsburgh, assistant professor of history, 1977-78; LeMoyne College, Syracuse, NY, assistant professor, 1978-82, associate professor, 1982-92, professor of history, 1992-, department head, 1988-91, 1992-95. **Publications:** Plehve: Repression and Reform in Imperial Russia, 1902-1904, 1983; Easter in Kishinev: Anatomy of a Pogrom, 1993; (with J.W. Langdon) A Hard and Bitter Peace: A Global History of the Cold War, 1996. EDITOR: (with J.Y. Simms Jr., and contrib.) Modernization and Revolution: Dilemmas of Progress in Late Imperial Russia, 1993; (and compiler with J.W. Langdon) The Cold War: A History through Documents, 1999. Contributor to history journals. **Address:** Department of History, LeMoyne College, Syracuse, NY 13214, U.S.A. **Online address:** judge@lemoyne.edu

JUDGE, Harry George. British, b. 1928. **Genres:** Education, History. **Career:** Fellow Brasenose College, Oxford, since 1973. Head Master, Banbury Grammar School, 1962-67, and Principal, Banbury Sch, 1967-73; Director, Dept of Educational Studies, Oxford University, 1973-88. **Publications:** Louis XIV, 1965; School is Not Yet Dead, 1974; Graduate Schools of Education in the United States: A View from Abroad, 1982; A Generation of Schooling: English Secondary Education since 1944, 1984; The University and the Teachers, 1994. **Address:** Brasenose College, Oxford OX1 4AJ, England.

JUDIS, John B. American, b. 1941. **Genres:** Biography. **Career:** Writer. **Publications:** William F. Buckley, Jr.: Patron Saint of the Conservatives, 1988; Grand Illusion, 1992; The Paradox of American Democracy, 1999. **Address:** 1428 Winding Waye Ln, Silver Spring, MD 20902-1452, U.S.A.

JUDKINS, Phil(lip Edward). British, b. 1947. **Genres:** Information science/Computers. **Career:** City of Bradford Metropolitan Council, Bradford, England, principal manpower services officer, 1975-77; Rank Xerox Ltd., London, England, manager of management services, 1977-87; Provincial Insurance plc, Kendal, England, director of resources, 1987-95; AXA Insurance, London, director, 1995-. **Publications:** (with D. West and J. Drew) Networking: The Rank Xerox Experiment, 1985; (with B. Sherman) Glimpses of Heaven, Visions of Hell: Virtual Reality and Its Implications, 1992; Licensed to Work, 1994. **Address:** AXA Insurance plc, 1 Aldgate, London EC3N 1RE, England. **Online address:** phil.judkins@axa-insurance.co.uk

JUDOVITZ, Dalia. American (born Romania), b. 1951. **Genres:** Art/Art history, Literary criticism and history, Philosophy. **Career:** University of Pennsylvania, Philadelphia, assistant professor of French, 1978-82; University of California, Berkeley, assistant professor of French, 1982-88; Emory University, Atlanta, GA, NEH Professor of French and Italian, 1988-. **Publications:** Subjectivity and Representation in Descartes: The Origins of Modernity, (ed. with T. Flynn) Dialectic and Narrative, 1993; Unpacking Duchamp: Art in Transit, 1995; The Culture of the Body: Genealogies of Modernity, 2001. **Address:** Department of French and Italian, Emory University, Atlanta, GA 30322, U.S.A. **Online address:** djudovi@emory.edu

JUDSON, John. American, b. 1930. **Genres:** Novellas/Short stories, Plays/Screenplays, Poetry, Autobiography/Memoirs. **Career:** University of Wisconsin-La Crosse, joined faculty, 1965, professor of English, now emeritus. Ed., Juniper Press, and Northeast literary mag., 1962-. **Publications:** (co-author) Two from Where It Snows, 1963; Surreal Songs, 1968; Within Seasons, 1970; (ed.) Voyages to the Inland Sea, 6 vols., 1971-76; Finding Worlds in Winter, 1973; West of Burnam, South of Troy (radio play, later stage play), 1973; Ash Is the Candle's Wick, 1974; Roots from the Onion's Dark, 1978; A Purple Tale, 1978; North of Athens, 1980; August on a Lone Bassoom, 1981; Letters to Jirac, II, 1980; Reasons Why I Am Not Perfect, 1982; The Carrabassett, Street William, Was My River (autobiography), 1982; Suite for Drury Pond, 1989; MUSE(SIC), 1992; The Inardo Poems, 1996; Three Years before the Braves Left Boston, 2000. **Address:** 1310 Shorewood Dr, La Crosse, WI 54601, U.S.A.

JUDT, Tony R(obert). British, b. 1948. **Genres:** History, Politics/Government. **Career:** King's College, Cambridge, fellow, 1972-78; University of California, Berkeley, assistant professor, 1978-80; St. Anne's College, Oxford, fellow, 1980-87; Institute of French Studies, New York University, NYC, professor of history, 1987-, Remarque Institute, director, 1995-. American Council of Learned Socs., fellow, 1980-81; Nuffield Foundation, fellow, 1986-87; Royal Historical Society, fellow, 1986; Guggenheim fellow, 1989-90;America Academy of Arts & Sciences, fellow, 1996-. Recipient of British Academy Award for Research, 1984. **Publications:** La Reconstruction du Parti Socialiste 1921-1926, 1976; (ed.) Conflict and Compromise: Socialists and Socialism in the Twentieth Century, 1976; Socialism in Provence, 1871-1914: A Study in the Origins of the Modern French Left, 1979; Marxism and the French Left: Studies in Labour and Politics in France, 1830-1981, 1986; (ed.) Resistance and Revolution in Mediterranean Europe, 1939-1948, 1989; Past Imperfect: French Intellectuals 1944-56, 1993; A Grand Illusion? An Essay on Europe, 1996; The Burden of Responsibility, 2000. **Address:** Remarque Institute, New York University, 53 Washington Sq S, New York, NY 10012, U.S.A.

JUDY, Dr. See KURIANSKY, Judith (Anne Brodsky).

JUHASZ, Anne McCreary. Canadian, b. 1922. **Genres:** Education, Sociology, Psychology. **Career:** Associate Professor of Education, University of British Columbia, Vancouver, 1962-67; Loyola University of Chicago, associate professor, 1967-70, professor, 1970-92, Professor Emerita, 1992.

Publications: Effective Study, 1968; (with G. Szasz) Adolescents in Society, 1969; (with E. A. Thorn, A. C. Smith and K. D. Munroe) The Gage Language Experience Reading Program, rev. ed. 1970; (with A. Ornstein and H. Talmage) A Handbook for Paraprofessionals, 1975. **Address:** Loyola University of Chicago, 6525 N. Sheridan Rd., Chicago, IL 60626, U.S.A.

JULIUS, Anthony (Robert). American, b. 1956. **Genres:** Art/Art history. **Career:** Attorney. Mishcon de Reya, London, England, 1981-, partner, 1984-, head of litigation, 1987-. Diana, Princess of Wales, Memorial Fund, trustee, 1997-, chairman, 1997-99, vice president, 2002-. **Publications:** T. S. Eliot: Anti-Semitism and Literary Form, 1995, reprinted with new preface, 2003; Idolizing Pictures: Idolatry, Iconoclasm, and Jewish Art, 2001; Transgressions: The Offences of Art, 2002. **Address:** Mishcon de Reya, Summit House, 12 Red Lion Sq., London WC1R 4QD, England. **Online address:** anthony.julius@mishcon.co.uk

JUNGER, Sebastian. American, b. 1962. **Genres:** Adult non-fiction. **Career:** Freelance writer. **Publications:** The Perfect Storm: A True Story of Men Against the Sea, 1997; Fire, 2001. Contributor to periodicals. **Address:** 315 W 36th St #14D, New York, NY 10018-6404, U.S.A.

JUNKER, Patricia. American, b. 1952. **Genres:** Art/Art history. **Career:** Toledo Museum of Art, Toledo, OH, fellow, 1976-77; Smith College, Northampton, MA, intern at art museum, 1978-80, curatorial assistant, 1980-82; University of Rochester, Rochester, NY, curator of American art and chief curator at Memorial Art Gallery, 198290; University of Wisconsin-Madison, curator of collections at Elvehjem Museum of Art, 1990-92; Fine Arts Museums of San Francisco, San Francisco, CA, assistant curator of American paintings, 1992-94, acting head of American art department, 1994-96, associate curator of American art, 1996-. **Publications:** Promoted to Glory: The Apotheosis of George Washington, 1980; The Course of Empire: The Erie Canal and the New York Landscape, 1825-1875, 1984; Winslow Homer in the 1890s: Prout's Neck Observed, 1990; John Steuart Curry: Inventing the Middle West, 1998; (coauthor) The Rockefeller Collection of American Art at the Fine Arts Museums of San Francisco. Author of exhibition catalogs. Contributor to books and periodicals. **Address:** M. H. de Young Memorial Museum, Fine Arts Museums of San Francisco, Golden Gate Park, San Francisco, CA 94118, U.S.A. **Online address:** pjunker@famsf.org

JUNKINS, Donald (Arthur). American, b. 1931. **Genres:** Poetry. **Career:** Emerson College, Boston, assistant professor, 1961; California State College, Chico, assistant professor, 1963-66; University of Massachusetts, Amherst, assistant professor, 1966-69, associate professor, 1969-74, director, Master of Fine Arts Program in English, 1970-78, 1989-90, professor of English, 1974-. **Publications:** The Sunfish and the Partridge, 1965; The Graves of Scotland Parish, 1968; Walden, 100 Years after Thoreau, 1968; And Sandpipers She Said, 1970; (ed.) The Contemporary World Poets, 1976; The Uncle Harry Poems and Other Maine Reminiscences, 1977; Crossing by Ferry, 1978; The Agamenticus Poems, 1984; Playing for Keeps: Poems, 1991; Journey to the Corrida (poems), 1999. **Address:** 63 Hawks Rd, Deerfield, MA 01342, U.S.A.

JURAGA, Dubravka. American (born Yugoslavia), b. 1956. **Genres:** Literary criticism and history. **Career:** Dnevnik (daily newspaper), Novi Sad, Yugoslavia, editor and translator, 1982-88; University of Arkansas, Fayetteville, copy editor and proof editor of Arkansas Traveler, 1988-89, editorial assistant for Meteoritics and Planetary Science, 1996; Northeastern Oklahoma State University, Tahlequah, adjunct instructor in English and in Russian language and culture, 1997-98; University of Arkansas, instructor in English, 1997-99; independent scholar, writer, and translator, 1999-. Private tutor in English as a second language, 1978-88; Workers University of Novi Sad, instructor, 1981-84; Institute of Neurology, Psychiatry, and Mental Health, Novi Sad, medical translator and instructor, 1981-88. University of Arkansas Press, editorial assistant, 1988-89. **Publications:** (with M.K. Booker) Bakhtin, Stalin, and Modern Russian Fiction: Dialogism, Carnival, and History, 1995; (with Booker) The Caribbean Novel in English: An Introduction, 1999. Contributor to books. Contributor of articles, stories, translations, and reviews to periodicals in Yugoslavia and the United States. **Address:** 1621 Terry Dr., Fayetteville, AR 72703, U.S.A. **Online address:** djuraga@comp.uark.edu

JURMAIN, Suzanne. American, b. 1945. **Genres:** Children's fiction, Young adult fiction. **Career:** Actress, beginning in 1949; University of California, Museum of Cultural History, Los Angeles, editor and public relations coordinator, 1968-77; free-lance writer and editor, 1978-. **Publications:** From Trunk to Tail: Elephants Legendary and Real (juvenile), 1989; Once

upon a Horse: A History of Horses and How They Shaped Our History (juvenile), 1989; Freedom's Sons: The True Story of the Amistad Mutiny (juvenile), 1998. **Address:** c/o Tracey Adams, McIntosh & Otis, Inc, 353 Lexington Ave Fl 15, New York, NY 10016, U.S.A.

JUSSAWALLA, Feroza. Indian, b. 1953. **Genres:** Literary criticism and history. **Career:** University of Texas at El Paso, professor of English, 1980-; Border Book Festival, member of board of directors. **Publications:** Family Quarrels: Towards a Criticism of Indian Writing in English, 1985; Excellent Teaching: Essays in Honor of Kenneth Eble, 1990; Interviews with Writers of the PostColonial World, 1992; (ed.) Conversations with V.S. Naipaul, 1997. **Address:** Department of English, University of Texas at El Paso, El Paso, TX 79968, U.S.A. **Online address:** fjussawa@mail.utep.edu

JUST, Ward. American, b. 1935. **Genres:** Novels, Novellas/Short stories. **Career:** Newsweek magazine, reporter, Chicago and Washington, 1959-62, London and Washington, 1963-65; The Reporter Magazine, Washington, 1962-63; The Washington Post, Washington and Saigon. **Publications:** NOVELS: A Soldier of the Revolution, 1970; The Congressman Who Loved Flaubert, 1973; Stringer, 1974; Nicholson at Large, 1975; A Family Trust, 1978; Honor, Power, Riches, Fame and the Love of Women, 1979; In the City of Fear, 1982; The American Blues, 1984; The American Ambassador, 1987; Jack Gance, 1989; The Translator, 1991; Ambition and Love, 1994; Echo House, 1996; A Dangerous Friend, 1999; Lowell Limpett, 2001; The Weather in Berlin, 2002. SHORT STORIES: Twenty-One: Selected Stories, 1990. OTHER: To What End, 1968; Military Men, 1970. **Address:** RFD 342, Vineyard Haven, MA 02568, U.S.A.

JUSTER, Norton. American, b. 1929. **Genres:** Children's fiction, Women's studies and issues, Songs/Lyrics and libretti, Architecture, Children's non-fiction, Picture/board books, Humor/Satire. **Career:** Architect, Juster and Gugliotta, New York, 1960-68; Adjunct Professor, Pratt Institute, NYC, 1960-70; Architect, Juster-Pope-Frazier Assocs., Shelburne Falls, Massachusetts, 1969-95, retired; Emeritus Professor of Design, Hampshire College, Amherst, Massachusetts. **Publications:** The Phantom Tollbooth, 1961; The Dot and the Line: A Romance in Lower Mathematics, 1963; Alberic the Wise and Other Journeys, 1965; Stark Naked: A Paranomastic Odyssey, 1969; So Sweet to Labor: Rural Women in America 1865-1895, 1980; Otter Nonsense, 1982; As: A Surfeit of Similes, 1989; (editor) A Woman's Place: Yesterday's Women in Rural America, 1996; Alberic the Wise, 1992; Picture Book Studio, As Silly as Knees, as Busy as Bees, 1998; The Phantom Tollbooth (opera), 1995. **Address:** 259 Lincoln Ave, Amherst, MA 01002, U.S.A.

JUSTICE, Donald (Rodney). See Obituaries.

JUSTICE, Keith LeRoy. American, b. 1949. **Genres:** Film, Local history/Rural topics, Politics/Government, Trivia/Facts, Bibliography. **Career:** Newton Record, Newton, MS, news editor, 1984-89, news editor, 1995-2003; Meridian Star, Meridian, MS, wire desk editor, 1989-92; Newton County Government, Newton, 911 and emergency management coordinator, 1992-95; East Central Community College, adjunct faculty member, 1998-99; Newton County Impact Mail, managing editor, 2003-. **Publications:** Adult Video Index '84, 1984; Public Office Index, 1985; Science Fiction Master Index, 1986; Science Fiction, Fantasy, and Horror Reference: An Annotated Bibliography of Works about Literature and Film, 1989; (ed. and contrib.) N. Williams, The History of Newton, 1989; (ed. and contrib.) Newton County and the Civil War, 1995; Bestseller Index: All Books, Publishers Weekly and the New York Times through 1990, 1998; Friends and Neighbors: Some of the People, a Few of the Places, and a Little of the History of Newton County and Surrounding Area, 1998; Presidents, Vice Presidents, Cabinet Members, Supreme Court Justices, 1789-2003: Vital and Official Data, 2003. **Address:** 11620 Hwy 492 E, Union, MS 39365, U.S.A. **Online address:** caboose@intop.net

JUSTISS, Julia. American. **Genres:** Romance/Historical. **Career:** Novelist and part-time high school French teacher; worked briefly as a business journalist; wrote newsletter for American Embassy in Tunis, Tunisia. **Publications:** The Wedding Gamble, 1998; A Scandalous Proposal, 2000; The Proper Wife, 2001; My Lady's Trust, 2002; My Lady's Pleasure, 2002; My Lady's Honor, 2002; Seductive Stranger, 2003; Wicked Wager, 2003. **Address:** Daingerfield, TX 75638, U.S.A. **Online address:** j.justiss@juno.com; www.juliajustiss.com

JWEID, Rosann. American, b. 1933. **Genres:** Education. **Career:** Elementary schoolteacher in Syracuse, NY, 1954; Scotia-Glenville Central School, Scotia, NY, library media specialist, 1967-93, department head, K-12

Library Department, 1982-92. Consultant. **Publications:** WITH M. RIZZO: The Library Classroom Partnership: Teaching Library Media Skills in the Middle and Junior High Schools, 1988, rev. ed., 1998; Building Character through Literature: A Guide for Middle School Readers, 2001; Building Character through Multicultural Literature: A Guide for Middle School Readers, 2004. **Address:** 707 Riverside Ave, Scotia, NY 12302, U.S.A.

K

KABIRA, Wanjiku Mukabi. Kenyan. **Genres:** Essays. **Career:** Editor and writer. **Publications:** The Oral Artist, 1983; (with K. Mutahi) Gikuyu Oral Literature, 1988; (with A.N. Ngoru) Gender Sensitivity in Bamako Initiative in Kisumu District: An Evaluation Report, 1992; (comp., with M. Masinjila), Gender and Development: The FEMNET Model for Gender Responsive Planning, Programming, Advocacy, and Sensitization, 1993; (with M. Gachago) Gender and Development: A FEMNET Manual for Trainers, 1993; (with E.A. Nzioki) Celebrating Women's Resistance: A Case Study of Women's Groups Movement in Kenya, 1993; (comp., with M. Masinjila and W. Njau) Needs Assessment Rusinga Island, 1993; Agikuyu (juvenile nonfiction), 1995; (with M. Masinjila) ABC of Gender Analysis: A Framework of Analysis for the Education Sector, 1995. EDITOR: (with A. Luvai and B. Muluka) Tender Memories, 1989; (with M. Karega and E. Nzioki) Our Secret Lives: An Anthology of Poems and Short Stories, 1991; (with A. Nzioki) They've Destroyed the Temple (stories and poems), 1992; (with J. Adhiambo-Oduol and M. Nzomo) Democratic Change in Africa: Women's Perspective, 1993; (with M. Masinjila and W. Mbugua) Delusions: Essays on Social Construction of Gender, 1994; (with W. Muthoni) The Road to Empowerment, 1994; (with W. Mbugua) With a Song in Our Hearts: A Collection of Poems on Women and Girls, 1996. **Address:** c/o Forum for African Women Educationalists, PO Box 30426, Nairobi, Kenya.

KACAPYR, Elia. American, b. 1956. **Genres:** Economics. **Career:** Ithaca College, Ithaca, NY, professor of economics, 1985-. **Publications:** Economic Forecasting, 1996; How to Prepare for the AP Macro/Micro Exam, 2001. **Address:** Dept of Economics, Ithaca College, Ithaca, NY 14850, U.S.A. **Online address:** kacapyr@ithaca.edu

KACHTICK, Keith. American. **Genres:** Novels. **Career:** Writer. Lineage Project, New York, NY, senior instructor. **Publications:** Hungry Ghost: A Novel, 2003. Contributor to periodicals. **Address:** c/o Author Mail, 10 East 53rd St., New York, NY 10022, U.S.A.

KACHUR, Lewis. American. **Genres:** Art/Art history. **Career:** S. R. Guggenheim Museum, New York City, curatorial assistant, 1982-84; freelance researcher, 1984-90; Kean College of New Jersey, Union, assistant professor of art history, 1990-. Fulbright lecturer in Osaka, Japan, 1992-93. **Publications:** Stuart Davis: An American in Paris, Whitney Museum, 1988; (with Karen Wilkin) The Drawings of Stuart Davis, Abrams, 1992. **Address:** Department of Fine Arts, Kean College of New Jersey, Union, NJ 07083, U.S.A.

KADARE, Ismail. Albanian, b. 1936. **Genres:** Novels, Novellas/Short stories, Poetry, Literary criticism and history. **Career:** Novelist, short story writer, and poet. **Publications:** NOVELS: Gjenerali i ushtrise se vdekur, 1963, trans. as The General of the Dead Army, 1971; Dasma, 1968, trans. as The Wedding, 1972; Kronike ne gur, 1971, trans. as Chronicle in Stone, 1987; Dimri i vetmise se madh (title means: The Great Winter), 1973, as Dimri i madh, 1981; Nentori i nje kryeqyti, 1975; Keshtjella, c. 1970, trans. as The Castle, c. 1980; Ura me tri harqe: triptik me nje intermexo, 1978, trans. as The Three-Arched Bridge, 1995; The Niche of Shame, 1978; Gjakftohtesia: Novela, 1980; Kush e solli Doruntinen, 1980, trans. as Doruntine, 1988; Viti I mbrapshte (The Dark Year), 1980; Krushqit jane te ngrire (The Wedding Procession Turned into Ice), 1980; Prilli I thyer, 1980, trans. as Broken April, 1990; Nenpunesi I pallatit te enderrave, 1980, trans. as The Palace of Dreams, 1993; Nje dosje per Homerin (also known as Dosja H),

1980, trans. as The File on H, 1998; Le crepuscule des dieux de la steppe (The Twilight of the Gods of the Steppe), 1981; La niche de la honte, trans., c. 1984; Koncert ne fund te dimrit, 1988, trans. as The Concert: A Novel, 1994; Perbindeshi (The Monster), 1991; Piramida, 1992, trans. as The Pyramid, 1996; Nata me hene (A Moonlit Night), 1985; Hija (The Shadow), 1994; Shkaba, 1996; La ville sans enseignes, 1996; Vie, jeu et maor de Lul Mazrek, 2002; La fille d'Agamemnon, 2003; Le Successeur, 2003. SHORT STORIES: Qyteti i jugut (title means: The Southern City), 1964; Sjellesi I fatkeqesise (Caravan of Veils), 1980; Invitation a un concert officiel et autre recits (Invitation to an Official Concert and Other Stories), 1985; La Grande Muraille, suivi de Le firman aveugle, 1993; Les Adieux du mal, 1996; Le Concours de beaute masculine, 1998; Trois chants funetres pour le Kosovo, 1998; L'envol du migrature, 2001. POETRY: Frymezimet djaloshare, 1954; Motive me diell: vjersha dhe poema, c. 1969; Koha: vjersha dhe poema, 1976; Buzeqeshje mbi bote, 1980; The Sixties; Insufficient Time. CRITICISM AND ESSAYS: Autobiografia e popullit ne vargje, 1980, trans. as The Autobiography of the People in Verse, 1987; Eskili, ky humbes i madh (title means: Aeschylus, the Great Loser), 1988; Ftese ne studio (Invitation to the Studio), 1990; Ardhja e Migjenit ne letersine shqipe (The Arrival of Migjeni in Albanian Literature), 1991; Pranvera shqiptare (The Albanian Spring), c. 1991; La legende des legendes (The Legend of Legends), 1995; Visage des Balkans (Visages of Balkans), 1995; Il a fallu ce deuil pour se retrouver, 2000. OTHER: Emblema e dikurshme: tregime e novela, 1977; Keshtjella dhe helmi: pjese teatrale, 1977; On the Lay of the Knights, 1979; Vepra letrare (title means: Works), 12 vols., 1981; Koha e shkrimeve: tregime, novela, pershkrime (Epoch of Writings: collection), 1986; Entretiens avec Eric Faye (Conversations with Eric Faye), 1991; Endrra mashtruese: tregime e novela, 1991; Spiritus: roman me kaos, zbulese dhe cmeers, 1996; Mauvaise saison sur l'Olympe (play), 1998; Lulet e ftohta te marsit, Froides flours d'avril, 2000. **Address:** c/o Librairie Artheme Fayard, 75 rue des Saints-Peres, F-75006 Paris, France.

KADEL, Andrew. American, b. 1954. **Genres:** Bibliography. **Career:** Ordained Episcopal priest, 1982; curate of Episcopal church in Lincoln, NE, 1981-83; vicar of Episcopal church in Kirksville, MO, 1983-85; Princeton University, Princeton, NJ, bibliographic specialist at university library, 1987-89; Mercy College, Dobbs Ferry, NY, reference librarian, 1989-90; Union Theological Seminary, NYC, reference and collection development librarian at Burke Library, 1990-. **Publications:** Matrology: A Bibliographby of Writings by Christian Women from the First to the Fifteenth Centuries, 1995. Contributor to Journal of Religious and Theological Information. **Address:** Burke Library, Union Theological Seminary, 13041 Broadway, New York, NY 10027, U.S.A.

KADIR, Djelal. Cypriot, b. 1946. **Genres:** Literary criticism and history. **Career:** Purdue University, West Lafayette, IN, professor of comparative literature and head of department, 1973-91; University of Oklahoma, Norman, distinguished professor of literature, 1991-94, Neustadt Professor of Comparative Literature, 1995-97; The Pennsylvania State University, Edwin Erle Sparks Professor of Comparative Literature, Director, Council on Inter-American Literary Cultures; lecturer at universities, foundations, institutes, and corporations. **Publications:** Juan Carlos Onetti, 1977; Questing Fictions, 1987; Columbus and the Ends of the Earth, 1992; The Other Writing, 1993. EDITOR: Triple Espera, 1976; (and trans) J. Cabral, Selected Poetry, 1937-1990, 1994. **Address:** Department of Comparative Literature, The Pennsylvania State University, 311 Burrowes Building, University Park, PA 16802-6203, U.S.A.

KADISH, Alon. Israeli/American, b. 1950. **Genres:** Economics, History, Military/Defense/Arms control. **Career:** University of London, England, research fellow at Institute of Historical Research, 1978-79; Hebrew University of Jerusalem, Israel, lecturer, 1980-84, senior lecturer in history, 1984-92, chairman, history department, 1995-97; University of Manchester, senior Simon research fellow, 1991-92, associate professor, 1992-2000, professor, 2000-; appointed to the Aryeh Ben-Eliezer Chair in National Literature Movements of the 19th and 20th Centuries, 1998. Merton College, Oxford, visiting research fellow, 2000. **Publications:** The Oxford Economists of the Late Nineteenth Century, 1982; Apostle Arnold: The Life and Death of Arnold Toynbee, 1986; Historians, Economists, and Economic History, 1989; (with K. Tribe) The Market for Political Economy: The Advent of Economics in British University Culture, 1850-1905, 1993; To Arms and Farms: The Hachsharot in the Palmach (Hebrew), 1995; (ed.) The Corn Laws: The Formation of Popular Economics in Britain, 6 vols., 1996; (with A. Sela and A. Golan) The Occupation of Lydda, July 1948 (Hebrew), 2000. **Address:** Department of History, Hebrew University of Jerusalem, Jerusalem, Israel.

KADUSHIN, Alfred. American, b. 1916. **Genres:** Sociology. **Career:** University of Wisconsin, Madison, School of Social Work, assistant professor, 1950-55, associate professor, 1955-58, professor of social work, 1959-90, emeritus professor, 1991-. **Publications:** (with J. Martin) Child Welfare Services, 1967, 4th ed., 1987; Child Welfare Services: A Research Source Book, 1969; Adopting Older Children, 1971; The Social Work Interview, 1972, 4th ed. (with G. Kadushin), 1997; Supervision in Social Work, 1976, 4th ed. (with D. Harkness), 2002; Consultation in Social Work, 1977; (with J. Martin) Child Abuse: An Interactional Event, 1981. **Address:** 4933 Marathon Dr, Madison, WI 53705, U.S.A.

KAEMMER, John E. American, b. 1928. **Genres:** Anthropology/Ethnology, Music. **Career:** Schoolteacher in Morrumbene, Mozambique, 1952-54, and Malange, Angola, 1957-61; Nyariri Teacher Training College, Mutoko, Zimbabwe, teacher, 1964-68; Indiana University-Bloomington, instructor in Independent Study Division, 1974-75; DePauw University, Greencastle, IN, assistant professor, 1975-81, associate professor, 1981-89, professor of anthropology, 1989-92, head of Department of Sociology and Anthropology, 1980-87; Zimbabwe College of Music, Harare, visiting lecturer, 1992-93. Conducted field research on music and social organization in Zimbabwe, 1971, 1972-73, and 1982. **Publications:** Music in Human Life: Anthropological Perspectives on Music, 1993. Work represented in anthologies. Contributor to music and anthropology journals. **Address:** 900 University St., Apt 11J, Seattle, WA 98101, U.S.A.

KAEMPFER, William H. American, b. 1951. **Genres:** Economics. **Career:** University of North Carolina at Greensboro, assistant professor of economics, 1978-79; University of Washington, Seattle, assistant professor of economics, 1979-81; Claremont McKenna College and Claremont Graduate School, Claremont, CA, 1985-90; University of Colorado, Boulder, assistant professor, 1981-89, associate professor, 1989-94, professor, 1994-. **Publications:** (with A.D. Lowenberg) International Economic Sanctions: A Public Choice Perspective, 1992; (with J. Marlow, J. Melvin and K. Maskus) International Trade: Theory and Evidence, 1995. **Address:** Department of Economics, University of Colorado, Boulder, CO 80309-0256, U.S.A.

KAFKA, F(rancis) L. American, b. 1926. **Genres:** Novels. **Career:** Writer. **Publications:** The Narrow Road, 1978; Tunnel to Glory, 1992. **Address:** 2011 Devon St., Colorado Springs, CO 80909, U.S.A.

KAFKA, Kimberly. American. **Genres:** Novels. **Career:** Writer; has taught writing workshops at the University of Michigan, Bennington College, and the University of Southern Maine. Wilderness emergency medical technician (EMT). **Publications:** True North, 2000. Contributor of short fiction to periodicals. **Address:** c/o Dutton, Division of Penguin Putnam Inc., 375 Hudson Street, New York, NY 10014, U.S.A.

KAFKA, Mitzi. *See* **PRELLER, James.**

KAGAN, Donald. American (born Lithuania), b. 1932. **Genres:** Classics, History. **Career:** Capital University, Columbus, OH, part-time instructor in history, 1957-58; Pennsylvania State University, University Park, instructor in history, 1959-60; Cornell University, Ithaca, NY, assistant professor, 1960-63, associate professor, 1964-67, professor of ancient history, 1967-69; Yale University, New Haven, CT, professor of history and classics, 1969-78, chairman, Classics Dept., 1972-75, master of Timothy Dwight College, 1976-78, Sterling Professor of History & Classics, 1978-, acting director of athletics, 1987-89, dean of Yale College, 1989-. **Publications:** The Great Dialogue: A History of Greek Political Thought from Homer to Polybius,

1965; The Outbreak of the Peloponnesian War, 1969; The Archidamian War, 1974; (with S. Ozment and F. Turner) The Western Heritage, 1979, 4th ed., 2003; The Peace of Nicias and the Sicilian Expedition, 1981; The Fall of the Athenian Empire, 1987; Pericles and the Triumph of Democracy, 1990; Pericles of Athens and the Birth of Democracy, 1991; On the Origins of War and the Preservation of Peace, 1995; (with F.W. Kagan) While America Sleeps: Self-Delusion, Military Weakness, and the Threat to Peace Today, 2000; The Pelopommesian War, 2003. EDITOR: The Decline and Fall of the Roman Empire in the West, 1962; Readings in Greek Political Thought, 1965; Problems in Ancient History, 1966; (with L.P. Williams and B. Teirney) Great Issues in Western Civilization, 1967, 3rd ed., 1976; Botsford and Robinson's Hellenic History, 5th ed., 1969; Studies in the Greek Historians: In Memory of Adam Parry, 1975. **Address:** Hall of Graduate Studies 215, Yale University, New Haven, CT 06520, U.S.A. **Online address:** donald.kagan@yale.edu

KAGAN, Elaine. American. **Genres:** Novels. **Career:** Actor in films and television productions. **Publications:** NOVELS: The Girls, 1994; Blue Heaven, 1996; Somebody's Baby, 1998; No Good-Byes, 2000; Losing Mr. North, 2002. **Address:** c/o Virginia Barber, William Morris Agency, 1325 Avenue of the Americas, New York, NY 10019, U.S.A.

KAGAN, Jerome. American, b. 1929. **Genres:** Psychology. **Career:** Professor of Psychology, Dept. of Psychology, Harvard University, Cambridge, Massachusetts, since 1964. **Publications:** (with Howard Moss) Birth to Maturity, 1962; Change and Continuity in Infancy, 1971; (with Richard Kearsley and Philip Zelazo) Infancy, 1978; The Second Year, 1981; The Nature of the Child, 1984; (with Paul Mussen, John Conger and Aletha Huston) Child Development and Personality (text), 6th ed., 1984; (with Julius Segal) Psychology: An Introduction (text), 7th ed., 1992; Unstable Ideas, 1989; Galen's Prophecy, 1994. **Address:** Dept. of Psychology, Harvard University, William James Hall, 33 Kirkland, Cambridge, MA 02138, U.S.A.

KAGAN, Shelly. American, b. 1954. **Genres:** Philosophy. **Career:** Educator and author. Yale University, Henry R. Luce Professor of Social Thought and Ethics, 1995-. Taught at the University of Pittsburgh and the University of Illinois at Chicago. **Publications:** The Limits of Morality, 1989; Normative Ethics, 1998. Contributor to periodicals. **Address:** Department of Philosophy, Yale University, New Haven, CT 06520, U.S.A. **Online address:** shelly.kagan@yale.edu

KAGARLITSKY, Boris. Russian, b. 1958. **Genres:** Area studies, International relations/Current affairs, Politics/Government. **Career:** Postal employee in Moscow, U.S.S.R., 1980-82; caretaker in Moscow, 1983-88; IMA Press News Agency, Moscow, political observer and journalist, 1988-90; Moscow Soviet, deputy, 1990-93. **Publications:** The Thinking Reed: Intellectuals and the Soviet State 1917 to the Present, 1988; The Dialectic of Hope, 1989; The Dialectic of Change, 1989; Farewell Perestroyka, 1990; The Disintegration of the Monolith, 1993; The Restoration in Russia, 1995; The Mirage of Modernization, 1995; The Square Wheels, 1995; New Realism, New Barbarism, 1999; The Twilight of Globalization, 2000; The Return of Radicalism, 2000; Russia under Yeltsin and Putin, 2002. **Address:** Krasnoarmeyskaya 29, Flat 43, 125319 Moscow, Russia.

KAGEL, John H(enry). American, b. 1942. **Genres:** Economics. **Career:** Texas A&M University, College Station, TX, began as assistant professor, became professor of economics, 1969-82; University of Houston, Houston, TX, professor of economics, 1982-88; University of Pittsburgh, Pittsburgh, PA, professor of economics and director of Economics Laboratory, 1988-99; University of Pittsburgh Graduate School of Business, Pittsburgh, professor of business administration, 1998-99; Ohio State University, Columbus, chaired professor of allied microeconomics and director of Economics Laboratory, 1999-. Served on the editorial boards of Behaviour Analysis Letters, 1981-83, American Economic Review, 1989-95, Journal of Experimental Economics, 1997-, and Management Science, 1999-. Consultant to various firms, including H. E. W., Division of Dentistry, Manpower Planning; the United States Air Force, Human Resources Laboratory; McQuary and Tagaropolis Law Firm; Solvay America; Tansco Pipeline; Reinhard and Anderson Law Firm; Munroe Consulting. Affiliate of Law and Economic Consulting Group. **Publications:** (editor, with Leonard Green) Advances in Behavioral Economics, Volumes 1-3, 1987-96; (with Raymond C. Battalio and Leonard Green) Economic Choice Theory: An Experimental Analysis of Animal Behavior, 1995; (editor, with A. Roth) The Handbook of Experimental Economics, 1995; (with Dan Levin) Common Value Auctions and the Winner's Curse, 2002. Contributor of numerous chapters to books and of articles to scholarly journals. **Address:** 4393 Donington Rd., Columbus, OH 43220, U.S.A. **Online address:** kagel@economics.sbs.ohio-state.edu

KAHAN, Alan S. American, b. 1959. **Genres:** History, Politics/Government. **Career:** Journal of Modern History, Chicago, IL, editorial assistant, 1983-84; Ecole des Hautes Etudes en Sciences Sociales, Paris, France, Lurcy fellow, 1984-85; University of Chicago, Chicago, lecturer in Western civilization, 1985, and social sciences, 1986-87, fellow of Olin Program in the History of Political Culture, 1987-88; Rice University, Houston, TX, Mellon assistant professor of history, 1988-92; Florida International University, Miami, assistant professor of history, 1992-. **Publications:** Aristocratic Liberalism: The Social and Political Thought of Jacob Burckhardt, John Stuart Mill, and Alexis de Tocqueville, 1992, 2nd ed., 2001; (trans.) A. de Tocqueville, The Old Regime and the Revolution, vol. 1, 1998, vol. 2, 1999; The Liberal Moment, forthcoming. Work represented in anthologies. Contributor of articles and reviews to history journals. **Address:** Dept of History, University Park DM-397, Florida International University, Miami, FL 33199, U.S.A. **Online address:** kahana@fin.edu

KAHL, Jonathan (D.). American, b. 1959. **Genres:** Meteorology/Atmospheric sciences. **Career:** National Oceanic and Atmospheric Administration, Boulder, CO, research associate, 1987-89; University of Wisconsin-Milwaukee, Milwaukee, WI, professor of atmospheric science, 1990-. **Publications:** Weatherwise: Learning about the Weather, 1992; Wet Weather: Rain Showers and Snowfall, 1992; Storm Warning: Tornadoes and Hurricanes, 1993; Thunderbolt: Learning about Lightning, 1993; Weather Watch: forecasting the Weather, 1996; Hazy Skies: Weather and the Environment, 1998; National Audubon Society First Field Field Guide to Weather, 1998. **Address:** 310 W. Lexington Blvd., Glendale, WI 53217, U.S.A. **Online address:** kahl@uwm.edu

KAHLENBERG, Richard D(awson). American, b. 1963. **Genres:** Education, Law, Politics/Government, Race relations, Autobiography/Memoirs. **Career:** Office of Senator Charles S. Robb, Washington, DC, legislative assistant, 1989-93; George Washington University, visiting associate professor, 1993-94; Center for National Policy, fellow, 1996-98; Century Foundation, senior fellow, 1998-. **Publications:** Broken Contract: A Memoir of Harvard Law School, 1992; The Remedy: Class, Race, and Affirmative action, 1996; All Together Now: Creating Middle-Class Schools through Public School Choice, 2001. EDITOR: A Notion at Risk: Preserving Public Education as an Engine for Social Mobility, 2000; Divided We Fail: Coming Together through Public School Choice, 2002; Public School Choice vs. Private School Vouchers, 2003; America's Untapped Resource: LowIncome Students in Higher Education, 2004. **Address:** 1333 H St NW 10th Fl, Washington, DC 20005, U.S.A. **Online address:** kahlenberg@tcf.org

KAHN, David. American, b. 1930. **Genres:** Military/Defense/Arms control. **Career:** Newsday, Melville, NY, reporter, 1955-63, assistant viewpoints editor, 1979-94, assistant editor, news, 1996-99, and member of Editorial Board, 1989-94, retired 1999; Herald Tribune, Paris, deskman, 1965-67; St. Antony's College, Oxford, sr. associate member, 1972-74; New York University, NYC, associate professor of journalism, 1975-79; adjunct professor of military intelligence, Yale, 1984, Columbia, 1985-89; SUNY Stony Brook, adjunct professor of journalism, 1991-94. Cryptologia, co-editor, 1977-. **Publications:** The Codebreakers, 1967; Hitler's Spies, 1978; Kahn on Codes, 1983; (trans. and ed.) Clandestine Operations, by Pierre Lorain (in U.K. as Secret Warfare), 1983; Seizing the Enigma, 1991; The Reader of Gentlemen's Mail, 2004. **Address:** 120 Wooleys Ln, Great Neck, NY 11023-2301, U.S.A. **Online address:** davidkahn1@aol.com

KAHN, John (Ellison). British (born Republic of South Africa), b. 1950. **Genres:** Novellas/Short stories, Advertising/Public relations, Communications/Media, Education, How-to books, Language/Linguistics, Speech/Rhetoric, Writing/Journalism, Translations. **Career:** Director of WordCraft Editing and Writing Ltd., London, England. Worked as newspaper reporter, reviewer, teacher, lexicographer, publisher's editor, and free-lance journalist and copywriter. **Publications:** (comp) The Right Word at the Right Time: A Guide to the English Language and How to Use It, 1985, rev. ed., 1986; What's in a Word? The Fascinating Stories behind Some Everyday Words, 1985; An Ear to the Ground: The Uncommon Origins of Some Common Expressions, 1986; (comp) Reader's Digest Reverse Dictionary, 1989; (ed.) How to Write and Speak Better, 1991; The Concise Oxford Dictionary of English Usage, forthcoming. **Address:** WordCraft Editing and Writing Ltd, 3 Mount Gardens, Leeds LS17 7QN, England. **Online address:** wordcraft@clara.net

KAHN, Michael A. American, b. 1952. **Genres:** Mystery/Crime/Suspense. **Career:** Blackwell Sanders Peper Martin (law firm), St. Louis, MO, partner, 1985-. **Publications:** RACHEL GOLD MYSTERIES: The Canaan Legacy, 1988, as Grave Designs, 1992; Death Benefits, 1992; Firm Ambitions, 1994;

Due Diligence, 1995; Sheer Gall, 1996; Bearing Witness, 2000; Trophy Widow, 2001. **Address:** Blackwell Sanders Peper Martin LLP, 720 Olive St Ste 2400, St. Louis, MO 63101, U.S.A. **Online address:** mkahn@blackwellsanders.com

KAHN, Peggy. See **KATZ, Bobbi.**

KAHN, Sharon. American, b. 1934. **Genres:** Children's fiction, Children's non-fiction, Mystery/Crime/Suspense. **Career:** Attorney, arbitrator, and writer. **Publications:** Kacy and the Space Shuttle Secret: A Space Adventure for Young Readers, 1996; (with R. Weingarten) Brave Black Women: From Slavery to the Space Shuttle, 1997. RUBY, THE RABBI'S WIFE MYSTERY SERIES: Fax Me a Bagel, 1998; Never Nosh a Matzo Ball, 2000; Don't Cry for Me, Hot Pastrami, 2001; Hold the Cream Cheese, Kill the Lox, 2002. **Address:** c/o Author Mail, Simon & Schuster, 1230 Avenue of the Americas, New York, NY 10020, U.S.A.

KAHNE, Joseph. American, b. 1964. **Genres:** Education. **Career:** Social studies teacher at public schools in NYC, 1986-88; University of Illinois at Chicago Circle, Chicago, assistant professor of education and policy studies, 1993-. **Publications:** Reframing Educational Policy: Democracy, Community, and the Individual, 1996. Contributor to books. Contributor of articles and reviews to education journals. **Address:** Dept of Education, Mills College, 5000 MacArthur Blvd, Oakland, CA 94613, U.S.A.

KAIM-CAUDLE, Peter (Robert). British (born Germany), b. 1916. **Genres:** Medicine/Health, Social sciences, Sociology. **Career:** Professor Emeritus of Social Policy, University of Durham, 1982- (Staff Tutor in Extra Mural Studies, 1950-63; Lecturer, 1963-68; Sr. Lecturer, 1968-75; Professor of Social Administration, 1975-79; Professor of Social Policy, 1979-82). Head of Dept. of Economic Studies, University College of Sierra Leone, 1954-55 and 1961; Research Professor, Economic and Social Research Institute, Dublin, 1968-70. Visiting appointments at University College Cork, University of Calgary, University of Monash, Australian National University, and Chung Hsing University, Taipei. **Publications:** Social Security in Ireland and Western Europe, 1964; Housing in Ireland: Some Economic Aspects, 1965; Social Policy in the Irish Republic, 1967; Dental Services in Ireland, Economic and Social Research Institute, 1969; Pharmaceutical Services in Ireland, 1970; Opthalmic Services in Ireland, 1970; (with J.G. Byrne) Irish Pension Schemes 1969, 1971; Comparative Social Policy and Social Security, 1973; (with G.N. March) Team Care in General Practice, 1975; (with J. Keithley) Aspects of Ageing, 1993; Biographical Note of H.J. Boyden, 2002. Contributor to journals in England and Ireland. **Address:** Beechwood, Princes St, Durham DH1 4RP, England.

KAIN, Philip J(oseph). American, b. 1943. **Genres:** Ethics, Philosophy, Politics/Government. **Career:** University of California, Santa Cruz, assistant professor of philosophy, 1974-82; Stanford University, Stanford, CA, lecturer in Western Culture Program, 1982-86; Santa Clara University, Santa Clara, CA, associate professor, 1988-94, Philosophy Dept, chairman, 1991-, professor of philosophy, 1994-. **Publications:** Schiller, Hegel, and Marx, 1982; Marx, Method, Epistemology, and Humanism, 1986; Marx and Ethics, 1988; Marx and Modern Political Theory, 1993. **Address:** Department of Philosophy, Santa Clara University, Santa Clara, CA 95053, U.S.A. **Online address:** pkain@scu.edu

KAINSDATTER, Marianne. See **MADSEN, Svend Aage.**

KAIRYS, David. American, b. 1943. **Genres:** Law, Civil liberties/Human rights, Novels. **Career:** Kairys & Rudovsky (law firm), Philadelphia, PA, partner, 1971-90; Temple University, Philadelphia, professor of law, 1990-. National Emergency Civil Liberties Committee, Philadelphia counsel, 1971-90. University of California, Santa Cruz, lecturer, 1975; University of Pennsylvania, fellow in community law and criminal litigation, 1968-71, lecturer in urban studies, 1972-79; adjunct professor of sociology, 1980-90. **Publications:** (ed. and contrib.) The Politics of Law: A Progressive Critique, 1982, 3rd ed, 1998; With Liberty and Justice for Some: A Critique of the Conservative Supreme Court, 1993. Work represented in anthologies. Contributor of articles and reviews to law journals, popular magazines, and newspapers. **Address:** Law School, Temple University, 1719 North Broad St., Philadelphia, PA 19122, U.S.A.

KAISER, David E. American, b. 1947. **Genres:** History, Politics/Government. **Career:** Harvard University, Cambridge, MA, lecturer and assistant professor of history, 1976-80; Carnegie-Mellon University, Pittsburgh, PA, associate professor of history, 1980-. **Publications:** Economic Diplomacy and the Origins of the Second World War, 1981; (with W. Young)

Postmortem: New Evidence in the Case of Sacco and Vanzetti, 1985; Politics and War: European Conflict from Philip II to Hitler, 1990; Epic Season, 1998; American Tragedy: Kennedy, Johnson, and the Origins of the Vietnam War, 2000. Contributor to periodicals. **Address:** Strategy and Policy Dept, Naval War College, 686 Cushing Rd, Newport, RI 02841-1207, U.S.A.

KAISER, Ken. American, b. 1945. **Genres:** Adult non-fiction. **Career:** Western Carolinas League, Minor League baseball umpire; American League, Major League baseball umpire, 1977-99. Worked as a bar bouncer, bank teller, and as the professional wrestler Hatchet Man. **Publications:** (with David Fisher) Planet of the Umps: A Baseball Life from behind the Plate, 2003. **Address:** c/o St. Martin's Press, Publicity Dept., 175 Fifth Ave, New York, NY 10010, U.S.A.

KAISER, Ward L(ouis). American/Canadian, b. 1923. **Genres:** Education, Geography, Social commentary, Theology/Religion. **Career:** Publishing consultant, college lectr., and workshop leader, 1986-. Minister, United Church of Canada, in Ontario, 1949-57; Associate, 1957-59, Ed., 1960-69, Sr. Ed., 1969-86, and Sr. Ed. and Executive Director, 1978-86, Friendship Press, National Council of Churches of Christ in the U.S.A. Minster, United Church of Christ in NJ, 1988-92, 1998-2000. Syndicated columnist, 1963-66. **Publications:** Focus: The Changing City, 1963; (with J.L.S. Shearman) Canada: A Study-Action Manual, 1966; Intersection: Where School and Faith Meet (student text and teacher's manual), 1969; The Challenge of a Closer Moon, 1969; Launching Pad: Literacy, 1970; (with C.P. Lutz) You and the Nation's Priorities, 1971; (gen. ed.) People and Systems, 1975; (with others) Forum: Religious Faith Speaks to American Issues, 1976; (trans.) The New Cartography, 1983; (trans.) Space and Time, 1984; A New View of the World: A Handbook to the World Map: Peters Projection, 1987, rev. ed., 1993; Live by Faith, Live by Risk, 1989; (with D. Wood) Seeing through Maps: The Power of Images to Shape Our World View, 2001. Contributor to magazines and journals. **Address:** 14706 Sugura Dr, Winter Garden, FL 34787, U.S.A. **Online address:** newmapper@aol.com

KALB, Jonathan. American, b. 1959. **Genres:** Theatre. **Career:** Hunter College and the CUNY Graduate Center, professor of theater, 1992-; New York Press, theater critic, 1997-. **Publications:** Beckett in Performance, 1989; Free Admissions: Collected Theater Writings, 1993; The Theater of Heiner Muller, 1998; Play by Play: Theater Essays and Reviews, 1993-2002, 2003. **Address:** Department of Theater, Hunter College, 695 Park Ave, New York, NY 10021, U.S.A.

KALBACKEN, Joan. American, b. 1925. **Genres:** Children's fiction, Poetry, Children's non-fiction. **Career:** Lincoln Junior High School, Beloit, WI, mathematics teacher, 1947-48; Pekin Community High School, Pekin, IL, algebra teacher, 1958-60; McLean County Unit Five Schools, Normal, IL, teacher of mathematics and French and foreign language supervisor, 1960-85; author of children's books, 1988-. **Publications:** (with E.U. Lepthien) Recycling, 1991; White-Tailed Deer, 1992; (with E.U. Lepthien) Wetlands, 1993; (with E.U. Lepthien) Foxes, 1993; The Menominee, 1994; Peacocks and Peahens, 1994; Isle Royale National Park, 1996; Badgers, 1996; Sheepskin and Morning Star, 1996; The Food Pyramid, 1998; Food Safety, 1998; Vitamins and Minerals, 1998. Contributor of articles and poems to periodicals. **Address:** 903 Ruston Ave, Normal, IL 61761, U.S.A. **Online address:** jokalb@earthlink.net

KALBERG, Stephen. American. **Genres:** Sociology. **Career:** Boston University, Boston, MA, associate professor of sociology, 1991-. **Publications:** Max Weber's Comparative-Historical Sociology, 1994. **Address:** Department of Sociology, Boston University, 96 Cummington St., Boston, MA 02215, U.S.A.

KALE, Steven D(avid). American, b. 1957. **Genres:** History. **Career:** Washington State University, Pullman, assistant professor of modern European history. **Publications:** Legitimism and the Reconstruction of French Society, 1852-1883, 1992. **Address:** Department of History, Washington State University, PO Box 644030, Pullman, WA 99164-4030, U.S.A. **Online address:** kale@wsu.edu

KALER, Anne K(atherine). American, b. 1935. **Genres:** Literary criticism and history, Mythology/Folklore, Popular Culture, Writing/Journalism. **Career:** Montgomery County Community College, Blue Bell, PA, part-time teacher, 1962-64; St. Francis College, Fort Wayne, IN, teacher, 1964-65; Gwynedd-Mercy College, Gwynedd Valley, PA, professor of English, 1966-2004; retired. **Publications:** The Picara: From Hera to Fantasy Heroine, 1991; Cordially Yours, Brother Cadfael, 1998; Romantic Conventions, 1999. **Address:** 27 Highland Ave, Lansdale, PA 19446-3249, U.S.A.

KALESNIKO, Mark G(aston). American (born Canada), b. 1958. **Genres:** Graphic Novels. **Career:** Graphic novelist; also works in the animation industry, Los Angeles, CA. **Publications:** GRAPHIC NOVELS: S.O.S., 1991; Alex, 6 vols, 1994-95; Why Did Pete Duel Kill Himself?, 1997; Mail Order Bride, 2001. **Address:** c/o Author Mail, Fantagraphics Books, 7563 Lake City Way NE, Seattle, WA 98115, U.S.A. **Online address:** kalesniko58@hotmail.com

KALETA, Kenneth C. American, b. 1948. **Genres:** Film. **Career:** Rowan University (formerly Rowan College of New Jersey), Glassboro, professor of film, 1977-. **Publications:** Asphodel, 1989; Occasional Papers, 1993; David Lynch, 1993; Hanif Kureishi: Postcolonial Storyteller, 1998. **Address:** Rowan University, 201 Mullica Hill Rd., Glassboro, NJ 08028, U.S.A. **Online address:** kaleta@rowan.edu

KALETSKI, Alexander. Russian, b. 1946. **Genres:** Novels. **Career:** Actor, musician, educator, artist, and author. Actor in films, theater, and television, Moscow, Soviet Union, 1965-69; songwriter, musician, and language instructor, United States, 1975-77; fabric designer, NYC, 1977-83; artist-illustrator, NYC, 1975-85; art exhibitions, 19852002; writer. **Publications:** Metro: A Novel of the Moscow Underground, 1985; Darkness of Light (novel), 2002. **Address:** 334 E 73rd St No 4C, New York, NY 10021, U.S.A.

KALFATOVIC, Martin R. American, b. 1961. **Genres:** Archaeology/Antiquities, Art/Art history, Bibliography. **Career:** Library of Congress, Washington, DC, collections assistant, 1983-86; Smithsonian Institution, Washington, DC, librarian for National Portrait Gallery-National Museum of American Art and Library, 1986-93, information access coordinator for the libraries, 1993-98, digital projects librarian, 1998-, head of New Media Office, 2001-. **Publications:** Nile Notes of a Howadji, 1992; The Fine Arts Projects of the New Deal, 1994; Creating a Winning Online Exhibition, 2002. Contributor of book reviews and articles to periodicals. **Address:** Libraries, Smithsonian Institution, Washington, DC 20560, U.S.A. **Online address:** kalfatovicm@si.edu

KALFUS, Melvin. American, b. 1931. **Genres:** History. **Career:** Hartford Courant, Hartford, CT, reporter, beginning in 1959; member of advertising staff at Polaroid Corp.; assistant manager at Westinghouse Electric Co.; assistant manager of presentations at Avco Research and Development; Tensor Corp., assistant marketing director, until 1967; Christopher Thomas/Muller Jordan Weiss, New York City, account supervisor, 1967-70, vice-president, 1968-73, management supervisor, 1970-79, senior vice-president, 1973-89, Instructor, History, New York University, summers, 1976 and 1980, Florida Atlantic University, 1990 and 1991; College of Boca Raton, (now Lynn University), 1991-97. **Publications:** Frederick Law Olmsted: The Passion of a Public Artist, New York University Press, 1990. **Address:** 6804 Via Regina, Boca Raton, FL 33433, U.S.A.

KALIA, Ravi. American (born India), b. 1947. **Genres:** History. **Career:** City College of the City University of New York, NYC, associate professor, 1993-. **Publications:** Chandigarh, 1987; Bhubaneswar, 1994. **Address:** City College of the City University of New York, History Department, 137th at Convent Ave, New York, NY 10031, U.S.A.

KALIN, Jim. American, b. 1959. **Genres:** Novels. **Career:** Writer. Also worked as a bartender. **Publications:** One Worm (novel), 1998. Contributor of short stories to anthologies. **Address:** c/o Russian Hill Press, 1250 17th St., no. 2, San Francisco, CA 94107, U.S.A.

KALLEN, Stuart A(rnold). American, b. 1955. **Genres:** Children's fiction, Young adult fiction, Children's non-fiction, Young adult non-fiction, Music, History, Civil liberties/Human rights, Environmental sciences/Ecology. **Career:** Freelance writer and musician. **Publications:** Recycle It! Once Is Not Enough, 1990. THE HISTORY OF ROCK 'N ROLL SERIES: Roots of Rock, two vols, 1989; Renaissance of Rock, two vols, 1989; Revolution of Rock, 1989; Retrospect of Rock, 1989. THE BUILDING OF A NATION SERIES: Newcomers to America, 1400-1650, 1990; Life in the 13 Colonies, 1650-1750, 1990; The Road to Freedom, 1750-1783, 1990; A Nation United, 1780-1850, 1990; A Nation Divided, 1850-1900, 1990; A Modern Nation, 1900-1990, 1990. BLACK HISTORY AND THE CIVIL RIGHTS MOVEMENT SERIES: The Lost Kingdoms of Africa, 1990; Days of Slavery, 1990; The Civil War and Reconstruction, 1990; The Twentieth Century and the Harlem Renaissance, 1990; The Civil Rights Movement, 1990; The Struggle into the 1990s, 1990. GHASTLY GHOST STORIES SERIES: How to Catch a Ghost, 1991; (and illustrator) Haunted Hangouts of the Undead, 1991; Phantoms of the Rich and Famous, 1991; Vampires, Werewolves, and Zombies, 1991; Monsters, Dinosaurs, and Beasts, 1991; Ghosts of the Seven

Seas, 1991; World of the Bizarre, 1991; Witches, Magic, and Spells, 1991. THE WORLD RECORD LIBRARY SERIES: Human Oddities, 1991; Spectacular Sports Records, 1991; Incredible Animals, 1991; Awesome Entertainment Records, 1991; Super Structures, 1991; Amazing Human Feats, 1991. THE SECOND REVOLUTION SERIES: Princes, Peasants, and Revolution, 1992; The Rise of Lenin, 1992; Stalin: Man of Steel, 1992; Khrushchev: The Coldest War, 1992; Brezhnev: Before the Dawn, 1992; Gorbachev-Yeltsin: The Fall of Communism, 1992. THE FABULOUS FUN LIBRARY SERIES: Ridiculous Riddles (Giggles, Gags, and Groaners), 1992; Tricky Tricks (Simple Magic Tricks), 1992; Mad Scientist Experiments (Safe, Simple Science Experiments), 1992; Math-a-magical Fun (Fun with Numbers), 1992; Puzzling Puzzles (Brain Teasers), 1992; Silly Stories (Funny, Short Stories), 1992; Funny Answers to Foolish Questions, 1992; The Giant Joke Book, 1992. TARGET EARTH SERIES: If the Clouds Could Talk, 1993; If Trees Could Talk, 1993; If the Sky Could Talk, 1993; If the Waters Could Talk, 1993; If Animals Could Talk, 1993; Eco-Games, 1993; Precious Creatures A-Z, 1993; Eco-Fairs and Carnivals, 1993; Earth Keepers, 1993; Eco-Arts & Crafts, 1993. I HAVE A DREAM SERIES: Maya Angelou: Woman of Words, Deeds, and Dreams, 1993; Arthur Ashe: Champion of Dreams and Motion, 1993; Martin Luther King Jr.: A Man and His Dream, 1993; Thurgood Marshall: A Dream of Justice for All, 1993. FAMOUS ILLUSTRATED SPEECHES AND DOCUMENTS SERIES: The Statue of Liberty: The New Colossus, 1994; The Gettysburg Address, 1994; Pledge of Allegiance, 1994; Star-Spangled Banner, 1994; Declaration of Independence, 1994. IF THE DINOSAURS COULD TALK … SERIES: Brontosaurus, 1994; Stegosaurus, 1994; Tyrannosaurus Rex, 1994; Pteranodon, 1994; Plesiosaurus, 1994; Triceratops, 1994. THE HOLOCAUST SERIES: The History of Hatred: 70 A.D. to 1932, 1994; The Nazis Seize Power: 1933-1939, 1994; The Holocaust: 1940-1944, 1994; The Faces of Resistance, 1994; Bearing Witness: Liberation and the Nuremberg Trials, 1994; Holocausts in Other Lands, 1994. OTHER: Beer Here: A Traveler's Guide to American Brewpubs & Microbreweries, 1995. Author of articles for magazines. **Address:** 4601 30th Ave. South, Minneapolis, MN 55406, U.S.A.

KALLEY, Jacqueline A(udrey). South African, b. 1945. **Genres:** Area studies. **Career:** History teacher at secondary schools, 1967-68 and 1970; Natal Provincial Library Services, staff member, 1972; University of the Witwatersrand, Johannesburg, South Africa, international affairs librarian at Jan Smuts Library, 1974-98, honorary research associate in politics, 1998-. Electoral Institute of Southern Africa, librarian, 1998-. Affiliated with Alexsan Library Centre, 1991-. South African Research Documentation Information User Service, coeditor of database, 1996-98. Murrayfield (community organization), chair of board of trustees, 1990-97 and 1999-2000. **Publications:** Transkeian Bibliography: 1945 to Independence, 1976; Index to the Union of South Africa Treaty Series, 1926-1960, 1978; The Transkei Region of Southern Africa, 1877-1978: A Select and Annotated Bibliography, 1980; South Africa's Foreign Relations, 1980-1984: A Select and Annotated Bibliography, 1984; South Africa by Treaty, 1806-1986: A Chronological and Subject Index, 1987; South Africa under Apartheid: A Select and Annotated Bibliography, 1987; Pressure on Pretoria: Sanctions, Boycotts, and the Disinvestment Campaign against South Africa; A Select and Annotated Bibliography, 1988; South Africa's Road to Change, 1987-1990: A Select and Annotated Bibliography, 1991; Apartheid in South African Libraries: The Transvaal Experience, 2000; South Africa's Treaties in Theory and Practice, 1806-1998, 2000. COMPILER: (with E. Schoeman and J. Willers) Letters to Smuts: Correspondence relating to the Personal Library of General J.C. Smuts, 1902-1950, 1980; (with others) Mandela's Five Years of Freedom: South African Politics and Economics, 1990-1995, 1996; (with others) Southern African Political History of Chronology of the Political Events from Independence to Mid-1997, 1999. Contributor to books. Contributor of articles and reviews to periodicals. **Address:** 317 Murrayfield, Corlett Dr., Illovo, Johannesburg 2196, Republic of South Africa.

KALLGREN, Beverly Hayes. American, b. 1925. **Genres:** Novels, Poetry, Children's non-fiction, History. **Career:** Schoolteacher in Litchfield, CT, 1947-53, 1959-64; guidance counselor in New Milford, CT, 1965-84; writer. **Publications:** (ed. with J.L. Crouthamel) "Dear Friend Anna": The Civil War Letters of a Common Soldier from Maine, 1992; Merry Christmas-And Then Some (poetry), 1993; Ministry of the First Congregational Church of Litchfield, Connecticut 1723-1999, 1999; Queen Anne's Lace (poetry); The Last Trolley Home (poetry); The House of Seven Secrets (novel), 2002; The Priest's Inn (novel), 2002; Tuesday Poems and the Maine Collection, 2002; A Goose Named Duck (children's nonfiction), 2004. Contributor to local newspapers. **Address:** 49 Goodhouse Rd, Litchfield, CT 06759, U.S.A.

KALLICH, Martin (Irvin). American, b. 1918. **Genres:** Literary criticism and history, History, Biography, Bibliography. **Career:** Professor Emeritus of English, Northern Illinois University, DeKalb, since 1979 (Professor, 1958-79). Member of faculty, Johns Hopkins University, Baltimore, Maryland, 1943-44, Wayne State University, Detroit, Michigan, 1945-49, and South Dakota State College, Brookings, 1949-58. **Publications:** The Psychological Milieu of Lytton Strachey, 1961; (co-author) The American Revolution Through British Eyes, 1962; Heav'n's First Law, Rhetoric and Order in Pope's Essay on Man, 1967; (co-author) Oedipus: Myth and Drama, 1968; The Other End of the Egg: Religious Satire in Swift's Gulliver's Travels, 1970; The Association of Ideas and Critical Theory in 18th Century England, 1970; Horace Walpole, 1971; (co-author) A Book of the Sonnet, 1972; British Poetry and the American Revolution: A Bibliographical Survey of Pamphlets, Journals, Newspapers, Prints, 1988; In progress: Benedict Arnold and the Poetry of the American Revolution: A Biography. **Address:** English Dept, Northern Illinois University, DeKalb, IL 60115, U.S.A.

KALMAN, Laura. American, b. 1955. **Genres:** Biography, Law. **Career:** Educator. University of California, Santa Barbara, professor of history. **Publications:** Legal Realism at Yale, 1927-1960, 1986; Abe Fortas (biography), 1990; The Strange Career of Legal Liberalism, 1996. **Address:** Department of History, University of California at Santa Barbara, Santa Barbara, CA 93106, U.S.A.

KALMAN, Maira. Israeli, b. 1949. **Genres:** Art/Art history, Children's fiction, Illustrations. **Career:** Writer and illustrator of children's books, 1986-. Designer, M & Co., NYC. **Publications:** Roarr: Calder's Circus, 1991. SELF-ILLUSTRATED FOR CHILDREN: Hey Willy, See the Pyramids, 1988; Sayonara, Mrs. Kackleman, 1989; Max Makes a Million, 1990; Ooh-la-la (Max in Love), 1991; Max in Hollywood, Baby, 1992; Chicken Soup, Boots, 1993; Swami on Rye: Max in India, 1995; Max Doll, 1995; Max Deluxe, 1996. Illustrator of abook by D. Byrne. **Address:** c/o Viking Children's Books, 375 Hudson St., New York, NY 10014, U.S.A.

KALSON, Albert E(ugene). American, b. 1932. **Genres:** Literary criticism and history, Theatre. **Career:** Purdue University, instructor, 1963-65, assistant professor, 1965-72, associate professor of English, 1972-93, professor, 1993-95, professor emeritus, 1995-. **Publications:** (with A.A. DeVitis) J.B. Priestley, 1980; Laughter in the Dark: The Plays of Alan Ayckbourn, 1993. **Address:** 19333 W Country Club Dr #125, Aventura, FL 33180, U.S.A.

KAMAKAHI, Jeffrey J(on). American, b. 1960. **Genres:** Cultural/Ethnic topics, Sociology. **Career:** University of Hawaii at Manoa, Honolulu, instructor in sociology, 1989-91; University of Central Arkansas, Conway, assistant professor of sociology, 1991-. Consultant and data analyst. **Publications:** (ed. with D.B.K. Chang, and contrib.) Social Control in Health and Law, 1992; Uncovering Sociology: A Primer, 1996; (with E. Fox and S. Capek) Come Lovely and Soothing Death: The Right to Die Movement in the U.S., 1999. Contributor to books and periodicals. **Address:** Department of Sociology, Simons Hall 116, St. Johns University, Collegeville, MN 56321-7155, U.S.A. **Online address:** jkamakahi@csbsju.edu

KAMAKARIS, Tina. (Athena). Canadian (born Greece). **Genres:** Novels, Education, Law. **Career:** George Brown College, Toronto, ON, professor of legal administration, 1973-74; Seneca College, Toronto, professor of legal administration, 1974-75, program director, 1976-81, professor, 1981-85, professor of English, 1986-. **Publications:** Legal Office Procedures, with book of simulations and instructor's manual, 1982, 5th ed., 2006; Legal Office Transcriptions Tapes & CDs, with student guide and answer key, 1995, 2006. **Address:** 63 Cheeseman Dr, Markham, ON, Canada L3R 3G3.

KAMAU, Kwadwo Agymah. American (born Barbados). **Genres:** Novels. **Career:** NYC Office for Economic Development, NYC, research assistant, 1983-85; NYC Department of Investigation, New York City, statistician, 1985-86; New York State Department of Taxation and Finance, senior economist in Office of Tax Policy Analysis, 1986-89; New Virginia Review, editorial assistant, 1991-92; Richmond Free Press, Richmond, VA, copy editor, 1992-93; free-lance copy editor and proofreader, 1993-94; writer, 1994-. Virginia Commonwealth University, adjunct professor, 1989-. Judge of writing contests. United Nations Secretariat, research assistant in international economic and social affairs, 1984. **Publications:** Flickering Shadows (novel), 1996; Pictures of a Dying Man (novel), 1999. Contributor of stories and articles to periodicals.

KAMEN, Henry. British, b. 1936. **Genres:** History, Translations. **Career:** Reader in History, University of Warwick, Coventry, since 1973 (Lecturer, 1966-71; Sr. Lecturer, 1971-73). Professor of History, Higher Council for Scientific Research, Barcelona, currently. **Publications:** (trans.) In the Interlude: Poems by Boris Pasternak 1945-1960, 1962; The Spanish Inquisition, 1965; The Rise of Toleration, 1967; The War of Succession in Spain 1700-1715, 1969; The Iron Century: Social Change in Europe 1550-1660, 1971; A Concise History of Spain, 1974; Spain in the Later Seventeenth Century 1665-1700, 1980; A Society in Conflict: Spain 1469-1714, 1983, 1991; European Society, 1500-1700, 1984; Inquisition and Society in Spain, 1985; Golden Age Spain, 1988; The Phoenix and the Flame, 1993; Philip of Spain, 1997; Philip V of Spain: The King Who Reigned Twice, 2001.

KAMENSKY, Jane. American, b. 1963. **Genres:** History. **Career:** Brandeis University, Waltham, MA, professor of history, 1993-. **Publications:** The Colonial Mosaic: American Women, 1600-1760, 1995; Governing the Tongue: The Politics of Speech in Early New England, 1997. **Address:** Brandeis University, Department of History Olin-Sang 215, Mail Stop 036, PO Box 9110, Waltham, MA 02454, U.S.A. **Online address:** kamensky@brandeis.edu

KAMIENIECKI, Sheldon. American. **Genres:** Environmental sciences/Ecology. **Career:** State University of New York at Buffalo, lecturer in environmental policy, 1977-78; California State University, San Bernardino, assistant professor of public administration, 1978-81, director of Paralegal Studies Program, 1979-81; University of Southern California, Los Angeles, assistant professor, 1981-86, associate professor, 1986-93, professor of global environmental issues and political attitudes and behavior, 1993-, director of Social Science Data Laboratory, 1981-87, vice-chair of Department of Political Science, 1989-, director of Environmental Studies Program, 1992-. **Publications:** Public Representation in Environmental Policymaking: The Case of Water Quality Management, 1980; Party Identification, Political Behavior, and the American Electorate, 1985; (ed. with M. Clarke and R. O'Brien, and contrib.) Controversies in Environmental Policy, 1986; (with H. Hahn) Referendum Voting: Social Status and Policy Preferences, 1987; (with S. Cohen) Environmental Regulation Through Strategic Planning, 1991; (ed. and contrib.) Environmental Politics in the International Arena: Movements, Parties, Organizations, and Policy, 1993; (ed. with G.A. Gonzalez and R.O. Vos) Flashpoints in Environmental Policymaking: Controversies in Achieving Sustainability, 1997. Work represented in anthologies. Contributor of articles and reviews to political science journals. **Address:** Department of Political Science, University of Southern California, Los Angeles, CA 90089, U.S.A.

KAMIL, Alan C(urtis). American, b. 1941. **Genres:** Psychology, Biology. **Career:** University of Massachusetts at Amherst, assistant professor, 1967-72, associate professor, 1972-79, professor of psychology, 1979-91; Visiting associate professor, University of California, Berkeley, 1976-77; University of Nebraska, Lincoln, professor of biological sciences and psychology, 1991-. **Publications:** Mastering Psychology: A Guide to Brown-Herrnstein's Psychology, 1975. EDITOR: (with N.R. Simonson) Patterns of Psychology: Issues and Prospects, 1973; (with T.D. Sargent) Foraging Behavior: Ecological, Ethological, and Psychological Approaches, 1981; (with J.R. Krebs and H.R. Pulliam) Foraging Behavior, 1987. **Address:** School of Biological Sciences, University of Nebraska, Lincoln, NE 68588-0118, U.S.A. **Online address:** akamil@unlserve.unl.edu

KAMM, Henry. American (born Germany), b. 1925. **Genres:** International relations/Current affairs. **Career:** New York Times, NYC, correspondent, 1949-96. Pulitzer Prize for international reporting, 1978. **Publications:** Dragon Ascending: Vietnam and the Vietnamese, 1996; Cambodia: Report from a Stricken Land, 1998. **Address:** Chemin du Riotord, 84800 Lagnes, France.

KAMMEN, Michael. American, b. 1936. **Genres:** History. **Career:** Cornell University, Ithaca, NY, assistant professor, 1965-67, associate professor, 1967-69, professor, 1969-73, chairman, Dept. of History, 1974-76, Newton C. Farr Professor of American History and Culture, 1973-. Children's Television Workshop, NYC, Chairman, Advisory Board, and Consultant for Our Story, 1974-76. **Publications:** A Rope of Sand: The Colonial Agents, British Politics, and the American Revolution, 1968; Deputyes and Libertyes, 1969; Empire and Interest: The American Colonies and the Politics of Mercantilism, 1970; People of Paradox: An Inquiry Concerning the Origins of American Civilization, 1972 (Pulitzer Prize for History); What Is the Good of History? Selected Letters of Carl L. Becker 1900-1945, 1973; Colonial New York, 1975; A Season of Youth, 1978; Spheres of Liberty, 1986; A Machine That Would Go of Itself: The Constitution in American Culture, 1986; Selvages and Biases: The Fabric of History in American Culture, 1987; Sovereignty and Liberty, 1988; Mystic Chords of Memory, 1991; Meadows of Memory, 1992; The Lively Arts: Gilbert Seldes and the Transformation of Cultural Criticism in the United States, 1996; In the Past Lane: Historical Perspectives on American Culture, 1997; Alexis de Toc-

queville and Democracy in America, 1998; American Culture, American Tastes, 1999; Rt. Gwathmey: The Life and Art of a Passionate Observer, 1999; A Time to Every Purpose: The Four Seasons in American Culture, 2004. EDITOR: (co) The Glorious Revolution in America, 1964; Politics and Society in Colonial America, 1967; The Past before Us, 1980; The Origins of the American Constitution, 1986; Contested Values: Democracy and Diversity in American Culture, 1995. **Address:** Dept of History, Cornell University, McGraw Hall, Ithaca, NY 14853, U.S.A. **Online address:** mgk5@cornell.edu

KAMPHOEFNER, Walter D. American, b. 1948. **Genres:** History. **Career:** University of Muenster, West Germany (now Germany), postgraduate research associate at Institute of Comparative Urban History, 1978-81; California Institute of Technology, Pasadena, Mellon postgraduate instructor, 1981-83; University of Miami, Coral Gables, FL, assistant professor, 1983-87, associate professor of history, 1987-88; Texas A&M University, College Station, assistant professor, 1988-90, associate professor of history, 1990-96, professor of history, 1996-. **Publications:** Westfalen in der Neuen Welt: Eine Sozialgeschichte der Auswanderung im 19. Jahrhundert, 1982; The Westfalians: From Germany to Missouri, 1987. EDITOR: (with W. Helbich and U. Sommer) Briefe aus Amerika: Deutsche Auswanderer schreiben aus der Neuen Welt, 1830-1930, 1988, trans. as News from the Land of Freedom: German Immigrants Write Home, 1991; (with W. Helbich) Deutsche im amerikanischen Burgerkrieg: Briefe von Front und Farm, 1861-1865, 2002 Work represented in anthologies. Contributor of articles and reviews to scholarly journals. **Address:** Department of History, Texas A&M University, College Station, TX 77843-4236, U.S.A. **Online address:** waltkamp@tamu.edu

KAN, Sergei. American (born Russia), b. 1953. **Genres:** Anthropology/Ethnology, Translations, History. **Career:** Northeastern University, Boston, MA, part-time assistant professor of anthropology, 1981-83; University of Michigan, Ann Arbor, assistant professor of anthropology, 1983-89; Dartmouth College, Hanover, NH, assistant professor, 1989-92, associate professor of anthropology, 1992-. **Publications:** (trans. from Russian, and author of intro and supplementary material) A. Kamenskii, Tlingit Indians, 1985; Symbolic Immortality: The Tlingit Potlatch of the Nineteenth Century, 1989; Memory Eternal: Tlingit Culture and Russian Orthodox Christianity Through Two Centuries, 1999. **Address:** Department of Anthropology, Dartmouth College, Hanover, NH 03755, U.S.A. **Online address:** sergei.kan@dartmouth.edu

KANAR, Stephen (Patrick). American, b. 1944. **Genres:** Law, Novels. **Career:** Partner of the firm of Fishback, Davis, and others, Orlando, FL, 1969-78; Troutman, Parrish & Kanar, Winter Park, FL, senior partner, 1978-79; Kanar Law Firm, Orlando, FL, senior partner, 1979-. Member of Bars of U.S. Court of Appeals, U.S. Court of Claims, U.S. Tax Court, and U.S. Supreme Court. Embry-Riddle Aeronautical University, adjunct professor of aviation, 1983. **Publications:** Aviation Law, 1983; The J Factor (novel), 2000. **Address:** 1200 Oakland Ln, Mount Dora, FL 32757, U.S.A. **Online address:** stephenkanar@aol.com

KANCHIER, Carole. Canadian. **Genres:** How-to books, Psychology, Self help. **Career:** Winnipeg Board of Parks and Recreation, Winnipeg, Manitoba, director of arts and crafts; geography teacher and director of physical education for women at collegiate school in Winnipeg; Royal Winnipeg Ballet, Winnipeg, director of publicity; high school director of guidance and counseling in Winnipeg; University of Calgary, Calgary, Alberta, instructor in educational psychology, 1980-82; University of Alberta, Edmonton, instructor in educational psychology, 1983-92; Private practice of psychology, 1981-. Syndicated columnist. **Publications:** Counsellor's Resource Book for Groups in Guidance, 1972; Career Guidance Model, 1976; Adult Education in Alberta, 1977; Native-oriented Adult Education Programs in the Prairie Provinces, 1977; Questers: Dare to Change Your Job-and Your Life, 1988, 3rd ed, 2000; The Self Discovery Series (in press); Open to change (in press). Contributor to magazines and journals worldwide.

KANDALL, Stephen R. American, b. 1940. **Genres:** Medicine/Health. **Career:** Yeshiva University, Albert Einstein College of Medicine, Bronx, NY, intern at Bronx Municipal Hospital Center, intern, 1965-66, assistant resident, 1966-67, senior resident, 1967-68, chief resident in pediatrics, 1968-69, assistant instructor at the medical college, 1968-69, assistant visiting pediatrician at Lincoln Hospital, 1969-76, assistant professor, 1972-76, lecturer in pediatrics, 1976-78, attending physician at Albert Einstein Hospital, 1972-76, associate director of Division of Neonatology and director of clinical neonatology, 1972-76; Mount Sinai School of Medicine of the City University of New York, NYC, assistant professor, 1976-77, associate professor, 1977-85, professor of clinical pediatrics, 1986-91, professor of pediatrics, 1991-94, assistant attending physician, 1976-85, attending physician, 1985-94; Yeshiva University, Albert Einstein College of Medicine, professor of pediatrics, 1994-; University of California, Medical Center, San Francisco, research fellow in neonatology, 1971-72; Tulane University, visiting scientist, 1969-71; guest lecturer at colleges, universities, and teaching hospitals in the United States and abroad; consultant. Guest on radio and television programs. **Publications:** Substance and Shadow: Women and Addiction in the United States, 1996; Women and Addiction in the United States, 1850 to the Present (monograph), 1998. Contributor to medical textbooks. Contributor of articles to professional journals. **Address:** Beth Israel Medical Center, First Ave. at 16th St., New York, NY 10003, U.S.A.

KANDEL, Michael. American, b. 1941. **Genres:** Science fiction/Fantasy, Children's fiction. **Career:** Editor at the Modern Language Association; Consultant science fiction editor for Harcourt; Translator of Stanislaw Lem. **Publications:** Strange Invasion, 1989; In between Dragons, 1991; Captain Jack Zodiac, 1993; Panda Ray, 1996. **Address:** Modern Language Association, 26 Broadway, New York, NY 10004-1789, U.S.A. **Online address:** michael.kandel@mla.org

KANE, Alex. See **LAZUTA, Gene.**

KANE, Gordon L. American, b. 1937. **Genres:** Physics, Sciences. **Career:** University of Michigan, Ann Arbor, professor of physics. **Publications:** Modern Elementary Particle Physics, 1987; (co) Higgs Hunter's Guide, 1990; The Particle Garden, 1995; Supersymmetry, 2000. EDITOR: Perspectives on Higgs Physics, 1992; Perspectives on Supersymmetry, 1998. **Address:** Randall Physics Laboratory, University of Michigan, Ann Arbor, MI 48105, U.S.A.

KANE, John. American, b. 1946. **Genres:** Novels. **Career:** Solters & Roskin, NYC, film publicist, 1977-80; unit film publicist, 1980-83; Home Box Office, NYC, director of publicity, 1983-90; independent film and television publicist, Los Angeles, CA, 1990-. **Publications:** Best Actress (novel), 1998. **Address:** c/o B.J. Robbins, 5130 Bellaire Ave., North Hollywood, CA 91607, U.S.A.

KANE, Leslie. American, b. 1945. **Genres:** Theatre, Literary criticism and history. **Career:** Massachusetts State College at Westfield, assistant professor, 1979-84, associate professor, 1985-89, professor of English, 1989-. Massachusetts Institute of Technology, adjunct professor, 1983; Babson College, visiting lecturer, 1985-86. **Publications:** The Language of Silence: On the Unspoken and the Unspeakable in Modern Drama, 1984; (ed. and contrib.) David Mamet: A Casebook, 1992; (ed. and contrib.) Israel Horovitz: Critical Approaches, 1993; (ed. and contrib.) Glengarry Glen Ross: Text and Performance, 1996; Weasels and Wisemen: Ethics and Ethnicity in the Work of David Mamet, 1999. **Address:** Department of English, Massachusetts State College at Westfield, Westfield, MA 01086, U.S.A.

KANE, Penny. Australian/British (born Kenya), b. 1945. **Genres:** Demography, Women's studies and issues. **Career:** Free-lance journalist, 1964-70; Family Planning Association, London, England, information officer, 1971-73; International Planned Parenthood Federation, London, press officer, 1973-75, deputy director, 1978-84; University of Wales, University College, Cardiff, information officer for Dept of Population Studies, 1975-78, visiting lecturer at Population Centre; consultant on health and population, 1984-; University of Melbourne, Office for Gender and Health, associate professor. **Publications:** (with M. Smith) The Pill Off Prescription, 1976; (ed.) B. Benjamin, The Decline in the Birthrate, 1978; (with B. Bewley and J. Cook) Choice Not Chance, 1978; The Which? Guide to Birth Control, 1983; A Decade of Partnership, 1974-1984, 1984; (with J. Porter) The Choice Guide to Birth Control, 1984, 2nd ed., 1988; (with S.S. Fader) Successfully Ever After, 1985; Famine in Selected Countries of the ESCAP Region, 1985; (ed. with D. Lucas) Asking Demographic Questions, 1985; (ed. with D. Davin and E. Croll, and contrib.) China's One-Child Family Policy, 1985; The Impact of Birth Spacing on Child Health, 1985; (ed. with L.T. Ruzicka) M. Rahman, Tradition, Development, and the Individual, 1986; (with M. Sparrow) Consumer Guide to Birth Control, 1986; (with L.T. Ruzicka) Mortality and Health Issues, 1987; (with L.T. Ruzicka) Australia's Population Trends and Their Social Implications, 1987; The Second Billion: People and Population in China, 1987; Ehkaisy (title means: Contraception), 1988; Famine in China, 1959-1961, 1988; (ed. with G. Wunsch and L.T. Ruzicka) Differential Mortality, 1989; Women's Health, 1990, 2nd ed., 1993; Victorian Families in Fact and Fiction, 1994; Women and Occupational Health, 1999. Contributor to books. **Address:** The Old School, Major's Creek, Braidwood, NSW 2622, Australia. **Online address:** pskane@braidwood.net.au

KANG, K. Connie. American (born Republic of Korea), b. 1942. **Genres:** Novels, Autobiography/Memoirs. **Career:** Democrat and Chronicle, Rochester, NY, reporter, beginning in 1964; Korea Times, Seoul, Korea, columnist, 1967-; San Francisco Examiner, San Francisco, CA, editorial writer, assistant metropolitan editor, reporter, and foreign correspondent, 1975-92; San Francisco Chronicle, staff reporter, 1976; Los Angeles Times, Los Angeles, CA, staff writer, 1992-. Haukuk University, assistant professor of international relations & English, 1967-70. **Publications:** Home Was the Land of Morning Calm: A Saga of a Korean American Family, 1995. **Address:** Los Angeles Times, 202 W 1st St, Los Angeles, CA 90012, U.S.A. **Online address:** connie.kang@latimes.com

KANIGEL, Robert. American, b. 1946. **Genres:** History, Literary criticism and history, Sciences, Technology, Travel/Exploration, Writing/Journalism, Biography, Essays. **Career:** Mechanical engineer, 1966-69; free-lance writer in Baltimore, MD, 1970-71, 1976-99, San Francisco, CA, 1971-74, New York City, 1975, and Cambridge, MA, 1999-. Johns Hopkins University, instructor in writing, 1985-91; University of Baltimore, Yale Gordon College of Liberal Arts, professor of English and senior fellow of the Institute for Language, Technology, and Publications Design, 1991-99; Massachusetts Institute of Technology, professor of science writing, director of Graduate Program in Science Writing, 1999-. **Publications:** Apprentice to Genius: The Making of a Scientific Dynasty, 1986; The Man Who Knew Infinity: A Life of the Genius Ramanujan, 1991; The One Best Way: Frederick Winslow Taylor and the Enigma of Efficiency, 1997; Vintage Reading, 1998; High Season, 2002. Author of articles, essays, reviews, book chapters. **Address:** c/o Vicky Bijur Literary Agency, 333 West End Ave, New York, NY 10023, U.S.A.

KANN, Mark E. American, b. 1947. **Genres:** Politics/Government. **Career:** Elementary school teacher in Chicago, Ill., 1968-71; University of Southern California, Los Angeles, assistant professor, 1975-81, associate professor, 1981-88, professor of political science, 1988-, director of graduate affairs, 1979-81, associate dean of Graduate Studies, 1990-93, Henry Salvatori professor of American Studies, 1992-. **Publications:** Thinking About Politics: Two Political Sciences, 1980; The American Left: Failures and Fortunes, 1982; Middle Class Radicalism in Santa Monica, 1986; On the Man Question: Gender and Civic Virtue in America, 1991. EDITOR & CONTRIBUTOR: (with J.P. Diggins) The Problem of Authority in America, 1981; The Future of American Democracy: Views From the Left, 1983. Contributor to books. **Address:** Department of Political Science, University of Southern California, University Park, Los Angeles, CA 90089-0044, U.S.A.

KANNUS, (Veli) Pekka. Finnish, b. 1959. **Genres:** Sports/Fitness, Medicine/Health. **Career:** Research Center for Sports Medicine, Tampere, Finland, resident physician, 1987-91, specialist in sports medicine, 1991-92; UKK Institute, Tampere, senior research fellow, 1992, chief physician and head of Accident and Trauma Research Center, 1993-; University of Jyvaeskylae, associate professor, 1991-95; University of Tampere, associate professor, 1995-99, professor, 2000-. University of Vermont, research fellow, 1989-90, visiting professor, 1994. Australian Conference of Science and Medicine in Sport, Vince Higgings Keynote Lecturer, 1995. **Publications:** Human Tendons: Anatomy, Physiology, and Pathology, 1997. Contributor to scientific journals. **Address:** Accident and Trauma Research Center, UKK Institute, Box 30, 33501 Tampere, Finland. **Online address:** klpeka@uta.fi

KANON, Joseph A. American, b. 1946. **Genres:** Novels, Mystery/Crime/Suspense. **Career:** Publishing executive and suspense novelist. Formerly executive vice president, Trade & Reference Publishing, Houghton Mifflin. **Publications:** NOVELS: Los Alamos, 1997; The Prodigal Spy, 1998; The Good German, 2001; Alibi, 2005. **Address:** 229 E 79 St, New York, NY 10021, U.S.A.

KANTARIS, Sylvia (Mosley). British, b. 1936. **Genres:** Poetry, Literary criticism and history, Women's studies and issues, Writing/Journalism, Essays. **Career:** English teacher, Withywood School, Bristol, 1958-59; English and French teacher, St. Paul's Way School, London, 1960-62; Tutor in French, University of Queensland, 1963-66; Open University Tutor, Southwest England, 1974-84; Extramural Lecturer, Exeter University, Devon, 1974-; Writer-in-the-Community, Cornwall, 1986; Freelance Writer/Performer/Tutor, 1986-. **Publications:** Time and Motion, 1975; Stocking Up, 1981; The Tenth Muse, 1983; (with D. M. Thomas) News from the Front, 1983; The Sea at the Door, 1985; (with Philip Gross) The Air Mines of Mistila, 1988; Dirty Washing: New and Selected Poems, 1989; Lad's Love, 1993. **Address:** 14 Osborne Parc, Helston, Cornwall TR13 8PB, England. **Online address:** sylvia@kantaris.com

KANTER, Lynn. American, b. 1954. **Genres:** Novels. **Career:** Center for Community Change, Washington, DC, writer, 1992-. **Publications:**

NOVELS: On Lill Street, 1992; The Mayor of Heaven, 1997. Work represented in anthologies. **Address:** Center for Community Change, 1000 Wisconsin Ave. N.W., Washington, DC 20007, U.S.A. **Online address:** LynnKanter@aol.com

KANUNGO, R(abindra) N. Canadian (born India), b. 1935. **Genres:** Administration/Management, Cultural/Ethnic topics, Social sciences, Business/Trade/Industry. **Career:** Ravenshaw College, India, lecturer, 1955-60; Indian Institute of Management, Calcutta, assistant professor, 1963-64; Indian Institute of Technology, Bombay, assistant professor and head of social science division, 1964-65; Dalhousie University, Halifax, NS, research associate, assistant professor and associate professor, 1965-69; McGill University, Montreal, PQ, associate professor, 1969-73, professor of management, 1974-, chair professor, chairman of department, 1988. University of California, Berkeley, visiting scholar, 1976-77; Indian Institute of Management, visiting professor, 1983-84. Guest on television and radio programs. Consultant. **Publications:** (with P. Misra) Introduction to the Child's Mind (in an Indian language), 1974; (with S. Dutta) Affect and Memory: A Reformulation, 1975; Biculturalism and Management, 1980; Work Alienation: An Integrative Approach, 1982; (with M. Mendonca) Compensation: Effective Reward Management, 1992; (with M. Mendonca) Ethical Dimensions of Leadership, 1996; (with J.A. Conger) Charismatic Leadership in Organizations, 1998. EDITOR & CONTRIBUTOR: (with H. Jain) Behavioral Issues in Management: The Canadian Context, 1977; (with M.D. Lee) Management of Work and Personal Life, 1984; South Asians in the Canadian Mosaic, 1984; (with J.A. Conger) Charismatic Leadership, 1988; (with A. Jaeger) Management in Developing Countries, 1990; (with R. Ghosh) South Asian Canadians, 1992; (with M. Mendonca) Work Motivation, 1994; Entrepreneurship and Innovation, 1998. **Address:** Faculty of Management, McGill University, 1001 Sherbrooke St. W, Montreal, QC, Canada H3A 1G5. **Online address:** kanungo@management.mcgill.ca

KAPFERER, Jean-Noel. French, b. 1948. **Genres:** Marketing, Administration/Management. **Career:** Procter & Gamble, Paris, France, became assistant product manager, 1970; H.E.C., Jouy-en-Josas, France, professor of business administration, 1975-. **Publications:** Rumors: Uses, Interpretations, and Images, 1991; Strategic Brand Management, 1994; Reinventing the Brand, 2001; The New Strategic Brand Management, 2004. **Address:** H.E.C. Graduate School of Management, 78350 Jouy-en-Josas, France. **Online address:** kapferer.com

KAPLAN, Alice Yaeger. American, b. 1954. **Genres:** Literary criticism and history. **Career:** Duke University, Durham, NC, associate professor to professor of Romance studies and literature, 1986-, Lehrman Professor of Romance Studies, 2003-. **Publications:** Reproductions of Banality: Fascism, Literature, and French Intellectual Life, 1986; Sources et citations dans "Bagatelles pour un massacre," 1988; French Lessons: A Memoir, 1993; The Collaborator: The Trial and Execution of Robert Brasillach, 2000. Contributor of articles and reviews to periodicals; translator of fiction from the French. **Address:** Program in Literature, 109 Art Museum, Duke University, Durham, NC 27708, U.S.A.

KAPLAN, Andrew. American, b. 1960. **Genres:** Young adult non-fiction, Business/Trade/Industry, Education. **Career:** Curriculum Concepts, NYC, editor and writer, 1982-85; freelance writer and editor, 1985-. **Publications:** Careers for Sports Fans, 1991; Careers for Computer Buffs, 1991; Careers for Artistic Types, 1991; Careers for Outdoor Types, 1991; Careers for Number Lovers, 1991; Careers for Wordsmiths, 1991; War of the Raven, 1991. **Address:** 25 Tudor City Pl., Apt. 1205, New York, NY 10017, U.S.A.

KAPLAN, Barbara Beigun. American, b. 1943. **Genres:** History. **Career:** University of Maryland at College Park, adjunct professor of history, 1981-, senior instructional designer at Center for Instructional Development and Evaluation, 1985-90, executive director of Program in Science, Technology, and Society Studies, 1988-91, coordinator of faculty development, 1993-. Gaithersburg Gazette, journalist, 1984; Applied Science Associates Inc., instructional technologist, 1985-90. **Publications:** Divulging Useful Truths in Physick: The Medical Agenda of Robert Boyle, 1993; Land and Heritage in the Virginia Tidewater: A History of King and Queen County, 1993. Work represented in anthologies. Contributor of articles and reviews to academic journals. **Address:** 5 Triple Crown Ct, Gaithersburg, MD 20878, U.S.A.

KAPLAN, Carter. (born United States), b. 1960. **Genres:** Literary criticism and history. **Career:** Yeshiva University, New York, NY, adjunct assistant professor, 1997; College of St. Elizabeth, Morristown, NJ, assistant professor, 1998-99; Shippensburg University, Shippensburg, PA, assistant professor, 1999-2000; Mountain State University, Beckley, WV, associate professor

of English and philosophy, 2001-. Architectural writer. **Publications:** Critical Synoptics: Menippean Satire and the Analysis of Intellectual Mythology, 2000. **Address:** Mountain State University, Beckley, WV 25802, U.S.A. **Online address:** kplnf@aol.com

KAPLAN, Edward S. American, b. 1942. **Genres:** Economics. **Career:** NYC Technical College of the City University of New York, Brooklyn, NY, professor, 1971-. **Publications:** (with T.W. Ryley) Prelude to Trade Wars: American Tariff Policy, 1890-1922, 1994; American Trade Policy, 1923-1995, 1996; U.S. Imperialism in Latin America: Bryan's Challenges and Contributions, 1900-1920, 1998; The Bank of the United States and the American Economy, 1999. Contributor to journals. **Address:** Social Science Department, NYC Technical College of the City University of New York, 300 Jay St, Brooklyn, NY 11201, U.S.A. **Online address:** ekaplan7@nyc.rr.com

KAPLAN, Elizabeth (A.). American, b. 1956. **Genres:** Children's non-fiction, Sciences. **Career:** Freelance writer and editor. Encyclopaedia Britannica, Chicago, IL, editorial indexer, 1980-82; Scott, Foresman and Company, Glenview, IL, associate editor, 1982-85; Gareth Stevens Books, Milwaukee, WI, editor, 1990-91. **Publications:** ASK ISAAC ASIMOV SERIES WITH ISAAC ASIMOV: How Do Airplanes Fly?, 1993; How Do Big Ships Float?, 1993; How Does a TV Work?, 1993; How Is Paper Made?, 1993; What Happens When I Flush the Toilet?, 1993. BIOMES SERIES: Tundra, 1995; Temperate Forest, 1995; Taiga, 1995. OTHER: Jewish Americans, 1995; (coauthor) Henry Hudson: Arctic Explorer and North American Adventurer. **Address:** 2626 North Farwell, Milwaukee, WI 53211, U.S.A.

KAPLAN, James. American, b. 1951. **Genres:** Novels, Novellas/Short stories, Plays/Screenplays, Business/Trade/Industry, Film, Writing/Journalism, Autobiography/Memoirs, Biography, Essays. **Career:** New Yorker, New York City, editorial typist, 1974-76; free-lance writer, 1976-; University of Southern Mississippi, Hattiesburg, assistant professor of English, 1978-79; Warner Bros., Burbank, CA, screenwriter, 1984-87. United Artists, screenwriter, 1986-87; Vanity Fair magazine, contributing editor, 1989-91; Entertainment Weekly Magazine, writer at-large, 1991-93; New York Magazine, contributing editor, 1993-99. **Publications:** Pearl's Progress (novel), 1989; The Airport (nonfiction), 1994; Two Guys from Verona (novel), 1998; (with J. McEnroe) You Cannot Be Serious, 2002. **Address:** c/o Joy Harris, Joy Harris Literary Agency, 156 Fifth Ave Ste 617, New York, NY 10010, U.S.A.

KAPLAN, Janet A(nn). American, b. 1945. **Genres:** Art/Art history, Communications/Media, Cultural/Ethnic topics, Women's studies and issues, Social commentary, Writing/Journalism, Biography. **Career:** Franconia College, Franconia, NH, faculty member and chair of art history department, 1976-78; University of New Hampshire, Plymouth, assistant professor of art history, 1978-79; Moore College of Art, Philadelphia, PA, assistant professor, 1980-86, associate professor, 1987-92, chair of liberal arts department, 1989-96, professor of art history, 1993-. Vermont College MFA in Visual Arts, graduate faculty, 1992-; New York University, Institute of Fine Arts, visiting professor, 2000. Art Journal, executive editor, 1996-2002. Reciepient of NEH, Rockefeller, and other grants and fellowships; art exhibition curator; consultant for artist's projects at Rosenbach Museum and Library; Philadelphia Redevelopment Authority, Arts Advisory Board. Frequent coordinator, panelist, and lecturer at conferences; guest on radio programs. **Publications:** Unexpected Journeys: The Art and Life of Remedios Varo, 1988, 3rd ed., 2000. Contributor to art catalogs and journals. **Address:** Moore College of Art and Design, Twentieth and the Parkway, Philadelphia, PA 19103, U.S.A. **Online address:** janetakaplan@earthlink.net

KAPLAN, Jerry. American, b. 1952. **Genres:** Business/Trade/Industry. **Career:** Stanford University, Stanford, CA, research associate in computer science; Lotus Development Corporation, principal technologist; TeKnowledge, cofounder and vice president of business development; GO Corporation, cofounder and chair, 1987-93; ONSALE, chief executive officer. **Publications:** Startup: A Silicon Valley Adventure, 1995. **Address:** ONSALE, 180 Montgomery St. Ste 2340, San Francisco, CA 94104-4226, U.S.A.

KAPLAN, Jonathan. South African, b. 1954. **Genres:** Autobiography/Memoirs. **Career:** Physician, journalist, author, and documentary filmmaker. **Publications:** The Dressing Station: A Surgeon's Chronicle of War and Medicine, 2002. **Address:** c/o Author Mail, Grove/Atlantic Inc., 841 Broadway, New York, NY 10003, U.S.A.

KAPLAN, Justin. American, b. 1925. **Genres:** Literary criticism and history, Biography. **Career:** Harvard University, Cambridge, MA, lecturer,

1969-70, 1972-73, 1976, 1978; College of the Holy Cross, Jenks Professor of Contemporary Letters, 1992-95. **Publications:** Mr. Clemens and Mark Twain, 1966; Lincoln Steffens: A Biography, 1974; Mark Twain and His World, 1974; Walt Whitman: A Life, 1980; (with A. Bernays) The Language of Names, 1997; (with A. Bernays) Back Then, 2002. EDITOR: Best American Essays, 1990; Bartlett's Familiar Quotations, 16th ed., 1992, 17th ed., 2002. **Address:** 16 Francis Ave, Cambridge, MA 02138, U.S.A. **Online address:** JKNames@aol.com

KAPLAN, Kalman J. American, b. 1941. **Genres:** Medicine/Health. **Career:** Wayne State University, Detroit, MI, assistant professor, 1967-73, associate professor, 1973-83, professor of psychology, 1984-, chair of Social Psychology Program, 1979-82, research associate at Institute of Gerontology, 1990. University of Illinois, College of Medicine, Chicago, adjunct professor, 1992-, clinical professor, 2001-. Personal Growth Services, therapist, 1982-84; Jensen Counseling Associates, intern, 1986-88, psychotherapist, 1988-92; Midwestern Educational Resources Center, psychotherapist, 1987-89; Joseph Counseling Services, clinical supervisor, 1990-92; Humana Michael Reese Hospital and Medical Center, attending clinical psychologist, 1990-, director of Suicide Research Center, 1994; Old Orchard Hospital, attending clinical psychologist, 1992-94; Highland Park Hospital, attending clinical psychologist, 1992-94; North Shore Center for Behavioral Medicine, psychotherapist, 1992-93; Psychological Assessments, codirector, 1994. Hebrew University of Jerusalem, visitor at Center for Cognitive Studies, 1975; Harvard University, research associate in psychology and social relations and visiting scholar at Divinity School, 1977-78, guest lecturer, 1978 and 1979. Guest lecturer. **Publications:** (with M.W. Schwartz and M.M. Kaplan) The Family: Biblical and Psychological Foundations, 1984; (with M.W. Schwartz) A Psychology of Hope, 1993; (with S. Emmons, C. Geiser, and M. Harrow) Living with Schizophrenia, 1997; TILT: Teaching Individuals to Love Together, 1998; (with M.W. Schwartz) Biblical Stories for Psychotherapy and Counseling, 2004. EDITOR: (with M.W. Schwartz) Jewish Approaches to Suicide, Martyrdom, and Euthanasia, 1998; Right to Die versus Sacredness of Life, 2000. Contributor to books. Contributor of articles and reviews to professional journals. **Address:** Dept of Psychology, Wayne State University, 204 Psychology Bldg, 71 W Warren Ave, Detroit, MI 48202, U.S.A. **Online address:** kalkap@aol.com; kkaplan@sun.science.wayne.edu

KAPLAN, Louise J. American, b. 1929. **Genres:** Psychology. **Career:** Private practice of psychoanalysis, 1966-68; Children's Day Treatment Center, NYC, chief psychologist, 1966-70; New York University, NYC, director of mother-infant research nursery, 1973-77; Margaret S. Mahler Research Foundation, Professional Advisory Board, 1980-; College of City University of New York, associate professor of psychology and director of child clinical services, 1977-80. Coeditor of American Imago. **Publications:** Oneness and Separateness: From Infant to Individual, 1978; Adolescence: The Farewell to Childhhood, 1984; The Family Romance of the Impostor-Poet Thomas Chatterton, 1987; Female Perversions: The Temptations of Emma Bovary, 1991; No Voice Is Ever Wholly Lost, 1995.

KAPLAN, Marion A. American, b. 1946. **Genres:** History, Women's studies and issues. **Career:** Queens College of the City University of New York, Flushing, NY, professor of history, 1985-2000; New York University, professor of Hebrew and Judaic studies, 2000-. **Publications:** The Jewish Feminist Movement in Germany: The Campaigns of the Juedischer Frauenbund, 1904-1938, 1979; The Making of the Jewish Middle Class: Women, Family, and Identity in Imperial Germany, 1991; Between Dignity & Despair: Jewish Life in Nazi Germany, 1998. EDITOR: (with R. Bridenthal and A. Grossmann) When Biology Became Destiny: Women in Weimar and Nazi Germany, 1984; The Marriage Bargain: Women and Dowries in European History, 1985.

KAPLAN, Morton A. American, b. 1921. **Genres:** International relations/Current affairs, Philosophy, Politics/Government. **Career:** Professor of Political Science, 1965-, and Distinguished Service Professor, 1989-, emeritus, 1991, University of Chicago (Assistant Professor, 1955-61; Associate Professor, 1961-65; Chairman, Committee on International Relations, 1959-85; Director, Ford Workshops Prgs. in International Relations, 1961-71; Director, Center of Strategic and Foreign Policy Studies, 1970-85). President, Professors World Peace Academy, 1984-. Advisory Board, Washington Times, 1983-. Ed. and Publr., The World and I, 1985-. Associate Ed., Journal of Conflict Resolution, 1961-81. **Publications:** US Foreign Policy 1945-1955, 1956; System and Process in International Politics, 1957, 1965; (with Katzenbach) Political Foundations of International Law, 1961; Macropolitics: Essays on the Philosophy and Science of Politics, 1969; Dissent and the State in Peace and War, 1970; On Historical and Political Knowing, 1971;

On Freedom and Human Dignity, 1973; The Rationale for NATO, 1973; Towards Professionalism in International Theory, 1979; Global Policy, Challenge of the '80s, 1984; Science, Language and the Human Condition, 1984; Law in a Democratic Society, 1993; Character & Identity, vol. 1, 1998, vol. 2, 2000. EDITOR: (and contrib.) New Approaches to International Relations, 1968; (and contrib.) Great Issues of International Politics, 1970; (and contrib.) SALT: Problems and Prospects, 1973; (and contrib.) Strategic Thinking and Its Moral Implications, 1973; (and contrib.) NATO and Dissuasion, 1974; (and contrib.) The Many Faces of Communism, 1978; Consolidating Peace in Europe, 1987; (co-ed.) The Soviet Union and the Challenge of the Future, 4 vols., 1988-89; (and contrib.) Morality and Religion, 1992; (and contrib.) The World of 2043, 1993. **Address:** 5446 S. Ridgewood, Chicago, IL 60615, U.S.A.

KAPLAN, Nelly. Also writes as Belen. French (born Argentina), b. 1936. **Genres:** Novels, Novellas/Short stories, Plays/Screenplays, Film, Biography. **Career:** Journalist for Argentine newspapers; Cythere Films, Paris, assistant director, 1957-64, director, 1967-; scriptwriter. **Publications:** FILM SCRIPTS: (with C. Makovski) La Fiancee du Pirate (title means: The Pirate's Fiancee; also known as Dirty Mary), 1969, in US as A Very Curious Girl, 1977; (with C. Makovski and R. Guyonmet) Papa les Petits Bateaux, 1971; (with C. Makovski) Il faut vivre dangereusement, 1974; (with J. Chapot) Nea (title means: New Woman), 1976, in US as Young Emanuelle! (with J. Chapot and C. Makovski) Charles et Lucie, 1979, in US as Charles and Lucie, 1982; Abel Gance et Son Napoleon, 1983; Pattes de Velours, 1986; Plaisir d'Amour, 1990; Ils furent une etrange comete, 2002. OTHER: Le Manifeste d'un Art Nouveau on "Magirama," Le Sunlight d'Austerlitz, 1960; Abel Gance's Napoleon (film history), 1994. SHORT STORIES AS BELEN: Le Reservoir des Sens; 1966; Le Collier de Ptyx, 1972; Un Manteau de Fou-Rire ou les Memoires d'une Liseuse de Draps, 1974 (A Coat of Laughter, or the Memoirs of a Lady Sheet Diviner); La Gardienne du Temps, 1995; Aux Orchidees Sauvage, 1998. **Address:** Cythere Films, 34 Champs Elysees, 75008 Paris, France.

KAPLAN, Rachel. French. **Genres:** Travel/Exploration. **Career:** French Links (a tourism service), Paris, founder and tour guide; international correspondent for American, French, British, and Czech publications. **Publications:** (trans) Manet: Painter of Modern Life, 1995; Little-known Museums in and Around Paris, 1996; Little-known Museums in and Around London, 1997. Contributor to periodicals. **Address:** c/o Harry N. Abrams Inc., 100 Fifth Ave., New York, NY 10011, U.S.A. **Online address:** kaplan@club-internet.fr

KAPLAN, Robert B. American, b. 1929. **Genres:** Language/Linguistics, Speech/Rhetoric. **Career:** University of Southern California, Los Angeles, Coordinator, English communication program for foreign students, 1961-65, assistant professor of English, 1963-65, associate professor, chairman, Linguistics Dept., and director, English Communication, 1965-72, professor, 1972-95, associate dean, continuing education, 1973-76, director, American Language Institute, 1986-91, emeritus professor, 1995-. National Association for Foreign Student Affairs, field service consultant, 1966-86, president, 1983; Association of Teachers of English as a Second Language, president, 1968; Annual Review of Applied Linguistics, general ed., 1981-90; Teachers of English to Speakers of Other Languages, president, 1990; American Association for Applied Linguistics, president, 1993-94; Meikai University, Japan, visiting professor, 1998-99; Current Issues in Language Planning, co-general editor, 1999-. **Publications:** The Anatomy of Rhetoric, 1971; Migrants in the Workplace, 1980; Language Planning in Nepal, Sweden, and Taiwan, 2000; Language Planning in Botswana, Hungary, Ivory Coast and Vanuatu, 2000. EDITOR: Reading and Rhetoric, 1963; On the Scope of Applied Linguistics, 1980; (co) Language Planning in Malawi, Mozambique and the Philippines, 1999; Oxford Handbook of Applied Linguistics, 2002. WITH OTHERS: Transformational Grammar: A Guide for Teachers, 1968; English at Your Fingertips, 1969; Exploring Academic Discourse, 1983; Writing across Languages, 1987; Introduction to Applied Linguistics, 1991; Theory and Practice of Writing, 1996; Language Planning from Practice to Theory, 1997; Language and Language-in-Education Planning in the Pacific Basin, 2002. Contributor to scholarly journals. **Address:** PO Box 577, Port Angeles, WA 98362, U.S.A. **Online address:** rkaplan@olypen.com

KAPLAN, Robert S. American, b. 1940. **Genres:** Administration/Management. **Career:** Carnegie-Mellon University, Pittsburgh, PA, member of industrial administration faculty, c. 1968-84, dean of Graduate School of Industrial Administration, 1977-83; Harvard University, Harvard Business School, Boston, MA, faculty member, 1984-, became Marvin Bower Professor of Leadership Development; Balanced Scorecard Collaborative, chairman. **Publications:** (with H.T. Johnson) Relevance Lost: The Rise and Fall of

Management Accounting, 1991; (ed.) Measures for Manufacturing Excellence, 1992; Measuring Corporate Performance (4-part videotape series), 1994; (with D. Norton) The Balanced Scorecard: Translating Strategy into Action, 1996; (with R. Cooper) Cost and Effect: Using Integrated Cost Systems to Drive Profitability and Performance, 1998; (with D. Norton) The Strategy-Focused Organization; coauthor of five other books. Contributor to business and management journals. **Address:** Harvard Business School, Morgan Hall 417, Boston, MA 02163, U.S.A.

KAPLAR, Richard T. American, b. 1951. **Genres:** Writing/Journalism. **Career:** Media Institute (nonprofit communications policy research organization), Washington, DC, vice-president, 1981-. **Publications:** The Financial Interest and Syndication Rules: Prime Time for Repeal, 1990; Advertising Rights, the Neglected Freedom: Toward a New Doctrine of Commercial Speech, 1991; (with P.D. Maines) The Government Factor: Undermining Journalistic Ethics in the Information Age, 1995; Cross Ownership at the Crossroads, 1997. EDITOR: Beyond the Courtroom: Alternatives for Resolving Press Disputes, 1991; Bad Prescription for the First Amendment: FDA Censorship of Drug Advertising and Promotion, 1993; Speaking Freely: The Public Interest in Unfettered Speech, 1995; The First Amendment and the Media, 1997, rev. ed., 2003. Contributor to periodicals. **Address:** Media Institute, 1800 N Kent St Ste 1130, Arlington, VA 22209, U.S.A.

KAPLOW, Robert. Also writes as Moe Moskowitz. American, b. 1954. **Genres:** Novels, Songs/Lyrics and libretti. **Career:** Radio producer, journalist, English teacher, and writer. **Publications:** Two in the City, 1979; Alex Icicle: A Romance in Ten Torrid Chapters, 1984; Alessandra in Love, 1989; Alessandra in Between, 1992; Steven Spielberg, Give Me Some of Your Money, 1994; Cancel My Subscription: The Worst of NPR, 2001; The Cat Who Killed Lilian Jackson Braun, 2003. **Address:** c/o Literary and Creative Artists, Inc., 3543 Albemarle St NW, Washington, DC 20008, U.S.A.

KAPOOR, L(achman) D(as). Indian, b. 1916. **Genres:** Medicine/Health. **Career:** Forest Department of Jammu and Kashmir, Baramulla, India, exploitation officer for the survey and collection of forest products, 1942-44; Drug Research Laboratory of Jammu and Kashmir, Jammu, India, botanist, 194455; CSIR, Regional Research Laboratory, Jammu, senior assistant director, 1958-64; CSIR, National Botanical Research Institute, Lucknow, India, deputy director, 1964-76; retired, 1976. Consulting scientist to Lupin Laboratories, Baidyanath Ayurved Pharmaceuticals, and Mehta Pharmaceuticals. **Publications:** (with R.N. Chopra, I.C. Chopra, and K.L. Handa) Chopra's Indigenous Drugs of India, rev. ed., 1958; (with Ramkrishnan) Advances in the Essential Oil Industry, 1977; The CRC Handbook of Ayurvedic Medicinal Plants, 1990; The Opium Poppy: Botany, Chemistry, and Pharmacology, 1995. Contributor to scientific journals. Some work appears under the name L.D. Kapur. **Address:** 11 Harvest Dr., Neshanic Station, NJ 08853, U.S.A.

KAPPES, Sister Marciann. American, b. 1947. **Genres:** Theology/Religion. **Career:** Schoolteacher in Oklahoma and California, 1968-87; St. Gregory's College, Shawnee, OK, member of theology faculty, 1992-. Carmelite Sisters of Saint Therese, Oklahoma City, OK, Roman Catholic nun, 1966-, and formation director. Oklahoma City University, teacher, 1981-84. **Publications:** Track of the Mystic: The Spirituality of Jessica Powers, 1994. Contributor to periodicals. **Address:** St. Gregory's College, 1900 West MacArthur Dr., Shawnee, OK 74801, U.S.A.

KAPSIS, Robert E. American, b. 1943. **Genres:** Film, Human relations/Parenting. **Career:** Brandeis University, Waltham, MA, assistant director of violence project for Lemberg Center for the Study of Violence, 1968-70; Queens College of the City University of New York, NYC, assistant professor, 1973-78, associate professor, 1979-92, professor of sociology, 1993-, director of neighborhood delinquency project, 1974-75, member of executive committee of council for media research, 1983-84, and film studies program, 1984-96. Rutgers University, consultant for sociology of adult education project, 1974; City University of New York faculty retrenchment study, principal investigator, 1976-83; Long Island University, adjunct professor on C. W. Post Campus, 1992; New School for Social Research, adjunct professor, 1992-; Graduate Center of the City University of New York, member of media and culture roundtable and salon, 1988-90. Museum of Modern Art, presenter of film series on the Cannes Film Festival, 1992. Hitchcock Project, principal investigator, 1984-92; Eastwood Project, principal investigator, 1991-. Multimedia Hitchcock Project, principal investigator, 1995-. Regular speaker at annual meetings of American Sociological Association, 1973-. **Publications:** (with others) The Reconstruction of a Riot: A Case Study of Community Tensions and Civil Disorder, 1970; Hitchcock: The Making of a

Reputation, 1992. Work represented in anthologies. Contributor to sociology and media-studies journals. **Address:** Department of Sociology, Queens College of the City University of New York, Flushing, NY 11367, U.S.A.

KAPUR, Manju. Indian. **Genres:** Novels. **Career:** Instructor at Delhi College, India. **Publications:** Difficult Daughters, 1998. **Address:** c/o Penguin Putnam, Publicity Department, 375 Hudson St., New York, NY 10014, U.S.A.

KARAMITROGLOU, Fotios. Greek, b. 1971. **Genres:** Language/Linguistics. **Career:** University of Athens, Athens, Greece, lecturer in translation methodology, 1998-. European Educational Organization, Athens, lecturer, 1999-. Greek Telecom, worked as teacher of English as a foreign language; Lumiere Hellas, worked as writer of subtitles for television movies and documentary films. **Publications:** Towards a Methodology for the Investigation of Norms in Audiovisual Translation, 2000. Contributor to periodicals. **Address:** Faculty of English Studies, University of Athens, Panepistimioupoli Zografou, 157 84 Athens, Greece. **Online address:** fotios@energy.gr

KARANIKAS, Alexander. American, b. 1916. **Genres:** Poetry, Literary criticism and history. **Career:** Emeritus Professor of English, University of Illinois at Chicago Circle, since 1982 (joined faculty, 1954). Instructor in English, Kendall College, 1952-53, and Northwestern University, 1953-54, both Evanston, Illinois. **Publications:** When a Youth Gets Poetic (poetry), 1934; In Praise of Heroes (poetry), 1945; Tillers of a Myth: The Southern Agrarians as Social and Literary Critics, 1966; (with Helen Karanikas) Elias Venezis (literary criticism), 1969; Hellenes and Hellions: Modern Greek Characters in American Literature, 1981; Nashville Dreams (musical comedy with songs by Larry Nestor), 1991; Stepping Stones (poetry), 1994. **Address:** 618 North Harvey Ave, Oak Park, IL 60302, U.S.A.

KARETZKY, Patricia E(ichenbaum). American, b. 1947. **Genres:** Art/Art history. **Career:** New York University, New York, NY, adjunct lecturer at Washington Square College, 1976-79, adjunct assistant professor of fine arts, 1979-87; Bard College, Annandale, NY, O. Munsterberg Professor of Asian Art, 1988-, adjunct of Graduate School of Decorative Arts, 1997-98. Fordham University, lecturer, 1988; School of Visual Arts, lecturer, 1991; Sarah Lawrence College, faculty member, 1992-93; Herbert H. Lehman College of the City University of New York, professor, 1994-. Metropolitan Museum of Art, curatorial research assistant in Asian art, 1989-90; curator of exhibitions at colleges, universities, and Hammond Art Gallery. Speaker at professional conferences and at public lectures. **Publications:** The Life of the Buddha: Pictorial and Scriptural Evidence in India, 1992; Court Art of the Tang Dynasty, 1996; Arts of the Tang Dynasty, 1996; Early Buddhist Narrative Art: Illustrations of the Life of the Buddha from Central Asia, China, Korea, and Japan, 2000. Author of exhibition catalogs. Contributor to academic journals. **Address:** 1530 Palisade Ave. No. 22L, Fort Lee, NJ 07024, U.S.A. **Online address:** karetzky@aol.com

KARETZKY, Stephen. American, b. 1946. **Genres:** Librarianship, Writing/Journalism. **Career:** Brooklyn Public Library, Brooklyn, NY, librarian, 1969-70; State University of New York-Buffalo, assistant professor of library and information studies, 1974-76; State University of New York-College at Geneseo, assistant professor of library and information studies, 1977-78; Haifa University, Haifa, Israel, associate professor of library and information studies, 1978-81; Shapolsky/Steimatzky Publishers, New York, NY, senior editor, 1981-82; San Jose State University, San Jose, CA, associate professor of library and information studies, 1982-85; Shapolsky Publishers, New York, NY, senior editor, 1985-86; Felician College, Lodi, NJ, associate professor of library and information studies and director of library, 1986-. **Publications:** Reading Research and Librarianship: A History and Analysis, 1982; The Cannons of Journalism, 1984; Not Seeing Red: American Librarianship and the Soviet Union, 1917-1960, 2002. EDITOR & CONTRIBUTOR: The Media's War against Israel, 1985; The Media's Coverage of the Arab-Israeli Conflict, 1989. Contributor of articles and reviews to periodicals. **Address:** Felician College Library, 262 South Main St., Lodi, NJ 07644, U.S.A. **Online address:** karetzkys@felician.edu

KARI, Daven M(ichael). American, b. 1953. **Genres:** Poetry, Literary criticism and history, Theology/Religion, Bibliography. **Career:** Jefferson Community College, Louisville, KY, lecturer, 1987-90; Spalding University, Louisville, lecturer, 1986-90; University of Louisville, lecturer, 1986-90; Missouri Baptist College, St. Louis, MO, assistant professor, 1991; California Baptist University, Riverside, professor and director of Christian Ministry Center, 1991-98, co-faculty adviser, The Banner, 1993-96; Washington Bible College, Lanham, MD, academic dean, 1998-2000; Baptist Christian School, Hemet, CA, administrator, 2000-01; Vanguard University, Costa Mesa, CA, professor of English, 2002-. Also an ordained Southern Baptist minister. **Publications:** T.S. Eliot's Dramatic Pilgrimage: Progress in Craft as an Expression of Christian Perspective, 1990; A Bibliography of Sources in Christianity and the Arts, 1995. EDITOR: (asst with J. Halpern, J. Kilborn and A. Lokke) Business Writing Strategies and Samples, 1988; (with D. Rayburn and D. Gwaltney) Baptist Reflections on Christianity and the Arts: Learning from Beauty, 1997. Contributor to books. Contributor of articles and poems to periodicals. **Address:** 23878 Bouquet-Cyn Pl, Moreno Valley, CA 92557, U.S.A. **Online address:** DavenMKari@aol.com

KARIER, Thomas. American, b. 1956. **Genres:** Economics. **Career:** Eastern Washington University, Cheney, professor of economics, 1981-. **Publications:** Beyond Competition, 1993; Great Experiments in American Economic Policy, 1997. **Address:** Department of Economics, Eastern Washington University, Cheney, WA 99004, U.S.A.

KARKALA, John A. Also writes as John B. Alphonso-Karkala. Indian, b. 1923. **Genres:** Novels, Poetry, Genealogy/Heraldry, Literary criticism and history, Bibliography, Biography. **Career:** Columbia University, NYC, teaching fellow, Oriental Studies Program, 1962-64, visiting professor of Oriental humanities, fall 1969, associate of university seminars: Shakespeare, Indology/South Asia, 1999-; State University of New York at New Paltz, assistant professor, 1964-65, associate professor, 1965-68, professor of literature, 1969-98, professor emeritus, 1999-. Member, Indian Foreign Missions, Geneva, London, and United Nations, NYC, 1953-60. **Publications:** Indo-English Literature in the Nineteenth Century, 1970; Passions of the Nightless Nights (novel), 1974; (with L. Karkala) Bibliography of Indo-English Literature, 1800-1966, 1974; Studies in Comparative Literature: Essays, 1974; Jawaharlal Nehru: A Literary Portrait, 1975; (with L. Karkala) When Night Falls (verse), 1980; Joys of Jayamagara (novel), 1981; (with L. Karkala) Indo-English Literature: Essays, 1994; (with L. Karkala) Teisko Ancestry: Record of Six Generations (Finland), 2001; Kurngaje Santan: Record of Six Generations (India), 2005. EDITOR: An Anthology of Indian Literature: Selections from Vedas to Tagore, 1972, rev. ed., 1987; Vedic Vision, 1980. **Address:** 100 Bennett Ave Apt 4E, New York, NY 10033-3045, U.S.A. **Online address:** jakarkala@aol.com

KARLE, Hellmut (William Arthur). British (born Germany), b. 1932. **Genres:** Psychology. **Career:** Aycliffe Hospital, Durham, England, clinical psychologist, 1954-56; North Wales Child Guidance Service, clinical psychologist, 1956-60; East Sussex County Council, educational psychologist, 1960-70; Lingfield Hospital School, educational psychologist, 1970-72; Guy's Hospital, London, England, principal psychologist, Department of Child and Adolescent Psychiatry, 1972-90, director of Linbury Research Project, 1981-86, acting head of Child Psychology Services, 1990-91; retired to breed pigs, 1994. Royal College of Midwives, visiting lecturer, 1963-78; Brighton Polytechnic, part-time lecturer, 1963-78; University of Sussex, field tutor, 1966-70; Medway and Maidstone College of Technology, part-time lecturer, 1970-76; Mayfield College, chairperson of board of governors, 1974-77. Consultant to Pestalozzi Children's Village Trust. **Publications:** (with J.H. Boys) Hypnotherapy: A Practical Handbook, 1987; Hypnosis and Hypnotherapy: A Patient's Guide, 1988, reprinted as Thorson's Introductory Guide to Hypnotherapy, 1992; The Filthy Lie: Discovering and Recovering from Childhood Sexual Abuse, 1992. Work represented in anthologies. Contributor to psychology journals. **Address:** c/o Free Association Books, 57 Warren St, London W1P 5PA, England.

KARLEN, Neal (Stuart). American, b. 1959. **Genres:** Music, Songs/Lyrics and libretti. **Career:** Columnist and freelance writer. Newsweek, NYC, staff writer and reporter, 1982-86; Rolling Stone, NYC, contributing editor, 1986-91. CBS News/America Tonight, NYC, on-air essayist, 1990; Minneapolis-St. Paul Magazine, Minneapolis, MN, columnist, 1990-; New York Times, NYC, contributing writer, 1992-. **Publications:** The Emperor's New Clothes (libretto), 1990; (with H. Youngman) Take My Life, Please, 1991; Babes in Toyland: The Making and Selling of a Rock and Roll Band, 1994. Contributor to periodicals. **Address:** c/o Times Books, 201 East 50th St., New York, NY 10022, U.S.A.

KARLIN, Daniel. British, b. 1953. **Genres:** Literary criticism and history. **Career:** Affiliated with Boston University, 2005-; writer. **Publications:** The Courtship of Robert Browning and Elizabeth Barrett, 1985; Browning's Hatreds, 1993; (with J. Woolford) Robert Browning, 1996; Proust's English, 2005. EDITOR: (and author of intro.) R. Kipling, The Jungle Books, 1987; Robert Browning and Elizabeth Barrett: The Courtship Correspondence, 1845-1846, 1989; (and author of intro.) R. Browning, Selected Poems, 1989; (with J. Woolford) The Poems of Robert Browning, 1991; (and author of intro.) H.R. Haggard, She, 1991; (and author of intro.) Penguin Book of

Victorian Verse, 1997; Rudyard Kipling, 1999. Contributor of articles and reviews to periodicals. **Address:** University Professors, Boston University, 745 Commonwealth Ave, Boston, 02215, U.S.A. **Online address:** d.karlin@ucl.ac.uk

KARLIN, Samuel. American, b. 1924. **Genres:** Mathematics/Statistics. **Career:** California Institute of Technology, Pasadena, Bateman research fellow, 1947-48, instructor, 1948-49, assistant professor, 1949-52, associate professor, 1952-55, professor of mathematics, 1955-56; Stanford University, Stanford, CA, professor of mathematics, 1956-, Robert Grimmett Professor, 1978-. Princeton University, visiting assistant professor, 1950-51, Wilks Lecturer, 1977; Weizmann Institute of Science, advisory dean of mathematics department, 1970-77; Cornell University, Andrew D. White Professor at Large, 1975-81; University of Massachusetts at Amherst, Commonwealth Lecturer, 1980; Indian Statistical Institute, Mahalanobis Memorial Lecturer, 1983; McMaster University, Britton Lecturer, 1990. **Publications:** (with K. Arrow and H. Scarf) Studies in the Mathematical Theory of Inventory and Production, 1958; Mathematical Methods and Theory in Games, Programming, and Economics, Vol I: Matrix Games, Programming, and Mathematical Economics, Vol II: The Theory of Infinite Games, 1959; (with H.M. Taylor) A First Course in Stochastic Processes, 1966, 2nd ed, 1975; (with W.J. Studden) Tchebycheff Systems: With Applications in Analysis and Statistics, 1966; Total Positivity, 1968; (with C.A. Micchelli, A. Pinkus, and I.I. Schoenberg) Studies in Spline Functions and Approximation Theory, 1976; (with Taylor) A Second Course in Stochastic Processes, 1980; (with Taylor) An Introduction to Stochastic Modeling, 1984; (with S. Lessard) Theoretical Studies on Sex Ratio Evolution, 1986. EDITOR & CONTRIBUTOR: (with Arrow and P. Suppes) Mathematical Methods in the Social Sciences, 1960; (with Arrow and Scarf) Studies in Applied Probability and Management Sciences, 1962; (with E. Nevo) Population Genetics and Ecology, 1976; (with T. Amemiya and L.A. Goodman) Studies in Econometrics, Time Series, and Multivariate Statistics, 1983; (with Nevo) Evolutionary Processes and Theory, 1986. Contributor to books. Contributor to mathematics journals and popular magazines. **Address:** Department of Mathematics, Stanford University, Stanford, CA 94305, U.S.A.

KARLIN, Wayne (Stephen). American, b. 1945. **Genres:** Novels, Novellas/Short stories, Autobiography/Memoirs. **Career:** Gannett Newspapers, White Plains, NY, reporter for the Reporter Dispatch, 1972; American College, Jerusalem, Israel, instructor in creative writing and director of student activities, 1973-75; freelance writer, Israel, 1973-75; Montgomery College, Rockville, instructor in English, 1982-84; College of Southern Maryland, LaPlata, MD, professor of language and literature, 1984-. First Casualty Press, president and coeditor, 1972-73; University of Massachusetts, visiting writer and faculty at the Joiner Center for the Study of War and Social Consequences, 1989-93; St. Mary's College, fiction director, Literary Festival, 1994-. **Publications:** NOVELS: Crossover, 1984; Lost Armies, 1988; The Extras, 1989; US, 1993; Prisoners, 1998; The Wished-For Country, 2002. TRANSLATOR: (with Phan Thanh Hao and C. Bacchi) Ho Anh Thai, Women on the Island, 2000; (and adaptor with Phan Thanh Hao) Ma Van Khang, Against the Flood, 2000; (and adaptor with Phan Thanh Hao) Nguyen Khai, Past Continuous, 2001. EDITOR: (with B.T. Paquet and L. Rottmann, and contrib.) Free Fire Zone: Short Stories by Vietnam Veterans, 1973; (with Le Minh Khue and Truong Vu, and contrib.) The Other Side of Heaven: Postwar Fiction by Vietnamese and American Writers, 1995; Le Minh Khue, The Stars, the Earth, the River, 1997; Ho Anh Thai, Behind the Red Mist, 1998; (with Ho Anh Thai) Love after War: Contemporary Fiction from Vietnam, 2003. OTHER: Rumors and Stones: A Journey, 1996. **Address:** PO Box 239, St. Marys City, MD 20686, U.S.A. **Online address:** waynek@csmd.edu

KARMEL, Peter Henry. Australian, b. 1922. **Genres:** Economics, Education. **Career:** University of Adelaide, professor of economics, 1950-62; University of Papua and New Guinea, Port Moresby, chairman of Interim Council, 1965-69, chancellor, 1969-70; Flinders University of South Australia, vice-chancellor, 1966-71; Australian University Commission, chairman, 1971-77; Interim Committee for Schools Commission, chairman, 1972-73; Australia Council, chairman, 1974-77; Commonwealth Tertiary Education Commission, chairman, 1977-82; Australian Council for Educational Research, president, 1979-99; Australian National University, Canberra, vice-chancellor, 1982-87, chairman of Board of the National Institute of the Arts, 1992-2003; Commonwealth Government Quality of Education Review Committee, chairman, 1984-85; Academy of the Social Sciences in Australia, president, 1987-90; Australian Institute of Health, chairman, 1987-91; Australian National Council on AIDS, chairman, 1988-92. **Publications:** Applied Statistics for Economists, 1957, rev. ed. (with M. Polasek), 1978; (with M. Brunt) Structure of the Australian Economy, 1962, 3rd ed., 1966; (with G.C. Harcourt and R.H. Wallace) Economic Activity, 1967. **Address:** 4/127 Hopetoun Circuit, Yarralumla, ACT 2600, Australia.

KARMILOFF-SMITH, Annette Dionne. British/French, b. 1938. **Genres:** Language/Linguistics, Psychology. **Career:** American University of Beirut, Lebanon, associate in psychology and research consultant at UNWRA/UNESCO Institute of Education, 1970-72; research collaborator of Jean Piaget at Centre International d'Epistemologie Genetique, Geneva, 1972-78; Geneva University, director of studies, 1979-80; Max Planck Institute, Nijmegen, Netherlands, research associate, 1979-82; Medical Research Council, London, England, senior scientist in Cognitive Development Unit, 1982-98; Institute of Child Health, professor and head of Neurocognitive Development Unit, 1998-. Visiting professor at US and European universities. British Academy, fellow, 1993; Academy of Medical Sciences, fellow, 1999. **Publications:** A Functional Approach to Child Language, 1979; (with W.M. Levelt and A. Mills) Child Language Research in ESF Countries, 1981; Beyond Modularity, 1992; Baby It's You, 1994; (with J. Elman and others) Rethinking Innateness; (with K. Karmiloff) Everything Your Baby Would Ask, if Only He or She Could Talk, 1999; (with K. Karmiloff) Pathways to Language, 2001. Work represented in anthologies. Contributor of articles and reviews to scholarly journals. **Address:** Neurocognitive Development Unit, Institute of Child Health, 30 Guildford St, London WC1N 1EH, England. **Online address:** a.karmiloff-smith@ich.ucl.ac.uk

KARNOW, Stanley. American, b. 1925. **Genres:** History. **Career:** Paris Correspondent, Time mag., 1950-57; North African Bureau Chief, 1958-59, Hong Kong Bureau Chief, 1959-62, and Special Correspondent, 1962-63, Time-Life, Inc.; Far East Correspondent, Saturday Evening Post, 1963-65; Far East Correspondent, 1965-71, and Diplomatic Correspondent, 1971-72, Washington Post; Associate Ed., New Republic, Washington, DC, 1973-75. **Publications:** Southeast Asia, 1963; Bitter Seeds: A Farmer's Story of the Revolution in China, 1964; Mao and China: From Revolution to Revolution, 1972, 3rd ed., 1990; (trans.) The Conspiracy and Death of Lin Bao, 1983; Vietnam: The War Nobody Won, 1983; Vietnam: A History, 1984; In Our Image: America's Empire in the Philippines, 1990 (Pulitzer Prize in History, 1990); Asian Americans in Transition, 1992; Paris in the Fifties, 1997; (author of intro.) The First Time I Saw Paris, 1999. **Address:** c/o Random House, 201 E 50th St, New York, NY 10022, U.S.A.

KARODIA, Farida. Canadian (born Republic of South Africa). **Genres:** Novels, Novellas/Short stories. **Career:** Short story writer, novelist, and scriptwriter for radio. Also worked as a teacher. **Publications:** NOVELS: Daughters of the Twilight, 1986; A Shattering of Silence, 1993; Other Secrets, 2000; Boundaries, 2003; Tiger Moon, forthcoming. SHORT STORIES: Coming Home and Other Stories, 1988; Against an African Sky and Other Stories, 1995. Work represented in anthologies. **Address:** c/o Penguin Publishers, PO Box 9, Parklands, Claremont, Johannesburg 2121, Republic of South Africa. **Online address:** fklll@telkomsa.net

KARON, Jan. American, b. 1937. **Genres:** Novels, Inspirational/Motivational Literature. **Career:** Various advertising agencies, copywriter; novelist. **Publications:** At Home in Mitford, 1994; A Light in the Window, 1996; These High, Green Hills, 1996; Out to Canaan, 1997; Miss Fannie's Hat, 1998; A New Song, 1999; Jeremy: The Tale of an Honest Bunny, 2000; A Southern Style Christmas: Holiday Treasures by Jan Karon, 2000; A Common Life: The Wedding Story, 2001; The Mitford Years (five-volume set), 2001; Father Timothy A. Kavanaugh, 2001; The Mitford Snowmen: A Christmas Story, 2001; (author of foreword) R.B. Graham, Never Let It End: Poems of a Lifelong Love, 2001; In This Mountain, 2002; Esther's Gift: A Mitford Christmas Story, 2002; The Trellis and the Seed, 2003; Shepherds Abiding, 2003; The Mitford Cookbook and Kitchen Reader, 2004. **Address:** c/o Viking Publicity, 375 Hudson Street, New York, NY 10014, U.S.A. **Online address:** www.mitfordbooks.com

KARP, Abraham J. American (born Poland), b. 1921. **Genres:** History, Theology/Religion. **Career:** Research Professor of American Jewish History and Bibliography, Jewish Theological Seminary of America, NYC, 1991-. Bernstein Professor of Jewish Studies, and Professor of History and Religious Studies, University of Rochester, New York, 1972-91. Member, Institute of Contemporary Jewry, Hebrew University, Jerusalem; former president, American Jewish Historical Society; former Rabbi, Congregation Beth El, Rochester, NY. **Publications:** New York Chooses a Chief Rabbi, 1955; The Jewish Way of Life, 1962; A History of the United Synagogue of America 1913-1963, 1967; Beginnings, 1975; Golden Door to America, 1976; The Jewish Way of Life and Thought, 1980; To Give Life, 1980; American Judaism, 1984; Haven and Home: A History of the Jews in America, 1985; Mordecai Manuel Noah: First American Jew, 1988; From the Ends of the Earth: Judaic Treasures at the Library of Congress, 1991; The Jews in America: A Treasury of Art and Literature, 1994; A History of the Jews in America, 1997; Jewish Continuity in America: Creative Survival in a Free Society,

1998. EDITOR: Conservative Judaism: The Heritage of Solomon Schechter, 1963; The Jewish Experience in America, 5 vols., 1969; (with M. Davis) Texts and Studies in American Jewish History, 1971. **Address:** 3333 Henry Hudson Parkway 22E, Bronx, NY 10463, U.S.A.

KARP, Larry. American, b. 1939. **Genres:** Medicine/Health, Novels. **Career:** Author. Physician, specializing in care of complicated pregnancy, labor, and delivery, and prenatal diagnosis, 1963-94. Founder, Prenatal Diagnosis Center, University of Washington, 1972, and Department of Perinatal Medicine, Swedish Hospital, Seattle, WA, 1982. **Publications:** Genetic Engineering: Threat or Promise?, 1976; The View from the Vue, 1977; The Enchanted Ear, 1995; The Music Box Murders, 1999; Scamming the Birdman, 2001; The Midnight Special, 2001. **Address:** c/o Write Way Publishing, 3806 South Fraser St., Aurora, CO 80014, U.S.A. **Online address:** larry@larrykarp.com

KARP, Robert J. American, b. 1941. **Genres:** Medicine/Health. **Career:** Pediatrician and nutritionist, 1971-94; State University of New York Brooklyn, NY, associate professor of pediatrics, 1994-. Associate director of Regional Center for Nutrition Education, Meany Academy of Medicine. **Publications:** Malnourished Children in the United States, 1994. **Address:** Kings County Hospital-CRW, Brooklyn, NY 11203, U.S.A.

KARR, Kathleen. American, b. 1946. **Genres:** Romance/Historical, Children's fiction, Young adult fiction. **Career:** Writer. Barrington High School, RI, English and speech teacher, 1968-69; curator, Rhode Island Historical Society Film Archives, 1970-71; American Film Institute, Washington, DC, archives assistant, 1971-72, member of catalog staff, 1972; Washington Circle Theatre Corp., general manager, 1973-78; Circle/Showcase Theatres, Washington, DC, advertising director, 1979-83, director of public relations, 1984-88; Circle Management Company/Circle Releasing, Washington, DC, public relations staff member, 1988-93. George Washington University, asst professor, 1979, 1980-81. Lecturer or instructor in film and communications at institutions and at film and writing conferences. **Publications:** FICTION FOR CHILDREN: It Ain't Always Easy, 1990; Oh, Those Harper Girls!, 1992; Gideon and the Mummy Professor, 1993; The Cave, 1994; In the Kaiser's Clutch, 1995; Go West, Young Women!, 1996; Phoebe's Folly, 1996; Spy in the Sky, 1997; Oregon, Sweet Oregon, 1998; Gold-Rush Phoebe, 1998; The Great Turkey Walk, 1998; The Lighthouse Mermaid, 1998; Man of the Family, 1999; Skullduggery, 2000; The Boxer, 2000; It Happened in the White House, 2000; Playing with Fire, 2001; Bone Dry, 2002; The 7th Knot, 2003; Gilbert & Sullivan Set Me Free, 2003; Exiled: Memoirs of a Camel, 2004. ROMANCE NOVELS FOR ADULTS: Light of My Heart, 1984; From This Day Forward, 1985; Chessie's King, 1986; Destiny's Dreamers, Book I: Gone West, 1993, Book II: The Promised Land, 1993. EDITOR: The American Film Heritage: Views from the American Film Institute Collection, 1972. Author of short films. Contributor to journals and texts. **Address:** c/o Tracey Adams, McIntosh & Otis, 353 Lexington Ave, New York, NY 10016, U.S.A. **Online address:** karr@bellatlantic.net

KARR, Mary. American. **Genres:** Poetry, Autobiography/Memoirs. **Career:** Syracuse University, Syracuse, NY, Jesse Truesdell Peck Professor of Literature. **Publications:** POETRY: Abacus, 1987; The Devil's Tour, 1993; Viper Rum, 1998. MEMOIRS: The Liars' Club: A Memoir, 1995; Cherry: A Memoir, 2000. Contributor to periodicals. **Address:** English Department, Syracuse University, Syracuse, NY 13244, U.S.A.

KARTTUNEN, Frances. American, b. 1942. **Genres:** Anthropology/Ethnology, History, Language/Linguistics, Race relations, Travel/Exploration, Women's studies and issues. **Career:** University of Texas at Austin, linguist, 1968-2000. **Publications:** (with J. Lockhart) Nahuatl in the Middle Years, 1976; An Analytical Dictionary of Nahuatl, 1982, 2nd ed., 1992; (with J. Lockhart) The Art of Nahuatl Speech: The Bancroft Dialogues, 1987; Between Worlds: Interpreters, Guides, and Survivors, 1994; The Other Islanders, 2005. **Address:** 67 N Centre St, Nantucket, MA 02554, U.S.A.

KASABOV, Nikola K(irilov). Bulgarian, b. 1948. **Genres:** Information science/Computers. **Career:** Technical University of Sofia, Bulgaria, lecturer to senior lecturer, 1976-87, associate professor, 1988-90; University of Essex, Colchester, England, senior lecturer, 1990-91; University of Otago, Dunedin, New Zealand, senior lecturer, 1992-95, associate professor of information science and director of graduate study and research, 1995-. International Graduate School for Artificial Intelligence, Sofia, director, 1987-91. Asia-Pacific Neural Network Assembly, president, 1997-. Holder of patents in the United States, England, France, Russia, and Bulgaria. **Publications:** (with Romanski) Computing, 1995; Foundations of Neural Networks, Fuzzy Systems, and Knowledge Engineering, 1996; (ed. with S. Awan)

Brain-Line Computing and Intelligent Systems, 1997; (ed. with R. Kozma) Neuro-Fuzzy Techniques for Intelligent Systems, 1998; Evolving Connectionist Systems, 2002. Contributor to periodicals. **Address:** School of Computing & Information Science, Auckland University of Technology, Private Bag 92006, Auckland 1020, New Zealand. **Online address:** nikola. kasabov@aut.ac.nz

KASCHAK, Ellyn. American, b. 1943. **Genres:** Psychology, Women's studies and issues. **Career:** George Washington University, Washington, DC, lecturer in psychology, 1965-66, research assistant at Arthritis Research Institute, 1968-69; District of Columbia General Hospital, Washington, psychology intern, 1966; school psychologist for public schools of Washington, DC, 1967-69; University Hospital, Columbus, OH, psychology intern, 1969-70; Ohio State University, Columbus, instructor in psychology, 1970-71; Veterans Administration Hospital, Palo Alto, CA, psychology intern, 1971-73; University of California, Berkeley, extension lecturer, 1972-74; San Jose State University, San Jose, CA, assistant professor, 1974-78, professor of psychology, 1983-, director of Family Counseling Service, 1975-, chairperson of Marriage, Family, and Child Counseling Program, 1985-. National Institute of Mental Health, research assistant, 1967-68; California State University, Hayward, administrative fellow, 1980-81; Pacific Graduate School, adjunct professor, 1983-85; Universidad Nacional de Costa Rica, senior research associate, 1985-88. Women & Therapy Journal, editor, 1998-. **Publications:** Engendered Lives: A New Psychology of Women's Experience, Basic Books, 1992. Work represented in anthologies. Contributor to psychology and women's studies journals. **Address:** Department of Psychology, San Jose State University, San Jose, CA 95192, U.S.A.

KASDORF, Julia. Also writes as Julia Spicher. American, b. 1962. **Genres:** Poetry, Local history/Rural topics. **Career:** Writer and educator. Pennsylvania Governors School for the Arts, instructor, 1984, 1985, 1987; New York University, NYC, writer, 1987-89, instructor, 1989-; Messiah College, Grantham, PA, assistant professor, 1996-2000; Pennsylvania State University, University Park, associate professor, 2000-. **Publications:** (as Julia Spicher) Moss Lotus (chapbook), 1983; Sleeping Preacher (poems), 1992; Eve's Striptease, 1998; Body and the Book, 2001; Fixing Tradition: Joseph W. Yoder, Amish American, 2002. Work represented in anthologies. Contributor to periodicals.

KASER, Michael Charles. British, b. 1926. **Genres:** Area studies, Economics. **Career:** H.M. Foreign Service, London and Moscow, Staff, 1947-51; U.N. Secretariat, Geneva, Economic Affairs Officer, 1951-63; Oxford University, Faculty Fellow, 1963-72, Lecturer in Soviet Economics, 1963-72, Latin Preacher, 1982, St. Antony's College, Professorial Fellow, 1972-83, Reader in Economics, 1972-83, Associate Fellow of Templeton College, 1983-, Director of the Institute for Russian, Soviet and E. European Studies, 1988-93, Emeritus Fellow, 1993-; Birmingham University, Institute for German Studies, Honorary Professor, 1994-. **Publications:** Comecon, 1965, 1967; Soviet Economics, 1970; (with J. Zielinski) Planning in East Europe, 1970; Health Care in the Soviet Union and Eastern Europe, 1976; (with S. Mehrotra) The Central Asian Economies since Independence, 1992; Privatization in the CIS, 1995; The Economies of Kazakstan and Uzbekistan, 1997. EDITOR: Economic Development for Eastern Europe, 1958; Soviet Affairs No. 4, 1966; (with R. Portes) Planning and Market Relations, 1971; (with H. Hohmann and K. Thalheim) The New Economic Systems of East Europe, 1975; (with A. Brown) The Soviet Union since the Fall of Khrushchev, 1975; (gen. ed.) Economic History of Eastern Europe 1919-1975, 3 vols., 1985-86; (co-) The Cambridge Encyclopedia of Russia and the Soviet Union, 1982, 2nd ed., 1994; (with A. Brown) Soviet Policy for the 1980s, 1982; (with E.A.G. Robinson) Early Steps in Comparing East-West Economies, 1992; (with D. Phillips) Education and Economic Change in Eastern Europe and the Former Soviet Union, 1992. **Address:** 31 Capel Close, Oxford OX2 7LA, England.

KASH, Don E. American, b. 1934. **Genres:** Politics/Government, Public/Social administration, Sciences, Technology. **Career:** Hazel Chair in Public Policy, George Mason University, Fairfax, Virginia, 1991-. Director, Program in Science and Public Policy, and Associate Professor of Political Science, Purdue University, Lafayette, Indiana, 1966-70; Director, Program in Science and Public Policy, 1970-78, and George Lynn Cross Research Professor of Political Science, and Research Fellow in Science and Public Policy, 1975-90, University of Oklahoma, Norman. **Publications:** The Politics of Space Cooperation, 1967; (co-author) North Sea Oil and Gas: Implications for Future United States Development, 1973; Energy under the Oceans, 1973; Energy Alternatives, 1975; Our Energy Future, 1976; U.S. Energy Policy: Crisis and Complacency, 1984; Perpetual Innovation: The New World of Competition, 1989; The Complexity Challenge: Technological Innovation for

the 21st Century, 1999. **Address:** School of Public Policy, George Mason University, Fairfax, VA 22030-4444, U.S.A. **Online address:** dkash@gmu. edu

KASINITZ, Philip. American, b. 1957. **Genres:** Urban studies. **Career:** New York University, New York City, instructor in metropolitan studies, 1986-87; Williams College, Williamstown, MA, assistant professor of sociology, 1987-93; Hunter College, Graduate Center of CUNY, associate professor, 1993-98, professor of sociology, 1999-. **Publications:** Caribbean New York, 1992. EDITOR: Metropolis, 1995; (co) Handbook on International Migration, 1999. Contributor to periodicals. **Address:** Dept of Sociology, CUNY Graduate Center, 365 5th Ave, New York, NY 10016, U.S.A. **Online address:** pkasinitz@gc.cuny.edu

KASISCHKE, Laura. American, b. 1961. **Genres:** Novels, Poetry. **Career:** Writer. University of Michigan, Ann Arbor, instructor of creative writing and literature, 1990-; University of Nevada, Las Vegas, associate professor, 1994-95. **Publications:** POETRY: Wild Brides, 1992; Housekeeping in a Dream, 1995. OTHER: Suspicious River, 1996; White Bird in a Blizzard, 1998; Fire and Flower, 1998; What It Wasn't, 2001; Dance and Disappear, 2002; Life before Her Eyes, 2002. Contributor of poems to periodicals.

KASPAROV, Garry (Kimovich). Russian (born Azerbaijan). **Genres:** How-to books. **Career:** Chess player and writer. Azerbaidzhan Champion chess player, 1975, USSR Junior Champion, 1975, International Master, 1979, International Grandmaster, 1980, World Junior Champion, 1980, USSR Champion, 1981, World Champion, 1985-. Gives chess exhibitions in countries throughout the world. **Publications:** (with R. Keene) Batsford Chess Openings, 1982; (with B. Wade) Fighting Chess: Kasparov's Games and Career, 1983; My Games, 1983; (with A. Nikitin) The Sicilian Scheveningen: Sicilian E6 and D6 Systems, 1983; (with A. Shakarov) Caro-Kann, 1984; New World Chess Champion: All the Championship Games with Annotations, 1986; The Test of Time, 1986; Kasparov Teaches Chess, 1987; (with D. Trelford) Child of Change: The Autobiography of Garry Kasparov, 1987; London-Leningrad Championship Games: Rematch Championship Games with Annotations by the World Champion, 1987; (with Trelford) Unlimited Challenge (autobiography), 1990; (with others) Kasparov v. Karpov 1990, 1991; (with Keene) Battle of the Titans: Kasparov-Karpov, 1991; On My Great Predecessors, 2003. **Address:** Krasnopresnenskaya nab. 12, Mezhdunarodnaya-2 Suite 1108, 123610 Moscow, Russia. **Online address:** maiavia@dol.ru

KASSLER, Jamie C(roy). American/Australian, b. 1938. **Genres:** Intellectual history, Music. **Career:** University of Sydney, Australia, postdoctoral research fellow in music, 1975-77; University of New South Wales, Kensington, Australia, research fellow in English and history and philosophy of science, 1979-93. Australian Academy of the Humanities, fellow, 1991-. **Publications:** The Science of Music in Britain, 1714-1830: A Catalogue of Writings, Lectures and Inventions, 2 vols., 1979; Inner Music: Hobbes, Hooke and North on Internal Character, 1995; Music, Science, Philosophy: Models in the Universe of Thought, 2001; The Beginnings of the Modern Philosophy of Music in England, 2004. EDITOR & CONTRIBUTOR: (with J. Stubington) Problems and Solutions: Occasional Essays in Musicology Presented to Alice M. Moyle, 1984; (with M. Chan) Roger North's Cursory Notes of Musicke (c. 1698-c. 1703): A Physical, Psychological, and Critical Theory, 1986; (with M. Chan) Roger North, The Musical Grammarian 1728, 1990; Metaphor: A Musical Dimension, 1991; (with M. Chan and J.D. Hine) Roger North's "Of Sounds" and Prendcourt Tracts: Digests and Editions with and Analytical Index, 2000. **Address:** 10 Wollombi Rd, Northbridge, NSW 2063, Australia.

KASTELY, James L. American, b. 1947. **Genres:** Literary criticism and history. **Career:** University of Hawaii at Manoa, Honolulu, assistant professor, associate professor of English, 1980-93; University of Houston, Houston, TX, associate professor of English, 1994-. **Publications:** Rethinking the Rhetorical Tradition: From Plato to Postmodernism, 1997. **Address:** Department of English, University of Houston, Houston, TX 77204, U.S.A. **Online address:** jkastely@jetson.uh.edu

KASZYNSKI, William. American, b. 1953. **Genres:** Travel/Exploration. **Career:** Self-employed lawyer in St. Paul, MN, 1981-99; freelance writer, 1997-. Waddell & Reed, St. Paul, MN, financial advisor, 2001-. **Publications:** (and photographer) The American Highway: The History and Culture of Roads in the United States, 2000. **Address:** 1132 East Magnolia Ave., St. Paul, MN 55106, U.S.A.

KATAGIRI, Yasuhiro. (born Japan), b. 1960. **Genres:** Area studies. **Career:** Japan Travel Bureau, Tokyo, sales representative, 1984-89; Kyoritsu

Women's University, Tokyo, research assistant, 1994-97; Tokai University, Kanagawa, Japan, assistant professor, 1997-2000, associate professor of American history and government, 2000-. **Publications:** (with Makoto Saito and others) Contemporary America (in Japanese), 1995; (with Tadao Umesao and others) Encyclopedia of Nations and Ethnic Relations (in Japanese), 1995; (with Kaname Saruya and others) One Hundred and One Important People in American History (in Japanese), 1997; The Mississippi State Sovereignty Commission: Civil Rights and States' Rights, 2002; (with Kaname Saruya and others) America (in Japanese), 2003. Contributor to periodicals. **Address:** 386-44 Sanada, Hiratsuka-shi, Kanagawa-ken 259-1206, Japan. **Online address:** katagiris@aol.com

KATO, Shuichi. Japanese, b. 1919. **Genres:** Art/Art history, Literary criticism and history. **Career:** Professor of Asian Studies, University of British Columbia, Vancouver, 1960-69; Professor of Japanology, Freie Universitaet, Berlin, 1969-73; Professor of Japanese Studies, Sophia University, Tokyo, 1976-85. Visiting Lecturer, Yale University, New Haven, Conn., 1974-76; Visiting Professor, Cambridge University, 1983, Universita degli Studio di Venezia, 1983-84; Guest Professor, Ritsvmeikam University, Kyoto, currently. **Publications:** Hitsuji No Uta (Song of a Sheep), 1968; Form, Style, Tradition: Reflexions on Japanese Art and Society, 1971; Genso Bara Toshi (Roses and Cities), 1973; 1974; The Japan-China Phenomenon, 1974; Six Lives Six Deaths: Portraits from Modern Japan, 1979; A History of Japanese Literature, 3 vols., 1979-83; Chosakushu (Collected Works) in 15 vols., 1978-79, Part II, in 9 vol., 1996-97; Japan Spirit & Form, 1994. **Address:** Setagaya-Ku, Kaminoge 1-8-16, Tokyo, Japan.

KATOUZIAN, Homa. Iranian/British, b. 1942. **Genres:** Area studies. **Career:** University of Leeds, lecturer in economics, 1968-69; University of Kent at Canterbury, lecturer, 1969-82; senior lecturer, 1982-86; University of Oxford, member, faculty of Oriental studies, 1999-; St. Antony's College, research fellow, 2004-; Princeton University, Institute for Advanced Studies, member of School of Historical Studies, 2001. Visiting professor at universities worldwide; consultant; Iranian Studies, editor; member of editorial boards. Has presented and spoken at lectures and conferences and given seminars at universities in Britain, the United States, and the European Union. **Publications:** IN ENGLISH: Ideology and Method in Economics, 1980; The Political Economy of Modern Iran, 1981; (ed. and trans.) Musaddiq's Memoirs: The End of the British Empire in Iran, 1988; Musaddiq and the Struggle for Power in Iran, 1990, 2nd ed., 1999; Sadeq Hedayat: The Life and Legend of an Iranian Writer, 1991; State and Society in Iran: The Eclipse of the Qajars and the Emergence of the Pahlavis, 2000; Iranian History and Politics: The Dialectic of 2003 State and Society, 2003. IN PERSIAN: 14 Essays on Literature, Sociology, Philosophy and Economics, 1996; A Song of Innocence (poetry), 1997, 2nd ed., 2003; Hedayat's The Blind Owl, 2nd ed., 1998; The Contradiction of State and Society in Iran, 2001; Arbitrary Rule, Democracy and the Popular Movement of Iran, 3rd ed., 2002; Satire and Irony in Hedayat, 2003; Jamalzadeh and His Literature, 2003. Contributor to books and periodicals. Translator of Persian-language poetry and nonfiction works. **Address:** Middle East Centre, St Antony's College, University of Oxford, Oxford OX2 6JF, England. **Online address:** h.katouzian@virgin.net

KATSH, M. Ethan. American, b. 1945. **Genres:** Law, Communications/Media. **Career:** Admitted to the Bar of New York State, 1970; University of Massachusetts at Amherst, assistant professor, 1970-76, chair, Legal Studies Department, 1993-94, adjunct professor of Judaic studies, 1986-, professor of legal studies, 1988-. Co-founder of University of Massachusetts at Amherst's Mediation Project, Director, Center for Information Technology and Dispute Resolution, 1997-, Director, Online Ombuds Office, 1996-. **Publications:** (ed with J.J. Bonsignore) Before the Law, 1974, 6th ed., 1998; Taking Sides: Clashing Views on Controversial Legal Issues, 1983, 8th ed, 1998; The Electronic Media and the Transformation of Law, 1989; Law in a Digital World, 1995. **Address:** Department of Legal Studies, University of Massachusetts at Amherst, Amherst, MA 01003, U.S.A. **Online address:** KATSH@Legal.UMass.edu

KATZ, Avner. Israeli, b. 1939. **Genres:** Children's fiction. **Career:** Artist and writer/illustrator of books for children and adults. Bezalel Academy of Art, Jerusalem, Israel, Avni Institute for Painting, Tel Aviv, Israel, and Hamidrasha for Painting, Tel Aviv, Israel, instructor, 1976-80; University of Haifa, Israel, instructor, 1978-, head of creative arts department, 1988-91, associate professor, 1993-. Solo exhibitions in Israel and the US. Group exhibitions in England, Israel, Czechoslovakia. **Publications:** SELECTED TITLES FOR CHILDREN; WRITTEN AND ILLUSTRATED BY KATZ. IN ENGLISH TRANSLATION: The King Who Was Not, 1989, originally published as Mishehu Motse Keter, 1979; My First Love, 1989, originally published as

Ahava Rishona, 1989; Tortoise Solves a Problem, 1993, originally published as Veaz Hatzav Bana lo Bai't, 1979; The Little Pickpocket, 1996, originally published as Hakayas Hakatan, 1979. IN HEBREW: Chamor Af (title means: The Flying Donkey), 1979; Mishehu Motse Perach (title means: Tommy and the Flower), 1979; Mishehu Motse Keter (title means: Tommy and the Crown), 1979; Shabtai Vehatsipor (title means: Shabtai and the Bird), 1985; Hutz Miprat Ze Oh Aher, Hacol Emet (title means: Apart From a Few Details, Everything is True), 1986. Illustrator of titles in Hebrew. Author and illustrator of twelve humorous horoscope books. Contributor of short stories and poems to anthologies. **Address:** 12 She'erit Israel St., 47201 Ramat-Hasharon, Israel.

KATZ, Bernard S. American, b. 1932. **Genres:** Economics. **Career:** Lafayette College, Easton, PA, professor of economics and business, 1967-91. Fulbright lecturer at Changchun University and Xiamen University, 1991-93; San Francisco State University, visiting professor. Consultant. **Publications:** (with R. Robbins) Modern Economic Classics: Evaluation through Time, 1988; Nobel Laureates in Economic Science, 1989; The Fountains of San Francisco, 1989. EDITOR: (with R. Sobel) Biographical Directory of the Council of Economic Advisors, 1988; (with R. Bukics) International Financial Management: A Handbook for Operation, Financial, and Treasury Professionals, 1990; Biographical Directory of the Governors of the Federal Reserve, 1991; (with S. Shojai) Oil in the Eighties: A Decade of Decline, 1992; (with R. Ahene) Investment in Africa, 1992; (with L. Rittenberg) The Economic Transformation of Eastern Europe: Problems and Prospects, 1992; (with D. Vencill) Biographical Dictionary of the United States Secretaries of the Treasury, 1789-1995, 1996. **Address:** 255 Shawnee Ave, Easton, PA 18042, U.S.A. **Online address:** katzbmee@yahoo.com

KATZ, Bobbi. Also writes as Barbara Gail, Emily George, Peggy Kahn, Della Maison, Don E. Plumme, Ali Reich. American, b. 1933. **Genres:** Children's fiction, Poetry, Children's non-fiction, Biography. **Career:** Former Ed., Random House Books for Young Readers, NYC. Former Creative Writing Consultant, Cornwall School Systems, New York; former Poetry Consultant, Harper and Row School Dept., NYC. **Publications:** Nothing but a Dog, 1972; I'll Build My Friend a Mountain, 1972; Upside Down and Inside Out: Poems for All Your Pockets, 1973; The Manifesto and Me-Meg, 1974; Rod and Reel Trouble, 1974; 1001 Words, 1975; Snow Bunny: Action on the Ice, 1976; Volleyball Jinx, 1977; (with others) The Cousteau Almanac, 1980; A Family Hanukkah, 1992; Meet Nelson Mandela, 1995; Poems Just for Us, 1995; Germs! Germs!, 1996; Could We Be Friends? Poems for Pals, 1997; Truck Talk: Rhymes on Wheels, 1997; American History Poems, 1998; Lots of Lice, 1998; Make Way for Tooth Decay, 1999; We the People, 2001; A Rumpus of Rhymes: A Book of Noisy Poems, 2001; Grammar Poems, 2003; Pocket Poems, 2004; Once around the Sun, Explorers, 2005. **Address:** 82 Riverview, Port Ewen, NY 12466, U.S.A. **Online address:** bobbikatz@aol.com; www.bobbikatz.com

KATZ, David. American, b. 1953. **Genres:** History. **Career:** Tel-Aviv University, Tel Aviv, Israel, lecturer, 1978-82, senior lecturer, 1982-87, associate professor, 1987-90, professor, department of history, 1990-, Abraham Horodisch chair for the history of books, 1994-. **Publications:** Philo-Semitism and the Readmission of the Jews to England, 1603-1655, 1982; Sabbath and Sectarianism in Seventeenth-Century England, 1988; The Jews in the History of England, 1485-1850, 1994. EDITOR: (with J.I. Israel) Sceptics, Millenarians and Jews, 1990; (with Y. Kaplan) Gerush ve-shivah: Yehude Angliyah be-Hilufe ha-Zemanim (title means:; Exile and Return: Anglo-Jewry Through the Ages), 1993; (with R.H. Popkin) Messianic Revolution: Radical Religious Politics to the End of the Second Millennium, 1998; (with J.E. Force) Everything Connects: Essays in Honor of Richard H. Popkin, 1998. **Address:** Tel-Aviv University, Department of History, 69978 Tel Aviv, Israel.

KATZ, Elia (Jacob). American, b. 1948. **Genres:** Novels, Novellas/Short stories, Plays/Screenplays. **Career:** Elia Katz Inc. (film and television production company), Venice, CA, president, 1984-. NetBack Inc. (online backup and registration service), co-founder and president. **Publications:** The Buster Stengrow Book. The End-of-the-World Chapter (novellas), 1969; Armed Love, 1971; Stengrow's Dad, 1995. Author of scripts for episodes of the television series Hill Street Blues, 1984-86, Simon & Simon, 1986, 1987, and Tour of Duty, 1988-90. **Address:** c/o Julie Popkin, Agent, 15340 Albright St, No. 204, Pacific Palisades, CA 90272, U.S.A.

KATZ, James Everett. American, b. 1948. **Genres:** Politics/Government. **Career:** Sociology educator, researcher, and author. Clarkson College, Potsdam, NY, associate professor, 1979-81; U.S. Senate, Washington, DC, professional staff member, 1981-83; LBJ School of Public Affairs, University of

Texas, Austin, assistant professor, 1983-86; Bell Communication Research, Morristown, NJ, researcher, 1986-; Rutgers University, New Brunswick, NJ, professor, School of Communication, Information, and Library Studies. **Publications:** (with I.L. Horowitz) Social Science and Public Policy in the United States, 1975; Presidential Politics and Science Policy, 1978; Congress and National Energy Policy, 1984; Connections: Social and Cultural Studies of the Telephone in American Life, 1999. EDITOR: (with O.S. Marwah) Arms Production in Developing Countries: An Analysis of Decision-Making, 1984; People in Space: Perspectives for a Star Wars Century, 1985; The Implications of Third World Military Industrialization: Sowing the Serpents' Teeth, 1986; (with R.E. Rice), The Internet and Health Communication: Experiences and Expectations, 2001; (with M.A. Aakhus) Perpetual Contact: Mobile Communication, Private Talk, Public Performance, 2002. Contributor to professional journals. **Address:** Rutgers University, Communication, 192 College Ave., New Brunswick, NJ 08901, U.S.A. **Online address:** jimkatz@scils.rutgers.edu

KATZ, Judith. American, b. 1951. **Genres:** Novels. **Career:** At the Foot of the Mountain Theatre, Minneapolis, MN, arts administrator, 1983-85; Great Midwestern Book Show, Minneapolis, arts administrator, 1985-86; University of Minnesota-Twin Cities, Minneapolis, adjunct member of women's studies faculty, 1986-; The Loft, writing teacher, 1988; Hamline University, MALS/MFA program, adjunct faculty, 1993-; Macalester College, visiting writer, 2002-03. **Publications:** NOVELS: Running Fiercely toward a High Thin Sound, 1992; The Escape Artist, 1997. **Address:** PO Box 7041, Minneapolis, MN 55407, U.S.A.

KATZ, Lawrence S(anford). American, b. 1947. **Genres:** Sports/Fitness. **Career:** Law clerk and associate of Gerald M. Lorence, Detroit, MI, 1971-73; Weingarden & Hauer, Berkley, MI, associate, 1973-74; Goldstein & Raznick, Warren, MI, associate, 1974-76; Goldstein, Raznick & Katz, Warren, MI, partner, 1977-78; private practice of law, Sterling Heights, MI, 1978-. State Bar of Michigan, member; Attorney Grievance Commission, special investigator, 1977-80; Attorney Grievance Commission, special counsel, 1980-81; Attorney Discipline Board, Hearing Panel, member, 1981-, chairperson, 1987-. Macomb County Circuit Court, domestic relations mediator, 1986-2001. Civic Searchlight Inc., director, 1993-95. Formerly performed in radio and television commercials. **Publications:** Baseball in 1939: The Watershed Season of the National Pastime, 1995. Contributor to books. **Address:** 38850 Van Dyke Ave Suite 102, Sterling Heights, MI 48312, U.S.A. **Online address:** GreatUncleLarry@aol.com

KATZ, Marshall P. American, b. 1939. **Genres:** Art/Art history. **Career:** Papercraft Corp., Pittsburgh, PA, chairperson and chief executive officer of a consumer household products company, 1962-91. **Publications:** Nineteenth-Century French Followers of Palissy, 1994; (with R. Lehr) Palissy Ware: Nineteenth-Century French Ceramists from Avisseau to Renoleau, 1996; Portuguese Palissy Ware, 1999. Contributor to magazines. **Address:** 4875 Ellsworth Ave, Pittsburgh, PA 15213-2843, U.S.A. **Online address:** palissy@usadr.net

KATZ, Michael Ray. American, b. 1944. **Genres:** Literary criticism and history, Translations. **Career:** Williams College, Williamstown, MA, assistant to associate professor of Russian, 1972-83; University of Texas, Austin, professor of Russian and chairman of Slavic languages dept., 1984-97; Middlebury College, VT, dean of language schools and schools abroad, 1998-. **Publications:** The Literary Ballad in Early 19th-Century Russian Literature, 1976; Dreams and the Unconscious in 19th-Century Russian Literature, 1984 (trans.) Who Is to Blame?, by Alexander Herzen, 1984; (trans.) What Is to Be Done?, by Nikolai Chernyshevsky, 1989; (trans.) Notes from the Underground, by Dostoevsky, 1989; (trans.) Tolstoy's Short Fiction, 1991; (trans.) Devils, by Dostoevsky, 1992; (trans.) Polinka Saks, by Druzhinin, 1992; Prologue, by Chernyshevsky, 1995; Antonina, by Tur, 1996; Sanin, by Artsybashev, 2001; The Five, by Jabotinsky, 2005. **Address:** Middlebury College, Middlebury, VT 05753, U.S.A. **Online address:** mkatz@middlebury.edu

KATZ, Molly. American. **Genres:** Mystery/Crime/Suspense. **Career:** Mystery novelist and former stand-up comedian. **Publications:** Nobody Believes Me, 1994. **Address:** c/o Andrews McMeel Publishing, 4520 Main St Ste 700, Kansas City, MO 64111, U.S.A.

KATZ, Ralph. American, b. 1944. **Genres:** Administration/Management. **Career:** Massachusetts Institute of Technology, Cambridge, professor of management, 1973-82; Northeastern University, Boston, MA, professor of management, 1982-. Massachusetts Institute of Technology, principal research associate at Sloan School of Management, 1982-. Independent management consultant. **Publications:** Career Issues in Human Resource Management, 1982; Managing Professionals in Innovative Organizations, 1988; The Human Side of Managing Technological Innovation, 1997. **Address:** College of Business, 304 Hayden Hall, Northeastern University, Boston, MA 02115, U.S.A. **Online address:** R.Katz@nunet.neu.edu

KATZ, Richard Stephen. American, b. 1947. **Genres:** Politics/Government. **Career:** City University of New York, assistant professor of political science, 1974-1976; Johns Hopkins University, Baltimore, MD, assistant professor of political science, 1976-1981, associate professor of political science, 1981-1985, professor of political science, 1985-; State University of New York, Buffalo, NY, professor of political science, 1995-1996; International School of Political Science, lecturer, 1993. **Publications:** (with K.V. Mulcahy) American Votes: What You Should Know About Election Today, 1976; A Theory of Parties and Electoral Systems, 1980; Democracies and Elections, Oxford University Press, 1997. EDITOR: (with M.C. Cummings, Jr.) The Patron State: Government and the Arts in Europe, North America, and Japan, 1987; (with P. Mair) Party Organizations in Western Democracies: 1960-1990: A Data Handbook, 1992; (with P. Mair) How Parties Organize: Change and Adaptation in Party Organization sin Western Democracies, 1994; (with S. Bowler and D.M. Farrell) Party Discipline and Parliamentary Government, 1998. Contributor to books. **Address:** Johns Hopkins University, Department of Political Science, Baltimore, MD 21218, U.S.A. **Online address:** Richard.Katz@jhu.edu

KATZ, Sanford N. American, b. 1933. **Genres:** Law. **Career:** Professor of Law, Boston College Law School, Newton Centre, MA, 1968-. Instructor, 1959-60, Assistant Professor, 1960-62, and Associate Professor of Law, 1963-64, Catholic University of America, Washington, DC; Professor of Law, University of Florida, Gainesville, 1964-68; Visiting Fellow, All Souls College, Oxford University, 1997. Director, Law and Child Protection, U.S. Dept. of Health, Education and Welfare, 1973-75. Ed.-in-Chief, Family Law Quarterly, 1971-84. **Publications:** When Parents Fail: The Law's Response to Family Breakdown, 1971; (ed.) The Youngest Minority: Lawyers in Defense of Children, 1974; (with Eekelaar) Family Violence, 1978; (with Meezan and Reisso) Adoptions without Agencies, 1978; (with Eekelaar) Marriage and Cohabitation, 1980; American Family Law in Transition, 1983; (with Eekelaar) The Resolution of Family Conflict, 1984; Negotiating to Settlement in Divorces, 1987; (with Weyrauch and Olsen) Cases and Materials on Family Law, 1994; (with Eekelaar and Maclean) Cross Currents, 2000; Family Law in America, 2003. **Address:** Boston College Law School, Newton Centre, MA 02459, U.S.A.

KATZ, Steve. Also writes as Stephanie Gatos. American, b. 1935. **Genres:** Novels, Novellas/Short stories, Plays/Screenplays, Poetry. **Career:** Professor of English, University of Colorado, Boulder, 1978- (Director of Creative Writing, 1978-81). Staff member, English Language Institute, Lecce, Italy, 1960; faculty member, University of Maryland Overseas, Lecce, 1961-62; Assistant Professor of English, Cornell University, Ithaca, New York, 1962-67; Lecturer in Fiction, University of Iowa, Iowa City, 1969-70; Writer-in-residence, Brooklyn College, 1970-71; Assistant Professor of English, Queens College, NYC, 1971-75; Associate Professor of English, Notre Dame University, Indiana, 1976-78. **Publications:** The Lestriad (novel), 1962; The Weight of Antony (poetry), 1964; The Exagggerations of Peter Prince (novel), 1968; Creamy and Delicious: Eat My Words (in Other Words) (short stories), 1970; (as Stephanie Gatos) Posh (novel), 1971; Saw (novel), 1972; Cheyenne River Wild Track (poetry), 1973; Moving Parts (novel), 1977; Wier and Pouce (novel), 1984; Stolen Stories, 1985; Florry of Washington Heights (novel), 1987; Journalism (poetry), 1990; 43 Fictions (new and selected stories), 1991; Swanny's Ways, 1995; Antonello's Lion, 2005. **Address:** 669 Washington St #602, Denver, CO 80203, U.S.A.

KATZ, Steven T(heodore). American, b. 1944. **Genres:** Philosophy, Essays. **Career:** Cambridge University, England, lecturer, 1971-72; affiliated with Dartmouth College, Hanover, NH, 1972-84, chairman of dept of religion, 1979-81; Cornell University, Ithaca, NY, professor of Near Eastern studies, 1984-96; Boston University, director, Center for Judaic Studies and professor of religion, 1996-. Hebrew University of Jerusalem, visiting research fellow, 1969-70, member of visiting faculty, 1971-73, visiting professor, 1976-77; Rutgers University, Summer Institute in Israel, instructor, 1971; University of Lancaster, visiting senior lecturer, 1974-75; visiting professor: University of Toronto, 1978, University of California, Santa Barbara, 1981, and Yale University, 1982; Harvard University, Center of Judaic Studies and Center for World Religions, visiting scholar, 1981-84, 2001-02; College of William and Mary, Mason Visiting Professor, 1983; University of Pennsylvania, Meyerhoff Professor of Jewish History, 1989-90. Modern Judaism, editor. **Publications:** Post Holocaust Dialogues, 1983; The Holocaust in Historical

Context, vol. 1, 1994, vols. 2 & 3, forthcoming; Mysticism and Language, 1992. EDITOR & CONTRIBUTOR: Jewish Philosophers: A History, 1975; Jewish Ideas and Concepts, 1977; Mysticism and Philosophical Analysis, 1978; Mysticism and Religious Traditions, 1983; The Essential Agus, 1997; Jacob Agus, American Rabbi, 1997; Mysticism & Sacred Scripture, 2000. EDITOR: Saadiah Gaon: Selected Essays, 1979; Collected Papers of Jacob Guttmann, 1979; Selected Writings of Julius Guttman, 1979; Studies by Samuel Horodesky, 1979; Maimonides: Selected Essays, 1979; Medieval Jewish Philosophy, 1979; Jewish Neo-Platonism: Selected Essays, 1979. FORTHCOMING: Cambridge History of Judaism, vol. 4; Comparative Mysticism Anthology. **Address:** Dept of Religion, Boston University, 745 Commonwealth Ave, Boston, MA 02215, U.S.A.

KATZ, Welwyn Wilton. Canadian, b. 1948. **Genres:** Novels, Children's fiction. **Career:** Writer. **Publications:** The Prophecy of Tau Ridoo, 1982; Witchery Hill, 1984; Sun God, Moon Witch, 1986; False Face, 1987; The Third Magic, 1988; Whalesinger, 1990; Come Like Shadows, 1993; Time Ghost, 1994; Out of the Dark, 1995; Beowulf, 1999.

KATZEN, Mollie. American, b. 1950. **Genres:** Food and Wine. **Career:** Artist, musician, and cook. Co-founder of the Moosewood Restaurant, Ithaca, NY, 1973. Cookbook author, 1974-. Has created and hosted television cooking shows. **Publications:** The Moosewood Cookbook, 1974, rev ed, 1992; The Enchanted Broccoli Forest: And Other Timeless Delicacies, 1982, rev ed, 1995; Still Life With Menu: Fifty New Meatless Menus With Original Art, 1988; (with A. Henderson) Pretend Soup and Other Real Recipes: A Cookbook for Preschoolers and Up, 1994. **Address:** c/o Mollie Katzen Productions, 609 Canon Dr., Kensington, CA 94708, U.S.A.

KATZENBACH, Jon R. American, b. 1932. **Genres:** Administration/ Management. **Career:** McKinsey & Company, New York, NY, director, 1959-98; Katzenbach Partners LLC, New York, NY, senior partner, 1998-. **Publications:** (with D. Smith) The Wisdom of Teams: Creating the High-Performance Organization, 1993; Teams at the Top: Unleashing the Potential of Both Teams and Individual Leaders, 1996; (with others) Real Change Leaders: How You Can Create Growth and High Performance at Your Company, 1997; (ed.) The Work of Teams, 1998; Peak Performance: Aligning the Hearts and Minds of Your Employees, 2000; (with D. Smith) The Discipline of Teams: A Mindbook-Workbook for Delivering Small Group Performance, 2001; Why Pride Matters More: The Power of the World's Greatest Motivational Force, 2003. **Address:** Katzenbach Partners LLC, 381 Park Ave., New York, NY 10016, U.S.A.

KATZMAN, Melanie A. American, b. 1958. **Genres:** Psychology, Medicine/ Health. **Career:** Devereux Center, Scottsdale, AZ, therapist, 1981-82; Good Samaritan Medical Center, Phoenix, AZ, therapist, 1982-83; Bulimia Therapy and Research Team, Phoenix, coordinator and consultant, 1983-84; New York University, Bellevue Medical Center, NYC, psychology intern, 1984-85; Institute for Behavior Therapy, NYC, part-time post-doctoral fellow, 1985-86; New York Hospital, Cornell Medical Center-Westchester Division, White Plains, NY, post-doctoral fellow, 1985-86; Regent Hospital, NYC, director of outpatient eating disorders services, 1986-87, clinical director of psychiatric outpatient services for Metropolitan Medical Group, 1988-89; Cornell University Medical Center, NYC, clinical assistant professor of psychology, 1987-; New York Hospital, NYC, assistant attending psychologist, 1987-; private practice, 1989-; The Business Practice, Hong Kong, director of corporate consultations, 1994-95. Chinese University of Hong Kong, scholar in residence, 1994-95; University of London's Institute of Psychiatry, lecturer, 1995-. Has presented papers at mental health association meetings, workshops, and conferences in the U.S. and abroad. **Publications:** (with L. Weiss and S.A. Wolchik) Treating Bulimia: A Psychoeducational Approach, 1985; (with Weiss and Wolchik) You Can't Have Your Cake and Eat It Too: A Self-Help Program for Controlling Bulimia, 1986; (ed. and contributor with P. Fallon and S. Wooley) Feminist Perspectives on Eating Disorders, 1994. Contibutor of articles to books. Contributor to professional journals and periodicals. **Address:** Institute of Psychiatry, De Crespigney Place, Denmark Hill, London SE5, England.

KAUFFMAN, Bill. (William J). American, b. 1959. **Genres:** Novels, Politics/Government, Travel/Exploration. **Career:** Senator D.P. Moynihan, Washington, DC, legislative assistant, 1981-83; Reason, Santa Barbara, CA/ Washington, DC, assistant editor, 1985-88; The American Enterprise, Washington, DC, associate editor, 1994-. **Publications:** Every Man a King (novel), 1989; Country Towns of New York (travel), 1994; America First! Its History, Culture, and Politics, 1995; With Good Intentions? Reflections on the Myth of Progress in America, 1998; Dispatches from the Muckdog Gazette: A Mostly Affectionate Account of a Small Town's Fight to Survive, 2003. **Address:** 28 Chapel St, PO Box 266, Elba, NY 14058, U.S.A.

KAUFFMAN, Donna. (born United States), b. 1960. **Genres:** Romance/ Historical. **Career:** Romance novelist. Previously worked as a hairdresser and competitive bodybuilder. **Publications:** Illegal Motion, 1993; Black Satin, 1994; Tango in Paradise, 1994; Bounty Hunter, 1994; Wild Rain, 1995; Bayou Heat, 1996; Tease Me, 1998; Her Secret Thrill, 2001; His Private Pleasure, 2002; Sean, 2003; Jingle Bell Rock, 2003; Against the Odds, 2003; Merry Christmas Baby, 2004. NOVELS; THREE MUSKETEERS SERIES: The Three Musketeers: Surrender the Dark, 1995; The Three Musketeers: Born to Be Wild, 1996; The Three Musketeers: Midnight Heat, 1996; NOVELS; DELGADO'S DIRTY DOZEN SERIES: Santerra's Sin, 1996; Silent Warrior, 1997; Light My Fire, 1997; Dark Knight, 1998. ANTHOLOGIES: (with others) Yours 2 Keep, 1999; (with Lori Foster and Janelle Denison) I Love Bad Boys, 2002; Men of Courage, 2003; (with Lori Foster and Janelle Denison) Bad Boys on Board, 2003; (with Lori Foster and Janelle Denison) Bad Boys, Next Exit, 2004. PARANORMAL NOVELS: The Legend MacKinnon, 1999; The Legend of the Sorcerer, 2000; Your Wish Is My Command, 2000; The Royal Hunter, 2001; The Charm Stone, 2002. CONTEMPORARY ROMANCE NOVELS: The Big Bad Wolf Tells All (formerly titled The Last Bridesmaid), 2003; The Cinderella Rules, 2004; Dear Prince Charming, 2004. **Address:** POB 541, Ashburn, VA 20146, U.S.A. **Online address:** donna@donnakauffman.com

KAUFFMAN, J. Howard. American, b. 1919. **Genres:** Sociology. **Career:** Goshen College, IN, instructor to professor of sociology, 1948-84, professor emeritus, 1984-, executive director of Social Research Service, 1967-84, director of research project Church Member Profile, 1971-75 and 1986-91, director of study-abroad programs in Belize, 1974-75, and China, 1981. **Publications:** (with L. Harder) Anabaptists Four Centuries Later: A Profile of Five Mennonite and Brethren in Christ Denominations, 1975; (with L. Driedger) The Mennonite Mosaic: Identity and Modernization, 1991. Work represented in books. Contributor to sociology and religious studies journals. **Address:** 1438 Greencroft Dr., Goshen, IN 46526, U.S.A. **Online address:** jhowardk@goshen.edu

KAUFFMAN, Janet. American, b. 1945. **Genres:** Novels, Novellas/Short stories, Poetry. **Career:** Jackson Community College, Michigan, professor, 1976-88; University of Michigan, Ann Arbor, visiting professor of English, 1984-85; Eastern Michigan University, professor, 1988-. **Publications:** POETRY: (with J. McCann) Writing Home, 1978; The Weather Book, 1981; Five on Fiction (poems), 2004. SHORT STORIES: Places in the World a Woman Could Walk, 1984; Obscene Gestures for Women, 1989; Characters on the Loose, 1997. NOVELS: Collaborators, 1986; The Body in Four Parts, 1993; Rot, 2001. **Address:** English Dept, Eastern Michigan University, 603 N Pray-Harrold, Ypsilanti, MI 48197, U.S.A.

KAUFFMAN, Stuart Alan. American, b. 1939. **Genres:** Biology. **Career:** University of Chicago, Chicago, IL, assistant professor of theoretical biology, 1969-73, became assistant professor of medicine, 1970-73; Laboratory of Theoretical Biology, National Cancer Institute, research associate, 1973-75; University of Pennsylvania College of Medicine, associate professor of biochemistry-biology, 1975-81, became associate professor of biochemistry and biophysics, 1981-; associated with the Santa Fe Institute. **Publications:** The Origins of Order: Self-Organization and Selection in Evolution, 1993; At Home in the Universe: The Search for Laws of Self-Organization and Complexity, 1995. Contributor to books. **Address:** Department of Biochemistry and Physiology, University of Pennsylvania College of Medicine, Philadelphia, PA 19104, U.S.A.

KAUFFMANN, Stanley. American, b. 1916. **Genres:** Novels, Plays/ Screenplays, Film, Literary criticism and history, Autobiography/Memoirs. **Career:** Critic, New Republic Mag., Washington, DC, 1958- (Film Critic, 1958-65, 1967-; Associate Literary Ed., 1966-67; Theatre Critic, 1969-79). Visiting Professor, Graduate Center, City University, NYC, 1977-92; Compere, The Art of Film Prog., 1963-67; Theatre Critic, New York Times, 1966, and Saturday Review Mag., 1979-85. Visiting Professor, Yale University School of Drama, New Haven, CT, 1967-73, 1977-86; Visiting Professor of Drama, Hunter College, City University of New York, 1990-2000; Distinguished Visiting Professor, Adelphi University, Garden City, NY, 1992-96. **Publications:** The Hidden Hero, 1949; The Tightrope, 1952; The Philanderer, 1953; A Change of Climate, 1954; Man of the World, 1956; If It Be Love, 1960; A World on Film, 1966; Figures of Light, 1971; (ed. with B. Henstell) American Film Criticism: From the Beginnings to Citizen Kane, 1973; Living Images, 1975; Persons of the Drama, 1976; Before My Eyes, 1980; Albums of Early Life, 1980; Theater Criticisms, 1984; Field of View, 1985; Distinguishing Features, 1994; Regarding Film, 2001. **Address:** 10 W 15th St, New York, NY 10011, U.S.A.

KAUFMAN, Bel. American (born Germany), b. 1911. **Genres:** Novels, Education, Essays. **Career:** Member, P.E.N. American Center, Authors

League; Commission on Performing Arts; Board, Sholom Aleichem Foundation and Phi Delta Kappa; Member, Advisory Council, Town Hall Foundation, NYC. Former Lecturer, New School for Social Research, NYC, English teacher in NYC high schs., and Assistant Professor, City University of New York. **Publications:** Up the Down Staircase, 1965; Love, etc., 1979. Author of short stories and articles. **Address:** 1020 Park Ave, New York, NY 10028, U.S.A. **Online address:** belkau@aol.com

KAUFMAN, Gerald (Bernard). British, b. 1930. **Genres:** Politics/Government, Humor/Satire. **Career:** House of Commons, National Heritage Committee, Chairman, 1992-97, Culture, Media and Sport Committee, Chairman, 1997-; Labour M.P. (U.K.) for Gorton Division of Manchester, 1983-; Member of Parliamentary Committee, 1980-92 (Labour M.P. for Ardwick Division, 1970-83; Under-Secretary of State, Dept. of the Environment, 1974-75, and Dept. of Industry, 1975; Minister of State, Dept. of Industry, 1975-79). On political staff, Daily Mirror, London, 1955-64; New Statesman, London, Political Correspondent, 1964-65; Labour Party, Parliamentary Press Liaison Officer, 1965-70, Executive Committee, Member, 1991-92. **Publications:** (with D. Frost, C. Booker and H. Sargent) How to Live Under Labour, 1964; (ed.) The Left, 1966; To Build the Promised Land, 1973; How to Be a Minister, 1980, rev. ed., 1997; (ed.) Renewal, 1983; My Life in the Silver Screen, 1985; Inside the Promised Land, 1986; Meet Me in St Louis, 1994.

KAUFMAN, Kenn. American, b. 1956?. **Genres:** Zoology. **Career:** Birder, artist, author, tour leader. Former associate editor, American Birds. **Publications:** (with L. Line and K.L. Garrett) The Audubon Society Book of Water Birds, 1987; (and illustrator) A Field Guide to Advanced Birding: Birding Challenges and How to Approach Them, 1990; Lives of North American Birds, 1996; (author of intro and bird notes) Porter, E., Vanishing Songbirds: The Sixth Order: Wood Warblers and Other Passerine Birds, 1996; Kingbird Highway: The Story of a Natural Obsession That Got a Little Out of Hand, 1997. **Address:** c/o Houghton Mifflin Co., 222 Berkeley St., Boston, MA 02116, U.S.A.

KAUFMAN, Lynne. (born United States). **Genres:** Law. **Career:** Playwright and author. University of California, Berkeley Extension, staff member for thirty years, became director of travel study programs. **Publications:** PLAYS: The Couch, 1998; Roshi, 1987; Speaking in Tongues, 1989; Our Lady of the Desert, 1991; Shooting Simone, 1994; Fifty/Fifty, 1994; Fakes, 1997; The Last Game Show, 2000; The Next Marilyn, 2003; Daisy in the Dreamtime, 2003; Picasso, 2003. OTHER: Slow Hands, 2003; Wild Women's Weekend, 2004. Contributor to periodicals. **Address:** Susan Gurman Agency, 865 West End Ave., #15A, New York, NY 10025, U.S.A.

KAUFMAN, Menahem. Israeli (born Germany), b. 1921. **Genres:** Area studies, History, Politics/Government. **Career:** Worked as a farmer in a kibbutz, Givat Zaid, Israel, 1940-50; Israel Defense Force, lieutenant colonel, 1952-69; Hebrew University of Jerusalem, The Institute of Contemporary Jewry, Jerusalem, Israel, administrative director, 1969-88, Senior Scholar, America-Holy Land Project, 1987-. **Publications:** America-Jerusalem Policy, 1947-1948, 1982; Non-Zionists in America and the Struggle for Jewish Statehood (in Hebrew), 1984; An Ambiguous Partnership: Zionists and Non-Zionists in America, 1939-45, 1991; Die hessischen Landjuden, 1933-45, 1991; The Magnes-Philby Negotiations, the Historical Record, 1998. EDITOR: (with M. Levine) Guide to America-Holy Land Studies, 1620-1948, Vol. 4: Resource Material in British, Israeli & Turkish Repositories, 1984; America and the Holy Land, the Foundation of a Special Relationship (in Hebrew), 1996. **Address:** Institute of Contemporary Jewry, Hebrew University of Jerusalem, Mount Scopus, 91905 Jerusalem, Israel.

KAUFMAN, Victor S(cott). (born United States), b. 1969. **Genres:** History. **Career:** Ohio University, Athens, instructor in history, 1997; Virginia Polytechnic Institute and State University, Blacksburg, instructor in history, 1997-98; Kennesaw State University, Kennesaw, GA, instructor in history, 1998-99; Southwest Missouri State University, Springfield, lecturer in history, 1999-2001; Francis Marion University, Florence, SC, assistant professor of history, 2001-. Georgia State University, instructor, 1998-99. **Publications:** Confronting Communism: U.S. and British Policies toward China, 2001. Contributor to periodicals. **Address:** 1349 Brittany Dr., Florence, SC 29501, U.S.A. **Online address:** vkaufman@fmarion.edu

KAUFMAN, Will. American, b. 1958. **Genres:** Literary criticism and history. **Career:** North Staffordshire Polytechnic, Stoke-on-Trent, England, parttime lecturer in English and American literature, 1986-88; Sriwijaya University, Palembang, South Sumatra, Indonesia, lecturer in English language and literature, 1988-90; Lancashire Polytechnic, England, lecturer in English and American studies, 1991-93; University of Central Lancashire, Preston, England, senior lecturer in English and American studies, 1993-; Crewe and Alsager College of Higher Education, part-time lecturer, 1987-88. **Publications:** The Comedian as Confidence Man, 1997. Contributor to books and periodicals. **Address:** Department of Cultural Studies, University of Central Lancashire, Preston, Lancashire PR1 2HE, England. **Online address:** w.kaufman@uclan.ac.uk

KAUFMANN, Dovid Yisroel Ber. American, b. 1951. **Genres:** Novels, Young adult fiction, Adult non-fiction, History, Ethics, Biography. **Career:** Tulane University, New Orleans, LA, instructor in English, 1985-89; Chabad House (Jewish student center), New Orleans, campus coordinator and teacher, 1985-. Tulane University, adjunct assistant professor of Hebrew and Israeli studies, 1994-96. **Publications:** The Silent Witness (novel), 1996; (with S. Zakar) Judaism OnLine: Confronting Spirituality on the Internet, 1998; (ed. and trans. with H. Greenberg) Besuros HeGeuloh, 1998. Contributor to periodicals. Some writings appear under the names David Kaufmann. **Address:** Chabad House, 7037 Freret St., New Orleans, LA 70118, U.S.A. **Online address:** kaufmann@tulane.edu

KAUFMANN, Myron (Stuart). American, b. 1921. **Genres:** Novels. **Career:** With Associated Press, 1947-60. **Publications:** Remember Me to God, 1957; Thy Daughter's Nakedness, 1968; The Coming Destruction of Israel (non-fiction), 1970; The Love of Elspeth Baker, 1982. **Address:** 59 Pond St, Sharon, MA 02067, U.S.A.

KAVALER, Rebecca. American, b. 1933. **Genres:** Novels, Novellas/Short stories, Poetry. **Publications:** STORIES: Further Adventures of Brunhild, 1978; Tigers in the Wood, 1986; A Little More Than Kin, 2002. NOVEL: Doubting Castle, 1984. **Address:** 425 Riverside Dr, New York, NY 10025, U.S.A. **Online address:** rkavaler@msn.com

KAVANAGH, Julie. South African, b. 1952. **Genres:** Biography. **Career:** Arts editor for the magazines Harper's & Queen, 1980-90; Vanity Fair, London editor, 1990-93; New Yorker, London editor, 1993-. **Publications:** Secret Muses: The Life of Frederick Ashton, 1997. Contributor to periodicals. **Address:** c/o New Yorker, 20 Vauxhall Bridge Rd., London S.W.1, England.

KAVANAGH, P(atrick) J(oseph). British, b. 1931. **Genres:** Novels, Children's fiction, Young adult fiction, Plays/Screenplays, Poetry, Autobiography/Memoirs. **Career:** Former Lecturer, British Institute, Barcelona, 1954-55, and University of Indonesia, Djarkarta; Staff member, British Council, 1957-59; Actor, 1959-70; Columnist, The Spectator, London, 1983-96; Times Literary Supplement, 1996-2002. Fellow, Royal Society of Literature, 1986. **Publications:** POETRY: One and One: Verse, 1959; On the Way to the Depot, 1967; About Time, 1970; Edward Thomas in Heaven, 1974; Life before Death, 1979; Selected Poems, 1982; Presences, 1987; An Enchantment, 1992; Collected Poems, 1992. NOVELS: A Song and Dance, 1968; A Happy Man, 1972; People and Weather, 1978; Only By Mistake, 1986. FOR CHILDREN: Scarf Jack, 1978; The Irish Captain, 1979, in U.K. as Rebel for Good, 1980. OTHER: The Perfect Stranger (autobiography), 1966; People and Places (essays), 1988; Finding Connections (travel), 1990; A Book of Consolations, 1992; Voices in Ireland, a Traveller's Literary Companion, 1994; A Kind of Journal (essays), 2003. EDITOR: Collected Poems of Ivor Gurney, 1982; (with J. Michie) The Oxford Book of Short Poems, 1984; The Essential G.K. Chesterton, 1985. **Address:** c/o PFD, Drury House, 34-43 Russell St, London WC2B 5HA, England.

KAVANAGH, Paul. See BLOCK, Lawrence.

KAVANAGH, Peter. Irish, b. 1916. **Genres:** Area studies, Mythology/Folklore, Theatre, Autobiography/Memoirs, Bibliography. **Career:** Schoolteacher in Dublin, Ireland, 1936-46; St. Francis College, Brooklyn, NY, assistant professor of English, 1946-47; Loyola University of Chicago, IL, assistant professor of English, 1947-49; Gannon College (now University), Erie, PA, assistant professor of English, 1949-50; editor and contributor to Encyclopedia Americana, Ireland, 1950-51; Kavanagh's Weekly, Dublin, publisher, 1952; Cementation Engineering Co., London, England, editor and writer, 1953-56; Peter Kavanagh Hand Press, NYC, owner, 1958-; Stout State University (now University of Wisconsin-Stout), professor, 1966-68. **Publications:** The Irish Theatre, 1946; The Story of the Abbey Theatre, 1950; A Dictionary of Irish Mythology, 1959; Garden of the Golden Apples: A Bibliography of Patrick Kavanagh, 1972; Beyond Affection: An Autobiography, 1977; Inniskeep: A Map, 1978; Savage Rock, 1978; Love's Tortured Headland, 1978; Sacred Keeper: A Biography of Patrick Kavanagh, 1980; The Dancing Flame, 1981; Piling up the Ricks (autobiography), 1989; The Complete Poems of Patrick Kavanagh with Extended Commentary, 1996; Pilgrimage of a Soul, 1996; Patrick Kavanagh: A Life Chronicle,

2000; Lough Derg, 2003. PLAYS: Saint Jerome: A Dissertation in Two Acts, 1961; Saint Patrick, 1961; John Scotus Eriugena, 1962; Saint Malachy, 1963; Oliver Plunkett, 1963. EDITOR: The John Quinn Letters, 1960; Lapped Furrows: Correspondence, 1933-1967, of Peter and Patrick Kavanagh, 1969; November Haggard: Uncollected Prose and Verse of Patrick Kavanagh, 1971; Complete Poems of Patrick Kavanagh, 1972; By Night Unstarred: An Autobiographical Novel, 1978; Patrick Kavanagh: Man and Poet, 1986; 10 Lectures on Poetry, 2004. **Address:** 35 Park Ave, New York, NY 10016, U.S.A. **Online address:** peterkavanagh@mindspring.com

KAVANAUGH, Andrea L(ee). American, b. 1951. **Genres:** Technology. **Career:** French American Bilingual School, instructor and administrative assistant, 1974-77; U.S. Department of Commerce, research assistant, 198485; Hollins College, Hollins College, VA, instructor in communications studies, 1989; Virginia Polytechnic Institute and State University, Blacksburg, research fellow, 1991-, instructor at Center for Programs in the Humanities, 1992, director of research for Blacksburg Electronic Village, 1993-, adjunct professor of communication studies, 1997-98, and fellow of Center for Human Computer Interaction. New Century Communications Network Inc., member of executive board, 1995-. Lecturer at educational institutions. **Publications:** (ed. with A. Cohill, and contrib.) Community Networks: Lessons from Blacksburg, Virginia, 1997; The Social Control of Technology in North Africa: Information in the Global Economy, 1998. Contributor to books. Contributor of articles and reviews to periodicals. **Address:** Blacksburg Electronic Village, Virginia Polytechnic Institute and State University, 840 University City Blvd. Suite 7, Blacksburg, VA 24060, U.S.A. **Online address:** Kavan@vt.edu

KAWAKAMI, Barbara Fusako. American (born Japan), b. 1921. **Genres:** Cultural/Ethnic topics, History, Local history/Rural topics, Biography, Documentaries/Reportage, Translations. **Career:** Professional dressmaker and designer, 1938-78; Leeward Community College, Community Services Program, sewing instructor, 1975-78; University of Hawaii, Manoa, Community Services Program, sewing instructor, 1978; Hawaii Public Television ARCHIVE Project, researcher, writer, associate producer, interviewer, translator, and costumer, 1985-89; Talk Story Festival, storyteller, 1989-96; Japanese American National Museum, Los Angeles, advisory council member, 1990-. Served as historical consultant for film Picture Bride, 1995; Niho-jima mura Museum, advisory council, historian, and researcher. **Publications:** Japanese Immigrant Clothing in Hawaii, 1885-1941, 1993. Contributor of poetry and fiction to newspapers and periodicals. **Address:** 94-421 Alapoai St, Mililani, HI 96789, U.S.A.

KAWATSKI, Deanna. Also writes as Deanna Barnhardt. Canadian, b. 1951. **Genres:** Poetry, Autobiography/Memoirs. **Career:** Freelance writer. **Publications:** (as Deanna Barnhardt) Bird, Bubble, and Stream (poems), 1980; Wilderness Mother, 1994; Clara and Me, 1996. Contributor to periodicals. **Address:** Box 84, Celista, BC, Canada V0E 1L0. **Online address:** deemay@mail.ocis.net

KAWIN, Bruce F. American, b. 1945. **Genres:** Plays/Screenplays, Poetry, Film, Literary criticism and history. **Career:** Professor of English and Film, University of Colorado, Boulder, since 1975. Teacher of Comparative Religion, Emanuel Temple Center, Beverly Hills, California, 1960-63; Producer and Anchorman, Literary Workshop, WKCR-FM, NYC, 1964-66; Ed., Columbia Review, NYC, 1966-67; Teaching Fellow, Cornell University, Ithaca, New York, 1967-70; Part-time Instructor, 1969-70, Assistant Professor of English and Director of Film Program, 1970-73, and Director, Creative Writing Program 1971-73, Wells College, Aurora, New York; Lecturer in English and Film, University of California at Riverside, 1973-75; Specialist in Film Analysis, Center for Advanced Film Studies, AFI, Beverly Hills, CA, 1974. **Publications:** Slides (poetry), 1970; Telling It Again and Again: Repetition in Literature and Film, 1972; Faulkner and Film, 1977; Mindscreen: Bergman, Godard, and First-Person Film, 1978; To Have and Have Not, 1980; The Mind of the Novel: Reflexive Fiction and the Ineffable, 1982; Faulkner's MGM Screenplays, 1982; How Movies Work, 1987; (revisor) Gerald Mast's A Short History of the Movies, 5th ed, 1992; 6th ed, 1995; 7th ed, 1999. **Address:** Dept of Eng & Film Studies, Denison 146A, Campus 226, University of Colorado, Boulder, CO 80309, U.S.A.

KAY, Alan N. American, b. 1965. **Genres:** Biography, Young adult nonfiction. **Career:** Lake Taylor Middle School, Norfolk, VA, civics teacher, 1989-92; Booker T. Washington High School, Norfolk, history teacher, 1992-93; Horace Mann Jr. High School, Brandon, FL, history teacher, 1993-94; King High International Baccalaureate School, Tampa, FL, advanced history teacher, 1994-97; Dunedin High School, Dunedin, FL, social studies teacher, 1997-. Media Projects Inc., consultant, 1993; Hillsborough, FL, History Day

coordinator, 1995-97; Pinellas County, FL, History Day coordinator, 1997-; presenter of workshops. **Publications:** YOUNG HEROES OF HISTORY SERIES: Send 'Em South, 2000; On the Trail of John Brown's Body, 2001; Off to Fight, 2002; Nowhere to Turn, 2002; No Girls Allowed, 2003. Author of classroom curriculum for grades 7-12. **Address:** 5471 Stallion Lake Dr., Palm Harbor, FL 34685, U.S.A. **Online address:** akay@youngheroesofhistory.com

KAY, George. British, b. 1936. **Genres:** Geography, Third World, Recreation. **Career:** Research Officer, Rhodes-Livingstone Institute, Zambia, 1959-62; Leverhulme Fellow in Commonwealth Studies and Lecturer in Geography, University of Hull, 1962-68; Professor of Geography, University of Zimbabwe, 1968-74; Professor of Geography, Staffordshire University, Stoke-on-Trent, 1976-2000. **Publications:** A Social Geography of Zambia, 1967; Rhodesia: A Human Geography, 1970; (with M. Smout) Salisbury: A Geographical Survey of the Capital of Rhodesia; Access for Countryside Walking, forthcoming. **Address:** Division of Geography, School of Sciences, Staffordshire University, Stoke-on-Trent ST4 2DE, England.

KAY, Guy Gavriel. Canadian, b. 1954. **Genres:** Science fiction/Fantasy, Novels. **Career:** Worked as editorial consultant on posthumous book by J.R.R. Tolkien, The Silmarillion, 1974-75; Canadian Broadcasting Corporation (CBC-Radio), Toronto, Ontario, writer and producer for drama department, 1982-89; writer. **Publications:** FANTASIES: The Summer Tree, 1984; The Wandering Fire, 1986; The Darkest Road, 1986; Tigana, 1990; A Song for Arbonne, 1992; The Lions of Al-Rassan, 1995; Sailing to Sarantium, 1998; Lord of Emperors, 2000. **Address:** c/o Westwood Creative Artists, 94 Harbord St, Toronto, ON, Canada M5S 1G6.

KAY, Jackie. (Jacqueline Margaret). Scottish, b. 1961. **Genres:** Poetry. **Career:** Writer. Writer-in-residence, Hammersmith, London, 1989-91. **Publications:** POETRY: The Adoption Papers, 1991; That Distance Apart (chapbook), 1991; Two's Company (for children), 1992; Three Has Gone (for children), 1994; Other Lovers, 1993; Bessie, 1997; Trumpet, 1998; Off Colour 1998; The Frog Who Dreamed She Was An Opera Singer, 1998. **Address:** c/o PFD, Drury House, 34-43 Russell Street, London WC2B 5HA, England.

KAY, John (A.). British, b. 1948. **Genres:** Business/Trade/Industry, Economics. **Career:** Oxford University, England, fellow in economics at St John's College, 1970-, lecturer in economics, 1971-78, Peter Moores Director, Said Business School, 1997-99. Institute for Fiscal Studies, research director, 1979-81, director, 1981-86; London Business School, professor, 1986-96, director of Centre for Business Strategy, 1986-91. **Publications:** (with L. Hannah) Concentration in Modern Industry, 1977; (with M.A. King) The British Tax System, 1978, 6th ed., 1997; (with A.W. Dilnot and C.N. Morris) The Reform of Social Security, 1984; (with Mayer and J. Edwards) The Economic Analysis of Accounting Profitability, 1987; Foundations of Corporate Success, 1993; Why Firms Succeed, 1995; The Business of Economics, 1996; The Truth about Markets, 2003; Culture & Prosperity, 2004; Everlasting Lightbulbs, 2004. EDITOR: The 1982 Budget, 1982; The Economy and the 1983 Budget, 1983; The Economy and the 1985 Budget, 1985; (with C.P. Mayer and D.J. Thompson) Privatisation and Regulation: The U.K. Experience, 1986; (with J.A. Fairburn) Mergers and Merger Policy, 1989; (with M. Bishop) European Mergers and Merger Policy, 1993; (with Bishop and Mayer) Privatisation and Economic Performance, 1994; (with Bishop and Mayer) The Regulatory Challenge, 1995. Contributor to books and academic journals. **Address:** johnkay.com Ltd, PO Box 4026, London W1A 6N2, England. **Online address:** johnkay@johnkay.com

KAYE, Barrington. Also writes as Henry Cooper, Tom Kaye. British, b. 1924. **Genres:** Novels, Poetry, Education, Sociology. **Career:** Professor of Education, University of the S. Pacific, Fiji, since 1983 (Reader, 1980-83). Lecturer in Education, 1951-54, and Social Research Fellow, 1955-56, University of Malaya; Sr. Lecturer in Education, University of the Gold Coast (now University of Ghana), 1956-62; Head, Dept. of Education, Redland College, Bristol, 1962-72; Chief Technical Adviser, Unesco, Paris, 1972-75; Head, Dept. of Education Studies, Bristol Polytechnic, 1975-80. **Publications:** The Song of my Beloved and Other Poems, 1951; (as Tom Kaye) It Had Been a Mild, Delicate Night (novel), 1957; (as Tom Kaye) Natten Hade Varit Mild Och Om (novel), 1959; Bugis Street Blues (poetry), 1960; (as Tom Kaye) Une Nuit, Douce, Fragile... (novel), 1960; The Development of the Architectural Profession in Britain, 1960; Upper Nankin Street, Singapore, 1960; (as Tom Kaye) David, From Where He Was Lying (novel), 1962; Bringing Up Children in Ghana, 1962; (as Tom Kaye) Dar David lag (novel), 1962; (with I. Rogers) Group Work in Secondary Schools, 1968; Participation in Learning, 1970; Tom Kaye's Love Poems, 1983; (as Henry

Cooper) Upcountry (novel), 1985; Tom Kaye's Other Love Poems, 1988; (as Tom Kaye) How I Write My Novels, chapter in After Narrative (ed. Subramani), 1990. **Address:** PO Box 4267, Samabula, Fiji.

KAYE, Elizabeth. American, b. 1945. **Genres:** Biography. **Career:** Writer. **Publications:** Mid-Life: Notes from the Halfway Mark, 1995; Nureyev: Portrait of a Dancer, in press. **Address:** 241 West 23rd St., New York, NY 10011, U.S.A.

KAYE, Geraldine. British, b. 1925. **Genres:** Children's fiction, Young adult fiction. **Career:** Taught for two years in Singapore; full-time writer. **Publications:** Annan and the Grass Village, 1965; Tawno, Gypsy Boy, 1968; Runaway Boy, 1971; Nowhere to Stop, 1972; To Catch a Thief, 1973; The London Adventure, 1973; Kofi and the Eagle, 1973; Marie Alone, 1973; The Rotten Old Car, 1973; Tim and the Red Indian Headdress, 1973; The Raffle Pony, 1974; Pegs and Flowers, 1974; The Yellow Pom-Pom Hat, 1974; Goodbye, Ruby Red, 1974; Joanna All Alone, 1974; Billy-Boy, 1974; Children of the Turnpike, 1975; A Different Sort of Christmas, 1976; Penny Black, 1977; Joey's Room, 1978; Week Out, 1979; King of the Knockdown Gingers, 1979; The Beautiful Take-Away Palace, 1980; The Day after Yesterday, 1981; The Plum Tree Party, 1982; The Sky-Blue Dragon, 1983; The Donkey Strike, 1984; Comfort Herself, 1984; The Biggest Bonfire in the World, 1985; The Call of the Wild Wood, 1986; The School Pool Gang, 1986; A Breath of Fresh Air, 1987; The Rabbit Minders, 1987; The Donkey Christmas, 1988; Great Comfort, 1988; A Dog Called Dog, 1990; Someone Else's Baby, 1990; A Piece of Cake, 1991; Snowgirl, 1991; Stone Boy, 1991; Hands off My Sister, 1993; Kelso's Carnival, 1994; Night at the Zoo, 1995; Late in the Day (adult fiction), 1997; Between Us (adult fiction), 1998; My Second Best Friend, 1999. **Address:** 39 High Kingsdown, Cotham, Bristol, Avon BS2 8EW, England.

KAYE/KANTROWITZ, Melanie. American, b. 1945. **Genres:** Novels, Cultural/Ethnic topics. **Career:** Harlem Education Project, NYC, instructor, 1963-65; University of California, Berkeley, instructor, 1971-72; Portland State University, OR, assistant professor, 1972-76, instructor, 1977-79; Goddard College, Plainfield, VT, adjunct professor, 1978-81; Norwich University, Vermont College Campus, Montpelier, adjunct professor, 1981-85, assistant professor, 1985-89, associate professor, 1989-. Visiting and adjunct faculty member at US colleges and universities. Queens College, CUNY, Worker Education Extension, director, 1999-. Sinister Wisdom Books, editor and publisher, 1984-88. **Publications:** We Speak in Code: Poems and Other Writings, 1980; My Jewish Face and Other Stories, 1990; The Issue Is Power: Essays on Women, Jews, Violence, and Resistance, 1992. EDITOR & CONTRIBUTOR: (with I. Klepfisz) The Tribe of Dina: A Jewish Women's Anthology, 1986, 2nd ed., 1989; (with Eber and I. Klepfisz) Action and Awareness: Handbook on Anti-Semitism, 1991. Some publications appear under the name Melanie Kaye. Work represented in anthologies. Contributor of poems, stories, essays, and reviews to periodicals. **Address:** 922 8th Ave, Brooklyn, NY 11215, U.S.A. **Online address:** mkk@netstep.net

KAYE, Marvin. American, b. 1938. **Genres:** Novels, Novellas/Short stories, Mystery/Crime/Suspense, Horror, Science fiction/Fantasy, Plays/Screenplays, Recreation. **Career:** GRIT newspaper, reporter, 1963-65, New York correspondent, 1970-; Toys Magazine, senior editor, 1966-70. **Publications:** The Histrionic Holmes, 1971; A Lively Game of Death, 1972; A Toy Is Born, 1973; The Handbook of Magic, 1973; The Grand Ole Opry Murders, 1974; Bertrand Russell's Guided Tour of Intellectual Rubbish (drama), 1974; The Handbook of Mental Magic, 1975; Bullets for Macbeth, 1976; Catalog of Magic, 1977; My Son, the Druggist, 1977; The Laurel and Hardy Murders, 1978; (with P. Godwin) The Masters of Solitude, 1978; The Incredible Umbrella, 1979; My Brother, the Druggist, 1979; Avon Calling (drama), 1980; The Possession of Immanuel Wolf and Other Improbable Tales, 1981; The Amorous Umbrella, 1981; (with P. Godwin) Wintermind, 1981; The Soap Opera Slaughters, 1982; (with P. Godwin) A Cold Blue Light, 1983; Ghosts of Night and Morning, 1987; Fantastique (novel), 1993; The Last Christmas of Ebenezer Scrooge, 2003. EDITOR: (and contrib.) Fiends and Creatures, 1974; (and contrib.) Brother Theodore's Chamber of Horrors, 1974; (and contrib.) Ghosts, 1981; Masterpieces of Terror and the Supernatural, 1985; Devils and Demons, 1987; Weird Tales, the Magazine That Never Dies, 1988; Witches and Warlocks, 1989; 13 Plays of Ghosts and the Supernatural, 1990; Haunted America, 1990; Lovers and Other Monsters, 1992; Sweet Revenge, 1993; Frantic Comedy, 1993; Masterpieces of Terror and the Unknown, 1993; The Game Is Afoot, 1994; Angels of Darkness, 1994; Readers Theatre, 1995; Page to Stage, 1996; The Definitive Dracula, 1996; The Resurrected Holmes, 1996; The Confidential Casebook of Sherlock Holmes, 1998; Don't Open this Book!, 1998; The Vampire Sextette, 2000; Incisions, 2000; The Ultimate Halloween, 2001; The Dragon Quintet, 2003.

KAYE, Peggy. American, b. 1948. **Genres:** Education. **Career:** Author and illustrator of children's books. Former teacher in New York, NY public and private elementary schools; private tutor in reading and math; educational consultant. **Publications:** SELF-ILLUSTRATED: Games for Reading: Playful Ways to Help Your Child Read, 1984; Games for Math: Playful Ways to Help Your Child Learn Math-from Kindergarten to Third Grade, 1987; Homework: Math, 6 vols (with teachers' guide), 1989; Homework: Reading (with teachers' guide), 1990; Games for Learning: Ten Minutes a Day to Help Your Child Do Well in School-from Kindergarten to Third Grade, 1991; Games for Writing: Playful Ways to Help Your Child Learn to Write, 1995; Afterwards: Folk and Fairy Tales with Mathematica Ever Afters, 2 vols, 1996-1997; Games with Books: Twenty-eight of the Best Children's Books and How to Use Them to Help Your Child Learn-from Preschool to Third Grade, 2002. Contributor to periodicals. **Address:** 55 West 86th St., New York, NY 10024, U.S.A. **Online address:** yggep1@aol.com

KAYE, Tom. See KAYE, Barrington.

KAYNAK, Erdener. American/Canadian (born Turkey), b. 1947. **Genres:** Marketing. **Career:** Hacettepe University, Ankara, Turkey, assistant professor, 1975-78; Acadia University, Wolfville, NS, assistant professor, 1978-79; Mount St. Vincent University, Halifax, NS, professor and department head, 1979-85; Chinese University of Hong Kong, visiting professor, 1985-86; Pennsylvania State University, Capital College, Middletown, professor of marketing, 1986-. Visiting professor: Bilkent University, 1989, 1991, Helsinki School of Economics and Business Administration, 1992, Norwegian School of Management, 1993, University of Hawaii at Manoa, Curtin University of Technology, University of Botswana. Cross-Cultural Marketing Services Inc., founder and president. **Publications:** Marketing in the Third World, 1982; (with R. Savitt) Comparative Marketing Systems, 1984; International Marketing Management, 1985; The Global Perspective in Marketing, 1985; World Food Marketing Systems, 1986; International Business in the Middle East, 1986; Marketing and Economic Development, 1986; Service Industries in Developing Countries, 1986; Transnational Retailing, 1988; (with K.-H. Lee) Global Business: Asia-Pacific Dimensions, 1989; The Management of International Advertising, 1989; Socio-Political Aspects of International Marketing, 1990; The Global Business: Four Key Marketing Strategies, 1993; Utilizing New Information Technology in the Teaching of International Business, 1993; (with P.N. Ghauri) Euromarketing, 1994; (coauthor) The Globalization of Consumer Markets, 1994; Guide to Publishing Opportunities in Business, Administration, and Management, 1995; International Marketing, 1995. Contributor to books. Contributor to academic professional journals. **Address:** School of Business Administration, E-355 Olmsted Bldg, Pennsylvania State University, Capital College, 777 W Harrisburg Pike, Middletown, PA 17057, U.S.A. **Online address:** k9x@psu.edu

KAYS, Scott A. American, b. 1960. **Genres:** Money/Finance. **Career:** Kays Financial Advisory Corp., Atlanta, GA, founder, president, and chief executive officer, 1985-. Ordained minister; Scott Kays Ministries Inc., founder, 1992; associate pastor of an interdenominational church in Atlanta, 1989-92, and a United Methodist church, 1994-96. Certified financial planner; host of investment seminars; guest on television programs. **Publications:** Achieving Your Financial Potential, 1999. **Address:** Kays Financial Advisory Corp., 1995 N Park Pl Ste 220, Atlanta, GA 30339, U.S.A. **Online address:** skays@ScottKays.com

KAYSEN, Susanna. American, b. 1948. **Genres:** Novels, Autobiography/Memoirs. **Career:** Writer. **Publications:** Asa, as I Knew Him, 1987; Far Afield, 1990; Girl, Interrupted, 1993; The Camera my Mother Gave Me, 2001. **Address:** c/o Jonathan Matson, Harold Matson Co, Inc, 276 Fifth Ave, New York, NY 10001, U.S.A.

KAZA, Stephanie. American, b. 1947. **Genres:** Essays. **Career:** High school science teacher in Santa Cruz, CA, and in the San Francisco Bay area, 1969-76; University of California-Santa Cruz, teaching assistant, 1976-79, lecturer in environmental studies, 1979-80; University of California-Berkeley, lecturer, 1988-89; Starr King School for the Ministry, Berkeley, CA, guest instructor, 1989-90; University of Vermont, Burlington, assistant professor of environmental studies, 1991-97, associate professor, 1997-; Schumacher College (Devon, Englad), guest instructor, 2001. **Publications:** The Attentive Heart: Conversations with Trees (essays), 1993. EDITOR: (with B.J. LeBoeuf) The Natural History of Año Nuevo, 1981; (with K. Kraft) Dharma Rain: Sources of Buddhist Environmentalism, 2000. **Address:** University of Vermont, 153 South Prospect St., Burlington, VT 05401, U.S.A. **Online address:** skaza@zoo.uvm.edu

KAZANTZIS, Judith. British, b. 1940. **Genres:** Novels, Poetry, Translations. **Career:** Poet, short fiction writer, novelist; painter, exhibitions,

1987-. **Publications:** Women in Revolt: The Fight for Emancipation: A Collection of Contemporary Documents, 1968. POETRY: Minefield, 1977; The Wicked Queen, 1980; (with M. Roberts and M. Wandor) Touch Papers, 1982; Let's Pretend, 1984; A Poem for Guatemala, 1988; Flame Tree, 1988; The Rabbit Magician Plate, 1992; Selected Poems 1977-92, 1995; Swimming through the Grand Hotel, 1997; The Odysseus Poems: Fictions of the Odyssey of Homer, 1999; Just after Midnight, 2004. NOVELS: Zones of Love and Terror, 2002. EDITOR: The Gordon Riots: A Collection of Contemporary Documents, 1966. TRANSLATOR: In Cyclops Cave, 2002. **Address:** PO Box 1671, Key West, FL 33041, U.S.A. **Online address:** jktropic@aol.com

KEAHEY, John. American. **Genres:** Travel/Exploration. **Career:** Salt Lake Tribune, news editor, reporter, 1989-. **Publications:** A Sweet and Glorious Land: Revisiting the Ionian Sea, 2000; Venice against the Sea: A City Besieged, 2002. **Address:** Salt Lake City Tribune, 143 South Main St., Salt Lake City, UT 84101, U.S.A. **Online address:** jkeahey@attbi.com

KEALEY, Edward J. American, b. 1936. **Genres:** History, Technology, Biography. **Career:** Ordained Catholic Priest, since 1989. Co-pastor, St. Sylvester Church, Medford, New York; Chairman, 1980-83, Professor of History, 1973-86, Associate Professor, 1966-73, Assistant Professor, 1962-66, Advisor for Graduate Studies, 1964-69, College of the Holy Cross, Worcester, Massachusetts; Lecturer, University of Massachusetts Labor Relations Research Center, Worcester, 1969-75. **Publications:** Roger of Salisbury, Viceroy of England, 1972; Medieval Medicus: A Social History of Anglo-Norman Medicine, 1981; Harvesting the Air: Windmill Pioneers in Twelfth Century England, 1987. **Address:** 68 Ohio Avenue, Medford, NY 11763, U.S.A.

KEANE, John. Australian/British, b. 1949. **Genres:** History, Politics/Government. **Career:** University of Westminster, London, England, professor of politics and director of Centre for the Study of Democracy. Guest on television and radio programs. **Publications:** The Media and Democracy, 1991; Tom Paine: A Political Life; Vaclav Havel: A Political Tragedy in Six Acts, 1999; eight other books. Contributor to magazines and newspapers. **Address:** Centre for the Study of Democracy, University of Westminster, 100 Park Village E, London NW1 3SR, England. **Online address:** csd@wmin.ac.uk

KEANEY, Brian. British, b. 1954. **Genres:** Young adult fiction, Young adult non-fiction. **Career:** Teacher in London, England, 1976-86; writer-in-residence in Redbridge, England, 1988-90, and in Merton, London, 1990-91; royal literary fellow, Goldsmith's College, University of London, 2001-02, London College of Fashion, 2002-03, and St Mary's College, University of Surrey. **Publications:** FOR YOUNG PEOPLE: Don't Hang About, 1985; Some People Never Learn, 1987; No Need for Heroes, 1989; If This Is the Real World, 1991; Boys Don't Write Love Stories, 1993; Family Secrets, 1997; The Private Life of Georgia Brown, 1998; Bitter Fruit, 1999; No Stone Unturned, 2001; Falling for Joshua, 2001; Where Mermaids Sing, 2004. **Address:** 111 Drakefell Rd, London SE4 2DT, England. **Online address:** brian.keaney@nt1world.com

KEARNS, Doris Helen. *See* **GOODWIN, Doris (Helen) Kearns.**

KEARNS, Josie. American, b. 1954. **Genres:** Poetry, Adult non-fiction. **Career:** University of Michigan, Ann Arbor, professor, 1994-. Ragdale Foundation, writer-in-residence, 1995-2002. **Publications:** New Numbers (poetry chapbook), 1999, expanded ed., 2000; Life after the Line (nonfiction). Poetry represented in anthologies. Contributor of poetry to journals. **Address:** 3262 Angell Hall, University of Michigan, Ann Arbor, MI 48109, U.S.A. **Online address:** jakearns@umich.edu

KEARNS, Lionel (John). Canadian, b. 1937. **Genres:** Poetry, Autobiography/Memoirs, Bibliography, Essays, History. **Career:** Writer and educator. **Publications:** Songs of Circumstance, 1963; Listen George, 1965; Pointing, 1967; By the Light of the Silvery McLune: Media Parables, Poems, Signs, Gestures, and Other Assaults on the Interface, 1969; About Time, 1974; The Birth of God (film poem), 1974; Negotiating a New Canadian Constitution (film poem), 1975; Poems for a Manitoulin Canada Day, 1976; Practicing Up to Be Human, 1978; Ignoring the Bomb: Poems New and Selected, 1982; Convergences, 1984; Universe, and Other Poems for the Screen, 1988. **Address:** 1616 Charles St, Vancouver, BC, Canada V5L 2T3.

KEARNS, Sheila M. American, b. 1955. **Genres:** Literary criticism and history. **Career:** University of Texas, Austin, assistant professor of English, 1985-94; University of Texas, Innovation, Creativity, and Capital Institute,

Austin, research associate, 1994-. **Publications:** Wordsworth, Coleridge, and Romantic Autobiography (literary criticism), 1995. **Address:** Innovation Creativity and Capital Institute, University of Texas, 2815 San Gabriel, Austin, TX 78705, U.S.A.

KEATES, Jonathan. British, b. 1946. **Genres:** Novellas/Short stories, Music, Biography, Travel/Exploration. **Career:** Travel, and short story writer. City of London School, London, England, teacher of English Literature. **Publications:** The Companion Guide to the Shakespeare Country, 1979;(with A. Hornak) Historic London, 1979; (with A. Hornak) Canterbury Cathedral, 1980; The Love of Italy, 1980; Allegro Postillions (short stories), 1983; Handel: The Man and His Music, 1985; Tuscany, 1989; Italian Journeys, 1992; Venice, 1994; Purcell: A Biography, 1995; Stendahl, 1995; Soon to Be a Major Motion Picture (short stories), 1997. Author of book reviews. **Address:** c/o Chatto & Windus, Random House UK, 20 Vauxhall Bridge Rd., London SW1V 2SA, England.

KEATING, AnaLouise. American, b. 1961. **Genres:** Literary criticism and history. **Career:** Eastern New Mexico University, Portales, associate professor, 1990-. **Publications:** Women Reading Women Writing: Self-Invention in Paula Gunn Allen, Gloria Anzaldua, and Audre Lorde, 1996. Contributor to books. Contributor to academic journals. **Address:** Department of Languages and Literature, Eastern New Mexico University, Portales, NM 88130, U.S.A. **Online address:** AnnLouise.Keating@enmu.edu

KEATING, Frank. American, b. 1944. **Genres:** Biography. **Career:** Federal Bureau of Investigation, Washington, DC, special agent, beginning c. 1969; worked as assistant district attorney of Tulsa, OK, until 1972; State of Oklahoma, member of House of Representatives, 1972-74, member of Senate, 1974-81, governor, 1995-2003; U.S. attorney for the northern district of Oklahoma, 1981-85; U.S. Department of the Treasury, Washington, DC, assistant secretary, 1985-; U.S. Department of Justice, Washington, DC, associate attorney general; U.S. Department of Housing and Urban Development, Washington, DC, general counsel and acting deputy secretary; American Council of Life Insurers, Washington, DC, president and chief executive officer, 2003-. **Publications:** Will Rogers: An American Legend, 2002. Contributor to periodicals. **Address:** American Council of Life Insurers, 101 Constitution Ave. N.W., Washington, DC 20001, U.S.A.

KEATING, H(enry) R(eymond) F(itzwalter). British, b. 1926. **Genres:** Novels, Novellas/Short stories, Mystery/Crime/Suspense, Literary criticism and history, Writing/Journalism. **Career:** Sub-Ed., Daily Telegraph, London, 1956-58, and The Times, London, 1958-60. Chairman, Crime Writers Association, London, 1970-71; Chairman, Society of Authors, 1983-84; President, Detection Club, 1986-2001; Fellow, Royal Society of Literature, 1990. **Publications:** Death and the Visiting Firemen, 1959; Zen There Was Murder, 1960; A Rush on the Ultimate, 1961; The Dog It Was That Died, 1962; Death of a Fat God, 1963; The Perfect Murder, 1964; Is Skin-Deep, Is Fatal, 1965; Inspector Ghote series, 1966-; The Strong Man, 1971; The Underside, 1974; A Remarkable Case of Burglary, 1975; Murder Must Appetize, 1975; A Long Walk to Wimbledon, 1978; The World of Sherlock Holmes, 1979; The Marks and Spencer Book of Great Crimes, 1982; The Lucky Alphonse, 1982; Mrs. Craggs, Crimes Cleaned Up, 1985; Writing Crime Fiction, 1986; The Bedside Companion to Crime, 1989; The Rich Detective, 1993; Cheating Death, 1994; Doing Wrong, 1995; The Good Detective, 1996; The Bad Detective, 1996; Asking Questions, 1996; In Kensington Gardens Once, 1997; The Soft Detective, 1998; Jack, the Lady Killer (verse), 1999; The Hard Detective, 2000; Breaking and Entering, 2000; A Detective in Love, 2001; A Detective under Fire, 2002; The Dreaming Detective, 2003. EDITOR: (and contrib.) Blood on My Mind, 1972; Agatha Christie: First Lady of Crime, 1977; Crime Writers, 1978; Whodunit, 1982. **Address:** 35 Northumberland Pl, London W2 5AS, England.

KEAY, John. British, b. 1941. **Genres:** Travel/Exploration, History. **Publications:** Into India, 1973; When Men and Mountains Meet, 1977; The Gilgit Game, 1979; India Discovered, 1981; Eccentric Travellers, 1982; Highland Drove, 1984; Explorers Extraordinary, 1985; The Honourable Company, 1991; Indonesia: From Sabang to Merauke, 1995; Last Post: The End of Empire in the Far East, 1997; India: A History, 2000; The Great Arc, 2000; Sowing the Wind, 2002; Mad about the Mekong, 2005; The Spice Route, 2005. EDITOR: The Royal Geographical Society's History of World Exploration, 1991; Collins Encyclopedia of Scotland, 1994. **Address:** Succoth, Dalmally, Argyll, Scotland.

KEE, Robert. British (born India), b. 1919. **Genres:** Novels, History, Autobiography/Memoirs. **Career:** Journalist; Television and radio broadcaster in U.K. **Publications:** A Crowd Is Not Company, 1947, new ed., 2000; The

Impossible Shore, 1949; A Sign of the Times, 1955; Broadstrop in Season, 1959; Refugee World, 1959; The Green Flag: A History of Irish Nationalism, 1972, new ed., 2000; Ireland: A History, 1980, rev. ed., 1995; The World We Left Behind, 1984; The World We Fought For, 1985; Trial and Error, 1986; Munich: The Eleventh Hour, 1988; Picture Post Album, 1989; The Laurel and the Ivy: Parnell and Irish Nationalism, 1993. **Address:** c/o Roger Coleridge and White, 20 Powis Mews, London W11 1JN, England.

KEEBLE, Neil H(oward). British, b. 1944. **Genres:** History, Literary criticism and history, Theology/Religion, Women's studies and issues, Biography. **Career:** University of Aarhus, Denmark, lecturer in English, 1969-74; University of Stirling, Scotland, lecturer, 1974-88, reader in English, 1988-95, professor of English, 1995-, deputy principal, 2001-. **Publications:** Richard Baxter: Puritan Man of Letters, 1982; The Literary Culture of Nonconformity in Later Seventeenth-Century England, 1987; (with G.F. Nuttall) Calendar of the Correspondence of Richard Baxter, 2 vols., 1991; "Loving and Free Converse": Richard Baxter in His Letters, 1991; The Restoration: England in the 1660s, 2002. EDITOR: The Autobiography of Richard Baxter, 1974; J. Bunyan, The Pilgrim's Progress, 1984; Handbook of English and Celtic Studies in the United Kingdom and the Republic of Ireland, 1988; John Bunyan: Conventicle and Parnassus; Tercentenary Essays, 1988; The Cultural Identity of Seventeenth-Century Woman: A Reader, 1994; L. Hutchinson, Memoirs of the Life of Colonel Hutchinson, 1995; Cambridge Companion to Writing of the English Revolution, 2001; John Bunyan: Reading Dissenting Writing, 2002; D. Defoe, Memoirs of the Church of Scotland, 2002; A. Marvell, Remarks upon a Late Disingenuous Discourse, 2003. **Address:** Deputy Principals' Office, University of Stirling, Stirling FK9 4LA, Scotland. **Online address:** n.h.keeble@stir.ac.uk

KEECH, Thomas (Walton). American, b. 1946. **Genres:** Novels, Law. **Career:** Maryland Department of Juvenile Services, juvenile probation officer, 1969-72; Legal Aid Bureau of Baltimore, Inc., staff attorney, 1975-81; Maryland Department of Economic and Employment Development, board of appeals chair, 1981-94; Office of the Attorney General, Baltimore, MD, assistant attorney general, 1994-. **Publications:** (with G. Abramson, J. Roberts, and L. Seaton) Unemployment Insurance Benefits, 1990; The Crawlspace Conspiracy (novel), 1995. **Address:** Office of the Attorney General, 300 West Preston St., Suite 302, Baltimore, MD 21201, U.S.A.

KEEFAUVER, Larry. American. **Genres:** Theology/Religion, Inspirational/Motivational Literature. **Career:** Pastor, teacher, and writer. Daily in God's Word (weekly television ministry), presenter; Your Ministries Consultation Services, executive director. **Publications:** (with J.D. Stone) Friend to Friend: How You Can Help a Friend through a Problem, 1983; Starting a Youth Ministry, 1984; Friends and Faith: Friendship Evangelism in Youth Ministry, 1986; Faith in the Workplace: A Four-Week Course to Help Adults Discover How to Live out Their Faith at Work, 1993; (with R. Cherry) The Doctor and the Word, 1996; Prayer and the Bible, 1996; Praying with Smith Wigglesworth, 1996; Welcoming the Presence of the Spirit, 1997; Receiving the Anointing of the Spirit, 1997; Blazing with the Fire of the Spirit, 1997; Hearing the Voice of the Spirit, 1997; Living the Spirit-Led Life, 1997; Operating in the Power of the Holy Spirit, 1997; Lord, I Wish My Husband Would Pray with Me, 1998; Carlton Pearson's Azuza Street Revival, 1998; Hugs for Grandparents: Stories, Sayings, and Scriptures to Encourage and Inspire, 1998; When God Doesn't Heal Now: How to Walk by Faith, Facing Pain, Suffering, and Death, 2000. EDITOR: Smith Wigglesworth on Faith: A Thirty-Day Devotional, 1996; Smith Wigglesworth on Healing: A Thirty-Day Devotional, 1996; The Original Smith Wigglesworth Devotional, 1997; The Original Azuza Street Revival Devotional, 1997; K. Kuhlman, Healing Words, 1997; The Original John G. Lake Devotional, 1997; The Original Maria Woodworth-Etter Devotional, 1997. **Address:** c/o Author Mail, Thomas Nelson Inc., 501 Nelson Pl., Nashville, TN 37214, U.S.A. **Online address:** drlarry@ymcs.org

KEEFE, Richard S(tanley) E(dward). American, b. 1958. **Genres:** Psychology, Medicine/Health. **Career:** Schizophrenia Biological Research Center, NYC, research coordinator, 1983-85, assistant research psychologist, 1985-89; Yale University, New Haven, CT, clinical psychology intern at Yale-New Haven Hospital, 1990, visiting scientist at Kidd Laboratory, 1990-92; Kraepelinian Schizophrenia Research Project, NYC, director of Neurocognitive Laboratories, 1990-95; Duke University, Durham, NC, assistant professor of psychiatry, 1995-. Beth Israel Medical Center, neuropsychology extern, 1987-88; Elmhurst Hospital, director of Diagnostic Assessment Service, 1990-95. Mount Sinai School of Medicine of the City University of New York, assistant professor, 1990-95; University of Utrecht, lecturer, 1994; guest on television and radio programs. **Publications:** (with P.D. Harvey) Understanding Schizophrenia: A Guide to the New Research on

Causes and Treatment, 1994. Contributor to books. Contributor of articles and reviews to professional journals, popular magazines, and newspapers. **Address:** Department of Psychiatry, Medical Center, Duke University, Durham, NC 27706, U.S.A.

KEEGAN, John E. American, b. 1943. **Genres:** Novels. **Career:** U.S. Department of Housing and Urban Development, Washington, DC, attorney; Office of the Prosecuting Attorney of King County, Seattle, deputy prosecutor; Davis Wright Tremaine, Seattle, partner. **Publications:** Clearwater Summer, 1994; Piper, 2001. Contributor to law journals and literary quarterlies. **Address:** 7722 22nd Ave NE, Seattle, WA 98115, U.S.A.

KEEGAN, Marcia. American, b. 1943. **Genres:** Area studies. **Career:** Albuquerque Tribune, Albuquerque, NM, journalist and photographer, 1963-64; Albuquerque Journal, Albuquerque, editor of "Home Living" Sunday supplement, 196468; freelance photographer, 1969-88; Clear Light Publishers, Santa Fe, NM, cofounder, 1988, president and book designer, 1988-. Lecturer and workshop presenter at educational institutions. Photographs of Native American and Tibetan cultures have been exhibited internationally in group and solo shows; work represented in permanent collections at major U.S. museums. **Publications:** AUTHOR AND PHOTOGRAPHER: Taos Pueblo and Its Sacred Blue Lake, 1972; Mother Earth, Father Sky, 1974; Southwest Indian Cookbook, 1977; We Can Still Hear Them Clapping, 1975; Oklahoma, 1979; The Dalai Lama's Historic Visit to North America, 1981; New Mexico, 1984; Enduring Culture, 1991; Pueblo Boy, 1991; Ancient Wisdom, Living Tradition, 1998; Pueblo People: Ancient Traditions, Modern Lives, 1998. PHOTOGRAPHER: Only the Moon and Me, 1968; Moonsong Lullaby, 1981; Ocean of Wisdom, 1989. Contributor to books and magazines. **Address:** 823 Don Diego, Santa Fe, NM 87501, U.S.A.

KEEGAN, William (James Gregory). British, b. 1938. **Genres:** Novels, Politics/Government, Economics. **Career:** Financial Times, London, England, economics correspondent, 1967-76; Bank of England, London, assistant to governor, 1976-77; Observer, London, economics editor, 1977-, assistant editor and business editor, 1981-83, associate editor, 1983-; member of advisory boards. Visiting professor of journalism, 1989, and honorary residential fellow, 1990, Sheffield University. **Publications:** FICTION: Consulting Father Wintergreen, 1974; A Real Killing, 1976. NONFICTION: (with R. Pennant-Rea) Who Runs the Economy?, 1979; Mrs. Thatcher's Economic Experiment, 1983; Britain without Oil, 1985; Mr. Lawson's Gamble, 1989; The Spectre of Capitalism: The Future of the World Economy after the Fall of Communism, 1992; 2066-and All That, 2000. Contributor to journals. **Address:** Observer, 119 Farringdon Rd, London EC1R 3ER, England.

KEELE, Alan (Frank). American, b. 1942. **Genres:** Literary criticism and history, Language/Linguistics, Translations. **Career:** Mormon missionary in Germany, 1962-64; Brigham Young University, Provo, UT, teacher of Germanic and Slavic languages, P.A. Christensen Memorial Lecturer, 1976, Honors Professor of the Year, 1992, Karl G. Maeser Professor, 1996, department head, and founding co-chairperson of Distance Learning Committee. **Publications:** Paul Schallueck and the Postwar German Don Quixote: A Case History Prolegomenon to the Literature of the Federal Republic, 1976; (with M.H. Folsom) Learn German, 1978; A German-English, English-German Glossary for Missionaries, 1982, 2nd ed. (with M.H. Folsom), 1983; The Apocalyptic Vision: A Thematic Exploration of Postwar German Literature, 1983; (with M.H. Folsom) German Core Vocabulary in Context: A Pedagogical Dictionary for Beginning Students of German, 1983; (with K.-H. Schnibbe and D.F. Tobler) The Price: The True Story of a Mormon Who Defied Hitler, 1984; Understanding Guenter Grass, 1988; (with R.L. Jones and F.J. Goertz) Wortindex zur "Blechtrommel" von Guenter Grass, 1990; (with Schnibbe and B. Holmes) Jugendliche gegen Hitler: Die Helmuth Huebener Gruppe in Hamburg, 1941-42, 1991; (with B. Holmes) When Truth Was Treason: German Youth against Hitler, 1995. TRANSLATOR: (with L. Norris) R.M. Rilke, Sonnets to Orpheus, 1989; (with N. Davis and G. Davis) W. Kempowski, Dog Days, 1991; (with L. Norris) Rilke, Duino Elegies, 1993. EDITOR: (with M.H. Folsom) P.P. Ashworth and C. Vigo, Learn Spanish, 1980; (with M.H. Folsom) C.W. Griggs and R. Stewart, Learn Greek, 1981, 2nd ed. (with M.F. Shelley), 1984; (with M.H. Folsom) M. Watabe, Learn Japanese, 1984. Contributor to books. Contributor of articles and reviews to journals. **Address:** 4082 JKHB, Brigham Young University, Provo, UT 84602, U.S.A. **Online address:** Alan_Keele@BYU.edu

KEELER, Robert F. American, b. 1944. **Genres:** Writing/Journalism. **Career:** New York Herald Tribune, NYC, copyperson and editorial assistant, 1965; Waterbury Republican, Waterbury, CT, journalist, 1969; Staten Island Advance, Staten Island, NY, journalist, 1969-71; Newsday, Melville, NY, reporter, 1971-, Albany bureau chief, 1978-81, editor of magazine, 1982-83, state editor, 1984, reporter on religion, ethics, and values, 1993-2001, editorial writer, 2001-. **Publications:** Newsday: A Candid History of the Respectable Tabloid, 1990; Parish!, 1997. **Address:** Newsday, 235 Pinelawn Rd, Melville, NY 11747, U.S.A. **Online address:** Bob.Keeler@newsday.com

KEELEY, Edmund. American (born Syrian Arab Republic), b. 1928. **Genres:** Novels, Novellas/Short stories, History, Literary criticism and history, Travel/Exploration, Translations. **Career:** Princeton University, NJ (joined faculty, 1954), Charles Barnwell Straut Professor of English Emeritus, Professor of English and Creative Writing Emeritus, Hellenic Studies Program, Director Emeritus. **Publications:** The Libation, 1958; The Gold-Hatted Lover, 1961; The Impostor, 1970; Modern Greek Poetry: Voice and Myth, 1983; A Wilderness Called Peace, 1985; The Salonika Bay Murder, 1989; School for Pagan Lovers, 1993; Albanian Journal, 1996; George Seferis and Edmund Keeley: Correspondence, 1951-1971, 1997; Inventing Paradise: The Greek Journey, 1937-47, 1999; On Translation: Reflections and Conversations, 2000; Some Wine for Remembrance, 2001. EDITOR: (with P. Bien) Modern Greek Writers, 1972; Voyage to a Dark Island, 1972; Cavafy's Alexandria, 1976; (with P. Sherrard) Odysseus Elytis: Selected Poems, 1981; (co) The Legacy of R.P. Blackmur: Essays, Memoirs, Texts, 1987; The Essential Cavafy, 1995. TRANSLATIONS: (with P. Sherrard) Six Poets of Modern Greece, 1960; (with M. Keeley) V. Vassilikos, The Plant, The Well, The Angel, 1964; (with P. Sherrard) Four Greek Poets, 1966; (with P. Sherrard) George Seferis: Collected Poems, 1967; (with G. Savidis) C.P. Cavafy: Passions and Ancient Days, 1971; (with P. Sherrard) C.P. Cavafy: Selected Poems, 1972; (with G. Savidis) Odysseus Elytis: The Axion Esti, 1974; (with P. Sherrard) C.P. Cavafy: Collected Poems, 1975; Ritsos in Parentheses, 1979; (with P. Sherrard) Angelos Sikelianos: Selected Poems, 1979; (with P. Sherrard) The Dark Crystal, Voices of Modern Greece, 1982, as A Greek Quintet, 1992; Yannis Ritsos: Exile and Return, Selected Poems 1967-1974, 1985; Yannis Ritsos: Repetitions, Testimonies, Parentheses, 1991. **Address:** 140 Littlebrook Rd, Princeton, NJ 08540, U.S.A. **Online address:** keeley@princeton.edu

KEEN, Ernest. American, b. 1937. **Genres:** Psychology. **Career:** Bucknell University, Lewisburg, Pa., assistant professor, 1964-69, associate professor, 1969-74, professor, 1974-2000, professor emeritus, 2000-. **Publications:** Three Faces of Being: Toward an Existential Clinical Psychology, 1970; Psychology and the New Consciousness, 1972; Primer in Phenomenological Psychology, 1975; Emotion, 1977; Drugs, Therapy, and Professional Power, 1998; Chemicals for the Mind, 2000; Ultimacy and Triviality in Psychotherapy, 2000; A History of Ideas in American Psychology, 2001. **Address:** 471 Knight Rd, Gettysburg, PA 17325, U.S.A. **Online address:** keen@bucknell.edu

KEEN, Sam. American, b. 1931. **Genres:** Human relations/Parenting, Philosophy, Psychology, Theology/Religion. **Career:** Writer. Louisville Presbyterian Theological Seminary, Louisville, KY, professor of philosophy of religion, 1962-68; Psychology Today, NYC, contributing editor, 1969-86. Western Behavioral Science Institute, National Institute of Mental Health postdoctoral fellow, 1969-70; Prescott College, professor of philosophy of the person, 1970; Humanistic Psychology Institute, professor, 1972; University of Florida Medical School, visiting professor of medical ethics, 1983. Lecturer, group leader, and consultant at colleges, universities, clinics, institutes, and corporations worldwide. Coproducer of TV documentary, with Bill Jersey, Faces of the Enemy, 1989. **Publications:** Gabriel Marcel, 1967; Apology for Wonder, 1969; To a Dancing God, 1970; (with A.V. Fox) Telling Your Story, 1973; Voices and Visions, 1974; Beginnings without End, 1975; (with J. Fowler) Life-Maps: Conversations on the Journey of Faith, 1978; What to Do When You're Bored and Blue, 1980; The Passionate Life: Stages of Loving, 1983; Faces of the Enemy, 1986, TV documentary, 1989; Fire in the Belly, 1991; Hymns to an Unknown God, 1994; To Love and Be Loved, 1997; Learning to Fly, 1999. **Address:** 16331 Norrbom Rd, Sonoma, CA 95476, U.S.A. **Online address:** www.SamKeen.com

KEENAN, Brian. Irish, b. 1950. **Genres:** Novels, Plays/Screenplays, Travel/Exploration, Biography. **Career:** Orangefield Boys School, Belfast, Northern Ireland, teacher, 1975-77; Belfast City Council, Belfast, comm. dev. officer, 1977-84; American University, Beirut, Lebanon, instructor in English, 1985-86; Trinity College, Dublin, Ireland, writer in resident, 1993-. **Publications:** An Evil Cradling: The Five-Year Ordeal of a Hostage, 1992; Blind Flight (screenplay), 1995; Between Extremes (travel), 1999; Turlough (novel), 2000. **Address:** Department of English, Trinity College, Dublin 1, Ireland.

KEENAN, Sheila. American, b. 1953. **Genres:** Children's fiction, Children's non-fiction. **Publications:** Good Morning, Monday, 1994; Frederick Dou-

glass: Portrait of a Freedom Fighter, 1995; The Scholastic Encyclopedia of Women in the United States, 1996, rev. ed., 2002; The Biggest Fish, 1996; More or Less a Mess, 1997; What Time Is It?, 1998; What's Up with that Cup?, 1999; Gods, Goddesses, and Monsters: An Encyclopedia of World Mythology, 2000; Lizzy's Dizzy Day, 2001; The Trouble with Pets, 2001; Scholastic Book of Outstanding Americans, 2003; O, Say Can You See, America's Symbols and Landmarks, 2004. ADAPTER, VOYAGES OF DISCOVERY SERIES: The History of Moviemaking, 1995; The Story of Flight, 1995; The World of Theater, 1995; What the Painter Sees, 1996; The Art of Making Books, 1996; The World of Insects, 1997; Bikes, Cars, Trucks, and Trains, 1997. **Address:** 75 Abbott Ave, Ocean Grove, NJ 07756, U.S.A.

KEENE, Ann T(odd). American, b. 1940. **Genres:** Young adult non-fiction. **Career:** Bloomington Montessori Association, Bloomington, IN, founder, 1968; Bloomington Montessori School, Bloomington, cofounder, 1969; Indiana University, Bloomington, instructor/adjunct professor, 1974-79; Business Horizons (magazine), Bloomington, managing editor, 1977-79; President's Select Commission on Immigration, Washington, DC, chief writer/editor, 1979-81; George Mason University, Fairfax, VA, adjunct professor of writing, 1982-83; E.P. Dutton, NYC, managing editor, 1984-85; freelance writer and editor, 1986-. **Publications:** NONFICTION FOR YOUNG ADULTS: Earthkeepers: Observers and Protectors of Nature, 1993; Willa Cather, 1994; Racism, 1995; Peacemakers: Winners of the Nobel Peace Prize, 1996. OTHER: (ed.) Encyclopedia of Psychoactive Drugs, rev. ed., 1992. Contributor to books. **Address:** 4 Jones Hill Rd., East Haddam, CT 06423, U.S.A.

KEENE, Carolyn. *See* WAGNER, Sharon Blythe.

KEENE, Dennis. British, b. 1934. **Genres:** Poetry, Literary criticism and history, Social commentary, Translations. **Career:** University of Malaya, Singapore and Kuala Lumpur, assistant lecturer, 1958-60; University of Kyoto, Japan, lecturer, 1961-63; Haile Selassie First University, Addis Ababa, Ethiopia, assistant professor, 1964-65; University of Kyushu, Fukuoka, Japan, lecturer, 1965-69; Japan Women's University, Tokyo, professor, 1970-81, 1984-93. **Publications:** Surviving (poems), 1980; Yokomitsu Riichi: Modernist, 1980; The Modern Japanese Prose Poem, 1980; Universe and Other Poems, 1984; (ed.) Earl of Surrey, Selected Poems, 1985; Wasurerareta Kuni Nippon (The Forgotten Country, Japan), 1995. Translator from Japanese to English of works by R. Yokomitsu, Y. Kurahashi, M. Nakamura, M. Kita, S. Maruya, N. Ikezawa. Also writes in Japanese. **Address:** 77 Staunton Rd, Headington, Oxford OX3 7TL, England.

KEENE, Donald. American, b. 1922. **Genres:** Area studies, Literary criticism and history, Translations. **Career:** Professor Emeritus and Shincho Professor of Japanese, Columbia University, NYC. Guest Ed., Asahi Shimbun, Tokyo, 1982-92. Lecturer, Cambridge University, 1948-53. Director, Japan Society, New York, 1979-82. Member, American Academy and Institute of Arts and Letters, 1987, and Japan Academy, 1989. **Publications:** The Battles of Coxinga, 1951; The Japanese Discovery of Europe, 1952; Japanese Literature: An Introduction for Western Readers, 1953; Living Japan, 1957; Bunraku, the Puppet Theatre of Japan, 1965; No: The Classical Theatre of Japan, 1966; Landscapes and Portraits, 1971; Some Japanese Portraits, 1978; World within Walls, 1978; Meeting with Japan, 1978; Travels in Japan, 1981; Dawn to the West, 1984; The Pleasures of Japanese Literature, 1988; Travelers of a Hundred Ages, 1989; Seeds in the Heart, 1993; On Familiar Terms, 1994; Modern Japanese Diaries, 1995; The Blue-Eyed Tarokaja, 1996; Emperor of Japan, 2002; Yoshimasa and the Silver Pavilion, 2003. EDITOR: Anthology of Japanese Literature, 1955; Modern Japanese Literature, 1956; Sources of Japanese Tradition, 1958; Twenty Plays of the No Theatre, 1970. TRANSLATOR: The Setting Sun, 1956; Five Modern No Plays, 1957; No Longer Human, 1958; Major Plays of Chikamatsu, 1961; The Old Woman, the Wife and the Archer, 1961; After the Banquet, 1965; Essays in Idleness, 1967; Madame de Sade, 1967; Friends, 1969; The Man Who Turned into a Stick, 1972; Three Plays by Kobo Abe, 1993; The Narrow Road of Oku, 1996; The Tale of the Bamboo Cutter, 1998; The Breaking Jewel. **Address:** 407 Kent Hall, Columbia University, New York, NY 10027, U.S.A.

KEENE, John (R.), (Jr.). American, b. 1965. **Genres:** Novels, Poetry. **Career:** University of Virginia, lecturer, managing editor of Callaloo, and member of board of directors, Global Studies for Teachers Program, all 1993-95; New York Times, fellow, 1995-96; NYU Wagner School, lecturer, 1997-2001; Northwestern University, assistant professor, 2002-. **Publications:** Annotations (novel), 1995; Seisuosis (cross-genre),2 003. Work represented in anthologies. Contributor of poems, essays, reviews, and stories to magazines and newspapers.

KEENE, Raymond D(ennis). British, b. 1948. **Genres:** Recreation, Sports/Fitness. **Career:** International Grandmaster in chess, 1976-; freelance author, c. 1968-; chess correspondent, Spectator, London, 1977, Times, London, 1985, and Sunday Times, 1997; Hardinge/Simpole Publishing, co-founder, 2001. OBE, 1985. **Publications:** NONFICTION: (as R.D. Keene) Flank Openings, 1967, rev. ed., 1970; (with L. Barden and W. Hartston) The King's Indian Defence, 1969, rev. ed., 1973; Yugoslav Attack, Dragon Variation, Sicilian Defence, 1969; (with D.N. Levy) Siegen Chess Olympiad, September 5th to September 26th 1970, c. 1970; (with G.S. Botterill) The Modern Defence, 1972; (with Levy) Chess Olympiad, 1972; (with Botterill) The Pirc Defence, 1973; Aron Nimzowitsch, 1974; (with W.G. Raines and A.K. Crombleholme) The European Team Championship, 1973; (with W.R. Hartston) Karpov-Korchnoi 1974, 1974; (with Levy) How to Play the Opening in Chess, 1974; (ed with R. Edwards) The Chess Player's Bedside Book, 1975; (ed.) Learn from the Grandmasters, 1975; Beginner's Guide to Chess, 1975; (with Levy) Chess Olympiad Nice 1974: World Team Championship, 1975; Leonid Stein: Master of Attack, 1976; (ed. with R.G. Wade and K.J. O'Connel) A. Suetin, A Contemporary Approach to the Middle Game, 1976; How to Play the King's Indian, Saemisch Variation, 1976; (with Levy) An Opening Repertoire for the Attacking Club Player, 1976, in US as An Opening Repertoire for the Attacking Player, 1977; (with Levy) Haifa Chess Olympiad, 1976, 1977; Nimzowitsch/Larsen Attack, 1977; Becoming a Grandmaster, 1977; The Chess Combination from Philidor to Karpov, 1977; Korchnoi vs. Spassky, 1978; World Chess Championship: Korchnoi vs. Karpov (in UK as Karpov-Korchnoi 1978), 1978; (with B. Ivkov and J. Kaplan) Nimzo-Indian Defence 1, 1979; (comp. with J.D.M. Nunn and R.G. Wade) 46th USSR Chess Championships, 1978, 1979; The Openings in Modern Theory and Practice, 1979; (with others) Caro-Kann Defence, 1980; (with S. Taulbut) French Defence: Tarrasch Variation, 1980; (with M. Chandler and L. Barden) English Chess Explosion: From Miles to Short, 1981; KarpovKorchnoi: Massacre in Merano, 1981; How to Play the Nimzo-Indian, 1982; (with G. Kasparov) Batsford Chess Openings, 1982; Dynamic Chess Openings, 1982; (with A. Whiteley) Ray Keene's Good Move Guide, 1982; London 1927, 1983; (with D. Goodman and R. Wade) USSR v Rest of the World Challenge Match, 1984; An Opening Repertoire for White, 1984, new ed. with B. Jacobs, 1995; The Evolution of Chess Opening Theory, 1985; (with Goodman) Maneuvers in Moscow: Karpov-Kasparov II, 1985; (ed. with B. Kazic and L.K. Ann) The Official Laws of Chess, 1985; (with R.G. Wade and A.J. Whiteley) The World Chess Championship: Botvinnik to Kasparov, 1986; (with Goodman) The Centenary Match Kasparov-Karpov III, 1986; Speed Chess Challenge Kasparov v Short: 1987, 1987; (with J. Plaskett and J. Tisdall) The English Defence, 1987; (with Taulbut) How to Play the Caro-Kann Defense, 1988; (with Goodman and D. Spanier) Showdown in Seville: Kasparov-Karpov IV, 1988; Kingfisher Pocket Book of Chess, 1988; The Simon & Schuster Pocket Book of Chess (juvenile), c. 1988; (with Kasparov) Batsford Chess Openings 2, 1989; (with N. Divinsky) Warriors of the Mind, 1989; Chess: An Illustrated History, 1990; Battle of the Titans: Kasparov-Karpov, 1991; Duels of the Mind, 1991; How to Beat Gary Kasparov, 1991; Winning Moves, 1991; Fischer-Spassky II, 1992; Discover Your Chess Strength, 1992; (with J. Speelman) Essential Chess Openings, 1992; (with Kasparov) Kasparov on the King's Indian, 1993; Gary Kasparov's Best Games, 1993; Nigel Short, 1993; Nigel Short's Best Games, 1993; Chess for Absolute Beginners, 1993; The Complete Book of Gambits, 1993; Kasparov v. Short 1993, 1993; (with E. Schiller) Winning with the Hypermodern, 1994; The Young Pretenders, 1994; (with T. Buzan) Buzan's Book of Genius, 1994; How to Win at Chess, 1995; (with Buzan) The Age Heresy, 1996; (with M. Gelb) Samurai Chess, 1997; (with Buzan) Buzan's Book of Mental World Records, 1997; Brain Games World Championship, 2000. **Address:** 86 Clapham Common North Side, London SW4 9SE, England. **Online address:** rdkobe@aol.com

KEENS-DOUGLAS, Richardo. West Indian (born Grenada), b. 1953. **Genres:** Plays/Screenplays. **Career:** Actor, writer, and storyteller. Member, Stratford Shakespearean Festival, 1978. Host, Cloud 9, CBC-Radio. Teacher, Children's Theatre, 1974-77; storyteller, performing throughout North America and overseas. **Publications:** The Obeah Man (musical), 1985; Caribbean Cindy (play), 1992; The Nutmeg Princess, 1992; La Diablesse and the Baby, 1994; Freedom Child of the Sea, 1995; Grandpa's Visit, 1996; The Trial of the Stone, 2000; The Nutmeg Princess (musical play), 2000. RADIO PLAYS: Once upon an Island; Tell a Tale. Contributor of short fiction to anthologies. **Address:** 10 Beaconsfield Ave. No. 4, Toronto, ON, Canada M6J 3H9. **Online address:** rkd38@hotmail.com

KEERY, James. British, b. 1958. **Genres:** Poetry. **Career:** High school English teacher in Wigan, England, 1980-86; Fred Longworth High School, Wigan, English teacher, 1986-95, head of English department, 1995-. Warrington District Council for the Protection of Rural England, chairperson, 1990-97. Gives readings from his works. **Publications:** That Stranger, the

Blues (poems), 1996; (ed.) Collected Poems of Burns Singer, 2001. Work represented in anthologies. Contributor of poems, articles, and reviews to books and periodicals. **Address:** 22 Chiltern Rd, Culcheth, Warrington, Cheshire WA3 4LL, England.

KEETER, (Charles) Scott. American, b. 1951. **Genres:** Politics/Government. **Career:** Union College, Schenectady, NY, visiting assistant professor of political science, 1978-79; Rutgers University, New Brunswick, NJ, assistant professor of political science, 1979-85; Virginia Commonwealth University, Richmond, assistant professor, 1986-88, associate professor, 1988-95, director of Survey Research Laboratory, 1988-91, professor of political science and head of Department of Political Science and Public Administration, 1995-. Served on University Committees; consultant. **Publications:** (with C. Zukin) Uninformed Choice: The Failure of the New Presidential Nominating System, 1983; (with M.X. Delli Carpini) What Americans Know about Politics and Why It Matters, 1996. Contributor to books on US elections. Contributor of articles and reviews to professional journals. Manuscript reviewer for periodicals and publishing companies. **Address:** Department of Political Science and Public Administration, Virginia Commonwealth University, Richmond, VA 23284, U.S.A. **Online address:** skeeter@vcu.edu

KEETON, Morris Teuton. American, b. 1917. **Genres:** Education, Philosophy. **Career:** Antioch College, Yellow Springs, OH, professor of philosophy and religion, 1956-77, vice president and provost, 1972-77; University of Maryland University College, College Park, director, Institute for Research on Adults in Higher Education, 1990-97, senior scholar, 1997-. American Association for Higher Education, president, 1972-73; Council for the Advancement of Experimental Learning, executive director, 1977-89, co-ed., CAEL Sourcebooks, 1978-83, president emeritus, 1990-. **Publications:** The Philosophy of Edmund Montgomery, 1950; Values Men Live By, 1960; Journey through a Wall, 1964; (with H. Titus) Ethics for Today, 4th ed., 1966, 5th ed., 1973; (with C. Hilberry) Struggle and Promise: Future for Colleges, 1969; Models and Mavericks: A Profile of Private Liberal Arts Colleges, 1971; Shared Authority on Campus, 1971; (co-author and ed.) Experiential Learning: Rationale, Characteristics, Assessment, 1977; (co-author and ed.) Learning by Experience: Who, What, How?, 1978; (co-author and co-ed.) Defining and Assuring Quality in Experiential Education, 1980; Employability in a High Performance Economy, Cael, 1993; (vol. ed.) Perspectives on Experiential Learning, 1994; (with B.G. Sheckley) Improving Employee Development, 1997; (with J. Griggs and B.G. Sheckley) Effectiveness and Efficiency in Higher Education for Adults, 2002. **Address:** 10989 Swansfield Rd, Columbia, MD 21044, U.S.A. **Online address:** mkeeton@atlantis.umuc.edu

KEFALA, Antigone. Australian (born Romania), b. 1935. **Genres:** Novels, Novellas/Short stories, Poetry. **Career:** Writer. New South Wales Department of Education, Sydney, teacher of English, 1961-68; University of New South Wales, administrative assistant, 1968-69; Australia Council for the Arts, Sydney, arts administrator, 1971-87. **Publications:** POETRY: The Alien, 1973; Thirsty Weather, 1978; European Notebook, 1988; Absence: New and Selected Poems, 1992, 2nd ed., 1998; Nepritomnost-Absence, 1998; Poems, 2000. NOVELS: The First Journey, 1975; The Island, 1984. OTHER: Alexia: A Tale of Two Cultures (for children), 1984; Summer Visit (novellas), 2002. **Address:** 12 Rose St., Annandale, NSW 2038, Australia.

KEGAN, Robert G. American, b. 1946. **Genres:** Philosophy. **Career:** Junior and senior high school teacher in St. Paul, MN, 1968-71; Harvard University, Cambridge, MA, instructor, 1975-76, lecturer, 1977-90, senior lecturer, 1990-98, professor of education, 1998-, William and Miriam Meehan Professor of Adult Learning and Professional Development, 2000-, senior counselor at Bureau of Study Counsel, 1976-79, Spencer research fellow, 1982-83, educational chair of Institute for Management and Leadership in Education, 1983-, codirector of Harvard-Macy Institute for the Reform of Medical Education, 1994-, codirector of Change Leadership Group, 2000-. Emmanuel College, visiting faculty member, 1972-77; Massachusetts School of Professional Psychology, member of teaching faculty, 1977-99; guest lecturer at other colleges and universities; workshop participant. **Publications:** The Sweeter Welcome, Voices for a Vision of Affirmation: Malamud, Bellow, and Martin Buber, 1976; The Evolving Self: Problem and Process in Human Development, 1982; In over Our Heads: The Mental Demands of Modern Life, 1994; (with L. Lahey) How the Way We Talk Can Change the Way We Work: Seven Languages for Transformation, 2001. Contributor to books. **Address:** Graduate School of Education, Harvard University, Cambridge, MA 02138, U.S.A. **Online address:** robert_kegan@gse.harvard.edu

KEHDE, Ned. American, b. 1940. **Genres:** Recreation, Politics/Government. **Career:** Free-lance writer, 1967-. University of Kansas, archivist, 1970-.

Publications: The American Left, 1955-1970, 1976. EDITOR: Dictionary of Contemporary Quotations, 1978; Index to "The Sporting News," 1992. Contributor to periodicals. **Address:** 1636 Learnard, Lawrence, KS 66044, U.S.A.

KEHLER, Dorothea. American, b. 1936. **Genres:** Literary criticism and history. **Career:** MacMurray College, Jacksonville, IL, instructor in English literature, 1964-65; Ohio University, Athens, lecturer, 1966-68; San Diego State University, CA, lecturer to professor of English literature, 1969-, now emerita. **Publications:** Problems in Literary Research: A Guide to Selected Reference 1975, 4th ed., 1997. EDITOR & CONTRIBUTOR: (with S. Baker) In Another Country: Feminist Perspectives on Renaissance Drama, 1991; A Midsummer Night's Dream: Critical Essays, 1998; (with L. Amtower) The Single Woman in Medieval and Early Modern England, 2003. Contributor to books. Contributor of articles and reviews to academic journals. **Address:** Dept of English and Comparative Literature, San Diego State University, San Diego, CA 92182-8140, U.S.A. **Online address:** dorothea_kehler@hotmail.com

KEIL, Charles. American, b. 1939. **Genres:** Poetry, Anthropology/Ethnology, Cultural/Ethnic topics, Education, Music, Sociology, Urban studies. **Career:** State University of New York at Buffalo, assistant professor, 1970-71, associate professor, 1971-83, professor of American studies, 1983-2000. Central Community School, co-founder, 1970; Trent University, visiting lecturer, 1982 and 1983; WBFO, cohost of The Beautiful River: A Green Variety Hour, 1989-91; Musicians United for Superior Education, Inc., president, 1990-99. **Publications:** Urban Blues, 1966, rev. ed., 1992; Tiv Song, 1979; (with A. Keil and R. Blau) Polka Happiness, 1992; (ed. with S. Crafts and D. Cavicchi) My Music, 1993; (with S. Feld) Music Grooves, 1994; (with A. Keil, R. Blau, and S. Feld) Bright Balkan Morning, 2002. **Address:** 22 Wells Hill Rd, Lakeville, CT 06039, U.S.A. **Online address:** musekids.org; 128path.org

KEILER, Allan Ronald. American, b. 1938. **Genres:** Music, Bibliography. **Career:** University of Michigan, Ann Arbor, MI, instructor, 1962-63, assistant professor of linguistics, 1963-66, associate professor of linguistics, 1967-73; psycholinguistics program chair, 1970-72; Association de Française de Linguistics, Appliquee, Grenoble, France, visiting lecturer, 1966; University of Washington, Seattle, WA, visiting assistant professor, 1966-67; University of Wisconsin, Madison, WI, visiting associate professor, summer 1971; Brandeis University, Waltham, MA, music professor. **Publications:** Marian Anderson: A Singer's Journey, 2000. **Address:** Brandeis University Music Department, Slosberg Hall MS051, 415 South St., Waltham, MA 02454, U.S.A. **Online address:** keiler@brandeis.edu

KEILLOR, Garrison (Edward). American, b. 1942. **Genres:** Novels, Novellas/Short stories, Humor/Satire. **Career:** Writer and host, A Prairie Home Companion radio show, 1974-87, 1993- (broadcast nationally from 1980); with American Radio Co., 1989-93; with Minnesota Public Radio, 1968-87. **Publications:** Happy to Be Here, 1982; Lake Wobegon Days, 1985; Leaving Home, 1987; We Are Still Married: Stories and Letters, 1989; WLT Radio Romance, 1991; The Book of Guys, 1993; Cat, You Better Come Home (for children), 1995; The Sandy Bottom Orchestra, 1996; The Old Man Who Loved Cheese, 1996; Wobegon Boy, 1997; Me, by Jimmy (Big Boy) Valente, as Told to Garrison Keillor, 1999; Lake Wobegon Summer 1956, 2001; Love Me, 2003. **Address:** Prairie Home Productions, 611 Frontenac Pl, St. Paul, MN 55104, U.S.A.

KEILLOR, Steven J(ames). American, b. 1948. **Genres:** History. **Career:** Writer, 1983-; Iowa State University, Ames, visiting assistant professor of history, 1996. Bethel College, St. Paul, adjunct professor of history; Minnesota Historical Society, consultant for Political Campaign Exhibit, 1994. Author of an independent study course for University of Minnesota. **Publications:** Hjalmar Petersen of Minnesota: The Politics of Provincial Independence, 1987; Prisoners of Hope: Sundry Sunday Essays, 1992; (with M. Gieske) Norwegian Yankee: Knute Nelson and the Failure of American Politics, 1860-1923, 1995; This Rebellious House: American History and the Truth of Christianity, 1996; Cooperative Commonwealth, 2000; Erik Ramstad and the Empire Builder, 2002; "A Splendid Affair": The Grand Excursion of 1854, 2004. EDITOR: No More Gallant a Deed, 2001. Contributor to history journals. **Address:** 34280 Degerstrom Rd, Askov, MN 55704, U.S.A.

KEIN, Sybil. (Consuela Provost). American, b. 1939. **Genres:** Plays/Screenplays, Poetry. **Career:** Educator, poet, dramatist, musician, lecturer, and performer specializing in Creole arts and culture; frequently gives poetry readings, musical performances, and lectures. Louisiana State University, New Orleans, LA, instructor in public speaking, 1970-72; Upward Bound,

New Orleans, LA, instructor in communications skills, 1971; University of Michigan at Flint, instructor in English and theater, 1972-75, assistant professor, 1975-78, associate professor, 1979-88, professor of English, 1988-. Children's Theater Touring Company, director, 1972-74; Consultant to Mc-Cree Theater, Flint, 1976-79; United Teachers of Flint, 1976-79; Pre-Congress Session on the Arts, Michigan Council for the Arts, 1978; and National Council of English, 1978-80. Consultant for PBS documentary film Storyville, 1993-94, and the documentary film Spirit Tides from Congo Square; producer and video-camera operator, Excerpts from the Jazz Funeral of James Black, 1988. Also musician; records, with brother, Charles Moore. **Publications:** PLAYS: Saints and Flowers, 1965; Projection One and The Black Box, 1967; The Christmas Holly, 1967; Deep River Rises, 1970; The Reverend, 1970; Get Together, 1970; When I Grow Up, 1973-74; Rouges Along the River Flint, 1977, revised as River Rouges, 1979. OTHER: Visions from the Rainbow, 1979; Gombo People: Poesies Creole de la Nouvelle Orleans (poetry in Creole and English), 1981; Delta Dancer, 1984; An American South (poetry), 1997. Contributor of poetry and essays to anthologies. Contributor of poems, articles, and book reviews to journals. **Address:** English Department, 326 French Hall, University of Michigan - Flint, 303 E. Kearsley St., Flint, MI 48502, U.S.A. **Online address:** sybkein@aol.com

KEITH, Caroline H(elen). American, b. 1940. **Genres:** Biography, Novellas/Short stories, Autobiography/Memoirs. **Career:** Richter McBride Productions Inc., NYC, researcher and writer, 1968-69; University of Maryland at College Park, editor, 1977-79; researcher for U.S. Senator Jacob K. Javits, Washington, DC, 1980; free-lance writer, 1980-. University of Maryland at College Park, speechwriter and author of editorials, 1988-89; Semmes & Semmes, legal researcher and preparer of legal briefs. **Publications:** "For Hell and a Brown Mule": The Biography of Senator Millard E. Tydings, 1991. Short fiction and memoirs represented in anthologies and literary journals. **Address:** 4816 Broad Brook Dr., Bethesda, MD 20814, U.S.A.

KEITH, Julie (Houghton). American/Canadian, b. 1940. **Genres:** Novellas/Short stories. **Career:** Writer. **Publications:** The Jaguar Temple and Other Stories, 1994; The Devil Out There (novella and stories), 2000. Work represented in anthologies. Contributor of stories to periodicals. **Address:** c/o Knopf Canada Ltd, 1 Toronto St, Toronto, ON, Canada M5C 2V6.

KEITH, William H(enry), Jr. American, b. 1950. **Genres:** Novels, Science fiction/Fantasy. **Career:** Writer. Designer of Games; worked as a lecturer and illustrator; science fiction paintings regularly exhibited at Confluence (a science fiction convention), Pittsburgh, PA. **Publications:** NOVELS: Renegades Honor, 1988; (with P. Jurasik) Diplomatic Act, 1997. Contributor to books. DOCTOR WHO SERIES: Doctor Who and the Rebel's Gamble, 1986; Doctor Who and the Vortex Crystal, 1986. BATTLETECH SERIES: Decision at Thunder Rift, 1986; Mercenary's Star, 1987; The Price of Glory, 1987; Tactics of Duty, 1995; Operation Excalibur, 1996. INVADERS OF CHARON SERIES: Nomads of the Sky, 1992; Warlords of Jupiter, 1993. SHARUG/STINGRAY SERIES: Sharuq, 1993; Stingray, 1994. WARSTRIDER SERIES: Rebellion, 1993; Warstrider, 1993; Jackers, 1994; Netlink, 1995; Symbionts, 1995; Battlemind, 1996. BOLO SERIES: Bolo Brigade, 1997; Bolo Rising, 1998. CD-ROM GAME GUIDES (with N. Barton): Spycraft: The Great Game, 1996; Titanic: Adventure out of Time, 1996; Toonstruck, 1996; Fallout, 1997; Lands of Lore: Guardians of Destiny, 1997; Riven, 1997. AS KEITH WILLIAM ANDREWS (with J.A. Keith): FREEDOM'S RANGERS SERIES: Freedom's Rangers, 1989; Raiders of the Revolution, 1989; Search and Destroy, 1990; Sink the Armada!, 1990; Treason in Time, 1990; Snow Kill, 1991. AS ROBERT CAIN: CYBERNARC SERIES: Cybernarc, 1991; Gold Dragon, 1991; Capo's Revenge, 1992; Island Kill, 1992; End Game, 1993; Shark Bait, 1993. AS IAN DOUGLAS: HERITAGE SERIES: Semper Mars, 1998; The Gray Shores of Luna, 1999. AS KEITH DOUGLASS. CARRIER SERIES: Carrier, 1991; Viper Strike, 1991; Armageddon Mode, 1992; Flame-Out, 1992; Maelstrom, 1993; Countdown, 1994; Afterburn, 1996. SEAL TEAM SEVEN SERIES: SEAL Team Seven, 1994; Nucflash, 1995; Specter, 1995. AS H. JAY RIKER. SEAL, THE WARRIOR BREED SERIES: Silver Star, 1993; Purple Heart, 1994; Bronze Star, 1995; Navy Cross, 1996; Medal of Honor, 1997; Marks of Valor, 1998; In Harm's Way, 1999. Also published under the name Bill Keith. **Address:** c/o Baen Books, PO Box 1403, Riverdale, NY 10471, U.S.A. **Online address:** whkeith@sgi.net

KELBAUGH, Gretchen. Canadian/American, b. 1956. **Genres:** Children's fiction, Plays/Screenplays, Biography. **Career:** High school science teacher in Quispamsis, NB, 1980-87; filmmaker, free-lance writer, 1987-. **Publications:** With All Her Might: The Life of Gertrude Harding, Militant Suffragette, 1998; Lollipopsicles (children's poetry), 2000; Can You Catch It Like a Cold?: A Story to Help Children Understand a Parent's Depression, 2002. **Address:** 277 Model Farm Rd, Quispamsis, NB, Canada E2E 4Z8. **Online address:** gretchk@rogers.com; www.storyfirstproductions.ca

KELEMEN, Julie. American, b. 1959. **Genres:** Theology/Religion, Children's non-fiction. **Career:** Central Institute for the Deaf, St. Louis, MO, technical writer/editor, 1986-87; Liguori Publications, Liguori, MO, associate editor, book and pamphlet department, 1987-90, associate editor, Parish Education Products, 1990-93. Adjunct English instructor at St. Louis Community College, St. Louis, and St. Charles County Community College, St. Peters, MO, 1993-95; Copy editor, Suburban Journals, St. Louis, MO, 1997-2003. **Publications:** Lent Is for Children, 1987; Advent Is for Children, 1988; Prayer Is for Children, 1992, rev. ed. as Learning to Pray: A Guide for Young People. **Address:** Meggers Hall, University of Wisconsin-Barron County, 1800 College Dr, Rice Lake, WI 54868-2497, U.S.A. **Online address:** jkelemen@uwc.edu

KELL, Richard (Alexander). Irish, b. 1927. **Genres:** Poetry. **Career:** Assistant Librarian, Luton Public Library, Beds., 1954-56, and Brunel College of Technology (now Brunel University), Uxbridge, Middx., 1956-59; Assistant Lecturer, 1960-65, and Lecturer in English, 1966-70, Isleworth Polytechnic, London; Sr. Lecturer, Newcastle upon Tyne Polytechnic, 1970-83. **Publications:** (Poems), 1957; Control Tower, 1962; (with others) Six Irish Poets, 1962; Differences, 1969; Heartwood, 1978; Humours, 1978; The Broken Circle, 1981; In Praise of Warmth, 1987; (with others) Five Irish Poets, 1990; Rock and Water, 1993; Collected Poems, 2001; Under the Rainbow, 2003. **Address:** 18 Rectory Grove, Gosforth, Newcastle upon Tyne NE3 1AL, England.

KELLEHER, Victor (Michael Kitchener). Also writes as Veronica Hart. Australian/British, b. 1939. **Genres:** Novels, Children's fiction, Young adult fiction, Novellas/Short stories, Horror. **Career:** Jr. Lecturer in English, University of Witwatersrand, 1969; Lecturer then Sr. Lecturer in English, University of South Africa, 1970-73; Lecturer in English, Massey University, Palmerstown North, New Zealand, 1973-76; Sr. Lecturer, 1976-83, and Associate Professor of English, University of New England, Armidale, New South Wales, 1984-87; full-time writer, currently. **Publications:** YOUNG ADULT FICTION: Forbidden Paths of Thual, 1979; The Hunting of Shadroth, 1981; Master of the Grove, 1982; Papio, 1984; The Green Piper, 1984; Taronga, 1986; The Makers, 1987; Baily's Bones, 1988; The Red King, 1989; Brother Night, 1990; Del-Del, 1991; To the Dark Tower, 1992; Where the Whales Sing, 1994; Parkland, 1994; Earthsong, 1995; Fire Dancer, 1996; Slow Burn, 1997; The Ivory Trail, 1999; Beyond the Dusk, 2000. NOVELS: Voices from the River, 1979; The Beast of Heaven, 1984; EM's Story, 1988; Wintering, 1990; Micky Darlin', 1992; Into the Dark, 1998. HORROR: Double God, 1994; The House That Jack Built, 1994; Storyman, 1996. OTHER: Africa and After (short stories), 1983, as The Traveller, 1987; Johnny Wombat (children's fiction), 1996; Collected Stories, 2000. **Address:** c/o Margaret Connolly, PO Box 945, Wahroonga, NSW 2076, Australia.

KELLENBERGER, James. American, b. 1938. **Genres:** Philosophy. **Career:** Cameroon College of Arts and Science, lecturer in logic, 1962-64; California State University, Northridge, assistant professor, 1967-71, associate professor, 1971-75, professor of philosophy, 1975-. Albion College, visiting professor, 1971-72; Claremont Graduate School, adjunct professor of religion, 1991; speaker at colleges and universities. **Publications:** Religious Discovery, Faith, and Knowledge, 1972; The Cognitivity of Religion: Three Perspectives, 1985; God-Relationships with and without God, 1989; (ed.) Inter-Religious Models and Criteria, 1993; Relationship Morality, 1995; Kierkegaard and Nietzsche: Faith and Eternal Acceptance, 1997; Moral Relativism, Moral Diversity, and Human Relationships, 2001. Contributor to books. Contributor of articles and reviews to journals. **Address:** Department of Philosophy, California State University, Northridge, CA 91330, U.S.A.

KELLER, Debra. American, b. 1958. **Genres:** Children's fiction. **Career:** Advertising copywriter in Los Angeles and San Francisco, CA, 1983-90; freelance copywriter, Sacramento, CA, 1990-. **Publications:** The Trouble with Mister, 1995.

KELLER, Edward B. (born United States), b. 1955. **Genres:** Marketing. **Career:** Yankelovich, Skelly & White, Inc., New York, NY, research associate, 1979-80, senior associate, 1980-82, vice president, 1982-86; Roper ASW, New York, NY, chief executive officer, 1986-. Member of advisory board, Annenberg School. **Publications:** (with Jon Berry) The Influentials, 2003. Contributor of articles to professional journals, magazines, and newspapers. **Address:** 300 W. 23rd St., New York, NY 10011, U.S.A. **Online address:** ekeller@roper.com

KELLER, Emily. American. **Genres:** Biography. **Career:** Math Association of America, started as editorial assistant, became chief copyeditor, 1977-84; high school English teacher, Buffalo and Niagara Falls, NY, 1960-90; Erie County Community College, Buffalo, instructor, 1989-91; Niagara County Community College, Niagara Falls, NY, writing instructor, 1990-91. **Publications:** Margaret Bourke-White: A Photographer's Life, 1996. Work represented in anthologies; poems published in journals. **Address:** 9354 Rivershore Dr., Niagara Falls, NY 14304, U.S.A.

KELLER, Joe. American, b. 1963. **Genres:** Antiques/Furnishings, Art/Art history. **Career:** Writer. **Publications:** all with D. Ross: Jadite: An Identification and Price Guide, 1999, 3rd ed, 2003; Russel Wright: Dinnerware, Pottery, and More: An Identification and Price Guide, 2000; Delphite and Jadite: A Pocket Guide, 2002; Fire-King: An Information and Price Guide, 2002. **Address:** PO Box 783, Melrose, MA 02176, U.S.A. **Online address:** JK3434@aol.com

KELLER, Laurent. Swiss, b. 1961. **Genres:** Zoology. **Career:** University of Lausanne, Lausanne, Switzerland, research assistant in zoology, 1983-85; University Paul-Sabatier, Toulouse, France, research associate in entomology, 1985-87; University of Lausanne, fellow in zoology, 1987-89, postdoctoral research associate, 1989-90; Harvard University, Cambridge, MA, research fellow at Museum of Comparative Zoology, 1990-92; University of Lausanne, fellow of Swiss Talents for Academic Research and Teaching (START), 1992-. University of Bern, START fellow, 1992-. **Publications:** (ed.) Queen Number and Sociality in Insects, 1993. **Address:** Institut de Zoologie et d'Ecologie Animale, University of Lausanne, 1015 Lausanne, Switzerland.

KELLER, Marian Jean. American, b. 1953. **Genres:** Education, Gerontology/Senior issues, Recreation. **Career:** Florida State University, Tallahassee, program administrator, 1975-78; Indiana University-Bloomington, visiting lecturer, 1978-79; University of Georgia, Athens, public service assistant & project director at Gerontology Center, 1979-84, public service associate of Institute of Community and Area Development and adjunct associate professor, 1984-89, acting department head, 1987-89; University of North Texas, Denton, associate professor, 1989-92, professor of recreation and leisure studies, 1992-, associate dean of academic affairs, 1993-97, dean of College of Education, 1997-. Grayson Community College, instructor, 1989-93; workshop presenter. Certified therapeutic recreation specialist; guest on media programs; consultant. **Publications:** Planning Social Group Activities for Older Adults, 1981; (with others) Helping Older Adults Develop Active Leisure Lifestyles, 1987; Activity Programming in Long-Term Health Care Facilities, 1989; (with B. Wilshite) Therapeutic Recreation, 1992, 2nd ed., 2000. EDITOR: Leisure Activities, 1985; Leisure Programming with Senior Citizens, 1985; (with N.J. Osgood) Dynamic Leisure Programming with Older Adults, 1987; Activities with Developmentally Disabled Elderly and Older Adults, 1991; Caregiving-Leisure and Aging, 1999. Contributor to books. Contributor of articles and reviews to professional journals. **Address:** Dean's Office 214 Matthews Hall, College of Education, University of North Texas, PO Box 311337, Denton, TX 76203-1337, U.S.A. **Online address:** JKeller@unt.edu

KELLER, William W(alton). American, b. 1950. **Genres:** International relations/Current affairs. **Career:** Congressional Office of Technology Assessment, analyst. **Publications:** The Liberals and J. Edgar Hoover: Rise and Fall of a Domestic Intelligence State, 1989; Arm in Arm: The Political Economy of the Global Arms Trade, 1995; (with P.N. Duremus, L.W. Pauly, and S. Reich) The Myth of the Global Corporation, 1999; (with R.J. Samuels) Crisis and Innovation in Asian Technology, 2002. **Address:** c/o Author Mail, Cambridge University Press, 40 West 20th St., New York, NY 10011, U.S.A.

KELLERMAN, Jonathan. American, b. 1949. **Genres:** Mystery/Crime/Suspense, Psychology. **Career:** Freelance illustrator, 1966-72; Children's Hospital of Los Angeles, staff psychologist, 1975-81, director, Psychosocial Program, 1976-81; University of Southern California School of Medicine, Los Angeles, assistant clinical professor, 1978-79, clinical associate professor, 1979-97, clinical professor, 1998-; Jonathan Kellerman Ph.D. and Assocs., Los Angeles, Head, 1981-88. Recipient: Mystery Writers of America Edgar Allan Poe Award, 1985; Anthony Boucher Award, 1986. **Publications:** Psychological Aspects of Childhood Cancer, 1980; Helping the Fearful Child: A Parent's Guide to Everyday and Problem Anxieties, 1981; When the Bough Breaks, 1985; Blood Test, 1986; Over the Edge, 1987; The Butcher's Theatre, 1988; Silent Partner, 1989; Time Bomb, 1990; Private Eyes, 1992; Devil's Waltz, 1993; Bad Love, 1994; Daddy, Daddy, Can You Touch the Sky?, 1994; Self-Defense, 1995; The Clinic, 1996; Survival of the Fittest, 1997; Billy Straight, 1998; Jonathan Kellerman's ABC of Weird Creatures,

1995; Billy Straight, 1998; Monster, 1999; Savage Spawn: Reflections on Violent Children, 1999; Dr. Death, 2000; A Cold Heart, 2003; The Conspiracy Club, 2004. **Address:** c/o Karpfinger Agency, 357 W 20th St, New York, NY 10011-3379, U.S.A.

KELLERT, Stephen R. American, b. 1944. **Genres:** Ethics. **Career:** Yale University, New Haven, CT, assistant professor, associate professor, professor, 1972-. **Publications:** Ecology, Economics, Ethics, 1991; The Value of Life, 1995; (coauthor) The Biophilia Hypothesis; Kinship to Mastery, 1997; (with T. Farnham) The Good in Nature and Humanity, 2002; (with P. Kahn) Children and Nature, 2002. **Address:** 205 Prospect St, New Haven, CT 06511, U.S.A.

KELLETT, Arnold. British, b. 1926. **Genres:** Poetry, History, Language/Linguistics, Theology/Religion, Travel/Exploration, Translations. **Career:** Mayor of Knaresborough, 1979-80, 1984-85; Honorary Citizen, 1996; Freeman of Knaresborough, 2001; Former Head of Modern Languages Dept., King James's School, Knaresborough, N. Yorks; Vice President of Yorkshire Dialect Society; writer, Dalesman magazine, 1994-. **Publications:** Isms and Ologies, 1965; (ed.) Maupassant: Contes du Surnaturel, 1969; (trans. and ed.) Tales of Supernatural Terror, 1972; The Knaresborough Story, 1972, rev. ed., 1990; Heros de France, 1973; (trans. and ed.) The Diary of a Madman and Other Tales of Horror, 1975; French for Science Students, 1975; Basic French, 1977; The Queen's Church, 1978; Know Your Yorkshire, 1980; Countryside Walks in the Harrogate District, 1983; Knaresborough in Old Picture Postcards, 1984; Exploring Knaresborough, 1985; Kellett's Christmas (poetry), 1988, rev. ed., 1998; The Dark Side of Maupassant, 1989; Historic Knaresborough, 1991; Basic Broad Yorkshire, 1991; The Yorkshire Dictionary, 1994, rev. ed., 2002; Knaresborough: Archive Photographs, 1995, rev. ed., 2003; Ee by Gum, Lord! (Yorkshire dialect gospels), 1996; On Ilkla Mooar baht 'at: The Story of the Song, 1998; Mother Shipton: Witch and Prophetess, 2002; King James's School, Knaresborough (1616-2003), 2003. **Address:** 22 Aspin Oval, Knaresborough, N. Yorkshire, England.

KELLEY, Alec E(rvin). American, b. 1923. **Genres:** Novellas/Short stories, Poetry, Autobiography/Memoirs, Translations. **Career:** Manhattan Project, Chicago, IL, chemist, 1944-46; University of Arizona, Tucson, assistant professor to professor of chemistry, 1952-86, professor emeritus, 1987-. Wesleyan University, Middletown, CT, professor, summers, 1967-68; Pennsylvania State University, Delaware County Campus, Media, professor, 1993. W.M. Symposia Inc., member of board of directors, 1992-99. Hospitality International (Tucson), member of board of directors, 1970-85; Humanist Community of Tucson, member of board of directors and "occasional president," 1958-92. **Publications:** (trans. with Alita Kelley) J. Promis, The Identity of Hispanoamerica, 1991; Take Me Away to Dreamland, 2001. **Address:** 154 Chandler Dr, West Chester, PA 19380-6805, U.S.A. **Online address:** kak7@psu.edu

KELLEY, (Kathleen) Alita. Also writes as C. A. de Lomellini. British, b. 1932. **Genres:** Poetry, Literary criticism and history, Translations. **Career:** Teacher of English as a second language in Lima, Peru, and Cuzco, Peru, 1962-68; teacher of English and French literature and civilization at schools in Lima, 1963-68; U.S. Embassy, Lima, teacher of Italian, 1967-68; Wiesman and Co., Tucson, AZ, commercial translator and office manager, 1969-92; Pennsylvania State University, Delaware County Campus, Media, assistant professor, 1992-98, associate professor of Spanish and French, 1998-. Hospitality International (Tucson), member of board of directors, 1970-85; Humanist Community of Tucson, program coordinator, 1970-92. **Publications:** (trans. with A.E. Kelley) Jose Promis, The Identity of Hispanoamerica, 1991; (trans.) C.M. Tatum, ed., New Chicana/Chicano Writing 2,s, 1992; (trans. with E. Grossman) Julio Ortega, Goodbye, Ayacucho and Moscow Gold (stories), 1994. AS C.A. DE LOMELLINI (POEMS): (trans.) J. Radcliffe, Lima Rooftops, 1978; Shared Images, 1981; Dreams of Samarkand , 1982; Ineffable Joys, 1983; Antimacassars, 1984; Target Practice, 1994; Northern Paranoia and Southern Comfort, 2003. Contributor of poems and articles on translation and Latin American literature to periodicals; translator of poems, short stories, and academic articles in journals, books, and anthologies. **Address:** Dept of Spanish and French, Pennsylvania State University Delaware County Campus, 25 Yearsley Mill Rd, Media, PA 19063, U.S.A. **Online address:** kak7@psu.edu

KELLEY, Douglas. American, b. 1957. **Genres:** Novels. **Career:** Novelist and corporate pilot. **Publications:** The Captain's Wife: A Novel, 2001. **Address:** c/o Author Mail, Dutton, 345 Hudson St., New York, NY 10014, U.S.A.

KELLING, Hans-Wilhelm. American (born Germany), b. 1932. **Genres:** History, Literary criticism and history, Translations. **Career:** Brigham Young University, Provo, UT, professor of Germanic languages, 1962-, chairman of dept., 1977-84, director of Foreign Language Housing and Summer Language Institute, 1985-. German South Mission, Church of Jesus Christ of Latter-day Saints, Munich, president, 1973-76; European Internship Program, director, 1986-, European Studies Program, director, 1992-. **Publications:** Deutsche Aufsatzhilfe, 1967; The Idolatry of Poetic Genius in German Goethe Criticism, 1970; Deutsch-Wie man's sagt und schreibt, 1972; Deutsche Kulturgeschichte, 1974, rev. ed., 2003; Avenues toward Christianity, 2001. TRANSLATOR: Mormon Doctrine, 1991; Kirchengeschichte, 1998. **Address:** German Dept, 4096 JKHB, Brigham Young University, Provo, UT 84602, U.S.A. **Online address:** hk@email.byu.edu

KELLNER, Bruce. American, b. 1930. **Genres:** Plays/Screenplays, Literary criticism and history, Bibliography, Biography. **Career:** Millersville University, PA, professor of English, 1969-91, emeritus professor, 1991-. Taught at Coe College, 1956-60, and Hartwick College, 1960-69. **Publications:** Carl Van Vechten and the Irreverent Decades, 1968; (comp.) A Bibliography of the Work of Carl Van Vechten, 1980; Friends and Mentors: Richmond's Carl Van Vechten and Mark Lutz, 1980; (with others) American Literature: Second Supplement to the University of Minnesota Monographs, 1981; The Harlem Renaissance: A Historical Dictionary for the Era, 1984, rev. ed., 1987; A Gertrude Stein Companion: Content with the Example, 1988; Donald Windham: A Bio-Bibliography, 1991; The Last Dandy: Ralph Barton, American Artist, 1991; Kiss Me Again: An Invitation to a Group of Noble Dames, 2002. PLAYS: Staying on Alone, 1998; Swimming on Concrete, 2000; Kiss Me Again, 2001. EDITOR: Keep a-Inchin' Along: Selected Writings about Black Arts and Letters, 1979; Letters of Carl Van Vechten, 1987; The Major Works of Gertrude Stein (16 vols.), 1993; Early Modern African American Writers, 1892-1922 (25 vols.), 1998; Letters of Charles Demuth, American Artist, 1883-1935; The Splendid Drunken Twenties: Selections from the Day Books, 1922-1930, of Carl Van Vechten, 2003. **Address:** 514 N School Ln, Lancaster, PA 17603, U.S.A. **Online address:** BruceKellnerB@aol.com

KELLOGG, Frederick. American, b. 1929. **Genres:** History. **Career:** Boise State University, Boise, ID, instructor, 1962-64, assistant professor, 1964-65, associate professor of history, 1966-67; University of Arizona, Tucson, instructor, 1967-68, assistant professor, 1969-71, associate professor of history, 1971-. University of Idaho, Moscow, visiting assistant professor, 1965. Idaho Historical Conference, founder, 1964; associated with the Idaho State Coordinating Committee in the National Coordinating Committee for the Promotion of History, 1983-. The Laws of Romania series, editor in chief; Southeastern Europe/L'Europe du sud-est, managing editor, 1974-. **Publications:** A History of Romanian Historical Writing (monograph), 1990; The Road to Romanian Independence, 1995; O istorie a istoriografiei romane, 1996; Drumul Romaniei spre independenta Iasi, 2002. Contributor to books. Contributor to history journals. **Address:** Dept of History, 215 Social Sciences Bldg, University of Arizona, Tucson, AZ 85721, U.S.A.

KELLOGG, Marjorie Bradley. American, b. 1946. **Genres:** Novels, Science fiction/Fantasy, Plays/Screenplays, Theatre. **Career:** Scenic designer for plays on and off-Broadway, regional theater productions, and films. Princeton University, visiting professor, 1983-84, 1985-86; Columbia University, adjunct professor, 1993-95; Colgate University, associate professor of design, 1995-. **Publications:** NOVELS: A Rumor of Angels, 1983; Lear's Daughters (science fiction), Vol. I: The Wave and the Flame, Vol. II: Reign of Fire, 1986; Harmony, 1991; The Book of Earth, 1995; The Book of Water, 1997; The Book of Fire, 2000; The Book of Air, 2003. OTHER: A Wrinkle in Time (stage adaptation), 1991; Livin' in the Garden (musical play), 1997. Contributor to magazines. **Address:** 205 Sanly Rd, Sidney Center, NY 13839, U.S.A. **Online address:** mkellogg@citlink.net

KELLOGG, Marne Davis. American, b. 1946. **Genres:** Mystery/Crime/Suspense. **Career:** People, assistant bureau chief in Colorado; Frontier Airlines, regional sales manager; Denver Center for the Performing Arts, Denver, CO, director of communications, 1976-78; The Kellogg Organization Inc., Denver, executive vice-president, 1981-. **Publications:** HUMOROUS MYSTERY NOVELS: Bad Manners, 1996; Curtsey, 1997; Tramp, 1998; Nothing But Gossip, 1999; Birthday Party, 2000; Insatiable, 2001. **Address:** The Kellogg Organization Inc., 825 E. Speer Blvd., Ste 100D, Denver, CO 80218, U.S.A.

KELLOGG, Steven. American, b. 1941. **Genres:** Children's fiction, Illustrations. **Publications:** SELF-ILLUSTRATED FOR CHILDREN: The Wicked Kings of Bloon, 1970; Can I Keep Him?, 1971; The Mystery Beast of Ostergeest, 1971; The Orchard Cat, 1972; Won't Somebody Play with Me?, 1972; The Island of the Skog, 1973; The Mystery of the Missing Red

Mitten, 1974, rev. ed. as The Missing Mitten Mystery, 2000; Much Bigger Than Martin, 1976; The Mysterious Tadpole, 1977; The Mystery of the Magic Green Ball, 1978; Pinkerton, Behave!, 1979; The Mystery of the Flying Orange Pumpkin, 1980; A Rose for Pinkerton, 1981; Tallyho, Pinkerton!, 1982; The Mystery of the Stolen Blue Paint, 1982; Ralph's Secret Weapon, 1983; Best Friends, 1986; Aster Aardvark's Alphabet Adventures, 1987; Prehistoric Pinkerton, 1987; The Christmas Witch, 1992; A Penguin Pup for Pinkerton, 2001; Millions to Measure, 2003; Clorinda, 2003; Santa Claus is Comin' to Town, 2004; Pinkerton and Friends: A Steven Kellogg Treasury, 2004. RETELLER: There Was an Old Woman, 1974; Paul Bunyan: A Tall Tale, 1984; Chicken Little, 1985; Pecos Bill, 1986; Johnny Appleseed, 1988; Jack and the Beanstalk, 1991; Mike Fink, 1992; Yankee Doodle, 1994; Sally Ann Thunder Ann Whirlwind Crockett: A Tall Tale, 1995; I Was Born about 10,000 Years Ago: A Tall Tale, 1996; The Three Little Pigs, 1997; A-Hunting We Will Go!, 1998; The Three Sillies, 1999; Give the Dog a Bone, 2000. Illustrator of books by others, including A. Brooks, A. Ehrlich, P. Glassman, R. Kinerk, R. Lindbergh, M. Mahy, B. Martin Jr., D.R. Massie, M. Mayer, G. Mendoza, T. Noble, P. Parish, T. Paxton, L. Robb, J. Ryder, D.M. Schwartz, J. Thurber, M. Twain, S. Williams. **Address:** c/o Author Mail, 7th Fl, HarperCollins Children's Books, 10 E 53rd St, New York, NY 10022, U.S.A. **Online address:** www.stevenkellogg.com

KELLY, Brian. American, b. 1954. **Genres:** Area studies, Documentaries/Reportage. **Career:** Georgetown Voice (college paper), Washington, DC, editor-in-chief, 197475; Daily Register (newspaper), Shrewsbury, NJ, reporter, 1975-76; Chicago Sun-Times, Chicago, reporter, 1976-84; freelance writer, 1984-; Regardies Business Magazine, Washington, editor, 1985; Washington Post, Washington, local editor of style section. Has given lectures and seminars in a variety of settings. **Publications:** NONFICTION: (with M. London) Amazon, 1983; (with London) The Four Little Dragons: Inside Korea, Taiwan, Hong Kong, and Singapore at the Dawn of the Pacific Century, 1989; Adventures in Porkland: How Washington Wastes Your Money and Why They Won't Stop, 1992. **Address:** c/o Raphael Sagalyn Agency, 7201 Wisconsin Ave, Ste 675, Bethesda, MD 20814-7213, U.S.A.

KELLY, Catriona (Helen Moncrieff). British, b. 1959. **Genres:** Literary criticism and history, Translations. **Career:** Oxford University, England, research fellow at Christ Church, 1987-93, university lecturer in Russian, 1996-, reader, 1997-2002, professor, 2002-; University of London, School of Slavonic and East European Studies, London, England, lecturer in Russian, 1993-96. **Publications:** Petrushka: The Russian Carnival Puppet Theatre, 1990; (trans.) E. Shvarts, Paradise, 1993; A History of Russian Women's Writing, 1820-1992, 1994. EDITOR: An Anthology of Russian Women's Writing, 1994; (ed. with D. Shepherd) Constructing Russian Culture in the Age of Revolution, 1998; An Introduction to Russian Cultural Studies, 1998; Utopias: Russian Modernist Texts 1905-1940, 1999; Russian Literature: A Very Short Introduction, 2001; Refining Russia: Advice Literature, Polite Culture, and Gender from Catherine to Yeltsin, 2001; Comrade Pavlik: The Rise and Fall of a Soviet Boy Hero, 2005. Translator of Russian works by L. Borodin, S. Kaledin, A. Prismanova, E. Shvarts, O. Sedakova, etc. Contributor of poems to periodicals. **Address:** New College, Oxford University, Oxford OX1 3BN, England.

KELLY, Chris. British, b. 1940. **Genres:** Novels. **Career:** Granada Television, Manchester, England, producer, 1965-70; Central Television, London, England, producer, 1989-92; Carlton Productions, London, producer, 1992-99; City Screen (Cambridge) Ltd, director, 1999-; United Productions, producer, 2000-01. **Publications:** NOVELS: The War of Covent Garden, 1989; The Forest of the Night, 1991; Taking Leave, 1995; A Suit of Lights, 2000. **Address:** 37 Camden Sq, London NW1 9XA, England.

KELLY, Clint. American, b. 1950. **Genres:** Novels, Inspirational/Motivational Literature. **Career:** Seattle Pacific University, Seattle, WA, communications specialist, 1988-. Writing instructor for Discover U and for writer's conferences; director of Seattle Pacific University Christian Writers Renewal; Presbyterian elder and teacher. **Publications:** FICTION: The Landing Place, 1993; The Lost Kingdom, 1994; The Aryan, 1995; Deliver Us from Evil, 1998; The Power and the Glory, 1999; Escape Underground (juvenile novel), 2001; Bruce the Spruce and the Christmas Goose (picture book). NONFICTION: The Fame Game: How You, Too, Can Become the Greatest, 1984; (with C. Bottemiller) The Everett Cartoon and Trivia Book, 1985; (with J.H. Hampsch) The Key to Inner Peace, 1985; Me Parent, You Kid! Taming the Family Zoo, 1993; How to Win Grins and Influence Little People, 1996; Dare to Raise Exceptional Children: Give Your Kids a Sense of Purpose, a Sense of Adventure, and a Sense of Humor, 2001. Contributor to anthologies and periodicals.

KELLY, Deirdre M. American/Canadian, b. 1959. **Genres:** Education, Sociology, Women's studies and issues. **Career:** High school music ap-

preciation teacher in Santa Clara, CA, 1988-89; University of British Columbia, Vancouver, associate professor of sociology of schooling, 1991-. **Publications:** Hard Work, Hard Choices: A Survey of Women in St. Lucia's Export-Oriented Electronics Factories, 1986; Last Chance High: How Girls and Boys Drop in and out of Alternative Schools, 1993; (co-ed.) Debating Dropouts, 1996; Pregnant with Meaning: Teen Mothers and the Politics of Inclusive Schooling, 2000. Work represented in anthologies. Contributor to periodicals. **Address:** Dept of Educational Studies, University of British Columbia, 2125 Main Mall, Vancouver, BC, Canada V6T 1Z4. **Online address:** dkelly@interchange.ubc.ca

KELLY, Fiona. See **JONES, Allan Frewin.**

KELLY, Fiona. See **OLDFIELD, Jenny.**

KELLY, Franklin (Wood). American, b. 1953. **Genres:** Art/Art history. **Career:** Virginia Museum of Fine Arts, Artmobile curator, 1975-76, curatorial assistant, 1976-77; Clark Art Institute, curatorial assistant, 1978-79; National Gallery of Art, Washington, DC, intern, 1980, Samuel H. Kress fellow at Center for Advanced Study in the Visual Arts, 1981-83, assistant curator of American art, 1985-87, curator of American art, 1987-88; curator of American and British paintings, 1990-; Minneapolis Institute of Arts, Minneapolis, MN, associate curator of paintings, 1983-85; Corcoran Gallery of Art, curator of collections, 1988-90. University of Delaware, lecturer, 1981; Rhodes College, Moss Lecturer, 1988; University of Maryland at College Park, visiting professor, 1990, adjunct associate professor, 1991-; Princeton University, visiting professor, 1991; University of Delaware, visiting scholar, 1995. Lecturer at colleges, universities, and museums. **Publications:** (with G.L. Carr) The Early Landscapes of Frederic Edwin Church, 1845-1854, 1987; Frederic Edwin Church and the National Landscape, 1988; (with J.A. Ryan, S.J. Gould, and D. Rindge) Frederic Edwin Church, 1989; (with M. Quick, J. Myers, and M. Doezema) The Paintings of George Bellows, 1992; (co-ed.) American Paintings from the Manoogian Collection, 1989; (co-author) Winslow Homer, 1995. Work represented in anthologies. Contributor to art journals. **Address:** Department of American and British Painting, National Gallery of Art, Washington, DC 20565, U.S.A.

KELLY, James Patrick. American, b. 1951. **Genres:** Science fiction/Fantasy. **Career:** Writer. **Publications:** Planet of Whispers, 1984; (with J. Kessel) Freedom Beach, 1985; Look into the Sun, 1989; Heroines, 1991; Wildlife, 1993; Think Like a Dinosaur, 1997; Strange, But Not a Stranger (stories), 2002. **Address:** c/o Ralph M. Vicinanza Ltd, 303 W 18th St, New York, NY 10011-4440, U.S.A. **Online address:** jim@jimkelly.net

KELLY, Joanne (W.). American, b. 1934. **Genres:** Librarianship, Bibliography. **Career:** Thomas Paine Elementary School, Urbana, IL, librarian, 1967; Urbana School District, Urbana, elementary librarian, 1968-92, coordinator of libraries, 1984-92. **Publications:** The Battle of Books, 1990; (with M. and K.V. Grabow) Rebuses for Readers, 1991; On Location: Settings from Famous Children's Books, 1992; Newbery Authors of the Eastern Seaboard: Integrating Social Studies and Literature, Grades 5-8, 1994. **Address:** 2110 Galen Dr., Champaign, IL 61821, U.S.A.

KELLY, Kevin (J.). American, b. 1952. **Genres:** Documentaries/Reportage. **Career:** Walking! Journal, Athens, GA, editor and publisher, 1982-84; Whole Earth Review, Sausalito, CA, editor and publisher, 1984-90; Wired, San Francisco, CA, executive editor, 1992-. **Publications:** (ed.) Signal: Communication Tools for the Information Age, 1988; Out of Control: The Rise of Neo-Biological Civilization, 1994; New Rules for the New Economy, 1998. Contributor to periodicals. **Address:** 149 Amapola Ave, Pacifica, CA 94044-3102, U.S.A.

KELLY, Lelia. American. **Genres:** Mystery/Crime/Suspense. **Career:** Writer; also worked in a banking job in Atlanta, GA. **Publications:** Presumption of Guilt, 1998; False Witness, 2000; Officer of the Court, 2001. **Address:** c/o Kensington Publishing Corp., 850 Third Ave., New York, NY 10022, U.S.A. **Online address:** leliakelly@mindspring.com

KELLY, Linda. British, b. 1936. **Genres:** Literary criticism and history, Theatre, Biography. **Career:** Vogue mag., travel editor, 1960-63. **Publications:** The Marvellous Boy: The Life and Myth of Thomas Chatterton, 1971; The Young Romantics: Paris 1827-1837, 1976; The Kemble Era: John Philip Kemble, Sarah Siddons and the London Stage, 1980; Women of the French Revolution, 1987; (ed. with Christopher Bland) Feasts, 1987; (with Laurence Kelly) Proposals, 1989; Juniper Hall, 1991; Richard Brinsley Sheridan: A Life, 1997; Susanna, the Captain and the Castrato, 2004. **Address:** 44 Ladbroke Grove, London W11 2PA, England.

KELLY, Louis Gerard. New Zealander/Canadian, b. 1935. **Genres:** Novellas/Short stories, Language/Linguistics, Literary criticism and history, Translations. **Career:** Professor of Linguistics and Classics, University of Ottawa, 1978-96 (Assistant Professor 1967-68; Associate Professor, 1969-78). Research Associate, Royal Commission on Bilingualism and Biculturalism 1965-67; former Lecturer in Phonetics and English, University Laval, Quebec. **Publications:** Twenty-Five Centuries of Language Teaching, 1969; The True Interpreter, 1979; Prorsus Taliter: The Latin Text of Kipling's Just-So Stories 1980; The Mirror of Grammar: Theology, Philosophy, and the Modistae, 2002. EDITOR: Descriptions and Measurement of Bilingualism, 1969; Basil Valentine: His Triumphant Chariot of Antimony, 1990; Michael de Marbasio, summa de Modis Significandi, 1995. **Address:** 306 Cherry Hinton Rd, Cambridge CB1 7AU, England.

KELLY, Maeve. Irish, b. 1930. **Genres:** Novels, Poetry, Humor/Satire. **Career:** Founder of shelter for victims of domestic violence, 1976; administrator of residential center for victims of domestic violence. **Publications:** A Life of Her Own, 1976; Necessary Treasons (novel), 1985; Resolution (poems), 1986; Florrie's Girls, 1989; Orange Horses, 1990; Alice in Thunderland. Works appear in anthologies.

KELLY, Richard. American, b. 1937. **Genres:** Literary criticism and history. **Career:** Lindsay Young Professor of English, University of Tennessee, Knoxville, 1974- (Assistant Professor, 1965-74). Instructor in English, University of North Carolina, Chapel Hill, 1964-65. Chairman of the 19-20th Century Section, 1976, and of the Advanced Composition Section, 1980, South Atlantic Modern Language Association. **Publications:** Douglas Jerrold, 1972; Lewis Carroll, 1977, 1990; George du Maurier, 1982; The Andy Griffith Show, 1982, 1984; Graham Greene, 1984; Daphne du Maurier, 1987; V.S. Naipaul, 1989; Graham Greene: A Study of the Short Fiction, 1992; The Carolina Watermen: Bug Hunters and Boatbuilders; The Art of George du Maurier, 1996. EDITOR: The Best of Mr. Punch: The Humorous Writings of Douglas Jerrold, 1970; (co-) Cartoons from 19th Century Punch, 1982; Alice's Adventures in Wonderland, 2000; A Christmas Carol, 2003. **Address:** Dept. of English, University of Tennessee, Knoxville, TN 37996, U.S.A. **Online address:** rmkelly2@att.net

KELLY, Robert. American, b. 1935. **Genres:** Novels, Poetry, Novellas/Short stories. **Career:** Director of the Writing Program, Milton Avery Graduate School, 1980-93; Asher B. Edelman Professor of Literature, Bard College, Annandale-on-Hudson, New York, since 1974 (Instructor in German, 1961-62; Instructor in English, 1962-64; Assistant Professor, 1964-69; Associate Professor, 1969-74). Director of the Writing Program, Milton Avery Graduate School 1980-1993 Ed., Matter mag. and Matter publishing co., NYC, later Annandale-on-Hudson, New York, since 1963. Ed., Chelsea Review, NYC, 1958-60; Founding Ed., Trobar mag., 1960-64, and Trobar Books, 1962-64; Contributor Ed., Caterpillar, NYC, 1969-73; Poet-in-Residence, California Institute of Technology, Pasadena, 1971-72, University of Kansas, Lawrence, 1975, and Dickinson College, Carlisle, Pa., 1976; Contributor Ed., Sulfur mag., Los Angeles, 1980-81. **Publications:** Armed Descent, 1961; Her Body Against Time, 1963; Round Dances, 1964; Tabula, 1964; Enstasy, 1964; Matter/Fact/Sheet/1, 1964; Matter/Fact/Sheet/2, 1964; The Well Wherein a Deer's Head Bleeds (play), 1964; Lunes, 1964; Lectiones, 1965; (ed. with P. Leary) A Controversy of Poets: An Anthology of Contemporary American Poetry, 1965; Words in Service, 1966; Weeks, 1966; Songs XXIV, 1967; Twenty Poems, 1967; Devotions, 1967; Axon Dendron Tree, 1967; Crooked Bridge Love Society, 1967; A Joining: A Sequence for H. D., 1967; The Scorpions (novel), 1967, 1985; Alpha, 1968; Finding the Measure, 1968; Songs I-XXX, 1968; Sonnets, 1968; From the Common Shore, Book 5, 1968; Statement, 1968; We Are the Arbiters of Beast Desire, 1969; A California Journal, 1969; The Common Shore, Books I-V: A Long Poems about American in Time, 1969; Kali Yuga, 1970; In time (essays), 1971; Eros and Psyche (chamber opera), 1971; Cities (novels), 1971; Flesh: Dream: Book, 1971; Ralegh, 1972; The Pastorals, 1972; Reading Her Notes, 1972; Sulphur, 1972; The Tears of Edmund Burke, 1973; Whaler Frigate Clippership, 1973; The Mill of Particulars, 1973; A Line of Sight, 1974; The Loom, 1975; Sixteen Odes, 1976; The Lady of, 1977; The Convections, 1978; Wheres, 1978; The Book of Persephone, 1978; The Cruise of the Pnyx, 1978; Kill the Messenger Who Brings Bad News, 1979; Sentence, 1980; Spiritual Exercises, 1981; The Alchemist to Mercury, 1982; Russian Tales, 1982; Mulberry Women, 1982; Under Words, 1983; Thor's Thrush, 1984; A Transparent Tree (short stories), 1985; Not This Island Music (poetry), 1987; The Flowers of Unceasing Coincidence (long poem), 1988; Doctor of Silence (short stories), 1988; Oahu (travel notation poems), 1988; Cat Scratch Fever (stories), 1991; Ariadne (long poem), 1991; A Strange Market (poetry), 1992; Queen of Terrors (stories), 1994; Mont Blanc (poem), 1994; Red Actions: Selected Poems 1960-1993, 1995. **Address:** Dept. of English, Bard College, Annandale on Hudson, NY 12504, U.S.A.

KELLY, Robert J. American, b. 1938. **Genres:** Criminology/True Crime, Sociology. **Career:** Brooklyn College of the City University of New York, Brooklyn, NY, professor of social science, 1968-, now Broeklundian Professor Emeritus; Graduate Center of the City University of New York, professor of sociology and criminology; consultant to New York Police Department, Pennsylvania Crime Commission, and New Jersey State Police; Robert Kelly Associates, Inc., president; Edward Sagarin Institute for the Study of Social Problems, president. **Publications:** Handbook of Organized Crime in the United States, 1995; African American Organized Crime, 1997; Hate Crimes: The Politics of Global Polarization, 1998; The Upperworld and the Underworld, 1999; Encyclopedia of Organized Crime in the United States, 2000; Organized Crime, Terrorism and Social Distress, 2003; Illicit Trafficking, forthcoming. Contributor to periodicals. **Address:** Dept of Educational Services, Brooklyn College of the City University of New York, 2900 Bedford Ave, Brooklyn, NY 11210, U.S.A. **Online address:** rkelly@brooklyn.cuny.edu

KELLY, Ronald. American, b. 1959. **Genres:** Novels, Novellas/Short stories. **Career:** Writer. **Publications:** NOVELS, EXCEPT WHERE NOTED: Hindsight, 1990; Pitfall, 1990; Something Out There, 1991; Moon of the Werewolf, 1991; Dark Dixie: Tales of Southern Horror (stories; audiobook), 1992; Father's Little Helper, 1992; Slocum and the Nightriders, 1993; The Possession, 1993; Fear, 1994; Slocum and the Gold Slaves, 1994; Blood Kin, 1996. Work represented in anthologies. Contributor of novellas and stories to magazines. **Address:** c/o Jabberwocky Literary Agency, PO Box 4558, Sunnyside, NY 11104-0558, U.S.A.

KELLY, Saul. American, b. 1957. **Genres:** History. **Career:** King's College London (at Joint Services Command and Staff College), England, lecturer in defence studies, 2001-. Previously worked as research associate, International Boundaries Research Unit, University of Durham, and research fellow, University of Westminster. **Publications:** (editor, with Anthony Gorst) Whitehall and the Suez Crisis, 2000; (with Charles Douglas-Home) Dignified and Efficient: The British Monarchy in the Twentieth Century, 2000; Cold War in the Desert: Britain, the United States, and the Italian Colonies, 1945-52, 2000; The Lost Oasis: The Desert War and the Hunt for Zerzura, 2002; Westview, 2003. Contributor of essays to books. **Address:** Defence Studies Department, Joint Services Command and Staff College, Faringdon Rd., Watchfield, Swindon, Wiltshire SN6 8TS, England. **Online address:** skelly@jscsc.org

KELMAN, Herbert Chanoch. American (born Austria), b. 1927. **Genres:** Ethics, International relations/Current affairs, Psychology, Social sciences. **Career:** Richard Clarke Cabot Professor of Social Ethics Ethics, Harvard University, Cambridge, MA, 2004- (Lecturer on Social Psychology, 1957-62; Richard Clarke Cabot Professor of Social Ethics, 1968-99; Director, Program on International Conflict Analysis and Resolution, Weatherhead Center for International Affairs, 1993-2003; Richard Clarke Cabot Research Professor of Social Ethics, 1999-2004). Research Psychologist, National Institute of Mental Health, Bethesda, MD, 1955-57; Professor of Psychology, and Research Psychologist, Center for Research on Conflict Resolution, University of Michigan, 1962-69. President, International Society of Political Psychology, 1985-86; President, Psychologists for Social Responsibility, 1990-92. **Publications:** (ed. and contrib.) International Behavior: A Social Psychological Analysis, 1965; A Time to Speak: On Human Values and Social Research, 1968; (with R.S. Ezekiel) Cross-National Encounters, 1970; (ed. with G. Bermant and D.P. Warwick) The Ethics of Social Intervention, 1978; (with V.L. Hamilton) Crimes of Obedience: Toward a Social Psychology of Authority and Responsibility, 1989. **Address:** Dept of Psychology, William James Hall, Harvard University, Cambridge, MA 02138, U.S.A. **Online address:** hck@wjh.harvard.edu

KELMAN, James. Scottish, b. 1946. **Genres:** Novels, Novellas/Short stories, Plays/Screenplays. **Career:** Novelist and short story writer. **Publications:** NOVELS: The Busconductor Hines, 1984; A Chancer, 1985; A Disaffection, 1989; How Late It Was, How Late, 1994 (Booker Prize); Translated Accounts, 2001. SHORT STORIES: An Old Pub Near the Angel, 1973; (with T. Leonard and A, Hamilton) Three Glasgow Writers, 1976; Short Tales from the Nightshift, 1978; Not Not While the Giro and Other Stories, 1983; (with A. Gray and A. Owens) Lean Tales, 1985; Greyhound for Breakfast, 1987; The Burn, 1991; Busted Scotch, 1997; The Good Times, 1998. PLAYS: The Busker, 1985; Le Rodeur (adaptation of the play by Enzo Cormann), 1987; In the Night, 1988; Hardie and Baird: The Last Days, 1991. OTHER: (ed.) An East End Anthology, 1988; The Return (screenplay), 1990. **Address:** 244 W. Princess St., Glasgow G4 9DP, Scotland. **Online address:** www.JamesKelman.co.uk

KELMAN, Judith (Ann). American, b. 1945. **Genres:** Mystery/Crime/Suspense. **Career:** Novelist. Valley Stream Public Schools, Valley Stream,

NY, teacher of mentally handicapped students, 1968-71; Camp A.N.C.H.O.R., Hempstead, NY, recreation supervisor of extracurricular activities for handicapped children, 1968-71; worked as a speech pathologist and educational consultant in public schools in Greenwich, CT; freelance writer, 1981-. **Publications:** MYSTERY/CRIME/SUSPENSE NOVELS: Prime Evil, 1986; Where Shadows Fall, 1988; While Angels Sleep, 1990; Hush Little Darlings, 1991; Someone's Watching, 1992; The House on the Hill, 1993; If I Should Die, 1994; One Last Kiss, 1995; More Than You Know, 1996; Fly Away Home, 1997. Contributor to anthologies and periodicals. **Address:** c/o Putnam Publicity, 375 Hudson St., New York, NY 10014, U.S.A. **Online address:** jkelman@jkelman.com; jkelman@aol.com.

KELNER, Toni L. P. American. **Genres:** Mystery/Crime/Suspense. **Career:** Writer. **Publications:** LAURA FLEMING MYSTERY NOVELS: Down Home Murder, 1993; Dead Ringer, 1994; Trouble Looking for a Place to Happen, 1995; Country Comes to Town, 1996; Tight as a Tick, 1998; Death of a Damn Yankee, 1999; Mad as the Dickens, 2001; Wed and Buried, 2003. Contributor of short stories to magazines and anthologies. **Address:** 285 Summer St, Malden, MA 02148, U.S.A. **Online address:** toni@tonilpkelner.com

KELSAY, Michael. (born United States), b. 1957. **Genres:** Novels. **Career:** Writer. **Publications:** Too Close to Call (novel), 2001; Basketball in Kentucky: Great Balls of Fire (documentary miniseries), 2002. Contributor to periodicals. **Address:** POB 423, 235 East 31st St., Lexington, KY 40588, U.S.A. **Online address:** m.kelsy@insightbb.com

KELTON, Elmer. Also writes as Tom Early, Alex Hawk, Lee McElroy. American, b. 1926. **Genres:** Westerns/Adventure, History. **Career:** Agricultural Ed., Standard-Times, San Angelo, Texas, 1948-63; Ed., Ranch Magazine, 1963-68; Associate Ed., W. Texas Livestock Weekly, 1968-90. **Publications:** Hot Iron, 1955; Buffalo Wagons, 1956; Barbed Wire, 1957; Shadow of a Star, 1959; The Texas Rifles, 1960; Donovan, 1961; Bitter Trail, 1962; Horsehead Crossing, 1963; Massacre at Goliad, 1965; Llano River, 1966; After the Bugles, 1967; Captain's Rangers, 1968; Hanging Judge, 1969; (as Alex Hawk) Shotgun Settlement, 1969; Bowie's Mine, 1971; The Day the Cowboys Quit, 1971; Wagontongue, 1972; The Time It Never Rained, 1973; (as Lee McElroy) Joe Pepper, 1975; (as Lee McElroy) Long Way to Texas, 1976; The Good Old Boys, 1978; The Wolf and the Buffalo, 1980; (as Lee McElroy) Eyes of the Hawk, 1981; Stand Proud, 1984; Dark Thicket, 1985; The Man Who Rode Midnight, 1987; (as Tom Early) Sons of Texas, 1990; Honor at Daybreak, 1991; Slaughter, 1992; Elmer Kelton Country, 1993; The Far Canyon, 1994; The Pumpkin Rollers, 1996; Cloudy in the West, 1997; The Smiling Country, 1998; The Buckskin Line, 1999; Badger Boy, 2001; The Way of the Coyote, 2002; Ranger's Trail, 2002; Texas Vendetta, 2003; Christmas at the Ranch, 2003; Jericho's Road, 2004. **Address:** 2460 Oxford, San Angelo, TX 76904-5433, U.S.A.

KEMMIS, Daniel (Orra). American, b. 1945. **Genres:** Urban studies, Regional/Urban planning. **Career:** Montana House of Representatives, Helena, MT, state representative, 1975-84, minority leader, 1981-82, speaker, 1983-84; admitted to the Bar of the state of Montana, 1978; Morrison, Jonkel, Kemmis & Rossbach, Missoula, MT, partner, 1978-80; Jonkel & Kemmis, MT, partner, 1981-84. Economic- and community-development specialist in Montana, 1984-; City of Missoula MT, mayor, 1990-96; Center for the Rocky Mountain West, University of Montana, Missoula, MT, director, 1996-; University of Montana, Missoula, MT, adjunct professor, 1988-89. **Publications:** Community and the Politics of Place, 1990; The Good City and the Good Life, 1995; This Sovereign Land: A New Vision for Governing the West, 2001. Contributor to professional journals and national publications. **Address:** 521 Hartman Ct #10, Missoula, MT 59802, U.S.A.

KEMNITZ, Thomas Milton, Jr. (born United States), b. 1984. **Genres:** Children's fiction. **Career:** Writer. **Publications:** (As Tom Kemnitz, Jr.) Space: The Race to the Moon, 2002. Also author of a book on problem-solving skills. **Address:** 247 High St., Monroe, NY 10950, U.S.A.

KEMP, Gene. British, b. 1926. **Genres:** Children's fiction. **Career:** Teacher, St. Sidwell's School, Exeter, 1962-74; Lecturer, Rolle College, 1963-79. **Publications:** Tamworth Pig series, 1972-92; The Turbulent Term of Tyke Tiler, 1977; Gowie Corby Plays Chicken, 1979; Dog Days and Cat Naps, 1980; The Clock Tower Ghost, 1981; No Place Like, 1983; Charlie Lewis Plays for Time, 1984; The Well, 1984; Jason Bodger and the Priory Ghost, 1985; McMagus Is Waiting For You, 1986; Juniper, 1986; I Can't Stand Losing, 1987; Room with No Windows, 1989; Just Ferret, 1990; Matty's Midnight Monster, 1991; The Mink War, 1992; Wanting a Little Black Gerbil, 1992; Roundabout (stories), 1993; Wacky World of Wessley Baker, 1994;

Zowey Corby's Story, 1995; Dog's Journey Home, 1996; Rebel Rebel, 1997; Tyke Tiler Terrible Joke Book, 1997; The Wishing Tower, 1998; The Hairy Hands, 1999. EDITOR: Ducks and Dragons, 1980; Puffin Book of Ghosts and Ghouls, 1992. **Address:** c/o Laurence Pollinger Ltd, 9 Staple inn, Holborn, London WC1V 7QH, England.

KEMP, Kenny. American, b. 1955. **Genres:** Romance/Historical, Plays/Screenplays, Essays. **Career:** Attorney, 1984-. Also works as a building contractor. **Publications:** Wildest Dreams (short film), 1987; Fedora (short film), 1995; 3/4 Inch Marine Ply (essay), 1996; I Hated Heaven (romance fiction), 1998; Dad Was a Carpenter (memoir), 2001; The Welcoming Door (historical fiction), 2002.

KEMP, Martin (John). Scottish (born England), b. 1942. **Genres:** Art/Art history, Sciences. **Career:** Dalhousie University, Halifax, NS, lecturer in history of art, 1965-66; University of Glasgow, lecturer in history of art, 1966-81; University of St. Andrews, Scotland, Faculty of the Arts, professor of fine arts, 1981-95, associate dean of graduate studies, 1983-87; Royal Scottish Academy, professor of history and hon. member, 1985-; University of Cambridge, Slade Professor of Fine Art, 1987-88; St. Leonard's College, provost, 1991-93; British Academy, Wolfson Research Professor, 1993-98; University of Oxford, professor of the history of art, 1995-. Princeton University, NJ, Institute of Advanced Study, fellow, 1984-85; New York University, NYC, Benjamin Sonnenberg Visiting Professor of Fine Arts, 1988; Association of Art Historians, chairman, 1989-92; University of North Carolina, Chapel Hill, Wiley Visiting Professor, 1993. **Publications:** Leonardo da Vinci: The Marvellous Works of Nature and Man, 1981; Geometrical Perspective from Brunelleschi to Desargues: Pictorial Means or an Intellectual End?, 1985; (co-author) Leonardo da Vinci, 1989; (ed.) Leonardo on Painting: An Anthology of Writings, 1989; The Science of Art, 1990; (co-ed.) The Altarpiece in the Renaissance, 1990; Behind the Picture: Art and Evidence in the Italian Renaissance, 1998; The Oxford History of Western Art, 2000; Visualizations: The "Nature" Book of Art and Science, 2000.

KEMP, Penn. Also writes as Penny Chalmers. Canadian, b. 1944. **Genres:** Novellas/Short stories, Plays/Screenplays, Poetry, Education, Theology/Religion, Cartoons, Translations. **Career:** High school English teacher in Ontario, 1966-70; writing teacher, 1973-; associated with artist-in-the-schools program of Ontario Arts Council, 1981-89. Writer in residence of Niagara/Erie Writers, Buffalo, NY, 1984, of Flesherton Public Library, Flesherton, ON, 1988, and in Bombay, India, 1995, 2000. Sound poetry performances in North America, Britain, Europe, and India. **Publications:** POEMS: Clearing, 1977; Toad Tales, 1980; Animus, 1983; Some Talk Magic, 1984; Binding Twine, 1984; Travelling Light, 1984; Eidoleons, 1988; Throo, 1990. ONE-ACT PLAYS: The Epic of Toad and Heron, 1977; Angel Makers, 1978; What the Ear Hears Last, 1994. POEMS AS PENNY CHALMERS: Bearing Down, 1972; Tranceform, 1976; Changing Place, 1978.

KEMP, (Bernard) Peter. British, b. 1942. **Genres:** Literary criticism and history. **Career:** Lecturer in English, Middlesex Polytechnic, 1968-88; Fiction Editor and Chief Fiction Reviewer of the Sunday Times. **Publications:** Muriel Spark, 1974; H.G. Wells and the Culminating Ape, 1982, 1996; (ed.) The Oxford Dictionary of Literary Quotations, 1997. **Address:** 61 Princes Ave, Finchley, London N3 2DA, England.

KEMP, Roger L. American, b. 1946. **Genres:** Administration/Management, Institutions/Organizations, Politics/Government, Public/Social administration, Regional/Urban planning, Urban studies. **Career:** City of Oakland, CA, assistant to the city manager, 1978-79; City of Seaside, CA, city manager, 1979-83; City of Placentia, CA, city administrator, 1983-87; City of Clifton, NJ, city manager, 1987-93; City of Meriden, CT, city manager, 1993-. Lecturer at colleges and universities. **Publications:** Coping with Proposition 13, 1980; Strategies for Hard Times, 1988. EDITOR: America's Infrastructure: Problems and Prospects, 1986; America's Cities: Strategic Planning for the Future, 1988; Privatization: The Private Provision of Public Services, 1991; Strategic Planning in Local Government: A Casebook, 1992; Strategic Planning for Local Government: A Handbook for Public Officials and Citizens, 1993; America's Cities: Problems and Prospects, 1995; Economic Development in Local Government, 1995; Urban Economic Development, 1995; Handbook of Strategic Planning, 1995; Managing America's Cities, 1998; Local Government Election Practices, 1999; Forms of Local Government, 1999; Main Street Renewal, 2000; The Inner City, 2001; How American Governments Work, 2002; Regional Government Innovations, 2003; Community Renewal through Municipal Investment, 2003; Model Government Charters, 2003; Homeland Security, 2003. **Address:** 421 Brownstone Ridge, Meriden, CT 06450, U.S.A. **Online address:** rlkbsr@snet.net

KEMPE, Frederick. American, b. 1954. **Genres:** Politics/Government, International relations/Current affairs. **Career:** Associated Press-Dow Jones, Frankfurt, Federal Republic of Germany (now Germany), bureau chief, 1978-79; Newsweek, Bonn, Federal Republic of Germany, correspondent, 1979-81; Wall Street Journal, roving correspondent in London, England, 1981-83, bureau chief in Vienna, Austria, 1984-86, diplomatic correspondent in Washington, DC, 1986-. **Publications:** Divorcing the Dictator: America's Bungled Affair with Noriega, 1990; Father/Land: A Personal Search for the New Germany, 1999. **Address:** Wall Street Journal Europe, Boulevard Brand Whitlock, 87, B-1200 Brussles, Belgium.

KEMPER, Steve. (born United States), b. 1951. **Genres:** Business/Trade/Industry. **Career:** Freelance journalist. Taught literature and writing at the University of Connecticut during the 1980s. **Publications:** Code Name Ginger: The Story behind Segway and Dean Kamen's Quest to Invent a New World, 2003. Contributor to periodicals. **Address:** c/o Author Mail, Harvard Business School, 60 Harvard Way, Boston, MA 02163, U.S.A. **Online address:** email@stevekemper.net

KEMPOWSKI, Walter. German, b. 1929. **Genres:** Novels, Adult nonfiction. **Career:** Teacher and archivist in Nartum, Germany, 1960-85; freelance writer, 1969; professor of literature and pedagogy at the University of Oldenburg, 1980-. **Publications:** NOVELS: Tadelloeser & Wolff, 1971; Uns Geht's Ja Noch Gold (title means: We're Still Doing Well), 1972; Ein Kapitel fuer Sich: Roman (title means: A Chapter in Itself), 1975; Aus Grosser Zeit: Roman, 1978, trans. as Days of Greatness, 1981; Schoene Aussicht (title means: Beautiful View), 1981; Herzlich Wilkommen (title means: Hearty Welcome), 1984; Hundstage: Roman, c. 1988, trans. as Dog Days, c. 1991; Mark und Bein: Eine Episode, c. 1992; Weltschmerz: Kinderszenen fast zu ernst, 1995; Bloomsday '97, 1997; Heil Welt, 1998. COMPILER: Haben Sie Hitler Gesehen? (nonfiction), 1973, trans. as Did You Ever See Hitler?, 1975; Immer so durchgemogelt (nonfiction; title means: Always Tricked My Way Through), 1974; Haben Sie Davon Gewusst? (nonfiction; title means: Did You Know About It?), 1979; Mein Lesebuch, 1979; Das Echolot: Ein kollektives Tagebuch, Januar und Februar 1943 (nonfiction; title means: The Echo-Sounder), c. 1993; Das Echolot: fuga furiosa: ein kollektives Tagebuch, Winter 1945, 1999; Der Roife Hahn: Dresden 1945, 2001. OTHER: Im Block (autobiography; title means: In the Block), 1969; Der Hahn im Nacken: Mini-Geschichten, 1973; Walter Kempowskis Harzreise erlaeutert (travel; title means: Walter Kempowski's Trip to the Harz Mountains), 1975; Alle Unter Einem Hut, 1976; Wer Will Unter die Soldaten?, 1976; Schnoor: Bremen zwischen Stavendamm und Balge, 1978; Unser Herr Boeckelmann, 1979; Kempowskis einfache Fibel, 1980; Beethovens Fuenfte und Moin Vaddr Laebt (manuscripts and notes for 2 radio plays), 1982; Herrn Boeckelmanns Schoenste Tafelgeschichten nach dem ABC Geordnet, 1983; Haumiblau: Kindergeschichten, 1986; Sirius: Eine Art Tagebuch (nonfiction), c. 1990; Alkor: Tagebuch, 2001; Das Echolot: Barbarossa '41, 2002. **Address:** Haus Kreienhoop, 27404 Nartum, Bundesrepublik, Germany.

KEMPRECOS, Paul. American. **Genres:** Mystery/Crime/Suspense. **Career:** Writer. The Cape Codder newspaper, Cape Cod, MA, reporter and managing editor; Cape Cod Business Journal, editor. **Publications:** ARISTOTLE SOCARIDES MYSTERY NOVELS: Cool Blue Tomb, 1991; Neptune's Eye, 1991; Death in Deep Water, 1992; Feeding Frenzy, 1993; The Mayflower Murder, 1996; Bluefin Blues, 1997. **Address:** 12 North St., Dennis Port, MA 02639-1418, U.S.A.

KEMSKE, Floyd. American, b. 1947. **Genres:** Novels, Advertising/Public relations, Writing/Journalism. **Career:** Weingarten Publications, Boston, MA, editor and editorial director, 1980-92; free-lance writer and graphic designer in Pepperell, MA, 1992-99; Novel Enterprises (writing workshops), Pepperell, MA, general partner, 1996-97; Kaplan College Online Education, editorial director, 2000-01. **Publications:** NOVELS: Lifetime Employment, 1992; The Virtual Boss, 1993; Human Resources, 1995; The Third Lion, 1997; Labor Day, 2000. OTHER: Write on Target (nonfiction), 1996. **Address:** PO Box 563, Pepperell, MA 01463, U.S.A. **Online address:** fkemske@thirdlion.com

KENAN, Randall (G.). American, b. 1963. **Genres:** Novels, Novellas/Short stories. **Career:** Alfred A. Knopf, New York City, editor, 1985-89; lecturer at Sarah Lawrence College, Bronxville, NY, 1989-, Vassar College, Poughkeepsie, NY, 1989-, and Columbia University, NYC, 1990-. **Publications:** A Visitation of Spirits (novel), 1989; Let the Dead Bury Their Dead and Other Stories, 1992; James Baldwin, 1994; Walking on Water, 1999. **Address:** c/o Tanya Bickley Enterprises, Inc., PO Box 1656, 249 Old Stamford Rd, New Canaan, CT 06840, U.S.A.

KENAZ, Yehoshua. Israeli, b. 1937. **Genres:** Novels, Novellas/Short stories, Essays. **Career:** Novelist, short-story writer, and translator. **Publications:** Ahare ha-hagim, 1964, trans. D. Bilu as After the Holidays, 1987; Ha-Isha ha-gedolah min ha-halomot (title means: Great Woman of the Dreams), 1973, rev. ed, 1986; Moment Musikali, 1980, trans. as Musical Moment and Other Stories, 1995; Ba-derekh el ha-hatulim, 1991, trans. D. Bilu as The Way to the Cats, 1994; Hitganvut yehidim, 1986; Mahazir ahavot kodmot, 1997, trans. D. Bilu as Returning Lost Loves, 2001; Nof 'im sheloshah 'etsim (title means: Landscape with Three Trees), 2000. **Address:** c/o Author Mail, Steerforth Press, PO Box 70, South Royalton, VT 05068, U.S.A.

KENDALL, Carol. American, b. 1917. **Genres:** Novels, Children's fiction, Translations. **Publications:** The Black Seven, 1946; The Baby-Snatcher, 1952; The Other Side of the Tunnel, 1956; The Gammage Cup (in U.K. as The Minnipins), 1959; The Big Splash, 1960; The Whisper of Glocken, 1965; (with Yao-wen Li) Sweet and Sour: Tales from China, 1979; The Firelings, 1982; Haunting Tales from Japan, 1985; The Wedding of the Rat Family, 1988. **Address:** 172 Chesterfield Rd., Leeds, MA 01053-9728, U.S.A.

KENDALL, Jane (F.). American, b. 1952. **Genres:** Children's fiction, Illustrations. **Career:** Free-lance illustrator of children's books, 1983-; feature writer and columnist, 1985-; Greenwich Magazine, senior writer, 1992-. **Publications:** SELF-ILLUSTRATED FOR CHILDREN: The Nutcracker: A Ballet Cut-Out Book, 1985; Miranda and the Movies, 1989; Miranda Goes to Hollywood, 1999. Illustrator of children's textbooks and books by L.S. Marcus. **Address:** c/o Greenwich Magazine, 39 Lewis St, Greenwich, CT 06830, U.S.A. **Online address:** jkendl@discovernet.net

KENDRICK, Stephen. American, b. 1954. **Genres:** Mystery/Crime/Suspense. **Career:** Previously affiliated with churches in Connecticut, Maryland, and Pennsylvania and with Unitarian chapels in England; First and Second Church, Boston, MA, minister. **Publications:** Holy Clues: The Gospel according to Sherlock Holmes, 1999; Night Watch: A Long-Lost Adventure in Which Sherlock Holmes Meets Father Brown, 2001. Contributor to periodicals. **Address:** First and Second Church, 66 Marlborough Street, Boston, MA 02116, U.S.A.

KENEALLY, Thomas (Michael). Australian, b. 1935. **Genres:** Novels, Children's fiction, Plays/Screenplays, Adult non-fiction, Writing/Journalism. **Career:** High sch. teacher, Sydney, 1960-64; University of New England, NSW, lecturer in drama, 1968-70; New York University, Inaugural Berg Professor, 1988; University of California, Irvine, writer-in-residence, 1985, distinguished professor, 1991-95. **Publications:** FICTION: The Place at Whitton, 1964; The Fear, 1965; Bring Larks and Heroes, 1967; Three Cheers for the Paraclete, 1968; The Survivor, 1969; A Dutiful Daughter, 1971; The Chant of Jimmie Blacksmith, 1972; Blood Red, Sister Rose, 1974; Gossip from the Forest, 1975; Season in Purgatory, 1976; Victim of the Aurora, 1977; Confederates, 1979; Passenger, 1979; The Cut-Rate Kingdom, 1980; Schindler's Ark (in US as Schindler's List), 1982; A Family Madness, 1985; The Playmaker, 1987; By the Line, 1988; To Asmara (in UK as Towards Asmara), 1989; Flying Hero Class, 1991; Woman of the Inner Sea, 1992; Jacko, 1993; A River Town, 1995; Bettany's Book, 2000; An Angel in Australia, 2002; Office of Innocence, 2002; Tyrant's Novel, 2004. NOVELS AS WILLIAM COYLE: Act of Grace, 1988; Chief of Staff, 1991. PLAYS: Halloran's Little Boat, 1968; Childermas, 1968; An Awful Rose, 1972; Bullie's House, 1981. SCREENPLAYS: Silver City, 1984. FOR CHILDREN: Ned Kelly and the City of Bees, 1968. NONFICTION: Moses: The Lawgiver, 1975; Outback, 1983; Australia: Beyond the Dreamtime, 1989; Now and in Time to Be: Ireland and the Irish, 1992; The Place Where Souls Are Born: A Journey to the Southwest, 1992; Memoirs from a Young Republic, 1993; The Utility Player, 1993; Our Republic, 1995; Homebush Boy: A Memoir, 1995; The Great Shame, 1998; American Scoundrel, 2002; Abraham Lincoln, 2002. **Address:** c/o Random House, Author Mail, 20 Alfred St, Milsons Point, NSW 2061, Australia.

KENISON, Katrina. American, b. 1958. **Genres:** Novellas/Short stories. **Career:** Houghton Mifflin Co., Boston, MA, editor, 1981-88, 1990-. **Publications:** (ed.) The Best American Short Stories, published annually, 1991-; (ed.) Mothers: Twenty Stories of Contemporary Motherhood, 1996. **Address:** Houghton Mifflin Co., 222 Berkeley St., Boston, MA 02116, U.S.A.

KENJO, Takashi. Japanese, b. 1940. **Genres:** Administration/Management, Engineering. **Career:** TEAC Corp., Musashino, Tokyo, Japan, researcher, 1964-65; Polytechnic University of Japan, Sagamihara, Kanagawa, Japan, lecturer, 1965-71, associate professor, 1971-81, professor of electric motors and their controls, 1981-. **Publications:** Stepping Motors and Their Microprocessor Controls, 1984, (with A. Sugawara) 2nd ed. 1994; (with S. Nagamori) Permanent-Magnet and Brushless DC Motors, 1985; Power Electronics for the Microprocessor Age, 1989; Electric Motors and Their

Controls, 1991; Upgrade Your English as a Japanese Scientist/Engineer and Manufacturing Motors; (with T.Sashida) An Introduction to Ultrasonic Motors, 1993; (with J. Lorriman) Japan's Winning Margins, 1994, 2nd ed. 1996. Editorial adviser to Oxford University Press.

KENKEL, William (Francis). American, b. 1925. **Genres:** Sociology. **Career:** University of Kentucky, Lexington, Professor of Sociology, now retired. President, National Council on Family Relations, 1967-68; Vice-President, North Central Sociological Association, 1980-81; President, Mid-South Sociological Association, 1988-89. **Publications:** (with J.F. Cuber) Social Stratification in the United States, 1954; (with J.F. Cuber and R. Harper) Problems of American Society, 2nd ed., 1964; The Family in Perspective, 5th ed., 1985; Society in Action (with E. Voland) 1975, sole author, 1980. **Address:** 2313 Shun Pike, Nicholasville, KY 40356-9405, U.S.A. **Online address:** wfkenkel@aol.com

KENNAN, George (Frost). American, b. 1904. **Genres:** History, International relations/Current affairs. **Career:** Professor Emeritus, Institute for Advanced Study, Princeton, New Jersey Joined U.S. Foreign Service, 1927; Vice Consul, Hamburg, 1927, Tallin, USSR, 1928; Third Secretary, Riga Kovno and Tallin, USSR, 1929; Language Officer Berlin, 1929; Third Secretary, Riga, 1931, Moscow, 1934; Consul, then Second Secretary, Vienna, 1935; Second Secretary, Moscow, 1935; with Dept. of State, Washington, 1937; Second Secretary, 1938; and Consul, 1939, Prague, Second Secretary, 1939, and First Secty, 1940, Berlin; Counsellor, Lisbon, 1942; Counsellor to U.S. Delegation, European Advisory Committee, London, 1944; Minister-Counsellor, Moscow, 1945; Deputy for Foreign Affairs, National War College, Washington, 1946; Member, Policy Planning Staff, Dept. of State, 1949-50; Chief, Policy Planning Staff, Dept. of State, on leave at Institute for Advanced Study, Princeton, 1950-51; Ambassador to the USSR 1952; visiting professorships, 1954-60; Ambassador to Yugoslavia, 1961-63; Professor, Princeton University, 1964-66; University Fellow in History and Slavic Civilizations, Harvard University, Cambridge, Massachusetts, 1966-70; Fellow, All Souls College, Oxford, 1969. President, National Institute of Arts and Letters, 1965-68, and American Academy of Arts and Letters, 1967-71. **Publications:** American Diplomacy 1900-1950, 1951; Das Amerikanisch-Russische Verhaltnis, 1954; Realities of American Foreign Policy, 1954; Soviet-American Relations, 1917-1920, vol. 1, Russia Leaves the War, 1956, vol. 2, The Decision to Intervene, 1958; Russia, The Atom and the West (Reith Lectures), 1958; Soviet Foreign Policy, 1917-1945, 1960; Russia and the West (Reith Lectures), 1958; Soviet Foreign Policy, 1917-1945, 1960; Russia and the West under Lenin and Stalin, 1961; On Dealing with the Communist World, 1963; Memoirs 1925-50, 1967; Democracy and the Student left, 1968; From Prague after Munich: Diplomatic Papers 1938-40, 1968; The Marquis de Custine and His Russia in 1839, 1971; Memoirs 1950-63, 1972; Cloud of Danger, 1978; The Decline of Bismarck's European Order: Franco-Russian Relations 1875-1890, 1979; The Nuclear Delusion, 1982; The Fateful Alliance, 1984; Sketches from a Life, 1989; Around the Cragged Hill, 1993; At a Century's Ending, 1996; An American Family. The Kennans: The First Three Generations, 2000. **Address:** Institute for Advanced Study, Princeton, NJ 08540, U.S.A.

KENNEALY, Jerry. American, b. 1938. **Genres:** Mystery/Crime/Suspense. **Career:** San Francisco Police Department, San Francisco, CA, police officer, 1961-65; private investigator in California, 1965-93; writer. **Publications:** NICK POLO MYSTERIES: Polo Solo, 1987; Polo, Anyone?, 1988; Polo's Ponies, 1988; Polo in the Rough, 1989; Polo's Wild Card, 1990; Green with Envy, 1991; Special Delivery, 1992; Vintage Polo, 1993; Beggar's Choice, 1994; All That Glitters, 1997. OTHER: Nobody Wins, 1977; The Conductor, 1995; The Forger, 1996; The Suspect, 1997; The Hunted, 1999; The Other Eye, 2000; Cashing Out, 2001. **Address:** 145 Madison Ave, San Bruno, CA 94066, U.S.A. **Online address:** jerrykennealy@hotmail.com

KENNEDY, A(lison) L. Scottish. **Genres:** Novels, Novellas/Short stories. **Career:** Writer. **Publications:** SHORT STORY COLLECTIONS: Night Geometry and the Garscadden Trains, 1990; Now That You're Back, 1995; Original Bliss, 1997; (ed. with H. White and M. Bateman) The Ghost of Liberace. NOVELS: Looking for the Possible Dance, 1993; So I am Glad, 1995; Everything You Need, 2001. **Address:** c/o Antony Harwood, Gillon Aitken Associates Ltd, 29 Fernshaw Rd, London SW10 0TG, England.

KENNEDY, Adrienne. American, b. 1931. **Genres:** Plays/Screenplays. **Career:** Yale University, New Haven, CT, lecturer in playwriting, 1972-73; Brown University, Providence, RI, visiting associate professor, 1979-80; Harvard University, Cambridge, MA, visiting lecturer, 1990-91. **Publications:** Funnyhouse of a Negro, 1964; (with J. Lennon and V. Spinetti) The Lennon Play: In His Own Write, 1967; Cities in Bezique: 2 One-Act Plays: The Owl

Answers and A Beast's Story, 1969; People Who Led to My Plays (memoirs), 1987; Adrienne Kennedy in One Act (collected works) 1988; Deadly Triplets (mystery), 1990; The Alexander Plays (collected works), 1992; Letter to My Students, Kenyon Review, 1993; (with A.P. Kennedy) Sleep Deprivation Chamber, 1996; Adrienne Kennedy Reader, 2001. Contributor to anthologies, 1969-87. **Address:** c/o Bridget Aschenberg, International Creative Management, 40 W 57th St, New York, NY 10019, U.S.A.

KENNEDY, David Michael. American, b. 1941. **Genres:** History. **Career:** Stanford University, California, assistant professor, 1967-72, associate professor, 1972-80, Donald J. McLachlan Professor of History, 1993-. **Publications:** Birth Control in America: The Career of Margaret Sanger, 1970; Over Here: The First World War and American Society, 1980, rev. ed., 2005; (with T.A. Bailey) The American Pageant, 8th ed., 1979, 13th ed. (with L. Cohen and T.A. Bailey), 2005; Freedom from Fear: The American People in Depression & War, 1929-1945, 1999 (Pulitzer Prize for History, 2000). EDITOR: (with P.A. Robinson) Social Thought in America and Europe, 1970; Progressivism: The Critical Issues, 1971; (with M. Parrish) Power and Responsibility: Case Studies in American Leadership, 1986. **Address:** Dept of History, Stanford University, Stanford, CA 94305, U.S.A. **Online address:** DMK@Stanford.edu

KENNEDY, Gavin. Scottish, b. 1940. **Genres:** Biography, Military/Defense/Arms control, Business/Trade/Industry. **Career:** National Defence College, Latimer, Part-time Lecturer in Economics; Brunel University, Uxbridge, Lecturer in Economics, 1972-74; University of Strathclyde, Sr. Lecturer in Economics, 1974-85; Heriot-Watt University, Edinburgh Business School, Professor, Esmee Fair Research Centre, Professorial Fellow, 1988-. **Publications:** The Military in the Third World, 1974; The Economics of Defence, 1975; The Death of Captain Cook, 1978; Bligh, 1978; Burden Sharing in NATO, 1979; (co-author) Managing Negotiations, 1980; Mathematics for Innumerate Economists, 1982; Everything Is Negotiable!, 1982; Defense Economics, 1982; Invitation to Statistics, 1983; Negotiate Anywhere, 1985; Superdeal, 1986; Macroeconomics, 1987; The Pocket Negotiator, 1987; Captain Bligh: The Man and His Mutinies, 1989; Negotiation, 1991; The Perfect Negotiation, 1992; Kennedy's Simulations for Negotiation Training, 1993; Kennedy on Negotiation, 1997; New Negotiating Edge, 1998; Profitable Negotiation, 1999; Influencing for Results, 2000. EDITOR: The Radical Approach, 1976; R.T. Gould's Captain Cook, 1978; Sir John Barrow's Mutiny of the Bounty, 1980; A Book of the Bounty, 1981. **Address:** 99 Caiyside, Edinburgh EH10 7HR, Scotland. **Online address:** gavin@negotiate.demon.co.uk

KENNEDY, John C. American, b. 1943. **Genres:** Anthropology/Ethnology. **Career:** Memorial University of Newfoundland, St. John's, professor of anthropology, 1973-. University of Bergen, exchange professor, 1995. Native People's Support Group, member; consultant on aboriginal issues. **Publications:** Holding the Line, 1982; People of the Bays and Headlands, 1995; Labrador Village, 1996. **Address:** Department of Anthropology, Memorial University of Newfoundland, St. John's, NL, Canada A1B 3X9.

KENNEDY, Kieran A. Irish, b. 1935. **Genres:** Economics. **Career:** Economic and Social Research Institute, Dublin, Sr. Research Officer, 1968-70, Director, 1971-96, Research Professor, 1996. Council Member, Statistical and Social Inquiry Society of Ireland, 1973-, Honorary Treasurer, 1980-87, President, 1989-92; Executive Officer, Office of the Comptroller and Auditor General, Dublin, 1954-55, and the Dept. of Industry and Commerce, Dublin, 1955-58; Administrative Officer, 1958-65, and Assistant Principal Officer, 1965-68, Dept. of Finance, Dublin; Economic Consultant, Central Bank of Ireland, Dublin, 1970-71; Founder Member and Council Member, Irish Council of the European League for Economic Co-operation, 1971-83; Member, National Economic and Social Council, 1973-77; Chairman, Royal Irish Academy National Committee for Economics and Social Sciences, 1984-88; Chairman, Swiss Irish Business Association, 1988-91. **Publications:** Productivity and Industrial Growth: The Irish Experience, 1971; (with R. Bruton) The Irish Economy, 1975; (with B.R. Dowling) Economic Growth in Ireland: The Experience since 1947, 1975; (ed. with D. Conniffe) Employment and Unemployment Policy for Ireland, 1984; (co-author) The Economic Development of Ireland in the Twentieth Century, 1988; Facing the Unemployment Crisis in Ireland, 1993; (ed.) From Famine to Feast: Economic and Social Change in Ireland 1847-1997, 1998. **Address:** ESRI, 4 Burlington Rd, Dublin 4, Ireland. **Online address:** kak@esri.ie

KENNEDY, Lawrence W. American, b. 1952. **Genres:** History, Regional/Urban planning, Urban studies. **Career:** Boston College High School, Boston, MA, teacher and department head, 1976-85; Boston Redevelopment Authority, Boston, consultant, 1987-92; University of Scranton, Scranton,

PA, assistant professor, 1992-98, associate professor of history, 1998-. Boston College, lecturer, 1987-92. **Publications:** Planning the City upon a Hill: Boston since 1630, 1992; Boston: A Topographical History, 3rd ed., 2000. **Address:** Department of History, University of Scranton, 800 Linden St, Scranton, PA 18510, U.S.A. **Online address:** Lawrence.Kennedy@scranton.edu

KENNEDY, Leigh. British (born United States), b. 1951. **Genres:** Novels, Novellas/Short stories, Science fiction/Fantasy. **Publications:** Faces, 1986; The Journal of Nicholas the American, 1986; Saint Hiroshima, 1989. **Address:** c/o Maggie Noach, 22 Dorville Crescent, London W6 0HJ, England.

KENNEDY, Liv. Canadian, b. 1934. **Genres:** Travel/Exploration. **Career:** Dalcraft Ltd., commercial artist, 1950-55; Grouse Mountain Resorts Ltd., ski instructor, 1955-63; free-lance writer and photographer, 1968-. Strasser Travel, professional tour escort and travel consultant, 1973-; Jib Set Sailing School, sailing instructor, 1974-78; Maritime Museum of Vancouver, coordinator of the annual series "Offshore Cruising Adventures," 1976-; Canadian Broadcasting Corp., yachting correspondent and broadcaster for Good Morning Radio, 1977-. Malaspina College, photojournalism teacher, 1992. **Publications:** (Co-author) Vancouver Once upon a Time, 1974; Coastal Villages, 1991. **Address:** 3600 Outrigger Rd., Nanoose Bay, BC, Canada V9P 9H3. **Online address:** kennmac@island.net; www.island.net/~kennmac/coastal

KENNEDY, Michael. British, b. 1926. **Genres:** Music, Biography. **Career:** Music Critic, Daily Telegraph, London, 1950- (Assistant Northern Ed., 1958-60; Northern Ed., 1960-86). Chief Music Critic, Sunday Telegraph, London, 1989-. **Publications:** The Halle Tradition, 1960; The Works of Ralph Vaughan Williams, 1964; Portrait of Elgar, 1968, 4th ed., 1993; Portrait of Manchester, 1970; History of the Royal Manchester College of Music, 1971; Barbirolli, 1971; Richard Strauss, 1976, rev. ed., 1995; Britten, 1981, rev. ed., 2000; Adrian Boult, 1987; Portrait of Walton, 1989; Music Enriches All: 21 Years of the Royal Northern College of Music, 1994; Richard Strauss, Man, Musician, Enigma, 1999; The Life of Elgar, 2004. EDITOR: Autobiography of Charles Halle; Mahler, 1974, rev. ed., 2000; Concise Oxford Dictionary of Music, 1980, rev. ed., 1995; Oxford Dictionary of Music, 1985, rev. ed., 1994. **Address:** The Bungalow, 62 Edilom Rd, Manchester M8 4HZ, England.

KENNEDY, Pagan. (Pamela). American, b. 1962. **Genres:** Novels, Novellas/Short stories, Horticulture. **Career:** Voice Literary Supplement, "zine" columnist, 1991-; freelance writer. Host of Boston-able cable television show. Recycling and antiwar activist. **Publications:** Stripping and Other Stories, 1994; Platforms: A Microwaved Cultural Chronicle of the 1970s, 1994; Spinsters (novel), 1995. Contributor to periodicals. **Address:** c/o Kim Witherspoon, 235 E 31st St., New York, NY 10016-6302, U.S.A.

KENNEDY, Paul Michael. British, b. 1945. **Genres:** History. **Career:** University of Oxford, Theodor Heuss Research Fellow, 1968-69; University of East Anglia, Norwich, lecturer, 1970-75, reader in history, 1975-83; Yale University, New Haven, CT, Dilworth Professor of History, 1983-. British Academy, fellow; CBE. **Publications:** Pacific Onslaught, 1972; Pacific Victory, 1973; The Samoan Tangle: A Study in Anglo-German-American Relations 1878-1900, 1974; The Rise and Fall of British Naval Mastery, 1976; The Rise and Fall of the Great Powers, 1988; Preparing for the Twenty-First Century, 1993. EDITOR: The War Plans of the Great Powers 1880-1914, 1979; The Rise of Anglo-German Antagonism 1860-1914, 1980; The Realities behind Diplomacy, 1981; Nationalist and Racialist Movements in Britain and Germany before 1914, 1981; Grand Strategies in War and Peace, 1991; Global Trends, 1994. **Address:** Dept of History, Yale University, New Haven, CT 06520, U.S.A. **Online address:** paul_kennedy@yale.edu

KENNEDY, Philip F. British (born Trinidad and Tobago). **Genres:** Literary criticism and history. **Career:** New York University, associate professor of Middle Eastern studies. Studies in Arabic and Middle Eastern Literature, editor. **Publications:** The Wine Song in Classical Arabic Poetry: Abu Nuwas and the Literary Tradition, 1997. Contributor to scholarly journals. **Address:** Department of Middle Eastern Studies, Kevorkian 202, New York University, 50 Washington Sq S, New York, NY 10012, U.S.A. **Online address:** philip.kennedy@nyu.edu

KENNEDY, Randall. American, b. 1954. **Genres:** Law. **Career:** Law professor and author. Admitted to Washington, DC bar, 1983. U.S. Court of Appeals, law clerk to Hon. Skelly Wright, 1982-83; U.S. Supreme Court, law clerk to Hon. Thurgood Marshall, 1983-84; Harvard University, Cambridge, MA, assistant professor of law, 1984-85, associate professor,

1985-89, professor, 1989-. **Publications:** Race, Crime and the Law, 1997. Contributor to scholarly journals. **Address:** Law School, Harvard University, Cambridge, MA 02138, U.S.A.

KENNEDY, Rick. American, b. 1935. **Genres:** Travel/Exploration. **Career:** Random House, NYC, editor, 1970-79; Sony Corp., Tokyo, Japan, editor, 1979-. **Publications:** Home Sweet Tokyo (essays), 1988; Good Tokyo Restaurants, 1992; Little Adventures in Tokyo, 1998; The Tokyo Q Guide to Tokyo, 1999. **Address:** 5-7-7 Takada Nishi, Kohoku-ku, Yokohama 223-0066, Japan. **Online address:** rok@ba2.so-net.ne.jp

KENNEDY, Robert Emmet, Jr. American, b. 1941. **Genres:** History, Philosophy. **Career:** George Washington University, Washington, DC, assistant professor, 1973-77, associate professor, 1977-82, professor of European History, 1982-. Instructor in History, Merrimack College, N. Andover, MA, 1964-66; Teaching assistant, Dept. of the History of Ideas, Brandeis University, Waltham, MA, 1968; Instructor, Kent State University, Ohio, 1968-69; Instructor in History, University of Toulouse-le-Mirail, France, 1969-73. American Council of Learned Socs. Fellow, 1977-78; Woodrow Wilson Fellow, 1983-84; International Congress on the history of the French Revolution, 1789-1989; International Lecturer; Guest Curator of Smithsonian, Documents of Liberty, exhibit, 1989. **Publications:** (ed. with J. Friguglietti) The Shaping of Modern France: Writings on French History since 1715, 1969; A Philosopher in the Age of Revolution: Destutt de Tracy and the Origins of Ideology, 1978; A Cultural History of the French Revolution, 1989; (with M.L. Netter, J.P. McGregor, and M.V. Olsen) Theatre, Opera and Audiences in Revolutionary Paris, Analysis and Repertory, 1996. Contributor to periodicals. **Address:** Dept. of History, George Washington University, Washington, DC 20052, U.S.A. **Online address:** EKennedy@gwu.edu

KENNEDY, William (Joseph). American, b. 1928. **Genres:** Novels, Plays/Screenplays. **Career:** Glen Falls Post Star, assistant sports ed., 1949-50; Albany Times-Union, reporter, 1952-56; Puerto Rico World Journal, San Juan, assistant managing ed., 1956; Miami Herald, reporter, 1957; correspondent, Time-Life Publications in Puerto Rico, and reporter, Knight Newspapers, 1957-59; San Juan Star, founding managing ed., 1959-61; Albany Times-Union, special writer, 1963-70; State University of New York at Albany, lecturer, 1974-82, professor of English, and founder, New York State Writers Institute, 1983-. **Publications:** The Ink Truck (novel), 1969; Legs (novel), 1975; Billy Phelan's Greatest Game (novel), 1978; Ironweed (novel), 1983 (Pulitzer Prize, 1984; National Book Critics Circle Award, 1984), (screenplay), 1987; O Albany! (non-fiction), 1983; (with F.F. Coppola) The Cotton Club (screenplay), 1983; (with B. Kennedy) Charlie Malarkey and the Belley Button Machine (children's book), 1986; Quinn's Book, 1988; Very Old Bones, 1992; Riding The Yellow Trolley Car (non-fiction), 1993; Charlie Malarkey and the Singing Moose, 1994; Grand View (play), 1996; An Albany Trio: Three Novels from the Albany Cycle, 1996; The Flaming Corsage, 1996; Rosco, 2002. **Address:** New York State Writers Institute, University at Albany, State University of New York, 1400 Washington Ave, Albany, NY 12222-0001, U.S.A.

KENNEDY, X. J. (Joseph Charles Kennedy). American, b. 1929. **Genres:** Children's fiction, Poetry, Literary criticism and history, Translations. **Career:** Tufts University, Medford, MA, assistant professor, 1963-67, associate professor, 1967-73, professor of English, 1973-79; Paris Review, poetry editor, 1962-64; Counter/Measures, co-editor, 1972-74. **Publications:** Nude Descending a Staircase, 1961, 2nd ed., 1994; An Introduction to Poetry, 1966, 11th ed. (with D. Gioia), 2005; Growing into Love, 1969; Breaking and Entering, 1972; Emily Dickinson in Southern California, 1974; One Winter Night in August, 1975; (with J.E. Camp and K. Waldrop) Three Tenors, One Vehicle, 1975; An Introduction to Fiction, 1976, 9th ed. (with D. Gioia), 2005; Literature, 1976, 9th ed. (with D. Gioia), 2005; The Phantom Ice Cream Man, 1979; Did Adam Name the Vinegarroon?, 1982; (with D.M. Kennedy) Knock at a Star: A Child's Introduction to Poetry, 1982, rev. ed., 1999; French Leave: Translations, 1984; Hangover Mass, 1984; The Forgetful Wishing Well: Poems for Young People, 1985; Cross Ties: Selected Poems, 1985; Brats, 1986; (with D.M. Kennedy) The Bedford Guide for College Writers, 1987, 7th ed. (with D.M. Kennedy, M.F. Muth, and S.A. Holladay), 2005; Ghastlies, Goops and Pincushions, 1989; Winter Thunder, 1990; Fresh Brats, 1990; The Kite That Braved Old Orchard Beach, 1991; (with D.M. Kennedy) Talking Like the Rain: A First Book of Poetry, 1992; The Beasts of Bethlehem, 1992; Dark Horses: New Poems, 1992; Drat These Brats!, 1993; The Minimus Poems, 1996; Uncle Switch, 1997; Elympics, 1999; Elefantina's Dream, 2002; The Purpose of Time, 2002; The Lords of Misrule: Poems, 1992-2001, 2002. EDITOR: (with J.E. Camp) Mark Twain's Frontier, 1963; (with J.E. Camp and K. Waldrop) Pegasus Descending, 1971,

2nd ed., 2004; Messages: A Thematic Anthology of Poetry, 1973; Tygers of Wrath, 1981; (with D.M. Kennedy) The Bedford Reader, 1982, 8th ed. (with D.M. Kennedy and J. Aaron), 2002; (with D. Gioia and M. Bauerlein) Handbook of Literary Terms, 2005. **Address:** 22 Revere St, Lexington, MA 02420-4424, U.S.A.

KENNELL, Nigel M. British, b. 1955. **Genres:** Classics. **Career:** Brock University, St. Catharines, Ontario, Canada, lecturer in classics, 1985-86; Memorial University, St. John's, Newfoundland, Canada, assistant professor, 1986-92, associate professor of classics, 1992-; Institute for Advanced Study, Princeton, NJ, research assistant, 1992-93; College de France, Paris, research associate, 1993. **Publications:** The Gymnasium of Virtue, 1996. Contributor to periodicals. **Address:** Classics Department, Memorial University, St. John's, NL, Canada A1C 5S7.

KENNELLY, (Timothy) Brendan. Irish, b. 1936. **Genres:** Novels, Poetry. **Career:** Trinity College, Dublin, jr. lecturer, 1963-66, lecturer, 1966-69, associate professor, 1969-73, chairman, English dept., 1973-76, professor of modern literature, 1973-. **Publications:** (with R. Holzapfel) Cast a Cold Eye, 1959; (with R. Holzapfel) The Rain, the Moon, 1961; (with R. Holzapfel) The Dark about Our Loves, 1962; (with R. Holzapfel) Green Townlands: Poems, 1963; Let Fall No Burning Leaf, 1963; The Crooked Cross (novel), 1963; My Dark Fathers, 1964; Up and At It, 1965; Collection One: Getting Up Early, 1966; Good Souls to Survive: Poems, 1967; The Florentines (novel), 1967; Dream of a Black Fox, 1968; Selected Poems, 1969; A Drinking Cup: Poems from the Irish, 1970; Bread, 1971; Love-Cry, 1972; Salvation, The Stranger, 1972; The Voices, 1973; Shelley in Dublin, 1974; A Kind of Trust, 1975; New and Selected Poems, 1976, 1978; Islandman, 1977; The Visitor, 1978; A Small Light, 1979; In Spite of the Wise, 1979; The Boats Are Home, 1980; The House That Jack Didn't Build, 1982; Cromwell, 1983; Selected Poems, 1985; Real Ireland, 1988; A Time for Voices: Selected Poems 1960-1990, 1990; The Book of Judas, 1991; Breathing Spaces, 1992; The Trojan Women, 1993; Journey into Joy, 1994; Poetry My Arse, 1995; Sophocles' Antigone, 1996; Words for Women (poems), 1997; Singing Tree, 1998; Man Made of Rain, 1998; Begin, 1999; Little Book of Judas, 2002; Between Innocence and Peace, 2002; Glimpses, 2001; Martial Art, 2003. EDITOR: The Penguin Book of Irish Verse, 1970, rev. ed., 1981; Ireland Past and Present, 1986; Landmarks of Irish Drama, 1988. **Address:** Dept of English, Trinity College, Dublin 2, Ireland. **Online address:** tknnelly@tcd.ie

KENNEMORE, Tim. British. **Genres:** Novellas/Short stories, Children's fiction. **Career:.** **Publications:** The Middle of the Sandwich, 1981; The Fortunate Few, 1981; Wall of Words, 1982; Here Tomorrow, Gone Today, 1983; Changing Times, 1984; Alice's Birthday Pig, 1995; Alice's World Record, 1996; Circle of Doom, 2001; Sabine, 2003. **Address:** c/o Andersen Press, 20 Vauxhall Bridge Rd, London SW1V 2SA, England.

KENNET, Lord. Also writes as Wayland Young, Wayland Kennet. British, b. 1923. **Genres:** Novels, History, International relations/Current affairs, Politics/Government, Social commentary, Travel/Exploration. **Career:** Member, House of Lords, 1960-99. Parliamentary Secretary, Ministry of Housing and Local Government, 1966-70; Labour Opposition Spokesman on Foreign Affairs and Science Policy, 1971-74; Social Democratic Party Spokesman on Foreign Affairs and Defence, 1981-90; Chief Whip, SDP, 1981-83. Chairman of International Parliamentary Conferences on the Environment, 1972-78; Vice President of the Parliamentary and Scientific Committee, 1988-99. Member, European Parliament, 1977-79. President of the UK Architecture Club, 1984-94; Vice President, Parliamentary Office of Science and Technology, 1990-93. **Publications:** AS WAYLAND YOUNG: The Italian Left, 1949; The Deadweight, 1952; Now or Never, 1953; (with E. Young) Old London Churches, 1956; The Montesi Scandal, 1957; Still Alive Tomorrow, 1958; Strategy for Survival, 1959; (with E. Young) The Socialist Imagination, 1960; (with E. Young) Disarmament: Finnegan's Choice, 1961; The Profumo Affair, 1963; Eros Denied, 1965; Thirty-four Articles, 1965; (ed.) Existing Mechanisms of Arms Control, 1965; (as Wayland Kennet) Preservation, 1972; The Futures of Europe, 1976; (with E. Young) Neither Red Nor Dead: The Case for Disarmament, 1981; The Rebirth of Britain, 1982; (with E. Young) London's Churches, 1986; (with E. Young) Northern Lazio, 1990; Parliaments and Screening, 1995. **Address:** 100 Bayswater Rd, London W2 3HJ, England.

KENNET, Wayland. See KENNET, Lord.

KENNEY, Catherine (McGehee). American, b. 1948. **Genres:** Novels, Literary criticism and history, Plays/Screenplays, Women's studies and issues, Humor/Satire. **Career:** Worked for a weekly newspaper; Thornton Community College, South Holland, IL, lecturer in English, 1974-76; Mun-

delein College, Chicago, IL, assistant professor, 1976-81, associate professor of English, 1981-91, chairman of department, 1978-85. Lecturer, Harper College, Palatine, IL, 1974-75. Member of Academic Humanists Advisory Board, Chicago Public Library, 1978-79; director of Lyceum Seminars, Newberry Library, 1981-. Consultant to American National Bank, Chicago Editorial Board and Board of Directors, Jane Austen Society. **Publications:** Thurber's Anatomy of Confusion, 1984; The Remarkable Case of Dorothy L. Sayers, 1990; Dorothy L. (play), 1993.

KENNEY, Charles. American, b. 1950. **Genres:** Documentaries/Reportage, Novels, Mystery/Crime/Suspense. **Career:** Boston Globe, Boston, MA, reporter and editor, 1978-94. **Publications:** (with R.L. Turner) Dukakis: An American Odyssey, 1988; Riding the Runaway Horse: The Rise and Decline of Wang Labs, 1992; Hammurabi's Code (novel), 1995; The Last Man (novel), 2001. **Address:** c/o Phillipa Brophy, Sterling Lord Literistic Inc., 65 Bleeker St., New York, NY 10012-2420, U.S.A.

KENNEY, Padraic (Jeremiah). American, b. 1963. **Genres:** Law. **Career:** University of Colorado, Boulder, assistant professor, 1992-99, associate professor, 1999-2003, professor of history, 2003-, associate chair and director of undergraduate studies, department of history. **Publications:** A Carnival of Revolution: Central Europe, 1989; (editor, with Gerd-Rainer Horn) Transnational Moments of Change: Europe 1945, 1968, 1989; Rebuilding Poland: Workers and Communists, 1945-1950, 1997. Contributor of articles, essays, and reviews to journals. Works represented in books by others. **Address:** Department of History, University of Colorado, Box 234, Boulder, CO 80309, U.S.A. **Online address:** padraic.kenney@colorado.edu

KENNEY, Richard (L.). American, b. 1948. **Genres:** Poetry. **Career:** Writer; University of Washington, Seattle, professor of English, 1987-. **Publications:** The Evolution of the Flightless Bird (poetry) 1984; Orrery (poetry), 1985; The Invention of the Zero, (poetry), 1993. **Address:** c/o Department of English, University of Washington, Seattle, WA 98195, U.S.A.

KENNEY, William Howland, III. American, b. 1940. **Genres:** Music, History. **Career:** Kent State University, Kent, OH, 1966-76, assistant professor, became associate professor, currently professor emeritus of American history and studies, 1976-. **Publications:** Chicago Jazz: A Cultural History, 1904-1930, 1993; Recorded Music in American Life: The Phonograph and Popular Memory, 1890-1945, 1999. EDITOR: Laughter in the Wilderness: Early American Humor to 1783, 1976; (with S. Deveaux) The Music of James Scott, 1993. Contributor to books and professional journals. **Address:** Department of History, Kent State University, 305 Bowman Hall, Kent, OH 44242, U.S.A. **Online address:** wkenney@kent.edu

KENNY, Sir Anthony (John Patrick). British, b. 1931. **Genres:** Intellectual history, Philosophy. **Career:** University of Oxford, Fellow of Balliol College, 1964-78, Wilde Lecturer on Natural Religion, 1969-72, Master, 1978-89, Pro-Vice-Chancellor for Development, 1998-2001; Warden of Rhodes House, 1989-99; British Academy, President, 1989-93; British Library, Chairman, 1993-97. **Publications:** Action, Emotion & Will, 1963; Descartes, 1968; The Five Ways, 1969; (trans.) Descartes: Philosophical Letters, 1969; (with C. Longuet-Higgins) The Nature of the Mind, 1972; Wittgenstein, 1973; Will, Freedom, and Power, 1975; The Aristotelian Ethics, 1978; Aristotle's Theory of the Will, 1979; The God of the Philosophers, 1979; Aquinas, 1980; Thomas More, 1982; Wyclif, 1985; The Legacy of Wittgenstein, 1984; The Ivory Tower, 1985; The Road to Hillsborough, 1986; Reason and Religion, 1987; The Heritage of Wisdom, 1987; God and Two Poets, 1988; The Metaphysics of Mind, 1989; The Oxford Diaries of Arthur Hugh Clough, 1990; Aristotle on the Perfect Life, 1992; Aquinas on Mind, 1993; Frege, 1995; A Life in Oxford, 1997; A Brief History of Western Philosophy, 1998; Essays on the Aristotelian Tradition, 2001; Aquinas on Being, 2002; The Unknown God, 2004. EDITOR: (and trans.) Blackfriars Edition of Aquinas' Summa Theologiae, 1964; Aquinas: A Collection of Critical Essays, 1969; Wyclif in His Times, 1986; The History of the Rhodes Trust, 2001. **Address:** 1A Larkins Ln, Old Headington, Oxford, England.

KENNY, Lorraine Delia. (born United States), b. 1961. **Genres:** Social sciences. **Career:** Visual Studies Workshop, Rochester, NY, intern, 1984-85, assistant editor, 1985-86, subscriptions coordinator, 1985-87, associate editor, 1987-89; National Council for Research on Women, New York, NY, coordinating editor, 1994-96; freelance copy editor and proofreader, 1996-97; Sarah Lawrence College, Bronxville, NY, member of anthropology guest faculty, 1997-2000; American Civil Liberties Union, New York, NY, public education coordinator for Reproductive Freedom Project, 2000-. University of California-Santa Cruz, instructor, 1992, 1993; LaGuardia Community College of the City University of New York, adjunct assistant professor, 1996,

1997; New School for Social Research, adjunct assistant professor at Eugene Lang College, 1997; also speaker at Free University of Amsterdam and University of California-Berkeley; workshop coordinator. **Publications:** Daughters of Suburbia: Growing Up White, Middle Class, and Female, 2000. Contributor to books and of articles and reviews to periodicals. **Address:** American Civil Liberties Union, 125 Broad St., New York, NY 10004, U.S.A. **Online address:** lkenny@aclu.org

KENNY, Maurice (Francis). American, b. 1929. **Genres:** Novellas/Short stories, Poetry, Literary criticism and history. **Career:** Writer. Associate professor at Paul Smith's College, Paul Smith's, NY; University of Victoria, BC, Canada; and North Country Community College, Saranac Lake, NY; visiting professor at University of Oklahoma, Norman; visiting poet, Lehigh University, spring, 1987. coordinator of the Robert Louis Stevenson Annual Writers Conference, summers 1987, 1988; SUNY, Potsdam, writer in residence. Has given lectures and readings throughout the country. **Publications:** Dead Letters Sent, and Other Poems, 1958; With Love to Lesbia, 1959; North: Poems of Home, 1977; Dancing Back Strong the Nation: Poems, 1979; I Am the Sun: A Lakota Chant, 1979; Only as Far as Brooklyn, 1979; Kneading the Blood, 1981, rev. ed., 1987; Blackrobe: Isaac Jogues, b. March 11, 1607, d. October 18, 1646: Poems, 1982; The Smell of Slaughter, 1982; Boston Tea Party, 1982; The Mama Poems, 1984; Rain and Other Fictions (short stories), 1985, rev. ed., 1990; Is Summer This Bear, 1985; Between Two Rivers: Selected Poems, 1987; Humors and/or Not So Humorous, 1987; Greyhounding This America: Poems and Dialog, 1988; Selections: Poems, 1988; The Short and the Long of It, 1990; Last Mornings in Brooklyn (chapbook), 1991; Tekonwatonti: Molly Brant (1735-1795): Poems of War, 1992, rev. ed., 2002; On Second Thought, 1995; Backward to Forward (essay), 1997; Tortured Skins & Other Fictions (short stories), 2000; In the Time of the Present (poetry), 2000; Carving Hawk (poetry). EDITOR: (and author of intro.) Wounds beneath the Flesh, 1983; Stories for a Winter's Night: Native American Fictions (short stories), 2000. Has composed poetry for TV programs. Contributor to periodicals. **Address:** Box 1029, Saranac Lake, NY 12983, U.S.A.

KENRICK, Tony. Australian, b. 1935. **Genres:** Mystery/Crime/Suspense. **Career:** Worked as an advertising copywriter in Sydney, Toronto, NYC, San Francisco, and London, 1953-72. **Publications:** The Only Good Body's a Dead One, 1970; A Tough One to Lose, 1972; Two for the Price of One, 1974; Stealing Lillian, 1975 (in U.K. as The Kidnap Kid, 1976); The Seven Day Soldiers, 1976; The Chicago Girl, 1976; Two Lucky People, 1978; The Nighttime Guy, 1979; The 81st Site, 1980; Blast, 1983; Faraday's Flowers, 1985; China White, 1986; Shanghai Surprise, 1986; Neon Tough, 1988; Glitterbug, 1991; The Return, 1996. **Address:** c/o Jean Naggar, 216 E. 75th St, New York, NY 10021, U.S.A.

KENT, Alan. *See* KINNEY, Arthur F.

KENT, Alexander. *See* REEMAN, Douglas (Edward).

KENT, Debra. American, b. 1952. **Genres:** Novels. **Career:** Writer. **Publications:** (ed.) The Kinsey Institute New Report on Sex: What You Must Know to Be Sexually Literate, 1990; The Diary of V: The Affair, 2001; The Diary of V: The Breakup, 2001; The Diary of V: Happily Ever After, 2001. Contributor to magazines. **Address:** c/o Author Mail, Warner Books, 1271 Avenue of the Americas, New York, NY 10020, U.S.A.

KENT, Helen. *See* POLLEY, Judith Anne.

KENT, Homer Austin, Jr. American, b. 1926. **Genres:** Theology/Religion. **Career:** Professor, Grace Theological Seminary and Grace College, Winona Lake, Indiana, 1951-98 (Dean, 1962-76; President, 1976-86). Consultant trans. of New International Version of the New Testament, 1968-73. **Publications:** The Pastoral Epistles, 1958; Ephesians: The Glory of the Church, 1971; Jerusalem to Rome, 1972; Epistle to the Hebrews: An Expository Commentary, 1972; Light in the Darkness, 1974; The Freedom of God's Sons, 1976; Treasures of Wisdom, 1978; A Heart Opened Wide, 1982; Faith That Works, 1986. **Address:** 305 6th St, Winona Lake, IN 46590, U.S.A.

KENT, James M. American, b. 1956. **Genres:** Marine sciences/Oceanography. **Career:** Litchfield County Times, New Milford, CT, reporter, 1980-81; The Advocate, Stamford, CT, reporter, 1982-83; Patient Care, Darien, CT, associate editor, 1983-85; Schlumberger Ltd, Ridgefield, CT, editor, 1985-96, NY, editor, 1997-2000; Thomson Corp., Stamford, CT, director of communications, 2000-02; Woods Hole Oceanographic Institution, director of communications, 2002-; writer. **Publications:** (with P.C.

Patton) A Moveable Shore: The Fate of the Connecticut Coast, 1992. **Address:** 246 Wild Harbor Rd, North Falmouth, MA 02556, U.S.A.

KENT, Joseph (P.). American, b. 1940. **Genres:** Poetry. **Career:** Writer. **Publications:** POETRY: White Wind, 1989; Streams, 1996. Contributor to books and periodicals. **Address:** 1372 Pine St, San Francisco, CA 94109, U.S.A. **Online address:** sunli8@msn.com

KENT, Richard G. American, b. 1951. **Genres:** Law, Sports/Fitness. **Career:** Attorney and writer. **Publications:** (with J. Steinbreder) Fighting for Your Children: A Father's Guide to Custody, 1998; (ed.) Inside Women's College Basketball: Anatomy of a Season, 2000, as Inside Women's College Basketball: Anatomy of Two Seasons, 2002. **Address:** 1115 Brood Ct., Bridgeport, CT 06601, U.S.A. **Online address:** bewbr@aol.com

KENT, Timothy J. American, b. 1949. **Genres:** Local history/Rural topics, History. **Career:** Silver Fox Enterprises, Ossineke, MI, writer and publisher. **Publications:** Birchbark Canoes of the Fur Trade, 2 vols, 1997; (ed.) Ft. Pontchartrain at Detroit: A Guide to the Daily Lives of Fur Traders, Military Personnel, Settlers, and Missionaries at French Posts, 2 vols, 2001; Tahquamenon Tales: Experiences of an Early French Trader and His Native Family, 2002. **Address:** Silver Fox Enterprises, 11504 U.S. 23 S., Ossineke, MI 49766, U.S.A.

KENTFIELD, J(ohn) A(lan) C. British, b. 1930. **Genres:** Engineering. **Career:** C.V.A. Kearney and Trecker Ltd., Brighton, England, trainee, 1950-52; Ricardo and Co. Ltd., Shoreham-by-Sea, England, assistant tester, 1952-56; University of London, Imperial College of Science and Technology, London, England, assistant lecturer in mechanical engineering, 1952-53; Curtiss-Wright Corp., Woodridge, NJ, project engineer, 1963-66; University of London, Imperial College of Science and Technology, lecturer in mechanical engineering, 1966-70; University of Calgary, Calgary, Alberta, associate professor, 1970-78, professor of mechanical engineering, 1978-, Killam resident fellow, 1980. Swiss Federal Institute of Technology, visiting professor, 1974-75; Naval Postgraduate School, Monterey, CA, visiting professor, 1990. Inventor, responsible for several patents; consultant to corporations in Canada and the United States. **Publications:** Nonsteady 1D: Internal Compressible Flows, 1993; The Fundamentals of Wind-Driven Water Pumpers, 1996. Contributor to scientific journals. **Address:** Department of Mechanical Engineering, University of Calgary, Calgary, AB, Canada T2N 1N4.

KENTON, Warren. Also writes as Zev ben Shimon Halevi. British, b. 1933. **Genres:** Novels, Paranormal, Theatre, Theology/Religion. **Career:** Freelance writer and lectr. Tutor, Architectural Association London, 1966-71; Lecturer Royal Academy of Dramatic Art, London, 1963-81; Wrekin Trust, lecturer; Temenos Academy, fellow; Way of Kabbalah courses in Europe, the Americas, Israel, founder. **Publications:** Stage Properties, 1964; As Above So Below, 1969; The Play Begins (novel), 1971; (as Zev ben Shimon Halevi) Tree of Life, 1972; Astrology, 1974; Adam and the Kabbalistic Tree, 1974; Way of Kabbalah, 1976; Kabbalistic Universe, 1977; Anatomy of Fate, 1978; Kabbalah: Tradition of Hidden Knowledge, 1979; Kabbalah and Exodus, 1979; Work of the Kabbalist, 1984; School of Kabbalah, 1985; Kabbalah and Psychology, 1986; The Anointed (novel), 1987; The Divine Plan: Kabbalah, 1996; Astrology and Kabbalah, 2001. Contributor to magazines. **Address:** 56 Torbay Rd, London NW6 7DZ, England.

KENWARD, Jean. (Jean Chesterman). British, b. 1920. **Genres:** Children's fiction, Poetry, Novellas/Short stories. **Career:** Part-time Lecturer in Creative Writing, Harrow School of Art, Middlesex, 1969-. **Publications:** A Book of Rhymes; Rain: A Flight of Words; The Forest; Old Mister Hotch Potch; (with B. Roe) Sing for Christmas; Ragdolly Anna Stories, 1979; Clutterby Hogg, 1980; Theme and Variations, 1981; Three Cheers for Ragdolly Anna, 1985; (adaptor) Aesop's Fables, 1986; The Hotchpotch Horse, 1987; Ragdolly Anna's Circus, 1987; The Odd Job Man and the Thousand Mile Boots, 1988; A Kettle Full of Magic, 1988; Seasons, 1989; Ragdolly Anna's Treasure Hunt, 1989. Contributor of poems to anthologies and school collections, and to radio. **Address:** 15 Shire Lane, Chorley Wood, Herts. WD3 5NQ, England.

KENWORTHY, Brian J(ohn). British, b. 1920. **Genres:** Literary criticism and history. **Career:** Translations. Teacher of Modern Languages, Cotham Grammar School, Bristol, 1943-46; Assistant Lecturer, 1947-52, Lecturer, 1952-68, and Sr. Lecturer in German, 1968-81, University of Aberdeen. **Publications:** George Kaiser, 1957; (co-trans.) The Drama of the Atom, 1958; (co-author) A Manual of German Prose Composition for Advanced Students, 1966; (ed.) George Kaiser: Die Koralle, Gas I and II, 1968 (also trans., 1971); (ed.) Hermann Sudermann: Litauische Geschichten, 1971; (ed.) George Kaiser: Plays, vol. 2, 1982. **Address:** 22 Upper Cranbrook Rd, Redland, Bristol BS6 7UN, England.

KENYON, Michael. Also writes as Daniel Forbes. American (born England), b. 1931. **Genres:** Novels, Mystery/Crime/Suspense, Travel/Exploration, Young adult fiction. **Career:** Regular contributor, Gourmet mag., NYC, since 1971. Reporter, Bristol Evening Post, 1955-58, News Chronicle, London, 1958-60, and Manchester Guardian, 1960-64. **Publications:** May You Die in Ireland, 1965; The Whole Hog (in U.S. as Trouble with Series Three), 1967; Out of Season, 1968; Green Grass, 1969; The 100,000 Welcomes, 1970; The Shooting of Dan McGrew, 1971; A Sorry State, 1973; Mr. Big, 1975; Brainbox and Bull (juvenile), 1975; The Rapist, 1977; Deep Pocket (in U.S. as The Molehill File), 1978; The Elgar Variation, 1981 (in U.S. as Daniel Forbes); Zigzag, 1981; The God Squad Bod (in U.S. as the Man at the Wheel), 1982; A Free-Range Wife, 1983; A Healthy Way to Die, 1986; Peckover Holds the Baby, 1988; Kill the Butler!, 1991; Peckover Joins the Choir, 1992; A French Affair, 1992; Peckover and the Bog Man, 1994. **Address:** 164 Halsey St, Southampton, NY 11968, U.S.A. **Online address:** harken2@optionline.net

KEOHANE, Dan. British (born Ireland), b. 1941. **Genres:** International relations/Current affairs, Politics/Government. **Career:** University of Keele, England, senior lecturer in international relations, 1977-2003, honorary research fellow, 2003-. **Publications:** Labour Party Defence Policy since 1945, 1993; (ed. with A. Danchev) International Perspectives on the Gulf Conflict, 1990-1991, 1994; Security in British Politics, 1945-99, 2000. **Address:** School of Politics, Intl Relations and the Environment, University of Keele, Keele, Staffs ST5 5BC, England. **Online address:** D.J.Keohane@Keele.ac.uk

KERBEL, Matthew Robert. American, b. 1958. **Genres:** Politics/Government, Communications/Media. **Career:** WNET/13 Public Television, NYC, news writer, 1980-82; University of Michigan, Ann Arbor, lecturer, 1987-88; Villanova University, Villanova, PA, assistant professor, 1988-95, associate professor, 1995-99, professor of political science, 1999-. **Publications:** Beyond Persuasion: Organizational Efficiency and Presidential Power, 1991; Edited for Television: CNN, ABC, and the 1992 Presidential Campaign, 1994; Remote and Controlled: Media Politics in a Cynical Age, 1995; If It Bleeds, It Leads: An Anatomy of Television News, 2000. Contributor of articles and reviews to political science journals. **Address:** Department of Political Science, Villanova University, Villanova, PA 19085, U.S.A.

KERBER, Linda K(aufman). American, b. 1940. **Genres:** History, Women's studies and issues. **Career:** Stern College for Women, Yeshiva University, NYC, lecturer, 1963-67, assistant professor, 1968; San Jose State College, CA, assistant professor, 1969-70; Stanford University, CA, visiting assistant professor, 1970-71; University of Iowa, Iowa City, associate professor, 1971-75, professor of history, 1975-85, May Brodbeck professor of liberal arts, 1985-. University of Chicago, IL, visiting professor, 1991-92. American Academy of Arts and Sciences, fellow; American Studies Association, president, 1988; Organization of American Historians, president, 1997; American Historical Association, president-elect, 2005. **Publications:** Federalists in Dissent: Imagery and Ideology in Jeffersonian America, 1970; Women of the Republic: Intellect and Ideology in Revolutionary America, 1980; Toward an Intellectual History of Women: Essays, 1997; No Constitutional Right to Be Ladies: Women and the Obligations of Citizenship, 1998. EDITOR: (with J. De Hart-Mathews) Women's America: Refocusing the Past, 1982, 6th ed., 2004; (with A. Kessler-Harris and K.K. Sklar) U.S. History as Women's History: New Feminist Essays, 1995. Contributor to professional journals. **Address:** Dept of History, University of Iowa, Iowa City, IA 52242, U.S.A.

KERBY, Mona. American. **Genres:** Children's fiction, Children's nonfiction, Librarianship. **Career:** Arlington, TX, kindergarten teacher, 1973-78; J.B. Little Elementary School, Arlington, librarian, 1978-93; writer of children's books, 1987-. Texas Woman's University, adjunct professor in library and information science, 1989-94; Western Maryland College, school library media program, coordinator 1994-. **Publications:** Investigating the Effectiveness of School Library Instruction, 1984; Friendly Bees, Ferocious Bees, 1987; Thirty-eight Weeks till Summer Vacation, 1989; Asthma, 1989; Beverly Sills: America's Own Opera Star, 1989; Cockroaches, 1989; Amelia Earhart: Courage in the Sky, 1990; Samuel Morse, 1991; Frederick Douglass, 1990; Yearbooks in Science 1950-59, 1997; Robert E. Lee, 1997; Reading Fun, 1998. **Address:** School Library Media Program, Thompson Hall, McDaniel College, Westminster, MD 21157-4390, U.S.A. **Online address:** rkerby@mcdaniel.edu

KERESZTY, Roch A. American (born Hungary), b. 1933. **Genres:** Theology/Religion. **Career:** University of Dallas, Texas, lecturer in theology, 1963-65, assistant professor of theology, 1965-70, chaplain, 1963-65, associate professor, 1970-78, adjunct professor of theology, 1978-; Cistercian Preparatory School, Irving, TX, instructor, 1969-, chairman of Theology Dept., 1972-. **Publications:** God Seekers for a New Age: From Crisis Theology to Christian Atheism, 1970; Krisztus, 1977; (with W.R. Farmer) Peter and Paul in the Church of Rome, 1990; Jesus Christ, Fundamentals of Christology, 1991, 2nd ed., 2002; (ed.) Rediscovering the Eucharist: Ecumenical Conversation, 2003. **Address:** Cistercian Abbey, 3550 Cistercian Rd, Irving, TX 75039, U.S.A. **Online address:** Fr-Roch@cistercian.org

KERET, Etgar. Israeli, b. 1967. **Genres:** Novels, Novellas/Short stories. **Career:** Author, journalist, and filmmaker. Columnist for a weekly newspaper in Jerusalem; comic strip writer for a Tel Aviv newspaper; comedy writer for Israeli television; lecturer at Tel Aviv University School of Film. Writer-in-residence, University of Iowa International Writing Program, 2001; participant in Sundance Institute Feature Film Program Screenwriters Lab, 2001. **Publications:** IN ENGLISH TRANSLATION: How to Make a Good Script Great, 1996; Jetlag, 1998; Selected Stories, 1998; The Bus Driver Who Wanted to Be God and Other Stories, trans. D. Bilu and M. Shlesinger, 2001. IN HEBREW: Tsinorot (short stories; title means: Pipelines), 1992; Ga'gu'ai le-Kising'er (title means: Missing Kissinger), 1994; (with R. Modan) Lo banu le-henot (comics; title means: Nobody Said It Was Going to Be Fun), 1996; (with A. Hanuka) Simta'ot ha-za'am (comics; title means: Streets of Rage), 1997; Ha-Kaitanah shel Kneler (novella; title means: Kneller's Happy Campers), 1998; (with J. Bar Giora) Entebbe (musical play). Author of teleplays; writer and director, with R. Tal, of short movie Skin Deep (also called Malka Red-Heart and Queen of Red Hearts). Keret's writings have been translated into fifteen languages. **Address:** c/o Author Mail, St. Martin's Press, 175 Fifth Ave., New York, NY 10010, U.S.A.

KERKHOFF, Blair. American, b. 1959. **Genres:** Sports/Fitness. **Career:** College sports reporter and author. Kansas City Star, Kansas City, MO, reporter, 1989-. **Publications:** Phog Allen: the Father of Basketball Coaching, 1996; A Century of Jayhawk Triumphs: The One Hundred Greatest Victories in the History of Kansas Basketball, 1997; The Greatest Book of College Basketball, 1998; Upon Further Review: Controversy in Sports Officiating, 2000. **Address:** Kansas City Star, 1729 Grand Blvd., Kansas City, MO 64108, U.S.A. **Online address:** bkerkhoff@kcstar.com

KERMAN, Joseph. American (born England), b. 1924. **Genres:** Music. **Career:** Professor of Music, University of California, Berkeley, 1952-. coed., 19th-Century Music, 1979-86; Heather Professor of Music, Oxford University, 1971-73. **Publications:** Opera as Drama, 1956, 1988; The Elizabethan Madrigal, 1962; The Beethoven Quartets, 1967; (with H. W. Janson) A History of Art and Music, 1968; (ed.) Beethoven: Autograph Miscellany (the Kafka Sketchbook), 1970; (with V. Kerman) Listen, 1972, 8th ed., 2003; The Masses and Motets of William Byrd, 1981; (with A. Tyson) The New Grove Beethoven, 1983; Contemplating Music, 1985; Write All These Down, 1994; Concerto Conversations, 1999; The Art of Fugue, 2005. **Address:** 107 Southampton Ave, Berkeley, CA 94707, U.S.A.

KERMODE, (John) Frank. British, b. 1919. **Genres:** Literary criticism and history, Autobiography/Memoirs. **Career:** Fellow of King's College, Cambridge, 1974-. General Ed., Modern Masters, Masterguides series, and Oxford Authors. John Edward Taylor Professor of English, Manchester University, 1958-65; Winterstoke Professor of English Literature, Bristol University, 1965-67; Lord Northcliffe Professor of Modern English Literature, University College London, 1967-74; King Edward VII Professor of English Literature, Cambridge University, 1974-82. **Publications:** Romantic Image, 1957; Wallace Stevens, 1960, 1989; Puzzles and Epiphanies, 1962; The Sense of an Ending, 1967; Continuities, 1968; Shakespeare, Spenser, Donne, 1971; Modern Essays, 1971; D.H. Lawrence, 1973; The Classic, 1975; The Genesis of Secrecy, 1979; The Art of Telling (essays), 1983; Forms of Attention, 1985; History and Value, 1988; An Appetite for Poetry, 1989; Poetry, Narrative, History, 1990; The Uses of Error, 1991; Not Entitled (memoir), 1995; Shakespeare's Language, 2000; Pleasing Myself, 2001; Pieces of My Mind, 2003. EDITOR: English Pastoral Poetry, 1952; Shakespeare: The Tempest, 1954; (and contrib.) The Living Milton, 1960; Discussions of John Donne, 1962; Edmund Spenser, 1964; Four Centuries of Shakespearean Criticism, 1965; Selected Poetry of Andrew Marvell, 1967; The Metaphysical Poets, 1969; King Lear: A Casebook, 1970; Poems of John Donne, 1970; (with R. Poirier) The Oxford Reader, 1971; (with J. Hollander) Oxford Anthology of English Literature, 1973; Selected Prose of T.S. Eliot, 1975; (with R. Alter) The Literary Guide to the Bible, 1987. **Address:** King's College, Cambridge CB2 1ST, England. **Online address:** frankkermode@lineone.net

KERN, Gregory. See TUBB, E(dwin) C(harles).

KERNER, Elizabeth. American. **Genres:** Science fiction/Fantasy. **Career:** Author. **Publications:** Song in the Silence: The Tale of Lanen Kaelar, 1997; The Lesser Kindred, 2001. **Address:** c/o Tor Books Author Mail, 175 Fifth Avenue, New York, NY 10010, U.S.A. **Online address:** Elizabeth@ elizabethkerner.com

KERNER, Fred. Also writes as Frederick Kerr, M. N. Thaler. Canadian, b. 1921. **Genres:** Novellas/Short stories, Songs/Lyrics and libretti, Children's non-fiction, Food and Wine, History, How-to books, Inspirational/ Motivational Literature, Medicine/Health, Inspirational/Motivational Literature, Medicine/Health, Psychology, Self help, Writing/Journalism, Humor/Satire, Reference. **Career:** President, Publishing Projects Inc, 1964-. Ed. Emeritus and Sr. Consulting Ed., Harlequin Enterprises Ltd., 1985- (Vice-President of Publishing, 1975-85). Newsman and Foreign Correspondent, 1942-56; Sr. Editor, Prentice-Hall, 1957-59; Ed.-in-Chief, Fawcett World Library, NYC, 1959-64; President and Ed.-in-Chief, Hawthorn Books, NYC, 1964-68; Editorial Director, Book and Educational Divs. Reader's Digest Association (Canada) Ltd., Montreal, 1968-75. **Publications:** (with L. Kotkin) Eat, Think and Be Slender, 1954; (with W. Germain) The Magic Power of Your Mind, 1956; (with J. Brothers) Ten Days to a Successful Memory, 1957; (anthologist) Love Is a Man's Affair, 1958; Stress and Your Heart, 1961; (as Frederick Kerr) Watch Your Weight Go Down, 1962; (with W. Germain) Secrets of Your Supraconscious, 1965; (comp.) A Treasury of Lincoln Quotations, 1965; (with D. Goodman) What's Best for Your Child and You, 1966; (with J. Reid) Buy High, Sell Higher!, 1966; (as M.N. Thaler) It's Fun to Fondue, 1968; (with I. Grumenza) Nadia, 1976; Mad about Fondue, 1986; Folles, Folles, Les Fondues, 1987; (with A. Willman) Prospering through the Coming Depression, 1988; (ed.) The Canadian Writer's Guide, 9th ed., 1985, 11th ed., 1991; The Home Emergency Handbook, 1990; Fabulous Fondues, 2000; Don't Count Calories, 2000; Los Mejores Fondues, 2000. **Address:** 1555 Finch Ave E Ste 1405, Willowdale, ON, Canada M2J 4X9. **Online address:** fkerner@pubproj.com

KERNFELD, Barry (Dean). American, b. 1950. **Genres:** Music. **Career:** Freelance writer and editor. Hamilton College, part-time lecturer, 1981-82; Cornell University, Ithaca, NY, lecturer, 1983-84. Part-time saxophonist, 1980-84, 1994-. Freelance writer, 1984-. **Publications:** What to Listen for in Jazz, 1995; Pop Song Piracy: Bootleg Song Sheets, Fake Books, and America's First Criminal Copyright Trials, forthcoming. EDITOR: (and contrib.) The New Grove Dictionary of Jazz, 2 vols., 1988, 2nd ed., 3 vols., 2001; The Blackwell Guide to Recorded Jazz, 1991, 2nd ed., 1995. **Address:** 506 W Foster Ave, State College, PA 16801-4039, U.S.A. **Online address:** bdk4@psu.edu

KERNS, Daniel R. See LICHTENBERG, Jacqueline.

KERNS, Thomas A. American, b. 1942. **Genres:** Ethics. **Career:** Educator and author. St. Ambrose College, Davenport, IA, instructor in philosophy, 1967-69; University of Portland, Portland OR, assistant professor of philosophy, 1970-71; St. Martin's College, Olympia, WA, assistant professor of philosophy and social science, 1973-76; North Seattle Community College, Seattle, WA, professor of philosophy, 1976-; Seattle University, adjunct professor of philosophy, 1991-. Member, ethics council of Group Health Cooperative (HMO), 1987-89; Chemical Injury Council, Seattle, WA, secretary, 1996-97. **Publications:** Ethical Issues in HIV Vaccine Trials, 1997; Jenner on Trial: The Ethics of Vaccine Research in the Age of Smallpox and the Age of AIDS, 1997; Environmentally Induced Illnesses: Ethics, Risk Assessment, and Human Rights, 2001. Contributor to journals. **Address:** POB 927, Yachats, OR 97498, U.S.A. **Online address:** tkerns@u.washington.edu

KERR, Alexander McBride. Australian, b. 1921. **Genres:** Economics. **Career:** Professor of Economics; Director, Challenge Bank, Vincent Corp., Nusantaqua Pte., National Oil N.L., Atlas Pacific Ltd., P.T. Cendana Pearls, P.T. Daya Sakti Baruna Nusantara Biomanagement Systems Pty and Development Analysis Pty. **Publications:** Personal Income of Western Australia, 1949; Northwestern Australia, 1962; Regional Income Estimation-Theory and Practice, 1963; The South West Region of Western Australia, 1965, 1966; Australia's North West, 1967; The Texas Reef Shell Industry, 1968. EDITOR: The Indian Ocean Region, 1981; We Flew, We Fell, We Survived, 1991. **Address:** 146 Alderbury St, Floreat, WA 6014, Australia.

KERR, Andrea Moore. American, b. 1940. **Genres:** Biography, Women's studies and issues, History. **Career:** Writer; women's historian. Worked as advertising copywriter, free-lance journalist, and teacher. **Publications:** Lucy Stone: Speaking Out for Equality, 1992. Contributor to books. **Address:** 153 E St. S.E., Washington, DC 20003, U.S.A.

KERR, Ann Zwicker. American, b. 1934. **Genres:** Autobiography/Memoirs. **Career:** American University, Beirut, Lebanon, instructor of English language and communications, 1983-84; American University, Cairo, Egypt, instructor of English language and communications, 1984-89; University of California, Los Angeles, Visiting Fulbright Scholar Program, coordinator, 1990-; speaker and teacher on the Middle East for university & community groups. **Publications:** Come with Me from Lebanon: An American Family Odyssey, 1994; Painting the Middle East, 2002. **Address:** 11288 Bunche Hall, University of California, Los Angeles, CA 90024, U.S.A. **Online address:** akerr@isop.ucla.edu

KERR, Carole. See CARR, Margaret.

KERR, Frederick. See KERNER, Fred.

KERR, Graham. American (born England), b. 1934. **Genres:** Food and Wine. **Career:** Past Manager, Royal Ascot Hotel, London; Chief Catering Adviser, Royal New Zealand Air Force; Presenter, The Galloping Gourmet television series, Take Kerr television series, Simply Marvellous, The Graham Kerr Show, Graham Kerr's Kitchen; The Gathering Place. **Publications:** Graham Kerr Cookbook by the Galloping Gourmet, 1970; Cooking with Graham Kerr, The Galloping Gourmet; The Galloping Gourmet's Kitchen Diary; The New Seasoning, 1976; The Love Feast, 1978; The Graham Kerr Step by Step Cookbook, 1982; Graham Kerr's Smart Cooking, 1991; Graham Kerr's Minimax Cookbook, 1992; Graham Kerr's Creative Choices, 1993; Graham Kerr's Kitchen, 1994; Graham Kerr's Best, 1995; Graham Kerr's Swiftly Seasoned, 1997; Gathering Place, 1997; Charting a Course to Wellness, 2004; My Personal Path to Wellness, 2004; Simply Splendid Cookbook, 2004. **Address:** 1020 N Sunset Dr, Camano Island, WA 98282-6665, U.S.A. **Online address:** www.grahamkerr.com

KERR, (Anne) Judith. British (born Germany), b. 1923. **Genres:** Children's fiction. **Career:** Secretary, Red Cross, London, 1941-45; Teacher and Textile Designer, 1948-53; Script Ed., and Script Writer, BBC-TV, London, 1953-58. **Publications:** The Tiger Who Came to Tea, 1968; Mog the Forgetful Cat, 1970; When Hitler Stole Pink Rabbit, 1971; When Willy Went to the Wedding, 1972; The Other Way Round, 1975; Mog's Christmas, 1976; A Small Person Far Away, 1978; Mog and the Baby, 1980; Mog in the Dark, 1983; Mog and Me, 1984; Mog's Family of Cats, 1985; Mog's Amazing Birthday Caper, 1986; Mog and Bunny, 1988; Look Out Mog! (in England as Mog and Barnaby), 1991; How Mrs. Monkey Missed the Ark, 1992; The Adventures of Mog, 1993; Mog on Fox Night, 1993; Mog in The Garden, 1994; Mog's Kittens, 1994; Mog and the Granny, 1995; Mog and the VeeEe Tee, 1996; The Big Mog Book, 1997; Birdie Halleluyah!, 1998; Hog's Bad Thing, 2000; The Other Goose, 2001; Goodbye Mog, 2002. **Address:** c/o HarperCollins Publishers, 77-85 Fulham Palace Rd, London W6 8JB, England.

KERR, K. Austin. American, b. 1938. **Genres:** History, Politics/ Government. **Career:** Professor of History, Ohio State University, Columbus, since 1984 (Instructor, 1965-68; Assistant Professor, 1968-71; Associate Professor, 1971-84). **Publications:** American Railroad Politics, 1914-1920, 1968; (ed.) The Politics of Moral Behavior, 1973; Organized for Prohibition: A New History of the Anti-Saloon League, 1985; (with M. Blackford) Business Enterprise in American History, 1986, 1990, 1994; (with A. Loveday and M. Blackford) Local Businesses: Exploring Their History, 1990; (with M. Blackford) BF Goodrich, Tradition and Transformation, 1870-1995, 1996. **Address:** Dept. of History, Ohio State University, Columbus, OH 43210, U.S.A. **Online address:** kerr.6@oso.edu

KERR, Katharine. American, b. 1944. **Genres:** Science fiction/Fantasy. **Career:** Fantasy game designer for TSR Inc., and contributing editor, Dragon magazine, early 1980s; freelance author since mid-1980s. **Publications:** FANTASY NOVELS. DEVERRY SERIES: Daggerspell, 1986, rev. ed, 1993; Darkspell, 1987, rev. ed 1994; The Bristling Wood, 1989, in UK as Dawnspell: The Bristling Wood; The Dragon Revenant, 1990, in UK as Dragonspell: The Southern Sea; A Time of Exile, 1991; A Time of Omens, 1992; Days of Blood and Fire, 1993, in UK as A Time of War: Days of Blood and Fire; Days of Air and Darkness, 1994, in UK as A Time of Justice: Days of Air and Darkness. OTHER NOVELS: Polar City Blues, 1991; Resurrection, 1992; Freeze Frames, 1995; (with M.A. Kreighbaum) Palace, 1996. Contributor to anthologies. **Address:** C/O Elizabeth Pomada, 1029 Jones St., San Francisco, CA 94109, U.S.A.

KERR, M. E. *See* **MEAKER, Marijane (Agnes).**

KERR, Margaret (H.). Canadian, b. 1954. **Genres:** Law. **Career:** Educator and author. Practicing attorney in Toronto, Ontario, Canada, 1988-94, 2000; Centennial College, Toronto, part-time professor, 1994-98; Seneca College, Toronto, part-time professor, 1994-98; York University, Toronto, executive officer. **Publications:** Canadian Tort Law in a Nutshell, 1997; (with J. Kurtz) The Complete Guide to Buying, Owning, and Selling a Home in Canada, 1997, 2nd ed, 2001; (with J. Kurtz) Make It Legal: What Every Canadian Entrepreneur Needs to Know about the Law, 1998; Legal Research: Step by Step, 1998; (with J. Kurtz) Facing a Death in the Family, 1999; (with J. Kurtz) Wills and Estates for Canadians for Dummies, 2000; (with J. Kurtz) Canadian Small Business Kit for Dummies, 2002. Contributor to books and periodicals. **Address:** Suite 716, Yonge St., Toronto, ON, Canada M4N 2N9. **Online address:** mhkerr@sympatico.co

KERR, Steven. American, b. 1941. **Genres:** Administration/Management. **Career:** College of Administrative Science, Ohio State University, assistant professor, 1970-74, associate professor, 1974-77; School of Business Administration, University of Southern California, professor of organizational behavior, 1977-82, chair, 1979-82, associate dean, 1982-85, professor of management and organization, 1982-92, director of Ph.D. program, 1985-88, Dean of Faculty, 1985-89, interim director entrepreneur program, 1988-89; General Electric Company, vice president of Leadership Development and Chief Learning Officer, 1994-. **Publications:** (with R.H. Filley) Managerial Process and Organizational Behavior, 1976; (ed., with others) Organizational Behavior, 1979; (with D.U. Ashkenas and T. Jick) The Boundaryless Organization, 1995; (ed.) Ultimate Rewards: What Really Motivates People to Achieve, 1997. Contributor to periodicals on the subjects of leadership and management. Book reviewer for journals. **Address:** 280 West St, Mount Kisco, NY 10549-3325, U.S.A.

KERRIGAN, John. *See* **WHITING, Charles (Henry).**

KERRY, Lois. *See* **DUNCAN, Lois.**

KERSAUDY, Francois. French, b. 1948. **Genres:** History, Military/Defense/Arms control. **Career:** University of Paris, Sorbonne, Paris, France, professor of international relations, 1981-; translator and writer. **Publications:** Strateges et Norvege 1940: les jeux de la guerre et du hasard, 1977; Churchill and de Gaulle, 1981; La Guerre du Fer 1940, 1987, trans. as Norway 1940, 1990; Vi stoler pa England, 1939-1949, 1991; Winston Churchill, le pouvoir de l'imagination, 2000. Contributor to periodicals. **Address:** University of Paris 1 - Pantheon - Sorbonne, 12 place du pantheon, 75231 Paris Cedex 05, France.

KERSENBOOM, Saskia. Dutch, b. 1953. **Genres:** Anthropology/Ethnology, Dance/Ballet, Music. **Career:** Royal Academy of Arts and Sciences, Amsterdam, Netherlands, researcher; University of Amsterdam, Amsterdam, associate professor of anthropology. Parampara: Traditional Arts of South India, founder, 1994, director, 1994; dancer and musician. **Publications:** Nitya-sumangali: Devadasi Tradition in South India, 1987, rev. ed., 1998; Word, Sound, Image: The Life of the Tamil Text, 1995. Contributor to books and periodicals. **Address:** Dept of Musicology, University of Amsterdam, Nwe Doelenstraat 16, 1012 CP Amsterdam, Netherlands. **Online address:** parapara@worldonline.nl

KERSHAW, Alex. American. **Genres:** Biography. **Career:** Writer. **Publications:** Jack London: A Life, 1997; The Bedford Boys, 2003. **Address:** c/o St. Martin's Press, 175 Fifth Ave., Rm. 1715, New York, NY 10010, U.S.A.

KERSHAW, Ian. British, b. 1943. **Genres:** History. **Career:** University of Manchester, England, assistant lecturer, 1968, lecturer in medieval history, 1970, senior lecturer, 1979-87, reader elect in modern history, 1987; University of Nottingham, Nottingham, England, professor and chair of modern history, 1987-89; University of Sheffield, England, professor and chair of modern history, 1989-. Ruhr-Universitaet Bochum, Germany, visiting professor of contemporary European history, 1983-84. **Publications:** Bolton Priory: The Economy of a Northern Monastery, 1286-1325, 1973; Der Hitler-Mythos: Volksmeinung und Propaganda im Dritten Reich, 1980, rev. ed. published in U.K. as The "Hitler-Myth": Image and Reality in the Third Reich, 1987; Popular Opinion and Political Dissent in the Third Reich: Bavaria: 1933-45, 1983; The Nazi Dictatorship: Problems and Perspectives of Interpretation, 1985, 4th ed., 2000; Hitler: A Profile in Power, 1991, 2nd ed., 2000; Hitler 1889-1936, 1998; Hitler, 1936-45: Nemesis, 2000; Making Friends with Hitler: Lord Londonderry and Britain's Road to War, 2004. EDITOR: Bolton Priory Rentals and Ministers' Accounts, 1473-1539, 1970;

Weimar: Why Did German Democracy Fail? 1990; (with M. Lewin) Stalinism and Nazism: Dictatorships in Comparison, 1997. **Address:** Dept of History, University of Sheffield, Sheffield S10 2TN, England.

KERSHAW, Peter. *See* **LUCIE-SMITH, (John) Edward (McKenzie).**

KERSHEN, (L.) Michael. American, b. 1982. **Genres:** Young adult fiction. **Career:** Student. **Publications:** Why Buffalo Roam, 1993. **Address:** 1000 Elmwood St, Norman, OK 73072-6113, U.S.A. **Online address:** lmkershen@ou.edu

KERTES, Joseph. Canadian (born Hungary). **Genres:** Novels, Children's fiction. **Career:** Teacher and writer. Director of Humber School for Writers, and Humber Comedy Workshop, Humber College, Toronto, Canada. **Publications:** NOVELS: Winter Tulips, 1988; Boardwalk, 1998. CHILDREN'S FICTION: The Gift, 1996; The Red Corduroy Shirt, 1998. **Address:** School of Creative and Performing Arts, Humber College, 3199 Lakeshore Blvd W, Toronto, ON, Canada M8V 1K8. **Online address:** joe.kertes@humber.ca

KERTESS, Klaus. American, b. 1940. **Genres:** Novellas/Short stories. **Career:** Bykert Gallery Inc., NYC, founder and director, 1966-75; Parrish Art Museum, Southampton, NY, Robert Lehman curator, 1983-89; Whitney Museum of American Art, NYC, adjunct curator of drawing, 1989-95, curator of 1995 Biennial, 1993-95. Guest curator, Celebrating Willem de Kooning, Guild Hall, 1994, and Alfonso Ossorio: Congregations, Parrish Art Museum, 1997. **Publications:** Roses Are Read, 1982; Brice Marden: Paintings and Drawings, 1992; Desire by Numbers, 1994; South Brooklyn Casket Company (short stories), 1997; Joan Mitchell, 1997. Contributor of short stories to periodicals. Contributor of art criticisms to periodicals. Author of essays for museum exhibition catalogs. **Address:** 4 E 8th St, New York, NY 10003, U.S.A.

KERTSCHER, Kevin M. American, b. 1964. **Genres:** Travel/Exploration. **Career:** Freelance film production work in Baltimore, Washington, DC, New York, and Los Angeles, 1987-93; documentary editor, Ken Burns/Florentine Films, Walpole, NH, 1994-96; independent documentary producer, Boston, MA, 1997-; writer. **Publications:** Africa Solo: A Journey across the Sahara, Sahel, and Congo, 1998. **Address:** c/o Steerforth Press, 105-106 Chelsea St., PO Box 70, South Royalton, VT 05068, U.S.A.

KERVEN, Rosalind. British, b. 1954. **Genres:** Children's fiction, Children's non-fiction, Mythology/Folklore. **Career:** Author, children's book reviewer, and consultant editor. **Publications:** Over 50 titles, including: FOR CHILDREN. FICTION: The Sea Is Singing, 1986; Who Ever Heard of a Vegetarian Fox?, 1988; Sorcery and Gold, 1998. NON-FICTION: Equal Rights for Animals, 1992; Saving Planet Earth, 1992; The Man Who Found America, 1999. MYTHS, LEGENDS, AND FOLK TALES: The Slaying of the Dragon, 1987; Earth Magic, Sky Magic, 1991; The Woman Who Went to Fairyland, 1992; In the Court of the Jade Emperor, 1993; The Rain Forest Storybook, 1994; Coyote Girl, 1996; Volcano Woman, 1996; The Weather Drum, 1996; The Mythical Quest, 1996; Enchanted Kingdoms, 1997; The Giant King, 1998; Aladdin and Other Tales from the Arabian Nights, 1998; King Arthur, 1998; The Enchanted Forest, 1999; How Did the World Begin, 2001; Do You Believe in Fairies?, 2003. FOR ADULTS: Traditional Stories: A Practical Guide for People Sharing Books with Children. **Address:** Swindonburn Cottage W, Sharperton, Morpeth, Northd. NE65 7AP, England.

KESSLER, Jascha (Frederick). American, b. 1929. **Genres:** Novels, Novellas/Short stories, Plays/Screenplays, Poetry, Songs/Lyrics and libretti, Translations. **Career:** University of Michigan, Ann Arbor, instructor, 1951-54; New York University, NYC, assistant professor, 1954-55; Hunter College, NYC, assistant professor, 1955-56; Harcourt, Brace and Co. Inc. publrs., NYC, Curriculum Research, assistant director, 1956-57; Hamilton College, Clinton, NY, assistant professor, 1957-61; University of California at Los Angeles, assistant professor, 1961-64, associate professor, 1964-70, professor of English and modern literature, 1961-. KUSC-FM, Los Angeles, Literature Program, reviewer, 1978-85; City of Santa Monica, CA, arts commissioner, 1990-96. **Publications:** An Egyptian Bondage and Other Stories, 1967, rev. ed., 2000; The Cave (libretto); Bearing Gifts, 1979; Lee Mullican, 1980; Death Comes for the Behaviorist: 4 Long Stories, 1983; Transmigrations: 18 Mythologems, 1985; Classical Illusions: 28 Stories, 1985; Siren Songs & Classical Illusions: 50 Stories, 1992; Collected Poems, 1998; Rapid Transit 1948: An Unsentimental Education, 2000; Christmas Carols & Other Plays, 1999; The Anniversary (libretto). POETRY: (ed. and contrib.) American Poems, 1964; Whatever Love Declares, 1969; After the Armies Have Passed, 1970; In Memory of the Future, 1976. TRANSLATOR: (with C. Rogers) G. Csath, The Magician's Garden: 24 Stories, 1980; (with A. Banani) Bride of

Acacias: The Poetry of Forugh Farrokhzad, 1983; (with C. Rogers) G. Csaath, Opium and Other Stories, 1983; (with G. Olujic) Rose of Mother-of-Pearl: A Fairytale, 1983; (with A. Shurbanov) N. Kantchev, Time as Seen from Above and Other Poems, 1984; Under Gemini: The Selected Poems of Miklos Radnoti, 1985; (with A. Shurbanov) Medusa: The Selected Poetry of Nicolai Kantchev, 1986; The Face of Creation: 23 Contemporary Hungarian Poets, 1988; (with M. Korosy) S. Rakos, Catullan Games, 1989; (with A. Banani) Look! The Guiding Dawn: Selected Poetry of Taaheraeh, 1993; King Oedipus, 1999; G. Olujic, Tataga's Children, 2000; O. Orban, Our Bearings at Sea, 2001; Traveling Light, 2001.

KESSLER, Judy. American, b. 1947. **Genres:** Communications/Media, Documentaries/Reportage. **Career:** People magazine, NYC, writer, 1974-80; The Today Show, NYC, producer, 1980-84; Entertainment Tonight, Los Angeles, CA, producer, 1984-86; Gorillas in the Mist (film), coproducer, 1987-88; Creative Affairs, Time Inc. Ventures, Los Angeles, vice-president. **Publications:** Inside Today: The Battle for the Morning, 1992; Inside People: The Stories behind the Stories, 1994. **Address:** Time Inc. Ventures, 11100 Santa Monica Blvd. Suite 1950, Los Angeles, CA 90025, U.S.A.

KESSLER, Julia Braun. Also writes as Julia Barrett. American, b. 1926. **Genres:** Novels, Romance/Historical, Young adult fiction, Gerontology/Senior issues, Ghost Writer. **Career:** Encyclopedia Americana, NYC, research editor, 1949-50; University of Michigan, Ann Arbor, editor at Institute for Social Research, 1951-54; Seventeen, NYC, features editor, 1954-57; University of California, Los Angeles, adjunct associate professor of humanities, 1964-69; University of Southern California, Los Angeles, editorial consultant at Ethel Percy Andrus Gerontology Center, 1971-74; free-lance writer, editor, and ghost writer, 1974-. **Publications:** Getting Even with Getting Old, 1980. AS JULIA BARRETT: (with G. Donnelly) Presumption: An Entertainment, 1993; The Third Sister: A Continuation of Jane Austen's "Sense and Sensibility," 1996; Charlotte: A Completion of Jane Austen's Last Work, 2000. Contributor of articles to magazines and newspapers. **Address:** 218 16th St, Santa Monica, CA 90402-2216, U.S.A. **Online address:** jbraun@ucla.edu

KESSLER, Leo. See **WHITING, Charles (Henry).**

KESSLER, Suzanne J. American, b. 1946. **Genres:** Psychology, Women's studies and issues. **Career:** State University of New York College at Purchase, assistant professor, 1972-81, associate professor, 1981-95, president of board of directors of Children's Center, 1986-89, professor of psychology, 1996-, dean, School of Natural and Social Sciences, 2004-. Bedford Hills Correctional Facility, coordinator of AIDS Education and Counseling Program, 1990. **Publications:** (with W. McKenna) Gender: An Ethnomethodological Approach, 1978; Lessons from the Intersexed, 1998. Contributor to books. Contributor of articles and reviews to periodicals. **Address:** School of Natural and Social Sciences, State University of New York, College at Purchase, 735 Anderson Hill Rd, Purchase, NY 10577-1400, U.S.A. **Online address:** skessler@purchase.edu

KESSNER, Thomas. American (born Germany), b. 1946. **Genres:** Novellas/Short stories, Cultural/Ethnic topics, History, Biography. **Career:** Professor of History, The Graduate Center, City University of New York, NYC (began as Instructor in 1971). Visiting Associate Professor, Brooklyn College, NY, 1980-81; Director, The Fiorello H. La Guardia Archives, La Guardia Community College, City University of New York, 1982-83. National Endowment for the Humanities Fellow, 1983-84; Rockefeller Foundation Research Fellow, 1985. **Publications:** The Golden Door: Italian and Jewish Immigrant Mobility in New York City, 1880-1915, 1977; (co-author) Ethnic Heritage: A Teacher's Manual, 1979; (co-ed.) Issues in Teaching the Holocaust: A Guide, 1981; (with B. Caroli) Today's Immigrants, Their Stories: A New Look at the Newest Americans, 1981; Fiorello H. La Guardia and the Making of Modern New York, 1989; (assoc. ed. and contrib.) The Encyclopedia of the City of New York, 1991; Capital City: New York City and the Men behind America's Rise to Economic Dominance, 1860-1900, 2003. **Address:** PhD Program in History, CUNY Graduate Center, 565 5th Ave, New York, NY 10016, U.S.A. **Online address:** TKessner@gc.cuny.edu

KETCHAM, Ralph Louis. American, b. 1927. **Genres:** History, Biography. **Career:** Syracuse University, NY, Professor of History and Political Science, 1963-97, Emeritus Professor, 1997-. University of Chicago, The Papers of James Madison, Ed., 1956-60; Yale University, New Haven, CT, Papers of Benjamin Franklin, Associate Ed., 1961-63. **Publications:** Benjamin Franklin, 1965; James Madison: A Biography, 1971; From Colony to Country: The Revolution in American Thought, 1750-1820, 1974; From Independence to Interdependence, 1975; Presidents Above Party: The First American

Presidency 1789-1829, 1984; Antifederalist Papers, 1986; Individualism and Public Life: A Modern Dilemma, 1987; (co-author) Participation in Government, 1988; Framed for Posterity: The Enduring Philosophy of the Constitution, 1993; The Idea of Democracy in the Modern Era, 2004. EDITOR: (with W. Hutchinson and W.M.E. Rachal) The Papers of James Madison, vols. I & II, 1962; (with L.W. Labaree) The Papers of Benjamin Franklin, vols. VI & VII, 1963; (with L.W. Labaree) The Autobiography of Benjamin Franklin, 1964; The Political Thought of Benjamin Franklin, 1965. **Address:** Maxwell School, Syracuse University, Syracuse, NY 13244, U.S.A. **Online address:** rketcham@syr.edu

KETCHUM, Richard M. American, b. 1922. **Genres:** History, Biography. **Career:** Editorial Director, Book Division, American Heritage Publishing Co., NYC, 1956-74; Ed., Blair & Ketchum's Country Journal, 1974-84. **Publications:** What Is Communism?, 1955; Male Husbandry, 1956; American Heritage Book of Great Historic Places, 1957; Four Days, 1964; Faces from the Past, 1970; The Secret Life of the Forest, 1970; The Winter Soldiers, 1973; Will Rogers, 1973; George Washington, 1974; Decisive Day, 1974; Second Cutting: Letters from the Country, 1981; The Borrowed Years, 1938-1941: America on the Way to War, 1989; Saratoga: Turning Point of the American Revolutionary War, 1997; Divided Loyalties, 2002. EDITOR: What Is Democracy?, 1955; American Heritage Book of the Revolution, 1958; American Heritage Book of the Pioneer Spirit, 1959; American Heritage Picture History of the Civil War, 1960; The Horizon Book of the Renaissance, 1961; The Battle for Bunker Hill, 1962; The Original Watercolor Paintings by John James Audubon for the Birds of America.

KETCHUM, William C., Jr. American, b. 1931. **Genres:** Antiques/Furnishings, Art/Art history, Crafts, Education. **Career:** New School of Social Research, NYC, instructor in collecting american antiques, 1971-88; NY University, instructor in art and art ed., 1984-; Museum of American Folk Art, curator of special projects, NYC, 1984-89; Marymount College, Tarrytown, NY, instructor in antiques, 1987-92; Folk Art Institute, NYC, faculty, 1990-; attorney, author. **Publications:** Early Potters and Potteries of New York State, 1970; The Pottery and Porcelain Collectors Handbook, 1971; American Basketry and Woodenware, 1974; A Treasury of American Bottles, 1975; Hooked Rugs, 1976; A Catalog of American Antiques, 1977; The Family Treasury of Antiques, 1978; Early American Crafts, 1979; The Catalog of American Collectibles, 1979; Western Memorabilia, 1980; Furniture II, 1980; Auction, 1980; The Catalog of World Antiques, 1981; Toys, 1981; Boxes, 1982; American Furniture: Cupboards, Chests and Related Pieces, 1982; Pottery and Porcelain, 1983; American Folk Art of 20th Century, 1983; Collecting American Bottles for Fun and Profit, 1985; Collecting American Toys, 1985; Collecting Sport Memorabilia, 1985; Collecting Items of the 40's and 50's, 1985; All American: Folk Art and Crafts, 1986; American Country Pottery, 1987; Holiday Collectibles, 1989; How to Run an Antiques Business, 1990; American Redware, 1991; American Stoneware, 1991; Country Wreaths & Baskets, 1991; Collecting the West, 1992; Western Memorabilia Identification and Price Guide, 1993; American Pottery & Porcelain, 1994; Marked American Furniture, 1995; American Folk Art, 1995; Grandma Moses, 1996; Simple Beauty: The Shakers in America, 1996; Art of the Golden West, 1996; Native American Art, 1997; Remington and Russell, 1997. Contributor to encyclopedias. **Address:** 241 Grace Church St, Rye, NY 10580, U.S.A.

KETNER, Kenneth Laine, (Sr.). American, b. 1939. **Genres:** History, Humanities, Philosophy, Biography. **Career:** Texas Tech University, Lubbock, professor, 1971-81, Charles Sanders Peirce Interdisciplinary Professor, 1981-99, Paul Whitfield Horn Professor, 1999-. National Endowment for the Humanities Fellowship, 1991-94. **Publications:** An Emendation of R.G. Collingwood's Doctrine of Absolute Presuppositions, 1973; Elements of Logic, 1990; A Thief of Peirce: The Letters of Kenneth Laine Ketner and Walker Percy, ed. Patrick Samway, 1995; His Glassy Essence: An Autobiography of Charles Sanders Peirce. EDITOR: (with J.E. Cook) Charles Sanders Peirce: Contributions to "The Nation", 4 vols, 1975-87; (co) Proceedings of the Charles Sanders Peirce Bicentennial International Congress, 1981; (with C.J. Kloesel) Peirce, Semeiotic, and Pragmatism: Essays by Max H. Fisch, 1986; (and coauthor of intro) Charles Sanders Peirce, Reasoning and the Logic of Things, 1992; Peirce and Contemporary Thought, 1995. Contributor of essays to professional journals. Contributor to anthologies. **Address:** Institute for Studies in Pragmaticism, Texas Tech University, Lubbock, TX 79409-0002, U.S.A.

KETRON, Larry. American, b. 1947. **Genres:** Plays/Screenplays. **Career:** Writer and actor, 1972-74; playwright, 1974-; screenwriter, 1983-. Playwright in residence at Workshop of the Players Art Theater (WPA), 1979-86; peer review panelist for New York Creative Artists Public Service Program, 1981-

82; guest artist at Aspen Playwrights Conference, 1982; panelist for Artists Foundation, Massachusetts state fellowship program for artists, 1983-84; guest lecturer at South Carolina Governor's School for the Arts, 1992. **Publications:** PLAYS: Cowboy Pictures, 1974; Augusta, 1975; Stormbound, 1975; Patrick Henry Lake Liquors, 1977; Quail Southwest, 1977; Rib Cage, 1978; The Frequency, 1979; Character Lines, 1980; A Tinker's Damn (also known as The Tricycle Trail), 1981; The Trading Post, 1981; Ghosts of the Loyal Oaks, 1982; Asian Shade, 1983; Eudora Welty's "The Hitch-Hikers" (adaptation), 1986; Fresh Horses, 1986; Rachel's Fate, 1987; No Time Flat, 1988; Sun Bearing Down, 1991; Laureen's Whereabouts, 1993. SCREEN-PLAYS: Westlander, 1984; Fresh Horses (adapted from play of same title), 1988; (with J. Fees and A. Liddle) Permanent Record, 1988; (with J. Stuart) Vital Signs, 1990; Asian Shade (adapted from play of same title), 1983; The Old Girlfriend (adapted from play Character Lines), 1995; The Only Thrill (adapted from play The Trading Post), 1996; The Retrievers, 2001; Ghost Cat, 2003. **Address:** 569 Lakeshore Dr., Pawleys Island, SC 29585, U.S.A. **Online address:** lketron@sc.rr.com

KETTELKAMP, Larry Dale. American, b. 1933. **Genres:** Children's non-fiction, Music, Paranormal, Psychology, Sciences, Sports/Fitness, Biography. **Career:** Garrard Publishing, Champaign, IL, art director, 1959-60; Highlights for Children, Honesdale, PA, layout and staff artist, 1962-67; Summy-Birchard Music, Princeton, NJ, director of publs., 1981-82; Rider University, Lawrenceville, NJ, instructor of graphic design, 1986-90; Bookarts Assocs., Cranbury, NJ, director, 1982-. Freelance writer, editor, music teacher, organist, composer, and lectr. **Publications:** Magic Made Easy, 1954; Spooky Magic, 1955; The Magic of Sound, 1956; Shadows, 1957; Singing Strings, 1958; Kites, 1959; Drums, Rattles and Bells, 1960; Gliders, 1961; Flutes, Whistles and Reeds, 1962; Puzzle Patterns, 1963; Spirals, 1964; Horns, 1964; Spinning Tops, 1966; Song, Speech and Ventriloquism, 1967; Dreams, 1968; Haunted Houses, 1969; Sixth Sense, 1970; Investigating UFOs, 1971; Religions East and West, 1972; Astrology, Wisdom of the Stars, 1973; Tricks of Eye and Mind, 1976; Hypnosis: The Wakeful Sleep, 1975; The Dreaming Mind, 1975; A Partnership of Mind and Body: Biofeedback, 1976; Investigating Psychics, 1977; The Healing Arts, 1978; Lasers, 1979; Mischievous Ghosts, 1980; Your Marvelous Mind, 1980; Electronic Musical Instruments, 1984; Starter Solos for Classical Guitar, 1984; Intermediate Etudes for Classical Guitar, 1984; The Human Brain, 1986; Modern Sports Science, 1986; Bill Cosby, 1987; Computer Graphics, 1989; Living in Space, 1993; ETs and UFOs, 1996. **Address:** 2 Wynnewood Dr, Cranbury, NJ 08512, U.S.A. **Online address:** bookartsandmusic@comcast.net

KEVILL-DAVIES, Sally. British, b. 1945. **Genres:** Antiques/Furnishings. **Career:** Sotheby's, London, England, cataloger and ceramics expert, 1965-74; Lecturer, broadcaster and writer. **Publications:** Price Guide to Eighteenth Century English Pottery, 1972; Jelly Moulds, 1982; Yesterday's Children, 1991. **Address:** 64A Flood Street, Chelsea, London SW3, England.

KEVLES, Bettyann Holtzmann. American, b. 1938. **Genres:** Animals/Pets, Art/Art history, Biology, Natural history, Travel/Exploration, Bibliography. **Career:** Los Angeles Times, contributor, 1981-2000; Yale University, Dept of History, lecturer, 2001-. **Publications:** Watching the Wild Apes: The Primate Studies of Goodall, Fossey, and Galdikas, 1976; Listening In, 1980; Thinking Gorillas, 1981; Females of the Species: Sex and Survival in the Animal Kingdom, 1986; Naked to the Bone: Medical Imaging in the Twentieth Century, 1997; Almost Heaven: The Story of Women in Space, 2003. **Address:** 37 Lincoln St, New Haven, CT 06511, U.S.A. **Online address:** Bettyann.Kevles@yale.edu

KEVLES, Daniel J. American, b. 1939. **Genres:** History, Sciences. **Career:** California Institute of Technology, Pasadena, Division of Humanities and Social Sciences, professor of the humanities (joined faculty, 1964); White House Staff, Member, 1964; Yale University, Dept of History, 2000-. **Publications:** The Physicists: The History of a Scientific Community in Modern America, 1978; In the Name of Eugenics: Genetics and the Uses of Human Heredity, 1985; (co-ed.) The Code of Codes: Scientific and Social Issues in the Human Genome Project; The Baltimore Case: A Trial of Politics, Science, and Character, 1998; (co-author) Inventing America: A History of the United States, 2002. **Address:** Dept of History, Yale University, PO Box 208324, New Haven, CT 06520-8324, U.S.A. **Online address:** daniel.kevles@yale.edu

KEYES, Daniel. American, b. 1927. **Genres:** Novels, Mystery/Crime/Suspense, Science fiction/Fantasy, Adult non-fiction, Psychology, Autobiography/Memoirs. **Career:** Wayne State University, Detroit, MI, instructor in English, 1961-66; Ohio University, Athens, lecturer, 1966-71; professor of English, 1972-99, professor emeritus, 2000-. **Publications:**

Flowers for Algernon, 1966; The Touch, 1968; The Fifth Sally, 1980; The Minds of Billy Milligan (nonfiction), 1981; Unveiling Claudia (nonfiction), 1986; Daniel Keyes Collected Stories, 1992; The Milligan Wars (nonfiction), 1994; Daniel Keyes Reader, 1995; Until Death...Sleeping Princess (fiction), 1999; Algernon, Charlie and I: A Writer's Journey (nonfiction), 1999.

KEYNES, Simon. British, b. 1952. **Genres:** History. **Career:** University of Cambridge, lecturer in Anglo-Saxon History, 1978-92, reader in Anglo-Saxon History, 1992-99, Elrington and Bosworth Professor of Anglo-Saxon, 1999-, fellow of Trinity College, 1976-. **Publications:** HISTORY: The Diplomas of King Aethelred The Unready (978-1016): A Study in Their Use as Historical Evidence, 1980; (trans, author of intro and notes, with M. Lapidge) Alfred the Great: Asser's Life of King Alfred and Other Contemporary Sources, 1983; Facsimiles of Anglo-Saxon Charters, 1991; The Liber Vitae of the New Minster and Hyde Abbey Winchester, 1996. EDITOR: (with D. Dumville) The Anglo-Saxon Chronicle: A Collaborative Edition, 1983-. **Address:** Trinity College, University of Cambridge, Cambridge CB2 1TQ, England. **Online address:** sdk13@cam.ac.uk

KEYS, Kerry Shawn. Also writes as Gopiah. American, b. 1946. **Genres:** Novellas/Short stories, Plays/Screenplays, Poetry, Songs/Lyrics and libretti, Translations. **Career:** US Peace Corps, volunteer agricultural assistant in South India, 1966-68; Pennsylvania State University, Mont Alto Campus, instructor, 1973; teacher of English as a second language and coordinator of a language laboratory in Rio de Janeiro, Brazil, 1974-77; Pine Press, Landisburg, PA, editor and publisher, 1977-; Harrisburg Area Community College, instructor, 1979-84; Dickinson College, instructor, 1980, associate fellow in English, 1981-; Vilnius University, Fulbright associate professor of English, 1998-2000. University of Iowa, International Writing Program, 1991, 1993; English-language officer for official visitors to the US, 1986-. **Publications:** POETRY: Swallowtails Gather These Stones, 1973; Jade Water, 1974; O Pintor e o Poeta: The Painter and the Poet, Jose Paulo Moreira da Fonseca (in English and Portuguese), 1976; Loose Leaves Fall: Selected Poems, 1977; Quingumbo: Nova Poesia Norte-Americana (bilingual anthology), 1980; Seams, 1985; (as Gopiah) A Gathering of Smoke, 1986; The Hearing, 1992; Fingerlings, 1993; Decoy's Desire, 1993; Fingerlings 2, 1994; Selected Poems (in Czech), 1996; Tao te ching Meditations, Bones & Buzzards; Conversations with Tertium Quid; and 27 books of poems and prose, 1994-2002. Translator of books by: J. Cabral de Melo Neto; L. Ivo; L. Katkus; S. Geda. Author of plays and a children's book. Contributor to periodicals. **Address:** Zemaitijas 3-15, 2001 Vilnius, Lithuania. **Online address:** kkeys@post.omnitel.net

KEYSER, James D. American, b. 1950. **Genres:** Anthropology/Ethnology. **Career:** Educator, archaeologist, and author. Field archaeologist affiliated with universities and with provincial parks of Alberta, Canada, 1973-76; State University of New York at Buffalo, assistant professor of anthropology, 1976-77; University of Tulsa, Tulsa, OK, assistant professor of anthropology, 1977-78; U.S. Forest Service, archaeologist with Minerals and Geology Group, Northern Region, 1978-80; regional archaeologist with Pacific Northwest Region, 1980-. Portland State University, lecturer, 1999-2000. Walking Softly Adventures, European rock art tour leader, 1999-2001. Plains Anthropological Conference, member of board of directors, 1985-88; International Scientific Advisory Committee for the Study of Chauvet Cave, member, 1999-2001. **Publications:** Indian Rock Art of the Columbia Plateau, 1992; Indian Petroglyphs of the Columbia Gorge: The Jeanne Hillis Rubbings, 1994; The Five Crows Ledger: Biographic Warrior Art of the Flathead Indians, 2000; (with M.A. Klassen) Plains Indian Rock Art, 2001. Contributor to books. Contributor of articles and reviews to anthropology journals. **Address:** c/o University of Utah Press, 260 South Central Campus Dr., Room 252, Salt Lake City, UT 84112, U.S.A.

KEYSERLINGK, Robert H. Canadian (born Germany), b. 1933. **Genres:** History. **Career:** Canadian Foreign Service, Ottawa, Ontario, foreign service officer in Germany and United Kingdom, 1957-61; University of Ottawa, Ottawa, instructor, 1963-64, assistant professor, 1964-67, associate professor, 1968-87, professor of history, 1987-. Military service: Royal Canadian Navy, 1954-59; became second lieutenant. **Publications:** Media Manipulation: Bismark and The Press in Imperial Germany, 1977; Austria in World War II, McGill-Queen's University Press, 1989. **Address:** 111 Wurtemburg St., Ottawa, ON, Canada K1N 8M1.

KHADDURI, Majid. American (born Iraq), b. 1908. **Genres:** International relations/Current affairs, Law, Law. **Career:** Middle East Institute, Washington, D.C., Director of Research and Education, 1950-95, Board of Governors, member, 1995-. President, Shaybani Society of International Law, since 1969. Professor in Baghdad, 1938-47; Visiting Professor, Indiana

University, Bloomington, 1947-48, and University of Chicago, 1948-49; Professor, 1949-70, and Distinguished Research Professor, 1970-80, Professor Emeritus, 1980-, School of Advanced International Study, Johns Hopkins University, Washington, D.C. **Publications:** Independent Iraq, 1951, 2nd ed. 1961; War and Peace in the Law of Islam, 1955; Islamic Jurisprudence: Shafi'i's Risala, 1961; Modern Libya, 1963; The Islamic Law of Nations: Shaybani's Siyar, 1966; Republican Iraq, 1969; Political Trends in the Arab World, 1970; Major Middle Eastern Problems in International Law, 1972; Arab Contemporaries, 1973; Socialist Iraq, 1978; Arab Personalities in Politics, 1981; The Islamic Conception of Justice, 1984; The Gulf War, 1988. **Address:** 4454 Tindall St NW, Washington, DC 20016-2718, U.S.A.

KHALID, Mansour. Sudanese, b. 1931. **Genres:** Area studies, International relations/Current affairs, Politics/Government. **Career:** Attorney in Khartoum, Sudan, 1957-59; United Nations (UN), NYC, legal officer, 1962-63, deputy resident representative in Algeria, 1964-65, president of UN security council, 1971-75, special consultant on coordination of UN information system, 1982; United Nations Educational, Scientific, and Cultural Organization (UNESCO), Paris, France, member of Bureau of Relations with member States, 1965-69; Government of Sudan, Khartoum, minister of youth and social affairs, 1969-71, chair of delegation of Sudan to UN General Assembly, special consultant and personal representative of UNESCO director-general for United Nations WRA fund-raising mission, 1970, permanent representative of Sudan to UN, 1971, minister of foreign affairs, 1971-75, 1977, minister of education, 197577, assistant to president for coordination and foreign affairs, 1976-77; Sudan Socialist Union, member of political bureau and assistant secretarygeneral, 1978, resigned all political posts, but remained member of general Congress, 1978; financial and investment consultant, 1980-. Visiting professor at the University of Colorado, 1968, and at the University of Khartoum, 1982; participant in many panel discussions. **Publications:** NONFICTION: Private Law in Sudan, 1970; The Nile Basin, Present and Future, 1971; Solution of the Southern Problem and its African Implications, 1972; The Decision-Making Process in Foreign Policy, 1973; Sudan Experiment With Unity, 1973; Diplomacy and Development, 1974; World Food Crisis: What After Rome?, 1975; Nimeiri and the Revolution of DisMay, 1985; (ed.) John Garang Speaks, 1987; The Government They Deserve: The Role of the Elite in Sudan's Political Evolution, 1990; (ed.) The Call for Democracy in Sudan, by J. Garang, 1992; Social-Cultural Aspects of Arab Diplomacy. Author of works in Arabic. **Address:** 9 Jubilee Palace, London SW3, England.

KHALVATI, Mimi. British (born Iran), b. 1944. **Genres:** Poetry. **Career:** Theatre Workshop, Tehran, Iran, actress and director; Theatre in Exile, co-founder. The Poetry School, London, coordinator. Free-lance tutor, workshop facilitator, and poetry translator. **Publications:** POETRY: Persian Miniatures/A Belfast Kiss, 1990; In White Ink, 1991; Mirrorwork, 1995; Entries on Light, 1997; Selected Poems, 2000; The Chine, 2002. EDITOR: Tying the Song, 2000. Poems included in anthologies.

KHAN, Adib. Australian (born Bangladesh), b. 1949. **Genres:** Literary criticism and history, Novels. **Career:** Writer. Ballarat Grammar School, teacher. **Publications:** Poetry Examined, 1984; Seasonal Adjustments, 1994; Solitude of Illusions, 1996. Contributor to periodicals and journals. **Address:** c/o Allen & Unwin Ltd., PO Box 8500, St. Leonards, NSW 1590, Australia.

KHAN, Badrul H(uda). American (born Bangladesh), b. 1960. **Genres:** Education. **Career:** Indiana University-Indianapolis, instructional developer and evaluation specialist at School of Medicine, 1993-94; University of Texas at Brownsville, assistant professor of educational technology and founding coordinator of graduate program in educational technology, 1994-97; George Washington University, Washington, DC, associate professor of educational technology and program director of EdTech Cohort Program at Alexandria, 1997-. Founder of BooksToRead.com and WebCourseReview. com; designer of AuthorWeb, a web-based authoring system; consultant to corporations and institutions. **Publications:** Web-Based Instruction, 1997; Instructional Multimedia Presentation with PowerPoint: A Practical Guide, 1997; Web-Based Training, 2001; E-Learning Strategies, 2002; E-Learning Checklist, 2002; Web-Based Learning, 2003. Contributor to periodicals. **Address:** George Washington University, 1775-B Duke St, Alexandria, VA 22314, U.S.A. **Online address:** khanb@BooksToRead.com; Badrulkhan@ Badrulkhan.com

KHAN, Hasan-Uddin. Pakistani/British, b. 1947. **Genres:** Architecture. **Career:** Payette Associates Inc., Boston, MA, assistant architect in London office, 1972-73; Gerald Shenstone and Partners, London, England, project architect, 1973-74; Unit 4 Architects and Planners, Karachi, Pakistan, partner, 1974-76; Aga Khan Award for Architecture (now Aga Khan Trust for

Culture), Philadelphia, PA, assistant convenor, 1977-79, convenor, 1980; consultant in Jakarta, Indonesia, 1981-84; Secretariat of the Aga Khan, Gouvieux, France, head of architectural activities, 1984-91; Massachusetts Institute of Technology, Department of Architecture, Cambridge, visiting associate professor, 1994-; Roger Williams University, Distinguished Professor of Architecture and Historic Preservation, 1999-. **Publications:** Charles Correa (monograph), 1987; (ed. with M. Frishman, and contrib.) The Mosque: History, Architecture, Development, and Regional Diversity, 1994; Contemporary Asian Architects (trilingual in English, French, and German), 1995; (with R. Holod) Contemporary Mosques: Clients, Designs, and Processes since 1950 (monograph), 1997; Internationalist Architecture, 1925-1965 (in English, German, Dutch, and French), 1997; The Middle East, 2000. Contributor to books. Contributor of articles and reviews to architecture journals and other periodicals.

KHAN, Mahmood H(asan). Canadian (born India), b. 1937. **Genres:** Third World. **Career:** Simon Fraser University, Burnaby, British Columbia, Canada, assistant professor, 1966-68, associate professor, 1969-79, professor of economics, 1980-. Consultant to organizations. **Publications:** Economics of the Green Revolution in Pakistan, 1975; Underdevelopment and Agrarian Structure in Pakistan, 1981; Rural Change in the Third World, 1992; Third World Sustainable Agriculture in Egypt, 1993; Egyptian Women in Agricultural Development, 1994; Climbing the Development Ladder with NGO Support, 1998; Public Policy and the Rural Economy of Pakistan, 1998; Community Organizations and Rural Development: Experience in Pakistan, 2001. Author of journal articles. **Address:** Dept. of Economics, Simon Fraser University, Burnaby, BC, Canada V5A 1S6. **Online address:** mkhan@sfu.ca

KHARE, R(avindra) S. Genres: Anthropology/Ethnology, Intellectual history, Literary criticism and history. **Career:** University of Virginia, Charlottesville, professor of anthropology. **Publications:** The Changing Brahmans: Associations and Elites among the Kanya-Kubjas of North India, 1970; Culture and Reality: Essays on the Hindu System of Managing Foods, 1976; The Hindu Hearth and Home, 1976; Normative Culture and Kinship: Essays on Hindu Categories, Processes and Perspectives, 1983; The Untouchable as Himself, 1984; Culture and Democracy: Anthropological Reflections on Modern India, 1985; Cultural Diversity & Social Discontent, 1998. EDITOR: (with D. Little) Leadership: Interdisciplinary Reflections, 1984; Food, Society and Culture: Aspects in South Asian Food Systems, 1986; The Eternal Food: Gastronomic Ideas and Experiences of Hindu and Buddhists, 1992; On and About the Postmodern Crisis: Writing/Rewriting, 1994; Perspectives on Islamic Law, 1999. **Address:** Dept. of Anthropology, University of Virginia, Brooks Hall, 305, PO Box 400120, Charlottesville, VA 22903, U.S.A. **Online address:** vsk3m@virginia.edu

KHAZANOV, Anatoly M. American, b. 1937. **Genres:** Anthropology/Ethnology. **Career:** Academy of Sciences of the USSR, junior scholar at Institute of Ethnography, 1967-75, senior scholar, 1975-81, acting junior scholar, 1980-85; Hebrew University of Jerusalem, Jerusalem, Israel, visiting professor, 1985-86, professor of sociology and social anthropology, 1986-90; Fellow of the British Academy, 1990-; University of Wisconsin-Madison, Ernest Gellner professor of anthropology, 1990-, fellow of Institute for Research in the Humanities, 1992. Centre for the Study of Nationalism, Prague, co-director, 1996. Moscow State University, senior lecturer, 1974, 1975, visiting professor, 1978, 1979; Chernigov Pedagogical Institute, senior lecturer, 1975; Kiev State University, visiting professor, 1976, 1979; Leningrad State University, visiting professor, 1977; Trenton State College, distinguished visiting professor, 1988-89; Victoria University of Manchester, honorary Lord Simon visiting professor, 1990; guest lecturer at colleges and universities around the world. Conducted anthropological field work throughout Eastern Europe and Asia. **Publications:** Nomads and the Outside World, 1984, rev. ed., 1994; Soviet Nationality Policy During Perestroika, 1991; (ed. with Ofer Bar Iosef, and intro of) Pastoralism in the Levant: Archaeological Materials in Anthropological Perspectives, 1992; After the USSR: Ethnicity, Nationalism, and Politics in the Commonwealth of Independent States, 1995. IN RUSSIAN: Essay on the History of the Sarmatian Military Act, 1971; (with V.P. Alexeev and L.A. Fainberg) Primitive Society: Main Problems of Evolution, 1975; The Gold of the Scythians, 1975; The Social History of the Scythians: Main Problems of Development of the Ancient Nomads of the Eurasian Steppes, 1975; (with A.I. Pershits, L.E. Koubel, and M.A. Chlenov) The Primitive Periphery of Class Societies, 1978. Contributor to books. Contributor of articles and reviews in English to anthropology journals in the United States and abroad. Contributor of articles in Russian to Russian and Ukrainian anthropology journals. **Address:** Department of Anthropology, 5240 Social Science Bldg., University of Wisconsin-Madison, 1180 Observatory Dr., Madison, WI 53706, U.S.A.

KHEIRABADI, Masoud. American (born Iran), b. 1951. **Genres:** Environmental sciences/Ecology, Geography, Humanities, International relations/Current affairs. **Career:** Taught at universities; Portland State University, International Studies Program, currently; Marylhurst University, Environmental Science Program, currently. **Publications:** Iranian Cities, 1991, rev. ed., 2000; Modern World Nations: Iran, 2003; Religions of the World: Islam, 2004. Contributor of articles on Islamic and Middle Eastern studies to scholarly journals, periodicals, and newspapers. **Address:** International Studies Program, Portland State University, Portland, OR 97207, U.S.A. **Online address:** kheirabadim@pdx.edu or masoud.kh@verizon.net

KHERDIAN, David. American, b. 1931. **Genres:** Novels, Children's fiction, Poetry, Literary criticism and history, Bibliography, Biography. **Career:** Literary consultant, Northwestern University, Evanston, IL, 1965; publisher, Giligia Press, 1967-73; poetry judge, Institute of American Indian Arts, Santa Fe, NM, 1968; ed., Ararat mag., 1970-71; poet-in-the-schools, State of New Hampshire, 1971; director, Two Rivers Press, 1978-86; ed., Forkroads magazine, 1995-96; editor, Stopinder: A Gurdjieff Journal for Our Time, 2000-. **Publications:** David Meltzer, 1965; A Bibliography of William Saroyan: 1934-1965, 1965; Gary Snyder, 1965; Six Poets of the San Francisco Renaissance, 1967; (with G. Hausman) Eight Poems, 1968; Six San Francisco Poets, 1969; On the Death of My Father and Other Poems, 1970; Homage to Adana, 1970; Looking over Hills, 1972; A David Kherdian Sampler, 1974; The Nonny Poems, 1974; Any Day of Your Life, 1975; Country Cat, City Cat, 1978; I Remember Root River, 1978; The Road from Home, 1979; The Farm, 1979; It Started with Old Man Bean, 1980; Finding Home, 1981; Beyond Two Rivers, 1981; Taking the Soundings on Third Avenue, 1981; The Farm: Book Two, 1981; The Song in the Walnut Grove, 1983; The Mystery of the Diamond in the Wood, 1983; Right Now; 1983; The Animal, 1984; Root River Run, 1984; Threads of Light, 1985; Bridger: The Story of a Mountain Man, 1987; A Song for Uncle Harry, 1988; The Cat's Midsummer Jamboree, 1990; The Great Fishing Contest, 1991; On a Spaceship with Beelzebub, 1991; The Dividing River/The Meeting Shore, 1991; Feathers and Tails, 1992; Juna's Journey, 1993; Friends: A Memoir, 1993; Asking the River, 1993; By Myself, 1993; My Racine, 1994; A Song for Emily, 1995; I Called It Home, 1997; The Rose's Smile: Farizad of the Arabian Nights, 1997; Seven Poems for Mikey, 1997; (reteller) The Golden Bracelet, 1998; Chippecotton: Root River Tales of Racine, 1998; The Revelations of Alvin Tolliver, 2001; Seeds of Light: Poems from a Gurdjieff Community, 2002; The Buddha: The Story of an Awakened Life, 2004. TRANSLATOR: The Pearl: Hymn of the Robe of Glory, 1979; Pigs Never See the Stars, 1982; The Song of the Stork: Early & Ancient Armenian Songs, 2004. EDITOR: (with J. Baloian) Down at the Santa Fe Depot: 20 Fresno Poets, 1970; Visions of America: By the Poets of Our Time, 1973; Settling America: The Ethnic Expression of 14 Contemporary Poets, 1974; Poems Here and Now, 1976; The Dog Writes on the Window with His Nose and Other Poems, 1977; Traveling America with Today's Poets, 1977; If Dragon Flies Made Honey, 1977; I Sing the Song of Myself, 1978; Beat Voices, 1995. **Address:** 5082 County Rte 7, Chatham, NY 12037, U.S.A. **Online address:** tavit@earthlink.net

KHILNANI, Sunil. Indian, b. 1960. **Genres:** Politics/Government. **Career:** Cambridge University, Cambridge, England, fellow of Christ's College, 1987-89; University of London, Birkbeck College, London, England, senior lecturer in politics, 1989-. **Publications:** Arguing Revolution: The Intellectual Left in Post-War France, 1993. Contributor to books. **Address:** Paul H. Nitze School of Advanced Intl Studies, 1740 Washington Ave NW, Washington, DC 20036-1983, U.S.A. **Online address:** khilnani@jhu.edu

KHOO THWE, Pascal. (born Myanmar), b. 1967. **Genres:** Autobiography/Memoirs. **Career:** Writer and political activist. **Publications:** From the Land of Green Ghosts: A Burmese Odyssey (memoir), 2002. **Address:** c/o Author Mail, HarperCollins, 10 East 53rd St., Seventh Floor, New York, NY 10023, U.S.A.

KHOROCHE, Peter (Andrew). British, b. 1947. **Genres:** Art/Art history, Theology/Religion, Translations. **Career:** University of London, England, lecturer in Sanskrit, 1970-74. **Publications:** (trans.) A Sura, Once the Buddha Was a Monkey, 1989; Ivon Hitchens, 1990; Ben Nicholson: Drawings and Painted Reliefs, 2002. **Address:** 51 Mawson Rd, Cambridge CB1 2DZ, England.

KHUSH, Gurdev S. Indian, b. 1935. **Genres:** Agriculture/Forestry, Horticulture. **Career:** Plant geneticist. Worked as a farmer and factory worker; University of California, Davis, researcher, 1960-67; International Rice Research Institute (IRRI), Manila, Philippines, 1967-2002. **Publications:** Cytogenetics of Aneuploids, 1973; (with N. Panda) Host Plant Resistance to Insects, 1995. EDITOR: (with G.H. Toenniessen) Rice Biotechnology, 1991; (with J. Bennett) Nodulation and Nitrogen Fixation in Rice: Potential and Prospects, 1992. Contributor to journals and periodicals. **Address:** Dept of Vegetable Crops, University of California, Davis, Davis, CA 95616, U.S.A. **Online address:** G.Khush@cgiar.org

KHWAJA, Waqas Ahmad. Pakistani, b. 1952. **Genres:** Poetry, Translations. **Career:** Emory University, Atlanta, GA, editorial assistant for Linguistic Atlas of the Gulf States, 1981-82; High Court, Lahore, Pakistan, lawyer/advocate, 1983-93; Agnes Scott College, Decatur, GA, assistant professor of English, 1995-. Quaid-e-Azam Law College, visiting professor, 1988-91; Punjab Law College, visiting professor, 1988-92; Lahore College for Arts and Sciences, visiting faculty, 1989-90; Punjab University, visiting faculty, 1990-91; Income Tax Directorate of Training, Lahore, visiting faculty, 1992-93; Emory University, visiting instructor, spring, 1995, and spring, 1996. Writers Group, Lahore, co-founder, 1984, convener and general editor of publications, 1984-92. **Publications:** Six Geese from a Tomb at Medum (poems), 1987; Writers and Landscapes (prose and poems), 1991; Miriam's Lament and Other Poems, 1992. EDITOR & TRANSLATOR FROM URDU: Cactus: An Anthology of Recent Pakistani Literature, 1984; Mornings in the Wilderness (prose and poems), 1988; Short Stories from Pakistan, 1992. Contributor of more than 70 articles to magazines and newspapers. **Address:** Department of English, Agnes Scott College, 141 East College Ave., Decatur, GA 30030, U.S.A.

KIAROSTAMI, Abbas. Iranian, b. 1940. **Genres:** Plays/Screenplays. **Career:** Scriptwriter, director of motion pictures and commercials, painter, and graphic artist. Filmmaking department, Institute for the Intellectual Development of Children and Young Adults, cofounder. **Publications:** Walking with the Wind: Poems, trans. by M.C. Beard and A. Karimi-Hakkak, 2002; (Photographer) Photographs, 2002. SCRIPTWRITER: Nan va koutcheh (short; title means: Bread and Alley), 1970; Zang-e tafrih (short; title means: The Breaktime), 1972; Mossafer (title means: The Traveler), 1974; Rangha (title means: The Colors), 1976; Gozaresh (title means: The Report), 1977; Behdasht-e dandan (title means: Dental Hygiene), 1980; Hamsarayan (title means: The Chorus), 1982; Hamshari (title means: Fellow Citizen), 1983; Khaneh-ye doust kojast?, 1987, released as Where Is the Friend's House?, 1987; Mashg-e shab (documentary), 1989, released as Homework; Nema-ye Nazdik, 1990, released as Close-Up, 1999; Va Zendegi edame darad, 1992, released as Life and Nothing More, re-released as And Life Goes On...; Zire derakhatan zeyton, 1994, released as Through the Olive Trees, re-released as Under the Olive Trees; Reperages (documentary), 1995; Safar, 1994, released as The Journey; Badkonake sefid, 1995, released as The White Balloon; Bid-o bad, 2000, released as Willow and Wind; Ta'm e guilass, 1997, released as Taste of Cherry, Zeitgeist Films, 1998; Bad ma ra khahad bord, 1999, released as The Wind Will Carry Us, 2000. **Address:** c/o Zeitgeist Films, 247 Centre St., 2nd Floor, New York, NY 10013, U.S.A.

KIBERD, Declan. Irish, b. 1951. **Genres:** Literary criticism and history. **Career:** Literary critic and educator. University College, Dublin, lecturer in English, professor of Anglo-Irish literature and drama. **Publications:** LITERARY CRITICISM: Synge and the Irish Language, 1979; Men and Feminism in Modern Literature, 1985; Idir Dha Chultur, 1993; Inventing Ireland: The Literature of the Modern Nation, 1996; Irish Classics, 2001. EDITOR: (with S. Dick), Omnium Satherum: Essays for Richard Ellmann, 1989; (with G. Fitzmaurice) An Crann Faoi Bhlath The Flowering Tree: Contemporary Irish Poetry with Verse Translations, 1991; The Student's Annotated Ulysses, 1992. **Address:** J203 Department of English, University College, Dublin, Ireland.

KIBLER, M. Alison. American. **Genres:** Theatre. **Career:** University of Wisconsin, Green Bay, past member of women's studies faculty; Australian National University, Canberra, visitor at Centre for Women's Studies. **Publications:** Rank Ladies: Gender and Cultural Hierarchy in American Vaudeville, 1999. **Address:** c/o Centre for Women's Studies, Australian National University, Box 4, Canberra, ACT 2600, Australia.

KIDD, Charles (William). British, b. 1952. **Genres:** Genealogy/Heraldry, Biography. **Career:** Burke's Peerage Ltd., London, England, assistant editor, 1972-77; Debrett's Peerage and Baronetage Ltd., London, assistant editor, 1977-80, editor, 1980-. **Publications:** (with P. Montague-Smith) Debrett's Book of Royal Children, 1982; Debrett Goes to Hollywood, 1986; (ed. with D. Williamson) Debrett's Peerage and Baronetage, 1985, rev. ed., 2003. **Address:** Debrett's Peerage Ltd, 1A Hammersmith, Broadway, London W6 9DL, England. **Online address:** peerage@debretts.co.uk

KIDD, Chip. American, b. 1964. **Genres:** Cartoons. **Career:** Graphic designer and writer. Alfred E. Knopf, New York, NY, book designer, 1986-;

Paris Review, consultant, 1995-; Pantheon, New York, NY, associate editor of comics division. Taught at the School of Visual Arts, New York, NY. **Publications:** Batman Collected, 1996, expanded ed, 2001; (with P. Dini) Batman Animated, 1998; (with L. Daniels) Superman, the Complete History, 1998; (with L. Daniels) Batman: The Complete History, 1999; (with L. Daniels) Wonder Woman: The Life and Times of the Amazon Princess, 2000; (with L. Daniels) Wonder Woman: The Golden Age, 2001; (commentary) C.M. Schulz, Peanuts: The Art of Charles M. Schulz, 2001; (with A. Spiegelman) Jack Cole and Plastic Man: Forms Stretched to Their Limits, 2001; The Cheese Monkeys: A Novel in Two Semesters, 2001. Contributor to periodicals. **Address:** Design Dept., Alfred E. Knopf, 201 East 50th St., New York, NY 10022, U.S.A.

KIDD, I(an) G(ray). British (born India), b. 1922. **Genres:** Classics, History, Philosophy. **Career:** University of St. Andrews, Scotland, lecturer, 1949-65, senior lecturer, 1965-73, professor of ancient philosophy, 1973-76, professor of Greek, 1976-87, professor emeritus, 1987-, provost of St. Leonard's College, 1978-83. Visiting professor at University of Texas at Austin, 1965-66; member of Institute for Advanced Study, Princeton, NJ, 1971-72, 1979-80. Chancellor's assessor at University Court, University of St. Andrews, 1989-99. Fellow of the British Academy, 1993. **Publications:** Posidonius, Vol. I: The Fragments, with Ludwig Edelstein, 1972, 2nd ed., 1989, Vol. II: The Commentary, 1988, Vol. III: The Translation of the Fragments, 1999; (with R. Waterfield) Plutarch, Essays, 1992. Contributor to books. **Address:** Ladebury, Lade Braes Lane, St. Andrews, Fife KY16 9EP, Scotland. **Online address:** igk@st-and.ac.uk

KIDD, Paul. Australian, b. 1963. **Genres:** Cartoons, Science fiction/Fantasy. **Career:** Melbourne House/Beam, Melbourne, Australia, senior designer of computer games, 1985-92; freelance scriptwriter for computer games, 1994-. **Publications:** How to Play "Lord of the Rings", 1987; Princess Karanam (comic book), 1993; Mus of Kerbridge (novel), 1995; Council of Blades (fantasy novel), 1996. Author of comic book series, including Tank Vixens, 1994-95, Fangs of K'aath, Cyberkitties, and Hive, all 1996-. Author of the interactive movie scripts Diskworld, Perfect Ten, 1995; and Cyberswine, Sega Australia, 1995. Designer and producer of computer games. Creator of paper games and board games. Contributor to periodicals. **Address:** P.O. Box 965, Eltham, VIC 3095, Australia.

KIDD, Richard. (born England), b. 1952. **Genres:** Children's fiction. **Career:** Artist and author. Exhibited regularly with the Rowan Gallery, London, England, 1977-93, in San Francisco, CA, and New York, NY, 1981-87, and in Europe. **Publications:** Almost Famous Daisy!, 1996; Monsieur Thermidor: A Fantastic Fishy Tale, 1998; Are We Nearly There Yet?, 1997; Lucinda Snodd-Gibbon's Scottish Collection, 1998; The Giant Goldfish Robbery, 1999; Deadly Famous, 2001; Lobsters in Love: A Whirlpool Romance, 2001; The Tiger Bone Thief, 2002; The Last Leg, 2003. **Address:** Caroline Walsh Associates, 5-8 Lower John St., Golden Square, London W1F 9HA, England.

KIDD, Sue Monk. American. **Genres:** Novels, Inspirational/Motivational Literature. **Career:** Author and nurse. Previously employed as a nurse, St. Joseph's Hospital, Fort Worth, TX, and instructor in nursing, Medical College of Georgia. Teacher of creative writing, speaker, and lecturer. **Publications:** NONFICTION: God's Joyful Surprise, 1988; When the Heart Waits, 1990; The Dance of the Dissident Daughter: A Journey from the Christian Tradition to the Sacred Feminine, 1996; Love's Hidden Blessings (essays). NOVELS: The Secret Life of Bees, 2001. Contributor of short stories to anthologies. Contributor to periodicals. **Address:** c/o Author Mail, Viking Press, 375 Hudson Street, New York, NY 10014, U.S.A.

KIDDER, Tracy. American, b. 1945. **Genres:** Novellas/Short stories, Adult non-fiction, Autobiography/Memoirs, Documentaries/Reportage. **Career:** Writer, 1974-. **Publications:** The Road to Yuba City: A Journey into the Juan Corona Murders, 1974; The Soul of a New Machine, 1981 (Pulitzer Prize and American Book Award, 1982); House, 1985; Among School Children, 1989 (Robert F. Kennedy Award, Christopher Award, Ambassador Book Award, 1990); Old Friends, 1993 (New England Book Award); Home Town, 1999; Mountains beyond Mountains, 2003 (Lettre Ulysses Award). **Address:** c/o Georges Borchardt Inc, 136 E 57th St, New York, NY 10022, U.S.A.

KIDMAN, Fiona (Judith). New Zealander, b. 1940. **Genres:** Novels, Novellas/Short stories, Poetry. **Career:** Writer. Worked as high-school librarian, 1961-62; writer, 1962-. Dame Commander of the NZ Order of Merit, 1999. **Publications:** NOVELS: A Breed of Women, 1979; Mandarin Summer, 1981; Paddy's Puzzle, 1983, in US as In the Clear Light, 1985; The Book of Secrets, 1987; True Stars, 1990; Ricochet Baby, 1996; The House Within, 1997; Songs from the Violet Cafe, 2003. SHORT STORIES: Mrs.

Dixon and Friends, 1982; Unsuitable Friends, 1988; The Foreign Woman, 1993; The Best of Fiona Kidman's Short Stories, 1998; A Needle in the Heart, 2002; (ed.) New Zealand Love Stories, an Oxford Anthology, 1999; (ed.) The Best New Zealand Fiction, 2004. POETRY: Honey and Bitters, 1975; On the Tightrope, 1978; Going to the Chathams, Poems: 1977-1984, 1985; Wakeful Nights: Poems Selected and New, 1991. OTHER: Search for Sister Blue (radio play), 1975; (with J. Ussher) Gone North (travel), 1984; (with G. Sheehan) Wellington, 1989; Palm Prints (biographical sketches), 1994. Contributor to periodicals. **Address:** 28 Rakau Rd, Hataitai, Wellington 3, New Zealand. **Online address:** fionakidman@compuserve.com

KIDWELL, Carol (Evelyn Beryl). Also writes as Carol Maddison. Canadian, b. 1923. **Genres:** Literary criticism and history, Biography. **Career:** Dean Emeritus, American College (now University) in Paris, 1978-, (Chairman, Humanities Division, and Professor of English, 1963-66; Dean, 1966-78). Assistant Professor of Classics, University of New Brunswick, Canada, 1946-49. **Publications:** Marullus: Soldier Poet of the Renaissance, 1989; Pontano: Poet and Prime Minister, 1991; Sannazaro and Arcadia, 1993; Pietro Bembo, Lover, Linguist, Cardinal, 2004. AS CAROL MADDISON: Apollo and the Nine: A History of the Ode, 1960; Marcantonio Flaminio: Poet, Humanist and Philosopher, 1964. Works appear in anthologies. **Address:** Sanderstead House, Rectory Park, Sanderstead, Surrey CR2 9JR, England.

KIDWELL, Clara Sue. American, b. 1941. **Genres:** History, Bibliography. **Career:** Kansas City Art Institute, MO, instructor in history, 1968-69; University of Washington, Seattle, coordinator of publications in Experimental Education Unit, 1970; Haskell Indian Junior College, Lawrence, KS, instructor in social sciences and chairperson of division, 1970-72; University of Minnesota-Twin Cities, Minneapolis, assistant professor of American Indian studies, 1972-74; University of California, Berkeley, associate professor to professor of Native American studies, 1974-96, head of Department of Ethnic Studies, 1974-75, 1978-79; University of Oklahoma, Norman, professor of history and director of Native American studies, 1995-. Visiting scholar, visiting associate professor, and lecturer at colleges and universities throughout the United States. National Museum of the American Indian, assistant director for cultural resources, 1993-95. Council of Graduate Schools, dean in residence, 1988-89. **Publications:** (with C. Roberts) The Choctaws: A Critical Bibliography, 1980; A Helsinki Record: Native American Rights, 1980; Choctaws and Missionaries in Mississippi, 1818-1918, 1995. Contributor to books. Contributor of articles and reviews to education, history, and Native American studies journals. **Address:** Native American Studies, 633 Elm Room 216, University of Oklahoma, Norman, OK 73019, U.S.A. **Online address:** cskidwell@ou.edu

KIEFER, Louis. Also writes as J. D. Mortmain. American, b. 1936. **Genres:** Self help. **Career:** Office of the Judge Advocate General, Washington, D.C., trial attorney in Litigation Division, 1964; Superior Court, Hartford, Conn., clerk in Family Relations Division, 1965-66; Resolute Insurance Co., Hartford, general counsel, 1966-67; Kiefer & Holtman, Simsbury, Conn., partner, 1967-70; private practice of law in Simsbury, 1970-80; Kiefer and O'Shea, P.C., private practice of law in Hartford, 1982-. Talk show host. **Publications:** How to Win Custody, 1982. **Address:** 21 Oak St Ste 310, Hartford, CT 06106-8002, U.S.A. **Online address:** LKiefer1@hotmail.com

KIELY, Benedict. Irish, b. 1919. **Genres:** Novels, Novellas/Short stories, History, Literary criticism and history, Autobiography/Memoirs, Essays. **Career:** Journalist in Dublin, 1939-64. **Publications:** Counties of Contention: Study of the Origins and Implications of the Partition of Ireland, 1945; Land without Stars, 1946; Poor Scholar: A Study of the Works and Days of William Carleton, 1794-1869, 1947; In a Harbour Green, 1949; Call for a Miracle, 1950; Modern Irish Fiction: A Critique, 1950; Honey Seems Bitter, 1952; The Cards of a Gambler: A Folktale, 1953; There Was an Ancient House, 1955; The Captain with the Whiskers, 1960; A Journey to the Seven Streams: 17 Stories, 1963; Dogs Enjoy the Morning, 1968; A Ball of Malt and Madame Butterfly: Stories, 1973; Proxopera, 1977; A Cow in the House and Other Stories, 1978; All the Way to Bantry Bay and Other Irish Journeys, 1978; The State of Ireland, 1980; The Small Oxford Book of Dublin, 1983; Nothing Happens in Carmin-Cross, 1985; My Trouble with Dracula and Other People, 1986; A Letter to Peachtree, 1987; Yeats' Ireland, 1989; Drink to the Bird (memoir), 1991; The Waves behind Us (memoir), 1999; A Raid into Dark Corners (essays), 1999; The Collected Short Stories of Benedict Kiely, 2001. EDITOR: The Various Lives of Keats and Chapman, by Flann O'Brien, 1976; The Penguin Book of Irish Short Stories, 1982. **Address:** 119 Morehampton Rd, Donnybrook, Dublin 4, Ireland.

KIELY, Robert (James). American, b. 1931. **Genres:** Literary criticism and history. **Career:** Harvard University, Cambridge, MA, instructor, 1962, assistant professor, 1964-66, associate professor, 1966-68, professor of English, 1968-, associate dean of Faculty of Arts and Sciences, 1972-75, master of Adams House, 1973-99, Loker Professor of English, 1985-, chairman, English Dept., 1987-90, Harvard College Professor, 2001-. Visiting professor at universities worldwide; member of boards. **Publications:** Robert Louis Stevenson and the Fiction of Adventure, 1964; The Romantic Novel in England, 1972; Beyond Egotism: The Fiction of James Joyce, Virginia Woolf, and D.H. Lawrence, 1980; Modernism Reconsidered, 1983; Reverse Tradition: Postmodern Fictions and the Nineteenth Century Novel, 1993; Still Learning, 2000. EDITOR: Man and Nature, 1966; The Good Heart, 1996. **Address:** 76 Rice St, Cambridge, MA 02140, U.S.A.

KIERNAN, Ben. Australian, b. 1953. **Genres:** History. **Career:** University of New South Wales, Sydney, Australia, tutor in history, 1975-77; University of Wollongong, Australia, senior lecturer in history, 1986-89; Yale University, New Haven, CT, associate professor, 1990-97, director of Cambodian Genocide Program, 1994-99, professor of history, 1997-, director of Genocide Studies Program, 1998-, A. Whitney Griswold Professor of History, 1999-. **Publications:** The Samlaut Rebellion, 1975; How Pol Pot Came to Power, 1985; Cambodia: The Eastern Zone Massacres, 1986; The Pol Pot Regime, 1996; Le genocide au Cambodge, 1998. EDITOR: Burchett, 1986; Genocide and Democracy in Cambodia, 1993; Conflict and Change in Cambodia, 2002; (co) The Specter of Genocide, 2003. **Address:** Department of History, Yale University, Box 208324, New Haven, CT 06520, U.S.A. **Online address:** www.yale.edu/gsp

KIERNAN, Brian. Australian, b. 1937. **Genres:** Literary criticism and history. **Career:** Associate Professor of English, University of Sydney, since 1972. Freelance journalist and lectr., in Italy, 1964-68, and Melbourne, 1968-72. Member, Committee of Mgmt, Australian Society of Authors, 1978-82; President, Associate for the Study of Australian Literature, 1980-83. **Publications:** Images of Society and Nature: Seven Essays on Australian Novels, 1971; Criticism, 1974; Patrick White, 1980; David Williamson: A Writer's Career, 1990, rev. ed. 1996; Studies in Australian Literary History, 1997. EDITOR: The Portable Henry Lawson, 1976, 1980; Considerations: New Essays on Kenneth Slessor, Judith Wright and Douglas Stewart, 1977; Douglas Stewart, 1977; The Most Beautiful Lies, 1977; The Essential Henry Lawson, 1982. **Address:** English Dept, University of Sydney, Sydney, NSW 2006, Australia.

KIERNAN, Caitlin R(ebekah). Irish, b. 1964. **Genres:** Romance/Historical. **Career:** Red Mountain Museum, Birmingham, AL associate paleontologist, 1985-86; San Diego State University, San Diego, CA, research associate, 1986-88. **Publications:** Candles for Elizabeth, 1998; Silk, 1998; Tales of Pain and Wonder, 2000. Contributor of short stories to anthologies also contributor of fiction to periodicals. **Address:** c/o Merrilee Heifetz, Writers House, 21 West 26th St., New York, NY 10010, U.S.A. **Online address:** cait@gothic.net

KIERNAN, Pauline. British. **Genres:** Theatre, Plays/Screenplays. **Career:** Playwright and Shakespearean scholar. University of Reading, Leverhulme research fellow, 1995-98. **Publications:** Actors (play), 1995; Shakespeare's Theory of Drama, 1996; Staging Shakespeare at the New Globe, 1999. **Address:** English Department, White Knights, PO Box 218, Reading, Bucks. RG6 6AA, England.

KIESSLING, Nicolas K. American, b. 1936. **Genres:** Literary criticism and history. **Career:** Washington State University, Pullman, WA, professor of English, 1967-. **Publications:** The Incubus in English Literature, 1977; The Library of Robert Burton, 1988; (co-ed) The Anatomy of Melancholy, Vol. I, 1989, Vol. II, 1990, Vol. III, 1994; The Legacy of Democritas Junior, Robert Burton, 1990. **Address:** Department of English, Washington State University, Pullman, WA 99164-5020, U.S.A. **Online address:** kiesslin@wsu.edu

KIEV, Ari. American, b. 1933. **Genres:** Psychiatry. **Career:** Clinical Associate Professor of Psychiatry, Cornell University Medical School, NYC, since 1967. **Publications:** (ed.) Magic, Faith and Healing, 1964; Curanderismo: Mexican American Folk Psychiatry, 1968; (ed.) Psychiatry in the Communist World, 1968; (ed.) Social Psychiatry, 1969; (with J. Argandona) Mental Health in the Developing World, 1972; Transcultural Psychiatry, 1972; A Strategy for Daily Living, 1973, rev. ed. 1997; A Strategy for Handling Executive Stress, 1974; (ed.) Somatic Aspects of Depressive Illness, 1974; The Drug Epidemic, 1975; The Suicidal Patient: Recognition and Management, 1976; A Strategy for Success, 1976; The Courage to Live, 1979; Active Loving, 1979; Riding Through the Downers, 1980; Recovery from Depression, 1982; How to Keep Love Alive, 1982; Breaking Free of Birth Order, 1993. **Address:** 150 E. 69th St., New York, NY 10021, U.S.A.

KIHN, Greg. American, b. 1952. **Genres:** Science fiction/Fantasy. **Career:** Writer. Rock musician and lead singer/guitarist for the Greg Kihn Band. **Publications:** Horror Show, 1996; Shade of Pale, 1997; Big Rock Beat, 1998. **Address:** c/o Tom Doherty Associates, 175 Fifth Ave., New York, NY 10010, U.S.A.

KIJEWSKI, Karen. American, b. 1943. **Genres:** Mystery/Crime/Suspense. **Career:** Writer. Former high school English teacher in Massachusetts, c. 1970-80; worked nights as a bartender, 1980-91. **Publications:** MYSTERY NOVELS: Katwalk, 1989; Katapult, 1990; Kat's Cradel, 1992; Copy Kat, 1992; Wild Kat, 1994; Alley Kat Blues, 1995; Honky Tonk Kat, 1996; Kat Scratch Fever, 1997. Contributor to anthologies. **Address:** c/o Deborah Schneider, Gelfman Schneider Literary Agents Inc., 250 West 57th St., New York, NY 10107, U.S.A.

KILBRACKEN, Lord. Also writes as John Raymond Godley. Irish (born England), b. 1920. **Genres:** Poetry, Art/Art history, Natural history, Autobiography/Memoirs, Biography. **Career:** Daily Mirror and Sunday Express, staff reporter, 1947-51; freelance writer for many publications, 1951-2001, including contracts with Evening Standard (as foreign corresp.) Daily Express and Tatler; active as Labour Peer in House of Lords, until disqualified, 1999; Editorial Director, Worldwatch Magazine, 1984-85. **Publications:** Even for an Hour (poetry), 1940; Tell Me the Next One, 1950; (ed.) Letters from Early New Zealand, 1951; The Master Forger (in U.S. as Master Art Forger), 1951; Living Like a Lord, 1955; A Peer behind the Curtain (in U.S. as Moscow Gatecrash), 1959; Shamrocks and Unicorns (essays), 1962; Van Meegeren, 1967; Bring Back My Stringbag, 1979; The Easy Way to Bird Recognition, 1982 (Times Educational Supplement's Senior Information Book Award 1983); The Easy Way to Tree Recognition, 1983; The Easy Way to Wild Flower Recognition, 1984. **Address:** Killegar, County Leitrim, Ireland. **Online address:** johnkilbracken@aol.com

KILEY, David. American, b. 1963. **Genres:** Business/Trade/Industry. **Career:** Automotive writer. USA Today, Detroit, MI, Detroit bureau chief, 2000-; has also worked as a communications consultant and as an automotive and advertising analyst for television programs. **Publications:** Getting the Bugs Out: The Rise, Fall, and Comeback of Volkswagen in America, 2001. Contributor to periodicals. **Address:** 1825 North Franklin Ct., Ann Arbor, MI 48103, U.S.A. **Online address:** dkiley@usatoday.com

KILHAM, Benjamin. American, b. 1953. **Genres:** Zoology. **Career:** Colt Firearms, Hartford, CT, former product engineer; gunsmith, woodsman, naturalist, and wildlife rehabilitator. **Publications:** (with E. Gray) Among the Bears: Raising Orphan Cubs in the Wild, 2002. **Address:** c/o Author Mail, Henry Holt and Company, 115 West 18th Street, New York, NY 10011, U.S.A.

KILIAN, Michael D. American, b. 1939. **Genres:** Novels, Politics/Government, Humor/Satire. **Career:** KNTV, San Jose, CA, writer, 1960-63; City News Bureau, Chicago, IL, reporter, 1965-66; Chicago Tribune, Chicago, IL, reporter and assistant political editor, 1966-71, member of the editorial board, 1971-, editorial writer, 1971-74, editorial page columnist, 1974-78, Washington, DC columnist, 1978-; CBS Radio, WBBM, Chicago, IL, commentator, 1973-82; WTTW Channel 11, Chicago, IL, commentator, 1975-78; National Public Radio, commentator, 1978-79; society, celebrity, arts, film, and theatre columnist and critic, 1986-; writer of the Dick Tracy comic strip; Irish Radio, commentator. **Publications:** NOVELS: The Valkyrie Project, 1981; Northern Exposure, 1983; Blood of the Czars, 1984; By Order of the President, 1986; Dance on a Sinking Ship, 1988; Looker, 1991; The Last Virginia Gentleman, 1992; The Big Score, 1993; Major Washington, 1998. NONFICTION: (with C. Fletcher and F.R. Ciccone) Who Runs Chicago?, 1979; (with A. Sawislak) Who Runs Washington?, 1982; (with J. Coates) Heavy Losses: The Dangerous Decline of American Defense, 1985. HUMOR: Flying Can Be Fun, 1985. **Address:** Chicago Tribune, Washington Office, 1325 G St. NW, Washington, DC 20005-3104, U.S.A.

KILLAN, Gerald. Canadian (born England), b. 1945. **Genres:** History, Local history/Rural topics, Biography. **Career:** University of Western Ontario, London, Canada, King's University College, faculty member, 1973-84, professor of history, 1984-, academic dean, 1992-97, principal, 1997-. **Publications:** Preserving Ontario's Heritage: A History of the Ontario Historical Society, 1976; David Boyle: From Artisan to Archaeologist, 1983; Protected Places: A History of Ontario's Provincial Parks System, 1993. **Address:** King's University College, University of Western Ontario, 266 Epworth Ave, London, ON, Canada N6A 2M3. **Online address:** gkillan@julian.uwo.ca

KILLDEER, John. See MAYHAR, Ardath (Hurst).

KILLHAM, Edward L(eo). American, b. 1926. **Genres:** International relations/Current affairs. **Career:** U.S. Department of State, Washington, DC, minister/counselor in U.S. Foreign Service, 1952-87, including service at U.S. embassies in Moscow, London, and Copenhagen, and with Office of Soviet Union Affairs and Office of Research and Intelligence, executive secretary at Treasury Department, 1961-63, deputy assistant secretary general of international staff, North Atlantic Treaty Organization, 1974-77, special adviser to U.S. delegation to strategic arms limitation talks in Geneva, Switzerland, 1977-78, ACDA representative on U.S. delegation to mutual balanced force reduction talks in Vienna, Austria, 1978-79, deputy chief of mission at U.S. embassy in Brussels, Belgium, 1979-82, deputy chairperson of U.S. delegation to Conference on Security and Cooperation in Europe (CSCE), Madrid, Spain, 1982-83, State Department adviser to Naval War College, 1983-85, deputy chairperson of U.S. delegation to CSCE Human Rights Conference, Ottawa, ON, 1985, director of Central African affairs, 1985-87; Killham Associates Consulting, Washington, DC, president, 1987-. Consultant to U.S. Department of Defense and U.S. Information Agency; Fulbright Professor, Copenhagen University, Denmark, 1996. **Publications:** The Nordic Way: A Path to Baltic Equilibrium, 1993. Contributor of articles and reviews to newspapers and professional journals. **Address:** Killham Associates Consulting, 3615 Winfield Lane N.W., Washington, DC 20007, U.S.A.

KILLOUGH, (Karen) Lee. American, b. 1942. **Genres:** Mystery/Crime/Suspense, Science fiction/Fantasy. **Career:** Freelance writer of SF short stories and novels. Radiologic technologist, St. Joseph Hospital, Concordia, KS, 1964-65, St. Mary Hospital, Manhattan, KS, 1965-67, 1969-71, and Morris Cafritz Memorial Hospital, Washington, DC, 1967-69; Kansas State University, KSU Veterinary Medical Teaching Hospital, Manhattan, chief radiologic technologist, 1971-2000. **Publications:** A Voice out of Ramah, 1979; The Doppelganger Gambit, 1979; The Monitor, the Miners, and the Shree, 1980; Aventine, 1981; Deadly Silents, 1981; Liberty's World, 1985; Spider Play, 1986; Blood Hunt, 1987; The Leopard's Daughter, 1987; Bloodlinks, 1988; Dragon's Teeth, 1990; Bloodwalk, 1997; Bridling Chaos, 1998; Blood Games, 2001; Wilding Nights, 2020. **Address:** PO Box 1167, Manhattan, KS 66505-1167, U.S.A. **Online address:** klkillo@flinthills.com

KILMER, Nicholas (John). American. **Genres:** Mystery/Crime/Suspense, Art/Art history, Plays/Screenplays, Poetry, Translations. **Career:** Teacher of art and Latin at school in Vienna, VA, 1960-62; Action for Boston Community Development, Boston, MA, writer in department of planning and evaluation, 1966-67; English teacher at private school in Beverly, MA, 1967-70; Swain School of Design, New Bedford, MA, associate professor of liberal arts, 1970-82, dean, 1979-82; affiliated with Art Research of Cambridge, Cambridge, MA, 1984-88; founder of Nicholas Kilmer Fine Art, 1988-. Painter, with exhibitions throughout the northeast US. **Publications:** (ed) Poems of Pierre de Ronsard, 1979; Thomas Buford Meteyard (exhibition catalogue), 1989; A Place in Normandy (memoir), 1996. CRIME NOVELS: Harmony in Flesh and Black, 1995; Man with a Squirrel, 1996; O Sacred Head, 1997; Dirty Linen, 1999. PLAYS: A Story for the Lost Seasons, 1977; The White House Wedding (three-act), 1977; A Ceremony for the Marriage of the Charles River and the Atlantic Ocean (musical event), 1978; One Swan Street (two-act), 1979; The Captain's Fancy (three-act), 1980. POETRY TRANSLATIONS: Poems of Pierre de Ronsard, 1979; F. Petrarch: Songs and Sonnets, 1981; Dante's Comedy: The Inferno, 1986. Contributor of poems, translations, and reviews to periodicals. **Address:** 14A Eliot St., Cambridge, MA 02138, U.S.A.

KILMISTER, Clive William. British, b. 1924. **Genres:** Mathematics/Statistics, Physics, Philosophy. **Career:** Assistant Lecturer, 1950-53, Lecturer, 1953-59, Reader, 1959-66, Professor of Mathematics, 1966-84, and Gresham Professor of Geometry, 1971-88, King's College, London. **Publications:** (with G. Stephenson) Special Relativity for Physicists, 1958; (with B. O. J Tupper) Eddington's Statistical Theory, 1962; Hamiltonian Dynamics, 1964; The Environment in Modern Physics, 1965; (with J. E. Reeve) Rational Mechanics, 1966; Men of Physics: Sir Arthur Eddington, 1966; Language, Logic and Mathematics, 1967; Lagrangian Dynamics, 1967; Special Theory of Relativity, 1970; The Nature of the Universe, 1972; General Theory of Relativity, 1973; Russell, 1984; Eddington's Search for a Fundamental Theory, 1995; (with T. Bastin) Combinatorial Physics, 1995. **Address:** Red Tiles Cottage, High St, Barcombe, Lewes BN8 5DH, England.

KILPATRICK, Alan Edwin. American. **Genres:** Anthropology/Ethnology. **Career:** University of California, Santa Cruz, lecturer at Oakes College, 1989-91; University of Minnesota-Twin Cities, Minneapolis, assistant professor of American Indian studies, 1991-93, McKnight Land Grant Professor, 1993; San Diego State University, San Diego, CA, professor of American

Indian studies, 1993-, department head, 1997. University of California, Los Angeles, extension lecturer in archaeology, 1989-90; speaker at colleges and universities; public speaker. **Publications:** The Night Has a Naked Soul: Witchcraft and Sorcery among the Western Cherokee, 1997. SCRIPTS: Paths to Progress (educational film), 1976; Knowledge (episodes), 1975-76. Contributor to books. Contributor of articles and reviews to periodicals. **Address:** Dept of American Indian Studies, San Diego State University, 5500 Campanile Dr, San Diego, CA 92182-5500, U.S.A. **Online address:** akilpatr@mail.sdsu.edu

KILPATRICK, Andrew. American, b. 1943. **Genres:** Money/Finance, Biography. **Career:** U.S. Peace Corps, volunteer in India, 1965-67; Raleigh News and Observer, Raleigh, NC, copy editor, 1971-72; Birmingham News, Birmingham, AL, reporter, 1972-84; Birmingham Post-Herald, Birmingham, business reporter, 1984-92; Prudential Securities Inc., Birmingham, stockbroker, 1992-. **Publications:** Warren Buffett: The Good Guy of Wall Street, 1992; Of Permanent Value: The Story of Warren Buffett, 1994, new ed., 2002; A Legacy of Leadership: The History of AmSouth Bank, 1996. **Address:** 2850 Cahara Rd Ste 210, Birmingham, AL 35223-2344, U.S.A. **Online address:** andyakpe@aol.com

KILPATRICK, Nancy. Also writes as Amarantha Knight. American, b. 1946. **Genres:** Horror, Novellas/Short stories. **Career:** George Brown College, Toronto, Ontario, Canada, writing teacher, 1985-95; freelance writer for newspapers and magazines. Guest on television and radio programs in Canada and the United States; gives readings from her works. **Publications:** Near Death (horror novel), 1994; Sex and the Single Vampire (part of the three-volume The Vampire Trilogies), 1994; (with D. Bassingwaithe) As One Dead (novel), 1996; Child of the Night (novel), 1996; Endorphins (tentative title; horror novel), 1996; Vampyr (tentative title; stories), 1996. Work represented in anthologies. Contributor to magazines and newspapers. AS AMARANTHA KNIGHT: The Darker Passions: Dracula (erotic horror novel), 1993; (ed., and contributor as Kilpatrick) Love Bites (anthology), 1994; The Darker Passions: Dr. Jekyll and Mr. Hyde (erotic horror novel), 1995; The Darker Passions: Frankenstein (erotic horror novel), 1995; The Darker Passions: The Fall of the House of Usher (erotic horror novel), 1995; (ed., and contributor as Kilpatrick) Flesh Fantastic (anthology), 1995; The Darker Passions: The Portrait of Dorian Gray (erotic horror novel), 1996; The Amarantha Knight Reader (excerpts from novels), 1996; (ed., and contributor as Kilpatrick) Sex Macabre (stories), 1996; (ed., and contributor as Kilpatrick) Seductive Spectres (stories), 1996. **Address:** c/o Ricia Mainhardt, 612 Argyle St., #L5, Brooklyn, NY 11230, U.S.A.

KILROY, Thomas. Irish, b. 1934. **Genres:** Novels, Plays/Screenplays. **Career:** Stratford College, Dublin, headmaster, 1959-64; University College, Dublin, lecturer, 1965-73; University College, Galway, professor of English, 1977-89. **Publications:** The Death and Resurrection of Mr. Roche, 1969; The O'Neill, 1969; The Big Chapel (novel), 1971; (ed.) Sean O'Casey: A Collection of Critical Essays, 1975; Tea and Sex and Shakespeare, 1976; Talbot's Box, 1979; Double Cross, 1986; That Man, Bracken, 1986; The Madame MacAdam Travelling Theatre, 1991; Gold in the Streets, 1993; The Secret Fall of Constance Wilde, 1997; The Shape of Metal, 2003; My Scandalous Life, 2004; Blake, 2004; Henry, 2005. ADAPTER: The Seagull, by Chekhov, 1981; Ghosts, by Ibsen, 1989; Six Characters in Search of an Author, 1996. **Address:** Kilmaine, Mayo, Ireland.

KILSON, Marion D. de B. American, b. 1936. **Genres:** Anthropology/Ethnology. **Career:** Harvard University, Cambridge, MA, research fellow in African ethnology, 1975-81, lecturer 1978-80; Radcliffe College, Cambridge, Bunting Institute, director, 1977-80; Emmanuel College, Boston, academic dean, 1980-86; Silver Burdett and Ginn, member, editorial staff, 1987-89; Salem State College, dean, School of Arts and Sciences, 1989-91, dean, Graduate School, 1991-2001. **Publications:** Kpele Lala, 1971; African Urban Kinsmen, 1974; Roal Antelope and Spider, 1976; Mary Jane Forbes Greene (1895-1910): Mother of the Japan Mission, 1991; Claiming Place: Biracial Young Adults of the Post-Civil Rights Era, 2001. **Address:** 4 Eliot Rd, Lexington, MA 02421, U.S.A. **Online address:** marion.kilson@worldnet.att.net

KILWEIN GUEVARA, Maurice. American (born Colombia), b. 1961. **Genres:** Poetry. **Career:** Indiana University of Pennsylvania, assistant professor, 1991-99, professor of English, 1999-. Also taught at University of Wisconsin and Marquette University. Has performed his work onstage. **Publications:** Postmortem: Poems, 1994; Poems of the River Spirit, 1996; Autobiography of So-and-So: Poems in Prose, 2001; The Last Bridge (play). Contributor to poetry anthologies and magazines. **Address:** Department of English, Sutton Hall 355, Indiana University of Pennsylvania, Indiana, PA 15705, U.S.A. **Online address:** Mauricio@iup.edu

KILWORTH, Garry. Also writes as F. K. Salwood, Garry Douglas. British, b. 1941. **Genres:** Novels, Novellas/Short stories, Romance/Historical, Science fiction/Fantasy, Children's fiction. **Career:** Freelance writer, 1982-. Served as a Signals Master in the Royal Air Force, 1959-74; Sr. Executive, Cable and Wireless, London and the Caribbean, 1974-82. **Publications:** In Solitary, 1977; The Night of Kadar, 1978; Split Second, 1979; Gemini God, 1981; A Theatre of Timesmiths, 1984; Witchwater Country, 1986; Spiral Winds, 1987; The Wizard of Woodworld, 1987; Voyage of the Vigilance, 1988; Cloudrock, 1988; Abandonati, 1988;The Rain Ghost, 1989; Hunter's Moon, 1989; Midnight's Sun, 1990; The Third Dragon, 1991; The Drowners, 1991; Standing on Shamsan, 1992; Frost Dancers, 1992; Angel, 1993; Billy Pink's Private Detective Agency, 1993; Archangel, 1994; The Phantom Piper, 1994; The Electric Kid, 1994; The Navigator Kings (trilogy), 1997, 1998, 1999; House of Tribes, 1996; A Midsummer's Nightmare, 1997; Crimean War (series, annually), 1998-. SHORT STORIES: The Songbirds of Pain, 1984; In the Hollow of the Deep-Sea Wave, 1989; Dark Hills, Hollow Clocks, 1990; In the Country of Tattooed Men, 1993; Hogfoot Right and Bird-Hands, 1993. AS GARRY DOUGLAS: Highlander, 1986; The Street, 1988. AS F.K. SALWOOD: The Oystercatcher's Cry, 1993; The Saffron Fields, 1994.

KIM, Byoung-lo Philo. Korean, b. 1960. **Genres:** Politics/Government. **Career:** Writer. **Publications:** Two Koreas in Development: A Comparative Study of Principles and Strategies of Capitalist and Communist Third World Development, 1992. WORKS IN KOREAN: The Bibliographical Explanation of the Work of Kim Il Sung, 1993; The Bibliographical Explanation of the Work of Kim Jong Il, 1993; Analysis on the Internalization of Juche Ideology, 1994. **Address:** SL Tobong, PO Box 22, Korea Institute for National Unification, Seoul 142-600, Republic of Korea. **Online address:** philo@ku.kinu.or.kr

KIM, Elaine H(aikyung). American, b. 1942. **Genres:** Literary criticism and history. **Career:** University of California, Berkeley, professor of Asian American Studies, assistant dean, College of Letters and Science, faculty assistant for the status of women, associate dean, graduate division. Fulbright Fellowship, 1987-88; Rockefeller Fellowship, 1991-92; Global Korea Award, 1998; White House Commission on Women in US History, 1998-. **Publications:** Asian American Literature: An Introduction to the Writings and Their Social Context, 1982; (with J. Otani) With Silk Wings: Asian American Women at Work, 1983; (co-author) Writing Self, Writing Nation: Essays on Theresa Hak Kyung Cha's DICTEE, 1994. CO-EDITOR: Making Waves: Writings by and about Asian American Women, 1989; East to America: Korean American Life Stories, 1996; Making More Waves: New Writing by Asian American Women, 1997; Dangerous Women: Gender and Korean Nationalism, 1998. Author of articles and essays. **Address:** Asian American Studies Program, 506 Barrows Hall, University of California, Berkeley, CA 94720, U.S.A.

KIM, Hakjoon. Korean, b. 1943. **Genres:** International relations/Current affairs. **Career:** Seoul National University, Korea, assistant professor to professor of political science, 1973-89, served as department head; Office of the South Korean President for Policy Research, chief assistant, 1989-91; Office of the South Korean President for the Press, chief secretary, 1991-93; Dankook University, Seoul, head of board of trustees. National Assembly of South Korea, member, 1985-88. **Publications:** Unification Policies of South and North Korea, 1945-1991, 3rd ed, 1992; Korea's Relations with Her Neighbors in a Changing World, 1994. **Address:** 97 Nonhyon-dong Kangnam-ku, Seoul 135-010, Republic of Korea.

KIM, In S(oo). Korean, b. 1943. **Genres:** History, Theology/Religion. **Career:** Presbyterian College and Theological Seminary, Seoul, Korea, professor of Graduate School of Ministry, 1982-, dean, 2000-02. Korea Association of the Accredited Theological Schools, general secretary, 1998-; Society of the Church History, president, 2000-02. **Publications:** Protestants and the Formation of Modern Korean Nationalism, 1996; History of the Christian Church in Korea, 1997; Brief History of the Christian Church in Korea, 1998; History of 100 Years of the Presbyterian College and Presbyterian Theological Seminary, 2002. **Address:** Presbyterian College and Theological Seminary, 353 Kwang Jang-dong, Kwang Jin-ku, Seoul 143-756, Republic of Korea. **Online address:** iskim@pcts.ac.kr

KIM, Myung Mi. American (born Republic of Korea), b. 1957. **Genres:** Poetry. **Career:** Poet and educator. Chinatown Manpower Project, New York, NY, English-as-a-second-language (ESL) teacher, 1981-82; Stuyvesant High School, New York, NY, English teacher, 1983-84; University of Iowa, teaching-writing fellow, 1984-86; Luther College, director of student support services, 1987-91; San Francisco State University, San Francisco, CA, assistant professor, 1991-. **Publications:** POETRY: Under Flag, 1991; The Bounty, 1996; Dura, 1998; Commons, 2002. Contributor to anthologies and to literary journals. **Address:** Department of Creative Writing, School of Humanities, San Francisco State University, 1600 Holloway Ave., San Francisco, CA 94132, U.S.A.

KIM, Richard E. American (born Republic of Korea), b. 1932. **Genres:** Novels. **Career:** President, Trans-Literary Agency, Shutesbury, Massachusetts, since 1985. Instructor in English, California State College, Long Beach, 1963-64; Assistant Professor, 1964-68, Associate Professor, 1968, and Adjunct Associate Prof of English, 1969-70, University of Massachusetts, Amherst; Visiting Professor of English, Syracuse University, New York, 1970-71; San Diego State University, 1975-77. **Publications:** The Martyred, 1964; The Innocent, 1968; Lost Names, 1970; In Search of Lost Years, 1985; In Russia and China: In Search of Lost Koreans (Photo-Essays), 1989. **Address:** 187 Leverett Rd, Shutesbury, MA 01072, U.S.A.

KIM, Young (Hum). American (born Republic of Korea), b. 1920. **Genres:** History, International relations/Current affairs. **Career:** Professor of History and Political Science, U.S. International University, San Diego, California, since 1961 (former Assistant Professor and Associate Professor). Former Assistant Secretary, U.S. Embassy, Seoul, Korea. **Publications:** East Asia's Turbulent Century, 1966; Patterns of Competitive Coexistence: USA vs. USSR, 1966; Twenty Years of Crises: The Cold War Era, 1968; Toward Rational View of China: The Vietnam War in Struggle Against History: U.S. Foreign Policy in an Age of Revolution, 1968; The Central Intelligence Agency: Problems of Secrecy in a Democracy, 1981; America's Frontier Activities in Asia: U.S. Diplomatic History in Asia in the Twentieth Century, 1981; The War of No Return, vol. 1, 1988, vol. 2, 1989; Woman's Liberation Issue in Korea, 1989; United States-Asian Relations in the 20th Century, 1996. **Address:** 3001 Conner Way, San Diego, CA 92117, U.S.A. **Online address:** ykim6@yahoo.com

KIMBALL, Cheryl. American, b. 1957. **Genres:** How-to books, Self help. **Career:** Heinemann (publisher), Portsmouth, NH, publisher in trade division, 1990-96; Chronimed Publishing, Minneapolis, MN, publishing director, 1996-98; Adams Media Corp., Avon, MA, acquisitions editor, 1998-2000; freelance writer and editor, 2000-. **Publications:** The Everything Horse Book: Buying, Riding, and Caring for Your Equine Companion, 2002; The Everything Get-out-of-Debt Book: Evaluate Your Options, Determine Your Course of Action, and Make a Fresh Start, 2002; Mindful Horsemanship: Increasing Your Awareness One Day at a Time, 2002; (with S.R. Turlington and C.A. Shea) The Everything Kid's Monsters Book: From Ghosts, Goblins, and Gremlins to Vampires, Werewolves, and Zombies: Puzzles, Games, and Trivia Guaranteed to Keep You up at Night, 2002; The Everything Home Decorating Book, 2003; (with M. Hammerly) What to Do When the Doctor Says It's PCOS, 2003; (with T. Lyons) What to Do When the Doctor Says It's Endometriosis: Everything You Need to Know to Stop the Pain and Heal Your Fertility, 2003; Outwitting Ants: 101 Truly Ingenious Methods and Proven Techniques to Prevent Ants from Devouring Your Garden and Destroying Your Home, 2003. **Address:** c/o Author Mail, Adams Media Corp., 57 Littlefield St., Avon, MA 02322, U.S.A. **Online address:** ckimball@worldpath.net

KIMBALL, John (Ward). American, b. 1931. **Genres:** Biology. **Career:** Instructor in Science, Noble and Greenough School, Dedham, MA, 1953-54; Project Officer, U.S. Air Force, Rome, NY, 1954-56; Instructor in Biology, Phillips Academy, Andover, MA, 1956-69; Special Research Fellow, National Institutes of Health, 1969-72; Assistant, then Associate Professor of Biology, Tufts University, Medford, MA, 1972-81; Visiting Lecturer, Harvard University, Cambridge, MA, 1982-86, 1990-91. **Publications:** Biology, 1965, 6th ed., 1994; Cell Biology, 1970, 3rd ed., 1984; Man and Nature: Principles of Human and Environmental Biology, 1975; Introduction to Immunology, 1983, 3rd ed., 1990. **Address:** 89 Prospect Rd, Andover, MA 01810-2227, U.S.A. **Online address:** jkimball@mcb.harvard.edu; biology-pages.info

KIMBALL, Meredith M. American, b. 1944. **Genres:** Psychology. **Career:** University of Minnesota-Twin Cities, St. Paul, research assistant, 196466; University of British Columbia, Vancouver, assistant professor of psychology, 1970-76; Simon Fraser University, Burnaby, British Columbia, assistant professor, 1976-82, associate professor, 1982-96, professor of psychology and women's studies, 1996-, head of women's studies department, 1991-93. Public speaker on women's and children's issues and on the ethics of justice and care; presents workshops. **Publications:** (with E. Gee) Women and Aging, 1987; Feminist Visions of Gender Similarities and Differences, 1995. Contributor to books. Contributor of articles and reviews to professional journals. **Address:** Department of Psychology, Simon Fraser University, Burnaby, BC, Canada V5A 1S6.

KIMBALL, Robert (Eric). American, b. 1939. **Genres:** Music, Theatre. **Career:** Yale Collection of Literature and American Musical Theatre, New Haven, CT, curator, 1967-71; New York Post, NYC, music and dance reviewer, 1973-87, chief classical music critic, 1987-88; Roxbury Records, president, 1988-; writer. Lecturer at Yale University, 1970 and 1974; senior research fellow and visiting professor of music at Brooklyn College of the City University of New York's Institute for Studies in American Music, 1974-75; lecturer in Drama at New York University, 1979-80; lecturer in music at Yale University, 1980-81. **Publications:** (with W. Bolcom) Reminiscing with Sissle and Blake, 1973; (with A. Simon) The Gershwins, 1973; (with T. Krasker) Catalog of the American Musical: Musicals of Irving Berlin, George and Ira Gershwin, Cole Porter, Richard Rodgers and Lorenz Hart, 1988. EDITOR: Cole, 1971; The Unpublished Cole Porter, 1975; The Complete Lyrics of Cole Porter, 1983; (with D. Hart) The Complete Lyrics of Lorenz Hart, 1986; The Complete Lyrics of Ira Gershwin, 1993. Contributor to Grove's Dictionary of Music. Contributor to periodicals. Contributor of notes-sometimes in collaboration with Alfred Simon-to recordings. **Address:** 180 W. 58th St., New York, NY 10019, U.S.A.

KIMBALL, Roger. American, b. 1953. **Genres:** Education. **Career:** Writer. Served as managing editor of New Criterion; held teaching posts at Yale University and Connecticut College. **Publications:** Tenured Radicals: How Politics Has Corrupted Our Higher Education, 1990, rev. ed., 1998; The Long March: How the Cultural Revolution of the 1960s Changed America, 2000; Experiments Against Reality: The Fate of Culture in the Postmodern Age, 2001; Lives of the Mind: The Use and Abuse of Intelligence from Hegel to Wodehouse, 2002; Art's Prospect: The Challenge of Tradition in an Age of Celebrity, 2003. **Address:** New Criterion, Foundation for Cultural Review, 900 Broadway Ste 602, New York, NY 10003, U.S.A. **Online address:** letters@newcriterion.com

KIMBRIEL, Katherine Eliska. American, b. 1956. **Genres:** Science fiction/Fantasy. **Career:** Science fiction and fantasy writer; technical writer; research aide; correspondence school instructor. Also worked as gold caster, janitor, and sales clerk. **Publications:** NOVELS. NUALA SERIES: Fire Sanctuary, 1986; Fires of Nuala, 1988; Hidden Fires, 1991. ALFREDA SORENSSON SERIES: Night Calls, 1996; Kindred Rites, 1997. Contributor of short stories to books. Contributor to periodicals. **Address:** c/o Author Mail, Seventh Floor, HarperCollins Publishers, 10 East 53rd St., New York, NY 10022, U.S.A. **Online address:** kkimbrie@flash.net

KIMBROUGH, S T, Jr. American, b. 1936. **Genres:** Music, Theology/Religion. **Career:** Writer, researcher, and singer, 1993-. United Methodist Church, General Board of Global Ministries, associate general secretary for mission evangelism, 1990-98. Charles Wesley Society, founding president; recording artist and performing vocalist in concerts, recitals, and operas. **Publications:** Israelite Religion in Sociological Perspective: The Work of Antonin Causse, 1978; Sweet Singer (musical play), 1985; Lost in Wonder: Charles Wesley, The Meaning of His Hymns Today, 1987; A Heart to Praise My God: Wesley Hymns for Today, 1996; Resistless Love: Christian Witness in the New Millennium, 2000; Anna Eklund: A Methodist Saint in Russia, 2001. EDITOR: Sweet Singer (hymns), 1984; (with O.A. Breckerlegge) The Unpublished Poetry of Charles Wesley, Vol. 1, 1988, Vol. 2: Hymns and Poems on Holy Scripture, 1990, Vol 3: Hymns and Poems for Church and World, 1992; (with J.C. Holbert and C.R. Young), Psalms for Praise and Worship: A Complete Liturgical Psalter, 1992; Charles Wesley: Poet and Theologian, 1992; Methodism in Russia and the Baltic States: History and Renewal, 1995; Global Praise 1, 1997, 2nd rev. ed. 2000; Charles Wesley, A Song for the Poor, 1997; Africa Praise Songbook: Songs from Africa, 1998; Global Praise 2: Songs for Worship and Witness, 2000; Orthodox and Wesleyan Spirituality, 2002; Orthodox and Wesleyan Spirituality, 2002; We Offer Them Christ, 2004. **Address:** 12 B Bridge Ave, Bay Head, NJ 08742, U.S.A.

KIMMEL, Eric A. American, b. 1946. **Genres:** Novels, Novellas/Short stories, Children's fiction. **Career:** Indiana University, South Bend, assistant professor of education, 1973-78; Portland State University, Oregon, professor of education, 1978-93; Shearwater Books, Ltd., president, 1993-. Contributor, Cricket, Spider. **Publications:** The Tartar's Sword, 1974; Mishka, Pishka and Fishka, 1976; Why Worry?, 1979; Nicanor's Gate, 1980; Hershel of Ostropol, 1981; (with R. Zar) In the Mouth of the Wolf, 1983; Anansi and the Moss-Covered Rock, 1988; The Chanukkah Tree, 1988; Charlie Drives the Stage, 1989; Hershel and the Hanukkah Goblins, 1989; I Took My Frog to the Library, 1989; The Chanukkah Guest, 1990; Nanny Goat and the Seven Kids, 1990; Four Dollars and Fifty Cents, 1990; Baba Yaga, 1991; Days of Awe, 1991; Bearhead, 1991; The Greatest of All, 1991; The Four Gallant Sisters, 1992; The Old Woman and Her Pig; Anansi Goes Fishing, 1992; Boots and His Brothers, 1992; The Spotted Pony and Other Stories, 1992;

The Tale of Aladdin and the Wonderful Lamp, 1992; The Gingerbread Man, 1993; Three Sacks of Truth, 1993; Asher and the Capmakers, 1993; The Witch's Face, 1993; I Know Not What, I Know Not Where, 1994; The Three Princes, 1994; Anansi and the Talking Melon, 1994; One Good Tern Deserves Another, 1994; Iron John, 1994; Bernal and Floridia, 1994; Bar Mitzvah, 1995; Count Silvernose, 1996; The Magic Dreidels, 1996; Billy Lazroe & the King of the Sea, 1996; Ali Baba & the Forty Thieves, 1996; One Eye, Two Eyes, & Three Eyes, 1996; Squash It, 1997; Sirko and the Wolf, 1997; Ten Suns, 1998; Easy Work, 1998; When Mindy Saved Hanukkah, 1998; A Hanukkah Treasury, 1998; Seven at One Blow, 1998; The Birds' Gift, 1999; Sword of the Samurai, 1999; The Rooster's Antlers, 1999; The Two Mountains, 2000; Montezuma and the Fall of the Aztecs, 2000; Grizz!, 2000; The Jar of Fools, 2000; The Runaway Tortilla, 2000; Gershon's Monster, 2000; A Cloak for the Moon, 2001; Robin Hook, Pirate Hunter, 2001; Website of the Warped Wizard, 2001; Zigazak!, 2001; Website of the Cracked Cookies, 2001; Anansi and the Magic Stick, 2001; Why the Snake Crawls on Its Belly, 2001; The Brass Serpent, 2002; The Erie Canal Pirates, 2002; Three Samurai Cats, 2003; Brother Wolf, Sister Sparrow (stories), 2003; Don Quixote and the Windmills, 2004; Wonders and Miracles, 2004; Cactus Soup, 2004; Castle of the Cats, 2004; Hayyim's Ghost, 2004; The Hero Beowulf, 2005; A Horn for Louis, 2005. **Address:** 2525 NE 35th Ave, Portland, OR 97212-5232, U.S.A. **Online address:** kimmels@comcast.net

KIMMEL, Jordan L. American, b. 1958. **Genres:** Money/Finance. **Career:** Morgan Stanley Dean Witter, Morristown, NJ, vice president for investment, 1994-97; First Montauk Securities, Red Bank, NJ, market strategist, 1997-. Magnet Investment Group, president and money manager, 1997-. **Publications:** Magnet Investing: Build a Portfolio and Pick Winning Stocks Using Your Home Computer, 1999. **Address:** Magnet Investment Group, 1201 Sussex Turnpike, Mount Freedom, NJ 07970, U.S.A.

KIMMEL, Michael S(cott). American, b. 1951. **Genres:** Sociology, Politics/Government. **Career:** Bryant College, Smithfield, RI, instructor in sociology, 1973; State University of New York College at Oneonta, instructor in sociology, 1973-74; University of California at Berkeley, instructor in sociology, 1974-76; University of California at Santa Cruz, visiting lecturer, 1977-81; Rutgers University, New Brunswick, NJ, assistant professor of sociology, 1982-86; State University of New York at Stony Brook, professor of sociology, 1987-; editor and writer. **Publications:** Absolutism and Its Discontent: State and Society in Seventeenth-Century France and England, 1988; (author of intro) Mundus Foppensis/The Levellers, 1988; Revolution: A Sociological Interpretation, 1990; Manhood in America: A Cultural History, 1996. EDITOR: Changing Men: New Directions in Research on Men and Masculinity, 1987; (with M.A. Messner) Men's Lives, 1989; Love Letters between a Certain Late Nobleman and the Famous Mr. Wilson, 1990; Men Confront Pornography, 1990; (with T.E. Mosmiller) Against the Tide: "Pro-Feminist" Men in the United States, 1776-1990, a Documentary History, 1992; The Politics of Manhood: Profeminist Men Respond to the Mythopoetic Men's Movement (and Mythopoetic Leaders Answer), 1995. Contributor of articles and reviews to periodicals. **Address:** Department of Sociology, State University of New York at Stony Brook, Stony Brook, NY 11794, U.S.A.

KIMMELMAN, Michael Simon. American, b. 1958. **Genres:** Art/Art history. **Career:** Harvard University, teaching fellow, 1982-84; Atlanta Journal-Constitution, art critic, 1984; Philadelphia Inquirer, art critic, 1985-87; U.S. News and World Report, Washington, culture editor, 1987; New York Times, art critic, 1988-90, chief art critic, 1990-. **Publications:** Portraits: Talking with Artists at Met, the Modern, the Louvre, and Elsewhere, 1998. **Address:** New York Times, 229 W 43rd St., New York, NY 10036, U.S.A.

KIMMERLING, Baruch. Israeli (born Romania), b. 1939. **Genres:** Politics/Government, Sociology. **Career:** Free-lance writer for newspapers and the Israeli Broadcasting Service, 1962-68; Hebrew University of Jerusalem, Israel, lecturer in department of sociology and anthropology, 1978-82, associate professor, 1982-87, professor, 1987-, director of Center for the Study and Documentation of Israeli Society, 1985-87. Massachusetts Institute of Technology, research fellow at Center for International Studies, 1978-79; Israel Foundation, trustee, 1983-85; University of Washington, research fellow, 1987-88, visiting associate professor at Henry Jackson School for International Studies, 1988-89; Israel Studies Association, member of board of directors, 1989. Journal of Applied Behavioral Science, consulting editor, 1980. **Publications:** Zionism and Territory: The Socioterritorial Dimensions of Zionist Politics, 1983; Zionism and Economy, 1983; The Interrupted System: Israeli Civilians in War and Routine Times, 1985; (ed.) The Israeli State and Society: Boundaries and Frontiers, 1989; (with J.S. Migdal) Palestinians: The Making of a People, 1993; The Sociology of Politics (textbook in Hebrew; title translated), 2 vols., 1993; Cultural Wars in Israel (in Hebrew), 2000. Contributor to anthologies. Contributor to periodicals. **Address:** Department of Sociology and Anthropology, Hebrew University of Jerusalem, 91 905 Jerusalem, Israel. **Online address:** mskimmer@mscc.huji. ac.il

KINCAID, Jamaica. American (born Antigua-Barbuda), b. 1949. **Genres:** Novels, Novellas/Short stories, Essays. **Career:** New Yorker mag., NYC, contributor, 1974-. **Publications:** At the Bottom of the River (short stories), 1984; Annie John (novel), 1985; A Small Place (essays), 1988; Lucy (novel), 1990; The Autobiography of My Mother; My Brother, 1997; My Garden (Book), 1999; Talk Stories, 2001; Mr. Potter, 2002. **Address:** c/o The New Yorker, 4 Times Sq, New York, NY 10036, U.S.A.

KINCHER, Jonni. American, b. 1949. **Genres:** Children's non-fiction, Psychology. **Career:** Author. Teacher; presenter at educational conferences. Founder of Inklusions, a rubber stamp company. **Publications:** Dreams Can Help, 1988; Psychology for Kids, 1990; The First Honest Book about Lies, 1992; More Psychology for Kids, 1994. **Address:** c/o Free Spirit Publishing, 217 5th Ave N Ste 200, Minneapolis, MN 55401-1299, U.S.A.

KINDL, Patrice. American, b. 1951. **Genres:** Young adult fiction. **Career:** Writer. **Publications:** YOUNG ADULT FANTASY: Owl in Love, 1993; The Woman in the Wall, 1997; Goose Chase, 2001; Lost in the Labyrinth, 2002. **Address:** 116 Middlefort Rd, Middleburgh, NY 12122-9601, U.S.A. **Online address:** patricekindl.com

KINEALY, Christine. Irish (born England), b. 1956. **Genres:** History. **Career:** Ulster Historical Foundation, Belfast, Northern Ireland, deputy director, 1987-90; University of Liverpool, England, deputy director of education program, 1990-92, fellow, 1992-. Historical consultant to Irish government, 1988-90. **Publications:** (ed. with C. Gallagher and T. Parkhill) Making Sense of Irish History: Evidence in Ireland for the Young Historian, 1990; Migration and Settlement: A Multi-Cultural Approach, 1992; The Glorious Revolution in Ireland, 1992; This Great Calamity: The Irish Famine, 1845-52, 1994; (with S. Sexton) The Irish: A Photohistory, 2002; The Great Irish Famine: Impact, Ideology and Rebellion, 2002. Contributor to books. Contributor to history and Irish studies journals. **Address:** 12 Marsden Rd, Southport, Merseyside PR9 9AE, England. **Online address:** ckinealy@uclan. ac.uk

KING, Alison. *See* MARTINI, Teri.

KING, Anita. American, b. 1931. **Genres:** Reference. **Career:** Graphic artist, writer/editor/researcher, music theorist, independent scholar, photographer. **Publications:** Quotations in Black, 1981; Candomble, 1987; Samba, 1989; Contemporary Quotations in Black, 1997. **Address:** 10 E138th St Apt 8E, New York, NY 10037, U.S.A.

KING, Anthony. Canadian, b. 1934. **Genres:** Politics/Government. **Career:** Professor of Government, University of Essex, Colchester, since 1969 (Sr. Lecturer, and Reader, 1966-69). Adjunct Scholar, American Enterprise Institute; Fellow of Magdalen College, Oxford, 1961-65. **Publications:** (with D.E. Butler) British General Election of 1964, 1965; (with D.E. Butler) British General Election of 1966, 1966; (with A. Sloman) Westminster and Beyond, 1973; British Members of Parliament: A Self-Portrait, 1974; Britain Says Yes: The 1975 Referendum on the Common Market, 1977; (with I. Crewe) SDP: The Birth, Life and Death of the Social Democratic Party, 1996; Running Scared: Why America's Politicians Campaign Too Much and Govern Too Little, 1997. EDITOR: British Prime Minister: A Reader, 1969, 1985; The New American Political System, 1978; Both Ends of the Avenue: Presidential-Congressional Relations in the 1980s, 1983; Britain at the Polls, 1992, 1992; New Labour Triumphs: Britain at the Polls, 1998. **Address:** Dept. of Government, University of Essex, Wivenhoe Park, Colchester, Essex CO4 3SQ, England.

KING, Bruce (Alvin). American, b. 1933. **Genres:** Intellectual history, Literary criticism and history, Biography. **Career:** Taught at Brooklyn College, 1960-61, University of Alberta, Calgary, 1961-62, University of Ibadan, 1962-65, University of Bristol, 1966-67, University of Lagos, 1967-70, University of Windsor, ON, 1970-73, Ahmadu Bello University, Zaria, Nigeria, 1973-76, University of Paris, 1977-78; Rockefeller Foundation Humanities Fellow, 1977-78; University of Stirling, Scotland, 1979; University of Canterbury, New Zealand, 1979-83; University of N Alabama, Albert S. Johnston Visiting Professor of Literature, 1983-86; visiting professor of English, Ben Gurion University of the Negev, Israel, 1987-89, University of Paris VII, 1990-91, and University of Angers, France, 1995. Fulbright Research Fellowship, India, 1988; National Endowment for the

Humanities, Interpretive Research Grant, 1990-93, 1995-97, Fellowship for Independent Scholars, 2001. **Publications:** Dryden's Major Plays, 1966; Marvell's Allegorical Poetry, 1977; The New English Literatures, 1980; Ibsen's A Doll's House, 1980; G.B. Shaw's Arms and the Man, 1980; Fielding's Joseph Andrews, 1981; History of 17th-Century English Literature, 1982; Modern Indian Poetry in English, 1987, 2nd ed., 2001; Coriolanus, 1989; Three Indian Poets: Ezekiel, Ramanujan and Moraes, 1991; V.S. Naipaul, 1993, 2nd ed., 2003; Derek Walcott and West Indian Drama, 1995; Derek Walcott: A Caribbean Life, 2000; The Internationalization of English Literature 1948-2000, 2004. EDITOR: 20th Century Interpretations of All for Love, 1968; Dryden's Mind and Art, 1969; Introduction to Nigerian Literature, 1971; Literatures of the World in English, 1974; (co) A Celebration of Black and African Writing, 1976; West Indian Literature, 1979, 2nd ed., 1995; Contemporary American Theatre, 1991; The Commonwealth Novel since 1960, 1991; Post-Colonial English Drama, 1992; The Later Fiction of Nadine Gordimer, 1993; New National and Post-Colonial Literatures, 1996. SERIES EDITOR: Modern Dramatists, 1982-92; English Dramatists, 1990-2004; Literature, Culture & Identity, 1999-2001. **Address:** 145 Quai de Valmy, 75010 Paris, France. **Online address:** 00acking@bsu.edu; king. adele@wanadoo.fr

KING, Carol Soucek. American, b. 1943. **Genres:** Architecture, Design, Homes/Gardens, Inspirational/Motivational Literature. **Career:** Santa Monica Evening Outlook, CA, drama critic; Los Angeles Herald Examiner, CA, editor of Lifestyle Section; Designers West, editor-in-chief, 1978-93; Designers World, editor-in-chief, 1991-93; Interior Expressions magazine, editor, 1998-99. Institute of Philosophy and the Arts, Pasadena, CA, founder. **Publications:** At Home and at Work: Architects' and Designers' Empowered Spaces, 1993; Furniture: Architects' and Designers' Originals, 1994; The Creative Touch: Designing with Glass, 1995; The Creative Touch: Designing with Wood, 1995; The Creative Touch: Designing with Tile, Stone and Brick, 1995; The Creative Touch: Designing with Textiles, 1995; Empowered Gardens, 1997; Gardenscapes, 1997; Designing with Light, 1998; Light Styling, 1999; Feng Shui at Home, 1999; Designing with Spirituality, 2000; The Art of Dramatic Living: Illuminations, 2005. **Address:** 60 El Circulo Dr, Pasadena, CA 91105, U.S.A. **Online address:** KingCarol@aol.com

KING, Cassandra. American, b. 1944. **Genres:** Novels. **Career:** Author. Taught college-level English and writing in Alabama. **Publications:** Making Waves in Zion, 1995; The Sunday Wife, 2002. **Address:** c/o Hyperion Books Author Mail, 77 West 66th Street, 11th Fl., New York, NY 10023, U.S.A.

KING, Cynthia. American, b. 1925. **Genres:** Novels, Novellas/Short stories, Children's fiction, Young adult fiction. **Career:** Writer; Editorial Consultant. Associate Ed., Hillman Periodicals, NYC, 1945-50; Managing Ed., Fawcett Publs., NYC, 1950-54; Teacher: Creative Writing in public and private schools, Houston, Texas, 1970-75; Coord., Exhibition of Children's Book Art, Cont. Art Museum, Houston, 1975; Resident, Michigan Council for the Arts Creative-Writer-in-the-Schools Program, 1976-84; Coord., Seminars on Book Proposals, 1981, and Writing for Children, 1982; Director, Short Story Symposium, 1985. **Publications:** In the Morning of Time: The Story of the Norse God Balder, 1970; The Year of Mr. Nobody, 1978; Beggars and Choosers, 1980; Sailing Home, 1982. Contributor of book reviews to newspapers. **Address:** 228 River St, Bethel, VT 05032, U.S.A. **Online address:** tonibking@adelphia.net

KING, Daniel (John). British, b. 1963. **Genres:** Recreation. **Career:** Writer. **Publications:** (with P. Ponzetto) Mastering the Spanish, 1992; Winning with the Najdorf, 1992; How Good Is Your Chess?, 1993; (with D. Trelford) World Chess Championship, Kasparov v. Short, 1993; World Chess Championships, 1993; How to Win at Chess: The Ten Golden Rules, 1995; World Chess Championships, 1995; (with P. Dove) Choose the Right Move, 1995; Kasparov v. Deeper Blue: The Ultimate Man vs. Machine Challenge, 1997; The Closed Sicilian, 1997; (with C. Duncan) Choose the Right Move, 1998; The English Defence, 1999; (with G. Kasparov) Kasparov against the World, 2000; Chess: From First Moves to Checkmate, 2000. **Address:** c/o Kingfisher Publications, New Penderel House, 283-288 High Holborn, London WC1V 7HZ, England. **Online address:** danieljohnking@ compuserve.com

KING, David. American, b. 1943. **Genres:** Art/Art history, Photography. **Career:** Photohistorian and art historian. Designer of retrospective on Alexander Rodchenko's work. **Publications:** NONFICTION: (with F. Wyndham) Trotsky: A Documentary, 1972; I Am King: A Photographic Biography of Muhammad Ali, 1975; (Designer) Alexander Rodchenko (catalog), 1979; (with C. Porter) Images of Revolution: Graphic Art from 1905 Russia, 1983 in UK as Blood and Laughter: Caricatures from the 1905 Revolution;

(Designer) David Elliot, New Worlds: Russian Art and Society, 1900-1937, 1986; Trotsky: A Photographic Biography, 1986; (Designer) Bruce Chatwin, Far Journeys: Photographs and Notebooks, 1993; The Commissar Vanishes: The Falsification of Photographs and Art in Stalin's Russia, 1997. **Address:** c/o Henry Holt and Company, 115 West 18th St., New York, NY 10011, U.S.A.

KING, (William) Dennis. American, b. 1941. **Genres:** How-to books, Writing/Journalism. **Career:** Our Town (weekly publication), New York, NY, journalist, 1978-81; free-lance writer. **Publications:** Lyndon LaRouche and the New American Fascism, 1989; Get the Facts on Anyone, 1992, 3rd ed., 1999. **Address:** 420 E 64th St, New York, NY 10021, U.S.A. **Online address:** Wdennisking@cs.com

KING, Francis (Henry). Also writes as Frank Cauldwell. British (born Switzerland), b. 1923. **Genres:** Novels, Poetry, Travel/Exploration. **Career:** Theatre reviewer, Sunday Telegraph, London, 1978-88; Regional Director, British Council, Kyoto, Japan, 1958-62; President, Intl P.E.N., 1985-89, vice president, 1989-; Spectator, literary reviewer, 1976-. **Publications:** To the Dark Tower, 1946; Never Again, 1947; An Air That Kills, 1948; The Dividing Stream, 1951; Rod of Incantation, 1952; The Dark Glasses, 1954; (as Frank Cauldwell) The Firewalkers: A Memoir, 1956; The Widow, 1957; (ed) Introducing Greece, 1957; The Man on the Rock, 1957; So Hurt and Humiliated, 1959; The Custom House, 1961; The Japanese Umbrella, 1964; The Last of the Pleasure Gardens, 1965; The Waves behind the Boat, 1967; The Brighton Belle, 1968; A Domestic Animal, 1970; Japan, 1970; Flights, 1973; A Game of Patience, 1974; The Needle, 1975; Christopher Isherwood, 1976; Hard Feelings, 1976; Danny Hill, 1977; E.M. Forster and His World, 1978; The Action, 1978; Indirect Method, 1980; Act of Darkness, 1983; Voices in an Empty Room, 1984; One Is a Wanderer, 1985; Frozen Music, 1987; The Woman Who Was God, 1988; Punishments, 1989; Visiting Cards, 1990; A Literary Companion to Florence, 1991; The Ant Colony, 1991; Secret Lives, 1991; Yesterday Came Suddenly, 1993; The One and Only, 1994; Ash on an Old Man's Sleeve, 1996; A Hand at the Shutter, 1996; Dead Letters, 1997; Prodigies, 2001; The Nick of Time, 2003. **Address:** 19 Gordon Pl, London W8 4JE, England. **Online address:** fhk@dircon.co.uk

KING, Francis P. American, b. 1922. **Genres:** Economics, Education, Money/Finance. **Career:** Sr. Research Officer, Teachers Insurance and Annuity Association, NYC, 1971-98 (Research Officer, 1954-71). Chairman of Board, Tuition Exchange, Allentown, Pa., 1972-88. **Publications:** Financing the College Education of Faculty Children, 1954; (with W.C. Greenough) Retirement and Insurance Plans in American Colleges, 1969; Benefit Plans in Junior Colleges, 1971; (with W.C. Greenough) Pension Plans and Public Policy, 1976; (with T.J. Cook) Benefit Plans in Higher Education, 1980. **Address:** 360 E. 72nd St, New York, NY 10021, U.S.A.

KING, Gary C. American. **Genres:** Mystery/Crime/Suspense. **Career:** Writer. **Publications:** TRUE CRIME ACCOUNTS: Blood Lust: Portrait of a Serial Sex Killer, 1992; Driven to Kill, 1993; Web of Deceit, 1994; Blind Rage, 1995; (with Don Lasseter) Savage Vengeance, 1996; The Texas 7, 2001; Murder in Hollywood, 2001; An Early Grave, 2001; Angels of Death, 2003; The Good Neighbor, 2004. Contributor to magazines in England and the United States. **Address:** c/o Peter Miller, PMA Literary and Film Management, 6th Floor Rear, 45 West 21st St., New York, NY 10010, U.S.A. **Online address:** garycking@earthlink.net

KING, Geoff. British, b. 1960. **Genres:** Film. **Career:** Writer and educator. Formerly worked as a journalist for newspapers and as a researcher; Brunel University, London, England, lecturer in film and television studies. **Publications:** Mapping Reality: An Exploration of Cultural Cartographies, 1996; Spectacular Narratives: Hollywood in the Age of the Blockbuster, 2000; (with T. Krzywinska) Science Fiction Cinema: From Outerspace to Cyberspace, 2000; New Hollywood Cinema: An Introduction, 2002; Film Comedy, 2002; (ed., with T. Krzywinska) ScreenPlay: Cinema/Videogame Interfaces, 2002. Contributor to periodicals. **Address:** Department of the Performing Arts, Brunel University, Uxbridge, Middlesex UB8 3PH, England. **Online address:** geoff.king@brunel.ac.uk

KING, Jeanette (Margaret). New Zealander, b. 1959. **Genres:** Poetry. **Career:** Teacher at a girls' high school in Christchurch, New Zealand, 1982-87; University of Canterbury, Christchurch, tutor, 1988-92; lecturer in Maori department, 1993-. **Publications:** E Pirangi Ana Koe?, 1994; E Haere Mai Ana Nga Manuhiri, 1994; One Sleepy Day, 1998; Te Pu Harakeke, 1998; Maramara (poems), 1999. Short stories written in Maori are represented in school anthologies. Contributor to periodicals. **Address:** Maori Department,

University of Canterbury, Private Bag 4800, Christchurch, New Zealand. **Online address:** j:king@maori.canterbury.ac.nz

KING, Jerry P. American, b. 1935. **Genres:** Mathematics/Statistics. **Career:** Lehigh University, Bethlehem, PA, assistant professor, 1962-65, associate professor, 1965-68, professor of mathematics, 1968-, associate dean of College of Arts and Sciences, 1979-81, dean of graduate school, 1981-87; writer. **Publications:** The Art of Mathematics, 1992. **Address:** Department of Mathematics, Lehigh University, 14 E Packer Ave, Bethlehem, PA 18015, U.S.A. **Online address:** jpk2@lehigh.edu

KING, Jonathon. American. **Genres:** Mystery/Crime/Suspense. **Career:** Journalist and writer. Philadelphia Daily News, Philadelphia, PA, reporter; South Florida Sun-Sentinel, Ft. Lauderdale, feature writer. **Publications:** MAX FREEMAN CRIME SERIES: The Blue Edge of Midnight, 2002; A Visible Darkness, 2003; Shadow Men, 2004. **Address:** c/o Dutton Publicity, 375 Hudson St., New York, NY 10014, U.S.A. **Online address:** jking@sun-sentinel.com

KING, Jonny. American, b. 1965. **Genres:** Music. **Career:** Associate with a law firm in Boston, MA, 1991-92; law clerk to Douglas P. Woodlock, Boston, 1992; Cowan, Liebowitz & Latman, NYC, special counsel, 1994-. Self-employed jazz pianist, 1980-, with three recorded albums; musical composer. **Publications:** What Jazz Is, 1997. **Address:** Cowan Liebowitz & Latman, 1133 Avenue of the Americas, New York, NY 10036, U.S.A. **Online address:** jonnyking@jazzcorner.com

KING, Kathryn R. American. **Genres:** Literary criticism and history. **Career:** Writer. University of Montevallo, Montevallo, AL, professor of English language and literature. **Publications:** Jane Barker, Exile: A Literary Career, 1675-1725, 2000. EDITOR: Thomas Hardy, Wessex Tales, 1991; The Poems of Jane Barker: The Magdalen Manuscript, 1998; (with A. Pettit) Eliza Fowler Haywood, The Female Spectator, 2001. **Address:** Dept of English, University of Montevallo, Comer Hall, Station 6420, Montevallo, AL 35115, U.S.A. **Online address:** kingk@montevallo.edu

KING, Laurie R. Also writes as Leigh Richards. American, b. 1952. **Genres:** Mystery/Crime/Suspense, Science fiction/Fantasy. **Career:** Writer. **Publications:** MYSTERIES: A Grave Talent, 1993; The Beekeeper's Apprentice, 1994; To Play the Fool, 1995; With Child, 1996; A Monstrous Regiment of Women, 1996; A Letter of Mary, 1997; The Moor, 1998; A Darker Place, 1999; O Jerusalem, 1999; Night Work, 2000; Folly, 2001; Justice Hall, 2002; Keeping Watch, 2003; The Game, 2004. SCIENCE FICTION: Califia's Daughters, 2004. **Address:** PO Box 1152, Freedom, CA 95019, U.S.A.

KING, Martha. American, b. 1937. **Genres:** Poetry, Novels. **Career:** Poet. **Publications:** Weather (poetry), 1978; Seventeen Walking Sticks (poetry and memoir), 1998; Little Tales of Family and War, 1990-1999 (fiction), 2000; (with others) Separate Parts: Six Memory Pieces, 2002; Imperfect Fit: Selected Poems, 2003. Contributor of poetry, prose, and criticism to magazines. **Address:** 326-A Fourth St., Brooklyn, NY 11215, U.S.A. **Online address:** martha.king@nmss.org

KING, Nicholas. British, b. 1947. **Genres:** Theology/Religion. **Career:** Priest, author, teacher. Entered Society of Jesus (Jesuits), 1970, ordained, 1980; St. Joseph's Theological Institute, Cedara, South Africa, dean of Biblical studies, 1989-1996; St. John Vianney Seminary, Pretoria, South Africa, spiritual director and lecturer. **Publications:** (trans.) J. Osuna, Friends in the Lord: A Study in the Origins and Growth of Community in the Society of Jesus from St. Ignatius' Conversion to the Earliest Texts of the Constitutions (1521-1541), 1974; What Is a Gospel?, 1981; Setting the Gospel Free, 1995; Jesuit Companions, 1997; Whispers of Liberation: Feminist Perspectives on the New Testament, 1998; The New Testament Freshly Translated, 2005. Contributor of reviews and articles to periodicals. **Address:** Campion Hall, Oxford OX1 1QS, England. **Online address:** nicholas.king@campion.ox.ac.uk

KING, Paul. *See* **DRACKETT, Phil(ip Arthur).**

KING, Philip J. American, b. 1925. **Genres:** Theology/Religion. **Career:** Boston College, Chestnut Hill, MA, professor of biblical studies, 1974-, faculty fellow, 1989. W. F. Albright Institute of Archaeological Research, Jerusalem, Israel, president, 1972-76; American Schools of Oriental Research, Jerusalem, member of board of trustees, 1973-90, president, 1976-82, honorary trustee, 1991-; American Research Center in Egypt, member of board of governors and executive committee, 1982-85, currently member; Palestine

Exploration Fund, member. Cambridge University, visiting fellow, 1989, life member of Clare Hall, 1990-. Conducted archaeological field research in Jordan, Israel, and Yemen, beginning in 1967. **Publications:** A Study of Psalm 45, 1959; The Book of Judges, 1960; The Book of Psalms, two parts, 1962; The Book of Numbers, 1966; American Archaeology in the Mideast: A History of the American Schools of Oriental Research, 1983; Amos, Hosea, Micah: An Archaeological Commentary, 1988; (ed.) Studies on the Mesha Inscriptions and Moab, 1989; Jeremiah: An Archaeological Companion, 1993. Editor, "Archaeology and Biblical Studies Series," 1985-91. Contributor to books. Contributor to theology and archaeology journals. **Address:** Department of Theology, Boston College, Chestnut Hill, MA 02467, U.S.A.

KING, Robert C(harles). American, b. 1928. **Genres:** Biology. **Career:** Northwestern University, Evanston, IL, joined faculty 1956, professor of genetics, 1964-. **Publications:** Genetics, 1962; Dictionary of Genetics, 1968, 6th ed., 2002; Ovarian Development in Drosophila Melanogaster, 1970; (ed.) Handbook of Genetics, vols. I-V, 1974-76; (ed. with H. Akai) Insect Ultrastructure, vol. I, 1982, vol. II, 1984. **Address:** Biochemistry Molecular Biology and Cell Biology Dept., Hogan Hall 2-100, 2153 N Campus Dr, Northwestern University, Evanston, IL 60208-3500, U.S.A.

KING, Roger (Frank Graham). British, b. 1947. **Genres:** Novels, Novellas/ Short stories, Plays/Screenplays, International relations/Current affairs. **Career:** Ahmadu Bello University, Zaria, Nigeria, lecturer and research fellow in agricultural economics and rural development, 1972-74; University of Reading, England, research officer in rural development, 1975-79; consultant in 20 countries for international development agencies, including United Nations International Fund for Agricultural Development, Rome, Italy, and Food and Agriculture Organization of the United Nations, Rome, 1978-90; Eastern Washington University, Spokane, visiting professor of English, 1990-91; San Francisco State University, associate professor of creative writing, 1994-97; writer. **Publications:** NOVELS: Horizontal Hotel, 1983; Written on a Stranger's Map, 1987; Sea Level, 1992; A Girl from Zanzibar, 2002. FILM: Still the Children Are Here, 2004. **Address:** 154 Shutesbury Rd, Leverett, MA 01054-9703, U.S.A. **Online address:** Rogerking1@aol.com

KING, Stephen. Also writes as Richard Bachman. American, b. 1947. **Genres:** Novels. **Publications:** Carrie, 1974; Salem's Lot, 1975; The Shining, 1977; Night Shift, 1978; The Stand, 1978, 1991; The Dead Zone, 1979; Firestarter, 1980; Danse Macabre, 1980; Cujo, 1981; The Dark Tower: The Gunslinger, 1982; Creepshow, 1982; Different Seasons, 1982; Christine, 1983; Pet Sematary, 1983; Cycle of the Werewolf, 1984; (with P. Straub) The Talisman, 1984; Skeleton Crew, 1985; It, 1986; The Eyes of the Dragon, 1987; Misery, 1987; The Dark Tower: The Drawing of the Three, 1987; The Tommyknockers, 1987; My Pretty Pony, 1988; The Dark Half, 1989; Dolan's Cadillac, 1989; Four Past Midnight, 1990; The Dark Tower: The Waste Lands, 1991; Gerald's Game, 1991; Needful Things, 1992; Dolores Claiborne, 1992; Nightmares and Dreamscapes, 1993; Insomnia, 1994; Desperation, 1996; The Green Mile (serial), 1996; The Two Dead Girls, 1996; Wizard and Glass 1997; Bag of Bones, 1997; The Girl Who Loved Tom Gordon, 1999; Hearts in Atlantis, 1999; Storm of the Century, 1999; Riding the Bullet, 2000; On Writing: A Memoir of the Craft (non-fiction), 2000; Dreamcatcher, 2001; Everything's Eventual, 2002; From a Buick 8, 2002; Journals of Eleanor Druse, 2004. AS RICHARD BACHMAN: Rage, 1977; The Long Walk, 1979; Roadwork, 1981; The Running Man, 1982; Thinner, 1984; The Regulators, 1996. **Address:** c/o Penguin USA, 375 Hudson St, New York, NY 10014, U.S.A. **Online address:** www.stephenking.com

KING, Teri. British, b. 1940. **Genres:** History, Recreation. **Career:** Astrologer, Daily Scottish Record, Weekend mag., and Sunday Mirror, London; freelance model, 1956-67. **Publications:** Love, Sex and Astrology, 1974; Business, Success and Astrology, 1974; Astrologers Diet Book, 1977; Your Child and the Zodiac, 1979; Marriage, Divorce, and Astrology, 1980; Further Love, Sex and Astrology, 1985; Sunrise, Sunset, 1988; Horrorscopes, 1989. Also author of 12 annual books.

KING, Thomas. Canadian, b. 1943. **Genres:** Novels, Children's fiction, Literary criticism and history. **Career:** Novelist and editor. Has also worked as a photojournalist. University of Lethbridge, Alberta, Canada, instructor, 1980-; University of Minnesota, professor. **Publications:** (ed. with C.D. Calver and H. Hoy) The Native in Literature, 1987; (ed.) All My Relations: An Anthology of Contemporary Canadian Native Fiction, 1990; Medicine River (fiction and teleplay), 1990; A Coyote Columbus Story (children's book), 1992; Green Grass, Running Water (fiction), 1993; Truth & Bright Water, 2000; Dreadful Water Shows Up, 2002. **Address:** School of English & Theatre Studies, University of Guelph, Guelph, ON, Canada N1G 2W1. **Online address:** thking@uoguelph.ca

KING, William Richard. American, b. 1938. **Genres:** Administration/ Management, Business/Trade/Industry, Information science/Computers. **Career:** University of Pittsburgh, Pa., Associate Professor, 1967-69, Director, Doctoral Program, 1971-74, Professor of Business Administration, 1969-85, Director, Strategic Mgmt. Institute, 1980-84, University Professor, 1986-; Case Western Reserve University, Assistant Professor of Operations Research, 1964-65; U.S. Air Force Institute of Technology, Assistant Professor of Statistics and Operations Research, 1965-67; Cleland-King, Inc., mgmt, consulting and research firm, Vice-President and Director, 1969-86. Management Science, Associate Ed., 1974-91; OMEGA, Member, Editorial Advisory Board, 1984-; International Journal on Policy and Information, Area Ed., 1981-; Management Information Systems Quarterly, Sr. Ed., 1982-85; Institute of Management Sciences, President, 1989-90; Association for Information Systems, Founding President, 1995-96. **Publications:** Quantitative Analysis for Marketing Management, 1967; Probability for Management Decisions, 1968; (co-author) Systems Analysis and Project Management, 1968, 3rd ed., 1983; (co-ed.) Systems, Organizations, Analysis, Management: A Book of Readings, 1969; (co-author) Management: A Systems Approach, 1972; Marketing Management Information Systems, 1977; (co-author) Strategic Planning and Policy, 1978; (co-ed.) Marketing Scientific and Technical Information, 1979; (co-author) The Logic of Strategic Planning, 1982; (co-ed.) Strategic Planning and Mgmt. Handbook, 1987; (co-ed.) Project Management Handbook, 1988; (co-ed.) Management of Information Systems, 1989, 2nd ed., 1994; (co-ed.) Organizational Transformation through Business Process Re-engineering, 1998. **Address:** Katz Graduate School of Business, University of Pittsburgh, Pittsburgh, PA 15260, U.S.A.

KING, Wilma. American, b. 1942. **Genres:** History. **Career:** Hampton University, Hampton, VA, associate professor, 1973-85; Indiana University of Pennsylvania, Indiana, associate professor, 1985-91; Michigan State University, East Lansing, associate professor of history, 1991-99; University of Missouri, Columbia, Strickland Professor of African American History, 1999-. National Endowment for the Humanities, principal investigator and co-director for Summer Seminars for College Teachers, Virginia, 1984; U.S. Department of Interior, Washington, DC, principal investigator and director of a feasibility study of the Frederick Douglass Home at Cedar Hill, 1985; public speaker on American and African-American history at universities and organizations, 1986-; member of Black History Advisory Board, Pennsylvania Historical and Museum Commission, 1990-91. **Publications:** (ed.) A Northern Woman in the Plantation South: Letters of Tryphena Blanche Holder Fox, 1856-1876, 1993; Stolen Childhood: Children and Youth in Bondage in the Nineteenth-Century, 1995; Toward the Promised Land, 1995; Children of the Emancipation (children's), 2000. Contributor to periodicals. **Address:** Department of History, 101 Read Hall, University of Missouri, Columbia, MO 65211, U.S.A.

KINGDON, Robert McCune. American, b. 1927. **Genres:** History. **Career:** University of Massachusetts, Amherst, instructor, and assistant professor of history, 1952-57; University of Iowa, Iowa City, assistant professor, and professor of history, 1957-65; University of Wisconsin, Madison, professor of history, 1965-98, director, Institute for Research in the Humanities, 1975-87, emeritus professor of history, 1998-. **Publications:** Geneva and the Coming of the Wars of Religion in France, 1956; Geneva and the Consolidation of the French Protestant Movement, 1967; The Political Thought of Peter Martyr Vermigli, 1980; Church and Society in Reformation Europe, 1985; Myths about the St. Bartholomew's Day Massacres, 1988; Adultery and Divorce in Calvin's Geneva, 1995. EDITOR: (with J.-F. Bergier) Registres de la Compagnie des Pasteurs de Geneve au temps de Calvin, 2 vols., 1962, 1964; William Cecil: Execution of Justice in England, and William Allen: A True, Sincere and Modest Defense of English Catholics, 1965; (with R.D. Linder) Calvin and Calvinism: Sources of Democracy?, 1970; Theodore de Beze: Du droit des magistrats, 1971; (and contrib.) Transition and Revolution: Problems and Issues of European Renaissance and Reformation History, 1974; Jean de Coras: Question politique, 1989; (with others) Registres du Consistoire de Geneve au temps de Calvin, vol. 1, 1996, vol. 2, 2002. **Address:** Institute for Research in the Humanities, University of Wisconsin, 1401 Observatory Dr, Madison, WI 53706, U.S.A.

KING-HELE, Desmond. British, b. 1927. **Genres:** Poetry, Air/Space topics, Earth sciences, Literary criticism and history, Meteorology/Atmospheric sciences, Sciences, Biography. **Career:** Deputy Chief Scientific Officer, Royal Aircraft Establishment, Farnborough, 1968-88; Ed., Notes and Records of the Royal Society, 1989-96. **Publications:** Shelley: His Thought and Work, 1960, 3rd ed., 1984; Satellites and Scientific Research, 1960; Erasmus Darwin, 1963; Theory of Satellite Orbits in an Atmosphere, 1964; Observing Earth Satellites, 1966, 2nd ed., 1983; The End of the Twentieth Century?, 1970; Poems and Trixies, 1972; Doctor of Revolution, 1977; Animal Spirits (poems), 1983; Erasmus Darwin and the Romantic Poets, 1986; Satellite Orbits in an Atmosphere, 1987; A Tapestry of Orbits, 1992; Erasmus Darwin: A Life of Unequalled Achievement, 1999; Antic and Romantic (poems), 2000. EDITOR: Essential Writings of Erasmus Darwin, 1968; Letters of Erasmus Darwin, 1981; The RAE Table of Earth Satellites 1957-89, 1990; John Herschel, 1992; C. Darwin, The Life of Erasmus Darwin, 2002. **Address:** 7 Hilltops Court, 65 North Lane, Buriton, Hants. GU31 5RS, England.

KINGMA, Daphne Rose. American, b. 1942. **Genres:** Human relations/ Parenting. **Career:** Author, psychotherapist, television talk show guest, public speaker, and workshop leader. Frequent guest television interview shows as an expert on relationships. **Publications:** The Men We Never Knew: Women's Role in the Evolution of a Gender, 1993; The Breakup Bible: Why Relationships End and Living through the Ending of Yours (sound recording), 1995, as Coming Apart: Why Relationships End and How to Live through the Ending of Yours, 1998; Weddings from the Heart: Contemporary and Traditional Ceremonies for an Unforgettable Wedding, 1995; Heart and Soul: Living the Joy, Truth, and Beauty of Your Intimate Relationship, 1995; Garland of Love: Daily Reflections on the Magic and Meaning of Love, 1995; To Have and to Hold: A Wedding Keepsake, 1997; The Future of Love: The Power of the Soul in Intimate Relationships, 1998; A Lifetime of Love: How to Bring More Depth, Meaning and Intimacy into Your Relationship, 1998; The Nine Types of Lovers: Why We Love the People We Do and How They Drive Us Crazy, 1999; The Book of Love, 2001; Finding True Love: The Four Essential Keys to Discovering the Love of Your Life, 2001; 365 Days of Love, 2002; The Many Faces of Love: Exploring New Forms of Intimacy (sound recording), 2002; True Love: How to Make Your Relationships Sweeter, Deeper and More Passionate, 2003. Author of introduction to books by D. Markova, A. Alvarez. **Address:** PO Box 5244, Santa Barbara, CA 93150, U.S.A. **Online address:** daphnekingma@yahoo.com

KINGMAN, (Mary) Lee. American, b. 1919. **Genres:** Children's fiction, Literary criticism and history. **Career:** Freelance writer and ed; former direct, councilmember, The Horn Book Inc, Boston; Massachusetts Children's Book Council, Houghton Mifflin Co., Boston, Massachusetts, 1944-46. **Publications:** Pierre Pidgeon, 1943; Ilenka, 1945; The Rocky Summer, 1948; The Best Christmas, 1949; Philippe's Hill, 1950; The Quarry Adventure (in U.K. as Lauri's Surprising Summer), 1951; Kathy and the Mysterious Statue, 1953; Peter's Long Walk, 1953; Mikko's Fortune, 1955; The Magic Christmas Tree, 1956; The Village Band Mystery, 1956; Flivver, the Heroic Horse, 1958; The House of the Blue Horse, 1960; The Saturday Gang, 1961; Peter's Pony, 1963; Sheep Ahoy!, 1963; Private Eyes, 1964; The Year of the Raccoon, 1966; The Secret of the Silver Reindeer, 1968; The Peter Pan Bag, 1970; Georgina and the Dragon, 1971; The Meeting Post: A Story of Lapland, 1972; Escape from the Evil Prophecy, 1973; Break a Leg, Betsy Maybe!, 1976; The Illustrator's Notebook, 1978; Head over Wheels, 1978; The Refiner's Fire, 1981; The Luck of the "Miss L," 1986; Catch the Baby!, 1990. EDITOR: Newbery and Caldecott Medal Books: 1956-1965, 1965; (with J. Foster and R.G. Lontoft) Illustrators of Children's Books: 1957-1966, 1968; Newbery and Caldecott Medal Books 1966-1975, 1975; (with G. Hogarth and H. Quimby) Illustrators of Children's Books 1967-1976, 1978; Newbery and Caldecott Medal Books: 1976-1985, 1986. **Address:** 105 High St., Gloucester, MA 01930, U.S.A.

KINGSBURY, Donald (MacDonald). Canadian (born United States), b. 1929. **Genres:** Science fiction/Fantasy. **Career:** McGill University, Montreal, lecturer in mathematics, 1956-86. **Publications:** Courtship Rite, 1982, in U.K. as Geta, 1984; The Moon Goddess and the Son, 1986; Psychohistorical Crisis, 2001. **Address:** c/o Eleanor Wood, 320 Central Park W Ste 1-D, New York, NY 10025, U.S.A. **Online address:** donaldkingsbury@sympatico.ca

KINGSLAND, Rosemary. (born India), b. 1941. **Genres:** Film. **Career:** Novelist, journalist, ghostwriter, and screenwriter. Has also worked as an independent olive-oil maker and merchant. **Publications:** Just a Gigolo (film novelization), 1979; A Saint among Savages, 1980; Hussy (film novelization), 1980; Treasure Islands, 1980; After the Ball Was Over, 1985; Cassata, 1987; Savage Seas, 1999; Hold Back the Night: Memoirs of a Lost Childhood, a Warring Family, and a Secret Affair with Richard Burton, 2003, published as The Secret Life of a Schoolgirl, 2003. **Address:** c/o Author Mail, Crown Publishers, 299 Park Ave., New York, NY 10171, U.S.A. **Online address:** rosekingsland@aol.com

KINGSLEY, April. American, b. 1941. **Genres:** Art/Art history. **Career:** Park Place Gallery, assistant director, 1965-66; Museum of Modern Art, NYC, curatorial assistant, 1969-71; Pasadena Art Museum, NY, associate curator, 1971-72; School of Visual Arts, NY, instructor, 1973-91; Sculpture Center, NY, curator, 1980-89; Franz Kline Catalogue Raisonnee, project director, 1986-; American Craft Museum, curator, 1993-97; Kresge Art Museum, curator, 1999-. Visiting lecturer at Pratt Institute, spring, 1979; adjunct faculty member at Rhode Island School of Design, 1982; City University of New York, adjunct professor, 1985-87, adjunct professor at Queens College, 1985. **Publications:** Afro-American Abstraction, 1981; Adolf Gottlieb: Works on Paper, 1985; The Turning Point: The Abstract Expressionists and the Transformation of American Art, 1992; Jean Miotte: Abstract Expressionist, 2000; The Paintings of Alice Dalton Brown, 2002. **Address:** Kresge Art Museum, Michigan State University, East Lansing, MI 48824-1119, U.S.A. **Online address:** akingsle@msu.edu

KINGSLEY, G. Thomas. American, b. 1936. **Genres:** Urban studies. **Career:** City planning consultant to the city and county of San Francisco, CA, 1961-62; Arthur D. Little, Inc., urban planner and economist, 1962-65; Ford Foundation, assistant chief physical planner for advisory planning group, Calcutta Metropolitan Planning Organization, 1965-67; University of Southern California, Los Angeles, assistant professor of urban and regional planning, 1967-68; Rand Institute, New York City, senior program analyst, 1968-69; New York City Housing and Development Administration, New York City, assistant administrator for fiscal and administrative services, 1969-73; Rand Corp., deputy director of Housing Studies Program and manager of field and program operations for Housing Assistance Supply Experiment, 1973-78, director of Housing and Urban Policy Program, 1978-82; United Nations Center for Human Settlements, chief adviser for Indonesia's National Urban Development Strategy Project, 1982-85; Urban Institute, Washington, DC, principal research associate, 1986-87, director of Center for Public Finance and Housing, 1987-. **Publications:** (with J.P. Telgarsky, I. Jackson, and M. Nanita-Kennett) Urbanization in the Caribbean: Prospects and Management Priorities, 1990; (with Telgarsky and G.E. Peterson) Urban Economies and National Development, 1991; (ed. with M.A. Turner) Housing Markets and Residential Mobility, 1993. Contributor to books. Contributor to planning journals. **Address:** 2100 M St. N.W., Washington, DC 20037, U.S.A.

KING-SMITH, Dick. British, b. 1922. **Genres:** Children's fiction. **Career:** Freelance writer, 1982-; served in the Grenadier Guards, 1941-46; farmer in Gloucestershire, 1947-67; Farmborough Primary School, Bath, teacher, 1975-82. **Publications:** The Fox Busters, 1978; Daggie Dogfoot, 1980, in US as Pigs Might Fly, 1982; The Mouse Butcher, 1981; Magnus Powermouse, 1982; The Queen's Nose, 1983; The Sheep-Pig, 1983, in US as The Gallant Pig, 1985; Harry's Mad, 1984; Lightning Fred, 1985; Saddlebottom, 1985; Noah's Brother, 1986; Dumpling, 1986; Yob, 1986; Pets for Keeps, 1986; E.S.P., 1986; H. Prince, 1986; The Hodgeheg, 1987; Friends and Brothers, 1987; Farmer Bungle Forgets, 1987; Cuckoobush Farm, 1987; Tumbleweed, 1987; Country Watch, 1987; Town Watch, 1987; Water Watch, 1988; George Speaks, 1988; Emily's Legs, 1988; The Jenius, 1988; Sophie's Snail, 1988; Martin's Mice, 1988; The Tobyman, 1989; The Trouble with Edward, 1989; Henry Pond the Poet, 1989; Dodos Are Forever, 1989; Jungle Jingles, 1990; The Water Horse, 1990; The Jolly Witch, 1990; The Wistling Piglet, 1990; Paddy's Pot of Gold, 1990; Ace, 1990; Alphabeasts, 1990; The Cuckoo Child, 1991; Sophies Tom, 1991; Find the White Horse, 1991; Horace and Maurice, 1991; Pretty Polly, 1992; Lady Daisy, 1992; The Ghost at Codlin Castle, 1992; The Animal Parade, 1992; The Topsy Turvy Story Book, 1992; The Finger-Eater, 1992; Blessu and Dumpling, 1992; Farm Tales, 1992; The Triffic Pig Book, 1992; The Guard Dog, 1992; All Pigs Are Beautiful, 1993; The Merry Thought, 1993; Dragon Boy, 1993; Horse Pie, 1993; The Invisible Dog, 1993; A Narrow Squeek and Other Animal Stories, 1993; Sophie Hits Six, 1993; The Swoose, 1994; Sophie in the Saddle, 1994; The Schoolmouse, 1994; Connie and Rollo, 1994; Harriet's Hare, 1994; Mr. Potter's Pet, 1994; The Excitement of Being Ernest, 1994; Clever Duck, 1996; Dirty Gertie Macintosh, 1996; Hogsel and Gruntel, 1996; The Stray, 1996; Dick King-Smith's Animal Friends, 1996; Treasure Trove, 1996; The Sheep-Pig, 1997; Thinderella and Other Topsy Turvy Stories, 1997; Mixed-Up Max, 1997; A Mouse Called Wolf, 1997; The Spotty Pig, 1997; Huge Red Riding Hood and Other Stories, 1997; Puppy Love, 1997; Smasher, 1997; The Merman, 1997; Mr Ape, 1998; How Green Was My Mouse, 1998; Animal Stories, 1998; Babe, 1998; Godhanger, 1999; The Witch of Blackberry Bottom, 1999; The Crowstarver, 1999; Charlie Muffin's Miracle Mouse, 1999; The Roundhill, 2000; Lady Lollipop, 2000; Billy the Bird, 2000; Spider Sparrow, 2000; The Mysterious Miss Slade, 2000; Funny Frank, 2001; Chewing the Cud, 2001; Titus Rules!, 2003; (with C. Pillo) Traffic, 2003; Nine Lives of Aristotle, 2003; Clever Lollipop, 2003; Golden Goose, 2005.

KINGSOLVER, Barbara. American, b. 1955. **Genres:** Novels, Novellas/ Short stories, Poetry, Natural history, Essays. **Career:** University of Arizona, Tucson, research assistant in department of physiology, 1977-79, technical writer in office of arid lands studies, 1981-85; free-lance journalist, 1985-87; full-time writer, 1987-. **Publications:** NOVELS: The Bean Trees, 1988; Animal Dreams, 1990; Pigs in Heaven, 1993; The Poisonwood Bible, 1998; Prodigal Summer, 2000. OTHER: Homeland and Other Stories, 1989; Holding the Line: Women in the Great Arizona Mine Strike of 1983 (nonfiction), 1989; Another America (poetry), 1992; High Tide in Tucson (essays), 1995; Small Wonder (essays), 2002; last Stand: America's Virgin Lands (natural history), 2002.

KINGSTON, Christina. Also writes as Christina Cordaire. American. **Genres:** Romance/Historical. **Career:** Novelist. **Publications:** Ride for the Roses, 2000; The Night the Stars Fell, 2001; Ride the Winter Wind, 2002; Ride the Wind Home, 2003. ROMANCES AS CHRISTINA CORDAIRE: Heart's Deception, 1992; Love's Triumph, 1993; Pride's Folly, 1993; Daring Illusion, 1994; Forgiving Hearts, 1994; Beloved Stranger, 1995; Loving Honor, 1995; Winter Longing, 1996; Spring Enchantment, 1996; Loving a Lowly Stranger, 1998. Contributor to anthologies. **Address:** PO Box 111, Violet Hill, AR 72584, U.S.A. **Online address:** chriscordaire@centurytel.net

KINGSTON, Maxine Hong. American, b. 1940. **Genres:** Novels, Poetry, Autobiography/Memoirs, Essays. **Career:** Teacher, Sunset High School, Hayward, CA, 1965-67, Kahuku High School, Hawaii, 1967-68, Drop-In School, Kahaluu, Hawaii, 1968-69, Kailua High School, Honolulu, 1969, Honolulu Business College, 1969-70, Mid-Pacific Institute, Honolulu, 1970-76, University of Hawaii, 1976-77, and Eastern Michigan University, 1986; University of California, Berkeley, senior lecturer, 1990-2003. **Publications:** The Woman Warrior: Memoirs of a Girlhood among Ghosts, 1976; China Men, 1980; Hawai'i One Summer, 1987; Through the Black Curtain, 1988; Tripmaster Monkey: His Fake Book, 1989; Conversations with Maxine Hong Kingston, 1998; (ed.) The Literature of California, 2001; To Be the Poet, 2002; The Fifth Book of Peace, 2003. **Address:** c/o Alfred A. Knopf Inc, 201 E 50th St, New York, NY 10022, U.S.A.

KINGTON, Miles (Beresford). British, b. 1941. **Genres:** Humor/Satire. **Career:** Freelance writer since 1963. Humour columnist, The Times, London, 1981-87, and The Economist, London, since 1987. **Publications:** (ed. and trans.) The World of Alphonse Allais, 1976; (ed.) Punch on Scotland, 1977; Let's Parler Franglais!, 1982; Let's Parler Franglais Again!, 1982; Miles and Miles, 1982; Let's Parler Franglais One More Temps, 1982; Moreover, 1982; Parlez-Vous Franglais?, 1983; Nature Made Ridiculously Simple: Or How to Identify Absolutely Everything, 1983; (with James Grainger) Vicarage Allsorts, 1985; Moreover, Too, 1985; The Franglais Lieutenant's Women, 1985; Un Four-Pack de Franglais, 1987; Welcome to Kington, 1989; Steaming through Britain, 1990; Jazz: An Anthology, 1992. **Address:** Lower Hayze, 40 Limply Stoke, Bath BA2 7FR, England.

KINKADE, Thomas. American, b. 1958. **Genres:** Art/Art history, Inspirational/Motivational Literature. **Career:** Artist and author; former background painter for animated film. Cofounder, Lightpost Publishing (now part of Media Arts Group Inc.). **Publications:** (with J. Gurney) The Artist's Guide to Sketching, 1982; Thomas Kinkade: Paintings of Radiant Light, 1995; Simpler Times, 1996; (with P. Kinkade) Chasing the Horizon: Our Adventures through the British Isles and France, 1997; Beyond the Garden Gate, 1997; Romantic Hideaways, 1997; I'll Be Home for Christmas, 1997; Spirit of America, 1998; Glory of Creation, 1998; Home Is Where the Heart Is, 1998; Hometown Memories, 1998; Seasons of Light, 1998; (with C. Miller) With Wings like Eagles: A Devotional, 1998; (with C. Miller) A Village Christmas: Personal Family Memories and Holiday Traditions, 1999; (with A.C. Buchanan and D. Klingsporn) Christ, the Light of the World: A Devotional, 1999; (with A.C. Buchanan) Lightposts for Living: The Art of Choosing a Joyful Life, 1999; The Home You Made for Me: Celebrating a Mother's Love, 2000; Thomas Kinkade: Masterworks of Light, 2000; Garden of Friendship, 2000; My Father's World: Masterpieces and Memories of the Great Outdoors, 2000; Let Your Light Shine, 2001; Off the Beaten Path: Devotionals, 2001; Warmth from the Windows, 2001; Thomas Kinkade's Romantic Europe, 2001; Thomas Kinkade's Sea to Shining Sea, 2001; (with N. Kinkade) The Many Loves of Marriage, 2001; A Book of Joy, 2002; Friends for Life, 2002; Joy of Fatherhood, 2002; Joy of Motherhood, 2002; Life's Little Blessings, 2002; Simple Little Pleasures, 2002; Finding a Peaceful Place, 2002; (compiler with A.C. Buchanan) Just around the Bend, 2002; (with K. Spencer) Cape Light, 2002. Illustrator of books by S. Hughes, D.K. McKelvey, S. Lloyd-Jones. **Address:** c/o Media Arts Group, 900 Lightpost Way, Morgan Hill, CA 95037, U.S.A.

KINKEAD-WEEKES, Mark. British (born Republic of South Africa), b. 1931. **Genres:** Literary criticism and history. **Career:** Fellow of the British Academy. University of Edinburgh, Assistant, then Lecturer, 1956-65;

University of Kent, Canterbury, Lecturer, then Sr. Lecturer, 1965-73, Pro Vice-Chancellor, 1974-78, Professor of English Literature, from 1974, now emeritus. **Publications:** (co-author) William Golding: A Critical Study, 1967; Samuel Richardson: Dramatic Novelist, 1973; D.H. Lawrence: Triumph to Exile 1912-1922, 1996; William Golding: A Critical Study of the Twelve Novels, 2002. EDITOR: (co) Alexander Pope, 1962; Twentieth Century Interpretations of the Rainbow, 1971; The Rainbow, 1990. **Address:** 5 Albion Pl, Ramsgate, Kent CT11 8HQ, England. **Online address:** mark. kinkead-weekes@virgin.net

KINNAMON, Keneth. American, b. 1932. **Genres:** Literary criticism and history, Bibliography. **Career:** University of Illinois at Urbana-Champaign, Assistant Professor, 1966-70, Associate Professor, 1970-73, Professor, 1973-82, Head of English Dept., 1977-82; University of Arkansas, Fayetteville, Ethel Pumphrey Stephens Professor of English, 1982-, now emeritus, Chairman of Dept, 1982-93. **Publications:** The Emergence of Richard Wright: A Study in Literature and Society, 1972; (with J. Benson, M. Fabre, and C. Werner) A Richard Wright Bibliography: Fifty Years of Criticism and Commentary, 1933-82, 1988. EDITOR: (with R.K. Barksdale) Black Writers of America: A Comprehensive Anthology, 1972; James Baldwin: A Collection of Critical Essays, 1974; New Essays on Native Son, 1990; (with M. Fabre) Conversations with Richard Wright, 1993; Critical Essays on Native Son. **Address:** Dept. of English, 333 Kimpel Hall, University of Arkansas, Fayetteville, AR 72701, U.S.A.

KINNELL, Galway. American, b. 1927. **Genres:** Novels, Poetry, Literary criticism and history, Translations. **Career:** Erich Maria Remarque Professor of Creative Writing, New York University, NYC; Former member of faculty, University of Grenoble, France; Poet-in-Residence, Juniata College, Huntingdon, Pa., and University of California, Irvine, 1968-69. **Publications:** (with A. Ostroff and W.T. Scott) 3 Self-Evaluations, 1953; What a Kingdom It Was, 1960; Flower Herding on Mount Monadnock, 1964; Black Light (novel), 1966; Poems of Night, 1968; Body Rags, 1968; The Poetics of the Physical World, 1969; The Hen Flower, 1970; First Poems, 1947-1952, 1970; The Book of Nightmares, 1971; The Shoes of Wandering, 1971; Body Rags, 1973; The Avenue Bearing the Initial of Christ into the New World: Poems 1946-1964, 1974; Walking down Stairs: Selections from Interviews, 1978; Mortal Acts, Mortal Words, 1980; Selected Poems, 1982; How the Alligator Missed Breakfast (for children), 1982; Thoughts Occasioned by the Most Insignificant of Human Events, 1982; The Fundamental Project of Technology, 1983; Remarks on Accepting the National Book Award, 1984; The Past, 1985; (ed) The Essential Whitman, 1987; When One Has Lived a Long Time Alone, 1990; Three Books, 1993; Imperfect Thirst, 1994; New Selected Poems, 2000. TRANSLATOR: R. Hardy, Bitter Victory, 1956; H. Lehmann, Pre-Columbian Ceramics, 1962; The Poems of Franccois Villon, 1965; Y. Bonnefoy, On the Motion and Immobility of Douve, 1968; Y. Goll, The Lackawanna Elegy, 1970; The Poems of Francois Villon, 1977; Y. Bonnefoy, Early Poems, 1947-1959, 1990; (with H. Leibmann) The Essential Rilke, 2000. **Address:** 1218 Town Highway 16, Sheffield, VT 05866-9762, U.S.A.

KINNEY, Arthur F. Also writes as Alan Kent. American, b. 1933. **Genres:** History, Literary criticism and history. **Career:** Yale University, New Haven, CT, instructor, 1963-66; University of Massachusetts, Amherst, assistant professor 1966-68, associate professor, 1968-73, professor of English, 1973-86, Thomas W. Copeland Professor of Literary History, 1986-, director of Massachusetts Center of Renaissance Studies, 1998-. Clark University, Worcester, MA, affiliate professor of English, 1971-; New York University, adjunct professor of English, 1991-. English Literary Renaissance, editor, 1971-; Huntington Library Fellow, 1973-74, 1983; Twayne English Author-Renaissance Books, editor, 1973-; Folger Shakespeare Library Fellow, 1974, 1990, 1992; Oxford University, England, Fulbright Fellow, 1977-78; NEH Senior Fellow, 1977-78, 1983-84, 1990, university research fellow, 1983-84; Massachusetts Studies in Early Modern Culture, editor, 1991-. **Publications:** On Seven Shakespearean Tragedies, 1968; On Seven Shakespearean Comedies, 1969; Titled Elizabethans, 1973; Rogues, Vagabonds, and Sturdy Beggars, 1973, 2nd ed., 1998; Elizabethan Backgrounds, 1974; Faulkner's Narrative Poetics, 1978; Dorothy Parker, 1978; Rhetoric and Poetic in Thomas More's Utopia, 1979; The Compson Family, 1982; Nicholas Hilliard's Art of Lymning, 1983; Flannery O'Connor's Library, 1985; The Sartoris Family, 1985; Humanist Poetics, 1986; Essential Articles for the Study of Sir Philip Sidney, 1986; John Skelton: Priest as Poet, 1987; Continental Humanist Poetics, 1989; The Coast of Illyria by Dorothy Parker and Ross Evans, 1990; The McCaslin Family, 1990; The Birds and Beasts of Shakespeare, 1990; Go Down, Moses: The Miscegenation of Time, 1996; The Sutpen Family, 1996; Dorothy Parker Revisited, 1997; Renaissance Drama, 1999; Lies Like Truth, 2001. EDITOR: H.R. Mythomystes, 1972; Markets of

Bawdrie, 1974; Sir Philip Sidney in Retrospect, 1986; Sir Philip Sidney's Achievement, 1990; Approaches to Teaching Faulkner's The Sound and the Fury, 1996; Classical, Renaissance, and Postmodernist Acts of the Imagination, 1996; Cambridge Companion to English Literature 1500-1600, 2000; Hamlet: New Critical Essays, 2001. CO-EDITOR: Bear, Man, and God, 1964; Symposium, 1969; Symposium on Love, 1970; 1576: Sir Philip Sidney and the Making of a Legend, 1986; Renaissance Historicism, 1988; Women in the Renaissance, 1990; Shakespeare: Text and Performance, 1999. **Address:** 25 Hunter Hill Dr, Amherst, MA 01002, U.S.A.

KINSELLA, Sophie. British. **Genres:** Novels. **Career:** Novelist. Former financial writer and journalist. **Publications:** The Secret Dreamworld of a Shopaholic, 2000, in US as Confessions of a Shopaholic, 2001; Shopaholic Abroad, 2001, in US as Shopaholic Takes Manhattan, 2002; Shopaholic Ties the Knot, 2002. **Address:** c/o Author Mail, Transworld Publishers Ltd./Black Swan, 61-63 Uxbridge Road, Ealing, London W5 5SA, England.

KINSELLA, Thomas. Irish, b. 1928. **Genres:** Poetry, Literary criticism and history, Translations. **Career:** Public administration: Irish Land Commission and Dept. of Finance, 1946-65. Poetry and Irish literature: Southern Illinois University, Carbondale, writer-in-residence, 1965-67, professor of English, 1967-70; Temple University, Philadelphia, PA, professor of English, 1970-90. Director, Dolmen Press, Dublin; Founder, Peppercanister publrs., Dublin, 1972. **Publications:** (trans.) Exile and Death of the Sons of Usnech, 1954; Poems, 1956; Another September, 1958, rev. ed., 1962; Moralities, 1960; Poems and Translations, 1961; Downstream, 1962; Wormwood, 1966; Nightwalker, 1967; Nightwalker and Other Poems, 1968; (trans.) The Tain, 1969; Tear, 1969; Davis, Mangan, Ferguson: Tradition and the Irish Writer, 1970; Butcher's Dozen, 1972; A Selected Life, 1972; Finistere, 1972; Notes from the Land of the Dead and Other Poems, 1972; New Poems 1973, 1973; Selected Poems 1956-1968, 1973; Vertical Man, 1973; The Good Fight, 1973; One, 1974; A Technical Supplement, 1976; Song of the Night and Other Poems, 1978; The Messenger, 1978; Fifteen Dead, 1979; One and Other Poems, 1979; Peppercanister Poems 1972-1978, 1979; Poems 1956-1973, 1979; One Fond Embrace, 1981; Songs of the Psyche, 1986; Her Vertical Smile, 1986; (ed) The New Oxford Book of Irish Verse, with translations, 1986; Out of Ireland, 1987; St. Catherine's Clock, 1987; Blood and Family, 1988; Selected Poems, 1962-1989, 1989; Poems from Centre City, 1990; Personal Places, 1990; Madonna, 1991; Open Court, 1991; From Centre City, 1994; The Dual Tradition: An Essay on Poetry and Politics in Ireland, 1995; The Collected Poems, 1956-1994, 1996; The Pen Shop, 1997; The Familiar, 1999; Godhead, 1999; Citizen of the World, 2000; Little Body, 2000.

KINSELLA, W(illiam) P(atrick). Canadian, b. 1935. **Genres:** Novels, Novellas/Short stories. **Career:** Full-time writer. University of Calgary, Dept. of English, assistant professor, 1978-83. **Publications:** Dance Me Outside, 1977; Scars, 1978; Shoeless Joe Jackson Comes to Iowa, 1980; Born Indian, 1981; Shoeless Joe, 1982; The Ballad of the Public Trustee, 1982; The Moccasin Telegraph, 1983; The Thrill of the Grass, 1984; The Iowa Baseball Confederacy, 1986; The Alligator Report, 1985; The Fencepost Chronicles, 1986; Five Stories, 1986; Red Wolf, Red Wolf, 1987; The Further Adventures of Slugger McBatt, 1988; The Miss Hobbema Pagent, 1988; The Art of Alan Sapp, 1990; Box Socials, 1992; A Series for the World, 1992; The Dixon Cornbelt League, 1993; Brother Frank's Gospel Hour (stories), 1994; The Winter Helen Dropped By (novel), 1995; If Wishes Were Horses, 1996; The Secret of the Northern Lights (stories), 1998; Magic Time (novel), 1998; (ed.) Baseball Fantastic: Stories, 2000; Japanese Baseball, and Other Stories, 2000. **Address:** Box 65, Yale, BC, Canada V0K 2J0. **Online address:** buzzard2_99@yahoo.com

KINZIE, Mary. American. **Genres:** Poetry, Literary criticism and history. **Career:** Northwestern University, Evanston, IL, director of creative writing program, 1975-, professor of English, 1990-; writer. **Publications:** POETRY: The Threshold of the Year: Poems, 1982; Summers of Vietnam and Other Poems, 1990; Masked Woman, 1990; Autumn Eros and Other Poems, 1991; Ghost Ship, 1996; Drift, 2003. CRITICISM: The Cure of Poetry in the Age of Prose, 1993; The Judge Is Fury, 1994; A Poet's Guide to Poetry, 1999. EDITOR: Prose for Borges, 1972; (with E. Anderson) The Little Magazine in America: A Modern Documentary History, 1978; The Tales of Arturo Vivante, 1990; A Poet's Prose: Selected Writings of Louise Bogan. Contributor of poetry and critical essays on poetry and fiction to periodicals. **Address:** Dept of English, Northwestern University, Evanston, IL 60208-2240, U.S.A. **Online address:** mkinzie@northwestern.edu

KIPNIS, Aaron R. American, b. 1948. **Genres:** Human relations/Parenting, Psychology, Social commentary, Sociology. **Career:** Gender Relations Institute, Santa Barbara, CA, director, 1988-; psychology professor, at universities including Pacifica Graduate Institute, CA, core faculty, 1995-; The Fatherhood Coalition, president, 1997-. **Publications:** Knights without Armor, 1991; What Women and Men Really Want, 1995; Angry Young Men, 1999. Contributor to journals and books; gives presentations and consultations nationwide on male psychology. **Address:** PO Box 4782, Santa Barbara, CA 93140, U.S.A. **Online address:** aaron@malepsych.com; malepsych.com

KIPP, Rita Smith. American, b. 1948. **Genres:** Anthropology/Ethnology, Sociology, Theology/Religion. **Career:** University of Pittsburgh at Johnstown, Johnstown, PA, instructor, 1971-72; Kenyon College, Gambier, OH, professor of anthropology, 1976-. Archaeological Tours, lecturer, 1987-90. **Publications:** (ed. with R.D. Kipp) Beyond Samosir, 1983; (ed. with S. Rodgers) Indonesian Religions in Transition, 1987; The Early Years of a Dutch Colonial Mission, 1990; Dissociated Identities, 1993. **Address:** Department of Anthropology, Kenyon College, Gambier, OH 43022, U.S.A. **Online address:** Kipp@Kenyon.edu

KIPPAX, Frank. See NEEDLE, Jan.

KIRALY, Marie. See BERGSTROM, Elaine.

KIRALY, Sherwood. American, b. 1949. **Genres:** Novels. **Career:** Writer. Worked 16 years at a national newspaper syndicate, through 4 name changes: Publishers-Hall, Field, News America, and North America Syndicate; positions included comics editor and managing editor. Served as syndicate editor for Ann Landers, Erma Bombeck, and Roger Ebert. Coauthor of episode of E/R, 1984. **Publications:** NOVELS: California Rush, 1990; Diminished Capacity, 1995; Big Babies, 1996; Who's Hot/Who's Not, 1998. Author of humorous articles for newspapers. **Address:** 2954 Alta Laguna Blvd, Laguna Beach, CA 92651-2066, U.S.A.

KIRBY, David Peter. British, b. 1936. **Genres:** History. **Career:** Professor in History, University College of Wales, Aberystwyth, 1993-96 (Lecturer, 1966-69; Sr. Lecturer, 1969-73; Reader, 1973-93). Assistant Lecturer, and Lecturer, University of Liverpool, 1962-66. **Publications:** The Making of Early England, 1967; (ed.) St. Wilfrid at Hexham, 1974; The Earliest English Kings, 1991, reprint, 1994; (with A. Williams and A.P. Smyth) A Biographical Dictionary of Dark Age Britain: England, Scotland and Wales, c.500 - c.1050, 1991; Bede's Historia Ecclesiastica Gentis Anglorum: Its Contemporary Setting, Jarrow Lecture, 1992; (ed. with J.L. Davies) The County History of Cardiganshire: vol. I: to 1081, 1994. **Address:** The Villa, The Launches, West Lulworth, Wareham BH20 5SF, England.

KIRBY, Gilbert Walter. British, b. 1914. **Genres:** Theology/Religion, Biography. **Career:** Principal, London, Bible College, Northwood, Middx., 1966-80. General Secretary, 1956-66, and President, 1979-83, Evangelical Alliance. **Publications:** The Protestant Churches of Britain, 1963; Pastor and Principal: E.F. Kevan, 1968; The Way We Care, 1973; Too Hot to Handle, 1978; Christian Living, 1979; All One in Christ Jesus?, 1984; Why All These Denominations?, 1988. EDITOR: Remember I Am Coming Soon, 1964; The Question of Healing, 1967; Evangelism Alert, 1972.

KIRBY, John R. Canadian, b. 1951. **Genres:** Education, Psychology. **Career:** University of Newcastle, Australia, lecturer to associate professor, 1976-87; Queen's University, Kingston, ON, Canada, associate professor to professor of education, 1987-. **Publications:** (with Das and Jarman) Simultaneous and Successive Cognitive Processing, 1979; (ed. with Biggs) Cognition, Development, and Instruction, 1980; (ed.) Cognitive Strategies and Educational Performance, 1984; (with Williams) Learning Problems: A Cognitive Approach, 1991; (co-author) Assessment of Cognitive Processes, 1994. Contributor to scientific journals. **Address:** Faculty of Education, Queen's University, Kingston, ON, Canada K7L 3N6. **Online address:** kirbyj@educ.queensu.ca

KIRBY, Michael Roger. British, b. 1957. **Genres:** Plays/Screenplays, Education, Philosophy, Social sciences. **Career:** Former teacher. Author, dramatist, editor, 1985-. **Publications:** Society Today, 1993; Education for Citizenship, 1993; Rights and Responsibilities, 1993; Sex Education in Schools, 1994; Philosophy, Religion and Ethics, 1995; Issues in Science, 1995; Art, Culture, and Aesthetics, 1995; Street Smarts, 1995; Understanding Democracy, 1997; Religious Studies Handbook, 1999; New Plays, 1999; Radio and Television Plays, 2001; Sociology in Perspective, 2002; Science and Technology Today, 2002; Sociology Explained, 2003; Collected Short Stories, 2003. **Address:** Penley House, Ellesmere Lane, Penley, Ellesmere, Shropshire SY12 0NG, England.

KIRCH, Patrick V(inton). American, b. 1950. **Genres:** Archaeology/Antiquities. **Career:** Associated with University of Hawaii at Manoa, Honolulu, beginning 1979, affiliated associate professor of anthropology, 1982-84; University of Washington, Seattle, associate professor, 1985-87, professor of anthropology, 1987-89, director of Thomas Burke Memorial Washington State Museum, 1984-89; University of California, Berkeley, professor of anthropology, 1989-, Class of 1954 Professor of Anthropology, 1995-, Hearst Museum of Anthropology, curator of oceanic archaeology 1989-, director, 1999-2002, Archaeological Research Facility, director, 1992-94. Bernice P. Bishop Museum, associate anthropologist, 1974-75, anthropologist, 1975-85, head of Division of Archaeology, 1983-84, research associate, 1984-; conducted archaeological and ethnographic field work in the Cook Islands, Samoa, Tonga, Papua New Guinea, the Marshall Islands, Tikopia, Anuta, the Solomon Islands, Wallis and Futura, the Loyalty Islands, and Hawaii. **Publications:** Marine Exploitation in Prehistoric Hawai'i, 1979; (with D. Yen) Tikopia: The Prehistory and Ecology of a Polynesian Outlier, 1982; (with J. Clark) Archaeological Investigations of the Mudlane-Waimea-Kawaihae Road Corridor, Island of Hawai'i, 1983; The Evolution of the Polynesian Chiefdoms, 1984; Feathered Gods and Fishhooks, 1985; Niuatoputapu: The Prehistory of a Polynesian Chiefdom, 1988; (with M. Sahlins) Anahulu: The Anthropology of History in the Kingdom of Hawaii, Vol. 1: Historical Ethnography, Vol. 2: The Archaeology of History, 1992; The Wet and the Dry, 1994; The Lapita Peoples, 1997; On the Road of the Winds, 2000; (with R. Green) Hawai'i-Ancestral Polynesia, 2001. EDITOR: (with M. Kelly) Prehistory and Ecology in a Windward Hawaiian Valley, 1975; Island Societies, 1986; (with T. Hunt) Archaeology of the Lapita Cultural Complex, 1988; Prehistoric Hawaiian Occupation in the Anahulu Valley, O'ahu Island, 1989; (with T. Hunt) Historical Ecology in the Pacific Islands, 1997; Lapita and Its Transformations in Near Oceania, 2001. Contributor to scientific journals. **Address:** Dept of Anthropology, 232 Kroeber Hall, University of California, Berkeley, CA 94720, U.S.A.

KIRCHNER, Bharti. American (born India), b. 1940. **Genres:** Novels, Food and Wine. **Career:** Bank of America, systems manager, 1980-84; IBM, advisory systems engineer, 1984-89; freelance writer, 1990-. **Publications:** NONFICTION: The Healthy Cuisine of India: Recipes from the Bengal Region, 1992; Indian Inspired: A New Cuisine for the International Table, 1993; The Bold Vegetarian: One Hundred Fifty Inspired International Recipes, 1995; Vegetarian Burgers, 1996. NOVELS: Shiva Dancing, 1998; Sharmila's Book, Darjeeling, 2002; Pastries, 2003. **Address:** 5217 Keystone Pl N, Seattle, WA 98103-6233, U.S.A. **Online address:** bhartik@aol.com

KIRCHNER, Emil J(oseph). German, b. 1942. **Genres:** Politics/Government. **Career:** University of Essex, England, temporary lecturer, 1974-76, director of Centre for European Studies, 1990-97, lecturer, professor, 1992-, coordinator of Jean Monnet European Centre of Excellence, 1999-; European Institute for European Community Policy Making, Brussels, director, 1981-86; European University Institute, Florence, Italy, Jean Monnet fellow, 1985-86; visiting professor: University of Connecticut at Storrs, 1986-87, Charles University, Prague, Centre for Economic Research and Graduate Education, 1997, 1998, Autonomous National University of Mexico, Social Sciences, 1998; Renmin University of China, Beijing, honorary guest professor, 2001-. Journal of European Integration, executive editor, 1997-. Honorary Jean Monnet Chair in European Political Integration, 1997. Cross of the Order of Merit, Germany, 2002. **Publications:** Trade Unions as a Pressure Group in the European Community, 1977; European Interest Groups and Their Relations with the Economic and Social Committee, 1980; (with K. Schweiger) The Role of Interest Groups in the European Community, 1981; The European Parliament: Performance and Prospects, 1984; Decision Making in the European Community, 1992; (with I. Budge and K. Newton) The Politics of the New Europe, 1998. EDITOR: (and contrib.) Public Service Unions and the European Community, 1983; (and contrib.) Liberal Parties in Western Europe, 1988; (with J. Sperling) The Federal Republic and NATO, 1949-1989, 1992; (with C. Bluth and J. Sperling) The Future of European Security, 1994; (with J. Sperling) Recasting the European Order, 1997; Decentralisation and Transition: The Visegrad Countries, 1999; (with T. Christiansen) Committee Governance in the European Union, 2000; (with L. Wenxiu and others) Studies on Policies and Policy Processes of the European Union, 2003. **Address:** Dept of Government, University of Essex, Wivenhoe Park, Wivenhoe Park, Colchester, Essex CO4 3SQ, England. **Online address:** emil@essex.ac.uk

KIRK, Donald. American, b. 1938. **Genres:** International relations/Current affairs. **Career:** Newspaper corresp., since 1965. **Publications:** Wider War: The Struggle for Cambodia, Thailand and Laos, 1971; Tell It to the Dead: Memories of a War, 1975, published as Tell It to the Dead: Stories of a War, 1996; Korean Dynasty: Hyundai and Chung Ju Yung, 1994; Looted: The

Philippines after the Bases, 1998; Korean Crisis, Unraveling of the Miracle in the IMF Era, 2000. **Address:** Washington, DC, U.S.A.

KIRK, Matthew. See WELLS, Angus.

KIRK, Pauline (M.). British, b. 1942. **Genres:** Novels, Poetry, Literary criticism and history. **Career:** Methodist Ladies College, Melbourne, Australia, teacher, 1965-66; Open University, tutor, counselor, assistant senior counselor, 1969-89; Department of Social Services, Leeds, England, senior officer and voluntary resource coordinator for city council, 1988-95; writer, 1995-. Tutor in adult education at Universities of London, Reading, and Leeds, 1969-89. Fighting Cock Press, partner. Performance poet and leader of creative writing workshops; judge of short story and poetry competitions; organizer of community arts festivals, 1980-. **Publications:** POETRY: Scorpion Days, 1982, 2nd ed, 1986; Red Marl and Brick, 1985; Rights of Way, 1990; Travelling Solo, 1995; Return to Dreamtime, 1996. NOVELS: Waters of Time, 1988; The Keepers, 1996. OTHER: (author of intro) Scathed Earth: The Collected Poems of Mabel Ferrett, 1996. Work represented in anthologies. Contributor of poems and articles to magazines and newspapers. **Address:** c/o David Grossman, David Grossman Literary Agency Ltd., 118b Holland Park Ave, London W11 4UA, England.

KIRK-GREENE, Anthony (Hamilton Millard). British, b. 1925. **Genres:** Area studies, History, Politics/Government. **Career:** University Lecturer, and Fellow, St. Antony's College, Oxford University, 1967-, and Director of the Foreign Service Programme, 1986-90. General Ed., Studies in African History, and Joint Ed., Colonial History Series. H.M. Colonial Service, Nigeria, 1950-57; Sr. Lecturer in Government, Institute of Administration, Zaria, Nigeria, 1957-62; Professor of Government, Ahmadu Bello University, Nigeria, 1962-65; Leverhulme Emeritus Fellowship, 1993. **Publications:** Adamawa Past and Present, 1958; (with C. Sassoon) The Cattle People of Nigeria, 1959; (with C. Sassoon) The River Niger, 1961; Barth's Travels in Nigeria, 1962; Principles of Native Administration in Nigeria, 1965; (with S.J. Hogben) The Emirates of Northern Nigeria, 1966; Hausa Proverbs, 1966; (with Y. Aliyu) A Modern Hausa Reader, 1967; Lugard and the Amalgamation of Nigeria, 1968; Crisis and Conflict in Nigeria, 1971; (with P. Newman) West African Narratives, 1972; (with C.H. Kraft) Teach Yourself Hausa, 1973; The Concept of the Good Man in Hausa, 1974; (with P. Ryan) Nigeria: Faces North, 1975; Biographical Dictionary of the British Colonial Governor, 1981; Stand by Your Radios, 1980; (with D. Rimmer) Nigeria since 1970, 1981; The Sudan Political Service, 1982; (with M. Adamu) Pastoralists of the Western Savanna, 1986; A History of the Corona Club, 1990; A Biographical Dictionary of the British Colonial Service, 1939-66, 1991; Diplomatic Initiative, 1994; (with J.H. Vaughan) The Diary of Hamman Yaji, 1995; On Crown Service, 1999; Britain's Imperial Administrators, 2000; Glimpses of Empire, 2001. EDITOR: The Making of Northern Nigeria, 1965; Language and People of Bornu, 1968; Gazetteers of Northern Nigeria, 1972; The Transfer of Power in Africa, 1978; Margery Perham: West African Passage, 1983; Margery Perham: Pacific Prelude, 1988; The Emergence of African History at British Universities, 1995; (with D. Rimmer) The British Intellectual Engagement with Africa, 2000. **Address:** St. Antony's College, Oxford OX2 6JF, England.

KIRK-GREENE, Christopher (Walter Edward). British, b. 1926. **Genres:** Language/Linguistics. **Career:** Assistant d'anglais, Lycee Berthollet, Annecy, France, 1948-49; Assistant Master 1949-86, and Head of Modern Languages Dept., 1962-78, Eastbourne College, Sussex. **Publications:** An Advanced French Vocabulary, 1958; Sixty Modern French Unseens, 1963; Les Mots Amis et Les Faux Amis, 1968; Lisez! Regardez! Repondez!, 1973; A First Book of French Idioms, 1973; Lectures Modernes, 1975; French False Friends, 1981 (as NTC's Dictionary of Faux Amis, 1990); Modern French Passages for Translation, 1984; Colloquial French, 1992; French Idioms and Expressions, 1997; Headlines-Colloquial English in Action, 2004. **Address:** 7 South Cliff, Eastbourne, E. Sussex BN20 7AF, England.

KIRKHAM, E. Bruce. American, b. 1938. **Genres:** Literary criticism and history. **Career:** Professor of English, Ball State University, Muncie, Indiana, since 1980 (Assistant Professor, 1968-74; Associate Professor, 1974-80). **Publications:** (ed. with John Fink) Indices to American Literary Annuals and Gift Books, 1825-1865, 1975; The Building of Uncle Tom's Cabin, 1977; A Concordance to the Olney Hymns of John Newton and William Cowper, 1983; A Concordance to the Plymouth Collection of Hymns and Tunes 1885, 1984. **Address:** Dept. of English, Ball State University, Muncie, IN 47306, U.S.A.

KIRKLAND, Martha. British. **Genres:** Romance/Historical. **Career:** Author of romance novels. **Publications:** ROMANCE NOVELS: The Marrying Season, 1995; The Secret Nabob, 1996; The Ruby Necklace, 1996; The Honorable Thief, 1996; The Gallant Gambler, 1997; Pratt's Landing, 1997; The Righteous Rogue, 1997; Three for Brighton, 1998; The Artful Heir, 1998; The Noble Nephew, 1998. Contributor to anthologies. **Address:** 4 Dunscome Rd., Warwick WK08, Bermuda.

KIRKLEY, Evelyn A(nne). American, b. 1961. **Genres:** Theology/Religion. **Career:** Educator and author. University of San Diego, San Diego, CA, associate professor of theology, 2001-. **Publications:** Rational Mothers and Infidel Gentlemen: Gender in American Atheism, 1865-1915, 2000. **Address:** Department of Theology, University of San Diego, 5998 Alcala Park, San Diego, CA 92110, U.S.A. **Online address:** ekirkley@sandiego.edu

KIRKMAN, William Patrick. British (born India), b. 1932. **Genres:** International relations/Current affairs. **Career:** Express & Star, Wolverhampton, editorial staff, 1955-57; Times, London, editorial staff, 1957-64 (commonwealth staff, 1960-64, and Africa correspondent, 1962-64); Oxford University Appointments Committee, assistant secretary, 1964-68; Wolfson College, Cambridge, fellow, 1968-2000, emeritus fellow, 2000-, vice-president, 1980-84, Press Fellowship Programme, director, 1982-96; Cambridge University Careers Service, secretary, 1968-92; Standing Conference of University Appointments Services, chairman, 1971-73; Journalists in Europe, U.K. Committee, 1985-98; Cambridgeshire Commonwealth Group, chairman, 1989-96; Cambridge Society, secretary & editor of Cambridge, 1992-2003; The Hindu, columnist, 1993-; Careers Research and Advisory Centre, newsletter, editor, 1997-98; American Friends of Cambridge University, Cambridge administrator, 2000-01. MBE, 1993. **Publications:** Unscrambling an Empire, 1966. **Address:** 14 George St, Willingham, Cambridge CB4 5LJ, England. **Online address:** wpk1000@cam.ac.uk.

KIRKPATRICK, Jeane (Duane Jordan). American, b. 1926. **Genres:** Politics/Government, International relations/Current affairs. **Career:** Georgetown University, Washington, D.C., Assistant Professor of Political Science, 1967-73, Professor, 1973-78, Leavey Professor in Foundations of American Freedom, 1978- (on leave 1981-85); American Enterprise Institute for Public Policy Research, Sr. Fellow, 1977- (on leave 1981-85). 20th Century Fund, Task Force on Presidential Elections Process, Co-Chairman. Member, National Committee on Party Structure and Presidential Nomination, Democratic National Committee, 1975 (Vice-Chairman, Committee on Vice-Presidential Selection, 1972-74). U.S. Representative to the United Nations, and Member of President Reagan's Cabinet, 1981-85. **Publications:** Foreign Students in the United States: A National Survey, 1966; Mass Behavior in Battle and Captivity, 1968; Leader and Vanguard in Mass Society: The Peronist Movement in Argentina, 1971; Political Woman, 1973; New Presidential Elite: Men and Women in National Politics, 1976; Dismantling the Parties: Reflections on Party Reform and Party Decomposition, 1978; Dictatorships and Doublestandards, 1981; The Reagan Phenomenon, 1983; Force and Freedom, 1987; Legitimacy and Force: State Papers and Current Perspectives 1981-1985, 2 vols., 1987; The Withering Away of the Totalitarian State: And Other Surprises, 1990. EDITOR: (and contrib.) Elections U.S.A., 1956; Strategy of Deception, 1963; The New Class, 1978; The New American Political System, 1978. **Address:** American Enterprise Institute, 1150 17th St. NW, Washington, DC 20036-4603, U.S.A.

KIRKUP, James (Falconer). British. **Genres:** Novels, Novellas/Short stories, Plays/Screenplays, Poetry, Children's non-fiction, Autobiography/Memoirs, Essays, Translations. **Career:** Fellow, Royal Society of Literature, 1964-. Gregory Fellow in Poetry, Leeds University, 1950-52; visiting poet and head of Dept. of English, Bath Academy of Art, Corsham, Wilts., 1953-56; travelling lecturer, Swedish Ministry of Education, Stockholm, 1956-57; professor of English, University of Salamanca, Spain, 1957-58, Tohoku University of Malaya, Kuala Lumpur, 1961-62, and Japan's Woman's University, Tokyo, 1963-70; literary ed., Orient/West Magazine, Tokyo, 1963-64; founder, Poetry Nippon, Japan, 1966; professor of English literature, Nagoya University, Japan, 1969-72; professor of comparative literature, Kyoto University of Foreign Studies, 1976-88. **Publications:** (with J. Ormond and J. Bayliss) Indications, 1942; (with R. Nichols) The Cosmic Shape, 1946; The Drowned Sailor and Other Poems, 1947; The Submerged Village and Other Poems, 1951; The Creation, 1951; A Correct Compassion and Other Poems, 1952; The Spring Journey and Other Poems of 1952-53, 1954; The Only Child, 1957; The Descent into the Cave and Other Poems, 1957; The Prodigal Son: Poems 1956-1959, 1959; Sorrows, Passions, and Alarms, 1959; The True Mistery of the Passion, 1960; These Horned Islands, 1962; Tropic Temper, 1962; The Love of Others (novel), 1962; Refusal to Conform, 1963; England, Now, 1964; Japan Industrial, 2 vols., 1964, 1965; Japan Marine, 1965; Japan Now, 1966; Frankly Speaking, 1966; Tokyo, 1966; Paper Windows, 1968; Filipinescas, 1968; Bangkok, 1968; One Man's

Russia, 1968; Japan Physical, 1969; (ed.) Shepherding Winds, 1969; Aspects of the Short Story, 1969; Streets of Asia, 1969; Hong Kong and Macao, 1970; Japan behind the Fan, 1970; White Shadows, Black Shadows, 1970; The Body Servant, 1971; Broad Daylight, 1971; A Bewick Bestiary, 1971; Transmental Vibrations, 1971; Heaven, Hell, and Hari-Kari, 1974; Zen Gardens, 1975; An Actor's Revenge (opera), 1978; Friends in Arms (opera), 1978; Zen Contemplations, 1978; Enlightenment, 1978; Scenes from Sesshu, 1978; Prick Prints, 1978; Steps to the Temple, 1979; Cold Mountain Poems, 1979; Modern Japanese Poetry, 1980; Scenes from Sutcliffe, 1981; Dengonban Messages, 1981; Ecce Homo: My Pasolini, 1982; No More Hiroshimas, 1982; The Damask Drum (opera), 1982, as play, 1984; When I Was a Child, 1983; To the Ancestral North, 1983; The Sense of the Visit, 1985; Fellow Feelings, 1986; The Mystery and the Magic of Symbols, 1987; I, of All People, 1988; The Best of Britain, 1989; Object Lessons (essays), 1990; Essays on Japanese Culture, 1990; A Poet Could not but Be Gay, 1991; Gaijin on the Ginza (novel), 1991; Throwback: Poems towards an Autobiography, 1992; Shooting Stars (haiku), 1992; First Fireworks, 1992; Words for Contemplation, 1993; Memoirs of a Misfit (autobiography), 1993; Queens Have Died Young and Fair (novel), 1993; Blue Bamboo, 1994; Look at It This Way, 1994; Strange Attractors, 1995; Formulas for Chaos, 1995; Counting to 9,999 (haiku), 1995; Noems, Koans and a Navel Display, 1995; The Genius of Haiku: R.S. Blyth (essays), 1995; Collected Longer Poems, Vol. I, 1995, Vol. II, 1997; Collected Shorter Poems, 1996; A Book of Tanka, 1996; Burning Giraffes, 1996; Figures in a Setting, 1996; The Patient Obituarist, 1996; Broad Daylight, 1996; UTSUSEMI, 1996; Child of the Tyne (autobiography), 1997; (with N. Matsubara) Tokonoma, 1999; One Man Band: Poems without Words, 1999; Tankalphabet, 2001; Modern Arab Poetry (anthology), 2000; Modern Arab Short Stories (anthology), 2000; A Tiger in Your Tanka, 2001; Victims and Tormentors, 2002; An Island in the Sky: Poems for Andorra, 2003. PLAYS: Upon this Rock, 1955; Masque: The Triumph of Harmony, 1955; The True Mystery of the Nativity, 1956; The Magic Drum, 1972; Ghost Mother, 1978; Two Classic German Plays, 1996. TRANSLATOR: The Meteor (play), 1956; The Physicists (play), 1963; Peer Gynt (play), 1972; Brand, by Ibsen, (play), 1972; Modern Japanese Poetry, 1978; To the Unknown God, 1982; The Bush Toads, 1982; An African in Greenland, 1982; Kawabata: Short Stories, 1982; Ito-san, 1991; A Room in the Woods, 1991; Painted Shadows, 1991; My Micheline, 1993; The Man in the Red Hat, 1993; Ceremonies of Difference, 1993; A Certain State of Mind: Haiku (essays), 1995; Being Blind, 1995; Paradise, 1995; State of Absence, 1995; Isabelle, 1995; How to Cook Women: Poems by Kyozo Takagi, 1997; Zhuangzi, He Dreamed He Was a Butterfly, 1997; F. Miura, Pages from the Seasons, 2001; F. Saito, In Thickets of Memory, 2001; Poems of Takahashi Mutsuo, 2004. **Address:** Atic D, Edifici les Bons, Avinguda de Rouillac, 7, Les Bons, Encamp, Andorra.

KIRKWOOD, Annie. American, b. 1937. **Genres:** Theology/Religion. **Career:** Employed by B and A Products, Bunch, OK. **Publications:** Mary's Message to the World, 1991; Messages to Our Family, 1994; Mary's Message of Hope, 1995; Instructions for the Soul, 1996. **Address:** B and A Products, Route 1, Box 100, Bunch, OK 74931, U.S.A.

KIRKWOOD, Dianna. American, b. 1946?. **Genres:** Self help. **Career:** Mercy Health Center, Dubuque, IA, director of marketing. **Publications:** (with J. Clemen, B. Schell, and D. Myerson) The Town That Lost a Ton: How One Town Used the Buddy System to Lose 3,998 Pounds-and How You Can Too!, 2002. **Address:** Mercy Health Center, 250 Mercy Dr., Dubuque, IA 52001, U.S.A. **Online address:** kirkwood@trinity-health.org

KIRKWOOD, Kathryn. See **FLUKE, Joanne.**

KIRSCH, George B(enson). American, b. 1945. **Genres:** History, Sports/Fitness, Urban studies. **Career:** Manhattan College, Riverdale, NY, assistant professor, 1972-80, associate professor, 1980-88, director of American Studies Program, 1975-85, professor of history, 1988-, department head, 1984-2001. **Publications:** Jeremy Belknap: A Biography, 1982; The Creation of American Team Sports: Baseball and Cricket, 1838-72, 1989; Voices from the Garden State: Documents in New Jersey History, 1993; The West in Global Context: A Documentary History, 1997; Baseball in Blue and Gray: The National Pastime during the Civil War, 2003. EDITOR: Sports in North America: A Documentary History, Vol. 3: 1841-1860, 1992, Vol. 4: Sport in War, Revival, and Expansion, 1860-1880, 1995; Encyclopedia of Ethnicity and Sports in the U.S., 2000. Contributor to books. Contributor of articles and reviews to periodicals. **Address:** Department of History, Manhattan College, Manhattan College Pky, Riverdale, NY 10471, U.S.A. **Online address:** George.Kirsch@manhattan.edu

KIRSCH, Jonathan. American, b. 1949. **Genres:** Novels, Biography. **Career:** Novelist, author of nonfiction, book reviewer, and attorney specializing in intellectual property rights. Los Angeles Times Book Review, book reviewer, 1968-; California magazine (formerly New West), editor, 1977-83; Newsweek, correspondent, 1979-80; Kirsch & Mitchell, Los Angeles, CA, attorney, 1988-. **Publications:** NOVELS: Bad Moon Rising, 1977; Lovers in a Winter Circle, 1978. NONFICTION: Kirsch's Handbook of Publishing Law: For Authors, Publishers, Editors, and Agents, 1995; The Harlot by the Side of the Road: Forbidden Tales of the Bible, 1997; Moses: A Life, 1998. Author of newspaper and magazine articles and book reviews. **Address:** Kirsch & Mitchell, 1875 Century Park E. Suite 1700, Los Angeles, CA 90067, U.S.A. **Online address:** ursts@aol.com

KIRSCHNER, Don S(tuart). American, b. 1928. **Genres:** History. **Career:** Drake University, Des Moines, IA, assistant professor of history, 1960-61; Roosevelt University, Chicago, IL, American history faculty, 1961-67; Simon Fraser University, Burnaby, British Columbia, professor of American history, 1967-93, professor emeritus, 1993-. **Publications:** City and Country, 1970; The Paradox of Professionalism, 1986; Cold War Exile, 1995. **Address:** History Department, Simon Fraser University, Burnaby, BC, Canada V5A 1S6.

KIRSCHNER, Ruth. *See* YOUNG, Ruth.

KIRSNER, Kim. Australian, b. 1941. **Genres:** Psychology. **Career:** University of Western Australia, Nedlands, professor of psychology, 1997-. **Publications:** (ed. with S. Lewandowsky and J. C. Dunn, and contrib.) Implicit Memory: Theoretical Issues, 1989; (ed. with M. Anderson, C. MacLeod, and others, and contrib) Implicit Processes in Psychological Science: Theory and Practice, 1998. Contributor to books and professional journals. **Address:** Department of Psychology, University of Western Australia, Nedlands, WA 6009, Australia. **Online address:** kimPsy.uwa.edu.au

KISSEL, Susan S. (Susan S. Adams). American, b. 1943. **Genres:** Literary criticism and history. **Career:** Teacher of English and Latin at public schools in Cincinnati, OH, 1964-65, substitute teacher, 1965-67; University of Cincinnati, instructor, 1967-69, adjunct instructor, 1975-78, lecturer in English, 1977-82; Northern Kentucky University, Highland Heights, adjunct instructor, 1975-78, assistant professor, 1978-83, director of women's studies, 1981-85, associate professor, 1984-92, professor of English, 1993-2003, emeritus professor, 2004-. Guest on radio programs. **Publications:** (ed. with M. Rouse) The Story of the Pewter Basin and Other Occasional Writings: Collected in Southern Ohio and Northern Kentucky, 1981; In Common Cause: The "Conservative" Frances Trollope and the "Radical" Frances Wright, 1993; Moving On: The Heroines of Shirley Anne Grau, Anne Tyler, and Gail Godwin, 1996. Contributor of articles and reviews to academic journals. **Address:** Dept of Literature and Language, Northern Kentucky University, Highland Heights, KY 41099, U.S.A.

KISSING, Steve. (born United States), b. 1963. **Genres:** Advertising/Public relations. **Career:** Writer, advertising copywriter, and editor. HSR Business to Business (advertising firm), Cincinnati, OH, associate creative director. **Publications:** Running from the Devil: A Memoir of a Boy Possessed, 2003. Also a contributing editor to Cincinnati magazine. **Address:** 8440 Lynnehaven Dr., Cincinnati, OH 45236, U.S.A.

KISSINGER, Henry (Alfred). American (born Germany), b. 1923. **Genres:** History, International relations/Current affairs, Politics/Government, Autobiography/Memoirs. **Career:** Founder and Chairman, Kissinger Assocs., Inc., NYC. Director, Harvard International Seminar, 1951-69, Director, Defense Studies Program, 1958-69, and Professor of Government, 1962-69, Harvard University, Cambridge, MA; Assistant to the President of the U.S. for National Security Affairs, 1969-75; U.S. Secretary of State, 1973-77. **Publications:** Nuclear Weapons and Foreign Policy, 1957; A World Restored: Castlereagh, Metternich and the Restoration of Peace, 1812-1822, 1957; The Necessity for Choice: Prospects of American Foreign Policy, 1961; The Troubled Partnership: A Reappraisal of the Atlantic Alliance, 1965; (ed.) Problems of National Security: A Book of Readings, 1965; American Foreign Policy, 1969, 3rd ed., 1977; White House Years (memoirs), 1979; For the Record: Selected Statements 1977-80, 1981; Years of Upheaval (memoirs), 1982; Observations: Selected Speeches and Essays 1982-1984, 1985; Diplomacy, 1994; Years of Renewal (memoirs), 1999; Does America Need a Foreign Policy?: Towards a Diplomacy for the 21st Century, 2001; Crisis, 2003; Ending the Vietam War, 2003. **Address:** Kissinger Assocs., Inc, 350 Park Ave, New York, NY 10022, U.S.A.

KISUBI, Alfred T(aligoola). American (born Uganda), b. 1949. **Genres:** Poetry. **Career:** Uganda Ministry of Information, Kampala, research officer at Nakasero Ministry of Information Headquarters, 1981-82; World Bank, research assistant in Uganda, 1981-82; high school teacher of English literature and religion in Kisii, Kenya, 1983-85; Johnson County Community College, Overland Park, KS, instructor, 1985-86; University of Missouri-Kansas City, instructor, 1986-90; Penn Valley Community College, Kansas City, instructor, 1989-92; University of Wisconsin-Oshkosh, associate professor of multicultural education and human services, 1992-. High school teacher of English, literature, political science, and history in Uganda; teacher at Pioneer College and Brown Mackie College. Missouri Story Telling Theater, storyteller; public speaker; consultant on multicultural topics and race relations. **Publications:** POETRY: Time Winds, 1988; Maybe It's a Dream, 1991; Storms: Poems of Azania, 1990; Hi, 1992. OTHER: (ed. with M.A. Burayidi) Race and Ethnic Relations in the First Person, 1998. Work represented in anthologies. Contributor of poems to periodicals. **Address:** School of Education and Human Services, University of Wisconsin-Oshkosh, 800 Algoma Blvd., Oshkosh, WI 54901, U.S.A. **Online address:** kisubi@uwosh.edu

KITA, Joe. American. **Genres:** Medicine/Health. **Career:** Author and motivational speaker. **Publications:** (ed.) Bicycling Magazine's Training for Fitness and Endurance, 1990; (with Lam Kam Chuen) Wisdom of Our Fathers: Timeless Life Lessons on Health, Wealth, God, Golf, Fear, Fishing, Sex, Serenity, Laughter, and Hope, 1999; The Father's Guide to the Meaning of Life: What Being a Dad Has Taught Me about Hope, Love, Patience, Pride, and Everyday Wonder, 2000; (foreword) Five Minutes to Orgasm Every Time You Make Love: Female Orgasm Made Simple, by D.C. Hutchins, 2000; Another Shot: How I Relived My Life in Less than a Year, 2001; Accidental Courage: Finding out I'm a Bit Brave after All, 2002. Author of articles on men's health. **Address:** c/o Rodale Press, 33 East Minor Street, Emmaus, PA 18098, U.S.A. **Online address:** jkita1@rodalepress.com

KITAJ, Karma. American, b. 1943. **Genres:** Biography. **Career:** Psychotherapist, author, and publisher. Psychotherapist in private practice, Brookline, MA. **Publications:** Women Who Could and Did: Lives of Twenty-six Exemplary Artists and Scientists, 2002. **Address:** Huckle Hill Press, PO Box 67273, Chestnut Hill, MA 02467, U.S.A. **Online address:** huckehillpress@attbi.com

KITCH, Sally L. American, b. 1946. **Genres:** Women's studies and issues. **Career:** Wichita State University, Wichita, KS, instructor, 1969-78, assistant professor, 1978-87, associate professor of women's studies, 1987-92, director of Center for Women's Studies, 1988-92; Ohio State University, Columbus, director of Center for Women's Studies, 1992-95, Dept of Women's Studies, professor, 1992-, chair, 1995-2000. **Publications:** (co-ed. and contrib.) Design for Equity: Women and Leadership in Higher Education, 1980; (co-author) The Source Book: An Inductive Approach to Composition, 1981; Chaste Liberation: Celibacy and Female Cultural Status, 1989; This Strange Society of Women: Reading the Letters and Lives of the Woman's Commonwealth, 1993; Women and Careers: Issues and Challenges, 1994; Higher Ground: From Utopianism to Realism in American Feminist Thought & Theory, 2000. **Address:** Department of Women's Studies, 286 University Hall, 230 N Oval Mall, Ohio State University, Columbus, OH 43210, U.S.A. **Online address:** kitch.1@osu.edu

KITCHELL, Webster (Lardner). American, b. 1931. **Genres:** Theology/Religion. **Career:** Unitarian minister and author. Ordained by Unitarian-Universalist Association, 1957; associate minister, Church of All Souls, NYC, 1957-60; minister, Eliot Unitarian Chapel, Kirkwood, MO, 1960-72, First Unitarian Church of Houston, Houston, TX, 1972-81, First Unitarian Church of Santa Fe, Santa Fe, NM, 1981-. **Publications:** God's Dog: Conversations with Coyote, 1991; Coyote Says…: More Conversations with God's Dog, 1996. Author of sermons, published online by Unitarian Church of Santa Fe. **Address:** 250 E Alameda St Apt 119, Santa Fe, NM 87501-2143, U.S.A.

KITCHEN, Bert. (Herbert Thomas). British, b. 1940. **Genres:** Children's fiction, Children's non-fiction. **Career:** Visiting lecturer in drawing and design at London Central School of Arts and Crafts, 1961-64, and City of London Polytechnic, 1964-; artist; author and illustrator of children's books, 1983-. Free-lance textile designer for Edinburgh Weavers, 1961-63; illustrator for Private Eye magazine, 1969-; artist of background paintings for feature and television films, 1975-85; artist for animation films, British Broadcasting Corporation (BBC-TV), and London Weekend Television, 1975-88; artist for advertising agencies, including J. Walter Thompson and McCann-Erikson. **Publications:** SELF-ILLUSTRATED FOR CHILDREN: Animal Alphabet, 1984; Mythical Creatures, 1986; Animal Numbers, 1987; Tenrec's Twigs, 1989; Gorilla Chinchilla, and Other Animal Rhymes, 1990; Pig in a Barrow (poems), 1991; Somewhere Today…, 1992; And So They

Build..., 1993; When Hunger Calls, 1994. **Address:** David Higham Associates, 5-8 Lower John St., Golden Square, London W1R 4HA, England.

KITCHEN, Judith. American, b. 1941. **Genres:** Poetry, Literary criticism and history, Essays. **Career:** State University of New York College at Brockport, lecturer in English, 1986-. University of Rochester, Eastman School of Music, artist at Aesthetic Education Institute, 1983-90; Wells College, writer in residence, 1986-87; Chautauqua Institution, writer in residence at Writers' Center, 1992, 1994; gives readings from her works. Worked as a secretary and in a carnival supply store. **Publications:** Upstairs Window (poetry chapbook), 1983; Perennials (poems), 1986; Understanding William Stafford, 1989; Only the Dance: Essays on Time and Memory, 1994. EDITOR: "Chapbook Series," 1981-; (with S.S. Rubin and E. Ingersoll) The Post-Confessionals: Conversations with Poets of the Eighties, 1989. Contributor of articles, poems, interviews, stories, and reviews to periodicals. **Address:** Department of English, State University of New York at Brockport, Brockport, NY 14420, U.S.A.

KITCHEN, Martin. British/Canadian, b. 1936. **Genres:** History. **Career:** Simon Fraser University, Burnaby, BC, University Professor, 1966-. **Publications:** The German Officer Corps 1890-1914, 1968; A Military History of Germany, 1974; Fascism, 1976; The Silent Dictatorship: The Politics of the German High Command under Hindenburg and Ludendorff, 1976; The Political Economy of Germany 1815-1914, 1978; The Coming of Austrian Fascism, 1980; Germany in the Age of Total War, 1981; British Policy towards the Soviet Union during the Second World War, 1986; Europe between the Wars, 1988; The Origins of the Cold War in Comparative Perspective, 1987; A World in Flames, 1990; Empire and After: A Short History of the British Empire and Commonwealth, 1994; Nazi Germany at War, 1994; The Cambridge Illustrated History of Germany, 1996; The British Empire and Commonwealth, 1996; Kaspar Hauser, 2001; The German Offensives of 1918, 2001. **Address:** Dept. of History, Simon Fraser University, Burnaby, BC, Canada V5A 1S6. **Online address:** kitchen@sfu.ca

KITCHEN, Paddy. British, b. 1934. **Genres:** Novels, Biography. **Career:** Art Critic, The Times and Country Life, 1977-96. **Publications:** Lying-in, 1965; A Fleshly School, 1970; Linsey-Woolsey, 1971; Paradise, 1972; A Most Unsettling Person (on Patrick Geddes), 1975; Gerard Manley Hopkins, 1978; A Pillar of Cloud, 1979; Poets' London, 1980; The Golden Veil, 1981; The Way to Write Novels, 1981; Barnwell, 1985; Blue Shoe, 1988. **Address:** 20 Benefield Rd, Oundle PE8 4ET, England. **Online address:** paddy.kitchen@tiscali.co.uk

KITELEY, Brian. American, b. 1956. **Genres:** Novels, Sciences, Autobiography/Memoirs, Autobiography/Memoirs. **Career:** Ohio University, assistant professor of English and creative writing, 1992-94; University of Denver, associate professor, English and creative writing, 1994-. Writer in residence at Yaddo, MacDowell, and Millay colonies; NEA Fellow, 1991; Guggenheim Fellow, 1992-93; Whiting Writers Award, 1996. **Publications:** Still Life with Insects, 1989; I Know Many Songs, but I Cannot Sing, 1996. **Address:** c/o Karpfinger Agency, 357 W 20th St., New York, NY 10011-3379, U.S.A. **Online address:** bkiteley@du.edu

KITFIELD, James C. American, b. 1956. **Genres:** Documentaries/Reportage. **Career:** Stars and Stripes, European Ed, Germany, intern; Overseas!, editor; National Journal Inc., Washington, DC, associate editor, 1989-. **Publications:** Prodigal Soldiers, 1995. Contributor to periodicals. **Address:** 4811 South 30th St., No. B-2, Arlington, VA 22206, U.S.A.

KITT, Sandra (E.). American, b. 1947. **Genres:** Novellas/Short stories, Romance/Historical, Librarianship, Illustrations. **Career:** Philip Gips Studios Inc., art assistant, 1970-72; NYC Board of Education, NYC, teacher in Cloisters Workshop Program, 1972-73; Information Specialist, NYC, librarian, 1974-92; American Museum of Natural History, NYC, manager of library services at Richard S. Perkin Library, Hayden Planetarium, 1992-. Museum of Contemporary Arts, assistant to the registrar and assistant coordinator at Children's Art Center, 1972-73; NYC Office of Cultural Affairs, teacher at Printmaking Workshop, 1974-80. Freelance graphic artist and illustrator, with work exhibited throughout the United States and represented in corporate collections. **Publications:** ROMANCE NOVELS: Rites of Spring, 1984; Adam and Eva, 1984; All Good Things, 1984; Perfect Combination, 1985; Only with the Heart, 1985; With Open Arms, 1987; An Innocent Man, 1989; The Way Home, 1990; Someone's Baby, 1991; Love Everlasting, 1993; Love Is Thanks Enough (also known as Friends, Families, and Lovers), 1993; Serenade, 1994; Sincerely, 1995; Significant Others, 1996; Between Friends, 1997; Family Affairs, 1998; Close Encounters, 2000; She's the One, 2001; Southern Comfort, 2004; The Next Best Things, 2005.

OTHER: The Color of Love (novel), 1995. Contributor of articles and reviews to museum and library journals. Contributor of short fiction to books. Illustrator of books by I. Asimov. **Address:** PO Box 403, New York, NY 10024, U.S.A. **Online address:** sandikitt@hotmail.com; author@sandrakitt.com

KITTINGER, Jo S(usenbach). American, b. 1955. **Genres:** Children's fiction, Natural history, Picture/board books. **Career:** Wood & the Works (fine crafts gallery), Alabaster, AL, co-owner and resident potter, 1977-80; freelance crafts designer, 1978-91; Mental Retardation & Developmental Disabilities Health Care Authority of Jefferson County, board member, 1996-; Society of Children's Book Writers and Illustrators, assistant regional adviser for the Southern Breeze region, 1999-. **Publications:** Dead Log Alive!, 1996; A Look at Rocks: From Coal to Kimberlite, 1997; A Look at Minerals: From Galena to Gold, 1998; Stories in Stone: The World of Animal Fossils, 1998; The Joy of Cats, 1999; Birds of North America East, 2001; Birds of North America West, 2001; Going to the Beach, 2002; Moving Day, 2003; A Lunch with Punch, 2003. Contributor to periodicals. **Address:** 1612 Colesbury Circle, Hoover, AL 35226, U.S.A.

KITTREDGE, William. Also writes as Owen Rountree. American, b. 1932. **Genres:** Novels, Novellas/Short stories, Westerns/Adventure, Essays. **Career:** University of Montana, Missoula, assistant professor, 1969-74, associate professor, 1974-79, professor of English, 1979-. **Publications:** SHORT STORIES: The Van Gogh Field and Other Stories, 1978; We Are Not in This Together, 1984; Phantom Silver, 1987. ESSAYS: Owning It All, 1987; Hole in the Sky, 1992; Who Owns the West, 1996; Taking Care, 1999; Balancing Water, 2000; The Nature of Generosity, 2000; Southwestern Homelands, 2002; The Best Stories of William Kittredge, 2003. EDITOR: (with S.M. Krauzer) Great Action Stories, 1977; (with S.M. Krauzer) The Great American Detective, 1978; (with S.M. Krauzer) Fiction into Film, 1979; Montana Spaces: Essays and Photographs in Celebration of Montana, 1988; (with A. Smith) The Last Best Place: A Montana Anthology, 1988; The Portable Western Reader, 1997. WESTERNS AS OWEN ROUNTREE (with S.M. Krauzer): Cord, 1982; Cord: The Nevada War, 1982; Cord: The Black Hills Duel, 1983; Cord: Gunman Winter, 1983; Cord: Hunt the Man Down, 1984; Cord: King of Colorado, 1984; Cord: Gunsmoke River, 1985; Cord: Paradise Valley, 1986; Cord: Brimstone Valley, 1986. **Address:** c/o Amanda Urban, ICM, 40 W 57th St, New York, NY 10019, U.S.A.

KITTS, Thomas M(ichael). American, b. 1955. **Genres:** Plays/Screenplays, Literary criticism and history. **Career:** Junior high school English teacher in NYC, 1977-79, high school teacher, 1979-80; St. Peter's College, Jersey City, NJ, adjunct assistant professor of English, 1980; St. John's University, Jamaica, NY, assistant director of alumni relations, 1980-83, director, 1983-91, adjunct instructor, 1980-91, assistant professor, 1991-97, associate professor of English, 1997-, chair, English/speech, 2000-. Speaker at colleges and conferences. **Publications:** The Theatrical Life of George Henry Boker, 1994; Gypsies (play), 1987; instructor's manual to accompany Literature: Reading Fiction, Poetry, Drama, and the Essay, by R. DiYanni, 4th ed., 1998, 5th ed., 2001; instructor's manual to accompany The American Tradition in Literature, by G. Perkins, 9th ed., 1999, 10th ed., 2002; (ed. with M. Kraus) Living on a Thin Line: Crossing Aesthetic Borders with the Kinks, 2002. Contributor to books and periodicals. **Address:** 648 20th St, Brooklyn, NY 11218-1045, U.S.A. **Online address:** TomKitts@aol.com

KITZINGER, Sheila. British, b. 1929. **Genres:** Medicine/Health, Social sciences, Women's studies and issues. **Career:** Social anthropologist, childbirth educator, and birth activist. Lecturer, Open University. Member, Board of Consultants, International Childbirth Education Association, 1972-. Hon. professor, Thames Valley University. Adviser: Miscarriage Association, Intl Cesarean Awareness Network, Maternity Alliance, Lactation Consultants' Association, Editorial Board, Midwives Information and Research Center. Researcher on race relations in Britain, University of Edinburgh, 1951-53. **Publications:** The Experience of Childbirth, 1962, 4th ed., 1973; Giving Birth, 1971, rev. ed., 1987; Education and Counselling for Childbirth, 1977; Women as Mothers, 1978, as Ourselves as Mothers, 1994; Birth at Home, 1979; The Good Birth Guide, 1979; The Experience of Breastfeeding, 1979; The Place of Birth, 1979; Pregnancy and Childbirth, 1980, as The Complete Book of Pregnancy and Childbirth, 1996; Some Women's Experience of Episiotomy, 1981; The New Good Birth Guide, 1983; Woman's Experience of Sex, 1983; Being Born, 1986; Freedom and Choice in Childbirth (in US as Your Baby Your Way), 1987; Some Women's Experiences of Epidurals, 1987; The Midwife Challenge, 1988; The Crying Baby, 1989; Breastfeeding Your Baby, 1989, as Breastfeeding, 1998; (with C. Kitzinger) Talking with Children about Things that Matter, 1989 (in US as Tough Questions, 1991); (with V. Bailey) Pregnancy Day by Day, 1990, 2nd ed., 1998; Home Birth and Other Alternatives to Hospital, 1991; The Year after Childbirth, 1994; Becoming a Grandmother, 1996; Rediscovering Birth, 2000; Birth Your Way, 2001; New Pregnancy and Childbirth, 2003; The New Experience of Childbirth, 2004. **Address:** Standlake Manor, Standlake nr Witney, Oxon. OX29 7RH, England. **Online address:** www.sheilakitzinger.com

KITZINGER, Uwe. British, b. 1928. **Genres:** Economics, International relations/Current affairs, Politics/Government. **Career:** Visiting Scholar, Harvard University, 1993-. Secretariat-General, Council of Europe, Strasbourg, France, 1951-58; Founding Ed., Journal of Common Market Studies, 1962; Research Fellow, 1958-62, Ford Fellow and Investment Bursar, 1962-76, Emeritus Fellow, 1976-, Nuffield College, Oxford; Adviser to Sir Christopher Soames, Vice-President, Commission of the European Communities, Brussels, 1973-75; Dean of the European Institute of Business Administration, Fontainebleau, France, 1976-80; Director, Oxford Centre for Management Studies, 1980-84; President, Templeton College, Oxford, 1984-91, Hon. Fellow, 2001. **Publications:** German Electoral Politics, 1960; The Challenge of the Common Market, 1961, rev. ed. as The Politics and Economics of European Integration, 1963; Britain, Europe and Beyond, 1964; The European Common Market and Community, 1967; Commitment and Identity, 1968; The Second Try, 1969; Diplomacy and Persuasion: How Britain Joined the EEC, 1973; Europe's Wider Horizons, 1975; (with D. Butler) The 1975 Referendum, 1976, 2nd ed., 1996; (with E. Frankel) Macro-Engineering and the Earth, 1998. **Address:** Standlake Manor, Near Witney, Oxon. OX29 7RH, England. **Online address:** kitzing@fas.harvard.edu

KIZAKI, Satoko. *See* HARADA, Masako.

KIZER, Carolyn. American, b. 1925. **Genres:** Poetry. **Career:** Founding Ed., Poetry Northwest, Seattle, 1959-65; Director of Literary Programs, National Endowment for the Arts, 1966-70; Professor, University of North Carolina, Chapel Hill, 1970-74; Professor, University of Maryland, College Park, 1976-77; Visiting Professor, Barnard College, Columbia University, Washington University, University of Iowa, University of Cincinnati, University of Louisville, State University of New York at Albany, Stanford University, University of Arizona, Princeton University, and others. **Publications:** The Ungrateful Garden, 1961; Knock upon Silence, 1965; Midnight Was My Cry: New and Selected Poems, 1971; YIN: New Poems, 1984; Mermaids in the Basement: Poems for Women, 1984; The Nearness of You, 1986; Carrying Over: Translations from Various Tongues, 1988; (with D. Finkel) Splintered Mirror (modern Chinese translations), 1991; Proses: Essays on Poets and Poetry, 1993; Picking and Choosing: Essays, 1995; Harping On: Poems 1985-1995, 1996; Pro Femina (chapbook), 2000; Cool, Calm & Collected Poems, 2000. EDITOR: The Essential Clare, 1993; 100 Great Poems by Women, 1995. **Address:** 19772 8th St. E, Sonoma, CA 95476, U.S.A.

KLAM, Matthew. American, b. 1964. **Genres:** Novellas/Short stories. **Career:** Journalist and author of short fiction. Teacher of creative writing at St. Albans School, American University, and Stockholm University. **Publications:** Sam the Cat, and Other Stories, 2000. Contributor of short fiction to periodicals. **Address:** c/o Author Mail, Random House, 299 Park Ave., New York, NY 10171, U.S.A. **Online address:** MattKlam@aol.com

KLAMMER, Martin (P.). American, b. 1957. **Genres:** Literary criticism and history. **Career:** Lutheran Council in the U.S.A., NYC, news and feature writer, 1983-84; University of Iowa, Iowa City, instructor in rhetoric and literature, 1984-90; Business and Professional People for the Public Interest, Chicago, IL, legal intern, 1990; Luther College, Decorah, IA, assistant professor of English and Africana studies, 1991-. **Publications:** Whitman, Slavery, and the Emergence of "Leaves of Grass", 1995. Contributor to books and periodicals. **Address:** Luther College, 700 College Dr., Decorah, IA 52101, U.S.A.

KLAPPERT, Peter. American, b. 1942. **Genres:** Poetry, Literary criticism and history. **Career:** Instructor, Rollins College, Winter Park, Florida, 1968-71; Briggs-Copeland Lecturer on English, Harvard University, Cambridge, Massachusetts, 1971-74; Lecturer, New College, Florida, 1972; Writer-in-Residence, 1976-77, and Assistant Professor, 1977-78, College of William and Mary, Williamsburg, Virginia; George Mason University, assistant professor, 1978-81, director, writing program, 1979-80, 1985-88, associate professor, 1981-91, professor, 1991-, Master of Fine Arts Program in Poetry, director, 1995-98. **Publications:** Lugging Vegetables to Nantucket, 1971; Circular Stairs, Distress in the Mirrors, 1975; Non Sequitur O'Connor, 1977; The Idiot Princess of the Last Dynasty, 1984; '52 Pick-Up: Scenes from the Conspiracy, A Documentary, 1984; Chokecherries: New & Selected Poems,

1966-99, 2000. **Address:** MSN 3E4, Dept. of English, George Mason University, Fairfax, VA 22030, U.S.A. **Online address:** pklapper@gmu.edu

KLARE, George Roger. American, b. 1922. **Genres:** Language/Linguistics, Mathematics/Statistics, Psychology. **Career:** Distinguished Professor of Psychology, Ohio University, Athens, since 1954 (Chairman, Dept. of Psychology, 1959-63; Dean, College of Arts and Sciences, 1965-71; Acting Dean, College of Arts and Sciences, 1984-85; Acting Associate Provost for Graduate and Research Progs., 1986-87), now emeritus. Research Associate and Language Program Director, Computer-Aided Instructional Laboratory, Harvard University, Cambridge, Massachusetts, 1968-69; Visiting Professor, University of Iowa, 1979-80, State University of New York, Stony Brook, 1971-72. **Publications:** (with B. Buck) Know Your Reader, 1954; The Measurement of Readability, 1963; (with P. A. Games) Elementary Statistics: Data Analysis for the Behavioral Sciences, 1967, instructors' manual, 1967; (with L. R. Campbell) Measuring the Readability of High School Newspapers, Parts I II, 1967; A Manual for Readable Writing, 1975, 4th ed., 1980; How to Write Readable English, 1984. **Address:** Dept. of Psychology, Ohio University, Athens, OH 45701, U.S.A. **Online address:** klare@ohiou.edu

KLARE, Michael T(homas). American, b. 1942. **Genres:** International relations/Current affairs, Military/Defense/Arms control. **Career:** Parsons School of Design, NYC, instructor in art history, 1967-70; North American Congress on Latin America, Berkeley, CA, research director, 1970-76; Princeton University, Princeton, NJ, visiting fellow at Center of International Studies, 1976-77; Institute for Policy Studies, Washington, DC, fellow and co-director of Program on National Security, 1977-84; Hampshire College, Amherst, MA, Five College Professor of Peace and World Security Studies and director of Five College Program in Peace and World Security Studies, 1985-. Visiting instructor at Tufts University Experimental College, 1973; visiting associate professor of peace studies, Wellesley College, 1992-93; associate research analyst at University of California at Berkeley Institute for International Studies, 1983. **Publications:** War without End: American Planning for the Next Vietnams, 1972; Supplying Repression: U.S. Support for Authoritarian Regimes Abroad, 1978, rev. ed., 1981; Beyond the "Vietnam Syndrome": U.S. Interventionism in the 1980s, 1981; American Arms Supermarket, 1984; (ed. with P. Kornbluh, and contrib.) Low Intensity Warfare: Counterinsurgency, Proinsurgency, and Antiterrorism in the Eighties, 1988; (ed. with D.C. Thomas) Peace and World Order Studies: A Curriculum Guide, 5th ed., 1989; (ed.) Peace and World Security Studies: A Curriculum Guide, 6th ed., 1994; (ed. with D.C. Thomas) World Security, 1991, 3rd ed. (ed. with Y. Chandrani), 1998; (ed. with J. Boutwell, and L. Reed, and contrib.) Lethal Commerce, 1995; Rogue States and Nuclear Outlaws, 1995; (with D. Anderson) A Scourge of Guns, 1996; (ed. with J. Boutwell, and contrib.) Light Weapons and Civil Conflict, 1999. Contributor to books. **Address:** Peace and World Security Studies, Hampshire College, Amherst, MA 01002, U.S.A. **Online address:** mklare@hampshire.edu

KLASS, David. American, b. 1960. **Genres:** Science fiction/Fantasy. **Career:** Novelist and screenwriter. Save Our Youth, board of directors; PEN Center USA West, board of directors. **Publications:** The Atami Dragons, 1984; Breakaway Run, 1986; A Different Season, 1988; Wrestling with Honor, 1989; Samuri Inc., 1992; California Blue, 1994; Danger Zone, 1995; You Don't Know Me, 2001. **Address:** c/o Aaron M. Priest Literary Agency, 708 Third Ave., 23rd floor, New York, NY 10017, U.S.A.

KLASS, Perri. American (born Trinidad and Tobago), b. 1958. **Genres:** Novels, Autobiography/Memoirs, Novellas/Short stories. **Career:** Pediatrician, writer. Author of Hers column, New York Times, 1984; Columninst, Discover mag., NYC. **Publications:** Recombinations (novel), 1985; I Am Having an Adventure (short stories), 1986; A not Entirely Benign Procedure: Four Years as a Medical Student, 1987; Other Women's Children (novel), 1990; Baby Doctor! A Pediatrician's Training, 1992. **Address:** c/o Maxine Groffsky, 853 Broadway, Ste. 708, New York, NY 10003, U.S.A.

KLASS, Sheila Solomon. American, b. 1927. **Genres:** Novels, Autobiography/Memoirs, Children's fiction, Young adult fiction. **Career:** City University of New York, Borough of Manhattan Community College, lecturer, 1965-67, instructor 1967-68, assistant professor, 1968-73, associate professor, 1973-82, professor of English, 1982-99, professor emerita, 2000-. **Publications:** Come Back on Monday, 1960; Everyone in This House Makes Babies, 1964; Bahadur Means Hero, 1969; A Perpetual Surprise, 1981; Nobody Knows Me in Miami, 1981; To See My Mother Dance, 1981; Alive and Starting Over, 1983; The Bennington Stitch, 1985; Page Four, 1986; Credit Card Carole, 1987; Kool Ada, 1991; Rhino, 1993; Next Stop: Nowhere, 1995; A Shooting Star: A Novel about Annie Oakley, 1996; In a

Cold Open Field, 1997; The Uncivil War, 1997; Little Women Next Door, 2000. **Address:** 900 W 190th St Apt. 2-0, New York, NY 10040, U.S.A.

KLAUCK, Hans-Josef. German, b. 1946. **Genres:** Theology/Religion. **Career:** University of Bonn, Germany, professor, 1981-82; University of Wurzburg, Germany, professor, 1982-1997; University of Munich, Germany, professor of the New Testament, 1997-2001; University of Chicago Divinity School, IL, professor of the New Testament and early Christian literature, 2001-. **Publications:** Allegorie und Allegorese in synoptischen Gleichnixtexten, 1978; Hausgemeinde und Hauskirche im fruhen Christentum, 1981; Herrenmahl und hellenistischer Kult: eine religionsgeschichtliche Untersuchung zum ersten Korintherbrief, 1982; Judas, ein Junger des Herrn, 1987; Der erste Johannesbrief, 1991; Alte Welt und neuer Glaube: Beitrage zur Religionsgeschichte, Forschungsgeschichte und Theologie des Neuen Testaments, 1994; Die religiose Umwelt des Urchristentums, 2 vols, 1995-1996, trans. B. McNeil as The Religious Context of Early Christianity: A Guide to Graeco-Roman Religions, 2000; Magie und Heidentum in der Apostelgeschichte des Lukas, 1996, trans. B. McNeil as Magic and Paganism in Early Christianity: The World of the Acts of the Apostles, 2000; Vorspiel im Himmel?: Erzahltechnik und Theologie im Markusprolog, 1997; Die Antike Briefliteratur und das Neue Testament, 1998; Dion von Prusa: Olympischerede, 2000; Apokryphe Evangelien eine Eintuhrung, 2002, trans. B. McNeil, in press. EDITOR: Monotheismus und Christologie: zur Gottesfrage im hellenistischen Judentum und im Urchristentum, 1992; Weltgericht und Weltvollendung: Zukunftsbilder im Testament, 1994. **Address:** Swift Hall 306D, University of Chicago Divinity School, 1025 E 58th St, Chicago, IL 60637, U.S.A.

KLAUSE, Annette Curtis. American (born England), b. 1953. **Genres:** Science fiction/Fantasy. **Career:** Silver Spring Community Library, Silver Spring, MD, children's librarian I, 1981; Montgomery County Department of Public Libraries, substitute librarian, 1981-82; Kensington Park Community Library, Kensington Park, MD, part-time children's librarian I, 1982-84; Bethesda Regional Library, Bethesda, MD, full-time children's librarian I, 1984-89; Olney Community Library, Olney, MD, head of children's services, 1989-91; Kensington Park Community Library, head of children's services, 1991-92; Aspen Hill Community Library, Rockville, Maryland, head of children's services, 1992-. Writer. **Publications:** The Silver Kiss, 1990; Alien Secrets, 1993; Blood and Chocolate, 1997. Author of short stories and poetry. Contributor of articles and reviews to professional journals. **Address:** c/o Bantam Doubleday Dell, 1540 Broadway, New York, NY 10036, U.S.A. **Online address:** human_oddity@juno.com

KLAVAN, Andrew. Also writes as Keith Peterson, Margaret Tracy. American. **Genres:** Novels. **Career:** Journalist, screenwriter, and novelist. **Publications:** NOVELS: Face of the Earth: A Novel, 1980; Darling Clementine, 1988; Son of Man, 1988; Don't Say a Word, 1991; The Animal Hour, 1993; Corruption, 1994; True Crime: The Novel, 1995; The Uncanny, 1998. NOVELS AS KEITH PETERSON: Eleanora, My Love, 1988; The Rain, 1988; There Fell a Shadow, 1988; The Trapdoor, 1989; Rough Justice, 1989; The Scarred Man, 1990. NOVELS AS MARGARET TRACY: Mrs. White, 1983. SCREENPLAYS: A Shock to the System, 1990. Contributor of poems to periodicals. **Address:** c/o Crown Publishing, 201 East 50th St., New York, NY 10022, U.S.A.

KLAVENESS, Jan O'Donnell. American, b. 1939. **Genres:** Children's fiction. **Career:** Children's book writer. University of Michigan, Ann Arbor, MI, assistant director of student organizations, 1963-65; Hofstra University, Hempstead, NY, assistant director of financial aid, 1979-82. Hillsborough School District, Hillsborough Gifted and Talented Program, mentor; College of NJ, lecturer, 2000; Harcourt Brace Educational Measurement Project, contributor, 2000-. **Publications:** A Funny Girl Like Me, 1980; The Griffin Legacy, 1983; Ghost Island, 1985; Keeper of the Light, 1990; Beyond the Cellar Door, 1991. **Address:** 41 Vliet Dr, Hillsborough, NJ 08844, U.S.A.

KLEBANOFF, Arthur. American, b. 1947. **Genres:** Business/Trade/Industry, Autobiography/Memoirs. **Career:** Worked at NYC Mayor's Office and as a White House aide after college. Morton L. Janklow Associates Inc., cofounder; Janklow, Traum, and Klebanoff, partner; International Management Group, vice president and head of publishing division, 1991; Scott Meredith Literary Agency, owner and president, 1993-; RosettaBooks (electronic publishing company), cofounder and CEO, 2001-. **Publications:** The Agent, 2002. **Address:** 200 W 57th St Ste 904, New York, NY 10019, U.S.A. **Online address:** aklebanoff@rosettabooks.com

KLECK, Gary. American, b. 1951. **Genres:** Criminology/True Crime. **Career:** Florida State University, Tallahassee, instructor, 1978-79, assistant professor, 1979-84, associate professor, 1984-91, professor of criminology

and criminal justice, 1991-. **Publications:** Point Blank: Guns and Violence in America, 1991; The Great American Gun Debate, 1997; Targeting Guns, 1997; Armed, 2001. **Address:** School of Criminology and Criminal Justice, Florida State University, Tallahassee, FL 32306-1127, U.S.A.

KLEH, Cindy (L.). (born United States), b. 1959. **Genres:** Sports/Fitness. **Career:** Summit Outdoors, San Francisco, CA, columnist, 1993-98; Ten Mile Times, San Francisco, writer, 1999-2001; freelance writer, 2000-. Worked as a bartender, tour guide in Hawaii, and teacher of snowboarding techniques. **Publications:** Snowboarding Skills: The Back-to-Basic Essentials for All Levels, 2002. Work represented in anthologies and contributor to periodicals. **Address:** 584 Montezuma Rd. No. 5, Dillon, CO 80435, U.S.A. **Online address:** ckleh63193@aol.com

KLEHR, Harvey. American, b. 1945. **Genres:** History, Politics/Government. **Career:** Emory University, Atlanta, professor of political science, 1971-. Historians of American Communism, president, 1985-87. **Publications:** Communist Cadre: The Social Background of the American Communist Party Elite, 1978; The Heyday of American Communism: The Depression Decade, 1984; Far Left of Center: The American Radical Left Today, 1988; The American Communist Movement: Storming Heaven Itself, 1992; The Secret World of American Communism, 1995; The Amerasia Spy Case, 1996; The Soviet World of American Communism, 1998; (with J.E. Haynes) Venona: Decoding Soviet Espionage in America, 1999. **Address:** Dept. of Political Science, Emory University, Atlanta, GA 30322, U.S.A. **Online address:** polshk@emory.edu

KLEIMAN, Ed. Canadian, b. 1932. **Genres:** Novellas/Short stories, Literary criticism and history. **Career:** University of Manitoba, Winnipeg, associate professor of English, 1961-96. Serves as judge at literary contests; gives public readings of his works, which have also been broadcast by Canadian Broadcasting Corporation (CBC). **Publications:** Leonard Cohen: "Blossom Show" in The Artist and His Critics (casebook), 1976; The Immortals (stories), 1980; A New-Found Ecstasy (stories), 1988; The World Beaters (stories), 1998. Works appear in anthologies. **Address:** 78 Queenston St, Winnipeg, MB, Canada R3N 0W5. **Online address:** Kleiman@ms.umanitoba.ca

KLEIMAN, Mark A. R. American, b. 1951. **Genres:** Politics/Government. **Career:** U.S. House of Representatives, Washington, DC, legislative assistant, 1974-75; Polaroid Corp., Cambridge, MA, special assistant to the chairman, 1975-76; City of Boston, Office of Management and Budget, Boston, MA, director of program analysis, 1977-79; U.S. Department of Justice, Criminal Division, Washington, DC, director of Office of Policy and Management Analysis, 1979-83; Harvard University, Cambridge, lecturer, 1987-92, associate professor of public policy, 1992; Botec Analysis Corporation, president; University of California, Los Angeles, professor of policy studies, 1996-. Drug Policy Analysis Bulletin, editor. **Publications:** Marijuana: Costs of Abuse, Costs of Control, 1989; Against Excess: Drug Policy for Results, 1992. **Address:** Department of Policy Studies, UCLA, School of Public Policy and Social Research, 3250 Public Policy Bldg., Los Angeles, CA 90095-1656, U.S.A. **Online address:** Kleiman@ucla.edu

KLEIN, Adam. American. **Genres:** Art/Art history. **Career:** Writer, musician, composer. Worked as a caseworker, San Francisco, CA; Roman Evening, band member, 1999-; Peace Corps, Bangladesh, 2003-. **Publications:** The Medicine Burns, 1995; (with Thomas Avena) Jerome: After the Pageant, 1996; Tiny Ladies, 2003. Stories have been published in various journals and magazines. **Address:** c/o Author Mail, Serpent's Tail, 4 Black Stock Mews, London N4 2BT, England.

KLEIN, Alan M. American, b. 1946. **Genres:** Sports/Fitness. **Career:** Northeastern University, Boston, MA, professor of sociology and anthropology. **Publications:** Sugarball: The American Game, The Dominican Dream, 1991; Little Big Men: Bodybuilding Subculture and Gender Construction, 1993; Baseball on the Border: A Tale of Two Laredos, 1997. **Address:** c/o Northeastern University, 360 Huntington Avenue, 517 Holmes Hall, Boston, MA 02115, U.S.A. **Online address:** a.klein@neu.edu

KLEIN, Allen. American, b. 1938. **Genres:** Medicine/Health, Psychology, Self help, Humor/Satire, Reference. **Career:** CBS-TV, New York City, scenic designer, 1962-71; owner of W.O.R.K.S. Silkscreen Studio, 1972-78; home health aide of State of California, 1979; Holistic Life Institute, San Francisco, director and teacher, 1979-82; seminar leader, speaker, and writer, 1983-. **Publications:** The Healing Power of Humor, 1989; Quotations to Cheer You Up When the World Is Getting You Down, 1991; Wing Tips, 1996; The Courage to Laugh, 1998; Up Words for Down Days, 1998; The Change-

Your-Life Quote Book, 2000; The Lift-Your-Spirits Quote Book, 2001; Winning Words, 2002; The Celebrate-Your-Life Quote Book, 2005.

KLEIN, Anne Carolyn. American. **Genres:** Theology/Religion. **Career:** Mary Washington College, Fredericksburg, VA, instructor in classics, philosophy, and religion, 1981; University of Virginia, Charlottesville, lecturer in religious studies, 1981-82; Harvard University, Cambridge, MA, research associate in women's studies and the history of religion at Harvard Divinity School, 1982-83; visiting scholar at Center for the Study of World Religions, 1983-84; Stanford University, Stanford, CA, lecturer, 1984-86, Jing Lyman Lecturer, 1986, acting assistant professor of religious studies, 1986-89; Rice University, Houston, TX, assistant professor, 1989-91, associate professor, 1989-95, professor of religious studies and head of department, 1995-. Fairfield University, annual visiting lecturer, 1991; Namgyal Monastery, adjunct faculty at Institute of Buddhist Studies, 1992-; University of Hawaii, Numata Distinguished Professor Lecturer, 1995. Conducted field studies in Tibet, India, Nepal, and China. Participates in retreats and public lectures. **Publications:** (assist. ed.) Tenzin Gyatso, The Buddhism of Tibet and the Key to the Middle Way (trans. by J. Hopkins, L. Rinbochay, and others), 1975; (assist. ed.) Nagarjuna, The Precious Garland and the Song of the Four Mindfulnesses (trans. by Hopkins and Rinbochay), 1975; (assist. ed.) Khensur Ngawang Lekden and Tsong-ka-ba, Compassion in Tibetan Buddhism (trans. by Hopkins), 1980; (ed. with Hopkins) Khetsun Sangpo, Tantric Practice in Nyingma (trans. by Hopkins), 1982; (ed.) Hopkins, The Tantric Distinction, 1984; Knowledge and Liberation: Tibetan Buddhist Epistemology in Support of Transformative Religious Experience, 1986; Knowing, Naming, and Negation: A Sourcebook on Tibetan Sautrantika, 1991; (ed. with L. Zahler) Geshe Gedun Lodro, Walking through Walls (trans. by Hopkins), 1992; Path to the Middle: Oral Madhyamika Philosophy in Tibet, the Spoken Scholarship of Kensur Yeshey Tupden, 1994; Meeting the Great Bliss Queen: Buddhists, Feminists, and the Art of the Self, 1995. Contributor to books. Contributor of articles and reviews to scholarly journals. **Address:** Department of Religious Studies, Rice University, Box 1892, Houston, TX 77251, U.S.A.

KLEIN, Cornelis. American (born Netherlands), b. 1937. **Genres:** Earth sciences. **Career:** Harvard University, Cambridge, MA, lecturer, 1965-69, associate professor of mineralogy, 1969-72, Allston Burr senior tutor at Leverett House, 1966-70; Indiana University-Bloomington, professor of mineralogy, 1972-84; University of New Mexico, Albuquerque, professor of geology, 1984-. **Publications:** (with Hurlbut) Manual of Mineralogy, 19th ed, 1977, 21st ed, 1993; (co-ed) The Proterozoic Biosphere. **Address:** Department of Earth and Planetary Sciences, University of New Mexico, Albuquerque, NM 87131, U.S.A.

KLEIN, Donald F. American, b. 1928. **Genres:** Medicine/Health, Psychology. **Career:** U.S. Public Health Service Hospital, Staten Island, NY, rotating intern, 1952-53; Creedmoor State Hospital, resident in psychiatry, 1953-54 and 1956-58; Creedmoor Institute for Psychobiologic Studies, research associate, 1957-59; Hillside Hospital, research associate, 1959-64, senior staff psychiatrist, 1965, director of research, 1965-70, medical director for evaluation, 1970-71; State University of New York at Stony Brook, professor of psychiatry, 1972-76; Columbia University, NYC, lecturer, 1976-78, professor of psychiatry, 1978-, director of Department of Therapeutics, 1976-, director of New York State Psychiatric Institute, 1976-. Qualified psychiatrist, State of New York; diplomate, National Board of Medical Examiners, American Board of Psychiatry and Neurology, and American Board of Clinical Pharmacology. Queens Hospital Center, psychiatrist in chief, 1970-71, full attending psychiatrist, 1972-85; Presbyterian Hospital, attending psychiatrist, 1977-. Long Island Jewish-Hillside Medical Center, director of research and evaluation in psychiatry, 1972-76; New York State Psychiatric Mental Health Clinical Research Center, director, 1978-. Queens College of the City University of New York, adjunct professor, 1969-92; visiting professor at University of Auckland, 1975, Albert Einstein College of Medicine, Yeshiva University, 1976-77, and University of Hawaii at Manoa, 1977, 1985, and 1986. **Publications:** (with J.M. Davis) Diagnosis and Drug Treatment of Psychiatric Disorders, 1969, 2nd ed (with R. Gittelman, F. Quitkin, and A. Rifkin) as Diagnosis and Drug Treatment of Psychiatric Disorders: Adults and Children, 1980; Psychiatric Case Studies: Treatment, Drugs, and Outcome, 1972; The Physicians Handbook on Depression, 1977; (with P.H. Wender) Mind, Mood, and Medicine: A Guide to the New Biopsychiatry, 1981; (with Wender) Do You Have a Depressive Illness?, 1988; (with Wender) Understanding Depression, 1993. EDITOR: (with R. Gittelman-Klein, and contrib.) Progress in Psychiatric Drug Treatment, Vol I, 1975, Vol II, 1976; (with R.L. Spitzer, and contrib.) Evaluation of Psychological Therapies: Psychotherapies, Behavior Therapies, Drug Therapies, and Their Interactions, 1976; (with Spitzer, and contrib.) Critical

Issues in Psychiatric Diagnosis, 1978; (with J.G. Rabkin, and contrib.) Anxiety: New Research and Changing Concepts, 1981; (with M.R. Liebowitz, A.J. Fyer, and J.M. Gorman) Modern Problems of Pharmacopsychiatry, Vol XXII: Anxiety, 1987. Work represented in books. Contributor of articles and reviews to medical journals. **Address:** 1016 5th Ave Apt 14D, New York, NY 10028, U.S.A.

KLEIN, George. Swedish (born Hungary), b. 1925. **Genres:** Medicine/Health. **Career:** Budapest University, Hungary, instructor in histology, 1945, instructor in pathology, 1946; Karolinska Institute, Stockholm, Sweden, research fellow, 1947-49, assistant professor of cell research, 1951-57, professor of tumor biology and department head, 1957-. Institute for Cancer Research, guest investigator, 1950; Stanford University, visiting professor, 1961; Harvard University, Dunham Lecturer, 1966; American Association of Cancer Research, Clowes Memorial Lecturer, 1967; Swedish Medical Association, Lennander Lecturer, 1967; Hebrew University, visiting professor, 1973-; University of Arizona, Donald Wae Waddel Lecturer, 1991. **Publications:** DNA-Virus Oncogenes and Their Action, 1983; Istallet for Hemland, 1984; Mechanisms of Neoplastic Transformation at the Cellular Level: Advances in Viral Oncology, 1984; Ateisten och den Heliga Staden, 1987; Pieta, 1989; Tumorigenic DNA Viruses, 1989; The Atheist and the Holy City: Encounters and Reflections, 1990; (with P. Ahlmark) Motstandet, 1991; Utvagen, 1992; (with L. Gyllensten) Hack i hal pa Minerva, 1993; Den Sjunde Dajvulen, 1995; Live Now, 1997. EDITOR: Viral Oncology, 1980; Oncogene Studies, 1982; The Transformation-Associated Cellular p53 Protein, 1982; Viruses as the Causative Agents of Naturally Occurring Tumors, 1985; Analysis of Multistep Scenarios in the Natural History of Human or Animal Cancer, 1987; Experimental Approaches to Multifactorial Interactions in Tumor Development, 1987. **Address:** MTC, Karolinska Institute, Box 280, 171 77 Stockholm, Sweden. **Online address:** georg.klein@mtc.ki.se

KLEIN, Josephine (F. H.). British, b. 1926. **Genres:** Psychiatry, Sociology, Theology/Religion. **Career:** Assistant Lecturer, and Lecturer in Social Psychology, University of Birmingham, 1949-62; Research Fellow, Nuffield College, Oxford, 1962-65; Reader in Social Relations, University of Sussex, 1965-70; Director, Community and Youth Work Training, Goldsmiths' College, University of London, 1970-74; private practice in psychotherapy. **Publications:** The Study of Groups, 1956; Working with Groups, 1961; Samples from English Cultures, 1965; Our Need for Others and Its Roots in Infancy, 1987; Doubts and Certainties in the Practice of Psychology, 1995; Jacob's Ladder: Essays on Experiences of the Ineffable in the Context of Psychotherapy, 2003. **Address:** 58 Roupell St, London SE1, England.

KLEIN, Kathleen Gregory. American, b. 1946. **Genres:** Women's studies and issues, Literary criticism and history, Mystery/Crime/Suspense. **Career:** Indiana University-Purdue University at Indianapolis, assistant professor, 1976-80, associate professor of English and women's studies, 1980-88, coordinator of Women's Studies Program, 1978-82; Southern Connecticut State University, New Haven, professor of English, 1991-, chairperson of department, 1988-91. **Publications:** The Woman Detective: Gender and Genre, 1988, 1995; (ed.) Great Women Mystery Writers: Classic to Contemporary, 1994; Women Times Three: Writers, Detectives, Readers, 1995; Diversity & Detective Fiction: Race, Gender, Ethnicity, 1999. **Address:** Department of English, Southern Connecticut State University, 501 Crescent St, New Haven, CT 06515, U.S.A. **Online address:** kleinrkr@aol.com

KLEIN, Marcus. American, b. 1928. **Genres:** Novellas/Short stories, Literary criticism and history. **Career:** State University of New York, Buffalo, professor of English, 1965-. **Publications:** After Alienation: American Novels in Mid-Century, 1964; Foreigners: The Making of Modern American Literature 1900-1940, 1981; Easterns, Westerns, and Private Eyes: American Matters 1870-1900, 1994. EDITOR: (with R. Pack) Innocence and Experience, 1966; (with R. Pack) Short Stories: Classic, Modern, Contemporary, 1967; The American Novel since World War II, 1969. **Address:** 12896 Rock Ridge Ln, Valley Center, CA 92082-5452, U.S.A.

KLEIN, Norman M. American, b. 1945. **Genres:** Art/Art history. **Career:** Educator and author. California Institute of the Arts, Valencia, CA, professor in European studies, popular culture, and writing, 1974-. KCET, Los Angeles, series advisor, Los Angeles History Project, 1989-90; Art Issues, contributing editor, 1989-; Smithsonian Institute, Washington, DC, associate curator of "Conflicting Promises" exhibition, 1994. **Publications:** Seven Minutes: The Life and Death of the American Animated Cartoon, 1993; The History of Forgetting: Los Angeles and the Erasure of Memory, 1997. EDITOR: (with R. Hertz) Twentieth-Century Art Theory: Urbanism, Politics, Mass Culture,

1990; (with M.J. Schiesl) Twentieth-Century Los Angeles: Power, Promotion, and Social Conflict, 1990. **Address:** School of Critical Studies, California Institute of the Arts, Valencia, CA 91355, U.S.A.

KLEIN, Philip Alexander. American, b. 1927. **Genres:** Economics. **Career:** National Bureau of Economic Research, NYC, New York City research staff, 1955-70, 1973-78; Pennsylvania State University, University Park, instructor, 1955-58, assistant professor, 1958-61, associate professor, 1961-68, professor of economics, 1968-2000, emeritus professor, 2000-; London School of Economics, academic visitor, 1973-74; Columbia University, Center for International Business Cycle Research, research associate, 1978-96; Econ Cycle Research Institute, NYC, senior research scholar, 1996-. **Publications:** Financial Adjustments to Unemployment, 1965; (with G.H. Moore) The Quality of Consumer Instalment Credit, 1967; (with R.L. Gordon) The Steel Industry and U.S. Business Cycles, 1971; The Cyclical Timing of Consumer Credit, 1920-1967, 1971; The Management of Market-Oriented Economics, 1973; (with G.H. Moore) Monitoring Business Cycles in Market-Oriented Countries, 1985; (ed.) Analyzing Modern Business Cycles, 1990; (with M.P. Niemira) Forecasting Financial & Economic Cycles, 1994; (ed.) The Role of Economic Theory, 1994; Beyond Dissent, Essays in Institutional Economics, 1994. **Address:** Dept of Economics, Pennsylvania State University, 516 Kern Graduate Bldg, University Park, PA 16802, U.S.A. **Online address:** pak11@psu.edu

KLEIN, Rachel S. American, b. 1953. **Genres:** Art/Art history, History. **Career:** Writer. **Publications:** (with L. Rexer) One-Hundred-Twenty-Five Years of Expedition and Discovery: The American Museum of Natural History, 1995; Moonlight and Music (juvenile art book), 1997. Contributor of fiction to journals. **Address:** 112 Park Pl., Brooklyn, NY 11217, U.S.A.

KLEIN, Richard. American, b. 1941. **Genres:** Food and Wine. **Career:** Yale University, New Haven, CT, instructor, 1966-68; Johns Hopkins University, Baltimore, MD, assistant professor, 1968-74, director of the graduate program in Paris, 1973-74; Cornell University, Ithaca, NY, associate professor, 1974-87, professor, 1988-, director of the Cornell in Paris program, 1986-87 and 1990-91, director of Cornell Abroad, 1990-91. **Publications:** Cigarettes Are Sublime, 1993; Eat Fat, 1996; Jewelry Talks, 2001. Contributor of articles to periodicals and academic journals. **Address:** Department of Romance Studies, Cornell University, Ithaca, NY 14853, U.S.A.

KLEIN, Robin (McMaugh). Australian, b. 1936. **Genres:** Children's fiction, Novellas/Short stories. **Publications:** The Giraffe in Pepperell, 1978; Honoured Guest, 1979; Sprung!, 1982; Things, 1982; Penny Pollard's Diary, 1983; Junk Castle, 1983; Oodoolay, 1983; People Might Hear You, 1984; Brock and the Dragon, 1984; Hating Alison Ashley, 1984; Penny Pollard's Letters, 1984; Ratbags and Rascals, 1984; Thalia the Failure, 1984; Thingnapped!, 1984; The Tomb Comb, 1984; Annabel's Ghost (stories), 1985; Good for Something (audio book), 1985; Snakes and ladders, 1985; Serve Him Right! (audio book), 1985; You're on Your Own, (audio book), 1985; The Enemies, 1985; Halfway across the Galaxy and Turn Left, 1986; Separate Places, 1985; Boss of the Pool, 1986; Games, 1986; Penny Pollard in Print, 1986; The Princess Who Hated It, 1986; Birk the Berserker, 1987; Get Lost, 1987; Christmas, 1987; Crookbook, 1987; Don't Tell Lucy, 1987; I Shot an Arrow, 1987; The Last Pirate, 1987; (with M. Dann) The Lonely Hearts Club, 1987; Parker-Hamilton, 1987; Laurie Loved Me Best, 1988; Dear Robin: Letters to Robin Klein, 1988; Penny Pollard's Passport, 1988; Against the Odds, 1989; The Ghost in Abigail Terrace, 1989; Come Back to Show You I Could Fly, 1989; Penny Pollard's Guide to Modern Manners, 1989; Tearaways, 1990; Boris and Borsch, 1990; All in the Blue Unclouded Weather, 1991; Dresses of Red and Gold, 1992; Amy's Bed, 1992; Seeing Things, 1993; Turn Right for Zyrgon, 1994; The Sky in Silver Lace, 1995; Thing's Concert, 1996; Thing's Birthday, 1996; Thing Finds a Job, 1996; Thingitis, 1996; The Listmaker, 1997; Bedtime Stories, 1997; Gabby's Fair, 1998; The Goddess, 1998. **Address:** c/o Author Mail, Curtis Brown Ltd, PO Box 19, Paddington, NSW 2021, Australia.

KLEIN, Sherwin. American, b. 1932. **Genres:** Ethics. **Career:** Rutgers University, New Brunswick, NJ, adjunct instructor in philosophy, 1960-64; Fairleigh Dickinson University, Edward Williams College, Hackensack, NJ, assistant professor, 1965-75, associate professor, 1975-82, professor, 1982-. Kean College of New Jersey, guest lecturer, 1976; part-time faculty member at Bergen Community College, Brooklyn College of the City University of New York, Long Island University, Montclair State College, and Seton Hall University. **Publications:** Business Ethics: Reflections from a Platonic Point of View, 1993, reprinted, 1995. Contributor to philosophy and business ethics journals. **Address:** New College for General and Continuing Studies, Fairleigh Dickinson University, 150 Kotte Pl., Hackensack, NJ 07601, U.S.A.

KLEIN, Zachary. American, b. 1948. **Genres:** Novels. **Career:** Worked for Volunteers in Service to America (VISTA), Chicago, IL; Chicago Peoples' School; Project Place, Boston, MA; and Sanctuary, Boston. Past member, Chicago Model City's Community Board. **Publications:** NOVELS: Still among the Living, 1990; Two Way Toll, 1991; No Saving Grace, 1994. **Address:** c/o Herb Katz, 151 E 83rd St, New York, NY 10028, U.S.A. **Online address:** ZacharyWKlein@aol.com

KLEINDIENST, Kris. American, b. 1953. **Genres:** Essays. **Career:** Left Bank Books, St. Louis, MO, co-owner, 1977-; writer; political activist. Booksellers advisory board member for Paris Review. **Publications:** (editor) This Is What Lesbian Looks Like: Dyke Activists Take on the Twenty-first Century, 1999. Also columnist for a newspaper. **Address:** 3631 Bellerive Blvd., St. Louis, MO 63116, U.S.A. **Online address:** kriski@primary.net

KLEINE-AHLBRANDT, William Laird. American, b. 1932. **Genres:** History. **Career:** Purdue University, Lafayette, IN, professor, 1963-. Ordre des Palmes Academiques, Chevalier, 1996. **Publications:** The Policy of Simmering: A Study of British Policy during the Spanish Civil War 1936-39, 1963; (ed.) The Appeasement of the Dictators Crisis Diplomacy, 1970; La Tosca, The Drama behind the Opera, 1990; Twentieth Century European History, 1992; Europe since 1945, from Conflict to Community, 1993; The Burden of Victory, France, Britain and the Enforcement of the Treaty of Versailles, 1919-1925, 1995; Bitter Prerequisites: A Faculty for Survival from Nazi Terror, 2001. **Address:** Dept. of History, Purdue University, West Lafayette, IN 47906, U.S.A. **Online address:** ferney@purdue.edu

KLEINER, Diana E. E. American, b. 1947. **Genres:** Art/Art history. **Career:** University of Virginia, Charlottesville, lecturer, 1975-76, assistant professor of the history of art, 1976-78; University of Massachusetts, Boston, visiting assistant professor of the history of art, 1979; Harvard University, Cambridge, MA, Mellon faculty fellow, 1979-80; Yale University, New Haven, CT, assistant professor, 1980-82, associate professor, 1982-89, professor of the history of art classics, 1989-, Dunham Professor of Classics and History of Art, 1995-, Deputy Provost for the Arts, 1995-2003. Member of advisory boards of professional journals and boards of directors of schools. **Publications:** Roman Group Portraiture, 1977; The Monument of Philopappos in Athens, 1983; Roman Imperial Funerary Altars with Portraits, 1987; Roman Sculpture, 1992. EDITOR: I Claudia: Women in Ancient Rome, 1996; I Claudia II: Women in Roman Art and Society, 2000. **Address:** History of Art Dept, Yale University, 56 High St, New Haven, CT 06520, U.S.A.

KLEINER, Fred S. American, b. 1948. **Genres:** Archaeology/Antiquities, Art/Art history. **Career:** American School of Classical Studies at Athens, Greece, Agora fellow, 1973-75; University of Virginia, Charlottesville, assistant professor, 1975-78; Boston University, MA, assistant professor, 1978-81, associate professor, 1981-86, professor of art history and archaeology, 1986-, chairperson, Department of Art History, 1981-85, director of graduate studies, 1979-81. American Journal of Archaeology, editor-in-chief, 1985-98; Yale University, visiting professor, 1997. **Publications:** Greek and Roman Coins in the Athenian Agora, 1976; The Early Cistophoric Coinage, 1977; Mediaeval and Modern Coins in the Athenian Agora, 1978; The Arch of Nero in Rome, 1985; (with R.G. Tansey) Gardner's Art through the Ages, 10th ed., 1996, 12th ed. (and with C.J. Mamiya), 2004. Contributor of articles and reviews to scholarly journals in the United States and abroad. **Address:** Art History Dept, Boston University, 725 Commonwealth Ave, Boston, MA 02215, U.S.A. **Online address:** fsk@bu.edu

KLEINMAN, Philip (Julian). British, b. 1932. **Genres:** Advertising/Public relations, Marketing. **Career:** Agence France-Presse, Paris, sub-editor, 1961-63; Daily Telegraph, London, England, sub-editor, 1964-68; Campaign, London, associate editor, 1968-72; Adweek, London, editor, 1972-74; freelance journalist and writer, 1974-; Admap magazine, market research columnist, 1986-. Chairman of Lagado Ltd, publishing and marketing consultancy company. **Publications:** Advertising Inside Out, 1977; Market Research: Head Counting Becomes Big Business, 1985; The Saatchi & Saatchi Story, 1987; World Advertising Review, 1983, 1984, 1985, 1986, 1988, 1989, 1990, 1991. **Address:** 18 Tremlett Grove, London N19 5JX, England.

KLEINSASSER, Lois. Also writes as Cait Logan, Cait London. American. **Genres:** Romance/Historical. **Career:** Novelist. **Publications:** AS CAIT LOGAN: Lady on the Line, 1986; Rugged Glory, 1986; Gambler's Lady, 1987; Lady's Choice, 1988; Lady's Desire, 1988; Tame the Fury, 1990; Wild Dawn, 1992; Night Fire, 1994; Delilah, 1995; The Wedding Gamble, 1996; Be Mine, 1997; Lady Desperado, 1997. AS CAIT LONDON: The Loving Season, 1989; Angel vs. Maclean, 1990; The Pendragon Virus, 1990; Midnight Rider, 1992; The Cowboy, 1993; Maybe No, Maybe Yes, 1993;

The Seduction of Jake Tallman, 1993; The Bride Says No, 1994; The Daddy Candidate, 1994; Fusion, 1994; Lightfoot and Loving, 1994; Every Girl's Guide to …, 1995; Miracles and Mistletoe, 1995; Mr. Easy, 1995; Every Groom's Guide to …, 1996; The Perfect Fit, 1998; Rafe Palladin: Man of Secrets, 1998; Scent of a Woman, 1998; Three Kisses, 1998; Blaylock's Bride, 1999. TALLCHIEF SERIES AS CAIT LONDON: The Cowboy and the Cradle, 1996; Tallchief's Bride, 1996; The Groom Candidate, 1997; Tallchief for Keeps, 1997; The Seduction of Fiona Tallchief, 1998. Contributor to books and periodicals. **Address:** c/o Silhouette Books, 233 Broadway Room 1001, New York, NY 10279-1001, U.S.A. **Online address:** caitlondon@7thgate.com

KLEMM, Barry. Australian, b. 1945. **Genres:** Novels. **Career:** Writer. **Publications:** NOVELS: The Tenth Hero, 1997; Last Voyage of the Albatross, 1998; Running Dogs, 2000. **Address:** Unit 20, The Clocktower, 255 Drummond St, Carlton 3053, Australia. **Online address:** barry@barryklemm.com

KLEMPNER, Joseph T(eller). American, b. 1940. **Genres:** Mystery/Crime/Suspense. **Career:** U.S. Treasury Department, Bureau of Narcotics, NYC, narcotics agent, 1964-66; Legal Aid Society, NYC, criminal defense attorney, 1966-68; self-employed criminal defense attorney, 1968-. **Publications:** Felony Murder (crime novel), 1995; Shoot the Moon, 1997; Change of Course, 1998; Flat Lake in Winter, 1999; Irreparable Damage, 2002; Fogbound, 2003. **Address:** PO Box 214, East Chatham, NY 12060, U.S.A. **Online address:** sandjklempner@taconic.net

KLEVEN, Elisa. Also writes as Elisa Schneider. American, b. 1958. **Genres:** Children's fiction, Illustrations. **Career:** Berkeley Hills Nursery School, Berkeley, CA, nursery school teacher, 1978-80; weaver and toy maker, 1980-84; Prospect School, El Cerrito, CA, fourth-grade and art teacher, 1984-86; writer and illustrator. **Publications:** (as Elisa Schneider) The Merry-Go-Round Dog, 1988; Ernst, 1989; The Lion and the Little Red Bird, 1992; (and illustrator) The Paper Princess, 1994; Hooray! A Pinata!, 1996; Puddle Pail, 1997; Monster in the House, 1998; Sun Bread, 2001; Dancing Deer and the Foolish Hunter, 2002. Illustrator of books by T. Brown, A. Dorros, K. Lotz, I. Wilner. **Address:** 1028 Peralta Ave, Albany, CA 94706-2402, U.S.A. **Online address:** EKleven@aol.com; www.elisakleven.com

KLIER, John Doyle. American, b. 1944. **Genres:** Cultural/Ethnic topics. **Career:** Fort Hays State University, Hays, KS, instructor, 1971-83, professor of history, 1983-89; University College London, London, England, Sidney and Elizabeth Corob Lecturer in Modern Jewish History, 1990-93, Sidney and Elizabeth Corob Reader in Modern Jewish History, 1993-95, head of department of Hebrew and Jewish Studies, 1993-2002, Sidney and Elizabeth Professor of Modern Jewish History, 1996-. Grant reviewer for U.S. Department of Education. **Publications:** Russia Gathers Her Jews: The Origins of the Jewish Question in Russia, 1772-1825, 1986; (ed. with S. Lambroza) Pogroms: Anti-Jewish Violence in Modern Russian History, 1991; Imperial Russia's Jewish Question, 1855-1881, 1995; (with H. Mingay) The Search for Anastasia: Solving the Mystery of the Lost Romanovs, 1995. Contributor to anthologies, periodicals, and radio programs. **Address:** Dept of Hebrew and Jewish Studies, University College London, Gower St, London WC1E 6BT, England. **Online address:** j.klier@ucl.ac.uk

KLIMAN, Bernice W. American, b. 1933. **Genres:** Literary criticism and history. **Career:** Long Island University, Greenvale, NY, instructor at C.W. Post College, 1964; State University of New York at Stony Brook, instructor, 1964-66; Long Island University, C.W. Post College, instructor, 1967-68; Queens College of the City University of New York, Flushing, NY, instructor, 1969-73; Bernard M. Baruch College of the City University of New York, NYC, assistant professor, 1974-75; Nassau Community College of the State University of New York, Garden City, professor, 1976-99, emeritus, 1999-. Yale University, visiting fellow at Davenport College, 1973, 1975, 1977, 1979; visiting scholar at Bowdoin College, 1989, and James Madison University, 1992; speaker at colleges and universities; co-founder and co-editor, Shakespeare on Film newsletter, 1976-92; coordinator and ed., new varionum Hamlet project. **Publications:** Hamlet: Film, Television, and Audio Performance, 1988; (ed. with P. Bertram) The Three-Text Hamlet: Parallel Texts of the First and Second Quartos and First Folio, 1991; Macbeth, 1992; The Enfolded Hamlet (monograph), 1996. Contributor to anthologies on Shakespeare. Contributor of articles and reviews to periodicals. **Address:** 70 Glen Cove Dr, Glen Head, NY 11545, U.S.A. **Online address:** bkliman@optonline.net

KLINE, Lisa Williams. American, b. 1954. **Genres:** Novels. **Career:** UNC-TV, Chapel Hill, NC, writer/researcher, 1976-78; Arthur Andersen Video Training, Division, Elgin, IL, video training writer, 1978-81; Gaithersburg, MD, freelance writer, 1981-. **Publications:** Eleanor Hill, 1999; The Princesses of Atlantis, 2002. **Address:** c/o Nancy Gallt, 273 Charlton Ave., South Orange, NJ 07079, U.S.A. **Online address:** lisa73154@aol.com

KLINE, Ronald R. American, b. 1947. **Genres:** History, Intellectual history, Biography. **Career:** IEEE Center for History of Electric Engineering, director, 1984-87; Cornell University, Ithaca, NY, assistant professor, 1987-93, associate professor, 1993-2001, professor of history of technology, 2001-. **Publications:** Steinmetz: Engineer and Socialist, 1992; Consumers in the Country, 2000. **Address:** 394 Rhodes Hall, Cornell University, Ithaca, NY 14850, U.S.A.

KLING, Christine. American. **Genres:** Marine sciences/Oceanography. **Career:** Seawoman, writer, and teacher. Worked as a bookstore clerk, deckhand, boat cook, windsurfing instructor, and charter boat operator. Broward County school system, Fort Lauderdale, FL, coordinator of magnet programs. **Publications:** Surface Tension, 2002; Cross Current, 2003. Contributor to periodicals. **Address:** c/o Author Mail, Random House, 1745 Broadway, New York, NY 10019, U.S.A.

KLINGENSTEIN, Susanne. American (born Germany), b. 1959. **Genres:** Cultural/Ethnic topics, Intellectual history, Literary criticism and history, Writing/Journalism, Essays. **Career:** University of Mannheim, Germany, assistant professor of English, 1986-87; Harvard University, Cambridge, MA, instructor, 1989-90, lecturer in English and American literature, 1990-92; Massachusetts Institute of Technology, Cambridge, assistant professor, 1993-96, associate professor of writing and humanistic studies, 1997-2001; Harvard-MIT Division of Health Sciences and Technology, lecturer, 2001-; Boston University, College of Communication, Dept of Journalism, lecturer, 2003-. Frankfurter Allgemeine Zeitung, cultural correspondent, 2000-. **Publications:** Jews in the American Academy, 1900-1940: The Dynamics of Intellectual Assimilation, 1991; Enlarging America: The Cultural Work of Jewish Literary Scholars, 1930-1990, 1998. **Address:** HST, E25-518, E14-333, Massachusetts Institute of Technology, Cambridge, MA 02139, U.S.A. **Online address:** sklingenstein@rcn.com

KLINGER, Eric. American (born Austria), b. 1933. **Genres:** Psychology. **Career:** University of Wisconsin, Madison, instructor in psychology, 1960-62; University of Minnesota, Morris, assistant professor, 1962-63, associate professor, 1963-69, professor of psychology, 1969-; University of Minnesota, Minneapolis, professor of psychology, 1978-. **Publications:** Structure and Functions of Fantasy, 1971; Meaning and Void: Inner Experience and the Incentives in People's Lives, 1977; Daydreaming, 1990. EDITOR: Imagery: vol. II: Concepts, Results and Applications, 1981; (with W.M. Cox) Handbook of Motivational Counseling, 2004. Contributor to books and periodicals. **Address:** Division of Social Sciences, University of Minnesota-Morris, Morris, MN 56267, U.S.A. **Online address:** klinger@umn.edu

KLITZMAN, Robert (L.). American, b. 1958. **Genres:** Gay and lesbian issues, Medicine/Health, Psychiatry, Sciences, Travel/Exploration. **Career:** National Institutes of Health, Bethesda, MD, research aide, 1980-81; Cornell University Medical Center, New York City, intern, 1985-86, resident, 1986-89; Columbia Presbyterian Medical Center, New York City, fellow, 1989-, assistant professor, 1996-. **Publications:** A Year-Long Night: Tales of a Medical Internship, 1989; In a House of Dreams and Glass: Becoming a Psychiatrist, 1995; Being Positive: The Lives of Men and Women with HIV, 1997; The Trembling Mountain: A Personal Account of Kuru, Cannibals and Mad Cow Disease, 1998. Contributor to periodicals. **Address:** c/o Kristine Dahl, International Creative Management, 40 W 57th St, New York, NY 10019, U.S.A.

KLUGER, Ruth. American (born Austria), b. 1931. **Genres:** Autobiography/Memoirs. **Career:** Educator. Princeton University, Princeton, NJ, professor and chair of German department; University of California-Irvine, professor of German, then emeritus. **Publications:** Weiter leben: eine jugend, 1992, trans. as Still Alive: A Holocaust Girlhood Remembered, 2001. **Address:** c/o Department of German, 400A Murray Krieger Hall, University of California, Irvine, CA 92697, U.S.A. **Online address:** rkluger@uci.edu

KLUGER, Steve. American, b. 1952. **Genres:** Novels, Plays/Screenplays, Adult non-fiction. **Publications:** FICTION: Changing Pitches, 1984; Bullpen, 1990; Last Days of Summer, 1998; Almost Like Being in Love, 2004. NON-FICTION: Lawyers Say the Darndest Things, 1990; Yank: World War II from the Guys Who Brought You Victory, 1990. PLAYS: Bullpen, 1984; Cafe 50's, 1988; Pilots of the Purple Twilight, 1989; After Dark, 1998. **Ad-**

dress: c/o Gail Hochman, Brandt & Hochman Literary Agents, 1501 Broadway Ste 2310, New York, NY 10036, U.S.A.

KLYZA, Christopher McGrory. American, b. 1959. **Genres:** Agriculture/Forestry, Politics/Government, Environmental sciences/Ecology, Natural history. **Career:** Minnesota Department of Natural Resources, Bureau of Land Management, St. Paul, research analyst, summers, 1984-85; University of Minnesota-Twin Cities, Minneapolis, instructor in political science, 1986-88, research analyst at Center for Urban and Regional Affairs, 1987-88; University of Vermont, Burlington, visiting instructor in political science, 1988-90; Middlebury College, Middlebury, VT, assistant professor, 1990-95, director of Program in Environmental Studies, 1994-97, 2000-, associate professor of political science, 1995-2000, professor of political science and environmental studies, 2000-. Lecturer at colleges and universities. **Publications:** (ed. with S.C. Trombulak, and contrib.) The Future of the Northern Forest, 1994; Who Controls Public Lands? Mining, Forestry, and Grazing Policies, 1870-1990, 1996; (with S.C. Trombulak) The Story of Vermont: A Natural and Cultural History, 1999; (ed.) Wilderness Comes Home: Rebuilding the Northeast, 2001. Contributor to books. Contributor of articles and reviews to political science and environmental journals. **Address:** Department of Political Science, Middlebury College, Middlebury, VT 05753, U.S.A.

KNAPP, Edward. *See* **KUNHARDT, Edith.**

KNAPP, Sara D. American, b. 1936. **Genres:** Librarianship. **Career:** Albany Medical Center, Albany, NY, social case work aide, 1958-63; New York State Library, Albany, assistant library supervisor in Division of Library Development, 1964-67; State University of New York at Albany, assistant librarian, 1967-70, associate librarian, 1970-79, librarian, 1979-, cataloger, 1967-68, head of Periodicals Section, 1968-69, head of Serials and Bindery Department, 1969-71, reference librarian, 1971-72, head of Bibliographic Services Unit, 1972, coordinator of Computer Search Service Unit, 1972-. Bibliographic Retrieval Services Inc., editor of the database BRS/TERM, 1983-89; consultant to Medical Reliance Co. and Bancroft Group. Capital District Library Council, member, 1969-, chairperson of Computer Based Reference Services Committee, Online Users Group, 1975-76. Colonie Public Library, volunteer, 1965-67; Clinton Square Neighborhood House, volunteer, 1965-67; Volunteers in Technical Assistance, volunteer for library research, 1967-; First Unitarian Church of Albany, chairperson of Channing Bookstore, 1966-68, 197071; Wheels to Independence, vice-president, 1974; Albany County Department of Social Services, member of advisory board of Infoline, 1979-85; member of Westlawn Neighborhood Improvement Association. **Publications:** BRS Training Workbook: An Introduction to Searching on the BRS System With Practice Exercises From the ERIC Database, Bibliographic Retrieval Services, 1979, revised edition, 1981; (Compiler) The Contemporary Thesaurus of Social Science Terms and Synonyms: A Guide for Natural Language Computer Searching, Oryx, 1993. Contributor of articles to library journals. Member of editorial board, College and Research Libraries, 1980-81. **Address:** University Library, State University of New York at Albany, 1400 Washington Ave., Albany, NY 12203, U.S.A.

KNAPPERT, Jan. Dutch, b. 1927. **Genres:** Mythology/Folklore, Anthropology/Ethnology, Literary criticism and history. **Career:** University of London, School of Oriental and African Studies, staff member, 1964-86; University of Louvain, Belgium, professor of sociolinguistics, 1971-96. Lecturer throughout world. **Publications:** Essai d'un dictionnnaire Alur-Francais-Anglais-Neerlandais, 1965; Traditional Swahili Poetry: An Investigation into the Concepts of East African Islam as Reflected in the Utenzi Literature, 1967; Un siecle de classification des langues Bantoues 1844-1945, 1970; (with J.D. Pearson and K. Ley) Encyclopaedia of Africa, 1978; (ed., translator and author of intro) Four Centuries of Swahili Verse: A Literary History and Anthology, 1979; Malay Myths and Legends, 1980; Namibia, Land and Peoples, Myths and Fables, 1981; Epic Poetry in Swahili and Other African Languages, 1983; Islamic Legends: Histories of the Heroes, Saints, and Prophets of Islam, 2 vols., 1985; (with A. Rippin) Textual Sources for the Study of Islam, 1986; Introduction to the Afrikaans Language, 1987; Proverbs from the Lamu Archipelago and the Central Kenya Coast, 1986; (ed. and translator, with A. Rippin) Textual Sources for the Study of Islam, 1986; The Encyclopaedia of Middle Eastern Mythology and Religion, 1993; East Africa: Kenya, Tanzania and Uganda, 1987; The A-Z of African Proverbs, 1989; The Aquarian Guide to African Mythology, 1991; Indian Mythology, 1991; Pacific Mythology, 1992; The A-Z of African Songs, 1997; Swahili Proverbs, 1997. COLLECTOR & TRANSLATOR: Myths and Legends of the Swahili, 1970; (and author of intro) Myths and Legends of the Congo, 1971; Swahili Islamic Poetry, 3 vols, 1971; An Anthology of Swahili Love Poetry, 1972, in UK as A Choice of Flowers: Chaguo la Maua;

An Anthology of Swahili Love Poetry; Tales of Mystery and Miracle from Morocco, 1976; Bantu Myths and Other Tales, 1977; Myths and Legends of Indonesia, 1977; Fables from Africa, 1980; Myths and Legends of Botswana, Lesotho, and Swaziland, 1985; Kings, Gods, and Spirits from African Mythology, 1986. **Address:** Tomakker 72, 5673 LG Nuenen, Netherlands.

KNAUFT, Bruce M. American, b. 1954. **Genres:** Anthropology/Ethnology. **Career:** University of California, San Diego, La Jolla, postdoctoral research fellow, 1983-85; Emory University, Atlanta, GA, assistant professor, 1985-90, associate professor of anthropology, 1990-. Conducted field research in Papua New Guinea. **Publications:** Good Company and Violence: Sorcery and Social Action in a Lowland New Guinea Society, 1985; South Coast New Guinea Cultures: History, Comparison, Dialectic, 1993. Work represented in anthologies. Contributor to anthropology journals. **Address:** Department of Anthropology, Emory University, Atlanta, GA 30322, U.S.A.

KNECHT, Heidi. American, b. 1961. **Genres:** Anthropology/Ethnology, Archaeology/Antiquities. **Career:** University of Miami, Coral Gables, FL, adjunct assistant professor, 1991-96; New York University, NYC, visiting scholar, 1996-. Thinking Strings, partner, 1998-. **Publications:** EDITOR & CONTRIBUTOR: (with A. Pike-Tay and R. White) Before Lascaux: The Complex Record of the Early Upper Paleolithic, 1993; Projectile Technology, 1998. Contributor to books and scholarly journals. **Address:** Thinking Strings, PO Box 537, South Orange, NJ 07079, U.S.A. **Online address:** hkatz@thinkingstrings.com

KNECHT, Robert Jean. British, b. 1926. **Genres:** History. **Career:** University of Birmingham, lecturer, 1959-68, sr. lecturer, 1968-77, reader, 1977-85, professor of French history, 1985-92, emeritus professor and honorary senior research fellow in modern history, 1993-. **Publications:** (ed.) The Voyage of Sir Nicholas Carewe, 1959; Renaissance and Reformation, 1967; Francis I and Absolute Monarchy, 1969; The Fronde, 1975; (co-ed.) Wealth and Power in Tudor England, 1978; Francis I, 1982; French Renaissance Monarchy: Francis I and Henry II, 1984, rev. ed., 1996; French Wars of Religion, 1989, rev. ed., 1996; Richelieu, 1991; Renaissance Warrior and Patron: The Reign of Francis I, 1994; The Rise and Fall of Renaissance France, 1996, 2nd ed., 2001; Richelieu, 1997; Un prince de la Renaissance: Francois 1et et son royaume, 1998; Catherine de' Medici, 1998; The French Civil Wars, 2000; The French Religious Wars, 1562-98, 2002. **Address:** 79 Reddings Rd, Moseley, Birmingham B13 8LP, England.

KNEELAND, Timothy (W). American, b. 1962. **Genres:** History. **Career:** Oklahoma Junior College, Oklahoma City, OK, Social & Behavior Science chair, 1989-93; Greenville College, Greenville, IL, assistant professor of history, 1996-2000; Nazareth College, Rochester, NY, assistant professor of history, 2000-. State & Science Study, researcher. **Publications:** PushButton Psychiatry: A History of Electroshock in America, 2002. Contributor to encyclopedias. Contributor of book reviews to periodicals. **Address:** Department of History, Nazareth College, 4245 E. Ave., Rochester, NY 14618, U.S.A. **Online address:** twkneela@naz.edu

KNEVITT, Charles (Philip Paul). British, b. 1952. **Genres:** Architecture. **Career:** Free-lance architectural journalist, 1974-78; What's New in Building, London, England, 1978-80; Sunday Telegraph, London, architecture correspondent, 1980-84; Times, London, architecture correspondent, 1984-. Editor of London Region Yearbook for Royal Institute of British Architects, 1980-82; program adviser for London Weekend Television, 1982, and Anglia Television, 1985; consultant to Thames Television News, 1983-; contributor to television and radio programs. **Publications:** Manikata: The Making of a Church, MPC Publications (Malta), 1980. Connections: The Architecture of Richard England, 196484, Lund, Humphries, 1984. Space on Earth: Architecture, People and Buildings, Methuen, 1985. (With Nick Wates) Community Architecture: How People Can Shape Their Own Environment, Penguin, 1986. (Editor) Monstrous Carbuncles: A Cartoon Guide to Architecture, Lund, Humphries, 1986. (Editor) Perspectives: An Anthology of 1001 Architectural Quotations, Lund, Humphries, 1986. **Address:** 200 Gray's Inn Rd., PO Box 7, London WC1X 8EZ, England.

KNIGHT, Alanna (Cleet). Also writes as Margaret Hope. British. **Genres:** Mystery/Crime/Suspense, Romance/Historical, Biography. **Career:** Society of Antiquaries, fellow. **Publications:** Legend of the Loch, 1969; The October Witch, 1971; This Outward Angel, 1972; Castle Clodha, 1972; Lament for Lost Lovers, 1972; The White Rose, 1973; A Stranger Came By, 1974; The Passionate Kindness, 1974; A Drink for the Bridge, 1976; The Wicked Wynsleys, 1977; The Black Duchess, 1980; Castle of Foxes, 1981; Colla's Children, 1982; The Clan, 1985; Estella, 1986; The Robert Louis Stevenson Treasury, 1986; RLS in the South Seas, 1987; Enter Second Murderer, 1988;

Blood Line, 1989; Deadly Beloved, 1989; Killing Cousins, 1990; A Quiet Death, 1991; To Kill a Queen, 1992; The Sweet Cheat Gone, 1992; Strathblair, 1993; This Outward Angel, 1993; (with E.S. Warfel) Bright Ring of Words: A Centennial Celebration of RLS, 1994; The Missing Duchess, 1994; The Bull Slayers, 1995; Murder by Appointment, 1996; The Coffin Lane Murders, 1998; Angel Eyes, 1998; The Royal Park Murder, 1998; The Monster in the Loch, 1999; Dead Beckoning, 1999; The Inspector's Daughter, 2000; The Dagger in the Crown, 2001; Dangerous Pursuits, 2002; The Final Enemy, 2002; Close & Deadly, 2002; An Orkney Murder, 2003; The Gowrie Conspiracy, 2003; Unholy Trinity, 2004; Ghost Walk, 2004. AS MARGARET HOPE: The Queen's Captain, 1978; Hostage Most Royal, 1979; The Shadow Queen, 1979; Perilous Voyage, 1983. **Address:** 24 March Hall Cres, Edinburgh EH16 5HL, Scotland. **Online address:** alanna.knight@virgin.net; www.alannaknight.com

KNIGHT, Amarantha. See KILPATRICK, Nancy.

KNIGHT, Bernard. Also writes as Bernard Picton. Welsh, b. 1931. **Genres:** Mystery/Crime/Suspense, Plays/Screenplays, Medicine/Health. **Career:** University of London, lecturer in forensic medicine, 1959-62; University of Wales, College of Medicine, lecturer, 1962-65, sr. lecturer, 1965-76, reader, 1976, professor and consultant in forensic pathology, 1989-96; University of Newcastle, sr. lecturer in forensic pathology, 1965-68. Medicine, Science and the Law, medical editor, 1960-63; Forensic Science International, editor, 1984-93. Crime Writer's Association Silver Dagger Award (non-fiction), adjudicator, 1999-2004. **Publications:** Murder, Suicide or Accident, 1971; Lion Rampant, 1972; Deg Y Dragwyddoldeb, 1972; Legal Aspects of Medical Practice, 1972, 5th ed., 1991; In the Dead, Behold the Quick (TV series), 1973; Edyfyn Brau, 1973; Autopsy 1977; Madoc, Prince of America, 1977; Discovering the Human Body, 1980; Forensic Radiology, 1981; Lawyer's Guide to Forensic Medicine, 1982, rev. ed., 1998; Sudden Death in Infancy, 1983; Coroner's Autopsy, 1983; Post-Mortem Technicians Handbook, 1984; Pocket Guide to Forensic Medicine, 1985; Forensic Medicine, 9th ed. (with K. Simpson), 1985, 11th ed., as Simpson's Forensic Medicine, 1997; Forensic Pathology, 1991, 3rd ed., 2004; Forensic Medicine documentary series, "Expert Witness," 1993; S4C TV Series "Dim Cliw," 1994; Crime Fiction Series HTV, "In at the Death," 1995; The Sanctuary Seeker, 1997; The Poisoned Chalice, 1998; Crowner's Quest, 1999; The Awful Secret, 2000; The Tinner's Corpse, 2001; The Grim Reaper, 2002; Fear in the Forest, 2003; Brennan, 2003; The Witch Hunters, 2004. AS BERNARD PICTON: The Lately Deceased, 1963; Thread of Evidence, 1965; Mistress Murder, 1966; Russian Roulette, 1968; Policeman's Progress, 1969; Tiger at Bay, 1970. **Address:** 26 Millwood, Cardiff CF14 0TL, Wales. **Online address:** knight@whodunnit.freeserve.co.uk

KNIGHT, D(avid) M(arcus). British. **Genres:** Intellectual history, Natural history, Sciences, Theology/Religion, Biography. **Career:** Professor in the History and Philosophy of Science, Dept. of Philosophy, University of Durham. General Ed., Cambridge Science Biographies; Ashgate series in history of science and technology. **Publications:** Atoms and Elements: A Study of Theories of Matter in England in the 19th Century, 1967; (ed.) Classical Scientific Paper: Chemistry, 1968, and Second Series, 1970; Natural Science Book in English 1600-1900, 1972; Sources for the History of Science 1660-1914, 1975; The Nature of Science: The History of Science in Western Culture since 1600, 1977; Zoological Illustrations: An Essay towards a History of Printed Zoological Pictures, 1977; The Transcendental Part of Chemistry, 1978; Ordering the World: A History of Classifying Man, 1981; The Age of Science, 1986; A Companion to the Physical Sciences, 1989; Ideas in Chemistry: A History of the Science, 1992; Humphry Davy: Science and Power, 1992; Science in the Romantic Era, 1998; Science and Spirituality: The Volatile Connection, 2004. **Address:** Dept. of Philosophy, University of Durham, 50 Old Elvet, Durham DH1 3HN, England. **Online address:** d.m.knight@durham.ac.uk

KNIGHT, David. See PRATHER, Richard Scott.

KNIGHT, Gareth. See WILBY, Basil Leslie.

KNIGHT, Hardwicke. British, b. 1911. **Genres:** History, Photography, Biography. **Career:** Chief Photographer, EMS Plastic Surgery Unit, Gloucester, England, 1941-46; Director of Medical Photography, Enfield Group Hospitals, England, 1948-57; Director of Medical Photography, University of Otago Medical School and Dunedin Hospital, 1957-78. President, New Zealand Institute of Medical Photographers, and Dunedin Film Society, 1966-77; Keeper of the Educational Photographic Collection, Otago Museum, Dunedin, New Zealand, 1971-91; Associate of the National Museum of New Zealand, 1990-. **Publications:** Archaeological Recording, 1960; Photography

in New Zealand: A Social and Technical Study, 1971; Dunedin Then, 1974; (with P. Coutts) Matanaka, 1975; History of Broad Bay School, 1977; Princes Street by Gaslight, 1976; Otago Peninsula, 1978, 3rd ed., 1980; (with S. Greif) Cutten, 1979; Burton Brothers, Photographers, 1980; The Ordeal of William Larnach, 1981; New Zealand Photographers, 1981; Otago Cavalcade, 7 vols., 1982-86; Hardwicke Knight, Photographer, 1983; Dunedin Early Photographs, 2 vols., 1984-85; Otago Early Photographs, 1988, 2 vols, 1988-1992; (with N. Wales) Buildings of Dunedin, 1988; Church Building in Otago, 1993; Morris Photography, 1994; Coxhead Brothers, Photographers, 1996; Joseph Weaver Allen, 1996; Russell Sedgfield: Pioneer Photographer, 2 vols., 1997. **Address:** Broad Bay, Dunedin, New Zealand.

KNIGHT, Harry Adam. See BROSNAN, John.

KNIGHT, Kathryn Lasky. See LASKY, Kathryn.

KNIGHT, Lynne. American, b. 1943. **Genres:** Novels. **Career:** Lowville Academy, Lowville, NY, English teacher and department head, 1970-90; Solano College, Suisun City, CA, and Contra Costa College, San Pablo, CA, part-time English instructor, 1990. **Publications:** Dissolving Borders, 1996; Snow Effects, 2000; The Book of Common Betrayals, 2002; Deer in Berkeley, 2004. Contributor of poetry to journals. **Address:** 1724 La Vereda Rd, Berkeley, CA 94709, U.S.A. **Online address:** lynneknight@yahoo.com

KNIGHTLEY, Phillip (George). Australian, b. 1929. **Genres:** History, Biography. **Career:** Copyboy, The Telegraph, Sydney, 1945-47; Reporter, the Northern Star, Lismore, 1948-49; Copra Trader and Assistant Ed., The Oceania Daily News, Fiji, 1950; Reporter, the Herald, Melbourne, 1952-54; Reporter, 1954-56, and Foreign Correspondent, 1956-60, The Daily Mirror, Sydney; Ed., Imprint, Bombay, 1960-62; with ABC, Sydney, 1963; Special Correspondent, The Sunday Times, 1965-85. **Publications:** (with B. Page and D. Leitch) Philby: The Spy Who Betrayed a Generation, 1968; (with H. Atkinson) The Games, 1968; (with C. Simpson) The Secret Lives of Lawrence of Arabia, 1969; The First Casualty: The War Correspondent as Hero Propagandist, and Myth-Maker, Crimea to Vietnam, 1975, rev. ed., 2000; Lawrence of Arabia, 1976; (with S. Fay) The Death of Venice, 1976; (ed.) Suffer the Children, 1979; The Vestey Affair, 1981; The Second Oldest Profession: The Spy as Bureaucrat, Patriot, Fantasist, and Whore, 1986; (with C. Kennedy) An Affair of State: The Profumo Case and the Framing of Stephen Ward, 1987; Philby: KGB Masterspy, 1988; A Hack's Progress, 1997; Australia: A Biography of a Nation, 2000. **Address:** 4 Northumberland Pl, London W2 5BS, England. **Online address:** phillipgk@aol.com

KNIPPENBERG, Joseph M. American, b. 1957. **Genres:** Politics/Government. **Career:** Oglethorpe University, Atlanta, GA, assistant professor, 1985-92, associate professor, 1992-; Boston College, visiting scholar, 1988-89; Emory University, Atlanta, GA, visiting associate professor, 1994. **Publications:** (ed., with P.A. Lawler) Poets, Princes, and Private Citizens: Literary Alternatives to Modern Politics, 1996. Contributor to periodicals. **Address:** Department of Political Science, Oglethorpe University, 4484 Peachtree Rd., Atlanta, GA 30319, U.S.A. **Online address:** jknippenbeg@ facstaff.oglethorpe.edu

KNOEPFLE, John. American, b. 1923. **Genres:** Poetry, Translations. **Career:** WCET Educational Television, Cincinnati, OH, Producer-Director, 1953-55; Ohio State University, Columbus, Assistant Instructor, 1956-57; Instructor, Southern Illinois University, East St. Louis, 1957-61, St. Louis University High School, 1961-62, and Mark Twain Institute, Clayton, Missouri, Summers 1962-64; Maryville College, St. Louis, Assistant Professor, 1962-66; Washington University College, St. Louis, Assistant Professor, 1963-66; St. Louis University, Associate Professor, 1966-72; Project Upward Bound, Washington, DC, Consultant, 1967-70; Sangmon State University, Springfield, IL, Professor of Literature, 1972-91. **Publications:** (trans. with R. Bly and J. Wright) Twenty Poems of Cesar Vallejo, 1961; Poets at the Gate, 1965; Rivers into Islands: A Book of Poems, 1965; Songs for Gail Guidry's Guitar, 1969; An Affair of Culture and Other Poems, 1969; After Gray Days and Other Poems, 1969; The Intricate Land: A Book of Poems, 1970; (with L. Mueller and D. Etter) Voyages to the Inland Sea: Essays and Poems, 1971; Dogs and Cats and Things Like That: A Book of Poems for Children, 1971; The Ten-Fifteen Community Poems, 1971; (trans. with R. Bly and J. Wright) Neruda and Vallejo: Selected Poems, 1971; Our Street Feels Good (for children), 1972; Whetstone: A Book of Poems, 1972; Deep Winter Poems, 1972; (with others) Regional Perspectives, 1973; Thinking of Offerings: Poems 1970-1973, 1975; A Gathering of Voices, 1978; (ed. with D. Jaffe) Frontier Literature: Images of the American West, 1979; A Box of Sandalwood: Love Poems, 1979; Poems for the Hours, 1979; Selected Poems, 1985; Poems from the Sangamon, 1985; (trans. with Wang Shou-yi) Tang

Dynasty Poems, 1985; (trans. with Wang Shou-yi), Sung Dynasty Poems, 1985; Dimtales, 1987; Begging an Amnesty, 1994; The Chinkapin Oak, 1995; The One Instant and Forever, 2001. **Address:** 2942 S Fillmore St, Springfield, IL 62704-4880, U.S.A. **Online address:** jackjohn@springnet1.com

KNOPP, Lisa. American, b. 1956. **Genres:** Essays. **Career:** Westside High School, Omaha, NE, English teacher, 1981-84; Western Illinois University, Macomb, teaching assistant, 1984-86; Valley High School, West Des Moines, IA, English teacher, 1986-88; University of Nebraska, Lincoln, teaching assistant, 1988-93, lecturer, 1994-95; Southern Illinois University, Carbondale, assistant professor, 1995-. **Publications:** Field of Vision (essays), 1996. Contributor of poems, articles and essays to newspapers, periodicals and anthologies. **Address:** English Department, Southern Illinois University, Carbondale, IL 62901, U.S.A.

KNOWLES, Dorothy. British (born Republic of South Africa), b. 1906. **Genres:** Film, Literary criticism and history. **Career:** Hon. Research Fellow, Royal Holloway and Bedford New College, University of London, since 1968. Lecturer in French, University of Liverpool, 1934-68. **Publications:** La Reaction idealiste au theatre depuis 1890, 1934; The Censor, the Drama and the Film 1900-1934, 1934; French Drama of the Inter-Wars Years 1918-1939, 1967; (co-author) Forces in Modern French Drama, 1972; Armand Gatti in the Theatre: Wild Duck against the Wind, 1989; Staging the Holocaust, 1998. Contributor to literary journals. **Address:** 48 Woodside Park Rd, London N12 8RS, England.

KNOWLES, Elizabeth. British, b. 1947. **Genres:** Language/Linguistics. **Career:** Oxford University Press, Oxford, England, staff member, then senior editor of English dictionary, 1983-93, publishing manager of Oxford quotation dictionaries, 1993-. **Publications:** EDITOR: Oxford Dictionary of New Words, 1997; Oxford Dictionary of Phrase, Saying, and Quotation, 1997; Oxford Dictionary of Twentieth Century Quotations, 1998; Oxford Dictionary of Quotations, 1999; Oxford Dictionary of Phrase and Fable, 2000; Oxford Dictionary of Modern Quotations, 2nd ed., 2002. **Address:** Oxford University Press, Great Clarendon St, Oxford OX2 6DP, England. **Online address:** elizabeth.knowles@oup.com

KNOWLES, Harry (Jay). American, b. 1971. **Genres:** Autobiography/Memoirs. **Career:** Founder of Web site Ain't It Cool News, 1996-; salesman of vintage film memorabilia. **Publications:** (with P. Cullum and M. Ebner) Ain't It Cool?: Hollywood's Redheaded Stepchild Speaks Out, 2002. **Address:** PO Box 180011, Austin, TX 78718, U.S.A. **Online address:** harry@aintitcool.com

KNOX, Bernard MacGregor Walker. American (born England), b. 1914. **Genres:** Classics, Literary criticism and history, Essays. **Career:** Professor of Classics, Yale University, New Haven, Conn., 1959-61; Director, Center for Hellenic Studies, Washington, D.C., 1961-85. Sather Lecturer, University of California, Berkeley, 1963; Nellie Wallace Lecturer, University of Oxford, 1975; Martin Lecturer, Oberlin College, Ohio, 1981; West Lecturer, Stanford University, California, 1984. Recipient: Guggenheim Fellowship, 1956-57; Award for Literature, National Institute of Arts and Letters, 1967; George Jean Nathan Award for Dramatic Criticism, 1978; NEH Jefferson Lecturer, 1992. **Publications:** Oedipus at Thebes, 1957; Oedipus the King, 1959; The Heroic Temper, 1964; Word and Action: Essays on the Ancient Theatre, 1979; Essays Ancient and Modern, 1989; The Oldest Dead White, European Males, 1993; (ed.) The Norton Book of Classical Literature, 1993; Backing into the Future, 1994. **Address:** 13013 Scarlet Oak Dr, Darnestown, MD 20878, U.S.A.

KNOX, Calvin M. See **SILVERBERG, Robert.**

KNOX, Elizabeth (Fiona). New Zealander, b. 1959. **Genres:** Novels, Plays/Screenplays. **Career:** Writer. Worked as tutor in film studies at Victoria University, 1989-95; worked as a clerk, printer, insurance underwriter, computer operator, editor, web page editor, publicity officer, and shop assistant. **Publications:** NOVELS: After Z-Hour, 1987; Paremata, 1989; Treasure, 1992; Pomare, 1994; Glamour and the Sea, 1996; Tawa, 1998; The Vintner's Luck, 1998; The High Jump, 2000; Black Oxen, 2001; Billie's Kiss, 2002. OTHER: The Dig (Un Certain Regard) (screenplay), 1994. Short stories represented in anthologies. Contributor to books and periodicals.

KNOX, George. British, b. 1922. **Genres:** Art/Art history. **Career:** University of British Columbia, Vancouver, professor of history of art, 1970-87, professor emeritus, 1987-; writer. **Publications:** Tiepolo Drawings in the Victoria and Albert Museum, 1960, 2nd ed., 1975; Domenico Tiepolo: Rac-

colta di Teste, 1970; Un Quaderno di Vedute di Giambattista Tiepolo e Figlio Domenico, 1974; Etchings by the Tiepolos: Domenico Tiepolo's Collection of the Family Etchings, from an Album in the Cooper-Hewitt Museum, 1976; Giambattista and Domenico Tiepolo: A Study and Catalogue Raisonne of the Chalk Drawings, 1980; (ed.) Piazzetta: A Tercentenary Exhibition of Drawings, Prints, and Books, 1983; (with J.B. Shaw) The Robert Lehman Collection, Volume VI: Italian Eighteenth-Century Drawings, 1988; Giambattista Piazzetta, 1682-1754, 1992; Antonio Pellegrini, 1675-1741, 1995; (with A. Gealt) Domenico Tiepolo: Master Draftsman, 1996. **Address:** 3495 W 11th Ave, Vancouver, BC, Canada V6R 2K1. **Online address:** gknox@interchange.ubc.cc

KNOX, Melissa. American, b. 1957. **Genres:** Biography. **Career:** St. Peter's College, Jersey City, NJ, associate professor of English, 1992-. **Publications:** Oscar Wilde: A Long and Lovely Suicide, 1994; Oscar Wilde in the 1990s, 2001. **Address:** Weinleite 8, 85072 Eichstatt, Germany. **Online address:** Sigmund@panix.com

KNOX, Robert Buick. See Obituaries.

KNOX-JOHNSTON, Sir Robin (William Robert Patrick). British, b. 1939. **Genres:** Recreation, Sports/Fitness. **Career:** Master mariner, writer. First person to sail solo nonstop around the world, June 1968-April 1969. International Yachtsman of the Year, 1995. **Publications:** A World of My Own, 1969; Robin Round the World 1970; Sailing, 1976; Last But Not Least, 1978; Twilight of Sail, 1978; Bunk Side Companion, 1982; Seamanship, 1986; The Boc Challenge, 1986; The Cape of Good Hope: A Maritime History, 1989; Yachting: The History of a Passion, 1990; The Columbus Venture, 1991; (with C. Bonington) Sea, Ice, Rock, 1992; Cape Horn, 1994; Beyond Jules Verne, 1995. **Address:** St. Francis College, Torbryan, Newton Abbot, Devon TQ12 5UR, England. **Online address:** rknoxjohnston@clipper-ventures.com

KNOX-MAWER, June. Welsh, b. 1930. **Genres:** Romance/Historical, History, Travel/Exploration, Autobiography/Memoirs. **Career:** Chester Chronicle, Chester, England, trainee reporter, 1947-50; Daily Express, correspondent and feature writer, 1952-57; free-lance journalist, 1957-. Presenter and radio interviewer for Fiji Broadcasting Commission in the 1960s; BBC-Radio, presenter and interviewer, including appearances on Woman's Hour, 1971-. **Publications:** The Sultans Came to Tea (travel diary), 1961; A Gift of Islands (travel diary), 1965; A World of Islands (history), 1968; Marama (historical novel), 1974; A South Sea Spell (travel diary), 1975; Marama of the Islands (historical novel), 1986; Tales from Paradise (oral history), 1986; Sandstorm (romance novel), 1991; The Shadow of Wings (novel), 1995; A Ram in the Well: A Welsh Homecoming (memoir), 2001. Contributor to magazines. **Address:** 6 H.S.B.C. Bank, Ruabon, N, Wales.

KNUDSEN, Margrethe June. Australian (born Wales), b. 1934. **Genres:** Gerontology/Senior issues, Travel/Exploration. **Career:** William Balmain College, Sydney, member of faculty, 1966-73; Australian Catholic University, Sydney, lecturer in English and education, 1974-97. Tour leader and organizer of cultural tours to Turkey and Scandinavia, 1987-; English Speaking Board, NSW, founding secretary; School Library Association, NSW, past secretary. **Publications:** (co-ed.) Quicksilver (3 books), 1965; Goldseekers, 1969. **Address:** 9 Best Rd, Middle Dural, NSW 2158, Australia. **Online address:** margrethe.knudsen@uts.edu.au

KNUDSON, Danny Alan. New Zealander, b. 1940. **Genres:** Education, History. **Career:** Principal, Otago Education Board, since 1978 (Deputy Principal, 1971-78). Ed., New Zealand Educational Institute, Yearbook of Education: The Creative Arts, 1973-74. **Publications:** The Story of Wakatipu, 1968; Goldfields Wonderland, 1974; (ed. with M. E. Fleming and R. H. Jarratt) The Creative Arts, 1975; Goldtown School, 1976; Standard V, 1892, 1982; The Road to Skippers, 1974. **Address:** 79 Centennial Ave, Wakari, Dunedin, New Zealand.

KNUTH, Donald E. American, b. 1938. **Genres:** Information science/Computers, Mathematics/Statistics, Theology/Religion. **Career:** Computer scientist and mathematician. California Institute of Technology, Pasadena, CA, assistant and associate professor of math, 1963-68; Stanford University, CA, professor of computer science, 1968-, now emeritus. Consultant, 1960-68; Guggenheim Foundation, fellow. **Publications:** The Art of Computer Programming, Vol. 1: Fundamental Algorithms, 1968, Vol. 2: Seminumerical Algorithms, 1969, Vol. 3: Sorting and Searching, 1973; Surreal Numbers, 1974; TeX and METAFONT: New Directions in Typesetting, 1979; (with D.H. Greene) Mathematics for the Analysis of Algorithms, 1981; The TeXbook, 1984; Computers and Typesetting, 5 vols., 1986; (with R.L. Graham and O. Patashnik) Concrete Mathematics: A Foundation for Computer Science, 1989; (with T. Larrabee and P.M. Roberts) Mathematical Writing, 1989; 3:16 Bible Texts Illuminated, 1990; Axioms and Hulls, 1992; Literate Programming, 1992; The Stanford GraphBase: A Platform for Combinatorial Computing, 1993; (with S. Levy) The CWEB System of Structured Documentation: Version 3.0, 1994; Selected Papers on Computer Science, 1996; Stable Marriage and Its Relation to Other Combinatorial Problems: An Introduction to the Mathematical Analysis of Algorithms, 1997; Digital Typography, 1999; MMIXware, 1999; Selected Papers on Analysis of Algorithms, 2000; Things a Computer Scientist Rarely Talks About, 2001; Selected Papers on Computer Languages, 2003; Selected Papers on Discrete Mathematics, 2003. **Address:** Stanford University, Computer Science Department, Stanford, CA 94305, U.S.A.

KNYE, Cassandra. See **DISCH, Thomas M(ichael).**

KOCH, Edward I(rving). American, b. 1924. **Genres:** Politics/Government, Autobiography/Memoirs, Biography. **Career:** Partner, Robinson, Silverman, Pearce, Aronsohn, and Berman (attorneys), since 1990. Practicing Lawyer, 1949-69; Member, NYC Council, 1967-68; Congressman, U.S. House of Representatives, Washington, D.C., 1969-77; Mayor of NYC, 1978-90. **Publications:** Mayor, 1984; Politics, 1985; (with John Cardinal O'Connor) His Eminence and Hizzoner, 1989; (with L.T. Jones) All the Best: Letters from a Feisty Mayor, 1990; (with D. Paisner) Citizen Koch, 1992; Ed Koch on Everything, 1994; (with H. Resnicow) Murder at City Hall, 1995; (with W.C. Staub) Murder on Broadway, 1996; (with D. Paisner) I'm Not Done Yet!, 2000. **Address:** Robinson, Silverman, Pearce, Aronsohn, and Berman, 1290 Avenue of the Americas, New York, NY 10104, U.S.A.

KOCHALKA, James. American, b. 1968. **Genres:** Graphic Novels. **Career:** Comic-book artist, writer, musician, songwriter. **Publications:** Magic Boy and Girlfriend, 1991; Paradise Sucks, 1997; Tiny Bubbles, 1998; Quit Your Job, 1998; Kissers, 1999; The Perfect Planet and Other Stories, 1999; Monkey vs. Robot, 2000; (editor, with others) Expo 2000, 2000; Sunburn, 2001; Pinky & Stinky, 2002; Fantastic Butterflies, 2002; Monkey vs. Robot and the Crystal of Power, 2003; Magic Boy and the Robot Elf, 2003; Fancy Froglin's Sexy Forest, 2003; Peanut Butter & Jeremy's Best Book Ever, 2003; American Elf: James Kochalka's Collected Sketchbook Diaries, 2004. Contributor to comic books, magazines, and anthologies. **Address:** POB 8321, Burlington, VT 05402, U.S.A.

KOCHAN, Miriam (Louise). British, b. 1929. **Genres:** History, Translations. **Career:** General Ed., Berg Women's Series; Sub-Ed., Reuters Economic Services, London, 1951-54. **Publications:** Life in Russia Under Catherine the Great, 1969; Catherine the Great, 1976; The Last Days of Imperial Russia, 1976; Prisoners of England, 1980; Britain's Internees in the Second World War, 1983. TRANSLATIONS: Greece, by Jeanne and Georges Roux, 1958; Gothic Cathedrals of France, by Marcel Aubert, 1959; Maya Cities, by Paul Rivet, 1960; The World of Archaeology, by Marcel Brion, 1961; Carthage, by Gilbert Picard, 1964; The Greek Adventure, by Pierre Leveque, 1968; Meiji 1868, by Paul Akamatsu, 1972; Capitalism and Material Life, by Fernand Braudel, 1973; History of Anti-Semitism vol. III, by Leon Poliakov, 1975; The Jewish Bankers and The Holy See, by Leon Poliakov, 1977; (with P. Engel) The Norm of Truth, by Pascal Engel, 1991; Anti-Semitism in France, by Pierre Birnbaum, 1992; A Social History of France in the 19th Century, by Christophe Charle, 1994; Haim Nahun, by Esther Benbassa, 1995. **Address:** 237 Woodstock Rd, Oxford, England.

KOCKA, Jürgen. German, b. 1941. **Genres:** History. **Career:** University of Munster, Germany, assistant professor of history, 1968-73; University of Bielefeld, Germany, professor of history, 1973-88; Free University of Berlin, professor of history, 1988-; Wissenschaftskolleg zu Berlin, permanent fellow, 1991-2000, Social Science Research Center, president, 2001-. Has had research fellowships and guest professorships worldwide. **Publications:** White-Collar Workers in America, 1890-1940, 1980; Facing Total War: German Society, 1914-1918, 1986; Bourgeois Society in Nineteenth Century Europe, 1993; Industrial Culture and Bourgeois Society: Business, Labor, and Bureaucracy in Modern Germany, 1999. **Address:** WZB, Reichpietschufer 50, D-10785 Berlin, Germany.

KODIS, Michelle R. American (born Germany), b. 1968. **Genres:** Food and Wine. **Career:** Gillette News-Record, Gillette, WY, reporter and feature writer, 1990; Colley Associates, Seattle, WA, health writer and editor, 1990; Willamette Falls Hospital, Oregon City, OR, public relations coordinator and health writer, 1991-93; Buzzworm's Earth Journal, Boulder, CO, assistant editor, 1993-94; Telluride Historical Museum, Telluride, CO, public relations and graphics coordinator, 1994; freelance writer and editor, 1992-. Healthy Communities (online news service), editor. Telluride Mountainfilm Festival, public relations and media director. **Publications:** The Telluride Cookbook: Recipes and Profiles of Telluride's Finest Restaurants and Caterers, 1995; Reach for Health: Regional, Environmental, and Community Health Guide, 1996; (with D. Moran and D. Hony) Love Scents: How Your Natural Pheromones Influence Your Relationships, Your Moods, and Who You Love, 1998. Contributor to periodicals. **Address:** PO Box 458, Telluride, CO 81435, U.S.A.

KOEGLER, Hans-Herbert. German, b. 1960. **Genres:** Literary criticism and history. **Career:** University of Frankfurt, Frankfurt, Germany, research fellow of Deutsche Forschungsgemeinschaft, 1986-88; University of Illinois at UrbanaChampaign, assistant professor of European philosophy, 1991-97, faculty associate of Programs in Arms Control, Disarmament, and International Security, 1994; University of North Florida, Jacksonville, assistant professor of language, 1997-. University of Catamarca, Argentina, honorary professor, 1996; Boston University, visiting scholar, 1997; lecturer at colleges and universities, including Babson College, Florida State University, and University of South Carolina-Columbia. Affiliated with Goethe-Institut in Germany. **Publications:** Die Macht des Dialogs: Kritische Hermeneutik nach Gadamer, Foucault, und Rorty, 1992, trans by P. Hendrickson as The Power of Dialogue: Critical Hermeneutics after Gadamer and Foucault, 1996; Michel Foucault: Ein Anti-Humanistischer Aufklaerer, 1994. Contributor to books. Contributor of articles and reviews to scholarly journals. **Address:** Department of History and Philosophy, University of North Florida, 4567 St. Johns Bluff Rd. S., Jacksonville, FL 32224, U.S.A. **Online address:** hkoegler@gw.unf.edu

KOELB, Clayton T. American, b. 1942. **Genres:** Literary criticism and history. **Career:** University of Chicago, Chicago, IL, assistant professor to professor of German, 1969-81; visiting professor at US universities; University of North Carolina, Guy B. Johnson Professor of German and comparative lit, 1991-. **Publications:** Thomas Mann's "Goethe and Tolstoy": Notes and Sources, 1984; The Incredulous Reader: Literature and the Function of Disbelief, 1984; Inventions of Reading: Rhetoric and the Literary Imagination, 1988; Kafka'a Rhetoric: The Passion of Reading, 1989. EDITOR: (with V. Lokke) The Current in Criticism: Essays on the Present and Future of Literary Theory, 1987; (with S. Noakes) The Comparative Perspective on Literature: Approaches to Theory and Practice, 1988; Nietzsche as Postmodernist: Essays Pro and Contra, 1990; (and trans) T. Mann, Death in Venice (critical edition), 1994. **Address:** Department of Germanic Languages, 414 Dey Hall, Univ. of North Carolina, Chapel Hill, NC 27599-3160, U.S.A.

KOENIG, Harold G. American, b. 1951. **Genres:** Medicine/Health, Human relations/Parenting. **Career:** Duke University, Durham, NC, clinical assistant professor, 1992-93, assistant professor, 1993-96, associate professor of psychiatry, 1996-, senior fellow at Aging Center, 1992-, and director of Center for the Study of Religion/Spirituality and Health. Federal Correctional Center, Butner, NC, research psychiatrist, 1992-93; Geriatric Evaluation and Treatment Clinic, director of psychiatric services; private practice of psychiatry. Shepherd's Centers of America, member of board of directors, 1997-. Speaker at colleges and universities; guest on media programs in the United States and abroad. **Publications:** (with M. Smiley and J. Gonzales) Religion, Health, and Aging, 1988; Aging and God: Spiritual Paths to Mental Health in Midlife and Later Years, 1994; Research on Religion and Aging, 1995; (with A.J. Weaver) Counseling Troubled Older Adults: A Handbook for Pastors and Religious Caregivers, 1997; (with T. Lamar and B. Lamar) A Gospel for the Mature Years: Finding Fulfillment by Knowing and Using Your Gift, 1997; Is Religion Good for Your Health? The Effects of Religion on Physical and Mental Health, 1997; (with Weaver) Pastoral Care of Older Adults, 1998; (ed. with Weaver and P. Roe) Reflections on Aging and Spiritual Growth, 1998; (ed.) Handbook of Religion and Mental Health, 1998; (with M. McConnell) The Healing Power of Faith, 1999; (with C. Tolson) The Healing Power of Prayer, 2003. Contributor to books, medical journals and popular magazines. **Address:** Center for the Study of Religion/Spirituality & Health, Duke University, Durham, NC 27708, U.S.A.

KOENIG, Karl P. American, b. 1938. **Genres:** Anthropology/Ethnology, Photography. **Career:** Stanford University, Stanford, CA, professor of psychology, 1964-66; University of New Mexico, Albuquerque, professor of psychology, 1966-75, and psychiatry, 1975-81; private practice of psychology, Albuquerque, 1981-. Photographer and print-maker. **Publications:** Gumoil Photographic Printing, 1994, 2nd ed., 1999. Contributor to photography, antiques, and psychology journals. **Address:** 6435 Nabor Rd NW, Albuquerque, NM 87107, U.S.A. **Online address:** kpkoe@swcp.com

KOENIGSBERGER, Helmut Georg. British/German (born Germany), b. 1918. **Genres:** History. **Career:** Lecturer in Economic History, Queen's

University, Belfast, 1948-51; Sr. Lecturer, University of Manchester, 1951-60; Professor of Modern History, University of Nottingham, 1960-66; Professor of European History, Cornell University, Ithaca, NY, 1966-73; Kings College, London, Professor of History, 1973-84, Fellow, 1999. Fellow, British Academy, 1989; Encomienda of the Order of Isabel the Catholic, 1997. **Publications:** The Government of Sicily under Philip II of Spain, 1951; (with G.L. Mosse and G.Q. Bowler) Europe in the Sixteenth Century, 1968; Estates and Revolutions, 1971; The Habsburgs and Europe 1516-1660, 1971; Politicians and Virtuosi, 1986; Medieval Europe 400-1500, 1987; Early Modern Europe 1500-1789, 1987; Monarchies, States Generals and Parliaments, 2001. EDITOR: Luther: A Profile, 1972; Republiken und Republikanismus im Europa der fruhen Neuzeit, 1988. **Address:** 116 Waterfall Rd, London N14 7JN, England.

KOERNER, Joseph Leo. American, b. 1958. **Genres:** Art/Art history. **Career:** Harvard University, Cambridge, MA, assistant professor of fine art, 1989-91, professor of fine art, 1991-. University of Constance, guest professor of literature, 1992. **Publications:** Die Suche nach dem Labyrinth: Der Mythos von Daedalus und Ikarus, 1983; Caspar David Friedrich and the Subject of Landscape, 1990; (with R. Crone) Paul Klee: Legends of the Sign, 1991. **Address:** Department of Fine Arts, Harvard University, Cambridge, MA 02138, U.S.A.

KOERNER, Lisbet. American. **Genres:** Adult non-fiction. **Career:** Harvard University, Cambridge, MA, Department of the History of Science, past associate; University of London, London, England, Centre for the History of Science, Technology, and Medicine, senior research investigator. **Publications:** (with D.B. Dick) Corroux, a History of a Sporting Estate, 1998; Linnaeus: Nature and Nation (biography), 1999. Contributor to books and professional journals. **Address:** Centre for the History of Science Technology and Medicine, Sherfield Building 446, Imperial College, London SW7 2AZ, England. **Online address:** l.koerner@ic.ac.uk

KOERTGE, Ron(ald). American, b. 1940. **Genres:** Young adult fiction, Poetry. **Career:** Pasadena City College, California, professor of English, 1965-2001. **Publications:** FOR YOUNG ADULTS. FICTION: Where the Kissing Never Stops, 1987; The Arizona Kid, 1988; The Boy in the Moon, 1990; Mariposa Blues, 1991; The Harmony Arms, 1992; Tiger, Tiger, Burning Bright, 1994; Confess-O-Rama, 1996; The Heart of the City, 1998; The Brimstone Journals, 2001; Stoner & Spaz, 2002; Margaux with an X, 2004. POETRY: Meat: Cherry's Market Diary, 1973; The Father Poems, 1974; The Hired Nose, 1974; My Summer Vacation, 1975; Men under Fire, 1976; Twelve Photographs of Yellowstone, 1976; How to Live on Five Dollars a Day, 1976; Cheap Thrills, 1976; Sex Object, 1979; The Jockey Poems, 1980; Diary Cows, 1982; Life on the Edge of the Continent: Selected Poems, 1982; High School Dirty Poems, 1991; Making Love to Roget's Wife, 1997; Geography of the Forehead, 2000. FOR ADULTS. The Boogeyman (novel), 1980. **Address:** 1115 Oxley St, South Pasadena, CA 91030, U.S.A.

KOESTENBAUM, Wayne. American, b. 1958. **Genres:** Poetry, Literary criticism and history. **Career:** Yale University, New Haven, CT, associate professor of English, 1988-1996; CUNY Graduate School, Professor of English, 1996-. **Publications:** Double Talk: The Erotics of Male Literary Collaboration, 1989; Ode to Anna Moffo and Other Poems, 1990; The Queen's Throat: Opera, Homosexuality, and the Mystery of Desire, 1993; Rhapsodies of a Repeat Offender, 1994; Jackie under My Skin: Interpreting an Icon, 1995; The Milk of Inquiry, 1999; Cleavage: Essays on Sex, Stars, and Aesthetics, 2000; Andy Warhol, 2001. **Address:** c/o Faith Hornby Hamlin, Sanford J. Greenburger Associates, 55 Fifth Ave, New York, NY 10003, U.S.A.

KOETZSCH, Ronald E. American, b. 1944. **Genres:** Food and Wine, Education. **Career:** Association of Waldorf Schools of North America, Fair Oaks, CA, editor, 1991-. **Publications:** Macrobiotics Yesterday and Today, 1983; Macrobiotics beyond Food, 1985; The Parents' Guide to Alternatives in Education, 1997. **Address:** Association of Waldorf Schools of North America, 3911 Bannister Rd., Fair Oaks, CA 95628, U.S.A.

KOFF, Richard M. American, b. 1926. **Genres:** Novels, Sciences. **Career:** Management consultant, since 1977. Design Engineer, American Hydromath Corp., 1949-55; Managing Ed., McGraw-Hill Publishing Co., NYC, 1955-66; Vice-President, Assistant Publr. and Business Manager, Playboy Enterprises, Chicago, 1966-77. **Publications:** (with J. J. Pippinger) Fluid Power Controls, 1958; How Does It Work?, 1961; Home Computers, 1979; The Home Electronics Catalog, 1979; Strategic Planning for Magazine Executives, 1981; Christopher (novel), 1981; Using Small Computers to Make Your Business Strategy Work, 1984; Increasing Your Wealth in Good

Times and Bad, 1985; Business Simulation: IBM-PC Version, 1985; Allocating and Managing Your Investment Assets, 1989. **Address:** 1600 Ben Crenshaw Way, Austin, TX 78746, U.S.A.

KOFORD, Kenneth J. American, b. 1948. **Genres:** Economics. **Career:** University of Delaware, Newark, assistant professor, associate professor, professor of economics and political science. **Publications:** EDITOR: (with J. Butkiewicz and J.B. Miller) Keynes' Economic Legacy: Contemporary Macro-Economic Theories, 1988; (with J.B. Miller) Social Norms and Economic Institutions, 1991. **Address:** Department of Economics, University of Delaware, Newark, DE 19716, U.S.A.

KOGAN, Norman. American, b. 1919. **Genres:** History, International relations/Current affairs. **Career:** University of Connecticut, Storrs, instructor, 1949-52, assistant professor, 1952-58, associate professor, 1958-63, professor, 1963-88, Director, Center for Italian Studies, 1967-75, professor Emeritus of Political Science, 1988-. Faculty associate, Columbia University, NYC, since 1966. Executive Secretary-Treasurer, Society for Italian Historical Studies, 1967-76; President, Conference Group on Italian Politics, 1975-77. **Publications:** Italy and the Allies, 1956; The Government of Italy, 1962; The Politics of Italian Foreign Policy, 1963; A Political History of Italy: The Postwar Years, 1983; Storia, Politica dell Italia Republicana, 2nd ed., rev., 1990. **Address:** 13 Westwood Rd, Storrs Mansfield, CT 06268, U.S.A.

KOGAWA, Joy Nozomi. Canadian, b. 1935. **Genres:** Novels, Poetry. **Career:** University of Ottawa, writer-in-residence, 1978. **Publications:** The Splintered Moon, 1967; A Choice of Dreams, 1974; Jericho Road, 1977; Obasan (novel), 1981; Woman in the Woods, 1985; Naomi's Road, 1986; Naomi no Michi, 1988; Itsuka (novel), 1992; The Rain Ascends (novel), 1995; A Song of Lilith, 2000; A Garden of Anchors, 2003.

KOGER, Lisa (Jan). American, b. 1953. **Genres:** Novels, Novellas/Short stories. **Career:** Free-lance writer, 1980-; Mississippi State University, Starkville, MS, visiting lecturer in fiction and poetry writing, 1990-91. Teacher of writing workshops at a variety of schools and institutions in the United States. **Publications:** Farlanburg Stories, 1990. **Address:** c/o Jane Gelfman, Schneider Literary Agents, Inc, 250 W 57th St, New York, NY 10107, U.S.A. **Online address:** hamlet@kih.net

KOHL, MaryAnn F(aubion). American, b. 1947. **Genres:** Art/Art history, Education. **Career:** Author, 1985-. Bright Ring Publishing, Bellingham, WA, founder and owner, 1985-. Former teacher in Ferndale, WA, and at Whatcom Community College and Bellingham Technical College; educational consultant. **Publications:** Mudworks: Creative Clay, Dough, and Modeling Experiences, 1989; (with C. Gainer) Good Earth Art: Environmental Art for Kids, 1990; (with J. Potter) ScienceArts: Discovering Science through Art Experiences, 1993; (with C. Gainer) MathArts: Exploring Math through Art for Three to Six Year Olds, 1996; (with J. Potter) Cooking Art: Easy Edible Art for Young Children, 1997; (with K. Solga) Discovering Great Artists: Hands-on Art for Children in the Styles of the Masters, 1997; (with J. Potter) Global Art: Activities, Projects, and Inventions from around the World, 1998; Making Make-Believe: Fun Props, Costumes, and Creative Play Ideas, 1999; The Big Messy Art Book: But Easy to Clean Up, 2000; (with J. Potter) Snacktivities: Fifty Edible Activities for Parents and Young Children, 2001; (with J. Potter) Storybook Art: Hands-on Art for Children in the Styles of One Hundred Great Picture Book Illustrators, 2002. CO-AUTHOR: Scribble Cookies: Independent Creative Art Experiences for Children, 1986, rev. ed. as Scribble Art: Independent Creative Art Experiences for Children, 1994; Preschool Art: It's the Process, Not the Product, 1994; Painting: Preschool Art (excerpted from Preschool Art), 2001; Clay and Dough: Preschool Art (excerpted from Preschool Art), 2001; Craft and Construction: Preschool Art (excerpted from Preschool Art), 2001; Drawing: Preschool Art (excerpted from Preschool Art), 2001; Collage and Paper: Preschool Art (excerpted from Preschool Art), 2001; First Art: Art Experiences for Toddlers and Twos, 2002. Contributor of short stories and essays to anthologies and periodicals. **Address:** PO Box 31338, Bellingham, WA 98228, U.S.A. **Online address:** maryann@brightring.com

KOHLER, Sandra. American, b. 1940. **Genres:** Poetry. **Career:** Poet and teacher. Prince of Wales College, Prince Edward Island, instructor in English, 1967-68; Bryn Mawr College, instructor, 1969-70, lecturer, 1970-72, assistant professor of English, 1972-77; The Curtis Institute, instructor in Literature, 1981, 1991-92; Main Line School Night, instructor in Literature and Writing, 1981-91; Susquehanna University, Selinsgrove, PA, member of English department faculty and faculty of the Writers Institute, 1994-. **Publications:** The Country of Women, 1995. Contributor to periodicals. **Ad-**

dress: Susquehanna University, Department of English, 514 University Avenue, Selinsgrove, PA 17870, U.S.A. **Online address:** kohler@susqu.edu

KOHN, Alan J(acobs). American, b. 1931. **Genres:** Zoology. **Career:** Hopkins Marine Station, laboratory assistant, 1951; Narragansett Marine Laboratory, junior assistant in marine biology, 1952; Marine Biological Laboratory, Woods Hole, MA, technician, 1953; Hawaii Marine Laboratory, associate in research, 1954, visiting collaborator, 1955-56; Yale University, New Haven, CT, W.W. Anderson fellow at Bingham Oceanographic Laboratory, 1958; Florida State University, Tallahassee, assistant professor of zoology, 1958-61; University of Washington, Seattle, assistant professor, 1961-63, associate professor, 1963-67, professor of zoology, 1967-98, adjunct professor at Quaternary Research Center, 1986-, professor emeritus, 1998-. Thomas Burke Memorial Washington State Museum, affiliate curator of malacology, 1965-70, adjunct curator, 1971-. Smithsonian Institution, National Research Council, senior postdoctoral research associate, 1967, research associate at National Museum of Natural History, 1985-, senior fellow of the museum, 1990; University of Hawaii at Manoa, visiting professor, 1968. Visiting investigator at Mid-Pacific Marine Laboratory, Enewetak, 1957 and 1971-73, Bernice P. Bishop Museum, 1961, and University of the Ryukyus, 1982-83; participant in Yale Seychelles Expedition to the Indian Ocean, 1957-58, and U.S. Biology Program of the International Indian Ocean Exped, 1963. **Publications:** A Chronological Taxonomy of Conus, 1758-1840, 1992; (ed. with F.W. Harrison) Microscopic Anatomy of Invertebrates, Vol 5: Mollusca I, 1994; (with F.E. Perron) Life History and Biogeography: Patterns in Conus, 1994; (with D. Rockel and W. Korn) Manual of the Living Conidae, 1995. Contributor to scientific journals. **Address:** Dept of Biology, Box 351800, University of Washington, Seattle, WA 98195, U.S.A. **Online address:** kohn@u.washington.edu

KOHN, Livia. German (born United States), b. 1956. **Genres:** Theology/Religion. **Career:** Kyoto University, Research Institute for Humanistic Studies, visiting scholar and research fellow, 1981-86, visiting scholar, 1991-93; University of Michigan, Center for Chinese Studies, Ann Arbor, MI, research fellow, 1986-87, adjunct lecturer in religious studies, 1987, Department of Asian Languages and Cultures, visiting assistant professor, 1987-88; Goettingen University, visiting assistant professor, 1988; Harvard University, John King Fairbank Center for East Asian Studies, Cambridge, MA, research associate, 1988-91; Boston University, Boston, MA, assistant professor, 1988-92, associate professor in Religion Department, 1992-. **Publications:** Leben und Legende des Ch'en T'uan, 1981; Seven Steps to the Tao, 1987; Taoist Mystical Philosophy, 1991; Early Chinese Mysticism, 1992; The Taoist Experience (anthology), 1993; (trans.) Laughing at the Tao: Debates among Buddhists and Taoists in Medieval China, 1994; God and the Dao, 1998; Daoism and Chinese Culture, 2001; Monastic Life in Medieval Daoism, 2003; (with C. Despeux) Women in Daoism, 2003The Daoist Monastic Manual, 2004; Cosmos and Community, 2004; Health and Long Life, 2005. EDITOR/CO-EDITOR: Taoist Meditation and Longevity Techniques, 1989; Lao-tzu and the Teo-te-ching, 1998; Daoism Handbook, 2000; (with H.D. Roth) Daoist Identity, 2002. **Address:** Dept of Religion, Boston University, 145 Bay State Rd, Boston, MA 02215, U.S.A. **Online address:** lkohn@bu.edu

KOHUT, Thomas A. American, b. 1950. **Genres:** History. **Career:** Williams College, Williamstown, MA, assistant professor, 1984-90, associate professor of history, 1990-96, Sue and Edgar Wochenheim Professor of History, 1996-. University of Munich and University of Siegen, guest professor. **Publications:** Wilhelm II and the Germans: A Study in Leadership, 1991. Work represented in anthologies. Contributor to periodicals. **Address:** Department of History, Williams College, Williamstown, MA 01267, U.S.A.

KOJA, Kathe. American, b. 1960. **Genres:** Science fiction/Fantasy. **Career:** Writer. **Publications:** The Cipher, 1991; Bad Brains, 1992; Skin, 1993; Strange Angels, 1994. **Address:** c/o Kristin Kaiser, Dell Publishing, 1540 Broadway, New York, NY 10036, U.S.A.

KOKORIS, Jim. American, b. 1958. **Genres:** Essays. **Career:** Advertising executive, 1982-90; Golin/Harris Communications, vice president, 1990-. **Publications:** The Rich Part of Life, 2001. Contributor of humorous pieces to publications. **Address:** 230 S Spring Ave, La Grange, IL 60525, U.S.A.

KOLATA, Gina. American, b. 1948. **Genres:** Medicine/Health, Sciences. **Career:** Science Magazine, Washington, DC, copy editor, 1973-74, writer, 1974-87; New York Times, NYC, reporter, 1987-. Columnist, Bild der Wissenschaft, 1984-87, Journal of Investigative Dermatology, 1985-87. **Publications:** (with others) Combatting the Number One Killer: The Scientific Report on Heart Disease, 1978; (with E.D. Freis) The High Blood Pressure

Book: A Guide for Patients and their Families, 1979; The Baby Doctors: Probing the Limits of Fetal Medicine, 1990; (with R.T. Michael, J.H. Gagnon, and E.O. Laumann) Sex in America: A Definitive Study, 1995; Clone: The Road to Dolly, and the Path Ahead, 1998. Contributor to periodicals, newspapers, and magazines. **Address:** New York Times Science Times, Section 229, West 43rd Street, New York, NY 10036, U.S.A.

KOLINSKY, Martin. British, b. 1936. **Genres:** International relations/Current affairs, Politics/Government, History. **Career:** Hebrew University of Jerusalem, Lecturer, 1970-72; University of Birmingham, Sr. Lecturer. **Publications:** Continuity and Change in European Society, 1974; (with M. Vaughan and P. Sheriff) Social Change in France, 1980; Law, Order and Riots in Mandatory Palestine, 1928-35, 1993; Britain's War in the Middle East: 1936-1942. EDITOR: (with W.E. Paterson) Social and Political Movements in Western Europe, 1976; Divided Loyalties, 1978; (with M.J. Cohen) Britain and the Middle East in the 1930s: Security Problems 1935-39, 1992; (with M.J. Cohen) Demise of the British Empire in the Middle East, 1998.

KOLKO, Joyce. Canadian (born United States), b. 1933. **Genres:** Economics, History, Politics/Government. **Career:** Writer. **Publications:** The Limits of Power: The World and United States Foreign Policy, 1945-1954 (with G. Kolko), 1972; America and the Crisis of World Capitalism, 1974; Restructuring the World Economy, 1988. **Address:** Wittenburgergracht 53, 1018 MX Amsterdam, Netherlands.

KOLLER, Jackie French. American, b. 1948. **Genres:** Children's fiction, Young adult fiction. **Career:** Author. **Publications:** FOR CHILDREN: Impy for Always, 1989; The Dragonling, 1990; Mole and Shrew, 1991; Fish Fry Tonight!, 1992; Mole and Shrew Step Out, 1992; A Dragon in the Family, 1996; No Such Thing, 1997; Dragon Quest, 1997; Mole and Shrew, All Year Through, 1997; Dragons of Krad, 1997; Dragon Trouble, 1997; Dragons and Kings, 1999; Bouncing on the Bed, 1999; One Monkey Too Many, 1999; Nickommoh!, 1999; Baby for Sale, 2002; Mole & Shrew Are Two, 2000; Mole & Shrew Have Jobs to Do, 2001; Mole & Shrew Find a Clue, 2001. FOR YOUNG ADULTS: Nothing to Fear, 1991; If I Had One Wish..., 1991; The Last Voyage of the Misty Day, 1992; The Primrose Way, 1992; A Place to Call Home, 1995; The Falcon, 1998; The Promise, 1999; Someday, 2002. Contributor of poems to anthologies. **Address:** c/o Curtis Brown Ltd, 10 Astor Pl, New York, NY 10003, U.S.A. **Online address:** jackiek@aol.com

KOLLER, James. American, b. 1936. **Genres:** Novels, Poetry, Essays. **Career:** Editor, Coyote Journal and Coyote Books, San Francisco, then New Mexico and Maine, 1964-. **Publications:** POETRY: Two Hands: Poems 1959-1961, 1965; Brainard & Washington Street Poems, 1965; Some Cows: Poems of Civilization and Domestic Life, 1965; The Dogs & Other Dark Woods, 1966; I Went to See My True Love, 1967; California Poems, 1971; Bureau Creek, 1975; Messages, 1976; Poems for the Blue Sky, 1976; (ed. and contrib.) Andiamo: Selected Poems by James Koller, Franco Beltrametti and Harry Hoogstraten, 1978; O Didn't He Ramble/O Ware Er Nicht Umhergezogen, 1981; Back River, 1981; One Day at a Time, 1981; Great Things Are Happening, 1984; Give the Dog a Bone, 1986; Openings, 1987; Fortune, 1987; (with F. Beltrametti) Graffiti Lyriques, 1987; (with others) A Gang of Four, 1989; Roses Love Sunshine, 1989; This Is What He Said, 1991; The Bone Show, 1999; Iron Bells, 1999; Close to the Ground, 2000; Crows Talk to Him, 2003; Looking for His Horses, 2003. NOVELS: If You Don't Like Me You Can Leave Me Alone, 1974; Shannon, Who Was Lost Before, 1975; (with F. Beltrametti) The Possible Movie, 1997. OTHER: Messages, 1972; Working Notes, 1985; The Natural Order (essays), 1990; Like It Was, 2000; (trans. with J. Monod and M. Cyprys) J. Monod, The Man Who Knows, 2003. **Address:** c/o Coyote Books, PO Box 629, Brunswick, ME 04011, U.S.A.

KOLLER, Kevin. *See* **LARSON, Muriel Koller.**

KOLODNY, Nancy J. American, b. 1946. **Genres:** Self help, Sex, Social work, Young adult non-fiction. **Career:** University City High School, University City, MO, English teacher, 1967-69; South Boston High School, MA, English teacher, 1970-71; Clayton High School, MO, English teacher, 1971-72; psychiatric social worker and eating disorder therapist, private practice, 1981-; Norwalk, CT; Keats Press, New Canaan, CT, editor, 1997-99; Silver Hill Hospital, New Canaan, therapist, 1999-2000; Renfrew Center, Wilton, CT, therapist, 2000-; "Closing the Gap," a high school parent-student communication program, New Canaan High School, creator/facilitator, 1987-89. Consultant; public speaker on eating disorders, adolescence and parenting. **Publications:** Instructor's Manual for "Human Sexuality" by Masters, Johnson, Kolodny, 1982, 3rd ed., 1988; (with F.E.F. Larocca) Anorexia and Bulimia Facilitator's Training Manual: A Primer, the BASH Approach, 1983;

(with R.C. Kolodny, T.E. Bratter, and C. Deep) How to Survive Your Adolescent's Adolescence, 1984; (with R.C. Kolodny and T.E. Bratter) Smart Choices: A Guide to Surviving at Home and in School, Dating and Sex, Dealing with Crises, Applying to College, and More, 1986; When Food's a Foe: How to Confront and Conquer Your Eating Disorder, 1987, rev. ed., 1998; The Beginner's Guide to Eating Disorders Recovery, 2003. Contributor to books. **Address:** 157 Silvermine Ave, Norwalk, CT 06850-1611, U.S.A. **Online address:** NJKolodny@aol.com

KOLPAN, Steven. American. **Genres:** Food and Wine. **Career:** Culinary Institute of America, Learning Resources Center, senior producer/writer, professor of wine studies and gastronomy. Wine and food consultant to establishments and corporations; faculty of Ulster County Community College, Stone Ridge, NY, State University of New York, College at New Paltz, and Ramapo College of New Jersey, Mahwah, NJ; art and media critic; executive director, Ulster County Council for the Arts. **Publications:** (with B.H. Smith and M.A. Weiss) Exploring Wine: The Culinary Institute of America's Complete Guide to Wines of the World, 1996; A Sense of Place: An Intimate Portrait of the Niebaum-Coppola Winery and the Napa Valley, 1999. Contributor of articles and reviews to magazines and periodicals. **Address:** The Culinary Institute of America, 1946 Campus Drive, Hyde Park, NY 12538-1499, U.S.A. **Online address:** s_kolpan@culinary.edu

KOLPAS, Norman. American. **Genres:** Food and Wine. **Career:** Williams-Sonoma Publishing, consulting editor, 1991-2001; University of California, Los Angeles, Writer's Program, nonfiction and cookbook-writing teacher; Wolfgang Puck Worldwide Inc., senior vice president of content. **Publications:** The Chocolate Lover's Companion, 1977; The Coffee Lover's Companion, 1977; Coffee, 1979; Mao, 1981; Abraham Lincoln, 1981; The Gourmet's Lexicon, 1982; (with J.R. Sedlar) Modern Southwest Cuisine, 1986; Britain: The Queen, Cricket, Sherlock Holmes, and Other Things Indubitably British, 1987; Breakfast and Brunch Book, 1988, as Breakfast and Brunch: Over Seventy Ideas and Menus for Starting the Day, 1993; Pasta Presto: One Hundred Fast & Fabulous Pasta Sauces, 1988; Pizza California Style: More than Eighty Fast and Easy Recipes for Delicious Gourmet Pizza, 1989; (with M. McCarty) Michael's Cookbook, 1989; Hors d'oeuvre: Festive and Elegant Party Menus, 1990; The Big Little Peanut Butter Cookbook: Fifty Recipes for Delicious, Easy-to-Make Desserts, Snacks, and Sandwiches, 1990; Pasta Light: Eighty Low-Fat, Low-Calorie, Fast and Fabulous Pasta Sauces, 1990; Sweet Indulgences, 1990, as Sweet Indulgences: Desserts for Every Occasion, 1993; (with G. Mahaffey) The Bel-Air Book of Southern California Food and Entertaining, 1991; The Chili Cookbook, 1991; Whole Meal Salads: One Hundred Fresh, Delectable Recipes for Easy One-Course Entrees, 1992; The World's Best Noodles, 1993; Pasta Menus, 1993; A Cup of Coffee: From Plantation to Pot, a Coffee Lover's Guide to the Perfect Brew, 1993; Gourmet Sandwiches, 1993; (recipes) Soups, 1993; Southwest the Beautiful Cookbook: Recipes from America's Southwest, 1994; Pasta Gusto: Fabulous Sauces & Flavored Pastas, 1994; More Pasta Light: Eighty Delicious, Low-Fat Sauces, 1995; Pizza Presto: Eighty Fast & Fabulous Recipes, 1996; Festive Desserts, 1996; Finger Food, 1996; Breakfast and Brunches, 1997; More Pasta Presto: One Hundred Fast and Fabulous Pasta Sauces, 1998; Main Dish Salads, 1998; Buongiorno! Breakfast and Brunch, Italian Style, 2001; The Quick Grill Artist: Fast and Fabulous Recipes for Cooking with Fire, 2002. EDITOR: (and compiler) Comforting Foods, 1996; Dinner Parties, 1996; C. Williams, Celebrating the Pleasure of Cooking, 1997. **Address:** c/o Author Mail, Random House/Clarkson Potter, 1540 Broadway, New York, NY 10036, U.S.A.

KOLPEN, Jana (Fayne). American, b. 1958. **Genres:** Romance/Historical. **Career:** Writer. **Publications:** The Secrets of Pistoulet (fiction), 1996; The Legend of the Villa della Luna, 1997. **Address:** c/o Sarah Jane Freyman, 59 West 71st St., New York, NY 10023, U.S.A.

KOMAIKO, Leah. American, b. 1954. **Genres:** Children's fiction, Picture/board books. **Career:** Writer. Involved in cause-related marketing projects for corporations and children. Has appeared on PBS's Reading Rainbow. **Publications:** PICTURE BOOKS: I Like the Music, 1987; Annie Bananie, 1987; Earl's Too Cool for Me, 1988; My Perfect Neighborhood, 1990; Where Can Daniel Be?, 1992; (Selfillustrated) A Million Moms and Mine, 1992; Leonora O'Grady, 1992; Aunt Elaine Does the Dance from Spain, 1992; Shoe Shine Shirley, 1993; Broadway Banjo Bill, 1993; Great-Aunt Ida and Her Great Dane, Doc, 1994; Just My Dad and Me, 1995; Fritzi Fox Flew in from Florida, 1995; On Sallie Perry's Farm, 1996. EASY-READERS: Annie Bananie Moves to Barry Avenue, 1996; Annie Bananie: Best Friends to the End, 1997; Annie Bananie and the People's Court, in press; Annie Bananie and the Pain Sisters, in press. **Address:** 13525 Huston St., Sherman Oaks, CA 91423-1401, U.S.A.

KOMP, Diane M. American, b. 1940. **Genres:** Medicine/Health, Inspirational/Motivational Literature. **Career:** Kings County Hospital, Brooklyn, NY, pediatric residency, 1965-67; University of Virginia School of Medicine, Charlottesville, VA, pediatric hematology/oncology fellowship, 1967-69, assistant professor, 1969-73, associate professor, 1973-76, professor of pediatrics, 1976-78, chief of hematology/oncology, 1970-78; American Academy of Pediatrics, fellow, 1971; Yale University School of Medicine, chief of hematology/oncology, 1978-85, professor of pediatrics, 1978-2000, professor emeritus, 2000-. **Publications:** A Window to Heaven: When Children See Life in Death, 1992; A Child Shall Lead Them: Lessons in Hope from Children with Cancer, 1993; Hope Springs from Mended Places: Images of Grace in the Shadows of Life, 1994; Children Are Breakfast for the Heart: Meditations to Nourish the Soul, 1996; Anatomy of a Lie: The Truth about Lies and Why Good People Tell Them, 1998; Bedtime Snacks for the Soul: Meditations to Sweeten Your Dreams, 2000; Why Me?: A Doctor Examines the Book of Job, 2001. Contributor to anthologies, textbooks, periodicals and journals. Contributor of scientific articles to journals. Author of editorials, book reviews, and abstracts of scientific presentations. **Address:** 88 Barker Hill Dr., Guilford, CT 06437, U.S.A. **Online address:** DoktorDi@aol.com

KOMUNYAKAA, Yusef. American, b. 1947. **Genres:** Poetry. **Career:** New Orleans Public Schools, elementary teacher; University of New Orleans-Lakefront, instructor in English and poetry; Indiana University at Bloomington, beginning in 1985, Ruth Lilly Professor, 1989-90, associate professor of arts and sciences. **Publications:** POETRY: Dedications and Other Darkhorses, 1977; Lost in the Bonewheel Factory, 1979; Copacetic, 1984; I Apologize for the Eyes in My Head, 1986; Dien Cai Dau, 1988; (ed. with S. Feinstein) The Jazz Poetry Anthology, 1991; Magic City, 1992; Neon Vernacular: New and Selected Poems, 1993; Thieves of Paradise, 1998; Talking Dirty to the Gods, 2000. Contributor to anthologies. Contributor of poetry and reviews to periodicals. **Address:** Princeton University, 210 185 Nassau St, Council of Humanities, Princeton, NJ 08544, U.S.A.

KONIGSBURG, E(laine) L(obl). American, b. 1930. **Genres:** Children's fiction. **Publications:** Jennifer, Hecate, Macbeth, William McKinley and Me, Elizabeth, 1967; From the Mixed-Up Files of Mrs. Basil E. Frankweiler, 1967 (Newbery Medal 1968); About the B'nai Bagels, 1969; (George), 1970; Altogether, One at a Time, 1971; A Proud Taste for Scarlet and Miniver, 1973; The Dragon in the Ghetto Caper, 1974; The Second Mrs. Giaconda, 1975; Father's Arcane Daughter, 1976; Throwing Shadows, 1979; Journey to an 800 Number, 1982, in U.K. as Journey by First Class Camel, 1983; Up from Jericho Tel, 1986; Samuel Todd's Book of Great Colors, 1990; Samuel Todd's Book of Great Inventions, 1991; Amy Elizabeth Explores Bloomingdale's, 1992; T-Backs, T-Shirts, COAT, and Suit, 1993; TalkTalk: A Children's Book Author Speaks to Grown-Ups, 1995; The View from Saturday, 1996 (Newbery Medal 1997); Silent to the Bone, 2000; Outcasts of 19 Schuyler Place, 2004. **Address:** c/o Atheneum Publishers, 1230 Avenue of the Americas, New York, NY 10020, U.S.A.

KONING, (Angela) Christina. British (born Brunei Darussalam), b. 1954. **Genres:** Novels. **Career:** Writer. Tate Gallery, worked in Publications Department, 1978; Transworld Publishers Ltd., member of export sales staff, 1978-81. Lecturer at educational institutions worldwide. Appeared on British television programs. **Publications:** A Mild Suicide (novel), 1992; The Good Reading Guide to Children's Books, 1997; Undiscovered Country (novel), 1998; Fabulous Time (novel), 2000. Work represented in anthologies. Contributor of articles, stories, and reviews to magazines and newspapers. **Address:** c/o Derek Johns, A.P. Watt Ltd., 20 John St, London WC1N 2DR, England. **Online address:** ckoning@interbase.co.uk

KONING, Hans. Also writes as Hans Koningsberger. American (born Netherlands), b. 1924. **Genres:** Novels, Plays/Screenplays, Politics/Government. **Publications:** Aquarel of Holland, 1950; The Golden Keys, 1956; The Blood-Red Cafe, 1958; The Affair, 1958; An American Romance, 1960; Walk with Love and Death, 1961, film, 1968; The Wind in the Pines (film), 1961; Hermione, 1962; I Know What I'm Doing, 1964; Love and Hate in China, 1966; The Revolutionary, 1967, screenplay, 1970; (as Hans Koning) The World of Vermeer, 1967; Along the Roads of the New Russia, 1968; The Future of Che Guevara, 1971; The Almost World, 1972; Death of Schoolboy, 1974; The Petersburg-Cannes Express, 1975; Columbus: His Enterprise, 1975, rev. ed. 1992; A New Yorker in Egypt, 1976; Amsterdam, 1977; America Made Me, 1979; The Kleber Flight, 1981; DeWitt's War, 1983; Nineteen Sixty Eight, 1987; Acts of Faith, 1988; The Iron Age, 1990; The Conquest of America, 1993; Pursuit of a Woman on the Hinge of History, 1998. **Address:** c/o Sterling Lord Literistic, 65 Bleecker St., New York, NY 10012, U.S.A.

KONINGSBERGER, Hans. *See* **KONING, Hans.**

KONRAD, Klaus. *See* **WHITING, Charles (Henry).**

KONZAK, Burt. (born United States), b. 1946. **Genres:** Children's fiction. **Career:** Toronto Academy of Karate and Judo, Toronto, Ontario, Canada, director and founder, 1970-; University of Toronto, assistant professor in the School of Physical and Health Education, 1973-94, instructor of Zen Buddhism and the Martial Arts, 1974-77; University of Guelph, Guelph, Ontario, Canada, instructor in sociology, 1980-81. Research associate at the Center for Comparative Political Research, State University of New York-Binghamton, 1969-70; research assistant at Harvard University, Cambridge, MA, 1970. Guest lecturer at colleges and universities in the United States and Canada. Teaches martial arts, self-defense, self-confidence, and fitness through workshops and demonstrations to schools, businesses, and other groups around the world. **Publications:** Noguchi the Samurai, 1994; Girl Power: Self-Defence for Teens, 1999; Samurai Spirit: Ancient Wisdom for Modern Life, 2002. Contributor of numerous articles to scholarly and popular journals. **Address:** 50 Poplar Plains Crescent, Toronto, ON, Canada M4V 1E8. **Online address:** boudreau@glendon.yorku.ca

KOOLHAAS, Rem. Dutch. **Genres:** Archaeology/Antiquities. **Career:** Writer. Has taught at Harvard, Columbia, UCLA, the Technical University of Delft, and London's Architectural Association. **Publications:** IN ENGLISH: Delirious New York: A Retroactive Manifesto for Manhattan, 1978, reprinted, 1994; (with B. Mau) S, M, L, XL: Office for Metropolitan Architecture, 1995; Rem Koolhaas: Conversations with Students, 1996; (with B. Mau) Living, 1999. UNTRANSLATED WORKS: (with others) Hoe Modern is de Nederlandse Architectuur?, 1990; Lille, 1990; Rem Koolhaas: Projectes Urbans (1985-1990), 1990; Six Projets/O.M.A., 1990. Contributor to periodicals. **Address:** Harvard Design School, 48 Quincy St, Cambridge, MA 02138, U.S.A. **Online address:** rkoolhaas@gsd.harvard.edu

KOONS, Carolyn. American, b. 1942. **Genres:** Adult non-fiction. **Career:** Azusa Pacific University, Azusa, CA, professor of Christian education, Institute for Outreach Ministries, executive director; author, writer, speaker; adjunct professor, Fuller Theological Seminary and Biola University. **Publications:** Tony, Our Journey Together, 1984; Beyond Betrayal, Healing My Broken Past, 1986; Single Adult Passages, Baker Book, 1991; Unstuck, Risking Change in Adult Life Passages, 1993. **Address:** Institute for Outreach Ministries, Azusa Pacific University, 901 E Alosta Ave, Azusa, CA 91702, U.S.A.

KOONS, James. *See* **PERNU, Dennis.**

KOONTZ, Dean R(ay). Also writes as David Axton, Brian Coffey, Deanna Dwyer, K. R. Dwyer, John Hill, Leigh Nichols, Owen West. American, b. 1945. **Genres:** Novels, Novellas/Short stories, Horror, Science fiction/Fantasy, Social commentary, Writing/Journalism. **Career:** Freelance writer, 1969-. **Publications:** Star Quest, 1968; The Fall of the Dream Machine, 1969; The Dark Symphony, 1970; Hell's Gate, 1970; Dark of the Woods, 1970; Beastchild, 1970; Anti-Man, 1970; Soft Come the Dragons (SF short stories), 1970; (with G. Koontz) The Pig Society (non-fiction), 1970; (with G. Koontz) The Underground Lifestyles Handbook (non-fiction), 1970; The Crimson Witch, 1971; The Flesh in the Furnace, 1972; A Darkness in My Soul, 1972; Time Thieves, 1972; Warlock, 1972; Starblood, 1972; Demon Seed, 1973; A Werewolf among Us, 1973; Hanging On, 1973; The Haunted Earth, 1973; Writing Popular Fiction (non-fiction), 1973; After the Last Race, 1975; Nightmare Journey, 1975; Night Chills, 1976; The Vision, 1977; Whispers, 1980; Phantoms, 1983; Darkness Comes (in US as Darkfall), 1984; Strangers, 1986; Watchers, 1987; Twilight Eyes, 1987; Oddkins, 1988; Servants of Twilight, 1988; Midnight, 1989; The Bad Place, 1990; Cold Fire, 1990; Dark Rivers of the Heart, 1994; Strange Highways, 1995; Tick-Tock, 1995; Intensity, 1995; Sole Survivor, 1997; Fear Nothing, 1998; Sieze the Night, 1999; Flase Memory, 2000; From the Corner of His Eye, 2001; One Door Away from Heaven, 2002; By the Light of the Moon, 2002; Face, 2003; Every Day's a Holiday, 2003; Robot Santa, 2004; Odd Thomas, 2004. AS DAVID AXTON: Prison of Ice (novel), 1976. NOVELS AS BRIAN COFFEY: Blood Risk, 1973; Surrounded, 1974; The Wall of Masks, 1975; The Face of Fear, 1977; The Voice of the Night, 1980. AS DEANNA DWYER: Demon Child, 1971; Legacy of Terror, 1971; Children of the Storm, 1972; The Dark Summer, 1972; Dance with the Devil, 1973. NOVELS AS K.R. DWYER: Chase, 1972; Shattered, 1973; Dragonfly, 1975. AS JOHN HILL: The Long Sleep, 1975. AS LEIGH NICHOLS: Key to Midnight, 1979; The Eyes of Darkness, 1981; House of Thunder, 1982; Twilight, 1984; Shadow Fires, 1987. AS OWEN WEST: The Funhouse (novelization of

screenplay), 1980; The Mask, 1981. **Address:** c/o Robert Gottlieb, Trident Media Group LLC, 41 Madison Ave 36th Fl, New York, NY 10010, U.S.A.

KOONTZ, Robin Michal. American, b. 1954. **Genres:** Children's fiction, Illustrations. **Career:** Production artist, illustrator, and writer. Worked as a veterinarian's assistant and nursing home activities director, 1974-76; Monterey Bay Publishing Co., Monterey, CA, typesetter, 1976-77; Express Press Printing, Eugene, OR, typesetter/camera, 1978-84; free-lance advertising production artist in Eugene, 1984-85; free-lance illustrator/writer, 1985-. Robin's Light-Arted Design Co., Noti, OR, owner; designer of gift tags, enclosures, and greeting cards, 1981-88. Conducts writing and illustrating workshops. **Publications:** Pussycat Ate the Dumplings, 1987; Dinosaur Dream, 1988; This Old Man, 1988; Chicago and the Cat: A Little Chapter Book, 1992; I See Something You Don't See: A Riddle-Me Picture Book, 1992; Chicago and the Cat: The Camping Trip, 1994; Chicago and the Cat: Halloween Party, 1994; Chicago and the Cat: The Family Reunion, 1996; Chicago and the Cat at the Country Fair, 1998; Complete Backyard Nature Activity Book, 1998; Why a Dog? By a Cat, 2000; How Is a Moose Like a Goose?, 2002. Illustrator of books by: B. Ayres, J. Hoffman, D. McNally, S. Tattler, E. Wilson. **Address:** PO Box 336, Noti, OR 97461, U.S.A. **Online address:** robink@rio.com

KOOPERMAN, Evelyn L. American, b. 1945. **Genres:** Local history/Rural topics. **Career:** San Diego Public Library, San Diego, CA, librarian, 1972-. **Publications:** San Diego Trivia, 1989; San Diego Trivia 2, 1993. **Address:** San Diego Public Library, 820 E St., San Diego, CA 92101, U.S.A.

KOOSER, Ted. (Theodore Kooser). American, b. 1939. **Genres:** Poetry, Adult non-fiction. **Career:** Vice President, 1994-98, now retired, Lincoln Benefit Life, Nebraska, (Sr. Underwriter, 1973-80, Associate Vice-President, 1980-94). Publisher, Windflower Press., Lincoln, 1967-. Part-Time Instructor in Creative Writing, University of Nebraska, Lincoln, 1970-. High School teacher, Madrid, Iowa, 1962-63; Correspondent, 1964-65, and Underwriter, 1965-73, Bankers Life Nebraska, Lincoln. **Publications:** Official Entry Blank, 1969; Grass County, 1971; Twenty Poems, 1973; A Local Habitation, and A Name, 1974; Shooting a Farmhouse; So This Is Nebraska, 1973; Not Coming to Be Barked At, 1976; Hatcher, 1978; Old Marriage and New, 1978; (with W. Kloefkorn) Cottonwood County, 1979; Sure Signs: New and Selected Poems, 1980; (ed.) The Windflower Home Almanac of Poetry, 1980; The Blizzard Voices, 1986; One World at a Time, 1985; Weather Central, 1994; Winter Morning Walks: 100 Postcards to Jim Harrison, 2000; Local Wonders: Seasons in the Bohemian Alps, 2002. **Address:** 1820 Branched Oak Rd, Garland, NE 68360, U.S.A.

KOPINAK, Kathryn. Canadian. **Genres:** Sociology. **Career:** King's University College, University of Western Ontario, Canada, professor of political sociology; writer. **Publications:** Desert Capitalism: Maquiladoras in North America's Western Industrial Corridor, 1996, as Desert Capitalism: What Are the Maquiladoras?, 1997. **Address:** Dept of Sociology, King's University College, 266 Epworth Ave, London, ON, Canada N6A 2M3. **Online address:** kopinak@uwo.ca

KOPIT, Arthur. American, b. 1937. **Genres:** Plays/Screenplays. **Publications:** Oh Dad, Poor Dad, Mama's Hung You in the Closet and I'm Feelin' So Sad: A Pseudoclassical Tragifarce in a Bastard French Tradition, 1960; The Day the Whores Came Out to Play Tennis and Other Plays (in U.K. as Chamber Music and Other Plays), 1965; Indians, 1968; An Incident in the Park, 1968; Wings, 1978; Secrets of the Rich, 1978; Good Help Is Hard to Find, 1982; Nine, 1983; Ghosts (adaptation), 1984; End of the World (with a Symposium to Follow), 1984; Road to Nirvana, 1991; Phantom (libretto), 1992; Three Plays, 1997; Y2K, 1999. **Address:** c/o William Morris Agency, 1325 Avenue of the Americas 15th Fl, New York, NY 10019, U.S.A.

KOPLEWICZ, Harold S. American, b. 1953. **Genres:** Human relations/Parenting. **Career:** Bronx Municipal Hospital Center, internship in pediatrics, 1978-79; New York Hospital, Westchester Division, residency in psychiatry, 1979-81; Columbia Presbyterian Medical Center, NYC, fellowship in child psychiatry, 1981-83, director of general residency training in child psychiatry, 1985-86; New York State Psychiatric Institute, NIMH research fellowship, 1983-85; Long Island Jewish Medical Center, New Hyde Park, NY, chief of division of child and adolescent psychiatry, 1986-96; New York University Medical Center, NYC, vice chair of department of psychiatry, 1996-, director of division of child and adolescent psychiatry, 1996-; New York University, School of Medicine, NYC, professor of clinical psychiatry, 1996-, Child Study Center, director, 1997-. **Publications:** It's Nobody's Fault: New Hope and Help for Difficult Children and Their Parents, 1996; Childhood Revealed: Art Expressing Pain, Discovery and Hope, 1999; Turbulent Times, Prophetic

Dreams: Art of Palestinian and Israeli Children, 2000; More Than Moody: Recognizing and Treating Adolescent Depression, 2002. **Address:** New York University, Child Study Center, 577 1st Ave, New York, NY 10016, U.S.A. **Online address:** harold.koplewicz@med.nyu.edu

KOPLOW, David A. (born United States), b. 1951. **Genres:** Law. **Career:** U.S. Arms Control and Disarmament Agency, Washington, DC, attorney and advisor, 1978-81; Georgetown University Law Center, Washington, DC, professor of law, 1981-, director of Center for Applied Legal Studies. U.S. Department of Defense, Washington, DC, Deputy General Counsel for International Affairs, 1997-99. **Publications:** Testing a Nuclear Test Ban: What Should Be Prohibited by a Comprehensive Treaty?, 1996; By Fire and Ice: Dismantling Chemical Weapons while Preserving the Environment, 1997; Smallpox: The Fight to Eradicate a Global Scourge, 2003. Contributor to books and scholarly journals. **Address:** 1032 Carper St., McLean, VA 22101, U.S.A. **Online address:** koplow@law.georgetown.edu

KOPPER, Lisa (Esther). American, b. 1950. **Genres:** Children's fiction. **Career:** Illustrator and author. **Publications:** SELF-ILLUSTRATED FOR CHILDREN: Daisy Thinks She Is a Baby, 1993; I'm a Baby, You're a Baby, 1994; My Pony Ride, 1995; Daisy Is a Mummy, 1996, in US as Daisy Is a Mommy, 1997; Daisy Knows Best, 1998. Illustrator of books by T. Harriott, L. Clark, H. Lewin, V. Whitehead, R. Silcock, C. Parker, M. Clarke, S. Lavelle, P. Bonnici, J. Older, O.N. Stanford and E.E. Mejias, K. Petty, L. Berg, Althea, S. Fraser, D. MacKinnon, C. Causley, M. Greaves, G. Hallworth. **Address:** 1 Peary Place, London, England.

KORDA, Michael (Vincent). American, b. 1933. **Genres:** Social commentary, Biography. **Career:** Simon and Schuster, publishers, NYC, editor-in-chief (joined co., 1958). **Publications:** NOVELS: Worldly Goods, 1982; Queenie, 1985; The Fortune, 1988; Curtain, 1991; The Immortals, 1992. OTHER: Male Chauvinism! How It Works, 1973; Power! How to Get It, How to Use It, 1975, as Power in the Office, 1976; Success! How Every Man and Woman Can Achieve It, 1977; Charmed Lives (biography of the Korda brothers), 1979; Man to Man: Surviving Prostate Cancer, 1996; Another Life, 1999; Country Matters, 2001. **Address:** c/o Simon and Schuster, 1230 Sixth Ave, New York, NY 10022, U.S.A.

KORDER, Howard. American, b. 1958. **Genres:** Plays/Screenplays. **Career:** Playwright. Worked as a story editor on the television series Kate and Allie for CBS. **Publications:** PLAYS: Middle Kingdom (one act), 1985; Episode 26 (two acts), 1985; Lip Service, 1985 (adapted by Korder for cable television), 1988; Fun (one act), 1987; Nobody (one act), 1987; Boys' Life, 1988; Wonderful Party! (one act), 1989; Search and Destroy, 1989; The Pope's Nose: Short Plays and Sketches, 1991; The Lights, 1993; Night Maneuver, 1995. **Address:** c/o Dramatists Play Service, 440 Park Ave. South, New York, NY 10016, U.S.A.

KORELITZ, Jean Hanff. American, b. 1961. **Genres:** Novels, Poetry. **Publications:** The Properties of Breath (poems), 1988; A Jury of Her Peers, 1996; The Sabbathday River (novel), 1999. **Address:** Pam Bernstein and Associates, 790 Madison Ave Ste 310, New York, NY 10021, U.S.A.

KORG, Jacob. American, b. 1922. **Genres:** Literary criticism and history, Biography. **Career:** Professor Emeritus of English, University of Washington, Seattle, 1965(Assistant and Associate Professor, 1955-65). Former staff member, English Dept., Bard College, Annandale-on-Hudson, New York, University of Maryland, College Park, and City College of New York. **Publications:** An Introduction to Poetry, 1959; George Gissing: A Critical Biography, 1963; Dylan Thomas, 1965, 2nd ed., 1992; (and ed.) The Force of Few Words, 1966; Language in Modern Literature, 1979; Browning and Italy, 1983; Ritual and Experiment in Modern Poetry, 1995; Winter Love: Ezra Pound and H.D., 2003. EDITOR: (with S. F. Anderson) Westward to Oregon, 1958; (with R.S. Beal) Thought in Prose, 1958, 3rd ed., 1966; London in Dickens' Day, 1960; (with R.S. Beal) The Complete Reader, 1961; George Gissing's Commonplace Book, 1962; Twentieth Century Interpretations of Bleak House, 1968; The Poetry of Robert Browning, 1971; Thyrza, by G. Gissing, 1974; The Unclassed, by G. Gissing, 1976; (with C. Korg) George Gissing on Fiction, 1978; George Gissing's Essay on Robert Burns, 1992. **Address:** Dept of English, Box 354330, University of Washington, Seattle, WA 98195, U.S.A. **Online address:** korg@u.washington.edu

KORMAN, Bernice. Canadian, b. 1937. **Genres:** Children's fiction. **Career:** Columnist for the Suburban (English-language weekly newspaper), 1964-81; Teleterm Inc., Markham, Ontario, executive assistant, 1980-. **Publications:** (with G. Korman) The D-Poems of Jeremy Bloom, 1992; (with G. Korman)

The LastPlace Sports Poems of Jeremy Bloom, 1993. **Address:** 20 Dersingham Crescent, Thornhill, ON, Canada L3T 4E7. **Online address:** gorkor@sympatico.ca

KORMAN, Gordon (Richard). American (born Canada), b. 1963. **Genres:** Children's fiction. **Career:** Writer, 1975-. **Publications:** CHILDREN'S FICTION: This Can't Be Happening at Macdonald Hall!, 1977; Go Jump in the Pool!, 1979; Beware the Fish!, 1980; Who Is Bugs Potter?, 1980; I Want to Go Home!, 1981; Our Man Weston, 1982; The War with Mr. Wizzle, 1982; Bugs Potter: Live at Nickaninny, 1983; No Coins, Please, 1984; Don't Care High, 1985; Son of Interflux, 1986; A Semester in the Life of a Garbage Bag, 1987; The Zucchini Warriors, 1988; Radio Fifth Grade, 1989; Losing Joe's Place, 1990; Macdonald Hall Goes Hollywood, 1991; (with B. Korman) The D- Poems of Jeremy Bloom, 1992; The Twinkie Squad, 1992; The Toilet Paper Tigers, 1993; Why Did the Underwear Cross the Road?, 1994; Something Fishy at Macdonald Hall, 1995; (with B. Korman) The Last Place Sports Poems of Jeremy Bloom, 1996; The Chicken Doesn't Skate, 1996; Liar, Liar, Pants on Fire, 1997; No More Dead Dogs, 2001; Son of the Mob, 2002; Maxx Comedy: The Funniest Kid in America, 2003; Jake, Reinvented, 2003; Son of the Mob: Hollywood Hustle, 2004; Born to Rock, 2006. MONDAY NIGHT FOOTBALL CLUB SERIES: Quarterback Exchange: I Was John Elway; Running Back Conversion: I Was Barry Sanders; Superbowl Switch: I Was Dan Marino; Heavy Artillery: I Was Junior Seau; Ultimate Scoring Machine: I Was Jerry Rice, 199798. SLAPSHOT SERIES: The Stars from Mars, The All-Mars All-Stars, The Face-Off Phony, Cup Crazy, 1999-2000. NOSEPICKERS SERIES: Nosepickers from Outer Space, Planet of the Nosepickers, Your Mummy Is a Nosepicker, Invasion of the Nosepickers, 1999-2001. ISLAND SERIES: Shipwreck, Survival, Escape, 2001. EVEREST SERIES: The Contest, The Climb, The Summit, 2002. DIVE SERIES: The Discover; The Deep; The Danger, 2003. ON THE RUN SERIES: Chasing the Falconers; The Fugitive Factor; Now You See Them-Now You Don't; The Stowaway Solution, 2005. **Address:** c/o Scholastic Inc, 555 Broadway, New York, NY 10012, U.S.A. **Online address:** gorkor@fci.broadband.com; www.gordonkorman.com

KORMONDY, Edward J(ohn). American, b. 1926. **Genres:** Biology, Environmental sciences/Ecology. **Career:** University of Michigan, instructor in zoology, 1955-57; Oberlin College, OH, assistant professor, associate professor, and professor of biology, 1957-68; American Institute of Biological Sciences, director, Commission on Undergrad. Education in the Biological Sciences, Washington, DC, 1968-71; Evergreen State College, Olympia, WA, member of the faculty, 1971-79, vice-president and provost, 1973-78; National Science Foundation, sr. professional associate, 1979; University of Southern Maine, Portland, provost and professor of biology, 1979-82; California State University, Los Angeles, vice-president, academic affairs, and professor of biology, 1982-86; University of Hawaii, Hilo, and University of Hawaii, W. Oahu (formerly West Oahu College), senior vice president, chancellor, and professor of biology, 1986-93; University of West Los Angeles, president, 1995-97; Pacific Oaks College, special assistant to the president, 2001-. **Publications:** Introduction to Genetics, 1964; Concepts of Ecology, 1969, 4th ed., 1995; (with T. Sherman) Biology: The Natural History and Integrity of Organisms, 1978; (with F. McCormick) Handbook of Contemporary Developments in World Ecology, 1981; (with B. Nebel) Environmental Science: The Way the World Works, 1981; (with B. Essenfeld) Biology, 1984; International Handbook of Pollution Control, 1989; (with P. Corcoran) Environmental Education, 1997; (with D. Brown) Fundamentals of Human Ecology, 1998; (with F. Inouye) University of Hawai'i-Hilo: A College in the Making, 2001. EDITOR: Readings in Ecology, 1965; General Biology, 2 vols., 1966; (with R. Leisner) Population, 1971; (with R. Leisner) Pollution, 1971; (with R. Leisner) Ecology, 1971. **Address:** 1388 Lucile Ave, Los Angeles, CA 90026-1520, U.S.A. **Online address:** ekor@aol.com

KORN, Marianne. See MACDONALD, Marianne.

KORNBLATT, Judith Deutsch. American, b. 1955. **Genres:** Mythology/Folklore, Cultural/Ethnic topics, Literary criticism and history, Philosophy, Intellectual history, Theology/Religion. **Career:** Columbia University, NYC, preceptor, 1982-85; Williams College, Williamstown, MA, visiting lecturer, spring, 1984; Columbia University, adjunct visiting assistant professor, spring, 1986; Indiana University-Bloomington, visiting assistant Professor, 1986-87; University of Wisconsin-Madison, visiting assistant professor, 1987-88, assistant professor, 1988-93, associate professor of Slavic languages, 1993-98, professor, 1998-, associate dean for humanities, graduate school, 1998-. **Publications:** The Cossack Hero in Russian Literature: A Study in Cultural Mythology, 1992; (co-ed. with R.F. Gustafson) Russian Religious Thought, 1996. Work represented in anthologies. Contributor of articles and reviews to periodicals. **Address:** Department of Slavic Languages, University of Wisconsin-Madison, 1220 Linden Dr., 720 VH, Madison, WI 53706, U.S.A.

KORNBLATT, Marc. American, b. 1954. **Genres:** Children's fiction, Plays/Screenplays. **Career:** Children's book author, playwright, teacher; began career as actor while working as a bartender, waiter, doorman, furniture mover, and typist. **Publications:** Flame of the Inquisition, 1986; (with S. Nanus) Mission to World War II, 1986; Paul Revere and the Boston Tea Party, 1987. PICTURE BOOKS: The Search for Sidney's Smile, 1993; Eli and the Dimplemeyers, 1994. CHILDREN'S NOVELS: Understanding Buddy, 2001; Izzy's Place, 2002. PLAYS: The Great Soul (for children), 1991; Plain Jane (for children), 1991; Bar Talk (one-act), 1992; Clifford's Voices, 1993; Last Days of a Translator, 1995; Dead Man on the Sidewalk Trilogy, 1996; Rope of Sand, 1998. Contributor of plays to the periodical Search, including Cold War Casualties, 1989; Biblical Warfare, 1990; Bloodbath at Cuyahoga, 1990; and The War at Home, 1990. Contributor of short stories and articles to periodicals. **Address:** 1108 Garfield St, Madison, WI 53711, U.S.A. **Online address:** members.home.net/mkornblatt

KORNBLITH, Hilary. American, b. 1954. **Genres:** Philosophy. **Career:** University of Vermont, Burlington, professor of philosophy and chairperson of department, 1979-. **Publications:** (ed.) Naturalizing Epistemology, 1985, 2nd 1994; Inductive Inference and Its Natural Ground, 1993. **Address:** Department of Philosophy, University of Vermont, Burlington, VT 05401, U.S.A.

KORNBLUH, Peter. American. **Genres:** International relations/Current affairs. **Career:** Writer. National Security Archive, senior analyst, 1986-, director of project on U.S.-Cuba relations; Columbia University, NYC, adjunct professor of international and public affairs, 1990-. **Publications:** Nicaragua, the Price of Intervention: Reagan's Wars against the Sandinistas, 1987; (ed., with M.T. Klare) Low-Intensity Warfare: Counterinsurgency, Pro-insurgency, and Antiterrorism in the Eighties, 1988; Nicaragua: The Making of U.S. Policy, 1978-1990 (microform), 1991; (ed. with M. Byrne) The Iran-Contra Affair: The Making of a Scandal, 1983-1988 (microform), 1992; (ed., with M. Byrne) The Iran-Contra Affair: A National Security Archive Documents Reader, 1992; (ed., with Byrne) The Iran-Contra Scandal: The Declassified History, 1993; (with J.G. Blight) Politics of Illusion: The Bay of Pigs Invasion Reexamined, 1998; (ed.) Bay of Pigs Declassified: The Secret CIA Report, 1998; (ed., with L. Chang) Cuban Missile Crisis, 1962: Including Recently Declassified Documents, 1998. Contributor to periodicals. **Address:** The National Security Archive, The Gelman Library, George Washington University, 2130 H Street NW Suite 701, Washington, DC 20037, U.S.A. **Online address:** pkorn@gwis2.circ.gwu.edu

KORNFIELD, Jack. American, b. 1945. **Genres:** Inspirational/Motivational Literature. **Career:** Meditation teacher, 1974-. Peace Corps volunteer in Thailand; cofounder, Insight Meditation Society, 1972; founder, Spirit Rock Center; Spiritwalk Foundation, instructor. **Publications:** (with S. Bhikkhu) A Brief Guide to Meditation Temples of Thailand, 1978; Living Buddhist Masters, 1977; (with J. Goldstein) Seeking the Heart of Wisdom: The Path of Insight Meditation, 1987; A Path with Heart: A Guide through the Perils and Promises of Spiritual Life, 1993; Buddha's Little Instruction Book, 1994; Living Dharma: Teachings of Twelve Buddhist Masters, 1996; (with Thieh Nhat, Bastan-Dzin-Rgya-Mtsho, and the Dalai Lama, Tenzin Gyatso) Buddhism in the West: Spiritual Wisdom for the Twenty-first Century, 1998; After the Ecstasy, the Laundry, 2000. EDITOR: (with P. Breiter) A Still Forest Pool: The Insight Meditation of Achaan Chah, 1985; (with G. Fronsdal) Teachings of the Buddha, 1993; (with C. Feldman) Soul Food: Stories to Nourish the Spirit and and the Heart, 1996. **Address:** Spiritwalk Foundation, PO Box 1022, Thousand Oaks, CA 91358, U.S.A.

KORNHEISER, Tony. American, b. 1948. **Genres:** Adult non-fiction. **Career:** Journalist and radio/television commentator. Newsday, Garden City, NY, reporter, 1970-75; New York Times, New York City, reporter, 1976-79; Washington Post, Washington, DC, reporter/columnist, 1979-. WJLA-TV, Washington, DC, host of The Tony Kornheiser Show, 1989; regular guest on The Sports Reporter, ESPN-TV; ESPN-Radio, host of The Tony Kornheiser Show. **Publications:** The Baby Chase, 1983; Pumping Irony; Bald as I Want to Be, 1997. **Address:** Washington Post, 1150 15th St. N.W., Washington, DC 20071, U.S.A.

KORNWOLF, James D. American. **Genres:** History, Architecture. **Career:** Educator, author, and art historian. Instructor at Rollins College and New Jersey Institute of Technology; College of William and Mary, Williamsburg, VA, professor of art history, 1968-c. 2002, now emeritus. Lecturer at colleges and universities. **Publications:** A History of American Dwellings, 1967; M.H. Ballie Scott and the Arts and Crafts Movement: Pioneers of Modern Design, 1972; (ed.) Modernism in America 1937-1941: A Catalog and Exhibition of Four Architectural Competitions: Wheaton College,

Goucher College, College of William and Mary, Smithsonian Institution, 1985; So Good a Design: The Colonial Campus of the College of William and Mary: Its History, Background, and Legacy, 1989; (with G.W. Kornwolf) Architecture and Town Planning in Colonial North America, 3 vols, 2002. Contributor of articles and book reviews to periodicals. Contributor to museum exhibition catalogues. **Address:** College of William and Mary, Department of Art and Art History, PO Box 8795, Williamsburg, VA 23187, U.S.A. **Online address:** jdkorn@wm.edu

KOROBKIN, Laura Hanft. American. **Genres:** Literary criticism and history. **Career:** Boston University, Boston, MA, assistant professor of English. **Publications:** Criminal Conversations: Sentimentality and Nineteenth-Century Legal Stories of Adultery, 1998. Contributor to professional journals and books. **Address:** Department of English, Boston University, 236 Bay State Rd., Boston, MA 02215, U.S.A. **Online address:** korobkin@bu.edu

KORT, Wesley A. American, b. 1935. **Genres:** Literary criticism and history, Theology/Religion. **Career:** University of Chicago, Divinity School, assistant to Perrin Lowry, Humanities Division, 1961-62, and Preston T. Roberts, 1962-63; Princeton University, NJ, Dept. of Religion, instructor, 1963-65; Duke University, Durham, NC, Dept. of Religion, assistant professor, 1965-70, member of Graduate Faculty of Religion, 1965-, associate professor, 1970-76, assistant dean of Graduate School, 1970-71, assistant provost, 1973-74, professor, 1976-. **Publications:** Shriven Selves: Religious Problems in Recent American Fiction, 1972; Narrative Elements and Religious Meaning, 1975; Moral Fiber: Character and Belief in Recent American Fiction, 1982; Modern Fiction and Human Time: A Study in Narrative and Belief, 1985; Story, Text, and Scripture: Literary Interests in Biblical Narratives, 1988; Bound to Differ: The Dynamics of Theological Discourses, 1992; "Take, Read": Scripture, Textuality, and Cultural Practice, 1996; C.S. Lewis Then and Now, 2001: Place and Space in Modern Fiction, 2004. **Address:** 308 Old Buggy Trail, Hillsborough, NC 27278, U.S.A. **Online address:** WKort@duke.edu

KORTH, Philip A. American, b. 1936. **Genres:** Organized labor, Local history/Rural topics, Anthropology/Ethnology. **Career:** Michigan State University, East Lansing, professor and associate dean, College of Arts & Letters; writer. **Publications:** (with M. Beegle) I Remember Like Today: The Auto-Lite Strike of 1934, 1988; Michigan: Visions of Our Past, 1990; Craftsmanship and the Michigan Union Carpenters, 1991; The Minneapolis Teamsters' Strike of 1934, 1995. Contributor to periodicals. **Address:** 4889 S Meadow Ridge Dr, Green Valley, AZ 85614, U.S.A. **Online address:** Korth@msu.edu

KORZENIK, Diana. American, b. 1941. **Genres:** Art/Art history, Education, Sociology. **Career:** Massachusetts College of Art, Boston, professor of art education, 1972-, now emerita, chairperson of department, 1972-87; writer and editor. Curator of exhibits; lecturer; consultant; American Antiquarian Society, advisor in American Art Education, 1992-93. **Publications:** Drawn to Art: A Nineteenth-Century American Dream, 1985; (co-author) Art-Making and Education, 1993; (co-ed.) The Cultivation of Artists in 19th Century America, 1997. Contributor to books and periodicals.

KOSCIELNIAK, Bruce. American, b. 1947. **Genres:** Children's fiction, Illustrations. **Career:** U.S. Postal Service, Adams, MA, clerk, 1977-91; writer and illustrator. **Publications:** FOR CHILDREN, SELF-ILLUSTRATED: Hector and Prudence, 1990; Hector and Prudence-All Aboard!, 1990; Euclid Bunny Delivers the Mail, 1991; Bear and Bunny Grow Tomatoes, 1993; Geoffrey Groundhog Predicts the Weather, 1995; Hear, Hear, Mr. Shakespeare, 1998; The Story of the Incredible Orchestra, 2000; Johann Gutenberg and the Amazing Printing Press, 2003. Illustrator of book by D. Fair. **Address:** 36 Summer St, Adams, MA 01220, U.S.A.

KOSHIRO, Yukiko. American (born Japan). **Genres:** Race relations. **Career:** Williams College, Williamstown, MA, visiting assistant professor; East Asian Institute at Columbia University, New York, NY, visiting scholar, 2001-02; University of Notre Dame, Notre Dame, IN, assistant professor of history; Vassar College, Poughkeepsie, NY, visiting professor; Bates College, Lewiston, ME, visiting professor in department of history, 2002-03. **Publications:** Trans-Pacific Racisms and the U.S. Occupation of Japan, 1999. **Address:** Department of History, Pettengill Hall, Bates College, Lewiston, ME 04240, U.S.A. **Online address:** ykoshiro@bates.edu

KOSKI, Mary B(ernadette). American, b. 1951. **Genres:** Children's fiction. **Career:** Welcome Home, Biwabik, MN, administrator, 1975-77; University of Minnesota-Duluth, instructor in accounting, 1981-82; Mesabi Community

College, Virginia, MN, instructor in accounting, 1982-92, acting viceprovost, 1985-87; Duluth Community College, Duluth, director and executive dean, 1992-95; Lake Superior College, Duluth, member of accounting and economics faculty, beginning in 1997. Certified public accountant. **Publications:** FOR CHILDREN: Impatient Pamela Calls 9-1-1, 1998; Pamela Asks: Why Are My Feet So Huge?, 2000; Impatient Pamela Wants a Bigger Family, 2002. **Address:** PO Box 948, Carefree, AZ 85377, U.S.A. **Online address:** mbkoski@aol.com

KOSS-CHIOINO, Joan D. American, b. 1935. **Genres:** Anthropology/ Ethnology, Psychiatry, Psychology. **Career:** Eastern Pennsylvania Psychiatric Institute, Philadelphia, research assistant, 1957; University of Pennsylvania, Philadelphia, instructor, 1964, lecturer in anthropology, 1964-65, lecturer in nursing, 1965-67; Temple University, lecturer and assistant professor, 1965-66, adjunct assistant professor, 1966-67; University of Puerto Rico, Rio Piedras, associate professor of anthropology, 1967-79; InterAmerican University, San Juan, Puerto Rico, visiting professor and head of Social Sciences Division, 1971-73; University of Puerto Rico, Dental Sciences lecturer in ecological sciences 1972-74; University of California, San Francisco, lecturer in psychiatry and postdoctoral fellow in international health, 1974-76, adjunct professor, 1975-87; California State University, Hayward, professor of anthropology, 1977-80; University of New Mexico, Albuquerque, associate professor, 1980-89, professor of psychiatry, 1989-92; Arizona State University, Tempe, professor of anthropology and women's studies, 1992-. Tulane University Medical Center, adjunct professor and visiting professor, 1989-. Government of Puerto Rico, Dept of Health, program director and researcher, 1976-79; consultant. Author of the film series "Alternative Paths to Healing," 1980-. **Publications:** Women as Healers, Women as Patients, 1992; (ed. with L. Vargas) Working with Culture, 1992; (with L. Vargas) Working with Latino Youth, 1999; (with T. Leatherman) Medical Pluralism in the Andes, 2003. Work represented in books. Contributor of articles and reviews to professional journals, until 1987 under the name Joan Koss. **Address:** 2011 I St NW #307, Washington, DC 20006, U.S.A. **Online address:** Joan.Koss@asu.edu

KOSSMAN, Nina. American (born Russia), b. 1959. **Genres:** Poetry, Autobiography/Memoirs, Translations. **Career:** Writer and translator. Worked as a language instructor in colleges, 1980-98. National Endowment for the Arts, fellowship panelist, 1994; oil paintings have appeared in group exhibitions in NYC. **Publications:** (trans.) M. Tsvetaeva, In the Inmost Hour of the Soul: Poems of Marina Tsvetaeva, 1989; (self-illustrated) Pereboii (poetry; title means: Syncopated Rhythms), 1990; Behind the Border: Memories of a Russian Childhood, 1994; Po Pravuyu Ruku Sna (poetry in Russian and English), 1996; (trans.) Tsvetaeva, Poem of the End: Selected Lyrical & Narrative Poetry, 1998; (ed.) Gods and Mortals: Modern Poems on Classical Myths (anthology), 2000. Contributor of short fiction to periodicals. Contributor of poetry to Russian periodicals. Contributor of poetry to anthologies. Translator of poetry appearing in anthologies.

KOSSOFF, David. British, b. 1919. **Genres:** Theology/Religion, Novellas/ Short stories. **Career:** Actor since 1945. Bible storyteller, BBC Radio and TV, since 1964. Former commercial artist, draughtsman, furniture designer, and technical illustrator. **Publications:** Bible Stories Retold, 1968; The Book of Witnesses, 1971; The Three Donkeys, 1972; The Voices of Masada, 1973; The Little Book of Sylvanus, 1975; You Have a Minute, Lord?, 1977; A Small Town Is a World, 1979; Sweet Nutcracker, 1985. **Address:** c/o Harper Collins Publishers, 77-85 Fulham Palace Rd, London W6 8JB, England.

KOSTELANETZ, Richard (Cory). American, b. 1940. **Genres:** Novels, Novellas/Short stories, Poetry, Art/Art history, Communications/Media, Dance/Ballet, Literary criticism and history, Music. **Career:** Assembling Press, Brooklyn, NY, co-compiler, assembling annual book, and co-director, 1970-82; John Jay College, City University of New York, program associate, thematic studies, 1972-73; Future Press, literary director, 1976-; Precisely, co-ed. and publisher, 1977-. University of Texas at Austin, visiting professor of American studies and English, 1977; American Writing Today, coordinator-interviewer, 1979-81. **Publications:** Music of Today, 1967; The Theatre of Mixed Means, 1968; Master Minds, 1969; And So Forth, 1969; Visual Language, 1970; The End of Intelligent Writing, 1974; I Articulations/Short Fictions, 1974; Recyclings: A Literary Autobiography, vol. I, 1974; Number One, 1974; Come Here, 1975; Extrapolate, 1975; Modulations, 1975; Word Prints, 1975; Portraits from Memory, 1975; Openings and Closings, 1975; Rain Rains Rain, 1976; Numbers: Poems and Stories, 1976; Constructs, 1976; Illuminations, 1977; Foreshortenings and Other Stories, 1978; Word-sand, 1978; Constructs Two, 1978; Grants and the Future of Literature, 1978; Tabula Rasa, 1978; Inexistencies, 1978; Twenties in the Sixties: Previously Uncollected Critical Essays, 1979; "The End" Appendix/"The End" Es-

sentials, 1979; Metamorphosis in the Arts, 1980; More Short Fictions, 1980; Exhaustive Parallel Intervals, 1980; Autobiographies, 1981; The Old Poetries and the New, 1981; Reincarnations, 1981; Turfs/Arenas/Fields/Pitches, 1983; Epiphanies, 1983; American Imaginations, 1983; Recyclings, 1984; The Old Fictions and the New, 1987; After Texts/Prose Pieces, 1987; The Grants-Fix, 1987; Conversing with Cage, 1988, 2nd ed., 2002; On Innovative Music(ian)s, 1989; Unfinished Business, 1990; The New Poetries and Some Old, 1991; Politics in the African-American Novel, 1991; WordWorks: Poems New and Selected, 1993; A Dictionary of the Avant-Gardes, 1993, 2nd ed., 2000; Minimal Fictions, 1994; On Innovative Performance(s), 1994; Morepartitions, 1994; Fillmore East: Recollections of Rock Theater, 1995; Crimes of Culture, 1995; An ABC of Contemporary Reading, 1995; One Million Words of Booknotes, 1996; John Cage (Ex)plain(ed), 1996; 30 Years of Critical Engagements with John Cage, 1996; Vocal Shorts: Collected Performance Texts, 1998; Political Essays, 1998; 3-Element Stories, 1998; 3 Canadian Geniuses, 2001; SoHo: The Rise and Fall of an Artists' Colony, 2003; More Openings & Closings, 2003; Autobiographies at 50, 2004; 35Years of Visible Writing, 2004; Autobiographies at 50, 2005; Film & Video: Alternative Views, 2005; Kaddish & Other Audio Writings, 2005. NOVELS: In the Beginning, 1971; One Night Stood, 1977. EDITOR/CO-EDITOR: On Contemporary Literature, 1964; (and contrib.) The New American Arts, 1965; Twelve from the Sixties, 1967; The Young American Writers, 1967; Beyond Left & Right, 1968; Assembling, 10 vols., 1970-81; Imaged Words & Worded Images, 1970; Possibilities of Poetry, 1970; Moholy-Nagy, 1970; John Cage, 1970; Social Speculations, 1971; Future's Fictions, 1971; Human Alternatives, 1971; Seeing through Shuck, 1972; In Youth, 1972; Breakthrough Fictioneers, 1973; The Edge of Adaptation, 1973; Essaying Essays, 1975; Language and Structure, 1975; Younger Critics in North America, 1976; Esthetics Contemporary, 1978; Assembling Assembling, 1978; Visual Literature Criticism, 1979; A Critical Assembling, 1979; Text-Sound Texts, 1980; Scenarios, 1980; Aural Literature Criticism, 1981; The Avant-Garde Tradition in Literature, 1982; American Writing Today, 1982; Pilot Proposals, 1982; Gertrude Stein Advanced, 1991; On Innovative Art(ist)s, Merce Cunningham: Dancing in Time and Space, 1992; John Cage, Writer, 1993; Writings about John Cage, 1993; Nicolas Slonimsky: The First 100 Years, 1994; A Portable Baker's Biographical Dictionary of Musicians, 1995; Classic Essays on 20th Century Music, 1996; A B.B. King Companion, 1997; A Frank Zappa Companion, 1997; Writings on Glass, 1997; AnOther E.E. Cummings, 1998; A Gertrude Stein Reader, 2002; Virgil Thomson: A Reader, 2002; Conceptual Dance; Aaron Copland Reader, 2003. Author of booklets, anthologies, essays, videotapes, films, and audio tapes. **Address:** Box 444, Prince St, New York, NY 10012-0008, U.S.A. **Online address:** RichardKostelanetz.com

KOSTELNIUK, James. (born Canada), b. 1946. **Genres:** Autobiography/ Memoirs. **Career:** Author of nonfiction. Worked various jobs; established janitorial business in Burnaby, British Columbia, Canada, c. 1970s; Winnipeg Transit, Winnipeg, Manitoba, Canada, bus operator, 1980-2001; retired. **Publications:** Wolves among Sheep: The True Story of Murder in a Jehovah's Witness Community, 2000. **Address:** 788 Scotland Ave., Winnipeg, Manitoba, Canada R3M 1X6.

KOSTERS, Marvin H(oward). American, b. 1933. **Genres:** Economics. **Career:** RAND Corp., Santa Monica, CA, economist, 1965-69; President's Council of Economic Advisers, Washington, DC, senior economist, 1969-71; U.S. Cost of Living Council, Washington, DC, associate director for economic policy, 1971-74; American Enterprise Institute for Public Policy Research, Washington, DC, resident scholar, 1974; Office of the Assistant to the President for Economic Affairs, Washington, DC, staff member, 1974-75; American Enterprise Institute for Public Policy Research, director of Center for the Study of Government Regulation, 1976-86, resident scholar and director of economic policy studies, 1987-. U.S. Department of Labor, Manpower Administration, associate administrator for policy, evaluation, and research, 1971, member of Task Force on Economic Adjustment and Worker Dislocation, 1975-76; Civil Aeronautics Board, member of advisory committee on procedural reform, 1975; consultant to U.S. Department of the Treasury and Council on Wage and Price Stability. Teacher at University of Chicago, summers, 1964-65, and University of California, Los Angeles, 1966-69. **Publications:** (with D. Ahalt) Controls and Inflation: The Economic Stabilization Program in Retrospect, 1975. EDITOR: (with T.B. Clark and J.C. Miller III) Reforming Regulation, 1980; (and contrib.) Workers and Their Wages: Changing Patterns in the United States, 1991; (and author of intro) Personal Savings, Consumption, and Tax Policy, 1992; Fiscal Politics and the Budget Enforcement Act, 1992. Work represented in anthologies. Contributor to periodicals. **Address:** 13120 Cedar Ridge Dr, Clifton, VA 20124, U.S.A. **Online address:** mkosters@aei.org

KOSTOFF, Lynn. American, b. 1954. **Genres:** Fashion/Costume. **Career:** Author and educator. Francis Marion University, Florence, SC, professor of

English, 1985-; previously taught at Indiana State University and University of Alabama. **Publications:** A Choice of Nightmares (novel), 1991; The Long Fall (novel), 2003. **Address:** c/o Author Mail, Carroll & Graf Publishers, William St., Sixteenth Floor, New York, NY 10038, U.S.A. **Online address:** LKostoff@fmarion.edu

KOSTORIS PADOA SCHIOPPA, Fiorella. Italian, b. 1945. **Genres:** Economics. **Career:** University of Rome, Italy, associate professor, 1977-80, professor, 1989-; University of Trieste, Italy, professor, 1980-83; Postgraduate School of Public Administration, Rome, professor, 1984-89; Institute for Economic Studies and Analyses, president, 1999-. Oxford University, Jemolo fellow at Nuffield College, 1992. **Publications:** IN ENGLISH: (ed.) Mismatch and Labour Mobility, 1991; Italy: The Sheltered Economy, 1993. IN ITALIAN: Scuola e classi sociali, 1974; La forza lavoro femminale, 1977; L'Economia sotto tutela, 1990; Squilibri erigidita nel mercato del lavoro italiano, 1992; Struttua di mercato e regolamentazione del tresporto aereo, 1995; (ed.) Pensioni e risanamento della finanza pubblica, 1996; (with F. Modigliani) Sostenibilita e solvibilita del pubblico in Italia, 1998. **Address:** Societa Editrice il Mulino Spa, Strada maggiore 37, 40125 Bologna, Italy. **Online address:** presidente@isae.it

KOSTOV, K. N. See **WHITING, Charles (Henry).**

KOTKER, Zane H. Also writes as Maggie Strong. American, b. 1934. **Genres:** Novels, Adult non-fiction, Medicine/Health, Self help. **Career:** Contributor, The New Republic, The National Review, and New York mags. Contributor Writer, Reader's Digest General Books, 1974-78; Associate Professor, Mount Holyoke College, South Hadley, Massachusetts, 1983; Professor, MFA Program, University of Massachusetts, Amherst, 1983; Visiting writer, Smith College, Northampton, MA, 1990, 1991. **Publications:** Bodies in Motion, 1972; A Certain Man, 1976; White Rising, 1981; (as Maggie Strong) Mainstay: For the Well Spouse of the Chronically Ill, 1988; Try to Remember (novel), 1997. **Address:** 45 Lyman Rd, Northampton, MA 01060, U.S.A. **Online address:** zane@crocker.com

KOTLER, Neil G. American, b. 1941. **Genres:** History, Marketing. **Career:** U.S. Peace Corps, volunteer teacher of Ethiopian history in Asmara, Ethiopia, 1964-66; De Paul University, Chicago, IL, instructor in American government and political science, 1967-71; Dartmouth College, Hanover, NH, instructor in American government and political science, 1971-73; University of Texas at Austin, instructor, 1974-75; U.S. House of Representatives, Washington, DC, legislative assistant to legislative director, 1975-84; Smithsonian Institution, Washington, DC, special assistant and program specialist, 1986-. Georgetown University, instructor, 1979. **Publications:** Democracy and Rights: One Citizen's Challenge (documentary videotape), 1989; Citizen Stories: Democracy and Responsibility in American Life (documentary videotape), 1991; (with P. Kolter) Museum Strategy and Marketing, 1998. EDITOR: Social Marketing: Strategies for Changing Public Behavior, 1989; Completing the Food Chain: Strategies for Combating Hunger and Malnutrition, 1989; Sharing Innovation: Global Perspectives on Food, Agriculture, and Rural Development, 1990; Frontiers of Nutrition and Food Security in Asia, Africa, and Latin America, 1992; (co-) The Statue of Liberty Revisited: Making a Universal Symbol, 1994. **Address:** Office of the Provost, Smithsonian Institution, Washington, DC 20560, U.S.A.

KOTLER, Philip. American, b. 1931. **Genres:** Marketing, Social sciences. **Career:** Northwestern University, Evanston, IL, assistant professor, 1962-64, associate professor, 1965-66, Johnson Distinguished Professor of International Marketing, formerly Harold T. Martin Professor of Marketing, 1967-. Director, School of the Art Institute of Chicago. **Publications:** Marketing Management: Analysis, Planning and Control, 1967, 11th ed., 2003; Marketing Models, 1971, 3rd ed., 1992; (co-ed.) Creating Social Change, 1972; (co-ed.) Simulation in the Social and Administrative Sciences, 1972; (co-ed.) Readings in Marketing Management, 1972; Strategic Marketing for Nonprofit Organizations, 1975, 6th ed., 2003; Principles of Marketing, 1980, 9th ed., 2001; Marketing Professional Services, 1984, 2nd ed., 2002; The New Competition, 1985; Strategic Marketing for Educational Institutions, 1985, 2nd ed., 1994; Marketing: An Introduction, 1987, 6th ed., 2002; Marketing for Health Care Organizations, 1987; Social Marketing, 1989, 2nd ed., 2002; Marketing for Congregations: Serving People More Effectively, 1992; Marketing Places: Attracting Investment, Industry, and Tourism to Cities, States, and Nations, 1993; Marketing for Hospitality and Tourism, 1996, 3rd ed., 2002; Standing Room Only: Strategies for Marketing the Performing Arts, 1996; The Marketing of Nations, 1997; Museum Strategy and Marketing, 1998; High Visibility, 2nd ed., 1998; Kotler on Marketing, 1999. **Address:** Kellogg School of Mgmt, Northwestern University, Evanston, IL 60208, U.S.A.

KOTLOWITZ, Alex. American, b. 1955. **Genres:** Social commentary, Documentaries/Reportage. **Career:** Worked on a cattle ranch in Oregon; producer of segments for the television series MacNeil/Lehrer NewsHour; reporter for Chicago Bureau of Wall Street Journal; free-lance writer. **Publications:** There Are No Children Here: The Story of Two Boys Growing up in the Other America, 1991; The Other Side of the River, 1998. **Address:** Wall Street Journal, Chicago Bureau, 1 South Wacker Dr. 21st Floor, Chicago, IL 60606, U.S.A.

KOTTER, John P(aul). American, b. 1947. **Genres:** Administration/Management. **Career:** Educator and management consultant. Harvard University Business School, Cambridge, MA, research fellow, 1972-73, assistant professor, 1973-77, associate professor, 1977-81, professor, 1981-90, Konusuke Matsushita Professor of Leadership, 1990-2002. **Publications:** (with P.R. Lawrence) Mayors in Action: Five Approaches to Urban Governance, 1974; (with V.A. Faux and C. McArthur) Self-Assessment and Career Development, 1978; Organizational Dynamics: Diagnosis and Intervention, 1978; (with L. Schlesinger and V. Sathe) Organization: Text, Cases, and Readings on the Management of Organizational Design and Change, 1979; Power in Management: How to Understand, Acquire, and Use It, 1979; The General Managers, 1982; Power and Influence: Beyond Formal Authority, 1985; The Leadership Factor, 1988; A Force for Change: How Leadership Differs from Management, 1990; (with J.L. Heskett) Corporate Culture and Performance, 1992; The New Rules: How to Succeed in Today's Post-Corporate World, 1995; Leading Change, 1996; Matsushita Leadership: Lessons from the Twentieth Century's Most Remarkable Entrepreneur, 1997; John P. Kotter on What Leaders Really Do, 1999; (with D.S. Cohen) The Heart of Change: Real-Life Stories of How People Change Their Organizations, 2002. **Address:** 975 Memorial Dr., Cambridge, MA 02138, U.S.A. **Online address:** jkotter@hbs.edu

KOTTLER, Jeffrey (A.). American, b. 1951. **Genres:** Self help, Psychology, Education. **Career:** University of North Alabama, Florence, assistant professor, 1976-81; Oakland University, Rochester, MI, adjunct professor, 1982-90; The Citadel, Charleston, SC, associate professor of counseling, 1990-91; Professor of Counseling, University of Nevada, Las Vegas, 1991-. **Publications:** (with W. Van Hoose) Ethical and Legal Issues in Counseling and Psychotherapy, 1977; Mouthing Off, 1980; Pragmatic Group Leadership, 1983; (with R. Brown) Introduction to Therapeutic Counseling, 1985, 3rd ed. 1996; On Being a Therapist, 1987; (with D. Blau) The Imperfect Therapist: Learning from Failure in Therapeutic Practice, 1989; Private Moments, Secret Selves, 1990; The Compleat Therapist, 1991; Compassionate Therapy: Working with Difficult Clients, 1992; (with S. Zehm) On Being a Teacher, 1993; (with E. Kottler) Teacher as Counselor, 1993; (with R. Hazler) The Emerging Professional Counselor: Student Dreams to Professional Realities, 1994; Beyond Blame: A New Way of Resolveing Conflict in Relationships 1994; (with Sexton and S. Whiston) Heart of Healing: Relationships in Therapy, 1994; (with R. Powell, and S. Zehm) Classrooms under the Influence: Counteracting Problems of Addiction, 1995; Growing a Therapist, 1995; The Language of Tears, 1996; (with R. Hazler) What You Never Learned in Graduate School, 1997; What's Really Said in the Teachers Lounge: Provocative Ideas about Cultures and Classrooms, 1997; Travel That Can Change Your Life, 1997. EDITOR: Finding Your Way as a Counselor, 1996; (with H. Forester-Miller) Issues and Challenges in Group Work, 1997. **Address:** Dept of Counseling, California State University, Fullerton, PO Box 6868, Fullerton, CA 92834-6868, U.S.A. **Online address:** jk@jeffreykottler.com; www.jeffreykottler.com

KOTZWINKLE, William. American, b. 1938. **Genres:** Novels, Science fiction/Fantasy, Children's fiction, Novellas/Short stories. **Career:** Freelance writer. **Publications:** SCIENCE FICTION: Hermes 3000, 1972; Doctor Rat, 1976; E.T.: The Extra-Terrestrial (novelization of screenplay), 1982; Superman III (novelization of screenplay), 1983; E.T.: The Book of the Green Planet, 1985; Jewel of the Moon (stories), 1986. NOVELS: The Fan Man, 1974; Night-Book, 1974; Swimmer in the Secret Sea, 1975; Fata Morgana, 1977; Herr Nightingale and the Satin Woman, 1978; Jack in the Box, 1980; Christmas at Fontaine's 1982; Queen of Swords, 1984; Exile, 1987; Hot Jazz Trio, 1989; Midnight Examiner, 1989; The Game of Thirty, 1994. FOR CHILDREN: The Fireman, 1969; The Ship That Came Down the Gutter, 1970; Elephant Boy: A Story of the Stone Age, 1970; The Day the Gang Got Rich, 1970; The Oldest Man and Other Timeless Stories, 1971; Return of Crazy Horse, 1971; The Supreme, Superb, Exalted, and Delightful, One and Only Magic Building, 1973; Up the Alley with Jack and Joe, 1974; The Leopard's Tooth, 1976; The Ant Who Took Away Time, 1978; Dream of Dark Harbor, 1979; The Nap Master, 1979; The Extra Terrestrial Storybook, 1982; Great World Circus, 1983; Trouble in Bugland: A Collection of Inspector Mantis Mysteries, 1983; Seduction in Berlin, 1985; The Book of the

Green Plant, 1985; Hearts of Wood, 1986; The World Is Big and I'm So Small, 1986; The Empty Notebook, 1990. OTHER: The Bear Went Over the Mountain, 1996. **Address:** c/o Doubleday, 1540 Broadway, New York, NY 10036, U.S.A.

KOUPAL, Nancy Tystad. American, b. 1947. **Genres:** History, Literary criticism and history, Women's studies and issues, Bibliography, Biography. **Career:** Morehead State University, teacher of composition, 1971-72; University of Wisconsin, teacher of American literature, 1972-74; South Dakota Department of Social Services, writer/editor, 1975-78; South Dakota State Library, library technician, 1978; freelance writer and editor for historical work on South Dakota women; South Dakota State Historical Society, director of the research and publishing program; South Dakota History, editor, 1979-; South Dakota State Historical Society Press, 1997-. **Publications:** South Dakota Women, 1850-1919: A Bibliography, 1975; (and coproducer) Dakota Women, 1978. EDITOR: The Woman Suffrage Movement in South Dakota, 2nd ed., 1975; The Way They Saw Us: The South Dakota State Historical Society Collection of Images from the Nineteenth-Century Illustrated Press, 1989; (and annotator) Our Landlady, 1996; Baum's Road to Oz: The Dakota Years, 2000; (regional ed.) Encyclopedia of the Great Plains, 2004. Contributor of historical articles, essays, and book reviews to periodicals. **Address:** Director Research and Publishing, South Dakota State Historical Society, 900 Governors Dr., Pierre, SD 57501, U.S.A. **Online address:** nancy. koupal@state.sd.us

KOURILSKY, Françoise. French, b. 1933. **Genres:** Plays/Screenplays, Theatre. **Career:** University of Paris, Sorbonne, France, associate professor of theater, 1968-74; Queens College of the City University of New York, Flushing, visiting professor of theater, 1974-75; State University of New York at Stony Brook, visiting professor of theater, 1975-76; New York University, NYC, professor of theater, 1976-78; Ubu Repertory Theater, NYC, founder, 1982, artistic director, 1982-2002. Stage director, including plays in the US, Canada, and Europe; Center for Theater Practice, co-founder, 1977, co-director, 1977-79; World Theatre Festival, director, 1981-82. **Publications:** Le Theatre aux Etats-Unis, 1967; Le Bread and Puppet Theatre, 1971. Co-author of three other books. Contributor to journals in the United States and abroad. TRANSLATOR: Jean-Paul Wenzel, Far from Hagondange (play), 1977; Michel Deutsch, Sunday (play), 1979; Griselda Gambaro, In the Country (play), 1983; EDITOR: Afrique: New Plays, 1987; The Paris Stage: Recent Plays, 1988; (co) Plays by Women, 1989; Gay Plays: An International Anthology, 1989; Theater and Politics, 1990; Afrique II, 1991; Ubu Repertory Theater, 1982-1992, 1992; New French-Language Plays, 1993; Plays by Women II, 1994; Monologues: Plays from Martinique, France, Algeria, and Quebec, 1995; Plays by Women III, 1996; Playwrights of Exile, 1997. **Address:** 61 Jane St Apt 15H, New York, NY 10014, U.S.A. **Online address:** frkourilsky@aol.com

KOVACH, Gay Haff. American, b. 1956. **Genres:** Children's fiction, Art/Art history, Children's non-fiction, Illustrations. **Career:** Sweet Art, SC, artist and illustrator, 1988-. **Publications:** Coastal Colors, 1995. **Address:** Sweet Art Studio, 221 First Creek Rd, Gaston, SC 29053, U.S.A. **Online address:** happytrailsfarmk@aol.com

KOVACH, Kenneth A. American, b. 1946. **Genres:** Administration/Management. **Career:** George Mason University, Fairfax, VA, professor of management, 1975-. American Council of Education, subject area specialist in personnel and labor relations, 1976-; Washington Personnel Administration, honorary member, 1979-; consultant to U.S. Department of Defense, Mitre Corp., and Zeiders Enterprises Inc. Guest on radio and television programs. American National Red Cross, chairperson of local personnel committee, 1979-. Military service: U.S. Marine Corps, 1968-70. **Publications:** Organization Size, Job Satisfaction, Absenteeism, and Turnover, 1977; Readings and Cases in Contemporary Labor Relations, 1980; Readings and Cases in Contemporary Personnel Management, 1981; Practical Labor Relations, 1986; Human Resource Management: A Diagnostic Approach, 1992; Labor Relations: A Diagnostic Approach, 1992; Strategic Human Resource Management, 1996; Strategic Labor Relations, 1997. Contributor to labor and management journals and newspapers. **Address:** School of Management, MSN 5F5, 218 Enterprise Hall, George Mason University, 4400 University Dr., Fairfax, VA 22030, U.S.A. **Online address:** KKOVACH@SOM.GMU. EDU

KOVACS, Deborah. American, b. 1954. **Genres:** Children's fiction, Children's non-fiction. **Career:** Children's Television Workshop, NYC, 1975-80, began as toy, game, and record developer for Sesame Street, became editor of Sesame Street Magazine; Scholastic Inc., NYC, magazine editor, 1980-85, founder and creative director of software division, 1985-97;

freelance writer for book, magazine, and computer software publishers; children's book author; Turnstone Publishing Group, Boston, MA, editor-in-chief, 1997-. **Publications:** Frazzle's Fantastic Day, 1980; When Is Saturday?, 1981; Battle of the Bands, 1987; A Day Underwater, 1987; The Hottest Group in Town, 1987; Moondreamers: The Evening Song, 1988; Woody's First Dictionary, 1988; (with J. Preller) Meet the Authors and Illustrators, Vol. 1, 1991, Vol 2, 1993; Brewster's Courage, 1992; Moonlight on the River, 1993; Beneath Blue Waters: Meetings with Remarkable Deep-Sea Creatures, 1996; Dive to the Deep Ocean, 2000; Off to Sea, 2000; Noises in the Night: The Habits of Bats, 2001. **Address:** 25 Jordan St., South Dartmouth, MA 02748, U.S.A.

KOVALSKI, Maryann. American, b. 1951. **Genres:** Children's fiction, Illustrations. **Career:** Author and illustrator. Vickers & Benson Advertising, Montreal, Canada, art director, 1974-75; freelance editorial illustrator, 1975-84; co-owner of Dinsmore Gallery, 1984-85. Work exhibited at galleries throughout Canada, Rome, and Paris. **Publications:** SELF-ILLUSTRATED FOR CHILDREN: Brenda and Edward, 1984; The Wheels on the Bus, 1987; Jingle Bells, 1988; Frank and Zelda, 1990, in US as Pizza for Breakfast, 1991; Take Me Out to the Ball Game, 1992; Queen Nadine, 1998; Omar on Ice, 1999; Rain, Rain, 1999. Illustrator of books by M. Atwood, D. Booth, P. Bourgeois, R.G. Gelman, L.K. Melmed, A. Morgan, E.O. Rael, R. Robart, R. Tregebov, T. Wynne-Jones. **Address:** 80 Belmont St, Toronto, ON, Canada M5R 1P8. **Online address:** maryann-kovalski@on.aibn.com

KOVEL, Joel. American, b. 1936. **Genres:** Politics/Government, Psychology, Race relations, Social commentary. **Career:** Alger Hiss Professor of Social Studies, Bard College, Annandale-on-Hudson, New York. Formerly Prof of Psychiatry, Albert Einstein College of Medicine, Bronx, New York, and psychoanalyst in private practice. **Publications:** White Racism: A Psychohistory, 1970; A Complete Guide to Therapy, 1976; The Age of Desire, 1982; Against the State of Nuclear Terror, 1984; The Radical Spirit (essays), 1988; In Nicaragua, 1988; History and Spirit, 1991; Red Hunting in the Promised Land, 1994; The Enemy of Nature, 2001. **Address:** Box 89, Willow, NY 12495, U.S.A. **Online address:** jkovel@prodigy.net

KOVEL, Ralph Mallory. American. **Genres:** Antiques/Furnishings, Plays/Screenplays. **Career:** Columnist with T.H. Kovel. Kovels: Antiques and Collecting, King Features syndicate, 1955-; Ask The Experts, House Beautiful 1979-2000. Ed. and Publisher, Kovels on Antiques and Collectibles, newsletter, 1974-, Kovels Sports Collectibles, newsletter, 1992-97; The Kovels on Collecting, Forbes Magazine, 2000-02. **Publications:** WITH T.H. KOVEL: Kovels' Dictionary of Marks: Pottery and Porcelain, 1953, rev. ed., 1995; A Directory of American Silver, Pewter, and Silver Plate, 1958; American Country Furniture, 1780-1875, 1963, Kovels' Know Your Antiques, 1967, rev. ed, 1993; Kovels' Antiques and Collectibles Price List, annual, 1968-; Kovels' Bottles Price List, 1971, 12th ed., 2002; Kovels' Price Guide for Collector Plates, Figurines, Paperweights and Other Limited Editions, 1974, 1978; Kovels' Collector's Guide to Limited Editions, 1974; Kovels' Collector's Guide to American Art Pottery, 1974; Kovels' Organizer for Collectors, 1978, rev. ed., 1983; Kovels' Illustrated Price Guide to Royal Doulton, 2nd ed., 1984; Kovels' Depression Glass and American Dinnerware, 1980, 8th ed., 2002; Kovels' Know Your Collectibles, 1981, 2nd ed., 1992; The Kovels' Book of Antique Labels, 1982; Kovels' Collector's Source Book, 1983; Kovels' New Dictionary of Marks, Pottery and Porcelain, 1850-1985, 1985; Kovels' Advertising Collectibles Price List, 1986; Kovels' Guide to Selling Your Antiques and Collectibles, 1987, 2nd ed., 1990; Kovels' American Silver Marks 1650 to the Present, 1989; Kovels' Antiques and Collectibles Fix-It Source Book, 1990; Kovels' Page-a-Day Collectibles Calendar, 1990, rev. ed. as Kovels' Antiques and Collectibles 2003 Day-at-a-Time Calendar; Kovels' American Art Pottery, 1993; Kovels' Guide to Selling, Buying and Fixing your Antiques and Collectibles, 1995; Kovels' Quick Tips: 799 Helpful Hunts on How to Care for Your Collections, 1995; The Label Made Me Buy It, 1998; Kovels' Yellow Pages, 1999, 2nd ed., 2003; Kovels' Bid, Buy and Sell Online, 2001; Kovels' Antiques and Collectibles, a 16-Month 2003 Calendar. **Address:** PO Box 22200, Beachwood, OH 44122, U.S.A. **Online address:** www.kovels.com

KOVEL, Terry Horvitz. American. **Genres:** Plays/Screenplays, Antiques/Furnishings. **Career:** Columnist with R. Kovel. Kovels: Antiques and Collecting, King Features syndicate, 1955-; Ask The Experts, House Beautiful, 1979-2000. Ed. and Publisher, Kovels on Antiques and Collectibles, newsletter, 1974-, Kovels Sports Collectibles, newsletter, 1992-97; The Kovels on Collecting, Forbes Magazine, 2000-02. **Publications:** WITH R. KOVEL: Kovels' Dictionary of Marks: Pottery and Porcelain, 1953, rev. ed., 1995; A Directory of American Silver, Pewter, and Silver Plate, 1958; American Country Furniture, 1780-1875, 1963; Kovels' Know Your Antiques, 1967, rev. ed, 1993; Kovels' Antiques and Collectibles Price List, annual, 1968-; Kovels' Bottles Price List, 1971, 12th ed., 2002; Kovels' Price Guide for Collector Plates, Figurines, Paperweights and Other Limited Editions, 1974, 1978; Kovels' Collector's Guide to Limited Editions, 1974; Kovels' Collector's Guide to American Art Pottery, 1974; Kovels' Organizer for Collectors, 1978, rev. ed., 1983; Kovels' Illustrated Price Guide to Royal Doulton, 2nd ed., 1984; Kovels' Depression Glass and Dinnerware, 1980, 8th ed., 2004; Kovels' Know Your Collectibles, 1981, 2nd ed., 1992; The Kovels' Book of Antique Labels, 1982; Kovels' Collector's Source Book, 1983; Kovels' New Dictionary of Marks, Pottery and Porcelain, 1850-1985, 1986; Kovels' Advertising Collectibles Price List, 1986; Kovels' Guide to Selling Your Antiques and Collectibles, 1987, 2nd ed., 1990; Kovels' American Silver Marks: 1650 to the Present, 1989; Kovels' Antiques & Collectibles Fix-It Source Book, 1990; Kovels' American Art Pottery, 1993; Kovels' Guide to Selling, Buying and Fixing Your Antiques and Collectibles, 1995; Kovels' Quick Tips: 799 Helpful Hints on How to Care for Your Collectibles, 1995; The Label Made Me Buy It, 1998; Kovels' Yellow Pages, 1999, 2nd ed., 2003; Kovels' Bid, Buy and Sell Online, 2001; Kovels' American Antiques, 1750-1900, 2004. **Address:** PO Box 22200, Beachwood, OH 44122, U.S.A. **Online address:** www.kovels.com

KÖVES, András. Hungarian, b. 1938. **Genres:** Economics. **Career:** Hungarian Ministry of Foreign Affairs, Budapest, Soviet desk officer and embassy in Moscow, 1960-73; Hungarian Academy of Sciences, Budapest, senior research fellow in economics, 1973-78; Kopint Institute for Economic and Market Research, Budapest, head of research department for international economics, 1978-87; Kopint-Datorg, Budapest, deputy general director of research, 1987-2002, adviser, 2002-. **Publications:** The CMEA Countries in the World Economy: Turning Inwards or Turning Outwards, 1985; (ed. with P. Marer) Foreign Economic Liberalization: Transformations in Socialist and Market Economies, 1991; Central and East European Economies in Transition: The International Dimension, 1992. **Address:** Kopint-Datorg, Csokonai u.3., H-1081 Budapest, Hungary. **Online address:** koves@mail.datanet.hu

KOWALESKI, Maryanne. American, b. 1952. **Genres:** History. **Career:** Fordham University, Bronx, NY, assistant professor, 1982-88, associate professor of history, 1988-96, professor of history, 1996-, director of graduate studies in history, 1988-93, head of department, 1993-, director of Center for Medieval Studies, 1998-. **Publications:** Local Markets and Regional Trade in Medieval Exeter, 1995. EDITOR: (with M. Erler) Women and Power in the Middle Ages, 1988; (and trans) The Local Customs Accounts of the Port of Exeter, 1266-1321, 1993. Contributor to books. Contributor of articles and reviews to history journals. **Address:** Department of History, Fordham University, Bronx, NY 10458, U.S.A.

KOWALEWSKI, Michael (John). American, b. 1956. **Genres:** Film, Literary criticism and history, Local history/Rural topics, Natural history, Travel/Exploration. **Career:** High school English teacher in Duluth, MN, 1978-79; Princeton University, Princeton, NJ, assistant professor of English, 1986-91; Carleton College, Northfield, MN, assistant professor of English, 1991-95; associate professor, 1995-2001, professor of English, 2001-, director of program in American studies, 2001-04. **Publications:** Deadly Musings: Violence and Verbal Form in American Fiction, 1993; Popular Classics of American Literature, 1996. EDITOR: Temperamental Journeys: Essays on the Modern Literature of Travel, 1992; Reading the West: New Essays on the Literature of the American West, 1996; Gold Rush: A Literary Exploration, 1998. **Address:** Department of English, Carleton College, Northfield, MN 55057, U.S.A. **Online address:** mkowalew@carleton.edu

KOWALKE, Kim H. American, b. 1948. **Genres:** Plays/Screenplays, Music, Theatre. **Career:** Neighborhood Music School, New Haven, CT, orchestra teacher, 1973-75; Occidental College, Los Angeles, CA, assistant professor, 1977-82, associate professor of music, 1982-86; University of Rochester, Rochester, NY, professor of music and chairman of music program, 1986-. Conductor, bassoonist, and pianist; conductor, 102nd National Guard Band, 1971-77; musical director, Yale Dramat and Yale Cabaret, 1973-74; conductor, Greater New Haven Youth Symphony, 1973-75; principal conductor, College Light Opera Company, Falmouth, MA, 1974, 1975, 1977, and 1979; conductor, Occidental Faculty Players and Collegiate Symphony Orchestra of Occidental College and California Institute of Technology, 1977-83. Principal commentator, "Kurt Weill and His Worlds," a series on National Public Radio Network, 1982. President of board of trustees, Kurt Weill Foundation for Music, 1981-. **Publications:** Kurt Weill in Europe, 1979; Speak Low (The Letters of Kurt Weill and Lotte Lenya), 1996. SCREENPLAYS: A Stranger Here Myself: Kurt Weill in American; Lenya: An Invention. Contributor to periodicals. EDITOR: A New Orpheus: Essays on Kurt Weill, 1986; A Stranger Here Myself: Kurt Weill Studien, 1993. **Address:** Music Program, 207 Todd, University of Rochester, Rochester, NY 14627, U.S.A.

KOWALSKI, Gary A. American. **Genres:** Inspirational/Motivational Literature. **Career:** Ordained Unitarian Universalist minister; writer. **Publications:** The Souls of Animals, 1991; Goodbye, Friend: Healing Wisdom for Anyone Who Has Ever Lost a Pet, 1997; Green Mountain Spring and Other Leaps of Faith, 1997. **Address:** c/o Skinner House Books, 25 Beacon St., Boston, MA 02108, U.S.A.

KOWALSKI, Kathiann M. American, b. 1955. **Genres:** Environmental sciences/Ecology, Children's non-fiction, Natural history, Politics/Government. **Career:** Squire, Sanders & Dempsey (law firm), Cleveland, OH, associate, 1979-88, partner, 1988-94; freelance writer, 1994-. **Publications:** Hazardous Waste Sites, 1996; Alternative Medicine: Is It for You?, 1998; Teen Rights: At Home, at School, Online, 2000; Campaign Politics: What's Fair? What's Foul?, 2000; The Everything Kids' Nature Book, 2000; The Everything Kids' Space Book, 2000. Contributor of articles, stories, and photographs to magazines. **Address:** 21255 S Park Dr, Fairview Park, OH 44126, U.S.A. **Online address:** kowalskikm@yahoo.com

KOYA, Tatsuhito. Japanese, b. 1964. **Genres:** Technology, Engineering. **Career:** Affiliated with Reynolds Metals Co., Richmond, VA. **Publications:** (with Toshio Mura) Variational Methods in Mechanics, Oxford University Press, 1992. **Address:** Reynolds Metals Co., Fourth and Canal Sts., Richmond, VA 23261, U.S.A.

KOZLOSKI, Lillian D. American, b. 1934. **Genres:** Air/Space topics, Local history/Rural topics. **Career:** National Air and Space Museum, Washington, DC, museum specialist, 1977-95; guest lecturer at Cornell University, New Jersey State Museum, and Clemson University; self-employed as lecturer, 1995-. James Monroe Museum, Mary Washington House, Gary Melchers-Belmont Museum and Apothecary, Fredericksburg, VA, docent, 2001-. **Publications:** U.S. Space Gear: Outfitting the Astronaut, 1994. Contributing writer and editor to World Book, Book of Days 1988, and Book of Days 1989-90. Contributor to periodicals. **Address:** 5035 Ridge Rd, Spotsylvania, VA 22553-6334, U.S.A. **Online address:** lillkoz@rcn.com

KOZOL, Jonathan. American, b. 1936. **Genres:** Education, Social commentary. **Career:** Teacher, Boston, 1964-65; Consultant, curriculum development, U.S. Office of Education, 1966-1968 Teacher, elementary sch., Newton, Massachusetts, 1966-68; began tutorial prog. for underprivileged children, Roxbury, Massachusetts, 1966, project developed into New School for Children; Educational Director, and Trustee, Storefront Learning Center, Boston area, 1968-74; Visiting Lecturer, colls. and univs. in U.S., 1969-96; Intr., Center for Intercultural Documentation, Cuernavaca, Mexico, 1969, 1970, 1974; Fellow, Ford, Rockefeller, and Guggenheim Foundations, 1970-83. **Publications:** Death at an Early Age: The Destruction of the Hearts and Minds of Negro Children in the Boston Public Schools, 1967; Free Schools, 1972, rev. ed. as Alternative Schools: A Guide for Educators and Parents, 1982; The Night Is Dark and I Am Far from Home, 1975, rev. ed. 1987; Children of the Revolution: A Yankee Teacher in the Cuban Schools, 1978; Prisoners of Silence: Breaking the Bonds of Adult Illiteracy in the United States, 1980; On Being a Teacher, 1981; Illiterate America, 1985; Rachel and Her Children: Homeless Families in America, 1988; Savage Inequalities: Children in America's Schools, 1991; Amazing Grace: The Lives of Children and the Conscience of a Nation, 1995; Ordinary Resurrections, 2000. **Address:** c/o Janklow and Nesbit, 445 Park Ave., Fl 13, New York, NY 10022, U.S.A.

KRAEHE, Enno Edward. American, b. 1921. **Genres:** History. **Career:** Corcoran Professor of History, University of Virginia, Charlottesville, 1977-91, (Professor, 1968-77). Professor of History, University of Kentucky, Lexington, 1963-64, and University of North Carolina, Chapel Hill, 1964-68. **Publications:** (co-author) Collectivization of Agriculture in Eastern Europe, 1958; Metternich's German Policy, vol. I: The Contest with Napoleon, 1799-1814, 1963, Volume II: The Congress of Vienna 1814-1815, 1983; (co-author, ed. and trans.) The Metternich Controversy, 1971. **Address:** 130 Bennington Rd, Charlottesville, VA 22901, U.S.A.

KRAEUTER, David W. American, b. 1941. **Genres:** Technology, Bibliography. **Career:** Washington and Jefferson College, Washington, PA, assistant librarian, 1968-92, associate librarian, 1992-2001. Pittsburgh Oscillator: Journal of the Pittsburgh Antique Radio Society, editor, 1986-95. **Publications:** Radio and Television Pioneers: A Patent Bibliography, 1992; British Radio and Television Pioneers: A Patent Bibliography, 1993; Radio and Electronics Pioneers: A Patent Bibliography, 1994; Index to Radio and Electronics Patents, 1995; Electronic Essays, 1996; Numerical Index to Radio and Electronics Patents, 1997; Radio Patent Lists and Index, 1830-

1980, 2001. Contributor to periodicals. **Address:** Library, Washington and Jefferson College, Washington, PA 15301, U.S.A. **Online address:** kraeuter@ sgi.net

KRAFT, Robert A(lan). American, b. 1934. **Genres:** History, Humanities, Theology/Religion. **Career:** Professor of Religious Studies Emeritus, University of Pennsylvania, Philadelphia, 2003- (Assistant Professor, 1963-68; Associate Professor, 1968-76;Professor of Religious Studies, 1976-2003). Assistant Lecturer in New Testament Studies, University of Manchester, England, 1961-63. **Publications:** The Apostolic Fathers: A New Translation and Commentary, vol. III, Barnabas and the Didache, 1965; (with P. Prigent) Epitre de Barnabe, 1971; (trans. and ed. with G. Krodel) W. Bauer and G. Strecker: Orthodoxy and Heresy in Earliest Christianity, 1971; Septuagintal Lexicography, 1972; (with A.-E. Purintun) Paraleipomena Jeremiou, 1972; (with others) Testament of Job, 1974; (with G. Nickelsburg) Early Judaism and Its Modern Interpreters, 1986. **Address:** University of Pennsylvania, Logan Hall, Philadelphia, PA 19104-6304, U.S.A. **Online address:** kraft@ccat. sas.upenn.edu; ccat.sas.upenn.edu/rs/rak/kraft.html

KRAFT, William F. American, b. 1938. **Genres:** Psychology. **Career:** Professor of Psychology, Carlow University , Pittsburgh, PA, 1969-. Psychologist in private practice. Director of Psychological Services, Somerset State Hospital, PA, 1965-68, and Dixmont State Hospital, Pittsburgh, 1968-70. Adjunct Professor, Duquesne University 1985-90. Consultant to Pittsburgh and Greensburg Catholic Diocese and religious communities. **Publications:** The Search for the Holy, 1971; A Psychology of Nothingness, 1974; Normal Modes of Madness, 1978; Sexual Dimensions of the Celibate Life, 1979; Achieving Promises: A Spiritual Guide for the Transitions of Life, 1982; A Whole and Holy Sexuality, 1989; The Search for the Holy, 1999; The Normal Alcoholic, 1999; Ways of the Desert, 2000; When Someone You Love Drinks Too Much, 2002. Contributor of many articles to professional journals and magazines.

KRAHN, Betina. American. **Genres:** Romance/Historical. **Career:** Former science teacher; writer. **Publications:** Hidden Fires, 1988; Midnight Magic, 1990; Caught in the Act, 1990; Behind Closed Doors, 1991; My Warrior's Heart, 1992; The Princess and the Barbarian, 1993; The Last Bachelor, 1994; The Perfect Mistress, 1995; The Unlikely Angel, 1996; The Mermaid, 1997; Passion's Treasure, 1998; The Soft Touch, 1999; Sweet-Talking Man, 2000; The Husband Test, 2001. **Address:** c/o Bantam Dell Publishing Group, Random House Inc., 1540 Broadway, New York, NY 10036, U.S.A.

KRAMER, Dale. American, b. 1936. **Genres:** Literary criticism and history, Bibliography, Biography. **Career:** Ohio University, Athens, instructor, 1962-63, assistant professor of English, 1963-65; University of Illinois, Urbana, assistant professor, 1965-67; associate professor, 1967-71, professor of English, 1971-96, emeritus, 1996-, associate dean of College of Arts and Sciences, 1992-95. Journal of English and German Philology, editor, 1972-95. **Publications:** Charles Maturin, 1973; Thomas Hardy: The Forms of Tragedy, 1975; Thomas Hardy: Tess of the d'Urbervilles, 1991. EDITOR: Critical Approaches to the Fiction of Thomas Hardy, 1979; The Woodlanders, by T. Hardy, 1981, 1985; The Mayor of Casterbridge, by T. Hardy, 1987; Critical Essays on Thomas Hardy: The Novels, 1990; The Cambridge Companion to Thomas Hardy, 1999.

KRAMER, Fritz W. German, b. 1941. **Genres:** Novels, Anthropology/Ethnology. **Career:** Free University of Berlin, Germany, assistant professor, 1974-77, professor of anthropology, 1977-83; freelance writer, 1983-89; Hochschule fuer bildende Kuenste, Hamburg, Germany, professor of art theory, 1989-. **Publications:** Literature among the Cuna Indians, 1970; Verkehrte Welten, 1977; Der rote Fes, 1987, published as The Red Fez, 1993; Zeitmarken, 1993; Bikini, 2000. Radio feature writer. Contributor to magazines and newspapers. **Address:** Friedhofsweg 42, D-22337 Hamburg, Germany.

KRAMER, Helen. American, b. 1946. **Genres:** Psychology. **Career:** Gestalt Associates, NYC, founder, 1975, supervisor, 1975-85; REAL Solutions, NYC, founder, 1990, director, 1990-. **Publications:** Liberating the Adult Within, 1994. **Address:** 222 Park Ave. S. No. 29, New York, NY 10003, U.S.A.

KRAMER, Hilton. American, b. 1928. **Genres:** Art/Art history. **Career:** Ed., New Criterion Magazine, NYC, 1982-. Art Critic, The New York Observer (weekly newspaper), 1987-. Associate Ed. and Feature Ed., Arts Digest, 1954-55; Managing Ed., 1955-58, and Ed., 1959-61, Arts Magazine; Art Critic, The Nation, 1962-63; Art Critic and Associate Ed., The New Leader, 1964-65; Art News Ed., from 1965, and Chief Art Critic, 1973-82,

The New York Times. **Publications:** The Age of the Avant-Garde: An Art Chronicle of 1956-1972, 1973; The Revenge of the Philistines: Art and Culture 1972-84, 1985; The Twilight of the Intellectuals: Culture and Politics in the Era of the Cold War, 1999. EDITOR: The New Criterion Reader: The First Five Years, 1988; (co) Against the Grain, 1995. **Address:** c/o New Criterion, 900 Broadway Ste 602, New York, NY 10003, U.S.A.

KRAMER, Linda Konheim. American, b. 1939. **Genres:** Art/Art history. **Career:** Solomon R. Guggenheim Museum, NYC, curator and administrator, 1963-79; Sotheby Parke-Bernet, NYC, part-time cataloger of modern drawings, 1980-82; Sotheby's, NYC, expert in modern drawings, 1982-85; Brooklyn Museum, Brooklyn, NY, curator of prints and drawings, 1985-94; independent curator and freelance writer, 1994-96; Nancy Graves Foundation, NY, executive director, 1996-. **Publications:** Selected Sculpture and Works on Paper, 1969; Prints from the Guggenheim Museum Collection, 1978; Milton Avery in Black and White: Drawings 1929-59, 1990; (with S. Faunce and K. Zieve) French Nineteenth-Century Drawings and Watercolors at the Brooklyn Museum, 1993; The Graphic Works of Philip Pearlstein, 1978-1994, 1995; The Pictographs of Adolph Gottlieb, 1995; The Prints of Janet Fish: A Catalogue Raisonne, 1997. Author of exhibition catalogs. Contributor to periodicals. **Address:** Nancy Graves Foundation, 450 W 31st St 2nd Fl, New York, NY 10001, U.S.A. **Online address:** LKramer561@aol. com

KRAMER, Lloyd S. American, b. 1949. **Genres:** History. **Career:** Stanford University, Stanford, CA, lecturer in history, 1983-84; Northwestern University, Evanston, IL, Mellon assistant professor of history, 1984-86; University of North Carolina at Chapel Hill, assistant professor, 1986-89, associate professor, 1989-95, professor of history, 1995-. **Publications:** Threshold of a New World: Intellectuals and the Exile Experience in Paris, 1830-1848, 1988; Lafayette in Two Worlds: Public Cultures and Personal Identities in an Age of Revolutions, 1996; Nationalism: Political Cultures in Europe and America, 1775-1865, 1998; (with R.R. Palmer and J. Colton) A History of the Modern World, 9th ed., 2002. EDITOR: Paine and Jefferson on Liberty, 1988; (with D. Reid and W. Barney) Learning History in America: Schools, Cultures, and Politics, 1994; (with S. Maza) A Companion to Western Historical Thought, 2002. **Address:** Department of History, CB-3195, University of North Carolina at Chapel Hill, Chapel Hill, NC 27599, U.S.A.

KRAMER, Lotte (Karoline Wertheimer). British (born Germany), b. 1923. **Genres:** Poetry. **Career:** Writer and painter. Volunteer worker, Peterborough Museum, Cambs., 1977-. Member, Writers in Schools, E. Anglia, 1982-. Laundry hand, Berhamsted, Herts., 1939-40, and Hampton, Middx., 1943-47; lady's companion, Oxford, 1940-43; dress shop asst., Richmond, Surrey, 1953-57. **Publications:** Scrolls, 1979; Ice-Break, 1980; Family Arrivals, 1981, 2nd ed., 1992; A Lifelong House, 1983; The Shoemaker's Wife and Other Poems, 1987; The Desecration of Trees, 1994; Earthquake and Other Poems, 1994; Selected & New Poems, 1997; Bilingual (German/English) Selection of Poems, 1999; The Phantom Lane, 2000. **Address:** 4 Apsley Way, Longthorpe, Peterborough, Cambs. PE3 9NE, England.

KRAMER, Martin. American/Israeli, b. 1954. **Genres:** International relations/Current affairs, History. **Career:** Tel Aviv University, Ramat Aviv, Israel, research associate at Moshe Dayan Center for Middle Eastern and African Studies, 1981-, director of the center, 1995-. Visiting professor at Cornell University, 1984, University of Chicago, 1990, 1991, and Georgetown University, 1994-95. **Publications:** Political Islam, 1980; Islam Assembled: The Advent of the Muslim Congresses, 1986; The Moral Logic of Hizballah, 1987; (ed.) Shiism, Resistance, and Revolution, 1987; Hezbollah's Vision of the West, 1989; (ed.) Middle Eastern Lives: The Practice of Biography and Self-Narrative, 1991; Arab Awakening and Islamic Revival: The Politics of Ideas in the Middle East, 1996; (ed.) The Islamism Debate, 1997; (ed.) The Jewish Discovery of Islam, 1999. Contributor of articles and reviews to professional journals. **Address:** Moshe Dayan Center, Tel Aviv University, 69978 Ramat Aviv, Israel. **Online address:** kramerm@ccsg.tau. ac.il

KRAMER, Peter (D.). American, b. 1948. **Genres:** Novels, Psychiatry. **Career:** George Washington University, instructor, 1980, assistant clinical professor of psychiatry, 1981-82; Brown University, assistant professor, 1982-85, assistant clinical professor, 1985-91, associate clinical professor, 1991-95, clinical professor of psychiatry, 1995-. Alcohol, Drug Abuse, and Mental Health Administration, Department of Health and Human Services, Rockville, MD, acting deputy director and acting director, Division of Science, 1980-81, special assistant for science to the administrator, 1981-82. **Publications:** Moments of Engagement: Intimate Psychotherapy in a

Technological Age, 1989; Listening to Prozac, 1993; Should You Leave?, 1997; Spectacular Happiness, 2001. Contributor to scientific journals and books. **Address:** 196 Waterman St, Providence, RI 02906, U.S.A.

KRAMNICK, Isaac. American, b. 1938. **Genres:** Politics/Government. **Career:** Harvard University, Cambridge, MA, instructor in government, 1965-66; Brandeis University, Waltham, MA, assistant professor of government, 1966-68; Yale University, New Haven, CT, associate professor of government, 1968-72; Cornell University, Ithaca, NY, professor of government, 1972-, associate dean of College of Arts and Sciences, 1986-89; writer. **Publications:** Bolingbroke and His Circle: The Politics of Nostalgia in the Age of Walpole, 1968; The Rage of Edmund Burke, 1978; (with F.M. Watkins) The Age of Ideology: Political Thought, 1750 to the Present, 2nd ed, 1979; Republicanism and Bourgeois Radicalism: Political Ideology in Late Eighteenth-Century England and America, 1991; Harold Laski-A Life on the Left, 1993; The Godless Constitution, 1996. EDITOR: W. Godwin, Enquiry Concerning Political Justice, 1976; (with M. Foot) The Thomas Paine Reader, 1987; James Madison et al., The Federalist Papers, 1987. **Address:** Department of Government, Cornell University, Ithaca, NY 14850, U.S.A.

KRANTZ, Hazel. American. **Genres:** Novels, Children's fiction, Children's non-fiction. **Career:** Elementary sch. teacher, Nassau County Schools, New York, 1957-68; Ed., True Frontier mag., 1969-71; Copy Ed., Sound Engineering Magazine, 1973-78. **Publications:** 100 Pounds of Popcorn, 1960; Freestyle for Michael, 1964; The Secret Raft, 1965; Tippy, 1968; A Pad of Your Own, 1973; The Complete Guide to Happiness and Success, 1980; Pink and White Striped Summer, 1982; None But the Brave, 1986; Daughter of My People: Henrietta Szold and Hadassah, 1987; For Love of Jeremy, 1990; Look to the Hills, 1995; Walks In Beauty, 1997. **Address:** 1306 Stoney Hill Dr, Ft. Collins, CO 80525, U.S.A. **Online address:** hkrantz600@aol.com

KRANTZ, Steven G. American, b. 1951. **Genres:** Mathematics/Statistics. **Career:** University of California, Los Angeles, assistant professor of mathematics, 1974-81; Pennsylvania State University, University Park, associate professor, 1980-84, professor of mathematics, 1984-86; Washington University, St. Louis, MO, professor of mathematics, 1986-. Visiting professor at univerisities and institutions worldwide; guest lecturer at colleges and universities in the U.S. and abroad. **Publications:** (with others) Freshman Calculus, 1971; (with Bonic and Cranford) Exercises and Sample Exams for Freshman Calculus, 1971; Function Theory of Several Complex Variables, 1982, 2nd ed., 1992; Complex Analysis: The Geometric Viewpoint (monograph), 1990; Real Analysis and Foundations, 1992; Partial Differential Equations and Complex Analysis, 1992; (with H.R. Parks) A Primer of Real Analytic Functions, 1992; Geometric Analysis and Function Spaces, 1993; How to Teach Mathematics, 1993; (with S. Sawyer) TEX for Scientists, 1994; The Elements of Advanced Mathematics, 1995; Techniques of Problem Solving, 1996; A Primer of Mathematical Writing, 1997; (with Greene) Function Theory of One Complex Variable, 1997; (with E. Gavosto and W. McCallum) Issues in Modern Mathematics Education, 1998; Handbook of Complex Variables, 1999; Handbook of Logic and Proof Techniques, 2001; (with H.R. Parker) The Implicit Function Theorem, 2002; Mathematical Apocrypha, 2002; A Mathematician's Survival Guide, 2003; Handbook of Typography for the Mathematical Sciences, 2001. EDITOR: Complex Analysis Seminar, 1987; (with others) Several Complex Variables and Complex Geometry, 3 vols., 1991; (with K. Rosen and D. Zwillinger) The Standard Book of Tables and Formulas, 1995. Contributor of articles and reviews to mathematics journals. **Address:** Department of Mathematics, Washington University, St. Louis, MO 63130, U.S.A. **Online address:** sk@math.wustl.edu

KRASHEN, Stephen D. American, b. 1941. **Genres:** Language/Linguistics, Writing/Journalism. **Career:** U.S. Peace Corps, Washington, DC, volunteer in Ethiopia, 1964-66; University of California, Los Angeles, postdoctoral fellow at Neuropsychiatric Institute, 1972-73; Queens College of the City University of New York, Flushing, NY, assistant professor of linguistics, 1973-75; University of Southern California, Los Angeles, associate professor, 1975-81, professor of linguistics, 1981-, professor of education, 1993-. **Publications:** Second Language Acquisition and Second Language Learning, 1981; Principles and Practice in Second Language Acquisition, 1982; (with H. Dulay and M. Burt) Language Two, 1982; (with T. Terrell) The Natural Approach: Language Acquisition in the Classroom, 1983; Writing: Research, Theory, and Application, 1984; The Input Hypothesis: Issues and Implications, 1985; (with D. Biber) On Course: Bilingual Education's Success in California, 1988; Foundations of Language Education, 1992; The Power of Reading, 1993; Under Attack, 1996; (foreign language ed.) The Easy Way, 1997; Condemned without Trial, 1999; Three Arguments against Whole

Language and Why They Are Wrong, 1999; Explorations in Language Acquisition and Use, 2003. **Address:** c/o A. R. Evans, Academic Study Associates Inc., 10 New King St. Ste 201, White Plains, NY 10604-1211, U.S.A.

KRASILOVSKY, Phyllis. American, b. 1926. **Genres:** Children's fiction, Travel/Exploration. **Publications:** The Man Who Didn't Wash His Dishes, 1950; The Very Little Girl, 1953; The Cow Who Fell in the Canal, 1957; Scaredy Cat, 1959; Benny's Flag, 1960; The Very Little Boy, 1961; Susan Sometimes, 1962; The Girl Who Was a Cowboy, 1965; The Very Tall Little Girl, 1969; The Shy Little Girl, 1970; The Popular Girls Club, 1972; L.C. Is the Greatest, 1975; The Man Who Tried to Save Time, 1979; The Man Who Entered a Contest, 1980; The First Tulips in Holland, 1982; The Man Who Cooked for Himself, 1982; The Happy Times Story Book, 1987; The Man Who Was Too Lazy to Fix Things, 1992; The Woman Who Saved Things, 1993. Contributor of travel and humorous articles to newspapers and magazines. **Address:** 235 Dolphin Cove Quay, Stamford, CT 06902, U.S.A.

KRASNOW, Iris. American, b. 1954?. **Genres:** Essays. **Career:** United Press International (UPI), Washington, DC, feature writer, 1984-; also worked as a journalism instructor. **Publications:** Surrendering to Motherhood: Losing Your Mind, Finding Your Soul, 1997. **Address:** c/o Hyperion Press, 47 Riverside Ave., PO Box 591, Westport, CT 06880, U.S.A.

KRATZ, Martin P. J. Canadian, b. 1955. **Genres:** Law, Information science/Computers. **Career:** Celanese Canada Ltd., Clover Bar, AB, chemical operator, 1974-76; Pitney Bowes Canada Ltd., Edmonton, AB, service representative, 1976-77; Texaco Exploration, Bonnie Glen, AB, engineering trainee, 1978; University of Stuttgart, Germany, research assistant at Institute fur Thermodynamik und Warmetechnik, 1979; Alberta Oil Sands Technology and Research Authority, Edmonton, engineer, 1980; Canadian Association of Fire Chiefs, consulting engineer, 1981; Alberta Court of Appeal and Court of Queen's Bench, Edmonton, law clerk, 1984-85; Ogilvie and Co., Edmonton, barrister and solicitor, 1985-88; Cruickshank Karvellas, Edmonton, barrister and solicitor, 1988-89, partner, 1989-91; Bennett Jones LLC, Calgary, lawyer, 1991-. University of Alberta, lecturer, 1986-; University of Calgary, assistant professor of law, 1987-; Osgoode Hall Law School, Toronto, law lecturer, 1999-; speaker at universities throughout Canada. Kratz Consulting, consultant, 1983-. **Publications:** (with P. Fites and A. Brebner) Control and Security of Computer Information Systems, 1988; (with P. Fites and P. Johnson) The Computer Virus Crisis, 1989, 2nd ed., 1992; Information Systems Security, 1994; Protection of Copyright and Industrial Design, 1994, 2nd ed., 1999; Obtaining Patents, 1995, 2nd ed., 1999; Internet Law, 1998. Contributor to professional journals. **Address:** Bennett Jones LLP, 855 2 St W, Calgary, AB, Canada T2A 6P1. **Online address:** kratzm@bennettjones.ca

KRAUS, Joanna Halpert. American, b. 1937. **Genres:** Novellas/Short stories, Children's fiction, Plays/Screenplays, Writing/Journalism. **Career:** Baltimore Children's Theatre, associate director, 1960-61; Clark Center for Performing Arts, assistant director, NYC, 1963-65; instructor, NYC Community College, 1966-69, Columbia University Teachers College, NYC, 1970-71, and State University of New York at Purchase, 1970-72; State University of New York at New Paltz, assistant professor, 1972-79; State University of New York at Brockport, associate professor, 1979-86, professor of theatre, 1986-95, emeritus, 1995-, coordinator of Arts for Children, 1981-90, graduate coordinator 1990-95. Children's Theatre Association of America, secretary, 1982-84; Quarante mag., theater critic, 1985-87. Columnist on children's books: Sunday Times, Downeast Coastal Press, Rossmoor News, 1996-. **Publications:** PLAYS: The Ice Wolf, 1967; Vasalisa, 1968; Mean to Be Free, 1968; The Dragon Hammer and Oniroku: Two Plays from the Far East, 1977; Circus Home, 1979; The Last Baron of Arizona, 1986; Kimchi Kid, 1987; The Shaggy Dog Murder Trial, 1988; Remember My Name, 1989; Mean to Be Free, 1990; (co-author) Tenure Track, 1993; Angel in the Night, 1996; Ms. Courageous: Women of Science, 1997; Sunday Gold, 1998; Women of Courage: 5 Plays, 2000. OTHER: Seven Sound and Motion Stories, 1971; The Great American Train Ride, 1975; Tall Boy's Journey, 1992. Contributor to books and newspapers.

KRAUSE, Jill A. *See* STEANS, Jill A.

KRAUSHAR, Peter Maximilian. British, b. 1934. **Genres:** Marketing. **Career:** President, KAE Development; Kraushar and Ramsay Intl, Partner; Chairman, Mintel International Group; Managing Director, D.F. Marketing Development Ltd., London, 1966-69; Chairman, KAE Group Ltd., 1969-89. Chairman, Marketing Society. **Publications:** New Products and Diversification, 1969, 1977; Practical Business Development: What Works, What Does Not?, 1985. **Address:** 2 Lauradale Rd, London N2 9LU, England.

KRAUSS, Bruno. *See* **BULMER, (Henry) Kenneth.**

KRAUSS, Clifford. American, b. 1953. **Genres:** Area studies. **Career:** United Press International, night editor at Mexico City bureau, 1977-79, reporter in New York City, 1979-80; Cox Newspapers, Mexico City, Mexico, Latin America correspondent, 1981-84; Wall Street Journal, New York City, Central America correspondent from Miami, FL, 1984-87; New York Times, New York City, State Department correspondent, 1990-91, congressional correspondent, 1991-94; New York City Police Department Bureau Chief, 1994-97. **Publications:** Inside Central America: Its People, Politics, and History, Summit Books, 1991. **Address:** c/o The New York Times, 229 W. 43rd St., New York, NY 10036, U.S.A.

KRAUSS, Lawrence M. American (born Canada), b. 1954. **Genres:** Astronomy, Physics. **Career:** Yale University, New Haven, CT, junior fellow, 1982-85, assistant professor, 1985-88, associate professor of physics and astronomy, 1988-93; Case Western Reserve University, Cleveland, OH, Ambrose Swasey Professor of physics and chair of department, 1993-. Carleton University, Nesbitt Lecturer, 1988, Chesley Lecturer, 1998; Catholic University, Herzfeld Lecturer, 1998; American Physical Society, Centennial Lecturer, 1999; lecturer at colleges and universities in the US and abroad. Harvard University, research fellow, 1982-85, associate in physics, 1987-; visiting researcher, Institute for Theoretical Physics (Santa Barbara, CA), 1984, 1985, 1988, 1989, 1992, and University of Chicago, 1989; visiting scientist, Boston University and Smithsonian Astrophysical Observatory, both 1985-86, Harvard-Smithsonian Center for Astrophysics, 1986-89, and CERN, Geneva, 1997; consultant to Ontario Science Centre. **Publications:** The Fifth Essence: The Search for Dark Matter in the Universe, 1989; Fear of Physics: A Guide for the Perplexed, 1993; The Physics of Star Trek, 1995; Beyond Star Trek, 1997; Atom, 2003; Hiding behind the Mirror: The Mysterious Allure of Extra Dimensions, 2005. EDITOR: (with F. Accetta) Cosmic Strings: The Current Status, 1988; (with S.J. Rey) Baryon Number Violation at the Electroweak Scale, 1992; Cosmic Microwave Background Anisotropies Two Years after COBE, 1994. Contributor of articles and reviews to scientific journals and popular magazines. **Address:** Dept of Physics, Rockefeller Bldg, Case Western Reserve University, 10900 Euclid Ave, Cleveland, OH 44106-7079, U.S.A. **Online address:** krauss@case.edu

KRAUSS, Nicole. American. **Genres:** Novels. **Career:** Poet and writer. **Publications:** NOVEL: Man Walks into a Room, 2002. Contributor of poetry and reviews to literary journals and other periodicals. **Address:** c/o Author Mail, Random House Canada, 2775 Matheson Blvd E, Mississauga, ON, Canada L4W 4P7.

KRAUSZ, Ernest. British, b. 1931. **Genres:** Race relations, Social sciences, Sociology. **Career:** Bar-Ilan University, Ramat-Gan, Israel, Professor, Chair of Sociology, 1972- (Rector, 1986-89), now emeritus. Member, Planning and Grants Committee, Council for Higher Education, Israel, 1990-96. Member, Israel Science Foundation, 1995-. Ed., Studies of Israeli Society, 1980-2002. Co-Editor, Sociological Papers, since 1992. Lecturer, 1967-70, Sr. Lecturer, 1970-72, and Reader, 1971-72, The City University, London. **Publications:** Sociology in Britain, 1969; Ethnic Minorities in Britain, 1971; (with S.H. Miller) Social Research Design, 1974; Sociological Research: A Philosophy of Science Perspective, 1986; The Limits of Science, 2000; (co-ed) Starting the 21st Century, 2002. **Address:** Dept. of Sociology, Bar-Ilan University, 52900 Ramat-Gan, Israel.

KRAUT, Richard. American, b. 1944. **Genres:** Philosophy. **Career:** University of Illinois at Chicago, professor of philosophy, 1969-95; Northwestern University, professor, 1995-. **Publications:** Socrates and the State, 1984; Aristotle on the Human Good, 1989; Aristotle Politics Books VII and VIII, 1997; Aristotle: Political Philosophy, 2002. **Address:** Department of Philosophy, Northwestern University, U.S.A.

KREBS, Nina Boyd. American, b. 1938. **Genres:** Psychology, Race relations. **Career:** Psychologist and author. California State University, counseling psychologist, 1971-76; Center for Family, Individual, and Organizational Development, Sacramento, CA, partner, 1976-83; psychologist in private practice in California, 1976-98. California State Board of Medical Quality Assurance, psychology examiner, 1978-93; U.S. Bureau of Reclamation, Mid-Pacific Region, independent contractor, 1979-; artist, 2001-. Consultant, lecturer, and presenter of workshops. **Publications:** (with R.D. Allen) Psychotheatrics: The New Art of Self-Transformation, 1979; Changing Woman, Changing Work, 1993; Edgewalkers: Defusing Cultural Boundaries on the New Global Frontier, 1999. **Address:** 4651 Breuner Ave, Sacramento, CA 95819, U.S.A.

KREFETZ, Gerald Saul. American, b. 1932. **Genres:** Economics, Money/Finance. **Career:** Prop., Krefetz Management & Research, NYC, 1985-. **Publications:** (with R. Marossi) Investing Abroad: A Guide to Financial Europe, 1965; (with R. Marossi) Money Makes Money and the Money Money Makes Makes Money, 1971; The Dying Dollar, 1972, 1975; The Book of Income, 1982; The Smart Investor's Guide: How to Make Money in the Coming Bull Market, 1982; Jews and Money: The Myths and the Reality, 1982; How to Read and Profit from Financial News, 1984, rev. ed. 1995; Leverage: How to Multiply Your Money, 1985; All about Saving, 1987; How to Pay for Your Children's College Education, 1988; The Basics of Investing, 1992; The Basics of Stocks, 1992; The Basics of Bonds, 1992; The Basics of Speculating, 1992; Paying for College, 1995; Parents Guide to Paying for College, 1999. **Address:** 55 Bethune St, New York, NY 10014, U.S.A. **Online address:** gkrefetz@nyc.rr.com

KREININ, Mordechai. American (born Israel), b. 1930. **Genres:** Economics. **Career:** University of Michigan, Survey Research Center, lecturer and study director, 1956-57; Michigan State University, East Lansing, assistant professor, 1957-59, associate professor, 1959-61, professor, 1961-89, University Distinguished Professor of Economics, 1990-. International Trade and Finance Association, president, 1993; Fulbright senior specialist, 2001-. Consultant, U.S. State Dept. 1970s, U.N., 1971-, and Brookings Institution, Washington, DC, 1972. Special Adviser on Policy and Research, U.N. Conference on Trade and Development, Geneva, Switz., 1971-73; Round-the-World lecturer for USIS, 1970-96. **Publications:** Israel and Africa: A Study in Technical Cooperation, 1964; Alternative Commercial Policies: Their Effects on the American Economy, 1967; International Economics, 1971, 9th ed., 2002; (co-author) The Monetary Approach to the Balance of Payments: A Survey, 1978; Economics, 1983, 1999; Can Australia Adjust?, 1988; International Commercial Policy: Issues for the 1990s, 1993; The U.S.-Canada Free Trade Agreement, 1999. **Address:** Dept. of Economics, Michigan State University, 101 Marshall Hall, East Lansing, MI 48824-1038, U.S.A. **Online address:** Kreinin@pilot.msu.edu

KREIT, Carol. American, b. 1936. **Genres:** Adult non-fiction. **Career:** Henry Dunay Designs Inc., New York, NY, vice president, 1973-92; Plumb Club of New York State Inc., New York, NY, executive director, 1982-95. Literacy Volunteers of America, English teacher. **Publications:** First Wives' Tool Kit, 2001. **Address:** 90 Chestnut St., Englewood, NJ 07631, U.S.A.

KREJČI, Jaroslav. Czech/British, b. 1916. **Genres:** International relations/Current affairs, Social sciences, Autobiography/Memoirs. **Career:** Institute of Philosophy of the Academy of Sciences, Centre for Research into Socio-Cultural Pluralism, Czech Republic, 1994-; Professor Emeritus, Lancaster University (formerly University of Lancaster), 1983- (Research Fellow, 1969-70, Visiting Lecturer, 1970-72, Lecturer, 1972-74, and Sr. Lecturer, 1974-76; Professor, School of European Studies, 1976-83). With State Planning Office, Prague, 1945-50, and State Bank, Prague, 1950-53; political prisoner, Czechoslovakia, 1954-60; Member, Production Co-operative, Prague, 1960-67, and Institute of Environment, Academy of Sciences, Prague, 1968. Teacher, Graduate School of Political and Social Science, Prague, 1948-50; External Associate Professor, Faculty of Economics, Technical University, Prague, 1950-52. **Publications:** Social Change and Stratification in Postwar Czechoslovakia, 1972; Social Structure in Divided Germany, 1976; (ed.) Sozialdemokratie und Systemwandel, 1978; (with V. Velimsky) Ethnic and Political Nations in Europe, 1981; National Income and Outlay in Czechoslovakia, Poland, and Yugoslavia, 1982; Great Revolutions Compared: The Search for a Theory, 1983; The Civilisations of Asia and the Middle East, Before the European Challenge, 1990; Czechoslovakia at the Crossroads of European History, 1990; The Human Predicament: Its Changing Image, 1993; Society in a Global Perspective, 1993; Great Revolutions Compared, the Outline of a Theory, 1994; (with P. Machonin) Czechoslovakia 1918-1992, A Laboratory for Social Change, 1996; Between Democracy and Dictatorship (memoirs in Czech), 1998; Intelligible Currents of History (in Czech), 2002. **Address:** Lonsdale College, Lancaster University, Bailrigg, Lancaster, England.

KREMENYUK, Victor (A.). Russian, b. 1940. **Genres:** International relations/Current affairs. **Career:** Institute for the USA and Canada, Moscow, USSR (now Russia), deputy director, 1970-. Also professor at Salzburg Seminar, Vienna Diplomacy Academy, and Marshall Center, Germany. **Publications:** (with V. Lukin and M. Nosov) U.S. Policy toward the Pacific, 1989; (with others) SSHA i regionalnye konflikty (title means: The USA and Regional Conflicts), 1990; Conflicts in and around Russia: Nation-Building in Difficult Times, 1994; (with others) Rossiya i SSHA posle kholodnoy voyny (title means: Russia and the USA after the Cold War), 1999. EDITOR & CONTRIBUTOR: International Negotiation: Analysis, Approaches, Issues,

1991, 2nd ed., 2002; (with I. W. Zartman) Cooperative Security: Reducing Third World Wars, 1995; (with S. Cross, I.A. Zevelev, and V.M. Gevorgian) Global Security beyond the Millennium: American and Russian Perspectives, 1999; (with G. Sjostedt) International Economic Negotiation: Models versus Reality, 2000; (with R. Avenhaus and G. Sjostedt) Containing the Atom: International Negotiations on Nuclear Security and Safety, 2002. **Address:** Institute for the USA and Canada, 2/3 Khlebny, 123995 Moscow, Russia. **Online address:** vkremenyuk@yahoo.com

KREMER, Marcie. *See* **SORENSON, Margo.**

KREML, William P. American, b. 1941. **Genres:** Philosophy, Politics/Government, Psychology. **Career:** Northern Illinois University, DeKalb, assistant professor of business law, 1965-66; University of Tennessee, Knoxville, assistant professor of business law, 1966-68; University of South Carolina-Columbia, assistant professor, 1971-77, associate professor, 1977-84, professor of government and international studies, 1984-96, distinguished professor emeritus, 1996-, vice-chairperson of department, 1991-93, interim chair of department, 1993. University of Peking, visiting professor, 1994, 1997; Mars Hill College, adjunct professor, 1998. Committee on the Constitutional System, co-founder and member; Concord Coalition, coordinator, 1995-. **Publications:** The Anti-Authoritarian Personality, 1977; The Middle Class Burden, 1979, rev. ed. as America's Middle Class: From Subsidy to Abandonment, 1998; Relativism and the Natural Left, 1984; A Model of Politics, 1985; Psychology, Relativism, and Politics, 1991; Losing Balance: The De-Democratization of America, 1991; The Constitutional Divide: The Private and Public Sectors in American Law, 1997; The Twenty-First Century Left, 2005. Contributor of articles and reviews to periodicals. **Address:** 111 Southwood Dr, Columbia, SC 29205, U.S.A. **Online address:** kreml@mindspring.com

KREMMER, Christopher. Australian, b. 1958. **Genres:** Area studies. **Career:** Journalist. Australian Broadcasting Corporation, writer. **Publications:** Stalking the Elephant Kings: In Search of Laos, 1997; The Carpet Wars: From Kabul to Baghdad: A Ten-Year Journey along Ancient Trade Routes, 2002. **Address:** c/o Author Mail, HarperCollins, 10 East 53rd Street 7th Floor, New York, NY 10022, U.S.A.

KRENTZ, Edgar Martin. American, b. 1928. **Genres:** Archaeology/Antiquities, Theology/Religion. **Career:** Concordia Seminary, St. Louis, MO, Instructor, 1953-56, Assistant Professor, 1956-63, Associate Professor, 1963-69, Professor of New Testament, 1969-75; Christ Seminary-Seminex, St. Louis, MO, Professor of New Testament, 1975-83; Lutheran School of Theology, Chicago, IL, Professor of New Testament, 1983-98, Professor Emeritus, 1998-. **Publications:** Biblical Studies Today, 1966; The Historical-Critical Method, 1975; Easter, Series B, Proclamation 3, 1985; Galatians, Augsburg New Testament Commentary, 1985. **Address:** 5433 S Ridgewood Ct, Chicago, IL 60615, U.S.A.

KREPS, Juanita M(orris). American, b. 1921. **Genres:** Economics. **Career:** Denison University, Granville, OH, instructor, 1945-46, assistant professor of economics, 1947-50; Hofstra University, Hempstead, NY, lecturer in economics, 1952-54; Queens College (now of the City University of New York), Flushing, NY, lecturer in economics, 1954-55; Duke University, Durham, NC, visiting instructor and assistant professor, 1958-62, associate professor, 1963-68, professor of economics, 1968-72, James B. Duke Professor of Economics, 1972-77, dean of Women's College and assistant provost, 1969-72, vice-president of the university, 1973-77; U.S. Department of Commerce, Washington, DC, secretary of commerce, 1977-79. Educational Testing Service, member of board of directors, 1971-77, chair of board of trustees, 1975-76. **Publications:** (ed with C.H. Kreps Jr.) Aid, Trade, and Tariffs, 1953; (ed.) Our Natural Resources 1955; (with C.E. Ferguson) Principles of Economics, 1962, 2nd ed., 1965; (ed.) Employment, Income, and Retirement Problems of the Aged, 1963; (with R. Laws) Automation and the Older Worker: An Annotated Bibliography, 1963; Automation and Employment, 1964; Taxation, Spending, and the National Debt, 1964; (ed.) Technology, Manpower, and Retirement Policy, 1966; Sex in the Marketplace: American Women at Work, 1971; Lifetime Allocation of Work and Income, 1971; (with G.G. Somers and R. Perlman) Contemporary Labor Economics, 1974, 2nd ed. as Contemporary Labor Economics and Labor Relations, 1981; (with R. Clark) Sex, Age, and Work: The Changing Composition of the Labor Force, 1975; (ed.) Women and the American Economy: A Look at the 1980s, 1976. **Address:** 2701 Pickett Rd, Durham, NC 27705-5688, U.S.A.

KRESSEL, Neil J. American, b. 1957. **Genres:** Law, Adult non-fiction, Politics/Government, Psychology, Social sciences. **Career:** Harvard University, sophomore tutor to teaching fellow, 1979-83; William Paterson

University of New Jersey, Wayne, assistant professor to professor of psychology and head of department, 1984-. New York University, adjunct assistant professor, 1989-91; Stevens Institute of Technology, adjunct associate professor, 1989-94. Private practice consultant, 1983-; Institute for Rational-Emotive Therapy, clinical psychologist, 1993-94. **Publications:** (ed.) Political Psychology: Classic and Contemporary Readings, 1993; Mass Hate: The Global Rise of Genocide and Terror, 1996, rev. ed., 2002; (with D.F. Kressel) Stack and Sway: The New Science of Jury Consulting, 2001. Contributor of articles and reviews to magazines and newspapers. **Address:** Department of Psychology, William Paterson University of New Jersey, Wayne, NJ 07470, U.S.A. **Online address:** kresseln@wpunj.edu

KRICH, Rochelle Majer. American (born Germany). **Genres:** Mystery/Crime/Suspense. **Career:** Writer and teacher. Department of English, Yeshiva High School, Los Angeles, CA, chair and teacher. **Publications:** MYSTERY NOVELS: Where's Mommy Now?, 1990; Till Death Do Us Part, 1992; Nowhere to Run, 1994; Speak No Evil, 1996; Fertile Ground, 1998. JESSIE DRAKE MYSTERY NOVELS: Fair Game, 1993; Angel of Death, 1994. **Address:** c/o Avon Books, 1350 Avenue of the Americas, New York, NY 10019, U.S.A.

KRICHER, John C. American, b. 1944. **Genres:** Environmental sciences/Ecology. **Career:** Ecologist and writer. Wheaton College, Norton, MA, began as assistant professor, became associate professor, 1970-80, professor of biology, 1980-. **Publications:** A Field Guide to Eastern Forests, North America, 1988; A Neotropical Companion: An Introduction to the Animals, Plants, and Ecosystems of the New World Tropics, 1989, rev. ed., 1997; Peterson First Guide to Dinosaurs, 1990; Peterson First Guide to Seashores, 1992; A Field Guide to the Ecology of Western Forests, 1993; A Field Guide to California and Pacific Northwest Forests, 1993, rev. ed., 1998; A Field Guide to Rocky Mountain and Southwest Forests, 1993, rev. ed., 1998; Peterson First Guide to Forests, 1994; Galapagos, 2002. **Address:** Department of Biology, Wheaton College, Norton, MA 02766, U.S.A.

KRICORIAN, Nancy. American, b. 1960. **Genres:** Novels. **Career:** Writer. Frost Poetry Festival, member of resident faculty, 1985; Queens College/City University of New York, lecturer in English, 1987-90; Barnard College, NYC, instructor in English and women's studies, 1988; literary scout for European publishers, 1989-. Visiting lecturer, Rutgers University, 1988, and Yale University, 1989, 1991. **Publications:** NOVELS: Zabelle, 1998; Dreams of Bread and Fire, 2003. Contributor of poetry and fiction to literary journals. **Address:** c/o Atlantic Monthly Press, 841 Broadway 4th Fl, New York, NY 10003-4793, U.S.A.

KRIEG, Joann P(eck). American, b. 1932. **Genres:** Biography, Local history/Rural topics. **Career:** Hofstra University, Hempstead, NY, associate professor of English, 1988-. Walt Whitman Birthplace Association, member of board of trustees and past president. **Publications:** Walt Whitman, Here and Now, Greenwood Press, 1985; To Know the Place: Teaching Local History, Long Island Studies Institute, 1986; Dwight D. Eisenhower: Soldier, President, Statesman, Greenwood Press, 1987; Evoking a Sense of Place, Heart of the Lakes Publishing, 1988; (with Paul Harper) John F. Kennedy, Greenwood Press, 1988; Long Island and Literature (monograph), Heart of the Lakes Publishing, 1989; Long Island Architecture, Heart of the Lakes Publishing, 1991; Epidemics in the Modern World, Twayne, 1992. **Address:** Department of English, Hofstra University, Hempstead, NY 11550, U.S.A.

KRIEG, Robert Anthony. American, b. 1946. **Genres:** Theology/Religion. **Career:** Entered Congregation of the Holy Cross, 1966, ordained Roman Catholic priest, 1973, resigned from the priesthood, 2000, laicized, 2002; King's College, Wilkes-Barre, PA, assistant professor of theology, 1975-77; University of Notre Dame, IN, assistant professor, 1977-85, associate professor of theology, 1985-, professor of theology, 1997-, director of field education for the ministry, 1978-84, director of Master's of Divinity Program, 1985-91, director of Ph.D. program, 1995-97. **Publications:** Story-Shaped Christology, 1988; Karl Adam: Catholicism in German Culture, 1992; Romano Guardini: A Precursor of Vatican II, 1997; Catholic Theologians in Nazi Germany, 2004. Contributor to theology journals. **Address:** Dept of Theology, 130 Malloy Hall, University of Notre Dame, Notre Dame, IN 46556-4619, U.S.A. **Online address:** Krieg.1@nd.edu

KRIEGEL, Leonard. American, b. 1933. **Genres:** Novels, Autobiography/Memoirs, Essays. **Career:** Assistant Professor to Professor of English, City College of New York, since 1961. **Publications:** The Long Walk Home, 1964; (ed.) Essential Works of the Founding Fathers, 1964; Edmund Wilson, 1971; Working Through, 1972; Notes for the Two-Dollar Window, 1976; (ed.) The Myth of American Manhood, 1978; On Men and Manhood, 1979;

Quitting Time, 1982; Falling into Life (essays), 1991; Flying Solo (memoir), 1999. **Address:** 355 8th Ave., New York, NY 10001-4838, U.S.A.

KRIEGER, Martin H. American, b. 1944. **Genres:** Business/Trade/Industry, Economics, Physics. **Career:** University of California, Berkeley, faculty member, 1968-73; Center for Advanced Study in the Behavioral Sciences, Palo Alto, CA, fellow, 1973-78; University of Minnesota-Twin Cities, Minneapolis, faculty member, 1974-80; Massachusetts Institute of Technology, Cambridge, faculty member, 1980-84; University of Southern California, Los Angeles, professor of planning, 1984-. National Humanities Center, fellow, 1978-79. **Publications:** Advice and Planning, 1981; Marginalism and Discontinuity: Tools for the Craft of Knowledge and Decision, 1989; Doing Physics: How Physicists Take Hold of the World, 1992; Constitutions of Matter, 1996; Entrepreneurial Vocations, 1996; What's Wrong with Plastic Trees?, 2000. **Address:** School of Policy Planning and Development, Ralph and Goldy Lewis Hall, University of Southern California, Los Angeles, CA 90089-0626, U.S.A. **Online address:** kreiger@usc.edu

KRIEGER, Melanie. American. **Genres:** Education. **Career:** Ward Melville High School, Melville, NY, teacher, 1979-86, academic teams coordinator, 1985-, research director for West Prep, 1986-; Stony Brook University, Stony Brook, NY, adjunct professor, 1984-96, co-director of Stony Brook High School Summer Research Institute and creator of mentor program linking high school students with college professors, 1984-96. **Publications:** How to Excel in Science Competitions, 1991; Means & Probabilities: Using Statistics in Science Projects, 1996. **Address:** 5 Deacon Court, Melville, NY 11747, U.S.A.

KRIEGER, Michael J. American, b. 1940. **Genres:** Travel/Exploration. **Career:** International Building Products Inc., San Francisco, CA, owner, 1964-69; Consolidated Foods Corporation, Geneva, Switzerland, European manager, 1969-74. Journalist and travel writer, 1974-. **Publications:** Tramp: Sagas of High Adventure in the Vanishing World of the Old Tramp Freighters, 1986; Conversations with the Cannibals: The End of the Old South Pacific, 1994. Contributor to periodicals; author of travel essays syndicated to newspapers by Universal Press Syndicate. **Address:** c/o Tom Wallace, The Wallace Agency, 177 East 70th St., New York, NY 10021, U.S.A.

KRIER, Léon. Luxembourger, b. 1946. **Genres:** Architecture. **Career:** James Stirling, London, assistant, 1968-70, 1973-74; J.P. Kleihues, Berlin, project partner, 1971-72; private practice, London, 1974-. Architectural Association School, London, lecturer, 1973-76; Royal College of Art, London, lecturer, 1977; Princeton University, lecturer, 1977; University of Virginia at Charlottesville, Jefferson Professor of Architecture, 1982; visiting scholar at University of Bologna, 1989, 1993; Yale University, Davenport Professor, 1990-91; Prince of Wales Summer School and Architecture Institute, 1990-93. Exhibitions of Krier's work have been mounted in Europe and the United States. **Publications:** Leon Krier: La Ricostruzione della Citta Europea, 1980; Leon Krier, Houses, Palaces, Cities, 1984; (ed.) Albert Speer: Architecture, 1932-1942, 1987; Leon Krier: Galerie der Stadt Stuttgart 27.2.-13.3.1988, 1988; Atlantis: International Centre for Culture, the Sciences, Politics, and Economics at Tenerife, Islas Canarias, 1988; Completar Santurce: Estudio Preliminar para el Plan Maestro de un Barrio, 1992; Leon Krier: Architecture and Urban Design, 1967-1992, 1992; Architecture: Choice or Fate, 1997. Contributor of articles to professional journals. **Address:** 8 Rue des Chapeliers, 83830 Claviers, France.

KRIESBERG, Louis. American, b. 1926. **Genres:** International relations/Current affairs, Sociology. **Career:** Columbia University, NYC, Dept. of Sociology, instructor, 1953-56; University of Chicago, Dept. of Sociology, sr. fellow in law and the behavioral sciences, 1957-58, research associate, 1958-62; National Opinion Research Center, sr. study director, 1958-62; Syracuse University, professor of sociology, 1966-97, director, Program on the Analysis and Resolution of Conflicts, 1986-94, Maxwell Professor of Social Conflict Studies, 1994-97, professor emeritus of sociology, 1997-, Maxwell Professor Emeritus of Social Conflict Studies, 1997-. **Publications:** Mothers in Poverty: A Study of Fatherless Families, 1970; Social Conflicts, 1973; Social Inequality, 1979; International Conflict Resolution, 1992; Constructive Conflicts, 1998, 2nd ed., 2003. EDITOR: Social Processes in International Relations, 1968; Research in Social Movements, Conflicts and Change, 14 vols., 1978-92; (with S. Thorsen and T. Northrup) Intractable Conflicts, 1989; (with S. Thorson) Timing the De-Escalation of International Conflicts, 1991. **Address:** Dept. of Sociology, 302 Maxwell Hall, Syracuse University, Syracuse, NY 13244, U.S.A. **Online address:** lkriesbe@maxwell.syr.edu

KRIMSKY, George A. American, b. 1942. **Genres:** Writing/Journalism. **Career:** Waterbury Republican-American, Waterbury, CT, reporter, 1966-69; Associated Press, New York, Beirut, Moscow, Los Angeles, correspondent and editor, 1969-85; International Center for Journalists, Washington, DC, president, 1985-96; independent media consultant, Washington, CT, 1996-. **Publications:** (with J.M. Hamilton) Hold the Press, 1996. Contributor of essays to periodicals. **Address:** 59 Old North Rd., Washington, CT 06793, U.S.A.

KRIN, Sylvie. *See* **FANTONI, Barry (Ernest).**

KRINARD, Susan. American. **Genres:** Romance/Historical. **Career:** Writer. **Publications:** Prince of Wolves, 1994; Prince of Dreams, 1995; Prince of Shadows, 1996; Twice a Hero, 1997; Body and Soul, 1998; Star Crossed, 1998; Touch of the Wolf, 1999; Once a Wolf, 2000. Contributor to books. **Address:** PO Box 51924, Albuquerque, NM 87181, U.S.A. **Online address:** skrinard@aol.com

KRISE, Thomas W(arren). American, b. 1961. **Genres:** Literary criticism and history. **Career:** U.S. Air Force regular officer, rose through ranks to lieutenant colonel, 1983-. U.S. Air Force Academy, Colorado Springs, CO, instructor in English, 1989-91, assistant professor of English, 1991-92, 1997-99; associate professor, 1999-2002, professor, 2002-; Air Force Humanities Institute, founding director. **Publications:** (ed., compiler, and author of intro and notes) Caribbeana: An Anthology of English Literature of the West Indies, 1657-1777, 1999; General editor, McNair Papers monograph series, numbers 41-57, 1995-97. Contributor to books and anthologies. **Address:** Air Force Humanities Institute (DFPY), 2354 Fairchild Dr, U.S. Air Force Academy, USAF Academy, CO 80840, U.S.A. **Online address:** thomas.krise@usafa.af.mil; krisetw@hotmail.com

KRISHER, Trudy (B.). American, b. 1946. **Genres:** Children's fiction, Young adult fiction, Writing/Journalism. **Career:** University of Dayton, OH, assistant professor and campus writing center coordinator, 1985-. **Publications:** Kathy's Hats: A Story of Hope, 1992; Spite Fences, 1994; Writing for a Reader, 1995; Kinship, 1997. **Address:** Multimedia Product Development, 410 S Michigan Ave Ste 460, Chicago, IL 60605, U.S.A.

KRISHNASWAMI, Uma. Indian, b. 1956. **Genres:** Children's fiction, Mythology/Folklore. **Career:** LEAP Inc., Silver Spring, MD, rehabilitation counselor, 1981-86; Epilepsy Foundation of America, Landover, MD, employment specialist/program administrator, 1986-88; University of Maryland, College Park, project coordinator in Special Education Department, 1988-97; freelance writer, 1997-. Leader of workshops, teacher of online writing courses for Writers on the Net, and codirector of local affiliate of National Writing Project. Writer-in-residence, Aztec Ruins National Monument. **Publications:** RETELLER: Stories of the Flood, 1994; The Broken Tusk: Stories of the Hindu God Ganesha, 1996; Shower of Gold: Girls and Women in the Stories of India, 1999. NONFICTION: Yoga Class, 2000; Beyond the Field Trip: Teaching and Learning in Public Places (for teachers), 2002; Holi, 2003. PICTURE BOOKS: Hello Flower, 2002; Chachaji's Cup, 2003; Monsoon, 2003. NOVEL: Naming Maya, 2004. Contributor of poems and stories to children's and adult's magazines. **Address:** 765 County Rd. 3000, Aztec, NM 87410, U.S.A. **Online address:** uma@umakrishnaswami.com

KRISKA, Laura J. American (born Japan). **Genres:** Novels. **Career:** Writer. Honda Motor Company, Tokyo, Japan, trainee and factory worker. **Publications:** The Accidental Office Lady, 1997. **Address:** c/o Charles E. Tuttle Co., Airport Industrial Park, RR1, Box 231-5, North Clarendon, VT 05759, U.S.A.

KRISLOV, Samuel. American, b. 1929. **Genres:** Social sciences. **Career:** Professor of Political Science, 1964-, and Adjunct Professor of Law, University of Minnesota, Minneapolis. Member of faculty, University of Oklahoma, Norman, 1957-60, and Michigan State University, East Lansing, 1960-64. **Publications:** The Supreme Court in the Political Process, 1965; The Negro in the Federal Bureaucracy, 1967; (with R. Dixon, A.S. Miller, and L. Huston) Roles of the Attorney General of the U.S., 1968; The Supreme Court and the Political Process, 1968; The Supreme Court and Political Freedom, 1968; (with M. Feeley and S. White) The Judicial Process and Constitutional Law (lab manual), 1972; Representative Bureaucracy, 1974; Representative Bureaucracy and the American Political System, 1981; American Constitutional Law, 1984; How Nations Choose Product Standards, 1997. EDITOR: (co-) American Government: The Clash of Issues, 1960, 8th ed., 1984; (with L. Musolf) The Politics of Regulation, 1964; (with K. Boyum, R. Schaffer, and S. White) Compliance: A Multi-Disciplinary Approach, 1972; (co-) Understanding Crime, 1977. **Address:** Dept of Political Science, Rm 1414 Social Sciences Bldg, University of Minnesota, 267 19th Ave S, Minneapolis, MN 55455, U.S.A. **Online address:** kris001@umn.edu

KRIST, Gary (Michael). American, b. 1957. **Genres:** Novels, Novellas/Short stories, Travel/Exploration. **Career:** Writer. Writer in residence at Millay Colony for the Arts, Austerlitz, NY, 1985; American Academy of Arts and Letters, Sue Kaufman Prize for First Fiction, 1989; NEA Creative Writing Grant 1989; Stephen Crane Award, 1999; Lowell Thomas Award Gold Medal for Travel Journalism, 2002. **Publications:** STORIES: The Garden State, 1988; Bone by Bone, 1994. NOVELS: Bad Chemistry, 1998; Chaos Theory, 2000; Extravagance, 2002.

KRISTAL, Efrain. American, b. 1959. **Genres:** Literary criticism and history. **Career:** University of California, Los Angeles, professor of Spanish and comparative literature. **Publications:** The Andes Viewed from the City: Literary and Political Discourse on the Indian in Peru, 1848-1930, 1987; (author of notes, with C.G. Beloya) Aves sin nido, by C. Matto de Turner, 1994; Temptation of the Word: The Novels of Mario Vargas Llosa, 1998. **Address:** Department of Spanish and Portuguese, University of California Los Angeles, PO Box 951532, 4319 Rolfe, Los Angeles, CA 90095, U.S.A. **Online address:** kristal@ucla.edu

KRISTEVA, Julia. Also writes as Julia Joyaux. Bulgarian, b. 1941. **Genres:** Novels, Language/Linguistics, Literary criticism and history. **Career:** Writer, educator, linguist, psychoanalyst, and literary theorist. Worked as a journalist in Bulgaria; Laboratoire d'anthropologie sociale, research assistant to Claude Levi-Strauss, 1967-73; University of Paris VII-Denis Diderot, instructor, 1972, professor of linguistics, 1973-; private psychoanalytic practice, Paris, 1978-. Visiting professor, Columbia University, 1974, University of Toronto, 1992. **Publications:** NONFICTION: Semeiotike, Recherce pour une sema-nalyse, 1969, abridged and trans. as Desire in Language, 1980; (as Julia Joyaux) Le Langage, cet inconnu,, 1969, as Julia Kristeva, 1981, trans. as Language: The Unknown, 1989; Le Texte du roman, 1970; Lapu Revolution du langage poetique, 1974, abridged trans. as Revolution in Poetic Language, 1984; Des Chinoises, 1974, trans. as About Chinese Women, 1977; (with others) La Traversee des signes, 1975; Polylogue, 1977, trans. in Desire in Language: A Semiotic Approach to Literature and Art, 1980; (with J.M. Ribettes) Folle Verite, verite et vraisemblance du texte psychotique, 1980; Pouvoirs de l'horreur, 1980, trans. as Powers of Horror, 1982; Histoires d'amour, 1983, trans. as Tales of Love, 1987; Au commencement etait l'amour, 1985, trans. as In the Beginning Was Love, 1987; A Kristeva Reader, 1986; Soleil noir, 1987, trans. as Black Sun, 1989; Etrangers a nous-memes, 1988, trans. as Strangers to Ourselves, 1991; Lettre ouverte a Harlem Desir, 1990, trans. as Nations without Nationalism, 1993; Les Nouvelles Maladies de l'ame, 1993, trans. as New Maladies of the Soul, 1995; Le Temps sensible, Proust et l'Experience litteraire, 1994, trans. as Time and Sense: Proust and the Experience of Literature, 1996; Sens et non-sens de la revolte, 1996; La Revolte intime, 1997; Contre la depression nationale: Conversation avec Philippe Petit, 1997; L'avenir d'une revolte, 1998; Visions capitales, 1998; (with C. Clement) Le Feminin et le Sacre, 1998; Le Genie feminin, vol. 1: Hannah Arendt, 1999, vol. 2: Melanie Klein, 2000, vol. 3: Colette, 2002; Lettre au president de la Republique sur les citoyens en situation de handicap, 2003; Meurtre a Byzance, 2004. NOVELS: Les Samourais, 1990, trans. as The Samurai, 1992; Le Vieil Homme et les loups, 1991, trans. as The Old Man and the Wolves, 1994; Possessions, 1996. EDITOR: (with T. Sebeok) Approaches to Semiotics, vol. 1, 1969; (with J.R. Debove and D.J. Umiker) Essays in Semiotics, 1971; Epistemologie de la linguistique. Hommage a Emile Benveniste, 1971; (with J.-C. Milner and N. Ruwet) Langue, discours, societe: pour Emile Benveniste, 1975. **Address:** Universite de Paris VII-Denis Diderot, UFR de Sciences des Textes et Documents 34-44 2e etage, 2 place Jussieu, 75005 Paris, France. **Online address:** kristeva@paris7.jussieu.fr

KRISTOF, Agota. Hungarian, b. 1935. **Genres:** Novels. **Career:** Writer. Worked at a textile factory in Hungary, 1954-56; at a watch factory in Switzerland, 1956-61, and as a dental assistant in Switzerland, 1980-88. **Publications:** Le grand cahier, 1986, trans. A. Sheridan as The Notebook, 1988; La preuve, Seuil, 1988, trans. D. Watson as The Proof, 1991; Le troisieme mensonge, 1991, trans. M. Romano as The Third Lie, 1996; Hier (title means: Yesterday), 1995. Also wrote pieces for the radio. **Address:** c/o Author Mail, Editions du Seuil, 27 rue Jacob, 75006 Paris, France.

KRISTOL, Irving. American, b. 1920. **Genres:** Politics/Government, Social commentary, International relations/Current affairs. **Career:** Ed., with Nathan Glazer, The Public Interest mag., Washington, D.C., since 1965. John M. Olin Distinguished Fellow, American Enterprise Institute, Washington, D.C., since 1988. Member, Council on Foreign Relations, NYC. Managing Ed., Commentary mag., NYC, 1947-52; Co-Founder and Ed., with Stephen Spender, Encounter mag., London, 1953-58; Ed., The Reporter mag., NYC, 1959-60; Executive Vice-President, Basic Books Inc., NYC, 1961-69.

Member, National Council on the Humanities, 1972-77; Member, President's Commission on White House Fellowships, 1981-84; John M. Olin Professor of Social Thought, Graduate School of Business Administration, New York University, NYC, 1983-88. **Publications:** (ed. with Daniel Bell) Confronta-tion: The Student Rebellion and the University, 1969; (ed. with Daniel Bell) Capitalism Today, 1971; On the Democratic Idea in America, 1972; (ed. with Nathan Glazer) The American Commonwealth, 1976; (ed. with Paul H. Weaver) The Americans: 1976, 1976; Two Cheers for Capitalism, 1978; (ed. with Daniel Bell) The Crisis in Economic Theory, 1981; Reflections of a Neoconservative, 1983; Neoconservatism: The Autobiography of an Idea, 1995. **Address:** 1112 16th St., NW, Suite 530, Washington, DC 20036, U.S.A.

KRITZ, Mary M. American. **Genres:** Demography, Sociology. **Career:** U.S. Peace Corps, volunteer community development worker and teacher in Dominican Republic, 1962-64; Experiment in International Living, group leader in Chile, 1965; Accion, community development specialist in Caracas, Venezuela, 1965-66; Venezuelan National Guard, developer of community-based projects in health and education for women and children, 1966-67; Purdue University, assistant professor of sociology and anthropology, 1972-74; Rockefeller Foundation, program associate, 1974, assistant director of social sciences, 1975-78, assistant director of population sciences, 1979-82, associate director of population sciences, 1983-88; Cornell University, as-sociate professor of rural sociology, 1989-98, senior research associate, 1999-, associate director of Population and Development Program, 1989-, as-sociate member of Latin American Studies Program, 1991-. International Union for the Scientific Study of Population, secretary-general and treasurer, 2002-. **Publications:** EDITOR: Migraciones internacionales en las Americas, 1980; (with C.B. Keely and S.M. Tomasi, and contrib.) Global Trends in Migration: Theory and Research on International Population Movements, 1981; U.S. Immigration and Refugee Policy: Global and Domestic Issues, 1983; (with L.L. Lim and H. Zlotnik, and contrib.) International Migration Systems: A Global Approach, 1992; (with D. Gurak) Immigration and a Changing America, 2004. **Address:** Population and Development Program, Dept of Development Sociology, Cornell University, Ithaca, NY 14853, U.S.A. **Online address:** mmk5@cornell.edu

KRITZER, Amelia Howe. American, b. 1947. **Genres:** Theatre, Women's studies and issues. **Career:** University of Wisconsin-Madison, research and editorial assistant for Theatre Journal, 1984-85, lecturer in English, 1989-90; University of Wisconsin-Milwaukee, lecturer in theater and dance, 1989; Indiana University-Bloomington, visiting assistant professor of theater and drama, 1990-91; West Virginia University, Morgantown, assistant professor of theater, 1991-95, and director of plays; University of St. Thomas, St. Paul, MN, associate professor of theater, 1997-, chair of theater dept, 1998-. University of Wisconsin Center, Rock County, guest director, 1992. **Publica-tions:** The Plays of Caryl Churchill: Theatre of Empowerment, 1991; Plays by Early American Women, 1775-1850, 1994. Work represented in anthologies. Contributor of articles and reviews to academic journals. **Ad-dress:** 1438 Berkeley Ave., St. Paul, MN 55105-2423, U.S.A.

KRIVICH, Mikhail. Russian. **Genres:** Criminology/True Crime. **Career:** Writer. **Publications:** (with O. Ol'gin) Comrade Chikatilo: The Psychopathol-ogy of Russia's Notorious Serial Killer, trans by T.P. Bludeau, 1993. **Ad-dress:** c/o Barricade Books, 185 Bridge Plaza N Ste 308-A, Fort Lee, NJ 07024, U.S.A.

KROEGER, Brooke. American, b. 1949. **Genres:** Biography. **Career:** United Press International, reporter in Chicago, IL, 1973-76, correspondent from Brussels, Belgium, 1977, London, England, 1978-79, and Tel Aviv, Israel, 1979-80, bureau chief in Tel Aviv, 1981-83, and editor for Europe, the Middle East, and Africa, 1983-84; Newsday-New York Newsday, NYC, United Nations correspondent and deputy metropolitan editor, 1984-87; New York University, associate professor of journalism; writer. **Publications:** Nel-lie Bly: Daredevil, Reporter, Feminist, 1994; Fannie: The Talent for Success of Writer Fannie Hurst, 1999; Passing: When People Can't Be Who They Are, 2003. Contributor to magazines and newspapers. **Address:** 1175 Park Ave, New York, NY 10128, U.S.A. **Online address:** brooke.kroeger@nyu.edu

KROETSCH, Robert (Paul). Canadian, b. 1927. **Genres:** Novels, Poetry. **Career:** Laborer and Purser, Yellowknife Transportation Co., N.W.T., 1948-50; Information Specialist, U.S. Air Force Base, Goose Bay, Labrador, 1951-54; Professor of English, State University of New York at Binghamton; Professor of English, University of Manitoba, Winnipeg, now retired. **Publi-cations:** But We Are Exiles, 1966; The Words of My Roaring, 1966; Alberta, 1968; The Studhorse Man, 1969 (Governor-General's Award); Gone Indian;

Badlands, 1975; What the Crow Said, 1978; The Sad Phoenician (verse), 1979; Field Notes (verse), 1981; Alibi, 1983; Advice to My Friends (verse), 1985; The Lovely Treachery of Words (essays), 1989; Completed Field Notes (verse), 1989; The Puppeteer, 1992; A Likely Story: The Writing Life, 1995; The Man from the Creeks: A Novel, 1998; The Hornbooks of Rita K (verse), 2001. **Address:** 4081 Cedar Hill Rd, Victoria, BC, Canada V8N 3C2.

KROHN, Claus-Dieter. German, b. 1941. **Genres:** History. **Career:** Free University of Berlin, Germany, assistant professor, 1973-76; University of Luneburg, Germany, professor of modern history, 1977-. **Publications:** Wissenschaft im Exil, 1987, trans. by R. and R. Kimber as Intellectuals in Exile: Refugee Scholars and the New School for Social Research, 1993. IN GERMAN: Stabilisierung und oekonomische Interessen, 1974; Wirtschaftstheorien als politische Interessen, 1981; (co-ed.) Handbuch der deutschsprachigen Emigration 1933-1945, 1998; (co-ed.) Biographisches Handbuch der deutschsprachigen wirtschaftswissenschaftlichen Emigration nach 1933, 1999. **Address:** University of Luneburg, 21332 Luneberg, Germany. **Online address:** cdkrohn@web.de

KROHN, Katherine E(lizabeth). American (born Germany), b. 1961. **Genres:** Children's fiction, Children's non-fiction, Biography. **Career:** Writer, 1991-. **Publications:** BIOGRAPHIES FOR CHILDREN: Lucille Ball: Pioneer of Comedy, 1992; Roseanne Arnold: Comedy's Queen Bee, 1993; Elvis Presley: The King, 1994; Marilyn Monroe: Norma Jean's Dream, 1996; Marcia Clark: Voice for the Victims, 1996; Princess Diana, 199; Rosie O'Donnell, 1999; Women of the Wild West, 2000; Ella Fitzgerald, 2001; Oprah Winfrey, 2003; Sojourner Truth, 2005; Madam C.J. Walker, 2005; Jane Goodall, 2006. OTHER: Everything You Need to Know about Birth Order, 2000; Everything You Need to Know about Living on Your Own, 2000; You and Your Parents' Divorce, 2001; Full House Michelle and Friends, 2001; Haunted Houses, 2005. **Address:** c/o Lerner Publications, 241 First Ave N, Minneapolis, MN 55401, U.S.A.

KROKER, Arthur (W.). Canadian, b. 1945. **Genres:** Art/Art history, Communications/Media, Information science/Computers, Literary criticism and history, Politics/Government. **Career:** University of Winnipeg, Winnipeg, Manitoba, assistant professor, 1975-80, director of Canadian studies, 1979-80, associate professor of political science, 1980-81; Concordia University, Montreal, Quebec, associate professor, 1981-87, professor of political science, 1987-. Associate fellow of Simone de Beauvoir Institute, 1984-85, research fellow at Concordia Centre for Broadcasting Studies, 1984-86. Detroit Institute of Arts, writer-in-residence, 1989; guest lecturer at colleges and universities; guest lecturer at art museums. Appeared on radio and television shows in Canada, the Netherlands, Austria, Italy, Germany, Norway, Finalnd, the United Kingdom, and France; organizes and chairs discussion panels at conferences. **Publications:** Technology and the Canadian Mind: Innis, McLuhan, and Grant, 1984, 2nd ed, 1987, 1985; (with D. Cook) The Postmodern Scene: Excremental Culture and Hyper-Aesthetics, 1986, 2nd ed, 1987; (with D. Cook and M. Kroker) Panic Encyclopedia: The Definitive Guide to the Postmodern Scene, 1989; The Possessed Individual: Technology and the French Postmodern, 1992; Spasm: Virtual Reality, Android Music, and Electric Flesh, 1993; (with M.A. Weinstein) Data Trash: The Theory of the Virtual Class, 1994; (with M. Kroker) Hacking the Future: Stories for the Flesh-Eating 90s, 1996. EDITOR: (with M. Verthuy, P. McCallum, and M. Kroker) Feminism Now: Theory and Practice, 1985; (with M. Kroker, and coauthor of intro) Body Invaders: Panic Sex in America, 1987; (with M. Kroker) The Hysterical Male: New Feminist Theory, 1991; (with M. Kroker) Ideology and Power in the Age of Lenin in Ruins, 1991; (with M. Kroker) The Last Sex: Feminism and Outlaw Bodies, 1993; (with M. Kroker) Digital Delirium, St. Martin's, 1997. Work represented in anthologies. Contributor of articles and reviews to periodicals. **Address:** Dept of Political Science, University of Victoria, 3800 Finnerty Rd Cornett A323, PO Box 3050 STN CSC, Victoria, BC, Canada V8W 3P5.

KROLL, Virginia L(ouise). Also writes as Melrose Cooper. American, b. 1948. **Genres:** Children's fiction, Children's non-fiction. **Career:** Fifth grade teacher in the Buffalo, NY, area, 1968-69 and 1980-81; Hamburg Memorial Youth Center, Hamburg, NY, recreation assistant, 1978-80. Medaille College, Buffalo, college instructor for Writing for Children course, 1993. **Publications:** PICTURE BOOKS: Helen the Fish, 1992; My Sister, Then and Now, 1992; Masai and I, 1992; Naomi Knows It's Springtime, 1993; Woodhoopoe Willie, 1993; Africa Brothers and Sisters, 1993; A Carp for Kimiko, 1993; When Will We Be Sisters?, 1993; Jaha and Jamil Went down the Hill, 1994; Hats Off to Hair!, 1994; I Wanted to Know All about God, 1994; Beginnings, 1994; Pink Paper Swans, 1994; Sweet Magnolia, 1994; The Seasons and Someone, 1994; New Friendt, True Friends, Stuck-Like-Glue Friends,

1994; Shelter Folks, 1995; Can You Dance, Dalila?, 1996; Motherlove, 1998; With Love, to Earth's Endangered Peoples, 1998; The Making of Angels, 1998; Butterfly Boy, 1997; Hands!, 1997; Faraway Drums, 1998; When God Made the Tree, 1999; Cat!, 1999; She Is Born!, 2000; Girl, You're Amazing, 2001. AS MELROSE COOPER: I Got a Family, 1994; I Got Community, 1995; Life Magic, 1996; Gettin' through Thursday, 1998; Life Riddles, 1994; Pets!, 1998; Kwanzaa, 1999. Contributor to periodicals. **Address:** c/o Publicity Director, Simon & Schuster Children's Books, 1230 Avenue of the Americas, New York, NY 10020, U.S.A.

KRONDORFER, Björn. German, b. 1959. **Genres:** Theology/Religion. **Career:** Lehigh University, Bethlehem, PA, adjunct lecturer in religion and history, 1990; St. Mary's College of Maryland, St. Mary's City, associate professor of religious studies, 1992-. Jewish-German Dance Theatre, co-founder and member, 1985-89. Series editor for Cultural Criticism Series, Oxford University Press, 1998-2003. **Publications:** Remembrance and Reconciliation: Encounters between Young Jews and Germans, 1995. EDITOR: Body and Bible: Interpreting and Experiencing Biblical Narratives, 1992; Men's Bodies, Men's Gods: Male Identities in a (Post) Christian Culture, 1996; (and author of afterword) E. Gastfriend, My Father's Testament: Memoir of a Jewish Teenager, 1938-45; (co-) Von Gott reden im Land der Tater: Theologische Stimmen der dritten Generation seit der Shoah, 2001; (co-) Das Vermachtnis annehmen: Kulturelle und biographische Zugange zum Holocaust, 2002. Contributor to books and periodicals. **Address:** Dept of Philosophy and Religious Studies, St. Mary's College of Maryland, St. Marys City, MD 20686, U.S.A. **Online address:** bhkrondorfer@smcm.edu

KRONEGGER, Maria Elisabeth. American (born Austria), b. 1932. **Genres:** Literary criticism and history. **Career:** Professor of French and Comparative Literature, Michigan State University, East Lansing, since 1970 (Assistant Professor, 1964-67; Associate Professor, 1967-70). Assistant Professor of French and Humanities, Hollins College, Virginia, 1962-64. **Publications:** James Joyce and Associate Image Makers, 1968; Impressionist Literature, 1973; Phaenomaenologie et Littaerature: l'origine de l'oeuvre d'art, 1987; The Life Significance of Baroque Poetry, 1988; Phenomenology and Esthetics: New Approaches to Comparative Literature, 1991. EDITOR: Allegory Old and New in Literature, the Fine Arts, Music and Theatre, and Its Continuity in Culture, 1994; Esthetique baroque et imagination creatice, 1998; (co-) Differentiation and Harmony: Vegetal, Animal, Human, 1998.

KRONEN, Steve. American, b. 1953. **Genres:** Poetry. **Career:** Winter Park Public Library, librarian. **Publications:** Empirical Evidence, 1992. **Address:** 2000 W Hampton Circle, Winter Park, FL 32792, U.S.A. **Online address:** skronen@mailcity.com

KRONENFELD, Jennie J(acobs). American, b. 1949. **Genres:** Medicine/Health. **Career:** University of Alabama, Birmingham, assistant professor to associate professor, 1975-80; University of South Carolina-Columbia, associate professor to professor of public health, 1980-90; Arizona State University, Tempe, professor of health administration and policy, 1990-. **Publications:** (ed. with E.D. Charles, Jr.) The Social and Economic Impact of Coronary Artery Disease, 1980; (with M.L. Whicker) U.S. Health Policy: An Analysis of the Federal Role, 1984; (with Whicker) Sex Role Changes: Technology, Politics, and Policy, 1986; (with Whicker) Captive Populations: Caring for the Young, the Sick, the Imprisoned, and the Elderly, 1990; Controversial Issues in Health Care Policy, 1993; (with Whicker and R.A. Strickland) Getting Tenure, 1993; (with Whicker) Confronting Ethical Dilemmas in Research and Technology, 1994. Work represented in anthologies. Contributor to sociology and health care journals. **Address:** Department of Sociology, Arizona State University, Tempe, AZ 85287-2101, U.S.A. **Online address:** jennie.kronenfeld@asu.edu

KRONINGER, Stephen. American. **Genres:** Art/Art history. **Career:** Graphic artist, illustrator, educator, and author. Illustrator of posters and album covers; cartoonist. Presents workshops and lectures at universities and colleges. Exhibits include Museum of Modern Art, New York; works included in permanent collection at National Portrait Gallery, Washington, DC. **Publications:** (And illustrator) If I Crossed the Road, 1997. ILLUSTRATOR: Dave Marsh, Fifty Ways to Fight Censorship: And Important Facts to Know about Censors, 1991; Ken Siman, The Beauty Trip, 1995; Barbara Park, Pssst! It's Me . . . the Bogeyman, 1998; Lenny Hort, Tie Your Socks and Clap Your Feet: Mixed-up Poems, 2000; Laura J. Garak, Cyberliteracy: Navigating the Internet with Awareness, 2001. Illustrations anthologized in books. **Address:** c/o Author Mail, Simon & Schusters, 1230 Avenue of the Americas, New York, NY 10020, U.S.A.

KROOTH, Richard. American, b. 1935. **Genres:** Earth sciences, History, Law, Organized labor, Politics/Government, Sociology. **Career:** Constitutional attorney, 1962-77; Law & Labor Research Group, Santa Barbara, CA, director, 1978-79; University of California, Santa Barbara & Riverside, professor, 1980-82; Riverside County Criminal Youth Div., CA, Diversion Team, academic director, 1980-82; Madison Area Technical College, visiting professor, 1983-84; California Institute of Management, Berkeley, professor, 1985-89, research associate, 1987-89; University of California, Berkeley, visiting scholar, 1985-86, research associate, 1989, 1993-; lecturer: San Francisco State University, 1990, Sonoma State University, Rohnert Park, CA, 1991-92; Golden Gate University, San Francisco, adjunct professor, 1993-; Harvest Publishers, CA, editor/publisher; speaker at colleges and universities. **Publications:** Empire: A Bicentennial Appraisal, 1975; Japan: 5 Stages of Development, 1976; The Great Social Struggle and the Foundations of Social Theory, 3 vols. 1978-80; Arms and Empire: Imperial Patterns before World War II, 1981; The Struggle for Grenada, 1984; The Dynamics of Enterprise in the American Milieu, Vol. 1: Socio-Economic Contours, 1985, Vol. 2: Legal Dimensions, 1988; Common Destiny: Japan & the US in the Global Age, 1990; (with H. Fukurai and E.W. Butler) Race and the Jury, 1993; (with B. Vladimirovitz) The Quest for Freedom, 1993; (with M. Moallem) The Middle East: A Geopolitical Study of the Region in the New Global Era, 1994; (with others) Anatomy of the McMartin Child Molestation Trial, 2000; (with H. Fukurai) Race in Jury Box, 2003; Gaia & the Fate of Midas, vol. 1, 2003, vol. 2, 2004; A Century Passing, 2004. Contributor to academic journals and anthologies. **Address:** PO Box 9515, Berkeley, CA 94709, U.S.A. **Online address:** krooth@yahoo.com

KROPP, Paul. Canadian/American, b. 1948. **Genres:** Children's fiction, Young adult fiction, Adult non-fiction. **Career:** Teacher, Burlington, ON, 1972-74; teacher, Hamilton, ON, 1974-94. **Publications:** FOR YOUNG ADULTS. FICTION: Wilted, 1980, rev. ed. as You've Seen Enough, 1992; Getting Even, 1986; Moonkid and Liberty, 1989; The Rock, 1989; Ellen, Elena, Luna, 1992; Moonkid and Prometheus, 1997; The Countess and Me, 2002. SERIES CANADA: Burn Out, 1979; Dope Deal, 1979; Hot Cars, 1979; Runaway, 1979; Fair Play, 1980; Dead On, 1980; Dirt Bike, 1980; No Way, 1980; Baby, Baby, 1982; Gang War, 1982; Snow Ghost, 1982; Wild One, 1982; Amy's Wish, 1984; Micro Man, 1984; Take Off, 1986; Get Lost, 1987; Head Lock, 1988; Tough Stuff, 1988; Split Up, 1989. SERIES 2000: Death Ride, 1986; Jo's Search, 1986; Not Only Me, 1987; Under Cover, 1987; Baby Blues, 1989; We Both Have Scars, 1990; The Victim Was Me, 1991; Riot on the Street, 1993; Blizzard, 1995. FOR CHILDREN: Justin, Jay-Jay and the Juvenile Dinkent, 1986 repr. as Fast Times with Fred, 1990; Cottage Crazy, 1988; Ski Stooges, 1992. FOR ADULTS. NONFICTION: The Reading Solution: Make Your Child a Reader, 1993 in US as Raising a Reader, 1996; (with L. Hodson) The School Solution: Getting Canada's Schools to Work for Your Children, 1995; I'll Be the Parent, You Be the Kid, 1998; How to Make Your Child a Reader for Life, 2000. **Address:** 391 Wellesley St E, Toronto, ON, Canada M4X 1H5.

KROUSE, Erika Dawn. American, b. 1969. **Genres:** Poetry, Novellas/Short stories. **Career:** University of Colorado-Denver, English instructor, 1994-96; Sniper Logic, Boulder, CO, editor, 1995-96; Cencorp, Boulder, CO, technical publications writer, 1996. Physician Reimbursement Systems, Denver, CO, technical writer. **Publications:** Calamity Jane (poetry), 1996; Come up and See Me Sometime (short stories), 2001. Contributor of short stories to periodicals. **Address:** PO Box 1645, Boulder, CO 80306, U.S.A. **Online address:** erika111@juno.com

KRUCKEBERG, Arthur R(ice). American, b. 1920. **Genres:** Homes/Gardens, Natural history, Botany. **Career:** University of Washington, Seattle, professor of botany, 1950-89, professor emeritus, 1989-, chairman of department, 1971-77. **Publications:** California Serpentines, 1981; Gardening with Native Plants of the Pacific Northwest: An Illustrated Guide, 1982; Natural History of Puget Sound Country, 1989. Contributor to scholarly journals and popular magazines. Editor, Douglasia. **Address:** Botany, Box 35-1330, University of Washington, Seattle, WA 98195-1330, U.S.A.

KRUEGER, Lesley. (born Canada). **Genres:** Novels. **Career:** Educator and fiction writer. Ryerson University, Toronto, Ontario, Canada, faculty member. Writer-in-residence, Tasmanian Writers' Centre and Varuna Writers' Centre. **Publications:** (with Dayv-James French and Rohinton Mistry) Coming Attractions, 1986; Hard Travel, 1989; Poor Player, 1993; Drink the Sky, 1999; Foreign Correspondences: A Traveler's Tales, 2000; The Corner Garden, 2004. **Address:** c/o Author Mail, Penguin Books Canada Ltd., 10 Alcorn Ave. Suite 300, Toronto, ON, Canada M4V 3B2.

KRUGER, Arnd. German, b. 1944. **Genres:** Sports/Fitness, History. **Career:** German Sports Federation, Frankfurt, managing editor, 1971-74; Berlin Teachers Training College, Berlin, Germany, university assistant, 1974-78;

University of Hamburg, Hamburg, Germany, associate professor, 1978-80; University of Goettingen, Goettingen, Germany, professor and department head, 1980-, and dean of School of Social Science. European Committee for Sport History, chairperson, 1995-97. **Publications:** Sport und Politik, 1975; Ritual and Record, 1991; The Story of Worker Sport, 1996; The 1936 Olympic Games in World Perspective, 1998. Author other books. Contributor to scholarly journals. **Address:** University of Goettingen, 2 Sprangerweg, 37075 Goettingen, Germany. **Online address:** akruege1@gwdg.de

KRUGER, Ehren. American, b. 1972. **Genres:** Film. **Career:** Screenwriter. Worked as an executive assistant at the Fox Broadcasting Company (Fox) and a script assistant for Sandollar Productions. **Publications:** SCREENPLAYS, EXCEPT AS INDICATED: Killers in the House (teleplay), 1998; Arlington Road, 1999; Scream 3, 2000; Reindeer Games, 2000; Texas Rangers, 2001; Impostor, 2002; The Ring, 2002. **Address:** c/o DreamWorks, 1000 Flower St., Glendale, CA 91201, U.S.A.

KRUH, David. American, b. 1956. **Genres:** History, Local history/Rural topics, Travel/Exploration, Novels, Plays/Screenplays, Songs/Lyrics and libretti. **Career:** WRAN-Radio, Dover, NJ, reporter and copywriter, 1978-80; WVNHRadio, Salem, NH, reporter and copywriter, 1980-81; WPIX-FM Radio, New York City, copywriter, 1981; WRKO/WROR-FM Radio, Boston, MA, staff engineer, 1981-87; Otocom Systems, Wilmington, MA, product manager, 1987-91; WEEIRadio, Boston, producer and writer for the Andy Moes Show, 1991-92; First Data Technology, Medford, MA, business writer, 1992-93; Central Artery Tunnel Project, Boston, MA, writer, spokesperson, webmaster, 1994-97; Analog Devices, Wilmington, MA, marketing communications manager, 1997-. **Publications:** Always Something Doing: A History of Boston's Infamous Scollay Square, 1990, 2nd ed., 1999; (with L. Kruh) Presidential Landmarks, 1992. **Address:** 3 Wescroft Rd., Reading, MA 01867, U.S.A. **Online address:** davekruh@ziplink.net

KRUH, Louis. American, b. 1923. **Genres:** History. **Career:** Began career as sales representative for weekly newspapers and a trade magazine; Batten, Barton, Durstine & Osborn Inc., NYC, marketing supervisor to senior account executive, 1954-70; New York Telephone, director of advertising, 1970-90; attorney in private practice, 1990-. Lecturer at colleges and universities, and to community and school groups. **Publications:** The Family Guide to Long Island, 1970, rev. ed. as The New Family Guide to Long Island, 1976; (co-author) Machine Cryptography and Modern Cryptanalysis, 1985; (co-ed.) Cryptology: Yesterday, Today, and Tomorrow, 1987; (co-ed.) Cryptology: Machines, History, and Methods, 1989; (with D.S. Kruh) Presidential Landmarks, 1992. **Address:** 17 Alfred Rd W, Merrick, NY 11566, U.S.A.

KRUMAN, Marc W. American, b. 1949. **Genres:** History. **Career:** Wayne State University, Detroit, MI, instructor to professor of history and chair of department, 1975-. **Publications:** Parties and Politics in North Carolina, 1836-1865, 1983; Between Authority and Liberty, 1997. **Address:** Department of History, 3094 F/AB, Wayne State University, Detroit, MI 48202, U.S.A. **Online address:** M.Kruman@wayne.edu

KRUPNICK, Karen. American, b. 1947. **Genres:** Children's non-fiction. **Career:** Author. Litel Elementary School, Chino Hills, CA, teacher of gifted students and mentor teacher, 1984-. **Publications:** The Great Race to Nome (for children), 1995; Kids@School.on.the.net, 1997; Teaching K-5 Social Studies Using the Internet. **Address:** 873 East 25th St., Upland, CA 91784-8337, U.S.A. **Online address:** kkrupnic@cyberg8t.com

KRUPP, Robin Rector. American, b. 1946. **Genres:** Children's fiction, Illustrations, Art/Art history, Travel/Exploration, Children's non-fiction, Astronomy. **Career:** Painter, author and illustrator of children's books; Pierce College, Woodland Hills, CA, instructor in art, 1971-85, 1988-93, 2001-02; Fashion Institute of Design and Merchandising, Los Angeles, CA, instructor in art, 1979-88; California State University, Northridge, instructor in writing and illustrating children's books, 1987-89; Metropolitan Cooperative Library System, artist for the Summer Reading Program, 1988 and 1990. **Publications:** SELF-ILLUSTRATED, JUVENILE: Get Set to Wreck!, 1988; Let's Go Traveling, 1992; Let's Go Traveling in Mexico, 1996. Illustrator of books by E.C. Krupp. **Address:** c/o Jane Jordan Browne, Multimedia Product Development, Inc, 410 S Michigan Ave Rm 724, Chicago, IL 60606-1465, U.S.A. **Online address:** rrkrapp@hotmail.com

KUBERSKI, Philip. American, b. 1952. **Genres:** Literary criticism and history, Autobiography/Memoirs. **Career:** Wake Forest University, Winston-Salem, NC, professor of English, 1989-. **Publications:** The Persistence of Memory: Organism, Myth, Text, 1992; A Calculus of Ezra Pound: Vocations of the American Sign, 1992; Chaosmos: Literature, Science, and Theory,

1994. **Address:** Department of English, Wake Forest University, Winston-Salem, NC 27109, U.S.A. **Online address:** kuberspf@wfu.edu

KUBEY, Robert W(illiam). American, b. 1952. **Genres:** Communications/Media. **Career:** University of Wisconsin-Madison, lecturer in psychology, 1980-81; University of Chicago, Chicago, IL, lecturer in Office of Continuing Education, 1984; University of California, Irvine, visiting lecturer in social ecology, 1984-85; Rutgers University, New Brunswick, NJ, associate professor of communication, 1991-, research director of Media Education Laboratory, 1995-97, director of Master's Program in Communication and Information Studies, 1997-, fellow of Rutgers College, 1985-, fellow at Center for the Critical Analysis of Contemporary Culture, 1986-87. Stanford University, assistant professor, 1985-91; Harvard University, member of faculty at Summer Institute on Media Education, 1993-94. Moderator and consultant for instructional videotapes on media education. National Committee for the Prevention of Child Abuse, member of board of directors of New Jersey chapter, 1988-90. **Publications:** (with M. Csikszentmihalyi) Television and the Quality of Life: How Viewing Shapes Everyday Experience, 1990; (ed. and contrib.) Media Literacy in the Information Age: Current Perspectives, 1997. Contributor of articles and reviews to professional journals and newspapers. **Address:** Department of Communication, Rutgers University, 4 Huntington St., New Brunswick, NJ 08901, U.S.A. **Online address:** kubey@scils.rutgers.edu

KÜBLER-ROSS, Elisabeth. *See* Obituaries.

KUBLICKI, Nicolas M. American. **Genres:** Documentaries/Reportage. **Career:** Office of Policy Development, assistant to deputy director, 1992-93; U.S. Department of Justice, assistant to senior trial attorneys of Environmental Enforcement section, 1993-94; Buchalter, Nemer, Fields & Younger Law Offices, Los Angeles, CA, associate, 1994-97; Ervin, Cohen & Jessup LLP, associate, 1997-2002, partner, 2002-03. Teaches real estate transactions at Pepperdine University School of Law and lectures to high schools, universities, and international policy groups. **Publications:** The Diamond Conspiracy, 2002. Author of articles for law publications. **Address:** Ervin Cohen & Jessup LLP, 9401 Wilshire Blvd., Ninth Floor, Beverly Hills, CA 90212, U.S.A. **Online address:** patcarlton@earthlink.net

KUCZKIR, Mary. Also writes as Fern Michaels. American, b. 1933. **Genres:** Novels, Romance/Historical, Humor/Satire. **Career:** Freelance writer. **Publications:** My Dish Towel Flies at Half Mast, 1979. ROMANCE NOVELS WITH R. ANDERSON AS FERN MICHAELS: Pride and Passion, 1975; Vixen in Velvet, 1976; Captive Passions, 1977; Valentina, 1978; Captive Embraces, 1979; Captive Splendors, 1980; The Delta Ladies, 1980; Golden Lasso, 1980; Sea Gypsy, 1980; Beyond Tomorrow, 1981; Captive Innocence, 1981; Whisper My Name, 1981; Without Warning, 1981; Nightstar, 1982; Paint Me Rainbows, 1982; Wild Honey, 1982; All She Can Be, 1983; Free Spirit, 1983; Tender Warrior, 1983; Cinders to Satin, 1984; Texas Rich, 1985; Ever the Empire, 1986; To Taste the Wine, 1987; Texas Heat, 1986; Texas Fury, 1989; Sins of Omission, 1989; Sins of the Flesh, 1990; For All Their Lives, 1991; Texas Sunrise, 1993; Desperate Measures, 1994; Serendipity, 1994; Seasons of Her Life, 1994; To Have and to Hold, 1994; Dear Emily, 1995; Vegas Rich, 1996; Wish List, 1996; Vegas Heat, 1997; Vegas Sunrise, 1997; White Fire, 1997; (with others) Heart of the Home, 1998; Finders Keepers, 1998; Sara's Song, 1998; Yesterday, 1999; Celebration, 1999; Annie's Rainbow, 1999; Guest List, 2000; Listen to Your Heart, 2000; What You Wish For, 2000; Plain Jane, 2001; Kentucky Rich, 2001; Charming Lily, 2001; Late Bloomer, 2002; Kentucky Sunrise, 2002; Kentucky Heat, 2002; Shattered Night, 2002. OTHER: Panda Bear Is Critical (novel), 1982. **Address:** c/o Kensington Publishing Corp., 850 3rd Ave, New York, NY 10022, U.S.A. **Online address:** fernmichaels@fernmichaels.com

KUCZMARSKI, Susan Smith. American, b. 1951. **Genres:** Education. **Career:** University of Illinois, Chicago, instructor, 1976-77; Rosary College, River Forest, IL, lecturer, 1977-78; Concordia University, River Forest, assistant professor, 1977-79; Constitutional Rights Foundation, Chicago, IL, educational director, 1979-81; Northwestern University, Evanston, IL, associate director of development and instructor, 1981-84; Kuczmarski & Associates, executive vice president, 1984-; National Louis University, Evanston, IL, instructor, 1986-88. **Publications:** (and ed.) Youth and Society: Rights and Responsibilities, 2nd ed., 1980; (with T.D. Kuczmarski) Values-Based Leadership: Rebuilding Employee Commitment, Performance, and Productivity, 1995; The Family Bond: Inspiring Tips for Creating a Closer Family, 2000. **Address:** 1165 North Clark St #700, Chicago, IL 60610, U.S.A.

KUCZMARSKI, Thomas D(ale). American, b. 1951. **Genres:** Administration/Management. **Career:** Served as brand manager for Quaker Oats; principal at Booz, Allen & Hamilton (international consulting firm); cofounder of Kuczmarski & Associates (consulting firm), 1984-. Adjunct professor and lecturer at universities. **Publications:** Managing New Products: The Power of Innovation, 1988; (with S.S. Kuczmarski) Values-Based Leadership: Rebuilding Employee Commitment, Performance, and Productivity, 1995; Creating an Innovation Mindset, 1995. **Address:** 428 W Roslyn Pl, Chicago, IL 60614, U.S.A.

KUDLINSKI, Kathleen V. American, b. 1950. **Genres:** Children's nonfiction. **Career:** Writer. Weekly columnist, The Naturalist, New Haven Register, New Haven, CT, 1988-. Has also worked as an elementary school classroom teacher; makes frequent visits to classrooms to talk about writing and book production. Chairperson, Guilford, CT Community Fund, 2003. **Publications:** Rachel Carson: Pioneer of Ecology, 1988; Juliette Gordon Low, America's First Girl Scout, 1989; Hero over Here: A Story of World War I , 1990; Pearl Harbor Is Burning: A Story of World War II, 1990; Animal Tracks and Traces, 1991; Night Bird: A Story of the Seminole Indians, 1993; Earthquake!: A Story of Old San Francisco, 1993; Lone Star: A Story of the Texas Rangers, 1994; Facing West: A Story of the Oregon Trail, 1994; Marie: An Invitation to Dance, 1996; Shannon: A Chinatown Adventure, 1996; Shannon: Lost and Found, 1997; Shannon: The Schoolmarm Mysteries, San Francisco, 1880, 1997; Popcorn Plants, 1998; Venus Flytraps, 1998; Dandelions, 1999; My Tree, 2000; My Body Is Changing: Now What Do I Do?, 2000; Rosa Parks, Young Rebel, 2001; Harriet Tubman, Freedom's Trailblazer, 2002; It's Not Easy Being Green, 2003; Food for Life!, 2003; Sojourner Truth, Voice of Freedom, 2003; The Spirit Catchers, 2004; What Do Roots Do?, 2004; Boy, Were We Wrong about Dinosaurs!, 2005; The Sunset Switch, 2005; Boy, Were We Wrong about the Solar System!, forthcoming. **Address:** 95 Alden Dr., Guilford, CT 06437, U.S.A. **Online address:** kathkud@aol.com

KUEHL, Stefan. German, b. 1966. **Genres:** History. **Career:** Civil service, 1986-88; independent consultant, 1990-94. **Publications:** The Nazi Connection: Eugenics, American Racism, and German National Socialism, 1994. **Address:** Amselweg 24, 25451 Quickborn, Germany.

KUENNE, Robert Eugene. American, b. 1924. **Genres:** Economics, Military/Defense/Arms control. **Career:** Professor of Economics, Princeton University, NJ, 1956-. Consultant, Institute for Defense Analyses, Arlington, VA, 1968-. Visiting Professor of Military Systems Analysis, U.S. Army War College, Carlisle Barracks, PA, 1967-84. **Publications:** (with G.B. Turner and R.D. Challener) National Security in the Nuclear Age, 1960; The Theory of General Economic Equilibrium, 1963; The Attack Submarine: A Study in Strategy, 1965; The Polaris Missile Strike: A General Economic Systems Analysis, 1966; Microeconomic Theory of the Market Mechanism: A General Equilibrium Approach, 1968; Eugen von Bohm-Bawerk, 1971; Rivalrous Consonance: A Theory of General Oligopolistic Equilibrium, 1986; (coauthor) Warranties in Weapon Systems Procurement, 1988; General Equilibrium Economics, 1992; The Economics of Oligopolistic Competition: Price and Nonprice Rivalry, 1992; Economic Justice in American Society, 1993; Price and Nonprice Rivalry in Oligopoly, 1998. EDITOR/CO-EDITOR: Monopolistic Competition Theory: Studies in Impact, 1967; New Directions in Regional Science, 1991; Dynamics and Conflict in Regional Structural Change, 1991; Microeconomics: Theoretical and Applied, 3 vols., 1991. **Address:** 63 Bainbridge St, Princeton, NJ 08540, U.S.A. **Online address:** kuenne@princeton.edu

KUH, Richard H. American, b. 1921. **Genres:** Law. **Career:** Lawyer, Warshaw Burstein Cohen Schlesinger & Kuh, LLP, NYC. District Attorney, New York County, 1974. **Publications:** Foolish Figleaves?: Pornography in, and out of, Court, 1967. **Address:** 14 Washington Pl, New York, NY 10003, U.S.A.

KUHRE, W. Lee. American, b. 1947. **Genres:** Technology, Information science/Computers, Environmental sciences/Ecology. **Career:** Anschutz Corp. (mining company), Denver, CO, environmental and safety manager, 1971-77; Kaiser Engineers, Oakland, CA, environmental and safety project manager, 1978-83; Pacific Bell, San Ramon, CA, environmental and safety manager, 1984-90; Seagate Technology (computer hardware manufacturer), Scotts Valley, CA, executive director of environmental health and safety, 1991-. University of San Francisco, senior lecturer, 1988-. Certified Hazardous Materials Manager; certified by AHERA; registered Environmental Assessor and Environmental Professional. **Publications:** Practical Management of Chemicals and Hazardous Waste, 1994; ISO 14001 Certification/Environmental Management Systems, 1995; ISO 14010s Environmental Auditing, 1996; ISO 14020s Environmental Labelling/Marketing, 1997. **Address:** Seagate Technology, 920 Disc Dr., PO Box 66360, Scotts Valley, CA 95067, U.S.A.

KUJOORY, Parvin. American (born Iran), b. 1936. **Genres:** Race relations, Reference. **Career:** University of Shiraz, Iran, began as assistant professor, became associate professor of English, 1967-83; Texas A&M University System, Prairie View, TX, reference librarian, 1985-87, assistant professor of media, 1987-89; University of the District of Columbia, Washington, DC, assistant professor to associate professor, 1990-97; Southern Methodist University, Dallas, TX, lecturer in English, 1998-99. Farsi Translation Bureau, Denton, TX, director, 1983-85; consultant to Wheaton Public Library; Choice, book reviewer, 1986-. **Publications:** Methods of Research, 1982; Black Slavery in America: An Annotated Mediagraphy, 1995; Shakespeare and Minorities: An Annotated Bibliography, 1970-2000, 2001. EDITOR: Readings in English: A Freshman English Textbook, 1974; (assoc.) Who's Who of the Nobel Prize Winners, 1986, 3rd ed., 1996. Contributor to periodicals. **Address:** 4565 Early Morn Dr, Plano, TX 75093, U.S.A. **Online address:** pkujoory@evi.net

KUKLIN, Susan. American, b. 1941. **Genres:** Children's non-fiction. **Career:** Photographer and writer. Work exhibited in group shows in and around New York City. **Publications:** FOR YOUNG PEOPLE (and photographer): Mine for a Year, 1984; Thinking Big, 1986; Reaching for Dreams, 1987; When I See My Doctor, 1988; When I See My Dentist, 1988; Taking My Cat to the Vet, 1988; Taking My Dog to the Vet, 1988; Fighting Back: What Some People Are Doing About AIDS, 1988; Going to My Ballet Class, 1989; Going to Nursery School, 1990; Going to My Gym Class, 1991; What Do I Do Now? Teenagers Talk about Sex and Pregnancy, 1991; How My Family Lives in America, 1992; Fighting Fires, 1993; Speaking Out: Teenagers Take on Race, Sex, and Identity, 1993; From Head to Toe: How a Doll is Made, 1994; After a Suicide: Young People Speak Up, 1994; Kodomo: Children of Japan, 1995; Fireworks: The Science, the Art, and the Magic, 1996; Irrepressible Spirit: Conversations with Human Rights Activists, 1996; (with B.T. Jones) Dance, 1998; Iqbal Masih and the Crusaders against Child Slavery, 1998; Trail: The Inside Story, 2000; Hoops with Swoopes, 2001; The Harlem Nutcracker, 2001; From Wall to Wall, 2002; All Aboard: A True Train Story, 2003. Photographer in books by: L. Atkinson, G. DeWeesse, B.T. Jones, R. Lacy, A. Michel, H. Terrace, P. Thompson, A. Zane. **Address:** c/o Hyperion Books for Children, 114 Fifth Ave, New York, NY 10011, U.S.A.

KUKREJA, Veena. Indian, b. 1960. **Genres:** Politics/Government. **Career:** University of Delhi, India, lecturer at Shivaji College, 1980-81, lecturer at Janaki Devi College, 1981-89, associate professor of political science, 1989-. **Publications:** Military Intervention in Politics: A Case Study of Pakistan, 1985; Civil-Military Relations in South Asia, 1991. Contributor to political science journals. **Address:** Department of Political Science, University of Delhi, Delhi 110 007, India.

KULIK, Boles. See COSTLEY, Bill.

KULKA, Richard A. American, b. 1945. **Genres:** Psychiatry, Psychology. **Career:** Institute for Social Research, Ann Arbor, MI, assistant study director at Survey Research Center, University of Michigan, 1973-75, assistant research scientist and study director, 1975-80; University of Michigan, lecturer, 1979-80; Research Triangle Institute, Research Triangle Park, NC, senior survey methodologist, 1980-88, chief scientist, 1980, research vice president, 1994-2000, senior research vice president, 2000-; University of North Carolina at Chapel Hill, research associate professor, 1981-88; National Opinion Research Center, University of Chicago, IL, associate director, 1989-93, senior vice president, 1994. **Publications:** (with J. Veroff and E. Douvan) The Inner American: Life, Work, and Mental Health from 1957 to 1976, 1981; (with Veroff and Douvan) Mental Health in America: Patterns of Help-Seeking from 1957 to 1976, 1981; (with J.E. McGrath and J. Martin) Judgment Calls in Research, 1982; (with others) Trauma and the Vietnam Generation: Report of Findings from the National Vietnam Veterans Readjustment Study, 1990. Contributor to books. **Address:** Research Triangle Institute, PO Box 12194, Research Triangle Park, NC 27709-2194, U.S.A. **Online address:** rak@rti.org

KULL, Andrew. American, b. 1947. **Genres:** Law, Botany, Travel/Exploration, History. **Career:** Paul, Weiss, Rifkind, Wharton & Garrison, New York City, attorney, 1977-80; Cleary, Gottlieb, Steen & Hamilton, New York City, attorney in New York and Paris, 1980-87; Emory University, Atlanta, GA, professor of law, 1987-; writer. **Publications:** Secrets of Flowers, Stephen Greene, 1966, revised edition, 1976; New England Cemeteries: A Collector's Guide, Stephen Greene, 1975; The Color-Blind Constitution, Harvard University Press, 1992. **Address:** School of Law, Emory University, Atlanta, GA 30322, U.S.A.

KULLING, Monica. Canadian, b. 1952. **Genres:** Children's fiction, Poetry, Children's non-fiction. **Career:** Researcher and developer of anthologies, Scholastic Canada, 1983-87, Ginn Publishing Canada, 1987-90, Houghton Mifflin Canada, 1990-92, and Prentice-Hall, 1992-. **Publications:** FICTION FOR CHILDREN: Little Peanut at the Zoo, 1983; I Hate You, Marmalade!, 1992; Waiting for Amos, 1992; (adaptor) Little Women, by L.M. Alcott, 1994; (adaptor) Les Miserables, by V. Hugo, 1995; (adaptor) The Adventures of Tom Sawyer, by M. Twain, 1995; (adaptor) Great Expectations, by C. Dickens, 1996; Marmee's Surprise: A Little Women Story, 1996; Edgar Badger's Balloon Day, 1996; Fairy Tale: A True Story (movie storybook), 1997, (novelization), 1997; Edgar Badger's Fix-It Day, 1997; The Body Snatcher (adaptation), 1998; Edgar Badger's Fishing Day, 1999; Edgar Badger's Butterfly Day, 1999. Contributor of short stories to magazines. POETRY: Go-Cart Getaway, 1993. Contributor of poetry to magazines and to anthologies. NONFICTION: Vanished! The Mysterious Disappearance of Amelia Earhart, 1996; Bears: Life in the Wild, 1998; Eleanor Everywhere: The Life of Eleanor Roosevelt, 1999; The Great Houdini: World-Famous Magician and Escape Artist, 1999; Sea of Ice: The Wreck of the "Endurance," 1999; Escape North! The Story of Harriet Tubman, 2000; Alligators: Life in the Wild, 2000. **Address:** c/o Random House, Books for Young Readers, 201 E 50th St 28th Fl, New York, NY 10022, U.S.A.

KULTERMANN, Udo. American (born Germany), b. 1927. **Genres:** Architecture, Art/Art history. **Career:** Washington University, St. Louis, professor, 1967-94, Ruth and Norman Moore Professor of Architecture, 1986-94, professor emeritus, 1994-. Museum Schloss Morsbroich, Leverkusen, West Germany, director, 1959-64. **Publications:** Architecture of Today, 1958; Hans und Wassili Luckhardt: Bauten und Entwuerfe, 1958; Dynamische Architektur, 1959; New Japanese Architecture, 1960; Der Schluessel zur Architektur von heute, 1963; Junge deutsche Bildhauer, 1963; New Architecture in Africa, 1963; New Architecture in the World, 1965; History of Art History, 1966, rev. ed., 2002; Architektur der Gegenwart: Kunst der Welt, 1967; The New Sculpture, 1967; Gabriel Grupello, 1968; The New Painting, 1969; New Directions in African Architecture, 1969; (with W. Hofmann) Modern Architecture in Color, 1970; Kenzo Tange: Architecture and Urban Design, 1970; Art and Life, 1970; New Realism, 1972; Ernest Trova, 1977; Die Architektur im 20. Jahrhundert, 1978, rev. ed., 2003; I Contemporanei (vol. XIV di Storia della Scultura del Mondo), 1979; Architecture in the Seventies, 1980; Architekten der Dritten Welt, 1980; Zeitgenoessische Architektur in Osteuropa, 1985; Kleine Geschichte der Kunsttheorie, 1987; Visible Cities-Invisible Cities, 1988; Kunst und Wirklichkeit, von Fiedler bis Derrida, 1991; Die Maxentius-Basilika-Ein Schluesselwerk spaetantiker Architektur, 1996; Contemporary Architecture in the Arab States-Renaissance of a Region, 1999; (ed.) World Architecture: A Critical Mosaic, Beijing and Vienna, Vol. VI: Architecture in Central and Southern Africa, 1900-2000, 2000; (ed.) St. James Modern Masterpieces, 1945, 1998; Thirty Years After, 2002; Architecture and Revolution, 2002. Contributor to books.

KUMAR, Alok. American (born India), b. 1954. **Genres:** Physics, Sciences, History. **Career:** California State University, Long Beach, lecturer in physics, 1980-92; State University of New York at Oswego, professor of physics, 1992-. NOVA/NASA Fellow, 2001. **Publications:** (trans. with S.I. Salem) Said Al-Andalusi, Science in the Medieval World: Book of the Categories of Nations, 1991; Laboratory Manual for College Physics, I, 2003, II, 2004. Work represented in anthologies. Contributor of research articles related to x-ray physics, atomic physics, history of science, and science education to scientific journals. **Address:** Dept of Physics, State University of New York at Oswego, Oswego, NY 13126, U.S.A. **Online address:** kumar@oswego.edu

KUMIGAI, Fumie. Japanese, b. 1943. **Genres:** Sociology. **Career:** University of New Hampshire, Durham, instructor, 1974-76; Hartwick College, Oneonta, NY, assistant professor of sociology, 1976-78; Sophia University, Tokyo, Japan, lecturer in sociology, 1978-81; Harvard University, Cambridge, MA, visiting scholar at Japan Institute, 1981-82; Stanford University, Stanford, CA, visiting scholar in sociology, 1982; University of British Columbia, Vancouver, visiting associate professor of home economics and fellow of Ohira Commemorative Research Program, 1982-83; International University of Japan, associate professor of sociology, 1983-87; Kyorin University, Tokyo, professor of sociology, 1988-. Lecturer at universities worldwide; guest speaker at colleges and universities. **Publications:** America no Kateinai Boryoku: Kodomo, Otto, Tsuma, Oya Gyakutai no Jittai (title means: Violence in the American Family: A Life Cycle Perspective), 1983; Marginalization no Seishun (title means: Marginalization: A Personal Account), 1985; Kaso to Kamitsu ni Ikiru San-Sedai no Hinonjin (title means: Three Generation Families in Rural and Urban Japan), 1987; Kokusaikajidai no Katei Kyoiku (title means: Japanese Family Education in the Era of Internationalization), 1988; Nihonteki Seisann Shisutemu in Yu-Esu-Ei: Masatsu kara Sogorikaihe (title means: Impacts of the Japanese Style of

Production System in the U.S.A.: From Friction to Friendship), 1996; Unmasking Japan Today: The Impact of Traditional Values on Modern Japanese Society, 1996; Degitaru Shakai no Shoyoso: Shakaigaku no Aratana Tenkai (title means: Issues in Digital Society: New Perspectives in Sociology), 1999. EDITOR: A Bridge across the Pacific: Japanese and American Society and Culture Today, 1977; (with Takashi Koyama and Kiyomi Morioka, and contrib) Family and Household in Changing Japan, 1980; Katei to Boryoku: Kazoku wo Meguru Ningenkankei (title means: Violence and the Family: Human Interactions in the Family), 1981; (with Haruo Matsubara) Konai Boryoku (title means: Violence in School), 1982; (with M. Hayasaka, J. Parochetti, and others) Social Problems of Internationalizing Societies: Comparative Analyses, 1992; (and contrib) Nihon no Kazoku to Chiikisei (title means: Japanese Family Structure and Regional Variations), Vol I: Higashi Nihon no Kazoku wo Chuushintoshite (title means: Special Emphasis on Eastern Japan), Vol II: Nishi Nihon no Kazoku wo Chuushintoshite (title means: Special Emphasis on Western Japan), 1997. Contributor to books, professional journals, and newspapers. **Address:** Department of Foreign Studies, Kyorin University, 476 Miyashita-cho, Hachioji, Tokyo 192-8504, Japan. **Online address:** n96287fk@sfc.keio.ac.jp; http://www.sfc.keio.ac.jp/~n96287fk

KUMIN, Maxine. American, b. 1925. **Genres:** Novels, Novellas/Short stories, Children's fiction, Young adult fiction, Poetry, Literary criticism and history. **Career:** Tufts University, Medford, MA, instructor in English, 1958-61, lecturer, 1965-68; Newton College, MA, lecturer in English, 1971-72; Columbia University, adjunct professor of writing, 1975; Hurst Professor of Literature: Brandeis University, Waltham, MA, 1975, Washington University, 1977; Library of Congress, consultant in poetry, 1981-82; Bucknell University, PA, poet-in-residence, 1983; Massachusetts Institute of Technology, visiting professor, 1984, visiting writer, 1986-87; Woodrow Wilson Visiting Fellow, 1979-84, 1991-94; Davidson College, NC, McGee Professor of Writing, 1997. Visiting Lecturer: University of Massachusetts, Amherst, 1972, Princeton University, 1977, 1979, 1981-82; Visiting Professor: University of Miami, FL, 1995, Pitzer College, Claremont, CA, 1996, Florida Intl University, Miami, 1998-2000, New England College, 2003-04. **Publications:** JUVENILE FICTION: Sebastian and the Dragon, 1960; Spring Things, 1961; Summer Story, 1961; Follow the Fall, 1961; A Winter Friend, 1961; Mittens in May, 1962; No One Writes a Letter to the Snail, 1962; Archibald the Traveling Poodle, 1963; Eggs of Things, 1963; (with A. Sexton) More Eggs of Things, 1963; Speedy Digs Downside Up, 1964; The Beach before Breakfast, 1964: Paul Bunyan, 1966; (with A. Sexton) The Wizard Tears, 1975; What Color Is Caesar, 1978. FOR ADULTS: Through Dooms of Love (in UK as A Daughter and Her Loves), 1965; The Passions of Uxport, 1968; The Abduction, 1971; The Designated Heir, 1974; To Make a Prairie (essays), 1979; Why Can't We Live Together Like Civilized Human Beings? (short stories), 1982; In Deep: Country Essays, 1987; Women, Animals, and Vegetable: Essays and Stories, 1994; Quit Monks or Die (mystery), 1999; Inside the Halo and Beyond (memoir), 2000; Always Beginning, 2000. POETRY: Halfway, 1961; The Privilege, 1965; The Nightmare Factory, 1970; Up Country, 1972; House, Bridge, Fountain, Gate, 1975; The Retrieval System, 1978; Our Ground Time Here Will Be Brief, 1982; The Long Approach, 1985; Nurture, 1989; Looking for Luck, 1992; Connecting the Dots, 1996; Selected Poems, 1960-1990, 1997; The Long Marriage, 2001; Bringing Together, Uncollected Early Poems, 1958-1988. **Address:** 40 Harriman Ln, Warner, NH 03278, U.S.A. **Online address:** montwid@aol.com

KUNDA, Gideon. Israeli, b. 1952. **Genres:** Engineering, Administration/Management, Anthropology/Ethnology, Sociology. **Career:** Massachusetts Institute of Technology, Cambridge, postdoctoral research fellow at Sloan School of Management, 1987-88; Tel Aviv University, Tel Aviv, Israel, lecturer, 1988-92, senior lecturer in department labor studies, 1992-. Consultant to Bell Communications Research, 1984-87, and Israeli Kibbutz Movement, 1989-91; Cornell University, visiting assistant professor at New York State School of Industrial and Labor Relations, 1988-89. **Publications:** Engineering Culture: Control and Commitment in a HighTech Corporation, 1992. Work represented in anthologies. Contributor of articles and reviews to academic journals. **Address:** Department of of Labor Studies, Tel Aviv University, 69978 Tel Aviv, Israel.

KUNHARDT, Edith. Also writes as Pine Grunewalt, Johnson Hill, Edward Knapp, Jessie Smith, Harry Coe Verr. American, b. 1937. **Genres:** Children's fiction, Children's non-fiction. **Career:** Golden Books, New York City, editor, 1974-86; children's book writer and illustrator, 1986-. **Publications:** FOR CHILDREN INCLUDING: I Want to Be a Farmer, 1989; I Want to Be a Firefighter, 1989; I'm Going to Be a Firefighter, 1989; Pat the Puppy, 1993; Honest Abe, 1993; I'm Going to Be a Police Officer, 1995; I'm Going to Be a Farmer, 1996; I'm Going to Be a Vet, 1996; Pat the Christmas Bunny, 1999; Pat the Pony; Tickle the Pig; Pat the Birthday Bunny, 2001; Bunny's Bath Time, 2002.

KUNITZ, Stanley (Jasspon). American, b. 1905. **Genres:** Poetry, Literary criticism and history, Essays. **Career:** Ed., Wilson Library Bulletin, NYC, 1928-43; member of faculty, Bennington College, VT, 1946-49; Professor of English, State University of New York, Potsdam, 1949-50; Lecturer, New School for Social Research, NYC, 1950-57; Director, YM-YWHA Poetry Workshop, NYC, 1958-62; Lecturer, 1963-67, and Adjunct Professor of Writing, 1967-85, Columbia University, NYC; 1st vice-president, Fine Arts Work Center, Provincetown, MA, 1968-; Ed., Yale Series of Younger Poets, Yale University Press, New Haven, CT, 1969-77. Visiting Professor, University of Washington, Seattle, 1955-56, Queens College, Flushing, NY, 1956-57, Brandeis University, Waltham, MA, 1958-59, Yale University, New Haven, 1970, Rutgers University, Camden, NJ, 1974, and Vassar College, Poughkeepsie, NY, 1981; Danforth Visiting Lecturer, US, 1961-63; Visiting Professor and Sr. Fellow in Humanities, Princeton University, NJ, 1978. Member, American Academy, 1963; Chancellor, Academy of American Poets, 1970-; Consultant in Poetry, Library of Congress, Washington, DC, 1974-76; President, Poets House, NYC, 1985-90; 10th Poet Laureate of the US, 2000-01. **Publications:** Intellectual Things: Poems, 1930; Passport to the War (poems), 1944; Selected Poems 1928-1958, 1958 (Pulitzer Prize, 1959); The Testing-Tree: Poems, 1971; The Terrible Threshold: Selected Poems, 1940-1970, 1974; (trans.) A. Voznesensky, Story under Full Sail, 1974; A Kind of Order, a Kind of Folly (essays), 1975; The Poems of Stanley Kunitz 1928-1978, 1979; The Wellfleet Whale and Companion Poems, 1983; Next-to-Last Things (poems and essays), 1985; Interviews and Encounters, 1992; Passing Through: The Later Poems, 1995; Collected Poems, 2000. EDITOR: (as Dilly Tante) Living Authors: A Book of Biographies, 1931; (with H. Haycraft and W.C. Hadden) Authors Today and Yesterday: A Companion Volume to Living Authors, 1933; (with H. Haycraft) British Authors of the 19th Century, 1936; (with H. Haycraft) American Authors, 1600-1900: A Biographical Dictionary of American Literature, 1938; (with H. Haycraft) Twentieth Century Authors: A Biographical Dictionary of Modern Literature, 1942; (with V. Colby) First Supplement, 1955; (with H. Haycraft) British Authors before 1800: A Biographical Dictionary, 1952; J. Keats, Poems, 1964; (with V. Colby) European Authors, 1000-1900: A Biographical Dictionary of European Literature, 1967; (and trans. with M. Hayward) Poems of Akhmatova, 1973; (and co-trans.) I. Drach, Orchard Lamps, 1978; The Essential Blake, 1987; (with D. Ignatow) The Wild Card: Selected Poems of Karl Shapiro, 1998. **Address:** 37 W 12th St, New York, NY 10011, U.S.A.

KUNTZ, Jerry. American, b. 1956. **Genres:** Information science/Computers. **Career:** Morris County Library, Whippany, NJ, systems librarian, 1984-89; Finger Lakes Library System, Ithaca, NY, automation manager, 1989-94; Ramapo Catskill Library System, Middletown, NY, electronic resources librarian, 1995-. **Publications:** (ed.) Library Technology Consortia: Case Studies in Design and Cooperation, 1994; The KidsClick! Web Searching Skills Guide (with CD-ROM), 2001. **Address:** Ramapo Catskill Library System, 619 Route 17M, Middletown, NY 10940, U.S.A. **Online address:** jkuntz@rcls.org

KUNTZ, John Kenneth. American, b. 1934. **Genres:** Theology/Religion. **Career:** Wellesley College, MA, instructor in biblical history, 1963-65, assistant professor, 1965-67; University of Iowa, Iowa City, Dept of Religious Studies, assistant professor, 1967-70, associate professor, 1970-76, professor of religion, 1976-. **Publications:** The Self-Revelation of God, 1967; The World of the Old Testament, 1968, 4th ed., 1988; The World of the New Testament, 1968, rev. ed., 1996; The People of Ancient Israel: An Introduction to Old Testament Literature, History, and Thought, 1974; Religion and Women: Images of Women in the Bible, 1978, rev. ed., 1995; Biblical Archaeology: Scratching the Surface in the Holy Land, 1982, rev. ed., 1995; Prophecy in Biblical Israel, 1991. **Address:** 321 Koser Ave, Iowa City, IA 52246, U.S.A. **Online address:** ken-kuntz@uiowa.edu

KUNZE, Michael. Czech, b. 1943. **Genres:** Adult non-fiction. **Career:** Lyric writer, record producer, playwright and librettist, and translator of musicals; historian, c. 1980-. **Publications:** Der Prozess Pappenheimer (nonfiction; title means The Pappenheimer Trial), 1980; Strasse ins Feure (nonfiction; title means Highroad into Fire), 1982; Highroad to the Stake: A Tale of Witchcraft (nonfiction), trans. by W.E. Yuill, 1987; Der Freiheit eine Gasse (title means Give Way to Freedom). Author of German-language television scripts. Author of musicals, including Elizabeth, Dance of the Vampires, and Mozart. **Address:** c/o Richard Roemer, Cavalier Entertainment Corp, 205 West End Ave #11M, New York, NY 10023, U.S.A. **Online address:** drkunze@ix.netcom.com

KUNZRU, Hari. British, b. 1971?. **Genres:** Novels. **Career:** Freelance journalist and editor. **Publications:** The Impressionist (novel), 2002.

Contributor to periodicals. **Address:** c/o Author Mail, Dutton, 375 Hudson St., New York, NY 10014, U.S.A. **Online address:** hari@dircon.co.uk

KUPCHAN, Charles A. American. **Genres:** Politics/Government. **Career:** Princeton University, assistant professor, 1986-93; U.S. Department of State, member of policy planning staff, 1992; The White House, National Security Council, director for European affairs, 1993-94; Georgetown University, associate professor, 1994-. Has also served as visiting scholar at Harvard University's Center for International Affairs, Columbia University's Institute for War and Peace Studies, International Institute for Strategic Studies in London, and the Centre d'Etudes et de Recherches Internationales in Paris. **Publications:** The Persian Gulf and the West: The Dilemmas of Security, 1987; The Vulnerability of Empire, 1994; (editor and contributor) Nationalism and Nationalities in the New Europe, 1995; (editor and contributor) Atlantic Security: Contending Visions, 1998; (Coeditor and contributor) Civic Engagement in the Atlantic Community, 1999; (with Emanuel Adler, Jean-Marc Coicaud, and Yen Foong Khong) Power in Transition: The Peaceful Change of International Order, 2001; The End of the American Era: U.S. Foreign Policy and the Geopolitics of the Twenty-first Century, 2002. Also author of several articles for scholarly publications. **Address:** Department of Government, ICC 6th Floor, Georgetown University, Washington, DC 20057, U.S.A. **Online address:** kupchane@georgeetown.edu

KUPER, Adam (Jonathan). British (born Republic of South Africa), b. 1941. **Genres:** Anthropology/Ethnology, Social sciences. **Career:** Makerere University, Uganda, Lecturer, 1967-70; University College, London, Lecturer, 1970-76; University of Leiden, Netherlands, Professor of African Cultural Anthropology, 1976-85; Brunel University, Professor of Social Anthropology, 1985-. **Publications:** Kalahari Village Politics: An African Democracy, 1970; (co-ed.) Councils in Action, 1971; Anthropologists and Anthropology: The British School 1922-1972, 1973; Changing Jamaica, 1976; (ed.) The Social Anthropology of Radcliffe-Brown, 1977; Wives for Cattle: Bridewealth and Marriage in Southern Africa, 1982; (co-ed.) The Social Science Encyclopaedia, 1985; South Africa and the Anthropologist, 1987; The Invention of Primitive Society: Transformations of an Illusion, 1988; (ed.) Conceptualizing Society, 1992; The Chosen Primate: Human Nature and Cultural Variation, 1994; Culture: The Anthropologists' Account, 1999; Among the Anthropologists, 1999. **Address:** Brunel University, Uxbridge, Middx UB8 3PH, England. **Online address:** Adam.Kuper@brunel.ac.uk

KUPER, Jenny Riva. American/British. **Genres:** Law. **Career:** B.M. Birnberg and Co., articled clerk, 1975-77; Camden Community Law Centre, solicitor, 1978-83; Children's Legal Centre, London, England, solicitor, 1983-93; British Red Cross, researcher on customary international humanitarian law, 1997; freelance legal researcher and consultant, 1998-; University of London, London School of Economics and Political Science, visiting research fellow. **Publications:** International Law concerning Child Civilians in Armed Conflict, 1997; Military Training Concerning Children in Armed Conflict, 2004. Contributor to books. Contributor of articles and reviews to periodicals. **Address:** Dept of Law and Development Studies Institute, London School of Economics and Political Science, University of London, Houghton St, London WC2A 2AE, England. **Online address:** J.Kuper@lse.ac.uk

KUPER, Peter. (born United States), b. 1958. **Genres:** Cartoons. **Career:** Comic-book artist, illustrator, graphic artist, editor. Cofounder of World War 3 Illustrated (political comix magazine), 1979; School of Visual Arts, New York, NY, instructor (alternative comix), 1987-; INX, art director. **Publications:** (Illustrator) Robert E. Howard, The Last Cat Book, Dodd, 1984; (Illustrator) Janice Prager and Arlene Lepoff, Why Be Different?: A Look into Judaism, 1986; (with Seth Tobocman) World War 3 Illustrated: 1980-1988, 1989; (Illustrator) Upton Beall Sinclair, 1991; Peter Kuper's Comic Strips: A Journal of Travels through Africa and Southeast Asia, 1992; Different Beat, 1994; (Illustrator) Franz Kafka, Give It Up!: And Other Short Stories, 1995; (with others) World War 3 Illustrated: Confrontational Comics, 1995; Stripped, 1995; The System, 1997; Topsy Turvy, 2000; Speechless, 2000; Mind's Eye: An Eye of the Beholder Collection, 2001; (Illustrator) Franz Kafka, The Metamorphosis, 2003; Comic Strip, 2003; Eye of the Beholder, 2003. Creator of comic strips. **Address:** c/o Author Mail, NBM, 555 Eighth Ave., Ste. 1202, New York, NY 10018, U.S.A. **Online address:** kuperart@aol.com

KUPPNER, Frank. Scottish, b. 1951. **Genres:** Poetry, Novels. **Career:** Engineer and writer. **Publications:** POETRY: A Bad Day for the Sung Dynasty, 1984; The Intelligent Observation of Naked Women, 1987; Everything Is Strange, 1994. NOVELS: Ridiculous! Absurd! Disgusting!, 1989; A Very Quiet Street, 1989; A Concussed History of Scotland, 1990; Something Very Like Murder, 1994. **Address:** c/o Polygon, 22 George Sq., Edinburgh EH8 9LF, Scotland.

KUREISHI, Hanif. British, b. 1954. **Genres:** Novels, Plays/Screenplays. **Career:** Royal Court Theatre, London, resident writer, 1981, 1985-86. **Publications:** PLAYS: Borderline, 1981; Birds of Passage, 1983; Outskirts, The King and Me, Tomorrow-Today!, 1983; Mother Courage (adapted from Brecht), 1984; Sleep with Me, 1999. SCREENPLAYS: My Beautiful Laundrette, 1986; Sammy and Rosie Get Laid, 1988; London Kills Me, 1989; Buddha of Suburbia, 1993; My Son the Fanatic, 1998. NOVELS: The Buddha of Suburbia, 1990; The Black Album, 1995; Intimacy, 1998; Gabriel's Gift, 2001. OTHER: (ed. with J. Savage) The Faber Book of Pop, 1995; Love in a Blue Time (stories), 1997; Midnight All Day (stories), 2000. **Address:** c/o Stephen Durbridge, The Agency, 24 Pottery Lane, Holland Park, London W11 4LZ, England.

KURIAN, George Thomas. American (born India), b. 1931. **Genres:** Reference. **Career:** George Kurian Reference Books, Baldwin Place, NY, president, 1972-. United Nations Studies Forum, director. **Publications:** Dictionary of Indian English, 1966; Children's Literary Almanac, 1973; Directory of American Book Publishing, 1975; Historical and Cultural Dictionary of India, 1976; Worldwide Markets for English-Language Books, 1977; Encyclopedia of the Third World, 3 vols., 1978, 4th ed., 1991; The Illustrated Book of World Rankings, 1979, 4th ed., 1996; Laurel Dictionary of Biography, 1980; World Press Encyclopedia, 2 vols., 1982; New American Gazetteer, 1984; Geo-Data: World Almanac Gazetteer, 1984; World Data, 1984; What's What in American Business, 1985; Sourcebook of Global Statistics, 1986; World Encyclopedia of Police Forces and Penal Systems, 1987; Yearbook of American Universities and Colleges, 1987; Global Guide to Medical Information, 1987; Handbook of Business Quotations, 1987; World Education Encyclopedia, 3 vols., 1988; Geo-Data: World Geographical Encyclopedia, 1989; Glossary of the Third World, 1989; (ed.) Teachers as Writers, 1989; Encyclopedia of the First World, 2 vols., 1990; The Benelux Countries, 1990; British Isles, 1990; North America, 1990; Scandinavia, 1990; Japan, 1990; Australia and New Zealand, 1990; Encyclopedia of the Second World, 1991; World Encyclopedia of Cities, 2 vols., 1993; Datapedia of the United States, 1993; Atlas of the Third World, 2nd ed., 1993; (with G.T.T. Molitor) Encyclopedia of the Future, 2 vols., 1995; Encyclopedia of Medical Media and Communications, 1996; Encyclopedia of the Democratic Party, 2 vols., 1996; Encyclopedia of the Republican Party, 2 vols., 1996; Timenglish, 1996; Global Data Locator, 1997; World Encyclopedia of Parliaments and Legislatures, 2 vols., 1997; The Dictionary of America, 1997; The World as It Should Be, 1997; Historical Guide to U.S. Government, 1998; (with D.B. Barrett and T.M. Johnson) World Christian Encyclopedia, 3 vols., 1998; (with J.D. Schultz) The Political Market Place, 1998; (with J.Y. Cole) Encyclopedia of the Library of Congress, 1999; (with Molitor) Compendium of the 21st Century, 1999; (with Schultz) The Chronicles of Christianity, 1999; The Nobel Scientists, 1999; Timetables of World Literature, 2002. **Address:** George Kurian Reference Books, PO Box 519, Baldwin Place, NY 10505, U.S.A. **Online address:** gtkurian@aol.com

KURIANSKY, Judith (Anne Brodsky). Also writes as Dr. Judy. American, b. 1947. **Genres:** How-to books, Psychology, Self help, Sex. **Career:** New York State Psychiatric Institute, NYC, senior research scientist, 1970-78; St. Luke's Hospital, NYC, intern in psychology, 1978-79; National Institute for Psychotherapies, sex therapy coordinator, 1977-79; Institutes of Religion and Health, NYC, lecturer, 1979-81; WABC-Radio, NYC, talk show host, 1981-84; Modern Satellite Network, Modern Life series, host, 1981; WCBS-TV, reporter, 1982-86; WOR-Radio, NYC, talk show host, 1987-88; Center for Marital and Family Therapy, therapist, 1987-; WPIX-TV, reporter, 1987-89; Alabama TV, Total Wellness for Women, cohost, 1988-89; ABC Talkradio Network, occasional host, 1988-94; NBC Consumer News and Business Channel, reporter and host, 1989-92; WHTZ Radio, host of syndicated Love Phones, 1992-99. Certified sex therapist by American Association of Sex Educators, Counselors, and Therapists. Public speaker and workshop leader; columnist for magazines and newspapers. **Publications:** Sex: Now That I've Got Your Attention, Let Me Answer Your Questions!, 1984; How to Love a Nice Guy, 1990; Generation Sex, 1995; The Complete Idiot's Guide to Dating, 1996, 3rd ed., 2003; Goodbye My Troubles, Hello My Happiness, 1997; The Complete Idiot's Guide to a Healthy Relationship, 1997, 2nd ed., 2001; The Complete Idiot's Guide to Tantric Sex, 2001; China Reproductive Health Hotline Professionals Solve Problems on Sex and Emotions, 2001. **Address:** c/o Pollack, 59 Commerce St, Staten Island, NY 10314, U.S.A. **Online address:** DrJudy411@aol.com

KURIEN, Christopher (Thomas). Indian, b. 1931. **Genres:** Economics, Sociology. **Career:** Madras Christian College, India, tutor, 1953-54; lecturer in economics, 1954-62; professor and head, Dept. of Economics, 1962-78; National Fellow in Economics, 1975-77; Madras Institute of Development Studies, director, 1978-88, professor, 1978-91, professor emeritus, 1991-.

Indian Council of Social Science Research, National Fellow, 1992-95. **Publications:** Our Five Year Plans, 1966; (ed. with S.V. Anantakrishnan, C.T.K. Chari and S. Rajiva) India Today, 1967; Indian Economic Crisis, 1969; A Theoretical Approach to the Indian Economy, 1970; (ed.) A Guide to Research in Economics, 1973; Poverty and Development, 1974; Poverty, Planning and Social Transformation, 1978; (with J. James) Economic Change in Tamil Nadu, 1979; Dynamics of Rural Transformation, 1981; (ed. with E.R. Prabhaker and S. Gopal) Economy Society and Development, 1991; The Economy: An Interpretative Introduction, 1992; On Markets in Economic Theory and Policy, 1993; Growth and Justice, 1992; Global Capitalism and the Indian Economy, 1994; Rethinking Economics, 1996 Economics, 1996. **Address:** 79 Second Main Rd, Gandhinagar, Madras 600 020, India.

KURLAND, Geoffrey. American, b. 1947. **Genres:** Autobiography/Memoirs. **Career:** Children's Hospital at Stanford University Medical Center, Stanford, CA, fellow, 1976-81; University of California, Davis, School of Medicine, assistant professor and director of pediatric pulmonology, 1981-88; University of Pittsburgh, professor of pediatrics, 1988-, director of pediatric flexible bronchoscopy service, 1990-, of pediatric pulmonary transplant program, 1992-, and of pediatric pulmonology fellowship, 1992-. **Publications:** My Own Medicine: A Doctor's Life as a Patient, 2002. Contributor to medical journals. **Address:** Division of Pediatric Pulmonology, Children's Hospital of Pittsburgh, 3705 Fifth Avenue, Pittsburgh, PA 15213, U.S.A. **Online address:** geoffrey.kurland@chp.edu

KURLAND, Michael (Joseph). Also writes as Jennifer Plum. American, b. 1938. **Genres:** Novels, Novellas/Short stories, Mystery/Crime/Suspense, Science fiction/Fantasy, Plays/Screenplays, Ghost Writer. **Career:** Ed., Pennyfarthing Press, San Francisco, 1976-80. News Ed., KPFK-Radio, Los Angeles, 1966; Teacher of English, Happy Valley School, Ojai, California, 1967; Ed., Crawdaddy, NYC, 1969; President, Computer Press Assn., 1985; also former play dir., road mgr. for a band, advertising copywriter, and freelance ghostwriter and writer of Mystery and SF short stories. **Publications:** (with Chester Anderson) Ten Years to Doomsday, 1964; Mission: Third Force, 1967; Mission: Tank War, 1968; A Plague of Spies (suspense), 1969; The Unicorn Girl, 1969; Transmission Error, 1970; (as Jennifer Plum) The Secret of Benjamin Square (suspense), 1972; The Whenabouts of Burr, 1975; Pluribus, 1975; Tomorrow Knight, 1976; The Princes of Earth (juvenile), 1978; The Infernal Device (suspense), 1979; (with S.W. Barton) The Last President, 1980; Psi Hunt, 1980; (with H.B. Piper) First Cycle, 1982; Death by Gaslight, 1982; Star Griffin, 1987; Ten Little Wizards, 1988; The Spymaster's Handbook, 1988; A Study in Sorcery, 1989; Button Right, 1989; Perchance, 1989; A Gallery of Rogues (true crime), 1993; How to Solve a Murder: The Forensic Handbook, 1995; Too Soon Dead (mystery), 1997; How to Try a Murder: The Handbook for Armchair Lawyers, 1997. EDITOR: The Redward Edward Papers, by Avram Davidson, 1978; The Best of Avram Davidson, 1979. **Address:** PO Box 2005, Petaluma, CA 94953-2005, U.S.A. **Online address:** michael@michaelkurland.com; www.michaelkurland.com

KURLANSKY, Mark. American, b. 1948. **Genres:** Documentaries/Reportage. **Career:** Chicago Tribune, Chicago, IL, reporter; Miami Herald, Miami, FL, reporter; Philadelphia Inquirer, Philadelphia, PA, reporter. **Publications:** A Continent of Islands: Searching for the Caribbean Destiny, 1992; A Chosen Few: The Resurrection of European Jewry, 1994; Cod: A Biography of the Fish That Changed the World, 1997; The White Man in the Tree and Other Stories, 2000; Salt: A World History, 2002; Choice Cuts, 2003; 1968: The Year that Rocked the World, 2004. Author of short stories and children's books; illustrator. Work represented in anthologies. Contributor to periodicals. **Address:** c/o Charlotte Sheedy, Charlotte Sheedy Literary Agency, 65 Bleeker St Fl 12, New York, NY 10012, U.S.A.

KUROKAWA, Mitsuhiro. Japanese, b. 1954. **Genres:** Children's fiction, Illustrations. **Career:** Author and illustrator of children's books. Has also worked at protecting author's copyrights, Japanese Board on Books for Young People. **Publications:** SELF-ILLUSTRATED IN ENGLISH TRANSLATION: Dinosaurs, 1989 (originally published as Kyoryu-tachi, 1987); Dinosaur Valley, 1992 (originally published as Kyoryu no Tani, 1991). SELF-ILLUSTRATED IN JAPANESE: Pompocoya-ai, 1988; Wa-a Kyoryu-da! (title means: Oh! Dinosaurs), 1990; Kyoryu Little Horn to Kyodai Yokuryu (title means: Little Horn and Big Pterosaur), 1992; Tatakac Kyoryu Torikeratopus, 1992; Kyoryu-tte Nandarou (book with paper slide-picture show; title means: What Are Dinosaurs), 1992; Daibouken Kyoryujima Mogura Hakase wo Sukue! (title means: The Adventure of Dinosaur Island), 1993; Kyoryu Torikeratopus to Kyodai Wani (title means: A Triceratops and a Big Crocodile), 1993; Chibi-chibi-saur to Kyofu no Tyrannosaur (title means: A Very Little Dinosaur and a Fierce Tyrannosaur), 1994; Genshi-jidai no Zetsumetsu Dobutsu (title means: Extinct Animals in the Primitive Ages), 1994; Kaettekonai Kyoryu-tachi (title means: Extinct Animals), 1994; Horobiyuku Nihon no Dobutsu tachi (title means: Extinct Animals in Japan), 1995; Sekai no Zetsumetsu Dobutsu (title means: Extinct Animals in the World), 1995; Kyoryu Torikeratopus to Tyranosaur (title means: A Triceratops and a Tyrannosaur), 1995; Horobiyuku Sekai no Kyoryu-tachi, 1996; Nihon no Zetsumetsu Dobutsu, 1996; Kyoryu Torikeratopus to Kyodai-game, 1996. Illustrator of books by others. Illustrator of yearly calendar Charles River, 1980-. **Address:** 16-21-203, Sekimachi Minami 4-chome, Nerima-ku, Tokyo 177, Japan.

KURSON, Ken. American, b. 1969. **Genres:** Money/Finance. **Career:** Journalist. Worth, staff writer; Source, money columnist; Money, staff member; Esquire, money columnist and contributing editor; Green, founder and editor-in-chief; CNN, Take It Personally (weekly program), commentator; National Public Radio Marketplace (program), regular commentator. Has appeared on financial programs on television. **Publications:** The Green Magazine Guide to Personal Finance: A No B.S. Book for Your Twenties and Thirties, 1998; (with D. Faber) The Faber Report: CNBC's "The Brain" Tells You How Wall Street Really Works and How You Can Make It Work for You, 2002; (with R. Giuliani) Leadership, 2002. **Address:** c/o Author Mail, Little Brown & Company, 1271 Avenue of the Americas, New York, NY 10020, U.S.A.

KURTZ, Don. American, b. 1951. **Genres:** Novels, Travel/Exploration. **Career:** New Mexico State University, Las Cruces, NM, associate professor of Spanish, 1981-2002. **Publications:** (with W.D. Goran) Trails of the Guadalupes (guidebook), 1978; South of the Big Four (novel), 1995. **Address:** PO Box 4182, Las Cruces, NM 88003, U.S.A. **Online address:** donkurtz@nmsu.edu

KURTZ, Donn M., II. American. **Genres:** Politics/Government. **Career:** University of Louisiana at Lafayette, faculty member, 1969-, Crocker Professor of Political Science, 1989-, department head, 1974-81. Duquesne University, fellow at African Institute, 1967. **Publications:** (ed.) The American Political Family, 1993; Kinship and Politics: The Justices of the United States and Louisiana Supreme Courts, 1997. Contributor to books and academic journals. **Address:** Department of Political Science, PO Box 41652, University of Louisiana at Lafayette, Lafayette, LA 70504, U.S.A.

KURTZ, Howard. American, b. 1953. **Genres:** Social commentary. **Career:** Bergen Record, Hackensack, NJ, reporter, 1975-76; Washington Star, Washington, DC, reporter, 1978-81; Washington Post, Washington, DC, reporter, 1981-. Guest on television programs. **Publications:** Media Circus, 1993; Hot Air, 1996; Spin Cycle, 1998; The Fortune Tellers: Inside Wall Street's Game of Money, Media, and Manipulation, 2000. Contributor to periodicals. **Address:** Washington Post, 1150 15th St. NW, Washington, DC 20071, U.S.A.

KURTZ, Jane. American, b. 1952. **Genres:** Novels, Local history/Rural topics. **Career:** Carbondale New School, Carbondale, IL, teacher/director, 1975-81; Trinidad Catholic High School, Trinidad, CO, teacher, 1984-89; University of North Dakota, Grand Forks, senior lecturer, 1995-2002. **Publications:** FICTION: I'm Calling Molly, 1990; Fire on the Mountain, 1994; Pulling the Lion's Tail, 1995; Miro in the Kingdom of the Sun, 1996; (with C. Kurtz) Only a Pigeon, 1997; Trouble, 1997; The Storyteller's Beads, 1998; Faraway Home, 1999; I'm Sorry, Almira Ann, 1999; River Friendly, River Wild, 2000; Jakarta Missing, 2001. PICTURE BOOKS: Water Hole Waiting, 2001; Rain Romp, 2002. NONFICTION: Ethiopia: The Roof of Africa, 1991; The American Southwest Resource Book: The People, 1996; Terrific Connections with Authors, Illustrators, and Storytellers, 1999; 35 Best Books for Teaching U.S. Regions, 2002. Contributor to journals. **Address:** 505 S Weaver Ave, Hesston, KS 67062, U.S.A.

KURTZ, Katherine. American, b. 1944. **Genres:** Novels, Romance/Historical, Science fiction/Fantasy. **Career:** Full-time writer. **Publications:** Deryni Rising, 1970; Deryni Checkmate, 1972; High Deryni, 1973; Camber of Culdi, 1976; Saint Camber, 1978; Camber the Heretic, 1981 Lammas Night, 1983; The Bishop's Heir, 1984; The King's Justice, 1985; The Quest for Saint Camber, 1986; The Deryni Archives, 1986; The Legacy of Lehr, 1986; The Harrowing of Gwynedd, 1989; Deryni Magic: A Grimoire, 1991; King Javan's Year, 1992; The Bastard Prince, 1994; Two Crowns for America, 1996; King Kelson's Bride, 2000; St. Patrick's Gargoyle, 2001; In the King's Service, 2003. ADEPT SERIES (with D.T. Harris): The Adept, 1991; #II: The Lodge of The Lynx, 1992; #III: The Templar Treasure, 1993; #IV: Dagger Magic, 1995; #V: Death of an Adept, 1996; The Temple and the Stone, 1998; The Temple and the Crown, 2001. ANTHOLOGY EDITOR:

Tales of the Knights Templar, 1995; On Crusade: More Tales of the Knights Templar, 1998; Crusade of Fire: Mystic Tales of the Knights Templar, 2002; Deryni Tales, 2002. **Address:** Holybrooke Hall, Bray, County, Wicklow, Ireland. **Online address:** kkurtz@iol.ie

KURZ, Ron. American, b. 1940. **Genres:** Novels. **Career:** Former Theatre Manager, Playhouse Theatre, Baltimore, Maryland. **Publications:** Lethal Gas, 1974; Black Rococo, 1976; Eyes of a Stranger (screenplay), 1981; Friday the 13th II (screenplay), 1981. **Address:** c/o Robert Eisenbach Inc, 6072 Franklin Ave Ste 203, Los Angeles, CA 90028, U.S.A.

KURZMAN, Dan. American, b. 1929. **Genres:** History, Biography, Documentaries/Reportage. **Career:** Washington Star, contributor, 1975-80; Independent News Alliance, contributor, 1979-84. Correspondent, International News Service, Paris, 1948; Feature Writer, Marshall Plan Information Office, Paris, 1948-49; Correspondent, National Broadcasting Co., Middle East, 1950-53; Bureau Chief, McGraw Hill World News Service, Tokyo, 1954-59; Correspondent, Washington Post, 1962-70; Newspaper Guild Front Page Award, 1964, George Polk Memorial Award, 1965. **Publications:** Kishi and Japan: The Search for the Sun (biography), 1960; Subversion of the Innocents, 1963, Overseas Press Club Award; Santo Domingo: Revolt of the Damned, 1965; Genesis 1948; The First Arab-Israeli War, 1970; The Race for Rome, 1975; The Bravest Battle: The Twenty Eight Days of the Warsaw Ghetto Uprising, 1976; Miracle of November: Madrid's Epic Stand 1936, 1980, OPC Cornelius Ryan Award; Ben-Gurion: Prophet of Fire (biography), 1983, National Jewish Book Award; Day of the Bomb: Countdown to Hiroshima, 1985; A Killing Wind: Inside Union Carbide and the Bhopal Catastrophe, 1987; Fatal Voyage: The Sinking of the U.S.S. Indianapolis, 1990; Left to Die: The Tragedy of the USS Juneau, 1994; Blood and Water: Sabotaging Hitler's Bomb, 1996; Soldier of Peace: The Life of Yitzhak Rabin, 1998; Disaster! The Great San Francisco Earthquake and Fire of 1906, 2001. **Address:** The Parker Imperial, 7855 Boulevard East, Apt. 23A, North Bergen, NJ 07047, U.S.A.

KURZWEIL, Allen. American, b. 1961?. **Genres:** Novels. **Career:** Freelance journalist. Yale University, New Haven, CT, visiting lecturer. **Publications:** NOVELS: A Case of Curiosities, 1992; The Grand Complication, 2000. Contributor to periodicals. **Address:** c/o The Ballantine Publishing Group, 201 East 50th St., New York, NY 10022, U.S.A.

KURZYDLOWSKI, Krzysztof Jan. Polish, b. 1954. **Genres:** Engineering. **Career:** University of Manitoba, Winnipeg, research associate, 1986-88; Warsaw University of Technology, Poland, associate dean, 1990-93, professor of materials science and engineering and vice rector for student affairs, 1993-99, dean of faculty, 1999-, chair of board of directors of Enterprise Development Center. Brunel University, researcher, 1994. State Committee for Scientific Research, vice chairman; Polish Business-Higher Education Forum, founding executive director. **Publications:** Theory of Dislocations (in Polish), 1984; Mechanics of Materials (in Polish), 1992; (co-author) The Quantitative Description of the Microstructure of Materials, 1996. Contributor to scientific books. Contributor to technical journals. **Address:** Department of Materials Science and Engineering, Warsaw University of Technology, Woloska 141, 02-507 Warsaw, Poland.

KUSHLAN, James A. American, b. 1947. **Genres:** Biology, Environmental sciences/Ecology, Natural history. **Career:** Everglades National Park, research biologist, 1975-84; Texas A&M University-Commerce, associate professor, 1984-87, professor of biology, 1987-88, director of Center for Water Resources Studies, 1986-88; University of Mississippi, University, professor of biology and chairperson of department, 1988-97; Patuxent Wildlife Research Center, director, 1994-2001; Smithsonian Institution, research associate, 1999-; U.S. Geological Survey, senior science adviser, 2001-02. **Publications:** (with J. Hancock) The Herons Handbook, 1984; (with J. Hancock and M.P. Kahl) Storks, Ibises, and Spoonbills of the World, 1992; (with H. Hafner) Heron Conservation, 2000; (with J. Hancock) The Herons, forthcoming. Work represented in anthologies. Contributor to biology and ornithology journals. **Address:** PO Box 1930, Edgewater, MD 21037, U.S.A. **Online address:** jkushlan@earthlink.net

KUSHNER, Ellen (Ruth). American, b. 1955. **Genres:** Science fiction/ Fantasy, Children's fiction, Plays/Screenplays. **Career:** Ace Books, NYC, editorial assistant, 1977-79; Pocket Books, NYC, associate editor, 1979-80; freelance copywriter, reviewer, and artist's representative, 1980-87; WGBH Radio, Boston, MA, producer/host, 1987-. **Publications:** FANTASY NOVELS: Swordspoint: A Melodrama of Manners, 1987; Thomas the Rhymer, 1990; (coauthor) The Fall of the Kings, 2002. NOVELS FOR CHILDREN: Outlaws of Sherwood Forest, 1985; The Enchanted Kingdom,

1986; Statue of Liberty Adventure, 1986; The Mystery of the Secret Room, 1986; Knights of the Round Table, 1988; St. Nicholas and the Valley Beyond, 1994. RADIO PLAYS: (coauthor) Which Way's Witch: A June Foray Halloween Spell, 1991; (also producer, director, and narrator) Festival of Liberation: The Passover Story in World Music, 1992; (also producer, director, and narrator) The Door Is Opened: A Jewish High Holiday Meditation, 1992; (also producer, director, and narrator) Beyond 1492: 500 Years of Jewish Song and Legend, 1992; (also producer and narrator) Esther: The Feast of Masks, 2002; (also producer and narrator) The Golden Dreydl: A Klezmer "Nutcracker" for Chanukah, 2001. EDITOR: Basilisk, 1980; (co-) The Horns of Elfland, 1997.

KUSHNER, Harold S. American, b. 1935. **Genres:** Theology/Religion. **Career:** Rabbi, Temple Israel of Natick, MA, 1966-90. President, New England Region, Rabbinical Assembly, 1972-74; President, Clergy Association of Natick, 1976-78; Ed., Conservative Judaism mag., 1980-84. **Publications:** When Children Ask about God, 1971; Commanded to Live (collected sermons), 1973; When Bad Things Happen to Good People, 1981; When All You've Ever Wanted Isn't Enough, 1986; Who Needs God, 1989; TO LIFE!, 1993; How Good Do We Have to Be?, 1996; Living a Life That Matters, 2001; The Lord Is My Shepherd, 2003. **Address:** 145 Hartford St, Natick, MA 01760, U.S.A.

KUSHNER, James A(lan). American, b. 1945. **Genres:** Demography, Ethics, Law, Politics/Government, Regional/Urban planning, Social commentary, Transportation, Urban studies. **Career:** Office of Economic Opportunity, Canton, OH, director of housing, 1969-70; Legal Aid of Western Missouri, Kansas City, managing attorney of Law Reform Project, 1970-73; University of California, Berkeley, project attorney, National Housing and Economic Development Law Project, 1973-75; Southwestern University School of Law, Los Angeles, CA, professor of law, 1975-. Temporary judge, of Los Angeles County Superior Court, 1981-86. Fair Housing Congress of Southern California, member of board of directors, 1981-86, president, 1984, chairman of board, 1986. **Publications:** Apartheid in America, 1980; Housing and Community Development, 1981, 3rd ed., 1999; Fair Housing, 1983, 2nd ed., 1995; Government Discrimination, 1988; Subdivision Law and Growth Management, 1991, 2nd ed., 2000; Land Use Regulation, 1999, 2nd ed., 2004; Comparative Urban Planning Law, 2003; The Post-Automobile City, 2004. **Address:** Southwestern University School of Law, 675 S Westmoreland St, Los Angeles, CA 90005, U.S.A. **Online address:** JKushner@swlaw.edu

KUSHNER, Lawrence. American, b. 1943. **Genres:** Theology/Religion. **Career:** Rabbi, teacher, author of books on Jewish spirituality. Congregation Solel, Highland Park, IL, rabbinic fellow-in-residence, 1969-71; Congregation Beth El, Sudbury, MA, rabbi, 1971-. Hebrew Union College-Jewish Institute of Religion, NYC, instructor, 1986-. **Publications:** The Book of Letters: A Mystical Hebrew Alef-Bait, 1975; Honey from the Rock: Visions of Jewish Mystical Renewal, 1977; The River of Light: Spirituality, Judaism, and the Evolution of Consciousness, 1981; (with D. Kerdeman) The Invisible Chariot: An Introduction to Kabbalah and Spirituality for Young Adults, 1986; The Book of Miracles: A Young Person's Guide to Jewish Spirituality, 1987; God Was in This Place and I, I Did Not Know: Finding Self, Spirituality and Ultimate Meaning, 1991; (trans. and editor) Sparks beneath the Surface: Selections from Itturay Torah on the Weekly Parasha, 1993; The Book of Words: Talking Spiritual Life, Living Spiritual Talk, 1993. **Address:** 1880 Vallejo St Apt 2, San Francisco, CA 94123-4932, U.S.A.

KUSHNER, Malcolm. American, b. 1952. **Genres:** Business/Trade/Industry. **Career:** California Workers Compensation Appeals Board, San Francisco, staff attorney, 1980-81; Graham & James (law firm), San Francisco, associate, 1981-82; Malcolm Kushner and Associates, Santa Cruz, CA, president, 1982-. Humor instructor, San Francisco Sheriff's Department; lecturer at Stanford University, University of Santa Clara, and University of California, Berkeley. Member of advisory board, Coast Commercial Bank. Member, Friends of the University of California, Santa Cruz, Library. **Publications:** The Light Touch: How to Use Humor for Business Success, 1990; Successful Presentations for Dummies, 1996. **Address:** Malcolm Kushner and Associates, P.O. Box 7509, Santa Cruz, CA 95061, U.S.A.

KUSHNER, Tony. American, b. 1956. **Genres:** Plays/Screenplays. **Career:** Theatre Communication Group, NYC, director of literary services, 1990-91; Juilliard School of Drama, NYC, playwright-in-residence, 1990-92. Guest artist at New York University Graduate Theatre Program, Yale University, and Princeton University, 1989-. **Publications:** PLAYS: Yes, Yes, No, No (juvenile), 1987; Stella, 1987; A Bright Room Called Day, 1991; Hydriotaphia, 1987; The Illusion, 1988; (with A. Dorfman) Widows, 1991; Angels in America: A Gay Fantasia on National Themes, Part One: Millennium Approaches, 1992, Part Two: Perestroika, 1992; Slavs!: Thinking about the Longstanding Problems of Virtue and Happiness, 1995; Dybbuk and Other Tales of the Supernatural, 1997; Death & Taxes, 2000; (with M. Sendak) Brundibar, 2003; Caroline, or Change, 2003. **Address:** c/o Joyce Ketay Agency, 1501 Broadway Ste 1908, New York, NY 10036, U.S.A.

KUSHNICK, Louis. American, b. 1938. **Genres:** Race relations. **Career:** Sociologist. Director of Ahmed Iqbal Ullah Race Relations Resource Centre, University of Manchester, Manchester, England. Institute of Race Relations, member of council. **Publications:** The Role of Management: Nondiscrimination or Affirmative Action?, 1968; Race, Class, and Struggle: Essays on Racism and Inequality in Britain, the United States, and Western Europe, 1998. EDITOR: (with J. Jennings) A New Introduction to Poverty: The Role of Race, Power, and Politics, 1999; (with B.P. Bowser and P. Grant) Against the Odds: Scholars Who Challenged Racism in the Twentieth Century, 2002. Contributor to books. **Address:** Ahmed Iqbal Ullah Race Relations Resource Centre, Dover Street, University of Manchester, Manchester M13 9PL, England. **Online address:** lou.kushnick@man.ac.uk

KUSKIN, Karla. Also writes as Nicholas Charles. American, b. 1932. **Genres:** Children's fiction. **Publications:** POETRY: Roar and More, 1956; James and the Rain, 1959; In the Middle of the Trees, 1958; The Animals and the Ark, 1958; Square as a House, 1960; The Bear Who Saw the Spring, 1961; All Sizes of Noises, 1962; Alexander Soames: His Poems, 1962; ABC-DEFGHIJKLMNOPQRSTUVWXYZ, 1963; The Rose on My Cake, 1964; Sand and Snow, 1965; In the Flaky Frosty Morning, 1969; Any Me I Want to Be: Poems, 1972; Near the Window Tree: Poems and Notes, 1975; A Boy Had a Mother Who Bought Him a Hat, 1976; Herbert Hated Being Small, 1979; Dogs and Dragons, Trees and Dreams, 1980; Night Again, 1981; Something Sleeping in the Hall, 1985; Soap Soup, 1992; Patchwork Island, 1994; City Dog, 1994; City Noise, 1994; Moon, Have You Met My Mother?, 2003. CHILDREN'S FICTION: Just Like Everyone Else, 1959; Which Horse is William?, 1959; The Walk the Mouse Girls Took, 1967; Watson, The Smartest Dog in the U.S.A., 1968; What Did You Bring Me?, 1973; The Philharmonic Gets Dressed, 1982; Thoughts, Pictures, and Words, 1995; The Sky Is Always in the Sky, 1998; I Am Me, 2000; Animals in the Ark, 2001; Dear Shell, You Smell, 2002; Under My Hood I Have a Hat, 2004; What Is It Like to Be a Cat?, 2005. SCREENPLAYS: What Do You Mean by Design?, 1973; An Electric Talking Picture, 1973. OTHER: A Space Story, 1978; The Dallas Titans Get Ready for Bed, 1986; Jerusalem, Shining Still, 1987; A Great Miracle Happened There: A Chanukah Story, 1993; Paul, 1994; The Upstairs Cat, 1997. POETRY AS NICHOLAS CHARLES: How Do You Get from Here to There?, 1962; Jane Ann June Spoon and Her Very Adventurous Trip to the Moon, 1966. **Address:** c/o Harriet Wasserman Literary Agency, 137 E 36th St, New York, NY 10016, U.S.A.

KUSUGAK, Michael (Arvaarluk). Canadian, b. 1948. **Genres:** Children's fiction, Children's non-fiction. **Career:** Worked in government positions for 15 years; worked as director of community programs for Arctic College. Full-time writer. **Publications:** FOR CHILDREN. FICTION: (with R. Munsch) A Promise Is a Promise, 1988; Baseball Bats for Christmas, 1990; Hide and Sneak, 1992; Northern Lights: The Soccer Trails, 1993. NON-FICTION: My Arctic 1,2,3, 1996; Arctic Stories, 1998; Who Wants Rocks?, 1999. **Address:** PO Box 572, Rankin Inlet, NU, Canada X0C 0G0. **Online address:** mkusugak@arctic.ca

KUTTNER, Robert. American. **Genres:** Economics, Politics/Government. **Career:** Washington Post, Washington, DC, national staff writer, early 1970s; American Prospect: A Journal for the Liberal Imagination, founder, c. 1990, editor (with others), c. 1990-; Village Voice, NYC, editor of Washington, DC, affairs; Working Papers for a New Society, editor-in-chief; New Republic, economics editor; Business Week, contributing columnist; also worked as a syndicated columnist. Has worked in noncommercial radio and television in California; instructor at Brandeis University and Boston University, both Boston, MA, the University of Massachusetts, and Harvard University's John F. Kennedy Institute of Politics, Cambridge, MA. Has served as chief investigator for the U.S. Senate Committee on Banking, Housing, and Urban Affairs, the executive director of U.S. president Jimmy Carter's National Commission on Neighborhoods, and as the founder and board member of the Economic Policy Institute. Has made appearances on National Public Radio (NPR), and on television programs. **Publications:** NONFICTION: Revolt of the Haves: Tax Rebellions and Hard Times, 1980; The Economic Illusion: False Choices between Prosperity and Social Justice, 1984; The Life of the Party: Democratic Prospects in 1988 and Beyond, 1987; Managed Trade and Economic Sovereignty, 1989; The End of Laissez

Faire: National Purpose and the Global Economy after the Cold War, 1991; (ed.) Ticking Time Bombs: The New Conservative Assaults on Democracy, 1996; Everything for Sale: The Virtues and Limits of Markets, 1997. Contributor to periodicals. **Address:** American Prospect, 5 Broad St, Boston, MA 02109, U.S.A. **Online address:** kuttner@prospect.org

KUVSHINOFF, Boris W. American, b. 1922. **Genres:** Novels, Young adult fiction, Poetry, Sciences, Translations. **Career:** Johns Hopkins University, Applied Physics Laboratory, Laurel, MD, translator of foreign scientific and technical literature, 1958-60, supervisor of document library, 1960-70, information section supervisor of Fire Problems Program, 1971-79, technical documentation analyst, 1980-85, program manager for U.S. Air Force Logistics Command Automated Warehouse Acquisition, 1986-87, manager of APL Business Systems Documentation, 1988-93, Stewart Janney fellow, 1990; writer, 1993-. **Publications:** (trans.) K.I. Shchelkin and Y.K. Troshin, Gas Dynamics of Combustion, 1965; (ed. and trans.) R.I. Soloukhin, Shock Waves and Detonations in Gases, 1965; (comp. and ed.) Fire Sciences Dictionary, 1977; (with R.A. Henle) Desktop Computers: In Perspective, 1992; Curse of the Firebirds Feather, forthcoming; The Tanana River Icebreakers, forthcoming. Work represented in anthologies. Contributor to professional journals. **Address:** 1103 Starway Ct, Baltimore, MD 21228-2728, U.S.A. **Online address:** B-Kuvshinoff@worldnet.att.net

KUYPER, Sjoerd. Dutch, b. 1952. **Genres:** Children's fiction. **Career:** Author of children's books, c. 1974-. **Publications:** Mooie Gedichten, 1974, trans. P. Nijmeijer as Aesthetic Poems, 1974; Ik herinner mij Klaas Kristiaan (poems), 1974; Handboek voor overleden knaagdieren, 1975; Dagen uit het leven, 1977; (ed.) Ontmoet de dichters, 1977; (with J.J. Diepstraten) Het nieuwe proza: interviews met jonge nederlandse schrijvers, 1978; Een kleine jongen en z'n beer, 1978; De glazen kamer: verhalen, 1979; (with J.J. Diepstraten) Dichters: interviews, 1980; Ratten en flamingo's, 1982; Een reisgenoot, 1985; (with J.J. Diepstraten) De verborgen steeg, 1986; De ogen van het paard, 1987; Het zand: verhalen, 1987; Majesteit, Uw ontbijt (juvenile), 1988; Nachtkind, 1992; Het zakmes (juvenile; title means: The Penknife), 1992; Robin en Suze, 1993; Zeepziederij de adelaar, 1994; Het eiland Klaasje (juvenile), 1995; Robin en God, 1997; (with A. van Häringen) Malmok, 1999. **Address:** c/o Author Mail, Uitgeverig Leopold BV, Postbus 3879, 1001 AR Amsterdam, Netherlands.

KUZNESKI, Chris. American, b. 1969. **Genres:** Mystery/Crime/Suspense. **Career:** Journalist, educator, and fiction writer. Pitt News, Pittsburgh, PA, sportswriter, 1988-91; Indiana Gazette, Indiana, PA, sportswriter, 1991-93; Franklin Area School District, Franklin, PA, English teacher, 1993-98. **Publications:** THRILLER: The Plantation, 2002. **Address:** c/o Paradox Publishing, PO Box 901, Wexford, PA 15090, U.S.A. **Online address:** Chris@chriskuzneski.com

KUZNETSOV, Nickolaj. Ukranian, b. 1955. **Genres:** Mathematics/Statistics, Information science/Computers. **Career:** Institute of Cybernetics, Kiev, Ukraine, junior researcher, 1979-84, senior researcher, 1984-89, leading researcher, 1989-. Alexander Humbold Foundation, KFA Julich and GR5, Munich, Germany, research grant, 1990-92, 1994-95. **Publications:** (with I.N. Kovalenko and V.M. Shurnkov) Random Processes, 1983; (with Kovalenko) Methods for the Evolution of Highly Reliable Systems, 1988; (with Kovalenko) The Mathematical Theory of Reliability of Time-Dependant Systems, with Practical Applications, 1987. **Address:** Institute of Cybernetics, Prospect Glushkova 40, 252207 Kiev, Ukraine.

KVASNOSKY, Laura McGee. American, b. 1951. **Genres:** Children's fiction, Illustrations. **Career:** Writer and illustrator. Graphic Designer, proprietor of one-person design shop, Seattle, WA, 1980-95; Vermont College, MFA in Writing for Children & Young People program, faculty, 2000-. **Publications:** SELF-ILLUSTRATED FOR CHILDREN: Pink, Red, Blue, What are You?, 1994; One, Two, Three, Play with Me, 1994; See You Later, Alligator, 1995; Mr. Chips!, 1996; What Shall I Dream?, 1996; Zelda and Ivy 1998; Zelda and Ivy and the Boy Next Door, 1999; Zelda and Ivy One Christmas, 2000; Frank and Izzy Set Sail, 2004. OTHER: One Lucky Summer (middlegrades novel), 2002. Illustrator of books by F.P. Jaques, K. Appelt, L. Hough. **Address:** c/o Author Mail, Candlewick Press Inc, 2067 Massachusetts Ave, Cambridge, MA 02140-1338, U.S.A. **Online address:** laura@lmkbooks.com

KWONG, Julia C. Hong Kong, b. 1946. **Genres:** Education. **Career:** St. Francois Canossian College, Hong Kong, teacher, 1967-69; University of Toronto, Toronto, Ontario, lecturer, 1975; St. Mary's University, Halifax, Nova Scotia, professor of sociology, 1975-76; University of Manitoba, Winnipeg, assistant professor, 1976-84, associate professor, 1984-89, professor of sociology, 1989-. University of Toronto, visiting professor, 1976; Harvard

University, research associate, 1980-81, visiting scholar, 1982-83 and 1991-92, corresponding research associate, 1992-93; Beijing University, visiting professor, summer, 1984. **Publications:** Chinese Education in Transition: Prelude to the Cultural Revolution, 1979; Sociolgy of Education, 1986; Cultural Revolution in China's Schools, 1988; (with I. Huffman) The Dream of Gold Mountain, 1989; The Political Economy of Corruption in China, 1997. Contributor of articles and reviews to academic journals. **Address:** Department of Sociology, University of Manitoba, Winnipeg, MB, Canada R3T 2N2.

KWONG, Peter. American. **Genres:** Cultural/Ethnic topics. **Career:** Writer. Director of the Asian American Studies Program at the City University of New York. **Publications:** Chinatown, New York: Labor and Politics, 1930-1950, 1980; The New Chinatown, 1987, rev. ed., 1996; Forbidden Workers: Illegal Chinese Immigrants and American Labor, 1998. **Address:** Hunter College, Asian American Studies Program, CUNY, 695 Park Ave., New York, NY 10021, U.S.A.

KYLE, Keith. British, b. 1925. **Genres:** Adult non-fiction. **Career:** English-Speaking Union, London, England, secretary of programs and publications department, 1951; British Broadcasting Corporation (BBC) radio, London, producer, 1951-53; The Economist, Washington, DC, chief U.S. correspondent, 1953-58, political and parliamentary correspondent, London, 1958-60; BBC television, London, reporter and newscaster in Nairobi, Kenya, 1960-64, and London, 1964-82; Royal Institute of International Affairs, London, head of meetings department, 1972-86, special assistant to director, 1987-90, research fellow, 1990-94; Visiting Professor of History, University of Ulster, 1993-99. Author of London column, New York Post, 1958-61; author of international affairs column, Listener, 1969-74; contributor to London Review of Books, 1979-94. John F. Kennedy School of Government, Harvard, fellow Institute of Politics, 1967-68. **Publications:** Cyprus, 1984; Suez, 1991; (joint ed.) Whither Israel?, 1993, rev. ed., 1994; Cyprus: In Search of Peace, 1998; The Politics of the Independence of Kenya, 1999; Suez: Britain's End of Empire in the Middle East, 2003. Contributor to books. **Address:** 25 Oppidans Road, London NW3 3AG, England. **Online address:** keithkyle@electra-tv.com

KYLE, Susan S(paeth). Also writes as Diana Blayne, Katy Currie, Diana Palmer. American, b. 1946. **Genres:** Novels, Romance/Historical, Science fiction/Fantasy. **Career:** Times, Gainesville, GA, district staff reporter, 1969-84; Tri-County Advertiser, Clarkesville, GA, staff reporter, 1972-82; Atlanta Constitution, district staff member, late 1970s; novelist, 1979-. **Publications:** NOVELS AS SUSAN KYLE: The Morcai Battalion (science fiction), 1980; Diamond Spur, 1988; Fire Brand, 1989; Night Fever, 1990; True Colors, 1991; Escapade, 1992; After Midnight, 1993. AS DIANA PALMER. NOVELS: Now and Forever, 1979; Storm over the Lake, 1979; To Have and

to Hold, 1979; Sweet Enemy, 1980; Bound by a Promise, 1980; Love on Trial, 1980; To Love and Cherish, 1980; Dream's End, 1980; If Winter Comes, 1981; At Winter's End, 1981; Heather's Song, 1982; The Cowboy and the Lady, 1982; Friends and Lovers, 1983; Fire and Ice, 1983; Snow Kisses, 1983; Darling Enemy, 1983; Diamond Girl, 1984; The Rawhide Man, 1984; Lady Love, 1984; Roomful of Roses, 1984; Heart of Ice, 1984; Passion Flower, 1984; Cattleman's Choice, 1985; Love by Proxy, 1985; The Australian, 1985; The Tender Stranger, 1985; Soldier of Fortune, 1985; Eye of the Tiger, 1986; Loveplay, 1986; Rawhide and Lace, 1986; After the Music, 1986; Champagne Girl, 1986; Unlikely Lover, 1986; Rage of Passion, 1987; Fit for a King, 1987; Betrayed by Love, 1987; Woman Hater, 1987; Enamored, 1988; Calhoun, 1988; Justin, 1988; Tyler, 1988; Sutton's Way, 1989; Hoodwinked, 1989; His Girl Friday, 1989; Reluctant Father, 1989; Hunter, 1990; Sweet Enemy/Love on Trial, 1990; Storm over the Lake/To Love and Cherish, 1990; If Winter Comes/Now and Forever, 1990; After the Music/Dream's End, 1990; Bound by a Promise/Passion Flower, 1990; To Have and to Hold/The Cowboy and the Lady, 1990; Ethan, 1990; Connal, 1990; Nelson's Brand, 1991; The Best Is Yet to Come, 1991; Harden, 1991; Evan, 1991; Lacy (historical), 1991; Donovan, 1992; The Case of the Mesmerizing Boss, 1992; The Case of the Confirmed Bachelor, 1992; The Case of the Missing Secretary, 1992; Emmett, 1993; Trilby (historical), 1993; Amelia (historical), 1993; Night of Love, 1993; King's Ransom, 1993; Calamity Mom, 1993; Secret Agent Man; (with D. Macomber and J. Duncan) To Mother with Love (stories); Nora, 1994; Noelle, 1995; Magnolia, 1996; Savage Heart, 1997; Once in Paris, 1998; Midnight Rider, 1998; Paper Rose, 1999; Callaghan's Bride, 1999; Beloved, 1999; Love with a Long, Tall Texan (short stories), 1999; Mercenary's Woman, 2000; Matt Caldwell, 2000; Lord of the Desert, 2000; The Winter Soldier, 2001; The Last Mercenary, 2001; The Texas Rose, 2001; After the Music, 2001; A Man of Means, 2002; Lionhearted, 2002; Desperado, 2002. AS DIANA BLAYNE. NOVELS: A Waiting Game, 1982; A Loving Arrangement, 1983; White Sand Wild Sea, 1983; Dark Surrender, 1983; Color Love Blue, 1984; Tangled Destinies, 1986; Denim and Lace, 1990. AS KATY CURRIE: Blind Promises, 1984. Contributor of short stories to anthologies. **Address:** PO Box 844, Cornelia, GA 30531-0844, U.S.A. **Online address:** www.dianapalmer.com

KYNASTON, David. British. **Genres:** History. **Career:** Author, editor, and historian. **Publications:** King Labour: The British Working Class, 1850-1914, 1976; The Secretary of State, 1978; The Chancellor of the Exchequer, 1980; Bobby Abel: Professional Batsman 1857-1936, 1982; Archie's Last Stand: M.C.C. in New Zealand, 1922-23: Being an Account of Mr. A.C. MacLaren's Tour and His Last Stand, 1984; The Financial Times: A Centenary History, 1988; WG's Birthday Party, 1990; The City of London, Vol. 1: A World of Its Own 1815-90, 1994, Vol. 2: Golden Years 1890-1914, 1995; (ed. with R. Roberts) The Bank of England 1694-1994: Money, Power, and Influence, 1995. **Address:** c/o Chatto & Windus, Random House, 20 Vauxhall Bridge Rd., London SW1V 25A, England.

L

LAAS, Virginia J(eans). American, b. 1943. **Genres:** History. **Career:** Classroom teacher in Joplin, MO, 1964-65; Pittsburg State University, Pittsburg, KS, lecturer in history, 1981-88; Missouri Southern State University, Joplin, lecturer, 1984-88, instructor, 1988-92, assistant professor, 1992-97, associate professor of history, 1997-. University of Wisconsin, intern at National Historical Publications and Records Commission Institute for the Editing of Historical Documents, 1986. **Publications:** (with Ritchie and D. Stewart) An Introduction to the Tri-State Mineral Museum, 1986; (with D.T. Cornish) Lincoln's Lee: The Life of Rear Admiral Samuel Phillips Lee, 1986; Love & Power in the 19th Century: The Marriage of Violet Blair, 1998. EDITOR: E. Ritchie, Guidebook to the Tri-State Mineral Museum, 1986; Wartime Washington: The Civil War Letters of Elizabeth Blair Lee, 1991; Bridging Two Eras: The Autobiography of Emily Newell Blair, 1977-1951, 1999. Contributor of reviews and articles to periodicals. **Address:** Missouri Southern State University, Joplin, MO 64801, U.S.A.

LABAND, John (Paul Clow). South African, b. 1947. **Genres:** History, Third World. **Career:** University of Natal, Pietermaritzburg, South Africa, temporary lecturer, 1972-73, lecturer, 1974-81, senior lecturer, 1982-89, associate professor, 1990-95, professor of history, 1996-, head of Department of Historical Studies, 1996-. **Publications:** (with J. Wright) King Cetshwayo kaMpande, 1983; Fight Us in the Open: The Anglo-Zulu War through Zulu Eyes, 1985; The Battle of Ulundi, 1988; (with J. Mathews) Isandlwana, 1992; Kingdom in Crisis: The Zulu Response to the British Invasion of 1879, 1992; Rope of Sand: The Rise and Fall of the Zulu Kingdom in the Nineteenth Century, 1995, in U.S. & U.K. as The Rise and Fall of the Zulu Nation, 1997; (with I. Knight) The War Correspondents: The Anglo-Zulu War, 1996. WITH P.S. THOMPSON: A Field Guide to the War in Zululand 1879, 1979; War Comes to Umvoti: The Natal-Zululand Border, 1878-9, 1980; Field Guide to the War in Zululand and the Defense of Natal 1879, 1983; The Buffalo Border 1879: The Anglo-Zulu War in Northern Natal, 1983; Kingdom and Colony at War: Sixteen Studies on the Anglo-Zulu War of 1879, 1990. EDITOR: (with R. Haswell) Pietermaritzburg 1838-1988: A New Portrait of an African City, 1988; (with D.C.F. Moodie) Moodie's Zulu War, 1988; (with Major Ashe and Captain E.V. Wyatt-Edgell) The Story of the Zulu Campaign, 1989; Lord Chelmsford's Zululand Campaign, 1878-1879, 1994. **Address:** Historical Studies, School of Human and Social Studies, University of Natal, Pietermaritzburg, Private Bag X01, Scottsville 3209, Republic of South Africa. **Online address:** Laband@history.unp.ac.za

LABANYI, Jo. British, b. 1946. **Genres:** Literary criticism and history. **Career:** University of London, Birkbeck College, London, England, professor of modern Spanish literature and cultural studies, 1971-. **Publications:** Ironia e historia en "Tiempo de silencio," 1985; Myth and History in the Contemporary Spanish Novel, 1989; (trans.) Galdos, Nazarin, 1993. EDITOR: Galdos, 1993; (with L. Charnon-Deutsch) Culture and Gender in Nineteenth Century Spain, 1995; (Co) Introduction to Spanish Cultural Studies: The Struggle for Modernity, 1995. Translator of Latin American novels and short stories. Contributor of articles and translations to literature and cinema journals. **Address:** University of Southampton, Avenue Campus, 3031, Level 3, Highfield, Southampton SO17 1BJ, England.

LA BERGE, Ann F. American, b. 1944. **Genres:** Sciences, Medicine/Health. **Career:** Virginia Polytechnic Institute and State University, Blacksburg, visiting assistant professor, 1979-81, assistant director of Center for the Study of Science in Society, 1981-85, program coordinator, 1985-86, visiting assistant professor of history, 1986-88, assistant professor of Center for Programs in the Humanities, 1989-, and Center for the Study of Science in Society, 1991-. STS Program, associate professor, 1994-. **Publications:** Mission and Method: The Early Nineteenth-Century French Public Health Movement, 1992. EDITOR: (with A. Donovan) Working Papers in Science and Technology Studies: Ethics in Engineering, 1982; (with D. Zallen) Readings in Humanities, Science, and Technology, 1992, 2nd 1995; (with M. Feingold, and contrib.) French Medical Culture in the Nineteenth Century, 1994. Contributor of articles and reviews to history journals. **Address:** Center for the Study of Science in Society, Lane Hall, Virginia Polytechnic Institute and State University, Blacksburg, VA 24061, U.S.A.

LABRIE, Ross. Canadian, b. 1936. **Genres:** Literary criticism and history. **Career:** University of Saskatchewan, Saskatoon, Canada, instructor in English, 1962-63; University of British Columbia, Vancouver, British Columbia, Canada, professor of English, 1963-2001; writer. **Publications:** The Art of Thomas Merton, 1979; Howard Nemerov, 1980; James Merrill, 1982; The Writings of Daniel Berrigan, 1989; The Catholic Imagination in American Literature, 1997; Thomas Merton and the Inclusive Imagination, 2001. Contributor to periodicals. **Address:** 592 E Carisbrooke Rd, North Vancouver, BC, Canada V7N 1N5. **Online address:** labrie@interchange. ubc.ca

LABRO, Philippe (Christian). French, b. 1936. **Genres:** Novels, Plays/Screenplays. **Career:** Journalist, filmmaker, novelist, and memoirist. Marie-France, journalist, 1958-59; France-Soir, journalist, 1959-; Director of films. Actor in films. **Publications:** Un Americain peu tranquille, 1960; Des Feux Mal Eteints (Poorly Extinguished Fires), 1967; Ce n'est qu'un debut, 1968, trans. as This Is Only a Beginning, 1970; Les barricades de Mai (The Barricades of May), 1968; L'heritier, 1973; Tous celebres, 1979; Des bateaux dans la nuit, 1982; Etudiant Etranger, 1986, trans. as The Foreign Student, 1988; Un ete dans l'Ouest, 1988, trans. as One Summer Out West, 1991; Le petit garcon, 1990, trans. as The Little Man, 1992; Quinze ans (Fifteen Years), 1992; Un debut a Paris (A Debut in Paris), 1994; La traversee, 1996; Dark Tunnel, White Light: My Journey to Death and Beyond, trans., 1997; Rendez-vous au Colorado (Rendezvous in Colorado), 1998; Manvella, 1999; Lettres d' Amerique, 2001; Je connais gens de toutes sortes, 2002. SCREENPLAYS: L'Heritier (The Inheritor), 1972; Sans mobile apparent (With Apparent Motive), 1972; L'Alpagueur, 1976; La Crime, 1983; Rive droite, rive gauche (Right Bank, Left Bank), 1984; Des feux mal eteints (Poorly Extinguished Fires), 1994; Foreign Student, 1994. **Address:** 5 rue Recamier, 75007 Paris, France.

LACEY, Nicola. British, b. 1958. **Genres:** Criminology/True Crime, Law, Women's studies and issues. **Career:** University of London, lecturer in law, 1981-84; New College, Oxford, fellow and tutor, 1984-95; Birkbeck College, University of London, professor of law, 1995-97; London School of Economics, professor of criminal law, 1998-. **Publications:** State Punishment: Political Principles and Community Values, 1988; (co-author) Reconstructing Criminal Law: Critical Perspectives on Crime and the Criminal Process, 1990, 3rd ed., 2003; (co-author) The Politics of Community, 1993; Unspeakable Subjects, 1998. **Address:** Law Department, London School of Economics, Houghton St, London WC2A 2AE, England. **Online address:** n.lacey@ lse.ac.uk

LACEY, Robert. British, b. 1944. **Genres:** History, Biography. **Career:** Sunday Times Magazine, London, assistant ed., 1969-73; Sunday Times,

Look! pages, ed., 1973-74; Cover Magazine, co-founder and co-editor, 1997-99. **Publications:** (author and ed.) The French Revolution, 2 vols., 1968; (author and ed.) The Rise of Napoleon, 1969; (author and ed.) The Peninsular War, 1969; (author and ed.) 1812: The Retreat from Moscow, 1969; Robert, Earl of Essex: An Elizabethan Icarus, 1971; The Life and Times of Henry VIII, 1972; The Queens of the North Atlantic, 1973; Sir Walter Raleigh, 1973; (author and ed.) Sir Francis Drake and the Golden Hinde, 1975; (ed. and contrib.) Heritage of Britain, 1975; Majesty: Elizabeth II and the House of Windsor, 1977; The Kingdom: Arabia and the House of Saud, 1981; Princess, 1982; Aristocrats, 1983; Ford: The Men and the Machine, 1986; God Bless Her, 1987; Little Man-Meyer Lansky and the Gangster Life, 1991; Grace, 1994; Sotheby's: Bidding for Class, 1998; (with D. Danziger) The Year 1000, 1999; Monarch, 2002; Great Tales from English History: Cheddar Man to the Peasants' Revolt, 2003, Chaucer to the Glorious Evolution, 2004. **Address:** c/o Curtis Brown Ltd, Haymarket House, 28/29 Haymarket 4th Fl, London SW1Y 4SP, England. **Online address:** robert@robertlacey.com

LACHMAN, Barbara. Also writes as Barbara L. Grant. American, b. 1938. **Genres:** Music. **Career:** Music teacher, 1972-82; teacher of Alexander Technique, 1982-92; College of Notre Dame, teacher at Women's Institute, 1993-97; Baltimore Curriculum Project, Baltimore, MD, writer, 1996-. Western Michigan University, annual lecturer, 1984-88; Sarah Lawrence College, guest lecturer, 1984, 1986; Trinity College, Hartford, CT, guest lecturer, 1986; Hartford College for Women, guest instructor, 1986-87; teacher at University of Puerto Rico and Sacred Heart University, San Juan, PR, 198892; Johns Hopkins University, teacher at Peabody Conservatory of Music, 1993-97; Calvert School, editor for home instruction department, 1993-96; Women's Chamber and Sight-Reading Chorus, conductor, 1972-82; Greater Hartford Academy for the Performing Arts, liaison counselor, 1986-87; La Casa del Libro (museum and library of rare books), San Juan, associate director, 1988-92. Also worked as a paralegal. **Publications:** The Journal of Hildegard of Bingen, 1993; Hildegard, the Last Year, 1997. Contributor of articles, translations, and reviews to periodicals and anthologies. Also writes under the name Barbara L. Grant. **Address:** 407 Spring Valley Rd., Lexington, VA 24450, U.S.A.

LACHMAN, Seymour P. American, b. 1933. **Genres:** Education, Cultural/Ethnic topics, Theology/Religion. **Career:** City University of New York (CUNY) Kingsborough Community College, Brooklyn, NY, dean and professor of history, 1963-69; CUNY Graduate School and University Center, NYC, professor of education, 1974-80; CUNY Baruch College, NYC, dean of community development, 1980-. NYC Board of Education, president, 1969-74; Conference on Public and Non-Public Schools, NYC, chair, 1975-, procedures editor, 1980-90; National Collaborative Public and Non-Public Schools, chair, 1988-; New York State Senate, senator from 22nd district, 1996-. National Committee on Middle East Studies of Greater New York, Conference on Soviet Jewry, chair, 1980-83. **Publications:** (with D. Bresnick and M. Polner) Black, White, Green, Red: The Politics of Education in Ethnic America, 1978; (with B.A. Kosmin) One Nation Under God: Religion in Contemporary American Society, 1993. **Address:** 406 Legislative Office Building, Albany, NY 12247, U.S.A. **Online address:** lachman@senate.state.ny.us

LACHNER, Dorothea. (Dorothea Knobloch). Austrian, b. 1951. **Genres:** Children's fiction. **Career:** Writer. Held a variety of jobs in Germany and Austria, 1969-72; worked as a teacher in Austria, 1972-74 and (with mentally impaired children) 1976-81. Worked with the mentally and physically impaired, 1987-95. **Publications:** Das grune Pferd im Himbeerbusch, 1995; Muensteraner autorenpreis fur Kinder-u-Jugend Theater, 2001; UA, 2003; Tonio und Giss Lif aus Leeds, 2005. WORK IN TRANSLATION: Andrew's Angry Words, 1995; The Gift from Saint Nicholas, 1995; Look Out, Cinder!, 1996; Smoky's Special Easter Present, 1996; Meredith, the Witch Who Wasn't, 1997; Meredith's Mixed-up-Magic, 2000; Danny, the Angry Lion, 2000; Meredith and Her Magical Book of Spells, 2003. Works have appeared in anthologies and have been adapted for radio programs in Austria. Has written plays for children's theater. **Address:** Badgasse 2/A-2721, Bad Fischau, Austria. **Online address:** dorla@utanet.at

LACHNIT, Carroll. American. **Genres:** Mystery/Crime/Suspense. **Career:** Writer. Orange County Register, worked as staff writer, 1984-92. Orange Coast magazine, managing editor, 1999-. **Publications:** MYSTERY NOVELS: Murder in Brief, 1995; A Blessed Death, 1996; Akin to Death, 1998; Janie's Law, 1999. Contributor to publications. **Address:** c/o Berkley Prime Crime, 375 Hudson St., New York, NY 10014, U.S.A.

LACHS, John. American, b. 1934. **Genres:** Poetry, Philosophy, Bibliography. **Career:** Professor of Philosophy, Vanderbilt University,

Nashville, Tennessee, 1967-93; Centennial Professor of Philosophy, 1993-; Assistant Professor, 1959-62; Associate Professor, 1962-66, and Professor, 1966-67, College of William and Mary, Williamsburg, Virginia. **Publications:** Animal Faith and Spiritual Life: Unpublished and Uncollected Works of George Santayana with Critical Essays on His Thought, 1967; Marxist Philosophy: A Bibliographical Guide, 1967; (ed. with S.M. Lachs) Physical Order and Moral Liberty: Previously Unpublished Essays of George Santayana, 1969; (trans. with P. Heath) J. G. Fichte: The Science of Knowledge, 1970; The Ties of Time (poetry), 1970; Intermediate Man, 1981; Mind and Philosophers, 1987; George Santayana, 1988; The Relevance of Philosophy to Life, 1995; In Love with Life, 1998; (with M. Hodges) Thinking in the Ruins, 1999. **Address:** Department of Philosophy, Vanderbilt University, Nashville, TN 37235, U.S.A.

LACKEY, Kris. American, b. 1953. **Genres:** Literary criticism and history. **Career:** University of New Mexico at Valencia County, instructor in English, 1982; University of Texas of the Permian Basin, Odessa, visiting assistant professor of English, 1983; Auburn University, Auburn, AL, instructor in English, 1983-86; University of New Orleans, New Orleans, LA, assistant professor, 1986-90, associate professor, 1990-97, associate chairperson of department, 1990-92, professor of English, 1997-. **Publications:** Roadframes: The American Highway Narrative, 1997. Contributor of articles, stories, and reviews to periodicals. **Address:** Department of English, University of New Orleans, Lakefront, New Orleans, LA 70148, U.S.A.

LACKEY, Mercedes R. American, b. 1950. **Genres:** Young adult fiction. **Career:** Artist's model in and near South Bend, IN, 1975-81; Associates Data Processing, South Bend, computer programmer, 1979-82; CAIRS, South Bend, surveyor, layout designer, and analyst, 1981-82; American Airlines, Tulsa, OK, computer programmer, 1982-. **Publications:** NOVELS FOR YOUNG ADULTS: Arrows of the Queen, 1987; Arrow's Flight, 1987; Arrow's Fall, 1988; Oathbound, 1988; Burning Water, 1989; Oathbreakers, 1989; Magic's Pawn, 1989; Reap the Whirlwind, 1989; (with E. Guon) A Knight of Ghosts & Shadows, 1990; Magic's Promise, 1990; Magic's Price, 1990; By the Sword, 1991; (with A. Norton) The Elvenbane: An Epic High Fantasy of the Halfblood Chronicles, 1991; Jinx High, 1991; Winds of Fate, 1991; Bardic Voices: The Lark & the Wren, 1992; (with L. Dixon) Born to Run, 1992; Children of the Night, 1992; (with E. Guon) Freedom Flight, 1992; (with Guon) Summoned to Tourney, 1992; Winds of Change, 1992; Winds of Fury, 1992; (with R. Emerson) Fortress of Frost & Fire: The Bard's Tale II, 1993; (with P. Anthony) If I Pay Thee Not in Gold, 1993; (with M.Z. Bradley) Rediscovery: A Novel of Darkover, 1993; (with A. McCaffrey) The Ship Who Searched, 1993; (with H. Lisle) When the Bough Breaks, 1993; The Robin & the Kestrel, 1993; Sacred Ground, 1994; (with L. Dixon) The Black Gryphon, 1994; Storm Warning, 1994; (with M.Z. Bradley and A. Norton) Tiger Burning Bright, 1995; The Eagle & the Nightingales, 1995; (with A. Norton) Elvenblood: An Epic High Fantasy, 1995; The Fire Rose, 1995; (with L. Dixon) The White Gryphon, 1995; Storm Rising, 1995; Firebird, 1996; (with L. Dixon) The Silver Gryphon, 1996; Storm Breaking, 1996; Four and Twenty Blackbirds, 1997; The Free Bards, 1997. **Address:** PO Box 2970, Claremore, OK 74018-2970, U.S.A.

LA CROIX, I(sobyl) F. Scottish, b. 1933. **Genres:** Botany, Horticulture. **Career:** Editor, The Orchid Review; The RHS Orchid Journal. **Publications:** Rhododendrons and Azaleas, 1973; Gardening in the Shade, 1978; Malawi Orchids: Epiphytes, 1983; Growing Scented Plants in Southern Africa, 1984; (co-author) Orchids of Malawi, 1991; (with E. la Croix) African Orchids in the Wild and in Cultivation, 1997. Contributor to horticultural and botanical journals. **Address:** 9 Port Henderson, Gairloch, Ross-shire IV21 2AS, Scotland. **Online address:** orchidrevieweditor@ths.org.uk

LACY, Allen. American, b. 1935. **Genres:** Homes/Gardens, Horticulture. **Career:** Professor of philosophy and gardening writer. Clemson College, Clemson, SC, instructor in English, 1961-62; James Madison University, Harrisonburg, VA, assistant professor, 1962-65, associate professor of philosophy and English, 1965-66; Michigan State University, East Lansing, assistant professor of humanities, 1966-68; Kirkland College, Clinton, NY, assistant professor, 1968-69, associate professor of philosophy and humanities, 1969-71; Richard Stockton College of New Jersey, Pomona, NJ, associate professor, 1971-72, professor of philosophy, 1972-. Founding editor, Allen Lacy's Homeground (quarterly journal), 1993-. Gardening columnist for Wall Street Journal, 1979-85, and for New York Times, 1986-93. **Publications:** Home Ground: A Gardener's Miscellany, 1984; Farther Afield: A Gardener's Excursions, 1986; The Garden in Autumn, 1990; The Glory of Roses, 1990; The Gardener's Eye and Other Essays, 1991; Gardening with Groundcovers and Vines, 1993; The Inviting Garden, 1998; In a Green Shade, 2000. EDITOR: (and trans., with M. Nozick and A. Kerrigan) Peace in War, by M. de Unamuno, 1983; (and trans. with others) The Private World, by Unamuno, 1984; Gardening for Love: The Market Bulletins, by E. Lawrence, 1987; The American Gardener: A Sampler, 1988; (with N. Goodwin) A Rock Garden in the South, by Lawrence, 1990. OTHER: (trans.) M. de Unamuno: The Rhetoric of Existence (philosophy), 1967. Author of gardening articles for periodicals. Contributor of book reviews and scholarly articles to periodicals. **Address:** 1511 Shore Rd., Linwood, NJ 08221, U.S.A.

LACY, Tira. See ESTRADA, Rita Clay.

LADD, Brian. American, b. 1957. **Genres:** History, Urban studies. **Career:** Free University of Berlin, Germany, postdoctoral fellow, 1986-88; University of Rhode Island, Kingston, lecturer in history, 1988-90; Oglethorpe University, Atlanta, GA, assistant professor of history, 1990-. **Publications:** Urban Planning and Civic Order in Germany, 1860-1914, 1990; Ghosts of Berlin, 1997. **Address:** Department of History, Tenbroeck 105, University at Albany, 1400 Washington Ave, Albany, NY 12222-0001, U.S.A. **Online address:** ladd@csc.albany.edu

LADD, Linda. American. **Genres:** Science fiction/Fantasy. **Career:** Writer. **Publications:** Wildstar, 1984; Moonspell, 1985; Fireglow, 1986; Dream Song, 1988; Frost Fire, 1990; Midnight Fire, 1991; Dragon Fire, 1992; White Lily, 1993; White Rose, 1994; White Orchid, 1995; Lilacs on Lace, 1996; Forever, My Love, 1997; A Love So Splendid, 1997; A Love So Fine, 1999; Running Scared, 2000; Midnight Fire; Silverswept. **Address:** c/o Author Mail, Doubleday Book Club, 401 Franklin Ave., Garden City, NY 11530, U.S.A. **Online address:** lindaladd@pbmo.net

LADD, Louise. American, b. 1943. **Genres:** Children's fiction, Young adult fiction, Inspirational/Motivational Literature, Medicine/Health, Autobiography/Memoirs, Essays, Ghost Writer. **Career:** Writer and freelance editor. Fairfield University, Fairfield, CT, teacher of the Writers' Workshop; also taught at Manhattanville College. Producer and actress, Connecticut Center Acting Ensemble for 19 years; also worked in the children's room at 2 local libraries, 14 years. **Publications:** CHILDREN'S FICTION: A Whole Summer of Weird Susan, 1987; The Double Fudge Dare, 1989. THE ANYWHERE RING SERIES: Miracle Island, 1995; Castle in Time, 1995; Lost Valley, 1996; Cherry Blossom Moon, 1996. THE DIAMOND DUDE RANCH SERIES, 2003: Call Me Just Plain Chris; The Wrangler's Secret; Prize-Winning Horse-Maybe; The Perfect Horse, 1998; Home for Christmas; Me, My Mare, and the Movie; Rodeo!; Belle's Foal. OTHER: (ed. with D. Taylor) Sandy Dennis: A Personal Memoir (biography), 1997. Contributor to periodicals.

LADD-TAYLOR, Molly. American. **Genres:** History. **Career:** Educator, writer. York University, Toronto, Canada, associate professor (history). **Publications:** Mother-Work: Women, Child Welfare, and the State, 1890-1930, 1994. EDITOR: Raising a Baby the Government Way: Mothers' Letters to the Children's Bureau, 1915-1932, 1986; (co) Root of Bitterness: Documents of the Social History of American Women, 1996; (with L. Umansky) "Bad" Mothers: The Politics of Blame in Twentieth-Century America, 1998. **Address:** Department of History, 2140 Vari Hall, York University, 4700 Keele St., Toronto, ON, Canada M3J 1P3. **Online address:** mltaylor@yorku.ca

LADELL, John L. Also writes as John Lindsay. Thai, b. 1924. **Genres:** Local history/Rural topics. **Career:** Forest Products Laboratory, Ottawa, Ontario, Canada, technical officer, 1950-67; Ontario Research Foundation (now Ortech), senior research scientist, 1961-72; writer, 1972-. **Publications:** (with M. Ladell) Inheritance: Ontario's Century Farms, Past and Present, 1979; (with Ladell) A Farm in the Family: The Many Faces of Ontario Agriculture Over the Centuries, 1985; They Left Their Mark: Surveyors and Their Role in the Settlement of Ontario, 1993. Contributor to scientific journals and popular magazines sometimes under the pseudonym John Lindsay. **Address:** 4276 Henderson Rd., Milton, ON, Canada L9T 2X5.

LADOW, Beth. American, b. 1957. **Genres:** History. **Career:** Historian; National Public Radio, Boston, MA, commentator. **Publications:** The Medicine Line: Life and Death on a North American Borderland, 2001. Contributor to books and periodicals. **Address:** 22 Lakeview Rd, Winchester, MA 01890, U.S.A.

LADUKE, Betty. American, b. 1933. **Genres:** Art/Art history. **Career:** Southern Oregon State College, Ashland, professor of art, 1964-96, now emeritus; artist and writer. Art works exhibited in institutions, museums, and galleries throughout the US. Works exhibited in one-person shows. **Publications:** Companeras: Women, Art, and Social Change in Latin America, 1985;

Africa through the Eyes of Women Artists, 1990; Women Artists: Multi-Cultural Visions, 1991; Africa: Women's Art, Women's Lives, 1997; Women Against Hunger, 1997. **Address:** 610 Long Way, Ashland, OR 97520, U.S.A. **Online address:** www.bettyladuke.com

LADUKE, Winona. American, b. 1959. **Genres:** Novels. **Career:** Social activist for the Chippewa people, MN. Worked as principal at a reservation school; founder, White Earth Land Recovery Project, c. 1988; leader of opposition to James Bay hydroelectric projects; founder and board co-chair, Indigenous Womens' Network; arrested during protest, 1994; organizer and host, Indigo Girls (music group) national "Honor the Earth" tour, 1995; member of board of directors, GreenPeace, USA, 1991-; program officer, Native American controlled foundation. **Publications:** Last Standing Woman, 1997. Contributor to books and periodicals. **Address:** White Earth Land Recovery Project, PO Box 327, White Earth, MN 56591, U.S.A.

LAFAVOR, Carole S. American. **Genres:** Mystery/Crime/Suspense. **Career:** Minnesota American Indian AIDS Task Force, Minneapolis, MN, nurse consultant, 1996, and past member of board of directors. Positively Native (national organization by and for Native American Indian, Alaskan, and Hawaiian natives with HIV/AIDS), member of board of directors and past administrator. Public speaker at schools and colleges, clinics, medical and nursing conferences, and tribal councils; guest on television and radio programs; subject of videotapes. **Publications:** OJIBWA MYSTERY NOVEL: Along the Journey River, 1996; Evil Dead Center, 1997. Contributor to periodicals. **Address:** 3932 Oakland Ave. S., Minneapolis, MN 55407, U.S.A. **Online address:** cslaf@aol.com

LAFAYE, A(lexandria R. T.). American, b. 1970. **Genres:** Young adult fiction, Novels, Children's fiction. **Career:** Roanoke College, Salem, VA, instructor in English, 1997-98; Plattsburgh State University, NY, assistant professor of English, 1998-. **Publications:** The Year of the Sawdust Man (juvenile historical novel), 1998; Edith Shay (young adult historical novel), 1998; Strawberry Hill (juvenile historical novel), 1999; Nissa's Place (juvenile historical novel), 1999. **Address:** c/o Marcia Wernick, Sheldon Fogelman Agency, 10 E 40th St, New York, NY 10016, U.S.A. **Online address:** alafaye@together.net

LAFEBER, Walter Frederick. American, b. 1933. **Genres:** History, International relations/Current affairs. **Career:** Cornell University, Ithaca, NY, Andrew and James Tisch University Professor, 2002-, Steven Weiss Presidential Teaching Fellow, 1994- (Assistant Professor, 1959-63; Associate Professor, 1963-67; Professor, 1967-68; Noll Professor of History, 1968-2002). Member, Editorial Board, Political Science Quarterly. Member, Advisory Committee, Foreign Relations of the United States series, U.S. Dept. of State, 1971-75; American Academy of Arts and Sciences, Guggenheim Fellow, 1990. **Publications:** The New Empire: An Interpretation of American Expansion, 1860-1898, 1963, 2nd ed., 1998; America, Russia and the Cold War, 1967, 9th ed., 2002; (co-author) Creation of the American Empire, 1973; (co-author) The American Century, 1974, 4th ed., 1997; The Panama Canal: The Crisis in Historical Perspective, 1978; The Third Cold War, 1981; Inevitable Revolutions: The U.S. in Central America, 1983; (co-author) America in Vietnam; The American Age: U.S. Foreign Policy at Home and Abroad from 1750 to Our Own Time, 1989, 2nd ed., 1994; The American Search for Opportunity, 1865-1913, Vol. II: The Cambridge History of American Foreign Relations, 1993; The Clash: U.S. Japan Relations throughout History, 1997; Michael Jordan and the New Global Capitalism, 1999, 2nd ed., 2000. EDITOR: John Q. Adams and American Continental Empire, 1965; America and Twenty Years Revolution, 1947-1967, 1969; Origins of the Cold War, 1941-1947, 1971; (co) Behind the Throne (essays in U.S. diplomatic history in honor of F.H. Harrington), 1993. **Address:** Dept of History, McGraw Hall, Cornell University, Ithaca, NY 14853-4601, U.S.A.

LAFEMINA, Gerry. American, b. 1968. **Genres:** Novellas/Short stories, Poetry. **Career:** Kirtland College, Roscommon, MI, professor, 1994-. Frostburg State University, distinguished poet in residence, 2004. **Publications:** 23 Below, 1994; A Print of Wildflowers (poetry), 1997; Shattered Hours: Poems 1988-94, 1997; Zarathustra in Love, 2001; Graffiti Heart, 2003; The Window Facing Winter, 2004. Contributor of short stories, poems, and essays to literary journals.

LAFERRIÈRE, Dany. Canadian (born Haiti), b. 1953. **Genres:** Novels. **Career:** Writer. Worked as a journalist in Haiti during the 1970s; later employed for five years in a tannery in Montreal, Quebec, Canada; affiliated with a Montreal television station, 1989-. **Publications:** Comment faire l'amour avec un Negre sans se fatiguer (novel), 1985, trans. D. Homel as

How to Make Love to a Negro, 1987; Eroshima (novel), trans. by Homel, 1991; L'odeur du cafe, 1991, trans. as An Aroma of Coffee, 1993; Le gout des jeunes filles, 1992, trans. as Dining with the Dictator, 1994; Cette grenade dans la main du jeune negre est-elle une arme ou un fruit?, 1993, trans. as Why Must a Black Writer Write about Sex?, 1994; Chronique de la derive douce (novel), 1994, trans. as Drifting Year, 1997; Pays sans chapeau, 1996, trans. as Down among the Dead Men, 1997; La chair du maitre, 1997; Le charme des apres-midi sans fin, 1997. **Address:** 4625 rue Cornwall, Saint-Hubert, QC, Canada J3Y 2S7.

LAFOREST, Gerard V. (J.). Canadian, b. 1926. **Genres:** Law. **Career:** Associate Professor of Law, 1956-63, and Professor, 1963-68, University of New Brunswick, Fredericton; Dean of Law, University of Alberta, Edmonton, 1968-70; Assistant Deputy Attorney General, Dept. of Justice, Ottawa, ON, 1970-74; Commissioner, Law Reform Commission of Can., 1974-79; Executive Vice-Chairman, Canada Bar Association Committee on the Constitution, 1977-78; Professor of Law and Director, Legislative Drafting Program, University of Ottawa, Common Law Section, 1979-81; Chairman, Special Inquiry on Kouchibouguac National Park, 1980-81; Professor of Law, University of Ottawa, 1971-79, McGill University, Montreal, 1972, 1977; Judge, New Brunswick Court of Appeal, 1981-85; Judge, Supreme Court of Canada, 1985-97; Distinguished Legal Scholar in Residence, University of New Brunswick, 1998-. **Publications:** Disallowance and Reservation of Provincial Legislation, 1955, 1970; Extradition to and from Canada, 1961, 1977, The Allocation of Taxing Power under the Canadian Constitution, 1967, 1981; Natural Resources and Public Property Under the Canadian Constitution, 1969; (with others) Le Territoire Quebecois, 1970; Water Law in Canada, 1973. **Address:** 320 University Ave, Fredricton, NB, Canada E3B 4J1.

LAFOREST, Guy. Canadian, b. 1955. **Genres:** History, Politics/Government. **Career:** Universite Laval, assistant professor, 1988-92, associate professor, 1992-96, professor of political science, 1996-, head of department of political science, 1997-2000. Canadian Journal of Political Science, coeditor, 1993-96. Institute of Intergovernmental Relations, Queen's University, Kingston, ONz, member of advisory board; Les Cahiers de droit, member of editorial board; Recherches sociographiques, member of editorial board. **Publications:** Trudeau et la fin d'un reve canadien, 1992, trans. as Trudeau and the End of a Canadian Dream, 1995; De la prudence, 1993; De l'urgence, 1995. EDITOR: (with L. Balthazar and V. Lemieux) Le Quebec et la restructuration du Canada, 1980-1992: Enjeux et perspectives, 1991; Charles Taylor, Reconciling the Solitudes, 1992; (with D.M. Brown) Integration and Fragmentation: The Paradox of the Late Twentieth Century, 1994; (with F. Blais and D. Lamoureux) Liberalismes et nationalismes: philosophie et politique, 1995; (with M. Elbaz and A. Fortin) Les frontieres de l'identite: modernite et postmodernisme au Quebec, 1996; (with R. Gibbins) Beyond the Impasse toward Reconciliation, 1998; Sortir de l'impasse: les voies de la reconciliation, 1998; (with P. De lara) Charles Taylor et l'interpretation de l'identite moderne, 1998. Contributor to books and scholarly journals. **Address:** Department of Political Science, Universite Laval, Ste-Foy, QC, Canada G1K 7P4. **Online address:** guy.laforest@pol.ulaval.ca

LA FORTUNE, Knolly Stephen. Trinidadian, b. 1920. **Genres:** Novels, Poetry. **Career:** A.T.C. Goldsmith's College, London University, 1954-56; F.R.G.S., 6th, December, 1976; Schoolmaster, I. L. E. A., since 1958 (Teacher in Charge, St. Paul's Roman Catholic School Library, 1968-69). Secretary, San Juan District Teacher's Association, 1954-55 and Art Teacher's Association, 1954-56; Education Officer, Trinidad and Tobago Association, London, 1967-68. **Publications:** Moments of Inspiration, 1947; Legend of T-Marie, 1968; Anthology of Caribbean Poets, 1969; Caribbean Folk-Lore, 1975-77; The Schoolmaster Remembers: Colonial Trinidad 1930, 1979; Trouble Make Monkey Eat Pepper (novel), 1984; Word Print, Longman's Caribbean Anthologies, 1990-92; Parnassus of World Poets, 1994. **Address:** 68 Arthurdon Rd, Brockley, London SE4 1JU, England.

LA FRENIERE, (B. Marie) Celine. Canadian/British (born Canada), b. 1950. **Genres:** Plays/Screenplays, Film, Writing/Journalism. **Career:** Professional actress on stage and screen, 1964-71; writer, 1969-. Radio and television interviewer and commentator for Canadian Broadcasting Corp. (CBC), 1969-70; production partner of film director Ronald Neame, 1980-87. **Publications:** The Arnaud Family, 1971, as A Propos, 1973; Chantez, 1972; (with J. Hill and D.P. Lewis) City on Fire (screenplay), 1979; Foreign Body (screenplay), 1986. Contributor of articles to periodicals. **Address:** Solar House, 50-56 Talacre Rd, London NW5 4LX, England. **Online address:** (agent) petercuming@blueyonder.co.uk

LAGATREE, Kirsten M. American, b. 1948. **Genres:** Homes/Gardens, How-to books. **Career:** Los Angeles Times, Los Angeles, CA, columnist.

Worked as reporter, news director, managing editor, producer, and broadcast journalist for public radio programs, 1981-93. **Publications:** Feng-Shui: Arranging Your Home to Change Your Life, 1996; (with A. Bredin) The Home Office Solution, 1998; Feng-Shui at Work, 1998; Checklists for Life; Sizzling Sex: 242 Sure-Fire Ways to Heat up Your Love Life. **Address:** c/o Andy McNicol, William Morris Agency, 1325 Avenue of the Americas, New York, NY 10019, U.S.A. **Online address:** kmlagatree@comcast.net

LAGRAND, Louis E. American, b. 1935. **Genres:** Education, Human relations/Parenting, Paranormal, Psychology. **Career:** Instr in Physical Education, Columbia University, NYC, 1958-62. SUNY Distinguished Service Professor, State University of New York, Potsdam, 1990- (Assistant Professor, 1962-65; Head Basketball Coach, 1962-70; Associate Professor, 1965-70; Professor of Health Science, 1970-90); Suffolk Community College, Adjunct Professor of Health Careers, 1995-. **Publications:** Coach's Complete Guide to Winning Basketball, 1967; Discipline in the Secondary School, 1969; Hatha Yoga in Health and Physical Education, 1974; Coping with Separation and Loss as a Young Adult, 1986; Changing Patterns of Human Existence, 1988; After Death Communication: Final Farewells, 1997; Messages and Miracles, 1999; Gifts from the Unknown, 2001. **Address:** 450 Fairway Isles Dr, Venice, FL 34292-3659, U.S.A. **Online address:** BL450@aol.com

LAGRAVENESE, Richard. American, b. 1960. **Genres:** Plays/Screenplays. **Career:** Screenwriter. **Publications:** SCREENPLAYS: Rude Awakening, 1989; The Fisher King, 1991; (with M. Weiss) The Ref, 1994; (with E. Chandler) The Little Princess, 1995; The Bridges of Madison County, 1995; Unstrung Heroes, 1995; The Mirror Has Two Faces, 1996; (with E. Roth) The Horse Whisperer, 1998; (with A. Ufia and A. Brooks) Beloved, 1998; Living Out Loud, 1998. **Address:** c/o Writers Guild of America, 7000 West 3rd St., Los Angeles, CA 90048, U.S.A.

LA GRECA, Annette M(arie). American, b. 1950. **Genres:** Psychology. **Career:** Catholic Home Bureau, NYC, Foster Care Division, caseworker 1972-73; school psychologist, Lafayette, IN, 1974-75; De Pauw University, Greencastle, IN, vocational and educational counselor, 1976-77; University of Miami, Coral Gables, FL, assistant professor, 1978-82, associate professor, 1982-86, professor of psychology and pediatrics, 1986-, coordinator of clinical child and pediatric training, 1982-86, director of clinical psychology at Mailman Center for Child Development, 1984-86, director of Child Psychology Division, 1987-, research consultant to Diabetes, Metabolic, and Lipid Disorders Unit, 1988-, fellow of Hecht Center, 1991-. St. Elizabeth's Hospital and Arnette Medical Clinic, pediatric psychology intern, 1976-77; University of North Carolina at Chapel Hill, clinical intern in pediatric and clinical child psychology, 1977-78; Montanari Residential Treatment Center, research consultant, 1979-82. Washington University, St. Louis, MO, visiting professor, 1990. **Publications:** (ed. and contrib.) Through the Eyes of the Child: Obtaining Self-Reports from Children and Adolescents, 1990; (ed. with L. Siegel, C.E. Walker, and J. Wallander, and contrib.) Advances in Pediatric Psychology: Stress and Coping in Child Health, 1992. Work represented in anthologies. Contributor of articles and reviews to psychology journals. **Address:** Department of Psychology, University of Miami, PO Box 248185, Coral Gables, FL 33124, U.S.A.

LAHIRI, Jhumpa. British, b. 1967. **Genres:** Adult non-fiction. **Career:** Writer. **Publications:** Interpreter of Maladies, 1999; (introduction) X. Zimbardo, India Holy Song (photography collection), 2000; The Namesake (novel), 2003. **Address:** c/o Houghton Mifflin, 222 Berkeley St., Boston, MA 02116, U.S.A.

LAHOOD, Marvin J(ohn). American, b. 1933. **Genres:** Literary criticism and history. **Career:** SUNY Distinguished teaching Professor of English, State University College of New York at Buffalo, since 1978. Academic Dean and Professor of English, Salem State College, Massachusetts, 1972-75; Dean of Faculty and Professor of English, D'Youville College, Buffalo, New York, 1975-78. **Publications:** (ed. with A. Rubulis) Latvian Literature, 1964; (ed.) Tender is the Night: Essays in Criticism, 1969; Conrad Richter's America, 1975; State University College at Buffalo: A History 1946-1972, 1980. **Address:** Buffalo State University, Ketchum Hall, 308, 1300 Elmwood Ave, Buffalo, NY 14222, U.S.A. **Online address:** lahoodmj@buffalostate.edu

LAHR, John (Henry). American, b. 1941. **Genres:** Novels, Plays/Screenplays, Theatre, Biography. **Career:** Literary adviser, Tyrone Guthrie Theatre, Minneapolis, MN, 1968, and literary adviser, Repertory Theatre, Lincoln Center, NYC, 1969-72; Grove Press, NYC, theatre editor, 1969-73; New Yorker, senior drama critic, 1992-. **Publications:** Notes on Cowardly

Lion, 1969; Up against the Fourth Wall, 1970; Acting Out America, 1970; Astonish Me, 1973; (with J. Price) Life-Show, 1973; The Autograph Hound, 1973; Hot to Trot (novel), 1974; Prick Up Your Ears: The Biography of Joe Orton, 1978; Coward: The Playwright, 1982; Automatic Vaudeville: Essays on Star Turns, 1984; Diary of a Somebody (play), 1989; The Manchurian Candidate (play), 1990; Dame Edna Everage and The Rise of Western Civilization, 1991; Light Fantastic, 1996; Sinatra: The Artist and the Man, 1997; Show and Tell, 2000; (co-author) Elaine Stritch at Liberty (play), 2002 (Tony Award). EDITOR: Showcase I, 1969; (with A. Lahr) Casebook on Harold Pinter's The Homecoming, 1971; (with J. Price) The Great American Life Show, 1974; Grove Press Modern Drama: Six Plays, 1975; The Complete Plays of Joe Orton, 1975; The Orton Diaries, 1986; Diaries of Kenneth Tynan, 2001. **Address:** 11A Chalcot Gardens, London NW3 4YB, England.

LAI, David Chuenyan. Canadian (born People's Republic of China), b. 1937. **Genres:** Geography. **Career:** University of Hong Kong, tutor, 1961-64, lecturer in geography, 1967-68; University of Victoria, British Columbia, visiting lecturer, 1968-69, assistant professor, 1969-73, associate professor, 1973-88, professor of geography, 1989-; writer. **Publications:** Arches in British Columbia, 1982; Chinatowns: Towns within Cities in Canada, 1988; The Forbidden City within Victoria: Myth, Symbol, and Streetscape of Canada's Earliest Chinatown, 1991; Land of Genghis Khan: The Rise and Fall of Nation - States in Chinese Northern Frontiers, 1995; Building and Rebuilding Harmony: The Gateway to Victoria's Chinatown, 1997; Canadian Steel, Chinese Government: No Chinese Labor, No Railway, 1998. **Address:** Department of Geography, University of Victoria, Victoria, BC, Canada V8W 3P5. **Online address:** dclai@uvvm.uvic.ca

LAI, Larissa. American, b. 1967. **Genres:** Novels. **Career:** Writer. Eric Cumine and Associates (architects and engineers), apprentice, 1989; CITR-Radio, host and producer of the series Air Aware, 1989; On Edge Productions, assistant curator, 1990; SAW Video Cooperative, coordinator, 1991; Banff Centre for the Arts, television and video associate in media arts department, 1992; Top Dollar Sisters, production manager for the film My Sweet Peony, 1992; Western Front Society, editor, 1994-95; Vancouver Art Gallery, gallery animateur, 1996-97. Cottages at Hedgebrook, resident, 1995; University of Calgary, MarkinFlanagan Distinguished Writer in Residence, 1997-98. Gives readings from her works. **Publications:** NOVELS: When Fox Is a Thousand, 1995; Salt Fish, 2002. Work represented in anthologies. Contributor of stories, poems, articles, and reviews to magazines. **Address:** c/o Dept of English, 2500 University Dr NW, University of Calgary, Calgary, AB, Canada T2N 1N4.

LAIDLER, Keith James. Canadian (born United Kingdom), b. 1916. **Genres:** Chemistry. **Career:** University of Ottawa, Ont., Professor, 1955-81, Professor Emeritus of Chemistry, 1981-. **Publications:** Chemical Kinetics, 1950, 3rd ed., 1987; Chemical Kinetics of Excited States, 1955; Chemical Kinetics of Enzyme Action, 1958, 2nd ed. (with P. S. Bunting), 1973; Reaction Kinetics, 1963; Theories of Chemical Reaction Rates, 1969; The Chemical Elements, 1970; Physical Chemistry with Biological Applications, 1978; (with J.H. Meiser) Physical Chemistry, 1982, 4th ed., 2002; The World of Physical Chemistry, 1993; To Light Such a Candle, 1998; Energy, Chance and Chaos, 2002. **Address:** 5 Arundel Ave, Ottawa, ON, Canada K1K 0B1. **Online address:** laidler@attcanada.ca

LAIMO, Michael. American, b. 1966. **Genres:** Adult non-fiction. **Career:** Writer, editor, and sales professional. Works as a sales representative for a swimwear company in New York, NY. Assistant fiction editor, Space and Time magazine. **Publications:** The Twilight Garden (chapbook), 1998; Demons, Freaks, and Other Abnormalities (short stories), 1999; Within the Darkness, Golden Eyes (chapbook), 1999; Dregs of Society (short stories), 2001; (editor) Bloodtype, 2001; Atmosphere (novel), 2002; Deep in the Darkness (novel), 2004. Contributor of short stories to periodicals. **Address:** c/o Author Mail, Adorchester Publishing/Leisure Books, 200 Madison Avenue, Ste. 2000, New York, NY 10016, U.S.A. **Online address:** michael@laimo.com

LAIN, Anna. See **LAMB, Nancy.**

LAIOU, Angeliki Evangelos. American/Greek, b. 1941. **Genres:** History. **Career:** Educator and historian. Harvard University, Cambridge, MA, assistant professor of history, 1969-72, professor of Byzantine history, 1981-; Brandeis University, Waltham, MA, associate professor, 1972-75; Rutgers University, New Brunswick, NJ, professor, 1975-79, distinguished professor, 1979-81. **Publications:** Constantinople and the Latins: The Foreign Policy of Andronicus II, 1282-1328, 1972; Peasant Society in the Late Byzantine

Empire: A Social and Demographic Study, 1977; (with M. Balard and C. Otten-Froux) Les Italiens a Byzance, 1987; Gender, Society, and Economic Life in Byzantium, 1992; Mariage, Amour et parente a Byzance aux XI-XIII siecles, 1992. EDITOR: Charanis Studies: Essays in Honor of Peter Charanis, 1980; (with H. Maguire) Byzantium: A World Civilization, 1992; Consent and Coercion to Sex and Marriage in Ancient and Medieval Societies, 1993; (with D. Simon) Law and Society in Byzantium: 9th-12th Centuries, 1994; (with E.R. May) The Dumbarton Oaks Conversations and the United Nations: 1944-1994, 1998; (with H. Ahrweiler) Studies on the Internal Diaspora of the Byzantine Empire, 1998; The Economic History of Byzantium, 2002. Contributor to books.

LAIRD, Ross. Australian, b. 1947. **Genres:** Communications/Media, Music. **Career:** Worked as a librarian, 1965-87; National Film and Sound Archive, Canberra, Australia, librarian and consultant, 1988-91; Wharf Cable Television, Hong Kong, senior manager of video library system, 1992-94; Ernst & Young, Hong Kong, manager of information and research unit, 1994-96; National Film and Sound Archive, sound archivist, 1997-. **Publications:** A Discography of Popular Music Recorded in Australia, 1924-1950, 1982; Tantalizing Tingles, 1995; Moanin' Low: Female Popular Vocals, 1920-1933, 1996; The First Wave: Australian Rock and Pop Recordings, 1955-1963, 1998; Sound Beginnings: A History of the Australian Record Industry to 1933, 1999. Contributor to books. **Address:** GPO Box 22, Canberra, ACT 2601, Australia. **Online address:** ra@netinfo.com.au

LAJE, Zilia L. (born Cuba), b. 1941. **Genres:** Novels. **Career:** Employed by Pittsburgh Plate Glass International, Havana, Cuba, 1959-60; Southeast Bank, Miami Springs, FL, corporate banking assistant, 1978-90; self-employed translator and writer, 1995-. **Publications:** La Cortina de bagazo (historical novel), 1995, translation published as The Sugar Cane Curtain, 2000; Cartas son cartas (novel), 2001, translation published as Love Letters in the Sand, 2002. Contributor to periodicals. **Address:** c/o Escritores Cubanos de Miami, POB 45-17321, Shenandoah Station, Miami, FL 33245, U.S.A. **Online address:** guarinapub@juno.com

LAKE, David (John). Australian (born India), b. 1929. **Genres:** Science fiction/Fantasy, Poetry, Literary criticism and history. **Career:** Lecturer, Sr. Lecturer, and Reader in English, University of Queensland, 1967-94. Assistant Master, Sherrardswood School, Welwyn Garden City, Herts., 1953-58, and St. Albans Boys Grammar School, Herts., 1958-59; Lecturer, in English, Saigon University, 1959-61, for the Thai Government, Bankok, 1961-63, and at Chiswick Polytechnic, London, 1963-64; Reader in English, Jadavpur University, Calcutta, 1965-67. **Publications:** John Milton: Paradise Lost, 1967; Greek Tragedy, 1969; Hornpipes and Funerals (poetry), 1973; The Canon of Thomas Middleton's Plays: Internal Evidence for the Major Problems of Authorship, 1975. SCIENCE FICTION NOVELS: Walkers on the Sky, 1976, 1978; The Right Hand of Dextra, 1977; The Wildings of Dextra, 1977; The Gods of Xuma, or, Barsoom Revisited, 1978; The Fourth Hemisphere, 1980; The Man Who Loved Morlocks, 1981; The Ring of Truth, 1983; Warlords of Xuma, 1983. FANTASY NOVELS: The Changelings of Chaan, 1985; West of the Moon, 1988. Several short stories. EDITOR: H.G. Wells, The First Men in the Moon, 1995; The Invisible Man, 1996. **Address:** Dept. of English, University of Queensland, St. Lucia, QLD 4067, Australia.

LAKE, Jo-Anne. (born Canada), b. 1941. **Genres:** Children's non-fiction. **Career:** Elementary schoolteacher in London, Ontario, Canada, 1961-63, and Oshawa, Ontario, Canada, 1963-65; University of Western Ontario, London, instructor in mathematics, 1965; elementary schoolteacher, 1968-80; middle-school teacher, 1981-83; teacher in a program for gifted students, 1983-85; Durham District Board of Education, Whitby, Ontario, Canada, consultant, 1986-90, administrator, 1991-2000; writer, public speaker, and educational consultant, 2000-. University of Toronto, instructor in elementary science. Sciencents, cofounder. Community volunteer. **Publications:** Imagine, 1993; Life Long Learning, 1997; Literature and Science Breakthroughs: Connecting Language and Science Skills in the Elementary Classroom, 2000. Contributor to education and library journals. **Address:** c/o Author Mail, Stenhouse Publishers, 477 Congress St. Suite 4B, Portland, ME 04101, U.S.A. **Online address:** joannelake@rogers.com

LAKE, M. D. (Allen Simpson). American, b. 1934. **Genres:** Mystery/Crime/Suspense. **Career:** Minnesota University, Minneapolis, MN, professor of Scandinavian languages and literature; writer. **Publications:** PEGGY O'NEILL MYSTERY NOVELS: Amends for Murder, 1989; Cold Comfort, 1990; A Gift for Murder, 1992; Poisoned Ivy, 1992; Murder by Mail, 1993; Grave Choices, 1995; Once upon a Crime, 1995; Flirting with Death, 1996; Ties of Blood, 1997; Midsummer Malice, 1997; Death Calls the Tune, 1999.

Work represented in anthologies. **Address:** c/o Author Mail, Avon Books, 10 East 53rd St., New York, NY 10022, U.S.A. **Online address:** mdlake1234@aol.com

LAKELAND, Paul. British, b. 1946. **Genres:** Theology/Religion. **Career:** Fairfield University, Fairfield, CT, assistant professor, 1981-84, associate professor, 1984-88, professor of religious studies, 1988-. Member of editorial board, Cross Currents; network editor, Religious Studies Review. **Publications:** Can Women Be Priests?, 1975; Free in Christ: The Challenge of Political Theology, 1984; The Politics of Salvation: The Hegelian Idea of the State, 1984; Theology and Critical Theory: The Discourse of the Church, 1990; Postmodernity, 1997. Contributor to professional journals. **Address:** Department of Religious Studies, Fairfield University, Fairfield, CT 06824, U.S.A. **Online address:** PFLakeland@fair1.fairfield.edu

LAKER, Rosalind. *See* OVSTEDAL, Barbara.

LAKOS, Amos. Canadian (born Romania), b. 1946. **Genres:** International relations/Current affairs, Bibliography. **Career:** University of Waterloo, Waterloo, Ontario, reference and collections development librarian, 1977-94, coordinator, management information services, 1994-. **Publications:** International Terrorism: A Bibliography, 1986; International Negotiations: A Bibliography, 1989; Terrorism, 1980-1990: A Bibliography, 1991. **Address:** Porter Library, University of Waterloo, Waterloo, ON, Canada N2L 3G1.

LAL, Brij V. Fijian, b. 1952. **Genres:** History, Politics/Government, Local history/Rural topics. **Career:** University of the South Pacific, Suva, Fiji, lecturer, 1976-83; University of Hawaii, Honolulu, assistant professor, then associate professor, 1983-91; Australian National University, Canberra, senior research fellow, 1990-93, senior fellow, 1993-97, professor, 1997-; Center for the Contemporary Pacific, director, 1998-. **Publications:** The Girmitiyas, 1983; Power and Prejudice, 1988; Broken Waves, 1992; (with P. Reeves and T.R. Vakatora) Fiji Islands, 1996; (with T.R. Vakatora) Fiji and the World, 1997; (with T.R. Vakatora) Fiji in Transition, 1997; Vision for Change, 1997; Another Way, 1998; Time to Change, 1999; Chalo Jahaji: On a Journey of Indenture in Fiji, 2000; Mr. Tulsi's Store: A Fijian Journey, 2001. EDITOR: (with J. McGuire and M. Borthwick) Problems and Methods of Enquiry in South Asian History, 1984; Politics in Fiji, 1986; Pacific Islands History, 1992; (with D. Munro and E.D. Beechert) Plantation Workers, 1993; (with K.R. Howe and R.C. Kiste) Tides of History, 1994; (with P. Larmour) Electoral Systems in Divided Societies, 1997; (with K. Fortune) Pacific Islands Encyclopedia, 2000. **Address:** Pacific and Asian History Division, Research School of Pacific and Asian Studies, Australian National University, H.C. Coombs Bldg 009, Canberra, ACT 0200, Australia. **Online address:** brij.lal@anu.edu.au

LALITA, K. Indian, b. 1953. **Genres:** Women's studies and issues. **Career:** Administrative College of India, Hyderabad, research associate, 1977-80; Rural Development Advisory Service, Hyderabad, director of women's programs, 1980-84; Osmania University, Anveshi Research Centre for Women's Studies, founder-coordinator, 1986-95; ThinkSoft Consultants, founder-director, 1993-. **Publications:** Manaku Teliyani Mana Charitra, 1986; We Were Making History: Life Histories of Women in the Telangana People's Struggle, 1989; Savalaksha Sandehalu, 1991; Women Writing in India, Vol. 1: 600 B.C. to the Early Twentieth Century, 1991, Vol 2: The Twentieth Century, 1992. **Address:** 1-2-16/11 First Street, Habsiguda, Hyderabad 500 007, Andhra Pradesh, India. **Online address:** vithal2@hd1.vsnl.net.in

LAM, Truong Buu. American (born Vietnam), b. 1933. **Genres:** History. **Career:** Institute of Historical Research, Saigon, director, 1957-64; State University of New York, Stony Brook, associate professor of history, 1968-71; University of Hawaii, Honolulu, associate professor of history, 1971-2000, professor, 2001-02, now retired. **Publications:** Patterns of Vietnamese Response to Foreign Intervention, 1967; New Lamps for Old, 1983; Resistance, Rebellion, Revolution in Vietnamese History, 1984; (with others) A Bibliographic Index, 1984; (ed.) Borrowings and Adaptations in Vietnamese Culture, 1987; Colonialism Experienced, 2000. **Address:** 189 Polihale Pl, Honolulu, HI 96825, U.S.A. **Online address:** lamb@hawaii.edu

LAMA, Dalai XIV. (Tenzin Gyatso). Tibetan, b. 1935. **Genres:** Theology/Religion, Autobiography/Memoirs. **Career:** Enthroned as fourteenth Dalai Lama of Tibet in Lhasa, 1940; named king, 1950; worked in China and Tibet to end Chinese domination of Tibet, 1950-59; escaped to India and began self-imposed exile, 1959; established Tibetan government-in-exile in Dharamsala, India; has traveled widely in Asia, Europe, and the US. Held several ceremonial political posts in China, including Honorary Chairman of the

Chinese Buddhist Association, 1953-59; delegate to the National People's Congress, 1954-59; and Chairman of the Preparatory Committee for the Autonomous Region of Tibet, 1955-59. **Publications:** The International Position of Tibet, 1959; My Land and My People (autobiography), 1962; An Introduction to Buddhism, 1965; The Opening of the Wisdom-Eye and the History of the Advancement of the Buddhadharma in Tibet, 1968; Happiness, Karma, and Mind, 1969; The Key to Madhyamika, 1974; The Buddhism of Tibet and the Key to the Middle Way, 1975; The Sadhana of the Inseparability of the Spiritual Master and Avalokiteshvara; A Mahayana Method for Accomplishment, 1975; Universal Responsibility and the Good Heart, 1976; Teachings of His Holiness the Dalai Lama, 1981; Four Essential Buddhist Commentaries (in English and Tibetan), 1982; The Collected Statements, Articles, and Interviews of His Holiness the Dalai Lama, 1982; Advice from Buddha Shakyamuni, 1982; Kindness, Clarity, and Insight, 1984; A Human Approach to World Peace, 1984; (with others) Emerging Consciousness for a New Humankind (conference papers), 1985; Opening the Eye of New Awareness, 1985; The Kalachakra Tantra, 1985; Transcendent Wisdom, 1988; The Bodhgaya Interviews, 1988; The Dalai Lama at Harvard, 1988; The Union of Bliss and Emptiness, 1988; Tibet, China, and the World (interviews), 1989; Oceans of Wisdom, 1989; Freedom in Exile (autobiography), 1990; The Meaning of Life, 1990; My Tibet, 1990; (with others) MindScience, 1991; Cultivating a Daily Meditation, 1991; Path to Bliss, 1991; (with T. Jinpa) The World of Tibetan Buddhism, 1995; Violence and Compassion, 1995; The Power of Compassion, 1995; Essential Teachings, 1995; The Path to Enlightenment, 1995; Beyond Dogma, 1996; The Good Heart, 1996; The Joy of Living and Dying in Peace, 1997; (with A. Berzin) The Gelug/Kagyu Tradition of Mahamudra, 1997; Awakening the Mind, Lightening the Heart, 1997; The Way to Freedom, 1997; The Heart of Compassion, 1997; The Buddha Nature, 1997; The Four Noble Truths, 1998; The Art of Happiness, 1998; Spiritual Advice for Buddhists and Christians, 1998; The Dalai Lama's Book of Wisdom, 1999; The Heart of the Buddha's Path,, 1999; (with A. Benson and F. Ouaki) Imagine All the People, 1999; The Transformed Mind, 1999; The Path to Tranquility, 1999; Stages of Meditation, 2000; A Simple Path, 2000; (with J.K. Rinpoche) Buddha Heart, Buddha Mind, 2000; Transforming the Mind, rev. ed. as The Dalai Lama's Book of Transformation, 2000; Ethics for the New Millennium, 2000; (with R. Matthieu) The Spirit of Tibet, 2001; Live in a Better Way, 2001; (M. Gee, comp.) Words of Wisdom: Selected Quotes from His Holiness the Dalai Lama, 2001; Dzogchen, 2001; An Open Heart, 2001. Contributor to books. **Address:** Thekchen Choeling, Mcleod Ganj 176219, Dharamsala, Himachal Pradesh, India. **Online address:** www.dalailama.com

LAMAR, Howard Roberts. American, b. 1923. **Genres:** History, Reference. **Career:** University of Massachusetts, Amherst, Instructor in History, 1945-46; Wesleyan University, Middletown, CT, Assistant in Instruction, 1948-49; Yale University, New Haven, CT, Instructor, 1949-54, Assistant Professor, 1954-59, Associate Professor, 1959-64, Professor of History, 1964-98, Dean of Yale College, 1979-85, Acting President, 1992-93, Sterling Professor of History Emeritus, 1998-. **Publications:** Dakota Territory, 1861-1889: A Study of Frontier Politics, 1956, rev. ed., 1997; The Far Southwest, 1850-1912: A Political History of the Territories of Arizona, Colorado, New Mexico and Utah, 1966, rev. ed., 2000; Texas Crossings: The Lone Star State and the American Far West, 1991; New Encyclopedia of the American West, 1998. EDITOR: The Cruise of the Portsmouth, 1845-1847: A Sailor's View of the Naval Conquest of California, by Joseph T. Downey, 1958; Reader's Encyclopedia of the American West, 1977; (with L. Thompson) The Frontier in History: North America and Southern Africa Compared, 1981. **Address:** Dept. of History, Yale University, PO Box 208324, New Haven, CT 06520, U.S.A.

LAMAY, Craig L. American. **Genres:** Communications/Media. **Career:** Columbia University, NYC, Freedom Forum Media Studies Center; American Academy of Arts and Sciences, Cambridge, MA, Public Service Television Project, associate director; writer. **Publications:** (with N.N. Minow) Abandoned in the Wasteland: Children, Television, and the First Amendment, 1995. EDITOR (with E.E. Dennis): Media and the Environment, 1991; America's Schools and the Mass Media, 1993; The Culture of Crime, 1995. **Address:** American Academy of Arts and Sciences, Public Service Television Project, Nortons Woods, 136 Irving St., Cambridge, MA 02138, U.S.A.

LAMB, Andrew (Martin). British, b. 1942. **Genres:** Music. **Career:** Cooperative Insurance Society Ltd., Manchester, England, actuarial student, 1963-69; Smiths Industries Ltd., London, England, investment manager, 1969-73; Lloyds Bank Ltd., London, investment manager, 1973; Philips Industries, London, assistant investment manager, 1973-76; MGM Assurance, Worthing, England, assistant general manager, 1976-88; Friends Provident Life Office, London, chief investment manager, 1988-2000. **Publications: Jerome Kern in Edwardian London, 1985; (with K. Ganzl) Ganzl's Book of the Musical Theatre, 1988; Skaters' Waltz: The Story of the Waldteufels, 1995; An Offenbach Family Album, 1997; Shirley House to Trinity School, 1999; 150 Years of Popular Musical Theatre, 2000; Leslie Stuart: Composer of Florodora, 2002; (with J. Myerscough) Fragson: The Triumphs and the Tragedy, 2004. EDITOR: The Moulin Rouge, 1990; Light Music from Austria, 1992; Leslie Stuart: My Bohemian Life, 2003. Contributor to books and periodicals. **Address:** 12 Fullers Wood, Croydon, Surrey CR0 8HZ, England. **Online address:** andrew-lamb@light-music.net

LAMB, Arnette. American. **Genres:** Romance/Historical. **Career:** Writer. **Publications:** HISTORICAL ROMANCE NOVELS: Highland Rogue, 1991; The Betrothal, 1992; Border Lord, 1993; Border Bride, 1993; (with A. Mills and R. Bitner) Cherished Moments, 1994; Chieftan, 1994; Maiden of Inverness, 1995. CLAN MACKENZIE TRILOGY: Betrayed, 1995; Beguiled, 1996; True Heart, 1997. **Address:** c/o Pocket Books, 1230 Avenue of the Americas, New York, NY 10020, U.S.A.

LAMB, Brian. American, b. 1941. **Genres:** Documentaries/Reportage, Communications/Media. **Career:** United Press International, radio reporter, late 1960s; press secretary for P.H. Dominick, U.S. Senator for Colorado, late 1960s; White House Office of Telecommunications Policy, assistant to the director, 1971-74; Media Reports editor and Cablevision Washington bureau chief, mid-1970s; Cable-Satellite Public Affairs Network (C-SPAN), founder, chairman, and CEO, 1977-. **Publications:** (with the staff of C-SPAN) America's Town Hall: C-SPAN, 1988; Booknotes: Writers and Their Stories from C-SPAN's Author Interviews, 1997. **Address:** C-SPAN, 400 North Capitol St., Washington, DC 20001, U.S.A.

LAMB, Connie. American, b. 1947. **Genres:** Genealogy/Heraldry, Librarianship, Bibliography. **Career:** University of Utah, Salt Lake City, technician at Air Pollution Laboratory, 1972-73; Utah State Library Commission, Salt Lake City, reference librarian and information retrieval specialist, 1977-79; Brigham Young University, Provo, UT, chair of Computer-Assisted Research Services Department, 1979-87, reference specialist in the Department of History and Religion, 1988-2000, reference specialist in Social Science/ Education Department, 2000-; Jerusalem Center, Israel, librarian, 1987-88; writer. **Publications:** EDITOR: (with R.D. Jensen and N.M. Smith) Agricultural and Animal Sciences Journal and Serials: An Analytical Guide, 1986; (with G. Cronin and B. Hall) Jewish American Fiction Writers: An Annotated Bibliography, 1991. Contributor to library and genealogy periodicals. **Address:** 1202 Harold B. Lee Library, Brigham Young University, Provo, UT 84602, U.S.A.

LAMB, Elizabeth Searle. American, b. 1917. **Genres:** Poetry, Children's non-fiction, Inspirational/Motivational Literature, Literary criticism and history. **Career:** President, Haiku Society of America, NYC, 1971. Ed., Frogpond: Quarterly Haiku Journal, 1984-91, 1994. Co-ed., Haiku Southwest, 1993. Honorary Curator, The American Haiku Archive, California State Library, Sacramento, CA, 1996-97. **Publications:** (with J. Bailey and P. Markun) The Pelican Tree and Other Panama Adventures, 1953; Today and Every Day, 1971; Inside Me, Outside Me, 1974; In this Blaze of Sun, 1975; Picasso's Bust of Sylvette, 1977; 39 Blossoms, 1982; Casting into a Cloud, 1985; Lines for My Mother, Dying, 1988; The Light of Elizabeth Lamb: 100 American Haiku, 1993 (trans. into Chinese by Haipinq Gong); Ripples Spreading Out: Poems for Bruce and Others, 1997; Platek Irysa/Petals of Iris, 1998 (trans. by A. Szuba); Across the Windharp: Collected and New Haiku, 1999. **Address:** 970 Acequia Madre, Santa Fe, NM 87505, U.S.A. **Online address:** eslamb@earthlink.net

LAMB, Karl A(llen). American, b. 1933. **Genres:** Novels, Novellas/Short stories, Politics/Government. **Career:** Faculty member, University of Michigan, Ann Arbor, 1958-63; Assistant Professor, to Professor of Politics, University of California, Santa Cruz, 1963-85; U.S. Naval Academy, dean and professor, 1985-99. **Publications:** (with J. Pierce and J.P. White) Apportionment and Representative Institutions: The Michigan Experience, 1963; (with N.C. Thomas) Congress: Politics and Practice, 1964; (with P.A. Smith) Campaign Decision-Making, 1968; (ed.) Democracy, Liberalism and Revolution, 1971; The People, Maybe, 1971, 3rd ed., 1978; As Orange Goes, 1974; The Guardians: Leadership Values and the American Tradition, 1982; Reasonable Disagreement: Two U.S. Senators and the Choices They Make, 1998. **Address:** 1300 Bonito Ct, Arnold, MD 21012-2302, U.S.A. **Online address:** lamb.arnold@erols.com

LAMB, Nancy. Also writes as R. G. Austin, Anna Lain, Pamela Ryder. American, b. 1939. **Genres:** Novels, Mystery/Crime/Suspense, Children's fiction, Young adult fiction, Poetry, Children's non-fiction, Essays. **Career:** Writer. **Publications:** (with R.G. Gelman) Vampires and Other Creatures of the Night (nonfiction), 1991; The Great Mosquito, Bull and Coffin Caper, 1992; (with M. Singer) The World's Greatest Toe Show, 1994; One April Morning: Children Remember the Oklahoma City Bombing, 1996. "WHICH WAY BOOKS" WITH R.G. GELMAN AS R.G. AUSTIN: The Castle of No Return, 1982; Vampires, Spies and Alien Beings, 1982; The Spell of the Black Raven, 1982; Famous and Rich, 1982; Lost in a Strange Land, 1982; The Curse of the Sunken Treasure, 1982; Cosmic Encounters, 1982; Creatures of the Dark, 1982; Invasion of the Black Slime and Other Tales of Horror, 1983; Trapped in the Black Box, 1983; Poltergeists, Ghosts and Psychic Encounters, 1984; The Shadow Stealers, 1984; Islands of Terror, 1985; Ten-Ton Monster, 1985. "SECRET DOOR BOOKS" WITH R.G. GELMAN AS R.G. AUSTIN: Wow! You Can Fly!, 1983; Giants, Elves and Scary Monsters, 1983; The Haunted Castle, 1983; The Secret Life of Toys, 1983; The Visitors from Outer Space, 1983; The Inch-High Kid, 1983; The Magic Carpet, 1983; Happy Birthday to You, 1983; The Monster Family, 1984; Brontosaurus Moves In, 1984; The Enchanted Forest, 1984; Crazy Computers, 1984. FOR ADULTS: Gentlemen Callers, 1978; The End of Summer, 1981; (as Pamela Ryder) Dakin Field, 1984; (as Anna Lain) Prism, 1988; (with C. Brod) The Creative Revolution and the Future of Japan (nonfiction), 1993. **Address:** c/o Andrea Brown Literary Agency, 1076 Eagle Dr, Salinas, CA 93905, U.S.A. **Online address:** nancy@nancylamb.com

LAMB, Patricia Clare. American, b. 1935. **Genres:** Poetry. **Career:** Poet. **Publications:** POETRY: Why Horatio, 1985; Dwelling, 1988; All Men by Nature, 1993; The Long Love: New and Collected Poems, 1957-1998, 1998. **Address:** 3614 Montrose Blvd., #405, Houston, TX 77006, U.S.A.

LAMB, Sharon. American, b. 1955. **Genres:** Psychology. **Career:** Clinical psychologist. Melrose-Mindoro High School, WI, English teacher, 1977-78; Greater Lawrence Mental Health Center, Lawrence, MA, intern, 1980; Greenhouse Inc., intern, 1980-81; Cambridgeport Problem Center, psychotherapist, 1981; Massachusetts General Hospital, clinical fellow, evaluator, 1982-88; Mt. Ida Junior College, Newton, MA, lecturer, 1984-85; Judge Baker Children's Center, MA, psychologist, 1988-89; Boston Institute for Psychotherapy, Boston, MA, instructor, 1989; Bryn Mawr College, Bryn Mawr, PA, assistant professor of psychology, 1989-96; Child Study Institute, psychologist, 1989-96; Network of Victim Assistance, consulting psychologist, 1993-; St. Michael's College, Colchester, VT, associate professor, 1996-; Creamery Associates (private practice), 1998-. **Publications:** The Trouble with Blame: Victims, Perpetrators, and Responsibility, 1996; The Secret Lives of Girls: The Real Feelings of Young Girls about Sex, Violence, Peer Pressure, and Morality, 2002. EDITOR: (with J. Kagan) The Emergence of Morality in Young Children, 1987; (and contrib) New Versions of Victims: Feminists Struggle with the Concept, 1999; (with J.G. Murphy) Before Forgiving: Cautionary Views of Forgiveness in Psychotherapy, 2002. Contributor of articles and reviews to newspapers and professional journals. Contributor to books. **Address:** The Creamery, Box 367, Shelburne Rd., Shelburne, VT 05482, U.S.A. **Online address:** slamb@smcvt.edu

LAMB, Wally. (Walter). American, b. 1950. **Genres:** Novels, Poetry, Humanities. **Career:** Norwich Free Academy, Norwich, CT, English teacher, 1972-88, writing center director, 1988-97; University of Connecticut, director of creative writing, 1997-99; writer. **Publications:** NOVELS: She's Come Undone, 1992; I Know This Much Is True, 1998. EDITOR: Always Begin Where You Are (poetry textbook), 1979; Couldn't Keep It to Myself: Testimonies from Our Imprisoned Sisters, 2003. **Address:** c/o Darhansoff, Verrill, Feldman Literary Agents, 226 W 26th St, New York, NY 10001, U.S.A.

LAMBDIN, Dewey (W.). American, b. 1945. **Genres:** Romance/Historical. **Career:** WMC-TV 5, Memphis, TN, assistant director, 1969-72, producer and director, 1972-81; WPTY-TV 24, Memphis, production manager, 1981-84; free-lance camera and light technician and director, Nashville, TN, 1984-87; Admark Advertising, Nashville, writer and producer, 1987; writer. **Publications:** HISTORICAL NOVELS: The King's Coat, 1989; The French Admiral, 1990; The King's Commission, 1991; The King's Privateer, 1992; The Gun Ketch, 1993; HMS Cockerel, 1994; For King and Country (compendium), 1995; A King's Commander, 1997; Jester's Fortune, 1999; King's Captain, 2000; Sea of Grey, 2002; Havoc's Sword, 2003. **Address:** 141 Neese Dr Apt G-20, Nashville, TN 37211, U.S.A.

LAMBERT, Angela Maria. British, b. 1940. **Genres:** Novels, History. **Career:** Lord and Lady Listowel, London, England, maid, 1961; Cassells (publisher), London, editor, 1961-62; Modern Woman (magazine), assistant editor, 1962; British Government, London, civil servant (personal assistant to a British cabinet minister), 1965-69; journalist, 1969-72; Independent Television News, London, presenter and reporter in current affairs, 1972-76; Thames Television, London, presenter and reporter, 1976-88; Independent (newspaper), London, chief feature writer and interviewer, 1990-96; Daily Mail (newspaper) London, 1996-2000; Sunday Telegraph, 2000-; volunteer worker for the British Labour Party; member of International Visitors Programme. **Publications:** NON-FICTION: Unquiet Souls: The Indian Summer of the British Aristocracy, 1880-1918, as Unquiet Souls: A Social History of the Illustrious, Irreverent, Intimate Group of British Aristocrats Known as "The Souls," 1984; Nineteen Thirty-Nine: The Last Season of Peace, 1989. NOVELS: Love among the Single Classes, 1989; No Talking after Lights, 1990; A Rather English Marriage, 1992; The Constant Mistress, 1994; Kiss and Kin, 1997; Golden Lads and Girls, 1999; The Property of Rain, 2001. **Address:** c/o A.P. Watt, Literary Agents, 20 John Street, London WC1N 2DR, England. **Online address:** angelalambert@compuserve.com

LAMBERT, Darwin. American, b. 1916. **Genres:** Novels, History, Natural history, Autobiography/Memoirs. **Career:** Freelance writer. Ed., Travel Lore mag., Luray, Virginia, 1937-42, Commonwealth Review newspaper, Luray, VA, 1947-49, Ely Daily Times, NV, 1956-61, and Daily Alaska Empire newspaper, Juneau, 1961-64; Co-Ed., Exploring Earthmans' World, 1970-76. **Publications:** Beautiful Shenandoah, 1937; Illustrated Guide to Shenandoah National Park, 1942; Gold Strike in Hell (novel), 1964; Herbert Hoover's Hideaway, 1971; The Earth-Man Story, 1972; Timberline Ancients, 1972; Administrative History of Shenandoah National Park, 1979; The Undying Past of Shenandoah National Park, 1989; Great Basin Drama, 1991; Earth Sweet Earth (autobiography), forthcoming. **Address:** 1050 Morning Star Rd, Luray, VA 22835-5720, U.S.A. **Online address:** dlambert@shentel.net

LAMBERT, Gavin. American (born England), b. 1924. **Genres:** Novels, Plays/Screenplays, Film. **Career:** Ed., Sight and Sound, London, 1950-55. **Publications:** The Slide Area, 1959; Inside Daisy Clover, 1963, screenplay, 1965; Norman's Letter, 1966; A Case for the Angels, 1968; The Goodby People, 1971; On Cukor, 1972; GWTW: The Making of Gone with the Wind, 1973; The Dangerous Edge, 1976; In the Night All Cats Are Grey, 1976; Running Time, 1982; Norma Shearer, 1990; Alla Nazimova, 1997; Mainly About Lindsay Anderson, 2000; Natalie Wood: A Life, 2004. SCREENPLAYS: (co-author) Sons and Lovers, 1960; The Roman Spring of Mrs. Stone, 1961; I Never Promised You a Rose Garden, 1977; Second Serve, 1986; Sweet Bird of Youth, 1989; Dead on the Money, 1991. **Address:** c/o Alfred A. Knopf, Inc, 201 E. 50th St, New York, NY 10022, U.S.A.

LAMBERT, Page. American, b. 1952. **Genres:** Novels, Novellas/Short stories, Animals/Pets, Environmental sciences/Ecology, Local history/Rural topics, Social commentary, Women's studies and issues, Autobiography/Memoirs, Essays. **Career:** Writer. Presents workshops; gives readings from her works. **Publications:** In Search of Kinship: Modern Pioneering on the Western Landscape, 1996; Shifting Stars (novel), 1997. Work represented in anthologies. Contributor to magazines and newspapers. **Address:** PO Box 624, Sundance, WY 82729, U.S.A.

LAMBI, Ivo Nikolai. Canadian (born Estonia), b. 1931. **Genres:** Military/Defense/Arms control, History. **Career:** University of Toronto, Toronto, Ontario, lecturer in history, 1958-60; University of Omaha, Omaha, NE, instructor in history, 1960-61; University of Saskatchewan, Saskatoon, assistant professor, 1961-, professor of history, 1967-, head of department, 1969-74. **Publications:** Free Trade and Protection in Germany, 1868-1879, 1963; The Navy and German Power Politics, 1862-1914, 1985. **Address:** Department of History, University of Saskatchewan, Saskatoon, SK, Canada.

LAMBRECHT, Bill. American. **Genres:** Sciences. **Career:** St. Louis Post-Dispatch, St. Louis, MO, Washington correspondent, 1984-. Co-founder, Bay Weekly (newspaper). **Publications:** Dinner at the New Gene Café: How Genetic Engineering Is Changing What We Eat, How We Live, and the Global Politics of Food, 2001. **Address:** c/o St. Martin's Press, 175 Fifth Ave., New York, NY 10010, U.S.A.

LAMIRANDE, Emilien. Canadian, b. 1926. **Genres:** History, Theology/Religion. **Career:** Professor Emeritus, Dept. of Religious Studies, University of Ottawa, Ont., since 1988 (Lecturer, Assistant Professor, 1954-65; Professor, 1971-88). Professor, 1965-70, Chairman, 1972-74, and Dean, 1967-69, Faculty of Theology, St. Paul University, Ottawa; Fellow, Royal Society of Canada, 1984. **Publications:** Un siecle et demi d'etudes sur l'ecclesiologie de saint Augustin, 1962; What Is the Communion of Saints, 1963; L'Eglise celeste selon saint Augustin, 1963; Dieu chez les hommes-La signification du Pavillon chretien, 1967; Etudes sur l'Ecclesiologie de saint Augustin, 1969; La situation ecclesiologique des Donatistes chez saint Augustin, 1972;

Church, State and Toleration: An Intriguing Change of Mind in Augustine, 1975; Le P.G. Simard: Un disciple de saint Augustin, 1981; Paulin de Milan et la "Vita Ambrosii," 1982; Elisabeth Bruyere, fondatrice des Soeurs de la Charite d'Ottawa, 1993, trans. as Elisabeth Bruyere: Foundress of the Sisters of Cahrity of Ottawa, 1995; Une figure meconnue: Damase Dandurand, 1996. **Address:** 6467 Tellier, Rock Forest, QC, Canada J1N 3B1.

LAMM, Leonard Jonathan. American, b. 1945. **Genres:** Psychology. **Career:** Clinical psychologist and psychotherapist in private practice, NYC. Associated with Spunk Fund Inc. **Publications:** The Idea of the Past, 1993. **Address:** Spunk Fund Inc., 780 Third Ave., 24th Floor, New York, NY 10017, U.S.A.

LAMMERS, Stephen E. American, b. 1938. **Genres:** Medicine/Health, Theology/Religion. **Career:** Lafayette College, Easton, PA, professor of religious studies, 1969-. **Publications:** On Moral Medicine, 1998. **Address:** Department of Religious Studies, Lafayette College, Easton, PA 18042, U.S.A. **Online address:** lammerss@lafayette.edu

LAMMERS, Wayne P. American, b. 1951. **Genres:** Language/Linguistics, Literary criticism and history, Translations. **Career:** University of Wisconsin, Madison, assistant professor of Japanese, 1984-90; Lewis and Clark College, Portland, OR, assistant professor of Japanese, 1990-92; Mangajin Inc., Atlanta, GA, translations editor, 1991-97; self-employed translator and consultant, 1991-. **Publications:** The Tale of Matsura: Fujiwara Teika's Experiment in Fiction, 1992. TRANSLATOR: Junzo Shono, Still Life and Other Stories, 1992; Shohei Ooka, Taken Captive: A Japanese POW's Story, 1996; Junzo Shono, Evening Clouds, 2000; Taichi Yamada, Strangers, 2003. **Address:** 14960 SW 92nd Ave, Tigard, OR 97224, U.S.A. **Online address:** wlammers@mac.com

LAMMING, George (Eric). Barbadian, b. 1927. **Genres:** Novels. **Publications:** In the Castle of My Skin, 1953; The Emigrants, 1954; Of Age and Innocence, 1958; Season of Adventure, 1960; The Pleasures of Exile, 1960; Natives of My Person, 1971; Water with Berries, 1972; New World Quarterly, 1990; Coming, Coming Home, 1995; Conversations: Essays, Addresses and Interviews 1953-1990, 1996; Coming Home II, 2000. EDITOR: Cannon Shot and Glass Beads: Modern Black Writing, 1974; On the Canvas of the World, 1999; Enterprise of the Indies, 1999. **Address:** c/o Author Mail, House of Nehesi Publishers, PO Box 460, Philipsburg, St. Martin, Netherlands Antilles.

LAMMON, Martin. American, b. 1958. **Genres:** Poetry, Travel/Exploration. **Career:** Juniata College, Huntingdon, PA, visiting instructor in English, 1988-91; Fairmont State College, Fairmont, WV, assistant professor to associate professor of English, 1991-97; Georgia College and State University, Milledgeville, professor of English, appointed to Fuller E. Callaway Endowed Flannery O'Connor Chair in Creative Writing, 1997-. Also taught at Ohio University and Pennsylvania State University. Arts & Letters Journal of Contemporary Culture, founding editor, 1999-; Association of Writers and Writing Programs, president, 2000-02. **Publications:** (ed.) Written in Water, Written in Stone: Twenty Years of Poets on Poetry, 1996; News from Where I Live: Poems, 1998. Contributor of poems and articles to periodicals. **Address:** Dept of English Speech and Journalism, Campus Box 44, Georgia College and State University, Milledgeville, GA 31061, U.S.A. **Online address:** martin.lammon@gcsu.edu

LAMONDE, Yvan. Canadian. **Genres:** History. **Career:** French-Canadian historian specializing in the history of ideas and of publishing in Quebec; professor at McGill University, Montreal. **Publications:** Historiographie de la philosophie au Quebec, 1853-1970, 1972; Guide d'histoire du Quebec, 1976; (with S. Simard) Inventaire chronologique et analytique d'une correspondance de Louis-Antoine Dessaulles (1817-1895), Ministere des affaires culturelles, 1978; Les bibliotheques de collectivites a Montreal (17e-19e siecle): sources et problemes, 1979; (with P-F Hebert) Le cinema qu quebec: essai de statistique historique, 1896 a nos jours, 1981; (with D. Olivier) Les Bibliotheques personnelles au Quebec: inventaire analytique et preliminaire des sources, 1983; Je me souviens: la litterature personnelle au Quebec, 1860-1980, 1983; (with R. Monpetit) Le parc Sohmer de Montreal, 1889-1919: un lieu populaire de culture urbaine, 1986; (with M. Fontin and F. Ricard) Guide de la litterature quebecoise, 1988; L'Histoire des idees au Quebec, 17601960: bibliographies des etudes, 1989; Gens de parole: conferences publiques, essais et debats a l'Institut canadien de Montreal, 1845-1871, 1990; Territoires de la culture quebecoise, 1991; La librairie et l'edition a Montreal, 1776-1920, 1991; Louis-Antoine Dessaulles, 1818-1895: un seigneur liberal et anticlerical, 1994. EDITOR: (and contrib) L'Imprime au Quebec: aspects historiques, 18e-20e siecles, 1983; (with G. Bouchard)

Quebecois et Americains: la culture quebecoise aux XIXe et XXe siecles, 1995. **Address:** Department of French, McGill @UNV, 845 Sherbrooke St. W., Montreal, QC, Canada H3A 2T5.

LAMONT, Michele. Canadian, b. 1957. **Genres:** Sociology. **Career:** Stanford University, postdoctoral research fellow in sociology, 1983-85; University of Texas at Austin, assistant professor of sociology, 1985-87; Princeton University, assistant professor, 1987-92, associate professor of sociology, 1993-, fellow of Wilson College, 1987-89, faculty associate of Center for International Studies, Woodrow Wilson School of Public and International Affairs, 1990-, fellow of Rockefeller College, 1990-. Harvard University, visiting fellow, Center for European Studies, 1987; Ecole des Hautes Etudes en Sciences Sociales (Paris), visiting fellow, Group for Political and Moral Sociology, 1992; New York Public Library, scholar in residence, Schomburg Center for Research in Black Culture, 1992; New York University, visiting fellow, Institute of French Studies, 1993; Russell Sage Foundation, fellow, 1996-97; John Simon Guggenheim Memorial Foundation, fellow, 1996-97; Institute for Advanced Study, visiting scholar, Spring 1997. Lecturer at Washington University, St. Louis, MO, Brooklyn College of the City University of New York, Centre Culturel de Cerisy-LaSalle, Cornell University, Harvard University, and Sorbonne, University of Paris; guest on Canadian radio programs. **Publications:** (ed. with Marcel Fournier) Cultivating Differences: Symbolic Boundaries and the Making of Inequality, 1992; Money, Morals, and Manners: The Culture of the French and the American Upper-Middle Class, 1992. Work represented in anthologies. Contributor of articles and reviews to sociology journals. **Address:** Department of Sociology, Princeton University, Princeton, NJ 08544, U.S.A.

LAMONT-BROWN, Raymond. British, b. 1939. **Genres:** History, Local history/Rural topics, Mythology/Folklore, Paranormal, Travel/Exploration, Biography. **Career:** Author and broadcaster. Lecturer, Continuing Education Dept., University of St. Andrews, 1977-, and University of Dundee, 1987-. Writers' Monthly, managing editor, 1984-86. Japanologist, 1965-. Justice of the Peace (Scotland). **Publications:** The History of St. Mark's Church, Dewsbury 1865-1965, 1965; Book of Epitaphs, 1967; The Rural District of Doncaster Official Guide and Industrial Handbook, 1968; Clarinda: The Intimate Story of Robert Burns and Agnes Maclehose, 1968; Sir Walter Scott's Letters on Demonology and Witchcraft, 1968; Robert Burns's Commonplace Book 1783-85, 1969; A Book of Superstitions, 1970; A Book of Proverbs, 1970; A Book of Witchcraft, 1971; Charles Kirkpatrick Sharpe's History of Witchcraft in Scotland, 1972; Phantoms, Legends, Customs and Superstitions of the Sea, 1972; General Trade in Berwick on Tweed 1894, 1972; Robert Burns's Tour of the Border, 1972; Robert Burns's Tours of the Highlands and Stirlingshire, 1973; A New Book of Epitaphs, 1974; The Magic Oracles of Japan, 1974; Casebook of Military Mystery, 1974; Epitaph Hunting, 1977; Scottish Epitaphs, 1978; Phantoms of the Theatre, 1978; Growing Up with the Highland Clans, 1979; Lothian and Border Walks for Motorists, 1980; East Anglian Epitaphs, 1980; My Fun Book of Scotland, 1980; Victorian and Edwardian Fife from Old Photographs, 1980; The Victorian and Edwardian Borderland from Rare Photographs, 1980; Victorian and Edwardian Dundee, 1981; Mary, Queen of Scots, 1982; Mysteries and Legends, 1982; A Visitor's Guide to St. Andrews, 1984; St. Andrews: City of Change, 1984; A Book of British Eccentrics, 1984; Victorian and Edwardian Perthshire, 1984; Victorian and Edwardian Angus, 1985; Irish Grave Humour, 1987; Discovering Fife, 1988; The Life and Times of Berwick-upon-Tweed, 1988; The Life and Times of St. Andrews, 1989; Scottish Superstitions, 1990; Royal Murder Mysteries, 1990; Scottish Traditions and Festivals, 1991; Famous Scots, 1992; Scottish Witchcraft, 1994; Scottish Folklore, 1996; Kamikaze, 1997; 100 Years Ago, 1997; Kempeitai, 1998; Edward VII's Last Loves, 1998; John Brown, 2000; Ships from Hell, 2002; Fife in History & Legend, 2002; The Villages of Fife, 2002; Humphry Davy, 2004; Andrew Carnegie, 2005. **Address:** 11, Seabourne Gardens, Broughty Ferry, Dundee DD5 2RT, Scotland.

LAMOTT, Anne. American, b. 1954. **Genres:** Food and Wine. **Career:** WomenSports, San Mateo, CA, staff writer, 1974-75; worked in a restaurant in Petaluma, CA; writer, 1980-; California Magazine, food reviewer, 1987-89; Mademoiselle magazine, book review columnist, 1990-92. **Publications:** NOVELS: Hard Laughter, 1980; Rosie, 1983; Joe Jones, 1985; All New People, 1989; Crooked Little Heart, 1997; Blue Shoe, 2002. OTHER: Operating Instructions: A Journal of My Son's First Year, 1993; Home and Other Stories: Catherine Wagner, 1993; Bird by Bird: Some Thoughts on Writing and Life, 1994; Traveling Mercies, 1999.

LAMPERT, Ada. Israeli, b. 1942. **Genres:** Psychology. **Career:** Ruppin Institute, Emek Hefer, Israel, professor of psychology, 1984-. Military

service: Israel Defense Forces. **Publications:** The Evolution of Love, 1997. Author of two books in Hebrew. **Address:** Ruppin Institute, 40250 Emek Hefer, Israel. **Online address:** alampert@ruppin.ac.il

LAMPHEAR, John. American, b. 1941. **Genres:** History. **Career:** Ohio University, Athens, visiting assistant professor, 1972-73; DePauw University, Greencastle, IN, director of African studies, 1973-79; University of Illinois at Urbana-Champaign, visiting assistant professor, 1979-80; University of Texas at Austin, professor of history, 1980-. **Publications:** The Traditional History of the Tie, 1976; The Scattering Time, 1992. **Address:** Department of History, University of Texas at Austin, Austin, TX 78712, U.S.A.

LAMPITT, Dinah. British, b. 1937. **Genres:** Novels, Romance/Historical, Mystery/Crime/Suspense. **Career:** Worked as junior writer for Woman magazine, assistant to the news editor of London Times, and assistant to the fiction editor of London Evening News, all during 1950s; free-lance writer, 1960s-1980s; full time writer 1980s-1990s. Director of plays and musicals for southern England theater groups. **Publications:** Sutton Place, 1983; The Silver Swan, 1984; Fortune's Soldier, 1985; To Sleep No More, 1987; Pour the Dark Wine, 1989; The King's Women, 1992; As Shadows Haunting, 1993; Banishment, 1994; Death in the Dark Walk, 1994; Death at the Beggar's Opera, 1995; Death at the Devil's Tavern, 1996; Death on the Romney Marsh, 1998. **Address:** c/o Darley Anderson, Estelle House, 11, Eustace Rd., London SW6 1JB, England.

LAMPLUGH, Lois. British, b. 1921. **Genres:** Children's fiction, Poetry, History, Autobiography/Memoirs, Biography, Local history/Rural topics, Photography. **Career:** Full-time writer. Member of the editorial staff, Jonathan Cape Ltd., London, England, 1947-57; served in the Auxiliary Territorial Service, 1939-43. **Publications:** The Stream Way (autobiography), 1948; The Old Navigator 1967; Honeyhill (for television), 1967-70; The Quarry Hare (adult verse), 1976; Barnstaple: Town on the Taw (history), 1983; A History of Ilfracombe, 1984; Minehead with Dunster (history), 1987; A Shadowed Man: Henry Williamson, 1895-1977 (biography), 1990; Take off from Chivenor (history), 1990; Lundy: Island without Equal (history), 1993; A Book of Georgeham and the Northwest Corner of Devon, 1995; Ilfracombe in Old Photographs, 1996; Two Rivers Meeting, 1998. FOR CHILDREN: The Pigeongram Puzzle, 1955; Nine Bright Shiners, 1955; Vagabonds' Castle, 1957; Rockets in the Dunes, 1958; The Sixpenny Runner, 1960; Midsummer Mountains, 1961; The Rifle House Friends, 1965; The Linhay on Hunter's Hill, 1966; The Fur Princess and the Fir Prince, 1969; Mandog (adaptation of TV serial), 1972; Sean's Leap, 1979; The Winter Donkey, 1980; Falcon's Tor, 1984; Sandrabbit, 1991. **Address:** c/ AP Watt, 20 John St., London WC1N 2DR, England.

LAMPPA, William R. American, b. 1928. **Genres:** Poetry. **Career:** Social Worker, Hennepin County Community Services, Minneapolis, Minnesota, 1964-87, retired. **Publications:** The Crucial Point and Other Poems, 1971; In Familiar Fields with Old Friends, 1972; The Ancient Chariot and Other Poems, 1973. **Address:** P. O. Box 81, Embarrass, MN 55732, U.S.A.

LAN, David. British (born Republic of South Africa), b. 1952. **Genres:** Plays/Screenplays, Anthropology/Ethnology, Translations. **Publications:** Painting a Wall, 1974; Bird Child, 1974; Homage to Been Soup, 1975; Paradise, 1975; Red Earth, 1976; The Winter Dancers, 1977; Sergeant Ola, 1979; Guns and Rain: Spirit Mediums and Guerrillas in Zimbabwe (nonfiction), 1985; (with C. Churchill) A Mouthful of Birds, 1986; Flight, 1986; The Ends of Earth, 1996; Tobias and the Angel (libretto), 1999; Collected Plays One, 1999. PLAYS/SCREENPLAYS: The Sunday Judge (TV), 1985; The Crossing (TV), 1988; Desire and Other Plays, 1990; Dark City (TV), 1990; Welcome Home Comrades (TV), 1990; Artist Unknown (TV), 1995; Charley Tango (radio), 1995; Royal Court Diaries (TV), 1996. ADAPTOR: J. Sobol, Ghetto, 1989; Euripides, Hippolytos, 1991; Euripides Ion, 1994; Verga, La Lupa, 1996; Chekhov, Uncle Vanya, 1998. **Address:** c/o Judy Daish Associates, 3 St. Charles Place, London W10 6EG, England.

LANCASTER, David. See **HEALD, Tim(othy Villiers).**

LANCASTER, Jane F(airchild). American, b. 1940. **Genres:** History. **Career:** Amory High School, Amory, MS, teacher of social studies and department head, 1969-73; homemaker and civic volunteer, Hamilton, MS, 1973-81; Mississippi State University, Mississippi State, teaching fellow, 1981-86; self-employed historian and author, 1986-. **Publications:** Removal Aftershock: The Seminoles' Struggles to Survive in the West, 1836-1866, 1994. BOOKLET: Hamilton Take Your Place in History As the First County Seat of Monroe, 1975. Contributor to books and encyclopedias; contributor of articles and reviews to periodicals.

LANCASTER, Michael (L.). British, b. 1928. **Genres:** Architecture, Homes/Gardens, Art/Art history, Design. **Career:** British Rail, assistant architect, 1948-57; architect in London, England, 1957-58; Fry, Drew, Drake & Lasdun, resident architect in Ibadan, Nigeria, 1958-61, architect in London, 1961-63; Derek Lovejoy and Partners, Colombo Plan adviser for the new capital city of Islamabad, West Pakistan, 1963-65; Gloucestershire College of Art and Design, senior/principal lecturer in landscape architecture, 1967-70; private practice in architecture, landscape architecture, and color consultancy, 1967-; Thames Polytechnic (now University of Greenwich), principal lecturer in landscape architecture and head of the division, 1970-91. London Borough of Richmond, member of Conservation Areas Advisory Committee, 1988-; lecturer in Europe, Russia, and the United States. **Publications:** Britain in View: Colour and the Landscape, 1984; (ed. with P. Goode, G. Jellicoe, and S. Jellicoe, and contrib.) The Oxford Companion to Gardens, 1986; The Colour Eye No. 5 (for TV), 1990; The Earthdwellers Guide No. 3 (for TV), 1991; The New European Landscape, 1994; Colourscape, 1996; Coloured Places, forthcoming. and. Contributor to books and periodicals. **Address:** 297 Lonsdale Rd., London SW13 9QB, England.

LANCASTER, Roger N(elson). American, b. 1959. **Genres:** Anthropology/Ethnology. **Career:** Evergreen State College, Olympia, WA, faculty member, 1987-88; George Mason University, Fairfax, VA, assistant professor of anthropology, 1988-93, associate professor, 1995-; Columbia University, NYC, associate professor of anthropology, 1993-95. **Publications:** Thanks to God and the Revolution: Popular Religion and Class Consciousness in the New Nicaragua, 1988; Life Is Hard: Machismo, Danger, and the Intimacy of Power in Nicaragua, 1992; (ed. with M. Di Leonardo) The Gender Sexuality Reader: Culture, History, Political Economy, 1997. Contributor to periodicals. **Address:** Department of Sociology and Anthropology, George Mason University, MS5, Fairfax, VA 22030-4444, U.S.A. **Online address:** cultural@gmu.edu

LANCASTER BROWN, Peter. British, b. 1927. **Genres:** Novels, Archaeology/Antiquities, Astronomy, Geography, Travel/Exploration. **Publications:** Twelve Came Back, 1957; Call of the Outback, 1970; What Star Is That?, 1971; Astronomy in Colour, 1972, 5th ed. 1983; Coast of Coral and Pearl, 1972; The Seas and Oceans in Colour, 1973; Comets, Meteorites and Men, 1973; Star and Planet Spotting, 1974, 1981; (ed. and co-author) The Lore of Sport Fishing, 1974; Megaliths, Myths, and Men, 1976; The Planet Earth, 1976; Megaliths and Masterminds, 1979; Fjord of Silent Men, 1982; Close Encounter Objects, 1983; The High Tatra Affair, 1983; Astronomy (Colour Library of Science), 1984; Halley and His Comet, 1985; Halley's Comet and the Principia, 1986; The Comet Man: Memoirs of Edmond Halley, 1987; The Man I Might Have Been: A Creative Autobiography of Jack London, 1988; Skywatch, 1993. **Address:** 10A St. Peter's Rd, Aldeburgh, Suffolk, England.

LANCE, James Waldo. Australian, b. 1926. **Genres:** Medicine/Health. **Career:** Neurologist, Prince Henry Hospital, Sydney, NSW, 1961-92; Professor of Neurology, University of New South Wales, Sydney, 1975-92, Associate Professor of Medicine, 1964-75; Consultant in Neurology, The Institute of Neurological Sciences, Prince of Wales Hospital, Sydney, 1992-. **Publications:** The Mechanism and Management of Headache, 1969, 6th ed., 1998; A Physiological Approach to Clinical Neurology, 1970, 3rd ed., 1981; The Golden Trout, 1978; Introductory Neurology, 1984, (co-author) 3rd ed., 1995; Migraine and Other Headaches, 1986. **Address:** Wales Medical Centre, Suite 5A, 66 High Street, Sydney, NSW 2031, Australia.

LANCE, Peter. American. **Genres:** Mystery/Crime/Suspense. **Career:** Daily News, Newport, RI, reporter; WNET, NYC, producer and reporter; Manhattan District Attorney's Office, trial preparation assistant; American Broadcast Company (ABC), NYC, field producer, 1978-1981, chief investigative correspondent, 1981-87; screenwriter and novelist. **Publications:** First Degree Burn, 1997. Author of scripts for Miami Vice; writer and consulting producer, Jag and The Sentinel. **Address:** c/o Berkley Publishing Group, 375 Hudson St., New York, NY 10014, U.S.A. **Online address:** netgraph@earthlink.net

LAND, Ben. See ROSENBERG, Robert.

LANDAU, Paul Stuart. American, b. 1962. **Genres:** History. **Career:** University of New Hampshire, Durham, assistant professor of African history, 1992-95; Yale University, New Haven, CT, assistant professor of African history, 1995-99; University of Maryland at College Park, associate professor, 1999-. **Publications:** The Realm of the Word: Language, Gender, and Christianity in a Southern African Kingdom, 1995. **Address:** Department of History, University of Maryland, College Park, MD 20742, U.S.A.

LANDAU, Susan. American, b. 1954. **Genres:** Information science/Computers. **Career:** Wesleyan University, Middletown, CT, assistant professor, 1983-89; University of Massachusetts at Amherst, research associate professor of computer science, 1989-99; Sun Microsystems, senior staff engineer, 1999-. **Publications:** (with W. Diffie) Privacy on the Line: The Politics of Wiretapping and Encryption, 1998. **Address:** Sun Microsystems, MSUBUR02-311, PO Box 4002, Burlington, MA 01803, U.S.A.

LANDER, Ernest McPherson, Jr. American, b. 1915. **Genres:** History. **Career:** Professor Emeritus of History, Clemson University, South Carolina (joined faculty, 1941). Fulbright Lecturer in American History, Jadavpur University, Calcutta, India, 1966-67, and University of Lagos, Nigeria, 1970-71. **Publications:** A History of South Carolina, 1865-1960, 1960; (ed. with C. M. McGee) A Rebel Came Home: The (Civil War) Diary of Florida Clemson, 1961, 1989; The Textile Industry in Antebellum South Carolina, 1969; South Carolina: The Palmetto State, 1970; (ed. with R.K. Ackerman) Perspectives in South Carolina History: The First 300 Years, 1973; (ed. with R.J. Calhoun) Two Decades of Change: The South since the Supreme Court's Desegregation Decision, 1975; Reluctant Imperialists: Calhoun, the South Carolinians, and the Mexican War, 1980; The Calhoun Family and Thomas Green Clemson: The Decline of a Southern Patriarchy, 1983; South Carolina: An Illustrated History of the Palmetto State, 1988; Tales of Calhoun Falls, 1991; From Clemson College to India in World War II, by a GI Who Never Saw the Enemy, 1992; The Life and Times of Ella Lorton, A Pendleton SC Confederate, 1996; Few Would Listen: A Clemson Professor's Memoir of Dissent, 1997. **Address:** 217 Riggs Dr, Clemson, SC 29631, U.S.A.

LANDER, Jack Robert. Canadian/British, b. 1921. **Genres:** History. **Career:** Professor Emeritus of History, University of Western Ontario, London, Ont. (Professor from 1965). Sr. Lecturer in History, University of Ghana, 1950-63; Associate Professor, Dalhousie University, Halifax, N. S., 1963-65. **Publications:** The Wars of the Roses, 1967; Conflict and Stability in Fifteenth Century England, 1969; Ancient and Medieval England: Beginnings to AD 1509, 1973; Crown and Nobility 1450-1509, 1976; Government and Community: England 1450-1509, 1980. **Address:** 5 Witherington Rd., London N5 1PN, England.

LANDES, Richard. American (born France), b. 1949. **Genres:** History. **Career:** Columbia University, NYC, postdoctoral fellow, 1984-86; University of Pittsburgh, PA, assistant professor of history, 1986-91; Boston University, MA, assistant professor to associate professor of history, 1991-. Center for Millennial Studies, director; also director of a project to publish the Opera Omnia of Ademar of Chabannes. **Publications:** Naissance d'Apotre: Les origines de la "Vita prolixior" de Saint Martial de Limoges au XIe siecle, 1991; Relics, Apocalypse, and the Deceits of History: Ademar of Chabannes, 989-1034, 1995. EDITOR: (with T. Head) The Peace of God: Social Violence and Religious Response in France Around the Year 1000, 1992; (with D. Van Meter) The Apocalyptic Year 1000: Studies in the Mutation of European Culture, in press. **Address:** Department of History, Boston University, 226 Bay State Rd., Boston, MA 02215, U.S.A.

LANDESMAN, Peter. American, b. 1965. **Genres:** Novels. **Career:** Author, painter, and journalist. **Publications:** NOVELS: The Raven, 1995; Blood Ace, 1999. Contributor to periodicals. **Address:** c/o Sloan Harris, ICM, 40 W 57th St, New York, NY 10019, U.S.A.

LANDIS, Geoffrey A(lan). American, b. 1955. **Genres:** Science fiction/Fantasy, Air/Space topics, Sciences. **Career:** Physicist and writer. Spire Corporation, Bedford, MA, staff scientist, 1977-82; Solar Energy Research Institute, Golden, CO, research associate, 1986-87; National Aeronautics and Space Administration (NASA) Lewis Research Center, Cleveland, OH, research associate, 1988-90; Ohio Aerospace Institute, Brook Park, OH, adjunct professor, 1990-92, senior research associate, 1995-2000; Sverdup Technology, Brook Park, OH, physicist, 1994-95; NYMA Inc., Brook Park, senior engineer, 1994-95; NASA John Glenn Research Center, physicist, 1999-. **Publications:** Myths, Legends, and True History, 1991; Mars Crossing (novel), 2000; Impact Parameter (short stories), 2001. EDITOR: Vision-21, Space Travel for the Next Millennium, 1991; Vision-21, Interdisciplinary Science and Engineering, 1993. Contributor to anthologies. Author of science fiction short stories; contributor to professional journals. **Address:** NASA John Glenn Research Center 302-1, 21000 Brookpark Rd, Cleveland, OH 44135, U.S.A.

LANDIS, Jill Marie. American, b. 1948. **Genres:** Romance/Historical. **Career:** Writer. Worked as a ride operator, sold shaved ice and cleaned condos and vacation rentals, elementary school educator for twelve years; teaches writing workshops and seminars. **Publications:** HISTORICAL-

ROMANCE NOVELS: Sunflower, 1988; Wildflower, 1989; Rose, 1990; Jade, 1991; Come Spring, 1992; Past Promises, 1993; Until Tomorrow, 1994; After All, 1995; Last Chance, 1995; Day Dreamer, 1996; Just Once, 1997. Author of novellas published in anthologies. **Address:** c/o Penguin/Putnam/ Berkley Publishing Group, 375 Hudson, New York, NY 10014, U.S.A.

LANDMAN, Jessica C. American, b. 1955. **Genres:** Environmental sciences/Ecology. **Career:** U.S. House of Representatives, Washington, DC, legislative aide, 1977-80; U.S. Department of Transportation, Washington, DC, honors attorney in office of the general counsel, 1984-86; Natural Resources Defense Council, Washington, DC, attorney, 1986-99, senior counsel, 2001-; Pew Oceans Commission, director of publications, 2000-01. Member of the Bars of the District of Columbia and the State of Maryland. **Publications:** Poison Runoff, 1989; (coauthor) The Clean Water Act Twenty Years Later, 1993; Prescription for Clean Water, 1997. Contributor to books. **Address:** 232 Park Ave, Takoma Park, MD 20912, U.S.A. **Online address:** j.landman@worldnet.att.net

LANDON, H(oward) C(handler) Robbins. American, b. 1926. **Genres:** Music. **Career:** University College, Cardiff, John Bird Professor of Music, from 1978. **Publications:** The Symphonies of Joseph Haydn, 1955; The Collected Correspondence and London Notebooks of Joseph Haydn, 1959; Beethoven, 1970; Haydn: Chronicle and Works (biography), 5 vols., 1976-80; Mozart and the Masons, 1982; Handel and his World, 1984; 1791: Mozart's Last Year, 1988; Mozart: The Golden Years, 1989; Mozart and Vienna, 1991; (with J. J. Norwich) Maestro: Five Centuries of Music in Venice, 1991; Vivaldi, 1993; The Mozart Essays, 1995; Horns in High C-A Memoir of Musical Discoveries and Adventures, 1999. EDITOR/CO-EDITOR: The Mozart Companion, 1956, 1970; Complete Symphonies, by Haydn, 1965-68; Complete String Quartets, by Haydn, 1968-83; Complete Piano Trios, by Haydn, 1970-78; The Mozart Compendium, 1990. **Address:** Foncoussieres, 81800 Rabastens (Tarn), France.

LANDON, Lucinda. American, b. 1950. **Genres:** Children's fiction, Illustrations. **Career:** Writer and Illustrator, Providence, Rhode Island, 1978-. Advertising Assistant, Boston Center for the Arts, 1974-75; special education teacher, Cambridge, Massachusetts, 1975-76. **Publications:** (also illustrator) Meg Mackintosh and the Case of the Missing Babe Ruth Baseball, 1986; Meg Mackintosh and the Case of the Curious Whale Watch, 1987; Meg Mackintosh and the Mystery at the Medieval Castle, 1989; Meg Mackintosh and the Mystery at Camp Creepy, 1990; Meg Mackintosh and the Mystery in the Locked Library, 1993; Meg Mackintosh and the Mystery at the Soccer Match, 1997; American History Mysteries, 1999; Meg Mackintosh and the Mystery on Main Street. Illustrator of books by W.V. Butler. **Address:** 26 Tucker Hollow, North Scituate, RI 02857, U.S.A.

LANDRUM, Gene N. American, b. 1935. **Genres:** Novels, Intellectual history, Psychology, Self help, Writing/Journalism, Biography. **Career:** Entrepreneur; started businesses, including the Chuck E. Cheese pizza chain; real estate business broker in Florida; Condyne Technology, Orlando, FL, president, c. 1993-. Speaker at colleges, universities, and organizations. **Publications:** Profiles of Genius: Thirteen Creative Men Who Changed the World, 1993; Profiles of Female Genius: Thirteen Creative Women Who Changed the World, 1994; Profiles of Power, 1995; Profiles of Black Success, 1997; Prometheus 2000, 1997; Eight Keys to Greatness, 1999; Profiles of Literary Genius, 2000; Sybaritic Genius, 2001; Entrepreneurial Genius, 2004; The Superman Syndrome, 2005; Empowerment, 2006. **Address:** 7897 Cocobay Dr, Naples, FL 34108-6510, U.S.A. **Online address:** Genie13@ compuserve.com

LANDSBERG, Brian K. American, b. 1937. **Genres:** Law. **Career:** U.S. Department of Justice, Civil Rights Division, Washington, DC, trial attorney and supervisory attorney, 1964-69, chief of Education Section, 1969-74, chief of Appellate Section, 1974-86; University of the Pacific, Sacramento, CA, visiting professor, 1984-85, professor of law, 1986-. Georgetown University, adjunct professor, 1981-84; University of California, Berkeley, visiting professor at Boalt Hall, 1995, 1997. U.S; Department of Justice, acting deputy assistant attorney general in Civil Rights Division, 1993-94; Lawyers Committee for Civil Rights under Law, member of board of trustees; member of U.S. Supreme Court Bar; inactive member of California State Bar and Bar of the District of Columbia. **Publications:** Enforcing Civil Rights: Race Discrimination and the Civil Rights Division, 1997; (ed.-inchief) Major Acts of Congress, 2004. Contributor of articles and reviews to periodicals. **Address:** McGeorge School of Law, University of the Pacific, 3200 Fifth Ave, Sacramento, CA 95817, U.S.A. **Online address:** blandsberg@uop.edu

LANDSBERG, Melvin. American, b. 1926. **Genres:** Literary criticism and history, Biography, Essays, Humor/Satire. **Career:** University of Kansas,

Lawrence, faculty member, 1961-, currently professor of English. **Publications:** Dos Passos' Path to U.S.A., 1972; (ed.) John Dos Passos' Correspondence with Arthur K. McComb, or, Learn to Sing the Carmagnole, 1991. **Address:** Department of English, University of Kansas, Lawrence, KS 66045, U.S.A.

LANDSBURG, Steven E(lliot). American, b. 1954. **Genres:** Economics. **Career:** Economics and mathematics educator. University of Iowa, Iowa City, assistant professor, 1981-85; Cornell University, Ithaca, NY, visiting assistant professor, 1983; University of Rochester, Rochester, NY, visiting assistant professor 1986-88; Colorado State University, Fort Collins, associate professor, 1989-; University of Rochester, visiting associate professor, 1991-. Visitor, Institute for Advanced Study, Princeton, NJ, 1982, 1983, 1988; research associate, Institute for Definitive Analysis, Princeton, NJ, 1987, and Queens University, Kingston, Ontario, Canada, 1986. Member, Rochester Center for Economic Research, Rochester, NY, 1987-. **Publications:** Price Theory and Applications, 1989, 1992, 1995, 1998; The Armchair Economist: Economics and Everyday Life, 1993; (with L.J. Feinstone) Macroeconomics, 1997; Fair Play: What Your Child Can Teach You about Economics, Values, and the Meaning of Life, 1997. Contributor to mathematics, philosophy, and economics journals. **Address:** Department of Economics, Harkness 225, University of Rochester, Rochester, NY 14627, U.S.A.

LANDY, Marcia. American, b. 1931. **Genres:** Film. **Career:** University of Pittsburgh, PA, assistant professor to professor of English and film studies, 1967-. **Publications:** Fascism in Film, 1986; British Genres, 1991; Imitations of Life, 1991; Queen Christina, 1996; Cinematic Uses of the Past, 1997; The Folklore of Consensus, 1998; Film, Politics, and Gramsci, 1994; Italian Film, 2000; The Historical Film: History and Memory in Cinema, 2001. **Address:** Department of English, 526 CL, University of Pittsburgh, Pittsburgh, PA 15260, U.S.A. **Online address:** mlandyt@pitt.edu

LANE, Abbe. American, b. 1935. **Genres:** Romance/Historical. **Career:** Entertainer and writer. **Publications:** But Where Is Love?, 1993.

LANE, Connie. See LAUX, Constance.

LANE, Dakota. American, b. 1959. **Genres:** Young adult fiction. **Career:** Freelance writer, c. 1996-. **Publications:** Johnny Voodoo (juvenile novel), 1996. Contributor to periodical. **Address:** PO Box 591, Woodstock, NY 12498, U.S.A.

LANE, Dixie. See SALAZAR, Dixie.

LANE, Harlan. American, b. 1936. **Genres:** Intellectual history, Psychology, Language/Linguistics. **Career:** University Distinguished Professor, 1988-, Professor, Dept. of Psychology, Northeastern University, Boston, 1974-88 (Chairman of the Dept., 1974-79). Assistant Professor, 1960-64, Associate Professor, 1964-67, and Professor of Psychology, 1967-71, University of Michigan, Ann Arbor; Professor of Linguistics, University of Paris-Sorbonne, 1969-73. **Publications:** (with D. Bem) A Laboratory Manual for the Control and Analysis of Behavior, 1964; (with G. Capelle) The World's Research in Language Learning, 1969; Introduction aa l'aetude du langage, 1972; The Wild Boy of Aveyron: A History of the Education of Retarded, Deaf and Hearing Children, 1976; The Wild Boy of Burundi: Psychological Catastrophies of Childhood, 1979; (trans. with F. Philip) Major Philosophical Works of Etienne Bonnot de Condillac, 1982; When the Mind Hears: A History of the Deaf, 1984; The Mask of Benevolence: Disabling the Deaf Community, 1992; (with R. Hoffmeister and B. Bahan) A Journey into the Deaf-World, 1996. EDITOR: (with F. Grosjean) Current Perspectives on American Sign Language, 1980; (with F. Philip) The Deaf Experience: Classics in Language and Education, 1984; (with C. Carroll) Diary of a Deaf Boy: The Youth of Laurent Clerc, 1991; (with R. Fischer) Looking Back: A Reader on the History of Deaf Communities and Their Sign Languages, 1993; Education and Access for Deaf People in France and the United States, 1994. **Address:** Psychology Dept, Northeastern University, 125 Nightingale Hall, 360 Huntington, Boston, MA 02115, U.S.A. **Online address:** lane@neu.edu

LANE, Nancy. American, b. 1947. **Genres:** Literary criticism and history. **Career:** Indiana University-Bloomington, associate instructor in French, 1969-76; University of South Carolina at Columbia, assistant professor, 1977-88, associate professor of French, 1988-, coordinator of French Division, 1984-85, 1986-88. Haverford College, visiting assistant professor, 1985. **Publications:** Understanding Eugene Ionesco, 1994. Contributor of articles and reviews to language and literature journals. **Address:** Department of French and Classics, University of South Carolina at Columbia, Columbia, SC 29208, U.S.A.

LANE, Nick. American. **Genres:** History. **Career:** Science writer, biochemist, freelance communications consultant, musician, and researcher. MRC Clinical Research Centre, scientific officer, 1988-91; Oxford Clinical Communications, medical writer, 1995-96; Medi Cine International, London, England, senior writer/producer, 1996-99; Adelphi Medi Cine, London, strategic director, 1999-2002. University College, University of London, honorary senior research fellow, 1997-. Fiddle player with the London-based Celtic band Probably Not. **Publications:** Oxygen: The Molecule That Made the World, 2002; (editor, with Erica E. Benson and Barry J. Fuller) Life in the Frozen State, 2004. **Address:** Caroline Dawnay, PFD, Drury House, 34-43 Russell St., London WC2B 5HA, England. **Online address:** n.lane@rfc.ucl.ac.uk

LANE, Simon. British, b. 1957. **Genres:** Novellas/Short stories. **Career:** Writer. **Publications:** May, In New York, and The Clipper Seamen's Bride (trilogy), 1985; The Hostage Returns, 1989; Le Veilleur, 1990; Still Life With Books, 1993; Fear, 1998. **Address:** Hotel la Louisiane, 60 rue de Seine, 75006 Paris, France.

LANE, Terry. Australian, b. 1939. **Genres:** Novels. **Career:** Radio broadcaster, minister, and writer. Australia Broadcasting Corporation (aBC), religious department, broadcaster, 1977, 1982-93; Methodist Department of Christian education, teacher; The National Interest (radio program), ABC, and Jon Faine's program, 3LO, 1993-. **Publications:** Famous Leaders Through the Ages (juvenile), 1966; As the Twig is Bent; GOD: The Interview, 1993; Hectic (novel), 1993; Tit for Tat, 1994; Sparrow's Fall (novel), 1995. Author of essays, articles and stories. **Address:** PO Box 93, Forest Hill, VIC 3131, Australia. **Online address:** lanet@alexia.net.au

LANG, Anthony E. Canadian, b. 1951. **Genres:** Medicine/Health. **Career:** Toronto Western Research Institute, Toronto, Ontario, Canada, senior scientist, 1985-; Toronto Western Hospital, director of Morton and Gloria Shulman Movement Disorder Clinic, 1993-; University of Toronto, Jack Clark Chair for Parkinson's Disease Research and professor of medicine and neurology, 2000-. **Publications:** WITH W.J. WEINER: Movement Disorders: A Comprehensive Survey, 1989; (L. Shulman) Parkinson's Disease: A Complete Guide for Patients and Families, 2001. EDITOR WITH W.J. WEINER: Drug-induced Movement Disorders, 1992; Behavioral Neurology of Movement Disorders, 1995. Author of studies in professional journals. Contributor to clinical reference books on movement disorders. **Address:** University of Toronto Movement Disorders Research Centre, The Toronto Hospital Western Division, MP11-306, 399 Bathhurst Street, Toronto., ON, Canada M5T 2S8.

LANG, Gladys Engel. American. **Genres:** Communications/Media, Sociology. **Career:** Professor of Communications, Political Science, and Sociology, University of Washington, Seattle, 1984-90, emeritus since 1990. Professor of Sociology, State University of New York, Stony Brook, 1970-84. **Publications:** (ed.) Mental Health, 1958; (with Kurt Lang) Collective Dynamics, 1961; (ed.) Old Age in America, 1961; (with Kurt Lang) Politics and Television, 1968; (with Kurt Lang) Voting and Nonvoting, 1968; (with Kurt Lang) The Battle for Public Opinion: The President, The Press, and the Polls During Watergate, 1983; (with Kurt Lang) Politics and Television Re-Viewed, 1984; (with Kurt Lang) Etched in Memory: The Building and Survival of Artistic Reputation, 1990. **Address:** 1249 20th Ave. E, Seattle, WA 98112, U.S.A.

LANG, Jenifer Harvey. American, b. 1951. **Genres:** Children's non-fiction, Food and Wine. **Career:** Restaurateur and writer. "21" Club Restaurant, New York City, cook, c. 1976-78; Nathans, Washington, DC, chef, 1978-; Cafe des Artistes, New York City, managing director, 1992-. Journalist; consumer spokesperson; has appeared on television programs. **Publications:** Tastings: The Best from Ketchup to Caviar, 1986; (ed. with others) Larousse Gastronomique, 1988, rev. ed., 1998; Jenifer Lang Cooks for Kids: 153 Recipes and Ideas for Good Food that Kids Love to Eat, 1991; Best of Kitchen Basics, 1996. **Address:** Cafe des Artistes, 1 W 67th St, New York, NY 10023, U.S.A.

LANG, Judith. British (born Egypt), b. 1939. **Genres:** Theology/Religion. **Career:** Writer. **Publications:** Ministers of Grace, 1989; (ed. with L. de Bruin) M. Casey, A Net in Water, 1994; The Angels of God, 1997. **Address:** Redwood, Colebatch, Bishop's Castle, Shropshire SY9 5JY, England.

LANG, King. See TUBB, E(dwin) C(harles).

LANG, Kurt. American (born Germany), b. 1924. **Genres:** Art/Art history, Communications/Media, Sociology. **Career:** Director, School of Communications, University of Washington, 1984-93, emeritus, 1993-. Research Sociologist, CBC, Ottawa, Ont., 1954-56; Instructor, 1956-59; Assistant Professor, 1959-62, and Associate Professor of Sociology and Chairman, 1963-64, Queens College of the City University of New York, NYC; Professor of Sociology, State University of New York, Stony Brook, 1964-84. **Publications:** (with G.E. Lang) Collective Dynamics, 1961; (with G.E. Lang) Voting and Nonvoting, 1968; (with G.E. Lang) Politics and Television, 1968; Military Institutions and Sociology of War, 1972; (with G.E. Lang) The Battle for Public Opinion, 1983; (with G.E. Lang) Politics and Television Re-Viewed, 1984; (with G.E. Lang) Etched in Memory: The Building and Survival of Artistic Reputation, 1990, rev. ed., 2001. **Address:** 1249 20th Ave E, Seattle, WA 98112, U.S.A. **Online address:** lang@u.washington.edu

LANG, Paul. American, b. 1948. **Genres:** Travel/Exploration. **Career:** Model High School, Roxbury, MA, instructor, 1977-78; worked in corporate writing, editing, and word processing, 1981-; freelance writer, 1991-. Organizer and leader of informal book discussions, Bridgewater State Correctional Institution, Bridgewater, MA, 1972; volunteer instructor, Cambodian Refugee Center, Chicago, IL, beginning 1984; tutor of English for Chinese immigrants, 1987-. **Publications:** (with S.S. Lang) Censorship, 1993; (with S. Lang) Teen Fathers, F. Watts, 1995; The English-Language Debate: Should America Have One Official Language?, 1995. **Address:** 1844 Commonwealth Ave. No. 8, Brighton, MA 02135, U.S.A.

LANG, Susan S. American, b. 1950. **Genres:** Medicine/Health, Psychology, How-to books, Adult non-fiction, Self help. **Career:** Post-Star, Glens Falls, reporter and photographer, 1975-77; Cornell University, Ithaca, NY, research assistant to astronomer Carl Sagan, author, senior manuscript editor of Icarus: Journal of Planetary Sciences, 1977-79; free-lance writer, 1977-; Cornell News Service, Ithaca, senior science writer, 1980-86, 1991-. **Publications:** Women without Children: Reasons, Rewards, Regrets, 1991; Extremist Groups in America, 1990; Teen Violence, 1991; Invisible Bugs and Other Creepy Creatures that Live With You, 1991; (with P. Lang) Censorship, 1993; (with R. Patt) You Don't Have to Suffer: A Complete Guide to Relieving Cancer Pain for Patients and Their Families, 1994; Nature in Your Backyard, 1994; (with P. Lang) Teen Fathers, 1995; Teens and Tobacco, 1996; More Nature in Your Backyard, 1999; (with L. Robbins) Headache Help: A Complete Guide to Understanding Headaches and the Medicines that Relieve Them, 2000. Author of articles. **Address:** 563 Ellis Hollow Creek Rd, Ithaca, NY 14850, U.S.A. **Online address:** SSL4@cornell.edu

LANG, William L. American, b. 1942. **Genres:** Local history/Rural topics. **Career:** Carroll College, Helena, MT, associate professor, 1970-78; Montana Historical Society, Helena, executive editor, 1978-89; Center for Columbia River History, Vancouver, WA, director, 1990-94; Portland State University, Portland, OR, professor of history, 1994-. **Publications:** Montana: A History of Two Centuries, 1991; Centennial West, 1991; Stories from an Open Country, 1995; Confederacy of Ambition, 1996; Great River of the West, 1999. **Address:** Department of History, Portland State University, Portland, OR 97207, U.S.A. **Online address:** langw@pax.edu

LANGA, Mandla. South African, b. 1950. **Genres:** Novels, Novellas/Short stories, Poetry. **Career:** African National Congress, cultural attache, London, England, beginning in 1995. **Publications:** NOVELS: Tenderness of Blood, 1987; A Rainbow on the Paper Sky, 1989; Memory of Stones (novel), 2000. SHORT STORIES: The Naked Song and Other Stories, 1996. Author of poems. Contributor to anthologies. **Address:** c/o David Philip Publishers, PO Box 23408 Claremont 7735, 208 Werdmuller Centre Newry St, Claremont, Cape Town 7700, Republic of South Africa. **Online address:** mlanga@icon.co.za

LANGBAUM, Robert (Woodrow). American, b. 1924. **Genres:** Literary criticism and history. **Career:** James Branch Cabell Professor of English and American Literature, University of Virginia, Charlottesville, 1967- (Associate Professor, 1960-63, and Professor, 1963-67); Instructor in English, 1950-55, and Assistant Professor, 1955-60, Cornell University, Ithaca, NY. Member, Editorial Board, Victorian Poetry, 1963-, New Literary History, 1969-, Bulletin of Research in the Humanities, 1977-, Studies in English Literature, 1978-, Southern Humanities Review, 1979-, Studies in Browning and His Circle, 1987-, Victorian Literature and Culture, 1991-, Browning Studies, 1993. **Publications:** The Poetry of Experience: The Dramatic Monologue in Modern Literary Tradition, 1957, 1986; The Gayety of Vision: A Study of Isak Dinesen's Art, 1964; The Modern Spirit: Essays on the Continuity of Nineteenth and Twentieth Century Literature, 1970; The Mysteries of Identity: A Theme in Modern Literature, 1977; The Word from Below: Essays on Modern Literature and Culture, 1987; Thomas Hardy in Our Time, 1995. EDITOR: The Tempest, by Shakespeare, 1964; The Victorian Age: Essays in History and in Social and Literary Criticism, 1967. **Address:** Dept. of English, University of Virginia, PO Box 400121, 219 Bryan Hall, Charlottesville, VA 22904, U.S.A. **Online address:** rwl8v@virginia.edu

LANGBEIN, John Harriss. American, b. 1941. **Genres:** History, Law. **Career:** University of Chicago Law School, assistant professor, 1971-73, associate professor, 1973-74, professor, 1974-80, Max Pam Professor of American and Foreign Law, 1980-90; Yale University, New Haven, CT, Chancellor Kent Professor, 1990-2001, Sterling Professor of Law and Legal History, 2001-. **Publications:** Prosecuting Crime in the Renaissance: England, Germany, France, 1974; Torture and the Law of Proof: Europe and England in the Ancien Raegime, 1977; Comparative Criminal Procedure: Germany, 1977; (with L. Waggoner) Selected Statutes on Trusts and Estates, 1987, 2001; (with B. Wolk) Pension and Employee Benefit Law, 1990, 3rd ed., 2000; (with R.H. Helmholz et al.) The Privilege against Self-Incrimination, 1997. **Address:** Yale Law School, PO Box 208215, New Haven, CT 06520-8215, U.S.A. **Online address:** john.langbein@yale.edu

LANGDON, E(sther) Jean Matteson. American, b. 1944. **Genres:** Anthropology/Ethnology. **Career:** Universidad del Cauca, Popayan, Colombia, part-time professor, 1973; John Jay College of Criminal Justice of the City University of New York, NYC, adjunct professor of anthropology, 1974-76; Cedar Crest College, Allentown, PA, associate professor, 1976-84; Universidade Federal de Santa Catarina, Santa Catarina, Brazil, professor of social anthropology, 1983-, vice coordinator of Pos-Graduacao de Ciencias Sociais, 1986-88, 1996-98. Indiana University-Bloomington, research associate; major field research includes interdisciplinary research in anthropology of health, shamanism, Indian health policy, and performance. **Publications:** (ed. with G. Baer, and contrib.) Portals of Power: South American Shamanism, 1992; (ed. with M. Cipoletti, and contrib.) Concepciones de la Muerte y el mas alla, 1992; Novas perspectivas de xamanismo no Brasil, 1994. Work represented in anthologies. Contributor to sociology and anthropology journals. **Address:** Pos-Graduacao em Antropologia, Universidade Federal de Santa Catarina, Florianopolis, 888040-970 Santa Catarina, Brazil. **Online address:** jean@cfh.ufsc.br

LANGDON, Philip. American, b. 1947. **Genres:** Architecture, Regional/Urban planning. **Career:** Freelance writer on architecture and design 1982-94, 1998-; Progressive Architecture Magazine, senior editor, 1994-96; Connecticut Conference of Municipalities, writer/editor, 1996-99; American Enterprise Magazine, associate editor, 1997-2000, contributing writer, 2000-; New Urban News, associate editor, 2002-03, senior editor, 2003-. **Publications:** Orange Roofs, Golden Arches: The Architecture of American Chain Restaurants, 1986; American Houses, 1987; Urban Excellence: 1989; (with S. Thomas) This Old House Kitchens, 1992; (with S. Thomas) This Old House Bathrooms, 1993; A Better Place to Live: Reshaping the American Suburbs, 1994; (ed. with J. King) The CRS Team and the Business of Architecture, 2002. **Address:** 178 E Rock Rd, New Haven, CT 06511, U.S.A.

LANGE, Arthur D. American, b. 1952. **Genres:** Literary criticism and history, Poetry. **Career:** Brilliant Corners: A Magazine of the Arts, publisher and editor, 1975-77; Chicago Council on Fine Arts, Chicago, IL, artist in residence, 1977-78; Columbia College, Chicago, instructor, 1979-. School of the Art Institute of Chicago, member of board of directors of Poetry Center, 1982-87; Jazz Institute of Chicago, member of board of directors, 1984-, past vice president; Chicago International Film Festival, judge, 1988-. **Publications:** (ed. with Nathaniel Mackey, and contrib.) Moment's Notice: Jazz in Poetry and Prose, 1993. POETRY: Needles at Midnight; Evidence; The Monk Poems; Glee: Song. Work represented in anthologies. Contributor of several hundred articles, poems, and reviews to magazines. **Address:** 6553 North Artesian, Chicago, IL 60645, U.S.A.

LANGE, James E(dward) T(homas). American. **Genres:** Criminology/True Crime, History, Law. **Career:** Lawyer practicing in Silver Spring, MD, 1983-. Metropolitan Washington Ear, volunteer broadcaster, 1976-; Montgomery County Chief Judge of Election, 1976-. **Publications:** (with K. DeWitt, Jr.) Chappaquiddick: The Real Story, 1993. Contributor to periodicals. **Address:** 10221 Menlo Ave, Silver Spring, MD 20910, U.S.A. **Online address:** langejameset@aol.com

LANGE, John. See CRICHTON, (John) Michael.

LANGENDOEN, D. Terence. American, b. 1939. **Genres:** Language/Linguistics. **Career:** Professor of Linguistics, University of Arizona, Tucson, 1988-. Assistant Professor, 1964-68, and Associate Professor, 1968-69, Ohio State University, Columbus; Professor, Brooklyn College and Graduate Center, City University of New York, 1969-88. **Publications:** The London

School of Linguistics, 1968; The Study of Syntax, 1969; Essentials of English Grammar, 1970; (with P.M. Postal) The Vastness of Natural Language, 1984. EDITOR: (with C.J. Fillmore) Studies in Linguistic Semantics, 1971; (with T.G. Bever and J.J. Katz) An Integrated Theory of Linguistic Ability, 1976; (with D.B. Archangeli) Optimality Theory: An Overview, 1997. **Address:** Dept of Linguistics, University of Arizona, PO Box 210028, Tucson, AZ 85721-0028, U.S.A. **Online address:** langendt@u.arizona.edu

LANGER, Erick D. American, b. 1955. **Genres:** History. **Career:** Carnegie-Mellon University, Pittsburgh, PA, assistant professor, 1984-90, associate professor of Latin American history, 1990-. University of Pittsburgh, adjunct associate professor, 1990-. **Publications:** (ed. with Zulema Bass Werner de Ruiz) Historia de Tarija: Corpus Documental, 1988; Economic Change and Rural Resistance in Southern Bolivia, 1880-1930, 1989; (ed. with R.H. Jackson) The New Latin American Mission History, 1995. Contributor to periodicals. **Address:** Department of History, Carnegie-Mellon University, 5000 Forbes Ave., Pittsburgh, PA 15213, U.S.A.

LANGFORD, David. British, b. 1953. **Genres:** Science fiction/Fantasy, Literary criticism and history. **Career:** Freelance writer, 1980-; managing director, Ansible Information, 1987-; columnist, Interzone, SFX and Fortean Times; weapons physicist, Atomic Research Establishment, 1975-80. **Publications:** SCIENCE FICTION. NOVELS: The Space Eater, 1982; The Leaky Establishment, 1984; (with J. Grant) Earthdoom!, 1987; (with J. Grant) Guts, 2001. STORY COLLECTIONS: The Dragonhiker's Guide to Battlefield Covenant at Dune's Edge: Odyssey Two, 1988; Irrational Numbers, 1994; (ed.) Maps: The Uncollected John Sladek, 2002; He Do the Time Police in Different Voices, 2003; Different Kinds of Darkness (stories), 2004. OTHER GENRES: (with others) The Necronomicon, 1978; War in 2080: The Future of Military Technology, 1979; An Account of a Meeting with Denizens of Another World 1871, 1979; (with C. Morgan) Facts and Fallacies: A Book of Definitive Mistakes and Misguided Predictions, 1981; (with P. Nicholls and B.M. Stableford) The Science in Science Fiction, 1982; (with C. Platt) Micromania (in US as The Whole Truth Home Computer Handbook), 1984; (with B.M. Stableford) The Third Millennium: The History of the World AD 2000-3000, 1985; The Unseen University Challenge, 1996; (ed. with J. Clute and J. Grant, contrib. ed.) The Encyclopedia of Fantasy, 1997; (with J. Kirby) A Cosmic Cornucopia, 1999; The Wyrdest Link, 2002. NON-FICTION COLLECTIONS: Critical Assembly, 1987; Critical Assembly II, 1992; Let's Hear It for the Deaf Man, 1992; The Silence of the Langford, 1996; Pieces of Langford, 1998; The Complete Critical Assembly, 2001; (ed.) Wrath of the Fanglord, 1998; Up through and Empty House of Stars, 2003; The SEX Column and Other Misprints, 2005. **Address:** 94 London Rd, Reading, Berks. RG1 5AU, England. **Online address:** ansible@cix.co.uk

LANGFORD, Gary R(aymond). New Zealander, b. 1947. **Genres:** Novels, Plays/Screenplays, Poetry, Novellas/Short stories. **Career:** Writer. Sr. Lecturer in Creative Writing, University of Western Sydney, 197?-. Ed., Macarthur Literary Review, 1984-. Ed., Ironbark, 1977-83; Co-Ed., Edge Literary Magazine, 1970-72; Director, Playhouse Theatre, 1982-86. **Publications:** POETRY: The Family, 1973; Four Ships, 1981; The Pest Exterminator's Shakespeare, 1984; Bushido, 1987; Strange City, 1988; Love at the Traffic Lights, 1990; Jesus the Galilee Hitch-Hiker, 1991; Confessions of a Nude Revolutionary, 2000. NOVELS: Death of the Early Morning Hero, 1976; Players in the Ballgame, 1979; The Adventures of Dreaded Ned, 1980; Vanities, 1984; Pillbox, 1986; A Classical Pianist in a Rock 'n Roll Band, 1989; Newlands, 1990, radio script, 1992; The Politics of Dancing, 1994; Friday Always Wanted to Be Tuesday, 1997. PLAYS: Lovers, 1977; Getting On, 1977; Reversals, 1978; I Didn't Ask to Grow Old, 1978; Superman, The True Story, 1979; Don't Jump Out That Window-You're Feeling Fine, 1982; Reunion, 1984; Who's Killing the Great Actors of Macbeth, 1984; Playing Moliere, 1984, radio script, 1993. MUSICALS: Flappers, 1982; Captain Australia, 1983; Doctor Repulsion's Rock 'n' Roll Horror Show, 1983; Soaps, 1984. EDITOR: Superbox, 1971; Shard, 1972. TELEVISION SCRIPTS: Quartet, 1973; Golden Handshake, 1974. STORIES: The Death of James Dean, 1978; A Library Is a Place of Love, 1989; Lunch in the Storyteller's Restaurant, 2001. RADIO SCRIPTS: The Couple Who BBQ Cats, 1995; Epicurean, 1996; A Family Hero, 1997. OTHER: The Writer's Dictionary (textbook), 1999. **Address:** c/o University of Western Sydney, Locked Bag 1797, Penrith South OC, NSW 1797, Australia. **Online address:** g.langford@uws.edu.au

LANGFORD, Gerald. See Obituaries.

LANGHOLM, Neil. See BULMER, (Henry) Kenneth.

LANGLEY, Andrew. British, b. 1949. **Genres:** Children's non-fiction. **Career:** Children's book author. Penguin Books, London, England, marketing assistant, 1974-78. **Publications:** FOR CHILDREN. NON-SERIES: Explorers on the Nile, 1981; Working in the Army: A Guide for Young People, 1983; The Superpowers, 1983; The First Men Round the World, 1983; Ian Botham (biography), 1983; Cleopatra and the Egyptians, 1985; Doctor, 1985; Energy, 1985; John F. Kennedy (biography), 1985; Librarian, 1985; The Making of the Living Planet, 1985; Peoples of the World, 1985; The Army, 1986; Combat Pilot, 1986; A Family in the Fifties, 1986; The Royal Air Force, 1986; The Royal Navy, 1986; Sailor, 1986; Airports, 1987; Cars, 1987; Genghis Kahn and the Mongols, 1987; Travel Games for Kids, 1987; The World of Sharks, 1987; Twenty Names in Pop Music, 1987; Travel Quizzes for Kids, 1988; Twenty Explorers, 1988; Twenty Names in Crime, 1988; (with M. Butterfield) People, 1989; Sport, 1989; Sport and Politics, 1989;(with T. Reynolds, T. Furniss, N. Hawkes, J. Sherwin, and V. Tulling) World Issues, 2 vols., 1990; Trucks and Trailers, 1991; Young Sailor, 1993; Grasslands, 1993; The Illustrated Book of Questions and Answers, 1993; Wetlands, 1993; The Industrial Revolution, 1994; The Age of Industry, 1994; Medieval Life, 1996; (with P. de Souza) The Roman News, 1996; Victorian Factories, 1996; Victorian Railways, 1996; The Search for Riches, 1996; Shakespeare and the Theatre, 1996; (with G. Wood) Life in a Victorian Steamship, 1997; Tudor Palaces, 1997; Food and Farming, 1997; Hans Christian Andersen, 1997; Alexander the Great: The Greatest Ruler of the Ancient World, 1997; Amelia Earhart: The Pioneering Pilot, 1997; Oxford First Encyclopedia, 1998; Trade and Transport, 1998. BEHIND THE SCENES SERIES: Radio Station, 1983; Hotel, 1983; Car Ferry, 1983; Football Club, 1983; Supermarket, 1983; Police Station, 1985; Post Office, 1985; Newspapers, 1985. ORIGINS SERIES: A Cup of Tea, 1982; The Meat in Your Hamburger, 1982; The Paper in Your Home, 1982. TOPICS SERIES: Great Disasters, 1985; Under the Ground, 1985; Television, 1986; Jungles, 1986. PASSPORT SERIES: Passport to Great Britain, 1985. FOCUS ON SERIES: Focus on Wool, 1985; Focus on Vegetables, 1985; Focus on Timber, 1986, in US as Spotlight on Timber, 1987; Focus on Vegetables, 1986. SPOTLIGHT ON SERIES: Spotlight on Airports, 1987; Spotlight on Aircraft, 1987; Spotlight on Dinosaurs, 1987; Spotlight on Aircraft, 1987, in the US as Aircraft, 1989; Spotlight on Spacecraft, 1987; Spotlight on the Moon, 1987, in the US. as The Moon, 1988; Spotlight on Trees, 1987. LET'S LOOK AT SERIES: Let's Look at Bikes, 1988, in the US as Bikes and Motorcycles, 1989; Let's Look at Trucks, 1988, in the US as Trucks, 1989; Let's Look at Circuses, 1989; Let's Look at Aircraft, 1989, in the US as Aircraft; Let's Look at Trains, 1989, in the US as Trains; Let's Look at Racing Cars, 1990, in the US as Racing Cars; Let's Look at Monster Machines, 1990, in the US as Monster Machines. THE STORY OF SERIES: (with S. Alcantara and J.D. Hofilena) The Story of the Philippines, 1989; The Story of Singapore, 1990; (with G. Bailey) The Story of India, 1990. RESOURCES SERIES: Copper, 1981; Paper, 1991; Steel, 1992. HISTORY OF BRITAIN SERIES: The Tudors, 1485 to 1603, 1993; The Stuarts, 1603 to 1714, 1993; Georgian Britain 1714 to 1837, 1994; Victorian Britain, 1837 to 1901, 1994; Modern Britain: 1901 to the 1990s, 1994; Queen Victoria, 1995; The Blitz, 1939-1945, 1995; The Home Front, 1995; Elizabeth I, 1996; Shakespeare and the Theatre, 1996. GREAT EXPLORERS SERIES: Discovering the New World: The Voyages of Christopher Columbus, 1994; Exploring the Pacific: The Expeditions of Captain Cook, 1994; The Great Polar Adventure: The Journeys of Roald Amundsen, 1994; Journey into Space: The Missions of Neil Armstrong, 1994. 100 GREATEST SERIES: 100 Greatest Tyrants, 1996; 100 Greatest Inventions, 1997; 100 Greatest Men, 1997; 100 Greatest Women, 1997; 100 Greatest Sports Champions, 1997; 100 Greatest Man-made Wonders, 1997; 100 Greatest Medical Discoveries, 1997; 100 Greatest Explorers, 1997; 100 Greatest Disasters, 1997; 100 Greatest Natural Wonders, 1997; 100 Greatest Amazing Animals, 1997; 100 Greatest Archaeological Discoveries, 1997. FOR ADULTS: (ed., with J. Utting) The Village on the Hill: Aspects of Colerne History, 1990; Glenfiddich: Made without Compromise since 1887, 1995; London Pride: 150 Years of Fuller, Smith and Turner, 1845-1995, 1995. **Address:** 8 Chapel Path, Colerne, Wilts. SN14 8DL, England.

LANGLEY, Charles P(itman), III. American, b. 1949. **Genres:** Children's fiction. **Career:** Shelby Medical Associates, physician (internal medicine), 1979-, president. **Publications:** Catherine and Geku: The Adventure Begins, 1996; Catherine, Anna, and Geku Go to the Beach, 1997; North, East, South, West: Catherine, Anna and Geku Take a Long Trip, 2001. **Address:** 82 Fairview Farms, Shelby, NC 28150, U.S.A. **Online address:** cplffarms@aol.com

LANGLEY, Lester D(anny). American, b. 1940. **Genres:** History, Politics/Government. **Publications:** The Cuban Policy of the United States: A Brief History, 1968; Struggle for the American Mediterranean: United States-European Rivalry in the Gulf Caribbean, 1976; The United States and the Caribbean 1900-1970, 1980, 1985; The Banana Wars: An Inner History of American Empire 1900-1934; Central America: The Real Stakes, 1985; Mex-America: Two Countries, One Future, 1988; America and the Americas: The

United States in the Western Hemisphere, 1989; The United States and the Caribbean in the 20th Century, 1989; Mexico and the United States: The Fragile Relationship, 1991; The Americas in the Age of Revolution, 1750-1850, 1996. EDITOR: The United States, Cuba and the Cold War: American Failure or Communist Conspiracy, 1970; (co-) The United States and Latin America, 1971.

LANGMEAD, Donald. Australian, b. 1939. **Genres:** Architecture. **Career:** University of Adelaide, South Australia Institute of Technology, Adelaide, Australia, lecturer, 1967-76, senior lecturer in architectural history, 1976-89, acting head of interior design, 1976-80; University of South Australia, Adelaide, principal lecturer, 1990-94, associate professor, 1995-98, professor of architecture, 1998-, professor of architectural history at Louis Laybourne Smith School of Architecture and Design, 1999, head of Louis Laybourne Smith School of Architecture, 1992-96, associate dean of research, 1998. University of Delft, guest lecturer, 1987; public speaker on architecture and architectural history; architectural history consultant. **Publications:** (with J.R. Schenk) Guide to the Architecture of Adelaide, 1982; (with D.L. Johnson) The Adelaide City Plan: Fiction and Fact, 1986; English Language Sources on Dutch Modern Architecture, 1900-1940: Monographs Not by Dutch Authors, 1986; English Language Sources on Dutch Modern Architecture, 1900-1940: Journal Articles Not by Dutch Authors, 1986; Dutch Modern Architecture, 1900-1940: Perceptions of Dutch Architects, Writers, and Editors, Illinois, 1987; Accidental Architect: G.S. Kingston, Pioneer and Builder, 1994; Willem Dudok: A Dutch Modernist, 1996; Dutch Modernism: Architectural Resources in the English Language, 1996; (with Johnson) Makers of Twentieth Century Modern Architecture, 1997; J.J.P. Oud and the International Style: A Bio-Bibliography, 1999; (with Johnson) Architectural Excursions: Frank Lloyd Wright, Holland, and Europe, 1999. Contributor to periodicals. **Address:** Louis Laybourne Smith School of Architecture and Design, University of South Australia, Adelaide, SA 5000, Australia. **Online address:** don.langmead@unisa.edu.au

LANGSTON, Douglas C. American, b. 1950. **Genres:** Philosophy. **Career:** New College of Florida, Sarasota, professor of philosophy and religion, 1977-. **Publications:** God's Willing Knowledge, 1986; Conscience and Other Virtues: From Bonaventure to MacIntyre, 2001. **Address:** New College of Florida, 5700 Tamiami Trail, Sarasota, FL 34243, U.S.A. **Online address:** langston@ncf.edu

LANGTON, Jane. American, b. 1922. **Genres:** Mystery/Crime/Suspense, Children's fiction. **Publications:** The Majesty of Grace, 1961, as Her Majesty, Grace Jones, 1972; The Diamond in the Window, 1962; The Transcendental Murder, 1964; The Swing in the Summer House, 1967; The Astonishing Stereoscope, 1971; The Boyhood of Grace Jones, 1972; Dark Nantucket Noon, 1975; Paper Chains, 1977; The Memorial Hall Murder, 1978; The Fledgling, 1980; Natural Enemy, 1982; Emily Dickinson Is Dead, 1984; The Fragile Flag, 1984; The Hedgehog Boy, 1985; Good and Dead, 1986; Murder at the Gardner, 1988; The Dante Game, 1991; God in Concord, 1992; Salt, 1992; Divine Inspiration, 1993; The String of Pearls, 1994; The Shortest Day, 1995; Dead as a Dodo, 1996; The Face on the Wall, 1998; The Thief of Venice, 1999; The Time Bike, 2000; Murder at Monticello, 2001; The Escher Twist, 2002; The Deserter, Murder at Gettysburg, 2003. **Address:** 9 Baker Farm Rd, Lincoln, MA 01773, U.S.A. **Online address:** janelangton@earthlink.net; www.janelangton.com

LANGUIRAND, Jacques. Canadian, b. 1931. **Genres:** Plays/Screenplays. **Career:** Playwright, essayist, and producer; professor at McGill University, Montreal, 1972-. **Publications:** PLAYS: Le Roi Ivre (The Drunken King), 1950; Les Insolites (The Unusual Ones), 1956; Les Grands Departs (Great Departure), 1958; Le Gibet, 1958; Les Insolites et Les Violons de L'Automne (The Usual Ones and Violins of Autumn), 1960; Les Cloisons (one-act dialogue), 1960; Diogene (one-act tragi-comedy), 1965; Klondyke (musical), 1965; L'Age de Pierre (multi-media show), trans. as Man Inc., 1970; L'Ecole du Rire (ballet-comedy), 1982. OTHER: Le Dictionnaire Insolite, 1962; Tout Compte Fait, 1963; De McLuhan a Pythagore, 1972; La Voie Initiatique, 1978; Vivre Sa Vie, 1979; Mater Materia, 1980. **Address:** 368 RTE 143, Ulverton, QC, Canada J0B 2B0.

LANGUM, David J. American, b. 1940. **Genres:** History, Biography. **Career:** Admitted to the California state bar, 1966. Private practice, San Francisco, CA, 1966-68, and San Jose, CA, 1968-78; Detroit College of Law, Detroit, MI, professor of law, 1978-83; Nevada School of Law, Reno, professor of law, 1983-85; Samford University, Birmingham, AL, Cumberland School of Law, professor of law, 1985-. **Publications:** (ed.) Law in the West, 1985; Law and Community on the Mexican California Frontier: Anglo-American Expatriates and the Clash of Legal Traditions, 1821-1846, 1987;

(with H. Hague) Thomas O. Larkin: A Life of Profit and Patriotism in Old California, 1990; Crossing over the Line: Legislating Morality and the Mann Act, 1994; (with H.P. Walthall) From Maverick to Mainstream: Cumberland School of Law, 1847-1997, 1997; William M. Kunstler: The Most Hated Lawyer in America, 1999. **Address:** Cumberland School of Law, Samford University, 800 Lakeshore Dr, Birmingham, AL 35229, U.S.A. **Online address:** djlangum@samford.edu

LANHAM, Richard Alan. American, b. 1936. **Genres:** Literary criticism and history, Writing/Journalism. **Career:** Emeritus Professor of English, University of California, Los Angeles, 1994- (Assistant Professor, 1965-69; Associate Professor, 1969-72; Professor, 1972-94; Director, 1979-82, and Executive Director, 1982-86, Writing Progs.). Instructor, and Assistant Professor, Dartmouth College, Hanover, New Hampshire, 1962-65. **Publications:** Sidney's Old Arcadia, 1965; A Handlist of Rhetorical Terms, 1968; 2nd ed. 1991; Tristram Shandy: The Games of Pleasure, 1973; Style: An Anti-Textbook, 1974; The Motives of Eloquence, 1976, repr., 2004; Revising Prose, 1979, 4th ed., 2000; Revising Business Prose, 1981, 4th ed., 2000; Analyzing Prose, 1983, 2nd ed., 2003; Literacy and the Survival of Humanism, 1983; The Electronic Word: Democracy, Technology, and the Arts, 1993. **Address:** Rhetorica, Inc., 927 Bluegrass Ln, Los Angeles, CA 90049, U.S.A.

LANIER, Sterling E(dmund). American, b. 1927. **Genres:** Science fiction/Fantasy, Children's fiction, Young adult fiction, Novellas/Short stories. **Career:** Full-time writer and sculptor since 1967. Research Historian, Winterthur Museum, Delaware, 1958-60; Ed., John C. Winston Co., 1961, Chilton Books, 1961-62, 1965-67, and Macrae-Smith Co., 1963-64. **Publications:** The War for the Lot (juvenile), 1969; The Peculiar Exploits of Brigadier Ffellowes (short stories), 1972; Hiero's Journey, 1973; The Unforsaken Hiero, 1983; Menace under Marwood, 1983; The Curious Quests of Brig. Fellowes, 1986. **Address:** c/o Curtis Brown Ltd, 10 Astor Place, New York, NY 10003, U.S.A.

LANIER, Virginia. See Obituaries.

LANKER, Brian T(imothy). American, b. 1947. **Genres:** Photography. **Career:** Phoenix Gazette, Phoenix, AZ, staff photographer, 1966-69; Capital-Journal, Topeka, KS, staff photographer, 1969-74; Register-Guard, Eugene, OR, chief photographer and director of graphics, 1974-82; contract photographer for magazines; affiliated with Lanker Inc; documentary film director, They Drew Fire: Combat Artists of WWII, 2000. **Publications:** I Dream a World: Portraits of Black Women Who Changed America, 1989, rev. ed., 1999. **Address:** Lanker Inc, 1993 Kimberly Dr, Eugene, OR 97405, U.S.A.

LANKFORD, Mary D. American, b. 1932. **Genres:** Children's fiction, Children's non-fiction. **Career:** Dover, DE, elementary school librarian, 1962-63; Walker Air Force Base, Roswell, NM, media services librarian, 1965-66; Irving Independent School District, Irving, TX, director of library and media services, 1966-; Texas Education Agency, Austin, assistant director of libraries; School of Library and Information Studies. **Publications:** Is It Dark? Is It Light?, 1991; Hopscotch around the World, 1992; Films for Learning, Thinking, and Doing, 1992; Educational Fieldtrips, 1992; Christmas Customs around the World, 1993; The Quinceanera, 1993; Dominoes around the World, 1994; Birthdays around the World, 2001; Jacks around the World, 2002. **Address:** 110 White Sands, Austin, TX 78734, U.S.A. **Online address:** mlankf2191@aol.com

LANKFORD, Nelson D. American, b. 1948. **Genres:** History, Biography. **Career:** American Historical Review, book review editor, 1978-83; Indiana University-Bloomington, Budget Office, 1983-84; Virginia Historical Society, Richmond, editor, 1984-, assistant director, 1990-. Conference of Historical Journals, president, 1989-91. **Publications:** An Irishman in Dixie, 1988; OSS against the Reich, 1991; The Last Aristocrat: David K.E. Bruce, 1898-1977, 1996; Eye of the Storm, 2000; Images from the Storm, 2001; Richmond Burning, 2002. **Address:** Virginia Historical Society, PO Box 7311, Richmond, VA 23221, U.S.A. **Online address:** nlankford@vahistorical.org

LANOUETTE, William (John). American, b. 1940. **Genres:** Communications/Media, History, Military/Defense/Arms control, Physics, Politics/Government, Writing/Journalism, Biography. **Career:** Newsweek, New York City, researcher and reporter, 1961-64; WVOX Radio, New Rochelle, NY, news editor, 1964; U.S. House of Representatives, Washington, DC, legislative assistant to John S. Monagan, 1967-68; National Observer, Washington, DC, staff writer, 1969-70, 1972-77; National Journal, Washington, DC, staff correspondent, 1977-82, contributing editor, 1982-83;

World Resources Institute, Washington, DC, communications director, 1983-85, senior associate, 1985; Bulletin of the Atomic Scientists, Chicago, IL, Washington correspondent, 1989-90; U.S. General Accounting Office, Washington, DC, senior analyst for energy and science issues, 1991-. Hansard Society for Parliamentary Government, American lecturer, 1965-66, 1970-71. **Publications:** (with B. Silard) Genius in the Shadows: A Biography of Leo Szilard, the Man behind the Bomb, 1992. Contributor to periodicals. **Address:** c/o F. Joseph Spieler, 154 W 57th St Rm 135, New York, NY 10019, U.S.A.

LANSDALE, Joe R(ichard). Also writes as Ray Slater. American, b. 1951. **Genres:** Novellas/Short stories, Mystery/Crime/Suspense, Horror, Science fiction/Fantasy, Westerns/Adventure. **Career:** Full-time writer, 1981-. Formerly a farmer, transportation mgr. for Goodwill Industries, and custodian, Stephen F. Austin State University, Nacogdoches, Texas, 1987-88. **Publications:** Act of Love, 1981; The Good, the Bad & the Indifferent (stories), 1983; Dead in the West, 1986; The Magic Wagon, 1986; The Nightrunners, 1987; The Drive-In, 1988; Cold in July, 1989; By Bizarre Hands (stories), 1989; The Drive-In 2: Not Just One of Them Sequels, 1990; Savage Season, 1990; Stories by Mama Lansdale's Youngest Boy, 1991; Batman: Captured by the Engines, 1991; Batman in Terror on the High Skies, 1992; Writer of the Purple Rage, 1994; Mucho MoJo, 1994; Two Bear Mambo, 1994; Electric Gumbo (stories), 1994; Fist Full of Stories, 1996; Bad Chili, 1997; Texas Night Riders (novel), 1997; (with L. Shiner) Private Eye Action as You Like It (stories), 1998; Rumble Tumble, 1998; The Boar, 1998; The Long Ones, 1999; Something Lumber This Way Comes, 1999; High Cotton, 2000; The Bottoms, 2000; Captains Outrageous, 2001; Zeppelins West, 2001. EDITOR: The Best of the West, 1986; New Frontiers: The Best of the West Two, 1989; (with J. LoBrutto) Razored Saddles, 1989; (with T. Knowles) The West That Was and The Wild West Show; (with R. Klaw) Weird Business, 1994; A Fine Dark Line, 2003. **Address:** c/o James C. Vines, 648 Broadway Ste 901, New York, NY 10012, U.S.A. **Online address:** www.joerlansdale.com

LANTIER, Patricia. American, b. 1952. **Genres:** Children's non-fiction, Young adult non-fiction. **Career:** Language arts teacher at elementary and high school levels, 1973-82; Marquette University, Milwaukee, WI, instructor in English, 1982-89; Gareth Stevens Publishing, Milwaukee, managing editor and director, creative department, 1990-2001; freelance writer and editor, 2001-02; Kalmbach Publishing Co, Astronomy magazine, managing editor, 2002-. **Publications:** Take Me Out to the Ball Game, 1994. ADAPTER: The Wonder of Loons, 1992; The Wonder of Whitetails, 1992; The Wonder of Wolves, 1992; Hurricane: The Rage of Hurricane Andrew, 1993; Guatemala Is My Home, 1993; Little Lost Fox Cub, 1993. THE ADVENTURES OF BUSTER THE PUPPY SERIES (picture books; English text): Buster Catches a Cold, 1991, in Japan as Ame No Hi No Korowan; Buster and the Little Kitten, 1991, in Japan as Korowan Wa Oniichan; Buster and the Dandelions, 1991, in Japan as Korowan To Fuwafuwa; Buster's First Snow, 1991, in Japan as Yuki No Hi No Korowan; Buster's Blustery Day, 1991, in Japan as Kaze No Hi No Korowan; Buster's First Thunderstorm, 1991, in Japan as Korowan To Gorogoro. PEOPLE WHO MAKE A DIFFERENCE SERIES (abridger): (with J. Bentley) Albert Schweitzer: The Doctor Who Devoted His Life to Africa's Sick, 1991; (with D. Winner) Desmond Tutu: Religious Leader Devoted to Freedom, 1991; (with B. Birch) Louis Braille: Bringer of Hope to the Blind, 1991. WINGS SERIES: Airplanes, 1994; Birds, 1994; Flying Animals, 1994; Flying Insects, 1994.

LANTRY, Mike. See TUBB, E(dwin) C(harles).

LANZA, Joseph. American, b. 1955. **Genres:** Music, Film. **Career:** Writer. **Publications:** Fragile Geometry: The Films, Philosophy, and Misadventures of Nicolas Roeg, 1989; Elevator Music: A Surreal History of Muzak, Easy-Listening, and Other Moodsong, 1994; The Cocktail: The Influence of Spirits on the American Psyche, 1995; Gravity: Tilted Perspectives on Rocketships, Rollercoasters, Earthquakes, and Angel Food, in press. **Address:** c/o St. Martin's Press, 175 Fifth Ave., New York, NY 10010, U.S.A.

LANZMANN, Claude. French, b. 1925. **Genres:** Cultural/Ethnic topics, Film, History, Literary criticism and history, Biography. **Career:** Filmmaker. Director of Les Temps Modernes in France; film director, Israel Why, 1973, Shoah, 1985, Tsahal, 1994, A Visitor from the Living, 1997, Sobibor, October 14th 1943, 16 pm, 2000. **Publications:** (ed.) The Bird Has No Wings: Letters of Peter Schwiefert, trans by Barbara Lucas, 1976; Shoah: An Oral History of the Holocaust, 1985; Shoah: The Complete Text of the Acclaimed Holocaust Film, 1995. **Address:** Les Films Aleph, 18 rue Marbeuf, 75008 Paris, France. **Online address:** clanzmann1@noos.fr

LAPIDES, Robert. American, b. 1940. **Genres:** History. **Career:** Manhattan Community College of the City University of New York, NYC, professor of English, 1973-; Hudson River, founding editor and editor-in-chief, 1982-. **Publications:** (ed. and compiler with A. Adelson) Lodz Ghetto: Inside a Community under Siege, 1989. Author of articles for periodicals. **Address:** Department of English, Manhattan Community College, 199 Chambers St., New York, NY 10007, U.S.A.

LAPIERRE, Laurier L. Canadian, b. 1929. **Genres:** Plays/Screenplays, History. **Career:** Senator, Canadian historian, radio and television broadcaster, educator, and author. School of Journalism, University of Regina, Bell Professor; University of Western Ontario, lecturer, 1960-62; McGill University, Toronto, ON, lecturer, 1963-64, associate professor of history, 1965-, became director of French-Canadian studies program; La Saberdache Quebecoise (collection), director. Host of radio and television programs. **Publications:** 1759: The Battle for Canada, 1990; Canada, My Canada: What Happened?, 1992; Sir Wilfrid Laurier and the Romance of Canada, 1996; Quebec, a Tale of Love, 2001. EDITOR: Four O'clock Lectures: French-Canadian Thinkers of the Nineteenth and Twentieth Centuries, 1966; Quebec: Hier et aujourd'hui, 1967; Essays on the Left: Essays in Honor of T.C. Douglas, 1971; If You Love this Country: Facts and Feelings on Free Trade, 1987. RADIO SCRIPTS: Genesis of a Nation: British North America, 1776-1867, 1966; The Apprenticeship: Canada from Confederation to the Eve of the First World War, 1967. **Address:** 28S Fairmont Ave, Ottawa, ON, Canada K1Y 1Y4. **Online address:** laurier.lapierre@sympatico.ca

LAPONCE, Jean Antoine. French/Canadian, b. 1925. **Genres:** Politics/Government. **Career:** University of British Columbia, Vancouver, assistant professor, 1956-61, associate professor, 1961-66, professor of political science, 1966-92, emeritus, 1992-; former instructor in political science, University of Santa Clara, California; University of Ottawa, Institute of Interethnic Relations, director, 1993-2001. **Publications:** The Protection of Minorities, 1961; The Government of France under the Fifth Republic, 1962; People vs. Politics, 1970; (ed. with P. Smoker) Experimentation and Simulation in Political Science, 1971; Left and Right: The Topography of Political Perceptions, 1981; Langue et Territoire, 1984, trans. as Languages and Their Territories, 1987. **Address:** Dept of Political Science, University of British Columbia, Vancouver, BC, Canada V6T 1Z1. **Online address:** jlaponce@interchange.ubc.ca

LAPPÉ, Frances Moore. American, b. 1944. **Genres:** Agriculture/Forestry, Economics, Education, Food and Wine, Human relations/Parenting, International relations/Current affairs, Politics/Government, Race relations, Social commentary, Social work, Urban studies, Writing/Journalism. **Career:** Author, lecturer. **Publications:** Diet for Small Planet, 1971, 1975, 1982; Great Meatless Meals, 1976; (with J. Collins) Food First, 1977; (with J. Collins) World Hunger, 1979; (with A. Beccar-Varela) Mozambique and Tanzania, 1980; (co-author) Aid as Obstacle, 1980; (co-author) What Can We Do? A Food, Land, Hunger Action Guide, 1980; (co-author) Casting New Molds, 1980; (co-author) Now We Can Speak, 1983; What Difference Could a Revolution Make? 1983; What to Do After You Turn Off the TV, 1985; (with J. Collins) World Hunger: Twelve Myths, 1986; (co-author) Betraying the National Interest, 1987; Rediscovering America's Values, 1989; (with R. Schurman) Taking Population Seriously, 1990; (with P.M. Dubois) The Quickening of America, 1994. **Address:** 6 Frost St, Cambridge, MA 02140-1503, U.S.A. **Online address:** flappe@americannews.com

LAPPING, Brian (Michael). British, b. 1937. **Genres:** Politics/Government, Public/Social administration, Social commentary. **Career:** Chief Executive, Brian Lapping Associates, television production company, since 1988. Productions include: Countdown to War (New York International Television Festival gold medal), The Second Russian Revolution (awards in US, UK etc), Watergate (du Pont, Emmey), Fall of the Wall, Question Time, The Death of Yugoslavia (du Pont, Peabody, Golden Gate and ten other awards). Television Producer, Granada Television Ltd., 1970-88; Executive Producer, World in Action, 1976-78, The State of the Nation, 1978-80, and End of Empire, 1980-85. Reporter, Daily Mirror, London, 1959-61; Reporter and Deputy Commonwealth Correspondent, The Guardian, London, 1961-67; Ed., Venture (Fabian Society monthly journal), 1965-69; Feature writer, Financial Times, London, 1967-68; Deputy Ed., New Society, London, 1968-70. **Publications:** (Co-ed.) More Power to the People, 1968; The Labour Government 1964-70, 1970; (ed.) The State of the Nation: Parliament, 1973; (ed.) The State of the Nation: The Bounds of Freedom, 1980; End of Empire, 1985; Apartheid: A History, 1986. **Address:** 61 Eton Ave., London NW3 3ET, England.

LA PUMA, Salvatore. American, b. 1929. **Genres:** Novels, Novellas/Short stories. **Career:** Writer. **Publications:** The Boys of Bensonhurst (stories), 1987; A Time for Wedding Cake (novel), 1990; Teaching Angels to Fly (stories), 1992. **Address:** 3226 Calle Pinon, Santa Barbara, CA 93105-2760, U.S.A.

LAQUEUR, Thomas Walter. American (born Turkey), b. 1945. **Genres:** History. **Career:** Concord College, instructor, 1968-69; University of California, Berkeley, assistant professor of history, 1973-. **Publications:** Religion and Respectability: Sunday Schools and Working Class Culture, 1780-1850, 1976; (ed. with C. Gallagher) The Making of the Modern Body: Sexuality and Society in the Nineteenth Century, 1987; Making Sex: Body and Gender from the Greeks to Freud, 1990. Contributor to books. Contributor of articles, essays, and reviews to periodicals. **Address:** Department of History, 3229 Dwinelle Hall, University of California, Berkeley, CA 94720, U.S.A. **Online address:** tlaqueur@library.berkeley.edu

LAQUEUR, Walter. American (born Germany), b. 1921. **Genres:** History, Politics/Government. **Career:** Institute of Contemporary History, and Wiener Library, London, director, 1964-91. Center of Strategic and International Studies, Research Council, Washington, DC, chairman. **Publications:** Communism and Nationalism in the Middle East, 1956; The Soviet Union and the Middle East, 1959; Young Germany, 1962; Russia and Germany, 1965; The Fate of the Revolution, 1967; The Road to War (in U.S. as The Road to Jerusalem), 1968; The Struggle for the Middle East, 1969; Europe since Hitler (in U.S. as Rebirth of Europe), 1970, 1982; Out of the Ruins of Europe, 1971; A History of Zionism, 1972, Confrontation: The Middle East War and World Politics, 1974; Weimar, 1974; Guerrilla, 1976; Terrorism, 1977; Terrible Secret, 1980; The Missing Years, 1980; Farewell to Europe, 1981; Germany Today, 1985; The Long Road to Freedom, 1989; Stalin-the Glasnost Revelations, 1991; Black Hundred, 1993; The Dream That Failed, 1994; Fascism, 1996; Generation Exodus, 2001. EDITOR: The Israel-Arab Reader, 1969, 1984; A Dictionary of Politics, 1971; A Readers Guide to Contemporary History, 1972; Fascism: A Reader's Guide, 1978. **Address:** CSIS, 1800 K St, Washington, DC 20006, U.S.A. **Online address:** laqueurw@csi.com

LARA, Adair. American, b. 1952. **Genres:** Essays. **Career:** Reader College of Marin, Kentfield, CA, 1976-83; freelance editor, 1983-86; San Francisco Focus Magazine, San Francisco, CA, managing editor, 1986-89; San Francisco Magazine, San Francisco, CA, executive editor, 1988-89; San Francisco Chronicle, San Francisco, CA, columnist, 1989-2002, reporter, 2002-. **Publications:** Welcome to Earth, Mom, 1992; Slowing Down in a Speeded-Up World, 1994; At Adair's House: More Columns from America's Favorite Former Single Mom, 1995; Hold Me Close, Let Me Go: A Mother, a Daughter, and an Adolescence Survived, 2001. **Address:** San Francisco Chronicle, 901 Mission St., San Francisco, CA 94103, U.S.A. **Online address:** alara@sfchronicle.com

LARDY, Nicholas R. American, b. 1946. **Genres:** Economics, International relations/Current affairs. **Career:** Yale University, New Haven, CT, assistant professor to associate professor of economics, 1975-83, assistant director of Economic Growth Center, 1979-82; University of Washington, Seattle, associate professor, 1983-85, professor of international studies, 1985-96, chair of China program, Jackson School of International Studies, 1984-89, director of Jackson School of International Studies, 1991-95; Brookings Institution, senior fellow, 1995-2003; Institute for International Economics, senior fellow, 2003-. **Publications:** Economic Growth and Distribution in China, 1978; Agriculture in China's Modern Economic Development, 1983; Agricultural Prices in China, 1983; Foreign Trade and Economic Reform in China, 1978-1990, 1992; China in the World Economy, 1994; China's Unfinished Economic Revolution, 1998; Integrating China into the Global Economy, 2002; (With Dan Rosen) Prospects for a US-Taiwan Free Trade Agreement, 2004. EDITOR: Chinese Economic Planning: Translations from Ching-Chi Yen-Chiu, 1978; (with K.R. Lieberthal) Chen Yun's Strategy for China's Development: A Non-Maoist Alternative, 1983. **Address:** Institute for International Economics, 1750 Massachusetts Ave NW, Washington, DC 20036-1903, U.S.A. **Online address:** nlardy@brook.edu

LARKIN, Joan. American, b. 1939. **Genres:** Plays/Screenplays, Poetry, Gay and lesbian issues, Inspirational/Motivational Literature, Women's studies and issues. **Career:** Brooklyn College of the City University of New York, NYC, assistant professor of English, 1969-94, adjunct professor of MFA writing program, 1997; Sarah Lawrence College, guest faculty, 1984-86, 1988, 1997-2004; Goddard College, MFA program in writing, 1994-96, 2002; New England College, MFA program in poetry writing, core faculty, 2002-. Bloom: Wueer Fiction, Art, Poetry & More, poetry editor, 2003-; University of Wisconsin Press, Living Out series editor (with D. Bergman). **Publications:** POETRY: Housework, 1975; A Long Sound, 1986; Cold River, 1997; (trans. with J. Manrique) Sor Juana's Love Poems, 1997. OTHER: Glad Day: Daily Meditations for Gay, Lesbian, Bisexual, and Transgender People, 1998; If You Want What We Have: Sponsorship Meditations, 1998. PLAYS: The AIDS Passion, 1996; The Living, 2001. EDITOR: (with E. Bulkin) Amazon Poetry, 1975; (with E. Bulkin) Lesbian Poetry,

1981; (with C. Morse) Gay and Lesbian Poetry in Our Time, 1988; A Woman Like That: Lesbian and Bisexual Writers Tell Their Coming Out Stories, 1999. **Address:** c/o Hazelden Foundation, 15251 Pleasant Valley Rd, PO Box 176, Center City, MN 55012, U.S.A. **Online address:** larkin7@earthlink.net

LAROCHE, Loretta. American, b. 1939. **Genres:** Medicine/Health, How-to books. **Career:** Stress management consultant, humorist, author, columnist, and lecturer. Television commentator; host of television specials on PBS. Loretta LaRoche & Company, Plymouth, MA, founder. Harvard Medical School, the Behavior Institute of Medicine, Cambridge, MA, adjunct faculty member. Producer of humorous stress-management videos. **Publications:** Relax-You May Only Have a Few Minutes Left: How to Use the Power of Humor to Defeat Stress in Your Life and Work, 1998; Life Is Not a Stress Rehearsal: Bringing Yesterday's Sane Wisdom into Today's Insane World, 2001. Contributor to magazines and newspapers. **Address:** Loretta LaRoche & Company, 50 Court St., Plymouth, MA 02360, U.S.A. **Online address:** loretta@lorettalaroche.com

LAROQUE, Francois G. French, b. 1948. **Genres:** Literary criticism and history. **Career:** Universite Paul Valery, Montpellier, France, assistant professor, 1973-80, associate professor, 1980-88, professor of English, 1988-90; Universite de Paris III (Sorbonne Nouvelle), Paris, France, professor of English, 1991-. **Publications:** Shakespeare et la fete, 1988, trans. as Shakespeare's Festive World: Elizabethan Seasonal Entertainment and the Professional Stage, 1991; (with A. Morvan and A. Topia) Anthologie de la litterature anglaise, 1991; Shakespeare comme il vous plaira, 1991; (with A. Morvan and F. Regard) Histoire de la litterature anglaise, 1997; (trans., notes and presentation) C. Marlowe, Doctor Faustus, 1997. **Address:** Institut du Monde Anglophone, Universite de Paris III, Sorbonne Nouvelle, 5 rue de l'Ecole-de-Medecine, 75006 Paris, France. **Online address:** flaroque@club-internet.fr

LA ROSA, Pablo. American (born Cuba), b. 1944. **Genres:** Novellas/Short stories. **Career:** Graceland College, Lamoni, IA, associate professor, 1972-78; Lowell H. Listrom Co., Kansas City, MO, margins analyst, 198388; Kansas State University, Manhattan, visiting instructor, 1988-89; Baker University, Baldwin City, KS, assistant professor, 1989-. Young Audiences of America, musical performer. **Publications:** Forbidden Fruit and Other Stories, 1996. **Address:** Baker University, PO Box 65, Baldwin City, KS 66006, U.S.A. **Online address:** LaRosa@harvey.bakeru.edu

LARRABEE, Lisa. American, b. 1947. **Genres:** Biography. **Career:** University of Kansas, Lawrence, KS, Department of Political Science, office manager, 1976-83; City of Lawrence, Lawrence, word processor, 1983-84; AAA Typing Service, Lawrence, owner and operator, 1983-87; University of Kansas, Department of Music, secretary, 1984-85; Rubins, Kase, Rubins, and Cambiano, PC, Kansas City, MO, legal secretary, 1985-87; University of Kansas, KU Psychological Clinic, office manager and bookkeeper, 1987-89; Poarch Creek Indians, Atmore, AL, office manager of WASG/WYDH radio stations, economic development assistant in the Tribal Chair's office, and administrative assistant in the Planning Department, 1989-93; Bender Shipbuilding and Repair Co. Inc., Mobile, AL, secretary, 1993-94; G5B Graphics, Perdido, AL, owner, writer, and artist, 1993-; ALTO Products Corp. AL, Atmore, office manager, 1994. **Publications:** Grandmother Five Baskets, 1993. **Address:** P.O. Box 179, Perdido, AL 36562, U.S.A.

LARSEN, Jeanne (Louise). American, b. 1950. **Genres:** Poetry, Translations, Novels. **Career:** Tunghai University, Taichung, Taiwan, lecturer in department of Western languages and literature, 1972-74; Mitsubishi Shipyard, UNESCO, and other institutions, Nagasaki, Japan, part-time instructor of English as a second language, 1978-80; Hollins University, Roanoke, assistant professor, 1980-86, associate professor, 1986-92, professor of English 1992-. **Publications:** POETRY: James Cook in Search of Terra Incognita: A Book of Poems, 1979; (trans.) Brocade River Poems: Selected Works of the Tang Dynasty Courtesan Xue Tao, 1987. NOVELS: Silk Road: A Novel of Eighth-Century China, 1989; Bronze Mirror, 1991; Manchu Palaces, 1996. **Address:** c/o Ray Lincoln, Elkins Park House, No. 107B, 7900 Old York Rd, Elkins Park, PA 19027-2318, U.S.A.

LARSEN, Torben B. Danish, b. 1944. **Genres:** Zoology. **Career:** International Planned Parenthood Federation, family planning specialist in Beirut, Lebanon, and London, England, 1970-84; Danish International Development Agency, New Delhi, India, family planning specialist, 1984-86; free-lance researcher and writer, 1986-. University of Florida, research associate; conducted entomological field studies in Nigeria, Spain, Morocco, Nigeria, Bulgaria, Jordan, Yemen, Papua New Guinea, India, Ecuador and the Galapagos Islands, Kenya, Botswana, and Ghana. **Publications:** Butterflies of Lebanon, 1974; (with K. Larsen) The Butterflies of Oman, 1980; The Butterflies of Saudi Arabia and Its Neighbours, 1984; The Butterflies of Egypt, 1990; The Butterflies of Kenya and Their Natural History, 1991; The Butterflies of Botswana and Their Natural History, forthcoming; The Butterflies of West Africa, forthcoming. Contributor to scientific journals. **Address:** 358 Coldharbour Lane, London SW9 8PL, England. **Online address:** torbenlarsen@compuserve.com

LARSGAARD, Chris. (born United States), b. 1967. **Genres:** Novels. **Career:** Writer. Private investigator, c. 1990-. **Publications:** The Heir Hunter (crime novel), 2000. **Address:** c/o Author Mail, Delacorte, 1745 Broadway, New York, NY 10019, U.S.A.

LARSON, Charles. American, b. 1922. **Genres:** Mystery/Crime/Suspense. **Career:** Producer, Columbia Pictures, 20th Century Fox, and QM Productions; California, 1964-73; Executive Producer, Nakia television series, Columbia Pictures Television, 1974; Co-Creator, Hagen television series, CBS, 1979-80. **Publications:** The Chinese Game, 1969; Someone's Death, 1973; Matthew's Hand, 1974; Muir's Blood, 1976; The Portland Murders, 1983. **Address:** 14205 S.E. 38th St., Vancouver, WA 98683, U.S.A.

LARSON, Edward J(ohn). American, b. 1953. **Genres:** Biology, History, Law. **Career:** Davis, Wright & Tremaine (law firm), Seattle, WA, attorney, 1979-82; U.S. House of Representatives, Washington, DC, associate counsel, 1982-86; University of Georgia, Athens, Richard B. Russell Professor of History and Law, 1987-. **Publications:** Trial and Error: The American Controversy over Creation and Evolution, 1985; Sex, Race, and Science: Eugenics in the Deep South, 1995; Summer for the Gods: The Scopes Trial and America's Continuing Debate over Science and Religion, 1997 (Pulitzer Prize for History, 1998); Evolution's Workshop: God and Science on the Galapagos Islands, 2002; Evolution: The Remarkable History of a Scientific Theory, 2004. **Address:** University of Georgia, Le Conte Hall, Athens, GA 30602, U.S.A. **Online address:** edlarson@uga.edu

LARSON, Gary. American, b. 1950. **Genres:** Humor/Satire, Cartoons. **Career:** Syndicated cartoonist since 1978. **Publications:** The Far Side, 1982; Beyond the Far Side, 1983; In Search of the Far Side, 1984; The Far Side Gallery, 1984; Bride of the Far Side, 1985; Valley of the Far Side, 1985; It Came from the Far Side, 1986; The Far Side Gallery II, 1986; The Far Side Observer, 1987; Hound of the Far Side, 1987; Night of the Crash-Test Dummies, 1988; The Far Side Gallery III, 1988; Pre-History of the Far Side: A Tenth Anniversary Exhibit, 1989; Wildlife Preserves: A Far Side Collection, 1989; Weiner Dog Art: The Far Side Collection, 1990; Unnatural Selections, 1991; Cow of Our Planet, 1992; The Chickens Are Restless, 1993; The Far Side Gallery 4, 1994; The Curse of Madame "C", 1994; The Far Side Gallery 5, 1995; Last Chapter and Worse, 1996; There's a Hair in my Dirt! A Worm's Story, 1998. ANIMATED FILMS: Gary Larson's Tales from the Far Side, 1994; Gary Larson's Tales from the Far Side II. **Address:** Universal Press Syndicate, 4520 Main St., Kansas City, MO 64111, U.S.A.

LARSON, Ingrid D(ana). American, b. 1965. **Genres:** Children's fiction. **Career:** Writer. Loretta Davis Promotional Agency, promotional model, 1984-. **Publications:** The Adventures of Herman and Hurby, 1995; The Adventures of Herman and Hurby and Family, 1997; Herman and Hurby, 2000. Poems represented in anthologies. **Address:** 486 W. Union St., East Bridgewater, MA 02333, U.S.A. **Online address:** idanalarson@aol.com

LARSON, Jennifer. American, b. 1965. **Genres:** Classics. **Career:** Kent State University, Kent, OH, assistant professor, 1994-. **Publications:** Greek Heroine Cults, 1995. Contributor to Greek, Roman, and Byzantine Studies. **Address:** Department of Modern and Classical Language Studies, Kent State University, Kent, OH 44242, U.S.A.

LARSON, Kirby. American, b. 1954. **Genres:** Children's fiction, Young adult fiction. **Career:** Children's book author and homemaker. **Publications:** Second-Grade Pig Pals, 1994; Cody and Quinn, Sitting in a Tree, 1996; The Magic Kerchief, 2000. SWEET VALLEY KIDS BOOKS: Scaredy-Cat Elizabeth, 1995; Elizabeth Hatches an Egg, 1996. **Address:** 8523 NE 147th Pl, Kenmore, WA 98028, U.S.A. **Online address:** Kirlane@aol.com

LARSON, Muriel Koller. Also writes as Kevin Koller. American, b. 1924. **Genres:** Theology/Religion. **Career:** Writer; counselor. **Publications:** Devotions for Women's Groups, 1967; How to Give a Devotion, 1967; Devotions for Children, 1969; Living Miracles, 1973; It Took a Miracle, 1974; You Are What You Think, 1974; God's Fantastic Creation, 1975; The Bible Says: Quiz Book, 1976; Are You Real, God?, 1976; I Give Up, God, 1978; Joy

Every Morning, 1979; What Happens When Women Believe, 1979; Living by Faith, 1984; Praise Every Day, 1984; Ways Women Can Witness, 1984; Me and My Pet Peeves, 1988; Petals of Praise, 1991. Contributor to periodicals. **Address:** 10 Vanderbilt Circle, Greenville, SC 29609-4009, U.S.A. **Online address:** MKLJOY@aol.com; doctormuriel@aol.com

LARSON, Sidner J. American, b. 1949. **Genres:** Literary criticism and history. **Career:** Kessler Law Office, Brookings, SD, attorney, 1985-88; University of Arizona, Tucson, instructor in English, 1989-92; Lewis-Clark State College, Lewiston, ID, director of American Indian studies, 1992-95; University of Oregon, Eugene, associate professor of American Indian literature, 1995-. **Publications:** NONFICTION: Catch Colt, 1995; Captured in the Middle, 2000. Contributor to professional journals. **Address:** Director, AISP, 347 Catt Hall, Iowa State University, Ames, IA 50011-1304, U.S.A.

LARSON, Stephanie Greco. American, b. 1960. **Genres:** Politics/Government, Communications/Media, Women's studies and issues. **Career:** George Washington University, Washington, DC, assistant professor of political science, 1986-92; Dickinson College, Carlisle, PA, assistant professor of political science, 1992-94; associate professor, 1994-. **Publications:** Creating Consent of the Governed: The Congressman and the Local Press, 1992. Work represented in anthologies. Contributor of articles to periodicals. **Address:** Department of Political Science, Dickinson College, Carlisle, PA 17013, U.S.A.

LARSON, Wendy. American. **Genres:** Literary criticism and history. **Career:** Professor of East Asian languages and literatures, University of Oregon. **Publications:** (trans., and author of introduction and critical essay) Wang Meng, Bolshevik Salute: A Modernist Chinese Novel, 1989; Literary Authority and the Modern Chinese Writer: Ambivalence and Autobiography, 1991; (ed., with A. Wedell-Wedellsborg) Inside Out: Modernism and Postmodernism in Chinese Literary Culture, 1993; Women and Writing in Modern China, 1998. **Address:** East Asian Languages and Literatures, University of Oregon, Eugene, OR 97403, U.S.A. **Online address:** wlarson@cas.uoregon.edu

LARUE, L. H. American, b. 1938. **Genres:** Law. **Career:** Washington and Lee University, Lexington, VA, professor of law, 1967-. **Publications:** A Student's Guide to the Study of Law, 1987, 2nd ed., 2001; Political Discourse: A Case Study of the Watergate Affair, 1988; (ed. with W. Holt) W.J. Ritz, Rewriting the History of the Judiciary Act of 1789, 1990; Constitutional Law as Fiction: Narrative in the Rhetoric of Authority, 1995. **Address:** School of Law, Washington and Lee University, Lexington, VA 24450, U.S.A.

LARZELERE, Alex. American, b. 1936. **Genres:** Military/Defense/Arms control. **Career:** U.S. Coast Guard, career officer as commander of patrol boats and cutters; served as aide to the president, 1971-73, chief of search and rescue in Miami, FL, and chief of staff for 7th Coast Guard District, Miami; served in Vietnam; retired as captain. **Publications:** The Coast Guard at War: Vietnam, 1965-1975, 1997; The 1980 Cuban Boatlift. **Address:** 5904 Mount Eagle Dr, Alexandria, VA 22303, U.S.A.

LA SALLE, Peter. American, b. 1947. **Genres:** Novels, Novellas/Short stories. **Career:** Professor of English, University of Texas at Austin, 1994- (Assistant Professor, 1980-86; Associate Professor, 1986-94). Lecturer in Creative Writing, Johnson State College, Vermont, 1974-76; Assistant Professor of English, Iowa State University, Ames, 1977-80. **Publications:** The Graves of Famous Writers and Other Stories, 1980; Strange Sunlight (novel), 1984; Hockey Sur Glace: Stories, 1996. **Address:** Dept. of English, University of Texas at Austin, Austin, TX 78712, U.S.A.

LA SALLE, Victor. See FANTHORPE, R(obert) Lionel.

LASENBY, Jack. New Zealander, b. 1931. **Genres:** Novels, Children's fiction, Novellas/Short stories. **Career:** Worked as deer culler, possum trapper, and teacher, c. 1950-68; New Zealand Department of Education, Wellington, editor of School Journal, 1969-75; Wellington Teachers' College, Wellington, senior lecturer in English, 1975-87; full-time writer, 1987-; Frank Sargeson Fellow, 1991; Writing Fellow: Victoria University of Wellington, 1993, Dunedin College of Education, 1995. **Publications:** CHILDREN'S FICTION: Charlie the Cheeky Kea, 1976; Rewi the Red Deer, 1976. NOVELS: The Lake, 1987; The Mangrove Summer, 1989; The Conjuror (young adult), 1992; Harry Wakatipu, 1993; Dead Man's Head, 1994; The Waterfall, 1995; The Battle of Poole Island, 1996; Because We Were the Travellers (young adult), 1997; Taur (young adult), 1998; The Shaman and the Droll, 1999; The Lies of Harry Wakatipu, 2000. SHORT STORIES: Uncle Trev, 1991;

Uncle Trev and the Great South Island Plan, 1991; Uncle Trev and the Treaty of Waitangi, 1992; Uncle Trev's Teeth, 1997. **Address:** 137 Aro St., Wellington 6006, New Zealand. **Online address:** jacklasenby@mac.com

LASH, N(icholas) L(angrishe) A(lleyne). British, b. 1934. **Genres:** Theology/Religion. **Career:** Cambridge University, Fellow of Clare Hall, Cambridge, 1987- (Fellow, 1969-85, and Dean, 1971-75, St. Edmund's House; Assistant Lecturer, 1974-78; Norris-Hulse Professor of Divinity, 1978-99). Oscott College, 1957-63; Assistant Priest, Slough, Bucks., 1963-68. **Publications:** His Presence in the World, 1968; Change in Focus, 1973; Newman on Development, 1975; Voices of Authority, 1976; Theology on Dover Beach, 1979; A Matter of Hope, 1982; Theology on the Way to Emmaus, 1986; Easter in Ordinary, 1988; Believing Three Ways in One God, 1992; The Beginning and End of "Religion," 1996. **Address:** Faculty of Divinity, St. John's St, Cambridge CB2 1TW, England.

LASKIER, Michael M. Israeli/American, b. 1949. **Genres:** History, International relations/Current affairs. **Career:** American Friends of the Alliance Israelite Universelle, NYC, associate director, 1978-80; Tel-Aviv University, lecturer at Diaspora Research Institute, 1980-88; Ben-Gurion University, visiting lecturer, 1980-82, history dept, teacher, 1998-2000; Herzliyya Military College, teacher, 1983-87; University of California, Los Angeles, visiting scholar, 1988-90; University of Judaism, Los Angeles, CA, visiting associate professor, 1988-90; Spertus College of Judaica, Chicago, Louis Susman Associate Professor of Jewish and Middle Eastern History, 1990-92, founder and director of Louis Susman Graduate Management-Base Jewish Communal Studies Program; University of Chicago, associate member of Center for Middle Eastern Studies, 1990-94; World Sephardic Educational Center, Los Angeles, executive director, 1992-94; University of Judaism, visiting professor, 1993-94; Bar-Ilan University, Ashqelon College, associate professor, 1994-, head of political science department, 1998-2002, Ramat-Gan, political science dept, teacher, 1998-2001, Dept of Middle Eastern History, 2001-. **Publications:** The Alliance Israelite Universelle and the Jewish Communities of Morocco, 1862-1962, 1983; North African Jewry in the Shadow of Vichy France and the Swastika (in Hebrew), 1992; The Jews of Egypt, 1920-1970: In the Midst of Zionism, Anti-Semitism, and the Arab-Israeli Conflict, 1992; North African Jewry in the Twentieth Century: A Political History of the Jews in Morocco, Tunisia, and Algeria, 1994, 2nd ed., 1997; The Jews of the Middle East and North Africa in Modern Times, 2003; Israel and the Maghreb: From Statehood to Oslo, 2004. Work represented in anthologies. Contributor to periodicals. **Address:** Shderot Lakhish 37, 82000 Qiryat Gat, Israel. **Online address:** michael_1949@barak-online.net

LASKIN, David. American, b. 1953. **Genres:** Horticulture, Humanities, Meteorology/Atmospheric sciences, Biography. **Career:** Freelance writer, 1979-. **Publications:** Getting into Advertising, 1986; The Parents Book for New Fathers, 1988; Eastern Islands, 1990; (with K. O'Neill) The Little Girl Book, 1992; A Common Life: Four Generations of American Literary Friendship and Influence, 1994; Braving the Elements, 1996; Rains All the Time, 1997; Partisans: Marriage, Politics, and Betrayal among the New York Intellectuals, 2000; Artists in Their Gardens, 2001. **Address:** 18757 Ridgefield Rd NW, Seattle, WA 98177, U.S.A. **Online address:** dlaskin@verizon.net

LASKIN, Pamela L. American, b. 1954. **Genres:** Children's non-fiction. **Career:** City College of the City University of New York, adjunct instructor in English, 1981-; Pratt Institute, Brooklyn, NY, adjunct instructor in creative writing and children's literature, 1989-; Gotham Writer's Workshop, instructor of children's writing. Tutors and performs poetry at a public school. **Publications:** A Little off the Top, 1985; Music from the Heart, 1989; (with A.A. Moskowitz) Wish upon a Star: A Story for Children with a Parent Who Is Mentally Ill, 1991; Dear Hades (chapbook), 1994; Heroic Horses, 1998; The Buried Treasure, 1998; Till Death Do Us Part, 2001; Trick or Treat, 2001; Getting to Know You, 2004; Other Stations, 2004. Contributor of poetry and short fiction to periodicals.

LASKY, Kathryn. Also writes as Kathryn Lasky Knight. American, b. 1944. **Genres:** Young adult fiction, Young adult non-fiction. **Career:** Writer. **Publications:** FOR YOUNG ADULTS. FICTION: The Night Journey, 1981; Beyond the Divide, 1983; Prank, 1984; Home Free, 1985; Pageant, 1986; The Bone Wars, 1988; Double Trouble Squared, 1991; Shadows in the Water, 1992; Voice in the Wind, 1993; Beyond the Burning Time, 1994; Memories of a Bookbat, 1994; A Journey to the New World: The Diary of Remember Patience Whipple, 1996; True North: A Novel of the Underground Railroad, 1996; Dreams of the Golden Country: The Diary of Zipporah Felman, 1998. FOR CHILDREN. FICTION: (with L. Floyd) Agatha's Alphabet, 1975; I Have Four Names for My Grandfather, 1976; Tugboats Never Sleep, 1977;

My Island Grandma, 1979; Jem's Island, 1982; Sea Swan, 1988; Fourth of July Bear, 1991; I Have an Aunt on Marlborough Street, 1992; The Tantrum, 1993; Cloud Eyes, 1994; The Solo, 1994; Pond Year, 1995; The Gates of the Wind, 1995; She's Wearing a Dead Bird on Her Head, 1995; Lunch Bunnies, 1996; Grace the Pirate, 1997; Marven of the Great North Woods, 1997; Hercules: The Man, the Myth, the Hero, 1997; Alice Rose and Sam, 1998. NONFICTION: Tall Ships, 1978; Dollmaker: The Eyelight and the Shadow, 1981; The Weaver's Gift, 1981; Sugaring Time, 1983; A Baby for Max, 1984; Puppeteer, 1985; Traces of Life: The Origins of Humankind, 1989; Dinosaur Dig, 1990; Surtsey: The Newest Place on Earth, 1992; Think Like an Eagle: At Work with a Wildlife Photographer, 1992; Monarchs, 1993; (with M. Knight) Searching for Laura Ingalls: A Reader's Journey, 1993; Days of the Dead, 1994; The Librarian Who Measured the Earth, 1994; The Most Beautiful Roof in the World: Exploring the Rainforest Canopy, 1997; Shadows in the Dawn: The Lemurs of Madagascar, 1998; A Brilliant Streak: The Making of Mark Twain, 1998; Vision of Beauty, 2001. NOVELS AS KATHRYN LASKY KNIGHT: Atlantic Circle, 1985; Trace Elements, 1986; The Widow of Oz, 1989; Mortal Words, 1990; Mumbo Jumbo, 1991; Dark Swan, 1994. **Address:** 7 Scott Street, Cambridge, MA 02138, U.S.A.

LASS, Roger. American, b. 1937. **Genres:** Language/Linguistics. **Career:** Indiana University, lecturer, 1964-65, assistant professor, 1965-66, associate professor of English and linguistics, 1967-73; University of Edinburgh, Scotland, visiting lecturer, 1969-70, lecturer, 1973-78, reader in linguistics, 1978-82; University of Cape Town, Rondebosch, South Africa, visiting lecturer, 1982, professor of linguistics, 1983-; member of extramural faculty of Fife County Council and summer school faculty at Hughes Hall, Cambridge; lecturer at universities worldwide. **Publications:** (ed.) Approaches to English Historical Linguistics, 1969; (with J.M. Anderson) Old English Phonology, 1975; English Phonology and Phonological Theory: Synchronic and Diachronic Studies, 1976; (trans.) Dieter Wunderlich, Foundations of Linguistics, 1979; On Explaining Linguistic Change, 1980; Phonology: An Introduction to Basic Concepts, 1984; The Shape of English, 1987; Old English: a Historical Linguistic Companion, 1994. **Address:** Department of Linguistics, University of Cape Town, Rondebosch 7700, Republic of South Africa. **Online address:** roger@beattie.uct.ac.za

LASSERRE, Philippe. French, b. 1939. **Genres:** Business/Trade/Industry. **Career:** French Foundation for Management Education, Paris, vice-general secretary, 1962-72; INSEAD, Fontainebleau, France, professor, 1975-. SNECMA, Paris, controller, 1963-69. **Publications:** Business Strategy and Management, 1986; Strategies for Asia Pacific, 1995, 2nd ed, 1999; Global Strategic Management, 2003. **Address:** INSEAD, Blvd. de Constance, 77309 Fontainebleau, France. **Online address:** philippe.lasserre@insead.edu

LASSITER, Mary. See HOFFMAN, Mary (Margaret).

LASSON, Kenneth. American, b. 1943. **Genres:** Law, Social commentary, Biography, Essays. **Career:** University of Baltimore School of Law, professor. **Publications:** The Workers: Portraits of Nine American Jobholders, 1971; Proudly We Hail: Profiles of Public Citizens in Action, 1975; Private Lives of Public Servants, 1978; Representing Yourself: What You Can Do without a Lawyer, 1983; Mousetraps and Muffling Cups, 1986; Trembling in the Ivory Tower, 2003. **Address:** University of Baltimore School of Law, 1420 N Charles St, Baltimore, MD 21201, U.S.A. **Online address:** klasson@ubalt.edu

LASSWELL, Marcia. American, b. 1927. **Genres:** Human relations/Parenting, Psychology. **Career:** California State University, Pomona, Professor of Psychology, 1960-; Clinical Professor in Graduate Program Training, Marriage and Family Therapists, and Co-Director, Human Relations Center, University of Southern California at Los Angeles; in private practice as Marriage and Family Counselor, 1959-. Member, Board of Dirs., Omega Foundation Member, Southern California Association of Marriage and Family Counselors (Vice President, 1971-72, and President, 1972-73). Lecturer, 1952-54, and Assistant Professor, 1959-60, Pepperdine College, Los Angeles. **Publications:** College Teaching of General Psychology (textbook), 1967; (with T. Lasswell) Love, Marriage and Family (textbook), 1973; (with N. Lobsenz) No-Fault Marriage, 1976; (with N. Lobsenz) Styles of Loving, 1980; (with N. Lobsenz) Equal Time, 1983; (with T. Lasswell) Love, Marriage and Family, 1983, 3rd ed., 1991. **Address:** 800 W. First St., No. 2908, Los Angeles, CA 90012, U.S.A. **Online address:** mlass@aol.com

LATEEF, Tolen S. See SANDERS, Clinton R.

LATEINER, Donald. American, b. 1944. **Genres:** Classics, Communications/Media, Industrial relations, Language/Linguistics, Literary criticism and history. **Career:** University of Pennsylvania, Philadelphia, assistant professor of classical studies, 1972-79; Ohio Wesleyan University, Delaware, OH, assistant professor, 1979-82, associate professor, 1982-87, professor of Humanities-Classics, 1987-92, John R. Wright Professor of Greek, 1992-. Lateiner Publishing, editor, 1985-. **Publications:** (ed.) Selected Papers of Lionel Pearson, 1983; The Historical Method of Herodotus, 1989, rev. ed., 1991; Sardonic Smile: Nonverbal Behavior in Homeric Epic, 1995. **Address:** c/o Judith Hallett, 5147 Westbard Ave, Bethesda, MD 20816, U.S.A. **Online address:** DGLatein@owu.edu

LATELL, Brian. American, b. 1941. **Genres:** International relations/Current affairs. **Career:** Georgetown University, Washington, DC, adjunct professor, 1978-. National Intelligence Council, Washington, DC, national intelligence officer for Latin America, 1990-94; Center for the Study of Intelligence, Washington, DC, director, 1994-98. **Publications:** Mexico at the Crossroads, 1986; Eye in the Sky, 1998. **Address:** 1530 North Key Blvd., Arlington, VA 22209, U.S.A.

LATHAM, Alison. American. **Genres:** Music. **Career:** Writer, editor, and music scholar. Previously publications editor at the Royal Opera House, Covent Garden, London, England. **Publications:** (editor, with Stanley Sadie) Stanley Sadie's Brief Guide to Music, 1986; (Assistant editor, with Stanley Sadie) The Norton/Grove Concise Encyclopedia of Music, 1988; (editor, with Roger Parker) Verdi in Performance, 2001; (editor, with Stanley Sadie) The Cambridge Music Guide, 2001; (editor) The Oxford Companion to Music, 2002; (editor) Sing, Ariel: Essays and Thoughts for Alexander Goehr's Seventieth Birthday, 2003; (editor) The Oxford Dictionary of Musical Works, 2004. **Address:** c/o Author Mail, Oxford University Press, 198 Madison Ave., New York, NY 10016, U.S.A.

LATHER, Patti. American, b. 1948. **Genres:** Women's studies and issues, Education. **Career:** Crawfordsville Indiana school system, Crawfordsville, IN, teacher of high school English, history, and American Studies, 1973-77; Mankato State University, Mankato, MN, assistant professor in women's studies department, 1983-88; Ohio State University, Columbus, OH, assistant professor, 1988-92, associate professor, 1992-97, professor of education, 1997-. Visiting professor, University of British Columbia, 1994, and University of Goteberg, Sweden, 1997. **Publications:** Getting Smart: Feminist Research and Pedagogy with/in the Postmodern, 1991; Feminist Research in Education: Within/Against, 1991; (with L. Richardson and L. Daisi) Big Talk: Academic Writing and Feminist Survival, 1991; (with C. Smithies) Troubling the Angels: Women Living with HIV/AIDS, 1997. Contributor to books. Contributor of articles to professional journals. **Address:** Ohio State University, 121 Ramseyer, 29 W. Woodruff, Columbus, OH 43210, U.S.A. **Online address:** lather.1@osu.edu

LATHEY, Gillian. British, b. 1949. **Genres:** Literary criticism and history. **Career:** Roehampton University, London, England, senior lecturer in language in education, 1990-99, deputy director of National Centre for Research in Children's Literature, 1999-, reader in children's literature, 2003-. Marsh Award for Children's Literature in Translation, administrator. **Publications:** The Impossible Legacy: Identity and Purpose in Autobiographical Children's Literature Set in the Third Reich and the Second World War, 1999. Contributor to books and professional journals. **Address:** National Center for Research in Children's Literature, Froebel College, Roehampton University, Roehampton Ln, London SW15 5PJ, England. **Online address:** G.Lathey@roehampton.ac.uk

LATOURELLE, René. Canadian, b. 1918. **Genres:** Theology/Religion. **Career:** Entered Societas Jesu (Society of Jesus), 1938; ordained Roman Catholic priest, 1950; University of Montreal, Montreal, Quebec, professor of fundamental theology, 1956-59; Pontifical Gregorian University, Rome, Italy, professor of fundamental theology, 1959-89, dean of faculty of theology, 1961-64, 1970-76, and 1981-84. **Publications:** Theology of Revelation, 1966; Theology: Science of Salvation, 1969; Christ and the Church: Signs of Salvation, 1972; Finding Jesus Through the Gospels: History and Hermeneutics, 1979; Man and His Problems in the Light of Jesus Christ, 1983; The Miracles of Jesus and the Theology of Miracles, 1988. EDITOR: (with G. O'Collins) Problems and Perspectives of Fundamental Theology, 1982; Vatican II, Assessment and Perspectives: Twenty-five Years After (1962-1987), 3 vols, 1988-89; Dictionary of Fundamental Theology, 1994. **Address:** Centre Vimont, 3200 Chemin de la Cote Ste-Catherine, Montreal, Canada H3T 1C1.

LATTANY, Kristin. Also writes as Kristin Hunter. American, b. 1931. **Genres:** Novels, Novellas/Short stories, Children's fiction, Plays/Screenplays. **Career:** Sr. Lecturer in English, University of Pennsylvania, Philadelphia, 1983-95 (Lecturer in Creative Writing, 1972-79; Adjunct Professor of

English, 1980-83). Copywriter, Lavenson Bureau of Advertising, Philadelphia, Pa., 1952-59; Research Assistant, School of Social Work, University of Pennsylvania, Philadelphia, 1961-62; Copywriter, Wermen Schorr, Philadelphia, 1962-63; Information Officer, City of Philadelphia, 1963-64 and 1965-66. **Publications:** AS KRISTIN HUNTER: God Bless the Child, 1964; The Double Edge (play), 1965; The Landlord, 1966; The Soul Brothers and Sister Lou, 1968; Boss Cat, 1971; The Pool Table War, 1972; Uncle Daniel and the Racoon, 1972; Guests in the Promised Land: Stories, 1973; The Survivors, 1975; The Lakestown Rebellion, 1978; Lou in the Limelight, 1981. AS KRISTIN LATTANY: Kinfolks, 1996; Do Unto Others, 2000; Breaking Away, 2003. **Address:** c/o Dystel and Goderich, 1 Union Sq W, New York, NY 10003, U.S.A.

LATTIMORE, Jessie. *See* **DRESSER, Norine.**

LATTIMORE, Jessie. *See* **FONTES, Montserrat.**

LATTIS, James M. American, b. 1954. **Genres:** Astronomy, History, Sciences, Theology/Religion. **Career:** Teacher of history of science and astronomy; University of Wisconsin-Madison, Space Astronomy Laboratory, staff member, Space Place, cofounder and director. **Publications:** Between Copernicus and Galileo, 1994; (with J. Tedeschi) The Italian Reformation of the 16th Century and the Diffusion of Renaissance Culture, 2000. **Address:** Space Astronomy Laboratory, University of Wisconsin-Madison, 1150 University Ave, Madison, WI 53706, U.S.A.

LATYNIN, Leonid (Aleksandrovich). (born Russia), b. 1938. **Genres:** Design. **Career:** Khudozhestvennaya Literatura Publishing House, radio commentator, Youth magazine, poetry division, 1962-74. Researcher of icons and local crafts in northern Russia, 1970s; translator of Central Asian poetry, 1980s. **Publications:** V chuzhom gorode: Grimer i Muza (novel), 1988; Obriad: Stikhotvoreniia, 1965-1991, 1993; Spiashchii vo vremia zhatvy (novel), 1993, translation by Andrew Bromfield and published as Sleeper at Harvest Time, 1994; The Face-Maker and the Muse, translated by Andrew Bromfield, 1999; Foneticheskii shum. Evgenii Vitkovskii: Dialogi, 2002; Russkaya Pravda, 2003. **Address:** c/o Russian Press Service, 1805 Crain St., Evanston, IL 60202, U.S.A. **Online address:** perova@glas.msk.su

LATZER, Barry. American, b. 1945. **Genres:** Criminology/True Crime. **Career:** John Jay College of Criminal Justice of the City University of New York, NYC, professor of law, 1978-. Graduate Center of the City University of New York, professor, 1978-; lecturer at colleges and universities. Member of State Bars of New York and New Jersey. Guest on television and radio programs. **Publications:** State Constitutions and Criminal Justice, 1991; State Constitutional Criminal Law, 1995, annual supplements, 1996-98; Death Penalty Cases: Leading U.S. Supreme Court Cases on Capital Punishment, 1998. Contributor to books. Contributor of articles and reviews to law journals. **Address:** Department of Government, John Jay College of Criminal Justice, City University of New York, 445 West 59th St., New York, NY 10019, U.S.A. **Online address:** proflatzer@aol.com

LAUBACH, David C. American. **Genres:** Literary criticism and history, Novels. **Career:** Educator and author. Loyalsock Township High School, Williamsport, PA, head of English department, 1960-69; St. Nicholas Grammar School, Northwood, England, English teacher, 1969-70; Westfield School District, Westfield, MA, director of English department, 1970-85; Colonial School District, Plymouth Meeting, PA, director of language arts and reading, 1985-87; Kutztown University, Kutztown, PA, associated professor of English, 1988-. Lycoming College, adjunct teacher, 1964-69; Williamsport Community College, drama instructor, 1966-69; Hampshire Lodge, teacher in humanities, 1967-68; Maxwell Vacation School, director 1971-77; University of Massachusetts, adjunct teacher in writing, 1977-85. **Publications:** Introduction to Folklore (nonfiction), 1989; Growing up Amish (novel), 1997. Contributor to books and periodicals. **Address:** English Department, Kutztown University, Kutztown, PA 19530, U.S.A.

LAUBENBACHER, Reinhard C. German, b. 1954. **Genres:** Mathematics/Statistics. **Career:** New Mexico State University, Las Cruces, NM, assistant professor, 1985-90, associate professor, 1990-96, professor of mathematics, 1996-. **Publications:** (ed. with B. Sturmfels, and trans.) Theory of Algebraic Invariants, 1993; (with D. Pengelley) Mathematical Expeditions, 1998. **Address:** Department of Mathematics, New Mexico State University, Las Cruces, NM 88003, U.S.A. **Online address:** reinhard@nmsu.edu

LAUBER, Volkmar. Austrian, b. 1944. **Genres:** Economics, Environmental sciences/Ecology, Politics/Government. **Career:** University of South Florida, Tampa, visiting instructor in political science, 1976-77; West Virginia Wes-

leyan College, Buckhannon, assistant professor of government and chairman of department, 1977-79; Johns Hopkins University, Bologna Center, Bologna, Italy, assistant professor of European studies, 1979-80; West Virginia Wesleyan College, assistant professor of government and chairman of department, 1980-82; University of Salzburg, Salzburg, Austria, professor of political science, 1982-, chairman of department, 1984-90. **Publications:** The Political Economy of France from Pompidou to Mitterrand, 1983; The Politics of Economic Policy: France, 1976-1982, 1983. EDITOR: (co-, and contrib.) Handbuch des Politischen Systems Osterreichs, 1991, 3rd ed., 1997; Contemporary Austrian Politics, 1996; (with A. Mol and D. Liefferink) Environmental Politics: The Voluntary Approach, 2000. Works appear in anthologies and journals. **Address:** Politikwissenschaft Rudolfskai 42, A-5020 Salzburg, Austria. **Online address:** volkmar.lauber@sbg.ac.at

LAUCK, Jon K. American. **Genres:** Agriculture/Forestry. **Career:** Intern for U.S. Senator Larry Pressler, summers, 1991-92; University of Iowa, Iowa City, IA, instructor, 1995-96; Davenport, Evans, Hurwitz & Smith (law firm), summer associate, 1999, associate, 2000-. University of Arkansas-Fayetteville, adjunct professor, summer, 2001; South Dakota State University, adjunct professor, 2001, 2002. **Publications:** American Agriculture and the Problem of Monopoly: The Political Economy of Grain Belt Farming, 1953-1980, 2000. Contributor of articles and reviews to law, history, and political science journals. **Address:** Davenport Evans Hurwitz & Smith, 513 South Main, Sioux Falls, SD 57101, U.S.A. **Online address:** jlauck@dehs.com

LAUDER, Robert E(dward). American, b. 1934. **Genres:** Philosophy, Theology/Religion. **Career:** Ordained Roman Catholic priest; Cathedral College of the Immaculate Conception, Douglaston, NY, instructor in philosophy, 1967-85; St. John's University, Jamaica, NY, professor of philosophy, 1985-. **Publications:** The Love Explosion: Human Experience and the Christian Mystery, 1979; The Priest as a Person: A Philosophy of Priestly Existence, 1981; Becoming a Christian Person, 1984; Rediscovering Myself and Others in God: The Never-Ending Dialogue, 1987; Loneliness Is for Loving, rev. ed., 1988; God, Death, Art, and Love: The Philosophical Vision of Ingmar Bergman, 1989; Nothing But Love; Walker Percy: Prophetic, Existentialist, Catholic Storyteller, 1996; Your Sacred Story, 1998. **Address:** Department of Philosophy, St. John's University, Jamaica, NY 11439, U.S.A.

LAUGHTON, Bruce (Kyle Blake). British/Canadian, b. 1928. **Genres:** Art/Art history. **Career:** University of London, Courtauld Institute of Art, London, England, teaching collection librarian, 1958-71; Queen's University, Kingston, Ontario, professor of art history, 1971-93, emeritus professor, 1993-. **Publications:** Philip Wilson Steer, 1860-1942, 1971; (with others) Roscoe Fisher, ed., The James Carling Illustrations to Edgar Allan Poe's "The Raven," 1982; The Euston Road School: A Study in Objective Painting, 1986; The Drawings of Daumier and Millet, 1991; Honore Daumier, 1996; William Coldstream 1908-1987, 2004. Contributor to books. **Address:** Department of Art, Queen's University, Kingston, ON, Canada K7L 3N6. **Online address:** BL5@post.queensu.ca

LAUNER, Donald. American, b. 1926. **Genres:** Marine sciences/Oceanography. **Career:** American Broadcasting Co., NYC, television master control engineer for forty years. Licensed captain, U.S. Coast Guard; Alliance for a Living Ocean, water quality tester; lecturer to boating groups. Good Old Boat magazine, contributing editor. **Publications:** A Cruising Guide to New Jersey Waters, 1995. Contributor to magazines. **Address:** 842 Spar Dr, Forked River, NJ 08731, U.S.A. **Online address:** launerdm@aol.com

LAUNIUS, Roger D. American, b. 1954. **Genres:** Air/Space topics, History. **Career:** Camp Moore State Commemorative Area, Tangipahoa, LA, museum manager, 1982; Military Airlift Command, Scott Air Force Base, IL, historian, 1982-84; Ogden Air Logistics Center, Hill Air Force Base, UT, chief of Office of History, 1984-86; Air Force Systems Command, Andrews Air Force Base, MD, deputy command historian, 1986-87; Military Airlift Command, command historian, 1987-90; National Aeronautics and Space Administration, Washington, DC, chief historian, 1990-. McKendree College, instructor, 1983-84; Weber State College, adjunct professor, 1985-86; Graceland College, adjunct professor, 1990-95; Florida Institute of Technology, Krieger Lecturer, 1993; University of Alabama, Huntsville, Honors Lecturer, 1994; Anne Arundel Community College, adjunct professor, 1995-; Loyola College, Baltimore, MD, History of Technology Lecturer, 1995. **Publications:** AEROSPACE HISTORY: NASA: A History of the U.S. Civil Space Program, 1994; Apollo 11 at Twenty-Five (electronic picture book), 1994. MORMON HISTORY: Zion's Camp: Expedition to Missouri, 1834, 1984; The Kirtland Temple: A Narrative History, 1986, 2nd ed., 1990; (with L.E. Braby) The Restoration: Themes of a Growing Faith, 1987; Invisible Saints: A History of

Black Americans in the Reorganized Church, 1988; Joseph Smith III: Pragmatic Prophet, 1988; Father Figure: Joseph Smith III and the Creation of the Reorganized Church, 1990. EDITOR: (with F.M. McKiernan) An Early Latter Day Saint History: The Book of John Whitmer, 1980; John Whitmer Historical Association Monograph Series, 1989-; (with McKiernan, and contrib.) Missouri Folk Heroes of the Nineteenth Century, 1989; New Series in NASA History, 1990-; (with W.B. Spillman) Let Contention Cease: The Dynamics of Dissent in the Reorganized Church of Jesus Christ of Latter Day Saints, 1991, 2nd ed., 1993; (with L. Thatcher) Differing Visions: Dissenters in Mormon History, 1994; History of Rocketry and Astronautics, 1994; Organizing for the Use of Space: Historical Perspectives on a Persistent Issue, 1995; (with J.E. Hallwas) Cultures in Conflict: A Documentary History of the Mormon War in Illinois, 1995; (with Hallwas) Kingdom on the Mississippi Revisited: Nauvoo in Mormon History, 1996. Contributor to books and magazines. **Address:** History Office, Headquarters National Aeronautics and Space Administration, Code Z, Washington, DC 20546, U.S.A.

LAURA, Dr. *See* **SCHLESSINGER, Laura.**

LAURENCE, Janet. Also writes as Julia Lisle. British, b. 1937. **Genres:** Mystery/Crime/Suspense, Food and Wine. **Career:** J. Walter Thompson (advertising agency), London, England, secretary, 1956-59; secretary in NYC and San Francisco, CA, 1959-60; Max Wilson (travel entrepreneur), personal assistant, 1960-65; Nielson, McCarthy (public relations firm), executive, 1965-70; free-lance public relations consultant; writer. Cooking instructor in own home, 1980-83. **Publications:** "DARINA LISLE" CRIME NOVELS A Deepe Coffyn, 1989; A Tasty Way to Die, 1990, 1991; Hotel Morgue, 1991; Recipe for Death, 1992; Death and the Epicure, 1993; Death at the Table, 1994; Death a la Provencale, 1995; Diet for Death, 1997; Appetite for Death, 1998; The Mermaid's Feast, 2000. HISTORICAL CRIME NOVELS: Canaletto & the Case of Westminster Bridge, 1997; Canaletto & the Case of the Privy Garden, 1999; Canaletto & the Case of Bonnie Prince Charlie, 2002. COOKBOOKS: A Little French Cookbook, 1989; A Little Scandinavian Cookbook, 1990; A Little Coffee Cookbook, 1992; Just for Two, 1992; Simply Delicious, 2001. OTHER: A Taste of Somerset Guide to Good Food and Drink, Books, 1989; To Kill The Past (suspense novel), 1994. Contributor of short stories to anthologies. AS JULIA LISLE: The Changing Years, 1993; A Perfect Match, 1996; Journeys from Home, 1997. **Address:** Conifers, Mayfield Close, Galhampton, Yeovil, Somerset BA22 7AX, England. **Online address:** Janetlaurence@compuserve.com

LAURENS, Jeannine. Belgian, b. 1950. **Genres:** History. **Career:** Provinciebestuur Oost-Vlaanderen, Ghent, Belgium, teacher, 1985-. **Publications:** (with R. Stallaerts) Historical Dictionary of the Republic of Croatia, 1995, 2nd ed., 2003. **Address:** Ellebogten 66, B-9070 Heusden, Belgium.

LAURENTS, Arthur. American, b. 1918. **Genres:** Novels, Plays/Screenplays. **Career:** Member of Council, Dramatists Guild, 1955-; Academy of Motion Picture Arts and Sciences; Screen Writers Guild; P.E.N.; Theatre Hall of Fame. Radio playwright, 1943-45; Director, Dramatists Play Service, NYC, 1961-66. Theater director: Invitation to a March, 1961; I Can Get It for Your Wholesale, 1961; Anyone Can Whistle, 1965; Gypsy, 1973; Scream, 1981; La Cage Aux Folles, 1983; Gypsy, 1989; Nick & Nora, 1991; Venecia, 2001; Hallelujah, Baby!, 2004. **Publications:** Home of the Brave (in U.K. as The Way Back), 1945; The Snake Pit (screenplay), 1948; Rope (screenplay), 1948; Caught (screenplay), 1949; The Bird Cage, 1950; The Time of the Cuckoo, 1953; Anastasia (screenplay), 1955; Bonjour Tristesse (screenplay), 1957; A Clearing in the Woods, 1957; West Side Story, 1958; Gypsy, 1959; Invitation to a March, 1961; Anyone Can Whistle, 1965; Do I Hear a Waltz?, 1966; Hallelujah, Baby!, 1967, rev. ed., 2004; The Way We Were (novel and screenplay), 1972; The Enclave, 1974; The Turning Point (novel and screenplay), 1977; Scream (play), 1981; A Loss of Memory (play), 1982; Nick & Nora, 1991; Jolson Sings Again, 1992; The Radical Mystique (play), 1995; My Good Name (play), 1997; Original Story By: A Memoir of Broadway and Hollywood, 2000; Big Potato (play), 2000; 2 Lives (play), 1999; Venecia (adaptation), 2001; The Vibrator, 2002; Attacks on the Heart (play), 2003; Selected Plays, 2004. **Address:** c/o Peter Franklin, William Morris Agency, 1325 Ave of the Americans, 15th Fl, New York, NY 10019, U.S.A.

LAURIE, Clayton D. American, b. 1954. **Genres:** History, Military/Defense/Arms control. **Career:** Public high school teacher in Council Bluffs, IA, 1977-84; U.S. Army Center of Military History, Washington, DC, military historian, 1986-. American University, adjunct lecturer, 1984-90; University of Maryland, Baltimore County, lecturer in history, 1991-. **Publications:** The Propaganda Warriors: America's Crusade Against Nazi Germany, 1996; The

Role of Federal Military Forces in Domestic Disorders, 1877-1945, 1996; The United States Army and Psychological Warfare Operations, 1918-1945, in press; (ed.) J.H. Ohly, The Emergency Operation of Industrial Facilities by the War Department During World War II, 1940-1945, in press. Contributor to journals. **Address:** 18302 Redbridge Ct., Olney, MD 20832-3032, U.S.A.

LAURIE, Edward James. American, b. 1925. **Genres:** Mystery/Crime/Suspense, Information science/Computers. **Career:** San Jose State University, CA (former Professor of Mgmt., Dept. Chairman, and Associate Dean), School of Business, Professor Emeritus of Marketing and Quantitative Studies, 1991-. **Publications:** Computer Applications in the U.S., 1960; Computers and How They Work, 1963; Computer and Computer Languages, 1966; Modern Computer Concepts, 1970; Computer, Automation and Society, 1979; The Borgia Blade, 2001; A Little Pinch of Death, 2001; The Detective Club, 2001; A Ladder of Death, 2001; The Seven Keys of Sara Seldon, 2001; One Murder for Money, 2002. **Address:** 1287 Pampas Dr, San Jose, CA 95120, U.S.A.

LAURIE, Hugh. British, b. 1959. **Genres:** Novels, Plays/Screenplays. **Career:** Actor and writer. Actor on stage. Directed an episode of Look at the State We're In, and a television commercial. Appeared music videos. Does voice over work for television commercials and animated films. Actor in television series, television movies, specials, and miniseries. Guest actor on television series. Actor in films. **Publications:** The Gun Seller (novel), 1996; (author of intro) P.G. Wodehouse, Jeeves and Wooster novels, 1996. TELEVISION PROGRAMS: Alfresco, 1982-83; The Crystal Cube, 1983; Saturday Live, 1986-87; Friday Night Live, 1988; A Bit of Fry and Laurie, 1987-95; Straight Talking, 1991; The Laughing Prisoner, 1993. **Address:** c/o The Gersh Agency, 232 N Canon Dr #201, Beverly Hills, CA 90210, U.S.A.

LAURIE, Peter. British, b. 1937. **Genres:** Adult non-fiction. **Career:** Journalist, editor, and software publisher. Freelance journalist for Vogue, Sunday Times (London), and other publications, 1962-79; Practical Computing, England, editor, 1979-82; Southdata Ltd. (software publishers), London, England, managing director, 1980-. **Publications:** Teenage Revolution, c. 1965; Drugs: Medical, Psychological and Social Facts, 1967; Beneath the City Streets: A Private Enquiry into the Nuclear Preoccupation of Government, 1970; Scotland Yard: A Personal Inquiry, 1970, in U.S. as Scotland Yard: A Study of the Metropolitan Police, 1971; Meet Your Friendly Social System, 1974; Electronics Explained, 1980; The Micro Revolution, 1980; The Computer Book, 1982; (with R. Bradbeer and P. De Bono) The Beginner's Guide to Computers, 1982; Joy of Computers, 1983; Databases: How to Manage Information on Your Micro, 1985; (with B. Laurie) Apache: The Definitive Guide, 1997. **Address:** Southdata Ltd., 166 Portobello Rd., London W11 2EB, England.

LAURIMORE, Jill Frances. American, b. 1947. **Genres:** Novels, Plays/Screenplays. **Career:** Playwright. **Publications:** PLAYS. TELEVISION: Family Tree, 1973; One's Company, 1974; (with H. Moore) The Georgian House, 1976. STAGE: Yours Most Affectionately, John Constable, 1976. NOVELS: Going to Pot, 1999; Dinosaur Days, 1999; The Bloody English Women of the Maison Puce, 2000; Cherry Ice, 2003. **Address:** c/o Simon Trewin, PFD, Drury House, 34-43 Russell St, London WC2B 5HA, England.

LAURSEN, John Christian. American, b. 1952. **Genres:** Politics/Government, Theology/Religion. **Career:** University of California, Riverside, professor of political science, 1991-. **Publications:** The Politics of Skepticism in the Ancients, Montaigne, Hume, and Kant, 1992. EDITOR/CO-EDITOR: New Essays on the Political Thought of the Huguenots of the Refuge, 1995; Difference and Dissent: Religious Toleration in Medieval and Early Modern Europe, 1996; Beyond the Persecuting Society: Religious Toleration before the Enlightenment, 1998; Religious Toleration: "The Variety of Rites" from Cyrus to Defoe, 1999; Carl Friedrich Bahrdt: The Edict of Religion and History and Diary of My Imprisonment, 2000; Millenarianism and Messianism in Early Modern European Culture, vol. 4: Continental Millenarians, 2001; Histories of Heresy in Early Modern Europe, 2002; Early French and German Defenses of Freedom of the Press, 2003. **Address:** Department of Political Science, University of California, Riverside, CA 92521, U.S.A.

LAUTERBACH, Ann. American, b. 1942. **Genres:** Poetry. **Career:** Poet, 1979-. Worked as an editor for art-book publisher Thames and Hudson, as editor of a monthly magazine on the history of modern art, and as publicity director of the Institute of Contemporary Arts in London, England, 1967-74. **Publications:** Many Times, But Then, 1979; Before Recollection, 1987; Clamor, 1991; And for Example, 1994; On a Stair, 1997; If in Time, 1975-

2000, 2001. **Address:** Department of English, Bard College, PO Box 5000, Annandale On Hudson, NY 12504, U.S.A.

LAUTERBORN, Robert F. American, b. 1936. **Genres:** Marketing, Advertising/Public relations. **Career:** Syracuse Herald Journal, Syracuse, NY, advertising sales representative, 1957-60; General Electric Co., worked in marketing and corporate communications, 1960-76; International Paper, NYC, director of marketing communications and corporate advertising, 1976-86; University of North Carolina at Chapel Hill, James L. Knight Professor of Advertising, 1986-. **Publications:** (coauthor) Integrated Marketing Communications, 1992; The New Marketing Paradigm, 1996. **Address:** CB 3365, University of North Carolina at Chapel Hill, Chapel Hill, NC 27599, U.S.A.

LAUTERSTEIN, Ingeborg. American (born Austria), b. 1933. **Genres:** Novels. **Career:** Director, Boston Author's Club, since 1983. **Publications:** The Water Castle, 1981; Vienna Girl, 1986. **Address:** 7 Pleasant St, Rockport, MA 01966, U.S.A.

LAUTURE, Denizé. American (born Haiti), b. 1946. **Genres:** Children's fiction, Poetry. **Career:** St. Thomas Aquinas College, Sparkill, NY, assistant professor of French and Spanish, 1980-. Performance poet; consultant on Haitian culture and language; children's book writer, 1980-. **Publications:** POETRY: The Blues of the Lightning Metamorphosis (in Creole), 1987; When the Denizen Weeps, 1989. PICTURE BOOKS: Father and Son, 1993; Running the Road to ABC, 1996; Mother and Twin Daughters, 2004. Contributor to periodicals. **Address:** St. Thomas Aquinas College, Rd 340, Sparkill, NY 10976, U.S.A. **Online address:** dlauture@stac.edu

LAUX, Constance. Also writes as Connie Deka, Zoe Daniels, Connie Lane. American, b. 1952. **Genres:** Young adult fiction, Romance/Historical, Horror. **Career:** Writer. **Publications:** ROMANCE NOVELS: Twilight Secrets, 1992; (as Connie Deka) Bright Promise, 1993; Moonlight Whispers, 1993; Earthly Delights, 1995; Touched by Magic, 1996; Devil's Diamond, 1998; Diamond Rain, 1999; Diamonds and Desire, 2000; (as Connie Lane) Reinventing Romeo, 2000. YOUNG ADULT HORROR: (as Zoe Daniels) Year of the Cat (trilogy), Book I: The Dream, Book II: The Hunt, Book III: The Amulet, 1995; Blood Moon (trilogy), Book I: The Curse, 1995, Book II: The Fortune Teller, 1995, Book III: The Reckoning, 1996; R.L. Stine's Ghosts of Fear Street, Book VII: Fright Knight, 1996. Work represented in anthologies. **Address:** c/o Writer's House, 21 W 26th St, New York, NY 10010, U.S.A.

LAVENDER, Abraham D(onald). American, b. 1940. **Genres:** Anthropology/Ethnology, Cultural/Ethnic topics, Genealogy/Heraldry, Local history/Rural topics, Politics/Government, Sex, Sociology. **Career:** University of Maryland, European Division, Izmir, Turkey, lecturer in psychology, 1967-68; St. Mary's College of Maryland, St. Mary's City, lecturer, 1972-73, assistant professor, 1973-74; University of Maryland at College Park, visiting assistant professor of sociology, 1974-77; University of Miami, adjunct faculty, summers, 1986-88, Coral Gables, FL, assistant professor, 1977-79, associate professor of sociology, 1979-83; Florida International University, Miami, adjunct, 1986-91, assistant professor, 1990-91, associate professor, 1991-97, professor of sociology and anthropology, 1997-. St. Thomas University, adjunct faculty, 1985-87; guest on radio and television programs; public speaker. **Publications:** Ethnic Women and Feminist Values: Toward a "New" Value System, 1986; French Huguenots: From Mediterranean Catholics to White Anglo-Saxon Protestants, 1990; (with C. Steinberg) Jewish Farmers of the Catskills: A Century of Survival, 1995; Miami Beach 1920: The Making of a Winter Resort, 2002. EDITOR: A Coat of Many Colors: Jewish Subcommunities in the United States, 1977; (with A. Newson) Black Communities in Transition: Voices from South Florida, 1996. Contributor to books. Contributor of articles and reviews to periodicals. **Address:** Dept of Sociology and Anthropology, Florida International University, Miami, FL 33199, U.S.A. **Online address:** lavender@fiu.edu

LAVERY, Bryony. British, b. 1947. **Genres:** Plays/Screenplays. **Career:** Artistic dir., Les Oeufs Malades, 1976-78, Extraordinary Productions, 1979-80, and Female Trouble, 1981-83, all London; Resident playwright, Unicorn Theatre for Children, London, 1985-87; Artistic Director, Gay Sweatshop, 1988-90; Tutor, M.A. Playwriting, Birmingham University, 1989-92. **Publications:** Uniforms and Uniformed, and Numerical Man (in Masks and Faces), 1984; Origin of the Species (Plays by Women, vol. 6), 1987; The Wild Bunch, 1989; Her Aching Heart & Other Plays, 1991; Nothing Compares to You, 1995; Goliath, 1997; Ophelia, 1997; Frozen, 1998; Wedding Story, 2000. **Address:** c/o St John Donald, PFD, Drury House, 34-43 Russell St., London WC2B 5HA, England.

LAVERY, David. American, b. 1949. **Genres:** Communications/Media, Film, Literary criticism and history. **Career:** College of St. Benedict, St. Joseph, MN, instructor in English, 1975-76; University of North Florida, Jacksonville, adjunct assistant professor of English, 1979-80; Seattle University, WA, visiting assistant professor of English, 1980-81; East China Normal University, Shanghai, foreign expert in English, 1981; University of Alabama, Huntsville, interim assistant professor of English, 1981-83; Northern Kentucky University, Highland Heights, assistant professor, 1983-87, associate professor of English, 1987-88; University of Memphis, TN, associate professor of communication and film studies, 1988-93; Middle Tennessee State University, Murfreesboro, professor of English, 1993-, department head, 1993-97. **Publications:** Late for the Sky: The Mentality of the Space Age, 1992; (co-author and co-producer) Owen Barfield: Man and Meaning (film), 1994. EDITOR & CONTRIBUTOR: Full of Secrets: Critical Approaches to Twin Peaks, 1994; (with A. Hague and M. Cartwright) Deny All Knowledge: Reading the X-Files, 1996; This Thing of Ours: Investigating the Sopranos, 2002; (with A. Hague) Teleparody: Predicting/Preventing the TV Discourse of Tomorrow, 2002; (with R.V. Wilcox) Fighting the Forces: What's at Stake in Buffy the Vampire Slayer, 2002. Contributor to books. Contributor of articles, poetry, short fiction, and reviews to periodicals. **Address:** Department of English, Middle Tennessee State University, Murfreesboro, TN 37132, U.S.A. **Online address:** dlavery@mtsu.edu; www. mtsu.edu/~dlavery

LAVIGNE, Louis-Dominique. Canadian. **Genres:** Plays/Screenplays. **Career:** Writer, director, and actor for film and television. Founding member of several contemporary theater troupes, including Theatre de Quartier. Teacher of creative writing, University of Quebec. **Publications:** PLAYS: As-tu peur des voleurs?, trans. by H. Beissel as Are You Afraid of Thieves?, 1978; On est capable (You Can Do It; juvenile), 1981; Parasol (juvenile), 1988; Le sous-sol des anges (juvenile), 1991; Rosemonde, trans. by M. Bromilow, 1997; Les petits orteils (juvenile), 1998, trans. as Ten Tiny Toes, 1998; Tu peux toujours danser (juvenile), 1998. PLAYS WITH J. DEBEFVE: Le voyage de Petit Morceau; L'Arche de Noe; La soupe au crapaud; Le piano sauvage; L'Ornithorynque; Desordres; La grande maison; Kobold!; Les Papas. **Address:** c/o Theatre Department, University of Quebec at Montreal, Case Postale 8888, Succursale Centre-Ville, Montreal, QC, Canada H3C 3P8.

LAVIN, Irving. American, b. 1927. **Genres:** Art/Art history. **Career:** Dumbarton Oaks, Fellow, 1957-1959; Vassar College, Poughkeepsie, NY, lecturer in art history, 1959-1962; New York University, NYC, associate professor of art history, became professor, 1963-1973; Institute for Advanced Study, Princeton, NJ, professor of historical studies, 1973-. Columbia University, NYC, Matthews Lecturer, 1957; Pierpont Morgan Library, NY, Franklin Jasper Walls Lecturer, 1975. **Publications:** Bernini and the Crossing of St. Peter's, 1968; Bernini and the Unity of the Visual Arts, 2 vols, 1980; (with P. Gordon, and others) Drawings by Gianlorenzo Bernini: From the Museum der Bildenden, (exhibition and catalogue), 1981; Bernin et l'Art de la Satire Social, 1987; Past-Present: Essays on Historicism in Art from Donatello to Picasso, 1993. EDITOR: (with J. Plummer) Studies in Late Medieval and Renaissance Painting in Honor of Millard Meiss, 2 vols, 1978; Gianlorenzo Bernini: New Aspects of his Art and Thought: A Commemorative Volume, 1986; World Art: Themes of Unity in Diversity: Acts of the XXVIth International Congress of the History of Art, 1986; (with W. Tronzo) Studies on Art and Archeology in Honor of Ernst Kitzinger on his Seventy-Fifth Birthday, 1987; Meaning in the Visual Arts: Views from the Outside: A Centennial Commemoration of Erwin Panofsky (1892-1968) (proceedings of a symposium), 1995; Three Essays on Style, by Erwin Panofsky, with a memoir by William S. Heckscher, 1996. Author of many scholarly papers. **Address:** School of Historical Studies, Institute for Advanced Study, Princeton, NJ 08540, U.S.A.

LAVIN, Maud. American, b. 1954. **Genres:** Design, History, Photography. **Career:** School of the Art Institute of Chicago, visual & critical studies & art history, associate professor. **Publications:** (with M. Teitelbaum and others) Montage and Modern Life, 1919-42, 1992; Cut with the Kitchen Knife: The Weimar Photomontages of Hannah Hoch, 1993; Clean New World, 2001; (with M. Archer and others) The Business of Holidays, 2004. **Address:** School of the Art Institute of Chicago, 112 S Michigan, Chicago, IL 60603-3103, U.S.A. **Online address:** mlavin@artic.edu

LAVINE, Steven D(avid). American, b. 1947. **Genres:** Art/Art history, Literary criticism and history. **Career:** University of Michigan, Ann Arbor, assistant professor of English and American literature, 1974-81; Rockefeller Foundation, NYC, assistant director for arts and humanities, 1983-86, associate director, 1986-88; California Institute of the Arts, Valencia, president, 1988-; writer. New York University, adjunct associate professor, 1984-85;

serves on boards of cultural institutions. **Publications:** EDITOR: (with H. Thomas) The Hopwood Anthology: Five Decades of American Poetry, 1981; (with I. Karp) Exhibiting Cultures: The Poetics and Politics of Museum Display, 1991; (with Karp and C.M. Kreamer) Museums and Communities: The Politics of Public Culture, 1992. Work represented in anthologies. Contributor of articles and reviews to academic journals. **Address:** Office of the President, California Institute of the Arts, 24700 McBean Parkway, Valencia, CA 91355, U.S.A.

LAW, Clara. Australian (born Macao), b. 1957. **Genres:** Plays/Screenplays. **Career:** Director and writer. **Publications:** SCREENPLAYS: (with E. Ling-Ching Fong) Floating Life, 1996; The Goddess of 1967, 2000. **Address:** c/o Southern Star Film Sales, Level 10 8 West St., North Sydney, NSW 2060, Australia.

LAW, John. British, b. 1946. **Genres:** Anthropology/Ethnology, Sociology. **Career:** University of Keele, Keele, England, became professor of sociology and social anthropology, 1973-. **Publications:** (with P. Lodge) Science for Social Scientists, 1984; (ed.) Power, Action, and Belief, 1986; (ed. with G. Fyfe) Picturing Power, 1988; (ed.) A Sociology of Monsters, 1991; (ed. with W.E. Bijker) Shaping Technology/Building Society, 1992; Organizing Modernity, 1994. **Address:** Department of Sociology, Centre for Science Studies, Cartmel College, Lancaster University, Lancaster LA1 4YL, England. **Online address:** j.law@lancaster.ac.uk

LAWDEN, Derek Frank. British, b. 1919. **Genres:** Mathematics/Statistics, Physics. **Career:** Head, Dept. of Mathematics, University of Canterbury, N. Z., 1956-67; Professor of Mathematics, University of Aston in Birmingham, 1967-83. **Publications:** Mathematics of Engineering Systems, 1954; Course of Applied Mathematics, 2 vols., 1960; Optimal Trajectories for Space Navigation, 1963; Mathematical Principles of Quantum Mechanics, 1967; Analytical Mechanics, 1972; Electromagnetism, 1973; Analytical Methods of Optimization, 1974; Introduction to Tensor Calculus, Relativity and Cosmology, 1982; Elements of Relativity Theory, 1985; Principles of Thermodynamics and Statistical Mechanics, 1986; Elliptic Functions and Applications, 1989. **Address:** Newhall, Church Bank, Temple Grafton, Alcester B49 6NU, England.

LAWLER, Nancy Ellen. American. **Genres:** Bibliography. **Career:** Historian. Oakton Community College, Des Plaines, IL, professor emeritus of economics and history. **Publications:** Soldiers of Misfortune: Ivoirien Tirailleurs of World War II, 1992; (editor, with John O. Hunwick) The Cloth of Many Colored Silks: Papers on History and Society, Ghanaian and Islamic, in Honor of Ivor Wilks, 1996; Soldiers, Airmen, Spies, and Whisperers: The Gold Coast in World War II, 2002. **Address:** c/o Author Mail, Ohio University Press, Scott Quadrangle, 1 Ohio University, Athens, OH 45701, U.S.A.

LAWLER, Patrick. American, b. 1948. **Genres:** Plays/Screenplays, Poetry. **Career:** Syracuse University, Syracuse, NY, teaching assistant and part-time instructor of writing courses, 1977-78, 1982-90; Onondaga Community College, Syracuse, tutor and adjunct instructor, 1978-; State University of New York, College of Environmental Science and Forestry, Syracuse, assistant professor of technical communications and writing project coordinator, 1990-; poet. Community Writers' Project, member of board of directors, 1988-89; held administrative and short-term teaching positions. **Publications:** PLAYS: (with S. Clark, K. Moore, and R. Estevez) What's Inside (performance piece), 1988; Voice/Box, 1988. POETRY: (ed. and contrib.) The Remembered Gate (anthology), 1979; A Drowning Man Is Never Tall Enough, 1990; Reading a Burning Book, 1994. **Address:** State University of New York, College of Environmental Science and Forestry, 1 Forestry Dr Rm 105 Moon, Syracuse, NY 13210, U.S.A. **Online address:** pjlawler@syr.edu

LAWLER, Peter Augustine. American, b. 1951. **Genres:** Politics/Government. **Career:** Educator and writer. Florida Southern College, Lakeland, instructor, 1978-79; Berry College, Mt. Berry, GA, assistant professor, 1979-83, associate professor of political science, 1983-; American Political Rhetoric, editor, 1982. **Publications:** The Restless Mind: Alexis de Tocqueville on the Origin and Perpetuation of Human Liberty, 1993; Under God with Liberty: The Religious Dimension of the American Idea of Liberty, 1994; A Question of Values: John Galtung's Peace Research, 1995; American Views of Liberty, 1997. EDITOR: American Political Rhetoric: A Reader, 1982, 2nd rev ed, 1995; Tocqueville's Political Science: Classic Essays, 1992; (with J. Alulis) Tocqueville's Defense of Human Liberty: Current Essays, 1993; (with R.M. Schaefer) The American Experience: Essays on the Theory and Practice of Liberty, 1994; (with J.M. Knippenberg) Poets, Princes,

and Private Citizens, 1996. **Address:** Department of Government & International Studies, Evans 115, Berry College, 2277 Martha Berry Hwy NW, Mt. Berry, GA 30149, U.S.A.

LAWLESS, John. *See* BEST, Don(ald M.).

LAWRENCE, Bruce B. American. **Genres:** Theology/Religion. **Career:** Religious historian. Duke University, professor (Islamic studies). **Publications:** RELIGIOUS HISTORY: Shahrastani on the Indian Religions, 1976; An Overview of Sufi Literature in the Sultanate Period, 1206-1526 A.D., 1979; Defenders of God: The Fundamentalist Revolt against the Modern Age, 1989; (trans. and annotator) Nizam ad-din Awliya: Morals for the Heart: Conversations of Shaykh Nizam ad-din Awliya Recorded by Amir Hasan Sijzi, 1992; Shattering the Myth: Islam beyond Violence, 1998. OTHER: The Complete Idiot's Guide to Religions Online, 2000; New Faiths, Old Icons: Muslims and Other Asian Immigrants in American Religious Life, 2002. EDITOR: Ibn Khaldun and Islamic Ideology, 1984; (with D. Gilmartin) Beyond Turk and Hindu: Rethinking Religions Ideologies in Islamicate South Asia, 2000. **Address:** Department of Religion, Duke University, Box 90964, Durham, NC 27708, U.S.A.

LAWRENCE, C(lifford) H(ugh). British, b. 1921. **Genres:** History, Theology/Religion. **Career:** University of London, Bedford College, London, England, lecturer, 1951-62, reader, 1962-70, professor of medieval history, 1970-87, head of department, 1980-85, professor emeritus, 1987-. Member of Press Council, 1977-81. Vice-chairman of Heythrop College, London, 1987-95. **Publications:** St. Edmund of Abingdon: A Study of History and Hagiography, 1960; Medieval Monasticism: Forms of Religious Life in Western Europe in the Middle Ages, 1984, 3rd ed., 2000; The Friars: The Impact of the Early Mendicant Movement on Western Society, 1994. EDITOR: (and contrib.) The English Church and the Papacy, 1965, 2nd ed., 1999; (and trans.) The Life of St. Edmund by M. Paris, 1996; (and trans.) The Letters of Adam Marsh, 2005. **Address:** 11 Durham Rd, London SW20 0QH, England.

LAWRENCE, Caroline. American. **Genres:** Children's fiction. **Career:** Writer; taught Latin, French and art at a small London primary school. **Publications:** ROMAN MYSTERY SERIES: Secrets of Vesuvius, 2001; The Thieves of Ostia, 2002; The Pirates of Pompeii, 2003; The Dolphins of Laurentum, 2003; The Assassins of Rome, 2003. **Address:** c/o Author Mail, Roaring Brook Press, 2 Old New Milford Rd., Brookfield, CT 06804, U.S.A. **Online address:** flaviagemina@hotmail.com; www.romanmysteries.com

LAWRENCE, Kathleen Rockwell. American. **Genres:** Novels, Novellas/Short stories, Essays. **Career:** Baruch College, English department. **Publications:** Maud Gone (novel), 1986; The Last Room in Manhattan (novel), 1988; The Boys I Didn't Kiss, and Other Essays, 1990. **Address:** 510 E 23rd St #13B, New York, NY 10010, U.S.A.

LAWRENCE, Louise. (Elizabeth Rhoda Holden). British, b. 1943. **Genres:** Science fiction/Fantasy, Young adult fiction. **Career:** Fulltime writer. Assistant Librarian, Gloucestershire County Library, 1960-64, and at Forest of Dean branches, 1969-71. **Publications:** Andra, 1971; The Power of Stars, 1972; The Wyndcliffe, 1975; Sing and Scatter Daisies, 1977; Star Lord, 1978; Cat Call, 1980; The Earth Witch, 1982; Calling B for Butterfly, 1982; Dram Road, 1983; Children of the Dust, 1985; Moonwind, 1986; The Warriors of Taan, 1986; Extinction Is Forever, 1990; Ben-Harran's Castle, 1992; Journey through Llandor, 1994; Road to Irriyan, 1995; Shadow of Mordican, 1996; Dreamweaver, 1996; The Crowlings, 1999. **Address:** c/o A.M. Heath, 79 St. Martin's Lane, London WC2N 4AA, England.

LAWRENCE, Martha C. American, b. 1956. **Genres:** Mystery/Crime/Suspense, Crafts. **Career:** Writer. Simon & Schuster, NYC, assistant editor, 198183; Harcourt Brace, San Diego, CA, acquisitions editor, 1983-87; business writer and astrologer, San Diego, CA, 1987-95. **Publications:** NONFICTION: Lightship Baskets of Nantucket, 1990; Scrimshaw: The Whaler's Legacy, 1993. MYSTERY NOVELS: Murder in Scorpio, 1995; The Cold Heart of Capricorn, 1997; Aquarius Descending, 1999. Contributor of short stories to magazines. **Address:** c/o Gina Maccoby Literary Agency, PO Box 60, Chappaqua, NY 10514, U.S.A. **Online address:** mysmartha@mlawrence.com

LAWRENCE, Michael. British, b. 1943. **Genres:** Children's fiction, Poetry. **Career:** Writer. Freelance photographer for publications and advertising agencies, pop music managements, and others. Worked as a graphic designer, antiques dealer, painter, sculptor, kibbutz worker, farmhand, copywriter, photographic printer, and press officer for a traveling circus. **Publications:**

Nudes and Victims (poetry collection), 1993; When the Snow Falls (novel), 1995; Finella Minella, 1998; Baby Loves, 1998; (with R. Ingpen) The Poppykettle Papers, 1999; The Caterpillar that Roared, 2000; Baby Loves Hugs and Kisses, 2000; Baby Loves Visiting, 2002; Young Dracula, 2002; Baby Loves Visiting, 2002; Milking the Novelty (memoir). JIGGY McCUE SERIES: The Poltergoose, 1999; The Killer Underpants, 2000; The Toilet of Doom, 2001; Maggot Pie, 2002. Contributor to juvenile anthologies. **Address:** c/o Author Mail, Dutton Children's Books, 345 Hudson St., New York, NY 10014, U.S.A.

LAWRENCE, P. *See* **TUBB, E(dwin) C(harles).**

LAWRENCE, Starling. American. **Genres:** Novels, Novellas/Short stories. **Career:** Editor and author. Crossroads Africa; Peace Corps, Cameroon, volunteer teacher of English, c. 1966-69; W.W. Norton, NYC, reader to editor-in-chief, 1970-. **Publications:** Legacies (short stories), 1996; Montenegro (novel), 1997. **Address:** W. W. Norton & Co., 500 Fifth Avenue, New York, NY 10110, U.S.A.

LAWRENCE, Steven C. (Lawrence Agustus Murphy). Also writes as C. L. Murphy. American, b. 1924. **Genres:** Westerns/Adventure, History. **Career:** Writer. English Teacher and Dept. Chairman, South Jr. High School, Brockton, Massachusetts, 1951-87. Instructor in Creative Writing, Stonehill College, North Easton, Massachusetts, 1967. **Publications:** The Naked Range, 1956; Saddle Justice, 1957; Brand of a Texan, 1958; The Iron Marshal, 1960; Night of the Gunmen, 1960; Gun Fury, 1961; With Blood in Their Eyes, 1961; Slattery, and Bullet Welcome for Slattery, 1961, Slattery published separately as The Lynchers, 1975; Walk a Narrow Trail, and a Noose for Slattery, 1962; Longhorns North, and Slattery's Gun Says No, 1962; A Texan Comes Riding, 1966; (as C.L. Murphy) Buffalo Grass (juvenile), 1966; That Man from Texas, 1972; Edge of the Land, 1974; Six-Gun Junction, 1974; North to Montana, 1975; Slattery Stands Alone, 1976; A Northern Saga: The Account of the North Atlantic-Murmansk, Russia, Convoys, 1976; Trial for Tennihan, 1976; Day of the Comancheros, 1977; Gun Blast, 1977; Slattery Stands Alone, 1979. **Address:** 30 Mercedes Rd, Brockton, MA 02301, U.S.A.

LAWRENCE-LIGHTFOOT, Sara. American. **Genres:** Education, Biography. **Career:** Harvard Graduate School of Education, Cambridge, MA, professor; writer. **Publications:** NONFICTION: Worlds Apart: Relationships between Families and Schools, 1978; (with J.V. Carew) Beyond Bias: Perspectives on Classrooms, 1979; The Good High School: Portraits of Character and Culture, 1983; Balm in Gilead: Journey of a Healer (biography), 1988; I've Known Rivers: Lives of Loss and Liberation, 1994. Author of articles, essays, and monographs. **Address:** Harvard Graduate School of Education, Dept. of Educational Administration, Harvard University, Cambridge, MA 02138, U.S.A.

LAWSON, Chet. *See* **TUBB, E(dwin) C(harles).**

LAWSON, James. American, b. 1938. **Genres:** Novels. **Career:** Sr. Vice President 1982-93, Creative Director, 1986-93, DDB Needham Worldwide, NYC (Associate Creative Director, 1982-86). Copywriter, McCann-Marschalk Advertising, 1961-62, J. Walker Thompson Advertising, NYC, 1963-64, and Al Paul Lefton Advertising, Philadelphia, 1964-66; Reporter, Aspen Times, Colorado, 1962; Vice-President and Copy Supvr., Doyle Dane Bernbach Advertising, NYC, 1966-78; Sr. Vice-President and Director of Creative Services, Doremus and Co., NYC., 1978-80; Vice President and Creative Director, Cunningham and Walsh Advertising, Los Angeles, 1980-82. **Publications:** NOVELS: Disconnections, 1968; The American Book of the Dead, 1972; Crimes of the Unconscious, 1974; The Girl Watcher, 1975; The Copley Chronicles, 1980; The Fanatic, 1980; Forgeries of the Heart, 1982; The Madman's Kiss, 1988, screenplay, 1992; The Reluctant God, 1993; Tales of Summer, 1997. SCREENPLAYS: The Age of Secrets, 1993; The Agency, 1993; Out of Bounds, 1994; Human Relations, 1994; Temporary Insanity, 1994; By Reason of Insanity, 1995; Going Nowhere, 1996; Why We're Here, 1997. OTHER: Andris in Isolation (play), 1993. **Address:** 151 Charles St., New York, NY 10014-2539, U.S.A.

LAWSON, JonArno Burhans. Canadian, b. 1968. **Genres:** Novels. **Career:** Beth Tikvah Group Home, Hamilton, Ontario, group home counselor, 1992-96; McCarthy-Tetrault Law Firm, Toronto, Ontario, library clerk, 1996-97; University of Toronto, Toronto, information services technician, 1997. **Publications:** Love Is an Observant Traveller, 1997. Contributor to periodicals. **Address:** 31 Hillside Ave., Dundas, ON, Canada L9H 4H7. **Online address:** amy.freedman@utoronto.ca

LAWSON, Linda. American, b. 1952. **Genres:** Writing/Journalism, Communications/Media. **Career:** Michigan Consumers Council, Lansing, MI, director of information, 1976-81; Ferris State University, Big Rapids, MI, instructor, 1981-82; Indiana University, Bloomington, assistant professor, 1988-95, associate professor, 1995-. **Publications:** Truth in Publishing: Federal Regulation of the Press's Business Practices, 1993. Contributor to periodicals. **Address:** Indiana University, School of Journalism, 200 Ernie Pyle Hall, Bloomington, IN 47405, U.S.A.

LAWSON, Philip. *See* **BISHOP, Michael.**

LAWSON, Philip. *See* **DI FILIPPO, Paul.**

LAWTON, Barbara (Perry). American, b. 1930. **Genres:** Horticulture. **Career:** Missouri Botanical Garden, manager of publications and editor of M.B.G. Bulletin, 1967-72; St. Louis Post-Dispatch, St. Louis, MO, weekly columnist, 1972-90; Gary Ferguson, (public relations), public relations counselor and partner, 1972-81; Daniel J. Edelman (public relations), St. Louis, account supervisor, 1981-84; Lawton & Associates (public relations and writing services), Kirkwood, MO, public relations counselor and writer, 1984-; writer and photographer. **Publications:** Improving Your Garden Soil, 1992; (with G.F. Van Patten) Organic Gardener's Basics, 1993; Seasonal Guide to the Natural Year-Illinois, Missouri, and Arkansas, 1994; The Magic of Irises, 1997. **Address:** c/o Timber Press, 133 SW 2nd Ave Ste 450, Portland, OR 97204, U.S.A.

LAWTON, John. British, b. 1949. **Genres:** Novels. **Career:** BBC Filmmaker, novelist. **Publications:** Black Out, 1995; Old Flames, 1997; A Little White Death, 1998. **Address:** c/o Viking Books Publicity, 375 Hudson St., New York, NY 10014, U.S.A.

LAX, Eric. American (born Canada), b. 1944. **Genres:** Film, Medicine/Health, Biography, Documentaries/Reportage. **Career:** Freelance writer. **Publications:** On Being Funny: Woody Allen and Comedy, 1975; Life and Death on 10 West, 1984; Woody Allen: A Biography, 1991; Paul Newman, 1996; (with A.M. Serber) Bogart, 1997. **Address:** 609 Trenton Dr, Beverly Hills, CA 90210-3102, U.S.A.

LAXDAL, Vivienne. Canadian, b. 1962. **Genres:** Plays/Screenplays. **Career:** Playwright and actor, premiering often in Ottawa by the Great Canadian Theatre Company and the National Arts Centre; Centaur Theatre (Montreal), Canadian Stage Company (Toronto), Odyssey Theatre (Ottawa), resident playwright. **Publications:** PLAYS: Blood-Brother, Step-Sister (juvenile), 1986; (with B. Lysnes) A Quantum Leap, 1987; Goose Spit, 1988; Ruby and the Rock, 1991; Karla and Grif, 1991; Personal Convictions, 1991; Angel's Goose, 1992; (with J.M. Dalpe) National CAPITALe Nationale, 1993; Cyberwomb, 1994; The Family Canoe, 1995; These Girls, 1999. PERFORMANCE PIECES: The Mother Beat; Ratiocination; Iron Maids. **Address:** RR#2, Box 206, Masham, QC, Canada J0X 2W0. **Online address:** laxdal@msn.com

LAYTON, Bentley. American. **Genres:** Theology/Religion. **Career:** Yale University, New Haven, CT, professor of religious studies. **Publications:** (ed.) The Gnostic Treatise on Resurrection from Nag Hammadi, 1979; Catalogue of Coptic Literary Manuscripts in the British Library Acquired since the Year 1906, 1987; The Gnostic Scriptures: A New Translation, 1987; (ed.) Nag Hammadi Codex II, 2-7: Together with XIII, 2, 1989; Coptic Grammar, 2000. **Address:** Dept. of Religious Studies, 451 College St, PO Box 208287, Yale University, New Haven, CT 06520-8287, U.S.A. **Online address:** bentley.layton@yale.edu

LAYTON, Irving (Peter). Canadian (born Romania), b. 1912. **Genres:** Novellas/Short stories, Poetry, Autobiography/Memoirs, Essays. **Career:** Professor of English Literature, York University, Toronto, 1969-. Associate Ed., First Statement, later Northern Review, Montreal, 1941-43; former Associate Ed., Contact mag., Toronto, and Black Mountain Review, North Carolina; Lecturer, Jewish Public Library, Montreal, 1943-58; high sch. teacher in Montreal, 1946-60; Part-time Lecturer, 1949-68, and Poet-in-Residence, 1965-66, Sir George Williams University, Montreal; Writer-in-Residence, University of Guelph, ON, 1968-69; Poet-in-Residence, University of Ottawa, ON, 1978-79; Writer-in-Residence, University of Toronto, 1981; Adjunct Professor, 1988, 1989, and Writer-in-Residence, 1989, Concordia University. **Publications:** Here and Now, 1945; Now Is the Place: Stories and Poems, 1948; The Black Huntsmen, 1951; (with R. Souster and L. Dudek) Cerberus, 1952; Love the Conqueror Worm, 1953; In the Midst of My Fever, 1954; The Cold Green Element, 1955; The Blue Propellor, 1955; The Bull Calf and Other Poems, 1956; Music on a Kazoo, 1956; The

Improved Binoculars: Selected Poems, 1956; A Laughter in the Mind, 1958; rev. ed., 1959; A Red Carpet for the Sun: Collected Poems, 1959; The Swinging Flesh, 1961; The Laughing Rooster, 1964; Collected Poems, 1965; Periods of the Moon: Poems, 1967; The Shattered Plinths, 1968; The Whole Bloody Bird (obs, aphs, and pomes), 1969; Selected Poems, 1969; Collected Poems, 1971; Nail Polish, 1971; Engagements: The Prose of Irving Layton, 1972; Lovers and Lesser Men, 1973; The Pole-Vaulter, 1974; Seventy-Five Greek Poems, 1974; Selected Poems, 2 vols., 1975; For My Brother Jesus, 1976; The Uncollected Poems 1936-59, 1976; The Poems of Irving Layton, 1977; The Covenant, 1977, Taking Sides: The Collected Social and Political Writings, 1977; The Tightrope Dancer, 1978; Droppings from Heaven, 1979; The Love Poems of Irving Layton, 1979; There Were No Signs, 1979; An Unlikely Affair: The Correspondence of Irving Layton and Dorothy Rath, 1979; For My Neighbors in Hell, 1980; Europe and Other Bad News, 1981; A Wild Peculiar Joy, 1982; The Gucci Bag, 1983; With Reverence and Delight: The Love Poems, 1984; A Spider Danced Cozy Jig, 1984; Where Burning Sappho Loved, 1985; Selected Poems, 1985; Waiting for the Messiah (memoirs), 1985; Dance with Desire, 1986; Final Reckoning: Poems 1982-86, 1987; Fortunate Exile, 1987; Wild Gooseberries: Selected Letters, 1989; Irving Layton and Robert Creeley: The Compete Correspondence, 1953-78, 1990; Fornalutx: Selected Poems 1928-1990, 1991. EDITOR: (with L. Dudek) Canadian Poems, 1850-1952, 1952; Panic: A Selection of Contemporary Canadian Poems, 1958; Poems for 27 Cents, 1961; Love Where the Nights Are Long: Canadian Love Poems, 1962; Anvil: A Selection of Workshop Poems, 1966; Poems to Colour, 1970; Anvil Blood (poems), 1973. Address: Maimonides Hosptial Geriatric Center, 4th Floor, Room D7, 5795 Caldwell Ave, Cote St. Luc, QC, Canada H4W 1W3.

LAZARUS-BLACK, Mindie. American. Genres: Anthropology/Ethnology, Law. Career: University of Illinois at Chicago Circle, Chicago, associate professor of criminal justice and affiliate assistant professor of anthropology, both 1990-. Conducted field work in Antigua, Barbados, and Trinidad, 1985-95. Publications: Legitimate Acts and Illegal Encounters: Law and Society in Antigua and Barbuda, 1994. EDITOR: (with P. Lange) Family Business in Dallas: A Matter of Values, 1982; (with S. Hirsch and contrib.) Contested States: Law, Hegemony and Resistance, 1994. Contributor to books. Contributor of articles and reviews to periodicals. Address: 624 Sheridan Sq, Apt 2, Evanston, IL 60202-4750, U.S.A.

LAZEBNIK, Claire Scovell. (born United States). Genres: Education. Career: Writer. Publications: Same As It Never Was (novel), 2003, published as Olivia's Sister, 2003; (with Lynn Kern Koegel) Overcoming Autism: Finding the Answers, Strategies, and Hope That Can Transform a Child's Life, 2004. Address: c/o Viking Press, 375 Hudson Street, New York, NY 10014, U.S.A. Online address: Claire@sameasitneverwas.com

LAZENBY, Edith P. American, b. 1945. Genres: Theology/Religion. Career: Evangelist. Publications: Tabernacle in the Wilderness, as It Relates to Jesus Christ, 1997. Address: PO Box 300928, JFK Airport Station, Jamaica, NY 11430-0928, U.S.A. Online address: exelsie@aol.com; hometown.aol.com/exelsie/myhomepage/index.html

LAZENBY, J(ohn) F(rancis). British (born India), b. 1934. Genres: Classics. Career: University of Newcastle upon Tyne, England, lecturer in ancient history, 1959-71, senior lecturer in ancient history, 1971-79, reader in ancient history, 1979-94, Department of Classics head, 1982-87, School of Humanities head, 1988-94, professor of ancient history, 1994-99, emeritus professor, 1999-. Publications: (with R.H. Simpson) The Catalogue of the Ships in Homer's Iliad, 1970; Hannibal's War: A Military History of the Second Punic War, 1978; The Spartan Army, 1986; The Defence of Greece 490-479 B.C., 1993; The First Punic War, 1996; The Peloponnesian War: A Military Study, 2004. Address: 15 Rectory Terrace, Gosforth, Newcastle upon Tyne NE3 1YB, England.

LAZER, Hank. (Henry Alan). American, b. 1950. Genres: Poetry. Career: University of Virginia, Charlottesville, instructor in English, 1975-77; University of Alabama, Tuscaloosa, 1977-, became professor of American literature, assistant dean for humanities and fine arts, 1991-. Publications: POETRY: Mouth to Mouth, 1977; INTER(R)RUPTIONS, 1992; Doublespace: Poems 1971-1989, 1992; Negation, 1994; Early Days of the Lang Dynasty, 1996; 3 of 10: H's Journal, Negation, and Displayspace, 1996; Opposing Poetries, 1996. EDITOR: C. Bernstein and others, On Equal Terms: Poems, 1984; What Is a Poet? Essays from the Eleventh Alabama Symposium on English and American Literature, 1987; On Louis Simpson: Depths beyond Happiness, 1988. Contributor of poems to magazines.Contributor to anthologies. Address: College of Arts and Sciences, University of Alabama, Box 870268, Tuscaloosa, AL 35487, U.S.A.

LAZERSON, Joshua N(athaniel). American, b. 1959. Genres: History, Reference, Biography. Career: American Bar Association, Chicago, IL, project manager, 1990-92; Northside HIV Treatment Center, project administrator, 1991-92; Urban Corps of San Diego, San Diego, CA, program developer, 1992-94; independent grant writer, San Diego, 1993-. Publications: Against the Tide: Whites in the Struggle Against Apartheid, 1994; (with K. Irvine) Dictionary of African Biography, Vol III: Southern Africa, 1995. Address: 1985 Country Grove Ln., Encinitas, CA 92024-1930, U.S.A.

LAZUTA, Gene. Also writes as Leo Axler, Alex Kane, Daniel Raven. American, b. 1959. Genres: Mystery/Crime/Suspense. Career: Kolodiy-Lazuta Funeral Home, Parma, OH, funeral director, 1982-. Publications: Blood Flies, 1990; Bleeder, 1991; Vyrmin, 1992; Forget Me Not, 1993. AS LEO AXLER: Final Viewing, 1993; Double Plot, 1994; Grave Matters, 1995. AS ALEX KANE: The Shinglo, 1989. AS DANIEL RAVEN: Happy Cage, 1990. Address: Kolodiy-Lazuta Funeral Home, 5677 State Rd., Parma, OH 44134, U.S.A.

LEA, James F(ranklin). American, b. 1945. Genres: Politics/Government. Career: Worked at Louisiana State Penitentiary, as an oil driller's helper in the Gulf of Mexico, and as a seaman in the Far East and South America; Livingston University, Livingston, AL, assistant professor of political science, 1971-75; University of Southern Mississippi, Hattiesburg, assistant professor, 1975-77, associate professor, 1977-81, professor of political science, 1981-. Lecturer at conferences and universities in U.S., Nigeria, Greece, Austria, Cyprus, Scotland, Wales; University of Wales of Swansea, visiting research professor, 1987. Publications: Kazantzakis: The Politics of Salvation, University of Alabama Press, 1979. Political Consciousness and American Democracy, University Press of Mississippi, 1982. (Editor) Contemporary Southern Politics, Louisiana State University Press, 1989. Address: Department of Political Science, University of Southern Mississippi, Box 5108, Southern Station, Hattiesburg, MS 39406, U.S.A.

LEAB, Daniel Josef. American, b. 1936. Genres: Film, Writing/Journalism, Bibliography. Career: Columbia University, NYC, instructor, and assistant professor of history, 1966-74; Seton Hall University, South Orange, NJ, professor of history, 1974-. Labor History, managing editor, 1974-2000; American Communist History, managing editor, 2001-. Publications: A Union of Individuals: The Formation of the American Newspaper Guild 1933-36, 1970; From Sambo to Superspade: The Black Motion Picture Experience, 1975; (with K.K. Leab) The Auction Companion, 1982; (with M. Neufield and D. Swanson) American Working Class History: A Representative Bibliography, 1984; "I Was a Communist for the FBI": The Unhappy Life & Times of Matt Cvetic, 2000. EDITOR: The Labor History Reader, 1985; (with P. Mason) Labor History Archives in the United States, 1992. Address: PO Box 1216, Washington, CT 06793, U.S.A. Online address: danleab@earthlink.net

LEACH, Douglas Edward. American, b. 1920. Genres: History. Career: Professor Emeritus of History, Vanderbilt University, Nashville, Tennessee (faculty member from 1956). Faculty member, Bates College, Lewiston, Maine, 1950-56. Publications: Flintlock and Tomahawk: New England in King Philip's War, 1956; (ed.) A Rhode Islander Reports on King Philip's War: The Second William Harris Letter of August, 1676, 1963; The Northern Colonial Frontier, 1607-1763, 1966; Arms for Empire: A Military History of the British Colonies in North America, 1607-1763, 1973; Roots of Conflict: British Armed Forces and Colonial Americans 1677-1763, 1986; Now Hear This: The Memoir of a Junior Naval Officer in the Great Pacific War, 1987. Address: Dept. of History, Vanderbilt University, Nashville, TN 37235, U.S.A.

LEACH, Penelope. British, b. 1937. Genres: Psychology, Social commentary. Career: Member of numerous commissions and councils relating to children's issues. British Psychological Society, fellow, 1988-; EPOCH, founder and parent education coordinator, 1989-; Child Magazine, consulting editor, 1995-; National Child Minding Association, president, 2000-; Tavistock Centre, London, and University of Oxford, sr. research fellow; Families, Children and Childcare Study, director. Publications: Babyhood: Infant Development from Birth to Two Years, 1974, rev. ed., 1983; Your Baby and Child, 1977, rev. ed., 1997; Who Cares? A New Deal for Mothers and Their Small Children, 1979; The Parents A-Z: A Handbook for Children's Health Growth and Happiness (in US as Your Growing Child), 1984, 2nd ed., 1987; The First Six Months: Coming to Terms with Your Baby, 1987; The Babypack, 1990; Children under Stress, 1992; Children First: What Society Must Do and Is not Doing - For Children Today, 1994. Contributor to both scholarly and popular periodicals. Address: 3 Tanza Rd, London NW3 2UA, England.

LEACH, William. American, b. 1944. **Genres:** History, Literary criticism and history. **Career:** Teacher at New York University, Columbia University, and the University of the South; Professor of History, Columbia University. **Publications:** True Love and Perfect Union: The Feminist Reform of Sex and Society, 1981, 2nd ed with new intro, 1989; Edith Wharton (biography), 1987; (author of commentary) L. Frank Baum, The Wonderful Wizard of Oz, 1991; Land of Desire: Merchants, Power, and the Rise of a New American Culture, 1993; 2nd Country of Exiles, 1999. **Address:** 225 West Shore Dr., Carmel, NY 10512, U.S.A.

LEACOCK, Elspeth. American, b. 1946. **Genres:** Geography. **Career:** Worked in publishing industry, 1979-. **Publications:** Hands-On Geography, 1993; Geography Brain Quest, 1997; (with S. Buckley) Journeys in Time; A New Atlas of American History, 2001; (with S. Buckley) Places in Time: A New Atlas of American History, 2001; The West, 2002; Journeys for Freedom: A New Atlas of American History, 2002; Children in Time: A New Atlas of American History, 2003. **Address:** 319 Bedford Ave., Brooklyn, NY 11211, U.S.A. **Online address:** elleacock@aol.com

LEADER, Darian. British. **Genres:** Psychology. **Career:** Psychoanalyst in private practice in London, England. Centre for Freudian Analysis and Research, co-founder. **Publications:** (with J. Groves) Lacan for Beginners, 1994; Why Do Women Write More Letters Than They Post?, 1996; Promises Lovers Make When It Gets Late, 1997; Freud's Footnotes, 2000. **Address:** c/o Centre for Freudian Analysis & Research, 60 Ivydale Rd, London SE1S 5BS, England.

LEADER, Mary. American, b. 1948. **Genres:** Poetry. **Career:** Oklahoma Attorney General, Oklahoma City, OK, assistant to Attorney General, 1980-81; Oklahoma Supreme Court, Oklahoma City, OK, referee, 1982-91; Emory University, Atlanta, GA, creative writing fellow for poetry and lecturer in literature and law. **Publications:** POETRY: Red Signature, 1997; The Penultimate Suitor, 2001. Contributor of poems to journals. **Address:** 916 Oakbrook Dr., Norman, OK 73072, U.S.A.

LEADER, Zachary. American, b. 1946. **Genres:** Literary criticism and history, Writing/Journalism. **Career:** Roehampton Institute, London, England, Professor of English Literature, 1977-; California Institute of Technology, visiting professor, 1991-93; Oxford University Press, revision and romantic authorship, 1996. **Publications:** Reading Blake's Songs, Routledge & Kegan Paul, 1981; Writer's Block, Johns Hopkins University Press, 1991. **Address:** Roehampton Institute, Roehampton Ln., London SW15 6PJ, England.

LEAHY, James E. American, b. 1919. **Genres:** Law. **Career:** Cupler, Tenneson, Serkland & Leahy, Fargo, ND, attorney, 1949-56; Merchants National Bank and Trust Co., Fargo, vice president and trust officer, 1956-64; California Western School of Law, San Diego, professor of law, 1964-85, professor emeritus, 1985-. Counsel to Jerry M. Leahy, 1985-. Member of North Dakota State House of Representatives, 1963-64, San Diego City Campaign Task Force, 1985-88, and San Diego County Grand Jury, 1986-87. **Publications:** The First Amendment, 1791-1991: Two Hundred Years of Freedom, 1991; With Liberty, Justice, and Equality for All, 1992; Freedom Fighters of The United States Supreme Court, 1996; Supreme Court Justices Who Voted with the Government, 1999; The North Dakota State Constitution, 2003. **Address:** 555 40th St S Apt 324, Fargo, ND 58103-1176, U.S.A. **Online address:** firstamend@att.net

LEAKEY, Richard (Erskine Frere). Kenyan, b. 1944. **Genres:** Anthropology/Ethnology, Autobiography/Memoirs. **Career:** Leader, Koobi Fora (formerly E. Rudolf) Research Project, 1968-, and W. Turkana Research Project, 1984-. Tour guide and trapper, 1951-65; leader of photographic safaris in E. Africa, 1965-68; co-leader of anthropological expeditions to Lake Natron, 1963-64, Lake Baringo, 1966, Omo River, 1967; National Museums of Kenya, administrative director, 1968-74, director, 1974-89; Kenya Wildlife Conservation and Management Dept., director, 1989-90; Kenya Wildlife Service, director, 1989-94, 1998-99; Richard Leakey & Associates Ltd, consultant, 2001-. **Publications:** (with R. Lewin) Origins, 1977; (with R. Lewin) People of the Lake, 1979; (with M. Leakey) Koobi Fora Research Project, vol. 1, 1979; The Making of Mankind, 1981; One Life (autobiography), 1981; Human Origins, 1982; (with R. Lewin) Origins Reconsidered, 1992; Man Ape-Ape Man, 1993; (with R. Lewin) The Sixth Extinction, 1995; (with R. Lewin) The Origins of Human Kind, 1995; Wildlife Wars, 2001. Contributor to professional journals. **Address:** PO Box 24926, Nairobi, Kenya. **Online address:** leakey@skyweb.co.ke

LEANING, Jennifer. American, b. 1945. **Genres:** Medicine/Health, Politics/Government. **Career:** Massachusetts General Hospital, Boston, intern and resident, 1975-78; Harvard Medical School, Boston, Mass., instructor in medicine, 1978-94; Assistant Professor of Medicine, 1994-; Harvard Community Health Plan, Brookline, chief of emergency services, 1984-92; Medical Director, Health Centers Division, 1992-; writer. **Publications:** (Editor with Langley Keyes) The Counterfeit Ark: Crisis Relocation for Nuclear War, Ballinger, 1984. **Address:** Harvard Pilgrim Health Care, 93 Worcester St., Wellesley, MA 02481-3609, U.S.A.

LEAR, Linda J(ane). American, b. 1940. **Genres:** Biography. **Career:** Vail Deane School, chair of department of history, 1963-65; National Cathedral School, chair of department of history, 1965-68; New Mexico State University, Las Cruces, NM, assistant professor, 1974-76; American Association of Retired Persons, project director and special assistant in humanities program, 1976-78; George Washington University, Washington, DC, assistant director experimental programs and associated professor, 1978-; Committee on Government Affairs, U.S. Senate, consultant in political science, 1976-. **Publications:** Harold L. Ickes: The Aggressive Progressive, 1874-1933, 1981; Rachel Carson: Witness for Nature, 1997. **Address:** c/o Henry Holt & Co., 115 West 18th St., 6th Fl., New York, NY 10011, U.S.A.

LEAR, Patricia. American, b. 1944. **Genres:** Novellas/Short stories. **Career:** Writer. **Publications:** Stardust, 7-Eleven, Route 57, A & W, and So Forth (short stories; includes "Powwow"), 1992. Contributor of articles and stories to magazines. Contributor to anthologies. **Address:** c/o Amanda Urban, International Creative Management, 40 W. 57th St., New York, NY 10019, U.S.A.

LEAR, Peter. See LOVESEY, Peter (Harmer).

LEASK, Nigel. Scottish, b. 1958. **Genres:** Literary criticism and history, Travel/Exploration. **Career:** Cambridge University, Queen's College, England, lecturer in English, 1989-. **Publications:** The Politics of Imagination in Coleridge's Critical Thought, 1988; British Romantic Writers and the East: Anxieties of Empire, 1992; Curiosity the Aesthetics of Travel Writing, 1770-1840: From an Antique Land, 2000. **Address:** Faculty of English, Queen's College, Cambridge University, Cambridge, England. **Online address:** njl1000@can.ac.uk

LEASOR, (Thomas) James. Also writes as Andrew MacAllan. British, b. 1923. **Genres:** Mystery/Crime/Suspense, History, Biography, Novels, Novellas/Short stories. **Career:** Director, Pagoda Films Ltd., 1959-. Director, Jason Love Ltd., 1964-. Reporter, Kentish Times, Sidcup, 1941-42; Reporter, and Columnist (as William Hickey), Feature Writer and Foreign Correspondent, Daily Express, London, 1948-55; Editorial Adviser and Consultant, George Newnes and C. Arthur Pearson Ltd., London, 1955-69; Director, Elm Tree Books Ltd., London, 1970-73. **Publications:** NOVELS: Not Such a Bad Day, 1946; The Strong Delusion, 1950; NTR: Nothing to Report, 1955; Follow the Drum, 1972; Mandarin-Gold, 1973; Jade Gate, 1976; The Unknown Warrior, 1980, in US as Code Name Nimrod, 1981. SUSPENSE NOVELS: Passport to Oblivion, 1964, Passport to Peril (in US as Spylight), 1966; Passport in Suspense, 1967 (in US as The Yang Meridian, 1968); Passport for a Pilgrim, 1968; They Don't Make Them Like That Any More, 1969; A Week of Love (short stories), 1969; Never Had a Spanner on Her, 1970; Love-All, 1971; Host of Extras, 1973; The Chinese Widow, 1975; Love and the Land Beyond, 1979; Open Secret, 1982; Ship of Gold, 1984; Tank of Serpents, 1986; Frozen Assets, 1989; Love Down Under, 1993; Speculator, 1993; Traders, 1994. OTHER: The Monday Story, 1951; Author by Profession, 1952; Wheels of Fortune: A Brief Account of the Life and Times of William Morris, Viscount Nuffield, 1954; The Serjeant Major: A Biography of R.S.M. Ronald Brittain, 1955; The Red Fort, 1956 (in UK, Mutiny at the Red Fort, 1959); (with K. Burt) The One That Got Away, 1956; The Millionth Chance: The Story of the R.101, 1957; War at the Top (in US as The Clock with Four Hands), 1959; (with P. Eton) Conspiracy of Silence (in US as Wall of Silence), 1960; The Plague and the Fire, 1961; Rudolf Hess, The Uninvited Envoy (in US as The Uninvited Envoy), 1962; Singapore: The Battle That Changed the World, 1968; Look Where I'm At! (play), 1971; Green Beach, 1975; Boarding Party, 1978; X-Troop, 1980; Who Killed Sir Henry Oakes?, 1983; The Marine from Mandalay, 1988; Cecil Rhodes and Barney Barnato, 1997. AS ANDREW MacALLAN: Succession, 1989; Generation, 1990; Diamond Hard, 1991; Fanfare, 1992. **Address:** Swallowcliffe Manor, Salisbury, Wilts. SP3 5PB, England.

LEATHERBARROW, W(illiam) J(ohn). British, b. 1947. **Genres:** Literary criticism and history. **Career:** University of Sheffield, England, professor of Russian, 1970-. **Publications:** Fedor Dostoevsky, 1981; (with D.C. Offord) A Documentary History of Russian Thought, 1987; Fyodor Dostoevsky: A Reference Guide, 1990; Fyodor Dostoyevsky: The Brothers Karamazov,

1992; (ed.) Fyodor Dostoyevsky, Crime and Punishment, 1992; Dostoevsky and Britain, 1995; Dostoevsky's The Devils, 1999; The Cambridge Companion to Dostoevskii, 2002. **Address:** Department of Russian, University of Sheffield, Sheffield S10 3QN, England.

LEAVELL, Linda. American, b. 1954. **Genres:** Literary criticism and history, Art/Art history, Biography. **Career:** Rhodes College, Memphis, TN, visiting assistant professor of English, 1985-86; Oklahoma State University, Stillwater, assistant professor, 1986-91, associate professor of English, 1991-. **Publications:** Marianne Moore and the Visual Arts: Prismatic Color, 1995. Contributor to periodicals. **Address:** Department of English, Oklahoma State University, Stillwater, OK 74078, U.S.A. **Online address:** leavell@okstate.edu

LEAVER, Ruth. *See* TOMALIN, Ruth.

LEAVITT, Caroline. American, b. 1952. **Genres:** Novels. **Career:** Writer and manuscript consultant. **Publications:** NOVELS: Meeting Rozzy Halfway, 1981; Lifelines, 1982; Jealousies, 1983; Family, 1987; Into Thin Air, 1993; Living Other Lives, 1995; Coming Back to Me, 2001. **Address:** PO Box 497, Hoboken, NJ 07030, U.S.A. **Online address:** TheLeav@aol.com

LEAVITT, David. American, b. 1961. **Genres:** Novels. **Career:** Viking-Penguin Inc., NYC, reader and educational assistant, 1983-84; University of Florida, professor of English, 2000-. **Publications:** Family Dancing, 1984; The Lost Language of Cranes, 1986; Equal Affections, 1989; A Place I've Never Been, 1990; While England Sleeps, 1993; (with M. Mitchell) Italian Pleasures, 1996; Arkansas, 1997; The Page Turner, 1998; Martin Bauman: Or, A Sure Thing, 2000; The Marble Quilt, 2001; Florence, a Delicate Case, 2002.

LEAVITT, Judith Walzer. American, b. 1940. **Genres:** History, Medicine/Health. **Career:** University of Wisconsin, Madison, assistant professor, 1975-81, associate professor, 1981-86, History of Medicine Department chair, 1981-93, permanent honorary member of history department, 1985-, professor, 1986-, Evjue-Bascom Professor of Women's Studies, 1990-95, School of Medicine, associate dean of faculty, 1996-; served on university committees. Participant in national committees and projects. Advisor to undergraduate and graduate students; organizer and participant in conferences, meetings, workshops, panels, and colloquii; member of grants review boards; has given national and international invited academic addresses; has appeared in radio presentations, interview, and talk shows. **Publications:** The Healthiest City: Milwaukee and the Politics of Health Reform, 1982; Women and Health in America: Historical Readings, 1984; Brought to Bed: Childbearing in America, 1750-1950, 1986; Typhoid Mary: Captive to the Public's Health, 1996. EDITOR: (with R.L. Numbers) Medicine Without Doctors: Home Health Care in American History, 1977; (with Numbers) Sickness and Health in America: Readings in the History of Medicine and Public Health, 1978; (with Numbers) Wisconsin Medicine: Historical Perspectives, 1981; (with M. Vogel) Health and Medicine in American Society (monograph series), 1988-95. Contributor to books. Author of articles and reviews published in periodicals. Manuscript reviewer for periodicals and publishing companies. **Address:** Department of the History of Medicine, University of Wisconsin, 1300 University Ave., Madison, WI 53706, U.S.A. **Online address:** jwleavit@facstaff.wisc.edu

LEAVY, Barbara Fass. American, b. 1936. **Genres:** Literary criticism and history. **Career:** Queens College of the City University of New York, Flushing, NY, professor of English. Cornell University, adjunct professor of English in psychiatry. **Publications:** La Belle Dame sans Merci and the Aesthetics of Romanticism, 1974; (with P.S. Jacobsen) Ibsen's Forsaken Merman: Folklore in the Late Plays, 1988; To Blights with Plague: Studies in a Literary Theme, 1992; In Search of the Swan Maiden: A Narrative on Folklore and Gender, 1993. Contributor of articles and reviews to literature journals. **Address:** Department of English, Queens College of the City University of New York, Flushing, NY 11367, U.S.A.

LEBEAU, Roy. *See* SMITH, Mitchell.

LEBOEUF, Michael. American, b. 1942. **Genres:** Business/Trade/Industry, Self help, Self help. **Career:** University of New Orleans, professor emeritus of management. **Publications:** Working Smart: How to Accomplish More in Half the Time, 1979; Imagineering: How to Profit from Your Own Creative Powers, 1980; The Productivity Challenge: How to Make it Work for America and You, 1982; The Greatest Management Principle in the World, 1985; How to Win Customers and Keep Them for Life, 1988; Fast Forward, 1994; The Perfect Business, 1996; The Millionaire in You, 2002.

LEBOVICS, Herman. Czech, b. 1935. **Genres:** History. **Career:** Historian and educator. Brooklyn College, Brooklyn, NY, instructor in European history, 1962-65; visiting assistant professor, Oberlin College, 1965-66; State University of New York, Stonybrook, assistant professor, 1966-69, associate professor of European history, 1969-. **Publications:** Social Conservatism and the Middle Classes in Germany, 1914-1933, 1969; The Alliance of Iron and Wheat in the Third French Republic, 1860-1914: Origins of the New Conservatism, 1988; True France: The Wars over Cultural Identity, 1900-1945, 1992; Mona Lisa's Escort: André Malraux and the Reinvention of French Culture, 1999. **Address:** Department of History, Social and Behavioral Sciences Building, State University of New York, Stonybrook, NY 11794, U.S.A. **Online address:** hlebovics@notes.cc.sunysb.edu

LEBOW, Eileen F. American (born Panama), b. 1925. **Genres:** Air/Space topics, Education, History, Military/Defense/Arms control, Transportation, Women's studies and issues. **Career:** Secondary school teacher in Montgomery County, MD, 1964-. **Publications:** Cal Rodgers and the Vin Fiz: The First Transcontinental Flight, 1989; A Grandstand Seat, 1998; The Bright Boys, 2000; Before Amelia: Women Pilots in the Early Days of Aviation, 2002. **Address:** 2821 29th St NW, Washington, DC 20008, U.S.A.

LEBOW, Jeanne. American, b. 1951. **Genres:** Poetry, Natural history. **Career:** Junior high school teacher of English and drama, 1973-77; worked in public relations for the Arts, 1977-81; Memphis State University, Memphis, TN, instructor in English, 1982-84; University of Ouagadougou, Ouagadougou, Burkina Faso, Fulbright lecturer, 1987-88; Northeast Missouri State University, Kirksville, assistant professor of English, 1988-91; free-lance writer; University of Southern Mississippi, grad. instructor, 1984-87, adjunct and visiting professor, 1992-95. Weekly nature column for local newspapers (Gautier Independent; Ocean Springs Record), 1991-2000; Bird-watchers Digest, writer, 1999-. **Publications:** The Outlaw James Copeland and the Champion-Belted Empress (poems), 1991. **Address:** PO Box 1295, Gautier, MS 39553, U.S.A. **Online address:** Shepart@datasync.com

LEBOWITZ, Albert. American, b. 1922. **Genres:** Novels, Law. **Career:** Lawyer: Partner, Murphy & Schlapprizzi, St. Louis, 1969-81; Partner, Murphy, Schlapprizzi & Lebowitz, 1981-86; Counsel, Donald L. Schlapprizzi, P. C., since 1986. **Publications:** Laban's Will, 1966; The Man Who Wouldn't Say No, 1969; A Matter of Days, 1989.

LE BRETON, Binka. British, b. 1942. **Genres:** Children's non-fiction, Civil liberties/Human rights, Environmental sciences/Ecology. **Career:** Concert pianist, 1974-89; Iracambi Rainforest Research Center, Brazil, director, 1999-; writer and lecturer on environmental affairs and human rights. Worked as a teacher of English as a foreign language in Nairobi, Jakarta, New Delhi, Recife, London, and Washington, D.C. **Publications:** Voices from the Amazon, 1993; The Rainforest, 1997; A Land to Die For, 1997; Todos Sabiam, 2000; Somebody Knows My Name, 2002; Vidas Roubadas, 2002; Trapped: Modern-Day Slavery in the Brazilian Amazon, 2003. **Address:** Fazenda Iracambi, Rosario da Limeira, 36887 Muriae M.G., Brazil. **Online address:** iracambi@iracambi.com

LEBRETON, J(ean) D(ominique). French, b. 1950. **Genres:** Biology. **Career:** Centre d'Ecologie Fonctionnelle et Evolutive, Montpellier, France, director of research, 1985-. **Publications:** (with others) Mathematiques pour biologistes: Exercices et problemes commentes (title means: Mathematics for Biologists: Exercises and Commentary on Problems), 1981; (ed., with C. Millier) Modeles dynamiques deterministes en biologie (title means: Dynamic Determinist Models in Biology), 1982; (ed., with others) Population Biology of Passerine Birds: An Integrated Approach, 1990; (ed., with P.M. North) Marked Individuals in the Study of Bird Population, 1992; (ed., with B. Asselain) Biometrie et Environnement (title means: Biometrics and Environment), 1993; (ed., with C.M. Perrins and G. J. M. Hirons) Bird Population Studies: Their Relevance to Conservation and Management, 1993. **Address:** CEFE/CNRS, BP 5051, Cedex II 3 Montpellier, France.

LEBSOCK, Suzanne (Dee). American, b. 1949. **Genres:** Mystery/Crime/Suspense, History, Women's studies and issues. **Career:** Rutgers University, New Brunswick, NJ, assistant to professor of history, 1977-92; University of North Carolina at Chapel Hill, 1992-95; University of Washington, Seattle, 19952003. Writer. **Publications:** "A Share of Honour": Virginia Women, 1600-1945 (essays), 1984; The Free Women of Petersburg: Status and Culture in a Southern Town, 1784-1860, 1984; (ed. with N.A. Hewitt) Visible Women: New Essays on American Activism, 1993; A Murder in Virginia: Southern Justice on Trial, 2003. Contributor to periodicals.

LE CARRÉ, John. (David John Moore Cornwell). British, b. 1931. **Genres:** Novels, Mystery/Crime/Suspense. **Career:** Tutor, Eton College, Berks.,

1956-58; member, British Foreign Service, 1960-64 (Second Secretary, Bonn, 1960-63; Consul, Hamburg, 1963-64); writer. **Publications:** Call for the Dead, 1960; A Murder of Quality, 1962; The Spy Who Came in from the Cold, 1963; The Looking-Glass War, 1965; A Small Town in Germany, 1968; The Naive and Sentimental Lover, 1971; Tinker, Tailor, Soldier, Spy, 1974; The Honourable Schoolboy, 1977; Smiley's People, 1980; The Quest for Karla (omnibus edition of Tinker, Tailor, Soldier, Spy; The Honourable Schoolboy; and Smiley's People), 1982; The Little Drummer Girl, 1983; A Perfect Spy, 1986; The Russia House, 1989; The Secret Pilgrim, 1991; The Night Manager, 1993; Our Game, 1995; The Tailor of Panama, 1996; Single & Single, 1999; The Constant Gardner, 2000; Absolute Friends, 2003. **Address:** c/o David Higham Assocs, 5-8 Lower John St, London W1R 4HA, England.

LECKEY, Andrew A. American, b. 1949. **Genres:** Money/Finance. **Career:** Oregon Statesman, Salem, OR, finance editor, 1975-76; Phoenix Gazette, Phoenix, AZ, statehouse reporter, 1976-78; finance columnist, Chicago Sun-Times, Chicago, IL, 1979-85, New York Daily News, New York, NY, 1985, Chicago Tribune, Chicago, IL, 1985-; writer. Finance commentator, WBEZ, Chicago, IL, 1981-83, WLS-TV, Chicago, IL, 1983; television reporter, Quicken.com Money Reports; financial anchor, CNBC-TV. University of California, Berkeley, instructor of business journalism. **Publications:** Make Money with the New Tax Laws, 1987; The 20 Hottest Investments for the 21st Century, 1994; The Morningstar Approach to Investing: Wiring into Mutual Fund Revolution, 1997; Global Investing: A Guide to the 50 Best Stocks in the World, 1999; (ed., with M. Loeb) The Best Business Stories of the Year: 2001 Edition, 2001; The Lack of Money Is the Root of All Evil: Mark Twain's Timeless Advice on Money, Wealth, and Investing, 2001. Syndicated finance columnist. **Address:** Tribune Media Services, 435 North Michigan Ave., Ste. 1500, Chicago, IL 60611, U.S.A.

LECKIE, Keith (Ross). Canadian, b. 1952. **Genres:** Novels, Plays/Screenplays. **Career:** Member of film production crews in Toronto, Ontario, 1975-79; film and television scriptwriter and director, 1979-; novelist, 1987-. Filmmaking teacher at Ontario high schools. Volunteer worker for Aid for Nicaragua. **Publications:** The Seventh Gate (novel), 1989. SCREENPLAYS FOR TELEVISION MOVIES/MINISERIES: Where The Spirit Lives, 1989; Lost in the Barrens, 1991; Journey into Darkness: The Bruce Curtis Story, 1992; The Price of Vengeance, 1993; Trail at Fortitude Bay, 1994; The Morrison Murders, 1996; The Arrow, 1996; The David Milgaard Story, 1998; Children of My Heart, 2000; Shattered City-The Halifax Explosion, 2003. FEATURE FILM SCREENPLAY: To Walk with Lions, 1998. **Address:** 590 Indian Rd, Toronto, ON, Canada M6P 2C2.

LECKIE, Ross. Scottish, b. 1957. **Genres:** Romance/Historical, Adult non-fiction. **Career:** Farmer, Perthshire, Scotland, 1981-83; Odeco, roughneck on North Sea oil rigs, 1983-86; free-lance journalist and copywriter, Edinburgh, Scotland, 1987-96; Martin Currie Investment Management, Edinburgh, director of corporate communications, 1996-. **Publications:** Bluff Your Way in the Classics, 1989; Grampian, 1991; The Gourmet's Companion, 1994. HISTORICAL NOVELS: Hannibal, 1995; Scipio, 1997; Carthage, 2000. **Address:** 16 Sayfield Sq, Edinburgh EH1 3NX, Scotland.

LECKIE, Shirley A(nne). American, b. 1937. **Genres:** History, Biography. **Career:** University of Toledo, OH, academic adviser, 1972-77, coordinator of adult liberal studies, 1974-77, director of external affairs and adult liberal studies, 1977-80, assistant dean of continuing education for business and professional seminars, 1980-81; Millsaps College, Jackson, MS, assistant professor of history and associate dean of continuing education, 1981-82; University of North Carolina at Asheville, director of continuing education and special programs, 1983-85; University of Central Florida, Orlando, assistant professor, 1985-88, associate professor of history, 1988-94, professor of history, 1995-. **Publications:** (with W.H. Leckie) Unlikely Warriors: General Benjamin H. Grierson and His Family, 1984; (ed.) The Colonel's Lady on the Western Frontier: The Correspondence of Alice Kirk Grierson, 1989; Elizabeth Bacon Custer and the Making of a Myth, 1993; Angie Debo: Pioneering Historian, 2000; (with W.H. Leckie) The Buffalo Soldiers: A Narrative of the Black Cavalry in the West, rev. ed. Work represented in anthologies. Contributor of articles and reviews to history and education journals. **Address:** Dept of History, University of Central Florida, Orlando, FL 32816, U.S.A. **Online address:** sleckie@pegasus.cc.ucf.edu

LECKY-THOMPSON, Guy W. British, b. 1974. **Genres:** Information science/Computers. **Career:** Computer programmer and author. **Publications:** (with M. DeLoura) Games Programming Gems, 2000; Infinite Games Universe: Mathematical Techniques, 2001; Infinite Game Universe: Level Design, Terrain, and Sound, 2002. Contributor to periodicals. **Address:** c/o

Author Mail, Charles River Media, 10 Downer Ave., Hingham, MA 02043, U.S.A. **Online address:** Guy_W@Lecky-Thompson.net

LECLAIRE, Anne D(ickinson). American, b. 1942. **Genres:** Novels, Essays. **Career:** Cape Cod Illustrated, Hyannis, MA, writer and associate editor, 1974-76; Cape Cod Times, Hyannis, reporter and op-ed writer, 1976-82; freelance writer, 1982-. WVLC-Radio, news reporter, 1974-76; Boston Globe, correspondent, 1979-82; also worked as an actor. **Publications:** NOVELS: Land's End, 1985; Every Mother's Son, 1987; Grace Point, 1992; Sideshow, 1994; Entering Normal, 2001; Leaving Eden, 2002. Work represented in anthologies. Contributor to magazines and newspapers. **Address:** 107 Deep Hole Rd, Box 656, South Chatham, MA 02659, U.S.A. **Online address:** www.anneleclaire.com

LECOMPTE, Mary Lou. American, b. 1935. **Genres:** History, Recreation. **Career:** St. Mary's College of Maryland, St. Mary's City, head of health, physical education, and recreation department, 1958-60; University of Texas at Austin, instructor to assistant professor, 1960-93, associate professor of physical education, 1993-. **Publications:** (with M.B. Alderson) Step Right In: Making Dance Fun for Boys and Girls, 1973; Cowgirls of the Rodeo: Pioneer Professional Athletes, 1993. Work represented in anthologies. Contributor of articles and reviews to physical education and history journals. **Address:** 12609 Dessau, No. A-143, Austin, TX 78754, U.S.A.

LECOMPTE, N(ancy) Jane. American, b. 1948. **Genres:** Novels. **Career:** Writer. **Publications:** Moon Passage (novel), Harper, 1989. **Address:** Jean V. Naggar, Jean V. Naggar Literary Agency, 216 East 75th St, New York, NY 10021, U.S.A.

LEDBETTER, Suzann. American, b. 1953. **Genres:** Biography, Novels, Humor/Satire. **Career:** Quassare Femina Inc., president. Southwest Missouri State University, instructor in continuing education department; guest on television programs; convention and workshop speaker, through Program Corp. of America. **Publications:** On the Edge of Forever, 1992; Nellie Cashman: Prospector and Trailblazer (biography), 1993; The Toast Always Lands Jelly-Side down and Other Tales of Suburban Life (humor), 1993; I Have Everything I Had Twenty Years Ago Except Now It's All Lower (humor), 1995; Trinity Strike (novel), 1996; Redemption Trail, 1996; Deliverance Drive, 1997; Colorado Reverie, 1997; Pure Justice, 1997; Klondike Fever, 1997. Author of the column Humor and contributing editor to Family Circle. Contributor to magazines. **Address:** P.O. Box 1032, Nixa, MO 65714, U.S.A.

LEDDY, Mary Jo. Canadian, b. 1946. **Genres:** History. **Career:** High school teacher, 1968-1970; Newman Center, Toronto, campus minister, 1976-1977; Catholic New Times, founding member, 1977, editor, 1977-1979, editorial team, 1981-1985; lecturer at University College, Toronto, Maryknoll Seminary, Higham, MA, and Regis College, Toronto; Toronto Star, columnist, 1979-1986; CBC TV, commentator. **Publications:** (ed., with M.A. Hinsdale) Faith that Transforms: Essays in Honor of Gregory Baum, 1987; Memories of War: Promises of Peace, 1989; Reweaving Religious Life: Beyond the Liberal Model, 1990; (with R. De Roo and D. Roche) In the Eye of the Catholic Storm: The Church Since Vatican II, 1992; At the Border Called Hope: Where Refugees are Neighbours, 1997. Contributor to periodicals. **Address:** 15 Oakmount Rd., Toronto, ON, Canada M6P 2M3.

LEDERBERG, Joshua. American, b. 1925. **Genres:** Biology, Medicine/Health. **Career:** Geneticist. University of Wisconsin, Madison, WI, assistant professor to associate professor of genetics, 1948-58; Stanford University, Stanford, CA, professor of genetics, 1959-78, became department chair; Rockefeller University, NYC, president, 1978-90, Sackler Foundation Scholar, 1990-; Columbia University, NYC, adjunct professor, 1990-. Recipient, Nobel Prize. **Publications:** Computations of Molecular Formulas for Mass Spectrometry, 1964; Papers in Microbial Genetics: Bacteria and Bacterial Viruses, 1951; (with others) Man and His Future, 1963; Health in the World of Tomorrow, 1969; (with others) The Excitement and Fascination of Science: Reflections by Eminent Scientists, Vol 3, Part 1, 1990. EDITOR: Encyclopedia of Microbiology, 4 vols, 1992; (with R.E. Shope and S.C. Oaks, Jr.) Emerging Infections: Microbial threats to Health in the United States, 1992. Contributor to journals and periodicals. **Address:** Rockefeller University, 1230 York Ave Ste 400, New York, NY 10021, U.S.A. **Online address:** lederberg@rockefeller.edu

LEDERER, Richard. American, b. 1938. **Genres:** Language/Linguistics. **Career:** St. Paul's School, Concord, N.H., English teacher and chairman of department, 1962-89; writer, 1987-. Language commentator for Public Radio stations; public speaker. **Publications:** Basic Verbal Skills, rev. ed., 1975; Anguished English: 1987; Get Thee to a Punnery, 1988; Crazy English,

1989; The Play of Words, 1990; The Miracle of Language, 1991; More Anguished English, 1993; Adventures of a Verbivore, 1993; Literary Trivia, 1994; Building Bridge, 1994; Nothing Risque, Nothing Gained, 1995; The Write Way, 1995; Pun and Games, 1996; Fractured English, 1996; The Word Circus, 1998; Sleeping Dogs Don't Lay, 1999; The Bride of Anguished English, 2000; The Circus of Words, 2001; Word Play Crosswords, Vol. 1, 2001, Vol. 2, 2002. **Address:** 9974 Scripps Ranch Blvd. #201, San Diego, CA 92131, U.S.A. **Online address:** richard.lederer@pobox.com; www.verbivore.com

LEDERMANN, Erich. British (born Germany), b. 1908. **Genres:** Medicine/Health, Psychiatry. **Career:** Homeopathic physician and psychiatrist. **Publications:** Natural Therapy, 1953; Philosophy and Medicine, 1970; Existential Neurosis, 1972; Good Health through Natural Therapy, 1976; Mental Health and Human Conscience: The True and False Self, 1984; Your Health in Your Hands: A Case for a Natural Medicine, 1989; Medicine for the Whole Person, 1997. **Address:** 13 Ardwick Rd, London NW2 2BX, England. **Online address:** drledermann@wholepersonmedicine.co.uk

LE DOEUFF, Michèle. French, b. 1948. **Genres:** Philosophy, Essays, Translations. **Career:** High school philosophy teacher, 1971-73; Ecole Normale Superieure de Fontenay, Fontenay, France, assistant professor, 1973-80, maitreassistante, 1980-86; Centre National de la Recherche Scientifique, Paris, France, researcher, 1986-93. Speaker for French Planned Parenthood Movement. **Publications:** L'Imaginaire philosophique, 1980, trans. as The Philosophical Imaginary, 1989; (with M. Llasera) Francis Bacon: La Nouvelle Atlantide, 1983; (trans.) Shakespeare: Venus et Adonis, 1986; L'Etude et le rouet: Des femmes, de la philosophie, etc., 1989, trans. as Hipparchia's Choice: An Essay Concerning Women, Philosophy, etc., 1991; Francis Bacon: Du Progres et de la promotion des savoirs, 1991; Sexe du Savoir, 1998. Contributor to periodicals. **Address:** 34 rue de Poitou, 75003 Paris, France.

LEDOUX, Joseph E. American. **Genres:** Psychology. **Career:** Author, editor, neurobiologist, and educator. New York University, Center for Neural Science, NYC, professor of neural science and psychology. **Publications:** (ed. with W. Hirst) Mind and Brain: Dialogues in Cognitive Neuroscience, 1986; The Emotional Brain: The Mysterious Underpinnings of Emotional Life, 1996; Synaptic Self: How Our Brains Become Who We Are, 2001. Contributor to periodicals. **Address:** Center for Neural Science, New York University, 4 Washington Place Room 809, New York, NY 10011, U.S.A.

LEDWIDGE, Michael. American, b. 1971. **Genres:** Novels. **Career:** Writer. **Publications:** The Narrowback, 1999; Bad Connection, 2001; Before the Devil Knows You're Dead, 2002. **Address:** c/o Pocket Books, 1230 Avenue of the Americas, New York, NY 10020, U.S.A.

LEE, A(rthur) Robert. British, b. 1941. **Genres:** Novels, Novellas/Short stories, Poetry, Area studies, Humanities, Literary criticism and history, Autobiography/Memoirs, Biography, Essays. **Career:** Princeton University, NJ, research fellow, 1965-66; California State University, Northridge, visiting asst professor, 1967; University of Kent at Canterbury, England, lecturer, 1967-87, senior lecturer, 1987-94, reader, 1994-96; Nihon University, Tokyo, Japan, professor of English, 1997-. Visiting lecturer/professor at universities throughout the US. **Publications:** Black American Literature since Richard Wright, 1983; Designs of Blackness, 1998; (with G. Vizenor) Postindian Conversations, 1998; Ethnics Behaving Badly, 2001; Multicultural American Literature: Comparative Black, Native, Latino/a and Asian American Fictions, 2003. EDITOR & CONTRIBUTOR: H. Melville, Moby-Dick, 1975, 3rd ed.; Black Fiction: New Studies in the Afro-American Novel since 1945, 1980; Nathaniel Hawthorne: New Critical Essays, 1982; Ernest Hemingway: New Critical Essays, 1983; Herman Melville: Reassessments, 1984; 19th-Century American Poetry, 1985; The 19th-Century American Short Story, 1985; Edgar Allan Poe: The Design of Order, 1986; First Person Singular: Studies in American Autobiography, 1988; Scott Fitzgerald: The Promises of Life, 1989; The Modern American Novella, 1989; William Faulkner: The Yoknapatawpha Fiction, 1990; (with M. Irwin and M. Kinkead-Weekes) Tensions and Transitions, 1990; A Permanent Etcetera, 1993; Typee, 1993; Billy Budd and Other Stories, 1993; Shadow Distance, 1994; Other British, Other Britain, 1995; (with W.M. Verhoeven) Making America, Making American Literature, 1995; The Beat Generation Writers, 1996; Loosening the Seams, 1999; Herman Melville: Critical Assessments, vols. 1-IV, 2001. Contributor to journals and volumes of literary criticism. **Address:** Dept of English, College of Humanities and Sciences, Nihon University, 3-25-40 Sakurajosui, Setagaya-ku, Tokyo 156-8550, Japan. **Online address:** arobertlee@hotmail.com

LEE, Ang. Taiwanese, b. 1954. **Genres:** Plays/Screenplays. **Career:** Director of films. **Publications:** SCREENPLAYS: Pushing Hands, 1991; (with N.

Peng and J. Schamus) The Wedding Banquet, 1993; (with H.L. Wang and J. Schamus) Eat Drink Man Woman, 1994. **Address:** c/o CAA, 9830 Wilshire Blvd., Beverly Hills, CA 90212-1804, U.S.A.

LEE, Bernie. American, b. 1926. **Genres:** Mystery/Crime/Suspense, Plays/Screenplays. **Career:** KMOX-Radio, St. Louis, MO, writer, c. 1949-53; writer and producer for advertising agencies in San Francisco, CA, including McCann-Erickson, Dancer-Fitzgerald-Sample, and Post-Keyes-Gardner, 1954-70; Cole & Weber Advertising, Portland, OR, writer and producer, 1970-72; free-lance writer, 1972-. **Publications:** MYSTERY NOVELS: Murder at Musket Beach, 1990; Murder without Reservation, 1991; Murder Takes Two, 1992. PLAY: Magic Lantern, 1995. Contributor to magazines. **Address:** 4626 NW Seblar Terr, Portland, OR 97210, U.S.A.

LEE, Chang-rae. Korean, b. 1965. **Genres:** Novels. **Career:** University of Oregon, Eugene, assistant professor of creative writing, 1993-. **Publications:** Native Speaker, 1995; Comfort Woman, in press; Gesture Life, 1999; Aloft, 2004. **Address:** c/o International Creative Management, 40 W. 57th Street, New York, NY 10019-4001, U.S.A.

LEE, Chin-Chuan. American (born Taiwan), b. 1946. **Genres:** Communications/Media, Writing/Journalism. **Career:** University of Minnesota-Twin Cities, Minneapolis, professor of journalism and mass communication, 1982-; Chinese University of Hong Kong, professor, 1994-98; City University of Hong Kong, chair professor, 2002-. **Publications:** Media Imperialism Reconsidered: The Homogenizing of Television Culture, 1980; (with J.M. Chan) Mass Media and Political Transition: The Hong Kong Press in China's Orbit, 1991; Money, Media, Power: Communication Patterns in Cultural China, 2000; Global Media Spectacle: News War over Hong Kong, 2002; Chinese Media Global Contexts, 2003. EDITOR: Voices of China: The Interplay of Journalism and Politics, 1990; China's Media, Media's China, 1994. **Address:** School of Journalism and Mass Communication, University of Minnesota-Twin Cities, Minneapolis, MN 55455, U.S.A. **Online address:** leexx010@umn.edu

LEE, Dennis (Beynon). Canadian, b. 1939. **Genres:** Children's fiction, Poetry, Literary criticism and history, Picture/board books. **Career:** House of Anansi Press, Toronto, editor, 1967-72; Poetry Program, McClelland and Stewart, publrs., Toronto, director, 1981-84. **Publications:** Kingdom of Absence, 1967; Civil Elegies, 1968; Civil Elegies and Other Poems, 1972; The Death of Harold Ladoo, 1976; Savage Fields: An Essay in Literature and Cosmology, 1977; The Gods, 1979; The Ordinary Bath (juvenile), 1979; The Difficulty of Living on Other Planets, 1987; Riffs, 1993; Nightwatch: New & Selected Poems, 1968-1996, 1996; Body Music (essays), 1998; Un, 2003. CHILDREN'S POETRY: Wiggle to the Laundromat, 1970; Alligator Pie, 1974; Nicholas Knock and Other People, 1974; Garbage Delight, 1977; Jelly Belly, 1983; Lizzie's Lion, 1984; The Ice Cream Store, 1991; Dinosaur Dinner with a Slice of Alligator Pie, 1997; Bubblegum Delicious, 2000; The Cat and the Wizard, 2001; Garbage Delight, Another Helping, 2002. EDITOR: (with R.A. Charlesworth) An Anthology of Verse, 1964, rev. ed. as A New Anthology of Verse, 1989; (with R.A. Charlesworth) The Second Century Anthologies of Verse, Book 2, 1967; (with H. Adelman) The University Game, 1968; T.O. Now: The Young Toronto Poets, 1968; The New Canadian Poets, 1970-1985, 1985. **Address:** c/o WCA, 94 Harbord St, Toronto, ON, Canada M5S 1G6.

LEE, Donald (Lewis). British, b. 1931. **Genres:** Zoology. **Career:** University of Leeds, Emeritus Professor, (Pro-Vice-Chancellor, 1987-89, professor of Agricultural Zoology, 1986-96). Research Fellow, 1958-63, and Fellow, 1963-71, Christ's College, Cambridge University; Head of Parasitology Dept., Houghton Poultry Research Station, 1966-71. Royal Society/Kan Tong Po Professor, University of Hong Kong, 1989-90; President, 1978-80, British Society of Parasitology. **Publications:** The Physiology of Nematodes, 1965, 2nd ed. with H.J. Atkinson, 1976; (ed. with D.H. Jennings) Symbiosis, 1976; The Biology of Nematodes, 2002. **Address:** School of Biology, University of Leeds, Leeds LS2 9JT, England.

LEE, Donald L(uther). See MADHUBUTI, Haki R.

LEE, Frances E. American, b. 1968. **Genres:** Politics/Government. **Career:** Case Western Reserve University, Cleveland, OH, assistant professor of political science, 1997-. **Publications:** (with B.I. Oppenheimer) Sizing Up the Senate: The Unequal Consequences of Equal Representation, 1999. Contributor of articles and reviews to periodicals. **Address:** Department of Political Science, Case Western Reserve University, Cleveland, OH 44106, U.S.A. **Online address:** fel@po.cwru.edu

LEE, Helen Elaine. American, b. 1959. **Genres:** Novels. **Career:** Novelist and attorney. **Publications:** NOVELS: The Serpent's Gift, 1994; Water Marked, 1999. **Address:** Massachusetts Institute of Technology, Program in Writing and Humanistic Studies, Cambridge, MA 02139, U.S.A.

LEE, Henry C(hang-Yuh). American (born China), b. 1938. **Genres:** Criminology/True Crime. **Career:** Taipei Police Department, Taiwan, lieutenant, 1960, captain, 1960-; worked as journalist, c. 1963-64; University of New Haven, New Haven, CT, assistant professor, 1975-76, associate professor and director of forensic science, 1976-78, director of center of applied research, 1976-, director of forensic science laboratory, 1977-, professor of forensic science, 1978-; director of State of Connecticut's State Forensic Science Laboratory, 1979-; writer, consultant, and visiting professor. **Publications:** (with P.R. De Forest and R.E. Gaensslen) Forensic Science: An Introduction to Criminalistics, 1983; (with R.E. Gaensslen) Procedures and Evaluations of Antisera for the Typing of Antigens in Bloodstains: ABH, Rh, MNSs, Kell, Duffy, and Kidd Blood Group Antigens and Gm/Km Serum Group Antigens, 1984; Dr. Henry C. Lee on Crime Scene Investigation and Reconstruction, 1988; (ed.) DNA and Other Polymorphisms in Forensic Science, 1990; (ed.) Advances in Fingerprint Technology, 1991. Editor of periodicals. **Address:** c/o Dept of Public Safety, 111 Country Club Rd, Middletown, CT 06457, U.S.A.

LEE, J. Cleo. See JOHNSON, Leland R(oss).

LEE, J(oseph) Edward. American, b. 1953. **Genres:** History. **Career:** University of North Carolina-Charlotte, professor of history, 1985-94; Winthrop University, Rock Hill, SC, professor of history, 1994-. **Publications:** Yorkville to York, 1997; White Christmas in April: The Collapse of South Vietnam, 1999; Gateway to the New South, 1999; Along the Catawba River, 1999; The Making of a Southern Eden, 2000; Nixon, Ford and the Abandonment of South Vietnam, 2000; South Carolina and the Civil War, 2000. **Address:** Department of History, Winthrop University, Rock Hill, SC 29733, U.S.A.

LEE, Jae. American, b. 1972. **Genres:** Graphic Novels. **Career:** Graphic artist. Illustrator for publishers. **Publications:** ILLUSTRATOR: The Sentry, written by Paul Jenkins, 2001; The Inhumans, written by Paul Jenkins, 2001; Fantastic Four: 1, 2, 3, 4 (Marvel Knights), 2004. Writer and illustrator of comic book series. **Address:** c/o Author Mail, Marvel Enterprises Inc, 10 East 40th St., New York, NY 10016, U.S.A. **Online address:** jaelle@aol.com

LEE, Jeanne M. Vietnamese, b. 1943. **Genres:** Mythology/Folklore. **Career:** Writer and illustrator. **Publications:** (Reteller and illustrator) Legend of the Milky Way, 1982; (Reteller and illustrator) Legend of the Li River: An Ancient Chinese Tale, 1983; (Reteller and illustrator) Toad is the Uncle of Heaven: A Vietnamese Folk Tale, 1985; Silent Lotus, 1991; The Song of Mu Lan, 1995; I Once Was a Monkey: Stories Buddha Told, 1999; Bitter Dumplings, 2002. Illustrator of books by L. Yep. **Address:** c/o Farrar Straus & Giroux, 19 Union Square W., New York, NY 10003, U.S.A.

LEE, Jennifer. (born Republic of Korea), b. 1968. **Genres:** Adult non-fiction. **Career:** University of California-Irvine, Irvine, assistant professor, 2000-02, associate professor of sociology, 2003-. Center for Advanced Study in the Behavioral Sciences, Palo Alto, CA, fellow, 2002-03. **Publications:** Civility in the City, 2002. **Address:** Department of Sociology, University of California Irvine, Irvine, CA 92697, U.S.A.

LEE, Joann Faung Jean. American (born Hong Kong). **Genres:** Cultural/Ethnic topics. **Career:** Chinese News, Taipei, Taiwan, freelance writer, 1972; China Lantern, Taipei, Taiwan, editor, 1972-73; KABC TV News, Los Angeles, CA, newswriter intern, 1974-75; KXTV News, Sacramento, CA, general assignment reporter, 1975-76; WLS TV News, Chicago, IL, general assignment reporter and newswriter, 1976-, WCAU TV News, Philadelphia, PA, general assignment reporter, 1977-79; WNEW TV News, New York, NY, general assignment reporter, 1979; Cable News Network, New York Bureau, correspondent, 1980-81; Columbia University, Graduate School of Journalism, New York, NY, assistant professor; Queen's College, associate professor, journalism director, 1991-95, re-appointed 1997. **Publications:** Asian Americans, 1992; Asian American Actors, 2000; Virtual Escape (www.onlineoriginals.com). **Address:** Queens College, CUNY, 65-30 Kissena Blvd., Flushing, NY 11367, U.S.A. **Online address:** joann_lee@qc.edu.

LEE, Josephine (D.). American. **Genres:** Theatre. **Career:** Princeton University, Princeton, NJ, lecturer in English, between 1984 and 1987; California State University, Northridge, assistant professor of English, 1987-89; Smith College, Northampton, MA, assistant professor of English, 1989-94; University of Minnesota-Twin Cities, associate professor of English, 1994-. **Publications:** Performing Asian America: Race and Ethnicity on the Contemporary Stage, 1997. Contributor to theatre books. Contributor to periodicals. **Address:** Department of English, 207 Lind Hall, University of Minnesota-Twin Cities, 207 Church St. S.E., Minneapolis, MN 55455-0134, U.S.A. **Online address:** leexx151@tc.umn.edu

LEE, Judith Yaross. American, b. 1949. **Genres:** Area studies, Cultural/Ethnic topics, Humanities, Literary criticism and history, Speech/Rhetoric. **Career:** Field Enterprises Educational Corp., Chicago, IL, traffic analyst for business research, 1971-73; Illinois Institute of Technology, Chicago, instructor in humanities, 1977; Long Island University, Brooklyn, NY, instructor to assistant professor of English and media arts, 1978-85, faculty admissions coordinator, 1980-81; University of Helsinki, Finland, visiting lecturer in American studies, 1986-87; Fiorello H. LaGuardia Community College of the City University of New York, Long Island City, NY, assistant professor of English, 1988-90; Ohio University, Athens, assistant professor of journalism and interpersonal communication, 1990-95, associate professor, 1995-2000, professor of interpersonal communication, 2000-, Central Region Humanities Center, co-director, 2001-; Bangkok University, Thailand, visiting professor, Doctoral Program in Interpersonal Communication, 1994. **Publications:** (ed. with J.W. Slade) Beyond the Two Cultures: Essays on Science, Technology, and Literature, 1990; Garrison Keillor: A Voice of America, 1991; Defining New Yorker Humor, 2000. Work represented in anthologies. Contributor of articles and reviews to periodicals. **Address:** Lasher Hall, Ohio University, Athens, OH 45701, U.S.A.

LEE, Laurel. See Obituaries.

LEE, Lily Xiao Hong. Australian (born China), b. 1939. **Genres:** Women's studies and issues. **Career:** University of Hong Kong, head of library serials department, 1965-71; University of Sydney, Sydney, New South Wales, Australia, 1982-, lecturer, 1993-98, coordinator of an M.A. course in translation and interpreting. **Publications:** Virtue of Yin: Studies on Chinese Women, 1994; (ed.-in-chief with A.D. Stefenowska) Biographical Dictionary of Chinese Women: The Qing Period, 1622-1911, 1998; (with S. Wiles) Women of the Long March, 1999; (ed.) Biographical Dictionary of Chinese Women: The Twentieth Century, 1912-2000, 2002. **Address:** Dept. of Chinese, University of Sydney, Sydney, NSW 2006, Australia. **Online address:** lily.lee@asia.usyd.edu.au

LEE, Li-Young. American (born Indonesia), b. 1957. **Genres:** Poetry. **Career:** Writer. **Publications:** POETRY: Rose, 1986; The City in Which I Love You, 1990. OTHER: The Winged Seed, 1995. **Address:** c/o Simon and Schuster, Simon and Schuster Bldg., 1230 Avenue of the Americas, New York, NY 10020, U.S.A.

LEE, M. Owen. American, b. 1930. **Genres:** Classics, Music. **Career:** Roman Catholic priest. University of St. Thomas, Houston, TX, professor of classics, 1968-72; Loyola University, Chicago, associate professor of classics, 1972-75; University of Toronto, professor of classics, 1975-, now emeritus. **Publications:** Word, Sound, and Image in the Odes of Horace, 1969; Fathers and Sons in Virgil's Aeneid, 1979; Death and Rebirth in Virgil's Arcadia, 1989; Wagner's Ring: Turning the Sky Round, 1990; First Intermissions, 1995; Virgil as Orpheus, 1996; The Olive Tree Bed and Other Quests, 1997; A Season of Opera, 1998; Wagner: The Terrible Man and His Truthful Art, 1999; Father Lee's Opera Quiz Book, 2000; The Operagoer's Guide, 2001; Athena Sings: Wagner and the Greeks, 2003. Author of articles. **Address:** 81 St. Mary St, Toronto, ON, Canada M5S 1J4.

LEE, Marie G. American, b. 1964. **Genres:** Novels, Young adult fiction, Adult non-fiction, Essays. **Publications:** Finding My Voice, 1992; If It Hadn't Been for Yoon Jun, 1993; Saying Goodbye, 1994; Necessary Roughness, 1996; F Is for Fabuloso, 1999. Contributor to anthologies. **Address:** c/o Charlotte Sheedy Literary Agency, 65 Bleecker St, New York, NY 10012, U.S.A. **Online address:** scdmarie@yahoo.com

LEE, Mark. (born United States), b. 1950. **Genres:** Military/Defense/Arms control. **Career:** Writer, journalist, and poet. **Publications:** The Lost Tribe, 1998; The Canal House, 2003. Contributor to periodicals. **Address:** c/o Author Mail, Algonquin Books, POB 225, Chapel Hill, NC 27515, U.S.A.

LEE, Mona. American, b. 1939. **Genres:** Novels. **Career:** State of Washington, Division of Vocational Rehabilitation, lead counselor. **Publications:** NOVELS: Alien Child, 1999; The Messenger. Contributor of short stories to magazines. **Address:** 3600 South Graham St., Seattle, WA 98118, U.S.A.

LEE, Norhm. *See* ANDERSON, Henry L(ee Norman).

LEE, Peter H. American (born Republic of Korea), b. 1929. **Genres:** Literary criticism and history, Translations. **Career:** Columbia University, NYC, Assistant Professor, 1960-62; University of Hawaii, Honolulu, Assistant Professor to Professor, 1962-87; University of California, Los Angeles, Professor of Korean and Comparative Literature, 1987-. **Publications:** Studies in Old Korean Poetry, 1959; Korean Literature: Topics and Themes, 1965; (trans.) Lives of Eminent Korean Monks, 1969; (ed.) Flowers of Fire, 1974, 1986; Songs of Flying Dragons: A Critical Reading, 1975; Celebration of Continuity: Themes in Classic East Asian Poetry, 1979; The Silence of Love: Twentieth Century Korean Poetry, 1980; Anthology of Korean Literature: From Early Times to the Nineteenth Century, 1981; A Korean Storyteller's Miscellany, 1989; Modern Korean Literature: An Anthology, 1990; Pine River and Lone Peak, 1991; Sourcebook of Korean Civilization, 2 vols., 1993-96; Sources of Korean Tradition, 1997-2000; The Record of the Black Dragon Year, 2000; Myths of Korea, 2000; The Columbia Anthology of Traditional Korean Poetry, 2002; A History of Korean Literature, 2003. TRANSLATOR & EDITOR: Kranich am Meer, 1959; Anthology of Korean Poetry, 1964; Poems from Korea, 1974. **Address:** Dept of Asian Languages and Cultures, Box 951540, University of California, Los Angeles, Los Angeles, CA 90095-1540, U.S.A. **Online address:** lee@humnet.ucla.edu

LEE, Rachel. Also writes as Sue Civil-Brown. American. **Genres:** Romance/ Historical. **Career:** Romance novel writer. **Publications:** Exile's End, 1992; An Officer and a Gentlemen, 1991; Serious Risks, 1991; Cherokee Thunder, 1992; Imminent Thunder, 1993; Ironheart, 1993; Lost Warriors, 1993; Thunder Mountain, 1994; Cowboy Cop, 1995; A Conard County Reckoning, 1996; A Fateful Choice, 1996; Caught, 1997; Nighthawk, 1997; The Catch of Conard County, 1998; Cowboy Comes Home, 1998; Before I Sleep, 1999; Boots and Badges, 1999; After I Dream, 2000; Snow in September, 2000; When I Wake, 2000; A January Chill, 2001; Under Suspicion, 2001; July Thunder, 2002; Last Breath, 2003; With Malice, 2003. AS SUE CIVIL-BROWN: Carried Away, 1997; Letting Loose, 1998; Chasing Rainbow, 1999; Catching Kelly, 2000; Tempting Mr. Wright, 2000; Next Stop, Paradise, 2001; Breaking All the Rules, 2002. OTHER NOVELS: Destination: Conard County; A Conard County Homecoming; Miss Emmaline and the Archangel; Lost Warriors; Point of No Return; A Question of Justice; Involuntary Daddy. **Address:** c/o Author Mail, Warner Books, 1271 Sixth Ave. 9th Fl., New York, NY 10020, U.S.A.

LEE, Sally. American, b. 1943. **Genres:** Children's non-fiction, Young adult non-fiction. **Career:** Special School District, St. Louis, MO, special education teacher, 1965-68; Spring Branch School District, Houston, TX, teacher, 1968-71; homemaker, 1971-90; Sugarland Properties, Inc., Sugar Land, TX, executive secretary, 1990-; writer. **Publications:** Donor Banks: Saving Lives with Organ and Tissue Transplants, 1988; Predicting Violent Storms, 1989; New Theories on Diet and Nutrition, 1990; The Throwaway Society, 1990; Pesticides, 1991; San Antonio, 1992; Hurricanes, 1993. **Address:** 3111 E Hickory Park Circle, Sugar Land, TX 77479-2616, U.S.A.

LEE, Sandra. *See* CUSICK, Heidi Haughy.

LEE, Sharon. American, b. 1952. **Genres:** Science fiction/Fantasy, Writing/ Journalism. **Career:** Science fiction writer. Worked in the secretarial field, 1970-76; University of Maryland Professional Schools, administrative aide to the Dean of the School of Social Work, 1976-78; Book Castle (a book store), founder and owner, 1978-80; also worked delivering tractor trailers, selling cider, and as an advertising copy writer. **Publications:** LIADEN UNIVERSE NOVELS (with S. Miller): Agent of Change, 1988; Conflict of Honors, 1988; Carpe Diem, 1989; Plan B, 1999; Partners in Necessity, 2000; Pilots Choice, 2001; I Dare, 2002; Balance of Trade, 2004. OTHER NOVELS: (with S. Miller) The Tomorrow Log, 2002; Barnburner, 2002. CHAPBOOKS: Variations Three; Endeavors of Will. CHAPBOOKS (with S. Miller): Two Tales of Korval; Fellow Travelers; Duty Bound; Certain Symmetry; Trading in Futures; Changeling; Loose Cannon; Quiet Magic; The Naming of Kinzel; Shadows and Shades; The Cat's Job; Master Walk; Quiet Knives. Contributor to periodicals. **Address:** c/o SRM Publisher, PO Box 0179, Unity, ME 04988-0179, U.S.A. **Online address:** sharonlee@korval.com

LEE, Sherman Emery. American, b. 1918. **Genres:** Art/Art history. **Career:** Adjunct Professor of Art, University of North Carolina at Chapel Hill, since 1983. Curator of Far Eastern Art, Detroit Institute of Art, Michigan, 1941-46; Advisor on Collections, Arts and Monuments Division Section, U.S. Army, Tokyo, 1946-48; Assistant Director, and Associate Director, Seattle Art Museum, Wash., 1948-52; Curator of Oriental Art, 1952-83, Assistant Director, 1956-57, Associate Director, 1957-58, and Director, 1958-83, Cleveland

Museum of Art, Ohio. Professor of Art, Case Western Reserve University, Cleveland, Ohio, 1962-83. **Publications:** Chinese Landscape Painting, 1954, 1962; (with Wen Fong) Streams and Mountains Without End, 1955; Rajput Painting, 1960; Japanese Decorative Style, 1961; Tea Taste in Japanese Art, 1963; History of Far Eastern Art, 1963, 1982; (with Wai-Kam Ho) Chinese Art Under the Mongols, 1968; Ancient Cambodian Sculpture, 1968; Asian Art, 1970; The Colors of Ink, 1974; (ed.) On Understanding Art Museums, 1975; Past, Present, East and West, 1983; Reflections of Reality in Japanese Art, 1983; The Sketchbooks of Hiroshige, 2 vols., 1984. **Address:** Carolina Meadows, Health Center 207, Chapel Hill, NC 27517, U.S.A.

LEE, Sky. Canadian, b. 1952. **Genres:** Novellas/Short stories, Novels. **Career:** Nurse and writer. **Publications:** (with P. Yee) Teach Me to Fly, Sky-fighter! and Other Stories, 1983; Disappearing Moon Cafe (novel), 1990; Bellydancer: Stories, 1994. **Address:** c/o Seal Press, PMB 375, 300 Queen Anne Ave N, Seattle, WA 98109-4512, U.S.A.

LEE, Wayne C. Also writes as Lee Sheldon. American, b. 1917. **Genres:** Westerns/Adventure, History. **Career:** Rural Mail Carrier, 1951-77. President, Western Writers of America, 1970-71, and Nebraska Writers Guild, 1974-76. **Publications:** Prairie Vengeance, 1954; Broken Wheel Ranch, 1956; Slugging Backstop, 1957; His Brother's Guns, 1958; Killer's Range, 1958; Bat Masterson, 1960; Gun Brand, 1961; Blood on the Prairie, 1962; Thunder in the Backfield, 1962; Stranger in Stirrup, 1962; The Gun Tamer, 1963; Devil Wire, 1963; The Hostile Land, 1964; Gun in His Hand, 1964; Warpath West, 1965; Fast Gun, 1965; Brand of a Man, 1966; Mystery of Scorpion Creek, 1966; Trail of the Skulls, 1966; Showdown at Julesburg Station, 1967; Return to Gunpoint, 1967; Only the Brave, 1967; (as Lee Sheldon) Doomed Planet, 1967; Sudden Guns, 1968; Trouble at Flying H, 1969; Stage to Lonesome Butte, 1969; Showdown at Sunrise, 1971; The Buffalo Hunters, 1972; Suicide Trail, 1972; Wind Over Rimfire, 1973; Son of a Gunman, 1973; Scotty Philip, the Man Who Saved the Buffalo, 1975; Law of the Prairie, 1975; Die Hard, 1975; Law of the Lawless, 1977; Skirmish at Fort Phil Kearney, 1977; Gun Country, 1978; Petticoat Wagon Train, 1978; The Violent Man, 1978. Ghost of a Gunfighter, 1980; McQuaid's Gun, 1980; Trails of the Smoky Hill (non-fiction), 1980; Shadow of the Gun, 1981; Guns at Genesis, 1981; Putnam's Ranch War, 1982; Barbed Wire War, 1983; The Violent Trail, 1984; White Butte Guns, 1984; War at Nugget Creek, 1985; Massacre Creek, 1985; The Waiting Gun, 1986; Hawks of Autumn, 1986; Wild Towns of Nebraska (non-fiction), 1988; Arikaree War Cry, 1992; Bad Men and Bad Towns (non-fiction), 1993; Deadly Days in Kansas (non-fiction), 1997. **Address:** PO Box 906, Imperial, NE 69033, U.S.A.

LEECH, Ben. *See* BOWKETT, Stephen.

LEECH, Geoffrey Neil. British, b. 1936. **Genres:** Language/Linguistics. **Career:** University College, London, lecturer, 1965-69; University of Lancaster, reader in English, 1969-74, professor of linguistics, 1974-. **Publications:** English in Advertising, 1966; A Linguistic Guide to English Poetry, 1969; Towards a Semantic Description of English, 1969; Meaning and the English Verb, 1971, 3rd ed., 2004; (with others) A Grammar of Contemporary English, 1972; Semantics, 1974, 2nd ed., 1981; (with J. Svartvik) A Communicative Grammar of English, 1975, 3rd ed., 2002; Explorations in Semantics and Pragmatics, 1980; (with M.H. Short) Style in Fiction, 1981; (with M. Deuchar and R. Hoogenraad) English Grammar for Today, 1982, 2nd ed., 2005; Principles of Pragmatics, 1983; (with R. Quirk, S. Greenbaum and J. Svartvik) A Comprehensive Grammar of the English Language, 1985; An A-Z of English Grammar and Usage, 1989; Introducing English Grammar, 1992; (with others) Longman Grammar of Spoken and Written English, 1999; (with D. Biber and S. Conrad) Longman Student Grammar of Spoken and Written English, and Workbook, 2002. EDITOR: (with S. Greenbaum and J. Svartvik) Studies in English Linguistics, 1980; (with C.N. Candlin) Computers in English Language Teaching and Research, 1986; (co) The Computational Analysis of English, 1987; (with E. Black and R. Garside) Statistically-Driven Computer Grammars of English, 1993; (with G. Myers and J. Thomas) Spoken English on Computer: Transcription, Mark-up and Application, 1995; (with R. Garside and A. McEnery) Corpus Annotation, 1997. **Address:** University of Lancaster, Bailrigg, Lancaster LA1 4YT, England.

LEECH, John. (Hans-Joachim Freiherr von Reitzenstein). British (born Germany), b. 1925. **Genres:** International relations/Current affairs, Military/ Defense/Arms control, Politics/Government, Third World. **Career:** L.G. Mouchel and Partners Ltd., London, England, articled pupil to special assistant to the chair, 1942-52; Bird and Co. Ltd., Calcutta, India, general manager and chief engineer for Indian Patent Stone Co., 1953-57; Britain in Europe/Europe House, London, director of activities for British membership of the European Community, 1958-61; Commonwealth Development Corp., London, general manager of Tanganyika Development Finance Co., 1965-67, head of external relations and member of management board, 1981-85; Rural Investment Overseas Ltd., London, chair, 1985-90, deputy chair, 1990-2000, European co-ordinator, West-West Agenda, 1988-. **Publications:** The NATO Parliamentarians' Conference, 1955-59, 1960; Europe and the Commonwealth, 1961; Aid and the Community, 1972; Halt! Who Goes Where? The Future of NATO in the New Europe, 1991; Asymmetries of Conflict: War without Death, 2002; (ed.) Whole and Free: NATO, EU Enlargement and Transatlantic Relations, 2002. Contributor to periodicals. **Address:** 8 Chester Square Mews, London SW1W 9DS, England. **Online address:** jleechvr@aol.com

LEECH, Kenneth. British, b. 1939. **Genres:** Medicine/Health, Sociology, Theology/Religion. **Career:** Curate, Holy Trinity, Hoxton, 1964-67, and St. Anne's, Soho, 1967-71, London; Chaplain, St. Augustines College, Canterbury, 1971-74; Rector, St. Matthew's Bethnal Green, London, 1974-81; Race Relations Field Officer, Church of England, 1981-87; Director, Runnymede Trust, 1987-90; M. B. Reckitt Urban Fellow, St. Botolph's Church, Aldgate, 1991-. **Publications:** (with B. Jordan) Drugs for Young People: Their Use and Misuse, 1967; Pastoral Care and the Drug Scene, 1970; Practical Guide to the Drug Scene, 1973; Keep the Faith Baby, 1973; Youthquake, 1973; Soul Friend, 1977; True Prayer, 1980; Brick Lane 1978; The Social God, 1981; What Everyone Should Know about Drugs, 1983; True God, 1985; Spirituality and Pastoral Care, 1986; Struggle in Babylon, 1988; Care and Conflict, 1990; The Eye of the Storm, 1992; We Preach Christ Crucified, 1994; The Sky Is Red, 1997, rev. ed., 2003; Drugs and Pastoral Care, 1998; Through Our Long Exile, 2001. **Address:** St. Botolph's Church, Aldgate, London EC3N 1AB, England. **Online address:** kenleech@aol.com

LEEDER, Elaine J. American, b. 1944. **Genres:** Biography, Human relations/Parenting. **Career:** Sheltering Arms Children's Service, NYC, caseworker, 1969-70; Elmira Psychiatric Center, Elmira, NY, psychiatric social worker, 1972-73; St. Joseph Hospital, Elmira, intake worker and group leader for Southern Tier Alcoholism Rehabilitation Service, 1973-77; Ithaca College, Ithaca, NY, associate professor of sociology and social work, 1977-, coordinator of Social Work Program, 1977-, and head of department, also member of Hillel board of directors. Chemung County Mental Health Clinic, psychiatric social worker, 1973-80; private practice of psychotherapy, 1980-91; worker in refugee assistance programs. Lecturer at colleges and universities; public speaker. **Publications:** The Gentle General: Rose Pesotta, Anarchist and Labor Organizer, 1993; Treating Abuse in Families: A Feminist and Community Approach, 1994. Work represented in anthologies. Contributor of articles and reviews to professional journals and popular journals. **Address:** Department of Sociology and Social Work, Muller 112, Ithaca College, Ithaca, NY 14850, U.S.A. **Online address:** leeder@ithaca.edu

LEEDS, Barry H. American, b. 1940. **Genres:** Literary criticism and history. **Career:** City University of New York, lecturer, 1963-64; University of Texas at El Paso, instructor, 1964-65; El Paso Herald Post, drama critic, 1965; Ohio University, Athens, teaching fellow, 1965-67; Central Connecticut State University, New Britain, assistant professor, 1968-71, associate professor, 1971-76, professor 1976-91, distinguished professor of English, 1991-. Choice Magazine, consultant and reviewer, 1968-; Connecticut Review, editor, 1989-93. **Publications:** The Structured Vision of Norman Mailer, 1969; Ken Kesey, 1981; The Enduring Vision of Norman Mailer, 2002. **Address:** 200 Blakeslee St Apt 121, Bristol, CT 06010, U.S.A.

LEEDS, (Sir) Christopher (Anthony). British, b. 1935. **Genres:** Economics, History, International relations/Current affairs, Politics/Government, Humor/Satire. **Career:** Assistant master, Merchant Taylors' School, Northwood, Middx., 1966-68, Christ's Hospital, Horsham, Sussex, 1972-75, and Stowe School, Bucks., 1978-81; University of Nancy II, France, lecturer, 1982-83, sr. lecturer, 1983-88, associate professor, 1988-2000; University of Kent of Canterbury, England, visiting research fellow, 2000-2001. **Publications:** Political Studies, 1968, 3rd ed., 1981; European History 1789-1914, 1971, 1980; Italy under Mussolini, 1972; (with R.S. Stainton and C. Jones) Management and Business Studies, 1974, 3rd ed., 1983; Unification of Italy, 1974; Historical Guide to England, 1976; British Government and Politics, 1981; Basic Economics Revision, 1982; Politics in Action, 1986; World History since 1900, 1987; Peace and War, 1987; English Humour, 1989. **Address:** 7 rue de Turique, 54000 Nancy, France. **Online address:** ChristopherLeeds400@hotmail.com

LEEDY, Paul D. See Obituaries.

LEEMAN, Richard W. American, b. 1955. **Genres:** Communications/Media. **Career:** University of North Carolina at Charlotte, professor of communication studies, 1989-. **Publications:** The Rhetoric of Terrorism and Counterterrorism, 1991; Do Everything Reform: The Oratory of Frances E. Willard, 1992; African-American Orators: A Biocritical Sourcebook, 1996; The Art and Practice of Argumentation and Debate, 1997. Contributor to academic journals. **Address:** Department of Communication Studies, University of North Carolina at Charlotte, Charlotte, NC 28223, U.S.A. **Online address:** rwleeman@email.uncc.edu

LEERBURGER, Benedict A. American. **Genres:** Librarianship, Self help, Technology. **Career:** Freelance writer, since 1979. Science Ed., Look Magazine, NYC, 1964-69; Director of Publs., New York Times, MCA, NYC, 1972-74; Ed. and Publr., Kraus-Thomson Organization Ltd., 1974-77; Publr., Film Review Digest, 1975-77; Ed.-in-Chief, McGraw-Hill Book Co., Webster Division, NYC, 1977-79. **Publications:** Josiah Willard Gibbs: American Theoretical Physicist, 1968; Marketing the Library, 1983; The Complete Consumer's Guide to the Latest Telephones, 1985; Insider's Guide to Foreign Study, 1988; The Complete Guide to Overseas Employment, 1991; Jobs Worldwide, 1995. **Address:** 338 Heathcote Rd, Scarsdale, NY 10583, U.S.A. **Online address:** Leerbs@cs.com

LEESE, Peter (Jeremy). American. **Genres:** Adult non-fiction. **Career:** Educator and author. Jagiellonian University, Krakow, Poland, assistant professor of English. **Publications:** (with C. Cook) St. Martin's Guide to Sources in Contemporary British History, 1994, published as The Longman Guide to Sources in Contemporary British History, 1994; (translation, with Elżbieta Wójcik-Leese) Włodzimierz Szturc, A Short History of Polish Literature, 1998; Shell Shock: Traumatic Neurosis and the British Soldiers of the First World War, 2002; (editor, with B. Piatek and I. Curyllo-Klag) The British Migrant Experience, 1700-2000: An Anthology, 2002; (editor, with W. Witalisz, and contrib.) PASE Papers in Cultural Literature: Proceedings of the Tenth International Conference of PASE, 2003. Contributor of papers and articles to publications. **Address:** English Department, Jagiellonian University, Al. Mickiewicza 9, 31-120 Krakow, Poland.

LEE SIX, Abigail (Etta). British, b. 1960. **Genres:** Literary criticism and history. **Career:** Cambridge University, Cambridge, England, research fellow in Spanish at Sidney Sussex College, 1986-88; University of London, London, England, lecturer in Hispanic studies at Queen Mary and Westfield College, 1988-. **Publications:** Juan Goytisolo: The Case for Chaos, 1990; Juan Goytisolo: Campos de Nijar, Critical Guides to Spanish Texts, 1995. **Address:** Dept of Hispanic Studies, Royal Holloway, University of London, Egham, Surrey TW20 0EX, England.

LEESON, Robert (Arthur). British, b. 1928. **Genres:** Children's fiction, Children's non-fiction, History, Literary criticism and history. **Career:** Journalist, 1944-; freelance editor and writer, 1969-. Literary and children's ed., Morning Star, London 1961-84; chairman, Writers' Guild, 1985-86. **Publications:** United We Stand, 1971; Strike: A Live History 1887-1971, 1973; Beyond the Dragon Prow, 1973; Maroon Boy, 1974; The Third Class Genie, 1975, as play, 2001; Bess, 1975; The Demon Bike Rider, 1976; The White Horse, 1977; Children's Books and Class Society, 1977; Silver's Revenge, 1978; The Cimaroons, 1978; Challenge in the Dark, 1978; Travelling Brothers, 1979; Grange Hill series, 4 vols., 1980-82; Harold and Bella, Jammy and Me, 1980; It's My Life, 1980; Forty Days of Tucker J, 1983; Candy for King, 1983; Genie on the Loose, 1984; Reading and Righting, 1985; Time Rope (serial novel), 4 vols., 1986; Reversible Giant, 1986; Wheel of Danger, 1986; Slambash Wangs of a Compo Gormer 1987; Never Kiss Frogs, 1988; Hey, Robin!, 1989; Burper, 1989; Jan Alone, 1990; Coming Home, 1991; One Frog Too Many, 1991; Pancake Pickle, 1991; April Fool at Hob Lane School, 1992; No Sleep for Hob Lane, 1992; Ghosts at Hob Lane, 1993; The Zarnia Experiment (serial novel) 6 vols., 1992-93; Karlo's Tale, 1993; The Last Genie, 1993; Smart Girls, 1993; Swapper, 1994; The Story of Robin Hood, 1994; The Dog Who Changed the World, 1994; Amazing Adventures of Idle Jack, 1995; Geraldine Gets Lucky, 1995; All the Gold in the World, 1995; Red White and Blue, 1996; Smart Girls Forever, 1996; Lucky Lad, 1997; Doomwater, 1997; Tom's Private War, 1998; Why's the Cow on the Roof?, 1998; Liar, 1999; Ruth (play, adaptation), 2000; Song of Arthur, 2000; My Sister Shahrqzad, 2000; Tom's War Patrol, 2001; Onda, Wind Rider, 2003; Partners in Crime, 2003. **Address:** 18 McKenzie Rd, Broxbourne, Herts., England.

LEESON, Ted. American, b. 1954. **Genres:** Novels. **Career:** Oregon State University, Corvallis, senior instructor, 1984-. **Publications:** The Habit of Rivers, 1994. **Address:** Moreland Hall, Oregon State University, Corvallis, OR 97331, U.S.A.

LEFCOURT, Peter. American, b. 1946. **Genres:** Novels, Plays/Screenplays. **Career:** Producer and writer. **Publications:** NOVELS: The Deal, 1991; The

Dreyfus Affair, 1992; Di and I, 1994; Abbreviating Ernie, 1997; Woody, 1998; Eleven Karens, 2003; The Manhattan Beach Project, 2005. STAGE PLAYS: Only the Dead Know Burbank, 1990; Sweet Talk, 1991; La Ronde de Lunch, 1992. EDITOR: The First Time I Got Paid for It, 2000. Has also written scripts for film and television. **Address:** c/o Ken Cross Management, 7720 Sunset Blvd, Los Angeles, CA 90046, U.S.A. **Online address:** lefcourt@earthlink.net

LEFEBURE, Leo D. American, b. 1952. **Genres:** Theology/Religion. **Career:** Roman Catholic priest in the Archdiocese of Chicago, 1978-. St. Stephen Protomartyr Church, DesPlaines, IL, associate pastor, 1978-82; Our Lady Help of Christians Church, Chicago, associate pastor, 1982-87; University of St. Mary of the Lake, Mundelein, IL, instructor of systematic theology, 1987-89, assistant professor, 1989-91, chair of department of systematic theology, 1989-92, associate professor, 1991-94, dean of ecclesiastical faculty, 1992-98, professor of systematic theology, 1994-99; Fordham University, visiting associate professor, 1999-2001, associate professor, 2001-. Chicago Studies, editor, 1999-2003. **Publications:** Toward a Contemporary Wisdom Christology: A Study of Karl Rahner and Norman Pittenger, 1988; Life Transformed: Meditations on the Christian Scriptures in Light of Buddhist Perspectives, 1989; The Buddha and the Christ: Explorations in Buddhist-Christian Dialogue, 1993; Revelation, the Religions, and Violence, 2000. Contributor to journals and periodicals. **Address:** 740 N Broadway, Yonkers, NY 10701-1543, U.S.A. **Online address:** lefebure@fordham.edu

LEFEBURE, Molly. British. **Genres:** Novels, Criminology/True Crime, Geography, Biography. **Career:** Professional Writer. **Publications:** Evidence for the Crown, 1955; Murder with a Difference, 1958; The Lake District, 1963; Scratch and Co., 1968; The Hunting of Wilberforce Pike, 1970; Cumberland Heritage, 1971; The Loona Balloona, 1974; Samuel Taylor Coleridge: A Bondage of Opium, 1974; Cumbrian Discovery, 1977; The Bondage of Love: A Life of Mrs. Samuel Taylor Coleridge, 1986; The Illustrated Lake Poets, 1987; Blitz!, 1988; Thunder in the Sky, 1991; Thomas Hardy's World, 1996. **Address:** c/o Watson Little Ltd, Capo di Monte, Windmill Hill, London NW3 6RJ, England.

LEFENS, Tim. American, b. 1953. **Genres:** History. **Career:** Author, painter, and art instructor. Artistic Realizations Technologies (A.R.T.), founder, 1995-; other jobs included tree cutter and house painter. **Publications:** Flying Colors: The Story of a Remarkable Group of Artists and the Transcendent Power of Art, 2002. **Address:** c/o Artistic Realizations Technologies, 11 Whippoorwill Way, Belle Mead, NJ 08502, U.S.A. **Online address:** art@artrealization.org

LEFF, Gordon. British, b. 1926. **Genres:** Intellectual history, Philosophy. **Career:** Freelance writer, lectr. and occasional broadcaster. King's College, Cambridge, Fellow, 1955-59; Manchester University, Lecturer, then Sr. Lecturer, 1956-65; University of York, Professor of History, 1965-88, Emeritus Professor, 1988-. **Publications:** Bradwardine and the Pelagians, 1957; Medieval Thought, 1958; Gregory of Rimini, 1961; The Tyranny of Concepts, 1961; Richard Fitzralph, 1963; Heresy in the Later Middle Ages, 2 vols., 1967; Paris and Oxford Universities in 13th and 14th Centuries, 1968; History and Social Theory, 1969; William of Ockham: The Metamorphosis of Scholastic Discourse, 1975; The Dissolution of the Medieval Outlook, 1976; Heresy, Philosophy and Religion in the Medieval West, 2002. **Address:** The Sycamores, 12 The Village, Strensall, York YO32 5XS, England.

LEFKOWITZ, Mary (Rosenthal). American, b. 1935. **Genres:** Classics. **Career:** Andrew W. Mellon Professor in the Humanities, Wellesley College, Wellesley, MA, 1979(Part-time Instructor in Greek, 1960-63; Assistant Professor, 1963-69; Associate Professor, 1969-75; Professor of Greek and Latin, 1975-79; Chairman, 1970-72, 1975-78, 1981-87; Director of Educational Research, 1978-79; Director of Pew Foundation Grant, 1986-). Visiting Professor, University of California, Berkeley, 1978; Visiting Fellow, St. Hilda's College, Oxford, 1979-80, Pembroke College, Oxford, 1986-87, and Corpus Christi College, Oxford, 1991; Honorary Fellow, St. Hilda's College, 1994-; Woodrow Wilson Fellow, 1957-58; American Council of Learned Socs. Fellow, 1972-73; National Endowment for the Humanities Fellow, 1979-80, 1991. **Publications:** The Victory Ode: An Introduction, 1976; Heroines and Hysterics, 1981; The Lives of the Greek Poets, 1981; Women in Greek Myth, 1986; First-Person Fictions: Pindar's Poetic "I," 1991; Not Out of Africa, 1996; Greek Gods, Human Lives, 2003. EDITOR: (with M.B. Fant) Women in Greece and Rome, 1977, rev. as Women's Life in Greece and Rome, 1982, 2nd ed., 1992; (with G.M. Rogers) Black Athena Revisited. **Address:** 15 W Riding St, Wellesley, MA 02482-6914, U.S.A. **Online address:** mlefkowitz@wellesley.edu

LEGATO, Marianne J. American, b. 1935. **Genres:** Medicine/Health. **Career:** Physician. Columbia University College of Physicians and Surgeons, instructor, 1968-69, associate, 1969-70, assistant clinical professor, 1970-73, assistant professor, 1973-77, associate professor of clinical medicine, 1977-98, professor of clinical medicine, 1998-; Partnership for Gender-Specific Medicine at Columbia, founder and director; Advisory Board of the Office of Research on Women's Health of the National Institutes of Health, charter member, 1995-; member of editorial boards. Producer of medical films. Lecturer at conferences throughout the U.S.; has appeared on television and radio programs. **Publications:** The Myocardial Cell for the Clinical Cardiologist, 1973; (with C. Colman) The Female Heart: The Truth about Women and Coronary Artery Disease, 1992; Gender-Specific Aspects of Human Biology for the Practicing Physician, 1997; What Women Need to Know: From Headaches to Heart Disease and Everything in Between, 1997; Eve's Rib, 2002. EDITOR: The Developing Heart: Clinical Implications of Its Molecular Biology and Physiology, 1985; The Stressed Heart, 1987. Contributor to medical journals, books, and newspapers. **Address:** 962 Park Ave, New York, NY 10028, U.S.A.

LEGG, Gerald. British, b. 1947. **Genres:** Zoology. **Career:** Museum biologist, researcher, and nonfiction author. Fourah Bay College, University of Sierra Leone, Freetown, lecturer in zoology and researcher, 1971-74; Booth Museum of Natural History, Brighton, England, keeper of natural sciences, 1974-. British Arachnological Society, council member; Institute of biology, member. **Publications:** FOR CHILDREN: Amazing Tropical Birds, 1991; The X-Ray Picture Book of Amazing Animals, 1993; Minibeasts, 1993; (with K. Barnham) Flyers Animals: Minibeasts, 1994; Monster Animals, 1994; The X-Ray Picture Book of Incredible Creatures, 1995; (with R. Matthews) Amazing Animal Facts, 1997; Sharks, 1997; Creepy Critters, 1997; Dragons, 1998; Bugs, 1998; Find out about Minibeasts, 2003. SCARY CREATURES SERIES: Bears, 2002; Alligators and Crocodiles, 2002; Rats, 2002. LIFECYCLES SERIES: From Caterpillar to Butterfly, 1997; From Egg to Chicken, 1997; From Seed to Sunflower, 1997; From Tadpole to Frog, 1997. HOW IT WORKS SERIES: The World of Animal Life, 1998; The World of Plant Life, 2000; The World of Insect Life, 2000. FOR ADULTS: (with R.E. Jones) Pseudoscorpions (Arthropoda, Arachnida): Keys and Notes for the Identification of the Species, 1988. Consultant to book series and natural history titles. Contributor of scientific papers, articles, and reviews to periodicals and journals. **Address:** c/o Booth Museum of Natural History, 194 Dyke Rd., Brighton, Sussex BN1 5AA, England. **Online address:** gerald@natura.uklinux.net

LEGGATT, Alexander. Canadian, b. 1940. **Genres:** Theatre, Literary criticism and history. **Career:** University of Toronto, University College, lecturer, 1965-67, assistant professor, 1967-71, associate professor, 1971-75, professor of English, 1975-. Guggenheim Fellowship, 1985-86; Killam Fellowship, 1995-97. **Publications:** Citizen Comedy in the Age of Shakespeare, 1973; Shakespeare's Comedy of Love, 1974; Ben Jonson: His Vision and His Art, 1981; English Drama: Shakespeare to the Restoration 1590-1660, 1988; Shakespeare's Political Drama, 1988; Harvester Twayne New Critical Introductions to Shakespeare: King Lear, 1988; Shakespeare in Performance: King Lear, 1991; Jacobean Public Theatre, 1992; English Stage Comedy 1490-1990, 1998; Introduction to English Renaissance Comedy, 1999; (ed.) The Cambridge Companion to Shakespearean Comedy, 2002. **Address:** University College, University of Toronto, Toronto, ON, Canada M5S 3H7.

LEGGE, John David. Australian, b. 1921. **Genres:** History, Politics/Government, Biography. **Career:** Lecturer, 1946-54, Sr. Lecturer, 1955-59, and Reader in History, 1960, University of Western Australia; Professor of History, 1960-78, Chairman of the Centre of Southeast Asian Studies, 1964-86, and Dean, Faculty of Arts, 1978-86, Monash University, Victoria. Director, Institute of Southeast Asian Studies, Singapore, 1969-70. President, Asian Studies Association of Australia, 1976-78; Chairman Victoria State Library/Museum Buildings Advisory Committee, 1985-88; Chairman, Editorial Advisory Board, Department of Foreign Affairs and Trade, 1985-96. **Publications:** (with F. Alexander and F.K. Crowley) The Origins of the Eastern Goldfields Water Scheme in Western Australia; Australian Colonial Policy, 1956; Problems of Regional Autonomy in Contemporary Indonesia, 1957; Britain in Fiji, 1858-1880, 1958; Central Authority and Regional Autonomy in Indonesia, 1961; Indonesia, 1964, 3rd ed., 1980; Sukarno: A Political Biography, 1972, 3rd ed., 2003; Intellectuals and Nationalism in Indonesia, 1988; (ed. with D. Bourchier) Indonesian Democracy: 1950s-1990s, 1994; Australian Outlook: A History of the Australian Institute of International Affairs, 1999. **Address:** 7 Eileen St, Armadale, VIC 3143, Australia.

LEGGETT, Richard G. (born England), b. 1953. **Genres:** Theology/Religion. **Career:** Anglican priest in Denver, CO, 1981-84, and South Bend,

IN, 1984-87; Vancouver School of Theology, Vancouver, British Columbia, Canada, professor, 1987-. **Publications:** A Companion to the Waterloo Declaration, 2000. Contributor of articles and reviews to periodicals. **Address:** 7249 Cypress St., Vancouver, BC, Canada V6P 5M2. **Online address:** rleggett@vst.edu

LEGRAIN, Philippe. American. **Genres:** Business/Trade/Industry. **Career:** Economist and journalist. Independent Economic Analysis (IDEA), new media writer, 1996; SBC Warburg Dillon Read, economic research, 1996-97; The Economist, correspondent 1997-2000; World Trade Organization (WTO), special adviser to the director-general, 2000-01; World Link, editor, 2002; Britain in Europe, chief economist, 2003-. **Publications:** Open World: The Truth about Globalisation, 2002, published as Open World: The Truth about Globalization, 2004. **Address:** Ivan R. Dee, Publisher, 1332 North Halsted Street, Chicago, IL 60622, U.S.A. **Online address:** philippe.legrain@ britainineurope.org.uk

LE GUIN, Ursula K(roeber). American, b. 1929. **Genres:** Novels, Novellas/ Short stories, Science fiction/Fantasy, Children's fiction, Young adult fiction, Poetry, Literary criticism and history. **Publications:** Rocannon's World, 1966; Planet of Exile, 1966; City of Illusion, 1967; A Wizard of Earthsea, 1968; The Left Hand of Darkness, 1969; The Tombs of Atuan, 1970; The Lathe of Heaven, 1971; The Farthest Shore, 1972; The Dispossessed, 1974; Very Far Away from Anywhere Else, 1976; The Word for World Is Forest, 1976; Orsinian Tales, 1976; The Language of the Night (criticism), 1979, rev. ed., 1992; Leese Webster, 1979; Malafrena, 1979; The Beginning Place (in U.K. as Threshold), 1980; The Adventure of the Cobbler's Rune, 1983; The Eye of the Heron, 1983; The Visionary, 1984; Always Coming Home, 1985; Buffalo Gals and Other Animal Presences, 1987; A Visit from Dr. Katz, 1988; Catwings, 1988; Fire and Stone, 1989; Catwings Return, 1989; Dancing at the Edge of the World (essays), 1989; Tenahu 1990; Fish Soup, 1992; A Ride on the Red Mare's Back, 1992; Wonderful Alexander, 1994; The Twins, the Dream, 1997; Tao te ching, 1997; Steering the Craft, 1998; Jane on Her Own, 1999; The Telling, 2000; Tom Mouse, 2001; Tales from Earthsea, 2001; The Other Wind, 2001; Gifts, 2004. SHORT STORIES: The Wind's 12 Quarters, 1975; The Compass Rose, 1982; A Fisherman of the Inland Sea, 1994; Four Ways to Forgiveness, 1995; Unlocking the Air, 1996; The Birthday of the World, 2002; Changing Planes, 2004. POETRY: Wild Angels, 1974; Hard Words, 1981; In the Red Zone, 1983; (with R. Dorband) Blue Moon over Thurman Street, 1993; Going Out with Peacocks, 1994; Sixty Odd, 1999. EDITOR: Nebula Award Stories XI, 1977; (with V. Kidd) Interfaces, 1980; (with V. Kidd) Edges, 1980; The Norton Book of Science Fiction: North American Science Fiction, 1993; Selected Stories of H.G. Wells, 2004. **Address:** c/o Virginia Kidd Agency Inc, Box 278, Milford, PA 18337, U.S.A.

LEGUIZAMO, John. American (born Colombia), b. 1965. **Genres:** Plays/ Screenplays, Humor/Satire. **Career:** Writer, actor, comedian. Emmy Award, for Freak. **Publications:** PLAYS: Mambo Mouth (solo show), 1991; Spic-O-Rama (solo show), 1992; Freak: A Semi-Demi-Quasi-Pseudo Autobiography, 1997. SCREENPLAYS: Mambo Mouth (TV), 1991; Spic-O-Rama (TV), 1993; The Pest, 1997; Freak (TV), 1998. **Address:** c/o William Morris Agency, 1 William Morris Pl, Beverly Hills, CA 90212, U.S.A.

LEHANE, Cornelius. American. **Genres:** Novels. **Career:** Rockland Community College, NY, professor of English; National Education Association, publications editor and writer. Worked as union organizer and bartender. **Publications:** Beware the Solitary Drinker, 2002. **Address:** c/o National Education Association, 1201 16th Street N.W., Washington, DC 20036, U.S.A. **Online address:** Clehane@nea.org

LEHANE, Dennis. American, b. 1965. **Genres:** Mystery/Crime/Suspense. **Publications:** MYSTERIES: A Drink Before the War, 1994; Darkness Take My Hand, 1996; Sacred, 1997; Gone, Baby, Gone, 1998; Prayers for Rain, 1999; Mystic River, 2001; Shutter Island, 2003. **Address:** c/o Ann Rittenberg, Ann Rittenberg Literary Agency, Inc., 1201 Broadway Ste 708, New York, NY 10001, U.S.A.

LEHMAN, Donna. American, b. 1940. **Genres:** Theology/Religion. **Career:** Private secretary for a church of the First Assembly of God, Fort Wayne, IN, 1959-61; Fort Wayne State Developmental Center, Fort Wayne, private secretary and office manager, 1961-65; Samaritan Pastoral Counseling Center, Fort Wayne, administrative assistant, 1984; free-lance writer, 1972-; Fort Wayne State Developmental Center, member of Human Rights Committee, 1991-96; Environmental Education Coalition, member of Northeast Indiana Speakers Bureau, 1991-96; Fort Wayne Parkinsons Support Group, co-

president, 1993-. **Publications:** What on Earth Can You Do? Making Your Church a Creation Awareness Center, 1993. Work represented in anthologies. Contributor to periodicals.

LEHMAN, Yvonne. American. **Genres:** Novels, Young adult fiction. **Career:** Blue Ridge Writers Conference, founder and director, 1986-92. **Publications:** NOVELS: Red Like Mine, 1970; Dead Men Don't Cry, 1973; Fashions of the Heart, 1981; In Shady Groves, 1983; Smoky Mountain Sunrise, 1984; Taken by Storm, 1985; More Than a Summer's Love, 1986; In Shady Groves, 1989, as Gomer, 1998; Drums of Shelomoh, 1993; Southern Gentleman, 1994; Mountain Man, 1995; A Whole New World, 1996; A la Mode Hawaiian Heartbeat, 1997; Name that Tune, 2003; Coffee Rings, 2004. YOUNG ADULT FICTION: Tornado Alley, 1996; Secret Storm, 1996; Mirror of Dreams, 1996; Picture Perfect, 1997; Swept Away, 1997; A Fighting Chance, 1997; After the Storm, 1998; Something Old Something New, 1998; The Gold Star, 1998; Call of the Mountain, 1998; Somewhere a Rainbow, 1999; Dear Jane, 1999; Whiter Than Snow, 1999; Going Home Again, 1999; Never Say Never, 1999; Catch of a Lifetime, 2000; Scrambled Eggs, 2000; Secret Ballot, 2000; Lily's Plight, 2000; Carolina, 2002; South Carolina, 2002; The Stranger's Kiss, 2002; Past the P's Please, 2002; On a Clear Day, 2003; His Hands, 2003. **Address:** PO Box 188, Black Mountain, NC 28711, U.S.A. **Online address:** YLehman@aol.com; www.YvonneLehman.com

LEHMANN, Geoffrey (John). Australian, b. 1940. **Genres:** Novels, Poetry. **Career:** Price Waterhouse, Sydney, partner. Qualified as a solicitor in 1963; C.R. Wilcox and Lehmann, Sydney, principal, 1969-76. **Publications:** (with L.A. Murray) The Ilex Tree, 1965; A Voyage of Lions and Other Poems, 1968; Conversation with a Rider, 1972; (ed.) Comic Australian Verse, 1972; From an Australian Country Sequence, 1973; A Spring Day in Autumn (novel), 1974; Australian Primitive Painters, 1977; Ross Poems, 1978; Nero's Poems: Translations of the Public and Private Poems of the Emperor Nero, 1981; (ed. with R. Gray) The Younger Australian Poets, 1983; (with C. Coleman) Taxation Law in Australia, 1989, 5th ed., 1998; Children's Games, 1990; Spring Forest, 1992; Collected Poems, 1997. **Address:** 8 Highfield Rd, Lindfield, NSW 2070, Australia.

LEHMBERG, Stanford Eugene. American, b. 1931. **Genres:** History. **Career:** University of Texas at Austin, Member of history faculty, 1956-69; University of Minnesota, Minneapolis, Professor of History, 1969-99, Professor Emeritus, 1999-. **Publications:** Sir Thomas Elyot, Tudor Humanist, 1960; (ed.) Sir Thomas Elyot's Book Named the Governor, 1962; Sir Walter Mildmay and Tudor Government, 1964; The Reformation Parliament, 1529-1536, 1970; The Later Parliaments of Henry VIII 1536-1547, 1977; The Reformation of Cathedrals, 1988; The Peoples of the British Isles, 1992; Cathedrals under Siege, 1996. **Address:** 1005 Calle Largo, Santa Fe, NM 87501, U.S.A.

LEHNE, Judith Logan. American, b. 1947. **Genres:** Children's fiction, Plays/Screenplays, Children's non-fiction, How-to books. **Career:** Matheny School for Cerebral Palsied Children, child care staff worker; Allstate Insurance, Berkeley Heights, NJ, rate clerk, 1967; McGraw-Hill Publishers, Hightstown, NJ, clerk, 1968; Mettler Instruments, Princeton, NJ, research and customer file coordinator, 1968-70; Geico Insurance, sales and service supervisor, 1970-72; Schneider Transport, Green Bay, WI, customer coordinator, 1978-79; Circle M Corral, Minocqua, WI, copywriter and advertising design coordinator for all publicity, 1988-91; freelance children's writer, presenter of workshops, and instructor for the Institute of Children's Literature, 1991-; school-to-work coordinator for Job Corps students, 1998-2000; consumer affairs specialist for mental health agency, 2000-. **Publications:** FOR CHILDREN. The Never-Be-Bored Book: Quick Things to Make When There's Nothing to Do, 1992; When the Ragman Sings, 1993; Coyote Girl, 1995; Kangaroos for Kids (nonfiction), 1997. PLAYS: Barney's Balloon, 1988; The Invasion of the Sugar Bugs, 1989; Train Ride to Adventure, 1990; A Special Gift for Matthew, 1991; Little Red Riding Dude, 1991; Reflections on Ice. Contributor to books. Contributor of stories to children's magazines. **Address:** Rhinelander, WI 54501, U.S.A. **Online address:** Scribe@newnorth.net

LEHRER, James (Charles). American, b. 1934. **Genres:** Novels, Plays/ Screenplays, Autobiography/Memoirs. **Career:** Co-partner, MacNeil-Lehrer Productions. Dallas Morning News, political reporter, 1959; Dallas Times Herald, court reporter, 1959-66, political columnist, 1966-68, and city editor, 1968-69; KERA-TV, Dallas, consultant, 1970, executive director of public affairs, 1970-72, editor and host of nightly news program; PBS, Washington, DC, first public affairs coordinator, 1972-73; National Public Affairs Center for Television, PBS news service, correspondent, 1973; The Robert MacNeil Report, co-anchor, 1975-76; The MacNeil/Lehrer Report, co-anchor and associate editor, 1976-83; The MacNeil/Lehrer NewsHour, co-anchor, 1983-95; The NewsHour with Jim Lehrer, anchor and executive editor, 1995-. **Publications:** NOVELS: Viva Max!, 1966; Kick the Can, 1988; Crown Oklahoma, 1989; The Sooner Spy, 1990; Lost and Found, 1991; Short List, 1992; Blue Hearts, 1993; Fine Lines, 1994; The Last Debate, 1995; White Widow, 1997; Purple Dots, 1998; The Special Prisoner, 2000; No Certain Rest, 2002; Flying Crows, 2004. MEMOIRS: We Were Dreamers, 1975; A Bus of My Own, 1992. PLAYS: Chili Queen, 1986; Church Key Charlie Blue, 1987; The Will and Bart Show, 1992. **Address:** NewsHour with Jim Lehrer, 3620 27th St S, Arlington, VA 22206, U.S.A.

LEHRER, Kate. American, b. 1939. **Genres:** Novels. **Career:** Writer. **Publications:** NOVELS: Best Intentions, 1987; When They Took Away the Man in the Moon, 1992; Out of Eden, 1996; Confessions of a Bigamist, 2004.

LEHRER, Stanley. American, b. 1929. **Genres:** Education, History, Sociology, Theology/Religion, Biography. **Career:** Youth Service Ed., Open Road Magazine, NYC, 1950-51; Managing Ed., 1953-68, and Publr., 1968-72, School & Society Magazine, NYC; Founder, Publr., Intellect Magazine, 1972-78; Founder, Publr. and Editorial Director, USA Today Magazine, 1978-99, Newsview, 1979-99, Your Health, 1980-99, and The World of Science, 1980-99. President, Society for the Advancement of Education, NYC, 1968-99. **Publications:** Leaders, Teachers, and Learners in Academe: Partners in the Educational Process, 1970; (co-author) Titanic: Fortune & Fate, 1998. EDITOR: The Countdown on Segregated Education, 1960; Religion, Government, and Education, 1961; John Dewey: Master Educator, 1961; A Century of Higher Education: Classical Citadel to Collegiate Colossus, 1962; Automation, Education, and Human Values, 1966; Conflict and Change on the Campus: The Response to Student Hyperactivism, 1970; Education and the Many Faces of the Disadvantaged: Cultural and Historical Perspectives, 1972. **Address:** 82 Shelbourne Ln, New Hyde Park, NY 11040-1044, U.S.A.

LEIB, Franklin A(llen). American. **Genres:** Novels. **Career:** Writer, 1985-. **Publications:** NOVELS: Fire Arrow, 1988; The Fire Dream, 1989; Sea Lion, 1990; Valley of the Shadow, 1991; The House of Pain, 1999; Behold a Pale Horse, 2000. **Address:** 5962 Amberwood Dr, Naples, FL 34110, U.S.A.

LEIBLUM, Sandra R. American. **Genres:** Medicine/Health, Psychology. **Career:** University of Medicine and Dentistry of New Jersey, Piscataway, professor of psychiatry at Robert Wood Johnson Medical School, 1988-. American Foundation for Urologic Disease, member of Sexual Function Health Council. **Publications:** (with J. Sachs) Getting the Sex You Want: A Woman's Guide to Becoming Pleased, Proud & Passionate in Bed, 2002. EDITOR: (with J. Gottman) How to Do Psychotherapy and How to Evaluate It: A Manual for Beginners, 1976; (with L. Pervin) Principles and Practices of Sex Therapy, 1980, 2nd ed. (with R.C. Rosen) as Principles and Practice of Sex Therapy: An Update for the 1990s, 1989, 3rd ed., 2000; (with R.C. Rosen, and contrib) Sexual Desire Disorders, 1988; (with R.C. Rosen, and contrib) Erectile Disorders: Assessment and Treatment, 1992; (with R.C. Rosen) Case Studies in Sex Therapy, 1996; (and contrib.) Infertility: Psychological Issues and Counseling Strategies, 1996. Contributor to books and periodicals. **Address:** Dept of Psychiatry, Robert Wood Johnson Medical School, University of Medicine and Dentistry of New Jersey, Piscataway, NJ 08854, U.S.A. **Online address:** leiblum@umdnj.edu

LEIDER, Richard J. American. **Genres:** Sex. **Career:** Consultant and writer. The Inventure Group, Minneapolis, MN, founding partner; Dorobo Fund, Tanzania, founder. **Publications:** (with J. Hagberg) The Inventurers: Excursions in Life and Career, 1978; Life Skills: Taking Charge of Your Personal and Professional Growth, 1994; (with D.A. Shapiro) Repacking Your Bags: Lighten Your Load for the Rest of Your Life, 1995, rev, 2002; The Power of Purpose: Creating Meaning in Your Life and Work, 1997; Working Naturally: A New Way to Maximize Individual and Organizational Effectiveness, 1999; (with D.A. Shapiro) Whistle While You Work: Heeding Your Life's Calling, 2001. Contributor to books and publications. **Address:** The Inventure Group, 601 Carlson Pkwy., Ste. 375, Minneapolis, MN 55305, U.S.A. **Online address:** inventuregrp@aol.com

LEIDNER, Alan C. American. **Genres:** Literary criticism and history. **Career:** University of Louisville, Louisville, KY, professor of German. **Publications:** The Impatient Muse: Germany and the Sturm und Drang, 1994; (with K.A. Wurst) Unpopular Virtues: The Critical Reception of J.M.R. Lenz, 1999. EDITOR: Sturm and Drang, 1992; (with H.S. Madland) Space to Act: The Theater of J.M.R. Lenz, 1993. **Address:** Department of Classical and Modern Languages, University of Louisville, Louisville, KY 40292, U.S.A. **Online address:** alan.leidner@louisville.edu

LEIDNER, Gordon. American, b. 1954. **Genres:** History. **Career:** Historian. President, Lincoln Group of the District of Columbia, 2002-03. Webmaster, Lincoln-institute.org, and abrahamlincoln.org. Member of board of directors, Abraham Lincoln Institute of the Mid-2000-. **Publications:** A Commitment to Honor: A Unique Portrait of Abraham Lincoln in His Own Words, 2000; Lincoln on God and Country, 2000; Abraham Lincoln: The Complete Book of Facts, Quizzes, and Trivia, 2001. Contributor to periodicals. **Address:** c/o Publicity Director, White Mane Publishing Co. Inc., PO Box 152, Shippensburg, PA 17257, U.S.A. **Online address:** ahistory@crosslink.com

LEIER, Mark. Canadian, b. 1956. **Genres:** Area studies. **Career:** Simon Fraser University, Burnaby, British Columbia, associate professor of Labour history, 1994-. **Publications:** Where the Fraser River Flows: The Industrial Workers of the World in British Columbia, 1990; Red Flags and Red Tape: The Making of a Labour Bureaucracy, 1995. **Address:** Department of History, Simon Fraser University, Burnaby, BC, Canada V5A 1S6. **Online address:** jleier@sfu.ca

LEIGH, David. British, b. 1946. **Genres:** Documentaries/Reportage. **Career:** Scotsman, Edinburgh, Scotland, staff journalist, 1970-74; Times, London, England, staff journalist, 1974-78; Guardian, London, staff journalist, 1978-82; Observer, London, chief investigative reporter, 1982-. **Publications:** (with P. Chippindale) The Thorpe Committal, 1979; The Frontiers of Secrecy: Closed Government in Britain, 1980; (with S. Hoggart) Michael Foot: A Portrait, 1982; High Time: The Shocking Life and Times of Howard Marks, 1984, rev. ed. as Drug Traffic in Cannabis: Howard Marks, 1988; (with others) The Worst Accident in the World: Chernobyl, the End of the Nuclear Dream, 1986; (with M. Linklater) Not with Honour: The Inside Story of the Westland Scandal, 1986; The Wilson Plot: How the Spycatchers and Their American Allies Tried to Overthrow the British Government, 1988, in UK as The Wilson Plot: The Intelligence Services and the Discrediting of a Prime Minister, 1988; Betrayed, 1993; Fergie, 1996; Sleaze, 1997; The Liar, 1999. **Address:** c/o The Guardian, 119 Farringdon Rd, London EC1R 3ER, England. **Online address:** David.Leigh@guardian.co.uk

LEIGH, Janet. See Obituaries.

LEIGH, Richard (Harris). American, b. 1943. **Genres:** History, Theology/Religion. **Career:** Simon Fraser University, Vancouver, British Columbia, special collections librarian, 1970-72; writer. **Publications:** WITH MICHAEL BAIGENT: (and H. Lincoln) The Holy Blood and the Holy Grail, 1982; (and Lincoln) The Messianic Legacy, 1986; The Temple and the Lodge, 1989; The Dead Sea Scrolls Deception, 1991; Secret Germany, 1994; Inquisition, 1999. **Address:** c/o Jonathan Clowes Ltd., 10 Iron Bridge House, Bridge Approach, London NW1 8BD, England.

LEIGH, Stephen. American, b. 1951. **Genres:** Science fiction/Fantasy. **Career:** Musician: vocalist and bassist in groups, 1969-; Sales Manager, Kelly Services 1988-. **Publications:** Slow Fall to Dawn, 1981; Dance of the Hag, 1983; A Quiet of Stone, 1984; The Bones of God, 1986; Crystal Memory, 1987; Dr. Bones & The Secret of the Lona, 1988; Robots & Aliens: Changling, 1989; The Abraxas Marvel Circus, 1989; Alien Tongue, 1991; Dinosaur World, 1992; Dinosaur Planet, 1993; Dinosaur and Samura, 1993; Dinosaur Warriors, 1994; (with J.J. Miller) Dinosaur Empire, 1995; Dinosaur Conquest, 1996; Dark Water's Embrace, 1998; Speaking Stones, 1999.

LEIGH FERMOR, Patrick (Michael). British. **Genres:** Novels, Travel/Exploration, Translations. **Publications:** The Traveller's Tree, 1950; A Time to Keep Silence, 1953; The Violins of Saint-Jacques, 1953; Mani, 1958; Roumeli, 1966; A Time of Gifts, 1977; Between the Woods and the Water, 1986; Three Letters from the Andes, 1993; Vanishing Greece, 1995; Words of Mercury, 2003. TRANSLATOR: Colette, Chance Acquaintances, 1951; The Cretan Runner, 1988. **Address:** c/o John Murray Ltd, 338 Euston Rd, London NW1 3BH, England.

LEIKEN, Robert S. American, b. 1939. **Genres:** International relations/Current affairs, Politics/Government. **Career:** Educational Services Inc., Cambridge, MA, consultant, 1964-65; Massachusetts Institute of Technology, Cambridge, assistant professor of humanities, 1968-71; Centro Investigacion y Documentacion, Mexico, professor of European history, 1971-72; National University of Mexico, Mexico City, professor of Mexican economic history, 1973; Centro Investigaciones y Docencias Economicas, Mexico City, researcher and professor, 1977-78; National Agricultural University of Mexico, Mexico City, professor of economics, 1978-80; National Endowment for the Humanities, reviewer of media program, 1981-; Georgetown University, Center for Strategic and International Studies, director of Soviet-

Latin American project, 1981-; author and editor, 1982-; Carnegie Endowment for International Peace, Washington, DC, senior associate, 1983-; Brookings Institution, Washington, DC, senior fellow, 1999-; Nixon Center, director of immigrative and national security, Washington, DC. **Publications:** Soviet Strategy in Latin America, 1982; The Melting Border, 2000; Why Nicaragua Vanished, 2003; Bearers of Global Jihad: Immigration and National Security after 9/11, 2004. EDITOR: Central America: Anatomy of Conflict, 1984; (with B. Rubin) The Central American Crisis Reader, 1987. Contributor to periodicals. **Address:** Nixon Center, 1615 L St NW, Washington, DC 20036, U.S.A. **Online address:** rsleiken@erols.com

LEINER, Katherine. American, b. 1949. **Genres:** Novels, Children's fiction. **Career:** Writer. Member of Heal the Bay, Pesticide Watch, Mothers against Drunk Driving, and Los Angeles Commission of Assaults against Women, SCBW, Authors Guild, PEN. **Publications:** Ask Me What My Mother Does, 1979; The Real Flash Gordon, 1980; The Greatest Show on Earth, 1980; The Steam Engine Lady, 1981; Both My Parents Work, 1986; Between Old Friends, 1987; The New Adventures of Pippi Longstocking, 1988; Something's Wrong in My House, 1988; Halloween, 1993; First Children, 1996; Mama Does the Mambo, 2001. FOR ADULTS: Digging Out (novel), 2004. **Address:** c/o Brentwood Management, 11812 San Vicente Blvd, Los Angeles, CA 90049, U.S.A. **Online address:** kathleiner@aol.com; KatherineLeiner.com

LEIRA, Arnlaug. Norwegian. **Genres:** Social sciences. **Career:** Researcher at Institute for Social Research, Oslo, Norway. **Publications:** Welfare States and Working Mothers: The Scandinavian Experience, 1992. **Address:** Institute for Social Research, Munthes Gate 31, 0260 Oslo, Norway.

LEISER, Gary. American, b. 1946. **Genres:** Area studies, History. **Career:** Cabrini College, Radnor, PA, visiting lecturer in Middle Eastern history, 1976; University of Utah, Salt Lake City, visiting instructor in Middle Eastern history, 1976-77; Food Development Corp., Pasco, WA, Middle East consultant, 1978; U.S. Department of Defense, staff interpreter and Middle East specialist at technical liaison office, Ankara, Turkey, 1980-83, Arabic linguist and analyst for Lebanon at Fort Meade, MD, 1983-84; U.S. Air Force in Turkey, civilian historian, 1984-89; Travis Air Force Base, CA, civilian historian, 1989-96, curator of Travis Air Museum, 1996-. University of Maryland, European Branch, instructor, 1981; Air University, instructor, 1995; lecturer at educational institutions; consultant to Brightstar Inc. **Publications:** (coauthor) A Brief History of Ankara, 2000. EDITOR/CO-EDITOR: Papers and Discussions: Turkiye Is Bankasi, 1984; (and trans., and author of intro.) A History of the Seljuks, 1988; (and trans.) M.F. Koprulu, Origins of the Ottoman Empire, 1992; (and trans.) Koprulu, Seljuks of Anatolia, 1992; (and trans., and author of intro.) Koprulu, Islam in Anatolia after the Turkish Invasion (Prolegomena), 1993; (and trans.) Vetluga Memoir: A Turkish Prisoner of War in Russia, 1995; (and trans., and author of intro.) Koprulu, Some Observations on the Influence of Byzantine Institutions on Ottoman Institutions, 1999; (and co-trans.) Questions and Answers for Physicians: A Handbook for Students, 2004. Contributor to encyclopedias and periodicals. Author of several classified publications for the U.S. Air Force. **Address:** 101 San Jose Ct, Vacaville, CA 95688, U.S.A. **Online address:** gleiser@juno.com

LEITCH, Maurice. British (born Northern Ireland). **Genres:** Novels, Novellas/Short stories, Plays/Screenplays. **Career:** Radio Drama Producer, BBC, London, 1970-89 (Features producer, Belfast, 1962-70). **Publications:** The Liberty Lad, 1965; Poor Lazarus, 1969; Stamping Ground, 1975; Silver's City, 1981; The Hands of Cheryl Boyd, 1987; Chinese Whispers, 1987; Burning Bridges, 1989; Gilchrist, 1994; The Smoke King, 1998; The Eggman's Apprentice, 2001. **Address:** 32 Windermere Ave, Queen's Park, London NW6 6LN, England.

LEITH, Linda Jane. Canadian (born Northern Ireland), b. 1949. **Genres:** Novels, Literary criticism and history, Translations. **Career:** Matrix magazine, publisher, editor, 1988-94; Vehicule Press, fiction editor 1989-94; Blue Metropolis International Literary Festival, president/festival director, 1998-. **Publications:** (ed.) Telling Differences: New English Fiction from Quebec, 1989; Introducing Hugh MacLennan's "Two Solitudes," 1990; Birds of Passage (novel), 1993; The Tragedy Queen (novel), 1995; (trans.) Travels with an Umbrella: An Irish Journey, 1999. **Address:** c/o Blue Metropolis Foundation, 1650 Lincoln #209, Montreal, QC, Canada H3H 1H1. **Online address:** info@blue-web.bleu.com

LEITHAUSER, Brad. American, b. 1953. **Genres:** Novels, Poetry. **Career:** Research Fellow, Kyoto Comparative Law Center, Japan, 1980-83; Guggenheim Fellow, 1982-83; MacArthur Foundation Research Fellow, 1983-87;

Visiting Writer, Amherst College, Massachusetts, 1984-85; Lecturer, Mount Holyoke College, S. Hadley, Massachusetts, 1987-88, 1990-. Recipient: Lavan Younger Poets Award, 1983. **Publications:** POETRY: Hundreds of Fireflies, 1982; A Seaside of Mountain: Eight Poems from Japan, 1985; Cats of the Temple, 1986; Between Leaps: Poems 1972-1985, 1987; The Mail from Anywhere, 1990. NOVELS: Equal Distance, 1985; Hence, 1989; Seaward, 1993; The Friends of Freeland, 1997; A Few Corrections, 2001. ESSAYS: Penchants and Places, 1996. **Address:** c/o Alfred A. Knopf, Inc, 201 E. 50th St, New York, NY 10022, U.S.A.

LEITNER, Isabella. Hungarian, b. 1924. **Genres:** Autobiography/Memoirs, Children's non-fiction. **Career:** Writer; lecturer on the Holocaust. **Publications:** Fragments of Isabella, 1978; (with I.A. Leitner) Saving the Fragments: From Auschwitz to New York, 1985; The Big Lie: A True Story (for children), 1992; (with I.A. Leitner) Isabella: From Auschwitz to Freedom, 1994.

LEITZ, Robert C(harles), III. American, b. 1944. **Genres:** Novellas/Short stories, Intellectual history, Literary criticism and history, Race relations, Social commentary. **Career:** Louisiana State University at Shreveport, assistant professor, 1973-77, associate professor, 1977-82, professor of English, 1982-, curator, J.S. Noel Collection, Noel Memorial Library, 1994-, Ruth Herring Noel Distinguished Professor, 2000-04, Ruth Herring Noel Endowed Chair, 2004-, American studies fellow, 1986, faculty senator, 1988-89. Huntington Library, Henry E. Huntington Research fellow, 1978, 1979; Texas A&M University, visiting professor, 1986. Derringdew Silky Terriers (kennel), owner. **Publications:** (with K.M. Price) Critical Essays on George Santayana, 1991. EDITOR: Selected Letters of W. D. Howells, vol. 3, 1980; (with E. Labor and I.M. Shepard) The Letters of Jack London, vol. 1: 1896-1905, vol. 2: 1906-1912, vol. 3: 1913-1916, 1988; (with Labor and Shepard) The Short Stories of Jack London: The Authorized Edition with Definitive Texts, 1990; (with Labor) The Call of the Wild, White Fang, and Other Dog Stories, 1990; (with E. Labor and M. Shepard) The Complete Short Stories of Jack London, 1993; (with J.R. McElrath Jr.) To Be an Author! Letters of Charles W. Chesnutt, 1889-1906, 1997; (with J.R. McElrath Jr. and J. Crisler) Charles W. Chesnutt: Essays and Speeches, 1999; (with K.L. Cope) The Eighteenth Century: A Current Bibliography, 2002; (with K.L. Cope) Imagining the Sciences, 2004. **Address:** Noel Memorial Library, Louisiana State University at Shreveport, Shreveport, LA 71115, U.S.A. **Online address:** rleitz@pilot.lsus.edu

LELCHUK, Alan. American, b. 1938. **Genres:** Novels. **Career:** Brandeis University, Waltham, Massachusetts, Professor and Writer-in-Residence, 1966-81; Amherst College, Massachusetts, Writer-in-Residence, 1982-84; Dartmouth College, Hanover, New Hampshire, Adjunct Professor, 1985-; CCNY, Visiting Writer, 1992; Steetforth Press, literary editor and founder, 1994-; Eofros Lorand University, Budapest, Hungary, Salgo Professor of American Studies, 1999-2000. Modern Occasions literary and cultural quarterly, Associate Ed., 1970-72. **Publications:** American Mischief, 1973; Miriam at Thirty-Four, 1974; Shrinking, 1978; (co-ed.) Eight Great Hebrew Short Novels, 1983; Miriam in Her Forties, 1985; On Home Ground, 1987; Brooklyn Boy, 1989; Playing the Game, 1995; Ziff: A Life?, 2003. **Address:** c/o Georges Borchardt Inc, 136 E 57th St, New York, NY 10022, U.S.A. **Online address:** Alan.Lelchuk@dartmouth.edu

LELLENBERG, Jon L. American, b. 1946. **Genres:** Mystery/Crime/Suspense, Literary criticism and history, Biography. **Career:** Defense policy analyst, national security strategist, and writer specializing in Sherlock Holmes. Office of the Secretary of Defense, board certified strategist; American agent administering Sherlock Holmes copyrights; writer. **Publications:** Nova 57 Minor: The Waxing and Waning of the 61st Adventure of Sherlock Holmes, 1990; Irregular Proceedings of the Mid 'Forties, 1995. EDITOR: (and author of intro.) Shylock Homes: His Posthumous Memoirs by John Kedrick Bangs, 1973; The Quest for Sir Arthur Conan Doyle: Thirteen Biographers in Search of a Life, 1987, 2nd ed. on CD-ROM as The Works of Arthur Conan Doyle, 1997; (with J. Nieminski) Dear Starrett-Dear Briggs: A Compendium of Correspondence, 1989; Irregular Memories of the Thirties, 1990; Irregular Records of the Early 'Forties, 1991; (with M.H. Greenberg and C.-L. Waugh) Holmes for the Holidays, 1996; Irregular Crises of the Late 'Forties, 1998; (with M.H. Greenberg and C.-L. Waugh) The New Adventure of Sherlock Holmes, 1999; (with M.H. Greenberg and C.-L. Waugh) More Holmes for the Holidays, 1999; (with M.H. Greenberg and D. Stashoven) Murder in Baker Street, 2001; (with M.H. Greenberg and D. Stashoven) Murder, My Dear Watson, 2002. Contributor to periodicals. **Address:** 3133 Connecticut Ave NW No 827, Washington, DC 20008, U.S.A. **Online address:** jlellenb@dgsys.com

LEMANN, Nicholas. American, b. 1954. **Genres:** Adult non-fiction, Business/Trade/Industry, History, Biography, Essays. **Career:** Washington

Monthly, Washington, DC, managing and contributing editor, 1976-; Texas Monthly, Austin, TX, associate, contributing, and executive editor, 1978-; Washington Post, Washington, DC, reporter, 1979-81; Atlantic Monthly, Boston, MA, national correspondent, 1983-; writer. **Publications:** (with C. Peters) Inside the System, 1978; The Fast Track: Texans and Other Strivers (essays), 1981; Out of the Forties (nonfiction), 1983; The Promised Land: The Great Black Migration and How It Changed America (nonfiction), 1990; Big Test, 1999. **Address:** 25 Harmon Ave, Pelham, NY 10803-1709, U.S.A.

LEMASTER, Carolyn Gray. American. **Genres:** Local history/Rural topics. **Career:** Homemaker and mother before college; University of Arkansas at Little Rock, editor of Forum (student newspaper), 1976-77, writer, editor, and director for the Office of Internal Communication, 1978-81, research assistant in archives, 1981-83; Arkansas Methodist Newspaper, Little Rock, AR, writer and editor's assistant, 1977; researcher and writer on Arkansas Jewish history, 1981-. Has also lectured frequently on the history of Jews in Arkansas, and on Biblical and post-Biblical Jewish history. Exhibited materials from the research for A Corner of the Tapestry in museums. **Publications:** A Corner of the Tapestry: A History of the Jewish Experience in Arkansas, 1820s-1990s, 1994; The Ottenheimers of Arkansas, 1995. Contributor of articles to periodicals. Contributor to books. **Address:** 24424 Maranatha Ln., Little Rock, AR 72223, U.S.A.

LEMASTER, J. R. American, b. 1934. **Genres:** Poetry. **Career:** Defiance College, Ohio, Professor of English, 1962-77; Baylor University, Waco, Texas, Professor of English, 1977-. **Publications:** The Heart Is a Gypsy, 1967; Children of Adam, 1971; Weeds and Wildflowers, 1975; (with M.W. Clarke) Jesse Stuart: Essays on His Work, 1977; Jesse Stuart: A Reference Guide, 1979; Jesse Stuart: Kentucky's Chronicler-Poet, 1980; First Person, Second, 1983; (with E.H. Long) The New Mark Twain Handbook, 1985; Purple Bamboo, 1986. EDITOR: Poets of the Midwest, 1966; (with S. Sternlicht) Symposia Poets, 1969; (with W. Chaney) There Comes a Time, 1971; (with C. Perrin) Certain Reconciliations, 1972; (with J. O'Kelley) On Weighing a Pound of Flesh, 1973; (with C. Winzeler) The Poem as Unidentified Flying Object, 1974; (with M.W. Clarke) The World of Jesse Stuart, 1975; Jesse Stuart: Selected Criticism, 1978; The Keeper of Juno's Swans, 1979; Making Sense of Grammar, 1980; The Builder and the Dream, 1980; Jesse Stuart on Education, 1992; (with J.D. Wilson) The Mark Twain Encyclopedia, 1993; (with D.D. Kummings) Walt Whitman: An Encyclopedia, 1998. **Address:** Dept. of English, Baylor University, Waco, TX 76703, U.S.A. **Online address:** J_R_LeMaster@baylor.edu

LE MAY, G(odfrey) H(ugh) L(ancelot). British (born Republic of South Africa), b. 1920. **Genres:** History, Politics/Government. **Career:** Assistant Ed., The Sudan Star, Khartoum, 1942-44; Sub-Ed., The Star, Johannesburg, 1944-46; Lecturer, Rhodes University, Grahamstown, S. Africa, 1947-48; Lecturer, Balliol College, Oxford, 1952-53; Professor, University of the Witwatersrand, Johannesburg, 1953-68; Fellow and Sr. Tutor, Worcester College, Oxford, 1968-90. **Publications:** British Government 1914-1953, 1955, 1964; British Supremacy in South Africa 1899-1907, 1965; Black and White in South Africa, 1973; The Victorian Constitution, 1979; The Afrikaners, 1995. **Address:** Worcester College, Oxford, England.

LEMAY, Shawna. Canadian, b. 1966. **Genres:** Poetry. **Career:** Writer. **Publications:** POETRY: All the God-sized Fruit, 1999; Against Paradise, 2001. **Address:** 470 Ormsby Rd., Edmonton, AB, Canada T5T 6B1. **Online address:** slemay@planet.eon.net

LEMIEUX, A(nne) C(onnelly). American, b. 1954. **Genres:** Children's fiction, Young adult fiction. **Career:** Freelance journalist, 1982-87; author, 1987-. Co-founder and co-moderator of the Children's Writer's Chat on America Online. **Publications:** The TV Guidance Counselor, 1993; Super Snoop Sam Snout: The Case of the Yogurt Poker, 1994; Super Snoop Sam Snout: The Case of the Stolen Snowman, 1994; Super Snoop Sam Snout: The Case of the Missing Marble, 1994; Fruit Flies, Fish and Fortune Cookies, 1994; Do Angels Sing the Blues?, 1995. Contributor to anthologies. **Address:** 1455 Durham Rd, Madison, CT 06443-1657, U.S.A.

LEMIRE, Beverly. Canadian, b. 1950. **Genres:** History, Fashion/Costume, Women's studies and issues. **Career:** Wilfrid Laurier University, Waterloo, Ontario, sessional instructor, 1985; University of Guelph, Ontario, sessional instructor, 1985; University of Lethbridge, Alberta, assistant professor, 1986-87; University of New Brunswick, Fredericton, assistant professor, 1987-91, associate professor, 1991-96, professor of history, 1996-. **Publications:** Fashion's Favourite: The Cotton Trade and the Consumer in Britain, 1660-1800, 1991; Dress, Culture and Commerce: The English Clothing Trade before the Factory, 1660-1800, 1997. Work represented in anthologies.

Contributor of articles and reviews to history and textile studies journals. **Address:** Department of History, University of New Brunswick, Fredericton, NB, Canada E3B 5A3.

LEMLIN, Jeanne. American, b. 1953. **Genres:** Food and Wine. **Career:** New York Cooking Center, NYC, cooking teacher, 1980-85; cookbook writer, 1985-. **Publications:** Vegetarian Pleasures, 1986; Quick Vegetarian Pleasures, 1992; Main-Course Vegetarian Pleasures, 1995; Simple Vegetarian Pleasures, 1998; Vegetarian Classics, 2001. Contributor to periodicals. **Address:** 15 Castle Hill Ave, Great Barrington, MA 01230, U.S.A.

LEMONCHECK, Linda. American, b. 1954. **Genres:** Women's studies and issues. **Career:** University of Southern California, Los Angeles, lecturer in Gender Studies Program; also taught at California State University, Long Beach, Occidental College, and University of California, Los Angeles; consultant to Pacific Clinics, Pasadena, and West End Family Counseling Services, Ontario, CA. Old Town Picture Show (art gallery), Pasadena, CA, owner, 1983-86; Long Beach Museum of Art, member of docent council. **Publications:** Dehumanizing Women: Treating Persons as Sex Objects, 1985; (with M. Hajdin) Sexual Harassment: A Debate, 1997; Loose Women, Lecherous Men: A Feminist Philosophy of Sex, 1997. Contributor to books. Contributor of articles and reviews to periodicals. **Address:** Gender Studies Program, SSM-116, University of Southern California, Los Angeles, CA 90089, U.S.A. **Online address:** llemon@msn.com

LEMONS, James Stanley. American, b. 1938. **Genres:** Cultural/Ethnic topics, History. **Career:** Professor of History, Rhode Island College, Providence, since 1976 (Assistant Professor, 1967-71; Associate Professor, 1971-76). Instructor, Ohio State University, Columbus, 1965-67. **Publications:** The Woman Citizen: Social Feminism in the 1920s, 1973; (ed.) Aspects of the Black Experience, 1975; (with G. Kellner) Rhode Island: The Independent State, 1982; The First Baptist Church in America, 1988; (with E.S. Adler) The Elect: Rhode Island's Women Legislators, 1922-1990, 1990; First: The History of the First Baptist Church in America, 2001. **Address:** Dept. of History, Rhode Island College, Providence, RI 02908, U.S.A. **Online address:** jlemons@ric.edu

LEMOS, Ramon Marcelino. American, b. 1927. **Genres:** Philosophy. **Career:** Professor of Philosophy, University of Miami, Coral Gables, Florida, 1967-, now emeritus (Instructor, 1956-58; Assistant Professor, 1958-62; Associate Professor, 1962-67; Chairman, 1971-84). **Publications:** Experience, Mind and Value: Philosophical Essays, 1969; Rousseau's Political Philosophy: An Exposition and Interpretation, 1977; Hobbes and Locke: Power and Consent, 1978; Rights, Goods and Democracy, 1986; Metaphysical Investigations, 1988; The Nature of Value: Axiological Investigations, 1995; A Neomedieval Essay in Philosophical Theology, 2001. **Address:** Dept. of Philosophy, University of Miami, Coral Gables, FL 33124, U.S.A.

LENAIL, Laura. *See* **ANDRE, Michael.**

LENDVAI, Paul. Austrian (born Hungary), b. 1929. **Genres:** History, Politics/Government, Biography. **Career:** Ed.-in-Chief, Europaeische Rundschau, Vienna, 1973-. Director, Radio Austria International, 1987-. Former Vienna Correspondent, Financial Times, London. **Publications:** Egypt, 1952; Greece, 1954; Eagles in Cobwebs: Nationalism and Communism in the Balkans, 1969; Anti-Semitism without Jews: Communist Eastern Europe, 1971; (with K.H. Ritschel) Kreisky: Portrait of a Statesman, 1972; The Limits to Change in the Danubian Region, 1977; The Bureaucracy of Truth: How Communist Governments Manage the News, 1981; The Lonely Albania, 1985; Hungary: The Art of Survival, 1988; Between Hope and Disenchantment: Reflections on the Change in Eastern Europe, 1994; Blacklisted-Memoirs of a Central European Journalist, 1996; The Hungarians-1000 Years of Victory in Defeat, 2002. **Address:** Ebendorferstrasse 6/4, 1010 Vienna, Austria.

LENG, Russell J. American, b. 1938. **Genres:** Politics/Government. **Career:** Middlebury College, Middlebury, VT, professor of political science and director of Program in International Politics and Economics, 1966-. **Publications:** Interstate Crisis Behavior, 1816-1980: Realism vs. Realpolitik, 1993; Bargaining and Learning in Recurring Crises, 2000. **Address:** Department of Political Science, Middlebury College, Munroe 221, Middlebury, VT 05753, U.S.A. **Online address:** leng@middlebury.edu

L'ENGLE, Madeleine. American, b. 1918. **Genres:** Novels, Science fiction/Fantasy, Children's fiction, Plays/Screenplays, Poetry, Autobiography/Memoirs. **Career:** Teacher, St. Hilda's and St. Hugh's Schools, NYC, 1960-2000; Cathedral of St. John the Divine, NYC, writer-in-residence and librarian, 1965-; Author's League of America, council member, 1976-; Author's Guild of America, president, 1985; author and lecturer. **Publications:** The Small Rain, 1945, as Prelude, 1969; Ilsa, 1946; And Both Were Young, 1949; Camilla Dickinson, 1951, as Camilla, 1964; A Winter's Love, 1957; A Wrinkle in Time, 1962; Meet the Austins, 1960; The Moon by Night, 1963; The 24 Days before Christmas, 1964; The Arm of the Starfish, 1965; The Love Letters, 1966; The Journey with Jonah (play), 1967; The Young Unicorns, 1968; Lines Scribbled on an Envelope (poetry), 1969; Dance in the Desert (short story), 1969; The Other Side of the Sun, 1971; A Circle of Quiet (autobiography), 1972; A Wind in the Door, 1973; The Summer of the Great-Grandmother (autobiography), 1974; Dragons in the Waters, 1976; The Irrational Season, 1977; A Swiftly Tilting Planet, 1978; The Weather of the Heart, 1978; Ladder of Angels, 1979; The Anti-Muffins, 1980; A Ring of Endless Light, 1980; Walking on Water, 1981; The Sphinx at Dawn, 1982; A Severed Wasp, 1983; And It Was Good, 1984; House Like a Lotus, 1984; Trailing Clouds of Glory, 1985; A Stone for a Pillow, 1986; Many Waters, 1986; A Cry Like a Bell, 1987; Two Part Invention, 1988; Sold into Egypt, 1988; From This Day Forward, 1988; An Acceptable Time, 1988; The Glorious Impossible, 1990; Certain Women, 1992; The Rock That Is Higher, 1993; Anytime Prayers, 1994; Troubling a Star, 1994; Penguins and Golden Calves, 1996; Glimpses of Grace, 1996; Wintersong: Christmas Readings, 1996; Mothers and Daughters, 1997; Bright Evening Star, 1997; (with L. Shaw) Friends for the Journey, 1997; Miracle on 10th Street, and Other Christmas Writings, 1998; My Own Small Place: Developing the Writing Life, 1999; A Full House: An Austin Family Christmas, 1999; Mothers & Sons, 1999; (with L. Shaw) A Prayerbook for Spiritual Friends, 1999; The Other Dog, 2000; (with G. Chase) Madeleine L'Engle Herself, 2001. **Address:** 924 West End Ave No. 95, New York, NY 10025, U.S.A.

LENNARD, John (Chevening). British, b. 1964. **Genres:** Poetry, Literary criticism and history, Theatre, Essays, Illustrations. **Career:** University of London, Royal Holloway and Bedford New College, Egham, England, tutor in English, 1990-91; Open University, tutor, 1990-92; Cambridge University, Trinity Hall, England, fellow and director of studies in English, 1991-98; Newton Trust Lecturer, Faculty of English, 1993-98; University of Notre Dame, London, assistant professor, 1998-2004; British-American Drama Academy, London, professor, 1998-2004, dean, Shakespeare Program, 2002-03; Leverhulme Research Fellow, 1999-2000; University of the West Indies, professor of British & American literature, 2005-. **Publications:** But I Digress: The Exploitation of Parentheses in English Printed Verse, 1991; The Poetry Handbook: A Guide to Reading Poetry for Pleasure and Practical Criticism, 1996, 2nd ed., 2005; (with M. Luckhurst) The Drama Handbook: A Guide to Reading Plays, 2002. Contributor of articles and reviews to periodicals. **Address:** Dept of Literatures in English, University of the West Indies, Mona, St. Andrew, Jamaica. **Online address:** john.lennard@uwimona.edu.jm

LENNON, Donald R. American, b. 1938. **Genres:** History. **Career:** Archives and History (North Carolina division), Raleigh, NC, archivist, 1964-67; East Carolina University, Greenville, NC, associate professor of history, director of East Carolina manuscript collection, and coordinator of special collections, 1967-2001. **Publications:** (ed. with I.B. Kellam) The Wilmington Town Book, 1743-1779, 1973; (with A.D. Watson and D.R. Lawson) Harnett, Hooper, and Howe: Revolutionary Leaders of the Lower Cape Fear, 1979; (with C.E. Bennett) A Quest for Glory: Major General Robert Howe and the American Revolution, 1991. **Address:** 201 Cherrywood Dr, Greenville, NC 27858, U.S.A. **Online address:** Donlen7@cs.com

LENNON, J. Robert. American, b. 1970. **Genres:** Novels. **Career:** Writer. **Publications:** NOVELS: The Light of Falling Stars, 1997; The Funnies, 1999. **Address:** c/o Riverhead Books, 375 Hudson St., New York, NY 10014, U.S.A.

LENNOX, John. Canadian, b. 1945. **Genres:** Literary criticism and history. **Career:** Educator and author. York University, Toronto, Ontario, Canada, lecturer in English, 1970-77, associate professor, 1977-90, director of graduate program, 1987-90, professor, 1991-, associate dean for faculty of graduate studies, 1996-99, acting dean, 1999-2000, dean, 2000-. Robarts Centre for Canadian Studies, director, 1985-88. **Publications:** (with C. Thomas) William Arthur Deacon: A Canadian Literary Life, 1982. EDITOR: (with M. Lacombe) Dear Bill: The Correspondence of William Arthur Deacon, 1988; (with J.M. Paterson) Challenges, Projects, Texts: Canadian Editing: Twenty-fifth Conference on Editorial Problems, 1993; Margaret Laurence-Al Purdy: A Friendship In Letters, 1993; (with R. Panofsky) Selected Letters of Margaret Laurence and Adele Wiseman, 1997. **Address:** Department of English, York University, 4700 Keele St, Toronto, ON, Canada M3J 1P3. **Online address:** jlennox@yorku.ca

LENNOX, Terry. See HARVEY, John B.

LENNOX-SMITH, Judith (Elizabeth). (Judith Lennox). British, b. 1953. **Genres:** Romance/Historical. **Career:** Civil Service, Staines, England, executive officer, 1975-76; writer. **Publications:** Reynardine (novel), 1989; Till the Day Goes Down (novel), 1991; The Glittering Strand (historical novel), 1991; The Italian Garden (historical novel), 1993. NOVELS AS JUDITH LENNOX: The Secret Years, 1994; The Winter House, 1996. **Address:** Maggie Hanbury, 27 Walcot Sq, London SE11, England.

LENO, Jay. American, b. 1950. **Genres:** Humor/Satire. **Career:** Rolls Royce auto mechanic and deliveryman; stand-up comedian; performed as opening act for other artists; Good Times, writer, 1974; Jay Leno and the American Dream, host and producer, 1986; The Tonight Show, exclusive guest host, 1987-92, host, 1992-. Appeared on television shows and in films, 1976-. **Publications:** (with B. Zehme) Leading with My Chin, 1996. EDITOR: Headlines: Real but Ridiculous Samplings from America's Newspapers, 1989; More Headlines: Real but Ridiculous Samplings from America's Newspapers, 1991; Headlines III: Not the Movie, Still the Book: Real but Ridiculous Samplings from America's Newspapers, 1991; Headlines IV: The Next Generation: More Outof-This World Headlines from the Bestselling Series, 1992; Jay Leno's Headlines. Books I, II, III, 1992; Jay Leno's Police Blotter: Real-life Crime Headlines from "The Tonight Show with Jay Leno", 1994. **Address:** PO Box 7885, Burbank, CA 91510, U.S.A.

LENT, John. Canadian, b. 1948. **Genres:** Novels. **Career:** Okanagan University College, professor of literature and creative writing, 1979-. Writer of poetry, fiction, non-fiction, and scholarly essays. **Publications:** A Rock Solid, 1978; Wood Lake Music, 1982; Frieze, 1984; The Face in the Garden (juvenile novel), 1990; Monet's Garden, 1996. **Address:** Okanagan University College, 7000 College Way, Vernon, BC, Canada V1B 2N5. **Online address:** jlent@junction.net

LENT, John A. American, b. 1936. **Genres:** Area studies, Communications/Media, Film, Third World, Women's studies and issues, Writing/Journalism, Bibliography, Cartoons, Humor/Satire, Reference. **Career:** West Virginia Institute of Technology, Montgomery, instructor, and director of Public Relations, 1960-62, 1965-66; De La Salle College, Manila, lecturer, 1964-65; Wisconsin State University, Eau Claire, assistant professor of journalism, 1966-67; Marshall University, Huntington, WV, assistant professor, 1967-69; University of Wyoming, Laramie, visiting associate professor, 1969-70; University of Iowa, Iowa City, International Communications Bulletin, teaching assistant, and associate ed., 1970-72; Universiti Sains Malaysia, Penang, Mass Communications Program, organizer and first professor, 1972-74; Temple University, Philadelphia, associate professor, 1974-76, professor of communications, 1976-; Third World Media Assocs., director, 1986-; University of Western Ontario, Rogers Distinguished Professor, 2000-; University of Shanghai, guest professor, 2002-05. **Publications:** Philippine Mass Communications Bibliography, 1966; Newhouse, Newspapers, Nuisances (biography), 1966; (co-author) Pied Type, a Load of Coal and the Laser Beam (filmstrip), 1969; Philippine Mass Communications, 1971; (ed.) Asian Newspapers' Reluctant Revolution, 1971; Asian Mass Communications, 1975, Supplement, 1978; Third World Mass Media and Their Search for Modernity, 1977; Broadcasting in Asia and the Pacific, 1978; Asian Newspapers, 1982; Comic Art, 1986; Global Guide to Communications, 1987; Videocassettes in the Third World, 1989; Asian Film Industry, 1990; Caribbean Popular Culture, 1990; Mass Communications in the Caribbean, 1990; Women and Mass Communications, 1991; Transnational Communications, 1991; Bibliographic Guide to Caribbean Mass Communications, 1992; Bibliography of Cuban Mass Communications, 1992; Animation, Caricature, Gag and Political Cartoons in the United States and Canada 1994; Cartoonometer, 1994; Comic Books and Comic Strips in the United States, 1994; Comic Art of Europe, 1994; Asian Popular Culture, 1995; A Different Road Taken, 1995; Comic Art in Africa, Asia, Australia, and Latin America, 1996; Global Productions, 1998; Themes and Issues in Asian Cartooning, 1999; Pulp Demons, 1999; Animation in Asia and the Pacific, 2001; Illustrating Asia, 2001; Comic Art of Europe through 2000, 2003; Comic Art in Africa, Asia, Australia, and Latin America through 2000, 2004. **Address:** 669 Ferne Blvd, Drexel Hill, PA 19026, U.S.A.

LENTIN, Ronit. Israeli/Irish, b. 1944. **Genres:** Novels, Adult non-fiction. **Career:** Israel Television, production assistant, 1968-69; Irish National Television (RTE), Dublin, Ireland, researcher, 1969-72; freelance newspaper journalist, Dublin, 1972-93; University of Limerick, Limerick, Ireland, lecturer in women's studies, 1993-94; Trinity College, Dublin, lecturer in sociology, 1994-, part-time lecturer at Centre for Women's Studies, 1995-97, course coordinator for graduate degree in ethnic and racial studies, 1997-.

Guest lecturer at other institutions. **Publications:** (with G. Niland) Who's Minding the Children?, 1981; Sichot im Nashim Palestiniot (title means: Conversations with Palestinian Women), 1982; Night Train to Mother (novel), 1989; Songs on the Death of Children (novel), 1996; Israel and the Daughters of the Shoah: Reoccupying the Territories of Silence, 2000. EDITOR & CONTRIBUTOR: In from the Shadows: The UL Women's Studies Collection, Vol. 1, 1995, Vol. 2, 1996; Gender and Catastrophe, 1997; (with A. Byrne) (Re)searching Women: Feminist Research and Practice in the Social Sciences in Ireland, 2000; (with N. Abdo) Women and Military Confrontation: Palestinian and Israeli Gendered Narratives of Dislocation, 2002; (with R. McVeigh) Racism and Anti-racism in Ireland, 2002. Contributor to books. Contributor of articles, short stories, and reviews to periodicals. **Address:** Department of Sociology, Trinity College, Dublin 2, Ireland. **Online address:** rlentin@tcd.ie

LENTZ, Harris M(onroe), III. American, b. 1955. **Genres:** Communications/Media, Biography. **Career:** Freelance writer and researcher, 1979-. Tennessee State General Assembly, Nashville, legislative assistant, 1972-76; St. Agnes Academy, Memphis, TN, librarian, 1973-74; file clerk and medical secretary for McCarthy DeMere, M.D., 1974-75; WMC-AM (radio station), co-host of weekly trivia program, 1991-94. **Publications:** Science Fiction, Horror, and Fantasy Film and Television Credits, 1983, supplemental vols, 1989, 1994; Assassinations and Executions: An Encyclopedia of Political Violence, 1865-1986, 1988; Heads of State and Governments: A Worldwide Encyclopedia of Over 2,300 Leaders, 1945 through 1992, 1994; Obituaries in the Performing Arts, 1995, published annually; Western and Frontier Film and Television Credits: 1903-1995, 1996; Biographical Dictionary of Professional Wrestling, 1997; Television Westerns Episode Guide, 1997; The Volcano Registry, 1999. **Address:** 3925 Appling Rd., Bartlett, TN 38135, U.S.A. **Online address:** hmliii@aol.com

LENTZ, John C(layton), Jr. American, b. 1957. **Genres:** Theology/Religion. **Career:** Associate pastor of a Presbyterian church in Winchester, VA, 1989-94; pastor and head of staff at a Presbyterian church in Cleveland Heights, OH, 1994-. **Publications:** Luke's Portrait of Paul, 1993. **Address:** 3031 Monticello Blvd., Cleveland Heights, OH 44118, U.S.A.

LENZ, Elinor. American, b. 1928. **Genres:** Education, Women's studies and issues. **Career:** Educational consultant, author, and lecturer. University of California at Los Angeles, coordinator of special programs for University Extension department of humanities and social sciences, 1960-71, director of Western Humanities Center, 1971-77. **Publications:** Second Wind (play), 1957; (ed. with A. LeBel) Land and the Pursuit of Happiness: A Bicentennial Anthology, 1975; (with M.H. Shaevitz) So You Want to Go Back to School: Facing the Realities of Reentry, 1977; (with L. Adams) Effectiveness Training for Women: E.T.W., 1979, reissued as Be Your Best: Personal Effectiveness in Your Life and Your Relationships, 1989; Creating and Marketing Programs in Continuing Education, 1980; Once My Child, Now My Friend, 1981; The Art of Teaching Adults, 1982; (with B.G. Myerhoff) The Feminization of America: How Women's Values Are Changing Our Public and Private Lives, 1985; Rights of Passage: How Women Can Find a New Freedom in Their Midyears, 1992. Author of television scripts and articles for periodicals.

LEO, Mabel R. American, b. 1937. **Genres:** Novels, Novellas/Short stories, Mystery/Crime/Suspense, Romance/Historical, Children's fiction, Autobiography/Memoirs, Biography. **Career:** Writer. Author of "Ethnic Cuisine," "Hints from Helpful Hanna," "Mystery Couple," and "Poem of the Month," all weekly columns for the local newspaper in New Port Richey, FL. **Publications:** The Saga of Jack Durant (biography), 1998; America: The Italian Dream (biography); Yahoodywho (for children); Because We Are Friends (short stories). NOVELS: Dear Sweetheart; Deadly Choices, 2002; Dark Secrets, 2004. Contributor to periodicals.

LEON, Nick. *See* GRANT, Graeme.

LEON, Sharon. Also writes as Sharon Heerboth. American, b. 1959. **Genres:** Film, Biography. **Career:** Ralph Wilson Plastics, Temple, TX, draftsperson, 1987-90; Siecor Corporation, Keller, TX, draftsperson, 1991-. Freelance writer, 1990-. **Publications:** (with D. Hitzeroth) The Importance of Isaac Newton, 1992; (with D. Hitzeroth) The Importance of Thurgood Marshall, 1997. AS SHARON HEERBOTH: (with D. Hitzeroth) Movies: The World on Film, 1991; (with D. Hitzeroth) The Importance of Galileo Galilei, 1992.

LEONARD, Constance. American, b. 1923. **Genres:** Mystery/Crime/Suspense, Children's fiction. **Publications:** The Great Pumpkin Mystery, 1971; The Other Maritha, 1972; Steps to Nowhere, 1974; Hostage in Illyria,

1976; Shadow of a Ghost, 1978; The Marina Mystery, 1981; Stowaway, 1983; Aground, 1984; Strange Waters, 1985. **Address:** 49 Kaufmann Dr., Peterborough, NH 03458, U.S.A.

LEONARD, Diana. British (born Trinidad and Tobago), b. 1941. **Genres:** Sociology, Education, Women's studies and issues. **Career:** Science teacher at public schools in London, England, 1964-67; University of Essex, Colchester, England, research assistant, 1973-75; University of London, Institute of Education, lecturer to senior lecturer in sociology, 1976-, professor, 1998-. Open University, member of faculty, 1980-83. **Publications:** (ed. with S. Allen) Sexual Divisions and Society: Process and Change, 1976; (ed. with S. Allen) Dependence and Exploitation in Work and Marriage, 1976; (trans. from French) N.-C. Mathieu, Ignored by Some, Denied by Others: The Social Sex Category in Sociology, 1977; (assoc. ed., with C.C. Harris and others) The Sociology of the Family, 1979; Sex and Generation: A Study of the Process and Ritual of Courtship and Wedding (monograph), 1980; (ed. with E. Whitelegg and others) The Changing Experience of Women, 1982; (with M.A. Speakman) The Family: Daughters, Wives, and Mothers (monograph), 1983; Moving Forwards (monograph), 1983; (trans., and author of intro.) C. Delphy, Close to Home: A Materialist Analysis of Women's Oppression, 1984; (with J. Hood-Williams) Families (monograph), 1988; (ed. with S. Allen) Sexual Division Revisited, 1990; (with C. Delphy) Familiar Exploitation: A New Analysis of Marriage, 1992. TELEVISION SCRIPTS: Working for Love, 1983; Women and Sport, 1983. Work represented in anthologies. Contributor to periodicals. **Address:** CREG Institute of Education, University of London, 20 Bedford Way, London WC1H 0AH, England. **Online address:** d.leonard@ioe.ac.uk

LEONARD, Dorothy. American, b. 1942. **Genres:** Administration/Management, Business/Trade/Industry. **Career:** U.S. Peace Corps, Washington, DC, volunteer university teacher, 1965-67; freelance journalist in Thailand, 1971-72; Djakarta Business Bulletin, Indonesia, founder and manager, 1972-75; SRI International, Stanford, CA, policy analyst, 1979-80; Massachusetts Institute of Technology, Cambridge, assistant professor, 1981-83; Harvard University, Harvard Business School, Boston, MA, assistant professor, 1983-89, associate professor, 1989-93, professor, 1993-94, William J. Abernathy Professor of Business Administration, 1994-. **Publications:** Wellsprings of Knowledge: Building and Sustaining Core Technological Capabilities, 1995; When Sparks Fly: Igniting Creativity in Groups, 1999; Deep Smarts, 2004. Contributor to books. Contributor of articles and reviews to academic journals. **Address:** Harvard Business School, Soldiers Field Rd, Boston, MA 02163, U.S.A.

LEONARD, Elmore. American, b. 1925. **Genres:** Novels, Mystery/Crime/Suspense, Westerns/Adventure. **Career:** Campbell Ewald advertising agency, Detroit, copywriter, 1950-61; writer of industrial and educational films, 1961-63; Elmore Leonard Advertising Co., director, 1963-66; full-time writer, 1967-. **Publications:** The Bounty Hunters, 1953; The Law at Randado, 1955; Escape from Five Shadows, 1956; East Stand at Saber River, 1959; in U.K. as Lawless River, 1959, 2nd U.K. ed. as Stand on the Saber, 1960; Hombre, 1961; Valdez Is Coming, 1969; The Big Bounce, 1969; The Moonshine War, 1969; Forty Lashes Less One, 1972; Mr. Majestyk (novelization of screenplay), 1974; Fifty-Two Pickup, 1974; Swag, 1976, as Ryan's Rules, 1976; The Hunted, 1977; Unknown Man No. 89, 1977; The Switch, 1978; Gunsights, 1979; City Primeval, 1980; Gold Coast, 1980; Split Images, 1982; Cat Chaser, 1982; Stick, 1983; La Brava, 1983; Glitz, 1985; Bandits, 1987; Touch, 1987; Freaky Deaky, 1988; Killshot, 1989; Get Shorty, 1990; Maximum Bob, 1991; Elmore Leonard Three Complete Works, 1992; Rum Punch, 1992; Pronto, 1993; Riding the Rap, 1995; Out of Sight, 1996; Cuba Libre, 1997; The Tonto Woman and Other Western Stories, 1998; Elmore Leonard's Western Roundup #1-3, 1998-99; Be Cool, 1999; Pagan Babies, 2000; Tishomingo Blues, 2002; When the Women Came out to Dance (stories), 2002; Mr. Paradise, 2004; Complete Western Stories, 2004; Coyote's in the House, 2004; Hot Kid, 2005. **Address:** c/o Random House, 1745 Broadway, 10th Floor, New York, NY 10019, U.S.A. **Online address:** www.elmoreleonard.com

LEONARD, Frances. American, b. 1939. **Genres:** Money/Finance. **Career:** Attorney in San Francisco, CA, 1979-88; Older Women's League, legal counsel, 1980-88. **Publications:** Women and Money, 1991; Money and the Mature Woman, 1993; Time Is Money, 1996. Contributor to periodicals. **Address:** c/o Sandra Dijkstra, 1155 Camino del Mar, No. 515, Del Mar, CA 92014, U.S.A.

LEONARD, Gerald. (born United States), b. 1960. **Genres:** History. **Career:** U.S. Court of Appeals for the Fourth Circuit, Chapel Hill, NC, law clerk to Judge J. Dickson Phillips, Jr., 1995-96; Boston University, Boston, MA, professor of law, 1996-. U.S. Supreme Court, law clerk to Justice David Souter, 1996-97. **Publications:** The Invention of Party Politics: Federalism, Popular Sovereignty, and Constitutional Development in Jacksonian Illinois, 2002. Contributor to books and law journals. **Address:** School of Law, Boston University, 765 Commonwealth Ave., Boston, MA 02215, U.S.A. **Online address:** gleonard@bu.edu

LEONARD, James S. American, b. 1947. **Genres:** Literary criticism and history. **Career:** Bost Engineering Co., city planner, 1968-70; Community Environment Consultants, vice president of English, 1970-73; City of Morristown, TN, city planning director, 1974-79; Clemson University, Clemson, SC, visiting assistant professor, 1980; The Citadel, Charleston, SC, assistant professor, 1983-88, associate professor, 1988-93, professor of English, 1993-. **Publications:** (as J.S. Leonard with C.E. Wharton) The Fluent Mundo: Wallace Stevens and the Structure of Reality, 1988; Afterword, A Tramp Abroad (The Oxford Mark Twain), 1996. EDITOR: (with T.A. Tenney and T.M. Davis) Satire or Evasion? Black Perspectives on Huckleberry Finn, 1992; (with R.M. Davis, J. Harris, and C.E. Wharton) Authority and Textuality: Current Views of Collaborative Writing, 1994; Making Mark Twain Work in the Classroom, 1999; (with G. McMichael and others) Anthology of American Literature, 2 vols., 2004. **Address:** Dept of English, The Citadel, Charleston, SC 29409, U.S.A. **Online address:** leonardj@citadel.edu

LEONARD, Karen Isaksen. American, b. 1939. **Genres:** Anthropology/Ethnology, History. **Career:** University of Michigan, Ann Arbor, associate of Center for South and Southeast Asian Studies, 1967-68, visiting lecturer in history, 1968; University of San Diego, San Diego, CA, lecturer in history, 1969; University of California, San Diego, lecturer in history, 1969-70; University of California, Irvine, assistant professor, 1972-78, associate professor, 1978-85, professor of anthropology, 1985-, director of women's studies, 1978-79. University of Virginia, visiting assistant professor, 1978. **Publications:** Social History of an Indian Caste: The Kayasths of Hyderabad, 1978; Making Ethnic Choices: California's Punjabi-Mexican-Americans, 1994; South Asian Americans, 1997. Book chapters. Contributor to professional journals. **Address:** Department of Anthropology, University of California, Irvine, CA 92697-5100, U.S.A. **Online address:** kbleonar@uci.edu

LEONARD, Stephen J. American, b. 1941. **Genres:** Local history/Rural topics. **Career:** Metropolitan State College, Denver, CO, assistant professor, 1966-74, associate professor, 1974-77, professor of history and head of department, 1977-. **Publications:** (with C. Abbott and D. McComb) Colorado: A History of the Centennial State, 1982, rev. ed., 1994; (with T.J. Noel) Denver: From Mining Camp to Metropolis, 1990; Trials and Triumphs: A Colorado Portrait of the Great Depression, 1993; (with D. Dines and S. Cuba) The Art of Charles Partridge Adams, 1993; (ed. with R. Baron and T.J. Noel) Thomas Hornsby Ferril and the American West, 1996; Lynching in Colorado, 1859-1919, 2002; (with T.J. Noel and D.L. Walker Jr.) Honest John Shafroth: A Colorado Reformer, 2003. Contributor to periodicals. **Address:** Dept of History, Box 27, Metropolitan State College, PO Box 173362, Denver, CO 80217-3362, U.S.A.

LEONARDI, Susan J. American, b. 1946. **Genres:** Gay and lesbian issues, Women's studies and issues, Autobiography/Memoirs, Biography. **Career:** High school English teacher in Belmont, Calif., 1971-76, and Ojai, Calif., 1976-79; University of California, Davis, lecturer in English, 1986-87; University of Maryland at College Park, assistant professor, 1987-90, associate professor of English, 1990-98, professor, 1999-. **Publications:** Dangerous by Degrees: Women at Oxford and the Somerville College Novelists, 1989; The Diva's Mouth: Body, Voice, Prima Donna Politics, 1997. **Address:** English Department, University of Maryland, College Park, MD 20742, U.S.A. **Online address:** sl18@umail.umd.edu

LEONE, Daniel. American, b. 1969. **Genres:** Medicine/Health. **Career:** Writer. **Publications:** The Spread of AIDS, 1997; Physician-Assisted Suicide, 1998. **Address:** c/o Greenhaven Press, 15822 Bernardo Center Dr, San Diego, CA 92127-2320, U.S.A.

LEONG, Russell (C.). Also writes as Wallace Lin. American, b. 1950. **Genres:** Novellas/Short stories, Poetry, Literary criticism and history. **Career:** Pacifica Public Radio, editor of KPFA Folio, 1975-76; University of California, Los Angeles, publications head for resource development and publications at Asian American Studies Center. Rockefeller American Generations Fellowship Program, coordinator, 1991-93. Editor and director of video documentaries. **Publications:** The Country of Dreams and Dust (poems), 1993; Asian American Sexualities: Dimensions of the Gay and Lesbian Experience, 1994; Phoenix Eyes and Other Stories, 2000. EDITOR: (with J.P. Yip) Him Mark Lai, A History Reclaimed: An Annotated Bibliography of

Chinese Language Materials on the Chinese of America, 1986; (with G. Nomura, R. Endo, and S. Sumida, and contrib.) Frontiers of Asian American Studies: Writing, Research, and Criticism, 1989; (and author of intro.) Moving the Image: Independent Asian Pacific American Media Arts, 1970-1990, 1991. Work represented in anthologies. Contributor of poems, articles, stories, and reviews to periodicals. **Address:** Dept of English, 2225 Rolfe Hall, Box 951530, University of California, Los Angeles, CA 90025-1530, U.S.A. **Online address:** rleong@ucla.edu

LEONHARDT, Alice. (born United States), b. 1950. **Genres:** Children's fiction. **Career:** Special education teacher, Howard County MD, 1976-94; writer, 1988-; Blue Ridge Community College, Weyers Cave, VA, adjunct instructor, 1995-; court-appointed special advocate for abused children, 1996-. **Publications:** Wild Cats, 1999; Mystery of the Vanishing Leopard, 1999; Why the Ocean Is Salty, 1999; Ocean Life: Tide Pool Creatures, 2000; Turtles Big Race, 2000; Save the Sea Turtles, 2000; The Princess and the Castle, 2000; Castles, Steck-Vaughn, 2000; Trash Is Dash, 2002; Animals You Will Never Forget, 2002; One Special Dog, 2002; Mystery at the White House, 2002; Presidents, 2002. UNDER PSEUDONYM ALISON HART: Shadow Horse, 1999; Shadow Horse, 2001; Chase: A Police Story, 2002; Rescue: A Police Story, 2002; Danger at the Wild West Show, 2003; Fires of Jubilee, 2003; Return of the Gypsy Witch, 2003. RIDING ACADEMY SERIES; UNDER PSEUDONYM ALISON HART: A Horse for Mary Beth, 1994; Andie out of Control, 1994; Jina Rides to Win, 1994; Mary Beth's Haunted Ride, 1994; Andie Shows Off, 1994; Jina's Pain-in-the-Neck Pony, 1995; The Craziest Horse Show Ever, 1995; Andie's Risky Business, 1995; Trouble at Foxhall, 1995; Foxhunt!, 1995; Lauren Rides to the Rescue, 1995; Haunted Horseback Holiday, 1996. LINDA CRAIG SERIES: Kathy in Charge, 1990; The Riding Club, 1990; A Horse for Jackie, 1990; The Glimmering Ghost, 1990; The Silver Stallion, 1990. THOROUGHBRED SERIES: Melanie's Last Ride, 1998; A Home for Melanie, 1998; Living Legend, 2000; The Bad Luck Filly, 2000; Perfect Image, 2000; Team Player, 2001; Racing Image, 2001; Perfect Challenge, 2002; Faith in a Long Shot, 2003. NEW ADVENTURES OF MARY-KATE AND ASHLEY SERIES: The Case of the High Seas Secret, 2001; The Case of the Jingle Bell Jinx, 2001; The Case of the Mall Mystery, 2002. **Address:** 174 Cider Mill Rd., Mt. Sidney, VA 24467, U.S.A. **Online address:** bbba@cfw.com

LEOPOLD, Christopher. *See* SYNGE, Allen.

LEPAGE, Robert. Canadian, b. 1957. **Genres:** Plays/Screenplays. **Career:** Actor, director, and playwright. Member of acting companies; National Arts Centre, Ottawa, artistic director of French Theatre, 1989-93; Ex Machina (theatre company), Quebec City, founder, 1994-; director of plays; actor on stage and screen. **Publications:** PLAYS: The Dragon's Trilogy, 1985; Vinci, 1986; (with M. Brassard) The Polygraph, 1987; Tectonic Plates, 1988; Needles and Opium, 1991; Le Confessional (screenplay), 1994; Elsinore, 1995; The Seven Streams of the River Ota, 1997; (with A. Morency) No (screenplay), 1998; (co-writer) Geometry of Miracles; Zulu, 1999; Far Side of the Moon, 2000. **Address:** 103 Dalhousie St, Quebec City, QC, Canada G1K 4B9. **Online address:** roleinc@attgolbal.net

LEPLIN, Jarrett. American, b. 1944. **Genres:** Philosophy. **Career:** University of North Carolina at Greensboro, professor of philosophy;. **Publications:** A Novel Defense of Scientific Realism, 1997. Editor of books. Contributor to philosophy journals. **Address:** Department of Philosophy, Box 26170, University of North Carolina at Greensboro, Greensboro, NC 27402, U.S.A. **Online address:** j_leplin@uncg.edu

LEPORE, Jill. American, b. 1966. **Genres:** History. **Career:** Yale University, acting instructor in American studies, 1993-95; University of California at San Diego, San Diego, assistant professor of history, 1995-96; Boston University, Boston, MA, assistant professor of history, 1996-. **Publications:** The Name of War: King Philip's War and the Origins of American Identity, 1998; The Age of Encounters: A History in Documents, in press; A is for American, 2001. Contributor of chapters to books. Contributor of articles and reviews to journals. **Address:** History Department, Boston University, 226 Bay State Rd., Boston, MA 02215, U.S.A. **Online address:** jlepore@bu.edu

LEPPEK, Christopher. American, b. 1954. **Genres:** Mystery/Crime/Suspense, Horror. **Career:** New Lyons Recorder, Lyons, CO, reporter, 1977; Intermountain Jewish News, Denver, CO, assistant editor, 1977-. **Publications:** The Surrogate Assassin (mystery novel), 1998; (with E. Isler) Chaosicon (horror novel), 2001. Contributor of articles and stories to magazines and newspapers. **Address:** 1016 S Washington St, Denver, CO 80209, U.S.A. **Online address:** RedRaven75@aol.com

LERMAN, Rhoda. American, b. 1936. **Genres:** Novels. **Publications:** Call Me Ishtar, 1972; Girl That He Marries, 1976; Eleanor: A Novel, 1979; Book of the Night, 1984; God's Ear, 1988; Animal Acts, 1994; In the Company of Newfies, 1996. **Address:** 135 Potter Hill Rd, Port Crane, NY 13833-1734, U.S.A.

LERNER, Barron H. American, b. 1960. **Genres:** Medicine/Health. **Career:** Historian, internist, writer, educator, and scholar. Columbia University, New York, NY, instructor, 1989-91, Mailman School of Public Health, assistant professor of medicine and public health, 1993-; Presbyterian Hospital, assistant physician, 1989-91, attending physician, 1993-; University of Washington, Seattle, WA, Instructor, 1991-93. **Publications:** Contagion and Confinement: Controlling Tuberculosis along the Skid Row, 1998; The Breast Cancer Wars: Hope, Fear, and the Pursuit of a Cure in Twentieth-Century America, 2001. Contributor to medical and historical journals, magazines, and newspapers. **Address:** Columbia University, Department of Medicine, Black Building 1-101, 630 West 168th St., New York, NY 10032, U.S.A. **Online address:** bhl5@columbia.edu

LERNER, Harriet. American, b. 1944. **Genres:** Children's non-fiction, Human relations/Parenting, Psychology. **Career:** Author, lecturer, consultant, and workshop leader. Private practice. Menninger Clinic, Topeka, KS, staff psychologist and psychotherapist, 1972-2001. **Publications:** FOR CHILDREN: (with S. Goldhor) What's So Terrible about Swallowing an Apple Seed?, 1996; (with S. Goldhor) Franny B. Kranny, There's a Bird in Your Hair!, 2001. FOR ADULTS: The Dance of Anger: A Woman's Guide to Changing the Patterns of Intimate Relationships, 1985; Women in Therapy, 1989; The Dance of Intimacy: A Woman's Guide to Courageous Acts of Change in Key Relationships, 1990; The Dance of Deception: Pretending and Truth-Telling in Women's Lives, 1993; Life Preservers: Good Advice When You Need It Most, 1997; The Mother Dance: How Children Change Your Life, 1998; The Dance of Connection: How to Talk to Someone When You're Mad, Hurt, Scared, Frustrated, Insulted, Betrayed, or Desperate, 2001. Author of audio tapes on adult topics. Contributor of articles on human relationships to popular and professional journals. **Address:** c/o Worley Shoemaker Artist Management, 215 W 53rd St, Kansas City, MO 64112-2815, U.S.A. **Online address:** jlworley@aol.com

LERNER, Henry M. American. **Genres:** Medicine/Health. **Career:** Physician and author. Newton-Wellesley Hospital, Newton, MA, private practice in obstetrics and gynecology; Women's Urinary Continence Center, Newton, director. Member of board of directors, ProMutual Insurance Company. **Publications:** Miscarriage: Why It Happens and How Best to Reduce Your Risks, 2003. **Address:** c/o Author Mail, Perseus Books Group, 387 Park Ave. S., New York, NY 10016, U.S.A.

LERNER, Laurence (David). British (born Republic of South Africa), b. 1925. **Genres:** Novels, Poetry, Literary criticism and history. **Career:** Professorial Fellow, University of Sussex, Brighton, 1985- (Lecturer then Reader, 1962-70; Professor of English, 1970-85). Schoolmaster, St. George's Grammar School, Cape Town, 1946-47; Assistant Lecturer then Lecturer in English, University College of the Gold Coast, Legon, Ghana, 1949-53; Extra-Mural Tutor then Lecturer in English, Queen's University of Belfast, 1953-62; Kenan Professor of English, Vanderbilt University, Nashville, TN, 1985-94. **Publications:** The Englishmen, 1959; Domestic Interior and Other Poems, 1959; The Truest Poetry, 1960; The Directions of Memory: Poems 1958-63, 1964; The Truthtellers: Jane Austen, George Eliot, and D.H. Lawrence, 1967; A Free Man, 1968; Selves, 1969; The Uses of Nostalgia, 1972; A.R.T.H.U.R.: The Life and Opinions of a Digital Computer, 1974; An Introduction to English Poetry, 1975; Love and Marriage, 1979; The Man I Killed, 1980; A.R.T.H.U.R. and M.A.R.T.H.A., 1980; The Literary Imagination, 1982; A Dialogue, 1983; Chapter and Verse: Bible Poems, 1984; Selected Poems, 1984; My Grandfather's Grandfather, 1985; Rembrandt's Mirror, 1987; The Frontiers of Literature, 1988; Angels & Absences: Child Deaths in the 19th Century, 1997; (trans.) Baudelaire: Selected Poems, 1999; Wandering Professor, 1999. EDITOR: Shakespeare's Tragedies, 1963; (with J. Holmstrom) George Eliot and Her Readers, 1966; Shakespeare's Comedies, 1967; (with J. Holmstrom) Thomas Hardy and His Readers, 1968; The Context of English Literature: The Victorians, 1978; Reconstructing Literature, 1983. **Address:** Abinger, 1-b Gundreda Rd, Lewes BN7 1PT, England.

LERNER, Martin. American, b. 1936. **Genres:** Art/Art history. **Career:** University of California, Santa Barbara, assistant professor, 1965-66; Cleveland Museum of Art, Cleveland, OH, assistant curator of Oriental art, 1966-72; Case Western Reserve University, Cleveland, adjunct assistant professor, 1968-72; Metropolitan Museum of Art, NYC, vice chair in charge

of Far Eastern art, 1972-75, curator of South and Southeast Asian art, 1978-; Columbia University, adjunct professor, 2004-. International lecturer and art consultant. **Publications:** Indian Miniatures from the Jeffrey Paley Collection, 1974; Bronze Sculptures from Asia, 1975; Blue and White: Early Japanese Export Ware, 1978; The Flame and the Lotus: Indian and Southeast Asian Art from the Kronos Collections, 1984; (with W. Felten) Thai and Cambodian Sculpture from the Sixth to the Fourteenth Centuries, 1989; (with Felten) Entdeckungen: Skulpturen der Khmer und Thai, 1989; (with S. Kossak) The Lotus Transcendent: Indian and Southeast Asian Art from the Samuel Eilenberg Collection, 1991; Ancient Khumer Sculpture, 1994. **Address:** Metropolitan Museum of Art, 1000 5th Ave, New York, NY 10028, U.S.A.

LERNER, Robert E(arl). American, b. 1940. **Genres:** History. **Career:** Princeton University, NJ, instructor in history, 1963-64; Western Reserve University, Cleveland, assistant professor of history, 1964-67; Northwestern University, Evanston, IL, assistant professor, 1967-71, associate professor, 1971-76, professor of history, 1976-, director of humanities, 1981-83, Peter B. Ritzma Professor in the Humanities. **Publications:** The Age of Adversity: Europe in the Fourteenth Century, 1968; The Heresy of the Free Spirit in the Later Middle Ages, 1972, 2nd ed., 1991; (co-author) One Thousand Years: Western Europe in the Middle Ages, 1974; The Powers of Prophecy, 1983; (co-author) World Civilizations, 1986, 9th ed., 1997; (co-author) Western Civilizations: Their History and Their Culture, 11th ed., 1988, 13th ed., 1998; (co-author) Johannes de Rupescissa, 1994; The Feast of Saint Abraham: Medieval Millenarians and the Jews, 2001. **Address:** Dept. of History, Northwestern University, Evanston, IL 60208, U.S.A. **Online address:** rlerner@northwestern.edu

LERNER, Steve. American, b. 1946. **Career:** Village Voice, NYC, staff writer, 1968-69; worked at tool factory, pottery, and orchard, and as carpenter in Vermont, 1971-75; Commonweal, research director, 1975-. **Publications:** The CY4 Report: Conditions of Life at the California Youth Authority, 1982; Bodily Harm: The Pattern of Fear and Violence at the California Youth Authority, 1986; State Raised Kids No One Wants, 1990; The Good News about Juvenile Justice, 1990; The Geography of Foster Care: Keeping Children in the Neighborhood, 1990; Earth Summit: Conversations with Architects of an Ecologically Sustainable Future, 1991; Beyond the Earth Summit: Conversations with Advocates of Sustainable Development, 1992; Eco-Pioneers, 1997. Contributor to periodicals. **Address:** 3512 35th St. NW, Washington, DC 20016, U.S.A. **Online address:** sdlerner@aol.com

LEROUX-HUGON, Hélène. French, b. 1955. **Genres:** Children's fiction, Art/Art history. **Career:** Illustrator and author of children's books, 1983-. Madeleine (private art school), Angers, France, teacher, 1978-86; Lycée St. Pierre la Joliverie, Nantes, France, art teacher, 1999-; Ravensburger (publisher), graphic artist and design director, 2000-; Artkids (children's art magazine), production supervisor, 2001-. **Publications:** J'AIME DESSINER SERIES IN ENGLISH AS I CAN DRAW ANIMALS SERIES: J'aime dessiner les animaux d'Afrique, 1997; J'aime dessiner les animaux de nos régions, 1997; J'aime dessiner les animaux du froid, 1999, trans. V.J. Weber as I Can Draw Polar Animals, 2001; J'aime dessiner les animaux de la forêt, 1998, trans. V.J. Weber as I Can Draw Forest Animals, 2001; J'aime dessiner les animaux sauvage, 1998, trans. V.J. Weber as I Can Draw Wild Animals, 2001; J'aime dessiner les animaux de la campagne, trans. V.J. Weber as I Can Draw Country Animals, 2001. SELF-ILLUSTRATED, IN FRENCH: Petits ateliers au fil des saisons, 1993; Gouache: jeux et décors peints, 1994; Fleurs fruits et couronnes, 1994; Masques en papiers pour jouer, 1996; Collages, 1996; Pochoirs: premiers pas, 1997; Vite on se déguise, 1997; Douces mousses, 1997; Ma ferme pâte à modeler, 1998; (with N. Seret) Déguisements pour tous, 1998. Illustrator of books by A. Rocard. Contributor to books. **Address:** 12 rue des Martyrs, 44100 Nantes, France. **Online address:** helene.lerouxhugon@caramail.com

LESCH, David W. American, b. 1960. **Career:** Northeastern University, Boston, MA, instructor in history, 1987; Johns Hopkins University, Baltimore, MD, instructor in history at extension school, 1988, 1989; University of Maryland, Baltimore County, Catonsville, instructor, 1990, adjunct professor of history, 1991; St. Mary's College of Maryland, St. Mary's City, visiting assistant professor of Middle East history, 1991-92; Johns Hopkins University, adjunct professor of Middle East history, 1992; Trinity University, San Antonio, TX, associate professor of Middle East history, 1992-, John Rogers faculty fellow, 1995-97. Guest speaker at colleges and universities; National Council on U.S.-Arab Relations, director of Summer in Syria Program, 1995-96. WMAR-TV, studio analyst during Persian Gulf crisis, 1990-91; Cable News Network (CNN), analyst, 1990-91; National Public Radio, regular commentator on Middle East issues. **Publications:**

Syria and the United States: Eisenhower's Cold War in the Middle East, 1992; (ed. and contrib.) The Middle East and the United States: A Historical and Political Reassessment, 1996. Contributor to books. Contributor of articles and reviews to academic journals and newspapers. **Address:** 807 Stoneway Dr., San Antonio, TX 78258, U.S.A. **Online address:** DLesch@trinity.edu

LESCH, John E(mmett). American, b. 1945. **Genres:** History. **Career:** University of California, Berkeley, assistant professor, 1977-84, associate professor, 1984-95, professor of history, 1995-. **Publications:** Science and Medicine in France: The Emergence of Experimental Physiology, 1790-1855, 1984; (ed.) German Chemical Industry in the 20th Century, 2000. **Address:** Department of History, University of California, Berkeley, CA 94720, U.S.A.

LESCROART, John T. American, b. 1948. **Genres:** Mystery/Crime/Suspense. **Career:** Professional singer and guitarist, Los Angeles and San Francisco, 1972-77; advertising director for "Guitar Player," Cupertino, CA, 1977-79; Guardians of the Jewish Homes for the Aging, Los Angeles, associate director, 1979-83; A.T. Kearney Inc., Alexandria, VA, associate consultant, 1982-85. **Publications:** NOVEL: Sunburn, 1982. CRIME AND MYSTERY: Son of Holmes, 1986; Rasputin's Revenge, 1987; Dead Irish, 1989; The Vig, 1990; Hard Evidence, 1993; The 13th Juror, 1994; A Certain Justice, 1995; Guilt, 1997; The Mercy Rule, 1998; Nothing but the Truth, 1999; The Hearing, 2001; The Oath, 2002; The First Law, 2003; The Second Chair, 2004; The Motive, 2004. **Address:** 426 D St, Davis, CA 95616-4131, U.S.A.

LESEUR, Geta. American (born Jamaica). **Genres:** Anthropology/Ethnology, Literary criticism and history, Third World, Women's studies and issues. **Career:** Indiana University-Bloomington, associate instructor in Afro-American studies, 1975-82; Colgate University, Hamilton, NY, assistant professor of English and Africana studies, 1984-85; University of California, Berkeley, fellow in African-American studies, 1985-86; University of Arizona, Tucson, adjunct professor of black studies, 1986-87; University of California, Berkeley, fellow in African-American studies, 1987-88; University of Missouri-Columbia, assistant professor, 1988-94, associate professor of English and women's studies and member of adjunct faculty in black studies, 1994-, Wakonse fellow, 1991. **Publications:** Ten Is the Age of Darkness: The Black Bildungsroman (literary criticism), 1995; Not All Okies Are White: The Lives of Black Cotton Pickers in Arizona, 2000. Contributor to books. Contributor of articles and reviews to periodicals. **Address:** Department of English, 107 Tate Hall, University of Missouri-Columbia, Columbia, MO 65211, U.S.A. **Online address:** LeSeurBrownG@missouri.edu

LESIKAR, Raymond Vincent. American, b. 1922. **Genres:** Writing/Journalism. **Career:** Emeritus Professor of Mgmt., Louisiana State University, Baton Rouge, 1977- (Associate Professor, 1954-59; Professor 1960-77). Assistant Professor, University of Texas, Austin, 1949-54; Professor, University of North Texas, Denton, 1979-87. **Publications:** (with R.D. Hay) Business Report Writing, 1957; (with W.P. Boyd) Productive Business Writing, 1959; Report Writing for Business, 1961, 10th ed., 1998; Business Communication: Theory and Application, 1968, 7th ed., 1993; (with W. Perlick) Introduction to Business: A Societal Approach, 1972, 3rd ed., 1979; How to Write a Report, 1974; Lesikar's Basic Business Communication, 1979, (with M. Flatley) 9th ed., 2002. **Address:** PO Box 7912, Horseshoe Bay, TX 78657, U.S.A. **Online address:** lesikar@tstar.net

LESLIE, John. American, b. 1944. **Genres:** Mystery/Crime/Suspense, Romance/Historical. **Career:** Writer, 1985-. **Publications:** NOVELS: Blood on the Keys, 1988; Bounty Hunter Blues, 1989; Killer in Paradise, 1991; Damaged Goods, 1991; Havana Hustle, 1993. NOVELS IN THE GIDEON LOWRY SERIES: Killing Me Softly, 1994; Night and Day, 1995; Love for Sale, 1996. **Address:** c/o Loretta Barrett Books Inc., 101 5th Ave., New York, NY 10003, U.S.A.

LESLIE, (Virginia) Kent A(nderson). American, b. 1942. **Genres:** Biography. **Career:** Queens College of the City University of New York, Flushing, NY, instructor in biology, 1961-64; Emory University, Atlanta, GA, instructor in preventive medicine, 1967-68; teacher of science and biology at a middle school in Bel Air, MD, 1968-69; high school science teacher in Marietta, GA, 1969-70; Emory University, teacher, 1991-92; Oglethorpe University, Atlanta, faculty member, 1993-, administrative director of women's studies, 1994-; guest lecturer at colleges and universities. **Publications:** Woman of Color, Daughter of Privilege: Amanda America Dickson, 1849-1893, 1995. Contributor to books. Contributor of articles and reviews to scholarly journals. **Address:** Oglethorpe University, 4484 Peachtree St. N.E., Atlanta, GA 30319, U.S.A.

LESLIE, Ward S. See **WARD, Elizabeth Honor.**

LESOURNE, Jacques. French, b. 1928. **Genres:** Economics, History, International relations/Current affairs, Social sciences. **Career:** Charbonnages de France, chief of economic dept, 1954-57; SEMA and METRA International Group, France, CEO, 1958-75; Conservatoire National des Arts et Metiers, Paris, professor of economics, 1975-91; Le Monde, Paris, CEO, 1991-94. Organization for Economic Cooperation and Development, director of Interfutures Project, 1976-79; French National Academy of Technologies, member of the board. **Publications:** Technique economique et gestion industrielle, 1958, trans. as Economic Analysis and Industrial Management, 1963; Economic Technique and Industrial Management, 1959; Le calcul economique, 1964, trans. as Cost-Benefit Analysis and Economic Theory, 1975; Du bon usage de l'etude economique dans l'entreprise, 1966; The Management Revolution, 1971; Modeles de croissance des entreprises, 1973; A Theory of the Individual for Economic Analysis, 1977; (with R. Loue) L'analyse des decisions d'amenagement regional, 1979; Demain, la France dans le monde, 1980; Colloque CNRS Analyse de systeme, 1980; Les mille sentiers de L'avenir, 1981, trans. as World Perspectives, 1982, rev. ed., 1986; Soirs et Lendemains de fete, 1984; L'entreprise et ses futurs, 1985; (with Loue) La gestion des villes, 1985; (with M. Godet) La fin des habitudes, 1985; Education et societe, 1988; (with B. Lecomte) De L'Atlantique a L'Oural, 1990, trans. as After Communism, 1991; Economie de L'ordre et du desordre, 1991, trans. as The Economics of Order and Disorder, 1992; Ou va L'Etat?, 1992; Un homme de notre siecle, 1999; Des avenirs qui n'ont pas en liere, 2001; (with A. Orlean and B. Wallises) Lecons de micro-ecunomie evolutionniste, 2003; Democratie, marche, gouvernance, quell avenice?, 2004. **Address:** 52 rue de Vangirard, 75006 Paris, France. **Online address:** jolesourne@wanadoo.fr

LESSER, Milton. See **MARLOWE, Stephen.**

LESSER, Wendy. American, b. 1952. **Genres:** Literary criticism and history. **Career:** Lesser & Ogden Associates (a public policy consulting firm), Berkeley, CA, partner, 1977-81; Threepenny Review, Berkeley, founding editor, 1980-; writer. **Publications:** The Life below the Ground: A Study of the Subterranean in Literature and History, 1987; His Other Half: Men Looking at Women through Art, 1991; (ed.) Hiding in Plain Sight: Essays in Criticism and Autobiography, 1993; Pictures at an Execution, 1994; A Director Calls, 1997; The Amateur: An Independent Life of Letters, 1999; Nothing Remains the Same: Rereading and Remembering, 2002. **Address:** Threepenny Review, PO Box 9131, Berkeley, CA 94709, U.S.A.

LESSING, Doris (May). Also writes as Jane Somers. British (born Persia), b. 1919. **Genres:** Novels, Novellas/Short stories, Science fiction/Fantasy, Plays/Screenplays, Poetry, Autobiography/Memoirs. **Career:** Writer. **Publications:** NOVELS: The Grass Is Singing, 1950; Martha Quest, 1952; A Proper Marriage, 1954; Retreat to Innocence, 1956; A Ripple from the Storm, 1958; The Golden Notebook, 1962; Landlocked, 1965; The Four-Gated City, 1969; Briefing for a Descent into Hell, 1971; The Summer before Dark, 1973; The Memoirs of a Survivor, 1974; Re Colonised Planet 5, Shikasta, 1979; The Marriages between Zones 3, 4, and 5, 1980; The Sirian Experiments, 1981; The Making of the Preresentative for Planet 8, 1982; The Sentimental Agents in the Volyen Empire, 1983; The Good Terrorist, 1985; The Fifth Child, 1988; Love Again, 1996; Mara and Dann, 1999; Ben, in the World, 2000; The Old Age of El Magnifico, 2001; The Sweetest Dream, 2001; The Grandmothers, 2003. SHORT STORIES: This Was The Old Chief's Country, 1951; Five, 1953; The Habit of Loving, 1957; A Man and Two Women, 1963; African Stories, 1964; Winter in July, 1966; The Black Madonna, 1966; The Story of a Non-Marrying Man and Other Stories, 1972; The Sun between Their Feet, 1973; Sunrise on the Veld, 1975; A Mild Attack of the Locusts, 1977; To Room Nineteen, 1978; The Temptation of Jack Orkney, 1978; London Observed: Stories and Sketches (in US as The Real Thing), 1992. NON-FICTION: Going Home, 1957, rev. ed., 1968; In Pursuit of the English, 1960; Particularly Cats, 1967; Prisons We Choose to Live Inside, 1987; The Wind Blows Away Our Words, 1987; Particularly Cats and More Cats, 1989; African Laughter: Four Visits to Zimbabwe, 1992; Under My Skin, 1994; Walking in the Shade, 1997. PLAYS: Each His Own Wilderness, 1958; Play with a Tiger, 1962; The Singing Door, 1973. OTHER: Fourteen Poems, 1959; A Small Personal Voice (essays & interviews), 1974; The Making of the Representative for Planet 8 (libretto for opera), 1988; Doris Lessing Reader, 1990; Putting the Questions Differently: Interviews with Doris Lessing, 1964-1994, 1996. AS JANE SOMERS: The Diary of a Good Neighbour, 1983; If the Old Could, 1984; The Diary of Jane Somers, 1984. **Address:** c/o Jonathan Clowes Ltd., 10 Iron Bridge House, Bridge Approach, London NW1 8BD, England.

LESSNOFF, Michael. British, b. 1940. **Genres:** Politics/Government. **Career:** University of Glasgow, Scotland, reader in politics, 1966-2003. **Publi-**

cations: The Structure of Social Science, 1974; Social Contract, 1986; (ed.) Social Contract Theory, 1990; The Spirit of Capitalism and the Protestant Ethic, 1994; Political Philosophers of the Twentieth Century, 1998; Ernest Gellner and Modernity, 2002. **Address:** Department of Politics, University of Glasgow, Glasgow G12 8QQ, Scotland. **Online address:** m.h.lessnoff@socsci.gla.ac.uk

LESTER, David. British/American, b. 1942. **Genres:** Psychiatry, Psychology. **Career:** Suicide Prevention & Crisis Service, Buffalo, NY, research director, 1969-71; Richard Stockton College, Pomona, NJ, professor of psychology, 1971-. **Publications:** Explorations in Exploration, 1969; (with G. Lester) Suicide: The Gamble with Death, 1971; Why People Kill Themselves, 1972, 4th ed., 2000; Comparative Psychology, 1973; A Physiological Basis for Personality Traits, 1974; Unusual Sexual Behavior, 1975; (with G. Lester) Crime of Passion, 1975; The Use of Alternative Modes for Communication in Psychotherapy, 1977; The Psychological Basis for Handwriting Analysis, 1980; (with B. Sell and K. Sell) Suicide: A Guide to Information Sources, 1980; Psychotherapy for Offenders, 1981; (with M. Murell) Introduction to Juvenile Delinquency, 1981; The Structure of the Mind, 1982; (with A. Levitt) Insanity and Incompetence, 1984; Gun Control, 1984; The Murderer and His Murder, 1986; The Death Penalty, 1987, 2nd ed., 1998; Suicide as a Learned Behavior, 1987; The Biochemical Basis of Suicide, 1988; Suicide from a Psychological Perspective, 1988; Why Women Kill Themselves, 1988; Can We Prevent Suicide?, 1989; Questions and Answers about Suicide, 1989; Suicide from a Sociological Perspective, 1989; (with R.V. Clarke) Suicide: Closing the Exits, 1989; Understanding and Preventing Suicide, 1990; Questions and Answers about Murder, 1991; Psychotherapy for Suicidal Clients, 1991; (with M. Braswell and P. Van Voorhis) Correctional Counseling and Rehabilitation, 2nd ed., 1992, 5th ed., 2004; (with B.L. Danto) Suicide behind Bars, 1993; The Cruelest Death, 1993; Suicide in Creative Women, 1993; Understanding Suicide, 1993; Patterns of Suicide and Homicide in America, 1994; Theories of Personality, 1995; Serial Killers, 1995; Patterns of Suicide and Homicide in the World, 1996; An Encyclopedia of Famous Suicides, 1996; Making Sense of Suicide, 1997; (with B. Yang) The Economy and Suicide, 1997; Suicide in American Indians, 1997; Suicide in African Americans, 1998; (with B. Yang) Suicide and Homicide in the 20th Century, 1998; Crime and the Native American, 1999; By Their Own Hand, 2000; Fixin' to Die, 2003; Mass Murder, 2004; (with M. Lindsay) Suicide by Cop, 2004. EDITOR: Crisis Intervention and Counseling by Telephone, 1973, 2nd ed., 2003; Gambling Today, 1979; The Elderly Victim of Crime, 1981; Suicide (annual), 1988-95; Current Concepts of Suicide, 1990; (with M. Tallmer) Now I Lay Me Down, 1994; Emile Durkheim: Le Suicide 100 Years Later, 1994; (with S. Canetto) Women and Suicidal Behavior, 1995; (with A. Leenaars) Suicide and the Unconscious, 1996; Suicide Prevention, 2001; Katie's Diary, 2004; (with R. Yufit) Assessment, Treatment, and Prevention of Suicidal Behavior, 2005. **Address:** Psychology Program, Richard Stockton College, Pomona, NJ 08240-0195, U.S.A. **Online address:** Lesterd@stockton.edu

LESTER, Julius. American, b. 1939. **Genres:** Children's fiction, Poetry, History, Literary criticism and history, Music, Mythology/Folklore, Autobiography/Memoirs, Novellas/Short stories, Young adult fiction, Novels. **Career:** Professor of Judaic Studies, University of Massachusetts, Amherst, 1971-. Musician and Singer. Director, Newport Folk Festival, Rhode Island, 1966-68; Contributor Ed., SING OUT, New York, 1964-69; Contributor Ed., Broadside of New York, 1964-70. **Publications:** (with P. Seeger) The 12-String Guitar as Played by Leadbelly: An Instructional Manual, 1965; The Mud of Vietnam (verse), 1967; Revolutionary Notes, 1969; Look Out Whitey! Black Power's Gon' Get Your Mama!, 1968; To Be a Slave, 1968; Black Folktales, 1969; Search for the New Land, 1969; The Knee-High Man and Other Tales, 1972; Long Journey Home, 1972; Two Love Stories, 1972; Who I Am, 1974; All Is Well (autobiography), 1976; This Strange New Feeling (short stories), 1982; Do Lord Remember Me, 1984; The Tales of Uncle Remus: The Adventures of Brer Rabbit, 1987; The Tales of Uncle Remus: Further Adventures of Brer Rabbit, 1988; Lovesong: Becoming a Jew (autobiography), 1988; How Many Spots Does a Leopard Have and Other Tales, 1989; Further Tales of Uncle Remus, 1990; Falling Pieces of the Broken Sky, 1990; The Last Tales of Uncle Remus, 1994; And All Our Wounds Forgiven (novel), 1994; John Henry, 1994; The Man Who Knew Too Much, 1994; Othello: A Novel, 1995; Sam and the Tigers, 1996; What a Truly Cool World, 1998; From Slave Ship to Freedom Road, 1998; Black Cowboy, Wild Horses: A True Story, 1998; When the Beginning Began, 1999; Uncle Remus, 1999; Pharoh's Daughter, 2000; Albidaro and the Mischievous Dream, 2000; Shining, 2000; Ackamarackus, 2001; When Dad Killed Mom, 2001; (with L. Cohen) The Blues Singers, 2001; Why Heaven is Far Away, 2002; Let's Talk About Race, 2004; Autobiography of God, 2004; Old African, 2004; Let's Talk about Race, 2005. EDITOR: (with M. Varela) To Praise Our Bridges: An Autobiography by Fanny Lou Hamer,

1967; (with M. Varela) Our Folk Tales, 1967; The Seventh Son: The Thought and Writings of W.E.B. Du Bois, 2 vols., 1971. **Address:** Department of Judaic and Near Eastern Studies, 744 Herter Hall, University of Massachusetts, Amherst, MA 01003, U.S.A. **Online address:** lester@judnea. umass.edu

LESTER, Margot Carmichael. American, b. 1962. **Genres:** Self help. **Career:** Blue Cross Blue Shield of North Carolina, editorial and administrative assistant, 1984-87, public affairs coordinator, 1987-88; University of North Carolina at Chapel Hill, publications director at Kenan-Flagler Business School, 1989-90, marketing director, 1990-93; Gurley Communications, founder and president, 1993-95; Universal Communications, managing partner, 1995-97; Word Factory, founder and president, 1997-; Glaxo Wellcome Inc., communications specialist, 1994-95. **Publications:** The Real Life Guide to Life after College, 1998; The Real Life Guide to Starting Your Career, 1998. Contributor to magazines. **Address:** 1728 Laurel Canyon Blvd, Ste B, Los Angeles, CA 90046-3128, U.S.A. **Online address:** verbtycoon@aol.com

LESTER, Mark. See **RUSSELL, Martin (James).**

LESTER, Richard K. American. **Genres:** Economics. **Career:** Massachusetts Institute of Technology, Cambridge, MA, MIT Industrial Performance Center, director and professor of nuclear engineering. **Publications:** (with M. Willrich and S.C. Greenberg) Radioactive Waste Management and Regulation, 1977; (with M.L. Dertouzos and R.M. Solow) Made in America: Regaining the Productive Edge, 1989; (ed., with S. Berger) Made by Hong Kong, 1997; The Productive Edge: How U.S. Industries are Pointing the Way to a New Era of Economic Growth, 1998. **Address:** Massachusetts Institute of Technology, Room E40-379, 77 Massachusetts Ave., Cambridge, MA 02139, U.S.A. **Online address:** rklester@mit.edu

L'ESTRANGE, Anna. See **ELLERBECK, Rosemary.**

LETCHFORD, Stanley. British, b. 1924. **Genres:** Mathematics/Statistics. **Career:** Jr. Lecturer, New College, Oxford University, 1950-52; Director of Mathematics Studies, Collier Macmillan Schools, 1962-82. **Publications:** Modern Arithmetic, 1970, 1975; Business Mathematics and Statistics, 1974, 3rd ed. 1984; The Economic System, 1975; Statistics: A Foundation Course, 1980; Statistics Workbook, 1982; (ed.) Quantitative Methods in Business, by Curwin and Slater, 1985; Statistics for Accountants, 1994. **Address:** 21 Gorringe Dr, Lower Willingdon, Eastbourne, Sussex BN20 9ST, England.

LETELLIER, Robert Ignatius. British (born Republic of South Africa), b. 1953. **Genres:** Literary criticism and history, Music, Bibliography. **Career:** University of Salzburg, Austria, member of Salzburg Centre for Research in the Early English Novel, Institut fuer Anglistik und Amerikanistik, 1990-. **Publications:** An Intensifying Vision of Evil: The English Gothic Novel (1764-1820) as a Self-Contained Literary Cycle, 1980; Kindred Spirits: An Assessment of the Interrelationship between the Romantic Novels of England and Germany, 1790-1820, 1982; A Bibliography of the English Novel from the Restoration to the French Revolution: A Checklist of Sources and Critical Materials, 1995; Sir Walter Scott and the Gothic Novel, 1995; Day in Mamre, Night in Sodom: A Study of Abraham and Lot in Genesis 18 and 19, 1995; The English Novel, 1660-1700: An Annotated Bibliography, 1997; The Diaries of Giacomo Meyerbeer, vol. 1, 1999, vol. 2, 2001, vol. 3, 2002, vol. 4, 2003; The English Novel, 1700-1740: An Annotated Bibliography, 2002; Meyerbeer Studies, 2005. **Address:** 7 Parker St, Cambridge CB1 1JL, England. **Online address:** r.letellier@ntlworld.com

LETESSIER, Dorothee. French, b. 1953. **Genres:** Novels, Plays/Screenplays. **Career:** Employed variously in a law office, 1974-76, and as a metallurgist, 1976-80; writer, 1980-. **Publications:** NOVELS: Voyage a Paimpol, 1980, trans. by M. Ward as A Breath of Air, 1985; Loica, 1983; La belle Atlantique (title means: The Beautiful Atlantic), 1986; Jean-Baptiste, ou, L'education vagabonde (title means: Jean-Baptiste: Learning to be a Wanderer), 1988; La reine des abeilles (title means: The Queen Bee), 1989; L'autocar, 1994. Author of scripts for television documentaries. **Address:** 7 rue Bovrgon, 75013 Paris, 13e, France.

LETHBRIDGE, Robert (David). British (born United States), b. 1947. **Genres:** Literary criticism and history. **Career:** Cambridge University, England, staff member, 1973-94, lecturer in French and fellow and senior tutor of Fitzwilliam College, 1982-94; University of London, professor of French Language and literature, director of Institute in Paris; writer. **Publications:** Maupassant "Pierre et Jean," 1984. EDITOR: (with T. Keefe) Zola and the Craft of Fiction, 1990; (with P. Collier) Artistic Relations: Literature and Visual Arts in Nineteenth-Century France, 1994; (with C. Lloyd) Maupassant, Conteur et Romancier, 1994; E. Zola, L'Assommoir, 1995; E. Zola, Pot-Bouille, 2000; E. Zola, La Debacle, 2000; G. de Maupassant, Bel-Ami, 2001; G. de Maupassant, Pierre et Jean, 2001. **Address:** University of London Institute in Paris, 9-11, rue de Constantine, 750007 Paris, France. **Online address:** r.lethbridge@ulip.lon.ac.uk

LETHEM, Jonathan (Allen). American, b. 1964. **Genres:** Novels. **Career:** Brazen Head Books, NYC, bookseller, 1977-80; Gryphon Books, NYC, bookseller, 1982-84; Pegasus Books, Berkeley, CA, bookseller, 1985-90; Moe's Books, Berkeley, bookseller, 1990-94; writer. **Publications:** NOVELS: Gun, with Occasional Music, 1994; Amnesia Moon, 1995; Motherless Brooklyn, 1999; As She Climbed across the Table, 1997; Girl in Landscape, 1998; This Shape We're In, 2001; The Fortress of Solitude, 2003. Contributor of short fiction to periodicals. **Address:** c/o Richard Parks Agency, 138 E 16th St No. 5B, New York, NY 10003, U.S.A.

LETNANOVA, Elena. Slovak, b. 1942. **Genres:** Music. **Career:** Piano soloist and accompanist, 1966-74 and 1985-; University of Jan Amos Komensky, Nitra, Czechoslovakia, lecturer to assistant professor, 1968-70; Slovconcert Agency, Bratislava, Czechoslovakia, concert pianist, 1970-74; State Conservatory of Music, Bratislava, professor of music, 1974-75; University of Jan Amos Komensky, Bratislava, assistant professor to associate professor in department of musicology, 1974-84; piano teacher in Rome, Italy, 1984-85; Barnes Constructural Engineers, Arlington, TX, draftsperson, 1985; teacher and concert performer in Texas and Colorado, 1985-87; University of Dayton, Dayton, OH, associate professor of piano and head of piano area, 1987-92; University of Jan Amos Komensky, assistant professor of English, 1992-93; free-lance artist and lecturer, 1993-96; teacher and concert performer. **Publications:** (trans.) Aleksandr I. Solzhenitsyn, Message from Exile, 1979; Piano Interpretation in the Seventeenth, Eighteenth, and Nineteenth Centuries: A Study of Theory and Practice Using Original Documents, 1991. **Address:** c/o Slovak Literary Agency, Partizansk 21, 81351 Bratislava, Slovakia.

LETTS, Billie. American, b. 1938. **Genres:** Novels. **Career:** Southeastern Oklahoma State University, Durant, instructor, 1975-95. **Publications:** Where the Heart Is, 1995; The Honk and Holler Opening Soon, 1998. **Address:** c/o Elaine Markson, Elaine Markson Literary Agency Inc., 44 Greenwich Ave., New York, NY 10011, U.S.A.

LEUPP, Gary P. American, b. 1956. **Genres:** History. **Career:** Tufts University, Medford, MA, assistant professor, 1988-95, associate professor of history, 1995-, adjunct professor of comparative religion, 1998-. **Publications:** Servants, Shophands, and Laborers in the Cities of Tokugawa Japan, 1992; Male Colors: The Construction of Homosexuality in Tokugawa Japan, 1995; Interracial Intimacy in Japan: Western Men and Japanese Women, 1543-1900, 2002. **Address:** Department of History, Tufts University, Medford, MA 02155, U.S.A. **Online address:** gleupp@granite.tufts.edu

LEV, Peter. American, b. 1948. **Genres:** Film. **Career:** University of Texas at Dallas, visiting assistant professor, 1980-82; Towson State University, MD, assistant professor to professor of mass communication, 1983-. **Publications:** Claude Lelouch, Film Director, 1983; The Euro-American Cinema, 1993. Contributor to periodicals. **Address:** Department of Mass Communication, Towson State University, Baltimore, MD 21252, U.S.A.

LEVANDOSKI, Rob. American, b. 1949. **Genres:** Novels. **Career:** Medina County Gazette, Medina, OH, reporter and city editor, 1970-74; Brunswick City Schools, Brunswick, OH, community relations director, 1974-79; Kings Court Communications, Brunswick, OH, editor, 1979-85; Advanstar Communications, Cleveland, OH, managing editor, 1985-93; University of Akron, Department of Continuing Education, Akron, OH, instructor in creative writing, 2000-. **Publications:** NOVELS: Going to Chicago, 1997; Serendipity Green, 2000; Fresh Eggs, 2002. **Address:** 185 West 130th St., Hinckley, OH 44233, U.S.A.

LEVAY, Simon. American (born United Kingdom), b. 1943. **Genres:** Biology, Gay and lesbian issues, Sex, Science fiction/Fantasy, Sciences. **Career:** Harvard Medical School, Boston, MA, 1971-84, assistant professor to associate professor of neurobiology, 1971-84; Salk Institute for Biological Studies, San Diego, CA, associate professor, 1984-92; Institute for Gay and Lesbian Education, West Hollywood, CA, chair of board of directors, 1992-96. University of California, San Diego, adjunct associate professor, 1984-92. **Publications:** The Sexual Brain, 1993; (with E. Nonas) City of Friends, 1995; Queer Science, the Use and Abuse of Research into Homosexuality, 1996; Albrick's Gold (novel), 1997; (with K. Sieh) The Earth in Turmoil,

Earthquakes and Volcanoes and Their Impact on Humankind, 1998; (with D. Koerner) Here Be Dragons, the Scientific Quest for Extraterrestrial Life, 2000.

LEVELT, Willem J(ohannes) M(aria). Dutch, b. 1938. **Genres:** Language/Linguistics, Psychology. **Career:** Harvard University, research fellow, 1965-66; University of Illinois at Urbana-Champaign, visiting professor, 1966-67; University of Groningen, Netherlands, professor of experimental psychology, 1967-71; University of Nijmegen, Netherlands, professor of experimental psychology, 1972-80, professor of psycholinguistics, 1980-; Max Planck Institute for Psycholinguistics, director, 1980-. Royal Netherlands Academy of Arts and Sciences, president, 2002-. **Publications:** On Binocular Rivalry, 1968; Formal Grammars in Linguistics and Psycholinguistics, 3 vols., 1974; Speaking: From Intention to Articulation, 1989. **Address:** Max Planck Institute for Psycholinguistics, Wundtlaan 1, 6525 XD Nijmegen, Netherlands.

LEVENE, Mark. British, b. 1953. **Genres:** History, International relations/Current affairs, Politics/Government, Biography. **Career:** University of Warwick, Coventry, England, lecturer in history, 1988-. Worked in peace movement; worked with young people. **Publications:** War, Jews, and the New Europe: The Diplomacy of Lucien Wolf, 1914-1919, 1992; (ed.) The Massacre in History, 1999. Contributor to professional journals. **Address:** Department of History, Rm 2055, University of Southampton, Highfield, Southampton S017 1BJ, England. **Online address:** M.Levene@sofon.ac.uk

LEVENTHAL, Bennett (L.). American, b. 1949. **Genres:** Psychology, Medicine/Health, Psychiatry. **Career:** Certified in psychiatry and child psychiatry, American Board of Psychiatry and Neurology. Charity Hospital at New Orleans, New Orleans, LA, house officer, 1974; Duke University, Durham, NC, resident in general psychiatry, 1974-78, senior fellow in pediatric psychiatry, 1976-77, chief fellow of division of child psychiatry, 1976-77, chief resident in psychiatry, 1977-78, clinical associate of medical center, 1978-80; University of Chicago, Chicago, IL, assistant professor, 1978-85, associate professor, 1985-90, professor of psychiatry and pediatrics and adjunct professor of psychology and biopsychology, 1990-, John Dewey Lecturer, 1982, associate chairman of department, 1985-, director of child psychiatry clinic, 1978-85, director of child and adolescent psychiatry, 1982-, medical director of child life and family education program, Wyler Children's Hospital, 1983-, director of Harris Center for Developmental Studies, 1983-89, acting director of student mental health service, 1986-87. Chicago Lakeshore Hospital, director of child and adolescent programs, 1986-. Smith College, clinical assistant professor, 1981-83; University of Illinois, visiting professor, 1984. **Publications:** (with N.L. Stein and T. Trabasso) Psychological and Biological Approaches to Emotion, 1990. **Address:** Department of Psychiatry, University of Chicago, 5841 South Maryland Ave, Chicago, IL 60637, U.S.A.

LEVER, (Tresham) Christopher (Arthur Lindsay). British, b. 1932. **Genres:** Antiques/Furnishings, Biology, Environmental sciences/Ecology, History, Natural history, Zoology. **Career:** Naturalist and writer. John Barran and Sons Ltd., director, 1956-64; Chairman, president, patron or trustee of nature conservation and animal welfare organizations. **Publications:** Goldsmiths and Silversmiths of England, 1975; The Naturalized Animals of the British Isles, 1977; Naturalized Mammals of the World, 1985; Naturalized Birds of the World, 1988; The Mandarin Duck, 1990; They Dined on Eland: The Story of the Acclimatisation Societies, 1992; Naturalized Animals: The Ecology of Successfully Introduced Species, 1994; Naturalized Fishes of the World, 1996; The Cane Toad: The History and Ecology of a Successful Colonist, 2001; Naturalized Reptiles and Amphibians of the World, 2003. **Address:** Newell House, Winkfield, Windsor, Berks. SL4 4SE, England.

LEVERE, Trevor H(arvey). Canadian (born England), b. 1944. **Genres:** Sciences, History. **Career:** University of Toronto, Toronto, ON, Canada, assistant professor, 1969-74, associate professor, 1974-81, professor of the history of science, 1981-, director of history of science program, 1981-86, 1993-98; Annals of Science, editor, 1999-. **Publications:** Affinity and Matter, 1971; (with G.L'E. Turner) Martinus Van Marum, Vol IV, 1973; Poetry Realized in Nature: Samuel Taylor Coleridge and Early Nineteenth-Century Science, 1981; Science and the Canadian Arctic: A Century of Exploration, 1818-1918, 1993; Chemists and Chemistry in Nature and Society, 1750-1878, 1994; Transforming Matter: A History of Chemistry, 2001. EDITOR: (with R. Jarrell) A Curious Field-Book, 1973; Editing Texts in the History of Science and Medicine, 1982; (with W. Shea) Nature, Experiment, and the Sciences, 1990. **Address:** Institute for the History & Philosophy of Science & Tech., Victoria College, University of Toronto, 73 Queen's Park Crescent E., Toronto, ON, Canada M5S 1K7.

LEVERT, Liberte E. *See* **BLEILER, Everett F(ranklin).**

LEVESQUE, John. Canadian, b. 1953. **Genres:** Novels, Essays. **Career:** North Bay Nugget, North Bay, Ontario, Canada, reporter, editor, and columnist, 1974-80; Hamilton Spectator, Hamilton, Ontario, Canada, writer, 1981-86, humor columnist, 1984-, film critic, 1986-93; writer. **Publications:** Rosseter's Memory (novel), 1991; Waiting for Aquarius (columns), 1993; Stranded on the Information Highway (columns), 1996; Geneva Farewell (novel), 1998. **Address:** Hamilton Spectator, 44 Frid St., Hamilton, ON, Canada L8N 3G3.

LEVEY, (Sir) Michael (Vincent). British, b. 1927. **Genres:** Novels, Art/Art history, Music. **Career:** Director, National Gallery, London, 1973-86 (Assistant Keeper, 1951-66; Deputy Keeper, 1966-68; Keeper, 1968-73); Slade Professor of Fine Art, Cambridge University, 1963-64; Slade Professor of Fine Art, Oxford University, 1994-95. **Publications:** Painting in XVIIIth Century Venice, 1959, rev. ed., 1994; From Giotto to Cezanne, 1962; Durer, 1964; Later Italian Pictures in the Collection of H. M. the Queen, 1964; Rococo to Revolution, 1966; Early Renaissance, 1967; The Life and Death of Mozart, 1971; Painting at Court, 1971; (with W.W. Kalnein) Art and Architecture of the 18th Century in France, 1972; High Renaissance, 1974; The World of Ottoman Art, 1976; The Case of Walter Pater, 1978; Sir Thomas Lawrence (exhibition catalog), 1979; The Painter Depicted, 1982; Tempting Fate, 1982; An Affair on the Appian Way, 1984; Giambattista Tiepolo, 1986; Men at Work, 1989; The Soul of the Eye (anthology), 1990; Florence, a Portrait, 1996; The Chapel Is on Fire (childhood memoir), 2000. **Address:** 36 Little Lane, Louth, Lincs. LN11 9DU, England.

LEVI, Anthony H. T. See Obituaries.

LEVI, Barbara Goss. American, b. 1943. **Genres:** Physics. **Career:** American Institute of Physics, College Park, MD, assistant editor, 1969-70, consulting editor, 1971-87, associate editor, 1987-88, senior associate editor, 1989-92, senior editor, 1992-. Princeton Unviersity, member of research staff, Center for Energy and Environmental Studies, 1981, 1983-87; Rutgers University, visiting professor, 1988-89. **Publications:** EDITOR: (with M. Sakitt and A. Hobson) Land-Based Strategic Missiles, 1989; (with D. Hafemeister and R. Scribner) Global Warming: Physics and Facts, 1992.

LEVI, Jan Heller. American, b. 1954. **Genres:** Poetry. **Career:** Poet and writer. Dell Publications, New York, NY, assistant editor, 1977-78; personal assistant to poet Muriel Rukeyser, New York, NY, 1978-80; Sarah Lawrence College, Bronxville, NY, director of public relations, 1981-83; ArtForum magazine, associate editor, 1988-90; New York Times, advertising account sales manager, 1990-96; freelance writer and teacher, 1997-. **Publications:** (ed.) A Muriel Rukeyser Reader, 1994; Once I Gazed at You in Wonder: Poems, 1999. Contributor of fiction and poetry to journals. **Address:** c/o University of Pittsburgh Press, Eureka Bldg 5th Fl, 3400 Forbes Ave, Pittsburgh, PA 15260, U.S.A.

LEVIANT, Curt. American. **Genres:** Novels. **Career:** Writer. **Publications:** NOVELS: The Yemenite Girl, 1977; Passion in the Desert, 1980; The Man Who Thought He Was Messiah, 1990; Partita in Venice, 1999; Diary of an Adulterous Woman: Including an ABC Directory That Offers Alphabetical Tidbits and Surprises, 2001; Ladies and Gentlemen, the Original Music of the Hebrew Alphabet, and, Weekend in Mustara: Two Novellas, 2002. EDITOR: (and intro.) Masterpieces of Hebrew Literature: A Treasury of 2,000 Years of Jewish Creativity, 1969. TRANSLATOR: S. Aleichem, From the Fair: The Autobiography of Sholom Aleichem, 1990; S. Aleichem, The Song of Songs, 1996; I.B. Singer, More Stories from My Father's Court, 2000; S. Aleichem, My First Love Affair and Other Stories, 2002. EDITOR & TRANSLATOR: S. Aleichem, Old Country Tales, 1966; (and intro.) S. Aleichem, Some Laughter, Some Tears: Tales from the Old World and the New, 1968; King Artus: A Hebrew Arthurian Romance of 1279, 1969, rev. ed., 2003; Avraham Reisen, The Heart-stirring Sermon: And Other Stories, 1992; Sholom Aleichem, Happy New Year! and Other Stories, 2000. Contributor to periodicals. **Address:** PO Box 1266, Edison, NJ 08818, U.S.A.

LEVIEUX, Eleanor. American, b. 1937. **Genres:** Language/Linguistics, Translations. **Career:** René Julliard (publisher), Paris, France, English adviser, 1960-64; International Chamber of Commerce, Paris, France, translator and editor, 1966-86; British Institute in Paris, Paris, France, assistant professor, 1984-; "Sciences Po" (political science institute), Paris, France, lecturer of English, 1985-88; University of Oregon, Eugene, professor in French department, summers, 1987, 1989-90, 1992-93, 1995, 1998. **Publications:** WITH M. LEVIEUX: Beyond the Dictionary in French, 1967, 7th rev ed as Cassell's Colloquial French, 1981; Année Bac: anglais 83, 1983; Année Bac: anglais 85, 1984; Insiders' French, 1999. TRANSLATOR: (with D. Coltman and P. Knight) Le Corbusier, The Radiant City, 1967; (with F.

Rosset) Sir K. Clark, Léonard de Vinci, 1967; Le Corbusier, The Nursery Schools, 1968; A. Memmi, The Scorpion, 1971; J. Soustelle, The Four Suns, 1971; Le Corbusier, Looking at City Planning, 1972; S. Alexandrian, Man Ray, 1973; S. Alexandrian and P. Waldberg, Max Ernst, 1973; P. Rossi, An Evening in Pisa, 1973; A. Terrasse, Paul Delvaux, 1973; R.F. Bruckberger, God and Politics, 1973; A. Memmi, Jews and Arabs, 1975; P. Gauguin, Oviri, 1977; V. Segalen, The Great Statuary of China, 1978; (with B. Thompson) G. Duby, The Age of the Cathedrals, 1981; C. Derouet, Kandinsky: 1934-44 (catalogue), 1985; J. and M. Guillaud, Rembrandt, 1986; J. and M. Guillaud, Fra Angelico, 1986; D. Abadie, Jean Dubuffet: The First Two Decades, 1986; (with B. Shuey) D. Marchesseau, The Intimate World of Alexander Calder, 1989; (with B. Shuey) J-P. Molinier, Private Gardens in Town, 1991; E. Zola, The Dreyfus Affair: "J'accuse!" and Other Writings, 1996. Contributor to books. **Address:** British Institute in Paris (University of London), 9-11 rue de Constantine, 75340 Paris Cedex 07, France.

LEVI-MONTALCINI, Rita. Italian, b. 1909. **Genres:** Medicine/Health. **Career:** University of Turin, Turin, Italy, assistant professor of anatomy, 1945-47; Washington University, St. Louis, MO, resident associate in Institute of Zoology, 1947-56, associate professor, 1956-58, professor, 1958-77, emeritus professor of neurobiology, 1977-; Institute of Neurobiology, National Research Council, Rome, Italy, founder and director. Nobel Prize for Medicine and Physiology, 1986. **Publications:** Elogio dell'imperfezione (autobiography), 1987, trans by L. Attardi published as In Praise of Imperfection: My Life and Work, 1988; Reti: Scienza, cultura, economia, 1993; Il tuo futurom, 1993. **Address:** CNR, Pizzale Aldo Moro, 7, 00185 Rome, Italy.

LEVIN, Amy K. Indian, b. 1957. **Genres:** Literary criticism and history. **Career:** Scarsdale High School, Scarsdale, NY, English teacher, 1978-80 and 1982-88; University of Colorado, Denver, senior instructor of English, 1989-90; Central Missouri State University, Warrensburg, associate professor of English, coordinator of Women's Studies, 1990-. Ford Foundation fellow at Center for the Study of Black Literature and Culture, University of Pennsylvania, 1992. **Publications:** The Suppressed Sister: A Relationship in Novels by Nineteenth and Twentieth-Century British Women, 1992. **Address:** Department of English, MAR 336, Central Missouri State University, Warrensburg, MO 64093, U.S.A.

LEVIN, Bernard. See Obituaries.

LEVIN, Betty (Lowenthal). American, b. 1927. **Genres:** Children's fiction. **Career:** Member of the faculty, Radcliffe Seminars, Cambridge, MA; also a sheep farmer. Research assistant, Museum of Fine Arts, Boston, 1951-52; part-time teaching fellow, Harvard Graduate School of Education, 1953; creative writing fellow, Radcliffe Institute, 1968-70; Massachusetts coordinator, McCarthy Historical Archive, 1969; instructor, Pine Manor Open College, Chestnut Hill, MA, 1971-75, and Emmanuel College, Boston, 1975; feature writer, Minute Man Publ., Lexington, MA, 1972; adjunct professor, Simmons College, Boston, 1975-87. **Publications:** The Zoo Conspiracy, 1973; The Sword of Culann, 1973; A Griffon's Nest, 1975; The Forespoken, 1976; Landfall, 1979; The Beast on the Brink, 1980; The Keeping Room, 1981; A Binding Spell, 1984; Put on My Crown, 1985; The Ice Bear, 1986; Julia MacRae Books, 1987; The Trouble with Gramary, 1988; Brother Moose, 1990; Mercy's Mill, 1992; Starshine and Sunglow, 1994; Away to Me, Moss, 1994; Fire in the Wind, 1995; Gift Horse, 1996; Island Bound, 1997; Look Back, Moss, 1998; Creature Crossing, 1999; The Banished, 1999; Shadow Catcher, 2000; That'll Do, Moss, 2002; Shoddy Cove, 2003. **Address:** Old Winter St, Lincoln, MA 01773, U.S.A.

LEVIN, Doron P. Israeli, b. 1950. **Genres:** Engineering, Biography. **Career:** St. Petersburg Times, St. Petersburg, Fla., reporter, 1977-81; Wall Street Journal, New York City, reporter in Pittsburgh, Pa., and Detroit, Mich., 1981-87; New York Times, New York City, bureau chief in Detroit, 1988-. Military service: Israel Defense Forces, 1973-76. **Publications:** Irreconcilable Differences: Ross Perot vs. General Motors, 1989; Behind the Wheel at Chrysler, 1995. **Address:** John Farquharson Ltd., 250 West 57th St., New York, NY 10107, U.S.A.

LEVIN, Gerald. American, b. 1929. **Genres:** Speech/Rhetoric, Biography, Literary criticism and history. **Career:** Professor Emeritus of English, University of Akron, Ohio. Instructor, University of Michigan, Ann Arbor, 1955-56; Instructor, University of Colorado, Boulder, 1956-57; Eastern Illinois University, Charleston, 1957-60. **Publications:** Prose Models, 1964, 10th ed. 1996; Brief Handbook of Rhetoric, 1966; The Short Story, 1967; (ed.) The Art of Rhetoric, by Francis Connolly, 1968; (with F. Connolly) Rhetoric Case Book, 1969; Styles for Writing, 1971; Sigmund Freud, 1975;

Short Essays, 1977, 7th ed. 1995; Richardson the Novelist, 1978; Writing and Logic, 1982; Macmillan College Handbook, 1987, 1991; The Educated Reader, 1988.

LEVIN, Igor. American (born Russia), b. 1931. **Genres:** Theatre. **Career:** Scientific researcher, 1954-65; college professor, 1965-75; developer of computer-based systems for aerospace applications, 1978-; writer. **Publications:** ALL WITH I. LEVIN: Methodology of Working on the Play and the Role, 1990; Working on the Play and the Role, 1992; The Stanislavsky Secret, 2002. Contributor to scientific journals. **Address:** 3315 Wisconsin Ave NW Apt. 102, Washington, DC 20016, U.S.A.

LEVIN, Ira. American, b. 1929. **Genres:** Novels, Plays/Screenplays. **Publications:** NOVELS: A Kiss before Dying, 1953; Rosemary's Baby, 1967; This Perfect Day, 1970; The Stepford Wives, 1972; The Boys from Brazil, 1976; Sliver, 1991; Son of Rosemary, 1997. PLAYS: (adapter) No Time for Sergeants, 1956; Critic's Choice, 1961; Veronica's Room, 1974; Deathtrap, 1979; Break a Leg, 1981; Cantorial, 1988. **Address:** Harold Ober Associates Inc, 425 Madison Ave #1D, New York, NY 10017, U.S.A.

LEVIN, Irina. American (born Russia), b. 1937. **Genres:** Theatre. **Career:** Theatre of Drama and Comedy, St. Petersburg, Russia, actress, 1958-73; performer of solo dramatic readings in concert programs, St. Petersburg, 1969-75; Theatre-Studio, St. Petersburg, drama teacher and director, 1970-75 Catholic University of America, Washington, DC, lecturer in acting and scene study, 1981-82; writer. **Publications:** ALL WITH I. LEVIN: Methodology of Working on the Play and the Role, 1990; Working on the Play and the Role, 1992; The Stanislavsky Secret, 2002. **Address:** 3315 Wisconsin Ave NW Apt 102, Washington, DC 20016, U.S.A.

LEVIN, Michael (Graubart). American, b. 1958. **Genres:** Novels, Theology/Religion, Autobiography/Memoirs. **Career:** Columbia Broadcasting System (CBS-TV), New York City, news researcher and writer, 1980-81; University of California, Los Angeles, teacher in Writer's Program, 1991-; writer. Member of Massachusetts bar; Authors Guild Foundation, treasurer, 1993-; Authors Guild, council member, 1994-; Stanchill College, visiting writer, 1993-94. **Publications:** Journey to Tradition: The Odyssey of a Born-again Jew (nonfiction), 1986; The Socratic Method (novel), 1987; Settling the Score (novel), 1989; Alive and Kicking, 1992; Guide to the Jewish Internet, 1996; Writer's Internet Sourcebook, 1997; What Every Jew Needs to Know about God, 1997; Where There's Smoke, There's Salmon, 2001; Complete Idiot's Guide to Jewish Spirituality and Mysticism, 2002; Complete Idiot's Guide to Your Civil Liberties, 2003; (with J. Cateau) Complete Idiot's Guide to the Pentagon, 2003. **Address:** c/o Writer2Author, 4265 Marina City Dr Ste 301, Marina Del Rey, CA 90292, U.S.A.

LEVIN, Michael Eric. American, b. 1943. **Genres:** Sciences, Women's studies and issues. **Career:** City College of the City University of New York, NYC, instructor to professor of philosophy, 1969-. **Publications:** Metaphysics and the Mind-Body Problem, 1979; Feminism and Freedom, 1987; Why Race Matters, 1997; (with L.M. Thomas) Sexual Orientation and Human Rights, 1999. **Address:** Dept of Philosophy, NAC S/144, City College of the City University of New York, Convent Ave at 138th St, New York, NY 10031, U.S.A.

LEVIN, Miriam (Ramsfelder). American, b. 1962. **Genres:** Novels. **Career:** Teacher, social worker, and author. **Publications:** In the Beginning, 1996. Contributor to Bergen Record. **Address:** 42-39 Herold Dr., Fair Lawn, NJ 07410, U.S.A. **Online address:** amejr999@optonline.net

LEVIN, Richard Louis. American, b. 1922. **Genres:** Literary criticism and history. **Career:** State University of New York, Stony Brook, professor of English, 1957-94, Dept. chairman, 1960-63, 1965-66, emeritus, 1994-. Joseph Crabtree Foundation, member, 1971-; advisory committee member, Modern Language Association, and advisory board member, World Center for Shakespeare Studies, both 1974-; member, Academic Council, Shakespeare Globe Theater Center, 1981-. University of Chicago, instructor, 1949-53, assistant professor, 1953-57. American Council of Learned Societies Fellowship, 1963-64; Shakespeare Association of America, trustee, 1977-80; National Endowment for the Humanities Senior Fellowship, 1974; Guggenheim Foundation Fellowship, 1978-79; Fulbright Lectureship, 1984-85; National Humanities Center Fellowship, 1987-88. **Publications:** The Multiple Plot in English Renaissance Drama, 1971; New Readings vs. Old Plays: Recent Trends in the Reinterpretation of English Renaissance Drama, 1979; Looking for an Argument: Critical Encounters with the New Approaches to the Criticism of Shakespeare and His Contemporaries, 2003. EDITOR: Tragedy: Plays, Theory, and Criticism, 1960; The Question of Socrates, 1961; Tragedy:

Alternate Edition, 1965; Thomas Middleton's Michaelmas Term, 1966. **Address:** English Dept, State University of New York, Stony Brook, NY 11794, U.S.A. **Online address:** rlevin@ms.cc.sunysb.edu

LEVIN, Ted. American, b. 1948. **Genres:** Environmental sciences/Ecology. **Career:** New York Zoological Society, Bronx, NY, educator, 1971-72, 1974; Montshire Museum of Science, adjunct naturalist in Norwich, VT, and Hanover, NH, 1977-92. Antioch New England Graduate School, adjunct faculty member, 1976-97; New England College, part-time faculty member, 1978-90; freelance nature photographer. Community of Thetford, VT, justice of the peace, Conservation Commission, 1996-. **Publications:** Backtracking: The Way of a Naturalist, 1987; Blood Brook: A Naturalist's Home Ground, 1992; Everglades National Park, 1995; (with F. Asch) Sawgrass Poems: A View of the Everglades, 1996; Cactus Poems: A View of the Desert, 1998; Songs of the North, 1999; Liquid Land: A Journey through the Florida Everglades, 2003. **Address:** PO Box 117, Thetford, VT 05074, U.S.A. **Online address:** Ted.Levin@valley.net

LEVINE, Alan J. American, b. 1950. **Genres:** History. **Career:** Writer, 1989-. **Publications:** The Soviet Union, the Communist Movement, and the World: Prelude to the Cold War, 1990; The Strategic Bombing of Germany, 1940-1945, 1992; The Missile and Space Race, 1994; The Pacific War, 1995; The United States and the Struggle for Southeast Asia, 1945-1973, 1995; Race Relations within Western Expansion, 1996; The War against Rommel's Supply Lines, 1942-1943, 1999. **Address:** 138-21 77th Ave., Kew Gardens Hills, NY 11367, U.S.A. **Online address:** LMHFL@aol.com

LEVINE, Allan. Canadian, b. 1956. **Genres:** Mystery/Crime/Suspense, History, Biography. **Career:** University of Manitoba, Winnipeg, instructor in education, 1983-84; St. John's-Ravenscourt School, Winnipeg, teacher of history, 1984-. Member of board of directors, Camp Massad, 1986-96; Member of board of directors, Winnipeg Board of Jewish Education, 1995-97. **Publications:** The Exchange: One Hundred Years of Trading Grain in Winnipeg, 1987; (ed. and contrib.) Your Worship: The Lives of Eight of Canada's Most Unforgettable Mayors, 1989; Scrum Wars: The Prime Ministers and the Media, 1993; Fugitives of the Forest: The Heroic Story of Jewish Resistance and Survival during the Second World War, 1998; Scattered among the Peoples: The Jewish Diaspora in Ten Portraits, 2002. HISTORICAL MYSTERIES: The Blood Libel, 1997; Sins of the Suffragette, 2000; The Bolshevik's Revenge, 2002. **Address:** St. Johns-Ravenscourt School, 400 South Dr, Winnipeg, MB, Canada R3T 3K5. **Online address:** levina@sjr.mb.ca

LEVINE, Barbara Hoberman. American, b. 1937. **Genres:** Human relations/Parenting, Inspirational/Motivational Literature, Language/Linguistics, Medicine/Health, Psychology, Self help, Speech/Rhetoric. **Career:** Author/Creative Director, WordsWork Press and Aslan Publishing, Fairfield, CT, owner. **Publications:** Your Body Believes Every Word You Say: The Language of the Body/Mind Connection, 1991, 2nd ed., 2000. **Address:** WordsWork Press and Aslan Publishing, 2490 Black Rock Turnpike No. 342, Fairfield, CT 06824, U.S.A. **Online address:** barbara@aslanpublishing.com; www.aslanpublishing.com

LEVINE, Gail Carson. American, b. 1947. **Genres:** Children's fiction. **Career:** Children's book author. New York State Department of Labor, NYC, employment interviewer, 1970-82; New York State Department of Commerce, NYC, administrative assistant, 1982-86; New York State Department of Social Services, NYC, welfare administrator, 1986-96; New York State Department of Labor, NYC, welfare administrator, 1986-. **Publications:** Ella Enchanted, 1997; Spacenapped (children's musical); The Two Princesses of Bamarre, 2001; Dave at Night, 1999; The Wish, 2000; The Princess Test, 1999; The Fairy's Mistake, 1999; Princess Sonora and the Long Sleep, 1999; Cinderellis and the Glass Hill, 2000; Betsy Who Cried Wolf, 2002; For Biddle's Sake, 2002; The Fairy's Return;, 2002.

LEVINE, Gustav. American, b. 1926. **Genres:** Mathematics/Statistics, Psychology. **Career:** Creedmoor Institute for Psychobiologic Studies, research scientist, 1958-66; Arizona State University, Tempe, associate professor of psychology, 1967-92. **Publications:** (with C.J. Burke) Mathematical Model Techniques for Learning Theories, 1972; Introductory Statistics: The Logic and the Methods, 1981; A Guide to SPSS for Analysis of Variance, 1991; (with S. Parkinson) Experimental Methods in Psychology, 1994. **Address:** 585 Indian Acres Ct, Tucker, GA 30084, U.S.A. **Online address:** guslevine@comcast.net

LEVINE, Jeffrey P. American, b. 1957. **Genres:** Business/Trade/Industry. **Career:** U.S. Department of Labor, Washington, DC, intern budget analyst,

1980-81; Ross Associates, Minneapolis, MN, manufacturer's representative, 1981-82; JPL Enterprises, Minnetonka, MN, owner of import and wholesale company, 1982-87; writer, 1988-. **Publications:** (with T. Crain) Doing Business in NYC, 1989; Doing Business in Chicago, 1990; Doing Business in Boston, 1994, 3rd ed., 1998; Pittsburgh Business Directory, 1995, 3rd ed., 2000; Ingram's Business Directory of Kansas City, 1997; Central Penn Business Directory, 1998, 2nd ed., 2002. **Address:** 10531 Cedar Lake Rd No 512, Minnetonka, MN 55305, U.S.A. **Online address:** jplauthor@hotmail. com

LEVINE, Joel S. American, b. 1942. **Genres:** Air/Space topics. **Career:** National Aeronautics and Space Administration, Langley Research Center, Hampton, VA, senior research scientist in Atmospheric Science Division, 1970-. College of William and Mary, adjunct professor of applied science and physics, 1992-, visiting professor of environmental science and policy, 1997-. Science Museum of Virginia, member of board of trustees, 1987-97. **Publications:** The Photochemistry of Atmosphere: Earth, the Other Planets, and Comets, 1985; Global Biomass Burning: Atmospheric, Climatic, and Biospheric Implications, 1991; Biomass Burning and Global Change, Volumes I-II, 1996. **Address:** Atmospheric Science Division Langley Research Center, National Aeronautics and Space Administration, Hampton, VA 23681, U.S.A. **Online address:** jslevine@widowmaker.com

LEVINE, John R. American, b. 1954. **Genres:** Information science/ Computers. **Career:** Interactive Systems, Boston, MA, 1979-84; Javelin Software, Cambridge, MA, senior engineer, 1984-87; Segue Software, Newton Center, MA, senior engineer, 1988-90, director, 1992-; writer and lecturer. **Publications:** (with M.L. Young and J.M. Young II) Understanding Javelin PLUS, 1987; (with D.C. Kay) Graphics File Formats, 1992; (with M.L. Young) UNIX for Dummies, 1993; (with C. Baroudi) The Internet for Dummies, 1993, 9th ed., 2003; (with M.L. Young) UNIX for Dummies Quick References, 1994; Programming for Graphic Files in C and C++, 1994; Linkers and Loaders, 2000; (with R. Everett-Church and G. Stebben) Internet Privacy for Dummies, 2002; (with R. Everett-Church and M.L. Young) Spam Fighting for Dummies, 2003. **Address:** I.E.C.C., PO Box 727, Trumansburg, NY 14886, U.S.A. **Online address:** writdir@johnlevine.com

LEVINE, Laura (Sue). American, b. 1943. **Genres:** Mystery/Crime/ Suspense. **Career:** Television film script and novel writer. Creator of the characters Count Chocula and Frankenberry for General Mills Cereal Co. **Publications:** (with D. Chodkowski) Mr. Wrong, A Guide to the Least-Eligible Bachelors in America, 1984. JAINE AUSTEN MYSTERY SERIES: This Pen for Hire, 2002; Last Writes, 2003. TELEVISION SCRIPTS (episodic): The Bob Newhart Show; Mary Hartman, Mary Hartman; Three's Company; Laverne and Shirley; The Jeffersons; Good Times. **Address:** c/o Author Mail, Kensington Books, 850 3rd Ave., New York, NY 10022, U.S.A.

LEVINE, Lawrence W(illiam). American, b. 1933. **Genres:** History. **Career:** City College of New York, NYC, lecturer, 1959-61; Princeton University, Princeton, NJ, instructor, 1961-62; University of California, Berkeley, assistant professor, 1962-67, associate professor, 1967-70, professor of history, 1970-84, Margaret Byrne Professor, 1984-. Visiting professor at University of East Anglia, Norwich, England, 1967-68, and Free University of Berlin, West Germany, 1977. **Publications:** Defender of the Faith: William Jennings Bryan; The Last Decade, 1915-1925, 1965; (ed. with R.M. Abrams) The Shaping of Twentieth-Century America: Interpretive Essays, 1965; (ed. with R. Middlekauff) The National Temper: Readings in American Culture and Society, 1968; Black Culture and Black Consciousness: Afro-American Folk Thought from Slavery to Freedom, 1978; Highbrow/ Lowbrow: The Emergence of Cultural Hierarchy in America, 1988. **Address:** Department of History, University of California, Berkeley, CA 94720, U.S.A.

LEVINE, Mortimer. American, b. 1922. **Genres:** History. **Career:** Joint General Ed., Archives of British History and Culture, Conference on British Studies, West Virginia University, since 1967; Member, Advisory Board, The Folger Library Ed. of the Works of Richard Hooker, Harvard University Press, since 1969. Lecturer in History, Brooklyn College, New York, 1954-55; West Virginia University, Morgantown, Instructor, 1955-57, Assistant Professor, 1957-61, Associate Professor, 1961-67, Professor of History, 1967-84, Professor Emeritus, 1984-. **Publications:** The Early Elizabethan Succession Question 1558-1568, 1966; Tudor England 1485-1603 (bibliography), 1968; Tudor Dynastic Problems 1460-1571, 1973. **Address:** 176 Fayette St, Morgantown, WV 26505-5533, U.S.A.

LEVINE, Norman. Canadian, b. 1924. **Genres:** Novels, Novellas/Short stories, Poetry, Travel/Exploration. **Career:** Employed by Dept. of National Defence, Ottawa, 1940-42; Royal Canadian Air Force, 1942-45; Head of

English Dept., Barnstaple Boys Grammar School, Devon, 1953-54; resident Writer, University of New Brunswick, Fredericton, 1965-66. **Publications:** The Tightrope Walker (verse), 1950; The Angled Road, 1952; Canada Made Me, 1958, 1979; One Way Ticket, 1961; (ed.) Canadian Winter's Tales, 1968; From a Seaside Town, 1970; I Don't Want to Know Anyone Too Well: 15 Stories, 1971; Selected Stories, 1975; I Walk by the Harbour, 1976; Thin Ice, 1979; Why Do You Live So Far Away?, 1984; Champagne Barn, 1984; Something Happened Here, 1991; By Frozen River, 2000.

LEVINE, Paul. American, b. 1948. **Genres:** Novels, Mystery/Crime/ Suspense, Plays/Screenplays, Law. **Career:** Miami Herald, FL, reporter, 1969-70; admitted to the Bar of Florida State, 1973, the Bar of U.S. Supreme Court, 1977, the Bar of the District of Columbia, 1978, and the Bar of the Commonwealth of Pennsylvania, 1989; attorney at law firms in Florida, 1973-77; Bartel, Levine & Shuford, FL, trial and appellate attorney and partner, 1977-78; Morgan, Lewis & Bockius, Miami, attorney and partner, 1978-87; Spence, Payne, Masington, Grossman & Needle, Miami, counsel or, 1987-88; Grossman & Roth, Miami, counselor, 1988-91; writer. University of Miami School of Law, adjunct faculty of communications law, 1978-80; You & The Law, creator, writer, and talent, 1978-82; previously legal commentator for WPLG-TV News and AM South Florida; CBS-TV, JAG, executive story editor, 1999-2001, First Monday, co-creator/coexecutive producer, 2002. **Publications:** What's Your Verdict?, 1980; To Speak for the Dead, 1990; Night Vision, 1992; False Dawn, 1993; Mortal Sin, 1994; Slashback, 1995; Fool Me Twice, 1996; Flesh and Bones, 1997; Nine Scorpions, 1998. **Address:** c/o Matt Loze, Course Management, 15159 Greenleaf St, Sherman Oaks, CA 91495, U.S.A. **Online address:** veritas5@ix.netcom.com

LEVINE, Philip. American, b. 1928. **Genres:** Poetry, Essays. **Career:** California State University, Fresno, professor of English, 1958-, now retired. American Academy of Arts & Letters, 1997; Academy of American Poets, chancellor, 2000; American Academy of Arts & Sciences, 2002; New York University, distinguished visiting poet. **Publications:** POETRY: On the Edge, 1963; Not this Pig, 1968; 5 Detroits, 1970; Thistles, 1970; Pili's Wall, 1971; Red Dust, 1971; They Feed They Lion, 1972; 1933, 1974; The Names of the Lost, 1976; Ashes, 1979 (National Book Award); 7 Years from Somewhere, 1979 (National Book Critics Circle Award); One for the Rose, 1981; Selected Poems, 1984; Sweet Will, 1985; (ed.) The Essential Keats, 1987; A Walk with Tom Jefferson, 1988; What Work Is, 1991 (National Book Award); New Selected Poems, 1991; The Simple Truth, 1994 (Pulitzer Prize for Poetry, 1995); The Mercy, 1999; Breath, 2004. ESSAYS: Don't Ask, 1981; The Bread of Time: Toward an Autobiography, 1994; So Ask, 2002. **Address:** 4549 N Van Ness Ave, Fresno, CA 93704, U.S.A.

LEVINE, Stuart George. Also writes as Esteban O'Brien Córdoba. American, b. 1932. **Genres:** Novellas/Short stories, Literary criticism and history. **Career:** University of Kansas, Lawrence, instructor, assistant professor, associate professor, 1958-69, professor, 1969-92, founding chairman, Dept. of American Studies, 1965-70, professor emeritus of English, 1992-. **Publications:** Materials for Technical Writing, 1963; (with N.O. Lurie) The American Indian Today, 1968; (ed.) C. Caffin, The Story of American Painting, 1970; Edgar Poe, Seer and Craftsman, 1972; (ed. with S.F. Levine) The Short Fiction of Edgar Allan Poe, 1975; The Monday-Wednesday-Friday Girl and Other Stories, 1994; (with S.F. Levine) Edgar Allan Poe/32 Stories, 2000; (with S.F. Levine) Eureka, 2004; Poe's Critical Theory: The Major Documents, forthcoming. Author of articles and short stories. **Address:** 1644 University Dr, Lawrence, KS 66044, U.S.A.

LEVINSON, Alan. British, b. 1943. **Genres:** Novellas/Short stories. **Career:** Solicitor of the Supreme Court of England, 1967-. Underwriter for Lloyd's, 1983-. **Publications:** Table for Four (short stories), 1995. **Address:** 9 Old Queen St., London SW1H 9JA, England.

LEVINSON, Harry. American, b. 1922. **Genres:** Administration/ Management, Psychology. **Career:** Chairman, The Levinson Institute, 1968-. Director, Division of Industrial Mental Health, The Menninger Foundation, Topeka, Kansas, 1954-68; Thomas Henry Carroll-Ford Foundation Distinguished Visiting Professor, Harvard Business School, Cambridge, Massachusetts, 1968-72; Clinical Professor, Dept. of Psychiatry, Harvard Medical School, Boston, 1972-92 (Laboratory of Community Psychiatry, 1972-85). **Publications:** (with W.C. Menninger) Human Understanding in Industry, 1956; (ed.) Toward Understanding Men, 2nd ed. 1957; (with C.R. Price, K.J. Munden, H.J. Mandl and C.M. Solley) Men, Management and Mental Health, 1962; Emotional Health: In the World of Work, 1964, 1984; (with P. Tournier, V. Frank, H. Thielicke, P. Lehman and S.H. Miller) Are You Nobody?, 1966; The Exceptional Executive, 1968; Executive Stress, 1969; (with A.G. Spohn and J. Molinari) Organizational Diagnosis, 1972; The Great Jackass Fallacy,

1973; Psychological Man, 1976; (with C. Lang) Executive, 1981; Casebook for Psychological Man, 1982; (with S. Rosenthal) CEO: Corporate Leadership in Action, 1984; (ed.) (with J. Robinson) Ready, Fire, Aim, 1986; Designing and Managing Your Career, 1988; Career Mastery, 1992. **Address:** 4889 Pineview Circle, Delray Beach, FL 33445-4318, U.S.A. **Online address:** hlevinson@worldnet.att.net

LEVINSON, Jay. American/Israeli, b. 1949. **Genres:** Criminology/True Crime, Travel/Exploration. **Career:** U.S. Central Intelligence Agency, 1972-81; Israel Police, 1981-2001; Freelance Writer and Speaker, 2001-. Guest lecturer in forensic science, law enforcement, and terrorism. **Publications:** Questioned Documents: A Lawyer's Handbook, 2000; (with H. Granot) Terror Bombing: The New Urban Threat, 2002; (with H. Granot) Transportation Disaster Response Handbook, 2002; Jewish Community of Cuba Until the Castro Revolution, forthcoming. Contributor to books and professional journals. **Address:** PO Box 23067, 91230 Jerusalem, Israel. **Online address:** Jay_Levinson@hotmail.com

LEVINSON, Jay Conrad. American. **Genres:** Marketing, Business/Trade/Industry. **Career:** Writer. Has taught marketing at University of California-Berkeley; former creative director in Europe for Leo Burnett Advertising; former senior vice-president of J. Walter Thompson, an advertising agency; cofounder of Guerrilla Marketing Inc.; founder of other businesses. **Publications:** Earning Money without a Job: The Economics of Freedom, 1979, rev ed, 1990; 555 Ways to Earn Extra Money, 1982, rev ed as 555 Ways to Earn Extra Money: Revised for the '90s, 1991; Guerrilla Marketing: Secrets for Making Big Profits from Your Small Business, 1984; An Earthling's Guide to Satellite TV, 1985; Quit Your Job: Making the Decision, Making the Break, Making It Work, 1987; Guerrilla Marketing Attack: New Strategies, Tactics, and Weapons for Winning Big Profits from Your Small Business, 1989; Guerrilla Marketing Weapons: One Hundred Affordable Marketing Methods for Maximizing Profits from Your Small Business, 1990; The Ninety-Minute Hour, 1990; (with B.J. Blechman) Guerrilla Financing: Alternative Techniques to Finance Any Small Business, 1991; (with B. Gallagher and O.R. Wilson) Guerrilla Selling: Unconventional Weapons and Tactics for Increasing Your Sales, 1992; Guerrilla Marketing Excellence: The Fifty Golden Rules for Small-Business Success, 1993; Guerrilla Marketing for the '90s: The Newest Secrets for Making Big Profits from Your Small Business, 1993; Guerrilla Advertising: Cost-Effective Techniques for Small-Business Success, 1994; (with S. Godin) The Guerrilla Marketing Handboook, 1994; (with C. Rubin) Guerrilla Marketing Online: The Entrepreneur's Guide to Earning Profits on the Internet, 1995; Guerrilla Marketing for the Home-Based Business, 1995; (with Rubin) Guerrilla Marketing Online Weapons: One Hundred Low-Cost, High-Impact Weapons for Online Profits and Prosperity, 1996; The Way of the Guerrilla: Achieving Success and Balance as an Entrepreneur in the 21st Century, 1996; (with Godin) Get What You Deserve: How to Guerrilla Market Yourself, 1997; (with Wilson and M.S.A. Smith) Guerrilla Trade Show Selling: New Unconventional Weapons and Tactics to Meet More People, Get More Leads, and Close More Sales, 1997; (with Wilson and Smith) Guerrilla Teleselling: New Unconventional Weapons and Tactics to Sell When You Can't Be There in Person, 1998. Columnist for magazines. Contributor to periodicals. **Address:** Guerrilla Marketing International, PO Box 1336, 260 Cascade Dr., Mill Valley, CA 94942, U.S.A.

LEVINSON, Jerrold. American, b. 1948. **Genres:** Essays, Philosophy. **Career:** State University of New York, Albany, NY, assistant professor, 1974-75; University of Maryland, College Park, assistant professor, 1976-81, associate professor, 1981-91, professor, 1991-. Visiting professor: University of London, 1991, Johns Hopkins University, 1993, Universite de Rennes, 1998, Columbia University, 2000; National Endowment for Humanities, summer institute, co-director, 1991, director, 2000. **Publications:** Music, Art, and Metaphysics (essays), 1990; The Pleasures of Aesthetics (essays), 1996; Music in the Moment (monograph), 1998; (ed.) Aesthetics and Ethics (essays), 1998; (co-ed.) Aesthetic Concepts (essays), 2000; (ed.) Oxford Handbook of Aesthetics, 2002. **Address:** Department of Philosophy, Skinner Building, University of Maryland, College Park, MD 20742, U.S.A.

LEVITIN, Sonia (Wolff). Also writes as Sonia Wolff. American (born Germany), b. 1934. **Genres:** Novels, Children's fiction. **Career:** Instructor, University of California, Los Angeles Extension prog., 1976-. Teacher, Writer's Program, Palos Verdes Peninsula, CA, 1978- (creative writing teacher, 1973-76). Elementary sch. teacher, Mill Valley, CA, 1956-57; adult education teacher, Daly City, CA, 1962-64, and Acalanes Adult Center, Lafayette, CA, 1965-72. **Publications:** Journey to America, 1970; Rita the Weekend Rat, 1971; Roanoke: A Novel of the Lost Colony, 1973; Who Owns the Moon?, 1973; Jason and the Money Tree, 1974; A Single Speckled

Egg, 1975; The Mark of Conte, 1976; Beyond Another Door, 1977; Reigning Cats and Dogs (novel), 1978; The No-Return Trail, 1978; A Sound to Remember, 1979; Nobody Stole the Pie, 1980; The Fisherman and the Bird, 1982; All the Cats in the World, 1982; (as Sonia Wolff) What They Did to Miss Lily (novel), 1982; The Year of Sweet Senior Insanity, 1982; Smile Like a Plastic Daisy, 1984; A Season of Unicorns, 1986; The Return, 1987; Incident at Loring Groves, 1988; Silver Days, 1989; The Man Who Kept His Heart in a Bucket, 1992; Annie's Promise, 1993; The Golem and the Dragon Girl, 1993; Adam's War, 1994; Escape from Egypt, 1994; Evil Encounter, 1996; Nine for California, 1996; A Piece of Home, 1996; Yesterday's Child, 1997; Boomtown, 1997; The Singing Mountain, 1998; The Cure, 1999; Taking Charge, 1999; Dream Freedom, 2000; Clem's Chances, 2001; When Elephant Goes to a Party, 2001; When Kangaroo Goes to School, 2001; Room in the Heart, 2003.

LEVOY, Myron. American, b. 1930. **Genres:** Novels, Children's fiction, Novellas/Short stories, Young adult fiction. **Publications:** A Necktie in Greenwich Village (novel), 1968; Penny Tunes and Princesses, 1972; The Witch of Fourth Street and Other Stories, 1972; Alan and Naomi, 1977; A Shadow Like a Leopard, 1981; Three Friends, 1984; The Hanukkah of Great-Uncle Otto, 1984; Pictures of Adam, 1986; The Magic Hat of Mortimer Wintergreen, 1988; Kelly 'N' Me, 1992; Eine Liebe in Schwarz-Weiss, 1999. **Address:** c/o Susan Cohen, Writers House Inc, 21 W 26th St, New York, NY 10010, U.S.A.

LEVY, Adrian. British, b. 1965. **Genres:** History. **Career:** Freelance writer, documentary film maker, and broadcaster. Sunday Times, London, investigative reporter to foreign correspondent; formerly theater director and theater reviewer. **Publications:** (with C. Scott-Clark) The Stone of Heaven: Unearthing the Secret History of Imperial Green Jade, 2002. **Address:** c/o Author Mail, Little Brown and Company, 1271 Avenue of the Americas, New York, NY 10020, U.S.A.

LEVY, Andrew (Gordon). American, b. 1962. **Genres:** Literary criticism and history. **Career:** Edgewood Teleservices, Plainsboro, NJ, systems analyst and software designer, 1984-86; Philadelphia College of Pharmacy and Science (now University of the Sciences), Philadelphia, PA, adjunct professor, 1989-92; Butler University, Indianapolis, IN, assistant professor, 1992-96, associate professor, 1996-, Edna Cooper Professor of English, 1998-, codirector of Writers' Studio, 1993-95 and 1997-, director of Fellows Program at Writers' Studio, 1993-. Speaker at colleges and universities. **Publications:** The Culture and Commerce of the American Short Story (monograph), 1993; (with F. Leebron) Creating Fiction: A Writer's Companion, 1995; (with Leebron and P. Geyh) Postmodern American Fiction: A Norton Anthology, 1997. Contributor to books. Contributor of stories, articles, and reviews to periodicals. **Address:** Department of English, Butler University, Indianapolis, IN 46208, U.S.A. **Online address:** alevy@butler.edu

LEVY, Barrie. American. **Genres:** Human relations/Parenting. **Career:** Therapist, consultant, and nonfiction author. **Publications:** NONFICTION: Skills for Violence-Free Relationships: Curriculum for Young People, Ages 13-18, 1984; (ed.) Dating Violence: Young Women in Danger, 1991; In Love and in Danger: A Teen's Guide to Breaking Free of Abusive Relationships, 1993; (with P.O. Giggans) What Parents Need to Know about Dating Violence, 1995; (with Giggans) 50 Ways to a Safer World, 1997. **Address:** c/o Seal Press, PMB 375, 300 Queen Anne Ave N, Seattle, WA 98109-4512, U.S.A.

LEVY, Constance. American, b. 1931. **Genres:** Poetry. **Career:** Webster Groves School District, Webster Groves, MO, teacher, 1952-53; Ritenour School District, St. Louis, MO, teacher, 1953-54; Washington University, St. Louis, MO, supervisor of student teachers, 1974-75; Missouri Arts Council, Writers in the Schools program, St. Louis, children's poet, 1975-81; Harris-Stowe State College, St. Louis, MO, adjunct instructor of children's literature, 1980-82. Freelance poet in schools, 1981-92; guest speaker in schools and educational conferences, 1991-. **Publications:** I'm Going to Pet a Worm Today and Other Poems, 1991; A Tree Place and Other Poems, 1994; When Whales Exhale, and Other Poems, 1996; A Crack in the Clouds and Other Poems, 1998; Splash!: Poems of Our Watery World, 2002; The Story of Red Rubber Ball, in press. Contributor to periodicals and anthologies. **Address:** 58 Frontenac Estates, St. Louis, MO 63131, U.S.A.

LEVY, Daniel S. American, b. 1959. **Genres:** Biography. **Career:** Writer. Time Magazine, NYC, staff reporter. **Publications:** Two-Gun Cohen: A Biography, 1997. Contributor to periodicals. **Address:** c/o Time Magazine, 1271 Avenue of the Americas, New York, NY 10020, U.S.A.

LEVY, David H. Canadian, b. 1948. **Genres:** Astronomy. **Career:** Writer, speaker, and amateur astronomer. University of Arizona, Tucson, instructional specialist, 1992-93, senior instructional specialist, 1993-97; Parade, science editor, 1997-. Planetary Science Institute, observer, 1982-92; International Halley Watch, assistant discipline specialist, 1985-89; Palomar Asteroid and Comet Survey, observer, 1989-96; Flandrau Science Center, Tucson, AZ, adjunct scientist and member of senior advisory board, 1991-. Cohost of weekly radio show Let's Talk Stars. **Publications:** The Joy of Gazing, 1982; The Universe for Children: How Astronomy-minded Adults Can Teach Children to Love the Sky, 1985; Observing Variable Stars: A Guide for the Beginner, 1989; The Sky: A User's Guide, 1991; Clyde Tombaugh: Discoverer of Planet Pluto, 1991; The Man Who Sold the Milky Way: A Biography of Bart Bok, 1993; The Quest for Comets: An Explosive Trail of Beauty and Danger, 1994; Skywatching, 1994; Impact Jupiter: The Crash of Comet Shoemaker-Levy 9, 1995; Stars and Planets, 1995; More Things in Heaven and Earth: Poets and Astronomers Read the Night Sky, 1997; Comets: Creators and Destroyers, 1998; Observing Variable Stars: A Guide for the Beginner, 1998; An Encyclopedia of the Universe, 1998; Shoemaker by Levy: The Man Who Made an Impact, 2000; (ed.) The Scientific American Book of the Cosmos, 2000; Starry Night: Astronomers and Poets Read the Sky, 2001; David Levy's Guide to the Night Sky, 2001. WITH OTHERS: (with S.J. Edberg) Observe-Comets, 1985; (with S.J. Edberg) Observe-Meteors, 1986; (with G.E. Tomlinson and R. Horgan) Astronomy Day: Bringing Astronomy to the People, 1993; (with T.B. Hunter) Medical Devices, Abbreviations, Acronyms, and Eponyms: A Pocket Guide, 1993; Comet Shoemaker-Levy 9 Slide Set, 1994; (with S.J. Edberg) An Observing Guide for Comets, Asteroids, Meteors, and Zodiacal Light, 1995; (with G. Bridges) Stars and Planets, 1996; (with L.A. Lebofsky and N.R. Lebofsky) Sharing the Sky: A Parent's and Teacher's Guide to Astronomy, 1997; (with S.J. O'Meara) Deep-Sky Companions: The Messier Object, 2000; (with W. Wallach-Levy), Exploring the Universe with Our Children: A Guide for Teachers and Parents, 2001; (with W. Wallach-Levy) Cosmic Discoveries: The Wonders of Astronomy, 2001. Contributor to books. Author of forewords for books. Author of columns. Contributor to periodicals. **Address:** c/o Prometheus Books, 59 John Glenn Drive, Amherst, NY 14228, U.S.A.

LEVY, Deborah. South African, b. 1959. **Genres:** Plays/Screenplays, Novels, Novellas/Short stories. **Career:** Playwright, novelist, and short story writer. **Publications:** PLAYS: Pax, 1984; Clam, 1985; Our Lady, 1986; Heresies and Eva and Moses: Two Plays, 1987. NOVELS: Beautiful Mutants, 1989; Swallowing Geography, 1993; The Unloved, 1994; Billy and Girl, 1999. OTHER: Ophelia and the Great Idea (short stories), 1988. **Address:** c/o George Capel, Simpson Fox, 52 Shaftesbury Ave., London W1V 7DE, England.

LEVY, Elizabeth. American, b. 1942. **Genres:** Children's fiction. **Career:** Writer since 1971. ABC, NYC, editor and researcher in news department, 1964-66; Macmillan Publishing Co., NYC, assistant editor, 1967-69; New York Public Library, NYC, writer in public relations, 1969; JPM Associates (urban affairs consultants), NYC, staff writer, 1970-71. **Publications:** FOR CHILDREN. FICTION: Nice Little Girls, 1974; Lizzie Lies a Lot, 1976; Frankenstein Moved in on the Fourth Floor, 1979; The Tryouts, 1979; Dracula Is a Pain in the Neck, 1980; Running Out of Time, 1980; Running Out of Magic with Houdini, 1981; The Computer that Said Steal Me, 1983; The Shadow Nose, 1983; Keep Ms. Sugarman in the Fourth Grade, 1992; Cheater, Cheater, 1993; Gorgonzola Zombies in the Park, 1993; Cleo and the Coyote, 1996; Wolfman Sam, 1996; My Life as a Fifth-Grade Comedian, 1997; Third Grade Bullies, 1998. SOMETHING QUEER MYSTERY SERIES: Something Queer Is Going On, 1973; Something Queer at the Ballpark, 1975; Something Queer at the Library, 1977; Something Queer on Vacation, 1980; Something Queer at the Haunted School, 1982; Something Queer at the Lemonade Stand, 1982; Something Queer in Rock 'n' Roll, 1987; Something Queer at the Birthday Party, 1990; Something Queer in Outer Space, 1993; Something Queer in the Cafeteria, 1994; Something Queer at the Scary Movie, 1995; Something Queer in the Wild West, 1997; Something Queer Under the Sea, 1999. MAGIC MYSTERIES SERIES: The Case of the Gobbling Squash, 1988; The Case of the Mind-Reading Mommies, 1989; The Case of the Tattletale Heart, 1990; The Case of the Dummy with Cold Eyes, 1991. THE GYMNASTS SERIES: The Beginners, 1988; First Meet, 1988; Nobody's Perfect, 1988; The Winner, 1989; Trouble in the Gym, 1989; Bad Break, 1989; Tumbling Ghosts, 1989; Captain of the Team, 1989; Crush on the Coach, 1990; Boys in the Gym, 1990; Mystery at the Meet, 1990; Out of Control, 1990; First Date, 1990; World Class Gymnast, 1990; Nasty Competition, 1991; Fear of Falling, 1991; Gymnasts Commandos, 1991; The New Coach, 1991; Tough at the Top, 1991; The Gymnast Gift, 1991; Go for the Gold, 1992; Team Trouble, 1992. BRIAN AND PEA BRAIN SERIES: Rude Rowdy Rumors, 1994; School Spirit Sabotage, 1994; A Mammoth Mix-Up, 1995. INVISIBLE INC. SERIES: The Schoolyard

Mystery, 1994; The Mystery of the Missing Dog, 1995; The Snack Attack Mystery, 1995; The Creepy Computer Mystery, 1996; The Karate Class Mystery, 1996; Parents' Night Fright, 1998. FOR YOUNG ADULTS. FICTION: Come Out Smiling, 1981; Double Standard, 1984; The Dani Trap, 1984; Night of Nights, 1984; All Shook Up, 1986; Cold as Ice, 1988; The Drowned, 1995. JODY AND JAKE MYSTERY SERIES: The Case of the Frightened Rock Star, 1980; The Case of the Counterfeit Race Horse, 1980; The Case of the Fired-Up Gang, 1981; The Case of the Wild River Ride, 1981; The Case of the Mile High Race, 1982. NONFICTION: The People Lobby: The SST Story, 1973; Lawyers for the People, 1974; By-Lines: Profiles in Investigative Journalism, 1975; (with R.H. Harris) Before You Were Three: How You Began to Walk, Talk, Explore, and Have Feelings, 1977; (with M. Miller) Doctors for the People: Profiles of Six Who Serve, 1977; (with E. & L. Hammond) Elephants in the Living Room, Bears in the Canoe: The Story of the Incredible Family Who Raise and Train Wild Animals in Their Home, 1977; (with T. Richards) Struggle and Lose, Struggle and Win: The United Mineworkers Story, 1977; (with E. & L. Hammond) Our Animal Kingdom, 1977; Politicians for the People: Six Who Stand for Change, 1979; If You Were There When They Signed the Constitution, 1987. PLAYS: Croon (one-act), 1976; Never Waste a Virgin (two-act), 1977; Lizzie Lies a Lot, 1978. OTHER: Marco Polo: The Historic Adventure Based on the Television Spectacular, 1982; Father Murphy's First Miracle, 1983; Return of the Jedi, 1983; A Different Twist, 1984; The Bride, 1985. FAT ALBERT AND THE COSBY KIDS SERIES: The Shuttered Window, 1981; Mister Big Time, 1981; Take Two, They're Small, 1981; Spare the Rod, 1981; Mom or Pop, 1981; The Runt, 1981. **Address:** 344 West 23rd Street, New York, NY 10011, U.S.A. **Online address:** LizMys@aol.com.

LEVY, Harry. American, b. 1944. **Genres:** Human relations/Parenting. **Career:** Physician, author, editor. PES Inc., NYC, founder and president, 1977-90; Health Opinion Research Inc., NYC, founder and president, 1984-91; Cyberounds, http://www.cyberounds.com, executive editor, 1996-. **Publications:** (with D. Caplovitz) Interreligious Dating Among College Students, 1966; Chain of Custody, 1998. Producer of film short and feature documentaries. **Address:** c/o Random House Publicity, 1745 Broadway #B1, New York, NY 10019-4305, U.S.A. **Online address:** levy@cyberounds.com

LEVY, Helen Fiddyment. American, b. 1937. **Genres:** Literary criticism and history. **Career:** University of Michigan, Ann Arbor, assistant director of Honors Program, 1982-85; George Mason University, Fairfax, VA, instructor in English, 1987-. Volunteer at mental health facilities and for political causes. **Publications:** Fiction of the Home Place, University Press of Mississippi, 1992. Contributor to scholarly journals. **Address:** Department of English, Mail Stop 3E4, George Mason University, 4400 University Dr., Fairfax, VA 22030, U.S.A.

LEVY, Jefery. American, b. 1958. **Genres:** Plays/Screenplays. **Career:** Director, producer, and screenwriter. University of Southern California, Los Angeles, professor of film. **Publications:** SCREENPLAYS: (with L. Bercovici) Ghoulies, 1985; (with L. Bercovici and C. Ver Wiel) Rockula, 1990; Drive, 1991; (with D. Rubin) S.F.W., 1994; Et tu Babe, 1998. MADE-FOR-TELEVISION MOVIES: The Chain, 1996; (with D. Bell and T. Raimi) Iggy Vile, M.D., 1999; (with M. Brandt and D. Haas) Invincible, 2001. **Address:** 9031 Hollywood Hills Rd., Los Angeles, CA 90046, U.S.A.

LEVY, Jill Meryl. American. **Genres:** Writing/Journalism, Reference. **Career:** Firebelle Productions, Campbell, CA, owner. Santa Clara County Fire Department, volunteer firefighter, 1980-. **Publications:** The First Responder's Pocket Guide to Hazardous Materials Emergency Response, 1996, 3rd ed. as The First Responder's Pocket Guide to Hazmat & Terrorism Emergency Response, 2003; Take Command of Your Writing, 1998;Hazmat Chemistry Study Guide, 2002;. **Address:** Firebelle Productions, 2 Timber Cove Dr, Campbell, CA 95008, U.S.A. **Online address:** jill@firebelleproductions.com

LEVY, JoAnn. American, b. 1941. **Genres:** Novels, History, Women's studies and issues, Biography. **Career:** Writer. Worked as editor and contributor to magazines. Frequent public speaker. **Publications:** Behind the Western Skyline, 1981; They Saw the Elephant: Women in the California Gold Rush, 1990; Unsettling the West: Eliza Farnham and Georgiana Kirby in Frontier California (biography), 2004. NOVELS: Daughter of Joy, 1998; For California's Gold, 2000. **Address:** PO Box 1809, Sutter Creek, CA 95685, U.S.A. **Online address:** joann@goldrush.com

LEVY, Leonard W(illiams). American (born Canada), b. 1923. **Genres:** History, Law, Politics/Government. **Career:** Andrew W. Mellon All-Claremont Professor Emeritus of Humanities, Claremont Graduate School, California, 1990- (William W. Clary Professor of History, 1970-74; Mellon

Professor and chairman, Graduate Faculty of History, 1974-90). Research assistant, Columbia University, NYC, 1950-51; member of faculty, Brandeis University, Waltham, MA, 1951-70 (Earl Warren Professor of American Constitutional History, 1958-70, dean of Graduate School of Arts and Sciences, 1958-63; dean of Faculty, 1963-66; chairman, Dept. of History, 1963-64, 1967-68; chairman, Graduate Program in the History of American Civilization, 1966-67, 1969-70). **Publications:** Law of the Commonwealth and Chief Justice Shaw, 1957; Legacy of Suppression, 1960; Jefferson and Civil Liberties, 1963; Origins of the Fifth Amendment, 1968 (Pulitzer Prize in History, 1969); Judgments: Essays on Constitutional History, 1972; Against the Law: The Nixon Court and Criminal Justice, 1974; Treason against God, 1981; Emergence of a Free Press, 1985; Constitutional Opinions, 1986; The Establishment Clause, 1986, rev, ed., 1994; Original Intent and the Framers' Constitution, 1990; Supplement I to Encyclopedia of American Constitution, 1992; Blasphemy: Verbal Offense against the Sacred, 1993; Encyclopedia of the American Presidency, 4 vols., 1993; Seasoned Judgments, 1994; A License to Steal, 1996; Origins of the Bill of Rights, 1999; Palladium of Justice, 1999; Ranters Run Amok, 2000; A Bookish Life, 2003; Aspects of Liberty, 2004; Facets of Freedom, 2004; A History of the Fourth Amendment, 2004. EDITOR: (with M.D. Peterson) Major Crises in American History, 1963; (with J.P. Roche) The American Political Process, 1963; (with Roche) The Presidency, 1964; (with Roche) The Congress, 1964; (with Roche) The Judiciary, 1964; (with Roche) Political Parties and Pressure Groups, 1964; Freedom of Press from Zenger to Jefferson, 1966; American Constitutional Law, 1966; Judicial Review and the Supreme Court, 1967; (co-) Freedom and Reform, 1967; Essays on the Making of the Constitution, 1969; The 14th Amendment and the Bill of Rights, 1971; The Supreme Court under Warren, 1972; Blasphemy in Massachusetts, 1973; Jim Crow Education, 1974; Essays on the Early Republic, 1974; (in-chief) Encyclopedia of the American Constitution, 4 vols., 1986. **Address:** 1025 Timberline Terr, Ashland, OR 97520, U.S.A.

LEVY, Marc. French, b. 1961. **Genres:** Novels. **Career:** Author. Former chief executive officer of architectural design firm in France. **Publications:** Et si c'était vrai, 1999, trans. as If Only It Were True, 2000. **Address:** c/o Publicity Director, Pocket Books, 100 Front St., Riverside, NJ 08075, U.S.A.

LEVY, Matthys. American (born Switzerland), b. 1929. **Genres:** Architecture, Children's non-fiction, Earth sciences, Engineering, Sciences. **Career:** Weidlinger Associates, NYC, principal, 1953-. Columbia University, adjunct professor of architecture, 1962-82. **Publications:** Structural Design in Architecture, 1967, 2nd ed., 1981; Why Buildings Fall Down, 1992, 2nd ed., 2002; Why the Earth Quakes, 1995; Earthquake Games, 1997; Engineering the City, 2000. **Address:** 40 College St Apt 702, Burlington, VT 05401-7316, U.S.A. **Online address:** levy@wai.com

LEVY, Peter B. American, b. 1956. **Genres:** History. **Career:** Rutgers University, Newark Campus, Newark, NJ, visiting assistant professor of history, 1986-88; York College, York, PA, associate professor of history, 1989-. **Publications:** (ed.) Let Freedom Ring: A Documentary History of the Modern Civil Rights Movement, 1992; The New Left and Labor in the 1960s, 1994; Encyclopedia of the Reagan-Bush Years, 1996; The Civil Rights Movement, 1998; America in the Sixties: Right, Left, and Center, in press. **Address:** Department of History, York College, York, PA 17405, U.S.A. **Online address:** plevy@ycp.edu

LEVY, Steven. American, b. 1951. **Genres:** Information science/Computers. **Career:** Freelance writer, critic, and publisher, 1975-. Columnist, MacWorld, 1985-; contributing writer, Wired, 1993-. Fellow, Freedom Forum Media Studies Center, 1994-95. **Publications:** Hackers: Heroes of the Computer Revolution, 1984; The Unicorn's Secret: Murder in the Age of Aquarius, 1988; Artificial Life: The Quest for a New Creation, 1992; Insanely Great: The Life and Times of Macintosh, the Computer That Changed Everything, 1994; Crypto: How the Code Rebels Beat the Government, 2000. Contributor to periodicals. **Address:** Columbia University, Freedom Forum Media Studies Center, 2950 Broadway, New York, NY 10026, U.S.A.

LEWES, Darby. American, b. 1946. **Genres:** Literary criticism and history. **Career:** Saint Xavier University, Chicago, IL, lecturer in English, 1986-90; University of Chicago, Chicago, instructor in literature, 1991-93; Lycoming College, Williamsport, PA, associate professor of English, 1993-. Loyola University of Chicago, lecturer, 1991-92, visiting assistant professor, 1992-93. **Publications:** Dream Revisionaries: Genre and Gender in Women's Utopian Fiction, 1870-1920, 1995; Nudes from Nowhere, 2000; A Brighter Morn, 2003. Contributor to periodicals. **Address:** Department of English, Lycoming College, Williamsport, PA 17701, U.S.A. **Online address:** lewes@lycoming.edu

LEWIECKI-WILSON, Cynthia. American, b. 1948. **Genres:** Literary criticism and history. **Career:** Miami University Middletown, Middletown, OH, assistant professor of English and affiliate of Women's Studies Program, 1990-. **Publications:** Writing Against the Family: Gender in Lawrence and Joyce, 1994; (with J. Sommers) From Community to College: Reading and Writing Across Diverse Contexts, 1995. **Address:** Miami University Middletown, 4200 East University Blvd., Middletown, OH 45042, U.S.A.

LEWIN, Michael Z. American/British (born United States), b. 1942. **Genres:** Novellas/Short stories, Mystery/Crime/Suspense, Plays/Screenplays. **Career:** High school science teacher, USA, 1966-69. **Publications:** How to Beat College Tests, 1970; Ask the Right Question, 1971; The Way We Die Now, 1973; The Enemies Within, 1974; The Next Man, 1975; Night Cover, 1976; The Silent Salesman, 1978; Outside In, 1980; Missing Woman, 1981; Hard Line, 1982; Out of Season (in U.K. as Out of Time), 1984; Late Payments, 1986; And Baby Will Fall (in U.K. as Child Proof), 1988; Called by a Panther, 1991; Underdog, 1993; (co-ed.) 1st Culprit, 1992; 2nd Culprit, 1993; 3rd Culprit, 1994; Telling Tails, 1994; Family Business, 1995; Rover's Tales, 1998; Cutting Loose, 1999; Family Planning, 1999; The Reluctant Detective and Other Stories, 2001; Eye Opener, 2004. **Address:** 15 Bladud Buildings, Bath BA1 5LS, England.

LEWIN, Moshe. French/American (born Poland), b. 1921. **Genres:** History, Politics/Government. **Career:** Professor of History, University of Pennsylvania, Philadelphia, 1978-. Director of Studies, Ecole Pratique des Hautes Etudes, Paris, 1965 and 1966; Sr. Fellow, Russian Institute, Columbia University, NYC, 1967-68; Professor in Soviet History and Politics, Centre for Russian and E. European Studies, University of Birmingham, 1968-78; member, Institute for Advanced Study, Princeton, New Jersey, 1972-73. **Publications:** Russian Peasant and Soviet Power, 1928-1930, 1966; Lenin's Last Struggle, 1967; Political Undercurrent in Soviet Economic Debates: From Bukharin to Modern Reformers, 1974; The Making of the Soviet System, 1985; The Gorbachev Phenomenon, 1988; Russia-USSR-Russia, 1994; (with I. Kershaw) Stalinism and Nazism-Dictatorships in Comparison, 1997; The Soviet Century, 2002. **Address:** Dept of History, 208 College Hall, University of Pennsylvania, Philadelphia, PA 19104, U.S.A.

LEWIN, Rhoda G. American, b. 1929. **Genres:** History, Literary criticism and history, Local history/Rural topics, Race relations, Writing/Journalism. **Career:** Free-lance writer and editor, 1956-; University of Minnesota Extension Division, instructor in communications, humanities, and creative writing, 1964-83; lecturer on Jewish, Holocaust, and oral history; book reviewer for Oral History Review and The Public Historian; American Jewish World, articles and column, "Around the Town," 1988-98; University of Minnesota, Elder Learning Institute, teacher, 2002-. **Publications:** Security: Everything You Need to Know about Household Alarm Systems, 1982; Witnesses to the Holocaust: An Oral History, 1990; Images of America: Jews of North Minneapolis, 2001; Reform Jews of Minneapolis, 2004. **Address:** 1200 Nicollet Mall #201, Minneapolis, MN 55403-2410, U.S.A. **Online address:** TRLewin@aol.com

LEWIN, Roger A. American, b. 1946. **Genres:** Psychology, Human relations/Parenting. **Career:** Sheppard and Enoch Pratt Hospital, Towson, MD, resident, 198185, psychiatrist, 1985-91, teacher and supervisor, 1991-. Private practice of psychiatry, Towson, 1981-. Harvard Volunteer Teachers for Africa, volunteer teacher in Tanzania at a training college for political leaders and at Kivukoni College in Dar es Salaam, 1967-69; Building Systems Inc., housing developer; conducted field work in Bahia, Brazil. Teacher and later director of a Quaker school in Cleveland, OH. **Publications:** (with C. Schutz) Losing and Fusing, 1992; Compassion, 1996; New Wrinkles (poems), 1996; Creative Collaboration in Psychotherapy, 1997. Contributor of the chapter "The Prospects for Ujamaa Villages" to Self-Reliant Tanzania; author of Why Produce?, a workbook for American high school students designed to engage them in thinking about Tanzanian social, political, and economic realities. **Address:** 139 Gibson Bldg., 652S North Charles, Towson, MD 21204, U.S.A. **Online address:** oaktree@home.com

LEWIS, Adrian R. American, b. 1952. **Genres:** Military/Defense/Arms control. **Career:** U.S. Army, Infantry, career officer, 1977-94 (retiring as major), including assignments as rifle platoon leader, support platoon leader, and company commander, assistant professor of military and American history at U.S. Military Academy, West Point, NY, 1987-90, course group director, 1990-91; University of California-Berkeley, Berkeley, CA, assistant professor, 1991-93, professor of military science and department chair, 1993-94; University of North Texas-Denton, associate professor of military history, 1995-, honor professor, 2000-01. Organizer and leader of tours of European battlefields and historic sites, 1988, 1989, and 1990; consultant to Encyclopaedia Britannica and to local area television and radio stations. **Publications:** Omaha Beach: A Flawed Victory, 2001. Contributor to books. Contributor of articles and reviews to journals. **Address:** Dept of History, University of North Texas, PO Box 310650, Denton, TX 76203-0650, U.S.A. **Online address:** alewis@unt.edu

LEWIS, Arnold. American, b. 1930. **Genres:** Architecture. **Career:** Educator and art historian. Wells College, Aurora, NY, 1962-64; College of Wooster, Wooster, OH, professor, 1964-96, professor emeritus of art history, 1996-. **Publications:** (ed.) Wooster in 1876, 1976; American Victorian Architecture: A Survey of the 70's and 80's in Contemporary Photographs, 1975; American Country Houses of the Gilded Age (Sheldon's Artistic Country Seats), 1982; Opulent Interiors and the Gilded Age (Sheldon's Artistic Houses), 1987; An Early Encounter with Tomorrow: Europeans, Chicago's Loop, and the World's Columbian Exposition, 1997. **Address:** 614 Kieffer St, Wooster, OH 44691, U.S.A. **Online address:** alewis@wooster.edu

LEWIS, Carol F. Ra. Also writes as Carol F. Ra. American, b. 1939. **Genres:** Poetry, Children's non-fiction. **Career:** Richmond City Schools, Richmond, IN, elementary school teacher, 1961-62; Vigo County Schools, Terre Haute, IN, elementary school teacher, 1962-64; Champaign Unit 4 Schools, Champaign, IN, teacher of gifted children, 1964-68; St. James Episcopal, Roanoke, VA, preschool director, 1973-74; Hollins College, Roanoke, lecturer in early childhood education and children's literature, 1974-; Herald News, Cayuga, IN, columnist, 1990-. **Publications:** AS CAROL F. RA: Trot, Trot to Boston: Play Rhymes for Baby, 1987; (with W.J. Smith) Behind the King's Kitchen: A Roster of Rhyming Riddles, 1992; (with Smith) The Sun Is Up, 1993. Contributor of poetry to literary magazines. Contributor to books. **Address:** 3654 W Mecca Rd, Rockville, IN 47872, U.S.A.

LEWIS, (Norman) Douglas. Welsh, b. 1940. **Genres:** Law, Politics/Government, Civil liberties/Human rights, Public/Social administration, Regional/Urban planning. **Career:** Called to the Bar at Lincoln's Inn, 1966; University of Sheffield, Sheffield, England, professor of public law, 1978-. **Publications:** (with B. Gateshill) The Comission for Local Administration, 1978; (with P. Kahn, R. Livock, and P. Wiles) Picketing, 1983; The Noble Lie, 1986; Complaints Procedures in Local Government, 1987; (with Burkinshaw and Harden) Government by Moonlight: The Hybrid Parts of the State, 1989; (with Burkinshaw) When Citizens Complain, 1993; Choice and the Legal Order: Rising above Politics, 1996. **Address:** Faculty of Law, University of Sheffield, Sheffield, England. **Online address:** N.D.Lewis@sheffield.ac.uk

LEWIS, Earl. Canadian. **Genres:** Race relations, History. **Career:** University of California-Berkeley, professor of Afro-American Studies, 1984-89; University of Michigan, Ann Arbor, 1989-, professor of history and African-American studies, director of the Center for African and African-American Studies, 1990-93, became vice provost for Academic Affairs-Graduate Studies and dean of the Rackham School of Graduate Studies, 1997-. Has served on editorial boards and on the boards of professional associations. Consultant and lecturer. **Publications:** In Their Own Interests: Race, Class, and Power in Twentieth-Century Norfolk, 1991; (with H. Ardizzone) Love on Trial: An American Scandal in Black and White, 2001. EDITOR: (with Robin D.G. Kelley) The Young Oxford History of African Americans, 11 vols, 1995-1997; (with J.W. Trotter) African Americans in the Industrial Age: A Documentary History, 1915-1945, 1996; (with Robin D.G. Kelley) To Make Our World Anew: A History of African Americans, 2000. **Address:** Horace H. Rackham School of Graduate Studies, University of Michigan, 915 East Washington St., Room 1004, Ann Arbor, MI 48109, U.S.A.

LEWIS, Gregg (Allan). American, b. 1951. **Genres:** Adult non-fiction. **Career:** David C. Cook Publishers, Elgin, IL, associate editor of youth publications, 1973-76; free-lance writer, 1976-77, 1987-; Campus Life, Carol Stream, IL, associate editor, 1977-79, editor, 1980-84, senior editor, 1984-87, editor at large, 1987-; Marriage Partnership, Carol Stream, senior editor, 1987-88, senior writer, 1988-. UPI Religious Radio Service, commentator, 1984-85. **Publications:** Telegarbage, 1977; (with M.M. Lewis) The Hurting Parent, 1979, rev. ed., 1990; (with R.L. Lewis) Inductive Preaching, 1983; (with S. Purl) Am I Alive?, 1986; Caught, 1987; (with B. Tirabassi) Just One Victory, 1987; (with M. Wazeter) Dark Marathon, 1989; (with S. Perry) In Sickness and in Health, 1989; (with D.S. Lewis) Motherhood Stress, 1989; (with R.L. Lewis) Learning to Preach Like Jesus, 1989; The Waters Run Deep, 1989; Beyond a Broken Promise, 1989; (with B. Tirabassi) The Life of the Party, 1990; (with T. Landry) Tom Landry, 1990; (with R.A. Seiple) A Missing Peace: Vietnam, 1992; (with C. and L. Wedemeyer) Charlie's Vic-

tory, 1993; (with D.S. Lewis) Did I Ever Tell You about When You Were Little?, 1994; (with D.S. Lewis) Did I Ever Tell You about When Your Parents Were Children?, 1994; (with D.S. Lewis) Did I Ever Tell You about When Your Grandparents Were Young?, 1994; (with D.S. Lewis) Did I Ever Tell You about How Our Family Got Started?, 1994; (with T. and C. Burke) Major League Dad, 1994; (with B. Thomas) Good Sports, 1994; (with C. Martin) I Can't Walk, So I'll Learn to Dance, 1994; (with D.S. Lewis) When You Were a Baby, 1995; Power of a Promise Kept, 1995; (with D. Gray) Yes, You Can, Heather!, 1995; (with D. Gray) Heather Whitestone, 1995; (with D. Jordan) Family First, 1996; (with H.F. Phillips) What Does She Want from Me, Anyway?, 1997; (with B. and K. McCaughey and D.S. Lewis) Seven from Heaven, 1998; (with D. Morris) Forgiving the Dead Man Walking, 1998; (with B. Carson) Big Picture, 1999; (with B. McCaughey and D.S. Lewis) Celebrating the Wonder of Motherhood, 1999; (with M. Akers) The Game and the Glory, 2000; (with H.G. Koenig) Healing Connection, 2000; (with B. Muzikowski) Safe at Home, 2001; (with D. Stevens) Jesus, M.D., 2001. EDITOR: (with T. Stafford) You Call This a Family?, 1986; H. and G. Taylor, Hudson Taylor's Spiritual Secret, 1990. Contributor of articles to religious and popular journals. **Address:** 237 River Ln SW, Rome, GA 30165-6546, U.S.A.

LEWIS, H. W. American, b. 1923. **Genres:** Physics. **Career:** University of California, Santa Barbara, professor, 1964-. **Publications:** Technological Risk, 1990; Why Flip a Coin?, 1997. **Address:** 4184 Cresta Ave., Santa Barbara, CA 93110, U.S.A. **Online address:** hlewis@physics.ucsb.edu

LEWIS, Herbert S. American, b. 1934. **Genres:** Anthropology/Ethnology. **Career:** Northwestern University, Evanston, IL, Instructor in Anthropology and Political Science, 1961-63; University of Wisconsin, Madison, Assistant Professor, 1963-67, Associate Professor, 1967-73, Professor of Anthropology, 1973-96, Emeritus Professor, 1996-. The Hebrew University, Jerusalem, Israel, Visiting Associate Professor, 1969-70. **Publications:** A Galla Monarchy: Jimma Abba Jifar, Ethiopia, 1830-1932, 1965; Leaders and Followers: Some Anthropological Perspectives, 1974; After the Eagles Landed: The Yemenites of Israel, 1989. **Address:** Dept of Anthropology, University of Wisconsin, 5135 Social Sci Bldg, 1180 Observatory Dr, Madison, WI 53706, U.S.A. **Online address:** hslewis@facstaff.wisc.edu

LEWIS, J(ohn) Parry. British, b. 1927. **Genres:** Economics, Mathematics/Statistics, Regional/Urban planning. **Career:** University of Exeter, Professor of Economics, 1965-67; University of Manchester, professor, 1967-82, Professor Emeritus of Economics of Regions and Towns, 1982-. **Publications:** Introduction to Mathematics for Students of Economics, 1959, 1969; Building Cycles and Britain's Growth, 1965; (with D.F. Medhurst) Urban Decay: An Analysis and a Policy, 1969; A Study of the Cambridge Sub-Region, 1973; Urban Economics, 1979; Freedom to Drink, 1985; (with A. Traill) Statistics Explained, 1998. **Address:** 36 Dartmouth Grove, Redcar, Cleveland TS10 2NX, England. **Online address:** jparrylewis@riter.freeserve.co.uk

LEWIS, J. Patrick. American, b. 1942. **Genres:** Children's fiction, Poetry. **Career:** Otterbein College, Westerville, OH, professor of economics, 1974-98, professor emeritus, 1998-; children's poet. **Publications:** FOR CHILDREN: The Tsar and the Amazing Cow, 1988; The Hippopotamusn't, 1990; Two-legged, Four-legged, No-legged Rhymes, 1991; Earth Verses and Water Rhymes, 1991; The Moonbows of Mr. B. Bones, 1992; The Fat-Cats at Sea, 1994; July Is a Mad Mosquito, 1994; The Frog Princess, 1994; The Christmas of the Reddle Moon, 1994; Black Swan/White Crow, 1995; Ridicholas Nicholas, 1995; Riddle-icious, 1996; The Boat of Many Rooms, 1997; The La-Di-Da Hare, 1997; Long Was the Winter Road They Traveled, 1997; The Little Buggers, 1998; Boshblobberbosh: Runcible Poems for Edward Lear, 1998; Doodle Dandies, 1998; The House of Boo, 1998; Riddle-Lightful, 1998; The Bookworm's Feast, 1999; Night of the Goat Children, 1999; At the Wish of the Fish, 1999; Earth & Sea and You & Me (in Japanese), 1999; Freedom Like Sunlight: Praisesongs for Black Americans, 2000; Isabella Abnormella and the Very, Very Finicky Queen of Trouble, 2000; Good Mousekeeping, 2001; A Burst of Firsts, 2001; Earth + Us: Continuous, 2001; The Shoe Tree of Chagrin, 2001; Arithmetickle, 2002; A World of Wonders, 2002; Earth and Me: Our Family Tree, 2002; The Last Resort, 2002; The Snowflake Sisters, 2003; Swan Songs: Poems of Extinction, 2003. **Address:** 104 Fairview Rd, Chagrin Falls, OH 44022, U.S.A. **Online address:** jplewis42@aol.com; www.jpatricklewis.com

LEWIS, J(ohn) R(oyston). Also writes as Roy Lewis, David Springfield. British, b. 1933. **Genres:** Mystery/Crime/Suspense, Law. **Career:** Teacher, Okehampton Secondary School, Devon, 1957-59; Lecturer, Cannock Chase Technical College, Staffordshire, 1959-61, Cornwall Technical College, Redruth, 1961-63, and Plymouth College of Technology, Devon, 1963-67; H.M. Inspector of Schools, Newcastle, 1967-75; Principal, Wigan College of Technology, 1981-2005; Managing Director, Templar North Publications Ltd. **Publications:** ON LAW: Cases for Discussion, 1965; Law for the Retailer, 1964 (as Law for the Retailer, 1974); An Introduction to Business Law, 1965; Law in Action, 1965; Questions and Answers on Civil Procedure, 1966; Building Law, 1966; Democracy: The Theory and the Practice, 1966; Managing within the Law, 1967; (with J.A. Holland) Principles of Registered Land Conveyancing, 1967; Company Law, 1967; Revision Notes for Ordinary Level British Construction, 1967; Civil and Criminal Procedure, 1968; Landlord and Tenant, 1968; Outlines of Equity, 1968; (with A. Redish) Mercantile and Commercial Law, 1969; (as David Springfield) The Company Executive and the Law, 1970; Law for the Construction Industry, 1976; Administrative Law for the Construction Industry, 1976; The Teaching of Public Administration in Further and Higher Education, 1979; The Victorian Bar 1837-1882, 1980; Certain Private Incidents, 1980; The Maypole, 1983. MYSTERY NOVELS AS ROY LEWIS: A Lover too Many, 1969; A Wolf by the Ears, 1970; Error of Judgment, 1971; The Fenokee Project, 1971; A Fool for a Client, 1972; The Secret Singing, 1972; Blood Money, 1973; Of Singular Purpose, 1973; A Question of Degree, 1974; Double Take, 1975; A Part of Virtue, 1975; Witness My Death, 1976; A Distant Banner, 1976; Nothing but Foxes, 1977; An Uncertain Sound, 1978; An Inevitable Fatality, 1978; A Violent Death, 1979; A Certain Blindness, 1980; Seek for Justice, 1981; A Relative Distance, 1981; Dwell in Danger, 1982; A Gathering of Ghosts, 1982; A Limited Vision, 1983; Once Dying, Twice Dead, 1984; Most Cunning Workmen, 1984; A Blurred Reality, 1985; A Trout in the Milk, 1986; Premium on Death, 1987; Men of Subtle Craft, 1987; The Salamander Chill, 1988; The Devil Is Dead, 1989; A Necessary Dealing, 1990; A Wisp of Smoke, 1991; A Secret Dying, 1992; Bloodeagle, 1993; The Cross Bearer, 1994; A Short Lived Ghost, 1995; Angel of Death, 1996; Suddenly as a Shadow, 1997; The Shape Shifter, 1998; The Ghost Dancers, 1999; An Assumption of Death, 2000; A Form of Death, 2000; Dead Secret, 2001; The Nightwalker, 2002; Phantom, 2002; The Ways of Death, 2003; Phantom, 2003; Dead Man Running, 2004; Headhunter, 2004. **Address:** Old Park, South Stainmore, Westmoreland, England. **Online address:** LewisR@tesco.net

LEWIS, Jack Pearl. American, b. 1919. **Genres:** Theology/Religion. **Career:** Professor Emeritus of Bible, Harding University Graduate School of Religion, Memphis, 1989- (Associate Professor, 1954-57; Professor, 1957-89). Minister in churches in Texas, Rhode Island and Kentucky, 1941-54. **Publications:** The Minor Prophets, 1966; The Interpretation of Noah and the Flood in Jewish and Christian Literature, 1968; Historical Backgrounds of Bible History, 1971; Archaeology and the Bible, 1975; The Gospel According to Mathew, 2 vols., 1976; The English Bible from the KJV to the N1V, 1981, 1991; Leadership Questions Confronting the Church, 1985; Exegesis of Difficult Passages, 1988; Questions You've Asked about Bible Translations, 1991; Major Prophets, 1999; The Ethics of the Prophets, 2001. EDITOR: The Last Things, 1972; Interpreting 2 Corinthians 5:14-21, 1989. **Address:** 1132 S Perkins Rd, Memphis, TN 38117-5533, U.S.A. **Online address:** jackplewis@juno.com

LEWIS, James R. American, b. 1949. **Genres:** Theology/Religion, Reference. **Career:** Religious studies scholar. University of Wisconsin-Stevens Point, lecturer in religious studies, 1999-. **Publications:** (with J.G. Melton) Sex, Slander, and Salvation, 1994; Seeking the Light, 1998; Doomsday Prophecies, 2000; Legitimating New Religions (monograph), 2003. REFERENCE WORKS: The Astrology Encyclopedia, 1994; Encyclopedia of Afterlife Beliefs and Phenomena, 1994; The Dream Encyclopedia, 1995; (with E. Oliver) Angels, A to Z, 1996; The Encyclopedia of Cults, Sects, and New Religions, 1998; Encyclopedia of New Religions, Cults, and Sects, 1998; Cults in America, 1998; Peculiar Prophets, 1999; Witchcraft Today, 1999; UFOs and Popular Culture, 2000; (with C. Skutsch) The Human Rights Encyclopedia (3 vols.; young adult), 2001; Satanism Today: An Encyclopedia of Religion, Folklore, and Popular Culture, 2001; Encyclopedic Sourcebook of UFO Religions, 2002. EDITOR: The Inner Life of Theosophy, 1990; The Unification Church, Vol. 3: Outreach, 1990; The Beginnings of Astrology in America, 1990; (with J.G. Melton) Perspectives on the New Age, 1992; (with J.G. Melton) Church Universal and Triumphant, 1994; From the Ashes, 1994; The Gods Have Landed, 1995; Magical Religion and Modern Witchcraft, 1996; Odd Gods, 2001; Oxford Handbook of New Religious Movements, 2004; (with J. Petersen) Controversial New Religions, 2005. FORTHCOMING: (with J. Petersen) Contemporary Religious Satanism; The Order of the Solar Temple. Contributor to books. Contributor of articles and book reviews to publications. **Address:** Dept of Philosophy, University of Wisconsin, Stevens Point, WI 54481, U.S.A. **Online address:** jlewis@uwsp.edu

LEWIS, Jeremy. British, b. 1942. **Genres:** Essays. **Career:** Writer. Chatto & Windus, London, editor, became director, 1979-89; London Magazine, deputy editor, 1991-94; Peters, Fraser & Dunlop, reader, 1994-2001; The Oldie, commissioning editor, 1996-. Has also worked as an editor for Andre Deutsch and Oxford University Press and as a literary agent. **Publications:** Playing for Time, 1987; (ed.) The Chatto Book of Office Life, or Love Among the Filing Cabinets, 1992, as The Vintage Book of Office Life, 1998; Kindred Spirits: Adrift in Literary London, 1995; Cyril Connolly: A Life, 1997; Tobias Smollett, 2003. **Address:** 3 Percival Rd, London SW14 7QE, England. **Online address:** jeremy.lewis5@btinternet.com

LEWIS, Johanna Miller. American, b. 1961. **Genres:** Art/Art history, History. **Career:** College of William and Mary, Williamsburg, VA, instructor, 1988, guest lecturer in history, 1990-91; University of Arkansas at Little Rock, chair and professor of history and associate coordinator of Public History Program, 1991-. Salem College, guest lecturer, 1985, 1989; lecturer at Clinch Valley State College and University of North Carolina at Greensboro. Old Salem, member of field crew, 1982; Gilmer-Smith Foundation, registrar and curator, 1984; Colonial Williamsburg, collections intern, 1986-90, curatorial intern at Abby Aldrich Rockefeller Folk Art Center, 1990-91; Jamestown-Yorktown Foundation, contract historian for Yorktown Victory Center, 1989-90; DeWitt Wallace Decorative Arts Gallery, curatorial intern, 1990; National Dunbar History Project, co-director, 1993-97; Central High Museum, project manager, 1996-97; A Gathering of Women: Arkansas Women, 1930-2000, project director, 1999-2000; Life Interrupted: The Japanese American Experience in World War II Arkansas, 2001-; So You Want to Start a Museum?, project director, 2002. **Publications:** Artisans in the North Carolina Backcountry, 1995. Contributor to books. Contributor of articles and reviews to magazines. **Address:** Department of History, University of Arkansas at Little Rock, 2801 S University, Little Rock, AR 72204, U.S.A. **Online address:** jmlewis@ualr.edu

LEWIS, Linda (Joy). American, b. 1946. **Genres:** Novels, Children's fiction, Business/Trade/Industry. **Career:** Broward County Schools, Fort Lauderdale, FL, school teacher, 1972-81; Simon & Schuster, New York City, writer, 1985-. **Publications:** LINDA SERIES: We Hate Everything but Boys, 1985; Is There Life after Boys?, 1987; We Love Only Older Boys, 1988; 2 Young 2 Go 4 Boys, 1988; My Heart Belongs to That Boy, 1989; All for the Love of That Boy, 1989; Want to Trade Two Brothers for a Cat?, 1989; Dedicated to That Boy I Love, 1990; Loving Two Is Hard to Do, 1990; Tomboy Terror in Bunk 109, 1991; Preteen Means in Between, 1993. **Address:** 810 Wolf Creek St, Clermont, FL 34711, U.S.A. **Online address:** linlewis22@aol.com

LEWIS, Margaret (B.). British, b. 1942. **Genres:** Biography. **Career:** University of Newcastle upon Tyne, England, public relations officer, 1984-96, tutor in English, 1989-90. Open University, tutor, 1970-93. Cofounder and copublisher, Flambard Press. **Publications:** Ngaio Marsh: A Life, 1991; Edith Pargeter: Ellis Peters, 1994, rev. ed., 2003; Josefina de Vasconcellos: Her Life and Art, 2002. **Address:** Stable Cottage, East Fourstones, Hexham, Northd. NE47 5DX, England.

LEWIS, Mervyn. *See* FREWER, Glyn Mervyn Louis.

LEWIS, Michael. American, b. 1960. **Genres:** International relations/Current affairs, Money/Finance, Politics/Government, Essays. **Career:** Salomon Brothers, NYC, bond salesman, 1985-88; writer. **Publications:** Liar's Poker: Rising through the Wreckage on Wall Street, 1989; Pacific Rift: Adventures in the Fault Zone between the U.S. and Japan, 1991; The Money Culture (articles and essays), 1991; The New Thing: A Silicon Valley Story, 1999; Next, 2001; Moneyball, 2003. **Address:** c/o Albert Zuckerman, Writers House, 21 West Twenty-sixth St., New York, NY 10010, U.S.A.

LEWIS, Norman. American, b. 1912. **Genres:** Language/Linguistics, Speech/Rhetoric. **Career:** City University of New York, Instructor, 1943-52; New York University, NYC, Associate Professor, 1955-64; Rio Hondo College, Whittier, CA, Professor of English, 1964- (Chairman, Communications Dept., 1964-75). **Publications:** (with W. Funk) 30 Days to a More Powerful Vocabulary, 1942; Power with Words, 1943; How to Read Better and Faster, 1944, 4th ed., 1978; Lewis English Refresher and Vocabulary Builder, 1945; Word Power Made Easy, 1949; Rapid Vocabulary Builder, 1951; How to Get More Out of Your Reading, 1951; 20 Days to Better Spelling, 1953; (ed.) New Roget's Thesaurus in Dictionary Form, 1961; Dictionary of Correct Spelling, 1962; Correct Spelling Made Easy, 1963; Dictionary of Modern Pronunciation, 1963; New Guide to Word Power, 1963; New Power with Words, 1964; 30 Days to Better English, 1964; How to Become a Better Reader, 1964; Modern Thesaurus of Synonyms, 1965; R.S.V.P.: Reading,

Spelling Vocabulary, Pronunciation, Books I-III, 1966, enlarged ed., Books I and II, 1982, Book III, 1983, Book A, 1985, Book B, 1986; See, Say, and Write: Spelling Texts, Books I and II, 1973; Instant Spelling Power, 1973; R.S.V.P. for College English Power, Books I-III, 1978; Instant Word Power, 1980; RSVP with Etymology, Books I-III, 1980-82; New American Dictionary of Good English, 1987. **Address:** c/o Dept. of English, Rio Hondo College, Whittier, CA 90608, U.S.A.

LEWIS, Padmore. *See* **LEWIS, Sandra Padmore.**

LEWIS, Peter (Elvet). British, b. 1937. **Genres:** Communications/Media, Literary criticism and history, Mystery/Crime/Suspense. **Career:** Reader in English, now Emeritus, University of Durham, since 1964. Member, Northern Arts Literature Panel, 1965-70, 1982-86. Managing Director, Flambard Press, 1991-. **Publications:** John Gay: The Beggar's Opera (criticism), 1976; John Le Carre, 1985; Fielding's Burlesque Drama, 1987; Eric Ambler, 1990. EDITOR: The Beggar's Opera, by John Gay, 1973; Poems '74, 1974; (co-) Implosions, by Deryck Cumming, 1977; Papers of the Radio Literature Conference 1977; Radio Drama, 1981; (co-) John Gay and the Scriblerians, 1988; Enduring to the End, 1990. Contributor of short crime fiction to anthologies. **Address:** Stable Cottage, East Fourstones, Hexham NE47 5DX, England.

LEWIS, Robert W. American, b. 1930. **Genres:** Literary criticism and history. **Career:** University of Nebraska, Lincoln, instructor in English, 1955-58; University of Texas at Austin, assistant professor of English, 1963-69; University of North Dakota, Grand Forks, associate professor, 1969-71, professor, 1971-90, Chester Fritz Distinguished Professor of English, 1990-. Fulbright professor at University of Catania, in Italy, 1967-68, and Ain Shams University, in Egypt, 1975-76. North Dakota Humanities Council, chair, 1982-84; North Dakota Quarterly, editor, 1982-; North Dakota Museum of Art, president of board of directors, 1990-92; Ernest Hemingway Foundation, president, 1987-92. **Publications:** Hemingway on Love, 1965; (ed.) Hemingway in Italy and Other Essays, 1990; A Farewell to Arms: The War of the Words, 1992. Contributor to periodicals. **Address:** Department of English, University of North Dakota, Grand Forks, ND 58202-7209, U.S.A.

LEWIS, Roy. *See* **LEWIS, J(ohn) R(oyston).**

LEWIS, Rupert. American, b. 1947. **Genres:** History, Politics/Government. **Career:** University of the West Indies, Kingston, Jamaica, lecturer, beginning c. 1972, reader in political thought, 1992-. Cornell University, Ithaca, NY, visiting scholar at Africana Studies and Research Center, 1993. **Publications:** Readings in Government and Politics of the West Indies, 1972; Garvey: Africa, Europe, the Americas, 1976; Marcus Garvey: Anti-Colonial Champion, 1988; Garvey: His Work and Impact, 1991; Political and Intellectual Study of Walter Rodney, 1994. **Address:** Department of Government, University of the West Indies, Mona Campus, Kingston 7, Jamaica.

LEWIS, Sandra Padmore. Also writes as Padmore Lewis. Barbadian, b. 1957. **Genres:** Essays, Poetry, Songs/Lyrics and libretti, Novellas/Short stories. **Career:** Port Authority of New York and New Jersey, NYC, accountant, 1994-. **Publications:** Some Things I Have Noticed, 1996. Some writings appear under the name Padmore Lewis. **Address:** 315 E. 23 Street, Brooklyn, NY 11226, U.S.A. **Online address:** SPLEWIS@PANYNJ.GOV

LEWIS, Shannon. *See* **LLYWELYN, Morgan.**

LEWIS, Sherry. American. **Genres:** Mystery/Crime/Suspense, Romance/Historical. **Career:** Novelist. Worked in florist and garden shops, a convenience store, an insurance agency, and a bank; worked as a bankruptcy paralegal; musician, performing with local bands. **Publications:** Call Me Mom, 1995; No Place for Secrets, 1995; No Place for Death, 1996; Keeping Her Safe, 1997; No Place for Sin, 1997. **Address:** c/o Berkley Publishing Group, 375 Hudson, New York, NY 10014, U.S.A. **Online address:** SLBWrites@aol.com

LEWIS, Stephen (C.). American, b. 1942. **Genres:** Romance/Historical, Mystery/Crime/Suspense. **Career:** Suffolk Community College, Brentwood, NY, professor of English, 1966-. **Publications:** Philosophy: An Introduction Through Literature, 1990; The Monkey Rope, 1990; And Baby Makes None, 1991; HISTORICAL MYSTERIES: The Dumb Shall Sing, 1999; The Blind in Darkness, 2000; The Sea Hath Spoken, 2001. **Address:** Suffolk Community College, Crooked Hill Rd., Brentwood, NY 11717, U.S.A. **Online address:** stevelew@yahoo.com

LEWIS, Sydney. American, b. 1952. **Genres:** Documentaries/Reportage. **Career:** Journalist and author. WBEZ, Chicago, IL, producer of Personal Essays series, 1997-. **Publications:** Hospital: An Oral History of Cook County Hospital, 1994; A Totally Alien Life-Form: Teenagers, 1996; Help Wanted: Tales from the First Job Front, 2000. **Address:** c/o The Fund for Independent Publishing, 38 Greene St., Fl 4, New York, NY 10013-2505, U.S.A.

LEWIS, Thomas H. American, b. 1919. **Genres:** Anthropology/Ethnology, Medicine/Health. **Career:** Physician. **Publications:** Forgotten Bottles along the Yellowstone, 1985; The Medicine Men: Oglala Sioux Ceremony and Healing, 1990. Contributor of articles and reviews to periodicals. **Address:** Box 162, Boyd, MT 59013, U.S.A.

LEWIS, Thomas P(arker). American, b. 1936. **Genres:** Children's fiction, Music. **Career:** President, Pro/Am Music Resources, White Plains, New York, since 1982. Coordinator, Institutional and Corporate Marketing Depts., Harper & Row, Publishers, Inc., NYC, 1964-82. National Writers' Union, Westchester/Fairfield Chapter, president. **Publications:** Hill of Fire, 1971; The Dragon Kite, 1974; Clipper Ship, 1978; A Call for Mr. Sniff, 1981; Mr. Sniff's Motel mystery, 1983; The Blue Rocket Fun Show, 1986; The Pro-Am Guide to U.S. Books about Music, 1987, 1988; Frida Cat, 1989; Something about the Music, 1990; A Source Guide to the Music of Percy Grainger, 1991; The Pro/Am Book of Music and Mythology, 1991. **Address:** Pro/Am Music Resources, 63 Prospect St., White Plains, NY 10606, U.S.A.

LEWIS, Trudy. American, b. 1961. **Genres:** Novels, Novellas/Short stories. **Career:** Saint Vincent Academy, Newark, NJ, English instructor, 1987-88; University of Missouri-Columbia, assistant professor of English, 1992-. Organized graduate student readings at both the University of Illinois at Chicago and the University of Missouri-Columbia. **Publications:** Private Correspondences (novel), 1994; The Bones of Garbo (short stories), 2003. Contributor of short stories to periodicals and anthologies. **Address:** 316-E Tate Hall, University of Missouri-Columbia, Columbia, MO 65211, U.S.A. **Online address:** LewisTr@missouri.edu

LEWIS, W(alter) David. American, b. 1931. **Genres:** Business/Trade/Industry, Economics, Engineering, History, Technology. **Career:** Hudson Professor of History and Engineering, Auburn University, Alabama, 1991-94, Distinguished University Professor, 1994-. Fellowship Coordinator, Eleutherian Mills-Hagley Foundation, Wilmington, Delaware, and Lecturer in History, University of Delaware, Newark, both 1959-65; Associate Professor of History, 1965-71, and Professor, 1971, State University of New York, Buffalo; Charles A. Lindbergh Professor of Aerospace History, National Air and Space Museum, Washington, D.C., 1993-94. Leonardo de Vinci Medal, Society for The History of Technology, 1993. **Publications:** From Newgate to Dannemora: The Rise of the Penitentiary in New York, 1796-1848, 1965; Iron and Steel in America, 1976; (with W.P. Newton) Delta: The History of an Airline, 1979; (with W.F. Trimble) The Airway to Everywhere: A History of All American Aviation 1937-1953, 1987; Sloss Furnaces and the Rise of the Birmingham District: An Industrial Epic, 1994. EDITOR: (with D.T. Gilchrist) Economic Change in the Civil War Era, 1965; (with B.E. Griessman) The Southern Mystique: Technology and Human Values in a Changing Region, 1977. **Address:** 708 Thach Hall, Auburn University, Auburn, AL 36849, U.S.A.

LEWIS, Ward B., (Jr.). American, b. 1938. **Genres:** Literary criticism and history. **Career:** University of Iowa, Iowa City, assistant professor of German, 1968-71; University of Georgia, Athens, assistant professor, 1971-73, associate professor of German, 1973-. Lecturer at University of South Carolina at Columbia, 1976, University of Houston, 1977, and University of Florida, 1982 and 1986. **Publications:** Poetry and Exile: An Annotated Bibliography of the Works and Criticism of Paul Zech, 1975; Eugene O'Neill: The German Reception of America's First Dramatist, 1984; (ed.) P. Zech, The Bird in Langfoot's Belfry, 1993; The Ironic Dissident: Frank Wedekind in the View of His Critics, 1997. Contributor of articles and reviews to academic journals. **Address:** Department of Germanic and Slavic Languages, University of Georgia, Athens, GA 30602, U.S.A. **Online address:** wlewis@arches.uga.edu

LEWIS-FERGUSON, Julinda. American, b. 1955. **Genres:** Dance/Ballet. **Career:** NYC Schools, NYC, grade school teacher in dance, computers, and creative writing, 1980-; taught dance at the high school and adult education level, Sunday school for Baptist church programs, and has served as a computer curriculum consultant. Coordinator of supplemental services, NYC Board of Education; consultant, National Endowment for the Arts, 1985. Guest host for cable television program, Eye on Dance, 1981-83. **Publications:** (ed.) Black Choreographers Moving: A National Dialogue, 1991;

Alvin Ailey, Jr.: A Life in Dance, 1994. Contributor of articles, sometimes under the name Julinda Lewis, to periodicals. **Address:** c/o New York City Board of Education, 65 Court Street, 12th Floor, Brooklyn, NY 11201, U.S.A.

LEWIS-SMITH, Anne. British, b. 1925. **Genres:** Poetry. **Career:** Member of Editorial Board, 1973-, and Main Ed., 1984-90, Envoi Publisher, Envoi Poets Publications; Ed. for BAFM Yearbook (Brit. Association of Friends of Museums) and member of BAFM Council. English Director, World Poetry Day, 1967; Vice President, Studie Scambi International, Italy; President, Amis des Musee des Ballon. Feature Writer, Women's Page, Stamford Mercury, 1964-70, and Cambridgeshire Life, and Northamptonshire Life, 1967-70. **Publications:** Seventh Bridge, 1964; The Beginning, 1966; Flesh and Flowers, 1967; Dandelion Flavour, 1970; Dinas Head, 1977; Places and Passions, 1986; In the Dawn, 1987; Circling Sound, 1996; Feathers, Fancies and Feelings, 2000. **Address:** Pen Ffordd, Newport, Pembrokeshire SA42 0QT, Wales.

LEYTON, Sophie. See **WALSH, Sheila.**

L'HEUREUX, John (Clarke). American, b. 1934. **Genres:** Novels, Novellas/Short stories, Poetry. **Career:** Entered the Society of Jesus, 1954; ordained a priest, 1966; requested laicization, 1970; Stanford University, California, professor of English, 1973-. The Atlantic, contributing editor, Boston, 1970-. **Publications:** NOVELS: Tight White Collar, 1972; The Clang Birds, 1972; Jessica Fayer, 1976; A Woman Run Mad, 1988; An Honorable Profession, 1991; The Shrine at Altamira, 1992; The Handmaid of Desire, 1996; Having Everything, 1999; The Miracle, 2002. POETRY: Quick as Dandelions: Poems, 1964; Rubrics for a Revolution, 1967; One Eye and a Measuring Rod: Poems, 1968; No Place for Hiding: Poems, 1971. STORIES: Family Affairs, 1974; Desires, 1981; Comedians, 1990. OTHER: Picnic in Babylon: A Priest's Journal, 1967. **Address:** Dept of English, Stanford University, Stanford, CA 94305, U.S.A.

LI, Leslie. American, b. 1945. **Genres:** Novels. **Career:** Writer. **Publications:** Bittersweet (novel), 1992. Work represented in anthologies. Contributor to periodicals. **Address:** c/o Kim Witherspoon, Witherspoon Associates, 235 E 31st St., New York, NY 10016, U.S.A.

LIATSOS, Sandra Olson. American, b. 1942. **Genres:** Poetry. **Career:** North Reading, MA, elementary school teacher, 1962-73; author, 1973-. **Publications:** FOR CHILDREN: Bicycle Riding, and Other Poems, 1997; Poems to Count On: 30 Terrific Poems and Activities to Help Teach Math Concepts, 1995. Contributor of poetry to textbooks, anthologies, and children's magazines. **Address:** 1210 Deer Trail Lane, Solvang, CA 93463, U.S.A.

LIBBY, Ronald T(heodore). American, b. 1941. **Genres:** Medicine/Health, Politics/Government, International relations/Current affairs. **Career:** University of California, Irvine, visiting research scholar, 1972; University of Botswana, Lesotho, and Swaziland, lecturer in political science, 1973-75; University of Malawi, Zomba, lecturer in political science, 1975-76; University of Zambia, Lusaka, lecturer in political science, 1976-79; University of Notre Dame, South Bend, IN, visiting assistant professor of political science, 1981-83; University of the West Indies, Mona, Kingston, Jamaica, senior lecturer in political science, 1983-85; Northwestern University, Evanston, IL, visiting associate professor of political science, 1985-86; Australian National University, Darwin, senior research fellow at research school of Pacific studies, 1986-87; Victoria University of Wellington, New Zealand, senior lecturer in political science, 1987-89; Southwest State University, Marshall, MN, professor of political science and head of department, 1989; St. Joseph's University, Dept of Political Science, professor and chair; University of North Florida, professor. **Publications:** Toward an Africanized U.S. Policy for Southern Africa, 1980; The Politics of Economic Power in Southern Africa, 1987; Hawke's Law: The Politics of Mining and Aboriginal Land Rights in Australia, 1989, 2nd ed., 1992; Protecting Markets: U.S. Policy and the World Grain Trade, 1992; Eco-Wars: Political Campaigns and Social Movements, 1999; The Police State of Medicine: The War on Doctors, 2004. Contributor to professional journals. **Address:** Dept of Political Science, University of North Florida, 4567 St John's Bluff Rd S, Jacksonville, FL 32224, U.S.A. **Online address:** rlibby@ unf.edu

LIBERA, Antoni. Polish. **Genres:** Plays/Screenplays, Novels. **Career:** Translator, theater director, essayist, playwright, opera librettist, and novelist. **Publications:** Eastern Promises (play), 1990; Madame, 1998, trans. A. Kolakowska, 2000. TRANSLATOR: Samuel Beckett: Pisma Proza, 1982; Waiting

for Godot, 1985. Has translated most of Samuel Beckett's dramas and prose into Polish, and has staged productions of Beckett's work internationally. Author of articles on Samuel Beckett; contributor to Polish literary journals. **Address:** c/o Farrar Straus & Giroux, 19 Union Square West, New York, NY 10003, U.S.A.

LIBERMAN, Rosette B. American. **Genres:** Writing/Journalism. **Career:** Amity Regional District, in Connecticut, high school English teacher, c. 1985-. Worked as a schoolteacher, from nursery school through university level, and as an educational administrator. **Publications:** Guide to Decision-making in Compliance with Section 504, 1988; (with G. Heyworth) The Writing and Revision Stylebook, 2000; The College Application Essay Bible, 2004. Contributor to books. **Address:** 141 Ramsdell St, New Haven, CT 06515, U.S.A. **Online address:** rbliberman@snet.net

LIBO, Kenneth (Harold). American, b. 1937. **Genres:** Cultural/Ethnic topics. **Career:** City College of the City University of New York, New York City, assistant professor of English, 1971-78; independent researcher and writer, 1978-80 and 1981-86; Jewish Daily Forward, New York City, editor, 1980-81; National Museum of American Jewish History, Philadelphia, PA, curator, 1986-89; Museum of Jewish Heritage, New York City, curator, 1989-. **Publications:** (with I. Howe) World of Our Fathers, 1976, in UK as The Immigrant Jews of New York, 1881 to the Present; (ed. with Howe) How We Lived: A Documentary History of Immigrant Jews in America, 1880-1930, 1979; (with Howe) We Lived There Too: In Their Own Words and Pictures-Pioneer Jews and the Westward Movement of America, 1984; All in a Lifetime, 1996; Sexias-Kursheedts and the Rise of Early American Jewry, 2001. **Address:** 40 Harrison St Apt 12 B, New York, NY 10013-2700, U.S.A. **Online address:** kenlibo@aol.com

LIBOV, Charlotte. American, b. 1950. **Genres:** Medicine/Health. **Career:** Volunteer English teacher in Ashdod, Israel, 1973-74; Milford Citizen, Milford, CT, general assignment reporter, 1974-76; volunteer counselor at a shelter for victims of domestic violence, Eugene, OR, 1977-79; Journal Inquirer, Manchester, CT, general assignment reporter, 1980-81; Springfield Daily News, Springfield, MA, bureau chief, 1981-84; Courant, Hartford, CT, restaurant reviewer, 1985-92; free-lance writer, 1992-. University of Connecticut, lecturer, 1982-83; Connecticut Public Television, freelance writer and producer, 1988-90; public speaker on women's health issues. **Publications:** (with F.J. Pashkow) The Women's Heart Book: The Complete Guide to Keeping a Healthy Heart, 1993, rev. ed., 2001; (with Pashkow) Fifty Essential Things to Do if the Doctor Says It's Heart Disease, 1995; Women: Hearts at Risk (television documentary), 1995; Migraine: 50 Essential Things to Do, 1998; Beat Your Risk Factors: A Woman's Guide to Reducing Her Risk for Cancer, Heart Disease, Stroke, Diabetes, and Osteoporosis. Contributor to magazines and newspapers. **Address:** 28 B Heritage Circle, Southbury, CT 06488, U.S.A. **Online address:** char@libov.com

LICHBACH, Mark Irving. American, b. 1951. **Genres:** Politics/Government. **Career:** Northwestern University, Evanston, IL, instructor in political science, 1977; University of Illinois at Chicago Circle, Chicago, assistant professor, 1978-84, associate professor of political science, 1984-91; University of Colorado, Boulder, associate professor, 1991-94, professor of political science, 1994-, and member of executive committee, Conflict and Peace Studies Program. Wissenschaftszentrum (Berlin, Germany), guest scientist, 1981. **Publications:** Regime Change and the Coherence of European Governments (monograph), 1985; The Rebel's Dilemma, 1995; The Cooperator's Dilemma, 1996. Contributor to books. Contributor of articles and reviews to journals. **Address:** Department of Political Science, University of Colorado, Campus Box 333, Boulder, CO 80309, U.S.A.

LICHT, H. William (Bill). Also writes as L. William Hermann, Mark Uno. American, b. 1915. **Genres:** Novels, Theology/Religion. **Career:** Pan American World Airlines, NYC, engineer, flight engineer, and co-pilot, 1942-53; Radio Corporation of America, Lancaster, PA, manufacturing design engineer, 1953-81. **Publications:** NOVELS: (as L. William Hermann) The Firestorm, 1993; Kingdom Age: Angels and Demons; Watchers: Kingdom Justice. OTHER: The Last 1260 Days. FORTHCOMING: Scenario of the Last Days; Commentary, Revelation. **Address:** 240 Brazil Ct, Sanford, FL 32771, U.S.A.

LICHTENBERG, Jacqueline. Also writes as Daniel R. Kerns. American, b. 1942. **Genres:** Science fiction/Fantasy. **Career:** Policy adviser, Star Trek Welcommittee. Former chairman, Science Fiction Writers of America Speakers Bureau; Monthly Aspectarian, science fiction review columnist, 1993-. **Publications:** House of Zeor, 1974, 3rd ed., 1981; (with S. Marshak and J. Winston) Star Trek Lives!, 1975; Unto Zeor, Forever, 1978; (with J. Lorrah)

First Channel, 1980; Mahogany Trinrose, 1981; Molt Brother, 1982; (with J. Lorrah) Channel's Destiny, 1982, Ren Sime, 1984; City of a Million Legends, 1985; Dushau, 1985; Farfetch, 1985; Outreach, 1986; (with J. Lorrah) Zelerod's Doom, 1986; Those of My Blood, 1988; Dreamspy, 1990; (with J. Lorrah) Simē Gen: The Unity Trilogy, 2003. AS DANIEL R. KERNS: Hero, 1993; Border Dispute, 1994.

LICHTENBERG, Peter A. American, b. 1959. **Genres:** Psychology, Gerontology/Senior issues. **Career:** University of Virginia, Western State Hospital, Charlottesville, staff member, 1986-90; Wayne State University, associate professor at the university, and training director and associate chief of Rehabilitation Institute of Michigan, 1991-. Mental Health and Aging Interest Group, coordinator, 1994-96; Psychologists in Long-Term Care, director, 1996-98; consulting neuropsychologist to Health Psychology Associates, Akron, OH, and West Bloomfield Nursing Home. **Publications:** A Guide to Psychological Practice in Geriatric Long-Term Care, 1994; (ed. with K. Anchor, J.T. Barth, and S. Hinderer) Advances in Medical Psychotherapy, Vol VII, 1994, Vol VIII, 1995. Contributor to psychology and gerontology journals and to newspapers. **Address:** 31817 Valley View St, Farmington, MI 48336, U.S.A. **Online address:** aa2275@wayne.edu

LICHTENBERG, Philip. American, b. 1926. **Genres:** Human relations/ Parenting, Psychiatry, Psychology, Social work. **Career:** Harvard University, Cambridge, MA, research fellow in clinical psychology, 1951-52; New York University, NYC, research assistant professor, 1952-54; Michael Reese Hospital, Chicago, research psychologist, 1954-57; New York State Mental Health Research Unit, Syracuse, research psychologist, 1957-61; Bryn Mawr College, PA, associate professor, 1961-68, professor, 1968-96, professor emeritus, 1996-. **Publications:** (with R. Kohrman and H. MacGregor) Motivation for Child Psychiatry Treatment, 1960; Psychoanalysis: Radical and Conservative, 1969; (with D.G. Norton) Cognitive and Mental Development in the First Five Years of Life, 1970; Lectures in Psychoanalysis for Social Workers, 1978; Getting Even: The Equalizing Law of Relationships, 1988; Undoing the Clinch of Oppression, 1990, as Community and Confluence, 1994; (with J. van Beuse-Kom and D. Gibbons) Encountering Bigotry: Befriending Projecting Persons in Everyday Life, 1997. **Address:** 26 Kendal Dr, Kennett Square, PA 19348, U.S.A. **Online address:** plichtenberg@erols.com

LICHTENSTEIN, Alex. American, b. 1962. **Genres:** History. **Career:** Florida International University, Miami, assistant professor of history, 1990-. Consultant to American Friends Service Committee. **Publications:** Twice the Work of Free Labor: The Political Economy of Convict Labor in the New South, 1996. Contributor to books. Contributor of articles and reviews to periodicals. **Address:** Department of History, Florida International University, Miami, FL 33199, U.S.A.

LICHTENSTEIN, Alice. American, b. 1958. **Genres:** Adult non-fiction. **Career:** Author; has taught at colleges throughout the northeastern United States. **Publications:** The Genius of the World, 2000. **Address:** c/o Miriam Altshuler Literary Agency, 53 Old Post Road North, Red Hook, NY 12571, U.S.A.

LICHTENSTEIN, Nelson. American, b. 1944. **Genres:** History, Biography, Organized labor. **Career:** Catholic University of America, Washington, DC, assistant professor, associate professor, 1981-89; University of Virginia, Charlottesville, professor, 1989-2001; University of California, Santa Barbara, professor, 2001-. **Publications:** Labor's War at Home: The CIO in World War II, 1982; Major Problems in the History of American Workers: Documents and Essays, 1991; The Most Dangerous Man in Detroit: Walter Reuther and the Fate of American Labor, 1995; State of the Union: A Century of American Labor, 2002. EDITOR: Political Profiles: The Johnson Years, 1976; Political Profiles: The Kennedy Years, 1976; (with S. Meyer) On the Line: Essays in the History of Auto Work, 1989; (with H.J. Harris) Industrial Democracy in America: The Ambiguous Promise, 1993. **Address:** Dept of History, University of California, Santa Barbara, CA 93106, U.S.A. **Online address:** nelson@history.ucsb.edu

LICKLIDER, Roy. American, b. 1941. **Genres:** International relations/ Current affairs. **Career:** Professor of Political Science, Rutgers University, New Brunswick, New Jersey, since 1989 (Assistant Professor, 1968-72; Associate Professor, 1972-89). Assistant Professor of Political Science, Tougaloo College, Mississippi, 1967-68; Program Officer, Exxon Education Foundation, 1977-78. **Publications:** The Private Nuclear Strategists, 1974; Political Power and the Arab Oil Weapon: The Experience of Five Industrial Nations, 1988; Stopping the Killing: How Civil Wars End, 1993. **Address:** Dept. of Political Science, Rutgers University, 89 George St, New Brunswick, NJ 08901-1411, U.S.A.

LIDCHI GRASSI, Maggi. Italian (born France), b. 1930. **Genres:** Novels, Novellas/Short stories, Mythology/Folklore. **Career:** Worked as art gallery manager, magazine editor, personal secretary, and teacher of English and creative writing at the Aurobindo Ashram; in charge of a school for village children, a home for abandoned children, and founder of an alternative medicine therapeutic center in Auroville; practicing homeopath. **Publications:** NOVELS: The Battle of Kurukshetra, 1985; Legs of the Tortoise, 1989; Great Sir and the Heaven Lady (non-fiction), 1993; The Light That Shone into the Dark Abyss (paranormal), 1994; The Great Golden Sacrifice of the Mahabharata, 2001. STORIES: Jitendra the Protector, 1986. NOVELS AS MAGGI LIDCHI: Earthman, 1967; The First Wife, 1981. **Address:** Sri Aurobindo Ashram, Pondicherry 605 002, India. **Online address:** suramama@satya.net.in

LIDDINGTON, Jill. British, b. 1946. **Genres:** Gay and lesbian issues, History, Local history/Rural topics, Women's studies and issues, Biography. **Career:** Leeds University, School of Continuing Education, lecturer, 1982-, reader, 1999-. Royal Historical Society, fellow. **Publications:** (with J. Norris) One Hand Tied behind Us: The Rise of the Women's Suffrage Movement, 1978, rev. ed., 2000; The Life and Times of a Respectable Rebel: Selina Cooper, 1864-1946, 1984; The Long Road to Greenham: Feminism and Anti-Militarism in Britain since 1820, 1989; Presenting the Past: Anne Lister of Halifax, 1791-1840, 1994; Female Fortune: Land, Gender and Authority: The Anne Lister Diaries, 1833-36, 1998. **Address:** c/o Rivers Oram Press, 144 Hemingford Rd, London N1 1DE, England. **Online address:** j.r.liddington@leeds.ac.uk

LIDDLE, Peter (Hammond). British, b. 1934. **Genres:** History. **Career:** Havelock School, Sunderland, History Teacher, 1957; Gateacre Comprehensive School, Liverpool, Head, History Dept., 1958-67; Notre Dame College of Education, Lecturer, 1967; Sunderland Polytechnic, Lecturer, 1967-70, Sr. Lecturer in History, 1970-87; University of Leeds, Keeper, The Liddle Collection, 1988-99, Associate Lecturer, School of History, 1995-99; Second World War Experience Centre, Leeds, Director, 1999-. Sunderland Industrial Archaeological Society, Chairman, 1969; British Audio-Visual Trust, Vice-President. The Poppy and the Owl, Founder/Editor/Contributor, 1990-99; Everyone's War, Founder/Editor/Contributor, 1999-. **Publications:** Men of Gallipoli, 1976; World War One: Personal Experience Material for Use in Schools, 1977; Testimony of War 1914-18, 1979; Sailor's War 1914-18, 1985; Gallipoli: Pens, Pencils and Cameras at War, 1985; 1916: Aspects of Conflict, 1985; (ed. and contrib.) Home Fires and Foreign Fields, 1985; The Airman's War 1914-18, 1987; The Soldier's War 1914-18, 1988; Voices of War, 1988; 1916: The Battle of the Somme, 1992; The Worst Ordeal, 1994; (ed. and contrib.) Facing Armageddon, 1996; Passchendaele in Perspective, 1997; At the Eleventh Hour, 1998; (co-ed., and contrib.) The Great World War 1914-45, Vol. 1, 2000, Vol. 2, 2001; (ed. with R.C. Begg) For Five Shillings a Day, 2000. **Address:** Prospect House, 39 Leeds Rd, Rawdon, Leeds LS19 6NW, England. **Online address:** enquires@war_experience.org

LIDDY, James. American (born Ireland), b. 1934. **Genres:** Poetry. **Career:** Professor of English, University of Wisconsin, Milwaukee, 1981- (joined faculty 1976). Staff member, San Francisco State College, 1967-69, State University of New York at Binghamton, 1969, Denison University, Ohio, 1971-72, University of Wisconsin, Parkside, 1972-73, and University College, Galway, 1973-74. **Publications:** A Life of Stephen Dedalus, 1959; A Munster Song of Love and War, 1960; Esau My Kingdom, 1962; In a Blue Smoke, 1964; Blue Mountain, 1968; Patrick Kavanagh, 1973; Baudelaire's Bar Flowers, 1975; Corca Bascinn, 1977; Comyn's Lay, 1979; Chamber Pot Music, 1982; Young Men Go Walking Out (novel), 1986; A White Thought in a White Shade: New and Selected Poems, 1987; Collected Poems, 1994; Gold Set Dancing, 2000; I Only Know That I Love Strength in My Friends and Greatness, 2003; The Doctor's House (autobiography), 2004. **Address:** 1924 E Park Place Apt E, Milwaukee, WI 53211, U.S.A.

LIDE, David R. American, b. 1928. **Genres:** Chemistry, Physics. **Career:** National Bureau of Standards, physicist, 1954-63, chief of Molecular Spectroscopy Section, 1963-69, director of Office of Standard Reference Data, 1969-88; consultant, 1988-. **Publications:** Basic Laboratory and Industrial Chemicals, 1993; (with G.W.A. Milne) Handbook of Data on Organic Compounds, 3rd ed., 1993; (with H.V. Kehiaian) CRC Handbook of Thermophysical and Thermochemical Data, 1994; (ed. in chief) CRC Handbook of Chemistry and Physics, 75th ed., 1994, 85th ed., 2004; Handbook of Organic Solvents, 1994; A Century of Excellence in Measurements, Standards, and Technology, 2001; The AIP Physics Desk Reference, 2002. Contributor to books and encyclopedias. Author of research papers, scientific reviews, and electronic databases. **Address:** 13901 Riding Loop Dr, North Potomac, MD 20878, U.S.A. **Online address:** drlide@mailaps.org

LIDE, Mary. Also writes as Mary Lomer, Mary Clayton. British. **Genres:** Novels, History, Mystery/Crime/Suspense. **Career:** Writer. Has worked as a historian and as an English and history teacher at universities and secondary schools in the United States and abroad; International Monetary Fund, Washington, DC, administrative assistant, 1981-84; The Writer's Center, Bethesda, MD, teacher of writing workshop, 1989-90. **Publications:** Ann of Cambray, 1984; Gifts of the Queen, 1985; A Royal Quest, 1987, in U.K. as Hawks of Sedgemont, 1988; Isobelle (in U.S. as Diary of Isobelle), 1988; Tregaran, 1989; Command of the King, 1990; The Legacy, 1991; (as Mary Lomer in U.K.) Fortune's Knave, 1992; The Homecoming (in U.S. as the Seascape), 1992; Polmena Cove, 1994; The Word Is Death, 1997; Death Is the Inheritance, 1998. AS MARY CLAYTON: Pearls before Swine, 1995; Dead Men's Bones, 1996; The Prodigal's Return, 1997. AS MARY LOMER: The Bait, 1961; Robert of Normandy, 1991. **Address:** c/o Goodman Associates, 500 West End Ave, New York, NY 10024, U.S.A.

LIE, John. American (born Republic of Korea), b. 1959. **Genres:** Sociology. **Career:** University of Illinois at Urbana-Champaign, Department of Sociology, department head, 1996-2001; University of Michigan, professor of sociology, 2001-. **Publications:** (ed. and trans.) The Impoverished Spirit in Contemporary Japan, 1993; (with N. Abelman) Blue Dreams, 1995; Sociology of Contemporary Japan, 1996; Han Unbound, 1998; Multiethnic Japan, 2001; (with R. Bryan) Sociology: Compass for a New Century, 2002. **Address:** Department of Sociology, University of Michigan, Ann Arbor, MI 48109, U.S.A.

LIEBER, Robert J. American. **Genres:** International relations/Current affairs. **Career:** Harvard University, Cambridge, MA, Dept. of Government, teaching fellow, 1966-68; University of California, Davis, assistant professor, 1968-72, associate professor, 1972-77, professor of political science, 1977-81, chairman of dept., 1975-76, 1977-80; Georgetown University, Washington, DC, professor of government, 1982-, dept. chairman, 1990-96. **Publications:** British Politics and European Unity: Parties, Elites, and Pressure Groups, 1970; Theory and World Politics, 1972; Oil and the Middle East War: Europe in the Energy Crisis, 1976; (co-author) Contemporary Politics: Europe, 1976; The Oil Decade, 1986; No Common Power: Understanding International Relations, 1988, 4th ed., 2001. EDITOR/CO-EDITOR: Eagle Entangled: U.S. Foreign Policy in a Complex World, 1979; Eagle Defiant: U.S. Foreign Policy in the 1980's, 1983; Eagle Resurgent? The Reagan Era in American Foreign Policy, 1987; Eagle in a New World: American Grand Strategy in the Post-Cold War Era, 1992; Eagle Adrift: American Foreign Policy at the End of the Century, 1997; Eagle Rules? Foreign Policy & American Primacy in 21st Century, 2002. **Address:** Dept of Government, Georgetown University, Washington, DC 20057-1034, U.S.A. **Online address:** lieberr@georgetown.edu

LIEBERMAN, Herbert. American, b. 1933. **Genres:** Novels, Plays/Screenplays. **Publications:** Matty and the Moron and Madonna, 1965; The Adventures of Dolphin Green, 1967; Crawlspace, 1971; The Eighth Square, 1973; Brilliant Kids, 1975; City of the Dead, 1976; The Climate of Hell, 1978; Night Call from a Distant Time Zone, 1982; Nightbloom, 1984; The Green Train, 1986; Shadow Dancers, 1989; Sandman, Sleep, 1993; The Girl with the Botticelli Eyes, 1996; The Concierge, 1998; Widdershins, 2003. **Address:** c/o Georges Borchardt Inc, 136 E 57th St, New York, NY 10017, U.S.A.

LIEBERMAN, Laurence (James). American, b. 1935. **Genres:** Poetry, Literary criticism and history. **Career:** Professor of English, University of Illinois, Urbana, 1970- (Associate Professor of English, 1968-70). Poetry Ed., University of Illinois Press, Urbana, 1971-. Former Poetry Ed., Orange County Illustrated, and Orange County Sun, California; taught at Orange Coast College, Costa Mesa, California, 1960-64, and College of the Virgin Islands, St. Thomas, 1964-68. **Publications:** POETRY: The Unblinding: Poems, 1968; The Osprey Suicides, 1973; God's Measurements, 1980; Eros at the World Kite Pageant: Poems 1979-82, 1983; The Mural of Wakeful Sleep, 1985; The Creole Mephistopheles, 1989; New and Selected Poems: 1962-92, 1993; The St. Kitts Monkey Feuds, 1995; Dark Songs: Slave House and Synagogue, 1996; Compass of the Dying, 1998; The Regatta in the Skies: Selected Long Poems, 1999; Flight from the Mother Stone (poems), 2000; Hour of the Mango Black Moon, 2004. OTHER: (ed.) The Achievement of James Dickey: A Comprehensive Selection of His Poems with a Critical Introduction, 1968; Unassigned Frequencies: American Poetry in Review 1964-77, 1977; Beyond the Muse of Memory: Essays on Contemporary American Poets, 1995. **Address:** Dept of English, University of Illinois, 608 S Wright St, Urbana, IL 61801, U.S.A.

LIEBERMAN, Susan (Abel). American, b. 1942. **Genres:** Human relations/Parenting. **Career:** Super Summers Inc., Houston, TX, executive director, 1993-. Rice University, director of Leadership Rice, 1998-. **Publications:** New Traditions: Redefining Celebrations for Today's Family, 1991; (with N.A. Bartle) Venus in Blue Jeans: Encouraging Candid Talk Between Mothers and Daughters on Sex, 1998; The Real High School Handbook, 1997; The KIDFUN Activity Book. **Address:** 1506 Driscoll St., Houston, TX 77019, U.S.A. **Online address:** susan@lieberman.net

LIEBERTHAL, Kenneth G. American, b. 1943. **Genres:** History, Politics/Government. **Career:** Swarthmore College, PA, instructor, 1972, assistant professor, 1972-75, associate professor, 1976-82, professor of political science and chairman of Social Science Division, 1982-83; University of Michigan, Ann Arbor, visiting professor, 1983, professor of political science, 1983-, Center for Chinese Studies, postdoctoral scholar, 1974-75, 1980, visiting associate research scientist, 1977, research associate, 1983-, director, 1986-89, faculty associate of Russian and East European Center, 1984-. Conducted research in Munich, Warsaw, and the USSR, 1963, Taipei, Hong Kong, and Tokyo, 1969-71, London, 1973, China, 1981, 1984-90, 1995-97, and India, 1997; social scientist at RAND Corp., 1975-76; foreign affairs commentator for WUOM-Radio, 1989-98; National Security Council, White House, special asst to the president and senior director for Asia, 1998-2001; Brookings Institution, visiting fellow, 2000; consultant. **Publications:** Research Guide to Central Party and Government Meetings in China, 1949-1976, 1976; Central Documents and Politburo Politics in China, 1978; Sino-Soviet Conflict in the 1970s, 1978; The Strategic Triangle, 1979; Revolution and Tradition in Tientsin, 1949-52, 1980; (ed. with N. Lardy and contrib.) Chen Yun's Strategy for China's Development, 1982; (with M. Oksenberg) Bureaucratic Politics and Chinese Energy Development, 1986; (with Oksenberg) Policy Making in China, 1988; (with M. Flynn and others) Paths to Sino-U.S. Cooperation in the Automotive Sector, 1989; (with B. Dixon) Research Guide to Central Party and Government Meetings in China, 1949-1986, 1989; (with J. Kallgren and others) Perspectives on Modern China, 1991; (with D.M. Lampton) Bureaucratic Politics and Decision Making in Post-Mao China, 1992; Governing China: From Revolution through Reform, 1995. **Address:** Center for Chinese Studies Annex, University of Michigan, 202 S Thayer, Ann Arbor, MI 48109, U.S.A.

LIEBESCHUETZ, John Hugo W(olfgang) G(ideon). British (born Germany), b. 1927. **Genres:** Archaeology/Antiquities, History, Theology/Religion. **Career:** Heanor Grammar School, Derbyshire, England, schoolteacher, 1957-63; University of Leicester, England, lecturer, 1963-74, senior lecturer, 1974-78, reader in classics, 1978-79; University of Nottingham, England, professor of classical and archaeological studies, 1979-92, professor emeritus, 1992-. British Academy, fellow, 1991; Princeton Institute of Advanced Study, member, 1993. **Publications:** Antioch: City and Imperial Administration in the Later Roman Empire, 1972; Continuity and Change in Roman Religion, 1979; Barbarians and Bishops: Army, Church, and State in the Age of Arcadius and Chrysostom, 1990; From Diocletian to the Arab Conquest: Change in the Late Roman Empire, 1990; The Decline and Fall of the Roman City, 2001. Contributor to classical journals. **Address:** Department of Classics, University of Nottingham, University Park, Notts. NG7 2RD, England. **Online address:** wolf@liebeschuetz5472.fsnet.co.uk

LIEBICH, Andre. British/Canadian, b. 1948. **Genres:** International relations/Current affairs, History, Politics/Government. **Career:** Harvard University, Cambridge, MA, teaching fellow, 1971-72, visiting scholar at Russian Research Center, 1979-80, 1986-87; Oxford University, Oxford, England, junior associate of St. Antony's College, 1972-73; Universite du Quebec a Montreal, assistant professor, 1974-78, associate professor, 1978-82, professor of political science, 1982-91; Graduate Institute of International Studies, Geneva, Switzerland, professor of international history and politics, 1989-; visiting professor at universities worldwide. **Publications:** Between Ideology and Utopia, 1979; Les Minorites Nationales en Europe Centrales et Orientale, 1997; From the Other Shore: Russian Social Democracy after 1921, 1997. EDITOR/CO-EDITOR: Selected Writings of August Cieszkowski, 1979; Le Liberalisme Classique, 1986; Les Minorites en Europe Centrale: Vers une Solution Europeenne?, 1993; Citizenship, East and West, 1995. **Address:** Graduate Institute of International Studies, Rue de Lausanne 132, CP 36, CH 1211 Geneva 21, Switzerland. **Online address:** liebich@hei.unige.ch

LIEBMAN, Herbert. American, b. 1935. **Genres:** Plays/Screenplays, Literary criticism and history. **Career:** College of Staten Island, Staten Island, NY, professor of English, 1966; Shakespeare Festival, member of Playwrights Unit, 1978-81; playwright and director. **Publications:** PLAYS: And Mrs. Casey Will Find Us in the Morning, 1977; The Breakers, 1979; Positions, 1984; Alex and Joanna, 1985; Midnight's Section, 1987. OTHER: Coney Island, 1991; The Dramatic Art of David Storey: The Journey of a Playwright, 1996.

Contributor of short stories to periodicals. **Address:** Department of English, College of Staten Island, 2800 Victory Blvd., Staten Island, NY 10314, U.S.A. **Online address:** hlieb35@aol.com

LIEBMANN, George W. American, b. 1939. **Genres:** Law. **Career:** Law clerk to Chief Judge F.W. Brune, Annapolis, MD, 1963-64; Frank, Bernstein, Conaway & Goldman, Baltimore, partner, 1964-67, 1969-79; Maryland State Law Department, Baltimore, assistant attorney general, 1967-69; executive assistant to Governor Harry Hughes, Annapolis, 1979-80; Liebmann & Shively, Baltimore, principal, 1980-. Visiting fellow at UK universities. Member of boards of directors. **Publications:** Maryland District Court Law and Practice, 1976; Maryland Circuit Court Forms, 1984; The Gallows in the Grove, 1995; The Little Platoons, 1997; Solving Problems without Large Government, 1999; Six Lost Leaders, 2001. **Address:** Liebmann & Shively, 8 W Hamilton St, Baltimore, MD 21201, U.S.A. **Online address:** george. liebmann2@verizon.net

LIEF, Judith L. American, b. 1946. **Genres:** Inspirational/Motivational Literature. **Career:** Shambhala International, Halifax, Nova Scotia, teacher, 1975-; Shambhala Publications, Boston, MA, editor, 1985-. Vajradhatu Publications, editor in chief, 1975-. Naropa Institute, dean and member of board of trustees; House Foundation, member of advisory board; Greyston Foundation, volunteer. **Publications:** Teachings of the Tibetan Book of the Dead, 1998. EDITOR: C. Trungda, Heart of the Buddha, 1991; Trungda, Transcending Madness, 1992; Trungda, Training the Mind, 1993; Trungda, The Art of Calligraphy, 1994; Trungda, Dharma Art, 1996. **Address:** 18 Belmont Terr., Yonkers, NY 10703, U.S.A. **Online address:** garudalake@aol. com

LIEVEN, Dominic. British. **Genres:** History. **Career:** Historian and political scientist. London School of Economics, London, England, professor of Russian history and politics. Visiting professor at Tokyo University and Harvard University; Humboldt fellow at Göttingen University and Munich University. **Publications:** Russia and the Origins of the First World War, 1983; (ed., with DC Watt) British Documents on Foreign Affairs: Reports and Papers from the Foreign Office Confidential Print: The Soviet Union, 1917-1939, 1985-86; Russia's Rulers under the Old Regime, 1989; The Aristocracy in Europe, 1993; Nicholas II: Emperor of All the Russias, 1993, in US as Nicholas II: Twilight of the Empire, 1994; Empire: The Russian Empire and Its Rivals, 2000. **Address:** Department of International History, London School of Economics, Houghton St., London WC2A 2AE, England. **Online address:** d.lieven@lse.ac.uk

LIFSHIN, Lyn. American, b. 1948. **Genres:** Poetry. **Career:** State University of New York, Albany, English instructor, 1968; writing consultant, New York State Mental Health Dept., 1969, and Empire State College, NY, 1973; Mansfield State College, poet-in-residence, PA, 1974; Albany Public Library Poetry Workshop, NY, director. **Publications:** Why Is the House Dissolving?, 1968; Black Apples, 1970; Leaves and Night Things, 1971; Femina Two, 1972; Moving by Touch, 1972; Merchurochrome Sun Poems, 1972; Tentacles, Leaves, 1972; Love Poems, 1972; Museum, 1974; Forty Days, Apple Nights, 1974; The Croton, 1974; Shaker Poems, 1974; The Old House, 1974; Wild Flowers Smoke, 1974; Green Bandages, 1974; All the Women Poets, 1974; Audley End Poems, 1974; Upstate Madonna, 1975; Some Madonna Poems, 1976; Leaning South, 1976; Plymouth Women, 1976; North, 1976; Glass, 1978; Paper Apples, 1978; Offered by Owner, 1979; Crazy Arms, 1979; 35 Sundays, 1980; Colors of Cooper Black, 1981; Hotel Lifshin, 1982; Mad Girl Poems, 1982; Blue Dust New Mexico, 1982; Reading Lips, 1982; Madonna Who Shifts for Herself, 1982; Want Ads, 1982; In the Dark with Just One Star, 1982; Kiss the Skin Off, 1985; Naked Charm, 1984; Blue Horses Nuzzle Thursday, 1985; Raw Opals, 1987; Many More Madonnas, 1988; Red Hair and the Jesuit, 1988; Unsealed Lips, 1989; Rubbed Silk, 1989; Not Made of Glass (film), 1989; The Doctor (poems), 1990; More Naked Charm, 1990; The Innocents, 1991; Reading Lips, 1992; Marilyn Monroe, 1994; Parade, 1994; Shooting Kodachromes, 1994; Appleblossoms, 1994; Feathers in the Wind, 1994; The 375 Poem about Me Comes in the Mail, 1994; Pointe Shoes, 1995; The Mad Girl Drives in a Daze, 1995; Color and Light, 1996; Mad Girls, Dead Men, 1996; More Mad Girls, 1996; My Mother's Fire, 1996; Autobiography, 1996; Jesus Alive in the Flesh, 1997; Cold Comfort, 1997; Caught in the Act, 1997; Flesh Dress, 1997; Before It's Light, 1999; Another Woman Who Looks Like Me (film). EDITOR: Tangled Vines, 1978, rev. ed., 1992; Ariadne's Thread, 1982.

LIGHTER, J(onathan) E. American, b. 1949. **Genres:** Language/ Linguistics. **Career:** University of Tennessee, Knoxville, research associate. **Publications:** (ed.) Historical Dictionary of American Slang, 1: A-G, 1994. Contributor of articles to American Speech, 1972-. **Address:** Department of English, 311 McClung Tower, University of Tennessee, Knoxville, TN 37996, U.S.A.

LIGHTFOOT, D. J. See SIZEMORE, Deborah Lightfoot.

LIGHTMAN, Alan P. American, b. 1948. **Genres:** Novels, Sciences. **Career:** Cornell University, Ithaca, NY, postdoctoral fellow in astrophysics, 1974-76; Harvard University, Cambridge, MA, assistant professor of astronomy, 1976-79, lecturer in astronomy and physics, 1979-89; Smithsonian Astrophysical Observatory, Cambridge, staff astrophysicist, 1979-89; Massachusetts Institute of Technology, Cambridge, John E. Burchard Professor of science and writing and senior lecturer in physics, 1989-2001, adjunct professor of humanities, 2001-; writer. American Academy of Arts and Sciences, fellow, 1996. **Publications:** Problem Book in Relativity and Gravitation (textbook), 1975; Radioactive Processes in Astrophysics (textbook), 1979; Time Travel and Papa Joe's Pipe: Essays on the Human Side of Science, 1984; A Modern Day Yankee in a Connecticut Court, and Other Essays on Science, 1986; (with R. Brawer) Origins: The Lives and Worlds of Modern Cosmologists, 1990; Ancient Light: Our Changing View of the Universe, 1991; Time for the Stars: Astronomy in the 1990s, 1992; Great Ideas in Physics, 1992; Einstein's Dreams, 1993; Good Benito, 1995; Dance for Two, 1996; The Diagnosis, 2000; Reunion, 2003. Contributor to periodicals. **Address:** Program in Writing and Humanistic Studies, Massachusetts Institute of Technology, Cambridge, MA 02139, U.S.A.

LIGON, Samuel. American. **Genres:** Sex. **Career:** Writer and teacher. **Publications:** Safe in Heaven Dead, 2003. Contributor to periodicals. **Address:** c/o Author Mail, HarperCollins, 10 East 53rd St., New York, NY 10022, U.S.A.

LILA, Kim. American, b. 1966. **Genres:** Food and Wine. **Career:** Kleinschmidt, Deerfield, IL, marketing manager, 1997-. **Publications:** Simply Casseroles, 1998. **Address:** Kleinschmidt, 450 Lake Cook, Deerfield, IL 60015, U.S.A. **Online address:** kcclila@ameritech.net

LILES, Maurine Walpole. American, b. 1935. **Genres:** Children's fiction, Children's non-fiction. **Publications:** FOR CHILDREN: Rebecca of Blossom Prairie, 1990; Kitty of Blossom Prairie, 1992; The Boy of Blossom Prairie Who Became Vice-President, 1993; Sam and the Speaker's Chair (biography), 1994. **Address:** PO Box 546, Floresville, TX 78114-0546, U.S.A.

LILIENFELD, Jane. American. **Genres:** Literary criticism and history. **Career:** Affiliated with Chicago State College, 1968-69; Lincoln University, currently associate professor of English. **Publications:** (author of intro) Virginia Woolf: Emerging Perspectives, 1994; (ed., with J. Oxford) The Languages of Addiction, 1999; Reading Alcoholisms: Theorizing Character and Narrative in Selected Novels of Thomas Hardy, James Joyce, and Virginia Woolf, 1999. **Address:** Department of English, Foreign Languages, 431 MLK Building, Lincoln University, Jefferson City, MO 65102, U.S.A. **Online address:** jlilienf@coin.org

LILLER, William. American, b. 1927. **Genres:** Astronomy. **Career:** Professional astronomer and writer. **Publications:** The Cambridge Guide to Astronomical Discovery, 1992. **Address:** Casilla 5022, Renaca, Chile.

LILLEY, Stephen R(ay). American, b. 1950. **Genres:** Children's non-fiction. **Career:** Schoolteacher in Winfield, MO, 1972-74; Lincoln County Schools, Elsberry, MO, teacher, 1974-. Northeast Missouri State University, adjunct faculty, 1977; Hannibal LaGrange College, adjunct faculty, 1989-92. Jazz musician and trumpet player. **Publications:** Hernando Cortes, 1996; The Conquest of Mexico, 1997; Fighters against American Slavery, 1999. Contributor to periodicals. **Address:** 274 Lilley Lane, Elsberry, MO 63343, U.S.A. **Online address:** trumpeter@lincolnco.net

LILLOY, Raul A. Argentine, b. 1953. **Genres:** Novels. **Career:** International Business Machines, computer programmer; teaches on the university level. **Publications:** Kolon 3492, 1996. **Address:** Parque del Recreo 2, 1-B, 4610 Cuevas del Almanzora, Dorrego, Argentina. **Online address:** rlilloy@raiz. uncu.edu.ar

LIM, Shirley Geok-lin. American (born Malaysia), b. 1944. **Genres:** Novels, Novellas/Short stories, Poetry, Literary criticism and history, Autobiography/ Memoirs. **Career:** University of Malaya, Kuala Lumpur, lecturer, 1967-69; Queens College, CUNY, Flushing, teaching fellow, 1972-73; Hostos Community College, CUNY, Bronx, assistant professor, 1973-76; Westchester College, SUNY, Valhalla, associate professor, 1976-90; University of California, Santa Barbara, professor of Asian American studies, 1990-94, professor of women's studies and English, 1994-. National University of Singapore, visiting fellow, 1982, writer-in-residence, 1985, Asia Foundation fellow at Centre for Advanced Studies, 1989; Graduate Center of CUNY, Mellon fellow, 1983, 1987; University of California, Irvine, minority discourses fellow at Interdisciplinary Research Center, 1993. East-West Center (Honolulu, HI), writer in residence, 1988; gives poetry readings and workshops. **Publications:** Another Country and Other Stories, 1982; Nationalism and Literature: English-Language Writers from the Philippines and Singapore, 1993; Writing South/East Asia in English, 1994; Life's Mysteries, 1995; Among the White Moon Faces (memoir), 1996; Two Dreams (stories), 1997; What the Fortune Teller Didn't Say, 1998; Joss and Gold, 2001. POETRY: Crossing the Peninsula, 1980; No Man's Grove, 1985; Modern Secrets, 1989;Monsoon History, 1994. EDITOR/CO-EDITOR: (and author of intro.) The Forbidden Stitch, 1989; Approaches to Teaching Kingston's The Woman Warrior, 1991; Reading Asian American Literatures, 1992; One World of Literature, 1992; Asian American Literature, 1999; Transnational Asia Pacific Gender, Representations and the Public Sphere, 1999; Power, Race, and Gender in Academe, 2000; Tilting the Continent, 2000; Moving Poetry, 2001. **Address:** Department of English, University of California, Santa Barbara, CA 93106, U.S.A. **Online address:** slim@english.ucsb.edu

LIMA, Robert (F.), (Jr.). American (born Cuba), b. 1935. **Genres:** Plays/Screenplays, Poetry, Literary criticism and history, Bibliography, Biography, Translations. **Career:** Hunter College, City University of New York, lecturer in Romance literatures, 1962-65; Pennsylvania State University, University Park, professor of Spanish and comparative literature, 1965-2002 (chairman, Dept. of Comparative Literature, 1970-75). University de San Marcos, Peru, poet-in-residence; Universidad Catolica, Peru, visiting professor, 1976-77; sr. Fulbright fellow, 1976-77. Modern International Drama, editorial associate, 1967-81; editorial boards: Lexis, 1977-, Estreno, 1989-, Journal of the Fantastic in the Arts, 2000-, Anuario Valle-Inclan, 2001-; fellow, Institute for the Arts & Humanities, 1986-2002. **Publications:** Episode in Sicily (play), 1959; The Theatre of Garcia Lorca, 1963; Ramon del Valle-Inclan, 1972; An Annotated Bibliography of Ramon del Valle-Inclan, 1972; (co-author) Poems of Exile and Alienation, 1976; Fathoms (poetry), 1981; (co-author) Dos Ensayos Sobre Teatro Espanol de Los Veinte, 1984; The Olde Ground (poetry), 1985; Valle-Inclan: The Theatre of His Life, 1988; Mayaland (poetry), 1992; Dark Prisms: Occultism in Hispanic Drama, 1995; Valle-Inclan: El Teatro De Su Vida, 1995; Ramon Del Valle-Inclan: An Annotated Bibliography, Vol. 1: Works, 1999; Sardinia/Sardegna (prose, poetry), 2000; Tracking the Minotaur (poetry), 2003; The Dramatic World of Valle-Inclan, 2003. EDITOR/CO-EDITOR: Seventh Street Anthology: Poems of "Les Deux Megots," 1961; Readers Encyclopedia of American Literature, rev. ed., 1962; Surrealism: A Celebration, 1975; Borges and the Esoteric, 1993; C. Pavonis, The Alchemical Art of Leonora Carrington, 2000. EDITOR & TRANSLATOR: Borges the Labyrinth Maker, 1965; Valle-Inclan: Autobiography, Aesthetics, Aphorisms, 1966; R. Valle-Inclan, The Lamp of Marvels, 1986; Savage Acts: Four Plays by Valle-Inclan, 1991. **Address:** 485 Orlando Ave, State College, PA 16803-3477, U.S.A. **Online address:** rxl2@psu.edu

LIMON, Jerzy. Polish, b. 1950. **Genres:** Novels, Literary criticism and history. **Career:** Adam Mickiewicz University, Poznan, Poland, Department of English, instructor, 1975-79, lecturer, 1979-80; University of Gdansk, Poland, Department of English, assistant professor, 1980-85; associate professor, 1985-93, professor, 1993-. **Publications:** Munchhauseniada (novel), 1980; Gentlemen of a Company: English Players in Central and Eastern Europe, 1590-1660, 1986; Dangerous Matter: English Drama and Politics in 1623-24, 1986; The Masque of Stuart Culture, 1990; Wieloryb (novel), 1998; Koncert niedzwiedzicy (novel), 1999; Miedzyniebem a scena, 2002. EDITOR: (with J.L. Halio) Shakespeare and His Contemporaries: Eastern and Central European Studies, 1993; (with M. Gibinska) Hamlet East and West, 1998. **Address:** Department of English, University of Gdansk, ul. Wita Stwosza 55., Gdansk-Oliwa, Poland. **Online address:** fthgedan@gdansk.sprint.pl

LIMON, Martin. American, b. 1948. **Genres:** Mystery/Crime/Suspense. **Career:** U.S. Army, career officer, serving in South Korea for ten years; freelance writer, c. 1992-. **Publications:** NOVELS: Jade Lady Burning, 1992; Slicky Boys, 1997; Buddha's Money, 1998. **Address:** c/o Bantam Books, 1540 Broadway, New York, NY 10036, U.S.A.

LIMONOV, Edward. French (born Russia), b. 1944. **Genres:** Novels, Poetry. **Career:** Writer, 1980-. **Publications:** Russkoe (poems), Ardis, 1979; Journal d'un rate (novel), 1982; It's Me, Eddie (novel), trans. from original manuscript, Eto ia, Edichka, 1983; Molodoi negodiai (novel), 1986, trans. as Memoir of a Russian Punk, 1990; His Butler's Story (novel), trans. from original manuscript, Istoria ego slugi, 1987; Le petit Salaud (title means: The

Young Scoundrel), 1988; Inostranets: Smutnoe vremia (novel), 1992; Podrostok Savenko: Povest', 1992; Stranac u rodnom gradu, 1993; Ubiistvo Chasovogo, 1993; U nas byla velikaia epokha, 1994; Limonov protiv Zhirinovskogo, 1994; Kon'iak Napoleon, 1995; 316, punkt V (novel), 1998; Sobranie sochinenii v trekh tomakh, 1998. Author of additional poetry volumes. Contributor to periodicals. **Address:** c/o Mary Kling, 7 rue Corneille, 75006 Paris, France.

LIN, Jami. American, b. 1956. **Genres:** Homes/Gardens. **Career:** Earth Design, Miami Shores, FL, president, 1983-. Professional interior designer and feng shui consultant. **Publications:** Feng Shui Today: Earth Design, the Added Dimension, 1995; The Feng Shui Anthology: Contemporary Earth Design, 1997; The Essence of Feng Shui: Balancing Your Body, Home, and Life with Fragrance, 1998; Basic Essentials, 2001; Earth Energies, 2001; Heaven Energies, 2001; Yearly + Monthly Energies, 2001. **Address:** Earth Design, PO Box 530725, Miami Shores, FL 33153, U.S.A. **Online address:** gp@JamiLin.com

LIN, Tan (Anthony). American, b. 1957. **Genres:** Poetry. **Career:** Whitney Museum of American Art, NYC, assistant for rights and reproductions, 1980-83; Martell and Co., NYC, writer and researcher in New York and in Louisville, KY, 1984-86; freelance writer, 1986-88; University of Virginia, Charlottesville, assistant professor of English, 1993; New Jersey City University. Formation Language School, Paris, France, instructor, 1981-82. Atlantic Center for the Arts, associate artist in residence, 1992; Centre College, Danville, KY, poet in residence, 1997; creator of and participant in performance projects, films, and videotaped performances; gives readings from his works. **Publications:** POETRY: Lotion Bullwhip Giraffe, 1996. Contributor to books. Work represented in anthologies. Contributor of poems and essays to magazines. **Address:** Department of English, New Jersey City University, John F Kennedy Blvd, Jersey City, NJ 07305, U.S.A. **Online address:** tananthonylin@hotmail.com

LIN, Wallace. See LEONG, Russell (C.).

LINCECUM, Jerry Bryan. American, b. 1942. **Genres:** Autobiography/Memoirs. **Career:** Austin College, Sherman, TX, assistant professor to professor, 1967-97, Henry L. and Laura H. Shoap Professor of English, 1997-. Telling Our Stories (autobiography writing project), director, 1990-; Center for Excellence in Liberal Arts Teaching and Faculty Development, director, 2002-. **Publications:** EDITOR: (with E.H. Phillips) Adventures of a Frontier Naturalist: The Life and Times of Dr. Gideon Lincecum, 1994; (with E.H. Phillips and P.A. Redshaw) Science on the Texas Frontier: Observations of Dr. Gideon Lincecum, 1997; (with E.H. Phillips and P.A. Redshaw) Gideon Lincecum's Sword: Civil War Letters from the Home Front, 2001; (with F.E. Abernethy and F.B. Vick) The Family Saga: A Collection of Texas Family Legends, 2003. **Address:** Dept of English, Austin College, 900 N Grand Ave, Sherman, TX 75090, U.S.A. **Online address:** jlincecum@austincollege.edu

LINCOLN, Geoffrey. See MORTIMER, Sir John (Clifford).

LIND, Levi Robert. American, b. 1906. **Genres:** Literary criticism and history, Translations. **Career:** University Distinguished Professor of Classics, University of Kansas, Lawrence, since 1964. **Publications:** Medieval Latin Studies: Their Nature and Possibilities, 1941; The Vita Sancti Malchi of Reginald of Canterbury, 1942; Epitaph for Poets and Other Poems, 1966 Twentieth Century Italian Poetry: A Bilingual Anthology, 1974; Gerontocomia, and Maximianus: Elegies, by Gabriele Zerbi, 1988; An Epitaph Years After, 1990; The Letters of Giovanni Garzoni, Bolognese Humanist and Physician (1419-1505), 1992. TRANSLATOR: The Epitome of Andreas Vesalius, 1949; Lyric Poetry of the Italian Renaissance, 1954; Ten Greek Plays in Contemporary Translations, 1957; Latin Poetry in Verse Translation, 1957; (ed.) Ecclesiale, by Alexander of Villa Dei, 1958; A Short Introduction to Anatomy, by Berengario da Carpi, 1959; Vergil's Aeneid, 1963; Aldrovandi on Chickens: The Ornithology of Ulisse Aldrovandi (1600), 1963; Problemata Varia Anatomica: The University of Bologna MS 1165, 1968; Roman Elegies and Venetian Epigrams, by Johann Wolfgang von Goethe, 1974; Studies in Pre-Vesalian Anatomy, 1974; Tristia, by Ovid, 1975; Elegies and Camille, by André Chénier, 1978; On the Fracture of the Skull or Cranium, by Bernardo da Carpi, 1990. **Address:** 4817 Baja Ct. NE, Albuquerque, NM 87111, U.S.A.

LIND, Michael. American, b. 1962. **Genres:** Politics/Government. **Career:** National Interest, executive editor; Harper's, NYC, senior editor, 1994-. **Publications:** The Next American Nation: The New Nationalism and the

Fourth American Revolution, 1995. Contributor to Dissent and the Wall Street Journal. **Address:** Harper's, 666 Broadway, 11th Floor, New York, NY 10012, U.S.A.

LINDBECK, (K.) Assar (E.). Swedish, b. 1930. **Genres:** Economics. **Career:** University of Stockholm, lecturer, 1959-60, Reader, 1962-63, Acting Professor of Economics, 1963-, Director of Institute for International Economic Studies, 1971-95, Professor of International Economics, 1995-. Chairman, Selection Committee for the Nobel Prize in Economic Sciences, Swedish Council for Economic Planning. Part-time Employee, 1953-54, and Member of Economic Secretariat, 1955-56, Treasury Dept., Stockholm; Rockefeller Foundation Fellow, Yale University, New Haven, CT, Federal Reserve Board, Washington, DC, and University of Michigan, Ann Arbor, 1957-59; Professor of Economics, Stockholm School of Economics, 1964-71; Wesley Clair Mitchell Research Professor, Columbia University, NYC, 1968-69; Ford Rotating Research Professor, University of California at Berkeley, 1969; Irving Fisher Visiting Professor, Yale University, 1976-77; Visiting scholar, Stanford University, 1977, Simon Fraser University, 1980, and Singapore University, 1987. Expert, Swedish Dept. of Domestic Affairs, 1964-66; Economic Adviser, Swedish Central Bank, 1964-68, 1971-73. **Publications:** The "New" Theory of Credit Control in the United States: An Interpretation and Elaboration, 1959; A Study of Monetary Analysis, 1963; Monetary-Fiscal Analysis and General Equilibrium, 1967; (with Gulbrandsen) The Economics of the Agriculture Sector, 1971; The Political Economy of the New Left: An Outsider's View, 1971; Swedish Economic Policy, 1972; Inflation: Global, International and National Aspects, 1980; (with Snower) The Insider-Outsider Theory of Employment and Unemployment, 1988; Unemployment and Macroeconomics, 1993; The Swedish Experiment, 1997. **Address:** Institute for International Economic Studies, Stockholm University, S-106 91 Stockholm, Sweden. **Online address:** assar@iies.su.edu

LINDELL, Colleen. American, b. 1963. **Genres:** Medicine/Health. **Career:** St. Croix Valley Memorial Hospital, St. Croix Falls, WI, registered nurse, 1984-85; St. John's Northeast Hospital, Maplewood, MN, registered nurse, 1985-87; St. Croix Valley Memorial Hospital, director of surgical services and coordinator of Diabetes Program, 1987-96; Med-Legal.net, Osceola, WI, president and consultant, 1996-. Medwave Inc., clinical coordinator, 1996-97; Magellan Medical Services, nurse consultant, 1996-; Fairview Lakes Regions Medical Center, registered nurse, 1996-2001. American Diabetes Association, camp nurse; Interfaith Caregivers, volunteer; national and local speaker. **Publications:** Internet Medical Guidebook (annual), 1998-2004. Contributor to periodicals. **Address:** Med-Legal.net, Inc., 1828 45th Ave Ste 104, Osceola, WI 54020-5403, U.S.A. **Online address:** lindell@med-legal. net; www.med-legal.net

LINDENBAUM, Pija. Swedish, b. 1955. **Genres:** Children's fiction, Illustrations. **Career:** Writer and illustrator. **Publications:** SELF-ILLUSTRATED: Else-Marie and Her Seven Little Daddies, 1991; Boodil My Dog, trans. by G. Charbonnet, 1992; Bridget and the Graywolfs, 2001; Bridget and the Muttonheads, 2002; Bridget and the Moose Brothers, 2003. IN SWEDISH: Britten och Prins Benny, 1996; Starke Arvid, 1997; Glossas Cafe, 1998. Illustrator of book by B. Lindenbaum. **Address:** Bjurholmsg.34, 11638 Stockholm, Sweden.

LINDENMUTH, Kevin J. American, b. 1965. **Genres:** Plays/Screenplays, Film. **Career:** Brimstone Media Productions, Brighton, MI, director/producer, 1992-. **Publications:** Making Movies on Your Own, 1998; The Independent Film Experience, 2002. SCREENPLAYS: Vampires & Other Stereotypes, 1993; Twisted Tales, 1994; Addicted to Murder, 1995; Alien Agenda, 1997; Screaming for Sanity, 1998; Creaturealm, 1998; Addicted to Murder 2, 1998; Rage of the Werewolf, 1999; Addicted to Murder: Blood Lust, 1999; Twisted Tales 2, 2000; Date with a Vampire, 2001; Alien Conspiracy, 2002; Werewolf Tales, 2002; Bites, 2003; Monstersdotcom, 2003; Goregoyles, 2003. **Address:** Brimstone Media Productions, 7900 State St, Brighton, MI 48116, U.S.A. **Online address:** infolindenmuth@aol.com; www.lindenmuth.com

LINDER, Marc. American, b. 1946. **Genres:** Economics, Law, Translations, History, Politics/Government, Industrial relations, Sociology. **Career:** Hohenheim University, Stuttgart, Germany, research associate of project on the industrialization of agrarian regions, 1973-74; Roskilde University Center, Denmark, lecturer in division of social sciences, 1974-77; National Autonomous University of Mexico, Mexico City, professor of economics, 1977; translator of German, Danish, Swedish, Norwegian, Polish, Dutch, Italian, French, and Spanish, 1977-80; Texas Rural Legal Aid, Weslaco, attorney in farmworker division, 1983-90; University of Iowa, Iowa City, visiting associate professor, 1990-92, associate professor of labor, 1992-94, professor, 1994-. **Publications:** (trans. from German) Johannes Bobrowski, I

Taste Bitterness (stories), 1970; Der AntiSamuelson, four volumes, 1974; Anti-Samuelson, two volumes, 1977; Reification and the Consciousness of the Critics of Political Economy: Studies in the Development of Marx's Theory of Value, 1975; (trans. from German) Fred Wander, The Seventh Well (novel), 1976; European Labor Aristocracies: Trade Unionism, the Hierarchy of Skill, and the Stratification of the Manual Working Class before the First World War, 1985; The Supreme Labor Court in Nazi Germany: A Jurisprudential Analysis, 1987; The Employment Relationship in Anglo-American Law: A Historical Perspective, 1989; Farewell to the Self-Employed: Deconstructing a Socioeconomic and Legal Solipsism, 1992; Migrant Workers and Minimum Wages: Regulating the Exploitation of Agricultural Labor in the United States, 1992; Projecting Capitalism: A History of the Internationalization of the Construction Industry, 1994; The Dilemmas at Laissez-Faire Population Policy in Capitalist Societies: When the Invisible Hand Controls Reproduction, 1997; Void Where Prohibited: The Regulation of Statutory Rest Breaks & the Right to Urinate "on Company Time", 1997. Work represented in anthologies. Contributor of articles and reviews to professional law and sociology journals. **Address:** College of Law, University of Iowa, Iowa City, IA 52242, U.S.A.

LINDER, Robert D. American, b. 1934. **Genres:** History. **Career:** Professor of History, Kansas State University, Manhattan, since 1973 (Assistant Professor, 1965-67; Associate Professor, 1967-73). **Publications:** The Political Ideas of Pierre Viret, 1964; (ed. with R. G. Clouse and R. V. Pierard) Protest and Politics: Christianity and Contemporary Affairs, 1968; (ed. with Robert M. Kingdon) Calvin and Calvinism: Sources of Democracy?, 1970; (ed.) God and Caesar: Case Studies in the Relationship of Christianity and the State, 1971; (ed. with Clouse and Pierard) The Cross and the Flag, 1972; (with Pierard) Politics: A Case for Christian Action, 1973; (ed. with others) Eerdman's Handbook to the History of Christianity, 1977; (with Pierard) Twilight of the Saints: Biblical Christianity and Civil Religion in America, 1978; (with Pierard) Civil Religion and the Presidency, 1988; (co-ed.) A Dictionary of Christianity in America, 1990; (co-ed.) The History of Christianity, 1990; (co-ed.) A Concise Dictionary of Christianity in America, 1995. **Address:** Dept. of History, Kansas State University, Manhattan, KS 66506, U.S.A.

LINDGREN, Barbro. Swedish, b. 1937. **Genres:** Children's fiction, Poetry. **Career:** Worked as a commercial artist and designer; author, 1965-. **Publications:** FOR CHILDREN: Mattias sommar (title means: Mattias's Summer), 1965, trans. as Hilding's Summer, 1967; Mera om Mattias (More about Mattias), 1966; Hej, hej Mattias (Hi, Hi, Mattias), 1967; I Vaestan Grind (Westwind Gate), 1968; Loranga, Masarin och Dartanjang, 1969; Loranga, Loranga, 1970; Nu har Kalle faat en liten syster (Kalle Now Has a New Little Sister), 1970; Jaettehemligt (Giant Secret), 1971; Goda goda: Dikter (Hello! Hello!: Poems), 1971, rev. ed., 1976; Nu aer vi gorillor lassas vi, 1971, trans. as Let's Be Gorillas!, 1976; Vaerldshemligt (World Secret), 1972; Alban: popmuffa foer sma hundar (Alban: A Muff Hat for Small Dogs), 1972, rev. ed., 2004, trans. as Alban, 1974; Bladen brinner (Burning Pages), 1973, rev. ed., 1978; Groengoelingen aer paa vaeg: Dikter foer barn och andra (The Green Woodpecker Is on His Way: Poems for Children and Others), 1974; Barbros pjaeser foer barn och andra (Barbro's Plays for Kids and Others), 1975, rev. ed., 1978; Vad tycker du? (What Do You Think?), 1976; Lilla Sparvel (Little Sparrow), 1976; Stora Sparvel (Big Sparrow), 1977; (with L. Westman) Hemliga laadans hemlighet (The Secret Box's Secrets), 1978; (with Westman) Jag har en tam myra (I Have a Tame Ant), 1978; (with Westman) Kom ner fraan traedet (Come down from the Tree), 1978; (with Westman) Var aer mina byxor? (Where Are My Pants?), 1978; (with Westman) Vaerldens laengsta korv (The World's Longest Hot Dog), 1978; (with Westman) Laesa med varandra (Reading with Each Other), 1978; Garderobsbio (The Movie Closet), 1978; Bara Sparvel (Just Sparrow), 1979; Sagan om den lilla farbrorn, 1979, trans. as The Story of the Little Old Man, 1991; Nils Pantaloni Penell, 1980; Fotograf Jag (Me, the Photographer), 1980; Mamman och den vilda bebin, 1980, adapted as The Wild Baby, 1981; Max nalle, 1981, trans. as Sam's Teddy Bear, 1982, in UK as Sam's Teddy, 1984; Max bil, 1981, trans. as Sam's Car, 1982; Max kaka, 1981, trans. as Sam's Cookie, 1982, in UK as Sam's Biscuit, 1984; Den vilda bebiresan, 1982, adapted as The Wild Baby Goes to Sea, 1983, in UK as The Wild Baby's Boat Trip, 1983; Max boll, 1982 trans. as Sam's Ball, 1983; Max lampa, 1982, trans. as Sam's Lamp, 1983, in UK as Bad Sam!, 1983; Max balja, 1982, trans. as Sam's Bath, 1983; Pompe badar I en a (Pompe Takes a Swim in the Stream), 1982; Pompe gar I skogen (Pompe Takes a Walk in the Woods), 1982; OBS! Viktigt! (Please Note! Important!), 1983, 2nd ed., 1990; Sagan om Karlknut, 1985, trans. as A Worm's Tale, 1988; Vilda bebin faar en hund, 1985, trans. as The Wild Baby's Dog, 1986, adapted as The Wild Baby Gets a Puppy, 1988; Max potta, 1986, trans. as Sam's Potty, 1986; Max dockvagn, 1986, trans. as Sam's Wagon, 1986, in UK as Sam's Cart, 1986; Vems lilla moessa flyger, 1987; Pellerell, 1987; Sunkan flyger (Sunkan

Flies), 1989, trans. as Shorty Takes Off, 1990; Korken flyger (The Cock Flies), 1990; Stackars Allan (For Allan), 1990; Pojken och stjarnan (The Boy and the Star), 1991; Titta Max grav (Sam's Grave), 1991; Jam-Jam Jb-Jb, 1992; Stora Syster, Lille Bror (Big Sister, Little Brother), 1992; Bara Boerje (Well Done Borje), 1992, trans. as Louie, 1994; Puss Puss Sant Sant, 1993; Gomorron Gud (Good Morning, Gud), 1994; Har ar Det Lilla Huset, 1994; Max Napp, 1994; Max Bloja, 1994; Svempa vill ha manga nappar, 1995; Lilla Lokomotivet Rosa, 1995, trans. as Rosa, Perpetual Motion Machine, 1996; Rosa Flyttar Till Stan, 1996; Rosa Pa Bal, 1997; Prinsessan Rosa, 1999; Na ar vi jobbarkaniner, 1997; Andrejs langtan, 1997, trans. as Andrei's Search, 2000; Namen Benny, 1998, trans. as Benny's Had Enough, 1999; Per och Pompe, 1998; Rosa pa dagis, 1999, trans. as Rosa Goes to Daycare, 2000; Angeln Gunnar dimper ner, 2000; Vi leker att du ar en humla, 2000; Jamen Benny, 2001, trans. as Benny and the Binky, 2002; Tre fugor av Bach, 2001; Graddbullarna Bulle och Rulle, Julia vill ha ett djur, 2002, trans. as Julia Wants a Pet, 2003; Rosas sanger (Songs of Rosa), 2004. FOR ADULTS: Genom ventilerna (Through the Ventilators), 1967; Felipe, 1970; Eldvin, 1972; Molnens broeder (The Celestial Brothers), 1975; Rapporter fraan marken: Dikter (Reports from the Ground: Poems), 1976; Det riktiga havet (The Real Ocean), 1979; En liten cyklist (The Little Cyclist), 1982; Elegi oever en doed raatta (poems; Elegy over a Dead Rat), 1983; Hunden med rocken: prosadikter (The Dog with the Overcoat: Prose and Poems), 1985; Vitkind: I ett barns hjaerta (In a Child's Heart), 1986; Nu aer du mitt barn (Now You Are My Child), 1988; Restauranten Ar Stangd, 1992; Jag sager bara Elitchoklad: Prosastycken (I Just Say Elite Chocolate), 1993; Kungsholmens Ros, 1995; Nar jag var prins utav Arkadien (When I Was a Prince of Arkadia), 2003; Det ar som i Rom: poems (It's Like in Rome: Poems), 2004. **Address:** c/o Eriksson & Lindgren AB, Hantverkargatan 87, Box 120 85, 102 23 Stockholm, Sweden. **Online address:** www.eriksson-lindgren.se

LINDGREN, David T(readwell). (born United States), b. 1939. **Genres:** Technology. **Career:** Central Intelligence Agency, Washington, DC, imagery analyst, 1964-66; Dartmouth College, Hanover, NH, professor of geography and department head, 1966-2001. Consultant to Central Intelligence Agency, National Aeronautics and Space Administration, and U.S. Department of the Interior. **Publications:** Land Use Planning and Remote Sensing, 1985; Trust but Verify: Imagery Analysis in the Cold War, 2000. **Address:** 3229 Klingle Rd. N.W., Washington, DC 20008, U.S.A. **Online address:** lindgren@uio.satnet.net

LINDGREN, James M. American, b. 1950. **Genres:** History. **Career:** Old Dominion University, Norfolk, VA, instructor in history, 1978-79, 1980; State University of New York at Plattsburgh, assistant professor, 1984-91, associate professor, 1991-94, professor of history, 1994-, department chair, 2001-. **Publications:** Preserving the Old Dominion: Historic Preservation and Virginia Traditionalism, 1993; Preserving New England: Preservation, Progressivism, and the Remaking of Memory, 1995. Contributor to history journals. **Address:** Department of History, State University of New York, Plattsburgh, NY 12901, U.S.A.

LINDHOLDT, Paul J. American, b. 1954. **Genres:** Literary criticism and history, Environmental sciences/Ecology, Poetry, Language/Linguistics. **Career:** Idaho State University, Pocatello, lecturer in English, 1984-87; University of Idaho, Moscow, visiting assistant professor of English, 1990-94; Eastern Washington University, assistant professor of English, 1994-; writer. **Publications:** John Josselyn, Colonial Traveler, 1988; Cascadia Wild: Protecting an International Ecosystem, 1993. Author of articles on American literature and culture, and environmental issues; journalism; and poems. **Address:** Department of English, Eastern Washington University, Cheney, WA 99004, U.S.A. **Online address:** plindholdt@ewu.edu

LINDISFARNE-TAPPER, Nancy. Also writes as Nancy Tapper. American/British, b. 1944. **Genres:** Novellas/Short stories, Anthropology/Ethnology. **Career:** Writer and educator. **Publications:** (as Nancy Tapper) Bartered Brides: Politics, Gender, and Marriage in an Afghan Tribal Society, 1991; (as Nancy Lindisfarne, ed. with A. Cornwall, and contrib.) Dislocating Masculinity: Comparative Ethnographies, 1993; (as Nancy Lindisfarne-Tapper, ed. with B. Ingham) Languages of Dress in the Middle East, 1997; (as Nancy Lindisfarne) Dancing in Damascus, 2000. Contributor to scholarly journals, from 1968-93 under the names Nancy Tapper, Nancy Lindisfarne-Tapper, and Nancy Lindisfarne. **Address:** Department of Anthropology and Sociology, London School of Oriental and African Studies, University of London, Thornhaugh St., Russell Sq., London WC1H 0XG, England.

LINDNER, Koenraad J(an). Canadian (born Netherlands), b. 1941. **Genres:** Medicine/Health. **Career:** State University of New York College at Brockport, assistant professor, 1973-74; University of Manitoba, Winnipeg, as-

sistant professor to associate professor, 1974-96; University of Hong Kong, lecturer to senior lecturer, 1993-. **Publications:** Epidemiology of Sports Injuries, 1996. **Address:** University of Hong Kong, PESSU, 111 Pokfulam Rd, Hong Kong, People's Republic of China. **Online address:** klindner@hku.hk; klindner@hotmail.com

LINDQUIST, N(ancy) J(ane). Canadian, b. 1948. **Genres:** Mystery/Crime/Suspense, Young adult fiction, Plays/Screenplays, Young adult non-fiction. **Career:** Secondary school teacher in Roblin, Manitoba, Canada, 1970-72; writer, editor, and columnist, Markham, Ontario, Canada, 1989-. Writing teacher at conferences and workshops. **Publications:** MYSTERY NOVEL: Shaded Light: A Manziuk and Ryan Mystery, 2000. NOVELS FOR YOUNG ADULTS: Best of Friends, 1991, rev. ed., 2000; In Time of Trouble, 1999; Friends Like These, 2000; Friends in Need, 2001. PLAY: Behind the News: Report form Bethlehem, 2001. NONFICTION: The Bridge, Vol. 1, 1998, Vol. 2, 1999; (coauthor) The New You, 2000. Contributor of stories and articles to magazines. **Address:** PO Box 487, Markham, ON, Canada L3P 3R1. **Online address:** author@njlindquist.com

LINDSAY, Frederic. Scottish, b. 1933. **Genres:** Novels, Plays/Screenplays, Poetry. **Career:** Annan Academy, instructor in English, 1960-66; Hamilton College of Education, lecturer in English and applied linguistics, 1966-78; writer, 1979-. **Publications:** And Be the Nation Again (poems), 1975. NOVELS: Brond, 1984; Jill Rips, 1987; A Charm against Drowning, 1988; After the Stranger Came, 1992; Kissing Judas, 1997; A Kind of Dying, 1998; Idle Hands, 1999; Death Knock, 2000; Darkness in My Hand, 2001. Author of radio plays for children, and of plays for Scottish Youth Theatre; author of several commissioned, but unproduced, film scripts. Adaptor of Brond into a three-part television work, 1987. **Address:** 28 The Green, Pencaitland, East Lothian EH34 5HE, Scotland. **Online address:** Frederic.Lindsay@hotmail.com

LINDSAY, Geoff. British. **Genres:** Education. **Career:** Sheffield Local Education Authority, Sheffield, England, senior educational psychologist; writer. **Publications:** EDITOR: Problems of Adolescence in the Secondary School, 1983; Screening for Children with Special Needs: Multidisciplinary Approaches, 1984; (with A. Miller) Psychological Services for Primary Schools, 1991; (with D. Thompson) Values into Practice in Special Education, 1997; (with M. Desforges) Baseline Assessment: Practice, Problems, and Possibilities, 1998. **Address:** c/o Taylor & Francis, 4 John St., London WC1N 2ET, England.

LINDSAY, John. See LADELL, John L.

LINDSAY, Maurice. Scottish, b. 1918. **Genres:** Novels, Poetry, Architecture, Biography, How-to books, Literary criticism and history, Natural history, Autobiography/Memoirs. **Career:** Director, 1967-83, and Consultant, 1983-, Scottish Civic Trust. Hon. Secretary-General, Europa Nostra, 1983-91. Drama Critic, Scottish Daily Mail, Edinburgh, 1946-47; Music Critic, Bulletin, Glasgow, 1946-60; freelance broadcaster, BBC, Glasgow, 1946-61; Program Controller, 1961-62, Production Controller, 1962-64, and Features Executive and Sr. Interviewer, 1964-67, Border Television, Carlisle. **Publications:** The Advancing Day, 1940; Perhaps Tomorrow, 1941; Predicament, 1942; No Crown for Laughter, 1943; Modern Scottish Poetry, 1946; The Enemies of Love, 1946; No Scottish Twilight, 1947; Hurlygush, 1948; The Scottish Renaissance, 1949; At the Wood's Edge, 1950; Ode for St. Andrew's Night and Other Poems, 1951; The Lowlands of Scotland: Glasgow and the North, 1953; Robert Burns: The Man, His Work, The Legend, 1954, 3rd ed., 1980; Dunoon, 1954; The Lowlands of Scotland: Edinburgh and the South, 1956; The Exiled Heart, 1957; (with D. Somervell) Killochan Castle, 1958; Clyde Waters, 1958; The Burns Encyclopedia, 1959, 3rd ed., 1980; Snow Warning, 1962; By Yon Bonnie Banks, 1962; Selected Poems of John Davidson, 1962; One Later Day, 1964; The Discovery of Scotland, 1964; This Business of Living, 1969; Comings and Goings, 1971; The Eye Is Delighted: Some Romantic Travellers in Scotland, 1971; Portrait of Glasgow, 1972, 1980; Selected Poems 1942-72, 1973; Scotland: An Anthology, 1974; Robin Philipson, 1975; A History of Scottish Literature, 1977; Walking without an Overcoat, 1977; Collected Poems, 1979; Lowland Scottish Villages, 1979; Francis George Scott and the Scottish Renaissance, 1979; A Net to Catch the Winds, 1981; (with A.F. Kersting) The Buildings of Edinburgh, 1981; Thank You for Having Me (autobiography), 1983; (with D. Handley) Unknown Scotland, 1984; The Castles of Scotland, 1986; The French Mosquitoes Woman, 1987; Count All Men Mortal: The History of the Scottish Provident Institution, 1987; Victorian and Edwardian Glasgow, 1987; Requiem for a Sexual Athlete, 1988; Glasgow, 1989; An Illustrated Guide to Glasgow 1837, 1989; Collected Poems, 1940-1990, 1990; (with D. Bruce) Edinburgh Past and Present, 1989; (with J. Lindsay) The Scottish Quotation Book, 1991;

(with J. Lindsay) The Music Quotation Book, 1992; (with J. Lindsay) The Theatre and Opera-Lovers Quotation Books, 1993; On the Face of It: Collected Poems, vol. 2, 1993; News of the World, 1995; (with J. Lindsay) Scottish Gardens, 1996; Speaking Likenesses, 1999; Worlds Apart, 2000; Glasgow: Fabric of a City, 2000. EDITOR: Sailing Tomorrow's Seas, 1944; (with H. MacDiarmid) Poetry Scotland, vol. I-III, and IV, 1945-53; (with F. Urquhart) Selected Poems by Sir Alexander Gray, 1948; (with H. Cruickshank) Selected Poems by Marion Angus, 1956; (with E. Morgan and G. Bruce) Scottish Poetry, 1966-72; (consultant) Voices of Our Kind, 1971; (with A. Scott and R. Watson) Scottish Poetry, 1974; Modern Scottish Poetry: An Anthology, 1976; As I Remember, 1979; Scottish Comic Verse 1425-1980, 1980; (with A. Scott) The Comic Poems of William Tennant, 1989; T. Hamilton, The Youth and Manhood of Cyril Thornton, 1990; (with J. Lindsay) The Scottish Dog, 1989. **Address:** 7 Milton Hill, Milton, Dunbarton, Scotland.

LINDSAY-POLAND, John. (born United States), b. 1960. **Genres:** Civil liberties/Human rights. **Career:** Fellowship of Reconciliation, San Francisco, CA, director of task force on Latin America and the Caribbean. Panama Update, editor and staff writer. **Publications:** (with Tom Barry, Marco Gandásequi, and Peter Simonson) Inside Panama: The Essential Guide to Its Politics, Economy, Society, and Environment, 1995; Emperors in the Jungle: The Hidden History of the U.S. in Panama, 2003. Contributor to periodicals. **Address:** Fellowship of Reconciliation, 2017 Mission St. No. 305, San Francisco, CA 94110, U.S.A.

LINDSEY, Johanna. American, b. 1952. **Genres:** Romance/Historical. **Publications:** Captive Bride, 1977; A Pirate's Love, 1978; Fires of Winter, 1980; Paradise Wild, 1981; Glorious Angel, 1982; So Speaks the Heart, 1983; Heart of Thunder, 1983; A Gentle Feuding, 1984; Brave the Wild Wind, 1984; Love Only Once, 1985; Tender Is the Storm, 1985; A Heart So Wild, 1986; When Love Awaits, 1986; Hearts Aflame, 1987; Secret Fire, 1987; Tender Rebel, 1988; Silver Angel, 1988; Defy not the Heart, 1989; Savage Thunder, 1989; Warrior's Woman, 1990; Gentle Rogue, 1990; Once a Princess, 1991; Prisoner of My Desire, 1991; Man of My Dreams, 1992; Angel, 1992; The Magic of You, 1993; Keeper of the Heart, 1993; Surrender My Love, 1994; You Belong to Me, 1994; Until Forever, 1995; Love Me Forever, 1995; Say You Love Me, 1996; Joining, 1999; The Heir, 2000; Home for the Holidays, 2000; Heart of a Warrior, 2001; The Pursuit, 2002; A Man to Call My Own, 2003.

LINDSKOLD, Jane M. American, b. 1962. **Genres:** Novels, Biography. **Career:** Lynchburg College, Lynchburg, VA, assistant professor, 1989-94; writer, 1994-. **Publications:** NONFICTION: Roger Zelazny, 1993. NOVELS: Brother to Dragons, Companion to Owls, 1994; Marks of Our Brothers, 1995; Pipes of Orpheus, in press. Also author of short stories. **Address:** Pimlico Agency, Inc., Po Box 20447, New York, NY 10021-0067, U.S.A.

LINDSTROM, Lamont (Carl). American, b. 1953. **Genres:** Anthropology/Ethnology. **Career:** Australian National University, Canberra, visiting research scholar, Research School of Pacific Studies, 1977-79; Southwestern at Memphis, Memphis, TN, visiting assistant professor, 1981-82; University of Tulsa, Tulsa, OK, assistant professor, 1982-88, associate professor, 1988-92, professor of anthropology, 1992-, department chair, 1991-96. East-West Center, fellow of Institute of Culture and Communication, 1987-88; National Endowment for the Humanities, seminar director, 1991 and 1993. Conducted anthropological field studies in Tanna, Vanuatu, 1978-79 and 1982-83; in Australia, Papua New Guinea, Fiji, Vanuatu, and the Solomon Islands, 1985; in Guadalcanal, the Solomon Islands, and Tanna, 1987; Vanuatu, 1988; and Port Moresby, Papua New Guinea, 1988-89. **Publications:** Kwamera Dictionary: Nikukua Savai Nagkiariien Nininife, 1986; Drugs in Western Pacific Societies: Relations of Substance (monograph), 1987; (ed. with G.M. White, and contrib.) The Pacific Theater: Island Recollections of World War II, 1989; (with G.M. White) Island Encounters: Black and White Memories of the Pacific War, 1990; Knowledge and Power in a South Pacific Society, 1990; (with V. Lebot and M. Merlin) Kava: The Pacific Drug, 1992; Cargo Cult: Strange Stories of Desire From Melanesia and Beyond, 1993. Work represented in books. Contributor of articles and reviews to anthropology journals. **Address:** Department of Anthropology, University of Tulsa, OK 74104, U.S.A. **Online address:** lamont-lindstrom@utulsa.edu

LINDVALL, Michael L(loyd). American, b. 1947. **Genres:** Theology/Religion, Documentaries/Reportage. **Career:** Drayton Avenue Presbyterian Church, Ferndale, MI, associate pastor, 1974-79; First Presbyterian Church of Northport, Long Island, NY, pastor, 1979-92; First Presbyterian Church of Ann Arbor, Ann Arbor, MI, senior pastor, 1992; Brick Presbyterian Church, NYC. **Publications:** The Good News from North Haven: A Year in the Life of a Small Town, 1991; Leaving North Haven, 2001; The Christian Life: A Geography of God. Contributor of short stories to periodicals. **Address:** Brick Presbyterian Church, 62 E 92nd St, New York, NY 10128, U.S.A.

LINE, David. See **DAVIDSON, Lionel.**

LINE, Maurice Bernard. British, b. 1928. **Genres:** Librarianship, Bibliography. **Career:** Professor Associate, University of Sheffield, 1977-. Visiting Professor, University of Loughborough, 1986-92. Sub-Librarian, University of Southampton, 1954-65; Deputy Librarian, University of Newcastle upon Tyne, 1965-68; Librarian, University of Bath, 1968-71; Librarian, National Central Library, London, 1971-73; Director-General, British Library Lending Division, 1974-85; Director-General, Science, Technology and Industry, British Library, 1985-88. **Publications:** Bibliography of Russian Fiction in English Translation to 1900 (excluding periodicals), 1963, 1972; The College Student and the Library, 1965; Library Surveys, 1967, 1982; (with K.P. Barr) Essays on Information and Libraries, 1975; (with J. Line) National Libraries, 1979, National Libraries 2, 1987; National Libraries 3, 1995; (with S. Vickers) Universal Availability of Publications, 1983; Academic Library Management, 1990. **Address:** 10 Blackthorn Ln, Burn Bridge, Harrogate, N. Yorkshire HG3 1NZ, England. **Online address:** mbl@hgte.demon.co.uk

LING, Amy. American (born China), b. 1939. **Genres:** Literary criticism and history, Cultural/Ethnic topics, Poetry. **Career:** Chengkung University, Tainan, Taiwan, lecturer in foreign languages and literatures, 1962-63; Lui, Paris, France, bilingual secretary, 1963; high school English teacher in Valley Stream, NY, 1963-65; Thomas Y. Crowell Co. (publisher), New York City, editorial assistant, 1965-66; City College of the City University of New York, New York City, lecturer in English, 1966-69; Brooklyn College of the City University of New York, Brooklyn, NY, instructor in English, 1969-72; Rutgers University, New Brunswick, NJ, assistant professor of English, 1972-88, coordinator of basic writing program at Livingston College, 1972-75; Georgetown University, Washington, DC, adjunct instructor in English, 1988-89; Queens College of the City University of New York, Flushing, NY, Rockefeller fellow in the humanities at Asian/American Center, 1989-90; Harvard University, Cambridge, MA, visiting associate professor of English, 1990; Trinity College, Hartford, CT, Visiting Allan K. Smith Associate Professor of Language and Literature, 1991; University of Wisconsin-Madison, associate professor of English and director of Asian American studies, 1991-94, professor 1994-. **Publications:** Chinamerican Reflections (chapbook of poems and paintings), 1984; (ed. with P. Lauter, J. Bruce-Novoa, J. Bryer, and others) Heath Anthology of American Literature, 1989; Between Worlds: Women Writers of Chinese Ancestry, 1990; (ed. with S. Hune, Hyung-chan Kim, and S. Fugita, and contrib.) Asian Americans: Comparative and Global Perspectives, 1991; (ed. with W. Brown) Imagining America: Stories from the Promised Land, 1991; (ed. with S. Lim) Reading the Literatures of Asian America, 1992; (ed. with W. Brown) Visions of America: Personal Narratives from the Promised Land, 1993; (ed. with C.N. Davidson, L. Wagner-Martin & others) The Oxford Companion to Women's Writing in the United States, 1995; (with A. White-Parks) Mrs. Spring Fragrance and other writings by Sui Sin Far, 1995. Author of television scripts. Work represented in anthologies. Contributor of articles, poems, and reviews to periodicals. **Address:** Department of English, University of Wisconsin, 600 North Park St., Madison, WI 53706, U.S.A.

LING, Peter J(ohn). British, b. 1956. **Genres:** Civil liberties/Human rights, History, Race relations, Technology, Transportation. **Career:** Lancashire Polytechnic, Preston, England, lecturer in history, 1984-86; Leicester Polytechnic, England, lecturer in history, 1986-88; Edge Hill College of Higher Education, Ormskirk, England, lecturer in history, 1988-89; University of Nottingham, England, lecturer, 1989-96, senior lecturer in American studies, 1996-. **Publications:** America and the Automobile, 1990; Gender in the Civil Rights Movement, 1999; TransAtlantic Encounters, 2000; Martin Luther King, Jr., 2002. **Address:** Department of American Studies, University of Nottingham, Nottingham NG7 2RD, England.

LING, Roger (John). British, b. 1942. **Genres:** Archaeology/Antiquities, Architecture, Art/Art history, Classics. **Career:** University College, Swansea, Wales, lecturer in classics, 1967-71; University of Manchester, lecturer, senior lecturer, reader in history of art, 1971-92, professor of classical art and archaeology, 1992-. Faculty member, British School at Rome, 1974-78, 1981-85. Member of council: Society for the Promotion of Roman Studies, 1978-81; Derbyshire Archaeological Society, 1981-90; Society of Antiquaries of London, 1988-91; Association Internationale pour l'Edude de la Mosaique Antique, 1999-2003. British Pompeii Project, director, 1978-86; Association Internationale pour la Peinture Murale Antique, secretary, 1989-95, president,

2001-02. **Publications:** The Greek World, 1976; (with T.C.B. Rasmussen) rev. ed. of A. Boethius: Etruscan and Early Roman Architecture, 1978; (with N. Davey) Wall Painting in Roman Britain, 1982; The Hellenistic World to the Coming of the Romans, 1984; Romano-British Wall Painting, 1985; rev. ed. of D.E. Strong: Roman Art, 1988; Classical Greece, 1988; Roman Painting, 1991; The Insula of the Menander at Pompeii I: The Structures, 1997; Ancient Mosaics, 1998; Stuccowork and Painting in Roman Italy, 1999; (ed.) Making Classical Art: Process and Practice, 2000.

LINGARD, Jeanette. Australian. **Genres:** Literary criticism and history. **Career:** University of Sydney (Australia), lecturer in Southeast Asian Studies; writer. **Publications:** (ed.) Diverse Lives: Contemporary Stories from Indonesia, 1996. **Address:** Department of Southeast Asian Studies, University of Sydney, Sydney, NSW 2006, Australia.

LINGARD, Joan (Amelia). British. **Genres:** Novels, Children's fiction, Plays/Screenplays. **Publications:** Liam's Daughter, 1963; The Prevailing Wind, 1964; The Tide Comes In, 1966; The Headmaster, 1968; The Lord on Our Side, 1970; The Twelfth Day of July, 1970; Across the Barricades, 1972; Into Exile, 1973; Frying as Usual, 1973; The Clearance, 1974; A Proper Place, 1974; Hostages to Fortune, 1975; The Resettling, 1975; The Pilgrimage, 1976; The Reunion, 1977; Snake among the Sunflowers, 1977; The Gooseberry, 1978; The Second Flowering of Emily Mountjoy, 1979; The File on Fraulein Berg, 1980; Greenyards, 1981; Maggie, 3 vols, 1982; Strangers in the House, 1981; The Winter Visitor, 1983; Sisters by Rite, 1984; Reasonable Doubts, 1986; The Freedom Machine, 1986; The Guilty Party, 1987; Rags and Riches, 1988; The Women's House, 1989; Tug of War, 1989; Glad Rags, 1990; Between Two Worlds, 1991; Hands off Our School, 1992; Night Fires, 1993; After Colette, 1993; Sulky Suzy, Jittery Jack, 1996; A Secret Place, 1998; Dark Shadows, 1998; John and the Treehouse, 1998; The Egg Thieves, 1999; Natasha's Will, 2000; Me and My Shadow, 1001; Tortoise Trouble, 2002; The Kiss, 2002; Tell the Moon to Come Out, 2003. **Address:** c/o David Higham Associates, 5-8 Lower John St, London W1R 4HA, England.

LINGEMAN, Richard. American, b. 1931. **Genres:** History, Literary criticism and history, Medicine/Health. **Career:** Executive Ed., The Nation, NYC, 1978-, senior editor, 1996-. Executive Ed., Monocle, NYC, 1960-66; Assistant Ed., New York Times Book Review, 1969-78. **Publications:** Drugs from A to Z: A Dictionary, 1969, 1974; Don't You Know There's a War On? (history), 1970; Small Town America: A Narrative History 1620 to the Present, 1980; Theodore Dreiser: At the Gates of the City 1871-1907, 1986; Theodore Dreiser: An American Journey 1908-1945, 1990; Sinclair Lewis: Rebel from Main Street, 2001. **Address:** c/o The Nation, 33 Irving Pl 8th Fl, New York, NY 10003, U.S.A.

LINGENFELTER, Richard Emery. American, b. 1934. **Genres:** Astronomy, History, Mythology/Folklore, Bibliography. **Career:** Research Physicist, Center for Astrophysics, University of California at San Diego, 1979-. Physicist, Lawrence Radiation Laboratory, Livermore, CA, 1957-62; Research Geophysicist, Institute of Geophysics and Planetary Physics, 1962-68, and Professor-in-Residence, Depts. of Astronomy and Planetary and Space Science, 1969-79, University of California at Los Angeles; Fulbright Research Scholar, Tata Institute for Fundamental Research, Bombay, India, 1968-69. **Publications:** (with R. Dwyer) The Nonpareil Press of T.S. Harris, 1957; First through the Grand Canyon, 1958; The Newspapers of Nevada, 1858-1958, 1964; The Rush of '89, 1967; Presses of the Pacific Islands, 1817-1867, 1967; The Hardrock Miners, 1973; Steamboats on the Colorado River, 1978; (with H. Hudson and D. Worrall) Gamma Ray Transients and Related Astrophysical Phenomena, 1982; (with K. Gash) Newspapers of Nevada 1854-1979, 1984; (with R. Dwyer) Lying on the Eastern Slope, 1984; Death Valley and the Amargosa, 1986; (with R. Dwyer) Dan DeQuille: The Washoe Giant, 1989; (with R. Rothschild) High Velocity Neutron Stars and Gamma Ray Bursts, 1996. EDITOR: The Cement Hunters, 1960; Washoe Rambles, 1963; (with R. Dwyer and D. Cohen) The Songs of the Gold Rush, 1964; (with R. Dwyer and D. Cohen) Songs of the American West, 1968; (with R. Dwyer) Death Valley Lore, 1988; (with R. Dwyer) Sagebrush Trilogy: Ida Meacham Strobridge and Her Works, 1990; The Mining West: A Bibliography and Guide to the History and Literature of Mining in the American and Canadian West, 2003. **Address:** Cass 0424, University of California, 9500 Gilman Dr, La Jolla, CA 92093-0424, U.S.A. **Online address:** rlingenfelter@ucsd.edu

LINK, Kelly. American. **Genres:** Novellas/Short stories. **Career:** Writer. Lady Churchill Rosebud Wristlet, co-editor; Small Beer Press, Northampton, MA, co-owner. Also teaches writing seminars. **Publications:** Stranger Things Happen (short stories), 2001. **Address:** Small Beer Press, 176 Prospect Ave., Northampton, MA 01060, U.S.A. **Online address:** info@kellylink.net

LINKIN, Harriet Kramer. American, b. 1956. **Genres:** Education, Literary criticism and history, Women's studies and issues. **Career:** University of Michigan, Ann Arbor, lecturer in English, 1985-86; New Mexico State University, Las Cruces, assistant professor, 1986-93, associate professor, 1993-2000, professor of English, 2000-. **Publications:** EDITOR & CONTRIBUTOR (with S.C. Behrendt): Approaches to Teaching British Women Poets of the Romantic Period, 1997; Romanticism and Women Poets: Opening the Doors of Reception, 1999. Contributor to books. Contributor of articles and reviews to periodicals. **Address:** Dept of English, New Mexico State University, Las Cruces, NM 88003, U.S.A. **Online address:** hlinkin@nmsu.edu

LINKLATER, Magnus (Duncan). Scottish, b. 1942. **Genres:** History, Politics/Government. **Career:** London Evening Standard, London, England, editor of "Londoner's Diary," 1966-69; Sunday Times, London, section editor, 1967-69, editor of "Spectrum" column, 1969-72, editor of magazine, 1972-75, news editor, 1975-79, features editor, 1979-83; Observer, London, managing editor, 1983-86; London Daily News, London, editor, 1986-87; The Scotsman, Edinburgh, Scotland, editor, 1988-94; The Times, columnist, 1994-; Radio Scotland, Presenter, 1994-97; Scottish Arts Council, Chairman, 1996-; Scotland on Sunday, columnist, 1998-. **Publications:** (with L. Chester and S. Fay) Hoax: The Inside Story of the Howard Hughes-Clifford Irving Affair, 1972; (with L. Chester and D. May) Jeremy Thorpe: A Secret Life, 1979, as The Secret Life of Jeremy Thorpe, 1980; Massacre: The Story of Glencoe, 1982; (with P. Eddy) War in the Falklands (in U.K. as The Falklands War), 1982; (with I. Hilton and N. Ascherson) The Nazi Legacy: Klaus Barbie and the International Fascist Connection (in U.K. as The Fourth Reich: Klaus Barbie and the Neo-Fascist Connection), 1984; (author of text) Scotland, 1984; (with D. Leigh) Not with Honour: The Inside Story of the Westland Scandal, 1986; (with C. Hesketh) For King and Conscience: John Graham of Claverhouse, Viscount Dundee, 1989; Highland Wilderness, 1993; (co-ed.) Anatomy of Scotland, 1992; People in a Landscape, 1997. **Address:** 5 Drummond Place, Edinburgh EH3 6PH, Scotland. **Online address:** magnus.linklater@blueyonder.co.uk

LINKLETTER, Art(hur Gordon). American (born Canada), b. 1912. **Genres:** Human relations/Parenting, Social commentary, Autobiography/Memoirs, Humor/Satire. **Career:** Television entertainer; Head, Linkletter Enterprises. **Publications:** People Are Funny, 1947; Kids Say the Darndest Things, 1957; (with A. Gordon) Secret World of Kids, 1959; (with D. Jennings) Confessions of a Happy Man, 1960; Kids Still Say the Darndest Things, 1961; Kids Sure Rite Funny, 1962; Oops!, 1967; Wish I'd Said That, 1968; Linkletter Down Under, 1968; Drugs at My Doorstep, 1973; How to Be a Super Salesman, 1973; Women Are My Favorite People, 1973; Yes, Can!, 1979; I Didn't Do It Alone, 1980; Hobo on the Way to Heaven, 1981; Public Speaking for Private People, 1981; Old Age Is Not for Sissies, 1988.

LINKS, Bo. American, b. 1949. **Genres:** Novels, Novellas/Short stories. **Career:** Jacobs, Blanckenburg, May & Colvin, San Francisco, CA, attorney, 1974-79; Colvin, Martin & Links, San Francisco, attorney, 1979-84; Dobbs, Berger, Molinari, San Francisco, attorney, 1985-94; Berger, Nadel & Vannelli, San Francisco, attorney, 1994-. **Publications:** Follow the Wind (fiction), 1995; Riverbank Tweed & Roadmap Jenkins, 2001. **Address:** Berger Nadel & Vannelli, 650 California St 25th Fl, San Francisco, CA 94108-2702, U.S.A. **Online address:** bolinks@lmi.net

LINN, Karen. American, b. 1957. **Genres:** Cultural/Ethnic topics, Music. **Career:** Smithsonian Institution, National Museum of American History, Washington, DC, researcher, 1988-91; Library of Congress, Washington, DC, archivist, 1991-. **Publications:** Register of the Sam DeVincent Collection of Illustrated American Sheet Music, 3 vols, 1989; That Half-Barbaric Twang: The Banjo in American Popular Culture, 1991. Contributor to journals. **Address:** 4816 44th St NW, Washington, DC 20016, U.S.A.

LINNEA, Ann. American, b. 1949. **Genres:** Environmental sciences/Ecology, Travel/Exploration. **Career:** Worked as a schoolteacher, forest service naturalist and journalist, 1971-82; Sense of Wonder Workshops, upper Midwestern America, cofounder, 1981-92; Peer Spirit, Langley, WA, cofounder, 1992-. **Publications:** (with M. Davis) Cache Trails (hiking guide), 1974; (with S. Datwyler) Cache Tours (skiing guide), 1977; (with M. Herman, J. Passineau and P. Treuer) Teaching Kids to Love the Earth, 1991; Deep Water Passage: A Spiritual Journey at Midlife, 1995; A Journey through the Maxwelton Watershed, 2002; Maxwelton Salmon Adventure. **Address:** Peer Spirit, PO Box 550, Langley, WA 98260, U.S.A. **Online address:** www.peerspirit.com

LINNELL, David. British, b. 1928. **Genres:** Literary criticism and history. **Career:** Actor in repertory and co-director of Minster Theatre Guild, 1950-

54; Elmira Little Theatre, Elmira, NY, co-director, 1954-55; advertising copywriter, 1956-67; Curtain Theatre, London, manager and administrator, 1967-89. **Publications:** Blake, 1994. **Address:** 6 Godstalls Lane, Steyning, W. Sussex BN44 3NE, England.

LINNEY, Peter. British, b. 1931. **Genres:** Local history/Rural topics. **Career:** Bradford Civil Engineers, Bradford, England, trainee civil engineer and drafter, 1948-57, work study assistant and senior assistant, 1957-64, assigned to movements department for the northeastern region of England, 1964-67; British Railways Board, Marylebone, senior work study consultant, 1967-70, member of business planning team, 1968-86, in charge of department, 1972-86, special assistant to the vice-chairperson and head of railways corporate planning, 1986-88. Transmark, producer of a corporate plan for Bangladesh Railways, 1990. Director of property development, container loading, and financial management companies. Transaid (transport consultants and organizers), co-founder, 1987, executive director and volunteer for Save the Children Fund in Africa, 1987-; Wainwright Society, secretary. **Publications:** (comp.) The Official Wainwright Gazetteer, 1993. **Address:** 3 Beech Close, Farnham, Knaresborough, N. Yorkshire, England. **Online address:** PeterLinney@compuserve.com

LINNEY, Romulus. American, b. 1930. **Genres:** Novels, Plays/Screenplays. **Career:** Actor and dir. in stock for 6 years; Stage Manager, Actors Studio, NYC, 1960; has taught at the University of North Carolina, Chapel Hill and Raleigh, University of Pennsylvania, Philadelphia, Brooklyn College, NYC, Columbia University, NYC, Connecticut College, New London, Princeton University, New Jersey, and Hunter College, NYC. **Publications:** (ed. with N.A. Bailey and D. Cascio) Ten Plays for Radio, 1954; (ed. with N.A. Bailey and D. Cascio) Radio Classics, 1956; Heathen Valley (novel), 1963; Slowly, by Thy Hand Unfurled (novel), 1965; The Sorrows of Frederick (play), 1966; Democracy and Esther, and The Love Suicide at Schofield Barracks, 1973; Holy Ghosts, and The Sorrows of Frederick, 1977; Old Man Joseph and His Family, 1978; Jesus Tales (novel), 1980; The Captivity of Pixie Shedman, 1981; Tennessee, 1981; Childe Byron, 1981; The Death of King Philip, 1983; Laughing Stock, 1984; Sand Mountain, 1985; A Woman without a Name, 1986; Pops, 1987; Heathen Valley, 1988; Juliet, Yancy and April Snow, 1989; Three Poets, 1990; "2," 1991; Ambrosio, 1992; Spain, 1993; Six Plays, 1993; True Crimes, 1996; Christmas Carol, 1996; Mountain Memory, 1997; Nine Adaptations for the American Stage, 2000. **Address:** c/o Peter Hagan, Writers & Artists, 19 W. 44th St #1000, New York, NY 10036, U.S.A.

LINOWES, David Francis. American, b. 1917. **Genres:** Administration/Management, Economics. **Career:** Boeschenstein Professor of Political Economy and Public Policy, University of Illinois, Urbana, 1976- (Distinguished Arthur Young Visiting Professor, 1973-74). Sr. Adviser, Institute of Government and Public Affairs. Member, Advisory Board, Office of Arms Control, Defense and International Security. Director, Chris-Craft Industries Inc., Saturday Review/World Magazine Inc., and Work in America Institute Inc. Consulting Founding Partner, Leopold and Linowes (now BDO Seidman), Washington, D.C., 1946-82; Chairman, U.S. Privacy Protection Commission, 1975-77; Chairman, Federal Commission on Fiscal Accountability of Nation's Energy Resources, 1981-82; Chairman, President's Commission on Privatization, 1988-89. **Publications:** Managing Growth through Acquisition, 1968; Strategies for Survival, 1973; The Corporate Conscience, 1974; Personal Privacy in an Information Society, 1977; (ed.) Impact of the Communication and Computer Revolution on Society, 1986; Socioeconomical Management, 1986; Privacy in America, 1989; Creating Public Policy: The Chairman's Memoirs of Four Presidential Commissions, 2000; The Most Productive Generation in History, 1946-1996. **Address:** 120 SE 5th Ave, Boca Raton, FL 33432, U.S.A.

LINSKY, Leonard. American, b. 1922. **Genres:** Language/Linguistics, Philosophy. **Career:** University of Illinois at Urbana-Champaign, began as assistant professor, became professor of philosophy, 1948-67; University of Chicago, Chicago, IL, professor of philosophy, 1967-93, chairman of department, 1968-74, professor emeritus, 1993-. Visiting professor at universities worldwide. **Publications:** Referring, Humanities, 1967; Names and Descriptions, 1977; Oblique Contexts, 1983. EDITOR: Semantics and the Philosophy of Language: A Collection of Readings, 1952; Reference and Modality, 1971. **Address:** 1413 E 57th St, Chicago, IL 60637, U.S.A.

LINSTRUM, Derek. British, b. 1925. **Genres:** Architecture. **Career:** Sr. Architect, West Riding Council, Yorks., 1958-66; Sr. Lecturer, Dept. of Architectural Studies, Leeds Polytechnic, 1966-71; Radcliffe Reader and Director of Conservation Studies, University of York, 1971-92. Hoffman Wood Professor of Architecture, University of Leeds, 1991-93. Architectural

Correspondent, The Yorkshire Post, 1966-94. **Publications:** Historic Architecture of Leeds, 1969; Sir Jeffry Wyatville: Architect to the King, 1972; Catalogue of the Drawings in the Collection of the Royal Institute of British Architects: The Wyatt Family, 1974; West Yorkshire Architects and Architecture, 1978; Towers and Colonnades: The Architecture of Cuthbert Brodrick, 1999. **Address:** 2 Wedgewood Grove, Roundhay, Leeds, W. Yorkshire LS8 1EG, England.

LINTON, Harold. American, b. 1947. **Genres:** Architecture, Design. **Career:** Lawrence Technological University, Southfield, MI, assistant dean of College of Architecture and Design, 1974-98, and department chair; Bradley University, Peoria, IL, professor of art and department chair, 1998-. University of Art and Design, Helsinki, Finland, co-founder of M.A. degree program in color and design and professor; guest lecturer at institutions. ColorDesign3D, chief executive officer; Harley Ellis Architecture, color and design consultant; painter, with work represented in public, private, and museum collections; guest on media programs; engages in civic activities related to the arts and design. **Publications:** Color Model Environments: Color and Light in Three-Dimensional Design, 1985; (with R. Rochon) Color in Architectural Illustration, 1989; (with R.J. Strickfaden) Architectural Sketching in Markers, 1991; Color Consulting: A Survey of International Color Design, 1991; (with S. Sutton) Sketching the Concept: Perspective Illustration for Architects, Designers, and Artists, 1993; Color Forecasting: A Survey of International Color Marketing, 1994; Portfolio Design, 1996, 2nd edition, 2000; Color in Architecture: Design Methods for Buildings, Interiors, and Urban Spaces, 1999. **Address:** Department of Art, Bradley University, 1501 West Bradley Ave., Peoria, IL 61625, U.S.A. **Online address:** linton@bradley.edu

LINTREY, Alan R. See GORDON, W. Terrence.

LINZER, Anna. American, b. 1950. **Genres:** Novels, Novellas/Short stories, Poetry, Money/Finance. **Career:** Author, poet, consultant. **Publications:** Ghost Dancing, 1998; (with R. Linzer) It's Simple!: Money Matters for the Nonprofit Board Member, 1999; (with R. Linzer) It's Easy!: Money Matters for Nonprofit Managers, 2001. Contributor of short fiction and poetry to periodicals. **Address:** PO Box 374, Indianola, WA 98342, U.S.A. **Online address:** rslinzer@earthlink.net

LINZEY, Andrew. British, b. 1952. **Genres:** Animals/Pets, Theology/Religion. **Career:** St. Augustine's College, Canterbury, England, deacon, 1975; ordained a priest of the Anglican Church, 1976; University of Essex, England, chaplain, 1981, director of studies at the Centre for the Study of Theology, 1987; Mansfield College, Oxford, England, senior research fellow, 1992; Oxford University, Oxford, member of faculty of theology, 1992. University of Prince Edward Island, visiting lecturer 1992; University of Nottingham, special professor in theology 1992-96; Saint Xavier University, Chicago, special professor 1996-; University of Birmingham, honorary professor, 1997-. **Publications:** Animal Rights: A Christian Assessment, 1976; (with E. Carpenter, H. Montefiore, T. Beeson, R. Harrison, and others) Animals and Ethics, 1980; (ed. with P.J. Wexler) Heaven and Earth: Essex Essays in Theology and Ethics, 1986; Christianity and the Rights of Animals, 1987; (with P.A.B. Clarke) Research on Embryos: Politics, Theology and Law, 1988; (ed. with Clarke) Theology, the University and the Modern World, 1988; (ed. with T. Regan) Animals and Christianity: A Book of Readings, 1988; (ed. with Regan) Compassion for Animals, 1989; (ed. with Regan) Song of Creation, 1989; (ed. with P.A.B. Clarke) Political Theory and Animal Rights, 1990; (ed.) The Sayings of Jesus, 1991; (ed. with Wexler) Fundamentalism and Tolerance: An Agenda for Theology and Society, 1991; Animal Theology, 1994; (ed. with Clarke) Dictionary of Ethics, 1995; (with D. Cohn-Sherbok) After Noah, 1997; (ed. with D. Yamamoto) Animals on the Agenda, 1998; Animal Gospel, 1998; Animal Rites, 1999. Contributor to encyclopedias, dictionaries, books, and periodicals. **Address:** Mansfield College, Oxford OX1 3TF, England. **Online address:** volinzey@aol.com

LIONEL, Robert. See FANTHORPE, R(obert) Lionel.

LIOU, K(uo-)N(an). Taiwanese, b. 1943. **Genres:** Meteorology/Atmospheric sciences. **Career:** Columbia University, NYC, research associate at Goddard Institute for Space Studies, 1970-72; University of Washington, Seattle, assistant professor, 1972-74; University of Utah, Salt Lake City, associate professor, 1975-80, professor of meteorology, 1980-, research professor, 1992-, adjunct professor of geology and geophysics, 1992-, director of Center for Atmospheric and Remote Sounding Studies, 1987-. National Center for Atmospheric Research, visiting scientist, 1975-76; National Aeronautics and Space Administration, visiting scientist at Ames Research Center, 1980-81. University of California, Los Angeles, visiting professor,

1981; Harvard University, visiting scholar, 1985; Peking University, visiting professor, 1989-; International Radiation Commission, member, 1992; Inner Mongolia Grassland Surface-Atmosphere Experiment, chairperson, 1992-. Consultant to White Sands Missile Range, Los Alamos National Laboratory, and Army Atmospheric Sciences Laboratory. **Publications:** An Introduction to Atmospheric Radiation, 1980; (ed.) Atmospheric Radiation: Progress and Prospects, 1987; Radiation and Cloud Processes in the Atmosphere: Theory, Observation, and Modeling (monograph), 1992. Contributor to scientific journals. **Address:** UCLA, Department of Atmospheric Sciences, 7163 Math Sciences, Los Angeles, CA 90095-1565, U.S.A.

LIPKIN, Randie. American, b. 1953. **Genres:** Novels. **Career:** Writer. **Publications:** Untitled (A Skier) (fiction), 1995; Without (fiction), 1998. **Address:** c/o Fugue State Press, PO Box 80, Cooper Station, New York, NY 10276, U.S.A. **Online address:** info@fuguestatepress.com

LIPKOWITZ, Myron A. American, b. 1938. **Genres:** Medicine/Health. **Career:** Lane Drugs, Lakewood, NJ, pharmacist and store manager, 1963-71; Uniontown, PA, Dept of Emergency Medicine, 1977-78; family practice, Uniontown and Markleysburg, PA, 1977778; Howell Medical Associates, Howell, NJ, family physician and allergist, 1979-95; Community Medical Associates, Howell, family physician and allergist, 1995-. Kimball Medical Center, affiliate, St Barnabas Health Care System, Lakewood, chair, Dept of Family Practice, 1979-; Jersey Shore Medical Center, Neptune, NJ, acting director, Dept of Family Practice, 1979-97. Newton Resource Group (for Pharmaceutical Marketing), Lambertville, NJ, consultant; Speaker's Bureau for several pharmaceutical companies. **Publications:** (with T. and J. Navarra) Therapeutic Communication, 1990; (with T. Navarra) Allergies A-Z, 1994; (with T. and J. Navarra) Encyclopedia of Vitamins, 1995. Contributor to journals. **Address:** c/o Sanford J. Greenberger, Inc., Attn: Faith Hamlin, 55 Fifth Ave, New York, NY 10003, U.S.A.

LIPMAN, David. American, b. 1931. **Genres:** Sports/Fitness. **Career:** Managing Editor, Post-Dispatch, St. Louis, Missouri, 1979-92 (Sports Reporter, 1960-66; Assistant Sports Ed., 1966-68; News Ed., 1968-71; Assistant Managing Ed., 1971-78; Chairman, Pulitzer/2000, 1992-97, Pulitzer Publishing Co., consultant, 1997-99. **Publications:** (as-told-to autobiography) Maybe I'll Pitch Forever, 1962, reissued 1995; Mr. Baseball: The Story of Branch Rickey, 1966; Ken Boyer, 1967; Joe Namath: A Football Legend, 1968; (co-author) The Speed King: Bob Hayes of the Dallas Cowboys, 1971; Bob Gibson, Pitching Ace, 1973; Jim Hart, Underrated Quarterback, 1977. **Address:** Creve Coeur, MO 63141, U.S.A. **Online address:** dlipman@post-dispatch.com

LIPMAN, Elinor. American, b. 1950. **Genres:** Novels, Novellas/Short stories. **Career:** Massachusetts Labor Relations Commission, Boston, public information officer, 1974-75; Massachusetts Teachers Association, Boston, managing editor, 1975-81; Simmons College, Boston, special instructor in communications, 1984-85; Hampshire College, Amherst, MA, visiting assistant professor of creative writing, 1988-89; writer. **Publications:** NOVELS: Then She Found Me, 1990; The Way Men Act, 1992; Isabel's Bed, 1995; The Inn at Lake Devine, 1998; The Ladies' Man, 1999; The Dearly Departed, 2001; The Pursuit of Alice Thrift, 2003. OTHER: Into Love and Out Again (stories), 1987. **Address:** c/o Suzanne Gluck, William Morris Agency, 1325 Avenue of the Americas, New York, NY 10019, U.S.A.

LIPMAN, Matthew. American, b. 1923. **Genres:** Art/Art history, Education, Philosophy, Writing/Journalism. **Career:** Montclair State University, Upper Montclair, NJ, professor of philosophy, 1972-, now emeritus, and director, Institute for the Advancement of Philosophy for Children; Thinking: The Journal of Philosophy for Children, contributing editor, 1978-. **Publications:** What Happens in Art, 1967; Discovering Philosophy, 1969, 1977; Contemporary Aesthetics, 1973; Harry Stottlemeier's Discovery, 1974; (with A.M. Sharp) Instructional Manual to Accompany Harry Stottlemeier's Discovery, 1975; Lisa, 1976, 1983; (with A.M. Sharp and F.S. Oscanyan) Ethical Inquiry, 1977, 1985; (with A.M. Sharp and F.S. Oscanyan) Philosophy in the Classroom, 1977, 1980; Suki, 1978; (ed. with A.M. Sharp) Growing Up with Philosophy, 1978; Mark, 1980; (with A.M. Sharp) Writing: How and Why, 1980; (with A.M. Sharp) Social Inquiry, 1980; Pixie, 1981; (with A.M. Sharp) Looking for Meaning, 1982, 1984; Kio and Gus, 1982; (with A.M. Sharp) Wondering at the World, 1986; Elfie, 1988; (with A. Gazzard) Getting Our Thoughts Together, 1988; Philosophy Goes to School, 1988; Thinking in Education, 1991, 2nd ed., 2003; Natasha, 1996. **Address:** Institute for the Advancement of Philosophy for Children, Montclair State University, Upper Montclair, NJ 07043, U.S.A. **Online address:** lipmanm@mail.montclair.edu

LIPMAN, Victoria M. American, b. 1949. **Genres:** Novels. **Career:** Writer. **Publications:** NOVELS: Leaving Alva, 1998. **Address:** c/o Publicity Director, Simon and Schuster Inc., 1230 Avenue of the Americas, New York, NY 10020, U.S.A.

LIPMAN-BLUMEN, Jean. American, b. 1933. **Genres:** Business/Trade/Industry. **Career:** Member of domestic policy staff under President Jimmy Carter; National Institute of Education Women's Research Program, assistant director, 1973-78; Office of the Assistant Secretary for Education, special assistant; Center for Advanced Study in the Behavioral Sciences, fellow, 1978-79; LBS International, president, 1979-84; University of Connecticut, visiting professor of sociology and organizational behavior; University of Maryland, visiting professor of sociology and organizational behavior; Claremont University, professor of public policy; Claremont Graduate University, Peter F. Drucker Graduate School of Management, Institute for Advanced Studies in Leadership, Claremont, CA, cofounder and director. Director, Achieving Styles Institute (consulting group). **Publications:** Sex Roles and Social Policy, 1979; Gender Roles and Power, 1984; The Connective Edge: Leading in an Interdependent World, 1996; (with H.J. Leavitt) Hot Groups: Seeding Them, Feeding Them, and Using Them to Ignite Your Organization, 1999. **Address:** Claremont Graduate University, Drucker Graduate School of Management, 1021 North Dartmouth Avenue, Claremont, CA 91711, U.S.A. **Online address:** jeanlipman@earthlink.net; jean.lipman-blumen@cgu.edu

LIPPI(-GREEN), Rosina. (Sara Donati). American, b. 1956. **Genres:** Novels, Language/Linguistics. **Career:** Professor, writer, and lecturer. Western Washington University, Bellingham, WA, associate professor. Formerly taught at University of Michigan, Ann Arbor. **Publications:** NOVELS: Homestead, 1998; (as Sara Donati) Into the Wilderness, 1998. ACADEMIC: AS ROSINA LIPPI-GREEN: Language Ideology and Language Change in Early Modern German: A Sociolinguistic Study of the Consonantal System of Nuremburg, 1994; English with an Accent: Language, Ideology, and Discrimination in the United States, 1997. Contributor of short fiction and academic articles to periodicals. **Address:** Western Washington University, Department of English, 341 Humanities Building, Bellingham, WA 98226, U.S.A. **Online address:** rlg@cc.wwu.edu

LIPPMAN, Thomas W. American, b. 1940. **Genres:** Documentaries/Reportage. **Career:** Washington Post, Washington, DC, reporter and foreign correspondent, 1965-99; freelance writer, 1999-. **Publications:** Understanding Islam, 1982, rev. ed, 1995; Egypt after Nasser, 1989; Madeleine Albright and the New American Diplomacy, 2000. Contributor of articles and reviews to periodicals. **Address:** 3925 McKinley St NW, Washington, DC 20015-2942, U.S.A. **Online address:** tw122@columbia.edu

LIPPY, Charles H(oward). American, b. 1943. **Genres:** Theology/Religion, Bibliography. **Career:** Oberlin College, OH, asst professor of religion, 1972-74; Miami University, Oxford, OH, visiting asst professor of religion and American studies, 1974-75; West Virginia Wesleyan College, Buckhannon, asst professor of Bible, religion, and humanities, 1975-76; Clemson University, SC, asst professor, 1976-80, associate professor, 1980-85, professor of religion, 1985-94, professor of history, 1985-88, acting head of department, 1988-89, director of Program in Philosophy and Religion, 1987-88; University of Tennessee at Chattanooga, LeRoy A. Martin distinguished professor of religious studies, 1994-; writer. University of North Carolina at Chapel Hill, visiting scholar, 1984; Emory University, visiting professor, 1990-91. **Publications:** Seasonable Revolutionary: The Mind of Charles Chauncy, 1981; A Bibliography of Religion in the South, 1985; The Christadelphians in North America, 1989; (with R. Choquette and S. Poole) Christianity Comes to the Americas, 1492-1776, 1992; Being Religious, American Style, 1994; Modern America Popular Religion, 1996; (with R. Krapohl) The Evangelicals, 1999; Pluralism Comes of Age, 2000. EDITOR & CONTRIBUTOR: Religious Periodicals of the United States, 1986; (with P.W. Williams) Encyclopedia of the American Religious Experience, 3 vols., 1988; Twentieth-Century Shapers of American Popular Religion, 1989; (with P.M. Fackler) Popular Religious Magazines of the United States, 1995; (with J. Topolewski and N. Topolewski) Where Rivers Run and Mountains Rise, 2002. **Address:** Department of Philosophy and Religion, #2753, University of Tennessee, 615 McCallie Ave, Chattanooga, TN 37403, U.S.A. **Online address:** Charles-Lippy@utc.edu

LIPSET, Seymour Martin. American, b. 1922. **Genres:** Politics/Government, Sociology. **Career:** Associate Professor of Sociology, Columbia University, NYC, 1950-56; Professor of Sociology, University of California, Berkeley, 1956-65; George Markham Professor of Government and Sociology, Harvard University, Cambridge, MA, 1965-75; Munro Professor of Political Science and Sociology, 1975-91, and Sr. Fellow, Hoover Institution, 1975-, Stanford University, California; George Mason University, Hazel Chair of Public Policy, 1991-. **Publications:** Agrarian Socialism, 1950; (with M. Trow and J.S. Coleman) Union Democracy, 1956; (with R. Bendix) Social Mobility in Industrial Society, 1959; Political Man, 1960; The First New Nation, 1963; Revolution and Counter-Revolution, 1965; (with E.

Raab) Politics of Unreason, 1970; Rebellion in University, 1972; (with D. Riesman) Education and Politics at Harvard, 1975; (with E.C. Ladd) The Divided Academy; (with I.L. Horowitz) Dialogues of American Politics, 1978; (with W. Schneider) The Confidence Gap, 1983; Conflict and Consensus, 1985; American Pluralism and the Jewish Community, 1990; Continental Divide: The Values and Institutions of the United States and Canada, 1990; (with E. Raab) Jews in The New American Scene, 1995; American Exceptionalism: A Double-Edged Sword, 1995; (with G. Marks) It Didn't Happen Here: Why Socialism Failed in the United States, 2000. **Address:** School of Public Policy, George Mason University, 3401 N Fairfax Dr MS3B1, Arlington, VA 22201, U.S.A. **Online address:** slipset@gmu.edu

LIPSYTE, Robert (Michael). American, b. 1938. **Genres:** Novels, Children's fiction, Sports/Fitness. **Career:** New York Times, sports columnist, 1957-71, city and sports columnist, 1991-2003; New York Post, columnist, 1977; CBS News, essayist, 1982-86; NBC News, correspondent, 1986-88; The Eleventh Hour television program, NYC, host, 1989-90. **Publications:** Nigger, 1964; The Masculine Mystique, 1966; The Contender, 1967; Assignment: Sports, 1970; (with S. Cady) Something Going, 1973; Liberty Two, 1974; Sportsworld: An American Dreamland, 1975; One Fat Summer, 1977; Free to Be Muhammed Ali, 1978; Summer Rules, 1981; Jock and Jill, 1982; The Summerboy, 1982; The Brave, 1991; The Chemo Kid, 1991; The Chief, 1993; (with G. Brown) Sports and Society; (with P. Levine) Idols of the Game, 1995; In the Country of Illness, 1998; Warrior Angel, 2003.

LIPTON, Eunice. American. **Genres:** Art/Art history, Women's studies and issues, Autobiography/Memoirs. **Career:** University of Rhode Island, Kingston, instructor in art history, 1965-67; Bard College, Annandale-on-Hudson, NY, instructor in art history, 1970-72; Hunter College of the City University of New York, lecturer to assistant professor of art history, 1973-78; Parsons School of Design, NYC, lecturer in art history, 1978-80; State University of New York at Binghamton, associate professor of art history, 1980-88. Williams College and Clark Art Institute, Robert Sterling Clark Visiting Professor, 1986; School of the Art Institute of Chicago, visiting artist, 1988. **Publications:** Picasso Criticism, 1901-1939: The Making of an Artist-Hero, 1976; Looking into Degas: Uneasy Images of Women and Modern Life, 1986; Alias Olympia: A Woman's Search for Manet's Notorious Model and Her Own Desire, 1993.

LIPTON, Peter. American, b. 1954. **Genres:** Philosophy, Sciences. **Career:** Oxford University, England, lecturer in external studies, 1979, tutor in philosophy of science, 1979-82; Clark University, Worcester, MA, assistant research professor, 1982-85; Williams College, Williamstown, MA, assistant professor, 1985-90; Cambridge University, England, lecturer in history and philosophy of science, 1991-97, professor, 1997-; King's College, Cambridge, fellow, 1994-; writer; lecturer at colleges and universities in the United States and Europe. **Publications:** Inference to the Best Explanation, 1991, rev. ed., 2004. **Address:** Dept of History and Philosophy of Science, Cambridge University, Free School Ln, Cambridge CB2 3RH, England. **Online address:** Peter.Lipton@kings.cam.ac.uk

LIQUORI, Marty. (Martin William, Jr). American, b. 1949. **Genres:** Sports/Fitness. **Career:** Athletic Attic (retail sporting goods store), Gainesville, Fla., founder and president, 1971-. Master of ceremonies at I.T.A. ProTrack, Los Angeles, Calif., 1971-73; commentator for ABC Sports, 1971-. President of Marty Liquori Sportswear, Inc.; vice-president of Athletic Lady; designer and promotional director for Brooks Shoe Co., Hanover, Pa., 1974-78; marketing consultant to Le Coq Sportif. Producer of ESPN-TV's "Running and Racing," 1986-. **Publications:** (with Skip Myslenski) On the Run: In Search of the Perfect Race, 1977; (with J.L. Parker, Jr.) Playboy's Elite Runner's Manual, 1980; (with J.L. Parker, Jr.) Playboy's Book of Real Running, 1980; (with Gerald Secor Couzens) Marty Liquori's Home Gym Workout, 1987. **Address:** 2915 NW 58th Blvd., Gainesville, FL 32606-8517, U.S.A.

LISANDRELLI, Elaine Slivinski. American, b. 1951. **Genres:** Education, Young adult non-fiction. **Career:** North Pocono Middle School, Moscow, PA, English teacher, 1973-; Marywood University, Scranton, PA, adjunct faculty member, 1986-. Member of Pennsylvania Writing Assessment Committee, Pennsylvania Department of Education, 1989. International Correspondence School, proofreader, summer, 1991; educational consultant. **Publications:** (co-author) Easywriter, Levels G and H, 1987; (with S.C. Bartoletti) The Study Skills Workout, 1988. YOUNG ADULT NONFICTION: Maya Angelou: More Than a Poet, 1996; Bob Dole: Legendary Senator, 1997; Ida B. Wells-Barnett: Crusader against Lynching, 1998; Ignacy Jan Paderewski: Polish Pianist and Patriot, 1999; Jack London: A Writer's Adventurous Life, 1999. Contributor to magazines. **Address:** North Pocono Middle School, Church St, Moscow, PA 18444, U.S.A. **Online address:** caleml@aol.com

LISBOA, Maria Manuel. Portuguese (born Mozambique), b. 1963. **Genres:** Literary criticism and history. **Career:** University of Newcastle upon Tyne, Newcastle upon Tyne, England, lecturer in Portuguese and Brazilian literature, 1988-93; Cambridge University, St. John's College, Cambridge, England, lecturer in Portuguese, Brazilian, and African (Lusopaone) literature, 1993-. Guest lecturer at universities. **Publications:** Machado de Assis and Feminism: Re-Reading the Heart of the Companion, 1996. Contributor to literature books. Contributor of stories, translations, articles, and reviews to periodicals. **Address:** St. John's College, Cambridge University, Cambridge CB2 1TP, England. **Online address:** MMGL100@ cam.ac.uk

LISCOMB, Kathlyn Maurean. American/Canadian, b. 1950. **Genres:** Art/Art history. **Career:** School of the Art Institute of Chicago, IL, visiting lecturer in art history and aesthetics, 1985; University of Victoria, British Columbia, assistant professor, 1986-91, associate professor, 1991-2000, professor of art history, 2000-. **Publications:** Learning from Mount Hua: A Chinese Physician's Illustrated Travel Record and Painting Theory, 1993; China and Beyond: The Legacy of a Culture (exhibition catalog), 2002. Contributor to academic journals. **Address:** Department of History in Art, University of Victoria, PO Box 1700, Victoria, BC, Canada V8W 2Y2. **Online address:** kliscomb@finearts.uvic.ca

LISK, Jill (Rosina Ann). British, b. 1938. **Genres:** History. **Career:** Head of History Dept. and House Mistress, Taunton School, Somerset. Former History Mistress, Barr's Hill Girls Grammar School, Coventry, La Sainte Union Convent Grammar School, Bath, and Bridgwater Girls Grammar School, Somerset. **Publications:** The Struggle for Supremacy in the Baltic 1600-1725, 1967; Essays in European History 1494-1789, 2 vols., 1988; Essays in European History 1494-1789, 2 vols., 1990. **Address:** 26 Northfield, Bridgwater, Somerset, England.

LISLE, Holly. American, b. 1960. **Genres:** Novels, Science fiction/Fantasy. **Career:** Writer. Worked as an advertising representative for a newspaper, sang in restaurants, taught guitar, did commercial artwork, and worked as a registered nurse for ten years, primarily in emergency and critical care units; became fulltime writer, 1993-. **Publications:** ARHEL NOVELS: Fire in the Mist, 1992; Bones of the Past, 1993; Mind of the Magic, 1995. GLENRAVEN NOVELS: (with M.Z. Bradley) Glenraven, 1996; (with M.Z. Bradley) Glenraven: In the Shadow of the Rift, in press. DEVIL'S POINT NOVELS: Sympathy for the Devil, 1996; (with W. Spence) The Devil and Dan Cooley, 1996; (with T. Nolan) Hell on High, 1997. BARD'S TALE NOVELS: (with A. Allston) Thunder of the Captains, 1996; (with A. Allston) Wrath of the Princes, 1997; Curse of the Black Heron, in press. OTHER NOVELS: Minerva Wakes, 1993; (with M. Lackey) When the Bough Breaks, 1993; (with S.M. Stirling) The Rose Sea, 1994; (with C. Guin) Mall, Mayhem and Magic, 1995; Hunting the Corrigan's Blood, 1997. Contributor of short stories to anthologies. **Address:** c/o Russell Galen, Scovil Chichak Galen Literary Agency, 381 Park Ave. S. Suite 1020, New York, NY 10016, U.S.A. **Online address:** Holly.Lisle@sff.net

LISLE, Janet Taylor. American, b. 1947. **Genres:** Children's fiction. **Career:** Writer. Has worked as a journalist in Georgia and New York. **Publications:** FOR CHILDREN: The Dancing Cats of Applesap, 1984; Sirens and Spies, 1985; The Great Dimpole Oak, 1987; Afternoon of the Elves, 1989; The Lampfish of Twill, 1991; Forest, 1993; The Gold Dust Letters, 1994; Looking for Juliette, 1994; A Message from the Match Girl, 1995; Angela's Aliens, 1996; The Lost Flower Children, 1999; The Art of Keeping Cool, 2000; How I Became a Writer and Oggie Learned to Drive, 2002. **Address:** c/o Penguin Putnam, Books for Young Readers, 345 Hudson St, New York, NY 10014, U.S.A.

LISLE, Julia. See LAURENCE, Janet.

LISLE, Laurie. American, b. 1942. **Genres:** Homes/Gardens, Biography, Essays. **Career:** Providence Journal and Evening Bulletin, Providence, RI, reporter, critic, 1965-66; Newsweek, New York City, researcher and reporter, 1970-77; freelance writer, 1978-; Long Island University, Southampton College, Southampton, NY, associate professor of English, 1981-82; Southern Connecticut Library Council, independent scholar, 1989-2002; NY Council for the Humanities, speaker, 2000-02. **Publications:** Portrait of an Artist: A Biography of Georgia O'Keeffe, 1980, rev. ed., 1986; Louise Nevelson: A Passionate Life, 1990; Without Child: Challenging the Stigma of Childlessness, 1996; Four Tenths of an Acre: Reflections on a Gardening Life, 2005. **Address:** PO Box 170, Ardsley On Hudson, NY 10503, U.S.A. **Online address:** llisle@ix.netcom.com

LISS, David. American, b. 1966. **Genres:** Adult non-fiction. **Career:** Writer and essayist. **Publications:** A Conspiracy of Paper, 2000; The Coffee Trader, 2003; A Spectacle of Corruption, 2004. Contributor of short stories to anthologies. **Address:** c/o Random House, 1745 Broadway #B1, New York, NY 10019-4301, U.S.A. **Online address:** lissd@davidliss.com

LISTER, R(ichard) P(ercival). British, b. 1914. **Genres:** Novels, Novellas/Short stories, Poetry, Travel/Exploration. **Publications:** The Way Backwards, 1950; The Oyster and the Torpedo, 1951; Rebecca Redfern, 1953; The Idle Demon, 1958; The Rhyme and the Reason, 1963; The Questing Beast, 1965; Journey in Lapland (in U.S. as The Hard Way to Haparanda), 1965; Turkey Observed (in U.S. as A Muezzin from the Tower of Darkness Cries), 1967; The Secret History of Genghis Khan (in U.S. as Genghis Khan), 1969; One Short Summer, 1974; Marco Polo's Travels, 1976; The Travels of Herodotus, 1980; The Albatross and Other Poems, 1986; Nine Legends, 1991; Two Northern Stories, 1996; Glimpses of a Planet, 1997; Me and the Holy Spirit, 1998. **Address:** Flat11, 42 St. James's Gardens, London W11 4RQ, England.

LITAN, Robert E(li). American, b. 1950. **Genres:** Economics, History, Sciences. **Career:** Brookings Institution, Washington, DC, research assistant, 1972-73; senior fellow, 1984-93; Yale University, New Haven, CT, instructor to lecturer in law and economics, 1975-77; President's Council of Economic Advisers, Washington, DC, regulation and energy specialist, 1977-79; Arnold & Porter, Washington, DC, associate, 1979-82; Powell, Goldstein, Frazer & Murphy, Washington, DC, associate, 1982-84, partner, 1984, counsel, 1985-90; Department Anti-trust Division, deputy assistant attorney general, 1993-. Visiting lecturer at Yale Law School, 1986, 1990; consultant. **Publications:** Energy Modeling for an Uncertain Future, 1978; (with W.D. Nordhaus) Reforming Federal Regulation, 1983; (with R. Lawrence) Saving Free Trade, 1986; What Should Banks Do?, 1987; (ed. with R.Z. Lawrence and C.L. Schultze) American Living Standards: Threats and Challenges, 1988; (ed. with C. Winston) Liability: Perspectives and Policy, 1988; (ed. with P. Huber) The Liability Maze, 1991; (ed. with R. Boltuck) Down in the Dumps, 1991; The Revolution in U.S. Finance, 1992; (with others) Physical Damage and Human Loss, 1992; (with J. Barth and R.D. Brumbaugh) The Future of American Banking, 1992; (with M. Baily and G. Burtless) Growth with Equity, 1993; (ed.) Verdict, 1993; (ed. with G.G. Kaufman) Assessing Bank Reform, 1993; (with R.J. Herring) Financial Regulation in the Global Economy, 1994; (with R.J. Herring) Financial Regulation in the Global Economy, 1995; (with R.W. Hahn) Improving Regulatory Accountability, 1997; (with J. Rauch) American Finance for the 21st Century, 1997; None of Your Business, 1998; (with W. Niskanen) Going Digital!, 1998; (ed. with A. Harwood and M. Pomerleano) Financial Markets and Development, 1999; (with others) Community Reinvestment Act after Financial Modernization, 2000; (ed. with C. Adams and M. Pomerleano) Managing Financial and Corporate Distress, 2000; (with P.J. Wallison) GAAP Gap, 2000; (ed. with A.M. Rivlin) Economic Payoff from the Internet Revolution, 2001. **Address:** Brookings Institution, 1775 Massachusetts Ave NW, Washington, DC 20036, U.S.A.

LITHGOW, John (Arthur). American, b. 1945. **Genres:** Children's fiction. **Career:** Stage, screen and television actor, director, singer, songwriter, and author. **Publications:** Under the Gun, 1972-1973; Kaufman at Large (solo show), 1981; Babysongs Presents John Lithgow's Kid-size Concert (video), 1990; Singin' in the Bathtub (children's musical album), 1999; The Remarkable Farkle McBride (children's book), 2000; Marsupial Sue (children's book; with compact disc), 2001; Farkle and Friends (children's musical album), 2002; Micawber (children's book; with compact disc), 2002; I'm a Manatee (children's book; with compact disc), 2003; Carnival of the Animals (with compact disc), 2004. **Address:** c/o Creative Artists Agency, 9830 Wilshire Blvd., Beverly Hills, CA 90212, U.S.A.

LITHMAN, Yngve Georg. Swedish, b. 1943. **Genres:** Anthropology/Ethnology, Area studies. **Career:** University of Stockholm, Stockholm, Sweden, affiliated with department of anthropology, 1978-. Visiting fellow in anthropology, University of London, 1985; professor, University of Manitoba, 1989-90; professor, University of Bergen, Norway, 1996-. **Publications:** The Practise of Underdevelopment and the Theory of Development, 1983; The Community Apart: A Case Study of a Canadian Indian Reserve Community, 3rd ed, 1986; (co-author) People and Land in Northern Manitoba, 1992. EDITOR: Nybyggarna I Sverige, 1986; (with W.T. Gerholm) The New Islamic Presence in Western Europe, 1988. **Address:** Centre for Social Research, University of Bergen, N-5007 Bergen, Norway.

LITTELL, Franklin H(amlin). American, b. 1917. **Genres:** Theology/Religion. **Career:** University of Michigan, Ann Arbor, director of Lane Hall, 1944-49; Office of the U.S. High Commissioner, Germany, member of religious affairs staff, 1949-51, chief Protestant adviser, 1953-58; Boston University, MA, dean of chapel, 1951-53; Emory University, Candler School of Theology, Atlanta, GA, professor of church history, 1958-60; Southern Methodist University, Perkins School of Theology, Dallas, TX, professor of church history, 1960-62; Chicago Theological Seminary, IL, professor of church history, 1962-69; Iowa Wesleyan College, Mount Pleasant, president, 1966-69; Temple University, Philadelphia, PA, professor of religion, 1969-86. University of Washington, Walker-Ames Professor, 1976; Institute for Contemporary Jewry, corresponding faculty member, 1973-; Stockton College, Ida E. King Distinguished Visiting Professor, 1989-91; Baylor University, Robert Foster Cherry Distinguished Visiting Professor, 1993-94; guest professor at universities. **Publications:** The Anabaptist View of the Church, 1952, 3rd ed. as The Origins of Sectarian Protestantism, 1964; The Free Church, 1957; Landgraf Philipp und die Toleranz:, 1957; The German Phoenix, 1960; A Tribute to Menno Simons, 1961; From State Church to Pluralism, 1962, rev. ed., 1971; The Church and the Body Politic, 1969; Wild Tongues: A Handbook of Social Pathology, 1969; The Crucifixion of the Jews, 1975; The Macmillan Atlas History of Christianity, 1976; (with I.G. Shur and M.E. Wolfgang) Reflections on the Holocaust, 1980; Selected Papers, 1981; (with M.S. Littell) A Pilgrim's Interfaith Guide to the Holy Land, 1981; (with A.L. Berger and H.G. Locke) What Have We Learned?, 1993; Historical Atlas of Christianity, 2001. EDITOR: Reformation Studies: Essays in Honor of Roland H. Bainton, 1962; Sermons to Intellectuals, 1963; (with H.G. Locke) The German Church Struggle and the Holocaust, 1974; Religious Liberties in the Crossfire of Creeds, 1978; A Half Century of Religious Dialogue, 1939-1989, 1989; Hyping the Holocaust, 1997. **Address:** PO Box 10, Merion Station, PA 19066-0010, U.S.A.

LITTELL, Robert. American, b. 1935. **Genres:** Novels. **Career:** Formerly an editor with Newsweek mag., based in Eastern Europe and the Soviet Union. **Publications:** (with R.Z. Chesnoff and E. Klein) If Israel Lost the War (non-fiction), 1969; (ed.) The Czech Black Book, 1969; The Defection of A. J. Lewinter, 1973; Sweet Reason, 1974; The October Circle, 1976; Mother Russia, 1978; The Debriefing, 1979; The Amateur, 1981; The Sisters, 1985; The Revolutionist, 1988; Once and Future Spy, 1991; An Agent in Place, 1994; The Visiting Professor, 1994; Walking Back the Cat, 1996; (with S. Peres) For the Future of Israel, 1998; The Company, 2002.

LITTEN, Dr. Harold. *See* BAHR, Robert.

LITTEN, Julian (William Sebastian). British, b. 1947. **Genres:** Art/Art history, History. **Career:** Victoria and Albert Museum, London, museum assistant, 1966-74, senior museum assistant, 1974-82, research assistant, 1983-88, curator, public affairs, 1988-98; Cathedrals Fabric Commission for England, 1986-; Society of the Faith, Court of Fellows, 1985-; General Synod of the Church of England, House of Laity, 1985-; Building Craft and Conservation Centre Trust, trustee, 1991-. **Publications:** St. Mary's Church, Woodford, Essex, 1977; Sir Gilbert Scott, 1978; Land for the Living: The Cremation Movement (film), 1989; The English Way of Death: The Common Funeral since 1450, 1991. **Address:** John Pawsey, 60 High St, Tarring, Worthing, W. Sussex BN14 7NR, England.

LITTLE, Anne Colclough. American, b. 1944. **Genres:** Literary criticism and history. **Career:** Auburn University at Montgomery, AL, assistant professor, 1989-95, associate professor of English, 1995-, director of Learning Center, 1995-99, director of composition, 1999-. **Publications:** (ed. with R.C. Evans) The Muses Female Are: Martha Moulsworth and Other Women Writers of the English Renaissance, 1995; (with R.C. Evans and B. Wiedemann) Short Fiction: A Critical Companion, 1997; (ed. with S. Paul) A Collection of Essays on the Poetry of Denise Levertov, 1999. Contributor to periodicals. **Address:** Dept of English and Philosophy, Auburn University at Montgomery, 7041 Senator's Dr, PO Box 244023, Montgomery, AL 36124, U.S.A. **Online address:** alittle@mail.aum.edu

LITTLE, Bentley. Also writes as Phillip Emmons. American, b. 1960. **Genres:** Horror. **Career:** Writer. Worked as a journalist. **Publications:** HORROR NOVELS: The Revelation, 1989; The Mailman, 1991; (as Phillip Emmons) Death Instinct, 1992, in UK under name Bentley Little as Evil Deeds, 1994; The Summoning, 1993; Night School, 1994, in US as University, 1995; Dark Dominion, 1995, in US as Dominion, 1996; The Store, 1996; Houses, 1997, in US as The House, 1998; The Ignored, 1997; Guests, 1997, in US as The Town, 1999; The Walking, 2000; The Association, 2001; The Return, 2002; The Policy, 2003; the Resort, 2004. OTHER: The Collection (short stories), 2002. Contributor of short stories to anthologies and periodicals. **Address:** c/o Dominick Abel, 146 W 82nd St Ste 1B, New York, NY 10024, U.S.A.

LITTLE, Douglas. Australian, b. 1942. **Genres:** Animals/Pets. **Career:** Self-employed architect, Sydney, NSW, Australia, 1966-; Arts Administration, manager of architectural competitions and national awards; AFS student exchange program, chapter president, 1985-88; guest speaker at primary schools, 1996-. **Publications:** Ten Little-Known Facts About Hippopotamuses, 1995. **Address:** 2/355 Maroubra Rd., Maroubra 2035, Australia.

LITTLE, (Flora) Jean. Canadian (born Taiwan), b. 1932. **Genres:** Children's fiction, Poetry. **Career:** Florida State University, Tallahassee, visiting instructor; Beechwood School for Crippled Children, Guelph, ON, specialist teacher; writer and lecturer, 1960-. **Publications:** Mine for Keeps, 1962; Home from Far, 1965; Spring Begins in March, 1966; Take Wing, 1968; When the Pie Was Opened: Poems, 1968; One to Grown On, 1969; Look through My Window, 1971; Kate, 1971; From Anna, 1972; Stand in the Wind, 1975; Listen for the Singing, 1977; Mama's Going to Buy You a Mockingbird, 1985; Lost and Found, 1986; Different Dragons, 1986; Hey, World, Here I Am: Poems, 1986; Little by Little, 1987; Stars Come Out Within, 1990; Once upon a Golden Apple, 1991; Jess Was the Brave One, 1992; The Revenge of the Small Small, 1992; His Banner over Me, 1995; Bats about Baseball, 1995; Gruntle Piggle Takes Off, 1997; The Belonging Place, 1997; Emma's Magic Winter, 1998; Jenny and the Hanukkah Queen, 1999; I Know an Old Laddie, 2000; Willow and Twig, 2000; Emma's Yucky Brother, 2000; What Will the Robin Do Then? (poetry), 2000; Orphan at My Door, 2001; Birdie for Now, 2002; Dear Canada, 2003; Brothers Far from Home, 2003; I Gave My Mom a Castle (poetry), 2003; Emma's Strange Pet, 2003; Pippin the Christmas Pig, 2003. **Address:** 91 Cambridge St, Guelph, ON, Canada N1H 2V3. **Online address:** jeanlittle@rogers.com

LITTLEFIELD, Bill. American, b. 1948. **Genres:** Novels, Sports/Fitness, Biography. **Career:** Curry College, Milton, MA, professor, 1976-; WBUR, host and writer of "Only a Game" radio program; freelance writer. **Publications:** Prospect, 1989; Champions: Stories of Ten Remarkable Athletes, 1993; Baseball Days: From the Sandlots to the Show, 1993; The Circus in the woods (novel), 2002; (ed.) Fall Classics: The Best Writing about the World Series' First 100 Years (anthology), 2004. Contributor to periodicals. **Address:** c/o Only a Game, WBUR, 890 Commonwealth Ave, Boston, MA 02215, U.S.A. **Online address:** blittlef@wbur.bu.edu

LITTLEFIELD, Holly. American, b. 1963. **Genres:** Novels, Travel/Exploration. **Career:** High school teacher in Osseo, MN, 1985-92; University of Minnesota-Minneapolis, researcher and teacher of communication, 1992-. **Publications:** FICTION: Fire at the Triangle Factory, 1996; NONFICTION: The Colors of Germany, 1997; The Colors of Japan, 1997; Colors of Ghana, 1999; Children of the Trail West, 1999; Colors of India, 2000; Children of the Indian Boarding Schools, 2001; Children of the Orphan Trains, 2001. **Address:** 1-105 Carlson School, University of Minnesota-Minneapolis, Minneapolis, MN 55455, U.S.A. **Online address:** littl009@umn.edu

LITTLEJOHN, Duffy. American, b. 1953. **Genres:** Travel/Exploration. **Career:** McCarthy, Flowers, and Roberts (law firm), San Francisco, CA, attorney, 1983-84; Meadows and Doris (law firm), San Francisco, attorney, 1984-85; San Francisco District Attorney's Office, assistant district attorney, 1985-87; Alameda County District Attorney's Office, Oakland, CA, senior deputy district attorney, 1987-89; self-employed criminal defense attorney, 1989-90, 1992-; semi-retired in Paris, France, from 1990-92; author. **Publications:** Hopping Freight Trains in America, 1993; Lonesome Whistle, 2002; Ridin' Free, 2002. **Address:** c/o Zephyr Rhoades Press, PO Box 1999, Silver City, NM 88062-1999, U.S.A. **Online address:** info@zrpress.com

LITTLETON, Mark (R.). American, b. 1950. **Genres:** Novels, Adult non-fiction, Children's fiction, Young adult fiction, Children's non-fiction, Young adult non-fiction. **Career:** Author of fiction and nonfiction books for children and adults; Annapolis Fellowship of Christian Writers, Annapolis, MD, leader, 1984-. **Publications:** NONFICTION: A Place to Stand: When Life Throws You off Balance, 1986; When God Seems Far Away: Biblical Insight for Common Depression, 1987; Lies We Like to Hear: Satan's Everyday Strategies, 1988; Submission Is for Husbands, Too (adult), 1988; Cool Characters with Sweaty Palms, 1989; What To Do When God Doesn't Follow Your Plan, 1989; The Terrible Plight of Oliver B., 1990; Delighted by Discipline, 1990; Escaping the Time Crunch, 1990; Battle Ready: Winning the War with Temptation, 1992; (with B. and A. Kelley) Stasia's Gift, 1993; The Storm Within, 1994; (with F. Minirth) You Can!, 1994. ADULT FICTION: Tales of the Neverending, 1990; Death Trip: A Novel, 1992; Before Eden, 1995. YOUNG ADULT NONFICTION: When They Invited Me to Fellowship I Thought They Meant a Cruise, 1992; The Basics: Nailing down What Builds You up, 1994. UP SERIES (young adult nonfiction): Beefin' Up: Daily Feed for Amazing Grazing, 1989; Tunin' Up: Daily Jammin' for Tight Relationships, 1991; Fillin' Up, 1993; Pairin' Up, 1995. ROCKY

CREEK ADVENTURES SERIES (young adult fiction): The Adventure at Rocky Creek, 1993; Tree Fort Wars, 1993; Trouble down the Creek, 1994. CRISTA CHRONICLES SERIES (young adult fiction): The Secret of Moonlight Mountain, 1992; Winter Thunder, 1992; Robbers on Rock Road, 1993; Escape of the Grizzly, 1994; Danger on Midnight Trail, 1994; Friends No Matter What, 1994. SPORTS HEROES SERIES: Baseball, 1995; Basketball, 1995; Football, 1995; Track and Field, 1995. **Address:** c/o Thomas Nelson Inc., 501 Nelson Place, Nashville, TN 37214, U.S.A.

LITTMAN, Jonathan (Russell). American, b. 1958. **Genres:** Information science/Computers. **Career:** PC World (magazine), San Francisco, CA, contributing editor, 1983-84; PC Week (magazine), Belmont, CA, staff reporter, 1984-86; Mac World (magazine), San Francisco, contributing editor, 1987-. Speaker at colleges and universities and on national television, 1985-. **Publications:** Once upon a Time in ComputerLand: The Amazing, Billion-Dollar Tale of Bill Millard, 1987; The Fugitive Game: Online with Kevin Mitnick, 1996. Contributor of articles and reviews to magazines. **Address:** c/o Little Brown and Co. Inc., 1271 Avenue of the Americas, New York, NY 10020, U.S.A.

LITWACK, Leon. American, b. 1929. **Genres:** History, Race relations. **Career:** Alexander F. and May T. Morrison Professor, 1987-, and Professor of History, 1971-, University of California, Berkeley (Faculty member, 1965-). Assistant to Associate Professor, University of Wisconsin, Madison, 1958-65. Member, Editorial Board, Journal of Negro History, 1974-79; President, 1986-87, Organization of American Historians; Executive Committee, American Council of Learned Societies, 1993-96; Executive Board, Southern Historical Association, 2002-05. Pulitzer Prize in History, 1980; American Book Award, History, 1981; Francis Parkman Prize, Society of American Historians, 1980. **Publications:** North of Slavery: The Negro in the Free States 1790-1860, 1961; (with others) The United States, 4th ed., 1976; Been in the Storm So Long: The Aftermath of Slavery, 1979; (with A. Meier) Black Leaders of the Nineteenth Century, 1988; Trouble in Mind, 1998; (co) Without Sanctuary: Lynching Photography in America, 2000. EDITOR: The American Labor Movement, 1962; (with K. Stampp) Reconstruction: An Anthology of Revisionist Writings, 1969; (gen.) The Harvard Guide to African-American History, 2001. **Address:** Dept. of History, University of California, Berkeley, CA 94720, U.S.A.

LIU, Eric. American, b. 1968. **Genres:** Literary criticism and history. **Career:** Next Progressive, Cambridge, MA, founder, 1991, editor, 1991-. Speechwriter for the White House and National Security Council, 1993-94. **Publications:** (ed.) Next: Young American Writers on the New Generation, 1994. **Address:** 11 Donald St., Lexington, MA 02420, U.S.A.

LIU, Timothy. American, b. 1965. **Genres:** Poetry. **Career:** University of California, Berkeley, Holloway lecturer, 1997; Cornell College, Mount Vernon, IA, Assistant Professor, 1994-98; William Paterson University, Hoboken, NJ, Assistant Professor, 1998-. **Publications:** A Zipper of Haze, 1988; Vox Angelica: Poems, 1992; Burnt Offerings, 1995; Say Goodnight, 1998; Hard Evidence, 2001; Of the I Sing, 2004. Contributor of poems to journals. **Address:** Dept of English, William Paterson University, 300 Pompton Rd, Wayne, NJ 07470, U.S.A. **Online address:** liut@wpunj.edu

LIVELY, Adam. Welsh, b. 1961. **Genres:** Novels, Politics/Government. **Career:** Writer, 1988-. **Publications:** NOVELS: Blue Fruit, 1988; The Burnt House, 1989; The Snail, 1991; Sing the Body Electric, 1993. OTHER: (ed. with J. Lively) Democracy in Britain: A Reader, 1994. **Address:** 69 Poet's Rd., London N5 25H, England.

LIVELY, Penelope. British (born Egypt), b. 1933. **Genres:** Novels, Novellas/Short stories, Children's fiction, Plays/Screenplays. **Publications:** CHILDREN'S FICTION: Astercote, 1970; The Whispering Knights, 1971; The Wild Hunt of Hagworthy, 1971; The Driftway, 1972; The Ghost of Thomas Kempe, 1973; The House in Norham Gardens, 1974; Going Back, 1975; The Boy without a Name, 1975; A Stitch in Time, 1976; Fanny's Sister, 1976; The Stained Glass Window, 1976; The Voyage of QV66, 1978; Fanny and the Monsters, 1978; Fanny and the Battle of Potter's Piece, 1980; The Revenge of Samuel Stokes, 1981; Uninvited Ghosts and Other Stories, 1984; Dragon Trouble, 1984; Debbie and the Little Devil, 1987; A House Inside Out, 1987; Judy and the Martian, 1992; The Cat, the Crow, and the Banyan Tree, 1994; Good Night, Sleep Tight, 1994; Two Bears and Joe, 1995; Goldilocks and the Three Bears, 1997; Ghostly Guests, 1997; One, Two, Three Jump!, 1998; In Search of a Homeland: The Story of the Aeneid, 2001. ADULT NOVELS: The Road to Lichfield, 1977; Treasures of Time, 1979; Judgement Day, 1980; Next to Nature, Art, 1982; Perfect Happiness, 1983; According to Mark, 1984; Moon Tiger, 1987; Passing On, 1989; City of the Mind, 1991; Cleopatra's Sister, 1993; Heat Wave, 1996; Spiderweb, 1999; The Photograph, 2003. STORIES: Nothing Missing but the Samovar and Other Stories, 1978; Corruption and Other Stories, 1984; Pack of Cards: Stories 1978-86, 1986; Beyond the Blue Mountains, 1997. OTHER: The Presence of the Past: An Introduction to Landscape History, 1975; Oleander, Jacaranda: A Memoir, 1994; A House Unlocked, 2001. **Address:** c/o David Higham Associates, Ltd., 5-8 Lower John St, Golden Sq, London W1R 4HA, England.

LIVINGSTON, Gordon (S.). American, b. 1938. **Genres:** Human relations/ Parenting. **Career:** Walter Reed General Hospital, Washington, DC, rotating intern, 1967-68; Johns Hopkins Hospital, Baltimore, MD, resident in psychiatry at Henry Phipps Psychiatric Clinic, 1969-72, fellow in child psychiatry, 1972-74; Columbia Medical Plan, Columbia, MD, psychiatrist, 1971-. Johns Hopkins University, assistant professor. Patuxent Medical Group, chief of psychiatry. **Publications:** Only Spring: On Mourning the Death of My Son, 1995. Contributor to medical journals, popular magazines, and newspapers. **Address:** Columbia Medical Plan, Knoll North 2, Columbia, MD 21045, U.S.A.

LIVINGSTON, Robert Henry. American, b. 1934. **Genres:** Songs/Lyrics and libretti, Plays/Screenplays. **Career:** Theater and television director, writer; and custom cabinet-maker. Gateway Playhouse, Belport, NY, stage manager, 1953-; Booth Theater, New York City, assistant stage manager, 1955-; CBS-TV, production assistant for Captain Kangaroo, 1959, worked as production assistant, assistant director, and director, 1960-63; free-lance director, CBS, NBC, ABC, and writer, 1963-. Directed theater and television productions. **Publications:** (Author of book) The Me Nobody Knows (musical), 1970; Taking My Turn (musical), 1984; Finkel's Follies, 1990. **Address:** 347 W. 39th St., New York, NY 10018, U.S.A.

LIVINGSTONE, J. B. See **JACQ, Christian.**

LLEWELLYN, Kate. Australian, b. 1940. **Genres:** Novels, Poetry, Travel/ Exploration, Autobiography/Memoirs, Essays. **Career:** Royal Adelaide Hospital, South Australia, trainee nurse, 1954-58; registered nurse, Adelaide, 1958-60; Llewellyn Galleries, Dulwich, coowner and director, 1968-75. **Publications:** POETRY: Trader Kate and the Elephants, 1983; Luxury, 1985; Honey, 1988; Figs, 1989; Selected Poems, 1992; Crosshatched, 1994; So False and Other Poems, 1999. OTHER: The Waterlily, 1986; Dear You, 1987; The Mountain, 1990; Angels and Dark Madonnas-Travels in Italy and India, 1991; Lilies Feathers and Frangipani, 1993; The Floral Mother and Other Essays, 1995; Gorillas Tea & Coffee-Travels in East Africa, 1995; (ed.) The Penguin Book of Australian Women Poets, 1986. **Address:** c/o Tim Curnow, Curtis Brown Literary Agents, 7 Union St, Paddington, NSW 2021, Australia.

LLEWELLYN, Sam. British, b. 1948. **Genres:** Novels, Mystery/Crime/ Suspense, Romance/Historical, Children's fiction, Marine sciences/ Oceanography. **Career:** Musician, writer, Campaigner. Director of Arch Books. **Publications:** THRILLERS: Dead Reckoning, 1988, Blood Orange, 1989; Death Roll, 1990; Dead Eye, 1991; Blood Knot, 1992; Riptide, 1994; Clawhammer, 1994; Maelstorm, 1995; Storm Force from Navarone, 1996; The Shadow in the Sands, 1998. CHILDREN'S BOOKS: Pegleg, 1989; Pig in the Middle, 1989; The Rope School, 1994; The Magic Boathouse, 1995; The Polecat Cafe, 1996; Neeson (nonfiction), 2004; Little Darlings, 2004; Bad, Bad Darlings, 2005; The Return of Death Eric, 2005. OTHER: Gurney's Revenge, 1978; Gurney's Reward, 1979; Gurney's Release, 1979; Hell Bay (novel), 1980; The Last Will and Testament of Robert Louis Stevenson, 1981; Yacky dar Moy Bewty!: A Phrasebook for the Regions of Britain (with Irish Supplement), 1985; Small Parts in History (nonfiction), 1985; The Worst Journey in the Midlands (nonfiction), 1985; Great Circle, 1987; The Sea Garden, 2000; The Malpas Legacy, 2001; Emperor Smith, the Man Who Built Scilly (nonfiction), 2005. **Address:** c/o LAW, 14 Vernon St, London W14 0RJ, England. **Online address:** samllewellyn@onetel.net.uk

LLITERAS, D. S. American, b. 1949. **Genres:** Novels, Poetry. **Career:** Has worked as a theatrical director, stage manager, actor, college instructor, deep sea diver; Norfolk Fire Department, professional firefighter, 1986-. **Publications:** POETRY: In a Warrior's Romance, 1991. NOVELS: In the Heart of Things, 1992; Into the Ashes, 1993; Half Hidden by Twilight, 1994; The Thieves of Golgotha, 1998; Judas the Gentile, 1999; 613 West Jefferson, 2001; Jerusalem's Rain, 2003. Contributor of haiku/poetry and short stories to periodicals and anthologies. **Address:** PO Box 5216, Virginia Beach, VA 23471, U.S.A.

LLOYD, A(lan) R(ichard). British, b. 1927. **Genres:** Novels, Science fiction/Fantasy, Animals/Pets, History, Biography. **Career:** Jersey Evening Post, journalist; freelance magazine writer; full-time author, 1962-. **Publications:** FANTASY NOVELS. "KINE SERIES": Kine, 1982, in UK as Marshworld, 1990; Witchwood, 1989; Dragonpond, 1990. OTHER NOVELS: The Eighteenth Concubine, 1972; Trade Imperial, 1979; The Last Otter, 1984, in US as The Boy and the Otter, 1985; The Farm Dog, 1986; Wingfoot, 1993. OTHER: The Drums of Kumasi, 1964; The Making of the King 1066 (in UK as The Year of the Conqueror), 1966; The Spanish Centuries, 1968; Franco, 1969; The King Who Lost America (in UK as Who Wickedest Age), 1971; The Maligned Monarch, 1972, in UK as King John, 1973; Marathon, 1973; The Scorching of Washington, 1974; The Taras Report, 1975; The War in the Trenches, 1976; The Hundred Years War, 1977; Destroy Carthage, 1977; The Great Prize Fight, 1977. **Address:** c/o HarperCollins, 77-85 Fulham Palace Rd, London W6 8JB, England.

LLOYD, Elisabeth A. American, b. 1956. **Genres:** Biology, Philosophy, Sciences, Sex, Women's studies and issues. **Career:** Harvard University, Cambridge, MA, visiting scholar in genetics, 1983-84; University of California, San Diego, La Jolla, visiting lecturer, 1984-85, assistant professor of philosophy, 1985-88; University of California, Berkeley, assistant professor, 1988-90, associate professor of philosophy, 1990-, associate professor, Program in Logic and Methodology of Science, 1992-. Harvard University, research associate at Museum of Comparative Zoology, 1989; University of California, Humanities Research Institute fellow, 1989, resident fellow, 1991; University of California, Davis, member of associated faculty, Program in History and Philosophy of Science, 1990-; Stanford University, consulting faculty, 1990; University of Auckland, visiting senior lecturer, 1990; lecturer at colleges and universities in the United States and Europe. **Publications:** The Structure and Confirmation of Evolutionary Theory, 1988, reissue, 1994; (ed. with E.F. Keller, and contrib.) Keywords in Evolutionary Biology, 1992; (ed) The Sciences in Human Perspective (series). Contributor of articles and reviews to philosophy and scientific journals. **Address:** Department of Philosophy, University of California, Berkeley, CA 94720, U.S.A.

LLOYD, Sir Geoffrey Ernest Richard. British, b. 1933. **Genres:** Philosophy. **Career:** Cambridge University, assistant lecturer, 1965-67, lecturer, 1967-74, sr. tutor of King's College, 1969-73, reader, 1974-83, professor of ancient philosophy and science, 1983-2000, master of Darwin College, 1989-2000. East Asian History of Science Trust, chairman, 1992-2002. **Publications:** Polarity and Analogy: Two Types of Argumentation in Early Greek Thought, 1966; Aristotle: The Growth and Structure of His Thought, 1968; Early Greek Science: Thales to Aristotle, 1970; Greek Science after Aristotle, 1973; Magic, Reason and Experience, 1979; Science, Folklore and Ideology, 1983; Science and Morality in Greco-Roman Antiquity, 1985; The Revolutions of Wisdom, 1987; Demystifying Mentalities, 1990; Methods and Problems in Greek Science, 1991; Adversaries & Authorities, 1996; Aristotelian Explorations, 1996; Greek Thought, 2000; The Ambitions of Curiosity, 2002; (with N. Sivin) The Way and the Word, 2002; In the Grip of Disease, 2003; Ancient Worlds, Modern Reflections, 2004. EDITOR: Hippocratic Writings, 1978; Aristotle on Mind and the Senses, 1978; (with J. Brunschwig) Le Savoir Grec, 1996. **Address:** Needham Research Institute, 8 Sylvester Rd, Cambridge CB3 9AF, England. **Online address:** gel20@hermes.cam.ac.uk

LLOYD, Levanah. See **PETERS, Maureen.**

LLOYD, Margaret Glynne. American (born England), b. 1946. **Genres:** Poetry, Literary criticism and history. **Career:** Poet; professor. Member of faculty at Springfield College. **Publications:** William Carlos Williams's "Paterson": A Critical Reappraisal, 1983; This Particular Earthly Scene (poetry), 1993. **Address:** 17 Lilly St., Florence, MA 01062, U.S.A.

LLOYD, P(eter) J(ohn). New Zealander, b. 1937. **Genres:** Economics. **Career:** New Zealand Department of Statistics, research officer, 1959; Victoria University of Wellington, Wellington, New Zealand, lecturer, 1962-64, senior lecturer, 1964-65; Michigan State University, East Lansing, assistant professor, 1965-68, associate professor of economics, 1969; Australian National University, Canberra, Australian Capital Territory, Australia, senior research fellow, 1969, senior fellow, 1970-81, professorial fellow, 1981-83, faculty chair of Research School of Pacific Studies, 1976, 1977; University of Melbourne, Parkville, Victoria, Australia, professor, 1983-, Ritchie Professor of Economics, 1995-, dean of Faculty of Economics and Commerce, 1988-93, director of Asian Business Centre, 1994-96, and Asian Economics Centre, 1997-99, acting director of Centre of Financial Studies, 2000-01. Member of research committees, editorial boards and commissions. **Publications:** International Trade Problems of Small Nations, 1968; Non-Tariff Barriers to Australian Trade, 1973; (with H. Grubel) Intra-Industry Trade, 1974; (with K. Vautier) International Trade and Competition Policy: CER, APEC, and the WTO, 1997; International Trade Opening and the Formation of the Global Economy: Selected Essays, 1999; (with K. Vautier) Promoting Competition in Global Markets: A Multi-national Approach, 1999; Intra-Industry Trade: Critical Writings in Economics, 2002. EDITOR; (and contrib) Mineral Economics in Australia, 1984; (with L. Pasinetti) Structural Change, Economic Interdependence, and World Development, 1986; (with Lim Chong-Yah; and contrib) Singapore: Resources and Growth, 1986; (with S. King) Economic Rationalism: Dead End or Way Forward?, 1993; (with L. Williams; and contrib) International Trade and Migration in the APEC Region, 1996; (with Xiao-guang Zhang) China in the Global Economy, 2000; (with Xiao-guang Zhang; and contrib) Models of the Chinese Economy, 2001; (with J. Nieuwenhuysen and M. Mead) Growth with Equity, 2001; (with Hyun-hoon Lee) Frontiers of Research in Intra-Industry Trade, 2002; (with H.G. Grubel) Intra-Industry Trade, 2003. Author of research monographs. Contributor to books and professional journals. **Address:** Department of Economics, Faculty of Economics and Commerce, University of Melbourne, Parkville, VIC 3010, Australia. **Online address:** pjlloyd@unimelb.edu.au

LLOYD, Peter Cutt. British, b. 1927. **Genres:** Anthropology/Ethnology, Gerontology/Senior issues, History, Sociology, Third World, Urban studies. **Career:** University of Sussex, Brighton, reader, 1967-78, professor, 1978-92, Emeritus Professor of Social Anthropology, 1992-. Hon. Director, International African Institute, London, 1988-91. Head, Dept. of Sociology, University of Ibadan, Nigeria, 1959-64; Sr. Lecturer, then Reader in West African Sociology, University of Birmingham, 1964-67. **Publications:** Yoruba Land Law, 1962; Africa in Social Change, 1967; Classes, Crises and Coups, 1971; The Development of Yoruba Kingdoms in the 18th and 19th Centuries, 1971; Power and Independence, 1974; Slums of Hope?, 1979; The "Young Towns" of Lima, 1980; A Third World Proletariat?, 1982. EDITOR: The New Elites of Tropical Africa, 1966; (with A. Mabogunje and B. Awe) The City of Ibadan, 1967; (with Philip Amis) Housing Africa's Urban Poor, 1990. **Address:** School of Social Sciences and Cultural Studies, University of Sussex, Brighton, E. Sussex BN1 9SN, England.

LLOYD, Rosemary. Australian, b. 1949. **Genres:** Literary criticism and history. **Career:** Cambridge University, England, fellow of New Hall, 1978-90, university lecturer, 1979-90; Indiana University-Bloomington, Rudy Professor of French, professor of gender studies, adjunct professor of comparative literature and English, 1990-. **Publications:** Baudelaire et Hoffmann: Affinites et influences, 1979; Baudelaire's Literary Criticism, 1981; Mallarme: Poesies, 1984; Flaubert's Madame Bovary, 1990; The Land of Lost Content: Childhood in 19th-Century French Literature, 1992; Closer & Closer Apart: Jealousy in Literature, 1995; Mallarme: The Poet and His Circle, 1999; Baudelaire's World, 2002; Shimmering in a Transformed Light: Writing the Still Life, 2004. EDITOR: (with L. Watson) Patterns of Evolution in Nineteenth-Century French Poetry, 1991; (co) T. de Banville, Oeuvres Completes, Vol. II, 1996; Banville, Roses de Noel, 1998. TRANSLATOR: Selected Letters of Charles Baudelaire, 1986; Selected Letters of Stephane Mallarme, 1988; Baudelaire: La Fanfarlo and Short Prose Poems, 1991; G. Sand, The Master Pipers, 1994; (and ed.) Revolutions in Writing: Nineteenth-Century French Prose, 1996. Contributor to periodicals. **Address:** Dept of French and Italian, 642 Ballantine Hall, Indiana University-Bloomington, Bloomington, IN 47405, U.S.A. **Online address:** rolloyd@indiana.edu

LLOYD, T(revor) O(wen). British/Canadian, b. 1934. **Genres:** History. **Career:** University of Toronto, Dept. of History, lecturer, 1959-63, assistant professor, 1963-67, associate professor, 1967-71, professor, 1971-97. **Publications:** The General Election of 1880, 1968; Canada in World Affairs, 1957-59, 1968; (ed. with J.T. McLeod) Agenda 1970, 1968; Empire to Welfare State: English History 1906-1967, 1970, 5th ed. (as 1906-2001), 2002; Suffragettes International, 1971; The Growth of Parliamentary Democracy in Britain, 1973; The British Empire 1558-1983, 1984, 2nd ed. (as 1558-1995), 1996; Empire, 2001. **Address:** Dept of History, University of Toronto, Toronto, ON, Canada M5S 3G3.

LLOYD-JONES, (Sir) (Peter) Hugh (Jefferd). British, b. 1922. **Genres:** Classics. **Career:** Regius Professor Emeritus of Greek, Oxford University, 1989- (Fellow and E. P. Warren Praelector in Classics, Corpus Christi College, 1954-60; Student of Christ Church and Regius Professor, 1960-89). Fellow of Jesus College, Cambridge, 1948-54; Assistant Lecturer, 1950-52, and Lecturer in Classics, 1952-54, Cambridge University. **Publications:** Appendix to the Loeb edition of Aeschylus, 1957; Menandri Dyscolus, 1960; Tacitus, 1964; The Justice of Zeus, 1971, 1983; Females of the Species: Semonides of Amorgos on Women, 1975; Myths of the Zodiac, 1978; (with M. Quinton) Imaginary Animals, 1980; (with P.J. Parsons) Supplementum Hellenisticum, 1983; Blood for the Ghosts, 1982; Classical Survivals, 1982; (with

N.G. Wilson) Sophoclis' Fabulae, 1990; (with N.G. Wilson) Sophoclea, 1990; Collected Academic Papers, 2 vols., 1990; Greek in a Cold Climate, 1991; Sophocles, 1-2, 1994, 3, 1996; Sophoclea: Second Thoughts, 1997. TRANSLATOR: Greek Metre, by Paul Maas, 1962; Aeschylus: Agamemnon, The Libation-Bearers, and The Eumenides, 1970, 2nd ed. 1979. EDITOR: The Greeks, 1962; Maurice Bowra: A Celebration, 1974. **Address:** 15 W Riding, Wellesley, MA 02482, U.S.A. **Online address:** mlefrowitz@wellesley.edu

LLOYD WEBBER, Andrew. British, b. 1948. **Genres:** Songs/Lyrics and libretti. **Career:** Composer, author, and producer. **Publications:** (with T. Rice) Evita: The Legend of Eva Peron, 1919-1952, 1978; Cats: The Book of the Musical, 1981; (with Rice) Joseph and the Amazing Technicolor Dreamcoat, 1982. **Address:** The Really Useful Group, 22 Tower St, London WC2H 9TW, England.

LLYWELYN, Morgan. Also writes as Shannon Lewis. Irish (born United States), b. 1947. **Genres:** Novels, Romance/Historical, Science fiction/Fantasy, Biography. **Career:** Full-time writer. **Publications:** The Wind from Hastings, 1978; Lion of Ireland: The Legend of Brian Boru, 1980; (as Shannon Lewis) Personal Habits, 1982; The Horse Goddess, 1982; Bard: The Odyssey of the Irish, 1984; Grania, She-King of the Irish Seas, 1986; Xerxes (biography), 1987; Red Branch, 1989; The Isles of the Blest, 1989; Druids, 1991; The Last Prince of Ireland, 1993; Finn Mac Cool, 1994; Silverhand, 1995; Graphic History of Ireland, 1995; Pride of Lions, 1996; "1916," 1998; Essential Library for Irish-Americans, 1999; Etruscans, 2000; "1921," 2001; "1949," 2003. **Address:** c/o Abner Stein, 10 Roland Gardens, London SW7 3PH, England.

LOADES, David Michael. British, b. 1934. **Genres:** History, Biography. **Career:** Lecturer in Political Science, University of St. Andrews, Scotland, 1961-63; Lecturer, 1963-71, Sr. Lecturer, 1971-77, and Reader in Modern History, 1977-80, University of Durham; Professor of History, University College of North Wales, Bangor, 1980-96; Honorary Research Professor, University of Sheffield, 1996-. **Publications:** Two Tudor Conspiracies, 1965; The Oxford Martyrs, 1970; Politics and the Nation 1450-1660, 1974, 5th ed., 1999; The Reign of Mary Tudor, 1979; The Tudor Court, 1986; Mary Tudor: A Life, 1989; Politics, Censorship and the English Reformation, 1991; Cranmer and The English Reformation, 1991; The Tudor Navy, 1992; The Mid-Tudor Crisis, 1992; Revolution in Religion, 1992; Essays in European History 1450-1650, 1993; The Politics of Marriage, 1994; Essays on the Reign of Edward VI, 1994; Power in Tudor England, 1996; John Dudley, Duke of Northumberland, 1996; Tudor Government, 1997; England's Maritime Empire, 2000; Chronicles of the Tudor Queens, 2002; Elizabeth I, 2003; Intrigue and Treason, 2004. EDITOR/COEDITOR: The Papers of George Wyatt, 1968; The End of Strife, 1984; Law and Government under the Tudors: Essays Presented to Sir Geoffrey Elton, 1988; Faith and Identity, 1989; The Chronicles of the Tudor Kings, 1990; John Foxe and the English Reformation, 1997; John Foxe: An Historical Perspective, 1999; The Anthony Roll, 2000; Letters from the Mary Rose, 2003; John Foxe: At Home and Abroad, 2004. **Address:** The Cottage, Priory Lane, Burford, Oxon. OX18 4SG, England.

LOBBAN, Richard A., Jr. American, b. 1943. **Genres:** Anthropology/Ethnology, Area studies, History. **Career:** Rhode Island College, Providence, professor of anthropology and African studies, 1972-, director of Program of African and Afro-American Studies, 1985-94. Worked as a professor at Bucknell University, Dartmouth College, and University of Pittsburgh; American University in Cairo, head of Urban Development Unit at Social Research Center, 1982-84. Sudan Studies Association, executive director; Rhode Island Black Heritage Society, vice president. **Publications:** Historical Dictionary of the Republics of Guinea-Bissau and Cape Verde, 1979, as Historical Dictionary of the Republic of Cape Verde, 3rd ed. (with M. Lopes), 1995; (with J. Forrest) Historical Dictionary of Guinea-Bissau, 1988, 3rd ed. (with P.K. Mendy), 1997; (with C. Fluehr-Lobban and J.O. Voll) Historical Dictionary of the Sudan, 2nd ed., 1992, 3rd ed. (with C. Fluehr-Lobban and R. Kramer), 2002; Cape Verde: Crioulo Colony to Independent Nation, 1995; (ed.) Middle Eastern Women in the Invisible Economy, 1998; Historical Dictionary of Ancient & Medieval Nubia, 2004. **Address:** Dept of Anthropology and African Studies, Rhode Island College, 600 Mt. Pleasant Ave, Providence, RI 02908-1991, U.S.A. **Online address:** rlobban@ric.edu

LOCHHEAD, Douglas (Grant). Canadian, b. 1922. **Genres:** Poetry, Literary criticism and history, Bibliography. **Career:** General Ed., Literature of Canada Series: Poetry and Prose in Reprint, 1972-, and Toronto Reprint Library of Canadian Prose and Poetry, 1973-, University of Toronto Press. Writer-in-Residence, Mount Allison University, Sackville, NB, 1987-90. Poet

Laureate of Sackville, New Brunswick, 2003-. **Publications:** The Heart Is Fire: Poems, 1959; Poems in Folio, no. 1 and no. 2, 1959, 1963; It Is All Around: Poems, 1960; Poet Talking, 1964; A&B&C&: An Alphabet, 1969; Millwood Road Poems, 1970; Prayers in a Field: Poems, 1974; The Full Furnace: Collected Poems, 1975; High Marsh Road, 1980; Battle Sequence, 1980; A E: A Long Poem, 1980; The Panic Field, 1984; Tiger in the Skull, 1986; Upper Cape Poems, 1989; Dykelands, 1989; Black Festival, 1991; Homage to Henry Alline, 1992; Breakfast at Mel's (poems), 1997; All Things Do Continue (poems), 1997; The Lucretius Poems, 1998; Cape Enrage: Poems on a Raised Beach, 2000; Yes, Yes, Yes! (poem), 2001; Weathers: Poems New and Selected, 2002; Orkney, October Diary (poem), 2002; Midgic: A Poem, 2003. EDITOR: (with N. Frye and J.A. Irving) T. McCulloch, The Stepsure Letters, 1960; (with R. Souster) Made in Canada: An Anthology of Contemporary Canadian Poetry, 1970; Bibliography of Canadian Bibliographies, rev. ed., 1972; (with R. Souster) 100 Poems of Nineteenth Century Canada, 1974; J.B. Hart, St. Ursula's Convent or The Nun of Canada, 1991. **Address:** 9 Quarry Ln, Sackville, NB, Canada E4L 4G3.

LOCHMAN, Jan Milic. Swiss (born Czech Republic), b. 1922. **Genres:** Theology/Religion. **Career:** Comenius Faculty, Prague, Professor of Theology, 1950-68; Union Theological Seminary, NYC, Professor of Theology, 1968-69; University of Basel, Switzerland, Professor of Systematic Theology, 1969-. **Publications:** The Church in a Marxist Society, 1970; (with H. Marcuse, R. Shaull and J. C. Bennett) Marxism and Radical Religion, 1970; Encountering Marx, 1977; Living Roots of Reformation, 1979; Reconciliation and Liberation, 1980; Signposts to Freedom, 1981; The Theology of Praise, 1982; The Faith We Confess, 1984; Christ and Prometheus?, 1988; The Lord's Prayer, 1990; Zeal for Truth and Tolerance, 1996. **Address:** Birmannsgasse 14, 4055 Basel, Switzerland. **Online address:** jmlochman@dplanet.ch

LOCHTE, Dick. (Richard S. Lochte). American, b. 1944. **Genres:** Novels, Novellas/Short stories, Mystery/Crime/Suspense, Plays/Screenplays. **Career:** Audio-tape fiction reviewer, 1989-99. Playboy Enterprises, Chicago, promotional copywriter, 1966-70; Playboy Enterprises, Los Angeles, West Coast promotional mgr., 1970-71; freelance writer, 1971; Los Angeles Free Press, film critic, 1971-74; Los Angeles Times, book columnist, 1974-85; Los Angeles mag., theater critic, 1975-96; Los Angeles Book Review, mystery fiction reviewer, 1996-. Recipient: Nero Wolfe Award, 1985. **Publications:** The Playboy Writer, 1968; Death Mask (novel), 1971; Escape to Athena (screenplay), 1979; Philip Strange (screenplay), 1985; Sleeping Dog (mystery), 1985; Laughing Dog (mystery), 1988; Sleeping Dog (screenplay), 1989; Blue Bayou (mystery), 1992; The Neon Smile (mystery), 1995; (with C. Darden) The Trials of Nikki Hill, 1999; (with C. Darden) L.A. Justice, 2001; Lucky Dog and Other Tales of Murder (short stories), 2001. **Address:** PO Box 5413, Santa Monica, CA 90409, U.S.A.

LOCK, Charles (John Somerset). British, b. 1955. **Genres:** Literary criticism and history. **Career:** Hoegskolan i Karlstad, Karlstad, Sweden, lecturer, 1980-82; University of Toronto, Toronto, Ontario, Canada, assistant professor, 1983-88, associate professor, 1988-93, professor of English, 1993-. **Publications:** Thomas Hardy, 1992. Contributor to periodicals. **Address:** Department of English, Erindale College, University of Toronto, Mississauga, ON, Canada L5L 1S6.

LOCK, Joan. British, b. 1933. **Genres:** Novels, Novellas/Short stories, Mystery/Crime/Suspense, Plays/Screenplays, Children's non-fiction, Criminology/True Crime, History, Women's studies and issues. **Career:** Queen Elizabeth Hospital, Gateshead, England, student nurse, 1950-54; Metropolitan Police, London, policewoman, 1954-60; British European Airways, London, reservations clerk, 1961-66; writer, 1966-; part-time jobs, freelance journalist for police and law periodicals, adviser on the history of British women police, 1966-; radio dramatist. **Publications:** Lady Policeman, 1968; Reluctant Nightingale, 1970; The British Policewoman: Her Story, 1979; Marlborough Street: The Story of a London Court, 1980; Tales from Bow Street, 1982; Blue Murder, 1986; Dreadful Deeds and Awful Murders: Scotland Yard's First Detectives, 1829-1878, 1990; Scotland Yard Casebook: The Making of the CID 1865-1935, 1993; Dead Image, 2000; Death in Perspective, 2001; Dead Born, 2002; Dead Letters, 2003; Dead End, 2004; Famous Trials; Famous Prisons; Protecting Yourself against Criminals. **Address:** c/o Severn House Publishers Ltd, 9-15 High St, Sutton, Surrey SM1 1DF, England. **Online address:** joanlock.co.uk

LOCKE, Christopher. American, b. 1947. **Genres:** Business/Trade/Industry, Marketing. **Career:** Fujitsu International Engineering, Ricoh Software Research Center, North-Holland/Elsevier Science Publishers, and Institute for

New Generation Computer Technology, Tokyo, Japan, technical editor, 1983-85; Carnegie Group, Pittsburgh, PA, director of corporate communications, 1985-91; Intelligent Technology Group, Pittsburgh, PA, vice president of corporate communications, 1985-91; Carnegie Mellon University Robotics Institute, Pittsburgh, PA, director of industrial relations, 1985-91; CIMLINC, Chicago, IL, director of corporate communications, 1991-92; Avalanche Development, Boulder, CO, vice president of business development, 1992-93; CMP Publications, Manhasset, NY, founding editor of Internet Business Report, 1993; MecklerWeb Corporation, Westport, CT, president, 1994; internetMCI, Reston, VA, editor and publisher, 1995; IBM, White Plains, NY, program director of online community development, 1995-96; Entropy Web Consulting, Boulder, CO, president, 1996-; Entropy Gradient Reversals, Boulder, CO, editor and publisher, 1996-; Displaytech, Boulder, CO, vice president of business development, 1996-97; personalization.com, Boulder, CO, editor-in-chief, 1999-2000; speaker. **Publications:** (with R. Levine, D. Searls, and D. Weinberger) The Cluetrain Manifesto: The End of Business as Usual, 2000; Gonzo Marketing: Winning Through Worst Practices, 2001; The Bombast Transcripts: Rants and Screeds of RageBoy, 2002. Contributor to periodicals. **Address:** 930-D West Moorhead Circle, Boulder, CO 80305, U.S.A. **Online address:** clocke@panix.com

LOCKE, Hubert G. American, b. 1934. **Genres:** History, Theology/Religion. **Career:** Professor of Public Affairs, University of Washington, Seattle, 1976-, now Emeritus (Associate Dean, 1976-77; Vice Provost, 1977-82; Dean, 1982-88). Director of Religious Affairs, 1957-62, Faculty Research Associate, Center for Urban Studies, and Adjunct Assistant Professor of Urban Education, 1967-69, Leo M. Franklin Memorial Professor of Human Relations, 1969-70, Wayne State University, Detroit; Special Assistant to the Commissioner of Police of Detroit, 1966-67; Dean, College of Public Affairs, University of Nebraska at Omaha, 1972-75. **Publications:** The Detroit Riot of 1967, 1969; The Care and Feeding of White Liberals, 1970; (ed. with Franklin H. Littell) The German Church Struggle and the Holocaust, 1974; The Church Confronts the Nazis, 1984; Exile in the Fatherland, 1987; The Black Antisemitism Controversy, 1994; Learning from History, 2000; Groping for God, 2002. **Address:** University of Washington, Box 353055, Seattle, WA 98195, U.S.A.

LOCKE, Maryel. American. **Genres:** Film, Literary criticism and history. **Career:** Radcliffe Quarterly, Cambridge, MA, editor, 1964-71; private practice of law, 1973-90. Commonwealth of Massachusetts, member of Board of Higher Education, 1976-80; Town of Weston, MA, chairperson of School Committee, 1965-68. Boston Museum of Fine Arts, member of steering committee for Friends of Film, 1987-; Harvard Institute for Learning in Retirement, leader, film studies courses, 1995-. **Publications:** (ed. with C. Warren) Jean-Luc Godard's Hail Mary: Women and the Sacred in Film, 1993. Work represented in anthologies. **Address:** 1 Longfellow Pl, Apt. 3312, Boston, MA 02114, U.S.A.

LOCKE, Robert R. American, b. 1932. **Genres:** Administration/Management. **Career:** University of Hawaii at Manoa, Honolulu, professor of history, business, and management, 1974-. Visiting professor at European Institute for Advanced Studies in Management, Brussels, Belgium, 1982-84, London School of Economics and Political Science, London, 1986-88, and University of Reading, 1988-. **Publications:** The End of the Practical Man, 1984; Management and Higher Education since 1940, 1989; The Collapse of the American Management Mystique, 1996; (ed.) Management Education, 1998; (with K.E. Schone) The Entrepreneurial Shift, 2004. **Address:** Dept of History, University of Hawaii at Manoa, 2530 Dole St, Honolulu, HI 96822, U.S.A. **Online address:** blocke@hawaii.edu

LOCKERBIE, D(onald) Bruce. American (born Canada), b. 1935. **Genres:** Plays/Screenplays, Administration/Management, Education, History, Literary criticism and history, Theology/Religion, Biography. **Career:** Stony Brook School, New York, scholar-in-residence, 1957-91; visiting consultant at American Schools in Asia and Africa, 1974-; PAIDEIA, Inc., chairman, 1984-. **Publications:** Billy Sunday, 1965; Patriarchs and Prophets, 1969; Hawthorne, 1970; Melville, 1970; Twain, 1970; Major American Authors, 1970; (with L. Westdahl) Success in Writing, 1970; Purposeful Writing, 1972; The Way They Should Go, 1972; The Liberating Word, 1974; The Cosmic Center: The Apostles' Creed, 1977; A Man under Orders: Lt. General William K. Harrison, 1979; Who Educates Your Child?, 1980; The Timeless Moment, 1980; Asking Questions, 1980; Fatherlove, 1981; In Peril on the Sea, 1984; The Christian, The Arts, and Truth, 1985; College: Getting In and Staying In, 1990; Take Heart, 1990; A Passion for Learning: A History of Christian Thought on Education, 1994; From Candy Sales to Committed Donors, 1996; Dismissing God: Modern Writers' Struggle against Religion, 1998; Thinking-and-Acting Like a Christian, 2001. **Address:** PO Box 26, Stony Brook, NY 11790, U.S.A.

LOCKLIN, Gerald Ivan. American, b. 1941. **Genres:** Novels, Novellas/ Short stories, Plays/Screenplays, Poetry, Literary criticism and history. **Career:** California State University, Los Angeles, instructor, 1964-65; California State University, Long Beach, professor of English, 1965-. **Publications:** POETRY: Sunset Beach, 1967; (with R. Koertge and C. Stetler) Tarzan and Shane Meet the Toad, 1970; Poop and Other Poems, 1972; Son of Poop, 1973; Toad's Europe, 1973; The Toad Poems, 1974; The Criminal Mentality, 1976; Toad's Sabbatical, 1978; Frisco Epic, 1978; Pronouncing Borges, 1978; Two Summer Sequences (& prose), 1979; Two Weeks on Mr. Stanford's Farm, 1980; The Last Toad, 1980; Two for the Seesaw and One for the Road, 1980; Scenes from a Second Adolescence and Other Poems, 1981; By Land, Sea, and Air, 1982; Why Turn a Perfectly Good Toad into a Prince? (& story), 1984; Gringo and Other Poems, 1985; (with R. Zepeda) We Love L.A.: The Olympic Boxing Poems, 1985; The Clubfoot Midget Shoots Pool, 1986; The English Mini-Tour, 1987; A Constituency of Dunces, 1988; The Death of Jean-Paul Sartre and Other Poems, 1988; (with others) Toad Comes to Cleveland, 1988; Return to Ronnie Scott's, 1988; On the Rack, 1988; Lost and Found, 1989; The Rochester Poems, 1990; The Illegitimate Son of Mr. Madman, 1991; The Return of the Prodigal Father, 1991; A Yank at Bangor 1991; (with R. Zepeda) The Lincoln, Nebraska Poems, 1991; The Firebird Poems, 1992; Outtakes, 1992; (with R. Zepeda) The Yellow Ford of Texas, 1993; Toad Writes Short Shorts, 1993; Big Man on Canvas, 1994; The Old Mongoose and Other Poems, 1994; (with R. Zepeda) The Durango Poems, 1994; (with R. Zepeda) Buying a Cabin: The Big Bear Poems, 1995; The Pittsburgh Poems, 1996; The Last Round-up, 1996; The Art Farmer Suite, and Other Poems, 1997; The Active Ingredient and Other Poems, 1997; More Jazz Poems, 1998; The Hospital Poems, 1998; Go West Young Toad, 1999; The Firebird Poems, 1999; The Back East Poems, 1999; This Sporting Life and Other Poems, 1999; Running into Ger, 1999; The Face of Chet Baker, 1999; The Iceberg Theory and Other Poems, 2000; Art and Life, 2000; Familiarities, 2001; Duke, Lester, Charles: The Sixth Jazz Chap, 2001; The Mystical Exercycle, 2002; The Life Force Poems, 2002; Young Chet, 2002; The Author's Not Quite Dead, 2002; Takes on Bill Evans, 2002; More Takes, 2003; Retirement Blues, 2003; The Modigliani/Montparnasse, Poems, 2003; 2 Jazz Poems, 2003; Music and Imagination, 2003; The Dorset Poems, 2003; The Ultimate Pessimist & Other Poems, 2003. SHORT STORIES/ NOVELLAS: Locked In, 1973; The Four-Day Work Week and Other Stories, 1977; A Weekend in Canada, 1979; The Case of the Missing Blue Volkswagen, 1985; The Gold Rush and Other Stories, 1989; The Conference, 1990; Candy Bars: Selected Stories, 2000; The Pocket Book, 2003. OTHER: The Chase: A Novel, 1976; The Cure: A Novel for Speedreaders, 1979; Children of a Lesser Demagogue, 1988; Locklin Biblio, 1991; Women Trouble (chapbook), 1994; The Cabo Conference, 1995; Two Jazz Sequences, 1995; The New Male, 1996; Charles Bukowski: A Sure Bet, 1996; The Macao/Hong Kong Trip, 1996; The First Time He Saw Paris, 1997; Down and Out: A Novel, 1999; Hemingway Colloquium: The Poet Goes to Cuba, 1999; A Simpler Time, a Simpler Place, 2000; Four Jazz Women: Toshiko, Claudia, June, and Jane, 2000. **Address:** English Dept, California State University-Long Beach, Long Beach, CA 90840, U.S.A. **Online address:** glocklin@csulb.edu

LOCKRIDGE, Larry. (Laurence S(hockley)). American. **Genres:** Novels, Literary criticism and history, Philosophy, Biography. **Career:** Harvard University, Cambridge, MA, teaching fellow, 1967-68; Rutgers University, New Brunswick, NJ, assistant professor of English, 1969-76; Northwestern University, Evanston, IL, visiting lecturer in English, 1977-78; New York University, NYC, associate professor, 1978-89, professor of English, 1989-. **Publications:** Coleridge the Moralist, 1977; The Ethics of Romanticism, 1989; Shade of the Raintree: The Life and Death of Ross Lockridge, Jr., 1994. EDITOR: (with J. Maynard and D. Stone) Nineteenth-Century Lives, 1989; R. Lockridge Jr., Raintree County, 1994. **Address:** Dept of English, New York University, 19 University Pl Rm 500, New York, NY 10003, U.S.A. **Online address:** laurence.lockridge@nyu.edu

LOCKWOOD, David. British, b. 1929. **Genres:** Sociology. **Career:** Professor of Sociology, since 1968, and Pro-Vice Chancellor, 1989-92, University of Essex, Colchester. Lecturer, London School of Economics, 1953-60; University Lecturer, Faculty of Economics, and Fellow, St. John's College, Cambridge University, 1960-68. Member, Social Science Research Council, 1973-76. **Publications:** The Blackcoated Worker: A Study in Class Consciousness, 1958, 1989; (with J. H. Goldthorpe, F. Bechhofer and J. Platt) The Affluent Worker: Industrial Attitudes and Behaviour, 1968; The Affluent Worker: Political Attitudes and Behaviour, 1968; The Affluent Worker in the Class Structure, 1969; Solidarity and Schism, 1992. **Address:** 82 High St, Wivenhoe, Essex CO7 9AB, England.

LOCKWOOD, Glenn. *See* **WHITEHEAD, David (Henry).**

LOCKYER, Judith. American, b. 1949. **Genres:** Literary criticism and history. **Career:** High school English teacher in Frankfort, KY, 1972-80; University of Michigan, Ann Arbor, instructor and associate director of composition, 1985; Albion College, Albion, MI, associate professor of English, 1985-. **Publications:** Ordered by Words, Southern Illinois University Press, 1991. **Address:** Department of English, Albion College, Albion, MI 49224, U.S.A.

LODGE, David. British, b. 1935. **Genres:** Novels, Plays/Screenplays, Literary criticism and history. **Career:** British Council, London, assistant, 1959-60; University of Birmingham, lecturer in English, 1960-71, sr. lecturer, 1971-76, professor, 1976-87, hon. professor of modern English literature, 1987-2000, emeritus professor of English literature, 2000-. **Publications:** The Picturegoers, 1960; Ginger, You're Barmy, 1962; (with M. Bradbury and J. Duckett) Between These Four Walls (revue), 1963; The British Museum Is Falling Down, 1965; Language of Fiction, 1966; Graham Greene, 1966; Out of the Shelter, 1970; The Novelist at the Crossroads and Other Essays on Fiction and Criticism, 1971; Evelyn Waugh, 1971; Changing Places, 1975; The Modes of Modern Writing, 1977; How Far Can You Go?, 1980; Working with Structuralism, 1981; Small World, 1984; Write On, 1986; Nice Work, 1988; After Bakhtin, 1990; The Writing Game (play), 1991; Paradise News, 1992; The Art of Fiction, 1993; Therapy (novel), 1995; The Practice of Writing, 1996; Home Truths (play), 1999, (novella), 1999; Thinks... (novel), 2001; Consciousness and the Novel, 2002; Author, Author, 2004. EDITOR: Jane Austen's Emma: A Casebook, 1968; Jane Austen: Emma, 1971; Twentieth Century Criticism: A Reader, 1972; Thomas Hardy: The Woodlanders, 1974; George Eliot: Scenes of Clerical Life, 1976; Henry James: The Spoils of Poyton, 1987; Modern Criticism and Theory 1989. **Address:** Dept. of English, University of Birmingham, Birmingham B15 2TT, England.

LODGE, Jeff. American, b. 1952. **Genres:** Novels. **Career:** Johns Hopkins University, Baltimore, MD, instructor at Center for Talented Youth, 1994-95; Virginia Commonwealth University, Richmond, adjunct instructor in English, 1995-, coordinator of graduate programs in English, 1996-. University of Richmond, adjunct instructor, 199596. **Publications:** Where This Lake Is (fiction), 1997. **Address:** Dept of English, Box 842005, Virginia Commonwealth University, Richmond, VA 23284, U.S.A. **Online address:** jalodge@vcu.edu

LOEB, Arthur L. American (born Netherlands), b. 1923. **Genres:** Sciences, Design, Mathematics/Statistics, Autobiography/Memoirs. **Career:** Harvard University, Cambridge, MA, senior lecturer in design science and visual mathematics, and honorary associate in visual and environmental studies. Soloist at Boston area churches; Collegium Iosquinum (ensemble for medieval and Renaissance music), founder and director. **Publications:** Electrical Double Layer, 1962; Introduction to Wave Mechanics, 1963; Color and Symmetry, 1973; Space Structures, Birkhauser, 1976; (trans. with C.I. Loeb) De Styl, 1985; (trans. with C.I. Loeb) Van Doesburg, c. 1989; Concepts and Images, 1992. Contributor to periodicals. **Address:** Carpenter Center, Harvard University, Cambridge, MA 02138, U.S.A.

LOEB, Jeph. (born United States), b. 1958. **Genres:** Cartoons. **Career:** Writer, screenwriter, comics creator, producer, and publisher. Screenplays include Teen Wolf, Commando, Burglar, and Firestorm; Awesome Entertainment, cofounder and publisher; Buffy the Vampire Slayer (animated television series), executive producer; Maurice Sendak's Seven Little Monsters (television series), Public Broadcasting Service (PBS), writer and producer; Smallville (television series), Warner Brothers, consulting producer. **Publications:** PLOTS AND SCRIPTS; SELECTED TITLES: Batman: Haunted Knight: The Legends of the Dark Knight Halloween Specials: Three Tales of Halloween in Gotham City, 1995; X-Men: The Age of Apocalypse, 1995; X-Men: Dawn of the Age of Apocalypse, 1996; Onslaught: To the Victor, 1997; Wolverine Gambit Victims, 1997; Batman: The Long Halloween (contains thirteen issues of the miniseries), 1998; Superman for All Seasons, 1999; Superman: No Limits, 2000; The Witching Hour, 2000; Batman: Dark Victory, 2001; Superman: Endgame, 2001; Superman: 'Til Death Do Us Part, 2002; Superman: Our Worlds at War, 2002; Superman: The Ultimate Guide, 2002; Superman: President Lex, 2003; Daredevil: Yellow, 2003; Spider-Man: Blue, 2003; Batman: Hush, Volume 1, 2003, Volume 2, 2004; Hulk: Gray, 2004. Writer for additional graphic novels and comic books for series and miniseries. **Address:** c/o Author Mail, DC Comics, 1700 Broadway, New York, NY 10019, U.S.A.

LOEB, Karen. American, b. 1946. **Genres:** Literary criticism and history, Novellas/Short stories, Poetry. **Career:** Columbia College, Chicago, IL, instructor in English, 1968-74; Eckerd College, St. Petersburg, FL, instructor in writing and composition, 1979-88; University of Wisconsin-Eau Claire, associate professor of English, 1988-. Gives readings from her works. **Publications:** Jump Rope Queen and Other Stories, 1993. Work represented in anthologies. Contributor of articles, stories, and poems to magazines and newspapers. **Address:** Department of English, University of Wisconsin-Eau Claire, Eau Claire, WI 54702, U.S.A.

LOEFFELHOLZ, Mary. American, b. 1958. **Genres:** Women's studies and issues, Literary criticism and history. **Career:** University of Illinois at Urbana-Champaign, assistant professor of English, women's studies, criticism, and interpretive theory, 1986-88; Northeastern University, Boston, MA, assistant professor of English, 1988-93, associate professor of English, 1993-. **Publications:** Dickinson and the Boundaries of Feminist Theory, University of Illinois Press, 1991; Experimental Lives: Women and Literature, 1900-1945, Twayne/Macmillan, 1992. Editor of Studies in American Fiction. **Address:** Department of English, Northeastern University, Boston, MA 02115, U.S.A.

LOEN, Raymond O(rdell). American, b. 1924. **Genres:** Administration/Management. **Career:** Uarco Inc., NYC and Philadelphia, PA, sales representative, sales trainer, and city sales manager, 1949-53; H.B. Maynard and Co. Inc., Pittsburgh, PA, staff consultant and senior consultant, 1953-59; Fibreboard Corp., San Francisco, CA, sales training manager and director of management services, 1959-63; R.O. Loen Co., Lake Oswego, OR, management consultant to large and small businesses throughout the United States, 1963-; Loen, Brandt Inc., founder and director, 1965-70; Swift Energy Co., founder and director, 1979-; Validity, Inc., director, 2002-. **Publications:** Manage More by Doing Less, 1971; Supervising by Objectives, 1971; Superior Supervision: The Ten Percent Solution, 1994. Contributor to professional journals. **Address:** R.O. Loen Co., 16 Becket St, Lake Oswego, OR 97035-1034, U.S.A. **Online address:** r.loen@comcast.net

LOENGARD, John. American, b. 1934. **Genres:** Illustrations, Photography. **Career:** Life (magazine), New York City, photographer and picture editor, 1961-. Became picture editor of Time, Inc. Magazine Development Group, 1972; founding picture editor of People (magazine). Teacher at International Center of Photography, New York City. Photographs represented in collections at George Eastman House, De Menil Foundation Collection, Vassar College Art Gallery, and International Center of Photography. **Publications:** Pictures under Discussion (photographs), 1987; Life Classic Photographs: A Personal Interpretation, 1988; Life Faces, 1991; Celebrating the Negative, 1994; Georgia O'Keeffe at Ghost Ranch, 1995; Life Photographers: What They Saw, 1998. **Address:** 20 W. 86th St., New York, NY 10024, U.S.A.

LOETHER, Herman John. American, b. 1930. **Genres:** Sociology. **Career:** California State University, Los Angeles, assistant professor, 1957-62, associate professor, 1962-66, professor, 1966-67; California State University, Dominguez Hills, professor of sociology, 1967-97, emeritus, 1997-. **Publications:** Problems of Aging, 1967, rev. ed., 1975; (with D.G. McTavish) Descriptive Statistics for Sociologists, 1974; (with D.G. McTavish) Inferential Statistics for Sociologists, 1974; (with D.G. McTavish) Statistical Analysis for Sociologists: A Student Manual, 1974; (with D.G. McTavish) Descriptive and Inferential Statistics: An Introduction, 1976, 4th ed., 1993; (with D.G. McTavish) Social Research, 1999, rev. ed., 2002; Social Impacts of Infectious Diseases in England, 1600-1900, 2000. **Address:** 6564 Monero Dr, Rancho Palos Verdes, CA 90275-3264, U.S.A. **Online address:** loether@csudh.edu

LOEVY, Robert D(ickinson). American, b. 1935. **Genres:** Politics/Government. **Career:** Goucher College, Baltimore, MD, assistant professor of political science, 1960-68; Colorado College, Colorado Springs, professor of political science, 1968-. **Publications:** (with others) American Government: We Are One, 1986; To End All Segregation: The Politics of the Passage of the Civil Rights Act of 1964, 1990; (with T. Cronin) Colorado Politics and Government: Governing the Centennial State, 1993; The Flawed Path to the Presidency, 1992: Unfairness and Inequality in the Presidential Selection Process, 1995; The Flawed Path to the Governorship, 1994: The Nationalization of a Colorado Statewide Election, 1996; (ed. and contrib) The Civil Rights Act of 1964: The Passage of the Law That Ended Racial Segregation, 1997; The Manipulated Path to the White House 1996: Maximizing Advantage in the Presidential Selection Process, 1998; Colorado College: A Place of Learning, 1874-1999, 1999. **Address:** Department of Political Science, Colorado College, Colorado Springs, CO 80903, U.S.A. **Online address:** bloevy@coloradocollege.edu

LOEWE, Michael. British, b. 1922. **Genres:** History, Bibliography. **Career:** University of London, England, lecturer in history of the Far East, 1956-63; Cambridge University, England, lecturer in Chinese studies, 1963-90; writer.

Publications: Imperial China: The Historical Background to the Modern Age, 1966; Records of Han Administration, Vol. 1: Historical Assessment, Vol. 2: Documents, 1967; Everyday Life in Early Imperial China during the Han Period, 202 BC-AD 220, 1968; Crisis and Conflict in Han China, 104 BC to AD 9, 1974; Ways to Paradise: The Chinese Quest for Immortality, 1979; Chinese Ideas of Life and Death: Faith, Myth, and Reason in the Han Period (202 BC-AD 220), 1982; The Pride That Was China (Great Civilizations series), 1990; Early Chinese Texts: A Bibliographical Guide, 1993; Divination, Mythology and Monarchy in Han China, 1994; A Biographical Dictionary of the Qin, Former Han and Xin Periods (221 BC-AD 24), 2000; The Men Who Governed Han China, 2004. EDITOR: (with C. Blacker) Ancient Cosmologies, 1975; (with C. Blacker) Divination and Oracles, 1981; (with D. Twitchett) The Cambridge History of China, Vol. 1: The Ch'in and Han Empires, 221 BC-AD 220, 1986; (with E. Shaughnessy) The Cambridge History of Ancient China, 1999. **Address:** Willow House, Grantchester, Cambridge CB3 9NF, England.

LOEWER, Jean. See JENKINS, Jean.

LOEWER, (Henry) Peter. American, b. 1934. **Genres:** Horticulture, Homes/Gardens, Young adult fiction, Illustrations, Natural history. **Career:** Free-lance artist and writer. Graphos Studio, Asheville, NC, owner and art director, 1963-. Upper Delaware, art director, 1979-80; Sullivan County Democrat, editor, 1979-81; Warwick Photo Advertiser, production manager, 1983-86. Host of The Wild Gardener for Asheville's public broadcasting station, WCQS. Illustrator, with work in permanent collection at Carnegie-Mellon University. **Publications:** The Indoor Water Gardener's How-to Handbook, 1973; Bringing the Outdoors In, 1974, 2nd ed, 1988; Seeds and Cuttings, 1975; Growing and Decorating with Grasses, 1977; Growing Plants in Water, 1980; Evergreens: A Guide for Landscape, Lawn, and Garden, 1981; The Month-by-Month Garden Almanac, 1983; Gardens by Design, 1986; The Annual Garden, 1988; American Gardens, 1988; A Year of Flowers, 1989; A World of Plants: The Missouri Botanical Garden, 1989; Letters to Sarah (juvenile), 1989; The Indoor Window Garden, 1990; The Inside-Out Stomach (juvenile), 1990; The Wild Gardener, 1991; Tough Plants for Tough Places, 1991; (with A. Halpin) Secrets of the Great Gardeners: The Brooklyn Botanic Garden, 1991; The Evening Garden, 1992; The New Small Garden, 1994; Thoreau's Garden, 1996; Seeds, 1996; The Winter Garden, 1998. EDITOR: (and photographer) Taylor's Guide to Annuals, 1986; Garden Ornaments, 1987; Ornamental Grasses, 1988. Illustrator of books by A.E. Simmons, B. Miles. **Address:** c/o Dominick Abel, 146 W 82nd St, New York, NY 10024, U.S.A. **Online address:** spicebush@aol.com

LOEWY, Erich H. Austrian/American (born Austria), b. 1927. **Genres:** Ethics, Medicine/Health. **Career:** Boston City Hospital, MA, intern, 1954-55; Case Western Reserve University, Cleveland, OH, resident, 1957-60, demonstrator, 1960-64, clinical instructor, 1964-70, senior clinical instructor in medicine, 1970-77; Union University, Albany Medical College, Albany, NY, clinical assistant professor of cardiology, 1977-81; University of Connecticut, School of Medicine, Farmington, assistant professor of medicine, 1981-84; University of Illinois, College of Medicine at Peoria, assistant professor, 1987-89, associate professor of clinical medicine, 1989-93, professor of medicine (ethics) 1993-. Adirondack Community College, lecturer, 1979-81; University of Illinois at Chicago Circle, assistant professor, 1984-89, associate professor of ethics, 1989-; visiting professor at University of Aarhus, 1989, 1991, 1992, Nordic School of Public Health, 1990, University of Marburg, 1990, 1992, Free University of Amsterdam, 1992, Converse College, 1992, and Erskine College, 1992; Universitat Wien, Gost professor, 1995; lecturer at colleges and universities in the United States and abroad. **Publications:** Ethical Dilemmas in Modern Medicine, 1986; A Textbook of Medical Ethics, 1989; Suffering and the Beneficent Community, 1991; Freedom and Community, 1993; Ethische Fragen in der Medizin, 1995; Textbook of Health Care Ethics, 1996, 2nd ed. (with R.A. Lowey); Moral Strangers, Moral Acquaintance and Moral Friends, 1996; (with R.A. Lowey) The Ethics of Terminal Care, 2000; (ed. with R.S. Lowey) Changing Health Care Systems from Ethical, Economic and Cross-Cultural Perspectives, 2001; (with R. Gronemeyer) Wohin mit den Sterbenden? Hospize in Europa, 2001. Work represented in anthologies. Contributor articles and reviews to medical and ethics journals. **Address:** 11465 Ghirardelli Ct, Gold River, CA 95670, U.S.A. **Online address:** ehloewy@ucdavis.edu

LOFAS, Jeannette. American, b. 1940. **Genres:** Human relations/Parenting, Psychology. **Career:** Atlas Magazine, NYC, cofounder and associate editor, 1959-61; Radio Free Europe, NYC, reporter, 1961-69; ABC-TV, NYC, on-air reporter, 1969; Ivan Tors Films, independent producer, 1970; Snowmass Arts Foundation, Aspen, CO, executive director, 197172; Family Matters cable television show, host, 1972-73; Stepfamily Foundation Inc., NYC, founder and president, 1975-. Also worked at KWTV, Oklahoma City, OK, as a television reporter and film critic; Metro Media, NYC, as on-air reporter. Whitney Museum, NYC, cofounder of New American Film Series. Public speaker on the topic of stepfamilies; has made guest appearances on television programs. Has also worked as a corporate consultant. **Publications:** (with R. Roosevelt) Living in Step (nonfiction), 1976; (with D.B. Sova) Stepparenting (nonfiction), 1985, rev. ed., 1995; How to Be a Stepparent (audio book), 1986; (with J. MacMillan) He's OK, She's OK: Honoring the Differences between Men and Women (psychology), 1995; Family Rules, 1998. **Address:** The Stepfamily Foundation Inc, 333 West End Ave, New York, NY 10023, U.S.A. **Online address:** stepfamily@aol.com; www. stepfamily.org

LOGAN, Anne. See **COLLEY, Barbara.**

LOGAN, Cait. See **KLEINSASSER, Lois.**

LOGAN, Chuck. American, b. 1942. **Genres:** Mystery/Crime/Suspense. **Career:** Writer. Formerly worked in automobile factories; St. Paul Pioneer Press, St. Paul, MN, former member of staff. U.S. Army, served in Vietnam; became paratrooper. **Publications:** Hunter's Moon, 1996; The Price of Blood, 1997; The Big Law, 1998; Absolute Zero, 2002; Vapor Trail, 2003. **Address:** c/o Author Mail, HarperCollins, 10 East 53rd St., 7th Fl., New York, NY 10012, U.S.A.

LOGAN, George M(eredith). Canadian/American (born United States), b. 1941. **Genres:** Literary criticism and history, Music, Philosophy. **Career:** Queen's University, Kingston, ON, assistant professor, 1967-74, associate professor, 1974-83, professor of English, 1983-95, head of department, 1985-94, James Cappon Professor of English, 1995-. Chair of Research Intensive Universities Steering Group for Humanities Computing, 1986-88; member of executive of Canadian Association of Chairs of English, 1986-89. **Publications:** The Meaning of More's Utopia, 1983; The Indiana University School of Music: A History, 2000. EDITOR: (with M.H. Abrams and others) The Norton Anthology of English Literature, 2 vols., 5th ed., 1986, 8th ed., 2005; (with R.M. Adams) T. More, Utopia, 1989, rev. ed., 2002; (with G. Teskey) Unfolded Tales: Essays on Renaissance Romance, 1989; (with R.M. Adams and C.H. Miller) Thomas More, Utopia: Latin Text and English Translation, 1995. **Address:** Dept of English, Queen's University, Kingston, ON, Canada K7L 3N6. **Online address:** logang@post.queensu.ca

LOGAN, Jake. See **RIEFE, Alan.**

LOGAN, Jake. See **RIFKIN, Shepard.**

LOGAN, Jake. See **SMITH, Martin Cruz.**

LOGAN, Matt. See **WHITEHEAD, David (Henry).**

LOGAN, Michael F. American, b. 1950. **Genres:** Regional/Urban planning, Urban studies. **Career:** University of Arizona, Tucson, history teacher, 1990-94; Oklahoma State University, Stillwater, assistant professor of history, 1994-. Pima Community College, teacher, 1992-94. **Publications:** Fighting Sprawl and City Hall: Resistance to Urban Growth in the Southwest, 1995. Contributor of articles and reviews to periodicals. **Address:** Department of History, 501 Life Sciences W., Oklahoma State University, Stillwater, OK 74078, U.S.A. **Online address:** mfl4925@okway.okstate.edu

LOGAN, Shirley Wilson. American, b. 1943. **Genres:** Literary criticism and history. **Career:** Schoolteacher, 1964-67; Howard University, Washington, DC, instructor in English, 1967-70; schoolteacher, 1970-74; Howard University, instructor in English, 1975-77; University of Maryland at College Park, instructor, 1980-92, assistant professor of English, 1992-, coordinator of Professional Writing Program Computer Laboratory, 1986-92, director of Professional Writing Program, 1992-. **Publications:** (ed.) With Pen and Voice: A Critical Anthology of Nineteenth-Century African-American Women, 1995. Contributor to books and periodicals. **Address:** Department of English, University of Maryland at College Park, College Park, MD 20742, U.S.A.

LOGAN, William. American, b. 1950. **Genres:** Poetry. **Career:** University of Florida, Gainesville, director of creative writing program, 1983-, assistant professor, 1983-87, associate professor, 1987-91, professor of English, 1991-; poet and poetry critic. **Publications:** POETRY: Sad-Faced Men, 1982; Difficulty, 1985; Sullen Weedy Lakes, 1988; Criticism: All the Rage, 1998; Vain Empires, 1998; Night Battle, 1999; Reputations of the Tongue, 1999; Desper-

ate Measures, 2002; Macbeth in Venice, 2003. **Address:** Department of English, Turlington Hall, University of Florida, Gainesville, FL 32611, U.S.A.

LOGSTON, Anne. American, b. 1962. **Genres:** Science fiction/Fantasy. **Career:** Writer. Has worked as a legal secretary. **Publications:** Shadow, 1991; Shadow Dance, 1992; Shadow Hunt, 1992; Greendaughter, 1993; Dagger's Edge, 1994; Dagger's Point, 1995; Wild Blood, 1995; Guardian's Key, 1996; Firewalk, 1997; Waterdance, 1999. **Address:** c/o Ace Publicity, 375 Hudson St., New York, NY 10014, U.S.A.

LOGUE, Christopher. British, b. 1926. **Genres:** Novellas/Short stories, Young adult fiction, Plays/Screenplays, Poetry, Documentaries/Reportage, Translations. **Career:** Writer. **Publications:** Wand and Quadrant, 1953; Devil, Maggot, and Son, 1955; (trans.) The Man Who Told His Love: Twenty Poems Based on Pablo Neruda's Los Cantos d'Amores, 1958; The Trial of Cob and Leach: A News Play, 1959; Songs, 1959; Trials by Logue (Antigone and Cob and Leach), 1960; Songs from The Lily-White Boys, 1960; Creon (play), 1961; True Stories, 1966; The Girls, 1969; New Numbers, 1969; Twelve Cards, 1972; Friday (play), 1972; Savage Messiah (screenplay), 1972; Puss-in-Boots Pop-Up, 1976; Ratsmagic (juvenile), 1976; The Crocodile (juvenile), 1976; Abecedary, 1977; The Magic Circus (juvenile), 1979; Bumper Book of True Stories, 1980; Ode to the Dodo: Poems 1953-1978, 1981; War Music: An Account of Books 16-19 of the Iliad, 1981; Kings: An Account of Books 1-2 of Homer's Iliad; The Husbands, An Account of Books 3-4 of Homer's Iliad; (with W. Green) Crusoe (screenplay), 1989; War Music: An Account of Books 1-4 and 16-19 of Homer's Iliad, 2001. EDITOR: True Stories from Private Eye, 1973; The Children's Book of Comic Verse, 1978; London in Verse, 1982; Sweet and Sour: An Anthology of Comic Verse, 1983; The Oxford Book of Pseuds, 1983; The Children's Book of Children's Rhymes, 1987. **Address:** 41 Camberwell Grove, London SE5 8JA, England.

LOGUE, John A(lan). American, b. 1947. **Genres:** Organized labor, Politics/Government. **Career:** Kent State University, Kent, OH, professor of political science, 1977-. Roskilde University Center (Denmark), professor, 1981-83. Ohio Employee Ownership Center, director, 1987-. **Publications:** Socialism and Abundance, 1982; (with E. Einhorn) Modern Welfare States: Politics and Policies in Social Democratic Scandinavia, 1989, 2nd ed. as Modern Welfare States: Scandinavian Politics and Policy in the Global Age, 2003; (with others) Participatory Employee Ownership: How It Works, 1998; (with J. Yates) The Real World of Employee Ownership, 2001. EDITOR: W.W. Winpisinger, Reclaiming Our Future: An Agenda for American Labor, 1989; (with D. Hancock and B. Schiller) Managing Modern Capitalism: Industrial Renewal and Workplace Democracy in the United States and Western Europe, 1991; (with S. Plekhanov and J. Simmons) Transforming Russian Enterprises: From State Control to Employee Ownership, 1995; (with M.D. Hancock) Transitions to Capitalism and Democracy in Russia and Central Europe: Achievements, Problems, Prospects, 2000. Work represented in anthologies. Contributor to professional journals and popular magazines. **Address:** Dept of Political Science, Kent State University, Kent, OH 44242, U.S.A.

LOGUE, Mary. American. **Genres:** Novels, Children's fiction, Children's non-fiction. **Career:** Poet, mystery novelist, editor, and author of children's books. **Publications:** (ed.) The Thief of Sadness/NorHaven Poetry Collective, 1979; (ed. with L. Sutin) Believing Everything, An Anthology of New Writing, 1980; Red Lake of the Heart (mystery), 1987; Discriminating Evidence (poetry), 1990; The Missing Statue of Minnehaha (children's novel), 1993; The Haunting of Hunter House (novel), 1993; Still Explosion: A Laura Malloy Mystery (novel), 1993; Forgiveness: The Story of Mahatma Gandhi (children's nonfiction), 1996; Elizabeth Barrett Browning: Love (children's nonfiction), 1996; Halfway Home: A Granddaughter's Biography, 1996; Settling (poetry), 1997. **Address:** c/o MidList Press, 4324 12th Avenue S., Minneapolis, MN 55407, U.S.A.

LOH, Sandra Tsing. American, b. 1962. **Genres:** Plays/Screenplays, Novels, Autobiography/Memoirs, Humor/Satire. **Career:** Writer and performance artist. Buzz magazine, Los Angeles, columnist, 1992-96; KCRW-Radio, Santa Monica, CA, commentator, 1997-; Commentator on National Public Radio (NPR); performer and composer of jazz music album, Pianovision, K2B2 Records, 1991. **Publications:** Depth Takes a Holiday: Essays from Lesser Los Angeles, 1996; Aliens in America (monologue), 1997; If You Lived Here, You'd Be Home by Now (novel), 1997; A Year in Van Nuys (humor), 2001. **Address:** c/o Sloan Harris, International Creative Management, 40 W 57th St, New York, NY 10019, U.S.A.

LOHANS, Alison. Canadian (born United States), b. 1949. **Genres:** Novels, Children's fiction, Young adult fiction. **Career:** Argenta Friends School, Argenta, BC, teacher, 1973-74; Regina Public Board of Education, Saskatchewan, instrumental music teacher, 1976-79; University of Regina, research assistant, Faculty of Education, 1986-88, 2001-; University of Regina Extension, instructor, 1990-95; Saskatchewan Writers Guild, 1995-2000; Regina Public Library, writer in residence, 2002-03. **Publications:** FOR YOUNG ADULTS: Who Cares about Karen?, 1983; Can You Promise Me Spring?, 1991; Foghorn Passage, 1992; Laws of Emotion, 1993; Don't Think Twice, 1997. FOR CHILDREN: Mystery of the Lunchbox Criminal, 1990; Germy Johnson's Secret Plan, 1992; Nathaniel's Violin, 1996; Getting Rid of Mr. Ribitus, 1998; Sundog Rescue, 1999; No Place for Kids, 1999; Skateboard Kids, 1999; Waiting for the Sun, 2001. **Address:** 76 Dolphin Bay, Regina, SK, Canada S4S 4Z8.

LOHREY, David T. (born United States), b. 1955. **Genres:** Plays/Screenplays. **Career:** Playwright. New Jersey City University, Jersey City, NJ, adjunct professor. **Publications:** PLAYS: Betterland, 2000; Jigsaw Confession, 2000; One, Two, Three, 2001; In a Newark Minute, 2001; Sperm Counts, 2002; Peace of Mind, 2002. **Address:** c/o New Jersey City University, 2039 Kennedy Blvd., Jersey City, NJ 07305, U.S.A. **Online address:** davlohrey@msn.com

LOMAS, Herbert. British, b. 1924. **Genres:** Poetry, Translations. **Career:** The Anargyrios School, Spetsai, Greece, teacher, 1950-51; University of Helsinki, Helsinki, Finland, lecturer to senior lecturer, 1952-65; West London Institute of Higher Education, London, England, lecturer to recognized teacher of London University and principal lecturer, 1966-83. **Publications:** POETRY: Chimpanzees Are Blameless Creatures, 1969; Private and Confidential, 1974; Public Footpath, 1981; Fire in the Garden, 1984; Letters in the Dark, 1986; Trouble, 1992; Selected Poems, 1995; A Useless Passion, 1999; The Vale of Todmorden, 2003 (in US as Troll: A Love Story, 2004). TRANSLATOR: (and ed.) Territorial Song: Contemporary Writing from Finland, 1981; (and ed.) Contemporary Finnish Poetry, 1991; E. Stenberg, Wings of Hope and Daring (poems), 1992; K. Nieminen, Fugue (poems), 1992; I. Tiihonen, Black and Red (poems), 1993; L. Krohn, The Eyes of the Fingertips Are Opening (poems), 1993; R. Ahti, Narcissus in Winter (poems), 1994; L. Otonkoski, Two Sequences for Kuhmo, 1994; A. Paasilinna, The Year of the Hare (novel), 1995; J. Rinnemaa, In Wandering Hall, 1995; Selected Poems: Eeva-Liisa Manner, 1997; Three Finnish Poets: Melleri, Ahti, Stenberg, 1999; Pentti Holappa: A Tenant Here: Selected Poems, 1999; Ilpo Tiihonen: Gaia, a Musical for Children, 2001; Johanna Sinisalo: Not before Sundown (novel), 2003. OTHER: (with others) A Handbook of Modern English for Finnish Students, 1957; Who Needs Money? (nonfiction), 1972. Contributor of reviews to periodicals. **Address:** North Gable, 30 Crag Path, Aldeburgh, Suffolk IP15 5BS, England.

LOMAS, Peter (Eric Samuel). British, b. 1923. **Genres:** Human relations/Parenting, Psychology. **Career:** Psychotherapist in private practice, 1959-. Mitcham Child Guidance Clinic, Surrey, Director, 1968-69. **Publications:** (ed.) The Predicament of the Family 1967; True and False Experience, 1973; The Case for a Personal Psychotherapy, 1981; The Limits of Interpretation, 1987; Cultivating Intuition, 1994; Personal Disorder and Family Life, 1998; Doing Good? Psychotherapy out of Its Depth. **Address:** 41 Beaulands Close, Cambridge, England.

LOMAX, Marion. See BOLAM, Robyn.

LOMER, Mary. See LIDE, Mary.

LOMNITZ, Cinna. Mexican (born Germany), b. 1925. **Genres:** Earth sciences, Sciences. **Career:** National University of Mexico, Mexico City, professor of seismology, 1968-. **Publications:** Global Tectonics and Earthquake Risk, 1974; (ed., with E. Rosenblueth) Seismic Risks and Engineering Descisions, 1976; Fundamentals of Earthquake Prediction, 1994. Contributor to professional journals and cultural monthlies. **Address:** Institute of Geophysics, National University of Mexico, 04510 Mexico City, DF, Mexico. **Online address:** cinna@prodigy.met.mx

LOMNITZ, Larissa Adler. Mexican (born France), b. 1932. **Genres:** Anthropology/Ethnology, Sociology. **Career:** Universidad Nacional Autonoma de Mexico, Mexico City, professor of socio-cultural anthropology, 1973-. Columbia University, Tinker Professor, 1985-86; City University of New York, distinguished visiting professor, 1987-88; American University, distinguished professor, 1989-90; Escuela Nacional de Antropologia y Historia, staff member, 1994-96; Tinker Professor, Chicago University, Chicago, IL, spring semester, 1996. **Publications:** Network and Marginality: Life in a Mexican Shantytown, 1977; (with M. Perez-Lizaur) A Mexican Elite Family, 1820-1980: Kinship, Class, and Culture, 1988; (with A. Melnick) Chile's

Middle Class: A Struggle for Survival in the Face of Neoliberalism, 1991; (with J. Fortes) Becoming a Scientist in Mexico: The Challenge of Creating a Scientific Community in an Underdeveloped Country, 1993; Redes Sociales Cultura y Poder: Ensayos de Antropologia Latinoamericana, 1994; (with A. Melnick) Chile's Political Culture & Parties, 2001. **Address:** Apdo. Postal 20-726, Admon. 20, Delegacion Alvaro Obregon, 01000 Mexico City, DF, Mexico. **Online address:** larissa@servidor.unam.mx

LOMONACO, Palmyra. American, b. 1932. **Genres:** Children's fiction, Education. **Career:** Teacher and writer in Durham, NC, 1954-84. New Mexico Department of Human Services, child-care specialist; Bernalillo County Mental Health-Mental Retardation Center, Albuquerque, NM, child care trainer; Albuquerque-Bernalillo County Economic Opportunity Board, director of child development and child care centers; University of New Mexico, adjunct instructor in on-site programs for Navajo and Apache early childhood education; University of Albuquerque, adjunct assistant professor of education; Duke University, play therapist in Department of Pediatrics; Durham Technical Community College, program director and instructor in Early Childhood Associate Program; consultant to early childhood education programs. **Publications:** Music and Motion: The Rhythmic Language of Children, 1976; Up from the Classroom, 1977; Halloween: Its Place in the Curriculum, 1988; Joey's Blanket, 1994; Night Letters, 1996. Contributor to magazines. **Address:** 4100 Five Oaks Dr No. 41, Durham, NC 27707, U.S.A.

LOMOSIA, Andrew. See STERN, Jay B.

LONDON, Cait. See KLEINSASSER, Lois.

LONDON, Herbert I. American, b. 1939. **Genres:** Education, Politics/Government, Social sciences. **Career:** New York University, NYC, professor of social studies, 1967-, dean of the Gallatin School, John M. Olin Professor of Humanities. Hudson Institute, consultant, 1969-, president, 1997-. **Publications:** Non-White Immigration and the White Australia Policy, 1970; Fitting In: Crosswise at Generation Gap, 1974; The Overheated Decade, 1976; The Seventies: Counterfeit Decade, 1979; Myths That Rule America, 1981; Closing the Circle: A Cultural History of the Rock Revolution, 1984; Why Are They Lying to Our Children?, 1984; Military Doctrine and the American Character, 1984; Armageddon in the Classroom, 1986; The Broken Apple: Notes on New York in the 1980s, 1989; From the Empire State to the Vampire State: New York in a Downward Transition, 1994; Decade of Denial, 2001. EDITOR & CONTRIBUTOR: Education in the Twenty-First Century, 1969; Social Science Theory, Structure and Application, 1975; A Strategy for Victory without War, 1988. **Address:** 2 Washington Sq. Village, New York, NY 10012, U.S.A. **Online address:** herb@hudson.org

LONDON, Joan. American, b. 1948. **Genres:** Novels. **Career:** Writer. **Publications:** Sister Ships, 1988; Letter to Constantine (short stories), 1993; Gilgamesh (novel), 2001; The New Dark Age, (collected stories), 2004. **Address:** Barbara Mobbs, POB 126, Edgecliff, New South Wales 2027, Australia.

LONEY, Glenn Meredith. American, b. 1928. **Genres:** Photography, Literary criticism and history, Theatre, Travel/Exploration, Speech/Rhetoric, Music, Design, Dance/Ballet, Art/Art history, Architecture. **Career:** Professor of Theatre, Brooklyn College and City University of New York Graduate Center, since 1961. Ed., The Modernist. Professor of English and Speech, University of Maryland Overseas, 1956-59; Professor of English and Speech, Hofstra University, Hempstead, New York, 1959-61. **Publications:** Briefing and Conference Techniques, 1959; (with P. McKay) The Shakespeare Complex, 1975; The Young Vic Scapino, 1975; Your Future in the Performing Arts, 1980; Twentieth Century Theatre, 1982; California Gold Rush Dramas, 1982; Unsung Genius, 1984; Musical Theatre in America, 1984; Creating Careers in Musical Theatre, 1988; Staging Shakespeare, 1990; Peter Brook: From Oxford to Orghast, 1997. EDITOR: Dramatic Soundings, 1968; (with R. Corrigan) Tragedy, 1971; (with R. Corrigan) Comedy, 1971; (with R. Corrigan) Forms of Drama, 1972; Peter Brook's Midsummer Night's Dream, 1974; The House of Mirth (play), 1981. **Address:** PhD Program in Theatre, City University Graduate Center, 365 Fifth Ave., New York, NY 10016, U.S.A.

LONG, A(nthony) A(rthur). British, b. 1937. **Genres:** Classics, Philosophy. **Career:** Professor of Classics, University of California, Berkeley, 1983-. Lecturer and Reader in Greek and Latin, University College, London, 1966-73; Professor of Greek, University of Liverpool, 1973-83; Joint Ed., Classical Quarterly, 1975-81. **Publications:** Language and Thought in Sophocles, 1968; (ed.) Problems in Stoicism, 1971; Hellenistic Philosophy, 1974, 1986; (co-ed.) Theophrastus of Eresus, 1985; (with D.N. Sedley) The Hellenistic

Philosophers, 1987; (co-ed.) The Question of Eclecticism, 1988; (co-ed.) Images and Ideologies, 1993; Stoic Studies, 1996; (ed.) The Cambridge Companion to Early Greek Philosophy.

LONG, Benjamin. American, b. 1967. **Genres:** Travel/Exploration. **Career:** Journalist and author. Idaho Statesman, Boise, reporter, 1988; Daily Idahonian, Moscow, ID, reporter, 1989-92; Daily Inter Lake, Kalispell, ID, reporter, 1992-98. **Publications:** Backtracking by Foot, Canoe, and Subaru along the Lewis and Clark Trail, 2000. **Address:** c/o Publicity Director, Sasquatch Books, 315 Second Ave. Ste. 260, Seattle, WA 98104, U.S.A. **Online address:** karenben@montanasky.net

LONG, Carolyn Morrow. American, b. 1940. **Genres:** History. **Career:** Vermont State Craft Center, Middlebury, artist-in-residence, 1973-80; Smithsonian Institution, Washington, DC, conservator at National Museum of American History, 1983-2001; writer, 2001-. **Publications:** Spiritual Merchants, 2001. **Address:** 3815 Alton Pl., Washington, DC 20016, U.S.A. **Online address:** carolynlong@earthlink.net

LONG, Cathryn J. American, b. 1946. **Genres:** Children's non-fiction, Archaeology/Antiquities, Young adult non-fiction. **Career:** Freelance writer, 1976-98; University of Cincinnati, cofounder of U-Kids, 1981-82, Center for the Electronic Reconstruction of Historic and Archaeological Sites, associate, 1998-; Curriculum Design for Tomorrow's World Inc., associate, 1982-. **Publications:** NONFICTION: (with R. Tretten) The Future of American Government: What Will It Be?, 1978; (with M.J. Turner, J.S. Bowes, and E.J. Lott) Civics: Citizens in Action, 1986, rev. ed., 1990; The Middle East in Search of Peace, 1994, rev. ed., 1996; Ohio: Past and Present, 1995; Crossword America, 4 vols., 1998-99; Earth Works: Ancient Newark, Ohio (screenplay), 1998; The Cherokee, 2000. OTHER: Out on the Town with Taft (children's play), 1983. **Address:** 362 Terrace Ave, Cincinnati, OH 45220, U.S.A.

LONG, D. Stephen. American, b. 1960. **Genres:** Theology/Religion. **Career:** Duke University, Durham, NC, director of continuing education at Duke Divinity School, 1990-95; St. Joseph's University, Philadelphia, PA, assistant professor of theology, 1995-. **Publications:** Living the Discipline: United Methodist Theological Reflections on War, Holiness and Civilization, 1991; Tragedy, Tradition, Transformism: The Ethics of Paul Ramsey, 1992. **Address:** St. Joseph's University, 5600 City Ave., Philadelphia, PA 19131, U.S.A.

LONG, Edward Leroy, Jr. American, b. 1924. **Genres:** Ethics, Theology/Religion. **Career:** James W. Pearsall Professor Emeritus of Christian Ethics and Theology of Culture, Drew University, Madison, NJ, 1986- (Professor, 1976-86). Minister to Students, Blacksburg Presbyterian Church, Virginia, 1951-54; Associate Professor of Philosophy and Ethics, 1951-54, and Associate Professor and Head of Dept. of Philosophy and Religion, 1955-57, Virginia Polytechnic Institute, Blacksburg; Associate Professor, 1957-65, and Professor of Religion, 1965-76, Oberlin College, Ohio. Series Ed., The Haddam House Series on the Christian in His Vocation, Association Press Publishers, 1960-64. **Publications:** Science and Christian Faith, 1950; The Christian Response to the Atomic Crisis, 1950; Religious Beliefs of American Scientists, 1952; Conscience and Compromise: An Approach to Protestant Casuistry, 1954; The Role of the Self in Conflicts and Struggle, 1962; A Survey of Christian Ethics, 1967; War and Conscience in America, 1968; (with J.T. Stephens) The Christian as a Doctor, 1960; (ed. with R.T. Handy) Theology and Church in Times of Change: Essays in Honor of John Coleman Bennett, 1970; A Survey of Recent Christian Ethics, 1982; Peace Thinking in a Warring World, 1983; Academic Bonding and Social Concern, 1984; Higher Education as a Moral Enterprise, 1992; To Liberate and Redeem: Moral Reflections on the Biblical Narrative, 1997; Patterns of Polity: Varieties of Church Governance, 2001; Facing Terrorism: Responding as Christian, 2004. **Address:** PO Box 10, Wicomico, VA 23184, U.S.A.

LONG, Elliot. See BENNETT, R(eginald) G(eorge) Stephen.

LONG, Eugene Thomas. American, b. 1935. **Genres:** Philosophy, Theology/Religion. **Career:** Randolph-Macon College, Ashland, VA, Assistant Professor to Professor of Philosophy, 1964-70; University of South Carolina, Columbia, Dept. of Philosophy, Associate Professor, 1970-73, Chairman, 1972-87, Professor, 1973-, Emeritus Professor, 2002-. Duke University, University of North Carolina Cooperative Program in the Humanities, Fellow, 1968-69. Metaphysical Society of America, Secretary-Treasurer, 1977-83, President, 1997-98; Society for Philosophy of Religion, President, 1980-81; American Philosophical Association, Secretary-Treasurer, 1985-94. International Journal for Philosophy of Religion, editor-in-chief,

1990-; Handbook of Contemporary Philosophy of Religion, editor, 1996-. **Publications:** Jaspers and Bultmann: A Dialogue between Philosophy and Theology in the Existentialist Tradition, 1968; Existence, Being and God, 1985; Twentieth Century Western Philosophy of Religion 1900-2000, 2000. EDITOR & CONTRIBUTOR: God, Secularization and History: Essays in Memory of Ronald Gregor Smith, 1974; Experience, Reason and God, 1980; (co-ed.) God and Temporality, 1984; (co-ed.) Being and Truth, 1986; Prospects for Natural Theology, 1992; God, Reason and Religions, 1995; Issues in Contemporary Philosophy of Religion, 2001. **Address:** Dept. of Philosophy, University of South Carolina, Columbia, SC 29208, U.S.A. **Online address:** longg@sc.edu

LONG, Jeff. American. **Genres:** Westerns/Adventure, History. **Career:** Novelist, historian, journalist, screenwriter, and stonemason. **Publications:** Outlaw: The True Story of Claude Dallas, 1985; Angels of Light, 1987; (foreword) Mountain Journeys: Stories of Climbers and Their Climbs, 1989; Duel of Eagles: The Mexican and U.S. Fight for the Alamo, 1990. NOVELS: The Ascent, 1992; Empire of Bones: A Novel of Sam Houston and the Texas Revolution, 1993; The Descent, 1999; Year Zero, 2002. **Address:** c/o Author Mail, Simon & Schuster-Pocket Books, 1230 Avenue of the Americas, New York, NY 10020, U.S.A.

LONG, Naomi Cornelia. See MADGETT, Naomi Long.

LONGBAUGH, Harry. See GOLDMAN, William.

LONGFELLOW, Layne (A.). American, b. 1937. **Genres:** Children's fiction, Poetry, Environmental sciences/Ecology. **Career:** Prescott College, Prescott, AZ, assistant professor of psychology, 1970-71, academic vice president, 1972-74; Menninger Foundation, Topeka, KS, director of executive seminars, 1975-78; Banff Centre, AB, Canada, wilderness seminars director, 1978-85; Lecture Theatre Inc., Prescott, president, 1981-; National Center for Preventive and Stress Medicine, seminar collaborator, 1983-86; Institute for Human Skills, director, 1985-; creator of psychological games for personal and professional use; composer of music; producer of videos; and author of speeches, seminars, and books. Author of and contributor to motivational and instructional videos and audio cassettes; creator of 2 games. **Publications:** The Mountain Waits (film), 1983; Visual Feast, 1995; Imaginary Menagerie, 1997; Longfellow Reads Longfellow, 2002. Contributor to books and recordings. **Address:** 1134 Haining St, Prescott, AZ 86305, U.S.A.

LONGLEY, Michael. Irish, b. 1939. **Genres:** Poetry. **Career:** Director for Literature and the Traditional Arts, Arts Council of Northern Ireland, Belfast, 1970-91; Assistant Master, Avoca School, Blackrock, 1962-63, Belfast High School and Erith Secondary School, 1963-64, and Royal Belfast Academical Institution, 1964-69. **Publications:** Ten Poems, 1965; (with S. Heaney and D. Hammond) Room to Rhyme, 1968; Secret Marriages: Nine Short Poems, 1968; (with B. Tebb and I. Crichton Smith) Three Regional Voices, 1968; No Continuing City: Poems 1963-68, 1969; Lares, 1972; An Exploded View: Poems, 1968-1972, 1973; Fishing in the Sky, 1975; Man Lying on a Wall, 1976; The Echo Gate: Poems 1975-1978, 1979; Selected Poems, 1963-1980, 1980; Patchwork, 1981; Poems 1963-1983, 1985; Gorse Fires, 1991; The Ghost Orchid, 1995; Broken Dishes, 1998; Selected Poems, 1998; (with S. Longley) Out of the Cold, 1999; The Weather in Japan, 2000. EDITOR: Causeway: The Arts in Ulster, 1971; Under the Moon, Over the Stars: Young People's Writing from Ulster, 1971; Selected Poems by Louis MacNeice, 1988; Poems by W.R. Rodgers, 1993. **Address:** 32 Osborne Gardens, Malone, Belfast 9, Northern Ireland.

LONGMAN, Jere. American. **Genres:** Sports/Fitness. **Career:** Sports writer, New York Times. **Publications:** The Girls of Summer: The U.S. Women's Soccer Team and How It Changed the World, 2000. **Address:** New York Times, 229 West 43rd Street, New York, NY 10036, U.S.A.

LONGMATE, Norman Richard. British, b. 1925. **Genres:** Mystery/Crime/Suspense, Education, History, Autobiography/Memoirs. **Career:** Fleet Street journalist, 1952-57; Administrative Officer, The Electricity Council, London, 1957-62; Chief Assistant, BBC Secretariat, London, 1965-83 (Radio Producer, 1963-65). **Publications:** Oxford Triumphant, 1955; Death Won't Wash, 1957; A Head for Death, 1958; Strip Death Naked, 1959; Vote for Death, 1960; Death in Office, 1961; Keith in Electricity, 1961; Electricity Supply, 1961; Electricity as a Career, 1964; King Cholera, 1966; The Waterdrinkers, 1968; Alive and Well: Medicine and Public Health 1830 to the Present Day, 1970; How We Lived Then, 1971; If Britain Had Fallen, 1972; The Workhouse, 1974; The Real Dad's Army, 1974; The GIs: The Americans in Britain 1942-45, 1975; Milestones in Working Class History, 1975; Air-

Raid: The Bombing of Coventry 1940, 1976; When We Won The War: The Story of Victory in Europe 1945, 1977; The Hungry Mills: The Story of the Lancashire Cotton Famine 1862, 1978; The Doodlebugs, 1981; The Bombers, 1982; The Breadstealers: The Fight against the Corn Laws 1838-1846, 1984; Hitler's Rockets, 1985; Defending the Island: From Caesar to the Armada, 1989; Island Fortress: The Defence of Great Britain 1603-1945, 1991; The Shaping Season: An Author's Autobiography. Childhood and Schooldays, 2000. EDITOR: A Socialist Anthology, 1953; Writing for the BBC, 1966; The Home Front, 1981. **Address:** c/o Hutchinson Ltd, Random House, 20 Vauxhall Bridge Rd, London SW1V 2SA, England. **Online address:** anharr@cybertours.com

LONGWORTH, Philip. British/Canadian, b. 1933. **Genres:** History. **Career:** McGill University, Montreal, professor of history, 1984-. **Publications:** (trans.) A Hero of Our Time, by Lermontov, 1962; The Art of Victory, 1965; The Unending Vigil, 1967, 1985; The Cossacks, 1969; The Three Empresses, 1971; The Rise and Fall of Venice, 1974; Alexis, Tsar of All the Russias, 1984; The Making of Eastern Europe, 1992/94, 2nd ed., 1997. **Address:** c/o A.M. Heath and Co Ltd, 79 St. Martin's Ln, London WC2N 4AA, England.

LONGYARD, William H(enry). American, b. 1958. **Genres:** Air/Space topics, History, How-to books, Language/Linguistics. **Publications:** How to Build and Fly Hydrogen and Hot Air Balloons, 1985; Who's Who in Aviation History: Five Hundred Biographies, 1995; Writer's Quick Fix, 2000; A Speck on the Sea: Epic Voyages in Improbably Small Vessels, 2003; Bugatti Blue (novel), forthcoming. **Address:** 2913 Bradenton Dr, Winston-Salem, NC 27103, U.S.A.

LONGYEAR, Barry B. American, b. 1942. **Genres:** Novels, Novellas/ Short stories, Mystery/Crime/Suspense, Science fiction/Fantasy, Self help, Writing/Journalism. **Career:** Freelance writer, 1977-. **Publications:** City of Baraboo, 1980; Manifest Destiny (stories), 1980; Circus World (stories), 1980; Elephant Song, 1981; The Tomorrow Testament, 1983; It Came from Schenectady, 1984; Sea of Glass, 1986; Saint Mary Blue, 1988; Naked Came the Robot, 1988; Enemy Mine, 1988; The God Box, 1989; Homecoming, 1989; Infinity Hold, 1990; The Change, 1994; The Last Enemy, 1997; Yesterday's Tomorrow, 1997; Silent Her, 2001. **Address:** PO Box 100, New Sharon, ME 04955-0100, U.S.A. **Online address:** bblongyr@tdstelme.net; BarryBLongyear.com

LOOBY, Christopher. American. **Genres:** Literary criticism and history. **Career:** University of Chicago, teacher, 1987-96; University of Pennsylvania, associate professor of English and graduate chair, 1996-. **Publications:** NONFICTION: (as Chris Looby) Benjamin Franklin, 1990; Voicing America: Language, Literary Form, and the Origins of the United States, 1996; (ed.) The Complete Civil War Journal and Selected Letters of Thomas Wentworth Higginson, 2000. **Address:** Department of English, University of Pennsylvania, 119 Bennett Hall, 3340 Walnut Street, Philadelphia, PA 19104, U.S.A. **Online address:** cloobyengineeringlish.upenn.edu

LOOMES, Brian. British, b. 1938. **Genres:** Crafts, Biography, Genealogy/ Heraldry, Natural history, Antiques/Furnishings. **Career:** Antique Dealer, since 1966. Formerly, Professional Genealogist. **Publications:** Yorkshire Clockmakers, 1972; Westmorland Clocks and Clockmakers, 1974; The White Dial Clock, 1974; Lancashire Clocks and Clockmakers, 1975; Country Clocks and their London Origins, 1976; Watch and Clock Makers of the World, vol. II, 1976; Complete British Clocks, 1978; The Early Clockmakers of Great Britain, 1982; Grandfather Clocks and Their Cases, 1985; Antique British Clocks: A Buyer's Guide, 1991; Antique British Clocks Illustrated, 1991; The Concise Guide to British Clocks, 1992; The Concise Guide to Tracing Your Ancestry, 1992; Bird Gardening, 1993; Painted Dial Clocks, 1995; The Clockmakers of Northern England, 1997; Brass Dial Clocks, 1998. **Address:** Calf Haugh Farm, Pateley Bridge, Yorks, England. **Online address:** clocks@ brianloomes.com; www.brianloomes.com

LOOMIE, Albert Joseph. American, b. 1922. **Genres:** History. **Career:** Emeritus Professor of History, Fordham University, NYC, 1993- (member of faculty since 1958; Professor, 1968-93). Member of the Jesuit Order since 1939. **Publications:** (with C. M. Lewis) The Spanish Jesuit Mission in Virginia, 1570-72, 1953; Toleration and Diplomacy: The Religious Issue in Anglo-Spanish Relations 1603-1605, 1963; The Spanish Elizabethans: The English Exiles at the Court of Philip II, 1964; Guy Fawkes in Spain, 1971; Spain and the Jacobean Catholics, vol. I, 1973, vol. II, 1978; Ceremonies of Charles I: The Notebooks of John Finet 1628-41, 1987; English Polemics at the Spanish Court: Joseph Creswell's Letter to the Ambassador from England, The English and Spanish Texts of 1606, 1993; Spain and the Early Stuarts 1585-1655, 1996. **Address:** Loyola Hall, Fordham University, Bronx, NY 10458, U.S.A.

LOOMIS, Christine. American. **Genres:** Children's fiction, Travel/ Exploration. **Career:** Author of children's books, family travel guides, and magazine articles. **Publications:** My New Baby-Sitter, 1991; At the Laundromat, 1993; At the Library, 1993; The Cleanup Surprise, 1993; At the Mall, 1994; In the Diner, 1994; One Cow Coughs: A Counting Book for the Sick and Miserable, 1994; We're Going on a Trip, 1994; The Hippo Hop, 1995; Fodor's Family Adventures, 1996, 2nd ed, 1998; Rush Hour, 1996; Cowboy Bunnies, 1997; Astro Bunnies, 1998; Simplify Family Travel, 1998. Contributor to magazines. **Address:** 4230 Gilpin Dr., Boulder, CO 80303-2530, U.S.A.

LOOMIS, Edward (Warren). American, b. 1924. **Genres:** Novels, Novellas/Short stories, Poetry, Cultural/Ethnic topics, Literary criticism and history, Documentaries/Reportage. **Career:** Professor Emeritus of English, University of California at Santa Barbara (Instructor, 1959-60; Assistant Professor, 1960-62; Associate Professor, 1962-66; Professor, 1966-). **Publications:** End of a War, 1958; The Charcoal Horse, 1959; Heroic Love (short stories), 1960; The Hunter Deep in Summer, 1961; The Mothers, 1962; Men of Principle, 1963; Vedettes: A Collection of Stories, 1964; On Fiction, Critical Essays and Notes, 1966; Four Women (short stories), 1967; Of Bank Burning: A Documentary Novel from Isla Vista, 1970; Creative Writing: The Art of Lying, 1971; Cancion of the Mayos (documentary film), 1978; Leader of the People (novella), 1988; The Tex-Mex Iliad (narrative poem), 1999; Heroic Spain; Sinners (novel); Clean and Sober (novel); Long Poems. **Address:** Dept. of English, University of California, Santa Barbara, CA 93106, U.S.A. **Online address:** ed910@home.com

LOOMIS, Jennifer A. American, b. 1942. **Genres:** Zoology. **Career:** Nurse, photographer, wildlife rehabilitator for the state of Maine. Work held in permanent collection at the Wells Public Library, ME, and Laudholm Farm Museum, Wells, ME. **Publications:** A Duck in a Tree, 1996. Photographs have appeared in periodicals. **Address:** Greenwood, ME 04255, U.S.A.

LOOMIS, Susan Herrmann. American, b. 1955. **Genres:** Food and Wine, Travel/Exploration. **Career:** Wenatchee World, Wenatchee, WA, reporter, 1977; North Central Washington Museum, Wenatchee, director of public relations, 1978; Cabrini Hospital, Seattle, WA, assistant director of public relations, 1979-80; Ecole de Cuisine La Varenne, Paris, France, member of editorial staff, 1981-82; Village Voice Cafe-Librairie, Paris, chef and manager, 1982-83; free-lance writer, 1983-84, 1986; International Association of Cooking Professionals, editor, 1985-86. **Publications:** (with P. Wells) The Food Lover's Guide to Paris, 1984; Paris in Your Pocket, 1985; The Great American Seafood Cookbook, 1988; Farmhouse Cookbook, 1991; Seafood Celebrations, 1993; French Farmhouse Cookbook, 1996; Italian Farmhouse Cookbook, 2000; On Rue Tatin, Living and Cooking in a Small French Town, 2001; Tarte Tatin, 2003. **Address:** 1 rue Tatin, 27400 Louviers, France.

LOON. See MARTIEN, Jerry.

LOONEY, Dennis (Oscar), (III). American, b. 1955. **Genres:** Literary criticism and history. **Career:** Educator and author. University of Pittsburgh, Pittsburgh, PA, assistant professor, 1986-93, associate professor of Italian, 1993-, chair of Department of French and Italian, beginning 1996, acting director of Center for West European Studies, secondary member in classics. City University of New York Latin/Greek Institute, instructor, summers, mid-1980s. **Publications:** Compromising the Classics: Romance Epic Narrative in the Italian Renaissance, 1996; (ed. with D. Shemek) Phaethon's Children: The Este Court and Its Culture in Early Modern France, 2003. Contributor to books. **Address:** Department of French and Italian, CL1328, University of Pittsburgh, Pittsburgh, PA 15260, U.S.A. **Online address:** looney@pitt.edu

LOONEY, Douglas S. American, b. 1942. **Genres:** Sports/Fitness. **Career:** Nashville Banner, Nashville, TN, general assignment reporter, 1965-68; Omaha World-Herald, Omaha, NE, bureau chief in Des Moines, IA, 1968-70; Better Homes & Gardens, Des Moines, special assignments editor, 1970; National Observer, Washington, DC, staff writer, 1970-75; Sports Illustrated, NYC, senior writer, 1975-. University of Colorado, adjunct professor of journalism and member of advisory board for school of journalism and mass communication; National Broadcasting Co., sports commentator; radio sports talk host. Established the Douglas S. Looney Professional-in-Residence endowment at the University of Colorado. **Publications:** (with D. Yeager) Under the Tarnished Dome: How Notre Dame Betrayed Its Ideals for Football Glory, 1993; (ed.) All for the Love of a Child, 1997. Contributor to books and anthologies. **Address:** c/o Sports Illustrated, Time & Life Bldg 18th Fl, 1271 Avenue of the Americas, New York, NY 10020, U.S.A.

LOORI, John Daido. American, b. 1931. **Genres:** Theology/Religion. **Career:** Zen Mountain Monastery, Mt. Tremper, New York, abbot and teacher, 1980-. Photographer and director of Dharma Communications. Was formerly a physical chemist. **Publications:** The Way of Everyday Life, 1979; Mountain Record of Zen Talks, 1988; The Eight Gates of Zen: Spiritual Training in an American Zen Monastery, 1992; Two Arrows Meeting in Mid-Air: The Zen Koan, 1994; The Still Point: A Beginner's Guide to Zen Meditation, 1996; The Heart of Being: Moral and Ethical Teaching of Zen Buddhism, 1996. **Address:** Zen Mountain Monastery, Old Route 28 Mt. Plank Rd., Mt. Tremper, NY 12457, U.S.A.

LOOSER, Devoney. American, b. 1967. **Genres:** Literary criticism and history. **Career:** Educator and author. State University of New York-Stony Brook, instructor in English, 1989-92; Indiana State University, Terre Haute, assistant professor of English, 1993-98; University of Wisconsin-Whitewater, assistant professor of women's studies, 1998-2000; Arizona State University, Tempe, visiting assistant professor of English, 2000-01; Louisiana State University, Baton Rouge, assistant professor of English, 2001-02, fellow at James Smith Noel Collection, 2002; University of Missouri-Columbia, assistant professor, 2002-, associate professor of English, 2004-. University of Wisconsin-Milwaukee, research associate at Center for 20th-Century Studies, 1996-97; University of California-Los Angeles, fellow at William Andrews Clark Memorial Library, 1997; Newberry Library, lecturer, 1997. Member of board of directors: Terre Haute Council on Domestic Abuse, 1997-98; Jane Austen Society of North America, 200002. **Publications:** British Women Writers and the Writing of History, 1670-1820, 2000. EDITOR: Jane Austen and Discourses of Feminism, 1995; (with E.A. Kaplan, and contrib.) Generations: Academic Feminists in Dialogue, 1997. Contributor to books and periodicals. **Address:** Dept of English, 107 Tate Hall, University of Missouri-Columbia, Columbia, MO 65211, U.S.A. **Online address:** looserd@missouri.edu

LOPACH, James J. American, b. 1942. **Genres:** Politics/Government. **Career:** High school English teacher in South Bend, IN, 1967-68; Pacific Telephone Co., assistant manager and manager in Palo Alto and Hayward, CA, 1968-69; South Bend Manpower Area Planning Council, South Bend, assistant director, 1971-73; University of Notre Dame, instructor, 1972-73; University of Montana, Missoula, director of local government projects for Bureau of Government Research, 1973-75, assistant professor, 1975-78, associate professor, 1978-83, professor of political science, 1983-, chair of department and director of Bureau of Government Research, 1977-87, acting director of Maureen and Mike Mansfield Center, 1984-85, associate dean of College of Arts and Science, 1987-88, special assistant to the president, 1988-92, associate provost, 1992-95; writer, expert witness. **Publications:** (with L.S. McKinsey) A State Mandates Local Government Review: The Montana Experience, 1979; (ed. and contrib.) We the People of Montana: The Workings of a Popular Government, 1983; (with K. Ford and D. O'Donnell) Planning Small Town America: Observations, Sketches, and a Reform Proposal, 1990; (with M.H. Brown and R.L. Clow) Tribal Government Today: Politics on Montana Indian Reservations, 1990, rev. ed., 1998. **Address:** Department of Political Science, University of Montana, Missoula, MT 59812, U.S.A.

LOPES, Dominic (M. McIver). British, b. 1964. **Genres:** Philosophy, Humor/Satire. **Career:** Indiana University at Kokomo, associate professor of philosophy, 1992-. **Publications:** Understanding Pictures, 1996; (ed. with D. Lopes) A Handful of Grams: Goan Proverbs, 1996. **Address:** Department of Philosophy, Indiana University at Kokomo, 2300 South Washington St., Kokomo, IN 46904, U.S.A. **Online address:** dlopes@indiana.edu

LOPEZ, Jack. (born United States), b. 1950. **Genres:** Essays. **Career:** Writer. Orange Coast College, Costa Mesa, CA, instructor, 1987; University of Redlands, Redlands, CA, instructor, 1988; California State University, Northridge, professor of English, 1989-. **Publications:** Cholos and Surfers: A Latino Family Album, 1998; Snapping Lines: Stories, 2001. Work represented in anthologies and contributor to periodicals. **Address:** c/o Author Mail, University of Arizona Press, 355 South Euclid Ave., Suite 103, Tucson, AZ 85719, U.S.A. **Online address:** jack.lopez@csun.edu

LOPEZ, Steve. American, b. 1953. **Genres:** Novels. **Career:** Worked at five California newspapers as sportswriter, mid-1970s; Oakland Tribune, Oakland, CA, news reporter, became columnist, 1977-83; San Jose Mercury News, San Jose, CA, columnist, 1983-85; Philadelphia Inquirer, columnist, 1985-96; Time Inc., columnist and writer-at-large, 1997-. **Publications:** Third and Indiana: A Novel, 1994; Land of Giants: Where No Good Deed Goes Unpunished, 1995; The Sunday Macaroni Club, 1997; In the Clear, 2002. **Address:** Los Angeles Times, 202 W 1st St, Los Angeles, CA 90012, U.S.A.

LÓPEZ-LUJÁN, Leonardo. Mexican, b. 1964. **Genres:** Archaeology/Antiquities, History. **Career:** Instituto Nacional de Antropologia e Historia,

Mexico City, Mexico, archaeologist and researcher, 1988-. Escuela Nacional de Antropologia e Historia, professor. **Publications:** The Offerings of the Templo Mayor of Tenochtitlan, 1994; Mexico: The Indian Past, 2000. IN SPANISH: Nomadas y Sedentarios, 1989; La recuperacion mexica del pasado teotihuacano, 1989; Xochicalco y Tula, 1995; Mito y realIdad de Zuyva, 1999. EDITOR: Atlas historico de Mesoamerica, 1989; Historia Antigua de Mexico, 1994. Contributor to archaeology journals. **Address:** Museo Templo Mayor, Guatemala 60, Centro, 06060 Mexico City, Mexico.

LÓPEZ-MORILLAS, Frances M. American, b. 1918. **Genres:** Translations. **Career:** Collins Radio Company, Cedar Rapids, IA, translator, 1940-43; Lincoln School, Providence, RI, teacher of Spanish, 1943-44; Mary C. Wheeler School, Providence, RI, teacher of French and Spanish, 1951-64; International Institute, Madrid, Spain, teacher of English as a foreign language, 1957-58; writer. **Publications:** TRANSLATOR: C.J. Cela, Journey to the Alcarria: Travels through the Spanish Countryside, 1964; J. Marias, Miguel de Unamuno, 1966; J. Vicens Vives, An Economic History of Spain, 1969; J. Marias, Jose Ortega y Gasset: Circumstance and Vocation, 1970; Spain in the Fifteenth Century, ed. by R. Highfield, 1972; A. Boulton, Cruz Diez, 1974; A. Boulton, Soto, 1974; A. de Orsua y Vela, Tales of Potosi, 1975; A. Boulton, Art in Aboriginal Venezuelan Ceramics, 1978; J. Lopez-Morillas, The Krausist Movement and Ideological Change in Spain, 1981; F. Savater, Childhood Regained, 1981; M. Delibes, The Hedge, 1983; J.L. Borges, Nine Essays on Dante, 1984; B. Perez Galdos, Torquemada, 1986; M. Delibes, Five Hours with Mario, 1988; C. Martin Gaite, Behind the Curtains, 1990; M. Delibes, The Stuff of Heroes, 1990; J. Marias, Understanding Spain, 1990; L. Weckmann, The Medieval Heritage of Mexico, 1992; Cabeza de Vaca, Castaways: The Narrative of Alvar Nunez Cabeza de Vaca, edited by E. Pupo-Walker, 1993; Selected Writings of Andres Bello, ed. by I. Jaksic, 1997; J. de Acosta, Natural and Moral History of the Indies (1590), 2002. OTHER: (ed. with E.K. Mapes) J.J. Fernandez de Lizardi, El periquillo sarniento, 1952. **Address:** 355 Blackstone Blvd Apt 106, Providence, RI 02906-4947, U.S.A. **Online address:** fmorillas@aol.com

LOPREATO, Joseph. American (born Italy), b. 1928. **Genres:** Sociology, Human relations/Parenting, Demography, Sex. **Career:** Professor of Sociology, University of Texas, Austin, since 1966 (Chairman, Dept. of Sociology, 1969-72). Assistant Professor of Sociology, University of Massachusetts, Amherst, 1960-62; Visiting Lecturer of Sociology, University of Rome, 1962-64; Associate Professor, University of Connecticut, Storrs, 1964-66. **Publications:** Vilfredo Pareto, 1965; Peasants No More, 1967; Italian Americans, 1970; (with L.E. Hazelrigg) Class, Conflict, and Mobility, 1972; (with L.S. Lewis) Social Stratification: A Reader, 1974; The Sociology of Vilfredo Pareto, 1975; Human Nature and Biocultural Evolution, 1984; Evoluzione e Natura Umana, 1990; Mai Più Contadini, 1990; (with T. Crippen) Crisis in Sociology: The Need for Darwin, 1999. **Address:** 1801 Lavaca St 10A, Austin, TX 78701, U.S.A. **Online address:** lopreato@mail.la.utexas.edu

LOPRESTI, Robert. American, b. 1954. **Genres:** Mystery/Crime/Suspense, Librarianship. **Career:** Wayne Public Library, Wayne, NJ, librarian, 1977-81; William Paterson College of New Jersey, Wayne, instructor to assistant professor, and worked as librarian, 1981-87; Western Washington University, Bellingham, assistant professor and government documents librarian, 1987-; writer. **Publications:** (ed.) James Thurber, Thurber on Crime, 1991. Columnist, Mystery Scene, Mudderous Intent Magazines. Contributor of stories to periodicals.

LORAINE, Philip. See ESTRIDGE, Robin.

LORBER, Judith. American, b. 1931. **Genres:** Medicine/Health, Sociology, Women's studies and issues. **Career:** New York State Pharmacist, NYC, assistant editor, 1953-55; copywriter for medical products for advertising agencies in NYC, 1955-64; Montefiore Hospital and Medical Center, Bronx, NY, project director in health services research, 1966-68; Bellevue Hospital, NYC, assistant research sociologist in Psychiatric Division, 1969-70; Fordham University, Bronx, instructor to assistant professor, 1970-72; Brooklyn College of the City University of New York, assistant professor to professor, 1972-95, professor emerita, 1995-; Mount Sinai Medical Center, adjunct associate professor, 1978-95; Graduate Center of the City University of New York, professor, 1981-95, coordinator of Women's Studies Certificate Program, 1988-91, professor emerita, 1995-; Bar Ilan University, lecturer, 1992-93; Ruhr University, Bochum, Germany, Marie Jahoda Professor, 1997; Dortmund University, Germany, visiting professor, 2003; Carl von Ossietzky University, Oldenburg, Germany, Fulbright senior specialist, 2004. **Publications:** Women Physicians: Careers, Status, and Power, 1984; Paradoxes of

Gender, 1994; Gender and the Social Construction of Illness, 1997, 2nd ed. (with L.J. Moore), 2002; Gender Inequality: Feminist Theories and Politics, 1998, 3rd ed., 2005; Breaking the Bowls: Degendering and Feminist Change, 2005. EDITOR: (with E. Freidson) Medical Men and Their Work, 1972; (with S.A. Farrell, and contrib.) The Social Construction of Gender, 1991; (with M.M. Ferree and B.B. Hess, and contrib.) Revisioning Gender, 1998. Contributor to books, encyclopedias, electronic data bases, and sociology and women's studies journals.

LORCA DE TAGLE, Lillian. American, b. 1914. **Genres:** Translations, Novellas/Short stories, Autobiography/Memoirs. **Career:** Ercilla, Santiago, Chile, translator and reporter, 1939-40; independent translator, 1936-49; Bacteriological Institute of Chile (epidemiology department), scientific translator, 1950-52; Organization of American States, Americas (magazine), assistant editor, 1952-54; League of Women Voters, Chattanooga, TN, public relations officer, 1956-62; U.S. Department of State, Washington, DC, escort interpreter, 1962-64; Voice of America, Washington, DC, chief of field services branch in American Republics Division, 1964-89, coordinator of evening air show, 1970-73, cultural affairs officer in Honduras, 1973-76; independent translator, 1989-. **Publications:** (trans.) R. de Vallbona, Flowering Inferno: Tales of Sinking Hearts, 1994; (trans.) J. Collyer, People on the Prowl, 1995; Honorable Exiles (memoir), 2000. Translator of books from English, French, and German into Spanish for publishers in Chile and Argentina. **Address:** 5006 Summer Forest Dr, Houston, TX 77091, U.S.A. **Online address:** lolarco@aol.com

LORD, Alison. See ELLIS, Julie.

LORD, Jeffrey. See ELLIS, Julie.

LORD, Jeffrey. See NELSON, Ray.

LORD, John Vernon. British, b. 1939. **Genres:** Children's fiction, Illustrations. **Career:** Brighton Polytechnic University, Head, Dept. of Visual Communication, 1974-81, Professor of Illustration, 1986-2000, Professor Emeritus, 2000-. CNAA Graphic Design Board, Chairman, 1981-84. **Publications:** (with J. Burroway) The Truck on the Track, 1970; (with J. Burroway) The Giant Jam Sandwich, 1972; The Runaway Roller Skate, 1973; Mr. Mead and His Garden, 1974; Who's Zoo, 1977; Miserable Aunt Bertha, 1980; Edward Lear's Nonsense Verse, 1984; Doodles and Diaries, 1985; (with J. Michie) Aesop's Fables, 1989; (with R. Craft) The Song That Sings the Bird, 1989; British Myths and Legends, 1998. Illustrator of book by R. Barber.

LORD, Nancy J. American, b. 1952. **Genres:** Novellas/Short stories, Local history/Rural topics, Natural history, Essays. **Career:** Writer and fisherman. State of Alaska, Homer and Juneau, legislative aide, 1979-84, 1988-89. University of Alaska, Homer and Anchorage, adjunct, visiting, and term instructor, associate professor of writing, 1991-. Commercial salmon fisherman, 1979-. **Publications:** The Compass Inside Ourselves: Short Stories, 1984; Survival: Stories, 1991; Darkened Waters: A Review of the History, Science, and Technology Associated with the Exxon Valdez Oil Spill and Cleanup, 1992; Fishcamp: Life on an Alaskan Shore (nonfiction), 1997; Green Alaska: Dreams from the Far Coast (nonfiction), 2000; The Man Who Swam with Beavers: Stories, 2001; The State of the Inlet (nonprofit agency report); Beluga Days: Tracking a White Whale's Truths (nonfiction), 2004. **Address:** PO Box 558, Homer, AK 99603, U.S.A. **Online address:** nancylord@alaskawriters.com; www.nancylord.alaskawriters.com

LORD, Tony. American, b. 1949. **Genres:** Homes/Gardens. **Career:** Research chemist; National Trust, England, gardens adviser, 1979-89; Royal Horticultural Society's Plant Finder, principal editor; author, photographer, horticultural consultant, lecturer. **Publications:** (Compiler of Historical Plant Lists) Roy C. Strong, Small Period Gardens: A Practical Guide to Design and Planting, 1992; Best Borders, 1994; (Photographer) Rosemary Verey, Rosemary Verey's Making of a Garden, with watercolors by Hilary Wills, 1995; Gardening at Sissinghurst, 1996, paperback edition published as Planting Schemes from Sissinghurst, 2003; (Photographer) George Plumptre, Classic Planting: Featuring the Gardens of Beth Chatto, Christopher Lloyd, Rosemary Verey, Penelope Hobhouse, and Many Others, 1998; Designing with Roses, 1999; Encyclopedia of Planting Combinations: The Ultimate Visual Guide to Successful Plant Harmony, 2002. **Address:** c/o Author Mail, Frances Lincoln Ltd., 4 Torriano Mews, London NW5 2RZ, England.

LORDAN, (Ellenora) Beth. American, b. 1948. **Genres:** Novels, Novellas/Short stories. **Career:** Southern Illinois University, assistant professor of English, 1991-93, associate professor, 1993-99, professor, 1999-. NEA, Fiction Fellow, 1993. **Publications:** August Heat, 1989; And Both Shall Row,

1998; But Come Ye Back, 2004. **Address:** Dept of English, Southern Illinois University at Carbondale, Carbondale, IL 62901, U.S.A.

LORENZ, Lee (Sharp). American, b. 1932. **Genres:** Illustrations, Children's fiction, Cartoons. **Career:** Artist, musician, and writer. New Yorker, NYC, staff cartoonist, 1958-, art editor, 1973-. Cornetist, 1955-. **Publications:** AND ILLUSTRATOR: Here It Comes: A Collection of Cartoons, 1968; Now Look What You've Done, 1977; Real Dogs Don't Eat Leftovers: A Guide to All that Is Truly Canine, 1983; The Golden Age of Trash: Cartoons for the Eighties, 1987. CHILDREN'S BOOKS, AND ILLUSTRATOR: Scornful Simkin (adapted from "The Reeve's Tale" in Geoffrey Chaucer's Canterbury Tales), 1980; Pinchpenny John (adapted from "The Miller's Tale" in Geoffrey Chaucer's Canterbury Tales), 1981; The Feathered Ogre, 1981; Big Gus and Little Gus, 1982; Hugo and the Space Dog, 1983; A Weekend in the Country, 1985; Dinah's Egg, 1990. ILLUSTRATOR Of ADULT BOOKS BY: B. Feirstein, S. Redman, J. Jillson, J. Hanson, and P. Marx. ILLUSTRATOR OF CHILDREN'S BOOKS BY: J.L. Collier, R.J. Margolis, J. Wahl, C. Keller, B. Pryor, D. Updike, J. Runcie. **Address:** P.O. Box 131, Easton, CT 06612, U.S.A.

LORRIMER, Claire. (Patricia Denise Clark). Also writes as Patricia Robins, Susan Patrick. British, b. 1921. **Genres:** Novellas/Short stories, Romance/Historical, Children's fiction, Young adult fiction, Poetry, Biography. **Career:** Woman's Illustrated mag., London, sub-editor, 1938-40. **Publications:** A Voice in the Dark, 1967; The Shadow Falls, 1974; Relentless Storm, 1975; The Secret of Quarry House, 1976; Mavreen, 1976; Tamarisk, 1978; Chantal, 1980; The Garden (cameo), 1980; The Chatelaine, 1981; The Wilderling, 1982; Last Year's Nightingale, 1984; Frost in the Sun, 1986; House of Tomorrow (biography), 1987; Ortolans, 1990; The Spinning Wheel, 1991; Variations (stories), 1991; The Silver Link, 1993; Fool's Curtain, 1994; Connie's Daughter, 1995; Beneath the Sun, 1996; The Reunion, 1997; The Reckoning, 1998; The Woven Thread, 1998; Second Chance, 1998; An Open Door, 1999; Never Say Goodbye, 2000; Search for Love, 2000; For Always, 2001; The Faithful Heart, 2002. AS SUSAN PATRICK: Statues of Snow (novel), 1948. NOVELS AS PATRICIA ROBINS: To the Stars, 1944; See No Evil, 1945; Three Loves, 1949; Awake My Heart, 1950; Beneath the Moon, 1951; Leave My Heart Alone, 1951; The Fair Deal, 1952; Heart's Desire, 1953; So This Is Love, 1953; Heaven in Our Hearts, 1954; One Who Cares, 1954; Love Cannot Die, 1955; The Foolish Heart, 1956; Give All to Love, 1956; Where Duty Lies, 1957; He Is Mine, 1957; Love Must Wait, 1958; Lonely Quest, 1959; Lady Chatterley's Daughter, 1961; The Last Chance, 1961; The Long Wait, 1962; The Runaways, 1962; Seven Loves, 1962; With All My Love, 1963; The Constant Heart, 1964; Second Love, 1964; The Night Is Thine, 1964; There Is But One, 1965; No More Loving, 1965; Topaz Island, 1965; Love Me Tomorrow, 1966; The Uncertain Joy, 1966; The Man behind the Mask, 1967; Forbidden, 1967; Sapphire in the Sand, 1968; Return to Love, 1968; Laugh on Friday, 1969; No Stone Unturned, 1969; Cinnabar House, 1970; Under the Sky, 1970; The Crimson Tapestry, 1972; Play Fair with Love, 1972; None But He, 1973; Forever, 1991; Fullfillment, 1993; Forsaken, 1994. JUVENILES AS PATRICIA ROBINS: The Adventures of the Three Baby Bunnies, 1934; Tree Fairies, 1945; Sea Magic, 1946; The Heart of a Rose, 1947; The 100 Reward, 1966. **Address:** Chiswell Barn, Marsh Green, Edenbridge, Kent TN8 5PR, England.

LOSADA (GOYA), Jose Manuel. Spanish, b. 1962. **Genres:** Literary criticism and history. **Career:** Spanish teacher at schools in Paris, France, 1986-88; University of Navarre, Navarre, Spain, associate professor of French, 1991-, assistant director of Department of Modern Languages, 1992-93. Complutense University of Madrid, associate professor, 1992-96; visiting scholar and guest speaker at colleges and universities. **Publications:** L'Honneur au Theatre: La Conception de l'Honneur dans le Theatre Espagnol et Francais du XVIIe Siecle, 1994; Tristan y su Angel: Diez Ensayos de Literatura General y Comparada, 1995; Los Violines de Viena (novel), 1996; Romancero General, 1998; Bibliographie Critique de la Litterature Espagnole en France au XVIIe Siecle: Presence et Influence, 1999. EDITOR: (with P. Brunel, and contrib.) Don Juan: Tirso, Moliere, Pouchkine, Lenau; Analyses et Syntheses sur un Mythe Litteraire, 1993; (and contrib.) Poeticas Francesas del Siglo XX: Poetiques Francaises du XXe Siecle, 1994; (and translator) V. Hugo, La Leyenda de los Siglos, 1994; (with K. Reichenberger and A. Rodriguez, and contrib.) De Baudelaire a Lorca, 1996; Don Juan y Sus Fantasmas, 1997; Bibliography of the Myth of Don Juan in Literary History, 1997. Contributor to books and to periodicals in French, Spanish, and English. **Address:** Grandpont House, Folly Bridge, Oxford OX1 4LD, England.

LOSCH, Richard R. American, b. 1933. **Genres:** Theology/Religion. **Career:** Episcopal priest, 1959-69; secondary school teacher, 1966-85; computer programmer and consultant, 1985-86; St. Timothy's School, Raleigh, NC, principal, 1986-88, math instructor, 1988-89; Cape Fear Academy, Wilmington, NC, math instructor, 1989-93; University of West Alabama, Livingston, AL, math instructor, 1994-2000, assistant professor of statistics, 2001-; St. James' Episcopal Church, Livingston, AL, rector, 1994-. **Publications:** The Many Faces of Faith: A Guide to World Religions and Christian Traditions, 2001. **Address:** PO Box 1560, Livingston, AL 35470, U.S.A.

LOSEFF, Lev. American (born Russia), b. 1937. **Genres:** Literary criticism and history. **Career:** Sakhalin Oil-Worker newspaper, USSR, journalist, 1959-60; freelance writer, Leningrad, USSR, 1961-62; Kostyor magazine, Leningrad, editor, 1962-75; Ardis Publishing House, Ann Arbor, MI, part-time editor, 1976-78. Michigan State University, East Lansing, MI, visiting professor, 1978-79; Dartmouth College, Hanover, NH, professor, 1979-. Also worked as a broadcaster for the Voice of America, Radio Liberty, the BBC, and Radio France. **Publications:** On the Beneficence of Censorship: Aesopian Language in Modern Russian Literature, 1984. EDITOR: Poetika Brodskogo: Sbornik Statei, 1986; (with V. Polukhina) Brodsky's Poetics and Aesthetics, 1990; Boris Pasternak: 1890-1990, 1991; (with P. Vail) Iosif Brodskii: trudy I dni, 1998; (with V. Polukhina) Joseph Brodsky: The Art of a Poem, 1998; (with B. Scherr) A Sense of Place: Tsarskoe Selo and Its Poets. Author of eight collections of poetry and prose in Russian. **Address:** Russian Department, Dartmouth College, 44 N. College Street, Hanover, NH 03755, U.S.A. **Online address:** lev.l.loseff@dartmouth.edu

LOSHITZKY, Yosefa. Israeli. **Genres:** Film. **Career:** Production assistant for Israeli television, 1977-78; Indiana University-Bloomington, associate instructor in comparative literature, 1982-85; Bowling Green State University, OH, visiting professor of radio, television, and film, 1985-86; Hebrew University of Jerusalem, Israel, lecturer to senior lecturer in communication, 1987-. Visiting scholar, visiting professor, and visiting fellow at universities worldwide; lecturer at educational institutions. **Publications:** The Radical Faces of Godard and Bertolucci, 1995; (ed.) Spielberg's Holocaust: Critical Perspectives on Schindler's List, 1997. Author of documentary film scripts for Israeli television. Contributor to books. Contributor of articles and reviews to periodicals. **Address:** Noah Mozes Department of Communication and Journalism, Hebrew University of Jerusalem, Mount Scopus, 91 905 Jerusalem, Israel. **Online address:** 106161.3211@compuserve.com

LOSSE, Deborah N(ichols). American, b. 1944. **Genres:** Literary criticism and history. **Career:** U.S. Peace Corps, Washington, DC, volunteer teacher of French and English as a second language at a government secondary school in Katsina, Nigeria, 1966-68; Arizona State University, Tempe, assistant professor, 1973-80, associate professor, 1980-92, professor of French, 1992-, chair, Dept of Languages & Literatures. **Publications:** Rhetoric at Play: Rabelais and Satirical Eulogy, 1980; Sampling the Book: Renaissance Prologues and the French Conteurs, 1994. Contributor to books. Contributor of articles and reviews to academic journals. **Address:** Department of Foreign Languages, Arizona State University, Tempe, AZ 85287-0202, U.S.A.

LOTCHIN, Roger W. American, b. 1935. **Genres:** Local history/Rural topics, History, Urban studies. **Career:** University of North Carolina at Chapel Hill, assistant professor, 1966-74, associate professor, 1974-79, professor of history, 1979-. **Publications:** San Francisco, 1846-1856: From Hamlet to City, 1974; (ed.) The Martial Metropolis: U.S. Cities in War and Peace, 1984; Fortress California, 1910-1961: From Warfare to Welfare, 1992. **Address:** Department of History, University of North Carolina at Chapel Hill, CB 3195, Chapel Hill, NC 27599, U.S.A.

LOTHIAN, (Thomas Robert) Noel. Australian, b. 1915. **Genres:** Horticulture, Homes/Gardens. **Career:** Sr. Lecturer in Horticulture, University of New Zealand, 1944-47; Director, Botanic Gardens, Adelaide, 1948-80. **Publications:** Practical Home Gardener; Commonsense Gardening; Complete Australian Gardener; (with I. Holliday) Growing Australian Plants. **Address:** P. O. Box 27A, Crafers, SA 5152, Australia.

LOTT, Bret. American, b. 1958. **Genres:** Novels, Novellas/Short stories, Adult non-fiction. **Career:** Big Yellow House Inc., Santa Barbara, CA, cook's trainer, 1977-79; RC Cola, Los Angeles, salesman, 1979-80; Daily Commercial News, Los Angeles, reporter, 1980-81; Ohio State University, instructor in remedial English, 1984-86; College of Charleston, SC, professor of English, 1986-; Vermont College of Norwich, member of faculty, M.F.A. Program, 1994-. **Publications:** NOVELS: The Man Who Owned Vermont, 1987; A Stranger's House, 1988; Jewel, 1991; Reed's Beach, 1993; The Hunt Club, 1998. SHORT STORY COLLECTIONS: A Dream of Old Leaves, 1989; How to Get Home, 1996. NONFICTION: Fathers, Sons, and Brothers: The Men in My Family, 1997. Works appear in anthologies. Contributor of

book reviews to periodicals. **Address:** Department of English, College of Charleston, Charleston, SC 29424, U.S.A.

LOTT, Eric. American, b. 1959. **Genres:** History, Humanities, Music, Race relations, Theatre. **Career:** Manhattan Community College, NYC, instructor, 1983-87; Columbia University, NYC, instructor, 1985-86; University of Virginia, Charlottesville, VA, instructor, 1988-89, assistant professor of English, 1990-96, associate professor, 1996-2000, professor of English, 2000-. **Publications:** Love and Theft: Blackface Minstrelsy and the American Working Class, 1993. Contributor to anthologies. Contributor to periodicals. **Address:** Department of English, Bryan Hall Box 400121, University of Virginia, Charlottesville, VA 22904-4121, U.S.A. **Online address:** ewl4p@virginia.edu

LOTTMAN, Herbert. American, b. 1927. **Genres:** Intellectual history, Biography. **Career:** The Bookseller, London, international correspondent. **Publications:** Detours from the Grand Tour, 1970; How Cities Are Saved, 1976; Albert Camus: A Biography, 1979; The Left Bank: Writers, Artists and Politics from the Popular Front to the Cold War, 1982; Petain, Hero or Traitor?, 1985; The Purge (in U.K. as People's Anger: Justice and Revenge after the Liberation of France), 1986; Flaubert: A Biography, 1988; Colette: A Life, 1991; The Fall of Paris: June 1940, 1992; The French Rothschilds, 1995; Jules Verne: An Exploratory Biography, 1997; Man Ray's Montparnasse, 2001; L'Ecrivain engage et ses ambivalences, 2003; The Michelin Men, 2003. **Address:** BP 214, 75264 Paris Cedex 06, France.

LOTZ, Anne Graham. (born United States), b. 1948. **Genres:** Theology/Religion, Self help, Inspirational/Motivational Literature. **Career:** Bible study instructor, 1976-88; founder of AnGeL Ministries, 1988-98; evangelist/speaker, 1988-98. **Publications:** The Vision of His Glory: Finding Hope through the Revelation of Jesus Christ, 1996; God's Story: Finding Meaning for Your Life in Genesis, 1997; Daily Light, 1998. **Address:** 5115 Hollyridge Dr., Raleigh, NC 27612-3111, U.S.A. **Online address:** AnGeLMnsty@aol.com

LOUBERE, Leo A(lbert). American, b. 1923. **Genres:** Food and Wine, History, Biography. **Career:** Professor Emeritus, Professor of History, State University of New York, Buffalo, since 1964 (Assistant Professor, 1957-63). Instructor to Assistant Professor, University of Tennessee, Knoxville, 1953-57. **Publications:** Louis Blanc: His Life and His Contribution to the Rise of French Jacobin-Socialism, 1961; Utopian Socialism: Its History since 1800, 1974; Radicalism in Mediterranean France: Its Rise and Decline, 1848-1914, 1974; The Red and the White: A History of Wine in France and Italy in the Nineteenth Century, 1978; The Vine Remembers, 1984; The Wine Revolution in France: The Twentieth Century, 1990; Nineteenth-Century Europe: The Revolution of Life, 1994. **Address:** University at Buffalo, History, 559 Park Hall, Buffalo, NY 14260-4130, U.S.A.

LOUD, G(raham) A(nthony). British, b. 1953. **Genres:** History. **Career:** University of Leeds, England, lecturer in history, 1978-92, senior lecturer, 1992-2000, reader in medieval Italian history, 2000-. McMaster University, consultant to Liri Valley Archaeological Survey, 1978-80. **Publications:** Church and Society in the Norman Principality of Capua, 1058-1197, 1985; Conquerors and Churchmen in Norman Italy, 1999; Montecassino and Benevento in the Middle Ages: Essays in South Italian Church History, 2000; The Age of Robert Guiscard: Southern Italy and the Norman Conquest, 2000. EDITOR: (with I. N. Wood) Church and Chronicle in the Middle Ages, 1991; (with T.E.J. Wiedemann) The History of the Tyrants of Sicily by Hugo Falcandus 1154-69, 1998; (with A. Metcalfe) The Society of Norman Italy, 2002. **Address:** School of History, University of Leeds, Leeds LS2 9JT, England. **Online address:** G.A.Loud@leeds.ac.uk

LOUD, Patricia Cummings. American. **Genres:** Art/Art history, Institutions/Organizations, Architecture. **Career:** University of Texas at Austin, teacher of children's art courses, 1950-51; Frederick County Board of Education, teacher in public school system, 1951-53; Radcliffe College, Resident Fellow, 1954-56; Brown University, Providence, RI, Ford fellow in college teaching, 1956-57, teaching associate in art history, 1957-60; Connecticut College, New London, lecturer and instructor in modern art and slide librarian, 1970-72; University of Connecticut, Southeastern Branch, Avery Point, lecturer in art history, 1970-71; Texas Christian University, Fort Worth, instructor in art history and humanities, 1972-76; Van Cliburn Foundation, executive assistant and coordinator of volunteers, 1980-81; Fort Worth Country Day School, scholar in residence, 1980; Kimbell Art Museum, Fort Worth, slide librarian and architectural historian, 1981-92, Curator of Architecture and Visual Resources, 1993; Curator of Architecture and Archivist, 1994-. **Publications:** The Art Museums of Louis I. Kahn, Duke

University Press, 1989; In Pursuit of Quality: The Kimbell Art Museum, A History of Its Art and Architecture, 1987. Contributor of essays to books. **Address:** Kimbell Art Museum, 3333 Camp Bowie Blvd, Fort Worth, TX 76107, U.S.A.

LOUDEN, Robert B. American, b. 1953. **Genres:** Philosophy. **Career:** Indiana University Northwest, Gary, adjunct lecturer, 1977-80; Barat College, adjunct lecturer, 1979-80; Iowa State University, Ames, visiting assistant professor of philosophy, 1980-82; University of Southern Maine, Portland, assistant professor, 1982-88, associate professor, 1988-96, chairman of department, 1988-89, 1992-96, 1998-2000, professor of philosophy, 1996-; Gottingen University, Germany, visiting professor, 1992; Emory University, visiting professor, 1995. Speaker at colleges and universities; guest on radio and television programs. **Publications:** Morality and Moral Theory: A Reappraisal and Reaffirmation, 1992; Kant's Impure Ethics: From Rational Beings to Human Beings, 2000. EDITOR: (with P. Schollmejer) The Greeks and Us, 1996; F. Schleiermacher, Lectures on Philosophical Ethics, 2002. FORTHCOMING: (with G. Zoeller) I. Kant, Anthropology, History, and Education; (with A.W. Wood) I. Kant, Lectures on Anthropology; Historical Dictionary of Ethics. Work represented in anthologies. Contributor to scholarly journals, newspapers, and books. **Address:** Department of Philosophy, University of Southern Maine, 96 Falmouth St, Portland, ME 04103, U.S.A. **Online address:** Louden@Maine.edu

LOUDON, David L. American, b. 1944. **Genres:** Economics, Marketing. **Career:** Louisiana State University, Baton Rouge, instructor in marketing, 1969-71; University of Rhode Island, Kingston, 1971-80, assistant professor to associate professor of marketing; University of Louisiana at Monroe (formerly Northeast Louisiana University), 1980-, associate professor to professor of marketing and head of Department of Management and Marketing. **Publications:** (with R. Stevens) Legal Services Marketing, 1989; (with R. Stevens and B. Warren) Marketing Planning Guide, 1991, 2nd ed. (and with B. Wrenn), 1997; (with R. Stevens) Marketing for Churches and Ministries, 1992; (with A. Della Bitta) Consumer Behavior, 4th ed., 1993; Strategic Planning for Churches and Ministries, 1994; Strategic Planning for Not-for-Profit Organizations, 1994; Fundamentals of Strategic Planning for Healthcare Organizations, 1997; Marketing Research: Text and Cases, 2002. **Address:** Dept of Management and Marketing, University of Louisiana at Monroe, 700 University Ave, Monroe, LA 71209, U.S.A.

LOUGHERY, John. American, b. 1953. **Genres:** Adult non-fiction, Gay and lesbian issues, History, Biography, Essays. **Career:** Columbia Grammar & Preparatory School, New York City, English teacher, 1977-93; free-lance art journalist, 1985-; Hudson Review, art critic, 1990-; biographer, historian, editor, and fiction writer. **Publications:** Alias S.S. Van Dine: The Man Who Created Philo Vance, 1992; (ed.) First Sightings: Stories of American Youth, 1993; John Sloan: Painter and Rebel, 1995; The Other Side of Silence: Men's Lives and Gay Identities, A Twentieth-Century Hisotry, 1998.

LOUGHLIN, James. Irish, b. 1948. **Genres:** History, International relations/Current affairs, Politics/Government. **Career:** Substitute teacher in local secondary schools, 1982-83; University of Ulster, Jordanstown, Northern Ireland, part-time lecturer in modern European and British history, 1984-86; Queen's University of Belfast, Northern Ireland, junior research fellow at Institute of Irish Studies, 1985, research associate, 1986-87, senior research fellow, 1987-88, part-time lecturer in modern history and politics, 1985-86; University of Ulster, Londonderry, lecturer, 1988-97, senior lecturer in history, 1997-99, reader in history, 1999-. **Publications:** Gladstone, Home Rule, and the Ulster Question, 1882-93, 1986; Ulster Unionism and British National Identity since 1885, 1995; The Ulster Question since 1945, 1998. Contributor to books and periodicals. **Address:** School of History and International Affairs, Magee College, University of Ulster, Londonderry BT48 7JL, Northern Ireland. **Online address:** JP.Loughlin@ulst.ac.uk

LOUIE, Andrea. American, b. 1966. **Genres:** Novels. **Career:** Novelist, journalist. Boston Globe, Boston, MA; San Jose Mercury News, San Jose, CA; Akron Beacon Journal, Akron, OH, reporter, 1989-92; Market News Service, New York, NY, freelance editor, 1993-2000; Brooklyn College, adjunct writer, 1996-; Asian American Writers' Workshop, publications director, 1998-2000. **Publications:** Moon Cakes (novel), 1995. **Address:** PO Box 582, Prince St Station, New York, NY 10012, U.S.A.

LOUIE, David Wong. American, b. 1954. **Genres:** Novels, Novellas/Short stories. **Career:** Writer. Worked in advertising in New York; teacher of creative writing and literature at University of California, Berkeley, 1988, Vassar College, 1988-92, and University of California, Los Angeles, 1992-. **Publications:** STORIES: Pangs of Love, and Other Stories, 1991; The

Barbarians Are Coming, 2000. Work represented in anthologies. Contributor to periodicals. **Address:** Department of English, University of California Los Angeles, Box 90095-1530, Los Angeles, CA 90095, U.S.A. **Online address:** louie@humnet.ucla.edu

LOUIS, Cindi. American, b. 1962. **Genres:** Romance/Historical. **Career:** Romance novelist. **Publications:** Crazy Thing Called Love, 2001; (with B. Jackson, F. Mason, and K. Perrin) The Best Man, 2003. **Address:** PO Box 411366, Dallas, TX 75241, U.S.A.

LOUIS, Pat. See FRANCIS, Dorothy Brenner.

LOUNSBERRY, Barbara. American, b. 1946. **Genres:** Adult non-fiction, Humanities, Writing/Journalism, Biography, Documentaries/Reportage, Essays. **Career:** University of Northern Iowa, Cedar Falls, news and feature writer at Office of Public Information, 1965-72, instructor of journalism, 1973-74, assistant professor of English, 1976-82, associate professor, 1983-89, professor of English, 1990-. **Publications:** The Art of Fact: Contemporary Artists of Nonfiction, 1990; The Writer in You, 1992; (ed. with G. Talese) Writing Creative Nonfiction: The Literature of Reality, 1996; The Tales We Tell: Perspectives on the Short Story, 1998; Time and Chance: An Iowa Mystery, 1998; 16,000 Suspects, 1999; Politics Is Murder: An Iowa Mystery, 2000. **Address:** Department of English, University of Northern Iowa, Cedar Falls, IA 50614-0502, U.S.A. **Online address:** Barbara.Lounsberry@uni.edu

LOURIE, Richard. American, b. 1940. **Genres:** Novels, Novellas/Short stories, Area studies, Translations. **Career:** Translator from Russian and Polish, literary critic, novelist. **Publications:** NOVELS: Sagittarius in Warsaw, 1973; First Loyalty, 1985; Zero Gravity, 1987. TRANSLATOR FROM RUSSIAN: U. Shulevitz, Soldier and Tsar in the Forest: A Russian Tale (for children), 1972; V. Voinovich, The Life and Extraordinary Adventures of Private Ivan Chonkin, 1977; V. Voinovich, In Plain Russian: Stories, 1979; V. Voinovich, Pretender to the Throne, 1981; E. Sevela, Why There Is No Heaven on Earth, 1982; A. Likhanov, Shadows across the Sun, 1983; (with D. Arthur and B. Barrett) E. Sevela, The Standard Bearer, 1983; V. Voinovich, The Anti-Soviet Soviet Union, 1986; V. Voinovich, Moscow 2042, 1987; A. Lvov, The Courtyard, 1988; (and author of intro.) A. Tertz, Goodnight, 1989; A. Sakharov, Memoirs, 1990; Autobiography of Joseph Stalin, 1999. TRANSLATOR FROM POLISH: C. Milosz, Visions from San Francisco Bay, 1982; T. Konwicki, The Polish Complex, 1982; T. Konwicki, A Minor Apocalypse, 1983; K. Brandys, A Warsaw Diary, 1984; J. Korczak, King Matt the First (for children), 1986; R. Spasowski, The Liberation of One: The Autobiography of R. Spasowski, 1986; E. Czarnecka and A. Fiut, Conversations with C. Milosz, 1987; (with J. Neugroschel) L. Dobroszycki, ed., The Chronicle of the Lodz Ghetto, 1941-1944, 1987; T. Konwicki, Moonrise, Moonset, 1987; (and ed.) A. Wat, My Century: The Odyssey of a Polish Intellectual, 1988; A. Hertz, The Jews in Polish Culture, 1988; T. Konwicki, Bohin Manor, 1990. OTHER: Letters to the Future, 1975; Russia Speaks, 1991; Predicting Russia's Future, 1991; Hunting the Devil, 1993. **Address:** 533 Canal St #6, New York, NY 10013-1328, U.S.A.

LOURY, Glenn C(artman). American, b. 1948. **Genres:** Race relations, Essays. **Career:** Northwestern University, Evanston, IL, assistant professor of economics, 1976-79; University of Michigan, Ann Arbor, associate professor, 1979-80, professor of economics, 1980-82; Harvard University, Cambridge, MA, professor of economics and Afro-American studies, 1982-84, professor of political economy, 1984-91; Boston University, Boston, MA, professor of economics, 1991-. American Enterprise Institute for Public Policy Research, Bradley Lecturer, 1992, 1994; visiting lecturer at colleges and universities in the United States and abroad; guest on television and radio programs; consultant to Federal Trade Commission, Center for Naval Analyses, and American Telephone & Telegraph Co. **Publications:** (ed. with J.Q. Wilson, and contrib.) From Children to Citizens, Vol III: Families, Schools, and Delinquency Prevention, 1987; One by One, from the Inside Out: Essays and Reviews on Race and Responsibility in America, 1995; Anatomy of Racial Inequality, 2002. Contributor to books. Contributor of articles and reviews to professional journals. **Address:** Department of Economics, Boston University, 270 Bay State Rd, Boston, MA 02215, U.S.A.

LOUV, Richard. American, b. 1949. **Genres:** Human relations/Parenting. **Career:** San Diego Union-Tribune, San Diego, CA, columnist; contributing editor to Parents Magazine; commentator for the Monitor Radio Network; consultant to the Benton Foundation; senior editor of KidsCampaigns website (www.kidscampaigns.org). Served as director of Project Concern's OPTION program; participated in conferences; delegate to Russia for People to People; has spoken before organizations and appeared on television and radio shows. **Publications:** America II, 1983; Childhood's Future, 1990; FatherLove, 1994; 101 Things You Can Do for Our Children's Future, 1994; The Web of Life: Weaving the Values that Sustain Us, 1996. Contributor to periodicals and newspapers. **Address:** c/o San Diego Union, PO Box 191, San Diego, CA 92112, U.S.A.

LOUX, Ann Kimble. American, b. 1943. **Genres:** Autobiography/Memoirs. **Career:** Writer. Associated with St. Mary's College, Notre Dame, IN. **Publications:** The Limits of Hope: An Adoptive Mother's Story, 1997. **Address:** 218 9th St., Salt Lake City, UT 84103-2524, U.S.A. **Online address:** aloux@saintmarys.edu

LOVE, (Kathleen) Ann. Canadian, b. 1947. **Genres:** Environmental sciences/Ecology, Children's non-fiction, Young adult non-fiction. **Career:** Pollution Probe, Toronto, Ontario, Canada, founder and education coordinator, 1969-72; Stroke, American Heart Association Journal, London, Ontario, and Dallas, TX, managing editor, 1980-86; teacher in Carcross, Yukon, Canada, 1972-75, and Buttonville, Ontario, 1991-. **Publications:** Taking Control, 1990; (with J. Drake) Take Action: An Environmental Book for Kids, 1992; (with Drake) The Kids' Cottage Book, 1993, in US as The Kids' Summer Handbook, 1994; Grizzly Dance (fiction), 1994. **Address:** c/o Ticknor & Fields, 215 Park Ave. S., New York, NY 10003, U.S.A.

LOVE, D. Anne. American, b. 1949. **Genres:** Children's fiction. **Career:** School administrator in Richardson, TX, 1974-88; University of North Texas, Denton, professor, 1989-91; Western Hills Area Education Agency, Sioux City, IA, consultant, 1994-96. **Publications:** JUVENILE FICTION: Bess's Log Cabin Quilt, 1995; Dakota Spring, 1995; My Lone Star Summer, 1996; Three against the Tide, 1998; I Remember the Alamo, 1999; A Year without Rain, 2000; The Puppeteer's Apprentice, 2003; The Secret Prince, 2005. **Address:** c/o Simon & Schuster Children's Publishing., 1230 Avenue of the Americas, New York, NY 10020, U.S.A.

LOVE, Douglas. American, b. 1967. **Genres:** Children's fiction, Plays/Screenplays, Children's non-fiction, Theatre. **Career:** Walden Family Playhouse, producing artistic director. **Publications:** PLAYS: (adapter with M. Thomas and others) Free to Be...You and Me, 1989; Broadway Bubbies, 1991; Be Kind to Your Mother (Earth), 1993; Blame It on the Wolf, 1993; So You Want to Be a Star (play production kit), 1993; Holiday in the Rain Forest, 1994; Kabuki Gift, 1994; Dieguito, 1994; Harmony Loves Harmony, 1995; Angelita, 1995; Three Onions, 1995; The Adventures of Cookie Cobalt, 1995; The Little House Christmas Theater Kit, 1995; Class Reunion, 2002. PLAYS/SCREENPLAYS/TELEPLAYS: Imagine That, 1996; Jammin' Animals, 2000. OUT OF THE BOX series-Hats Off, 1998; Jungle, 1998; Blowin' in the Wind, 2000; Treasures, 2000; Animal Antics, 2000; Shadow Fun, 2000; Rainbow Colors, 2000. OTHER: Imagination Station: 99 Games to Spark Your Imagination, 1995; Great American Kids Slumber Party Book, 1997; Great American Kids Backyard Campout Book, 1997; Disney Do-It-Yourself Costume & Face Painting Kit, 1997; Disney's Face Painting & Costume Book II, 2002. **Address:** c/o Nancy Rose, Schreck, Rose & Dapello, 660 Madison Ave, New York, NY 10021, U.S.A. **Online address:** dlove@waldenfamilyplayhouse.com

LOVE, Ronald S(cott). Canadian, b. 1955. **Genres:** History. **Career:** University of Alberta, Edmonton, Alberta, Canada, Isaac Walton Killam fellow, 1988-90; University of Saskatchewan, Saskatoon, Saskatchewan, Canada, instructor and Canada research fellow, 1990-99; State University of West Georgia, Carrollton, associate professor of history, 1999-. **Publications:** Blood and Religion: The Conscience of Henri IV, 1553-1593, 2002; (ed. with G.J. Ames) Distant Lands and Diverse Cultures: The French Experience in Asia, 1600-1700, 2003; SaskTel: The Biography of a Crown Corporation and the Development of Telecommunications in Saskatchewan, 2003, as Dreaming Big: A History of SaskTel, 2003. **Address:** Department of History, State University of West Georgia, Carrollton, GA 30118, U.S.A.

LOVE, Susan M. American, b. 1948. **Genres:** Medicine/Health. **Career:** Beth Israel Hospital, Boston, MA, intern in surgery, 1974-75, surgical resident, 1975-79, surgical coordinator, 1979, clinical fellow in pathology, 1980; Harvard Medical School, Boston, clinical fellow in surgery, 1977-78, clinical instructor, 1980-87, assistant clinical professor of surgery, 1987-92; University of California, Los Angeles, associate professor of clinical surgery, 1992-96, adjunct associate professor, 1996-97, adjunct professor of general surgery, 1997-, holder of Revlon Chair in Women's Health, 1995-96, director of Revlon/UCLA Breast Center, 1992-96. Guy's Hospital, London, England, visiting registrar, 1977-78; Beth Israel Hospital, assistant in surgery, 1980-87, director of Breast Clinic, 1980-88, associate surgeon, 1987-92; director of research at Faulkner Breast Center, 1992; Dana Farber Cancer Institute, clinical associate, 1981-92; Santa Barbara Breast Cancer Institute, director of

research, 1995-, medical director, 1996-. **Publications:** (with K. Lindsey) Dr. Susan Love's Breast Book, 1990, rev ed, 1995; (with W. Silen and W.E. Matory) Atlas of Techniques in Breast Surgery, 1996; (with Lindsey) Dr. Susan Love's Hormone Book: Making Informed Choices about Menopause, 1997. Contributor to medical textbooks. Contributor of articles and reviews to medical journals. **Address:** 16593 Via Floresia, Pacific Palisades, CA 90272, U.S.A. **Online address:** slove@earthlink.net

LOVEGROVE, James (Matthew Henry). British, b. 1965. **Genres:** Novels. **Career:** Novelist. **Publications:** The Hope, 1990; (with P. Crowther) Escardy Gap, 1996; Days, 1998; The Web: Computopia, 1998; (as J.M.H. Lovegrove) Krilov Continuum, 1998; (as J.M.H. Lovegrove) The Berserker, 1999. Contributor to books. Contributor of short fiction to periodicals. **Address:** c/o Antony Harwood, Aitken Stone & Wylie Ltd., 29 Fernshaw Rd., London SW10 0TG, England.

LOVELACE, Earl. Trinidadian, b. 1935. **Genres:** Novels, Novellas/Short stories, Plays/Screenplays. **Career:** Jamaican Civil Service, agricultural assistant. **Publications:** While Gods Are Falling, 1965; The Schoolmaster, 1968; The Dragon Can't Dance, 1979, play, 1986; The Wine of Astonishment, 1982; A Brief Conversion and Other Stories, 1986; Salt (novel), 1997; Growing in the Dark, 2003. PLAYS: The New Boss, 1962; My Name Is Village, 1976; Pierrot Ginnard, 1977; The New Hardware Store, 1980; Jestina's Calypso and Other Plays, 1984; The Wine of Astonishment, 1987. **Address:** c/o Andre Deutsch, Carlton Publishing Group, Unit 2, Wenta Business Cntr Colneway, Watford, Hertfordshire WD24 4ND, England.

LOVELACE, Merline (A.). American, b. 1946. **Genres:** Romance/Historical, Westerns/Adventure. **Career:** Entered U.S. Air Force in 1968, commissioned, 1968, retired at the rank of colonel, 1991; novelist, 1991-. Lecturer on women in the military at national and local level. **Publications:** ROMANCE NOVELS: Bits and Pieces, 1993; Maggie and Her Colonel (novella), 1994; Alena, 1994; Sweet Song of Love, 1994; Dreams and Schemes, 1994; Siren's Call, 1994; Somewhere in Time, 1994; His Lady's Ransom, 1995; Lady of the Upper Kingdom, 1996; Line of Duty, 1996; Beauty and the Bodyguard, 1996; Halloween Honeymoon, 1996; Thanksgiving Honeymoon, 1996; Valentine's Honeymoon, 1997; Duty and Dishonor, 1997; Above and Beyond, 1997; Countess in Buckskin, 1997; White Tiger/Green Dragon, 1997. CODE NAME: DANGER SERIES: Night of the Jaguar, 1995; Cowboy and the Cossack, 1995; Undercover Man, 1996; Perfect Double, 1996. Contributor to anthologies. **Address:** 2325 Tuttington, Oklahoma City, OK 73170, U.S.A. **Online address:** lovelace@iamerica.net

LOVELL, (Sir) (Alfred Charles) Bernard. British, b. 1913. **Genres:** Astronomy. **Career:** Professor of Radio Astronomy, and Director of Nuffield Radio Astronomy Labs. at Jodrell Bank, University of Manchester, 1951-81. President, Royal Astronomical Society, 1969-71. **Publications:** Science and Civilization, 1939; World Power Resources and Social Development, 1945; (with J. A. Clegg) Radio Astronomy, 1952; Meteor Astronomy, 1954; (with R. Hanbury Brown) The Exploration of Space by Radio, 1957; The Individual and the Universe, 1959; The Exploration of Outer Space, 1962; (with M. Joyce Lovell) Discovering the Universe, 1963; Our Present Knowledge of the Universe, 1967; The Story of Jodrell Bank, 1968; Out of the Zenith: Jodrell Bank, 1957-70, 1973; The Origins and International Economics of Space Exploration, 1973; Man's Relation to the Universe, 1975; P. M. S. Blackett: A Biographical Memoir, 1976; In the Center of Immensities, 1978; Emerging Cosmology, 1981; The Jodrell Bank Telescopes, 1985, Voice of the Universe, 1987; (with F. Graham Smith) Pathways to the Universe, 1988; Astronomer by Chance, 1990; Echoes of War, 1991. **Address:** Jodrell Bank, Macclesfield, Cheshire, England.

LOVELL, Glenville. American, b. 1955. **Genres:** Novels. **Career:** Novelist, playwright, and actor. Has traveled extensively with theatrical companies. **Publications:** NOVELS: Fire in the Canes, 1995. Also author of plays. **Address:** c/o Soho Press, 853 Broadway, New York, NY 10003, U.S.A.

LOVELL, Marc. *See* **MCSHANE, Mark.**

LOVELL, Mary S(ybilla). British, b. 1941. **Genres:** Novels, History, Local history/Rural topics, Travel/Exploration, Biography. **Career:** Worked as an accountant and business director, 1963-83, and as a technical writer and documentation manager, 1983-86; full-time writer, 1986-. **Publications:** A Hunting Pageant, 1981; Cats as Pets, 1982; Straight on till Morning: The Biography of Beryl Markham, 1987; (ed.) B. Markham, The Splendid Outcast (stories), 1987; The Sound of Wings: The Life of Amelia Earhart, 1989; Cast No Shadow: The Life of the American Spy Who Changed the Course of World War II, 1992; Rebel Heart, the Biography of Jane Digby, 1995; A

Rage to Live: Biography of Sir Richard F. Burton and Isabel (Lady) Burton, 1998; The Sisters (biography), 2001; Bess of Hardwick, 2004; One More Spring, in progress; Deadlier than the Male: Women Adventurers (anthology), in progress. **Address:** c/o Robert Ducas Literary Agent, The Barn House, 244 Westside Rd, Norfolk, CT 06058, U.S.A. **Online address:** marylovell2002@yahoo.com

LOVESEY, Peter (Harmer). Also writes as Peter Lear. British, b. 1936. **Genres:** Novellas/Short stories, Mystery/Crime/Suspense, Sports/Fitness. **Career:** Hammersmith and West London College, London, head of General Education Dept., 1969-75. **Publications:** The Kings of Distance, 1968; (with T. McNab) The Guide to British Track and Field Literature, 1275-1968, 1969; Wobble to Death, 1970; The Detective Wore Silk Drawers, 1971; Abracadaver, 1972; Mad Hatter's Holiday, 1973; Invitation to a Dynamite Party (in U.S. as The Tick of Death), 1974; A Case of Spirits, 1975; Swing, Swing Together, 1976; (as Peter Lear) Goldengirl, 1977; Waxwork, 1978; The Official Centenary History of the Amateur Athletic Association, 1979; (as Peter Lear) Spider Girl, 1980; The False Inspector Dew, 1982; Keystone, 1983; Butchers and Other Stories of Crime, 1985; (as Peter Lear) The Secret of Spandau, 1986; Rough Cider, 1986; Bertie and the Tinman, 1987; On the Edge, 1989; Bertie and the Seven Bodies, 1990; The Last Detective, 1991; Diamond Solitaire, 1992; Bertie and the Crime of Passion, 1993; The Crime of Miss Oyster Brown and Other Stories, 1994; The Summons, 1995; Bloodhounds, 1996; Upon a Dark Night, 1997; Do Not Exceed the Stated Dose, 1998; The Vault, 1999; The Reaper, 2000; An Athletics Compendium, 2001; The Sedgemoor Strangler and Other Stories, 2001; Diamond Dust, 2002; The House Sitter, 2003. **Address:** c/o Vanessa Holt Ltd, 59 Crescent Rd, Leigh-on-Sea, Essex SS9 2PF, England.

LOVETT, Sarah. American, b. 1953. **Genres:** Travel/Exploration, Children's non-fiction, Zoology, Mystery/Crime/Suspense. **Career:** Office of the Attorney General, Santa Fe, NM, legal researcher; New Mexico State Penitentiary, Santa Fe, forensic researcher; writer, 1989-. Has also worked as a theater director, dancer, playwright, gas station attendant, upholstery assistant, and bartender. **Publications:** MYSTERIES: Dangerous Attachments, 1995; Acquired Motives, 1996; A Desperate Silence, 1997; Dantes' Inferno, 2001. EXTREMELY WEIRD SERIES; Extremely Weird Frogs, 1991; Extremely Weird Reptiles, 1991; Extremely Weird Primates, 1991; Extremely Weird Birds, 1992; Extremely Weird Endangered Species, 1992; Extremely Weird Fishes, 1992; Extremely Weird Insects, 1992; Extremely Weird Sea Creatures, 1992; Extremely Weird Mammals, 1993; Extremely Weird Micro Monsters, 1993; Extremely Weird Snakes, 1993; Extremely Weird Spiders, 1996; Encyclopedia of Extremely Weird Animals, 1997; Extremely Weird Animal Defenses, 1997; Extremely Weird Animal Disguises, 1997; Extremely Weird Animal Hunters, 1997; Extremely Weird Bats, 1997. TRAVEL BOOKS: Kidding around London: A Family Guide to the City, 1989; Kidding around London: A Young Person's Guide to the City, 1989; Kidding around NYC: A Young Person's Guide to the City, 1989; Kidding around the Hawaiian Islands: A Young Person's Guide, 1990; Kidding around the National Parks of the Southwest: A Young Person's Guide, 1990; Unique Colorado: A Guide to the State's Quirks, Charisma, and Character, 1993; Unique Florida: A Guide to the State's Quirks, Charisma, and Character, 1993; Unique New Mexico: A Guide to the State's Quirks, Charisma, and Character, 1993; Unique New England: A Guide to the Region's Quirks, Charisma, and Character, 1994; Unique Texas: A Guide to the State's Quirks, Charisma, and Character, 1994. **Address:** PO Box 6692, Santa Fe, NM 87502, U.S.A. **Online address:** author@sarahlovett.com

LOW, Anthony. American, b. 1935. **Genres:** Literary criticism and history. **Career:** Professor of English, since 1978, New York University (Assistant Professor, 1968-71; Associate Professor, 1971-78; Dept. Chairman, 1989-95). Assistant Professor, Seattle University, Wash., 1965-68. **Publications:** Augustine Baker, 1970; The Blaze of Noon: A Reading of Samson Agonistes, 1974; Love's Architecture: Devotional Modes in Seventeenth-Century English Poetry, 1978; (ed.) Urbane Milton: The Latin Poems, 1984; The Georgic Revolution, 1985; The Reinvention of Love: Poetry, Politics and Culture from Sidney to Milton, 1993. **Address:** Dept. of English, New York University, 19 University Pl Rm 521, New York, NY 10003, U.S.A. **Online address:** low@compuserve.com

LOW, Kathleen. American. **Genres:** Librarianship. **Career:** University of California, Davis, cataloger, 1980-83; CLASS, San Jose, CA, online coordinator, 1983-84; California State Library, Sacramento, online reference librarian, 1984-88, database specialist, 1988-89, outreach manager, 1989-92, principal librarian, 1992-. **Publications:** Legislative Reference Services and Sources, 1995; (ed. and contrib.) The Roles and Responsibilities of Reference Librarians, 1996; Recruiting Library Staff, 1999. Contributor to

magazines. **Address:** California State Library, PO Box 942837, Sacramento, CA 94237-0001, U.S.A. **Online address:** klow@library.ca.gov

LOW, Setha M. American, b. 1948. **Genres:** Cultural/Ethnic topics. **Career:** San Francisco State College (now University), San Francisco, CA, instructor in anthropology, 1971; University of Pennsylvania, Philadelphia, assistant professor, 1976-82, associate professor of landscape architecture and regional planning, anthropology, and city planning, 1982-88, associate faculty of Center for the Study of Aging, 1982-87, and Leonard Davis Institute of Health Economics, 1984-87; Graduate School and University Center of the City University of New York, NYC, professor of environmental psychology and anthropology, 1987-, director of Public Space Research Group, 1988-. Universidad de Costa Rica, honorary professor, 1986-87; York University, Toronto, Ontario, visiting professor, 1991; University of Pennsylvania, visiting lecturer, 1992-95; New York University, visiting professor, 1995; speaker at Yale University and Columbia University. Conducted anthropological field work in Costa Rica, El Salvador, Guatemala, Japan, Spain, Mexico, France, Cuba, Venezuela, and the United States; consultant. **Publications:** Culture, Politics, and Medicine in Costa Rica, 1985; (with F. Johnston) Children of the Urban Poor: The Sociocultural Environment of Growth, Development, and Malnutrition in Guatemala City, 1995. EDITOR: (with E. Chambers) Housing, Culture, and Design: A Comparative Perspective, 1989; (with D. David) Gender, Health, and Illness: The Case of Nerves, 1989; (with I. Altman) Place Attachment, 1992. Contributor to books. Contributor of articles and reviews to scholarly journals. **Address:** Graduate Center of the City University of New York, 33 West 42nd St., New York, NY 10036, U.S.A.

LOWBURY, Edward (Joseph Lister). British, b. 1913. **Genres:** Poetry, Literary criticism and history, Biography. **Career:** Physician and writer. Hospital Infection Research Laboratory, Birmingham, hon. director, 1960-79; University of Aston, Birmingham, visiting professor, 1979-88. **Publications:** Fire: A Symphonic Ode, 1934; Port Meadow, 1936; Crossing the Line, 1946; Metamorphoses, 1955; (with T. Heywood) Facing North (miscellany), 1960; Time for Sale, 1961; New Poems, 1965; Daylight Astronomy, 1968; Figures of Eight, 1969; (with T. Salter and A. Young) Thomas Campion: Poet, Composer, Physician, 1970; Green Magic, 1972; Two Confessions, 1973; The Night Watchman, 1974; Poetry and Paradox, 1976; (with J. Press and M. Riviere) Troika, 1977; Selected Poems, 1978; The Ring, 1979; A Letter from Masada, 1982; Goldrush, 1984; Birmingham, Birmingham!, 1985; Flowering Cypress, 1986; Variations on Aldeburgh, 1987; A Letter from Hampstead, 1987; Apocryphal Letters, 1989; Selected and New Poems, 1935-1989, 1990; First Light, 1991; Collected Poems, 1993; Hallmarks of Poetry (essays), 1994; Mystic Bridge, 1997; (with A. Young) To Shirk No Idleness: A Critical Biography of Andrew Young, 1998; Blind Man's Buff, 2001; (with others) Three Voices, Three Visions, 2002. EDITOR: Widening Circles, 1976; Night Ride and Sunrise, 1978; (with Alison Young) The Poetical Works of Andrew Young, 1985; Apollo: An Anthology of Poems by Doctor-Poets, 1990; (with A. Young) Selected Poems of Andrew Young, 1998. **Address:** c/o 25 Churston Gardens, London N11 2NJ, England.

LOWDEN, Desmond Scott. British, b. 1937. **Genres:** Mystery/Crime/Suspense, Plays/Screenplays. **Publications:** Bandersnatch, 1969; The Boondocks, 1972; Bellman and True, 1975; Boudapesti 3, 1979; Sunspot, 1981; Cry Havoc, 1984; The Shadow Run, 1989 (Crime Writers' Association Silver Dagger Award); Chain, 1990. **Address:** c/o Rogers, Coleridge and White, 20 Powis Mews, London W11 1JN, England.

LOWE, Ben(no P.). American, b. 1956. **Genres:** History, Philosophy. **Career:** Barry University, Miami Shores, FL, assistant professor of history, 1990-93; Florida Atlantic University, Boca Raton, assistant professor, 1993-96, associate professor of history, 1996-. Duke University, scholar in residence, 1992. **Publications:** Imagining Peace: A History of Early English Pacifist Thought, 1340-1560, 1997. Contributor to books. Contributor of articles and reviews to scholarly journals. **Address:** Department of History, Florida Atlantic University, 777 Glades Rd, Boca Raton, FL 33431, U.S.A. **Online address:** bplowe@fau.edu

LOWE, Mick. Canadian (born United States), b. 1947. **Genres:** Adult nonfiction. **Career:** Daily Nebraskan, staff writer and columnist, 1966-68; Lincoln Daily Star, Lincoln, NE, staff writer, 1967-68; Georgia Straight, Vancouver, staff writer and columnist, 1970-72; The Grape, Vancouver, cofounder, 1972; Gauntlet, editor, 1973-74; Globe & Mail, Toronto, freelance correspondent, 1974-76, 1979-87; CBC Radio News, staff reporter, 1977-78; CBC radio Morning North Sudbury, founding producer, 1978; Cambrian College, lecturer in journalism, 1988-90. **Publications:** Conspiracy of Brothers: A True Story of Murder, Bikers, and the Law, 1988; One Woman Army: The Life of Claire Culhane, 1992. Contributor to publications. **Address:** 32 Onwatin Lake Rd., East Hanmer, ON, Canada P3P 1J4.

LOWE, Rodney. British, b. 1946. **Genres:** History. **Career:** Heriot-Watt University, Edinburgh, Scotland, lecturer in history, 1972-78; University of Bristol, Bristol, England, professor of contemporary history, 1979-. Australian National University, visiting research fellow, 1994. **Publications:** Adjusting to Democracy, 1986; Economic Planning in Britain, 1943-51, 1992; The Development of the Welfare State, 1939-51, 1992; The Welfare State in Britain since 1945, 1993, 2nd ed., 1999; Welfare Policy under the Conservatives, 1998; Welfare Policy in Britain, 1999; From Beveridge to Blair, 2002. **Address:** Department of Historical Studies, University of Bristol, Bristol BS8 1TB, England. **Online address:** R.Lowe@bristol.ac.uk

LOWE, Stephen. British, b. 1947. **Genres:** Plays/Screenplays. **Career:** Artistic dir., Meeting Ground Theatre Co., Nottingham, since 1984. Actor and dir., Stephen Joseph Theatre-in-the-Round, Scarborough, Yorks., 1975-78; Sr. Lecturer, Dartington College of Arts, Devon, 1978-82. **Publications:** Touched, 1977, 1981; The Ragged Trousered Philanthropists, 1978, 1983; Tibetan Inroads, 1981; Cards, 1983; Moving Pictures: Four Plays, 1985; (ed.) Peace Plays, 2 vols., 1985, 1989; Divine Gossip, 1989; (trans.) William Tell, 1989. **Address:** Judy Daish Assocs. Ltd, 2, St. Charles Place, London W10 6EG, England.

LOWE-EVANS, Mary. American, b. 1941. **Genres:** Literary criticism and history. **Career:** University of West Florida, Pensacola, assistant professor, 1987-91, associate professor, 1991-94, professor of English, 1994-. Modern Language Association, regional delegate, 1990-93; University of West Florida, chair of Women Faculty Equity Commission, 1991-, associate dean of College of Arts and Sciences, 1993-, director of Women's Studies Program, 1993-. **Publications:** Crimes Against Fecundity: Joyce and Population Control, 1989; Frankenstein: Mary Shelley's Wedding Guest, 1993. Contributor to books and periodicals. **Address:** College of Arts and Social Sciences, University of West Florida, Pensacola, FL 32514, U.S.A.

LOWENBERG, Anton D(avid). American (born Republic of South Africa), b. 1957. **Genres:** Economics. **Career:** California State University, Northridge, assistant professor, 1984-92, professor of economics, 1992-. **Publications:** (with W.H. Kaempfer) International Economic Sanctions: A Public Choice Perspective, 1992; (with W.H. Kaempfer) The Origins and Demise of South African Apartheid: A Public Choice Analysis, 1998. **Address:** Department of Economics, California State University, 18111 Nordhoff St., Northridge, CA 91330-8374, U.S.A.

LOWENBERG, Susan. American, b. 1957. **Genres:** Literary criticism and history, Reference. **Career:** Bradley University, Peoria, IL, librarian, 1981-86; California State University Library, Northridge, chair of circulation department, 1986-89; University of Colorado, Boulder, head of access services department, 1989-90, science librarian and curator of Map Library, 1991-92; California Institute of the Arts, Santa Clarita, librarian of information resources and theatre/dance, 1993-99, associate dean, 1999-. **Publications:** C.S. Lewis: A Reference Guide, 1972-1988, 1993. **Address:** California Institute of the Arts, 24700 McBean Parkway, Santa Clarita, CA 91355, U.S.A.

LOWENSTEIN, Michael W. American, b. 1942. **Genres:** Business/Trade/Industry, Administration/Management, Marketing. **Career:** Customer Retention Associates, Collingswood, NJ, managing director, 1995-. **Publications:** Customer Retention, 1995; (co-author) Redefining Consumer Affairs, 1996; The Customer Loyalty Pyramid, 1997; Customer Win Back, 2001. Contributor to periodicals, newsletters, and CRM portal sites. **Address:** 302 Lees Ave, Collingswood, NJ 08108-3108, U.S.A. **Online address:** mlowenstein@p3.net; www.customerloyalty.org

LOWENTHAL, Cynthia J. American, b. 1952. **Genres:** Literary criticism and history. **Career:** Tulane University, New Orleans, LA, associate professor of English, 1987-. **Publications:** Lady Mary Wortley Montagu and the Eighteenth Century Familiar Letter, 1994. **Address:** Department of English, Tulane University, New Orleans, LA 70118, U.S.A.

LOWERY, Robert G. American, b. 1941. **Genres:** Essays, Biography. **Career:** Sean O'Casey Review, Long Island, N.Y., publisher, 1974-82; Irish Literary Supplement, Long Island, publisher, 1982-. Free-lance typesetter, editor, and book designer. **Publications:** (comp) An Annotated Index to Sean O'Casey's Autobiographies, 1983. EDITOR: (with D. Krause) Sean O'Casey: Centenary Essays, 1980; Essays on Sean O'Casey's Autobiographies, 1981; From Times Past: Brooks Atkinson on Sean O'Casey, 1982; A Whirlwind in Dublin: The Plough Riots, 1984; (with P. Angelin) My Very Dear Sean: George Jean Nathan on Sean O'Casey-Letters and Reviews, 1984. **Address:** 2592 N. Wading River Rd., Wading River, NY 11792, U.S.A. **Online address:** RLowery2592@cs.com

LOWING, Anne. See GEACH, Christine.

LOWRY, Bullitt. American, b. 1936. **Genres:** History, Adult non-fiction. **Career:** Converse College, Spartanburg, SC, assistant professor of history, 1960-64; University of North Texas, Denton, associate professor to professor of history, 1964-. Wylie College, visiting professor, 1968. U.S. Congressional Office, Washington, DC, research assistant for 4th District, Texas, 1978. Denton County Historical Commission, vice-chair, 1976-85, chair, 1985-89; Denton City Landmark Commission, chair. **Publications:** (co-ed) The Red Virgin: Memoirs of Louise Michel, 1981; (co-author) World History, 2 vols, 1991; Causes and Consequences of World War I, 1996; Armistice-1918, 1996. **Address:** Department of History, University of North Texas, Denton, TX 76203, U.S.A. **Online address:** blowry@unt.edu

LOWRY, Lois (Hammersberg). American, b. 1937. **Genres:** Children's fiction, Young adult fiction, Literary criticism and history. **Publications:** Black American Literature, 1973; Literature of the American Revolution, 1974; Values and the Family, 1977; A Summer to Die, 1977; Find a Stranger, Say Goodbye, 1978; Here in Kennebunkport, 1978; Anastasia Krupnik, 1979; Autumn Street, 1980, in UK as The Woods at the End of Autumn Street, 1987; Anastasia Again!, 1981; Anastasia at Your Service, 1982; The One Hundredth Thing about Caroline, 1983; Taking Care of Terrific, 1983; Anastasia, Ask Your Analyst, 1984; Us and Uncle Fraud, 1984; Anastasia on Her Own, 1985; Switcharound, 1985; Anastasia Has the Answers, 1986; Anastasia's Chosen Career, 1987; Rabble Starkey, 1987, in UK as The Road Ahead, 1988; All about Sam, 1988; Number the Stars, 1989 (Newbery Medal, 1990); Your Move, J.P.!, 1990; Anastasia at This Address, 1991; The Giver, 1993 (Newbery Medal, 1994); Anastasia Absolutely, 1995; See You Around Sam, 1996; Stay: Keepers Story, 1997; Looking Back: A Book of Memories, 1998; Zooman Sam, 1999; Gathering Blue, 2000; Goony Bird Greene, 2002; The Messenger, 2004; The Silent Boy, 2003. **Address:** 205 Brattle St, Cambridge, MA 02138-3345, U.S.A.

LOWRY, Ritchie Peter. American, b. 1926. **Genres:** Sociology. **Career:** Professor of Sociology, Boston College, Chestnut Hill, Massachusetts, since 1966 (Chairman, Dept. of Sociology, 1967-70). Founder, President, Good Money, Inc., New Hampshire, 1982-. Instructor to Associate Professor of Sociology, California State University at Chico, 1955-64; Sr. Research Scientist and Associate Professor of Research, Special Operations Research Office, American University, Washington, D.C., 1964-66. **Publications:** Who's Running This Town? Community Leadership and Social Change, 1965, 1968; (ed.) Problems of Studying Military Roles in Other Cultures: A Working Conference, 1967; (with R.P. Rankin) Sociology: The Science of Society, 1969, rev. ed. 1972; Social Problems: A Critical Analysis of Theory and Public Policy, 1974; (with R.P. Rankin) Sociology: Social Science and Social Concern, 1977; Information Flow in Government Agencies, 1977; Looking Different Ways, 1977; Bridging the Gap: Public, Scientific, and Policy Views of Rape, 1978; A Meta-Analysis of Research Grant Applications Assigned to the NIMH Work and Mental Health Program, 1984; Good Money: A Guide to Socially Responsible Investing for the '90s, 1991, 1993. **Address:** Dept. of Sociology, Boston College, Chestnut Hill, MA 02467, U.S.A. **Online address:** GOODMONEY1@aol.com

LOWRY, William R. American, b. 1953. **Genres:** Politics/Government. **Career:** OSCO Drug Stores, assistant manager, 1979-81; Washington University, St. Louis, MO, joined staff, 1988-, professor of political science. Washington University, member of campus youth board of directors, 1991-92, traveling speaker for alumni association, 1992. **Publications:** The Dimensions of Federalism: State Governments and Pollution Control Policies, 1992; The Capacity for Wonder, 1994; Preserving Public Lands for the Future, 1998; Dam Politics, 2003. **Address:** Department of Political Science, Washington University, St. Louis, MO 63130, U.S.A.

LOXLEY, James. Scottish, b. 1968. **Genres:** Literary criticism and history. **Career:** University of Edinburgh, Edinburgh, Scotland, lecturer. **Publications:** Royalism and Poetry in the English Civil Wars: The Drawn Sword, 1997. Contributor to books and scholarly journals. **Address:** Department of English Literature, University of Edinburgh, David Hume Tower, George Square, Edinburgh EH8 9JX, Scotland. **Online address:** James.Loxley@ed.ac.uk

LOY, Rosetta. Italian, b. 1931. **Genres:** Novels. **Career:** Writer. Also worked as a publicist, 1975-. **Publications:** La parole ebreo, 1997 trans. as First Word, 2000. NOVELS: La bicicletta, 1974; La porta dell'acqua, 1976, 2nd ed., 2000; L'estate di Letuque, 1982; All'insaputa della notte, 1984, 2nd ed., 1990; Le strade di polvere, 1987, trans. as The Dust Roads of Monferrato, 1991; Sogni di inverno, 1992; Cioccolata da Hanselmann, 1995 trans.

as Hot Chocolate at Hanselmann's, 2003; Ahi, Paloma, 2000; Uero e l'albers de ricorsli, allurre l'arie, 2004. **Address:** Via di IV Peperino 1, 00188 Rome, Italy.

LOZA, Steven (Joseph). American. **Genres:** Music. **Career:** University of Chile, School of Music, 1989; Kanda University of International Studies, Japan, 1996-97; University of California, Los Angeles, associate professor, then professor of ethnomusicology; UCLA Latin American Center, associate director, research, and director of music department. Latin jazz performer and producer. **Publications:** Barrio Rhythm: Mexican American Music in Los Angeles, 1993; (ed.) Selected Reports in Ethnomusicology 10: Musical Aesthetics and Multiculturalism in Los Angeles, 1994; Tito Puente and the Making of Latin Music, 1999. **Address:** UCLA Department of Ethnomusicology, 2539 Schoenberg Hall, 405 Hilgard Ave., Los Angeles, CA 90095, U.S.A. **Online address:** sloza@ucla.edu

LOZOWICK, Lee. American, b. 1943. **Genres:** Poetry, Theology/Religion, Inspirational/Motivational Literature. **Career:** Self-employed coin and stamp dealer in Milburn, NJ, 1965-70; gave seminars in the Silva Method (motivational seminars) in Tabor, NJ, 1970-75; singer and lyricist for rock band, liars, gods, and beggars, in Prescott, AZ, 1989-97; singer and lyricist for Blues Band, SHR1, the Blues Sensation, 1995-. **Publications:** SPIRITUALITY: In the Fire, 1978; Laughter of the Stones, 1979; Acting God, 1980; The Book of Unenlightenment; The Yoga of Enlightenment, 1980; The Cheating Buddha, 1980; The Only Grace Is Loving God, 1982; Living God Blues, 1984; In Praise of Rumi, 1989; (as Lee Khepa Baul) Derisive Laughter from a Bad Poet, 1993; Poems of a Broken Heart (poetry), 1993, Vol. Two, 1997; (ed. with R. Ryan) In Praise of Japanese Love Poetry, 1994; The Alchemy of Love and Sex, 1995; The Alchemy of Transformation, 1996; Conscious Parenting, 1997. Has also written the song lyrics for the ten albums of liars, gods, and beggars. **Address:** PO Box 4272, Prescott, AZ 86301, U.S.A.

LU, Ning. Chinese, b. 1955. **Genres:** Politics/Government. **Career:** Government of China, analyst, 1975-87; International Center, Washington DC, fellow, 1988-93; Atlantic Council, Washington, DC, senior fellow, 1994-95; SPH (newspaper), Singapore, China, senior correspondent, 1995-. Consultant to World Bank. **Publications:** Flashpoint Spratlys, 1995; The Dynamics of Foreign-Policy Decision Making in China, 1997. **Address:** 338 G St. N.E., Washington, DC 20002, U.S.A. **Online address:** luming@sph.com.sg; luming@vocleet.mail.com

LUBAR, David. American, b. 1954. **Genres:** Young adult fiction. **Career:** Creative Computing magazine, editor, 1980-82; has also worked as a video-game designer, programmer, and translator for companies such as GameBoy and Atari, 1982-. **Publications:** (with T. Riley and K. Riley) Computer Controller Cookbook, 1983; (compiler) It's Not a Bug, It's a Feature!: Computer Wit and Wisdom, 1995; The Unwilling Witch (young adult), 1997; The Psychozone: The Witch's Monkey and Other Tales, 1997; The Psychozone: Kidzilla and Other Tales, 1997; The Wavering Werewolf (young adult), 1997; The Vanishing Vampire (young adult), 1997; The Gloomy Ghost (young adult), 1998; Hidden Talents (young adult), 1999; Monster Road (young adult), 1999; The Trouble with Heroes, 2002; Dunk, 2002; Wizards of the Game, 2003. Contributor to anthologies. **Address:** 4695 Oakwood Ln., Nazareth, PA 18064, U.S.A. **Online address:** davidlubar.com

LUBAR, Joel F. American, b. 1938. **Genres:** Biology, Psychology. **Career:** Regional Ed., International Journal of Physiology and Behavior, 1969-88. Associate Ed., Biofeedback and Self-Regulation, since 1990. Professor of Psychology, University of Tennessee, Knoxville, since 1971 (Associate Professor, 1967-71). Assistant Professor, Dept. of Psychology, University of Rochester, New York, 1963-67. **Publications:** Biological Foundations of Behavior, 1969; (with R. L. Isaacson, L. Schmaltz and R. Douglas) A Primer of Physiological Psychology, 1971; First Reader in Physiological Psychology, 1972; Biological Foundations of Behavior, 1974; (with W. Deering) Behavioral Approaches to Neurology, 1981; Physiological Bases of Behaviour, 1982. **Address:** Dept. of Psychology, University of Tennessee, Knoxville, TN 37996, U.S.A.

LÜBBREN, Nina. (born Germany), b. 1962. **Genres:** Cultural/Ethnic topics. **Career:** Anglia Polytechnic University, Cambridge, England, senior lecturer in art history, 1995-. **Publications:** Rural Artists' Colonies in Europe, 1870-1910, 2001; (editor, with David Crouch) Visual Culture and Tourism, 2002. **Address:** Anglia Polytechnic University, East Rd., Cambridge CB1 1PT, England. **Online address:** n.lubbren@apu.ac.uk

LUBIN, Bernard. American, b. 1923. **Genres:** Psychology, Bibliography, Administration/Management, Institutions/Organizations. **Career:** Professor of Psychology, University of Missouri, Kansas City, since 1976 (Chairman of the Dept., 1976-83). Member, Editorial Board, American Journal of Community Psychology, Journal of Community Psychology, and International Journal of Group Psychotherapy. Consultant Reader, Psychological Reports. Professor, 1967-74, and Director of Psychology Training, 1969-74, University of Missouri School of Medicine, Kansas City; Professor and Director of Clinical Training, Dept. of Psychology, University of Houston, 1974-76. **Publications:** (with M. Zuckerman) Multiple Affect Adjective Check List: Manual, 1965, 1986; (with A.W. Lubin) Group Psychotherapy: A Bibliography of the Literature from 1956 through 1964, 1966; (with E.E. Levitt) The Clinical Psychologist: Background, Roles and Functions, 1967; Depression Adjective Check Lists: Manual, 1967, 1994; (with E.E. Levitt) Depression: Concepts, Controversies and Some New Facts, 1975, 1983; (with L.D. Goodstein and A.W. Lubin) Organizational Change Source Book, vols. I and II, 1979; (with W.A. O'Connor) Ecological Approaches to Clinical and Community Psychology, 1983; (with A.W. Lubin) Comprehensive Index to Group Psychotherapy Writings, 1987; (with R. Gist) Psychosocial Aspects of Disaster, 1988; (with R.V. Whitlock) Homeless in America, 1893-1992; (with P.G. Hanson) Answers to Most Frequently Asked Questions about Organization Development, 1995; (with C.D. Wilson, S. Petren, and A. Polk) Research on Group Treatment Methods, 1996. **Address:** Dept. of Psychology, University of Missouri, 5319 Holmes St, Kansas City, MO 64110, U.S.A.

LUCADO, Max (Lee). American, b. 1955. **Genres:** Inspirational/Motivational Literature, Theology/Religion. **Career:** Minister, radio personality, and author of religious nonfiction and fiction; ordained in Church of Christ. Central Church of Christ, Miami, FL, associate minister, 1979-82; Tijunca-lareja de Cristo, Rio de Janeiro, Brazil, missionary, 1983-88; Oak Hills Church of Christ, San Antonio, TX, pulpit minister, 1988-. Lecturer on a daily radio program. **Publications:** NONFICTION: No Wonder They Call Him the Savior, 1986; God Came Near, 1987; Six Hours One Friday, 1989; The Applause of Heaven, 1990, abridged ed., 1993; In the Eye of the Storm, 1991; And the Angels Were Silent, 1992, portions as The Final Week of Jesus, 1994; He Still Moves Stones, 1993; Walking with the Savior, 1993; On the Anvil, 1994; A Gentle Thunder, 1995; In the Grip of Grace, 1996; (with J. Countryman) God's Inspirational Promise Book, 1996; The Great House of God, 1997; Just Like Jesus; When Christ Comes; He Chose the Nails; Traveling Light; A Love Worth Giving, 2002. FICTION: When God Whispers Your Name, 1994; Cosmic Christmas; The Christmas Cross. JUVENILE FICTION: Just in Case You Ever Wonder, 1992; Tell Me the Story, 1992; Tell Me the Secrets, 1993; (with J., A., and S. Lucado) The Children of the King, 1994; (with J., A., and S. Lucado) The Crippled Lamb, 1994; The Song of the King, 1995; Alabaster's Song, 1996; You Are Special; Because I Love You; Jacob's Gift; Just the Way You Are; All You Ever Need; Small Gifts in God's Hands; With You All the Way; You Are Mine; He Chose You; If I Only Had a Green Nose. OTHER: (gen. ed.) The Inspirational Study Bible, 1995. **Address:** Oak Hills Church of Christ, 19595 IH-10 W, San Antonio, TX 78257-9508, U.S.A.

LUCAN, Medlar. See MARTIN, Alex.

LUCAS, Barbara. (Mrs. Bernard Wall). British, b. 1911. **Genres:** Novels, Plays/Screenplays, Theology/Religion, Autobiography/Memoirs. **Publications:** Stars Were Born, 1934; The Trembling of the Sea, 1936; Anna Collett, 1946; Growing Up, 1956; Prelude to a Wedding, 1964; (with B. Wall) Thaw at the Vatican, 1964; More Ado About Nothing, 1969; Widows and Widowers, 1979; Poor Wilfred (radio play), 1984; Rene Hague: A Personal Memoir, 1989. **Address:** Swan Cottage, Rackham, Pulborough, W. Sussex, England.

LUCAS, Celia. British, b. 1938. **Genres:** Children's fiction, Biography. **Career:** Freelance writer. Editorial Assistant, George Rainbird Ltd., London, 1962-65; Art Ed., W. H. Allen Ltd., London, 1965-66; Researcher, 1966-68 and Reporter, 1968-71, Daily Mail, London and Manchester; Partner, 1971-74, and Director, 1974-86, Welsh Border News Agency. **Publications:** Prisoners of Santo Tomas, 1974; Steel Town Cats, 1987; (with I. Skidmore) Glyndwr Country, 1988; Anglesey Rambles, 1989; The Adventures of Marmaduke Purr Cat, 1990; The Terrible Tale of Tiggy Two, 1995; Madoc's Prickly Problem, 2000. **Address:** Aberbraint, Llanfairpwll, Anglesey, North LL61 6PB, Wales.

LUCAS, Craig. American, b. 1951. **Genres:** Plays/Screenplays, Songs/Lyrics and libretti. **Career:** Writer. Actor in stage productions; chorus singer in Broadway musicals. **Publications:** PLAYS: Missing Persons, 1981; Reckless, 1983, screenplay, 1995; Blue Window, 1984, screenplay, 1987; Prelude to a Kiss, 1988, screenplay, 1992; God's Heart, 1997; The Dying Gaul; Savage Light. MUSICALS: Three Postcards, 1986; Marry Me A Little, 1980. SCREENPLAYS: Longtime Companion, 1990. OPERA LIBRETTI: Orpheus in Love, 1993; Breedlove. Author of one-act plays. Contributor to periodicals and anthologies. **Address:** Peter Franklin, William Morris Agency, 1325 Avenue of the Americas, New York, NY 10019, U.S.A.

LUCAS, Eileen. American, b. 1956. **Genres:** Children's non-fiction. **Career:** Writer of juvenile nonfiction books. **Publications:** The Everglades, 1994; The European Conquest, 1995; Trade, 1995; Civil Rights, 1996; The Complete Library of U.S. Presidents: The Eisenhower, Kennedy, Johnson Years, 1997; The Nixon, Ford, Carter Years, 1997; The Reagan, Bush, Clinton Years, 1997; Vincent Van Gogh, 1997; Contemporary Human Rights Activists, 1997; Cracking the Wall, 1997; Elizabeth Dole, 1998; The Eighteenth and Twenty-First Amendments, 1998; The U.S. Postal Service, 1999; Prudence Crandall: Teacher for Equal Rights, 2001; The Aaron Burr Treason Trial, 2003. **Address:** 167 Fontana Ave, PO Box 543, Fontana, WI 53125, U.S.A.

LUCAS, John. British, b. 1937. **Genres:** Poetry, Literary criticism and history, Biography. **Career:** University of Nottingham, former reader in English studies; Loughborough University, former professor of English; Nottingham Trent University, research professor. **Publications:** (with J. Goode and D. Howard) Tradition and Tolerance in 19th Century Fiction, 1966; The Melancholy Man, 1970; About Nottingham, 1971; Chinese Sequence, 1972; A Brief Bestiary, 1972; Arnold Bennett: A Study of His Fiction, 1974; Tim and the Quarry Affair, 1974; Egil's Saga, 1975; The Literature of Change, 1977; The 30's: A Challenge to Orthodoxy, 1978; Romantic to Modern: Essays on Ideas and Culture 1750-1900, 1982; The Days of the Week, 1983; Moderns and Contemporaries, Novelists, Poets, Critics, 1985; (with B. Haynes) The Trent Bridge Battery, 1985; Modern English Poetry: From Hardy to Hughes, 1986; Studying Grosz on the Bus, 1989; England and Englishness: Poetry and Nationhood 1688-1900, 1989; Charles Dickens: The Major Novels, 1992; Flying to Romania, 1992; John Clare, 1994; One for the Piano, 1997; The Radical Twenties: Aspects of Writing, Politics & Culture, 1997; William Blake, 1998; (with J. Goodridge) Selected Poems of Robert Bloomfield, 1999; On the Track, 2000; The Good That We Do, 2001; Ivor Gurney, 2001; Starting to Explain: Essays on Poetry, 2002; A World Perhaps: New & Selected Poems, 2002; The Long and the Short of It, 2004. EDITOR: Poems of George Crabbe, 1967; Jane Austen's Mansfield Park, 1971; Literature and Politics in the 19th Century, 1971; W.H. Mallock's The New Republic, 1974; Poems of G.S. Fraser, 1981; Oliver Goldsmith, 1988; Writing and Radicalism, 1996. **Address:** 19 Devonshire Ave, Beeston, Nottingham, England.

LUCAS, John A. American, b. 1927. **Genres:** Sports/Fitness. **Career:** Track and field coach at high schools, preparatory schools, and universities, 1949-72; Pennsylvania State University, University Park, senior research and teaching professor of sport history, 1961-95. International Olympic Committee Consultant, member of subcommittees and official Olympic lecturer. **Publications:** (with R. Smith) Saga of American Sports, 1977; The Modern Olympic Games, 1980; Future of the Olympic Games, 1992. Contributor to journals in the United States and abroad. **Address:** 645 Berkshire Dr., State College, PA 16803, U.S.A.

LUCAS, John Randolph. British, b. 1929. **Genres:** Philosophy. **Career:** Fellow, Merton College, Oxford University, 1960-96 (Jr. Research Fellow, 1953-56). Fellow, Corpus Christi College, Cambridge, 1956-59; member, Archbishop's Commission on Christian Doctrine, 1967-72. Fellow of the British Academy, 1988. **Publications:** The Principles of Politics, 1966; The Concept of Probability, 1970; The Freedom of the Will, 1970; (co-author) The Nature of Mind, 1972; A Treatise on Time and Space, 1973; (co-author) The Development of Mind, 1974; Democracy and Participation, 1976; Freedom and Grace, 1976; On Justice, 1980; Space, Time and Causality, 1985; The Future, 1989; (co-author) Space, Time and Electromagnetism, 1990; Responsibility, 1993; (co-author) Ethical Economics, 1997; The Conceptual Roots of Mathematics, 1999; (co-author) An Engagement with Plato's Republic, 2003. **Address:** Lambrook House, East Lambrook, Somerset TA13 5HW, England. **Online address:** john.lucas@merton.ox.ac.uk; users.ox.ac.uk/~jrlucas

LUCASHENKO, Melissa. Australian, b. 1967. **Genres:** Documentaries/Reportage. **Career:** Foundation for Aboriginal and Islander Research Action, Brisbane, Australia, newspaper editor. Yugambeh Corporation for Culture, member. **Publications:** Steam Pigs, 1997; Killing Darcy, 1998; The Orphan, in press. **Address:** c/o University of Queensland Press, PO Box 42, St. Lucia, QLD 4076, Australia. **Online address:** supergin27@bigpond.com.au

LUCHETTI, Cathy. American. **Genres:** Food and Wine. **Career:** Writer. **Publications:** The Hot Flash Cookbook: Delicious Recipes for Health and WellBeing through Menopause, 1997. **Address:** 6120 Lawton St., Oakland, CA 94618, U.S.A.

LUCIE-SMITH, (John) Edward (McKenzie). Also writes as Peter Kershaw. British (born Jamaica), b. 1933. **Genres:** Poetry, Art/Art history, Photography, Translations, Novellas/Short stories. **Career:** Freelance author, journalist, and broadcasting. Education Officer, RAF, 1954-56; Co-Founder, Turret Books, London, 1965. **Publications:** (Poems), 1954; A Tropical Childhood and Other Poems, 1961; (with J. Clemo and G. MacBeth) Penguin Modern Poets 6, 1964; Confessions and Histories, 1964; Fir-Tree Song, 1965; Jazz for the NUF, 1965; A Game of French and English, 1965; Three Experiments, 1965; Mystery in the Universe: Notes on an Interview with Allen Ginsberg, 1965; Gallipoli-Fifty Years After (poetry), 1966; Cloud Sun Fountain Statue, 1966; Op Art, 1966; What Is a Painting?, 1966; Silence, 1967; Heureux Qui, Comme Ulysse…, 1967; Borrowed Emblems, 1967; Towards Silence, 1968; Teeth and Bones, 1968; Six Kinds of Creature, 1968; Thinking about Art: Critical Essays, 1968; (as Peter Kershaw) A Beginner's Guide to Auctions, 1968; Snow Poem, 1969; Egyptian Ode, 1969; Movements in Art since 1945 (in U.S. as Late Modern: The Visual Arts since 1945), 1969; Six More Beasts, 1970; Lovers, 1970; The Rhino, 1971; A Girl Surveyed, 1971; The Yak, The Polar Bear, The Dodo, The Goldfish, The Dinosaur, The Parrot, 1971; A Concise History of French Painting, 1971; Eroticism in Western Art, 1972; Symbolist Art, 1972; The First London Catalogue: All the Appurtenances of a Civilised, Amusing and Comfortable Life, 1974; The Well-Wishers, 1974; The Invented Eye: Masterpieces of Photography, 1839-1914, 1975; Joan of Arc, 1976; (with C. Dars) How the Rich Lived, 1976; (with C. Dars) Work and Struggle, 1977; Art Today, 1977; Fantin-Latour, 1977; The Dark Pageant (novel), 1977; Outcasts of the Sea, 1978; A Concise History of French Painting 1978; Super-Realism, 1979; Furniture: A Concise History, 1979; Cultural Calendar of the Twentieth Century, 1979; The Story of Craft, 1981; The Body, 1981; Bertie and the Big Red Ball (for children), 1982; A History of Industrial Design, 1983; Art Terms: An Illustrated Dictionary, 1984; Beasts with Bad Morals (poetry), 1984; Art of the 1930's, 1985; Lives of the Great 20th Century Artists, 1986; Sculpture since 1945, 1987; Obsert Lancaster, 1988; (co-author) The New British Painting, 1988; Art in the 1980s, 1990; Art Deco Painting, 1990; Fletcher Benton, 1990; Jean Rustin, 1990; Harry Holland, 1991; Wendy Taylor, 1992; Andres Nagel, 1992; Alexander, 1992; Art and Civilization, 1992; 20th Century Latin American Art, 1993; Race, Sex and Gender in Contemporary Art, 1994; Elisabeth Frink: A Portrait, 1994; John Kirby, 1994; American Realism, 1994; Visual Arts in the 20th Century, 1996; The Art of Albert Paley, 1996; Lin Emery, 1996; Art Erotica, 1997; Adam, 1998; Zoo, 1998; Women in Art, 1999; Judy Chicago, 2000. EDITOR: Rubens, 1961; Raphael, 1961; (with P. Hobsbaum) A Group Anthology, 1963; The Penguin Book of Elizabethan Verse, 1965; The Liverpool Scene, 1967; A Choice of Browning's Verse, 1967; The Penguin Book of Satirical Verse, 1967; Holding Your Eight Hands: A Book of Science Fiction Verse, 1969; (with P. White) Art in Britain, 1969-1970, 1970; British Poetry since 1945, 1970; (with S. Watson-Taylor) French Poetry Today: A Bi-Lingual Anthology, 1971; Primer of Experimental Poetry, 1870-1922, 1971; Masterpieces from the Pompidou Centre, 1983; The Faber Book of Art Anecdotes, 1992. TRANSLATOR: Manet, by R. Rey, 1962; Jonah: Selected Poems of Jean-Paul de Dadelsen, 1967; (with P. Claudel) Five Great Odes, 1970; The Muses, by P. Claudel, 1967. **Address:** c/o Rogers, Coleridge and White, 20 Powis Mews, London W11, England.

LUCIUK, Lubomyr Y(aroslav). Canadian, b. 1953. **Genres:** Area studies, Geography, History. **Career:** Royal Ontario Museum, summer field assistant, 1967-71; Ontario Ministry of Natural Resources, researcher, 1972-77; University of Alberta, Edmonton, research assistant in geography, 1979-80, research assistant in oral history at Canadian Institute of Ukrainian Studies, 1982-84; University of Toronto, ON, postdoctoral fellow in geography, 1984-88; Queen's University, Kingston, ON, assistant professor of geography, 1988-90, became adjunct professor; Royal Military College of Canada, Kingston, Dept of Politics and Economics, professor. Ukrainian Canadian Civil Liberties Association, director of research. **Publications:** Ukrainians in the Making, 1980; (with B.S. Kordan) A Delicate and Difficult Question, 1986; (with B.S. Kordan) Anglo-American Perspectives on the Ukrainian Question, 1938-1951, 1987; (with M. Carynnyk and B.S. Kordan) The Foreign Office and the Famine, 1988; A Time for Atonement, 1988; (with B.S. Kordan and G. J. Matthews) Creating a Landscape: A Geography of Ukrainians in Canada, 1989; (with A. Chyczij) Memorial, 1989; (with M. Carrynnyk) Between Two Worlds: The Memoirs of Stanley Frolick, 1990; Welcome to Absurdistan, 1994; (with R. Sorobey) Konowal, 1995; Searching for Place, 2000; In Fear of the Barbed Wire Fence, 2002. EDITOR: (and author of intro.) Heroes of Their Day: The Reminiscences of Bohdan Panchuk, 1983; (with N. Hillmer and B.S. Kordan) On Guard For, 1988; (with S.M. Hryniuk) Canada's Ukrainians, 1991; Righting and Injustice, 1994. **Address:** Dept of Politics and Economics, Royal Military College of Canada, Kingston, ON, Canada K7K 7B4.

LUCKETT, Dave. Australian, b. 1951. **Genres:** Children's fiction. **Career:** Teacher at secondary schools in Western Australia, 1974-75; federal public servant, Perth, Australia, 1977-97. **Publications:** The Adventures of Addam, 1995; Night Hunters, 1995; The Best Batsman in the World, 1996; The Wizard and Me, 1996; The Last Eleven, 1997; A Dark Winter, 1998; A Dark Journey, 1999. **Address:** 69 Federal St., Tuart Hill, WA 6060, Australia.

LUDBROOK, John. Australian (born New Zealand), b. 1929. **Genres:** Medicine/Health. **Career:** Sr. Principal Research Fellow, University of Melbourne, since 1989. Professor Emeritus of Surgery, University of Adelaide, since 1980 (Professor, 1969-80). Sr. Lecturer in Surgery, University of Otago, 1959-63; Professor of Surgery, University of New South Wales, 1964-68; Associate Director, Baker Medical Research Institute, Melbourne, 1981-88. **Publications:** (with G. J. Fraenkel and H. A. F. Dudley) Guide to House Surgeons, 8th ed. 1961-85; (with R. G. Elmslie) Introduction to Surgery: 100 Topics, 1971-77; Analysis of the Venous System, 1972; (with V. C. Marshall) Clinical Science for Surgeons, 1988. **Address:** 349 Canning St, North Carlton, VIC 3054, Australia. **Online address:** ludbrook@unimelb.edu.au

LUDLOW, Howard Thomas. American, b. 1921. **Genres:** Administration/Management, Industrial relations. **Career:** Professor Emeritus of Industrial Relations, Seton Hall University, South Orange, New Jersey, since 1990 (Instructor, 1949-52; Assistant Professor, 1952-56; Associate Professor, 1956-58; Professor, 1958-90). **Publications:** Business Management, 1965; Labor Economics, 1966. **Address:** 32135 River Cove Dr, Orange Beach, AL 36561, U.S.A.

LUDWICKSON, John. American, b. 1948. **Genres:** Archaeology/Antiquities. **Career:** North Dakota Historical Society, Bismarck, archaeologist, 1976-77; Nebraska State Historical Society, Lincoln, archaeologist, 1978-. **Publications:** (with G.H. Smith) Fort Manuel: The Archaeology of an Upper Missouri Trading Post of 1812-1813, 1981; (with J. O'Shea) Archaeology and Ethnohistory of the Omaha Indians, 1992.

LUDWIG, Jack. Canadian, b. 1922. **Genres:** Novels, Novellas/Short stories, Plays/Screenplays, Literary criticism and history. **Career:** State University of New York at Stony Brook, professor of English, 1961-. Stony Brook Poetry Center, director, 1993-94. Member of faculty, Williams College, Williamstown, MA, 1949-53; Bard College, Annandale-on-Hudson, NY, 1953-58, and University of Minnesota, Minneapolis, 1958-61; Harvard University International Seminar, Humanities Group, chairman, 1963-66; University of Toronto, ON, Canada, writer-in-residence, 1968-69; Banff Centre, Banff, AB, Canada, writer-in-residence, 1974. **Publications:** (ed. with R. Poirier) Stories British and American, 1953; (ed. with S. Bellow and K. Botsford) The Noble Savage, 1960-62; Recent American Novelists, 1962; Confusions (novel), 1963, 1965; Above Ground (novel), 1968, 1974; Bustout (play), 1969; Ubu Rex (play), 1970; (ed. with A. Wainwright) Soundings: New Canadian Poets, 1970; Hockey Night in Moscow, 1972; A Woman of Her Age (novel), 1973; the Great Hockey Thaw, 1974; Homage to Zolotova (poetry), 1974; Games of Fear and Winning, 1976; The Great American Spectaculars, 1976; Five Ring Circus, 1977. **Address:** PO Box 112, Shoreham, NY 11786-0112, U.S.A. **Online address:** yanklud@yahoo.com

LUDWIKOWSKI, Rett R. American (born Poland), b. 1943. **Genres:** Law, Politics/Government. **Career:** Jagiellonian University, Cracow, Poland, senior lecturer in political science, 1967-71; adjunct professor, 1971-76, assistant professor of politics, 1976-81, associate professor of law, 1981, chairman, Div. of Business, 1976-80, Dept of Modern Political Movements and Ideas, 1976-82, and Div. of Law, 1980-81; Marguerite Wilbur Foundation, Santa Barbara, CA, senior fellow, 1981-82; Hoover Institution on War, Revolution, and Peace, Stanford, CA, visiting scholar, 1983; Catholic University of America, Washington, DC, visiting professor, 1984-85, professor of law, 1985-, director of Institute of Comparative and International Law, 1987. Visiting professor at Alfred University and Elizabethtown College, both 1983; Max-Planck-Institut fuer auslandisches und internationales Privatrecht, visiting scholar, 1990. **Publications:** The Conservatism of the Kingdom of Poland during the Inter-Insurrectional Period, 1976; Black Radicalism in the United States, 1976; (with J. Wolenski) John Stuart Mill, 1979; Essays on Galician Political Movements, 1848-1892, 1980; Polish Political Culture (monograph), 1980; Main Currents of Polish Political Thought, 1815-1890, 1982; Will the Crisis of Communism Begin in Poland? (monograph), 1983; The Crisis of Communism, 1986; Continuity and Change in Poland, 1991; (ed. with K. Thompson) Constitutionalism and Human Rights, 1991; America and the World of Business, 1991; I-God (in Polish), 1992; (with W. Fox) The Beginning of the Constitutional Era, 1993; International Trade and Business Regulations, Vol. 1 (in Polish), 1996, (ed. and co-author) International Trade and Business Transactions, Vol. 2, 1998;

Constitution-Making in the Region of Former Soviet Dominance, 1996; Comparative Constitutional Law, 2002; Comparative Human Rights nad Fundamental Freedoms, Vol. 1, 2002. Contributor to law and political studies journals. **Address:** Law School, Catholic University of America, Washington, DC 20064, U.S.A. **Online address:** Ludwikowski@law.edu

LUEBBERMANN, Mimi. American (born Venezuela), b. 1945. **Genres:** Horticulture, How-to books. **Career:** Writer. Tasting of Summer Produce, development director, 1988-90; Organic Farming Research Foundation, coordinator of Celebration of the Organic Harvest, 1992; Sonoma County Chefs' Tasting, coordinator, 1998. **Publications:** (with G. Brennan) Beautiful Bulbs, 1993; (with G. Brennan) Little Herb Gardens, 1993; Paydirt: Growing Specialty Vegetables and Herbs for Serious Cash, 1994, rev. ed., 1997; Miscarriage Grief, 1994; Terrific Tomatoes, 1994; Climbing Vines, 1995; Easy Orchids, 1996; Salad Gardens, 1996; The Williams-Sonoma Wedding Planner, 1996; The Country Baker's Book of Baking with Herbs, 1996; Heirloom Gardens, 1997; Cactus and Succulent Gardens, 1997; Little Potted Gardens, 1998; Homegrown Fruit, 1998; Shade Gardens, 1999. EDITOR: (with J. Bennett) Where the Heart Is: A Celebration of Home, 1995; (contrib) Smith and Hawken's Book of Outdoor Gardening, 1997. **Address:** Windrush Farm, 2263 Chileno Valley Rd., Petaluma, CA 94952, U.S.A.

LUEBKE, Frederick Carl. American, b. 1927. **Genres:** History. **Career:** University of Nebraska, Lincoln, associate professor 1968-72, professor, 1972-87, director, Center for Great Plains Studies, 1983-88, Charles Mach Distinguished Professor of History, 1987-94, emeritus, 1994-. **Publications:** Immigrants and Politics, 1969; Bonds of Loyalty: German Americans and World War I, 1974; Germans in Brazil: A Comparative History of Cultural Conflict During World War I, 1987; Germans in the New World: Essays in the History of Immigration, 1990; A Harmony of the Arts: The Nebraska State Capitol, 1990; Nebraska: An Illustrated History, 1995. EDITOR: Ethnic Voters and the Election of Lincoln, 1971; The Great Plains: Environment and Culture, 1979; Ethnicity on the Great Plains, 1980; Vision and Refuge: Essays on the Literature of the Great Plains, 1981; (co) Mapping the North American Plains, 1987; European Immigrants in the American West, 1998. **Address:** 4650 Crescent Ridge Ln, Eugene, OR 97405-7036, U.S.A. **Online address:** fcluebke@alltel.net

LUELLEN, Valentina. *See* **POLLEY, Judith Anne.**

LUFT, Lya Fett. Brazilian, b. 1938. **Genres:** Poetry, Essays. **Career:** Translator, poet, essayist, novelist, teacher, 1964-. **Publications:** POETRY AND ESSAYS: Cancoes de limiar, 1964; Flauta doce: Tema e variacoes, 1972; Materia do cotidiano, 1978; Mulher no palco, 1984; O lado fatal, 1988. NOVELS: As parceiras, 1980; A asa esquerda do anjo, 1981; Reuniad do familia, 1982; O quarto fechado, 1984, trans. by C.C. McClendon and B.J. Craige as The Island of the Dead, 1986; Exilio, 1987, trans. by G. Pontiero as The Red House, 1994. Translator of German- and English-language works of fiction into Portuguese. **Address:** c/o Carcanet Press, Fourth Floor, Conavon Ct., Blackfriars St., Manchester M3 5BQ, England.

LUGGER, Phyllis M. American, b. 1954. **Genres:** Astronomy. **Career:** Northwestern University, Evanston, IL, postdoctoral fellow in physics and astronomy, 1981-82; University of Illinois at Urbana-Champaign, Urbana, visiting research associate in physics and astronomy, 1982-83; University of Missouri-Columbia, assistant professor of physics and astronomy, 1983-84; Indiana University-Bloomington, assistant professor, 1984-88, associate professor, 1988-94, professor of astronomy, 1995-. **Publications:** (ed. and contrib.) Asteroids to Quasars: A Symposium Honouring William Liller, 1991. Work represented in anthologies. Contributor to journals. **Address:** Department of Astronomy, Indiana University-Bloomington, Bloomington, IN 47405, U.S.A.

LUHRMANN, T(anya) M(arie). American, b. 1959. **Genres:** Anthropology/Ethnology. **Career:** Cambridge University, Cambridge, England, resident fellow in Christ's College, 1985-89; University of California, San Diego, La Jolla, asst professor, 1989-92, associate professor, 1992-98, professor of anthropology, 1998-2000; University of Chicago, professor, 2000-. Frequent lecturer at conferences and seminars. **Publications:** Persuasions of the Witch's Craft: Ritual Magic in Contemporary England, 1989; The Good Parsi: The Fate of a Postcolonial Indian Elite; Of Two Minds: The Growing Disorder in American Society, 2000. **Address:** Committee on Human Development, 5730 S Woodlawn Ave, Chicago, IL 60637, U.S.A. **Online address:** tluhrmann@midway.uchicago.edu

LUIS, William. American, b. 1948. **Genres:** Literary criticism and history. **Career:** Dartmouth College, Hanover, NH, lecturer, 1979-80, assistant professor, 1980-85, associate professor, 1985-88; State University of New York at Binghamton, visiting associate professor, 1988-89, associate professor, 1989-91, acting director of Latin American and Caribbean Area Studies Program, 1988-89, director, 1989-90; Vanderbilt University, Nashville, TN, member of Latin American and Iberian Studies Program, 1991-, associate professor, 1991-96, professor, 1996-; Washington University, St. Louis, MO, visiting associate professor, 1988; Yale University, visiting professor, 1998. **Publications:** Literary Bondage: Slavery in Cuban Narrative, 1990; Dance between Two Cultures: Latino-Caribbean Literature Written in the United States, 1997; Culture and Customs of Cuba, 2001; Lunes de Revolucion: Literatura y cultura en los primeros anos de la Revolucion Cubana, 2003. EDITOR: (with E. Desnoes) Los Dispositivos en la Flor, 1981; (and contrib) Voices from Under: Black Narrative in Latin America and the Caribbean, 1984; (with J. Rodriguez-Luis, and contrib) Translating Latin America: Culture as Text, 1991; Dictionary of Literary Biography, Volume 113: Modern Latin American Fiction Writers, First Series, 1992; (with A. Gonzalez) Dictionary of Literary Biography, Volume 145: Modern Latin American Fiction Writers, Second Series, 1994. Contributor to books. Contributor of articles and reviews to professional journals. **Address:** Department of Spanish and Portuguese, 302 Furman Hall, Vanderbilt University, Nashville, TN 37235, U.S.A. **Online address:** William.Luis@vanderbilt.edu

LUKACS, John (Adalbert). American (born Hungary), b. 1924. **Genres:** History. **Career:** Retired professor of history. **Publications:** The Great Powers and Eastern Europe, 1953; (ed. and trans.) European Revolution and Correspondence with Gobineau, by Alexis de Tocqueville, 1959; A History of the Cold War, 1961 (3rd ed. as A New History of the Cold War, 1966); Decline and Rise of Europe, 1965; Historical Consciousness, 1968, 1985, 1994; The Passing of the Modern Age, 1970; The Last European War, 1939-1961, 1976; 1945: Year Zero, 1978; Philadelphia: Patricians and Philistines, 1900-1950, 1981; Outgrowing Democracy: A History of the United States in the Twentieth Century, 1984; Immigration and Migration, 1986; Confessions of an Original Sinner, 1989; Budapest, 1990: A Historical Portrait of a City and Its Culture, 1988; The Duel: May 10-July 31, 1994. The Struggle between Churchill and Hitler, 1991; The End of the 20th Century and the End of the Modern Age, 1993; Destinations Past, 1994; George F. Kennan and the Origins of Containment 1944-46: The Kennan-Lukacs Correspondence, 1997; The Hitter of History, 1997; A Thread of Years, 1998; Four Days in London, May 1940, 1999; A Student's Guide to the Study of History, 2000; Churchill, 2002. **Address:** 129 Valley Park Rd, Phoenixville, PA 19460, U.S.A.

LUKER, Nicholas (John Lydgate). British, b. 1945. **Genres:** Literary criticism and history, Translations. **Career:** University of Nottingham, England, lecturer, 1970-88, senior lecturer in Russian, 1988-. Visiting lecturer: Victoria University of Wellington, New Zealand, 1976, 1996; Dartmouth College, George Washington University, and Luther College, 1978, 1985, University of Auckland, 1991, 1993, 1996, 1998, 2000, 2002, 2004; University of Otago, New Zealand, 1993, 1996, 1998, 2000; University of Canterbury, Christchurch, 1998, 2000. Visiting fellow: Department of Russian, University of Otago, Dunedin, New Zealand, 1991; Victoria University of Wellington, 1991. **Publications:** Alexander Grin, 1973; (trans. with B. Scherr) A. Grin, The Seeker of Adventure (selected stories), 1978; A. I. Kuprin, 1978; The Forgotten Visionary, 1982; In Defence of a Reputation: Essays on the Early Prose of Mikhail Artsybashev, 1990. EDITOR: (trans., and author of intro.) An Anthology of Russian Neo-Realism: The Znanie School of Maxim Gorky, 1982; (and author of intro.) Fifty Years On: Gorky and His Time (critical essays), 1987; (trans., and author of intro.) Alexander Grin: Selected Short Stories, 1987; (trans., and author of intro.) From Furmanov to Sholokhov: An Anthology of the Classics of Socialist Realism, 1988; (and contrib.) The Russian Short Story, 1900-1917 (critical essays), 1991; (co-trans., and author of intro.) Y. Miloslavsky, Urban Romances (stories), 1994; (and contrib.) After the Watershed, Russian Prose, 1917-1927 (critical essays), 1996; (and contrib.) Out of the Shadows (critical essays), 2003. Contributor to books.

LUKES, Steven M. British, b. 1941. **Genres:** Philosophy, Politics/Government, Sociology. **Career:** European University Institute, Florence, professor of social and political theory, 1988-. Archives Europaeennes de Sociologie, editorial board, member; International Sociological Association, Research Committee on the History of Sociology, vice-president; Nuffield College, Oxford, research fellow, 1964-66; Balliol College, Oxford, fellow and tutor in sociology and politics, 1966-88. **Publications:** Emile Durkheim, His Life and Work, an Historical and Critical Study, 1973; Individualism, 1973; Power: A Radical View, 1974; Essays in Social Theory, 1977; (with I. Galnoor) No Laughing Matter, 1985; Marxism and Morality, 1985; Moral Conflicts and Politics, 1991; The Curious Enlightenment of Professor Carilat, 1995; Multicultural Questions, 1999. CO-EDITOR: (with A. Arblaster) The

Good Society-A Book of Readings, 1970; Durkheim and the Law, 1984. Contributor to books. **Address:** New York University, 269 Mercer Street, 439, NYU mail code 0831, New York, NY 10003, U.S.A. **Online address:** steven.lukes@nyu.edu

LUKKEN, Miriam. (born United States), b. 1960. **Genres:** Adult nonfiction. **Career:** Worked as a schoolteacher, 1983-92; writer, 1992-. Troup County Humane Society, past president; LaGrange Junior Service League, member. **Publications:** Read This Book before Your Child Starts School, 1994; (editor) Southern Born and Bread (cookbook), 1996; Mrs. Dunwoody's Excellent Instructions for Homekeeping, 2003. **Address:** Joann Davis, Redbridge Inc, 700 Washington St., New York, NY 10014, U.S.A. **Online address:** mimilukken@char ter.net

LUMPKIN, Aaron. American, b. 1951. **Genres:** How-to books. **Career:** Department of Veterans Affairs, Nashville, TN, program supporter at veterans' hospital, 1985-. Motivational speaker. **Publications:** You Can Be Positive, Confident, and Courageous, 20021; Becoming All That You Are Capable of Being (audio cassette), 2001. **Address:** 1020 Preston Dr., Nashville, TN 37206, U.S.A. **Online address:** jaaronlump@aol.com

LUMPKIN, Betty S(tewart). American, b. 1934. **Genres:** Librarianship, Education. **Career:** Elementary schoolteacher in Chattanooga, TN, 1966-67; junior high school English teacher and curriculum coordinator in Chattanooga, 1967-74; middle school librarian in Ooltewah, TN, 1974-75; substitute teacher at public schools in Simsbury, CT, 1975-79; Ooltewah High School, Ooltewah, head librarian and head of library department, 1979-. **Publications:** (with B.H. Sorrow) CD-ROM for Librarians and Educators, 1993. **Address:** P.O. Box 659, Harrison, TN 37341, U.S.A.

LUMSDEN, Linda J. American, b. 1953. **Genres:** History. **Career:** Western Kentucky University, Bowling Green, associate professor of journalism, 1996-. **Publications:** Rampant Women: Suffragists and the Right of Assembly, 1997; The Inez: The Life and Times of Inez Milholland, 2004. **Address:** School of Journalism and Broadcasting, Western Kentucky University, Bowling Green, KY 42104, U.S.A. **Online address:** linda.lumsden@wku.edu

LUNAN, Duncan. British, b. 1945. **Genres:** Science fiction/Fantasy, Air/Space topics, Astronomy. **Career:** Full-time writer. Association in Scotland to Research into Astronautics (ASTRA), treasurer, 1965-66, 1977-78, 1990-91, 1997-, president, 1966-72, 1978-85, 1991-97, vice-president, 1972-76, secretary, 1985-89; Glasgow SF Circle, chairman, 1969-75, co-chairman, 1986-92; Glasgow Herald, science fiction critic, 1971-85; European Space Association, vice-president, 1977-79; Glasgow Parks Dept. Astronomy Project, manager, 1978-79; Airdrie Observatory, assistant curator, 1987-97, 2002-; tutor in English literature & language, international correspondence schools, 1995-. **Publications:** Man and the Stars, 1974; New Worlds for Old, 1979; Man and the Planets, 1983; (ed.) Starfield, Science Fiction by Scottish Writers, 1989. Contributor of short stories and articles to books and periodicals. **Address:** Flat 65, Dalriada House, 56 Blythswood Ct, Anderston, Glasgow G2 7PE, Scotland. **Online address:** astra@dlunan.freeserve.co.uk

LUND, Gerald N. American, b. 1939. **Genres:** Novels, Romance/Historical, Theology/Religion. **Career:** Church of Jesus Christ of Latter-day Saints, Salt Lake City, Utah, Church Education System, zone administrator, retired (instructor, curriculum writer and director, 1965-99). **Publications:** The Coming of the Lord, 1971; This Is Your World, 1973; One in Thine Hand, 1982; The Alliance, 1983; Leverage Point, 1985; The Freedom Factor, 1987; The Work and the Glory (series): vol. 1, 1990, vol. 2, 1991, vol. 3, 1992, vol. 4, 1993, vol. 5, 1994, vol. 6, 1995, vol. 7, 1996, vol. 8, 1997, vol. 9, 1998; Jesus Christ: Key to the Plan of Salvation, 1991; Fire of the Covenant, 1999; Kingdom and the Crown, vol. 1, 2000, vol. 2, 2001, vol. 3, 2002. **Address:** c/o LDS Church, 50 E North Temple St, Salt Lake City, UT 84150, U.S.A.

LUND, Michael. American, b. 1945. **Genres:** Novels, Literary criticism and history. **Career:** Longwood College, Farmville, VA, instructor, 1974-76, assistant professor, 1976-83, associate professor, 1983-90, professor of English, 1990-. **Publications:** Reading Thackeray, 1988; (with L.K. Hughes) The Victorian Serial, 1991; America's Continuing Story: An Introduction to Serial Fiction, 1850-1900, 1993; (with L.K. Hughes) Victorian Publishing and Mrs. Gaskell's Work, 1999; Growing Up on Route 66 (novel), 2000. Work represented in anthologies. Contributor of articles and reviews to academic journals. **Address:** Department of English, Longwood College, Farmville, VA 23909, U.S.A. **Online address:** mlund@longwood.lwc.edu

LUNDBERG, George D. American, b. 1933. **Genres:** Medicine/Health. **Career:** Pathologist, editor, and author. Chief pathologist at a teaching hospital, El Paso, TX; Los Angeles County/University of Southern California Medical Center, Los Angeles, professor of pathology and associate director of laboratories for ten years; University of California, Davis, professor and chair of pathology for five years; American Medical Association, Chicago, IL, editor of Journal of the American Medical Association, editor-in-chief of Scientific Information and Multimedia Group, 1982-99; Medscape (online medical information), founder and editor-in-chief of Medscape General Medicine, 1999-; emeritus editor-in-chief, 2002-; special advisor to CEO and chair, WebMD, 2002-; CBS HealthWatch.com, founder and editor-in-chief. Adjunct professor at Northwestern University, Chicago, IL, and Harvard School of Public Health, Boston, MA. **Publications:** (with J. Stacey) Severed Trust: Why American Medicine Hasn't Been Fixed, 2001. EDITOR: (and contrib) Managing the Patient-focused Laboratory, 1975; (with B.H. Woolley) Pathology for the Practicing Pharmacist, 1976; The Professional and Community Role of the Pathologist in Alcohol Abuse, 1976; Using the Clinical Laboratory in Medical Decision-making, 1983; (with H.S. Meyer) Fifty-one Landmark Articles in Medicine: The JAMA Centennial Series, 1985; (with H.M. Cole) AIDS, from the Beginning, 1986. **Address:** c/o WebMD Medscape Health Network, 224 W 30th St, New York, NY 10001-5399, U.S.A. **Online address:** glundberg@webmd.net

LUNDE, David (Eric). American, b. 1941. **Genres:** Poetry, Literary criticism and history, Translations. **Career:** State University of New York College at Fredonia, instructor, 1967-69, assistant professor, 1969-72, associate professor, 1972-78, professor of English, 1978-2001, professor emeritus, 2001-. Drama and Theatre, managing editor, 1968-71; Basilisk Press, editor and publisher, 1970-85. **Publications:** POETRY: Sludge Gulper 1, 1971; Calibrations, 1981; Blues for Port City (science fiction poems), 1995; Heart Transplants & Other Misappropriations, 1996; Nightfishing in Great Sky River, 1999. **Address:** 2480 13th St, North Bend, OR 97459, U.S.A. **Online address:** davelunde@prodigy.net

LUNDEBERG, Philip (Karl). American, b. 1923. **Genres:** History, Bibliography. **Career:** Curator Emeritus of Naval History, National Museum of American History, Smithsonian Institution, Washington, DC, 1984- (Associate Curator, 1959-61; curator, 1961-84). Assistant to the Historian of U.S. Naval Operations in World War II, Division of Naval History, U.S. Navy Dept., 1950-53; Assistant Professor of History, St. Olaf College, Northfield, Minnesota, 1953-55, and U.S. Naval Academy, Annapolis, MD, 1955-59. Vice President, 1968-71, and President, 1971-73, American Military Institute; Chairman, International Congress of Maritime Museums, 1972-73; Chairman, Council of American Maritime Museums, 1974-76; Vice-President, 1974-79, and President, 1980-83, U.S. Commission on Military History; Secretary, International Committee on Museum Security, 1975-79. **Publications:** American Anti-Submarine Operations in the Atlantic, May 1943-May 1945 (dissertation, 1954), 1998; (co-author) Sea Power, 1960, 1981; The Continental Gunboat "Philadelphia," 1966, 1995; (ed.) Bibliographie de l'Histoire des Grandes Routes Maritimes: Etats-Unis d'Amerique, 1971; Samuel Colt's Submarine Battery, 1974. **Address:** Armed Forces History Collections, National Museum of American History, Smithsonian Institution, Washington, DC 20560, U.S.A.

LUNDESTAD, Geir. Norwegian, b. 1945. **Genres:** Politics/Government. **Career:** University of Oslo, history department, research fellow, 1970-73; University of Tromsø, associate professor of history, 1974-79, professor of American civilization, 1979-88, professor of history, 1988-90; director of Norwegian Nobel Institute and secretary of the Norwegian Nobel Committee, 1990-; adjunct professor of international history, University of Oslo, 1991-. Visiting scholar, Center for International Affairs, Harvard University, 1983; frequent commentator on Norwegian television and radio; head of a committee to reorganize the foreign policy institutes in the Oslo area, 1993-94. Member of the advisory council for Arms Control and Disarmament, Norwegian Foreign Office, 1986-; member of the Norwegian Defense Commission, 1990-92. **Publications:** The American Non-Policy towards Eastern Europe, 1943-1947, 1975; America, Scandinavia, and the Cold War, 1945-1949, 1980; East, West, North, South: Major Trends in International Politics since 1945, 1987, 4th ed, 1999; The American "Empire" and Other Studies of U.S. Foreign Policy in Comparative Perspective, 1991; "Empire" by Integration: The United States and European Integration, 1945-1997, 1998; EDITOR: (with O.A. Westad) Beyond the Cold War: New Dimensions in International Relations, 1993; The Fall of Great Powers, Peace, Stability, and Legitimacy, 1994; No End to Alliance: The United States and Western Europe: Past, Present, and Future, 1998. Contributor to English-language anthologies and periodicals. Author of books and articles in Norwegian on Norwegian history and foreign policy after 1945. **Address:** Norwegian Nobel Institute, Drammensun. 19, 0255 Oslo, Norway. **Online address:** gl@nobel.no

LUNDMAN, Richard J. American, b. 1944. **Genres:** Sociology. **Career:** University of Delaware, Newark, assistant professor of sociology, 1972-74; Ohio State University, Columbus, assistant professor, 1975-77, associate professor, 1978-83, professor of sociology, 1984-, chairperson of graduate studies, 1985-89. **Publications:** (ed. with M.D. Ermann) Corporate and Governmental Deviance: Problems of Organizational Behavior in Contemporary Society, 1978, 6th ed., 2002; Police and Policing, 1980; (ed. and contrib.) Police Behavior: A Sociological Perspective, 1980; (with Ermann) Corporate Deviance, 1982; Prevention and Control of Juvenile Delinquency, 1984, 3rd ed., 2001. **Address:** Department of Sociology, Ohio State University, 388 Bricker Hall, 190 N Oval Mall, Columbus, OH 43210, U.S.A. **Online address:** lundman.1@osu.edu

LUNDSTROM, John B(ernard). American, b. 1948. **Genres:** History, Military/Defense/Arms control. **Career:** Milwaukee Public Museum, Milwaukee, WI, curator of history, 1974-86, assistant curator of Americana, 1986-89, curator of American and military history, 1989-2004, senior curator, 2004-. **Publications:** The First South Pacific Campaign: Pacific Fleet Strategy, December, 1941-June, 1942, 1976; The First Team: Pacific Naval Air Combat from Pearl Harbor to Midway, 1984, rev. ed., 1990; The First Team and the Guadalcanal Campaign: Naval Fighter Combat from August to November, 1942, 1994; (with S. Ewing) Fateful Rendezvous: The Life of Butch O'Hare, 1997. Contributor to periodicals. **Address:** Milwaukee Public Museum, 800 W Wells St, Milwaukee, WI 53233, U.S.A. **Online address:** jl@mpm.edu

LUNGE-LARSEN, Lise. Norwegian, b. 1955. **Genres:** Mythology/Folklore, Children's fiction. **Career:** Children's book author and storyteller, 1980-. College of St. Catherine, St. Paul, MN, instructor in English and director of English as a Second Language Program, 1981-87; Hamline University, St. Paul, MN, adjunct faculty member, 1982-90; University of Minnesota, Duluth, instructor in children's literature, 1990, 1994. **Publications:** (reteller, with M. Preus) The Legend of the Lady Slipper: An Ojibwe Tale, 1999; (reteller) The Troll with No Heart in His Body, and Other Tales of Trolls from Norway, 1999; The Race of the Birkebeiners, 2001; Tales of the Hidden Folk: Stories of Fairies, Gnomes, Selkies, and Other Hidden Folk, 2004. **Address:** 2011 Lakeview Dr., Duluth, MN 55803, U.S.A. **Online address:** LLL@chartermi.net

LUNN, Janet (Louise Swoboda). Canadian (born United States), b. 1928. **Genres:** Children's fiction, History. **Career:** Children's book consultant, Ginn and Co., Scarborough, ON, 1968-78; Children's ed., Clarke Irwin, Toronto, 1972-75; Writer-in-Residence, Regina Public Library, ON, 1982-83; Chairwoman, Writers Union of Canada, 1984-85; Writer-in-Residence, Kitchener Public Library, ON, 1988; Writer-in-Residence, University of Ottawa, 1993. **Publications:** (with R. Lunn) The County, 1967; Double Spell, 1968, 1985, in U.S. as Twin Spell, 1969; Larger Than Life, 1979; The Twelve Dancing Princesses (retelling), 1979; The Root Cellar, 1983; Shadow in Hawthorn Bay, 1986; Amos's Sweater, 1988; One Hundred Shining Candles, 1989; Duck Cakes for Sale, 1989; (with C. Moore) The Story of Canada, 1992, rev. ed., 2000; Come to the Fair, 1997; The Hollow Tree, 1997; The Umbrella Party, 1998; Charlotte, 1998; Laura Secord, 2001; Double Spell, 2003. EDITOR: The Unseen (anthology), 1994; The Unseen: Scary stories, 1997. **Address:** 115-3260 Southgate Rd, Ottawa, ON, Canada K1V 8W9. **Online address:** janetlunn@sympatico.ca

LUNNEBORG, Patricia W(ells). American, b. 1933. **Genres:** Business/Trade/Industry, Human relations/Parenting. **Career:** Professor and writer. University of Washington, Seattle, associate professor of psychology, 1967-87. **Publications:** The Vocational Interest Inventory, VII: Manual, 1981; To Work: A Guide for Women College Graduates, 1982; Women Police Officers: Current Career Profile, 1989; Women Changing Work, 1990; Abortion: A Positive Decision, 1992; OU Women: Undoing Educational Obstacles, 1994; OU Men: Work through Lifelong Learning, 1997; The Chosen Lives of Childfree Men, 1999; (ed., with B.W. Ryan) Food, Drink, and the Female Sleuth, 2002. **Address:** 11930 Riviera Place NE, Seattle, WA 98125, U.S.A. **Online address:** lunneborg@comcast.net

LUPER, Steven. American, b. 1956. **Genres:** Philosophy. **Career:** Trinity University, San Antonio, TX, professor of philosophy, 1982-. Methodist Hospital, member of Bioethics Committee. **Publications:** Invulnerability: On Securing Happiness, 1996; Living Well, 2000; A Guide to Ethics, 2001; The Skeptics, 2002. EDITOR: The Possibility of Knowledge: Nozick and His Critics, 1987; Problems of International Justice, 1988; (with C. Brown) The Moral Life, 1991, 2nd ed., 1997; (with Brown) Drugs, Morality, and the Law, 1994; Social Ideals and Policies: Readings in Social and Political Philosophy, 2000; Essential Knowledge, 2004. **Address:** Department of

Philosophy, Trinity University, 715 Stadium Dr, San Antonio, TX 78212, U.S.A. **Online address:** sluper@trinity.edu

LUPICA, Mike. American, b. 1952. **Genres:** Mystery/Crime/Suspense, Sports/Fitness, Autobiography/Memoirs. **Career:** Boston Globe, Boston, MA, correspondent, 1970-74; Boston Phoenix, Boston, columnist, 1971-75; Boston magazine, Boston, columnist, 1974-75; Washington Star, Washington, DC, feature writer, 1974-75; New York Post, NYC, basketball writer and columnist, 1975-76; New York News, NYC, columnist, 1977-81; New York Daily News, NYC, columnist, 1980-. Writer for World Tennis, 1974-81, and columnist for the National (daily sports newspaper) and Esquire. Broadcast sports journalist for CBS Morning News, 1982-84, ESPN, 1982-83, WCBS-TV, 1983, and WNBC Radio. **Publications:** SPORTS AUTOBIOGRAPHIES: (with R. Jackson) Reggie: The Autobiography, 1984; (with B. Parcells) Parcells: Autobiography of the Biggest Giant of Them All, 1987; (with F. Imus) Fred Book, 1998. "PETER FINLEY" MYSTERIES: Dead Air, 1986; Extra Credits, 1988; Limited Partner, 1990; Jump, 1995; Bump and Run, 2000; Full Court Press, 2001; Wild Pitch, 2002; Red Zone, 2003. OTHER: Shooting from the Lip (nonfiction), 1988; (with W. Goldman) Wait till Next Year, 1988; Mad as Hell: How Sports Got Away from the Fans and How We Got It Back, 1996; Summer of '98, 1999. **Address:** New York Daily News, 450 W 33rd St Fl 3, New York, NY 10001, U.S.A. **Online address:** mike@lupica.com

LUPOFF, Richard A(llen). American, b. 1935. **Genres:** Novellas/Short stories, Mystery/Crime/Suspense, Science fiction/Fantasy, Young adult fiction, Literary criticism and history. **Career:** Broadcaster and Interviewer, KPFA-FM, 1977-. Technical Writer, Sperry Univac, NYC, 1958-63; Ed., Canaveral Press, NYC, 1962-70; Film Producer, IBM, NYC and Poughkeepsie, New York, 1963-70; Ed., Xero fan mag., 1963; West Coast Ed., Crawdaddy, 1970-71, and Changes, 1971-72; Ed., Organ, 1972; Book Ed., Algol, 1973-79; Ed., Canyon Press, 1986-87; Contributing Ed., Science Fiction Eye, 1987-89. **Publications:** (ed.) The Reader's Guide to Barsoom and Amtor, 1963; Edgar Rice Burroughs, Master of Adventure (criticism), 1965, 1968; One Million Centuries, 1967; (ed. with D. Thompson) All in Color for a Dime, 1970; Sacred Locomotive Flies, 1971; Into the Aether, 1974; (ed. with D. Thompson) The Comic-Book Book, 1974; The Crack in the Sky, 1976, in U.K. as Fool's Hill, 1978; Lisa Kane (juvenile), 1976; Sandworld, 1976; The Triune Man, 1976; Barsoom: Edgar Rice Burroughs and the Martian Vision (criticism), 1976; Sword of the Demon, 1977; Space War Blues, 1978; (with R.E. Howard) The Return of Skull-Face, 1978; Nebogipfel at the End of Time, 1979; The Ova Hamlet Papers (short stories), 1979; (ed.) What If? Stories That Should Have Won The Hugo, 1980; Stroka Prospekt, 1982; Sun's End, 1984; Circumpolar, 1984; Lovecraft's Book, 1985; The Digital Wristwatch of Philip K. Dick, 1985; Countersolar, 1987; Galaxy's End, 1988; The Forever City, 1988; The Black Tower, 1988; The Comic Book Killer, 1988; The Final Battle, 1990; The Classic Car Killer, 1991; Night of the Living Gator, 1992; The Bessie Blue Killer, 1994; The Sepia Siren Killer, 1994; The Cover Girl Killer, 1995; Silver Chariot Killer, 1996; Radio Red Killer, 1997; (co-ed.) All in Color for a Dime, 1997; (ed.) Investigations of Avram Davidson, 1999; The Great American Paperback, 2001; Claremont Tales, 2001; Claremont Tales II, 2002. Works appear in anthologies. **Address:** 3208 Claremont Ave, Berkeley, CA 94705, U.S.A.

LURAGHI, Raimondo. Italian, b. 1921. **Genres:** History. **Career:** Professor of history at a junior college in Torino, Italy, 1954-64; University of Genoa, Genoa, Italy, professor of American history, 1964-96, professor emeritus, 1996-. Visiting professor at colleges and universities. **Publications:** The Rise and Fall of the Plantation South, 1976; (ed.) La Guerra Civile Americana, 1976; Storia della Guerra Civile Americana, 1984; A History of the Confederate Navy, 1997. **Address:** Corso Regina Margherita 155, 10122 Torino, Italy. **Online address:** rlurag@libero.it

LURIE, Alison. American, b. 1926. **Genres:** Novels, Fashion/Costume, Literary criticism and history, Mythology/Folklore. **Career:** Cornell University, Ithaca, NY, lecturer in English, 1969-73, professor of English, 1976-. **Publications:** V.R. Lang: A Memoir, 1959; Love and Friendship, 1962; The Nowhere City, 1965; Imaginary Friends, 1967; Real People, 1969; The War between the Tates, 1974; Only Children, 1979; The Heavenly Zoo (juvenile), 1979; Clever Gretchen (juvenile), 1980; Fabulous Beasts (juvenile), 1981; The Language of Clothes, 1982; Foreign Affairs, 1984; The Truth about Lorin Jones, 1988; Don't Tell the Grown Ups: Subversive Children's Literature, vol. 1, 1990; Women and Ghosts, 1994; The Last Resort, 1998; (reteller) The Black Geese: A Baba Yaga Story from Russia (juvenile), 1999; Familiar Spirits: A Memoir of James Merrill and David Jackson, 2001; Boys and Girls Forever, 2003. EDITOR: Oxford Book of Modern Fairy Tales, 2002. **Address:** 1409 Hanshaw Rd, Ithaca, NY 14850-2730, U.S.A.

LURIE, Jonathan. American, b. 1939. **Genres:** History, Law, Politics/Government. **Career:** Teacher of social science at high schools in Oak Park and River Forest, IL, 1962-65; Rutgers University, Newark Campus, Newark, NJ, instructor, 1969-70, assistant professor, 1970-76, associate professor of history and law, 1976-84, associate dean, Graduate School of Newark, 1976-80, professor of history and adjunct professor of law, 1985-. U.S. Military Academy, visiting professor of law, 1994-95; historian to the U.S. Court of Military Appeals, 1987-2001. **Publications:** The Chicago Board of Trade, 1859-1905: The Dynamics of Self Regulation, 1979; Law and the American Nation, 1865-1912, 1983; The Constitution and Economic Change, 1989; Arming Military Justice: The Origins of the U.S. Court of Military Appeals, 1992; Pursuing Military Justice: The History of the Court of Military Appeals, 1951-1980, 1998; Military Justice in America, 2001; (with R. Labbe) Reconstruction, Regulation and the Fourteenth Amendment, 2003; The Chase Court, 2004. **Address:** Dept of History, Conklin Hall Rm 330, Rutgers University, 175 University Ave, Newark, NJ 07102, U.S.A. **Online address:** jlurie@andromeda.rutgers.edu

LURIE, Morris. Australian, b. 1938. **Genres:** Novels, Novellas/Short stories, Children's fiction, Plays/Screenplays, Essays. **Career:** Full-time writer, Melbourne, 1973-. **Publications:** NOVELS: Rappaport, 1966; The London Jungle Adventures of Charlie Hope, 1968; Rappaport's Revenge, 1973; Flying Home, 1978; Seven Books for Grossman, 1983; Madness, 1991. SHORT STORIES: Happy Times, 1969; Inside the Wardrobe: 20 Stories, 1975; Running Nicely, 1979; Dirty Friends, 1981; Outrageous Behaviour, 1984; The Night We Ate the Sparrow: A Memoir and 14 Stories, 1985; Two Brothers, Running (and screenplay), 1988; The String, 1995; Welcome to Tangier, 1997; The Secret Strength of Children, 2001. FOR CHILDREN: The 27th Annual African Hippopotamus Race, 1969; Arlo the Dandy Lion, 1971; Toby's Millions, 1982; The Story of Imelda, Who Was Small, 1984; Night-Night!, 1986; What's That Noise? What's That Sound?, 1991; Racing the Moon 1993; Boy in a Storm at Sea, 1997; Zeeks Alive!, 1997. ESSAYS: The English in Heat, 1972; Hack Work, 1977; Public Secrets: Blowing the Whistle on Australia, England, France, Japan, the US, and Places Worse, 1981; Snow Jobs, 1985; My Life as a Movie, 1988. OTHER: Waterman: Three Plays, 1979; Whole Life (autobiography), 1987; When and How to Write Short Stories and What They Are (textbook), 2000; 17 Versions of Jewishness: 20 Examples, 2001. **Address:** c/o Penguin Books, PO Box 701, Hawthorn, VIC 3122, Australia.

LUSTBADER, Eric Van. American, b. 1946. **Genres:** Novels, Mystery/Crime/Suspense, Westerns/Adventure, Science fiction/Fantasy. **Publications:** The Sunset Warrior, 1976; Shallows of Night, 1977; Dai-San, 1978; Beneath an Opal Moon, 1978; The Ninja, 1980; Sirens, 1982; Black Heart, 1983; The Miko, 1984; Jian, 1985; Shan, 1986; Zero, 1988; French Kiss, 1989; White Ninja, 1990; Angel Eyes, 1991; Black Blade, 1993, The Kaisho, 1993; Floating City, 1994; Dark Homecoming, 1997; Ring of Five Dragons, 2001; Art Kills, 2001; The Veil of a Thousand Tears, 2002. Contributor to anthologies. **Address:** c/o Henry Morrison Inc., PO Box 235, Bedford Hills, NY 10507, U.S.A.

LUSTED, Marcia Amidon. American, b. 1962. **Genres:** Novels, Architecture, History. **Career:** Writer. **Publications:** Time's Passage (fiction), 2000; Building History: The Holy City of Jerusalem, 2002; Building History: Hoover Dam, 2003; Building History: The Canals of Venice, 2003; Building History: A Nuclear Power Plant, 2004; Building History: The Empire State Building, 2004. **Address:** c/o Author Mail, Lucent Books, 15822 Bernardo Center Dr, San Diego, CA 92127-2320, U.S.A. **Online address:** mglusted@prexar.com

LUSTIG, Nora Claudia. Argentine, b. 1951. **Genres:** Business/Trade/Industry, Economics. **Career:** El Colegio de Mexico, Mexico City, professor of economic studies, 1975-91; Brookings Institution, Washington, DC, senior fellow of Foreign Policy Studies Program, 1993-. Massachusetts Institute of Technology, visiting scholar, 1982; University of California, Berkeley, visiting professor, 1984. Mexican National System of Research, fellow, 1987-91; Washington Exchange, co-director, 1990-. **Publications:** Mexico: The Remaking of an Economy, 1992, rev. ed., 1998; (ed. with B. Bosworth and R. Lawrence) North American Free Trade: Assessing the Impact, 1992. Contributor to professional journals. Also writes in Spanish. **Address:** 7020 W Greenvale Pky, Chevy Chase, MD 20815, U.S.A.

LUSTIG, T(imothy) J(ohn). British, b. 1961. **Genres:** Novels, Area studies, Literary criticism and history. **Career:** University of Keele, Keele, England, lecturer in American literature, 1993-. **Publications:** Doubled Up, 1990; (ed.) Henry James, "The Turn of the Screw" and Other Stories, 1991; Henry James and the Ghostly, 1994. **Address:** Department of American Studies, University of Keele, Keele, Staffs ST5 5BG, England. **Online address:** t.j.lustig@ams.keele.ac.uk

LUTTWAK, Edward (Nicolae). American/Romanian, b. 1942. **Genres:** History, International relations/Current affairs, Military/Defense/Arms control, Politics/Government. **Career:** Research professor, Johns Hopkins University, Baltimore, 1975-78, and Georgetown University, Washington, DC, 1978-82; Center of Strategic and International Studies, Washington, DC, associate, 1978-89, senior fellow, 1989-. **Publications:** Coup D'Etat, 1968; Dictionary of Modern War, 1971; The Strategic Balance 1972, 1972; The US-USSR Strategic Balance, 1974; The Political Uses of Sea Power, 1974; (co-author) The Israeli Army, 1975; The Grand Strategy of the Roman Empire, 1977; Strategy and Politics, 1980; The Grand Strategy of the Soviet Union, 1983; The Pentagon and the Art of War, 1985; Strategy and History: Collected Essays, 1985; (co-author) Yearbook of International Politics 1983-84, 1984, 1984-85, 1985; Strategy: The Logic of War and Peace, 1987, rev. ed., 2002; The Endangered American Dream, 1993; Turbo-Capitalism: Winners and Losers in the Global Economy, 1999; La Renaissance du poivoir aerienne, 2000. **Address:** CSIS, 1800 K St NW, Washington, DC 20006, U.S.A.

LUTZ, Catherine A. American, b. 1952. **Genres:** Anthropology/Ethnology. **Career:** State University of New York at Binghamton, assistant professor, 1981-89, associate professor of anthropology, 1989-92; University of North Carolina at Chapel Hill, associate professor, 1992-96, professor of anthropology, 1996-2003; Brown University, professor, 2003-. **Publications:** Unnatural Emotions, 1988; (with J. Collins) Reading National Geographic, 1993; Homefront, 2001. EDITOR: (with L. Abu-Lughod) Language and the Politics of Emotion, 1990; (with T. Schwartz and G. White) New Directions in Psychological Anthropology, 1993. **Address:** Dept of Anthropology, Brown University, Providence, RI 02912-1970, U.S.A.

LUTZ, John (Thomas). American, b. 1939. **Genres:** Novellas/Short stories, Mystery/Crime/Suspense, Plays/Screenplays, Writing/Journalism. **Career:** Full-time writer, 1975-. President, Private Eye Writers of America, 1987, 1988, and Mystery Writers of America, 1991. **Publications:** The Truth of the Matter, 1971; Buyer Beware, 1976; Bonegrinder, 1977; Lazarus Man, 1979; Jericho Man, 1980; The Shadow Man, 1981; (with B. Pronzini) The Eye, 1984; Nightlines, 1984; The Right to Sing the Blues, 1986; Tropical Heat, 1986; Ride the Lightning, 1987; Scorcher, 1987; Dancer's Debt, 1988; Better Mousetraps (short stories), 1988; Kiss, 1988; Shadowtown, 1988; Time Exposure, 1989; Flame, 1990; SWF Seeks Same, 1990; Diamond Eyes, 1990; Bloodfire, 1991; Hot, 1992; Dancing with the Dead, 1992; Spark, 1993; Thicker than Blood, 1993; Torch, 1994; Shadows Everywhere (short stories), 1994; Burn, 1995; Death by Jury, 1995; Lightning, 1996; The Ex, 1996, film (with L. Cohen), 1998; Oops!, 1998; (with D. August), Final Seconds, 1998; Until You Are Dead (short stories), 1998; The Nudger Dilemmas (short stories), 2001; The Night Caller, 2001; The Night Watcher, 2003. **Address:** 880 Providence Ave, Webster Groves, MO 63119, U.S.A. **Online address:** JLutz65151@aol.com

LUTZ, Tom. (Thomas M). American. **Genres:** History, Adult non-fiction, Literary criticism and history. **Career:** Writer and educator. University of Iowa, Iowa City, professor of English. **Publications:** American Nervousness, 1903: An Anecdotal History, 1991; (ed., with S. Ashton) These "Colored" United States: African American Essays from the 1920s, 1996; Crying: The Natural and Cultural History of Tears, 1999; Cosmopolitan Vistas, 2004. **Address:** University of Iowa, Department of English, Iowa City, IA 52242, U.S.A. **Online address:** tom-lutz@uiowa.edu

LUX, Maureen K. (born Canada), b. 1956. **Genres:** Adult non-fiction. **Career:** Federation of Saskatchewan Indian Nations, historical consultant, 1999-2002; University of Saskatchewan, Saskatoon, Saskatchewan, Canada, assistant professor of history, 2002-. **Publications:** Medicine That Walks: Disease, Medicine, and Canadian Plains Native People, 1880-1940, 2001. **Address:** Department of History, University of Saskatchewan, Campus Dr., Saskatoon, Saskatchewan, Canada. **Online address:** mlux@sympatico.ca

LUXON, Thomas H. American, b. 1954. **Genres:** Literary criticism and history. **Career:** University of Chicago, Chicago, IL, William Rainey Harper Instructor, 1984-85; St. Lawrence University, Canton, NY, visiting assistant professor of English, 1985-86; Franklin and Marshall College, Lancaster, PA, assistant professor of English, 1987-88; Dartmouth College, Hanover, NH, associate professor of English, 1988-, vice chair of department, 1994-96. **Publications:** Literal Figures: Puritan Allegory and the Reformation, 1995. Contributor to books. **Address:** Department of English, HB6032, Dartmouth College, Hanover, NH 03755, U.S.A.

LUZBETAK, Louis J(oseph). American, b. 1918. **Genres:** Anthropology/Ethnology, Language/Linguistics, Theology/Religion. **Career:** Professor of Cultural Anthropology, Catholic University of America, and Georgetown University, both Washington, D.C., 1956-65, now retired; Executive Director, Center for Applied Research in the Apostolate, Washington, D.C. 1965-73; President, Divine Word College, Epworth, Iowa, 1973-78; Ed., Anthropos: International Review of Ethnology and Linguistics, 1979-82; member, Pontifical Council for Culture, Vatican City, 1987-89. **Publications:** Marriage and the Family in Caucasia, 1951; Middle Wahgi Dialects, 1954; Tabare Dialect, 1954; Middle Wahgi Phonology, 1954; The Church and Cultures: An Applied Anthropology for the Religious Worker, 1963; The Church in the Changing City, 1966; The Church and Cultures: New Perspectives in Missiological Anthropology, 1988. Contributor of articles on church-related research to periodicals. **Address:** Divine Word Residence, PO Box 6000, 1901 Waukegan Rd., Techny, IL 60082-6000, U.S.A.

LYCETT GREEN, Candida. British, b. 1942. **Genres:** Homes/Gardens, Horticulture, Plays/Screenplays, Children's fiction. **Career:** Writer of nonfiction and children's books, and broadcaster. **Publications:** (with C. Booker) Goodbye London: An Illustrated Guide to Threatened Buildings, 1972; The Front Garden, 1979; English Cottages, 1982; Brilliant Gardens, 1989; The Perfect English Country House, 1991; England: Travels through an Un-wrecked Landscape, 1996; Country Life's One Hundred Favorite Houses, 1999; (with HRH the Prince of Wales) The Garden at Highgrove, 2000; Over the Hills and Far Away: An English Odyssey, 2003. EDITOR: John Betjeman: Letters, Vol. One: 1926-1951, 1994, Vol. Two: 1951-1984, 1995; John Betjeman, Coming Home: An Anthology of His Prose, 1997; Betjeman's Britain: An Anthology of Prose and Verse, 1999. DOCUMENTARY SCREENPLAYS: The Front Garden, 1979; The English Woman and the Horse, 1981; A Cottage in the Country, 1983. FOR CHILDREN: Hadrian the Hedgehog, 1969, in US as The Adventures of Hadrian the Hedgehog, 1970; Hadrian in the Orient, 1971. Contributor to periodicals. **Address:** c/o Desmond Elliott, 403 Carrington House, Hertford St., London W1Y 7TD, England.

LYDECKER, John. See GALLAGHER, Stephen.

LYDEN, Jacki. American, b. 1954. **Genres:** Autobiography/Memoirs. **Career:** National Public Radio, Washington, DC, reporter, 1981-, worked as reporter from Chicago Bureau and as Middle East and European correspondent from London Bureau, currently senior correspondent and substitute host of the series Weekend All Things Considered. University of Chicago, Benton fellow in Middle East Studies, 1991-92. **Publications:** Daughter of the Queen of Sheba (memoir), 1997; Landmarks and Legends of Uptown. Contributor to magazines. **Address:** National Public Radio, 635 Massachusetts Ave. N.W., Washington, DC 20001, U.S.A.

LYFTOGT, Kenneth L. American, b. 1951. **Genres:** Local history/Rural topics. **Career:** Lecturer at University of Northern Iowa, Iowa City, and for the Iowa Public School System and Iowa Humanities Board. **Publications:** Road Freaks of Trans-Amerika, 1975; (with A. Sunseri) The Sullivan Family of Waterloo (booklet), 1988; (ed.) Left for Dixie: The Civil War Diary of John Rath, 1991; Highway 13, 1991; From Blue Mills to Columbia: Cedar Falls and the Civil War, 1993. **Address:** 205 Seerley Bldg., University of Northern Iowa, Cedar Falls, IA 50614, U.S.A.

LYKINS, Jenny. American. **Genres:** Romance/Historical. **Career:** Writer. **Publications:** FICTION: Lost Yesterday, 1997; Echoes of Tomorrow, 1997; Waiting for Yesterday, 1997; Distant Dreams, 1998. Contributor to books. **Address:** c/o Jove Publications Inc. Publicity, 375 Hudson St., New York, NY 10014, U.S.A. **Online address:** JenLykins@aol.com

LYMAN, Darryl (Dean). American, b. 1944. **Genres:** History, Language/Linguistics, Writing/Journalism, Bibliography. **Career:** Writer. Instructional Objectives Exchange, author of educational materials, 1978-82; School Research and Service Corp., author of educational materials, 1981-83. **Publications:** (with M.D. Lewis) Essential English: Solving Common Writing Problems, 1981; The Animal Things We Say, 1983, rev. ed. as Dictionary of Animal Words and Phrases, 1994; Great Jews in Music, 1986, rev. ed., 1996; Great Jews on Stage and Screen, 1987, rev. ed., 1994; The Jewish Comedy Catalog, 1989, rev. ed., 1996; Civil War Wordbook, 1994; Civil War Quotations, 1995; Jewish Heroes and Heroines: Their Unique Achievements, 1996; Great Jewish Families, 1996. Contributor to periodicals. **Address:** Enslow Publishers, Inc., 40 Industrial Rd Box 398, Berkeley Heights, NJ 07922-0398, U.S.A.

LYNCH, Allen C. American, b. 1955. **Genres:** Politics/Government, International relations/Current affairs. **Career:** Institute for East-West Security Studies, NYC, research associate and deputy director of studies,

1984-89; Columbia University, NYC, assistant director of W. Averill Harriman Institute for Advanced Study of the Soviet Union, 1989-92; University of Virginia, Charlottesville, associate professor of government and foreign affairs, 1992-. RFE-RL Research Institute (Munich), visiting fellow, 1993-94. **Publications:** (ed. with F.S. Larrabee and R.B. Byers) Confidence-Building Measures and International Security, 1986; Political and Military Implications of the "Nuclear Winter" Theory, 1987; The Soviet Study of International Relations, 1987, rev ed, 1989; Gorbachev's International Outlook: Intellectual Origins and Political Consequences, 1989; The Soviet Breakup and U.S. Foreign Policy, 1992; The Cold War Is Over-Again, 1992; (ed. with K.W. Thompson) Soviet and Post-Soviet Russia in a World of Change, 1994; (with R. Lukic) Europe from the Balkans to the Urals: The Disintegration of Yugoslavia and the U.S.S.R. and International Politics, in press. **Address:** Department of Government and Foreign Affairs, 232 Cabell Hall, University of Virginia, Charlottesville, VA 22901, U.S.A.

LYNCH, Chris. American, b. 1962. **Genres:** Young adult fiction. **Career:** Writer. Teacher of writing at Emerson University, 1995, and Vermont College, 1997-. Proofreader of financial reports, 1985-89. Conducted a writing workshop at the Boston Public Library, summer, 1994. **Publications:** Shadow Boxer, 1993; Iceman, 1994; Gypsy Davey, 1994; Slot Machine, 1995; Political Timber, 1996; Freewill, 2001. BLUE-EYED SON SERIES: Mick, 1996; Blood Relations, 1996; Dog Eat Dog, 1996. HE-MAN WOMAN-HATERS CLUB SERIES (for young readers): Johnny Chest Hair, 1997; Babes in the Woods, 1997. Contributor of stories and articles to anthologies and periodicals. **Address:** c/o Fran Lebowitz, Writers House, 21 West 26th St., New York, NY 10010, U.S.A.

LYNCH, Daniel. American, b. 1946. **Genres:** Novels. **Career:** Philadelphia Inquirer, Philadelphia, PA, political writer, 1970-74; Newsday, Long Island, NY, Queens editor, 1974-79; Times Union, Albany, NY, managing editor and columnist, 1979-. New York State Associated Press, president, 1994-95. **Publications:** Deadly Ernest, 1986; A Killing Frost, 1987; Deathly Pale, 1988; Brennan's Point, 1988; Bad Fortune, 1989; Yellow, 1992. **Address:** Times Union, Box 15000, Albany, NY 12212, U.S.A.

LYNCH, Frances. See COMPTON, D(avid) G(uy).

LYNCH, John. British, b. 1927. **Genres:** History. **Career:** University of Liverpool, lecturer in History, 1954-61; University of London, lecturer, reader and professor of Latin American History, University College, 1961-74, professor of Latin American History and Director of Institute of Latin American Studies, 1974-87, emeritus professor, 1987-. **Publications:** Spanish Colonial Administration, 1782-1810: The Intendant System in the Viceroyalty of the Rio de la Plata, 1958; Spain Under the Habsburgs, 2 vols., 1964-69; (ed. with R. A. Humphreys) The Origins of the Latin American Revolutions 1808-1826, 1965; The Spanish American Revolutions 1808-1826, 1973; Argentine Dictator: Juan Manuel de Rosas 1829-1852, 1981; (with others) The Cambridge History of Latin America, vol. 3, 1985, vol. 4, 1986; Bourbon Spain 1700-1808, 1989; Caudillos in Spanish America 1800-1850, 1992; Latin American Revolutions, 1808-1826: Old and New World Origins, 1994; Massacre in the Pampas, 1872: Britain and Argentina in the Age of Migration, 1998; Latin America between Colony and Nation, 2001. **Address:** 8 Templars Cres, London N3 3QS, England. **Online address:** johnlynch53@msn.com

LYNCH, Michael. Scottish, b. 1946. **Genres:** History. **Career:** Writer. University College of North Wales, Bangor, lecturer in history, 1971-79; University of Edinburgh, Scotland, lecturer, 1979-88, senior lecturer in Scottish history, 1988-92, Sir William Fraser professor of Scottish history and palaeography, 1992-. **Publications:** Edinburgh and the Reformation, 1981; Scotland: A New History, 1992; (with E.P. Dennison and D. Ditchburn) Aberdeen before 1800: A New History, 2002. EDITOR: The Early Modern Town in Scotland, 1986; (with G. Stell and M. Spearman) The Scottish Medieval Town, 1987; Mary Stewart: Queen in Three Kingdoms, 1989; (with A.A. MacDonald and I.B. Cowan) The Renaissance in Scotland: Studies in Literature, Religion, History, and Culture Offered to John Durkhan, 1994; (with D. Broun and R.J. Finlay) Image and Identity: The Making and Re-making of Scotland through the Ages, 1998; (with J. Goodare) The Reign of James VI, 2000; (with H.T. Dickinson) The Challenge to Westminster: Sovereignty, Devolution and Independence, 2000; Oxford Companion to Scottish History, 2001. **Address:** Dept of Scottish History, University of Edinburgh, 17 Buccleuch Pl, Edinburgh EH8 9LN, England. **Online address:** m.lynch@ed.au.ek

LYNCH, Michael P(atrick). American, b. 1966. **Genres:** Philosophy. **Career:** University of Mississippi, University, assistant professor, 1995-2000;

Connecticut College, New London, assistant professor, 2000-2001, associate professor of philosophy, 2002-. **Publications:** Truth in Context: An Essay on Pluralism and Objectivity, 1998. EDITOR: The Nature of Truth: Classic and Contemporary Perspectives, 2001; (with H. Battaly) Perspectives on the Philosophy of William P. Alston, in press. Contributor to periodicals. **Address:** Department of Philosophy, Connecticut College, 270 Mohegan Avenue, New London, CT 06320-4196, U.S.A. **Online address:** mplyn@conncoll.edu

LYNCH, Patrick. See SINGTON, Philip.

LYNCH, Peter S. American, b. 1944. **Genres:** Economics, Money/Finance. **Career:** Fidelity Investments, Boston, MA, research analyst, 1969-74, research director, 1974-77, manager of Fidelity Magellan Fund, 1977-90, trustee, Fidelity Investment, 1990-. Guest lecturer, Boston College. **Publications:** (with J. Rothchild) On Up on Wall Street: How to Use What You Already Know to Make Money in the Market, 1989; (with Rothchild) Beating the Street: How to Pick Winning Stocks and Develop a Strategy for Mutual Funds, 1993; (with Rothchild) Learn to Earn: A Beginner's Guide to the Basics of Investing and Business, 1996. **Address:** 27 State St., Boston, MA 02109, U.S.A.

LYNCH, Thomas. American, b. 1948. **Genres:** Poetry, Novels. **Career:** Writer and funeral director. **Publications:** Skating with Heather Grace, 1986; Grimalkin and Other Poems, 1994; The Undertaking: Life Studies from the Dismal Trade, 1997; Bodies in Motion and at Rest, 2000. **Address:** 404 East Liberty, Milford, MI 48381, U.S.A. **Online address:** thoslynch@aol.com

LYND, Staughton (Craig). American, b. 1929. **Genres:** History, Novellas/Short stories. **Career:** Writer, activist, and attorney; admitted to the Bar of the State of Ohio, 1976. University Settlement House, New York City, tenant organizer and community worker, 1957-58; Spelman College, Atlanta, GA, history instructor, 1961-64; Yale University, New Haven, CT, assistant professor of history, 1964-67; Chicago State College, Chicago, IL, associate professor of history, 1967-68; attorney in Youngstown, OH, 1976-78; Legal Services Corp., Youngstown, attorney, 1978-96. Head of Council of Federated Organizations' Freedom Schools in Mississippi, 1964. **Publications:** NONFICTION: Anti-Federalism in Dutchess County, New York: A Study of Democracy and Class Conflict in the Revolutionary Era, 1962; Class Conflict, Slavery, and the United States Constitution (essays), 1966; (ed.) Nonviolence in America: A Documentary History, 1966, rev. ed. (co-ed. with A. Lynd) 1995; (with T. Hayden) The Other Side, 1967; Intellectual Origins of American Radicalism, 1968; (with M. Ferber) The Resistance, 1971; (ed.) Personal Histories of the Early C.I.O., 1973; (with G. Alperovitz) Strategy and Program: Two Essays towards a New American Socialism, 1973; (ed.) American Labor Radicalism: Testimonies and Interpretations, 1973; (ed. with A. Lynd) Rank and File: Personal Histories by Working-Class Organizers, 1973; Labor Law for the Rank and Filer, 1978, rev. ed. 1993; The Fight against Shutdowns: Youngstown's Steel Mill Closings, 1982; (ed. with S. Bahour and A. Lynd) Homeland: Oral Histories of Palestine and Palestinians, 1994; (ed.) "We Are All Leaders": The Alternative Unionism of the Early 1930s, 1996; Living inside Our Hope; A Steadfast Radical's Thoughts on Rebuilding the Movement, 1997. **Address:** 1694 Timbers Court, Niles, OH 44446, U.S.A.

LYNDS, Dennis. Also writes as William Arden, Nick Carter, Michael Collins, John Crowe, Carl Dekker, Maxwell Grant, Mark Sadler. American. **Genres:** Novels, Novellas/Short stories, Mystery/Crime/Suspense, Science fiction/Fantasy, Children's fiction, Young adult fiction. **Career:** Full-time writer, 1967-. Assistant Ed., Chemical Week, NY, 1951-52; Editorial Director, American Institute of Management, NYC, 1952-53; Associate Ed., then Managing Ed., Chemical Engineering Progress, NYC, 1954-60; Ed., Chemical Equipment and Laboratory Equipment, NYC, 1962-66; Instructor, Santa Barbara City College, Adult Education Division, CA, 1966-67. **Publications:** Combat Soldier (novel), 1962; Uptown Downtown (novel), 1963; Why Girls Ride Sidesaddle (short stories), 1980; Talking to the World (stories & novella), 1995. MYSTERY NOVELS: Charlie Chan Returns (novelization of TV play), 1974; S.W.A.T.-Crossfire (novelization of TV play), 1975. MYSTERY NOVELS AS WILLIAM ARDEN: A Dark Power, 1968; Deal in Violence, 1969; The Goliath Scheme, 1971; Die to a Distant Drum, 1972, in UK as Murder Underground, 1974; Deadly Legacy, 1973. JUVENILE MYSTERY NOVELS AS WILLIAM ARDEN: The Mystery of the Moaning Cave (Laughing Shadow, Shrinking House, Blue Condor, Dead Man's Riddle, Dancing Devil, Headless Horse, Deadly Double, Purple Pirate, Smashing Glass, Wrecker's Rock), 11 vols., 1968-86; The Secret of the Crooked Cat, 1970; The Secret of Phantom Lake, 1973; The Secret of Shark Reef, 1979; Crimebusters #1: Hot Wheels, 1989. MYSTERY NOVELS AS NICK

CARTER: The N3 Conspiracy, 1974; The Green Wolf Connection, 1976; Triple Cross, 1976. MYSTERY NOVELS AS MICHAEL COLLINS: Act of Fear, 1967; The Brass Rainbow, 1969; Night of the Toads, 1970; Walk a Black Wind, 1971; Shadow of a Tiger, 1972; The Silent Scream, 1973; Blue Death, 1975; The Blood-Red Dream, 1976; The Nightrunners, 1978; The Slasher, 1980; Freak, 1983; Minnesota Strip, 1987; Red Rosa, 1988; Castrato, 1989; Chasing Eights, 1990; The Irishman's Horse, 1991; Cassandra in Red, 1992; Crime Punishment and Resurrection (short stories and novella) 1992; The Cadillac Cowboy, 1995; Fortunes' World (stories), 2000; Spies and Thieves, Cops and Killers, Etc. (stories), 2002. SCIENCE FICTION NOVELS AS MICHAEL COLLINS: Lukan War, 1969; The Planets of Death, 1970. MYSTERY NOVELS AS JOHN CROWE: Another Way to Die, 1972; A Touch of Darkness, 1972; Bloodwater, 1974; Crooked Shadows, 1975; When They Kill Your Wife, 1977; Close to Death, 1979. MYSTERY NOVEL AS CARL DEKKER: Woman in Marble, 1973. MYSTERY NOVELS AS MAXWELL GRANT: The Shadow Strikes, 1964; Shadow Beware, 1965; Cry Shadow, 1965; The Shadow's Revenge, 1965; Mark of the Shadow, 1966; Shadow-Go Mad!, 1966; The Night of the Shadow, 1966; The Shadow-Destination: Moon, 1967. MYSTERY NOVELS AS MARK SADLER: The Falling Man, 1970; Here to Die, 1971; Mirror Image, 1972; Circle of Fire, 1973; Touch of Death, 1983; Deadly Innocents, 1986. **Address:** 12 St Anne Dr, Santa Barbara, CA 93109, U.S.A. **Online address:** dennislynds@cox.net; dennislynds.com

LYNDS, Gayle (Hallenbeck). Also writes as Gayle Stone, G. H. Stone. American. **Genres:** Novels, Mystery/Crime/Suspense. **Career:** Arizona Republic, Phoenix, reporter; General Electric TEMPO, Santa Barbara, CA, editor; Santa Barbara magazine, Santa Barbara, editor-in-chief; Prime magazine, Santa Barbara, editor. **Publications:** Masquerade (thriller), 1996; Mosaic, 1998; Mesmerized, 2001; The Coil, 2003. WITH R. LUDLUM: The Hades Factor, 2000; The Paris Option, 2002; The Altman Code, 2003. Author of 5 novels featuring the character Nick Carter. NONFICTION AS GAYLE STONE: (with C.E. Crowther) Intimacy: Strategies for Successful Relationships, 1986. JUVENILE FICTION AS G.H. STONE: Rough Stuff, 1989; Reel Trouble, 1989; Fatal Error, 1990.

LYNN, Adele B. American, b. 1953. **Genres:** Human relations/Parenting. **Career:** Mon Valley Progress Council, Belle Vernon, PA, community developer, 1977-80; Federal Reserve Bank, Pittsburgh, PA, trainer, 1980-82; Lynn Learning Labs, Belle Vernon, owner, 1982-. Author of "Understanding EFAA," a monthly column for American Bankers Association, 1988, and "In Search of Honor," a monthly column in Illinois Banker, 1998. **Publications:** Mentoring: Passing on the Torch, 1997; In Search of Honor: Lessons from Workers on How to Build Trust, 1998; The Emotional Intelligence Activity Book, 2001. **Address:** Lynn Learning Labs, 609 Broad Ave, Belle Vernon, PA 15012, U.S.A. **Online address:** LynnLabs@westol.com

LYNN, John A(lbert). American, b. 1943. **Genres:** History, Military/Defense/Arms control. **Career:** Indiana University, visiting assistant professor of history, 1972-73; University of Maine at Orono, assistant professor of history, 1973-77; University of Illinois at Urbana-Champaign, assistant professor of history, 1978-83, associate professor of history, 1983-91, professor of history, 1991-. **Publications:** The Bayonets of the Republic: Motivation and Tactics in the Army of Revolutionary France, 1791-94, 1984, rev. ed., 1996; (ed.) The Tools of War: Ideas, Instruments, and Institutions of Warfare, 1445-1871, 1990; (with G. Satterfield) A Guide to Sources in Early Modern European Military History in Midwestern Research Libraries, 1991, 2nd ed., 1994; (ed.) Feeding Mars: Logistics in Western Warfare from the Middle Ages to the Present, 1993; Giant of the Grand Siecle: The French Army, 1610-1715, 1997; The Wars of Louis XIV, 1667-1714, 1999. **Address:** Department of History, University of Illinois at Urbana-Champaign, 309 Gregory Hall, 810 South Wright, Urbana, IL 61801, U.S.A.

LYNN, Jonathan. British, b. 1943. **Genres:** Novels, Plays/Screenplays. **Career:** Director, writer, actor. **Publications:** (with G. Layton) Doctor in Charge, Doctor at Sea, Doctor on the Go (television series), 1971-74; (with G. Layton) My Name Is Harry Worth (television series), 1973; On The Buses (television series); Pig of the Month (play), 1974; (with B. Levinson) The Internecine Project (screenplay), 1974; (with G. Layton) My Brother's Keeper (2 television series), 1975, 1976; A Proper Man (novel), 1976; (with A. Jay) Yes Minister (television series), 1980-83, as paperback, 3 vols., 1981-83, as (hardback) The Complete Yes Minister, 1984; Clue (screenplay), 1985; Yes Prime Minister, 2 series, 2 vols., 1986-87; Nuns on the Run (screenplay), 1990; Mayday (novel), 1993. **Address:** c/o PFD, Drury House, 34-43 Russell Street, London WC2B 5HA, England.

LYNN (RUIZ), Kathryn. Also writes as Kathryn Belle, Kate McPhail, Lynn Mohundro. American, b. 1953. **Genres:** Education. **Career:** Chemeketa

Community College, Salem, OR, master tutor in English and writing, 1992-97; Falls City Child Care Center, Falls City, OR, teacher, 1997-98; Kidz Korner Educational Center, Dallas, OR, owner, director, and teacher, 1998-. **Publications:** Outside-Looking In (flash cards), 1997; Reflections (poems on CD-ROM), 1999. Contributor of poems and stories to magazines, using the names Kate McPhail and Kathryn Lynn. Some writings also appear under the names Kathryn Belle and Lynn Mohundro. **Address:** PO Box 659, Dallas, OR 97338, U.S.A. **Online address:** Kathrynly@aol.com

LYNN, Richard. British, b. 1930. **Genres:** Psychology. **Career:** Professor of Psychology, University of Ulster, Coleraine, since 1972. Lecturer, Exeter University, Devon, 1956-67; Professor of Psychology, Economic and Social Research Institute, Dublin, 1967-72. **Publications:** Arousal, Attention and the Orientation Reaction, 1966; Personality and National Character, 1971; Introduction to the Study of Personality, 1971; (ed.) The Entrepreneur, 1974; Dimensions of Personality, 1981; Educational Achievement in Japan, 1987; The Secret of the Miracle Economy, 1991; Dysgenius, 1997; Eugenics, 2001; (with T. Vanhanen) IQ and the Wealth of Nations, 2002. **Address:** 4 Lungwood House, Clevedon Road, Bristol BS8 3TL, England. **Online address:** Lynnr540assistantaol.com

LYNTON, Norbert (Casper). British (born Germany), b. 1927. **Genres:** Art/Art history. **Career:** Professor Emeritus of the History of Art, University of Sussex, Brighton, 1989- (Professor, 1975-89; Dean, School of European Studies, 1985-88). Lecturer in the History of Art and Architecture, Leeds College of Art, 1950-61; Sr. Lecturer, then Head of the Dept. of Art History and General Studies, Chelsea School of Art, London, 1961-70; Director of Exhibitions, Arts Council of Great Britain, 1970-75. London Correspondent, Art International, 1961-66; Art Critic, The Guardian, London, 1965-70. **Publications:** (with others) Simpson's History of Architectural Development, vol. 4, The Renaissance, 1962; Kenneth Armitage, 1962; Paul Klee, 1964; The Modern World, 1968; The Story of Modern Art, 1980; Looking at Art, 1981; (with others) Looking into Paintings, 1985; Victor Pasmore: Paintings and Graphics 1980-92, 1992; Ben Nicolson, 1993;Jack Smith, 2000; William Tillyer: Against the Grain, 2000; (with E. Langmuir) The Yale Dictionary of Art and Artists, 2000. Contributor to books, journals, and exhibition catalogs. **Address:** 4/14 Clifton Terrace, Brighton BN1 3HA, England.

LYON, Annabel. Canadian, b. 1971. **Genres:** Novellas/Short stories. **Career:** Writer. **Publications:** Oxygen, 2000.

LYON, Bentley. American, b. 1929. **Genres:** Mystery/Crime/Suspense. **Career:** U.S. Forest Service, worked in prevention and control of forest fires, seasonally, 1947-52, full time, 1952-85; USMC, 1952-54; writer. **Publications:** (ed. & comp.) Wildland Fire Management Terminology, 1985; White Crow, 1989; Summer Stalk, 1992. **Address:** PO Box 1900, Porterville, CA 93258-1900, U.S.A.

LYON, David. Canadian (born Scotland), b. 1948. **Genres:** Philosophy, Sociology, Technology, Theology/Religion. **Career:** High school English teacher, Surrey, England, 1972; lecturer at secondary schools in Bradford, 1972-74, and Bingley, England, 1975-78; senior lecturer in sociology at secondary schools, Ilkley, England, 1978-90; Queen's University, Kingston, ON, Canada, associate professor, 1991-94, professor of sociology and head of department, 1994-. Wilfrid Laurier University, visiting assistant professor, 1976-77, visiting professor, 1984; Regent College, Vancouver, BC, visiting lecturer, 1976; Calvin College, research fellow, 1981-82; University of Leeds, Television Research Centre, visiting research fellow, 1984-85; London Institute for Contemporary Christianity, associate faculty member, 1985-90; New College, Berkeley, CA, visiting professor, 1986; Open University, course tutor in sociology of technology, 1987-90; Ecole Des Hautes Etudes en Sciences Sociales, Paris, Professeur invite, 1996; Monash University and the University of Melbourne, Australia, visiting scholar, 1999-2000. **Publications:** Christians and Sociology, 1975; Karl Marx: An Assessment of His Life and Thought, 1979; Sociology and the Human Image, 1983; Future Society, 1984; The Silicon Society, 1986; The Information Society, 1988; Postmodernity, 1994, 2nd ed., 1999; The Electronic Eye, 1994; (ed. with E. Zureik) Computers, Surveillance, and Privacy, 1995; Living Stones, 1995; Jesus in Disneyland, 2000; Surveillance Society, 2001; (ed.) Surveillance as Social Sorting, 2003; Surveillance after September 11, 2003. Contributor to books. Contributor of articles and reviews to scholarly journals and popular magazines. **Address:** Department of Sociology, Queen's University, Kingston, ON, Canada K7L 3N6. **Online address:** lyond@post.queensu.ca

LYON, Elinor. (Elinor Wright). British, b. 1921. **Genres:** Children's fiction. **Publications:** Hilary's Island, 1948; Wishing Watergate, 1949; The House in

Hiding, 1950; We Daren't Go A Hunting, 1951; Run Away Home, 1953; Sea Treasure, 1955; Dragon Castle, 1956; The Golden Shore, 1957; Daughters of Aradale, 1957; Riders' Rock, 1958; Cathie Runs Wild, 1960; Carver's Journey (in U.S. as The Secret of Hermit's Bay), 1962; Green Grow the Rushes, 1964; Echo Valley, 1965; The Dream Hunters, 1966; Strangers at the Door, 1967; The Day That Got Lost, 1968; The Wishing Pool, 1970; The King of Grey Corrie, 1974; The Floodmakers, 1976. **Address:** Bron Meini, Harlech, Wales.

LYON, George Ella. (George Ella Vernon). American, b. 1949. **Genres:** Novels, Children's fiction, Young adult fiction. **Career:** University of Kentucky, Lexington, instructor in English and creative writing, 1977-; Centre College of Kentucky, visiting assistant professor, 1979-80, writer in residence, 1985; Transylvania University, lecturer, 1984-86; Radford University, visiting faculty, 1986. **Publications:** POETRY: Mountain, 1983; Growing Light, 1987; Catalpa, 1993. YOUNG ADULT NOVELS: Borrowed Children, 1988; Red Rover, Red Rover, 1989; Here and Then, 1994. PICTURE BOOKS: Father Time and the Day Boxes, 1985; A Regular Rolling Noah, 1986; A B Cedar: An Alphabet of Trees, 1989; Together, 1989; Come a Tide, 1990; Basket, 1990; Cecil's Story, 1991; The Outside Inn, 1991; Who Came Down That Road, 1992; Dreamplace, 1993; Mama Is a Miner, 1994; Five Live Bongos, 1995; A Day at Damp Camp, 1996; Ada's Pal, 1996; A Wordful Child, 1996; A Sign, 1998; Counting on the Woods: A Poem, 1998; A Traveling Cat, 1998; One Lucky Girl, 2000. OTHER: Braids (play), 1985; Choices: Stories for Adult New Readers, 1989; (ed. with B.H. Baber and G. Norman) Old Wounds, New Words: Poems from the Appalachian Poetry Project, 1994; With a Hammer for My Heart (novel), 1997; Where I'm from, Where Poems Come From, 1999. **Address:** 913 Maywick Dr, Lexington, KY 40504-3121, U.S.A.

LYON, Janet. American. **Genres:** Literary criticism and history. **Career:** University of Illinois at Urbana-Champaign, teacher of English and women's studies. **Publications:** Manifestoes: Provocations of the Modern, 1999. Contributor to books and academic journals. **Address:** Department of English, University of Illinois at Urbana-Champaign, 608 South Wright, Urbana, IL 61801, U.S.A. **Online address:** jwlyon@uiuc.edu

LYON, Jeff(rey R.). American, b. 1943. **Genres:** Medicine/Health, Sciences. **Career:** Miami Herald, Miami, FL, reporter, 1964-66; Chicago Today, Chicago, IL, reporter, 1966-74; Chicago Tribune, Chicago, columnist and feature writer, 1974-. Columbia College of Chicago, creative writing teacher, 1987, director of science communication program, 1988-. Recipient, Pulitzer Prize, 1987. **Publications:** Playing God in the Nursery, 1985; (with P. Gorner) Altered Fates: The Promise of Gene Therapy, 1995. **Address:** c/o Chicago Tribune, 435 N Michigan Ave, Chicago, IL 60611, U.S.A.

LYONS, David (Barry). American, b. 1935. **Genres:** Philosophy, Law. **Career:** Cornell University, 1964-95, Susan Linn Sage Professor of Philosophy emeritus and professor of law emeritus; Boston University, professor of law, 1995-, professor of philosophy, 1998-. **Publications:** Forms and Limits of Utilitarianism, 1965; In the Interest of the Governed: A Study in Bentham's Philosophy of Utility and Law, 1973; Ethics and the Rule of Law, 1984; Moral Aspects of Legal Theory, 1993; Rights, Welfare, and Mill's Moral Theory, 1994. EDITOR: Rights, 1979; Mill's Utilitarianism: Critical Essays, 1998. **Address:** Boston University, 765 Commonwealth Ave, Boston, MA 02215, U.S.A. **Online address:** dbl@bu.edu

LYONS, Louis. British, b. 1937. **Genres:** Mathematics/Statistics, Physics, Sciences. **Career:** Oxford University, England, university lecturer in nuclear physics, 1970-, Jesus College, tutor and fellow, 1969-, senior tutor, 1980-83, vice-principal, 1992-95. Royal Society visiting professor, 1987-89, 1996. Initiator of conferences on Statistics and Particle Physics, CERN, Geneva, 2000, FermiLab, 2000, Durham, UK, 2002, and Stanford, 2003; Proceedings, editor. **Publications:** Statistics for Nuclear and Particle Physicists, 1986; A Practical Guide to Data Analysis for Physical Science Students, 1991; All You Wanted to Know about Mathematics but Were Afraid to Ask, 1995; Contributor to scientific journals. **Address:** Dept of Physics, Denys Wilkinson Bldg, Oxford University, Keble Rd, Oxford OX1 3RH, England. **Online address:** l.lyons@physics.ox.ac.uk

LYONS, Nick. American, b. 1932. **Genres:** Literary criticism and history, Sports/Fitness, Business/Trade/Industry. **Career:** President, The Lyons Press, NYC, 1978-. Professor of English, Hunter College, City University of New York, 1961-88; Executive Ed., Crown Publishers, 1964-74. **Publications:** (ed.) Jones Very: Selected Poems, 1966; Fisherman's Bounty, 1970; The Seasonable Angler, 1970; Fishing Widows, 1974; The Sony Vision, 1976; Bright Rivers, 1978; Locked Jaws, 1979; Confessions of a Fly-Fishing Addict, 1989; Spring Creek, 1992; A Flyfisher's World, 1996; My Secret Fishing Life, 1999; Full Creel, 2000. **Address:** 342 W 84th St, New York, NY 10024, U.S.A.

LYONS, Paul. American, b. 1942. **Genres:** Sociology. **Career:** Temple University, Philadelphia, PA, instructor in history, 1967-71; history teacher at a middle school, Philadelphia, 1971-80; Stockton College, Pomona, NJ, professor of social work, 1980-. **Publications:** Philadelphia Communists, 1936-1956, 1982; Class of 66: Living in Suburban Middle America, 1994; New Left, New Right, and the Legacy of the Sixties, 1996. Contributor to books and academic journals. **Address:** Stockton College, Pomona, NJ 08240, U.S.A. **Online address:** plyons@stockton.edu

LYONS, Thomas Tolman. American, b. 1934. **Genres:** Civil liberties/Human rights, History, Race relations. **Career:** Mount Hermon School, history teacher, 1958-63; Phillips Academy, Andover, MA, history teacher, 1963-, now emeritus. Dartmouth College, Hanover, NH, visiting fellow in history, 1968-69. **Publications:** Black Leadership in American History, 1970; The Supreme Court in Contemporary American Life, 1975; The Expansion of the Federal Union, 1978; After Hiroshima, 1979, 3rd ed., 1991. EDITOR: Presidential Power in the Era of the New Deal, 1964; Realism and Idealism in Wilson's Peace Program, 1965; Reconstruction and the Race Problem, 1968; The President: Teacher, Preacher, Salesman, 1984. **Address:** 8 Oak St, Newburyport, MA 01950, U.S.A. **Online address:** lyons.et@comcast.net

LYONS, William (Edward). Australian, b. 1939. **Genres:** Philosophy. **Career:** University of Glasgow, lecturer in philosophy, 1973-85; Trinity College, Dublin, Ireland, head of School of Mental and Moral Science, 1985-95, professor of moral philosophy, 1985-. **Publications:** Gilbert Ryle: An Introduction to His Philosophy, 1980; Emotion, 1980; The Disappearance of Introspection, 1986; (ed.) Modern Philosophy of Mind, 1995; Approaches to Intentionality, 1995; Matters of the Mind, 2001. **Address:** Arts Building, Trinity College, Dublin 2, Ireland. **Online address:** wlyons@tcd.ie

LYSAUGHT, Jerome P. American, b. 1930. **Genres:** Education, Medicine/Health. **Career:** Professor of Pediatrics and Nursing, University of Rochester, New York, since 1969 (Assistant Professor, 1963-66; Associate Professor, 1966-69; Professor Emeritus of Education, 1990-). Ed., Education Administration Qtly., since 1985. Coordinator, Rochester Clearinghouse on Self-Instructional Materials for Health Care Facilities, River Campus Station, Rochester, New York Assistant Manager, Educational Microfilm Systems, Eastman Kodak Co., 1954-61; Director, National Commission for the Study of Nursing and Nursing Education, 1967-73. **Publications:** (with C.M. Williams) A Guide to Programmed Instruction, 1963; An Abstract for Action: Report of the National Commission for the Study of Nursing and Nursing Education, 1970, appendices, 1971; From Abstract into Action: Implementation of the Recommendations of the National Commission for the Study of Nursing and Nursing Education, 1973; A Luther Christmas Anthology, 1978; Action in Affirmation: Toward an Unambiguous Profession of Nursing, 1980. EDITOR: Programmed Learning: Evolving Principles and Industrial Applications, 1961; Programmed Instruction in Medical Education, 1965; (with H. Jason) Self-Instruction in Medical Education, 1968; Individualized Instruction in Medical Education, 1968; Instructional Systems for Medical Education, 1971; Technology in Medical Education, 1973; Action in Nursing: Progress in Professional Purpose, 1974. Author of journal articles, monographs, and book chapters. **Address:** 17 Bretton Woods Dr, Rochester, NY 14618, U.S.A. **Online address:** jlys@son.rochester.edu

LYTLE, Elizabeth Stewart. American, b. 1949. **Genres:** Children's nonfiction, Homes/Gardens. **Career:** Freelance magazine writer, 1984-. News-Herald, Franklin, PA, feature writer and consumer editor, 1971-86; English teacher in Franklin, 1990-; Meridian International, Ogden, UT, magazine contributing editor, 1993-. Communications consultant. **Publications:** Careers in the Construction Industry, 1992, 2nd ed., 1994; Careers as an Electrician, 1993, 3rd ed., 1999; Careers in Plumbing, Heating, Ventilation, and Air Conditioning, 1994; Careers in Cosmetology, 1999. Contributor of articles on home improvement and home design topics to magazines; contributor of monographs to the Institute for Research career series (Chicago), 1984-2000. **Address:** 128 Belmar Rd, Franklin, PA 16323, U.S.A. **Online address:** lizlytle@usa.choice.com

ISBN 1-55862-552-6